D1758261

Hertfordshire

Not For
Loan

CSU

522 203 99X

International WHO'S WHO in

Popular MUSIC

2016

International WHO'S WHO in

2016

Popular

MUSIC

18th Edition

Routledge
Taylor & Francis Group

LONDON AND NEW YORK

Eighteenth edition published 2016
by Routledge
2 Park Square, Milton Park, Abingdon, Oxon., OX14 4RN, United Kingdom

and by Routledge
711 Third Avenue, New York, NY 10017, USA

www.routledge.com

Routledge is an imprint of the Taylor & Francis Group, an informa business

© 2016 Routledge

All rights reserved. No part of this book may be reprinted or reproduced or utilised in any form or by any electronic, mechanical, or other means, now known or hereafter invented, including photocopying and recording, or in any information storage or retrieval system, without permission in writing from the publishers.

Trademark notice: Product or corporate names may be trademarks or registered trademarks, and are used only for identification and explanation without intent to infringe.

First published 1996

ISBN: 978-1-85743-817-8
ISSN: 1740-0163

Typeset in Frome by Data Standards Limited

Senior Editor: Robert J. Elster
Editorial Researchers: Shubha Banerjee (Deputy Team Leader), Herina Gangmei (Editorial Researcher), Meer Hussain (Editorial Researcher), Puja Kumari (Editorial Researcher)
Consulting Editors: Gerard Delaney, Annabella Gabb, Sue Leckey, Justin Lewis
Editorial Assistant: Eleanor Simmons
Editorial Director: Paul Kelly

The Publishers make no representation, express or implied, with regard to the accuracy of the information contained in this book and cannot accept any legal responsibility for any errors or omissions that may take place.

Printed and bound in Great Britain by
TJ International Ltd, Padstow, Cornwall

FOREWORD

The 18th edition of the INTERNATIONAL WHO'S WHO IN POPULAR MUSIC provides biographical information on more than 7,000 prominent people from pop, rock, folk, jazz, rap, dance, world, blues, gospel and country music, including instrumentalists, singers, writers, producers and managers. The biographies include information on career, recordings, compositions, publications, honours and, where available, personal and contact details.

For each edition entrants are given the opportunity to make necessary amendments and additions to their biographies. Supplementary research is done by the editorial department in order to ensure that the book is as up to date as possible on publication.

In addition to the biographical information, the directory section provides appendices of music festivals, music organizations, music awards and digital music. The names of entrants whose death has been reported over the past year are included in the obituary.

Readers are referred to the book's companion title in The Europa Biographical Reference Series, the INTERNATIONAL WHO'S WHO IN CLASSICAL MUSIC, for a comprehensive collection of information on the most prominent people in the fields of classical and light classical music.

The biographical information contained in this edition, as well as information on past entrants, deceased entrants and entrants from the wide range of other Europa biographical sources, is provided online in WORLD WHO'S WHO. Using the product's sophisticated search functions, researchers can easily and quickly access the rich biographical data in the comprehensive Europa biographical database. As well, online users can take advantage of the quarterly updating cycle that ensures the data is as current as possible. Details of this resource are available at www.worldwhoswho.com

The assistance of the individuals and organizations included in this publication in providing up-to-date material is invaluable, and the editors would like to take this opportunity to express their appreciation.

March 2016

ALPHABETIZATION AND THE TRANSCRIPTION OF NAMES

The list of names is alphabetical, with the entrants listed under their family name. If part of an entrant's family name is in parentheses, indicating that this part is not usually used, this will be ignored for the purposes of the alphabetical listing.

If an entrant's name is spelt in a variety of ways, a cross-reference is provided. An entrant who is known by a pseudonym or by an abbreviation of their name is either listed under this name or a cross-reference is provided. Multiple pseudonyms are cross-referenced where considered necessary.

Titles as part of a pseudonym, such as DJ, are ignored for the purposes of the alphabetical listing. Pseudonyms that include numbers as part of the name are listed alphabetically under the spelling of that number.

All names beginning Mc and Mac are listed as if they began Mac, e.g. McDevitt before MacDonald.

In the case of surnames beginning De, Des, Du, van or von the entries are normally found under the prefix. Names beginning St are listed as if they began Saint, e.g. St Germain before Salamun.

It should be noted that in some countries (including The People's Republic of China, The Republic of Korea, The Democratic People's Republic of Korea, Cambodia and Viet Nam) the family name is given first, followed by the given name; however, this does not affect alphabetization.

In Indonesia some people have only one name, under which their entries are alphabetized. In Thailand people often have two names, but these do not always equate to Western usage. We alphabetize the entries under the better-known name, providing the full name in the entry and cross-references where considered necessary.

Arabic names have been transliterated from the written form, rather than from pronunciation (which can vary from place to place). However, in Arabic pronunciation, when the word to which the definite article, al, is attached begins with one of certain letters called 'Sun-letters', the l of the article changes to the initial letter in question, e.g. al-shamsu (the sun) is pronounced ash-shamsu. Accordingly, where the article is attached to a name beginning with a Sun-letter, it has been rendered phonetically. Names beginning with 'Moon-letters', however, retain the l of the definite article. Names with Arabic prefixes are alphabetized after the prefix, unless requested otherwise by the entrant.

In a few cases consistency of transliteration has been sacrificed in order to avoid replacing a familiar and accepted form of a name by another which, although more accurate, would be unrecognizable.

CONTENTS

ABBREVIATIONS

AA — Associate in Arts
AAA — Agricultural Adjustment Administration
AAAS — American Association for the Advancement of Science
AAF — Army Air Force
AASA — Associate of the Australian Society of Accountants
AB — Aktiebolag
AB — Alberta
AB — Bachelor of Arts
ABA — American Bar Association
ABC — American Broadcasting Company
ABC — Australian Broadcasting Corporation
ABRSM — Associated Board for the Royal Schools of Music
AC — Companion of the Order of Australia
ACA — American Composers' Alliance
ACA — Associate of the Institute of Chartered Accountants
Acad. — Académie, Academy
Acad. — Académie
Acad. — Academy
ACCA — Associate of the Association of Certified Accountants
Accad. — Accademia
accred — accredited
ACIS — Associate of the Chartered Institute of Secretaries
ACLS — American Council of Learned Societies
ACM — Academy of Country Music
ACP — American College of Physicians
ACS — American Chemical Society
ACT — Australian Capital Territory
ADB — African Development Bank
ADC — Aide-de-camp
Adm. — Admiral
Admin. — Administration, Administrative, Administrator
Admin — Administration
Admin. — Administrative
Admin. — Administrator
AE — Air Efficiency Award
AERE — Atomic Energy Research Establishment
AF — Air Force
AFC — Air Force Cross
affil. — affiliated
AFL — American Federation of Labor
AFM — Air Force Medal
AFofM — American Federation of Musicians
AFTRA — American Federation of Television and Radio Artists
AG — Aktiengesellschaft (Joint Stock Company)
AGMA — American Guild of Musical Artists
Agric. — Agriculture
a.i. — ad interim
AIA — American Institute of Architects, Associate of the Institute of Actuaries
AIA — American Institute of Architects
AIA — Associate of the Institute of Actuaries
AIAA — American Institute of Aeronautics and Astronautics
AIB — Associate of the Institute of Bankers
AICC — All-India Congress Committee
AICE — Associate of the Institute of Civil Engineers
AIChE — American Institute of Chemical Engineers
AIDS — Acquired Immune Deficiency Syndrome
AIEE — American Institute of Electrical Engineers
AIME — American Institute of Mining Engineers, Associate of the Institution of Mining Engineers
AIME — American Institute of Mining Engineers
AIME — Associate of the Institution of Mining Engineers
AIMechE — Associate of the Institution of Mechanical Engineers
AIR — All-India Radio
AK — Alaska
AK — Knight of the Order of Australia
aka — also known as
Akad. — Akademie
AL — Alabama
Ala — Alabama
ALCS — Authors' Lending and Copyright Society
ALS — Associate of the Linnaean Society
Alt. — Alternate
AM — Albert Medal, Alpes Maritimes, Master of Arts, Member of the Order of Australia
AM — Albert Medal
AM — Alpes Maritimes

AM — amplitude modulation
AM — Master of Arts
AM — Member of the Order of Australia
Amb. — Ambassador
AMICE — Associate Member of the Institution of Civil Engineers
AMIEE — Associate Member of the Institution of Electrical Engineers
AMIMechE — Associate Member of the Institution of Mechanical Engineers
ANC — African National Congress
ANU — Australian National University
AO — Officer of the Order of Australia
AP — Andhra Pradesh (India)
Apdo — Apartado (Post Box)
APEC — Asia and Pacific Economic Co-operation
approx. — approximately
appt — appointment
apptd — appointed
APRA — Australian Performing Rights Association
apt — apartment
apto — apartamento
A&R — Artists and Repertoire
AR — Arkansas
ARA — Associate of the Royal Academy
ARAM — Associate of the Royal Academy of Music
ARAS — Associate of the Royal Astronomical Society
ARC — Agriculture Research Council
ARCA — Associate of the Royal College of Art
ARCM — Associate of the Royal College of Music
ARCO — Associate of the Royal College of Organists
ARCS — Associate of the Royal College of Science
ARIBA — Associate of the Royal Institute of British Architects
Ariz. — Arizona
Ark. — Arkansas
ARSA — Associate of the Royal Scottish Academy, Associate of the Royal Society of Arts
ARSA — Associate of the Royal Scottish Academy
ARSA — Associate of the Royal Society of Arts
ASCAP — American Society of Composers, Authors and Publishers
ASEAN — Association of South-East Asian Nations
ASLIB — Association of Special Libraries and Information Bureaux
ASME — American Society of Mechanical Engineers
Asoc. — Asociación
Ass. — Assembly
Asscn — Association
Assoc. — Associate
ASSR — Autonomous Soviet Socialist Republic
Asst — Assistant
ATD — Art Teacher's Diploma
ATV — Associated Television
Aug. — August
autobiog. — autobiography
Avda — Avenida (Avenue)
AZ — Arizona

b. — born
BA — Bachelor of Arts, British Airways
BA — Bachelor of Arts
BA — British Airways
BAAS — British Association for the Advancement of Science
BAC&S — British Academy of Composers and Songwriters
BAFTA — British Academy of Film and Television Arts
BAgr — Bachelor of Agriculture
BAgrSc — Bachelor of Agricultural Science
BAO — Bachelor of Obstetrics
BAOR — British Army of the Rhine
BArch — Bachelor of Architecture
Bart — Baronet
BAS — Bachelor in Agricultural Science
BASc — Bachelor of Applied Science
BASCA — British Association of Songwriters, Composers and Authors (now BAC&S)
BBA — Bachelor of Business Administration
BBC — British Broadcasting Corporation
BC — British Columbia
BCC — British Council of Churches
BCE — Bachelor of Civil Engineering
BChir — Bachelor of Surgery
BCL — Bachelor of Canon Law, Bachelor of Civil Law

viii

BCL	Bachelor of Canon Law
BCL	Bachelor of Civil Law
BCom	Bachelor of Commerce
BComm	Bachelor of Commerce
BCS	Bachelor of Commercial Sciences
BD	Bachelor of Divinity
Bd	Board
BDS	Bachelor of Dental Surgery
Bdwy	Broadway
BE	Bachelor of Education, Bachelor of Engineering
BE	Bachelor of Education
BE	Bachelor of Engineering
BEA	British European Airways
BEcons	Bachelor of Economics
BEd	Bachelor of Education
Beds.	Bedfordshire
BEE	Bachelor of Electrical Engineering
BEM	British Empire Medal
BEng	Bachelor of Engineering
Berks.	Berkshire
BET	Black Entertainment Television
BFA	Bachelor of Fine Arts
BFI	British Film Institute
BIM	British Institute of Management
biog.	biography
BIS	Bank for International Settlements
BJ	Bachelor of Journalism
BL	Bachelor of Laws
BLA	Bachelor of Landscape Architecture
Bldg	Building
BLit	Bachelor of Letters
BLit	Bachelor of Literature
BLit(t)	Bachelor of Letters
BLitt	Bachelor of Letters
BLitt	Bachelor of Literature
BLL	Bachelor of Laws
BLS	Bachelor in Library Science
blvd	boulevard
BM	Bachelor of Medicine
BM	Bachelor of Music
BMA	British Medical Association
BME	Bachelor of Music Education
BMEd	Bachelor of Music Education
BMI	Broadcast Music Incorporated
BMus	Bachelor of Music
Bn	Battalion
BNOC	British National Oil Corporation
BOAC	British Overseas Airways Corporation
BP	Boîte Postale (Post Box)
BPA	Bachelor of Public Administration
BPharm	Bachelor of Pharmacy
BPhil	Bachelor of Philosophy
Br.	Branch
Brig.	Brigadier
BS	Bachelor of Science, Bachelor of Surgery
BS	Bachelor of Science
BS	Bachelor of Surgery
BSA	Bachelor of Scientific Agriculture
BSc	Bachelor of Science
BSE	Bachelor of Science in Engineering (USA)
BSFA	British Science Fiction Association
Bt	Baronet
BTh	Bachelor of Theology
BTI	British Theatre Institute
Bucks.	Buckinghamshire
c.	circa
c.	child(ren)
c/o	care of
CA	California
CA	Chartered Accountant
Calif.	California
Cambs.	Cambridgeshire
CAMI	Columbia Artists Management International
Cand.	Candidate, Candidature
Cand.	Candidate
Cand.	Candidature
Cantab.	of Cambridge University
Capt.	Captain
Cards.	Cardiganshire
CB	Companion of (the Order of) the Bath
CBC	Canadian Broadcasting Corporation
CBE	Commander of (the Order of) the British Empire
CBI	Confederation of British Industry
CBIM	Companion of the British Institute of Management
CBiol	Chartered Biologist

CBS	Columbia Broadcasting System
CBSO	City of Birmingham Symphony Orchestra
CC	Companion of the Order of Canada
CChem	Chartered Chemist
CCMA	Canadian Country Music Association
CCMI	Companion of the Chartered Management Institute (formerly CIMgt)
CCP	Chinese Communist Party
CD	Canadian Forces Decoration, Commander Order of Distinction
CD	Canadian Forces Decoration
CD	Commander Order of Distinction
CD	compact disc
Cdre	Commodore
CD-ROM	compact disc read-only memory
CDU	Christlich-Demokratische Union
CE	Chartered Engineer, Civil Engineer
CE	Chartered Engineer
CE	Civil Engineer
CEAO	Communauté Economique de l'Afrique de l'Ouest
Cen.	Central
CEng	Chartered Engineer
CENTO	Central Treaty Organization
CEO	Chief Executive Officer
CERN	Conseil (now Organisation) Européen(ne) pour la Recherche Nucléaire
CFR	Commander of the Federal Republic of Nigeria
CGM	Conspicuous Gallantry Medal
CGT	Confédération Général du Travail
CH	Companion of Honour
Chair.	Chairman, Chairwoman, Chairperson
Chair.	Chairman
Chair.	Chairperson
Chair.	Chairwoman
ChB	Bachelor of Surgery
CHB	Companion of Honour of Barbados
Chem.	Chemistry
ChM	Master of Surgery
CI	Channel Islands
CIA	Central Intelligence Agency
Cia	Compagnia, Companhia (Company)
Cía	Compañía (Company)
CID	Criminal Investigation Department
Cie	Compagnie (Company)
CIE	Companion of (the Order of) the Indian Empire
CIEE	Companion of the Institution of Electrical Engineers
CIMgt	Companion of the Institute of Management (now CCMI)
C-in-C	Commander-in-Chief
CIO	Congress of Industrial Organizations
CIOMS	Council of International Organizations of Medical Science
circ.	circulation
CIS	Commonwealth of Independent States
CLD	Doctor of Civil Law (USA)
CLit	Companion of Literature
CM	Canada Medal, Master of Surgery
CM	Canada Medal
CM	Master of Surgery
CMA	Country Music Association
CMEA	Council for Mutual Economic Assistance
CMG	Companion of (the Order of) St Michael and St George
CNAA	Council for National Academic Awards
CNRS	Centre National de la Recherche Scientifique
CO	Chamber Orchestra
CO	Colorado
CO	Commanding Officer
Co.	Company, County
Co.	Company
Co.	County
COI	Central Office of Information
Col	Colonel
Col.	Colonia, Colima (hill)
Coll.	College
Colo	Colorado
COMECON	Council for Mutual Economic Assistance
COMESA	Common Market for Eastern and Southern Asia
Comm.	Commission
Commdg	Commanding
Commdr	Commander, Commandeur
Commdr	Commander
Commdr	Commandeur
Commdt	Commandant
Commr	Commissioner
CON	Commander of Order of Nigeria
Conf.	Conference
Confed.	Confederation
Conn.	Connecticut

ABBREVIATIONS

Contrib.	contribution, Contributor
Contrib.	contribution
Contrib.	Contributor
COO	Chief Operating Officer
Corp.	Corporate
Corpn	Corporation
Corresp.	Correspondent, Corresponding
Corresp.	Correspondent
Corresp.	Corresponding
CP	Caixa Postal (Post Box), Communist Party
CP	Caixa Postal, Case Postale, Casella Postale (Post Box)
CP	Communist Party
CPA	Certified Public Accountant
CPA	Commonwealth Parliamentary Association
CPhys	Chartered Physicist
CPP	Convention People's Party (Ghana)
CPPCC	Chinese People's Political Consultative Conference
CPSU	Communist Party of the Soviet Union
cr.	created
CRNCM	Companion of the Royal Northern College of Music
CSc	Candidate of Sciences
CSCE	Conference on Security and Co-operation in Europe
CSI	Companion of (the Order of) the Star of India
CSIRO	Commonwealth Scientific and Industrial Research Organization
CSSR	Czechoslovak Socialist Republic
CStJ	Commander of (the Order of) St John of Jerusalem
CT	Connecticut
Cttee	Committee
CUNY	City University of New York
CV	Commanditaire Vennootschap
CVO	Commander of the Royal Victorian Order
CWA	(British) Crime Writers' Association
d.	daughter(s)
DArch	Doctor of Architecture
DB	Bachelor of Divinity
DBA	Doctor of Business Administration
DBE	Dame Commander of (the Order of) the British Empire
DC	District of Columbia
DC	Distrito Central
DCE	Doctor of Civil Engineering
DCL	Doctor of Canon Law, Doctor of Civil Law
DCL	Doctor of Canon Law
DCL	Doctor of Civil Law
DCM	Distinguished Conduct Medal
DCMG	Dame Commander of (the Order of) St Michael and St George
DCnL	Doctor of Canon Law
DComm	Doctor of Commerce
DCS	Doctor of Commercial Sciences
DCT	Doctor of Christian Theology
DCVO	Dame Commander of the Royal Victorian Order
DD	Doctor of Divinity
Dd'ES	Diplôme d'études supérieures
DDR	Deutsche Demokratische Republik (German Democratic Republic)
DDS	Doctor of Dental Surgery
DE	Delaware
Dec.	December
DEcon	Doctor of Economics
DEd	Doctor of Education
DEFRA	Department for Environment, Food and Rural Affairs
Del.	Delaware, Delegate, Delegation
Del.	Delaware
Del.	Delegate
Del.	Delegation
Denbighs.	Denbighshire
DenD	Docteur en Droit
DEng	Doctor of Engineering
DenM	Docteur en Medicine
Dep.	Deputy
Dept	Department
DES	Department of Education and Science
Desig.	Designate
DèsL	Docteur ès Lettres
DèsSc	Docteur ès Sciences
Devt	Development
DF	Distrito Federal
DFA	Diploma of Fine Arts, Doctor of Fine Arts
DFA	Diploma of Fine Arts
DFA	Doctor of Fine Arts
DFC	Distinguished Flying Cross
DFM	Distinguished Flying Medal
DH	Doctor of Humanities
DHist	Doctor of History
DHL	Doctor of Hebrew Literature

DHSS	Department of Health and Social Security
DHumLitt	Doctor of Humane Letters
DIC	Diploma of Imperial College
DipAD	Diploma in Art and Design
DipAgr	Diploma in Agriculture
DipArch	Diploma in Architecture
DipEd	Diploma in Education
DipEng	Diploma in Engineering
DipMus	Diploma in Music
DipScEconSc	Diploma of Social and Economic Science
DipTh	Diploma in Theology
Dir	Director
Dist	District
DIur	Doctor of Law
DIurUtr	Doctor of both Civil and Canon Law
Div.	Division, Divisional
Div.	Division
Div.	Divisional
DJ	disc jockey
DJur	Doctor of Law
DK	Most Esteemed Family (Malaysia)
DL	Deputy Lieutenant
DLit	Doctor of Letters
DLit	Doctor of Literature
DLit(t)	Doctor of Letters, Doctor of Literature
DLitt	Doctor of Letters
DLitt	Doctor of Literature
DLS	Doctor of Library Science
DM	Doctor of Medicine (Oxford)
DM	Doctor of Music
DMA	Doctor of Musical Arts
DMD	Doctor of Dental Medicine
DME	Doctor of Musical Education
DMEd	Doctor of Musical Education
DMedSc	Doctor of Medical Science
DMilSc	Doctor of Military Science
DMinSci	Doctor of Municipal Science
DMS	Director of Medical Services
DMus	Doctor of Music
DMusEd	Doctor of Music Education
DMV	Doctor of Veterinary Medicine
DN	Distrito Nacional
DO	Doctor of Ophthalmology
DPH	Diploma in Public Health
DPhil	Doctor of Philosophy
DPM	Diploma in Psychological Medicine
DPS	Doctor of Public Service
dpto	departamento
Dr	Doctor
Dr(a)	Doctor(a)
Dr rer. nat	Doctor of Natural Sciences
Dr rer. pol	Doctor of Political Science
DrAgr	Doctor of Agriculture
DrIng	Doctor of Engineering
DrIur	Doctor of Laws
DrMed	Doctor of Medicine
DrOecPol	Doctor of Political Economy
DrOecPubl	Doctor of (Public) Economy
DrPhilNat	Doctor of Natural Philosophy
DrSc	Doctor of Sciences
DrSci	Doctor of Sciences
DrScNat	Doctor of Natural Sciences
DS	Doctor of Science
DSC	Distinguished Service Cross
DSc	Doctor of Science
DSci	Doctor of Sciences
DScS	Doctor of Social Science
DSM	Distinguished Service Medal
DSO	Companion of the Distinguished Service Order
DSocSc	Doctor of Social Science
DSocSci	Doctor of Social Science
DST	Doctor of Sacred Theology
DTech	Doctor of Technology
DTechSc	Doctor of Technical Sciences
DTechSci	Doctor of Technical Sciences
DTh	Doctor of Theology
DTheol	Doctor of Theology
DTM	Diploma in Tropical Medicine
DTM&H	Diploma in Tropical Medicine and Hygiene
DUniv	Doctor of the University
DUP	Diploma of the University of Paris
DVD	digital versatile disc
E	East, Eastern
EBRD	European Bank for Reconstruction and Development
EC	European Commission, European Community

ABBREVIATIONS

EC	European Commission
EC	European Community
ECA	Economic Commission for Africa, Economic Co-operation Administration
ECA	Economic Commission for Africa
ECA	Economic Co-operation Administration
ECAFE	Economic Commission for Asia and the Far East
ECE	Economic Commission for Europe
ECLA	Economic Commission for Latin America
ECLAC	Economic Commission for Latin America and the Caribbean
ECO	Economic Co-operation Organization
Econ.	Economic
Econ(s)	Economic(s)
Econs	Economics
ECOSOC	Economic and Social Council
ECSC	European Coal and Steel Community
ECWA	Economic Commission for Western Asia
ED	Doctor of Engineering (USA), Efficiency Decoration
ED	Doctor of Engineering (USA)
ED	Efficiency Decoration
ed	educated
ed.	edited, editor
ed	edited
Ed.	Editor
ed.	editor
EdD	Doctor of Education
Edif.	Edificio (Building)
Edin.	Edinburgh
EdM	Master of Education
Edn	Edition
edn	edition
Educ.	Education
EEC	European Economic Community
EFTA	European Free Trade Association
e.g.	exempli gratia (for example)
eh	Ehrenhalben (Honorary)
EIB	European Investment Bank
EM	Edward Medal, Master of Engineering (USA)
EM	Edward Medal
EM	Master of Engineering (USA)
Emer.	Emerita, Emeritus
EMI	Electrical and Musical Industries
Eng	Engineering
EngD	Doctor of Engineering
ENO	English National Opera
EP	extended-play (record)
EPLF	Eritrean People's Liberation Front
ESA	European Space Agency
ESCAP	Economic and Social Commission for Asia and the Pacific
ESCWA	Economic and Social Commission for Western Asia
esq.	esquina (corner)
est.	established
etc.	et cetera
ETH	Eidgenössische Technische Hochschule (Swiss Federal Institute of Technology)
Ets	Etablissements
EU	European Union
EURATOM	European Atomic Energy Community
eV	eingetragener Verein
Exec.	Executive
Exhbn	Exhibition
Ext.	Extension
f.	founded
FAA	Fellow of the Australian Academy of Science
FAAS	Fellow of the American Association for the Advancement of Science
FAATS	Fellow of the Australian Academy of Technological Sciences
FACC	Fellow of the American College of Cardiology
FACCA	Fellow of the Association of Certified and Corporate Accountants
FACE	Fellow of the Australian College of Education
FACP	Fellow of the American College of Physicians
FACS	Fellow of the American College of Surgeons
FAHA	Fellow of the Australian Academy of the Humanities
FAIA	Fellow of the American Institute of Architects
FAIAS	Fellow of the Australian Institute of Agricultural Science
FAIM	Fellow of the Australian Institute of Management
FAO	Food and Agriculture Organization
FAS	Fellow of the Antiquarian Society
FASE	Fellow of the Antiquarian Society of Edinburgh
FASSA	Fellow of the Academy of Social Sciences of Australia
FBA	Fellow of the British Academy
FBI	Federal Bureau of Investigation
FBIM	Fellow of the British Institute of Management
FBIP	Fellow of the British Institute of Physics

FCA	Fellow of the Institute of Chartered Accountants
FCAE	Fellow of the Canadian Academy of Engineering
FCGI	Fellow of the City and Guilds of London Institute
FCIA	Fellow of the Chartered Institute of Arbitrators
FCIB	Fellow of the Chartered Institute of Bankers
FCIC	Fellow of the Chemical Institute of Canada
FCIM	Fellow of the Chartered Institute of Management
FCIS	Fellow of the Chartered Institute of Secretaries
FCMA	Fellow of the Chartered Institute of Management Accountants
FCO	Foreign and Commonwealth Office
FCSD	Fellow of the Chartered Society of Designers
FCT	Federal Capital Territory
FCWA	Fellow of the Institute of Cost and Works Accountants (now FCMA)
FDGB	Freier Deutscher Gewerkschaftsbund
FDP	Freier Demokratische Partei
Feb.	February
Fed.	Federal, Federation
Fed.	Federal
Fed.	Federation
FEng	Fellow(ship) of Engineering
FFCM	Fellow of the Faculty of Community Medicine
FFPHM	Fellow of the Faculty of Public Health Medicine
FGCM	Fellow of the Guild of Church Musicians
FGS	Fellow of the Geological Society
FGSM	Fellow of the Guildhall School of Music and Drama
FIA	Fellow of the Institute of Actuaries
FIAL	Fellow of the International Institute of Arts and Letters
FIAM	Fellow of the International Academy of Management
FIAMS	Fellow of the Indian Academy of Medical Sciences
FIAP	Fellow of the Institution of Analysts and Programmers
FIArb	Fellow of the Institute of Arbitrators
FIB	Fellow of the Institute of Bankers
FIBA	Fellow of the Institute of Banking Associations
FIBiol	Fellow of the Institute of Biologists
FICE	Fellow of the Institution of Civil Engineers
FIChemE	Fellow of the Institute of Chemical Engineers
FID	Fellow of the Institute of Directors
FIE	Fellow of the Institute of Engineers
FIEE	Fellow of the Institution of Electrical Engineers
FIEEE	Fellow of the Institute of Electrical and Electronics Engineers
FIFA	Fédération Internationale de Football Association
FIJ	Fellow of the Institute of Journalists
FilLic	Licentiate in Philosophy
FIM	Fellow of the Institute of Metallurgists
FIME	Fellow of the Institute of Mining Engineers
FIMechE	Fellow of the Institute of Mechanical Engineers
FIMI	Fellow of the Institute of the Motor Industry
FInstF	Fellow of the Institute of Fuel
FInstM	Fellow of the Institute of Marketing
FInstP	Fellow of the Institute of Physics
FInstPet	Fellow of the Institute of Petroleum
FIPM	Fellow of the Institute of Personnel Management
FIRE	Fellow of the Institution of Radio Engineers
FITD	Fellow of the Institute of Training and Development
FL	Florida
FLA	Fellow of the Library Association
Fla	Florida
FLN	Front de Libération Nationale
FLS	Fellow of the Linnaean Society
FM	frequency modulation
FMA	Florida Music Association
FMedSci	Fellow of the Academy of Medical Sciences
fmr	former
fmrly	formerly
FNI	Fellow of the National Institute of Sciences of India
FNZIA	Fellow of the New Zealand Institute of Architects
FRACP	Fellow of the Royal Australasian College of Physicians
FRACS	Fellow of the Royal Australasian College of Surgeons
FRAeS	Fellow of the Royal Aeronautical Society
FRAI	Fellow of the Royal Anthropological Institute
FRAIA	Fellow of the Royal Australian Institute of Architects
FRAIC	Fellow of the Royal Architectural Institute of Canada
FRAM	Fellow of the Royal Academy of Music
FRAS	Fellow of the Royal Asiatic Society, Fellow of the Royal Astronomical Society
FRAS	Fellow of the Royal Asiatic Society
FRAS	Fellow of the Royal Astronomical Society
FRBS	Fellow of the Royal Society of British Sculptors
FRCA	Fellow of the Royal College of Anaesthetists
FRCM	Fellow of the Royal College of Music
FRCO	Fellow of the Royal College of Organists
FRCOG	Fellow of the Royal College of Obstetricians and Gynaecologists
FRCP	Fellow of the Royal College of Physicians (UK)

ABBREVIATIONS

FRCPath	Fellow of the Royal College of Pathologists
FRCP(E)	Fellow of the Royal College of Physicians (Edinburgh)
FRCPE	Fellow of the Royal College of Physicians, Edinburgh
FRCPGlas	Fellow of the Royal College of Physicians (Glasgow)
FRCPI	Fellow of the Royal College of Physicians of Ireland
FRCR	Fellow of the Royal College of Radiology
FRCS	Fellow of the Royal College of Surgeons
FRCS(E)	Fellow of the Royal College of Surgeons (Edinburgh)
FRCSE	Fellow of the Royal College of Surgeons, Edinburgh
FRCVS	Fellow of the Royal College of Veterinary Surgeons
FREconS	Fellow of the Royal Economic Society
FREng	Fellow of the Royal Academy of Engineering
FRES	Fellow of the Royal Entomological Society
FRFPS	Fellow of the Royal Faculty of Physicians and Surgeons
FRG	Federal Republic of Germany
FRGS	Fellow of the Royal Geographical Society
FRHistS	Fellow of the Royal Historical Society
FRHortS	Fellow of the Royal Horticultural Society
FRIBA	Fellow of the Royal Institute of British Architects
FRIC	Fellow of the Royal Institute of Chemists
FRICS	Fellow of the Royal Institute of Chartered Surveyors
FRMetS	Fellow of the Royal Meteorological Society
FRNCM	Fellow of the Royal Northern College of Music
FRPS	Fellow of the Royal Photographic Society
FRS	Fellow of the Royal Society
FRSA	Fellow of the Royal Society of Arts
FRSAMD	Fellow of the Royal Scottish Academy of Music and Drama
FRSC	Fellow of the Royal Society of Canada, Fellow of the Royal Society of Chemistry
FRSC	Fellow of the Royal Society of Canada
FRSC	Fellow of the Royal Society of Chemistry
FRSE	Fellow of the Royal Society of Edinburgh
FRSL	Fellow of the Royal Society of Literature
FRSM	Fellow of the Royal Society of Medicine
FRSNZ	Fellow of the Royal Society of New Zealand
FRSS	Fellow of the Royal Statistical Society
FRSSA	Fellow of the Royal Society of South Africa
FRTS	Fellow of the Royal Television Society
FSA	Fellow of the Society of Antiquaries
FSIAD	Fellow of the Society of Industrial Artists and Designers
FTCL	Fellow of Trinity College London
FTI	Fellow of the Textile Institute
FTS	Fellow of Technological Sciences
FWAAS	Fellow of the World Academy of Arts and Sciences
FZS	Fellow of the Zoological Society
GA	Georgia
Ga	Georgia
GATT	General Agreement on Tariffs and Trade
GB	Great Britain
GBE	Knight (or Dame) Grand Cross of (the Order of) the British Empire
GC	George Cross
GCB	Knight Grand Cross of (the Order of) the Bath
GCIE	Knight Grand Commander of (the Order of) the Indian Empire
GCMG	Knight (or Dame) Grand Cross of (the Order of) St Michael and St George
GCSI	Knight Grand Commander of (the Order of) the Star of India
GCVO	Knight (or Dame) Grand Cross of the Royal Victorian Order
GDR	German Democratic Republic
Gen.	General
GHQ	General Headquarters
GLA	Greater London Authority
Glam.	Glamorganshire
GLC	Greater London Council
Glos.	Gloucestershire
GM	George Medal
GmbH	Gesellschaft mit beschränkter Haftung (Limited Liability Company)
GMT	Greenwich Mean Time
GOC	General Officer Commanding
GOC-in-C	General Officer Commanding-in-Chief
Gov.	Governor
Govt	Government
GP	General Practitioner
GPO	General Post Office
Grad.	Graduate
GRSM	Graduate of the Royal School of Music
GSMD	Guildhall School of Music and Drama, London
GSO	General Staff Officer
Hants.	Hampshire
hc	honoris causa
HE	His Eminence, His (or Her) Excellency
HE	His Eminence
HE	His (or Her) Excellency
Herefords.	Herefordshire
Herts.	Hertfordshire
HH	His (or Her) Highness
HHD	Doctor of Humanities
HI	Hawaii
HIV	human immunodeficiency virus
HLD	Doctor of Humane Letters
HM	His (or Her) Majesty
HMS	His (or Her) Majesty's Ship
Hon.	Honorary, Honourable
Hon.	Honorary
Hon.	Honourable
Hons	Honours
Hosp.	Hospital
HQ	Headquarters
HRH	His (or Her) Royal Highness
HS	Heraldry Society
HSH	His (or Her) Serene Highness
HSP	Hungarian Socialist Party
HSWP	Hungarian Socialist Workers' Party
Hunts.	Huntingdonshire
IA	Iowa
Ia	Iowa
IAAF	International Association of Athletics Federations
IAEA	International Atomic Energy Agency
IATA	International Air Transport Association
IBA	Independent Broadcasting Authority
IBRD	International Bank for Reconstruction and Development (World Bank)
ICAO	International Civil Aviation Organization
ICC	International Chamber of Commerce
ICE	Institution of Civil Engineers
ICEM	Intergovernmental Committee for European Migration
ICFTU	International Confederation of Free Trade Unions
ICI	Imperial Chemical Industries
ICOM	International Council of Museums
ICRC	International Committee for the Red Cross
ICS	Indian Civil Service
ICSID	International Centre for Settlement of Investment Disputes
ICSU	International Council of Scientific Unions
ID	Idaho
Ida	Idaho
IDA	International Development Association
IDB	Inter-American Development Bank
i.e.	id est (that is to say)
IEA	International Energy Agency
IEE	Institution of Electrical Engineers
IEEE	Institution of Electrical and Electronic Engineers
IFAD	International Fund for Agricultural Development
IFC	International Finance Corporation
IGAD	Intergovernmental Authority on Development
IISS	International Institute for Strategic Studies
IL	Illinois
Ill.	Illinois
ILO	International Labour Organization
IMC	International Music Council
IMCO	Inter-Governmental Maritime Consultative Organization
IMechE	Institution of Mechanical Engineers
IMF	International Monetary Fund
IMMIE	Indian Music Excellence (award)
IMO	International Maritime Organization
IN	Indiana
Inc.	Incorporated
incl.	including
Ind.	Independent, Indiana
Ind.	Independent
Ind.	Indiana
Insp.	Inspector
Inst.	Institute, Institution
Inst.	Institute
Inst.	Institution
Int.	International
INTERPOL	International Criminal Police Organization
INTUC	Indian National Trades Union Congress
IOC	International Olympic Committee
IPC	Institute of Professional Critics
IPU	Inter-Parliamentary Union
IRCAM	Institut de Recherche et Coordination Acoustique/Musique
ISCM	International Society for Contemporary Music
ISM	Incorporated Society of Musicians
ISO	Companion of the Imperial Service Order
ITA	Independent Television Authority
ITN	Independent Television News
ITU	International Telecommunications Union

xii

ABBREVIATIONS

ITV	Independent Television
IUPAC	International Union of Pure and Applied Chemistry
IUPAP	International Union of Pure and Applied Physics
Jan.	January
JCB	Bachelor of Canon Law
JCD	Doctor of Canon Law
JD	Doctor of Jurisprudence
JMK	Johan Mangku Negara (Malaysia)
JP	Justice of the Peace
Jr	Junior
JSD	Doctor of Juristic Science
Jt	Joint
Jtly	Jointly
JuD	Doctor of Law
JUD	Juris utriusque Doctor (Doctor of both Civil and Canon Law)
JUDr	Juris utriusque Doctor (Doctor of both Civil and Canon Law), Doctor of Law
Kan.	Kansas
KBE	Knight Commander of (the Order of) the British Empire
KC	King's Counsel
KCB	Knight Commander of (the Order of) the Bath
KCIE	Knight Commander of (the Order of) the Indian Empire
KCMG	Knight Commander of (the Order of) St Michael and St George
KCSI	Knight Commander of (the Order of) the Star of India
KCVO	Knight Commander of the Royal Victorian Order
KG	Royal Knight of the Most Noble Order of the Garter
KGB	Committee of State Security (USSR)
KK	Kaien Kaisha
KLM	Koninklijke Luchtvaart Maatschappij (Royal Dutch Airlines)
km	kilometre(s)
KNZM	Knight of the New Zealand Order of Merit
KP	Knight of (the Order of) St Patrick
KS	Kansas
KStJ	Knight of (the Order of) St John of Jerusalem
Kt	Knight
KT	Knight of (the Order of) the Thistle
KY	Kentucky
Ky	Kentucky
LA	Los Angeles
LA	Louisiana
La	Louisiana
Lab.	Laboratory
LAMDA	London Academy of Music and Dramatic Art
Lancs.	Lancashire
LDP	Liberal Democratic Party
LDS	Licentiate in Dental Surgery
LEA	Local Education Authority
Legis.	Legislative
Leics.	Leicestershire
LenD	Licencié en Droit
LèsL	Licencié ès Lettres
LèsSc	Licencié ès Sciences
LG	Lady of (the Order of) the Garter
LHD	Doctor of Humane Letters
LI	Long Island
LicenDer	Licenciado en Derecho
LicenFil	Licenciado en Filosofia
LicenLet	Licenciado en Letras
LicMed	Licentiate in Medicine
Lincs.	Lincolnshire
LittD	Doctor of Letters
LLB	Bachelor of Laws
LLC	Limited Liability Company
LLD	Doctor of Laws
LLL	Licentiate of Laws
LLM	Master of Laws
LLP	Limited Liability Partnership
LM	Licentiate of Medicine, Licentiate of Midwifery
LM	Licentiate of Medicine
LM	Licentiate of Midwifery
LN	League of Nations
LP	long-playing (record)
LPh	Licentiate of Philosophy
LPO	London Philharmonic Orchestra
LRAM	Licentiate of the Royal Academy of Music
LRCP	Licentiate of the Royal College of Physicians
LRSM	Licentiate of the Royal Schools of Music
LSE	London School of Economics and Political Science
LSO	London Symphony Orchestra
Lt	Lieutenant
LTCL	Licentiate of Trinity College of Music, London
Ltd	Limited

Ltd(a)	Limited, Limitada
Ltda	Limitada
LTh	Licentiate in Theology
LVO	Lieutenant, Royal Victorian Order
LW	long wave
LWT	London Weekend Television
m.	marriage, married, metre(s)
m.	marriage
m.	married
m.	metre(s)
MA	Massachusetts
MA	Master of Arts
MAgr	Master of Agriculture (USA)
Maj.	Major
MALD	Master of Arts in Law and Diplomacy
Man.	Management, Manager, Managing, Manitoba
Man.	Management
Man.	Manager
Man.	Managing
Man.	Manitoba
MArch	Master of Architecture
Mass	Massachusetts
MAT	Master of Arts and Teaching
Math.	Mathematical, Mathematics
Math.	Mathematical
Math.	Mathematics
MB	Bachelor of Medicine
MB	Manitoba
MBA	Master of Business Administration
MBE	Member of (the Order of) the British Empire
MBS	Master of Business Studies
MC	master of ceremonies
MC	Military Cross
MCC	Marylebone Cricket Club
MCE	Master of Civil Engineering
MCh	Master of Surgery
MChD	Master of Dental Surgery
MCL	Master of Civil Law
MCom	Master of Commerce
MComm	Master of Commerce
MCP	Master of City Planning
MD	Doctor of Medicine
MD	Maryland
Md	Maryland
MD	Music Director
MDiv	Master of Divinity
MDS	Master of Dental Surgery
Me	Maine
ME	Maine
ME	Myalgic Encephalomyehtis
MEconSc	Master of Economic Sciences
MEd	Master of Education
mem.	member
MEng	Master of Engineering (Dublin)
MEngSc	Master of Engineering
MEP	Member of European Parliament
Met	Metropolitan Opera House, New York
MFA	Master of Fine Arts
Mfg	Manufacturing
Mfrs	Manufacturers
Mgr	Monseigneur, Monsignor
Mgr	Monseigneur
Mgr	Monsignor
MHRA	Modern Humanities Research Association
MHz	megahertz (megacycles)
MI	Marshall Islands
MI	Michigan
MIA	Master of International Affairs
MICE	Member of the Institution of Civil Engineers
Mich.	Michigan
MIChemE	Member of the Institution of Chemical Engineers
Middx	Middlesex
MIDI	Musical Instrument Digital Interface
MIEE	Member of the Institution of Electrical Engineers
Mil.	Military
MIMarE	Member of the Institute of Marine Engineers
MIMechE	Member of the Institution of Mechanical Engineers
MIMinE	Member of the Institution of Mining Engineers
Minn.	Minnesota
MInstT	Member of the Institute of Transport
Miss.	Mississippi
MIStructE	Member of the Institution of Structural Engineers
MIT	Massachusetts Institute of Technology
MJ	Master of Jurisprudence

MLA	Master of Landscape Architecture, Member of the Legislative Assembly	NE	North East
MLA	Master of Landscape Architecture	NEA	National Endowment for the Arts
MLA	Member of the Legislative Assembly	Neb.	Nebraska
MLA	Modern Language Association	NEDC	National Economic Development Council
MLC	Member of the Legislative Council	NEH	National Endowment for the Humanities
MLitt	Master of Letters	NERC	Natural Environment Research Council
MLitt	Master of Literature	Nev.	Nevada
MLS	Master of Library Science	NF	Newfoundland
MM	Master of Music	NFSPS	National Federation of State Poetry Societies
MM	Military Medal	NGO	non-governmental organization
MME	Master of Music Education	NH	New Hampshire
MMEd	Master of Music Education	NHK	Nippon Hoso Kyokai (Japanese broadcasting system)
MMus	Master of Music	NHS	National Health Service
MN	Minnesota	NI	Northern Ireland
MNOC	Movement of Non-Aligned Countries	NIH	National Institutes of Health
MO	Missouri	NJ	New Jersey
Mo.	Missouri	NL	Newfoundland and Labrador
MOBO	Music of Black Origin	NM	New Mexico
MOH	Medical Officer of Health	NME	New Musical Express
Mon.	Monmouthshire	no.	number
Mont.	Montana	Northants.	Northamptonshire
Movt	Movement	Notts.	Nottinghamshire
MP	Madhya Pradesh (India), Member of Parliament	Nov.	November
MP	Madhya Pradesh (India)	NPC	National People's Congress
MP	Member of Parliament	nr	near
MP3	MPEG-1 Audio Layer-3 (audio compression format)	NRC	Nuclear Research Council
MPA	Master of Public Administration (Harvard)	NRK	Norsk Rikskringkasting (Norwegian broadcasting system)
MPEG	Moving Picture Experts Group	NS	Nova Scotia
MPh	Master of Philosophy (USA)	NSAI	Nashville Songwriters' Association International
MPhil	Master of Philosophy	NSF	National Science Foundation
MPolSci	Master of Political Science	NSW	New South Wales
MPP	Member of Provincial Parliament (Canada)	NT	Northern Territory
MRAS	Member of the Royal Asiatic Society	NT	Northwest Territories
MRC	Medical Research Council	NU	Nunavut Territory
MRCP	Member of the Royal College of Physicians	NUJ	National Union of Journalists
MRCP(E)	Member of the Royal College of Physicians (Edinburgh)	NV	Naamloze Vennootschap
MRCPE	Member of the Royal College of Physicians, Edinburgh	NV	Nevada
MRCS	Member of the Royal College of Surgeons of England	NW	North West
MRCSE	Member of the Royal College of Surgeons, Edinburgh	NWT	North West Territories
MRCVS	Member of the Royal College of Veterinary Surgeons	NY	New York (State)
MRI	Member of the Royal Institution	NYPO	New York Philharmonic Orchestra
MRIA	Member of the Royal Irish Academy	NYSO	New York Symphony Orchestra
MRIC	Member of the Royal Institute of Chemistry	NZ	New Zealand
MRP	Mouvement Républicain Populaire	NZIC	New Zealand Institute of Chemistry
MS	manuscript	NZSA	New Zealand Society of Authors
MS	Master of Science, Master of Surgery	O	Ohio
MS	Master of Science	OAPEC	Organization of Arab Petroleum Exporting Countries
MS	Master of Surgery	OAS	Organization of American States
MS	Mississippi	OAU	Organization of African Unity
MSA	Memphis Songwriters' Association	OBE	Officer of (the Order of) the British Empire
MSc	Master of Science	OC	Officer of the Order of Canada
MScS	Master of Social Science	Oct.	October
MSO	Melbourne Symphony Orchestra	OE	Order of Excellence (Guyana)
MSP	Member Scottish Parliament	OECD	Organisation for Economic Co-operation and Development
MT	Montana	OEEC	Organization for European Economic Co-operation
MTh	Master of Theology	Of.	Oficina (Office)
MTS	Master of Theological Studies	OFS	Orange Free State
MTV	Music Television	OH	Ohio
MUDr	Doctor of Medicine	OHCHR	Office of the United Nations High Commissioner for Human Rights
MusB	Bachelor of Music		
MusBac	Bachelor of Music	OIC	Organization of the Islamic Conference
MusD	Doctor of Music	OJ	Order of Jamaica
MusDoc	Doctor of Music	OK	Oklahoma
MusM	Master of Music (Cambridge)	Okla	Oklahoma
MVD	Master of Veterinary Medicine	OM	Member of the Order of Merit
MVO	Member of the Royal Victorian Order	ON	Ontario
MW	Master of Wine	ON	Order of Nigeria
MW	medium wave	Ont.	Ontario
MWA	Mystery Writers of America	ONZ	Order of New Zealand
		ONZM	Officer of the New Zealand Order of Merit
N	North, Northern	OP	Ordo Praedicatorum (Dominicans)
NABOB	National Association of Black-Owned Broadcasters	OPCW	Organization for the Prohibition of Chemical Weapons
NARAS	National Academy of Recording Arts and Sciences	OPEC	Organization of the Petroleum Exporting Countries
NAS	National Academy of Sciences (USA)	OPM	Office of Production Management
NAS	National Academy of Songwriters	OQ	Officer National Order of Québec
NASA	National Aeronautics and Space Administration	OR	Oregon
Nat.	National	Ore.	Oregon
NATO	North Atlantic Treaty Organization	Org.	Organization
Naz.	Nazionale	ORTF	Office de Radiodiffusion-Télévision Française
NB	New Brunswick	OSB	Order of St Benedict
NBC	National Broadcasting Company	OSCE	Organization for Security and Co-operation in Europe
NC	North Carolina	OST	original soundtrack
ND	North Dakota	Oxon.	of Oxford University, Oxfordshire
NDD	National Diploma in Design	Oxon.	of Oxford University
NE	Nebraska	Oxon.	Oxfordshire

ABBREVIATIONS

PA	Pennsylvania
Pa	Pennsylvania
Parl.	Parliament, Parliamentary
Parl.	Parliament
Parl.	Parliamentary
PBS	Public Broadcasting Service
PC	Privy Councillor
PCC	Provincial Congress Committee
PdB	Bachelor of Pedagogy
PdD	Doctor of Pedagogy
PdM	Master of Pedagogy
PDS	Partei des Demokratischen Sozialismus
PE	Prince Edward Island
PEI	Prince Edward Island
Pembs.	Pembrokeshire
PEN	Poets, Playwrights, Essayists, Editors and Novelists (Club)
Perm.	Permanent
PETA	People for the Ethical Treatment of Animals
PF	Postfach (Post Box)
PGCE	Postgraduate Certificate of Education
PharmD	Docteur en Pharmacie
PhB	Bachelor of Philosophy
PhD	Doctor of Philosophy
PhDr	Doctor of Philosophy
Phila	Philadelphia
PhL	Licentiate of Philosophy
PLA	People's Liberation Army, Port of London Authority
PLA	People's Liberation Army
PLA	Port of London Authority
PLC	Public Limited Company
PLO	Palestine Liberation Organization
PMB	Private Mail Bag
pnr	partner
PO	Philharmonia Orchestra
PO	Post Office
PO Box	Post Office Box
POB	Post Office Box
POW	Prisoner of War
PPR	Polish Workers' Party
PPRA	Past President of the Royal Academy
PPRNCM	Professsional Performer of the Royal Northern College of Music
PQ	Province of Québec
PR	Puerto Rico
PR(O)	Public Relations (Officer)
PRA	President of the Royal Academy
Pref.	Prefecture
Prep.	Preparatory
Pres.	President
PRI	President of the Royal Institute (of Painters in Water Colours)
PRIBA	President of the Royal Institute of British Architects
Prin.	Principal
Priv Doz	Privat Dozent (recognized teacher not on the regular staff)
PRO	Public Relations Officer
Proc.	Proceedings
Prod.	Producer
Prof.	Professor
promo	promotional
Propr	Proprietor
Prov.	Province, Provincial
Prov.	Province
Prov.	Provincial
PRS	Performing Right Society
PRS	President of the Royal Society
PRSA	President of the Royal Scottish Academy
PSM	Panglima Setia Mahkota (Malaysia)
pt	part
Pty	Proprietary
Publ.	Publication
publ.	publication
Publr	Publisher
Publ(s)	Publication(s)
Publs	Publications
publs	publications
Pvt.	Private
PZPR	Polish United Workers' Party
QC	Province of Québec
QC	Queen's Counsel
QEH	Queen Elizabeth Hall, London
QGM	Queen's Gallantry Medal
Qld	Queensland
QPM	Queen's Police Medal
QSO	Queen's Service Order
QSO	Queensland Symphony Orchestra
q.v.	quod vide (to which refer)
RA	Royal Academician, Royal Academy, Royal Artillery
RA	Royal Academician
RA	Royal Academy
RA	Royal Artillery
RAAF	Royal Australian Air Force
RAC	Royal Armoured Corps
RACP	Royal Australasian College of Physicians
RADA	Royal Academy of Dramatic Art
RAF	Royal Air Force
RAFVR	Royal Air Force Volunteer Reserve
RAH	Royal Albert Hall, London
RAI	Radio Audizioni Italiane
RAM	Royal Academy of Music
RAMC	Royal Army Medical Corps
RAOC	Royal Army Ordnance Corps
R&B	Rhythm and Blues
RC	Roman Catholic
RCA	Radio Corporation of America, Royal Canadian Academy, Royal College of Art
RCA	Radio Corporation of America
RCA	Royal Canadian Academy
RCA	Royal College of Art
RCAF	Royal Canadian Air Force
RCM	Royal College of Music
RCO	Royal College of Organists
RCP	Romanian Communist Party
RCP	Royal College of Physicians
RCPI	Royal College of Physicians of Ireland
Regt	Regiment
REME	Royal Electric and Mechanical Engineers
Rep.	Representative, Represented
Rep.	Representative
Rep.	Represented
Repub.	Republic
resgnd	resigned
retd	retired
Rev.	Reverend
rev. edn	revised edition
RFH	Royal Festival Hall, London
RGS	Royal Geographical Society
RI	Rhode Island
RIAS	Radio im Amerikanischen Sektor
RIBA	Royal Institute of British Architects
RLPO	Royal Liverpool Philharmonic Orchestra
RMA	Royal Military Academy
RMA	Royal Musical Association
RN	Royal Navy
RNCM	Royal Northern College of Music (formerly Royal Manchester College of Music)
RNLI	Royal National Life-boat Institution
RNR	Royal Naval Reserve
RNVR	Royal Naval Volunteer Reserve
RNZAF	Royal New Zealand Air Force
RO	Radio Orchestra
ROC	Rock Out Censorship
ROH	Royal Opera House, London
RP	Member Royal Society of Portrait Painters
rpm	revolutions per minute
RPO	Royal Philharmonic Orchestra
RPR	Rassemblement pour la République
RSA	Royal Scottish Academy, Royal Society of Arts
RSA	Royal Scottish Academy
RSA	Royal Society of Arts
RSAMD	Royal Scottish Academy of Music and Drama
RSC	Royal Shakespeare Company, Royal Society of Canada
RSC	Royal Shakespeare Company
RSC	Royal Society of Canada
RSDr	Doctor of Social Sciences
RSFSR	Russian Soviet Federative Socialist Republic
RSL	Royal Society of Literature
RSNO	Royal Scottish National Orchestra (formerly SNO)
RSO	Radio Symphony Orchestra
RSPB	Royal Society for Protection of Birds
Rt Hon.	Right Honourable
Rt Rev.	Right Reverend
RTÉ	Radio Telefís Éireann
RTF	Radiodiffusion-Télévision Française
RTS	Royal Television Society
RVO	Royal Victorian Order
RWS	Royal Society of Painters in Water Colours
S	South, Southern
S.	San
s.	son(s)

ABBREVIATIONS

SA	Sociedad Anónima, Société Anonyme, South Africa
SA	Sociedad Anónima (Limited Company)
SA	Société Anonyme (Limited Company)
SA	South Africa
SA	South Australia
SAARC	South Asian Association for Regional Co-operation
SACEM	Société d'Auteurs, Compositeurs et Editeurs de Musique
SADC	South African Development Community
SAE	Society of Aeronautical Engineers
SAG	Screen Actors' Guild
Salop.	Shropshire
SALT	Strategic Arms Limitation Treaty
Sask.	Saskatchewan
SATB	soprano, alto, tenor, bass
SB	Bachelor of Science (USA)
SC	Senior Counsel
SC	South Carolina
SCAP	Supreme Command Allied Powers
ScB	Bachelor of Science
ScD	Doctor of Science
SD	South Dakota
SDak	South Dakota
SDLP	Social and Democratic Liberal Party
SDP	Social Democratic Party
SE	South East
SEATO	South East Asia Treaty Organization
SEC	Securities and Exchange Commission
Sec.	Secretary
Secr.	Secretariat
SED	Sozialistische Einheitspartei Deutschlands (Socialist Unity Party of the German Democratic Republic)
Sept.	September
S-et-O	Seine-et-Oise
SFWA	Science Fiction and Fantasy Writers of America
SGA	Songwriters' Guild of America
SHAEF	Supreme Headquarters Allied Expeditionary Force
SHAPE	Supreme Headquarters Allied Powers in Europe
SJ	Society of Jesus (Jesuits)
SJD	Doctor of Juristic Science
SK	Saskatchewan
SL	Sociedad Limitada
SLD	Social and Liberal Democrats
SM	Master of Science
SO	Symphony Orchestra
SOAS	School of Oriental and African Studies
Soc.	Société, Society
Soc.	Société
Soc.	Society
SOCAN	Society of Composers, Authors and Music Publishers of Canada
SOSA	State Opera of South Australia
SpA	Società per Azioni
SPD	Sozialdemokratische Partei Deutschlands
SPNM	Society for the Promotion of New Music
Sr	Senior
SRC	Science Research Council
Srl	Società a responsabilità
SSM	Seria Seta Mahkota (Malaysia)
SSR	Soviet Socialist Republic
St	Saint
Sta	Santa
Staffs.	Staffordshire
STB	Bachelor of Sacred Theology
STD	Doctor of Sacred Theology
Ste	Sainte
STL	Licentiate of Sacred Theology
STM	Master of Sacred Theology
str.	strasse
SUNY	State University of New York
Supt	Superintendent
SVSA	South West Virginia Songwriters' Association
SW	short wave
SW	South West
SWAPO	South West Africa People's Organization
TA	Territorial Army
TCL	Trinity College of Music, London
TD	Teachta Dála (mem. of the Dáil), Territorial Decoration
TD	Teachta Dála (mem. of the Dáil)
TD	Territorial Decoration
Tech.	Technical, Technology
Tech.	Technical
Tech.	Technology
Temp.	Temporary
Tenn.	Tennessee
Tex.	Texas

ThB	Bachelor of Theology
ThD	Doctor of Theology
THDr	Doctor of Theology
ThM	Master of Theology
TLS	Times Literary Supplement
TN	Tennessee
trans.	translated
Trans.	Translation, translator
Trans.	Translation
Trans.	translator
Treas.	Treasurer
TU(C)	Trades Union (Congress)
TV	television
TX	Texas
u.	utca (street)
UAE	United Arab Emirates
UAR	United Arab Republic
UCLA	University of California at Los Angeles
UDEAC	L'Union Douanière et Economique de l'Afrique Centrale
UDR	Union des Démocrates pour la République
UED	University Education Diploma
UHF	ultra-high frequency
UK	United Kingdom (of Great Britain and Northern Ireland)
UKAEA	United Kingdom Atomic Energy Authority
ul.	ulitsa (street)
UMIST	University of Manchester Institute of Science and Technology
UMNO	United Malays National Organization
UN(O)	United Nations (Organization)
UNA	United Nations Association
UNCED	United Nations Council for Education and Development
UNCHS	United Nations Centre for Human Settlements (Habitat)
UNCTAD	United Nations Conference on Trade and Development
UNDCP	United Nations International Drug Control Programme
UNDP	United Nations Development Programme
UNDRO	United Nations Disaster Relief Office
UNEF	United Nations Emergency Force
UNEP	United Nations Environment Programme
UNESCO	United Nations Educational, Scientific and Cultural Organization
UNFPA	United Nations Population Fund
UNHCR	United Nations High Commissioner for Refugees
UNICEF	United Nations International Children's Emergency Fund
UNIDO	United Nations Industrial Development Organization
UNIFEM	United Nations Development Fund for Women
UNITAR	United Nations Institute for Training and Research
Univ.	University
UNKRA	United Nations Korean Relief Administration
UNRRA	United Nations Relief and Rehabilitation Administration
UNRWA	United Nations Relief and Works Agency
UNU	United Nations University
UP	United Provinces, Uttar Pradesh (India)
UP	United Provinces
UP	Uttar Pradesh (India)
UPU	Universal Postal Union
Urb.	Urbanización (urban district)
US	United States
USA	United States of America
USAAF	United States Army Air Force
USAF	United States Air Force
USAID	United States Agency for International Development
USN	United States Navy
USNR	United States Navy Reserve
USPHS	United States Public Health Service
USS	United States Ship
USSR	Union of Soviet Socialist Republics
UT	Utah
UWI	University of the West Indies
VA	Virginia
Va	Virginia
VC	Victoria Cross
VHF	very high frequency
VI	(US) Virgin Islands
Vic.	Victoria
Vol.	Volume
vol.	volume
Vol(s)	Volume(s)
Vols	Volumes
vols	volumes
VSO	Victoria State Opera
VSO	Voluntary Service Overseas
VT	Vermont
Vt	Vermont

ABBREVIATIONS

W	West, Western	WNO	Welsh National Opera
WA	Washington (State)	WOMAD	World of Music, Arts and Dance
WA	Western Australia	Worcs.	Worcestershire
Warwicks.	Warwickshire	WRAC	Women's Royal Army Corps
Wash.	Washington (State)	WRNS	Women's Royal Naval Service
WCC	World Council of Churches	WTO	World Trade Organization
WCMD	Welsh College of Music and Drama, Cardiff	WV	West Virginia
WCT	World Championship Tennis	WVa	West Virginia
WEU	Western European Union	WWF	World Wildlife Fund
WFP	World Food Programme	WY	Wyoming
WFTU	World Federation of Trade Unions	Wyo.	Wyoming
WHO	World Health Organization		
WI	Wisconsin		
Wilts.	Wiltshire	YMCA	Young Men's Christian Association
WIPO	World Intellectual Property Organization	Yorks.	Yorkshire
Wis.	Wisconsin	YT	Yukon Territory
WMO	World Meteorological Organization	YWCA	Young Women's Christian Association

INTERNATIONAL TELEPHONE CODES

To make international calls to telephone and fax numbers listed in the book, dial the international code of the country from which you are calling, followed by the appropriate country code for the organization you wish to call (listed below), followed by the area code (if applicable) and telephone or fax number listed in the entry.

	Country code	+ or − GMT*
Abkhazia	7	+4
Afghanistan	93	$+4\frac{1}{2}$
Åland Islands	358	+2
Albania	355	+1
Algeria	213	+1
American Samoa	1 684	−11
Andorra	376	+1
Angola	244	+1
Anguilla	1 264	−4
Antigua and Barbuda	1 268	−4
Argentina	54	−3
Armenia	374	+4
Aruba	297	−4
Ascension Island	247	0
Australia	61	+8 to +10
Austria	43	+1
Azerbaijan	994	+5
Bahamas	1 242	−5
Bahrain	973	+3
Bangladesh	880	+6
Barbados	1 246	−4
Belarus	375	+2
Belgium	32	+1
Belize	501	−6
Benin	229	+1
Bermuda	1 441	−4
Bhutan	975	+6
Bolivia	591	−4
Bonaire	599	−4
Bosnia and Herzegovina	387	+1
Botswana	267	+2
Brazil	55	−3 to −4
British Indian Ocean Territory (Diego Garcia)	246	+5
British Virgin Islands	1 284	−4
Brunei	673	+8
Bulgaria	359	+2
Burkina Faso	226	0
Burundi	257	+2
Cabo Verde	238	−1
Cambodia	855	+7
Cameroon	237	+1
Canada	1	−3 to −8
Cayman Islands	1 345	−5
Central African Republic	236	+1
Ceuta	34	+1
Chad	235	+1
Chile	56	−4
China, People's Republic	86	+8
Christmas Island	61	+7
Cocos (Keeling) Islands	61	$+6\frac{1}{2}$
Colombia	57	−5
Comoros	269	+3
Congo, Democratic Republic	243	+1
Congo, Republic	242	+1
Cook Islands	682	−10
Costa Rica	506	−6
Côte d'Ivoire	225	0
Croatia	385	+1
Cuba	53	−5
Curaçao	599	−4
Cyprus	357	+2
Czech Republic	420	+1
Denmark	45	+1
Djibouti	253	+3
Dominica	1 767	−4
Dominican Republic	1 809	−4
Ecuador	593	−5
Egypt	20	+2
El Salvador	503	−6
Equatorial Guinea	240	+1
Eritrea	291	+3
Estonia	372	+2
Ethiopia	251	+3
Falkland Islands	500	−4
Faroe Islands	298	0
Fiji	679	+12
Finland	358	+2
France	33	+1
French Guiana	594	−3
French Polynesia	689	−9 to −10
Gabon	241	+1
Gambia	220	0
Georgia	995	+4
Germany	49	+1
Ghana	233	0
Gibraltar	350	+1
Greece	30	+2
Greenland	299	−1 to −4
Grenada	1 473	−4
Guadeloupe	590	−4
Guam	1 671	+10
Guatemala	502	−6
Guernsey	44	0
Guinea	224	0
Guinea-Bissau	245	0
Guyana	592	−4
Haiti	509	−5
Honduras	504	−6
Hong Kong	852	+8
Hungary	36	+1
Iceland	354	0
India	91	$+5\frac{1}{2}$
Indonesia	62	+7 to +9
Iran	98	$+3\frac{1}{2}$
Iraq	964	+3
Ireland	353	0
Isle of Man	44	0
Israel	972	+2
Italy	39	+1
Jamaica	1 876	−5
Japan	81	+9
Jersey	44	0
Jordan	962	+2
Kazakhstan	7	+6
Kenya	254	+3
Kiribati	686	+12 to +13
Korea, Democratic People's Republic (North Korea)	850	+9
Korea, Republic (South Korea)	82	+9
Kosovo	381†	+3
Kuwait	965	+3
Kyrgyzstan	996	+5
Laos	856	+7
Latvia	371	+2
Lebanon	961	+2
Lesotho	266	+2
Liberia	231	0
Libya	218	+1
Liechtenstein	423	+1
Lithuania	370	+2
Luxembourg	352	+1

INTERNATIONAL TELEPHONE CODES

	Country code	+ or − GMT*		Country code	+ or − GMT*
Macao	853	+8	Seychelles	248	+4
Macedonia, former Yugoslav republic	389	+1	Sierra Leone	232	0
Madagascar	261	+3	Singapore	65	+8
Malawi	265	+2	Sint Eustatius	1721	−4
Malaysia	60	+8	Sint Maarten	1721	−4
Maldives	960	+5	Slovakia	421	+1
Mali	223	0	Slovenia	386	+1
Malta	356	+1	Solomon Islands	677	+11
Marshall Islands	692	+12	Somalia	252	+3
Martinique	596	−4	South Africa	27	+2
Mauritania	222	0	South Ossetia	7	+4
Mauritius	230	+4	South Sudan	211	+2
Mayotte	262	+3	Spain	34	+1
Melilla	34	+1	Sri Lanka	94	+5½
Mexico	52	−6 to −7	Sudan	249	+2
Micronesia, Federated States	691	+10 to +11	Suriname	597	−3
Moldova	373	+2	Svalbard	47	+1
Monaco	377	+1	Swaziland	268	+2
Mongolia	976	+7 to +9	Sweden	46	+1
Montenegro	382	+1	Switzerland	41	+1
Montserrat	1 664	−4	Syria	963	+2
Morocco	212	0	Taiwan	886	+8
Mozambique	258	+2	Tajikistan	992	+5
Myanmar	95	+6½	Tanzania	255	+3
Nagornyi Karabakh	374	+4	Thailand	66	+7
Namibia	264	+2	Timor-Leste	670	+9
Nauru	674	+12	Togo	228	0
Nepal	977	+5¾	Tokelau	690	+15
Netherlands	31	+1	Tonga	676	+13
New Caledonia	687	+11	Transnistria	373	+2
New Zealand	64	+12	Trinidad and Tobago	1 868	−4
Nicaragua	505	−6	Tristan da Cunha	290	0
Niger	227	+1	Tunisia	216	+1
Nigeria	234	+1	Turkey	90	+2
Niue	683	−11	'Turkish Republic of Northern Cyprus'	90 392	+2
Norfolk Island	672	+11½	Turkmenistan	993	+5
Northern Mariana Islands	1 670	+10	Turks and Caicos Islands	1 649	−5
Norway	47	+1	Tuvalu	688	+12
Oman	968	+4	Uganda	256	+3
Pakistan	92	+5	Ukraine‡	380	+2
Palau	680	+9	United Arab Emirates	971	+4
Palestinian Territories	970 or 972	+2	United Kingdom	44	0
Panama	507	−5	United States of America	1	−5 to −10
Papua New Guinea	675	+10	United States Virgin Islands	1 340	−4
Paraguay	595	−4	Uruguay	598	−3
Peru	51	−5	Uzbekistan	998	+5
Philippines	63	+8	Vanuatu	678	+11
Pitcairn Islands	872	−8	Vatican City	39	+1
Poland	48	+1	Venezuela	58	−4½
Portugal	351	0	Viet Nam	84	+7
Puerto Rico	1 787	−4	Wallis and Futuna Islands	681	+12
Qatar	974	+3	Yemen	967	+3
Réunion	262	+4	Zambia	260	+2
Romania	40	+2	Zimbabwe	263	+2
Russian Federation	7	+3 to +12			
Rwanda	250	+2			
Saba	599	−4			
Saint-Barthélemy	590	−4			
Saint Christopher and Nevis	1 869	−4			
Saint Helena	290	0			
Saint Lucia	1 758	−4			
Saint-Martin	590	−4			
Saint Pierre and Miquelon	508	−3			
Saint Vincent and the Grenadines	1 784	−4			
Samoa	685	+13			
San Marino	378	+1			
São Tomé and Príncipe	239	0			
Saudi Arabia	966	+3			
Senegal	221	0			
Serbia	381	+1			

* The times listed compare the standard (winter) times in the various countries. Some countries adopt Summer (Daylight Saving) Time—i.e. +1 hour—for part of the year.

† Mobile telephone numbers for Kosovo use either the country code for Monaco (377) or the country code for Slovenia (386).

‡ The Republic of Crimea and the city of Sevastopol were placed in the time zone GMT+4 following their annexation by Russia in 2014.

Note: Telephone and fax numbers using the Inmarsat ocean region code 870 are listed in full. No country or area code is required, but it is necessary to precede the number with the international access code of the country from which the call is made.

OBITUARY

Anderson, Lynn Rene	30 July 2015
Béart, Guy	16 September 2015
Bickerton, Wayne	29 November 2015
Bley, Paul	3 January 2016
Bowie, David	10 January 2016
Brazier, Graham Philip	4 September 2015
Bregovic, Goran	28 June 2015
Brown, Errol	6 May 2015
Brown, (James Edward) Jim Ed	11 June 2015
Bryce, Owen	8 October 2015
Cole, Natalie Maria	31 December 2015
Coleman, Ornette	11 June 2015
Dehaven, Penny Charlotte	23 February 2014
Diamond, Jim	8 October 2015
Divljan, Vladimir	5 March 2015
Doonican, (Michael Valentine) Val	1 July 2015
Forrester, John	24 November 2015
Fox, John	10 February 2015
Frey, Glenn	18 January 2016
Horner, James	22 June 2015
Howard, Rex	7 November 2012
James, Sonny	22 February 2016
Jennings, John	16 October 2015
Kantner, Paul	28 January 2016
Keepnews, Orrin	1 March 2015
Khan, Sabri	1 December 2015
King, Benjamin (Ben) Earl Nelson	30 April 2015
Lane, Stevens	22 August 2015
Last, James Hans	9 June 2015
Lemmy	28 December 2015
Lisak, Ivan-Vanja	2 July 2015
Masondo, David	5 July 2015
Mavian, Robert A.	20 April 2013
Mbande, Venacio Notico	25 June 2015
Napoleon, Marty	27 April 2015
Ngcobo, Patrick	1 February 2015
Ondreicka, Karol Michal	18 April 2013
Pitch, Harry	15 July 2015
Quibel, Robert Henri Maurice	17 January 2013
Rankin, Dusty	24 September 2015
Rendell, Don	20 October 2015
Renbourn, John	26 March 2015
Richcrath, Gary	13 September 2015
Roar, Finn	7 January 2015
Robertson, Donald Irwin	16 March 2015
Rose, Doudou N'Diaye	19 August 2015
Royal, Billy Joe	6 October 2015
Shportko, Victor	29 January 2015
Sjösten, Lars	19 October 2011
Smith, Daniel W.	19 December 2015
Squire, Chris	27 June 2015
Summers, Jazz	14 August 2015
Sylvestre, Frédéric	27 August 2014
Taylor, John Michael (Mike)	18 February 2016
Toussaint, Allen	10 November 2015
Weiland, Scott	3 December 2015
White, Andy	9 November 2015
White, Maurice	3 February 2016
Woods, Philip (Phil) Wells	29 September 2015

Biographies

A

A-MEI (see Chang Hui-mei)

AALTONEN, Juhani (Junnu); Finnish musician (saxophone, flute); b. 12 Dec. 1935. *Education:* Sibelius Acad., Helsinki, Berklee Coll. of Music, Boston, USA. *Career:* played with drummer Edward Vesala 1965–; played with Arils Andersen's quartet 1970s; work in radio, television and studio recordings; featured soloist, Suomi (jazz suite), Heikki Sarmanto; Crossing, Jukka Linkola; played in reed section, UMO (New Music Orchestra) 1975–; fmr mem., jazz rock group Tasavallan Presidentti; concentrated on flute as beneficiary of government grant, late 1980s–; formed duo with pianist-composer Heikki Sarmanto; also formed Juhani Aaltone Trio. *Recordings:* with Arild Andersen: Shimri 1977, Green Shading into Blue 1978; with Edward Vesala: Nana 1970, Na Madol 1974, Rodina 1976, Satu 1976, Mau Mau 1982; with Heikki Sarmanto: Flowers in the Water 1969, Counterbalance 1971, Like a Fragonard 1971, Everything Is It 1972, Onnen aika 1973, Moment Musical 1978, Pohjola Suite 1980, Passions of a Man 1986, Kalevala Fantasy 1986, Man with a Sax 1987, Pohjoisia Kuvia 1988, Felix the Great 1988, Salakuljetettu Ikoni 1989, The Traveler 1990, Tales of Max 1991, Perfect Harmony 1991, Hearts 1995, Carrousel 1996; solo: Etiquette 1974, Springbird 1979, Prana 1981, Suomi Sinfonia 1983, Pan Fantasy 1990, Distant Dreams 1990, I Love You, Lord 1991, O Lord You're Beautiful 1993, Silver Spell 1996; with Juhani Aaltonen Trio: Mother Tongue 2003, Illusion of a Ballad 2006. *Honours:* Finnish Jazz Federation Yrjö Award 1968. *Address:* Kukintie 10, 01620 Vantaa, Finland (office). *E-mail:* junnu@juhaniaaltonen .com (office). *Website:* juhaniaaltonen.com.

AARONSON, Paul, BA, MBA; American sales and marketing director; b. 16 March 1955, Queens, NY; m. Sharon Stern 1994. *Education:* Univ. of Florida, St John's Univ. *Career:* salesman, Record Shack, New York 1978–81; Sales Man., Important Record Distributors 1981–86; owner, One Up Promotions 1987–90; Dir of Marketing, Domino Records 1991–92; Dir Sales and Marketing, Viceroy Music 1992–. *Recordings:* albums: with John Mooney: Testimony 1992; with Cowboy Mouth: Mouthing Off 1993; with Sunset Heights: Texas Tea 1994; with Savoy Brown: Bring It Home 1995; Rattlesnake Guitar, The Music Of Peter Green 1995. *Address:* Viceroy Music Group, 547 W 27th Street, Sixth Floor, New York, NY 10001, USA (office).

ABA YAZEED, Mohamed Mounir; Egyptian singer and actor; b. 10 Oct. 1954, Aswan. *Education:* studied cinematography. *Career:* mem. Syndicate of Musicians, Syndicate of Actors. *Films include:* Bitter Day Sweet Day, An Egyptian Story, Destiny. *Plays:* The King is the King, King of the Beggars, Goodnight Egypt. *Television:* Tales of the Stranger (TV film). *Recordings include:* Windows 1981, Talk 1985, In the Middle of the Circle 1987, From First Touch 1996. *Honours:* Second Prize, Festival of Arab Television 1995–96. *Address:* 13 al-Bergass Street, Garden City, Cairo, Egypt.

ABAD, Marina 'La Canillas'; Spanish singer and musician (percussion); b. Valencia. *Career:* fmr mem. Agüita Troop all-female theatre co.; lead singer Ojos de Brujo (group that fuses gypsy and flamenco music with Latin American, punk, hip hop, reggae and electronic influences); f. own label La Fábrica de Colores 2001 and since then have operated as ind. org.; several tours in Europe, Latin America and USA; collaborations with Nitin Sawhney, Asian Dub Foundation. *Recordings:* albums: Vengue 1999, Barí 2002, Barí: Remezclas de la Casa 2003, Techarí 2006, Aocaná 2009; other: Girando Barí (DVD) 2005. *Honours:* World Music Award for Europe, BBC Radio 3 2004. *E-mail:* marina@ojosdebrujo.com (office). *Website:* www.ojosdebrujo.com.

ABADIE, Claude; French musician (clarinet) and bandleader; b. 15 Jan. 1920, Paris; m. Chantal Bertin 1958; two s. one d. *Education:* studied engineering. *Career:* leader, first Dixieland Revival Band, France early 1940s; modern jazz musician, late 1960s; leader, own jazz dectet; mem. Union des Musiciens de Jazz. *Recordings:* albums: Blues Pour Boris, Revival New Orleans Sur Seine, Vivement Le 15 Novembre. *Publications:* À Propos de Jazz (series of articles for La Jaune et la Rouge) 1978–85, Le Jazz: Comment ça fonctionne 1994. *Address:* 16 Domaine des Hocquettes, 92150 Suresnes, France (home). *Telephone:* 1-42-04-65-96 (home). *Fax:* 1-42-04-65-96 (home).

ABATE, Gregory; American musician (saxophone, flute), composer and arranger; b. 31 May 1947, Fall River, Mass; two s. one d. *Education:* Berklee Coll. of Music. *Career:* began career as lead alto-saxophone with Ray Charles Orchestra 1976–78; formed own group Channel One 1978; played tenor sax with Artie Shaw Orchestra under leadership of Dick Johnson 1986–87; post hard bop soloist at jazz festivals, socs and clubs across USA, Canada, Europe, UK, also Georgia and Russia; workshops and masterclasses; Adjunct Prof. of Jazz Studies, Rhode Island Coll. *Recordings include:* with Greg Abaté Quartet (James Williams, Rufus Reid and Kenny Washington): Bop City Live At Birdland 1991; with Greg Abaté Quintet: Straight Ahead 1993, Dr Jekyll and Mr Hyde 1994, Bop Lives! 1998, Happy Samba 2000; with Greg Abaté and Friends: My Buddy 1997, It's Christmastime 1997, Broken Dreams 2000, Evolution 2002, Horace is Here 2004, Monsters in the Night 2005, Birds of a Feather (with Alan Barnes Quartet) 2008, Monterey Live 2009, First Encounter (with Gary Smulyan) 2010, The Greg Abate Quintet Featuring Phil Woods 2012; as sideman: Bird Lives (with Red Rodney) 1993, Samba Manhattan Style (with Claudio Ruditi) 1996, Blue Chip Jazz (with Mark Soskin, Harvie Swartz). *Publications include:* contrib. to Jazz Times, Penguin Guide To Jazz, Sax Journal, other trade and national newspapers. *Honours:* Arts International Grant 1992. *E-mail:* contact@gregabate.com. *Website:* www .gregabate.com.

ABBAS, Hisham Mohammad, MechEng; Egyptian singer; b. 13 Sept. 1963, Cairo. *Education:* American Univ. of Cairo. *Career:* fmr mem., Aliaa Saleh; mem., Pats Band 1977–78; solo artist 1978–. *Recordings include:* albums: Hisham 1992, Zay el-aol 1995, Ya Leila 1997, Ainy 1997, Kalam el-leil 1999, Habibi dah 2000, Gowwa fi albi 2002, Sebha tehebbak 2004, Ya habibi... ta'ala gamby 2007, Matbataliesh 2009. *Honours:* Orbit Arabic Song Award 1997. *Address:* c/o Alam el-Phan, Cairo, Egypt (office). *Website:* www.hishamabbas .net.

ABBEY, John E.; British record company executive; b. 8 July 1945, London. *Career:* Ed. and founder, Blues and Soul magazine, London 1966–85; Pres. and founder, Contempo Records, London 1971–78; Pres. and co-founder, Ichiban Records Inc. (now Ishi Records) 1985–. *Address:* Ishi Records, Kala Entertainment Group, 500 East Rope Mill Lane, Canton, GA 30115, USA (office). *E-mail:* info@KalaEntertainmentGroup.com. *Website:* www .KalaEntertainmentGroup.com.

THE ABBOTT (see RZA)

ABBOTT, Jacqueline (Jacqui); British singer; b. 10 Nov. 1973, Whiston, Merseyside. *Career:* mem., The Beautiful South 1994–2000, reformed with Paul Heaton in duo 2014–. *Recordings:* albums: with The Beautiful South: Miaow 1994, Blue Is The Colour 1996, Quench 1998, Painting It Red 2000; with Paul Heaton: What Have We Become? 2014, Wisdom, Laughter and Lines 2015. *Website:* paulheaton.co.uk.

ABDOU, Saabou; Niger musician; b. 28 Dec. 1963, Maradi; m. Hassana Abdou; five s. two d. *Career:* live concerts; mem. ANACIM. *Compositions:* Saadou, Bori, Carnaval, Tchoun Koussouma. *Recordings:* Carnaval, Tchoun Koussouma. *Honours:* Best Musician of the Year 1998, Certificate of Honour 1997. *Current Management:* c/o Band Leader, Carnaval Maradi, Maradi, Niger.

ABDOULAHI, Alhousseini, (Abdalla); Malian singer, songwriter and musician (guitar); b. 1968, In-Lamawene. *Career:* mem. Touareg group, Tinariwen. *Recordings include:* albums: The Radio Tisdas Sessions 2000, Amassakoul 2004, Aman Iman: Water is Life 2007, Imidiwan (Uncut Music Award) 2009, Tassili (Grammy Award for Best World Music Album 2012) 2011. *Honours:* BBC Radio 3 Award for World Music (Africa) 2005. *Address:* c/o Independiente Ltd, 40 Adam and Eve Mews, London W8 6UJ, England. *Telephone:* (20) 7368-2241. *Fax:* (20) 7937-9642. *E-mail:* info@independiente .co.uk. *Website:* www.tinariwen.com; www.independiente.co.uk.

ABDUL, Paula Julie; American singer and choreographer; b. 19 June 1962, San Fernando, Calif.; d. of Harry Abdul and Lorraine Abdul; m. 1st Emilio Estevez 1992 (divorced 1994); m. 2nd Brad Beckerman 1996 (divorced 1998). *Education:* Van Nuys High School, Northridge Coll. California State Univ. *Career:* choreographer, LA Laker basketball cheerleaders; choreographer for several bands, including Duran Duran, Toto, The Pointer Sisters, ZZ Top; scenes in films Bull Durham, Coming To America, The Waiting Game, The Doors, Touched By Evil, Junior High School; City of Crime video (from film Dragnet); worldwide performances as singer include tours throughout USA, UK, Japan and Far East; f. Co Dance (dance co.); series judge, various TV series including: American Idol: The Search for a Superstar 2002–09, The X Factor (USA) 2011–12, So You Think You Can Dance 2014–. *Choreography includes:* pop videos: The Jacksons and Mick Jagger's Torture, George Michael's Monkey, Janet Jackson's Control, Nasty (MTV Video Award for best choreography 1987), When I Think Of You, What Have You Done For Me Lately; television: Dolly Parton Christmas Special, Tracey Ullman Show (Emmy Award for best choreography) 1989. *Television includes:* as series judge: American Idol: The Search for a Superstar 2002–09, Live to Dance 2011, The X Factor (USA version) 2011–12, So You Think You Can Dance (Australian version) 2014, (USA version) 2015–. *Recordings include:* albums: Forever Your Girl 1989, Shut Up And Dance (The Dance Mixes) 1990, Spellbound 1991, Head Over Heels 1995, Greatest Hits 2000. *Honours:* Rolling Stone Award for Best Female Singer 1989, American Music Awards for Favorite Pop/Rock Female Vocalist 1989, 1992, Billboard Magazine Top Female Pop Album 1990, Grammy Award for Best Music Video (for Opposites Attract) 1991, Starlight Foundation Humanitarian of the Year, Los Angeles 1992. *Website:* www.paulaabdul.com.

ABERCROMBIE, John; American jazz musician (guitar); b. 16 Dec. 1944, Portchester, NY. *Education:* Berklee Coll. of Music. *Career:* musician with Johnny 'Hammond' Smith, Dreams (with Michael and Randy Brecker), Chico Hamilton Band, Gil Evans, Gato Barbieri, Billy Cobham's Spectrum; founder of own trio, Timeless; founder of trio, Gateway (with Jack DeJohnette and Dave Holland) 1975; leader of own quartet 1978; also worked with Ralph Towner, Michael Brecker, Jan Garbarek, Jack DeJohnette's New Directions, Jan Hammer. *Recordings include:* albums: Timeless 1974, Works 1974, Gateway 1975, Gateway 2 1977, Characters 1977, Arcade 1978, Straight Flight 1979, M 1980, Solar 1982, Night 1984, Current Events 1985, Getting There 1987, John Abercrombie, Marc Johnson and Peter Erskine 1988,

Animato 1989, Upon a Time 1989, While We're Young 1992, November 1992, Speak Of The Devil 1993, Nosmo King 1994, Gateway: Homecoming 1994, In the Moment 1994, Farewell 1995, Tactics Live 1996, Open Land 1999, The Hudson Project 2000, Cat 'N' Mouse 2002, Class Trip 2004, Structures 2006, The Third Quartet 2007, Coincidence 2008, Topics 2008, Tales (with Robert Balzar) 2009, Wait Til You See Her 2009, Within A Song (with Joe Lovano, Drew Gress and Joey Baron) 2012, 39 Steps (with Marc Copland, Drew Gress and Joey Baron) 2013; numerous other collaborative albums. *Current Management:* c/o Maurice Montoya Music Agency, 11 Island Avenue, Suite 1711, Miami, FL, 33139, USA. *Telephone:* (212) 229-9160; (305) 763-8961. *Fax:* (305) 831-4472. *E-mail:* info@mmmusicagency.com. *Website:* www.mmmusicagency.com. *E-mail:* john@johnabercrombie.com (home). *Website:* www.johnabercrombie.com.

ABILDGAARD, Bertel; Danish musician, songwriter and actor; b. 2 April 1955, Soborg; m. 1984; one s. two d. *Career:* mem. cabaret group, 5XKAJ 1982–; solo artist 1995–; mem. Danske Populærautorer. *Television:* Room Service (main character, Tony, comedy series), many television, radio plays. *Film:* Kajs Fosdeldag 1990. *Recordings:* Kajsynger Pop 1984, Agte Kærlighed 1987, Alle Bornene 1991, Krumme Tær-sang 1992. *Honours:* Se Og Hors Humor Pris 1988. *Current Management:* Erik Morbo/Vagn Moller, Dansk Dirma Og Hotel, Underholding Aps, Rosenyparken 81, 2670 Greve, Denmark; c/o Avenue Music, Dkovvænget 22, 4862 Guldborg, Denmark. *Telephone:* (70) 20-05-34; (40) 20-11-85. *E-mail:* info@avenuemusic.dk; guitarkaj@gmail.com. *Website:* www.avenuemusic.dk; www.guitarkaj.dk.

ÅBORG, Carl Anders, MA; Swedish musician, journalist, radio producer and teacher; *Museum Educationalist, Statens Försvarshistoriska Museer*; b. 24 March 1952, Malmö; m. 1st (divorced); two s. one d.; m. 2nd; one s. *Education:* degree in ethnology, Swedish and media communication. *Career:* mem. Aston Reymers Rivaler 1979–85, Drömpojkarna, OJJ!600, Prins Lätt, Klarskinn, Hugh Scott Band II; currently works in Educ. Dept, Armémuseum, Stockholm. *Theatre appearance:* Roskilde 1982. *Compositions:* Håll mig hårt, Vi bygger om, Rosa-Lill and 90 other songs. *Films:* Alska mig 1984, Magister Flykt 1984, Herr Bohm och sillen 1986, Olssons pastejer 1988. *Television:* own show 1981, Nygammalt 1982. *Recordings include:* with Aston Reymers Rivaler: Från Myggjagare till foträta 1979, Krääl 1980, Tvål 1981, Aston! 1983, I grodornas land 1984, Mästerverk 1995; with Drömpojkarna: Drömpojkarna 1978; with OJJ!600: OJJ!600 1986; with Prins Lätt: Nåt att gnaga på 1999; with Klarskinn: Klarskinn 2004, Tretton 2007, Fyra nya melodier 2012; with Hugh Scott Band II: Bryndwr Road Vol. 1 2006. *Honours:* Munich Youth Prize for Film Animation 1988. *Address:* Per Lindeströms väg 72, 12146 Johanneshov, Sweden (home). *E-mail:* anders.aborg@armemuseum.se (office); anders.aborg@gmail.com (home).

ABOU-KHALIL, Rabih; Lebanese composer, arranger and musician (flute, oud); b. 17 Aug. 1957, Machghara. *Education:* Acad. of Music, Munich, Germany. *Career:* numerous collaborations, including Sonny Fortune, Glen Valez, Milton Cardona, Howard Levy, Glen Moore, Steve Swallow, Quartet Balanescu. *Recordings:* albums: Compositions and Improvisations 1981, Bitter Harvest 1984, Between Dusk and Dawn 1986, Bukra 1988, Nafas 1988, Roots and Sprouts 1990, Al-Jadida 1990, Blue Camel 1992, Tarab 1992, The Sultan's Picnic 1994, Arabian Waltz 1995, Odd Times 1998, Yara 1998, The Cactus of Knowledge 2000, Il Sospiro 2002, Morton's Foot 2003, Journey to the Centre of an Egg 2005, Songs for Sad Women 2007, Em Portugues 2008, Selection 2009, Trouble in Jerusalem 2010. *Honours:* German Critics' Award 2003. *Current Management:* c/o Boris Jourdain, soundsurveyor, Domaine de Bezons, 1 rue Jean Carrasso, 95870 Bezons, France. *Telephone:* (9) 66-93-97-72. *E-mail:* boris@soundsurveyor.com. *Website:* www.soundsurveyor.com; www.rabihaboukhalil.com.

ABRAHAMS, Mick; British musician (guitar); b. 7 April 1943, Luton. *Career:* guitarist with Neil Christian; Dickie Pride; Toggery Five; McGregor's Engine; mem., Jethro Tull, 1967–69; numerous concerts, festival appearances; founder, Blodwyn Pig, re-formed 1988; solo artist 1971–; financial consultant 1970s–80s. *Recordings include:* with Jethro Tull: This Was, 1968; Love Story, 1969; with Blodwyn Pig: Ahead Rings Out, 1969; Getting To This, 1970; All Said And Done, 1991; Lies (A New Day), 1993; Solo albums: Mick Abrahams, 1971; A Musical Evening With Mick Abrahams, 1971; At Last, 1982, One 1996, See My Way 2000, Leaving Home Blues 2005, Mick's Back 2008, Times Have Changed 2009. *Publication:* What is a Wommett: The Autobiography of Mick Abrahams 2008. *Current Management:* Serious Bob Promotions, 250 West 85th Street, Suite 11D, New York, NY 10024, USA. *E-mail:* mickaby2@btinternet.com (home). *Website:* www.squirrelmusic.com (home).

ABRAMS, Muhal Richard; American composer, musician (piano, clarinet) and educator; b. (Richard Abrahams), 19 Sept. 1930, Chicago, Ill. *Education:* Chicago Musical Coll., Governors State Univ. *Career:* composer and arranger for Walter 'King' Fleming Jazz Orchestra 1955; performer with numerous soloists, including James Moody, Eddie Harris; co-founder, MJT+3 1955; formed the Experimental Band 1961; toured and recorded as soloist and with others, various Muhal Richard Abrams groups 1970s; moved to New York 1977; composer and performer with numerous ensembles, including the Muhal Richard Abrams Sextet 1977–; taught at Banff Centre, Canada, Columbia Univ., , California Inst. for the Arts, Syracuse Univ., , BMI Composers' Workshop; Co-founder and first Pres. Asscn for the Advancement of Creative Musicians (AACM) 1965, Founder AACM School of Music 1969, Pres. New York chapter; fmr panellist Nat. Endowment for the Arts and New York State Council on the Arts; mem. Bd of Dirs Nat. Jazz Service Org., Meet the Composer. *Compositions include:* Egypic 1955, End Of The Line 1955, The Bird Song 1967, Levels and Degrees Of Light 1967, Wise In Time 1969, Young At Heart 1969, Zambezi Dance 1972, Aleph The Fool 1973, Afrisong 1975, Ballad for New Souls 1975, Ballad for Old Souls 1975, Blues for M 1975, Two Over One 1975, Arhythm Songy 1977, Balladi 1977, Charlie in the Parker 1977, Excerpts 1977, B Song 1978, Bud P 1978, D Song 1978, Duo 1 1978, Duo 2 1978, Balu 1980, Fafca 1980, Ancient & Future Reflections 1981, Blues Forever 1981, Chambea 1981, Cluster for Many Worlds 1981, Duet for One World 1981, Quintet for soprano, piano, harp, cello and violin 1982, Down The Street From The Gene Ammons Public School 1982, Du King 1982, The Fairness Of Life 1982, Improvisation Structures I-II-III-IV-V-VI for piano 1983, Blessed Be The Heavens At 12 1983, Bloodline 1983, Trio for piano 1984, Down At Peppers 1984, Odyssey of King for orchestra 1984, String Quartet No. 2 1985, Saturation Blue for orchestra 1986, Piano Duet No. 1 for piano (four hands) 1986, Duet for Violin and Piano 1986, C.C.'s World 1986, Colors in Thirty-Third 1986, Direflex 1986, Drumman Cyrille 1986, Continuous Variation 1988, Folk Tales '88 for orchestra 1988, Big T 1989, Fanfare 1989, Fortex 1989, Hearinga Suite 1989, Blu Blu Blu 1990, Cycles Five 1990, Petsrof 1990, Plus Equal Minus Balance 1990, Ode To The Imagination 1990, Scenes and Colors 1990, Septone 1990, One For The Whistler 1990, What A Man for Orchestra 1991, Nusped 1991, Transversion 1 1991, String Quartet No. 3 1992, Strings & Things 1992, Familytalk 1993, DizBirdMonkBudMax (A Tribute) 1993, Illuso 1993, Meditation 1993, Before and After 1994, The Harmonic Veil 1994, The Junction 1994, Crossbeams 1994, Encore 1994, Scaledance 1994, Saxophone Quartet No. 1 1994, New Horizons 1995, Ensemble Song 1995, The Prism 3 1995, Eleven Over Four 1995, Hydepth 1995, Textures 95 1995, Tribute to Julius Hemphill and Don Pullen 1995, Think All Focus One 1995, One Line Two Views 1995, One Merger 1996, Over The Same Over 1996, Dabadubada 1996, GMBR 1996, Linetime 1996, Marching With Honor 1996, Imagine 1996, Song For All 1996, Steamin' Up The Road 1996, Blues For You 1997, The Visibility of Thought 2001, Streaming 2005, Vision Towards Essence 2007, Spectrum 2010, numerous other collaborative albums. *Honours:* Danish Jazz Center Int. JazzPar Award, Copenhagen, Denmark 1990, Nat. Endowment for the Arts Jazz Master Award 2010. *E-mail:* info@pirecordings.com. *Website:* www.pirecordings.com.

ACE; British musician (guitar); b. (Martin Ivor Kent), 30 March 1967, Cheltenham. *Career:* Founder mem., Skunk Anansie 1994–2001, 2009–; numerous headlining tours, festival appearances, television and radio shows; solo artist 2001–. *Recordings include:* albums: Paranoid And Sunburnt 1995, Stoosh 1996, Post Orgasmic Chill 1999, Smashes and Trashes 2009, Wonderlustre 2010, Black Traffic 2012. *Website:* www.skunkanansie.net.

ADAMS, Bryan, OC; Canadian/British rock singer, songwriter, musician (guitar) and photographer; b. 5 Nov. 1959, Kingston, Ont.; pnr Alicia Grimaldi; two d. *Career:* numerous world-wide tours. *Recordings:* albums: Bryan Adams 1980, You Want It You Got It 1981, Cuts Like A Knife 1983, Reckless 1984, Into The Fire 1987, Waking Up The Neighbours 1991, So Far So Good 1992, Live! Live! Live! 1995, 18 'Til I Die 1996, MTV Unplugged 1987, On A Day Like Today 1998, The Best Of Me 2000, Spirit: Stallion of Cimarron (film soundtrack) 2002, Room Service 2004, 11 2008, Bare Bones 2010, Tracks of My Years 2014, Get Up! 2015. *Photography exhibitions:* Toronto, Montréal, Saatchi Gallery, London, Royal Jubilee Exhbn, Windsor Castle 2002. *Publications:* Bryan Adams: The Official Biography 1995, Made in Canada (photographs by Bryan Adams). *Honours:* 15 Juno Awards, Recording Artist of the Decade, Canada, Grammy Award, American Music Award, Gov.-Gen's Performing Arts Award for Lifetime Artistic Achievement 2010. *Current Management:* The Leighton-Pope Organisation, 8 Glenthorne Mews, 115a Glenthorne Road, Hammersmith, London, W6 0LJ, England. *Telephone:* (20) 8741-4453. *Fax:* (20) 8741-4289. *E-mail:* info@l-po.com. *Address:* 425 Carrall Street, Suite 520, Vancouver, BC V6B 6E3, Canada (office). *E-mail:* info@bryanadams.com (office). *Website:* www.bryanadams.com.

ADAMS, Faye Ann, BSc, MEd; American voice teacher and music teacher (piano, band and orchestra); b. 24 March 1952, Allentown, Pa; m. Ronald G. Adams 1974; two d. *Education:* Kutztown State Univ., Mansfield State Univ. School of Music. *Career:* soprano, piano accompanist, proprietor and instructor, Willing Hearts, Hands and Voices Music Studio; former head music specialist, Reading City School Dist; solo vocalist in Pennsylvania German dialect, German Festival (Heemt Fescht). *Publications:* Events at Allemangel: Historic Research on Berks County History 1995, There is a Place (musical score, instrumental and vocal parts) 2004. *Honours:* Zeswitz Music Award for Music Achievement 1973, 1974.

ADAMS, H. Leslie, MusM, PhD; American composer; b. 30 Dec. 1932, Cleveland, OH. *Education:* Glenville High School, Oberlin Coll. Conservatory of Music, OH, California State Univ., Long Beach, Ohio State Univ., Univ. of Kansas, Cleveland Inst. of Music. *Career:* piano accompanist for ballet and dance companies in New York, numerous performances of his compositions 1957–62; Assoc. Musical Dir Karamu House, Cleveland, OH 1964–65, Composer-in-Residence 1979–80; Musical Dir Kaleidoscope Players, Raton, NM 1967–68; Composer-in-Residence, Cuyahoga Community Coll., Cleveland 1980, Cleveland Music School Settlement 1981–82; Founder and Pres. Accord Assocs. Inc. 1980–86, Exec. Vice-Pres. and Composer-in-Residence 1986–92; Exec. Vice-Pres. and Composer-in-Residence, Creative Arts Inc. 1997–; teacher, Soehl Jr High School, Linden, NJ 1962–63, secondary schools in Raton, NM 1966–67; Asst Prof. of Music, Florida A&M Univ., Tallahassee

1968; Assoc. Prof. of Music, Dir of the Univ. Choir and Dir of Choral Clinics, Univ. of Kansas, Lawrence 1970–78; mem. Advisory Council, Musical Arts Asscn (Cleveland Orchestra) 1982; mem. American Choral Dirs Asscn, American Guild of Organists. *Compositions:* Hark, to the Shouting Wind! 1951, I Hear A Voice 1951, Night 1951, The Constant Lover 1951, Break, Break, Break 1951, Teach Me, O Lord (from Psalm 119) 1951, Turn Away Mine Eyes 1951, Four Pieces for piano 1951, Pastorale for violin and piano 1952, Asperges Me for chorus 1952, Two Vachel Lindsay Songs 1952–53, Of Man's First Disobedience (from Paradise Lost) 1953, On the Sea 1953, Seven Amen Chorale Responses 1953, Intermezzo for violin and piano 1953, Theme and Variations in A-flat Major (or Variations on a Serious Theme) 1953, A Kiss in Xanadu (ballet) 1954, The Congo 1955, Romance for orchestra 1960, Five Songs on Texts by Edna St Vincent Millay (or Five Millay Songs) 1960, Six Songs (on Texts by African-American Poets) 1961, A White Road 1961, Sonata for violin and piano 1961, Three Preludes for piano 1961, Sonata for horn and piano 1961, Contrasts for piano 1961, Concerto for piano and orchestra (or CitiScape) 1964, All the Way Home 1965, Madrigal for chorus 1969, Love Song for chorus 1969, Hosanna to the Son of David for chorus 1969, Psalm 121 for chorus 1969, Under the Greenwood Tree for chorus 1969, Psalm 23 for chorus 1970, There Was an Old Man for chorus 1970, Vocalise for chorus 1973, Man's Presence: A Song of Ecology for chorus 1975, Trombone Quartet 1975, Sonata for cello and piano 1975, Etude in G Minor 1977, Prelude and Fugue for organ 1979, Ode to Life for orchestra 1979, Dunbar Songs (or Three Songs on Texts of Paul Laurence Dunbar) 1981, Christmas Lullaby 1983, Night Song for flute and harp 1983, Symphony No. 1 1983, The Righteous Man: A Cantata to the Memory of Dr Martin Luther King Jr (or Cantata No. 1) 1985, Blake (opera) 1986, The Wider View 1988, Hymn to Freedom 1989, Love Expressions 1990, Love Memory 1990, What Love Brings 1991, A Christmas Wish for chorus 1991, Offering of Love for organ 1991, Amazing Grace 1992, Song of the Innkeeper's Children 1992, Song to Baby Jesus 1992, Christmas Lullaby for orchestra with chorus 1993, Song of Thanks 1993, Love Request 1993, Lullaby Eternal 1993, Anniversary Song 1993, Flying 1993, Midas, Poor Midas 1994, From a Hotel Room 1994, Daybirth 1994, Western Adventure for orchestra 1994, Hymn to All Nations for chorus 1997, Slaves (a drama with music) 2005. *Publications:* contrib. articles The Mahlerian Mystique 1969, The Problems of Composing Choral Music for High School Use 1973. *Honours:* Nat. Asscn of Negro Women Inc. Composition Competition, New York 1963, Nat. Educ. Defense Act Fellowship 1969–70, Christian Arts Inc. Nat. Award for Original Composition for Choral Ensemble, New York 1974, Nat. Endowment for the Arts Award 1979, Rockefeller Foundation Study and Conference Center, Bellagio Italy 1979, Yaddo Artists Colony, Saratoga Springs NY 1980, 1984, Cleveland Foundation Fellow 1980, Jennings Foundation Fellow 1981, 'Meet The Artist' Cleveland Ohio Public Schools, Nat. Opera Asscn Legacy Award 2006, Distinguished Alumnus Award, California State Univ., Long Beach 2006, Gems of Cleveland Award 2007. *Current Management:* Creative Arts Inc., 9409 Kempton Avenue, Cleveland, OH 44108; Avava Artists Management, 229 West 134th Street, New York, NY 10030, USA. *E-mail:* CreativeArtsInc@webtv.net; avidw@avavaartists.com. *Telephone:* (212) 502-0306 (office). *E-mail:* HLeslieAdams@webtv.net (home). *Website:* www.hleslieadams.com.

ADAMS, Justin Alexander; British musician (guitar) and producer. *Career:* fmr mem. Jah Wobble's Invaders of the Heart; producer Lo'jo 1996–; Founding mem. Justin Adams & The Wayward Sheikhs; Founding mem. Les Triaboliques; other collaborations include Brian Eno, Daniel Lanois, Sinead O'Connor, Billy Bragg, Peter Gabriel, Nusrat Fateh Ali Khan, Robert Plant, Chaka Demus and Pliers, Baaba Maal, Moodswings, Davy Spillane, Iarla O'Lionaird, Angelique Kidjo, Adrian Sherwood, Jakie Liebezeit, Frank Chickens, Blyth Power, Natacha Atlas, Abdel Ali Slimani, Juldeh Camara; television work for BBC, ITV, Channel 4, MTV. *Film scores include:* The Kitchen Child 1990, When the Red Wind Blows 1999, Amor 2009, Sex and the City 2 2010. *Recordings include:* albums: with Jah Wobble: Invaders of the Heart: Rising Above Bedlam 1991, Without Judgement 1993, Take Me To God 1993; solo: Desert Road 2000, Kin 2001; with Juldeh Camara: Soul Science (BBC Radio 3 World Music Award for Culture Crossing 2008) 2007, Tell No Lies 2009; with Les Triaboliques: rivermudtwilight 2009; as producer for Lo'jo: Mojo Radio 1997, Bohême de Cristal 2000, Au cabaret sauvage/L'une des siens 2002. *Address:* c/o Sasa Music, 309 Aberdeen House, 22–24 Highbury Grove, London, N5 2EA, England (office). *E-mail:* rab@sasa.demon.co.uk (office). *Website:* www.sasamusic.com (office).

ADAMS, Oleta; American singer; b. Seattle, WA. *Career:* leader, own trio, 1980s; cabaret singer, Kansas; singer with Tears For Fears, album and tours, 1987; solo artist, 1990–. *Recordings:* albums: Circle Of One (1990; Evolution, 1993; Never Knew, 1995; Movin' On, 1995; Come Walk With Me, 1997; The Very Best Of…, 1998; All The Love, 2001, Christmas Time with Oleta 2006, Let's Stay Here 2009; singles: Rhythm Of Life, 1990; Get Here, 1991; Circle Of One, 1991; Don't Let The Sun Go Down On Me, 1992; I Just Had To Hear Your Voice, 1993; with Tears For Fears: Woman In Chains, Badman's Song, on album The Seeds Of Love, 1989. *Current Management:* c/o Chevy Nash, ENGINE Entertainment, 209 10th Avenue South, Suite 429B, Nashville, TN 37203, USA. *Telephone:* (615) 248-3335. *E-mail:* chevynash@comcast.net; engineentertainment@comcast.net. *Website:* www.oletaadams.com.

ADAMS, Pierrette; Republic of the Congo singer; b. 5 May 1962, Pointe-Noire. *Career:* solo artist 1994–. *Recordings include:* albums: Journal Intime 1994, Mal de mère 1996, Je vous salue maris 1999, Absolument 2001,

Anesthésie 2003, Coma profond 2007, 7e Jour 2012. *Address:* c/o X-Pol Music, 5 rue Montebelo, Vitry sur Seine 94400 Paris, France. *E-mail:* info@pierrette-adams.com. *Website:* www.pierrette-adams.com.

ADAMS, (David) Ryan; American singer, songwriter and musician (guitar, piano); b. 5 Nov. 1974, Jacksonville, NC; m. Mandy Moore 2009. *Career:* mem., Patty Duke Syndrome; mem., alternative country band Whiskeytown 1994–97; tribute album to Gram Parsons with Emmylou Harris; solo artist 2000–, with band The Cardinals 2004–09. *Recordings include:* albums: with Whiskeytown: Faithless Street 1996, Strangers Almanac 1997, Rural Free Delivery (with Emmylou Harris) 1997, Pneumonia 2001; with The Cardinals: Cold Roses 2005, Jacksonville City Nights 2005, Follow the Lights 2007, Cardinology 2008; solo: Heartbreaker 2000, Gold 2001, Demolition 2002, Answering Bell 2002, Rock N Roll 2003, Love Is Hell 2004, 29 2005, Easy Tiger 2007, Orion 2010, Ashes & Fire 2011, Ryan Adams 2014. *Publications include:* poetry: Infinity Blues 2008, Hello Sunshine 2009. *Honours:* NME Award for Best Solo Artist 2003, Q Merit Award 2007. *Website:* www.ryan-adams.com.

ADE, King Sunny; Nigerian singer; b. 1 Sept. 1946, Oshogbo. *Career:* played with semi-professional juju bands in Nigeria; lead guitarist, Rhythm Dandies 1964; also played with Tunde Nightingale; formed the Green Spots 1966, renamed the African Beats late 60s; formed own label, Sunny Alade Records 1975; est. Ariya, own juju nightclub, Lagos, Nigeria; also owns an oil firm, a mining co. and a film and video production co.; f. King Sunny Ade Foundation for young musicians and performers, Lagos; formed supergroup The Way Forward 1996; tours include UK, USA and Japan; formed group, Golden Mercury. *Film appearances:* Juju Music 1988, Live At Montreux 1990, Roots of Rhythm 1997. *Recordings include:* albums: Alanu Loluwa 1967, Sunny Ade Live Play 1976, In London 1977, Festac 77 1978, The Message 1981, Ariya Special 1982, Conscience 1982, Juju Music 1982, Synchro System 1983, Aura 1984, Otito 1985, Saviour 1986, Funmilayo 1989, Live At The Hollywood Palace 1992, E Dide 1995, Odu 1998, Seven Degrees North 2000, Dr Sehindemi 2003, Omo Wunmi 2003, Seven Degrees North 2009, Bábá mo Túndé 2010. *Honours:* Award for Outstanding Contribution to World Music 2008. *Address:* c/o Mesa/Bluemoon Recordings, 2276 Plover Court, Arroyo Grande, CA 93420, USA (office). *E-mail:* info@mesabluemoon.com (office). *Website:* mesabluemoon.com (office).

ADEBIMPE, Tunde; American singer. *Education:* New York Univ. *Career:* fmr computer animator in Brooklyn; Founder-mem., TV on the Radio 2001–; artist, working with stop-motion animation. *Recordings include:* albums: Desperate Youth, Bloodthirsty Babes 2004, Return to Cookie Mountain 2006, Dear Science 2008, Nine Types of Light 2011, Seeds 2014. *Honours:* Shortlist Music Prize 2004. *Address:* c/o 4AD, 17–19 Alma Road, London, SW18 1AA, England (office). *E-mail:* 4ad@4ad.com (office). *Website:* www.4ad.com (office); www.tvontheradio.com.

ADEDAYO, Olu Shola, BSc, RN, HND, MA; British singer and actress; *Managing Director, Taurus Records (UK) Ltd;* b. 27 April 1971, Nigeria. *Education:* trained as a nurse, midwife and health visitor. *Career:* many ventures with African band Leke Leke 1990–93; mem. all-girl dance band, Orage; Man. Dir Taurus Records (UK) Ltd; currently DJ, African radio station programme, Shola's Your Health; mem. Musicians' Union, British Acad. of Composers and Songwriters, Music of Black Origin (MOBO); has appeared in print advertisements for Learn Direct, Tower Hamlets Coll.; now owns Private Health Visitor and also works as a wedding planner. *Film appearances:* Secrets 2001, Temptation 2002, Oke Ga J'oke 2003, In Your Dreams 2006. *Recordings:* albums: with Leke Leke: Leke Leke; solo: Seun Re Re 2004. *Television:* advertisements for Nigerian TV, UK adverts. *Telephone:* (20) 8697-2181 (office). *Fax:* (20) 8697-2181 (home). *E-mail:* shola020@hotmail.co.uk (home). *Website:* www.privatehealthvisitor.com (office); www.designerweddingplanner.com (office).

ADELE, MBE; British singer and songwriter; b. (Adele Laurie Blue Adkins), 5 May 1988, London, England. *Education:* BRIT School for Performing Arts and Tech. *Career:* professional solo artist 2008–; tours in UK, USA, Canada; worked with Jim Abiss, Eg White and Mark Ronson; recorded with the Raconteurs, sang with Burt Bacharach at BBC Electric Proms 2008. *Television:* Ushi Says: Hi 2001, Saturday Night Live 2008, Ugly Betty 2009. *Recordings include:* albums: 19 2008, 21 (Grammy Awards for Album of the Year 2012, for Best Pop Vocal Album 2012, Mastercard British Album of the Year, BRIT Awards 2012, Billboard Music Award for Top Pop Album 2013) 2011, 25 2015. *Honours:* Critics' Choice Award, BRIT Awards 2008, BRIT Award for Best British Female Solo Artist 2012, Grammy Awards for Best Female Pop Vocal Performance 2008, for Best New Artist 2008, for Record of the Year 2012, for Song of the Year 2012, for Best Pop Solo Performance 2012, for Best Short Form Music Video 2012, for Best Pop Solo Performance 2013, for Best Song Written for Visual Media (for Skyfall) 2014 Songwriter of the Year, Ivor Novello Awards 2012, Ivor Novello Award for Most Performed Work of 2011 (for Rolling in the Deep) 2012, Golden Globe Award for Best Original Song in a Motion Picture (for Skyfall) 2013, Academy Award for Best Original Song (with Paul Epworth) (for Skyfall) 2013. *Address:* c/o XL Recordings, 1 Codrington Mews, London, W11 2EH, England. *E-mail:* info@septembermanagement.com. *Website:* www.xlrecordings.com; www.adele.tv.

ADKINS, (Tracy Deryl) Trace; American country singer and musician (guitar); b. 13 Jan. 1962, Sarepta, La; two d. *Education:* Louisiana Technical Univ. *Career:* worked on an oil rig for several years before deciding to pursue musical career; joined gospel quartet the New Commitments; solo career early

1990s–. *Recordings include:* albums: with New Commitments: The New Commitment Quartet 1979, with Meat Loaf (guest vocalist) Hell in a Handbasket 2012; solo: Dreamin' Out Loud 1996, Big Time 1997, More Trace Adkins 1999, Chrome 2001, Comin' On Strong 2003, Songs About Me 2005, Honky Tonk Badonkadonk 2006, American Man: Greatest Hits Volume II 2007, Dangerous Man 2006, X 2008, Cowboy's Back in Town 2010, Love Will 2013, The King's Gift 2013. *Publication:* A Personal Stand: Observations and Opinions from a Freethinking Roughneck 2007. *Honours:* winner People's Choice Ark-La-Tex Male Gospel Vocalist of the Year 1980, ACM Award for New Male Vocalist 1997, ACM Award for Best Single (for You're Gonna Miss This) 2009. *E-mail:* fans@traceadkins.com. *Website:* www.traceadkins.com.

ADOLFSSON, Jörgen; Swedish musician and composer; b. 14 March 1951, Hallingeberg; m. Vered Adolfsson Mann 1994; one s. one d. *Education:* Stockholm Univ. *Career:* mem. Archimedes Badkar 1974–80, duo Karl Brothers 1976–, ISKRA 1980–92, Vargavinter 1976, Bitter Funeral Beer Band 1980–86; performed with Kenneth Kvarnstrom Danscompany 1989–91, Cristina Caprioli Danscompany 1992–93, and for modern choreographers Bogdan Szyber, Carina Reich, Greta Lindholm, Efva Lilja; TV and radio productions; performed with Don Cherry, Mongezi Feza, Johnny Dyani, Jon Rose, Lars Gullin, Raymond Strid, Tommy Adolfsson; mem. STIM, FSJ, SKAP, Fylkingen. *Recordings include:* with Archimedes Badkar: Badrock för barn i alla åldrar 1975, II 1976, Tre 1977; with ISKRA: Jazz i Sverige 1975, Allemansrätt 1977, Besvärjelser 1979, Fantasies 1984, Luft 1990; with Vargavinter: Vargavinter 1976; with Bitter Funeral Beer Band: Bitter Funeral Beer 1981, Praise Drumming 1986; with Karl Brothers: Air Change 1995. *Honours:* Grand Prix Int. Video Danse/Carina Ari 1992.

ADOLFSSON, Tommy C.; Swedish musician and composer; b. 21 Oct. 1953, Ljusdal, Halsingland; m. Cecilia Johansson; one d. *Education:* Music School, Economy Coll., Stockholm Music Conservatory, Sussex Univ., Birkagarden Music Coll., studied in music England, Sweden, Tanzania, Malawi, Zambia, Madagascar, Bali and Java, India. *Career:* mem. Archimedes Badkar 1974–80, duo Karl Brothers 1976–, ISKRA 1980–92, Bitter Funeral Beer Band 1980–86, Half Nelson 1985–88, DAST Quartet (South African music and poetry) 1985–90, Swedish Radio jazz group 1990–94, Peter Bryngelsson Project 1992, jazz group Krakatau, Finland 1995–96; performed with Kenneth Kvarnstrom Danscompany 1989–91, Cristina Caprioli Danscompany 1992–93; performed with Tuomo Hapaalas Waterorchestra (at Stockholm Waterfestival) 1994; mem. STIM, SAMI, SKAP. *Recordings include:* with Archimedes Badkar: Badrock för barn i alla åldrar 1975, II 1976, Tre 1977; with Iskra: Jazz i Sverige 1975, Allemansrätt 1977, Besvärjelser 1979, Fantasies 1984, Luft 1990; with Bitter Funeral Beer Band: Bitter Funeral Beer 1981, Praise Drumming 1986; with Karl Brothers: Air Change 1995. *Honours:* Acad. of Art Awards 1985, 1991, 1993, 1994, 1997, STIM Award 1995.

AD-ROCK, (King Adrock); American rap artist and musician (guitar); b. (Adam Horowitz), 31 Oct. 1966, New York. *Career:* mem. The Young and the Useless 1979; mem. rap/rock group, Beastie Boys 1983–2014; numerous tours and festival appearances. *Films include:* Krush Groove 1985, Tougher Than Leather 1988, Lost Angels 1989, Long Road Home 1991, A Kiss Before Dying 1991, Roadside Prophets 1992, Cityscapes: Los Angeles 1994, Godspeed 2007. *Television appearance include:* The Equalizer (series). *Recordings include:* albums: Licensed To Ill 1986, Paul's Boutique 1989, Check Your Head 1992, Ill Communication 1994, Root Down 1995, The In Sound From Way Out 1996, Hello Nasty 1998, Sounds Of Science 1999, To The 5 Boroughs 2004, The Mix-Up (Grammy Award for Best Pop Instrumental Album 2008) 2007, Hot Sauce Committee, Pt. 2 2011. *Honours:* elected to Rock and Roll Hall of Fame (as mem. of Beastie Boys) 2012. *Website:* www.beastieboys.com.

AERTS, Raymond Benedict Charles; Dutch theatre and concert producer and artist agent and manager; b. 12 April 1966, Amsterdam; m. Sarah Frances Kate Reÿs-Smith 1992. *Education:* studied marketing communications and piano. *Career:* with Charles Aerts Theatre Productions International, concert and theatre productions for: Liza Minelli; Ray Charles; Shirley Bassey; Bold and Beautiful In Concert; Lionel Hampton; Don McLean; Oklahoma!; Elvis; Annie Get Your Gun; Maria de Lourdes; artists represented include: Charles Aznavour; Gilbert Bécaud; Nana Mouskouri; Julien Clerc; Lionel Hampton; Maria Callas; Don McLean; Shirley Bassey; mem. Vecta. *Honours:* (with Charles Aerts Theatre Productions Int.) Ridder, Orde van Oranje Nassau, The Netherlands; Chevalier, Ordre des Arts et des Lettres, France; Vecta mem. of honour; cultural awards and honours from Brazil, Hungary, Bulgaria and Indonesia.

AFANASIEFF, Walter; American producer, musician (keyboards, drums, guitar) and songwriter; b. 10 Feb. 1958, Brazil; pnr; three c. *Career:* played keyboards with violinist Jean-Luc Ponty; formed band The Warriors with Joaquin Lievano; became prod. for Sony Music; collaborations with Christina Aguilera, Clay Aiken, All-4-One, Allure, Marc Anthony, Babyface, Regina Belle, George Benson, Michael Bolton, Boyz II Men, Mariah Carey, Coco, Céline Dion, Destiny's Child, Kenny G., Josh Groban, Whitney Houston, Michael Jackson, Leona Lewis, Trey Lorenz, Ricky Martin, *NSYNC, Aaron Neville, New Kids on the Block, Lionel Richie, Savage Garden, Barbra Streisand, Luther Vandross, Narada Michael Walden, Mika, Johnny Mathis, Rhydian, Brian McKnight. *Honours:* Grammy Award for Producer of the Year 2000. *Address:* Sony BMG Music Entertainment, 550 Madison Avenue, New York, NY 10022-3211, USA (office). *Telephone:* (212) 833-8000. *Fax:* (212) 833-4818. *Website:* www.sonymusic.com.

AG ALHABIB, Ibrahim, (Abreybone); Malian singer, songwriter and musician (guitar); b. 1958, Tessalit. *Career:* founder mem. Touareg group, Tinariwen 1982–. *Recordings include:* albums: The Radio Tisdas Sessions 2000, Amassakoul 2004, Aman Iman: Water is Life 2007, Imidiwan (Uncut Music Award) 2009. *Honours:* BBC Radio 3 Award for World Music (Africa) 2005. *Address:* c/o Independiente Ltd, The Drill Hall, 3 Heathfield Terrace, London W4 4JE, England (office). *E-mail:* tinariwen@apartment22.com (office); info@independiente.co.uk (office). *Website:* www.tinariwen.com.

AG AYAD, Said; Malian musician (percussion); b. 1979, Abeibara. *Career:* mem. Touareg group, Tinariwen. *Recordings include:* albums: The Radio Tisdas Sessions 2000, Amassakoul 2004, Aman Iman: Water is Life 2007, Imidiwan (Uncut Music Award) 2009. *Honours:* BBC Radio 3 Award for World Music (Africa) 2005. *Address:* c/o Independiente Ltd, The Drill Hall, 3 Heathfield Terrace, London W4 4JE, England (office). *E-mail:* tinariwen@apartment22.com (office); info@independiente.co.uk (office). *Website:* www.tinariwen.com.

AG HAMID, Elaga; Malian musician (guitar). *Career:* mem. Touareg group, Tinariwen. *Recordings include:* albums: The Radio Tisdas Sessions 2000, Amassakoul 2004, Aman Iman: Water is Life 2007, Imidiwan (Uncut Music Award) 2009. *Honours:* BBC Radio 3 Award for World Music (Africa) 2005. *Address:* c/o Independiente Ltd, The Drill Hall, 3 Heathfield Terrace, London W4 4JE, England (office). *E-mail:* tinariwen@apartment22.com (office); info@independiente.co.uk (office). *Website:* www.tinariwen.com.

AG LECHE, Eyadou; Malian singer and musician (guitar); b. 1978, Kidal. *Career:* mem. Touareg group, Tinariwen. *Recordings include:* albums: The Radio Tisdas Sessions 2000, Amassakoul 2004, Aman Iman: Water is Life 2007, Imidiwan (Uncut Music Award) 2009. *Honours:* BBC Radio 3 Award for World Music (Africa) 2005. *Address:* c/o Independiente Ltd, The Drill Hall, 3 Heathfield Terrace, London W4 4JE, England (office). *E-mail:* tinariwen@apartment22.com (office); info@independiente.co.uk (office). *Website:* www.tinariwen.com.

AGERSKOV, Flemming Michael; Danish musician (trumpet); b. 29 Sept. 1963, Holstebro; two d. *Education:* Conservatory of Århus, studied in Kyoto, Japan. *Career:* played with Marc Johnson, Eliane Elias, Marilyn Mazur, Jonas Johansen, Jon Balke, Martin France, Joakim Milder, Fredrik Lundin, Ray Charles, Iain Ballamy, Josefine Cronholm, Kresten Osgood, Egberto Gísmonti; formed own group, Face to Face, with Martin France, Julian Argüelles, Jesper Nordenstroem and Hans Andersson 1997; Binocular with pianist Makiko Hirabayashi and accordionist Francesco Cali. *Recordings:* CV Joergensen: Sjaelland, Fraklip fra det fjrrne, Kim Kristensen: A Jazzpar 93 Project on Storyville, Flemming Agershov: Face to Face 1999, Josefine Cronholm/Ibis: Wild Garden, Peter Danemo: Alive. *Publication:* The Two Rooms 2000. *Honours:* Trumpet Player of the Year 1991, Danish Music Award, Push To Participate, Takuan 2001. *Address:* Esthersvej 8, 2, 2900 Hellerup, Denmark (home). *Telephone:* 33-93-04-71 (office); 29-91-80-09 (office). *E-mail:* agerskov@email.dk (home).

AGGETT, Piers Sean, BSc (Hons); British electronic musician (keyboards), songwriter and record producer; b. 1987. *Education:* Leeds Metropolitan Univ. *Career:* Founder-mem. Rudimental 2010–; released debut single Deep in the Valley 2011; collaborations with MC Shantie, Adiyam, MNEK and Syron, John Newman, Alex Clare, Angel Haze, Ella Eyre, Emeli Sandé, Nas, Foxes. *Recordings:* album: with Rudimental: Home (MOBO Award for Best Album 2013) 2013. *Current Management:* c/o Coda Music Agency LLP, CODA House, 56 Compton Street, Clerkenwell, London, EC1V 0ET, England. *Telephone:* (20) 7017-2500. *Fax:* (20) 7017-2555. *Website:* www.codaagency.com; www.rudimental.co.uk.

AGHILI, Shadmehr; Iranian singer, musician, composer, producer and actor; b. 27 Jan. 1973, Tehran. *Education:* Tehran Conservatory of Music. *Career:* singer and writer of popular songs; emigrated to Canada, but now lives in Los Angeles; live concert, Las Vegas Dec. 2014. *Film:* Par e Parvaz (also composed soundtrack). *Recordings include:* albums: Bahar e Man 1997, Fasl e Ashenayi 1998, Mosaafer 1998, Dehati 1999, Mashgh e Sokoot 1999, Naghmeha ye Mashreghi 1999, Par e Parvaz 2001, Doori o Pashimani 2003, Khiali Nist 2003, Adam Foroush 2004, Popcorn 2005, Taghdir 2009, Tarafdaar 2012. *E-mail:* info@shadmehraghili.net. *Website:* www.shadmehraghili.net.

AGNES; Swedish singer and songwriter; b. (Agnes Emilia Carlsson), 6 March 1988, Vänersborg. *Career:* winner of Swedish Idol 2005; began live performances 2006–; int. career 2009–; performed duet with Björn Skifs at wedding of Victoria, Crown Princess of Sweden and Prince Daniel 2010. *Recordings include:* albums: Agnes 2005, Stronger 2006, Dance Love Pop 2008, Veritas 2012, Collection 2013. *Honours:* MTV Europe Music Award for Best Swedish Act 2009, Swedish Music Publrs Asscn Award for Song of the Year (for Release Me) 2009, QX Award for Artist of the Year 2010, Radio Regenbogen Award for Newcomer of the Year 2010, NowNowNext Brink of Fame: Music Artist Award 2010. *Current Management:* c/o Rec Sthlm. Mäster Samuelsgatan 54, SE-111 21 Stockholm, Sweden. *Telephone:* (8) 788-49-82. *E-mail:* dita@recsthlm.com. *Website:* www.recsthlm.com; agnescarlsson.se.

AGNES MONICA; Indonesian singer, actress, songwriter and record producer; b. (Agnes Monica Muljoto), 1 July 1986, Jakarta; d. of Ricky Muljoto and Jenny Siswono. *Education:* Pelita Harapan Senior High School, Pelita Harapan Univ., Oregon State Univ., USA. *Career:* began as a child singer 1992, recorded three albums; TV presenter for children's programmes in

1990s; TV actress 1999–; further solo albums 2003–; collaborations include Michael Bolton; appointed Asian anti-drug ambassador by Drug Enforcement Administration and Int. Drug Enforcement Conf. Far East Region 2007; first solo concert held in Kuala Lumpur, Malaysia 2007; represented Indonesia at Asia Song Festival 2008, 2009; appointed MTV EXIT (End Exploitation and Trafficking) Ambassador 2010. *Television includes:* as TV presenter: children's programmes during 1990s including Video Anak Anteve, Diva Romeo, Tralala-Trilili; as actress: Lupus Millennia (soap opera) 1999, Mr Hologram (soap opera) 1999, Pernikahan Dini (soap opera) 2001, Ciuman Pertama 2002, Kejar Daku Kau Ku Tangkap 2002, Amanda 2002, Cinta Selembut Awan 2002, Cewekku Jutek (lead role) 2003, Bunga Perawan (lead role) 2004, Cantik (lead role) 2004; The Hospital (drama) 2005, Romance in the White House (drama) 2005, Ku Tlah Jatuh Cinta (soap opera) 2005, Pink (soap opera) 2006, Kawin Muda (soap opera) 2006, Jelita (soap opera) 2008, Pejantan Cantik 2010, Mimo Ketemu Poscha 2012; other: Indonesian Idol (talent show judge) 2010, 2012. *Recordings include:* albums: Si Meong 1992, Yess! 1995, Bala-Bala 1996, And the Story Goes 2003, Whaddup A..'?! 2005, Sacredly Agnezious (Anugerah Musik Indonesia Awards for Best Pop Album 2010, for Best of the Best Album 2010) 2009. *Honours:* Panasonic Awards for Favorite Presenter of Children's Programs 1999, 2000, for Favorite Actress 2001, 2002, 2003, SCTV Awards for Popular Actress 2002, for Famous Actress 2004 Anugerah Musik Indonesia Awards for Best Female Solo Pop Artist 2004, 2009, 2010, for Best Dance/Techno Production 2004, for Best Duo/Group (for duet with Ahmad Dhani) 2004, for Best Female Pop Artist 2006, for Best R&B Production 2006, Anugerah Planet Muzik Award for Best Female Newcomer 2004, MTV Indonesia Awards for Most Favorite Female 2006, 2008 Asia Song Festival Best Asian Artist Award 2008, 2009, AMI Award for Best Pop Female Singer 2011, Mnet Asian Music Award for Best Asian Artist Indonesia 2012. *Address:* c/o Aquarius Musikindo, Aquarius Pustaka Musik, Jalan Batu Tulis 13 No. 17, Jakarta, Pusat 10120, Indonesia (office). *Telephone:* (21) 3807236 (office). *Website:* www.aquarius-musikindo.com (office); www.agnesmonicaofficial.com.

AGNEZ MO; Indonesian singer, songwriter, actress and record producer; b. (Agnes Monica Muljoto), 1 July 1986, Jakarta; d. of Ricky Muljoto and Jenny Siswono. *Education:* Pelita Harapan High School, Pelita Harapan Univ. *Career:* recorded three albums for children as Agnes Monica 1992–96; children's TV presenter 1996–2000; began acting in TV soap operas 1999; returned to music 2002; numerous collaborations including Yana Julio, Ahmad Dhani, Keith Martin, Michael Bolton; opening act for Boyz II Men concert 2007; represented Indonesia at Asia Song Festival, Seoul 2008; changed professional name to Agnez Mo 2013; released debut international single Coke Bottle (featuring Timbaland and T.I.) 2013; producer and mentor for The Freaks singing group 2015; producer for Chloe X 2015. *Television includes:* as presenter: Video Anak Anteve, Tralala-Trilili (Panasonic Awards for Favorite Presenter of Children's Program 1999, 2000), Diva Romeo; as actress: Lupus Millenia 1999, Mr Hologram 1999, Pernikahan Dini (Panasonic Awards for Favorite Actress 2001, 2002, SCTV Famous Actress Award 2002) 2000–02, Ciuman Pertama 2002, Kejar Daku Ku Tangkap 2002, Amanda 2002, Cewekku Jutek 2003, Bunga perawan 2004, Cantik 2004, The Hospital 2005, Romance in the White House 2005, Ku T'lah Jatuh Cinta 2005, Pink 2005, Kawin Muda 2006, Jelita 2008, Kawin Masal 2008, Pejantan Cantik 2010, Marisa 2011, Mimo Ketemu Poscha 2012; as mentor and judge: Indonesian Idol 2010–11, Nez Academy 2012. *Recordings include:* albums: as Agnes Monica: Si Meong 1992, Yess! 1995, Bala-Bala 1996, And the Story Goes (three Anugerah Musik Awards 2004) 2003, Whaddup A...'?! (two Anugerah Musik Awards 2006) 2005, Sacredly Agnezious (Anugerah Musik Awards for Best Pop Album and Best of the Best Album 2010) 2009; as Agnez Mo: Agnez Mo 2013. *Honours:* Panasonic Award for Favorite Actress 2003, Anugerah Planet Muzik Award for Best Female Newcomer 2004, SCTV Award for Famous Actress 2004, MTV Indonesia Awards for Favorite Female 2006, 2008, for Best Female Solo Pop Artist 2009, 2010, 2011, 2012, Mnet Asian Music Awards for Best Artist from Indonesia 2012. *Current Management:* c/o Johnny Wright, Wright Entertainment Group, 7680 Universal Boulevard, Suite 565, Orlando, FL 32819, USA. *Telephone:* (407) 826-9100. *Website:* www.wegmusic.com; www.agnezmo.com.

AGOSSI, Mina; French jazz singer and bandleader; b. 6 Jan. 1972, Besancon. *Education:* studied in France, Niger, Morocco; masterclasses with Sheela Jordan in Boston, Jeanne Lee in France. *Career:* performing with a swing and New Orleans-style jazz band, Brittany 1993; formed own trio 2001; performances in Europe and USA; generally sings accompanied only by bass and drums/percussion; known for her experimental approach to jazz standards; collaborations with Spirit of Life Ensemble, Archie Shepp, Adam Pieronscyk, Mukta; recordings with Eric Jacot (bass) and Ichiro Onoe (drums) 2006–09; currently in quartet with Phil Reptil. *Dance:* version of Ain't Misbehavin' used in Pina Bausch's Sweet Mambo 2009. *Television includes:* Mina Agossi une voix Nomade... (documentary film by Jean Henri Meunier); numerous appearances. *Recordings include:* albums: Voice and Bass 1997, Alkemi 2000, EZ-Pass to Brooklyn 2002, Carousel 2003, Zaboum! 2004, Well You Needn't 2005, Who Wants Love? (Live) 2007, Simple Things? 2008, Just Like a Lady 2010, Red Eyes (with Archie Shepp) 2012. *Honours:* Hon. Citizen, Bayonne; FNAC young self-produced artists prize 1997, Best Newcomer, Adami Awards. *Address:* c/o Naïve Productions, Paris, France. *E-mail:* contact@naive.fr; agossi@dbmail.com. *Website:* www.naive.fr; www .minaagossi.com.

ÅGREN, Björn Sten; Swedish musician (guitar); b. 1979. *Career:* guitarist with rock band Razorlight 2002–10. *Compositions:* To The Sea, I Can't Stop This Feeling I've Got (co-writer). *Recordings:* albums: Up All Night 2004, Razorlight 2006, Slipway Fires 2008. *Television:* The Mighty Boosh. *Address:* Vertigo Records, Mercury Music Group, 364–366 Kensington High Street, London, W14 8NS, England (office). *E-mail:* vertigo@umusic.com (office). *Website:* www.vertigorecords.co.uk (office); www.razorlight.co.uk.

AGUILAR, Pepe; American singer; b. San Antonio, Tex.; s. of Antonio Aguilar and Flor Silvestre. *Career:* began singing aged three; solo artist; collaborations include Rocio Durcal, Vikki Carr; produced for Jose Julian, Guadalupe Pineda, Antonio Aguilar. *Recordings include:* Recuérdame Bonito 1992, Chiquilla Bonita 1995, Con Tambora 1995, Que Bueno Mariachi 1995, Exitos con Banda 1997, Por mujeres como tu 1998, Por el Amor de Siempre, por una mujer bonita (Grammy Award for Best Mexican/Mexican American Album 2000) 1999, Grande de los Grande 2000, Mejor de Nosotros, Tambora 2: Cautiva y Triste 2001, Historias de mi Tierra (Latin Grammy Award for Best Ranchero Album 2006, Grammy Award for Best Mexican/Mexican-American Album 2007) 2006, Enamorado (Latin Grammy Award for Best Ranchero Album 2007) 2007, 100% Mexicano (Grammy Award for Best Mexican/Mexican-American Album 2008) 2008, Bicentenario 1810/1910/2010 (Grammy Award for Best Regional Mexican Or Tejano Album 2012) 2010, Lastima que sean ajenas (Latin Grammy Award for Best Ranchero Album 2014) 2013; EPs: Negociaré Con La Pena 2011, Más de un Camino 2012 (Latin Grammy Award for Best Ranchero Album 2012), MTV Unplugged 2014. *E-mail:* contacto@pepeaguilar.com.mx. *Website:* www.pepeaguilar.com.

AGUILERA, Christina Maria; American singer; b. 18 Dec. 1980, Staten Island, New York; m. Jordan Bratman 2005 (divorced); one s. *Career:* appeared on US Star Search TV talent show aged eight; joined cast of Orlando-based TV show, The New Mickey Mouse Club aged 12; intensive worldwide promotional touring 1997–; solo artist 1998–; coach and judge, The Voice (US TV show) 2011–13; apptd WFP Amb. Against Hunger. *Film:* Burlesque 2010. *Recordings include:* albums: Christina Aguilera 1999, Mi Reflejo (Billboard Latin Music Award for Best Pop Album of the Year 2001) 2000, My Kind Of Christmas 2000, Just Be Free 2001, Stripped 2002, Back to Basics 2006, Bi-On-Ic 2010, Lotus 2012. *Honours:* Grammy Award for Best New Artist 2000, American Latino Media Arts (ALMA) Award for Best New Entertainer 2000, Billboard Award for Female Vocalist of the Year 2000, Q Award (for Dirrty) 2003, Grammy Awards for Best Female Pop Vocal Performance (for Beautiful) 2004, (for Ain't No Other Man) 2007, for Best Pop Duo/Group Performance (for Say Something, with A Great Big World) 2015, MTV Europe Music Award for Best Female Artist 2006, Special Achievement Award, ALMA Awards 2012, George McGovern Leadership Award 2012. *Current Management:* Irving Azoff, Azoff Management, 3500 West Olive Avenue, Suite 600, Burbank, CA 91505, USA. *Website:* www .christinaaguilera.com.

AHERNE, Jonathon David; Australian bass guitarist and songwriter. *Career:* mem. The Temper Trap 2005–; released debut EP The Temper Trap 2006; group relocated to London 2008; released debut album 2009. *Recordings:* albums: with The Temper Trap: Conditions 2009, The Temper Trap (ARIA Music Award for Best Rock Album 2012) 2012. *Honours:* with The Temper Trap: ARIA Music Awards for Best Group 2010, 2012, for Most Popular Australian Single (for Sweet Disposition) 2010. *Current Management:* c/o Lunatic Entertainment, Level 1, 490 Crown Street, Surry Hills, NSW 2010, Australia. *E-mail:* info@lunaticentertainment.com. *Website:* www .lunaticentertainment.com. *Address:* c/o Liberation Music, 9 Dundas Lane, Albert Park, Vic. 3206, Australia (office). *Telephone:* (3) 9695-7899 (office). *Fax:* (3) 9690-8665 (office). *E-mail:* info@liberationmusic.net (office). *Website:* www.liberationmusic.net (office); www.thetempertrap.com.

AHISKALI, Fatih; Turkish musician (oud); b. 1976, Antalya. *Education:* ITU Turkish Music State Conservatory. *Career:* mem. Yeni Türkü 1997–; concerts worldwide. *Recordings by band:* albums (does not play on all): 'Yeni', Her Dem Yeni, Telli Telli Remixes, Süper Baba (film music), Ask Yeniden, Rumeli Konseri, Külhani Şarkilar, Vira Vira, Yeşilmişik?, Günebakan: Dünyanin Kapilari, Akdeniz Akdeniz. *E-mail:* info@fatihahiskali.com (office). *Website:* www.fatihahiskali.com.

AHLIN, Tina; Swedish musician (piano), singer, arranger and composer; b. 6 July 1967, Stockholm. *Career:* several big pop acts and pop tours around Scandinavia, with Lisa Wilsson, Orup, Tomas Dileva; worked with several television productions and television orchestra; wrote arrangements to Swedish Radio Symphony Orchestra, choirs, big bands; work with lots of jazz and pop concerts. *Recordings:* Det går bra ändå 2002, Sommarkort 2005. *Current Management:* FTS Showbusiness AB, Calle Gustavsson, Gamlestagsvägen 2-4 B3, 415 02 Göteborg, Sweden. *Telephone:* (31) 21-18-16. *Fax:* (31) 21-18-21. *E-mail:* calle@fts.se. *Website:* www.fts.se. *E-mail:* tina.ahlin@telia.com. *Website:* www.tinaahlin.se.

AHMAD, Salman; American composer, songwriter, musician (guitar) and medical doctor; b. 12 Dec. 1963, Lahore, Pakistan; s. of Ejaz Ahmad and Shahine Khan; m. Samina Haq. *Education:* Tappan Zee High School, King Edward Medical Coll., MBBS. *Career:* early childhood spent travelling the world; returned to Pakistan to study medicine 1982; began musical career in band Vital Signs 1991; founder mem., Junoon (with Ali Azmat and Brian O'Connell) 1990–, banned by Pakistani authorities for criticism of govt corruption early 1990s; upon invitation of UN Sec.-Gen., Kofi Annan, performed at UN Gen. Ass. (first band to play at Gen. Ass.); tours throughout Asia, N America, Middle E and Europe; UN Goodwill Amb. on the issue of HIV/AIDS 2001; appearances in Pakistani TV dramas; currently lives in New York; Jazbe-e-Junoon selected as official song of cricket world cup, hosted by Pakistan 1996. *Television:* The Rockstar and the Mullah (producer, VH1 documentary) 2002. *Recordings include:* albums: with Junoon: Junoon 1990, Talaash 1993, Inquilaab 1995, Khashmakash 1996, Azaadi 1997, Parvaaz 1999, Andaz 2001, The Millennium Edition (compilation) 2000, Daur-e-Junoon 2002, Dewaar 2003; solo: Infiniti 2005. *Publication:* Rock and Roll Jihad: A Muslim Rock Star's Revolution for Peace 2009. *Honours:* Channel V Music Award for Int. Group 1998, UNESCO Award for Outstanding Achievement in Music and Peace 1999, BBC Asia Award 1999. *Current Management:* Junoon Inc., 210 Old Tappan Road, Tappan, NY 10983, USA. *E-mail:* saminadr@gmail.com. *E-mail:* info@junoon.com. *Website:* www .junoon.com.

AHMAD, Saeen Zahur; Pakistani singer; b. 1937, Okara. *Career:* Sufi musician, plays the traditional instrument ektara; performed at shrines in Ojara; first concert performance at All Pakistan Music Conference 1989. *Recording:* album: Awazay 2006. *Soundtracks include:* Khuda Ke Liye 2007, West Is West 2011. *Honours:* BBC Best Voice of the Year in Asia/Pacific Region 2006.

AHMED, Mahmoud; Ethiopian singer; b. 8 May 1941, Addis Ababa. *Career:* made his name singing with the Imperial Body Guard Band, performing in hotels and at official state events –1974; sang with numerous bands in Ethiopia including the Ibex Band, the Venus Band, the Walias Band, the Idan Raichel Project, the Roha Band; opened own music store in Addis Ababa during 1980s; many of his recordings reissued as part of Ethiopiques series on French record label Buda Musique 1999–; performed at WOMAD Festival, UK 2005. *Recordings include:* Almaz 1973 (reissued, Ethiopiques Vol. 6 1999), Erè Mèla Mèla 1975 (reissued Ethiopiques Vol. 7 2000), Soul of Addis 1997, Slow Collections 1998, Yitbarek 2003, Alèmeyé (Ethiopiques Vol. 19) 2005. *Honours:* Winner (Africa), BBC Radio 3 World Music Awards 2007. *Address:* Buda Musique, 188 Boulevard Voltaire, 75011 Paris, France (office). *Telephone:* 1-40-24-01-03 (office). *E-mail:* contact@budamusique.com (office). *Website:* www.budamusique.com (office).

AHO, Susan; Finnish singer and musician (accordion). *Education:* Sibelius Acad. *Career:* mem. as accordionist, Värttinä 1996, singer 1998–; additional collaborations with Vaeltajat and the puppet theatre, Sampo; represented Finland in Eurovision Song Contest with Johanna Virtanen as Kuunkuiskaajat 2010. *Music for theatre:* co-wrote score to stage musical, The Lord of the Rings (with A. R. Rahman) (Princess of Wales Theatre, Toronto) 2006. *Recordings include:* albums: Kokko 1996, Vihma 1998, Ilmatar 2000, 6.12 2001, iki 2003, Miero 2006. *Current Management:* c/o Phillip Page, Hoedown Arts Oy, Neitsytpolku 9 F 81, 00140 Helsinki, Finland. *Telephone:* (50) 5692982. *Fax:* (9) 628950. *E-mail:* pap@hoedown.com. *Address:* c/o Real World Records Limited, Mill Lane, Box, Wiltshire, SN13 8PL, England. *Telephone:* (845) 146-1733. *Website:* www.realworldmusic.com; www.varttina.com.

AHROLD, Robert (Robbin) Liam, BSc; American copyright executive; b. 29 Sept. 1943, Washington; m. Kyle Warren 1972, two d. *Education:* Georgetown University. *Career:* reporter, Time Magazine, 1967–71; various positions, Home Box Office, including Director, Special Programming; Director, Corporate Public Relations, 1974–82; Producer, Executive producer, Celebration, first pay television Rock Series, 1975; Vice-President, Corporate Relations, RCA Records, 1982–87; various pay television music specials for HBO including: Country In New York, 1976; Vice-President, Corporate Relations, Broadcast Music Inc. 1987–; Ed. and Publisher, Musicworld (quarterly membership magazine for BMI); Vice-President, Board of Governors, New York Chapter, NARAS; mem. NATAS; Country Music Asscn; Gospel Music Asscn; National Academy Popular Music. *Address:* Broadcast Music Inc., 320 W 57th Street, New York, NY 10019, USA (office). *Telephone:* (212) 586-2000. *Fax:* (212) 397-0789. *Website:* www.bmi.com.

AHVENLAHTI, Olli; Finnish composer and musician (piano, keyboards); b. 6 Aug. 1949, Finland. *Education:* Sibelius Acad., Berklee Coll. of Music, Boston, USA, Helsinki Univ. *Career:* first jazz concert with Hasse Walli-Make Lievonen Sextet, 1969; collaborated with Mike Koskinen, Pekka Pöyry, Esko Rsnell; founding mem., The Group, 1970s; represented Finland, Nordring radio contest; formed quintet with trumpeter Markku Johansson, 1970s; chief conductor, TV 1, Finnish Broadcasting Company, 1990–; pianist, backing singer Vesa-Matti Loiri. *Compositions include:* composer, arranger for UMO (New Music Orchestra); Music for theatre, film, television dramas; Piece based on texts from Hermann Hesse's Glass Bead Game. *Recordings include:* albums: Bandstand 1975, The Poet 1976, Based on a Novel 1981, Lasihelmipeli 1984, The Way You Walk 1986, Kaksi Ihoa (with Tommy Tabermann, Pepe Willberg and Johanna Iivanainen) 2007. *Honours:* Finnish Jazz Federation Yrjö Award 1975. *Telephone:* 0400-427116 (mobile) (office). *Fax:* (09) 791412 (office). *E-mail:* ahvenlahti.music@kolumbus.fi. *Website:* www.olliahvenlahti.com.

A.I.; Japanese singer and rapper; b. (Ai Carina Uemura), 2 Nov. 1981, Los Angeles, Calif., USA. *Education:* Los Angeles County High School for the Arts. *Career:* participated in Mary J. Blige concert, Universal Amphitheater, Los Angeles 1998; dancer in Janet Jackson music video 1998; mem. girl group SX4 1999; offered contract with BMG Funhouse 2000; debut single release 2000; signed with Def Jam Japan 2002; numerous collaborations including Namie

Amuro, Ken Hirai, The Jacksons, Miliyah Kato, Mao Denda, Sphere of Influence, Suite Chic, Anna Tsuchiya, Exile Atsushi, MC2, K'naan, Thelma Aoyama. *Recordings:* albums: My Name is Ai 2001, Original Ai 2003, 2004 Ai 2004 , Mic-a-holic Ai 2005, What's Goin' On Ai 2006, Don't Stop Ai 2007, Viva Ai 2009, The Last Ai 2010, Independent 2012. *Address:* c/o EMI Music Japan, Akasaka Biz Tower, 3-1, Akasaka Gochome, Minato, Tokyo, 107-6327, Japan (office). *Telephone:* (3) 6830-8300 (office). *Website:* ai.emimusic.jp/en/index .html (office).

AILEE; American singer and actress; b. (Amy Lee), 30 May 1989, Denver, Colo. *Education:* Scotch Plains-Fanwood High School, Pace Univ. *Career:* raised in New Jersey; fmr artist for Muzo Entertainment, relocated to S Korea 2010; K-pop recording artist for YMC Entertainment 2010–; numerous collaborations including Wheesung, Decipher 2011; solo debut release Heaven 2012; released debut mini-album 2012; first solo concert, Olympic Hall, Olympic Park, Seoul 2015. *Television includes:* Dream High 2012, Laws of the City 2014, One Fine Day 2014. *Recordings:* album: VIVID 2015. *Honours:* numerous awards including Asia Song Festival New Artist Award 2012, MelOn Music Awards for Best New Artist 2012, for Top 10 2014, Mnet Asian Music Award for Best New Female Artist 2012, for Best Female Vocal Performance (for U&I) 2013, (for Singing Got Better) 2014, (for Mind Your Own Business) 2015, Golden Disk Award for Best New Artist 2013, for Digital Bonsang (for U&I) 2014, (for Don't Touch Me) 2015. *Website:* ailee-jp.net.

AINLAY, Chuck; American engineer and producer. *Career:* partner, Back-Stage Studio, Nashville, Tenn.; f. METAlliance; worked with Mark Knopfler, George Strait, Vince Gill, Trisha Yearwood, The Dixie Chicks, Emmylou Harris, Peter Frampton, Steve Earle, Dire Straits, James Taylor, Wynonna, Travis Tritt, Everclear, Willie Nelson, Sugarland, Taylor Swift, Lee Ann Womack. *Honours:* Grammy Award for Best Surround Sound Album 2006, for Best Pop Instrumental 2007, for Best Country Album 2008; ACM Award for Best Engineer 2013. *Address:* BackStage Studio, c/o Sound Stage Studios, 10 Music Circle S, Nashville, TN 32703, USA (office). *Telephone:* (615) 256-2676 (office). *Fax:* (615) 259-2942 (office). *E-mail:* ainlaycj@aol.com. *Website:* www.soundstagestudios.com (office); www.chuckainlay.com.

AIREY, Don; British musician (keyboards), arranger and conductor; b. 21 June 1948, Sunderland, England; m. Doris Airey 1977; two s. one d. *Education:* Nottingham Univ., Royal Manchester Coll. of Music. *Career:* mem. Colosseum II 1975–78, Rainbow 1978–81, Ozzy Osbourne 1982–85, Jethro Tull 1986–87, Whitesnake 1988–90, Gary Moore Blues Band 1990–91; session player, arranger 1992–95; ELO 1996–97; mem. Deep Purple 2001–; mem. BAC&S, PRS. *Recordings include:* albums: Down To Earth (with Rainbow), Blizzard Of Oz (with Ozzy Osbourne), Whitesnake 87 (with Whitesnake), Still Got The Blues (with Gary Moore Blues Band), 20 Years Of Jethro Tull (with Jethro Tull) 1988, Back To The Light (with Brian May) 1993; with Deep Purple: Bananas 2003, Deep Purple And Friends 2003, Total Abandon 2004, Rapture Of The Deep 2005; solo: K2, Tales Of Triumph And Tragedy, A Light in the Sky 2008. *E-mail:* info@deep-purple.com. *Website:* www.deep-purple.com; www.donairey.com.

AITKEN, Matt; British songwriter and producer; b. 25 Aug. 1956. *Career:* mem. pop band, Agents Aren't Aeroplanes 1980s; mem. songwriting/production team, Stock Aitken Waterman 1984–93, producing artists, including Rick Astley, Big Fun, Brother Beyond, Hazell Dean, Divine, Jason Donovan, Mel and Kim, Kylie Minogue, Robson and Jerome, Sinitta, Sonia, Donna Summer; co-founder, PWL label 1988; co-prod., Love This Records 1994–. *Honours:* BRIT Award for Best Producer (Stock Aitken Waterman) 1988.

AJRAM, Nancy; Lebanese singer; b. 16 March 1983, al-Ashrafia, Beirut; d. of Nabil Ajram and Rimonda Ajram; m. Fadi Hachem 2008; one d. *Television:* won nat. entertainment show Noujoum Al-Moustakbal. *Recordings include:* albums: Mehtagalak 1999, Sheel Oyounak Anni (Take Your Eyes Away From Me) 2001, Ya Salam (How Fantastic) 2003, Ah We Noss 2004, Ya Tabtab...Wa Dallaa 2006, Shakhbat Shakhbit 2007, Betfakkar Fi Eih?! 2008, N7 2010, Nancy 8 2014. *Honours:* UNICEF Regional Amb. for Middle East & North Africa 2009; Arab Music Award for Best Newcomer 2004, Murez d'Or Awards for Best Female Lebanese Singer 2003, Best Female Arab Singer 2006, World Music Award for best-selling Middle East artist 2008, named by Arabian Business amongst Power 100: World's Most Influential Arabs (90th) 2010, Best Female artist, OTV Awards 2013, Murex d'Or Most popular female artist 2012/13, Best female artist, BIAF 2015. *Address:* c/o EMI Music Arabia, PO Box 61003, Dubai, United Arab Emirates (office). *E-mail:* info@ emimusicarabia.com (office). *Website:* www.nancyajram.com.

AKABU (see Lee, Dave)

AKALA; British rapper; b. (Kingslee Daley), brother of Ms Dynamite. *Career:* fmr football player with Wimbledon FC and West Ham United youth teams; collaborations with Jammer, Baby Blue, Earz. *Recordings:* albums: It's Not A Rumour 2006, Freedom Lasso 2007. *Honours:* Best Hip Hop Artist, MOBO Awards 2006. *E-mail:* info@illastate.com (office). *Website:* www.akalamusic .com (office).

AKENDENGUE, Pierre Claver, PhD; Gabonese psychologist and musician; b. 25 April 1943, Aouta; m. Michelle Ossouach 1997; six s. three d. *Education:* Univ. of Orléans, Petit Conservatoire de la Chanson de Mireille, Paris. *Career:* moved to France to finish educ. 1965, founded Ntche record label 1978–82; returned to Gabon 1985; cultural adviser to Pres. Omar Bongo; many compositions and recordings; concerts world-wide including Africa, Europe,

Canada, West Indies, Japan; founder, Gabonese Asscn of Artists and Performers. *Recordings*: albums: Nandipo 1974, Africa Obota 1976, Eseringuila 1978, Owende 1979, Mengo 1980, Awana W'Afrika 1982, Mando 1983, Réveil de l'Afrique 1984, Sarraouinia 1986, Espoir à Soweto 1988, Silence 1990, Lambarena 1993, Maladalite 1995, Carrefour Rio 1996, Obakadences 2000, Ekunda-Sah 2004, Gorée 2006, La Verité d'Afrique 2008. *Honours:* Young Singers Prize, SACEM 1976, Best Film Music Award, FESCAPO 1985, RFI Trophy 1989, Prix d'Excellence, Africa Music Awards 1997. *Current Management:* c/o Jacques Hupin, Agora Spectacles, 13, place des Chartreux, 76140 Petit Quevilly, France. *Telephone:* 35-03-32-30. *Fax:* 35-72-11-98. *E-mail:* j.hupin@wanadoo.fr. *Website:* www.akendengue.com.

AKGÜL, Ferman; German singer and musician; b. 25 Dec. 1979, Ankara, Turkey. *Education:* Gazi Univ. *Career:* mem., alternative rock band, maNga 2002–; concerts, festivals include Sziget Festival, Mannheim Turkish Rock Festival, also London. *Recordings:* albums: maNga 2004, Şehr-i Hüzün 2009. *Honours:* MTV Europe Music Award for Best European Act 2009. *Current Management:* c/o Hadi Elazzi, GRGDN, Mübayacı sok. 5, Rumelihisarı, 34470 İstanbul, Turkey. *Telephone:* (212) 2876287. *Fax:* (212) 2876216. *E-mail:* manga@grgdn.com. *Website:* www.grgdn.com. *Address:* c/o Sony Music Entertainment, Sony Music Türkiye, Ticaret A.Ş. Oteller Sokak 1/5, Tepebaşı, 34430 İstanbul, Turkey (office). *Website:* manga.web.tr.

AKIL; American rap artist. *Career:* mem., Jurassic 5 1993–2007; solo artist (as Akil the MC) 2007–; numerous live performances. *Recordings include:* albums: with Jurassic 5: Jurassic 5 (EP) 1997, Quality Control 2000, Power in Numbers 2002, Feedback 2006; as Akil the MC: Sound Check 2009. *Current Management:* c/o Jamal Drew, Risky Cereal Management, Bandwidthmusic.com, Houston, TX 77054, USA. *Telephone:* (832) 495-6323. *E-mail:* jamaldrew@riskycereal.com. *Website:* www.bandwidthmusic.com; www.myspace.com/akilthe1mc.

AKINMUSIRE, Ambrose; American jazz trumpeter; b. 1 May 1982, Oakland, Calif. *Education:* Manhattan School of Music, Univ. of Southern California, Thelonious Monk Inst. of Jazz, Los Angeles. *Career:* mem. Berkeley High School Jazz Ensemble; hired for Steve Coleman's Five Elements band for European tour; studied trumpet with Laurie Frink, Lew Soloff, Terence Blanchard; released debut recording 2007; has performed with numerous musicians including Vijay Iyer, Esperanza Spalding, Jason Moran, Aaron Parks; participant, Jason Moran's multimedia concert, My Mind: Monk at Town Hall 2009. *Recordings:* albums: as leader: Prelude to Cora 2007, When the Heart Emerges Glistening 2011, The Imagined Savior is Far Easier to Pain 2014; as sideman: Resistance is Futile, Steve Coleman 2001, Shadows, Aaron Parks 2002, In What Language?, Vijay Iyer and Mike Ladd 2003, Casually Introducing, Walter Smith III 2006, Anti Social Club, Alan Pasqua 2007, Return to You, Sara Cazarek 2007, New Constellations: Live in Vienna, Josh Roseman 2007, Consequences, John Escreet 2008, Esperanza, Esperanza Spalding 2008, Form, Danny Grissett 2008, House Without a Door, Le Boeuf Brothers 2009, Don't Fight the Inevitable, John Escreet 2010, III, Walter Smith III 2010, Barefooted Town, David Binney 2011, Graylen Epicenter, David Binney 2011, Nights On Earth, Vince Mendoza 2011, Sound Travels, Jack DeJohnette 2012, That Nepenthetic Place, Dayna Stephens 2013, Life Forumn, Gerald Clayton 2013. *Honours:* Winner, Thelonious Monk Int. Jazz Competition 2007, Carmine Caruso Int. Jazz Trumpet Solo Competition 2007, Jazz Journalists' Asscn Jazz Award for Trumpeter of the Year 2012, 2015, North Sea Jazz Festival Paul Acket Award 2014. *Current Management:* c/o Mariah Wilkins Artist Management LLC, 315 East 86th Street, Suite #2EE, New York, NY 10028, USA. *E-mail:* mariahwilkins@me.com. *Website:* www.mariahwilkins.com/index.html; www.ambroseakinmusire.com.

AKIYOSHI, Toshiko; Japanese/American musician (piano) and composer; b. 12 Dec. 1929, Dairen, Manchuria, People's Republic of China; m. 1st Charlie Mariano; m. 2nd Lew Tabackin. *Education:* Berklee College of Music, USA. *Career:* successful jazz pianist in Japan; recorded for Norman Granz; moved to USA 1956; mem. various groups, including Charlie Mariano, Charles Mingus; became composer, especially for big bands; worked with saxophonist Lew Tabackin, Los Angeles in early 1970s, formed Toshiko Akiyoshi Jazz Orchestra 1973. *Recordings include:* Toshiko's Piano 1953, Toshiko 1953, The Toshiko Trio 1954, Toshiko Akiyoshi: Her Trio, her Quartet 1956, Amazing Toshiko Akiyoshi 1957, The Many Sides Of Toshiko 1957, United Nations 1958, Toshiko Mariano 1960, Toshiko Mariano Quartet 1963, Toshiko Meets Her Old Pals 1961, Country And Western Jazz Pianos (with Steve Kühn) 1963, Toshiko and Modern Jazz 1964, Toshiko Mariano and her Big Band 1965, At The Top Of The Gate 1968, Toshiko Akiyoshi Quartet Vols I–III 1970–71, Solo Piano 1971, Kogun 1974, Long Yellow Road 1974, Tales Of A Courtesan 1975, Road Time 1976, Dedications 1976, Insights 1976, March Of The Tadpoles 1977, Tribute to Billy Strayhorn 1978, Finesse 1978, Salted Ginko Nuts 1978, Notorious Tourist from the East 1978, Sumi-e 1978, Farewell To Mingus 1980, Tanuki's Night Out 1981, European Memoirs 1982, Ten Gallon Shuffle 1984, Wishing Peace 1986, Interlude 1987, Remembering Bud, Cleopatra's Dream 1990, Carnegie Hall Concert Live 1991, From Toshiko With Love 1981, Carnegie Hall Concert Live 1991, Desert Lady/Fantasy 1993, Live At Maybeck Recital Hall 1994, Dig 1999, Night and Dream 1999, Sketches of Japan 1999, Toshiko plays Toshiko 1999, Yes I have No 4BEAT Today 1999, 1961 2001, Four Seasons of Morita Village 2001, Monopoly Game 2001, Shio Ginnan 2001, Solo Piano 2006, Miwaku No Jazz 2006, Toshiko Meets Old Pal 2007, From Toshiko With Love 2007, Dedications, Vol. (1,2,3) 2009. *Publications include:* Life with Jazz 1995. *Honours:* Shijah sh (Japan)

1999, Order of the Rising Sun, Gold Rays with Rosette (Japan) 2004; Japan Foundation Award, Asahi Award 2005, Jazz Master Award, Swing Journal Special Award 2006, Nat. Endowment for the Arts 2007. *Current Management:* Berkeley Agency, 2608 9th Street, #301, Berkeley, CA 94710, USA. *Telephone:* (510) 843-4902. *Fax:* (510) 843-7271. *E-mail:* mail@berkeleyagency.com. *Website:* www.berkeleyagency.com.

AKKERMAN, Jan; Dutch musician (guitar, lute), composer and arranger; b. 24 Dec. 1946, Amsterdam. *Education:* Music Lyceum, Amsterdam. *Career:* mem. Johnny and The Cellar Rockers 1958, The Hunters, Brainbox 1969, Focus 1969–76; solo artist 1973–; periodic reunions with Focus; mem. side project, Forcefield (with Ray Fenwick and Cozy Powell) 1988–89. *Recordings include:* albums: with Focus: In And Out Of Focus 1971, Moving Waves 1971, Focus III 1972, At The Rainbow 1973, Hamburger Concerto 1974, Mother Focus 1975, Focus Con Proby 1977, House Of The King 1983, Pass Me Not 1995; solo: Profile 1973, Tabernakel 1974, Eli 1977, Jan Akkerman 1978, Arunjuez 1978, Live 1979, 3 1980, It Could Happen To You 1985, Can't Stand Noise 1986, Pleasure Point 1987, The Noise Of Art 1990, Heartware 1991, Puccini's Cafe 1993, Blues Hearts 1994, Focus In Time 1996, 10,000 Clowns On A Rainy Day (two vols) 1997, Passion (acoustic) 1999, C.U. 2004, Fromage a Trois 2006; with Forcefield: The Talisman 1988, To Oz And Back 1989. *Honours:* Melody Maker Poll Winner for Best Guitarist 1973, Conamus Golden Harp for Musical Career 2005. *Address:* c/o Bert Bijlsma, P/A Hamrikkerweg 4, 9943 TB, NW Scheemda, The Netherlands (office). *Telephone:* (598) 446357 (office). *E-mail:* info@bertbijlsma.com (home). *Website:* www.bertbijlsma.com (home); www.janakkerman.com (home).

AKON; American/Senegalese singer, songwriter and producer; b. (Aliaune Thiam), 1981, St Louis, Mo.; s. of Mor Thiam. *Career:* grew up in Senegal, returned to USA aged seven; served a three-year prison sentence; released debut album Trouble 2004; Founder Konvict Muzik, Kon Live Distribution, Konvict Clothing; guest vocal appearances with Young Jeezy, Gwen Stefani, Chamillionaire, Bone Thugs-n-Harmony, Three 6 Mafia, Fabolous, 50 Cent, Mario; has produced tracks for Daddy Yankee, Kardinal Offishall; collaborations with Eminem, Snoop Dogg, Styles P, Young Jeezy, Savage, Michael Jackson, David Guetta, JRandall, Vishal-Shekhar, Dr Dre, Pitbull, Whitney Houston and others. *Recordings include:* albums: Trouble 2004, Konvicted 2006, Freedom 2008, Akonic 2010, Stadium 2013; singles: Lonely 2005, Moonshine 2005, We Are the World: 25 for Haiti 2010. *Honours:* American Music Award for Favorite Male Soul/R&B Artist 2007, cited among 40 Most Powerful Celebrities in Africa (5th) 2011. *Address:* c/o Universal/Motown, 2220 Colorado Avenue, Santa Monica, CA 90401, USA (office). *Website:* www.umrg.com (office).

AKYÜZ, Osman Refik; Turkish recording engineer, producer, singer and musician (bass guitar, keyboards); b. 16 June 1974, Istanbul. *Education:* Capital Univ., The Recording Workshop, USA, Ulster Co. Coll., Timur Selcuk Music School. *Career:* indie musician, performed as atonall 1986–, also as iksir (with Borga Parlar); co-f. 2013 Records 2006; numerous TV and radio jingles, video clip for Say; appeared on Number One TV, Dream TV, Genç TV, Dinamo FM, Bogaziçi University Radio; featured in Yuxexes, Bant Magazine, SABAH Newspaper and Hürriyet. *Compositions include:* All the Stars, The Lake Girl, Happy, Aydede, Let Me Be, Sunday Morning, The Land of Sand, Ascend, A Sail To Sky, Say, Kokorec Mania, Was Not, Supermeen, Sen Beni Sevmiyorsun. *Recordings:* as atonall: Ancient Melodies 1996, Big Time Bomb 2003, Waiting for That Day 2006, Sen Beni Sevmiyorsun, O Günü Beklerken (ABI Gold Diploma Medal 2007); as iksir (with Borga Parlar): Vardir 1999. *Honours:* one of Outstanding Musicians of the 20th Century, IBC 2000. *Address:* Zergerdan SOK No. 22, 34467 Emirgan, Istanbul, Turkey. *Telephone:* (212) 277-6369. *E-mail:* atonall@yahoo.com (home).

ALABINA, Ishtar; Israeli/French singer; b. (Eti Zach), 10 Nov. 1968, Kiryat Atta. *Career:* fmr backing singer for flamenco bands; lead singer, Alabina (backed by band Los Niños de Sara) 2000–; simultaneous solo career; sings in Arabic, Hebrew, French and Spanish. *Recordings include:* albums: with Alabina: Alabina 1996, Sahara (aka The Album II) 1998, L'Essentiel 2000; solo: La Voix d'Alabina 2000, Truly Emet 2003, Je sais d'ou je viens 2005, The Best Of lshtar Alabina 2009, lshtar Alabina 7 2012. *E-mail:* michelabihssira@aol.com. *E-mail:* contact@ishtaralabina.net. *Website:* www.ishtaralabina.net.

ALADE, Yemi Eberechi; Nigerian Afropop singer and songwriter; b. 13 March 1989, Abia State; d. of James Alade and Helen Uzoma. *Education:* Victory Grammar School, Lagos, Univ. of Lagos. *Career:* fmr mem. Noty Spices 2005; winner, Peak Talent Show 2009; achieved int. hits with Bamboo 2013, Johnny 2013; numerous collaborators including Lace, M.I. Waje, Timi Dakolo, Burna Boy, Selebobo, Falz. *Recordings:* album: King of Queens 2014. *Honours:* MTV Africa Music Award for Best Female Artist 2015. *Website:* www.yemialadeworld.com.

ALAINA, Lauren; American country music singer and songwriter; b. (Lauren Alaina Kristine Suddeth), 8 Nov. 1994, Rossville, Ga; d. of J.J. Suddeth and Kristy Suddeth. *Education:* Lakeview-Fort Oglethorpe High School. *Career:* series runner-up, American Idol (season 10) 2011; toured as part of American Idols LIVE! tour 2011; numerous public and TV appearances; toured with Jason Aldean 2012, Sugarland 2012. *Television:* American Idol (series runner-up) 2011. *Recordings:* album: Wildflower 2011. *Honours:* American Country Award for New Artist of the Year 2012. *Current Management:* c/o XIX Entertainment, 1604 17th Avenue South, Nashville, TN 37212, USA. *Telephone:* (615) 244-0019. *Fax:* (615) 463-7519. *E-mail:* info@

xixentertainment.com. *Website:* www.xixentertainment.com; www .laurenalainaofficial.com.

ALAKOTILA, Timo Pekka; Finnish musician (piano, harmonium), composer, arranger and producer; b. 15 July 1959. *Education:* Conservatory of Helsimes. *Career:* mem., JPP, 1982–; teacher of composition and music theory, Helsinki Pop and Jazz Conservatory; teacher, Folk Music Dept, Sibelius Academy; Mem., Maria Kalaniemi's Aldargaz ensemble, 1994–; mem., Troka; mem., Luna Nova; numerous tours world-wide; worked with: Värttinä, Hannu Ilmolahti, Järvelän Näppärit, Feeniks, Tallari, Hannu Seppänen, Burlakat, Loituma, Kaira, Halo. *Compositions:* Folkmoods West; Having Myself A Time, 1998. *Recordings:* albums: with JPP: Laitisen Mankeliska; JPP; I've Found A New Tango; Pirun Polska; Kaustinen Rhapsody; String Tease; History; with Aldargaz: IHO; AHMA; Harmonia Mundi; with Troka: Troka; Smash; as producer: Loituma, Things of Beauty 2006, Duo Milla Viljamaa and Johnna Juhola, Mi Retorno 2007. *Honours:* with JPP: Folk Music Group Championship, 1982; Band of the Year, Kastinen Festival, 1986; Finnish Radio Tunnustus Prize, 1988; Album of the Year, Helsingin Sanomat, 1988; with Aldargaz: Prize of Finland, Award for Artistic Achievement, 1996. *Current Management:* Hoedown, Laivurinrinne 2, 00120 Helsinki, Finland. *Website:* www.hoedown.com; www.myspace.com/timoalakotila.

ALAMA, Ragheb Subhi; Lebanese singer and songwriter; b. 7 June 1962, Beirut; m. Jihan al-Ali 1997; two s. *Education:* music conservatory. *Career:* appeared on Studio el-Phan 1980; solo artist 1980–. *Recordings include:* albums: Ya Rayt 1986, Al Hadiya 1987, Dawa el Leil 1988, Ma Y'gooz 1989, Alby Ashe'ha 1991, Ya Hayati 1993, Taw'am Ruhy 1995, Alamteeny 1996, Sayedati el Gameela 1996, Bravo 'Alaiky 1997, Habeeby Ya Nasy 1999, Saharooni el Leil 2001, Tab Leh? 2002, El Hob el Kebeer 2004, Baa'sha'ak 2008, Seneen Rayha 2010. *Honours:* Key to Detroit (USA), Key to Sydney (Australia); Platinum Award, Studio El Fan, Academy Award for video clip (for Alamtini), Arabian World Gold Lion Award for Best Arabic Male Singer 1998. *Address:* PO Box 25-330, Beirut, Lebanon (office). *Telephone:* (1) 784500 (office). *Fax:* (1) 805116 (office). *E-mail:* khodr@ragheb-alama.com (office). *Website:* ragheb-alama.com.

ALAN, Mark, BSc; American artist manager and agent; b. 14 Sept. 1939, Elizabeth, New Jersey; one s. one d. *Career:* Premier Talent Agency, New York 1965–68; President, New Beat Management, New York 1968–71; artists included: Tommy James and the Shondells; The Illusion; Robin McNamara; The Sidekicks; Exile; worked with Jeff Barry and Tommy James; manager, Andre Cymone; Airkraft; Zwarte; President and owner, National Talent Associates, Minneapolis; President, Mark Alan Agency, 1988–; manager for Illerazzum, Every Mother's Nightmare and Peter Phippen. *Address:* Mark Alan Agency, PO Box 21323, St Paul, MN 55121, USA. *Telephone:* (612) 686-5094.

ALAR; Estonian musician (guitar). *Career:* mem., Tuberkuloited 1988–. *Recordings include:* albums: Klassiöhtu 1992, Lilleke rohus 1993, Religioon 1995, Õhtupimedas 1997, Seitseteist lillekest rohus 1999, D-Tuur, Vol. 6 1999, Kiirteel 2000, Wiimane 2001, Tuberkuloited unplugged 2001, Estraadialbum 2003, Põlevad väljad 2004, Miss a teed 2007. *Current Management:* MMM Agentuur OÜ, Risti 2-21, 11624 Tallinn, Estonia. *E-mail:* mm@mmagentuur .ee. *Website:* www.mmagentuur.ee. *E-mail:* Alar@aigro.ee. *Website:* www .tuberkuloited.ee.

ALBARN, Damon, OBE; British singer, musician (keyboards) and songwriter; b. 23 March 1968, Whitechapel, London, England; s. of Hazel Albarn and Keith Albarn. *Education:* Stanway Comprehensive, Colchester, East 15 Drama School, Debden. *Career:* mem. and lead singer, Blur (fmrly named Seymour) 1989–; live appearances and tours world-wide; Founder-mem. and Musical Dir of 'virtual band', Gorillaz 1998–, collaborating with numerous guest artists; Founder-mem. The Good The Bad and The Queen 2006–. *Film:* Face 1997. *DVD includes:* with Gorillaz: Phase One: Celebrity Take Down 2002, Phase Two: Slow Boat to Hades 2006. *Compositions:* wrote film scores for Ravenous (with Michael Nyman) 1998, Ordinary Decent Criminal 1999, 101 Reykjavík (with Einar Örn Benediktsson) 2000; wrote theatre score for Monkey: Journey to the West 2007; wrote libretto and score for opera Dr Dee 2011. *Recordings include:* albums: with Blur: Leisure 1991, Modern Life Is Rubbish 1993, Parklife (Best Album, Q Awards 1994, BRIT Awards, Best Single, Best British Video, BRIT Awards 1995, Best Album, NME Awards 1995) 1994, The Great Escape (Best Album, Q Awards 1995) 1995, Blur 1997, 13 1999, The Best Of Blur 2000, Think Tank (Best Album, Q Awards 2003, Best Album, South Bank Show Awards 2003) 2003, Midlife 2009, The Magic Whip 2015; with Gorillaz: Gorillaz 2001, G-Sides 2002, Laika Come Home 2002, Demon Days 2005, D-Sides 2007, Plastic Beach 2010, Dr Dee 2012; solo: Mali Music (various contributors) 2002, Democrazy 2003, Everyday Robots 2014; with The Good The Bad and The Queen: The Good The Bad and The Queen 2007; with DRC Music: Kinshasa One Two 2011; with Rocket Juice and the Moon: Rocket Juice and the Moon 2012; with Africa Express: Maison des Jeunes 2013. *Honours:* with Blur: BRIT Awards for Best Single, Best Video, Best Album, Best Band 1995, for Outstanding Contrib. to Music 2012, Best Alternative Band, Smash Hits Awards 1994, Best band and Best Live Act, NME Awards 1995, Best Act in the World Today, Q Awards 1999, Best Band, Best Single (Tender), NME Awards 2000, NME Award for Best Live Event (Blur at Hyde Park) 2010; with Gorillaz: Q Awards for Best Video, for Best Producer 2005, Digital Music Award for Top Online Band, for Best Use of Digital Platforms 2005, MTV Europe Music Award for Best Group 2005,

Grammy Award for Best Pop Collaboration with Vocals (for Feel Good Inc.) 2006, NME John Peel Music Innovation Award 2006, Ivor Novello Award for Songwriter of the Year 2006, Q Inspiration Award 2007; other: Ivor Novello Awards – Best Songwriters (shared with Noel Gallagher) 1996, PRS for Music Heritage Award 2009, Inspiration Award, MOJO Awards 2009. *Current Management:* c/o Eleven Management, Suite B, Park House, 206–208 Latimer Road, London, W10 6QY, England. *Telephone:* (20) 8749-1177. *E-mail:* info@ elevenmgmt.com. *Website:* elevenmgmt.com; www.blur.co.uk; www.gorillaz .com; www.thegoodthebadandthequeen.com; www.damonalbarnmusic.com.

ALBERSTEIN, Chava; Israeli singer, songwriter and musician (guitar); b. 1948, Szczecin, Poland; m. Nadav Levitan. *Career:* moved to Israel aged four. *Films include:* Too Early to be Quiet, Too Late to Sing (documentary) 1999. *Recordings include:* albums: solo: Hine Lanu Nigun 1967, Tza'atzueiah Shel Osnat 1967, Perach Halilach 1967, Mot Haparpar 1968, Mirdaf 1968, Chava Alberstein Beshirei Rachel 1969, Margaritkalach 1969, Mishirei Eretz Ahavati 1970, Chava Betochnit Yachid Vol. 1 1971, Chava Betochnit Yachid Vol. 2 1971, Isha Ba'avatiach 1971, Chava Veoded Be'eretz Haksamim 1972, Chava Vehaplatina 1972, Lu Yehi 1973, K'mo Tzemach Bar 1975, Tzolelet Tzabarit 1975, Lehitei Hazahav 1975, Elik Belik Bom 1976, Halaila Hu Shirim 1977, Karusella 1–3 1977, Shirei am Beyiddish 1977, Hitbaharut 1978, Chava Vehagitara 1979, Ma Kara Beretz Mi 1979, Shir Bematana 1980, Ani Holechet Elai 1980, Kolot 1982, Shiru Shir Im Chava 1982, Nemal Bait 1983, Avak Shel Kochavim 1984, Mehagrim 1986, Od Shirim Beyiddish 1987, Hatzorech Bamilah, Hatzorech Bashtika 1988, Chava Zingt Yiddish 1989, London 1989, Ahava Mealteret 1991, Ha'chita Zomachat Shuv 1992, The Man I Love 1992, Derech Achat 1995, Yonat Ha'ahava 1996, Adaber Itcha 1997, Shanachie 1998, Techef Ashuv 1999, Chava Alberstein: Yiddish Songs 1999, Foreign Letters 2001, End of the Holiday 2003, Coconut 2005, The Man I Love 2006, I'll Be Right Back 2006, Improvised Love 2006, The Milky Way–Songs for Children 2007, Human Nature 2008; with The Klezmatics: The Well 1998. *Honours:* Dr hc (Tel-Aviv Univ.); YIVO Inst. Jewish Research Lifetime Achievement Award 2004, six Kinor David Prizes. *Current Management:* c/o Aviv Productions Inc., 10418 East Meadowhill Drive, Scottsdale, AZ 85255, USA. *Telephone:* (480) 659-1568. *E-mail:* itzik@aviv2.com. *Website:* www .aviv2.com/chava.

ALBERTINI, Paul-René; French record company executive. *Career:* Pres. and CEO Sony Music Entertainment France 1995–98; Exec. Vice-Pres. Sony Music Europe 1998–2000; Pres. Warner Music Europe 2000–02; Pres. Warner Music Int. 2002–04, Chair. and CEO 2004–06; mem. Bd Dirs IFPI, Harvest Entertainment 2007–; Chairman, Sushi Venture Partners 2007–; Consultant, Square Media International 2008–.

ALBINI, Steve; American singer, musician (guitar) and record producer. *Career:* founder, Big Black, 1982–88; founder, Rapeman, 1988; member, Shellac 1992–; co-founder Electrical Audio Studios, Chicago; record producer, for artists including The Pixies; The Wedding Present; Tad; The Breeders; Formed Shellac with Bob Weston and Todd Trainer, 1993. *Recordings include:* albums: with Big Black: Racer X, 1985; Atomizer, 1986; The Hammer Party, 1986; Sound Of Impact, 1987; Big Black, Live, 1989; Rich Man's Track, 1989; Pigpile, 1992; with Rapeman: Two Nuns And A Pack Mule, 1988; with Shellac: At Action Park, 1994; Terraform, 1998; 1000 Hurts, 2000, Excellent Italian Greyhound 2007; numerous productions including: Surfer Rosa, The Pixies; Pod, The Breeders; Salt Lick, Tad; Seamonsters, The Wedding Present; Bush; Storm And Stress; Melt Banana; PW Long. *Address:* c/o Electrical Audio Studios, 2621 West Belmont Avenue, Chicago, IL 60618, USA. *Telephone:* (773) 539-2555. *Fax:* (773) 539-4495. *E-mail:* info@electrical.com. *Website:* www.electrical.com.

ALBORÁN, Pablo; Spanish Latin singer and musician (guitar, piano); b. (Pablo Moreno de Alborán Ferrándiz), 31 May 1989, Malaga; s. of Salvador Moreno de Alborán Peralta and Elena Ferrándiz Martínez. *Career:* composed first songs 2001; recorded early demo with Manuel Illán; first full tour of Spain 2011; performed at Latin Grammy Awards with Demi Lovato 2011. *Recordings:* album: Pablo Alborán 2011. *Address:* Hablemos de Música, EMI Music Iberia, Alcalá 44, 3ª, 28014 Madrid, Spain (office). *Telephone:* (91) 2109800 (office). *E-mail:* hablemosdemusica@emimusic.com (office). *Website:* www .emimusic.es (office); www.pabloalboran.es.

ALBOROSIE; Italian singer, musician (guitar, bass, drums, keyboards), DJ and producer; b. (Alberto D'Ascola), 4 July 1977, Marsala, Sicily. *Career:* Founder-mem. Reggae National Tickets 1993–2000; moved to Jamaica and embarked on solo career 2001; became producer and engineer, Geejam Studios; co-founded Forward Recordings with Jon Baker; numerous collaborations including with Beenie Man, Etana, Dean Frazer, Lutan Fya, Gentleman, Jewel, Mario, No Doubt, Les Nubians, Sisqo, Angie Stone, Wyclef. *Recordings include:* albums: with Reggae National Tickets: Squali 1996, Un affare difficile 1997, Lascia un po' di te 1998, La Isla 1999, Roof Club 2000; solo: Rough Tune 2007, Soul Pirate 2008, Escape from Babylon 2009, Escape from Babylon to the Kingdom of Zion 2010, Alborosie, Specialist and Friends 2010, Dub Clash 2010, 2 Times Revolution 2011. *Honours:* MOBO Award for Best Reggae Act 2011. *Address:* c/o Greensleeves Records, VP Records Jamaica, 1 Upper Sandringham Avenue, Kingston 10, Jamaica (office); c/o VP Records and Greensleeves United Kingdom, Unit 14, Metro Centre, St John's Road, Isleworth, Middlesex, TW7 6NJ, England (office). *Telephone:* (20) 8758–0564 (UK) (office). *Fax:* (876) 968–8461 (Jamaica) (office); (20) 8758-0811 (UK) (office). *E-mail:* press@vprecords.com (office). *Website:* www.greensleeves.net (office); www.alborosiemusic.com (home).

ALBRIGHT, Gerald, BS; American jazz musician (saxophone, bass guitar), producer and songwriter; b. 30 Aug. 1957, Los Angeles; m. Glynis Albright; one s. one d. *Education:* Univ. of Redlands. *Career:* recorded with Patrice Rushen, Anita Baker, Ray Parker, Jr, Lola Folana, Atlantic Starr, The Winans, Olivia Newton-John, The Temptations and Maurice White; also toured with musicians including Les McCann, Rodney Franklin, Jeff Lorber, Teena Marie, Marlene Shaw, Debra and Eloise Laws, Quincy Jones, Whitney Houston, Phil Collins; numerous appearances at clubs and jazz festivals; collaborations with contemporary jazz stars including Will Downing, Jonathan Butler, Hugh Masekela, Chaka Khan, and Rachelle Ferrell; performed as featured saxophonist at US President Bill Clinton's inauguration ceremony. *Recordings include:* solo: Just Between Us 1987, Bermuda Nights 1988, Dream Come True 1990, Live At Birdland West 1991, Smooth 1994, Giving Myself to You 1995, Live to Love 1997, Groovology 2002, Kickin' It Up 2004, New Beginnings 2006, Sax for Stax 2008, Pushing the Envelope 2010. *Current Management:* c/o Steve Chapman, Chapman Management, 14011 Ventura Blvd, Sherman Oaks, CA 91423, USA. *Telephone:* (818) 788-9577. *E-mail:* info@chapmanmanagement.com. *Website:* www.chapmanmanagement.com; www.geraldalbright.com.

ALDEAN, Jason; American country singer and songwriter; b. (Jason Aldine Williams), 28 Feb. 1977, Macon, Ga; m. 1st Jessica Ussery 2001 (divorced); two d.; m. 2nd Brittany Kerr 2015. *Recordings include:* albums: Jason Aldean 2005, Relentless 2007, Wide Open 2009, My Kinda Party (Country Music Asscn Country Album of the Year 2011) 2010, Night Train 2012, Old Boots New Dirt (Billboard Music Award for Top Country Album 2015) 2014. *Honours:* Acad. of Country Music Awards for Top New Male Vocalist 2006, for Single Record of the Year (with Kelly Clarkson for Don't You Wanna Stay) 2012, for Vocal Event of the Year (with Kelly Clarkson for Don't You Wanna Stay) 2012, for Male Vocalist of the Year 2013, 2014, for Vocal Event of the Year (with Luke Bryan and Eric Church for The Only Way I Know) 2013, American Country Award 2011, Billboard Music Award for Top Country Song (for Burnin' It Down) 2015. *Current Management:* c/o Buddy Lee Attractions, 38 Music Square East, Suite 300, Nashville, TN 37203, USA. *Telephone:* (615) 244-4336. *Website:* www.buddyleeattractions.com. *Address:* Broken Bow Records, Cummins Station, 209 10th Avenue South, Suite 230, Nashville, TN 37203, USA. *E-mail:* info@brokenrecords.com (office). *Website:* www.jasonaldean.com.

ALDERETE, Juan; American musician (bass); b. (John Alderete), 5 Sept. 1963, Los Angeles, Calif. *Career:* mem. Racer X 1985–89, 1999–; mem. The Mars Volta 2003–. *Recordings include:* albums: with Racer X: Street Lethal 1986, Second Heat 1987, Technical Difficulties 1999, Superheroes 2000, Getting Heavier 2002; with The Mars Volta: De-Loused in the Comatorium 2003, Frances the Mute 2005, Amputechture 2006, The Bedlam in Goliath 2008, Octahedron 2009, Noctourniquet 2012; has appeared with numerous other artists on their recordings. *Film:* The Sentimental Engine Slayer (co-producer). *Honours:* Grammy Award for Best Hard Rock Performance (for Wax Simulacra) 2009. *Address:* c/o Warner Bros. Records Inc., 3300 Warner Blvd, Burbank, CA 91510, USA. *Website:* www.racerxband.com; www.themarsvolta.com.

ALDRIDGE, Chris, (Beebe), BA (Hons); British musician (saxophones, flute, EWI (electric wind instrument), vocals), composer and teacher; b. 14 March 1976, Walsall, West Midlands, England; s. of Robert Aldridge and Carole Aldridge; m.; two d. *Education:* Univ. of Wolverhampton. *Career:* apprentice lead alto saxophonist, Walsall Jazz Orchestra, Midland Youth Jazz Orchestra; performed at London Marathon 1997, London Jazz Festival, Reading Rock Festival 1998, Montreux Jazz Festival 1989; appearances at Ronnie Scott's, Rock City and Royal Liverpool Philharmonic Hall; collaborations include Ben E. King, Gary U.S. Bonds, Tony Christie, Marcus Collins, Jimmy James, Climax Blues Band, Gerard Presencer, Bud Shank, John Dankworth, Kenny Baker, Victor Mendoza, Bobby Shew, Roy Wood, Hot Chocolate, The Christians, US3, Surinder Sandhu, Ian Parker, Bizarre Inc, Geno Washington, Mother, Gold Blade, Angie Brown, Jaki Graham; also support to McCoy Tyner, Joe Lovano, Blue, Rancid, My Life Story, 911, Tony Hadley, Boney M, Odyssey, Sonia, Will Young, Gareth Gates, The Supremes; mem. Musicians' Union. *Radio includes:* various interviews and live performances, including Paul Jones Blues Show, Radio 2 Janice Long Show, Radio One DJ Spoony Show (teaching him saxophone) 2005. *Films include:* performed on soundtracks to Intimate With A Stranger, Chemical Wedding 2008. *Compositions include:* original music for The Biome Dome (prize-winning entry at BBC Gardeners' World Live 2000), Intimate With A Stranger (contrib. to film soundtrack). *Television includes:* Doctors (BBC), The One Show, Alan Titchmarsh Show, Midlands Today, Pointless. *Recordings include:* with Mother: Waddaman, with Gold Blade: Home Turf, with Divine Sounds: 1,000 Nudes, with Bizarre Inc: Stereoman, featured soloist on Montreux Jazz Festival compilation 1999, with Earthlab: Element 2008, with Surinder Sandhu: The Fictionist 2009, Alexander Shulgin's Songbook 2009; solo: Chris Aldridge 1997, as Beebe: Holy Island 2001, Xplain 2006, Twisted 2007, The Zig Zag Theory 2009, Smoove 2013. *Publications include:* Funky Recorders series of books. *Honours:* winner, BBC Big Band Competition (with Walsall Jazz Orchestra) 1995. *Address:* 2 Wych Elm Road, Clayhanger, Brownhills, West Midlands, WS8 7QP, England (home). *Telephone:* (1543) 360966 (home);

(7711) 781831 (office). *E-mail:* beebeinfo@yahoo.com (office). *Website:* www.beebeplanet.com (office).

ALDRIDGE, Roger Merle, MA; American jazz composer, musician (clarinet, flute, saxophone) and data warehouse consultant; b. 18 Sept. 1946, Kansas City, Mo.; m. Nancy Sherwood 1999; one s. two d. *Education:* Berklee Coll. of Music, Washington Univ., McKendree Univ., Highlands Univ., Inst. for the Certification of Computer Professionals. *Career:* performed with Smokey Robinson, Diahann Carroll 1970–72; composed multimedia theatre music and jazz works 1972–77; Instructor of Music, Fontbonne Coll. 1974–77; Adjunct Prof., Montgomery Coll. 1988–99; works composed include contemporary jazz pieces, tangos, sambas, rags, blues, traditional style fiddle tunes and music for wind ensemble 1989–; mem. BMI, American Music Center, American Composers Forum, Int. Sax On The Web, Chesapeake Bay Foundation. *Compositions:* over 600 compositions including Appalachian Awakening, Salt Marsh Rag, Blues for Lester, Carla Sings Us a Lullaby, A Samba Named Nancy, Baltimore Row House, October Joy, PI Why, Toads, Goodbye to Summer, Sleepy Creek Samba, Rainy Afternoon, Rubber Chicken Rag, Salt Marsh Rag, Blues for a Forgotten Ancient Music, Connecticut Avenue SUVs, New Tango No. 1, Buzzards in Love (for wind ensemble), Ups and Downs. *Recordings include:* Earth's Essence, A Celtic Portrait, Michigan's Heritage, Buzzards in Love, Appalachian Awakening, Spirit Journeys. *Honours:* Research Grant, Inst. of Scientific Studies 1973, Montie Award, Best Music in a Video 1992, Award and Grant, Fannie Mae Foundation 1994, Award, Chesapeake Bay Foundation 1995. *Address:* 4205 Gelding Lane, Olney, MD 20832-1708, USA (home). *E-mail:* nancyandrog@verizon.net (office). *Website:* www.rogeraldridge.com.

ALEMAÑY (CASTRILLO), Jesús; Cuban musician (trumpet) and composer; b. 14 Oct. 1962, Guanabacoa. *Education:* Conservatoire Guillermo Tomas, Guanabacoa. *Career:* began studying trumpet at the Conservatoire, aged 13; invited to join Sierra Maestra, Cuba's leading contemporary ensemble specializing in the roots style of salsa known as son, featuring the trumpet as solo instrument, aged 16; played with Sierra Maestra for over a decade, recording 11 albums; relocated to London 1992; organized (with Paris-based Cuban pianist Alfredo Rodriguez) a Descarga jam session in Paris to honour percussionist Patato Váldez 1994; band leader and mem. ¡Cubanismo!; subsequent releases were a straight Latin album, Reencarnación, and a collaboration with New Orleans musicians, Mardi Gras Mambo. *Recordings include:* albums: with Sierra Maestra: Son Highlights From Cuba 1993, ¡Dundunbanza! 1994; with ¡Cubanismo!: Jesús Alemañy's ¡Cubanismo! 1996, Malembe 1997, Reencarnación 1998, Mardi Gras Mambo 2000, The Very Best of Mucho Gusto 2001, Greetings from Havana 2007. *Current Management:* c/o Susie Lopez, Alafia Music, 4 Westfield Road, Benson, Oxon, OX10 6NH, England. *Telephone:* (1491) 835038. *E-mail:* cubanismo@talktalk.net.

ALEXANDER, Gregg; American singer, musician (guitar), songwriter and producer; b. 4 May 1970, Grosse Point, MI. *Career:* solo artist; mem. and lead singer, The New Radicals 1998–99; songwriter, songs recorded by: Danielle Brisebois, Geri Halliwell, Ronan Keating, Rod Stewart, Sophie Ellis-Bextor, Santana, Boyzone. *Recordings:* albums: solo: Save Me From Myself, Michigan Rain 1989, Intoxifornication 1992; with The New Radicals: Maybe You've Been Brainwashed Too, 1998. *Current Management:* c/o McDaniel Entertainment, Santa Monica, CA, USA. *Telephone:* (424) 238-5711. *Website:* mcdanielentertainment.com.

ALEXANDER, John Eric, BFA; American composer; b. 10 Feb. 1962, Elizabeth, New Jersey; m. Ellen Greiss 1986; one s. *Education:* Parsons School of Design. *Career:* Associate Producer, Iris Films Inc, New York, 1975–83; Producer, Sam Alexander Productions, New York, 1983–86; John Eric Alexander Music Inc, New York, 1986–; mem, AFofM. *Compositions:* Composer, music producer, film soundtracks: The Fly, 1986; Red Heat, 1987; Predator, 1987; The Mosquito Coast, 1987; Witches of Eastwick, 1988; Flatliners, 1990; Lethal Weapon II, 1990; Bird On A Wire, 1990; Die Hard II, 1990; Silence of The Lambs, 1991; Point Break, 1991; Ricochet, 1991. *Honours:* Cannes Film Festival Award, Witches of Eastwick, 1988.

ALEXANDER, Phil; British editor; *Editor-in-Chief, Mojo. Career:* Man. Ed. Kerrang! –2002; Man. Ed. Q magazine 2002; Ed.-in-Chief Mojo magazine 2003–, Q Magazine 2014–; Assoc. Publr, Bauer Media 2011–. *Television includes:* presenter of rock show, Raw Power 1990, presenter of Popped In, Crashed Out (series) 1999. *Address:* MOJO, Endeavour House, 189 Shaftesbury Avenue, London, WC2H 8JG, England (office). *Telephone:* (20) 7208-3443 (office). *E-mail:* mojo@bauermedia.co.uk (office). *Website:* www.mojo4music.com.

ALI, Nadia; Pakistani/American singer and songwriter; b. 3 Aug. 1980, Libya. *Career:* relocated to New York with family aged five; debut single Rapture became international hit 2001; singer with duo iiO 2001–05; solo career 2006–; solo debut album 2009; numerous recording collaborations including Armin van Buuren, Rosko, Tocadisco, Serge Devant, Schiller, Chris Reece, Sultan & Ned Shepard, Starkillers & Alex Kenji, Alesso, Spencer & Hill, Sander van Doom and Sidney Samson, EDX, BT and Arty. *Recordings include:* albums: with iiO: Poetica (as member) 2005, Exit 110 (as guest vocalist) 2011; solo: Embers 2009. *Honours:* International Dance Music Awards for Best Progressive House Track (for Pressure, with Alesso) 2012, for Best Trance Track (for Feels So Good) 2012. *Current Management:* c/o Steven Haddad, Hashtag Management, 157 South Detroit Street, Los Angeles, CA 90036, USA. *Website:* www.hashtagmanagement.com; www.nadiaali.com.

ALIFANTIS, Nicu; Romanian singer, composer and musician (guitar); b. 31 May 1954, Braila. *Education:* National Univ. of Theater and Film I.L. Caragiale. *Career:* wrote music for theatre (118 plays) and film soundtracks (17); numerous recital concerts and tours. *Recordings include:* albums: Cintec de Noapte 1976, Dupa Melci 1979, Nicu Alifantis 1984, Mitica Popescu 1984, Piata Romana n.9 1988, Risipitorul de Iubire 1990, Decembre 1992, Ia Toji Baladist 1993, Voiaj 1995, Nichita 1996, Nicu Alfantis 25 1999, Cadavrul Viu 2001, Neuitatele Femei 2002, Sah Mat 2004, Simphonicu 2006, Vinyl Collection 2007, Asta seara stau acasa 2009, Cantece de semineu 2010, Quindecennial Alifantis & Zan 2011, Nevestele vesele din Windsor 2011, Mozaic 2013, Mitica Popescu (editie aniversara) 2014. *Honours:* Cultural Merit Order 2004; Theatre Music Awards 1986, 1991, 1993, Singer of the Year 1993. *Telephone:* (74) 2269054 (office). *E-mail:* alifantis@alifantis.ro. *Website:* www.alifantis.ro.

ALIZÉE; French singer; b. (Alizée Jacote), 21 Aug. 1984, Ajaccio, Corsica; m. Jérémy Chatelain 2003; one d. *Career:* discovered on French TV show 'Graines de stars' 2000. *Recordings include:* albums: Gourmandises 2000, Mes Courantes Electriques 2003, Psychédélices 2007; singles: Moi Lolita 2000, L'Alizée 2000, Parler tout bas 2001, Gourmandises 2001, J'en ai marre 2003, J'ai pas vingt ans 2003, A contre-courant 2003. *Honours:* M6 Award, NRJ Music Award, World Music Award 2002. *Address:* RCA Music Group, Song BMG Music France, 20–26 rue Morel, 92110 Paris, France (office). *Website:* www.rcsmusic.fr (office); www.alizee-officiel.com.

ALLEN, Duane David, BS; American singer and songwriter; b. 29 April 1943, Taylortown, TX; m. Norah Lee Stuart 1969; two s. *Education:* East Texas Univ. *Career:* radio DJ, Paris, Texas 1963–65; lead singer of gospel/country group, Oak Ridge Boys 1966–; mem. CMA, Gospel Music Asscn, AFTRA, Nat. Acad. Recording Arts and Sciences, Acad. of Country Music. *Compositions:* He Did It All For Me; Here's A Song For The Man; How Much Further Can We Go; I Will Follow The Sun. *Recordings include:* albums: with Oak Ridge Boys: International 1971, Light 1972, Hymns 1973, Street Gospel 1973, Gospel Gold Heartwarming 1974, Oak Ridge Boys 1974, Super Gold 1974, Sky High 1975, Old Fashioned... 1976, Y'All Come Back Saloon 1977, Room Service 1978, The Oak Ridge Boys Have Arrived 1979, Together 1980, Fancy Free 1981, Bobbie Sue 1982, Oak Ridge Boys Christmas 1982, Friendship 1983, American Made 1983, The Oak Ridge Boys Deliver 1984, Step On Out 1985, Seasons 1985, Christmas Again 1986, Where the Fast Lane Ends 1986, Monongahela 1987, New Horizons 1988, American Dreams 1989, Unstoppable 1991, The Long Haul 1992, Revival 1997, Voices 1999, From the Heart 2001, Colors 2003, The Journey 2004, Common Thread 2005, Front Row Seats 2006, A Gospel Journey 2009, The Boys Are Back 2009. *Publication:* The History of Gospel Music (co-author) 1971. *Honours:* Grammy Awards 1970–77, 12 Gospel Music Asscn Dove Awards, American Music Award for Best Country Group of the Year 1982, Country Music Asscn Award for Vocal Group of the Year 1978, Acad. of Country Music Award for Best Vocal Group 1977, 1979. *Address:* 88 New Shackle Island, Hendersonville, TN 37075, USA (office). *Telephone:* (615) 824-4924 (office). *Website:* www.oakridgeboys.com.

ALLEN, Geri, MMus; American jazz musician (piano) and composer; *Associate Professor of Jazz and Contemporary Improvisation, University of Michigan*; b. (Geri Antoinette Allen), 1957, Pontiac, Mich.; d. of Mount Allen and Barbara Allen; three c. *Education:* Cass Technical High School, Detroit, Howard Univ., Univ. of Pittsburgh. *Career:* fmr Asst Prof. of Music, Howard Univ.; taught at New England Conservatory and The New School; currently Assoc. Prof. of Jazz and Contemporary Improvisation, Univ. of Michigan; formed own trio with Ron Carter, Tony Williams, also performs with The Detroit 3; also played with Ornette Coleman, Wallace Roney, Jack DeJohnette, Betty Carter, Dave Holland, Marcus Belgrave, Charlie Haden, Jimmy Cobb, Paul Motian, Dewey Redman, Ravi Coltrane, Lester Bowie, Charles Lloyd, and numerous others. *Recordings include:* The Printmakers, Twilight Time, The Nurturer, Maroons, Twenty One, Etudes And Segments (with Charlie Haden, Paul Motian), Feed The Fire (with Betty Carter, Jack DeJohnette, Dave Holland), Sound Museum 1996, Gathering 1998, Eyes in the Back of your Head, Timeless Portraits and Dreams, Flying Towards the Sound, A Child is Born 2011, Grand River Crossings: Motown and Motor City Inspirations 2013. *Honours:* Benny Golson Award, Distinguished Alumni Award, Distinguished Prof. Award, Howard Univ., SESAC Special Achievement Award, Eubie Blake Award, Downbeat Critics Poll, Talent Deserving Wider Recognition, 1993, 1994, African American Classical Music Award, Spelman Coll., Jazzpar Prize, Lady of Soul Award, Key to Cambridge. *Current Management:* c/o Ora Harris Ross, Clayton Productions, 5090 East Lakeshore Drive, San Ramon, CA 94582, USA. *Telephone:* (925) 804-6232. *E-mail:* pianospaces@aol.com; rossclytn@aol.com. *Address:* School of Music, Theatre and Dance, University of Michigan, E.V Moore Building, 1100 Baits Drive, Ann Arbor, MI 48109-2085, USA (office). *Telephone:* (734) 764-0583 (office). *Fax:* (734) 763-5097 (office). *E-mail:* gaallen@umich.edu (office). *Website:* www.music.umich.edu; www.geriallen.com.

ALLEN, Henry Kaleialoha; American musician (Hawaiian steel guitar, jazz guitar, ukulele), songwriter and producer; b. 11 June 1933, Hilo, Hawaii; s. of Henry Kameau Allen and Martha Mersberg; m. Sherron Allen 1971; one s. three d. *Education:* Hawaiian Music Inst., studied in Los Angeles. *Career:* Founder, Hawaiian Music Inst.; f. own record label, Rainbow Records; mem. ASCAP, HSGA, Musicians Asscn of Hawaii. *Film appearances include:* (music parts) Hawaiian Eye, Blue Hawaii, Barnaby Jones, Mama's Family. *Compositions include:* Lahaina, Walking in the Sand, Hookipa (Jazz) Noalani, Koele Mist, We Say Aloha, Goodbye, Lanikai, Hawaii: Islands in the Sky, Kalele, Swinging, Sands. *Recordings include:* albums: A Lei of Stars, Blue Hawaii, Magic of Steel Guitar, Europa, Equinox, Legacy, Mauna Kea Hawaiian Steel Guitar 2008, East of the Sun West of the Moon 2009, Step Into My Life 2013. *Publications include:* Learning to Play the Hawaiian Way 1991, Book of Songs, Hawaiian Steel Guitar 1993, Ukulele: Pila Li'i Li'i Hana 2006. *Honours:* State Foundation for Culture and the Arts Award 1995, 1996, Master Artist grants, ASCAP Award 1996, 1997, County of Maui grant for music work, Gov.'s Recognition and Fine Arts Award 2004, Hawaii State Senate Award 2004, Mayor of Maui Lifetime Achievement Award 2005. *Address:* c/o Polynesian Promotions, 5161-D, Kohi Street, Lahaina, Maui, HI 96761, USA. *Telephone:* (808) 669-6189. *Fax:* (808) 559-6189. *E-mail:* henrykallen@aol.com (home).

ALLEN, Kevin; American musician (guitar); b. 17 July 1979. *Career:* fmr mem., ...And You Will Know Us By The Trail Of Dead. *Recordings include:* albums: ...And You Will Know Us By The Trail Of Dead 1998, Madonna 1999, Source Tags and Codes 2002, The Secret of Elena's Tomb 2003, Worlds Apart 2005, So Divided 2006, The Century of Self 2009, Tao of the Dead 2011, Lost Songs 2012.

ALLEN, Lily; British singer and songwriter; b. 2 May 1985, Hammersmith, London; d. of Keith Allen and Alison Owen; m. Sam Cooper; two d. *Career:* signed recording contract with Warner Music 2002, left without releasing any music; signed to Regal Records/Parlophone 2005; gained initial popularity by posting music on MySpace social networking website; collaborations with Basement Jaxx, Robbie Williams, Jamie T, Dizzee Rascal, Mark Ronson; launched fashion label Lily Loves 2007. *Recordings include :* albums: Alright, Still 2006, It's Not Me, It's You 2009, Sheezus 2014. *Film:* Elizabeth 1998. *Television includes:* Lily Allen and Friends (BBC 3) 2008, Neighbours 2009, Lily Allen: From Riches to Rags 2011. *Honours:* Revelation of the Year, Oye Awards, Mexico 2007, Ivor Novello Awards for Best Song (for The Fear) 2010, for Most Performed Work (for The Fear) 2010, for Songwriter of the Year 2010. *Current Management:* c/o Todd Interland, 21st Artists, 1 Blythe Road, London W14 0HG, England. *Telephone:* (20) 7348-4801. *Address:* c/o Regal, Parlophone Records, EMI House, 43 Brook Green, London W6 7EF, England. *Telephone:* (20) 7605-5000. *E-mail:* james@regal.co.uk. *Website:* www.regal.co.uk; www.lilyallenmusic.com.

ALLEN, Peter Raymond; British musician, bandleader, broadcaster and event organizer; *Owner, Pete Allen Music*; b. 23 Nov. 1954, Newbury, Berks., England; m. Christine Allen. *Education:* Downs School, Compton, nr Newbury. *Career:* formed Pete Allen Jazz Band 1978; numerous one-night shows at theatres, clubs and festivals throughout UK and abroad; regular appearances on BBC Radio 2 plays and for local radio and numerous network and regional TV shows for BBC and ITV; also appears as a guest soloist and presents own solo music show; mem. Performing Right Soc. *Compositions:* Beau Sejour, Mystic Gypsy, St Louis Street Stomp, Riverside Rag, Springtime Swing, Black Lion Rag, At the Upton Mardi Gras, Never Without You, Movin On, Movin On Again, Something Different, Clarinet Clarinade. *Recordings:* Turkey Trot 1978, Down in Honky Tonk Town 1979, Gonna Build A Mountain 1980, Beau Sejour 1987, Big Chief, Loose Tie 1996, All Aboard for Alabama 1997, Oh Play That Thing 1998, Reeds 'n' Rhythm 1998, Movin' On 1999; as Just Pete Allen: Clarinade of Music 2003, Merry Christmas 2004, Wine and Dine 2004; with Pete Allen Jazz Band: Chinatown My Chinatown 2004, Bechet's Walk 2005, Free and Easy 2007, 30 Years On 2008, Playing for Time 2009, Live at the Brewhouse 2009, Amapola 2011, Something Different 2012, Jazzalikes 2012, Live in Nyborg 2013, Solitude 2013, Reeds Strings & Ivories 2013. *Honours:* Hon. Citizen of New Orleans 1992; World Wide All Stars, Sacramento, Calif. 1984, European Top Eight Jazz Band (Germany). *Address:* 1 Tamarind, Willand Cullompton, Devon, EX15 2SR, England. *Telephone:* 7899-925194 (mobile). *E-mail:* peteallenjazz@tiscali.co.uk. *Website:* www.peteallenjazz.com.

ALLEN, Richard (Rick) John Cyril; British rock musician (drums); b. 1 Nov. 1963, Sheffield, England; m. Lauren; one c. *Career:* mem. Def Leppard 1978–; numerous concerts and tours worldwide, festival appearances; lost left arm in car crash 1984, returned to perform with custom-built drum kit 1985. *Recordings include:* albums: The Def Leppard EP 1978, On Through the Night 1980, High 'n' Dry 1981, Pyromania 1983, Hysteria 1987, Adrenalize 1992, Retro Active 1993, Vault 1980–95 1995, Slang 1996, Euphoria 1999, X 2002, Yeah 2006, Songs from the Sparkle Lounge 2008, Def Leppard 2015. *Television:* Behind the Music (documentary series, VH1) 1998, Storytellers (documentary, VH1), Hysteria: The Def Leppard Story (documentary, VH1), Ultimate Albums (documentary, VH1). *Honours:* American Music Awards for Favorite Heavy Metal Album, for Favorite Heavy Metal Artist 1989. *Address:* c/o Primary Wave Music, 116 East 16th Street, 9th Floor, New York, NY 10003, USA. *E-mail:* info@primarywave.com. *Website:* www.defleppard.com.

ALLEN, Tony; Nigerian musician (drums); b. 12 Aug. 1940, Lagos. *Career:* self-taught drummer; worked as an engineer for radio station in Lagos; played claves and later drums with 'Sir' Victor Olaiya's highlife band, also played with Agu Norris and the Heatwaves, Nigerian Messengers, Melody Makers; mem. Fela Kuti's Koola Lobitos highlife band 1964–79, band later renamed Africa '70, became music dir as well as drummer; formed own band 1980; collaborations with musicians including King Sunny Ade, Ray Lema, Manu Dibango, Roy Ayers, Air; mem. The Good, The Bad and The Queen 2006–; has lived in Lagos, London and Paris. *Recordings include:* albums: with Fela Kuti/

Africa '70: Fela's London Scene 1970, Roforofo Fight 1972, Shakara 1972, Afrodisiac 1973, Gentlemen 1973, Confusion 1974, He Miss Road 1974, Alagbon Close 1975, Everything Scatter 1975, Excuse O 1975, Expensive Shit 1975, Monkey Banana 1975, Noise For Vendor Mouth 1975, Ikoyi Blindness 1976, Na Poi 1976, Unnecessary Begging 1976, Upside Down 1976, Yellow Fever 1976, Fear Not For Man 1977, No Agreement 1977, Opposite People 1977, Sorrow Tears And Blood 1977, Stalemate 1977, Zombie 1977, Unknown Soldier 1979, V.I.P. 1979, Music Of Many Colours (with Roy Ayers) 1980, I Go Shout Plenty 1986, The Two Sides Of Fela-Jazz and Dance 1999; solo: Jealousy 1975, Progress 1977, No Accommodation For Lagos 1979, No Discrimination 1980, Never Expect Power Always (N.E.P.A) 1988, Ariya 1998, Black Voices 1999, Homecooking 2002, Every Season 2002, Eager Hands & Restless Feet 2002, Live 2004, Lagos No Shaking 2006, Secret Agent 2009; others: The Good, The Bad & The Queen 2007, Inspiration Information 4 2009, Rocket Juice and the Moon 2012. *Website:* www.thegoodthebadandthequeen.com (office).

ALLEN OF KENSINGTON, Baron (Life Peer), cr. 2013, of Kensington in the Royal Borough of Kensington and Chelsea; **Charles Lamb Allen,** Kt, CBE, FRSA, FCMA; British business executive and broadcaster; *Chairman, Global Radio*; b. 4 Jan. 1957. *Career:* accountant, British Steel 1974–79; Deputy Audit Man. Gallaghers PLC 1979–82; Dir Man. Services Grandmet Int. Services Ltd 1982–85, Group Man. Dir Compass Vending, Grandmet Innovations Ltd 1986–87, Man. Dir Grandmet Int. Services Ltd 1987–88, Man. Dir Compass Group Ltd 1988–91, Chief Exec. Leisure Div., Granada Group 1991–92; Chair. Granada Leisure and Services 1993–2000, CEO LWT (following takeover by Granada) 1994–96 (Chair. 1996), CEO Granada Group PLC 1996–2000, Chair. GMTV 1996–2000, Jt Deputy Chair. Granada Compass PLC 2000, Exec. Chair. Granada PLC 2000–03, CEO ITV PLC (after merger of Granada and Carlton) 2003–07; Chair. Yorkshire Tyne Tees TV 1997–; Chair. M2002 Ltd (Manchester Commonwealth Games); Chair. Global Radio (Heart, Capital, Classic FM, LBC, Gold, XFM, Choice) 2007–, Exec. Bd of the Labour Party 2012–, British Red Cross 2013–, 2 Sisters food Group, ISS A/S 2013–; Chair. (non-exec.) EMI Music 2009–10, CEO 2010–11; Sr Adviser, Goldman Sachs Capital Partners 2008–; Vice-Chair. London 2012 Ltd (effort to bring 2012 Olympics to London); Dir (non-exec.) Tesco plc 1999–2010, Endemol 2008–, Virgin Media 2008–, GET A/S 2009–; mem. (Labour), House of Lords 2013–. *Honours:* Hon. DBA (Manchester Metropolitan) 1999, (Salford) 2002; named as Mayor of the Olympic Village, London for the duration of the Games May 2012. *Address:* Global Radio, 30 Leicester Square, London, WC2H 7LA (office); House of Lords, Westminster, London, SW1A 0PW, England. *Telephone:* (20) 7766-6000 (office); (20) 7219-5353. *Fax:* (20) 7766-6111 (office). *E-mail:* info@thisisglobal.com (office); contactholmember@parliament.uk. *Website:* www.thisisglobal.com/radio (office); www.parliament.uk/biographies/lords/lord-allen-of-kensington/4304.

ALLEYNE, Cheryl Louise; British musician (drums); b. 4 Sept. 1963, N London, England. *Education:* Coll. of Arts and Tech., Newcastle upon Tyne. *Career:* drummer with The Jazz Warriors, Loose Tubes, Courtney Pine Septet, Steve Williamson Quintet; house drummer for Richard Blackwood's Club Class Comedy (Five); MTV Spring Break Jams, Us3, San Diego 1994; moved to USA to work on jazz circuit 2000; show band drummer on cruise liners 2001, 2003. *Recordings include:* Ashley Slater's The Human Groove 1989, The Jazz Warriors' Chameleon 1993, Keith Waithe's Magic Of Olmec 1995, Gail Thompson's Jazz Africa 1995, Ciyo's Somewhere Out There 1996, Kevin Haynes's Tomorrows Path 1997, Alex Wilson's Afro-Saxon 1998. *Honours:* Most Promising Musician of the Year, Edinburgh Jazz Festival 1986. *E-mail:* cherrydrums@hotmail.com.

ALLISON, Ben, BA; American musician (bass), producer, composer and arranger; b. 1966, New Haven, Conn. *Education:* New York Univ., Yale Univ. *Career:* f. groups including Man Size Safe, Peace Pipe, Medicine Wheel; tours throughout the USA, Canada, Europe, Brazil; f. Jazz Composers Collective 1991; co-leader, Herbie Nichols Project 1994–; has appeared on over 40 albums by various artists; also music for film, TV and radio; featured artist, Jazz Sinfonica Orchestra of São Paulo 2005, 2008. *Music for film/TV includes:* theme: On the Media (Nat. Public Radio); scores: Two Days (play), Play Name (film). *Recordings include:* solo: Seven Arrows 1996, Medicine Wheel 1998, Third Eye 1999, Riding the Nuclear Tiger 2001, Peace Pipe 2002, Buzz 2004, Cowboy Justice 2006, Little Things Run the World 2008, Think Free 2009, Action-Refraction 2011; with Herbie Nichols Project: Love Is Proximity 1997, Dr. Cyclops' Dream 1999, Strange City 2001; with Steven Bernstein's Millennial Territory Orchestra: Vol. 1 2006, We Are MTO 2008. *Honours:* grants from Chamber Music America, Mary Flagler Cary Charitable Trust, Nat. Endowment for the Arts, Aaron Copland Foundation, Meet the Composer, American Composers Forum, numerous SESAC Awards for Top 5 National Radio Airplay, Bird Award, Netherlands, 2005. *E-mail:* ben@benallison.com. *Website:* www.benallison.com.

ALLISON, Bernard; American musician (guitar), singer, arranger and composer; b. 26 Nov. 1965, Chicago; one d. *Career:* documentary film, The Next Generation; France, Grand de Sable, Paris Premier; Live at the New Morning; mem, SCEM. *Recordings:* The Next Generation 1990, No Mercy 1994, Hang On 1994, Funkifino 1995, Keepin' the Blues Alive 1997, Born with the Blues 1997, Times Are Changing 1998, Across the Water 2000, Storms of Life 2002, Higher Power 2005, Triple Fret 2005, Chills and Thrills 2007, The Otherside 2010. *Honours:* New Artist of the Year, Atlanta, Georgia, 1998. *Current Management:* Intrepid Artists, 1300 Baxter Street, Suite 405, Charlotte, NC 28204, USA. *Telephone:* (704) 358-4777. *Fax:* (704) 358-3171. *E-mail:* staff@intrepidartists.com. *Website:* www.intrepidartists.com. *Address:* c/o Jazzhaus Records, Gluemerstrasse 2b, 79102 Freiburg i Br., Germany. *Telephone:* (761) 7919-780. *Fax:* (761) 72935. *E-mail:* ilg@jazzhausrecords.com. *Website:* www.jazzhausrecords.com; www.bernardallison.com.

ALLISON, James (Jim) H.; American songwriter, music publisher and producer; b. 13 Feb. 1959, Gettysburg, Pennsylvania, USA. *Education:* Master's Penn State University, Gettysburg College, BA. *Career:* Began writing songs aged 13; High school English teacher for 2 years; Musician and bandleader for 20 years; Set up own music publishing and production company, 1985; Studio owner and producer; Recorded and helped launch country music career of Billy Ray Cyrus; mem, CMA. *Compositions:* What Am I Gonna Do About You, Reba McEntire; Fade To Blue, LeAnn Rimes; Cowboys Don't Cry, Daron Norwood. *Recordings:* Razzy Bailey; Earl Thomas Conley; Mickey Gilley; Brenda Lee; Jo Dee Messina; Del Reeves; Connie Smith; Jett Williams; Lee Ann Womack. *Publications:* 1001 Song Ideas Vols 1 and 2, 1999; Million Dollar Ideas: Inventions Creations and Opportunities, 2000. *Honours:* Nashville Songwriters Assn award, What Am I Gonna Do About You, 1987; Billboard Song Contest, Nobody Loves Me Like The Blues, Winner, 1992. *Address:* AlliSongs Inc, 1603 Horton Avenue, Nashville, TN 37212, USA. *Telephone:* (615) 943-0995. *E-mail:* Stephanie@allisongs.com. *Website:* www.allisongs.com.

ALLISON, Mose; American singer, jazz and blues musician (piano), lyricist and composer; b. 11 Nov. 1927, Tippo, Miss. *Career:* influenced by Louis Jordan, Louis Armstrong and Nat 'King' Cole, started out playing trumpet then switched to piano; after college and the army, appeared professionally for the first time 1950; returned to college shortly after; recorded with Al Cohn and Bobby Brookmeyer for Prestige Records 1956; signed own record deal 1957; joined Columbia in 1960 for two years before a 14-year record deal with Atlantic; after a six-year recording hiatus re-emerged briefly on Elektra before signing with Blue Note; tours extensively throughout N America, UK and Europe. *Compositions include:* Ain't You A Mess, Ask Me Nice, Autumn Song, Back Country Sketches, Back Down South, Back on the Corner, Barefoot Dirt Road, Benediction, Big Brother Cabaret, Card Carnival, Certified Senior Citizen, Children of the Future, City Home, Creekbank Suite, Crepuscular Air, Cruise Control, Crush, Cuttin' Out Days Like This Devil in the Cane Field, Dinner on the Ground, Do It, Don't Forget to Smile, Dr. Jekyll and Mr. Hyde, Echo, Ever Since I Stole the Blues, Ever Since the World Ended, Everybody Cryin' Mercy, Finale, Foolkiller, Gettin' There, Gimcracks and Gewgaws, Gotham Day Gotham Night, Hello There Universe, High Jinks, Highway 49, Hittin' On One, How Does it Feel, How Much Truth?, Hymn to Everything, I Don't Love You No More, I Don't Want Much, I Don't Worry About a Thing, I Feel So Good, I Looked in the Mirror Today, I Know You Didn't Mean It, Idyll, If You Live, If You Only Knew, If You Really Loved Me, If You're Goin' to the City, I'm Alive, I'm Not Talkin', Ingénue, It Didn't Turn Out That Way, January, Just Like Livin', Kiddin' on the Square, Let It Come Down, Local Color Suite, Long Song, Look Here, Look What You Made Me Do, Meadows, MJA Jr., Middle Class White Boy, Mockingbird, Modest Proposal, Mojo Woman, Monsters of the Id, Moon and Cypress Mountains, Mule, My Backyard, My Brain, Natural Born Malcontent, Nevermore, New Ground, New Parchman, Nightclub, Nightride, Nightwatch, No Exit, No Matter, No Trouble, Livin' Now You See It, Numbers On Paper, Ole' Man John, Old Man Blues, On The Run, One of These Days, Parchman Farm, Perfect Moment, Powerhouse Promenade, Puttin' Up With Me, Ramble, Renegade, Saritha, Saturday Scamper, Sentimental Fool I'm Smashed, Sob Story, Somebody Gonna Have to Move Spires, Spring Song, Standby, Stop This World, Swingin' Machine, Tai Che Life, Tell Me Something, Texanna, The Chaser, The Earth Wants You, The Fires of Spring, The Gettin' Paid Waltz, The Hills, The Minstrel, The More You Get, The News, The Path, The River, The Way of the World, The Well, This Ain't Me, Top Forty, Town Train, Variation on Dixie, Warhorse, Warm Night Was, Western Man, What a Shame, What Do You Do After You've Ruined Your Life, What Will It Be?, What's With You?, What's Your Movie?, Who Am I?, Who's In, Who's Out?, Wild Man on the Loose, You Can Count on Me To Do My Part, You Can't Push People Around, Young Man Blues, Your Mind is On Vacation, Your Molecular Structure. *Recordings include:* albums: The Al Cohn Quintet 1956, Stan Getz Quartet – Live in 1956/57, Stan Getz Quartet: The Soft Swing 1957, Jazz Alive! A Night at the Half Note 1959, Al Cohn & Zoot Sims Quartet 1960, Al Cohn & Zoot Sims Quartet: You 'N' Me 1960; as Mose Allison: Back Country Suite 1957, Local Color 1957, Young Man Mose 1958, Ramblin' with Mose 1958, Creek Bank 1958, Autumn Song 1959, Tranfiguration of Hiram Brown 1959, I Love the Life I Live 1960, Takes to the Hills 1961, I Don't Worry 'Bout a Thing 1962, Swingin' Machine 1963, Mose Allison Sings 1963, The Word from Mose 1964, Mose Allison Alive! 1965, Wild Man on the Loose 1965, Down Home Piano 1965, Mose Allison Plays for Lovers 1966, V-8 Ford Blues 1966, Mose Goes 1968, Hello There Universe 1969, The Best of Mose Allison 1970, Western Man 1971, Retrospective 1971, Mose in Your Ear 1972, Seventh Son 1973, I've Been Doin' Some Thinkin' 1968, Your Mind is on Vacation 1976, Middle Class White Boy 1982, Lessons In Living 1982, Ever Since the World Ended 1987, The Best of Mose Allison 1988, Greatest Hits 1988, My Backyard 1989, At His Best 1990, Sings and Plays 1991, The Earth Wants You 1993, Pure Mose 1994, High Jinks! 1994, Allison Wonderland 1994, The Sage of Tippo, Gimcracks and Gewgaws 1998, The London Chronicles Vol. 1 2001, The London Chronicles Vol. 2 2002, The Way of the World 2010; compilations: Hot Rods

& Custom Classics, Live From the Mountain Stage Lounge, Jazz Profile, Nighttime Jazz, Smooth and Cool Music to Install Windows 98, Borders Classic Jazz, Atlantic Jazz Classics, Atlantic Jazz Vocal Classics, Cocktail Mix, Vol. 2: Martini Madness, Drivin' Blues, Essential Jazz, Great Moments in Jazz, Night Time Jazz, The Whole Nine Yards Motion Picture Soundtrack, Voices of Cool. *Current Management:* c/o The Blues Agency, 323 Beale Street, Suite 2000, Memphis, TN 38103, USA. *E-mail:* info@moseallison.com (home). *Website:* www.moseallison.com.

ALLMAN, Gregg; American musician; b. 8 Dec. 1947, Nashville, TN; m. Cher Bono 1975 (divorced 1979); one c. *Career:* co-founder, Hour Glass; support to Eric Burdon and the Animals, 1967; co-founder, singer, Allman Brothers (with brother Duane), 1969–76, 1978–81, 1989–; solo artist 1973–; also recorded with wife, Cher 1976–79; numerous live appearances, festivals; actor in film, Rush 1991. *Recordings:* Albums with Hour Glass: Hour Glass, 1967; Power Of Love, 1968; with The Allman Brothers: Allman Brothers Band, 1970; At Fillmore East, 1971; Eat A Peach, 1972; Brothers And Sisters, 1973; Win Lose Or Draw, 1975; The Road Goes On Forever, 1976; Wipe The Windows, Check The Oil, Dollar Gas, 1976; Enlightened Rogues, 1979; Brothers Of The Road, 1981; The Best Of The Allman Band, 1981; Dreams, 1989; Seven Turns, 1989; Shades Of Two Worlds, 1991; Second Set, 1995; Fantastic Allman Brothers Original Hits, 1999; solo albums: Laid Back, 1973; The Gregg Allman Tour, 1974; Playin' Up A Storm, 1977; I'm No Angel, 1987; Just Before The Bullets Fly, 1988; Searchin' For Simplicity, 1997; with Cher: Allman And Woman, 1976; Two The Hard Way, 1977. *Publications:* My Cross to Bear (memoir) 2012. *Website:* www.greggallman.com.

ALLOUCHE, Joël; Musician (drums, percussion); b. 6 Nov. 1960, Bougie, Algeria; m. 1988; one s. one d. *Career:* professional musician with pop bands, singers 1975–; jazz 1980–; played in Japan, Canada, USA, Africa, UK, India; worked with musicians including John Surman, Kenny Wheeler, Palle Danielsson, Enrico Rava, Urs Leimgruber, Don Friedman, Maurice Magnoni, Marc Ducret, François Jeanneau, Michel Portal, Doudou Gouirand, Don Cherry, Antonello Salis; concerts, festivals with Coïncidence, the Llabador brothers group 1980–; international concerts with Philippe Caillat's guitar trio, in Berlin, Copenhagen, Hamburg, Hungary; mem. Reflexionen 1983, Maurice Magnoni Quintet 1987, Marc Ducret Trio 1988, Pandémonium, François Jeanneau Quartet, Michel Portal's New Unit 1990, Nguyen Lê's guitar trio 1992, Soriba Kouyaté's trio; currently based in Montpellier, collaborations with Michel Marre, Doudou Gouirand, Gérard Pansanel, in trio with Serge Lazarevitch and Eric Barret; teaches masterclasses at conservatoires and music schools. *Recordings include:* French Connection (with Philippe Caillat) 1981, Fire Brigade (with Philippe Caillat) 1982; with J. P. Llabador: Coincidence 1984, Brussels 1987; Forgotten Tales (with Doudou Gouirand and Don Cherry) 1985; with Urs Leimgruber: Reflexionen 1986, Live 1986, Remember To Remember 1987; Andata Senza Ritorno (with Maurice Magnoni) 1988, Superbe Déménagement 1989, Gris (with Marc Ducret) 1990, Lato Sensu (with Philippe Gareil) 1991, Beatles Stories (with Gérard Pansanel and Antonello Salis) 1992, Maloya Transit (with François Jeanneau and Trio Tambours) 1992, Paolo Damiani (with Kenny Wheeler) 1992, Dominique Pifarely (with Ricardo del Fra), F. Couturier 1993, Birds Can Fly, J. P. Llabador 1995, Orchestra Improvista, Nino Rota-Fellini (with Gouirand, Pansanel) 1995, Tales From Vietnam (Nguyen Lê) 1996, Few Notes (with Jean Bardy) 1998, Tamborea, Engergypsy 1999, Kanakassi, W. P. Fresu 1999, Bamana (with Soniba Kouyaté) 2001, Live in Montreux (with Soriba Kouyaté) 2002, A Jamais (with Joshua Breakstone) 2003, Boléro (with Doudou Gouiram) 2006, L'Arbre Pleure (with Nathalie Loriers) 2006, Give me Five (with Jean Pierre Llabador) 2007, Zapping (with Furio Di Castri) 2008, Electrip Vol. 2 (with Michel Prandi) 2010; solo: Close Meeting 2007. *Address:* 8 bis rue du Professeur Lombard, 34000 Montpellier, France (home). *E-mail:* joel.allouche@tele2.fr (home); contact@joel-allouche.com (home). *Website:* www.myspace.com/joelallouche (home).

ALLPASS, Soma; Danish musician (cello, piano, guitar), singer, songwriter and arranger; b. 9 July 1968, Copenhagen. *Education:* Royal Academy of Music, Copenhagen. *Career:* cellist and backing singer, Trains and Boats and Trains, rock band, 1989–94; co-arranger, Roskilde Festival, 1992, 1993, 1994; tours in Denmark, Norway, Sweden, Germany, England, Finland and New York; New Music Seminar, 1992; mem. KODA; Danish Musicians' Union. *Recordings:* albums: Trains And Boats And Trains, 1990; Hum (mini album), 1990; Engulfed, 1991; Minimal Star, 1992; solo: Lucky Angel 2001, Sway 2007. *Honours:* Rodovre Music Prize 1996. *E-mail:* somaallpass@hotmail.com. *Website:* www.myspace.com/somaallpass; www.somaallpass.dk.

ALLSTAR FRESH, (DJ Guan); Dutch producer, DJ and remixer; b. 1 Aug. 1965, Amsterdam. *Career:* producer under the name King Bee; DJ 1979–, now at Club iT, Amsterdam; owner record label, Model Records. *Recordings include:* albums: as Allstar Fresh: Back By Dope Demand 1990, Royal Jelly 1990, Must Be The Music; singles: as Allstar Fresh: Everybody In The Place, Demesshuffle 1988, Listen To The Sound Of The Drum and Bass 1988, Up The Par 1990, Here We Go Again 1993, Love Thing 1999; as DJ Guan: They Don't Understand, Get Ready, Damn Who The Hell Are You, It's Gonna Be Alright (remix), Lift Your Hands Up (remix), You're My Inspiration (remix), Trip To India (with Eric Nouhan). *Honours:* Dance Artist Awards 1991, 1992. *Address:* c/o Club iT, Amstelstraat 24, 1017 Amsterdam, The Netherlands. *E-mail:* info@allstarfresh.com. *Website:* www.allstarfresh.com; www.dj-guan .com.

ALLWRIGHT, (Sydney) Graeme; French singer, writer and composer; b. 7 Nov. 1926, Lyall Bay, New Zealand; m. Catherine Dasté 1951; three s. one d. *Career:* moved to France 1948; 30 years professional stage work, television, radio; concerts include Nyons Festival, Switzerland, Le Printemps de Bourges; Les Francofolies à la Rochelle, France; L'Olympia, Palais des Sports; mem. SACEM, ADAMI. *Recordings include:* Le Trimardeur 1965, Joue, joue, joue 1966, Le jour de clarté 1968, Recollections 1970, Jeanne d'Arc 1972, Graeme Allwright chante Leonard Cohen 1973, De Passage 1975, Questions 1978, Condamnés 1979, Ombres 1981, Limière 1992, Live 1994, With the Glenn Ferris Quartet 2000, Talents 2006, Des Inédits Pour le Plaisir 2008, Light 2010, Sings Brassens. *Address:* 13 place Aligre, 75012 Paris, France (home). *Website:* www.mga.asso.fr.

ALLYSON, Karrin; American singer and pianist; b. (Karrin Allyson Schoonover), 27 July 1962, Great Bend, KS. *Education:* Univ. of Nebraska. *Recordings:* albums: I Didn't Know About You 1992, Sweet Home Cookin' 1993, Azure-Te 1994, Collage 1996, Daydream 1996, From Paris To Rio 1999, Ballads: Remembering John Coltrane 2001, In Blue 2002, Wild For You 2004, Footprints 2006, Imagina: Songs of Brasil 2008, By Request: The Best of Karrin Allyson 2009, 'Round Midnight 2011. *Telephone:* (201) 928-0513. *E-mail:* amsala@aol.com. *Website:* www.amsartists.com. *E-mail:* fantalk@ karrin.com (office). *Website:* www.karrin.com.

ALMOND, (Peter) Marc; British singer and lyricist; b. 9 July 1959, Southport, Lancashire, England. *Education:* coll. in Southport, Leeds Polytechnic. *Career:* Founder mem. Soft Cell (with David Ball) 1979–84, re-formed 2001; Founder, Marc & the Mambas 1982–84; Founder, The Willing Sinners 1984; solo artist 1984–. *Recordings include:* albums: with Soft Cell: Non-Stop Erotic Cabaret 1981, Non-Stop Ecstatic Dancing 1982, The Art Of Falling Apart 1983, This Last Night In Sodom 1984, Down In The Subway 1994, Cruelty Without Beauty 2002, Live 2003, At The BBC (live) 2003; with Marc & the Mambas: Untitled 1982, Torment & Toreros 1983; with the Willing Sinners: Vermin In Ermine 1984, Stories of Johnny 1985, A Woman's Story 1986; solo: Some Bizarre 1981, Mother Fist And Her Five Daughters 1987, Singles 1984–1987 1987, Stars We Are 1988, Jacques 1990, Enchanted 1990, The Tenement Symphony 1991, Twelve Years Of Tears (live) 1993, Treasure Box 1995, Fantastic Star 1996, Absinthe: The French Album 1996, Slut 1998, Live in Concert 1998, Open All Night 1999, Stranger Things 2001, Little Rough Rhinestones Vol. 1 2002, Willing Sinner: Live in Berlin 2003, In Session Vol. 1 2003, Heart on Snow 2003, In Session Vol. 2 2003, Stardom Road 2007, Variété 2010, Feasting with Panthers 2011. *Honours:* Best Selling Single of the Year (for Tainted Love) 1981, BRIT Award for Best British Single (for Tainted Love) 1982, Billboard Magazine New Wave Band of the Year 1982, Mojo Hero Award 2010, Edinburgh Festival Fringe First 2011, Ivor Novello Inspiration Award 2013, Attitude Icon Award 2013. *Address:* c/o Cherry Red Records, Power Road Studios, 114 Power Road, London, W4 5PY, England (office). *Telephone:* (20) 8996-3120. *Fax:* (20) 8747-4030. *E-mail:* ma .management@yahoo.com (office); infonet@cherryred.co.uk (office). *Website:* www.marcalmond.co.uk.

ALMQVIST, Peter ('Howlin' Pelle); Swedish singer; b. 1979. *Career:* mem. and lead singer, The Hives 1993–. *Recordings include:* albums: Barely Legal 1997, Veni Vidi Vicious 2000, Your New Favourite Band (compilation) 2001, Tyrannosaurus Lives 2004, The Black and White Album 2007, Lex Hives 2012. *Honours:* NME Award for Best Int. Band 2003. *Address:* The Hives, Regnbågsvägen 46, 737 43 Fagersta, Sweden. *E-mail:* hives@innocent.com; TheHives@goldve.com. *Website:* www.myspace.com/thehives; www .thehivesbroadcastingservice.com.

ALPERT, Herb; American musician (trumpet), songwriter and record industry executive; b. 31 March 1935, Los Angeles; s. of Louis Alpert and Tillie Goldberg; m. 1st Sharon Mae Lubin 1956 (divorced); two c.; m. 2nd Lani Hall; one d. *Education:* Univ. of Southern Calif. *Career:* co-owner and fmr Pres. Carnival record co., later renamed A&M Record Co., Co-Chair. 1962–94; founder and Co-Chair. Almo Sounds 1994–2002; leader, arranger, own music group, Tijuana Brass 1962–; tours world-wide and numerous concert appearances; f. Herb Alpert Foundation. *Recordings include:* albums: The Lonely Bull 1962, Tijuana Brass 1963, Tijuana Brass Vol. 2 1963, South Of The Border 1964, Whipped Cream & Other Delights 1965, Going Places 1965, What Now My Love 1965, S.R.O. 1966, Sounds Like Us 1967, Herb Alpert's Ninth 1967, Beat Of The Brass 1968, Christmas Album 1968, Warm 1969, The Brass Are Comin' 1969, Summertime 1971, Solid Brass 1972, Four Sider 1973, You Smile, The Song Begins 1974, Coney Island 1975, Just You And Me 1976, Herb Alpert/Hugh Masekela 1978, Rise 1979, Keep Your Eyes On Me 1979, Beyond 1980, Magic Man 1981, Fandango 1982, Blow Your Own Horn 1983, Noche De Amor 1983, Bullish 1984, Wild Romance 1985, Keep Your Eye On Me 1987, Under A Spanish Moon 1988, My Abstract Heart 1989, North On South Street 1991, Midnight Sun 1992, Second Wind 1996, Passion Dance 1997, Colors 1999, Definitive Hits 2001, Lost Treasures 2005, Whipped Cream & Other Delights Rewhipped 2006, Anything Goes (with Lani Hall) 2009, I Feel You (with Lani Hall) 2011, Steppin' Out (Grammy Award for Best Pop Instrumental Album 2014) 2013. *Honours:* Lifetime Achievement Award (non-performer), Rock and Roll Hall of Fame Foundation 2005, Nat. Medal of Arts 2012. *Address:* c/o Herb Alpert Foundation, 1414 Sixth Street, Santa Monica, CA 90401, USA. *Telephone:* (424) 272-7082. *Website:* www.herbalpert.com.

ALSOU; Russian singer; b. (Alsou Tenisheva), 27 June 1983, Bugulma, Tatarstan; m. Yan Abramov 2006; two d. *Career:* solo artist 1998–, numerous concerts and live appearances; appearance at Eurovision Song Contest (second place) 2000; collaborations with Enrique Iglesias; hosted Eurovision Song Contest 2009. *Films:* as actor: Spirit Trap 2005. *Recordings include:* albums: Alsou 1999, I Had an Autumn Dream 2002, 19 2003, Samoe Glavnoe 2008, Tugan Tel/Rodnaya Rech 2008. *Website:* www.alsou.ru.

ALTERHAUG, Bjorn; Norwegian academic, jazz musician (bass) and composer; *Professor of Jazz, Norwegian University of Science and Technology;* b. 3 June 1945, Mo i Rana; m. Anne-Lise Alterhaug 1968; one s. one d. *Education:* Music Inst. of Science, Trondheim, Niels-Henning Orsted Pedersen. *Career:* played as jazz soloist with Ben Webster, Lucky Thompson, Chet Baker, Clark Terry; numerous television and radio broadcasts; festival composer, Silver Jubilee of North Norway Festival 1989; currently Prof. of Jazz, Norwegian Univ. of Science and Tech.; mem. Norwegian Jazz Federation, NOPA, Royal Norwegian Soc. of Science and Letters. *Recordings include:* solo albums: Moments 1979, A Ballad 1986, Constellations 1991, Songlines 2009. *Publications:* contrib. articles on improvisation and communication. *Honours:* Norwegian Jazz Federation Buddy Award 1989, Sør-Trøndelag County Culture Prize 2011. *Address:* Norwegian University of Science and Technology, 7491 Trondheim, Norway (office). *Telephone:* 73-59-65-68 (office). *Fax:* 73-59-65-88 (office). *E-mail:* bjorn.alterhaug@hf.ntnu.no (office). *Website:* www.hf.ntnu.no/hf/Musikk (office).

ALTMAN, John Neville Rufus, BA; British composer, conductor, arranger, orchestrator and musician (saxophone); b. 5 Dec. 1949, London; m. Rita Pukacz 1977; three s. one d. *Education:* University of Sussex, Birkbeck College, London. *Career:* recorded as keyboard player with Eric Clapton; Sting; Phil Collins; Saxophonist with Muddy Waters; Little Richard; Ben E King; Jimmy Page; John Lennon; Dr John; Slim Gaillard; Musical Director for Van Morrison, late 1970s; Regular conductor, Royal Philharmonic Orchestra; mem. PRS; ASCAP; BAC&S; ASMAC. *Compositions:* Films include: Funny Bones; Bhaji On The Beach; Hear My Song; Bad Behaviour; Devlin; Camilla; Titanic; RKO 281; The Lost Empire; Fidel; Beautiful Joe; Television includes: Peak Practice; Miss Marple; Shadowlands; First and Last; Comic Relief, 1995; By The Sword Divided; Composer, arranger, producer of over 3000 commercials including: British Airways; ATandT; Pan Am; General Motors; Stella Artois; Rover; Intercity; British Telecom; Films as arranger, orchestrator, conductor include: Monty Python's Life of Brian; Erik The Viking; Just A Gigolo; Foreign Bodies; The Sheltering Sky; Leon (aka The Professional); Golden Eye; Little Voice. *Recordings:* Arranger, conductor, producer: Singles: Downtown Train, Rod Stewart; Kissing A Fool, George Michael; That Ole Devil Called Love, Alison Moyet; Always Look On The Bright Side Of Life, Monty Python; Walking In The Air, Aled Jones; Love Is On Our Side, Tom Jones; It's Oh So Quiet, Björk; Albums: Streetfighting Years, Simple Minds; Hey Manhattan, Prefab Sprout; A Very Special Season, Diana Ross; Wildest Dreams, Tina Turner; Closing credits, song for film: Innocent Lies, Patricia Kaas; albums include: Shaking the Blues Away 2004, You Started Something 2004; with John Altman Orchestra: Sure Thing 2002. *Honours:* TRIC Award, 1995; Primetime Emmy Award, Outstanding Music Composition for a Drama or Miniseries, RKO 281, 2000. *Current Management:* c/o SMA Talent Limited, The Cottage, Church Street, Fressingfield, Suffolk, IP21 5PA, England. *Telephone:* (1379) 586734. *Fax:* (1379) 586131. *E-mail:* carolynne@smatalent .com. *Website:* www.smatalent.com.

AMA, Shola; British singer; b. (Mathurin Campbell), 8 March 1979, Willesden, London. *Career:* solo artist 1997–; numerous television appearances, tours. *Recordings include:* Albums: Much Love, 1997; In Return, 1999, Supersonic 2002; Singles: You Might Need Somebody, 1997; You're The One That I Love, 1997; Who's Loving My Baby, 1997; Much Love, 1998; Taboo (with Glamma Kid), 1999; Imagine, 2000. *Honours:* MOBO Awards, Best R&B Artist, Best Newcomer, 1997; BRIT Award, Best Female, 1998. *Current Management:* c/o MN2S, 4-7 Vineyard Borough, London, SE1 1QL, England.

AMADOR, Diego; Spanish singer and musician (piano, guitar); b. 1973, Seville. *Career:* solo artist in the flamenco style. *Recordings include:* albums: Anticipo Flamenco 1994, El Aire de lo puro 2001, Piano Jondo 2007, Rio de los Cansteros 2008. *Telephone:* 609451218 (Spain) (office). *Fax:* 934666300 (Spain) (office). *E-mail:* juanestrada@diegoamador.es (office). *Website:* www .diegoamador.es.

AMAR, Moustafa; Egyptian singer, composer and actor; b. (Moustafa Ahmed Mohammad Hassan Qamar), 22 Sept. 1966; m. 1993; two s. *Education:* Univ. of Alexandria. *Career:* solo artist 1990–. *Films:* El-batal 1997, El-hob el-awal 2000, As'hab walla business 2001, Alb garee' 2002, Bahebbak wana kaman 2003, Hobbak nar 2004, Hareem kareem 2005, Ali ya Weeka (TV series), Esabet el-Doctor Omar 2007, Mafeesh Faida 2008. *Recordings include:* albums: Wassaf 1990, Layaleki 1993, Seket el-ashe'en, Eftekerney, Ela man yehomo el-amr, Tal el-leil, Nar el-hob, Enaek wahshaney, Aisheen, Haiaty, Monaya, Rohy Feek 2003, Ensa 2004, Lesa habayeb 2006, Heya 2010. *Address:* c/o Alam el-Phan, Cairo, Egypt (office). *Website:* www.moustafaamar .com.

AMARANTOS, Gaby; Brazilian singer; b. (Gabriela Amaral dos Santos), 1 Aug. 1978, Jurunas, Belém, Pará. *Career:* numerous TV appearances and live shows; recorded theme song for football World Cup (with Monobloco) 2014. *Recording:* album: Treme 2012. *Honours:* Prêmio Multishow New Hit Award 2012, MTV Video Music Brazil Awards for Best Female Act 2012, for Artist of the Year 2012. *Website:* gabyamarantos.com.

AMBROSE, Edmund David; British record company executive and musician (bass); b. 11 Dec. 1945, Highgate, London; m. Angela 1975; two s. one d. *Education:* Brymshaw College of Art; London College of Printing. *Career:* musician with: Shotgun Express; Julie Driscoll; Brian Auger and Trinity; Arthur Brown; Cat Stevens; numerous television and radio broadcasts; concerts include: Royal Albert Hall and Fairfield Hall; Director of Planet 3 Records; Publishing for: Sex Pistols; Vapors; Dexy's Midnight Runners; Duran Duran; Pet Shop Boys; Transvision Vamp; Love City Groove; mem, Chelsea Arts Club; Rye Art Gallery. *Recordings:* with Shotgun Express: Shotgun Express, 1969; with Brian Auger and The Trinity: Open, 1967; Definitely What, 1968; Steetnoise, 1968; Befour, 1970; Genesis, 1975. *Honours:* Brightest Hope, Best Record with Brian Auger and The Trinity. *Address:* 71 Finlay Street, Fulham, London SW6 6HF, England.

AMBROSIUS, Marsha, (The Songstress); British singer and songwriter. *Education:* Brit School for Performing Arts, Croydon. *Career:* mem., Floetry 1997–2007; solo artist 2007–; co-songwriter for Michael Jackson, Alicia Keys, Jill Scott and Jazz (Dru Hill); featured on several songs, incl. Busta Rhymes 'Get You Some'. *Recordings include:* albums: with Floetry: Floetry Floetic (Soul Train Lady of Soul Award for Best Album 2003) 2002, Floetry Floacism 2003, Flo'Ology 2005; solo: Late Nights and Early Mornings 2011. *Address:* c/o J Records LLC, RCA Music Group, 745 Fifth Avenue, New York, NY 10151, USA (office). *Telephone:* (646) 840-5600. *Fax:* (646) 840-5729. *Website:* www .rcamusicgroup.com; www.marshaambrosiusmusic.com.

AMBUSH, Scott; American musician (bass); b. 28 April 1960, Frederick, Md; s. of Webster Ambush and Jeanette Lofton Ambush. *Education:* Univ. of Maryland. *Career:* mem. Spyro Gyra 1992–. *Recordings include:* albums with Spyro Gyra: Three Wishes 1992, Dreams Beyond Control 1993, Love & Other Obsessions 1995, Heart of the Night 1996, 20/20 1997, Road Scholars 1998, In Modern Times 2001, Original Cinema 2003, The Deep End 2004, Wrapped in a Dream 2006, Good to Go-Go 2007, Down the Wire 2009, A Foreign Affair 2011, The Rhinebeck Sessions 2013; with Mindset: Mindset 1991. *Current Management:* c/o Phil Brennan, Crosseyed Bear Productions, 270 Olympic Avenue, Buffalo, NY 14215, USA. *Telephone:* (716) 831-1511. *E-mail:* info@ philbrennan.com. *Website:* www.spyrogyra.com.

AMENT, Jeff; American musician (bass); b. 10 March 1963. *Career:* musician in Seattle SubPop scene in 1980s; mem. Green River 1987–89, Mother Love Bone 1989, Pearl Jam 1990–; mem. Temple of the Dog project 1991; numerous contributions and collaborations with various artists. *Recordings include:* albums: with Green River: with Pearl Jam: Ten 1991, Vs. 1993, Vitalogy 1994, Merkin Ball 1995, No Code 1996, Yield 1998, Live on Two Legs 1998, Binaural 2000, Riot Act 2002, Pearl Jam 2006, Backspacer 2009; with Mother Love Bone: Apple 1990, Alternative Moments 2001, The Road Mix: Music from the Television Series One Tree Hill, Volume 3 2007; with Temple of the Dog: Temple Of The Dog 1992; with Brad: Shame 1993, Interiors 1997, Welcome To Discovery Park 2002; with Deranged Diction: Life Support/No Art, No Cowboys, No Rules 2009; with Tres Mts.: Three Mountains 2011; with RNDM: Acts 2012; solo: Tone 2008, While My Heart Beats 2012. *Honours:* American Music Award for Favorite New Artist 1993, Rolling Stone Readers Awards for Best New American Band, Best Video 1993. *Address:* Pearl Jam, POB 81429, Seattle, WA 98108-1329, USA. *E-mail:* contact@vandenbergcom .com. *Website:* www.pearljam.com.

AMERIE, BFA; American singer; b. (Amerie Mi Marie Rogers), 12 Jan. 1980, Fitchburg, Mass; m. Lenny Nicholson 2011. *Education:* Georgetown Univ. *Career:* musical collaborations with Nas, Bow Wow, LL Cool J. *Film appearances include:* Maid in Manhattan 2002, Deliver Us from Eva 2003, First Daughter 2004. *Television appearance:* The Center 2003. *Recordings include:* albums: All I Have 2002, Touch 2005, Because I Love It 2007, Playlist: The Very Best of Amerie 2008, Best 15 Things 2009, In Love and War 2009, Cymatika Vol. I 2013; singles: Why Don't We Fall in Love 2002, Why R U 2009, Heard 'Em All 2010. *Honours:* Soul Train Music Award for Best R&B/Soul or Rap New Artist 2003, Lady of Soul Aretha Franklin Award for Entertainer of the Year 2005. *Address:* c/o Island Def Jam Records, Worldwide Plaza, 825 Eighth Avenue, 28th Floor, New York, NY 10019, USA. *Telephone:* (212) 333-8000. *Website:* www.islanddefjam.com.

AMES, Roger; Trinidad and Tobago music company executive; *CEO International, Ticketmaster Inc.;* b. 1949. *Career:* with EMI UK 1975–79; staff A & R Dept, Phonogram, PolyGram UK 1979–83, Chair. and CEO PolyGram UK 1991–94, Group Exec. and Vice-Pres. PolyGram Int. Ltd 1996–99, Pres. PolyGram Music Group 1996–99; Gen. Man. London Records 1983, later Man. Dir, purchased back-catalogue of Factory Records; Pres. Warner Music Int. 1999, Chair. and CEO Warner Music Group 1999–2004; Sr Advisor, Time Warner, EMI Music 2005–07; Pres. EMI Music, North America 2007–08, Pres. EMI Music, UK Jan.–May 2008; CEO Int., Ticketmaster Inc. 2009–; Advisor, Ingenious VCT Funds;. *Address:* Ticketmaster UK, 48 Leicester Square, London, WC2H 7LR, England (office). *Telephone:* (20) 7344-4000 (office). *Fax:* (20) 7915-0411 (office). *Website:* www.ticketmaster.co .uk (office).

AMIGO, Vicente; Spanish musician (guitar); b. 25 March 1967, Guadalcanal, Seville. *Career:* flamenco guitarist; has performed with Camarón, Sting, Alejandro Sanz, Rosario, Carmen Linares, Manolo Sanlúcar, Khaled, Miguel Bosé, John McLaughlin, Al DiMeola, Milton Nascimento. *Compositions include:* De mi corazón al aire 1991, Poeta, Concierto flamenco para un marinero en tierra, Vivencias imaginadas 1995. *Recordings include:* De mi

Corazón al Aire 1991, Vivencias Imaginadas 1995, Poeta 1997, Ciudad de las ideas (Latin Grammy Award for Best Flamenco Album 2001) 2000, Un Momento en el Sonido 2005, Paseo de Gracia 2009, Tierra 2013. *Honours:* winner, Concurso Internacional de Guitarra Flamenca 1988, Concurso Nacional del Cante de las Minas de la Unión 1989, Ramón Montoya Prize for Concert Guitar 1989, Premio de la Música 1998, 1999, Ondas Award 2002. *Current Management:* Intercambio de Cultura y Arte, C/Carretas 14-5°-I 5, Madrid, 28012, Spain. *Telephone:* (91) 5312440. *Fax:* (91) 5315936. *E-mail:* amigomusica@icart.es. *Website:* www.icart.es. *Address:* Riff Producciones S.L, C/ Marqués de Boil, 514008, Córdoba, Spain. *Telephone:* (95) 7497501. *E-mail:* info@riffmusic.org. *Website:* www.riffmusic.es; www.vicente-amigo.com.

AMIN-SMITH, Milan Neil; British musician (violin, piano) and songwriter; b. 1988. *Education:* Westminster School, Jesus Coll., Cambridge. *Career:* formerly violinist in string quartet at Univ. of Cambridge (with Grace Chatto); Founder-mem. Clean Bandit 2009–; released debut single A+E 2012; toured UK with Disclosure 2013; released single Rather Be (with Jess Glynne) 2014; numerous collaborations with other artists including Noonie Bao, Sharna Bass, Gorgon City, Love Ssega, Kandaka Moore and Nikki Cislyn, Stylo G. *Recordings:* albums: with Clean Bandit: New Eyes 2014. *Honours:* Grammy Award for Best Dance Recording (for Rather Be) 2015. *Current Management:* c/o Machine Management, Studio 16, London Fields Studios, 11–17 Exmouth Place, London, E8 3RW, England. *Telephone:* (20) 7923-3502. *E-mail:* info@machinemanagement.co.uk. *Website:* machinemanagement.co.uk; cleanbandit.co.uk.

AMINA; Tunisian singer and actress; b. (Amina Annabi), 5 March 1962, Carthage; one d. *Career:* moved to France 1975; sang French entry, Eurovision Song Contest 1991. *Films:* Maman 1989, The Sheltering Sky 1990, La Belle histoire 1992, The Hour of the Pig 1993, La nuit sacrée 1993, The Advocate 1995, Cleopatra 1999, La Mecanique des femmes 2000, Inch'Alla dimanche 2001, Philosophale 2001, Dream of Trespass 2002, Les Marins perdus 2003, Il était une fois dans l'oued 2005, Comme tout le monde 2006. *Recordings include:* albums: Yalil 1989, IP5 (soundtrack) 1992, Wa Di Ye 1992, Annabi 1999. *Honours:* Le prix Piaf 1991.

AMIRKHAS ADEH, Ninef, BSc; Iranian conductor, arranger and musician (keyboard); b. 1975, Tehran. *Education:* Azad Univ. *Career:* mem. The Arian Band (first officially sanctioned mixed-gender pop band in Iran); arranger of instrumental album, Palace of Dreams, by Siamak Khahani. *Recordings include:* albums: Sunflower, And But Love!, Till Eternity, Without You With You 2008, singles: Here Comes Nowrooz, Here Comes Spring 2009, The Footsteps of Hope 2010. *Current Management:* c/o Mr Mohsen Rajabpour, Taraneh Sharghee Cultural & Artistic Co., Apartment No. 26, Seventh Floor, Suite 22, Second Alley, Shahnazari Street, Mohseni Square, Mirdamad Avenue, Tehran 1547914415, Iran. *Telephone:* (21) 22223513. *Fax:* (21) 22223670. *E-mail:* info@taranehsh.com. *Website:* www.taranehsh.com; www.arianmusic.com.

AMOR, Amir; British musician, songwriter and record producer; b. (Amir Izadkhah), 1985. *Career:* Co-founder Major Toms recording studio 2009; Founder-mem. Rudimental 2010–; released debut single Deep in the Valley 2011; collaborations with MC Shantie, Adiyam, MNEK and Syron, John Newman, Alex Clare, Angel Haze, Ella Eyre, Emeli Sandé, Nas, Foxes. *Recordings:* album: with Rudimental: Home (MOBO Award for Best Album 2013) 2013. *Current Management:* c/o Coda Music Agency LLP, CODA House, 56 Compton Street, Clerkenwell, London, EC1V 0ET, England. *Telephone:* (20) 7017-2500. *Fax:* (20) 7017-2555. *Website:* www.codaagency.com; www.rudimental.co.uk; www.majortoms.co.uk.

AMOROSI, Vanessa; Australian singer; b. 8 Aug. 1981, Melbourne. *Career:* solo artist 1997–; performed at opening ceremony of Olympic Games, Sydney 2000; patron Variety Club. *Recordings:* albums: The Power 2000, Turn to Me 2001, Somewhere in the Real World 2008, Hazardous 2009, V 2012. *Honours:* APRA Award for Most Performed Australian Work (for Shine) 2001, PPCA Award for Most Played Song in All Media 2001, Young Entertainer of the Year, Variety Club 2001, Gov.-Gen.'s Award 2002, Best New Artist on Commercial Radio, Fed. of Australian Broadcasters 2002, Young Victorian of the Year 2002, Career Achievement Award, Nat. Australia Day Council 2003, Best Int. Newcomer, Viva Comet Awards, Germany 2003, Centenary Medal 2003, ARIA No.1 Chart Awards (for This is Who I Am) 2010. *Current Management:* Ralph Carr, Ralph Carr Management, Lennox House, 229 Lennox Street, Richmond, Vic. 3121, Australia. *Telephone:* (3) 9428-4862. *Fax:* (3) 9429-9137. *E-mail:* rc@ralphcarr.com. *Website:* www.ralphcarr.com; www.vanessaamorosi.com.

AMOROSO, Alessandra; Italian singer; b. 12 Aug. 1986, Galatina, Lecce. *Career:* contestant and series winner, Amici di Maria De Filippi 2008; released debut single Stupida 2009; first headlining tour 2009. *Television:* Amici di Maria De Filippi (series winner) 2008. *Recordings:* albums: Senza nuvole 2009, Il mondo in un secondo 2010, Cinque passi in più 2011, Amore Puro 2013, Vivere a colori 2015. *Honours:* Wind Music Awards 2009, 2010, 2011, MTV Europe Music Award for Best Europe South Act 2014. *Website:* alessandraamoroso.it.

AMOS, Tori; American singer, songwriter and musician (piano); b. (Myra Ellen Amos), 22 Aug. 1963, Newton, NC; d. of Edison Amos and Mary Ellen Amos; m. Mark Hawley 1998; one d. *Education:* Peabody Inst., Baltimore. *Career:* singer in piano bars as teenager; solo artist 1987–; numerous tours,

television and radio appearances. *Recordings include:* albums: Y Kant Tori Read 1988, Little Earthquakes 1991, Under The Pink 1994, Boys For Pele 1995, From The Choirgirl Hotel 1998, Star Profile 1998, To Venus & Back 1999, Maximum Tori 2000, Strange Little Girls 2001, Scarlet's Walk 2003, Tales Of A Librarian 2003, The Beekeeper 2005, The Collection 2006, American Doll Posse 2007, Abnormally Attracted to Sin 2009, Midwinter Graces 2009, Night of Hunters (ECHO Klassik-Ohne-Grenzen Prize 2012) 2011, Gold Dust 2012, Unrepentant Geraldines 2014. *Publication:* Piece by Piece (autobiog. with Ann Powers) 2005. *Honours:* Q Award for Best New Act 1992. *Address:* Spivak Entertainment, 11845 West Olympic Blvd, Suite 1125, Los Angeles, CA 90064, USA (office). *Website:* www.toriamos.com.

AMRAM, David Werner, BA, MusD, LLD; American composer, conductor, musician and academic; b. 17 Nov. 1930, Philadelphia, Pa; one s. two d. *Education:* Oberlin Conservatory of Music, Manhattan School of Music, George Washington Univ., Moravian Coll., , Muhlenberg Coll., Univ. of Hartford, St Lawrence Univ. *Career:* pioneer of French horn in jazz and Latin music during late 1940s, played French horn with Nat. Symphony Orchestra 1951–52; world tours as a jazz player, multi-instrumentalist, folklorist, composer and conductor; Dir of Music, New York Shakespeare Festival 1956–67, Lincoln Center Theater 1963–65; Composer-in-Residence, New York Philarmonic Orchestra 1966–67; Dir of Music for Young People's Concerts and Parks Concerts, Brooklyn Philharmonic 1971–98; Composer-in-Residence, Democratic Nat. Convention, Denver 2008; fmr Leo Block Chair of Arts and Humanities, Univ. of Denver; work commissioned to celebrate opening of Jefferson Wing of Library of Congress 1995; guest conductor with more than 75 symphony orchestras around the world; composer of 110 orchestral compositions for symphony orchestras and chamber music groups; collaborated with Jack Kerouac 1956–69, Leonard Bernstein, Arthur Miller, Lionel Hampton, Elia Kazan, Bob Dylan, Dizzy Gillespie, Archibald MacLeish, Pete Seeger, Charles Mingus, Eugene Ormandy, Jacques d'Amboise, Titi Puente, Joseph Papp, Odetta, Alan Ginsberg, Paquito d'Rivera, John Frankenheimer, Betty Carter, Lawrence Ferlinghetti; mem. BMI. *Compositions include:* Ode to Lof Buckley for orchestra, The Final Ingredient (opera), 12th Night (opera), A Little Rebellion: Thomas Jefferson for narrator and orchestra, American Dance Suite, Trombone Alone 1996, Kokopelli: A Symphony in Three Movements 1997, Giants of the Night (flute concerto for James Galway) 2000, This Land: Symphonic Variations on a Song by Woody Guthrie 2007, Greenwich Village Portraits 2014. *Compositions for film and television:* Pull My Daisy 1958, The Turn of the Screw (TV series episode 'Startime') 1959, Cry Vengeance! (TV film) 1961, The Young Savages 1961, Splendor in the Grass 1961, The Manchurian Candidate 1962, The Arrangement 1969, Medea (TV film) 1983, Pigeon Feathers (TV film) 1987, The Beat Generation: An American Dream 1987, Frog Crossing 1996, The Source 1999, Boys of Winter (documentary) 2001, The Frontier Gandhi: Badsha Khan (documentary) 2009, 333 (documentary) 2012, Isn't it Delicious 2013. *Dance:* composed music for many Jacques d'Amboise choreographed pieces. *Plays include:* JB, After the Fall, The Passion l of Joseph D, Tartuffe. *Recordings include:* Triple Concerto 1970, No More Walls 1971, An American Original 1993, Hava New York 1995, Three Concertos 1995, The Final Ingredient 1996, At Home/Around the World 1996, Visions of Cody 1996, Southern Stories 2000, Back to My Roots (with Lil Greenwood) 2007, Songs of the Soul 2007. *Publications include:* Vibrations: The Musical Times of David Amram 1968, Offbeat: Collaborating with Kerouac 2002, Upbeat: Nine Lives of a Musical Cat 2007. *Honours:* six hon. degrees; Obie Award, Jay McShann Lifetime Achievement Award 2011, Bruce Ricter Lifetime Film Achievement Award 2012, Pete and Toshi Seeger Power of Song Award 2012. *Current Management:* c/o Douglas Yeager, 300 West 55th Street, Suite 15E, New York, NY 10019, USA. *Telephone:* (212) 245-0240. *Fax:* (212) 245-6576. *E-mail:* yeagerprod@aol.com. *E-mail:* amramdavid@aol.com. *Website:* www.davidamram.com.

AMSALLEM, Franck, MMus; French musician (piano), composer, singer and producer; b. 25 Oct. 1961, Oran, Algeria; m. Thérèse Walsh; one d. *Education:* Nice Conservatory of Music, Berklee Coll. of Music, Manhattan School of Music. *Career:* performed with Gerry Mulligan, Charles Lloyd, Bobby Watson, Joe Chambers, Harry Belafonte, Blood Sweat and Tears, Bob Belden, Tim Ries, Peter King, Didier Lockwood; featured on French nat. radio. *Compositions:* Out A Day, Chanson Triste, After, Running After Eternity, Nuits, Is That So, In Second Thought, Summer Times, A Week in Paris, Place du Temps. *Recordings:* Out A Day 1992, Regards 1993, Is That So 1996, Years Gone By 1998, New York Stories, On Second Thoughts, 2000, Summer Times 2003, A Week in Paris 2005, Amsallem Sings 2009. *Honours:* Fondation de la Vocation, 1989; NEA Competition Fellowship, 1990; ASCAP Award for Young Composers, 1991. *Address:* 100 Ocean Parkway #6K, Brooklyn, NY 11218, USA. *E-mail:* sallemjazz@numericable.com. *Website:* perso.numericable.com/franck.amsallem/index.html; www.myspace.com/amsallem.

AMURO, Namie; Japanese singer; b. 20 Sept. 1977, Okinawa; m. Sam Maruyama. *Education:* Okinawa Actor's School. *Career:* mem. of group Super Monkeys 1992, left group for short period, returned in 1994; solo artist 1995–. *Singles include:* (with Super Monkeys) Paradise Train, Try Me, Tiayo No Season, (solo) Stop the Music, Body Feels Exit, Chase the Chance, Don't Wanna Cry, You Are My Sunshine, Sweet 19 Blues, Can You Celebrate. *Albums include:* (solo) Sweet 19 Blues 1996, Concentration 20 1997, 181920 1998, Genius 2000 2000, Break the Rules 2000, Style 2003, Queen of Hip-Pop 2005, Play 2007, Past<Future 2009, Uncontrolled 2012, Feel 2013. *Honours:* Japan Records Award 1996. *Address:* c/o Avex Trax, Room 3608-10, Windsor

16

House, 311 Gloucester Road, Causeway Bay, Hong Kong Special Administrative Region, People's Republic of China. *Website:* namieamuro.jp; avex.jp/amuro.

AMYOT, Robert; French musician (French bagpipes), singer and storyteller; b. 25 July 1953, Montreal, Canada; s. of David Reid and Elizabeth McKinnon; m. Chrystel Amyot. *Education:* Diplôme d'Etat, Professeur de musique traditionnelle. *Career:* played with Jean Blanchard and Evelyne Girardon in Beau-Temps-Sur-La-Province, and with Eric Montbel; mem. La Grande Bande de Cornemuse, Le Quintette de Cornemuse; performed at folk and storytelling festivals worldwide; music teacher offering piping and singing concerts world-wide; Pres. of Jury, St-Chartier Festival 1990–96; mem. Asscn of Professional Music Therapists. *Play:* La Nuit des Rois (writer, with Hélène Vincent). *Compositions include:* Le Brandevin, Le Loriot de Baltimore, Le Harfang des Neiges, Marie Miville, L'Anniversaire and numerous other pipe tunes and songs in the traditional style. *Recordings include:* Su'l Tempo, In cerco di grana, 30 ans, Musicalpina, Compagnons Savoyards, La Cantate des Alpes, Fleur de terre (Trio Berger, Blanchard, Amyot), Trappeur Courtois, Sur la vignolon, Le quintette de cornemuses (Prix choc de la musique), La grande bande de cornemuses (Prix Nouvelle Acad. Palmares), Le grand festin, Valheirmeil, Penn ar bed, Del Piemont als Pirineus. *Honours:* First Prize for Cornemuse, Anost, France 1987. *Address:* 14 route de Dampierre, , 74130 Vailly sur Sauldre, France (home). *Telephone:* (2) 48-58-01-50 (office). *E-mail:* robert.amyot@wanadoo.fr (home). *Website:* www.robert-amyot.com (home); www.lady-chrystel-kilts.com (home).

AMZAH, Shila; Malaysian singer and musician (keyboards, guitar); b. (Nur Shahila binti Amir Amzah), 13 Aug. 1990, Kuala Lumpur; d. of N.D. Lala. *Career:* fmr child singer (under the name Shila Tekno) and teenage artist (as Sha-hila); collaborations include Atilia Heron, Dafi, RAN, Ning Baizura and Jaclyn Victor (as trio). *Television includes:* One in a Million (participant; runner-up) 2007, Asian Wave (reality show for Chinese TV; series winner) 2012. *Recordings include:* albums: solo: Terima Kasih Guru 2000, Sha-hila 2005, Ost 5 Jingga 2008, Bebaskan 2009; with Ning Baizura and Jaclyn Victor: 3 Suara (Anugerah Planet Muzik Award for Best Duo/Group 2010, Anugerah Industri Muzik Award for Best Duo or Group Vocal Performances 2011, Anugerah Bintang Popular Berita Harian Award for Popular Duo/Group Artists 2011) 2010. *Honours:* Gold Award/Champion and Best Song (for Memori Tercipta), Asia New Singer Competition 2008, Anugerah Industri Muzik Awards for Best Song Award and Best Pop Song Award (both for Patah Seribu) 2012, Shout! Power Vocal Award 2012, Anugerah Planet Muzik Award for Best Female Artist 2012. *Address:* c/o Sony Music Entertainment Malaysia Sdn. Bhd., A1-3-07 Solaris Dutamas, No 1 Jalan Dutamas 1, Kuala Lumpur, WP 50480, Malaysia (office). *Telephone:* (3) 62079898 (office). *Fax:* (3) 62079595 (office). *Website:* www.sonymusic.com (office); www.myspace.com/sh4hil469.

ANANDA PROJECT (see Brann, Chris)

ANASTACIA; American singer and songwriter; b. (Anastacia Newkirk), 17 Sept. 1973, Chicago, Ill.; m. Wayne Newton 2007 (divorced 2010). *Education:* Professional Children's School, Manhattan. *Career:* worked as a dancer on pop videos and TV prior to being discovered as vocalist on MTV talent show, The Cut; career developed in Europe prior to US success; performed alongside Michael Jackson at historic United We Stand benefit concert 2001; established Anastacia Fund, through the Breast Cancer Research Foundation 2004. *Recordings include:* albums: Not That Kind 2001, Freak of Nature 2002, Anastacia 2004, Pieces of a Dream – The Greatest Hits 2005, Heavy Rotation 2008, It's a Man's World 2012, Resurrection 2014. *Honours:* World Music Award for Best New Int. Artist 2001, MTV Europe Music Award for Best Pop Act 2001, Echo Award for Best Int. Female Pop and Rock Artist, Germany 2005. *Website:* www.anastacia.com.

ANCHEV, Emil; Bulgarian singer; b. 17 Aug. 1962. *Career:* Founder–mem. and lead singer, Konkurent 1986–; numerous concerts, TV and radio programmes. *Recordings:* Konkurent 1989, Something Wet 1995, Escape from Paradise 2002, Give me Time 2007. *Honours:* First prizes: Top Rock Band, Youth Festival Vidin 1989, Rock Ring, Sofia 1990, Top Rock Composition: The Cavalry 1991, Top Rock Singer, Bulgaria 1994, Group of the Year, The Darik Radio Countdown 1994. *E-mail:* emil.anchev@abv.bg (office). *Website:* www.konkurentrockband.com.

ANDERSEN, Arild; Norwegian jazz musician (double bass), bandleader and composer; b. 27 Oct. 1945, Oslo. *Career:* touring musician with George Russell, Jan Garbarek, Jon Christensen, Karin Krog, Edward Vesala, 1966–73; also worked with Don Cherry; Stan Getz; Sam Rivers; Paul Bley; Leader, own quartet, 1974; Leader, Norwegian quintet Masquelero 1982–92; own group SAGN with Kirsten Bråten Berg 1990–97; co-leader with Markus Stockhausen of several groups 1997–2003; trio with Tommy Smith, Paolo Vinaccia 2007–; recorded 20 albums in own name for ECM, working with Paul Motian, Bill Frisell, Alphonse Mouzon, Kenny Wheeler, Jon Christensen, Vasillis Tsabroupolos, Kirsten Bråten Berg, Bugge Wesseltoft, Nana Vasconcelos, Ralph Towner, John Scofield, Pat Metheny. *Recordings:* albums: Clouds In My Head 1975, Shimri 1976, Green Shading Into Blue 1978, Lifelines 1980, Molde Concert 1981, Masquelero 1983, Bande A Part 1985, Aero 1988, Re-Enter 1989, Sagn 1993, If You Look Far Enough (with Nana Vasconcelos, Ralph Towner) 1993, Arv 1993, Kritin Lavransdatter 1995, Sommerbrisen 1995, Hyperborean 1997, Achirana 2000, Karta 2000, The Sign 2002, Joyosa 2004, Moon Water (with Carsten Dahl) 2004, The Triangle 2004, Electra 2004, In

House (with John Etheridge and John Marshall) 2007, Live at Bellville (with Tommy Smith and Paolo Vinaccia) 2008, Green in Blue 2010, Celebration 2012. *Honours:* Prix du Musicien Européen, Acad. du Jazz (France) 2008. *Current Management:* c/o Kjell KalleKlev Management, Georgernes Verft 12, 5011 Bergen, Norway. *Telephone:* 55-55-76-37. *Fax:* 55-55-76-31. *E-mail:* kjell@kalleklev.no. *Website:* www.kalleklev.no. *Address:* Holmensv. 43 A, 0376 Oslo, Norway (home). *Telephone:* 4-8060000 (mobile). *E-mail:* arild@arildandersen.com (home). *Website:* www.arildandersen.com.

ANDERSEN, Torfinn Nergaard; Norwegian music company executive. *Career:* Dir, Groovy Management; Owner, record label, Rec 90 (Norway); man. for Butterfly Garden (Norway); mem. FONO. *Address:* Rec 90, PO Box 1291, Nøstegt 50, 5811 Bergen, Norway (office). *Telephone:* 55-32-34-10 (office). *Fax:* 55-31-18-75 (office). *E-mail:* rec90@rec90.com (office). *Website:* www.rec90.com (office).

ANDERSON, Adam David; British musician (synthesizer), songwriter and producer; b. 14 May 1984, Manchester. *Career:* fmr mem. Bureau 2006–07, Daggers 2007–09; mem. Hurts 2009–; supported Scissor Sisters on UK tour 2010; recorded with Kylie Minogue 2010, first full European tour 2011. *Recordings:* albums: Happiness (Fonogram Best Int. Album Award, Hungary 2011) 2010, Exile 2013, Surrender 2015. *Honours:* BAMBI Award for Best Int. Newcomer 2010, Musikexpress Best Int. Performer Style Award 2010, Bamby Shooting-Star Award, Germany 2010, NME Best New Band Award 2011, Best Int. Newcomer, ECHO Awards, Germany 2011. *Address:* c/o RCA Records, RCA Label Group UK, 9 Derry Street, London, W8 5HY, England (office). *Website:* www.informationhurts.com.

ANDERSON, Beth, BA, MA, MFA; American composer and musician (piano); b. 3 Jan. 1950, Lexington, KY; m. Elliotte Rusty Harold. *Education:* Univ. of California at Davis with Larry Austin and John Cage, Mills Coll., Oakland with Terry Riley and Robert Ashley. *Career:* founder Ear Magazine, New York 1975; solo performer as vocalist and piano accompanist at dance studios; producer Women's Work series, Greenwich House Arts, New York; mem. New York Women Composers, Int. Alliance of Women in Music, Poets and Writers. *Compositions include:* April Swale for viola and harpsichord, August Swale for woodwind quintet, Belgian Tango, Brass Swale for brass quintet, Elizabeth Rex: Or The Well Bred Mother Goes To Camp (musical), Flute Swale for harpsichord, German Swale for tape, Guitar Swale for guitar duet, January Swale for string quartet, Joan (oratorio), March Swale for string quartet, May Swale for viola solo, Minnesota Swale for orchestra, Mourning Dove Swale for string orchestra, Net Work, New Mexico Swale for chamber ensemble, Nirvana Manor (musical), Pennyroyal Swale for string quartet, Queen Christina (opera), Revel for orchestra, Rhode Island Swale for harpsichord, Riot Rot (text-sound piece), Rosemary Swale for string quartet, Saturday/Sunday Swale for brass quintet, September Swale for mandolin and guitar, Soap Tuning (musical), The Fat Opera (musical), Three Swales for string orchestra, Trio: Dream In 'D'. *Recordings include:* Peachy Keen-O 2003, Swales and Angels 2004, Quilt Music 2005. *Publications:* Beauty is Revolution, The Internet for Women in Music. *Honours:* Nat. Endowment for the Arts Grant, Nat. Public Radio Satellite Program Development Fund Grant. *Current Management:* Jeffrey James Arts Consulting, 45 Grant Avenue, Farmingdale, NY 11735, USA. *Telephone:* (516) 586-3433. *Fax:* (516) 586-3433. *E-mail:* jamesarts@worldnet.att.net. *Website:* www.jamesarts.com. *E-mail:* beth@beand.com (office). *Website:* www.beand.com.

ANDERSON, William (Billy) John; British musician (piano-accordion), composer and broadcaster; b. 5 March 1946, Colinsburgh, Fife; m. Elizabeth W. Hannah 1966; three s. one d. *Education:* Madras Coll., St Andrews. *Career:* broadcaster with BBC radio, television 1969–; freelance presenter with Radio Tay, Dundee 1984–; tours to USA, Canada, United Arab Emirates, Oman, Brunei, North Malaysia, Germany, Netherlands, Italy, Australia; mem. Musicians' Union, PRS. *Recordings include:* seven albums with Albany (own group); Scotland Now 1982, Sonas 1999, Origins 2002, Music, Song and Dance 2005, Old Comrades 2014. *Address:* 4 Kingsloan Court, Largoward, Leven, Fife KY9 1JH, Scotland. *Telephone:* (1334) 840469. *E-mail:* billyandersonmusic@gmail.com. *Website:* www.billyanderson.co.uk.

ANDERSON, Brett; British singer and songwriter; b. 29 Sept. 1967, Haywards Heath, London. *Education:* Univ. Coll. London. *Career:* Founder mem. Geoff 1985, Suave and Elegant 1989; Founder mem. Suede 1989–2004, 2010–; numerous television appearances, concerts and festivals; tours of Europe, America and Japan; Founder mem. The Tears 2004–05; solo artist 2006–. *Recordings include:* albums: with Suede: Suede (Mercury Music Prize 1993) 1993, Dog Man Star 1994, Coming Up 1996, Sci-Fi Lullabies 1997, Head Music 1999, Sessions CD (fan club release) 2000, A New Morning 2002, Bloodsports 2013, Night Thoughts 2016; with The Tears: Here Come The Tears 2005; solo: Brett Anderson 2007, Wilderness 2008, Slow Attack 2009, Black Rainbows 2011, singles: Love Is Dead 2007, A Different Place 2008, The Hunted 2009, Brittle Heart 2011, Crash About to Happen 2011. *Honours:* with Suede: Q Awards for Best New Act 1993, Q Magazine Icon Award 2013. *Current Management:* Quietus Management Limited, 13 Bramley Road, 2nd Floor Phoenix Brewery, London, W10 6SP, England. *Telephone:* (20) 3220-0310. *Website:* www.quietusmanagement.com; www.brettanderson.co.uk; www.suede.co.uk.

ANDERSON, Carleen; American/British singer and songwriter; b. 10 May 1957, Houston, TX; one s. *Education:* University of Southern California, Los Angeles City College. *Career:* country and western session singer 1976–79;

joined Black Widow as lead singer 1976–77; joined Family Funkton as lead singer 1978; worked as bank teller and office clerk; singer and songwriter, Young Disciples 1990–92; solo work; work with Paul Weller, Bryan Ferry, Doctor John, Courtney Pine, Johnny Cash, Massive Attack, Ocean Colour Scene, Paul McCartney, Incognito, Jocelyn Brown; joined Brand New Heavies 1999; Head of Vocal Dept, Brighton Inst. of Modern Music 2002–07. *Recordings:* albums: with Young Disciples: Road to Freedom 1991; solo: True Spirit 1994, Blessed Burden 1998, Alberta's GrandDaughter 2002, Soul Providence 2005. *Current Management:* c/o Jim Lane. *Telephone:* (1389) 764548. *E-mail:* jimmusic801@hotmail.com. *Website:* www.carleenanderson .net.

ANDERSON, Christopher (Chris) William; American musician (guitar), singer and songwriter; b. 22 Sept. 1956, Los Angeles, Calif.; m. Sharon Ann Cooper 1991; one s. one d. *Career:* leader, Chris Anderson Group; tours with artists including Allman Brothers, Stevie Ray Vaughan, Double Trouble, Lynyrd Skynyrd, Bad Company, Government Mule, Outlaws, Marshall Tucker, Charlie Daniels, Wet Willie; mem. AFTRA, AFofM. *Recordings include:* Old Friend with Chris Anderson Group, Trouble On The Tracks with Double Trouble, Right On Time, Grinder Switch with Floyd Miles. *E-mail:* chrisandersongroup@hotmail.com (office). *Website:* www.myspace.com/ chrisandersongroup.

ANDERSON, Emma Victoria Jane, BA; British musician (guitar) and songwriter; b. 10 June 1967, Wimbledon, London, England. *Education:* Ealing Coll. of Higher Education. *Career:* bass player, The Rover Girls 1986–88; lead guitarist and songwriter, Lush 1988–96, 2015–; world-wide tours, festival appearances; guitarist and songwriter, Sing-Sing 1998–2008; mem. PRS, Musicians' Union, PAMRA. *Recordings include:* albums: with Lush: Scar (mini album) 1989, Gala 1990, Spooky 1992, Split 1994, Lovelife 1996, Ciao! Best Of Lush 2000; with Sing-Sing: The Joy Of Sing-Sing 2001, Sing-Sing and I 2006. *Current Management:* Jonathan Morley, Northern Lights Management. *E-mail:* jonathan@northernlightsmgt.co.uk. *Website:* www .northernlightsmgt.co.uk; lushofficial.com.

ANDERSON, Ernestine; American singer; b. 11 Nov. 1928, Houston, Tex. *Career:* entered talent contest and hired by trumpeter Russel Jacquet to sing with big band aged 12; toured with Johnny Otis band 1946–47; recorded songs with GiGi Gryce, New York 1955; toured Scandinavia 1955, recorded first album in Sweden 1958; performed Monterey Jazz Festival 1958. *Recordings include:* albums: Ernestine Anderson: The Toast of the Nation's Critics (Hot Cargo) 1958, The New Sound of Ernestine Anderson 1963, Hello Like Before 1977, Live From Concord to London 1978, Sunshine 1980, Never Make Your Move Too Soon 1981, Big City 1983, When the Sun Goes Down 1985, Live at the Alley Cat 1987, Be Mine Tonight 1987, A Perfect Match (with George Shearing) 1988, Live at the 1990 Concord Jazz Festival Third Set 1990, Boogie Down 1991, Great Moment with Ernestine Anderson 1993, Now and Then 1994, Blues, Dues & Love 1997, Isn't It Romantic 1998, I Love Being Here With You 2002, Love Makes the Changes 2003, A Song for You 2009. *Honours:* Best New Vocal Star, Down Beat 1959. *Current Management:* c/o AMI, PO Box 534, New York, NY 10014, USA. *Website:* www.ernestineanderson.com.

ANDERSON, Ian; British writer, broadcaster and musician (guitar, slide guitar); b. 26 July 1947, Weston-Super-Mare; m. Hanitra Rasoanaivo 1990; one step-d. *Career:* solo musician, 1967–72; member of duo Hot Vultures, 1972–79; English Country Blues Band, 1979–83; Tiger Moth, 1983–89; Editor of Folk Roots Magazine (now fROOTS), 1979–; radio presenter, BBC and ILR, 1984–. *Recordings:* five solo albums include: Stereo Death Breakdown, 1969; three albums with Hot Vultures include: Up The Line, 1979; two albums with English Country Blues Band, compiled as Unruly, 1993; two albums with Tiger Moth, compiled as Mothballs, 1995; with Blue Blokes: Stubble 2008. *Address:* c/o fROOTS, PO Box 337, London, N4 1TW, England. *Telephone:* (20) 8340-9651. *Fax:* (20) 8348-5626. *E-mail:* ian@frootsmag.com. *Website:* www .frootsmag.com.

ANDERSON, Ian Scott, MBE; British musician and songwriter; b. 10 Aug. 1947, Dunfermline, Scotland; s. of James Anderson; m. 1st Jennie Franks 1970; m. 2nd Shona Anderson 1976; one s. one d. *Career:* mem. Jethro Tull; numerous radio and TV appearances; mem. PRS, Composers' Guild. *Compositions include:* Living In The Past, Aqualung, Thick As A Brick. *Recordings include:* Living In The Past 1969, Aqualung 1971, Thick As A Brick 1972, Minstrel In The Gallery 1975, The Best Of Jethro Tull, Songs From The Wood, Heavy Horses 1978, Celtic Experience, Living With The Past 2002, The Secret Language of Birds 2000, Rupi's Dance 2003, Thick as a Brick 2 2012; solo: Walk into Light 1983, Divinities: Twelve Dances with God 1995, The Secret Language of Birds 2000, Rupi's Dance 2003, Homo Erraticus 2014. *Honours:* Dr hc (Heriot Watt Univ.) 2006, (Univ. of Abertay, Dundee) 2011; Grammy Award 1988, Ivor Award for Int. Achievement in Music 2006. *Current Management:* c/o Brad Goodman, WME Entertainment, 9601 Wilshire Blvd, Suite 300, Beverly Hills, CA 90210, USA. *Telephone:* (310) 285-9000. *Fax:* (310) 285-9010. *E-mail:* BGoodman@wmeentertainment.com. *Website:* www .wmeentertainment.com; jethrotull.com.

ANDERSON, James Noel, BS; American recording engineer, producer and radio consultant; *Professor of Recorded Music, Clive Davis Department of Recorded Music, Tisch School of the Arts, New York University;* b. 23 Dec. 1951, Butler, Pennsylvania; m. Phoebe Ferguson 1982; two s. *Education:* Duquesne University, Eastman School of Music, studied audio engineering in Berlin. *Career:* audio engineer, radio stations, Pittsburgh, Washington,

1973–80; President, James Anderson Audio (radio consultant), New York, 1980; radio programmes: Taylor Made Piano, with Billy Taylor, 1981; co-producer, Segovia! (radio documentary), 1983 television programme: Segovia At The White House, with Andres Segovia, 1980; independent audio engineer and producer 1980–; Chair., Audio Engineering Soc. 1999–2000, Pres. 2008–09; currently Prof. of Recorded Music, Clive Davis Dept of Recorded Music, Tisch School of the Arts, New York Univ., Chair. 2004–08; mem. Audio Engineering Soc., Chair. 1999–2000, Pres. 2008–09; mem. NARAS; Audio Independents in Radio. *Recordings:* albums as recording engineer: Live At Fat Tuesdays, Pepper Adams, 1983; Sweet And Lovely, James Moody, 1989; Uptown/Downtown, McCoy Tyner, 1989. *Honours:* Peabody Award, Taylor-Made Piano, 1982; EBU Prix Futura Award, 1986. *Address:* c/o Clive Davis Department of Recorded Music, Tisch School of the Arts, New York University, 194 Mercer Street, 5th Floor, New York, NY 10003, USA. *Telephone:* (212) 992-8400. *E-mail:* tisch.recorded.music@nyu.edu. *Website:* www.tisch.nyu.edu.

ANDERSON, James William (Bill), III; American country singer, songwriter, musician (guitar, harmonica) and actor; b. 1 Nov. 1937, Columbia, SC. *Career:* began career as sports writer; later DJ in Commerce, Georgia; after early writing success, signed by Decca Records as a performer 1958; joined the Grand Ole Opry 1961; US country and pop successes for five decades as both writer and performer; written hits for artists including Ivory Joe Hunter, Jerry Lee Lewis, Dean Martin, Ray Price, Collin Raye, Debbie Reynolds, Connie Smith, Porter Wagoner, Steve Wariner, Lawrence Welk, Kitty Wells, Faron Young, Ken Dodd; as artist, over 80 Billboard country chart singles 1958–91; hosted own TV show 1968, also game shows The Better Sex 1977–78, Fandango 1983–89; host, Opry Backstage; idiosyncratic monologues on record earned the nickname Whispering Bill. *Films:* Forbidden Island 1959, Gold Guitar 1966, Las Vegas Hillbillies 1966, Forty Acre Feud 1968, From Nashville With Love 1969. *Compositions include:* Cincinnati Ohio, City Lights, Eight By Ten, Face To The Wall, Five Little Fingers, Get A Little Dirt On Your Hands, Happy Birthday To Me, Happy State of Mind, I Can't Remember, I Don't Love You Anymore, I Get The Fever, I Love You Drops, I May Never Get To Heaven, I Missed Me, I Never Once Stopped Loving You, I've Enjoyed As Much of This As I Can Stand, If It's All The Same To You, Losing Your Love, Mama Sang A Song, My Life (Throw It Away If I Want To), Nobody But A Fool Would Love You, Once A Day, Peel Me A Nanner, Po' Folks, River Boat, Saginaw Michigan, Still, That's What It's Like To Be Lonesome, Then and Only Then, Tip of My Fingers, Two Teardrops, Walk Out Backwards, We All Missed You, When Two Worlds Collide, Wild Weekend, Wish You Were Here, You and Your Sweet Love. *Recordings include:* albums: Country Heart Songs 1962, Still 1963, Bill Andersen Sings 1964, Showcase 1964, From This Pen 1965, Bright Lights and Country Music 1965, I Love You Drops 1966, Get It While the Gettin's Good 1967, I Can't Do Nothing Alone 1967, Country Style 1968, For Loving You (with Jan Howard) 1968, Wild Weekend 1968, Happy State of Mind 1968, Story 1969, My Life/But You Know I Love You 1969, Christmas 1969, If It's All the Same to You (with Jan Howard) 1970, Love is a Sometimes Thing 1970, Where Have All Our Heroes Gone 1970, Always Remember 1971, Bill and Jan or Jan and Bill (with Jan Howard) 1972, Singing His Praise (with Jan Howard) 1972, Just Plain Bill 1972, For All the Lovely Women in the World 1972, Don't She Look Good 1972, Bill 1973, Whispering 1974, Turn the Radio On/Talk to Me Ohio 1975, Sometimes (with Mary Lou Turner) 1976, Peanuts and Diamonds and Other Jewels 1976, Scorpio 1977, Billy Boy and Mary Lou (with Mary Lou Turner) 1977, Love and Other Sad Stories 1978, Lady's Choice 1979, Nashville Mirrors 1980, Southern Fried 1983, Yesterday, Today and Tomorrow 1984, Country Music Heaven 1991, Country 1994, I Wonder if God Like Country Music 1995, Fine Wines 1998, Lot of Things Different 2001, Whisperin Bluegrass 2007. *Publications:* I Hope You're Living As High On The Hog As The Pig You Turned Out To Be (anecdotes) 1983, Whispering Bill (autobiography) 1989. *Honours:* Nashville Songwriters Hall of Fame 1975, Georgia Music Hall of Fame 1985, Vocal Event of the Year, Too Country (with Brad Paisley, George Jones and Buck Owens) 2001, Country Music Hall of Fame 2001. *Current Management:* Intune Entertainment, 19 Music Square W, Suite E, Nashville, TN 37203, USA. *Telephone:* (615) 301-1822. *E-mail:* leew@ intuneentertainment.com. *Website:* www.intuneentertainment.com. *E-mail:* whisper@billanderson.com (office). *Website:* www.billanderson.com.

ANDERSON, John; American country singer, songwriter and musician (guitar, harmonica); b. 13 Dec. 1954, Orlando, FL. *Career:* formed bands the Weed Seeds and the Living End during teens; moved to Nashville and sang with sister Donna, 1972; staff writer for Al Gallico Music; first recorded for Ace of Hearts, 1974. *Compositions include:* Swingin'; Goin' Down Hill; I Wish I Could've Been There. *Recordings:* Wild And Blue 1982, Blue Skies Again 1987, 10 1988, Too Tough to Tame 1990, Seminole Wind 1992, Sold Ground 1993, You Can't Keep a Good Memory Down 1994, Christmas Time 1994, Country 'til I Die 1994, Swingin' 1995, Paradise 1996, Takin' the Country Back 1997, The Encore Collection 1997, Nobody's Got It All 2001, Somehow Someway Someday 2002, Country Legends 2002, Anthology 2002, Mississippi Rainstorm 2003, Country Masters 2004, I Just Came Home to Count the Memories 2005, Easy Money 2007, Bigger Hands 2009. *Honours:* CMA, Horizon Award, 1983; CMA, Single of the Year, Swingin', 1983. *Current Management:* The Bobby Roberts Company Inc, PO Box 1547, Goodlettsville, TN 37072-1547, USA. *Telephone:* (615) 859-8899. *Fax:* (615) 859-2200. *E-mail:* info@ bobbyroberts.com. *Website:* www.bobbyroberts.com; www.johnanderson.com.

ANDERSON, Jon; British singer; b. 25 Oct. 1944, Accrington, Lancashire, England. *Career:* mem. The Warriors late 1960s; Co-founder progressive rock group Yes 1968–80, 1983–89, formed group Anderson Bruford Wakeman Howe 1989, then re-adopted the name Yes 1991–; solo artist 1967–; formed duo with Vangelis as Jon & Vangelis 1980–84; numerous concerts, festivals and tours in the UK and USA. *Recordings include:* albums: with Yes: Yes 1969, Time And A Word 1970, The Yes Album 1971, Fragile 1971, Close To The Edge 1972, Yessongs 1973, Tales From The Topographic Oceans 1973, Relayer 1974, Yesterdays 1975, Going For The One 1977, Tormato 1978, 90125 1983, The Solos 1985, Big Generator 1987, Union 1991, Yesstory 1991, Symphonic Music Of Yes 1993, History Of The Future 1993, Talk 1994, An Evening Of Yes Music Plus 1994, Keys To Ascension 1996, Open Your Eyes 1997, Something's Coming 1998, The Ladder 1999, House Of Yes: Live From House Of Blues 2000, Magnification 2001, Keystudio 2001, Yestoday 2002, Yes Remixes 2003, Yes And Friends 2003, Re(Union) 2004, Yes, Friends and Relatives 1998, In a Word: Yes (1969–) 2002, The Word Is Live 2005, Live at Montreux 2003 2007, Union Live 2011; with Anderson Bruford Wakeman Howe: Anderson Bruford Wakeman Howe 1989; as Jon & Vangelis: Short Stories 1980, The Friends of Mr Cairo 1981, Private Collection 1983, Page of Life 1991, Chronicles 1994; solo: Olias Of Sunhillow 1976, Song Of Seven 1980, Animation 1982, Three Ships 1985, In The City Of Angels 1988, Change We Must 1994, Deseo 1994, Angels Embrace 1995, Toltec 1996, Earth-MotherEarth 1997, The Promise Ring 1997, The More You Know 1998, Simply Christmas 2001, Survival & Other Stories 2010. *Honours:* Grammy Award for Best Rock Instrumental Performance (for Cinema) 1985. *Current Management:* c/o Trudy Green, HK Management, 9200 Sunset Blvd, Suite 530, Los Angeles, CA 90069, USA. *Telephone:* (310) 550-5240. *E-mail:* yes@yesworld .com. *Website:* www.yesworld.com; www.jonanderson.com.

ANDERSON, Laurie P., MFA; American performance artist, musician (keyboards, violin) and writer; b. 5 June 1947, Wayne, Ill.; d. of Arthur T. Anderson and Mary Louise Anderson (née Rowland); m. Lou Reed 2008 (died 2013). *Education:* Columbia Univ., Barnard Coll. *Career:* instructor in Art History, City Coll., CUNY 1973–75; freelance critic, Art News, Art Forum; composer and performer in multi-media exhbns; Artist-in-Residence, ZBS Media 1974, NASA 2002–04; Distinguished Artist-In-Residence, Experimental Media and Performing Arts Center, Rensselaer Polytechnic Inst. 2012–; fmr Artist-In-Residence High Performance Rodeo, Calgary, Alberta, UCLA Center for the Art of Performance; residencies at Yaddo (retreat for writers and artists) 2011, 2012, 2014, American Acad. in Rome; Guest Dir Brighton Festival, UK 2016; Guggenheim Fellow 1983. *Exhibitions include:* solo shows: Barnard Coll. 1970, Harold Rivkin Gallery, Washington 1973, Artists' Space, New York 1974, Holly Solomon Gallery, New York 1977, 1980–81, Museum of Modern Art 1978, Queen's Museum, New York 1984, Barbican, London 2002, Vito Schnabel Gallery, New York 2012; numerous group exhbns 1972–. *Other projects:* New York Social Life, Voices From The Beyond, Talk Normal, Natural History, Songs and Stories for Moby Dick 1999, Happiness 2002, The End of the Moon (performance piece) 2004, Homeland (performance piece) 2006, Delusion (performance piece) 2010. *Film performances:* Carmen, Personal Service Announcements, Beautiful Red Dress, Talk Normal, Alive From Off Center, What You Mean We?, Language Is A Virus, This Is The Picture, Sharkey's Day, Dear Reader, Home of the Brave (writer, dir, performer) 1986, Puppet Motel (CD-ROM) 1995, Heart of a Dog 2015. *Recordings include:* O Superman 1981, Big Science 1982, United States 1983, Mister Heartbreak 1984, Strange Angels 1989, Bright Red 1994, The Ugly One With The Jewels And Other Stories 1995, Life on a String 2001, Live At Town Hall, New York City 2002, Homeland 2010; film scores: Home Of The Brave 1986, Swimming To Cambodia, Monster In A Box. *Publications include:* The Package 1971, October 1972, Transportation, Transportation 1973, The Rose and the Stone 1974, Notebook 1976, Artifacts at the End of a Decade 1981, Typisch Frac 1981, United States 1984, Empty Places: A Performance 1989, Laurie Anderson's Postcard Book 1990, Stories from the Nerve Bible 1993, Night Life 2007. *Honours:* Dr hc (Art Inst. of Chicago), (Philadelphia Coll. of the Arts); Gish Prize 2007, Pratt Inst. Honorary Legends Award 2011, Yaddo Artist Medal 2015. *Current Management:* Curtis R. Priem Experimental Media and Performing Arts Center, Rensselaer Polytechnic Institute, 110 8th Street, Troy, NY 12180, USA. *Telephone:* (518) 276-3921 (office). *E-mail:* studio@difficultmusic.com. *Website:* empac.rpi.edu (office); www .laurieanderson.com.

ANDERSON, Moira, OBE; British singer; b. 5 June 1940, Kirkintilloch, Scotland. *Career:* singer, traditional Scottish folk music; also interpretations of popular standards and light operatic works; regular UK television appearances. *Recordings include:* albums: Moira Anderson's Scotland 1970, This is Moira Anderson 1971, The Auld Scotch Songs 1975, Someone Wonderful 1978, Golden Memories 1981, The Love of God 1986, A Land for all Seasons 1988, 20 Scottish Favourites 1990. *E-mail:* ajblackb@monaco.mc (office); info@moiraanderson.co.uk (office). *Website:* www.moiraanderson.co .uk (office).

ANDERSON, Terry Randall; American songwriter and musician (drums, guitar); b. 25 Dec. 1956, Louisberg, North Carolina; m. Grace Brummett 1989; two s. *Education:* Sandhills Community College, Southern Pines, NC. *Career:* drums with: Don Dixon; Marti Jones; mem. Terry Anderson and the Olympic Ass-Kickin Team 2005–; mem. ASCAP. *Compositions:* Battleship Chains, recorded by Georgia Satellites; I Love You Period; co-wrote 4 songs on Dan Baird's solo record. *Recordings:* albums: solo: Minn, Minn, You Don't Like Me

1995, What Else Can Go Right 1996, I'll Drink to That 2001; with Olympic Ass-Kickin Team: Terry Anderson and the Ass-Kickin Team 2005, When the Oakteam Comes to Town 2007, National Champions 2009. *Address:* 5214 Western Blvd, Raleigh, NC 27606; Doublenaught Records, 411 Morrison Avenue, Raleigh, NC 27608, USA. *Website:* www.doublenaughtrecords.com; www.myspace.com/olympicasskickinteam.

ANDERSSON, Göran Bror (Benny); Swedish composer and musician (keyboards); b. 16 Dec. 1946, Stockholm; m. 1st Frida Lyngstad 1978 (divorced 1981); m. 2nd Mona Nörklit 1981; two s. one d. *Career:* keyboard player and songwriter, the Hep Stars 1964–69; songwriter with Björn Ulvæus 1966–; partner in production with Ulvæus at Polar Music 1971; mem. pop group, ABBA 1972–82; winner, Eurovision Song Contest 1974; worldwide tours; concerts include Royal Performance, Stockholm 1976, Royal Albert Hall, London 1977, UNICEF concert, New York 1979, Wembley Arena 1979; reunion with ABBA, Swedish TV This Is Your Life 1986; continued writing and producing with Ulvæus 1982–; produced musical Mamma Mia! with Ulvæus, West End, London 1999–; founder and bandleader, BAO (Benny Anderssons Orkester) and Benny Andersson Band 2001–; also composer for many other artists including Gemini, Ainbusk, Josefin Nilsson; mem., Royal Swedish Acad. of Music 2007. *Films:* as composer: ABBA: The Movie (also performer) 1977, Mio in the Land of Faraway 1987, Songs from the Second Floor 2000, You, the Living 2007, Mamma Mia! 2008, Palme (Guildbagge Award 2013) 2012. *Compositions include:* ABBA songs (with Ulvaeus); musicals: Chess (with lyrics by Tim Rice) 1983, Kristina Från Duvemåla (based on Vilhelm Moberg's epic novels, Utvandrarna) 1995, Mamma Mia! (with Ulvaeus) 1999. *Recordings:* albums: with the Hep Stars: We and Our Cadillac 1965, The Hep Stars 1966, Jul med Hep Stars 1967, It's Been a Long Long Time 1968, Songs We Sang 68 1968; with Ulvaeus: Lycka 1970; with ABBA: Ring Ring 1973, Waterloo 1974, ABBA 1975, Greatest Hits 1976, Arrival 1977, The Album 1978, Voulez-Vous 1979, Greatest Hits Vol. 2 1979, Super Trouper 1980, The Visitors 1981, The Singles: The First Ten Years 1982, Thank You For The Music 1983, Absolute ABBA 1988, ABBA Gold 1992, More ABBA Gold 1993, Forever Gold 1998, The Definitive Collection 2001; with BAO: Benny Anderssons orkester 2001, BAO! 2004, BAO 3 2007, Story of a Heart 2009, O klang och jubeltid 2011, Tomten har àkt hem 2012; singles include: with ABBA: Ring Ring 1973, Waterloo 1974, Mamma Mia 1975, Dancing Queen 1976, Fernando 1976, Money Money Money 1976, Knowing Me Knowing You 1977, The Name Of The Game 1977, Take A Chance On Me 1978, Summer Night City 1978, Chiquitita 1979, Does Your Mother Know? 1979, Angel Eyes/Voulez-Vous 1979, Gimme Gimme Gimme (A Man After Midnight) 1979, I Have A Dream 1979, The Winner Takes It All 1980, Super Trouper 1980, On And On And On 1981, Lay All Your Love On Me 1981, One Of Us 1981, When All Is Said And Done 1982, Head Over Heels 1982, The Day Before You Came 1982, Under Attack 1982, Thank You For The Music 1983. *Publication:* Mamma Mia! How Can I Resist You? (with Björn Ulvaeus and Judy Craymer) 2006. *Honours:* Dr hc (Stockholm Univ. Faculty of Humanities) 2007, (Luleå Tekniska Univ. Faculty of Humanities and Social Sciences) 2012; World Music Award for Best Selling Swedish Artist 1993, Ivor Novello Special International Award (with Björn Ulvaeus) 2002, inducted into Rock and Roll Hall of Fame (with ABBA) 2010. *Address:* c/o Mono Music AB, Stockholm (office); Södra Brobänken 41A, 111 49 Stockholm, Sweden. *Telephone:* (8) 555-19-600 (office). *E-mail:* info@monomusic.se (office). *Website:* www.monomusic.se (office); www.abbasite.com; www .bennyanderssonorkester.se; www.bennyanderssonband.com.

ANDERSSON, Mats Lennart; Swedish musician (drums); b. 2 Jan. 1964, Stockholm. *Career:* mem. bob hund 1991–; numerous concerts in Scandinavia, including Roskilde, Lollipop, Ruisrock, Quartfestivalen and Hultsfred festivals; mem. STIM, SAMI. *Compositions include:* I Stället för Musik: Förvirring 1996, Düsseldorf 1996. *Recordings include:* bob hund 1993, Edvin Medvind, 7 1994, I Stället för Musik: förvirring 1996, Omslag: Martin Kann 1996, Düsseldorf 3:53 1996, Ett fall och en lösning 1997, Nu är det väl revolution på gång? 1998, Jag rear ut min själ! Allt skal bort!!! 1998, Helgen V.48 1999, Sover aldrig 1999, Stenåldem kan börja 2001, Ingenting 2002. *Honours:* Swedish Grammy Awards for Best Live Act 1994, Best Lyrics 1996. *Website:* www.bobhund.nu.

ANDRADE, Mayra; Cabo Verde singer; b. 1985, Havana, Cuba. *Career:* solo artist 2001–. *Recordings include:* albums: Navega 2006, Stória, stória 2008, Studio 105 2010, Lovely Difficult 2013. *Honours:* winner Jeux de la Francophonie songwriting contest 2001, Preis der Deutschen Schallplattenkritik 2007, BBC Radio 3 World Music Award for Best Newcomer 2008, Cubadisco Int. Award 2008. *Address:* c/o Sony BMG Music Entertainment (France), 52–54 rue de Châteaudun, 75342 Paris Cedex 09, France. *E-mail:* mayra@mayra-andrade.com. *Website:* www.mayra-andrade.com.

ANDRE 3000, (Dré); American rap artist, singer and actor; b. (Andre Benjamin), 27 May 1975, Georgia; s. of Lawrence Walker and Sharon Benjamin Hodor. *Education:* Tri-City High School, Atlanta. *Career:* mem. Outkast (with Big Boi) 1992–, signed to LaFace Records; mem. production Co. A Band Apart 2006; designed Outkast Clothing line Benjamin Bixby 2008; f. Moxie Turtle. *Recordings include:* albums: Southernplayalisticadillacmuzik 1994, ATLiens 1996, Aquemini 1998, Stankonia 2000, Big Boi And Dre Present... 2002, Speakerboxxx/The Love Below (Grammy Awards for Album of the Year, Best Rap Album 2004, American Music Award for Best Rap/Hip-Hop Album 2004) 2003, My Life In Idlewild 2005, Idlewild 2006, 3 Stacks 2008, Alter Ego: The Mixtape 2008, Andre Benjamin Presents: Andre 3000

Is... 2009. *Films include:* Hollywood Homicide 2003, Be Cool 2005, Revolver 2005, Four Brothers 2005, OutKast: Idlewild 2006, Battle in Seattle 2007, Fracture 2007, Semi Pro 2008, The After Party: The Last Party 3 2010, All is by My Side 2013. *Television includes:* Families, The Shield 2004, 2008, Class of 3000 2006–07, About a Girl 2008. *Honours:* Source Award for Best New Rap Group of the Year 1995, American Music Awards for Best Hip Hop/R&B Group 2003, 2004, Grammy Award for best urban/alternative performance 2004, World Music Awards for Best Group, Best Pop Group, Best Rap/Hip-Hop Artist 2004, MTV Europe Best Group Award 2004, Best Song Award, Best Video Award (both for Hey Ya) 2004. *Current Management:* William Morris Endeavor Entertainment, 9601 Wilshire Blvd, Beverly Hills, CA 90210, USA. *Website:* www.outkast.com.

ANDREA, Mihallaq; Albanian musician (guitar, organ) and composer; b. 17 July 1949, Korce; m. Irena Cironaku 1988; one s. one d. *Career:* appearances at nat. festivals, Kenget e Stines, Serenata Korcare Festival; Chair. Musical Society. *Recordings:* Margarita; Serenata; Kitare E Dashur; Eja, Eja; Ne Kinema; Fatkeqesia. *Honours:* First Place, the music of the drama, The Geologist, 1984; First Place, Serenata Korcare Festival, 1999. *Address:* Petro Saro, No. 9 Lagjja 3, Korce, Albania.

ANDREA, Nanni; Italian producer and promoter; b. 20 May 1963, Porretta Terme; m. Cristina Baisi 1998; one c. *Career:* Music Producer, mainly Soul, Funk and R&B; recordings for many labels.

ANDREASSEN, Preben; Danish organist, choir director and composer; *Organist and Choir Leader, Nygårdskirkens Gospelkor;* b. 23 Aug. 1944, Ålborg; s. of Christian Andreassen and Anna Andreassen; two s. *Education:* Royal Danish Music Acad., Copenhagen, Church music educ., studied with Gospel pianist Jackie LaVaree Johnson in Los Angeles and with choir dir Jester Hairston. *Career:* organist, pianist, choir dir and composer, Brøndby-vester Church 1975–; also Nygårdskirkens Gospelkor; concerts in Germany, Sweden, Norway, The Netherlands, Greece, USA and Denmark; Danish television DR1: Youth Services 1991, 1992, Before Sunday 1995, Christmas Services 1993, Gospel Services 1998, 2000, 2002; mem. Dansk Organist og Kantor Samfund. *Compositions include:* choral works: Before Sunday 1992, Christmas Songs 1994, New Danish Hymn Book 1994, Music for Meditation 1998; hymns in various collections. *Radio:* Danish Broadcasting 2000, 2006, 2014. *Television:* Danish Channel 1, Before Sunday 1992, 1993, 1998, Danish Christian TV. *Recordings include:* albums: Christmas Music 1982, Before Sunday 1992, Livet er levende 1993 (Life is Living) 1992, Gospel Music 1997, 1998, Sing Along CD with Christmas Carols 2000, SKG Unplugged Gospel 2010. *Publications include:* Brondbyvester Church Organ History 1987, Christmas Songs 1994, Swedish Hymns book 2008; music in song books: Egtved, Unitas, Melody in Swedish choral book. *Honours:* First Prize, Int. Choir Fest, Veldhoven, Netherlands 1989. *Address:* Kirkebjerg Allé 178, 2605 Brøndby, Denmark (home). *Telephone:* 27-20-23-08 (office). *E-mail:* preben .andreassen@mail.dk. *Website:* www.azusagospelchoir.webbyen.dk (office); www.nygaardskirkensgospelkor.webbyen.dk (office).

ANDREWS, Bob 'Derwood'; British musician (guitar) and songwriter; b. (Robert Ian Andrews), 17 June 1959, Fulham, London, England. *Career:* mem. and guitarist punk band Generation X 1976–79; Founder mem. Empire in early 1980s, Westworld 1986–91, Moondogg 1994–; mem. PRS, BMI. *Recordings include:* albums: with Generation X: Generation X 1978, Valley Of The Dolls 1979, KMD: Sweet Revenge 1998; with Westworld: Where the Action Is 1987, Beatbox Rock 'N' Roll 1988, Movers And Shakers 1991, Beatbox Rock 'N' Roll 1997; with Empire: Expensive Sound 1981, Expensive Sound 2003; with Jimmy Pursey: Imagination Camouflage 1980; with Moondogg: Fat Lot Of Good 1996, God's Wallop 2001, A.T.L.I.T.W. 2004; with Speedtwinn: California 2002; with Derwood: Tone Poet 2007; with Bowleg: Mojave Full Circle 2007; solo: Cover Yer Arse 2010. *Address:* c/o D.O.R., POB 1797, London, E1 4TX, England. *E-mail:* contact@dor.co.uk. *Website:* www.dor.co .uk.

ANDREWS, Dame Julie Elizabeth, DBE; British actress and singer; b. (Julia Wells), 1 Oct. 1935, Walton-on-Thames, Surrey, England; m. 1st Tony Walton 1959 (divorced 1968); one d.; m. 2nd Blake Edwards 1969 (died 2010); one step-s. one step-d. and two adopted d. *Education:* voice lessons with Lillian Stiles-Allen. *Career:* first stage appearance aged 12 as singer, London Hippodrome; played in revues and concert tours; debut in Starlight Roof, London Hippodrome 1947; work for UN Devt Fund for Women. *Theatre:* Starlight Roof (London Hippodrome) 1947, Cinderella (London Palladium), The Boy Friend (Broadway) 1954, My Fair Lady 1956–60, Camelot (Broadway) 1960–62, Putting it Together 1993, Victor, Victoria 1995–96. *Films:* Mary Poppins (Academy Award for Best Actress 1964) 1963, The American-ization of Emily 1964, The Sound of Music 1964, Hawaii 1965, Torn Curtain 1966, Thoroughly Modern Millie 1966, Star! 1967, Darling Lili 1970, The Tamarind Seed 1973, 10 1979, Little Miss Marker 1980, S.O.B. 1980, Victor/ Victoria 1981, The Man Who Loved Women 1983, That's Life 1986, Duet For One 1986, The Sound of Christmas (TV) 1987, Our Sons (TV) 1991, Relative Values 1999, The Princess Diaries 2001, Shrek 2 (voice) 2004, The Princess Diaries 2: Royal Engagement 2004, The Cat That Looked at a King 2004, Shrek the Third (voice) 2007, Enchanted (voice) 2007, The Tooth Fairy 2010, Shrek Forever After (voice) 2010, Despicable Me (voice) 2010. *TV appearances include:* High Tor 1956, The Julie Andrews Hour 1972–73, Great Perform-ances Live in Concert 1990, The Julie Show (ABC) 1992, Eloise at the Plaza 2003, Eloise at Christmastime 2003. *Recordings:* albums: My Fair Lady

(Broadway cast recording) 1956, The Lass With The Delicate Air 1957, Julie Andrews Sings 1958, Rose Marie 1958, Camelot (Broadway cast recording) 1960, Don't Go In The Lion's Cage Tonight 1962, Heartrending Ballads and Raucous Ditties 1962, Julie & Carol at Carnegie Hall (with Carol Burnett) 1962, Mary Poppins (film soundtrack) 1964, The Sound Of Music (film soundtrack) 1965, A Christmas Treasure 1968, Star! 1968, Darling Lili 1969, TV's Fair Julie 1972, The Secret of Christmas 1977, Christmas With Julie Andrews 1982, Love Me Tender 1983, Broadway's Fair Julie 1984, Love Julie 1989, At The Lincoln Center (with Carol Burnett) 1989, The King And I (studio cast) 1992, Broadway: The Music of Richard Rodgers 1994, Here I'll Stay: The Words of Alan Jay Lerner 1996, Nobody Sings It Better 1996. *Publications:* Mandy (as Julie Andrews Edwards) 1972, Last of the Really Great Whangdoodles 1973, The Great American Mousical (as Julie Andrews Edwards, with Emma Walton Hamilton) 2006, Home (autobiog.) 2008. *Honours:* three Golden Globe Awards 1964, 1965, Emmy Award 1987, BAFTA Award 1989, Kennedy Center Honor 2001, Screen Actors' Guild Lifetime Achievement Award 2006. *Current Management:* c/o WME Entertainment, 9601 Wilshire Boulevard, 3rd Floor, Beverly Hills, CA 90210, USA. *Telephone:* (310) 850-4550; (310) 285-9000. *Fax:* (310) 248-5650; (310) 285-9010. *E-mail:* jcolbert@wmeentertainment.com; ndavid@wmeentertainment.com. *Website:* www.wma.com.

ANDRIES, Alexandru Braesti, PhD; Romanian singer, songwriter, musi-cian (electric guitar, acoustic guitar, keyboards, harmonica), architect and lecturer; b. 13 Oct. 1954, Brasov, Romania. *Education:* Inst. of Architecture. *Career:* guest, most Romanian jazz festivals including Sibiu, Costinesti, Cluj, Constanta, Bucharest, 1979–; tours throughout Romania; concerts include Palace Hall Bucharest, Polivalenta Hall Bucharest; special guest, concerts at American Cultural Center, Bucharest; guest, British Council, 1989; appear-ances, most jazz and blues clubs in Romania, including Club A Bucharest, Constanta, Timisoara, Tirgu-Mures, Iasi; special guest star, Golden Stag Festival, Brasov Romania, with Kylie Minogue, Dionne Warwick, 1993; guest, most Romanian radio stations including ProFM, Contact, Total, independent television stations; Assoc. Prof., Ion Mincu Univ. of Architecture and Urban Planning, Bucharest; mem., Romanian Union of Composers, Romanian Union of Writers, Romanian Union of Architects, The Mickey Mouse Club. *Video film:* Damen Tano et La Légion Etrangère. *Television:* Blues Alive 2002. *Recordings:* albums: Interiors 1 1984, Interiors 2 1985, Country And Western Greatest Hits 1986, Rock 'n' Roll 1987, On Distance 1988, Three Mirrors 1989, Censored 1990, Today 1991, Appetite Rises Eating 1992, My She-Neighbours 1, 2, 3 1992, How Far Away 1993, Nothing New On The Eastern Front 1993, Slow Burning Down 1994, Alexandru Andries 1994, Hocus Pocus 1995, White Album 1996, Home 1996, Ungra 1996, Silence Of The Heart 1996, In Concert 1997, All By Myself 1997, Bluntly 1998, Secret Colours 1998, Black And White 1999, Texteriors 1999, Songs For The Princess 1999, Bad Weather (Best Jazz and Blues Album 2001) 2000, Live 2001, Divorce Music (Best Jazz and Blues Album 2002) 2001, Ready Made Songs 2002, Blues Expert 2003, 50/30/20 2004, Special Order 2005, Nothing Turns Out The Way You Wanted It 2006, La Legion Etrangere - Original Soundtrack 2007; singles: Waiting For Maria 1990, Wait 'Til Tomorrow 1992, Dream With Angels 1994, Watercolours 1999, Bingo Romania 2000, Special Edition 2006; videos: How Far Away 1992, 3 Video Moments 1994, 21 Decembrie 1995, Teatrul Bulandra 1996, In Concert 1997, Blues Alive, The Most Beautiful Day 2000, Live 2001, I Can't Help It, Really Like You 2002, 50/30/20 2004, Tenderness ... 2005, Special Edition 2006, Videoarchive Vols 1, 2 and 3 2007. *Publications:* Waiting For Maria 1990, Happy Birthday Mr Dylan (Romanian translations from Bob Dylan's songs) 1991, Home Alone (short stories) 1992. *Honours:* Best Singer/ Songwriter, Vox, Pop, Rock (Romanian musical newspaper) 1990, Golden Record Award 1991, Best Singer 1992, Best Singer, Songwriter, The Pro FM Contact Radio Awards 1994, Best Jazz and Blues Album 2001, 2002, Special Award Union of Music Critics of Romania 2004, Radio Romania Special Award for Recording Achievements 2005. *Current Management:* Aurel Mitran Management, Calea Victoriei 48–50, Sc.B, Apt 73, Sector 1, Bucharest 70102, Romania. *Address:* Soseaua Stefan Cel Mare 26, Blvd 24A, Apt 26, Sector 2, Bucharest 71158, Romania. *Website:* www.alexandries.free.fr.

ANDRST, Lubos; Czech jazz and blues musician (guitar) and composer; b. 26 July 1948, Prague; two c. *Career:* musician with J. Stivín, E. Viklicky, R. Dasek, M. Svoboda, V. Misik, M. Prokop, among others; founder, Energit 1973; founder, Lubos Andrst Blues Band 1980; founder, Lubos Andrst Group 1993; accompanied Paul Jones, Katy Webster 1998, 2000; teaches course in jazz music, Prague Conservatory. *Compositions:* some 80 compositions incl. Capricornus, November, Ikebana, La Bodeguita Dez Medio, Imprints, Encountering, White Landscape, Follow Your Heart, Europe Blues, Wide-Open Door. *Recordings include:* albums: Energit 1975; Piknik, 1978; Capricornus, 1981; Plus-Minus Blues, 1988; Imprints, 1992; L. Andrst With Friends, 1996; Acoustic Set, 1996; Blues Time, 1998; Man With A Guitar, 1999. *Publications:* Jazz Rock Blues, 1988; Redaction, 1995. *Address:* c/o ARTA Music, Lublanska 57, 120 00 Prague 2 (office); Matousova 6, 150 00 Prague 5, Czech Republic. *E-mail:* jazzblues@seznam.cz; 2hp@arta.cz. *Website:* www.lubosandrst.cz.

ANDRUSZKOW, Life, BA, MA; Danish/Polish musician, singer, composer and film and music producer, director, writer and teacher; *CEO, cityzenz film:media:communication;* b. 22 Sept. 1955, Copenhagen, Denmark; two s. *Education:* Univ. of Copenhagen, Univ. of Cambridge, UK, Univ. of Lund, Sweden; pvt. lessons in classical music on trumpet and cornet by conductor

Jorgen Clausen, on piano by Prof. Anker Blyme; pvt. lessons in rock-pop music, on vocal by tutors Jens Christian Smith and Cathrine Sadolin, Denmark and Ian Adams, London; studied rock-pop-guitar at Musicians' Inst., London and film-score composition at Ebeltoft Int. Film Coll.; master-classes at DMF, Copenhagen, Musicians' Inst., London. *Career:* guitarist 1967–; singer 1981–; autodidactive composer and lyricist 1974–; performed and recorded with various bands, including The Law, Box de Viola, Art Exist, La Violenza, The Act, LÍFE, Human Dolls 1979–2008; composer and producer of music for CD, musicals and film 1981–2008; writer/director and producer of short films and music videos 1987–2010; teacher of music, The Rhythmic Evening School of Copenhagen 1982–85, The Rhythmic Centre of Copenhagen 1999–2001; teacher of English and web design, AOF Copenhagen 1999–2000; Lecturer in European Film and Philosophy, Copenhagen Senior High School 2011; coach in cultural entrepreneurialism, CBS 2011; CEO cityzenz film:media:communication. *Actor:* Flying Images (musical) 1986, Tones of an Outsider 1989, Paradise of Fools 1998. *Short films:* Tones Of An Outsider 1989, Blason Dédoré 1993, Yellow Tapestry 2007. *Music videos:* Dream Without Reality 1988, Heaven Cries For No One 1988, People Like Us (live) 1988, Dancing In Burning Silhouettes (live) 1989, Promises 1998, Like A Love In The Haze 2001, Beautiful 2005, I Don't Know Why 2010. *Film scores:* Vertical Travels 1995, Paradise of Fools 1998, The Heaven Is My Ceiling 2000. *Musicals:* Sincerely Yours (cabaret), various theatres, Copenhagen 1983–84, Flying Images, Copenhagen 1986, The Ballad of Suzy, New York 2000. *Lyrics for:* Michael Westwood Band on CDs: Bromzkij Garden 1994, Live For It All 1996, Blossom from the Dirt 1998, No Time At All 2001, Assemblage 2002, Stockholm Sessions 2003. *Radio:* Sincerely Yours, Danish Nat. Radio (DR) 1984. *Recordings:* EPs: Aubaude Dolorose 1985, Europe After The Rain 1995, Is This Life? 1996, Promises 1997, Infant Faces Of A Ruling Class (live) 2002, I've Found You Now (live) 2003, Men Without Shadows 2006; albums; We're Only Strangers Now 1980, Sham Rules 1981, False Truth 1982, Retrograde 1984, Burning Silhouettes 1989, If They See The Bridges Broken 2007, On The Verge Of Surrender 2008; singles: Beautiful 2003, Praha 2003, Misery Loves Company 2004. *Publications include:* The Existentialism in Ingmar Berg-man's Smultronstället 2011, The Existentialism in Krzysztof Kieslowski's Trois couleurs: bleu, blanc, rouge 2012. *Address:* cityzenz film:media:com-munication, Sankt Pauls Gade 42, 1313 Copenhagen, Denmark (office). *Telephone:* 20-34-70-07 (office). *E-mail:* info@cityzenz.eu (office). *Website:* www.cityzenz.eu (office).

ANDRUZZI, Gabriel (Gabe); American musician (saxophone, keyboards, percussion). *Career:* mem. The Rapture 2001–14. *Recordings include:* albums: Out Of The Races And Onto The Tracks 2001, Echoes 2003, Pieces of People We Love 2006, In the Grace of Your Love 2011. *Current Management:* Principle Management, 30–32 Sir John Rogerson's Quay, Dublin 2, Ireland. *Website:* therapturemusic.com.

ANDY, Horace; Jamaican singer; b. (Horace Keith Hinds), 19 Feb. 1951, Kingston. *Career:* made debut recordings 1967; changed name 1970; released numerous recordings at Studio One 1970–74; freelance recording artist 1974–77; emigrated to Connecticut, USA 1977, to London 1985; collaborations with Massive Attack on Blue Lines 1991, Protection 1994, Mezzanine 1998. *Recordings include:* albums: Skylarking 1972, You Are My Angel 1973, In The Light 1977, Bim Sherman Meets Horace Andy & U Black (with Bim Sherman) 1980, Unity Showcase (with Errol Scorcher) 1981, Dance Hall Style (aka Exclusively) 1982, Showcase 1983, Sings For You & I 1985, Confusion (with Patrick Andy Clash) 1985, Elementary 1985, Reggae Superstars Meet (with Dennis Brown) 1986, From One Extreme To Another (with John Holt) 1986, Big Bad Man 1987, Haul & Jack Up 1987, Fresh 1988, Shame & Scandal 1988, Everyday People 1988, Life Is For Living 1995, Roots & Branches 1997, See & Blind 1999, Living In The Flood 1999, Zion Gate 2002, Mek It Bun 2003, This World 2005, Livin' It Up 2007, Two Phazed People 2009, Serious Times 2010, Broken Beats 2013.

ANGEL ALBA, Adolfo; Mexican musician (keyboards), songwriter and producer; b. 1 Sept. 1963, Fresnillo, Zacatecas. *Career:* mem. La Brisa 1977–83; mem. Los Temerarios 1983–; formed Angel Records, later renamed AFG Sigma 1990–96, producing for other artists. *Film:* Sueño y realidad 1993. *Recordings include:* albums: Los 14 grandes éxitos de Los Temerarios 1983, Los Temerarios en las alturas 1984, Cumbias y norteñas 1985, Pero no 1986, Los Temerarios 1988, Incontenibles 1989, Los Temerarios internacionales y románticos 1990, Te quiero 1991, Mi vida eres tú 1992, Tu ultima canción 1994, Camino del amor 1995, Nuestras canciones 1995, Nuestras canciones (vol. II) 1997, Como te recuerdo 1998, En la madrugada se fue (Latin Grammy Award 2001) 2000, Baladas rancheras 2001, Una lagrima no basta (Billboard Latin Music Award for Regional Mexican Album of the Year by a Male Group 2003) 2002, Tributo al amor 2003, Veintisiete 2004, Regalo de amor 2004, Sueño de amor 2005, www.lostemerarios.net.

ANGEL ALBA, Gustavo; Mexican singer, songwriter and musician (guitar); b. 1 May 1968, Fresnillo, Zacatecas. *Career:* mem. La Brisa 1977–83; mem. Los Temerarios 1983–; formed Angel Records, later renamed AFG Sigma 1990–96, producing for other artists. *Film:* Sueño y realidad 1993. *Recordings include:* albums: Los 14 grandes éxitos de Los Temerarios 1983, Los Temerarios en las alturas 1984, Cumbias y norteñas 1985, Pero no 1986, Los Temerarios 1988, Incontenibles 1989, Los Temerarios internacionales y románticos 1990, Te quiero 1991, Mi vida eres tú 1992, Tu ultima canción 1994, Camino del amor 1995, Nuestras canciones 1995, Nuestras canciones (vol. II) 1997, Como te

recuerdo 1998, En la madrugada se fue (Latin Grammy Award 2001) 2000, Baladas rancheras 2001, Una lagrima no basta (Billboard Latin Music Award for Regional Mexican Album of the Year by a Male Group 2003) 2002, Tributo al amor 2003, Veintisiete 2004, Regalo de amor 2004, Sueño de amor 2005, Recuerdos del alma 2007, Si tú te vas 2008. *Website:* www.lostemerarios.net.

ANGELLO, Steve; Swedish DJ, songwriter and record producer; b. (Steven Angello Josefsson Fragogiannis), 22 Nov. 1982, Athens, Greece; m. Isabel Adrian; two d. *Career:* raised in Stockholm, Sweden; remixer of numerous artists including Eurythmics, Robin S; has collaborated with Sebastian Ingrosso on many productions under aliases including Buy Now, Fireflies, Mode Hookers, The Sinners, Outfunk, General Moders; collaborated with Eric Prydz (as A&R Project) and with Axwell (as Supermode); mem. Swedish House Mafia (electronic dance music trio) 2007–13, numerous collaborations including Laidback Luke, Pharrell, Tinie Tempah, John Martin, Knife Party; remixers for Coldplay (Every Teardrop is a Waterfall). *Films:* Take One (documentary) 2010. *Recordings:* albums: with Swedish House Mafia: Until One 2010, Until Now 2012. *Honours:* with Swedish House Mafia: MTV Europe Music Award for Best Swedish Act 2010, 2011. *Current Management:* c/o ATM Artists, 55 Kentish Town Road, London, NW1 8NX, England. *E-mail:* amy@ atmartists.com. *Website:* www.atmartists.com; www.swedishhousemafia.com; www.steveangello.tv.

ANGELOPULO, Charles; South African singer and composer; b. 8 Dec. 1954, Pretoria; m. 1978; one s. one d. *Career:* title role, Jesus Christ Superstar 1990; lead singer Web, Cafe Society, Blasé; currently Head of Composition and Marketing, Eclipse Music; mem. SAMRO, ASAMI. *Compositions:* over 65 recorded and released titles include: Helen of Troy, The Rock Opera; I Love Africa; Good Time Girls; When You Gonna Love Me; Nothing Anybody Can Say. *Address:* 433 16th Avenue, Rietfontein, Pretoria 0084, South Africa. *Telephone:* (73) 220-6934. *E-mail:* info@eclipsemusic.co.za. *Website:* www .eclipsemusic.co.za.

ANGER, Darol; American musician (violin, mandolin, guitar), producer, writer and educator; *Associate Professor, Berklee College of Music;* b. 7 May 1953, Seattle, Wash.; m. Emy Phelps. *Education:* Univ. of California, Santa Cruz, studied with David Grisman, David Baker and Billy Taylor. *Career:* Leader, Republic of Strings, Turtle Island String Quartet; Co-Leader (with Mike Marshall), Psychograss, The Duo (with Mike Marshall), Co-founder The Fiddlers 4, Anger/Marshall Band, the Montreux Band, The David Grisman Quintet (DGQ); solo artist, performing with artists including Stéphane Grappelli, Bela Fleck, Sam Bush, Edgar Meyer, Bill Evans, Tony Rice, David Grisman, Vassar Clements, Peter Rowan, Michael Doucet, Regina Carter, Billy Taylor, Mark O'Connor, Bill Keith, Mike Marshall, Tony Trischka, Todd Phillips, Aoife O'Donovan; producer and arranger for other artists, including Natalie MacMaster; performances world-wide since 1975, including Carnegie Hall, Lincoln Center, Town Hall, New York, Cambridge Folk Festival, Palau Música Catalana, Montreux Jazz Festival, Montreal Jazz Festival, Telluride & Rockygrass Bluegrass Festivals, Vancouver Folk Festival, Detroit Sym-phony Hall, Seattle Symphony Hall, Davies Symphony Hall, Great American Music Hall San Francisco, Sanders Theatre Boston, São Paulo Hall, etc.; various seminars and clinics at US colls; instructor, Mark O'Connor Fiddle Confs; currently Assoc. Prof., Berklee Coll. of Music; f. String Resource Bd of Int. Asscn of Jazz Educators; mem. American String Teachers Asscn. *Films include:* Chops and Groves, Blues On The Fiddle (instructional videos); contrib. to soundtracks of films Best Offer, A Shock To The System, Country, various HBO features. *Recordings include:* Darol Anger & Republic of Strings Ensemble (two recordings), Fiddlers 4, The Duo: Woodshop at Home & On the Range, Diary of a Fiddler, Heritage, A Christmas Heritage; with Mike Marshall: Brand New Can, Comotion, Jam, Chiaroscuro; with the Turtle Island String Quartet: TISQ Retrospective, By the Fireside, A Week In Detroit, Spider Dreams, On the Town, Skylife, Metropolis, Now Hear This (with Psychograss), Like Minds. *Producer:* Blueprint (Natalie MacMaster), Sweet Loam (Joe Walsh), Song of Deligh (Maeve Gilchrist); string arrange-ments for Marc-Andre Fortin. *Publications:* Darol Anger Original Fiddle Tunes, Darol Anger's Bluegrass Fiddle. *Honours:* MacDowell and Ucross Fellow. *Address:* One Forest Avenue, Portland, ME 04101, USA (office). *E-mail:* darolfm@earthlink.net (office). *Website:* www.darolanger.com.

ANGGUN; Indonesian singer; b. (Anggun Cipta Sasmi), 29 April 1974, Jakarta; d. of Darto Singo; m. Michel Georgea. *Career:* at seven years old recorded album of children's songs; at 12 years old recorded successful rock album, Dunia Aku Punya (World of Mine); extensive touring through Asia; moved to France 1994; various tours and concerts. *Recordings include:* albums: Dunia Aku Punya 1986, Anak Putih Abu Abu 1991, Nocturno 1992, Anggun C. Sasmi… Lah!!! 1993, Yang Hilang 1994, Au nom de la lune (aka Anggun) 1997, Snow on the Sahara 1998, Desirs Contraires 2000, Chrysalis 2000, Luminescence 2005, Elevation 2008. *Address:* c/o Carosello Records, Galleria del Corso 4, 20100 Milan, Italy (office). *E-mail:* info@carosellorecords .com (office). *Website:* www.anggun.com.

ANGHAM; Egyptian singer and songwriter; b. (Angham Mohammad Sulei-man), 19 Jan. 1972, Alexandria; d. of Mohammad Ali Suleiman and Mageda abd el-Aaleem; m. 1st Magdy Aref 1999 (divorced 2000); one s.; m. 2nd Fahd 2004 (divorced 2008); one s. *Education:* Cairo Conservatory. *Career:* solo artist 1987–. *Recordings include:* albums: Fil rokn el-baeed el-hadi 1987, Awal gawab 1988, Lalili lali 1989, Layek 1989, Etafakna 1990, Bibasata kida 1991, Enta el-alam 1992, Ella ana 1993, Boalak eih 1995, Akdar 1996, Shay daa

1996, Betheb meen 1997, Khally bokra li bokra 1998, Wahdaniya 1999, Leih Sebtaha 2001, Omry maak 2003, Bahibbik wahashteeny 2005, Kolma n'arrab 2007, Nefsy Ahebbak 2009, Alhekaya Almohamadia 2010, Mahadesh Yehasebni 2010. *Honours:* Egypt's Number 1 Female Artist 2001, Alexandria National Music Festival Sawt el-Hob Award 2006, Nile Entertainment Best Egyptian Female Artist 2007. *Address:* c/o Rotana, al-Mohandeseen, 13 Mohammad Shafik Road, Cairo, Egypt. *Website:* www.angham.webs.com.

ANGUS, Colin; British musician; b. 24 Aug. 1961, Aberdeen. *Education:* Aberdeen University. *Career:* mem. Alone Again Or; Founder mem. The Shamen 1986–. *Recordings include:* albums: Drop 1987, In Gorbachev We Trust 1989, Phorward 1989, En-Tact 1990, Progeny 1991, Boss Drum 1992, SOS 1993, Axis Mutatis 1995, Hempton Manor 1996, UV 1998, On Air, The BBC Sessions (compilation) 1998; singles include: Christopher Mayhew Says 1987, Jesus Loves Amerika 1988, Pro Gen 1990, Move Any Mountain 1991, L.S.I. 1992, Ebeneezer Goode 1992, Boss Drum 1992, Phorever People 1992, Destination Eschaton 1995, Hemp 1996, Universal 1998, U Nations 1998. *Current Management:* Moksha Management, PO Box 102, London, E15 2HH, England. *Website:* www.moksha.co.uk.

ANITTA; Brazilian singer, songwriter and actress; b. (Larissa de Macedo Machado), 30 March 1993, Rio de Janeiro; d. of Mauro Machado and Miriam Machado. *Career:* signed with Furacão 2000 record label 2010, with Warner Music label 2013. *Films:* as actress: Copa de Elite 2014, Didi e O Segredo dos Anjos 2014, Breaking Through 2015. *Recordings:* albums: Anitta 2013, Meu Lugar (MTV Latin Music Award for Best Live Album 2015) 2014, Ritmo Perfeito 2014, Bang! 2015. *Honours:* Melhores do Ano for Best Song (for Show das Poderosas) 2013, Kids Choice Award for Best Brazilian Act 2015, MTV Europe Music Awards for Best Brazilian Act 2014, 2015, for Best Latin America Act 2015. *Current Management:* Juliana Mattoni or Paulo Pimenta, Ju Mattoni, Rio de Janeiro, Brazil. *Telephone:* (21) 996673005. *E-mail:* Juliana@jumattoni.com; Paulo@jumattoni.com. *Website:* www.jumattoni.com. *E-mail:* contato@anittaoficial.com. *Website:* anittaoficial.com.

ANKA, Paul, OC; Canadian/American singer, songwriter and actor; b. 30 July 1941, Ottawa, Ont.; m. Marie Ann Alison de Zogheb 1963 (divorced); five d. *Career:* numerous TV appearances world-wide, live performances; mem. BMI. *Films:* Girls Town 1959, The Private Lives of Adam and Eve 1960, Look in Any Window 1961, The Longest Day 1962, Captain Ron 1992, Ordinary Magic 1993, Mad Dog Time 1996, 3000 Miles to Graceland 2001. *Television:* The Paul Anka Show (series host) 1982, Perry Mason: The Case of the Maligned Mobster 1991. *Compositions:* theme for The Tonight Show 1962, theme music for films, The Longest Day, No Way Out, Atlantic City, and contrib. of songs to numerous other films; some 900 songs, including It Doesn't Matter Anymore (for Buddy Holly) 1959, My Way (for Frank Sinatra) 1969, She's A Lady (for Tom Jones) 1971, Puppy Love (for Donny Osmond); other songs performed by artists including Elvis Presley, Barbra Streisand, Linda Ronstadt, The Sex Pistols, Nina Simone, Gipsy Kings and Robbie Williams. *Recordings include:* albums: The Fabulous Paul Anka And Others 1956, Paul Anka 1958, My Heart Sings 1959, Paul Anka Sings His Big 15 1959, Vol. II 1962, Vol. III 1962, Paul Anka Swings For Young Lovers 1959, Anka At The Copa 1960, It's Christmas Everywhere 1960, Diana 1962, Young Alive & In Love! 1962, Let's Sit This One Out 1962, Our Man Around the World 1963, Three Great Guys (with Sedaka and Cooke) 1963, Songs I Wish I'd Written 1963, Paul Anka 1964, Paul Anka Italiano 1964, A Casa Nostra 1964, Strictly Nashville 1966, Goodnight My Love 1969, Sincerely 1969, Life Goes On 1969, Paul Anka 70s 1970, Jubilation 1972, My Way 1974, Anka 1974, Feelings 1975, Remember Diana 1975, She's A Lady 1975, Times Of Your Life 1976, The Painter 1977, The Music Man 1977, Listen To Your Heart 1978, Headlines 1979, Both Sides Of Love 1981, Walk A Fine Line 1983, Freedom for the World 1987, Somebody Loves You 1989, Face in the Mirror 1993, After All 1995, Amigos (with others) 1996, A Body Of Work 1998, Rock Swings 2005, Classic Songs, My Way 2007, Songs of December 2011, Duets 2013. *Publications:* My Way (autobiography) 2014. *Honours:* Chevalier, Ordre des Arts et des Lettres. *Address:* Paul Anka Productions, 10960 Wilshire Blvd, 5th Floor, Los Angeles, CA 90024, USA (office). *Telephone:* (310) 858-0797 (office). *Fax:* (310) 553-5930 (office). *Website:* www.paulanka.com.

ANNA R.; German singer, songwriter and musician; b. (Andrea Natalie Rosenbaum), 25 Dec. 1969, Berlin; m. Nilo Neuenhofen 2002. *Career:* grew up in East Berlin; fmrly worked as laboratory assistant, music seller; Founder mem. Rosenstolz 1991–, released debut album 1992. *Recordings:* albums: with Rosenstolz: Soubrette werd' ich nie 1992, Nur einmal noch 1994, Sanfte Verführer 1994, Mittwoch is' er fällig 1995, Objekt der Begierde 1996, Die Schlampen sind müde 1997, Zucker 1999, Kassengift 2000, Macht Liebe 2002, Herz 2004, Das grosse Leben 2006, Die Suche geht weiter 2008, Wir sind am Leben 2011. *Honours:* ECHO Award for Best Nat. Rock/Pop Group 2012. *Current Management:* Pop-out Management, Forster Strasse 5, 10999 Berlin, Germany. *Website:* www.rosenstolz.de.

ANNIE (see Berge Strand, Anne Lilia)

ANNIES, Nicholas Charles; British artist manager, photographer and graphic artist; b. 23 Jan. 1971, Kettering; m. Lauren Kelly Behan 1996; one d. *Career:* Manager, record labels: Reality Recordings, c. 1990; ADI Records, 1991; Paradise Records, 1992; Co-manager, Village of Experimental Sound Studios, Cambridge; PA Engineer, including Caister Weekenders, 1987–91; Graphic Designer; Professional website designer; Managing Director: Once Click Solutions Ltd; founder. VectorFunk; mem. Musicians' Union; Society of Amateur Artists; Media Records Italy. *Recordings:* Singles: Armageddon (12), co-produced by Shades Of Rhythm, 1991; with 39 Orbits: 2 12 releases, 1993–94; Music For A Mono Nation, due 2002. *Publications:* Underworld, monthly magazine, Peterborough City, 1990–93. *Address:* 70 Fenton Road, Warboys, Huntingdon, Cambs., PE28 2SL, England. *E-mail:* nick@vectorfunk .co.uk. *Website:* www.vectorfunk.co.uk; www.djnickannies.co.uk.

ANNISETTE (see Annisette Koppel)

ANOUK; Dutch singer; b. (Anouk Teeuwe), 8 April 1975, The Hague; m. 1st Edwin Jansen (divorced 1998); m. 2nd Remon 2004 (divorced 2008); three s. one d. *Recordings include:* albums: Together Alone 1997, Urban Solitude 1999, Lost Tracks 2001, Graduated Fool 2003, Update 2004, Hotel New York 2004, Anouk is Alive 2006, Who's Your Mamma? 2007, Live at Gelredome 2008, For Bitter or Worse 2009, To Get Her Together 2011, Sad Singalong Songs 2013. *Honours:* TMF Belgium Awards for Best Female Int. Artist, Best Int. Album, Best Int. Video 2005, MTV Europe Music Award for Best Dutch & Belgian Act 2005, 2006, TMF Dutch Award for Best Female Artist, Best Rock Act, Best Video 2006. *E-mail:* management@anouk.nl. *Website:* www.anouk .com.

ANSELMO, Phil; American rock singer and songwriter. *Career:* lead singer and lyricist heavy rock group, Pantera 1987–2003; lead singer, Down 1991–. *Recordings:* albums: with Pantera: Power Metal 1988, Cowboys From Hell 1990, A Vulgar Display Of Power 1992, The Great Southern Treadkill 1996, Reinventing the Steel 2000; with Down: Nola 1995, Down II – A Bustle in your Hegerow 2002, Down III – Over the Under 2007. *Address:* c/o McGhee Entertainment, 8730 Sunset Boulevard, Suite 200, West Hollywood, CA 90069, USA. *Telephone:* (310) 432-2250. *E-mail:* info@mcgheela.com. *Website:* www.mcgheela.com. *Address:* Down LLC, PO Box 51887, Phoenix, AZ 85076, USA (office). *Website:* www.down-nola.com.

ANSEMS, Tony; American musician (guitar) and songwriter; b. 9 March 1940, Tilburg, Netherlands; m. Darlene. *Education:* American College, Bryn Mawr, Pennsylvania. *Career:* fmr mem., bands including Sundown, Foggy Valley Boyz; guitarist with Breakaway; currently mem. of classic country band Doty Island Railroad; songwriter; founder and Pres., Songwriters of Wisconsin; mem., NSA; NAS; ASCAP. *Address:* Songwriters of Wisconsin International, PO Box 1027, Neenah, WI 54957-1027, USA (office). *Telephone:* (920) 725-5129 (office). *Fax:* (920) 720-0195 (office). *E-mail:* tonyansems@ gmail.com (office). *Website:* www.songwritersofwisconsin.org/ (office); www .tonyansems.com (home).

ANSTICE-BROWN, Sam, BMus; British musician (drums) and arranger; b. 24 July 1963, Sherborne, Dorset, England. *Education:* Berklee College of Music, Boston, USA. *Career:* tours, gigs with: Georgie Fame; Barbara Thompson; Mornington Lockett; Guy Barker; Jean Toussant; Iain Ballamy; Tony Wjan; John Etheridge; Zoot Money; Dick Morissey; Don Weller; Dave Newton; Alan Skidmore; Bobby Wellins; presenter, Music, Mind and Mastery lectures and workshops; mem, Musicians' Union. *Recordings:* Take It Or Leave It, Giladatzmon; Back To Square One, Organix. *Address:* 2 Church Street, Kingsbury, Martock, TA12 6AU, England. *E-mail:* sam@sambrown.co .uk. *Website:* www.sambrown.co.uk.

ANT, Adam; British singer, songwriter and actor; b. (Stuart Leslie Goddard), 3 Nov. 1954, Marylebone, London, England; m. 1st Carol Mills 1975 (divorced), m. 2nd Lorraine Gibson (divorced); one d. *Career:* Founder and lead singer, Adam and the Ants 1977–82; numerous tours, television and radio appearances; solo artist 1982–86, 1992–; mem. all-star Peace Choir 1991. *Film appearances include:* 15 films, including World Gone Wild, Sunset Heat. *Television appearances include:* Northern Exposure, The Equalizer. *Compositions include:* numerous songs with co-writer Marco Pirroni. *Recordings include:* albums: with Adam and the Ants: Dirk Wears White Sox 1979, Kings Of The Wild Frontier (BRIT Award for Best British Album 1982) 1980, Prince Charming 1981; solo: Friend Or Foe 1982, Strip 1983, Vive Le Rock 1985, Hits 1986, Manners And Physique 1990, Wonderful 1995, Antbox (career box set) 2001, Adam Ant is the Blueblack Hussar in Marrying The Gunner's Daughter 2010; featured tracks on film soundtracks including: Jubilee, Metropolis. *Publication:* Stand and Deliver: The Autobiography 2006. *Honours:* Ivor Novello Award, Songwriters of Year, with Pirroni 1982, Q Idol Award 2008. *Current Management:* Neil O'Brien Entertainment, 26 Eastcastle Street, London, W1W 8DQ, England. *Telephone:* (20) 7631-5168. *E-mail:* info@ neilobrienentertainment.com. *Website:* www.adam-ant.net.

ANTHONY, Julie, OBE, AM; Australian actress and singer; b. 23 Aug. 1951, Galga, S Australia; d. of D. L. Lush and B. Lush; m. Eddie Natt 1976; two d. *Career:* began singing with a local band and won an amateur TV talent quest 1970; regular appearances on Adelaide Tonight Show; moved to Sydney, regular TV appearances and performances on club and cabaret circuit; lead role in Australian production of Irene 1973; starred in UK version at Adelphi Theatre 1976; returned to Australian TV and appeared in three nat. specials 1977; tours to USA, worked with Bill Cosby, Roy Clarke and Merv Griffin; invited to sing with the re-formed Seekers at 1988 World Expo, Brisbane, joined group as lead singer 1988–89; sang nat. anthem at official opening of Australia's new Parl. House 1988; returned to the stage in I Do!, I Do! 1988; teamed up with jazz musician Don Burrows for tours 1994, also appearance at Jazz and Blues Festival, Gold Coast International Hotel 1995; returned to cabaret with season at Tilbury Hotel, Sydney 1996. *Stage role:* Maria in The Sound Of Music, Sydney 1983, toured major and regional centres. *Film:*

Paradise Road (cameo role as band singer) 1997. *Albums include:* Sings Just For You 1982, I Dreamed A Dream 1988, You And I 1995, Live From The Tilbury Hotel 1996. *Honours:* Best Newcomer (Actress) Award, The Play and Players of London 1976, Australian Variety Club Awards for Best Female Vocalist 1976, 1977, 1978, 1980, 1982, 1986, 1988, Entertainer of the Year 1977, 1978, 1982, Sammy and Penguin Awards for Best Television Variety Performer 1977, Most Popular Female Entertainer 1988, Best TV Variety Entertainer (Female) 1978, Best Newcomer, Plays and Players (London) 1976, Female Vocal Variety Performer of the Year (MO Awards) 1994, 1996. *Address:* c/o ATA Allstar Artists, Locked Bag 5, Haymarket, NSW 1240, Australia.

ANTHONY, Marc; American singer, songwriter and actor; b. (Marco Antonio Muñiz), 16 Sept. 1968, New York; m. 1st Dayanara Torres Delgado 2000 (divorced 2004); two s. one d.; m. 2nd Jennifer Lopez 2004 (divorced 2012); one s. one d. *Career:* sang back-up on demos and TV commercials, aged 12; started writing songs in high school, including Boy I've Been Told, a hit for SaFire 1988; teamed up with film score composer, Louie Vega; album When the Night is Over featured many Latin musicians, awakening interest in salsa; signed to Sony and released first solo album 1993. *Films include:* East Side Story 1988, Carlito's Way 1993, Natural Causes 1994, Hackers 1995, Big Night 1996, The Substitute 1996, Bringing Out the Dead 1999, Con la música por dentro 1999, Feelin' So Good (voice) 2000, In the Time of the Butterflies 2001, Man on Fire 2004, El Cantante 2007. *Theatre includes:* The Capeman (Broadway musical) 1998. *Recordings include:* albums: Rebel 1988, When The Night Is Over (with Louie Vega) 1991, Otra Nota 1993, Todo a su tiempo 1995, Contra la corriente 1997, Marc Anthony 1999, Desde un Principio: From the Beginning 1999, Libre 2001, Mended 2002, Amar sin mentiras (Latin Grammy Award for Best Latin Pop Album 2005) 2004, Valió la Pena (Latin Grammy Award for Best Tropical Album 2005) 2004, Sigo Siendo Yo 2006, El Cantante (Latin Grammy Award for Best Salsa Album 2008) 2007, Iconos 2010, 3.0 (Billboard Music Award for Top Latin Album 2014, Latin Grammy Award for Best Salsa Album 2014) 2013. *Honours:* 16 Premio Lo Nuestro Awards, Latin Grammy Awards for Best Latin/Tropical Performance (for Contra la Corriente) 1998, for Song of the Year (for Dímelo) 1999, for Record of the Year (for Vivir Mi Vida) 2013, Billboard Latin Music Telemundo Star Award 2005, American Music Award for Favorite Latin Artist 2013, Billboard Music Awards for Top Latin Artist 2014, for Top Latin Song (for Vivir Mi Vida) 2014. *Address:* c/o Sony Music Latin, Sony Music Entertainment, 550 Madison Avenue, New York, NY 10022, USA (office). *Telephone:* (212) 833-8000 (office). *Fax:* (212) 833-5828 (office). *Website:* www.sonymusiclatin.com (office); www.marcanthonyonline.com/us.

ANTHONY, Michael; American musician (bass); b. 20 June 1955, Chicago, IL. *Career:* mem., Snake; mem. of rock group, Van Halen 1974–2006; toured as mem. of The Other Half 2006; mem. Chickenfoot 2009–; numerous tours worldwide, festival appearances; co-host radio show with Sammy Hagar, Radio Westwood One 1992. *Recordings include:* albums: with Van Halen: Van Halen 1978, Van Halen II 1979, Women and Children First 1980, Fair Warning 1981, Diver Down 1982, 1984 1984, 5150 1986, OU812 1988, For Unlawful Carnal Knowledge 1991, Right Here Right Now 1993, Balance 1995, Van Halen 3 1998; with Chickenfoot: Chickenfoot 2009. *Honours:* Grammy Award for Best Hard Rock Performance 1992, MTV Music Video Awards 1984, 1992, American Music Award for Favorite Album 1992. *Address:* Mad Anthony Cafe, PO Box 192, Lagunitas, CA 94938, USA. *E-mail:* media@madanthonycafe.com. *Website:* www.madanthonycafe.com; www.chickenfoot.us.

ANTILL, Danny Terrance; South African musician (keyboards, flute), producer and arranger; b. 8 Sept. 1959, Johannesburg; m. 1982; one s. two d. *Education:* Royal Academy of Music. *Career:* toured with Stingray throughout South Africa; appeared on national television 1, 2, 3; solo piano albums released throughout Europe; mem, SAMRO. *Recordings:* Stingray, Danny Antill, Amaduduzo, Siyabamukela, Amaduduzo, Exotic Voices And Rhythms; solo albums include: In Moments Like These 1996, Heavenly Moments 1997, Quiet Moments 1998, Intimate Moments 2002. *Address:* Brettian Productions, 51 David Draper Road, Bruma, Johannesburg 2026, South Africa. *Telephone:* (11) 622-3356. *Fax:* (11) 616-5874. *E-mail:* info@brettian.com. *Website:* www.brettian.com.

ANTOINE THE SWAN (see Kiedis, Anthony)

ANTON, Alan; Canadian musician (bass guitar); b. (Alan Alizojvodic). *Career:* mem. Hunger Project 1979; mem. Germinal –1984; Founder mem. Cowboy Junkies 1985–; formed independent label Lament 1986–88, 1998–. *Recordings include:* albums: Whites Off Earth Now! 1986, The Trinity Session 1988, The Caution Horses 1989, Black Eyed Man 1992, Pale Sun, Crescent Moon 1993, 200 More Miles 1996, Studio: Selected Studio Recordings 1996, Lay It Down 1996, Miles From Our Home 1998, Waltz Across America 2000, Open 2001, Radio Sessions 2002, Open Road 2002, In The Time Before Llamas 2003, One Soul Now 2004, Early 21st Century Blues 2005, At the End of Paths Taken 2007, Renmin Park 2010, Demons: The Nomad Series, Vol. 2 2011, Sing in My Meadow: The Nomad Series, Vol. 3 2011, The Wilderness: The Nomad Series, Vol. 4 2012. *Music for film:* Big Nothing 2006. *Music for television:* Other Voices: Songs from a Room 2005. *Address:* c/o Cooking Vinyl, PO Box 1845, London, W3 0ZA, England. *Telephone:* (20) 8600-9200. *Fax:* (20) 8743-7448. *E-mail:* info@cookingvinyl.com; junkieinfo@aol.com. *Website:* www.cookingvinyl.com; www.cowboyjunkies.com.

ANTONACCI, Biagio; Italian singer, songwriter and musician (guitar); b. 9 Nov. 1963, Milan; pnr Marianna Morandi; two s. *Recordings include:* albums: Sono cose che capitano 1989, Adagio Biagio 1991, Liberatemi 1992, Biagio Antonacci 1994, Il mucchio 1996, Mi fai stare bene 1998, 9 Novembre 2001 2001, Convivendo – Parte I 2004, Convivendo – Parte II 2005, Vicky Love 2007, Inaspettata 2010, Sapessi dire no 2012. *Address:* c/o IRIS SRL, Universal Music Italia, Universal Music Group, via Benigno Crespi 19, 20159 Milan, Italy (office). *Telephone:* (03) 802730154 (office). *E-mail:* iris@antonacci.it (office). *Website:* www.universalmusic.it/pop (office); www.biagioantonacci.it.

ANTONOFF, Jack; American guitarist and singer; b. 31 March 1984, Bergenfield, NJ. *Education:* Professional Children's School, New York. *Career:* fmr mem. punk rock band Outline; Founder mem. Steel Train 2002–13; Founder mem. fun. 2008–; toured with Jack's Mannequin 2008, 2010; support act for Vedera, Paramore, Panic at the Disco; first single release 2009; collaborations include Janelle Monáe (We Are Young). *Recordings include:* albums: with Steel Train: Twilight Tales from the Prairies of the Sun 2005, Trampoline 2007, Steel Train 2010; with fun.: Aim and Ignite 2009, Some Nights 2012. *Honours:* with fun.: Teen Choice Awards for Choice Rock Group 2012, for Choice Single by a Group (for We Are Young) 2012, Grammy Award for Song of the Year (We Are Young), for Best New Artist (Fun.) 2013, Billboard Music Award for Top Rock Artist 2013, Grammy Award for Album of the Year (as producer with Taylor Swift for 1989) 2016. *Address:* Fueled by Ramen Records, 1290 Avenue of the Americas, 28th Floor, New York, NY 10104 (office); Warner Music Group, 75 Rockefeller Plaza, New York, NY 10019, USA (office). *Telephone:* (212) 275-2000 (office). *Website:* www.wmg.com (office); www.fueledbyramen.com (office); www.ournameisfun.com; www.steeltrain.net.

ANTUNES, Arnaldo; Brazilian singer, songwriter, poet and writer; b. (Arnaldo Augusto Nora Antunes Filho), 2 Sept. 1960, São Paulo; s. of Arnaldo Augusto Nora Antunes and Dora Leme Ferreira Antunes; m. 1st Go Antunes 1980; m. 2nd Zaba Moreau 1987; four c. *Education:* Pontifical Catholic Univ. of Rio de Janeiro. *Career:* mem. Titãs do IêIê 1981–92; solo artist 1992–; mem. Tribalistas (with Carlinhos Brown and Marisa Monte) 2002–03. *Recordings include:* albums: with Titãs do IêIê: Titãs 1984, Televisão 1985, Cabeça Dinossauro 1986, Jesus não tem Dentes no País dos Banguelas 1987, Go Back 1988, Õ Blesq Blom 1989, Tudo as Mesmo Tempo Agora 1991, Acústico MTV (as guest singer) 1991, Sacos Plásticos (as guest songwriter) 2009; solo: Nome 1993, Ninguém 1995, O Silêncio 1996, Um som 1998, O Corpo 2000, Paradeiro 2001, Saiba 2004, Qualquer 2006, Iê-Iê-Iê 2009, Acústico MTV 2012; with Tribalistas: Tribalistas 2003. *Publications include:* poetry: Ou E 1983, Psia 1986, 2 ou + corpos no mesmo espaço 1997, Doble Duplo 2000, Outro 2001, ET et Tu 2003, Antologia 2006; other: Tudos 1990, As Coisas 1992, Nome 1993, 40 escritos 2000, Palavra Desordem 2002, Frases do Tomé aos Três Anos 2006, Como é que chamo o Nome Disso 2006. *Website:* www.arnaldoantunes.com.br.

APACHE INDIAN; British singer; b. (Steven Kapur), Birmingham. *Career:* solo artist 1992–; int. tours. *Recordings include:* albums: No Reservations 1992, Make Way For The Indian 1995, Real People 1998, Wild East 1998, Karma 2002, Time For Change 2005, Sadhu – The Movement 2007. *Honours:* UK Asian Music Awards: Best Int. Success 2003, Outstanding Achievement 2005, Lifetime Achievement Award 2011. *Current Management:* c/o Steve Hughes, BHX Management, 306F The Big Peg, 120 Vyse Street, Birmingham, B18 6NF, England. *Telephone:* (121) 251-5544 (office). *Fax:* (870) 127-5120 (office). *E-mail:* musicmgmt@hotmail.com. *Telephone:* (121) 236-6635. *E-mail:* apachesbar@hotmail.co.uk. *Website:* www.karmasound.com; www.apachesbar.com; www.myspace.com/apachei.

APELBAUM, Morris Moishe, BSc, BA, DipEd, DipAdmin; producer and engineer; b. 13 July 1957, Haifa, Israel; m.; one s. *Career:* mem. CARAS; SOCAN. *Recordings:* Producer: Oliver Jones: Many Moods; Lights Of Burgundy; Tim Brady: Scenarios; Imaginary Guitars; Inventions; Double Variations. *Honours:* Juno Award. *Address:* 3880 Clark Street, Montréal, QC H2W 1W6, Canada.

APHEX TWIN (see James, Richard David)

APHROHEAD (see Felix Da Housecat)

APL DE AP; American rap artist. *Career:* fmr mem., Atban Klann; founder mem., Black Eyed Peas 1995–. *Recordings include:* albums: Behind The Front 1998, Bridging The Gap 2000, Elephunk (NRJ Music Award for Best Int. Album, France 2005) 2003, Monkey Business (Juno Award for Int. Album of the Year 2006, American Music Award for Favorite Rap/Hip-Hop Album 2006) 2005, The E.N.D. (Grammy Award for Best Pop Vocal Album 2010) 2009, The Beginning 2010. *Honours:* MTV Europe Award for Best Pop Act 2004, 2005, Australian MTV Awards for Best R&B Video, for Sexiest Video (both for Hey Mama) 2005, American Music Award for Favorite Pop/Rock Band, Duo or Group 2005, 2009, for Favorite Rap/Hip-Hop Band, Duo or Group 2005, 2006, 2009, Grammy Award for Best Rap Performance by a Duo or Group (for Don't Phunk with my Heart) 2006, MOBO Award for Best Group 2006, American Music Award for Favorite Soul/R&B Band, Duo or Group 2006, Grammy Awards for Best Pop Performance by a Duo or Group with Vocal (for My Humps) 2007, (for I Gotta Feeling) 2010. *Website:* www.apldeap.com; www.blackeyedpeas.com.

APPLE, Fiona; American singer and songwriter; b. 13 Sept. 1977, New York; d. of Brandon Maggart and Diane McAfee. *Career:* released debut album Tidal aged 19 years; collaborations with Johnny Cash. *Recordings:* albums: Tidal 1996, When the Pawn . . . 1999, Extraordinary Machine 2005, The Idler Wheel Is Wiser Than the Driver of the Screw and Whipping Cords Will Serve You More Than Ropes Will Ever Do 2012. *Honours:* Best New Artist, MTV Music Video Awards 1997, Grammy Award for Best Female Rock Vocal Performance 1998, Best Female Vocalist, Calif. Area Music Awards 2000. *Address:* Epic Records, Sony BMG, 550 Madison Avenue, 24th Floor, New York, NY 10022-3211, USA (office). *Telephone:* (212) 833-8870 (office). *Website:* www .epicrecords.com (office); www.fiona-apple.com.

APPLESEED (see Seate, Tshepo)

APPLETON, Nicole Marie; British/Canadian singer; b. 7 Dec. 1974, Hamilton, Ont.; sister of Natalie Appleton-Howlett; m. Liam Gallagher (divorced); one s. *Career:* mem. All Saints 1995–2001, 2006–; mem. Appleton 2001–04; co-presenter, The Hot Desk 2007–, pesenter, Cover Me Canada 2011, apptd adviser to Louis Walsh on X-Factor 2013. *Film:* Honest 2000. *Recordings include:* albums: with All Saints: All Saints 1997, Saints and Sinners 2000, Studio 1 2006; with Appleton: Everything's Eventual 2003. *Publication:* Together (autobiography, with Natalie Appleton-Howlett) 2002. *Honours:* BRIT Award for Best Single (for Never Ever) 1997. *Current Management:* c/o Fascination Management, 1st Floor, 6 South Hill Park, London, NW3 2SB, England. *Telephone:* (20) 7586-6457. *E-mail:* info@ fascinationmanagement.com. *Website:* www.fascinationmanagement.com.

APPLETON-HOWLETT, Natalie Jane; British/Canadian singer; b. 14 May 1973, Toronto; sister of Nicole Appleton; one d.; m. Liam Howlett. *Career:* mem. All Saints 1995–2001, 2006–; mem. Appleton 2001–04. *Film:* Honest 2000. *Recordings include:* albums: with All Saints: All Saints 1997, Saints and Sinners 2000, Studio 1 2006; with Appleton: Everything's Eventual 2003. *Television includes:* I'm a Celebrity...Get Me Out of Here! Season 4 2004. *Publication:* Together (autobiography, with Nicole Appleton) 2002. *Honours:* BRIT Award for Best Single (for Never Ever) 1997. *Current Management:* c/o Fascination Management, 1st Floor, 6 South Hill Park, London, NW3 2SB, England. *Telephone:* (20) 7586-6457. *E-mail:* info@fascinationmanagement .com. *Website:* www.fascinationmanagement.com.

APRIL, Johnny; American musician (bass guitar); b. 27 March 1965, Enfield, Connecticut. *Career:* fmr mem. Maniax, Mostly Holy; mem. Staind 1995–. *Recordings include:* albums: Tormented 1996, Dysfunction 1999, Break The Cycle 2001, 14 Shades of Grey 2001, Chapter V 2005, The Illusion of Progress 2008, Staind 2011. *Honours:* VH-1 'Your Song Kicked Ass But Was Played Too Damn Much' Award 2001. *Current Management:* c/o The Firm Inc., 9100 Wilshire Blvd, Suite 400W, Beverly Hills, CA 90212, USA. *Website:* www .staind.com.

AQUAMANDA, BA; British singer, musician (keyboards), writer and producer; b. (Amanda Greatorex), Matlock, Derbyshire. *Education:* Leicester. *Career:* vocalist, lyricist, Knights of The Occasional Table; Breathe track on compilation album Shamanarchy In The UK; Album and cover design, Knees Up Mother Earth, 1993; Session on John Peel, 1994; Now solo as Aquamanda; Runs record label Fairy Cake Universe with partner Dr Tony Hare; mem, PRS; MCPS; PPL; Musicians' Union. *Compositions:* lyricist, vocalist, composer, Knees Up Mother Earth. *Recordings:* Album: Knights Of The Occasional Table, 1993; Solo single: Free Your Spirit (12 vinyl), 1995; Love is my Language; Cosmic Disco; Diary. *E-mail:* info@aquamanda.net (office). *Website:* www.aquamanda.net (office).

ARATA, Tony; American songwriter; b. Savannah, GA; m. Jaymi. *Education:* Georgia Southern University. *Career:* songs recorded by: Suzy Bogguss, Garth Brooks, Philip Claypool, Patricia Conroy, Helen Darling, Chris Gaines, Jim Glaser, Emmylou Harris, Sylvia Hutton, Michael James, Hal Ketchum, Dave Koz, Patty Loveless, Ruby Lovett, Delbert McClinton, Reba McIntire, Barra MacNeils, Oak Ridge Boys, Lee Roy Parnell, Ronna Reeves, Allen Reynolds, Dan Seals, David Slater, Jo-El Sonnier, Randy Travis, Tanya Tucker, Clay Walker, Don Williams, George Winston, Trisha Yearwood. *Compositions include:* Anonymous; Black And White And Blue; The Change; The Dance; Don't Forget Who You're Talking To; Don't Let Her See Me Fall; Dreaming With My Eyes Open; Everybody's Equal; Face To Face; Fairytale; Handful Of Dust; Here I Am; I Don't Want To Go Out Wondering; I Hear A Call; I Used To Worry; I Wish Hearts Would Break; I've Been Down Too Long; I'll Be Your Fool Tonight; I'm Holding My Own; In The Wink Of An Eye; Kickin' And Screamin'; Long Stretch Of Lonesome; Love Every Time; Love Is Stronger; The Man In The Mirror; Nothing But Love; One Of My Reasons; Part Of Me; Pretend; Right Where It Hurts; Same Old Story; Satisfied Mind; Slower; Someday I Will Lead The Parade; Stand By The Road; Standing By The River; Tell The Truth; That's The Way I Remember It; This Is My Prayer For You; What Else Can I Do; Why Ain't I Running; You Can't Get There From Here; You Were Gone. *Recordings:* albums: Songwriters On Beale Street 1999, Changes; The Names Behind The Artist; Way Back When 2000, Such is Life 2005. *Honours:* Acad. of Country Music Song of the Year (for The Dance). *Address:* Little Tybee Records, PO Box 41142, Nashville, TN 37204, USA. *E-mail:* tony@tonyarata.com. *Website:* www.tonyarata.com.

ARBEIT, Jochen; German singer and musician (guitar). *Career:* mem. Die Haut 1984–97; mem. experimental band, Einstürzende Neubauten 1997–; mem. ABQ 2008–. *Recordings include:* albums: with Einstürzende Neubauten: Silence is Sexy 2000, Perpetuum Mobile 2004, Grundstück 2005, Jewels 2008; solo: Solo 2008. *E-mail:* jochenarbeit@freenent.de. *Website:* www .jochenarbeit.com.

ARCARI, Dave; British musician (guitar), songwriter, producer, publicist and photographer; *Touring Musician, Buzz Records/Dixiefrog Records;* b. (David Vincent Arcari), 14 Aug. 1964, Glasgow, Scotland; partner Margaret McDonald. *Education:* Fife Coll. *Career:* mem. band Summerfield Blues – 1996; numerous live sessions for BBC radio; TV appearances, European Cable Shows; mem. the Radiotones 1997–2007; now solo performing artist and songwriter world-wide; mem. Musicians' Union, Asscn of Ind. Music. *Compositions:* Ain't Crying 1993, 24 Hours 1993, Uncle Jack 1995, Journeytime is Over 1997, You Oughta Know 1997, Good Friend Blues 1998, Gravel Road 1998, Pomegranate Heart 1998, Devil Got My Woman 1998, Don't Stop 1999, Close To The Edge 2000, She's Gone 2000, Wherever I Go 2000, No More Mister Nice Guy 2000, One Side Blind 2000, Day Job 2000, Bring My Baby Back 2001, Bound To Ride 2002, Small World 2003, Troubled Mind 2003. *Recordings:* with Summerfield Blues: Devil And The Freightman, Let's Scare The Posh People, Little Miss Behavin'; with Denim Elliots: Gooseberry Rain; with Radiotones: Gravel Road 1999, Whiskey'd Up 2000, Bound To Ride 2003; solo: Blue Country Steel 2004, Come with Me 2007, Got Me Electric 2009, Devil's Left Hand 2010, Nobody's Fool 2012. *Honours:* Scottish Blues Band of the Year 1993. *Current Management:* c/o Buzz Records, PO Box 15, Drymen, Glasgow, G63 0WR, Scotland. *Telephone:* (1360) 870248. *E-mail:* studio@thebuzzgroup.co.uk. *Website:* www.thebuzzgroup.co.uk; www .davearcari.com.

ARCH, David; British composer, arranger and musician (keyboards); b. 25 Oct. 1962, Watford; m. Katherine Arch 1991; two c. *Education:* King James Coll., Henley; Guildhall School of Music, GGSM. *Career:* musical dir, keyboard player, arranger and composer for films, television and albums; joined Joe & Co in 1987, working with producer Mark Campbell, to compose advertisements; Musical Dir for Strictly Come Dancing, The One and Only, Just the Two of Us, Dance X, Strictly Dance Fever, The World's Greatest Elvis; extensive arrangements, principally in the popular music field; worked on numerous film soundtracks; mem. Performing Right Soc., Mechanical Copyright Protection Soc., British Acad. of Composers and Songwriters. *Compositions for television include:* Night and Day, GMTV, Strange But True. *Address:* c/o One More Music Company Limited, Soho Recording Studios, The Heals Building, 22-24 Torrington Place, London, WC1E 7HJ, England (office). *Telephone:* (20) 7636-4474. *Website:* www.onemoremusiccompany.com (office).

ARCHER, Gem; British musician (guitar) and singer. *Career:* fmr mem., Heavy Stereo; mem., Oasis 1999–2010; numerous concert and festival appearances; regular tours UK, Europe and USA; mem. Beady Eye 2010–14. *Recordings include:* albums: with Heavy Stereo: Deja Voodoo; with Oasis: Familiar To Millions (live) 2001, Heathen Chemistry 2002, Don't Believe The Truth (Q Award for Best Album) 2005, Stop the Clocks 2006, Dig Out Your Soul 2008; with Beady Eye: Different Gear, Still Speeding 2011, BE 2013. *Honours:* NME Awards for Best UK Band, Artist of the Year 2003, Q Award for Best Act in the World Today 2006, BRIT Award for Outstanding Contribution to Music 2007. *Current Management:* Ignition Management, 54 Linhope Street, London, NW1 6HL, England. *Telephone:* (20) 7298-6000. *Fax:* (20) 7258-0962. *E-mail:* mail@ignition-man.co.uk. *Website:* www.oasisinet .com; www.beadyeyemusic.com.

ARCHER, Martin Walker, LLB; British musician (saxophone, electronics) and composer; b. 9 March 1957, Sheffield. *Education:* Univ. of Nottingham. *Career:* leader, composer, Hornweb 1983–93; current mem., Transient v Resident, ASK; owner of Discus Record Label. *Recordings:* albums: with Hornweb Saxophone Quartet: Kinesis, 1986; Sixteen, 1987; Universe Works, 1989; Solo recordings: Wild Pathway Favourites (Wire Magazine World Top 25 album) 1988; Ghost Lily Cascade, 1996; 88 Enemies, 1998; Winter Pilgrim Arriving, 2000, English Commonflowers 2003, Heritage and Ringtones 2004, Artefacts (with Neil Carver) 2006, The Inclusion Principle (with Hervé Perez) 2006, In Stereo Gravity 2008, Ghosts of Gold (with Julie Tippetts) 2009, The Leaf Factory (with Hervé Perez) 2010, Tales of FiNiN (with Julie Tippetts) 2011; with Transient v Resident: Electrical Shroud, 1995; Dharma Day, 1998; WKCR, 1999; Medulla, 1999; with Simon H. Fell: Pure Water Construction, 1999; with ASK: Disconnected Bliss 1998, The Formulary of Curses 2004; with Outward Sound Ensemble: Cloudburst 2004; with Masayo Asahara: Saint Agnes Foundation 1974, Saint Catherine Torment 2005; with Geraldine Monk: Angel High Wires, 2001, Fluvium 2003; Compiler Of The Network miniatures series: Vol. I, 1994; Vol. II, 1995; The Music is Silent, 1996; Sound Gallery, 1997. *Current Management:* Discus, PO Box 658, Sheffield S10 3YR, England. *E-mail:* huckleberry@discus-music.co.uk (office). *Website:* www .discus-music.co.uk (office).

ARCHER, Richard; British singer, songwriter and musician (guitar); b. 18 Jan. 1977, Staines. *Education:* Kingston Univ. *Career:* fmr lead singer with band Contempo; Founder mem., lead singer and main songwriter with band Hard-Fi 2003–. *Recordings include:* albums: Stars of CCTV 2005, Once Upon a Time in the West 2007, Kalashnik Love 2008, Friendship 2009, Killer Sounds 2011; other: In Operation (DVD) 2006. *Current Management:* c/o Necessary Records, PO Box 28362, London, SE20 7WH, England. *Telephone:* (7832) 141503. *E-mail:* info@necessaryrecords.com. *Website:* www.necessaryrecords .com; www.hard-fi.com.

ARCHER, Tasmin Angela; British singer and songwriter; b. 3 Aug. 1963, Bradford, England. *Career:* solo artist 1992–; tours of USA, UK, Europe; mem.

Musicians' Union. *Recordings include:* albums: Great Expectations 1992, Bloom 1995, Singer/Songwriter 2004, On 2006. *Honours:* BRIT Award for Best Newcomer 1993. *E-mail:* t.a.enquiries@tasminarcher.com. *Website:* www.tasminarcher.com.

ARDEN-GRIFFITH, Paul, GRSM, GRNCM, ARMCM; British singer (tenor); *Associate Director and Musical Director, Make It So*; b. 18 Jan. 1952, Stockport, Greater Manchester, England; s. of Jack Griffith and Alma Griffith (née Arden); partner Ken Spencer. *Education:* Royal Manchester Coll. of Music, Royal Northern Coll. of Music, Cantica Voice Studio, London. *Career:* debut as Puck in Benjamin Britten's Midsummer Night's Dream, Sadler's Wells Theatre, London 1973; other performances include Franz Lehar's The Merry Widow, Henze's We Come to the River, Britten's Paul Bunyan, Carlisle Floyd's Of Mice and Men, Carl Orff's Carmina Burana, Prokofiev's The Duenna, Count Almaviva in Rossini's Barber of Seville, Puccini's Il Tabarro, Rossini's The Count Ory, Verdi's La Traviata, Mozart's Die Zauberflöte, Lloyd Webber's Phantom of the Opera, The Legendary Lanza, Babes in the Wood, Lloyd Webber's Sunset Boulevard, That Old Minstrel Magic; concerts and cabarets include London Dorchester Hotel, Hyde Park Intercontinental, Piccadilly Theatre, The Belfry Club, Savoy Hotel, Tramshed, Theatre Royal Drury Lane, The Limelight Club, Royal Artillery House; worldwide concert tours, festival appearances, master-classes and lecture tours of UK, Netherlands, Hong Kong, USA music colls and arts faculties; founder-mem. Arts Council's Opera 80 Touring Co.; Pres. Barezzi Theatre School; Assoc. Dir and Musical Dir, Make It So; performances include Strauss' Die Fledermaus with White Horse Opera 2001, Puccini's La Bohème with Somerset Opera 2003, Sondheim's Sweeney Todd, Covent Garden 2003–04, Strauss' Die Fledermaus with Opera Holland Park, London 2004, The Pocket Orchestra (The Unlikely Lives of the Great Composers) at Trafalgar Studio 2, West End, London 2006, City Varieties, Leeds 2006, 42nd Street, West Side Story, Honk!, Stagedoor Manor Performing Arts Center, New York 2007, Guys and Dolls, The Music Man, Phantom, Stagedoor, New York 2008, A Little Night Music, Me and My Girl, The Mikado, Stagedoor, New York 2009, The Great American Songbook, UK tour 2009, Eric Wetherell's A Foreign Field, Redgrave Theatre, Bristol 2010, Aladdin, Assembly Rooms, Derby 2010, The Mystery of Edwin Drood, Woman in White, Annie, Stagedoor, New York 2011, Aladdin, Playhouse Theatre, Weston-Super-Mare 2011, Gala Concert, Lincoln Cathedral 2012, Aladdin, Plaza Theatre, Stockport 2012, Dick Whittington, Plaza Theatre, Stockport 2013, Cinderella, Plaza Theatre, Stockport 2014; Intimate Opera (MD), London 2015, Cinderella, Middlesbrough Theatre 2015. *Recordings include:* The Song Is You 1986, Phantom Of The Opera (original cast recording) 1987, An Evening With Alan Jay Lerner 1987, Minstrel Magic (cast soundtrack) 1993, A Minstrel On Broadway 1994, Encore! 1995, The Classic Collection 1995, Accolade! 1996. *Publications include:* contrib. to Phantom of the Opera: The First Year Backstage by Marcus Tyler. *Honours:* Gwilym Gwalchmai Jones Scholarship for Singing 1974. *Current Management:* c/o MBA, Concorde House, 18 Margaret Street, Brighton, BN2 1TS, England. *Telephone:* (1273) 685970. *Fax:* (1273) 685971. *E-mail:* info@mbagency.co.uk. *Website:* www.mbagency.co.uk. *Address:* Make It So, 18 Margaret Street, Brighton, BN2 1TS, England (office). *Telephone:* 7800-810349 (mobile) (office). *E-mail:* pag@makeitso.gb.com (office). *Website:* www.makeitso.gb.com (office).

ARENA, Tina; Australian singer and songwriter; b. (Filippina Arena), 1 Nov. 1967, Melbourne; m. Ralph Carr (divorced 1999); one s. *Education:* St Columba's Coll. *Career:* fmr mem. Young Talent Time; other performances include Nine 1987, Soul Dynamite 1989, Joseph and his Amazing Technicolor Dreamcoat 1992, Cabaret 2000, Notre Dame de Paris 2002, Chicago: the Musical 2007. *Recordings include:* albums: Tiny Tina 1977, Strong As Steel 1990, Don't Ask (Aria Album of the Year) 1994, In Deep 1998, Just Me 2001, Un Autre Univers 2005, Songs of Love and Loss 2007, 7 Vies 2008, The Onstage Collection 2010. *Honours:* Performer and Rock Performer of the Year MO Awards 1996, Aria Female Artist of the Year 1995, Variety Club Entertainer of the Year 1995, Advance Australia Foundation Award 1996, World Music Award for World's Highest Selling Female Artist, Highest Selling Female Artist in Australian History 1996, 2000. *E-mail:* bruce@barbian.co.uk. *Website:* www.barbian.co.uk; www.tinaarena.com.

ARGENT, Rod; British musician (keyboards) and singer; b. 14 June 1945, St Albans. *Career:* founder, The Zombies 1963–69; founder own group, Argent 1970s; also solo artist and record producer; numerous live appearances, tours; production partnerships with Chris White and Peter Van Hooke 1980s; toured as part of Ringo Starr's All-Star Band 2006–. *Recordings:* albums: with the Zombies: The Zombies, 1965; Begin Here, 1965; Odyssey And Oracle, 1967; with Argent: Argent, 1970; Ring Of Hands, 1971; All Together Now, 1972; In Deep, 1973; Nexus, 1974; Encore, 1974; Circus, 1975; Counterpoints, 1975; Anthology, 1976; Hold Your Head Up, 1978; Rock Giants, 1982; Music From The Spheres, 1991; Solo: Moving Home, 1978; Ghosts, 1982; Shadowshow, 1985; Red House, 1988; Rescue, 1991; with Nanci Griffith: Late Night Grande Hotel, 1991; MCA Years, 1993; also: Into The West, 1993; Painted Desert Serenade, 1993; Sun Ain't Gonna Shine Anymore, 1994; Healing Bones, 1994; On Nights Like This, 1996; Martyrs And Madmen, 1997; Dick Bartley Presents.., 1998; Salty Heaven, 1999, As Far As I Can See 2004; singles include: with the Zombies: She's Not There (No. 2, USA), 1964; Tell Her No, 1965; with Argent: Hold Your Head Up, 1971; God Gave Rock And Roll To You, 1973; with Colin Blunstone: Sanctuary, 2001; Co-producer, debut album by Tanita Tikaram, 1988. *Website:* www.rodargent.com; www.myspace.com/colinblunstoneandrodargent.

ARGÜELLES, Julian; British musician (saxophones, woodwinds) and composer; b. 28 Jan. 1966, Birmingham. *Career:* mem. various youth bands; mem. Loose Tubes, including a BBC Proms performance; mem. Mike Gibbs Orchestra, Kenny Wheeler Big Band, Chris McGregor's Brotherhood of Breath, The Very Big Carla Bley Band, Hermeto Pascoal, Django Bates' Delightful Precipice; performed Concerto for piano, percussion and saxophone, by Mario Lagina; mem. Face to Face, NDR Bid Band, HR Big Band, RAM Big Band; comm. by BBC Radio 3 for Octet; regular positions at Trinity Coll. of Music, London, Royal Northern Coll. of Music, Manchester; Ensemble in Residence, Univ. of York. *Recordings include:* Phaedrus (with Julian Argüelles Quartet), Home Truths (with Julian Argüelles Quartet), Scapes (with Steve Argüelles) 1996, Skull View (with Julian Argüelles Octet) 1997, Escapade (with Julian Argüelles Octet) 1999, As Above, So Below (with Julian Argüelles Octet) 2004, Partita 2006, Momenta 2009, Ground Rush (with Tom Rainey and Mickael Formanek) 2010. *Honours:* Pat Smyth Award, various BBC Awards, Jazz Composers Alliance Julius Hemphill Award (USA) 1999, Best Instrumentalist Award, Scottish Jazz Awards 2012. *Address:* 3 Preston Cottages, East Linton, East Lothian, EH40 3DS, Scotland (home). *E-mail:* arg.jul@gmail.com; Jularg@tiscali.co.uk. *Website:* www.julianarguelles.com; www.thick-skinned.com.

ARIE, India; American singer, songwriter and musician; b. (India Arie Simpson), 3 Oct. 1975, Denver, Colo. *Education:* Savannah Coll. of Art and Design. *Career:* musical collaborations include Stevie Wonder, Cassandra Wilson, John Cougar Mellencamp; contrib. to film soundtracks, including Bamboozled 2000, We Were Soldiers 2002, American Dreams 2003, A Shark Tale 2004. *Television appearances include:* American Dreams (mini-series, NBC) 2003. *Recordings include:* albums: Acoustic Soul 2001, Voyage to India (Grammy Award for Best R&B Album 2003) 2002, Testimony Vol. 1: Life & Relationships 2006, Testimony Vol. 2: Love and Politics 2009, Songversation 2013. *Honours:* Vibe Magazine Award for Best New Artist 2001, Billboard Video Award 2001, Essence Award 2002, BET Award for Best Female R&B Artist 2002, 2003, Grammy Award: for Best Urban/Alternative Performance 2003, 2010, for Best R&B Album 2003, Best Pop Collaboration with Vocals 2010. *Current Management:* c/o Tom Storms, Suretone Entertainment, 54 Music Square East, Suite 300, Nashville, TN 37203, USA. *Telephone:* (615) 864-7400. *E-mail:* tomstorms@suretone.com. *Website:* www.indiaarie.com.

ARIYASU, Momoka; Japanese singer; b. 15 March 1995, Saitama. *Career:* mem. Sister Rabbits 2004–09; backing dancer for boy band Exile 2004; mem. all-female group Power Age 2009; mem. Momoiro Clover Z 2009, renamed Momoiro Clover Z 2011–; first national tour 2009; debut single 2009; numerous live and TV appearances; int. concert appearances in Germany, Malaysia, France. *Television:* French Potato Cup 1999, Saturday Drama Special 2001, Suntory Mystery Prize 2001, Monday Mystery Theater 2001, SMAPxSMAP 2002, Ponkikkids (children's TV series) 2004–05, Friday Entertainment 2006, Drama 30 2006. *Films:* Gin no Angel 2004, Shirome 2010, Momodora 2012. *Recordings:* albums: Battle and Romance (CD Shop Award for Best CD 2012) 2011, 5th Dimension 2013, Iriguchi no Nai Deguchi 2013. *Honours:* MTV Video Music Award Japan for Best Choreography 2013, MTV Europe Music Award for Best Japanese Act 2013. *Current Management:* c/o Stardust Promotion, 2F Takeda-Dai2 Bldg, 2-3-3 Ebisu-nishi, Shibuya, Tokyo, 150-0021, Japan. *Website:* www.stardust.co.jp; starchild.fm/special/en/momoclo.

ARJONA, Ricardo; Guatemalan singer, songwriter, musician (piano, guitar) and record producer; b. (Edgar Ricardo Arjona Morales), 19 Jan. 1964, Jocotenango; s. of Ricardo Arjona Moscoso and Mimi Morales. *Education:* School of Communication Sciences, Universidad de San Carlos de Guatemala. *Career:* participant at Festival Infantil Juventud 74 (with song Gracias al Mundo); fmrly played basketball for Guatemalan national team; fmr schoolteacher; recording career 1985–; songwriter for artists including Yuri; collaborations include Marta Sánchez, Panteón Rococó, Marc Anthony, Eros Ramazzotti, Sandró, Gaby Moreno; many international tours. *Recordings include:* albums: Decir que te amo 1985, Jesús, verbo no sustantivo 1988, Del otto lado del sol 1991, Animal nocturno 1993, Historias 1994, Si el norte fuera el sur (Billboard Latin Music Award for Rock Album of the Year 1997) 1996, Sin daños a terceros (Billboard Latin Music Award for Rock Album of the Year 1999) 1998, Vivo 1998, Galeria Caribe 2000, Santo pecado (Lo Nuestro Award for Pop Album of the Year 2004) 2002, Adentro (Latin Grammy Award for Best Male Pop Vocal Album 2006, Grammy Award for Best Latin Pop Album 2007) 2005, 5to Piso 2008, Poquita Ropa 2010, Independiente 2011. *Honours:* Rafael Álvarez Ovalle Order for International Accomplishments 1993, ASCAP Awards for Pop/Contemporary Song (for Te Conozco) 1995, (for Detrás de mi ventana 1995), for Pop/Ballad Song of the Year (for El Problema) 2004, (for Por qué de tan cruel el amor) 2006, (for A Ti) 2007, (for Quiero) 2008, (for Sin Ti... Sin Mi) 2010, for Pop Song (for El Amor) 2012, ASCAP Latin Heritage Award 2006, Orgullosamente Latino Award for Latin Soloist of the Year 2006, for Latin Trayectory of the Year 2010, Billboard Latin Music Awards for Male Latin Pop Airplay Song of the Year (for A Ti) 2007, for Latin Tour of the Year 2010, Premios Juventud Supernova Award 2009. *Address:* c/o Metamorfosis Records, Warner Music Latina, Warner Music Group, 75 Rockefeller Plaza, New York, NY 10019, USA (office). *Telephone:* (212) 275-2000 (office). *Website:* www.wmg.com (office); www.ricardoarjona.com.

ARMAN, Hossein; Afghan singer, composer and musician (harmonium); one s. (Khaled Arman). *Career:* forced into exile, moved to Switzerland; Founder mem., Ensemble Kaboul 1995–. *Recordings include:* albums: Nastaran 2001,

Mahwash. Radio Kabul: Tribute To Afghan Composers (with Ustad Mahwash) 2003, Afghan Music 2010. *Honours:* BBC Radio 3 World Music Award (Asia Category) 2003. *Address:* c/o Khaled Arman, 10 chemin Adolphe Pasteur, 1209, Geneva, Switzerland (office). *E-mail:* khaledarman@swissonline.ch (office); ESchoenlei@aol.com. *Website:* www.adem.ch (office).

ARMAN, Khaled; Afghan musician (guitar, violin, rubab); s. of Hossein Arman. *Education:* studied in Prague, Czechoslovakia and Paris, France. *Career:* fmr guitarist, Orchestra of Radio Kabul; mem., Ensemble Kaboul 1995–. *Recordings include:* albums: Nastaran 2001, Mahwash. Radio Kabul: Tribute To Afghan Composers (with Ustad Mahwash) 2003. *Honours:* BBC Radio 3 World Music Award (Asia Category) 2003. *Address:* 10 chemin Adolphe Pasteur, 1209, Geneva, Switzerland (office). *E-mail:* khaledarman@ swissonline.ch (office). *Website:* www.adem.ch (office).

ARMAN, Osman; Afghan musician (flute, tubak). *Career:* mem., Ensemble Kaboul 1995–. *Recordings include:* albums: Nastaran 2001, Mahwash. Radio Kabul: Tribute To Afghan Composers (with Ustad Mahwash) 2003. *Honours:* BBC Radio 3 World Music Award (Asia Category) 2003. *Address:* c/o Khaled Arman, 10 chemin Adolphe Pasteur, 1209, Geneva, Switzerland (office). *E-mail:* khaledarman@swissonline.ch (office). *Website:* www.adem.ch (office).

ARMAOU, Lyndsay Gael Christian; Irish singer, musician (piano, guitar), songwriter and actor; b. 18 Dec. 1980, Athens, Greece; m. Lee Brennan 2006. *Career:* mem. B*Witched 1998–2002; currently owner, Popstars Acad., Richmond; mem. Clayton 2007–; numerous tours and television appearances. *Recordings include:* albums: B*Witched 1998, Awake and Breathe 1999. *Address:* c/o Grantham Hazeldine, Suite 315, The Linen Hall, 162–168 Regent Street, London, W1B 5TD, England. *Telephone:* (20) 7038-3737. *E-mail:* caroline@granthamhazeldine.com. *Website:* www.lindsayarmaou.com.

ARMATAGE, John Sinclair; British musician (drums); b. 5 Aug. 1929, Newcastle upon Tyne; m. Ann Johnston 1975. *Career:* mem. Wally Fawkes Band, Bruce Turner Jump Band, Alan Elsdon Band, Pete Allen Band, Terry Lightfoot Band; tours with Don Byas, Ben Webster, Earl Hines, Red Allen, Pee Wee Russell; numerous television and radio appearances. *Film appearances:* Living Jazz 1962, Plenty. *Recordings include:* albums with Bruce Turner, Alan Elsdon, Bud Freeman, Terry Lightfoot. *Current Management:* c/o Ann Armatage, 1 Keable Road, Wrecclesham, Farnham, GU10 4PW, England.

ARMATRADING, Joan, MBE, BA; British singer and songwriter; b. 9 Dec. 1950, St Kitts, West Indies; d. of Amos Ezekiel Armatrading and Beryl Madge Benjamin. *Education:* Open Univ. *Career:* moved to Birmingham, UK 1958; began professional career in collaboration with lyric-writer Pam Nestor 1972; tours worldwide. *Recordings include:* albums: Whatever's For Us 1973, Back To The Night 1975, Joan Armatrading 1976, Show Some Emotion 1977, Me Myself I 1980, Walk Under Ladders 1981, The Key 1983, Secret Secrets 1985, The Shouting Stage 1988, Hearts and Flowers 1990, The Very Best of 1991, Square the Circle 1992, What's Inside 1995, Lovers Speak 2003, Into the Blues 2007, This Charming Life 2010, Live at Royal Albert Hall 2011, Starlight 2012. *Honours:* Hon. Fellow, John Moores Univ. 2000, Univ. of Northampton 2003; Hon. DLitt (Aston Univ.) 2006; Hon. DMus (Birmingham) 2002, (Royal Scottish Acad. of Music and Drama) 2008, (Open Univ.) 2013; BASCA Gold Badge Award 2011, Lifetime Achievement Award, British Folk Festival 2012. *Address:* c/o JABA, 72 New Bond Street, London, W1S 1RR, England (office). *Website:* www.joanarmatrading.com (office).

ARMSTRONG, Billie Joe; American singer and musician (guitar); b. 17 Feb. 1972, San Pablo, Calif.; m. Adrienne Nesser 1994; two s. *Career:* Founding mem., Sweet Children, renamed Green Day 1989–; numerous tours and television appearances; side projects include Pinhead Gunpowder, Screeching Weasel, The Network and Foxboro Hot Tubs. *Recordings include:* albums: with Green Day: 39/Smooth 1990, Kerplunk 1991, Dookie 1994, Insomniac 1994, Nimrod 1997, Warning 2000, International Superhits (compilation) 2001, Shenanigans 2002, American Idiot (Grammy Award for Best Rock Album 2005, MTV Europe Music Award for Best Album 2005, American Music Award for Favorite Pop/Rock Album 2005, BRIT Award for Best Int. Album 2006) 2004, 21st Century Breakdown (Grammy Award for Best Rock Album 2010) 2009, ¡Uno! 2012, ¡Dos! 2012, ¡Tres! 2012; with The Network: Money Money 2020 2003; with Foxboro Hot Tubs: Stop Drop and Roll!!! 2008. *Honours:* Australian MTV Awards for Best Group 2005, for Best Rock Video (for American Idiot) 2005, MTV Award for Best Rock Video, Best Group Video (both for Boulevard of Broken Dreams), Best Group, MTV Viewer's Choice Award 2005, Kerrang! Awards for Best Band on the Planet, Best Live Act 2005, NME Award for Best Video (for American Idiot) 2005, MTV Europe Music Awards for Best Rock Act 2005, 2009, 2013, Billboard 200 Album Group of the Year 2005, Billboard Music Awards for Pop Group of the Year, for Hot 100 Group of the Year, for Rock Artist of the Year, for Rock Song of the Year (for Boulevard of Broken Dreams), for Modern Rock Artist of the Year 2005, Grammy Award for Record of the Year (for Boulevard of Broken Dreams) 2006, BRIT Award for Best Int. Group 2006, ASCAP Awards for Creative Voice, and for Song of the Year (for Boulevard of Broken Dreams) 2006, American Music Award for Favorite Rock Artist 2009. *E-mail:* info@greenday .com (office). *Website:* www.greenday.com.

ARMSTRONG, Craig, OBE; British composer; b. 1959, Shettleston, Scotland. *Education:* Royal Acad. of Music. *Career:* resident student composer, London Contemporary Dance Theatre 1980; music and dance specialist, Strathclyde Council 1982; founder of performance music, theatre and dance group 1988;

fmr mem., Hipsway, The Big Dish, The Kindness of Strangers, Texas; worked with Björk, Evan Dando, Massive Attack, Madonna, McAlmont, Luciano Pavarotti, Tina Turner, U2; f. Winona (with Scott Fraser) 2007–. *Recordings include:* albums: Hope 1993, The Space Between Us 1998, As If To Nothing 2002, Piano Works 2004, Memory Takes My Hand 2008; with Winona: Rosebud 2008. *Compositions for films include:* Daddy's Gone 1994, Close 1995, Fridge 1995, A Good Day for the Bad Guys 1995, Romeo and Juliet (Ivor Novello Award, Anthony Asquith Award, BAFTA Award) 1996, Orphans 1997, Best Laid Plans 1998, Plunkett & Macleane 1998, One Day in September (documentary) 1999, The Bone Collector (ASCAP Award) 1999, Moulin Rouge! (Golden Globe for Best Original Music 2001, IF Award 2001) 2000, Kiss of the Dragon 2001, The Quiet American 2002, Love Actually 2003, The Clearing 2004, Ray 2004, Fever Pitch 2005, Must Love Dogs 2005, Ray (Grammy Award for Best Score Soundtrack Album for Motion Picture, Television or Other Visual Media 2006) 2005, The Incredible Hulk 2008, Wall Street: Money Never Sleeps 2010, In Time 2011, The Great Gatsby 2013; contrib. music to Mission Impossible, Goldeneye, Batman Forever, Spider-Man 2 (Escape). *Compositions for television include:* Encounters (BBC2) 1991, Tartan Shorts (STV) 1994, London Bridge (Carlton) 1995. *Other compositions:* 7 Stations 1985, String Quartet 1988, Crow 1988, Losing Alec 1988 score to Macbeth (Tron Theatre) 1993, score to The Broken Heart (RSC, Barbican) 1994, If Time Must Pass 1999, When Morning Turns To Light 2000, My Grandmother's Love Letters 2000, Visconti 2001, Northern Sounds...Islands 2002, One Minute 2005, Immer (violin concerto) 2007, The Lady from the Sea (opera) 2012. *Honours:* GLAA Young Jazz Musician of the Year 1980, World Soundtrack Award for Discovery of the Year 2001, American Film Inst. Award for Composer of the Year 2001, Grammy Award for Best Score Soundtrack Album for Motion Picture, Television or Other Visual Media 2005. *Current Management:* IE Music Ltd., 111 Frithville Gardens, London W12 7JQ, England. *Telephone:* (20) 8600-3400. *Fax:* (20) 8600-3401. *E-mail:* info@ iemusic.co.uk. *Website:* www.iemusic.co.uk. *E-mail:* contact@ craigarmstrongonline.com (office). *Website:* www.craigarmstrong.com.

ARMSTRONG, Dido Florian Cloud de Bounevialle (see Dido)

ARMSTRONG, Roland (Rollo); British producer; brother of Dido. *Career:* prod. of British house music; established own label Cheeky Records 1991; produced Felix's single, Don't You Want Me 1992; began remixing numerous artists, including Pet Shop Boys, Gabrielle, M People, Wonder Stuff, Ian Wright, Björk, Simply Red; produced hit singles for Out Tribe and High on Love; founding mem., Faithless 1995–. *Recordings as producer/remixer:* Pet Shop Boys: Absolutely Fabulous (remixer), Disco 2 (remixer), Can You Forgive Her (remixer); Black Grape: Get Higher (remixer); Olive: You're Not Alone (producer/remixer); Sliding Doors (film soundtrack, producer/remixer); Dido: No Angel (co-producer) 2001. *Recordings:* albums: with Faithless: Reverence 1996, Reverence/Irreverance, Sunday 8pm 1998, Saturday 3am 1999, Back to Mine (compilation of other artists' work) 2001, Outrospective 2001, Reperspective 2002, No Roots 2004, To All the New Arrivals 2006, The Dance 2010; solo: Dusted: Safe From Harm 2005. *Address:* Faithless Live Ltd, PO Box 17336, London, NW5 4WP, England (office). *E-mail:* info@faithless.co.uk (office). *Website:* www.faithless.co.uk.

ARMSTRONG, Timothy (Tim) Lockwood; American singer, musician (guitar) and producer; b. 1966; m. Brody Armstrong 1998. *Career:* fmr mem., Operation Ivy, Downfall; Founder mem., Rancid (with Matt Freeman); started own record label, HellCat Records 1996; produced numerous albums. *Recordings include:* albums: with Rancid: Rancid 1993, Let's Go 1994, And Out Come The Wolves 1995, Life Won't Wait 1998, Rancid 2000, Indestructible 2003, B Sides and C Sides 2008, Let the Dominoes Fall 2009; with Transplants: Transplants 2002, Haunted Cities 2005, In a Warzone 2013; solo: A Poet's Life 2007, Tim Timebomb's Rocknroll Theater 2012. *Address:* c/o HellCat Records, 2798 Sunset Blvd, Los Angeles, CA 90026, USA (office). *Telephone:* (213) 355-5000. *E-mail:* info@hell-cat.com (office). *Website:* www .hell-cat.com (office); www.ratsinthehallway.com; www.rancidrancid.com.

ARMSTRONG, Timothy Paul; New Zealand singer and songwriter; b. 10 Feb. 1961, Birmingham, England. *Career:* mem. The Politicians 1981–86, Tim Armstrong band 1987–; numerous TV appearances. *Recordings include:* albums: Relationships 1992, Breaking Hearts 1993, Wondering Why 1995, Tomorrow 2011, Before my time 2014, Life is Just a Lesson 2015. *Honours:* Waikato Rock Award for Best Male Vocalist, Best Recorded Work. *Address:* 483 Hauraki Road, RD4, Thames, 3574, New Zealand (home). *Telephone:* (7) 867-5414 (office). *E-mail:* kiwibandits@xtra.co.nz (office). *Website:* www .timarmstrongband.com (office).

ARNESEN, Dag S.; Norwegian musician (piano) and composer; b. 3 May 1950, Bergen; m. Wenche Gausdal 1986. *Education:* Music Conservatory, Bergen. *Career:* Norwegian television (NRV) appearances with own group, Ny Bris; project for Vossa Jazz, eight-piece band including Elvin Jones (drums), Jon Surman (saxophone), Palle Danielson (bass); with Joe Henderson, Woody Shaw Quintet; extensive touring with own trio; mem. FNJ, NOPA, GRAMART. *Recordings include:* albums: Ny Bris 1982, Renascent 1984, The Day After 1990, Photographs 1992, Movin' 1994, Wandering Around Grieg 1996, Inner Lines 1998, Time Enough 2005, Norwegian Song 2007, Norwegian Song 2 2008, Norwegian Song 3 2010. *Honours:* Vossa Jazz Prize 1992, Grieg Prize 1994, Statoil/Sildajazz Prize 2003, Buddy Award 2009. *Address:* Gutenbergs V6 18, 5034 Bergen, Norway. *E-mail:* dag@mulemusic .no. *Website:* www.mulemusic.no.

ARNOLD, Cheryl Christine; American country singer; b. 23 April 1951, Seattle; m. Michael Stipek 1979; three s. (triplets). *Education:* Washington Univ. *Career:* country singer 1980–; support act for country artistes including: Lorrie Morgan 1982, Hoyt Axton 1984, Loretta Lynn 1984, Ricky Nelson 1985, Johnny Cash 1988, Reba McEntire 1989, Glen Campbell 1990; co-f. Blue Mariah Band; mem. Acad. of Country Music, Country Music Asscn. *E-mail:* info@bluemariahband.com. *Website:* www.bluemariahband.com.

ARNOLD, David; British composer; b. 1962, Luton, England. *Career:* mem. British Academy of Songwriters, Composers and Authors (BASCA); collaborations with musical acts including Cast, The Cardigans, Kaiser Chiefs, Massive Attack, Pulp, and solo artists Natasha Bedingfield, Melanie C, Björk, Chris Cornell, Shirley Manson, Mark Morriss; apptd Musical Dir for 2012 Olympic Games and 2012 Paralympic Games, London. *Compositions for film and TV include:* The Young Americans 1993, Stargate 1994, Last of the Dogmen 1995, Independence Day (Grammy Award) 1996, Stargate SG-1 (TV theme) 1997, The Visitor (TV theme) 1997, A Life Less Ordinary 1997, Tomorrow Never Dies 1997, Godzilla 1998, Wing Commander (theme) 1999, The World is Not Enough 1999, Randall & Hopkirk (TV) 2000, Shaft 2000, Baby Boy 2001, The Musketeer 2002, Little Britain (TV theme), Casino Royale 2006, Amazing Grace 2006, Quantum of Solace 2008, How to Lose Friends & Alienate People 2008, Sherlock (TV theme) 2010. *Film appearance:* The Young Americans 1993. *Television appearances include:* The League of Gentlemen 2000, Little Britain 2003. *Current Management:* Blue Focus Management, 15233 Ventura Blvd, Suite 200, Sherman Oaks, CA 91403, USA. *Website:* www.davidarnold.com.

ARNOLD, Kristine; American singer; b. 28 Nov. 1956, Torrance, Calif.; m. Leonard Arnold; two d. *Career:* mem. duo, Sweethearts of the Rodeo (with sister Janis Gill) 1975–, winners, Wrangler Country Showcase 1985. *Recordings include:* Sweethearts of The Rodeo 1986, One Time One Night 1988, Buffalo Zone 1990, Sisters 1992, Rodeo Waltz 1993, Beautiful Lies 1996. *Honours:* Vocal Duo, Country Music Asscn (nine consecutive years), Music City News Award, Best Vocal Duo, Viewer's Choice Awards, The Nashville Network (TNN), Favourite Group, Nat. Asscn of Ind. Record Distributors (NAIRD) Award for Best Country Album 1994. *Current Management:* c/o Tony Conway, Ontourage Management, 1625 Broadway Suite, 500 Nashville, TN 37203, USA. *Telephone:* (615) 724-1813. *Fax:* (615) 724-1813. *E-mail:* info@conwayent.com. *Website:* www.conwayent.com.

ARNOLD, P. P.; American soul singer; b. (Patricia Ann Cole), 1946, Los Angeles, CA; m. David Arnold; one s. one d. *Career:* singer in church choirs; mem. of Ike and Tina Turner's backing group, The Ikettes 1966; mem. of backing trio, The Nice 1966; solo artist 1967–; numerous live and television appearances; toured as session singer with the Beatmasters, Dr John, Freddie King, Nils Lofgren, Oasis, Ocean Colour Scene, Primal Scream, Small Faces, Roger Waters, Paul Weller; formed Band of Angels 1999. *Musicals:* Catch My Soul 1969, Jesus Christ Superstar 1970, Starlight Express 1984, Once on this Island 1994. *Recordings include:* albums: First Lady of Immediate 1967, Kafunta 1968, The First Cut 1998, Different Drum 1998, Salobrena 2000, Temptation 2001; with Imagination: Body Talk 1981, In the Heat of the Night 1982, Night Dubbing 1983, Scandalous 1983, Angel 1986, Imagination 1989; with Dr Robert: Five in the Afternoon 2007. *Current Management:* Elizabeth H. McLean, 6 Homedale Place, Prudhoe, Northumberland NE42 5AZ, England. *E-mail:* contact@pparnold.com. *Website:* www.pparnold.com.

ARRIALE, Lynne, BMus, MMus; American jazz musician (piano), composer and educator; *Associate Professor of Jazz Studies and Director of Small Ensembles, University of North Florida, Jacksonville;* b. 29 May 1957, Milwaukee, Wisconsin. *Education:* Wisconsin Conservatory of Music. *Career:* tour of Japan with 100 Golden Fingers (featuring Tommy Flanagan, Hank Jones, Monty Alexander, Cedar Walton, etc.); extensive int. festival and concert tours, including Mary Lou Williams Jazz Festival at the Kennedy Center, The Gilmore, Spoleto Arts, Montreux, Montreal, Monterey, North Sea, Burghausen, Stuttgart, Pori, San Francisco, Ottawa, Zagreb, Perth and Brisbane Jazz Festivals and in S Africa with full symphony orchestra; featured on Profile of a Recording Artist (PBS), on numerous Nat. Public Radio (NPR) programmes and in Billboard, Downbeat, JazzTimes; live media appearances include CNN/FN' Biz, NPR's Jazz Piano Christmas – Live from The Kennedy Center, and radio/TV interviews throughout USA, UK and Europe, including BBC, Radio France and German Nat. Television; headline performance at Jazz Educ. Network Convention with her quartet, featuring Randy Brecker 2011; has worked with Montreux Jazz Competition, American Pianists Asscn Fellowship Awards, The Kennedy Center's Mary Lou Williams Competition, Jacksonville Piano Competition; Assoc. Prof. of Jazz Studies and Dir of Small Ensembles, Univ. of North Florida, Jacksonville; Faculty mem. Jamey Aebersold Summer Jazz Workshops, Centrum Port Townsend Jazz Workshop, Thelonious Monk Inst., Aspen, Colo; featured mentor at The Mary Lou Williams Emerging Artist Workshop at the Kennedy Center; conducts educational clinics and master-classes world-wide; invited as one of Yamaha Artists in Educ. 2011. *Television:* multiple live concerts for NDR, including Live at Burghausen, Live at the Stuttgart Jazz Festival. *Recordings include:* albums: The Eyes Have It 1994, When You Listen 1995, With Words Unspoken 1996, A Long Road Home 1997, Melody 1998, Live At Montreux (Critic's Choice Reader's Guide Magazine—Neil Tesser) 2000, Inspiration (Jazz Week Radio #1, New Yorker Magazine's Best CDs 2003, German Record Critics Award) 2002, Arise (Billboard #20, Jazz Week Radio #1, Jazz Review Editor's Choice) 2002, Come Together (Billboard #17, UPI's Best Jazz CDs

2003, #1 Jazz Week Radio) 2004, Lynne Arriale Trio LIVE (German Record Critics Award) 2005, Nuance (CD of the month for the three German audio magazines, CD of the Month Audio, CD of the Month Stereo, Star of the Month Fono Forum, SESAC Nat. Performance Activity Award) 2008, Convergence (in top 50 CDs of 2011, JazzTimes, in top 10 CDs of 2011, Ken Franckling's Jazz Notes) 2011. *Publications:* articles in Downbeat, JazzED Magazine, Jazz Inside Magazine, JazzTimes. *Honours:* Winner, Great American Jazz Piano Competition 1993, German Record Critics Award, SESAC Nat. Performance Award. *Address:* 4300 South Beach Parkway 2107, Jacksonville Beach, FL 32250, USA (office). *Telephone:* (813) 944-9186 (office). *E-mail:* arriale@aol.com (office). *E-mail:* lynne@lynnearriale.com. *Website:* www.lynnearriale.com.

ARSON, Nicholaus; Swedish musician (guitar); b. (Nicholaus Almqvist), 1977. *Career:* mem., The Hives 1993–. *Recordings:* albums: Barely Legal 1997, Veni Vidi Vicious 2000, Your New Favourite Band (compilation) 2001, Tyrannosaurus Lives 2004, The Black and White Album 2007, Lex Hives 2012. *Honours:* NME Award for Best Int. Band 2003. *Address:* The Hives, Regnbågsvägen 46, 737 43 Fagersta, Sweden. *E-mail:* TheHives@goldve.com. *Website:* www.myspace.com/thehives; www.thehivesbroadcastingservice.com.

ARTHUR, Davey; Irish musician (multi-instrumentalist), singer, composer, arts consultant and music publisher; b. (David Arthur), 24 Sept. 1954, Donegal; s. of David Arthur and Brigit Connaghan; m. Jo-Ann Arthur; four s. five d. *Education:* Univ. of Edinburgh, UK. *Career:* appeared with The Buskers, Tam Linn; Founder-mem. The Fureys and Davey Arthur 1980, The Davey Arthur Band, Davey Arthur and Fionnuala Gill; Dir, Humblebum Publishing; Founder-mem. Bd Culture Ireland (Irish state agency). *Recordings:* The Cisco Special 1960, Songs Of Woody Guthrie 1961, I Ain't Got No Home 1962, The Sound Of The Fureys And Davey Arthur 1981, When You Were Sweet Sixteen 1982, Steal Away 1983, In Concert 1984, Golden Days 1984, At The End Of A Perfect Day 1985, The First Leaves Of Autumn 1986, The Fureys Finest 1987, The Fureys Collection 1989, The Scattering 1989, The Very Best Of 1991, The Winds Of Change 1992, Celtic Sidesaddle 2000, Cut to the Chase 2002, The Reel Years 2005, Common Ground 2010, Into the Light 2011. *Address:* Celtic Works, Cloghane, Linehan, Cahersiveen, Co. Kerry, Ireland. *Telephone:* 87-1420305 (mobile); (76) 6025455 (office). *E-mail:* daveyarthur@eircom.net (home); info@daveyarthur.net. *Website:* www.daveyarthur.ie; www.myspace.com/daveyarthur.

ARTHUR, Joseph Lyburn; American singer, musician (guitar) and songwriter; b. 28 Sept. 1972, Akron, Ohio. *Career:* sings with backing band, The Lonely Astronauts. *Film appearance:* The Dream Catcher 1999. *Film music:* Pigeonholed (composer) 1999, Shrek 2 (contrib.) 2004. *Television includes:* contribs: The O.C. 2003, True Blood 2008, House M.D. 2008, Hung 2009, Numb3rs 2009, Late Night with Jimmy Fallon 2010, Conan 2010. *Recordings include:* albums: Big City Secrets 1997, Come to Where I'm From 2000, Redemption's Son 2002, Our Shadows Will Remain 2004, Nuclear Daydream 2006, Let's Just Be 2007, Temporary People 2008, The Graduation Ceremony 2011, Redemption City 2012. *Current Management:* c/o Peter Wark, Wark DKD Management, 4446 Blvd, St-Laurent, Suite 801, Montreal, PQ H2W 1Z5, Canada. *Telephone:* (514) 939-3775. *Fax:* (514) 904-0626. *E-mail:* peter@dkd.com. *E-mail:* jaquestions@josepharthur.com. *Website:* www.josepharthur.com.

THE ARTIST (see Prince)

ARVANITAKI, Eleftheria; Greek singer; b. 16 Oct. 1958, Athens; m. George Hadjimichalis; two c. *Career:* mem., Opisthodromiki Kompania 1980–85; solo artist 1984–. *Recordings include:* albums: with Opisthodromiki Kompania: Stis Xanthis, sto Aiginitio, sto Armatagogo Kos 1982, Mia Nichta me tin Opisthodromiki Kompania 1983, Sti Mesi tis Kompanias 1984; solo: Eleftheria Arvanitaki 1984, Contraband 1986, Tanirama 1989, Meno Ektos 1991, I Nichta Kateveni 1993, The Bodies and the Knives 1994, Ta Kormia ke ta Maheria (with Ara Dinkjian) 1994, Tragoudia gia tous mines 1996, Off the Road 1998, Broadcast 2001, Live at the Gyalino Mousiko Theatro 2003, Live 2003, Three Songs 2004, Ola sto fos 2004, Dromoi Parallhoi 2005, Stis akres ap'ta matia sou 2006, Grigora I wra perase 2006, Dynata 1986–2007 2007, Mirame 2008, Mercury 2010. *Television:* Leoforos A 1987. *Honours:* two Greek Music Awards for Best Female Singer of the Year. *Current Management:* 41 Kapodistriou Avenue, 152 37 Athens, Greece. *Telephone:* (210) 6813411. *Fax:* (210) 6828613. *E-mail:* oinoi1@otenet.gri. *Website:* www.arvanitaki.gr.

ARVIZU, Reginald 'Fieldy Snuts'; American musician (bass guitar). *Career:* Founder mem., L.A.P.D. (Love and Peace, Dude) 1989, renamed KoRn 1992–; numerous tours and live appearances; formed Fieldy's Dreams 2000–. *Recordings include:* albums: with L.A.P.D.: Love And Peace, Dude (EP) 1989, Who's Laughing Now 1991, L.A.P.D. 1997; with KoRn: Korn 1994, Life Is Peachy 1996, Follow The Leader 1998, Issues 1999, Untouchables 2002, Take A Look In The Mirror 2003, See You On The Other Side 2005, Untitled 2007, Korn III: Remember Who You Are 2010, The Essential Korn 2011, The Path of Totality 2011, Paradigm Shift 2013; solo: Fieldy's Dreams: Rock 'N' Roll Gangster 2002. *Publication:* Got the Life: My Journey of Addiction, Faith, Recovery, and Korn (autobiography) 2009. *Website:* www.korn.com.

AS ONE (see Degiorgio, Kirk)

ÁSGÍMSSON, Andri; Icelandic musician (keyboards). *Career:* mem., Leaves 2004–. *Recordings include:* albums: Breathe 2002, The Angela Test 2005, We Are Shadows 2009. *E-mail:* leaves@leaves.is. *Website:* www.leaves.is.

ASHANTHI; Sri Lankan R&B and hip hop singer, rapper, songwriter and record producer; b. (Ashanthi de Alwis). *Career:* fmr singer with Bathiya and Santhush; mem. of duo Ashanthi'n'Ranidu 2003–05, first R&B/hip-hop artist from Sri Lanka to sign to an int. record label; solo artist 2006–; collaborator with Dinesh K, Benny Dayal, Randhir, Reshmonu; f. Ashanthi's School of Music professional music school 2009. *Television:* Yes Superstar (judge) 2010, Sirasa Mega Sangeeth (Sri Lankan version of The Voice) (judge and mentor) 2011–12. *Recordings include:* with Ashanthi'n'Ranidu: Obe Magemai 2003; solo: Sandawathuren 2006, Daas Panawa 2011, Rock the World 2012. *Honours:* Shanghai Asia Music Festival Winner of Most Promising Singer Award, China 2000, Golden Clef Music Award for Song of the Year (for Angel) 2003, Derana Music Video Awards for Best Hip Hop Video (for Alwanthiyak) 2008, for Best Baila Music Video of the Year (for Papare) 2011, IndieGo Music Asia Awards for Best Female Singer (Gold) 2011, for Best Pop Act of Asia (Silver), for Best Hip Hop Act of Asia 2011 and Honorary Award for Most Creative and Innovative Act 2011, Bite My Music Global Award for Best Pop Act (Gold) 2011, Junior Chamber of Commerce TOYP (Ten Outstanding Young Personalities) Award for Contribution to the Arts 2012. *Address:* c/o Ashanthi's School of Music, 304/14 Park Road, Colombo, 5, Sri Lanka (office). *E-mail:* management@ashanthi.com. *Website:* www.ashanthi.com.

ASHANTI; American hip-hop and R&B singer, songwriter and actress; b. (Ashanti Douglas), 13 Oct. 1980, Glen Cove, New York; d. of Ken-Kaide Thomas Douglas and Tina Douglas. *Career:* signed record deal when 14 years old; guest vocalist with artists, including Big Punisher, Ja Rule, J. Lo, Big Pun, Fat Joe, Notorious B.I.G.; solo artist 2002–. *Television appearances:* Polly (musical film), American Dreams (one episode) 2002, Buffy the Vampire Slayer (one episode) 2003, The Muppets' Wizard of Oz (TV film) 2005. *Film appearances:* Bride & Prejudice 2004, Coach Carter 2005, John Tucker Must Die 2006, Resident Evil: Extinction 2007. *Recordings include:* albums: Ashanti 2002 (Grammy Award for Best Contemporary R&B Album 2003), Foolish/Unfoolish: Reflections on Love 2002, Chapter II 2003, Ashanti's Christmas 2003, Concrete Rose 2004, The Declaration 2008, Braveheart 2014. *Honours:* Music of Black Origin (MOBO) Award for Best R&B Act 2002, American Music Awards for Best New Pop/Rock Artist, Best New Hip Hop/R&B Artist 2003, Nat. Asscn for the Advancement of Colored People (NAACP) Image Award, Comet Award, Teen Choice Award, Nickelodeon's Kid Choice Award. *Website:* ashantithisisme.com.

ASHCROFT, Richard; British singer, songwriter and musician (guitar); b. 11 Sept. 1971; m. Kate Radley; one s. *Career:* Founder mem. and lead singer Verve 1989, renamed The Verve 1994–99, 2007–09; numerous festival performances; solo artist 2000–, Founder mem. United Nations of Sound 2009–. *Recordings include:* albums: with The Verve: A Storm in Heaven 1993, No Come Down 1994, A Northern Soul 1995, Urban Hymns (BRIT Award for Best British Album 1998, Q Award for Classic Album 2007) 1997, Forth 2008; solo: Alone With Everybody 2000, Human Conditions 2002, Keys To The World 2006; with United Nations of Sound: United Nations of Sound 2010. *Honours:* BRIT Award for Best British Group (with The Verve) 1998. *Current Management:* Big Life Management, 67–69 Chalton Street, London NW1 1HY, England. *Telephone:* (20) 7554-2100. *Fax:* (20) 7554-2101. *Website:* biglifemanagement.com; www.richardashcroftonline.com.

ASHER, James; British composer, producer and musician (keyboard, drums); b. 4 Sept. 1950, Eastbourne, Sussex. *Education:* Grade VI violin. *Career:* sound engineer, R. G. Jones studio, London; mem. APC, REPRO. *Compositions:* wrote and recorded over 20 albums library music; films and television include: La Filiere Chinoise (Cinema Euro Group), Gems (Thames Television), The Boat Show (BBC2), The Plant (Screen One); television station idents for: Central, Granada, MTV USA, Future Television Lebanon, European Superchannel; television themes for: Ulster Television news, Channel 4 rugby programme. *Recordings:* albums: The Great Wheel 1990, Globalarium 1993, Dance of the Light 1995, Rivers of Life 1996, Feet in the Soil 1996, Tigers of the Raj 1998, Raising the Rhythms 1999, Feet in the Soil 2 2000, Colours of Trance (with harpist Madeleine Doherty) 2000, Kali Thunder 2001, Atlantean Chants 2001, Sounding the Stones (with Arthur Hull) 2003, Drums of Fire (with Sivamani) 2003, Words Within the Wheel 2004, Lotus Path 2004, Bravado Masala (with Mahesh Vinayakram) 2008, Dev-Aura Chronicles Volume 1 2010; as drummer: Empty Glass, Pete Townshend; single: Peppermint Lump (produced by Pete Townshend); producer for: Ritchie, John 'Rabbit' Bundrick, Asha. *Address:* 44 Milton Road, Eastbourne, Sussex BN21 1SW, England. *E-mail:* jamesa@jamesasher.co.uk (home). *Website:* www.james-asher.co.uk (home).

ASHER, Peter, CBE; British manager, record producer, singer and musician (guitar); b. 22 June 1944, London, London; m. Wendy Worth 1983; one d. *Education:* King's Coll., London. *Career:* mem. duo, Peter and Gordon 1964–68; Head of A&R, Apple Records 1968–70; produced, signed, James Taylor; Founder Peter Asher Management, USA; management, production of Linda Ronstadt; Sr Vice-Pres. Sony Music Entertainment 1995–2002, Consultant 2002–; Co-Pres. Sanctuary Artist Man. Inc. 2002–05, Pres. Sanctuary Artist Man. North America 2005–; representation includes Peter Blakeley, Chicano Soul'n Power, Iris DeMent, The Innocence Mission, Little Feat, Kirsty MacColl, Maria Fatal, Mariachi Los Campaneros de Nati Cano, Randy Newman, Over The Rhine, Linda Ronstadt, Laura Satterfield, James Taylor, Williams Brothers, Warren Zevon; dept for management of major record producers, engineers, including Phil Ramone, George Massenburg. *Recordings include:* albums produced include: with 10,000 Maniacs: In My Tribe 1987, Blind Man's Zoo 1989; with Linda Ronstadt: Canciones de mi padre 1987, Cry Like A Rainstorm, Howl Like The Wind 1989, Frenesi 1992; with Mary's Danish: American Standard 1992; with Neil Diamond: The Christmas Album 1992, The Christmas Album Vol. 2 1994; with Randy Newman: Faust 1995; with Chantal Kreviazuk: Under These Rocks and Stones 1997; with Julia Fordham: Collection 1999; with Amanda Marshall Everybody's Got a Story 2002; with Wilson Phillips: California 2004; with Diana Ross: I Love You 2006; with Carole King and James Taylor: Live at the Troubadour 2010; with Steve Martin and Edie Brickell: Love Has Come for You 2013; albums or tracks for: Paul Jones, Barbara Keith, Tony Kosinec, Jo Mama, John Stewart, Kate Taylor, Tony Joe White, Andrew Gold, John David Souther, Bonnie Raitt, Ronin, Cher, Peter Blakeley, Maria McKee, Williams Brothers, Diana Ross, Julia Fordham, Ringo Starr, Olivia Newton-John, Laura Satterfield, Dixie Chicks. *Honours:* Grammy Award for Producer of the Year 1978, 1989, Grammy Award for Best Spoken Comedy Album (Live 2002) 2002. *Telephone:* (720) 220-8742. *E-mail:* rkputney@gmail.com; KPutney@aol .com. *Website:* keithputneyproductions.com; peterashermusic.com.

ASHER, Phil; British producer, remixer and DJ; b. 3 Jan. 1966, London. *Career:* world-wide DJ; compiler of Jazz In The House album series for Kickin' Music; mem., Restless Soul, Pascal's Bongo Massive, Two Shiny Heads, Electric Soul; collaborations: Orin Walters, Luke McCarty, Nathan Haine. *Recordings:* Albums: Sound Travels (with Nathan Haines), 2001; Singles: Pascal's Bongo Massive Vol. 1, 1991; Vol. 2, 1992; Vol. 3, 1993; Let Go (with Two Shiny Heads), 1992; Dub House Disco (with Two Shiny Heads), 1992; Mama (with Restless Soul), 1997; Psykodelik (with Restless Soul), 1997; Phlash 3000 Parts 1 and 2 (as Phlash), 2000; Earth Is The Place (with Nathan Haines), 2001. *Current Management:* c/o Phlash Music, Suite B, 2 Tunstall Rd, London SW9 2DA, England. *E-mail:* info@restlesssoul.co.uk. *Website:* www .restlesssoul.co.uk.

ASHILAAKO BILANSO MBO, Djonimbo; Democratic Republic of the Congo country singer, musician (guitar, flute), composer and artist; b. 3 July 1969, Bolobo; two s. *Education:* degree in secondary studies. *Career:* numerous appearances on nat. TV and radio 1984–; playing character in stories for the Francophone Photo Magazine, Amina; singer with Planete Lolingo Band, 1976; Tout Grand Nania Band, 1979; Credo Band; 1980; Fa-Sol Band, 1983–; mem, National Society of Artists. *Compositions:* Si Bonne, Si Belle, Si Compliquée... La Vie, 1989; Bosso Bikali, 1993. *Recordings:* La Vie est Belle et Compliquée, 1996. *Honours:* First Prize, Radio Challenge for Family Planning, 1986; Third Prize, poetry and song challenge, Goethe Institute, 1987; First Prize, National Song Festival, 1991; Second Prize, Song Festival, French Embassy, 1998. *Address:* BP 18525, Kinshasa 13, Democratic Republic of the Congo.

ASHLEY, Steve Frank, BA, DipAD; British singer, songwriter and musician (guitar, bouzouki, harmonica, whistle); b. 1946, London; m. Elizabeth Mary Holborow; one s. one d. *Education:* Ealing Coll. of Art, Maidstone Coll. of Art. *Career:* Founder mem. Albion Country Band 1972; formed Ragged Robin 1973; solo tours of Europe and USA; tv and radio appearances 1974–79, including Family Album (performed with members of Fairport Convention); Peace Songs for CND; formed Steve Ashley Band 1983; tours of Europe, including festivals at Glastonbury, Cambridge and Cropredy; mem. Mechanical-Copyright Protection Soc., Performing Right Soc., Performing Artists Media Rights Asscn, PPL. *Compositions include:* songs: Fire and Wine, Candlemas Carol, Spirit of Christmas, Duke of Cambridge, The Rough With The Smooth, Once in a While, Feelin' Lazy, Say Goodbye, Gog and Magog, Ships of Shame, This Old English Town, Best Wishes, People in Love, That's Why, In Your Heart. *Television includes:* music for Roger Deakin's TV documentaries: Ballad of the Ten Rod Plot 1991, Stable Lads (for Anglia) 1993. *Recordings include:* albums: Stroll On (Contemporary Folk Album of the Year, Folk Review) 1974, Speedy Return 1975, Demo Tapes 1980, Family Album 1981, More Demo Tapes 1983, Mysterious Ways 1990, The Test Of Time 1999, Stroll on Revisited 1999, Everyday Lives 2001, Live In Concert 2006, Time and Tide 2007, This Little Game 2015. *E-mail:* steve@steveashley.co.uk. *Website:* www .steveashley.co.uk.

ASHTON, William (Bill) Michael, OBE, MBE, BA, DipEd; British musician (saxophones, clarinet), composer, bandleader, songwriter and journalist; *Founding Musical Director, National Youth Jazz Orchestra;* b. 6 Dec. 1936, Blackpool; m. Kay Ashton (née Watkins); three c. *Education:* St Peter's Coll., Oxford. *Career:* Founder univ. dance band, The Ambassadors; OU Big Band; Founder, Sec., OU Modern Jazz Club; Taught in France 1960–61; played US bases with The Stardust Combo, Caveau Des Fouleurs, Chateaudun, France; worked in Red Bludd's Bluesicians, London; Co-founder with Pat Evans, The London Schools Jazz Orchestra, later renamed The London Youth, then The Nat. Youth Jazz Orchestra (NYJO); worked full-time with NYJO 1973–, fmr Chair., currently Founding Musical Dir, played world-wide, made numerous television appearances, and recorded over 45 albums; Royal Variety Performance 1978; toured twice with Shorty Rogers, John Dankworth, John Williams, and many singers; Founder publishing co., Stanza Music 1967; numerous compositions for NYJO; Fellow, Leeds Coll. of Music 1995. *Recordings include:* with National Youth Jazz Orchestra, Live at London Weekend Television 1975, These Are The Jokes 1996, View From The Hill 1996, In Control 1999.

Publications include: Ed., News from NYJO (quarterly magazine). *Honours:* Inter-Univ. Jazz Band Competition Award 1962, Critics Choice 1992, 1995, British Jazz Award, Best British Big Band 1993, 1995, 2002, BBC Radio 2 Award, Services to Jazz 1995, Special Award, All-Party Parliamentary Jazz Group. *Address:* National Youth Jazz Orchestra, 11 Victor Road, Harrow, Middlesex, HA2 6PT, England (office). *Telephone:* (20) 8863-2717 (home). *Fax:* (20) 8863-8685 (home). *E-mail:* info@nyjo.org.uk (office); bill.ashton@virgin .net (home). *Website:* www.nyjo.org.uk (office).

ASHWORTH, Stephanie; Australian musician (bass guitar); b. Perth, WA. *Career:* mem. Sandpit 1995; mem. trio Something For Kate 1998–. *Recordings include:* albums: with Sandpit: On Second Thought (compilation) 1998; with Something For Kate: Beautiful Sharks 1999, QandA With Dean Martin (compilation) 2000, Echolalia 2001, The Official Fiction 2003, Elsewhere for Eight Numbers 2004, Phantom Limbs 2004, Desert Lights 2006, The Murmur Years 2007. *Honours:* Australian Music Industry Critics Award for Album of the Year 2000, Australian Live Music Award for Best Live Act 2000, JJJ Listeners' Poll for Best Album 2001. *Address:* PO Box 2235, Prahran, Vic. 3181, Australia (office). *E-mail:* stephanie@somethingforkate.com (office). *Website:* www.somethingforkate.com (office).

ASLAM, Atif; Pakistani singer and actor; b. 12 March 1983, Wazirabad. *Education:* Univ. of Central Punjab. *Career:* fmr mem. band Jal; solo artist 2004–; has toured in USA and Canada. *Recordings include:* albums: Jalpari 2004, Doorie (Best Album, Lux Style Awards 2006) 2006, Meri Kahani 2008, The Dreamer Awakes 2011. *Films include:* Bol (actor and singer) 2011; as singer: Zeher 2005, Kalyug 2005, Bas Ek Pal 2006, Race 2008, Kismat Konnection 2008, Ajab Prem Ki Ghazab Khahani 2009, Prince 2010, Spanish Beauty 2010, F.A.L.T.U 2011. *Honours:* Indus Music Award (Best Lyrics, Best Song, Best Composition for song Aadat) 2005, Sahara Sangeet Award (Best Playback Singer) 2005, Musik Award (Most Wanted Male) 2006, 2008, Lycra MTV Style Award (Most Stylish Person in Music) 2007, Tamgha-e-Imtiaz 2008. *Telephone:* (50) 9208679. *E-mail:* info@aadeez.com. *Website:* www .aadeez.com.

ASQUITH, Stuart Andrew; British songwriter and musician (keyboard); b. 23 Sept. 1971, Wakefield. *Education:* studied piano and keyboard. *Career:* made White Label dance record under name, Mind Vacation 1992, changed name to Lost In Process; signed to Ouch! Records 1995; mem. Musicians' Union. *Recordings:* Ain't We Funky/Sustain The Pressure 1995, Pacemaker/ We Can Do This 1995, Rock On 1995, Made In Rio 1995.

ASSAF, Mohammed; Palestinian singer; b. 1 Sept. 1989, Misrata, Libya. *Education:* Gaza City's Palestine Univ. *Career:* relocated with parents to Gaza 1993; made television debut 2000; series winner, Arab Idol 2013. *Television:* Arab Idol (series winner) 2013. *Recordings:* album: Assaf 2014. *Honours:* MTV Europe Music Award for Best Africa/India/Middle East Act 2014. *Address:* c/o Platinum Records, MBC Group, Dubai, United Arab Emirates (office). *Website:* www.mbc.net/en.html (office); www.mohammedassaf442.com.

ASTATKE, Mulatu; Ethiopian composer, arranger and musician (vibraphone, conga, organ); b. 1943, Jimma. *Education:* Lindisfarne Coll. and Trinity Coll. of Music, Berklee Coll. of Music, USA. *Career:* credited as being the founder of 'Ethio-jazz', a fusion of traditional Ethiopian music with jazz and Latin influences; performed with numerous official state bands in Ethiopia during 1960s and 1970s; performed with Duke Ellington on his visit to Ethiopia 1971; int. concerts include the Kennedy Center, Washington, DC, Lincoln Center, New York, Beethoven-Haus, Bonn, Barbican Centre, London; Fellow, Radcliffe Inst., Harvard Univ. 2007–08. *Film soundtracks:* Broken Flowers 2005. *Recordings include:* Mulatu of Ethiopia, Ethio Jazz, From New York City to Addis Ababa: The Best of Mulatu Astatke, Assiyo Bellema, Ethiopiques Vol. 4, Inspiration Information, Mulatu Steps Ahead 2010, Timeless: Live at Luckmann Theatre, LA 1 Feb 2009 2010, Sketches of Ethiopia 2013. *Honours:* Hon. DMus (Berklee Coll. of Music) 2012; Red Sea Medal for Fine Arts, Ethiopia 1986, Soc. of Ethiopians Established in Diaspora Award 2006, Berklee Achievement Award. *Address:* c/o Buda Musique, 37 rue des Vignerons, 94300 Vincennes, France. *Telephone:* 1-41-74-02-09. *E-mail:* contact@budamusique.com. *Website:* www.budamusique.com; www.ethiojazz .com.

ASTBURY, Ian; British singer; b. 14 May 1962, Heswall, Merseyside, England. *Career:* founder, Southern Death Cult 1982, re-named Death Cult 1983, re-named The Cult 1984–95, re-formed 1999–; formed Holy Barbarians 1996–99; numerous tours in UK, Europe, N America, Japan; also festival appearances; singer, The Doors of the 21st Century tour 2002–03. *Recordings:* albums: with The Cult: Southern Death Cult 1983, Dreamtime 1984, Love 1985, Electric 1987, Sonic Temple 1989, Ceremony 1991, Pure Cult 1993, The Cult 1994, Ghost Dance 1996, High Octane Cult 1996, Cream 1996, Celebrity Deathmatch 1999, Zen Mafia 1999, Beyond Good And Evil 2001, Born Into This 2007, Choice of Weapon 2012. *Current Management:* Tom Vitorino Management Inc., 11606 Vimy Road, Granada Hills, CA 91344, USA. *Telephone:* (818) 368-9060. *Fax:* (818) 368-9061. *Website:* www.thecult.us.

ASTLEY, Jon; British record producer; b. 22 Jan. 1951, Manchester, England; two d. *Career:* producer 1978–, for The Who, Eric Clapton, Corey Hart, Debbie Harry, Pete Townshend, LSO and LPO; remixing and remastering extensive catalogues of The Who, Eric Clapton, Pete Townshend, Tori Amos, Abba, Level 42, Ash, Judas Priest, Slade, Relish, Hothouse Flowers, Bon Jovi, Jools Holland, Emmylou Harris, Rolling Stones, Tears For Fears, George Harrison, Led Zeppelin; solo artist, songwriter 1986, 1988; mem. MCPS, PRS. *Recordings include:* albums: Everyone Loves The Pilot (Except The Crew) 1987, The Compleat Angler 1988. *Honours:* Cedar Award for Best CD Remastering for Led Zeppelin, George Harrison and 'Who's Next' by The Who, V.S.D.A Award for The Who Live at Royal Albert Hall, DVD2002 Surround Music Award for Pete Townshend's Music From Lifehouse concert. *Address:* 2 Embankment, Twickenham, TW1 3DH, England. *Telephone:* (20) 8892-9236. *Website:* www.closetotheedge.biz (office).

ASTLEY, Rick; British singer and songwriter; b. 6 Feb. 1966, Warrington, Cheshire. *Career:* drummer in school band, Give Way 1982; lead singer, FBI 1984; apprenticeship, Stock/Aitken/Waterman 1985; tape operator, PWL Studios 1986; solo artist 1987–; presenter, weekly show, Magic 105.4 2010–; numerous concerts and tours. *Recordings include:* albums: Whenever You Need Somebody 1987, Hold Me In Your Arms 1988, Free 1991, Body And Soul 1992, Keep It Turned On 2001, Love Songs 2004, Portrait 2005, Together Fovever: The Best of Rick Astley 2007, The Very Best of Rick Astley 2008, Whenever You Need Somebody Deluxe Edition 2010, Hold Me In Your Arms Deluxe Edition 2010. *Honours:* BRIT Award for Best British Single (for Never Gonna Give You Up) 1988, two Billboard Awards 1988. *Current Management:* c/o The Agency Group, 361–373 City Road, London, EC1V 1PQ, England. *E-mail:* neil@rickastley.co.uk. *Website:* www.rickastley.co.uk.

ASTON, Michael Philip; British musician, artist and singer; b. 22 Aug. 1957, Bridgend, Wales; m. Margaret La Guardia 1992. *Career:* lead singer, Gene Loves Jezebel; tours, radio and television broadcasts. *Film appearance:* She's Having a Baby 1986. *Recordings:* albums: with Gene Loves Jezebel: Promise 1983, Immigrant 1985, Discover 1986, House Of Dolls 1988, From The Mouth Of Babes; Love Lies Bleeding 1999, Voodoo Dollies, Giving Up the Ghost 2001, Exploding Girls 2003; with Edith Grove: Edith Grove, 1995; solo: Why Me Why This Why Now, 1995. *Honours:* T. J. Martel MVP 1995, Song of Year, Desire, College USA 1986. *Address:* 1419 N Hayworth Ave, Los Angeles, CA 90046, USA. *E-mail:* michaelphilip@sbcglobal.net. *Website:* www .genelovesjezebel.com.

ASTRAUSKAS, Rimantas, MA, DH; Lithuanian ethnomusicologist and producer; *Associate Professor of Ethnomusicology, Lithuanian Academy of Music and Theatre;* b. 9 April 1954, Kaunas. *Education:* Kaunas J. Gruodis Higher Music School, Lithuanian State Conservatoire, Lithuanian Acad. of Music, Univ. of Oxford, UK, Danish Folk Song Archives, Copenhagen, Bergen Univ., Norway, Univ. of Tampere. *Career:* Producer, Lithuanian State TV and Radio Cttee 1978–88; Lecturer, Lithuanian Acad. of Music and Theatre 1988–95, Assoc. Prof. of Ethnomusicology 1995–; Chair. Council for the Protection of Ethnic Culture, Lithuanian Parl. 2000–02; UNESCO Expert on Intangible Cultural Heritage; mem. Int. Org. of Folk Art, Int. Council for Traditional Music, European Seminar in Ethnomusicology, Lithuanian Composers' Union. *Compositions:* author of more than 500 TV and radio broadcasts on various musical topics and events; documentary film: Išaudes Šokio Rašta (co-author). *Publications:* Typological Classification of Tunes (ed.) 1996, Ritual and Music (ed.) 1999, Folk Culture at the Beginning of the Third Millennium (ed.) 2001, Ethnic Relations and Musical Folklore (ed.) 2002, Traditional Music and Research in the Baltic Area – New Approaches in Ethnomusicology (ed.) 2005, Almanac 'M. K. Ciurlionis and the World' (ed.) 2005; more than 30 articles on Lithuanian traditional music. *Honours:* Special Award, Best Broadcast at Int. Contest of Musical Broadcasts, Kishinew 1982. *Address:* Gedimino pr. 42, 01110 Vilnius (office); V. Grybo 1/29-11, 10313 Vilnius, LT 55, Lithuania (home). *Telephone:* (5) 2612691 (office); (5) 2711106 (home). *Fax:* (5) 2120093 (office); (5) 2711106 (home). *E-mail:* astram@delfi.lt. *Website:* www.lma.lt (office).

ASTRO; British musician (trumpet), singer and MC; b. (Terence Wilson), 24 June 1957, Birmingham. *Education:* Golden Hillock comprehensive school. *Career:* mem. reggae group UB40 1978–; numerous concerts, tours. *Recordings include:* albums: Signing Off 1980, Present Arms 1981, The Singles Album 1982, UB44 1982, Labour of Love 1983, Live 1983, More UB40 Music 1983, Geffery Morgan 1984, Baggariddim 1985, Little Baggaridim 1985, UB40 File 1985, Rat In The Kitchen 1986, CCCP: Live In Moscow 1987, UB40 1988, Labour of Love II 1990, Promises and Lies 1993, Anansi 1995, Guns In The Ghetto 1997, Labour of Love III 1998, Presents The Dancehall Album 1998, Homegrown 2003, Who You Fighting For? 2005, TwentyFourSeven 2008. *Current Management:* c/o Part Rock Management Limited, 1 Conduit Street, London, W1S 2XA, England. *Telephone:* (20) 8207-1418. *E-mail:* stewartyoung@mindspring.com. *Address:* UB40, PO Box 15345, Birmingham, B9 9GJ (office); DEP International Limited, PO Box 117, Birmingham, B5 5RG, England (office). *E-mail:* info@ub40.co.uk (office). *Website:* www.ub40.co .uk (office).

ATB; German producer, remixer and DJ; b. (Andre Tanneberger), 1973, Freiberg. *Recordings:* eight studio albums, six 'in the mix' compilations, two Sunset Beach DJ Session compilation and four DVDs. *Current Management:* c/o Dancefield Office, Raiffeisenstrasse 2A, 53639 Königswinter, Germany. *Telephone:* (2244) 9181500. *Fax:* (2244) 9181555. *E-mail:* info@dancefield.com. *Website:* www.dancefield.com; www.atb-music.com.

ATKINS, Bobby Lee; American musician (guitar, banjo), singer and songwriter; b. 22 May 1933, Shoals, North Carolina; m. Judy Smit 1961; six s. one d. *Career:* began with Bill Monroe and the Bluegrass Boys; played with Charlie Monroe, Flint Hill Playboys; played with Joe Stone for 15 years; played with Joe and the Dixie Mountaineers; formed own band, Bobby Atkins and The Countrymen 1967; songwriter, composer, arranger Bob's Special Music Publishing Co.; performed on stage with Mac Wiseman, Clyde Moody, Jim Fanes; on radio with Flatt and Scruggs, Don Reno, Red Smiley; mem. Country and Bluegrass Music Asscn. *Recordings include:* over 100 albums and two film scores including: Crimes Of The Heart, Gold Hill Gold, The Best Of Bobby Atkins, Mark Albin And The Country, The Country Side of Bobby Atkins, We Do It For You. *Address:* PO Box 251, Summerfield, NC 27358, USA (office). *Telephone:* (334) 274-3301 (office).

ATKINS, Juan, (Model 500, Infiniti); American producer, remixer and DJ; b. 12 Sept. 1962, Detroit. *Career:* techno innovator; contributed to the establishment of the techno genre as part of the Belleville Three (with Derrick May and Kevin Saunderson); mem. Cybotron; collaborations: Derrick May, Kevin Saunderson, Maurizio. *Film:* High Tech Soul 2006. *Recordings include:* albums: Enter (with Cybotron) 1983, Sonic Sunset 1994, Deep Space 1995, Skynet (as Infiniti) 1998, Mind And Body 1999, The Berlin Sessions 2005; singles: Clear (with Cybotron) 1983; as Model 500: No UFO's 1985, Night Drive (Thru Babylon) 1985, Technicolor 1986, Sound Of Stereo 1987, Interference 1988, The Chase 1989, Ocean To Ocean 1990, Jazz Is The Teacher 1993, The Flow 1995, I Wanna Be There 1996, Game One (as Infiniti) 1996, Be Brave 1999, OFI/Huesca 2010. *Current Management:* Deejay Booking, 144 Rue de Livourne, 1000 Brussels, Belgium. *Telephone:* (2) 647-96-74. *Fax:* (2) 644-18-20. *E-mail:* info@deejaybooking.com. *Website:* www .deejaybooking.com.

ATKINS, Mark; Australian musician (didgeridoo, guitar, harmonica, drums), composer, artist and storyteller; b. 1959, WA. *Career:* collaborator with numerous composers and musicians, including Philip Glass, Jimmy Page, Robert Plant, Dónal Lunny, Peter Sculthorpe, James Morrison, Jenny Morris, John Williamson; current mem. The Black Arm Band. *Recordings include:* albums: solo: Didgeridoo Concerto 1994, Plays Didgeridoo 1995, City Circles 1996, The Sound of Gondwana 1997, Didgeridoo Dreamtime 1999, Didge Odyssey (with Parris and Pu-Yu Macleod) 2004, Creeper Vines and Times 2005, Didge Odyssey 2006, The Reason To Breathe 2006, The Bushman 2010, Dreamtime 2011; with Ankala: Rhythms from the Outer Core 1997; with Ankala & The World Orchestra: Didje Blows the Games 2000. *Honours:* Winner, Golden Didgeridoo Competition 1990. *Current Management:* c/o Marguerite Pepper Productions, PO Box 1711, Potts Point, NSW 1335, Australia. *Telephone:* (2) 9357-7857. *E-mail:* info@mpproductions.com.au. *Website:* www.mpproductions.com.au. *E-mail:* markdatkins@hotmail.com (office).

ATLAS, Natacha; Belgian singer and dancer; b. 20 March 1964, Brussels. *Career:* fmrly a singer in various bands in Northampton, England; returned to Belgium and worked in Arabic and Turkish nightclubs; singer with Mandanga, Belgian salsa band; singer on projects with ¡Loca! and Jah Wobble 1991–; mem., Trans-Global Underground (TGU); numerous live and festival appearances internationally; worked with musicians, including Apache Indian, Peter Gabriel, David Arnold. *Recordings include:* albums: with Trans-Global Underground: International Times; solo: Diaspora 1995, Halim 1998, Gedida 1999, The Remix Collection 2000, Ayeshteni 2001, Something Dangerous 2003, Mish Maoul 2006, Ana Hina 2008, Mounqaliba 2010; other: Habibi: Classics and Collaborations 2013, Expressions: Live in Toulouse 2013. *Honours:* Nuit de Clip Award (for video of Amulet), Tunisia. *Address:* c/o World Village Music, 1117 Chestnut Street, Burbank, CA 91506, USA. *E-mail:* lisa@redozmusic.com (office); info-wvm@worldvillagemusic.com. *Website:* www.worldvillagemusic.com.

ATTISSO, Barthélemy; Togolese musician (guitar) and lawyer. *Career:* mem. Star Band, Club Miami, Dakar, Senegal 1968–70; Founder mem. and orchestral dir, Orchestra Baobab 1970–85, originally at Club Baobab to 1977, then Jandeer Club, Balafon Club to 1978, time spent in Paris, then at Ngalam Club to 1985; Orchestra Baobab re-formed 2001–, resident at Club 4U Club, Dakar; full-time lawyer, Togo. *Recordings include:* albums: M'Beugene 1972, Hommage à Lay M'Boop 1974, Orchestre Baobab '75 1975, Guy Gu Rey Gi 1975, Senegaal Sunugaal 1975, Visage du Sénégal 1975, Aduna Jarul Naawoo 1975, N'Deleng N'Deleng 1977, Une Nuit Aun Jandeer 1978, Baobab à Paris Vols 1 and 2 1978, Gouygui Dou Daanou 1979, Mohamadou Bamba 1980, Sibou Odia 1980, Ken Dou Werente (re-released as Pirate's Choice 2001) 1982, On Verra Ça: The 1978 Paris Sessions 1992, Bamba 1993, Specialist in All Styles (BBC Radio 3 Awards for World Music Critic's Award for Album of the Year 2003) 2002, A Night at Club Baobab 2006, Made in Dakar 2007, La Belle Epoque 2009, The Rough Guide to Psychedelic Africa 2012. *Honours:* BBC Radio 3 Awards for World Music, Africa Region 2003. *Address:* c/o World Circuit Records, First Floor, Shoreditch Stables, 138 Kingsland Road, London, E2 8DY, England. *E-mail:* post@worldcircuit.co.uk. *Website:* www .worldcircuit.co.uk.

ATZMON, Gilad; Israeli musician (saxophone, clarinet) and producer; b. 9 June 1963; m.; one d. *Education:* Rubin Acad. of Music, Jerusalem and Univ. of Sussex, UK. *Career:* producer for numerous Israeli jazz, dance and rock artists; toured with numerous major int. jazz artists, including Memphis Slim, Jack De Johnette, Richie Byrach; toured with Jazz Africa, joined Ian Dury And The Blockheads (later The Blockheads) as saxophonist 1998. *Recordings:* albums: with Spiel: Spiel 1993, The Spiel Acid Jazz Band 1995, Both Sides 1995; with The Gilad Atzmon Trio: Take It Or Leave It 1999; with DJ Face: Juizz Music 1999; with The Orient House Ensemble: Gilad Atzmon And The Orient House Ensemble 2000, Nostalgico 2001, Exile (BBC Jazz Award for

Best Album) 2003, Musik: Rearranging the 20th Century 2004, Refuge 2007, In Loving Memory of America 2009, The Tide Has Changed 2010; with The Blockheads: Where's the Party? 2004, Staring Down the Barrel 2009; solo: For the Ghosts Within (with Robert Wyatt and Ros Stephen) 2010. *Publications include:* Guide to the Perplexed 2002, My One and Only Love 2004. *Honours:* HMV Top Dog Award Birmingham Int. Jazz Festival 1996. *Address:* c/o Enja Records, PO Box 190333, 80603 Munich, Germany (office). *E-mail:* giladatzmon@mac.com (office). *Website:* www.gilad.co.uk; www.theblockheads .com.

AUBUT, Lise; Canadian songwriter; b. 29 Aug. 1943, Lévis, Quebec. *Education:* Coll. of Gen. and Vocational Educ. *Career:* songwriter, 15 musical albums and over 150 songs; mem. SPACQ, SODRAC, SACEM. *Compositions include:* hit songs: Paquetville, sung by Edith Butler; Un Million de Fois Je T'aime. *Honours:* three Felix Awards. *Address:* 86 Côte Ste Catherine, Outremont, PQ H2V 2A3, Canada (office). *Telephone:* (514) 270-9556 (office). *Fax:* (514) 270-4252 (office). *E-mail:* info@liseaubut.com (office). *Website:* liseaubut.com.

AUCH, Greg; American country musician (drums) and singer; b. 28 Jan. 1967, Charlotte, NC; m. Linda Auch; three s. *Career:* mem., The Moody Brothers, 1987–98; played guitar and drums, Disneyland Paris, 1992–98; fmr mem. Rocky Yelton and the Hired Guns; mem. National Academy of Recording Arts and Sciences. *Address:* 5900 Oakwielde Court, Charlotte, NC 28227, USA. *Website:* www.myspace.com/gregauch.

AUERBACH, Daniel (Dan) Quine; American singer, songwriter, producer and musician (guitar, bass guitar, keyboards); b. 14 May 1979, Akron, Ohio; s. of Charles Auerbach and Mary Little Quine. *Career:* fmr mem. The Barnburners; Founder-mem. The Black Keys 2001–. *Recordings include:* albums: with The Black Keys: The Big Come Up 2002, Thickfreakness 2003, Rubber Factory 2004, Magic Potion 2007, Attack & Release 2008, Blakroc (collaboration with Damon Dash and several rap artists) 2009, Brothers (Grammy Awards for Best Alternative Music Album and Best Recording Package 2010) 2010, El Camino (Grammy Award for Best Rock Album 2013) 2011, Turn Blue 2014; solo: Keep It Hid 2009; as producer and contributor: Radio Moscow, Radio Moscow 2007, Guts of Steel, Brimstone Howl 2007, Why Don't You Give it to Me?, Nathaniel Mayer 2007, Every Hour is a Dollar Gone, Patrick Sweany 2007, Let it Ride, Buffalo Killers 2008, With Blasphemy So Heartfelt, Jessica Lea Mayfield 2008, Why Won't You Let Me Be Black?, Nathaniel Mayer 2009. *Honours:* Grammy Award for Best Rock Performance by a Duo or Group with Vocals 2011, for Best Rock Performance, for Best Rock Song (Lonely Boy), for Producer of the Year (Non Classical) 2013, BRIT Award for Best Int. Group 2014. *Address:* c/o Nonesuch Records, Warner Music Group, 75 Rockefeller Plaza, New York, NY 10019, USA (office). *E-mail:* info@ nonesuch.com (office). *Website:* www.nonesuch.com (office); www .theblackkeys.com (home).

AUGÉ, Gaspard; French musician and producer; b. 21 May 1979, Besançon. *Career:* mem. Justice 2003–. *Recordings include:* albums: Waters of Nazareth 2005, Phantom 2007, DANCE 2007, † 2007, DVNO 2008, Audio, Video, Disco 2011, Access All Arenas 2013. *Honours:* MTV Europe Music Award for Best Video (for We Are Your Friends) 2006, (for DANCE) 2007, for Best French Act 2007, Victoires de la Musique for Best Electronic/Dance Act 2008, Grammy Award for Best Remixed Recording (for Electric Feel, MGMT) 2009. *Address:* c/o Ed Banger Records, Headbangers Entertainment, 10 rue Ramey, 75018 Paris, France. *Telephone:* 1-42-52-92-04. *E-mail:* contact@edbangerrecords .com. *Website:* www.edbangerrecords.com.

AUGER, Brian Albert Gordon; British musician (organ, piano), composer and producer; b. 18 July 1939, London, England; m. Ella Natale 1968; one s. two d. *Education:* Coll. of Marin, San Francisco, Calif., USA. *Career:* professional musician 1963–; performed with Brian Auger Trinity, Brian Auger's Oblivion Express, Eric Burdon/Brian Auger Band; worldwide tours; major TV shows in UK, Europe, USA, Japan, Czechoslovakia, Hungary, Greece; radio appearances world-wide. *Recordings:* No. 1 single: This Wheel's On Fire 1968; albums: Brian Auger Trinity And Julie Driscoll: Open 1967, Definitely What 1968, Streetnoise 1969, Brian Auger Trinity: Befour 1970: Brian Auger's Oblivion Express: Oblivion Express 1970, A Better Land 1971, Second Wind 1972, Closer To It 1973, Straight Ahead 1974, Reinforcements 1975, Live Oblivion, Vol. 1 1975, Vol. II 1976, Happiness Heartaches 1977, Encore 1978, Planet Earth Calling 1981, Here And Now 1983, Keys To The Heart 1987, Eric Burdon/Brian Auger Band: Access All Areas 1993, The Best Of Brian Auger 1997, Voices Of Other Times 2000, Looking in the Eye of the World 2005. *Honours:* Poll Winner, Jazz Piano and New Star categories, UK Melody Maker magazine 1963, German Rock and Folk Best Jazz and Best Rock Organist 1970, Best Jazz Organist, USA Keyboard Magazine 1976, 1977. *Current Management:* c/o Available Entertainment, 7095 Hollywood Boulevard, Suite 428, Hollywood, CA 90028, USA. *Telephone:* (213) 949-4801. *Fax:* (213) 710-6806. *E-mail:* info@availableentertainment.com. *Website:* www .availableentertainment.com. *E-mail:* info@brianauger.com (home). *Website:* www.brianauger.com (home).

AUSERÓN, Santiago, (Juan Perro); Spanish songwriter, singer and writer; b. 25 July 1954, Zaragoza; m. Catherine François 1979. *Education:* Universidad Complutense de Madrid, Université de Vincennes, Paris. *Career:* songwriter, singer, Radio Futura 1980–92; frequent travels to Cuba, seeking roots of Afro-hispanic sound 1984–; released historic compilation of traditions Semilla del Son 1991–92; began touring as Juan Perro, with flamenco, jazz, rock musicians 1993–; founder, La Fábrica de Tonadas 2003–; mem, Spanish Asscn of Interpreters and Authors, Independent Production Office, La Huella Sonora. *Recordings include:* with Radio Futura: Música Moderna 1980, La Estatua del Jardín Botánico 1982, La Ley del Desierto, La Ley del Mar 1984, De Un País En Llamas 1985, La Cancion de Juan Perro 1987, Escuela de Calor 1989, Veneno En La Piel 1990, Tierra Para Bailar 1992; solo (as Juan Perro): Raices Al Viento (including Spanish, Cuban, British musicians) 1995, La Huella Sonora 1997, Mr Hambre 2000, Cantares de Vela 2002; solo (as Santiago Auserón): Las Malas Lenguas (with Luis Auserón) 2006, Canciones de Santiago Auserón con la Original Jazz Orquestra 2008, Río Negro 2011. *Publications:* La Imagen Sonora 1998, Canciones de Radio Futura 1999; articles on music, art and philosophy, to newspapers and magazines. *Honours:* Medalla de Oro Santa Isabel de Portugal 2002; Radio Futura acclaimed as Best Spanish Rock Band of the 1980s (voted by radio stations, rock magazines), Premio Max de las Artes Escénicas 2001, Premio Trovador a las Artes Escénicas, Festival de Los Castillos 2007, Premio al mérito rockero. *Address:* Corazón de Maria, 6, 8° 1, 28002 Madrid, Spain (office). *Telephone:* (91) 4152525 (office). *Fax:* (91) 4169627 (office). *E-mail:* lhs@lahuellasonora.es (office). *Website:* www.lahuellasonora.com.

AUSTEN, Ed; British musician (guitar, bass, mandolin) and singer; b. (Edward John Roberts), 22 Dec. 1942, London, England. *Education:* studied classical guitar. *Career:* worked with: The Who, Free, Derek and The Dominoes, Eric Clapton, The Hollies, Dave Dee, Cliff Bennett, Robert Fripp, Andy Summers; many artists on country music circuit; mem Musicians' Union. *Address:* 417 Wimbourne Road E, Ferndown, Dorset BH22 9LZ, England (home). *Telephone:* (7950) 214295 (home).

AUSTIN, Dallas; American producer and songwriter; b. 29 Dec. 1970, Columbia, GA. *Career:* songwriter and producer for numerous artists including TLC, Madonna, Michael Jackson, Boyz II Men, Aretha Franklin, Sugababes, McFly, Gwen Stefani; founder, Rowdy Records 1992–. *Recordings include:* Troop, Attitude, musician, producer, 1989; Oooooooh... On The TLC Tip, arranger, producer, 1992; White Men Can't Jump, producer, drummer, 1992; DJ Jazzy Jeff And The Fresh Prince, Code Red, composer, producer, 1993; Hi Five, Faithful, producer, 1993; Joi, Pendulum Vibe, vocalist, producer, 1994; Madonna, Bedtime Stories, producer, 1994; Berry Gordy, Music, The Magic, The Memories, producer, 1995; Michael Jackson, History: Past, Present And Future, keyboards, producer, 1995; Boyz II Men, II: Yo Te Voy A Amar, producer, 1995; Fishbone, Chim Chim's Bad Ass Revenge, producer, 1996; Nutty Professor soundtrack, producer, 1996; Indigo Girls, Shaming Of The Sun, vocals, 1997; Michael Jackson, Blood On The Dance Floor, keyboards, producer, 1997; Aretha Franklin, Rose Is Still A Rose, arranger, producer, 1998; Brandy, Never Say Never, producer, 1998; N'Dea Davenport, producer, 1998; Monica, Boy is Mine, producer, 1998; TLC, Fanmail, arranger, vocals, 1999. *Address:* Rowdy Records, 75 Marietta Street, 6th Floor, Atlanta, GA 30305; DARP Studio Inc., 582 Trabert Avenue NW, Atlanta, GA 30309-2260, USA. *Telephone:* (404) 351-3736. *Website:* www .myspace.com/dallasaustin.

AUSTIN, Patti; American singer; b. 10 Aug. 1948, California. *Career:* child performer from age 3; appearances included Sammy Davis, Jr television show; theatre performances: Lost In The Stars; Finian's Rainbow; Tours with Quincy Jones, age 9; Harry Belafonte, age 16; recording debut, age 17; singer, television jingles, session work, 1970s; worked with: Paul Simon; Billy Joel; Frankie Valli; Joe Cocker; George Benson; Roberta Flack; Marshall Tucker; Steely Dan; The Blues Brothers. *Recordings include:* albums: End Of A Rainbow 1976, Havana Candy 1977, Live At The Bottom Line 1979, Body Language 1980, Every Home Should Have One 1981, Patti Austin 1984, Gettin' Away With Murder 1985, The Real Me 1988, Love's Gonna Get You 1990, Carry On 1991, Live 1992, That Secret Place 1994, In And Out Of Love 1998, Street Of Dreams 1999, On The Way To Love 2001, For Ella 2002, Church: Songs of Soul and Inspiration 2003, Baby Come to Me and Other Hits 2005, Love Collection 2005, Intimate Patti Austin 2007, Avant Gershwin (Grammy Award for Best Jazz Vocal Album 2008) 2007, Baby Come To Me 2009, I Really Don't Want Much for Xmas 2009, Sound Advice 2011; guest vocalist, album George Gershwin songs, Hollywood Bowl Orchestra 1992. *Honours:* Grammy Award (for The Dude) 1982. *Website:* www.pattiaustin .com.

AVALON, Frankie; American singer, musician (trumpet) and actor; b. (Francis Avallone), 18 Sept. 1939, Philadelphia; m. Kay Avalon; four s. four d. *Career:* began playing trumpet with Rocco and The Saints; numerous TV and live appearances. *Film appearances include:* Jamboree 1957, Guns of The Timberland 1960, The Alamo 1960, Sail A Crooked Ship 1962, Voyage To The Bottom of The Sea 1962, Beach Party 1963, Bikini Beach 1964, Muscle Beach Party 1964, The Carpetbaggers 1964, Beach Blanket Bingo 1965, I'll Take Sweden 1965, Sergeant Deadhead 1966, Fireball 500 1966, How To Stuff A Wild Bikini 1966, Skidoo 1968, The Take 1974, Grease 1978, Back To The Beach 1987, Troop Beverly Hills 1989, Twist 1992, The Stoned Age 1994, Casino 1995, Charlie Gracie Fabulous 1997, The Wages of Spin 2007, Mr Warmth: The Don Rickles Project 2007. *Recordings include:* De De Dinah 1957, Venus 1959, Bobby Sox To Stockings 1959, A Boy Without A Girl 1959, Just Ask Your Heart 1959, Why 1960, When The Good Guys Used To Win 1999; albums include: Swingin' On A Rainbow 1960, A Whole Lotta Frankie 1961, Frankie Avalon's Christmas Album 1962, Venus 1978, Fabulous Frankie Avalon 1991, Good Guys 1999. *Current Management:* c/o Alan Morell, Creative Management Partners, 433 North Camden Drive, 6th Floor, Beverly Hills, CA 90210, USA. *Telephone:* (508) 292-7900. *Website:* creativemanagementpartners.com; www.frankieavalon.com.

AVELLA, Vicente G.; Venezuelan Composer and Musician (piano); b. 27 Nov. 1970, Caracas; m. Kirsten Sollek-Avella, 27 Dec. 1996. *Education:* BM, Piano Performance, Indiana University, 1995; MM, Composition, Eastman School of Music, 1998. *Career:* Score to animations, A Spring Day, 1997, Up The Tree, 1999, by Glenn Ehlers; Outdone, by Dan Pejril; Score to independent film, A Night Less Ordinary, by John Rockefeller, 1999; Score to industrial video by The Greater Rochester Visitors Association; Performances by ALEA III, Boston, 1997, and Academic Octet of Caracas, Venezuela, 1998; Score to animation by Val Perkins, Bibbily Bobbily Job, 2000; Score to animation by Shaun Forster, The Diestmobile, 2000; Score to short film by E. Hannois, The Shell, 2001; mem, ASCAP; The Society of Composers and Lyricists. *Television:* as orchestrator: American Dad! 2008–09, Family Guy 2008–. *Compositions:* Different Beginnings, concerto for 2 drums and orchestra, 1998; Vegetaciones and In the Forestial Depths of the Day, songs for mezzo-soprano and chamber ensemble; String Quartet; Winter's Cold Light, for brass quintet; Songs of Sand, a set of songs for mezzo-soprano and piano, 2000. *Honours:* Second Place, 15th International Composition Competition for Young Composers, 1997; Bernard and Rose Sernoffsky Competition Prize, 1998. *Current Management:* Westwood Entertainment Group, 162 Chestnut Street, Suite 2, Rutherford, NJ 07070, USA. *Telephone:* (818) 505-8851. *E-mail:* vicente@ pandorasboombox.com. *Website:* www.pandorasboombox.com.

AVICII; Swedish DJ, record producer, remixer and musician (keyboards); b. (Tim Bergling), 8 Sept. 1989, Stockholm. *Career:* remixer and producer of dance tracks 2007–; debut release Manman issued via Pete Tong's record label Bedroom Bedlam; signed to At Night Management 2008; international hit singles with Levels 2011, Silhouettes 2012, Wake Me Up! 2013; collaborations with numerous artists including DJ Ralph, Sebastien Drums, Norman Doray, Oliver Ingrosso, Otto Knows, Leona Lewis, Lenny Kravitz, Eric Turner, Nicky Romero, David Guetta, Madonna, Björn Ulvaeus and Benny Andersson, Aloe Blacc; first DJ to headline Radio City Music Hall, New York 2012; co-founder, House for Hunger charity 2011. *Recordings include:* albums: as compiler: Avicii Presents Strictly Miami 2011, The Singles 2011; solo: True 2013, Stories 2015. *Honours:* American Music Award for Favorite Electronic Dance Music Artist 2013, MTV Europe Music Award for Best Electronic Act 2013, Billboard Music Award for Top Dance/Electronic Song (for Wake Me Up!) 2014, iHeartRadio Music Award for EDM Song of the Year (Wake Me Up!) 2014. *E-mail:* info@atnightmgmt.com. *Website:* www.atnightmgmt.com; www.avicii .com.

AVON, Alan; British singer, actor and songwriter; b. 25 Dec. 1945. *Education:* studied music and drama privately. *Career:* backing and session vocalist, London 1960s; lead singer, Hedgehoppers Anonymous; toured Europe, Southern Africa, UK 1965–72; solo artist 1972–; numerous radio, television, and live appearances; mem. Equity, British Acad. of Songwriters, Composers and Authors. *Recordings include:* album: Hey!; singles: Hey!, Song For Pete, Over The Rainbow; compositions featured on other artists' albums. *Honours:* SARI Awards for Best Male Vocalist, Best Album, Best British Group 1972. *Current Management:* c/o Dinosaur Promotions, 5 Heyburn Crescent, Westport Gardens, Stoke on Trent, Staffordshire ST6 4DL, England. *E-mail:* alan@alanavon.com. *Website:* www.alanavon.com.

AWADI, Didier; Senegalese rap artist and producer; b. 1969, Dakar. *Career:* pioneer of African hip-hop movt; co-f. group Positive Black Soul (PBS) 1989 (now PBS Radikal0); f. Studio Sankara, producing artists including Carlou D, Baye Souleye, Big D, Da Brains, Doug E Tee, Assane Gaye, Khady Mbaye. *Recordings include:* albums: with Positive Black Soul: Boul Faalé 1994, Run Cool 1997, Saalam, New York-Paris-Dakar 2003; solo: Kaddu Gor (Parole d'honneur) (Radio France Int. World Music Award 2003) 2002, Un Autre Monde Est Possible 2005, Présidents d'Afrique 2008, Sunugaal 2008. *Honours:* Chevalier des Arts et des Lettres 2005; RFI World Music award 2003, Best African Rapper, Tamani Awards (Mali) 2004. *Current Management:* c/o Studio Sankara, Sicap Amitie 3, N°4098, derrière hôpital Gaspard Camara, Dakar Fann, Senegal. *Telephone:* (8) 242024. *E-mail:* awadioffice@ yahoo.fr. *Website:* www.studiosankara.com.

AWOYINKA, Shiji, BEng, MSc; British singer, songwriter and musician (keyboards, percussion); b. 23 Oct. 1969, London. *Career:* Finalist, Sony Dance Music Search, 1993; Concerts: Ronnie Scott's, 1995; Orange, 1995; WKD, 1995; various pubs, clubs and cafés, New York City, 2003; collaborations with Salif Keita, Osunlade, Calvin Gaines, Alix Alvarez, Frenchie Thompson, The Platters, Vinia Mojica, Wunmi; mem. MCPS, PRS, Musicians' Union, ASCAP. *Recordings:* albums: God-given; singles: Facets (EP), My Lover's Embrace 1997, Feels Like, Sanctuary. *Address:* 15 Reynardsons Court, High Road, London N17 9HX, England; 330 Lenox Road, Apt 4u, Brooklyn, New York, NY 11226, USA (home). *Telephone:* (718) 675-7643. *E-mail:* shiji01@hotmail.com.

AXEL, Ian; American singer, songwriter and musician (piano, ukulele); b. 30 March 1985, Fair Lawn, New Jersey. *Education:* Fair Lawn High School, New York Univ. *Career:* Founder-mem. A Great Big World 2011–; collaborated with Christina Aguilera on second version of song Say Something 2013. *Recordings include:* albums: This is the New Year 2011; with A Great Big World: Is There Anybody Out There? 2013, When the Morning Comes 2015. *Honours:* Grammy Award for Best Pop Duo/Group Performance (for Say Something, with Christina Aguilera) 2015. *Current Management:* c/o Works Entertainment, 215 South La Cienega Boulevard, Suite 210, Beverly Hills, CA 90211,

USA. *E-mail:* luke@worksentertainment.com. *Website:* worksentertainment .com; ianaxel.com; www.agreatbigworld.com.

AXELROD, David; American composer, arranger and record producer; *Composer and Arranger, Local 47 AFM/RMALA;* b. 17 April 1936, Los Angeles, CA; s. of Morris Axelrod and Pearl Plaskow; m. Terry Axelrod; 3 s. (one deceased), one d. *Education:* Dorsey High School. *Career:* producer at Capitol Records 1960s–70s for numerous artists, including Lou Rawls, Stan Kenton, Harold Land, Hampton Hawes, Cannonball Adderley, Electric Prunes; solo artist; arranger and remixer, U.N.K.L.E; performed at Royal Festival Hall, London. *Films:* Cannonball, Vision's Playhouse. *Recordings:* 14 solo albums, including: Songs of Innocence 1968, Song of Experience 1969, Earth Rot 1970, David Axelrod's transcription of Handel's Messiah 1971, The Auction 1972, Heavy Axe 1974, Seriously Deep 1975, Strange Ladies 1977, Marchin' 1980, Requiem: The Holocaust 1993, The Big Country 1995, An Axelrod Anthology 1999. *Honours:* Grammy Awards (for Lou Rawls' Dead End Street) 1967, (for Cannonball Adderley's Mercy, Mercy, Mercy) 1967. *Current Management:* c/o Lisa Haugen, 28th Paradigm Management, PO Box 1000, Mill Valley, CA 94942, USA. *Telephone:* (415) 388-8545. *Fax:* (415) 388-8545. *E-mail:* LH@28thparadigm.com. *Website:* www.28thparadigm.com; www.davidaxelrodmusic.com.

AXWELL; Swedish DJ, songwriter and record producer; b. (Axel Christofer Hedfors), 18 Dec. 1977, Lund. *Career:* several singles as Quazar 1995–97, as OXL 1995–2001, as Soulplayaz 2001–05; collaborated with Isabel Fructuoso (as Mambana) 2001–05; worldwide hit song with Feel the Vibe 2004; worked with Steve Angello (as Supermode) 2006; also recorded under other aliases including Jetlag, Mahogany People, Starbeach, Axer; many collaborators including StoneBridge, Robbie Rivera, Evelyn Thomas, Errol Reid, Max'C, Cyndi Lauper, Dirty South, Bob Sinclar; numerous remixes for artists including Usher, N*E*R*D, Madonna, Nelly Furtado, Stonebridge, Deep Dish, Pharrell, Adele, The Temper Trap, Roger Sanchez, Hard Fi; mem. Swedish House Mafia (electronic dance music trio) 2007–13, numerous collaborations including Laidback Luke, Pharrell, Tinie Tempah, John Martin, Knife Party; remixers for Coldplay (Every Teardrop is a Waterfall). *Films:* Take One (documentary) 2010. *Recordings:* albums: solo: Axwell Presents Axtone 2010, Axtone Presents Thomas Gold Compilation 2012; with Swedish House Mafia: Until One 2010, Until Now 2012. *Honours:* Beatport Music Awards for Best House Artist 2008, 2009, for Best Remix (for remix of Dirty South's Let It Go) 2008; with Swedish House Mafia: MTV Europe Music Award for Best Swedish Act 2010, 2011. *Current Management:* c/o ATM Artists, 55 Kentish Town Road, London, NW1 8NX, England. *E-mail:* amy@atmartists.com. *Website:* www.atmartists.com; www.swedishhousemafia.com; www.axwell.co.uk.

AYACH, Ramy; Lebanese singer and songwriter; b. 18 Aug. 1980, Baakleen. *Career:* solo artist 1997–. *Recordings include:* albums: Rae'h 1997, Moujiza 1998, Walaah 1999, Diwan al-Hob 2000, Albi mal 2002, Ya msahar ayni 2004, Habbaytak ana 2006. *Honours:* Arab Music Award for Best Music Video (for Albi mal) 2002. *Address:* c/o Rotana, Burj al-Ghazal, 11th Floor, al-Tabaris, Achrafieh, Beirut, Lebanon (office). *E-mail:* info@rotana.net (office). *Website:* www.rotana.net (office); www.ramyayach.com.

AYACHE, Jennifer; French singer, songwriter; b. 9 Nov. 1983, d. of Chantal Lauby. *Career:* mem. Superbus 1998–; formed Wonderama project 2011. *Recordings include:* albums: Aéromusical 2002, Pop'N'Gum 2004, Wow 2006, Lova Lova 2009, Sunset 2012; Wonderama project: Make the Rules 2011. *Honours:* MTV Europe Music Award Best French Act 2005. *Website:* www .superbus.fr.

AYALA, Jose, (Joey Ayala), AB (Econ); Philippine singer-songwriter, performer, musician, arranger and producer; *President, Bagong Lumad Artists Foundation Inc.;* b. (Jose Inigo Homer Lacambra Ayala), 1 June 1956, M. Fortich, Bukidnon; s. of Jose V. Ayala, Jr and Tita A. Lacambra; m. Maria Jessie G. Sorongon; two s. *Education:* Ateneo de Manila, Elementary & High School, Ateneo de Davao, Asian Inst. of Man. *Career:* musical artist with theatre background; music production; popular education, environment/cultural icon; currently Pres. Bagong Lumad Artists Foundation Inc.; Chair. Nat. Cttee on Music 2008–10, Vice-Chair. 2011–13. *Films:* music for Brutus, Bagong Buwan, Donsol. *Compositions:* modern dance, Encantada 1992, Noche Buena 1995, I Hotel/The Fall 1997, Labaw Donggon, Mga Kuwento ni Lola Basyang. *Recordings:* Panganay Ng Umaga 1982, Magkabilaan 1986, Mga Awit ng Tanod-lupa 1991, Lumad Sa S'yudad 1992, Lupa't Langit 1997, Organik, Sita at Rama, 16 Love Songs 2003, Basta May Saging, Joey Ayala RAW, Mga Awit ng Magdaragat, Palay Bigas Kanin. *Publications:* SiningBayan: The Art of Nation-Building, Core Book: Palay Bigas Kanin. *Honours:* title of Mandiriwa; Ten Outstanding Young Men 1991, Awit Awards 1992, 1993, 1997, Katha Award 1997, City Govt of Davao Datu Bago Award 1998, Benigno Aquino Social Artistry Award 2009, MAGIS Award. *Telephone:* (2) 456-7665 (home). *E-mail:* joeyayala@blafi.org (office); mjessiea@yahoo.com (home). *Website:* www.blafi.org (office); www.joeyayala.com (home).

AYDIN, Emre; Turkish singer and songwriter; b. 2 Feb. 1981, Isparta; s. of Şaban Aydın and Nermin Aydın. *Education:* Dokuz Eylül Univ. *Career:* lead singer, 6.Cadde 1999–2003; now solo performer. *Recordings include:* with 6 Cadde: 6.Cadde 2003; solo: Afili Yalnizlik 2006, Kağıt Evler 2010, Beni Biraz Böyle Hatırla 2012. *Honours:* MTV Europe Music Award for Best European Act 2008. *Current Management:* c/o Hadi Elazzi, GRGDN, Mübayaci Sok No.5, 34470 Rumelihisari, Istanbul, Turkey. *Telephone:* (212) 2876287. *Fax:* (212)

2876216. *E-mail:* management@grgdn.com. *Website:* www.grgdn.com. *E-mail:* emreaydin@grgdn.com (home). *Website:* www.emreaydin.org.

AYERS, Nigel, BA; British composer and visual artist; b. 3 July 1957, Tideswell, Derbyshire. *Career:* f. pioneering multimedia performance group Nocturnal Emissions 1978; business ventures include record labels Sterile Records 1978, Earthly Delights 1987–; tours of Europe, USA, Canada, including performances with Butch Dance Company: Poppo and the GoGo Boys; exhibitions of video work in Tate Gallery and ICA, London; soundtracks for film work by Charlotte Bill; mem. MCPS, PRS, PPL. *Recordings include:* Tissue Of Lies 1978, Drowning In A Sea Of Bliss 1982, Viral Shedding 1983, Befehlsnotstand 1984, Spiritflesh 1988, Magnetized Light 1993, Glossalalia 1994, Imaginary Time 1995. *Publications include:* Network News, Vegetation Flesh 1995. *Honours:* Meet the Composer, New York 1992. *Address:* PO Box 2, Lostwithiel, PL22 OYY, England. *E-mail:* ayers.nigel@virgin.net. *Website:* www.nigelayers.com.

AYERS, Roy; American musician (vibraphone); b. 10 Sept. 1940, Los Angeles; m. Argerie J. Ayers 1973; two s. one d. *Career:* live performances and TV broadcasts; live film, Ronnie Scott's Jazz House London; mem., ASCAP; Local 802; American Federation of Musicians. *Compositions include:* Everybody Loves The Sunshine, Running Away, Love Will Bring Us Back, Searching. *Recordings include:* recorded 80 albums including: Wayne Henderson 1980, Music Of Many Colors 1980, Pre-Mixture 1981, Center Of The World 1981, Feeling Good 1982, Lots Of Love 1983, Silver Vibrations 1983, Drivin' On Up 1983, In The Dark 1984, You Might Be Surprised 1985, I'm The One 1987, Searchin' 1991, Drive 1992, Vibesman Live At Ronnie Scott's 1995, Essential Groove Live 1996, Spoken Word 1998, Juice 1999, For Café Après-midi 2002, Virgin Ubiquity: Unreleased Recordings 1976-1981 2004, Virgin Ubiquity II: Unreleased Recordings 1976-1981 2005, Virgin Ubiquity Remixed 2006, Perfection 2006; singles include: Get On Up Get On Down 1978, Heat Of The Beat (with Wayne Henderson) 1979, Don't Stop The Feeling 1980, Poo Poo La La 1984, Expansions (with Scott Grooves) 1998, Our Time is Coming 2001, Good Vibrations 2003. *Honours:* New Star on Vibes Downbeat Magazine 1966, American Music Award 1977, Louis Armstrong Award 1978, Best Song of Year for Get Money 1997. *Current Management:* Universal Attractions, 135 West 26th Street, 12th Floor, New York, NY 10001, USA. *Telephone:* (212) 582-7575. *Fax:* (212) 333-4508. *E-mail:* jepstein@universalattractions.com. *Website:* www.universalattractions.com; www.royayers.com.

AYICK, Paul; American musician (trumpet) and composer; b. 28 May 1947, Paterson, New Jersey; m. Rose Marie Kissel 1984; one d. *Education:* New York College of Music, New York University. *Career:* trumpeter with Ray Fernandez, 1972–75; Hugh Brodie, 1975–78; leader, Paul Ayick Quintet, 1978–88; co-leader with Ira Sullivan, 1990; also appeared with: Les Elgant; Ray Anthony; John Spider Martin; Little Anthony; Paul Cohen; Gene Krupa Band; mem, AFofM. *Address:* 4800 SW 70th Terrace, Davie, FL 33314, USA. *Telephone:* (954) 321-9368. *E-mail:* bulos@earthlink.net. *Website:* www .paulayickvintagebrass.com.

AYLLÓN, Eva; Peruvian singer; b. (María Angélica Ayllón Urbina), 6 Feb. 1956, Lima; m.; two c. *Career:* appeared with various groups, early 1970's, including Rinconcito Monsefuano, La peña de los Ugarte, Los Mundialistas o Callejón; lead singer, Los Kipus 1973–75; began touring internationally 1979; Founder mem., Los Hijos del Sol 1989; moved to USA 2003. *Recordings include:* albums: solo: Los Kipus y Eva 1977, Al ritmo de Eva Ayllón 1980, Cuando hacemos el amor 1982, Eva Ayllón en escena 1984, Para mi gente 1985, Huellas 1987, Lando de la vida y yo 1989, Eva siempre Eva 1990, Concierto de gala en vivo 1992, Gracias a la vida 1993, Para tenerte 1994, 25 años 25 éxitos 1995, Ritmo color y sabor 1996, Juntos llevamos la paz 1999, Eva! Leyenda Peruana 2004, Kimba fá 2009, Canta a Chabuca Granda 2010, Celebra 40 Años Enamorada Del Perú 2010; with Los Hijos del Sol: To My Country 2002. *E-mail:* jmori55@aol.com. *Website:* www.evaayllon.net.

AYRES, Ben; British musician (multi-instrumentalist) and songwriter. *Career:* mem., General Havoc –1991; founding mem., Cornershop 1992–; mem. Clinton; founder, owner, Meccico label 1998–. *Recordings:* Albums: with Cornershop: Hold On It Hurts 1994, Woman's Gotta Have It 1995, When I Was Born For The 7th Time 1997, Handcream For A Generation 2002, Judy Sucks a Lemon for Breakfast 2009, Urban Turban 2012; with Clinton: Disco And The Halfway To Discontent 1998. Singles: with Cornershop: In The Days Of Ford Cortina (EP) 1993, Lock Stock & Double Barrel (EP) 1993, Readers' Wives (EP) 1993, Born Disco, Died Heavy Metal 1994, Jullander Shere 1995, Wog (The Western Oriental Mixes) 1996, Butter The Soul 1996, Good Ships 1997, Brimful of Asha 1997, Sleep on the Left Side 1998, Lessons Learned from Rocky I to Rocky III 2002; with Clinton: Jam Jar 1995, Superloose 1996, Superloose (The Automator Remixes) 1997, David D. Chambers, Buttoned Down Disco, People Power in the Disco Hour. *Address:* c/o Oasis Productions, 36 W 20th Street, New York, NY 10011, USA. *E-mail:* info@cornershop.com. *Website:* www.cornershop.com.

AYRES, Mark Richard, BSc; British composer; b. 28 Dec. 1960, London; m. Nicola Jane 1993; two s. *Education:* University of Keele. *Career:* composer of music for films including: The Innocent Sleep; television including: Doctor Who, BBC, 1988–89; mem, British Academy of Composers and Songwriters; Musicians' Union; PRS; MCPS. *Compositions:* soundtracks: The Innocent Sleep, for soprano, orchestra; Doctor Who; numerous arrangements of film, television themes, for album release. *E-mail:* Mark_Ayres@compuserve.com (home). *Website:* ourworld.compuserve.com/homepages/Mark_Ayres (home).

AZALEA, Iggy; Australian rapper and songwriter; b. (Amethyst Amelia Kelly), 7 June 1990, Sydney, NSW; d. of Brendan Kelly and Tanya Kelly. *Career:* moved to USA 2006; issued first mixtape 2011; signed to T.I.'s record label Grand Hustle 2012; released first EP Glory 2012; opening act for Rita Ora UK tour 2013, for Nas European tour 2013, for Beyonce's tour of Australia 2013; several hit collaborations including T.I. (on Change Your Life), Ariana Grande (on Problem) and Charli XCX (on Fancy); other collaborations include Rita Ora, Jennifer Lopez. *Recordings:* mixtapes: Ignorant Art 2011; album: The New Classic (American Music Award for Favorite Rap/Hip-Hop Album 2014) 2014. *Honours:* American Music Award for Favorite Rap/Hip-Hop Artist 2014, ARIA Music Award for Breakthrough Artist 2014, MTV Video Music Award for Best Pop Video (for Problem, with Ariana Grande) 2014, MTV Europe Music Award for Best Song (for Problem) 2014, Billboard Music Awards for Top Rap Artist 2015, for Top Rap Song (for Fancy) 2015, for Top Streaming Artist 2015. *Current Management:* c/o Sarah Stennett, Turn First Artists, Grove Studios, Adie Road, London, W6 0PW, England. *Telephone:* (20) 8742-6700. *E-mail:* info@turnfirstartists.com. *Website:* www.turnfirstartists .com; iggyazalea.com.

AZMAT, Ali; Pakistani musician; b. 20 April 1970, Lahore. *Education:* Ashfield Business School, Sydney, Australia. *Career:* began musical career in band Jupiters, Lahore 1990; Founder-mem. Junoon (with Salman Ahmad and Brian O'Connell) 1990–, banned by Pakistani authorities for criticism of govt corruption early 1990s; upon invitation of UN Sec.-Gen., Kofi Annan, performed at UN Gen. Ass. (first band to play at Gen. Ass.) 2001; tours throughout Asia, N America, Middle East and Europe; Jazbe-e-Junoon selected as official song of cricket world cup, hosted by Pakistan 1996; simultaneous solo career 2002–. *Film music:* Paap (directed by Pooja Bhatt), Jism-2 2012. *Recordings include:* albums: with Junoon: Junoon 1990, Talaash 1993, Inquilaab 1995, Khashmakash 1996, Azaadi 1997, Parvaaz 1999, Andaz 2001, The Millennium Edition (compilation) 2000, Daur-e-Junoon 2002, Dewaar 2003; solo: Social Circus 2005, Klashinfolk 2008, Josh-E-Junoon 2010, Bum Phatta 2011, Chalta Mein Jaaon 2011, Josh 2012, Waar 2013, Babu Bhai 2014, Sawal 2014; singles: with Junoon: Jazbe-e-Junoon 1996, Saeein, Ehtesaab 1996, Sayonee 1997, Taara jala. *Honours:* Channel V Music Award for International Group 1998, UNESCO Award for Outstanding Achievement in Music and Peace 1999, BBC Asia Award 1999, Indus Music Award for Best Rock Band 2004. *Current Management:* Samina Ahmad, Junoon Inc., 210 Old Tappan Road, Tappan, NY 10983, USA. *E-mail:* saminadr@gmail.com (office). *Website:* aliazmat.com.

AZNAVOUR, Charles; French/Armenian film actor, singer and diplomatist; *Armenian Ambassador to Switzerland;* b. (Shahnour Vaghenag Aznavourian), 22 May 1924, s. of Mischa Aznavourian and Knar Baghdasaryan; m. 1st Micheline Rugel 1946; m. 2nd Evelyne Plessis 1955; m. 3rd Ulla Thorsel 1967; five c. *Education:* Ecole Centrale de T.S.F., Centre de Spectacle, Paris. *Career:* with Jean Dasté Company 1941; Man. Dir French-Music 1965–; Roving UNESCO Amb. to Armenia 1995–; Hon. Pres. Belgrade Film Festival 2003; numerous song recitals in Europe and USA; film music includes: Soupe au lait, L'île du bout du monde, Ces dames préfèrent le mambo, Le cercle vicieux, De quoi tu te mêles Daniela, Douce violence, Les Parisiennes; also author and singer of numerous songs; composer of operetta Monsieur Carnaval 1965, Douchka 1973; Armenian Amb. to Switzerland and Amb. and Perm. Rep. of Armenia to UNESCO, Paris 2009–. *Recordings include:* albums: Jazznavour 1998, Aznavour 2000, Colore ma vie 2007, Tú pintas mi vida 2008, Charles Aznavour et ses amis au Palais Garnier 2008. *Films and television include:* La tête contre les murs 1959, Tirez sur le pianiste 1960, Un taxi pour Tobrouk, Le testament d'Orphée, Le diable et les dix commandements, Haute-infidélité 1964, La métamorphose des cloportes 1965, Paris au mois d'août 1966, Le facteur s'en va-t-en guerre 1966, Candy 1969, Les intrus 1973, Sky Riders, Intervention Delta, Folies bourgeoises, Dix petits nègres 1976, The Twist 1976, The Tin Drum 1979, Qu'est-ce qui a fait courir David? 1982, Les fantômes du chapelier 1982, La montagne magique 1983, Vive la vie 1984, Mangeclous 1988, Il Maestro 1992, Les Années Campagne 1992, Pondichéry Dernier Comptoir des Indes 1996, Les Mômes 1999, Judaicaë I 2000, Laguna 2001, Angelina (TV) 2002, Passage du bac (TV) 2002, Ararat 2002, Le Père Goriot 2004, Emmenez-moi 2005. *Honours:* Commdr, Légion d'honneur 2004, Commdr des Arts et des Lettres, Russian Foreign Ministry's Badge 2014; Dr hc (Univ. of Montréal) 2009; numerous prizes including Grand Prix nat. de la chanson 1986, César d'honneur 1997, Time Magazine Entertainer of the Century 1998, Molière amical 1999, MIDEM Lifetime Achievement Award 2009, Grigor Lusavorich Award (Nagorno-Karabakh Republic) 2009. *Address:* Embassy of Armenia, Avenue du Mail 28, 1205 Geneva, Switzerland (office). *Telephone:* (22) 320-11-00 (office). *Fax:* (22) 320-61-48 (office). *E-mail:* mission .armenia@bluewin.ch (office). *Website:* www.switzerland.mfa.am (office); www.charlesaznavour-lesite.fr.

AZRAK, Janice; American record company executive; *Owner, EyeCon Productions;* b. 12 Dec. 1951, Brooklyn, New York. *Career:* publicist, MCA Records, New York 1971–76, SIR Productions, New York 1976–77; Vice-Pres., Creative Services/Artist Development, Warner Brothers Records, Nashville 1977–2004; currently Owner, EyeCon Productions; Vice-Pres. Bd of Dirs, Acad. of Country Music 1985–86. *Address:* EyeCon Productions, 7206 Elbert, Houston, TX 77027, USA (office).

AZZI, María Susana, MBA; Argentine cultural anthropologist; b. 12 Oct. 1952, Buenos Aires. *Education:* Colegio Mallinckrodt, Buenos Aires, Departamento de Letras, Universidad Católica Argentina, Buenos Aires, ESEADE, Buenos Aires. *Career:* Prof., Bd mem., Asoc. Reina de la Plata, Buenos Aires; Cultural Anthropologist, Facultad de Filosofia y Letras, Universidad de Buenos Aires; Bd mem. Fundación Astor Piazzolla, Buenos Aires; Lecturer on Argentina, the Tango, Astor Piazzolla's life and music, immigration to Argentina and on Antarctica, in Argentina, USA, Europe, Australia, Mexico and Korea; radio and TV appearances in Argentina, Australia, France, Italy, UK and USA; consultant for Sony Classical (USA), Dance Perspectives Foundation and Metropolitan Museum of Art, New York, Smithsonian Institution, Washington DC, Fundación Astor Piazzolla and Instituto Nacional de Antropología y Pensamiento Latinoamericano, Buenos Aires, Nat. Geographic Soc.; mem. Club del Progreso, Soc. for Ethnomusicology, American Anthropological Asscn, Int. Council for Traditional Music, Latin American Studies Asscn. *Publications include:* Italian Immigration and Their Impact on the Tango in Argentina 1997, Tango Argentino 1999, Le Grand Tango, The Life & Music of Astor Piazzolla (with Simon Collier) 2000 (translations in Spanish, Japanese, Korean and Polish), Pioneers of Argentine Industry 2008; album liner notes for Tango album by Yo-Yo Ma 1997, Pablo Ziegler's Asphalt 1998, Marcelo Alvarez's Carlos Gardel 1999, Gidon Kremer's album on Piazzolla's music 1999. *Address:* Posadas 1612 8°, Buenos Aires 1112, Argentina. *E-mail:* msa@mariasusanaazzi.com. *Website:* www .mariasusanaazzi.com.

B

B, Bela; German musician (drums), singer and songwriter; b. (Dirk Albert Felsenheimer), 14 Dec. 1962, Berlin. *Career:* comic book publisher and owner, Extrem Erfolgreich Enterprises –2006; mem. Attac (anti-globalisation movement) 2007–; Co-Founder and mem. punk rock band, Die Ärzte 1982–88, 1993–; Co-founder and mem. Depp Jones 1988–93; also solo career; numerous film and TV appearances. *Recordings include:* albums: Debil 1984, Im Schatten der Ärzte 1985, Die Ärzte 1986, Nach uns die Sintflut 1988, Das ist nicht die ganze Wahrheit ... 1988, Die Ärzte früher! 1989, Die Bestie in Menschengestalt 1993, Planet Punk 1995, Le Frisur 1996, 13 1998, Satanische Pferde 1999, Wir wollen nur deine Seele 1999, Runter mit den Spendierhosen, Unsichtbarer! 2000, Männer haben kein Gehirn 2001, 5, 6, 7, 8 - Bullenstaat 2001, Rock'n'Roll Realschule 2002, Geräusch 2003, Jazz ist anders 2007, Lied vom Scheitern 2008, auch 2012; solo: Bingo 2006, Code B 2009, Altes Arschloch Liebe 2009. *Address:* BPX 1992, Four Music Production GmbH, Schlegelstrasse 26b, 10115 Berlin, Germany (office). *E-mail:* impressum@bela-b.de (office). *Website:* www.bela-b.de; www.bademeister .com.

B., Eric; American DJ and MC; b. (Louis Eric Barrier), 8 Nov. 1965, Elmhurst, New York. *Career:* part of duo Eric B. & Rakim 1985–92; Owner, 95th Street (record label). *Recordings include:* albums: as Eric B. & Rakim: Paid In Full 1987, Follow The Leader 1988, Let The Rhythm Hit 'Em 1990, Don't Sweat The Technique 1992; solo: Eric B. 1995; singles: as Eric B. & Rakim: Eric B Is President 1986, Just A Beat 1988, Let The Rhythm Hit 'Em 1990, Move The Crowd 1990, Mahogany 1990, In The Ghetto 1990, What's On Your Mind 1991, Juice 1992, Don't Sweat The Technique 1992, Casualties Of War 1992, Microphone Fiend 1992, Eric B. Is President 1997, I Ain't No Joke 1997, I Know You Got Soul 1997.

B., Primož, BSc; Slovenian musician (guitar) and songwriter; b. (Primož Benko), 14 March 1977. *Career:* mem., Siddharta 1995–. *Recordings include:* albums: Id 1999, Nord 2001, Silikon Delta 2002, Rh- 2003, Petrolea 2006, Maraton 2007, Saga 2009. *Honours:* Viktor Award for Best Act 2003, 2004, 2006, for Special Achievement 2003, MTV Europe Music Award 2005. *Current Management:* Siddharta, PO Box 179, 1236 Trzin, Slovenia. *Telephone:* (4) 1382192. *E-mail:* info@siddharta.net. *Website:* www.siddharta.net.

B REAL; American singer and rap artist; b. (Louis Freese), 2 June 1970, South Gate, Los Angeles, Calif. *Career:* Founder-mem., DVX 1986, renamed Cypress Hill 1988–; host, Breal.tv. *Recordings include:* albums: with Cypress Hill: Cypress Hill 1991, Black Sunday 1993, Cypress Hill III: Temples of Boom 1996, IV 1998, Skull & Bones 2000, Live at the Fillmore 2000, Stoned Raiders 2001, Till Death Do Us Part 2004, Rise Up 2010, Cypress X Rusko 2012; solo: The Gunslinger, Vol. I 2004, Smoke N Mirrors 2009. *E-mail:* ebarkho@gmail .com; applesz6@aol.com. *Website:* www.cypresshill.com.

B-ROCK (see Litrell, Brian Thomas)

BABULJAK, Karel; Czech musician (keyboards, zither, guitar, drums), composer and poet; b. 5 Oct. 1957, Prague; m. 1st Barbora 1982; m. 2nd Tereza 1996; two s. two d. *Career:* musician and composer in rock, reggae, new age styles; Founder mem. of groups Relaxace 1979–, Mama Bubo 1983–, Vopruz 1983–, Sajkedelik Sraml Band 1992, Karel Babuljak and his Band of Dreams 1999, Kapela SNOO 1999; mem. of groups Babalet 1983–, Hypnotix 1988–90, Boothill 1998, Dreams (later changed to Snoo) 1999, Prvni Republika 2001–; collaboration with Theatre Prague 5, film Prague 5. *Recordings include:* albums: solo: Ha Ha Ha 1989, The Best of 89–90, A Way of Man 1991, A Mass Of Lany 1991, Organ Meditation 1991, Here and There 1991, Eryjon 1991, Kings Blues 1991, Bubol & Slon: I Have To Go 1992, Bubala 1993, Billiard Blues 1996, Bubol's Shouts from Darkness 1996, A Man with a Knapsack 1996, Oversmoked Blue Spirit 1997, Bubol's Collected Writings 1997, The Meeting 1997, Eastern Europe 1997, Teas 1999, Father Bubo 1999, The Bubol's Good While 2000, Bubol's Dreams 2001, Bubol in Myto 2001, Cehun Dub Rasta Music 2001, Morning in Unhosti 2002, Organ Sutra 2002, Sirloin 2002, Vakinu 2002, A Man Plays Zither 2002; with groups: Mama Bubo vol. one 1983, At the Macha's Sea 1984, Strange Things 1984, Rakishma 1985, Ball-Shapedness 1983–85, Planet Haj 1985, So That They Love One Another, Vopruz: Tedium 1983, Partochale Tumul 1984, Rakishma 1985, Relaxace: Relaxace 1987, Music of Spheres 1988, Silence 1990, Morning Prayer 1992, Czech Koan 1996, Indian Variations 2000, Dhjana 1991, Kadael 1993, Flower Reggae 1995, Sound and Silence 1996, Kapela SNOO: No Ceremonies 2002, Babalet: Green 1987, African Woman 1989, Babalet 1990, Ali Baba & Babalet Live 1993, Flowers Reggae 1996, Tomorrow the Sun will Shine 1998, Hypnotix: Rastaman in Prague 1988, Boothill: Sister 1999, Soundtrack 2000, Prvni Republica (with David Vavra) Cau hele! 1996. *Current Management:* Lubos Fendrych, Nad Koulkon 21, 15000 Prague 5, Czech Republic. *Address:* Na'drazni 213, Myto 33805, Czech Republic. *E-mail:* karel.babuljak@ c-box.cz. *Website:* www.ceskyhudebnislovnik.cz.

BABY U (see U-God)

BABYDADDY; American musician (multi-instrumentalist); b. (Scott David Hoffman), 1976. *Career:* mem., Scissor Sisters 2001–. *Recordings include:* albums: Scissor Sisters (BRIT Award for Best Int. Album 2005) 2004, Ta-Dah 2006, Night Work 2010, Magic Hour 2012. *Honours:* BRIT Awards for Best

Int. Group, Best Int. Breakthrough Act 2005, Meteor Ireland Music Award for Best Int. Group 2007. *Current Management:* c/o Dave Holmes, 3–D Management, 1901 Main Street #3, Santa Monica, CA 90405, USA. *Telephone:* (310) 314-6276. *E-mail:* info@3dmgmt.com. *Website:* www.3dmgmt.com. *E-mail:* sisters@scissorsisters.net (office). *Website:* www.scissorsisters.com.

BACA DE LA COLINA, Susana; Peruvian singer; b. Chortillos, Lima; m. Ricardo Pereira. *Career:* formed experimental group combining poetry and song; took part in int. Agua Dulce Festival in Lima; with husband f. Instituto Negrocontinuo 1992; first US performance in Brooklyn 1995; one US and six European tours; Minister of Culture July–Dec. 2011; Pres. OAS Comm. of Culture 2011–13. *Albums include:* Susana Baca 1997, Del Fuego y del Agua 1999, Eco de Sombras 2000, Lamento Negro (early Cuban recordings, Latin Grammy Award for Best Folk Album) 2001, Espiritu Vivo 2002, Travesias 2006, Cantos de Adoración 2010, Afrodiaspora 2011. *Publication:* The Cultural Importance of Black Peruvians (co-author with Richard Pereira) 1992. *Honours:* Ordre des Arts et Lettres, Order of Merit (Peru). *Address:* c/o Iris Musique, 5 Passage St-Sebastien, 75011 Paris, France. *Telephone:* (1) 4769933 (office). *Website:* www.luakabop.com/susana_baca.

BACAR, Zena; Mozambican singer and songwriter; b. Ilha de Mocambique. *Career:* Founding mem. and lead singer, Eyuphuro 1981; recorded the first int. release for a Mozambican group, Mama Mosambiki 1989–early 1990s, reformed 1998–. *Recordings include:* albums: Parado de Sucessos, Mama Mosambiki 1990, Yellela 2001, 25 Anos 2005, Watana 2006. *E-mail:* post@ worldmusic.net. *Website:* www.worldmusic.net.

BACCHUS, Brian Michel, AB; American record company executive, record producer and academic; *Instructor in Recorded Music Tisch School of Arts, New York;* b. 8 Aug. 1957, New York. *Education:* Syracuse Univ. *Career:* National Jazz Promotions Co-ordinator, Polygram Records, New York 1986–87; Man., National Jazz Promotions 1987–88; Dir, Jazz Promotion 1988–90; Dir Antilles Records/Island Records, New York 1990–92; Sr Dir of A&R, EMI Blue-Note Records 1997–2001; co-f. SoulFeast Music 2001–; currently also Instructor in Recorded Music, Tisch School of Arts, New York Univ. *Recordings include:* producer of albums: Remembrance, The Harper Brothers 1990, Music Inside, Joyce 1990, Amazon Secrets, Ricardo Silveira 1990, Kenny Drew Jr 1991; with Randy Weston: Spirits Of Our Ancestors 1991, Volcano Blues 1993, Khepara 1998; other: Sanctified Shells, Steve Turre 1992, Ann Dyer and The No Good Time Fairies 1995, Timepeace, Terry Callier 1998, Spirit! The Power of Music 2003; with Steve Turre: The Spirits Up Above 2004, Keep Searchin' 2006; with Gregory Porter: Be Good 2012, Liquid Spirit 2013. *Honours:* Billboard Award, Top Jazz Album, Remembrance 1990. *Address:* Clive Davis Department of Recorded Music, Tisch School of Arts, 194 Mercer Street, 5th Floor, New York, NY 10012, USA (office). *Telephone:* (212) 992-8400. *E-mail:* tisch.recorded.music@nyu.edu (office). *Website:* clivedavisdept.tisch.nyu.edu (office).

BACH, Leroy Frederick; American musician (guitar, keyboard), composer and music producer; b. 1964, Chicago, Ill. *Career:* mem. 5ive Style 1994–99, Wilco 1999–2004, The Dishes, Uptighty; Co-founder Low Tide Trio; session work with artists, including Liz Phair; worked in Rainbo Club Chicago 1995–2010; apptd Artist-in-Residence, Center for the Study of Race Politics and Culture, Univ. of Chicago 2012. *Recordings include:* albums: with 5ive Style: 5ive Style 1995, Miniature Portraits 1999; with Wilco: Summerteeth 1999, Yankee Hotel Foxtrot (Wired Rave Award 2003) 2002, More Like the Moon (EP) 2003, A Ghost is Born (Grammy Award for Best Alternative Music Album 2005) 2004, Kicking Television 2005. *Film:* I Am Trying To Break Your Heart 2002. *Website:* www.leroybach.com.

BACH, Sebastian; American rock singer, lyricist and actor; b. (Sebastian Bierk), 3 April 1968, Bahamas; m. Maria Aquinar 1992. *Career:* lead singer of rock group, Skid Row 1987–96, Founder mem. The Last Hard Men 1996–97; numerous live appearances, tours and festival appearances. *Stage appearance:* title role in production of Jekyll and Hyde (Broadway) 2000, The Rocky Horror (The Musical) 2001. *Recordings include:* albums: with Skid Row: Skid Row 1989 (American Music Award for Hard Rock New Artist 1990), Slave To The Grind 1991, B-Sides Ourselves (EP) 1992, Subhuman Race 1995, Scream 1996, Working Man 1996, 12 Picks 1997, Forty Seasons... 1998, Loaded Deck 1998, Thickskin 2003, Revolutions per Minute 2006, United World Rebellion: Chapter One (EP) 2013; solo: Bring 'Em Bach Alive 1999, Bach 2: Basics 2001, Angel Down 2007, Kicking & Screaming 2011, ABachalypse Now 2013. *Honours:* American Music Award for Favorite New Hard Rock Artist 1990. *Address:* c/o Reverbnation, 555 8th Avenue, Suite 909, New York, NY 10018, USA. *E-mail:* info@reverbnation.com. *Website:* www.reverbnation.com/ sebastianbach; www.sebastianbach.com.

BACH YEN, (Blanche Hirondelle); Vietnamese pop and folk singer; b. (Bach Yen Tran), 12 June 1942, Soc Trang; m. Tran Quang Hai 1978; one d. *Career:* began performing in Paris in the style of Edith Piaf 1961; tour of Europe including Belgium, Austria and Germany; visited USA 1965; appeared on Ed Sullivan TV Show; appearances on other TV shows and appearances with Bing Crosby, Joey Bishop, Mike Douglas, Pat Boone; toured in 46 US states and also visited Canada, Mexico, Caracas, Panama, Bogotá, Curaçao, alongside Jimmy Duranti, Liberace and Frankie Avalon; returned to Paris;

met musician and ethnomusicologist Tran Quang Hai and worked with traditional Vietnamese folk music; more than 2,000 concert performances; sings in Hebrew and several European languages as well as Vietnamese. *Films:* sang for John Wayne film, The Green Berets (uncredited) 1968, Universal Soldier (performed song Qua Cau Gio Bay) 1992. *Television:* Toast of the Town (series) 1965, The Bob Hope Show (series) 1966, The Joey Bishop Show (series) 1967. *Recordings:* seven albums with Tran Quang Hai, including Dreams & Reality 1988. *Honours:* Grand Prix du Disque, Acad. Charles Cros 1983. *Address:* 12 rue Gutenberg, 94450 Limeil-Brévannes, France.

BACHARACH, Burt; American composer, arranger, conductor and musician (piano); b. 12 May 1928, Kansas City, MO; m. 1st Paula Stewart 1953 (divorced 1958); m. 2nd Angie Dickinson 1965 (divorced 1980), one d. (deceased); m. 3rd Carole Bayer Sager 1982 (divorced 1990), one s.; m. 4th Jane Hansen 1993, two c. *Education:* McGill Univ., Montréal, Music Acad. West, Santa Barbara. *Career:* jazz musician 1940s; accompanist, arranger, conductor for various artists, including Vic Damone, Marlene Dietrich, Joel Gray, Steve Lawrence; writer of songs, film music and stage musicals; regular collaborations with Hal David 1962–70, Carole Bayer Sager from 1981. *Film appearance:* Magic of Marlene (TV) 1965. *Film scores:* What's New, Pussycat? 1965, After the Fox 1966, On the Flipside 1966, Casino Royale 1967, Butch Cassidy and the Sundance Kid 1969, Lost Horizon 1973, Arthur 1981, Night Shift 1982, Arthur 2 On the Rocks 1988, Grace of My Heart 1996, My Best Friend's Wedding 1997. *Compositions include:* Promises, Promises (musical) 1969; with Hal David: The Story of My Life, Magic Moments, Tower of Strength, Wives and Lovers, 24 Hours From Tulsa, What The World Needs Now Is Love, Walk On By, Trains and Boats and Planes, Do You Know The Way To San Jose?, Alfie, Anyone Who Had A Heart, There's Always Something There To Remind Me, Make It Easy On Yourself, What's New Pussycat?, This Guy's In Love With You, Raindrops Keep Fallin' On My Head, Close To You; with Carole Bayer Sager: Making Love, Heartlight, That's What Friends Are For, On My Own; with Carole Bayer Sager, Peter Allen and Christopher Cross: Arthur's Theme. *Recordings include:* albums: Searching Wind 1958, Brigitte Bardot 1961, Move It On The Backbeat (with The Backbeats) 1961, Saturday Sunshine 1963, Don't Go Breaking My Heart 1965, Hit Maker! 1965, The Man 1965, Nikki 1966, Alfie 1967, Reach Out 1967, The Bell That Couldn't Jingle 1968, I'll Never Fall In Love Again 1969, Make It Easy On Yourself 1969, All Kinds of People 1971, Burt Bacharach 1971, Portrait In Music 1971, Living Together 1973, Saturday Sunshine 1973, Futures 1977, Painted from Memory 1998, One Amazing Night 1998, Isley Meets Bacharach – Here I Am (with Ronald Isley) 2003, At This Time (Grammy Award for Best Pop Instrumental Album 2006) 2005. *Publications:* Anyone Who Had a Heart (autobiography) 2013. *Honours:* Cue Magazine Entertainer of the Year (with Hal David) 1969, three Acad. Awards, four Grammy Awards, two Emmy Awards, one Tony Award, Royal Swedish Acad. of Music Polar Music Prize 2001, Gershwin Prize for Popular Song (with Hal David), US Library of Congress 2012. *Current Management:* c/o Tina Brausam, 8033 Sunset Boulevard #996, Los Angeles, CA 90046, USA. *Address:* c/o Sony BMG, 550 Madison Avenue, New York, NY 10022, USA.

BACHCHAN, Amitabh, BSc; Indian actor, singer and television presenter; b. 11 Oct. 1942, Allahabad, Uttar Pradesh; s. of Harivansh Rai and Teji Bachchan; m. Jaya Bachchan; one s. one d. *Education:* Sherwood Coll. Nainital, Delhi Univ. *Career:* mem. Lok Sabha (Parl.) 1984–87; re-launched film co. AB Corpn 2003; Goodwill Amb. for UNICEF 2003–. *Films include:* Saat Hindustani (Nat. Award 1970) 1969, Anand (Filmfare Award) 1971, Parwaana 1971, Bombay to Goa 1972, Zanjeer 1973, Namak Haraam (Filmfare Award) 1973, Abhimaan 1973, Majboor 1974, Deewar 1975, Sholay 1975, Chupke Chupke 1975, Kabhi Kabhie 1976, Imaan Dharam 1977, Amar Akbar Anthony (Filmfare Award) 1977, Don (Filmfare Award) 1978, Kasme Vaade 1978, Mr. Natwarlal 1979, Jurmana 1979, Ram Balram 1980, Shaan 1980, Barsaat Ki Ek Raat 1980, Manzil 1981, Lawaaris 1981, Silsila 1981, Nammak Halal 1982, Shakti 1982, Coolie 1983, Mahaan 1983, Sharaabi 1984, Mard 1985, Aakhree Raasta 1986, Kaun Jeeta Kaun Hara 1987, Shahenshah 1988, Jadugar 1989, Agneepath (Nat. Award 1991) 1990, Hum (Filmfare Award) 1991, Ajooba 1991, Khuda Gawah 1992, Insaniyat 1994, Bade Miyan Chote Miyan 1998, Tumhare Liye 1999, Sooryavansham 1999, Mohabbatein (IIFA 2001, Filmfare Award) 2000, Aks (Filmfare Award) 2001, Kabhi Khushi Kabhi Gham 2001, Kaante 2002, Baghban 2003, Khakee 2004, Veer-Zaara 2004, Ab Tumhare Hawale Watan Saathiyo 2004, Waqt 2005, Sarkar 2005, Black 2005 (Nat. Award, Filmfare Award) 2006, Kabhi Alvida Naa Kehna (Never Say Goodbye) 2006, Eklavya – The Royal Guard 2007, Nishabd 2007, Zamaanat 2007, Cheeni Kum 2007, The Last Lear (Stardust Award) 2008, Paa 2009, Rann 2009, Teen Patti 2010, The Great Gatsby 2013. *Television:* presenter, Kaun Banega Crorepati? (Who Wants To Be A Millionaire?). *Honours:* Hon. Citizen, Deauville, France 2003–; Chevalier, Ordre nat. de la Légion d'honneur 2006; Dr hc (Jhansi Univ.) 2004, (Delhi Univ.) 2006, (De Montfort Univ., UK) 2006, (Leeds Metropolitan Univ.) 2007, (Queensland Univ. of Tech., Australia) 2009; Avadh Samman, Govt of UP 1980, Padma Shri 1984, Greatest Star of the Millennium (result of BBC online poll) 1999, Special Hon. Award, Int. Indian Film Acad. Awards 2000, Star of the Century Award, Alexandria Int. Film Festival 2001, Yash Bharati Samman, Govt of UP 1995, Padma Bhushan 2001, named Most Powerful Actor in Bollywood, Forbes magazine 2001, Dayawati Modi Award 2002, Kishore Kumar Award, Madhya Pradesh Govt 2002, Raj Kapoor Award, Govt of Maharashtra 2002, Living Legend Award, Fed. of Indian Chambers of Commerce and Industry 2004,

Shyam Sunder Dyay Kishan Munshi Lifetime Achievement Award 2004, Deenanath Mangeshkar Award 2005, Special Award, Mumbai Acad. of Moving Image Int. Film 2007, Visit London Special Award for Outstanding Achievement 2007, Crystal Award, World Econ. Forum 2009, Asian Film Cultural Award 2009, Life OK Screen Lifetime Achievement Award 2014, Padma Vibhushan 2015; numerous other nat. and int. awards. *Address:* Pratiksha, 10th Road, JVPD Scheme, Mumbai, 400 049, India (home). *Telephone:* (22) 6207579 (home); (22) 6206162 (home).

BACHIRI, Isam; Danish producer, musician and songwriter; b. 1 Aug. 1977, Morocco. *Education:* Islands-Brygge School, Denmark. *Career:* mem. Outlandish 1997–. *Recordings include:* albums: Outland's Official (Danish Music Award for Best Hip-Hop Album) 2000, Beats, Rhymes & Life 2004, Bread & Barrels of Water 2003, Closer than Veins 2005, Sound of a Rebel 2009; singles: Institution 2007, 2200 Carmen 2009. *Current Management:* c/o Thomas Borresen, Soulcamp Entertaiment, Gasvaerksvej 15 d, 1 sal 1656 Copenhagen v, Denmark. *E-mail:* thomas.borresen@soulcamp.dk. *Website:* www .soulcampentertainment.com.

BACHMAN, Randy, OC; Canadian singer, songwriter, musician (guitar) and producer; b. 27 Sept. 1943, Winnipeg, Man.; m. 1st Lorayne Stevenson 1966 (divorced 1977); m. 2nd Denise McCann 1982; one s. (Tal Bachman). *Career:* mem. The Guess Who, re-formed 1984 to tour; Founder mem. Brave Belt 1970, re-formed as Bachman-Turner Overdrive 1972–76; solo artist 1977–79, 1981–; Founder mem. Ironhorse 1979, Union 1981. *Compositions include:* You Ain't Seen Nothing Yet. *Television:* First Time Around on CBC and PBS (TV concert as Bachman-Cummings). *Radio:* host: Randy's Vinyl Tap (Silver Medal Int. Radio Conf. 2009) 2006–. *Recordings include:* albums: with Bachman-Turner Overdrive: Bachman-Turner Overdrive 1973, Bachman-Turner Overdrive 2 1974, Not Fragile 1974, BTO As Brave Belt 1975, Four-Wheel Drive 1975, Head On 1976, Bachman-Turner Overdrive 1984; solo: Axe 1972, Survivor 1978, Any Road (featuring Neil Young) 1992, Bob's Garage 1993, Songbook 1998, Every Song Tells a Story 2002, JazzThing 2006, JazzThing II 2007, Jukebox 2007, Takin' Care Of Christmas 2008; with Ironhorse: Ironhorse 1979, Everything Is Grey 1979; with Union: on Strike 1981, Merge 1996; with Bachman & Cummings: First Time Around 2006. *Honours:* Order of Manitoba 2005; Hon. DMus (Brandon Univ.) 2003; Prairie Music Hall of Fame, Manitoba 1999, Lt-Gov's Performing Arts Award, Ottawa 2004. *Current Management:* c/o Gilles Paquin, Paquin Entertainment, 468 Stradbrook Avenue, Winnipeg, Man., R3L 0J9, Canada. *Telephone:* (204) 988-1120. *Fax:* (204) 988-1135. *E-mail:* info@paquinentertainment.com. *Website:* www .paquinentertainment.com; www.randybachman.com (home).

BACHMAN, Talbert (Tal) Charles Robert; Canadian singer, songwriter and musician; b. 13 Aug. 1968, Vancouver, BC; s. of Randy Bachman; m. Tracy Bachman, seven c. *Television appearances include:* Melrose Place 1999. *Recordings include:* albums: Tal Bachman 1999, Staring Down the Sun 2004. *Honours:* BMI's Song of the Year Award (She's So High) 2000, Juno Awards for Top New Solo Artist and Top Producer 2000. *Current Management:* c/o Paquin Entertainment, 468 Stradbrook Avenue, Winnipeg, Man., R3L 0J9, Canada. *Telephone:* (204) 988-1120. *Fax:* (204) 988-1135. *E-mail:* info@paquinentertainment.com. *Website:* www.paquinentertainment.com.

BACKER, Matthew de Bracey, BA; American musician (guitar), singer and songwriter; b. New Orleans, Louisiana; m. Elisa Richards 1994. *Education:* University of Warwick, Berklee College of Music, Boston, USA. *Career:* recordings, performances, television appearances with: Sinéad O'Connor; Elton John; Marcella Detroit; Aimee Mann; Emmylou Harris; Mica Paris; Joe Cocker; Swing Out Sister; Beautiful South; Sarah Jane Morris; Michael Ball; Suzanne Rhatigan; Jools Holland; Kate St John; Daniel Cartier, ABC, Belinda Carlisle; Soundtrack work for television programmes including Equinox; Cracker; Spitting Image; Knowing Me Knowing You; Rory Bremner; Solo and collaborative singing/songwriting, and session work; mem, Musicians' Union. *Recordings:* albums: solo: Is That All? 2002, The Impulse Man 2004. *Telephone:* (20) 8962-9413. *E-mail:* ian.shaw@warmfuzz.com. *Website:* www .warmfuzz.com. *E-mail:* matt@mattbacker.com (office). *Website:* www .mattbacker.com.

BADALAMENTI, Angelo, (Andy Badale, Angelo Bagdelamenti); American composer; b. 22 March 1937, New York. *Education:* Eastman School of Music. *Career:* composed pop songs (under name Andy Badale); collaborations with artists, including Julee Cruise, Jocelyn West, Tim Booth, Marianne Faithfull, the Pet Shop Boys; worked as orchestrator and conductor on many movies; some cameo appearances in films and TV. *Compositions for films:* Gordon's War (as Andy Badale) 1973, Law and Disorder (as Andy Badale) 1974, Blue Velvet 1986, A Nightmare on Elm Street 3: Dream Warriors 1987, Weeds 1987, Tough Guys Don't Dance 1987, Parents 1989, Cousins 1989, National Lampoon's Christmas Vacation 1989, Wait Until Spring, Bandini 1989, Wild at Heart 1990, The Comfort of Strangers (BFI Anthony Asquith Award 1991) 1990, Twin Peaks: Fire Walk With Me 1992, Naked in New York 1994, La cité des enfants perdus 1995, Lost Highway 1997, The Blood Oranges 1997, Arlington Road 1999, La fille sur le pont (song Who Will Take My Dreams Away?) 1999, The Straight Story 1999, Holy Smoke 1999, Forever Mine 1999, Story of a Bad Boy 1999, The Beach 2000, A Piece of Eden 2000, Julie Johnson 2001, Mulholland Drive 2001, Cet amour-là 2001, Suspended Animation 2001, Secretary 2002, L'Adversaire 2002, Cabin Fever 2002, Auto Focus 2002, Resistance 2002, Mysteries of Love 2002, Darkened Room 2002, Rabbits 2002, Son frère (theme) 2003, The Company (song) 2003, Indoor Fireworks 2003,

Push 2004, Evilenko 2004, Napola 2004, Un long dimanche de fainçailles 2004, Dark Water 2005, The Wicker Man 2006, The Edge of Love 2007, 44 Inch Chest 2009, Secretariat 2010, A Woman Poster 2010, A Butterfly Kiss 2011, Life of Pi 2012. *Compositions for television:* Twin Peaks (Grammy Award, Independent Spirit Award, Saturn Award, BPI Best Album 1991) 1990, Industrial Symphony No. 1: The Dream of the Broken Hearted 1990, On the Air 1992, David Lynch's Hotel Room 1993, Witch Hunt 1994, Inside the Actor's Studio (as Angelo Bagdelamenti) 1994, Profiler 1996, Cracker (aka Fitz) 1997, Mario Puzo's The Last Don 1997, Lathe of Heaven 2002, Undefeated 2003, Les Liaisons dangereuses 2003, Fortid til salg 2004, Frankenstein 2004. *Honours:* eight ASCAP awards, Composer of the Year Award 2005, Lifetime Achievement Award 2008, Henry Mancini Lifetime Achievement Award 2011. *Current Management:* c/o Kraft-Engel Management, 15233 Ventura Blvd, Suite 200, Los Angeles, CA 91403, USA. *Telephone:* (818) 380-1918. *E-mail:* info@kraft-engel.com. *Website:* www.kraftengel.com; www.angelobadalamenti.com.

BADIHI, Borzouyeh (Borzou); Iranian musician (percussion, tonbak, tempo); b. 1977, Tehran; m. *Education:* Azad Univ. *Career:* veterinary surgeon; mem. The Arian Band (the first officially sanctioned mixed-gender pop band in Iran). *Recordings include:* albums: Sunflower 2000, And But Love! 2001, Till Eternity 2004, Without You With You 2008; single: Here Comes Spring 2009, The Footsteps of Hope 2010 (Certificate of Appreciation from World Food Programme). *Current Management:* c/o Mr Mohsen Rajabpour, Taraneh Sharghee Cultural & Artistic Co., Apt No. 26, Seventh Floor, Suite 22, Second Alley, Shahnazari Street, Mohseni Square, Mirdamad Avenue, Tehran 1547914415, Iran. *Telephone:* (21) 22223513 (office). *Fax:* (21) 22223670 (office). *E-mail:* president@taranehsh.com (office). *Website:* www.taranehsh.com (office); www.arianmusic.com.

BADLEY, Bill; British musician (guitar, banjo, mandolin, lute) and singer; b. Wiltshire, England. *Education:* Exeter University, Royal College of Music. *Career:* played with: The Consort of Musicke; The New London Consort; The Dufay Collective; Own group, Arcadia; Film work includes: Lady Jane; Caravaggio; Member, The Carnival Band, 1984–; First performance, Burnley Canalside Festival, 1984; Play material from: Sweden; Croatia; USA; Bolivia; Spain; UK; France; appearances include: festivals, arts theatres and centres; Barbican Centre; Glasgow Cathedral; Birmingham Symphony Hall; Assistant producer, Thames Television; currently music teacher, Malmesbury School. *Recordings include:* album with Maddy Prior: Christmas Carols. *Address:* c/o Malmesbury School, Corn Gastons, Malmesbury, Wilts., SN16 0DF, England. *Telephone:* (1666) 829700. *Fax:* (1666) 829701. *E-mail:* admin@malmesbury.wilts.sch.uk. *Website:* www.malmesbury.wilts.sch.uk.

BADLY DRAWN BOY; British singer, musician (guitar, keyboards) and songwriter; b. (Damon Gough), 2 Oct. 1970, Bolton, England. *Career:* collaborated with UNKLE 1998; ran Twisted Nerve record label with Andy Votel, currently runs One Last Fruit record label. *Films:* as composer: About a Boy 2002, The Fattest Man in Britain 2009, Being Flynn 2012. *Recordings include:* albums: The Hour Of Bewilderbeast (Mercury Music Prize) 2000, About A Boy OST 2002, Have You Fed The Fish? 2002, One Plus One Is One 2004, Born in the UK 2006, Is There Nothing We Could Do? 2009, It's What I'm Thinking: Part 1 - Photographing Snowflakes 2010, Being Flynn OST 2012. *Current Management:* Biglife Management, 67–69 Chalton Street, London, NW1 1HY, England. *Telephone:* (20) 7554-2100. *Fax:* (20) 7554-2101. *E-mail:* reception@biglifemanagement.com. *Website:* www.biglifemanagement.com; www.badlydrawnboy.co.uk.

BADU, Erykah; American R&B singer, songwriter, actress and record producer; b. (Erica Abi Wright), 26 Feb. 1972, Dallas, Tex.; one s. two d. *Education:* Grambling State Univ. *Career:* performances with cousin Free, in Erykah Free; turned solo, obtained recording deal; support slots to numerous artists, including Wu Tang Clan; collaborations with Omar, OutKast, Guru. *Films include:* Blues Brothers 2000, The Cider House Rules 1999, House of D 2004, Before the Music Dies 2006, Dave Chappelle's Block Party 2006. *Recordings include:* albums: Baduizm (Best R&B Album 1998) 1997, Live 1997, Heartache 1998, Mama's Gun 2000, Worldwide Underground 2003, New AmErykah, Part One 2008, New AmErykah, Part Two: Return of the Ankh 2010. *Honours:* Grammy Award for Best Female R&B Vocal Performance (for On & On) 1998, Grammy Award for Best Rap Performance by Duo or Group (for You Got Me, with The Roots) 2000, Best R&B Song, BET Awards for Video of the Year (for Love of My Life) 2003. *E-mail:* erykahbaducom@gmail.com. *Website:* www.erykahbadu.com.

BAEKHYUN; South Korean singer; b. (Byun Baekhyun), 6 May 1992, Bucheon, Gyeonggi Prov. *Education:* Jungwon High School. *Career:* mem., K-pop boy band Exo 2012–; mem. sub-group Exo-K 2012–; debut single 2012; numerous TV and live appearances. *Television:* EXO's Showtime 2013–. *Recordings:* albums: Mama 2012, XOXO (Mnet Asian Music Award for Album of the Year 2013) 2013. *Honours:* numerous awards including: for Exo: Mnet Asian Music Award for Best New Asian Artist/Group 2012, MTV Europe Music Award for Best Japan/Korea Act 2013, MelOn Music Award for Song of the Year (for Growl) 2013; for Exo-K: Golden Disk Newcomer Award 2012. *Address:* c/o SM Entertainment, 521 Apgujeong 2-dong, Gangnam-gu, Seoul, South Korea (office). *Telephone:* (2) 6240-9800 (office). *Website:* www.smtown.com (office); exo.smtown.com (home).

BAEZ, Joan Chandos; American folk singer; b. 9 Jan. 1941, Staten Island, NY; d. of Albert V. Baez and Joan Baez (née Bridge); m. David Harris 1968 (divorced 1973); one s. *Education:* School of Fine and Applied Arts, Boston Univ. *Career:* began career as singer in coffee houses, appeared at Ballad Room, Club 47 1958–68, Gate of Horn, Chicago 1958, Newport, RI, Folk Festival 1959–69, Town Hall and Carnegie Hall, New York 1962, 1967, 1968; gave concerts in black colls in southern USA 1963; toured Europe and USA 1960s–90s, Democratic Repub. of Viet Nam 1972, Australia 1985; recordings with Vanguard Records 1960–72, A & M Record Co. 1972–76, Portrait Records 1977–80, Gold Castle Records 1987–89, Virgin Records 1990–93, Guardian Records 1995–, Grapevine Label Records 1995–; awarded eight gold albums, one gold single; many TV appearances; began refusing payment of war taxes 1964; detained for civil disobedience opposing conscription 1967; speaking tour of USA and Canada for draft resistance 1967–68; Founder and Vice-Pres. Inst. for Study of Non-Violence (now called Resource Center for Non-Violence) 1965–; Founder Humanitas Int. Human Rights Comm. 1979–92. *Recordings include:* albums: Joan Baez 1960, Joan Baez, Vol. 2 1961, In Concert, part 2 1963, 5 1964, Farewell Angelina 1965, Noel 1966, Joan 1967, Baptism 1968, Any Day Now 1968, David's Album 1969, One Day At A Time 1969, First Ten Years 1970, Carry It On (soundtrack) 1971, Ballad Book 1972, Come From The Shadows 1972, Where Are You Now My Son? 1973, Hits, Greatest and Others 1973, Gracias A La Vida 1974, Contemporary Ballad Book 1974, Diamonds and Rust 1975, From Every Stage 1976, Gulf Winds 1976, Blowin' Away 1977, Best Of 1977, Honest Lullaby 1979, Very Early Joan 1982, Recently 1987, Diamonds and Rust In The Bullring 1989, Speaking Of Dreams 1989, Play Me Backwards 1992, Rare Live and Classic 1993, Ring Them Bells 1995, Gone from Danger 1997, Dreams 1997, Best Of... 1997, 20th Century Masters: The Millennium 1999, Dark Chords on a Big Guitar 2003, Bowery Songs 2005, Day After Tomorrow 2008, How Sweet the Sound 2009. *Publications include:* Joan Baez Songbook 1964, Daybreak 1968, Coming Out (with David Harris) 1971, And Then I Wrote... (songbook) 1979, And a Voice to Sing With 1987. *Honours:* Chevalier, Légion d'honneur; Gandhi Memorial Int. Foundation Award 1988. *Address:* Diamonds and Rust Productions, PO Box 1026, Menlo Park, CA 94026-1026, USA (office). *Telephone:* (650) 328-0266 (office). *Fax:* (650) 917-1020 (office). *E-mail:* jbwebpages@aol.com (office). *Website:* www.joanbaez.com (home).

BAGAYOKO, Amadou; Malian singer, musician and composer; b. 24 Oct. 1954; m. Mariam Doumbia; three c. *Education:* Inst. for Young Blind People. *Career:* fmr mem., Ambassadeurs du Motel de Bamako; mem., duo, Amadou & Mariam; apptd Amb. Against Hunger, WFP and EU. *Recordings include:* albums: Vols 1–5 (five albums on cassette), Sou ni tilé 1998, Se te djon ye (reissue on CD of first two cassette recordings) 1999, Tje ni Mousso 1999, Wati 2002, Dimanche à Bamako (Victoires de la Musique Award 2004, BBC Radio 3 Award for World Music Album of the Year 2006) 2004, Welcome to Mali 2008, The Magic Couple 2009, Folila 2012. *Honours:* BBC Radio 3 Award for World Music (Africa) 2006. *Website:* www.amadou-mariam.com.

BAHRI, Mamdouh; Tunisian musician (guitar); b. 31 July 1957, Sfax; m. Geva Nouyrit 1993, one s. one d. *Education:* Swiss Jazz School; Seminars with Joe Diorio, Jim Hall, John Abercrombie. *Career:* Festival Jazz D'O-Beziers 1989, Bastia Festival 1990, Carthage Music Festival, Tunisia 1991, Blue Note, New York 1992, 1995, Romans Festival 1993, Pori Jazz Festival, Finland 1995, Sweet Basil 1995; appearances in USA including in New York, Alabama, Connecticut, Maryland; mem. SACEM, SPEDIDAM, ADAMI. *Recordings include:* From Tunisia With Love, The Spirit Of Life Ensemble 1992, Mamoudh Bahri, Nefta 1993, Inspirations 1993, Feel The Spirit 1994, Live At The S Spot 1995, African Flame 1998. *Website:* mamdouh.bahri.free.fr.

BAHTIYAR, Cem; Turkish musician (bass); b. 18 Jan. 1979, Denizli. *Career:* mem. alternative rock band, maNga 2002–; concerts, festivals include Sziget Festival, Mannheim Turkish Rock Festival, also London. *Recordings include:* albums: maNga 2004, Şehr-i Hüzün 2009, We Could Be the Same (EP) 2010, Fly to Stay Alive (single) 2011, e-akustik (Blue Jean Award for Album of the Year) 2012. *Honours:* MTV Europe Music Award for Best European Act 2009. *Current Management:* c/o Hadi Elazzi, GRGDN, Mübayacı sok. 5, Rumelihisarı, 34470 İstanbul, Turkey. *Telephone:* (212) 2876287. *Fax:* (212) 2876216. *E-mail:* manga@grgdn.com. *Website:* www.grgdn.com. *Current Management:* c/o Sony Music Entertainment, Sony Music Türkiye, Ticaret A.Ş. Oteller Sokak 1/5, Tepebaşı, 34430 İstanbul, Turkey. *Website:* manga.web.tr.

BAIKIE, Pete; British composer, writer, comedian, musician (guitar, piano) and actor; b. 17 April 1957, Edinburgh, Scotland. *Education:* Edinburgh Univ. *Career:* actor, writer, BBC Radio 4 series In Other Words... The Bodgers 1985; Actor, singer/musician, BBC Radio 4 series Bodgers, Banks and Sparkes 1986; actor, singer, musician, writer, CH 4 television series, Absolutely 1989–93; actor, writer, CH 4 television series, Squawkie Talkie 1995; actor (role of bandleader) Swing Kids (Disney film); producer, HTV/Paramount television series Barry Welsh Is Coming 1996–; bandleader/musician, Channel 5 UK television series The Jack Docherty Show 1997; Co-presenter, BBC Radio 2 series Saturday Night Jack 2000–01; Co-founder, Absolutely Productions 1989–, currently mem. Bd of Dirs; mem. Musicians' Union, British Acad. of Composers & Songwriters (BAC&S). *Compositions include:* television themes for: It's Only TV But I Like It (BBC 1), Vic and Bob's Shooting Stars, Two Fat Ladies, Bang Bang It's Reeves and Mortimer, Stressed Eric (all BBC 2), Barbara, 2DTV (both ITV1), Absolutely, mr don and mr george, Squawkie Talkie, Teenage Health Freak (all CH4), Radio themes for: Labour Exchange, If You're So Clever, The Preventers, BBC Radio 4. *Address:* c/o Board of Directors, Absolutely Productions Limited, Unit 19, 77 Beak Street, London W1F 9DB, England. *Telephone:* (20) 7644-5575. *Website:* www.absolutely.biz.

BAILEY, Philip; American singer, musician (percussion) and producer; b. 8 May 1951, Denver, Colo. *Career:* Music Dir gospel group, The Stovall Sisters; mem. Friends and Love; mem. Earth, Wind and Fire 1972–84, 1987–; live performances and tours include numerous special effects; solo artist 1983–86. *Recordings include:* albums: with Earth, Wind and Fire: Last Days And Time 1972, Head To The Sky 1973, Open Our Eyes 1974, That's The Way Of The World (soundtrack) (Grammy Award) 1975, Gratitude 1975, Spirit 1976, All 'N' All 1977, I Am 1979, Faces 1980, Raise! 1981, Secret Messages 1982, Powerlight 1983, Electric Universe 1983, Touch The World 1987, Heritage 1990, Millennium 1993, In The Name Of Love 1997, Take Two 2001, The Promise 2003, Avatar 2003, Illumination 2005; solo: Chinese Wall 1984, The Wonders Of His Love 1984, Triumph 1985, Inside Out 1986, Wonders Of Love 1988, Family Affair 1990, Philip Bailey 1994, Dreams 1999, Life and Love 2002, Soul on Jazz 2002. *Honours:* American Music Award for Favorite Soul/Rhythm and Blues Band 1977, 1979, Grammy Award for Best R&B Vocal Performance (for All 'N' All) 1979, (for After The Love Has Gone) 1980, Best R&B Instrumental (for Boogie Wonderland) 1980, MTV Music Video Award 1985, Ivor Novello Award (for Easy Lover) 1986, Grammy Award for Best Gospel Performance 1987. *E-mail:* band@earthwindandfire.com. *Website:* www.earthwindandfire.com; www.philipbailey.com.

BAILEY, Roy, MBE, BA, FRSA; British folk singer, musician (guitar) and academic; *Professor Emeritus, Sheffield Hallam University;* b. (Roy Smith), 20 Oct. 1935, London, England; m. Val Turbard 1963; one s. one d. *Education:* Univ. of Leicester. *Career:* professional singer 1960–; radio and TV broadcasts, tours in UK, Switzerland, Canada, USA, Australia; appearances include festivals in UK, Canada, Switzerland, Belgium, Australia; Prof. of Sociology and Social Work, Sheffield Hallam Univ. 1988–90, Prof. Emer. 1990–; retd, now freelance singer/musician; mem. Anti-Capitalist Roadshow; Patron, Towersey Village Festival, Shepley Spring Festival, Music on the Marr, Cumbria (Festival). *Recordings include:* Smoke and Dust Where The Heart Should Have Been 1965, Oats and Beans and Kangaroos 1966, Cobweb Of Dreams 1969, Roy Bailey 1970, That's Not The Way It's Got To Be (with Leon Rosselson) 1975, New Bell Wake 1976, Love Loneliness and Laundry (with Leon Rosselson) 1977, If I Knew Who The Enemy Was (with Leon Rosselson) 1978, Hard Times 1982, Freedom Peacefully 1985, Leaves From A Tree 1989, Why Does It Have To Be Me 1990, Never Leave A Story Unsung 1992, What You Do With What You've Got 1993, Business As Usual 1994, Rhythm and Reds (with Band of Hope) 1994, New Directions in the Old 1997, Past Masters 1998, CODA (with Karen Tweed, Andy Cutting, Ian Carr) 1999, Up the Wooden Hill 2001, Sit Down and Sing (with Martin Simpson and John Kirkpatrick) 2005, Below the Radar 2009, Tomorrow 2011. *Publications include:* Contemporary Social Problems in Britain (with Jock Young) 1973, Radical Social Work (with Mike Brake) 1975, Radical Social Work and Practice (with Mike Brake) 1980, Theory and Practice in Social Work (with Phil Lee) 1982. *Current Management:* c/o Alan Bearman Music, The Music Base, Kings Place, 90 York Way, London, N1 9AG, England. *Telephone:* (20) 7014-2821. *E-mail:* ABM.Alan@btinternet.com. *Website:* www.alanbearmanmusic.co.uk. *E-mail:* roy@roybailey.net (home). *Website:* www.roybailey.net.

BAIN, Aly, MBE; Scottish musician (violin); b. 15 May 1946, Lerwick, Shetland. *Education:* studied with Tom Anderson. *Career:* mem. Boys of the Lough 1988; formed duo with Phil Cunningham. *Television:* presenter, Down Home (series on spread of fiddle music from Scotland and Ireland to N America, Channel 4) 1991, The Shetland Set (series, BBC) 1991, When Nicola Benedetti Met Aly Bain 2009, Fishing for Poetry 2010. *Recordings include:* with Phil Cunningham: The Pearl 1995, The Ruby 1997, Another Gem 2000, Spring the Summer Long 2003, Roads Not Travelled 2006, Portrait 2010, Five and Twenty 2012, Best of Aly and Phil Vol. 2 2013; Aly Bain-Mike Whelans 1971, The Silver Bow (with Tom Anderson) 1976, Shetland Folk Fiddling Vol. 2 (with Tom Anderson) 1978, Aly Bain 1985, Down Home Vol. 1 1986, Down Home Vol. 2 1986, Aly Meets The Cajuns 1988, Lonely Bird 1992, Aly Bain and Friends 1994, Follow The Moonstone 1996, Aly Bain and Young Champions 2005, Beyond the Stacks (with Ale Möller) 2007, The Best of Aly Bain: Vol. 1: A Fiddler's Tale 2008. *Publications include:* Fiddler on the Loose (autobiography) 1993. *Honours:* BBC Radio 2 Folk Awards for Best Duo (with Phil Cunningham) 2005, for Lifetime Achievement 2013. *Website:* www.firefly-productions.co.uk; www.philandaly.com.

BAINES, Nick; British musician (keyboards); b. 21 March 1978. *Career:* Founder-mem. Runston Parva 1997, renamed Parva, renamed Kaiser Chiefs 2003–. *Recordings include:* albums: Employment (Meteor Ireland Music Award for Best Int. Album 2006, NME Award for Best Album 2006, Ivor Novello Award for Best Album 2006) 2005, Yours Truly, Angry Mob 2007, Off With Their Heads 2008, The Future Is Medieval 2011, Education, Education, Education and War 2014. *Honours:* Meteor Ireland Music Award for Best Int. Group 2006, BRIT Awards for Best British Rock Act, Best British Live Act, Best British Group 2006, Nordoff-Robbins Silver Clef Award for Best Group 2006, Q Award for Best Video (for 'Ruby') 2007. *Telephone:* (20) 7377-4320. *E-mail:* james.sandom@redlightmanagement.com; jessica.lord@redlightmanagement.com. *Website:* redlightmanagement.com; www.kaiserchiefs.com.

BAIO, Christopher (Chris) Joseph; American musician (bass guitar, keyboards) and songwriter; b. 29 Oct. 1984, Bronxville, NY. *Education:* Columbia Univ. *Career:* fmr mem. Midnight Hours, Underrated; worked as DJ; Founder-mem. Vampire Weekend 2006–, signed to XL Recordings 2007; numerous festival appearances and tours. *Recordings:* albums: with Vampire Weekend: Vampire Weekend 2008, Contra 2010, Modern Vampires of the City (Grammy Award for Best Alternative Music Album 2014) 2013. *Honours:* with Vampire Weekend: NME Award for Best New American Alternative/Indie Band 2008, Q Magazine Award for Best Video (for Giving Up the Gun) 2011, for Best Act in the World Today 2013. *Current Management:* c/o Ian Montone, Monotone, Inc., 820 Seward Street, Hollywood, CA 90038, USA. *Telephone:* (323) 308-1818. *Address:* c/o Kris Chen, XL Recordings, 304 Hudson Street, 7th Floor, New York, NY 10013, USA (office). *Telephone:* (212) 995-5882 (office). *E-mail:* krischen@xlrecordings.com (office); vampireweekend@gmail.com (home). *Website:* www.xlrecordings.com (office); www.vampireweekend.com.

BAIOCCHI, Regina Harris, BA, MM, PR Cert.; American composer and musician; b. 16 July 1956, Chicago, Ill.; d. of Egie Harris, Sr and Lanzie Harris (née Belmont); m. Gregory D. Baiocchi. *Education:* Richards Vocational High School, Chicago, Paul Laurence Dunbar Vocational High School, Roosevelt Univ., Illinois Inst. of Tech., Inst. of Design, Chicago, New York Univ., DePaul Univ. *Career:* began composing aged ten; Orchestral Suite performed at Detroit Symphony Orchestra/Unisys Corpn Symposium 1992; composer-in-residence, Mostly Music Inc. 1992; guest composer, Wayne State Univ., Detroit 1993–94; guest composer/public relations lecturer, Northeastern Ill. Univ., Chicago 1993–94; guest composer, Columbia Coll., Chicago 1995, Northwestern Univ., Evanston 1996; composer, Musical Dir, Steppenwolf Theatre, Chicago 1997; 'Miles Per Hour' performed by Chicago Symphony Orchestra 1989; 'Muse' performed by Detroit Symphony Orchestra 1997; commissioned by Evanston Township High School to write orchestral 'ETHS Fanfare' for 150th anniversary; premiered 'Congregational Mass', 'Caint see to caint see' (spiritual) and 'Doxology' for pipe organ at Rockefeller Chapel, Univ. of Chicago 2011. *Compositions:* Equipoise by Intersection for piano 1978, Realizations for strings 1978, Chasé 1979, Who Will Claim The Baby? for chorus 1984, Send Your Gifts for chorus 1984, Father We Thank You for chorus 1986, Zora Neale Hurston Songs 1989, Psalm 138 for chorus 1990, We Real Cool for jazz ensemble 1990, Miles Per Hour (Jazz Sonatina) for trumpet 1990, Autumn Night for flute 1991, Crystal Stair for vocal ensemble 1991, Foster Pet 1991, Langston Hughes Songs 1991, Orchestral Suite 1991–92, Sketches for piano trio 1992, Shadows 1992, A Few Black Voices 1992, Teddy Bear Suite for orchestra 1992, Legacy 1992, Bwana's Libation 1992, QFX 1993, Much in Common for vocal ensemble 1993, Nobody's Child for chorus 1993, Mason Room 1993, Three Pieces for Greg 1994, Deborah for percussion 1994, Liszten, My Husband is Not a Hat for piano 1994, After the Rain 1994, Friday Night 1995, Darryl's Rose 1995, Gbeldahoven: No One's Child (opera) 1996, African Hands for orchestra with soloists 1997, Skins for percussion 1997, Dreamhoppers 1997, Nikki Giovanni 1997, Muse for orchestra 1997, Message to My Muse 1997, Dream Weaver 1997, Déjà Vu, for solo piano 1999, Communion, for marimba and strings 1999, HB4A, for piano, bass, drums and saxophone 2000, Karibu, for B-flat clarinet 2007, Congregational Mass for SATB 2011, Caint see to caint see (SATB spiritual) 2011, Doxology for pipe organ 2011. *Publications:* books: Indigo Sound 2003, Urban Haiku and Other Selected Poems 2004, Blues Haiku and Other New Poems 2005; online Study Guides for Chicago Humanities Festival 2012. *Honours:* City of Chicago Dept of Cultural Affairs CAAP grant 1992–94, 1996, AT&T grant 1994, Nat. Endowment for the Arts/Randolph Street Gallery Regional Artist Program grant 1995, Chicago Music Assen Award 1995, ASCAP Special Awards grants 1996, 1997, Art Inst. of Chicago and the Lila Wallace/Reader's Digest Fund Award 1997, 3Arts Foundation Award 2011. *Address:* PO Box 450, Chicago, IL 60605, USA (office). *Telephone:* (312) 253-7453 (home). *Fax:* (312) 922-3978 (office). *E-mail:* Regina@ReginaHarrisBaiocchi.com. *Website:* www.reginaharrisbaiocchi.com.

BAIYEWU, Tunde; British singer; b. (Babatunde Emanuel Baiyewu), 25 Nov. 1968, London; step-s. of Olusegun Obasanjo; m. Tope Adeshina 2007. *Education:* Univ. of Newcastle. *Career:* Founder-mem. (with Paul Tucker) and lead singer, The Lighthouse Family 1993–2001; solo artist 2004–. *Recordings include:* albums: with The Lighthouse Family: Ocean Drive 1995, Postcards From Heaven 1997, Whatever Gets You Through The Day 2001; solo: Tunde 2004. *Current Management:* c/o Independent Sound Management, 3rd Floor, 39 Margaret Street, London, W1G 0JQ, England. *Telephone:* (20) 7493-9200. *Fax:* (20) 7493-9111. *E-mail:* alexis@independentsound.net.

BAJAKIAN, Clint; American music and entertainment executive and composer; *Music Manager, Sony Computer Entertainment America;* b. (Clinton James Bajakian), 1962, Bryn Mawr, Pa; s. of Vincent Bajakian and Amy Bajakian; m. Deniz Ince; one s. one d. *Education:* New England Conservatory, Univ. of Mich. *Career:* composer and sound supervisor, LucasArts Entertainment Co. 1991–2000; composer for over 80 games titles; Co-Man. The Bay Area Sound Dept 2000–04; Co-creator iMUSE System; currently Music Man., Sony Computer Entertainment America; Vice-Pres. Game Audio Network Guild; mem. Cttee Interactive Audio Special Interest Group; mem. Acad. of Interactive Arts and Sciences; lecturer at events, including The Game Developer's Conf. *Compositions include:* scores or contributions to video game soundtracks: Monkey Island 2: LeChuck's Revenge 1991, Indiana Jones and the Fate of Atlantis 1992, Day of the Tentacle 1993, Star Wars: Dark Forces 1994, Star Wars: Tie Fighter Collector's CD-ROM 1995, The Dig 1995, Outlaws 1997, Indiana Jones and the Infernal Machine 1999, Escape from Monkey Island 2000, Star Wars: Knights of the Old Republic 2003, Rise to Honor 2003, Unreal II: The

Awakening 2003, The Lord of the Rings: The Return of the King 2003, James Bond 007: Everything or Nothing 2004, The Bard's Tale 2004, Psychonauts 2005, God of War 2005, SOCOM 3: Navy Seals 2005, Uncharted: Drake's Fortune 2007. *Honours:* Computer Gaming World magazine Outstanding Achievement Award 1996, Game Audio Network Guild Award for Best Interactive Score, for Music of the Year 2003, Best Original Score, Acad. of Interactive Arts and Sciences 2006. *Address:* Sony Computer Entertainment America, 919 E Hillsdale Boulevard, Second Floor, Foster City, CA 94404, USA (office). *Website:* www.scea.sony.com (office).

BAJTALA, Janos, DipMus; Hungarian singer, composer, arranger and musician (piano); b. 5 Dec. 1944, Budapest; one s. *Education:* Jazz Academy, Budapest. *Career:* formed Jazz/Soul Trio, 1965; television and radio shows in Hungary, 1965–71; tours with soul bands The Bandwagon, Foundation, 1974; co-arranger, West End hit musical, The Black Mikado, 1975–76; tours with reggae group Chosen Few, 1981–88; tours with Boney M, 1991–98; tours with Jimmy Ruffin (Motown), 1999–; currently keyboard player, Guy Tortora Band; mem. PRS. *Recordings:* Gipsy Girl (own composition), charted in Hungary, 1968; Keyboards, Black Mikado cast album, 1975; Keyboards on album Bad Weathers, Vivian Weathers, 1980; Various recordings with Chosen Few, 1981–88. *Honours:* first prize, nationwide pop and jazz contest, 1967; Best soloist, Hugarian International Jazz Festival, 1971. *E-mail:* janosbajala@hotmail.com; info@guytortora.com. *Website:* www.guytortora.com.

BAKALA, Bretislav, DipTech; Czech musician (keyboard); b. 18 June 1957, Brno; m. Marta Srvtova 1984, one s. one d. *Education:* College of Technology, Brno, Folk Art School. *Career:* keyboard player of jazz duo in Brno; Good Company, Dancing 19, in Norway, Germany, Switzerland, Mallorca, Austria, 1987–97; composer and keyboard player, Sound Studio. *Compositions:* Warum Lieb'ich Dich Allein; Lift Me Up; You're Crossing My Life; New Day; Zeit, Du Heilst Wunden. *Recordings include:* albums: Immer Wieder 1994, Just Friends 1996.

BAKER, Anita; American singer; b. 26 Jan. 1958, Detroit, Mich.; m. Walter Bridgeforth Jr 1988 (divorced); two s. *Career:* mem. funk band, Chapter 8 1976–80; worked as receptionist, Detroit 1980–82; solo singer and songwriter 1982–. *Recordings include:* albums: with Chapter 8: I Just Wanna Be Your Girl 1980; solo: The Songstress 1983, Rapture (Grammy Award for Best Rhythm and Blues Vocal Performance 1987) 1986, Giving You the Best That I Got (Grammy Awards for Best Rhythm and Blues Song, Best Rhythm and Blues Performance by a Female Artist 1988, Best Album 1989, Soul Train Award for Best R&B Album 1989, American Music Award for Favorite Female Soul/R&B Album 1988) 1988, Compositions (Grammy Award for Best Rhythm and Blues Performance, NAACP Image Award for Best Album of the Year) 1990, Rhythm of Love 1994, My Everything 2004, Christmas Fantasy 2005, Only Forever 2013. *Honours:* Soul Train Awards for Best Single by a Female Artist 1987, for Best R&B Single, Best R&B Song 1989, American Music Award for Favorite Female Soul/R&B Artist 1988, 1990, NAACP Image Award for Best Female Vocalist 1990. *Current Management:* c/o WME, 9601 Wilshire Blvd, Beverly Hills, CA 90210, USA. *Telephone:* (310) 285-9000. *Fax:* (310) 285-9010. *Website:* www.wma.com; www.anitabaker.com.

BAKER, Arthur; American producer and remixer; b. 22 April 1955, Boston, Mass. *Career:* worked as producer with Afrika Bambaataa, Ash, Lee Coombs, Felix da Housecat, Mansun, Timo Mass, New Order, Senser, Hall & Oates, numerous others; worked as remixer with David Bowie, Bob Dylan, Fleetwood Mac, Morcheeba, The Pet Shop Boys, Rolling Stones, Bruce Springsteen, Talking Heads, Mariah Carey, Black Eyed Peas, Diana Ross. *Films include:* Fried Green Tomatoes 1989, Listen Up - 1989, The Lives Of Quincy Jones 1989. *Current Management:* Stephen Budd Management, 10 Greenland Street, Camden, London, NW1 0ND, England. *Telephone:* (70) 4040-9533. *Fax:* (20) 7688-8999. *E-mail:* enquiries@record-producers.com. *Website:* www .record-producers.com.

BAKER, Carroll Anne, OC; Canadian country singer and songwriter; b. 4 March 1949, Nova Scotia. *Career:* British tour with Slim Whitman; recorded duets with daughter Candace; Eddie Eastman; Jack Scott; Roger Whittaker; Concert with Canada Pops Orchestra; Television includes: 3 Carroll Baker super specials, CBC; Mini-series, seven half-hour shows, CBC; guest appearances: Hee Haw; New Country; Nashville Now; The Tommy Hunter Show; Lifetime; Canada AM; headlined for Regent Holiday Tours, Carroll Baker's Country Cruise, 1989; mem. AFofM; ACTRA; SOCAN. *Compositions include:* I'm An Old Rock and Roller (Dancin' To A Different Beat). *Recordings include:* I Should Have Put A Hold On Love 1990. *Honours:* Entertainer of the Year, Country Award, Canada; 3 Platinum, 6 Gold albums; 5 Gold Singles; JUNO Awards: 1975–78; Big Country Awards, 1975–81; 1987; BMI Award, 1977; RPM Programmer Award, 1978, 1981; Procan Award, 1983; 14 consecutive No. 1 singles, Canadian country charts, 1975–81; Top Country Female, Canadian Country Music, 1985; Martin Guitar Award, 1989; Lifetime Achievement, Canadian Country Music Awards, 1991; Inductee, Canadian Country Music Hall of Honour, 1992. *Address:* c/o John Beaulieu, Carroll Baker Enterprises, 210 Dimson Street, Guelph, ON N1G 3C8, Canada. *Telephone:* (519) 822-2732. *Fax:* (519) 822-2732. *E-mail:* rejean158@sympatico .ca. *E-mail:* carroll.baker@carrollbakersinger.ca. *Website:* www .carrollbakersinger.ca.

BAKER, David Nathaniel, BMusEd, MMusEd; American composer, musician (tuba, trombone, cello, bass) and academic; *Distinguished Professor of Music and Chair, Jazz Department, Jacobs School of Music, Indiana University*; b.

21 Dec. 1931, Indianapolis, Ind.; m. Lida Baker. *Education:* Crispus Attucks High School, Indiana Univ.-Bloomington, Berklee School of Music, Boston, School of Jazz, Lenox. *Career:* professional musician 1948–; played in bands with Maynard Ferguson, Quincy Jones, George Russell, Wes Montgomery and Lionel Hampton; teacher, Lincoln Univ., Jefferson City, MO 1956–57; public schools in Indianapolis 1958–59; private teacher 1960–66; teacher, Ind. Central Coll. 1963–64; Distinguished Prof. of Music, Chair. of the Jazz Dept, Dept of Jazz Studies, Indiana Univ. 1966–; also taught at Indiana State Univ., New England Conservatory of Music, San Diego State Coll., Chicago State Univ., Wichita State Univ.; Conductor and Artistic Dir Smithsonian Jazz Masterworks Orchestra; Pres., Jazz Action Coalition; Chair., Jazz Advisory Panel, Kennedy Center; Chair., Jazz, Folk and Ethnic Advisory Panel, Nat. Endowment for the Arts; Pres., Nat. Jazz Service Org. *Compositions include:* Le roi for jazz ensemble 1957, Kentucky Oysters for jazz ensemble 1958, Stereophrenic for jazz ensemble 1959, Lunacy for jazz ensemble 1959, April B for jazz ensemble 1959, Terrible T for jazz ensemble 1962, Three Jazz Moods 1963, Blues for string orchestra 1966, Coltrane in Memoriam for jazz ensemble 1967, The Beatitudes (oratorio) 1968, Abyss 1968, Black America: To the Memory of Martin Luther King Jr (cantata) 1968, Catholic Mass for Peace (Votive Mass for Peace) for chorus 1969, Le Chat qui pêche for jazz ensemble 1969, Five Short Pieces for piano 1970, Jazz Suite for sextet in Memory of Bob Thompson (In Memoriam: Freedom) 1971, Adumoratio for jazz ensemble 1971, Suite (Sweet) Louis: A Tribute To Louis Armstrong for percussion 1971, Songs of the Night (for voice with instrumental ensemble) 1972, Sonata for violoncello and piano 1973, The Black Experience 1973, Levels: A Concerto for solo contrabass, jazz band, flute quartet, horn quartet and string quartet 1973, Aulil for jazz ensemble 1973, Lacypso for jazz ensemble 1974, An Evening Thought for jazz ensemble 1974, Bebop Revisited for jazz ensemble 1974, Le Miroir noir for jazz ensemble 1974, Six poèmes noir pour flûte et piano 1974, Two Improvisations for orchestra and jazz combo 1974, Sangre Negro (ballet) 1974, Give and Take (for voice with instrumental ensemble) 1975, Electric Stere-Opticon for cello 1975, Roots 1976, The Triplet Blues 1976, Contrasts 1976, Jazz Suite for violin and piano 1979, Singers of Songs/Weavers of Dreams: Homage to My Friends 1980, Sonata for violin, cello and four flutes 1980, Concerto for fours 1980, Cahaphi for jazz ensemble 1982, Lerma Samba for jazz ensemble 1982, Lima Beba Samba for jazz ensemble 1982, Lorob for jazz ensemble 1982, The Aebersold Strut for jazz ensemble 1982, AlMaCo for jazz ensemble 1982, Birdsong for jazz ensemble 1984, Bourne for jazz ensemble 1984, Groovin' For Diz for jazz ensemble 1984, The Five M Calypso for jazz ensemble 1984, Rouge et noir 1985, Suite for French horn, string quartet and contrabass 1985, Reflections on a Summer's Day for strings 1986, Through This Vale of Tears (for voice with instrumental ensemble) 1986, Sonata for French horn and jazz quartet 1986, Suite for French horn and jazz combo 1986, Sonata for jazz violin and string quartet 1987, two cello string quartets 1987, Inspiration for flute 1987, Ellingtones: A Fantasy for saxophone and orchestra 1987, Life Cycles for orchestra 1988, Impressions for two cellos 1988, Jazz Dance Suite for piano 1988, Homage: Bartok, Bird and Duke for jazz ensemble 1988, Duo for clarinet and cello 1988, To Dizzy With Love for jazz ensemble 1988, Shapes for percussion 1988–89, Concertpiece for viola 1989, Sonata for solo cello 1990, Sonata for clarinet and piano 1990, Alabama Landscape for orchestra 1990, Duet for alto saxophones 1990, Suite in Folk Style 1990, Soleil Impromptu 1990, Witness: Six Original Compositions in Spiritual Style 1990, Faces of the Blues: A Fantasy for alto saxophone and saxophone quartet 1990, Kirsten's First Song for jazz ensemble 1990, Steppin' Out for jazz ensemble 1990, An After Hours Lament for jazz ensemble 1990, Autumn's Dreams for jazz ensemble 1990, Miami Suite for jazz ensemble 1991, Concert Piece for viola and orchestra 1991, Concertpiece for trombone and strings 1991, Jazz Suite for clarinet and symphony orchestra: Three Ethnic Dances 1992, Truckin' for jazz ensemble 1992, Roots II 1992, Parallel Planes for orchestra 1992, Refractions for cello quartet 1993, Shades of Blue for orchestra 1993, Images, Shadows and Dreams: Five Vignettes for chorus 1993, Homage à l'histoire 1994, Images of Childhood for orchestra 1994, Eclipse for jazz ensemble 1996, Kirsten and her Puppy Katie for jazz ensemble 1996, Everybody's Song for jazz ensemble 1996, Illegal Entrance for jazz ensemble 1996, To The Fore for jazz ensemble 1996, Velvet Rose for jazz ensemble 1996. *Publications include:* Charlie Parker, Alto Saxophone 1978, Miles Davis, Trumpet 1978, J. J. Johnson, Trombone 1979, Jazz Pedagogy: A Comprehensive Method of Jazz Education for Teacher and Student 1979, Contemporary Patterns 1979, A Creative Approach to Practising Jazz 1994, Jazz Treble Clef Expressions and Explorations 1995, How To Learn Tunes: A Jazz Musician's Survival Guide 1997. *Honours:* Dr hc (Wabash Coll.), (Oberlin Coll.), (New England Conservatory of Music); Nat. Asscn of Negro Musicians Outstanding Musician Award 1968, Special Award 1976, Ind. Distinguished Citizen Award 1976, Nat. Asscn of Jazz Educators Hall of Fame Award 1981, Leadership Devt Center Outstanding Achievement in Business and the Professions Award 1983, Pres. Award for Distinguished Teaching, Indiana Univ., James Smithson Medal, Smithsonian Inst. 2002, American Jazz Masters Award, Nat. Endowment for the Arts 2000, Emmy Award 2003, Living Jazz Legend Award, Kennedy Center 2007. *Address:* Jacobs School of Music, Merrill Hall, MU218, Indiana University, Bloomington, IN 47405-2200, USA (office). *Telephone:* (812) 855-8546 (office). *E-mail:* bakderd@indiana.edu (office). *Website:* www.indiana.edu (office); www .davidbakermusic.org.

BAKER, Peter (Ginger); British musician (drums); b. 19 Aug. 1939, Lewisham, London. *Career:* drummer with Terry Lightfoot, Acker Bilk, Alexis

Korner's Blues Incorporated 1962, Graham Bond Organisation 1964–65; mem. Cream 1966–68, Blind Faith 1968–69, Airforce 1970–72, Salt (Nigeria), Baker-Gurvitz Army, Energy; short spells with Atomic Rooster and Hawkwind; Ginger Baker's Nutters; solo recording artist, and leader of own trio (with Bill Frisell and Charlie Haden); collaboration with Masters of Reality 1993; numerous performances with Cream and with Blind Faith. *Recordings include:* albums: with Cream: Fresh Cream 1967, Disraeli Gears 1967, Wheels Of Fire 1968, Goodbye 1969, The Best Of Cream 1969, Live Cream 1970, Live Cream Vol. 2 1972, Heavy Cream 1972, 20th Century Masters (compilation) 2000; with Blind Faith: Blind Faith 1969; with Airforce: Airforce 1970, Airforce 2 1972, Offen Bach 1970 2010; solo: The Best Of 1973, 11 Sides Of Baker 1977, From Humble Origins 1983, Horses and Trees 1986, Ginger Baker's African Force 1987, Middle Passage 1990, Unseen Rain 1992, Ginger Baker's Energy 1995, African Force 2001, African Force: Palanquin's Pole 2006; with Ginger Baker Trio: Going Back Home 1995, Falling Off The Roof 1995, Do What You Like 1998, Coward Of The County 1999. *Website:* www .gingerbaker.com.

BAKER, Rob; Canadian musician (guitar). *Career:* mem., The Tragically Hip 1983–. *Recordings include:* albums: Up to Here 1989, Road Apples 1991, Fully Completely 1992, Day for Night 1994, Trouble at the Henhouse 1996, Live Between Us 1997, Phantom Power 1998, Music @ Work 2000, In Violet Light 2002, In Between Revolution 2004, World Container 2006, We Are the Same 2009. *Honours:* inducted into the Canadian Music Hall of Fame 2005; Juno Music DVD of the Year Award 2006. *Address:* c/o Universal Music, 2450 Victoria Park Avenue, Suite 1, Toronto, ON M2J 5H3 (office); The Tragically Hip, PO Box 98130, 970 Queen Street East, Toronto, ON M4M 1J0, Canada. *E-mail:* TTH@thehip.com. *Website:* www.thehip.com.

BAKER, Ronald, BA; American musician (trumpet) and singer; b. 21 Nov. 1968, Baltimore, Maryland; m. Patricia Labeau 1994; one d. *Career:* Founder, Ronald Baker Quintet 1998; broadcasts on Radio France; played in film, Le Nouveau Monde; opened concerts for: André Ceccarelli; Black Label; Roy Haynes; Benny Waters; major festivals include: Montlouis; Montpellier; Orléans. *Recordings include:* Oberlin Jazz Ensemble; Perry-Boulanger Duo; Oppossum Gang; albums: with Ronald Baker Quintet: Five for Fun 2003, Endless Story 2007.

BALD HEAD SLICK (see Guru)

BALDAN, Bebo; Italian producer, musician (drums, percussion, electronics), arranger and composer; *Producer, Exit World Music Productions*; b. 16 April 1966, Venice. *Education:* studied with Percussione Ricerca Ensemble (members of Orchestra La Fenice–Conservatory of Venice); also studied with Nana Vasconcelos, Trilok Gurtu. *Career:* performed at festivals and venues in England, France (Les Printemps du Bourges, Tranmusicales-Rennes), Switzerland, Curaçao Jazz Festival, Estonia (Tallin Jazz Festival), Italy (Interzone Festival, RAI Television, Videomusic Television), USA (New York and KPEL Radio, Berkeley, California); played with Eugenio Bennato, DMA, Max M'Bass Ado, Andrea Braido, Luis Rizzo, Estasia, Duck Baker, Tolo Marton, Eddy C Campbell, Pitura Freska, also at Wim Wenders' Electronic Paintings exhibition, Venice; collaborated with Stephen James and David Torn and composed for Jon Hassell, Steven Brown, Steve Reich, Michael Nyman, Wim Mertens, David Torn, Ryuichi Sakamoto, Frank Zappa; Artistic co-Dir, UNESCO Festival, S.Giorgio, Venice 2002; mem. SIAE. *Film soundtracks:* Macbeth (Claudio Misculi), Aqua Nostra Igniset (Anselmo de Filippis), First Light, La Notte dei Foghi,. *Recordings:* worked on over 120 albums: as composer: Bebo Baldan: Vapor Frames 1991, Soniasikri (with Stephen James) 1991, Interzone (featuring Jon Hassell, Steve Reich, Wim Mertens, Michael Nyman) 1993, Sonora 4 (featuring Ryuichi Sakamoto, Frank Zappa, Hector Zazou) 1994, Diving Into The World (with David Torn) 1995, Earthbeat (with David Torn and Stephen James) 1995, Jaya (featuring Narah) 1996, Light from the Abyss (with P. Zennaro and Carolyn Carlson) 1997, Tantra: Life is Here (featuring David Torn) 1998, Maya 2000, Tantra Transensuality 2001, Flying Fishes 2004, Tantratribe: Radio Indye 2005, Quello Che Il Pubblico... (with Gilberto Gil and Moni Ovadia) 2005, Ghassan Mawlawi Sufi Memories 2006, Bebo Best & super lounge orchestra 2007. *Address:* Exit Productions, Via Metauro 21, 30174 Mestre, Venice, Italy (office). *Telephone:* (347) 1664821 (office). *E-mail:* exitworldmusic@gmail.com (office). *Website:* www.tantratribe .com (office); www.bebo.best.cd (office).

BALDOUS, Bernard; French musician (acoustic bass); b. 12 Dec. 1951, Montpellier. *Education:* Conservatoire de Musique, Montpellier, Berklee College of Music, Boston, USA. *Career:* plays bass with R. Anouillez, S. Baldous, J. Blanton, J. Benayoun, V. Espinieto, Fanfan Sanchez, E. Goldstein, M. Levine, A. Marcos, C. McBride, J. Neves, F. Nicolas, J. Peiffer, V. Perez, P. Pellegati, D. Ragot, G. Reilles, P. Rosengoltz, Sega Seck, P. Torreglosa, F. Urtado, S. Wilson, A. Woygnet; mem. Jazz Action Montpellier. *Compositions:* Fantome; Gigi; BB Blues. *Recordings:* Bernard Baldous Trio, 1993; Concerto for Jazz Band and Symphony Orchestra, 1994; Instant Jazz Quintet, 1995. *Website:* www.myspace.com/bernardbaldous.

BALIARDO, Diego; French musician (guitar). *Career:* guitarist with The Gipsy Kings; group was formed in Arles (originally named Los Reyes) 1976; performed throughout Europe and N Africa; collaborations with Ruben Blades, Joan Baez, Bananarama; group performs style of music known as Rumba Flamenca or Rumba Catalana; pioneered the introduction of drum kits, electronic bass, electronic keyboards, pop and reggae rhythms and modern recording techniques into flamenco music. *Film:* Tierra Gitana (Gipsy

Ground) 1996. *Recordings include:* albums: Gitan Poete (as Los Reyes) 1977, Allegria 1982, Luna de Fuegos 1983, Gipsy Kings 1988, Mosaique 1989, Allegria US Version 1990, Este Mundo 1991, Live 1992, Love and Liberté (Best Pop Album of the Year, Latin Grammy Awards) 1993, Greatest Hits 1994, The Best of the Gipsy Kings 1995, Estrellas 1995, Tierra Gitana 1996, Compas 1997, Cantos de Amor 1998, Volare: The Very Best of the Gipsy Kings 1999, Somos Gitanos 2001, Tonino Baliardo 2003, Roots 2004, Pasajero 2006, Savor Flamenco (Grammy Award for Best World Music Album 2014) 2013. *Current Management:* c/o Impact Artist Management, 42 Hamilton Terrace, New York, NY 10031, USA. *Telephone:* (212) 280-0800. *E-mail:* info@ impactartist.com. *Website:* www.impactartist.com; www.gipsykings.com.

BALIARDO, Paco; French musician (guitar). *Career:* guitarist with The Gipsy Kings; group was formed in Arles (originally named Los Reyes) 1976; performed throughout Europe and N Africa; collaborations with Ruben Blades, Joan Baez, Bananarama; group performs a style of music known as Rumba Flamenca or Rumba Catalana; pioneered the introduction of drum kits, electronic bass, electronic keyboards, pop and reggae rhythms and modern recording techniques into flamenco music. *Film:* Tierra Gitana (Gipsy Ground) 1996. *Recordings include:* albums: Gitan Poete (as Los Reyes) 1977, Allegria 1982, Luna de Fuegos 1983, Gipsy Kings 1988, Mosaique 1989, Allegria US Version 1990, Este Mundo 1991, Live 1992, Love and Liberté (Best Pop Album of the Year, Latin Grammy Awards) 1993, Greatest Hits 1994, The Best of the Gipsy Kings 1995, Estrellas 1995, Tierra Gitana 1996, Compas 1997, Cantos de Amor 1998, Volare: The Very Best of the Gipsy Kings 1999, Somos Gitanos 2001, Tonino Baliardo 2003, Roots 2004, Pasajero 2006, Savor Flamenco (Grammy Award for Best World Music Album 2014) 2013. *Current Management:* c/o Impact Artist Management, 42 Hamilton Terrace, New York, NY 10031, USA. *Telephone:* (212) 280-0800. *E-mail:* info@ impactartist.com. *Website:* www.impactartist.com; www.gipsykings.com.

BALIARDO, Tonino; French musician (guitar) and composer. *Career:* lead guitarist with The Gipsy Kings and composer of the group's instrumentals; group was formed in Arles (originally named Los Reyes) 1976; performed throughout Europe and N Africa; collaborations with Ruben Blades, Joan Baez, Bananarama; group performs a style of music known as Rumba Flamenca or Rumba Catalana; pioneered the introduction of drum kits, electronic bass, electronic keyboards, pop and reggae rhythms and modern recording techniques into flamenco music. *Film:* Tierra Gitana (Gipsy Ground) 1996. *Recordings include:* albums: Gitan Poete (as Los Reyes) 1977, Allegria 1982, Luna de Fuegos 1983, Gipsy Kings 1988, Mosaique 1989, Allegria US Version 1990, Este Mundo 1991, Live 1992, Love and Liberté (Best Pop Album of the Year, Latin Grammy Awards) 1993, Greatest Hits 1994, The Best of the Gipsy Kings 1995, Estrellas 1995, Tierra Gitana 1996, Compas 1997, Cantos de Amor 1998, Volare: The Very Best of the Gipsy Kings 1999, Somos Gitanos 2001, Tonino Baliardo 2003, Roots 2004, Pasajero 2006, Savor Flamenco (Grammy Award for Best World Music Album 2014) 2013. *Current Management:* c/o Impact Artist Management, 42 Hamilton Terrace, New York, NY 10031, USA. *Telephone:* (212) 280-0800. *Fax:* (212) 280-0808. *E-mail:* info@impactartist.com. *Website:* www.impactartist.com; www .gipsykings.com.

BALKE, Jon Georg; Norwegian musician (piano, keyboards, percussion), conductor and composer; *Administrator, Magnetic Music*; b. 7 June 1955, Ringsaker; m.; two d. *Career:* began professional career with Arild Andersen's quartet 1974; tours of Europe; recordings for ECM Records; later established as composer for groups such as Oslo 13, Masqualero, Jokleba, Magnetic North Orchestra, Batagraf, Siwan; also composer of chamber music and theatre; mem. Norwegian Composers' Assen, Norwegian Jazz Forum. *Exhibitions:* works with Kjell Bjorgeengen,Tone Myskja, Dag Thoresen and others. *Dance:* works with Francesco Scavetta and Giorgio Rossi. *Stage performances:* The Palm Wine Drinkard 1981, Spinn 1994, Explo 97 1997. *Television:* Magnetic North live in Bruxelles (SVT) 1996, I Løse lufta (NRK) 2001, Magnetic Musician (NRK, SVT) 2006, Siwan (NRK) 2008. *Recordings:* albums: Nonsentration 1992, Further 1994, Rotor 1998, Solarized 1999, Saturation 1998, Kyanos 2002, Diverted Travels 2004, Book of Velocities 2008, Siwan 2009, Say and Play Batagraf 2011. *Honours:* Buddy Award, Norwegian Jazz Fed. 1985, Jazz Musician of Year 1994, Edvard Prize for Composition 2000, Rolf Gamleng Prize 2008, Jahrespreis den Deutschen Schallplattenkritik 2009. *Website:* www.magnetic.no (home); www.siwan.no (home); www .batagraf.org (home).

BALL, David (Dave); British musician (synthesizer) and composer; b. 3 May 1959, Blackpool, Lancashire; m. Ginny. *Career:* Founder-mem. Soft Cell (with Marc Almond) 1979–84, re-formed 2001; mem. The Grid (with Richard Norris) 1990–; Founder-mem. Nitewreckage (with Celine Hispiche, Rick Mulhall and Terry Neale) 2010–; written and produced for Kylie Minogue, Billie Ray Martin. *Compositions include:* score for stage revival, Suddenly Last Summer 1983. *Recordings include:* albums: with Soft Cell: Non-Stop Erotic Cabaret 1981, Non-Stop Ecstatic Dancing 1982, The Art Of Falling Apart 1983, This Last Night In Sodom 1984, Down In The Subway 1994, Cruelty Without Beauty 2002, Live 2003, At The BBC (live) 2003; with The Grid: Electric Head 1990, 456 1992, Evolver 1994, Music For Dancing 1995, Doppelgänger 2008; with Nitewreckage: Take Your Money And Run 2011; solo: In Strict Tempo 1983. *Honours:* Billboard Award for New Wave Band of the Year 1981, BRIT Award for Best British Single (for Tainted Love) 1982. *Website:* www .celineandnitewreckage.com.

BALL, Ian E.; British musician (guitar, bass, percussion, harmonica), singer, songwriter and producer; b. 1974, Southport, England. *Career:* Founding mem. Gomez 1996–; mem. Operation Aloha; numerous concerts, festival, radio and television appearances. *Films include:* La Cucina (composer) 2007. *Recordings include:* albums: Bring It On 1998, Liquid Skin 1999, Abandoned Shopping Trolley Hotline 2000, In Our Gun 2002, Out West: Live at the Fillmore 2005, How We Operate 2006, A New Tide 2009, Whatever's on Your Mind 2011, Unfold Yourself 2013. *Honours:* Mercury Music Prize 1998. *Current Management:* c/o Marc Allan, Red Light Management, 321 East Main Street, Charlottesville, VA 22902, USA. *Website:* www.redlightmanagement .com. *E-mail:* gomez@gomeztheband.com (office). *Website:* www .gomeztheband.com.

BALL, Malcolm, LRAM; British musician (percussion, keyboards) and composer; *Instrumental Advisor and Senior Examiner, Trinity College London;* b. 8 Aug. 1953, Ilford, Essex, England; m. Jack Ball. *Education:* Royal Coll. of Music. *Career:* specializes in contemporary music of all kinds; BBC Radio broadcasts with Geoff Warren Quartet for Jazz in Britain, Jazz Today; Arts Council tours of Hungary, Yugoslavia; workshops with Graham Collier; Head of Percussion and Contemporary Studies, London Borough of Redbridge; Instrumental Advisor and Sr Examiner, Trinity Coll. London (fmrly Trinity Guildhall); writer for contemporary music magazine Avant; webmaster for Olivier Messaien website; mem. Royal Soc. of Musicians of GB, Musicians' Union, Stockhausen Soc., British Harry Partch Soc. *Compositions:* Close Your Eyes and See, for orchestra 1995, O-taiko-Do, Terror Nova, for percussion ensemble. *Achievements include:* plays ondes Martenot. *Publications:* Percussive Perspectives, Trinity College London Drum Kit Publications; articles on Stockhausen and Messiaen on the internet. *Address:* 102 Victoria Chase, Colchester, Essex, CO1 1WW, England (home). *Telephone:* (1206) 510384 (office). *E-mail:* rechants1@yahoo.co.uk (home). *Website:* www .malcolmball.co.uk; www.oliviermessiaen.org.

BALL, Michael Ashley, OBE; British actor, singer and broadcaster; b. 27 June 1962, Bromsgrove, Worcs., England; s. of Anthony George Ball and Ruth Parry Ball (née Davies); partner Cathy McGowan. *Education:* Plymouth Coll., Farnham Sixth Form Coll., Guildford School of Acting. *Career:* numerous nat. and int. concert tours; co-founder and patron Research into Ovarian Cancer. *Theatre includes:* Judas/John the Baptist in Godspell (debut), Aberystwyth 1984, Frederick in The Pirates of Penzance, Manchester Opera House 1984, Marius in Les Misérables, London 1985–86, Raoul in The Phantom of the Opera, London 1987–88, Alex in Aspects of Love, London 1989–90, New York (debut) 1990, Giorgio in Passion, London 1996, Alone Together (part of Divas Season), London 2001, Caractacus Potts in Chitty Chitty Bang Bang, London 2002–04, The Woman in White 2005, Hairspray (Olivier Award for Best Actor in a Musical) 2008, Sweeney Todd - The Demon Barber of Fleet Street (Olivier Award for Best Actor in a Musical) 2012. *Film:* England My England 1995. *Television:* represented UK in Eurovision Song Contest 1992, own TV series 'Michael Ball' 1993, 1994, Royal Variety performances, Michael Ball in Concert (video) 1997, An Evening with Michael Ball 1998, Lord Lloyd Webber's 50th Birthday 1998, Michael Ball at Christmas 1999. *Radio:* Sunday Night with Michael Ball (BBC Radio 2) 2014–. *Recordings include:* albums: Rage of the Heart 1987, Michael Ball 1992, Always 1993, One Careful Owner 1994, The Best of Michael Ball 1994, First Love 1996, Michael Ball – The Musicals 1996, Michael Ball – The Movies 1998, Christmas 1999, Live at the Royal Albert Hall 1999, This Time It's Personal 2000, Centre Stage 2001, Music 2005, One Voice 2006, Back to Bacharach 2007, Past and Present 2009, Songs of Love 2009, Encore 2010, Heroes 2011, Both Sides Now 2013, If Everyone Was Listening 2014; stage show cast recordings include Les Miserables 1986, Aspects of Love 1989, West Side Story 1993, Passion 1996, Chitty Chitty Bang Bang 2002, Sweeney Todd: The Demon Barber of Fleet Street 2012. *Honours:* Dr hc (Plymouth); Variety Club of Great Britain Most Promising Artiste Award 1989, The Variety Club Best Recording Artiste 1998, Theatregoers Club of Great Britain Most Popular Musical Actor 1999. *Current Management:* c/o Phil Bowdery, Live Nation (Music) UK Ltd, Regent Arcade House, 19-25 Argyll Street, London, W1F 7TS, England. *Telephone:* (20) 7009-3333. *Fax:* (20) 7009-3211. *E-mail:* sarah.donovan@livenation.co.uk. *Website:* www.livenation.co.uk. *E-mail:* mbe@michaelball.co.uk (office). *Website:* www .michaelball.co.uk; www.mbfc.co.uk (office).

BALL, Tom; American singer, musician (harmonica, guitar) and writer; b. 24 Oct. 1950, Los Angeles, Calif.; s. of James H. Ball and Lolita M. Ball (née Mecham); m. Laurie Linn 1983; one d. *Education:* Santa Monica Coll. *Career:* singer, harmonica player Yerba Buena Blues Band 1965–67; freelance musician 1968–79; mem. duo Tom Ball and Kenny Sultan 1979–; business venture: Good Time Blues Pub (BMI); studio work on 250 recordings, films, TV shows; mem. NARAS, AFTRA, AFofM. *Recordings include:* albums: Confusion 1981, Who Drank My Beer 1983, Bloodshot Eyes 1986, Guitar Music 1988, Too Much Fun 1990, Filthy Rich 1993, Double Vision 1996, 20th Anniversary – Live! 2000, 18 Pieces for Solo Steel-string Guitar 2003, Solo Guitar Music from Films 2007, Tis the Season 2009, Nagasaki Sails from Uranus 2011. *Publications include:* author: Blues Harmonica 1993, Nasty Blues 1995, Sonny Terry Licks 1997, Little Walter/Big Walter Licks 2000, The Marty Graw Book 2002, Dropped D Tuning 2003. *Honours:* Telly Award Winner 1994. *Address:* PO Box 20156, Santa Barbara, CA 93120, USA (home). *Website:* www.tomball.us.

BALLAMY, Iain Mark; British musician (saxophone) and composer; b. 20 Feb. 1964, Guildford. *Career:* collaborations with Loose Tubes, Bill Bruford's Earthworks, Balloon Man, New York Composers' Orchestra, Dewey Redman, Gil Evans, George Coleman, Mike Gibbs, Hermeto Pascoal, Sankalpam 1982–; mem. Django Bates' groups Human Chain and Delightful Precipice; appeared in Out There, musical theatre production 1995–96; specialist tutor, Royal Acad. of Music, Trinity Coll. of Music; mem., Musicians' Union, PRS; MCPS; GVL. *Compositions:* Commissions for Apollo Saxophone Quartet, Salford College, Birmingham Jazz, Food Cheltenham Jazz Festival, Bath International Festival. *Recordings include:* Balloon Man 1989, All Men Amen 1995, The Little Radio, Food (1), Food (2), Food (3), Pepper Street Interludes 2000, Signal to Noise, Acmé, Three Windows; with Django Bates: Quiet Nights, Like Life, Good Evening, Here is the News, Winter Truce (and Homes Ablaze), Summer Fruits (and Unrest), You Live and Learn, More Jazz 2007, Mercurial Balm 2012, Quercus 2013; with Loose Tubes: Loose Tubes, Delightful Precipice, Open Letter, with Bill Bruford's Earthworks: Earthworks, Dig, All Heaven Broke Loose, Stamping Ground, Heavenly Bodies. *Honours:* John Dankworth Cup 1985, BT British Jazz Award for Best Ensemble 1995, BBC Radio 3 Award for Innovation, British Jazz Awards 2001. *E-mail:* iain@ ballamy.com. *Website:* www.ballamy.com.

BALLARD, Glen, BA; American songwriter, record producer, arranger, musician (piano, guitar) and programmer and screenwriter; b. 1 May 1953, Natchez, MS. *Education:* Univ. of Mississippi. *Career:* joined Elton John's organization, Los Angeles; songwriter, MCA Music Publishing 1978; independent songwriter late 1980s; formed Java Records 1996, later part of Island/ Def Jam; as prod. and songwriter, worked with Paula Abdul, Aerosmith, Anastacia, Backstreet Boys, Philip Bailey, George Benson, Natalie Cole, Dave Matthews Band, Céline Dion, Earth Wind & Fire, Sheena Easton, Aretha Franklin, Michael Jackson, Al Jarreau, Quincy Jones, Alanis Morissette, Stevie Nicks, No Doubt, K. T. Oslin, Wilson Phillips, Pointer Sisters, Seal, Shakira, George Strait, Curtis Stigers, Barbra Streisand, Van Halen, Jack Wagner. *Contributed songs for films:* Two of a Kind 1983, The Slugger's Wife 1985, Clubland 1999, Titan A.E. (also prod.) 2000, The Mummy Returns 2001, Shallow Hal 2001, xXx 2002, The Matrix Reloaded 2003, The Polar Express (Grammy Award for Best Song Written for Motion Picture, Television or Other Visual Media, with Alan Silvestri 2006) 2004. *Recordings:* numerous albums as producer or contributor including: Michael Jackson, Thriller 1982, Pointer Sisters, Break Out 1983, Michael Jackson, Bad 1987, Paula Abdul, Forever Your Girl 1989, Wilson Phillips, Wilson Phillips 1990, Curtis Stigers, Curtis Stigers 1991, Alanis Morissette, Jagged Little Pill 1995, The Corrs, Talk on Corners 1997, No Doubt, Return of Saturn 2000, Anastacia, Anastacia 2004, Annie Lennox, Songs of Mass Destruction 2007, Anouk, Who's Your Momma 2007, Wilson Phillips, Christmas in Harmony 2010, Stevie Nicks, In Your Dreams 2011. *Honours:* Grammy Awards, incl. Best Rock Song 1990, Best Rock Album, Album of the Year, Video of the Year; National Acad. of Songwriters Songwriter of the Year 1997, ASCAP Songwriter of 1997, NARAS Governor's Award 1997. *E-mail:* info@glenballard.com. *Website:* www .glenballard.com.

BALLARD, Kaye; American actress and singer; b. 20 Nov. 1926, Cleveland, OH. *Career:* numerous television appearances; concerts include: two Royal command performances; Hello Dolly; Nymph Errant; stage performances include: Nunsense; Gypsy; Annie Get Your Gun; High Spirits; Odd Couple; Ziegfield Follies (touring companies); Top Bananas; Three To Make Ready; Touch and Go; Wonderful Town; She Stoops To Conquer; Golden Apple; Carnival; Molly (Broadway); One woman shows: Working 42nd Street At Last; Hey Ma; mem. SAG; AFTRA; Equity. *Recordings include:* Nymph Errant; Songs From Hey Ma; Fanny Brice; Then and Again; Unsung Sondheim; Ladies Who Wrote The Lyrics; Long Time Friends; Golden Apple; Gershwin Rarities; Follies; Peanuts. *Address:* c/o Mark Sendroff, Sendroff and Baruch LLC, 1500 Broadway, Suite 2001, New York, NY 10036-4015, USA. *Telephone:* (212) 840-6400. *Fax:* (212) 840-6401. *E-mail:* msendroff@ sendroffbaruch.com. *Website:* www.sendroffbaruch.com. *E-mail:* info@ kayeballard.com. *Website:* www.kayeballard.com.

BALSAMO, Terry; American musician (guitar). *Career:* fmr mem., Cold 1995–2003, 2009; mem. rock band, Evanescence 2003–. *Recordings include:* albums: with Cold: 13 Ways to Bleed on Stage 2000, Year of the Spider 2003; with Evanescence: Anywhere But Home (live) 2004, The Open Door 2006, Evanescence 2011. *Honours:* Grammy Award for Best New Artist 2003, Grammy Award for Best Hard Rock Performance (for Bring Me To Life) 2003. *Address:* c/o Wind-up Records, 72 Madison Avenue, New York, NY 10016, USA. *E-mail:* evanescence@winduprecords.com. *Website:* www.evanescence .com.

BALTAZANIS, Kostas, BMus; Greek musician (guitar), music educator and writer; b. 20 Feb. 1965, Patras. *Education:* Berklee College of Music, Boston, USA. *Career:* Artistic Director, Nakas Conservatory, Athens, Greece; Studio musician, clinician for Berklee College of Music; Writer of music education books. *Publications:* Jazz Harmony; Music Theory and Ear Training; Electric Guitar. *Website:* www.myspace.com/kostasbaltazanis.

BALVIN, J; Colombian reggaeton and hip hop singer; b. (José Álvaro Osorio Balvin), 7 May 1985, Medellin. *Career:* moved to USA 2002; released first mixtape and first single 2012; toured USA supporting Enrique Iglesias and Pitbull; co-headlined USA tour with Becky G 2015. *Recordings include:* albums: Real 2009, El Negocio 2011, La Familia (Premio Lo Nuestro Urban Album of the Year 2015) 2013. *Honours:* Latin Grammy Award for Best Urban Song (for Ay Vamos) 2015, Premios Lo Nuestro for Urban Artist of the Year

2015, for Best Urban Song and Best Urban Collaboration of the Year (for 6AM, with Farruko) 2015, MTV Europe Music Award for Best Latin America Central Act 2015. *E-mail:* management@jbalvinelnegocio.com. *Website:* jbalvin.com.

BANDARA, Asela; Sri Lankan musician (bass guitar). *Education:* Trinity Coll., Kandy. *Career:* Founder mem., rock group Paranoid Earthling 2000–, debut live performance 2001; released several EPs and singles 2005–, including Rock'n'Roll is My Anarchy, Playtime Music 2007, Bringing Down the Sun 2008; live performances in India 2009, Afghanistan 2012. *Recordings include:* several EPs and singles. *E-mail:* manager@paranoidearthling.com (office); manager.paranoidearthling@gmail.com (office). *Website:* www.paranoidearthling.com.

BANDIER, Martin N., BA, LLD; American lawyer and entertainment business executive; *Chairman and CEO, Sony/ATV Music Publishing*; b. 21 July 1941, New York, NY; m. Dorothy Bandier; three c. *Education:* Syracuse Univ., Brooklyn Law School. *Career:* began career with law firm in Manhattan; joined legal dept at LeFrank Organisation, becoming Sr Vice-Pres.; Co-f. Entertainment Co. 1975, Entertainment Music Co. 1985, SBK Entertainment World 1987; Vice-Chair. Thorn EMI 1989–91, CEO EMI Music Publishing 1991–2007, Chair. 1992–2007, mem. Bd of Dirs EMI Group plc 1998–2006; Chair. and CEO, Sony/ATV Music Publishing LLC 2007–; mem. Bd of Dirs United Jewish Appeal, City of Hope, Songwriter's Hall of Fame, Nat. Music Publrs' Asscn, Rock and Roll Hall of Fame; Trustee, T.J. Martell Foundation, Syracuse Univ.; mem. Metropolitan New York Advisory Bd, Nat. Acad. of Recording Arts and Sciences; f. music and entertainment industry degree programme at Syracuse Univ. named The Bandier Program for Music and Entertainment Industries 2006. *Honours:* Abe Olman Publisher Award 1990, Arents Award 1994, Patron of the Arts inductee, Songwriters Hall of Fame 2003. *Address:* Sony/ATV Music Publishing LLC, 550 Madison Avenue, Fifth Floor, New York, NY 10022, USA (office). *Telephone:* (212) 833-8000 (office). *Fax:* (212) 833-5552 (office). *E-mail:* info@sonyatv.com (office). *Website:* www.sonyatv.com (office).

BANDY, Marion (Moe); American country singer and musician (guitar); b. 12 Feb. 1944, Meridian, Mississippi. *Career:* played guitar in father's band The Mission City Playboys, San Antonio, Texas; Rodeo rider; Debut single Lonely Lady, Satin Records, 1964; Regular on San Antonio TV show Country Corner, 1973; Signed to GRC Records, 1974; Many Billboard country hits mostly on Columbia Records, including some with Joe Stampley, 1974–89; Moe and Joe collaborations included controversial parody of Boy George, Where's The Dress, 1984; Americana, 1988, used by George Bush Sr as presidential theme song; Opened own 900 seater Moe Bandy Americana Theatre in Branson, Missouri. *Recordings:* albums: I Just Started Hatin' Cheatin' Songs Today 1974, It Was Always So Easy (to Find an Unhappy Woman) 1975, Hank Williams You Wrote My Life, 1976; Just Good Ol' Boys (with Joe Stampley), I Cheated Me Right Out Of You, It's A Cheatin' Situation, 1979; She's Not Really Cheatin' (She's Just Getting' Even), 1982, Many Mansions 1989, Too Old to Die Young 2005, Souvenirs 2009. *Honours:* CMA, Vocal Duo of the Year (with Joe Stampley), 1980. *Address:* Sweetsong Nashville, 1021 16th Avenue South, Nashville, TN 37212, USA (office). *Telephone:* (615) 329-3187 (office). *Fax:* (615) 327-4454 (office). *E-mail:* info@sweetsongnashville.com (office). *Website:* www.sweetsongnashville.com (office). *Address:* Bullrope Production (Moe Bandy Music), PO Box 1035, Branson, MO 65615, USA. *Telephone:* (417) 252-4663. *E-mail:* info@MoeBandy.com. *Website:* www.moebandy.com.

BANERJEE, Chandrani, BA; Indian singer and songwriter; b. 27 Oct. 1973, Chandernagore; d. of Dr K. M. Das and Sandhyarani Das; m. Vikramjit Banerjee 1993. *Education:* Gokhale Memorial Coll., Calcutta (now Kolkata). *Career:* mem. Krosswindz 1990–, lead vocalist 1999–; performed for Great Indian Rock Festival 1996; performed with Gautam Chatterjee and Mohiner Ghoraguli 1998–99; performed and recorded with Calcutta folk band Bhoomi 1999–2001; sang on two Bhoomi albums: Jatra Shurn and Udaan; regular Krosswindz tours in Indian sub-continent, also USA 2007; Calcutta Corresp., RSJ music magazine 1994–98. *Films:* The Way Back Home, Amra Ebong. *Recordings include:* albums: The Singles 1994, Abar Bochor Kuri Pore 1995, Gir 1995, Gir Vol. 2 1996, Poth Gache Beke 1996, Khyaper Gan 1999, One World 2002, Bhebe Dekhecho Ki 2002, Music Of The Globe 2003, Jhiko Jhiko 2004, Misiki Misiki 2005, Krosswindz Dhowan 2006, Phire Dekha (Mirchi Music Award for Album of the Year 2012) 2011; several recordings with Saregama India Ltd. *Publications include:* numerous articles on Indian music scene for RSJ magazine. *Honours:* Best Female Vocals Award, St Xavier's Coll. Festival 1991, Presidency Coll. 1992. *Address:* Flat 1B Kanak Appartment, 174/10 N. S. C. Bose Road, Kolkata 700 040, India (home). *Telephone:* (98) 30156148 (mobile); (33) 24814125 (home). *E-mail:* tukiguitarman@gmail.com (office). *Website:* www.krosswindz.com (office).

BANERJEE, Ratanjit (Mickey), BA, MBA; Indian musician (keyboards); b. 27 Aug. 1974, Dhanbad; brother of Vikramjit Banerjee. *Education:* Jawaharlal Nehru Univ., Jadavpur Univ. *Career:* mem. Krosswindz 1990–, keyboard player 2001–. *Recordings include:* albums: The Singles 1994, Abar Bochor Kuri Pore 1995, Poth Gache Beke 1996, Khyaper Gan 1999, One World 2002, Bhebe Dekhecho Ki 2002, Music Of The Globe 2003, Jhiko Jhiko 2004, Misiki Misiki 2005, Krosswindz Dhowan 2006, Phire Dekha (Mirchi Music Award for Album of the Year 2012) 2011. *Address:* Flat 1B Kanak Appartment, 174/10 N. S. C. Bose Road, Kolkata 700 040, India (home). *Telephone:* (33) 24813877 (home); (98) 30022578 (mobile). *E-mail:* ratanjitbanerjee77@yahoo.com (office). *Website:* www.krosswindz.com (office).

BANERJEE, Vikramjit (Tuki), BA; Indian musician (guitar), backing singer, composer and producer; *Leader, Krosswindz*; b. 11 Oct. 1971, Calcutta (now Kolkata); brother of Ratanjit Banerjee; m. Chandrani Banerjee 1993. *Education:* St Xavier's Coll., Calcutta. *Career:* Band Leader, Lead Guitarist and Music Dir Krosswindz 1990–; played with jazz fusion band Chlorophyll Dreams 1989–99; performed with Gautam Chatterjee and Mohinder Ghoraguli 1998–99; played guitar with folk band Bhoomi 1999–2001; Krosswindz USA tour 2007, 2009; certified as enlisted recording artist for AIR. *Films:* The Way Back Home, Calcutta Blues, Amra Ebong, Madly Bengali, Ujaane Poddo Bhashe, Khasi Kotha. *Radio:* Mirchi, Aamar FM, Red FM, BBC Asia, PBS Melbourne, live radio unplugged concert for Sandusky Radio, Seattle. *Recordings include:* albums: The Singles 1994, Abar Bochor Kuri Pore 1995, Poth Gache Beke 1996, Khyaper Gan 1999, One World 2002, Bhebe Dekhecho Ki 2002, Music Of The Globe 2003, Jhiko Jhiko 2004, Misiki Misiki 2005, Tribute to Eric Johnson 2004, Dhowa 2006, Phire Dekha 2011. *Publication:* Eternal Portraits – The International Library of Poetry 2005. *Honours:* AIR Recording Artist 1990, St Miguel Scholarship for Music, St Mary's Coll., Minn., USA 1992, Berklee Scholarship Cttee Award 1992, Album of the Year (Band), Mirchi Awards 2012. *Address:* Flat 1B Kanak Appartment, 174/10 N.S.C. Bose Road, Kolkata 700 040, India (home). *Telephone:* 98-30156148 (mobile); (33) 23814125 (home). *E-mail:* tukiguitarman@yahoo.com (office); vikramjit.banerjee@yahoo.com (office); tukiguitarman@gmail.com (home). *Website:* www.krosswindz.com (office); www.cdbaby.com/krosswindz (home).

BANFIELD, William (Bill) Cedric, BMus, MA, DMA; American composer, academic and musician (guitar); *Professor of Liberal Arts, Berklee College of Music*; b. 24 March 1961, Detroit, MI. *Education:* Cass Tech. High School, New England Conservatory of Music, Boston, Tufts Univ., Medford, Boston Univ., Univ. of Mich. at Ann Arbor. *Career:* mem. Detroit bands, including Cool Breeze and The Sapphire from age 12; f. Bill Banfield Quintet 1980; founder and operator, B Magic Operations, Boston 1984–88; guest guitar soloist with Detroit Metropolitan Orchestra 1984, 1989; conductor, La Chorale des Martyrs de L'Ouganda (Senegalese Choir and Orchestra) 1988; f. Undine Smith Moore Collection, Ind. Univ. 1993; teacher public schools, Boston 1980–86; Musical Dir, Days in the Arts Program, Tanglewood Music Festival, Tanglewood, MA 1984–88; Minister of Educ., Union United Church, Boston 1984–88; Program Co-ordinator, Boston Theological Inst. 1985–88; founder and Dir, Young Artists Devt Inc., Boston 1985–88, Boston Music Community Center 1986–88; guitar instructor, Univ. of Mich. at Ann Arbor 1988–89, jazz instructor 1988–90; private instructor in composition, arranging and guitar pedagogy 1988–92; instructor, Hartford Biblical Studies Inst., Detroit, MI 1989–92; Asst Prof., Dept of Afro-American Studies, Ind. Univ. at Bloomington 1992–97; Prof. of Music, Ind. Univ./Purdue Univ., Indianapolis 1992–97; Dir and composer-in-residence, Soul Revue/Black Popular Arts Ensemble, Afro-American Arts Inst., Ind. Univ. 1992–97; witness series, composer-in-residence, Plymouth Music Series, Minneapolis, MN 1993–95; visiting artist and scholar at numerous insts., including Univ. of Mich. at Ann Arbor 1994, Carleton Coll. 1995, St Augustine Coll. 1995, Tufts Univ. 1995, Univ. of Mass at Amherst 1995, Univ. of Minneapolis 1995, Butler Univ. 1996, Duke Univ. 1996, Univ. of Akron 1996; W. E. B. Dubois Fellow, Harvard Univ. 2001; Endowed Chair Humanities and Fine Arts, Univ. of St Thomas, St Paul 1997–2006, also Dir American Cultural Studies Program and Assoc. Prof.; Prof. of Liberal Arts, Berklee Coll. of Music 2006–; mem. American Guild of Organists, Nat. Advisory Council, ASCAP, Coll. Music Soc., Minn. Composers' Forum, Nat. Asscn of Negro Musicians. *Compositions include:* for solo instruments: Warmly Embraced for piano 1980, A Stroll in Lydian for piano 1981, Reversed Roles for piano 1981, One Segment Samba for piano 1981, Belshazzar for guitar 1981, Hanaha for guitar 1981, A Little Look At Me for piano 1982, I V bVIII 5b7 b7 for piano 1982, Karla for guitar 1982, Song for Earl for guitar 1983, Song for Mic for guitar 1983, Gibbit for oboe 1985, Fantasy for piano 1987, Mead 28 for piano 1989, Waggussyduke for piano 1989, Suite for Richard for trumpet 1990, Two Tall Tales for bassoon 1992; for small instrumental ensembles: Derwin E.: Six Minutes for String Quartet No. 1 1983, Susan: String Quartet No. 2 1985, El Dia de Derber: Wedding Suite for string quartet and piano 1985, Bobby's Theme 1985, Brass Belly 1988, Spirituals 1988, Zola 1988, Cone Tone: String Quartet No. 3 1989, Four Persons 1991, For Bass Wrapped in Pita Pocket with Ketchup, Mayo and a Dash of Hot Mustard 1991, Can We All Get Along? 1992, Dance Like The Wind for woodwind 1995; for jazz ensemble: The Dream Suite 1980, Carla 1983, Straightline 1983, A Friend's Advice 1984, Just A Note From Sam 1988, Her Embrace 1990, Last Night She Had a Really Good Dream 1992, Blues for Anne 1992, Lisa 1993, Magdalene 1993, Rachel 1993, Derry Alan 1993, Brooke 1993, And What Would You Like to Hear Little Lady? 1995, TIM (Time in Motion) 1995, She Made It Crystal Clear 1995, Song for George 1996, Three Late Night Discussions 1996, Bill's Blue 1996, Brookes Way 1997, A Prayer 1997; for concert band: Concerto for Wind Symphony 1995, The Seed: Fanfare for Wind Symphony 1998; for full orchestra: Fantasy for Orchestra on Themes from Shakespeare 1989, Symphony No. 1: Brevities of Experience 1990, Dreams Realized/Nightmare Resolved 1992, Symphony No. 5: Five Shades of a Woman in Black 1993, Four Songs for Five American Voices: Symphony No. 6 1993, Essay for orchestra 1995; for orchestra with soloists: Marsheila 1982, Baroque Suite for guitar and string orchestra 1987, Susej Moments for guitar and string orchestra 1987, Three Movements and Themes on Shakespeare 1988, Jenny Festival for guitar and orchestra 1989, Moods and Colors concerto for trombone and orchestra 1991, You Can Tell the World 1992, Delancey Street 1994, Symphony No. 7: Reveries, A Summer's Circle 1997; for orchestra with chorus: Guide Us Through the Years 1988, Visions: Symphonic Songs for orchestra and double chorus 1988, Job's Song: Symphony No. 3 1992, Life Suite 1995; vocal: Pleasing Thought 1979, I'm Won 1984, Are You Thinking About Me? 1984, Baby You 1984, All I Gotta Do 1984, Unmistakable You 1985, Steadfast Love: Psalm 118 for chorus 1986, Harp Song 1989, Summer Lies 1989, The Prophetess 1989, Steadfast Love: Psalm 138 for chorus 1989, I Love You My Life 1990, Momma Why?: Questions of a Young American (opera) 1991, Spiritual Songs 1991, Desire: Langston Living Amongst the Poets Unknown 1992, The Prophetess II 1992, Eyes (musical) 1995, Luyala (opera) 1997, Fisherman's Dock (opera) 1997. *Recordings:* albums: with Bill Banfield Band: Spring Forward 2009. *Publications:* Musical Landscapes in Color: Conversations with Black American Composers 2003, Black Notes: Essays of a Musician writing in a Post-Album Age 2004; contrib. numerous articles. *Honours:* Chrysler Corpn Scholarship, Youth of Understanding 1978, Boston Foundation Artist Award 1987, winner Savannah Symphony American Symphony Orchestra League nat. search for black talent 1994, McKnight Foundation Composers-in-Residence Fellowship from the American Composers Forum, Carleton Coll., Univ. of St Thomas 1995–96, Detroit Symphony/UNISYS Award 1995. *Address:* Department of Liberal Arts, Berklee College of Music, 1140 Boylston Street, Boston, MA 02215, USA (office). *Telephone:* (617) 747-2552 (office). *Website:* www.berklee.edu (office); www.billbanfield.com.

BANGALTER, Thomas; French producer, remixer and DJ; b. 1 Jan. 1975, Paris. *Career:* fmr mem. Darling; Co-founder, Daft Punk 1992–; f. record label, Roulé; collaborations with Bob Sinclair, Alan Braxe; remixed Gabrielle, Ian Pooley, Chemical Brothers. *Film:* score: Tron: Legacy 2010. *Recordings include:* albums: with Daft Punk: Homework 1996, Discovery 2001, Alive 1997 2001, Human After All 2005, Musique Vol. 1 1993–2005 2006, Alive 2007 (Grammy Award for Best Electronic/Dance Album 2009) 2007, Random Access Memories (Grammy Awards for Album of the Year 2014, for Best Dance/Electronica Album 2014, Billboard Music Award for Top Dance/Electronic Album 2014) 2013; solo: Together 2000, numerous albums produced. *Honours:* Grammy Award for Best Dance Recording (for Harder Better Faster Stronger) 2009, Grammy Awards for Record of the Year, for Best Pop Duo/Group Performance (both for Get Lucky) 2014, Billboard Music Award for Top Dance/Electronic Artist 2014. *Current Management:* Primary Talent International, The Primary Building, 10-11 Jockey's Fields, London, WC1R 4BN, England. *Telephone:* (20) 7400-4500. *Fax:* (20) 7400-4501. *E-mail:* PeterE@primary.uk.com. *Website:* www.primary.uk.com; www.daftpunk.com.

BANHART, Devendra; American singer, guitarist and artist; b. 30 May 1981, Houston, Tex. *Career:* raised in Venezuela; folk/rock singer-songwriter; fmr mem. Vetiver; Co-founder Gnomonsong record label 2005; collaborations with Vashti Bunyan, Bert Jansch, Yoko Ono, and Rodrigo Amarante from Los Hermanos. *Exhibitions:* Devendra Banhart: Drawings 1999–2006, Emilio Mazzoli Galleria D'arte Contemporanea, Modena, Italy 2007. *Recordings include:* Oh Me Oh My 2003, The Black Babies 2003, Rejoicing in the Hands 2004, Niño Rojo 2004, Cripple Crow 2005, Devendra Banhart/Jana Hunter 2005, Smokey Rolls Down Thunder Canyon 2007, What Will We Be 2009, Mala 2013. *Address:* XL Recordings, 304 Hudson Street, 7th Floor, New York, NY 10013, England. *E-mail:* xl@xlrecordings.com. *Website:* www.xlrecordings.com/devendrabanhart; devendrabanhart.com.

DR BANJO (see Wernick, Peter)

BANKOLE, Kayus; British rapper, singer and songwriter; b. Edinburgh, Scotland. *Education:* Boroughmuir High School, Edinburgh. *Career:* raised in Maryland, USA, Nigeria, Edinburgh; fmr mem. 3 Style; mem. Young Fathers 2008–. *Recordings:* albums: with Young Fathers: Inconceivable Child... Conceived 2009, Dead (Mercury Music Prize 2014) 2014, White Men Are Black Men Too 2015; mixtapes: Tape One 2011, Tape Two 2013. *Address:* Big Dada Records, Big Dada HQ, PO Box 4296, London, SE11 4WW, England (office). *E-mail:* info@bigdada.com (office); youngfathers@googlemail.com (home). *Website:* www.bigdada.com (office); www.young-fathers.com.

BANKS, Mike, (Mad Mike); American musician and producer; b. Detroit, Mich. *Career:* founder Underground Resistance (techno collective and label), Submerge Distribution; collaborations with Jeff Mills, Robert Hood, Suburban Knight, L'Homme Van Renn, Octave One; mem. Members of The House, Galaxy 2 Galaxy. *Recordings include:* albums: Sonic Destroyer (as X101) 1991, BXA (as X102) 1992, Interstellar Fugitives (with Underground Resistance) 1998, Shifting Gears: DJ C1 2002, Vibrations (with DJ Rolando) 2003, Get Lost, Vol.6 (with Totally Enormous Extinct Dinosaurs) 2013; singles: as Underground Resistance: Final Frontier 1991, Nation To Nation 1991, Living For The Night (featuring Yolanda Reynolds) 1991, Riot EP 1991, World To World 1991, Galaxy 2 Galaxy 1992, Codebreaker 1997, Turning Point 1998, Hi-Tech Dreams 2007, Electronic Warfare 2.0 2008. *Current Management:* c/o Alter Ego Management and Booking, PO Box 32468, Detroit, MI 48232, USA. *E-mail:* cornelius@alteregomgt.com. *Website:* www.alteregomgt.com.

BANKS, Nick; British musician (drums); b. 28 July 1965, Rotherham, Yorkshire, England. *Career:* mem., Pulp 1987–2002, 2011–; numerous tours, television appearances and festival dates. *Recordings include:* albums: Freaks 1987, Separations 1992, His 'N' Hers 1994, Different Class 1995, This is Hardcore 1998, We Love Life 2001, Hits 2002. *Honours:* Mercury Music Prize 1995, BRIT Award 1996. *Website:* www.pulppeople.com.

BANKS, Paul, (Julian Plenti); American singer and musician (guitar); b. 3 May 1978, Clacton-on-Sea, Essex. *Career:* mem. and lead singer, Interpol 1998–. *Recordings include:* albums: Turn On The Bright Lights 2002, Antics 2004, Our Love to Admire 2007, Interpol 2010; solo: Julian Plenti is Skyscraper 2009, Julian Plenti Lives (EP) 2012, Banks 2012, Everybody on My Dick Like They Supposed to Be 2013. *Current Management:* c/o Matador Records, 304 Hudson Street, 7th Floor, New York, NY 10013, USA. *E-mail:* info@interpolny.com. *Website:* www.bankspaulbanks.com; www.julianplenti.com; www.interpolnyc.com.

BANKS, Paul; British musician (guitar); b. 1973, England. *Career:* mem., Shed Seven 1996–2000, 2007–; numerous television appearances and live tours; filmmaker 2000–, founder of Digifish Media Productions 2003; mem. Albion 2006–07. *Recordings include:* albums: with Shed Seven: Change Giver 1996, A Maximum High 1996, Let It Ride 1998. *Telephone:* (1759) 318803. *E-mail:* paul@digifish.co.uk; info@digifish.co.uk. *Website:* www.digifish.co.uk; www.shedseven.com.

BANKS, Tony; British musician (keyboards); b. 27 March 1950. *Career:* mem., Genesis 1970–; solo artist 1979–99, 2006–; numerous worldwide tours. *Recordings include:* albums: with Genesis: Foxtrot 1972, Selling England by the Pound 1973, Genesis Live 1973, The Lamb Lies Down on Broadway 1974, Trick of the Tail 1976, Wind and Wuthering 1977, Seconds Out 1977, And Then There Were Three 1978, Duke 1980, Abacab 1981, Three Sides Live 1982, Genesis 1983, Invisible Touch 1986, We Can't Dance 1991, Genesis Live 1992, Calling All Stations 1997, Archives Vol. 1 1998, Not About Us 1998, Demo Mix Down On Broadway 1998, Turn It On Again 1999, Archive Vol. 2 2001; solo: A Curious Feeling 1979, The Fugitive 1983, The Wicked Lady 1983, Soundtracks 1986, Bankstatement 1989, Still 1992, Strictly Inc 1995, Seven: a Suite for Orchestra 2004. *Publication:* Genesis: Chapter and Verse (with other band mems) 2007. *Honours:* inducted into Rock and Roll Hall of Fame 2010. *E-mail:* info@genesis-music.com. *Website:* www.genesis-music.com.

BANNISTER, Brian; British singer and musician (banjo, mandolin, harmonica). *Career:* founder mem., Salty Dog; Winner, Birmingham songwriting competition; Performed official Olympic bid record; Resident topical songwriter for John Tainton Show, BBC; mem., The Debonairs, including television and radio appearances; Founder member, Mack and The Boys, 1989; Member, The New Bushbury Mountain Daredevils, 1992–; band mem. Harvey Andrews Band; work includes: Backing vocalist, Slade album; Producer, songwriter, dance artists. *Recordings:* with The Debonairs: Hoochey Coochey Man; with Sub Zero: Out Of The Blue; with The Balti Brothers: Balti; with Mack and The Boys: Mack and The Boys; Downtime Love; with The New Bushbury Mountain Daredevils: Bushwacked; The Yellow Album; Bushbury Mountain. *Website:* www.myspace.com/newbushburymountaindaredevils.

BANNISTER, Michael; British musician (keyboards) and programmer. *Career:* fmr studio engineer for bands, including Belle & Sebastian, Mogwai, Aberfeldy; mem. Texas 2005–. *Recordings include:* album: Red Book 2005. *Current Management:* c/o G. R. Management Limited, 974 Pollockshaws Road, Glasgow, G41 2HA, Scotland. *Telephone:* (141) 632-1111. *E-mail:* dirk@texasindemand.com (office). *Website:* www.texas.uk.com (office).

BANTON, Buju; Jamaican reggae and dancehall singer; b. (Mark Anthony Myrie), 15 July 1973, Salt Lane, nr Kingston. *Recordings include:* albums: The Ruler 1986, Stamina Daddy 1991, Mr Mention 1991, Voice Of Jamaica 1993, Buju Banton Meets Garnett Silk And Tony Rebel 1993, Til Shiloh 1995, Chanting Down The Walls Of Bab (with Anthony B) 1997, Inna Heights 1997, Unchained Spirit 2000, Rudeboys Inna Ghetto 2000, Dubbing With The Banton 2000, The Best Of The Early Years 1990–95 2001, Want It 2002, Friends For Life 2003, Buju And Friends 2004, Too Bad 2006. *Honours:* Tamika Reggae Album of the Year Award, Songwriter of the Year Award, Nelson Mandela Award (New York) 1998. *Address:* c/o Gargamel Music, Inc., 10 Carlisle Avenue, Kingston 8, Jamaica (office). *Website:* www.gargamelmusic.com (office).

BANTON, Pato; British reggae singer and songwriter; b. (Patrick Murray), 5 Oct. 1961, London; s. of Lillian Murray. *Career:* began career as MC in Birmingham; mem. reggae band Crucial Music 1980–85; tours throughout USA and South America with own eight-piece group, The Reggae Revolution; also solo artist; CEO, Gwarn International Agency & Recordings. *Recordings include:* albums: Mad Professor Recaptures Pato Banton 1986, Never Give In 1987, Visions Of The World 1989, Wize Up! 1990, Live and Kickin' All Over America 1991, Universal Love 1992, Collections 1994, Stay Positive 1996, Life is a Miracle 2000, The Words of Christ 2006, Positive Vibrations (with Mystic Roots Band) 2007, Pato Banton and Friends 2008, Destination Paradise 2008. *Honours:* BBC Lifetime Achievement Award, Black Music Award for Lifetime Achievement, Birmingham Museum Reggae Hall of Fame. *Address:* 9854 National Blvd #353, Los Angeles, CA 90034, USA (office). *Telephone:* (323) 877-6502 (office). *E-mail:* gwarninternational@gmail.com (office). *Website:* www.patobanton.com (office).

BAPA, Sayan; Russian (Tuvan) singer. *Career:* mem. folk singing quartet, Huun-Huur-Tu 1992–. *Recordings include:* albums: 60 Horses in My Herd 1993, The Orphan's Lament 1994, If I'd Been Born an Eagle 1997, Where Young Grass Grows 1999, Malerija 2003, Eternal 2009, Ancestors Call 2010. *Address:* c/o JARO Record Company, Bismarckstrasse 43, 28203 Bremen, Germany; c/o Electrofone Music, 453 South Spring Street, Suite 320, Los

Angeles, CA 90013, USA. *E-mail:* info@electrofone.com; hhtmanagement@gmail.com; mail@jaro.de. *Website:* www.electrofone.com; www.huunhuurtu.com.

BAPTISTE, Denys Leigh; British musician (jazz saxophone); b. 14 Sept. 1969, London. *Education:* West London Inst., Brunel Univ., Guildhall School of Music, London. *Career:* joined Gary Crosby's Nu Troop 1992; mem. The Jazz Warriors 1993; toured with Bheki Mseleku, performed with Julian Joseph, Jason Rebello, Omar, Orphy Robinson and others 1993–94; recorded with Jazz Jamaica, Ernest Ranglin, Gregory Isaacs, Juliet Roberts, Montage, J-Life, Nu Troop, Martin Taylor, McCoy Tyner UK All Stars, Manu Dibango Afro Funk Orchestra, Jazz Jamaica All-Stars. *Recordings include:* albums: Be Where You Are 1999, Alternating Currents 2001, Let Freedom Ring (with Ben Okri) 2003, Identity By Subtraction 2010. *Honours:* Int. Band Competition Best Ensemble Award at Jazz á Vienne Int. Festival France 1998, Malibu Music Of Black Origin (MOBO) Award for Best Jazz Act 1999, British Jazz Award for Rising Star 2000. *Current Management:* c/o Dune Music, First Floor, 73 Canning Road, Harrow, HA3 7SP, England. *Telephone:* (20) 8424-2807. *Fax:* (20) 8861-5371. *E-mail:* info@dune-music.com. *Website:* www.dune-music.com; www.denysbaptiste.com.

BAQWA, Tshawe, (Kapricon); Norwegian singer; b. 6 Jan. 1980, Germany. *Career:* mem. Madcon 1992–; co-presenter, The Voice of Madcon (The Voice TV channel) 2005. *Recordings include:* albums: It's All a Madcon (Spellemannprisen for Best Hip Hop Album) 2004, So Dark the Con of Man 2007, Conquest 2009, Contraband 2010, Contakt 2012, Icon 2013. *Honours:* Spellemannprisen for Best Song (for Beggin') 2008. *Current Management:* c/o Peter Peters, Friendly Entertainment, Majorstuveien 17, PO Box 1042, 0367 Oslo, Norway. *Telephone:* 48-40-19-98. *E-mail:* peter.peters@friendly.no. *Website:* www.friendly.no; www.madconlive.com.

BARÂT, Carl Ashley Raphael; British singer and guitarist; b. 6 June 1978, Basingstoke; pnr Edie Langley; two s. *Career:* mem. The Libertines 2001–04, 2014–, Dirty Pretty Things 2005–08; solo artist 2005–, The Jackals 2014–; collaborated with Reverend and the Makers 2012, Benjamin Biolay 2012, Vanessa Paradis 2013. *Film:* Telstar 2008. *Recordings include:* with The Libertines: Up the Bracket 2002, The Libertines 2004, Anthems for Doomed Youth 2015; with Dirty Pretty Things: Waterloo to Anywhere 2006, Romance at Short Notice 2008; solo: Carl Barât 2010, with the Jackals: Let it Reign 2015. *Publication:* Threepenny Memoir: The Lives of a Libertine 2010. *Honours:* Dr hc (Univ. of Winchester) 2012; with the Libertines: NME Award for Best British Band 2005, Q Award for Best Track (for Gunga Din) 2015. *Current Management:* c/o James Whitting, Coda Music Agency LLP, CODA House, 56 Compton Street, Clerkenwell, London EC1V 0ET, England. *Telephone:* (20) 7017-2500. *Fax:* (20) 7017-2555. *E-mail:* james@codaagency.com. *Website:* www.codaagency.com.

BARBA, Reyli; Mexican singer and composer; b. 12 April 1972, Juárez, Chiapas. *Career:* songwriter for Alejandro Fernández and Beyoncé Knowles; Founder-mem. Elefante 1997–2003, represented Mexico at Viña del Mar Festival, Chile; solo artist 2003–. *Recordings:* with Elefante: El Que Busca Encuentra 2001, Lo Que Andábamos Buscando 2001, solo: En la Luna (On the Moon) 2004, Fe (Faith) 2007, Bien Acompanado 2011. *Television:* theme songs for Rubi, Big Brother (Mexican version). *Address:* c/o Sony Music Norte, Sony Music Entertainment, 550 Madison Avenue, 23rd Floor, New York, NY 10022-3211, USA (office). *Telephone:* (55) 5249-3200 (Mexico) (office). *Website:* www.sonymusic.com.mx (office); www.reyli.com.mx.

BARBER, (Daniel) Christopher, OBE; British jazz musician (trombone, trumpet, horn, double bass), bandleader and composer; b. 17 April 1930, Welwyn Garden City. *Education:* Guildhall School of Music. *Career:* leader, various amateur jazz bands; formed first band with Lonnie Donegan, Monty Sunshine 1940s; leader, Chris Barber Jazzband (later changed to Chris Barber Jazz, Blues Band and Big Chris Barber Band) 1954–; international tours and concerts include 1954 line-up re-formed for 40th Anniversary concerts, Royal Festival Hall, 100 Club, Netherlands, Germany 1994; also played with Ken Colyer, Joe Harriott, Wild Bill Davis, Mac Rebenneck; helped promote US artists in UK including Brownie McGhee, Muddy Waters, Louis Jordan. *Compositions include:* numerous works with Richard Hill, including Jazz Elements, Concerto For Jazz Trombone (both premiered in Berlin). *Recordings include:* albums: Ragtime 1960, Getting Around 1963, Live In East Berlin 1968, Sideways 1974, Take Me Back To New Orleans 1980, Everybody Knows 1987, Stardust 1988, Essential Chris Barber 1990, Get Yourself To Jackson Square 1990 and several EPs. *Current Management:* c/o Wim Wigt Productions Limited, 98 Arundel Avenue, Croydon, CR2 8BE, England. *Telephone:* (20) 8662-1235. *Fax:* (20) 8654-2120. *Website:* www.chrisbarber.net.

BARBER, Tony; musician (guitar, bass, drums, synthesizer) and producer; b. 20 April 1963, Edmonton, London, England; m. Nathalie; one d. *Career:* mem., Lack of Knowledge 1979–85, Boys Wonder 1987–88, Buzzcocks 1992–; solo recordings as Airport; appeared on records by other artists 1986–; mem. PRS, PAMRA, PPL. *Compositions:* Sirens are Back, with Lack of Knowledge, 1984; Lift Off with Airport, as Airport, 2000. *Recordings include:* with Buzzcocks: All Set 1996, Modern 1999, Time's Up 2000, (untitled) 2003, Flat-Pack Philosophy 2006; with Airport: Lift Off with Airport 2000. *Current Management:* c/o Brent Smith, One William Morris Place, Beverly Hills, CA 90212, USA. *Telephone:* (310) 859-4299. *Fax:* (310) 859-4440. *Website:* www.buzzcocks.com.

BARBIER, Denis, (Alexandre Abremski); French composer and musician (flute); b. 22 April 1954, Paris; m. Silvana di Martino; one s. one d. *Education:* conservatories of Paris arrdt 9è, Montreuil and Vincennes. *Career:* flute soloist, Orchestre National de Jazz 94/97 with Laurent Cugny; US tour with Big Band Lumière 1991; tour, Europe, with Gil Evans and Big Band Lumière 1986; concerts on Radio France with Lumière, Orchestre National de Jazz, Chute Libre, Moravagine, Le Green, Flute Unlimited; France Culture with Shi Pei Pou (Peking); mem. SACEM, SACD, UCMF, ADAMI. *Compositions include:* music for contemporary dance, theatre and films, Jazz on the Moon for symphonic orchestra and solo alto saxophone 1996, Capriccio for flute and harp 1987, From the Sea to the Land for two harps 1988, Exotiques for Celtic harp 2001, Petit Prélude for clarinet and harp 2002, Petit Lotus for flute and piano 2002, Stella Donna for equal voices 2010, Flute and Hammond Organ (Jazz Duo with Hervé Saint Guirons) 2014. *Recordings include:* Un Sueno, Piece for soprano voice, cordes & Hautbois 1998, Sous Le Signe Du Cheval (wind quintet and piano) 1995, Work for 30 musicians and rhythm section in four movements 1995, Flute Unlimited 2004; film music: L'Alibi En Or (with Charles Aznavour) 1993, Fausto (A La Mode, USA) 1993, Bosna 1994, Milice, Film Noir 1996, Slogans 2001, La Fille du Juge 2006; music for television serial 1984–; documentaries: From the Sea to the Land for two harps (with Serge Moati) 1996, Brook par Brook 2002; television films: Barbe Bleue (with Samy Frey), Prune Becker 2004; jazz albums: PRAO (with Mino Cinelu and Brothers), Denis Barbier Jazz Group, Chute Libre and Moravagine (with Mino Cinelu), Orchestre National de Jazz. *Honours:* Prix Boris Vian de l'académie du jazz; Médaille Hommage de la SACEM 2005. *Address:* 12 rue Georges Bizet, 33320, Le Taillan Médoc, France (home). *Telephone:* 5-56-57-59-71 (home); 6-83-58-19-09. *E-mail:* denis.barbier@live.fr.

BARBIERI, Richard; British musician (keyboards) and songwriter; b. 30 Nov. 1957, London, England. *Career:* Founder mem. Japan 1974–83, The Dolphin Brothers (with Steve Jansen) 1987, Rain Tree Crow (with mems of Japan) 1991, Porcupine Tree 1993–; mem. Medium Productions (with Steve Jansen and Mick Karn) 1993; record producer, Swedish group Lustans Lakejer 1982. *Recordings include:* albums: with Japan: Adolescent Sex 1978, Obscure Alternatives 1978, Quiet Life 1979, Gentlemen Take Polaroids 1980, Tin Drum 1981, Oil On Canvas 1983; with Steve Jansen: Worlds In A Small Room 1986, Stone To Flesh 1995, Changing Hands 1998; with The Dolphin Brothers: Catch The Fall 1987; with Rain Tree Crow: Rain Tree Crow 1991; with Steve Jansen and Mick Karn: Beginning to Melt 1994, Seed 1994, Playing in a Room with People 2001; with Steve Jansen and N. Takemura: Changing Hands 1997; with Porcupine Tree: The Sky Moves Sideways 1995, Signify 1996, Metanoia 1998, Stupid Dream 1999, Voyage 34: The Complete Trip 2000, Lightbulb Sun 2000, Recordings 2001, In Absentia 2002, Deadwing 2005, Fear of a Blank Planet 2007, The Incident 2010, Octane Twisted 2012; with Steve Hogarth: Not the Weapon But the Hand 2012. *Website:* www.porcupinetree.com.

BARBOSA, Chris; American producer and remixer; b. Bronx, New York; m.; two c. *Education:* All Hallows Inst., Elizabeth Seton Coll. *Career:* Co-founder and record producer, engineer, arranger, songwriter for Ligosa 1983–2006; Dir Multimedia Services, Wyckoff Heights Medical Center 2006–12; produced or performed production remixes for many artists including Shannon, Robin Gibb, Billy Idol, George Michael, New Kids on the Block, The Spinners, Lisa Fischer, George Lammond, Nolan Thomas, Andru Donalds, Safire, Cynthia, Judy Torres, Monet, Alisha. *Recordings include:* Bad Of The Heart, George Lamond 1978, Hot Power Mixes 1987, I Wasn't Born Yesterday, Safire 1990, No More Games, New Kids On The Block 1991, Best Of Freestyle 1992, Bass Bomb: Latin Hip Hop 1993, Freestyle Greatest Hits 1994, Essential, Shannon 1995, Wherever The Rhythm Takes Me, Alisha 1996, Absolutely: The Very Best Of... 1997, Freestyle Explosion 1998, Bodrum Hits 1998, White Party 2000 2000, Black Box 2000 (as producer), Party Monster 2003, Wedding Party 2006, Electro House XL 2009, Ultra Dance 11 2010, Pop Princesses 2010 2010. *Honours:* ASCAP Pop Award.

BARD, Alexander, MSc; Swedish music producer, songwriter, artist, author and philosopher and lecturer; *Managing Director, Bullgod Kommunikation AB;* b. 17 March 1961, Vaestra Ny. *Education:* Stockholm School of Econs. *Career:* Co-founder Stockholm Records, SoFo Records; Man. Dir Bullgod Kommunikation AB; fmr mem. Army of Lovers, Vacuum, BWO (Bodies Without Organs); Producer, Alcazar, Midi Maxi & Efti; mem. Gravitonas; mem. Bd Swedish Zoroastrian Soc. *Recordings include:* albums: with Army of Lovers: Disco Extravaganza 1990, Massive Luxury Overdose 1991, The Gods Of Earth And Heaven 1993, Glory Glamour And Gold 1994, Les Greatest Hits 1995, Le Grand Docu-Soap 2000; with Vacuum: The Plutonium Cathedral 1996, Seance At The Chaebol 1998; with BWO: Prototype 2005, Halcyon Days 2006, Fabricator 2007, Pandemonium 2008, Big Science 2009. *Publications:* The Netocrats (with Jan Soderqvist) 2002, The Global Empire (with Jan Soderqvist) 2005, The Body Machines (with Jan Soderqvist) 2009, Syntheism – Creating God in the Internet Age (with Jan Soderqvist) 2014. *Address:* Bullgod Kommunikation AB, Skaanegatan 61, 11637 Stockholm, Sweden. *E-mail:* bardissimo@gmail.com (home).

BARDY, Jean; French musician (bass, guitar, trumpet) and composer; b. 3 March 1957, Soisy, Montmorency. *Education:* Conservatoire de Musique d'Eubonne. *Career:* professional jazz bass player, playing Be-Bop in clubs including: River Bop, Petit Opportun, Cardinal Paf, Throughout France; Played with artists including: Guy Lafitte, René Urtreger, Martial Solal, Laurent Cugny, Barney Wilen, Laurent de Wilde, Pepper Adams, Roy

Haynes, Steve Grossman, Sonny Stitt, Chet Baker (one year in France, Europe), Nat Adderley, Johnny Griffin, Harold Danko, Dee Dee Bridgwater; composer for les Affranchis 2000–. *Recordings include:* Live In Paris, Antoine Hervé, Sud, Antoine Illouz, Naif, Rhythm-A-Ning, Laurent Cugny, Gil Evans 1987, Samya Cynthia, François Chassagnite, César Le Chien, Chansons, Jean Bardy 1991, Anna Livia Plurabelle, André Hodeir. *Honours:* Prix Django Reinhardt for: Live In Paris, Rhythmning, Prix de l'Academie du Disque, Léonard de Vinci Grant 1990. *Website:* www.jeanbardy.com.

BARE, Robert (Bobby) Joseph; American country singer and songwriter; b. 7 April 1935, Ironton, Ohio. *Career:* recording artist 1955–; numerous club, television and radio station appearances. *Television includes:* Grand Ole Opry; Host, Bobby Bare and Friends. *Films:* A Distant Trumpet 1964. *Recordings include:* singles: All American Boy, Detroit City (Grammy), 500 Miles Away From Home, Miller's Cave, A Dear John Letter, Come Sundown, Please Don't Tell Me How The Story Ends, Marie Laveau, Daddy What If, The Jogger, Tequila Sheila, Numbers, numerous albums: Detroit City 1963, 500 Miles Away From Home 1963, The Travelling Bare 1964, Tender Years 1965, Talk Me Some Sense 1966, Folsom Prison Blues 1968, Lincoln Park Inn 1969, This Is Bare Country 1970, I'm A Long Way From Home 1971, What Am I Gonna Do 1972, Memphis Tennessee 1973, Lullabys, Legends and Lies 1974, Cowboys and Daddys 1975, The Winner and Other Losers 1978, Bare 1979, Down and Dirty 1980, Drunk and Crazy 1980, As Is 1981, Ain't Got Nothing To Lose 1982, Bobby Bare–The Mercury Years 1970–72 1987, Country Store 1988, I Love An Old Fashioned Christmas 1995, Hard Time Hungrys 1998, Live At Gilley's 1999, The Moon Was Blue 2005, Down & Dirty...Plus 2006, Darker Than Light 2012; with Skeeter Davis: Tunes For Two 1965, Your Husband, My Wife 1970; with The Hillsiders: The English Countryside 1967; with Norma Jean and Liz Anderson: The Game Of Triangles 1967; with Bill Parsons: Buddies with the Blues 1956-1961 2013. *Current Management:* c/o The Bobby Roberts Company, Inc., POB 1547, Goodlettsville, TN 37070, USA. *Telephone:* (615) 859-8899. *Fax:* (615) 859-2200. *E-mail:* info@bobbyroberts .com. *Website:* www.bobbyroberts.com.

BAREILLES, Sara Beth; American singer, songwriter and musician (piano); b. 7 Dec. 1979, Eureka, Calif.; d. of Paul Bareilles and Bonnie Halvorsen (née Capellas). *Education:* Univ. of California, Los Angeles. *Career:* has collaborated with Ingrid Michaelson, Weezer; selected by US First Lady Michelle Obama to perform at the G-20 summit, Pittsburgh 2009. *Recordings:* albums: Careful Confessions 2004, Little Voice 2007, Kaleidoscope Heart 2010, The Blessed Unrest 2013, What's Inside: Songs from Waitress 2015. *Honours:* Billboard Year End Awards for Hot Adult Contemporary Song and Hot Adult Digital Song Awards 2008. *Current Management:* Career Artist Management, 1100 Glendon Avenue, Suite 1100, Los Angeles, CA 90024, USA. *Telephone:* (310) 776-7640. *E-mail:* sarab@camanagement.com. *Website:* www.camanagement.com; www.sarabmusic.com.

BARGELD, Blixa; German singer, musician (guitar) and composer; b. (Christian Emmerich), 12 Jan. 1959, Berlin. *Career:* mem., Einstürzende Neubauten 1980–; guitarist, Nick Cave & The Bad Seeds 1984–2003; Founder mem. anbb 2007. *Recordings include:* albums: Kollaps 1981, Zeichnungen des Patienten O. T. 1983, Halber Mensch 1985, Fünf Auf der Nach Oben Offenen Richterskala 1987, Haus der Lüge 1989, Tabula Rasa 1993, Ende Neu 1996, Silence is Sexy 2000, Perpetuum Mobile 2004, Grundstück 2005; solo: Elementarteilchen 2001, Blixa Bargeld liest Bertolt Brecht Erotische Gedichte 2006. *Website:* www.blixa-bargeld.com.

BARKER, Aaron G., Sr; American songwriter; b. 3 May 1953, San Antonio, Tex. *Career:* mem. Country Music Asscn, Nashville Songwriters Asscn International (NSAI), Acad. of Country Music. *Compositions include:* for George Strait: Baby Blue 1988, Love Without End 1990, Easy Come, Easy Go 1990, I Know She Still Loves Me 1995, I'd Like To Have That One Back 1995, I Can Still Make Cheyene 1997, Peace of Mind 1998, Christmas Cookie 1999, Old Time Christmas 1999; for Doug Supernaw: Honky Tonkin' Fool 1993, Not Enough Hours in the Night 1995; for Clay Walker: Watch This 1997, You're Beginning to Get to Me 1998; for Bill Enquall: I Am a Cowboy 1998, for Lonestar: What About Now 1998; for Kelly Atkin: What About Now. *Recordings include:* albums: The Taste of Freedom 1977, Straight From the Horse's Mouth 1998, Echoes 2006, Lifelines 2006. *Honours:* Songwriters Award, Music City News 1990. *E-mail:* aaronbarker@comcast.net. *Website:* www.aaronbarker.com.

BARKER, Guy Jeffery, MBE; British jazz musician (trumpet), composer and arranger; b. 26 Dec. 1957, Chiswick, London, England. *Education:* Royal Coll. of Music. *Career:* began playing the trumpet aged 12; mem. Nat. Youth Jazz Orchestra; major concerts include Cleveland Jazz Festival 1978, South Bank Jazz Festival 1989; leader own quintet, UK tour 1978; also played with Gil Evans, John Dankworth, Chris Hunter, Stan Tracey's Hexad, Hubbard's Cubbard, Ornette Coleman, Peter King, Jim Mullen, Jack Sharpe Big Band, Sting, Quincy Jones; featured soloist, London Symphony Orchestra; played in backing groups with artists, including Sammy Davis Jr, Mel Tormé, Liza Minnelli, Lena Horne, Frank Sinatra, Georgie Fame; tribute tours to Chet Baker and Bix Beiderbecke; Founder Guy Barker's Int. Septet and Guy Barker Jazz Orchestra; Presenter, Guy Barker's World Café, BBC World Service 2003; arranged music for Chicago Symphony Orchestra, Britten Sinfonia and the film The Talented Mister Ripley; Musical Dir/Arranger for the opening gala concert 'Jazz Voice: Celebrating a Century of Song', London Jazz Festival 2008–14, on several BBC Radio 2 Friday Night is Music Night

shows featuring the Guy Barker Jazz Orchestra with the BBC Concert Orchestra, celebrating the music of Billie Holiday/Duke Ellington and Billy Strayhorn/Ella Fitzgerald, Aretha Franklin and Dusty Springfield/Jazz Royalty to celebrate the wedding of Prince William and Kate Middleton; Assoc. Composer, BBC Concert Orchestra 2013–15. *Compositions:* The Spirit of Django, orchestral suite (co-composer) (premiered at BBC Proms 2012) 2011, That Obscure Hurt, suite for orchestra, jazz ensemble, male vocalist and actress (premiered at Aldeburgh Festival 2013) 2012. *Recordings include:* albums: solo: Holly J 1989, Isn't It 1991, Into the Blue 1994, What Love Is 1998, The Talented Mr. Ripley 1999, Timeswing 2000, Soundtrack 2001, The Amadeus Project 2007; with Hubbard's Cubbard: Hubbard's Cubbard 1983, Nip It In The Bud 1985; with Clark Tracey: Suddenly Last Tuesday 1986, Stiperstones 1987; with Peter King: Brother Bernard 1988. *Honours:* BBC Jazz Awards Best Band 2003, BASCA/PRS Gold Badge 2013. *Address:* c/o Provocateur Records, Friendly Hall, 31 Fordwich Road, Fordwich, Canterbury, Kent CT2 0BW, England (office). *Telephone:* (1227) 712021 (office). *E-mail:* jazz@provocateurrecords.co.uk (office); guy@guybarker.co.uk (office). *Website:* www.provocateurrecords.co.uk (office); www.guybarker.co.uk.

BARKER, Paul; American musician (bass, keyboards); b. 8 Feb. 1950, Palo Alto, CA. *Career:* mem., Ministry 1986–2004; mem. U.S.S.A. 2006–; founder mem. Flowering Blight 2007–; numerous side projects including Pigface, including Steve Albini, Jello Biafra, Chris Connelly and Dwayne Goettell; co-founder Malekko Heavy Industry Corpn. *Recordings include:* albums: with Ministry: Twitch, 1985; The Land Of Rape and Honey, 1988; The Mind Is a Terrible Thing to Taste, 1989; In Case You Didn't Feel Like Showing Up (Live), 1990; Psalm 69: The Way To Succeed and the Way to Suck Eggs, 1992; Filth Pig, 1996; Dark Side Of the Spoon, 1999; with U.S.S.A.: The Spoils 2007; with Flowering Blight: The Perfect Pair 2008. *Address:* c/o Malekko Heavy Industry Corporation, 814 SE 14th Avenue, Portland, OR 97214, USA. *Telephone:* (503) 236-8155. *Website:* www.malekkoheavyindustry.com; www .floweringblight.com.

BARKER, Sophie Alexandra Jessica; British singer; b. 5 Nov. 1971. *Career:* featured vocalist with Zero 7; also recorded with Groove Armada, The Egg, Muki, Bliss; solo artist 2004–. *Recordings include:* albums: with Zero 7: Simple Things 2001, When It Falls 2004; other appearances include: Groove Armada, Vertigo 1999, Muki, Quiet Riot 2000, The Egg, Forwards 2001, Bliss, Quiet Letters 2004; solo: Lullaby 2004, Earthbound 2005, Seagull 2011, A Forest/Say Goodbye 2011. *E-mail:* sophie@sophiebarker.com; info@ sophiebarker.com; chloelander@gmail.com. *Website:* www.sophiebarker.com.

BARKER, Travis Landon; American musician (drums); b. 14 Nov. 1975, Fontana, CA. *Career:* fmr mem., punk-pop groups The Vandals, The Aquabats; mem., Blink-182 1998–2005, 2009–; numerous TV appearances and concerts worldwide; mem., Boxcar Racer 2001–03; mem., Transplants 1999; founder mem., (+44) 2006–. *Film appearance:* American Pie 1999. *Recordings include:* albums: with Blink-182: Enema Of The State 1999, The Mark, Tom And Travis Show (The Enema Strikes Back) 2000, Take Off Your Pants And Jacket 2001, Blink-182 2003; with Boxcar Racer: Boxcar Racer 2002; with Transplants: Transplants 2002; with (+44): When Your Heart Stops Beating 2006. *Current Management:* International Talent Booking, First Floor, Ariel House, 74a Charlotte Street, London, W1T 4QJ, England. *Telephone:* (20) 7637-6979. *Fax:* (20) 7637-6978. *E-mail:* info@itb.co.uk. *Website:* www.itb.co.uk; www.blink182.com; www.boxcarracer.com; www .plusfortyfour.com; www.travisbarker.com.

BARLOW, Andrew; British producer. *Career:* Founder-mem. Lamb 1994–2004, Hoof 2004–, Luna Seeds; Prof. of Music Tech., Leeds Coll. of Music; produced music for theatre, TV and commercials. *Recordings include:* albums: with Lamb: Lamb 1996, Fear of Fours 1999, What Sound 2001, Between Darkness and Wonder 2003, Best Kept Secrets: The Best of Lamb 1996–2004 2004. *E-mail:* andy_barlow@mac.com (office). *Website:* andybarlow .net.

BARLOW, Eric; singer and musician (guitar). *Education:* classical training. *Career:* mem., The New Bushbury Mountain Daredevils, 1992–; backing vocals, Slade; Producer, songwriter for various dance artists. *Compositions include:* songs recorded by artists including Jaki Graham; Asia Blue; Several songs at number 1, Europe and Africa, including: Heartbreaker, Rozalla. *Recordings:* solo: You Betta Run; with Rozalla: Heartbreaker; Sunny; The Perfect Kiss; Spirit Of Africa; with Mack and The Boys: The Unknown Legends; with The New Bushbury Mountain Daredevils: Bushwacked; The Yellow Album; Bushbury Mountain; Banjo Spiders, 1999. *Address:* c/o PR Promotions, PO Box 200, Belper, Derbyshire, DE56 2ZL, England. *Telephone:* (1773) 853428. *E-mail:* reelmusic@btinternet.com. *Website:* www .prpromotions.org.uk; www.myspace.com/thebushburymountaindaredevils.

BARLOW, Gary, OBE; British singer, songwriter and producer; b. 20 Jan. 1971, Frodsham, Cheshire, England; m. Dawn Barlow 2000; one s. two d. *Career:* mem. Take That 1990–96, 2006–; solo artist 1996–; numerous live appearances and tours; songwriter, with songs recorded by artists including Charlotte Church and Delta Goodrem; acting debut in ITV 1 drama Heartbeat 2000; judge, The X Factor (ITV 1) 2011–13; asked by HM Queen Elizabeth II to organize her 86th birthday and Diamond Jubilee celebrations in 2012. *Recordings include:* albums: with Take That: Take That and Party 1992, Everything Changes 1993, Nobody Else 1995, Beautiful World 2006, The Circus 2008, Progress 2010, III 2014; solo: Open Road 1997, Twelve Months Eleven Days 1999, Since I Saw You Last 2013. *Publication:* My Take 2006.

Honours: Nordoff Robbins Silver Clef Award for Best Band 1995, 2009, Golden Camera Award (Berlin), Golden Otto Award for best band, MTV Award for Best Group in Europe, seven Smash Hits Awards, BRIT Award for Best British Single 1994, (for Patience) 2007, (for Shine) 2008, for Best British Live Act 2008, for Best British Group 2011, Ivor Novello Awards for Most Performed Work and Best Selling Song 1996, Q Idol Award (with Take That) 2006, GQ Awards for Man of the Year 2007, Ivor Novello Award for most Performed Song (for Shine) 2008, The Sun Newspaper's Lord of the Year 2009, Blue Peter Gold Badge 2010, Q Award for Best Collaboration (for Shame) 2011, Q Award for Classic Songwriter 2011. *Current Management:* c/o Jonathan Wild, 10 Management, c/o Polydor Records, 364–366 Kensington High Street, London, W14 8NS, England. *Telephone:* (20) 7467-0602. *E-mail:* jonathan@10management.com. *Website:* www.garybarlow.com; www .takethat.com.

BARLOW, Louis (Lou) Knox; American singer and musician (guitar, bass); b. 17 July 1966, Dayton, OH. *Career:* Founder mem. Dinosaur (with J. Mascis) 1984, renamed Dinosaur, Jr 1987–89, 2007–; Founder mem. Sebadoh 1987, Sentridoh 1991, Folk Implosion 1994. *Recordings include:* albums: with Dinosaur/Dinosaur, Jr: Dinosaur 1985, You're Living All Over Me 1987, Bug 1988, Beyond 2007, Farm 2009, I Bet on Sky 2012; with Sebadoh: Weed Forestin' 1989, The Freed Man 1990, Sebadoh III 1991, Bubble and Scrape 1993, Bakesale 1994, Harmacy 1996, The Sebadoh 1999, Defend Yourself 2013; with Sentridoh: Lou Barlow and his Sentridoh 1995; with Folk Implosion: Kids (OST) 1995, Dare to be Surprised 1997, One Part Lullaby 1999, The New Folk Implosion 2003; solo: Emoh 2005, Goodnight Unknown 2009. *Current Management:* c/o Brian Schwartz, Bleemusic Inc., 2401 Broadway, Boulder, CO 80304, USA. *Telephone:* (303) 998-0001. *Fax:* (303) 447-2484. *E-mail:* brian@bleemusic.com; schwartz@7smgmt.com. *Website:* www.bleemusic.com; www.dinosaurjr.com; www.loobiecore.com.

BARLOW, Thomas, BA, PGCE; musician (saxophone); b. 30 Sept. 1961, Manila, Philippines. *Education:* Univ. of Kent and De Montfort Univ. *Career:* founder mem., The Larks; mem., Aztec Camera –1996; formed Tommy Barlow Quartet; mem., Butterfield 8; founder mem., Deptford Dance Orchestra (later Jools Holland Big Band); mem., Swordfish; mem. Monkey Chuckle; mem. Musicians' Union, PRS. *Recordings include:* 3 singles, 1 EP, with The Larks; recording sessions with: Aztec Camera, 1988; Jools Holland; Deptford Dance Orchestra; BBC Education Programme; Swordfish. *Website:* www.myspace .com/monkeychuckle.

BARMAN, Tom; Belgian singer and musician (guitar); b. 1 Jan. 1972. *Career:* Founder-mem. dEUS 1991–. *Film:* Any Way the Wind Blows (writer and dir). *Recordings include:* albums: Worst Case Scenario 1994, My Sister = My Clock 1995, In A Bar, Under The Sea 1997, The Ideal Crash 1999, Pocket Revolution 2005, Vantage Point 2008, Keep You Close 2011, Following Sea 2012. *Current Management:* c/o Christian Pierre, Musickness Bvba, Rozenlaan 57, 2970 Gravenwezel, Belgium. *E-mail:* christian.pierre@musickness.be. *Website:* www.musickness.be; www.deus.be.

BARNARD, Robert Graeme, AO; Australian musician and bandleader; b. 24 Nov. 1933, Melbourne; m. Danielle Ann Barnard 1993; two s. one d. *Career:* regular appearances on variety television; co-compere for ABC TV jazz programme; featured soloist, Queensland Symphony Orchestra; tours extensively; mem. Professional Musicians Club. *Compositions:* many pieces recorded over the years. *Recordings include:* New York Notes 1996, Wholly Cats 2003; Lord of the Rings (with John Sangster); many with Graeme Bell, with Strings and several LPs and EPs. *Honours:* Hon. Life Mem. Victorian Jazz Archive 2008; Queen Elizabeth Jubilee Medal 1977, Australian Jazz Critics Award 1990, 1991, 1992, , inducted into Montsalvat Hall of Fame 1988, Australian Legends of Jazz 1991, Advance Australia Award 1991, inducted into Australian Jazz Hall of Fame 1993, MO Awards 1993, 1997. *Address:* 8–9 Hume Street, Wollstonecraft, NSW 2065, Australia (home). *Telephone:* (4) 1043-8149; (2) 9438-1495 (home). *Fax:* (2) 9438-1379 (home). *E-mail:* barnard@acay.com.au (home).

BARNES, Alan Leonard, DipMus; British musician (saxophone, clarinet); b. 23 July 1959, Altrincham, Cheshire, England; m. Clare Hirst 1995; one s. one d. *Education:* Leeds Music Coll. *Career:* mem. Pasadena Roof Orchestra 1980–82, Tommy Chase Quartet 1983–86, Coled Jazz Renegades 1986–88, Humphrey Lyttelton Band 1988–92, freelance musician with bands formed by Mike Westbrook, Kenny Baker, Don Weller, Warren Vaché, Freddie Hubbard, John Dankworth; own quartet and duo with David Newton; f. own jazz label, Woodville Records 2003–; formed Alan Barnes All Stars 2003–; Fellow, Leeds Coll. of Music 2003; mem. Martin Taylor's Spirit of Django 2009–. *Compositions include:* Blues on the Beach, The Hawk, Side-Steppin', Freedom Samba, Below Zero, The Sherlock Holmes Suite 2002. *Recordings include:* Below Zero (with David Newton Trio), Like Minds, Trouble 1996, Thirsty Work, Days Of Wine and Roses (with Tony Coe) 1998, A Dotty Blues, Shine (with Warren Vaché), Memories Of You, Manhattan (with Conte Candoli), If You Could See Me Now (with Jim Watson Trio), The Marbella Jazz Suite (with Alan Barnes All Stars) 2004, Blessing in Disguise 2006, Zootcase (with Scott Hamilton) 2006, Birds of a Feather (with Greg Abaté) 2009, Doodle Oodle (with Ken Poplowski) 2009, Last Train to Hauteville (with Spirit of Django) 2010, Hi-Ya (with Scott Hamilton) 2010, The London Session (with Warren Vaché) 2011, The Jazz Age (with Bryan Ferry) 2012. *Honours:* British Jazz Awards for Alto Sax 1995, 1997, 1999, 2001, Clarinet 1994, 1996, 1998, Baritone Sax 1998,

2000, 2002, BBC Jazz Instrumentalist of the Year 2001, 2006. *Address:* info@alanbarnesjazz.com (office). *Website:* www.alanbarnesjazz.com.

BARNES, Jimmy; Australian musician (guitar) and singer; b. Scotland. *Career:* lead singer, Cold Chisel 1979–83, 1998, 2009–; solo artist 1984–; mem. Living Loud 2004. *Recordings include:* albums: with Cold Chisel: Breakfast At Sweethearts 1979, East 1980, Circus Animals 1982, The Last Wave Of Summer 1998; solo: Body Swerve 1984, Jimmy Barnes 1985, Freight Train Heart 1987, Barnestorming 1988, Two Fires 1990, Heat 1993, Psychlone 1995, Love and Fear 1999, Soul Deeper 2000, Double Happiness 2005, Out in the Blue 2007, The Rhythm and the Blues 2008, Rage and Ruin 2010; with Living Loud: Living Loud 2004. *Address:* c/o Liberation Music, 9 Dundas Lane, Albert Park, Melbourne, Vic. 3206, Australia. *Telephone:* (3) 9695-7899. *Fax:* (3) 9690-8665. *E-mail:* info@liberationmusic.net. *Website:* www.liberationmusic .net; www.jimmybarnes.com.

BARNES, Neil; British producer and remixer; b. 6 Aug. 1960, London, England. *Career:* Co-founder, Hard Hands Records (with Paul Daley); world-wide DJ; mem. Leftfield 1995–2002, 2010–; collaborations with Djum Djum, Afrika Bambaataa, Roots Manuva, John Lydon. *Recordings include:* albums: with Leftfield: Leftism 1995, Rhythm and Stealth 1999, A Final Hit 2005, Tourism 2012, Alternative Light Source 2015. *Website:* www.leftfieldmusic .com.

BARNETT, Courtney Melba; Australian singer, songwriter and musician (guitar); b. 3 Nov. 1987, Sydney, NSW. *Education:* St Michael's Collegiate School, Tasmanian School of Art. *Career:* fmr guitarist, Melbourne band Rapid Transit 2010–11; mem. Immigrant Union 2011–13; formed own record label Milk! Records 2012; released debut EP 2013; released debut album 2015. *Recordings include:* album: Sometimes I Sit and Think, and Sometimes I Just Sit (ARIA Award for Best Independent Release 2015) 2015. *Honours:* ARIA Awards for Breakthrough Artist 2015, for Best Female Artist 2015. *Current Management:* c/o Nick O'Byrne, Look Out Kid Management, 191 Stanley Street, West Melbourne, Vic. 3003, Australia. *Website:* www.lookoutkid.com; courtneybarnett.com.au (home).

BARNHOLDT, Ole, MA; composer; b. 14 Feb. 1958, Hvorup, Denmark. *Education:* Dick Grove School of Music, Los Angeles, USA, Univ. of Ålborg, Denmark. *Career:* scored various film, television, video projects 1986–; mem. The Jazz Police; mem. KODA (Denmark). *Compositions:* for Denmark's Radio Symphony Orchestra: Valley Heart, Siciliano for Maria. *Publication:* Music Design. *Telephone:* (20) 424-054. *E-mail:* ole@jazzpolice.dk. *Website:* www .jazzpolice.dk.

BARON COHEN, Erran; British DJ, producer, musician (trumpet) and songwriter. *Career:* founder mem. world fusion group, Zöhar. *Films:* as composer: Appelfeld's Table 2004, Borat: Cultural Learnings of America for Make Benefit Glorious Nation of Kazakhstan 2006, Brüno 2009, The Infidel 2010, The Dictator 2012. *Recordings include:* albums: Zöhar: One. Three. Seven 2001, Do You Have Any Faith? 2007; solo: Songs in the Key of Hanukkah 2008. *Honours:* World Music Peace Award 2003. *Current Management:* Embargo Management, 9–10 Jew Street, Brighton, East Sussex BN1 1UT, England. *E-mail:* sumit@embargomanagement.com. *Website:* www .embargomanagement.com; www.zoharmusic.com.

BARRET, Eric; French musician (saxophone) and composer; b. 5 May 1959, Le Havre. *Career:* played with J. P. Mas, A. Ceccarelli 1983, with Barret, Romano Texier 1985, Orchestre National de Jazz 1986, D. Humair 1988, Quartet with M. Ducret 1988, Eric Barret Trio, with Serge Lazarevitch, Joel Allouche; also played with: A. Hervé, R. Urtreger, S. Swallow, J. Griffin, K. Wheeler, A. Farmer, L. Bennett, S. Grossman, F. Hubbard; apptd Prof., Bagneux Music Conservatory 1991; mem. Roy Haynes Quartet 1997, Orchestre National de Jazz 1997. *Recordings include:* Barret, Romano Texier 1987, Eric Barret Quartet 1989, L'Echappe Belle 1992, L'attente des femmes 2012. *Publications include:* Etudes Jazz Pour Saxophone, Gammes Et Arpèges Pour Le Jazz 1987. *Honours:* Boris Vian Price, Bien débuter le saxophone 1997.

BARRETT, Andrew, MusB; American musician (keyboards), arranger and composer; b. 19 Aug. 1953, Oceanside, NY; m. Kathleen Anna McGinley 1980. *Education:* Indiana Univ. *Career:* musician, arranger for various artists, including Diana Ross, Irene Cara, Sister Sledge 1981–82; consultant, Cats Shubert Organization 1982–; synthesizer consultant, New York stage productions, including Cats 1987, Me and My Girl 1987, Les Misérables 1988, Phantom of the Opera 1988, Miss Saigon 1989; mem. ASCAP, NARAS. *Compositions:* contrib. to film soundtracks: Nightmare On Elm Street 3: Dream Warriors 1987, National Lampoon's Christmas Vacation 1990, Shattered 1991, Twist of Fate 1999, Julie Johnson 2001, Cet Amour-La 2001, Auto Focus 2002, Undefeated 2003, Imaginary Witness: Hollywood and the Holocaust 2004, The Flooded Playground 2005. *E-mail:* andy@ andrewbarrett.com. *Website:* www.andrewbarrett.com.

BARRETT, Brian; American musician and songwriter; b. 9 Feb. 1968, Murfreesboro, Tenn.; m. Katrina Startin Barrett. *Education:* Hardin-Simmons Univ. *Career:* numerous live and television appearances; mem. Gospel Music Assn. *Recordings include:* albums: Brian Barrett 1993, Nailed In Stone 1995; also appeared on: Child's Christmas, Revel Players 1993, Tribute: The Songs Of Andrae Crouch 1996, Should've Been Gone, Empty Grave 1999. *Honours:* CCM Readers Awards, Favourite Country Artist,

Favourite Country Album. *Address:* 180 Wallace Road, Apartment S5, Nashville, TN 37211-4634, USA (home).

BARRETT, James Charles; musician (bass guitar) and programming; b. 4 Dec. 1970, London, England. *Career:* founder mem. of rock/dance group, Senser 1989–99, 2003–; numerous television and radio appearances, toured extensively throughout Europe, USA, Japan; numerous festivals. *Recordings include:* albums: with Senser: Stacked Up 1994, Asylum 1998, SCHEMAtic 2004, How to Do Battle 2009. *Address:* c/o Imprint Music, 17c Northwold Road, London, N16 7DH; 24 Gibson Gardens, Stoke Newington, London, N16 7HB, England. *E-mail:* maurice@imprintmusic.co.uk. *Website:* www.imprintmusic.co.uk; www.senser.co.uk.

BARRETT, Mark Vincent; musician (guitar) and sound engineering; b. 27 Jan. 1959, Bishops Stortford, England; one s. one d. *Education:* Stourbridge Coll. of Art; Acton Guitar Inst. *Career:* mem., East Orange 1983; Q Lazzarus 1988; guitarist for Janey Lee Grace; radio broadcasts and television appearances; mem. Musicians' Union. *Recordings:* with Q Lazzarus: Don't Let Go; Goodbye Horses; Mexico 70; albums: Dust Has Come To Stay; Sing When You're Winning. *Address:* Fox and Punch Bowl, Burfield Road, Old Windsor, Berkshire, England.

BARRETT, Paul, MusB; Irish producer, musician (keyboards, brass), composer and arranger; b. 8 Aug. 1954, Dublin. *Education:* Trinity Coll., Dublin, Royal Irish Acad. of Music, Blackrock Coll. *Career:* played trombone, RTÉ Symphony Orchestra 1970–74; musical arranger, EMI Records 1973–75; orchestrator, keyboardist, trombonist, Noel Pearson Productions 1973–81; trombonist, orchestrator, keyboardist, RTÉLO 1974–82; keyboards, arranger, composer, trombonist, RTÉ TV and radio 1975–89; Founder-mem. Sleepless Knights 1976–77, Metropolis 1979–82, Junta 1982; CEO STS Studio 1982–99; Founder 24 track studio with Fairlight CMI, STS 1983–; fmr producer, sound engineer, orchestrator, keyboardist, programmer, brass player with band U2: producer, arranger, keyboardist, RSC 1989–90; performed with artists including Marianne Faithfull, Sinead O'Connor, Brian Eno, Tom Robinson, Hazel O'Connor, Steve Lillywhite, Luka Bloom, Flood, Hothouse Flowers, Bill Whelan, Christy Moore; film music composer; producer for artists including Hazel O'Connor, Hothouse Flowers, Luka Bloom, The Stars of Heaven, Carole King, Coosh, Equation, Quincy Jones, Boyzone; mem. Performing Right Soc., Mechanical-Copyright Protection Soc., Performing Artists Media Rights Asscn, AYIC. *Website:* paulbarrettmusic.com.

BARRETT, Paul Franklyn, (Earl Fuggle); Welsh booking agent, promoter and personal manager; b. (Paul Francis Barrett), 14 Dec. 1940, Blackwood, Caerphilly, Wales; s. of David John Barrett and Hazel Lillian Barrett (née Radford); m. Lorraine Jayne Booth 1972; one s. one d. *Education:* King's Coll., London. *Career:* Owner Paul Barrett Rock 'n' Roll Enterprises; promoter, booking agent, personal man., representing, among others, The Jets, Crazy Cavan and the Rhythm Rockers, Matchbox, Jean Vincent, Wee Willie Harris, Jack Scott, Charlie Gracie, Robert Gordon 1960–; numerous personal appearances, TV, radio; mem. Performing Right Soc., Mechanical-Copyright Protection Soc. *Film appearances:* Blue Suede Shoes, Bloody New Year. *Recordings:* Spirit of Woodstock, I Told You So, Punk, Girl Please Stay, solo vocals on Superstar, featured on Gold album. *Publication:* Shakin' Stevens (with Hilary Hayward) 1983. *Address:* 21 Grove Terrace, Penarth, CF64 2NG, Wales (office). *Telephone:* (29) 2070-4279 (office). *E-mail:* barrettrocknroll@ntlworld.com (office).

BARRON, Chris; American singer; b. 5 Feb. 1968. *Education:* New School, NY. *Career:* Founder mem. funk/rock group, The Spin Doctors 1988–; tours, performances, television appearances. *Recordings include:* albums: Homebelly Groove 1990, Pocket Full Of Kryptonite 1992, Turn It Upside Down 1994, You've Got To Believe In Something 1996, Here Comes The Bride 1999, Just Go Ahead Now (compilation) 2000, Nice Talking to Me 2005, Pancho and the Kid (with Chris Barron) 2009 Casino Logic (with ZO2) 2009, Essential: The 90s 2010, John Popper & the Duskray Troubadours (with John Popper) 2011, Suzie Cracks the Whip (with Blues Traveler) 2012, If the River Was Whiskey 2013; solo: Shag 2001. *Current Management:* c/o Jason Richardson, DAS Communications, 83 Riverside Drive, New York, NY 10024, USA. *E-mail:* jason@dasgroup.com; contactspindoctors@dasgroup.com. *Website:* www.spindoctors.com.

BARRON, Christine Angela, PGCA; British composer, musician, writer, music teacher and adjudicator; b. 9 May 1949, Birmingham, England. *Education:* Moseley School of Art, Birmingham, School of Contemporary Pop and Jazz, London, Univ. of Leeds. *Career:* began as freelance percussionist, including work with Birmingham Symphony Orchestra; theatre, cabaret musician with top entertainers, including Bruce Forsyth, Des O'Connor, Leslie Crowther, Val Doonican; part-time lecturer in percussion and composition, North Warwickshire and Hinkley Coll. of Tech. and Art, Nuneaton, Warwickshire; well known in the UK for innovative percussion workshops and masterclasses featuring percussion; mem., British Acad. of Composers and Songwriters, British Fed. of Festivals for Music, Dance and Speech (also adjudicator), Int. Fed. of Festivals for Music, Dance and Speech (also adjudicator). *Compositions include:* TV signature tunes: Shut That Door (also released as single), Where Are They Now; commissioned by Chappell Music Library for album, short pieces as jingles, theme, incidental music for TV, radio, films (distributed world-wide); collaboration with Boosey and Hawkes Music Publishers on albums, including album recorded by Royal Philharmonic Orchestra; also wrote for their educational catalogue under

pseudonyms: Chris Barron, Christine Barron. *Television includes:* Shut That Door, Where Are They Now. *Publications include:* comprehensive tutors with cassette for Learn As You Play series: Learn As You Play Drums (new CD edn 2006), Learn As You Play Tuned Percussion and Timpani, Learn As You Play Drums Cassette, Drum Styles Made Easy 2009. *Address:* c/o Boosey & Hawkes Music Publishers, First Floor, Aldwych House, 71–91 Aldwych, London, WC2B 4HN, England. *E-mail:* composers@boosey.com. *Website:* www.boosey.com; www.christine-barron.com.

BARRON, Kenny, BA; American jazz pianist; b. 9 June 1943, Philadelphia, Pa. *Education:* Empire State Coll. *Career:* pianist with younger brother Bill Barron 1961–63, Dave Burns 1962, Perry Robinson 1962, Dizzy Gillespie 1963–66, Stanley Turrentine 1967, Booker Erwin 1967, Joe Henderson 1967, Freddie Hubbard 1969, James Moody 1969; co-leader, Sphere 1982–, Classical Jazz Quartet; recorded with Stan Getz 1987–91; other recording sessions include Buddy Rich, George Benson, Elvin Jones, Chet Baker; Ron Carter; taught piano and keyboard harmony at Rutgers Univ., then at Juilliard School of Music; Fellow, American Acad. of Arts and Sciences 2009. *Recordings include:* albums: as leader: You Had Better Listen (with Barron-Jimmy Owens Quintet) 1968, Sunset to Dawn 1973, Peruvian Blue 1974, Lucifer 1975, In Tandem 1976, Innocence 1978, Golden Lotus 1980, Green Chimneys 1983, 1+1+1 1984, Autumn in New York 1985, New York Attitude 1985, Scratch 1985, What If 1986, Two as One 1986, Rhythm-a-ning 1989, Invitation 1990, The Only One 1990, Lemuria – Seascape 1991, Confirmation 1991, The Moment 1991, Quickstep 1991, People Time 1992, Other Places 1993, Sambao 1993, Things Unseen 1993, Wanton Spirit 1994, Swamp Sally 1996, Night and the City 1998, Freefall 2001, Canta Brazil 2002, Peace 2003, Images 2004, The Traveler 2008, Minor Blues 2009, Thrasher Dream Trio 2013, The Art of Conversation (with Dave Holland) (Jazz Journalists' Asscn Award for Record of the Year 2015) 2014; with Yusef Lateef: The Blue Yusef Lateef 1968, The Gentle Giant 1972; solo: At the Piano 1981, Spiral 1993; with Sphere: Four in One 1982, Flight Path 1983, Four for All 1987; with Stan Getz: Voyage 1986; numerous other appearances including: The Kicker, Joe Henderson 1967, Natural Essence, Tyrone Washington 1967, Tex Book Tenor, Booker Ervin 1968, Now!, Bobby Hutcherson 1969, Re-Entry, Charles Sullivan 1975, Piccolo, Ron Carter 1977, Naima, Marvin Peterson 1978, Dedicated to Tadd, Charles Davis 1979, Mad About Tadd, Continuum 1980, The Angels of Atlanta, Marvin Peterson 1981, Jazz French Horn, Tom Varner 1985, All That Jazz, Ella Fitzgerald 1989, Bossas & Ballads – The Lost Sessions, Stan Getz 1989, Struttin', Ron Holloway 1995, Kamau, Charles Sullivan 1995, The Observer, Jon Irabagon 2009. *Honours:* Jazz Masters Award 2010, Jazz Journalists' Asscn for Pianist of the Year 2015, for Trio or Duo of the Year (with Dave Holland) 2015. *Current Management:* c/o Karen Kennedy, 24/ Seven Artist Development, 6 Richmond Street, Newark, NJ 07103, USA. *Telephone:* (973) 230-3160. *Fax:* (973) 353-9477. *E-mail:* kk24seven@aol.com. *Website:* www.kennybarron.com.

BARROW, Geoff; British musician (keyboards, drums), programmer, producer, arranger and songwriter; b. 9 Dec. 1971, Walton in Gordano, Bristol, England. *Career:* tape operator, Coach House Studio, Bristol; worked on Massive Attack's Blue Lines; wrote track for Neneh Cherry's Home Brew album; remixed work for Primal Scream, Paul Weller, Depeche Mode, Massive Attack, Earthling; mem., Portishead 1991–, Beak 2009–, Quakers 2012–; f. Australian record label, Invada Records (with Katalyst's Ashley Anderson) 2001, Invada UK (with Fat Paul) 2003; opened art gallery, The Friend & Co Gallery, Bristol 2008. *Films include:* To Kill A Dead Man (short feature, also projected on MI5 building, London) 1995, Exit through the Gift Shop 2010. *Recordings include:* albums: Dummy (Mercury Music Prize for Best Album) 1994, Herd Of Instinct 1995, Portishead 1997, PNYC (live) 1998, Glory Times 1998, Roseland, New York (DVD) 2002, Third 2008, Beak 2009, Quakers 2012, Drokk: Music Inspired by Mega-City One 2012. *Current Management:* Fruit, Ground Floor, 37 Lonsdale Road, London, NW6 6RA, England. *Telephone:* (20) 7326-0848. *Fax:* (20) 7326-8078. *E-mail:* fruitmanagement@btconnect.com. *Website:* www.portishead.co.uk.

BARRY, Mark Anthony Luke; British singer and songwriter; b. 26 Oct. 1978, Manchester. *Career:* Co-founder and mem. BBMak pop group 1996–2003; various tours and live shows. *Recordings include:* albums: with BBMak: Sooner Or Later 2000, Into Your Head 2002.

BARTHOLOMEW, Dave Louis; American musician (trumpet), composer, arranger and producer; b. 24 Dec. 1920, Edgard, La. *Career:* mil. service as Tech Sergeant, Army, played trumpet in the 196th Army Ground Force Band, France 1942–46; as composer and performer played around New Orleans, toured world-wide with the big bands of Jimmy Lunceford, Claiborne Williams, Ernie Fields, Papa Celestine, Joe Robicheaux, Clyde Kerr Sr, Fats Domino; played with Fats Pichon's band 1938–42, led band 1940–42; f. and led Dave Bartholomew Big Band from 1946; songwriter, arranger, producer and A&R Dir Imperial Record Co. 1952–63; co-writer songs sung by artists, including Fats Domino, Chuck Berry, Elvis Presley. *Compositions include:* The Fat Man (with Fats Domino) 1949, She's My Baby Blues (with Fats Domino) 1950, Boogie Woogie Baby 1950, Korea Blues 1950, Every Night About This Time (with Fats Domino) 1951, Poor Me (with Fats Domino) 1952, How Long (with Fats Domino) 1952, My Ding-A-Ling (with Todd Rhodes) 1952, Goin' To The River 1953, Rose Mary (with Fats Domino) 1953, Something's Wrong (with Fats Domino) 1953, Love Me (with Fats Domino) 1954, You Done Me Wrong 1954, Where Did You Stay 1954, You Can Pack Your Suitcase 1954, Thinking Of You 1954, I Hear You Knockin'

46

(with Pearl King) 1955, Blue Monday 1955, Don't You Know I Love You (with Fats Domino) 1955, All By Myself (with Fats Domino) 1955, Ain't That A Shame (with Fats Domino) 1955, Bo Weevil (with Fats Domino) 1955, I'm In Love Again (with Fats Domino) 1956, One Night (with Pearl King) 1956, Wait And See 1957, I'm Walkin' (with Fats Domino) 1957, Valley Of Tears (with Fats Domino) 1957, When I See You (with Fats Domino) 1957, The Big Beat (with Fats Domino) 1957, Yes, My Darling (with Fats Domino) 1957, Little Mary (with Fats Domino) 1958, Young School Girl (with Fats Domino) 1958, Be My Guest (with Fats Domino) 1959, I Want To Walk You Home (with Fats Domino) 1959, I Want You To Know (with Fats Domino) 1959, My Girl Josephine (with Fats Domino) 1960, Walkin' To New Orleans (with Fats Domino and Robert Guidry) 1960, The Monkey 1985, Bad Habit 1991, The Golden Rule 1991, High Flying Women 1991. *Recordings include:* albums: solo: Fats Domino Presents Dave Bartholomew 1961, New Orleans House Party 1963, Jump Children 1984, Monkey 1985, In The Alley 1991, King Sides 2004; with The Maryland Jazz Band: Walking To New Orleans 1995. *Honours:* inducted into Rock and Roll Hall of Fame (as non–performer) 1991, winner Rhythm & Blues Foundation Pioneer Award 1996, Grammy Trustees Award 2012. *Address:* 4732 Odin Street, New Orleans, LA 70126, USA.

BARTHOLOMEW, Simon James, BA; British musician (guitar); b. 16 Oct. 1965, Woolwich, London. *Education:* Polytechnic of East London. *Career:* guitarist, The Brand New Heavies 1985–, The Akimbo Band; session musician for Mother Earth, Jamiroquai, Samuel Purdey, Mr X; mem. Musicians' Union, MCPS, PRS. *Recordings include:* albums: with The Brand New Heavies: The Brand New Heavies 1991, The Heavy Rhyme Experience 1992, Brother Sister 1994, Shelter 1997, Allaboutthefunk 2004, Get Used to It 2006, Take It to the Streets! 2008, Live In London 2009, Best Of 20 Years 2011. *E-mail:* nick@constituo.co.uk. *Website:* www.thebrandnewheavies.net (office).

BARTLETT, Thomas Wayland, (Doveman); American pianist, singer and record producer; b. 13 Oct. 1981, Brattleboro, Vt. *Career:* fmrly studied piano in London; co-f. folk band Popcorn Behavior (with Sam Amidon), later renamed Assembly 1990s; music critic, Salon.com 2001; performed with groups Chocolate Genius and Elysian Fields 2001; solo artist (as Doveman) 2005–; Founder of Burgundy Stain Sessions nights at Poisson Rouge club 2011–; Founder-mem. and producer, The Gloaming 2011–; musician with numerous artists live and on record including Antony and the Johnsons, Joshua Bell, David Byrne, The National, Bebel Gilberto, Glen Hansard, Miho Hatori, Marisa Monte, Angus & Julia Stone, Martha Wainwright, Rufus Wainwright; producer for many artists including Sam Amidon, Bell X1, Anna Calvi, Hannah Cohen, Glen Hansard, Dawn Landes, Julia Stone, Trixie Whitley. *Recordings:* albums: as Doveman: The Acrobat 2005, With My Left Hand I Raise the Dead 2007, The Conformist 2009; with The Gloaming: The Gloaming 2014. *E-mail:* m@barquemgmt.com. *Website:* barquemgmt.com; tommydove.tumblr.com; thegloaming.net.

BARTON, Bart; American songwriter, record producer and artist manager; m. Pat McKool 1975. *Career:* Pres. Canyon Creek Records, Bekool Music Group, Lemon Square Music, Dallas, Tex.; mem. Country Music Asscn, Canadian Country Music Asscn, GMA, Canadian Acad. of Recording Arts and Sciences, Nat. Acad. of Recording Arts and Sciences. *Recordings include:* She's Sitting Pretty 1989; contrib. to Super Country 89 Album 1989; Co-producer and writer of four songs on album, A Tribute to the American Veterans. *Honours:* Canadian Country Music Asscn, Outstanding International Support Award. *Address:* Bekool Music Group, 11347 Park Central Plaza, Dallas, TX 75230, USA.

BARTON, Lou Ann; American singer; b. 17 Feb. 1954, Fort Worth, Tex. *Career:* numerous live concerts, television appearances; mem. Fabulous Thunderbirds 1975, Triple Threat Review, Double Trouble 1977–80; solo artist with Lou Ann Barton Band 1981–95. *Recordings include:* Old Enough 1982, Austin Rhythm and Blues Christmas 1983, Forbidden Tones 1988, Read My Lips 1989, Dreams Come True with Angela Strehli, Marcia Ball 1990, Sugar Coated Love 1998, Thunderbroad 2001, Someday 2002. *Honours:* four-times winner, Austin Chronicle Music Awards including three-time winner, Female Vocalist of Year. *Current Management:* c/o LutherWolf Management, POB 162078, Austin, TX 78716-2078, USA. *Telephone:* (512) 448-3065. *Fax:* (512) 448-3067. *E-mail:* wayne@lutherwolf.com. *Website:* www.lutherwolf.com.

BARTOSCH, Patrik; Swedish musician (guitar), composer and arranger; b. Lomma. *Career:* Founder-mem. Eggstone 1986–; the band est. Tambourine Studios (with Tore Johansson and Anders Nordgren) 1991–, Vibrafon Records 1995–; studios used by artists, including St Etienne and The Cardigans. *Recordings include:* albums: In San Diego 1992, Somersault 1994, Vive La Difference 1997, Spanish Slalom 1998, Ça chauffe en Suede! 1999, Swan Lee 2005, Victorious 2007, The Old Terminal 2008, Celebrations 2008. *Address:* Tambourine Studios, Sofielundsvägen 57, 214 34 Malmö, Sweden (office). *Telephone:* (40) 87-08-8 (office). *Fax:* (40) 87-08-0 (office). *E-mail:* info@tambourinestudios.com (office). *Website:* www.tambourinestudios.com (office).

BARZEN, Dietmar, Dipl-kfm, Dr rer pol; German producer and composer; b. 18 Oct. 1958, Oberhausen; m. 1994; one d. *Career:* Owner, ind. record label, BME Records Germany; mem. Marketing Club. *Compositions include:* Songs into the Light, Chris Sutton, Friday Night, Kent, Sky High, Far Side Gallery, Piano Dreams, David Warwick, Number One, SES. *Recordings include:* some 150 published and released titles. *Address:* BME Records Germany, Obere Dorfstr. 41B, 50829 Cologne, Germany (office).

BASA, Andrej; Slovenian composer, musician (keyboards), producer and arranger; *Art Director, Melodies of Istria and Kvarner Festival;* b. 10 Feb. 1950, Ljubljana; m. 1977; one s. *Education:* Acad. of Music, Ljubljana. *Career:* Art Dir, The Croatian Children's & Youth Festival, New York, Karnevalfest (Croatia), Melodies of Istria and Kvarner Festival; over 1,200 compositions, 3,200 arrangements. *Recordings include:* suite for orchestra, music for three films; album: Between The Sky and The Earth (instrumental music); as producer, arranger, sound engineer: over 180 albums with various artists. *Honours:* Eurovision Song Contest 1993; 32 festival awards. *Address:* 51215 Kastav, Rubesi 139A, Croatia (home).

BASIA; Polish singer and songwriter; b. (Basia Trzetrzelewska), 1954, Jaworzno. *Career:* singer, Matt Bianco, 1982–86, 2004; solo artist 1986–, with composer Danny White. *Recordings:* albums: solo: Time And Tide 1986, London, Warsaw, New York 1990, The Sweetest Illusion 1994, Basia On Broadway 1995, Clear Horizon—The Best Of Basia 1997, It's That Girl Again 2009, From Newport To London: Greatest Hits Live... And More 2011; with Matt Bianco: Whose Side Are You On 1984, Matt's Mood 2004. *Current Management:* c/o Carl Leighton Pope, LPO, 8 Glenthorne Mews, 115a Glenthorne Road, Hammersmith, London W6 0LJ, England. *Telephone:* (20) 8741-4453. *Fax:* (20) 8741-4289. *E-mail:* carl@l-po.com. *Website:* www.l-po.com; www.basiasongs.com.

BASS, (James) Lansten (Lance); American singer; b. 4 May 1979, Laurel, Miss. *Career:* aged 11 joined local community choir; first engagement with the Mississippi Show Stoppers; toured USA with Attache choir; mem., 'N SYNC vocal quintet 1995–2002; signed to BMG Ariola Munich 1997; first headline US tour 1998; created own pop and country record label, Free Lance Entertainment 2000; created own film production company, Lance Bass Productions, released films, On The Line 2001, Lovewrecked; started boy band Heart2Heart 2011–; host of radio show Dirty Pop with Lance Bass (SiriusXM) 2012–. *Play:* Hairspray 2007. *Recordings include:* albums: 'N SYNC 1998, Home For The Holidays 1998, The Winter Album 1998, No Strings Attached 2000, Celebrity 2001; with Heart2Heart: Facebook Official (debut single) 2011. *Publication:* Out of Sync 2007. *Honours:* presented with keys to City of Orlando 2000, American Music Award, Favorite Pop/Rock Band, Duo or Group 2002, Human Rights Campaign Visibility Award 2006. *Website:* www.lancebass.com.

BASSEY, Dame Shirley Veronica, DBE; British popular singer; b. 8 Jan. 1937, Tiger Bay, Cardiff, Wales; d. of Henry Bassey and Eliza Bassey (née Mendi); one d.; m. 1st Kenneth Hume 1961 (divorced 1965; deceased); m. 2nd Sergio Novak 1971 (divorced 1981); one d. (deceased) one adopted s. *Career:* sang at Astor Club, London; signed up for Such is Life by impresario Jack Hylton 1955; started making records 1956; appeared in cabaret in New York 1961; Artist for Peace, UNESCO 2000; Int. Amb., Variety Club 2001. *Film:* La Passione 1996. *Albums include:* Born to Sing the Blues 1958, And I Love You So 1972, Magic is You 1978, I Am What I Am 1984, Sassy Bassey 1985, New York, New York 1991, Great Shirley Bassey 1999, Thank You For the Years 2003, Get the Party Started 2007, The Performance 2009, Hello Like Before 2014. *Singles include:* Banana Boat Song, As I Love You, Kiss Me Honey Honey Kiss Me, As Long As He Needs Me, theme song for film Goldfinger 1964, Diamonds Are Forever 1971. *Honours:* Chevalier, Légion d'honneur 2010; numerous awards, including 20 Gold Discs and 14 Silver Discs for sales in UK, Netherlands, France, Sweden and other countries; Best Female Singer (TV Times) 1972, 1973, (Music Week) 1974, Best Female Entertainer (American Guild of Variety Artists) 1976, Britannia Award for Best Female Singer 1977. *Address:* 31 Avenue Princesse Grace, 98000 MC, Monaco (office). *E-mail:* burnmycandle@monaco.mc (office). *Website:* www.dameshirleybassey.com.

BASSHUNTER; Swedish producer and singer; b. (Jonas Erik Altberg), 22 Dec. 1984, Halmstad. *Career:* began producing music under Basshunter pseudonym 1999–. *Recordings include:* albums: The Old Shit 1999, The Bassmachine 2004, LOL <(^^,)>2006, Now You're Gone: The Album 2008, Bass Generation 2009, Every Morning 2009, The Early Bedroom Sessions 2013, Calling Time 2013. *Honours:* European Border Breakers Award 2008. *Current Management:* Extensive Music, POB 3166, 200 22 Malmö, Sweden. *Telephone:* (40) 680-21-50. *Fax:* (40) 680-21-51. *E-mail:* henrik@extensivemusic.com. *Website:* www.extensivemusic.com; www.basshunter.se.

BASSIMA; Lebanese singer; b. Beirut. *Career:* solo artist 1998–; collaborations with Marwan Khoury, Samir Sfeir, Tareq Madkoor, Boudi Naoum. *Recordings include:* albums: Dawwabni dob 1999, Andi su'al 2001, Ein yamo 2003, Shou raja'ak 2004, Shou 'a bali 2005, Helm at-tuyour 2008. *Address:* c/o Rotana, Burj al-Ghazal, 11th Floor, al-Tabaris, Achrafieh, Beirut, Lebanon (office). *E-mail:* info@rotana.net (office).

BASTOS, Waldemar; Angolan singer and songwriter; b. 1954, Sao Salvador do Congo. *Career:* began performing 1961; formed Jovial in Kabinda. *Recordings:* Estamos Juntos (featuring Chico Buarque and Martinho da Vila), 1983; Angola Minha Namorada (featuring Jorge Degas), 1990; Pitanga Madura, 1992; Pretaluz, 1998, Renascence 2004, Love is Blindness 2008, Classics of My Soul 2010. *E-mail:* management@waldemarbastos.com. *Website:* www.luakabop.com; www.waldemarbastos.com; www.myspace.com/waldemarbastos.

BAT FOR LASHES; British singer, songwriter and musician; b. (Natasha Khan), 25 Oct. 1979, d. of Rehmat Khan. *Education:* Univ. of Brighton. *Career:*

fmr nursery school teacher; began solo career 2006–. *Recordings:* albums: Fur and Gold 2006, Two Suns 2009, The Haunted Man 2012. *Honours:* ASCAP Vanguard Award 2007, UK Asian Music Award for Best Alternative Act 2010, Ivor Novello Award for Best Contemporary Song 2010. *E-mail:* dickodell@ hotmail.com (office). *Address:* c/o Parlophone Records, Warner Music Group, 28 Kensington Church Street, London, W8 4EP, England (office). *E-mail:* info@batforlashes.com (office). *Website:* www.parlophone.co.uk (office); www .batforlashes.com.

BATES, Django Leon; British musician (keyboards, horn) and composer; b. 2 Oct. 1960, Beckenham, Kent, England; m. Beverley Hills 1988; one s. one d. *Education:* Morley Coll. *Career:* played with Human Chain 1981, Loose Tubes 1983, First House 1986–89, Bill Bruford's Earthworks; solo artist 1990–; toured over 30 countries with these bands and others; mem. Delightful Precipe (Orchestra), Dedication Orchestra; f. Circus Umbilicus. *Recordings include:* albums: with Human Chain: Human Chain 1986, Cashin' In 1988; with Loose Tubes: Loose Tubes 1985, Delightful Precipice 1986, Open Letter 1988; with First House: Erendira 1986, Cantalina 1989; with Bill Bruford's Earthworks: Earthworks 1987, Dig? 1989, All Heaven Broke Loose 1991, Stamping Ground 1994; solo: Music For The Third Policeman 1990, Summer Fruits (And Unrest) 1993, Autumn Fires (And Green Shoots) 1994, Winter Truce (And Homes Blaze) 1995, Good Evening. . . Here Is The News 1996, Like Life 1998, Quiet Nights 1998, You Live And Learn... (Apparently) 2004, Spring is Here (Shall we Dance?) 2008, Beloved Bird 2010, Confirmation 2012. *Honours:* three UK Wire Awards 1987, German Stern Des Jahres 1993, French Academie du Jazz 1994, Mercury Music Award 1997, Jazzpar Prize 1997. *Current Management:* Django Bates Management, c/o Jeremy Farnell, 21 St John's Church Road, London, E9 6EJ, England. *Website:* www .djangobates.co.uk.

BATES, Simon Dominic, BA, LGSM; British musician (saxophone, clarinet, flute, wind synthesizer), programmer, teacher, composer and arranger; *Professor of Saxophone, Royal Marines School of Music;* b. 24 Aug. 1964, London; m.; two d. *Education:* Colchester Inst., Guildhall School of Music and Drama. *Career:* Yamaha Saxophone and Wind Synthesizer endorsee and clinician; musician with: Simon Bates Quartet, Jamie Cullum, Emma Bunton, Elvis Costello, Rick Wakeman, Kylie Minogue, Bananarama, Alvin Stardust, Jason Donovan, Tony Hadley, Dizzee Rascal, Sax Appeal, Peter Erskine, Chaka Khan, Lulu, Billy Ocean, D:Ream, Eddie Floyd; Musical Dir for Rick Astley, Bette Midler, Alexander Armstrong, Johnny Vaughan Tonight, The Big Breakfast; Prof. of Saxophone, Royal Marines School of Music 2004–; mem. Musicians' Union. *Television:* Johnny Vaughan Tonight, Parkinson, The Big Breakfast etc.. *Recordings include:* TV, radio, library sessions; albums and singles with many different artists. *Address:* c/o musicSHmusic, Glendale House, Guildford Road, Loxwood, West Sussex, RH14 0SE, England (office). *Telephone:* (1403) 752954 (office). *E-mail:* simon@musicshmusic.com (office). *Website:* www.musicshmusic.com (office); www.simonbates.net.

BATISAH, Taufik; Singaporean singer, songwriter and record producer; b. (Muhammad Taufik Bin Batisah), 10 Dec. 1981. *Education:* Jurong Secondary School, Singapore Polytechnic. *Career:* fmr singer with group Bonafide; contestant in TV series Singapore Idol 2004 (series winner); signed recording contract with Sony BMG 2005; numerous live performances. *Television:* Singapore Idol (series winner) 2004, Shooting Stars 2005, Stage: Fried Rice Paradise – the Musical 2010. *Recordings include:* albums: Blessings 2005, All Because of You 2006, Teman Istimewa 2007, Suria Hatiku (AnugeraHitz.sg Award for Best Album 2010) 2008, Kenangan Di Hari Raya 2011. *Honours:* Nickelodeon Kids' Choice Wannabe Awards (Singapore) 2006, 2007, MTV Asia Award for Favourite Artist Singapore 2006, Anugerah Planet Muzik Awards for Most Popular Male Artiste 2006, for Most Popular Singapore Artiste 2007, 2008, 2009, 2012, for Most Popular Singapore Song (for Usah Lepaskan) 2007, (for Berserah) 2008, for Best Local Singapore Song (for Usah Lepaskan) 2007, for Best Singapore Artiste 2008, for Most Popular Regional Artiste 2012, for Best Collaboration (with Rossa) (for Aku Bersahaja) 2012, Pesta Perdana Award 2007, Singapore Youth Award for Arts and Culture 2008, Composers and Authors Society (Compass) Award for Top Local Malay Pop Song (for Useh Lepaskan) 2009, Manja Star Award 2010, AnugeraHitz.sg Awards for Best Artiste 2010, for Best Composer 2010, for Popular Song 2010, for Most Popular Ariste 2010, Yahoo! Singapore 9 Entertainment Award 2011, Mnet Award for Best Asian Artist Singapore 2012. *Current Management:* c/o ArtisteNetworks Management, Hype Records Pte Limited, Henderson Building, 221 Henderson Road (S), 159557, Singapore. *Telephone:* 6375-3755. *E-mail:* hype@ hyperecords.com. *Website:* www.hyperecords.com; www.taufikbatisah.net.

BATMANGLIJ, Rostam; American musician (keyboards), songwriter and record producer; b. 28 Nov. 1983, Washington, DC; s. of Mohammad Batmanglij and Najmieh Batmanglij. *Education:* Columbia Univ. *Career:* mem. duo Discovery 2005–; Founder-mem. Vampire Weekend 2006–, signed to XL Recordings 2007; also collaborations with other musicians and groups including Converse, Hamilton Leithauser; numerous festival appearances and tours. *Recordings:* albums: with Vampire Weekend: Vampire Weekend 2008, Contra 2010, Modern Vampires of the City (Grammy Award for Best Alternative Music Album 2014) 2013; with Discovery: LP 2009. *Honours:* with Vampire Weekend: NME Award for Best New American Alternative/Indie Band 2008, Q Magazine Award for Best Video (for Giving Up the Gun) 2011, for Best Act in the World Today 2013. *Current Management:* c/o Ian Montone, Monotone, Inc., 820 Seward Street, Hollywood, CA 90038, USA. *Telephone:* (323) 308-1818. *Address:* c/o Kris Chen, XL Recordings, 304 Hudson Street,

7th Floor, New York, NY 10013, USA (office). *Telephone:* (212) 995-5882 (office). *E-mail:* krischen@xlrecordings.com (office); vampireweekend@gmail .com (home). *Website:* www.xlrecordings.com (office); www.vampireweekend .com.

BATT, Mike; British songwriter, composer, producer, arranger and singer; *Chairman, Dramatico Entertainment Limited;* b. 6 Feb. 1950, Southampton. *Career:* began as A&R Man. for Liberty/UA Records, producing Groundhogs, Big Joe Williams, leaving to pursue independent career as artist, writer and producer; produced Linda Lewis, Steeleye Span (All Around My Hat), Elkie Brooks (Lilac Wine), David Essex (Oh What a Circus); wrote, sang and produced The Wombles and solo albums Schizophonia, Tarot Suite and others; produced Phantom of the Opera single (with Steve Harley and Sarah Brightman); produced and composed for Vanessa Mae's album, The Violin Player 1995; worked with Bond and Becky Taylor 2000–01; produced and composed for classic-pop octet, The Planets 2002; produced first album for Katie Melua 2003; CEO Dramatico; Deputy Chair. BPI 2007–; mem. Performing Right Soc. (Council), British Acad. of Composers and Songwriters (Vice-Pres.). *Compositions include:* Caravans (film score), Bright Eyes (for Art Garfunkel), A Winter's Tale (David Essex), I Feel Like Buddy Holly (Alvin Stardust), Please Don't Fall in Love (Cliff Richard); solo hit singles: Summertime City, The Ride to Agadir, Lady of the Dawn, The Winds of Change; composer of many commissioned pieces, including the opening of the Channel Tunnel for HM the Queen, also for HM the Queen's Golden Wedding Anniversary 1997, One Minute Silence 2002, The Closest Thing to Crazy (for Katie Melua) 2003. *Recordings include:* Schizophonia 1977, Tarot Suite 1979, Waves 1980, Six Days in Berlin 1981, Zero Zero 1982, The Hunting of the Snark 1987, Songs of Love and War 1988, Arabesque 1995, A Songwriter's Tale 2008. *Theatrical project:* The Hunting of the Snark. *Address:* Dramatico Entertainment Limited, PO Box 214, Farnham, Surrey, GU10 5XZ, England. *Website:* www.dramatico.com (office); www.mikebatt.com.

BATTLE, Nicholas Nigel; British music publisher, musician and manager; b. 14 Aug. 1957, Dartmouth, Devon; m. Lynn 1989. *Career:* fmrly led Sheffield Youth Orchestra; bass player, After The Fire; bass player, Writz; also worked with Godley and Creme, Kajagoogoo; Gen. Man., Windswept Pacific Music Ltd; mem. PRS, BAC&S, MPA Pop Publishers Cttee, IPA Council. *Recordings include:* songs recorded by Cliff Richard, First Date, Front Page, Producer, Falling In Love Again, Techno Twins. *Current Management:* c/o Windswept Music Ltd, Hope House, 40 St Peter's Road, London W6 9BH, England.

BAUER, Johannes; German musician (trombone); b. 22 July 1954, Halle, East Germany. *Education:* studied in Berlin. *Career:* freelance improvisational musician 1979–; duo with Barry Guy, trio with Annick Nozati and Fred Van Hove Doppelmoppel (with Konrad Bauer, Joe Sachse, Uwe Kropinski) Slawterhaus (with Dietmar Diesner, Jon Rose, Peter Hellinger), Ulrich Gumpert Trio, Peter Brötzmann Alarm Orchester, März Combo, Tony Oxley's Contemporary Music Ensemble, Globe Unity Orchestra, Derek Bailey's Company, Cecil Taylor European Big Band; leader of various workshop bands. *Recordings:* albums: solo: Organo Pleno 1993; other appearances include: Alarm, Peter Brötzmann 1981, In the Tradition, Alan Silva 1993, Bauer Bauer, Conrad Bauer 1993, The Wild Man's Band, The Wild Man's Band 1997, Aventure Quebecoise, Conrad Bauer 1999, Second Edition, Sweethearts in a Drugstore 2000, Inscape... Tableaux, Barry Guy 2001, Globe Unity Orchestra 2002, Globe University Orchestra 2003, New Horse for the White House, Ken Vandermark 2006, Family Affairs, Conrad Bauer 2008, Outside This Area, DoppelMoppel 2008. *Address:* c/o Intakt Records, PO Box 468, 8024 Zurich, Switzerland. *Telephone:* (44) 383-82-33. *Fax:* (44) 383-82-33. *E-mail:* intakt@intaktrec.ch. *Website:* www.intaktrec.ch; www.johannes -bauer.net.

BAUER, Judah; American musician (guitar, harmonica); b. 1973, Appleton, WI. *Career:* fmr mem., Twenty-Miles; mem., Jon Spencer Blues Explosion 1990–. *Recordings include:* albums: Jon Spencer Blues Explosion, 1992; Crypt Style, 1992; Extra Width, 1993; Mo' Width, 1994; Orange, 1994; Experimental Remixes, 1995; Now I Got Worry, 1996; Controversial Negro, 1997; Rocketship, 1997; ACME, 1998; Magical Colours, 2000; Plastic Fang, 2002, Damage 2004; other credits: Jukebox, Cat Power 2008. *Address:* c/o Majordomo Records, Shout! Factory, 2034 Armacost Avenue, 1st Floor, Los Angeles, CA 90025, USA. *Telephone:* (310) 979-5880. *E-mail:* info@shoutfactory.com. *Website:* www.majordomorecords.com; www.thejonspencerbluesexplosion .com; www.myspace.com/jsbluesexplosion.

BAY, Hans Henrik; Danish musician (guitar) and composer; b. 26 Dec. 1963, Copenhagen; m. Susanne Bechmann; one s. one d. *Education:* Rhythmic Music Conservatory, Copenhagen. *Career:* tour of Denmark with Jorgen Emborg 1988–89, mem. Ensemble NEW and Billy Cobham 1997–; played with James Moody, Ed Neumeister, Jukkis Outtila, Tomas Franck, Bob Rockwell and Jesper Lundgaard; mem., Danish Music Union, Danish Jazz Beat Folk Autorer. *Compositions include:* Crescent 434, 6/8, In the Bar, Chasing the Hawk, Wine and Woman, Bays Blues, Cruising. *Recordings include:* Jorgen Emborg Septet: Keyword 1989, Ensemble New with Billy Cobham 1998, Hope Street, Well, Obviously 2000, Chasing the Hawk 2002. *Address:* Bredager 32, 7120 Vejle Ø, Denmark (home). *E-mail:* post@hanshenrikbay.dk; info@ reverbnation.com. *Website:* www.hanshenrikbay.dk; www.reverbnation.com.

BAY, James Michael; British singer, songwriter and guitarist; b. 4 Sept. 1990, Hitchin, Herts., England. *Education:* Hitchin Boys' School, British and Irish Modern Music Inst. *Career:* released first EP 2013; opening act for

Rolling Stones Hyde Park concert 2013; toured with Hozier 2014; first UK headlining tour 2014; opening act on European leg of Taylor Swift world tour 2015; performed on Pyramid Stage at Glastonbury Festival 2015. *Recording:* album: Chaos and the Calm 2015. *Honours:* BRIT Awards Critics' Choice Award 2015, Q Award for Best New Act 2015. *Current Management:* c/o Closer Artists Management and Publishing, Matrix Complex, 91 Peterborough Road, London, SW6 3BU, England. *Telephone:* (20) 7384-6438. *E-mail:* info@closerartists.com. *Website:* www.closerartists.com; jamesbaymusic.com.

BAYLIS, Christopher Edward, BSc; producer and musician (guitar); b. 7 July 1954, Reading, Berkshire, England. *Education:* University of Surrey. *Career:* founder mem., Siam 1980; formed The Guitar Orchestra 1989; production credits include Maddy Prior, Davey Arthur, Automatic Dlamini; mem. PRS, MCPS, Musicians' Union. *Recordings:* The Guitar Orchestra 1991, Interpretations, The Guitar Orchestra 1994. *Address:* c/o Park Records, PO Box 651, Oxford OX2 9RB, England. *Telephone:* (1865) 241717. *E-mail:* info@parkrecords.com. *Website:* www.parkrecords.com; www.myspace.com/theguitarorchestra.

BAYNE, Iain; British musician (drums, percussion, piano); b. 22 Jan. 1960, St Andrews, Fife, Scotland. *Career:* mem. of folk group, Runrig 1980–; numerous concerts. *Recordings include:* albums: Recovery 1981, Heartland 1985, The Cutter and The Clan 1987, Searchlight 1989, The Big Wheel 1991, Amazing Things 1993, Mara 1995, In Search of Angels 1999, The BBC Archives 1999, The Stamping Ground 2001, Proterra 2003, Everything You See 2007. *E-mail:* mike@runrig.co.uk (office). *Website:* www.runrig.co.uk (office).

BAYNTON-POWER, David; British musician (drums); b. 29 Jan. 1961, Kent, England. *Career:* mem., James 1990–2002, re-formed 2007–; numerous tours, festival dates and TV appearances; freelance TV sound engineer 2002–. *Recordings include:* albums: Gold Mother 1990, Seven 1992, Laid 1993, Wah Wah 1994, Whiplash 1997, The Best Of James 1998, Millionaires 1999, B-Sides Ultra 2001, Pleased To Meet You 2001, Getting Away With It 2002, Hey Ma 2008, The Night Before 2010, The Morning After 2010, The Gathering Sound 2011, La Petite Mort 2014. *Website:* www.wearejames.com.

BEACHILL, Peter C.; British musician (trombone); b. 1 Feb. 1961, Barnsley, Yorkshire. *Education:* Leeds College of Music. *Career:* studio musician; Prin. Trombone, London Metropolitan, London Philharmonic, Royal Philharmonic, London Sinfonietta orchestras; various television shows including Royal Variety, Barrymore, BAFTA Awards, BBC, LWT Shows; tours with James Last, Natalie Cole, Shirley Bassey, Pete Townshend, Cliff Richard, Chris Rea, Eric Clapton, Oasis; mem, Royal Society of Musicians. *Recordings:* albums with: Paul McCartney, Sting, Pet Shop Boys, Diana Ross, Rod Stewart, James Last, Shirley Bassey, Cliff Richard, Peter Gabriel, Eric Clapton, Grace Jones, Pink Floyd, Led Zeppelin, Pete Townshend. *Honours:* BBC Don Lusher Trombone Award. *Address:* c/o London Metropolitan Orchestra, Timbers, Woburn Hill, Weybridge, Surrey KT15 2QG, England (office).

BEAKER, Norman; British musician (guitar, piano, bass, harp), singer, composer and producer; b. 21 June 1950, Manchester; m. 1977 (divorced 1985); one s. *Education:* Royal Northern Coll. of Music. *Career:* formed Norman Beaker Band 1982–; solo concerts with Alexis Korner, Eric Clapton, Jack Bruce, B. B. King, Lowell Fulsom, Graham Bond, Buddy Guy; numerous television and radio broadcasts; mem. PRS, MCPS. *Recordings include:* albums: Bought in the Act 1986, Modern Days Lonely Nights 1988, Into the Blues 1989, The Older I Get, The Better I Was 1999, Who's He Calling Me Him? 2002, Live at the Tivoli 2010. *Publications include:* freelance writer on R&B, various magazines and journals. *Honours:* Blues Guitarist of the Year 1989. *E-mail:* admin@normanbeakerband.com (office). *Website:* www.normanbeakerband.com.

BEANS, AD; American rapper and musician; b. (Robert Edward Stewart II), 3 July 1971, White Plains, NY; s. of Robert E. Stewart and Janet Mearle London Stewart; one d. *Education:* American Coll. for the Applied Arts, Coll. of Art, Greenwich, Conn. *Career:* mem. The Anti-Pop Consortium 1997–2002, 2007–; solo artist 2002–; f. Adored and Exploited record label; collaborations with Arto Lindsey, Vernon Reid, Alec Empire, Gang of Four (remix), Attica Blues, Bill Laswell, Dabrye, Dj Krush, Prefuse 73, Ratatat, Terranova. *Recordings include:* albums: with The Anti-Pop Consortium: Tragic Epilogue 2000, Shopping Carts Crashing 2001, Diagnol Rhyme Gargantula 2001, Ends Against the Middle 2002, Arrhythmia 2002, Fluorescent Black 2009, Knives from Heaven 2011; solo: Tomorrow Right Now 2003, Now, Soon, Someday 2004, Shock City Maverick 2004, Only 2006, Thorns 2008, End It All 2011. *Current Management:* c/o Joseph N Noon, Spectrum Music, 235 Nassau Avenue, Suite 2L, Brooklyn, NY 11222, USA. *Telephone:* (718) 383-2313. *Fax:* (718) 383-2373. *E-mail:* joseph@spectrummusic.net. *Website:* www.spectrummusic.net.

BEARD, Frank; American musician (drums); b. 11 June 1949, Frankston, Tex. *Career:* mem. The Warlocks 1967, name changed to The American Blues 1968; Founder-mem. ZZ Top 1970–. *Recordings include:* albums: with The American Blues: American Blues Is Here 1967, The American Blues Do Their Thing 1969; with ZZ Top: ZZ Top's First Album 1970, Rio Grande Mud 1972, Tres Hombres 1973, Fandango 1975, Takin' Texas To The People 1976, Tejas 1976, Deguello 1979, El Loco 1981, Eliminator 1983, Afterburner 1985, Recycler 1990, Antenna 1994, Rhythmeen 1996, XXX 1999, Mescalero 2003, Eliminator 2008, Texicali 2012, La Futura 2012. *Honours:* Nordoff-Robbins

Music Therapy Foundation Silver Clef Award 1992. *E-mail:* info@zztop.com (office). *Website:* www.zztop.com.

BEARD, Susan (Sue) Stephanie, BA; British jazz singer, songwriter, musician (piano, oboe, ukelele), actress and writer; b. 25 Feb. 1961, London. *Education:* Bristol Univ., York Univ. *Career:* comic/satirical jazz singer; numerous radio and television broadcasts; concerts include Live at London's Comedy Store, Ronnie Scott's, Pizza On The Park, Astoria, One Woman Show Tour including Edinburgh Festival, Kuala Lumpur, Arezzo, Paris. *Compositions include:* Spooks! (children's musical) 1995; composer, performer, many topical, satirical and jazz songs for radio, television, live performances. *Current Management:* Nick Young, Crawfords, 2 Conduit Street, London W1R 9TG, England.

BEASLEY, Walter; American musician (alto, soprano saxophones) and songwriter; b. California. *Career:* Jazz Explosion's Just the Sax tour. *Recordings:* Albums: Walter Beasley, 1988; Just Kickin' It, 1989; Intimacy, 1992; Private Time, 1995; Live and More, 1996; Tonight We Love, 1997; For Your Pleasure, 1998; Won't You Let Me Love You, 2000; Rendez Vous, 2002; For Her 2005, Ready for Love 2007, Free Your Mind 2009, Backatcha! 2010; singles: Call Me; I'm So Happy; Jump On It; Nothin' But A Thang; On The Edge; Tenderness; Where; You Are The One; If You Ever Loved Someone; Don't Say Goodbye. *Address:* c/o Shanachie Records, Dept. WWW, 37 East Clinton Street, Newton, NJ 07860, USA. *Website:* www.shanachie.com; www.walterbeasley.com.

BEATTY, Marc; British musician (bass guitar); b. Croydon. *Career:* mem., Brakes 2002–; numerous live performances; fmr resident producer, Mockingbird Studios, Brighton. *Recordings include:* albums: Give Blood (Best album of the year by the influential Rough Trade Shops) 2005, The Beatific Visions 2006, Touchdown 2009, Rock Is Dodelijk (Live Album) 2009.

BEAUFORD, Carter; American musician (drums); b. 2 Nov. 1957. *Education:* Shenandoah Conservatory, Winchester, VA. *Career:* son of a jazz trumpeter; session player, including guest appearance on a Carlos Santana album; first gig aged 9, with jazz-fusion outfit led by Big Nick Nicholas; mem. band, Secrets 1984–90; four-year residency as pianist, Ramsey Lewis' Bet on Jazz show; mem., Dave Matthews Band 1991–; numerous tours and live appearances world-wide; first album released on group's own Bama Rags label. *Recordings:* albums: Remember Two Things 1993, Under The Table And Dreaming 1994, Crash 1996, Live At Red Rocks 8.15.95 1997, Before These Crowded Streets 1998, Listener Supported (live) 1999, Everyday 2001, Live In Chicago 12.19.98 2001, Busted Stuff 2002, Live At Folsom Field, Boulder, Colorado 2002, Central Park Concert 2003, Live Trax, Vol 1–12 2004–08, The Gorge 2004, Stand Up 2005, Big Whiskey and the GrooGrux King 2009, Away from the World 2012. *Honours:* Grammy Awards for Best Rock Performance by a Duo or Group with Vocal 1997, VH-1 Awards for Favorite Group, Must Have Album, Song of the Year 2001. *E-mail:* fanmail@davematthewsband.com (office). *Website:* www.davematthewsband.com.

BEAUPRE, Jhan; American songwriter and musician (guitar); b. 29 April 1950, Dallas, TX; m. Joyce Ann Beaupre 1983, six d. *Education:* Southwestern Union College. *Career:* founder mem., The Sound System aged 15; played with various bands for seven years; business venture, Sound Illusions, promoting and recording new artists and songwriters; mem. BMI, Austin Song Writers Group, Johnson County Asscn (sec.), Song Writers of Wisconsin, Fort Bend SW Group. *Compositions include:* She Can Make A Man Cry; A Good Guitar; There's A Flame. *Address:* Listen Loud Music Publishing, 4761, CR 305, Grandview, TX 76050, USA. *Telephone:* (817) 641-0735. *E-mail:* listenloudpublisher@gmail.com.

BEAUSSIER, Daniel Gérard Jacques; French musician, composer, teacher and producer; b. 2 June 1957, Valenciennes, Nord; m. Aesa Sigurjonsdottir 1987; three s. one d. *Education:* ICAM. *Career:* tour, Europe, with Carla Bley 1988; with Nana Vasconcellos, Paris Jazz Festival 1991, Hozan Yamamato 1995, Monica Passos, Charlélie Couture, Shiro Daimon, Astrolab Collectif; collaborations with D Beaussier (150 concerts); mem UMJ, FNEIJ, IAJS; Director, EDIM, Creative Music School, Paris. *Recordings:* Fleur Carnivore, Carla Bley, Lueurs Bleues, Daniel Goyone, Trilok Gurtu, Sans(e)krit, Daniel Beaussier, Casamento, Monica Passos, Chambre 13, Lydia Domancich, You Are Here, Uman. *Honours:* First prize, CNR, Lille, France. *Address:* 24 Ave d'Alembert, 92160 Antony, France (home).

BEBE; Spanish singer, songwriter and actress; b. (Maria Nieves Robolledo Vila), 9 May 1978, Valencia; one d. *Career:* fmr mem. Vanagloria; solo artist 2004–. *Films:* Al sur de Granada 2003, El oro de Moscú 2003, Busco 2006, La educación de las hadas 2006, Caótica Ana 2006. *Recordings:* albums: Pafuera Telarañas 2004, Y 2009. *Honours:* Latin Grammy Award for Best New Artist 2005. *E-mail:* info@belledejourmanagement.com. *Website:* www.belledejourmanagement.com; www.labebebellota.com.

BEBEK, Zeljko; Bosnia and Herzegovina singer; b. 16 Dec. 1945, Sarajevo; m. 1st Sandra Bebek 1982 (divorced); m. 2nd Ružica Bebek 2002; three d., one s. *Education:* Univ. of Civil Rights. *Career:* mem. Eho 61 1961, Kodeski 1966–70, Novi Kodeski 1970–72, Bijelo Dugme 1974–85. *Recordings include:* (singing in Croatian language) Skoro da Smo Isti, Bosanac, Selma, Na Zadnjem Sjedistu, Da Je Srece Bilo, Dabogda Te Voda Odnijela, Sta Je Meni Ovo Trebalo, A Svemir Miruje, Odlazim, Tijana; solo albums: Mene Tjera Neki Vrag, 1984, Armija B 1985, Niko Više Ne Sanja 1989, Pjevaj Moj Narode 1989, Gori Svijet...Ti Ceš Ga Ugasiti 1994, Puca Mi U Glavi 1995, S Tobom I Bez

Tebe 1999, Ošini po prašini 2000, Kad poljubac pomiješaš sa vinom 2012. *Website:* www.zeljkobebek.com.

BÉCHAMP, Debbie; Canadian singer; b. 5 Feb. 1958, Chapeau, PQ; m. Peter Komisar Jr; one s. three d. *Education:* studied classical guitar. *Career:* numerous live and TV appearances; concerts as support act for artists including Garth Brooks, Lee Greenwood, Eddie Rabbitt; two seasons of musical theatre 2006–09; mem. AFofM. *Television:* hosted variety music shows on CBC TV. *Recordings include:* albums: Time To Move Along, Mixed Emotions, See the Sunshine. *Honours:* winner, Canadian Open Country Singing Contest (three consecutive years), winner, CBC TV Contest, Look Out World Here We Come. *Address:* 075339 Side Road 24-25, Grand Valley, ON L9W 0K2, Canada (home). *Telephone:* (519) 928-2257 (home). *E-mail:* debbie .bechamp,komisar@bell.net; debbie@debbiebechamp.com. *Website:* www .debbiebechamp.com.

BECK; American musician, singer and producer; b. (Bek David Campbell), 8 July 1970, Los Angeles, CA; s. of David Campbell and Bibbe Hansen; m. Marissa Ribisi 2004; one s. one d. *Career:* early performances at local parties in Los Angeles; worked with producers Karl Stephenson, and later the Dust Brothers; numerous tours and live appearances; collaborated with Snoop Doggy Dogg, Air; remixed Air, Jon Spencer Blues Explosion, Bjork, David Bowie. *Exhibitions:* Beck & Al Hansen: Playing With Matches, Santa Monica Museum of Art then to galleries in New York City and Winnipeg, Manitoba, Canada). *Recordings include:* albums: Mellow Gold 1994, Stereopathic Soul Manure 1994, One Foot in the Grave 1994, Odelay (Grammy Award for Alternative Music Performance 1997) 1996, Mutations (Grammy Award for Alternative Music Performance 2000) 1998, Midnite Vultures 1999, Sea Change 2002, Guero 2005, Guerolito 2006, The Information 2006, Modern Guilt 2008, Morning Phase (Grammy Awards for Album of the Year 2015, for Best Rock Album 2015) 2014. *Honours:* Grammy Award for Best Rock Vocal Performance Male 1997, BRIT Award for Best International Solo Artist 2000. *Current Management:* c/o Silva Artist Management. *E-mail:* info@ sammusicbiz.com. *Website:* www.sammusicbiz.com; www.beck.com.

BECK, Jeff; British musician (guitar), composer and singer; b. 24 June 1944, Surrey; m. Sandra Cash 2005. *Education:* Wimbledon Art Coll. *Career:* fmr mem. Screaming Lord Sutch, The Tridents; guitarist, The Yardbirds 1965–66; leader, Jeff Beck Group 1967–72, Beck, Bogert & Appice 1972–74, with numerous concerts and festival appearances, tours; Patron, Folly Wildlife Rescue Trust. *Recordings include:* albums: with the Yardbirds: For Your Love 1965, Having A Rave Up With The Yardbirds 1965, The Yardbirds with Sonny Boy Williamson 1966, Yardbirds 1966, Over Under Sideways Down 1966, Birdland 2003, Rave Up With the Yardbirds 2006; with Jeff Beck Group/solo: Truth 1968, Beck-Ola 1969, Rough and Ready 1971, Jeff Beck Group 1972, Beck, Bogert and Appice 1973, Beck, Bogert and Appice, Live in Japan 1974, Blow By Blow 1975, Wired 1976, Jeff Beck With The Jan Hammer Group Live 1977, There and Back 1980, Flash 1985, Jeff Beck's Guitar Shop With Terry Bozzio and Tony Hymas 1989, Crazy Legs 1993, The Best Of Beck 1995, Who Else! 1999, You Had It Coming 2001, Jeff 2003, Live at B.B King's 2005, Bootleg Album 2006, Emotion and Commotion 2010, Live and Exclusive from the Grammy Museum 2010, Jeff Beck's Rock 'N' Roll Party: Honoring Les Paul 2011; contrib.: Jon Bon Jovi, Blaze of Glory 1990, Roger Waters, Amused to Death 1992, Tribute to Muddy Waters 1993, Stone Free – A Tribute to Jimi Hendrix 1993, Luciano Pavarotti, Ti Adoro 2003, Cyndi Lauper, The Body Acoustic 2005, Imogen Heap, Speak for Yourself 2005, Crossroads 2007. *Honours:* Dr hc (Univ. of the Arts London and Univ. of Sussex) 2011; Grammy Award for Best Rock Instrumental Performance 1985, 1989, 2001, 2003, 2010, BAFTA Award for Best Original Television Music (for Frankie's House, with Jed Leiber) 1993, Ronnie Scott Award for Blues Artist of the Year 2007, Grammy Award for Best Pop Instrumental Performance (Nessun Dorma) 2011, Grammy Award for Best Rock Instrumental Performance (Hammerhead) 2011, Ivor Novello Award for Outstanding Contribution to British Music 2014. *Website:* www.jeffbeckofficial.com.

BECKENSTEIN, Jay; American band leader, musician (saxophone) and producer; b. 14 May 1951, Brooklyn, New York; three d. *Education:* State Univ. of New York, Buffalo with Edward Yadzinski, also with John Sadola. *Career:* owned BearTracks Studios; sideman in several blues and R&B bands; f. and leader, jazz band Spyro Gyra 1977–. *Recordings include:* albums with Spyro Gyra: Spyro Gyra 1978, Morning Dance 1979, Catching the Sun 1980, Carnaval 1980, Freetime 1981, Incognito 1982, City Kids 1983, Access All Areas 1984, Alternating Currents 1985, Breakout 1986, Stories Without Words 1987, Rites of Summer 1988, Point of View 1989, Fast Forward 1990, Three Wishes 1992, Dreams Beyond Control 1993, Love & Other Obsessions 1995, Heart of the Night 1996, 20/20 1997, Road Scholars 1998, Got the Magic 1999, In Modern Times 2001, Original Cinema 2003, The Deep End 2004, Wrapped in a Dream 2006, Good to Go-Go 2007, A Night Before Christmas 2008, Down the Wire 2009, A Foreign Affair 2011; solo: Eye Contact 2000. *Website:* www.spyrogyra.com.

BECKER, Irene, CandPhil; Danish musician (piano) and composer; b. 30 March 1951, Ålborg; m. Pierre Dorge 1985. *Education:* Univ. of Copenhagen. *Career:* mem. Pierre Dorge's New Jungle Orchestra 1980–; mem. of trio, Dorge, Becker, Carlsen; performs with singer Sainkho Namtclylak, Austria; composer of film music; has composed music for several TV documentary films, including Pigebørn (DR/TV-fakta) 1992, Som sendt fra Regnbuen 2000, At Digte i Guld og Sølv 2003, Ylva og Dragen 2005; various jingles for DR-TV;

has also composed music, with husband Pierre Dørge, for films: Bryllupsfoto-grafen 1993, Love and Hate – European Stories 1994, The Letter 1994, Pigs and Pearls 1997, Holger Danske 1997, Eva Och Adam; mem. DJBFA, Danish Musicians' Union. *Address:* Ermelundsvej 115, 2820 Gentofte, Denmark. *Telephone:* 31-69-43-73. *E-mail:* irene@newjungleorchestra.com. *Website:* www.irenebecker.com; www.newjungleorchestra.com.

BECKER, Jason; American rock musician (guitar). *Education:* classical guitar. *Career:* mem. of rock group, Cacophony 1986–90; also solo artist; guitarist with David Lee Roth 1991. *Recordings:* albums: with Cacophony: Speed Metal Symphony, 1987; Go Off, 1989; solo: Perpetual Burn, 1988; Perspective, 1996; Raspberry Jams, 1999, Blackberry Jams 2003, Collection 2008; with David Lee Roth: A Little Ain't Enough, 1991. *Address:* PO Box 70513, Point Richmond, CA 94807, USA. *Website:* www.jasonbeckerguitar .com.

BECKER, Walter; American musician (guitar, bass) and record producer; b. 20 Feb. 1950, New York; one s. two step-s. *Career:* founder mem. Steely Dan 1972–81, 1993–; record producer 1980–; solo recording artist; tours of USA, Japan, Europe, Australia. *Recordings:* albums: Can't Buy A Thrill 1972, My Sportin' Life 1973, Countdown To Ecstasy 1973, Pretzel Logic 1974, Katy Lied 1975, The Royal Scam 1976, Aja 1977, Greatest Hits 1979, Metal Leg 1980, Gaucho 1981, Reelin' In The Years 1985, Do It Again 1987, Remastered: The Best Of Steely Dan 1993, Citizen Steely Dan 1972–80 1993, Alive In America 1995, Two Against Nature 2000, Everything Must Go 2003; solo: 11 Tracks Of Whack 1995, Circus Money 2008; jazz recordings for LeeAnn Ledgerwood, Andy Laverne, Jeff Beal, Jeremy Steig, David Kikosi, Lorraine Feather, Sam Butler, Donald Fagen. *Honours:* Grammy Awards. *Address:* c/o Sonic360 Inc., 9461 Charleville Boulevard 527, Beverly Hills, CA 90212, USA (office). *Website:* www.sonic360.com (office); www.walterbecker.com.

BECKERS, Ludo (Lazy Lew); Belgian musician (harmonica); b. 27 March 1957, Molenstede, Belgium; m. 1981; one s. one d. *Education:* Halewÿnstichting, Antwerp. *Career:* harmonica player (sometimes singer), The Zoots 1984–86, The Sultans 1987, Medford Slim Band 1990–94, Brothers in Blues 1990–96; European tours with Zora Young, R L Burnside, Big Lucky Carter, Calvin Jackson; mem. Société Belge des Auteurs, Compositeurs et Editeurs (SABAM). *Recordings include:* with The Zoots: Live at the Banana Peel 1984, Blues at the Farmhouse 1984, Bad Days Are Gone 1986; with The Sultans: Little by Little 1987; with Medford Slim Band: Too Much is Never Enough 1991, Come and Get It! 1994. *Address:* 77 Te Boelaarlei, 2140 Antwerp, Belgium (home). *Website:* www.overblow.com/ludo.

BECKETT, Steve; British record company executive; *Managing Director, Warp Records.* *Career:* fmr mem. of punk band with the late Rob Mitchell, later opened record store with Mitchell, Warp Records, Sheffield, England 1987; co-founder and Man. Dir, Warp Records label for electronic music 1989–; first release, WAP 001, Track With No Name, by Forgemasters 1989; released compilations of various artists 1993–; artists signed include Anti-Pop Consortium, Aphex Twin, Autechre, Black Dog, Boards of Canada, Broadcast, LFO, Nightmares on Wax, Plaid, Plone, Red Snapper, Sabres of Paradise, Squarepusher, Maxïmo Park; founder, Warp Films 2000–, downloads website Bleep.com 2004–. *Address:* Warp Records Ltd, Spectrum House, 32–34 Gordon House Road, London, NW5 1LP, England. *Telephone:* (20) 7284-8350. *Fax:* (20) 7284-8360. *E-mail:* info@warprecords.com. *Website:* www.warprecords .com.

BECKHAM, Victoria Caroline; British singer, model, actress, fashion designer and business executive; b. 17 April 1974, Harlow, Essex, England; d. of Tony Adams and Jackie Adams; m. David Beckham 1999; three s. one d. *Education:* St Mary's High School, Cheshunt, Herts., Jason Theatre School, Laine Arts Theatre Coll. *Career:* mem. Touch, later renamed the Spice Girls 1993–2001, as 'Posh Spice', reunion tour 2007–08; solo artist 2000–; launched her dvb Denim collection in New York 2007, also unveiled new eye-wear range, launched Intimately Beckham perfume 2007, debut cosmetics line V-Sculpt launched in Tokyo 2008; the face of Marc Jacobs for his Spring collection 2008; own fashion collection debuted during New York Fashion Week at the Waldorf Hotel 2008; appeared on covers of British Vogue April 2008, Indian Vogue Nov. 2008, Russian Vogue Feb. 2009; launched a secondary line, Victoria by Victoria Beckham 2011; guest judge, Project Runway 2008, Germany's Next Topmodel 2009, American Idol 2010; spokesperson for the Ban Bossy campaign advocating leadership roles for girls 2014–. *Films:* Spiceworld: The Movie 1997, Ugly Betty (episode, A Nice Day for a Posh Wedding) 2007, Spongebob Squarepants (voice of Queen Amphitrite) 2010. *Television:* documentaries: Victoria's Secrets 2000, Being Victoria Beckham 2002, The Real Beckhams 2003, Full Length & Fabulous, Victoria Beckham: Coming to America 2007, Giving You Everything 2007. *Recordings include:* albums: with The Spice Girls: Spice 1996, Spiceworld 1997, Forever 2000, Greatest Hits 2007; solo: Victoria Beckham 2001, Not Such An Innocent Girl 2004. *Publications:* Learning to Fly (autobiog.) 2001, That Extra Half an Inch 2006. *Honours:* two Ivor Novello songwriting awards 1997, Smash Hits Award for Best Band 1997, BRIT Awards for Best Single (for Wannabe) 1997, for Best Video (for Say You'll Be There) 1997, for Best Performance of the last 30 years 2010, three American Music Awards 1998, Special BRIT Award for Int. Sales 1998, Glamour Magazine Awards for Woman of the Year and for Entrepreneur of the Year 2007, Walpole Award 2011, assessed by Woman's Hour (BBC Radio 4) as one of the 100 most powerful women in fashion in UK 2013, named by Management Today magazine as Britain's most successful entrepreneur of 2014. *Current Management:* c/o 19 Entertainment, Unit 33, Ransomes Dock, 35–37 Parkgate, London, SW11 4NP, England. *Website:* www.victoriabeckham.com.

BEDER, Mark; British record producer, music publisher and artist manager; b. 16 Nov. 1959, London; one s. one d. *Career:* with A & R Dept, Carlin Music Publrs; A & R Man., Polydor and Virgin Records; Man. Dir for Pumphouse Music, Pumphouse Sounds, Pumphouse Songs, FXU Records; Man. of D:ream, X-Avia, Tri, Siren, D J Peer; mem. PRS, MCPS, MPA, IMF. *Honours:* Best Newcomers, Best Dance Act, Radio One Tune of the Year 1992.

BEDINGFIELD, Daniel; British singer and songwriter; b. 1980, New Zealand; s. of Molly Bedingfield; brother of Natasha Bedingfield. *Career:* solo artist; mem. Bd Global Angels. *Recordings include:* albums: Gotta Get Thru This 2002, Second First Impression 2004, Stop the Traffik – Secret Fear 2012; several EPs. *Honours:* Interactive Music Award People's Choice 2002, BRIT Award for British Male Solo Artist 2004. *Website:* www.danielbedingfield.com.

BEDINGFIELD, Natasha; British singer and songwriter; b. 1981, London; sister of Daniel Bedingfield; m. Matthew Robinson 2009. *Career:* solo artist 2004–. *Recordings include:* albums: Unwritten 2004, N.B. 2007, Strip Me 2010. *Honours:* Smash Hits Award for Hot New Talent 2005. *Website:* www .natashabedingfield.com.

BEDNAREK, Kamil; Polish reggae singer and songwriter; b. 10 May 1991, Brzeg. *Career:* lead singer, Star Guard Muffin 2008–12; contestant, TV series Mam talent! 2010; Founder-mem. and lead singer, Bednarek 2012–. *Recordings:* albums: with Star Guard Muffin: Szanuj 2010; with Bednarek: Jestem 2012. *Television:* Mam talent! (participant) 2010, Bitwa na glossy (mentor) 2012. *Honours:* MTV Europe Music Awards for Best Polish Act 2013, for Best East European Act 2013. *Website:* www.sgmband.com (home); kamilbednarek .pl (home).

BEEBY, John; British musician (guitar), songwriter and producer; b. 18 Nov. 1945, Nuneaton, Warwickshire; m. 1974; one s. *Career:* toured Germany 1963–64; with The Zephyrs 1964; toured with Del Shannon, Jerry Lee Lewis, Billy Fury, Pretty Things, Count Prince Miller 1968, Tony Gregory, Horace Faith; television appearances include Ready Steady Go, Top of the Pops, Scene At 6.30, Wogan, Pebble Mill; film appearances: Be My Guest (with Jerry Lee Lewis, Steve Marriott), Primitive London, Ice Cream Dream, Business Ventures: John Beeby's Music Place 1975; worked freelance with various artists; worked with Eurythmics' Dave Stewart as songwriter, producer 1980s; co-writer, Dreamtime, with Daryl Hall 1986; co-writer, producer, with Brian Hodgson, Why Do I Always Get It Wrong (UK entry, Eurovision Song Contest) 1989; worked in Nashville, USA, with various artists including Robert Ellis Orral, Larry Henley, Roger Cook 1989; mem. Performing Right Soc., British Acad. of Composers & Songwriters. *Recordings include:* She's Lost You 1964, Wonder What I'm Gonna Do 1965, A Little Bit Of Soap 1965, Dreamtime 1986, Why Do I Always Get It Wrong 1989, Take A Chance On Me 1989, Hinterland 1995. *Honours:* BMI Dreamtime, USA and UK .

BEEDLE, Ashley, (Daddy Ash, Black Jazz Chronicles, Delta House of Funk); British producer, remixer and DJ; b. 25 Nov. 1962, Hemel Hempstead, England. *Career:* worked in record shops Black Market and Flying Records in London; mem., Ballistic Brothers, Black Science Orchestra, Disco Evangelists; founder mem., X-Press 2 1993–; founder, Afro Art Records; collaborations with David Holmes, Marc Woolford; mem. MCPS/PRS. *Recordings include:* albums: Walter's Room (with Black Science Orchestra) 1994, Ballistic Brothers vs The Eccentric Afros 1995, London Hooligan Soul (with Ballistic Brothers) 1995, Future Juju (as Black Jazz Chronicles) 1998, Muzikizum 2002, Makeshift Feelgood (with X-Press 2) 2006, Inspiration Information Volume 2 (with Horace Andy) 2009, Mavis 2010. *Honours:* Muzik Award for Best Producer (with X-Press 2) 2001. *Address:* Think Espionage, 71 St. John Street, London, EC1M 4NJ, England. *E-mail:* ad@thinkespionage.com. *Website:* www.xpress2 .com.

BEENIE MAN; Jamaican reggae artist and DJ; b. (Anthony Moses Davis), 22 Aug. 1973, Kingston; m. Michelle D'Angel Downer 2006 (divorced 2007). *Career:* first prize, nat. Teeny Talent contest at age of eight, recording single 'Too Fancy'; DJ at Unlimited, Prince Jammy and Volcano sound systems 1983–; solo artist, with numerous collaborations, from the age of 10. *Recordings include:* albums: The Invincible Beenie Man, Guns Out (with Bounty Killer), Defend It 1994, Dis Unu Fi Hear 1994, Beenie Man Meets Mad Cobra 1995, Blessed 1995, Maestro 1996, Guns Out 1997, Many Moods Of Moses 1997, Doctor 1999, Y2K 1999, Art And Life (Grammy Award for Best Reggae Album 2001) 2000, Youth Quake 2001, The Magnificent 2002, Heavyweight Dancehall Clash 2002, Tropical Storm 2002, Street Life 2004, Back To Basics 2004, Concept of Life 2006, Hundred Dollar Bag 2006, Undisputed 2006, Monsters of Dancehall 2007, The Legend Returns 2009. *Honours:* DJ of the Year Award 1993, Lifetime Achievement Award 2011.

BEERS, Garry William; Australian musician (bass guitar); b. 22 June 1957, Manly, NSW; two d. *Career:* fmr mem., Doctor Dolphin; founder mem., The Farriss Brothers 1977, renamed INXS 1979–; collaborations with other artists; owner Mangrove Studios; side project Mudhead. *Recordings include:* albums: INXS 1980, Underneath The Colours 1981, Shabooh Shoobah 1982, The Swing 1984, Listen Like Thieves 1985, Kick 1987, X 1990, Live Baby Live 1991, Welcome To Wherever You Are 1992, Full Moon Dirty Hearts 1993, Elegantly Wasted 1997, Switch 2006, Original Sin 2010. *Honours:* Brit Award for Best Int. Group 1991, World Music Award for Outstanding Contribution

To The Music Industry 1992. *Address:* c/o Petrol Records, PO Box 7754, 2026 Sydney, Australia. *E-mail:* info@inxs.com. *Website:* www.inxs.com.

BEGGS, Nick; British musician (bass guitar, chapman stick), producer, writer and arranger; b. 15 Dec. 1961, Winslow, Bucks; one d. *Career:* f. Art Nouveau 1979, Kajagoogoo 1982–85, 2008–, Ellis, Beggs and Howard 1987, Iona 1989; mem., Musicians' Union, MCPS, PPL, PRS; A&R Man. Phonogram Records 1993–94; recorded and toured with ABC, Alphaville, Belinda Carlisle, Celtus, China Crisis, Cliff Richard, Cozi, Curiosity Killed The Cat, Howard Jones, John Paul Jones, Kim Wilde, Steven Wilson. *Compositions:* White Feathers 1983, Islands 1984, Crazy People's Right to Speak 1985, Homelands 1988, The Book of Kells 1992, Beyond These Shores 1993. *Recordings include:* Big Bubbles No Troubles (with Ellis Beggs and Howard) 1988, A Woman and a Man (with Belinda Carlisle) 1996, The Thunderthief (with John Paul Jones) 2001; solo albums: Stick Insect 2002, The Maverick Helmsman 2004. *E-mail:* info@nickbeggs.co.uk. *Website:* www.nickbeggs.co.uk.

BEGLEY, Séamus; Irish singer and musician (button accordion); b. Dingle, County Kerry; brother of Eilín Begley, Maire Begley, Seosaimhin Ni Bheaglaoich and Breandan Begley. *Career:* started playing for local dances aged 14; long-term collaboration with Steve Cooney as Begley & Cooney; formed duo with guitarist, Jim Murray. *Recordings include:* albums: An Ciarraíoch Mallaithe (with Maire Begley) 1972, Plancstaí Bhaile Na Buc (with Maire Begley) 1989, Meitheal (with Steve Cooney) 1997, Ragairne (with Jim Murray) (Hot Press Magazine Folk and Trad Album of the Year Award, Traditional Album of the Year Award, The Irish Times) 2001, Éirí go lá (with Jim Murray) 2009, Disgrace Notes (with Tim Edey). *Honours:* Nat. Entertainment Award for Most Popular Traditional Act (with Steve Cooney) 1997. *E-mail:* seamusbegleyandjimmurray@gmail.com. *Website:* www .seamusbegleyandjimmurray.ie.

BEIJBOM, Lars; Swedish composer, arranger and musician (drums, piano); b. 1 Aug. 1950, Svarta; one s. *Education:* Berklee Coll. of Music, USA. *Career:* co-leader Beijbom Kroner Big Band; composer and arranged music for large number of radio/television programmes, Big Bands Symphony Orchestra's, arranged and composed music for artists including: George Russell, Dorothy Donegan, Dee Dee Bridgewater, Dionne Warwick, Benny Anderson, Tomas Ledin, Maritza Horn, Tre Damer, The Swedish Radio Jazz Group, The Danish Radio Big Band, NDR-band; musical arranger, Danish star Stig Rossen; leader of new band Orchestra Six 2013; mem. STIM, SKAP, SAMI. *Compositions:* Three for Daniel, The Swinging Triangle, In the Long Run, Eat Your Heart Out, Up Your Alley, The Goose is Out, Sweet Sadness, The Fire Within, Alpha and Omega, 11 Peterborough Street. *Recordings:* Subway Baby 1977, White Orange 1980, Bright Orange: The Goose is Out 1983, Beijbom Kroner Big Band, Live in Copenhagen (Jazz CD of the Year, Danish Jazz Special Critics Choice 1997) 1996, Beijbom Kroner Big Band, Opposites Attract 1998, Tredamer, Duke, We Love You Madly 1999. *Honours:* SKAP Award 2009. *Address:* Flygelv 4, 22472 Lund, Sweden (home). *Telephone:* (733) 96-39-11 (office). *E-mail:* lars.beijbom@gmail.com (home).

BEINS, Burkhard; German musician (percussion); b. 22 Oct. 1964, Celle. *Career:* mem. various punk bands and experimental music for taped material and percussion 1980–90; numerous concerts and festival appearances; mem. ensembles, including Perlonex, Activity Center, Polwechsel, The Sealed Knot, Phosphor, Trio Sowari; collaborations with Keith Rowe, Sven-Åke Johansson, John Bisset, Orm Finnendahl, Charlemagne Palestine and others. *Recordings include:* Relay III: Random Play 1995, Nunc 1996, Yarbles 1997, The Answering Machine Solution 1997, Möwen & Moos (with Activity Center) 1999, Bad Alchemy (with Perlonex) 2000, The Sealed Knot (with Rhodri Davies and Mark Wastell) 2000, Perlon (with Perlonex) 2000, Chapel/Kapell (with John Bisset) 2001, Grain (with Keith Rowe) 2001, Hörstücke II 2001, Peripherique (with Perlonex) 2001, Relay Eight 2001, Phosphor 2002, Nmperign + Dörner 2002, Lidingö (with Andrea Neumann) 2002, Surface/ Plane (with The Sealed Knot) 2003, Perlonex 2003, Labor 2003, Santa Fé (with Sven-Åke Johansson) 2003, Misiiki (with Dirk Marwedel and Michael Vorfeld) 2003, Berlin Drums (with Tony Buck, Steve Heather and Eric Schaefer) 2004, Keith Rowe/Burkhard Beins (live) 2004, Unwanted Object (with The Sealed Knot) 2004, Activity Center and Phil Minton 2005, Three Dances (with Trio Sowari) 2005, Zur Stabilen Stützung eines Körpers ist es Notwendig (with Serge Baghdassarians and Boris Baltshun) 2006, Tension (with Perlonex) 2006, Disco Prova 2007, SLW (with Lucio Capece, Rhodri Davies and Toshimaru Nakamura) 2009. *E-mail:* sound@burkhardbeins.de (office). *Website:* www.burkhardbeins.de.

BELAFONTE, Harry; American singer, composer and actor; b. (Harold George Belafonte Jr.), 1 March 1927, New York; s. of Harold George Belafonte Sr and Malvene Love Wright; m. 1st Marguerite Byrd 1948 (divorced); two c.; m. 2nd Julie Robinson 1957 (divorced); one s. three d.; m. 3rd Pamela Frank. *Education:* George Washington High School, New York. *Career:* in Jamaica 1935–39; service with US Navy 1943–45; student, American Negro Theater, then at Manhattan New School for Social Research Dramatic Workshop 1946–48; first engagement at the Vanguard, Greenwich Village; European tours 1958, 1976, 1981, 1983, 1988; Pres. Belafonte Enterprises Inc.; Goodwill Amb. for UNICEF 1987; Host of Nelson Mandela Birthday Concert, Wembley, UK 1988; concerts in USA, Europe 1989, Canada 1990, USA and Canada 1991, N America, Europe and Far East 1996; mem. Bd New York State Martin Luther King Jr Inst. for Nonviolence 1989–; mem. Bd of Trustees, Inst. for Policy Studies. *Achievements include:* RCA album Calypso made him the first artist in industry history to sell over one million LPs. *Recordings include:* Calypso 1956, An Evening with Belafonte 1957, Belafonte at Carnegie Hall 1959, Belafonte Returns to Carnegie Hall 1960, Jump Up Calypso 1961, To Wish You a Merry Christmas 1962, The Midnight Special 1962, The Many Moods of Belafonte 1962, An Evening with Belafonte/Mouskouri 1966, Belafonte and Miriam Makeba 2003. *Films include:* Bright Road 1953, Carmen Jones 1954, Island in the Sun 1957, The World, the Flesh and the Devil 1959, Odds Against Tomorrow 1959, The Angel Levine 1970, Buck and the Preacher 1972, Uptown Saturday Night 1974, White Man's Burden 1995, Kansas City 1996, Bobby 2006, Motherland 2009, Sing Your Song 2011. *Publication:* My Song: A Memoir 2011. *Honours:* Hon. DHumLitt (Park Coll., Mo.) 1968, Hon. Dr Arts, New School of Social Research, New York 1968, Hon. DCL (Newcastle) 1997, numerous other hon. doctorates; Grammy Award 1985, Kennedy Center Honors 1989, Golden Acord Award, Bronx Community Coll. 1989, Mandela Courage Award 1990, Nat. Medal of the Arts 1994, New York Arts and Business Council Award 1997, Award of Excellence, Ronald McDonald House Charities 2000, Grammy Lifetime Achievement Award 2000, Distinguished American Award, John F. Kennedy Library, Boston 2002, BET Humanitarian Award 2006, Andrew Goodman Foundation Lifetime Achievement Award 2011, Humanitarian Oscar 2014. *Address:* c/o The Agency Group Ltd, 1880 Century Park East, Suite 711, Los Angeles, CA 90067, USA. *Telephone:* (310) 385-2800. *Fax:* (310) 385-1220. *Website:* www .theagencygroup.com.

BELCHEV, Mikhail Ivanov; Bulgarian singer, composer, lyricist and musician (guitar); b. 13 Aug. 1946, Sofia; m. Christina Konstantinova Belcheva 1988; one s. *Education:* Bodra Smyana Bulgarian Nat. Youth Choir. *Career:* solo artist 1967–; tours in Italy 1970, Spain 1982, France 1983, West Berlin 1986, USA 1987, Canada 1988, USSR, Germany, Poland, Czechoslovakia, Romania; mem. Bulgarian Artist Asscn; mem. Bd of Dirs The Music Author. *Recordings include:* albums: Where Are Your Friends 1972, Counterpart 1977, Re-Qualification 1988, Cricket On The Pavement 1993, Man To Hug (lyrics by Mikhail Belchev) 1994; television biographical musical films: Where Are You Friends 1973, Counterpart 1977. *Publications include:* poetry: At First Cock-Crow 1987, A Man To Hug 1994. *Honours:* Cyril and Methodius Order; Golden Orpheus Festival Awards, Bratislava and Sopot Festival Awards.

BELEW, Adrian; American musician (guitar), singer, songwriter and producer; b. (Robert Steven Belew), 23 Dec. 1949, Covington. *Career:* session musician 1980s; singer, guitarist, King Crimson 1981–84, 1993–; solo artist 1982–; Founder, The Bears 1986–; producer, Jars of Clay 1966. *Recordings include:* albums: solo: Lone Rhino 1982, Twang Bar King 1983, Mr Musichead 1989, Young Lions 1990, Inner Revolution 1990, Desire Caught By The Tail 1991, Here 1994, The Acoustic Adrian Belew 1995, Op Zop Too Wah 1996, Belewprints 1998, Salad Days 1998, Coming Attractions 1999, Side One 2005, Side Two 2005, Side Three 2006, Side Four 2007, e 2009; with King Crimson: Discipline 1981, Beat 1982, Three Of A Perfect Pair 1984, Vroom 1995, Thrak 1995, B'Boom 1995; with The Bears: The Bears 1987, Car Caught Fire 2001, Eureka 2007; as session musician: with Laurie Anderson: Mister Heartbreak 1984, Home Of The Brave 1986; with David Bowie: Stage 1978, Lodger 1979, Another Face 1981; with Talking Heads: Remain In Light 1980, The Name Of This Band Is 1982; with Frank Zappa: In New York 1978, Sheik Yerbouti 1979, Yer Are What You Is 1982, You Can't Do That On Stage Anymore 1988, The Key, Joan Armatrading 1983, The Catherine Wheel, David Byrne 1981, Maybe It's Live, Robert Palmer 1982, Zoolook, Jean-Michel Jarre 1984, True Colors, Cyndi Lauper 1986, Strange Little Girls, Tori Amos 2001. *Honours:* Cammy Lifetime Achievement Award 2001. *Address:* Adrian Belew Presents, PO Box 956, Mount Juliet, TN 37121-0956, USA (office). *E-mail:* mgt@ adrianbelew.net (office). *Website:* www.adrianbelew.net.

BELL, Andy; British singer and songwriter; b. 25 April 1964. *Career:* singer, Void; lead singer, Erasure 1985–; numerous UK and Int. tours, TV appearances. *Recordings include:* albums: Wonderland 1986, The Circus 1987, The Two-Ring Circus 1987, The Innocents 1988, Wild! 1989, Chorus 1991, Pop!— The First 20 Hits 1992, I Say I Say I Say 1994, Erasure 1995, Cowboy 1997, Loveboat 2000, Other People's Songs 2003, Nightbird 2005, Electric Blue 2005, Union Place 2006, On The Road To Nashville 2007, Light at the End of the World 2007, Erasure The First 40 Hits 2009, Andy Bell Non-Stop 2010, Tomorrow's World 2011, Snow Globe 2013, The Violet Flame 2014. *Honours:* BRIT Award for Best British Group 1989, Ivor Novello Award for Most Performed Work (for Blue Savannah) 1991. *Address:* Erasure Information Service, 1 Albion Place, London, W6 0QT, England (office). *E-mail:* info@mute .co.uk (office). *Website:* www.mute.com (office); www.erasureinfo.com.

BELL, Andrew (Andy) Piran; British musician (guitar), songwriter and singer; b. 11 Aug. 1970, Cardiff, Wales; m. 1st Idha Övelius 1992; m. 2nd Shiarra Bell; one s., one d. *Education:* Banbury Art School. *Career:* mem. rock band Ride 1988–96, 2014–; session musician with Idha 1992–; mem. Hurricane #1 1997–99, Oasis 1999–2010, Beady Eye 2010–14. *Recordings include:* with Ride: Nowhere 1990, Going Blank Again 1992, Carnival Of Light 1994, Tarantula 1996, OX4 2001; with Idha: Melody Inn 1994; with Hurricane #1: Hurricane #1 1997, Only The Strongest Will Survive 1999; with Oasis: Familiar To Millions (live) 2001, Heathen Chemistry 2002, Don't Believe The Truth (Q Award for Best Album) 2005, Stop the Clocks 2006, Dig Out Your Soul 2008; with Beady Eye: Different Gear, Still Speeding 2011, BE 2013. *Honours:* NME Awards for Best UK Band, Artist of the Year 2003, Q Award for Best Act in the World Today 2006, BRIT Award for Outstanding

Contribution to Music 2007. *Current Management:* c/o Mr Marcus Russell, Ignition Management, 54 Linhope Street, London, NW1 6HL, England. *Telephone:* (20) 7298-6000. *Fax:* (20) 7258-0962. *E-mail:* info@ignition.co.uk. *Website:* www.ignition.co.uk; www.ridemusic.net.

BELL, Chris; British musician (drums); b. 26 Aug. 1960, London. *Career:* mem. Thompson Twins 1979–82; numerous live appearances; mem. Spear of Destiny 1982–83; work with Specimin 1985; mem. Gene Loves Jezebel 1986–91; toured USA, Japan, Europe, South America; numerous television appearances; tours, recordings, television with Big Country 1991–92; tour and recording with Nan Vernon 1992; tours with Hugh Cornwell 1993, 1994; live work with Phantom Chords 1994–95; various sessions 1995. *Recordings include:* albums: with Thompson Twins: A Product Of 1981, Set 1982; with Nan Vernon 1993, with Hugh Cornwell 1995.

BELL, Colin Stewart, BA, MA; British record company executive and artist manager; b. 11 Sept. 1952, Carrickfergus, County Antrim, Northern Ireland. *Education:* Queen Mary Coll., King's Coll., Univ. of London. *Career:* publicist, Rogers and Cowan; Man., Tom Robinson Band; Head of Press, Phonogram UK Ltd; Man. Dir, London Records 1991–98; fmr Man., Elton John; Clore Leadership Fellow 2004. *Honours:* Leslie Perrin PR Award, Music Week Marketing Award. *Address:* c/o The Clore Leadership Programme, South Building, Somerset House, Strand, London, WC2R 1LA (office); 53 Hillgate Place, London, SW12 9ES, England (home). *Telephone:* (20) 8673-7603 (home).

BELL, Dennis Lawrence, BM, MA; American record producer, musician (keyboards), arranger, songwriter and conductor and music educator; b. 4 Dec. 1941, New York; m. Claudette Washington 1979; one s. d. *Education:* New York Univ., City Univ. of New York, Queens Coll. *Career:* Founder and CEO, City Slicker Productions, Mark of Aries Music, GuavaJamm Entertainment (record label); produced records for Doug E. Fresh, Dave Valentin, New Voices of Freedom, U2, Touché and others; wrote dance scores/compositions for modern dance/ballet; played and recorded albums with Marcus Miller, Buddy Williams, Nick Brignola, Jimm Owens, Dave Grusin, Buddy Morrow, Sal Salvador, Dave Valentin, Noel Pointer, Steve Jordan, U2, Lenny Kravitz, Celia Cruz, Billy Preston and others; currently Prof. of Music and Music Tech., Mercy Coll., Westchester Co.; fmrly Conductor, Bronx Boro-Wide Chorus and teacher, LaGuardia High School of Music and Art and Performing Arts; mem. BMI, Nat. Asscn Entertainment. *Recordings include:* solo: I, Myself and Me 2002, Musique pour la Danse Moderne 2008; numerous albums with others. *Publication:* Music Alive. *Honours:* Boystown Award for Public Service, Bronx Boro President's Award for Community Service. *Address:* GuavaJamm Entertainment Inc., PO Box L, Inwood Station, New York, NY 10034, USA (office). *Telephone:* (212) 567-0411 (office). *E-mail:* dennis@guavajamm.net (office). *Website:* www.guavajamm.net (office); www.cityslickerproductions .net (office).

BELL, Eric; Northern Irish musician (guitar), singer and songwriter; b. 3 Sept. 1947, Belfast. *Career:* musician with Van Morrison, Northern Ireland 1967; founder mem. of rock group, Thin Lizzy 1969–74; co-arranger, Whiskey in the Jar; television appearances; mem., Noel Redding Band 1976–78; fmr. member, Mainsqueeze; mem. Eric Bell Band. *Recordings include:* with Thin Lizzy: Whiskey In The Jar; The Rocker; Collection; Soldier Of Fortune; Dedication: The Very Best...; Remembering; with Eric Bell Band: Irish Boy 1998. *E-mail:* contact@eric-bell.com. *Website:* www.eric-bell.com.

BELL, Madeline; British/American singer; b. 23 July 1942, Newark, New Jersey, USA; d. of Henry Bell and Evelyn Bell; m. Barry Reeves (deceased). *Education:* South Side High School, New York. *Career:* began as gospel singer; toured north-eastern USA with The Glovertones; joined The Bradford Singers 1961; toured Europe with original cast of Black Nativity 1962–63; moved to London 1963; worked as session singer; solo artist 1968–; joined Blue Mink 1969. *Recordings include:* albums: I'm Gonna Make You Love Me 1968, Comin' Atcha 1974, This is One Girl 1976, Beat Out That Rhythm on a Drum 1998, Blessed 2000, Tribute to Ray Charles; with Blue Mink: Our World 1969, Melting Pot 1970, Real Mink 1970, A Time of Change 1972, Blue Mink 1973, Only When I Laugh 1973, Have You Met Miss Bell 1993, Girl Talk 1995, Yes I Can 1997, Blessed 1999, Soulmates, Blue Christmas 2005–07, This is Love 2011. *Honours:* Hackney Empire UK Black Woman of the Year 1994, British Acad. of Songwriters, Composers and Authors Award 1995, Int. Alliance for Women in Music 1999, Heritage Foundation Lifetime Achievement Award 2003. *Telephone:* (7751) 606892 (office). *E-mail:* madeline@madelinebell.com (office). *Website:* www.madelinebell.com (office).

BELL, Thom; American producer, songwriter, arranger and musician (keyboards); b. 27 Jan. 1943, Kingston, Jamaica. *Career:* mem. Gamble's Romeos, MFSB (Mother, Father, Sister, Brother) band; Producer and arranger, Cameo records –1968, Philly Groove 1968–69; formed songwriting team with Linda Creed; Ind. producer, arranger, songwriter; worked with Delfonics, Ronnie Dyson, Phyllis Hyman, Elton John, Johnny Mathis, O'Jays, Showstoppers, The Spinners, Stylistics, Deniece Williams. *Compositions include:* Betcha By Golly Wow, Break Up to Make Up, Didn't I Blow Your Mind This Time, Ghetto Child, I'll Be Around, I'm Coming Home, I'm Doing Fine Now, I'm Stone In Love With You, La-La Means I Love You, Mesmerized, One Man Band, Rockin' Roll Baby, Rubberband Man, You Are Everything, You Make Me Feel Brand New, Then Came You 1974, They Just Can't Stop It the (Games People Play) 1975, Are You Ready for Love 1979, Silly 1981, It's Gonna Take a Miracle 1982, I Don't Have the Heart 1990. *Honours:* Grammy

Award for Best Producer of the Year 1975, inducted into Songwriters Hall of Fame 2006.

BELLAMY, David; American singer and songwriter; b. 16 Sept. 1950, Darby, FL. *Career:* played R&B clubs, backing Eddie Floyd, Percy Sledge, Little Anthony and the Imperials; played throughout Southeast USA, with own band, Jericho; cut demos with Neil Diamond's band; formed Bellamy Brothers with brother Howard, later formed Bellamy Brothers Records; tours with Loggins and Messina; Doobie Brothers; Beach Boys; Conway Twitty; collaborated as songwriter with Costas, Don Schlitz and Bobby Braddock; mem. ASCAP, AFTRA, AFofM. *Compositions include:* Spiders and Snakes; Sugar Daddy; Do You Love As Good As You Look; Old Hippie; Kids of The Baby Boom. *Recordings include:* 28 albums 1976–2007 including: Lonely Planet 1999, Reason for the Season 2002, Jesus is Coming 2007. *Honours:* Record of the Year (for If I Said You Had A Beautiful Body) 1979, CMT Independent Video of the Year (for Cowboy Beat). *Telephone:* (352) 588-3628. *E-mail:* blmymusic@aol.com. *Website:* www.bellamybrothers.com.

BELLAMY, Gina, (Gina Bellamy-Loren), BA; American record company executive, record producer, singer and songwriter; *President, Scootertunes Inc.;* b. (Gina Lynn Bellamy), 23 April 1957, Dallas, Tex. *Education:* Univ. of Texas, Arlington. *Career:* began recording, singing career aged 13; duet concerts with some radio and TV appearances; stand-in actor on TV series, Dallas; organized Scootertunes Inc. (currently Pres.), Scooter Records, Scooter Productions and J. B. Quantum Music; participated in live radio broadcast of Willie Nelson's Farm Aid 1994; mem. American Fed. of Music, The American Soc. of Composers, Authors and Publrs, BMI, Nat. Acad. of Recording Arts and Sciences. *Recordings include:* True Love Conquers All, Gina Bellamy 1994, The Fever, The Fever (contemporary country group) 1995, Feelings of Christmas/Santa's All Star Revue 1996, Lavender Blue 1997, Wild Honey 1999, Some Favorites and 2 Christmas Songs 2013, My Songs 2014, Jalapeno Heat 2015, Changes on the Wind 2016. *Address:* Scootertunes Inc., PO Box 610166, Dallas, TX 75261, USA (office). *Telephone:* (972) 986-5582 (office). *E-mail:* scootune1@verizon.net (office). *Website:* www.scootertunes.com (office).

BELLAMY, Howard; American singer and songwriter; b. 2 Feb. 1946, Darby, FL; m. Ilona. *Career:* played R&B Clubs, backing Eddie Floyd, Percy Sledge, Little Anthony and the Imperials; played Southeast USA with own band, Jericho; became Jim Stafford's road manager; cut demos with Neil Diamond's band; formed The Bellamy Brothers (with brother, David), later formed Bellamy Brothers Records; toured USA with Loggins and Messina; Doobie Brothers; Beach Boys; Conway Twitty; collaborated with Costa, Don Schlitz and Bobby Braddock; mem. ASCAP, AFTRA, AFofM. *Recordings include:* 28 albums 1976–2007 including: Lonely Planet 1999, Reason for the Season 2002, Jesus is Coming 2007. *Honours:* Record of the Year (for If I Said You Had A Beautiful Body) 1979, CMT Independent Video of the Year (for Cowboy Beat) 1992. *Telephone:* (352) 588-3628. *E-mail:* blmymusic@aol.com. *Website:* www.bellamybrothers.com.

BELLAMY, Matthew James; British singer and musician (guitar); b. 9 June 1978. *Career:* formed group Gothic Plague aged 13, group became Rocket Baby Dolls before finally settling on name Muse 1997–; released two 1,000-copy EPs on UK ind. label, Dangerous; numerous festival appearances, broadcasts. *Recordings include:* albums: Showbiz 1999, Origin Of Symmetry 2001, Hullabaloo 2002, Absolution (Kerrang! Award for Best Album 2004) 2003, Time Is Running Out 2004, Black Holes and Revelations 2006, The Resistance (Grammy Award for Best Rock Album 2011) 2009, The 2nd Law 2012, Drones (Grammy Award for Best Rock Album 2016) 2015. *Honours:* NME Awards for Best New Band 2000, for Best Live Band 2005, 2008, 2009, for Best British Band 2007, 2010, 2011, Kerrang! Awards for Best British Band 2001, for Best British Live Act 2002, for Best Live Act 2006, Q Awards for Innovation in Sound 2003, for Best Live Act 2004, 2006, 2007, for Best Act in the World Today 2009, 2012, MTV Europe Music Awards for Best Alternative Act 2004, 2006, for Best UK and Irish Act 2004, 2007, for Headliner 2007, BRIT Awards for Best Live Act 2005, 2007, American Music Award for Favorite Alternative Artist 2010, Ivor Novello Award for International Achievement 2011. *Website:* www.muse.mu.

BELLAMY, Thomas (Tom) Rhys; British musician (guitar, keyboards); b. 21 Jan. 1978. *Career:* mem. The Cooper Temple Clause late 1998–2007; developed side project as DJ, Rhysmix; collaborated with Pure Reason Revolution 2010; mem. Losers; worked on project Mutation (with Ginger Wildheart) 2012. *Recordings include:* albums: with Cooper Temple Clause: See This Through And Leave 2002, Kick Up The Fire And Let The Flames Break Loose 2003, Make This Your Own 2007; with Pure Reason Revolution: Hammer and Anvil 2010.

BELLOTTE, Peter; British songwriter, producer and musician (guitar); b. 28 Aug. 1943. *Career:* collaborations with Giorgio Moroder 1972–84; Co-founder Say Yes Productions; worked with Donna Summer, Roberta Kelly, Chicory Tip, Sparks, Irene Cara, Elton John, Blondie, Janet Jackson, Melba Moore, France Joli, Marty Wilde, Munich Machine, Gonzalez; fmr mem. Trax (with Keith Forsey). *Television includes:* South Park 2004, Being Erica 2010, Late Night with Jimmy Fallon 2011. *Films include:* soundtracks for: Scarface 1983, Metropolis 1984, The Full Monty 1997. *Honours:* inducted into Dance Music Hall of Fame, New York 2004. *E-mail:* info@petebellotte.com. *Website:* www.petebellotte.com.

BELLOW, Roger David, BA; American musician (guitar, violin, mandolin, banjo, bass) and teacher; b. 15 April 1950, Chicago, IL; m. Judy Golombeck 1977 (divorced). *Education:* University of Tennessee, Antioch College, studied in Bogotá, Colombia, Old Town School of Folk Music, Chicago. *Career:* Cas Walker, TV Show, Knoxville, Tennessee, 1968–70; Kennedy Center Concert, Washington, DC, 1976; Kaustinen International Folk Festival, Finland, 1981; Belize Tour, 1983; University of Chicago, Folk Festival, 1986; Faculty of Augusta Heritage Center, Elkins, W Virginia, 1989–; SC Arts Comm Resident Artist, 1987–; Host, Vintage Country Radio Program, public radio, 1987–2001; Japan Tour, 1993; University of Chicago Folk Festival, 1999; performed at the Encuentro de dos Tradiciones in Mexico 2000; performance on Radio México, 2001; currently mem. Roger Bellow and the Troubadours; mem. AFofM, Reunion of Professional Entertainers. *Recordings:* with Revonah: Get In Line Brother, 1980; with Flying Fish: Success Street, 1988; On The Road To Prosperity, 1991; (Japanese recording) The Bay Quintet, 1993; with Augusta Faculty Band: Zombies Of Swing, 1994; Allons a Grand Kaplan, with Paul Dudley Kershaw, 1998; Cross Country Swing, with Paul Anastasio, 1999; Sentimental Journey, with Ann Caldwell, 2001. *Publications:* research published in Bluegrass Unlimited and Journal of Country Music. *Honours:* South Carolina Folk Heritage Award, 1995; SC Grant for Research in Country Music. *E-mail:* Max@MandoMaxMusic.com. *Website:* www.mandomaxmusic.com/trouba.

BELMONDO, Lionel; French musician (saxophones, flute); b. 19 Aug. 1963, Hyères. *Education:* Conservatory de Toulon. *Career:* Dir School of Music, Centre Vas; teacher in other schools 1982–90; moved to Paris 1990; side man for concerts with Michel Legrand, Phil Woods, Toots Thielemans, Dee Dee Bridgewater, Horace Silver, Lew Tabackin; formed quintet, Belmondo (with brother, Stéphane); numerous TV appearances; currently with Lionel Belmondo Trio. *Recordings include:* albums: with Belmondo Quintet: For All Friends 1994, Infinity 1999, Hymne au Soleil (Prix Victoire for Best Jazz Album 2004) 2003, Influence (with Yusef Lateef) (Best Album for French Victoires du Jazz 2006) 2005, Milton Nascimento and Belmondo 2008, Live Infinity 2009, Clair Obscur 2011. *Honours:* Prix Django Reinhardt for Best French Musician (with brother) 1994. *Address:* c/o Muriel Vandenbossche, 40, rue Coriolis, 75012 Paris, France. *Website:* lionelbelmondo.com.

BELMONDO, Stéphane; French musician (trumpet, flugelhorn); b. 8 July 1967, Hyères; m. Elisabeth Kontomanou; one s. *Education:* Conservatory de Toulon. *Career:* mem. Big Band Lumiere; side man in concerts with Michel Legrand Big Band, Chet Baker, Tom Harrell, David Liebman, Dee Dee Bridgewater, Horace Silver; formed quintet, Belmondo (with brother, Lionel); numerous television appearances. *Recordings include:* albums: with Belmondo Quintet: For All Friends 1994, Infinity 1999, Hymne au Soleil (Prix Victoire for Best Jazz Album 2004) 2003, Influence (with Yusef Lateef) (Best Album for French Victoires du Jazz 2006) 2005, Milton Nascimento and Belmondo 2008, Infinity Live 2009, The Same As It Never Was Before 2011; solo: Ameskery (with Sylvain Luc) 1999, Wonderland 2004. *Honours:* Django Reinhardt Award for Best French Musician (with brother Lionel) 1994. *Website:* stephanebelmondo.artiste.universalmusic.fr.

BELTRAMI, Marco; American composer; b. 7 Oct. 1966, Long Island, New York. *Education:* Brown Univ., Yale School of Music, composer scholarship with Jerry Goldsmith. *Career:* composer of film/TV scores; has worked with Robert Rodriquez, Luis Mandoki, John Dahl, Jodie Foster, David E. Kelley and Marilyn Manson; concert music performances with Oakland East Bay Symphony Orchestra, São Paulo State Orchestra, Chicago Civic Symphony Orchestra, Le Nouvel Ensemble Moderne, Montréal, Bacchanalia Chamber Festival, New York, Italy, Moscow, Fornero Camerata, Italy; mem. Int. Piano Duo Asscn, Tokyo, BMI. *Compositions include:* Death Match 1994, The Bicyclist 1994, Land's End (TV) 1995, The Whispering 1996, The Incorporated 1996, Scream 1996, Stranger in My Home (TV) 1997, Mimic 1997, Scream 2 1997, Halloween H20: Twenty Years Later (additional music) 1998, The Faculty 1998, Nightwatch (additional music) 1998, 54 1998, David and Lisa (TV) 1998, The Minus Man 1999, The Florentine 1999, Deep Water (TV) 1999, Scream 3 2000, Goodbye, Casanova 2000, The Crow: Salvation 2000, The Watcher 2000, Highway 395 2000, Dracula 2000 2001, Angel Eyes 2001, Joy Ride 2001, Blade 2: Bloodlust 2002, Resident Evil (with others) 2002, The Dangerous Lives of Altar Boys 2002, I Am Dina 2002, The First $20 Million Is Always the Hardest 2002, The Practice (TV) 2003–04, Terminator 3 2003, Cursed 2004, Hellboy 2004, I, Robot 2004, Flight of the Phoenix 2004, Cursed 2005, xXx: State of the Union 2005, Underworld Evolution 2005, Red Eye 2005, The Three Burials of Melquiades Estrada 2005, The Omen 2006, Captivity 2007, Vikaren 2007, The Invisible 2007, Live Free or Die Hard 2007, 3:10 to Yuma 2007, The Eye 2008, In the Electric Mist 2008, The Woman In Black 2012, The Sessions 2012, Deadfall 2012, Trouble With the Curve 2012. *Current Management:* Kraft-Engel Management, 15233 Ventura Blvd., Suite 200, Sherman Oaks, CA 91403, USA. *Website:* www.MarcoBeltrami.com.

BEN, Jorge, (Jorge Duílio Menezes, Jorge Ben Jor); Brazilian singer, musician (guitar), composer and songwriter; b. 1940, Rio de Janeiro. *Career:* fuses different musical traditions, both Brazilian and int.; music is rhythmically very creative with an African feel combined with rock, samba, baião (music based on northeastern Brazilian folkloric forms) and maracatu (an Afro-Brazilian processional dance); career started in the early 1960s, when bossa nova was the dominant music, but gained more recognition during MPB (Música Popular Brasileira) era when experimentation and fusing of styles was more accepted; solo artist 1969–72; toured internationally many times and has worked with artists, including King Sunny Ade, Os Mutantes, Timbalada. *Recordings include:* albums: Samba Esquema Novo, 1963; Sacundin Ben Samba, 1964; O Bidú, 1967; Jorge Ben, 1969; Forca Bruta, 1970; Ben, 1972; Dez Anos Depois, 1973; A Tabú De Esmerelda, 1974; Samba Nova, 1975; Africa Brasil, 1976; A Banda Do Ze Pretinho, 1978; Salve Simpatia, 1979; Alo Alo Como Vai?, 1980; Dadiva, 1983; Benjor, 1989; Ao Vivo No Rio, 1992; 23, 1993; Homo Sapiens, 1995; Musicas Para Tocar Em Elevador, 1997; Puro Suingue, 2000, Reactivus Amor Est (Turba Philosophorum) 2004, Recuerdos de Asunción 443 2007. *Telephone:* (11) 2885-7676. *E-mail:* shows@benjor.com.br. *Website:* www.jorgeben.com.br.

BENATAR, Pat; American singer; b. (Pat Andrejewski), 1953, Brooklyn, New York; m. Neil Giraldo; one c. *Career:* Grammy Awards for Best Female Rock Vocal Performance 1981, 1982, 1983, 1984. *Recordings include:* albums: In the Heat of the Night 1979, Crimes of Passion 1980, Precious Time 1981, Get Nervous 1982, Live From Earth 1983, Tropico 1984, Seven the Hard Way 1985, Wide Awake in Dreamland 1988, Best Shots 1989, True Love 1991, Gravity's Rainbow 1993, All Fired Up: The Very Best of Pat Benatar 1994, Best of Pat Benatar Vols 1 and 2 2001, Christmas In America 2001, Go 2003. *Publication:* Between a Heart and a Rock Place 2010. *Website:* benatargiraldo .com.

BENDIX, Nicky; Danish musician (piano, keyboard), music teacher, composer and arranger; b. 22 March 1969, Odense. *Education:* studied piano. *Career:* started composing and playing aged 15; performed in jazz/fusion settings with the Danish Radio Big Band, Rudi Smith, Jorge Degas, Uffe Markussen, Henrik Bolberg and Bent Jædig; own composition, Suite for Mankind, performed on TV2, Denmark 1997; since 1993 has composed and performed music for contemporary dance and multimedia events; multimedia performer, The Pillar of Shame 1997; composed and recorded the music score for the film En Sidste gang, by Jesper Bernt; mem. Dansk Musiker Forbund. *Recordings:* albums: Trancework, 1994; with Sunset Yellow: Sunset Yellow, 1995; with Sunzet: Sunzet, 1998. *Honours:* Jazz Musician of the Year, FYN 1995. *E-mail:* nickybendix@yahoo.dk. *Website:* www.nickybendix.com.

BENDZKO, Tim; German singer and songwriter; b. 9 April 1985, Berlin. *Career:* began writing songs at age 16; won talent competition 2009; appeared at Berlin Waldbühne before 20,000 spectators 2009; support act to Silly on tour 2010; released debut album 2011; supported Elton John and Joe Cocker at live dates in Germany. *Recordings:* album: Wenn Worte meine Sprache wären (If Words Were My Language) 2011. *Honours:* Winner, Bundesvision Song Contest 2011, Bambi Award for Best Newcomer 2011, Audi Generation Award for Music 2011, 1Live Krone Award for Best Single 2011, Wild and Young Award 2011, ECHO Award for Best Nat. Newcomer 2012, Regenbogen Award 2012, MTV Europe Music Award for Best German Act 2012. *Address:* Sony Music Entertainment GmbH, Neumarkter Strasse 28, 81673 Munich, Germany (office). *Website:* www.sonymusic.de (office); www.timbendzko.de.

BENÉT, Eric; American singer; b. 15 Oct. 1966, Milwaukee, Wis.; m. 1st (deceased) one d.; m. 2nd Halle Berry 2001 (divorced); m. 3rd Manuela Testolini 2011. *Career:* began career as part of Gerard during late 1980s; formed Benet 1992; solo career 1999–; collaborations with Faith Evans, Tamia, Roy Ayers, Me'Shell Ndegeocello. *Recordings include:* albums: Benet (with Benet) 1992, True To Myself 1996, A Day In The Life 1999, Hurricane 2005, Love and Life 2008, Lost in Time 2010, The One 2012. *Website:* www .ericbenet.net.

BÉNEY, Jean-Christophe; French jazz musician (saxophone); b. 2 Oct. 1969, Boulogne, Billancourt. *Education:* Conservatoire Nat. Supérieure de Musique, Paris. *Career:* Le Pom (Scene et Marnaise de Création Musicale); orchestra co-directed by François Jeanneau, Patrice Caratini, Philippe Macé, Andy Emler; formed Jean-Christophe Béney Quartet (with Pierre de Bethmann, Jules Bikoko, Benjamin Hénocq); mem., Laurent Coq Quartet, Belmondo Big Band, Antoine Hervé Big Band, Nicolas Folmer Quintet; mem. SACEM, ADAMI, SPEDIDAM. *Recordings:* Hard Scores, Patrice Caratini, 1996; Le Pom, 1997; Sérénade, Philippe Sellam, 1997; Le Pom, 1997; Jaywalker, with Laurent Coq Quartet, 1998, with Jean-Christophe Béney Quartet: Tenor Joke 1998, The Link 2010; solo: Casiopée 2002, Polychromy 2004, Pop Up 2007. *Honours:* Concours Nat. de Jazz de la Défense Prix de Soloiste 1995. *Address:* c/o Pure Song Management, 43 rue de la Rochefoucauld, 75009 Paris, France. *Telephone:* (1) 53-21-06-97. *Fax:* (9) 56-79-06-97. *E-mail:* contact@puresong.fr. *Address:* 2 rue Cyrano de Bergerac, 75018 Paris, France; c/o FairJazz, 5051 Berri #405, Montreal, Quebec, H2J 2S1, Canada. *Telephone:* (514) 903-5192. *E-mail:* info@fairjazz.com; info@ jeanchristophebeney.com. *Website:* www.jeanchristophebeney.com.

BENNETT, Brian Laurence, OBE; British musician (drums) and composer; b. 9 Feb. 1940, London; m. Margaret Tuton; two s. one d. *Career:* backed Gene Vincent, Eddie Cochran on tour; drummer, Cliff Richard and The Shadows 1961–; session drummer 1970s–80s; Brian Bennett Band support to Cliff Richard, UK, Japan, USSR 1970s; composer of film and television music; arranger, producer; played with Hank Marvin as The Shadows, Knebworth 1990; British tour, joined by Hank Marvin, also s. Warren Bennett on keyboards; mem. PRS, MCPS, APC, MPA, SODS. *Compositions for film:* themes: Summer Holiday (three Ivor Novello Awards) 1962, Wonderful Life, Finders Keepers, The Harpist 1997; score: The Boys, French Dressing, The American Way, Terminal Choice. *Compositions for television:* soundtracks: Dallas, Knots Landing, Ruth Rendell Mysteries (Best TV Theme Award) 1989, Nomads of The Wind (BBC 2), Pulaski, The Knock, The Sweeney, Minder,

Global Sunrise (BBC) 1997, Living Britain (BBC 2), Dirty Work (ITV) 2000, Murder in Mind (BBC) (Craft & Design Award, Royal Television Soc. for Best Original Title Music) 2001–03, Great Natural Wonders of the World (BBC) 2002, Moon Power (BBC) 2003, New Tricks (BBC) 2007–08. *Honours:* 25 Years in British Music 1983, Gold Badge Award, British Acad. of Composers & Songwriters Soc. 2001. *Address:* c/o Bucks Music Limited, Onward House, 11 Uxbridge Street, London W8 7TQ, England. *E-mail:* info@bucksmusicgroup .co.uk. *Website:* www.brianbennettmusic.co.uk.

BENNETT, Easther; British singer; b. 11 Dec. 1972, London; m. Shane Lynch 1998. *Career:* mem. Eternal 1992–99. *Recordings include:* albums: Always and Forever 1993, Power Of a Woman 1995, Before The Rain 1997, Greatest Hits 1998, Eternal, 1999, Essential Eternal (compilation) 2001. *Honours:* Smash Hits Award, Ind. Dance Award, Dance Act of the Year 1995.

BENNETT, Phil; Australian singer, songwriter and musician (keyboards); b. 28 Sept. 1958, Singapore; m. Fifi 1992. *Career:* mem., Helicopters mid 1980s, Love Bites 1990s, Witness 1997, PillBox 1998; numerous tours and live appearances; mem. Australian Performing Rights Asscn. *Compositions:* Eyewitness, 1997; Carved in Stone, 1997. *Recordings include:* albums: The Helicopters, 1982; Great Moments in Aviation, 1984; Never Seen Eyes, solo, 1990; Kiss the Feet, 1995; Stories from the South, Witness, 1998. *Honours:* Sonics Magazine on Cue Award 1990, Australia Day Award 1993.

BENNETT, Richard; American musician (guitar), producer, arranger and writer; b. 1951, Chicago, Ill. *Education:* studied with Forrest Skaggs. *Career:* record producer, musician, session and touring; recording and touring with Neil Diamond in Los Angeles 1971–88. *Recordings include:* The Red Road, Bill Miller 1994, Raven In the Snow, Bill Miller 1995, A Native Suite, Bill Miller 1995, Kim Richey, Kim Richey 1995, Silvertone, Steve Earle 1995, Capitol, High and Dry, Marty Brown, Wild Kentucky Skies, Marty Brown, Cryin', Lovin', Leavin', Marty Brown, Hillbilly Rock, Marty Stuart, Tempted, Marty Stuart, This One's Gonna Hurt You, Marty Stuart, Come on Joe, Jo-El Sonnier, Have A Little Faith, Joe-El Sonnier, Lost and Profound, Lost and Profound, Memory Thieves, Lost and Profound, A Joyful Noise, The Sullivans, Music Makin' Mama, Jim Silvers, Everybody Knows, Prairie Oyster, Plectrasonics, Nashville Mandolin Ensemble, Sessions: Billy Pilgrim 1994, Mark Knopfler and Neil Diamond 1995. *Recordings include:* albums: solo: Themes from a Rainy Decade 2004, Code Red Cloud Nine 2008, Valley of the Sun 2010, For the Newly Blue 2013. *E-mail:* moderneshellac@comcast.net. *Website:* www.richard-bennett.com.

BENNETT, Tony, MusD; American singer and entertainer; b. (Anthony Dominick Benedetto), 3 Aug. 1926, Astoria; s. of John Benedetto and Anna Suraci; m. 1st Patricia Beech 1952 (divorced 1971); two c.; m. 2nd Sandra Grant 1971 (divorced 1984); two d.; m. 3rd Susan Crow 2007. *Education:* American Theatre Wing, NY and Univ. of Berkeley. *Career:* frequent appearances on TV and in concert; owner and recording artist with Improv Records; paintings exhibited at Butler Inst. of American Art, Youngstown, Ohio 1994; f. Frank Sinatra School of the Arts 2001. *Recordings include:* The Art of Excellence 1986, Bennett/Berlin 1988, Astoria: Portrait of the Artist 1990, Perfectly Frank (Grammy Award for Best Traditional Vocal Performance) 1992, Steppin' Out (Grammy Award for Best Traditional Pop Vocal) 1993, The Essence of Tony Bennett 1993, MTV Unplugged (Grammy Award for Album of the Year, Best Traditional Pop Vocal) 1994, Here's to the Ladies 1995, The Playground 1998, Cool (Grammy Award) 1999, The Ultimate Tony 2000, A Wonderful World (with kd lang) (Grammy Award for Best Traditional Pop Vocal Album) 2003, The Art of Romance (Grammy Award for Best Traditional Pop Vocal Album 2006) 2005, Duets: An American Classic (Grammy Award for Best Traditional Pop Vocal Album 2007) 2006, Tony Bennett Sings the Ultimate American Songbook, Vol. 1 2007, A Swingin' Christmas 2008, Body and Soul (Grammy Award for Pop Duo/Group Performance with the late Amy Winehouse 2012) 2011, Duets II (Grammy Award for Traditional Pop Vocal Album 2012) 2011, Viva Duets 2012, Cheek to Cheek (with Lady Gaga) (Grammy Award for Best Traditional Pop Vocal Album 2015) 2014, The Silver Lining: the Songs of Jerome Kern (with Bill Charlap) (Grammy Award for Best Traditional Pop Vocal Album) 2016. *Publication:* The Good Life: The Autobiography of Tony Bennett 1998, Life is a Gift: The Zen of Bennett 2012. *Honours:* Grammy Award for Best Traditional Pop Vocal Performer 1998, Kennedy Center Honor 2005, Billboard Century Award 2006, Nat. Endowment for the Arts Jazz Masters Award 2006, Grammy Award for Best Pop Collaboration with Vocals (with Stevie Wonder) 2007, Ronnie Scott Lifetime Achievement Award 2007, inducted into New Jersey Hall of Fame 2011. *Address:* 130 West 57th Street, Apartment 9D, New York, NY 10019, USA. *Website:* www.tonybennett.com.

BENNETT, Vernie; British singer; b. 17 May 1971. *Education:* studied law. *Career:* mem. Eternal 1992–99. *Recordings include:* albums: Always and Forever 1993, Power Of a Woman 1995, Greatest Hits 1997, Before The Rain 1997, Power Of a Woman 1998, Eternal 1999, Essential Eternal (compilation) 2001. *Honours:* Smash Hits Award.

BENNETT, Warren; British composer and musician; b. 4 July 1962, Palmers Green, London, England; m. Jane Catherine 1991, two d. *Career:* mem. The Vibratos; music for television includes Wuthering Heights, London's Burning, Ambassador, The Knock, Staying Alive, Birds of a Feather; arranger, Hank Marvin albums Into the Light, Heartbeat, Plays Cliff, Plays Holly, Plays Lloyd Webber and Tim Rice; arranger, Darren Day album Summer Holiday; concert tours with Hank Marvin, 1994, 1995, 1997, 1998. *Recordings:* solo: Secrets Of

The Heart; Pathways To Love, La Mort de Henri 2006; Close to the Hedge, with Mark Griffiths 1996; with The Vibratos: Tornado Alley 2004; Classical Guitar Moods, with Mirage. *Address:* c/o Leo's Den Direct, PO Box 4088, Sturminster Newton, Dorset, DT10 1YP, England. *Telephone:* (1258) 821341. *E-mail:* orders@leosden.co.uk. *Website:* www.leosden.co.uk; www.btinternet .com/~shadows_archive/shadows/Warren/Warren.html.

BENNETT-LAW, Michael, (Law), MA, LRAM; British musician (piano), singer, music director, composer and lecturer; *Musical Director, The Piccadilly Dance Orchestra*; b. (Michael Charles Ewan Law), 30 March 1960, Dar-Es-Salaam, Tanzania; s. of Sir Eric and Lady Law. *Education:* Gonville and Caius Coll., Cambridge, Royal Coll. of Music. *Career:* Music Dir, Piccadilly Dance Orchestra 1988–; numerous radio and TV appearances, concerts and tours, including UK/Far East tour with Sheridan Morley 1999; mem. Performing Right Soc., Mechanical-Copyright Protection Soc. *Compositions:* Play Me An Elegant Song, I'm Singin' A Swing Song Now. *Films:* Last Orders (The Piccadilly Dance Orchestra. *Radio:* for BBC Radio 2: Radio 2 Arts Programme, Friday Night is Music Night, Desmond Carrington, Tribute to Noel Coward 1999; concert from Wigmore Hall (BBC Radio 3), Loose Ends (BBC Radio 4). *Recordings include:* five albums with The Piccadilly Dance Orchestra 1989, 1993, 1995, 1997, 1999; An Evening with Sheridan Morley and Michael Law 2003. *Telephone:* (845) 370-0178 (office). *E-mail:* mail@pdo .org.uk (home). *Website:* www.pdo.org.uk (office); www.michaellaw.org.uk.

BENNINGTON, Chester; American singer; b. 20 March 1976, Phoenix, AZ; m. Samantha. *Career:* fmr singer, Grey Daze; mem., Linkin Park 1999–; founder mem., Dead by Sunrise 2005–; numerous int. concerts. *Recordings include:* albums: with Grey Daze: Wake Me 1994, No Sun Today 1997; with Linkin Park: Hybrid Theory (Rock Bear Awards for Best Int. Album 2001) 2000, Reanimation 2002, In The End: Live & Rare 2002, Meteora 2003, Live in Texas 2003, Collision Course (with Jay-Z) 2004, Minutes to Midnight 2007, A Thousand Suns 2010, Living Things 2012, The Hunting Party 2014; with Dead by Sunrise: Out of Ashes 2009. *Honours:* Billboard Award for Best Modern Rock Artist 2001, Rock Bear Award for Best Int. Band 2001, Kerrang! Award for Best Int. Newcomer 2001, Rolling Stone Award for Best Hard Rock/ Metal Band 2001, World Music Awards for Best Selling Rock Group 2002, 2003, 2007, MTV Awards for Best Group, Best Hard Rock 2002, MTV Europe Awards for Best Rock Act 2004, 2011, 2012, 2014, for Best World Stage Performance 2009, 2013, for Best Live Act 2010, Grammy Award for Best Rap/ Sung Collaboration (for Numb/Encore, with Jay-Z) 2006, MTV Europe Music Award for Best Band 2007, American Music Awards for Favorite Alternative Rock Music Artist 2007, 2008, 2012. *Current Management:* Andy Gould Management, 8484 Wilshire Boulevard, Suite 425, Beverly Hills, CA 90211, USA. *Website:* www.linkinpark.com.

BENOIT, Tab; American blues, rock singer and musician (guitar, harmonica); b. 17 Nov. 1967, Baton Rouge, Louisiana. *Career:* guitarist with various country, rock and blues bands, Houma, La 1986–89; solo career, New Orleans 1990–; appears on Strike a Deep Chord compilation album, 1991; TV debut on Baywatch Nights 1993; songs featured on TV in Melrose Place, Party of Five, Northern Exposure, Beverly Hills 90210, Baywatch; mem. Screen Actors Guild. *Recordings include:* Strike a Deep Chord: Blues Guitars for the Homeless 1991, Nice and Warm 1992, What I Live For 1994, Standing on the Bank 1995, Live: Swampland Jam 1997, Homesick for the Road 1999, Wetlands 2002, Whiskey Store 2002, Sea Saint Sessions 2003, Whiskey Store Live 2004, Fever for the Bayou 2005, Voice of the Wetlands 2005, Brother to the Blues 2006, Power of the Pontchartrain 2007, Night Train To Nashville 2008, Medicine 2011, Box of Pictures–Voice of the Wetlands Allstars 2011. *Current Management:* c/o Thunderbird Management Group, PO Box 1686, LaRose, LA 70373, USA. *Telephone:* (985) 798-5665. *E-mail:* thunderbird@ cajunnet.com. *Website:* www.tabbenoit.com (home).

BENOÎT BLUE BOY; French singer and musician (harmonica, guitar); b. (Benoît Billot), 24 May 1946, Paris; two d. *Education:* Ecole des Beaux Arts, Paris. *Career:* played harmonica for Stevie Wonder, Carole King, James Taylor, Albert King 1970–72; played with Zachery Richard 1972; Founder-mem. Benoît Blue Boy and The Tortilleurs 1978; mem. Soc. des auteurs, compositeurs et éditeurs de musique (SACEM), Admin des droits des artistes et musiciens interprètes (ADAMI). *Recordings:* Benoît Blue Boy 1978, Original 1979, Le Blues du Vendeur de Blues 1981, Plaisir Simple 1982, Tortillage 1986, BBB et les Toit Cleurs 1988, Parlez Vouz Français? 1990, Plus Tard Dans la Soirée 1992, Couvert de Bleus 1994, Lent ou Rapide 1997, Benoît Blue Boy en Amérique 2001, Maux d'absence 2004, Mic Mac 2008, Funky Aloo 2011, Papa, fais pas ça 2013. *Current Management:* c/o Denis Leblond, Tempo Spectacle, 99 avenue de Clichy, 75017 Paris, France. *Telephone:* 1-42-26-03-03. *Fax:* 1-42-26-03-13. *E-mail:* tempo.spectacle@ wanadoo.fr. *Website:* www.myspace.com/tempospectacle; blueboy.free.fr.

BENSON, Brendan; American singer, songwriter and musician (guitar, keyboard); b. 14 Nov. 1970, Royal Oak, Mich. *Career:* solo artist; Founder mem., The Raconteurs 2006–. *Recordings include:* albums: solo: One Mississippi 1996, Lapalco 2002, The Alternative to Love 2005, My Old, Familiar Friend 2009, What Kind of World 2012; with The Raconteurs: Broken Boy Soldiers 2006, Consolers of the Lonely 2008. *Current Management:* c/o Monotone Management, 820 Seward Street, Hollywood, CA 90038, USA; c/o Paul Boswell, The Free Trade Agency, Free Trade House, Chapel Place, Rivington Street, London, EC2A 3DQ, England (office). *E-mail:*

brendanbensoninfo@crownmusic.co.uk (office). *Website:* www.brendanbenson .com; www.theraconteurs.com.

BENSON, George; American musician (guitar) and singer; b. 22 March 1943, Pittsburgh, Pa. *Career:* session musician in Pittsburgh; guitarist with Brother Jack McDuff; session work with Herbie Hancock, Wes Montgomery 1966; solo artist 1966–; regular world-wide tours, concerts and festivals. *Recordings include:* albums: It's Uptown 1966, Benson Burner 1966, Giblet Gravy 1967, Tell It Like It Is 1969, The Other Side Of Abbey Road 1970, Beyond The Blue Horizon 1972, Good King Bad 1973, Bad Benson 1974, Supership 1975, Breezin' 1976, Benson And Farrell (with Joe Farrell) 1976, George Benson In Concert: Carnegie Hall 1977, In Flight 1977, Weekend In LA 1978, Livin' Inside Your Love 1979, Give Me The Night 1981, George Benson Collection 1981, In Your Eyes 1983, 20/20 1985, The Love Songs 1985, While The City Sleeps 1986, Collaboration 1987, Twice The Love 1988, Tenderly 1989, Big Boss Band 1990, Midnight Moods: The Love Collection 1991, Love Remembers 1993, The Most Exciting New Guitarist On The Jazz 1994, Take Five 1995, Live and Smokin' 1995, California Dreamin' 1996, That's Right 1996, Lil' Darlin' 1996, Talkin' Verve 1997, Essentials 1998, Standing Together 1998, Masquerade 1998, Masquerade Is Over 1999, Love And Jazz 1999, Live At Casa Caribe 2000, Absolute Benson 2000, All Blues 2001, Irreplaceable 2004, Givin' It Up 2006, Songs and Stories 2009, Guitar Man 2011, Inspiration: A Tribute to Nat King Cole 2013. *Honours:* Grammy Awards for Best R&B Instrumental 1976, 1980, Record of the Year 1976, Best Pop Instrumental 1976, 1984, Best R&B Male Vocal Performance 1978, 1980, Best Jazz Vocal Performance 1980, Best Jazz Instrumental Performance 1991, Grammy Award for Best Pop Instrumental Performance (for Mornin') 2007, for Best Traditional R&B Vocal Performance (for God Bless the Child) 2007. *Current Management:* c/o Stephanie Gonzalez, Apropos Management & Marketing, 365 Avenida de los Arboles, Suite 220, Thousand Oaks, CA 91360, USA. *E-mail:* stephanie@aproposmanagement.com. *Website:* www .georgebenson.com.

BENSON, Ray; American musician (guitar), singer, record producer, actor and artist manager; b. 16 March 1951, Philadelphia, Pa; m. Diane Carr 1983; two s. *Education:* Antioch Coll. *Career:* lead singer, Asleep At The Wheel for 25 years; producer of nine Asleep At The Wheel albums 1973–93; also producer for George Strait, Ricky Van Shelton, Sweethearts of the Rodeo, k d lang, Aaron Neville and Rob Wasserman, Bruce Hornsby and Willie Nelson, Darden Smith, Don Walser; eight film scores, commercials; actor in four music videos; numerous TV appearances; Exec. Dir and Co-Producer Texas Festival, Kennedy Centre 1991; mem. Bd of Dirs Rhythm and Blues Foundation, KLRU Public TV, St David's Community Health Foundation, Health Alliance for Austin Musicians; Trustee NARAS. *Theatre:* A Ride With Bob (actor, writer and musical dir). *Recordings include:* albums: Coming Right At Ya 1973, Asleep At The Wheel 1974, Texas Gold 1975, The Wheel 1977, Served Live 1979, Framed 1980, Drivin' 1980, Pasture Prime 1985, Asleep At The Wheel 10 1987, Western Standard Time 1988, Keepin' Me Up Nights 1990, Live and Kickin' 1992, Route 66 1992, The Swingin' Best Of Asleep At The Wheel 1992, Tribute To The Music Of Bob Wills and The Texas Playboys 1993, Still Swingin' 1994, The Wheel Keeps On Rollin' 1995, Minstrel Man From Georgia 1996, Texas Top Hand 1996, Way Out West 1996, Swing 1997, Live Back to the Future Now 1997, Down At The Sky-Vue Drive In 1998, Horse Whisperer 1998, Songs Of Forbidden Love 1998, Fiddle Fire 1998, Global Voices 1998, More 1999, Ride With Bob (Grammy Award for Best Country Instrumental and Best Package Design) (Regional Emmy for The Making of Ride With Bob) 1999, Take Me Back to Tulsa 2003, Remembers the Alamo 2003, Reinventing the Wheel 2007, Santa Loves to Boogie 2007, Willie and the Wheel (with Willie Nelson) 2009, It's a Good Day 2010, Time Can Change 2012, Deep in the Heart: Big Songs for Little Texans Everywhere 2012. *Honours:* Acad. of Country Music Award 1977, Buddy Award 1985, nine Grammy Awards, Western Swing Soc. Hall of Fame 1994, Texas State Musician 2004, six Austin Music Awards (with Asleep at the Wheel) 2007, Texan of the Year 2011, Texas Medal of the Arts Award for Multimedia 2011, TEC Les Paul Award 2011, Lifetime Achievement Award, Americana Music Association 2011. *Current Management:* c/o Bismeaux Records, PO Box 463, Austin, TX 78767, USA. *Telephone:* (512) 444-9885. *Fax:* (512) 444-4699. *E-mail:* bismeaux@austin.rr.com; info@bismeauxrecords.com. *Website:* www .raybenson.com; www.bismeauxrecords.com; asleepatthewheel.com.

BENSUSAN, Pierre; French musician (guitar), singer and composer; b. 30 Oct. 1957, Oran, French Algeria; m. Doatea Cornu 1985; one s. *Career:* festivals include Montreux, Nyon (Switzerland), Musiques Métisses d'Angouleme (France); jazz festivals include Montreal, Edmonton, Brussels, Lugano; guitar festivals include Liège, Grand, Milwaukee, Boston, Tel-Aviv, Paris, Nice, Festival Inter-Celtic de Lorient, Zenith-Paris; Stockfish tour (Germany), Bern, Lanzburg, Eppalinges, London Summer Banks Festival, Vancouver, Toronto, Polymusicales de Bollène, Bergamo, Rotterdam, Flanders Festival; appeared with or played with artists including Suzanne Vega, Jacques Higelin, Paco de Lucia, Carla Bley, Larry Coryell, Philip Catherine, Doc Watson, John Renbourn, David Bromberg, Nana Vasconcelos, Oregon, Uzeb, Taj Mahal, Alan Stivell, Al Stewart, Bobby Thomas, Didier Malherbe, Guinga, Tommy Emmanuel etc. *Recordings:* Près de Paris, Pierre Bensusan 2, Musiques, Solilai, Spices, Wu Wei, Live in Paris, Nice Feeling, Intuite, Altipanos, An Evening with IGN, Vividly, Encore. *Publications:* The Guitar Book; Dagad Music; three videos: The Guitar of Pierre Bensusan, Vols 1 and 2; Pierre Bensusan in Concert; A World of Celtic Fingerstyle Guitar. *Honours:*

Grand Prix du Disque, Montreux Festival 1976, AFIM Award for best acoustic album 1983, Best World Music Guitar Player, Guitar Payer Magazine Readers Choice (USA) 2008. *Address:* BP 10232, 02406 Chateau Thierry Cedex, France. *Telephone:* admindadgadfr@orange.fr. *Website:* www.pierrebensusan .com.

BENTLEY, Dierks; American country music singer and songwriter; b. 20 Nov. 1975, Phoenix, Ariz.; m. Cassidy Black; two d. *Education:* Vanderbilt Univ. *Career:* moved to Nashville, Tenn. aged 19 years; worked at The Nashville Network tv channel; completed first solo US tour 2006; frequent concerts with Cross Canadian Ragweed; collaborations with Del McCoury Band; mem. Grand Ole Opry 2005–. *Recordings include:* albums: Don't Leave Me In Love 2001, Dierks Bentley 2003, Modern Day Drifter 2005, Long Trip Alone 2006, Feel that Fire 2009, Up on the Ridge 2010, Home 2012, Country & Cold Cans 2012, Love for Levon: A Benefit to Save the Barn 2013, Riser 2014. *Honours:* ACM Award for Top New Artist 2004, CMA Horizon Award 2005, Country Music Asscn Award for Music Video of the Year (for Drunk on a Plane) 2014. *Current Management:* Rogue Music Group, 346 21st Avenue North, Nashville, TN 37203, USA. *Website:* www.dierks.com.

BENTZON, Nikolaj, DipMus; Danish jazz musician (piano) and composer; b. 21 Feb. 1964, Copenhagen; m. Agnethe Koch 1993, one s. two d. *Education:* Berklee College of Music, Boston, USA. *Career:* mem., Danish Radio Jazz Orchestra 1990–; Leader, Nikolaj Bentzon Trio 1989, Nikolaj Bentzon and The Scandinavian Connection 1992–, The Nikolaj Bentzon Brotherhood 1995, Nikolai Bentzon Constitution 1997; mem., Ernie Wilkin's Almost Big Band three years; debut performance of Bob Brookmeyer's November Music, written for Nikolaj Bentzon 1994, Radio House, Copenhagen. *Recordings include:* albums: with Nikolaj Bentzon Trio: Pianoforte, Between Us, Triskelos, Nexus; one album with Nikolaj Bentzon and The Scandinavian Connection; one album with Nikolaj Bentzon Brotherhood; one album featuring Mike Clark and Paul Jackson; album featuring Paul Jackson, Mike Clarke 1998. *Honours:* Dunkerque Jazz Festival best soloist 1983, Jacob Gade Award 1983, Oscar Peterson Jazz Award 1985, Danish Society for Jazz, Rock and Folk Music Hon. Award 1991. *Address:* c/o Dacapo Records, Gråbrødretorv 16, 1154 Copenhagen, Denmark. *Telephone:* 32960602. *Fax:* 32962602. *E-mail:* music@dacapo-records.dk. *Website:* www.nikolajbentzon .com.

BERAUD, Marie Laure; Belgian singer; b. 22 Jan. 1959, Lyon, France; two s. *Career:* solo artist; numerous tours and television appearances; mem. Société des auteurs, compositeurs et éditeurs de musique (SACEM). *Recordings include:* album: Turbigo 12–12 (Academie Charles Cros First Album Prize) 1992. *E-mail:* info@marie-laure-beraud.be. *Website:* www.marie-laure -beraud.be.

BERENGUER, José, PhD; Spanish musician (guitar); b. 21 Oct. 1955, Barcelona. *Career:* composer of computer, electroacoustical music; played at Autumno Musicale, Como, Italy; Internationale Fenienkurse-Danmstadt, Germany; Synthèse, Bourges, France; Festival International de Músicadel Segle XX, Barcelona, Spain; Puntope encuentro, Madrid, Spain; Para Lelo Madrid; Chair., Ascociacion de Musica Electroacoustica de España; Vice-Chair., Associaó Catalana de Compositors; mem. International Electroacoustic Music Academy of Bourges. *Recordings include:* Klängé, 1993; Antropometria Don Quichotte; Spira; Constellacions; Silence. *Honours:* TIME of CIM/UNESCO; Electroacoustic Music Prize, Bourges.

BERESFORD, Steve, BA; British musician (piano); *Senior Lecturer in Music, University of Westminster;* b. 6 March 1950, Wellington, Shropshire. *Education:* York University. *Career:* worked on a large number of film soundtracks, concerts, recordings; numerous collaborations including: The Portsmouth Sinfonia, The Slits, Lol Coxhill, Ivor Cutler, Frank Chickens, John Zorn, Evan Parker, Nigel Coombes; Conductor and pianist, London Improvisers Orchestra 2001–; currently Sr Lecturer in Music, Univ. of Westminster; mem. PRS, MCPS, PAMRA, MU. *Compositions:* I Was There; Unremarkable; Thanks to Minnie; My Hawaiian Bath Tub Melody; Pentimento; Avril Brisé. *Recordings:* Cue Sheets; Short in the UK; The Bath Of Surprise; Museum of Towing and Recovery; Fish Of the Week; recent albums include: Trap Street 2002, Ointment 2003, Check for Monsters 2008. *Honours:* Paul Hamlyn Award for Composers 2012. *Address:* School of Media, Arts and Design, University of Westminster, Watford Road, Northwick Park, Middx, HA1 3TP, England. *Telephone:* (20) 7911-5000 ext 4650. *E-mail:* s.beresford@ amserve.com; S.Beresford@westminster.ac.uk. *Website:* www.efi.group.shef .ac.uk; www.westminster.ac.uk.

BERG, Shelton Glen, MMus; American musician (piano), academic, composer and arranger; *Dean, Phillip and Patricia Frost School of Music, University of Miami;* b. 18 Aug. 1955, Cleveland, Ohio. *Education:* Univ. of Houston. *Career:* Chair. of Instrumental Music, San Jacinto Coll., North Shore 1979–81, Chair. of Instrumental and Commercial Music San Jacinto Coll., Pasadena 1981–91; fmr McCoy/Sample Endowed Prof. of Jazz Studies, Thornton School of Music, Univ. of Southern California, also Chair. of Jazz Studies 1991–2002; Dean, Phillip and Patricia Frost School of Music, Univ. of Miami 2007–; Pres. International Asscn of Jazz Educ. 1996–98; mem. Nat. Asscn for Music Educ. (fmrly Music Educators Nat. Conf.). *Compositions include:* commission: Theme Song of 1986 Olympia Festival; for television: Fudge (ABC), A League of Their Own (CBS); numerous compositions for jazz combos, chorus and Big Band. *Recordings as pianist:* The Joy (with Bill Watrons) 1994, A Time for Love, Space Available. *Publications include:* Jazz

Improvisation: The Goal-Note Method 1989; numerous articles in Jazz Educators Journal and Piano and Keyboard Magazines. *Honours:* seven ADDY Awards, Lawrence Berk Leadership Award 2002, Educator of the Year Award, Los Angeles Jazz Soc. 2003.

BERG, Terje; Norwegian musician (bass); b. 24 Jan. 1972, Trondheim. *Education:* college. *Career:* founder mem., Hedge Hog 1989; toured Europe 1994, 1995. *Recordings:* Erase, 1992; Surprise, 1992; Primal Gutter, 1993; Mercury Red, 1994; Mindless, 1994; The Healing EP, 1995; Thorn Cord Wonder, 1995. *Website:* www.myspace.com/terjeberg.

BERGE, Svein; Norwegian musician; b. 17 Feb. 1976, Tromso. *Career:* mem. Aedena Cycle 1994–99, Röyksopp 2002–; remix projects with Coldplay, Lady Gaga, Depeche Mode, Beck, Robyn. *Recordings include:* albums: Melody AM 2002, The Understanding 2005, Röyksopp's Night Out 2006, Back to Mine 2007, Junior 2009, Senior 2010, Late Night Tales 2013, Do It Again (with Robyn) 2014, The Inevitable End 2014. *Current Management:* c/o Deutsch-Englische Freundschaft, 51 Lonsdale Road, Queens Park, London, NW6 6RA, England. *E-mail:* info@d-e-f.com. *Website:* www.d-e-f.com; www.royksopp .com.

BERGE STRAND, Anne Lilia, (Annie); Norwegian singer and DJ; b. 21 Nov. 1977, Trondheim. *Career:* sings and DJs her electronic pop music worldwide; debut album 2004–05; hits with Chewing Gum and Heartbeat. *Recordings include:* album: Anniemal 2004, DJ Kicks 2005, Don't Stop 2009. *Honours:* Spellemannprisen for Best Newcomer 2005, two Alarm Awards (Norway) 2005. *E-mail:* anniemelodymusic@gmail.com. *Website:* www .anniemelody.com.

BERGGREN, Jenny Cecilia; Swedish singer and songwriter; b. 19 May 1972, Gothenburg; d. of Göran Berggren and Birgitta Berggren; sister of Jonas Berggren; m. Jakob Petrén 2004; one s. one d. *Career:* mem. Ace of Base 1990–, lead singer 1998–; Amb. of Voi-project 2010. *Recordings include:* albums: The Sign 1993, The Bridge 1995, Cruel Summer 1998, Flowers 1998, Lucky Love 2001, Da Capo 2002, The Golden Ratio 2010; solo: My Story 2010. *Publications:* Vinna hela världen (autobiography). *Current Management:* c/o Warner/ Chappell Music Scandinavia, Box 5164, 102 44, Stockholm, Sweden. *Telephone:* (8) 622-09-00. *Fax:* (8) 755-15-96. *E-mail:* info.sweden@warnerchappell .com. *Website:* www.aceofbase.com. *Address:* Voi Lutheran Mission, POB 757, 80300, Voi, Kenya. *E-mail:* info@aceofbase-music.de. *Website:* www .jennyberggren.com.

BERGGREN, Jonas (Joker); Swedish musician (keyboards), songwriter and singer; b. 21 March 1967, Göteborg; s. of Göran Berggren and Birgitta Berggren; m. Birthe Haugland; four c. *Career:* mem. Ace of Base 1990–. *Recordings include:* albums: Happy Nation 1993, The Bridge 1995, Flowers/ Cruel Summer 1998, Hallo Hallo 2000, Life Is a Flower 2001, Da Capo 2002, Unspeakable 2002. *Current Management:* Hagenburg Management, Kyrko-gatan 31, 411 08 Gothenborg, Sweden. *Website:* www.aceofbase.com.

BERGGREN, Malin (Linn); Swedish singer; b. 1970, sister of Jonas Berggren and Jenny Berggren. *Career:* mem., Ace of Base 1990–2005. *Recordings:* albums: Happy Nation 1993, The Bridge 1995, Flowers/Cruel Summer 1998, Da Capo 2002.

BERGMAN, Alan, BA; American lyricist and writer; b. Brooklyn, New York; m. Marilyn Keith, two d. *Education:* University of North Carolina. *Career:* collaborated with Marilyn Bergman; Michel Legrand; Dave Grusin; Marvin Hamlisch; Henry Mancini; Johnny Mandel; John Williams; David Shire: Neil Diamond; James Newton Howard; Quincy Jones; Lew Spence; Sammy Fain; Billy Goldenberg; Lalo Schifrin; Norman Luboff; Sergio Mendes; mem. ASCAP; AMPAS; Songwriters Guild of America; Society of Composers and Lyricists. *Compositions:* songs include: That Face; Yellow Bird; Nice 'n' Easy; The Windmills of Your Mind; The Way We Were; The Summer Knows; What Are You Doing The Rest of Your Life?; Summer Me, Winter Me; So Many Stars; You Must Believe In Spring; Places That Belong To You; You Don't Bring Me Flowers; Little Boy Lost; In The Heat of The Night; The Hands of Time; I Love To Dance; I Believe In Love; Sweet Gingerbread Man; The Last Time I Felt Like This; I'll Never Say Goodbye; Make Me Rainbows; Like A Lover; The Island; All His Children; Marmalade, Molasses and Honey; If We Were In Love; It Might Be You; How Do You Keep The Music Playing; Papa Can You Hear Me? The Way He Makes Me Feel; Ordinary Miracles; Where Do You Start? Most of All You; The Girl Who Used To Be Me; Michel Legrand Album; Live At Donte's; Broadway scores: Something More; Ballroom; Film/ TV scores: Yentl; Queen of The Stardust Ballroom; Sybil; TV themes: Maude; Good Times; Alice; Brooklyn Bridge; The Powers That Be. *Recordings:* albums: Lyrically, Alan Bergman 2007. *Honours:* three Acad. Awards, two Emmy Awards, two Golden Globes, two Grammy Awards. *E-mail:* info@ alanandmarilynbergman.com. *Website:* www.alanandmarilynbergman.com.

BERGMAN, Barry, BS; American artist manager and music publisher; b. 24 Aug. 1944, New York. *Education:* New York Univ. *Career:* Vice-President, Marks Music 1975–79; Vice-President, Creative Affairs, United Artists Music 1979–81; Owner, Barry Bergman Man. 1982–, Ellymax Music 1985–, Wood Monkey Music 1986–; artist man. for Keven Jordan, Marc Ribler, Rob Friedman, Kings Country; publr of music by Cher, Kiss, Michael Bolton, Kathy Mattea; mem. ASCAP, Broadcast Music Inc.; Founder and Pres. Int. Mans Forum, Free Enterprise Music Company. *Honours:* ASCAP Pop Award 1989. *Current Management:* c/o Barry Bergman Management, 350 East 30th Street, Suite 3R, New York, NY 10016, USA. *Telephone:* (212) 213-8787 (office). *Fax:* (212) 213-9797 (office). *E-mail:* barrybergman@earthlink.net (office). *Website:* www.barrybergman.com.

BERGMAN, Marilyn; American lyricist and writer; b. 10 Nov. 1929, Brooklyn, New York; m. Alan Bergman 1958, one d. *Education:* High School of Music and Art, New York Univ. *Career:* collaborations with Alan Bergman, Michel Legrand, Dave Grusin, Marvin Hamlisch, Henry Mancini, Johnny Mandel, John Williams, David Shire, Neil Diamond, James Newton Howard, Quincy Jones, Lew Spence, Sammy Fain, Billy Goldenberg, Lalo Schifrin, Norman Luboff, Sergio Mendes; Pres. and CEO, American Soc. of Composers, Authors and Publishers (ASCAP) 1994–2009; mem. AMPAS, Soc. of Composers and Lyricists, Songwriters Guild of America. *Compositions include:* Yellow Bird; Nice 'n' Easy; The Windmills of Your Mind (Academy & Golden Globe Awards); The Way We Were (Academy, Golden Globe and Grammy Awards); The Summer Knows; What Are You Doing For The Rest of Your Life?; Summer Me Winter Me; So Many Stars; You Must Believe In Spring; Places That Belong To You; You Don't Bring Me Flowers; Little Boy Lost; In The Heat of The Night; The Hands of Time; I Love To Dance; I Believe In Love; Sweet Gingerbread Man; The Last Time I Felt Like This; I'll Never Say Goodbye; Make Me Rainbows; Like a Lover; The Island; All His Children; Marmalade, Molasses and Honey; If We Were In Love; It Might Be You; How Do You Keep The Music Playing; Papa Can You Hear Me?; The Way He Makes Me Feel; Ordinary Miracles (Emmy Award); Where Do You Start?; Most of All You; The Girl Who Used To Be Me; Portrait Edition; Michel Legrand Album; Live At Donte's; Broadway scores: Something More; Ballroom; Film/TV scores, Yentl; Queen of The Stardust Ballroom (Emmy Award); Sybil (Emmy Award). *Honours:* Dr hc (Berklee Coll. of Music) 1995, (Univ. of Massachusetts) 2009; Women in Film Crystal Award 1986, Clooney Foundation Singers Salute to the Songwriter Award 1986, Songwriter's Guild Aggie Award 1987, National Academy of Songwriters Lifetime Achievement Award 1995, Songwriters Hall of Fame Johnny Mercer Award 1997, Cultural Medal of Honour in Spain 1998, National Music Publishers Association Lifetime Achievement Award 2000, Governor's Award from the National Association of Recording Arts & Sciences (NARAS) 2002, Johnny Mercer Foundation Lifetime Achievement Award 2003, World Soundtrack Lifetime Achievement Award (Flanders Film Festival) 2004. *E-mail:* info@alanandmarilynbergman.com (office). *Website:* www.alanandmarilynbergman.com.

BERGSMAN, Victoria, (Taken by Trees); Swedish singer and songwriter; b. 4 May 1977. *Career:* mem., The Concretes 1999–2006; band f. label, Licking Fingers; with Taken by Trees 2007–. *Recordings include:* albums: Boyoubetterunow 2000, The Concretes 2003, Layourbattleaxedown 2005, In Colour 2006, Hey Trouble 2007; solo: Open Field 2007, East of Eden 2009, Other Worlds 2012. *Current Management:* c/o Secretly Canadian, 1499 West Second Street, Bloomington, IN, 47403, USA. *E-mail:* anh@iamsoundrecords.com (office). *Website:* takenbytreesofficial.tumblr.com.

BERLIN, Steve; American musician (saxophone, keyboards) and record producer; b. 14 Sept. 1955, Philadelphia, Pa. *Career:* fmr mem. Top Jimmy & The Rhythm Pigs, The Flesh Eaters; mem. Los Lobos 1973–; mem. The Blasters 1979–; collaborated with Paul Simon, Sheryl Crow, Faith No More, The Tragically Hip, Great Big Sea, The Bridge, Nathan Wiley, and John Lee Hooker. *Recordings include:* albums: De Este De Los Angeles 1978, How Will The Wolf Survive 1984, By the Light of the Moon 1987, La Pistola y El Corazón 1988, The Neighborhood 1990, Kiko 1992, Colossal Head 1996, This Time 1999, Good Morning Aztlán 2002, The Ride 2004, The Town and the City 2006, Los Lobos Goes Disney 2009, Tin Can Trust 2010; Disconnected in New York City 2013; with The Blasters: The Blasters 1981, Non-Fiction 1983, Hard Line 1985, Trouble Bound 2002, Going Home 2004; with The Flesh Eaters: Dragstrip Riot 1991, Crucified Lovers in Woman Hell 1993, Ashes of Time 1999, Miss Muerte 2004. *Current Management:* c/o Chris Tetzeli, Red Light Management, 124 12th Avenue South, Nashville, TN 37203-3146, USA. *Telephone:* (615) 279-3784. *Website:* www.loslobos.org; ww.flesheaters.com.

BERLIOZ, Gérard; French Musician (percussion, tympanon, cymbalum) and Music Educator; b. 15 March 1943, Paris; m. 1964, 1 s., 1 d. *Education:* Prix de Percussion du Mans; Prix de Percussion, Conservatoire National Supérieur de Music de Paris. *Career:* Professor, several conservatoires in Paris region; Worked with symphony orchestras: Radio-France; Radio-Moscow; Leningrad; Prague; Music Hall concerts at Moulin Rouge; Casino de Paris; Olympia; Theatres, operas, ballet companies include: Paris; Rouen; Vichy; Nice; Toulouse; Grenoble (others in France); Monte Carlo; Canada; Japan; Festivals all over France; International tours with: Mikis Theodorakis; Lorin Maazel; Jerry Lewis (Europe, North Africa, South Africa, USA, Canada, Japan, Thailand, South America, Israel, Australia); Musician accompanying: Claude Bolling; Tom Jones; Ginger Rogers; Ray Charles; Charles Aznavour; Gilbert Bécaud; Mireille Mathieu; Catherine Ribeiro; Music for films, musical comedies and recordings with: Michel Legrand; Maurice Jarre; Claude Nougaro; Mikis Theodakiris; Jean Claude Naude; Guy Defatto; Mireille Mathieu; Catherine Ribeiro; mem, L'Ordre National Des Musiciens. *Publications:* Director, Percussion Collection; Chronicler, Journal: Tam Tam Percussion; Author, several instruction manuals; Author, numerous articles on percussion.

BERMAN, Jason (Jay); American music industry executive. *Career:* fmr rep. for Warner Music, Recording Industry Asscn of America (RIAA) Bd – 1987, Pres. RIAA 1987–92, Chair. 1992–98; Chair. and CEO Int. Federation for the Phonographic Industry (IFPI) 1998–2004; est. anti-piracy consultancy,

Berman Rosen Global Strategies; US Special Counsel for Trade to President Clinton 1998; Bd mem. Loudeye Corpn. *Address:* c/o Loudeye Corpn, 1130 Rainier Avenue, South Seattle, WA 98144, USA.

BERNARD, Alain, DipCIM; French musician (piano, electric keyboard), composer, arranger and teacher; b. 8 Sept. 1952. *Education:* pvt. piano and harmony lessons with Bernard Maury; orchestration, arrangement, composition studies at CIM, Paris with Yvan Julien; master-classes with various teachers, including F. Janneau and D. Humair. *Career:* jazz/soul/Latin/variety musician 1977–; sideman for French musicians, including J. L. Longnon, Gérard Badini Swing Machine, Ornicar big-band; also American musicians, including F. Foster, E. L. Davis, H. S. Edison, J. Henderson, J. Newman, B. Tate, D. D. Bridgewater, J. Witherspoon, J. L. Wilson; jazz festivals at Nice, Vienne, Marciac, Dresden, Geneva, Brussels; founder of own trio 1987; plays with own and various bands in France, Germany, Belgium, the Netherlands; writer for Orchestre Régional de Jazz de Bretagne, Peter Butler and Alain Bernard Quartet; also composes and arranges for singers, combos, big bands; numerous radio and TV programmes; mem. SACEM, SPEDIDAM, ADAMI. *Films:* La Rumba, Mayrig. *Recordings include:* Mais Où Est Donc Ornicar (with Joe Henderson), Mr Swing Is Still Alive (Gérard Badini Super Swing Machine), Jazz Cartoon, L'Incroyable Huck, Sing Feeling & Screaming (with J. Hawkins), Invitation (with E. Lelann), Horizons (with Orchestre Jazz Bretagne), Jazz me a New Song (Peter Butler and Alain Bernard Quartet), Hot House, R'n'Big Band (Orchestre de Jazz de Bretagne), Romaric Sextet. *Telephone:* (2) 97-58-00-43 (home). *E-mail:* alanbernard@orange.fr (home). *Website:* www.myspace.com/alainbernard (home).

BERNARD, Claude Camille; French musician (alto saxophone) and bandleader; b. 5 Oct. 1945, Paris; m. (deceased); two s. two d. *Education:* Conservatoire Artistique Cardinal Lemoine; alto saxophone with Jean Ledieu, Conservatoire Nat., Nancy. *Career:* festival appearances at Chateauvallon 1976, Vansovin 1977, Suse den Netherlands, Yugoslavia, Turkey 1994, People's Republic of China, Africa 1995; played with Steve Lacy, Michael Smith, Lavelle, Mickey Baker, Wei Wei; Olympic Games Atlanta centennial with Wei Wei and Michael Smith Band 1996; specializes in improvisation, solo and accompanied; mem., Syndicat des Chefs d'Orchestre, Société des auteurs, compositeurs et éditeurs de musique (SACEM), SACD, Centre International de Musicotherapie. *Recordings include:* Quebella Promenade, Brin de Laine, Facett'vega.

BERNARDI, Alessandro; Italian singer and musician (guitar); b. 26 Nov. 1959, Venice; s. of Mario Bernardi and Giuseppina Scarpa. *Education:* Pacinotti Industrial Coll., Venice. *Career:* with Los Primos, tour of Japan 1988; with Ole, Italy 1989, 1994; also to Australia, Singapore, Hong Kong, Russia, Canada; toured UK with solo show, 'Passion, Grace, Fire'; composed music for TV advertisements, Royal Shakespeare Co., Queen's Golden Jubilee 2002, Manchester Commonwealth Games etc.; mem. Musicians' Union. *Recordings include:* albums: A Different Story 2001, Songs to Protest About (with The Native Hipsters) 2006; with Los Primos: Paul's Lurking Grapefruit, Latino-comedy. *Honours:* Time Out Magazine Pick of The Fringe 1989, winner Covent Garden Street Festival 1989, British Gas Best Newcomer, Edin. Festival 1992, Scottish Daily Express New Name Award, Edin. Festival 1992, Best Music Act, Bournemouth 1993. *Address:* Alessandro Passion Grace & Fire, 14B Vicarage Grove, Camberwell, London, SE5 7LW, England (home). *E-mail:* alessandrovenice@aol.com (office).

BERNINGER, Matt; American singer and songwriter; b. 13 Feb. 1971, Ohio; m. Carin Besser; one d. *Education:* Univ. of Cincinnati. *Career:* mem., The National 1999–. *Recordings include:* albums: The National 2001, Sad Songs For Dirty Lovers 2003, Alligator 2005, Boxer 2007, High Violet 2010, Trouble Will Find Me 2013. *Current Management:* c/o Dawn Berger, Post Hoc Management, 750 Grand Street, 7S, Brooklyn, NY 11211, USA. *E-mail:* info@americanmary.com (office). *Website:* www.americanmary.com.

BERRABAH, Amelle; British singer; b. 22 April 1984, Aldershot, Hants. *Career:* mem., Sugababes 2005–13; solo career 2012–. *Recordings include:* Change 2007, Catfights and Spotlights 2008, Sweet 7 2010. *Current Management:* c/o Crown Music Management, 91 Peterborough Road, London SW6 3BU, England. *E-mail:* info@crowntalentgroup.com. *Website:* crowntalentgroup.com.

BERRY, (William Thomas) Bill; American musician (drums); b. 31 July 1958, Hibbing, Minn. *Career:* Founder-mem. R.E.M. 1980–97; numerous int. tours and festival appearances; mem. side project, Hindu Love Gods 1986–90; became a farmer late 1990s. *Recordings include:* albums: with R.E.M.: Chronic Town 1982, Murmur 1983, Reckoning 1984, Fables Of The Reconstruction 1985, Life's Rich Pageant 1986, Dead Letter Office 1987, Document 1987, Eponymous 1988, Green 1988, Out Of Time (Billboard Award for Best World Album, Q Award for Best Album) 1991, Automatic For The People (Grammy Award for Best Alternative Music Album, Atlanta Music Award for Rock Album, Q Award for Best Album, Rolling Stone Critics Award for Best Album 1993) 1992, Monster 1994, New Adventures In Hi-Fi 1996; with Hindu Love Gods: Hindu Love Gods 1990. *Honours:* numerous MTV Music Video Awards, Earth Day Award 1990, Billboard Award for Best Modern Rock Artist 1991, BRIT Awards for Best Int. Group 1992, 1993, 1995, Grammy Awards for Best Pop Performance, Best Music Video 1992, Atlanta Music Awards for Act of the Year, Video of the Year 1992, IRMA Award for Int. Band of the Year 1993, Rolling Stone Critics Award for Best Band 1993.

BERRY, (Charles Edward Anderson) Chuck; American singer and composer; b. 18 Oct. 1926, St Louis, Mo.; m. Thermetta Suggs 1948; four c. *Career:* plays guitar, saxophone, piano; concert and TV appearances 1955–. *Albums include:* After School Sessions 1958, One Dozen Berrys 1958, New Juke Box Hits 1960, Chuck Berry 1960, More Chuck Berry 1960, On Stage 1960, You Can Never Tell 1964, Greatest Hits 1964, Two Great Guitars 1964, Chuck Berry in London 1965, Fresh Berrys 1965, St Louis to Liverpool 1966, Golden Hits 1967, At the Fillmore 1967, Medley 1967, In Memphis 1967, Concerto in B Goods 1969, Home Again 1971, The London Sessions 1972, Golden Decade 1972, St Louis to Frisco to Memphis 1972, Let the Good Times Roll 1973, Golden Decade (Vol. II) 1973, (Vol. V) 1974, Bio 1973, Back in the USA 1973, I'm a Rocker 1975, Chuck Berry 75 1975, Motorvatin' 1976, Rockit 1979, Chess Masters 1983, The Chess Box 1989, Missing Berries 1990, Rarities 1990, On the Blues Side 1993, Anthology 2000. *Films include:* Go, Johnny Go, Rock, Rock, Rock 1956, Jazz on a Summer's Day 1960, Let the Good Times Roll 1973, Hail! Hail! Rock 'n' Roll 1987. *Publication:* Chuck Berry: The Autobiography 1987. *Honours:* inducted into Int. Hall of Fame, Nashville Songwriters Asscn 1982, Grammy Award for Life Achievement 1984, inducted into Rock and Roll Hall of Fame 1985, Broadcast Music, Inc. (BMI) Icon Award 2002, Polar Music Prize 2014. *Website:* www.chuckberry .com.

BERRY, John; American singer and songwriter; b. 14 Sept. 1959, Aiken, SC; m. Robin Calvert; two s. one d. *Career:* moved to Nashville 1990; tours, concerts with own band; numerous television appearances; mem. AFofM, CMA, NARAS, ACM. *Recordings:* Albums: John Berry, 1995; Standing On The Edge, 1995; O Holy Night, 1995; Faces, 1996; Better Than A Biscuit, 1998; Wildest Dreams, 1999; All The Way To There, 2001, I Give My Heart 2004, Those Were the Days 2008; Singles: Your Love Amazes Me (No. 1); Standing On The Edge Of Goodbye; I Think About It All The Time; If I Had Any Pride Left At All, 1995; Change My Mind, 1996; She's Takin' A Shine, 1997. *Honours:* Grammy Awards for Best Male Country Performance 1995, 1996. *Telephone:* (225) 395-9673. *E-mail:* circletmanagement@gmail.com. *Address:* John Berry Inc., Clear Sky Records Inc., 1720 Epps Bridge Road, Suite 108, Athens, GA 30606, USA. *Telephone:* (706) 769-2402. *Fax:* (706) 769-7852. *Website:* johnberry.musiccitynetworks.com/index.htm.

BERRY, Mark 'Bez'; British musician (percussion) and dancer; b. 18 April 1964, Manchester, England. *Career:* mem., Happy Mondays 1985–93, 1999–2000, 2004–; numerous tours and festival appearances; founder mem., Black Grape 1993–98; mem. Domino Bones 2006–. *Recordings include:* albums: with Happy Mondays: Squirrel and G-Man Twenty-Four Hour Party People Plastic Face Carnt Smile (White Out) 1986, Bummed (Q Magazine Classic Album Award 2013) 1988, Pills 'n' Thrills and Bellyaches 1990, ...Yes Please! 1992; with Black Grape: It's Great When You're Straight... Yeah! 1995, Stupid, Stupid, Stupid 1997, Uncle Dysfunktional 2007. *Publications:* Freaky Dancin' 1998. *Honours:* DMC World DJ Award for Best Indie Act 1991. *Current Management:* c/o Warren Askew Management, Woodhead House, 44/46 Market Street, Hyde, Cheshire, SK14 1AH, England. *Telephone:* (7818) 888368. *E-mail:* weaentertainment@gmail.com. *Website:* www.myspace.com/dominobones; www.happymondaysonline.com.

BERRYMAN, Guy; British musician (bass guitar) and songwriter; b. 12 April 1978, Fife, Scotland. *Education:* University Coll., London. *Career:* mem. Coldplay 1998–. *Recordings include:* albums: Parachutes (BRIT Award for Best Album 2001, Grammy Award for Best Alternative Album 2002) 2000, A Rush Of Blood To The Head (BRIT Award for Best British Album 2003, NME Award for Best Album 2003) 2002, X&Y (MasterCard British Album, BRIT Awards 2006, Juno Award for Int. Album of the Year 2006) 2005, Viva la Vida (Grammy Award for Best Rock Album 2009) 2008, Mylo Xyloto (Billboard Music Award for Top Rock Album 2012) 2011, Ghost Stories (Billboard Music Award for Top Rock Album 2015) 2014, A Head Full of Dreams 2015. *Honours:* BRIT Awards for Best British Group 2001, 2003, 2012, for Best British Single (for Speed of Sound) 2006, for Best Live Act 2014, MTV Europe Music Awards for Best UK and Ireland Act 2002, for Best Song (for Speed of Sound) 2005, for Best Rock Act 2015, Billboard Music Awards for Group of the Year 2002, for Top Rock Artist 2012, for Top Alternative Artist 2012, Ivor Novello Awards for Songwriters of the Year 2003, for Best Selling British Song (for Viva la Vida) 2009, Grammy Awards for Record of the Year (for Clocks) 2004, for Best Rock Vocal Performance by a Duo or Group (for In My Place) 2004, for Song of the Year 2009, for Best Pop Performance by a Duo or Group (both for Viva la Vida) 2009, Q Awards for Best Act in the World 2005, 2011, Digital Music People's Choice Award for best official site, for Best Digital Music Community (for Coldplay.com) 2005, American Music Award for Favorite Alternative Music Artist 2005, Echo Award for Best Int. Group, Germany 2006, ASCAP Award for Song of the Year (for Speed of Sound) 2006, World Music Award for Best Rock Act 2008. *Address:* c/o Dave Holmes, 3-D Management, 1901 Main Street, #3000, Los Angeles, CA 90405, USA. *Telephone:* (310) 314-1390. *Website:* www.coldplay.com.

BERRYMAN, Peter Anthony; British musician (guitar), composer and teacher; b. 22 June 1945, Redruth, Cornwall, England; two s. one d. *Career:* tours with Famous Jug Band 1969–71; Mormos, Africa 1973; Julie Felix, Australasia 1974; Bridget St John, UK 1976; Brenda Wootton, France 1985–90; Blue Ticket, 1987–93; solo tours of UK, Europe 1972–; numerous radio broadcasts and television and festival appearances; guitar teacher 1982–; composer of music for Kneehigh Theatre, Theatre Rotto, The Barneys; mem. PRS. *Recordings:* Spiral Staircase, 1968; Sunshine Possibilities, 1969;

Chameleon, 1970; Legendary Me; Magical Flight; Sky In My Pie; Past, Present and Future; Under A Summer Sky; Best Of British Folk; Picture Rags; The Electric Muse; Duet, with Adrian O'Reilly, 1999, The Return 2007, The Ghosts of May 2010. *Publication:* Silver Harvest 1998. *E-mail:* peteberryman1@yahoo.co.uk; pete@peteberryman.com. *Website:* www .peteberryman.com.

BERTHELSEN, Claus Gymoese, BEcons; Danish singer, songwriter and author; b. 28 Sept. 1958, Copenhagen; one d. *Education:* with Copenhagen Boys Choir. *Career:* founder of own group, Naïve; several live performances in Denmark, including Roskilde Festival, television appearances; actor in Gangway I Tyrol; mem. DJBFA. *Compositions:* songs: Carry On; Marble Afternoon. *Recordings include:* albums with Naïve: Fish, Careless, Absolution Music. *Website:* www.myspace.com/naive.

BERTRAM, Dominique; Algerian musician (electric bass); b. 8 Aug. 1954, Algiers; m. Florence Faisan 1991, one s. one d. *Career:* worked with singers: Michael Jonasz; Veronique Sanson; Catherine Lara; Patrick Bruel; Al Jarreau, Nicolle Croisille; performed with Magma; co-creator, the ZAM; mem. SACEM, Spedidam, ADAMI. *Recordings:* Michael Jonasz; Veronique Sanson; Dominique Bertram: Chinese Paradise, 1985; Bass Now, 1992. *Publications:* Method Up Bass 1990, Jouer de la Basse c'est façile 1994. *Address:* c/o Zampower, 2 chemin Goeb, 67000 Strasbourg, France. *E-mail:* contact@zampower.com. *Website:* www.zampower.com/en.

BERTRAM, Hans-Dieter 'Sherry'; German musician (drums, percussion); b. 20 May 1936, Leipzig; m. Dagmar 1969; two s. *Education:* Berlin Conservatory. *Career:* freelance musician; graphic designer, moderator for Rias radio station 1957–89; concerts and recordings, Berlin Philharmonic Orchestra 1962, Deutsche Oper Berlin 1962, 1967, 1972, 1993–95; musicals and music for theatre; studio musician for television, radio, films, jingles, records, Rias Live talk show 1969–89; CA 1000 programmes; jazz drummer with own groups, big bands; drum and percussion teacher, Leo-Borchard Music School, Berlin 1987–; Music Dir, Orchester Bertram 1976–; mem. Landesmusikrat Berlin, Jazz Department. *Address:* Bertram Music Entertainment, Rudolstaedter Strasse 123, 10713 Berlin, Germany (office). *Telephone:* (30) 8242972 (office); (30) 8237991 (home). *Fax:* (30) 8245059 (office). *E-mail:* sherry@bme-berlin.de. *Website:* www.bertram-music-entertainment .de (office).

BERTRAND, Plastic; Belgian musician, singer, songwriter and writer, producer, editor and television presenter; b. (Roger Allen François Jouret), 24 Feb. 1954, Brussels; m. Evelyne van Daele 1979; one s. one d. *Education:* studied music theory and percussion at Music Acad., Brussels, studied design at Saint-Luc Inst., studied music theory, percussion and music history at Conservatoire Royal de Musique de Bruxelles. *Career:* singer and drummer in Buffalo Scouts Band (formed with Boy Scouts aged nine) 1963–73, performed covers of Rolling Stones songs; then formed The Pelicans to perform at parties, later changed name to Passing the Time, performed in bars, clubs and at festivals along the Dutch and Belgian coast; hired by pirate radio station Radio Veronica; formed the band Hubble Bubble 1974, credited as songwriter, singer and drummer under the name Roger Junior; also worked as a stage manager at Théâtre des Galeries; began solo career as the credited artist of the int. hit single Ça plane pour moi 1977, though in fact the song had been sung and produced by its composer Lou Deprijck; toured Europe, Japan, Australia and N America with Lou Deprijck, becoming one of the few French-speaking artists to appear in the Billboard chart; appeared on several TV shows, presenting Jackpot (TF1), Destination Noël (France 2), Due per tutti (RAI2), Supercool (RTBF) (also producer); lived in Milan 1982–85, featured in a photo-story; recorded, with Daniel Balavoine and ABBA's Anni-Frid Lyngstad, Abbacadabra (a musical tale for children); co-wrote, with Vladimir Cosma, several film scores, including Astérix et la surprise de César (Asterix Versus Caesar); represented Luxembourg in Eurovision Song Contest with the song Amour Amour 1987; formed company MMD with Pierrette Broodthaers, produced two albums for David Janssen and a single for Noël Godin; est., with Pierrette Broodthaers, Broodthaers & Bertrand art gallery, collaborations with Museum of Contemporary Art, Valenciennes and Belgian artist Jacques Charlier to produce 120 Andy Warhol-style portraits; presented fortnightly TV show Duel (RTBF) for two seasons; tours in Belgium, France and Switzerland and again in Germany for a new series of concert 2001–05; appeared in Eurotrash (Channel 4); guest on Clarkson (BBC 2); manager Star Academy contest show on RTL-TVI Sept.–Nov. 2002; concert at Cirque Royal, Brussels to celebrate 25 years since start of solo career 2003; presented daily TV show Hit Story (France 3) July–Sept. 2003; participant in TV show La ferme célébrité 2 (TF1) 2004; performed with symphony orchestra for the 175th anniversary of Belgian independence 2005; presented culinary show Voulez vous diner avec moi? (BETV) 2005; appeared on a special 1980s edn of Le Maillon Faible (French equivalent of The Weakest Link); appeared at the Countdown Spectacular 2 Tour in all major capital cities of Australia Aug.–Sept. 2007; concert with the Porn Flakes band to celebrate 400th anniversary of Quebec city 2008; cr. the Pink Show (new stage arrangement) for a six-day open air tour in Belgium with RTBF 2009; concert in Vancouver for opening ceremony of the Winter Olympic Games 2010; worked on a new cosmetic products line Pogo Pogo; numerous concerts in France, Belgium and Switzerland 2010; appeared in French TV shows, including Taratata; concert at Paris Olympia 2010. *Films:* Légitime Violence, Baoum (short) early 1980s, Casablanca Driver 2004, Le bénévole 2006, J'ai kidnappé Plastic Bertrand (short) 2009. *Television:* TF1 Jackspot 1980, Ivre mort pour la patrie (film)

1998, Si j'avais dix trous de cul (short) 1999, Eurotrash 2001, Due per tutti, I migliori anni 2008, Vivement dimanche (co-presenter), RTL Disco Show 2 2009, Supercool RTBF, History France 3. *Recordings:* albums: with Hubble Bubble: Hubble Bubble 1975; solo: AN1 1979, J'te Fais un Plan 1980, L'album 1981, Plastiqeuz vos Baffles 1981, Grands succès/Greatest Hits 1981, Chat Va...Et Toi? 1988, Pix 1988, Suite Diagonale 1994, Plastic Hits (compilation) 1998, Bertrand – Compilation Hubble Bubble 2002, Ultra Terrestre 2002, Dandy Bandit 2009; singles: New Promotion/You'll Be The One 1975, Ça plane pour moi/Pogo Pogo 1977, Bambino/Le Petit Tortillard 1978, Super Cool/ Affection 1978, Sha La La La Lee/Naif Song 1978, Tout petit la planète/C'est le Rock'N'Roll 1978, Tout petit la planète /J'te fais un plan/Hit 87 1979, Sentimentale moi/Quais Quais Quais Quais 1979, Sentimental me/Sentimentale moi 1979, Le Monde est merveilleux/ J'te fais un plan 1979, Sans Amour/ Plastic Boy 1979, Téléphone à téléphone mon bijou/Stop ou encore 1979, Téléphone à téléphone mon bijou /Kangourou Kangourou 1980, Hula Hoop/ Amoureux fou de toi 1980, Jaques Cousteau/Paradis 1981, La Star à pécole/ Baby Doll/Coeur D'acier 1981, L'amour Ok/New York/Coeur d'acier/Stop ou encore 1982, Ping Pong/Coeur D'Acier 1982, Duo Avec Nathalie 1982, Arret d'autobus/Mon Nez, mon nez 1983, Chat/Fou des Fifties 1983, Major Tom/ Miss Italie 1983, Gueule d'amour/Down Town 1983, Astérix est Là/Le Secret du druide 1985, Je l'jure/La Fille du premier rang 1986, Let's Slow Again/ Toujours plus haut 1986, Amour, Amour 1987, Démente a la menthe 1988, Slave To The Beat/Plastiiic Acid Mix 1989, Sex Tabou 1990, House Machine/ Club Control feat. Plastic Bertrand 1990, Les Joueurs de Tchik Tchik 1994, Play Boy/Canape 2002, Plastcubration/Tous, Touchez-vous 2003, Machine/ Remixes 2005. *Publications:* Ça plane...délires et des larmes 2008. *Honours:* Chevalier, Ordre de la Couronne 2004; 15 gold records, five platinum records, Billboard Award (USA), acclaimed by MTV as the "most wanted comeback" artist 2000, Grand Prix de l' Acad. Française du Disque, Prix Sabam (Belgium), Rolls Royce Cup (Italy), Grand Prix du Disque Midem. *Current Management:* c/o Pierrette Broodthaers, MMD, 14 avenue H. Boulenger, 1180 Brussels, Belgium. *Telephone:* (2) 534-60-00. *E-mail:* procontact@ plasticbertrand.com. *Website:* www.plasticbertrand.com.

BESIAKOV, Ben; Danish musician (piano, organ); b. 27 Oct. 1956, Copenhagen; one s. *Career:* mem. Danish Musicians' Asscn. *Compositions:* Choo Choo (with Lennart Ginman and Mike Clark). *Recordings:* You Stepped Out Of A Dream 1990, Raney (with Doug Raney) 1996, The Red Light (with Bent Jaedig) 1996, When Granny Sleeps (with Dave Liebman) 1995, Human Beat Boxer (with Niclas Knudsen and Adam Nussbaum) 1997, Aviation (with George Garzone, Billy Hart, Ray Drummond and Jens Winther) 1999, Hey Why Don't We Play (with George Garzone) 2001, Style of Glamour (with Rikke Lie) 2003, A prima vez (with Christina von Bülow-Bau Besiakov) 2005. *Honours:* Ben Webster Prize 1990, Jasa Prize 1993. *Address:* Gl. Vartovvej 21, 2900 Hellerup, Denmark (office). *Telephone:* 28-10-23-30 (office); 39-62-11-00 (home). *Fax:* 39-62-11-00 (home). *E-mail:* ben@benbesiakov.com; tjuutjuu@ hotmail.com. *Website:* www.benbesiakov.com.

BEST, Matthew; British musician (drums, keyboards), DJ and record producer; b. 26 Jan. 1961, London, England. *Education:* West London Inst. of HE. *Career:* studio drummer, Captain Sensible 1977–80; formed Carcrash International 1983–84; played live for UK Subs and Anti-Nowhere League; formed Urban Dogs; Pressure Point (featuring P. P. Arnold); simultaneously mem. of Psychic TV 1986–; formed Greedy Beat Syndicate; plays live with techno band, Yum Yum; mem. Musicians' Union. *Recordings:* two albums with Urban Dogs, 12 albums with Psychic TV, two albums with Greedy Beat Syndicate. *Address:* 19 Irving Street, London, WC2H 7AU, England.

BETHÂNIA VIANNA TELLES VELLOSO, Maria; Brazilian singer; b. 18 June 1946, Santa Amaro da Purificacão; d. of José Telles Velloso and Claudionor Vianna Telles Velloso; sister of Caetano Veloso. *Career:* became musical pnr of theatre dir Álvaro Guimarães aged 16; composed soundtrack for short film Moleques de Rua (Dir Álvaro Guimarães); performed as a cappella, Boca de Ouro musical production 1963; organizer Nós por Exempio (popular music show), opening of Teatro Vila Velha, Salvador 1964; performed in Mora na Filosofia musical production (Dirs Caetana Veloso and Gilberto Gil) 1964; substitute performer in show Opinião 1965; performer Carcara 1985; signed to RCA label 1965; opened show Recital at Cangaceiro nightclub, Rio 1966, Rosa Dos Ventas at Teatro de Praia, Rio 1971, Drama al Luz da Noite 1973, A Cena Muda 1974, Pássaro da Manhã 1977, A Hora da Estrela 1984, Dadaya: As Sete Moradas 1989; performed at MIDEM, Cannes, France 1971; appeared in film Quando o Carnaval Chegar 1972. *Recordings include:* more than 30 albums including: Edu Lobo e Maria Bethânia 1967, Maria Bethânia 1969, Maria Bethânia Ao Vivo 1970, A Tua Presenda 1971, Rosa Dos Ventas 1971, Drama 1973, Chico Buarque a Maria Bethânia Gravado ao Vivo 1975, Pássaro Proibido 1976, Passaro da Manhã 1977, Álibi 1978, Mel 1979, Alteza 1981, A Beira e o Mar 1984, Dezembros 1987, Maria 1988, Memoria da Pele 1990, Olho D'água 1992, As Canções Que Você Fez Para Mim 1993, Âmbar 1997, Imitação da Vida 1997, Diamante Verdadeiro 1998, Maricotinha 2002, Brasileirinho 2003, Que falta você me faz 2005, Pirata 2006, Mar de Sophia 2006, Dentro do Mar tem Rio 2007, Omara Portuondo e Maria Bethânia 2007, Encantaria 2009, Tua 2009, Amor, Festa, Devoção 2010. *Honours:* Prêmio Shell de Música 2008. *Address:* Quitanda Produções Artísticas, rua Sarapuí 8, Botafogo, 22260-170 Rio de Janeiro, Brazil (office). *Telephone:* (21) 2266-9300 (office). *E-mail:* anabasbaum@terra.com.br (office). *Website:* www.mariabethania.com.br (home).

BETTENCOURT, Nuno Duarte Gil Mendes; musician (guitar) and producer; b. 20 Sept. 1966, Azores, Portugal; m. Suze DeMarchi 1994; two c. *Career:* fmr mem., Overseas, Myth, Viking, Ruin, Sinful; mem. funk/rock group, Extreme 1985–96, 2008–; tours and worldwide appearances; mem., Mourning Widows 1999; mem., Population 1 2002–, renamed DramaGods 2005; touring guitarist for Rihanna 2010–11. *Recordings include:* albums: Extreme 1989, Extreme II Pornograffitti 1991, III Sides To Every Story 1992, Very Special Christmas Vol. 2 1992, Shaved and Dangerous 1993, Ultimate Rock Vol. 1 1993, There Is No God 1994, Kiss My Ass 1994, Honey 1994, Waiting for the Punchline 1995, Flesh 1995, Saudades de Rock 2008; solo: Schizophonic 1997; with Mourning Widows: Mourning Widows 1999, Furnished Souls for Rent 2000; with Population 1: Population 1 2002; with DramaGods: DramaGods 2005. *Honours:* Boston Music Awards for Act of Year, for Outstanding Rock Single (for Hole Hearted), for Outstanding Pop Single, for Outstanding Song/Songwriter (for More Than Words), for Outstanding Instrumentalist 1992. *Website:* www.nuno-bettencourt.com/ myspace; extreme-band.com/site.

BETTIS, John; American lyricist; b. 24 Oct. 1946, Long Beach, CA. *Career:* co-founder, The Carpenters from 1970; worked with artists, including Michael Jackson, Madonna, Whitney Houston, Diana Ross. *Compositions include:* Top of The World; Yesterday Once More; Only Yesterday; Goodbye To Love; Human Nature; Crazy For You; Slow Hand; One Moment In Time; When You Tell Me That You Love Me. *Honours:* Academy Award, Golden Globe, Emmy Award. *Address:* John Bettis Music, PO Box 668, Sunset Beach, CA 90742-0668, USA. *E-mail:* info@johnbettismusic.com. *Website:* www.johnbettismusic .com.

BEVAN, Alonza; musician (bass guitar); b. 24 Oct. 1970, London. *Career:* founder mem. The Objects of Desire (with Crispian Mills and Paul Winterhart) renamed The Kays; founder mem., Kula Shaker (with Jay Darlington) 1995–; mem. Johnny Marr & The Healers 2000–; f. Tumbleweed with wife Audrey Evans 2011; numerous TV appearances and appearances at rock festivals. *Recordings include:* albums: with Kula Shaker: K 1996, Peasants, Pigs and Astronauts 1999, Strangefolk 2007, Pilgrim's Progress 2010; with Johnny Marr & The Healers: Boomslang 2003; with Tumbleweed: Sinnerman 2011. *Address:* StrangeF.O.L.K. LLP, 6 Lansdowne Mews, London, W11 3BH, England. *E-mail:* kulashakerofficial@googlemail.com. *Website:* www.kulashaker.co.uk.

BEVAN, Beverley; British musician (drums); b. 24 Nov. 1946, Birmingham. *Career:* member, groups: Carl Wayne and The Vikings; Denny Laine and The Diplomats; Danny King and The Mayfair Set; Drummer, The Move, 1966–72; Appearances include: National Jazz and Blues Festival, 1966; Support to The Rolling Stones, Paris, 1967; Art Festival Ball, Brighton, 1967; Isle of Wight Festival, 1968; Reading Festival, 1972; Drummer, Electric Light Orchestra (ELO), 1972–; Concerts include: Heartbeat '86 benefit, Birmingham, 1986; Brief spell, drummer, Black Sabbath, including Reading Festival, 1983. *Recordings:* Albums: with the Move: Move, 1968; Shazam, 1970; Looking On, 1970; Message From The Country, 1971; Great Move: The Best Of The Move, 1993; with ELO: Electric Light Orchestra, 1972; On The Third Day, 1973; Eldorado, 1974; The Night The Light Went On In Long Beach, 1974; Face The Music, 1975; Olé ELO, 1976; A New World Record, 1976; Out Of The Blue, 1977; Discovery (No. 1, UK), 1979; ELO's Greatest Hits, 1979; Xanadu (film soundtrack), 1980; Time, 1981; Secret Messages, 1983; Balance Of Power, 1986; Greatest Hits, 1989; Afterglow, 1990; Electric Light Orchestra, 1991; Moment Of Truth, 1994; One Night Live In Australia, 1997; Live At Wembley '78, 1998; Flashback 2000; Also appears on: Twang! A Tribute, 1996; Supernatural Fairy Tails, 1996; Under Wheels Of Confusion, 1996; Singles: with the Move include: I Can Hear The Grass Grow; Flowers In The Rain; Fire Brigade; Blackberry Way (No. 1, UK); Hello Susie; Curly; Brontosaurus; California Man; with ELO: Roll Over Beethoven; Showdown; Can't Get It Out Of My Head; Strange Magic; Evil Woman; Lovin' Thing; Rockaria!; Do Ya; Telephone Line; Turn To Stone; Mr Blue Sky; Wild West Hero; Shine A Little Love; Don't Bring Me Down; Xanadu (No. 1, UK); Hold On Tight; Rock 'n' Roll Is King; Calling America; Solo: Let There Be Drums. *Honours:* Outstanding Contribution to British Music, Ivor Novello Award, 1979. *Address:* c/o Brian Yeates Entertainment, Home Farm House, Canwell, Sutton Coldfield, West Midlands, B75 5SH, England. *Telephone:* (121) 323-2200. *Website:* www .brianyeates.co.uk; www.bevbevan.com.

BEVAN, Jack William; British musician (drums) and songwriter; b. 4 Oct. 1985, Wycombe, Leics., England. *Career:* fmr mem. The Edmund Fitzgerald; Founder-mem. Foals 2005–. *Recordings:* albums: with Foals: Antidotes 2008, Total Life Forever 2010, Holy Fire 2013, What Went Down 2015. *Honours:* with Foals: NME Awards for Best Track (for Spanish Sahara) 2011, (for Inhaler) 2013, Q Magazine Awards for Best Live Act 2013, for Best Act in the World Today 2015. *Current Management:* c/o Steve Matthews, Q Prime Management, 729 Seventh Avenue, #1600, New York, NY 10019, USA. *Telephone:* (212) 302-9790. *E-mail:* info@qprime.com. *Website:* www.qprime .com; www.foals.co.uk.

BEX, Emmanuel Jean; French musician (Hammond organ, piano) and composer; b. 8 June 1959, Caen; m. Sophie Simon 1991. *Education:* Conservatory of Caen, Conservatory of Paris. *Career:* mem. The Bex'tet quintet 1991; sideman with Babick Reinhardt, Barney Wilen, Philippe Catherine; founder mem., Steel Bex (with E. Bex and Steel Band) 1997, Bex Machine, E. Bex Quartet 1997, Bex trio (with Philip Catherine and Aldo Romano) 1998, BFG (with Glenn Ferris and Simon Goubert) 2000, 2006, Open Gate Trio (with Francesco Bearzatti and Simon Goubert) 2009. *Compositions include:* Esperanto Cantabile Cconcerto for Hammond organ and symphony orchestra 2007, Requiem in Colours 2011. *Recordings:* Bex and Jouvelet In Public, 1983; with Ray Lema: Bwana Zoulu, 1987; with Bex, Pino, Teslard: Triple Idiome, 1988; with Xavier Jouvelet: Blues Congo, 1988; with La Bande à Badauld: Vacances Au Soleil, 1988; Caravanserail, 1989; with Bertrand Renaudin: Interplay, 1990; Miscellaneous Song, 1991; with Carl Schlosser: Texas Sound, 1992; with Babick Reinhardt: Histoire Simple, 1992; with Marais, Bex, Romano: Poissons Nageurs, 1993; with Bex'tet: Enfance, 1991; Organique, 1993; Rouge Et Or, 1995; with Barney Wilen: Nitty Gritty, 1993; Steel Bex, Emmanuel Bex, 1996; Due des Lowbards, Christian Escoudé Trio, 1997; '3' with trios: Bex/Romano/Catherine, Bex/Huchard/Barthelmy, Bex/Ceccareli/Lagrene, 1997; Mauve, 2000; Here and Now, Bex/Ferris/Goubert 2001, Organ Song (with Mônica Passos) 2006, Concerto for Hammond Organ and Symphonic Orchestra 2007, Third String (with J. Renard and J.P. Feiss) 2008, Open Gate (with Francesco Bearzatti and Simon Goubert) 2009, Open Gate feat Béla Bartók – Concerto pour trio et orchestre 2011. *Honours:* Acad. du Jazz Prix Django Reinhardt 1995, Grand Prix de l' Acad. Charles Cros (for BFG) 2000, Choc de l'année Jazzman 2000, Acad. du Jazz Prix Boris Vian (for BFG) 2000, Les Victoires du Jazz/Django d'Or (for BFG) 2002, Django d'Or for Musician of the Year 2003. *Current Management:* Puls'action, 8 Atelier E02, 2 rue Denfert Rochereau, 93200 Saint-Denis, France. *Telephone:* 9-53-51-04-23 (office). *E-mail:* pulsaction@sfr.fr. *Website:* www.emmanuelbex.net.

BEY, Andrew W. (Andy); American jazz singer and musician (piano); b. 28 Oct. 1939, Newark, NJ. *Career:* Founder-mem., family trio Andy and the Bey Sisters 1956–67, debut recordings 1961; solo career 1967–; numerous collaborations including Louis Jordan, Horace Silver, Gary Bartz, Dee Dee Bridgewater. *Recordings:* albums: with Bey Sisters: Now! Hear 1964, Round Midnight 1965; with Max Roach: Members, Don't Git Weary 1968; solo: Experience and Judgement 1974, As Time Goes By 1991, Ballads, Blues and Bey 1996, Shades of Bey 1998, Tuesdays in Chinatown 2001, Chillin' 2003, American Song 2004, Ain't Necessarily So 2007, The World According to Andy Bey 2013, Pages from an Imaginary Life 2014. *Honours:* Jazz Journalists Asscn Jazz Vocalist of the Year 2003. *Address:* c/o High Note Records, Jazz Depot, 106 West 71st Street, New York, NY 10023, USA (office). *Telephone:* (212) 873-2020 (office). *Fax:* (212) 877-0407 (office). *Website:* www.jazzdepot.com (office); www.myspace.com/andybey (home).

BEYONCÉ; American singer, songwriter, actress and producer; b. (Beyoncé Giselle Knowles), 4 Sept. 1981, Houston, Tex.; d. of Mathew Knowles and Tina Knowles; m. Jay-Z (Shawn Carter) 2008; one d. *Career:* Founding mem. GirlsTyme (with Kelly Rowland, later joined by LaTavia Roberson and LeToya Luckett), group renamed Something Fresh, then The Dolls before settling on Destiny's Child 1989–2005; numerous live performances, tours; solo artist 2001–; est. clothing label Touch of Couture; Amb. for World Humanitarian Day campaign 2012. *Recordings include:* albums: with Destiny's Child: Destiny's Child 1998, The Writing's On The Wall 1999, Survivor (American Music Award for Favorite Pop/Rock Album 2002) 2001, Eight Days Of Christmas 2001, Destiny Fulfilled (Lady of Soul Award for Best Group Album 2005, American Music Award for Favorite Soul/R&B Album 2005) 2004; solo: Soul Survivors 2002, Dangerously in Love (Grammy Award for Best Contemporary R&B Album 2004) 2003, Live At Wembley 2004, B-Day (Grammy Award for Best Contemporary R&B Album 2007) 2006, I Am... Sasha Fierce (Grammy Award for Best Contemporary R&B Album 2010) 2008, 4 2011, Beyoncé (American Music Award for Favorite Soul/R&B Album 2014) 2013. *Films include:* Austin Powers in Goldmember 2002, The Fighting Temptations 2003, The Pink Panther 2006, Dreamgirls 2006, Cadillac Records (also exec. producer) 2008, Obsessed (also exec. producer) 2009, Epic (voice) 2013. *Television includes:* Carmen: A Hip Hopera (film) 2001, Wow! Wow! Wubbzy! (series) 2009, Robins (series) 2010. *Honours:* (with Destiny's Child) Billboard Award for Artist of the Year, Group of the Year, Hot 100 Singles Artist of the Year, Hot 100 Group of the Year 2000, NAACP Image Award for Outstanding Duo or Group (for Say My Name) 2001, MTV Video Award for Best R&B Video (for Say My Name) 2001, American Music Award for Favorite Soul/R&B Group 2001, Soul Train Sammy Davis Jr Award for Entertainer of the Year 2001, American Music Award for Favorite Pop/Rock Band, Duo or Group 2002, BRIT Award for Best Int. Group 2002, MOBO Award for Best Gospel Act 2002, World Music Award for World's Best Pop Group 2005, Lady of Soul Award for Best Group Single (for Soldier) 2005, American Music Award for Favorite Soul/R & B Band, Duo or Group 2005; (solo) Billboard Awards for New Female Artist of the Year, New R&B Artist, Hot 200 Female Artist 2003, Female R&B/Hip Hop Artist of the Year 2006, Female Artist of the Decade 2009, Radio Artist of the Decade 2009, Millennium Award 2011, BRIT Awards for Best Int. Female Solo Artist 2004, Billboard R&B/Hip Hop Awards for Top Female Artist, New Artist 2004, Grammy Awards for Best R&B Song, Best R&B Performance by a Duo or Group with Vocal (for Say My Name) 2001, for Best R&B Performance by a Duo or Group with Vocals (for Survivor) 2002, for Best R&B Song, Best Rap/Sung Collaboration (for Crazy in Love, with Jay-Z) 2004, for best R&B performance by a duo or group (for The Closer I Get To You, with Luther Vandross) 2004, for Best Female R&B Vocal Performance (for Dangerously In Love) 2004, (for Single Ladies) 2010, for Best R&B Performance by a Duo or Group with Vocals (for So Amazing, with Stevie Wonder) 2006, for Song of the Year (for Single Ladies) 2010, for Best Female Pop Vocal Performance (for Halo) 2010, for Best Traditional R&B Vocal Performance (for At Last) 2010, for Best R&B Song (for Single Ladies) 2010, for Best Traditional R&B Performance (for Love on Top) 2013, for Best R&B Performance, for Best R&B Song (both for Drunk in Love, with Jay-Z) 2015, Billboard Music Award for R&B/Hip-Hop Group of the Year 2005, MOBO Awards for Best Song and Best Video (both for Deja Vu), for Best Int. Female 2006, Soul Train Award for Best Single by a Female (for Irreplaceable) 2007, for Best Dance Performance (for Run the World (Girls)) 2011, BET Award for Best R&B Female 2007, for Video of the Year (for Irreplaceable) 2007, MTV Video Music Award for Best Collaboration (for Beautiful Liar with Shakira) 2007, MTV Europe Music Awards for Best Female 2009, for Best Song (for Halo) 2009, for Best Live Act 2013, for Best Song with a Social Message 2014, American Music Awards for Favorite Female Soul/Rhythm and Blues Artist 2009, 2014, named to VH1's list of the 100 Greatest Artists of All Time 2010, ranked by Forbes magazine amongst The World's 100 Most Powerful Women (ninth) 2010, (18th) 2011, (32nd) 2012, (17th) 2013–14, (21st) 2015, ranked third on VH1's 100 Greatest Women in Music 2012, Writing Award, New York Asscn of Black Journalists 2012, MTV Video Music Award for Best Collaboration (for Drunk in Love featuring Jay Z) 2014, for Best Video with a Social Message (for Pretty Hurts) 2014. *Current Management:* c/o Music World Entertainment, 1505 Hadley Street, Houston, TX 77002-8927, USA. *Telephone:* (713) 772-5175. *Website:* musicworldent.com; www.beyonceonline.com; www.destinyschild.com.

BFC (see Craig, Carl)

BHAMRAH, Kulwant Singh; Indian bhangra singer and songwriter; b. 11 Feb. 1955; m. Satvinder Bhamrah 1979; one s. one d. *Education:* civil engineering. *Career:* singer in bhangra folk Punjabi band, Apna Sangeet; performances, television appearances and radio broadcasts worldwide; mem. PRS, MCPS, Musicians' Union, British Actor's Equityl. *Recordings include:* albums: Apna Sangeet 1986 (Upcoming Band Award 1986/87, Best Band Award, UK Asian Pop Awards 1987/88), Tour India 1987, Mera Yaar 1988, Overdrive 1992 (Best Lyricist, UK Asian Pop Awards 1992), Chack Dey Phattay; Desi Rytham; Musicblasters; Ragga Blasters, Mini Blasters; Mister Blasters; Hi-Kiddaw, The Return 2006, The Sounds of UK Bhangra 2009. *Honours:* Asian Pop Award for Best Songwriter 1992, for Best Live Band 1994. *Address:* VIP Records Ltd, PO Box 4768, Coventry, CV6 9FD, England (office). *Telephone:* (797) 445 3595 (office); (131) 657 9779 (office). *Website:* enquiries@viprecords.co.uk (office); www.viprecords.co.uk (office).

BHATIA, Anjali, BTec, BA; British singer, musician (guitar, drums) and songwriter; b. 15 Oct. 1968, Chiswick, London, England. *Education:* Kingsway Princeton College, Goldsmiths College, Islington Music Workshop. *Career:* fmr mem. Voodoo Queens 1992–99; festival appearances include Reading, Phoenix; radio broadcasts; solo artist, producer and engineer; mem. PRS, Musicians' Union. *Recordings include:* albums: with Voodoo Queens: Chocolate Revenge 1994, Sheer Witchery 1999; solo: Anjali 2000, The World of Lady A 2003. *Telephone:* (20) 7490-8990. *E-mail:* kalpna_mata@hotmail.com. *E-mail:* jack@ec1music.com. *Website:* www.anjali.org.uk.

BHATTACHARYA, Pandit Debashish, BSc; Indian musician (slide guitar), guitar designer; *Executive Director, Bhattacharya's School of Universal Music*; b. 12 Jan. 1963, Kolkata; s. of Sunil Kumar Bhattacharya and Manjushree Bhattacharya; m. Tripti Bhattacharya; one s. one d. *Education:* Calcutta Univ.; studied Indian vocal styles with Pandit Ajay Chakraborty, guitar training with Pandit Brij Bhushan Kabra. *Career:* debut public performance at age four broadcast on All India Radio; has invented his own 'Trinity of Guitars' with the 22-stringed Chaturangi, the 14-stringed Ghandarvi and the 4-stringed Anandi; developed own three-fingered style of playing; numerous tours and recordings with John McLaughlin's group Shakti and Bob Brozman, other collaborations with Ustad Zakir Hussain, Rene Lacaille, Takashi Hiriyasu, Lieu Fang, Julian Kytasty; numerous tours of India, Europe and USA; has written a syllabus on Indian classical guitar; f. Trideb Int. Guitar Co. to design and produce Chaturangui, Gandharvi and Anandi musical instruments; founder Bhattacharya's School of Universal Music, to promote art and artisans in Kolkata 2003–, also Exec. Dir; formed NGO to save guitar mfrs in Kolkata; performed in American, Canadian, European and African Jazz, World Music and Folk Festivals, Nat. Slide Guitar Festival, Int. Guitar Festivals and numerous others. *Recordings include:* Sheer Magic, Hindustani Slide, Debashish Bhattacharya Guitar (with Bob Brozman, Martin Simpson, Mike Auldridge, John Fahe), Remember Shakti (with John Mclaughlin, Zakir Hussain, U. Sriniwas, Selvaganesh, Shiva Mani), Sunrise, Calcutta To California, Hindustani Slide Guitar, Reflection of Love, Young Masters, Call of the Desert, Raga Pahadi Jhinjhoti, Inside Afghanistan, Raga Saraswati 2000, Magams of Syria 2002, Mahima (with Bob Brozman) 2003, Calcutta Slide Guitar 3 2005, Calcutta Chronicles: Indian Slide Guitar Odyssey 2008, O'Shakuntala 2009. *Honours:* Pres. of India Award, All India Radio Nat. Music Competition 1984, Top Grade Award, Prasar Bharati, Ministry of Information and Broadcasting, Asiatic Soc. Gold Medal 2005, Winner (Asia/Pacific), BBC Planet Award for World Music 2007. *Address:* 204/1 Regent Colony, Kolkata 700 040, India (office). *Telephone:* (33) 24849131 (home); (33) 24286886 (office). *Fax:* (33) 24713250 (office). *E-mail:* hindslide_dev@yahoo.com (home); debashishguitar@gmail.com (home); info@debashishbhattacharya.com (office). *Website:* www.debashishbhattacharya.com.

BHEAGLAOICH, Seosaimhín Ní, BA; Irish singer and broadcaster; b. West Kerry, Gaeltacht. *Education:* Trinity College, Dublin. *Career:* presenter, television series The Mountain Lark, RTE; broadcaster with Raidio-Na-Gaeltachta; numerous television appearances, RTE, Ireland; presenter, As I

Roved Out, BBC Ulster. *Recordings include:* solo album: Taobh Na Gréine (Under The Sun), Gael-Linn. *E-mail:* eolas@gael-linn.ie.

BHOSLE, Asha; Indian singer, composer and restaurateur; b. 8 Sept. 1933, Sangli, Maharashtra; d. of Dinanath Mangeshkar; m. 1st Ganpatrao Bhosle (divorced); m. 2nd Rahul Dev Burman 1980 (died 1994); two s. one d. *Career:* Indian film playback singer; has recorded over 12,000 songs in 18 languages; first film Chunaria 1948; first solo in Raat Ki Rani 1949; sang in styles influenced by Latin American and American Big Band Jazz; worked extensively with Kishore Kumar 1970s; owns restaurants in several cities worldwide. *Recordings include:* albums (soundtracks): Dus Lakh 1967, Shikhar 1968, Hare Rama Hare Krishna 1972, Naina 1973, Pran Jaye Par Vachan Na Jaye 1974, Don 1977, Umrao Jaan 1981, Ijazat 1986, Dilwale Dulhania Le Jayeng 1995, Rangeela 1996; solo: Songs of My Soul – Rare and Classic Vols 1 and 2 2001, You've Stolen My Heart (with the Kronos Quartet) 2005, 75 Years of Asha 2008. *Film:* Mai (as actress) 2013. *Honours:* Dr hc (Univ. of Amravati), (Univ. of Jalgaon), DLitt (Jodhpur Nat. Univ.); Filmfare Award 1967, 1968, 1971, 1972, 1973, 1974, 1977, 1996, Nat. Award 1981, 1986, Nightingale of Asia 1987, Lata Mangeshkar Award, Madhya Pradesh Govt 1989, Maharashtra Govt 1999, Filmfare Special Award, Rangeela Re 1996, Screen Videocon Award 1997, MTV Contribution to Music Award 1997, five Channel V Awards, Singer of the Millennium, Dubai 2000, Kolhapuri Bhushan Award 2000, Sangli Bhushan Award 2000, Omega Excellence Lifetime Achievement Award 2000, Filmfare Lifetime Achievement Award 2001, Dada Saheb Phalke Award 2001, Dayawati Modi Award 2001, BBC Mega Mela Lifetime Achievement Award 2002, Swaralaya Yesudas Award 2003, Living Legend Award, Fed. of Indian Chamber of Commerce and Industry 2004, MTV Immies 2005, Padma Vibhushan 2008, Freddie Mercury Award. *Address:* 1st Floor, Prabhu Kunj Apartment, Pedder Road, Mumbai 400 026, India (home). *Telephone:* (22) 64938070. *E-mail:* info@ashasrestaurants.com. *Website:* www .ashasrestaurants.com.

BIAZZI, Marco; Italian musician (guitar); b. 3 April 1977, Milan. *Career:* mem. metal band, Lacuna Coil 1999–. *Recordings include:* albums: In A Reverie 1999, Unleashed Memories 2001, Comalies 2002, Karmacode 2006, Shallow Life 2009, Dark Adrenaline (Female Metal Voices Fest Award for Best Album) 2012. *Current Management:* Riot Rock Management, 639 Dupont Street, Unit 216, Toronto, ON M6G 1Z4, Canada. *Website:* www.lacunacoil.it.

BIBB, Eric; American musician (guitar); b. 15 Aug. 1951, New York, NY; s. of folk singer Leon Bibb; m. Sari Matinlassi-Bibb. *Career:* grew up among artists of 1960s New York folk scene; relocated to Europe; worked as music teacher in Sweden; performed at folk and blues festivals around Europe; relocated to London 2002. *Recordings include:* albums: as solo artist or band leader: Rainbow People 1977, Songs For Peace 1982, Golden Apples Of The Sun 1983, Spirit And The Blues 1994, Good Stuff 1997, Me To You 1997, Home To Me 1999, Roadworks 2000, Just Like Love 2000, Painting Signs 2001, Natural Light 2003; with Cyndee Peters: Olikalikadant 1978, Collection 1993; with Bert Deivert: April Fools 1979, River Road 1980, Hello Stranger 1983; with Leon Bibb: A Family Affair 2002, A Ship Called Love 2005, Praising Peace 2006, Diamond Days 2006, Get Onboard 2008, Booker's Guitar 2009. *Current Management:* c/o Sandy Waring, Solo Music Management, 39 Ashley Road, Salisbury, Wilts., SP2 7DD, England. *Telephone:* 7799-116085 (mobile). *E-mail:* sandy@solomanagement.co.uk. *Website:* www.solomanagement.co .uk; www.ericbibb.com.

BICKERSTETH, John Dennis; British musician (piano, keyboards), singer and composer; b. 27 June 1954, Constantine, Cornwall, England. *Education:* choral scholar Truro Cathedral, studied with John Winter and Guillaume Ormond. *Career:* mem., Cruiser, Ian and The Muscletones, The Barneys, Ian Dunlop's Babylon Babies, Daniel Rovai and Friends; performances at Ton and Kirschen Theatre (Potsdam), Chip Bray Show (Amsterdam Lido); MD, Back On Stage, UFA Fabrik, Berlin; MD, Stewart and Ross; M'Toto; J B Band; Botticelli Angels; mem. Musicians' Union. *Recordings include:* album: Ian and The Muscletones. *Address:* Tregarth, Bissoe, Truro, Cornwall TR4 8RJ, England.

BICKNELL, Robert David, BMus; British singing teacher; b. 7 Dec. 1957, Jersey, St Helier, Channel Islands. *Education:* Goldsmiths Coll., Redroofs Theatre School. *Career:* many pantomimes; singing coach, Faking It (Channel 4), Celebrity Stars in Their Eyes (Granada), The Lesley Garrett Show (BBC) Hidden Talents (LWT), Popstars (Germany) and (Switzerland), Liverpool Nativity (BBC), Manchester Passion (BBC) Richard and Judy (Granada) Goldies band By Royal Appointment (BBC), Born to Shine (ITV), The Voice UK (BBC); Robert's celebrity clients include Natalie Imbruglia, Kirsty Young, Denise Welsh, Tim Vincent, Billy Bragg, Cheryl Baker, Ben Freeman, David Ginola, Josie Lawrence etc. *Television includes:* Robin Hood, Lenny Henry Show, Doctor Who, Saturday Night Live, as singing coach on The Big Breakfast (Channel 4) 6 months, 1–3 (Sky One), DJ Kat Show, Richard & Judy, Looking Good (BBC), O Zone (BBC), This Morning (ITV), The Big E (Channel 4), Give Your Mate a Break (Granada), Popstars (Germany), Popstars (Switzerland), Spiegel TV (Germany), MTV (Germany). *Recordings include:* Love Can Build a Bridge, The Matchmaker (film), No Angels (Germany) (Double-Platinum Disc), Tears (Switzerland) (Double-Gold Disc). *Contributions to:* Daily Mail, The Stage and publs in Germany and Switzerland. *Address:* 69 Lower Flat, Acre Lane, London, SW2 5TN, England. *Telephone:* (20) 7733-8669. *E-mail:* mail@robertbicknell.co.uk. *Website:* www .singingteacher.co.uk.

BIDDLE, Elizabeth (Liz) Rosina, BA, MA; Welsh record producer, artist agent and musician (bassoon); *Senior Partner, Upbeat Management*; b. 29 April 1952, Pontypridd. *Education:* Aberystwth Univ., Guildhall School of Music and Drama, City Univ. *Career:* Dir of Music, Comprehensive School 1984; bassoon tutor at Christ's Hospital, Horsham 1984–99; Founder and Sr Partner, Upbeat Man. 1984–, Upbeat Recordings 1984–; writer for Musical Opinion for three years; mem. International Artist Man.'s Asscn, British Phonographic Industry. *Recordings include:* Producer for The Temperance Seven, Terry Lightfoot, Ken Colyer, Carey Blyton, Lonnie Donegan. *Address:* Upbeat Management, Larg House, Woodcote Grove, Coulsdon, Surrey, CR5 2QQ, England (office). *E-mail:* liz@upbeat.co.uk (office). *Website:* www.upbeat .co.uk (office).

BIDER, Les; American music industry executive. *Education:* Wharton Business School, Univ. of Pennsylvania. *Career:* joined Warner Bros. Music, Chair. 1987–2005, CEO Warner/Chappell Music Inc. 1988–2005; Exec.-in-Residence of media investment co., Elevation Partners 2006–. *Address:* Elevation Partners, 70 E 55th Street, 12th Floor, New York, NY 10022, USA (office). *Telephone:* (212) 317-6555. *Fax:* (212) 317-6556. *E-mail:* info@ elevation.com (office). *Website:* www.elevation.com (office).

BIEBER, Justin; Canadian singer; b. (Justin Drew Bieber), 1 March 1994, London, Ont.; s. of Jeremy Bieber and Pattie Mallette. *Career:* discovered by Scooter Braun after posting videos of his performances on YouTube 2008, came to the attention of Usher who signed him to a recording contract; professional solo artist 2009–; tours: Urban Behavior Tour 2009, My World Tour 2010–11, Believe Tour 2012–13. *Recordings include:* albums: My World 2.0 (Teen Choice Award for Best Pop Album 2010, American Music Award for Favorite Pop/Rock Album 2010, Billboard Music Award for Top Pop Album 2011, Juno Award for Pop Album of the Year 2011) 2009, Under the Mistletoe 2011, Believe (American Music Award for Favorite Pop/Rock Album 2012) 2012, Complete My Journals 2013, Purpose 2015; singles: Where Are Ü Now 2015, What Do You Mean? 2015. *Honours:* Queen Elizabeth II Diamond Jubilee Medal 2012; numerous awards including: TRL Award for Best Int. Act 2010, Teen Choice Awards for Best Male Artist, for Best Breakout Male Artist 2010, MTV Video Music Awards for Best New Artist 2010, for Best Male Video (U Smile) 2011, MTV Europe Music Awards for Best Male 2010, 2011, 2012, 2013, 2014, 2015, for Best Push Act 2010, for Best Pop Act 2011, 2012, for Best World Stage Performance 2012, for Best North America Act 2015, for Biggest Fans 2015, for Best Look 2015, for Best Collaboration (for Where Are Ü Now?, with Skrillex and Diplo) 2015, Young Hollywood Awards Newcomer of the Year 2010, American Music Awards for Artist of the Year 2010, 2012, for Favorite Pop/Rock Male Artist 2010, 2012, for T-Mobile Breakthrough Artist 2010, for Collaboration of the Year (for Where Are Ü Now?) 2015, BRIT Award for Best Int. Breakthrough Act 2011, Juno Fan Choice Awards 2011, 2012, Billboard Music Awards for Top New Artist 2011, for Top Social Artist 2011, 2012, for Top Streaming Artist 2011, for Top Digital Media Artist 2011, Billboard Music Awards for Top Male Artist 2013, for Top Social Artist 2013, 2014, 2015, Much Music Award for Favorite Artist 2014, Grammy Award for Best Dance Recording (for Where Are Ü Now?) 2016. *Current Management:* c/o Scott Braun, SB Projects, Worldwide Plaza, 825 Eighth Avenue, 28th Floor, New York, NY 10019, USA. *E-mail:* info@scooterbraun.com. *Website:* scooterbraun.com; www.justinbiebermusic.com.

BIET, Remi; French musician (saxophones, flute); b. 1 Oct. 1958, Dieppe; m. Brigitte Tailleux; two d. *Education:* Ecole Normale d'Instituteurs. *Career:* tours worldwide and TV appearances; mem. UMJ. *Recordings:* ONJ: Badault; A Plus Tard, 1991; Mingus, Monk Ellington, 1992; Bouquet Final, 1993, Par delà le miroir 1998, L'Ode d'Ulysse 2007. *Address:* 31 rue de Neuvillette, 76240 Le Mesnil-Esnard, France. *Telephone:* (2) 35-80-48-93. *E-mail:* remi .biet@sfr.fr. *Website:* remi.biet.free.fr.

BIG BOI; American rap artist; b. (Antoine André Patton), 1 Feb. 1975, Savannah, Ga. *Education:* Tri-City High School, Atlanta. *Career:* mem., Outkast (with Andre 3000, aka Dré) 1992–, signed to LaFace Records; designed Outkast Clothing line; also solo artist; numerous collaborations including Mary J. Blige, Cutty, Missy Elliott, Fantasia, Janelle Monáe, Raekwon, Kelly Rowland, Trick Daddy. *Recordings include:* albums: with Outkast: Southernplayalisticadillacmuzik 1994, ATLiens 1996, Aquemini 1998, Stankonia 2000, Big Boi And Dre Present... 2002, Speakerboxxx/The Love Below (Grammy Awards for Album of the Year, Best Rap Album 2004, American Music Award for Best Rap/Hip-Hop Album 2004) 2003, My Life In Idlewild 2005, Idlewild 2006; solo: Sir Lucious Left Foot: The Son of Chico Dusty 2010, Vicious Lies and Dangerous Rumors 2012. *Honours:* Source Award for Best New Rap Group of the Year 1995, American Music Awards for Best Hip Hop/R&B Group 2003, 2004, Grammy Award for best urban/ alternative performance 2004, World Music Awards for Best Group, Best Pop Group, Best Rap/Hip-Hop Artist 2004, MTV Europe Best Group Award 2004, Best Song Award, Best Video Award (both for Hey Ya) 2004. *Current Management:* c/o Career Artist Management, 9350 North Civic Center Drive, Beverly Hills, CA 90210, USA. *Telephone:* (310) 776-7640. *Fax:* (424) 230-7839. *Website:* camanagement.com. *Address:* c/o Epic Records, 550 Madison Avenue, New York, NY 10022, USA (office). *Telephone:* (212) 833-8000 (office). *Website:* www.epicrecords.com (office); www.outkast.com; www.bigboi.com.

BIG SEAN; American rapper, singer and songwriter; b. (Sean Michael Leonard Anderson), 25 March 1988, Santa Monica, Calif. *Education:* Detroit Waldorf School, Cass Technical High School. *Career:* raised in Detroit, Mich.;

signed to Kanye West's GOOD Music label 2007; collaborations with numerous artists including 2 Chainz, Chiddy Bang, John Legend, Wiz Khalifa, Nicki Minaj, Nas, Rick Ross, Kanye West, Pharrell Williams. *Recordings include:* mixtapes: Finally Famous: The Mixtape 2007, UNKNOWBIGSEAN 2009, Finally Famous Volume 3: BIG 2010, Detroit (BET Hip Hop Award for Best Mixtape 2013) 2012; albums: Finally Famous (BET Hip Hop Award for Album of the Year 2011) 2011, Hall of Fame 2013, Dark Sky Paradise 2015. *Honours:* BET Award for Best New Artist 2012, BET Award for Best Collaboration, Duo or Group (for Blessings, with Drake and Kanye West) 2015, MTV Video Music Award for Best Video with a Social Message (for One Man Can Change the World, with Kanye West and John Legend) 2015. *Current Management:* c/o Roc Nation, 9348 Civic Center Drive, Beverly Hills, CA 90210, USA. *Telephone:* (310) 975-6854. *Website:* rocnation .com; uknowbigsean.com.

BIG YOUTH; Jamaican reggae DJ and record company executive; b. (Manley Augustus Buchanan), 19 April 1949, Kingston. *Career:* fmr cab driver and mechanic; leading reggae DJ, Kingston during 1970s; Founder, Negusa Nagast and Augustus Buchanan record labels 1973. *Recordings include:* albums: Screaming Target 1973, Reggae Phenomenon 1974, Dreadlocks Dread 1975, Natty Cultural Dread 1976, Hit The Road Jack 1976, Isaiah First Prophet Of Old 1978, Everybody Skank: the Best Of Big Youth 1980, Some Great Big Youth 1981, The Chanting Dread Inna Fine Style 1983, Live at Reggae Sunsplash 1984, A Luta Continua 1985, Manifestation 1988, Jamming In the House Of Dread 1991, Higher Ground 1997; also appears on: Escape Artist 1981, Holy Ground 1990, Legends Of Reggae Music 1998.

MR BIGGS (see Isley, Ronald)

BÍLÁ, Lucie; Czech singer; b. (Hana Zaňáková), 7 April 1966, Otvovice; d. of Josef Zaňák; fmr partner Petr Kratochvíl; one s.; fmr partner Vaclav Noid Barta. *Career:* co-owner Theatre Ta Fantastika, Prague; has toured throughout Western Europe; has performed in charity concerts in Czech Repub. *Recordings include:* albums: Missariel 1993, Lucie Bílá 1994, Hvezdy jako hvezdy (Stars as Stars) 1998, Uplne naha (Totally naked) 1999, Jampadampa 2003, Laska je laska (Love is love - Best Of) 2004, Koncert (Concert) 2006, Woman 2007, Bang Bang! 2009, Bíle Vánoce 2010, Modi 2012, Recital 2013. *Theatre includes:* Les Misérables 1992, Dracula 1995, Rat-Catcher 1996, Joan of Arc (Thalia Prize) 2000, Love is Love 2004, Elixir Zivota 2006, Carmen 2008, Aida 2012, Addams Family 2014. *Films include:* Horká kaše 1988, Divoká srdce 1989, Volná noha 1989, Praákům, těm je hej 1990, Zkoušové obdobi 1990, Fontána pro Zuzanu 2 1993, Princezna ze miejna 1994, King Ubu 1996, Čas dluhů 1998, V peřině, Babověsky. *Publications include:* Nyní ji to vim (Now I Know It Already) 1999, Jen kratka navsteva potesi (Just short visit delights) 2007. *Honours:* numerous awards including Czech Grammy Prize 1992–96, Most Popular Singer (Czech Repub.) 1994–2007, Czech Musical Acad. Prize 1997, Czech Nightingale Trophy 1996–2004, 2007–14. *Address:* Agentura 44, s.r.o. Karlova 8, 110 01 Prague 1, Czech Republic. *E-mail:* produkce@luciebila.com (office). *Website:* www.luciebila.com.

BÍLÁ, Věra; Czech singer; b. 22 May 1954, Rokycany, Bohemia; d. of Karol Giňa; m.; one adopted s. *Career:* singer with Romany band Kale; subject of documentary Cerna a bila v barve (Black and White in Colour) 1999, concerts include Hollywood Bowl 1999, Central Park, New York 2000, Barbican Centre, London 2001, Cinque d'Hiver, Paris 2002, Womad, Transmusical de Rennes Festival, Printemps de Bourges Festival. *Recordings include:* Me la na kamav (I Don't Want Her), Ara, more (Go Away), Miro rom hin ternoro (My Husband is Too Young), Ma dara (Don't Be Afraid), Rom-Pop 1996, Kale Kalore 1999, Queen of Romany 2000, Rovana 2001, C'est Comme Ca 2005.

BILAL; American singer and songwriter; b. (Bilal Sayeed Oliver), 23 Aug. 1979, Philadelphia, Pa. *Education:* Mannes Music Conservatory, New York. *Career:* approached by Moyo Entertainment, moved to Brooklyn and started gigging; demo tape heard by Erykah Badu, contributed to her Mama's Gun album; mem., Soulaquarians collective, which includes Talib Kweli, D'Angelo, Jill Scott, Questlove, James Poyser; collaborations with Common, Erykah Badu, Mos Def, Guru. *Recordings include:* albums: First Born Second 2001, Love for Sale 2006, Airtight's Revenge 2010, A Love Surreal 2013. *Website:* www.bilalmusic.com.

BILÁN, Díma; Russian singer, songwriter and actor; b. 24 Dec. 1981, Ust-Dzheguta, Karachay-Cherkessia. *Education:* Gnesins Musical Coll. *Career:* placed fourth, Russian/Latvian New Wave festival 2002; released debut album 2003; represented Russia at Eurovision Song Contest, placed second 2006, Winner 2008; collaborated with Anastacia on the song Safety 2010. *Recordings:* albums: Ya Nochnoy Huligan (I'm a Night Hooligan) 2003, Na Beregu Neba (At the Sky's Shore) 2004, Vremva reka (Time-River) (Muz-TV Award for Album of the Year 2007, ZD Award for Album of the Year 2007) 2006, Protiv pravil (Against the Rules) 2008, Believe (ZD Award for Album of the Year 2009) 2009, Mechtatel (Dreamer) 2011. *Films:* Not Born Beautiful 2005, Club 2006, The Adventures of Pinocchio 2006, Star Break 2007, Kingdom of Crooked Mirrors 2007, Goldfish 2008, Pinocchio 2009, Theatre of the Absurd 2011. *Honours:* numerous awards including: ZD Awards for Sexiest Artist 2003, for Singer of the Year 2004, 2009, for Soloist of the Year 2007, 2008, Golden Gramophone Awards 2005, 2006, 2007, 2008, MTV Russia Music Awards for Best Performer 2005, for Best Artist 2005, 2006, 2007, for Best Song 2006, 2007, for Best Video 2008, for Best Singer 2008, for Pop Project 2008, MTV Europe Music Awards for Best Russian Act 2005, 2006, 2007, 2008, 2009, 2010, 2012, for Best European Act 2012, World Music Award for Best

Selling Russian Artist 2006, Glamour Magazine Awards for Man of the Year 2006, 2009, Honoured Artist of Kabardino-Balkaria 2006, of Chechnya 2007, of Ingushetia 2008, Muz-TV Awards for Song of the Year 2007, for Best Performer 2007, 2008, 2010, 2011, 2012, for Best Ringtone 2008, for Best Video 2009, for Best Song 2009, People's Artist of Kabardino-Balkaria Award 2008. *Address:* c/o Universal Records Russia, Kutuzovskiy prospect 36, bld. 23, office 418, 121170 Moscow, Russia (office). *Website:* www.universalmusic.ru/ en (office); www.bilandima.ru/enghtml.

BILEZIKJIAN, John, AA, BA; American musician (oud) and composer; b. 1 Feb. 1948, Calif.; m. Helen Louise Bilezikjian. *Education:* Los Angeles Valley Coll. *Career:* mem. Musicians' Union; collaborations with Leonard Cohen, Robert Palmer, Luis Miguel, Judy Frankel, Brothers of the Baladi, Armen Chakmakian Roupen Altiparmakian and Andy Madadian. *Compositions include:* Preludio Primo, Jemilleh, Eastern Fantasy, Ansial, Taksim Opus 10, Taksim Opus 20, The Land of Noah's Ark, I Love You Baby; music for film, television and stage: Mission Impossible, I Spy, Apples Way, The Postman Always Rings Twice, Anastasia, Schindler's List, The Prince of Egypt. *Recordings include:* America's Oud Virtuoso, The Art Of The Oud, The Neo Classical Oud, The Magic Of John Bilezikjian, Music Of the Armenian Diaspora, Dantz Fever, Armenian Connection, Moonlight Sonata, 1001 Nights, Dream Of Scheherazade, Sirocco, Tapestry Of the Dance, Sounds of the Middle East, The Magic Of. *Publication:* Hal Leonard Oud Method 2006. *Address:* Dantz Records, PO BOX 2434, Laguna Hills, CA 92654-2434, USA (office). *Telephone:* (949) 581-5664. *E-mail:* DantzRec@aol.com. *Website:* www .dantzrecords.com.

BILGI, Furkan; Turkish musician (kemençe); b. 1979, Adana. *Education:* Istanbul Tech. Univ. (ITU) Turkish Music State Conservatory. *Career:* mem. Yeni Türkü 1997–; concerts world-wide. *Recordings by band:* albums (does not play on all): "Yeni", Her Dem Yeni, Telli Telli Remixes, Süper Baba (film music), Ask Yeniden, Rumeli Konseri, Külhani Şarkilar, Vira Vira, Yeşilmişik?, Günebakan: Dünyanin Kapilari, Akdeniz Akdeniz. *E-mail:* furkan@ yeniturku.com. *Website:* www.yeniturku.com.

BILLINGTON, Scott Thomas; American record producer and musician (harmonica); *Vice-President, A&R, Rounder Records;* b. 27 Oct. 1951, Melrose, Mass; m. Johnette Downing. *Career:* produced more than 100 albums of roots-orientated music for labels including Rounder, Columbia, Sire, Real World, In-Akustik; Vice-Pres., A&R, Rounder Records; mem. Nat. Acad. of Recording Arts and Sciences, Broadcast Music, Inc. (BMI). *Recordings include:* Alright Again (Clarence Gatemouth Brown), Pictures and Paintings (Charlie Rich), Voodoo (The Dirty Dozen Brass Band), Turning Point (Buckwheat Zydeco), One Foot in the Blues (Johnny Adams) 1996, Beau Jocque and the Zydeco Hi-Rollers 1996, You'll Never Get to Heaven (Bill Morrissey) 1996, R&B = Ruth Brown 1997, The Story Of My Life (Irma Thomas) 1997, Sing It! (Irma Thomas, Marcia Ball and Tracy Nelson) 1998, The B-3 and Me (Davell Crawford) 1998, A Good Day for the Blues (Ruth Brown) 1999, Allons en Louisiane – The Rounder Records Guide to Cajun Music, Zydeco and South Louisiana 2000, Down Home on Dog Hill (Boozoo Charis) 2001, From Daybreak to Heartbreak (Blues Company) 2003, Tangle Eye, Alan Lomax's Southern Journey Remixed 2004, Daily Bread 2005, After the Rain (Irma Thomas) 2006, Simply Grand (Irma Thomas) 2008, My Dusty Road (Woody Guthrie) 2009, Unlock Your Mind (Soul Rebels) 2012, Twenty Dozen (Dirty Dozen Brass Band) 2012. *Honours:* two Grammy Awards, Grand Prix Du Disque, two W. C. Handy Awards, Offbeat Magazine's Producer of the Year Award, New Orleans 1997, Sweet Soul Music Award, Poretta (Italy) 2008, The Blues Foundation's Keeping the Blues Alive Award for Producer, Best of the Beat (New Orleans) Lifetime Achievement Award 2012. *E-mail:* sbillington@ rounder.com (office). *Website:* www.scottbillington.net.

BILOUS, Edward, BM, MM, DMA; American composer and conductor. *Education:* Manhattan School of Music, Juilliard School. *Career:* joined Juilliard School, Music, Drama, Liberal Arts Department, Lincoln Center Institute; Co-chairman of Literature, Music Department at Juilliard; Artistic Director of Music Advancement Program; Director, Consultant of Music Education programme by Juilliard and Berkley Learning Technologies. *Compositions:* film, television music: Le Bain; Tribeca; Anna Sorror; Urban Fairy Tales; The Last Romantic; Theme for Monaco Film Festival, 1993; Orchestrator, arranger for: Carnegie Hall Tribute to Pete Townshend (with Roger Daltrey, Alice Cooper, Sinead O'Connor, The Spin Doctors, Eddie Vedder); CD-ROM tour of Beauborg Museum, Pompidou Center, Paris; Juilliard Music Adventure; Educational Adventure Game; Circus!. *Films:* as composer: Sleepaway Camp 1983, Minor Details 1998, Dead broke 1998, Mixing Nia 1998, The Naked Man 1998, Just One Time 1999, Scottsboro: An American Tragedy 2000, Two of a Kind 2004, Kylie Goldstein, All American 2005, Shoot Down 2007, Where the Ocean Meets the Sky 2008, All About Prints 2009. *Television:* as composer: The American Experience 2001–08, Frontier House 2002, Frontline 2002–03, Carrier 2008. *Honours:* Joseph Machlis Award for Excellence, Juilliard School; Best Public Service Announcement Award (Elephant Slaughter), Cannes, 1989. *E-mail:* Rachel@cubeventures.com. *E-mail:* Edward@edwardbilous.com. *Website:* www.edwardbilous.com.

BILY, Antonin; Czech composer, arranger and musician (piano); b. 7 May 1939, Prague; m. Jitka Bila 1972, two s. *Education:* Conservatory of Prague and J. Jezek Conservatory. *Career:* pianist and composer, Traditional Jazz Studio, Prague 1960–; teacher and Head of Composition/Conducting Section,

J. Jezek Conservatory, Prague 1986–; mem. Asscn of Music Artists and Scientists; Czech Music Society; Czech Jazz Society. *Compositions:* Metamorphoses of Time, 1986; Modus Vivendi, 1991; Fine Stagione; A Town So Strange; On the Seventh Floor. *Recordings:* some 20 albums with Traditional Jazz Studio, some recorded with Benny Waters, Tonny Scot, Albert Nicholas, Beryl Breyden. *Honours:* first prize Jazz Festival Düsseldorf 1968, first prize International Contest of Composition for Jazz Bigband, Barga, Italy 1989. *Address:* Korunní 29, 120 00 Prague 2, Czech Republic.

BIMBIM; Indonesian musician (drums); b. (Bimo Setiawan Almachzumi Sidharta), 25 Dec. 1966, Jakarta; s. of Sidharta M. Soemarno and Iffet Vececha; m. Reny Setiawati; one d. *Education:* Perguruan Cikini High School. *Career:* formed band while at school, playing mainly Rolling Stones songs 1983; band adopted name Slank in late 1980s; best-selling Indonesian rock band of 1990s; band formed own record label and promotions co., Pulau Biru Productions and tabloid Koran Slank. *Recordings include:* albums: Suit...-Suit...He...He... 1991, Kampungan 1992, Piss! 1993, Generasi Biru 1994, Minoritas 1995, Lagi Sedih 1996, Tujuh 1997, Mata Hati Reformasi 1998, 999 09 1999, Virus 2001, Satu Satu (Best Pop Rock Album, SCTV Music Awards 2003) 2003, Road to Peace 2004, Plur 2004, Slankissme 2006, Slow but Sure 2007, Anthem for the Broken Hearted 2008. *Video:* Terbunuh Sepi (Favourite Video Clip, dari VMI—Video Musik Indonesia 1994/1995), Best Video Clip 1995/1996. *Honours:* BASF Best Selling Album for 1990/1991 Award for Rock category, BASF Best Selling Album for 1991/1992 Award for Pop Rock category, BASF Best Selling Album for 1993/1994 Award for Rock/Alternative category, BASF Best Selling Album for 1994/1995 for Rock category (Double Platinum Album Category), Best Song and Best Selling Album and Best Pop/Rock Band, Anugerah Musik Indonesia (AMI) Awards 1998, Best Rock Album, AMI Awards 1999, Best Video Clip Model and Best Video Clip Director, MTV Indonesia Music Awards 2002, Best Rock Song, AMI Awards 2002, World Peace Music Award 2003, Best Rock Album, Best Rock Group, Best Rock Album Producer, AMI Awards 2003, Best Rock Album, Best Rock Song, AMI Awards 2004. *Current Management:* Jl. Potlot 14, Duren Tiga, Jakarta 12760, Indonesia. *Telephone:* (21) 7919-6819. *Fax:* (21) 7919-3437. *E-mail:* mgt@slank .com. *Website:* www.slank.com.

BINDING, Philip Robert; British composer, producer, writer and musician (piano, synthesizer); *Managing Director, Boom! Music Ltd;* b. 20 March 1960, Barry, South Wales; m. Helen Garnett 1990; one d. *Education:* Ravensbourne Art Coll. *Career:* sound engineer 1980–91; formed Boom Productions with Simon Moore, producing music for TV, film 1991, Man. Dir Boom! Music Ltd 1999–; mem. Musicians' Union, British Acad. of Songwriters, Composers and Authors, Performing Right Soc., Mechanical-Copyright Protection Soc. *Compositions:* TV themes, incidental music includes Gladiators, The West Wing, Saturday Night Live, International Gladiators, You Bet, Pop Quiz, What's My Line, ITV Sport, Missing, Expert Witness, Strange But True, Beadle's About, Love and Marriage, ITV Promotions, World Cup '98 theme tune, C5 News, Moment of Truth, Gladiators, Survivor, HTV News. *Address:* Boom! Music Ltd, Tanglewood, 16 Blackwood Close, West Byfleet, Surrey, KT14 6PP, England (office). *E-mail:* info@boommusic.tv (office). *Website:* www .boommusic.tv (office).

BINDZI, Lucien; Cameroonian artist manager and music promoter; *Founder and President, Institut Culturel, Scientifique et Environnemental Bindzi Mimbolo;* b. Emana. *Education:* industrial electricity diploma. *Career:* fmr artist manager and music promoter; Founder and Pres., Africa Music Int. 1986, F. Bindzi Mibolo Schools of Art 1997, renamed Institut Culturel, Scientifique et Environnemental Bindzi Mimbolo 2007–. *Address:* Institut Bindzi Mimbolo, 15 rue Charles Gounod, 56100 Lorient, France (office). *Telephone:* 2-97-83-38-75 (office). *Fax:* 2-97-83-38-75 (office). *E-mail:* institut .bindzi.mimbolo@hotmail.fr (office); gaelle.tonje@laposte.net (office).

BINESH-PAJOOH, Shahkar, PhD; Iranian rap artist, composer, academic and poet; b. 13 Dec. 1972, Tehran. *Career:* solo artist; musical collaborations with Alireza Assar, Shadmehr Aghili. *Recordings include:* albums: Banooyeh sharghi 1997, Eskenas 2000. *Publications:* I Like Your Hands 1999, Kafe naderi 2003, Eternity of a Kiss 2004. *E-mail:* info@shahkar.com; shahkar@shahkar.com. *Website:* www.shahkar.com.

BINGHAM, (George) Ryan; American singer, songwriter and musician (guitar); b. 31 March 1981, Hobbs, NM; m. Anna Axster. *Career:* Founder and performer with group The Dead Horses; composed multi-award winning song The Weary Kind for the film Crazy Heart 2009. *Film:* Crazy Heart (soundtrack and actor) 2009. *Recordings:* albums: Mescalito 2007, Roadhouse Sun 2009, Junky Star 2010; also appears on soundtrack to Crazy Heart (Golden Globe Award for Best Original Song, Academy Award for Best Original Song, Grammy Award, Annual Americana Music Asscn Award for Song of the Year 2010) 2009. *Honours:* Critics' Choice Award, Satellite Award, BMI Award. *Current Management:* c/o Kyle Wilensky, Creative Artists Agency, 2000 Avenue of the Stars, Los Angeles, CA 90067, USA. *Telephone:* (424) 288-2000. *Fax:* (424) 288-2900. *E-mail:* kwilensky@caa.com. *Website:* www.caa.com; www.binghammusic.com.

BINNS, Henry; British producer and remixer; b. 1971, London. *Career:* started as studio engineer; began remixing with pnr, Sam Hardaker, under the name Zero 7, later producing own material 1999–; collaborations with Sia Furler, Sophie Barker, Mozez; remixed Terry Callier, Radiohead, Lenny Kravitz, Lambchop, NERD; mem. PRS. *Recordings include:* albums: Simple Things 2001, Another Late Night 2002, When It Falls 2004, The Garden 2006,

Yeah Ghost 2009, We Are Born (with Sia) 2010, Before I Sleep (with Bo Bruce) 2013; singles: EP 1 1999, EP 2 2000, Destiny (featuring Sia and Sophie) 2001, I Have Seen (featuring Mozez) 2001, In the Waiting Line (featuring Sophie) 2001, Distractions (featuring Sia) 2002, Somersault 2004. *Honours:* Muzik Award for Best New Artist 2001. *Current Management:* Solar Management Ltd, Unit 10 Union Wharf, 23 Wenlock Road, London, N1 7SB, England. *Telephone:* (20) 7794-3388. *Fax:* (20) 7794-5588. *E-mail:* info@ solarmanagement.co.uk. *Website:* www.solarmanagement.co.uk; www.zero7 .co.uk.

BINSON, Bussakorn Sumrongthong, BA, MA, PhD, DPhil; Thai academic; *Professor of Music, Faculty of Fine and Applied Arts, Chulalongkorn University;* b. 29 Nov. 1962, Bangkok; d. of Thongplew Sumrongthong. *Education:* Chulalongham Univ., Univ. of York. *Career:* Bd of Graduate, Faculty of Fine and Applied Arts, Chulalongkorn Univ., later Assoc. Prof. of Music, currently Prof.; Co-Dir Urban Research Plaza Osaka City Univ. & Chulalongkorn Univ.; Liaison Officer, Int. Council of Traditional Music (Thailand); Dir Intermusic Center Thailand, Center of Excellence in Thai Music & Culture Chulalongkorn Univ. *Compositions include:* Hudan Mus-Javanese Piece On Thai Xylophone, Homnong Sakura: Composition for the New Millennium, The Thai and European Perspective Concert- Rapport of Thailand and Norway. *Recordings include:* Manmongkol. *Honours:* First Prize, Best Thai Xylophone Player 1984, Best Teaching Award 2010, SAGE Best Paper Award 2012. *Address:* Music Department, Faculty of Fine and Applied Arts, Chulalongkorn University, Phayathai, Bangkok 10330, Thailand (office). *Telephone:* (2) 218-4582 (office). *Fax:* (2) 249-8190 (office). *E-mail:* bsumrongthong@yahoo.com (office). *Website:* pioneer.chula.ac.th/~sbussako (office).

BIRCH, Robert Charles, (Rob B); British singer and rap artist; b. 11 June 1961, Nottingham. *Career:* Co-founder, Gee Street studio and record label; Founder-mem. Stereo MCs 1987–; numerous live performances with extended band and extra vocalists; numerous remixes, including U2, PM Dawn, Queen Latifah, Disposable Heroes of Hiphoprisy, Monie Love, Electronic, Madonna, Frozen, Jungle Brothers. *Recordings include:* albums: 33 45 78 1989, Supernatural 1990, Connected (BRIT Award for Best British Album 1994) 1992, Stereo MCs 1993, Deep Down and Dirty 2001, Paradise 2005, Double Bubble 2008, Emperor's Nightingale 2011. *Honours:* BRIT Award for Best British Group 1994. *E-mail:* info@stereomcs.com. *Website:* www.stereomcs .com.

BIRGÉ, Jean-Jacques Gaston; French composer, musician (keyboard, electronics, reed trumpet, Tenori-on, flute etc.), writer, film director and multimedia author; b. 5 Nov. 1952, Paris; one d. *Education:* IDHEC Diploma, Nat. Film School. *Career:* plays many different kinds of rare acoustic and electronic instruments; f. GRRR record label; live music on silent films, including Caligari, Fall of the House of Usher, Jeanne d'Arc, The Man With The Camera…, J'Accuse, Le K (with Richard Bohringer), Il Etait Une Fois La Fête Fotaine; The Extraordinary Museum (Japan), Jours de cirque (Monaco), EuroPrix (Austria), The Alphabet (CD-ROM) (Grand Prix Möbius Int. 2000, Prix Multimedia SACD 2000) 1999, Leonardo da Vinci's Dream Machine (iPad); mem. Un Drame Musical Instantané; Musical Dir The Evenings of Rencontres d'Arles de la Photographie, Plays with Vincent Segal, Sacha Gattino, Birgitte Lyregaard, Antonin-Tri Hoang, videast Jacques Perconte…. *Exhibition:* Nabaz'mob (Centre Pompidou, Paris, world tour). *Films:* La nuit du phoque 1974, The Sniper 1994, 12 shorts on USA 1968 tour détour deux enfants 2013. *Radio:* USA: Le complot, La peur du vide, Improvisation mode d'emploi. *Television:* Idir and Johnny Clegg a capella 1993. *Recordings:* Trop D'Adrénaline Nuit 1977, Rideau! 1980, A Travail Égal Salaire Égal 1981, Carnage 1985, L'Hallali 1988, Qui Vive? 1990, Kind Lieder 1991, Urgent Meeting 1992, Opération Blow Up 1993, Sarajevo Suite 1994, Carton (enhanced CD) 1997, Machiavel (enhanced CD) 1998, Défense De (also DVD) 2003, Establissement d'un ciel d'alternance (with poet Michel Houellebecq) 2007; 95 hours of unissued music (drame.org) 2011–13. *Publications:* La corde à linge (novel) 2011, USA 1968 tour détour deux enfants (novel) 2013. *Honours:* British Acad. Award for TV Arts 1994, Jury Prize at Locarno Festival for Sarajevo, A Street Under Siege (collective), First Prize CineKid, Netherlands 2000, Giga Maus, Germany 2000, First Prize, MMCA, Japan 2000, SCAM Prize for Best Internet Site (for Le Ciel est bleu) 2001–02, Narrow Cast Award 2002, Flash Festival Prix Spécial Centre Pompidou (for Flying Puppet) 2002, Senef Jury Prize 2003, Prix Interactive Création, SACD (for Somnambules.net) 2004, Prix Ars Electronica NetVision/Net Excellence Hon. Mention (for Somnambules.net) 2004, Prix de la Création Nouveaux Médias Videoformes, Prix Ars Eletronica Award of Distinction Digital Music 2009. *Address:* 60 rue René Alazard, 93170 Bagnolet, France (home). *Telephone:* 1-43-63-76-92 (home). *E-mail:* jjbirge@drame.org. *Website:* www.drame.org; www.nabazmob.com; www.somnambules.net; www.lecielestbleu.com; davincidream.surletoit.com.

BIRGISSON, Jón Þor (Jónsi); Icelandic singer and musician (guitar). *Career:* founder mem. and lead singer, Sigur Rós 1994–; co-founder, Jónsi & Alex 2003–; also solo artist 2009–; numerous tours. *Recordings include:* albums: with Sigur Rós: Von, Ágœtis Byrjun 2000, ( ) 2002, Takk... 2005, Hvarf-Heim 2007, Með Suð I Eyrum Við Spilum Endalaust 2008, Valtari 2012; DVD: Heima 2007; with Jónsi & Alex: Riceboy Sleeps 2009; solo: Go 2010. *Honours:* Shortlist Music Prize 2001. *Address:* c/o Smekkleysa Records, PO Box 1263, 121 Reykjavík, Iceland (office). *E-mail:* contact@jonsi.com (office). *Website:* www.sigur-ros.com; www.jonsiandalex.com; www.jonsi.com.

BIRKBY, Peter Richard; British composer and musician (percussion); b. 30 Nov. 1957. *Education:* Leeds College of Music. *Career:* numerous radio and television broadcasts; tours with Shirley Bassey; Vic Damone; Gene Pitney; Dave Willetts; Jesus Christ Superstar; mem. PRS, MCPS, Musicians' Union. *Compositions include:* over 80 pieces for percussion (solo and ensemble), six for orchestra, 20 for jazz orchestra. *Recordings:* Three Movements for Orchestra, Queen Elizabeth Hall, 1994; with own group, Legends: Special Edition, 1986. *Address:* PRBP, PO Box 7, South Kirkby, Pontefract, West Yorkshire WF9 3XJ, England. *Telephone:* (1977) 648645. *Website:* www.prbp .co.uk.

BIRKETT, Chris; British record producer, composer, musician (guitar) and singer; b. 14 April 1953, Aldershot, Hampshire; m. Janet Susan Hewett 1981; one s. one d. *Career:* guitarist with: Ann Peebles, Rufus Thomas, Gene Knight, Love Affair; singer with Omaha Sherif; producer for Sinead O'Connor, Buffy Sainte-Marie, Talitha MacKenzie; television: Wogan, Pebble Mill, BBC News; radio: Radio 1, GLR, Capital; mem PRS, MCPS, Musicians' Union. *Compositions include:* Albums: Men From The Sky 1993, Freedom 2009. *Recordings include:* as producer/mixer/writer: Sinead O'Connor: Nothing Compares 2U; solo: album: I Do Not Want, Kiss Of Life, Mandinka/Put 'Em On Me, Siedah Garrett, Copperhead Road, Steve Earle; with Five Star: Silk and Steel, Luxury Of Life, Love Letters/That Old Devil, Alison Moyet, Nothing But Flowers, Talking Heads, Movements, Osibisa, Johnny Come Lately, Pogues, Holding Up Half The Sky: Voices Of Celtic Women; also with artists: Sting, Buffy Sainte-Marie, Laurie Freelove, Darden Smith, Cry Sisco, The Bible, Randy Remet, Hernandez, Mango Grove, Mr Big, Ice Cold In Alice, Richard Jon Smith, John Otway, Roman Holiday, Precious Wilson, John Kongos, Siobhan McCarthy, Mondino, The Soul Brothers, Talitha MacKenzie, Guo Yue, Jyoti Hirota, Etran Finatawa. *Publications include:* articles in Billboard, Studio Engineer. *Honours:* Ampex Golden Reel Awards: Gold Star and Mango Grove, platinum discs: Nothing Compares 2U, Sinead O'Connor. *Address:* Chris Birkett Production, 12, rue Adolphe Chérioux, 92130 Issy Les Moulineaux, France (office). *Telephone:* 6-25-47-68-77 (office). *Fax:* 4-77-13-85-68 (office). *E-mail:* chrisbirkett@free.fr (office); chrisbirkett@yahoo.com. *Website:* chrisbirkett.free.fr.

BIRKIN, Jane, OBE; French (b. British) actress and singer; b. 14 Dec. 1946, London; d. of David Birkin and Judy Campbell; m. John Barry (divorced); one d.; one d. with the late Serge Gainsbourg (Charlotte Gainsbourg); one s. with Jacques Doillon. *Theatre includes:* Carving a Statue 1964, Passion Flower Hotel 1965, La Fausse suivante 1985, L'Aide-Mémoire 1993, Créatrice et Interprète de Oh! pardon tu dormais 1999, Electra by Sophocles. *Films include:* The Knack 1965, Blow Up 1966, Les Chemins de Katmandou 1969, Je t'aime moi non plus 1976, Mort sur le Nil 1978, Jane B par Agnès V 1988, Oh pardon! Tu dormais 1992, Noir comme le souvenir 1995, La fille d'un soldat ne pleure jamais 1999, The Last September 2000, Ceci est mon corps 2001, Reines d'un jour 2001, Merci Docteur Rey 2002, Mariées mais pas trop 2003, Boxes (actor and dir) 2007, 36 Views from the Pic Saint-Loup 2009, Thelma, Louise et Chantal 2010, Twice Born 2012, Quai d'Orsay 2013. *Recordings include:* albums: Je t'aime (Beautiful Love) 1970, Lolita Go Home 1975, Ex Fan des Sixties 1978, Baby Alone in Babylone 1983, Lost Song 1987, Au Bataclan 1987, Je Suis Venue Te Dire Que Je M'en Vais 1992, Jane B., Vol. 1 1993, Concert Integral à l'Olympia 1997, Je t'aime moi non plus 1998, Quoi Générique TV 1998, Jane Birkin Coffret 1998, Ballade de Johnny 1998, A la Légère 1998, Jane en Concert au Japan 2001, Jane Birkin et Serge Gainsbourg 2001, Arabesque 2003, Rendez-Vous 2004, Fictions 2006, Enfants d'Hiver 2008; singles: (songs by Serge Gainsbourg) C'est la vie qui veut ça, La Baigneuse de Brighton, Je t'aime moi non plus (Le Métier trophy 1970), Di doo dah, Le Canari est sur le balcon, Baby Song, Si ça peut te consoler, Tu n'es pas le premier garçon, Lolita Go Home, Love for Sale, La Ballade, Ex-fan des sixties, Baby Alone in Babylone (Grand Prix du disque, Acad. Charles-Cros). *Publication:* Oh pardon! Tu dormais 1999. *Honours:* Chevalier des Arts et des Lettres; Gold Leaf Award Canada 1968, Triomphe du cinéma 1969, 1973, Victoire de la musique (for best female singer) 1992. *Current Management:* c/o Olivier Gluzman, Les Visiteurs du Soir, 40 rue de la Folie Regnault, 75011 Paris, France. *Telephone:* (1) 44-93-02-02. *Fax:* (1) 44-93-04-40. *E-mail:* ogluzman@visiteurdusoir.com. *Website:* www.visiteursdusoir.com; www .janebirkin.net/uk.

BIRO, Daniel Andrew; French composer, songwriter and musician (piano); b. 29 Jan. 1963, Johannesburg, South Africa. *Education:* Jazz Conservatory, Monaco and Nice University, France. *Career:* as keyboard player, world tours with: The Truth, 1987; Big Bam Boo, 1989; bandleader, songwriter with L'Orange, 1993–; arranger, musicals by Henry Lewis include: Joan of Kent; The End of The World Show; co-founder, Lust, multi-arts performance organization; record label, Sargasso Records (experimental new music); mem. Musicians' Union, SACEM, SPNM. *Compositions:* for dance: Beauty and The Beast, 1992; Desert, 1995; for film: Lessons In How To Wear Red, 1994; Mu, 1995; other: Through The Mirror, 1993; The Pinocchio Tapes, 1994; Beba In White, 1995. *Recordings include:* albums: Soho Square, 1993; The Comparative Anatomy Of Angels, 1996; Elegant Enigmas, 1999, L'Orange 2002, The Long Journey Home 2004, Mysteries of the Revolution 2007, A Still, Thin Sound 2009. *Address:* c/o Sargasso, PO Box 221, Baldock, SG7 6WZ, England. *Telephone:* (20) 8458-0440. *E-mail:* info@sargasso.com. *Website:* www .danielbiro.com.

BIRTLES, Gary; British musician (saxophone), singer and music promoter; b. 10 June 1955, Leicester, England; two s. *Career:* singer, own band, The Swinging Laurels; saxophone session player for Fun Boy 3; mem. brass section, The Beautiful South 1990–2007; singer in country/pop band, Yellow-belly; numerous television appearances; mem. PRS. *Recordings:* singles with The Swinging Laurels: Peace Of Mind 1980, Rodeo 1982, Lonely Boy 1983, Zoom 1984. *Website:* www.beautifulsouth.co.uk; www.thedonkeybar.com.

BISCUIT BOY (see Heaton, Paul David)

BISHOP, Michael Joseph; American recording engineer and record producer; b. 14 June 1951, Santa Monica, Calif.; m. Wendy LaTessa 1979; two d. *Career:* record producer, recording engineer 1972–; mem. Audio Engineering Soc., Nat. Acad. of Recording Arts and Sciences (NARAS), MPGA, American Soc. of Composers, Authors and Publrs (ASCAP), AQHA, NRHA. *Recordings include:* as recording engineer: Play That Funky Music, Wild Cherry 1986, Live At Carnegie Hall, Liza Minnelli 1987, The Sound Of Music, Cincinnati Pops Orchestra 1988, Big Band Hit Parade, Dave Brubeck/Cab Calloway/Gerry Mulligan/Doc Severensen 1988, To Diz with Love, Dizzy Gillespie 1992, The Great Fantasy Adventure Album, Cincinnati Pops Orchestra 1995, Seven Steps to Heaven, Ray Brown Trio 1996, Come On In This House, Junior Wells 1996, Live at Buddy Guys, Junior Wells 1997, Copland: Music Of America, Cincinnati Pops Orchestra 1997, Tribute at Town Hall, Oscar Peterson 1996, So What's New?, Dave Brubeck 1998. *Honours:* eight Grammy Awards.

BISMUT, Michel; French composer and musician (contrebass); b. 20 April 1954, Tunis, Tunisia; m. Agnes Berger 1992, one s. one d. *Education:* Classical Conservatoire. *Career:* jazz festivals and clubs throughout France, also UK, Germany, Spain, Israel; television appearances and broadcasts on national radio; mem. Société des auteurs, compositeurs et éditeurs de musique (SACEM). *Recordings:* Socco 1991, UR 1996, Porte Bonheur 2002. *Address:* Compagnie Bismut, Condorcet Créations, 42, rue Adam de Craponne, 34000 Montpellier, France. *Telephone:* 4-67-58-63-89. *Fax:* 6-70-71-33-23. *E-mail:* cie -bismut@orange.fr. *Website:* www.compagnie-bismut.com.

BISSET, John, BFA; British musician (guitar); b. 3 Nov. 1960, Stockport; two s. *Education:* Ravensbourne Coll. of Art. *Career:* improviser, composer and arranger; work with London Electric Guitar Orchestra; toured England with Billy Jenkins; appearances at Relay, live shows; performances at 2:13 Club run with Burkhard Beins, 1994–98; Brush 'n' Strings with Rhodri Davies and Marcus Heesch, improvised music with live painting; Tha Arc, English tour, 1999; Go! daily radio show for children compiled by John Bisset and presented with children; arranger and performer, Happy Happy; arranger of Purcell for dance piece Vivre d'Amour; invited artist, Real Time Music Meeting, Hamburg, 1998; tours with Burkhard Beins on drums; Fairplay '98 Festival; mem. PRS. *Recordings include:* Flying Fish (without wings); Funny Old World; Ralay OOO Random Play 2; Kneel Down Like A Saint Gorilla and Stop; Dervish; Holly; 13 Lumps Of Chease, with London Electric Guitar Orchestra, Chapel/Kapell 2001, Smithy 2004.

BIXLER-ZAVALA, Cedric; Mexican/American singer, songwriter and musician (guitar); b. 4 Nov. 1974, Calif.; m. Chrissie Carnell 2009; two s. *Career:* Founding mem. At the Drive-In 1993–2001, 2011–12; Founding mem. The Mars Volta 2001–12; Founding mem. Zavalaz 2013–. *Recordings include:* albums: with At the Drive-In: Acrobatic Tenement 1996, In Casino Out 1998, Relationship of Command 2000; with The Mars Volta: De-Loused in the Comatorium 2003, Frances the Mute 2005, Amputechture 2006, The Bedlam in Goliath 2008, Octahedron 2009, Noctourniquet 2012. *Honours:* Grammy Award for Best Hard Rock Performance (for Wax Simulacra) 2009. *Website:* www.themarsvolta.com.

BJARNI; Icelandic musician (guitar). *Career:* mem. rock band, Mínus 1998–. *Recordings include:* albums: Hey Johnny! 1999, Jesus Christ Bobby 2001, Halldor Laxness 2004, The Great Northern Whalekill 2008. *Address:* c/o Smekkleysa Records, PO Box 1263, 121 Reykjavík, Iceland. *Website:* www .minusonline.com.

BJELLAND, Kat; American singer and musician (guitar); b. 8 Dec. 1963, Woodburn, Ore.; one s. *Career:* Founder-mem. of all-girl rock groups, Babes in Toyland 1987–97; currently mem. Katastrophy Wife. *Recordings include:* albums: with Babes in Toyland: Spanking Machine 1990, To Mother (mini album) 1991, Fontanelle 1992, Peel Sessions 1992, Painkiller 1993, Nemesisters 1995, Devil (compilation) 2000, Viled 2000, Natural Babe Killers 2000, Minneapolism 2001; with Katastrophy Wife: Amusia 2001, All Kneel 2004. *E-mail:* arockj@gmail.com. *Website:* www.katastrophywife.com.

BJERRE, Jonas; Danish singer; b. 21 Sept. 1976. *Career:* Founder mem., Mew 1996–; the band formed record label, Evil Office 2000–; mem. Apparatjik 2008–. *Recordings include:* albums: with Mew: A Triumph For Man 1997, Half The World Is Watching Me 2000, Frengers (Danish Music Critics Award for Album of the Year) 2003, Mew And The Glass Handed Kites 2005, No More Stories 2009; with Apparatjik: We Are Here 2010, Square Peg in a Round Hole 2012; solo: Skyscraper 2011. *Honours:* Danish Music Critics Award for Band of the Year 2003, MTV Europe Music Award for Best Danish Act 2005. *E-mail:* hq@evil-office.net. *Website:* www.evil-office.net; www.mewsite.com.

BJÖRK; Icelandic singer, songwriter, musician, record producer and actress; b. (Björk Guðmundsdóttir), 21 Nov. 1965, Reykjavík; m. Thór Eldon (divorced); one s., one d. *Career:* first solo release aged 11; fmr singer for various Icelandic groups, including Exodus, Tappi Tikarras; singer, Kukl, later renamed The Sugarcubes 1986–92; solo artist 1992–. *Films:* Dancer in the Dark (Cannes Film Festival Best Actress Award 2000) 2000, Drawing

Restraint 9 2005, Anna and the Moods (voice) 2007. *Recordings include:* albums: with The Sugarcubes: Life's Too Good 1988, Here Today, Tomorrow Next Week 1989, Stick Around For Joy 1992, It's It 1992; solo: Björk 1977, Debut 1993, Post 1995, Telegram 1996, Homogenic 1997, Selmasongs 2000, Vespertine 2001, Dancer in the Dark 2001, Greatest Hits 2002, Family Tree 2002, Medúlla 2004, Army of Me: Remixes and Covers (charity album) 2005, Drawing Restraint 9 (OST) 2005, Volta 2007, Voltaic 2009, Biophilia 2011, Vulnicura 2015. *Honours:* BRIT Award for Best Int. Newcomer 1994, MTV European Music Award for Best Int. Female Artist 1994, 1996, 1997, Q Inspiration Award 2005, MOJO Inspiration Award 2007, Polar Music Prize 2010. *Current Management:* Quest Management, 36 Warple Way, Unit 1D, London, W3 0RG, England. *Telephone:* (20) 8749-0088. *Fax:* (20) 8749-0080. *E-mail:* info@quest-management.com. *Website:* www.quest-management.com. *Address:* c/o Nonesuch Records, Warner Music Group, 75 Rockefeller Plaza, New York, NY 10019, USA (office). *Telephone:* (212) 275-2000 (office). *E-mail:* info@nonesuch.com (office). *Website:* www.nonesuch.com (office); www.bjork .com.

BJÖRKENHEIM, Raoul Melvin; American musician (guitar); b. 11 Feb. 1956, Los Angeles, Calif.; m. Päivi Björkenheim (Määttä); one s. *Education:* Helsinki Conservatory, Berklee Coll. of Music, Boston. *Career:* Founder-mem. of own jazz groups, Arbuusi and Roommushklahn 1980–83; mem. Edward Vesala's Sound and Fury 1984–86; with Sielun Veljet 1989; mem. Krakatau 1987–, Scorch Trio 1998–; tours throughout Finland. *Compositions include:* for big band: Other Places, Some, Primal Mind; for symphony orchestra: Whales, Ballando; for electric guitar orchestra: Apocalypso. *Recordings include:* with Edward Vesala: Bad Luck Good Luck, Kullervo, Lumi; with Krakatau: Ritual 1988, Alive 1990, Volition 1992, Matinale 1994; with Scorch Trio: Luggunt 2004, Brolt 2008; with Markus Holkko: From Circuits, with Love 2010; with Anders Nilsson and Gerald Cleaver: Kalabalik 2010. *Honours:* Finnish Jazz Federation Yrjö Award 1984, Emma Prize for Best Jazz Record (for Volition) 1993. *E-mail:* rosebud@raoulbjorkenheim.com. *Website:* www.raoulbjorkenheim.com.

BJORNS, Siggi; Icelandic musician (guitar, harmonica); b. 26 June 1955. *Career:* fmr fisherman 14 years; professional musician 1988–; performed in clubs and halls in more than 20 countries; television appearances in Denmark and Iceland; radio broadcasts in Denmark, Iceland, Norway and New Zealand; mem. Dansk Musikerforbund (Danish Musicians' Union), KODA, GRAMEX, DJBIA. *Compositions:* Bubbinn; Kotturinn; Beitningartremmi; One Gentle Touch. *Recordings:* albums: Blues On Both Sides, 1993; Live At Sorens, 1993; Bisinn a Trinidad, 1994; Smoke 'n' Perfume, 1995; Road, 1998. *Address:* Brammersgade 2A-3, 8000 Århus C, Denmark. *E-mail:* siggibook@hotmail .com. *Website:* www.siggib.com.

BJØRNSTAD, Ketil; Norwegian musician (piano), composer and writer; b. 25 April 1952, Oslo. *Education:* studied piano with Amalie Christie and Robert Riefling, Oslo, further studies in London and Paris. *Career:* professional debut with Oslo Philharmonic 1969; performed with experimental Svein Finnerud Trio 1971; music and literary critic, Aftenposten 1972–98; first recording of own music Åpning 1973; collaborations with numerous Norwegian and int. musicians from fields of jazz, folk, rock, avant-garde and classical music, including Ole Paus, Jon Christensen, Terje Rypdal, David Darling, Cornelis Vreeswijk, Randi Stene, Lars Anders Tomter, Anneli Drecker, Nora Taksdal, Lill Lindfors; has toured in Europe, Asia and USA and performed at jazz festivals in Frankfurt, Neuwied, Ingolstadt, Hamburg, Stans, Vienna, Voss, Molde, Modena, Ravenna, Nancy, Porto, Montreal, Shanghai, Warsaw and London; UK tour with Contemporary Music Network 2006; has published over 20 novels, also poetry, essays, literary and music criticism. *Recordings include:* Åpning 1973, Berget det blå (Spellemannsprisen) 1974, Tredje dag 1975, Lise Madsen, Moses & de Andre (with Ole Paus) 1975, Finnes du noensteds ikveld 1976, Selena 1977, Musikk for en lang natt 1977, Leve Patagonia 1978, Svart Piano 1979, Tidevann 1980, Och människor ser igen (with Lill Lindfors) 1980, 30-års-krigen (with Stavangerenseblet) 1981, Engler i sneen 1982, Bjørnstad/Paus/Hamsun 1982, Aniara (with Lindfors/ Fristorp) 1983, Mine dager i Paris 1983, Preludes Vol. 1 1984, Människors makt (with Lill Lindfors) 1985, Natten (with Sissel I. Andersen) 1985, Preludes Vol. 2 1986, Three Ballets 1987, Karen Mowat-suite 1988, The Shadow (with Randi Stene) 1990, Odyssey 1991, Rift 1991, Messe for en såret jord (with Randi Stene and Lars Anders Tomter) 1992, Løsrivelse (with Kari Bremnes) 1993, Water Stories 1993, For den som elsker 1994, Sanger fra en klode 1995, Salomos Høysang 1995, The Sea 1995, Haugtussa 1996, The River (with David Darling) 1997, Reisetid 1997, The Sea II 1997, Ett Liv (with Lill Lindfors) 1998, The Rosenborg Tapes Vol. 1 1998, The Rosenborg Tapes Vol. 2 1999, Himmelrand – Tusenårsoratoriet 1999, Epigraphs (with David Darling) 2000, Grace 2001, Old 2001, The Nest 2003, Seafarer's Song 2004, Floating 2005, Rainbow Sessions 2007, Devotions 2007, Life in Leipzig 2008, The Light: Songs of Love and Fear 2008, Coastlines (with Lill Lindfords) 2008, Remembrance 2010, Hvalenes Sang 2010, Night Song 2011, Early Piano Music 2011. *Compositions:* Minotauros (ballet) 1997, IZZAT (youth opera) 2006. *Film soundtracks:* Engler i sneen 1983, Forever Mozart 1996, Nous sommes tous encore ici 1997, Emporte moi 1999, Museum of Modern Art 1999, Histoire du Cinéma 1999, Eloge d'Amour 2001, Trofast 2004, Ae Fond Kiss 2005, Samotnosc W Sieci 2006. *Plays:* Ildlandet (musical) 1984, Spill 1995, Forestillinger 1997, Minotauros 1997. *Publications include:* fiction: Nattsvermere 1974, Kråker og Krigere 1975, Pavane 1976, Vinterbyen 1977, Landet på andre siden 1979, Bingo 1981, Oda! 1983, Det personlige motiv

1985, G-moll-balladen 1986, Oppstigning fra det usynlig 1988, Stormen 1989, Skumringsmulighetene 1990, Villa Europa 1992, Historien om Edvard Munch 1993, Barnevakt 1994, Drift 1996, Drømmen om havet 1996, Veien til Dhaka 1997, Nåde (Riksmålsprisen) 1998, Fall 1999, Ludvig Hassels tusenårsskifte 2000, Jæger 2001, Mannen som gikk på jorden (jtly) 2002, Tesman 2003, Til Musikken 2004, Elven 2007, Damen i Dalen 2009, De udødelige (novel) 2011, Drømmemesteren - Bendik Riis 2011, Belonging 2011, Verdens Ende (novel) 2012; poetry: Alene ut 1972, Nærmere 1973; non-fiction: Reisen til Gallia (essays, with Ole Paus) 1998, Flammeslukeren (biog.) 2005, Liv Ullmann: Livslinjer (biog.) 2005, Historier om sårbarhet (with Catherine Jacobsen) 2007, Elven 2007, Kolbein Falkeid - et naerbilde (biog.) 2008, Damen i Dalen 2009, De udødelige 2011. *Honours:* Priz des Lecteurs, France 2008. *Current Management:* Kjell Kalleklev Management, Georgernes Verft 3, 5011 Bergen, Norway. *Telephone:* 55-55-76-30. *Fax:* 55-55-76-31. *E-mail:* kjell@kalleklev .no. *Website:* www.kalleklev.no; www.ketilbjornstad.com.

BJOSSI; Icelandic musician (drums). *Career:* mem. rock band, Mínus 1998–. *Recordings include:* albums: Hey Johnny! 1999, Jesus Christ Bobby 2001, Halldor Laxness 2004, The Great Northern Whalekill 2008. *Address:* c/o Smekkleysa Records, PO Box 1263, 121 Reykjavík, Iceland. *Website:* www .minusonline.com.

BLACHMAN, Thomas; Danish musician (drums), composer, bandleader, producer and label manager; b. 2 April 1963, Copenhagen; s. of Henning Blachman and Annie Blachman. *Education:* Berklee Coll. of Music, USA. *Career:* Co-founder jazz quintet, Page One; tours of Europe, USA 1986–90; played drums for Lee Konitz, Joe Henderson; solo artist 1991–. *Recordings include:* albums: with Page One: Beating Bop Live 1988, Live At Ronnie Scott's 1989; solo: Love Boat 1991, Blachman Meets Al and Remee 1994, Blachman Introduces Standard Jazz and Rap Vol. 1, Billie Koppel 1995, Caroline Henderson 1995, Shiny Shoes and a Stiffy 1999. *Television:* judge on The X Factor 2008–, Blachman (series) 2013–, Mentor 2013. *Publication:* The Colossal Human (co-author) 2008. *Honours:* three Grammy Awards 1991, 1995. *E-mail:* thomas@blachman.com (office). *Website:* www.blachman.com.

BLACK, Barry; British musician (drums, percussion); b. 1 July 1950, Newcastle upon Tyne, England; m. Barbara Ann; one s. one d. *Education:* LTCL, LGSM. *Career:* mem., John Miles Band, 1973–83; tours of Europe, USA, Canada; support tours with: Elton John; Fleetwood Mac; Aerosmith; Jethro Tull; Tour with Beckett (later renamed Back Street Crawler); 2 albums, with Splinter; television appearances; mem. PRS, Equity, Musicians' Union. *Compositions:* Do It Anyway, John Miles; Madness Money and Music, Sheena Easton; Take My Love and Run, The Hollies. *Recordings:* all John Miles albums and singles, up to early 1980s; Barry Black, 1995; Tragic Animal Stories, 1997. *Address:* c/o Alias Records, 10153 1/2 Riverside Drive, Suite 115, Toluca Lake, CA 91602, USA. *E-mail:* alias@aliasrecords.com. *Website:* www .aliasrecords.com.

BLACK, Charlie; American country music songwriter; b. Cheverly, MD. *Career:* staff writer, Terrace Music, Nashville 1970–; songwriter, Warner Chappell Music, 1977–88; own company, Five-Bar-B Songs, 1989–; songs recorded by: Roy Orbison; Anne Murray; Paul Anka; Dan Seals; Kenny Rogers; K. T. Oslin; Eddy Raven; Bobby Bare; Bellamy Brothers; Charlie Rich; mem. ASCAP Southern Advisory Board. *Compositions:* Anne Murray: Shadows In The Moonlight; A Little Good News; Blessed Are The Believers; Reba McEntire: You Lie; K. T. Oslin: Come Next Monday; T. G. Shepard: Slow Burn; Strong Heart; Bellamy Brothers: Do You Love As Good As You Look; Tommy Overstreet: I Don't Know You Anymore; Earl Thomas Conley: Honor Bound; Gary Morris: 100% Chance of Rain. *Honours:* Country Music Writer of Year, SESAC, 1979; Country Music Writer of Year, ASCAP 1983, 1984; Elected to NSAI Songwriters Hall of Fame, 1991. *Address:* 1618 16th Avenue S, Nashville, TN 37212, USA.

BLACK, Clint; American singer, songwriter and producer; b. 4 Feb. 1962, USA; m. Lisa Hartman 1991. *Career:* television appearance in an episode of Wings; numerous live performances. *Films:* as actor: Maverick 1994, Going Home 2000, Anger Management 2003, Flicka 2 2010. *Recordings:* Killing Time, 1989; Put Yourself In My Shoes, 1990; The Hard Way, 1992; No Time To Kill, 1993; One Emotion, 1994; Nothin' But the Taillights, 1997; D'Lectrified, 1999, Spend My Time 2004, Christmas with You 2004, Drinkin' Songs and Other Logic 2005, The Love Songs 2007. *Honours:* CMA's Horizon Award, 1989; CMA's Top Male Vocalist, 1990; AMA's Favourite New Country Artist, 1990; Music City News: Star of Tomorrow, Album of the Year, 1990; ACM's Album of the Year, Single of the Year; Best New Vocalist; Best Male Vocalist, 1990. *Address:* c/o Sony Music Entertainment, 555 Madison Avenue, 10th Floor, New York, NY 10022-3211. *Telephone:* (615) 301-4300. *Website:* www .sonymusic.com; www.clintblack.com.

BLACK, Don, OBE; British lyricist; b. (Donald Blackstone), 21 June 1938, London; s. of Morris Blackstone and Betsy Blackstone; m. Shirley Berg 1958; two s. *Education:* Cassland Road School, London. *Career:* writer, NME 1955; lyric writer 1960–; worked with Charles Aznavour, John Barry, Elmer Bernstein, Ron Grainer, Marvin Hamlisch, Christopher Hampton, Maurice Jarre, Quincy Jones, Michel Legrand, Andrew Lloyd Webber, Henry Mancini, Charles Strouse, Jule Styne; mem. and Chair. BAC&S 1986–94. *Compositions:* songs: To Sir With Love, I'll Put You Together Again, Walk Away, Ben (with Walter Scharf) 1972; musicals: Billy 1974, Tell Me On Sunday 1980, The Little Prince and the Aviator 1982, Song and Dance 1982, Aspects of Love 1989, Sunset Boulevard 1993, The Goodbye Girl 1997, Bombay Dreams 2001,

Romeo and Juliet 2002, Dracula 2002, Bonnie and Clyde 2009, Stephen Ward The Musical 2013; title songs to films: Thunderball 1965, Born Free (Acad. Award 1966) 1966, To Sir With Love 1967, True Grit 1969, Diamonds Are Forever 1971, The Man With The Golden Gun 1974, The Italian Job, Tomorrow Never Dies, The World Is Not Enough, The Worst Witch 1986. *Honours:* Hon. DArts (City of London Univ.) 2005; Golden Globe, six Ivor Novello Awards, two Tony Awards, Sunset Boulevard 1995, Platinum, Gold, Silver discs, Ivor Novello Acad. Fellowship 2009; inducted into Songwriters Hall of Fame 2007. *Current Management:* c/o John Cohen, Clintons Solicitors, 55 Drury Lane, Covent Garden, London, WC2B 5RZ, England. *E-mail:* donlyric@aol.com. *Website:* www.donblack.co.uk.

BLACK, Frances; Irish singer; b. 25 June 1960, Dublin; m. Brian Allen, one s. one d. *Education:* Rathmines College. *Career:* mem., Arcady, Woman's Heart Tour; toured with Kieran Goss; solo career; tours of USA, Australia, England, Ireland. *Recordings include:* albums: with The Black Family: The Black Family, 1986; Time For Touching Home, 1988; What A Time, 1996; with Arcady: After the Ball, 1991; with Kieran Goss: Black and Goss, 1994, 1995; solo: Talk to Me, 1994; The Sky Road, 1995; Smile on Your Face, 1996; Don't Get Me Wrong, 1998, How High the Moon 2003, This Love Will Carry 2006. *Honours:* Most Popular Irish Entertainer; National Entertainment Awards, 1995; Best Female, 1995, 1996, IRMA. *Telephone:* (87) 9831617. *E-mail:* brianallen@ireland.com. *Telephone:* (87) 7584249. *E-mail:* francesblackpr@eircom.net. *Website:* www.frances-black.net.

BLACK, Frank, (Black Francis); American singer, songwriter and musician (guitar); b. (Charles Michael Kitteridge Thompson), 6 April 1965, Long Beach, Calif. *Education:* Univ. of Massachusetts. *Career:* formed the Pixies with Joey Santiago, as 'Black Francis' 1986–93, 2004–; recorded demo, The Purple Tape 1987; solo artist as 'Frank Black' 1992–, some releases with band The Catholics. *Recordings include:* albums: with the Pixies: Come On Pilgrim (EP) 1987, Surfer Rosa 1988, Doolittle 1989, Bossanova 1990, Trompe Le Monde 1991, Death To The Pixies 1987–1991 1997, Live At The BBC 1998, Complete B-Sides 2001, Pixies (DVD) 2004, Wave of Mutilation: The Best of the Pixies 2004, Indie Cindy 2014; solo: Frank Black 1993, Teenager Of the Year 1994, The Cult Of Ray 1996, Frank Black and The Catholics 1998, Pistolero 1999, Dog In The Sand 2001, Black Letter Days 2002, The Devil's Workshop 2002, Show Me Your Tears 2003, Honeycomb 2005, Fastman/Raiderman 2006, Christmass 2006, Bluefinger 2007, Svn Fngrs 2008, The Golem 2010, NonStopErotik 2010, Abbabubba 2011, Paley & Francis 2011. *Current Management:* Richard Jones, Key Music Management Limited, 56A Bramhall Lane South, Bramhall, Stockport, SK7 1AH, England. *Telephone:* (161) 440-0670. *E-mail:* contact@keymusicmanagement.com. *Website:* www.keymusicmanagement.com; www.pixiesmusic.com.

BLACK, Jake, (The Very Reverend Dr D. Wayne Love); British vocalist. *Career:* Founder mem. and vocalist Alabama 3 1988–; band known as A3 in USA. *Recordings include:* albums: Exile on Coldharbour Lane 1997, La Peste 2000, Power In The Blood 2002, The Last Train To Mashville 2003, Outlaw 2005, M.O.R. 2007, Revolver Soul 2010, Essential (with Nas). *Honours:* American Society of Composers, Authors and Publishers (ASCAP) Award 2004. *Website:* www.alabama3.co.uk.

BLACK, Mary; Irish folk singer and songwriter; b. 23 May 1955, Dublin; m. Joe O'Reilly; three c. *Career:* singer with traditional and contemporary Irish groups; fmr mem. De Dannan; solo artist; numerous tours. *Recordings include:* albums: Mary Black 1983, Collected 1984, Without The Fanfare 1985, The Black Family, with the Black Family 1986, By The Time It Gets Dark 1987, Time For Touching Home (with the Black Family) 1989, No Frontiers 1989, Babes In The Wood 1991, The Best Of Mary Black 1991, The Collection 1992, The Holy Ground (Irish Rock Music Award for Best Album 1994) 1993, Circus 1995, Looking Back 1995, One and Only 1997, Shine 1997, Song For Ireland 1999, Songs Of The Irish Whistle 1999, Speaking With The Angel 2000, The Full Tide 2006, Twenty-five Years—Twenty-five Songs: The Best of Mary Black 2008, Stories from the Steeples 2012. *Honours:* Irish Ind. Arts Award 1983, Nat. Entertainment Award for Best Female Artist 1986, Irish Rock Music Award for Best Female Artist 1987, 1988, 1992, 1994, 1996, Hot Press Award for Best Irish Solo Artist 1993, Nat. Entertainment Award for Personality of the Year 1993, Belfast Telegraph EMA Award for Best Irish Solo Artist 1994, Irish Music Magazine Award for Best Female Folk Artist 2000, 2001, 2005, Irish Music Magazine Award for Best Contemporary Female Artist 2003, The Irish Post Lifetime Achievement Award 2006. *Current Management:* c/o Joe O'Reilly, The Music Plant, Unit F5, South City Business Park, Whitestown Way, Dublin 24, Ireland; c/o Paul Charles, Asgard, 125 Parkway, London, NW1 7PS, England. *E-mail:* pc@asgard-uk.com. *Website:* www.mary-black.net.

BLACK FRANCIS (see Black, Frank)

BLACK JAZZ CHRONICLES (see Beedle, Ashley)

BLACK SHELLS (see Tomiie, Satoshi)

BLACKBURN, Paul, (Blackie); British musician (guitar, bass, percussion, omnichord); b. 1974, Southport. *Career:* Founding mem., Gomez 1996–; numerous concerts, festival, radio and television appearances. *Recordings include:* albums: Bring It On 1998, Liquid Skin 1999, Abandoned Shopping Trolley Hotline 2000, In Our Gun 2002, Out West: Live at the Fillmore 2005, How We Operate 2006, A New Tide 2009, Whatever's on Your Mind 2011. *Honours:* Mercury Music Prize 1998. *Current Management:* c/o Jason Colton,

Red Light Management, 321 East Main Street, Charlottesville, VA 22902, USA. *E-mail:* gomez@gomeztheband.com (office). *Website:* www.gomeztheband.com.

BLACKMON, Odie, BA; American songwriter, producer and academic; *Lecturer in Music, Blair School of Music, Vanderbilt University;* b. El Dorado, Ark. *Education:* Middle Tennessee State Univ. *Career:* writer of numerous country music hits, songs have been recorded by Lee Ann Womack, George Strait, Rachel Proctor, Gary Allan, Cyndi Thomson, Jason McCoy, Aaron Tippin, Tammy Cochran; production work with Jason McCoy, Brice Long, Gary Allan; currently Lecturer in Music, Blair School of Music, Vanderbilt Univ.; fmr mem. Songwriting Faculty, William's Syndrome Camp, Vanderbilt Kennedy Center. *Compositions include:* I May Hate Myself In The Morning, Learning To Fall, Days Like This, She'll Leave You With A Smile, Let's Be Naughty (And Save Santa The Trip), I'm the One, Baby I Will, I Don't Look Back, There Goes The Boy, Broke Down, And I Love You, I Believe. *Honours:* Country Music Asscn (CMA) Award for Single of the Year (I May Hate Myself In The Morning by Lee Ann Womack) 2005, three Performance Awards, American Soc. of Composers, Authors and Publrs (ASCAP), three Achievement Awards, Nashville Songwriters Asscn International (NSAI). *Address:* Vanderbilt University, Blair School of Music, 2400 Blakemore Avenue, Nashville, TN 37212-3499, USA (office). *Telephone:* (615) 322-7651 (office). *E-mail:* odie.blackmon@vanderbilt.edu (office). *Website:* blair.vanderbilt.edu/bio/odie-blackmon (office).

BLACKMORE, Richard (Ritchie) Hugh; British rock musician (guitar), composer, producer and arranger; b. 14 April 1945, Weston-Super-Mare, Avon, England. *Education:* Thompson School of Music. *Career:* session musician, toured with Mike Dee and The Jaywalkers 1961–62, Screaming Lord Sutch and his Savages 1962, Gene Vincent, Jerry Lee Lewis, The Outlaws, The Musketeers, The Dominators, The Wild Boys 1964, Neil Christian's Crusaders, The Roman Empire, Mandrake Root 1967; Foundermem. rock group Deep Purple 1968–74, 1984–94, Rainbow 1975–84, 1994–98, Blackmore's Night 1995–; mem. ASCAP, BMI, PRS. *Recordings include:* albums: with Deep Purple: Shades Of Deep Purple 1968, The Book Of Taliesyn 1969, Deep Purple 1969, Concerto For Group And Orchestra 1969, Deep Purple In Rock 1970, Fireball 1971, Machine Head 1972, Who Do We Think We Are? 1973, Burn 1974, Stormbringer 1974, Perfect Strangers 1985, Fireworks 1985, The House Of Blue Light 1987, Slaves And Masters 1990, The Battle Rages On 1992; with Rainbow: Ritchie Blackmore's Rainbow 1975, Rising 1976, On Stage 1977, Long Live Rock 'n' Roll 1978, Down To Earth 1979, Difficult To Cure 1981, Straight Between The Eyes 1982, Bent Out Of Shape 1983, Stranger in Us All 1998; with Blackmore's Night: Shadow Of The Moon 1998, Under A Violet Moon 1999, Fires At Midnight 2001, Minstrels And Ballads 2001, Past Times With Good Company 2003, Ghost Of A Rose 2003, Castles And Dreams (DVD) 2005, Village Lanterne 2005, Winter Carols 2006, Paris Moon 2007, Secret Voyage 2008, Autumn Sky 2010. *Address:* c/o Carole Stevens, Blackmore Productions, PO Box 735, Nesconset, NY 11767-0735, USA. *Telephone:* (631) 979-8199. *Fax:* (631) 979-6987. *E-mail:* mnstrelhal@aol.com. *Website:* www.blackmoresnight.com.

BLACKSTOCK, Narvel Wayne; American artist manager and entertainment company executive; b. 31 Aug. 1956, Fort Worth, Tex.; m. Reba McEntire 1989; four c. (three from previous marriage). *Career:* personal Man.: Pres., Starstruck Entertainment, Nashville 1988–; mem. Nat. Acad. of Recording Arts and Sciences (NARAS), Country Music Asscn, Acad. of Country Music. *Address:* Starstruck Entertainment, 40 Music Square West, Nashville, TN 37203, USA (office). *Telephone:* (615) 259-5400 (office). *Fax:* (615) 259-5401 (office). *Website:* www.starstruck.net (office).

BLACKSTONE, Richard; music industry executive; *Chief Creative Officer for North America, BMG Rights Management.* *Education:* attended law school. *Career:* produced music for TV programmes; Dir of Business Affairs, Zomba Publishing co. 1989, later apptd Head of Creative and Business Affairs, then Pres. 2002–05; Chair. and CEO Warner/Chappell Music (part of Warner Music Group—WMG) 2005–07; Sr Adviser to the Chair. and CEO of WMG, Edgar Bronfman Jr. 2007–10; Chief Creative Officer for North America, BMG Rights Management 2010–. *Address:* c/o BMG Rights Management (US) LLC, 6 East 32nd Street, 11th Floor, New York, NY 10016, USA (office). *Telephone:* (212) 561-3000 (office). *E-mail:* info.us@bmg.com. *Website:* www.bmgrights.com.

BLACKWELL, Chris; British entertainment company executive; b. 22 June 1937, London, England. *Career:* Founder, Island Pictures, Mango Records; Founder and Chair. Island Records 1962–97 (sold to Polygram); issued masters from Jamaican producers; signings to Island include Jimmy Cliff, Bob Marley, Millie Small, Spencer Davis Group, Steve Winwood, John Martyn, Robert Palmer, Nick Drake, Cat Stevens, Free, Mott The Hoople, Spooky Tooth, Fairport Convention, B-52's, Toots and The Maytals; Founder audio/visual entertainment co. Palm Pictures 1998–. *Honours:* Order of Jamaica 2004; named most influential UK-based industry exec., Jamaican Musgrave Medal 2003, Music Week Awards 2009, inducted in the Rock and Roll Hall of Fame 2001. *Address:* Palm Pictures, 110 East 25th Street, New York, NY 10010, USA (office). *Telephone:* (646) 790-1211 (office). *Website:* www.palmpictures.com (office).

BLACKWOOD, Sarah; British singer; b. Halifax, England. *Career:* mem., Dubstar 1994–2000, 2010–; mem. Client 2002–. *Recordings include:* albums: with Dubstar: Disgraceful 1995; Goodbye 1997, Make It Better 2000; with

Client: Client 2003, City 2004, Heartland 2007, Command 2009, Authority 2014. *E-mail:* info@dubstar.com. *Website:* www.dubstar.org.uk; www.eblackwood.com.

BLADES, Jack; American singer and musician (bass guitar); b. 24 April 1954, Palm Desert, CA. *Career:* mem., Night Ranger, 1981–88, 1996–; numerous live concerts; mem., Damn Yankees, 1989–94; mem. of side project, Shaw Blades (with Tommy Shaw), 1995–. *Recordings include:* albums: with Night Ranger: Dawn Patrol, 1982; Midnight Madness, 1983; Seven Wishes, 1985; Big Life, 1987; Man In Motion, 1988; Live In Japan, 1990; Neverland, 1997; Seven, 1998, Hole in the Sun 2007; with Damn Yankees: Damn Yankees, 1991; Don't Tread, 1992; with Shaw Blades: Hallucination, 1995, 7 Deadly Zens, 1998, Influence 2007; solo: Jack Blades 2004; with Tak Matsumoto Group: TMG I 2004. *Honours:* Motor City Music Award for Outstanding National Rock Pop Single, 1992. *Website:* www.nightranger.com.

BLADES, Rubén, MA; Panamanian singer, bandleader, composer, actor and fmr government official; b. 16 July 1948, Panama City; m. Luba Mason. *Education:* Univ. of Panama, Harvard Law School, USA. *Career:* singer, Conjunto Latino 1966–67, Los Salvajes del Ritmo 1967–69; Asst, Legal Dept, Nat. Bank of Panama 1973–74; moved first to Miami 1974, then to New York; joined Ray Barreto's band 1975, later with Guarare; worked with Willie Colón 1976–81; mem., Fania All-Stars 1976–80; songwriter for numerous Latin artists during late 1970s; leader, Son del Solar 1983–93; collaborated with Editus, and Editus Ensemble, from Costa Rica 1999–2003; Minister of Tourism of Panama 2004–09; currently sings backed by Roberto Delgado and Orchestra, from Panama. *Film appearances include:* The Last Fight 1983, Crossover Dreams 1985, Critical Condition 1987, Fatal Beauty 1987, The Milagro Beanfield War 1988, Homeboy 1988, Disorganized Crime 1989, Heart of the Deal 1990, Mo' Better Blues 1990, The Lemon Sisters 1990, The Two Jakes 1990, Crazy from the Heart 1991, The Josephine Baker Story 1991, Color of Night 1993, A Million to Juan 1994, Scorpion Spring 1996, The Devil's Own 1997, Chinese Box 1997, Cradle Will Rock 1999, All the Pretty Horses 2000, Gideon's Crossing (TV) 2000–01, Assassination Tango 2002, Once Upon a Time in Mexico 2003, Imagining Argentina 2003, Spin 2003, Secuestro Express 2005, Spoken Word 2009, For Greater Glory: The True Story of Cristiada 2012, Safe House 2012, The Counselor 2013, Hands of Stone 2014. *Recordings include:* albums: with Pete Rodríguez: De Panama a Nuevo York 1970; with Ray Barretto: Barretto 1975, Barretto Live: Tomorrow 1976; with Fania All-Stars: Tribute To Tito Rodríguez 1976, Anthology 2012; with Larry Harlow: La Raza Latina 1977; with Louie Ramírez: Louie Ramírez y Sus Amigos 1978; with Willie Colón: The Good, The Bad, The Ugly 1975, Metiendo Mano! 1977, Siembra 1978, Maestra Vida (parts 1 and 2) 1980, Canciones del Solar de los Aburridos 1981, The Last Fight 1982, Tras la Tormenta 1995; solo: Seis del Solar 1982, El Que La Hace La Paga 1983, Buscando America 1984, Mucho Mejor 1984, Crossover Dreams (film soundtrack) 1985, Escenas (Grammy Award) 1985, Agua de Luna 1987, Doble Filo 1987, Nothing But The Truth 1988, With Strings 1988, Antecedente (Grammy Award) 1988, Rubén Blades y Son del Solar... Live! 1990, Caminando 1991, Amor y Control 1992, Mucho Mejor 1995, La Rosa de los Vientos 1996, Tiempos 1999, Mundo (Grammy for Best World Music album and Latin Grammy Award for Best Contemporary Tropical Album) 2002, Across 110th Street (Latin Grammy Award for Best Salsa/Merengue Album 2005) 2005, Cantares del Subdesarrollo (Latin Grammy Award for Best Singer-Songwriter Album 2010) 2009, Todos Vuelven Parts 1 and 2 (Latin Grammy Award for Best Salsa Album 2011), Dos Clásicos 2011, Eba Say Aja 2012, Frente a Frente 2013, Tangos (Latin Grammy Award for Best Tango Album 2015, Grammy Award for Best Latin Pop Album 2015) 2014, Son de Panama (Latin Grammy Award for Best Salsa Album 2015, Grammy Award for Best Tropical Latin Album 2016) 2015. *Honours:* Dr hc (Berklee Coll. of Music) 2005, (Lehman Coll.), (Univ. of Berkeley); Pablo Neruda Order (Chile), Culture Order (Ecuador); ACE Award for Best Actor in Cable TV Industry (for Dead Man Out) 1989, Latin New York magazine Award for Composer of the Year 1976, ASCAP Founders Award 2005, Harry Chapin Humanitarian Award, ASCAP 2011. *Current Management:* c/o Relentless Agency, 261 East 134th Street, 2nd Floor, South Bronx, NY 10454, USA. *E-mail:* info@therelentlessagency.com. *Address:* Ruben Blades Productions Inc., 135 West 50th Street, 12th Floor, New York, NY 10020-1299, USA (office). *Website:* www.rubenblades.com.

BLAIR, David Chalmers Leslie, Jr, BA; American/British writer, composer and artist; b. 8 April 1951, Long Beach, Calif.; descendant of 13th Earl of Rothes, Scotland. *Education:* California State Univ. at Long Beach, Univ. of Aix-en-Provence; teaching certificate, English as a Second Language. *Career:* music has been performed in California and New York and worldwide in Denmark, Sweden, Ukraine and elsewhere. *Recordings:* 109 albums, including Her Garden of Earthly Delights, Sir Blair of Rothes, The Jack, Danish Pastry, San Francisco, Peace on the White House Lawn, Holocaust in Waco, Europe, St Luke Passion, The Seduction of Inga, My Only Link with Reality, Her Sexual Banquet, Journey of a Poor Man, Psychedelico Band, Brave New Girl, First Day of University. *Publications include:* Death of an Artist 1982, Vive la France 1993, Death of America 1994, Mother 1998, Evening in Wisconsin 2001, The Girls (& Women) I Have Known 2001, A Small Snack Shop in Stockholm-Sweden 2002, Beautiful Women – Flags of the World (large print series). *Address:* 19331 105th Avenue, Cadott, WI 54727, USA (home). *Telephone:* (715) 703-9671 (home).

BLAIS, Julien; Canadian musician (drums); b. 1979, Rimouski, Québec. *Career:* fmr mem. XLarge, Reset; mem. The Stills 2005–10; has toured with

Melissa auf der Maur, Loser, Megan McCauley; currently drummer for Coeur de Pirate, Jeremy Fisher, The Sainte Catherines. *Recordings include:* albums: with The Stills: Without Feathers 2005, Oceans Will Rise (Juno Award for Best Alternative Album of the Year 2009) 2008, Great Canadian Song Quest 2010, La Reine, Coeur de Pirate 2010, Coeur de Pirate 2011, Un matin Sans Bruit 2011. *Honours:* Juno Award for Best New Group of the Year 2009. *Website:* www.coeurdepirate.com.

BLAKE, Adam James Wyndham; British singer, songwriter, musician (guitar, bass) and teacher; b. 30 July 1960, Lincoln, England; m. Catherine Ramage 1991, one d. *Career:* played with many groups including: The Cannibals; Treatment; Mumbo-Jumbo; The Hipshakers; Raw, 1976–; Bassist, Natacha Atlas; guitarist, Errol Linton; mem. PRS; Musicians' Union; PAMRA. *Recordings:* Restless; Put You Behind Me; Waiting For Love; Even If You Hadn't; Friends. *E-mail:* adamblake77@hotmail.com.

BLAKE, Ian; British/Australian composer, producer and musician (woodwinds, keyboards, bass); b. 9 Dec. 1955, London. *Education:* Australian Nat. Univ. *Career:* mem. London Boy Singers 1968–71; tours and recording with Pyewackett 1980–88; with Mike Jackson 1988–93; backing musician for June Tabor, Michelle Shocked, Eric Bogle; musician, National Theatre, London 1987; tours with Mellstock Band 1988; writer and musician, The Crusades, Barossa Festival 1992; Lecturer in Contemporary Music Production, Canberra Inst. of Tech. 1997–98; sings with The Pocket Score Co.; mem. APRA, MEAA. *Compositions include:* Spirit of Place 1996, The Gathering of the Animals 1998, Big Bird for solo contrabass recorder 2000, Verklärter Bungalow for four cellos and voices 2001, Earth Loops for recorders, marimbas and percussion 2002, Rockface for cello, voice and computer 2003, Lucy for bass clarinet, soprano saxophone and loop pedal 2006, Starling for clarinet quartet 2006, Masque for small string orchestra 2006, Eidola for chamber choir and digital pipe organ 2008, The River Daughter for voice, bassoon and electronic textures 2008. *Recordings include:* producer and musician, Eric Bogles' Small Miracles 1997, Endangered Species 2000; writer, producer, musician, over 20 children's albums; contributor, albums by Martin Simpson, Andrew Cronshaw, June Tabor, Gjallarhorn, Mary McLaughlin, Les Barker. *Publications:* The Really Easy Cello Book 1989. *E-mail:* ian@ianblake.net (office). *Website:* www.ianblake.net.

BLAKE, James, (Harmonimix); British singer, songwriter, musician (keyboards, programming, samplers) and record producer; b. (James Blake Litherland), 26 Sept. 1988, Enfield, Middx, England; s. of James Litherland. *Education:* Latymer School, Edmonton, Goldsmiths Coll., Univ. of London. *Career:* debut single release Air & Lack Thereof 2009; placed second in BBC's Sound of 2011 poll; runner-up, BRIT Awards' Critics' Choice 2010; collaborations with Bon Iver, RZA, Brian Eno. *Recordings:* albums: James Blake 2011, Overgrown (Barclaycard Mercury Prize 2013) 2013. *Honours:* Ivor Novello Award for Best Contemporary Song (for Retrograde) 2014. *Current Management:* c/o Lucy Dickins, International Talent Booking, Ariel House, 74a Charlotte Street, London, W1T 4QJ, England. *Telephone:* (20) 7637-6979. *Fax:* (20) 7637-6978. *E-mail:* lucy@itb.co.uk. *Website:* www.itb.co.uk; www.jamesblakemusic.com.

BLAKE, Karl Antony, BA; British musician, filmmaker and lyricist; b. 5 Dec. 1956, Reading, Berkshire, England. *Career:* founder mem., Lemon Kittens 1978; joined as duo by Danielle Dax 1979–82; founder mem., Shock Headed Peters 1982–87, 1990–; mem., Alternative TV 1985–86; solo, as The Underneath 1986–87; founder mem., British Racing Green 1987–91; founder mem., Evil Twin 1987–; toured and recorded with Left Hand Right Hand 1988–2004; bass guitarist for live shows, Gae Bolg and the Church of Fand; bass guitarist and drummer, Seven Pines. *Film appearances:* Chariots of Fire, Caravaggio, Voice of Silence. *Recordings include:* albums: with Lemon Kittens: We Buy A Hammer For Daddy, The Big Dentist; with Shock Headed Peters: Not Born Beautiful 1985, Fear Engine 1988, Several Headed Enemy 1992, Fear Engine II 1993, Tendercide 1996; with The Underneath: Lunatic Dawn of the Dismantler 1987; with Evil Twin: The Black Spot 1992; solo album 1987. *Website:* www.myspace.com/karlblake.

BLAKE, Norman; British musician (guitar) and singer; b. 20 Oct. 1965, Bellshill, Scotland; one d. *Career:* fmr mem., The Boy Hairdressers; Founder mem., Teenage Fanclub 1989–; mem. BMX Bandits 1986–1991, The Reindeer Section 2002–. *Recordings include:* albums: with Teenage Fanclub: A Catholic Education 1990, Bandwagonesque 1991, The King 1991, Thirteen 1993, Grand Prix 1995, Songs From Northern Britain 1997, Howdy! 2000, Words Of Wisdom And Hope 2002, Man-Made 2005, Shadows 2010; with The Reindeer Section: Son Of Evil Reindeer 2002. *Website:* www.teenagefanclub.com.

BLANCHARD, Pierre; French musician (violin), composer and arranger; b. 24 May 1956, Saint-Quentin; one s. *Education:* Conservatoire de St Quentin; Université Musicale International de Paris; studied in New York. *Career:* Prof., CIM 1979–81; violinist, Martial Solal's Big Band 1981–86; played throughout Europe; played with Stéphane Grappelli, Antibes and Paris Festivals 1988; formed Gulf String 1989; Dir of Jazz Class, CNR D'Aubervilliers: La Courneuve 1992–; formed Quintette A Cordes de Pierre Blanchard 1994; performed compositions with Metropole Orchestra (Amsterdam) conducted by Vince Mendoza 1996; formed Arcollectiv 1998; formed Appassionato quartet 2009. *Recordings include:* solo albums: Each One Teach One 1985, Music For String Quartet, Jazz Trio, Violin and Lee Konitz 1987, Gulf String 1993, Volutes 1999; two albums with Martial Solal Big Band 1982, 1984; with Raphael Fays: Voyages 1988, Gipsy Touch 1991; with Pierre Michelot: Bass and Bosses 1989; with Dorado Schmitt: Rendezvous – Tribute to Stéphane Grappelli 2004; other albums with René Urtreger, Eric Le Lann, Post Image, Jazzogene Big Band, Thomas Dutronc. *Publications:* Jazz Violin Method, Vol. 1 2004, Jazz Violin Methos, Vol. II 2007. *Current Management:* c/o Cornolti Production, 119 State Road, 54700 Montauville, France. *Telephone:* 3-83-80-94-08. *E-mail:* thierry@cornolti-production.com. *Website:* www.cornolti-production.com. *Address:* 12 rue Léon Loiseau, Montreuil, France (home). *Telephone:* 1-55-86-29-03 (home); (8) 71-72-43-52 (office).

BLANCHARD, Terence Oliver; American musician (trumpet); *Artistic Director, Thelonius Monk Institute of Jazz Performance, Loyola University*; b. 13 March 1962, New Orleans; s. of Joseph Oliver Blanchard and Wilhelmina Ray Blanchard; m. Robin Regina Blanchard; two s. *Education:* New Orleans Center of Creative Arts, Rutgers Univ., studied jazz with Ellis Marsalis, classical trumpet with George Jensen. *Career:* toured with Lionel Hampton 1980; joined Art Blakey and the Jazz Messengers, worldwide tours 1982; formed Harrison-Blanchard 1990; worked on Spike Lee's film Malcolm X, made first screen appearance; tours throughout USA, Canada, Japan and Europe 1991; Artistic Dir Thelonious Monk Inst. of Jazz Performance, Loyola Univ., New Orleans 2000–; Artistic Dir, Henry Mancini Inst., Univ. of Miami Frost School of Music 2011–; Monterey Jazz All Star Tour 2008; Herbie Hancock Tour 2008. *Film scores:* Malcolm X 1993, Clockers 1995, Summer Of Sam 1999, Caveman's Valentine 2001, Original Sin 2001, Glitter 2001, Jim Brown – All American 2002, People I Know 2002, Barbershop 2002, The 25th Hour 2002, Dark Blue 2003, She Hate Me 2004, Waist Deep 2006, When the Levees Broke 2006, Inside Man 2006, Talk to Me 2007, Miracle At St. Anna 2008, Cadillac Records 2008, Bunraku 2010, Red Tails 2012, Black or White 2014, Chi-Raq 2015. *Recordings include:* with Art Blakey: Dr Jeckyle 1992, New Year's Eve At Sweet Basil 1992, Art Blakey's Jazz Messengers: Live In Leverkeusen 1995; as Harrison-Blanchard: New York Second Line 1984, Discernment 1986, Crystal Stair 1987, Black Pearl 1988; solo: Mo' Better Blues 1990, Terence Blanchard 1991, Simply Stated 1992, Malcolm X Jazz Suite 1993, Billie Holliday Songbook 1994, Romantic Defiance 1995, The Heart Speaks 1995, Jazz In Film 1999, Let's Get Lost 2001, Wandering Moon 2001, Bounce 2003, Illuminations (with McCoy Tyner, Gary Bartz, Christian McBride and Lewis Nash) (Grammy Award 2005) 2004, Flow 2005, A Tale of God's Will: A Requiem for Katrina (Grammy Award for Best Large Jazz Ensemble Album 2008) 2007, Choices 2009, Magnetic 2013, Champion (opera) 2013, Breathless 2015. *Publications:* contribs of articles to professional journals and magazines; Contemporary Cat: Terence Blanchard with Special Guests by Anthony Magro. *Honours:* Grand Prix du Disque 1984, 2009, Grammy Award Winner 2004, 2007, 2008, Grammy Awards for Best Jazz Instrumental Solo (for Be-Bop) 2009, for Best Improvised Jazz Solo (for Dancin' 4 Chicken) 2010, Jazz Journalists' Asscn Award for Trumpeter of the Year 2014. *Current Management:* c/o 6110 St Charles Avenue, New Orleans, LA 70118, USA. *Fax:* (504) 897-1267 (office). *E-mail:* robin@burgessmgmt.com (office). *E-mail:* info@burgessmgmt.com (office). *Website:* www.terenceblanchard.com.

BLANCO, Benny; American songwriter, record producer, rapper and musician; b. (Benjamin Levin), 8 March 1988, Reston, Va. *Career:* collaborated with rapper Spank Rock on EP Bangers & Cash 2007; with record producer Dr Luke 2008; songwriter or producer for numerous acts 2008– including Christina Aguilera, 3OH!3, Taio Cruz, Gym Class Heroes, Ke$ha, Maroon 5, Bruno Mars, Katy Perry, Rihanna, Snoop Dogg, Trey Songz, Britney Spears, Wiz Khalifa. *Compositions include:* as co-writer: Blah Blah Blah (for Ke$ha), California Gurls (for Katy Perry), Circus (for Britney Spears), Diamonds (for Rihanna), Don't Trust Me (for 3HO!3), Dynamite (for Taio Cruz), Moves Like Jagger (for Maroon 5 featuring Christina Aguilera), Teenage Dream (for Katy Perry), Tik Tok (for Ke$ha). *Recordings include:* albums as producer or songwriter include: Circus, Britney Spears 2008, One of the Boys, Katy Perry 2008, Identified, Vanessa Hudgens 2008, Animal, Ke$ha 2010, Teenage Dream, Katy Perry 2010, Cannibal, Ke$ha 2010, The Papercut Chronicles II, Gym Class Heroes 2011, Overexposed, Maroon 5 2012, Unapologetic, Rihanna 2012. *Honours:* BMI Pop Award for Songwriter of the Year 2012.

BLAND, Bill; British musician (African and Latin percussion); b. 6 Feb. 1962, Wirral, Merseyside, England. *Education:* School of Oriental and African Studies, studied Cuban percussion with Oscar Valdes and African percussion with Emmanuel Tagoe. *Career:* radio and TV appearances with Ebo Iye, with Peter Badejo 1991, Roberto Plas's Latin Ensemble 1992, Orquesta la Clave featuring Jesus Alemany 1993, London Afro Blok, Commonwealth Games, Canada 1994, Palenke 1996, Yoruba Jazz People 1998, Kevin Haynes Grupo Elegoua 1999; mem. London Lucumi Choir. *Recordings include:* Alex Wilson, Afro Saxon.

BLANT, David, Cert. Ed, ALCM; British musician (bass guitar, accordion, piano) and teacher; b. 21 Nov. 1949, Burton-on-Trent, Staffs., England; s. of Peter Blant and Renée Blant; m. Jennifer Gow 1971; one s. one d. *Education:* Dartington Coll. of Arts. *Career:* various bands from age 13; mem. of indie bands Yeah Jazz, R Cajun and the Zydeco Brothers 1985–; Founder-mem. The Zydeco Hot Rods 1993–; mem. The Vice-Bishops' Blues Band, The Vice-Bishops' Ceili Band, The Zydeco Brothers' Band; radio broadcasts; mem. Musicians' Union, Performing Right Soc. *Films:* Room for Romeo Brass, This is England. *Radio:* The Folk Show. *Recordings include:* with Steve Womack: Northern Comfort 1984; with R.Cajun & the Zydeco Brothers: Pig Sticking in Arcadia 1987, Out of the Swamp 1989, Don't Leave the Floor 1991, No Known Cure 1993, That Cajun Thing 1994, Get Up Get Down 2000; with The Vice-Bishops of Uttoxeter: Dances & Dirges 1995, Airs and Disgraces; with Yeah Jazz (aka Big Red Kite): Short Stories 1996, Songs from Biscuit Town 2000; with The Vice-Bishops' Blues Band: House of Cards 2000, Caught in the Crossfire 2004; with Marsden, Blant and Squire: Trio 2003. *Address:* c/o Fred Hopwood, Smalltown Music, 17 Colne Mount, Uttoxeter, Staffs., ST14 7QR; PO Box 94, Derby, DE22 1XA, England. *Telephone:* (1889) 563123. *E-mail:* fred@smalltownmusic.co.uk. *Website:* www.smalltownmusic.co.uk.

BLATNÝ, Pavel, Magister; Czech composer, conductor, musician (piano) and musicologist; b. 14 Sept. 1931, Brno; m. Danuse Spirková 1982; one s. one d. *Education:* Brno Conservatory, Univ. of Brno, Berklee Coll. of Music, Boston, USA. *Career:* more than 2,000 recitals of piano music, often in a third-stream mode, mixing jazz and classical techniques; conductor of many concerts in the fmr Czechoslovakia; Chief of the Music Div., Czech television 1971–92; Prof., Janáček Acad. of Musical Arts, Brno 1979–90; Pres. Club of Moravian Composers. *Compositions include:* Music for Piano and Orchestra 1955, Concerto for Orchestra 1956, Concerto for Jazz Orchestra 1962–64, Twelfth Night (based on Shakespeare's play) 1975, Forest Tales: The Well and Little House (television opera for children) 1975, The Willow Tree (cantata with orchestra) 1980, The Bells, symphonic movement 1981, Christmas Eve (cantata with orchestra) 1982, The Midday Witch (cantata with orchestra) 1982, Two Movements for Brasses 1982, Hommage à Gustav Mahler for orchestra 1982, Prologue for mixed choir and jazz orchestra 1984, Ring a Ring o' Roses, for solo piano 1984, Signals for Jazz Orchestra 1985, Confrontation (written with his son, Marek Blatný), for rock group and symphony orchestra 1995, Play Rock, Play New Music (written with his son, Marek Blatný) 1997, Meditation 1999, Symphony Erbenia'da 2003, An old song, antivariations for symphony orchestra on song of Thomas Aquin 2008; other music for wind instruments, for piano. *Recordings:* Pavel Blatný – Jazz in Modo Classico 1980, Jubileum 2006. *Honours:* winner, Composition Prize, Prague Jazz Festival 1966, 1967, Leoš Janáček Prize 1984, Anfiteatro d'Argento, Naples, Italy 1989, Lifetime Achievement Award, Brno 2000. *Address:* Absolonova 35, 62400 Brno, Czech Republic (home). *Telephone:* (5) 4122-3062 (home). *E-mail:* pblatny@atlas.cz.

BLATT, Melanie; British singer; b. 25 March 1975. *Career:* founder mem. female vocal group, All Saints 1993–2000, 2006–; collaboration with Artful Dodger; solo artist 2003–05. *Film:* Honest 2000. *Recordings include:* albums: with All Saints: All Saints 1997, Saints and Sinners 2000, Studio 1 2006; solo: Do Me Wrong 2003. *Honours:* BRIT Award for Best Single (for Never Ever) 1998. *Current Management:* c/o Fascination Management, 1st Floor, 6 South Hill Park, London, NW3 2SB, England. *Telephone:* (20) 7586-6457. *E-mail:* info@fascinationmanagement.com. *Website:* www.fascinationmanagement.com.

BLEGVAD, Peter; American singer, songwriter and cartoonist; b. 14 Aug. 1951, New York. *Career:* Founder-mem. Slapp Happy 1971–; collaborations with Henry Cow, Faust, Golden Palominos, John Greaves, Chris Cutler, Lisa Herman; creator of Leviathan cartoon strip, Independent on Sunday 1992–99. *Recordings include:* albums: with Slapp Happy: Sort Of 1973, Slapp Happy 1974, Ça Va 1998; with Slapp Happy and Henry Cow: Desperate Straights, In Praise Of Learning; solo: Kew Rhône (with John Greaves and Lisa Herman) 1977, Smell of a Friend by The Lodge (with John Greaves), Dr Huelsenbeck's Mentale Heilmethode (with John Greaves) 1992, The Naked Shakespeare 1983, Knights Like This 1985, Downtime 1989, King Strut & Other Stories 1990, Unearthed (with John Greaves) 1995, Just Woke Up (with John Greaves and Chris Cutler) 1995, Hangman's Hill 1998, Choices Under Pressure 2001, Orpheus the Lowdown (with Andy Partridge) 2004, Gonwards (with Andy Partridge) 2012. *Publications include:* Headcheese 1994, The Book of Leviathan 2001, The Bleaching Stream 2011, Kew. Rhone 2014. *Website:* www.leviathan.co.uk.

BLEY, Carla Borg; American jazz composer; b. 11 May 1938, Oakland, Calif.; d. of Emil Carl Borg and Arlene Anderson; m. 1st Paul Bley 1959 (divorced 1967); m. 2nd Michael Mantler 1967 (divorced 1992); one d. *Career:* freelance composer 1956–; pianist, Jazz Composers Orchestra, New York 1964–; European concert tours with Jazz Realities 1965–66; founder, WATT 1973–; toured Europe with Jack Bruce Band 1975; leader, Carla Bley Band, touring USA and Europe 1977–; Cultural Council Foundation grantee 1971, 1979; Guggenheim Fellow 1972; Nat. Endowment for Arts grantee 1973. *Music:* composed and recorded: A Genuine Tong Funeral 1967, Escalator Over the Hill (opera) 1970–71 (Oscar du Disque de Jazz 1973), Tropic Appetites 1973; composed chamber orchestra 3/4 1974–75, Mortelle Rautonnée (film score) 1983; recordings include: Dinner Music 1976, The Carla Bley Band–European Tour 1977, Music Mecanique 1979, Fictitious Sports 1980, Social Studies 1980, Carla Bley Live! 1981, Heavy Heart 1984, I Hate to Sing 1984, Night Glo 1985, Sextet 1987, Live 1987, Duets 1988, Fleur Carnivore 1989, The Very Big Carla Bley Band 1991, Go Together 1993, Big Band Theory 1993, Songs with Legs 1995, Goes to Church 1996, Fancy Chamber Music 1998, Are We There Yet? 1999, 4×4 2000, Looking for America 2003, The Lost Chords 2004, The Lost Chords find Paolo Fresu 2008, Appearing Nightly 2008. *Honours:* winner, int. jazz critics' poll, Down Beat magazine seven times (1966, 1971, 1972, 1978, 1979, 1980, 1983), Best Composer of Year, Down Beat readers' poll 1984 and Composer/Arranger of Year 1985–92, Best in Field Jazz Times critics' poll 1990, Prix Jazz Moderne for The Very Big Carla Bley Band (Acad. du Jazz) 1992, Best Arranger Down Beat critics' poll 1993, 1994. *Current Management:* c/o Laurel Wicks, Ted Kurland Associates, 173 Brighton Avenue, Boston, MA 02134-2003, USA. *Telephone:* (617) 254-0007.

Fax: (617) 782-3524. *E-mail:* agents@tedkurland.com. *Website:* www
.tedkurland.com. *Address:* c/o Watt Works, PO Box 67, Willow, NY 12495,
USA (office). *Website:* www.wattxtrawatt.com (office).

BLICHFELDT, Anders; Danish singer and musician (guitar); b. 9 Nov.
1963, Copenhagen; m. Marina 1988; two s. *Career:* lead singer, Big Fat Snake;
numerous concerts, including Roskilde Festival, Midfyn Festival, Skander-
borg Festival, several nat. TV and radio shows; mem. DJBFA, Dansk Artist
Forbund. *Recordings include:* Big Fat Snake 1991, Born Lucky 1992,
Beautiful Thing 1994, Midnight Mission 1995, Uno 2001, Club CAJ 2002,
Born to Be Blue 2005. *Honours:* Grammy Award 1998.

BLIGE, Mary J.; American singer and songwriter; b. 11 Jan. 1971, Bronx,
New York; m. Kendu Isaacs 2003. *Career:* solo artist; numerous tours and live
appearances; has collaborated with numerous musicians, including George
Michael, Lauryn Hill; Co-founder Foundation for the Advancement of Women
Now. *Films:* I Can Do Bad All By Myself 2009. *Recordings include:* albums:
What's The 411? 1992, My Life 1994, Mary Jane 1995, Share My World 1997,
The Tour 1998, Mary 1999, No More Drama 2001, Ballads 2001, Love & Life
2003, The Breakthrough (American Music Award for Favorite Soul/R&B
Album 2006, Grammy Award for Best R&B Album 2007, Best R&B/Soul
Album by a Female Artist, Soul Train Awards 2007) 2005, Growing Pains
(Grammy Award for Best Contemporary R&B Album 2009) 2007, Stronger
with Each Tear 2009, My Life II: The Journey Continues 2011, Think Like a
Man Too 2014, The London Sessions 2014. *Honours:* American Music Award
for Favorite Female Hip-Hop/R&B Artist 2003, for Favorite Female Soul/R&B
Artist 2006, Grammy Award for Best Pop Collaboration with Vocals (jtly)
2004, BET Award for Best Female R&B Artist 2006, nine Billboard Awards
2006, Grammy Award for Best Female R&B Vocal Performance (for Be
Without You) 2007. *Current Management:* Steve Lucas Associates, 156 West
56th Street, New York, NY 10019, USA. *Website:* www.maryjblige.com.

BLILIE, Hannah; American musician (drums). *Career:* has performed with
bands including Sarah Dougher, Chromatics, Stiletto, Mr Yuk, The Lumpies,
Vade, The Vogue, Soiled Doves; mem. Gossip 2003–; currently also mem. band
Shoplifting. *Recordings:* albums: Standing in the Way of Control 2006, Music
for Men 2009; with Gossip: Standing in the Way of Control 2006, Music for
Men 2009, A Joyful Noise 2012. *Website:* www.gossipyouth.com.

BLOMSTROM, John Paul, Sr; American insurance executive and fmr
artist agent and musician (drums); b. 19 April 1949, Miami, OK; m. Cheryl
Ann Byrd 1978; one s. two d. *Career:* artist manager for The Tonyans (family
group), 1970s; Vince Vance and the Valiants; Lic and Stiff, 1980; First
promoter to bring Pat Benatar to Houston; also promoter of artists including
Muddy Waters; Hall and Oates; Prince; The Police; Agent for artists including
Madam X; Appeared in film, Robocop II; fmrly ran American Bands
Management agency; founder John Blomstrom Enterprises insurance com-
pany. *Publications:* Writer for Music News. *Address:* John Blomstrom
Enterprises, 3300 South Gessner Suite 207, Houston, TX 77063, USA.
Telephone: (713) 785-3700. *Fax:* (713) 785-4641. *E-mail:* johnblomstrom@aol
.com. *Website:* www.johnblomstrom.com.

BLONDIN, Ludivine Josette Edmee; French actress, singer and model; b.
10 Oct. 1958, Lyon; partner John Phil Wayne; one d. *Career:* singer, musical
act/films: L'Art de la Fugue with Bernard Haller and Maurice Biraud; William
Tell with Will Lyman; Drole D'Endroit Pour Une Rencontre, with Gerard
Depardieu; La Petite Maison Dans La Prairie, with Michael Landon;
Interview of John Phil Wayne for France 3 TV and TLM TV; introduction
portrait of John Phil Wayne as video; mem. AZ Production. *Recordings
include:* Fairy Tales For Fauve; recording for French radio and TV as
animator: Les Jeux de 20 Heures, Les Jeux Du Dimanche, La Soupiere a Des
Oreilles, Maurice Bejart à Arles.

BLONDY, Alpha; Côte d'Ivoirian reggae singer, composer and bandleader; b.
(Seydou Koné), 1 Jan. 1953, Dimbokro. *Education:* Columbia Univ., USA.
Career: West African reggae vocalist and band leader during 1980s-; UN Amb.
of Peace for Côte d'Ivoire 2005. *Recordings include:* albums: Jah Glory 1982,
Cocody Rock 1984, Apartheid is Nazism 1985, Jerusalem 1986, Revolution
1987, The Prophets 1989, Masada 1992, Live Au Zenith 1992, SOS Tribal War
1993, Dieu 1994, Grand Bassam Zion Rock 1996, Yitzhak Rabin 1998, Elohim
1999, Merci (2002, Akwaba 2005, Jah Victory 2007, Vision 2011, Mystic Power
2013. *Current Management:* c/o Michel Jovanovic, Mediacom, BP 231, 51058
Reims, France. *Telephone:* 3-26-40-96-71. *Fax:* 3-26-40-23-13.

BLOOM, Eric; American singer and musician (guitar, keyboards); b. 1 Dec.
1944. *Career:* mem. of rock group, Blue Öyster Cult 1971–; regular tours and
festival appearances. *Recordings include:* albums: Blue Öyster Cult, 1972;
Tyranny and Mutation, 1973; Secret Treaties, 1974; Live On Your Feet Or On
Your Knees, 1975; Agents Of Fortune, 1976; Spectres, 1978; Some Enchanted
Evening, 1978; Mirrors, 1979; Cultosaurus Erectus, 1980; Fire Of Unknown
Origin, 1981; ETL (Extra-Terrestrial Live), 1982; The Revolution By Night,
1983; Club Ninja, 1986; Imaginos, 1988; Career Of Evil: The Metal Years,
1990; Bad Channels, 1992; Live 1976, 1994; Cult Classic, 1994; Summerdaze,
1997, Heaven Forbid 1998, Curse of the Hidden Mirror 2001. *Address:* c/o
Steve Schenck, Paradise Artists, 216 East 75th Street #PE, New York, NY
10021, USA. *Telephone:* (212) 879-5900. *Fax:* (212) 879-0668. *Website:* www
.blueoystercult.com; www.ericbloom.net.

BLOOM, Jane Ira, BA; American jazz musician (soprano saxophone),
composer and teacher; *Faculty Member, New School for Jazz and Contem-*

porary Music; b. 12 Jan. 1955, Boston, Mass; d. of Joel Bloom and Evelyn
Bloom; m. Joseph Grifasi 1974. *Education:* Yale Univ., Yale School of Music.
Career: relocated to New York City; first musician and composer commis-
sioned by NASA Art Program 1989; currently mem. Faculty, New School for
Jazz and Contemporary Music, New York; numerous collaborations including
Bob Brookmeyer, Jay Clayton, Mark Dresser, Ethel Ennis, Gloria Feidman,
David Friedman, Jerry Granelli, Frederick Hand, Fred Hersch, Ron Horton,
Daniel Humair, Jin Hi Kim, Klaus Konig, David Lahm, Cleo Laine, M'Lumbo,
Ivo Perlman, Bobby Previte, Julian Priester, Kenny Wheeler, Annabelle
Wilson, Min Xiao-Fen. *Recordings:* albums: We Are 1978, Second Wind 1980,
Mighty Lights 1982, As One 1984, Modern Drama 1987, Slalom 1988, Art and
Aviation 1992, The Nearness 1995, The Red Quartets 1997, 1999, Sometimes
the Magic 2000, Chasing Paint 2002, Like Silver, Like Song 2004, Mental
Weather 2008, Popular Science 2013, Sixteen Sunsets 2013. *Honours:* Charlie
Parker Fellowship Award for Jazz Innovation 1997, New York Foundation for
the Arts Fellowship 1998, Int. Women in Jazz Jazz Masters Award 2001, Jazz
Journalists Asscn Award for Soprano Saxophonist of the Year 2001, 2003,
2006, 2008, 2011, 2012, 2014, 2015, Guggenheim Fellowship in Music
Composition 2007, Mary Lou Williams Women in Jazz Award for Lifetime
Service to Jazz 2007. *Address:* The New School for Jazz and Contemporary
Music, Arnhold Hall, 55 West 12th Street, Room 519, New York, NY 10011,
USA (office). *Telephone:* (212) 229-5896 ext 4576 (office). *E-mail:* bloomj@
newschool.edu (office); outline@tuna.net. *Website:* www.newschool.edu
(office); www.janeirabloom.com.

BLUE, Barry; British songwriter, producer and singer; b. 4 Dec. 1950,
London; m. Lynda Blue 20 May 1974; one s. two d. *Education:* St Marleybone
Grammar, London. *Career:* first television appearance, Stubby Kaye's Silver
Star Show, age 11; first major concert, Split Festival, Yugoslavia singing his
own composition, 1969; first radio appearance, bassist, Spice (later became
Uriah Heep), John Peel Show; first major tour, solo singer with Queen and
Status Quo, 1973; Staff Producer, CBS Records 1976–78; Man. Dir Favored
Nations Music Publishing 2000–11; CEO Purple City Records 2003–06;
producer, composer, numerous hit records for artists including Bananarama,
Five Star, Heatwave, Diana Ross, Céline Dion, The Saturdays, Pixie Lott;
opened Aosis Recording Studios, where albums produced for artists including
Sinead O'Connor, Bronski Beat, Depeche Mode, Fine Young Cannibals,
1984–88; owner of Escape Records; Councillor, BAC&S; mem. PRS, Writer-Dir
2010–. *Recordings include:* Dancin' On A Saturday Night, Sugar Me, Lynsey
de Paul, Boogie Nights, Heatwave, Always and Forever, Heatwave; over 30
UK Chart singles as singer, producer and writer. *Honours:* Carl Allan Award
1973, Producer of the Year 1977, six BMI, ASCAP Awards, 28 Platinum, Gold
and Silver Sales Awards. *Address:* c/o Favored Nations Music Publishing, PO
Box 31, Bushey, Hertfordshire, WD2 2PT, England.

BLUMBERG, Stuart Lester, AA; American musician (trumpet); b. 27 Oct.
1947, Detroit, MI; m. Dorothy Ebeling; one s. *Education:* Los Angeles Valley
College, California State Univ., Northridge. *Career:* toured with Don Ellis;
Louis Bellson; first trumpet, numerous Broadway performances; Music
Contractor, Shubert Theatre, Los Angeles, 1991; recorded numerous televi-
sion and radio commercials, film soundtracks; mem. NARAS. *Recordings:* with
various artists including: Frank Sinatra; Barbra Streisand; Lou Rawls; Lionel
Richie; The Osmonds; Joe Cocker; Dionne Warwick; The Rolling Stones; Barry
Manilow; Beach Boys; The Commodores; The Pointer Sisters; Steppenwolf;
Jermaine Jackson; Carly Simon; Talking Heads; Air Supply; Blood, Sweat and
Tears.

BLUMENTHAL, Laurent Pierre; French musician (saxophone); b. 21 Dec.
1964, Paris; m. Marianne 1992; two d. *Education:* CNR Lyon and Eastman
School of Music, Rochester, New York. *Career:* tour of USSR with La Velle and
Orj 1991; tour of Québec 1991, Festival de Montréal 1992, both with
Tourmaline; tours of Germany, Italy, Portugal and France with Orchestre
Nat. de Jazz 1993–94; tour of Germany with Dimitri Naiditch/Laurent
Blumenthal Duo 1995; played all French jazz festivals 1990–; performed with
own quintet, septet, and artists including Johnny Griffin, Ernie Watts, Michel
Colombier, ORJ, Henri Texier, Daniel Humair, Mario Stanchev; Orchestre
Nat. de Jazz with Denis Badault; also performed with Tito Puente, Nicole
Croisille, Louis Sclavis. *Recordings include:* Il Était Une Fois La Révolution,
ORJ 1988, Shakok, Shakok 1989, Johnny Griffin et l'ORJ, ORJ 1990, Sozopol,
Mario Stanchev 1990, Parcours, Aira Works 1990, Kaleidoscope, Mario
Stanchev 1992, Monk Mingus Ellington, ONJ Badault 1993, Bouquet Final,
ONJ Badault 1994. *Honours:* first prize Nat. Saxophone Competition 1987,
first prize Festival de Vienne (with Shakok) 1988, first prize Festival de
Sorgues 1993, second prize (soloist), third prize (group, with Dimitri Naiditch)
Concours de la Défense 1993. *Address:* c/o Association Continuum, 7 rue des
Carmes du Palais, 34000 Montpellier, France.

BLUNSTONE, Colin; British singer; b. 24 June 1945, Hatfield, Hertfordshire, England. *Career:* singer, The Zombies, 1963–67, re-formed 1991–; solo
career, 1969–; numerous live appearances. *Film appearance:* Bunny Lake is
Missing 1966. *Recordings include:* albums: with The Zombies: The Zombies
1965, The Zombies: Begin Here 1965, Odyssey and Oracle 1967, New World
1991; solo: One Year 1971, Ennismore 1973, Journey 1974, Planes 1976,
Never Even Thought 1978, Late Nights In Soho 1979, I Don't Believe In
Miracles 1982, Echo Bridge 1995, Live At The BBC 1996, Light Inside 1998;
with Rod Argent: Out of the Shadows 2001, As Far As I Can See 2004. *Current
Management:* c/o John Waller, The Old Truman Brewery, 91 Brick Lane,

London, E1 6QL, England. *Telephone:* (20) 7247-1057. *E-mail:* john@johnwaller.net. *Website:* www.colinblunstone.co.uk.

BLUNT, James; British singer, songwriter and musician (guitar); b. Tidworth. *Education:* Univ. of Bristol and Royal Mil. Acad., Sandhurst. *Career:* in British army –2002; solo artist 2003–. *Recordings include:* albums: Back to Bedlam 2004, Chasing Time: The Bedlam Sessions 2006, All the Lost Souls 2007, Some Kind of Trouble 2010, Moon Landing 2013. *Honours:* Q Award for Best New Artist 2005, Digital Music Award for Best Pop Artist 2005, MTV Europe Music Award for Best New Act 2005, BRIT Award for Best Pop Act, Best British Male Solo Artist 2006, Echo Award for Best Int. Newcomer, Germany 2006, Ivor Novello Awards for Most Performed Song, and for hit. Hit of the Year (both for You're Beautiful) 2006, Regenbogen Awards (Germany) Best Int. Male Artist 2011. *Current Management:* Twenty-First Artists Ltd, 1 Blythe Road, London, W14 0HG, England. *Telephone:* (20) 7348-4800. *E-mail:* info@wabbie.com. *Website:* www.jamesblunt.com.

BLUNT, Martin; musician (bass guitar); b. May 1964. *Career:* fmr mem., Makin' Time; founding mem., The Charlatans 1990–; numerous tours, festivals, television and radio appearances. *Recordings include:* albums: Some Friendly 1990, Between 10th And 11th 1992, Up To Our Hips 1995, The Charlatans 1995, Tellin' Stories 1997, Us And Us Only 1999, Songs From The Other Side 2000, Wonderland 2001, Live It Like You Love It 2002, Up At The Lake 2004, Simpatico 2006, You Cross My Path 2008, Who We Touch 2010, Modern Nature 2015. *Current Management:* Big Life Management, 67–69 Chalton Street, London, NW1 1HY, England. *Telephone:* (20) 7554-2100. *Fax:* (20) 7554-2101. *E-mail:* tim@biglifemanagement.com. *Website:* www .biglifemanagement.com. *Address:* The Charlatans, PO Box 134, Sandbach, Cheshire CW11 1AE, England. *E-mail:* info@thecharlatans.net (office). *Website:* www.thecharlatans.net.

BoA; South Korean singer; b. (Boa Kwon), 5 Nov. 1986, Kyung Gi Do. *Career:* signed recording contract aged 13; achieved success in Japan; records in Korean, Japanese and English. *Recordings include:* albums: Listen To My Heart 2002, Jumping Into The World 2002, ID Peace B 2002, No. 1 2002, Peace B Remixes 2002, Valenti 2003, Next World 2003, Atlantis Princess 2003, Love & Honesty 2004, My Name 2004, The Face 2008, BoA 2009, Mamoritai: White Wishes 2009, Identity 2010. *Honours:* several music awards. *Address:* c/o Avex Inc., Sumitomo Seimei Aoyama Bldg, 3-1-30 Minami-Aoyama, Minato-ku, Tokyo 107-8577, Japan. *Website:* www.avexnet.or.jp/boa.

B.O.B.; American rapper, singer, songwriter, musician (keyboards, guitar) and record producer; b. (Bobby Ray Simmons Jr), 15 Nov. 1988, Winston-Salem, North Carolina. *Education:* Columbia High School, Decatur, Ga. *Career:* signed to Atlantic Records and Rebel Rock Records 2006; released singles including Haterz Everywhere (with Wes Fif) 2007, I'll Be in the Sky 2008; toured USA with The SHOOTiN for Stars Tour 2010; appeared at MTV Video Music Awards 2010; support act on Paramore's UK tour 2010; numerous collaborations including T.I., Giggs, Bruno Mars, Hayley Williams, Playboy Tre, Janelle Monáe, Lil Wayne, Nelly, André 3000, Haley Reinhart, Taylor Swift. *Recordings include:* albums: The Adventures of Bobby Ray 2010, Strange Clouds 2012, Underground Luxury 2013, Psycadelik Thoughtz 2015; mixtapes: The Future 2007, Cloud 9 2007, Hi! My Name is B.o.B. 2008, Who the F#*k is B.o.B.? 2008, B.o.B. vs. Bobby Ray 2009, May 25 2010, No Genre 2010, E.P.I.C. (Every Play is Crucial) 2011, Fuck 'Em We Ball 2012. *Honours:* Soul Train Award for Best Song (for Nothin' On You, with Bruno Mars) 2010, Teen Choice Award for Best Hook-Up Song (for Airplanes, with Hayley Williams) 2010. *Address:* c/o Atlantic Records, Warner Music Group, 75 Rockefeller Plaza, New York, NY 10019, USA (office). *E-mail:* bobbeats@gmail .com; ContactUs@bobatl.com. *Website:* www.wmg.com (office); www.bobatl .com.

BOBINEC, Ivica; Croatian radio station executive; b. 16 Sept. 1937, Zagreb; m. Visnja Kolina 1961; one s. one d. *Education:* University of Zagreb, Musical Academy, Zagreb. *Career:* singer, bass guitar player, Combo 5 (orchestra), 1973–86; international concert tours across Europe, 1966–69; Split Festival, Zagreb Festival of Popular Music, 1971–77; radio and television appearances 1958–95, including Eurovision Song Contest, Luxembourg, 1984; Bergen, Norway, 1986; General Manager, Cibona Radio Station; mem, Glazbena Unija (Music Society of Croatia). *Compositions:* Cibona (music and lyrics), anthem of Croatian National Basketball Team, 1990. *Recordings:* Solo: Pijem Da Zaboravim Nju, 1973.

DJ BOBO; Swiss musician, producer and DJ; b. (René Baumann), 5 Jan. 1968, Kölliken; m. Nancy Rentzsch 2002; two c. *Recordings include:* albums: Dance With Me 1993, There is a Party 1994, Just for You 1995, World in Motion 1996, Magic 1998, Level 6 1999, Planet Colors 2001, Celebration 2002, Visions 2003, Chihuahua 2003, Pirates of Dance 2005, Greatest Hits 2006, Vampires 2007, Olé Olé-The Party 2008, Fantasy 2010, Dancing Las Vegas 2011. *Honours:* Prix Walo 1995, 1996, 1997, 1998, World Music Award for bestselling Swiss recording artist 1995, 1996, 1997, 1998, 2000, 2002, 2003, 2004, 2005, German DJ Award for Best Male Pop Act 2003, Golderner Lollipop 2004. *Current Management:* c/o Yes Music AG/DJ BoBo Management, Breitenweg 6, 6370 Stans, Switzerland. *Telephone:* (41) 6191350. *Fax:* (41) 6191369. *E-mail:* yesmusic@yes.ch. *Website:* www.djbobo.ch.

BOCELLI, Andrea; Italian singer (tenor); b. 22 Sept. 1958, Lajatico, Pisa; s. of the late Alessandro Bocelli and of Edi Bocelli; m. 1st Enrica Cenzatti 1992; two s.; m. 2nd Veronica Berti 2014; one d. *Education:* Univ. of Pisa. *Career:*

began piano lessons aged six, later learned to play the flute, saxophone, trumpet, trombone, harp, guitar and drums; became blind following a football accident aged 12; won first song competition, Margherita d'Oro in Viareggio with O sole mio aged 14; earned money performing in piano bars; completed law school and spent one year as a court-appointed lawyer; won Newcomers section of Sanremo Music Festival 1994; has recorded 13 solo studio albums, of both pop and classical music, two greatest hits albums and nine complete operas; biggest-selling solo artist in history of classical music; duet with Celine Dion, The Prayer, for animated film The Quest for Camelot, won Golden Globe for Best Original Song 1999. *Recordings include:* albums: Bocelli 1995, Viaggio Italiano 1995, Romanza 1997, Aria 1998, Sacred Arias 1999, Sogno 1999, Verdi 2000, La Bohème 2000, Verdi Requiem 2001, Cieli di Toscana 2001, Sentimento (Classical BRIT Award for Best Album 2003) 2002, Tosca 2003, Aria: The Opera Album 2005, MW 2006, Vivere 2007, Incanto 2008, My Christmas 2009, Andrea Chénier 2010, Carmen: Duets & Arias 2010, Concerto: One Night in Central Park 2011, Notte Illuminata 2011, Opera 2012, Roméo et Juliette 2012. *Publications:* The Music of Silence: A Memoir (La musica del silenzio) (autobiog.) 2000 (reworked 2010). *Honours:* Grande Ufficiale, Ordine al merito della Repubblica Italiana 2006, Grand Officer, Orden al Mérito de Duarte, Sánchez y Mella (Dominican Repub.) 2009; named one of People Magazine's 50 Most Beautiful People 1998, honoured with a star on Hollywood Walk of Fame 2010, World Music Award for World's Best-selling Classical Artist 2010, America Award, Italy-USA Foundation 2012, Classic BRIT Award for Int. Artist of the Year in association with Raymond Weil 2012. *Current Management:* c/o Michele Torpedine, MT Opera and Blues Production and Management, via Mario Musolesi, 40138 Bologna, Italy. *Telephone:* (51) 251117. *Fax:* (51) 251123. *E-mail:* mtorped@tin.it. *Website:* www.mt -operaandblues.it; www.andreabocelli.org.

BOCOUM, Afel; Malian singer, musician (guitar) and songwriter; b. 1955, Niafunké. *Education:* govt agricultural coll., Mali. *Career:* began by accompanying father to his performances; at 13 joined Ali Farka Toure's band, ASCO 1968; agricultural advisor by profession; joined Orchestre Diaba Regional 1982; played with Ensemble Niafunké; toured internationally with Toure since 1991; formed Alkibar in early 1980s; contributed to Damon Albarn's Mali Music project 2002. *Recordings include:* with Ensemble Niafunké: Radio Mali; with Ali Farka Toure: The Source 1992; solo: Alkibar 1999, The Rough Guide To The Music Of Mali and Guinea 2000, The Music Of Mali 2001, Niger (with Alkibar) 2006, Tabital Pulaaku 2009. *Honours:* second place Mali Biennale 1972. *Current Management:* Contre Jour, Voye d'En Haut, 41 Vodelée, Doische 5680, Belgium. *Telephone:* (82) 66 74 70. *Fax:* (82) 66 74 72. *E-mail:* info@contrejour.com. *Website:* www.contrejour.com.

BODEN, Jonathan (Jon), BA, MMus; British singer, composer and musician (fiddle); b. 1977, Chicago, Ill., USA; pnr Fay Hield; one s. one d. *Education:* Univ. of Durham, London Coll. of Music. *Career:* fmr teacher, Stagecoach Theatre Arts, Oxford; composer and company founder, Tailor-Made Musicals; mem. Spiers & Boden duo (with John Spiers); mem. Eliza Carthy and the Ratcatchers –2007; founding mem. Bellowhead 2004–; solo artist 2006–; f. The Remnant Kings 2009–. *Recordings:* albums: with Spiers & Boden: Through and Through 2001, Bellow 2003, Tunes 2005, Songs 2005, Vagabond 2008, The Works 2011; with Bellowhead: E.P. Onymous 2004, Burlesque 2006, Matachin 2008, Hedonism 2010, Broadside (BBC Radio 2 Folk Award for Album of the Year 2013) 2012, Revival 2014; with Eliza Carthy and the Ratcatchers: Rough Music 2005; solo: Painted Lady 2006, Songs from the Floodplain 2009. *Honours:* BBC Radio 2 Folk Award for Folk Singer of the Year 2010. *Address:* c/o Tom Rose, Navigator Records, The New Powerhouse, Gateway Business Centre, Kangley Bridge Road, London, SE26 5AN, England (office). *Telephone:* (870) 444 0799 (office). *E-mail:* info@navigatorrecords.co.uk (office); glassceilingpr@btconnect.com (office). *Website:* www.navigatorrecords.co.uk (office); www.spiersandboden.com; www.bellowhead.co.uk; www.jonboden .com.

BODILSEN, Jesper Vejbaek; Danish Musician (double bass, electric bass); b. 5 Jan. 1970, Haslev. *Education:* Rhythmical Diploma Degree, Royal Academy of Music, Århus; Played Cornet in Balleskolens Brass Band, 1980–89; Lessons in Big Band Arranging, Line Writing. *Career:* Pori Jazz, Beijing Jazz Festival, Scandinavian Jazz Quartet, 1994; Concerts with Ed Thigpen, Duke Jordan, Janusz Carmello, Bent Jaedig, 1994; James Moody, 1996; Fred Wesley, 1996; Horace Parlan, 1996; Ulf Wakenius, 1997; Tours with Beibom/Kroner Big Band, 1996–97; Katrine Madsen, 1998; Stig Rossen, 1997; Member, Ed Thigpen Trio, 1997; Jazzpar Concerts with Erling Kroner, Dino Saluzzi, 1998. *Compositions:* Dedication, 1994. *Recordings:* Contributor, albums: Come Rain Or Come Shine, Hanne Romer, 1994; New Deal, Scandinavian Jazz Quartet, 1994; A Night in Bilbao, Scandinavian Jazz Quartet, 1996; Giving It Away, Helle Hansen, 1995; Red Letter Days, Harvest Moon, 1995; I'm Old Fashioned Katrine Madsen, 1996; Dream Dancing, Katrine Madsen, 1997, Close to You, Katrine Madsen 2004, Gleda: Songs from Scandinavia, Stefano Bollani 2004, 117 Ditmas Avenue, Kasper Villaume 2005, Supernatural Love, Katrine Madsen 2006, Love List, Kaya Bruel 2008, Stone in the Water, Stefano Bollani 2009, Simple Life, Katrine Madsen 2009; solo: Short Stories for Dreamers 2010. *Address:* c/o Sundance Music Limited, Gothersgade 107, 1123 Copenhagen; Godthaabsvej 36 B, 2 TV, 2000 Frederiksberg, Denmark. *Telephone:* (33) 33-87-20. *Fax:* (33) 15-02-06. *E-mail:* sundance@sundance.dk. *Website:* www.sundance.dk.

BØE, Erik Glambek; Norwegian singer and musician (guitar); b. 25 Oct. 1975, Bergen; m. Ina Grung; one s. *Career:* mem. Skog 1995–97, 2006–;

Founder mem. (with Erlend Øye) Kings of Convenience 2000–. *Recordings include:* albums: The Kings of Convenience 2000, Quiet Is The New Loud 2001, Versus 2001, Riot On An Empty Street 2004, Declaration of Dependence 2009. *Address:* Kirkeveien 10, 5072 Bergen, Norway. *E-mail:* management@ kingsofconvenience.com. *E-mail:* eirik@kingsofconvenience.com (office). *Website:* www.kingsofconvenience.org.

BOESEL, Jason; American musician (guitar, drums, percussion) and singer; b. Oahu, Hawaii. *Career:* mem. Evergreen 1990s, Rilo Kiley 2001–, The Elected 2004–06, Bright Eyes 2005–07, Conor Oberst and the Mystic Valley Band 2007–10; also solo artist 2009–; has also collaborated with The Lassie Foundation, Jenny Lewis and the Watson Twins, Jakob Dylan, The Young Veins and others. *Recordings:* albums: with Rilo Kiley: Execution of All Things 2002, More Adventurous 2004, Under the Blacklight 2007; with The Elected: Me First 2004, Sun, Sun, Sun 2006; with Bright Eyes: I'm Wide Awake, It's Morning 2005, Digital Ash in a Digital Urn 2005, Cassadaga 2007; with Conor Oberst and the Mystic Valley Band: Conor Oberst 2008, Outer South 2009; other appearances: El Dorado, The Lassie Foundation 2001, Trouble is Real, Johnathan Rice 2005, Rabbit Fur Coat, Jenny Lewis and the Watson Twins 2006, Acid Tongue, Jenny Lewis 2008, The Way That It Was, Pierre de Reeder 2008, Elephants... Teeth Sinking Into Heart, Rachael Yamagata 2008, Seeing Things, Jakob Dylan 2008, White Water, White Bloom, Sea Wolf 2009, Devil's Made a New Friend, Jarrod Gorbel 2010, Take a Vacation!, The Young Veins 2010, I'm Having Fun Now, Jenny and Johnny 2010; solo: Hustler's Son 2010. *Current Management:* c/o Jessica Massa, Press Here Publicity, 138 West 25th Street, 9th Floor, New York, NY 10001, USA. *Telephone:* (212) 246-2640. *Fax:* (212) 582-6513. *E-mail:* jessica@pressherepublicity.com. *Website:* www .pressherepublicity.com. *Address:* c/o Brant Weil, Warner Bros. Records Inc., 3300 Warner Boulevard, Burbank, CA 91505-4694, USA (office). *E-mail:* brant .weil@wbr.com (office). *Website:* www.warnerbrosrecords.com (office); www .rilokiley.com.

BOGGUSS, Suzy Kay; American country singer; b. 30 Dec. 1956, Aledo, Ill.; d. of Charles Bogguss and B.J. Bogguss; m. Doug Crider; one s. *Education:* Illinois State Univ. *Career:* discovered singing at Dolly Parton's theme park Dollywood; solo country singer 1986–; collaborations with Ray Benson, Chet Atkins, Steve Dorff, Matraca Berg, Pat Bunch. *Recordings:* albums: Somewhere Between 1989, Moment Of Truth 1990, Aces 1991, Voices In The Wind 1992, Somethin' Up My Sleeve 1993, Simpatico (with Chet Atkins) 1994, Give Me Some Wheels 1996, Nobody Love, Nobody Gets Hurt 1998, Suzy Bogguss 1999, Have Yourself a Merry Little Christmas 2001, Swing 2003, Sweet Danger 2007. *Honours:* CMA Horizon Award, Most Promising Artist 1992. *Current Management:* Lotos Nile Media, PO Box 90245, Nashville, TN 37209-0245, USA. *Telephone:* (615) 298-1144. *E-mail:* Kissyblack@lotosnile.com. *Website:* www.lotosnile.com. *E-mail:* info@suzybogguss.com (office). *Website:* www.suzybogguss.com.

BOGLE, Eric, AO; Scottish/Australian singer, songwriter and musician (guitar); b. 23 Sept. 1944, Peebles, Scotland; m. Carmel 1972. *Career:* accountant –1980; full-time musician 1980–; various tours, television appearances; full mem. Australasian Performing Right Asscn (APRA). *Recordings include:* albums: Scraps Of Paper 1981, When The Wind Blows 1985, Singing In The Spirit Home 1987, Something Of Value 1988, Song Book 1990, Voices In The Wilderness 1991, I Wrote This Song 1995, Hard Hard Times 1997, Emigrant And The Exile 1997, Small Miracles 1998, At This Stage 2005, The Dreamer 2009. *Publications:* five song books since 1980. *Honours:* UN Peace Medal 1986, APRA Gold Award 1986. *Current Management:* c/o Arthur & Pat Laing Entertainment, 35 Montague Street, Goulburn, NSW 2580, Australia. *Telephone:* (2) 6292-4550. *E-mail:* peter@laing-entertainment.com.au. *Website:* www.laing-entertainment.com.au. *Address:* PO Box 1037, Unley, SA 5061, Australia (office). *E-mail:* info@ericbogle.net (office). *Website:* www .ericbogle.net.

BOGLIUNI, Mario; Croatian composer, musician (piano) and arranger; b. 24 May 1935, Svetvincenat-Pula; m. Maria Adler 1973; one s. *Education:* Conservatorium of Music Art. *Career:* concerts and tours, Croatia; European countries; Australia, 1969; USA, 1970; Russia, 1974; editor, several series on pop music; compositions for theatre and film; mem. Music Asscn of Croatia (DHS). *Compositions:* songs: Running Out of World; Why Do I Love You; Sailors Cha Cha Cha; Three Friends; Serenade. *Honours:* 25 Croatian and international festival awards. *Address:* Sestinski Dol 121 A, 41000 Zagreb, Croatia.

BOIC, Drazen, MD; Croatian musician (piano), composer and arranger; b. 11 April 1931, Zagreb; m. Anita 1967, one s. one d. *Education:* Secondary Music School, Zagreb and studied medicine. *Career:* jazz musician, commercial music; Leader, own trio, quartet, quintet, sextet; Croatian Zagreb Radio Orchestra, 1954–58; playing for US Air Forces, 1957–64; tours in Russia, 1967–80; pianist, ballet school, Zagreb, 1980–90; piano player, Hotel Esplanade, Zagreb, 1980–; mem. Croatian Musicians' Union, Zagreb. *Compositions include:* Tiho i Mirno; Ljetni Ritam; Anita Fedor; Petra.

BOIĆ, Fedor; Croatian composer, producer and musician (keyboards); b. 17 Oct. 1968, Zagreb. *Career:* playing in theatre, Komedija; With Tereda Kesouija: ITD Band; Aerodrom; Novi Fosili; many Croatian television and radio shows; Currently playing keyboards in Prijavo Kazaliste; Producer, sound engineer, JM Sound Studio-Zagreb on over 30 LPs for artists including: ITD Band; Jasna Zlokic; Sanja Dolezal; Novi Fosili; Jasmin Stauros; Venera; Vesna Ivic; Duka Caic; Prljavo Kazaliste; HDS, Croatian Composer Society;

HGU, Croatian Musician Society. *Publications:* Suzy; Jugoton; Ofej. *Address:* Brace Cvijica 17, 41000 Zagreb, Croatia.

BOJSEN-MOLLER, Cai; Danish composer and musician (drums, keyboards); b. 7 March 1966, Copenhagen; m. Anna Reumert 1986; one s. one d. *Career:* Musician, Gangway; Musician for Busstop, Paris-Paris, Naive, Lisa Nilsson and Louise Hoffsten; Composer, Solo Performer, 1990; International concerts in England, Japan and Germany; Performed Roskilde Festival, 1997. *Compositions:* Solo albums: A Bit of Something, 1997; Super Sonic Jazzy Session, 1998; Singles: A Night in the Pit, 1996; Revertrhythm, 1996; Bits, 1997. *Recordings:* Compilations: Get Lost, 1996; Past, Present and Future, 1997; Further Adventures in Techno Soul, 1998. *Publications:* Film/Art Videos: Talk Like Whales, 1994; Pets, 1995. *Honours:* four Grammy Awards, Gangway, 1993.

BOLAM, Frank, LRAM; British musician (guitars) and teacher; b. 22 April 1949, Glasgow, Scotland; divorced, one s. one d. *Education:* studied with Iain McHaffie and Ron Moore. *Career:* professional since age 21; major productions, theatre, musicals including: Hair, Glasgow Metropole Theatre; West Side Story; Chess; numerous television appearances, radio broadcasts and recording sessions; extensive professional and session work; full-time instrumental music teacher, Glasgow, Renfrewshire and N Ayrshire schools; set exam syllabus for the Scottish Qualification Authority; teacher, Lecturer, Strathclyde Univ.; mem. Glasgow Society of Musicians, Musicians' Union, EIS. *Recordings include:* The Jazz Train. *Publications:* complete guitar and bass guitar courses (all styles and levels) for exam syllabus for Glasgow, Renfrew and N Ayrshire Education Depts. *Honours:* Yamaha Scottish Instrumental Teacher of the Year 2003. *Address:* 47 Coltmuir Street, Parkhouse, Glasgow, G22 6LU, Scotland. *Telephone:* (141) 336-6739.

BOLGER, Leslie William Patrick; British musician (guitar), arranger and teacher; b. 11 Aug. 1947, Liverpool, England; m. Claire Holland 1970; three d. *Education:* Univ. of Manchester, studied with George Gola in Australia. *Career:* jazz performances with artists, including Martin Taylor, Louis Stewart, Ben Clatworthy, Ike Isaacs, Gary Potter; arranger, music adviser, Granada Television; session guitarist, arranger, Piccadilly Radio and Radio Merseyside; backing guitarist for many cabaret artists, including Tony Christie, The Nolans, Gerard Kenny, Joe Longthorne, Bob Monkhouse; currently Head of Guitar Studies, Univ. of Salford, Liverpool Arts Centre; mem. Musicians' Union. *Honours:* numerous honours for Les Bolger Jazz Guitar Ensemble. *Address:* 12 Firbank Close, Daresbury View, Runcorn, Cheshire WA7 6NR, England (home). *E-mail:* l.bolger1@ntlworld.com (office).

BOLLING, Claude; French jazz pianist, composer and band leader; b. 10 April 1930, Cannes; s. of Harry Bolling and Geneviève Brannens; m. Irène Dervize-Sadyker 1959; two s. *Education:* Nice Conservatory, studied with pvt. music teachers, including Bob Colin, Earl Hines, Maurice Duruflé, Willie 'The Lion' Smith, André Hodeir. *Career:* worked with Dizzy Gillespie, Stéphane Grappelli, Rex Stewart, Roy Eldridge, Sidney Bechet, Albert Nicholas, Lionel Hampton, The Ellingtonians, Carmen McRae, Jo Williams; formed groups Les Parisiennes, Claude Bolling Big Band. *Compositions include:* piano solos, duos, trios and all instrumental combinations, including jazz, big band and symphony orchestra; written and recorded with Jean-Pierre Rampal (Suite for Flute), Alexandre Lagoya (Guitar Concerto), Maurice André (Toot Suite), Pinchas Zukerman (Suite for Violin), Yo-Yo Ma (Suite for Cello). *Compositions for film:* more than 100 film soundtrack scores, including Le Jour et l'Heure 1963, Borsalino 1970, Le Magnifique 1973, Flic Story 1975, California Suite 1978, L'Homme en Colère 1979, The Awakening 1980, Willie and Phil 1980, La Mandarine, Le Mur de l'Atlantique, On ne meurt que deux fois 1985, Netchaiev est de retour 1991, Hasards ou coïncidences 1998. *Compositions for television include:* Jazz Memories, Les Brigades du Tigre (series) 1974–83, Chantecler 1977, Claudine à l'école 1978, L'étrange monsieur Duvallier (series) 1979, Georges Dandin 1980, Le calvaire d'un jeune homme impeccable 1981, Panurge 1982, Les Dalton en cavale 1983, Lucky Luke (series) 1984, La garçonne 1988, Renseignements généraux (series) 1989–90, L'amant de ma soeur 1991, Ce que savait Maisie 1995, Antoine 1996, Maintenant ou jamais 1997, Letter from an Unknown Woman 2001. *Honours:* Hon. Citizen of Los Angeles; Commdr, Ordre des Arts et des Lettres 2006, Chevalier, Ordre nat. du Mérite, Officier Légion d'honneur 2010; Médaille d'or Maurice Ravel, SACEM Gold Medal and Grand Prix 1984. *Address:* CAID Music, 20 avenue de Lorraine, 92380 Garches, France (office). *Telephone:* (1) 47-41-41-84 (office). *Fax:* (1) 47-01-03-63 (office). *E-mail:* bollingclaude@yahoo.fr. *Website:* www.claude-bolling.com (home).

BOLO, Yami, (Roland MacLean); Jamaican reggae singer; b. 1970, Kingston. *Career:* singer with Sugar Minott's Youth Promotion sound system; solo singer 1985–; founder, Yam Euphony record label, 1992. *Recordings include:* albums: Ransom, 1989; Jah Made Them All, 1989; Who Knows It Feels It, 1991; Up Life Street, 1992; Cool and Easy, 1993, Yami Bolo Meets Lloyd Hemmings 1994, Fighting for Peace 1994, Star of Love 1995, War Monger 1996, Jah Love 1998, Wisdom Cry 1998, Freedom and Liberation 1999, Say a Prayer 1999, Wonders and Sign 2000, Healing of All Nations 2001, 4 Rebels 2001, Forces of Nature Volume 2 2002, Rebelution 2003, The Ministry 2005, Love the Unbreakable Resolve 2006, Crucial Duets Volume 1 2009. *Address:* Yam Euphony Music Inc., PO Box 1413, Bronx, New York, NY 10466, USA. *Telephone:* (917) 548-9185. *Fax:* (718) 528-0108. *E-mail:* info@yamibolo.com. *Website:* www.yamibolo.com.

BOLTON, Michael; American singer, songwriter and producer; b. (Michael Bolotin), 26 Feb. 1953, New Haven, Conn.; three d. *Career:* singer for rock group Blackjack 1978–82; collaborator, Glasnost album as mem. of US songwriting team in Moscow 1988; solo recording artist, fmrly under name Michael Bolotin; numerous live appearances and tours; songwriter for Barbra Streisand, Cher, KISS, Kenny G and Peabo Bryson; collaborations with Bob Dylan, Lady Gaga, Diane Warren, Desmond Child, David Foster, A.R. Rahman, Phil Ramone, Ne Yo, Billy Mann, Kanye West, Jay Z, John Legend; numerous television appearances; mem. BMI. *Compositions include:* How Am I Supposed To Live Without You, Laura Branigan 1983, I Found Someone, Cher 1988; Co-writer (with Paul Stanley), Forever, Kiss 1990, Steel Bars (with Bob Dylan) 1992. *Recordings include:* albums include: Michael Bolton 1983, Everybody's Crazy 1985, The Hunger 1987, Soul Provider 1989, Time Love and Tenderness 1991, Timeless: The Classics 1992, The One Thing 1993, All That Matters 1997, My Secret Passion 1998, Timeless Vol. 2 1999, Greatest Hits 1985–95 1995, Go The Distance (theme from Disney film Hercules), This Is The Time: The Christmas Album 1996, All That Matters 1997, My Secret Passion 1998, Timeless: The Classics Vol. 2 1999, Only A Woman Like You 2002, Vintage 2004, Bolton Swings Sinatra 2006, A Swinging Christmas 2007, One World One Love 2009, Home for Christmas 2010, Gems: The Duets Collection 2011, Ain't No Mountain High Enough: A Tribute to Hitsville 2013. *Publication:* The Secret of the Lost Kingdom (juvenile) 1997. *Honours:* New York Music Award, Best R&B Vocalist 1988, ASCAP Airplay Awards 1989, Pollstar Tour of the Year 1990, Grammy Awards for Best Pop Vocal Performance 1990, 1992, American Music Awards for Favourite Male Pop/ Rock Artist, Favourite Album 1992, 1993, BMI Song of the Year 1991, Hitmakers Award, National Songwriters Hall of Fame 1995, five times winner, BMI Million Performance Song Award. *Current Management:* c/o Levin/Nelson Entertainment, 130 West 57th Street, Suite 7B, New York, NY 10019, USA. *Telephone:* (212) 489-5738. *Fax:* (212) 489-6319. *E-mail:* info@ levinnelson.com. *Website:* www.levinnelson.com. *E-mail:* boltoninfo@aol.com. *Website:* www.michaelbolton.com.

BOLVIG, Palle P. S.; Danish musician (trumpet, flugelhorn), composer and arranger; b. 25 Nov. 1932, Copenhagen; m. Jytte 1969; one s. three d. *Career:* mem. Ib Glindemann Orchestra 1951–61, Int. Band, Newport Festival 1958, Danish Radio Big Band, 1964–97, Ernie Wilkins Almost Big Band 1980–, Allan Bo Band 1997–; mem. The Danish Trumpet Socs. *Compositions include:* Easy Mood 1961, Gosty Day 1970, Zabacoot 1970, Portrait Of Cordoba 1971, Back To Tenderness 1971, Child Of Pain 1985, Blue January 1999. *Recordings include:* Newport International Band 1958, Brownsville Trolley Line, Danish Radio Big Band 1969, Ben Webster and the Danish Radio Big Band 1970, Thad Jones and the Danish Radio Big Band 1978, Ernie Wilkins Almost Big Band 1981, Aura, Miles Davis 1985; with the Danish Radio Band: Little Bit Of Duke 1994, First British Tour 1995, Suite For Jazz Band 1995; other: Captain Coe's Famous Racearound 1996, Like Life, Django Bates 1998, Impulsive, The Danish Radio Jazz Orchestra 1997, Ways Of Seeing, The Danish Radio Jazz Orchestra 1999, Blues, Blues and All That Jazz, Allan Bo Band 1999, Sahib Shihab — the Danish Radio Jazz Group 2001, Stan Kenton, with the Danish Radio Big Band 2002, Putte Wickman & Ernie Wilkins Almost Big Band 2005, Out of this World with Bobo Moreno and Ernie Wilkins Almost Big Band 2007. *Address:* Holmevaenget 3, Gundsømagle, 4000 Roskilde, Denmark (home).

BOM; South Korean singer; b. (Park Bom), 24 March 1984, Seoul. *Education:* Gould Acad., Bethel, Lesley Univ., Berklee Coll. of Music, USA. *Career:* has sung with Big Bang, Lexy, Kim Ji-Eun, Red Roc, GD&TOP, Lee Hyo Ri, G-Dragon and Park Myung Soo; mem. 2NE1 2009–; launched solo career 2009. *Film:* Girlfriends 2009. *Television includes:* 2NE1 TV 2009–11; also appearances on Inkigayo (SBS) 2009-11, M! Countdown (Mnet) 2009–11, Music Bank (KBS) 2009–11. *Recordings:* albums: with 2NE1: To Anyone (Melon Music Award for Album of the Year 2010, Mnet Asian Music Award for Album of the Year 2010, Korean Music Award for Best Dance and Electronic Album 2011) 2010, Crush 2014. *Honours:* numerous awards for 2NE1 including: Asia Song Festival Asian Newcomer's Award 2009, Melon Music Awards for New Artist and Top 10 2009, for Top 10 2010, Mnet 20's Choice Awards for Hot New Star 2009, Hot CF Star 2009 and Hot Online Song 2009, Mnet Asian Music Awards for Best New Female Artist 2009, for Music Portal Award 2009, for Song of the Year 2009, for Best Music Video 2009, 2010, for Best Female Group 2010, for Artist of the Year 2010, Rhythmer Awards for R&B Artist of the Year and Rookie of the Year 2009 Style Icon Best Female Singer Awards 2009, 2010, MTV Daum Music Fest Award for Artist of the Year 2011, MYX Music Favorite K-pop Video Award 2011; also numerous Cyworld Digital Music Awards including Top Selling Artist Award 2009, Newcomer of the Year 2010, Bonsang Award 2010, Artist of the Year Award 2010, Song of the Year 2010; solo award: Mnet Asian Music Awards for Best Digital Single 2010. *Address:* c/o YG Entertainment, 397–5 YG Building, Hapjeong-Dong, Mapo-Gu, Seoul 109-819, South Korea (office). *Telephone:* (2) 3143-1105 (office). *Fax:* (2) 544-1546 (office). *E-mail:* web@ygmail.net (office). *Website:* eng.ygfamily.com/ main/main.html (office); www.yg-2ne1.com (home).

BOM-BANE, Jane, BA (Hons), PGCE; British singer, composer, lyricist and musician (harmonium); *Performer/Restaurateur, Bom-Bane's*; b. (Jane Bayley), 11 Sept. 1953, Leek, Staffs., England; m. André Schmidt 1982 (divorced); one s. *Education:* Univ. of Warwick. *Career:* fmr singer with The Swinging Cats; solo artist: 1994–; performances at Edinburgh Festival 1994, 1997, 1999, 2001, 2002, 2004, 2005, 2012; Owner/performer, Bom-Bane's (music café) 2006–; radio and TV appearances on BBC, Channel 4 and internationally. *Musicals:* original musicals written and performed in Bom-Bane's: Bom-Bane's: The Musical, A Musical History of 24 George Street, Brighton, Bom-Bane's Christmas Musical: Merrily on High. *Exhibitions:* Aqua Annie's and My Guy (story-poems illustrated by pastel-painter Tom Walker); site specific tours: Jane Bom-Bane's House, The Crossword House. *Recordings include:* albums: Round-a-way Wrong Songs 1995, It Makes Me Laugh 1996, Underwonderworld 1997, I've Got a Goldfish Bowl on my Head 1998, soundtrack: The Man From Porlock 1995, Rotator 2002, Bom-Bane's: The Musical (soundtrack). *Honours:* Spirit of the Fringe Music Award, Edinburgh Festival 2005, Three Weeks' Editor's Award 2007. *Address:* Bom-Bane's, 24 George Street, Brighton, BN2 1RH, England (office). *Telephone:* (1273) 606400 (office). *E-mail:* janebombane@yahoo.co.uk (office). *Website:* bombanes.com (office).

BON JOVI, Jon; American singer, songwriter, musician (guitar), record producer and actor; b. (John Francis Bongiovi, Jr), 2 March 1962, Perth Amboy, NJ; m. Dorothea Hurley 1989; three s. one d. *Career:* singer in local bands Raze, Atlantic City Expressway; Founder-mem. and lead singer in rock group Bon Jovi 1983–88, 1992–; solo artist 1988–; numerous tours, radio, TV and live appearances world-wide; soundtrack for numerous films; Owner man. co. BJM; Owner record label Jambco; Founder and primary Owner Philadelphia Soul of the Arena Football League 2004–. *Films include:* Young Guns II: Blaze of Glory (uncredited) 1990, Moonlight and Valentino (Motion Picture Club Premier Performance Award) 1995, The Leading Man 1996, Little City 1997, Destination Anywhere (video) 1997, No Looking Back 1998, Homegrown 1998, Row Your Boat 1998, U-571 2000, Pay It Forward 2000, Ally McBeal 2001–02, Vampires: Los Muertos 2002, Cry Wolf 2005, Pucked 2006, New Year's Eve 2011. *Television includes:* Unsolved Mysteries 1988, Sex and the City (series) 1999, Ally McBeal (series) 2002. *Recordings include:* albums: with Bon Jovi: Bon Jovi 1984, 7800° Fahrenheit 1985, Slippery When Wet 1986, Bon Jovi Live 1987, New Jersey 1988, Keep The Faith 1991, Cross Road (compilation) 1994, These Days 1995, Crush 2000, One Wild Night 1985–2001 (live) 2001, Tokyo Road: Best of Bon Jovi (compilation) 2001, Bounce 2002, Distance 2003, This Left Feels Right (compilation) 2003, Have a Nice Day 2005, Lost Highway 2007, The Circle 2009, Greatest Hits (compilation) 2010, What About Now 2013, Burning Bridges 2015; solo: Young Guns II: Blaze of Glory 1990, Destination Anywhere 1997; box set: 100,000,000 Bon Jovi Fans Can't Be Wrong 2004. *Honours:* American Music Awards for Favorite Pop/Rock Band 1988, for Favorite Pop/Rock Single 1991, Nordoff-Robbins Music Therapy Silver Clef 1990, Golden Globe Award for Best Original Song from a Motion Picture (for Blaze of Glory) 1991, BRIT Award for Best Int. Group (with band) 1995, VH-1 Award for Favorite Video (for It's My Life) 2000, Grammy Award for Best Country Collaboration with Vocals (with Jennifer Nettles) 2007, Billboard Music Award for Top Touring Artist 2014. *Current Management:* c/o Bon Jovi Management, PO Box 237040, New York, NY 10023, USA. *Telephone:* (212) 336-9413. *Fax:* (212) 336-5385. *Website:* www.bonjovi.com.

BONAPARTE, Bonny, (Bonny B); American musician (drums, percussion, vocals); b. Trinidad and Tobago. *Career:* played with local groups in Trinidad such as USA The Trinidad Troubadours; f. own band Trinity; performed/ recorded with artists including Peter Tosh, Bob Marley, Yellowman, The Mighty Sparrow, Crazy, Calypso Rose, Tony Ricardo, Earl Rodney and Friends, Kid Creole and the Coconuts; now lives in Las Vegas; also toured and recorded with Bruce Hornsby; mem., jazz band Spyro Gyra 2007–11. *Recordings include:* Good to Go-Go 2007, A Night Before Christmas 2008, Down the Wire 2009, A Foreign Affair 2011. *Honours:* George Benson Lifetime Achievement Award, Canadian Smooth Jazz Awards 2007 (with Spyro Gyra). *Current Management:* c/o Phil Brennan, Crosseyed Bear Productions, 270 Olympic Avenue, Buffalo, NY 14215-3258, USA. *Telephone:* (716) 831-1511. *E-mail:* phil@philbrennan.com.

BONDS, Gary 'US'; American singer, songwriter and producer; b. (Gary Anderson), 6 June 1939, Jacksonville, Fla. *Career:* mem. group The Turks; solo artist 1960–; co-writer, producer with Bruce Springsteen and Steve Van Zandt 1978; mem. Global Village Champions Foundation. *Recordings include:* albums: Quarter to Three 1961, Twist Up Calypso, Dedication 1978, On The Line 1982, Standing In The Line Of Fire 1984, Take Me Back To New Orleans 1995, King Biscuit Flower Hour Presents Gary US Bonds Live 2001, Back in 20 2004, Let Them Talk 2009; producer for artists including Johnny Paycheck, ZZ Hill. *Honours:* inducted into Long Island Music Hall of Fame 2006, Global Village Champion of the Decade Award 2009. *Website:* www.garyusbonds .com.

BONE, Greg; British musician (guitar); b. 21 Jan. 1962, Hartlepool, England; one s. *Career:* played with Terry Ronald; support tours with Hall and Oates, 1990; Robert Palmer, 1991; television and radio broadcasts, particularly with Band of Thieves (now known as Thieves Like Us); mem. Musicians' Union. *Recordings include:* with the Pet Shop Boys: Discography, 1991; Was It Worth It? 1991; DJ Culture, 1991; Bilingual, 1996; Clive Griffin, Clive Griffin, 1993; Nobody Else, Take That, 1995; Sole Purpose, Secret Life, 1995; Warehouse Grooves Vol. 5, 1998; Love and The Russian Winter, Simply Red, 1999; Reload, Tom Jones, 1999; Killing Time, Tina Cousins, 2000; Steptacular, Steps, 2000.

BONET, Maria del Mar; Spanish singer, songwriter and musician (guitar); b. 27 April 1947, Palma, Mallorca. *Career:* began singing with Els Setze Jutges, Barcelona, 1967; live performances worldwide; recorded and toured, France and Spain, with Ensemble de Musique Traditionelle de Tunís, 1985;

toured Spain, with Brazilian Milton Nascimiento, 1986; presented Arenal, with choreographer, dancer, Nacho Duato, 1988; International Peralada Music Festival, 1992; performed show, The Greece of Theodorakis, 1993; performed in Cants d'Abelone, 1994; performed show, Merhaba, Summer Festival, Barcelona, 1994; Edinburgh International Festival, 1995; mem. Societat General d'Autors i Editors (SGAE), Associació de Cantants i Intèrprets Professionals en Llangua Catalana (ACIC). *Recordings include:* Maria del Mar Bonet, 1974; A L'Olympia, 1975; Maria del Mar Bonet, 1976; Cançons de Festa, 1976; Alenar, 1977; Saba de Terrer, 1979; Quico-Maria del Mar, 1979; Cançons de la Nostra Mediterranea, 1980; L'Aguila Negra, 1981; Jardí Tancat, 1981; Sempre, 1981; Breviari d'Amor, 1982; Maria del Bonet, 1983; Anells d'Aigua, 1985; Gavines i Dragons, 1987; Ben A Prop, 1989; Bon Viatge Faci la Cadernera, 1990; Coreografies, with Nacho Duato, 1990; Ellas, Maria del Mar Bonet Canta a Theodorakis, 1993; Salmaia, 1995; El Cor el Temps, 1997; Cavall de Foc, 1999. *Publications:* Antología de la Nova Cançó Catalana, 1968; Maria del Mar Bonet, 1976; La Nova Cançó, 1976; Tretze que Cantan, 1982; Veinte Años de Canción en España, 1984; Una Història de la Cançó, 1987; 25 Anys de Cançó a Mallorca, 1987; Secreta Veu (poems and watercolours), 1987; Maria del Mar Bonet (biography), Joan Manresa, 1994; Quadern de Viatge, poems and watercolours, 1998. *Honours:* French Government Charles Cross Academy Award, Best Foreign Record, 1984; Cross of St George, Catalan Government Prize, 1984; Catalan Government National Prize, 1992. *Telephone:* (650) 563-9280. *Fax:* (650) 563-9266. *E-mail:* hrmusic@hrmusic.com. *Website:* www.hrmusic.com/artists/bonetart.html.

BONFILS, Tony; French musician (bass guitar, double bass) and singer; b. 27 Jan. 1948, Nice; three s. one d. *Education:* Licence de Psychologie. *Career:* bass player with: Dee Dee Bridgewater; Sacha Distel; Charles Aznavour; also studio musician. *Honours:* Prix de Contre Basse; Medaille de Solfege. *Telephone:* (1) 30-76-63-26. *Fax:* (1) 30-76-92-82. *E-mail:* bonfils.tony@free.fr. *Website:* www.1212.com/a/bonfils/tony.html.

BONGA, Ntshukumo (Ntshuks), BSc; South African musician (alto saxophone, clarinet) and engineer; b. 1 Oct. 1963, Johannesburg. *Career:* appearances include Reithalle, Berne, Switzerland, Purcell Room, South Bank Centre, London Jazz Festival 1994, London ICA 1996, WOMAD Festival 1997; performances with Robyn Hitchcock; mem. Musicians' Union, PRS, London Musicians Collective. *Recordings include:* albums: Urban Ritual 1995, Ntshuks Bonga's Tshisa, Moss Elixir, Robyn Hitchcock, FJQ 1998. *Address:* 81a Glengall Road, London NW6 7ES, England (home). *E-mail:* ntshuks@gmail.com. *Website:* www.ntshuksbonga.com.

BONHAM, Jason; British musician (drums, percussion); b. 1967, England; s. of John Bonham; m. Jan Charteris 1990. *Education:* studied with his father. *Career:* mem., Airrace 1984; founder mem., Virginia Wolf 1986; worked with members of Led Zeppelin, 1987–88, 2007; Concert, Atlantic Records 40th Anniversary concert, Madison Square Garden, 1988; US tour with Jimmy Page, 1988; founder of own group, Bonham 1989–; has also performed with UFO, Foreigner, Damnocracy, Virginia Wolf; Joe Bonamassa; mem. Black Country Communion 2010–. *Recordings include:* albums: with Airrace: Shaft Of Light, 1984; with Virginia Wolf: Virginia Wolf, 1986; with Jimmy Page: Outrider, 1988; with Bonham: The Disregard Of Timekeeping, 1989; Madhatter, 1992; with Motherland: Peace For Me, 1994; with Red Blooded Blues: Red Blooded Blues, 1995; with Black Country Communion: Black Country 2010. *Address:* J&R Adventures, 1060 Holland Drive Ste K, Boca Raton, FL 33433, USA. *Telephone:* (561) 994-2344. *Fax:* (561) 994-27079. *E-mail:* info@bccommunion.com. *Website:* www.bccommunion.com; www.jasonbonham.net.

BONHAM, Tracy; American singer and musician (piano, violin); b. 16 March 1967, Eugene, Ore.; m. 1st Steve Slingeneyer (divorced 2001); m. 2nd Jason Fine. *Education:* Univ. of Southern California, Berklee Coll. of Music. *Career:* began singing at age five, playing violin at age nine and piano at age 14. *Recordings include:* albums: The Burdens of Being Upright 1996, Down Here 2000, Blink the Brightest 2005, In The City + In The Woods (EP) 2006, Masts of Manhatta 2010. *Current Management:* MAD Management, 4844 Riverton Avenue, Suite 104, North Hollywood, Los Angeles, CA 91601, USA. *Telephone:* (323) 596-1280. *Website:* Michael.Dutcher@gmail.com; www.tracybonham.com.

BONIN, Nathalie; American/Canadian musician (violin); b. 17 Nov. 1971, San Francisco, CA. *Education:* Aaron Copland School of Music, McGill University. *Career:* composer, Director, Ca Se Soigne, 1998; Producer Co-ordinator, String Festival 1998; Duke Ellington Tribute Concert, 1998; Valentino Orchestra, 1998; Said Mesnaoui, Arabic Violin and Percussion, 1998; mem. AFM, SOCAN. *Recordings:* Moist; Excentricus; Cineparc; Clair de Lune; Mendelssohn: Concerto for Violin Nos 1 and 2; Beethoven Symphony No. 3; Verismo; Enfants Retour; Prokofieff: Pierre et le Loup; Korngold, Ciel de Lune, Katjar 1997; Risque et Pendule, Ensemble Pierre Labbé 2003, La Espada de la Noche, Ted Nash and ODEON 2005, Magic Numbers, Quinsin Nachoff 2006, Horizons, Quinsin Nachoff 2008, Portrait in Seven Shades, Wynton Marsalis and the Jazz at Lincoln Center Orchestra 2010. *Honours:* Québec Arts Council Grant; Deans Honour List, McGill; First Prize Winner, Darius Milhaud Competition; Winner Canadian Music Competition; First Prize Winner, CW Post Summer Chamber Music Festival Concerto Competition. *E-mail:* nathalie.bonin@videotron.ca; nathalie@nathaliebonin.com. *Website:* www.nathaliebonin.com.

BONN, Stanley; American record label executive, publishing company executive and producer; b. 3 Feb. 1924, Freeport, Ill.; m. Eva L. Bonn 1947; one s. one d. *Career:* Owner, ESB Records, Gather Round Music, Bonnfire Publishing; worked with Bobby Lee Caldwell, John P Swisshelm, Rob Lynn, Jeff Ashbaker, Eddie Sheppard; mem. Country Music Asscn of America, California Country Music Asscn, Greater Southern Country Music Asscn. *Compositions:* The Sounds of the Universe. *Recordings include:* The Gold in this Ring, Janie's Song, Highway 44, She's a Dance Hall Lady, Don't Watch Me Fall Apart, West Texas Lady, Ten Minutes After Five, The Sounds Of the Universe, All the Tears, Toe Tappin' Country Man, Three Reasons, 2nd Wind, First Date Blues. *Honours:* Song of the Year Award (five times), Record Label of the Year Award 1991, 1992, 1994, Golden Eagle Award, California Country Music Asscn 1994.

BONNEY, Simon; Australian singer and songwriter; b. 3 June 1961, Sydney; m. 1984, one s. one d. *Career:* performed in film Wings of Desire (Wim Wenders), with Crime and the City Solution; contributor to film scores: To The Ends of The World (Wim Wenders); Faraway So Close (Wim Wenders); Gas Food and Lodgings (Alison Anders); Underworld (Roger Christian); mem. PRS. *Recordings include:* albums: with Crime and the City Solution: Just South Of Heaven, 1985; Room Of Lights, 1986; Shine, 1988; The Bride Ship, 1989; Paradise Discotheque, 1990; The Adversary: Live; solo: Forever, 1992; Everyman, 1995. *Website:* www.myspace.com/simonbonney.

BONNIE 'PRINCE' BILLY (see Oldham, Will)

BONO; Irish rock singer, songwriter and humanitarian; *Lead Singer, U2*; b. (Paul Hewson), 10 May 1960, Dublin; m. Alison Stewart 1982. *Education:* Mount Temple School. *Career:* Founder-mem. and lead singer, the Feedback 1976, renamed the Hype, finally renamed U2 1978–; numerous concerts, including Live Aid Wembley 1985, Self Aid Dublin, A Conspiracy of Hope (Amnesty International Tour) 1986, Smile Jamaica (hurricane relief fundraiser) 1988, Very Special Arts Festival, White House, Washington, DC 1988; numerous tours world-wide. *Plays include:* Spider-Man: Turn Off The Dark (music and lyrics by Bono and The Edge), Broadway, New York 2011–14. *Films include:* Rattle and Hum 1988, The Million Dollar Hotel (co-writer) 2000. *Recordings include:* albums: Boy 1980, October 1981, War 1983, Under a Blood Red Sky 1983, The Unforgettable Fire 1984, Wide Awake In America 1985, The Joshua Tree (Grammy Award for Album of the Year, Best Rock Performance by a Duo or Group with Vocal) 1987, Rattle and Hum 1988, Achtung Baby (Grammy Award for Best Rock Performance by a Duo or Group with Vocal 1992) 1991, Zooropa (Grammy Award for Best Alternative Music Album) 1993, Passengers (film soundtrack with Brian Eno) 1995, Pop 1997, The Best Of 1980–90 1998, All That You Can't Leave Behind (Grammy Award for Best Rock Album 2001) 2000, The Best Of 1990–2000 2002, How To Dismantle An Atomic Bomb (Meteor Ireland Music Award for Best Irish Album 2006, Grammy Awards for Album of the Year, for Best Rock Album 2006) 2004, No Line on the Horizon 2009, Songs of Innocence 2014. *Honours:* Foreign Hon. Fellow, American Acad. of Arts and Sciences 2009; Portuguese Order of Liberty 2005; Hon. KBE 2007; 22 Grammy Awards with U2, including Best Rock Performance by a Duo or Group with Vocal (for Desire) 1988, BRIT Awards for Best Int. Act 1988–90, 1992, 1998, 2001, Best Live Act 1993, Outstanding Contribution to the British Music Industry 2001, JUNO Award 1993, World Music Award 1993, Grammy Award for Song of the Year, Record of the Year, Best Rock Performance by a Duo or Group with Vocal (all for Beautiful Day) 2000, Grammy Awards for Best Pop Performance by a Duo or Group with Vocal (for Stuck In A Moment You Can't Get Out Of), for Record of the Year (for Walk On), for Best Rock Performance by a Duo or Group with Vocal (for Elevation) 2001, American Music Award for Favourite Internet Artist of the Year 2002, Ivor Novello Award for Best Song Musically and Lyrically (for Walk On) 2002, Golden Globe for Best Original Song (for The Hands That Built America, from film Gangs of New York) 2003, Grammy Awards for Best Rock Performance by a Duo or Group with Vocal, Best Rock Song, Best Short Form Music Video (all for Vertigo) 2004, TED Prize 2004, Nordoff-Robbins Silver Clef Award for lifetime achievement 2005, Q Award for Best Live Act 2005, Digital Music Award for Favourite Download Single (for Vertigo) 2005, Meteor Ireland Music Award for Best Irish Band, Best Live Performance 2006, Grammy Awards for Song of the Year, for Best Rock Performance by a Duo or Group with Vocal (both for Sometimes You Can't Make it on Your Own), for Best Rock Song (for City of Blinding Lights) 2006, Ambassadors of Conscience Award, Amnesty International 2006, Liberty Medal 2007, Visionary Award, Palm Springs Film Festival 2014, Golden Globe Award for Best Original Song (Ordinary Love in Mandela: Long Walk to Freedom) 2014. *Current Management:* c/o Principle Management, 30–32 Sir John Rogersons Quay, Dublin 2, Ireland. *E-mail:* nadine@numb.ie. *Website:* www.u2.com.

BONSALL, Joseph Sloan, Jr; American singer and author; b. 18 May 1948, Philadelphia, Pa; s. of Joe Bonsall, Sr and Lillie Bonsall; m. Mary Ann Bell 1982; two d. *Education:* Frankford High School, Philadelphia. *Career:* mem. of gospel singing groups 1966–73; mem. country group The Oak Ridge Boys 1973–; mem. Grand Ole Opry, Acad. of Country Music, Nat. Acad. of Recording Arts and Sciences, American Fed. of Television and Radio Artists, Country Music Asscn, Gospel Music Asscn. *Recordings:* singles: Y'All Come Back Saloon, I'll Be True To You, Leavin' Louisiana In The Broad Daylight, Trying To Love Two Women, Elvira, Bobbie Sue, American Made, Love Song, I Guess It Never Hurts To Hurt Sometime, Come On In, Make My Life With You; albums: Oak Ridge Boys 1974, Sky High 1975, Old Fashioned... 1976,

Live 1977, Y'All Come Back Saloon 1977, Room Service 1978, The Oak Ridge Boys Have Arrived 1979, Together 1980, Greatest Hits 1980, Fancy Free 1981, Bobbie Sue 1982, Christmas 1982, Very Best 1982, American Made 1983, The Oak Ridge Boys Deliver 1983, Friendship 1983, Greatest Hits II 1984, Seasons 1985, Step On Out 1985, Where The Fast Lane Ends 1986, Christmas Again 1986, Monogahela 1987, New Horizons 1988, American Dreams 1989, Greatest Hits III 1989, Unstoppable 1991, The Long Haul 1992, Revival 1997, Voices 1999, From the Heart 2001, Colors 2003, The Journey 2004, Common Thread 2005, Front Row Seats 2006, A Gospel Journey 2009, The Boys Are Back 2009, It's Only Natural 2011. *Publications:* eight books, including the Molly the Cat series, G.I. Joe & Lillie: Remembering a Life of Love & Loyalty, An American Journey (Oak Ridge Boys autobiog.), From My Perspective 2010. *Honours:* induced into Philadelphia Music Hall of Fame, Gospel Music Hall of Fame, five Grammy Awards 1970–77, four Acad. of Country Music Awards (including the Cliffie Stone Pioneer Award for Lifetime Achievement and Best Vocal Group 1977, 1979), four Country Music Asscn Awards, numerous Gospel Music Asscn Dove Awards, Country Music Asscn Vocal Group of the Year 1978, American Music Award for Best Country Group 1982, Gold and multi-Platinum discs. *Current Management:* c/o Jim Halsey, The Halsey Company, 720 North 136th Road, Mounds, OK 74047, USA. *Telephone:* (918) 827-6529. *Fax:* (918) 827-6533. *E-mail:* jim@jimhalsey.com. *E-mail:* josephsbonsall@aol.com. *Website:* www.oakridgeboys.com (office); www.josephsbonsall.com.

BOOBA; French rapper; b. (Élie Yaffa), 9 Dec. 1976, Boulogne-Billancourt. *Career:* mem. of duo Lunatic 1994–2003; solo artist 2000–; most legally downloaded artist in French music history; numerous collaborations including Kayna Samet, Léya Masry, Trade Union & Mister Rudie, Diddy, 2Chainz, Philly Poe, Shay, Rim'K. *Recordings include:* albums: with Lunatic: Mauvais œil 2000; solo: Temps mort 2002, Panthéon 2004, Ouest Side 2006, 0.9 2008, Lunatic 2010, Futur 2012; several mixtapes. *Address:* c/o Universal Music France S.A.S., 20/22 rue des Fossés Saint Jacques, 75005 Paris, France (office). *Telephone:* 1-44-41-91-91 (office). *E-mail:* uol@umusic.com (office). *Website:* www.universalmusic.fr (office); www.boobalunatic.com.

BOOHORISHVILI, Mehab; Georgian folk singer and musician (guitar); b. 15 June 1972, Batumi. *Education:* Batumi Music Coll. *Career:* Turkey Folklore Festival, 1995; Eshme, group, Spain; Legames International Folklore Festival, 1997; GIEZA International Folk Festival, Spain, 1997; Bravo Festival, Tblisi, Georgia, 1998; Ariola, Otello, Turker; Festival of Arpendos; leader, Folk Song Trio; mem., Batume folk song group; singer, Batumi State Opera. *Recordings:* interpretations of major Georgian folk songs with Batumi State folk song group. *Honours:* Prize, GIEZA Festival, Spain, 1997; Prize, Spara Festival, 1997.

BOOM, Paddy; American musician (drums); b. (Patrick C. Seacor), 6 Sept. 1968, Singapore. *Career:* mem., Scissor Sisters 2001–08. *Recordings include:* albums: Scissor Sisters (BRIT Award for Best Int. Album 2005) 2004, Comfortably Numb 2004, Ta-Dah 2006. *Honours:* BRIT Awards for Best Int. Group, Best Int. Breakthrough Act 2005, Meteor Ireland Music Award for Best Int. Group 2007. *Website:* www.paddyboom.com.

BOONE, Deborah (Debby) Ann; American singer and actress; b. 22 Sept. 1956, Hackensack, NJ; d. of Pat Boone and Shirley Boone; m. Gabriel Ferrer 1979; two s. two d. *Career:* singer with (father) Pat Boone and family group 1970–; recording artist 1977–. *Television:* numerous television appearances include Sins of The Past (ABC) 1984. *Plays:* Seven Brides For Seven Brothers, national tour 1981–82, Sound of Music, national tour 1987–88, Grease, Meet Me in St Louis, The King and I. *Recordings include:* You Light Up My Life 1977, Midstream 1978, Love Has No Reason 1980, With My Song ...I Will Praise Him 1980, Savin' It Up 1981, Surrender 1983, Choose Life 1985, Friends For Life 1987, Home For Christmas 1993, Greatest Hymns 2000, You Light Up My Life: Greatest Inspirational Songs 2001, Reflections of Rosemary 2005, With My Song/Friends for Life 2008, Surrender/Choose Life 2008. *Publications include:* So Far; Bedtime Hugs For Little Ones (children's book) 1988, Tomorrow Is A Brand New Day (co–author) 1989, The Snow Angel 1991, Welcome to This World 1996, Nightlights 1997, Counting Blessings 1998. *Honours:* American Music Award for Song of the Year, Grammy Award for Best New Artist 1977, CMA Best New Country Artist 1977, Singing Star of Year, AGVA 1978, Dove Awards 1980, 1984, Best Inspirational Performance 1980, Best Gospel Performance (with Phil Driscoll) 1983, Keep The Flame Burning 1984, Best New Personality, National Asscn Theatre Owners. *Current Management:* c/o Susan Munao, Lighthouse Entertianment Group, 13542 Ventura Boulevard, Suite 327, Sherman Oaks, CA 91423, USA. *Telephone:* (818) 505-1230. *Website:* www.debbyboone.net.

BOONE, Pat; American singer and actor; b. 1 June 1934, Jacksonville, FL; m. Shirley Foley 1953, four d. *Education:* North Texas State Teachers' College, David Liscomb College, Columbia Univ. *Career:* numerous live and TV appearances; own television show, 1957; owner, Lamb and Lion Records. *Film appearances:* Bernadine, 1957; April Love, 1957; Mardi Gras, 1958; Journey To The Centre of The Earth, 1959; All Hands On Deck, 1961; State Fair, 1962; Main Attraction, 1962; Yellow Canary, 1963; Greatest Story Ever Told, 1965; Perils of Pauline, 1967; The Cross and The Switchblade, 1971. *Recordings include* Twixt Twelve and Twenty, 1958; Between You, Me and the Gatepost, 1960; The Real Christmas, 1961; Care and Feeding of Parents, 1967; A New Song, 1971; Joy, 1973; A Miracle A Day Keeps The Devil Away; My Faith, 1976; Pat Boone Devotional Book, 1977; The Honeymoon Is Over, 1977; Together: 25 Years With The Boone Family, 1979; Pray To Win: God Wants You To Succeed, 1980, In a Metal Mood: No More Mr. Nice Guy 1997, We Are Family: R&B Classics 2006. *Address:* PBGL Inc., 9220 Sunset Boulevard, Suite 310, Los Angeles, CA 90069, USA. *Telephone:* (310) 858-5900. *Fax:* (310) 858-5935. *E-mail:* info@patsgold.com. *Website:* www.patboone.com.

BOOTH, Sean Anthony; British programmer and producer; b. 1972. *Career:* mem. Lego Feet 1987–; mem. Autechre 1991–; involved in Gescom projects 1991–. *Films include:* Basscadet 1993, Second Bad Vilbel 1995, Pi 1998, Gantz Graf 2001. *Radio:* co-host IBC pirate radio show 1987–93, Disengage, Kiss FM Manchester 1993–98. *Recordings include:* albums: with Autechre: Incunabula 1993, Amber 1994, Tri Repetae 1995, Chiastic Slide 1997, LP5 1998, Confield 2001, Draft 7.30 2003, Untilted 2005, Quaristice 2008, Oversteps 2010; with Gescom: Minidisc (ARS Electronica Distinction) 1998; with Hafler Trio/Autechre: æ^{3}o & h^{3}æ 2003, æo^3 & ^{3}hæ 2005; singles: with Autechre: Cavity Job 1991, Basscadet 1994, PIOB 1994, Anti 1994, Garbage 1995, Anvil Vapre 1995, We R Are Why 1996, Envane 1997, Cichlisuite 1997, To Day 1998, The Peel Sessions 1999, EP7 1999, Split Rmx 12 1999, Peel Sessions Vol. 2 2001, Gantz Graf 2002; with Gescom: Gescom 1994, Gescom 2 1994, Motor (EP) 1994, The Sounds Of Machines Our Parents Used 1995, Keynell 1996, This 1998, That 1998, Minidisc 1998, Iss:sa 2003. *Current Management:* c/o Warp Records, Spectrum House, 32–34 Gordon House Road, London NW5 1LP, England. *Telephone:* (20) 7284-8350. *Fax:* (20) 7284-8360. *E-mail:* info@warprecords.com. *Website:* www.warprecords.com.

BOOTH, Tim; British singer and lyricist; b. 4 Feb. 1960, Leeds, England; one s. *Education:* Univ. of Manchester. *Career:* founder mem. and lead singer, James 1982–2002, re-formed 2007–; numerous tours, festival dates and TV appearances; solo artist 2002–; screenwriter, dance teacher and actor 2002–. *Film appearance:* Batman Begins 2005. *Recordings include:* albums: with James: Stutter 1986, Strip Mine 1988, One Man Clapping 1989, Gold Mother 1990, Seven 1992, Laid 1993, Wah Wah 1994, Whiplash 1997, The Best Of James 1998, Millionaires 1999, B-Sides Ultra 2001, Pleased To Meet You 2001, Getting Away With It 2002, Hey Ma 2008, The Night Before 2010, The Morning After 2010, La Petite Mort 2014; solo: Booth And The Bad Angel (with Angelo Badalamenti) 1996, Bone 2004. *Address:* c/o Mercury Records, 364–366 Kensington High Street, London W14 8NS, England (office). *Website:* www.wearejames.com.

BORDEN, David, BM, MM, MA; American composer and musician (piano, synthesizer); *Composer and Director, Mother Mallard's Portable Masterpiece Company*; b. 25 Dec. 1938, Boston, Mass; s. of Raymond Borden and Natalie Mallard Borden; m. 2nd Rebecca Godin 1994; one s. *Education:* Eastman School of Music, Harvard Univ., Hochschule für Musik, Berlin, Germany. *Career:* fmr Dir, Digital Music Program, Cornell Univ.; performances at WBAI Free Music Store, The Kitchen, The Knitting Factory, Dance Theatre Workshop, Town Hall, Lincoln Center, Roulette, Issue Project Room (all New York), Gatherings (Philadelphia), Tivoli Konzert Halle (Copenhagen), Barbican Centre (London), Portsmouth Festival (England), New Music America (Montreal, Canada); Composer and Dir, Mother Mallard's Portable Masterpiece Co.; mem. Herbert F. Johnson Museum of Art, Ithaca, New York, Brown Univ., Providence, Duquesne, Pittsburgh, MOOG FEST, Asheville, New Music USA, Berlin Atonal, Germany 2015. *Film soundtrack:* The Exorcist (part) 1973. *Compositions:* for synthesizer ensemble: The Continuing Story of Counterpoint, Easter, Enfield in Winter, Cayuga Night Music, Variations on a Theme of Philip Glass, Angels, Heaven-kept Soul for piano and two laptop computers, Smart Hubris for electric violin and three laptop computers, K216.01 for electric violin and three laptop computers, Vienna for electric guitars and wind, Tribute to Ruth St Denis and Ted Shawn for four laptops and video projection, Viola Farber in seven movements, Earth Journeys for four laptops; for two pianos: Unjust Malaise, Double Portrait, The FOTH Variations, TCSOC Part 2, TCSOC Part 88.01, TCSOC Part 11, I Trill Tunes. *Recordings include:* The Continuing Story of Counterpoint, Place, Times and People, Mother Mallard's Portable Masterpiece, Like a Duck to Water, Cayuga Night Music, ... It's Gone (DVD), Variations on a Theme of Philip Glass 2014; recordings on Cuneiform, New World, , Arbiter, Spectrum Spools. *Publications include:* Dialogues for Trumpet and Trombone, Heaven-Kept Soul for solo piano and laptops. *Honours:* Foundation for Contemporary Arts Grant, Award for Innovative Teaching, Cornell Univ. *Address:* 227 Enfield Falls Road, New York, NY 14850, USA (office). *Telephone:* (607) 277-4155 (office). *E-mail:* drb4@cornell.edu (office); davidborden@mac.com. *Website:* www.mothermallard.com; www.davidborden.org.

BORLAND, Wes; American musician (guitar); b. 7 Feb. 1975, Nashville, Tenn.; m. Heather McMillan 1998. *Education:* Douglas Anderson School of the Arts. *Career:* sang and played guitar in own band in Jacksonville; mem., Limp Bizkit 1994–2001, 2004–06, 2009–; has worked with side-project group Big Dumb Face; co-f. Black Light Burns 2005–. *Films:* Underworld: Awakening (Original Soundtrack) 2012, Resident Evil (guitar soundtrack) 2012. *Recordings include:* albums: with Limp Bizkit: Three Dollar Bill Y'All 1997, Significant Other 1999, Chocolate Starfish And The Hotdog Flavored Water 2000, New Old Songs 2001, The Unquestionable Truth (Part 1) 2005, Gold Cobra 2010; with Big Dumb Face: Duke Lion Fights the Terror! 2001; with Black Light Burns: Cruel Melody 2007, Cover Your Heart and the Anvil Pants Odyssey 2008, The Moment You Realize You're Going to Fall 2012, Lotus Island 2013. *Honours:* American Music Award for Favorite Alternative Artist 2002. *Current Management:* c/o Peter Katsis, The Firm, 9100 Wilshire Blvd, Suite 400 West, Beverly Hills, CA 91212, USA. *Telephone:* (310) 246-9000.

Fax: (310) 246-1999. *Website:* www.limpbizkit.com; www.blacklightburnsofficial.com; www.theborlandgallery.com.

BORRELL, Johnny; British singer and musician (guitar); b. (Jonathan Edward Borrell), 4 April 1980, Muswell Hill, London. *Career:* Founding mem. and front-man rock band Razorlight 2002–. *Recordings include:* albums: Up All Night 2004, Razorlight 2006, In the Morning 2006, Slipway Fires 2008, Revolver Soul 2010, Borrell 1 2013. *Television:* The Mighty Boosh. *Address:* Vertigo Records, Mercury Music Group, 364–366 Kensington High Street, London, W14 8NS, England. *E-mail:* vertigo@umusic.com. *Website:* www.vertigorecords.co.uk; www.razorlight.co.uk.

BORŠCAK, Mario; Croatian musician (bass guitar). *Career:* mem., Pipschips&videoclips 1992–. *Recordings include:* albums: Shimpoo Pimpoo 1993, Dernjava 1995, Fred Astaire (Porin Award for Best Rock Album) 1997, Bog (Porin Award for Best Rock Album 2000) 1999, Drveće i rijeke 2003. *Address:* c/o Menart Records, Bencekovićeva 19, 10 000 Zagreb, Croatia. *Website:* www.pipschipsvideoclips.com.

BORUM, Stefan; Danish composer and musician (piano); b. 21 Aug. 1954, Viborg; two s. one d. *Education:* Creative Music Studio, Woodstock, NY, USA. *Career:* mem., Blue Sun 1975–78, Lost Kids 1979–80; created Sun Quartet; numerous concerts, tours and festival appearances; mem., Shades of Blue 1987–; mem. DMF (Danish Musicians' Union), DJFBA. *Recordings:* It's All Money Johnny, Blue Sun, 1976; Sun Quartet, Sun Quartet, 1987; On A Mission From Muddy Waters, Shades Of Blue, 1992.

BOSCO (DE FREITAS MUCCI), João; Brazilian singer, musician (guitar) and composer; b. 13 July 1946, Ponte Nova, Minas Gerais. *Education:* Ouro Preto Univ. *Career:* Univ. collaboration with lyricist Vinicius de Morais; began long association with ex-psychiatrist Aldir Blanc late 1970s–late 1980s; supplied Elis Regina with much of her best material; after her early death, became known as a performer of own material; struggled with censorship during military dictatorship in Brazil; 1977 composition O Bebaido e a Equilibrista (The Drunkard and the Tightrope Walker) became Amnesty International theme song; influenced by many styles including samba, jazz, African, Cuban, rock; in addition to Portuguese, lyrics use languages including English, French, Spanish, Yoruban. *Recordings include:* João Bosco 1973, Caca A Raposa 1975, Galos De Briga 1976, Tiro De Misericordia 1977, Linha De Passe 1979, Bandalhismo 1980, Essa É A Sua Vida 1981, Comissão De Frente 1982, Ao Vivo 100th Apresentacao 1983, Gagabirô 1984, Cabeca De Nego 1986, AiAiAi De Mim 1987, Bosco 1989, Zona De Fronteira 1991, Acústico 1992, Na Onda que Balança 1994, Da Licença Meu Senhor 1996, As Mil e Uma Aldeias 1997, Benguelê 1998, Na Esquinha 2000, Malabaristas do Sinal Vermelho 2003, Obrigado Gente! 2006, Não vou para o céu, mas já não vivo no chão 2008, Senhoras Do Amazonas 2010, Festa 2012. *Website:* www.joaobosco.com.br.

BOSÉ, Miguel; Spanish/Italian singer and actor; b. (Luis Miguel Luchino González Bosé), 3 April 1956, Panama City, Panama; s. of Luis Miguel Dominguín and Lucia Bosé. *Career:* screen actor 1971–; professional singer 1975–, popular in Italy, Spain and Southern Europe; recorded Latin American int. hit Amante bandido 1985; numerous albums and tours; recorded duets albums Papito 2010 and Papitwo 2012 with numerous collaborators including Ricky Martin, Shakira, Michael Stipe, Paulina Rubio, Julieta Venegas, Amaia Montero, Alejandro Sanz, Fangoria, Pablo Alborán, Malú, Penélope Cruz, Juan Luis Guerra, Tiziano Ferro, Jovanotti. *Films include:* Gli eroi 1973, Vera, un cuento cruel 1974, La orca 1976, Giovannino 1976, Garofano rosso 1976, Retrato de familia 1976, Suspiria 1977, Oedipus orca 1977, La gabbia 1977, California 1977, Sentados al borde de la mañana con los pies colgando 1978, La borgata dei sogni 1978, Cosa de locos 1981, El caballero del dragón 1985, En penumbra 1987, Shangay Lily 1989, L'avaro 1990, Lo más natural 1991, High Heels 1991, La nuit sacrée 1993, Mazeppa 1993, La reine Margot 1994, Enciende mi pasión 1994, Gazon maudit 1995, Amor digital 1996, Libertarias 1996, Oui 1996, Lorca 1998, La Mirada del otro 1998. *Television:* Due di tutto 1982, Il segreto del Sahara (mini-series) 1988, Detrás del dinero 1995. *Recordings:* albums: Linda 1978, Miguel Bosé 1978, ¡Chicas! 1979, Miguel 1980, Más allá 1981, ¡Bravo, muchachos! 1982, Made in Spain 1983, Bandido (with Giorgio Vanni and Tomato) 1984, Salamandra 1986, XXX (with Giorgio Vanni and Tomato) 1987, Los chicos no lloran 1990, Directo 90 1990, Bajo el signo de Cain 1993, Laberinto 1996, 11 maneras de ponerse un sombrero 1998, Lo major de Bosé 1999, Girados (with Ana Torroja) 2002, Sereno (Latin Grammy Award for Best Male Pop Performance 2003) 2002, Por vos muero 2004, Velvetina 2005, Papito 2007, Cardio 2010, Papitwo 2012. *Honours:* Hon. Citizen of Colombia 2010; Festivalbar winner (three times), Latin Recording Acad. Person of the Year 2013. *Address:* c/o Clara Heyman y Paloma Fernández, Calle Príncipe de Vergara, 202. 6° C., 28002 Madrid, Spain (office). *E-mail:* info@heymanfernandez.com (office). *Website:* miguelbose.com.

BOSÉ, Dominguín; Spanish/Italian singer, songwriter and actor; b. 3 April 1956, Aries, Panama; s. of the late Luís Miguel Domnguín and of Lucia Bosé. *Career:* solo artist; collaborations with Pablo Alborán, Juan Luis Guerra, Tiziano Ferro, Shakira, Julieta Venegas, Jovanotti, Malú, Joaquín Sabina, Ximena Sariñana Ricky Martin and Dani Martín. *Film appearances:* Gli Eroi 1972, Vera, un Cuento Cruel 1973, Retrato de Familia 1976, Oedipus Orca 1976, Giovannino 1976, Garofano Rosso 1976, Suspiria 1977, La Gabbia 1977, California 1977, Sentados al Borde de la Mañana con los Pies Colgando 1978, En Penumbra 1985, El Caballero del Dragón 1985, Shangay Lily 1989, L'Avaro 1989, Lo Más Natural 1990, Tacones Lejanos 1991, La Nuit Sacrée

1993, Mazeppa 1993, Enciende mi Pasión 1994, La Reine Margot 1994, Gazon Maudit 1995, Amor Digital 1996, Libertarias 1996, Oui 1996, Lorca 1998, La Mirada del Otro 1998. *Recordings include:* albums: Linda 1977, Miguel Bosé 1978, Chicas 1979, Miguel 1980, Madrid 1980, Más Allá 1981, Bravo Muchachos 1982, Made In Spain 1983, Bandido 1984, Salamandra 1986, XXX 1987, Los Chicos No Lloran 1990, Directo '90 1990, Bajo El Signo De Cain (aka Under The Sign Of Cain) 1994, De Partisano A Duende 1994, Pedro Y El Lobo 1994, Laberinto 1995, Personalidad 1996, Mordre Dans Ton Coeur 1997, 11 Maneras De Ponerse Un Sombrero 1998, Sereno (Latin Grammy Award for Best Male Pop Vocal Album 2003) 2002, Por vos Muero 2003, Velvetina 2005, Papito 2007, Cardio 2010, Papitwo 2012. *Honours:* Latin Recording Acad. Person of the Year 2013. *Current Management:* c/o RLM Management, C/ Puerto de Santa Maria 65, 28043, Madrid, Spain. *Telephone:* (91) 7216440. *Fax:* (91) 3889822. *E-mail:* rlm@rlm.es. *Website:* www.rlm.es; www.miguelbose.com.

BOSKOV, Ole; Danish musician (piano, acoustic guitar, keyboards), singer and songwriter; b. 31 Aug. 1963, Copenhagen; m. Tina Boskov 1992; one s. *Career:* singer/songwriter 1980–; No. 1 hit single in Denmark with Danish version of MC Hammer's Can't Touch This; currently CEO Positive Music; mem., Danish Songwriters Guild. *Compositions include:* Listen To The Wind, Pennsylvania, Going Crazy. *Recordings include:* backing vocals for Ester Brohus; solo albums: Listen To The Wind 1996, Going Crazy 2005, Songs in Black and White 2005, Piano Improvisations, Ride My Limousine. *Address:* Boskov Tømrer og Snedker, Store Torvegade 139, 3700 Rønne, Denmark. *Telephone:* 51-96-65 44. *E-mail:* oleibboskov@hotmail.com. *Website:* www.boskov.dk.

THE BOSS (see Morales, David)

BOSTOCK, Chris; British songwriter, producer and musician (bass, keyboards); b. 23 Nov. 1962, Hillingdon, London. *Career:* songwriter and bassist with Vic Godard's Subway Sect 1981–82, JoBoxers 1983–86; toured with Dave Stewart and Spiritual Cowboys 1990–92; collaborated with OMD, Shakespears Sister, Style Council, Sandie Shaw; produced albums for Savage World 1993, Clint Bradley 1997; mem. Re-Pro, PRS, Musicians' Union. *Recordings include:* Boxerbeat 1983, Just Got Lucky 1983, Johnny Friendly 1983, Is This Really the First Time 1985, Essential Boxerbeat 1996; appeared on Spiritual Cowboys and Honest albums by Dave Stewart and the Spiritual Cowboys, Goodbye Cruel World, Shakespears Sister, Cafe Bleu, Style Council.

BOTAN, Nazê; Iraqi (Kurdish) singer; b. 1968, Georgia; m. Newroz Botan. *Career:* started singing at the age of eleven; formed own band in Georgia; emigrated to Denmark 1991; worked on various music cassettes with her husband; performs regularly with own band Nazê and the Botans and with Oriental Mood; numerous folk and world music festival appearances in Denmark, Sweden, Norway, Netherlands, Germany, Italy, Pakistan. *Recordings include:* Ax Kurdistan 1996, Kurdistan: The Forgotten World 1998; with Oriental Mood: Oriental Garden 1997, Greatest Hits plus 2 1999. *Address:* Blokland 88 Street. TV, 2620 Albertslund, Denmark. *Telephone:* 43-64-64-93. *Fax:* 43-64-64-93.

BOTH, Robert (Bob) Allen; American recording engineer, producer and musician; *Owner, Twain Recording;* b. 10 Nov. 1952, Montclair, New Jersey; m. Karen Sue Cody 1977; one s. *Education:* Art School, Ridgewood. *Career:* A&R Dept, Polydor Records, New York 1971–72; A&R Dir, recording engineer, producer, James Brown Enterprises, New York 1972–76; staff engineer, Delta Recording 1976–77, Quad Recording 1979; Owner and Chief Engineer, Twain Recording, New Jersey 1976–; audio instructor, Ramapo Coll. of New Jersey 1993–2006, William Paterson Univ., New Jersey 1995–2005, County Coll. of Morris, New Jersey 1997–2000; mem. Music Producers Guild of America. *Recordings include:* with The JB's: Doin' It to Death 1973, Damn Night 1974, Breakin' Bread 1974, Hustle with Speed 1975, JB's Reunion 1999, Soul Of the Funky Drummers 1999; with Maceo Parker, USA 1974; with James Brown: Get On The Good Foot 1972, Black Caesar 1973, Slaughters Big Rip Off 1973, Reality 1974, The Payback 1974, Hell 1974, Sex Machine Today 1975, Everybody's Doin' The Hustle 1975, Hot 1976, Body Heat 1977; with Lyn Collins: Check Me Out 1975; with Fred Wesley: Funk For Your Ass 2007. *Publications:* contrib. of articles in the music press, EQ, Pro Sound News, Pro Music. *Honours:* three RIAA Gold Records Awards for work with James Brown. *Address:* Twain Recording, 18 Hiawatha Pass, West Milford, NJ 07480, USA (office). *Telephone:* (973) 697-7540 (office). *E-mail:* contact@twainrecording.com (office). *Website:* www.twainrecording.com (office).

BOTSCHINSKY, Allan; Danish musician (trumpet, flugelhorn), composer and producer; b. 29 March 1940, Copenhagen; s. of Berl Botschinsky and Gudrun Verona Botschinsky; m. Marion Kaempfert 1990. *Education:* Royal Danish Conservatory, Manhattan School of Music, New York with Cecil Collins, studied with Prof. Svend Erik Werner and Bo Holten. *Career:* professional aged 16, playing in leading groups of Copenhagen's Jazz Scene, with, among others, Ib Glindeman, Bent Axen, Oscar Pettiford, Stan Getz, Mal Waldron, Dexter Gordon, Thad Jones and Ben Webster; mem. Jazz Quintet '60 and the Danish Radio Jazz Group; played with and conducted The Danish Radio Big Band; regular tours and recordings with Peter Herbolzheimer's Rhythm Combination and Brass and Ali Haurand's European Jazz Ensemble and European Trumpet Summit; Co-founder MA Music Int. jazz label; Founder First Brass Ensemble; producer, The Bert Kaempfert Orchestra. *Compositions and arrangements include:* Sentiments: suite for large orchestra, Dronning Dagmar for orchestra, Patchwork for chamber orchestra,

Turnus for orchestra, Unexpected Move for orchestra, Lost and Found for two jazz soloists and orchestra, The River and the Blue Hippopotamus for jazz soloist and chamber orchestra, A Jazz Sonata for trumpet and piano, Colours for solo clarinet, Colours for solo cello, Colours for solo flute, Colours for solo viola, Für Berl for three bassoons and contrabassoon, Highland Fantasies for trumpet and organ, Jazz Antiphony for brass octet, Parati-Para, Nemo Nostrum for mixed choir and horn. *Recordings include:* Allan Botschinsky Quintet Stunt, After The War, Iron Office, Ambience, Twilight Music, Oscar Pettiford & Lee Gaines, Jazz Quintet, Jazz Quintet 60, Blue Bros, Sahib Shihab And The Danish Radio Jazz Group, Tricotism, Ben Webster No Fool No Fun-The Danish Radio Big Band, Live At Montmartre, A Good Time Was Had By All, Short Story, Brass Galore, The George Gruntz Concert, Jazz Galaconcert 79, Bigband Bebop, European Jazz Ensemble - Live, First Brass, Allan Botschinsky, Derek Watkins, Bart & Erik van Lier, Duologue, Allan Botschinsky, Niels-Henning Ørsted Pedersen, The Night, Allan Botschinsky Quintet, feat. Ove Ingemarsson, Thomas Clausen, Lars Danielsson, Victor Lewis, Last Summer, Allan Botschinsky Quartet, feat. Dave Stryker, George Mraz, Victor Lewis, European Jazz Ensemble, At The Philharmonic Cologne, I've Got Another Rhythm, Allan Botschinsky Quartet, feat. Dave Stryker, Charles Fambrough, Victor Lewis, The Bench, Allan Botschinsky Quintet. *Honours:* Ben Webster Prize 1983. *Current Management:* c/o Marion Kämpfert Music, Gartenstrasse 2, PF 42, 6301 Zug, Switzerland. *Telephone:* (41) 7812100. *Fax:* (41) 7472189. *E-mail:* mkaempfert@mac.com. *E-mail:* allan@allanbotschinsky.com. *Website:* www.allanbotschinsky.com.

BOTTUM, Roddy; American musician (keyboards); b. 1 July 1963, Los Angeles, CA. *Education:* classically-trained pianist. *Career:* mem. rock group, Faith No More 1980–98, 2009–; leader alternative pop band, Imperial Teen 1995–; numerous festival appearances and tours. *Film music:* Totally Sexy Loser 2003, Put the Camera on Me 2003, Adam & Steve 2005. *Recordings include:* albums: with Faith No More: Faith No More 1985, Introduce Yourself 1987, The Real Thing 1989, Live At Brixton Academy 1991, Angel Dust 1992, King For A Day... Fool For A Lifetime 1995, Album of the Year 1997, Sol Invictus 2015; with Imperial Teen: Seasick 1996, What Is Not To Love 1998, On 2002, The Hair the TV the Baby and the Band 2007, Feel the Sound 2012. *Honours:* Bammy Awards for Outstanding Group, for Best Keyboardist 1991, MTV Video Award for Best Special Effects 1991, Bay Area Award for Outstanding Keyboardist 1993. *Website:* www.imperialteen.com; www.fnm .com.

BOTWIN, Will; American music executive; *President and CEO, Red Light Management. Education:* Arizona State Univ. *Career:* Founder, Side One Management 1982–97; Gen. Man., then Exec. Vice-Pres. Columbia Records 1998–2001; Pres. Columbia Records Group 2002–06; Pres. and CEO Red Light Management and ATO Records 2006–. *Address:* Red Light Management, 44 Wall Street, 22nd Floor, New York, NY 10005, USA (office). *E-mail:* info@ redlightmanagement.com (office). *Website:* www.redlightmanagement.com (office).

BOUBLIL, Alain Albert; French (b. Tunisian) writer and dramatist; b. 5 March 1941, Tunis, Tunisia; four s. *Career:* emigrated to France age 18; worked for several years in music publishing; wrote libretto and lyrics for La Révolution Française 1973, Les Misérables 1980, Abbacadabra 1984, Miss Saigon 1989, Martin Guerre 1996, The Pirate Queen 2006, Marguerite 2008; Le Journal d'Adam et Eve (play) 1994. *Honours:* two Tony Awards, Two Grammy Awards, two Victoire de la Musique Awards, Molière Award (all for Les Misérables), Evening Standard Drama Award (for Miss Saigon), Laurence Olivier Award (for Martin Guerre).

BOULIANE, Daniel G.; Canadian producer, composer, musician (keyboards, drums, percussion) and singer; b. 26 Oct. 1963, Hull, Québec; m. Lise Roy 1981; one s. one d. *Education:* Université du Québec; Coll. Alexandre. *Career:* over 300 soundtracks for film and TV; soundtracks for Moving the Mountain; soundtracks for many nat. ads; composer and music producer, Onde-Spirale 2001–11; mem. Academic of Canadian Cinema and Television. *Films include:* soundtracks include: Le Dernier des Franco-Ontariens 1996, Letters to a Street Child 1999, Enfer et contre tous! 1999, Hank and Mike 2000, Lord Kurt 2001, Unexpected 2001, Straight 2002, The Last Just Man 2002, Greg and Gentillon 2005. *Television include:* soundtracks include: Jewel on the Hill 2000, Chunkydorey 2001, Une Mission à partager 2001. *Recordings include:* New World 1994, Nomad 1994, Remember 1998, Tagayet 2002. *Publication:* Titles of Dak: New World 1994.

BOURASSA, François, BMus, MMus; Canadian jazz musician (piano) and composer; b. 26 Sept. 1959, Montréal; s. of fmr Québec Premier Robert Bourassa. *Education:* McGill Univ., New England Conservatory of Music, Boston. *Career:* concerts in Canada, USA, Europe (France, Belgium, Spain), China, Japan, Korea, Russia, Mexico; Canadian tours of jazz festivals; concert with Dave Brubeck, Wayne Shorter, Dave Holland, Dizzy Gillespie, Stan Getz; celebration of 50th anniversary of Canadian Gov. Gen. Office; celebration of Charles Dutoit's birthday, Radio France, Radio Canada. *Compositions:* Reflet 1, Jeune Vieux Jeune, Echo, Tour of France, Indefinite Time. *Recordings:* albums: Reflet 1 1986, Jeune Vieux Jeune 1993, Echo 1996, Cactus 1998, Trio François Bourassa Et André LeRoux – Live 2001 (JUNO Winner, OPUS Prize), Indefinite Time (FÉLIX Winner, OPUS Prize) 2003, Rasstones 2007, Idiocyncrasie 2011. *Honours:* New York Artist Residency (CALQ), Canada and Québec Arts Council Compositions Grants, Winner, Montréal Int. Jazz Festival's Competition 1985, OPUS Prize for Performance, Oscar Peterson

Prize, Montreal Jazz Festival 2007. *Current Management:* c/o F.A.M Group, 4102 St-Urbain, Montréal, QC H2W IV3, Canada. *Telephone:* (514) 844-7312. *Fax:* (514) 844-9989. *E-mail:* info@famgroup.ca. *Website:* www.famgroup.ca; www.francoisbourassa.com.

BOURDE, Hervé; French musician (saxophone, flute, piano) and composer; b. 12 July 1951, Marseilles; one d. *Career:* tours of Europe from age 15; concepts for jazz festivals; mem. SPEDIDAM, ADAMI. *Recordings:* six solo albums, ten as soloist, composer; recent albums include: Un Certain Trio 2009. *Honours:* first prize City of Marseilles Conservatoire. *E-mail:* musiqueur@ hervebourde.com. *Website:* www.hervebourde.com.

BOURDON, Rob; American musician (drums); b. 20 Jan. 1979, Calabasas, CA. *Career:* founding mem., Xero 1996, renamed Hybrid Theory, later renamed Linkin Park 1999–; numerous int. concerts. *Recordings include:* albums: Hybrid Theory (Rock Bear Awards for Best Int. Album 2001) 2000, Reanimation 2002, In The End: Live & Rare 2002, Meteora 2003, Live in Texas 2003, Collision Course (with Jay-Z) 2004, Minutes to Midnight 2007, A Thousand Suns 2010, Living Things 2012, The Hunting Party 2014. *Honours:* Billboard Award for Best Modern Rock Artist 2001, Rock Bear Award for Best Int. Band 2001, Kerrang! Award for Best Int. Newcomer 2001, Rolling Stone Award for Best Hard Rock/Metal Band 2001, World Music Awards for Best Selling Rock Group 2002, 2003, 2007, MTV Awards for Best Group, Best Hard Rock 2002, MTV Europe Awards for Best Rock Act 2004, 2011, 2012, 2014, for Best World Stage Performance 2009, 2013, for Best Live Act 2010, Grammy Award for Best Rap/Sung Collaboration (for Numb/Encore, with Jay-Z) 2006, MTV Europe Music Award for Best Band 2007, American Music Awards for Favorite Alternative Rock Music Artist 2007, 2008, 2012. *Current Management:* Andy Gould Management, 8484 Wilshire Boulevard, Suite 425, Beverly Hills, CA 90211, USA. *Website:* www.linkinpark.com.

BOURGOIN, Patrick G.; French musician (saxophones, flute, clarinet); b. 16 Dec. 1948, Paris. *Career:* played with many French artists, including Gino Vanelli in Paris and Manu Dibango on world tour 1971–; mem. Société des auteurs, compositeurs et éditeurs de musique (SACEM), Société de Perception et de Distribution des Droits des Artistes-Interprètes (SPEDIDAM). *Recordings include:* Super Kumba (with Manu Dibango) 1974, Call on the White Line (with Yann Linhart) 1980, All Your Love (Neilo-Feel) 1982, Love is a Game (Iren Bochenko) 1987, Big Thing (with Duran Duran) 1988, Le Meilleur De Sol En Si-Sol En Si 2005. *Address:* 80 boulevard Gambetta, 94130 Nogent sur Marne, France (home).

BOURREAU, Guillaume; French booking agent and production manager. *Career:* booking agent and talent buyer for 3C 1997–; manager for Zenzile 1997–2010; music programmer, Les Invites de Villeurbanne festival 2005–. *Address:* 3C Tour – Les Jardins de Gambetta – tour n° 3, 74 rue Georges Bonnac, 33000 Bordeaux, France (office). *Telephone:* (5) 57-53-02-48 (office). *Fax:* (5) 57-53-02-40 (office). *E-mail:* guillaume.bourreau@3ctour.com (office). *Website:* www.3ctour.com.

BOUSSAGUET, Pierre-Michel-André; French jazz musician (string bass player), composer and arranger; b. 12 Nov. 1962, Albi; m. (divorced); two d. *Career:* with Guy Lafitte, 1986–; tours worldwide with artists, including Wynton Marsalis, Joe Pass, Didier Lockwood, Monty Alexander; mem. SACEM, UMJ. *Compositions:* Impressions III, Creation for symphonic orchestra and jazz quartet; Symphonic and jazz pieces, 1997. *Recordings:* 2 Bass hits (with Ray Brown), 1988–; P. Boussaguet Quintet featuring Tom Harrell, 1992; Charme, 1998; duet with Guy Lafitte, Crossings, 1999; current trio featuring H. Sellin and A. Queen, Charme, 1999. *Address:* c/o International Jazz Productions SCCL, La Gleva 42–44, oficina 5, 08006 Barcelona, Spain. *Telephone:* (932) 117259. *Fax:* (934) 186246. *Website:* inter-jazz.com/ web. *Address:* 52 rue Pierre Mourgues, 81000 Albi, France.

BOUTROS, Julia; Lebanese singer; b. 1 April 1968, Beirut; m. Elias Abu Saeb 1996, one c. *Career:* solo artist 1991–. *Recordings include:* albums: Ghabet shams el-hak 1991, Wayn msafer 1992, Hikayet atab 1993, Ya Ossas 1994, El-karar 1996, Chi gharib 1998, Bisaraha 2001, Lab ahlamak 2004, Et-tawadna alayk 2006. *Address:* Asda'a Public Relations, Spectrum Building, Second Floor, Suite 212, PO Box 28063, Dubai, United Arab Emirates (office). *Telephone:* (4) 3344550 (office). *Fax:* (4) 3344556 (office). *E-mail:* info@asdaa .com (office). *Website:* www.asdaa.com; www.juliaboutros.net.

BOVA, Jeffrey Stephen; American musician (keyboards) and composer; b. 22 June 1953, District of Columbia. *Education:* Berklee College of Music, Manhattan School of Music. *Career:* musician, composer 1975–; asst composer, arranger, Herbie Hancock 1987–88; Cyndi Lauper, 1987–89; Ryuichi Sakamoto, 1988–89; musician, composer, Distance 1988–; keyboard player on albums by Billy Joel, Cyndi Lauper, Aztec Camera, Michael Bolton, Cher, Tina Turner, Eric Clapton, Meat Loaf, Céline Dion, The Bee Gees, Average White Band, Ian Hunter, Robert Hart, Hall and Oates, Mick Jones; mem. ASCAP. *Compositions and arrangements for film:* Colors, 1989; The Handmaid's Tale, 1990; Pretty Woman, 1990.

BOVEE, Robert (Bob), BA; American musician (guitar, harmonica, banjo, autoharp) and singer; b. 17 Feb. 1946, Omaha, NE; m. Gail A. Heil 1988. *Education:* University of Nebraska. *Career:* regular tours of Western Europe, USA, radio broadcasts, festival appearances. *Recordings include:* Pop Wagner and Bob Bovee 1977, The Roundup 1979, For Old Time's Sake 1985, Behind The Times 1986, Come All You Waddies 1988, Rebel Voices 1988, Come Over and See Me 1991, Rural Route 2 1996, When the Cactus is in Bloom 2000, Bluff

Country Gathering 2005. *Publications:* contrib. numerous articles, reviews on American traditional music in The Old Time Herald, Inside Bluegrass. *Address:* 18287 Gap Drive, Spring Grove, MN 55974, USA (office). *Telephone:* (507) 498-5452 (office). *E-mail:* bobngail@springgrove.coop (office). *Website:* www.boveeheil.com.

BOWEN, Lorraine, BMus; British musician, performer and songwriter; b. 31 Oct. 1961, Gloucestershire. *Education:* Univ. of Surrey. *Career:* singing teacher to Billy Bragg; writer, singer, The Lorraine Bowen Experience; songwriter and performer of lounge hits and comedy songs; mem. MCPS, Musicians' Union, PRS. *Compositions:* Julie Christie, Crumble Song, Bicycle Adventure, I Love London, Space, Spinach. *Recordings include:* with The Dinner Ladies: These Knees Have Seen The World 1989; with Billy Bragg: The Internationale 1990, Don't Try This At Home 1991, William Bloke 1997; with The Lorraine Bowen Experience: Greatest Hits Vol. I 1995, Vol. II 1998, Bossy Nova 2001, Oh! What A Star! 2002, Songs from the Living Room 2002, Vital Organs 2006, Suburban Exotica 2010. *Telephone:* (12) 7332-4147. *E-mail:* info@lorrainebowen.co.uk. *Website:* www.lorrainebowen.co.uk.

BOWEN, Tim; British music industry executive. *Career:* Head of Business Affairs, Sony Music UK, then Head, Sony Music Publishing Int., New York 1982–86; Man. Dir CBS/Columbia Records UK 1986–91; Sr Vice-Pres. Marketing and Business Affairs, Universal Music Int. 1994–99, Exec. Vice-Pres. 1999–2001; COO BMG Europe 2002–03, Chair. BMG Entertainment, UK and Ireland 2003–04, Chair. Sony BMG UK & Ireland, Canada, Australia, New Zealand, South Africa 2004–06, COO Sony BMG 2006–08; currently Prin., BPM Entertainment, London. *Website:* www.bpmentertainment.co.uk.

BOWLES, Coy; American musician (guitar, organ); b. 20 Feb. 1979, Thomaston, Ga; s. of Barney Bowles and Janis Bowles. *Education:* Georgia State Univ. *Career:* founder mem. Coy Bowles and the Fellowship 2004–; mem. Zac Brown Band 2006–; f. Coy Cares Foundation 2010. *Recordings:* albums: with Coy Bowles and the Fellowship: Into the Distance 2007; with Zac Brown Band: The Foundation 2008, You Get What You Give 2010. *Publications:* Southern Ground Cook Book (with Zac Brown) 2008. *Honours:* Acad. of Country Music Award for Top New Vocal Duo or Group 2009, for Vocal Event of the Year (for As She's Walking Away, featuring Alan Jackson) 2011, Grammy Award for Best New Artist 2010, CMA New Artist of the Year 2010. *Current Management:* ROAR, 9701 Wilshire Boulevard, Eighth Floor, Beverly Hills, CA 90212, USA. *Telephone:* (310) 586-8222. *E-mail:* zbb@roar.la. *Website:* www.roar.la. *E-mail:* coy@zacbrownband.com (office); info@coybowles.com (office). *Website:* www.coybowles.com; www.zacbrownband .com.

BOWLS, Richard (Ric) John; American recording engineer and musician (violin, guitar, keyboards); b. 13 July 1950, Rantoul, Ill. *Education:* Univ. of California, Riverside. *Career:* touring musician 1975–77; ind. sound engineer 1977–; sound engineer, Total Expereince Records 1986–88; sound engineer, programmer, MIDI Studio Systems 1988; technical consultant, Music Suite 1992; designer, builder, various recording studios and keyboard systems; Owner/designer, Sendit Electronics; Owner, It's Only Plastic, music recording studios 1999; apptd Chief Engineer, Entertainment 2001; recording engineer for films: Apocalypse Now, Darkman, Halloween, The Fog; television credits as engineer and/or synth programming include: War and Remembrance, Knots Landing, Dallas, The Incredible Hulk, Little House On The Prairie, Wonder Woman, Love Boat, Hawaii 5–0, Moonlighting, Baywatch, Star Trek: The Next Generation, Mission Impossible, Brady Bunch; mem. Nat. Acad. of Recording Arts and Sciences (NARAS). *Recordings include:* 11 albums with Giorgio Moroder, five albums with Donna Summer, Cher, Michael Nesmith, Berlin, Gap Band, Oingo Boingo, Ahmad Jamal, Yarborough and Peoples, ELO, Deniece Williams, Earth Wind and Fire, The Crusaders, Frank Zappa, Stephen Stills, Barbra Streisand, George Clinton, David Bowie, Carl Palmer, Jean Luc-Ponty, Aretha Franklin, Peter Frampton, Sly Stone, Tom Jones, Lalo Schifrin, Cityscrapes film score; co-productions with Carmine Appice. *Honours:* Acad. Award (for Apocalypse Now), Grammy Award for Best Music Video (for Michael Nesmith), Emmy Award, Golden Globe, People's Choice Award (all for War and Rememberance) 1989.

BOWN, Alan; British musician (trumpet); b. 21 July 1942, Slough, Berkshire; m. Jean Bown 1964; one s. one d. *Education:* S/M/RAF School of Music. *Career:* started playing with The John Barry Seven; RAF bandsman 1956–60; recorded five albums over 10 years with own band, The Alan Bown Set; A&R Man. CBS Records; tours with The Who, Yes, Moody Blues, Cream; numerous television appearances; mem. PRS. *Recordings include:* all compositions on own albums: Live At The Marquee 1963, Outward Bown 1967, Listen 1970, Stretching Out 1971. *Address:* 71 Shaggy Calf Lane, Slough, SL2 5HN, England.

BOWN, Andrew Steven; British musician (keyboards, bass guitar, guitar, harmonica) and singer; b. 22 March 1946, London; m. 1st Caroline Attard 1971; one s. one d.; m. 2nd Veronica Bown 2004. *Career:* musician with The Herd 1969, Judas Jump, Pink Floyd, Status Quo 1976–; mem. Musicians' Union, PRS, Equity. *Recordings include:* albums: with The Herd, Pink Floyd; with Status Quo: Ma Kelly's Greasy Spoon 1970, Dog of Two Heads 1971, Piledriver 1973, Hello! 1973, Quo 1974, Encore 1974, On The Level 1975, Pop Chronik 5 1975, Blue For You 1976, Live 1977, Rockin' All Over The World 1977, If You Can't Stand The Heat 1978, Whatever You Want 1979, Just Supposin' 1980, Never Too Late 1981, Now Hear This 1981, 1+9+8+2 1982, Live At The N.E.C. 1984, Status Quo 1984, To Be Or Not To Be 1983, Back To

Back 1983, In The Army Now 1986, Ain't Complaining 1988, Rock 'Til You Drop 1991, Live Alive Quo 1992, The Other Side Of Status Quo 1995, Thirsty Work 1995, Don't Stop 1996, Whatever You Want 1997, Under The Influence 1999, Famous In The Last Century 2000, Rockin' And Rollin' 2001, Heavy Traffic 2002, The Party Ain't Over Yet 2005, In Search of the Fourth Chord 2007, Pictures 2008, Quid Pro Quo 2011: Solo: Unfinished Business 2011, Bula Quo 2013, Aquostic 2014. *Honours:* with Status Quo: Nordoff-Robbins Music Therapy Centre Silver Clef Award 1981, Ivor Novello Award 1983, BRIT Award for Outstanding Contribution to the British Music Industry 1991, World Music Award for Outstanding Contribution to Music 1991. *Current Management:* Duroc Media Ltd, Riverside House, 10–12 Victoria Road, Uxbridge, Middlesex, UB8 2TW, England. *Telephone:* (1895) 810831. *Fax:* (1895) 231499. *E-mail:* info@durocmedia.com. *Website:* www.statusquo.co.uk.

BOX, Mick; British singer and musician (guitar); b. 8 June 1947, Walthamstow, London, England. *Career:* founder mem. of rock band, Uriah Heep 1970–; extensive int. tours; first western heavy rock group to perform in Moscow, 1987. *Recordings include:* albums: Very 'Eavy, Very 'Umble, 1970; Salisbury, 1971; Look At Yourself, 1971; Demons and Wizards, 1972; The Magician's Birthday, 1972; Uriah Heep Live, 1973; Sweet Freedom, 1973; Wonderworld, 1974; Return To Fantasy, 1975; High and Mighty, 1976; The Best Of Uriah Heep, 1976; Firefly, 1977; Innocent Victim, 1978; Fallen Angel, 1978; Conquest, 1980; Abnominog, 1982; Head First, 1983; Equator, 1985; Anthology, 1986; Live In Moscow, 1988; Raging Silence, 1989; The Uriah Heep Story, 1990; Still 'Eavy, Still Proud, 1990; Different World, 1991; Rarities, 1991; Sea Of Light, 1995; Time Of Revelation, 1996; Classic Heep, 1998; Spellbinder, 1999; Future Echoes Of The Past, 2001; Electrically Driven (with Ian Anderson), 2001, Wake the Sleeper 2008, Celebration 2009. *E-mail:* qedg@btinternet.com. *Website:* www.uriah-heep.com.

BOY GEORGE; British singer, songwriter and DJ; b. (George O'Dowd), 14 June 1961, Eltham, Kent. *Career:* fmr singer, Bow Wow Wow (under name Lieutenant Lush); Founder mem., lead singer, In Praise of Lemmings, renamed Sex Gang Children, then Culture Club 1981–87, 1998–2002; solo artist 1987–; numerous tours world-wide; numerous songwriting collaborations with John Themis; est. fashion label, B Rude. *Theatre:* Taboo (composer and actor, musical) West End 2002–03, Broadway 2003–04. *Television:* The Voice UK 2015–. *Recordings include:* albums: with Culture Club: Kissing To Be Clever 1982, Colour By Numbers 1983, Waking Up With The House On Fire 1984, From Luxury To Heartache 1986, Don't Mind If I Do 1999, 12 Mixes Plus 2003; solo: Sold 1987, Tense Nervous Headache 1988, Boyfriend 1989, High Hat 1989, The Martyr Mantras 1991, Devil In Sister 1994, Cheapness And Beauty 1995, Galaxy Weekend 1999, Galaxy Mix 1999, Everything I Own 1999, BoyGeorgeDJ.com 2001, Lucky For Some 2001, A Night Out 2002, U Can Never B 2 Straight 2002, In & Out With Boy George: A DJ Mix 2002, Ordinary Alien 2010, This Is What I Do 2013; singles: with Culture Club: Do You Really Want To Hurt Me 1982, Time (Clock of the Heart) 1982, Church Of The Poisoned Mind 1983, Victims 1983, It's A Miracle 1983, Karma Chameleon (BRIT Award for Best-Selling British Single 1984) 1983, The War Song 1984, The Medal Song 1984, Move Away 1986, I Just Wanna Be Loved 1998, Your Kisses Are Charity 1999, Cold Shoulder 1999; solo: Il Adore, Everything I Own 1987, You Found Another Guy 1989, The Crying Game (film theme, with Pet Shop Boys) 1992, Funtime 1995, Same Thing In Reverse 1995, Love Is Leaving 1997, When Will You Learn 1998, Police & Thieves 1998. *Publications include:* Take It Like A Man 1995, Boy George 2003, Straight (with Paul Gorman) 2005. *Honours:* BRIT Awards for Best British Newcomer 1983, Best British Group 1984. *Current Management:* c/o MAK Management GmbH, Klingler GmbH, Hötzendorfplatz 4 A 6060, Austria. *Fax:* (5) 223 20-49-20-34. *E-mail:* managementboygeorge@yahoo.co.uk (office); anna@mak-management.com. *Website:* www.mak-management.com. *E-mail:* cultureclub@music3w.com. *Website:* www.culture-club.co.uk.

BOYD, Brandon; American singer and musician (percussion); b. 15 Feb. 1976, Van Nuys, Calif. *Career:* Founder-mem., Incubus 1991–, Sons of the Sea 2013–; tours and other live appearances. *Recordings include:* albums: Fungus Amongus 1995, S.C.I.E.N.C.E. 1997, Make Yourself 1999, Morning View 2001, A Crow Left of the Murder 2004, Light Grenades 2006, Monuments and Melodies 2009, If Not Now, When? 2011, The Essential Incubus 2012; solo album: The Wild Trapeze 2010. *Honours:* Billboard Award for Modern Rock Single of the Year 2001. *Website:* www.enjoyincubus.com.

BOYD, Will; American musician (bass guitar). *Career:* mem. rock band, Evanescence 2002–06; mem. American Princes 2006–. *Recordings include:* albums: with Evanescence: Origin 2002, Fallen 2003, Anywhere But Home (live) 2004, The Open Door 2006; with American Princes: Other People 2008. *Honours:* Grammy Award for Best New Artist 2003, Grammy Award for Best Hard Rock Performance (for Bring Me To Life) 2003. *Address:* c/o Yep Roc Records, 449-A Trollingwood Road, Haw River, NC 27258, USA. *Telephone:* (877) 733-3931. *E-mail:* americanprinces@gmail.com. *Website:* www .americanprinces.com.

BOYLAN, John Patrick, BA; American producer; b. 21 March 1941, New York. *Education:* Bard Coll. *Career:* Exec. Producer, CBS Records 1976–80, Vice-Pres. 1980–86; f. Great Eastern Music Co 1986, Adjunct Prof. of Recording Arts and Music, Citrus Coll., Glendora Calif. 2005–; mem. National Acad. of Recording Arts and Sciences, American Fed. of Television and Radio Artists, American Fed. of Musicians, Audio Eng Soc. *Recordings as producer:* numerous acts including Boston, The Charlie Daniels Band, Linda Ronstadt,

Little River Band, Nelson, Carly Simon; film soundtracks Nightshift, Urban Cowboy, Footloose, Born On The Fourth Of July, The Simpsons Sing The Blues. *Address:* Citrus College, 1000 West Foothill Boulevard, Glendora, CA 91741, USA (office). *Website:* www.citruscollege.edu.

BOYLE, Diarmuid (Dee); British musician (drums); b. Rotherham. *Career:* mem. Chakk 1985–88, The Longpigs –1999. *Recordings include:* singles: Happy Again, She Said 1995, Jesus Christ 1995, Far 1996, On and On 1996, Lost Myself 1996, Blue Skies 1999; albums: The Sun Is Often Out 1996, Mobile Home 1999.

BOYLE, Susan; British singer; b. 1 April 1961, West Lothian, Scotland. *Career:* contestant and runner-up on reality tv show Britain's Got Talent 2009; debut album was the biggest-selling of the year throughout the world 2009. *Recordings:* albums: I Dreamed a Dream 2009, The Gift 2010, Someone to Watch Over Me 2011, Standing Ovation: the Greatest Songs from the Stage 2012, Home for Christmas 2013, Hope 2014. *Current Management:* c/o Andy Stephens, Andy Stephens Management, Unit 6, Utopia Village, 7 Chalcot Road, London, NW1 8LH, England. *Address:* c/o Sony Music Entertainment, 9 Derry Street, London, W8 5HY, England (office). *E-mail:* contact@susanboylemusic.com (office). *Website:* www.susanboylemusic.com.

BOZIC, Petar Vedran; Croatian singer and musician (guitars, piano, harp); b. 21 May 1947, Zadar; m. Majstorovic-Bozic Nada 1972, one s. *Education:* studied mathematics and music. *Career:* played piano, amateur groups, 1963; played guitar professionally, 1965; played in Croatian groups: Gresnici, Roboti, Wheels of Fire, MI, BP Convention, Time, Boomerang, Parni Valjak; countless stage, TV, radio appearances; toured all over Europe; studio musician, Telephon Blues Band (formerly Call 66); mem. HGU (Croatian Musicians' Union). *Recordings:* over 200 albums 1972–. *Honours:* HGU Status Prize for Guitar Player of the Year 2000; Stari Macak (critics' award), Lifetime Achievement in Rock and Roll Music, 2001.

BRAAM, Michiel, BMA; Dutch musician (piano), composer, bandleader and educator; *Head of Jazz & Pop Department, ArtEZ Conservatorium; Artistic Leader, Bik Bent Braam Foundation;* b. 17 May 1964, Nijmegen. *Education:* Conservatory ArtEZ Arnhem. *Career:* leader, pianist, composer, Flex Bent Braam, eBraam, Trio BraamDeJoodeVatcher, Solo Braam, Michiel Braam's Hybrid 10tet, All Ears; variety of projects in the field of modern jazz and improvisation; many radio and TV appearances worldwide; Head of Jazz & Pop Dept, ArtEZ Conservatorium. *Compositions:* Het XYZ Der Bik Bent Braam, Second Coolbook, Foamy Wife Hum, Colors, Growing Pains, Bonsai, The Hobbit, Change This Song, Nopera, Extremen, Serendipities, On The Move, Lucebert, 3, Exit, Non-Functionals. *Recordings:* with Bik Bent Braam: Howdy, Het XYZ Der Bik Bent Braam, Black/White, Bik Bent Braam Goes Bonsai, Extremen, Serendipities; with All Ears: Foamy Wife Hum, Line; with Bentje Braam: BB, Playing The Second Coolbook; with Trio BraamDeJoode-Vatcher: Monk Materials, Colors, Change This Song; solo: Oeps, Michiel vs Braam; with eBraam: Hosting Changes, NonFunctionals, 3; with Hybrid 10tet: On The Move. *Publications:* reviews and interviews in books, jazz-oriented and other magazines, and newspapers world-wide, including Tetterettet 1996, New Dutch Swing 1998. *Honours:* Podium Prize 1989, Boy Edgar Prize 1996–97. *Website:* www.michielbraam.com.

BRADFIELD, James Dean; Welsh musician (guitar) and singer; b. 21 Feb. 1969, Pontypool, Gwent; m. Mylène Halsall 2004; one d. *Education:* Oakdale Comprehensive School. *Career:* founder mem., Betty Blue 1986, renamed Manic Street Preachers 1988–; numerous tours, festival appearances, TV and radio appearances; first Western group to play concert in Cuba since 1979, February 2001; musical collaborators include Tom Jones, 808 State, Kylie Minogue. *Recordings include:* albums: with Manic Street Preachers: Generation Terrorists 1992, Gold Against The Soul 1993, The Holy Bible 1994, Everything Must Go (BRIT Award for Best British Album 1997) 1996, This Is My Truth, Tell Me Yours (BRIT Award for Best British Album 1999) 1998, Know Your Enemy 2001, Forever Delayed 2002, Lipstick Traces: A Secret History Of Manic Street Preachers 2003, Lifeblood 2004, Send Away the Tigers 2007, Journal for Plague Lovers 2009, Postcards from a Young Man 2010, Rewind the Film 2013, Futurology 2014; solo: The Great Western 2006. *Honours:* numerous including: with Manic Street Preachers: BRIT Awards for Best British Group 1997, 1999, Q Awards for Best Live Act 2001, for Best Track (for Your Love Alone is Not Enough) 2007, for Best Video (for Show Me the Wonder) 2013, MOJO Maverick Award 2009. *Current Management:* Gillian Porter, Hall or Nothing Independent Publicity, 2 Archer Street, Soho, London, W1D 7AW, England. *E-mail:* gillian@hallornothing.com. *Website:* www.hallornothing.com; www.manicstreetpreachers.com; www.jamesdeanbradfieldofficial.com.

BRADFIELD, Marian; Irish singer, songwriter and musician (guitar); b. 31 Dec. 1953, Waterford; m. Robert Bradfield 1974, two d. *Career:* began career with Young Generation Choir, Waterford; formed own group Peace; performed at George Doherty's Folk Club, Donegal; numerous concerts, television appearances, radio broadcasts. *Recordings include:* albums: Marian, 1993; Tonight Is Just For Us, 1994; The Emperor's Field, 1998, Secret Life of a Woman 2007. *Address:* c/o Oscar Music Agency, 14 Inchmurrin Drive, Glasgow, G73 5RT, Scotland. *Telephone:* (141) 634-1095. *E-mail:* oscarsfolk@aol.com. *Website:* www.oscarmusic.co.uk; www.marianbradfield.com.

BRADFORD, Carmen; American jazz singer and academic; b. 19 July 1960, Austin, Tex.; d. of Bobby Bradford and Melba Joyce. *Education:* Huston-Tillotson Coll., Austin. *Career:* singer with Count Basie Orchestra 1982–91; other collaborations include Shelly Berg, George Benson, Dori Caymmi, Kamau Daa'ood; fmr Adjunct Asst Prof. of Jazz Studies, Thornton School of Music, Univ. of Southern Calif. *Recordings include:* albums: Finally Yours 1992, With Respect 1995, Home With You (with Shelly Berg) 2004. *Honours:* two Grammy Awards (with Count Basie Orchestra). *Telephone:* (770) 972-0279. *E-mail:* txgurlmusic@yahoo.com. *Website:* www.carmenbradford.com.

BRADY, Paul; Northern Irish folk singer, songwriter and musician (multi-instrumentalist); b. 19 May 1947, Strabane, County Tyrone. *Career:* singer and performer with various groups including The Inmates, The Kult, Rootzgroop, Planxty; fmr mem. folk group The Johnstons; solo artist 1978–; tours and festival appearances. *Compositions include:* songs: Crazy Dreams (recorded by Roger Chapman, Dave Edmunds), Night Hunting Time (recorded by Santana), Steel Claw, Paradise is Here (both recorded by Tina Turner), Luck of the Draw, Bonnie Raitt 1991, Cal (film soundtrack with Mark Knopfler), Faith in the Future (theme music to TV series) 1995. *Recordings include:* albums: Andy Irvine/Paul Brady 1976, The High Part Of The Road (with Tommy Peoples) 1976, Welcome Here Kind Stranger 1978, Hard Station 1981, True For You 1983, Full Moon 1984, Back To The Centre 1986, Molloy, Brady, Peoples (with Matt Molloy, Tommy Peoples) 1986, Primitive Dance 1987, Paradise Is Here 1989, Trick Or Treat 1991, Spirits Colliding 1995, Oh What A World 2001, Say What You Feel 2005, Hooba Dooba 2010. *Honours:* Hon. DLitt (Univ. of Ulster) 2009; Belfast Telegraph Entertainment Media and Arts Award for Best Solo Rock Artist 1991, Irish Music Award for Best Irish Male Artist 1993, Irish Music Award 2002, BBC Radio 2 Folk Award 2006, National Concert Hall Lifetime Achievement Award 2015. *E-mail:* peebeemusic@gmail.com (home). *Website:* www.paulbrady.com.

BRAGG, Stephen William (Billy); British singer, songwriter and musician (guitar); b. 20 Dec. 1957, s. of Dennis Frederick Austin Bragg and Marie Victoria D'Urso; m. Juliet Wills; one s. *Career:* Founder-mem. Riff Raff –1981; solo artist 1981–; Co-founder musicians' collective, Red Wedge; Founder-mem. The Blokes 1999–. *Recordings include:* albums: Life's A Riot with Spy vs Spy 1983, Brewing Up With Billy Bragg 1984, Talking With the Taxman About Poetry 1986, Back To Basics 1987, Workers' Playtime 1988, The Internationale 1990, You Woke Up My Neighbourhood 1991, Don't Try This at Home 1991, William Bloke 1996, Still Looking for a New England 1997, Bloke on Bloke 1997, Mermaid Avenue (with Wilco) 1998, Reaching to the Converted 1999, Mermaid Avenue Vol. 2 (with Wilco) 2000, England, Half English (with The Blokes) 2002, Must I Paint You A Picture? 2003, Mr Love and Justice 2008, Fight Songs 2011, Mermaid Avenue III (with Wilco) 2012, Tooth & Nail 2013. *Publication:* The Progressive Patriot 2006. *Honours:* Q Classic Songwriter Award 2007, BBC Radio 2 Folk Roots Award 2013, XFM Inspiration Award 2014. *Address:* Bragg Office, PO Box 6830, Bridport, DT6 9BH, England. *E-mail:* office@braggcentral.com (office). *Website:* www.billybragg.co.uk.

BRAHEM, Anouar; Tunisian musician (oud), composer and filmmaker; b. 20 Oct. 1957, Tunis. *Education:* studies with Ali Sriti at the Nat. Conservatory of Music, Tunis. *Career:* based in Paris, France 1981–85, composed music for film and theatre, collaborated with Maurice Béjart on his ballet Thalassa Mare Nostrum and with Gabriel Yared as lutist for Costa Gavras' film Hanna K.; returned to Tunisia 1985, created a project for Carthage Festival collaborating with musicians including Abdelwaheb Berbech, the Erköse brothers, François Jeanneau, Jean-Paul Celea, François Couturier; Dir, City of Tunis Musical Ensemble (EMVT) 1987–90, productions included Leïlatou Tayer 1988, El Hizam El Dhahbi 1989, Rabeb 1989, Andalousiat 1990; carried out research into Arab classical music; recorded debut album Barzakh for ECM Records 1991; as well as being a master of traditional Arab musical forms has also worked in collaboration with numerous musicians from other disciplines including Norwegian saxophonist Jan Garbarek, Pakistani tabla master Shaukat Hussain, French jazz pianist François Couturier, French accordionists Jean-Louis Matinier and Richard Galliano, Romany clarinettist Barbaros Erköse, British musicians John Surman (saxophone) and Dave Holland (bass); participated in creation of Centre for Arab and Mediterranean Music, Sidi Bou Saïd 1992; has performed concerts throughout Europe, USA and Middle East. *Film:* Words in the Wake of War 2006. *Film and theatre soundtracks:* Sabots en Or and Bezness by Nouri Bouzid, Halfaouine by Ferid Boughedir, Les Silences du Palais and La saison des hommes by Moufida Tlatli, Wannas el kloub by Mohamed Driss, El Amel, Borj El hammam and Bosten Jamalek by Theatre Phou. *Recordings:* Barzakh 1991, Conte de l'incroyable amour 1992, Madar 1994, Khomsa 1995, Thimar (Jazz Album of the Year, Jazz Wise magazine, Preis der Deutschen Schallplattenkritik) 1998, Astrakan Café 2000, Le Pas du Chat Noir 2002, Charmediterranéen (with Orchestre Nat. de Jazz) 2002, Vague 2003, Le Voyage de Sahar 2006, The Astounding Eyes of Rita 2009, Souvenance 2014. *Honours:* Grand Nat. Prize for Music, Tunisia 1985. *Address:* c/o ECM, Amtsgericht München HRB, 53950 Munich, Germany (office). *E-mail:* contact@anouarbrahem.com (office); ecm@ecmrecords.com (office). *Website:* www.ecmrecords.com (office); www.anouarbrahem.com.

BRAKE, Marita, BS; American singer, songwriter and musician (guitar); b. Springfield, IL; m. Gil Moore 1982. *Education:* Illinois State University. *Career:* community concerts tour; Carnegie Hall; Canterbury Festival, Canterbury, England; television broadcasts on BBC and PBS; performance for Presidential inauguration, 1997; mem. Nashville Songwriters' Asscn, Folk Alliance, Gospel Music Asscn. *Compositions:* The Marita Brake In Concert Song Book, 1997. *Recordings include:* albums: The Road I Took To You, 1989; Gypsy Moon, 1996, The Celtic Rose 2005. *Publications:* contrib. articles in magazines and reviews. *Honours:* Woman of Distinction Award for Excellence in the Arts. *Telephone:* (309) 663-1589. *E-mail:* mbrake@maritabrake.net. *Website:* www.maritabrake.net.

BRAMERIE, Thomas; French musician (acoustic bass); b. 18 Sept. 1965, Bergerac; m. Edith Vuillon 1992. *Career:* sideman with various international jazz musicians in Europe, 1987–; played with: Chet Baker; Toots Thielemans; Johnny Griffin; Frank Wess; Tom Harrell; Joshua Redman; European tour, with Jimmy Scott, 1994; festival appearances: Nice; Montreux; Newport; Northsea; mem., Belmondo Quintet, Michele Hendricks Quintet, Dédé Ceccarelli Quartet; regular mem., Dee Dee Bridgewater's Band 1997; several world tours. *Recordings:* Live In Paris, Teddy Edwards Quartet, 1994; For All Friends, Belmondo Quintet, 1994; From The Heart, Dédé Ceccarelli Quartet, 1996; Ted Nash European Quartet, 1996. *E-mail:* info@nuevamusic.com. *Website:* www.nuevamusic.com.

BRANCH, Alan; British sound engineer, musician (guitar), producer, programmer and music technology journalist; b. 22 Jan. 1962, London; m. 1988; three d. *Education:* Lime Grove Coll., Goldsmiths Univ. *Career:* live, session guitarist; tape operator at Topic Records; engineer at The Works Studio; engineer at Roundhouse Studios; Chief Engineer, Roundhouse Recording Studios; freelance engineer; mem. Musicians' Union. *Recordings include:* artists: Jeff Beck, U2, M People, De La Soul, D:ream, Jamiroquai, Living Colour, Ruby Turner, Boy George, Omar, On U Sound, Adrian Sherwood, Primal Scream, Lighthouse Family, Eternal, Simply Red, Depeche Mode, Nine Inch Nails, Sinead O'Connor, The Popes, Jordi Camell, Sharon Corr, Joss Stone; various other artists. *Honours:* Grammy Award (for A Day in the Life by Jeff Beck) 2010. *Telephone:* (7973) 719572. *E-mail:* alan@alanbranch.com; boomer68@mac.com. *Website:* www.alanbranch.com.

BRANCH, Michelle; American singer and musician (guitar); b. 2 July 1983, Ariz. *Career:* began playing guitar and writing songs aged 14 years; released first album through independent label aged 16; formed music duo with Jessica Harp, The Wreckers 2005 (disbanded 2007); spotted supporting Hanson and offered recording contract. *Recordings include:* albums: The Spirit Room 2001, Hotel Paper 2003, Stand Still Look Pretty 2006; singles: Everywhere (Viewers' Choice Award, MTV Video Music Awards) 2001, All You Wanted 2001, Goodbye To You 2002, Are You Happy Now 2003, Breathe 2003. *Honours:* Grammy Award for Best Pop Collaboration (for Santana's The Game Of Love) 2002. *Address:* c/o Maverick Recording Company, 9348 Civic Center Drive, Beverly Hills, CA 90210, USA. *Website:* www.michellebranch.net.

BRANCO, Cristina; Portuguese singer; b. 1972; m.; one s. *Career:* performs in the traditional fado style, incorporating elements of folk and pop into her work. *Recordings include:* albums: Cristina Branco in Holland 1997, Murmúrios 1999, Post Scriptum 1998, O Descobridor 2001, Corpo Iluminado 2003, Sensus 2003, Ulisses 2005, Perfil 2007, Abril 2008, Kronos 2009, Não há só tangos em Paris 2011. *Address:* c/o ONC, Rua Veloso Salgado, 23–2° Drt., 4100-497 Porto, Portugal. *Telephone:* (22) 6188503. *Fax:* (22) 6189126. *E-mail:* oncproducoes@netcabo.pt. *Website:* www.oncproducoes.com. *Address:* c/o Universal Music Portugal, 12D Rua Prof. Reinaldo dos Santos, Lisbon 1549-006, Portugal. *Website:* www.cristinabranco.com.

BRANCOWITZ, Laurent; French musician (guitar) and songwriter; b. (Laurent Mazzalai), 1974, Versailles; brother of Christian Mazzalai. *Career:* mem. Darlin' 1992–95; mem. Phoenix 1997–. *Recordings:* albums: United 2000, Alphabetical 2004, It's Never Been Like That 2006, Wolfgang Amadeus Phoenix (Grammy Award for Best Alternative Album 2010) 2009. *Address:* c/o Glassnote Music, 770 Lexington Avenue, New York, NY 10065, USA (office). *E-mail:* info@glassnotemusic.com (office). *Website:* www.glassnotemusic.com (office); www.wearephoenix.com.

BRAND, Oscar, BS; Canadian composer, folk singer, musician (guitar) and writer; b. 7 Feb., Winnipeg, MB; m. Karen Grossman 1970, three s. one d. *Education:* Brooklyn College, Fairfield University. *Career:* presenter, Folk-song Festival, New York Public Radio, (oldest continuous radio show in history), 1945–; on credits of 75 documentary films; hundreds of radio and television shows; Music Dir, Sunday Show, NBC; Exploring; Treasure Chest; host, composer, First Look; Spirit of '76, NBC; performer for children on television, records and film; mem. advisory panel which created television programme, Sesame Street; Curator of Songwriters' Hall of Fame; Pres., Gypsy Hill Music; Lecturer on Dramatic Writing, Hofstra Univ., Hempstead, NY; Artistic Dir, Project America, 1998–2000; mem. SAG, AFTRA, ACTRA, Dramatists' Guild, AFofM. *Compositions include:* songs for: Doris Day; Ella Fitzgerald; Harry Belafonte; The Smothers Brothers; Mormon Tabernacle Choir; scripted, scored ballets for Agnes DeMille and Michael Bennett; commercials include: Maxwell House; Oldsmobile; Log Cabin; Rival; songs in films: The Fox; Sybil; The Long Riders; Blue Chips; music for: In White America; score for: How To Steal An Election; music and lyrics with Paul Nassau for Broadway shows: A Joyful Noise; The Education of Hyman Kaplan; wrote, scored Kennedy Center's bicentennial musical, Sing America Sing. *Recordings include:* over 90 albums, including: I Love Cats, 1994; Get A Dog, 1995; Campaign Songs 1789–1996, 1999. *Publications:* When I First Came To This Land, The Ballad Mongers (autobiog.), Party Songs, Singing Holidays, Bawdy Songs, Songs of '76, Western Guitar, Celebrate, Bridge of

Hope. *Honours:* Peabody Awards, 1982, 1996; Hon. PhD, University of Winnipeg, 1989; Radio Pioneers of America, 1991; awards for film credits: Venice, Edinburgh, Golden Reel, Valley Forge, Freedoms Foundation; Scholastic; Golden Lion; Peabody; Ohio State; Edison; Emmy. *Address:* Gypsy Hill Music, PO Box 1362, Manhasset, NY 11030, USA. *Fax:* (516) 487-2010. *E-mail:* OscrBrand@aol.com. *Website:* www.oscarbrand.com.

BRANDY; American R&B singer; b. (Brandy Norwood), 11 Feb. 1979, McComb, Miss.; d. of Willie Norwood Sr and Sonja Norwood; m. Robert Smith 2001 (divorced); one d. *Education:* Pepperdine Univ. *Career:* began singing when a child in local church; competed in numerous talent shows; obtained record deal aged 14; numerous live and TV appearances. *Television:* Thea (series) 1993, Moesha (series) 1996, Cinderella (film) 1997, Double Platinum (film) 1999. *Films:* I Still Know What You Did Last Summer 1998, Osmosis Jones (voice) 2001, Sesame Beginnings: Beginning Together 2006. *Recordings include:* albums: Brandy 1994, De Falda Cortita 1995, Never Say Never 1998, Full Moon 2002, Afrodisiac 2004, Human 2008; singles: Make It Right 1990, I Wanna Be Down 1994, Sittin' Up In My Room 1995, Baby 1995, Best Friend 1995, Brokenhearted 1995, Missing You 1996, The Boy Is Mine (with Monica) 1998, Top Of The World 1998, Have You Ever 1998, Almost Doesn't Count 1999, Everything I Do 1999, U Don't Know Me 1999, Never Say Never 2000, Another Day In Paradise 2001, What About Us 2002, Full Moon 2002, Talk About Our Love 2004, Afrodisiac 2004, Who Is She 2 U 2004, Human 2008, Two Eleven 2012. *Website:* www.foreverbrandy.com.

BRANN, Chris, (P'Taah, Feral, Ananda Project); American producer, remixer and DJ; b. Atlanta, Ga. *Career:* formed Wamdue Kids 1994, also Wamdue Project, Ananda Project. *Recordings include:* albums: as Wandue Kids: Wamdue Works 1996, These Branching Moments 1996; as Wamdue Project: Resource Toolbox Vol. 1 1996, Program Yourself 1998, Compendium 1999; as Ananda Project: Release 2000, Morning Light 2003, Relight 2005, Fire Flower 2007, Night Blossom 2008; as P'Taah: Compressed Light 1999, De'compressed 2001, Staring at the Sun 2003, Perfumed Silence 2011. *Website:* www.chrisbrann.com.

BRANNIGAN, Paul; journalist. *Education:* Univ. of Ulster. *Career:* free-lancer on Kerrang! magazine from 1994, later News Ed., Features Ed. and Deputy Ed., Ed. 2005–09. *Publications:* collection of Lemmy's great platitudes 2009, This is a Call: The Life and Times of Dave Grohl 2011, Birth School Metallica Death (co-written with Ian Winwood) 2013.

BRANSON, Sir Richard Charles Nicholas, Kt; British business executive; *Chairman, Virgin Group Ltd;* b. 18 July 1950, Blackheath, London; s. of Edward James Branson and Eve Branson; m. 1st Kristen Tomassi 1969 (divorced 1979); m. 2nd Joan Templeman 1989; one s. one d. *Education:* Stowe School. *Career:* set up Student Advisory Centre (now Help) 1970; f. Virgin mail-order co. 1969, first Virgin record shop 1971, recording co. 1973, nightclub (The Venue) 1976, Virgin Atlantic Airlines 1984; f. and Chair. Virgin Retail Group, Virgin Communications, Virgin Travel Group, Voyager Group; took Virgin Music Group public 1986, bought back shares 1988 (rotating chairmanship 1991, Chair. 1991–92, now Life Pres. after sale of shares 1992); Group also includes publishing, broadcasting, construction, heating systems, holidays; Chair. UK 2000 1986–88, Pres. 1988–; Dir Intourist Moscow Ltd 1988–90; f. The Healthcare Foundation 1987, Virgin Books 1989 (sold to Random House 2007), Virgin Radio 1993, Virgin Rail Group Ltd 1996, Virgin Express 1996 (merged with SN Brussels Airlines forming Brussels Airlines 2006), V2 Records 1997 (sold to Universal Music Group 2007), Virgin Mobile (sold to NTL/NTL:Telewest 2006 and re-launched as Virgin Media 2007) 1999, Virgin Blue (Australia) 2000, Virgin Galactic (space tourism co.) 2004, Virgin Comics 2006, Virgin Animation 2006, Virgin Health Bank 2007, Virgin Nigeria 2007, Virgin America 2007, Virgin Fuels 2009; launched Virgin Cola (drink) 1994, Babylon (restaurant) 2001, Virgin Vodka (drink); crossed Pacific in hot air balloon with Per Lindstrand 1991; world record for fastest crossing of the Channel in amphibious vehicle 2004; made unsuccessful attempt with his children at eastbound record crossing of Atlantic Ocean under sail in 99ft (30m) sloop, Virgin Money (also known as Speedboat) 2008; Chair. jury of first Picnic Green Challenge 2007; set up global science and tech. prize, The Virgin Earth Challenge 2007; hosted environmental gathering at his pvt. island, Necker Island (part of British Virgin Islands) in Caribbean with several prominent entrepreneurs, celeb-rities and world leaders to discuss global warming-related problems March 2008; Patron Int. Rescue Corps, Prisoners Abroad; Commr Broadband Comm. for Digital Devt 2010, Global Comm. on Drug Policy 2011. *Film and TV appearances:* Friends, Baywatch, Birds of a Feather, Only Fools and Horses, Goodness Gracious Me, Tripping Over, Live & Kicking, The Rebel Billionaire 2004, Around the World in 80 Days 2004, Casino Royale 2006, Superman Returns 2006, Rabbit Fever 2006. *Publications:* Losing My Virginity (auto-biography) 1998, Screw It, Let's Do It 2006, Business Stripped Bare: Adventures of a Global Entrepreneur 2008, Reach for the Skies: Ballooning, Birdmen and Blasting into Space 2010, Screw Business as Usual 2011, Like a Virgin: Secrets They Won't Teach You at Business School 2013, The Virgin Way: How to Listen, Learn, Laugh and Lead 2014. *Honours:* Hon. DTech (Loughborough) 1993; Dr hc (Kaunas Technology Univ.) 2013; Blue Riband Title for Fastest Atlantic Crossing 1986, Segrave Trophy 1987, ranked No. 85 on list of 100 Greatest Britons (BBC) 2002, ranked No. 86 on list of 100 Worst Britons (Channel 4) 2003, ranked by Time Magazine amongst Top 100 Most Influential People in the World 2007, UN Correspondents Asscn Citizen of the World Award 2007, German Media Prize 2011, Pres.'s Merit Award, Nat.

Acad. of Recording Arts and Sciences 2012, Business for Peace Foundation Award 2014. *Address:* Virgin Group Ltd, 120 Campden Hill Road, London, W8 7AR, England (office). *Telephone:* (20) 7229-1282 (office). *Fax:* (20) 7727-8200 (office). *Website:* www.virgin.com (office).

BRANT, Claudia; Argentine singer and songwriter; b. (Claudia Alejandra Menkarski), 21 July 1968, Buenos Aires; m. (divorced); one s., one d. *Education:* studied architecture. *Career:* solo recording artist 1989–; composed songs for numerous artists including Marc Anthony, Michael Bublé, Christian Castro, Chayanne, Lara Fabian, Alejandro Fernández, Luis Fonsi, Gisela, Josh Groban, Il Divo, Kenny G, La Ley, Playa Limbo, Jennifer Lopez, Victor Manuelle, Edith Márquez, Ricky Martin, Sandra Mihanovich, Germán Montero, Tito Nieves, Natalia Oreiro, Milly Quezada, Paulina Rubio, Carlos Santana, Barbra Streisand, Olga Tañón, Diego Torres; 2013; Sr Vice-Pres. Latin Songwriters Hall of Fame 2013–, also Vice-Chair. Educ. Cttee. *Recordings include:* albums: as solo artist: Enfonces Vale la Pena 1989, Claudia Brant 1991, Tu Marca en el Alma 1995, Por Capricho 2006, Manuscrito 2011. *Films:* compositions for: Ladron Que Roba a Ladron (Lions Gate) 2006, Despicable Me 2009, Hop 2011. *Honours:* as songwriter: winner OTI Song Festival, Mexico 1991, winner Viña Del Mar Song Festival, Chile 1994, four ASCAP Awards 2004, LA Music Award for Best Latin Artist 2004, SESAC Latina Awards for Songwriter of the Year and Publisher of the Year (Nana Maluca Music) 2007–09, Latin Grammy Award for Song of the Year 2009, Monitor Latino Pop Awards for Publisher of the Year and Songwriter of the Year 2009, Premios OYE (Mexico) Award for Song of the Year 2009, Premios Lo Nuestro Pop Song of the Year Award 2009. *E-mail:* brantones@ hotmail.com. *Website:* www.claudiabrant.com.

BRAUN, Rick; American musician (trumpet), composer and producer; b. 6 July 1955, Allentown, Pa; m. Laura Hunter 1992. *Education:* Eastman School of Music. *Career:* Founder own group, Auracle; performed at numerous jazz festivals, tours; mem. BMI, American Fed. of Musicians (AFofM). *Compositions:* co-writer, Here With Me, REO Speedwagon 1989. *Recordings include:* Intimate Secrets 1993, Night Walk 1994, Christmas Present 1994, Beat Street 1995, Body and Soul 1997, Full Stride 1998, Best Of Braun 1999, Shake It Up 2000, Kisses in the Rain 2001, Groovin' 2002, Esperanto 2003, Sessions, Vol. 1 2004, Your's Truly 2006, RnR 2006, Peter White Christmas with Mindi Abair and Rick Braun 2007, All It Takes 2009, Sings with Strings 2011. *Honours:* BMI Top 100 Songs of the Year (for Here With Me) 1990. *E-mail:* contactus@ rickbraun.com. *Website:* www.rickbraun.com.

BRÄUNINGER, Jürgen, MA, DMus; German composer and electronic instrumentalist; *Associate Professor, School of Arts, University of KwaZulu-Natal;* b. 13 Sept. 1956, Stuttgart; m. Brigitte Keck 1985. *Education:* San Jose State Univ., Calif., USA, Staatliche Hochschule für Musik und darstellende Kunst, Stuttgart, Univ. of Natal, S Africa. *Career:* Staatlich gepruefter Musiklehrer; tutor 1977–82; Musical Dir Theatre Tri Buehne, Stuttgart 1980–82; mem. Musica Nova, Bd Dirs Soc. for New Music and New Jazz 1981–85; Co-organizer New Music Concert Series 1984–85; Lecturer, Staatliche Akad. der bildenden Künste, Stuttgart 1984–85, Staatliche Hochschule für Musik und darstellende Kunst, Stuttgart 1984–85; Lecturer in Composition and Dir Electronic Music Studio, Univ. of KwaZulu-Natal 1985–, Sr Lecturer 1991–, Assoc. Prof. 1997–; Distinguished Visiting Composer, San Jose State Univ. 1988–89; mem. Bd Dirs Durban Music School 2004–; mem. Gesellschaft für musikalische Aufführungs- und mechanische Vervielfältigungsrechte (GEMA). *Compositions include:* The Tam Tam Tape, Elektronische Musik, Ornament 1982, Saxomanie, D-Art S and Bass-Auf, all 1984, on Vibraphony-Saxonomie Ornament, Xherone 1986, . . . anywhere far 1991, Ahimsa-Ubuntu 1995, Yinkosi Yeziziba 2002. *Recordings include:* Durban Noise and Scraps Works 1999, . . . anywhere far 2004, Limes X 2004, The Bow Project 2005; Contributing Composer and complete score realization motion picture soundtrack: The Lawnmower Man, New Line Cinema Corporation, USA 1991; orchestration and additional music motion picture soundtrack: The Dead Pit, Skouras Picture, USA 1989, Insurrections: a musical dialogue between Indian and South African artists, South African History Online 2012. *Publications include:* As Producer: Mandela Peace Rally 1990, Music for Liberation 1990, Celebrating Oral Tradition: Bandlululondini 1992, Art Gecko 1993, Gathering Forces I 1994, Old World, New World, Third World Studios, proceedings of the International Computer Music Conference, San Jose, California 1992, Gumboots to the Rescue, South African Journal of Musicology 1998, Southern Cones, Leonardo Music Journal Vol. 10 2000. *Address:* University of KwaZulu-Natal, School of Arts, Durban 4041, South Africa (office). *Telephone:* (31) 260-1349 (office). *E-mail:* brauning@ukzn.ac.za (office). *Website:* music.ukzn.ac.za (office).

BRAVE CAPTAIN (see Carr, Martin)

BRAXTON, Anthony; American jazz musician (alto saxophone, clarinet); b. 4 June 1945, Chicago, Ill. *Education:* Wilson Jr Coll. *Career:* played clarinet and alto saxophone whilst serving in US Army; joined musician's co-operative, AACM, Chicago 1966; formed own group, The Creative Construction Company (CCC) 1968; Co-founder, Circle (with Chick Corea, Dave Holland, Barry Altschul) 1970; played in France with various European improvisers; mem. Globe Unity Orchestra; performed at Derek Bailey's Company Festivals; performed with own quartet; duo with drummer Max Roach 1970s; teacher, Wesleyan Coll. during 1980s–; Founder and Artistic Dir The TriCentric Foundation. *Compositions include:* series of 12 operas, Trillium, Quartet (London) 1985, Quartet (Birmingham) 1985, Quartet (Willisau) 1991.

Recordings include: over 70 albums as bandleader; appeared on numerous other recordings by artists, including Joseph Jarman, George Lewis, Max Roach, Derek Bailey, Muhal Richard Abrams, CCC, ROVA Saxophone Quartet, London Jazz Composers Orchestra. *Publications include:* Tri-axium Writings 1985, Composition Notes (five Vols) 1988. *Honours:* Jazz Masters Award 2014. *Address:* c/o The TriCentric Foundation, Music Department, Wesleyan University, Middletown, CT 06459; 36 Mansfield Terrace, Middletown, CT 06457, USA. *Telephone:* (860) 685-2650. *Fax:* (860) 685-2651. *E-mail:* music@wesleyan.edu. *Website:* www.wesleyan.edu/music/braxton.

BRAXTON, Tamar Estine; American R&B and soul singer and songwriter; b. 17 March 1977, Severn, Md; d. of Michael Braxton and Evelyn Braxton; m. Vincent Herbert 2008; one s. *Career:* mem. of family group The Braxtons 1989–98; backing singer for elder sister Toni Braxton 1997, 2000–02; solo artist 1998–; reunited with Braxtons for TV series Braxton Family Values 2011–12; launched own fashion range, Get Your Life 2012; numerous collaborations including Amil, Jermaine Dupri, Silk, Tank. *Television includes:* Braxton Family Values 2011–12, The Soul Man 2012, The Real (co-presenter) 2013. *Recordings:* albums: with the Braxtons: So Many Ways 1996; solo: Tamar 2000, Love and War 2013, Winter Loversland 2013. *Publication:* Love and War (co-author) 2013. *Honours:* BET Centric Award 2013, Soul Train Awards for Best R&B/Soul Female Artist 2013, for Song of the Year (for Love and War) 2013. *Address:* c/o Streamline Records, Interscope Records, Universal Music Group. 2220 Colorado Avenue, Santa Monica, CA 90404, USA (office). *Telephone:* (310) 865-5000 (office). *Website:* www .interscope.com (office); www.tamarbraxton.com.

BRAXTON, Toni; American singer; b. 7 Oct. 1967, Philadelphia, Pa; m. Keri Lewis (divorced 2012); two s. *Career:* mem. of female vocal group, with sisters Tamar, Trin and Tavanda 1990; solo artist 1993–. *Recordings include:* solo albums: Toni Braxton 1993, Secrets 1996, The Heat 2000, Snowflakes 2001, More Than a Woman 2002, Libra 2005, Pulse 2010, Love, Marriage & Divorce (with Babyface) (Grammy Award for Best R&B Album 2015) 2014. *Publications:* Unbreak My Heart: A Memoir 2014. *Honours:* Grammy Award for Best Female R&B Vocal Performance (for He Wasn't Man Enough) 2001, American Music Award for Favorite Soul/R&B Female Artist 2001. *Current Management:* Int. Creative Man., 10250 Constellation Blvd, Los Angeles, CA 90067, USA. *Website:* www.tonibraxton.com.

BRAZIER, Roy; British bandleader, musician (saxophone, blues harp) and singer; b. 28 Jan. 1965, Walthamstow, London, England. *Career:* founder mem., Darktown 1987, for parties, functions; performed for Williams Grand Prix Engineering; numerous concerts, television appearances; mem. Musicians' Union. *Recordings:* albums: with Darktown: Blues, Jazz and Other Animals 1997; solo: The Blues Brother 2004. *Honours:* Voted in Top Ten Blues Harp players, UK, 1995; Certificate of Excellence for Blues Harmonica at the European Harmonica Festival, Germany, 1996. *Telephone:* (7941) 775952. *E-mail:* Roy@thebluesbrother.co.uk. *Website:* www.southx.biz/ thebluesbrother/.

BRECHIN, Sandy, MA; British musician, composer and record label owner; *Director, Brechin All Records;* b. 20 April 1969, Edinburgh, Scotland. *Education:* Daniel Stewart's & Melville Coll., Univ. of Edinburgh. *Career:* toured worldwide with bands Burach, Seelyhoo and Sandy Brechin Band, as well as a variety of teaching and session work; Founder, Brechin All Records; mem. Musicians' Union, Equity, Mechanical-Copyright Protection Soc., Performing Right Soc., Traditional Music and Song Asscn of Scotland. *Theatre:* The Wedding 2002, Accidental Death of an Accordionist 2002, 2008, The Miniatures 2003. *Television includes:* numerous appearances on BBC TV and Radio, STV and Channel 4, including The Lottery Show Live: A Song for Britain 1997, Boxed Set (STV, with Donnie Munro and Karen Mathieson) 2000, Tartan Jam (Channel 4, with Martyn Bennet and Natalie Macmaster) 2000, Reporting Scotland 2003, 2007; several appearances on European TV and radio, and in the USA and Far East. *Video:* Learn Scottish Accordion with Sandy Brechin 2000. *Recordings include:* albums: with Burach: The Weird Set 1995, Born Tired 1997, Deeper 2000, Unstoppable 2006; with The Sandy Brechin Band: Out Of His Box 1996, Out Of His Tree 1999; with Seelyhoo: The First Caul 1995, Leetera 1998; The Complete Songs of Robert Tannahill Vol 1 2005; with The Sensational Jimi Shandrix Experience: Ceilidh Band: Electric Landlady 2006; The Accidental Death of an Accordionist 2008; MacGregor, Brechin & ÓhEadhra's Sonas 2008, Ewan Wilkinson's Lost In The Day 2009; with Donnie Munro's On the West Side 2000, Across The City And The World 2002, An Turas 2008; more than 50 other albums and compilations. *Publication:* Out of His Mind (own compositions) 2001. *Address:* Brechin All Records, 16/2 Panmure Place, Tollcross, Edinburgh EH3 9JJ, Scotland (office). *Telephone:* (131) 466-6559 (office). *Fax:* (131) 466-6559 (office). *E-mail:* info@ brechin-all-records.com (office). *Website:* www.brechin-all-records.com (office).

BRECKER, Randall (Randy) Edward; American musician (trumpet, saxophone, horns) and arranger; b. 27 Nov. 1945, Philadelphia, Pa; brother of the late Michael Brecker; m. Eliane Elias; one d. *Education:* Indiana Univ. *Career:* professional trumpeter 1966–; freelance musician; played with Blood, Sweat and Tears, Horace Silver, Art Blakey, Clark Terry, Janis Joplin, Stevie Wonder, James Brown, Larry Coryell, Billy Cobham, Charles Mingus, Lew Tabakin; bandleader/arranger 1975–; Founder-mem., Dreams; mem., The Brecker Brothers 1987–; leader, Randy Brecker Band; arranger for numerous artists, including George Benson, Diana Ross, Chaka Khan; clinician, Nat.

Asscn of Jazz Educators; mem. AFofM. *Recordings include:* albums: with The Brecker Brothers: The Brecker Brothers 1975, Back To Back 1976, Don't Stop The Music 1977, Heavy Metal Be-Bop 1978, Detente 1980, Straphangin' 1981, Blue Montreux 1989, Collection Vol. I 1990, Vol. II 1992, Big Idea 1992, Return Of The Brecker Brothers 1992, Out Of The Loop 1994, Some Skunk Funk (Grammy Award for Best Large Jazz Ensemble Album 2007) 2006, The Brecker Brothers Band Reunion 2013; solo: Toe To Toe 1989, In The Idiom 1991, Live At Sweet Basil 1992, Score 1993, Into The Sun 1995, Hanging In The City 2001, 34th N Lex 2003, Both/And (with Marc Copland) 2006, Randy in Brasil (Grammy Award for Best Contemporary Jazz Album 2009) 2008; with Horace Silver: You Gotta Take A Little Love 1969; with Billy Cobham: Crosswinds 1974, Total Eclipse 1974, Shabazz 1975, A Funky Thide To Sings 1975, Inner Conflicts 1978; with Charles Mingus: Me, Myself and Eye 1978. *Current Management:* c/o Darryl Pitt, Depth of Field Management, 1501 Broadway, Suite 1304, New York, NY 10036, USA. *Telephone:* (212) 302-9200. *Fax:* (212) 382-1639. *E-mail:* breck27@randybrecker.com. *Website:* www .randybrecker.com.

BREGVADZE, Nani Georgievna; Georgian singer; b. 21 July 1938, Tbilisi; d. of Georgi Efremovich Bregvadze and Olga Aleksandrovna Mikeladze; m.; one d. *Education:* Tbilisi Conservatoire (pianoforte class under Machutadze). *Career:* soloist with Orchestra of Tbilisi Politechnical Inst. 1956, with Georgian State Philharmonia 1959–, with Orchestra 'Rero' 1959–64, with 'Orera' 1964–80; specializes in Georgian music and Russian romances; has toured abroad on numerous occasions; mem. Women for Peace Asscn, Metekhi Women Club; fmr mem. Soviet Woman Soc. *Films:* Veri Neighborhood Melodies, Encounter in the Mountains, Shores, Flooding, Light in the Window, The Warmth of Your Hands, Teksel, Orera, Go Forward!, Baker's Wife, Necklace for My Loved One. *Television:* Orera, sruli svlit 1967, Primite vyzov, senyory! 1982. *Honours:* Hon. Citizen of Tbilisi 1995, Hon. Citizen of Benalmadena, Spain 1996; Orden Pocheta Gruzii 1997; Honored Artist (Zasluzhennaya artistka) of Georgia 1968, People's Artist of Georgia 1974, People's Artist of USSR 1983, Order of Honour 1995, State Prize of Georgia 1997, Shota Rustaveli Prize Winner 2000. *Address:* Irakly Abashidze str. 18A, Apt 10, 380079 Tbilisi, Georgia. *Telephone:* (32) 22-37-22.

BRENNAN, Dave, CEng, MechE; British bandleader, musician (banjo, guitar, parade drums), singer, broadcaster and master of ceremonies; b. 24 Dec. 1936, Rotherham, England; m. 1st; two s.; m. 2nd Val Hudson 1996. *Education:* Rotherham Grammar School. *Career:* military service in Malayan Emergency 1959–60; presented own jazz programme, BBC Radio Sheffield, 17 years; bandleader, 1960–; leader: Jubilee Jazz Band; Jubilee New Orleans Brass Band; Heritage New Orleans Brass Band; Big Easy New New Orleans Parade Band; toured widely including: USSR (twice), Russia and Siberia; toured Europe with the International Jazz Band, 1997; mem. Musicians' Union; MI Mech E; Labour Party; SIMA. *Recordings:* Mardi Gras in New Orleans; Take Me To The Mardi Gras; Rags, Stomps and Dreamy Melodies; Inn Swinger; Amazing Grace; Bouncing Around; Let's Get This Show On The Road with Alton Purnell; Swinging At Swinden, with Louis Nelson; International Jazz Band; Several recordings with Chris Blount Jazz Band, Ken Colyer and Sarah Spencer's Rue Conti Jazz Band. *Honours:* GSM, Pingat Jasi Malaysian Medal;Vice-Pres., Swanage Jazz Festival. *Address:* Tanglewood, Marcliff Lane, Wickersley, Rotherham, S66 2AZ, England. *Telephone:* (1709) 700440. *E-mail:* DaveBrennanUK@hotmail.com. *Website:* www.davebrennanjazz.com.

BRENNAN, John Wolf, BA, MA; Irish/Swiss musician (piano, organ, melodica), composer and arranger; *Teacher of Piano, Arrangement and Improvisation, Gymnasium Immensée, Hochschule Luzern, ETH Zurich*; b. 13 Feb. 1954, Dublin, Ireland; s. of Hans Wolf and Una Wolf Brennan; m. Béatrice Brennan, three d. *Education:* University of Fribourg, Lucerne Conservatory with Eva Serman, Academy of School and Church Music, CMS Woodstock, NY with Karl Berger, Royal Irish Academy of Music, Dublin with James Wilson, masterclasses with Edison Denisov, Ennio Morricone, Klaus Huber, Heinz Holliger, Hanspeter Kyburz. *Career:* concert tours in Western and Eastern Europe, Russia, Japan, China, Canada and USA; recording projects include: Pago Libre (pan-European jazz quartet with Arkady Shilkloper, Tscho Theissing and Tom Götze); Triangulation (with Christy Doran, Patrice Héral and Bruno Amstad); TwinKeys (with Esther Flückiger); Melos Montis (with Franziska Wigger and Hanspeter Wigger); Broken Dreams (with Alexandra Prusa and Peter Gossweiler); Pipelines (with Hans Kennel); Momentum (with Thomas K. J. Mejer and Gerry Hemingway); collaborations include: James Galway, Christian Zehnder, Julie Tippetts, Evan Parker, Yang Jing, Chris Cutler, Peggy Lee, Dylan van der Schyff, Eddie Prévost, Alex Cline, Agnes Heginger, Gabriele Hasler, Eveline Hasler, Thomas Hürlimann, Daniel Mezger, Hanna Johansen, Norma Winstone, Robert Dick, Daniele Patumi, Urs Leimgruber, Magda Vogel, Urs Blöchlinger, Corin Curschellas, Lindsay Cooper; has composed two operas, vocal music and many works for chamber ensembles, piano solo, glockenspiel, choir, alphorn, pipa; Teacher of Piano, Arrangement and Improvisation, Gymnasium Immensée, Hochschule Luzern, ETH Zurich; mem. AIC, CMC, STV, SMS, SMPV. *Compositions include:* Night.Shift, Güdelmäntig, Wurzelklänge/Sonic Roots, State of Flux, The Well-Prepared Clavier, Wolkenpumpentango, SILK/ST/RINGS, Immram, Triple Stipple, Silly Blooze, Equilibrium precario, Sonata Pentatonica, KLA4, Ng-l, Zigfing, Frictions, Euratorium, Bestiarium, Through The Ear of a Raindrop, Sculptural Sonorities, Morgenstern Hat Gold Im Mund, Géo métrique ment, Epithalamium, Alef Bet – An Oriental Peace Piece, A Golly Gale's Way To Galway Bay, Nearly Charming, Treiblinge,

Rhap.s.odie, Capriccio. *Recordings include:* solo: The Beauty of Fractals 1989, Iritations 1991, Text, Context, Co-Text & Co-Co-Text 1993, The Well-Prepared Clavier 1998, Flügel 2002, Pictures in a Gallery 2006, The Speed of Dark 2009; with Pago Libre: Extempora 1990, Pago Libre 1996, Wake Up Call 1999, Cinémagique 2001, Phoenix 2003, Shooting Stars & Traffic Lights 2006, Stepping Out 2006, platzDADA! 2008, Fake Folk 2009; with Triangulation: Triangulation 2004, Whirligigs 2010; with Momentum: Momentum 1999, Momentum 2 2000, Momentum 3 2001; with HeXtet: Through the Ear Of a Raindrop 1998, Minute Age 1999, Momentum 1999, Entropology - The Science Of Sonic Poetry 2000, Pipelines 2000, Momentum 2 2000, Momentum 3 2001, Momentum 4 – Rising Fall 2005, Poya 2012. *Publication:* Wurzelklänge/Sonic Roots 2010, 2011. *Honours:* Werkjahr, Dienemann Foundation, Lucerne 1989, Förderpreis, Sarna Jubilee Foundation 1991, Fellowship of BINZ39 Art Foundation, Zurich 1993, Prize, Nat. Flute Asscn, USA 1993, Award, Jubilee Foundation of Union Bank of Switzerland 1994, Miglior Disco Del Anno, MusicaJazz 1994, Album of the Year, Jazzthetik 1996, comm. from Hindemith Foundation 1997, London Fellowship, Zuger Kulturstiftung Landis & Gyr 1997, Prix de la Fondation Suisa 2002, Markant Foundation Fellowship and opera comm. 2007, Pro Helvetia Priority Award 2007–09, Award, UBS Culture Foundation 2008, Deutscher Schallplattenpreis 2009. *Address:* Hofmattstrasse 5, 6353 Weggis, Lucerne, Switzerland (home). *Telephone:* (41) 3902777 (office). *E-mail:* johnwolf@brennan.ch (home). *Website:* www.pagolibre.com; www.brennan.ch.

BRENNAN, Moya, (Máire Ni Bhraonain); Irish singer and musician (harp); b. 4 Aug. 1952, Dublin. *Career:* founder mem., singer, harpist of folk group, Clannad 1970–; regular Irish and int. tours, concert and festival appearances. *Compositions include:* television and film music: Harry's Game (ITV) 1982, Robin of Sherwood (ITV) 1984, The Atlantic Realm (BBC1) 1988. *Recordings include:* albums: with Clannad: Magical Ring 1983, Legend 1984, Macalla 1986, Sirius 1987, Atlantic Realm 1989, Pastpresent 1989, Clannad The Collection 1989, Anam 1993, Banba 1993, Lore 1996, Landmarks 1998; solo: Maire 1992, Misty-Eyed Adventures 1995, Perfect Time 1998, Whisper to the Wild Water 1999, Two Horizons 2003, An Irish Christmas 2005, Signature 2006, Heart Strings 2008; with Cormac de Barra: My Match is a Makin' 2010; with T with the Maggies: T with the Maggies 2010. *Publications:* The Other Side of the Rainbow 2000. *Honours:* International Ambassador, Christian Blind Mission Ireland 2003; Ivor Novello Award for Best Theme from a Television or Radio Production (for Theme from Harry's Game) 1983, British Acad. Award for Best Soundtrack of the Year (for Robin of Sherwood) 1985, Meteor Ireland Music Awards Lifetime Achievement Award 2007. *Current Management:* Upfront Management, 4 Windmill Lane, Dublin 2, Ireland. *E-mail:* info@moyabrennan.com. *Website:* www.clannad.ie; www.moyabrennan.com.

BRESLIN, Paul; French singer, composer, lyricist and musician (guitar); b. 27 June 1950; m. Cathy Liegeois 1989, one s. *Education:* Reed College. *Career:* bandleader, on stage and live television, for Percy Sledge, 1994–95; bandleader for Billy Paul, Europe, 1995; played all major French jazz festivals with Eddy Louiss (Hammond organ); musician on recordings by Gilbert Becaud; Serge Gainsbourg; Michel Columbier; Françoise Hardy; Catherine Deneuve; Eddy Louiss; France Gall; Michel Berger. *Compositions:* music and lyrics for Ray Charles: Separate Ways; Good Thang. *Recordings:* solo albums: Hot Lunch; Rikitikitak.

BRETT, Martin; British musician (bass guitar, guitar, piano); b. 29 March 1959, Dorking, Surrey, England; two s. *Career:* bass guitar, Voice of the Beehive 1986–95; worldwide tours; television appearances; songwriting partnership with Voice of the Beehive; formed own music production company, Brett Dempsey Music, with Michael Dempsey; bass guitar, I, Ludicrous 2008–; studio in Sussex; composer for films, television and commercials; mem. PRS; PAMRA; Musicians' Union; MCPS. *Recordings:* albums: Let It Bee 1988, Honey Lingers 1991, Sex and Misery 1995. *E-mail:* info@bdmmusic.com. *Website:* www.iludicrous.co.uk; www.bdmmusic.com.

BREWIS, David; British musician (guitar, bass, keyboards), record producer and songwriter; b. 3 June 1957, Sunderland, England. *Education:* Newcastle Coll. *Career:* fmr mem., Kane Gang; UK and European tours; numerous television appearances; co-writer of theme for BAFTA Award-winning children's series, Byker Grove (Zenith for BBC TV, 1989–2006); mem. Field Music 2005–; performs solo work as School of Language; mem, PRS; BMI. *Recordings:* albums: with the Kane Gang: Bad and Lowdown World 1985, Miracle 1987; with Field Music: Field Music 2005, Write your own History 2006, Tones of Town 2007, Field Music 2010; solo (as School of Language): Sea from Shore 2008; as producer: with Prefab Sprout: Swoon 1984; as guitarist: Ocean Drive, Lighthouse Family 1995, Andromeda Heights, Prefab Sprout 1997. *Address:* c/o Memphis Industries, 8 Ripplevale Grove, London, N1 1HU, England (office). *E-mail:* info@memphis-industries.com (office). *Website:* www.memphis-industries.com (office); www.field-music.co.uk.

BREWSTER, Cori; Canadian musician (guitar) and singer; b. 1960. *Career:* major Canadian festivals, television shows. *Recordings include:* albums: One More Mountain 1994, Stones 1998, Large Bird Leaving 2007, Buffalo Street 2009. *Address:* Shadow Lake Music, Box 8027, Canmore, Alberta, Canada. *Telephone:* (403) 609-0693. *E-mail:* info@coribrewster.com. *Website:* www.coribrewster.com.

BREZOVSKÝ, Ali; Slovak composer; b. 26 Feb. 1940; m. Vlasta Brezovska 1963, one s. one d. *Education:* Univ. of Bratislava. *Career:* various projects including scores to Slovak films, Smoliari, 1978; Losers, Zázracny Autobus,

1981; Magic Bus; Scores to theatre plays, many songs (pop and rock) and instrumental compositions; mem. Slovak Music Asscn; Soza/Slovak Union of Authors. *Compositions:* Rozpravkovi Stopari, fairy-tale; Hitchhikers (children's); Cengá Do Triedy (School Bell is Ringing); Let/Flight: Songs for album of a popular Slovak Rock Group. *Recording:* Soundtracks of Ali Brezovsky 1996. *Honours:* Third Place, International Music Festival, Bratislavska, Lyra, 1974, 1985; Award for Original Soundtrack, 1978; Smoliari; Summer Film Festival.

BRICE, Lee; American country music singer and songwriter; b. 10 June 1979, Sumter, South Carolina; m. Sara Nanette Reeveley 2013; two c. *Education:* Clemson Univ. *Career:* songwriter for many country music artists including Jason Aldean, Cowboy Crush, Keith Gattis, Adam Gregory, Garth Brooks, Cory Morrow, Kenny Chesney, Tim McGraw, Blake Shelton 2007–; signed to Curb Records label 2007, released debut single 2007. *Recordings:* albums: Lee Brice 2010, Hard 2 Love 2012, I Don't Dance 2014. *Honours:* Acad. of Country Music Award for Song of the Year (for I Drive Your Truck) 2014. *Address:* c/o Digital Dreamz LLC, 1227 17th Avenue South, Unit 4, Nashville, TN 37212 (office); c/o Curb Records, 49 Music Square East, Nashville, TN 37203, USA (office). *Telephone:* (615) 915-3727 (Digital Dreamz) (office); (615) 321-5080 (Curb) (office). *E-mail:* david@digital-dreamz.net (office). *Website:* www.digital-dreamz.net (office); www.curb.com (office); www.leebrice.com.

BRICKMAN, James (Jim); American musician (piano) and singer; b. 20 Nov. 1961, Cleveland, Ohio. *Education:* Cleveland Inst. of Music. *Career:* began writing incidental music for Henson Assocs and Sesame Street TV series, 1981; f. Brickman Arrangement, company specializing in music for TV and radio advertising; worked as motivational speaker before releasing first album. *Recordings include:* albums: No Words 1994, By Heart 1995, Picture This 1997, The Gift 1997, Visions Of Love 1998, If You Believe 1999, Destiny 1999, My Romance 2000, Simple Things 2001, Love Songs And Lullabies 2002, Peace 2003, The Romance of Jim Brickman 2004, Grace 2005, The Disney Songbook 2005, Escape 2006, Christmas Romance 2006, Hope 2007, Homecoming 2007, Valentine 2008, Unspoken 2008, Beautiful World 2009, Home 2010, All Is Calm: Peaceful Christmas Hymns 2011. *Publications include:* Simple Things 2001. *Honours:* twice Songwriter of the Year, SESAC, Canadian Country Music Award (for Best Vocal/Instrumental Collaboration), Dove Award, Gospel Music Asscn. *Address:* Brickman Music, 23800 Commerce Park, Suite G, Beachwood, OH 44122, USA (office). *Website:* www.jimbrickman.com.

BRIDGEMAN, Duncan; British producer and musician; b. Essex, England. *Education:* Bancrofts School, Woodford Green. *Career:* mem. of soul band I-Level early 1980s; became producer, working with artists including Duran Duran, Eurythmics, Paul McCartney, Shakespear's Sister, Take That; joined and toured with Tribal Drift 1990s; co-produced, co-directed and co-wrote Grammy nominated film and album projects 1 Giant Leap 2001, What About Me? 2007; wrote, produced and directed feature film Hecho en Mexico 2011; collaborated with artists including Asha Bohsle, Baaba Maal, Michael Franti, Michael Stipe and Robbie Williams. *Recordings:* albums: with I-Level: I-Level 1982, Shake 1985; with Tribal Drift: Priority Shift 1996; with 1 Giant Leap: 1 Giant Leap 2001; singles: with I-Level: Give Me; with 1 Giant Leap: Braided Hair 2001, My Culture 2001. *Address:* 8A Hollybush Lane, Sevenoaks, Kent, TN13 3UN, England (office). *E-mail:* db1@me.com (office). *Website:* www.1giantleap.tv (office).

BRIDGEWATER, Dee Dee; American singer, actress, producer and radio host; *President, DDB Productions Inc.;* b. (Denise Garrett), 27 May 1950, Memphis, Tenn.; d. of Matthew Garrett and Marion Holiday, step-d. of Shed Hudspeth; m. 1st Cecil Bridgewater 1970 (divorced); m. 2nd Gilbert Moses 1975 (divorced); m. 3rd Jean-Marie Durand 1991 (divorced); one s. two d. *Education:* Michigan State Univ. *Career:* sang with Univ. of Illinois Big Band; New York debut as lead vocalist with Thad Jones-Mel Lewis Band 1970; toured and recorded with stars including Sonny Rollins, Dizzy Gillespie, Dexter Gordon, Max Roach and Roland Kirk; moved to France; also performed in Soviet Union, Tokyo, Paris and London; returned to prominence in USA after signing contract with Verve; Founder DDB Records, currently Pres. DDB Productions Inc.; presenter, NPR's Jazzset with Dee Dee Bridgewater; apptd Amb., FAO 1999; mem. Haut Conseil de la Francophonie. *Plays:* The Wiz, 1940s Radio Hour, Sophisticated Ladies, Cosmopolitan Greetings, Carmen Jazz, Black Ballad, Lady Day. *Musicals:* The Wiz (Tony Award for Best Featured Actress in a Musical 1975), Lady Day 1987, Black Ballad, Carmen Jazz, Cabaret. *Films include:* The Fish that Saved Pittsburgh 1979, The Brother from Another Planet 1984. *Radio:* Jazzset with Dee Dee Bridgewater (NPR) (New York Festivals Gold Medal 1997, New York AIR Award 1998, 1999). *Television:* Benson 1980, Another Life 1982, Night Partners 1983, Highlander 1993, It's Not About Love 1998. *Recordings:* albums: Afro Blue 1974, Dee Dee Bridgewater 1976, Just Family 1977, Bad For Me 1979, Dee Dee Bridgewater 1980, Live In Paris (Jazz Academy Awards Billie Holiday Award for Best Jazz Vocal 1988) 1987, Victim Of Love 1990, Dee Dee Bridgewater In Montreux 1991, Keeping Tradition (Django d'Or 1994) 1993, Love And Peace (Jazz Academy Awards Billie Holiday Award for Best Jazz Vocal) 1995, Prelude To A Kiss 1996, Dear Ella (Grammy Awards for Best Jazz Vocal and Best Arrangement for Vocal 1998) 1997, Victoires de la Musique Award for Best Jazz Vocal Album 1998) 1997, Live At Yoshi's 2000, This Is New 2002, J'ai Deux Amours 2005, Red Earth 2007, Eleanora Fagan (1915–1959): To Billie with Love from Dee Dee (Grammy Award) 2010,

Midnight Sun 2011, Dee Dee's Feathers 2015. *Honours:* Chevalier, Ordre nat. du Mérite, Officier des Arts et des Lettres; Dr hc (Univ. of Michigan), (Berklee Coll. of Music); JJA Jazz Award 2011. *Current Management:* DDB Productions Inc., 137 North Larchmont Blvd, #642, Los Angeles, CA 90004; 3278 Wilshire Blvd, 6th Floor, Los Angeles, CA 90010, USA (office). *Telephone:* (310) 494-4008. *Fax:* (310) 494-4014. *E-mail:* tulani@ddbprods.com (office); info@ddbprods.com. *Website:* www.ddbprods.com; www.deedeebridgewater.com.

BRIGHT, Anna Lia; American songwriter, singer and poet; b. 25 Feb. 1952, West Palm Beach, Fla. *Career:* appearances on Danish television and radio; singer in piano bars, clubs, cafés and concert halls in Holland, Spain, Scandinavia and the Canary Islands; songwriter for various artists; tours schools with her show Stand Up Poetry (poetry, song and storytelling); mem. KODA, Nat. Broadcasting Co. (NCB), DJBFA. *Recordings include:* as songwriter: Wind and Fire by Frank Ryan, You Better Believe by Zapp Zapp, Walk The Walk; as singer and songwriter: That's Lambada, To This Planet. *Publications include:* Undiscovered Days (poems) 1996, Liquid Heat (novel), Borderless (novel). *Honours:* Hon. Mention for short stories entered in Daily City Short Story Contest; Editor's Choice Award for Outstanding Achievement in Poetry, Nat. Library of Poetry 1997, Music Aid Int. Award for Best Songwriter (Denmark). *Website:* annaliabright.com.

BRIGHTMAN, Sarah; British actress and singer; d. of Grenville Brightman and Pauline Brightman (née Hall); m. Andrew Lloyd Webber 1984 (divorced 1990). *Career:* fmr mem. Pan's People and Hot Gossip groups; concerts worldwide. *Performances include:* Cats, Requiem, The Phantom of the Opera, Aspects of Love (music all by Andrew Lloyd Webber), I and Albert, The Nightingale, The Merry Widow, Trelawney of the Wells, Relative Values, Dangerous Obsession, The Innocents. *Recordings:* albums include: As I Came of Age 1990, Sarah Sings the Music of Andrew Lloyd Webber 1992, Dive 1993, Surrender 1995, Fly 1995, Timeless 1997, Eden 1999, La Luna 2000, Classics 2001, Harem 2003, Diva 2006, Symphony 2008, A Winter Symphony 2008. *Address:* c/o Claudia Dorrell, Dorrell Management, 2nd Floor, Lyme Wharf, 191 Royal College Street, London, NW1 0SG, England. *Telephone:* (870) 420-5088. *Fax:* (870) 420-5188. *E-mail:* claudia@dorrellmanagement.com. *Website:* www.sarah-brightman.com (home).

BRINCK, Lars, BA (Arts), BA (Science), PhD; Danish musician (keyboards), composer and arranger; *Associate Professor, Head of Research and Assistant Principal, Rhythmic Music Conservatory, Copenhagen;* b. (Lars Brinck-Jensen), 30 March 1957, Copenhagen; s. of Erik Brinck-Jensen and Gudrun Elise Kamstrup Larsen; m. Karen-Lis Kristensen 1984; four s. *Education:* Royal Acad. of Music, Århus, Aarhus Univ., Aalborg Univ. *Career:* keyboard player/composer/arranger/producer for Poul Krebs, Arvid Hunter 1982–89, Thomas Kellerup 1990–92, Gary Snider 1992, Erik Grip 1993–97, Lene Siel 1994–95, Jette Torp 1995–98, Jens Jefsen 1997–, Lars Brinck Sextet 1998–; currently also Assoc. Prof., Head of Research and Asst Prin., Rhythmic Music Conservatory, Copenhagen; teacher at acads of music and univs in Denmark; researcher and author; Bd mem. Nat. Assessment, Ministry of Culture, Danish Inst. of Evaluation; Fellow, Aalborg Univ. *Recordings:* Lars Brinck 1997, Traveloque 1998. *Address:* Rhythmic Music Conservatory, Leo Mathisens Vej 1, Holmen, 1437 Copenhagen, Denmark (office). *Telephone:* 32-68-67-00 (office). *E-mail:* lb@rmc.dk (office). *Website:* www.larsbrinck.com.

BRISLIN, Kate Young, BA; American singer and musician (guitar, banjo, keyboards, bass); b. (Kathryn Ann Young), 19 Feb. 1946, Portsmouth, Ohio; m. 1st Tom Brislin 1968; m. 2nd Jody Stecher 1987. *Education:* Univ. of Guam. *Career:* appearance, Prairie Home Companion 1994; as backing singer with Jane Voss: An Album of Songs 1974, Farther Down the Road 1999; with Laurie Lewis: Restless Rambling Heart 1986, Earth and Sky 1997; with Mike Seeger: Third Annual Farewell Reunion 1994; with Alice Gerrard: Pieces of My Heart 1994, Songs of Love and Loss 2003; with Gail Fratar: Come Away 1997; with Kathy Kallick: Use a Napkin Not Your Mom 1995, My Mother's Voice 2002; with Alan Senauke: Wooden Man 2002, Everything is Broken 2011; with Jody Stecher: Going Up On The Mountain 1976, Rasa 1980, Out On The Rolling Sea 1994, Oh The Wind and The Rain 1999, Dark Was the Night 2000, Shining Bright 2002, Wonders and Signs 2011; mem. IBMA, North American Folk Alliance. *Recordings include:* with Arkansas Sheiks: Whiskey Before Breakfast 1975; with The Blue Flame Stringband 1982; with the Any Old Time Stringband 1978, Ladies Choice 1980, I Bid You Goodnight 1996, Duets with Jody Stecher: A Song That Will Linger 1989, Blue Lightning 1991, Our Town 1993, Stay Awhile 1995, Heart Songs 1997, Songs of the Carter Family 2000, Return 2010; Duet with Katy Moffatt: Sleepless Nights 1996; also appears on: Young Fogies Vol. 2 1995, American Fogies Vol. 2 1996, Rounder Bluegrass Guitar 1996. *Address:* 133 Lake Street, San Francisco, CA 94118, USA (home). *Telephone:* (415) 387-9648 (home). *Fax:* (415) 974-1520 (office). *E-mail:* kbrislin@comcast.net. *Website:* jodyandkate.com.

BRITT, Michael Wayne; American country singer and musician (guitar); b. 15 June 1966, Fort Worth, TX. *Education:* Univ. of Texas. *Career:* received first guitar aged 15, played in various school bands; fmr mem., Santa Fe; mem., Canyon 1988–90; founder mem., Texasee 1992, became resident house band at the Wildhorse Saloon, Nashville, name changed to Lonestar 1995–. *Recordings include:* albums: Lonestar 1995, Crazy Nights 1997, Lonely Grill 1999, This Christmas Time 2000, I'm Already There 2001, Let's Be Us Again 2004, Coming Home 2005, Mountains 2006, My Christmas List 2007. *Address:*

c/o BNA Records, Sony BMG, 1400 18th Avenue, South Nashville, TN 37212, USA (office). *Website:* www.lonestarnow.com.

BRITTON, Reginald L.; American musician (drums); b. 19 Nov. 1964; three c. *Career:* mem. Black Magic Johnson; played with Young Americans, Tash and Country Magic, Eddie Snow's Snow Flakes, G Sharp Band, Tom Irwin Band, Oysters Rockefeller; mem. Central Illinois Blues Club, American Fed. of Musicians. *Compositions include:* 63 Blues, Mind My Own Business, Hooked on Something, Too Stupid, Little Bit Crazy, Every Now and Then, Gone to Long, Loving Ways. *Recordings include:* Past and Present, Oysters Rockefeller. *Publications include:* 63 Blues 1996, Mind Your Own Business 1998, Hooked on Something 1998, Every Now and Then 1998.

BRITTON, Simon, (Red Rhythm); British record producer, songwriter, musician, actor and music consultant; b. 22 Feb. 1970, Bristol. *Career:* collaborated with numerous artists including Ashanti, Aaliyah, Boyz II Men, Sean Paul, Run DMC, Liberty X, Kool & The Gang, Eminem, Aggro Santos, Kimberly Wyatt, Chaka Demus & Pliers, Chris Brown, Beverley Knight, Melanie C, Jimmy Cliff, Michelle Williams, Ginuwine, Peter Andre, Missy Elliott, Sting, Talib Kweli, Timbaland, Usher, Michael Jackson, Leona Lewis; has written and produced movie soundtracks for Disney, Touchstone Pictures, New Line Cinema, Universal Pictures. *Honours:* winner, 2010/11 British TV Advertising Awards for Best Use of Recorded Music 2010/2011 (for PUMA Hardchorus TV advertising campaign), Cannes Gold Award (for PUMA Hardchorus TV Advertising Campaign) 2011, Clio Gold Award (for PUMA Hardchorus TV Advertising Campaign) 2011, Clio Gold Award for Online (for PUMA Hardchorus TV Advertising Campaign) 2011, Emmy Award for Outstanding Reality Program (for Queer Eye For The Straight Guy). *E-mail:* simon@simonbritton.tv. *Website:* www.simonbritton.tv.

BROCHET, Marc; French composer, musician and teacher; b. 3 April 1956, Soissons, Aisne; m. Dominique Hemard 1981, one s. two d. *Education:* Conservatoire Superieur de Paris. *Career:* concerts with vocal jazz group Vox Office; festivals include: Nice; Vienna; Tel-Aviv; televised concert for M6; teacher in composition, Conservatoire National d'Enseignement Superieur de Poitiers. *Compositions:* music for theatre and dance. *Recordings:* Boppin' in French, Vox Office. *Publications:* for television and radio. *E-mail:* marc .brochet@free.fr. *Website:* marc.brochet.free.fr.

BROCK, Dave; British singer, songwriter and musician (guitar); b. Isleworth, Middx, England. *Career:* Founder and leader of rock group, Hawkwind 1969–; regular UK, European and US tours; concerts and festival appearances. *Recordings include:* albums: Hawkwind 1970, In Search Of Space 1971, Doremi Fasol Latido 1972, Space Ritual 1973, Hall Of The Mountain Grill 1974, Warrior On The Edge Of Time 1975, Astounding Sounds and Amazing Music 1976, Road Hawks 1976, Masters Of The Universe 1977, Quark Strangeness and Charm 1977, 25 Years On 1978, PXR-5 1979, Levitation 1980, Sonic Attack 1981, Church Of Hawkwind 1982, Choose Your Masques 1982, The Chronicle Of The Black Sword 1985, Angels Of Death 1987, Spirit Of The Age 1988, The Xenon Codex 1988, Space Bandits 1990, Stasis 1990, Electric Tepee 1992, It Is The Business Of The Future 1993, The Business Trip 1994, New World's Fair 1995, In Your Area 1999, Weird Tapes Vols 1–6 2000, Spacebrock 2001, Yuleritual 2001, Canterbury Fayre 2002, Spaced Out in London 2004, Take Me to Your Leader 2005, Take Me to Your Future 2006, Blood of the Earth 2010, Onward 2012, Stellar Variations 2012, Looking for Love in the Lost Land of Dreams 2012. *Honours:* Mojo Maverick Award 2010. *Address:* Hawkwind, PO Box 28, Honiton, Devon, EX14 1PB, England (office). *Telephone:* (1404) 831871 (office). *Fax:* (20) 7681-2270 (office). *E-mail:* management@hawkwind.com (office); contact@hawkwind.com (office). *Website:* www.hawkwind.com (office).

BRODY, Lane; American singer, songwriter, actress and fmr model; *Chairman and CEO, Walden's Puddle Wildlife Rehabilitation and Education Center;* b. (Lynn Connie Voorlas), Oak Park, Ill.; d. of Gust Harry Voorlas and Demetra Jane Ellis; m. Edward H. Bayers Jr 1994. *Education:* private study. *Career:* sang commercial jingles; has toured world-wide with John Anderson, Willie Nelson, Steve Wariner, Tom Bresh, Lee Greenwood; appearances on numerous TV shows, recently Country's Family Reunion; actively recording and songwriting; Chair. and CEO Walden's Puddle Wildlife Rehabilitation and Educ. Center, Joelton, Tenn.; mem. SAG, AFTRA, NARAS, CMA. *Compositions include:* Tough Enough, Hottest Night of the Year, Anne Murray (co-wrote), All The Unsung Heroes, Yellow Rose of Texas (co-wrote), and numerous others. *Recordings include:* Tender Mercies theme, The Gift Of Life theme, Country Gold soundtrack, Yellow Rose title track, All The Unsung Heroes title song, Tough Enough, title track, Pieces of Life, On the Wings of Songs, Thanks For What You Did, He's Taken, More Nights, It's Another Silent Night, Alibis. *Television:* Taxi, Heart of The City, USO Special, Lee Greenwood TV Special, Today Show, Austin City Limits, Country's Family Reunion, and numerous other appearances. *Honours:* Hon. mem. 101st Airborne; BMI Award for Yellow Rose, American Film Festival Video Documentary of the Year, numerous awards for philanthropic work for children, veterans/mil. and animals, including Darryl Waltrip 'Hometown Hero' Award. *Address:* Lane Brody Global Fan Club, 5543 Edmondson Pike, Suite 87, Nashville, TN 37211, USA (office). *E-mail:* lane@lanebrody.com (office). *Website:* www.lanebrody.com.

BRODY, Neville; British magazine designer, typographer and album cover designer; *Head of Communication Art and Design Department, Royal College of Art;* b. 23 April 1957, London, England. *Education:* Hornsey Coll., London

Coll. of Printing. *Career:* designed record sleeves for Rocking Russian and Stiff Records; Art Dir, Fetish Records early 1980s, The Face magazine 1981–86, Arena magazine 1987–90; design work for City Limits, Lei, Per Lui, Actuel, The Observer; founder and Dir typographic design agencies, FontWorks and FontShop International 1990–; founder and Dir, Research Studios 1994–; involved in launch of FUSE quarterly design forum and publication; Head of Communication Art and Design Department, Royal College of Art 2011–. *Publications:* The Graphic Language of Neville Brody Vol. 1 (with Jon Wozencroft) 1988, Vol. 2 1994, G1: New Dimensions in Graphic Design (with Lewis Blackwell) 1996. *Address:* Research Studios, 94 Islington High Street, London, N1 8EG (office); Royal College of Art, Kensington Gore, London, SW7 2EU, England. *Telephone:* (20) 7590-4444. *Fax:* (20) 7590-4500. *E-mail:* info@ researchstudios.com; info@rca.ac.uk. *Website:* www.researchstudios.com; www.rca.ac.uk.

BROEMEL, Carl; American musician (guitar, pedal steel guitar). *Career:* mem. My Morning Jacket 2004–; also solo artist 2010–. *Recordings include:* albums: with My Morning Jacket: Z 2005, Okonokos 2006, Evil Urges 2008, Circuital 2011; solo: All Birds Say 2010. *Address:* c/o RCA Records, 1540 Broadway, New York, NY 10036, USA (office). *E-mail:* carlbroemel@ mymorningjacket.com (office); info@carlbroemel.com (office). *Website:* www .mymorningjacket.com; carlbroemel.com/web.

BROKOP, Lisa; Canadian singer, songwriter and musician (guitar, keyboards); b. 6 June 1973, Surrey, BC. *Career:* singer, rhythm guitarist, keyboardist, Marty Gillan and the Sweetwater Band 1988; formed own band 1989; toured with Clay Walker and George Strait; film role: Harmony Cats; performed CCMA Awards Show, Canada and CMA Awards Show Nashville 1992; mem. SOCAN, CCMA, CMA, ACM, AFofM. *Recordings include:* albums: My Love 1993, Harmony Cats 1993, Every Little Girl's Dream, 1994; Lisa Brokop, 1996, When You Get to Be You 1999, Undeniable 2000, Hey Do You Know Me? 2005, Beautiful Tragedy 2008. *Honours:* Horizon Award (Best New Artist), Gospel Performer of Year, British Columbia Country Music Assn (BCCMA) 1990, Princess Margaret Order of Lion, Special Ambassador 1991, CKWX Songwriter's Contest 1991, Female Vocalist of Year, BCCMA 1992, Youth Achievement Award, Vocal Excellence YTV 1992, Female Vocalist of Year, International Achievement Award, BCCMA 1993, Vocal Collaboration Award with Johner Brothers, Saskatchewan Country Music Assn 1994, Worldfest Houston Gold Award 1994, Female Vocalist of Year, International Achievement Award, Single of Year, BCCMA 1994. *E-mail:* dean@lisabrokop .com. *Website:* www.lisabrokop.com.

BROM, Rafael; Czech singer, musician (multi-instrumentalist), composer, producer and publisher and art director; *President, Cosmotone Records;* b. 13 Aug. 1952, Prague; s. of Libor Brom. *Education:* studied graphic art, fine art, computer graphics, graphic design, exploration drafting and web design. *Career:* lived in Prague 1952–63, moved to Sarajevo 1963; moved to USA 1979; appearances on radio stations, USA, Canada; currently Pres. Cosmotone Records, Cosmotone Music; mem. The American Soc. of Composers, Authors and Publrs (ASCAP). *Art exhibitions:* Rafael's Art Gallery. *Recordings include:* albums: Rafael Brom 1 1983, Lord Hamilton-Padre Pio 1985, Peace Of Heart 1986, The Sounds Of Heaven 1989, Dance For Padre Pio 1991, The True Measure Of Love 1992, Music For Peace Of Mind 1993, The Christmas Songs, You'll Never Walk Alone, Angelophany 2002, All My Love To You Jesus 2002, Rafael Brom Unplugged 2004, Life is Good, Enjoy it While You Can 2008, Change 2008, The Peanut Regatta 2009, Refugee from Socialism 2009, Move Your Ass 2010, The Best of Rafael Brom – 4 Volumes Album 2011, Ineptocracy 2012, Ascension 2013, At the Gates of Heaven 2013, The Best of Rafael Brom-Volume V 2014, Destined for Heaven 2014, Democrats 2015, The Best of Rafael Brom-Volume VI 2015, Equilibrium 2015. *Dance:* Dance for Padre Pio. *Radio:* US Main FM, coll. and Public Radio stations. *Honours:* ASCAP Special Awards. *Current Management:* c/o marianland.com, 2951 Marina Bay Drive, Suite 130, PMB 501, League City, TX 77573-2733, USA. *Telephone:* (281) 538-7360. *Fax:* (281) 538-0815. *E-mail:* marianland@ earthlink.net. *Website:* www.marianland.com/music14.html; www.rafaelbrom .com.

BRONFMAN, Edgar Miles, Jr; American business executive; b. 16 May 1955, Montreal; s. of the late Edgar Miles Bronfman; m. 1st Sherri Brewer 1979 (divorced 1991); three c.; m. 2nd Clarissa Alcock 1994; three c. *Career:* began career working in British and US film industries as producer; joined family firm Seagram as Asst to Pres. 1982, Man. Dir Seagram Europe in London 1982–84, Pres. House of Seagram 1984–88, Exec. Vice-Pres. US Operations 1988–89; Pres. and COO J.E. Seagram Corpn New York 1989–94; Pres. and CEO Seagram Co. Ltd 1994–2000 (after merger with Vivendi to form Vivendi Universal), Vice-Chair. Bd of Dirs Vivendi Universal 2000–03; attempted to buy back Seagram assets in 2003 but failed; Chair. and CEO Lexa Pnrs LLC, then with Thomas H. Lee Pnrs acquired Warner Music Group, Chair. and CEO 2004–11, Chair. 2011–12; fmr Acting Pres. MCA Inc.; mem. Bd of Dirs French & Associates 2001–; Chair. Bd of Dirs Endeavor (nonprofit); Gen. Pnr, Accretive Tech. Pnrs LLC (venture capital firm); Chair. Governing Bd, World Jewish Congress 2007–. *Website:* www.endeavor.org.

BRONZE, David; British musician (bass); b. 2 April 1952, Billericay, Essex; m. Julie; one s. one d. *Career:* mem. Procol Harum, Robin Trower Band, Dr Feelgood, Art of Noise, Duane Eddy Band, Barbara Dickson Band, Mickey Jupp Band, Chris Farlowe and The Thunderbirds, Eric Clapton Band, Paul Carrack Band; numerous concerts and live performances; mem. Performing

Right Soc., Musicians' Union, Performing Artists Media Rights Asscn. *Recordings include:* with Dr Feelgood, as producer, mixer, musician: Down At The Doctors 1994, On The Road Again 1996; as musician: with Eric Clapton: From The Cradle 1994, Pilgrim 1998; with Procol Harum: Prodigal Stranger 1991; with Paul Carrack: Beautiful World 1997; with Gary Barlow: Open Road 1997; with Nik Kershaw: 1997, 15 Minutes 1999, To Be Frank 2001; with Eric Bibb: Home To Me 1997, Painting Signs 2001, Natural Light (also producer) 2003; with S.A.S. Band: Show 2001; with Gordon Haskell: Shadows On The Wall 2002; Amy Wadge 'Woj' Album (producer); Concert For George 2002; many sessions with various artists. *Honours:* Blueprint magazine Best UK Bassist 2000–02.

BROOK, Michael; Canadian composer, producer and musician (guitar); b. 1952, Toronto. *Education:* York Univ., Toronto. *Career:* studied Indian music with LaMonte Young; guitarist with Flivva 1976–77; guitarist, The Everglades 1977–78; house engineer, Grant Avenue Studios, Hamilton; occasional touring guitarist, Martha & The Muffins; collaborated with Brian Eno, developing video sculpture and sound installations in Italy, Canada, Germany, Sweden, Australia, Japan and USA 1984–89; other collaborations include Pieter Nooton, U. Srinivas, Nusrat Fateh Ali Khan, Tenores di Bitti, Gasparayan, Hukwe Zawose; producer for Roger Eno, Youssou N'Dour, Nusrat Fateh Ali Khan, Cheb Khaled, The Pogues, U. Srinivas, Gasparayan, Julia Fordham; world tour with Robert Fripp and David Sylvian 1993. *Music for film:* Captive 1986, The Fires of Kuwait 1992, Albino Alligator 1997, Affliction 1999, India: Kingdom of the Tiger 2002, An Inconvenient Truth 2006, Into the Wild 2007, Country Strong 2010, The Perks of Being a Wallflower 2012. *Recordings include:* albums: with Flivva: The Name Is Schreibman 1977; solo: Hybrid 1985, Cobalt Blue 1992, Live at the Aquarium London Zoo 21 May 1992 1993, Shona 1996, RockPaperScissors 2006; with Divan Gasparyan: Black Rock 1998, Penumbra 2008; with Hukwe Zawose: Assembly 2002. *Honours:* Grammy Award for Best New Age Album 1998.

BROOKE, Ally; American singer; b. (Allyson Brooke Hernandez), 7 July 1993, San Antonio, Tex.; d. of Jerry Hernandez and Patricia Hernandez. *Career:* mem. Love You Like a Sister, named 1432, then renamed Fifth Harmony (or 5H) 2012–; contestants on US version of The X Factor (finished in third place) 2012; signed with Syco Music and Epic Records 2012; issued debut EP Better Together 2013; opening act on Cher Lloyd's I Wish tour 2013, on Demi Lovato's Neon Lights Tour 2014, on Austin Mahone's tour of North America and Brazil 2014; headlining act, MTV Artists to Watch concert 2014. *Television:* The X Factor (contestant on US series) 2012. *Recordings:* album: with Fifth Harmony: Reflection 2015. *Honours:* Teen Choice Single: Group Award 2014, MTV Video Music Artist to Watch Award 2014, MTV Europe Music Awards for Best North America Act, for Best US Act and for Best Worldwide Act 2014. *Address:* c/o Syco Music, Syco Entertainment, 9830 Wilshire Blvd, Beverly Hills, CA 90212, USA. *Website:* www .sycoentertainment.com; www.fifthharmonyofficial.com.

BROOKLYN FRIENDS (see Morales, David)

BROOKS, Clyde Scott; American musician (percussion, drums) and record producer; b. 16 Jan. 1948, Milwaukee, Wis.; m. Geri Brooks 1988. *Education:* Berklee Coll. of Music, Boston. *Career:* fmr mem. Sunset Road; fmr Pres. NotStock/EMI Music; session musician for Dolly Parton, Kenny Rogers, Ronnie Milsap, Don Henley, Oak Ridge Boys, Johnny Winter, Jerry Lee Lewis, Barbara Mandrell, George Strait, Ted Nugent, Little Richard, B J Thomas, Tanya Tucker, Kenny Chesney; record producer for recordings by Lois Lane, Jason and the Scorchers, Nancy Brooks, Lynn Anderson, The Headlights, B B Watson, Ronna Reeves; mem. American Fed. of Television and Radio Artists (AFTRA), Country Music Asscn, American Fed. of Musicians (AFofM). *Publication:* The Recording Drummer 1974. *Telephone:* (615) 390-9375 (office). *E-mail:* clyde-brooks@att.net (office). *Website:* www .clydebrooks.com.

BROOKS, Elkie; British singer; b. (Elaine Bookbinder), 25 Feb. 1946, Salford, Manchester. *Career:* toured with Eric Delaney Band 1960s; joined jazz-rock act, Dada, later became Vinegar Joe 1970–74; solo artist 1974–. *Recordings include:* albums: Rich Man's Woman 1975, Two Days Away 1977, Shooting Star 1978, Live and Learn 1979, Pearls 1981, Pearls II 1982, Minutes 1984, Screen Gems 1984, No More The Fool 1986, The Early Years 1964–66 1987, Bookbinder's Kid 1988, Inspiration 1989, Round Midnight 1993, Pearls III 1993, Circles 1995, Circles 1995, Amazing 1996, Nothin' But The Blues 1996, From The Heart 1996, Pearls Concert Live 1999, We've Got Tonight 2000, Shangri-La 2002, Trouble in Mind 2002, Electric Lady 2005, Live With Friends 2006, Powerless 2010. *Current Management:* c/o Eventful Productions, Coachmans Cottage, Spreacombe, Braunton, EX33 1JA, England. *Telephone:* (1271) 870127. *E-mail:* jam.music@virgin.net. *Address:* Elkie Shop, 8 Mears Close, Penistone, Sheffield, S36 6EZ, England (office). *E-mail:* mail@elkiebrooks.net (office). *Website:* www.elkiebrooks.net.

BROOKS, (Troyal) Garth, BS; American country singer, songwriter and musician (guitar); b. 7 Feb. 1962, Tulsa, Okla; s. of Troyal Raymond and Colleen Carroll Brooks; m. 1st Sandra Mahl 1986; three c.; m. 2nd Trisha Yearwood 2005. *Education:* Oklahoma State Univ. *Career:* mem. American Soc. of Composers, Authors and Publrs (ASCAP), Country Music Asscn, Acad. of Country Music. *Recordings include:* albums: Garth Brooks 1989, No Fences (Acad. of Country Music Album of the Year 1991, CMA Award for Best Album 1991) 1990, Ropin' The Wind 1991, Beyond The Season 1992, The Chase 1992, In Pieces 1993, The Hits 1994, Fresh Horses 1995, Sevens 1997, In The Life Of

Chris Gaines 1999, Garth Brooks & The Magic Of Christmas 1999, Double Live (American Music Award for Favorite Country Album 2001) 2000, Scarecrow 2001, The Entertainer 2006, Man Against Machine 2014; singles: If Tomorrow Never Comes 1989, The Dance (Acad. of Country Music Song of Year, CMA Award for Best Single) 1991, Friends in Low Places (Acad. of Country Music Single Record of Year) 1991, If Tomorrow Never Comes (American Music Country Song of Year) 1991, Tour EP 1994, To Make You Feel My Love 1998, One Heart At A Time 1998, Lost In You 1999, Call Me Claus 2001, The Thunder Rolls, We Shall Be Free, Somewhere Other Than The Night, Learning to Live Again. *Television specials:* This is Garth Brooks 1992, This is Garth Brooks Too 1994, Garth Brooks: The Hits 1995, Garth Brooks Live in Cen. Park 1997. *Honours:* Acad. of Country Music Entertainer of the Year 1991, 1992, 1993, 1994, Male Vocalist of the Year Award 1991, Horizon Award 1991, Country Music Asscn Entertainer of the Year award 1991, 1992, Grammy Award for Best Male Country Vocalist 1992, Best Male Country Music Performer 1992, 1993, Best Male Musical Performer, People's Choice Awards 1992–95, Country Music Award for Artist of the Decade 1999, American Music Award for Favorite Country Artist 2000, Special Award of Merit 2002, inducted into Country Music Hall of Fame 2012, 50th Anniversary Milestone Award, Acad. of Country Music Awards 2015. *Current Management:* c/o Bob Doyle, Major Bob Music, 1111 17th Avenue S, Nashville, TN 37212, USA. *Telephone:* (615) 329-4150. *Fax:* (615) 329-1021. *Website:* majorbob.com; www.garthbrooks.com.

BROOKS, Leon Eric (Kix), III; American country singer, musician (guitar) and songwriter; b. 12 May 1955, Shreveport, La. *Career:* solo artist and staff songwriter with Tree Publishing; mem., duet Brooks & Dunn (with Ronnie Dunn) 1988–2010. *Compositions include:* Brand New Man; I'm Only In It For The Love; My Next Broken Heart; That Ain't No Way To Go; Whiskey Under The Bridge; You're Gonna Miss Me When I'm Gone. *Recordings include:* albums: solo: Kix Brooks 1989, New to This Town 2012; as Brooks & Dunn: Brand New Man 1991, Hard Workin' Man 1993, Waitin' On Sundown 1994, Borderline 1996, If You See Her 1998, Tight Rope 1999, Steers and Stripes 2001, It Won't Be Christmas Without You 2002, Red Dirt Road 2003, Hillbilly Deluxe 2005, Cowboy Town 2007. *Honours:* Country Music Asscn (CMA) Vocal Duo of the Year 1993–98, 2004, 2005, 2006, ACM Awards for Best Vocal Duo 2004, 2005, 2006, 2007, 2010, for Song of the Year (for Believe) 2006, four American Music Awards for Favorite Country Band, including 2005, CMA Award for Single of the Year, Music Video of the Year (both for Believe) 2006, 50th Anniversary Milestone Award, Acad. of Country Music (with Ronnie Dunn) 2015. *Website:* www.kixbrooks.com.

BROOKS, Meredith; American singer, songwriter and musician (guitar); b. Corvallis, OR. *Career:* mem. of all-female group, The Graces 1990; solo artist 1991–. *Recordings include:* albums: Blurring the Edges, 1997; See It Through My Eyes, 1997; Deconstruction, 1999, Bad Bad One 2002, If I Could Be... 2007. *Address:* c/o Jody Nachtigal, Arcadia Group Management, 11400 West Olympic Boulevard, 2nd Floor, Los Angeles, CA 90064, USA. *Telephone:* (310) 445-8888. *E-mail:* jody@arcadia-us.net. *Website:* www.meredithbrooks .com.

BROOKS, (Nichola) Nikki, BPharm; British musician (keyboards, bass guitar, clarinet) and singer; b. Bristol. *Education:* Guildhall School of Music. *Career:* lead vocalist, McCoy 1985; lead vocalist, Wild! 1986–87; lead and backing vocalist, bass, keyboards in various covers bands; vocalist, Madame Arthur 2003; bass guitarist, No Quarter 2004–05; currently mem. Uncensored; played with mems of Gillan, Iron Maiden, UFO, Wild Horses, Pat Travers Band, Gary Moore Band; tours, festivals in UK and Europe; vocal sessions include Dreamboys, LA Centrefold Videos; currently writing material with songwriting partner; mem. Musicians' Union, PRS. *Recordings include:* wrote and recorded four song session for BBC Radio 1 Rock Show (Tommy Vance). *E-mail:* nikki@nikkibrooks.com (office). *Website:* www.nikkibrooks .com.

BROSCH, Christopher; German promoter and agent; b. 9 April 1957, Munich; m. Kerstin Estherr Brosch 1991, one d. *Education:* studied law in Cologne. *Career:* freelance tour manager for various German tour promoters, 1980–85; talent booker for Peter Rieger Koncertagentur, Cologne, acts include: Peter Gabriel; Joe Cocker; Run-DMC; Beastie Boys; changed to Hamburg based company, Blinffish Promotion, as talent booker for new bands; started own company: Bizarre Productions 1992; acts promoted include: Beastie Boys; Portishead; Hole; Cocteau Twins; Oasis; Foo Fighters; Daft Punk.

BROUDIE, Ian; British singer, songwriter, musician (guitar) and producer; b. 4 Aug. 1958, Liverpool. *Career:* mem., Original Mirrors, late 1970s, Big In Japan 1977; mem. duo, Care, mid-1980s; Founder-mem., The Lightning Seeds 1990–2000, 2006–; also solo artist 2004–; numerous television and radio appearances, concert and festival appearances; singer, songwriter, Three Lions (Official England Squad's Euro '96 theme), with David Baddiel and Frank Skinner 1996; record producer 1980s–, for numerous artists, including Echo and The Bunnymen, The Fall, Wah!, Icicle Works, The Primitives, Alison Moyet, Frank and Walters, Dodgy, Sleeper. *Recordings include:* albums: with The Lightning Seeds: Cloudcuckooland 1991, Sense 1992, Jollification 1994, Dizzy Heights 1996, Like You Do... 1996, The Best Of 1997, Tilt 1999, Four Winds 2009; solo: Tales Told 2004. *Website:* www.lightningseeds.net.

BROUGHTON, Bruce; American composer and academic; *Adjunct Professor of Scoring for Motion Pictures and Television, Thornton School of Music,*

University of Southern California; b. 8 March 1945, Los Angeles, Calif. *Education:* Univ. of Southern California. *Career:* mem. ASCAP (Bd of Dirs), Motion Picture Acad. (Bd of Govs), Soc. of Composers and Lyricists (fmr Pres.); currently Adjunct Prof. of Scoring for Motion Pictures and Television, Thornton School of Music, Univ. of Southern California, taught film composition in Advanced Film Music Studies program; Guest Lecturer, Dept of Music, UCLA. *Compositions include:* for film: Silverado 1985, Young Sherlock Holmes 1985, The Boy Who Could Fly 1986, Harry and the Hendersons 1987, The Presidio 1988, Narrow Margin 1990, The Rescuers Down Under 1990, Homeward Bound 1993, Tombstone 1993, Baby's Day Out 1994, Miracle on 34th Street 1994, Infinity 1996, Shadow Conspiracy 1997, Krippendorf's Tribe 1998, Lost in Space 1998, Damaged Care 2002, Bobbie's Girl 2002, Last Flight Out 2004, Mickey, Donald, Goofy: The Three Musketeers 2004, Warm Springs 2005, Bambi II 2006, Doughboy 2011, A Christmas Tree Miracle 2013, Alone Yet Not Alone 2013; for television: Hawaii Five-O 1968, Barnaby Jones 1973, Dirty Sally 1974, Police Woman 1974, Khan! 1975, Three for the Road 1975, Spencer's Pilots 1976, Quincy 1976, The Andros Targets 1977, Logan's Run 1977, The Oregon Trail 1977, How the West Was Won 1978, Dallas 1978, The Runaways 1978, The Paradise Connection 1979, Hart to Hart 1979, Buck Rogers in the 25th Century 1979, The Return of Frank Cannon 1980, Desperate Voyage 1980, Skag 1980, Killjoy 1981, The Girl, the Gold Watch & Dynamite 1981, One Shoe Makes It Murder 1982, Desperate Lives 1982, The Blue and the Gray 1982, This Girl for Hire 1983, M.A.D.D.: Mothers Against Drunk Driving 1983, Cowboy 1983, Two Marriages 1983, Passions 1984, The Master of Ballantrae 1984, The First Olympics: Athens 1896 1984, The Cowboy and the Ballerina 1984, Stormin' Home 1985, Amazing Stories 1985, The Thanksgiving Promise 1986, George Washington II: The Forging of a Nation 1986, Sorry, Wrong Number 1989, Tiny Toon Adventures 1990, The Old Man and the Sea 1990, Capitol Critters 1992, O Pioneers! 1992, JAG (theme) 1995, Glory & Honor 1998, Night Ride Home 1999, Jeremiah 1999, The Ballad of Lucy Whipple 1999, First Monday 2002, Rough It 2002, Damaged Care 2002, Bobbie's Girl 2002, The Locket 2002, Eloise at the Plaza 2003, Warm Springs 2005, The Dive from Clausen's Pier 2005, Safe Harbor 2009, Hollywood in Vienna 2011 2011. *Honours:* eight Emmy Awards, for Dallas, Buck Rogers, The First Olympics, Tiny Tune Adventures, O Pioneers!, Glory and Honor. *Current Management:* c/o WME Entertainment, 9601 Wilshire Blvd., 3rd Floor Beverly Hills, Los Angeles, CA 90210, USA. *Address:* Thornton School of Music, Univ. of Southern California, Los Angeles, CA 90089-0851, USA (office). *Telephone:* (213) 740-6935 (office). *Fax:* (213) 740-3217 (office). *E-mail:* smptv@usc.edu (office); info@brucebroughton.com. *Website:* www.usc.edu/schools/music/private/faculty/bbrough.php (office); www.brucebroughton.com.

BROUWER, Leovigildo (Leo); Cuban composer, conductor and classical guitarist; b. 1 March 1939, Havana. *Education:* studied with Isaac Nicola, Peyrellade Conservatoire, Havana, Juilliard School, , USA with Stefan Wolpe and Vincent Persichetti, Hartt Coll. with Isadore Freed. *Career:* debut 1956; Dir Music Dept, Instituto Cubano 1960; teacher, Nat. Conservatory, Havana 1961–67, Dir experimental dept of Cuban film music from 1967; created the Experimentación de Sonidos (with Silvio Rodriguez and Pablo Milanes) 1968; many tours as guitar soloist; guitar competition founded in his honour, Japan 1984; fmr conductor, Orquesta de Cuba; Co-founder, Orchestra de Córdoba, Spain 1992. *Compositions for film:* Historias de la revolución 1960, Papeles son papeles 1966, La Muerte de un burócrata 1966, Hanoi, martes 13 1967, Las Aventuras de Juan Quin Quin 1967, Memorias del subdesarrollo 1968, La Primera carga al machete 1969, La Bataille des dix millions 1971, Un Día de noviembre 1972, Una Pelea cubana contra los demonios 1972, Ustedes tienen la palabra 1973, El Extraño caso de Rachel K 1973, El Hombre de Maisinicú 1973, Rancheador 1975, La Cantata de Chile 1975, El Otro Francisco 1975, La Última cena 1976, Destino manifiesto 1977, Son o no son 1978, El Recurso del método 1978, No hay sábado sin sol 1979, Los Sobrevivientes 1979, La Viuda de Montiel 1979, Una y otra vez 1982, Cecilia 1982, Alsino y el cóndor 1982, Tiempo de amar 1983, Los Refugiados de la cueva del muerto 1983, Amada 1983, La Rosa de los vientos 1983, Hasta cierto punto 1983, La Segunda hora de Esteban Zayas 1984, Jíbaro 1984, Tiempo de morir 1985, Visa USA 1986, Como agua para chocolate 1992, Mátame mucho 1998, Ficción sin ficción 2002, Memorias de Lucía 2003, Lucía y el tiempo 2004, La Persistence de la memoria 2004, Kordavision 2005. *Compositions include:* Homenaje a Manuel de Falla 1958, Sonograms for prepared piano 1963, Balada for flute and orchestra 1963, Tropos for orchestra 1967, Hexahedron for six players 1969, Flute Concerto 1972, Homenaje a Lenin for electronics, five guitar concertos 1972–92, Doble Concierto for violin, guitar and orchestra 1995, Lamento for Rafael Orozco for clarinet and strings 1996, Concierto No.7 La Habana 1998, Concierto No.8 Concierto Cantata de Perugia 1999, Viaje a la Semilla 2000, La Danza Imposible for orchestra 2001, Pictures of Another Exhibition 2001, An Idea 2001, Nuevos Estudios Sencillos 2002, Concierto de Benicassim for guitar and orchestra 2002, La Ciudad De Las Columnas 2004, Paisaje Cubano con fiesta 2007, many smaller pieces for guitar. *Honours:* Latin Grammy Award for Best Classical Album (for Integral Cuartetos de Cuerda) 2010. *Current Management:* c/o Chester Music and Novello & Co., 14–15 Berners Street, London, W1T 3LJ, England.

BROWN, Alex; British singer and musician (piano, trumpet, guitar, drums); b. 17 Jan. 1967, Glynde. *Career:* lead singer, Macho Frog 1985–88; UK (South East) tour 1987; signed to Brown Bear Records 1990–; tours in Austria, Germany, Belgium, England; numerous live appearances; mem. PRS, Musicians' Union, PPL, VPL, Umbrella. *Recordings include:* That's What It Takes 1993, Supernatural Love 1994, Life Is Just Worth Living 1994, Halfway To Heaven 1994, Too Far Away 1995, What I Like 1995, I've Been Missing You 1995.

BROWN, Andy; New Zealand singer and songwriter; b. 1 Nov. 1968, Auckland. *Career:* Mainstage NZ Festival, 1991; Shelterbelt Festival, 1992; New Zealand Tour; Australian Tour, 1993; Parachute Music Festivals, 1992, 1994, 1995; New Zealand tour, three months; Tear Fund, Hope and Justice Tour, 1995; world tour, Europe and USA, 1996; mem. Australasian Performing Rights Asscn. *Recordings include:* albums: Surge, 1991; Nice Moon, 1994; Merge, 1996; Pakajam, 1998. *Honours:* Nice Moon, 10 Best of '94, Audio Video magazine, NZ.

BROWN, Angie; singer and actor; b. 13 June 1963, Clapham, London, England. *Education:* studied singing with Annette Batram. *Career:* solo singer, with numerous television appearances; lead singer, Ramona 55; guest and featured singer, Bizarre Inc. 1992, Motiv8 1994, Northside Connection 2000, Eric S 2002; mem. Equity, PRS, Musicians' Union, PAMRA. *Recordings include:* album: An Album I Thought I Could Only Dream Of! (with Ramona 55) 1994. *Address:* LJE, 32 Willesden Lane, Kilburn, London NW6 7ST, England. *Website:* www.angie-brown.com.

BROWN, Bobby; American singer; b. 5 Feb. 1969, Roxbury, MA; m. Whitney Houston 1992 (divorced 2007); one d. *Career:* founder mem., New Edition 1981–85, re-formed 1995; solo artist 1985–; established Bosstown recording studio and record label; mem. Heads of State 2008–; collaborations with Ja Rule, Damian Marley, Macy Gray. *Film appearances:* Ghostbusters II 1989, Nora's Hair Salon 2004, Lucky Number Slevin 2005, Nora's Hair Salon II 2008. *Television:* Being Bobby Brown (documentary series, Bravo) 2005. *Recordings include:* albums: solo: King Of Stage 1986, Don't Be Cruel 1989, Dance… Ya Know It! 1989, Bobby 1992, B Brown Posse 1993, NBA Jam Session 1993, Remixes N The Key Of B 1993, Forever 1997, The Masterpiece 2011. *Honours:* SKC Boston Music Awards 1989–, Soul Train Music Award for Best R&B/Urban Contemporary Album of the Year, American Music Awards 1990–; Grammy Award for Best Male R&B Vocal Performance (for Every Little Step) 1990, Coca-Cola Atlanta Music Award for Outstanding Male Vocalist 1992. *Current Management:* c/o Tommy Brown, 2160 N Central Road, Fort Lee, NJ 08014, USA. *Website:* www.bobbybrownonline.com.

BROWN, Carlinhos; Brazilian singer, songwriter and musician (percussion); b. (Antônio Carlos Santos de Freitas), 1962, Salvador, Bahia. *Career:* began recording and production career writing jingles, WR radio station, Salvador 1980; joined Caetano Veloso's group, Banda Nova 1985; formed Timbalada (drum band of over 120 musicians and singers) 1990; mem. Tribalistas with Marisa Monte and Arnaldo Antunes 2002–03; collaborations with Gilberto Gil, Gal Costa, João Gilberto, Djavan, João Bosco. *Compositions:* over 200 songs including Segue o Seco, Maria de Verdade, Arrepio, Magamalabares recorded by Marisa Monte, Rapunzel, Rímas Irmãs by Daniela Mercury, Lavanda by Daúde, Visão do Ciclope by Luís Caldas, Meia Luna Inteira by Caetano Veloso, others by recorded Sérgio Mendes, Gal Costa, Cássia Eller, Sepultura. *Recordings:* albums: solo: Alfagamabetizado 1996, Omelete Man 1998, Bahia do Mundo – Mito e Verdade 2000, Carlito Marrón 2004, Candombless 2005, A Gente Ainda Não Sonhou 2007; with Timbalada: Cada Cabeça É Um Mundo 1995, Andei Road 1996, Mineral 1997, Mãe de Samba 1997, Pense Minha Cor 1999, Timbalismo 2001, Motumba Bless 2002, Serviço de Animacão Popular 2004, Alegria Original 2007; with Tribalistas: Tribalistas 2003. *Website:* www.carlinhosbrown.com.br.

BROWN, Christopher (Chris); American R&B singer; b. 5 May 1989, Tappahannock, Va. *Career:* solo artist 2004–. *Recordings include:* albums: Chris Brown 2005, Exclusive 2007, Graffiti 2009, F.A.M.E. (Grammy Award for Best R&B Album 2012) 2011, Fortune 2012, X 2014, Fan of a Fan (with Tyga) 2015, Royalty 2015. *Honours:* Soul Train Music Award for Best R&B/Soul New Artist 2006, BET Award for Best New Artist 2006, Billboard Awards for Artist of the Year, New Artist of the Year 2006, MTV Video Music Award for Best Male Video (for With You) 2008, MOBO Awards for Best Int. Act 2008, for Best R&B/Soul Artist 2008, American Music Award for Artist of the Year 2008, Best Hip-Hop Video, Best Collaboration (with Busta Rhymes), People's Champ Award, BET Hip Hop Awards 2011. *Address:* c/o Jive Records, Sony Music Entertainment, 555 Madison Avenue, 10th Floor, New York, NY 10022-3211, USA. *Website:* www.chrisbrownworld .com.

BROWN, Christopher (Chris) M.; American composer, producer, recording engineer and teacher; b. 1 July 1954, Evanston, Ill. *Education:* Oberlin Coll. Conservatory of Music. *Career:* long affiliation with Paul Winter and The Winter Consort; scores for tv, film, industrial videos; recorded, edited or mixed numerous albums, films and video scores; teacher, Faculty of Music, Wooster School, Danbury; mem. Nat. Acad. of Recording Arts and Sciences, AFofM. *Recordings include:* Prayer for the Wild Things, Paul Winter 1995. *Honours:* Grammy Award 1995. *Address:* 1401 Route 35, South Salem, NY 10590; 16 High Street, Bethel, CT 06801, USA. *Telephone:* (914) 391-5766. *E-mail:* christopherbrown@earthlink.net. *Website:* christopherbrownmusic.com.

BROWN, (Andrew John) Drew; American musician (guitars, keyboards) and songwriter; b. 9 Jan. 1984. *Career:* mem. Republic 2002–, renamed OneRepublic; support act to many artists including Bon Jovi, P!nk, Maroon 5; collaborated with Timbaland on track Apologize 2008. *Recordings:* albums: with OneRepublic: Dreaming Out Loud 2007, Waking Up 2009, Native 2013;

other appearances: Echo, Leona Lewis 2009, Shock Value II, Timbaland 2009. *Honours:* with OneRepublic: Teen Choice Music Award for Rock Track (for Stop and Stare) 2008, MTV Asia Award for Best Hook Up (for Apologize – with Timbaland) 2008, ESKA Music Award (Poland) for Band of the Year (Int.) 2010. *Address:* c/o Patriot Records, Interscope Records, 1755 Broadway, New York, NY 10019, USA (office). *Telephone:* (212) 841-8000 (office). *Website:* www.patriotrecords.com (office); www.onerepublic.net.

BROWN, Foxy; American rap artist; b. (Inga DeCarlo Fung Marchand), 6 Sept. 1979, Brooklyn, New York; m. Ricardo Brown 1999. *Education:* Brooklyn Coll. Acad. High School, New York. *Career:* guest appearances on songs by LL Cool J, BLACKstreet, Toni Braxton, Case, Jay-Z, Method Man, Total; sentenced to one year imprisonment on assault charges 2007–08. *Film appearance:* Woo 1998. *Recordings include:* albums: Ill Na Na 1996, Chyna Doll 1998, Broken Silence 2001, Brooklyn's Don Diva 2008.

BROWN, Gregory (Greg); American singer and songwriter; b. 2 July 1949, Ia; m. 3rd Iris Dement 2002. *Career:* won contest to support touring artist in Ia; relocated to New York; organized folk nights; worked as songwriter for artists including The Platters; returned to Ia; worked as musician for Iowa Arts Council; temporarily retired from music; regular guest on Garrison Keillor radio show 1980; f. Red House Records 1980–; toured extensively; subject of tribute album Going Driftless 2002. *Recordings include:* albums: Hacklebarney 1974, Iowa Waltz 1981, 44&66 1981, One Night… 1983, In The Dark With You 1985, Songs Of Innocence And Experience 1986, One More Goodnight Kiss 1988, One Big Town 1989, Down In There 1990, Dream Café 1992, Friend Of Mine 1993, Bathtub Blues 1993, The Poet Game 1994, The Live One 1995, Further In 1996, Slant Six Mind 1997, Solid Heart 1999, Covenant 2000, Over And Under 2000, Down In The Valley 2001, Milk Of The Moon 2002, Live At The Black Sheep 2003, If I Had Known (compilation) 2003, In the Hills of California (Live from the Kate Wolf Music Festival 1997–2003) 2004, The Evening Call 2006, Yellow Dog 2007, Live from the Big Top 2007, Dream City: Essential Recordings Vol. 2, 1997–2006 2009, Freak Flag 2011, Hymns to What Is Left 2012. *Address:* Red House Records, POB 4044, St Paul, MN 55104, USA (office). *Telephone:* (651) 644-4161 (office). *Fax:* (651) 644-4248 (office). *Website:* www.redhouserecords.com (office); www.gregbrown .org.

BROWN, Ian George; British singer, songwriter and musician (bass guitar); b. 20 Feb. 1963, Ancoats, Greater Manchester; m. Fabiola Quiroz-Brown. *Career:* formed Patrol 1980, name changed to English Rose 1983, later the Stone Roses 1984–96; numerous tours worldwide with the Stone Roses; solo artist 1997–. *Recordings include:* albums: with the Stone Roses: The Stone Roses 1989, Turn Into Stone 1992, Second Coming 1994, The Very Best Of The Stone Roses 2002; solo: Unfinished Monkey Business 1998, Golden Greats 1999, Music Of The Spheres 2001, Remixes Of The Spheres 2002, Solarized 2004, The Greatest 2005, The World is Yours 2007, My Way 2009, Cream Chilled Electronic 2011, Seriously 90's 2013. *Honours:* NME Godlike Genius Award 2006, Q Legend Award 2007. *Website:* www.ianbrown.co.uk.

BROWN, James Kofi; Ghanaian musician (guitar), singer, composer and arranger; b. 15 Feb. 1949, Kumasi, Kwadaso; m. Comfort Peprah Aman Fo 1992, three s. *Career:* many concerts in Ghana and in France; various radio and television broadcasts; mem. SACEM; SDRM French Musical Society. *Recordings:* Time Is So Hard; Riot (That's Too Bad); I'm In The Mood For Love; Life Is A Stage; Be My Girl; I've Found A New Lover (Georgina); Let's Be Together. *Honours:* Best video clip, festival in Paris, France.

BROWN, James Lee; American musician (saxophones, keyboards); b. 7 Oct. 1953, Rocky Mount, North Carolina; m. Angela Y. Brown 1982; two s. two d. *Recordings include:* Saxophonic Praises; Manifestation. *Honours:* ASCAP Award for Songwriting. *Current Management:* Saxophonic Praises Inc., 4714 Keppler Place, Temple Hills, MD 20748, USA. *Telephone:* (301) 423-1395. *E-mail:* j.brown@visto.com; saxophonicprais@aol.com.

BROWN, (James) Jimmy; British musician (drums); b. 20 Nov. 1957. *Education:* Moseley School of Art. *Career:* mem. reggae group UB40 1978–; numerous concerts, tours. *Recordings include:* albums: Signing Off 1980, Present Arms 1981, The Singles Album 1982, UB44 1982, Labour of Love 1983, Live 1983, More UB40 Music 1983, Geffery Morgan 1984, Baggariddim 1985, Little Baggariddim 1985, UB40 File 1985, Rat In The Kitchen 1986, CCCP: Live In Moscow 1987, UB40 1988, Labour of Love II 1990, Promises and Lies 1993, Anansi 1995, Guns In The Ghetto 1997, Labour of Love III 1998, Presents The Dancehall Album 1998, Homegrown 2003, Who You Fighting For? 2005, TwentyFourSeven 2008. *Current Management:* c/o Part Rock Management Limited, 1 Conduit Street, London, W1S 2XA, England. *Telephone:* (20) 8207-1418. *E-mail:* stewartyoung@mindspring.com. *Address:* UB40, PO Box 15345, Birmingham, B9 9GJ, England (office). *E-mail:* info@ ub40.co.uk (office). *Website:* www.ub40.co.uk (office).

BROWN, Kevin John; musician (saxophone); b. 19 July 1960, Nottingham, England. *Career:* fmr mem. The Beautiful South; numerous tours, TV and radio broadcasts, and live performances; Head, Glasshouse Loan Music Project, Alloa, Scotland 2010–; mem. Musicians' Union. *Recordings include:* albums: with The Beautiful South: Choke 1990, 0898 1992, Carry On Up The Charts 1994; other: Rubaiyat (Elektra Records 40th anniversary) 1990, Imperial 66 (with The Miracle Drug) 1993.

BROWN, Melanie Janice; British singer; b. 29 May 1975, Leeds, England; m. 1st Jimmy Gulzar 1998 (divorced); two d.; m. 2nd Stephen Belafonte 2007.

Career: mem. Touch, later renamed The Spice Girls 1993–2001, as Melanie B (later Melanie G) or 'Scary Spice', reunion tour 2007–08; numerous tours, concerts, television and radio appearances; world tours include UK, Europe, India, USA; solo artist 1998–. *Film includes:* Spiceworld: The Movie 1997. *Television includes:* as presenter This is My Moment (ITV 1) 2001; as judge: The X Factor (ITV) 2014–. *Recordings include:* albums: with The Spice Girls: Spice 1996, Spiceworld 1997, Forever 2000, Greatest Hits 2007; solo: Hot 2003, LA State of Mind 2005. *Honours:* two Ivor Novello songwriting awards 1997, Smash Hits Award for Best Band 1997, BRIT Awards for Best Single (for Wannabe), for Best Video (for Say You'll Be There) 1997, for Best Performance of the last 30 years 2010, three American Music Awards 1998, Special BRIT Award for Int. Sales 1998. *Website:* www.melaniebrown.com.

BROWN, Michael; songwriter and musician (saxophone, bass guitar, keyboards); b. 29 April 1968, Grimsby, South Humberside, England. *Career:* mem., Illustrious GY 1988–93, with tours, tv appearances and radio broadcasts; Founder mem., Giant Killers (as songwriter) 1995–; mem. Musicians' Union. *Recordings include:* album with Illustrious GY: No, No, No 1993.

BROWN, Norman; American musician (guitar); b. Shreveport, Los Angeles. *Education:* Musicians' Inst., Hollywood. *Career:* worldwide touring, worldwide radio airplay; mem. of jazz trio Brown-Whalum-Braun (BWB). *Recordings include:* albums: Just Between Us 1992, After The Storm 1994, Better Days Ahead 1996, Celebration 1999, Just Chillin' (Grammy Award for Pop Instrumental Album 2003) 2002, West Coast Coolin' 2004, Stay with Me 2007, Sending My Love 2010; with BWB: Groovin' 2002. *Honours:* Soul Train Award for Best Jazz Album 1995. *Address:* c/o Peak Records Inc., 100 North Crescent Drive, Suite 275, Beverly Hills, CA 90210, USA. *Telephone:* (310) 385-4040. *Fax:* (310) 385-4050. *E-mail:* PeakRecordsUSA@gmail.com. *Website:* www .peakrecords.com.

BROWN, Robert (Rob) John; British programmer and producer; b. 1970. *Career:* mem. Autechre 1991–; involved in Gescom projects 1995–. *Recordings include:* albums: with Autechre: Incunabula 1993, Amber 1994, Tri Repetae 1995, Chiastic Slide 1997, Autechre 1998, Confield 2001, Draft 7.30 2003, Untilted 2005, Quaristice 2008, Oversteps 2010; with Gescom: Minidisc 1998; singles: with Autechre: Cavity Job 1991, Basscadet 1994, Anti 1994, Garbage 1995, Anvil Vapre 1995, Keynell 1996, Envane 1997, Cichlisuite 1997, To Day 1998, The Peel Sessions 1999, EP7 1999, Split Rmx 12 1999, Peel Sessions Vol. 2 2001, Gantz Graf 2002; with Gescom: Gescom 1994, Gescom 2 1994, Motor (EP) 1994, The Sounds Of Machines Our Parents Used 1995, Keynell 1996, This 1998, That 1998, Iss:sa 2003. *Current Management:* c/o Warp Records, Spectrum House, 32–34 Gordon House Road, London NW5 1LP, England. *Telephone:* (20) 7284-8350. *Fax:* (20) 7284-8360. *E-mail:* info@warprecords .com. *Website:* www.warprecords.com.

BROWN, Selwyn 'Bumbo'; British musician (keyboards). *Career:* mem., Steel Pulse; numerous TV appearances, world-wide tours. *Recordings include:* albums: Handsworth Revolution 1978, Tribute To The Martyrs 1979, Caught You (aka Reggae Fever) 1980, True Democracy 1982, Earth Crisis 1984, Reggae Refreshers 1985, Babylon The Bandit (Grammy Award) 1985, State of Emergency 1988, Victims 1991, Rastafari Centennial 1992, Smash Hits 1993, Vex 1994, Rastanthology 1996, Rage & Fury 1997, Sound System: The Island Anthology 1996, Living Legacy 1999, African Holocaust 2004. *Address:* c/o Richard Hermitage, Steel Pulse Ltd, 33 Kersley Road, London, N16 0NT, England. *Telephone:* (121) 622-6857. *Website:* www.steelpulse.com (office).

BROWN, (Anthony) T. Graham; American country singer and songwriter; b. 30 Oct. 1954, Arabi, Ga. *Career:* Founder, Rio Diamond 1976; Founder, T. Graham Brown's Rock of Spam 1979; demo singer, Nashville 1982; recorded commercials; solo artist 1985–. *Recordings include:* albums: I Tell It Like It Used To Be 1986, Brilliant Conversationalist 1987, Come As You Were 1988, Bumper To Bumper 1990, You Can't Take It With You 1991, Don't Go To Strangers 1996, Wine into Water 1998, Lives 2001, The Next Big Thing 2003, The Present 2006, Deja Vu All Over Again 2007. *E-mail:* showtgbiz@gmail .com. *Website:* www.tgrahambrown.com.

BROWN, Tony Ersic; American record company executive, songwriter, producer and musician (keyboards); b. 11 Dec. 1946, Greensboro, North Carolina; m. 1st Janie Levin (divorced); m. 2nd Anastasia Pruitt 1999 (divorced 2009); m. 3rd Jamie Antee 2013; two c. *Career:* songwriter, Silverline Music 1972; musician with Oak Ridge Boys 1972–75, Elvis Presley 1975–77, Emmylou Harris 1977–80, Roseanne Cash 1980–83; A&R Exec., RCA Records 1978–84; A&R Exec., MCA Records 1984, later Pres.; Co-founder Universal South Records 2002–06; mem., NARAS, Nashville Entertainment Asscn, CMA, ACM, Gospel Music Asscn. *Recordings include:* albums include: with Emmylou Harris: Blue Kentucky Girl 1979, Christmas Album 1979, Evangeline 1981, Cimarron 1981, White Shoes 1983; with Guy Clark: Better Days 1983; also appears on: Guitar Town 1986, Pontiac 1987, Little Love Affairs 1988, Lyle Lovett and His Large Band 1989, Hardin County Line 1990, For My Broken Heart 1991, Love and Danger 1992, Reba McEntire Greatest Hits Vol. 2 1993, 8 Seconds 1994, Strait Out Of The Box 1995, Step Right Up 1996, Horse Whisperer 1998. *Honours:* Dove Award, Gospel Music Asscn 1972, Grammy Awards 1980, 1983, 1985, Producer of the Year, NARAS 1991, AMA Lifetime Achievement Award for Producer/Engineer 2008.

BROWN, Zac; American country music singer and guitarist; b. Cumming, GA. *Education:* West Georgia Coll., Carrolton, Univ. of West Georgia. *Career:* Founder mem. Zac Brown Band 2002–; released debut single 2003; co-founder,

Zac's Place music club and restaurant 2004. *Recordings include:* albums: with Zac Brown Band: Far from Einstyne 2004, Home Grown 2005, The Foundation 2008, You Get What You Give 2010, Uncaged (Grammy Award for Best Country Album 2013) 2012, Jekyll + Hyde 2015. *Honours:* with Zac Brown Band: Acad. of Country Music Awards for Top New Vocal Duo or Group 2009, for Top Vocal Event of the Year (with Alan Jackson) 2011, Country Music Television Music Awards for USA Weekend Breakthrough Video of the Year 2009, for Performance of the Year (with Jimmy Buffet) 2011, Grammy Awards for Best New Artist 2010, for Best Country Collaboration with Vocals (with Alan Jackson) 2011, Country Music Asscn Award for New Artist of the Year 2010. *Current Management:* c/o ROAR Management, 9701 Wilshire Boulevard, 8th Floor, Beverly Hills, CA 90212, USA. *Address:* c/o Lynn Oliver, Southern Ground Artists, 1700 Marietta Blvd, Atlanta, GA 30318-3639, USA (office). *E-mail:* lynn@southerngroundartists.com (office). *Website:* www .southerngroundartists.com (office); www.zacbrownband.com.

BROWNE, Jackson; American singer, songwriter and musician (guitar, piano); b. 9 Oct. 1948, Heidelberg, Germany; m. 1st Phyllis Major 1975 (died 1976); one s.; m. 2nd Lynne Sweeney 1981 (divorced 1983); one s. *Career:* fmr mem., Nitty Gritty Dirt Band 1966; solo singer, songwriter, musician 1967–; Co-founder Musicians United for Safe Energy (MUSE), Nukefree.org, Success through the Arts Foundation; numerous tours and concerts, festival appearances and benefit concerts. *Compositions include:* songs recorded by Tom Rush, Nico, Linda Ronstadt, The Eagles; co-writer with Glenn Frey, Take It Easy. *Recordings include:* albums: Jackson Browne 1972, For Everyman 1973, Late For The Sky 1974, The Pretender 1976, Running On Empty 1978, Hold Out 1980, Lawyers In Love 1983, Lives In The Balance 1987, World In Motion 1989, I'm Alive 1993, Looking East 1996, The Naked Ride Home 2002, Solo Acoustic Vol. 1 2005, Solo Acoustic Vol. 2 2008, Time the Conqueror 2008, Love Is Strange: En Vivo Con Tino (with David Lindley) 2010, Standing in the Breach 2014. *Honours:* Hon. DMus (Occidental Coll.) 2004; John Steinbeck Award 2002, inducted into Rock and Roll Hall of Fame 2004, Songwriters Hall of Fame 2007, NARM Harry Chapin Humanitarian Award 2008. *Address:* Inside Recordings, Los Angeles, USA (office). *Telephone:* (818) 506-0898 (office). *Website:* www.insiderecordings.com (office); www.jacksonbrowne.com.

BROWNE, Michael Jerome; Canadian singer and musician (guitar, banjo, fiddle, mandolin, harmonica); b. 9 April 1960, Indiana. *Career:* solo artist, coffee houses and street corners, Canada, USA, UK, 1974–84; lead singer, guitarist, Stephen Barry Band 1984–99; accompanist, Vann Walls and visiting blues artists; mem. American Federation of Musicians. *Compositions:* (co-written with B. A. Markus): Blacktop; You're For Me; Children; The Path You Leave Behind; May You Come And Stay; Cancer Ward Blues; Guitar Mama. *Recordings:* In The Evening (with Vann Walls), 1997; Michael Jerome Browne, 1998; Drive On, 2001, Michael Jerome Browne and the Twin Rivers String Band 2004, Double 2007, This Beautiful Mess 2008. *Honours:* Real Blues Award, Best Canadian Acoustic Blues Artist, 1998; Maple Blues Award, Acoustic Artist of the Year, 2001. *Address:* c/o The Borealis Recording Company Limited, 290 Shuter Street, Toronto, Ont., M5A 1W7, Canada. *Telephone:* (416) 530-4288. *Fax:* (416) 530-0461. *E-mail:* info@borealisrecords .com; hokeypokeypro@yahoo.com. *Website:* www.borealisrecords.com; www .michaeljeromebrowne.com.

BROWNE, Nichola; British journalist; *Head, Commercial Content Hub, Time Inc.. Career:* began career as staff writer, J-17 magazine; News Ed., Kerrang!, later Features Ed. 2002–09, Ed. 2009–11; Sr Account Man., Sports Vision (now Vision Nine) 2011–12; Head, Commercial Content Hub, Time Inc. UK 2014–. *Address:* Time Inc., Blue Fin Building, 110 Southwark Street, London, SE1 0SU, England (office). *Telephone:* (20) 3148-5000 (office). *Website:* www.timeincuk.com (office).

BROZA, David; Israeli/Spanish/American singer and songwriter; b. 4 Sept. 1955, Haifa, Israel; m.; three c. *Education:* studied in England and Spain. *Career:* fmr graphic artist; fmr Artist-in-Residence, Bennington Coll., USA; apptd Goodwill Amb. for UNICEF. *Recordings include:* albums: Sikhot Salon 1977, Hakeves Ha Shisha Asar 1978, David Broza 1978, Klaf 1981, Haisha Sheiti 1983, Broza 1984, A Poet in New York 1987, Away from Home 1989, First Collection 1990, Neshika Gnuva 1992, Time of Trains 1993, Masada Live 1994, Elements of Love 1994, Second Street 1994, Stonedoors 1994, Sodot Gdolim 1995, Matchil Linshom 1999, Isla Mujeres 2000, Spanish Heart 2001, Painted Postcard 2002, Todo O Nada 2002, Parking Completo 2004, Night Dawn, The Unpublished Poetry of Townes Van Zandt 2010, Third Language 2011. *Current Management:* Aviv Productions Inc., 10418 East Meadowhill Drive, Scottsdale, AZ 85255, USA. *Telephone:* (480) 659-1568. *Fax:* (602) 659-1581. *E-mail:* itzik@aviv2.com. *Website:* www.aviv2.com; www.davidbroza .net.

BRUCE, Hal Nelson; Canadian musician (guitar, piano, harmonica, bass, percussion), singer and songwriter; b. 27 May 1952, Halifax, Nova Scotia; one s. one d. *Career:* began playing in first rock 'n' roll band aged 14; full-time player 1982–; entertained three years running on Canadian Country Awards Show; performed in Halifax, Vancouver, Nashville, USA and London, UK; three consecutive performances as only solo performer, International Beatle Week, Liverpool, UK; mem. Atlantic Fed. of Musicians, Nova Scotia Country Music Asscn, Songwriters Asscn of Nova Scotia, Canadian Country Music Asscn, Music Industry Asscn of Nova Scotia. *Recordings include:* The First Time 1988, Goin' Home 1992, Cover-Up 1995, I''ll Be On My Way 1998, On Our Way 1998, In My Life 2002, I Will 2004, Thank You Girl 2006, All You

Need Is Love 2008. *Honours:* Male Vocalist of the Year 1991, Nova Scotia, winner, talent search, Nova Scotia, winner, Entertainer, Male Vocalist, Band, Video, Songwriter of the Year, Nova Scotia Country Music Awards, Vocalist and Band of the Year, CHFX Radio, Best of Texas Award for Songwriting, inducted to Hall of Fame, International Beatle Week Festival 2008. *Address:* Cavern Music, 18 Bellefontaine Court, Lawrencetown, NS B2Z 1L3, Canada (office). *Telephone:* (902) 435-7410 (office). *E-mail:* halbruce@halbruce.com (office). *Website:* www.halbruce.com.

BRÜCKNER, Thomas, (Tomcraft); German producer, musician (electronics) and DJ; b. 12 June 1975, Munich. *Career:* began DJing in Munich; remixed artists, including Dave Gahan, Pet Shop Boys, Sonique. *Recordings include:* albums: All I Got 2001, MUC 2003, Hyper Sexy Conscious 2006, For the Queen 2007. *Current Management:* c/o Great Stuff GmbH, Weissenburgerstrasse 19, 81667 Munich, Germany. *E-mail:* management@greatstuff.eu. *Website:* www .greatstuff.eu; www.tomcraft.de.

BRUEL, Patrick; French actor and singer; b. 14 May 1959, Tlemcen, Algeria. *Career:* actor 1979–; solo recording artist 1982–. *Films include:* Le Coup de Sirocco 1979, Ma femme s'appelle reviens 1982, Les Diplômés du dernier rang 1982, Le Bâtard 1983, Le Grand carnaval 1983, Marche à l'ombre 1984, La Tête dans le sac 1984, P.R.O.F.S. 1985, Suivez mon regard 1986, La Mémoire tatouée 1986, Attention bandits 1987, Un homme amoureux 1987, La Maison assassinée 1988, L'Union sacrée 1989, Force majeure 1989, Il y a des jours... et des lunes 1990, Toutes peines confondues 1992, Profil Bas 1993, Sabrina 1995, Les Cent et une nuits 1995, Hommes femmes mode d'emploi 1996, Le Jaguar 1996, K 1997, Paparazzi 1998, Hors jeu 1998, The Misadventures of Margaret 1998, Lost and Found 1999, Le Lait de la tendresse humaine 2001, Les Jolies choses 2001, Une vie à t'attendre 2004, El Lobo 2004, L'Ivresse du pouvoir 2006, O Jerusalem 2006, Un secret 2007. *Recordings include:* albums: Deux Faces, 1986; Olympia '87–A Tout A L'heure (live), 1987; Alors Regarde, 1989; Tour '91–Si Ce Soir... (live), 1991; Trois, 1994; Tour '95–On S'etait Dit... (live), 1995; Juste Avant, 1999; Rien Ne S'efface (live), 2001; Entre Deux, 2002, Des Souvenirs devant 2006. *E-mail:* opendisc@patrickbruel.com. *Website:* www.patrickbruel.com.

BRUFORD, Bill; British musician (drums, percussion), lecturer and composer; b. 17 May 1949, Sevenoaks, Kent, England; m. Carolyn Bruford 1973; two s. one d. *Education:* Univ. of Leeds and pvt tuition with Lou Pocock of Royal Philharmonic Orchestra. *Career:* mem. progressive rock group, Yes 1968–72, formed group, Anderson Bruford Wakeman Howe 1989, then re-adopted the name Yes 1991; mem., Genesis, UK, King Crimson, Gong; solo artist with group Bill Bruford's Earthworks 1986–; worldwide tours and appearances; compositions as writer for BBC TV and Buddy Rich Orchestra; f. Summerfold and Winterfold Records (as divs of Bill Bruford Productions 1972) 2004; Lecturer, Univ. Kingston, Acad. of Contempory Music, Guildford; mem. Percussive Arts Soc., Performing Right Soc., British Acad. of Composers and Songwriters; retd from public performing 2009. *Recordings include:* albums: with Yes: Yes 1969, Time And A Word 1970, The Yes Album 1971, Fragile 1971, Close To The Edge 1972, Yessongs 1973, Union 1991, Yesstory 1991; solo: Feels Good To Me 1978, One Of A Kind 1978, Gradually Going Tornado 1980, The Bruford Tapes 1980, Music For Piano And Drums 1983, Flags 1984, Earthworks 1987, Dig? 1989, All Heaven Broke Loose 1991, Symphonic Music Of Yes 1993, Stamping Ground: Bill Bruford's Earthworks Live 1994, Heavenly Bodies 1997, If Summer Had Its Ghosts 1997, A Part And Yet Apart 1999, Sound Of Surprise 2001, Upper Extremities 2001, Footloose And Fancy Free 2002, Random Acts Of Happiness 2004, Every Step A Word, Every Word A Song 2004, Earthworks Underground Orchestra 2006, World Drummers Ensemble 2006, In Two Minds 2007, Skin and Wire 2009. *Publications include:* When In Doubt, Roll!, Bill Bruford: The autobiography 2009; contrib. to numerous magazine articles. *Honours:* inducted into Modern Drummer magazine Hall of Fame 1990. *Telephone:* (1483) 276841 (office). *Fax:* (1483) 276841 (office). *E-mail:* info@billbruford.com (office); www.billbruford .com (office).

BRUN, Christian, MSc; French musician (guitar) and composer; b. 24 Dec. 1965, Antibes. *Education:* studied with Tal Farlow, music teacher degree. *Career:* performances with Lou Bennett, Manu Katche, Diane Tell, Laurent De Wilde, Christian Escoude, Kirk Lightsey, San Severino, Dee-Dee Bridgewater, etc.; recordings with Sonny Fortune, David Kikoski, Ray Drummond, Lonnie Plaxico, etc.; performed at festivals: Marciac, Albijazz, Jazz sur son 31, Jazz Sous les Pommiers; collaboration with DJ Yann Lebreuilly on Sofa Attitude et Clyb Foster productions; mem. Soc. des auteurs, compositeurs et éditeurs de musique (SACEM), Soc. de Perception et de Distribution des Droits des Artistes-Interprètes de la Musique et de la Danse (SPEDIDAM), Admin des droits des artistes et musiciens interprètes (ADAMI). *Recordings:* Houseful 1991; Samantha's Dance, with Steve Mabry; Brooklyn Session, with D. Kikoski, L. Plaxico, T. Campbell 1995, Melodik 1999, French Songs 2001; many collaborations including: Docteur Boris & Mister Vian (with Diane Tell) 2009, Movements (with Alex Tassel) 2009, Heads or Tails (with Alex Tassel) 2010, La Paz/Congo (with Quartier Sud) 2010. *Honours:* Winner, Radio France Competition 1991. *Address:* 19 avenue Secrétan, 75019 Paris, France. *Telephone:* 6-11-90-51-93 (mobile). *E-mail:* brun.chris@free.fr; info@ christianbrun.com. *Website:* www.christianbrun.com.

BRUNBORG, Tore; Norwegian jazz musician (tenor, soprano saxophone); b. 20 May 1960, Trondheim; two s. one d. *Education:* Music Conservatory, Trondheim. *Career:* toured, recorded with Masqualero 1982–92; currently mem. Tore Gustavsen Ensemble, Manu Katche Group, Mats Eilertsen Quartet, Bjørnstad/Christensen/Brunborg; currently leader or co-leader, Tore Brunborg Trio, Meadow, Scent of Soil; mem. Norwegian Musicians' Union. *Compositions:* commission for Vossa Jazz 1989, music for big bands, small groups. *Recordings:* three albums with Masqualero, others with Bo Stieff, Rita Marcotulli, Jon Balke, Arild Anderson, Anders Jormin, Chick Lyall, Billy Cobham; contrib. to Bande A Part 1985, Aero 1988, Re-enter 1991, Nonsentration 1992, Tid 1993, Hyperborean 1997, North Story 1998, Gravity 2003; with Geir Lysne Esemble: The Grieg Code 2009; with Manu Katche: Third Round 2010; with Ketil Bjørnstad: Remembrance 2010. *Honours:* Reenskaugprisen, Spelemannsprisen (three times, with Masqualero). *Address:* Bekkeveien 52, 1396 Billingstad, Norway. *Telephone:* 9164-9909. *E-mail:* tore.brunborg@broadpark.no; brunborg@me.com. *Website:* www .torebrunborg.com.

BRUNDTLAND, Torbjörn; Norwegian musician; b. 10 May 1975, Tromso. *Career:* mem., Aedena Cycle 1994-95, Röyksopp 2002–. *Recordings include:* albums: Melody AM 2002, The Understanding 2005, Röyksopp's Night Out 2006, Back to Mine 2007, Junior (Spellemannsprisen Best Composer and Best Electronic Album 2010) 2009, Senior 2010, Late Night Tales 2013, Do It Again (with Robyn) 2014. *Current Management:* c/o DEF Limited, 51 Lonsdale Road, London, NW6 6RA, England. *Telephone:* (20) 7328-2922. *E-mail:* info@d-e-f .com. *Website:* d-e-f.com. *E-mail:* news@royksopp.com. *Website:* www .royksopp.com.

BRUNEAU, Thierry; French musician (bass clarinet, bassoon, flute, alto, tenor and baritone saxophones); b. 28 July 1949, Paris; m. Päivi Hernala 1971. *Education:* CIM (jazz school); private lessons with Allen Eager, Buddy Collette, Chris Woods; Conservatoire of Music. *Career:* mem. Big Bands: Alan Silva Celestrial Communication Orchestra, Laurent Cugny Big Band Lumiere, Quintet with Charles Tyler, 1987; Tours: Scandinavia 1989–90, Japan 1989, Europe with local rhythm sections, Mal Waldron 1988–93, Ken McIntyre 1990–92, 1996, Anthony Ortega 1991–92, 1995; Concerts with: Richard Davis 1990, Dennis Charles 1994; Also played with: Duke Jordan, Han Bennink, Frank Lowe; Scriptwriter, actor, composer, film Last Date (Hans Hylkema's film about Eric Dolphy); Founder, own record label, Serene 1989; Released some Eric Dolphy material (the Uppsala Concert); Played festivals at: Turku, Finland, Gothenburg, Sweden, Vienne, Tourcoing, Montpellier, TBB, Jazz Valley (France). *Recordings include:* Live At De Kave, Thierry Bruneau Quartet featuring Mal Waldron; Tribute, Ken McIntyre/Thierry Bruneau Quintet featuring Richard Davis; Anthony Ortega/Thierry Bruneau: 7 Standards and A Blues, Anthony Ortega.

BRUNET, Alain, MA; French musician (trumpet); b. 6 March 1947, Saint Sorlin, Drome. *Education:* Sorbonne University, Paris National Conservatory. *Career:* founder, Module, 1974; founder, Alain Brunet Quartet; Played with: Martial Solal; René Utreger; Jean-Louis Chautemps; Lee Konitz; Sonny Stitt; Georges Wein; Swing Limited Corporation; Machi-oul Big Band; Michel Graillier; Richard Raux; Al Grey; Stéphane Grappelli; Bernard Lubat; Didier Lockwood; Festivals: Vienna, 1983; Paris, 1984; Montpellier, 1988–90; Nevers, 1988; Nice, 1989–90, 1992–93; Montreux, 1992; New Orleans, 1992; Midem, 1993; Halle That Jazz Paris, 1993; Montréal, 1993; Newport, Saratoga, 1993; Invited to numerous international festivals including: East Africa; Tunisia; Greece; Belgium; Germany; Italy; Russia; Poland; Finland; Appearances on French television, 1975–; Hosted with Eve Ruggieri, Musiques Au Coeur (Jazz News), France 2 TV; Adviser to President, Fifth TV Channel; Tour, USA includes: Boston, San Francisco, Los Angeles, 1995; Appeared Midem, Cannes, 1994; mem, SACEM. *Recordings:* with Machi-oul Big Band, 1975; Module, 1982; Rominus, with Didier Lockwood, 1990; Alain Brunet Plays Serge Gainsbourg, 1993; French Melodies in LA 1995, Alain Brunet, 1997, Alain Brunet and Strings Plays Charles Trenet 2003. *Website:* www.alainbrunet.net.

BRUNI, Carla; Italian/French model and singer; b. (Carla Gilberta Bruni Tedeschi), 23 Dec. 1967, Turin; fmr partner of Raphaël Enthoven; one s.; m. Nicolas Sarközy de Nagy Bocsa 2008; one d. *Education:* Univ. of Paris. *Career:* began career as model, City Models, Paris 1986; appeared in GUESS? advertising campaigns 1987; catwalk model for Chistian Dior, Paco Rabanne, Chanel, Givenchy, Yves Saint Laurent and John Galliano 1990s; listed as one of world's top 20 highest-paid models, Business Age 1998; retd from catwalk modelling 1998; signed to Versace to model fragrance advertisements 1998; signed to record label Naïve, launched singing career 2002; First Lady of France (as wife of Pres. of French Repub.) 2008–12; f. Carla Bruni-Sarkozy Foundation 2009. *Films include:* Prêt-à-Porter 1994, Unzipped (uncredited) 1995, Catwalk 1996, Paparazzi 1998, Yves Saint Laurent: His Life and Times 2002, La caravane des enfoirés 2007, Starko! 2008, (500) Days of Summer 2009, Midnight in Paris 2011. *Film music:* En la ciudad (song Tout le monde) 2003, Le divorce (song Quelqu'un m'a dit) 2003, In the City (writer and performer Tout le monde) 2003, Conversations with Other Women (music Le Plus Beau du Quartier, J'en connais, L'excessive) 2005, The Lake House (performer La Noyée 1970) 2006, Colors en sèrie: Rosa: Enganxós o diví (song and lyrics and performer Quelqu'un m'a dit) 2007. *Television includes:* Die Schönsten Frauen der Welt – Carla Bruni 1995, Ombre et lumière 2003, Lo + plus 2003, Qui veut gagner des millions? 2004, Vivement dimanche prochain 2005, 2008, 2009, 2010, Le grand journal de Canal+ 2005, 2008, 2009, Campus, le magazine de l'écrit: Nouveau campus en direct! 2006, Turin 2006: XX Olympic Winter Games (mini-series) 2006, Symphonic show spécial Sidaction 2007, Stars of Europe 2007, Tenue de soirée: Cannes 2007, Later

with Jools Holland 2008, Wetten, dass...? 2008, Somebody Told Me About... Carla Bruni (documentary) 2008, Late Show with David Letterman 2008, Sidaction 2009 2009, Chuck: Chuck vs First Class 2010, Melody Gardot: The Accidental Musician 2010. *Recordings include:* albums: Quelqu'un m'a dit 2002, No Promises 2007, Comme si de rien n'était 2008, Little French Songs 2013. *Honours:* ranked by Forbes magazine amongst The World's 100 Most Powerful Women (35th) 2010. *Website:* www.carlabrunisarkozy.org/en; www .carlabruni.com.

BRUNTON, Gary; British jazz musician (double bass); b. 9 March 1968, Burnley, Lancashire, England; m. Beatrice Welter 1993. *Education:* University College, Swansea, studied with Thierry Barbé, Henri Texier, Pierre Michelot, Ray Brown, Dave Holland, and with Gary Peacock at Paris Conservatory. *Career:* with Upper Space Group: Duc des Lombards; Sunset; Festival de Django Reinhardt, 1995; with Edouard Ferlet Trio: Petit Opportun; Festival de Jazz de Parthenay, 1994; Hotel Adagio; Hotel Lutecia; Trilogie: Salle André Marechal, 1994; with Guitar Hell: Tours, Germany, 1994, 1995; Sunset; Hot Club de Lyon; La Tour Rose; Performances with: Trio Bojan Zulfikarpasic: Radio France Inter; with Trio Michel Grailler: Le Petit Journal Montparnasse; Le Houdon; with Jonathan Lewis Quartet: Jazz Parade, BBC Radio; Brecon Jazz Festival, Tour, Britain, 1990; Elizabeth Kontamanu Quartet, Rumanian tour, 1992; Stephanie Crawford Quartet; Michelle Hendricks; Paulo Fresu; Stéphane Belmondo; François Théberge; Pete Osbourne; Jeannot Rabeson; Patrice Galas; Philippe Soirat; Simon Goubert; Sangoma Everett; Olivier Hutman; Charles Bellonzi; Craig Handy; mem, UMJ (Union Musiciens de Jazz). *Recordings:* Lucide Beausonge; Laure Milena; Bruno Joubrel; Patrick Husson; Commercial television; Film track, Tom Est Tout Seul, La Bande Son, Canal+. *E-mail:* www.myspace.com/ garybrunton.

BRUNTON, Richard McNaughton; British musician (guitars, keyboards) and composer; b. 3 Oct. 1949, Newcastle upon Tyne; one s. two d. *Career:* performed in own R&B band, Newcastle 1964–68; moved to London, freelance guitarist 1969; recorded over 200 records for artists including Gerry Rafferty, Dr John, Barbara Dickson, Greg Lake, Pete Sinfield; numerous television and film soundtracks; mem. Musicians' Union, PRS, BAC&S. *Recordings include:* with Peter Sinfield: Still 1973, Stillusion 1993; with Gerry Rafferty: Night Owl 1979, Snakes and Ladders 1980, Best Of... 1989, City to City/Night Owl 2007; with Steve Jolliffe: Journeys Out Of The Body 1982, Doorways To The Soul 1988, Richard Thompson, Sweet Talker 1992, Supernatural Fairy Tales 1996; with Greg Lake: From The Beginning 1997.

BRYAN, David; American musician (keyboards); b. (David Bryan Rashbaum), 7 Feb. 1962, Sayreville, NJ. *Career:* founder mem. rock group Bon Jovi 1983–88, 1992–; simultaneous solo career 1995–; numerous tours, television, radio and live appearances worldwide. *Recordings include:* albums: with Bon Jovi: Bon Jovi 1984, 7800° Fahrenheit 1985, Slippery When Wet 1986, Bon Jovi Live 1987, New Jersey 1988, Keep The Faith 1992, Cross Road 1994, These Days 1995, Crush 2000, One Wild Night 1985–2001 2001, Bounce 2002, Distance 2003, This Left Feels Right 2003, Have A Nice Day 2005, Lost Highway 2007, The Circle 2009, What About Now 2013, Burning Bridges 2015; solo: On A Full Moon 1995, Lunar Eclipse 2000. *Honours:* American Music Awards for Favorite Pop/Rock Band 1988, for Favorite Pop/Rock Single 1991, Nordoff-Robbins Music Therapy Silver Clef 1990, BRIT Award for Best Int. Group (with band) 1995, VH-1 Award for Favorite Video (for It's My Life) 2000, Billboard Music Award for Top Touring Artist 2014. *Current Management:* Bon Jovi Management, PO Box 237040, New York, NY 10023, USA. *Telephone:* (212) 336-9413. *Fax:* (212) 336-5385. *Website:* www.bonjovi.com.

BRYAN, Kelle; British singer, entrepreneur and actress; b. 1976. *Career:* mem. of all-female vocal group, Eternal 1992–98; founder and Dir and CEO, Red Hot Entertainment 2000–; Amb. St Thomas Lupus Trust. *Recordings include:* albums: with Eternal: Always and Forever 1993, Power of a Woman 1995, Before The Rain 1997, Greatest Hits 1998, Essential Eternal (compilation) 2001; solo: Breakfast In Bed 2000. *Honours:* Smash Hits Award, Int. Dance Award for Dance Act of the Year 1995. *Telephone:* (20) 7635-0403. *Fax:* (20) 7635-8988. *E-mail:* info@redhotentertainment.biz; andy@kellebryan.co .uk. *Website:* www.redhotentertainment.biz; kelle.so-addictive.co.uk.

BRYAN, (Thomas Luther) Luke; American country music singer, songwriter and musician (guitar); b. 17 July 1976, Leesburg, Ga; m. Caroline Boyer 2006; two s. *Education:* Lee County High School, Georgia Southern Univ. *Career:* songwriter for Billy Currington, Travis Tritt; signed to Capitol Records Nashville 2007; released debut album 2007; duetted with Jason Aldean and Eric Church 2012; debut tour as headline act 2013. *Recordings include:* albums: I'll Stay Me 2007, Doin' My Thing 2009, Tailgates & Tanlines 2011, Spring Break...Here to Party 2013, Crash My Party (Billboard Music Award for Top Country Album 2014) 2013, Kill the Lights 2015. *Honours:* Acad. of Country Music Awards for Top New Solo Vocalist 2010, for Top New Artist 2010, for Vocal Event of the Year 2015, Country Music Television Awards for USA Weekend Breakthrough Video of the Year 2010, for Video of the Year, Male 2012, for Entertainer of the Year 2013, for Vocal Event of the Year (for 'The Only Way I Know' with Jason Aldean and Eric Church) 2013, for Male Video of the Year 2015, American Music Awards for Favorite Male Country Artist 2012, 2013, 2014, 2015, American Country Awards for Artist of the Year 2013, for Artist of the Year: Male 2013, for Touring Artist of the Year 2013, Billboard Music Award for Top Country Artist 2014, Country Music Asscn Awards for Entertainer of the Year 2014, 2015. *Current Management:*

c/o Red Light Management, 124 12th Avenue South, #600, Nashville, TN 37203, USA. *Telephone:* (615) 279-3784. *Website:* www.redlightmanagement .com. *Address:* c/o Capitol Records Nashville, 3322 West End Ave #1100, Nashville, TN 37203, USA. *Website:* www.capitolnashville.com (office); www .lukebryan.com.

BRYANT, Dana, BA; American spoken word artist; b. 2 May 1965, New York, NY. *Education:* Brandeis Univ. *Career:* has performed at jazz festivals in Vienna, Berlin Jazz, Brighton Jazz Bop; TV appearances include Fighting Wordz, MTV, Spoken Word Unplugged, The South Bank Show, The Girlie Show; mem. ASCAP. *Recordings include:* Dominican Girdles Heat 1993, Wishing From The Top 1996; also appears on: Quiet Revolution 1993, Time and Love 1997, Adventures Of Bread and Butter 1998, Jazzonia 1998, Future 2 Future 2001, Smokin Beats 2002, Nu Jazz Cool: Blue Beats and Chilled Jazz Grooves 2003. *Publication:* Song of The Siren 1995.

BRYANT, Gerry; British musician (bass guitar); b. 30 April 1965, Portsmouth. *Career:* bass guitarist in group, Mega City Four, touring throughout Europe including Scandinavia, Japan, USA and Canada 1988–96; various television and radio broadcasts, concerts and festival appearances; sound engineer and tour man. 1996–; Dir, The Rooms Rehearsal Studios Ltd 2001–; mem. Musicians' Union. *Recordings include:* with Mega City Four: Tranzophobia 1988, Who Cares Wins 1989, Terribly Sorry Bob 1990, Sebastopol Road 1992, Inspiringly Titled. . . (live album) 1992, Magic Bullets 1993, Soulscraper 1996; with Serpico: Everyone Vs Everyone 2001. *Address:* The Rooms Rehearsal Studios, Lynchford Lane, North Camp, Farnborough, GU14 6JD (office); 12 Orwell Close, Farnborough, GU14 9LR, England. *E-mail:* therooms@hotmail.co.uk (office). *Website:* theroomsrehearsalstudios.co.uk (office).

BRYANT, Michael James; British programmer and producer; b. 1 May 1960, High Wycombe, Buckinghamshire, England. *Career:* mem. Fluke 1988–, 2 Bit Pie 2005–; contributed remixes for Talk Talk, Björk, Simple Minds, Smashing Pumpkins, The Rolling Stones, Yello, New Order and others. *Recordings include:* albums: The Techno Rose Of Blighty 1990, Out 1991, Six Wheels On My Wagon 1993, Oto 1995, Risotto 1997, Progressive History X (compilation) 2001, Puppy 2003, 2Pie Island 2006; singles: Thumper 1989, Joni 1989, Philly 1990, Slid 1993, Electric Guitar 1993, Groovy Feeling 1993, Bubble 1994, The Peel Sessions 1994, Bullet 1995, Tosh 1995, Atom Bomb 1996, Absurd 1997, Squirt 1997, Pulse 2002, Hang Tough 2003, Switch 2003. *Address:* c/o One Little Indian Records, 34 Trinity Crescent, London, SW17 7AE, England. *Telephone:* (20) 8772-7600. *Fax:* (20) 8772-7603. *E-mail:* info@ indian.co.uk. *Website:* www.indian.co.uk.

BRYANT, Terl; British musician (drums, percussion); b. 2 May 1961, Walgrave, Northamptonshire; m. Juliet Bryant 1992, one d. *Career:* mem. Iona 1992–; Founder and Dir Psalm Drummers Asscn 1995–2009; toured, recorded with artists from UK and USA including: Steve Taylor, Cliff Richard, Darrell Mansfield, Sheila Walsh, Lies Damned Lies, Ben Okafor, Graham Kendrick, Ishmael, Phil and John (The Woodthieves), Richard Darbyshire, Martin Smith, Noel Richards, Dave Bilbrough, Adrian Snell, Paul Field; others including six years with Peter Murphy (ex-Bauhaus), including three albums, extensive tours, USA, Japan, Israel, Europe; mem. Musicians' Union. *Recordings include:* Love Hysteria 1987, Deep 1989, Don't Look Now 1989, Iona 1990, Holy Smoke 1991, Book Of Kells 1992, Beyond These Shores 1994, Journey Into The Morn 1995, Heaven's Bright Sun 1997, Arms Of Mercy 1998; solo: Psalm 1995, Timbrel 1999, Rhythms of Fire 2007, Drums of Hope 2008. *Publication:* A Heart to Drum 2006. *Honours:* Gospel Music Awards (GMA) International Artist Award (for The Book of Kells) 1993. *Address:* c/o Psalm Drummers Association, 86 London Road, Colchester, CO3 9DW, England. *Website:* terlbryant.com.

BRYAR, Robert (Bob); American musician (drums); b. 31 Dec. 1979, Chicago, Ill. *Career:* mem. rock band, My Chemical Romance 2004–10. *Recordings include:* albums: I Brought You My Bullets, You Brought Me Your Love 2002, Three Cheers for Sweet Revenge 2004, The Black Parade 2006, Danger Days: The True Lives of the Fabulous Killjoys 2010. *Honours:* Kerrang! Award for Best Int. Band 2006, 2007, NME Award for Best Int. Band 2007. *Website:* www.mychemicalromance.com.

BRYDON, Mark; British producer, arranger, remixer, composer and musician (multi-instrumentalist); b. 22 Dec. 1960, Sheffield, England. *Career:* fmr mem. Cloud 9; mem. Moloko 1995–2004. *Recordings include:* albums: Do You Like My Tight Sweater? 1995, I Am Not A Doctor 1998, Things To Make And Do 2000, Statues 2002, Casual Lounge 2005.

BRYDOY, Eivind, MSc (Business); Norwegian artist manager and record company executive; *Manager, Artist Vision*; b. 20 June 1964, Levanger; s. of Sverre Brydoy and Oddrun Brydoy; m. Katherine DePaul; one d. *Education:* Norwegian School of Econs, Univ. of New Orleans, USA. *Career:* fmr controller, Stageway Record Co.; with Agency Dept, Stageway for two years; started Artistpartner and worked for four years; guest teacher in Music Man., Høgskolen i Hedmark, Rena; Vice-Chair. IMMF 2003; currently Chair. MMF Norway; fmr Gen. Sec., NEMAA, now mem. Bd; currently Owner and Man., Artist Vision; Consultant, Believe Digital Norway. *Publication:* Eureka Collaborative Agreements: A Strategic Analysis 1992. *Honours:* Hit Awards-Manager award Norway 2001. *Address:* Artist Vision, Dicksvei 12, 1366 Oslo, Norway (office). *Telephone:* 45-50-04-44 (office). *Fax:* 21-54-72-88 (office). *E-mail:* eivind@artist.vision (office). *Website:* www.artist.vision (office).

BRYNGELSSON, Hans Inge Peter; Swedish musician and composer; b. 17 Sept. 1955, Vetlanda; m. Anita Malmguist Bryngelsson 1986; one s. *Education:* Vallehilde Folkhojskole Dramatic Inst. *Career:* leader, Ragnarö 1972–84, Triangulus 1985–89; mem. Urban Turban 1993–; composed music for film, theatre, expositions, radio and TV; mem. Svenska Tonsättares Internationella Musikbyrå (STIM), SKAP, SAMI. *Compositions:* Via 1990, Happy Starr 1992, Sound of Glass 1995, Guitarrsis for 10 guitarists, Katabasis for five bass instruments. *Recordings include:* Ragnarö 1976, King Tung 1979, Via 1990, Urban Turban 1994, Urban Turban Overtime 1996, Astro Turf 1998. *Television:* Ode to the Stone (film) 1991, The Other Shore Michael Wiström (film) 1992, Snalast (film) 1997. *Honours:* STIM Musical Prize, SKAP Musical Prize.

BRYSON, David; American musician (guitar); b. 5 Oct. 1961, San Francisco, Calif. *Career:* formed acoustic duo with Adam Duritz, joined by others to form Counting Crows 1993–; numerous tours and live appearances. *Recordings include:* albums: August & Everything After 1993, Recovering the Satellites 1996, Across a Wire: Live in New York 1998, This Desert Life 1999, Hard Candy 2002, Saturday Nights and Sunday Mornings 2008, August and Everything After: Live at Town Hall 2011, No One Knows What Happens Next 2012, Underwater Sunshine 2012, Somewhere Under Wonderland 2014. *Current Management:* c/o International Talent Booking, First Floor, Ariel House, 74a Charlotte Street, London, W1T 4QJ, England. *Website:* www .countingcrows.com.

BRYSON, Jeanie; American jazz singer; b. 10 March 1958, d. of Dizzy Gillespie and Connie Bryson; m. Coleman Mellett (died 2009). *Education:* Rutgers Univ., Livingston Coll. *Career:* solo artist, guest vocalist on numerous albums. *Recordings include:* albums: I Love Being Here With You 1993, Tonight I Need You So 1994, Some Cats Know 1995, Deja Blue 2001. *Current Management:* c/o Michael Mazur, Mazur Entertainment, Inc., PO Box 2425, Trenton, NJ 08607, USA. *Website:* www.jeaniebryson.com.

BRYSON, (Robert) Peabo; American soul singer and producer; b. 13 April 1951, Greenville, South Carolina. *Career:* fmr mem. Moses Dillard, Tex-Town Display, Michael Zager's Moon Band 1976–78; solo artist 1979–. *Recordings include:* albums: Reaching For The Sky 1978, Crosswinds 1978, We're The Best Of Friends (with Natalie Cole) 1979, Live–and More (with Roberta Flack) 1980, Paradise 1980, I Am Love 1981, Turn The Hands Of Time 1981, Don't Play With Fire 1982, Born To Love (with Roberta Flack) 1983, The Peabo Bryson Collection 1984, Straight From The Heart 1984, Quiet Storm 1986, Take No Prisoners 1987, Positive 1988, All My Love 1989, Can You Stop The Rain 1991, Tonight I Celebrate My Love 1992, Through The Fire 1994, Peace On Earth 1997, Family Christmas 1998, Unconditional Love 1999, Missing You 2007; singles: Closer Than Close, Lost In The Night, Shower You With Love, Why Goodbye, How Wonderful We Are, Light The World; with Michael Zager's Moon Band: Reaching For The Sky, I'm So Into You; solo: If Ever You're In My Arms Again 1984, Duets: Gimme Some Time, with Natalie Cole 1979, Tonight I Celebrate My Love, with Roberta Flack 1983, Beauty and The Beast, with Céline Dion (Grammy Award 1992) 1992; other duets with Melissa Manchester, Regina Belle; other collaborations include Kenny G, Barry Mann, Minnie Riperton; contrib. Color and Light: Jazz Sketches On Sondheim 1995. *Address:* Guardian Angel Music, 1720 Peachtree Street Northwest, Atlanta, GA 30309, USA. *Website:* peabobryson.net.

BRYSON, William Shields; American musician (bass) and singer; b. 10 Nov. 1946, Evanston, IL; m. Anne Jeanine Bailey 1976. *Career:* bass player, Bluegrass Cardinals; Country Gazette; Doug Dillard Band; The Long Riders with Ry Cooder, 1980–84; The Desert Rose Band, 1985–94, 2008–, Grateful Dudes 1988–, Laurel Canyon Ramblers; mem. Screen Actors' Guild; AFTRA; AFofM. *Recordings include:* albums: What A Way Earn A Living, Country Gazette, 1977; Long Riders (film soundtrack), Ry Cooder, 1980; Jackrabbit, Doug Dillard, 1980; Home Coming and Family Reunion, The Dillards, 1980; with The Desert Rose Band: The Desert Rose Band, 1987; Running, 1988; Pages Of Life, 1990; True Love, 1991; A Dozen Roses, 1991; with Laurel Canyon Ramblers: Rambler's Blues 1995, Blue Rambler 2 1996, Back on the Street Again 1998. *Honours:* ACM Award for Bass Player of the Year 1990, Touring Band of the Year (with Desert Rose Band) 1988–90. *Address:* c/o Sugar Hill Records, 120 31st Avenue North, Nashville, TN 37203-1248. *Telephone:* (615) 297-6890. *E-mail:* info@sugarhillrecords.com; bill@grateful -dudes.net. *Website:* www.sugarhillrecords.com; www.grateful-dudes.net.

BRZEZICKI, Mark; musician (drums, percussion); b. 21 June 1957, Slough, Berkshire, England. *Education:* Brooklands Technical Coll. *Career:* mem., Big Country 1981–89, 1993–, with tours, festival appearances, television broadcasts; founder mem. Casbah Club 2004–; has also performed with: The Cult, Procol Harum, Pete Townshend, Ultravox, Roger Daltrey, The Pretenders; mem. Thunderclap Newman 2010–; mem. From The Jam (with Bruce Foxton) 2010–; mem. Prince's Trust, GISM, PRS. *Recordings include:* albums: with Big Country: The Crossing, 1983; Steeltown, 1984; The Seer, 1986 and seven others; also five albums with Pete Townshend; three with Midge Ure; with Casbah Club: Venustraphobia 2006; with Thunderclap Newman: Beyond Hollywood 2010. *Honours:* Zildjian Musician Poll, Best Rock/Pop mainstream drummer UK 1988–90; Making Music Poll 1988; Pearl Drummers Club, Best UK Rock/Pop drummer 1990; Prince's Trust Award 1984. *E-mail:* nigel .morton@moneypennymusic.co.uk. *Address:* Owl House, Byers Lane, South Godstone, Surrey RH9 8JL, England. *Website:* www.casbahclub.co.uk; www .thunderclapnewmanmusic.com; www.casbahclub.co.uk.

BT, (Libra, Elastic Chakra); American producer and remixer; b. (Brian Transeau), Washington, DC. *Education:* Berklee Coll. of Music, Boston. *Career:* played synthesizer on a Salt 'N' Pepa album; started producing for Deep Dish's label; began remixing, notably on his reworking of Tori Amos' Blue Skies; collaborations with Deep Dish, Sasha, Tsunami One; remixed Billie Ray Martin, Madonna, Seal, Mike Oldfield; solo artist 1996–. *Recordings include:* albums: Ima 1996, ESCM 1997, Movement in Still Life 1999, Emotional Technology 2003, This Binary Universe 2006, These Hopeful Machines 2010. *Address:* c/o Twenty4seven Management, PO Box 7042, 4800 GA Breda, The Netherlands. *Telephone:* (76) 521-53-64. *Fax:* (76) 513-84-36. *Website:* www.twenty4sevenmanagement.com. *Address:* c/o DTS Europe, No. 5 Tavistock Estate, Ruscombe Lane, Twyford, Berkshire, RG10 9NJ, England. *E-mail:* webmaster@btmusic.com. *Website:* www.btmusic.com.

BUARQUE, Chico; Brazilian singer, songwriter, musician (guitar), writer and poet; b. (Francisco Buarque de Hollanda), 19 June 1944, Rio de Janeiro; s. of Sérgio Buarque de Hollanda and Maria Amélia Cesário de Hollanda; brother of vocalist Miucha, uncle of Bebel Gilberto. *Career:* left Univ., of São Paulo to absorb local Bossa Nova scene and began writing songs; came to prominence when compositions recorded by singer Nara Leao. *Recordings include:* albums: Pedro Pedriero 1965, Chico Buarque de Hollanda 1966, Morte e Vida Severina 1966, Umas e outras 1969, Chico Buarque na Itália 1969, Apesar de você 1970, Per un pugno di samba 1970, Construção 1971, Quando o carnaval chegar 1972, Caetano e Chico juntos e ao vivo 1972, Chico canta 1973, Sinal fechado 1974, Chico Buarque & Maria Bethânia ao vivo 1975, Meus caros amigos 1976, Cio da Terra 1977, Os saltimbancos 1977, Gota d'água 1977, Chico Buarque 1978, Ópera do malandro 1979, Vida 1980, Show 1° de Maio 1980, Almanaque 1981, Saltimbancos trapalhões 1981, Chico Buarque en espanhol 1982, Para viver um grande amor 1983, O grande circo místico 1983, Chico Buarque 1984, O Corsário do rei 1985, Ópera do malandro 1985, Malandro 1985, Melhores momentos de Chico & Caetano 1986, Francisco 1987, Dança da meia-lua 1988, Chico Buarque ao vivo Paris Le Zenith 1990, Paratodos 1993, Uma palavra 1995, Terra 1997, As Cidades 1998, Chico ao Vivo 1999, Cambaio 2001, Chico Buarque Duetos 2002, Carioca 2006, Carioca ao Vivo 2007, Chico 2011, Na Carreira 2012. *Film music:* Anjo assassino 1966, Garota de Ipanema 1967, Roda Vida (play, also score) 1968, Quando o carnaval chegar 1972, Os saltimbancos trapalhões 1981, Ópera do malandro 1985, Ed Mort 1996, O mandarim 1995, Budapeste 2009. *Publications:* A Banda (songbook) 1966, Fazenda modelo (novel) 1974, Chapeuzinho Amarelo (poems) 1979, A bordo do Rui Barbosa 1981, Estorvo (novel) 1991, Benjamim (novel) 1995, Budapeste 2003, Leite Derramado 2009. *Address:* c/o Discmedi SA, Ronda Guinardó, 59 Bis, Baixos, 08024 Barcelona, Spain. *Website:* www.chicobuarque.com.br.

BUARQUE DE HOLLANDA, Anna Maria, (Ana de Hollanda); Brazilian singer, songwriter and politician; b. 12 Aug. 1948, São Paulo; d. of Sérgio Buarque de Hollanda and Maria Amélia Alvim Buarque de Hollanda. *Education:* Int. School of Theater of Latin America and the Caribbean, Cuba. *Career:* stage debut aged 16 at Coll. of Rio Branco; Dir Centro Cultural São Paulo 1983–85; Sec. of Culture, City of Osasco 1986–88; musical tours throughout Brazil and Angola, Cuba, Uruguay 1988–2000; Dir Centro de Música da Funarte (Fundação Nacional de Artes) 2003–07; Minister of Culture 2011–12; fmr mem. Partido Comunista Brasileiro. *Recordings:* solo albums: Tão Simples 1995, Um Filme 2001, Só na Canção 2009. *Website:* www.anadehollanda.com.

BUBLÉ, Michael; Canadian singer and actor; b. 9 Sept. 1975, British Columbia; m. Luisana Lopilato; two s. *Career:* solo artist; collaborations with Tony Bennett, The Bee Gees, Nelly Furtado. *Recordings include:* albums: Babalu 2001, Michael Bublé 2003, Come Fly With Me 2004, It's Time (Juno Awards for Album of the Year, Pop Album of the Year 2006, Echo Music Award 2006, Canadian Smooth Jazz Album of the Year 2006) 2005, Call Me Irresponsible (Grammy Award for Best Traditional Pop Vocal Album 2008) 2007, Michael Bublé Meets Madison Square Garden (Grammy Award for Best Traditional Pop Vocal Album 2010) 2010, Crazy Love (Juno Awards for Album of the Year 2010, for Pop Album of the Year 2010) 2009, Christmas (Juno Award for Album of the Year 2012) 2011, To Be Loved (Grammy Award for Best Traditional Pop Vocal Album 2014) 2013. *Films include:* Duets 2000, Totally Blonde 2001, The Snow Walker 2003, Kath and Kim 2005. *Honours:* Much More Music Award 2004, Juno Awards for New Artist of the Year 2004, for Artist of the Year 2006, for Single of the Year (for Home) 2006, (for Haven't Met You Yet) 2010, Canadian Radio Music Award for Best Solo Artist 2006, Socan Songwriter of the Year Award (for Home) 2006, Canadian Smooth Jazz Award for Male Vocalist of the Year 2006, Much More Music Award (for Save the Last Dance for Me) 2006, Juno Fan Choice Award 2008, 2010, 2015, Canadian Smooth Jazz Artist of the Year Award 2008, Canadian Smooth Jazz Award for Best Original Composition (for Everything) 2008, Meteor Awards Int. Male Solo Artist 2010. *Address:* c/o Bruce Allen Talent, Suite 500, 425 Carrall Street, Vancouver, BC V6B 6E3, Canada (office); Reprise Records, Warner Bros Records Inc., 3300 Warner Blvd, Burbank, CA 91505, USA (office). *Website:* www.michaelbuble.com.

BUCHANAN, Keisha; British singer and songwriter; b. 30 Sept. 1984, London. *Career:* Founder-mem. Sugababes 1998–2009; mem. Mutya Keisha Siobhan 2012–. *Recordings include:* One Touch 2000, Angels With Dirty Faces 2002, Three 2003, Taller In More Ways 2005, Change 2007, Catfights and Spotlights 2008, All or Nothing (with Jay Sean) 2009; single: with Mutya Keisha Siobhan: Flatline 2013. *Honours:* Q Award (for Freak Like Me) 2002, BRIT Award for Best Dance Act 2003. *Website:* www.mutyakeishasiobhan.com.

BUCK, Peter; American musician (guitar) and producer; b. 6 Dec. 1956, Berkeley, CA. *Career:* founder mem., R.E.M. 1980–2011; numerous int. tours, live appearances; mem. side-project, Hindu Love Gods 1986–90; mem. collective, The Minus 5; mem. project, Tired Pony 2009–. *Recordings include:* albums: with R.E.M.: Chronic Town 1982, Murmur 1983, Reckoning 1984, Fables Of The Reconstruction 1985, Life's Rich Pageant 1986, Dead Letter Office 1987, Document 1987, Eponymous 1988, Green 1988, Out Of Time (Billboard Award for Best World Album, Q Award for Best Album) 1991, Automatic For The People (Grammy Award for Best Alternative Music Album, Atlanta Music Award for Rock Album, Q Award for Best Album, Rolling Stone Critics Award for Best Album 1993) 1992, Monster 1994, New Adventures In Hi-Fi 1996, Up 1998, Star Profiles 1999, Reveal 2001, Bad Day Pt 1 and 2 2003, Glastonbury 1999 2003, Around The Sun 2004, Accelerate 2008, Collapse into Now 2011; with Hindu Love Gods: Hindu Love Gods 1990; with The Minus 5: At The Organ 2005, The Gun Album 2006; with Tired Pony: The Place we Ran From 2010; solo: Peter Buck 2012, I Am Back to Blow Your Mind Once Again 2014. *Honours:* numerous MTV Music Video Awards, Earth Day Award 1990, Billboard Award for Best Modern Rock Artist 1991, BRIT Awards for Best Int. Group 1992, 1993, 1995, Grammy Awards for Best Pop Performance, Best Music Video 1992, Atlanta Music Awards for Act of the Year, Video of the Year 1992, IRMA Award for Int. Band of the Year 1993, Rolling Stone Critics Award for Best Band 1993. *Current Management:* REM/Athens Ltd, 250 W Clayton Street, Athens, GA 30601, USA. *Website:* www.remhq.com; www.tiredpony.com.

THE BUCKETHEADS (see Gonzalez, Kenny)

BUCKINGHAM, Lindsey; American musician (guitar), singer and songwriter; b. 3 Oct. 1947, Palo Alto, Calif. *Career:* mem. rock band, Fritz 1960s; mem. duo, Buckingham Nicks (with Stevie Nicks) 1971–74; mem. Fleetwood Mac 1975–87; solo artist 1978–. *Recordings include:* albums: with Buckingham Nicks: Buckingham Nicks 1973; with Fleetwood Mac: Fleetwood Mac 1975, Rumours (Billboard Award for Album of the Year 1977, American Music Award for Favorite Pop/Rock Album 1978, Grammy Award for Album of the Year 1978) 1977, Tusk 1978, Fleetwood Mac Live 1980, Mirage 1982, Tango In The Night 1987, The Dance 1997, Say You Will 2003, Pious Bird Of Good Omen 2004; solo: Law and Order 1981, Go Insane 1984, Out Of The Cradle 1992, Under the Skin 2006, Gift of Screws 2008, Live at the Bass Performance Hall 2008, Seeds We Sow 2011. *Honours:* American Music Award for Favorite Pop/Rock Group 1978. *Current Management:* c/o Sanctuary Artist Management, 15301 Ventura Blvd, Building B, Suite 400, Sherman Oaks, CA 91403, USA. *E-mail:* jessica@lindseybuckingham.com. *Website:* www.lindseybuckingham.com; www.fleetwoodmac.com.

BUCKLAND, Jonny; British musician (guitar) and songwriter; b. 11 Sept. 1978, Mold, Wales; m. Chloe Evans 2009; one s. one d. *Education:* University Coll., London. *Career:* mem. Coldplay 1998–. *Recordings include:* albums: Parachutes (BRIT Award for Best Album 2001, Grammy Award for Best Alternative Album 2002) 2000, A Rush Of Blood To The Head (BRIT Award for Best British Album 2003, NME Award for Best Album 2003) 2002, X&Y (MasterCard British Album, BRIT Awards 2006, Juno Award for Int. Album of the Year 2006) 2005, Viva la Vida (Grammy Award for Best Rock Album 2009) 2008, Mylo Xyloto (Billboard Music Award for Top Rock Album 2012) 2011, Ghost Stories (Billboard Music Award for Top Rock Album 2015) 2014, A Head Full of Dreams 2015. *Honours:* BRIT Awards for Best British Group 2001, 2003, 2012, for Best British Single (for Speed of Sound) 2006, for Best Live Act 2014, MTV Europe Music Awards for Best UK and Ireland Act 2002, for Best Song (for Speed of Sound) 2005, for Best Rock Act 2015, Billboard Music Awards for Group of the Year 2002, for Top Rock Artist 2012, for Top Alternative Artist 2012, Ivor Novello Awards for Songwriters of the Year 2003, for Best Selling British Song (for Viva la Vida) 2009, Grammy Awards for Record of the Year (for Clocks) 2004, for Best Rock Vocal Performance by a Duo or Group (for In My Place) 2004, for Song of the Year 2009, for Best Pop Performance by a Duo or Group (both for Viva la Vida) 2009, Q Awards for Best Act in the World 2005, 2011, Digital Music People's Choice Award for best official site, for Best Digital Music Community (for Coldplay.com) 2005, American Music Award for Favorite Alternative Music Artist 2005, Echo Award for Best Int. Group, Germany 2006, ASCAP Award for Song of the Year (for Speed of Sound) 2006, World Music Award for Best Rock Act 2008. *Current Management:* c/o Dave Holmes, 3-D Management, 1901 Main Street, #3000, Los Angeles, CA 90405, USA. *Telephone:* (310) 314-1390. *Website:* www.coldplay.com.

BUCKLER, Rick; British musician (drums); b. 6 Dec. 1955, Woking, Surrey. *Career:* founder mem., The Jam 1972–82; founder mem., From The Jam 2007–09. *Recordings include:* albums: with The Jam: In the City 1977, This is the Modern World 1977, All Mod Cons 1978, Setting Sons 1979, Sound Affects 1980, The Gift 1982. *Publication:* Our Story (autobiog. of The Jam, with Bruce Foxton) 1994. *E-mail:* rick@thejamfan.net. *Website:* www.thejamfan.net.

BUCKLEY, Steve, BSc; British musician (saxophones, bass clarinet, tin whistle); b. 6 Jan. 1959, Orpington, Kent. *Education:* Univ. of Leeds. *Career:* tours, recordings with Loose Tubes, Delightful Precipice, Human Chain; numerous radio and TV appearances with these bands; long association with South American, African London-based bands; other projects include BBC Award-winning 'Big Air', co-led by Chris Batchelor and featuring Myra

Melford, Jim Black and Oren Marshall. *Recordings:* Open Letter, Loose Tubes; Third Policeman, Django Bates; Summer Fruits, Delightful Precipice; Winter Truce, Delightful Precipice; Whole and The Half, Buckley Batchelor; Pyrotechnics, Human Chain; Live At Bad Gleichenberg; Noble, Marshall, Buckley Bud Moon; Noble Marshall Buckley; Life as We Know It, Buckley Batchelor; Barrel Organ Far From Home, Huw Warren; Big Air, Buckley Batchelor; Bumping, Massoukos; Waitless, Empty Boat. *E-mail:* altobuck59@yahoo.co.uk.

BUCKMAN, Mirshad; Sri Lankan singer, songwriter and musician (guitar). *Education:* Trinity Coll., Kandy. *Career:* Founder mem., rock group Paranoid Earthling 2000–, debut live performance 2001; released several EPs and singles 2005–, including Rock'n'Roll is My Anarchy, Playtime Music 2007, Bringing Down the Sun 2008; live performances in India 2009, Afghanistan 2012. *Recordings:* several EPs and singles. *E-mail:* manager@paranoidearthling.com (office); manager.paranoidearthling@gmail.com (office). *Website:* www.paranoidearthling.com.

BUDD, Stephen; British music manager; b. 25 Dec. 1958, London; m. 1986; one d. one s. *Career:* started Torch Records 1979; signed The Sound, The Cardiacs, Big Sound Authority; Manager: The Sound, Big Sound Authority; Sally Oldfield, 1980–85; Managed producers, Tony Visconti, Arthur Baker, 1985–88; Started Stephen Budd Management, managing producers: Martyn Ware; Mike Hedges; Rick Nowels; Rafe McKenna, Arthur Baker, Steve Levine, Charlie Rapino, Gary Katz and others 1988–; Formed Morrison Budd Music Publishing, with partner Bryan Morrison, 1993–; Formed Supervision Management with Paul Craig, for artists Lloyd Cole, Heaven 17, The Webb Brothers, Dark Flower, Seventh Son, Screaming Orphans, Sherena Dugani, 1999–; mem. Int. Managers' Forum (Bd mem.), Producer Managers Group (Chair.). *Address:* Stephen Budd Management, 59-65 Worship Street, London, EC2A 2DU, England. *Telephone:* (20) 7688-8995. *Fax:* (20) 7688-8999. *E-mail:* info@record-producers.com. *Website:* www.record-producers.com.

BUDDE, Martin; Danish musician (drums, organ); b. 25 Oct. 1966, Aarhus. *Career:* drummer, Godless Wicked Creeps 1991–; organist, The Defectors 1997–; mem. Danish Music Soc. *Recordings include:* with Godless Wicked Creeps: Victim Of Science, Hellcoholic, Hystereo, Smile; with The Defectors: Allright Girl; albums: Let Me, Baby Gimme Love, Turn Me On, Live At Gutter Island, Snot Dum, Bruised & Satisfied 2007, Bloody Bloody Mary 2009, Takin' Out the Trash 2009. *Address:* Mollevangs Allé 196, 8200 Århus N, Denmark (home). *Website:* www.thedefectors.com.

BUDTS, Danny; Belgian musician (guitar, synthesizer), singer, songwriter, composer and producer; b. 12 May 1958, Wilrijk; m. Machteld de Muynck 1982; two s. *Career:* lead guitar, Cold Turkey 1970s; solo career 1990– (as Syndromeda, 1994–); founded own midi studio 1990. *Recordings include:* as Syndromeda: Mind Trips 1997, Circles Of Life 1997, The Legacy Of God 1998, Birth Of a Black Hole 1999, The Alien Abduction Phenomenon 2001, In Touch With The Stars 2001, Creatures From The Inner 2003, Metaphysical Experiences 2005, A Day in the Fields 2005, Last Days on Earth 2006, Attack! 2006, The Resurrection 2006, Von Haulshoven Meets Syndromeda 2007, Amin-Sadhana 2007, Mythical Pursuit 2008, Syndromeda in C.H.A.O.S. 2009, The Twilight Conjunction 2009, Waiting for the Second Sun 2010, The Second Intelligent Lifeform 2010. *E-mail:* info@syndromeda.be. *Website:* syndromeda.be/index.html.

BUDWEISEROVA, Irena; Czech singer; b. 8 Nov. 1957, Rokycany; m. Pavel Barta 1986, one d. *Education:* conservatoire. *Career:* mem. of folk/jazz group, Spiritual Kvintet 1980–; own jazz, blues, soul band, Budweiserova and Friends 1988–; performed in five musicals, two on stage in Prague 1993–; Speak About the Music, Czech Radio 1997–98; Prof., Conservatoire of Jaroslav Jezek, Prague 1998–; concerts, tours of Europe, Canada, USA, South America, Australia; mem. Federation of Authors in Interprets, Czech Jazz Company. *Recordings include:* 15 albums with Spiritual Kvintet; with own group: Blue Soul 1993, Moment 1995, Taking Of the Skin 1996, Crustaceans Of The Time 2000, Sometimes I Feel Like a Friend 2003; two albums with Rangers; two albums from musicals Bastard and Babylon. *Honours:* Female Vocalist of the Year 1983, Thalia Prize 1998. *Address:* c/o Martin Bárta, PO Box 17, 190 16 Prague, Czech Republic (office). *Telephone:* (2) 34705536 (office). *E-mail:* pbag@centrum.cz (office). *Website:* www.budweiserova.com.

BUENA, Mutya; British singer; b. 21 May 1984, London, England; one d. *Career:* founder mem., Sugababes 1998–2005, mem. Mutya Keisha Siobhan (group reformed) 2012–; solo artist 2007–; collaborations on tracks with Asher D 2009, Agent X 2009, Tah Mac 2009, NightShift 2009, City Boy Soul 2011, Paul Morrell 2011. *Recordings include:* albums (with Sugababes): Angels With Dirty Faces 2002, Three 2003, Taller In More Ways 2005; solo: Real Girl 2007. *Honours:* Q Award (for Freak Like Me) 2002, BRIT Award for Best Dance Act 2003. *Website:* www.mutyakeishasiobhan.com.

BUENDÍA, Elfego; Mexican singer and musician (guitar). *Career:* mem. Café Tacvba; contrib. to film soundtracks, including Y tu mamá también, Vivir Mata, Amores Perros; collaborations with artists, including Celso Piña, El Gran Silencio, Inspector, Kronos Quartet, Ofelia Medina, David Byrne. *Recordings:* albums: Café Tacuba 1992, Re 1994, Avalancha de Éxitos (EP) 1996, Reves/YoSoy (Latin Grammy Award for best rock album) 1999, Tiempo Transcurrido 2001, Vale Callampa (EP) 2002, Cuatro Caminos (Latin Grammy Award for best alternative music album 2004) 2003, SiNo 2007. *Honours:* Latin Grammy Awards for Best Rock Song (for Esta Vez) 2008, for

Best Alternative Song (for Volver a Comenzar) 2008. *Address:* Universal Music Latino, 1425 Collins Avenue, Miami Beach, FL 33139, USA (office). *Website:* www.cafetacuba.com.mx.

BUFFETT, Jimmy, BS; American country singer and songwriter; b. 25 Dec. 1946, Pascagoula, Miss.; m. Jane Slagsvol 1977. *Education:* Univ. of Southern California. *Career:* fmr freelance journalist, Inside Sports Outside magazine; Billboard magazine; solo artist 1970s–; formed Coral Reef Band 1975; f. Margaritaville Records 1993, Mailboat Records 1999; Founder-mem. Cousteau Society. *Compositions include:* Railroad Lady (recorded by Merle Haggard), He Went to Paris (recorded by Waylon Jennings), Margaritaville, Come Monday, Cheeseburger in Paradise. *Recordings include:* albums: Down to Earth 1972, High Cumberland Jubilee 1972, A White Sport Coat and A Pink Crustacean 1973, Living and Dying In 3/4 Time 1974, A1A 1974, Rancho Deluxe (film soundtrack) 1975, Havana Daydreaming 1976, Changes in Latitudes, Changes in Attitudes 1977, Son of a Son of a Sailor 1978, You Had to Be there 1978, Volcano 1979, Coconut Telegraph 1980, Somewhere over China 1981, One Particular Harbour 1983, Riddles in the Sand 1984, Last Mango in Paris 1985, Songs You Know by Heart 1986, Floridays 1986, Hot Water 1988, Off to See the Lizard 1989, Live Feeding Frenzy 1991, Before the Beach 1993, Fruitcakes 1994, Margaritaville Cafe 1995, Barometer Soup 1995, Late Night Gumbo 1995, Banana Wind 1996, Christmas Island 1996, Don't Stop the Carnival 1998, Beach House On the Moon 1999, Tuesdays, Thursdays, Saturdays 1999, Far Side of the World 2002, Meet Me in Margaritaville 2003, License to Chill 2004, Take the Weather with You 2006, Buffet Hotel 2009, Encores 2010, Welcome to Fin City 2012, Songs from St. Somewhere 2013. *Publication:* Tales from Margaritaville 1989. *Honours:* Hon. Dir, Greenpeace; Country Music Asscn Award for Vocal Event of the Year (with Alan Jackson) 2003, Acad. of Country Music Award for Single of the Year 2003. *Current Management:* c/o Mailboat Records, 10866 Wilshire Blvd, Suite 200, Los Angeles, CA 90024, USA. *E-mail:* info@mailboatrecords.com (office). *Website:* www.mailboatrecords.com; www.margaritaville.com.

BUGG, Jake; British singer, songwriter and musician (guitar); b. (Jacob Edwin Kennedy), 28 Feb. 1994, Nottingham, England. *Career:* appeared on BBC Introducing Stage, Glastonbury Festival 2011; support act to Noel Gallagher's High Flying Birds 2012; numerous live, TV and radio appearances. *Recordings:* albums: Jake Bugg 2012, Shangri La 2013. *Honours:* Q Magazine Award for Best New Act 2013. *Current Management:* c/o Kirk Sommer, William Morris Entertainment, Centre Point, 103 New Oxford Street, London, WC1A 1DD, England. *Telephone:* (20) 7534-6800. *Fax:* (20) 7534-6900. *E-mail:* ksommer@wmeentertainment.com. *Website:* www.wma.com.

BUGSY, Stomy; French rap artist, composer, producer and actor; b. (Gilles Georges Duarte), 21 May 1972, Sarcelles, Paris; one s. *Career:* co-f. Ministère AMER 1989–; solo artist 1996–. *Recordings:* albums: with Ministère AMER: Traitres 1989, Pourquoi tant de haine 1992, 95200 1994; solo: Le Calibre Qu'il Te Faut 1996, Quelques balles de plus pour...Le Calibre Qu'il Te Faut 1998, Gangster d'Amour 1999, Trop Jeune Pour Mourir 2000, 3 Zéros (soundtrack) 2002, 4ème Round 2003, Rimes Passionnelles 2007. *Films include:* Le Marquis 2000, De l'Amour 2001, Les jolies choses 2001, Le boulet 2002, 3 zéros 2002, Le Fleuve 2003, Gomez et Tavarès 2003, Nèg Maron 2005, The Shadow Dancer 2005, Arthur et les Minimoys 2006, Gomez vs Tavarès 2007, Bollywoogie 2007, Cold Blood 2008, It Will Not Be Possible 2008, Aliker 2008, La Glisse 2011, Bye Bye Blondie 2012.

BÜHLER, Urs; Swiss singer (tenor); b. 19 July 1971, Willisau. *Education:* Sweelinck Conservatorium, The Netherlands. *Career:* mem., Il Divo 2003–. *Recordings include:* albums: Il Divo 2004, Ancora 2005, The Christmas Collection 2005, Siempre 2006, The Promise 2008, Wicked Game 2011. *Website:* www.ildivo.com.

BUHRER, Rolf Marcel; Swiss musician (valve-bone, upright string bass); b. 28 June 1932, Zurich; one s. *Career:* mem. of bands Laferrière, Claude Luter, Mixim Saury; played with Albert Nicolas, Mezz Mezzrow, Harry 'Sweets' Edison, Eddie Davis, Moustache; tours France, Germany, North Africa; numerous recordings; mem. Union Musician de Jazz.

BUIKA, Concha; Spanish singer; b. 11 May 1972, Palma de Mallorca. *Career:* solo artist 2005–. *Recordings include:* albums: Buika 2005, Mi Niña Lola (Premio al Mejor Album de Canción Española 2007) 2006, Niña de Fuego 2008, El Último Trago (with Chucho Valdés) (Latin Grammy Award for Best Traditional Tropical Album 2010) 2009, En Mi Piel 2011, La Noche Más Larga 2013. *Current Management:* c/o Mariana Gyalui, Calle Covarrubias, 3 3° Izq., 28010 Madrid, Spain. *Website:* www.conchabuikamusic.com.

BUIRETTE, Michèle Jeanne; French musician (accordion); b. 4 March 1949, Boulogne Sur Seine, France; one d. *Education:* Maitrise de Psychologie. *Career:* Jazz Festivals: Le Mans; Berlin; Grenoble; Tours, Europe: Germany; Netherlands; Switzerland; Italy; Croatia; Slovenia; mem, SACEM. *Recordings:* with Pied de Poule: Indiscretion 1989; Café Noir 1991; Jamais Tranquille! 1995, Confection et artiles divers 1998; solo: La Mise En Plis 1985, Le Panapé de Caméla 2006, Le géant du Néant 2008, Île et elle 2009. *Address:* c/o Florence Lecordier, Cie la Margoulette, 23 Quai Duguay-Trouin, 35600 Redon, France. *Telephone:* (6) 67-43-47-84. *E-mail:* infos@lamargoulette.org. *Telephone:* (6) 78-00-77-64. *E-mail:* mbuirette@club-internet.fr. *Website:* www.michele-buirette.com; www.michelebuirette/myspace.com.

BÜLBÜLOĞLU, Polad, PhD; Azerbaijani composer, singer, film actor and diplomatist; *Ambassador to Russia*; b. 4 Feb. 1945, Baku; s. of Bul-Bul. *Education:* Azerbaijan State Conservatory. *Career:* head of pop-music ensembles 1975–87; Head of Azerbaijan State Philharmonic 1987–88; apptd Minister of Culture 1988; elected mem. Milli-Medjlis 1995; Dir-Gen. Int. Org. TURKSOI 1994; Prof., Int. Humanitarian Acad.; currently Amb. to Russia. *Music:* symphonic works, chamber and instrumental music, musical, vocal cycles, incidental music, pop-songs. *Honours:* Hon. Prof., Azerbaijan Univ. of Culture and Arts; Om emerit al (Moldova) 2005, Order of Independence 2005, Order of Friendship (Russia) 2005; Song of the Year Award (for Will Be Delighted by the Sun Again 1977, I am In Love 1978, Beloved Country 1979, Tell Your Eyes 1980), People's Artist of Azerbaijan 1982, Kazakhstan Nat. Award of Peace and Progress 2010. *Address:* Embassy of Azerbaijan, 125009 Moscow, Leontyevskii per. 16, Russia (office); Fioletova street 6/8, Apartment 53, Baku, Azerbaijan (home). *Telephone:* (495) 629-43-3 (office); (12) 4932177 (home). *Fax:* (495) 202-50-72 (office). *E-mail:* embassy@azembassy.msk.ru (office). *Website:* www.azembassy.ru (office).

BULOW, Harry Timothy, BA, MA, PhD, Lic. Dip.; American composer, conductor, musician (saxophone) and academic; *Professor and Head, Rueff School of Visual and Performing Arts, Purdue University*; b. 19 Feb. 1951, Des Moines, Ia; m. Ellen Bulow 1992, one s., one d. *Education:* San Diego State Univ., Univ. of California, Los Angeles, Trinity Coll. of Music, London, UK. *Career:* composer of film scores, popular songs and jazz; currently Prof. of Music and Head, Rueff School of Visual and Performing Arts, Purdue Univ.; mem. American Soc. of Composers, Authors and Publrs (ASCAP), Soc. of Composers, Southeastern Composers League. *Compositions:* film music: The Burglar, Agatha; popular songs: Touch My Life, The Goodbye Song, All Jazz: Kickback, Crystal Cove, Milpas Street Blues, Sola Street Strut, Hilo Bay, Distant Memory; classical music: Concerto for alto saxophone and orchestra, Concerto for flute and chamber orchestra, Pillars for orchestra, Textures for wind ensemble, Legacy for band, Kakkazan for band; chamber music: Lines, Curves and Voluminous Variations, Indiana Dunes. *Publications:* Textures for Wind Ensemble, Kakkazan for Band, Legacy for Band. *Honours:* Henry Mancini Award for Film Music Composition, First Prize, Int. Composers Competition, Trieste, Italy, Oscar Espla Prize, City of Alicante, Spain, 35 annual awards from ASCAP, Nat. Endowment for the Arts Fellowship (USA). *Address:* Division of Music, Patti and Rusty Rueff School of Visual and Performing Arts, Purdue University, Yue-Kong Pao Hall, 552 West Wood Street, West Lafayette, IN 47907, USA (office). *Telephone:* (765) 494-3056 (office). *E-mail:* hbulow@purdue.edu (office); htbulow@comcast.net (home). *Website:* www.cla.purdue.edu/music (office); www.harrybulow.com.

BUNDRICK, John 'Rabbit' Douglas; American musician (keyboards, piano, hammond organ) and composer; b. 21 Nov. 1948, Baytown, TX; m. Susan Elizabeth Vickers 1989. *Education:* music at school and coll. *Career:* Musical Dir, composer, Johnny Nash, Sweden 1971; moved to UK 1971; mem., Free 1972, Eric Burdon 1975; co-founder, Crawler 1976–79; mem., The Who 1979–84; prolific session musician; mem. PRS, Musicians' Union. *Recordings include:* albums: with The Who: The Kids Are Alright (live) 1979, Face Dances 1981, Hooligans 1982, It's Hard 1982, Once Upon A Time 1983, Who's Last (live) 1984, Two's Missing 1987, Joined Together (live) 1990, Live At The Isle Of Wight Festival 1970 1996, The BBC Sessions 2000; with Free: Heartbreaker, Free Story, The Best Of Free; with Pete Townshend: Rough Mix, Empty Glass, Psychoderelict, White City; with Andy Fairweather-Low: La Booga Rooga, Be Bop 'N' Holla; with Rabbit: Dream Jungle, Broken Arrows, Dark Saloon, Run For Cover, Same Old Story; solo: Broken Arrows 1973, Dark Saloon 1974, Moccasin Warrior 1997, Moccasin Warrior II 1998, Echoes Of Africa 1999, The Fairy Garden 1999, Welcome To America 2001. *Address:* c/o David Clayton, 39 Staverton Road, Bilborough, Nottingham NG8 4ET, England. *E-mail:* mail@rabbittwo.com. *Website:* www.rabbitwho.com.

BUNFORD, Huw 'Bunf;' Welsh musician (guitar); b. 15 Sept. 1967, Cardiff. *Career:* mem. Super Furry Animals 1993–; recorded two EPs on indie label, then obtained major indie label deal; numerous tours in the UK and abroad; began as techno outfit but became more psychedelic and progressive rock; appearances at numerous festivals. *Recordings include:* albums: Fuzzy Logic 1996, Radiator 1997, Guerrilla 1999, Mwng 2000, Rings Around The World 2001, Phantom Power 2003, Love Kraft 2005, Hey Venus 2007, Dark Days/ Light Years 2009. *E-mail:* info@superfurry.com. *Website:* www.superfurry .com.

BUNTON, Emma Lee; British singer; b. 21 Jan. 1976, London, England; pnr Jade Jones; one s. *Career:* actress, including appearances in EastEnders; mem. Touch, later renamed The Spice Girls 1993–2001, as 'Baby Spice', reunion tour 2007–08; numerous tours, concerts, television and radio appearances; world tours include UK, Europe, India, USA; presenter on TV and radio including BBC Radio 1 and satellite TV show; solo artist 1999–. *Television:* judge, Dancing on Ice (ITV) 2010. *Film:* Spiceworld: The Movie 1997. *Recordings include:* albums: with The Spice Girls: Spice 1996, Spiceworld 1997, Forever 2000, Greatest Hits 2007; solo: A Girl Like Me 2001, Free Me 2004, Life in Mono 2006. *Honours:* two Ivor Novello songwriting awards 1997, Smash Hits Award for Best Band 1997, BRIT Awards for Best Single (for Wannabe), for Best Video (for Say You'll Be There) 1997, for Best Performance of the last 30 years 2010, three American Music Awards 1998, Special BRIT Award for Int. Sales 1998. *Address:* c/o 19 Entertainment, Unit 33 Ransomes Dock Business Centre, 35-37 Parkgate Road, London SW11 4NP; c/o Virgin Records Ltd, 553–579 Harrow Road, London, W10 4RH, England. *Website:* www.emmabuntonofficial.com; www.spicegirlsforever.co.uk.

BURCH, Bruce; American musician (guitar) and songwriter; *Director, Music and Entertainment Business (MEBUS) Certificate Program, Kennesaw State University*; b. Georgia; m. Cindy. *Education:* College degree, University of Georgia. *Career:* Football Coach, Gainsville High School; Signed to Combine Music, Nashville, to develop songwriting, then Famous Music; Co-founder, Burch Brothers Music (with brother David); founded Undergraduate Music Program, Terry Coll. of Business, Univ. of Georgia 2005; Dir, Music and Entertainment Business (MEBUS) Certificate Program, Kennesaw State Univ. 2010–; mem. SESAC. *Compositions:* Hits include: Reba McEntire: Rumor Has It; T Graham Brown: The Last Resort; Billy Joe Royal: Out of Sight and On My Mind; Other songs recorded by: Reba McEntire; Aaron Tippin; George Fox; Dan Seals; Barbara Mandrell; Oak Ridge Boys. *Address:* c/o Coles College of Business, Kennesaw State University, 1000 Chastain Road, BB 255, Kennesaw, GA 30144, USA. *Telephone:* (770) 423-6425. *Website:* www.kennesaw.edu; www.myspace.com/bruceburchmusic.

BURCHILL, Charlie; British musician (guitar, violin) and songwriter; b. 27 Nov. 1959. *Career:* Founder-mem. rock group, Simple Minds 1978–; worldwide tours and festival appearances. *Recordings include:* albums: Life In A Day 1979, Real To Real Cacophony 1980, Empires and Dance 1980, Sons and Fascinations 1981, Sister Feelings Call 1981, Celebration 1982, New Gold Dream 1982, Sparkle In The Rain 1984, Once Upon A Time 1985, Live In The City of Light 1987, Street Fighting Years 1989, Themes (four vols) 1990, Real Life 1991, Glittering Prize 81–92 1992, Good News From The Next World 1995, Neapolis 1998, Neon Lights 2001, Cry 2002, Black & White 2005, Graffiti Soul 2009, Celebrate: Greatest Hits 2013, Big Music 2014. *Honours:* Q Award for Best Live Act 1991. *Current Management:* c/o OJK Limited, 5th Floor, 61 Mosley Street, Manchester, M2 3HZ, England. *Telephone:* (161) 300-6000. *Fax:* (161) 237-5163. *E-mail:* info@ojk.co.uk. *Website:* www.ojk.co.uk; www.simpleminds.com.

BURDON, Eric; American (b. British) singer; b. 11 May 1941, Walker, Newcastle, Tyne and Wear; m. 3rd Marianna Burdon. *Education:* Newcastle Coll. of Art and Industrial Design. *Career:* mem. The Pagans; mem. The Animals 1963–67, renamed Eric Burdon and The New Animals 1968; formed Eric Burdon and War 1970; solo artist 1971–; leader, Eric Burdon Band; tours worldwide, festival appearances. *Film appearances:* Top Gear 1965, Stranger in the House 1967, Joe vs The Volcano 1990. *Recordings include:* albums: with The Animals: The Animals 1964, Animal Tracks 1965, The Animals On Tour 1965, The Best Of The Animals 1966, The Most Of The Animals 1966, Animalisms 1966, Animalization 1966, Help Me Girl 1967, When I Was Young 1967, Best Of (Vol. 2) 1967, Winds Of Change 1967, The Twain Shall Meet 1968, Every One Of Us 1968, Love Is 1969, Before We Were So Rudely Interrupted 1977, Ark 1983, Rip It To Shreds 1984; with Eric Burdon and War: Eric Burdon Declares War 1970, Black Man's Burdon 1971; solo, with Eric Burdon Band: Eric Is Here 1967, Guilty 1971, Ring Of Fire 1974, Sun Secrets 1975, Stop (with Jimmy Witherspoon) 1975, Survivor 1978, Gotta Find My Baby 1979, Last Drive 1980, Live 1982, Comeback 1982, I Used To Be An Animal 1988, Wicked Man (with Jimmy Witherspoon) 1988, Crawling King Snake 1992, Lost Within The Halls Of Fame 1995, Misunderstood 1995, Soldier Of Fortune 1997, The Ultimate Comeback 2001, Soul Of A Man 2006, 'Til Your River Runs Dry 2013. *Publications:* I Used To Be An Animal, But I'm All Right Now (autobiog.) 1986, Don't Let Me Be Misunderstood: A Memoir 2001. *Current Management:* c/o Marianna Burdon, PO Box 1477, Ojai, CA 93024, USA. *Telephone:* (760) 406-1950. *E-mail:* marianna@ ericburdon.com. *Website:* www.ericburdon.com.

BURGESS, Brio, BA; American composer, dramatist, poet and jazz singer; b. 27 April 1943, San Francisco, CA. *Education:* Russell Sage Coll. *Career:* various clerical positions at federal, state, city and county agencies 1972–; performances in Saratoga Springs, NY, San Francisco, San Mateo, CA, Albany, NY, and Troy, NY, of music and words (original works) in various formats; presentation of Street Kids on Radio WRPI, NY and Play with Music, 1992, Radio Free America Broadcast. *Compositions:* Suite for Picasso; Escape, ballet, for Piano, Harp, Feet and Chains; Girl on a Ball, Children's Dance and Toys, piano tunes; Sound Dreams, piano music; Space Visions, including The Painter's Song; Hippy Children's Concentration Camp Blues, for Piano, Harp and Words; Tin Angel Blues, 1990; Purple Hood Suite, 1991–92. *Recordings:* Clear, 1978; Briomindsound, 1979; Ulysses Dog No. 9, 1980; Gathered Hear, 1980; Still, 1981; Ringade, 1982; Grate, 1982; Ether, 1982; Zen Meditations, 1987. *Publications:* poems in Poetalk Publications and BAPC Anthologies, 1989–95; Outlaw Blues, eight song-poems, 1992; Poem in Open Mic: The Albany Anthology, 1994; Street Kids and Other Plays, four opera-musical libretto, 1995, Wail!: An American Journey 2007. *Current Management:* Gail G. Tolley, 5 Cuyler Street, Albany, NY 12202, USA. *E-mail:* streetkids2@aol .com.

BURGESS, John Edward; British record producer and studio owner (retd); b. 8 March 1932, London; m. Jean Horsfall 1964; three s. *Education:* Ealing Grammar School. *Career:* Press, promotion, publicity, EMI Records, 1951; Production Asst to Norman Newell; Founder mem., AIR Group of Companies with George Martin, 1965; AIR Studios opened 1969; Merged with Chrysalis, 1974; Man. Dir, Air Studios, Montserrat, West Indies, 1979; Man. Dir, Air Studios, London, 1969–90, Lyndhurst, 1990–94. *Recordings:* Producer for: Adam Faith; Manfred Mann; Peter and Gordon; Freddie and the Dreamers;

John Barry Seven; George Martin Orchestra; Cast albums: Barnum; Guys and Dolls. *Address:* 2 Sudbury Hill, Harrow on the Hill, Harrow, Middlesex, HA1 3SB, England. *Fax:* (20) 8422-5000 (home). *E-mail:* johnboy@gangu.fsnet.co .uk (home).

BURGESS, Tim; British singer; b. 30 May 1967, Salford, Manchester, England. *Career:* fmr mem., Electric Crayons; founding mem. and lead singer, The Charlatans 1989–; numerous tours, festivals, television and radio appearances. *Recordings include:* albums: with The Charlatans: Some Friendly 1990, Between 10th And 11th 1992, Up To Our Hips 1995, The Charlatans 1995, Tellin' Stories 1997, Us And Us Only 1999, Songs From The Other Side 2000, Wonderland 2001, Live It Like You Love It 2002, Up At The Lake 2004, Simpatico 2006, You Cross My Path 2008, Who We Touch 2010, Modern Nature 2015; solo: I Believe 2003, Oh No I Love You 2012. *Current Management:* Big Life Management, 67–69 Chalton Street, London, NW1 1HY, England. *Telephone:* (20) 7554-2100. *Fax:* (20) 7554-2101. *E-mail:* tim@ biglifemanagement.com. *Website:* www.biglifemanagement.com. *Address:* The Charlatans, PO Box 134, Sandbach, Cheshire CW11 1AE, England (office). *E-mail:* info@thecharlatans.net (office). *Website:* www.thecharlatans .net.

BURKE, Lena; Cuban singer, songwriter, musician (piano) and actor; b. 18 Feb. 1978, La Hubana; d. of Rey Nerio and Malena Burke. *Career:* studied guitar and classical piano as a child; solo artist 2005–09; mem. Alex, Jorge y Lena 2010–, recorded album with singer, songwriter and producer Aureo Baqueiro; performed at Lo Nuestro Awards 2011. *Recordings:* solo: Lena 2005, La Mala (soundtrack) 2009; with Alex, Jorge y Lena: Alex, Jorge y Lena (Latin Grammy Award for Best Pop Album by a Duo or Group with Vocals 2011) 2010. *Films:* as actor: La Mala 2009. *Address:* c/o Warner Music Latina, 3400 West Olive Avenue, Burbank, CA 91505-5538, USA (office). *Telephone:* (818) 953-2600 (office). *Website:* www.alexjorgeylena.com.

BURLEY, Philip (Pip) George; British musician (keyboards), composer and television producer; b. 31 Dec. 1943, Croydon; m. Christine Komaromy 1974; three d. *Career:* freelance keyboard player, composer, arranger; played with Sydney Lipton, Joe Loss, Ken Mackintosh; cabaret with The Semitones; television producer 1987–; credits include Darling Buds of May, A Touch of Frost, Pride of Africa; mem. PRS, Chief Barker, Variety Clubs of Great Britain 1999–. *Compositions:* music for television includes Musicround, Darling Buds of May, score for Romeo and Juliet 1993, The Comedy of Errors 1995. *Honours:* Ivor Novello Award 1991.

BURMAKA, Maria; Ukrainian musician; b. 16 June 1970, Kharkiv; m. Dmytro Nebesiftchuk 1993; one d. *Education:* Kharkiv State Univ. *Career:* won Grand Prix at various Ukrainian festivals including Oberig, Chervona Ruta, Lutsk; solo artist 1992–. *Recordings include:* albums: Maria 1992, Znovu lyublyu (trans. as In Love Again) 1998, Mia 2001, Iz yangolom na plechi (trans. as With an Angel on my Shoulder) 2001, Maria Burmaka, Number 9 2004. *Telephone:* (50) 575-94-98. *E-mail:* vet34@kiev.ua. *Website:* www .burmaka.com.ua.

BURN, Chris, BMus, MMus; British musician (piano); b. 13 March 1955, Epping, Essex, England. *Education:* Surrey Univ. *Career:* British tours, festival appearances, including Bochum, Berlin, Copenhagen, Ulrichsberg, Cologne, Victoriaville; radio and TV broadcasts; fmr mem. of Instrumental Staff, Music Dept, Colchester Inst.; mem. PRS, MCPS. *Recordings include:* A Fountain Replete, Ensemble 1988, A Henry Cowell Concert 1993, Music for Three Rivers 1997, Horizontals White 2001, The Middle Distance 2009, Wandlerweiser Und So Weiter 2013. *Honours:* ACGB 1988, 1990, 1992, 1994. *E-mail:* enquiries@chrisburnmusician.co.uk (home). *Website:* www .chrisburnmusician.com (home).

BURNEL, Jean-Jacques; British singer and musician (bass); b. 21 Feb. 1952, London, England. *Education:* Bradford Univ. *Career:* founder mem. rock group, Stranglers 1974–; tours of Europe, USA, Canada, festival appearances; also solo artist. *Recordings include:* albums: with Stranglers: Rattus Norvegicus 1977, No More Heroes 1978, Black and White 1978, Live (X Cert) 1979, The Raven 1979, Themeninblack 1981, La Folie 1982, The Collection 1982, Feline 1983, Aural Sculpture 1984, Dreamtime 1986, All Live and All of the Night 1988, 10 1990, In the Night 1992, Saturday Night, Sunday Morning 1993, About Time 1995, Written in Red 1997, The Hit Men 1997, 5 Live 01 2001, Suite XVI 2006; solo: Euroman Cometh 1979. *Honours:* Ivor Novello Award for Most Performed Work (for Golden Brown) 1983. *E-mail:* martin@costellomusic.co.uk. *E-mail:* jjburnelshidokan@hotmail.com. *Website:* www.shidokan.org.uk; www.stranglers.net; www.stranglers.co.uk.

BURNETT, T Bone; American musician (guitar), singer, songwriter and producer; b. (John Henry Burnett), 18 Jan. 1945, St Louis, Mo. *Career:* touring musician with Delaney and Bonnie, B-52 Band, Bob Dylan's Rolling Thunder Revue 1970s; Founder-mem., Alpha Band 1976–79; solo artist 1972, 1980–; producer for artists, including Joseph Arthur, Autolux, BoDeans, Peter Case, Clay Pigeons, Bruce Cockburn, Elvis Costello, Counting Crows, Marshall Crenshaw, Eels, Jimmie Dale Gilmore, Emmylou Harris, Joe Henry, Tonio K., Leo Kottke, The Ladykillers, Los Lobos, Natalie Merchant, Nitty Gritty Dirt Band, Roy Orbison, Sam Phillips, David Poe, Spinal Tap, Ralph Stanley, The Surfers, Daniel Tashian, Wallflowers, Gillian Welch, Cassandra Wilson. *Recordings include:* albums: with B-52 Band: The B-52 Band & The Fabulous Skylarks 1972; with Alpha Band: Alpha Band 1976, Spark In The Dark 1977, Statue Makers Of Hollywood 1978; solo: Truth Decay 1980, Trap Door (EP)

1982, Proof Through the Night 1983, Behind the Trap Door (EP) 1984, T Bone Burnett 1986, The Talking Animals 1988, The Criminal Under My Own Hat 1992, Twenty Twenty: The Essential T Bone Burnett 2006, The True False Identity 2006, Tooth of Crime 2008; as producer: several albums including Time Step 1983, The Turning 1987, Mystery Girl 1989, Go Slow Down 1993, Raising Sand 2007, The Secret Sisters 2010, The Union 2010, Voice of Ages 2012, Storm & Grace 2012, Glad Rag Doll 2012. *Film soundtracks:* Until the End of the World 1991, O Brother, Where Art Thou? 2000, Divine Secrets of the Ya-Ya Sisterhood 2002, Cold Mountain (Anthony Asquith Award, BAFTA with Stephen Bruton for Achievement in Film Music 2010) 2003, Don't Come Knocking 2005, Walk the Line 2005. *Television includes:* as producer: Nashville 2012. *Films:* A Midnight Clear (music arranger) 1992, The Big Lebowski (musical archivist) 1998, O Brother, Where Art Thou? (music producer) 2000, Down from the Mountain (music dir) 2000, Cold Mountain (exec. music producer) 2003, The Ladykillers (exec. music producer) 2004, Walk the Line (exec. music producer) 2005, All the King's Men (exec. music producer) 2006, Across the Universe (music producer) 2006, Crazy Heart (Grammy Award for Best Compilation Soundtrack Album 2011) 2009, Happy Feet Two 2011, The Hunger Games 2012. *Honours:* 12 Grammy Awards including Grammy Award for Best Song Written For Motion Picture, Television or Other Visual Media (for The Weary Kind) 2011, (for Safe & Sound) 2013. *Website:* www.tboneburnett.com.

BURNS, Christian Anthony; British singer, musician (guitar) and songwriter; b. 18 Jan. 1976, Wigan; s. of Tony Burns. *Career:* Co-founder, BBMak pop group 1996–2003; numerous TV appearances, live concerts. *Recordings include:* albums: with BBMak: Sooner Or Later 2000, Into Your Head 2002; Rock 'n' Rave 2008, These Hopeful Machines 2010, Mirage–The Remixes 2011.

BURNS, Robert George Henry, BA (Hons), PhD, FLCM, FHEA; British musician (bass guitar), composer and educator; *Senior Lecturer in Contemporary Performance, Music Department, University of Otago;* b. 24 Feb. 1953, London, England; m. Elizabeth Chennells 1991; one s. *Education:* Guildhall School of Music and Drama, Brunel Univ., London Coll. of Music, Otago Univ., NZ. *Career:* tours, live appearances and recordings with Sam and Dave, Edwin Starr, Lene Lovich, Isaac Hayes, Pete Townshend, Eric Burdon, David Gilmour, Albert Lee, James Burton, Jerry Donahue, Viv Stanshall, Zoot Money; formed Robert Burns Music 1987; Prin. Examiner in bass guitar, Trinity Coll. of Music 1992; Head of Bass Guitar Studies, Basstech/Thames Valley Univ. 1994; mem. Subject2Change; Sr Lecturer in Contemporary Performance, Dept of Music, Univ. of Otago 2001–. *Compositions:* soundtracks for clients, including Lonrho, Sunday Times, IBM, MTV, P&O. *Recordings include:* for TV: Red Dwarf, Mr Bean, 2 Point 4 Children, Alas Smith and Jones, Lenny Henry, Blackadder III, Not the Nine O'Clock News, Three of a Kind. *Publications:* The Rock File, Transforming Folk 2012; columnist for Bassist and Musician magazines; numerous articles in academic journals. *Address:* University of Otago, 364 Leith Walk, Dunedin 9054, New Zealand (office). *Telephone:* (3) 479-8444 (office). *E-mail:* rob.burns@stonebow.otago.ac .nz (office). *Website:* www.otago.ac.nz/music (office); www.myspace.com/ subject2changenz.

BURNSTEIN, Cliff; manager; b. 1953. *Career:* jt Founder and head, with Peter Mensch, Q-Prime Management; managed artists and groups, including AC/DC, Tal Bachman, Crazy Town, Def Leppard, Dokken, Fountains of Wayne, Garbage, Nina Gordon, Hole, Bruce Hornsby, Ivy, Madonna, Metallica, Queensryche, Red Hot Chili Peppers, Rush, Shania Twain, Smashing Pumpkins, Tesla, Veruca Salt, Warrior Soul; Q-Prime Management acquired part-ownership, with Zomba Music Publishing, of Volcano Records 1998. *E-mail:* info@qprime.com. *Website:* www.qprime.com.

BURONFOSSE, Marc; French musician (upright acoustic bass and electric bass); *Teacher, Conservatoire à Rayonnement Régional de Paris;* b. 6 May 1963, Soissons, France; m. Jennifer Forse 1993; one d. *Career:* Japanese tour with Les Solistes de Versailles (chamber orchestra); Fellowship to study at the New School of Music, New York; Tour of Central Africa with Sylvain Kassap Quartet; European tours with Sylvain Kassap Quartet and Bojan Z Quartet; currently Teacher, Conservatoire à Rayonnement Régional de Paris; mem. Marc Buronfosse Sounds Quartet; TV and radio appearances; mem. ADAMI, SACEM, SPEDIDAM. *Recordings include:* Sylvain Kassap Quartet Quixote, Bojan Z Quartet with Marc Buronfosse Sounds Quartet: Before the Second Round 2010. *Honours:* First prize, Concours de la Défense 1992, Concours Etrechy 1995. *E-mail:* contact@marcburonfosse.com. *Website:* www .marcburonfosse.com.

BURRELL, Kenny, BMus; American jazz musician (guitar) and academic; *Professor, Department of Music and Ethnomusicology, Herb Alpert School of Music, University of California, Los Angeles;* b. 31 July 1931, Detroit, Mich. *Education:* Wayne State Univ., Detroit. *Career:* apptd Dir Jazz Studies Program, Dept of Ethnomusicology, Herb Alpert School of Music, UCLA 1996, currently Prof., Dept of Music and Ethnomusicology; played with Candy Johnson Sextet, Yusef Lateef, Tommy Flanagan, Dizzy Gillespie 1951, Oscar Peterson Trio 1955, Hampton Hawes Trio 1956, Benny Goodman 1957; association with organist, Jimmy Smith; leader own trio. *Recordings include:* albums: The Cats 1957, Kenny Burrell–John Coltrane 1958, At The Five Spot Cafe Vol. 1 1959, Midnight Blue 1960, Live At The Village Vanguard 1960, Guitar Forms 1965, For Charlie Christian and Benny Goodman 1967, Handcrafted 1978, Kenny Burrell In New York 1981, Night Song 1982, Listen To The Dawn 1983, Bluesin' Around 1984, A La Carte 1986,

Generations 1987, Blue Lights Vols 1 and 2 1989, Togethering 1989, Recapitulation 1989, Guiding Spirit 1989, Sunup To Sundown 1991, Soulero 1996, Love Is The Answer 1998, Ballad Essentials 2005, A Night at the Vanguard 2008. *Honours:* Dr hc (William Paterson Coll.); Jazz Master Award, Nat. Endowment for the Arts (NEA) 2005. *Address:* University of California, Los Angeles, Herb Alpert School of Music, Department of Music 2539, Schoenberg Music Building, Box 951616, Los Angeles, CA 90095-1616, USA (office). *Telephone:* (310) 206-1044 (office). *Fax:* (310) 206-4738 (office). *E-mail:* kburrell@arts.ucla.edu (office). *Website:* www.music.ucla.edu (office).

BURROUGHS, Gary Stuart; British musician (drums, percussion), singer, songwriter, producer and engineer; b. 3 April 1953, Doncaster; m. Lyn Acton 1976; one s. *Education:* Hull Technical Coll. *Career:* drummer with Soul Image, The Pink, Listen, The Weazles, Johnny Duncan and the Bluegrass Boys, Rock and Roll Circus, Rock Orchestrals, Johnny Johnson and the Bandwagon, Snake Eye, The Killers, Jackal, Buster Crab, Sarah Gordan's All American Soul Show, Sheer Elegance, Roy Wood: Wizzo, Christie, Nosmo King, Luggage, Export, Earthman Liberation, What Katy Did Next, Tiffanys, Gimmex, Stork Club, Bertice Reading, Lionel Bart, Simon Townshend, Resistdance, Marino, NGO, Fila Brazillia, Derek Bailey, Naked Orange 1968–; tour man. for Limmie and The Family Cookin' 1976; sound engineer, Fairview Music 1979; lead singer, Techno Pop, Marino, Listen, Blitzkrieg, The Weazles, The Choirboys, NGO; support to numerous artists on tour; television appearances; prod. for Smash live, Top of the Pops (BBC 1) 1994; business ventures include DIG for music, Midem 1991, Wall 2 Wall Records 1990, Wall 2 Wall Studios 1992; mem. PRS, Equity. *Recordings include:* solo album: Sacred Places. *Honours:* Blues Album of the Year, Paris, France 1992.

BURROWS, Andy; British musician (drums); b. 30 June 1979, Winchester. *Career:* mem. rock band Razorlight 2004–09, We Are Scientists 2009–; Founder-mem. I Am Arrows 2009–; collaborations with Tom Smith as Smith & Burrows, Tom Odell and Delilah. *Recordings include:* album: with Razorlight: Razorlight 2006, Slipway Fires 2008; solo: The Colour of My Dreams 2008, Company 2012; with We Are Scientists: Barbara 2010; with I Am Arrows: Sun Comes Up Again 2010; with Tom Smith: Funny Looking Angels 2011. *Website:* www.wearescientists.com.

BURTON, Gary; American jazz musician (vibraphone, piano); b. 23 Jan. 1943, Anderson, Ind. *Education:* Berklee Coll. of Music, Boston. *Career:* mem. George Shearing's Group 1963; played with Stan Getz for two years; formed own bands 1960s–; leader various bands featuring artists, including Larry Coryell, Roy Haynes, Pat Metheny, Eberhard Weber; also recorded with Stéphane Grappelli, Carla Bley, Keith Jarrett, Chick Corea, Michael Brecker, Peter Erskine; teacher, Berklee Coll. of Music 1971–. *Recordings include:* albums: Duster 1967, Lofty Fake Anagram 1967, A Genuine Tang Funeral (with Carla Bley) 1968, Country Roads and Other Places 1968, Paris Encounter (with Stéphane Grappelli) 1969, Green Apple 1969, Gary Burton and Keith Jarrett (with Keith Jarrett) 1970, Crystal Silence (with Chick Corea) 1972, Ring (with Eberhard Weber) 1974, Hotel Hello 1974, Matchbook 1974, Dreams So Real 1975, Passengers (with Eberhard Weber) 1976, Slide Show (with Ralph Towner) 1976, Duet (with Chick Corea) (Grammy Award for Best Jazz Instrumental Album 1979) 1978, Easy As Pie 1980, Picture This 1983, Real Life Hits 1984, Whiz Kids 1986, Times Like These 1988, Reunion (with Pat Metheny) 1989, Cool Nights 1990, Right Time Right Place (with Paul Bley) 1991, Six Pack 1993, Face To Face (with Makoto Ozone) 1995, Live In Cannes 1996, Astor Piazzolla Reunion 1996, Native Sense: The New Duets (with Chick Corea) 1997, Departure 1997, Like Minds (Grammy Award for Best Jazz Instrumental Album 2000) 1998, Libertango: The Music Of Astor Piazzolla 2000, For Hamp, Red, Bags and Cal 2001, Selected Recordings 2002, Virtuosi (with Makoto Ozone) 2002, Songs & Lullabies (with Fred Hersch and Norma Winstone) 2005, Next Generation 2005, The New Crystal Silence (with Chick Corea) (Grammy Award for Best Jazz Instrumental Album 2009) 2008, Quartet Live 2009, Common Ground 2011, Hot House (with Chick Corea) 2012. *Honours:* Grammy Awards for Best Jazz Performance (for Alone at Last) 1972, for Best Jazz Instrumental Solo (for Rhumbata) 1998, for Best Improvised Jazz Solo (with Chick Corea) (for Hot House) 2013. *Address:* c/o Concord Records, Concord Music Group, Inc., 23307 Commerce Park Road, Cleveland, OH 44122, USA (office). *Website:* www.concordmusicgroup.com; www.garyburton.com.

BURTON, (Patrick Henry) Paddy; British musician (percussion) and musical instrument maker; b. 19 Aug. 1961, Stockport, Cheshire; two mem. *Education:* Newcastle Univ. *Career:* Musical Dir for theatre companies; performing musician with local bands 1978–86, Pineapple Agogo 1986–90; Musician-in-Residence, City of Edinburgh District Council 1990–92; player with Amadeus 1993–, Jack Drum Arts, Dodgy Clutch, The Fabulous Salami Brothers; musical instrument maker (slitdrums, multiplayer giant xylophones); mem. Musicians' Union, Sound Sense, Equity. *Recordings include:* Trashcan Gamelan Edinburgh 1992, Black Diamonds, Black Gold 1993, Fish Xylophone 1994. *Address:* 43–44 Gladstone Terrace, Sunniside, Bishop Auckland, DL13 4LS, England (home).

BURULCICH, Anthony; American musician (drums). *Career:* mem. The Bravery 2003–; drummer with Morrissey 2012–. *Recordings include:* albums: Unconditional (EP) 2004, The Bravery 2005, The Sun and the Moon 2007, Stir the Blood 2009. *E-mail:* petegalli@cybercom.net. *Address:* c/o Island Records, 364–366 Kensington High Street, London W14 8NS, England (office). *Website:* www.thebravery.com.

BURWELL, Carter; American composer; b. 18 Nov. 1955, New York, NY. *Education:* Harvard Univ. *Career:* Chief Computer Scientist, Cold Spring Harbor Laboratory 1979–81; Computer Modeler and Animator, later Dir, Digital Sound Research 1982–87; film-score composer; mem. ASCAP. *Compositions:* for television: Framed (additional music) 1990, And the Band Played On 1993, Children Remember the Holocaust 1995; for film: Blood Simple 1984, Psycho III 1986, Raising Arizona 1986, A Hero of Our Time 1986, The Beat 1987, Pass the Ammo 1987, It Takes Two 1988, Checking Out 1988, Miller's Crossing 1990, Scorchers 1991, Doc Hollywood 1991, Barton Fink 1991, Storyville 1991, Waterland 1992, Buffy the Vampire Slayer 1992, Kalifornia 1992, This Boy's Life 1992, A Dangerous Woman 1993, Wayne's World 2 1993, And the Band Played On 1993, The Hudsucker Proxy 1993, Airheads 1994, It Could Happen to You 1994, The Celluloid Closet 1995, Bad Company 1995, Rob Roy 1995, A Goofy Movie 1995, Two Bits 1995, Fear 1995, The Chamber 1996, Fargo 1996, Joe's Apartment 1996, Picture Perfect 1997, Locusts 1997, Girls Night Out 1997, Assassins 1997, Conspiracy Theory 1997, Jackal 1997, Velvet Goldmine 1998, Gods and Monsters 1998, The Big Lebowski 1998, The Spanish Prisoner 1998, The Hi Lo Country 1998, Being John Malkovich 1999, The Corruptor 1999, The General's Daughter 1999, The Hi-Lo Country 1999, Mystery Alaska 1999, Three Kings 1999, What Planet Are You From? 2000, Hamlet 2000, O Brother, Where Art Thou? 2000, Book of Shadows: Blair Witch 2 2000, Before Night Falls 2000, A Knight's Tale 2001, The Man Who Wasn't There 2001, Simone 2002, The Rookie 2002, Adaptation 2002, Intolerable Cruelty 2003, The Ladykillers 2004, The Alamo 2004, Fur: An Imaginary Portrait of Diane Arbus 2006, The Hoax 2006, Moving Gracefully Toward the Exit 2006, No Country for Old Men 2007, Before the Devil Knows You're Dead 2007, In Bruges 2008, Burn After Reading 2008, Twilight 2008, Seven Psychopaths 2012, Twilight: Breaking Dawn 2012. *Address:* The Body Inc., 105 Hudson Street, Suite 10N, New York, NY 10013, USA (office). *Telephone:* (917) 512-1240 (office). *Fax:* (212) 219-8483 (office). *E-mail:* carter@thebodyinc.com (office). *Website:* www.carterburwell.com.

BUSCKE, Phil; New Zealand musician (guitar); b. Cambridge. *Career:* Founder-mem. Trinket 1996, renamed The Datsuns 1997–; Owner, Hell Squad Records. *Recordings include:* albums: The Datsuns 2002, Outta Sight Outta Mind 2004, Smoke & Mirrors 2006, Head Stunts 2008. *E-mail:* enquiries@thedatsuns.com. *Website:* www.thedatsuns.com.

BUSH, John; American singer; b. 24 Aug. 1963, Los Angeles, CA. *Career:* lead singer, Armored Saint 1982–92, 1999–, Anthrax 1992–2005, 2009–10; numerous live appearances; mem. AFTRA. *Recordings include:* albums: with Anthrax: Sound Of White Noise, 1993; Stomp 442, 1995; Vol. VIII: The Threat Is Real, 1998; Madhouse: The Very Best Of Anthrax, 2001, We've Come for You All 2003, The Greater of Two Evils 2004; with Armored Saint: March Of The Saint, 1984; Delirious Nomad, 1985, Raising Fear 1987, Symbol Of Salvation, 1991, Revelation 2000, Nod to the Old School 2001, La Raza 2010. *Address:* c/o Metal Blade Records USA, 5737 Kanan Road, #143, Agoura Hills, CA 91301, USA. *E-mail:* metalblade@metalblade.com. *Website:* www .metalblade.com; www.myspace.com/armoredsaint; www.armoredsaint.com.

BUSH, Kate, CBE; British singer, songwriter, musician and record producer; b. 30 July 1958, Bexleyheath, Kent, England; pnr Danny McIntosh; one s. *Career:* numerous live and TV appearances; Dir Novercia Ltd; Founder Fish People label; guest and backing vocalist for numerous artists, including Peter Gabriel, Roy Harper, Prince, Midge Ure. *Film:* The Line, The Cross and The Curve (writer, dir and actor) 1993. *Stage:* live shows: The Tour of Life 1979, Before the Dawn (Evening Standard Theatre Editor's Award 2014) 2014. *Recordings include:* albums: The Kick Inside 1978, Lionheart 1978, Never for Ever 1980, The Dreaming 1982, Hounds of Love 1985, The Whole Story 1986, The Sensual World 1989, This Woman's Work 1990, The Red Shoes 1993, Aerial 2005, Director's Cut 2011, 50 Words for Snow (South Bank Sky Arts Award 2012) 2011. *Honours:* BPI Awards for Best Vocalist 1979, 1987, Ivor Novello Award for Outstanding British Lyrics (for The Man With The Child In His Eyes) 1979, BRIT Award for Best Female Artist 1987, Q Magazine Award for Best Classic Songwriter 2001, Ivor Novello Award for Outstanding Contribution to British Music by a Songwriter 2002. *E-mail:* admin@ katebush.com. *Website:* www.katebush.com.

BUSH, Kristian Merrill; American country music singer, songwriter, record producer and musician (guitar, mandolin, harmonica); b. 14 March 1970, Knoxville, Tenn.; m. Jill Bush; one s., one d. *Education:* Avon Old Farms Boarding School. *Career:* solo artist 1987–90, 2001–02; formed folk-rock duo Billy Pilgrim with Andrew Hyra 1990–2001; mem. Sugarland 2002–, toured with Brad Paisley 2005, Kenny Chesney 2006–07, Keith Urban 2008; guest appearance on USA for Haiti charity single We Are the World 25 for Haiti 2010; record producer for several artists including Chuck Brodsky, Beth Wood, Shawn Mullins; session musician on numerous recordings including ones for Shawn Mullins, Kristen Hall, Ellis Paul. *Recordings:* albums: solo: Heroes 1987, Saturday 1989, Politics and Pocketchange 1990, Paint it All 2002; with Billy Pilgrim: St. Christopher's Crossing 1992, Words Like Numbers 1993, Billy Pilgrim 1994, Bloom 1995, Snow Globe 1999; with Sugarland: Twice the Speed of Life 2004, Enjoy the Ride 2006, Love on the Inside 2008, Gold and Green 2009, The Incredible Machine 2010. *Honours:* with Sugarland: American Music Award for Favorite Breakthrough Artist 2005, Country Music Television Awards for Collaborative Video of the Year 2006, for Duo Video of the Year 2011, Country Music Association Awards for Vocal Duo of the Year 2007, 2008, 2011, Grammy Awards for Best Collaboration (with Bon Jovi) 2007, for Best Country Song 2009, for Best Country

Performance by a Duo or Group 2009, Academy of Country Music Awards for Song of the Year 2008, Milestone Award 2009, for Vocal Duo of the Year 2009, 2011. *Current Management:* c/o Gail Gellman Management, 22917 Pacific Coast Highway, Suite 920, Malibu, CA 90265-4879, USA. *E-mail:* gail@ gellmanmgmt.com. *Website:* www.gellmanmgmt.com. *Address:* c/o Mercury Nashville, Universal Music Group, 2220 Colorado Avenue, Santa Monica, CA 90265-4879, USA (office). *Website:* www.sugarlandmusic.com.

BUSHWACKA!; British producer, remixer and DJ; b. (Matthew Stuart Benjamin), 2 Aug. 1972, London, England. *Career:* DJ with Ratpack; resident DJ at The End, London; engineer at Mr C's Watershed Studio, London; mem., Makesome Breaksome, Mashupheadz; mem., Layo & Bushwacka! (with Layo Paskin); collaborations with Nathan Coles; co-founder Plank/Oblong Records (with Lewis Copeland) 1995. *Recordings include:* albums: Wak'd (as Plantastik) 1998, Low Life (with Layo) 1999, Cellar Dwellas 2000, Night Works (with Layo) 2002, Feels Closer (with Layo) 2006, Rio de Janeiro – GU33 2008, Rising & Falling (with Layo) 2012. *Address:* Plank Records, 9 the Shaftesbury Centre, 85 Barlby Road, London, W10 6BN, England. *E-mail:* bushwacka@plank.co.uk. *Website:* www.bushwacka.com; www .layoandbushwacka.com.

BUSTA RHYMES; American rap artist and producer; b. (Trevor Tahiem Smith), 20 May 1972, Brooklyn, New York; two s. (one deceased). *Career:* Co-founder, Leaders of the New School 1990; guest on albums by artists, including Boyz II Men, Mary J. Blige, TLC and A Tribe Called Quest; solo artist 1996–; formed own record co., Flipmode Entertainment 2004 (Conglomerate Records 2011–); started own clothing line, Bushi; several tours and live appearances. *Films include:* Who's the Man? 1993, Strapped (TV) 1993, Higher Learning 1995, The Rugrats Movie (voice) 1998, Shaft 2000, Finding Forrester 2000, Narc 2002, Halloween: Resurrection 2002, Death of a Dynasty 2003, Full Clip 2004, Strong Arm Steady 2004, Breaking Point 2009, The Unforgiven 2011. *Recordings include:* albums: with Leaders of the New School: Future Without A Past 1991, T.I.M.E. 1993; solo: The Coming 1996, When Disaster Strikes 1997, Extinction Level Event 1998, Anarchy 2000, Genesis 2001, It Ain't Safe No More 2002, The Big Bang 2006, Back on my B.S. 2009, Year of the Dragon 2012. *Current Management:* c/o Flipmode Records, Universal Music Group, 1755 Broadway, New York, NY 10019, USA. *Website:* www.universalmusic.com.

BUTCHER, John Bernard; British musician (saxophone) and composer; b. 25 Oct. 1954, Brighton, England. *Education:* PhD. *Career:* originally a physicist –1982; work includes improvisation, composition, multi-tracked saxophone pieces, explorations with feedback and extreme acoustics and large instrumental ensembles; has collaborated and recorded with musicians including Derek Bailey, John Stevens, Gerry Hemingway, The EX, Rhodri Davies, John Edwards, Gino Robair, Toshimaru Nakamura and Steve Beresford; groups include John Butcher Group, Anemone Quintet, The Apophonics, The Contest of Pleasures, Thermal and Way Out Northwest; also solo performer, tours and broadcasts in Europe, Japan, North America and Australia; festival appearances include Berlin Total Music Meeting, Du Maurier Jazz (Canada), Knitting Factory (New York), Company (London), Huddersfield Contemporary Music Festival; has composed works for ensembles including Polwechsel (Austria), Elision Ensemble (Australia), Rova Saxophone Quartet (USA); f. ACTA Records, Weight of Wax CD label. *Television:* Date with an Artist (BBC). *Compositions include:* somethingtobesaid 2008, Penny Wands and Native String for eight reconstructed futurist intonarumori 2009. *Recordings:* solo: 13 Friendly Numbers 1992, London & Cologne 1998, Fixations (14) 2000, Invisible Ear 2003, Cavern with Nightlife 2002, The Geometry of Sentiment 2006, Resonant Spaces 2006, Bell Trove Spools 2011; with others: Fonetiks 1985, Conceits 1987, News From The Shed 1989, Cultural Baggage 1990, Spellings 1993, Respiritus 1995, Concert Moves 1995, Scrutables (with Derek Bailey and Gino Robair) 2000, The White Spot 2008, Buffalo Pearl (with Gerry Hemingway) 2008, Carliol (with Rhodri Davies) 2008, Under the Roof (with Claudia Ulla Binder) 2010, Dusted Machinery (with Toshimaru Nakamura) 2010. *Honours:* Paul Hamlyn Award 2011. *E-mail:* info@johnbutcher.org.uk. *Website:* www.johnbutcher.org.uk.

BUTCHER, Simon David, (Simon York), BA (Hons); British songwriter, composer, singer and musician (guitar, bass, violin, keyboards), artist, actor and graphic designer; b. 21 Dec. 1975, Mansfield, Notts., England. *Education:* Clarendon Coll., Nottingham Trent Univ. *Career:* mem. of band Delirium, signed recording contract with Roadrunner Records 1997, band later changed name to D-ELZ; currently lead mem. and songwriter, Luxury Stranger; mem. PRS, MCPS, PPL, PRC, Equity, AURA. *Compositions include:* Soon You Will, Next Stage, Roadrunner, Better Place, Bring Me An Ocean, Defy, Don't Forget…, Dream Scheme, Ettey, Fantasy Love, Flesh and Blood, For You, God, It's So Easy…, Haunting, Ice Maiden, I Need You, I Hate You, I Need Your Light, Loretta, Love The Dealer, Martyr, Rhyme, Sleep, The Boy With The Thumb In His Mouth, The Day Project (Introduction), The Dream, The Wrong Time, To Cling To, Urban Love Song, Walkin' Around, White Dove, Won't Be Long Now. *Art exhibition:* Automatic Orchestra, multi-media installation, Nottingham city centre. *Television:* The Real Jack and the Beanstalk, Playing the Field, Peak Practice. *Recordings include:* Dual Carriageway, Bitch, Indignant, Soon You Will, Next Stage, Roadrunner. *Honours:* Band of the Year 1995. *Current Management:* c/o David Butcher, First Step Management, 96 George Street, Mansfield, Notts., NG19 6SB, England. *E-mail:* first.step@tesco.net. *E-mail:* info@luxurystranger.net. *Website:* www.luxurystranger.net.

BUTLER, Bernard; British musician (guitar, keyboards) and songwriter; b. 1 May 1970, Stamford Hill, London; m. Elisa Butler. *Education:* Queen Mary Coll., London, studied violin and piano. *Career:* mem., Suede 1992–95; numerous live and TV appearances; tours of Europe, America, Japan; mem. duo, McAlmont and Butler (with David McAlmont) 1994–95, 2001–; solo artist 1998–; recorded with Bryan Ferry, Edwyn Collins, Aimee Mann, Sparks, Eddi Reader, Neneh Cherry, Duffy; Founder-mem., The Tears 2005–. *Recordings include:* albums: with Suede: Suede 1993, Dog Man Star 1994; with McAlmont and Butler: The Sound Of McAlmont And Butler 1995, Bring It Back 2002; solo: People Move On 1998, Friends and Lovers 2000; with The Tears: Here Come The Tears 2005. *Honours:* Mercury Music Prize 1993, Producer of the Year, Music Producers' Guild Awards 2009, BRIT Award for Best British Producer of the Year 2009. *E-mail:* infobb@bernardbutler.com. *Website:* www .bernardbutler.com.

BUTLER, Chad; American musician (drums); b. 24 March 1974, Amsterdam, The Netherlands; m. Tina Butler 1999; three c. *Education:* Univ. of California, San Diego. *Career:* mem., Switchfoot 1997–. *Recordings include:* albums: The Legend of Chin 1997, New Way to be Human 1999, Learning to Breathe 2000, The Beautiful Letdown (GMA Dove Award for Album of the Year 2004) 2003, Nothing is Sound 2005, Oh! Gravity 2006, Hello Hurricane 2009, Vice Verses (GMA Dove Award for Rock Album of the Year 2012) 2011. *Current Management:* c/o Bruce Flohr, Red Light Management, 9200 Sunset Blvd, Los Angeles, CA 90069, USA. *E-mail:* switchfoot@redlightmanagement.com. *Website:* www.redlightmanagement.com; www.switchfoot.com.

BUTLER, Edith, OC, BA, MA; Canadian singer and musician (guitar); b. 27 July 1942, Paquetville, New Brunswick. *Career:* tours of Canada, USA, Japan, France; television and radio shows; mem. SOCAN, SACEM, SODRAC. *Recordings include:* 28 albums, including Le Retour 2013. *Publication:* La fille de Paquetville. *Honours:* Ordre National du Mérite 1998, Order of New-Brunswick; Hon. DLit (Univ. of Acadia), Hon. DMus (Université de Moncton), (Université of New-Brunswick); three Felix Awards, Nelly Award, Charles-Cros Award, Helen Creighton Acheivement Award, Gov. Gen.'s Performing Arts Award for Lifetime Artistic Achievement 2009, Lt Gov.'s Award. *Address:* 1441 Chemin Gendron, Canton Stanstead, Stanstead, PQ, J1X 3W4, Canada (office). *Telephone:* (819) 843-4959 (office). *E-mail:* butlere@globetrotter.net (home). *Website:* www.edithbutler.net.

BUTLER, (Terry) Geezer; British musician (bass); b. 17 July 1949, Birmingham; m. Gloria Butler. *Career:* bass player, UK heavy rock group Black Sabbath, 1967–; leader GZR band; band mem. Heaven & Hell 2006–10; numerous concerts world-wide. *Recordings include:* albums: Black Sabbath 1970, Paranoid 1970, Master of Reality 1971, Black Sabbath, Vol. 4 1972, Sabbath Bloody Sabbath 1973, Sabotage 1975, Technical Ecstasy 1976, Never Say Die! 1978, Heaven and Hell 1980, Mob Rules 1981, Born Again 1983, Seventh Star 1986, The Eternal Idol 1987, Headless Cross 1989, Tyr 1990, Dehumanizer 1992, Cross Purposes 1994, Forbidden 1995, Reunion 1998, Past Lives 2002; with Ozzy Osbourne: Just Say Ozzy 1990, Ozzmosis 1995; as GZR: Plastic Planet 1995, Black Science 1997, Ohmwork 2005; with Heaven & Hell: Live from Radio City Music Hall 2007, The Devil You Know 2009, Neon Nights: 30 Years of Heaven & Hell 2010. *Honours:* with Black Sabbath: Grammy Award for Best Metal Performance (for God is Dead?) 2014. *Current Management:* c/o Gloria Butler Management, 8899 Beverly Blvd Suite, 905 West Hollywood, Los Angeles, CA, 90048, USA. *Website:* www.blacksabbath .com; www.geezerbutler.com.

BUTLER, Jonathan Kenneth; South African musician (guitar), singer and songwriter; b. 10 Oct. 1961, Cape Town; m. Barenese Vanessa 1983, two d. *Career:* solo artist, with extensive tours of USA, Japan, Europe, South America, South Africa, TV appearances; mem. Musicians' Union, PRS, AFTRA. *Recordings include:* albums: Introducing Jonathan Butler, 1977; Jonathan Butler, 1987; More Than Friends, 1988; Heal Our Land, 1990; Head To Head, 1994; Do You Love Me? 1997; Story Of Life, 1999; The Source, 2000. *Honours:* NAACP Award, five ASCAP Awards. *Current Management:* c/o Sohayla Cude, Associated Talent Management, 2800 Olympic Blvd, 1st Floor, Santa Monica, CA 90404, USA. *Website:* www.jonathanbutler.com.

BUTLER, LaVerne; American jazz singer; b. Shreveport, La; d. of Scott Butler. *Education:* Univ. of New Orleans. *Career:* moved to New York 1984; fmr English teacher. *Recordings include:* albums: No Looking Back 1992, Day Dreamin' 1994, Blues In The City 1999, A Foolish Thing To Do 2001. *Current Management:* c/o John Belmont, Belmont Agency, Inc., 15620 30th Avenue, SE, Mill Creek, MA 98012-5892, USA. *Telephone:* (425) 357-0101. *Fax:* (425) 357-0103. *E-mail:* john@belmontagency.com. *Website:* www.belmontagency .com.

BUTLER, Nigel; British songwriter, producer and programmer; b. 12 Sept. 1966; m. Angela Dial. *Career:* worked as prod. and songwriter with Bardot, B*Witched, Hear'say, Steps, theaudience; worked as programmer with Alisha's Attic, The Charlatans, Erasure, Patricia Kaas, Manic Street Preachers, The Orb, Travis, Ronan Keating. *Address:* c/o Bucks Music Group, Onward House, 11 Uxbridge Street, London, W8 7TQ, England. *Telephone:* (20) 7221-4275. *Fax:* (20) 7229-6893. *E-mail:* info@bucksmusicgroup.co.uk. *Website:* www.bucksmusicgroup.co.uk.

BUTLER, William (Will); Canadian musician (synthesizer, bass guitar, percussion); brother of Win Butler; m. Jenny Shore 2008. *Career:* founder mem., Arcade Fire 2003–. *Films:* as composer: Her 2014. *Recordings include:*

albums: with Arcade Fire: Funeral 2004, Neon Bible (Juno Award for Alternative Album of the Year 2008) 2007, The Suburbs (Grammy Award for Album of the Year 2011) 2010, Reflektor (Juno Awards for Album of the Year and Alternative Album of the Year 2014) 2013; solo: Policy 2015. *Current Management:* Quest Management, 1D–36 Warple Way, London, W3 0DY, England. *Telephone:* (20) 8749-0088. *Fax:* (20) 8749-0080. *E-mail:* info@quest-management.com. *Website:* www.quest-management.com; www.arcadefire.com.

BUTLER, Win; American singer, songwriter and musician (guitar, bass guitar, keyboards, harmonica); b. Texas; brother of William Butler; m. Régine Chassagne. *Education:* Phillips Exeter Acad. *Career:* founder mem. and lead singer, Arcade Fire 2003–. *Recordings include:* albums: Funeral 2004, Neon Bible (Juno Award for Alternative Album of the Year 2008) 2007, The Suburbs (Grammy Award for Album of the Year 2011) 2010, Reflektor (Juno Awards for Album of the Year and Alternative Album of the Year 2014) 2013. *Address:* Quest Management, 1D–36 Warple Way, London, W3 0DY, England. *Telephone:* (20) 8749-0088. *Fax:* (20) 8749-0080. *E-mail:* info@quest-management.com. *Website:* www.quest-management.com; www.arcadefire.com.

BUXTON, Felix; British DJ, producer and songwriter; b. 1971. *Career:* Founder-mem., Basement Jaxx 1994–; Co-founder and Owner, Atlantic Jaxx records 1994–; remixes for acts, including Pet Shop Boys, Roger Sanchez, Lil' Mo Yin Yang; worked with vocalist Corrina Josephs. *Recordings include:* albums: Atlantic Jaxx (compilation) 1997, Remedy 1999, Rooty 2001, Kish Kash (Grammy Award for Best Electronic/Dance Album 2005) 2003, The Singles 2005, Crazy Itch Radio 2006, Scars 2009, Zephyr 2009, Junto 2014. *Honours:* BRIT Awards for Best British Dance Act 2002, 2004. *Address:* c/o XL Recordings, One Codrington Mews, London, W11 2EH, England (office). *Telephone:* (20) 8870-7511. *Website:* www.xlrecordings.com; www.basementjaxx.co.uk.

BYERS, Rodney, (Roddy Radiation); British musician (guitar); b. (Roderick James Byers), 5 May 1955, Keresley. *Career:* mem. The Wild Boys, The Specials; Founder-mem. The Skabilly Rebels 2003–; formed own record label, 2-Tone; numerous tours and television appearances. *Recordings include:* albums include: with The Specials: The Specials 1979, More Specials 1980, Today's Specials 1996, Guilty 'Til Proved Innocent! 1998, Conquering Ruler 2001; with The Skabilly Rebels: Duff Guide to Ska 2011, Skabilly Rebel: The Roddy Radiation Anthology 2003. *Address:* ReverbNation, 115 North Duke Street, Suite 2A, Durham, NC 27701, USA. *E-mail:* info@reverbnation.com. *Website:* www.thespecials.com; www.roddyradiation.com.

BYRNE, Benjamin (Ben) Michael James; British musician (drums); b. 8 March 1977, Warrington, Cheshire. *Career:* mem. Starsailor 2000–. *Recordings include:* albums: Love Is Here 2001, Silence Is Easy 2003, On the Outside 2005, All the Plans 2009. *Honours:* NME Awards for Brightest New Hope Award 2001. *Website:* www.starsailor.net.

BYRNE, David; American musician, songwriter, composer, director and writer; b. 14 May 1952, Dumbarton, Scotland; s. of Thomas Byrne and Emily Anderson Byrne (née Brown); m. Adele Lutz 1987; one c. *Education:* Rhode Island School of Design, Maryland Inst. Coll. of Art. *Career:* Founder-mem. Talking Heads 1974–92; solo artist, musician, composer, producer 1980–; producer for artists, including B-52s, Fun Boy 3, Margareth Menezes; producer Index Video 1983–; dir videotapes 1981–; designer stage sets, lighting, album covers and posters 1977–; f. Luaka Bop label 1988; Curator,

Meltdown festival, Southbank Centre, London 2015. *Compositions for film, television and theatre include:* Stop Making Sense 1984, The Knee Plays 1984, Alive from Off Center 1984, Dead End Kids 1986, True Stories 1986, Tribute 1986, The Kitchen Presents Two Moon July 1986, True Stories 1986, The Forest 1986, Something Wild 1986, The Last Emperor (Acad. Award for Best Music, Original Score 1988, Golden Globe Best Original Score - Motion Picture 1988, Grammy Award for Best Album of Original Instrumental Background Score Written for a Motion Picture or Television 1988, Los Angeles Film Critics Asscn Award for Best Music 1987) 1987, Married to the Mob 1988, A Rustling of Leaves: Inside the Philippine Revolution 1988, The Catherine Wheel 1988, Magicians of the Earth: The Giant Woman and The Lightning Man (TV) 1990, Magicians of the Earth: A Young Man's Dream and a Woman's Secret (TV) 1990, Blue in the Face 1995, In Spite of Wishing and Wanting 2002, Young Adam 2003, This Must be the Place (David di Donatello Award for Best Music and Best Song 2012) 2011. *Films include:* Stop Making Sense (actor) 1984, True Stories (actor, dir and co-screenwriter) 1986, Checking Out 1988, This Must Be the Place (as himself) 2011. *Recordings include:* albums: with Talking Heads: Talking Heads '77 1977, More Songs About Buildings And Food 1978, Fear Of Music 1979, Remain In Light 1980, The Name Of This Band Is Talking Heads 1982, Speaking In Tongues 1983, Stop Making Sense 1984, Little Creatures 1985, True Stories 1986, Naked 1988, Popular Favourites: Sand In The Vaseline 1992; solo: My Life In The Bush Of Ghosts (with Brian Eno) 1981, The Knee Plays 1985, The Forest 1988, Rei Momo 1989, Uh-Oh 1992, David Byrne 1994, Feelings 1997, Look Into The Eyeball 2001, Grown Backwards 2004, Big Love: Hymnal 2008, Everything that Happens will Happen Today (with Brian Eno) 2008, Here Lies Love (with Fatboy Slim) 2010, Love This Giant (with St Vincent) 2012, Caetano Veloso And David Byrne: Live At Carnegie Hall 2012. *Publications include:* Stay Up Late 1987, What the Songs Look Like 1987, Strange Ritual 1995, Bicycle Diaries 2009, How Music Works 2012. *Honours:* Film Critics Award for Best Documentary 1985, MTV Video Vanguard Award 1985, Music Video Producers Asscn Award 1992, inducted into Rock and Roll Hall of Fame 2002. *Current Management:* Maine Road Management, 195 Chrystie Street, Suite 901F, New York, NY 10002, USA. *Telephone:* (212) 979-9004. *Fax:* (212) 979-0985. *E-mail:* mailbox@maineroadmanagement.com. *Website:* www.maineroadmanagement.com; www.davidbyrne.com.

BYRNE, Nicholas (Nicky) Bernard James Adam; Irish singer and songwriter; b. 9 Oct. 1978, Dublin; m. Georgina Ahern 2003; three c. *Career:* mem., Westlife 1999–2012; numerous tours, festivals and TV appearances. *Recordings include:* albums: Westlife 1999, Coast to Coast 2000, World of our Own 2001, Unbreakable - The Greatest Hits 2002, Turnaround 2003, Face to Face 2005, The Love Album 2006, Back Home 2007, Where We Are 2009, Gravity 2010. *Honours:* BRIT Awards for Best Pop Act 2001, 2002, Meteor Ireland Music Award for Best Irish Pop Act 2005, 2006, 2007, 2008, 2009, 2010. *E-mail:* meryl@merylhoffmanmanagement.com. *Website:* www.merylhoffmanmanagement.com; www.nickybyrne.com.

BYWATER, (Richard) Buzby; British musician (string bass). *Career:* Founder-mem. Mack and The Boys, tours throughout Europe 1990–93; mem. The New Bushbury Mountain Daredevils 1992–; backing vocals for Slade; producer and songwriter for dance artists; topical songs for radio. *Recordings include:* with Mack and The Boys: Mack and The Boys, Downtime Love, The Unknown Legends; with The New Bushbury Mountain Daredevils: Bushwacked, The Yellow Album, Bushbury Mountain.

C

MR C; British rap artist, singer, musician (guitar), actor and record producer; b. (Richard West), 2 Jan. 1968, London. *Career:* joined The Shamen 1991–99; f. Plink Plonk record label 1992; Owner and DJ, The End dance club 1996–. *Recordings include:* albums: with The Shamen: Boss Drum 1992, Different Drum 1994, Axis Mutatis 1995, Hempton Manor 1996, UV 1998; solo: X-Mix,Vol. 6: The Electronic Storm 1996, DJ Collection, Vol. 3: Back to the Old School 1997, Mr C. Presents Subterrain 100% Unreleased 2000, Change 2002 Hip-no-tized 2003, Hold Up 2005, Superfreq Express 2007, Smell the Coffee 2013; singles: Make It Mine 1992, LSI (Love Sex Intelligence) 1992, Ebeneezer Goode 1992, Boss Drum 1992, Phorever People 1994, Transamazonia 1995, Destination Eschaton 1995, Hemp 1996, Move Any Mountain 1996, Universal 1998, U Nations 1998, A Thing Called Love 1998, Because 1998, The Birds and the Bees 1999, Nice 'n' Nasty 2001, Click 2002, The Club 2002, Circles of Love 2002, More Than Just a Dream 2003, You Are a Freak 2004, Lunar 2010, Something Strange 2012. *Address:* The End Ltd, Beaumount House, 47 Mount Pleasant, London, WC1X 0AE, England (office). *E-mail:* info@endclub.com (office). *Website:* www.endclub.com (office).

C, Melanie (see Chisholm, Melanie)

CABAS ROSALES, Andrés Mauricio; Colombian musician; b. 7 Oct. 1977, Barranquilla; m. Johana Bahamón 2007. *Career:* solo artist 2000–. *Recordings include:* albums: Cabas 2000, Contacto (MTV Latin Award for Best Rock Album) 2003, Puro Cabas 2005, De la Sombra a la Luz 2006, Amores Difíciles 2008, Pantaleón y las visitadoras 2010. *Honours:* MTV Latin Award for Best Rock Interpretation, Lo Nuestro Award for Best Rock Video, Lo Nuestro People's Award. *Telephone:* (786) 467-8461. *E-mail:* rizoalvaro@hotmail.com; alvaro.rizo@cabasmusic.com.

CABBLE, Lise; Danish songwriter, singer and musician (guitar); b. 10 Jan. 1958, Copenhagen. *Career:* Founder-mem. all-girl punk band, Clinic Q 1981; Founder-mem. singer, guitarist, songwriter rock band, Miss B Haven 1986–97; solo artist 1997–. *Recordings include:* with Miss B Haven: Miss B Haven 1987, Ice On Fire 1987, On Honeymoon 1988, Nobody's Angel 1990, Mellem hjerter og spar 1991, Suk and Stads 1994, Marta Marta 1996. *Honours:* Danish songwriter and singer awards, several awards with Miss B Haven.

CABELLO, (Karla) Camila; American singer; b. 3 March 1997, Cojimar, Cuba; d. of Alejandro Cabello and Sinuhe Cabello. *Career:* raised in Havana and Mexico; relocated to USA with parents aged five; when. Love You Like a Sister, renamed 1432, then renamed Fifth Harmony (or 5H) 2012–; contestants on US version of The X Factor (finished in third place) 2012; signed with Syco Music and Epic Records 2012; issued debut EP Better Together 2013; opening act on Cher Lloyd's I Wish tour 2013, on Demi Lovato's Neon Lights Tour 2014, on Austin Mahone's tour of North America and Brazil 2014; headlining act, MTV Artists to Watch concert 2014. *Television:* The X Factor (contestant on US series) 2012. *Recordings:* album: with Fifth Harmony: Reflection 2015. *Honours:* Teen Choice Single: Group Award 2014, MTV Video Music Artist to Watch Award 2014, MTV Europe Music Awards for Best North America Act, for Best US Act and for Best Worldwide Act 2014. *Address:* c/o Syco Music, Syco Entertainment, 9830 Wilshire Blvd, Beverly Hills, CA 90212, USA. *Website:* www.sycoentertainment.com; www .fifthharmonyofficial.com.

CABRA MARTÍNEZ, Eduardo José, (Visitante); Puerto Rican musician, producer and composer; b. 10 Sept. 1978, Santurce; half-brother of René Pérez Joglar (aka Residente). *Education:* Manolo Acosta School of the Arts, Univ. of Puerto Rico. *Career:* fmr mem. rock group Bayanga; formed Calle 13 with half-brother René Pérez Joglar, music combines influences from hip hop, reggaeton, cumbia, tango, electronica; collaborations with Voltio, Three 6 Mafia, Nelly Furtado, Alejandro Sanz. *Recordings include:* albums: Calle 13 (Latin Grammy Award for Best Urban Music Album 2006) 2005, Residente O Visitante (Latin Grammy Award for Best Urban Music Album 2007, Grammy Award for Best Latin Urban Album 2008) 2007, Los de Atrás Vienen Conmigo (Latin Grammy Awards for Best Album, for Best Urban Album 2009, Grammy Award for Best Latin Urban Album 2010) 2008, Entren Los Que Quien 2010 (Latin Grammy Award for Album of the Year 2011, Best Urban Music Album 2011), Multi Viral (Grammy Award for Best Latin Pop, Rock or Urban Album 2015) 2014. *Films include:* My Block, Puerto Rico (documentary) 2006, Singer, An Intimate Journey (documentary) 2009, Sin Mapa 2009. *Honours:* Best New Artist, MTV Latin Awards 2006, Best Urban Artist 2007, 2009, Latin Grammy Awards for Best New Artist and Best Short Form Music Video 2006, for Best Urban Song (for Pal Norte with Panasuyo and Orishas) 2007, for Best Recording (for No Hay Nadie Como Tú) 2009, for Best Alternative Song (No Hay Nadie Como Tú) 2009, for Best Short Form Music Video (La Perla) 2009, for Best Alternative Song (Calma Pueblo) 2011, for Best Urban Song (Baile de los Pobres) 2011, for Record of the Year (Latinoamérica) 2011, for Song of the Year (Latinoamérica) 2011, for Best Tropical Song (Vamo' a Portarnos Mal) 2011, Producer of the Year (with Rafael Arcaute) 2011, Best Short Form Music Video (Calma Pueblo) 2011. *Address:* c/o Sony Music Latin, 555 Madison Avenue, New York, NY 10022-3211, USA (office). *E-mail:* polo.lacalle13@ gmail.com; elvecindariocalle13@gmail.com. *Website:* lacalle13.com.

CACCIOTTOLO, Neil J., (Neil 'Guitar Man' Cacci), BA; Italian/American studio musician, arranger, producer, publisher and music educator; *Senior Editor, The Chicago Municipal News (CNN);* b. 9 Nov. 1953, Evergreen Park, Ill.; s. of Neil Cacciottolo and Marie Cacciottolo. *Education:* Southwest Coll., Omega School of Communications, Carnvale School of Music, Chicago, American Conservatory of Music, Chicago, Blackstone Law, Certified Legal Specialist for Copyright Law. *Career:* consults songwriters and artists, prepares budgets, various recording projects; music supervisor in all aspects of studio production; public relations services for major and independent artists; studio musician, involved with recording background music, demo production for song catalogues, commercial recordings; professional career 1969–; Publr, Harry Fox Agency; Sr Ed. Chicago Municipal News; Dir of Media, The Sunset Media Group; Chair. Chicago Music Partners (NFP); mem. American Fed. of Musicians, Local 47 Hollywood, CA, Production Signatory, City Club of Chicago; Voter-mem. NARAS; writer/publr ASCAP, top 2000 musicians of the 20th Century. *Radio:* plays for various Internet radio stations; local, regional and int. radio stations. *Television:* Synchronization Licensing; sound library for commercial announcements and synchronization for soundtrack movie trailers. *Recordings:* Part Time Love, Rhonda Lee, Bye Bye Baby, Lonely Highway, Love's Touch, Enchanted Meadow, Country Life, The Happy Traveller, Melinda; as producer: Regeneration (Reunion of Nashville's 'A' Team) 2004, Production Signatories, American Fed. of Musicians, Rock-A-Billy Friends, Anthology. *Publications:* The Do's and Don'ts of the Music Industry, Music Curriculum for Advanced Students. *Honours:* Hon. Dr of Letters in Music; CMA Record Promoter and Co. of the Year Award 1992, Int. Indie Gold Record Awards, Music Educational Speaker Award 2007, Producer's Award (NARAS). *Address:* 3400 West 111th Street, Unit 600, Chicago, IL 60655, USA (office). *Telephone:* (708) 371-9533 (office). *E-mail:* sunsetpromogrp@comcast.net (office). *Website:* www.sunsetchicago.com (office); legal.sunsetchicago.com (office). *Current Management:* c/o Sunset Management, Div. of Sunset Promotions of Chicago, Inc., 3400 West 111th Street, Unit 600, Chicago, IL 60655, USA. *Telephone:* (708) 371-9533. *E-mail:* twistedsoundrecords@gmail.com.

CACIA, Paul Scott; American musician (trumpet), bandleader and producer; b. 20 June 1956, Santa Ana, Calif.; m. Janine Cameo 1978; two d. *Education:* studied with Claude Gordon. *Career:* musician with: Calvin Jackson 1972, Louis Bellson Big Band 1973, Stan Kenton College Neophonic 1974, Buddy Miles Express 1975, Don Ellis Electric Orchestra 1976, Ray Anthony 1978, Al Hirt Big Band 1979; ind. musician and producer 1979–84; bandleader, The New Age Orchestra 1984–; Dir, Don Ellis Estate 1984–87; apptd Lecturer, Besson trumpets 1984; Chair., Stan Kenton Scholar Fund; mem. American Fed. of Musicians. *Recordings include:* albums: Unbelievable 1977, Disco 1979, Starting Now 1980, All in Good Time 1981, Believe It 1983, A Portrait in Time 1984, Quantum Leap 1984, Alumni Tribute Kenton 1987, The Symphony Album 2001, Opening Act 2004, Portrait 2004, Legacy 2006. *Current Management:* c/o Empressario, LLC, 10153 1/2 Riverside Drive, Suite 409, Toluca Lake, CA 91602, USA. *E-mail:* contact@paulcacia.com (office). *Website:* www.paulcacia.com.

CACTUS, Françoise; French singer, musician (guitar, drums), writer and artist; b. Sens. *Career:* fmr mem. Lolitas; Founder-mem. Stereo Total 1993–. *Recordings include:* albums: Oh Ah! 1995, Monokini 1997, Juke-Box Alarm 1999, My Melody 1999, Musique Automatique 2001, Do The Bambi 2005, Discotheque 2006, Paris-Berlin 2007, No Controles 2009, Baby Ouh! 2010. *Art exhibitions:* Hyäryllistä-gallery, Turku, Finland 2000, 'Girls & Animals' (with Stu Mead), Galerie Katze 5, Berlin 2001, 'Lolitas', Galerie Interconti, Hamburg 2002. *Publications:* novels: Autobigophonie 1997, Abenteuer einer Provinzblume 1999, Zitterparties 2000, Mitzi 2000, Neurosen zum Valentinstag 2004. *Current Management:* c/o Mathias Schwarz, Powerline Agency, Kastanienallee 29/30, 10435 Berlin, Germany. *E-mail:* ms@powerline-agency .com. *Website:* www.powerline-agency.com. *E-mail:* stereototal@flirt99.com. *Website:* www.stereototal.de.

CADBURY, Richard (Dik) Benjamin; British musician (bass, guitar), singer and composer; b. 12 June 1950, Selly Oak, Birmingham; m. Barbara 1979; two d. *Career:* toured, recorded with Decameron 1973–76; mem. Steve Hackett (bass and vocals) 1978–80, Mike D'Abo's Mighty Quintet, Top Catz 1991–, Dave Harper Band; tours include Reading Festival 1976, UK, Europe, North America 1980; owner, Millstream Recording Studio 1978–88; mem. Musicians' Union, PRS. *Compositions include:* Saturday, for Third Light (with Dave Bell). *Recordings:* albums: with Decameron: Mammoth Special 1974, Third Light 1975, Tomorrow's Pantomime 1976, Parabola Road 2004; with Steve Hackett: Spectral Mornings 1979, Defector 1980; solo: About Time 1999. *E-mail:* dik@dikcadbury.com (office). *Website:* www.dikcadbury.com.

CAENS, Thierry; French musician (trumpet); b. 24 Sept. 1958, Dijon; three c. *Education:* Paris Nat. Superior Conservatory with Maurice André. *Career:* fmr solo trumpet with Orchestre National de Lyon 1975; f. Quintette Arban (with Jean-Paul Leroy) 1976; fmr solo cornet with Paris Opera Orchestra 1982; Prof., Conservatory of Dijon 1985; apptd Dijon Cultural Amb. of the City of Dijon 2014; tours of Japan; creator, William Sheller Trumpet Concerto, Pleyel, Paris 1992; soloist, Cyrano, B O Music by Jean-Claude Petit; duo with Jean Guillou, Organ; Artistic Dir, Camerata de Bourgogne 1987; columnist,

Burgundy Magazine, France Bleu Bourgogne. *Recordings include:* Albums: Alla Francese 1993, Tangos and Milongas: The Heart of Argentinian Tango 1995, Haydn, Bach Brandenburg Concerts, Haydn, Jericho, La Belle Epoque 1998, Baroque Concertos and Suites, Cyrano, Honegger, Discovery, The Golden Age for Music for Winds, L'Art du Cornet a Pistons 1996, Absurd Machine 2000, Portrait of a Trumpeter 2000, Ten of the Best 2000, Impressions for Trumpet, From the Ground 2005, 3ème Souffle: Works for Trumpet & Orchestra 2006, Ostinato 2007, The Brass 3 2009, Le chant Libre 2012. *Honours:* Chevalier des Arts et Lettres; First prize, Paris Conservatory. *E-mail:* martine.croce@instantpluriel.com. *Address:* Thierry Caens Vivartis Association, 7 Rue de l'Ecole de Droit Porte X, Dijon 21000, France. *Telephone:* 3-80-53-00-45. *E-mail:* vivartis@thierrycaens.com. *Website:* www .thierrycaens.com.

CAFFEY, Charlotte Irene; American singer, musician (guitar, keyboards, bass) and songwriter; b. 21 Oct. 1953, Santa Monica, Calif.; d. of Ann Caffey and Michael Caffey; m. Jeff Mcdonald; one d. *Education:* Immaculate Heart Coll. *Career:* mem., the Go-Go's (formerly The Misfits) 1978–85; backing singer for Belinda Carlisle; songwriter and session musician for Belinda Carlisle; formed the band Graces (with Meredith Brooks and Gia Campbell) 1988; formed band Astrid's Mother after Graces split The Go-Go's re-formed briefly for PETA benefit concert 1990; mem., re-formed Go-Go's 1994, performed at numerous shows (with Jane Wiedlin) 1997; shows in Las Vegas; The Go-Go's re-formed 2000–, for an album and tours, including US tour with B-52's; Founder and Owner, Five Foot Two Records 2002; numerous collaborations with various artists. *Recordings include:* albums: with the Go-Go's: Beauty And The Beat 1981, Vacation 1982, The Go-Go's 1982, Talk Show 1984, Return To The Valley Of The Go-Go's 1994, God Bless The Go-Go's 2001; with the Graces: Perfect View 1989; other: played piano in Foolish Games (by Jewel), But for the Grace of God (with Keith Urban and Jane Wiedlin). *Plays:* Lovelace: A Rock Musical (West Garland Award for Best Musical Score, for Best Music Direction with Anna Waronker, Stage Scene LA Award for Best World Premier Musical). *Current Management:* c/o Direct Management, 947 North La Cienega Blvd, Los Angeles, CA 90069, USA. *Telephone:* (310) 854 3535. *E-mail:* info@directmanagement.com. *Website:* directmanagement.com. *E-mail:* gogos@beyondmusic.com (office). *Website:* www.gogos.com (office).

CAFFREY, Leon; British musician (drums). *Career:* member, The Farm; Hunkpapa; played with Squeeze and China Crisis; joined Space, 1998–2005; numerous tours and television appearances. *Recordings:* singles: The Ballad of Tom Jones (with Cerys Matthews), 1998; Begin Again, 1998; Bad Days, 1998; Diary of a Wimp, 2000; albums: Tin Planet, 1998; Greatest Hits, 2002, Suburban Rock 'N' Roll 2004.

CAHILL, Dennis M.; American guitarist and composer; b. 16 June 1954, Chicago, Ill. *Education:* Chicago Music Coll. *Career:* regular collaborator with fiddler Martin Hayes since mid-1980s; Founder-mem. The Gloaming 2011–; performer with musicians including Kevin Burke, Liz Carroll, Seamus Egan, P.J. Hayes, Eileen Ivers, Arty McGlynn, Laurence Nugent, Iarla Ó Lionáird, Liam O'Flynn, Laura Risk. *Recordings:* albums: with Martin Hayes: The Lonesome Touch 1997, Live in Seattle 1999, Welcome Here Again 2008; with The Gloaming: The Gloaming 2014. *E-mail:* m@barquemgmt.com. *Website:* barquemgmt.com; thegloaming.net.

CAILLAT, Colbie; American singer, songwriter and musician (guitar); b. 28 May 1985, Newbury Park, Calif.; d. of Ken Caillat. *Career:* began writing songs with Mikal Blue 2004; began professional singing career after posting songs on Myspace 2005–. *Recordings:* albums: CoCo 2007, Breakthrough 2009. *Honours:* BMI Pop Awards for Songwriter of the Year 2009, for Song of the Year (for Bubbly) 2009, Grammy Award for Best Pop Collaboration with Vocals (for Lucky with Jason Mraz) 2010. *Current Management:* c/o Chad Jensen, The Fitzgerald Hartley Company, 34 North Palm Street, Suite 100, Ventura, CA 93001, USA. *Telephone:* (805) 641-6441. *Fax:* (805) 641-6444. *E-mail:* cjallclear@earthlink.net. *Website:* www.fitzhart.com; www .colbiecaillat.com.

CAIN, Jonathan; American musician (keyboards, guitar, harmonica), songwriter, producer and singer; b. (Jonathan Leonard Friga), 26 Feb. 1950, Chicago, Ill.; m. Elizabeth Yvette Fullerton 1989; three c. *Education:* Chicago Conservatory of Music. *Career:* mem. The Babys; mem. Journey 1981–87, 1995–; mem. Bad English 1988–91; mem. Hardline 1992–; also solo artist; numerous concerts, festival appearances and tours; contributed to solo albums of Neal Schon. *Recordings include:* albums: with Babys: The Babys 1977, Broken Heart 1977, Head First 1979, Union Jacks 1980, On the Edge 1980, Anthology 1981; with Journey: Journey 1975, Look into the Future 1976, Next 1977, Infinity 1978, Evolution 1979, Departure 1980, Escape 1981, Frontiers 1983, Raised On Radio 1986, Greatest Hits 1989, Trial By Fire 1996, When You Love A Woman 1996, Remember Me 1998, Arrival 2001, Generations 2005, Revelation 2008, Eclipse 2011; with Bad English: Bad English 1989, Backlash 1991; with Hardline: Double Eclipse 1992, II 2002, Leaving the End Open 2009; solo albums: Windy City Breakdown 1977, Back To The Innocence 1995, Piano With A View 1997, Body Language 1997, For A Lifetime 1998, Namaste 2001, Anthology 2001, Animated Movie Love Songs 2002, Bare Bones 2004, Where I Live 2006. *Honours:* BMI Songwriter Award (Open Arms and Who's Crying Now?). *Address:* PO Box 1393, Franklin Park, IL 60131 USA. *E-mail:* jonathan@jonathancain.com. *Website:* www.jonathancain.com; www.journeymusic.com.

CAINE, Uri; American jazz pianist and classical composer; b. 8 June 1956, Philadelphia; s. of Burton Caine. *Education:* Univ. of Pennsylvania. *Career:* began studying piano with Bernard Pfeiffer; played in bands led by Philly Joe Jones, Johnny Coles, Odean Pope, Hank Mobley, Grover Washington, Mickey Roker and Jymmie Merritt during high school; studied music composition with George Crumb and George Rochberg at Univ. of Pennsylvania and performed with Joe Henderson, Donald Byrd, J. J. Johnson, Stanley Turrentine, Lester Bowie and Freddie Hubbard; Composer-in-Residence, Los Angeles Chamber Orchestra 2006–09, Mannes Coll. 2013–14; performed in groups led by Don Byron, Dave Douglas, John Zorn, Terry Gibbs and Buddy DeFranco, Clark Terry, Rashid Ali, Arto Lindsay, Sam Rivers and Barry Altschul, Bobby Watson, Annie Ross, The Enja Band, Global Theory, The Woody Herman Band, The Master Musicians of Jajouka; performed at What is Jazz? Festival, New York, North Sea Jazz Festival, The Hague, Montréal Jazz Festival, Jazz Across the Borders, Berlin, Texaco Jazz Festival, NY, Umbria Jazz Festival, Gustav Mahler Festival, Toblach, Italy, Vittoria Jazz Festival, San Sebastian Jazz Festival, Newport Jazz Festival, Salzburg Festival, Munich Opera, Holland Festival, Israel Festival, IRCAM and others; numerous recordings with piano trio, Bedrock trio and versions of music by Mahler, Mozart,Verdi and others. *Compositions include:* ballet composed for Vienna Volksoper 2000, version of Diabelli Variations for Concerto Köln 2001, Mahler Reimagined, London 2002. *Recordings include:* 25 CD recordings including albums: Sphere Music 1993, Toys 1995, Urlicht/Primal Light 1996, Wagner e Veneza 1997, Blue Wail 1998, Sidewalks of New York 1999, Love Fugue 2000, The Goldberg Variations 2000 (performed by Pennsylvania Ballet 2001), Solitaire 2001, Rio 2001, Bedrock3 2001, Shelf-Life (with Bedrock) 2005, Closure (with Mark O'Leary and Ben Perowsky) 2006, Things (with Paolo Fresu) 2006, Uri Caine Ensemble Plays Mozart 2006, Pure Affection (with Gust Tsillis) 2007, The Othello Syndrome 2008, Secrets (with Mark Feldman, Greg Cohen and Joey Baron) 2009, Think (with Paolo Fresu and Alborada String Quartet) 2009, Plastic Temptation (with Bedrock) 2009, Twelve Caprices (with Arditti String Quartet) 2010, Siren 2011, Sonic Boom (with Han Bennink) 2012, Rhapsody in Blue 2013, Callithump 2014, Present Joys (with Dave Douglas) 2014. *Honours:* Toblacher Komponierhäuschen Award for Best Mahler CD 1997. *E-mail:* uricaine@verizon.net. *Website:* www .uricaine.com.

CAINES, Ronald Arthur; British musician (saxophonist); b. 13 Dec. 1939, Bristol; m. Susan Weaver 1958, one s. two d. *Education:* West of England Coll. of Art. *Career:* worked extensively in Europe, especially France, Switzerland, UK college circuit; played in Keith Tippett's Big Band, Ark; also with: Julie Tippett; Evan Parker 1970s; f. East of Eden band; played improvised and Latin based music, led modern jazz quartet; mem. Performing Right Soc., Musicians' Union (delegate). *Compositions include:* Northern Hemisphere; Bathers of Lake Balaton; Isadora; music for film Laughter in the Dark 1969. *Recordings:* Mercator Projected; SNAFU; The World of East of Eden. *E-mail:* roncainesweb@aol.com. *Website:* www.roncaines.co.uk; www .eastofedentheband.com.

CAIRNS, Andy; Irish singer and musician (guitar); b. 22 Sept. 1965, Ballyclare. *Career:* Founder-mem. rock group Therapy? 1989–; numerous live appearances. *Recordings include:* albums: Babyteeth 1991, Pleasure Death 1992, Nurse 1992, Troublegum 1994, Infernal Love 1995, Semi-Detached 1998, Suicide Pack – You First 1999, So Much For The Ten Year Plan 2000, Shameless 2001, High Anxiety 2003, Never Apologise Never Explain 2004, One Cure Fits All 2006, Crooked Timber 2009, A Brief Crack of Light 2012. *E-mail:* churchofnoise@therapyquestionmark.co.uk. *Website:* www .therapyquestionmark.co.uk.

CALAMARO, Andrés; Argentine musician and composer; b. (Andrés Calamaro Masel), 22 Aug. 1961, Buenos Aires. *Career:* formed Elmer Band; fmr mem. Raíces, Los Abuelos de la Nada, Los Rodríguez 1991–97; solo artist 1984–; producer for other bands and soloists; tours around Latin America, Spain. *Recordings include:* albums: with Raíces: B.O.V. Dombe 1978; with Abuelos de la Nada: Los Abuelos de la Nada 1982, Vasos y Besos 1983, Himno de mi Corazón 1984, En Directo desde el Opera 1985; with Los Rodríguez: Buena Suerte 1991, Disco Pirate 1992, Disco Pirata 1992, Sin Documentos 1993, Palabras Más, Palabras Menos 1995, Hasta Luego 1997; solo: Hotel Calamaro 1984, Vida cruel 1985, Por mirarte 1988, Nadie sale vivo de aquí 1990, Grabaciones encontradas volumen uno 1993, Caballos salvajes (soundtrack) 1995, Live en Ayacucho 1994, Caballos salvajes 1995, Grabaciones encontradas volumen dos 1996, Alta suciedad 1997, Las otras caras de Alta Suciedad 1998, Honestidad brutal 1999, El salmón 2000, El cantante 2004, El regreso 2005, Tinta roja 2006, El palacio de las flores 2006, La lengua popular (Latin Grammy Award for Best Rock Solo Vocal Album 2008) 2007, Dos son Multitud 2008, Nada se Pierde 2009, On the Road 2010, Bohemio 2014; singles: Tristeza de la Ciudad. *Honours:* Premio Gardel de Oro 2006, 2008, Latin Grammy Award for Best Rock Song 2014. *Website:* www.calamaro.com.

CALAZANS, Teca; Brazilian composer and singer; b. 27 Oct. 1940, Vitoria, Espirito Santo; m. Philippe Lesage 1991; one d. *Career:* former actress; performed at Olympia, with Claude Nougaro; lieved in France for 10 years, returned to Brazil 1979–88; compère television show for three years; numerous live appearances, festivals. *Compositions:* Côco Verde, Gabriel, Caíco (sung by Milton Nascimento), Firuliu (sung by Nara Leâo), Atras da luminosidade (sung by Gal Costa). *Recordings include:* Musiques et Chants du Brasil 1974, Caminho das Aguas 1975, Cade o Povo 1975, Desafio de Viola 1978, Povo Daqui 1980, Eu Nao Sou Dos 1981, Teca Calazans 1982, Mário

Trezentos 350 1983, Jardin Exotique 1983, Mina do Mar 1985, Teca Calazans Chante Villa Lobos 1990, Pizindim 1991, Intuiçao 1993, O Samba dos Bambas 1994, Firoliu 1997, Forro de Cara Nova 1998, Alma De Tupi 2000, Cantoria Brasileira (with Elomar, Xangai, Pena Brance, Renato Teixeira), Teca Calazans & Heraldo Do Monte 2003, Impressões sobre Mauricio Carrilho & Meira 2007. *Publications:* Nordeste' Song 2002, Brazil: Cantadores and Repentistas 2002. *E-mail:* tecalazans@wanadoo.fr; info@tecacalazans.com. *Website:* www.tecacalazans.com.

CALCANHOTTO, Adriana, (Adriana Partimpim); Brazilian singer and songwriter; b. 3 Oct. 1965, Porto Alegre; d. of Carlos Calcanhotto and Morgada Assumpção Cunha; pnr Suzana de Morães. *Career:* began career singing in bars around Porto Alegre; professional solo singer 1984–; collaborated with Wally Salomão, António Cicero. *Compositions include:* Tua, performed by Maria Bethânia (Latin Grammy Award for Best Brazilian Song 2010). *Recordings:* Enguiço 1990, Senhas 1992, A Fábrica do Poema 1994, Maritmo 1998, Público 2000, Cantada 2002, Adriana Partimpim (Latin Grammy Award for Best Album for Children) 2004, Maré 2008, Adriana Partimpim Dois 2009. *Publications:* Algumas Letras 2003, Saga Lusa: O Relato de uma Viagem 2008. *E-mail:* jleonard@uol.com.br (office). *Website:* www.adrianacalcanhotto .com.

CALDER, Clive; South African/British music company executive; b. 1946, Johannesburg; m.; two c. *Career:* Founder CCP Records, South Africa 1972; Founder Chair. and CEO, Zomba Music Group mid-1970s–2002; Founder Jive Records, Zomba Books, Zomba Man., Zomba Music Publrs; sold Zomba Music Group to BMG Music 2002, remained in advisory role to the co. *Address:* c/o Zomba Music Group, BMG Music, Times Square, 1540 Broadway, New York, NY 10036, USA.

CALE, John; British singer, musician (bass, keyboards, viola) and producer; b. 9 March 1942, Garnant, Wales. *Education:* classical music training. *Career:* mem., The Dream Syndicate; founder mem., The Velvet Underground 1964–68, 1993; solo artist 1970–; residency, Café Bizarre, Greenwich Village 1966; house band, Andy Warhol's Factory arts collective, New York 1966; Reunion, with Lou Reed, Nico 1972; reunion with Velvet Underground, European tour 1993; prod. for artists, including Nico, Iggy Pop, Patti Smith, Jonathan Richman, Squeeze, Happy Mondays, Siouxsie and The Banshees. *Recordings include:* albums: with The Velvet Underground: The Velvet Underground and Nico 1967, White Light, White Heat 1968, Live MCMXCIII 1993; solo: Vintage Violence 1970, Church of Anthrax 1971, Academy in Peril 1972, Paris 1919 1973, Fear 1974, June 1 1974 1974, Slow Dazzle 1975, Helen of Troy 1975, Guts 1977, Animal Justice 1977, Sabotage 1979, Honi Soit 1981, Music For A New Society 1982, Caribbean Sunset 1984, Comes Alive 1984, Artificial Intelligence 1985, Words For The Dying 1989, Fragments of a Rainy Season 1992, Walking on Locusts 1996, Dance Music 1998, Le Vent de la Nuit 1999, Close Watch 1999, Black Acetate 2005, Circus Live 2006; with Lou Reed: Songs For Drella 1990; with Brian Eno: Wrong Way Up 1991; with Bob Neuwirth: Last Day On Earth 1994. *Film scores:* Sid and Nancy 1982, Paris S'Eveille 1991, La Naissance de l'Amour 1993, Antartida 1995, N'oublie pas que tu vas mourir 1996, I Shot Andy Warhol 1997, Eat and Kiss 1997. *Honours:* Hon. Fellow Goldsmiths Coll., London 1997. *Website:* www.myspace .com/johncaleofficialsite.

CALHOUN, William (Will); American musician (drums); b. 22 July 1964, Brooklyn, New York. *Education:* Berklee College of Music. *Career:* mem. Living Colour 1984–95, 2000–; mem. band Stone Raiders; also played with Jungle Funk and HeadFake; appeared as Sideman with Pharoah Sanders, B.B. King, Herb Alpert, Dr. John, Jaco Pastorius, Wayne Shorter and others. *Recordings:* albums: with Living Colour: Vivid 1988, Time's Up 1990, Biscuits 1991, Stain 1993, Collideøscope 2003, The Chair in the Doorway 2009; with Stone Raiders: Truth to Power 2012; solo: Live at the Blue Note 2000, Native Lands 2005, Life in this World 2012. *Honours:* Buddy Rich Jazz Masters Award (for outstanding performance as drummer), Best New Drummer 1988 and Number One Progressive Drummer 1989, 1991, 1992, Modern Drummer Magazine, International Rock Awards Elvis Award for Best New Band 1989, MTV Award for Best New Artist, for Best Group Video, for Best Stage Performance 1989, Grammy Awards for Best Hard Rock Performance (for Cult of Personality) 1990, (for Time's Up) 1991, Rolling Stone Critics Poll Winner for Best Band 1991 and Best Drummer of 1990, International Rock Award for Best Rock Band (Living Colour) 1991. *Address:* Too Fly Productions, Inc., POB 857, Baychester Station, Bronx, New York, NY 10469, USA. *Website:* www.willcalhoun.com; livingcolour.com.

CALIX, Mira; South African composer, producer and artist; b. (Chantal Francesca Passamonte), 1974, Durban. *Career:* fmr publicist, Warp Records; solo artist 1996–. *Art installations:* My Secret Heart (British Composers Award for Best Community or Educational Project 2009), Chorus, Natures, Strata, Nothing Is Set In Stone, Passage, Inside There Falls, Ada project, Moving Museum 35. *Play:* The Oresteia. *Film soundtracks:* Transparent Roads, Onibus, Strata #2 2009, Fables – A Film Opera, The Adventures of Prince Achmed – Lotte Reineger 2010, Champagne – Alfred Hitchcock 2012. *Film:* The More That You Appear (video art). *Commissions:* Sonnet 130 for Royal Shakespeare Company, Dead Wedding for Opera North and Manchester Int. Festival, Elephant and Castle for Aldeburgh Festival, Ort Oard and Rock Remix for London Sinfonietta, Natures for Faster Than Sound Festival, Nunu for the Ether Festival, Chorus for United Visual Artists, My Secret Heart for Streetwise Opera (Royal Philharmonic Soc. Award), Nunu Wadudu

mix for BMIC, She'll Be Around for the ICA, Strata #2 (Best Original Soundtrack, Rencontres Audiovisuelles) 2009, Fables – A Film Opera 2011, Field Recordings – Bang on a Can 2012, He Fell Amongst Roses 2013, If Then While For 2014. *Recordings include:* albums: One on One 2000, Vol. 4: Skimskitta 2003, 3 Commissions 2004, Eyes Set Against the Sun 2007, The Elephant In The Room: three commissions 2008. *Honours:* Quercus Lamu Bursary, Grant for the Arts 2009, Royal Philharmonic Soc. Award 2009, British Composer Award 2009, Prix Ars Electronica – Award of Distinction 2010. *Current Management:* c/o Warp Records, PO Box 25378, London, NW5 1GL, England. *Telephone:* (20) 7284-8350. *E-mail:* info@warprecords.com. *E-mail:* carpel@miracalix.com. *Website:* www.miracalix.com.

CALLE, Eduardo (Ed) Joaquin, MMus, EdD; American musician (saxophone), composer, arranger and teacher; *Associate Professor of Music Business and Production, Miami Dade College*; b. 10 Aug. 1959, Caracas, Venezuela; m. Sari Calle; three c. *Education:* Univ. of Miami, Nova Southeastern Univ. *Career:* solo artist; recorded and toured with int. artists including Frank Sinatra, Gloria Estefan, Vikki Carr, Julio Iglesias, Arturo Sandoval, Regina Belle; currently Assoc. Prof. of Music Business and Production, Miami Dade Coll.; mem. PALO!, Miami Saxophone Quartet, World Music 5. *Recordings include:* solo albums (original compositions and arrangements): Nightgames 1985, Tenderfly 1994, Double-talk 1996, Sunset Harbor 1999, Colors of the World: Bolero and Jazz 1999, Jam Miami 2000, Playboy Jazz 2001, Ed. Calle plays Santana 2004, In the Zone 2006, Dr Ed Calle Presents Mamblue (Latin Grammy Award for Best Instrumental Album 2015) 2015. *Publications include:* Music as a Branch of Mathematics 2007, Remedial Mathematics: Online vs. Face-to-Face: Comparison of Online and Traditional Community College Math Remediation 2012; numerous teaching books for the saxophone. *Current Management:* c/o The Jazz Agency, 18375 Ventura Blvd, Suite 430, Tarzana, CA 91356, USA. *Telephone:* (818) 813-5299. *E-mail:* info@thejazzagency.com. *Website:* www.thejazzagency.com. *Address:* School of Entertainment and Design Studies, Commercial Music Department, Miami Dade College, Room 8213-2, 11011 SW 104th Street, Miami, FL 33176, USA (office). *Telephone:* (305) 237-0593 (office). *Fax:* (305) 237-2772 (office). *E-mail:* ecalle@mdc.edu (office); dredcalle@gmail.com. *Website:* www.drcalle .com (office); www.edcalle.com.

CALLEROS, Juan Diego; Mexican bass guitarist and songwriter; b. 19 April 1962, Guadalajara. *Career:* mem. Sombrero Verde 1978–85; Founder mem. Maná 1986–; group f. Salva Negra Foundation (financing and supporting projects to protect environment) 1995–; over 25 million records sold worldwide; numerous int. tours. *Recordings:* albums: with Sombrero Verde: Sombrero Verde 1981, A Tiempo de Rock 1983; with Maná: Falta Amor 1990, ¿Dónde Jugarán Los Niños? 1992, Cuando los Ángeles Lloran 1995, Sueños Liquidos (Grammy Award for Best Latin Rock/Alternative Performance 1999, Premio Lo Nuestro for Pop Album of the Year 1999) 1997, Maná MTV Unplugged (Ritmo Latino Music Award for Album of the Year 2000) 1999, Revolución de Amor (Billboard Latin Music Awards for Latin Rock Album of the Year 2003, for Latin Pop Album of the Year – Duo or Group 2003, Grammy Award for Best Latin Rock/Alternative Album 2003, Latin Grammy Award for Best Rock Album by a Duo or Group 2003, Premio Lo Nuestro for Rock Album of the Year 2003, Ritmo Latino Music Award for Album of the Year 2003) 2002, Amar es Combatir (Billboard Latin Music Award for Latin Rock/Alternative Album of the Year 2007, Grammy Award for Best Latin Rock/Alternative Album 2007, Premio Lo Nuestro for Rock Album of the Year 2007) 2007, Arde el Cielo (Billboard Latin Music Awards for Latin Pop Album of the Year – Duo or Group 2009, for Latin Rock/Alternative Album of the Year 2009) 2008, Drama y Luz (Latin Grammy Award for Best Rock Album 2011, Premio People en Español Award for Best Album 2011, Grammy Award for Best Latin Pop, Rock or Urban Album 2012, Premio Lo Nuestro Award for Rock/Alternative Award of the Year 2012) 2011, Cama Incendiada (Latin Grammy Award for Best Pop/Rock Album 2015) 2015; other contribs include: Supernatural, Santana 1999. *Honours:* apptd FAO Goodwill Amb. 2003; with Maná: Premios Lo Nuestro for Best Pop Group 1997, 1999, 2000, for Pop Song of the Year (for Mariposa Traicionera) 2004, for Rock Song of the Year (for Labios Compartidos) 2007, (for Bendita Tu Luz) 2008, for Rock Artist of the Year 2007, 2008, for Lifetime Achievement 2011, for Rock/Alternative Artist of the Year 2012, Ritmo Latino Music Award for Best Solo or Rock Group Artist 1999, Premios Oye! Special Social Prize to Music 2002, Award for Best Solo or Group Artist 2003, Mexican Public Commercial Award 2004, MasterTone Award (for Labios Compartidos) 2007, Latin Grammy Awards for Record of the Year 2000, for Best Rock Performance by a Duo or Group (both with Santana, for Corazón Espinado) 2000, for Best Pop Performance by a Duo or Group with Vocal (for Se Me Olvidó Otra Vez) 2000, Latin Grammy Special Award for Musical Accomplishments 2006, Billboard Latin Awards for Pop Airplay Song of the Year – Duo or Group (for Labios Compartidos) 2007, for Latin Tour of the Year 2008, for Hot Latin Song of the Year – Duo or Group (for Si No Te Hubieras Ido) 2009, for Latin Pop Airplay Song of the Year – Duo or Group (for Si No Te Hubieras Ido) 2009, for Latin Duet or Group Songs 2012, for Latin Duet or Group Album 2012, for Latin Pop Duet or Group of the Year Songs 2012, for Latin Pop Duet or Group of the Year Album 2012, Premio Juventud Supernova Award 2006, Premios Juventud for Favorite Rock Artist 2007, 2008, 2009, 2011, 2012, World Music Awards for World's Best Selling Latin Group 2007, for Best Selling Latin American Artist 2007, Los Premios 40 Principales for Best Concert/Tour 2007, 2011, Pan American Health Org. Champions of Health (for Salva Negra Foundation), World Health Day 2008, Premios Telehit for Best Int. Mexican Band 2011, Premio People en Español

Award for Best Rock Artist or Group 2011, Premio Cadena Dial 2011, Premio Casandra Internacional 2012. *Address:* c/o Warner Music Mexico, SA de C.V. Leibnitz 32 Col., Nueva Anzures, México, DF 11590, Mexico (office). *Telephone:* (55) 5279-3800 (office). *Website:* www.warnermusic.com.mx (office); www.mana.com.mx.

CALLIS, (John William) Jo; British musician and songwriter; b. 2 May 1951, Rotherham, Yorkshire. *Education:* Edinburgh Coll. of Art. *Career:* mem. of several bands, including The Human League, The Rezillos, Shake, Boots for Dancing; co-writer with many other artists; mem. BAC&S. *Recordings include:* albums: with The Human League: Reproduction 1979, Dare 1981, Love and Dancing 1982, Hysteria 1984, Crash 1986, Romantic? 1990, Octopus 1995, Greatest Hits 1996, Secrets 2001, The Very Best of the Human League 2003, Credo 2011, Sight and Sound 2012, All the Best 2013, Greatest Ever! Electric Eighties 2013; with The Rezillos: Can't Stand The Rezillos 1978, Mission Accomplished...But the Best Goes On 1979, Can't Stand the Rezillos: The (Almost) Complete Rezillos 1993; with Shake: Culture Shock (EP) 1979. *Honours:* BRIT Award for Best British Breakthrough Act 1982, Q Award for Innovation in Sound 2004 (The Human League), ASCAP Award (for Don't You Want Me), (Keep Feeling) Fascination) 2008. *Address:* 3A Rochester Terrace, Edinburgh, EH10 5AA, Scotland. *Telephone:* (131) 447-6273. *E-mail:* mjcallis08@btinternet.com. *Website:* www.rezillos.com (office); www .thehumanleague.co.uk (office).

CALZADO, David; Cuban singer, songwriter, musician (violin) and producer, bandleader, music director and vocalist; b. (Sergio David Calzado Almenares), 1957. *Education:* Escuela Nacional de Arte. *Career:* played with father's band and Orquesta Ritmo Oriental; produced records for Cuban record co., Egrem; became first violin at Tropicana in Havana; formed band for summer season at Sporting Club of Monaco, La Charanga Habanera 1988–, supporting artists, including Whitney Houston, Barry White, Charles Aznavour; band re-launched with new line up 1993–97; re-formed band with new mems. *Recordings include:* albums: Me Sube La Fiebre 1992, Hey You, Loca! 1994, Pa'Que Se Entere la Habana 1995, Love Fever 1996, Tremendo Delirio 1997, El Charanguero Mayor 2000, Chan Chan Charanga 2001, Marina, quiere bailar! 2003, Soy Cubano, Sou Popular 2003, Charanga Light 2004, El Ciclón de la Habana 2005, Light 2006, El Rey de Los Charangueros 2007, Pa Que Se Entere La Habana 2007, La Caratula 2009. *Current Management:* c/o COVENT — Consulting Marketing and Advertising, Leguario Avenue 49, office 5 Parla, Madrid, Spain. *Telephone:* (91) 0052096. *E-mail:* comunicacion@covent.es. *Website:* www.covent.es. *E-mail:* info@ charangahabanera.net. *Website:* www.charangahabanera.net.

CAMARA DE LANDA, Enrique Guillermo, PhD; Argentine/Spanish ethnomusicologist; *Professor (Catedrático de Universidad), University of Valladolid;* b. 3 May 1951, Buenos Aires. *Education:* Argentinian Catholic Univ., Buenos Aires, Univ. of Valladolid. *Career:* Prof. of Ethnomusicology, Univ. de Valladolid; mem, Vice-Pres., SIbE (Soc. de Etnomusicología); SEdEM (Soc. Española de Musicología): IASPM-LA; AAM (Asociación Argentina de Musicología). *Publications include:* books: La música de la baguala del Noroeste argentino 1994, Etnomusicología 2003, De Huahuaca a La Quiaca: identidad y mestizaje en la música de un carnaval andino 2006; books (ed.): Approaches to African Music 2006, Sangita y Natya: Música y artes escénicas de la India 2006; CD-ROMs: Manual de Transcripción y Análisis de la Música de Tradición Oral, La Universidad en el Cambio de Siglo 2006, El Espacio Europeo de Educación Superior 2006, Patrocinio, mecenazgo y gerencia en la Universidad del Siglo XXI 2006; DVDs: Sitar 2006, Mridangam 2006, Vina 2006, Canto carnático 2006; CDs: Calypsos 1988, Argentina: Charanda y chamamé 1992, Argentina: Carnaval 1994, Passione argentina: tanghi italiani degli anni 30 1999; also dir of audiovisual collections; contrib. chapters to books and articles in int. journals and magazines. *Address:* Historia y Ciencias de la Música, Facultad de Filosofía, y Letras. Universidad de Valladolid, Plaza del Campus, 47011 Valladolid, Spain. *Telephone:* (98) 3423000 (office). *Fax:* (98) 34233596 (office). *E-mail:* engcamara@gmail.com (home); camara@fyl .uva.es (home). *Website:* www.musicologiahispana.com (home).

CAMBUZAT, François R.; Spanish singer, musician (guitar) and composer. *Career:* mem. ATTAC. *Recordings include:* with the Kim Squad: Young Bastards 1987; solo: Notre-Dame des Naufragés 1988, Uccidiamo Kim 1990; with Il Gran Teatro Amaro: Port-Famine 1991, Hôtel Brennesel 1993, Piazza Orphelins 1995; with F R Cambuzat et les Enfants Rouges: Swinoujscie-Tunis 1995, Reus-Ljubljana 1998, Taurisano-Cajarc 1998, Reus-Ljubljana 1998; with L'Enfance Rouge: Davos-Legros 1999, Rostock-Mamur 2002, Krsko-Valencia 2005, Tràpani-Al Halq Waady 2008, Bar-Bari 2011; various compilations. *E-mail:* info@enfancerouge.org. *Website:* www.enfancerouge.net.

CAMERON, Chris; British musician (keyboards), arranger and producer. *Career:* worked with Hot Chocolate, Wham!, George Michael (also his music dir), Stevie Nicks, Terence Trent D'Arby, Breathe, Take That, Presumptos Implicados, Pepsi and Shirlie, A1, Gary Barlow, Joe Cocker, Randy Crawford, Chris De Burgh, Will Downing, Stephen Duffy, Elton John, John Martyn, 911, Pet Shop Boys, Steps, Tina Turner. *Address:* c/o Richard Muhammed, 30 Great Portland Street, London, W1W 8QU, England (office).

CAMERON, Kate; British singer, songwriter and musician (piano, French horn); b. 14 Nov. 1965, Hemel Hempstead, Hertfordshire, England. *Education:* Univ. of Sussex, Middlesex Univ. *Career:* lead vocalist, backing vocalist, vocal arranger, writer with GMT 1990–92; worked with Doug Wimbish, Bob Jones, John Waddell, Q; Host of Singers Nightclub; Musical Dir, Minx, all-

female cabaret a cappella group 1993–95; session singer for artists including Norman Cook 1994; Head of Vocals, Brighton Inst. of Modern Music 2002–; mem., Musicians' Union, Variety Artist's Asscn. *Recordings include:* P.A.S.S.I.O.N., Jon Of The Pleased Wimmin 1995, with Freak Power (backing vocals), Rush, Get In Touch 1994. *Address:* Brighton Institute of Modern Music, 38-42 Brunswick Street, Hove, BN3 1EL, England (office). *Telephone:* (44) 264-6666 (office). *E-mail:* info@bimm.co.uk (office). *Website:* www.bimm .co.uk (office).

CAMERON, Matt; American musician (drums), singer and songwriter; b. 28 Nov. 1962, San Diego, Calif.; m. April Acevez; one s. one d. *Career:* mem. heavy rock group, Soundgarden 1986–97, 2010–; mem. Temple of the Dog 1992, Hater 1993, Wellwater Conspiracy 1998–, Pearl Jam 1998–; numerous tours and festival appearances. *Film compositions include:* Attack of the Killer Tomatoes (Puberty Love) 1978, Spider-Man (Hero) 2002. *Recordings include:* albums: with Soundgarden: Ultramega OK 1988, Louder Than Love 1989, Badmotorfinger 1991, Superunknown 1994, Down On The Upside 1996, A-Sides 1997, King Animal 2012; with Temple of the Dog: Temple Of The Dog 1992; with Hater: Hater 1993, The 2nd 2007; with Wellwater Conspiracy: Declaration Of Conformity 1997, Brotherhood Of Electric: Operational Directives 1999, The Scroll and Its Combinations 2001, Wellwater Conspiracy 2003; with Pearl Jam: Binaural 2000, Riot Act 2002, Pearl Jam 2006, Backspacer 2009, Lightning Bolt 2013; other: compilation album with Half Japanese, Adil Omar and Penn Jillette 2010, Fingerprints (with Peter Frampton) 2006. *Honours:* Grammy Award (for Black Hole Sun) 1994. *Website:* www.pearljam.com; soundgardenworld.com.

CAMILLE; French singer; b. (Camille Dalmais), 1978, Paris. *Education:* Institut d'Etudes Politiques, Paris. *Career:* performed with Nouvelle Vague 2004–05; performed Benjamin Britten's A Ceremony of Carols and a new a cappella work God is Sound (The 12 World Prayers), L'église Saint-Eustache, Paris 2007; collaborations with Seb Martel, Franck Monnet, Gerard Manset, Jean-Louis Murat. *Music for film:* Flight of the Red Balloon 2006. *Recordings:* albums: Le Sac des Filles 2002, Le Fil (Prix Constantin, Revelation of the Year, Victoires de la Musique 2006) 2005, Music Hole 2008. *Honours:* BBC Radio 3 Awards for World Music (Winner, Europe) 2007, Best Female Artist, Victoires de la Musique 2009. *Current Management:* c/o Blonde Music, 29 avenue Mac Mahon, 75017 Paris, France. *Telephone:* 1-56-60-45-45. *E-mail:* blonde@blondemusic.com. *Website:* www.blondemusic.com; www.camille-lefil .com.

CAMILO, Michel; Dominican Republic jazz musician (piano) and composer; b. 4 April 1954, Santo Domingo; m. Sandra Camilo 1975. *Education:* Nat. Conservatory, Santo Domingo, Mannes and Juilliard School of Music, New York. *Career:* mem. Nat. Symphony Orchestra, Santo Domingo 1970, conductor 1987; moved to New York 1979; debut at Carnegie Hall with trio 1985; Musical Dir Heineken Jazz Festival, Dominican Rep. 1987–92; guest soloist with numerous orchestras 1994–; Co-Artistic Dir Latin-Caribbean Music Festival, Washington, DC 1998; toured internationally with Paquito D'Rivera; Prof. Emer., Univ. Autónoma de Santo Domingo 1992; mem. AfofM, RMA, American Music Center. *Recordings include:* albums: The Goodwill Games (theme) (Grammy Award), Calle 54 (OST), Amo mi cama rica (OST) 1970, Why Not! (Grammy Award) 1986, Suntan/Michel Camilo in Trio 1987, Michel Camilo 1988, On Fire 1991, On The Other Hand 1991, Amo tu cama rica (OST) 1992, Rhapsody for two pianos 1992, Suntan 1992, Rendezvous 1993, Los Peores años de nuestra vida (OST) 1994, One More Once 1994, Two Much (OST) 1996, Hands of Rhythm (with Giovanni Hidalgo) 1997, Thru My Eyes 1997, Piano Concerto and Suite 1998, Spain (with Tomatito) 2000, Calle 54 2001, Triangulo 2002, Concerto for piano and orchestra 2002, Solo 2005, Live at the Blue Note 2005, Rhapsody in Blue 2006, Spain Again (with Tomatito) 2006, Spirit of the Moment 2007, Mano a Mano 2011, What's Up? (Latin Grammy Award for Best Latin Jazz Album 2013) 2013. *Honours:* Dr hc (Univ. Tecnológica de Santiago) 1994, (Berklee Coll. of Music) 2000; Clearwater Jazz Holiday Int. Jazz Award 1993, Emmy Award 1986; Kt Heraldic Order of Christopher Columbus, Silver Cross of the Order of Duarte, Sanchez y Mella 2001. *Address:* c/o Sandra Camilo, Redondo Music & Management Co., PO Box 216, Katonah, NY 10536, USA (office). *Telephone:* (914) 234-6030 (office). *Fax:* (914) 205-3082 (office). *E-mail:* Mijazz@ix.netcom.com (office). *Website:* www.michelcamilo.com.

CAMISON, Mathias (Mat); composer, arranger and musician (keyboard); b. 5 Aug. 1941, Algeria. *Career:* musician on tour with All French stars, Jimmy Cliff, The Four Tops, Film (France), Black and White In Color; numerous hits in England, USA as Pepper Box; television music for Canal, Sport, Music on France 1; mem. Société des auteurs, compositeurs et éditeurs de musique (SACEM), Société de Perception et de Distribution des Droits des Artistes-Interprètes, ADAMI. *Recordings include:* Hits with Pepper Box: Love Me Baby, Sheila B Devotion, We've Got A Feeling (with Chris Waddle and B Boli). *Honours:* Academy Award, Molière.

CAMOZZI, Christopher Alan; American musician (guitar); b. 1 May 1957, Burlingame, California. *Education:* Private musical study. *Career:* Musician for Michael Bolton tours: Soul Provider; Time, Love and Tenderness; Timeless, The Classics; The One Thing tours; Television: Tonight Show; Arsenio Hall; Billboard Music Awards; American Music Awards; VH-1 Honours: Oprah Winfrey Show; Donahue; NBC TV; Specials; VH2 Unplugged; with Mariah Carey: Grammy Awards; Tonight Show; mem, Musicians' Union. *Recordings:* with Michael Bolton: Soul Provider; Time, Love and Tenderness;

Timeless, The Classics; with Mariah Carey: Mariah Carey; with Barbra Streisand: Greatest Hits and More; with Whitney Houston: I'm Your Baby Tonight. *Publications:* Guitar Player; Peavey Monitor. *Address:* c/o Associated Entertainment Consultants Inc., 2 Dwight Road, Burlingame, CA 94010, USA. *Telephone:* (650) 348-7972. *Fax:* (650) 348-5629. *E-mail:* gig@associatedentertainment.com. *Website:* www.associatedentertainment.com.

CAMP, Manel; Spanish musician (piano), arranger, composer and music director; b. 20 April 1947, Manresa, Barcelona. *Education:* Berklee Coll. of Music, Boston. *Career:* as solo pianist: Int. festivals: Grenoble, France, Brirstonas, Lithuania, Cheboksari and Yaroslav, Russia, Buenos Aires, Argentina, Caracas, Venezuela, Boston, USA, Barcelona, Madrid, San Sebastian and Granada, Spain; mem. Associacion Catalana de Compositors, Asociación de Musica de Jazz de Catalunya. *Compositions include:* Petita Suite, Simbols, Canigo, Ressorgir, El Llibre de les Besties. *Recordings include:* Minorisa, Fusion, Poesia Secreta, Primer Viatge, La Meva Petita Terra, Escàndols, El Complot Dels Anells, Viu; Ben A Prop, Diàlegs, Ressorgir, Duets, Contrast, Coratge, Rosebud, Complicitats, Canço, Canigo, L'Ultime Frontera. *Honours:* Best Recording Composition, Generalitat de Catalunya 1985, Best Musical Performance, Radio Nacional 1988, Best Soloist, Int. Festival Jazz, San Sebastian 1986, Nat. Cinematography Award, Generalitat 1992, Premi Altaveu 1996, Premi, Iniciativa 1997. *Address:* c/o de la Mel, 23, 2n, 08240 Barcelona, Spain. *Website:* www.manelcamp.cat.

CAMPBELL, Alistair (Ali); British singer, musician (guitar) and songwriter; b. 15 Feb. 1959, Birmingham, England; brother of Robin Campbell. *Career:* Founding mem. and lead singer, UB40 1979–2008; also solo artist; numerous concerts, tours. *Film:* Dance With the Devil 1988. *Recordings include:* albums: with UB40: Signing Off 1980, Present Arms 1981, The Singles Album 1982, UB44 1982, Labour of Love 1983, Live 1983, More UB40 Music 1983, Geffery Morgan 1984, Baggariddim 1985, Little Baggaridim 1985, UB40 File 1985, Rat In The Kitchen 1986, CCCP: Live In Moscow 1987, UB40 1988, Labour of Love II 1990, Promises and Lies 1993, Anansi 1995, Guns In The Ghetto 1997, Labour of Love III 1998, Presents The Dancehall Album 1998, UB40 Present The Fathers Of Reggae 2002, Homegrown 2003, Who You Fighting For? 2005, TwentyFourSeven 2008; solo: Big Love 1995, Running Free 2007, Flying High 2009, Great British Songs 2010, Silhouette 2014. *Publications:* Blood and Fire: The Autobiography of Ali and Robin Campbell 2006, Just Get on with It! 2010. *Current Management:* Part Rock Management Ltd, 1 Conduit Street, London, W1S 2XA, England. *Telephone:* (20) 8207-1418. *E-mail:* stewartyoung@mindspring.com. *Website:* www.alicampbell.net.

CAMPBELL, David; British musician (drums, percussion), songwriter, music arranger and producer; b. 22 Oct. 1969, Glasgow. *Education:* Clydebank Coll. *Career:* drummer, percussionist, writer, arranger, producer with Parksorch 1987–88, Kiss 'N' Tell 1988–92, Ragged Laughter 1992–94, Raglin Street Rattle 1994–; concerts and tours include Beat The Clyde 1987, Prince of Wales Gala Concert 1989; solo American tour of Southern states 1993, US Coast to Coast tour 1994, TV Special, Live at The Festival 1988; mem. PRS. *Compositions include:* Need A Lover 1992, State of Confusion 1993, On Brilliant Wings 1994, She Called My Name 1995, Seize the Day, Moment in White 1999. *Recordings include:* Cava Sessions 1988, The Word Is Out... The Time Is Now 1992, Raglin Street Rattle 1995, Dog on Wheels, (EP with Belle and Sebastian) 1996, Year Zero 1999.

CAMPBELL, Eddie; Scottish musician (keyboards); b. 6 July 1965, Glasgow. *Career:* mem. Texas 1989–2000; numerous tours, festival and TV appearances. *Recordings include:* albums: Southside 1989, Mother's Heaven 1991, Rick's Road 1993, White on Blonde 1997, The Hush 1999, The Greatest Hits 2000, Careful What You Wish For 2003, Return to Bliss 2009.

CAMPBELL, Erica Atkins; American gospel singer and songwriter; b. 29 April 1972, Stamford, Conn.; d. of Eddie Atkins and Thomasina Atkins; m. Warryn Campbell 2001, one d. *Education:* El Camino Coll. *Career:* appeared on Bobby Jones Gospel show on BET; joined Michael Matthews travelling gospel shows Mama I'm Sorry 1995, and Sneaky; also backing singer with various R&B artists; mem. Mary Mary (with sister Tina Campbell) 1998–. *Recordings include:* albums: Thankful (Grammy Award for Best Contemporary Gospel Album) 2000, Incredible 2002, Mary Mary (Dove Award for Contemporary Gospel Album of the Year 2006) 2005, The Sound 2008, Something Big 2011, Go Get It 2012, Help (Grammy Award for Best Gospel Album 2015) 2014. *Publications include:* Transparent (autobiography) 2003, Be U (with sister Tina Campbell) 2011. *Honours:* MOBO Award for Best Gospel Act 2000, 2001, NAACP Award for Best Gospel Artist 2009, BET Award for Best Gospel Artist 2009, Grammy Awards for Best Gospel Performance (for Get Up) 2009, for Best Gospel Song (for God In Me) 2010, (for Go Get It) 2013, American Music Award for Favorite Contemporary Inspirational Artist 2009. *Website:* www.mary-mary.com.

CAMPBELL, Glen Travis; American singer and musician (guitar); b. 22 April 1936, Delight, Ark.. *Career:* mem. Dick Bills Band 1954; Founder Glen Campbell and The Western Wranglers 1958; session musician, Los Angeles; replaced Brian Wilson touring with the Beach Boys 1964–65; film appearances include True Grit 1969, Norwood 1970; Host, Glen Campbell Goodtime Hour (TV show) 1969–72. *Recordings include:* albums: Too Late To Worry, Too Late To Cry 1963, The Astounding 12-String Guitar of Glen Campbell 1964, Gentle On My Mind (Grammy Award for Best Country and Western Recording 1967, Grammy Hall of Fame Award 2008) 1967, By The Time I Get To Phoenix 1967,

Hey Little One 1968, A New Place In The Sun 1968, Galveston 1969, Try A Little Kindness 1970, Oh Happy Day 1970, Norwood (soundtrack) 1970, The Last Time I Saw Her 1971, Anne Murray/Glen Campbell 1971, I Knew Jesus (Before He Was A Star) 1973, Reunion (The Songs of Jimmy Webb) 1974, Rhinestone Cowboy 1975, Bloodline 1976, Southern Nights 1977, Basic 1978, Somethin' About You Baby I Like 1980, It's The World Gone Crazy 1981, Old Home Town 1983, Letter To Home 1984, Just A Matter of Time 1986, No More Night 1988, Still Within The Sound of My Voice 1988, Walkin' In The Sun 1990, Unconditional Love 1991, Favourite Hymns 1992, Somebody Like That 1993, Phoenix 1994, Christmas with Glen Campbell 1995, Branson City Limits 1998, In Concert (live) 1999, Meet Glen Campbell 2008, Ghost on the Canvas 2011. *Honours:* inducted into Country Music Hall of Fame 2005, Q Legend Award 2008, Grammy Lifetime Achievement Award 2012, Grammy Award for Best Country Song (for I'm Not Gonna Miss You) 2015. *Address:* Glen Campbell Enterprises, 1888 Century Park East, Suite 900, Los Angeles, CA 90067, USA. *Website:* www.glencampbellshow.com.

CAMPBELL, Isobel, BA; British singer, musician (cello) and songwriter; b. 27 April 1976, Glasgow, Scotland. *Career:* mem., Belle & Sebastian 1996–2002, The Gentle Waves 1998–; solo artist 2002–; collaborations with Arab Strap, Snow Patrol, Kinobe, Future Pilot, Green Peppers, Mark Lanegan, Eugene Kelly, Alasdair Roberts, Howe Gelb, Bill Wells. *Recordings include:* albums: with Belle & Sebastian: Tigermilk 1996, If You're Feeling Sinister 1996, The Boy With The Arab Strap 1998, Fold Your Hands Child, You Walk Like A Peasant 2000, Storytelling 2002; with The Gentle Waves: The Green Fields of Foreverland 1999, Swansong For You 2000; solo: Ghost Of Yesterday (with Bill Wells) 2002, Amorino 2004, Ballad Of The Broken Seas (with Mark Lanegan) 2005, Milk White Sheets 2006, Sunday at Dirt Devil (with Mark Lanegan) 2008, Hawk (with Mark Lanegan) 2010. *Honours:* BRIT Award for Best Newcomer (with Belle & Sebastian) 1999. *Current Management:* c/o Midnight to Six Management Limited, 5 Harley Place, Harley Street, London, W1G 8QD, England. *E-mail:* harper@midnighttosix.com. *Website:* www.isobelcampbell.co.uk.

CAMPBELL, John; music publisher and artist manager; b. 16 April 1953, Reigate, Surrey, England; m. Sue 1984. *Career:* Chair., JC Music; Publisher, Man. for Richard Feldman, Nick Trevisick, Jeff Paris, Michael Graves, Mike Moran, Howard New, Lowcraft, Akure, Santessa, Bachelor Number One, Mikey Graham; Artist Man. for Marcella Detroit, Shakespears Sister, Lena Fiagbe, Oui 3, Clementines, Nut; mem. Pegs Club, Liberal Party, Groucho Club.

CAMPBELL, Robin; British musician (guitar) and singer; b. 25 Dec. 1954, Birmingham; brother of Ali Campbell. *Career:* mem. reggae group UB40 1978–; numerous concerts, tours. *Film:* Dance With the Devil 1988. *Recordings include:* albums: Signing Off 1980, Present Arms 1981, The Singles Album 1982, UB44 1982, Labour of Love 1983, Live 1983, More UB40 Music 1983, Geffery Morgan 1984, Baggariddim 1985, Little Baggariddim 1985, UB40 File 1985, Rat In The Kitchen 1986, CCCP: Live In Moscow 1987, UB40 1988, Labour of Love II 1990, Promises and Lies 1993, Anansi 1995, Guns In The Ghetto 1997, Labour of Love III 1998, Presents The Dancehall Album 1998, UB40 Present The Fathers of Reggae 2002, Homegrown 2003, Who You Fighting For? 2005, Dub Sessions 2007, TwentyFourSeven 2008, Love Songs 2009, Best Of Labour Of Love 2009, Dub Sessions II 2009, Labour Of Love IV 2010, Dub Sessions III 2010. *Publication:* Blood and Fire: the autobiography of Ali and Robin Campbell 2006. *Current Management:* c/o Part Rock Management Limited, 1 Conduit Street, London, W1S 2XA, England. *Telephone:* (20) 8207-1418. *E-mail:* stewartyoung@mindspring.com. *Address:* UB40, PO Box 15345, Birmingham, B9 9GJ, England (office). *E-mail:* info@ub40.co.uk (office). *Website:* www.ub40.co.uk (office).

CAMPBELL, Simon John, BSc, FRGS; British musician (guitar), singer, producer and songwriter; b. 9 Jan. 1958, Bury, Lancashire; m. 1st Angela Mary Campbell 1982; two s.; m. 2nd Suzy Starlite 2014. *Education:* Univ. of Salford. *Career:* mem. rock band Whitefire 1975–81; national tours with R&B band Roadrunner 1981–85; tours with pop band Gilt Edge, Cutting Edge 1985–86; int. tours, Little Brother 1986–89, Disciples 1990–92; The Method 1992–94, Simon Campbell Band 1994–95; formed band Very Very Bad Men; f. Erskine Design (with Simon Collison) 2006, Supertone Records Residential Recording Studio, Valencia 2015; formed Starlite-Campbell band 2015; mem., Musician's Union (UK), Audio Eng Soc., PRS for Music, Phonographic Performance Ltd (PPL). *Recordings include:* albums: with Whitefire: Parades the Glory 1978; with Little Brother: Survival 1992; solo: ThirtySix 2011, The Knife 2014. *E-mail:* joern.braun@musikreflex.de. *Website:* musikreflex.de. *E-mail:* simon@supertonerecords.com (office). *Website:* www.simoncampbell.com.

CAMPBELL, Tina; American gospel singer and songwriter; b. 1 May 1974, Stamford, Conn.; d. of Eddie Atkins and Thomasina Atkins; m. Teddy Campbell 2000; two d. *Education:* El Camino Coll. *Career:* appeared on Bobby Jones Gospel show on BET; joined Michael Matthews travelling gospel shows Mama I'm Sorry 1995, and Sneaky; also backing singer with various R&B artists; mem. Mary Mary (with sister Erica Atkins Campbell) 1998–. *Recordings include:* albums: Thankful (Grammy Award for Best Contemporary Gospel Album) 2000, Incredible 2002, Mary Mary (Dove Award for Contemporary Gospel Album of the Year 2006) 2005, The Sound 2008, Something Big 2011, Go Get It 2012. *Honours:* MOBO Award for Best Gospel Act 2000, 2001, NAACP Award for Best Gospel Artist 2009, BET Award for

Best Gospel Artist 2009, Grammy Awards for Best Gospel Performance (for Get Up) 2009, for Best Gospel Song (for God In Me) 2010, (for Go Get It) 2013, American Music Award for Favorite Contemporary Inspirational Artist 2009. *Website:* www.mary-mary.com.

CAMPBELL, Vivian Patrick; Northern Irish rock musician (guitar) and singer; b. 25 Aug. 1962, Belfast; m. Julie Campbell; two c. *Career:* mem. Dio 1983–87, Whitesnake 1987–88, Trinity, Riverdogs, Shadow King 1991; mem. Def Leppard 1992–; numerous concerts and tours worldwide, festival appearances; solo artist as singer 2006–. *Recordings include:* albums: with Dio: Holy Diver 1983, The Last In Line 1984, Sacred Heart 1985; with Whitesnake: Whitesnake 1987; with Shadow King: Shadow King 1991; with Def Leppard: Adrenalize 1992, Retro Active 1993, Vault 1980–95 1995, Slang 1996, Euphoria 1999, X 2002, Yeah 2006, Songs from the Sparkle Lounge 2008, Mirrorball: Live And More 2011; solo: Two Sides of If 2006. *Television:* Behind the Music (documentary series, VH1) 1998, Storytellers (documentary, VH1), Hysteria: The Def Leppard Story (documentary, VH1), Ultimate Albums (documentary, VH1). *Current Management:* c/o Primary Wave Music, 116 East 16th Street, 9th Floor, New York, NY 10003, USA. *E-mail:* info@primarywave.com. *Website:* www.defleppard.com; www.viviancampbell.com.

CAMPI, Ray, (Ramblin' Ray); American musician (guitar, bass, dobro steel, mandolin); b. 20 April 1934, New York, NY. *Education:* BFA, Univ. of Texas, 1957. *Career:* TV appearances on Austin City Limits, Tomorrow Show (NBC), Texas Saturday Night (BBC 2) 1991, BBC radio 1977, Echo's Show; mem., Austin Federation of Musicians, Hemsby Festival UK; mem. Rockabilly Hall of Fame. *Compositions:* Rockin' At the Ritz, Caterpillar, A Little Bit of Heartache, Kick Da Bukkit, Christmas Cheer, Let the New Year in Your Heart, Somebody Took My Teeth (on Christmas Evening). *Recordings:* music tracks on over 65 albums 1956–, including The Ultimate Jimmie Skinner Songbook, Woody, Favorite Country Kings, Road to Rockabilly, Friends Along the Way. *Publications:* Rolling Stone 1980, Dynamite 1995, Now Dig This 1996, Blue Suede News 2002, 2003. W. K. Rock & Roll 2012. *Current Management:* Paul Barrett, Rock 'n' Roll Enterprises, 2872½ W Avenue 35, Los Angeles, CA 90065, USA. *Telephone:* (323) 255-7868 (office). *Website:* www.rockabillyhall.com. *Address:* c/o Real Music, PO Box 250425, Glendale, CA 91225-0425. *Website:* www.electricearl.com.

CANIBOL, Heinz, BEcons; German record company executive; *Managing Partner, 105music;* b. 3 July 1951, Gelsenkirchen; m. Brigitte Canibol 1984. *Career:* Product Man. and Marketing Dir, CBS Records, Germany 1977–89; Man. Dir, Sony Music, Austria 1989–91; Man. Dir and Vice-Pres. G/A/S, MCA Music Entertainment, Germany 1992–99, Vice-Pres. Germany, Switzerland, Austria division 1994–99; Pres. and CEO, Germany, Swutzerland, Austria division, EMI 1999–2002; Man. Partner, 105music record label 2003–. *Address:* 105music, Hopfensack 20, 20457 Hamburg, Germany (office). *Telephone:* (40) 82221510 (office). *Fax:* (40) 822215225 (office). *E-mail:* info@105music.com (office). *Website:* www.105music.com (office).

CANN, Judith Leonie, BA; Australian composer and musician (keyboard); b. 3 April 1958, Perth, WA; m. David George Hunt 1986; one s. one d. *Education:* Australian Film and Television School, Nat. Film School and Univ. of Surrey, UK. *Career:* composed, performed synthesized scores and music for use in the film, TV, video industry; mem. Performing Right Soc., Musicians' Union. *Recordings:* 25 library tracks with Chappell, 175 library tracks with Carlin, scored music for 1492 The Shattered Utopia (short film), Making Ends Meet, Network Europe, Channel Tunnel videos; TV series: A Tale of 4 Market Towns; World In Action; laser, video, fireworks display in People's Repub. of China. *Publications:* article in APV magazine, Videomaker. *Honours:* Stemra Award for Most Impressive Use of Library Music (Netherlands) 1994. *Address:* 10 Queen Street, Pitstone, Bucks., LU7 9AU, England (home). *E-mail:* judecannhunt@hotmail.co.uk (office).

CANNING, Brendan; Canadian singer, songwriter and musician (bass guitar); b. 1969. *Career:* mem. hHead 1991–97; mem. By Divine Right 1999; mem. Blurtonia 1999–2002; founder and mem. Broken Social Scene 1999; mem. Valley of the Giants 2002–04. *Recordings:* albums: with hHead: Fireman 1992, Jerk 1994, Ozzy 1996; with By Divine Right: Bless This Mess 1999; with Broken Social Scene: Feel Good Lost 2001, You Forgot It in People (Juno Award for Alternative Album of the Year 2003) 2002, Bee Hives 2003, Broken Social Scene (Juno Award for Alternative Album of the Year 2006) 2005, Forgiveness Rock Record 2010, Lo-Fi for the Dividing Nights 2010; with Blurtonia: Blurtonia 2002; with Valley of the Giants: Valley of the Giants 2004; solo: Something for All of Us 2008. *Current Management:* Canvas Media, 460 Richmond Street West, Suite 402, Toronto, ON M5V 1Y1, Canada. *Telephone:* (416) 203-2217. *Fax:* (416) 203-2209. *E-mail:* press@canvasmedia.ca. *Website:* www.canvasmedia.ca. *E-mail:* raiseyourhands@arts-crafts.ca (office). *Website:* www.brokensocialscene.ca; www.brendancanning.com.

CANO, José María; Spanish composer, arranger, songwriter, musician (guitar) and producer; b. 21 Feb. 1959, Madrid; brother of Nacho Cano. *Career:* mem. Mecano 1980–93; simultaneous solo career 1992–; music producer. *Recordings include:* albums: with Mecano: Mecano 1982, ¿Dónde Está El País De Las Hadas? 1983, Ya Viene El Sol 1984, En Concierto 1985, Lo Ultimo De Mecano 1986, Entre El Cielo Y El Suelo 1986, Descanso Dominical 1988, Aidalai 1991, Ana José Nacho 1998; solo: Luna (opera) 1997, José Cano 2000. *Website:* www.josecano.com.

CANO, Nacho; Spanish composer, arranger, songwriter, musician (keyboards, synthesizer) and producer; b. 26 Feb. 1963, Madrid; brother of José Cano. *Career:* mem. Mecano 1980–93; simultaneous solo career 1992–; music producer. *Recordings include:* albums: with Mecano: Mecano 1982, ¿Dónde Está El País De Las Hadas? 1983, Ya Viene El Sol 1984, En Concierto 1985, Lo Ultimo De Mecano 1986, Entre El Cielo Y El Suelo 1986, Descanso Dominical 1988, Aidalai 1991, Ana José Nacho 1998; solo: Un Mundo Separado Por El Mismo Dios 1994, El Lado Femenino 1996, Amor Humor 1999, Nacho Cano 2001. *Website:* www.nachocano.com.

CANONGE, Mario-Laurent, Bac et licence; French musician (piano, keyboards), composer and arranger; b. 5 Sept. 1960, Fort-de-France, Martinique; two d. *Education:* Conservatoire Hauts de Seine, Université musicologie. *Career:* formed group Ultramarine 1983, Chic Hot, Sakiyo, Sakesho and others; tours world-wide. *Compositions include:* Pei Mwen Jodi, Pogo, Yélé Congo, Lésé Palé, Si On Sa Révé, Vidé Bo Kay, Echapaya, Dimanoua, Non Musieu, Sé Kon Sa, Bam Ti Bonjou, Sé ou Ki Lanmou, Madikera, Plein Sud, Lueur éteinte, Poésie du Chaos, A Fleur de Terre, Entre la Pelée et l'Ararat, Half Way There, Ska du Cap, Noel filao. *Recordings:* albums: Retour Aux Sources 1991, Trait D'Union 1993, Hommage A Marius Cultier 1994, Aromes Caraibes 1995, Chawa 1997, Punch en Musique 1 1999, Carte Blanche 2001, Les Plus Belles Chansons de Noël 2001, Rhizome 2004, Punch en Musique 2 2007, Rhizome Tour 2008, Mitan 2011. *Television:* Sur le Pont des Artistes, Rien a Cine, France Inter, Top Live, Europe I, Cerde de Minuit, Pintenne 2, Jazz 6, Jazz a Vienne. *Honours:* Best Pianist, Prix de la Défense 1983, Best Album, Best Composer, SACEM Martinique 1992–94, Best Album 1996, Musical Research Prize 1995. *Current Management:* c/o Enzo Productions, 6 place George Sand, 91130 Ris Orangis, France. *E-mail:* enzoproductions@enzoproductions.com. *Website:* www.mariocanonge.net (home).

CANOVILLE, Katherine; British music company executive and music manager; b. 13 Jan. 1965, Hillingdon, Middlesex; m. Stephen Carrington 1995. *Career:* concert promoter 1979–81; Artist Man. 1981–95; Man. Dir, Buzz Magazine 1986–89; Co-founder, Nation Records 1988, Man. Dir 1990–98; sole trader, QFM Promotions 1994; currently music consultant, FULL 36IXTY; fmr writer for Oracle/Teletext world music page –1992; mem. BMIA BRIT Award Cttee. *E-mail:* katherine.frontline@blueyonder.co.uk.

CANTRELL, Blu; American singer; b. (Tiffany L. Cobb), 1 Oct. 1976, Providence, Rhode Island. *Career:* fmr model; fmr backing singer for Faith Evans, P Diddy, Gerald Levert. *Recordings include:* albums: So Blu 2001, Bittersweet 2003.

CANTRELL, Jerry; American musician (guitar) and vocals; b. 18 March 1966, Tacorna, WA. *Career:* mem. Alice in Chains; numerous tours and TV appearances including MTV Unplugged session. *Recordings:* albums: Facelift 1990, Dirt 1992, Sap 1992, Jar of Flies 1994, Alice in Chains 1995, I Stay Away 1995, Unplugged 1996, Nothing Safe 1999, Music Bank 1999, Live 2000, Greatest Hits 2001, Black Gives Way to Blue 2009; solo: Boggy Depot 1998, Degradation Trip 2002. *Current Management:* Velvet Hammer Management, 9014 Melrose Avenue, West Hollywood, CA 90069, USA. *Telephone:* (310) 657-6161. *Fax:* (310) 657-0310. *Website:* www.velvethammer.net; www.aliceinchains.com.

CANTÚ, Paty; Mexican singer, songwriter and actress; b. (Patricia Giovanna Cantú Velasco), 25 Nov. 1983, Houston, Tex., USA. *Career:* raised in Guadalajara, Mexico; Founder-mem., duo Lu (with Mario Sandoval) 2000–07; solo career 2008–; support act on tour to Aleks Syntek 2008; debut solo single 2008. *Television:* as actress: El Pantera 2009. *Recordings:* with Lu: Lu 2004; solo: Me Quedo Sola 2009, Afortunadamente No Eres Tú 2010, Corazón Bipolar 2012. *Honours:* Premios MTV Award for Best New Artist – North 2009. *E-mail:* ventas@seitrack.com.mx. *Website:* seitrack.com.mx; patycantu.com (home); www.myspace.com/patycantu (home).

CANYON, George; Canadian country singer and songwriter; b. (Frederick George Lays Jr), 1971, New Glasgow, NS; m. Jennifer; two c. *Television:* competed in Nashville Star 2004. *Recordings include:* albums: Ironwolf 1996, George Canyon 1999, One Good Friend 2004, Home for Christmas 2005, Somebody Wrote Love 2006, What I Do 2008. *Honours:* Music Industry of Nova Scotia Award for New Artist Recording of the Year, Country Recording of the Year 2004, Canadian Country Music Award for Top Entertainer, Top Male Artist, Top Single, Top Songwriter (with Gordie Sampson) 2005, Humanitarian Award 2008, JUNO Award for Country Recording of the Year 2005, 2007, Canadian Radio Music Award for Best New Country Group or Solo Artist 2005. *Current Management:* c/o Anya Wilson, Promotion and Publicity, 401 Richmond Street W, Suite 220, Toronto, ON M5V 1X3, Canada. *Telephone:* (416) 977-7704 (office). *Fax:* (416) 977-7719 (office). *E-mail:* anya@anyawilson.ca (office). *Website:* www.georgecanyon.com.

CAPERS, Valerie Gail, MS; American composer, arranger and musician (piano); b. 24 May 1935, New York; d. of Alvin Capers. *Education:* New York Inst. for the Educ. of the Blind, Juilliard School of Music, New York. *Career:* composer and arranger, Mango Santamaria Afro-Cuban band; formed own trio; frequent panellist, lecturer, clinician and performer at conferences; teacher, Hunter Coll. 1959–60, Manhattan School of Music, New York 1968–75, High School of Music and Art, New York 1971; Prof. Dept of Music and Art, Bronx Community Coll., CUNY 1985–95, Chair 1987–95, Prof. Emer. 1995–. *Compositions include:* Sing About Love for chorus 1974, Portraits in Jazz for piano 1976, In Praise of Freedom for chorus 1976, Psalm 150 for chorus 1980, Sojourner for chorus and jazz ensemble 1981, Organum for jazz ensemble 1982, The Gift of Song for chorus 1982, Duke Ellington Suite for chorus 1984, Escenas Afro-Cubanas 1985, Song of the Seasons 1987, El Toro for jazz ensemble 1990, The Ring Thing for jazz ensemble 1993, Odyssey for jazz ensemble 1995. *Recordings include:* albums: Portrait In Soul 1967, Affirmation 1982, On Come On Home 1995, Wagner Takes The A-Train 1999, Limited Edition 2001. *Publication:* Portraits in Jazz 2000. *Honours:* Hon. DFA (Susquehanna Univ.) 1996, (Doane Coll., Nebraska) 2004, (Bloomfield Coll., New Jersey) 2004; New York City Creative Arts Service Award 1974, Nat. Endowment for the Arts grant 1976, CUNY Research Foundation grant 1983, Bronx Borough Pres.'s Award for Outstanding Artistic Contributions to Community 1992, Nat. Endowment for the Arts Special Project 1994–95, Jazz Heritage Award 1997. *E-mail:* RowanAndrewDavid@aol.com. *Website:* www .valeriecapers.com.

CAPPADONNA; American MC and rap artist; b. (Darryl Hill), 18 Sept. 1969. *Career:* Guest Assoc., later full mem. Wu-Tang Clan 1995–; solo artist 1998–; associated with rapper collective Theodore Unit. *Recordings include:* albums: with Wu-Tang Clan: Enter The Wu-Tang (36 Chambers) 1993, Wu-Tang Forever 1997, The W 2000, Iron Flag 2001, Disciples Of The 36 Chambers: Chapter 1 (live) 2004; solo: The Pillage 1998, The Yin And The Yang 2001, Struggle 2003, The Cappatalize Project 2008, Slang Prostitution 2009, The Pilgrimage 2011. *Website:* www.wutang-corp.com.

CAPTAIN HOLLYWOOD; American singer, rap artist and producer; b. (Tony Dawson-Harrison), 9 Aug. 1962, Newark, New Jersey. *Career:* choreographer, major German television programme; artist, performing and producing for The Mixmaster, Twenty 4 Seven 1986–90, Captain Hollywood Project 1991–95; mem. GEMA, Germany. *Recordings include:* albums: Street Moves 1990, Love Is Not Sex 1993, Animals or Human 1995, The Afterparty 1996; singles: More and More 1991, All I Want 1993, Only With You 1993, Rhythm of Life 1994, Danger Sign 2001, Axel F. 2003, More and More Recall 2008. *Publications include:* Grand Piano, I Can't Stand It, More and More. *Current Management:* c/o Armin Rahn Agency and Management, reimühlenstr. 7, 80469 Munich, Germany. *Telephone:* (49) 89775044. *Fax:* (89) 7250660. *E-mail:* info@arminrahn.com; jl@cpthollywood-management.com. *Website:* www.arminrahn.com; www.captain-hollywood.com.

CAPTAIN SENSIBLE; British singer and musician (guitar, bass guitar); b. (Ray Burns), 24 April 1954, Balham, London. *Education:* Stanley Technical School. *Career:* fmr mem., Johnny Moped band; Founder mem. punk rock band, The Damned 1976–77, 1979–84, 1996–; mem. Dead Men Walking; solo artist 1982–; mem. PRS, Musicians' Union; toured with his punk band Punk Floyd. *Recordings include:* with The Damned: Damned, Damned, Damned 1977, Machine Gun Etiquette 1979, The Black Album 1980, Live At Shepperton 1980 1982, Strawberries 1982, Live At Newcastle 1983, Damned But Not Forgotten 1985, Live 1991, Ballroom Blitz 1992, Music For Pleasure 1995, Eternally Damned 1995, Fiendish Shadows 1996, Not of This Earth 1996, Testify 1997, Eternal Damnation Live 1999, Molten Lager 2000, Grave Disorder (also co-wrote) 2001, So, Who's Paranoid? 2008; solo: Women and Captain First 1982, Power of Love 1983, Revolution Now 1989, Live at the Milky Way 1995, Meathead 1995, The Universe of Geoffrey Brown 1998, Mad Cows and Englishmen 1996. *Address:* Allied Autonomy, 118 Oldham Road, Manchester, M4 6AG, England. *Telephone:* (12) 0042-8087. *E-mail:* info@captainsensible.com. *Website:* www.captainsensible.com.

CARA, Irene; American singer, actor and dancer; b. 18 March 1959, Bronx, New York. *Career:* collaborations with George Duke, The Brecker Brothers, Oleta Adams, Giorgio Moroder; formed group Hot Caramel 2007; mem. Equity, Screen Actors' Guild. *Stage appearances include:* stage appearances: Maggie Flynn, Broadway, 1968; The Me Nobody Knows, 1970; Via Galactica, New York, 1972; Got To Go Disco, 1979; Ain't Misbehavin'. *Film appearances:* Aaron Loves Angela, 1975; Sparkle, 1976; Fame, 1980; DC Cab, 1980; City Heat, 1984; A Certain Fury, 1985; Busted Up, 1986; Killing 'Em Softly, 1985; The Man In 5-A. *Recordings include:* albums: Anyone Can See, 1982; What A Feelin', 1983; Carasmatic, 1987. *Honours:* Obie Award, Academy Award for Best Song (for Fame), (for Flashdance… What a Feeling). *Address:* Betty McCormick, Midwest Talent, 4821 Lankershim Boulevard, Suite F149, North Hollywood, CA 91601, USA. *Telephone:* (818) 765-3785. *Fax:* (818) 484-3500. *E-mail:* betty@midwesttalent.com. *Website:* www.midwesttalent.com; www .irenecara.com.

CAREY, Mariah; American singer and songwriter; b. 22 March 1970, Long Island, NY; m. 1st Tommy Mottola 1993 (divorced 1998); m. 2nd Nick Cannon 2008 (divorced 2014); two s. *Career:* fmr backing singer, Brenda K. Starr, New York 1988; solo artist 1988–; f. Crave record label 1997; f. Camp Mariah holiday project for inner-city children. *Recordings include:* albums: Mariah Carey (Soul Train Award for Best Album by a Female Artist) 1990, Emotions 1991, MTV Unplugged (EP) 1992, Music Box 1993, Merry Christmas 1994, Daydream 1995, Butterfly 1997, #1s 1998, Rainbow 1999, Glitter 2001, Charmbracelet 2002, The Remixes 2003, The Emancipation of Mimi (Lady of Soul Award for Best Solo R&B/Soul Album, Vibe Award for Album of the Year, Grammy Award for Best Contemporary R&B Album 2006, Image Award for Best Album 2006) 2005, E=MC2 2008, Memoirs of an Imperfect Angel 2009, Merry Christmas II You 2010, Me. I Am Mariah… The Elusive Chanteuse 2014. *Television includes:* judge, American Idol 2013. *Films include:* The Bachelor 1999, Glitter (also soundtrack) 2001, WiseGirls 2002, State Property 2 2005, Tennessee 2008, Precious 2009, The Butler 2013. *Honours:* Grammy

Awards for Best New Artist, Best New Pop Vocal by a Female Artist 1990, Soul Train Awards for Best New Artist, Best Single by a Female Artist 1990, Rolling Stone Award for Best Female Singer 1991, eight World Music Awards 1991–95, seven Billboard Awards 1991–96, four American Music Awards 1992–96, Int. Dance Music Award for Best Solo Artist 1996, American Music Awards Special Award of Achievement 2000, Lady of Soul Award for Best Solo R&B/Soul Single (for We Belong Together) 2005, Vibe Awards for Artist of the Year, for R&B Voice of the Year, for Best R&B Song (for We Belong Together) 2005, American Music Award for Favorite Female Soul/R&B Artist 2005, Female Billboard 200 Album Artist of the Year 2005, Billboard Music Awards for Hot 100 Song of the Year, Hot 100 Airplay of the Year, Rhythmic Top 40 Title of the Year (all for We Belong Together) 2005, Billboard Music Award for Female R&B/Hip-Hop Artist of the Year 2005, Grammy Award for Best Female R&B Vocal Performance (for We Belong Together) 2006. *Website:* www .mariahcarey.com.

CARGILL, James; British musician (bass) and producer; b. England. *Career:* founder mem., Broadcast 1995–; signed recording contract with Duophonic label 1996, moved to Warp Records 1997. *Recordings include:* albums: Work and Non Work 1997, The Noise Made By People 2000, HAHA Sound 2003, Tender Buttons 2005, The Future Crayon 2006, Broadcast and the Focus Group Investigate Witch Cults of the Radio Age 2009. *Current Management:* c/o Martin Pike, Associated London Management, PO Box 3787, London, SE22 9DZ, England. *Telephone:* (20) 7821-9823. *Fax:* (20) 7262-9928. *E-mail:* info@duophonic.com. *Website:* www.duophonic.com. *Address:* c/o Warp Records Limited, Spectrum House, 32–34 Gordon House Road, London, NW5 1LP, England. *Telephone:* (20) 7284-8350. *E-mail:* editor@warp.net. *Website:* www .warp.net; futurecrayon.blogspot.com.

CARIBOU, (Daphni), PhD; Canadian musician (synthesizer, drums, guitar, bass guitar), composer and record producer; b. (Daniel Victor Snaith), 1978, Dundas, Ont. *Education:* Imperial Coll., London, UK. *Career:* recorded as Manitoba 2001–04, renamed Caribou 2004–. *Recordings include:* as Manitoba: Start Breaking My Heart 2001, Up in Flames 2003; as Caribou: The Milk of Human Kindness 2005, Andorra (Polaris Music Prize 2008) 2007, Swim (Juno Award for Electronic Album of the Year 2011) 2010, Our Love (IMPALA Album of the Year Award 2015, Juno Award for Electronic Album of the Year 2015) 2014; as Daphni: Jiaolong 2012. *Honours:* Mixmag Essential Mix of the Year 2014. *E-mail:* cariboutheband@gmail.com. *Website:* www.caribou.fm.

CARLÀ, Ermanno (Erma); Italian musician (bass guitar); b. 26 Oct. 1980, Lecce, Apulia. *Career:* mem. Negramaro 2002–. *Recordings include:* albums: Negramaro 2003, 000577 2004, Mentre Tutto Scorre 2005, La Finestra 2007, Casa 69 2010, La Rivoluzione Sta Arrivando 2015. *Honours:* MTV Europe Music Award Best Italian Act 2005. *E-mail:* management@negramaro.com. *Website:* www.negramaro.com.

CARLISLE, Belinda; American singer and songwriter; b. 17 Aug. 1958, Hollywood, Calif.; m. Morgan Mason 1986; one s. *Career:* fmr mem. The Germs, Black Randy, Metro Squad; Founder mem. and lead singer, The Go-Go's (formerly The Misfits) 1978–85, re-formed briefly for PETA benefit concert 1990, re-formed 1994 for shows in Las Vegas, re-formed 2000 for an album and tours; solo artist 1986–94. *Recordings include:* albums: with the Go-Go's: Beauty and the Beat 1981, Vacation 1982, Talk Show 1984, Return to the Valley of The Go-Go's 1994, God Bless The Go-Go's 2001; solo: Belinda 1986, Heaven On Earth 1987, Runaway Horses 1989, Live Your Life Be Free 1991, Real 1993, A Woman and a Man 1996, Runaway Live 2000, Voila 2007. *Film appearances:* Swing Shift 1984. *Stage appearances:* Grease 1983, Hairspray (London) 2009–10. *Publication:* Lips Unsealed: A Memoir 2010. *E-mail:* gogos@beyondmusic.com (office). *Website:* www.gogos.com; www .belindacarlisle.tv.

CARLOS, Roberto; Brazilian singer and songwriter; b. 19 April 1941, Cachoeiro de Itapemirim; s. of Robertino Braga and Laura Moreira Braga; m. 1st Cleonice Rossi 1968 (divorced 1978); one d.; m. 2nd Myrian Rios 1980 (divorced 1989); m. 3rd Maria Rita Simões Braga 1996 (died 1999); two s. one d. *Education:* Conservatório Musical de Cachoeiro. *Career:* started performing professionally in 1958; has presented numerous radio and TV programmes; pioneered Jovem Guarda movt in 1970s, influenced by American rock and roll; numerous tours in South America; has performed with Maria Bethânia, Tom Jobim, Chico Buarque, Caetano Veloso, Dorival Caymmi. *Recordings include:* Louco por Você 1961, O Inimitável 1968, À Janela, A Distância e Por Amor 1971, Honestly 1981, Se Diverte e já não Pensa em Mim 1988, Amor sem limite 2000, Pra sempre 2003; over 45 albums including Para Sempre Ao Vivo No Pacaembu (Latin Grammy Award for Best Brazilian Romantic Album), Roberto Carlos 2006 (Latin Grammy Award for Best Brazilian Romantic Album), Roberto Carlos-En Vivo 2008, Elas Cantam Roberto Carlos 2009, Esse Cara Sou Eu 2012. *Honours:* First Prize, San Remo Festival 1968, Latin Grammy Awards for Best Singer 1989, for Best Brazilian Romantic Album 2005, for Best Brazilian Song 2013. *Address:* c/o Sony BMG Brasil, Rua Lauro Muller 116, 4º Andar, Conjunto 4001 a 4003, Botafogo, 22290-160 Rio de Janeiro, Brazil. *Telephone:* (21) 2128-0600 (office). *Website:* www .robertocarlos.com.

CARLOS, Wendy, AB, MA; American composer, synthesist and recording engineer; b. 14 Nov. 1939, Pawtucket, RI. *Education:* Brown Univ., Columbia Univ. *Career:* worked as a recording engineer, associating with Robert Moog in the development of the Moog Synthesizer 1964; pioneer in utilising the resources of the synthesizer; has delivered papers at New York Univ., Audio

Engineering Soc. Digital Audio Conference, Dolby New York City Surround Sound demonstration and panel, and at other music/audio conferences; mem. Audio Engineering Soc., Soc. of Motion Picture and Television Engineers, Nat. Acad. of Recording Arts and Sciences. *Compositions include:* Noah (opera) 1964. *Recordings include:* albums: Switched-on Bach (three Grammy Awards) 1968, The Well-Tempered Synthesizer 1969, Sonic Seasonings 1972, A Clockwork Orange (soundtrack) 1972, Switched-on Bach II 1974, By Request 1975, Switched-on Brandenburgs 1979, The Shining (soundtrack) 1980, Tron (soundtrack) 1982, Digital Moonscapes 1984, Beauty In the Beast 1986, Secrets of Synthesis 1987, Peter and the Wolf (with Al Yankovic) 1988, Switched-On Bach 2000 1992, Tales of Heaven and Hell 1998, Switched-On Boxed Set 1999, Rediscovering Lost Scores 2005. *Website:* www.wendycarlos.com.

CARLOTTI, Jan-Mari; singer, musician (guitar), writer and composer; b. 23 June 1948, Meknès, Morocco. *Career:* singer, solely in Occitan (Provençal language); formed Mont Jóia, 1974–83; solo artist, 1983; also worked with Anita/Anita, Michel Marre. *Recordings include:* five albums with Mont Jóia, six albums as solo artist or in other groups, including Chants des Troubadours, with Michel Marre 1995. *Publications include:* Anthologie de la Nouvelle Chanson Occitaine 1984. *Honours:* Grand Prix, Academie Charles Cros, 1978, 1994; First Prize, International Artist, Turin Folk Competition, 1989; Best Solo Artist, Trad Magazine, 1991. *Address:* 2 bis Imp Fleury-Proudhon, 13200 Arles, France.

CARLSSON, Maurits; Swedish musician (drums) and composer; *Executive Director, Tambourine Studios;* b. Lomma, nr Malmö. *Career:* Founder-mem. Eggstone 1986–; the band est. Tambourine Studios (with Tore Johansson and Anders Nordgren) 1991– (now Exec. Dir), Vibrafon Records 1995–; studios used by artists, including St Etienne and The Cardigans. *Recordings include:* albums: In San Diego 1992, Somersault 1994, Vive La Différence 1997, Spanish Slalom 1998, Ça chauffe en Suede! 1999. *Address:* Tambourine Studios, Sofielundsvägen 57, 214 34 Malmö, Sweden (office). *Telephone:* (40) 87-08-8 (office). *Fax:* (40) 87-08-0 (office). *E-mail:* info@tambourinestudios.com (office). *Website:* www.tambourinestudios.com (office).

CARLSTROEM, Vigilante; Swedish musician (guitar); b. 1978. *Career:* mem. The Hives 1993–. *Recordings:* albums: Barely Legal 1997, Veni Vidi Vicious 2000, Your New Favourite Band (compilation) 2001, Tyrannosaurus Lives 2004, The Black and White Album 2007, Lex Hives 2012. *Honours:* NME Award for Best Int. Band 2003. *Address:* The Hives, Gold Village Entertainment, 72 Madison Avenue, 8th Floor, New York, NY 10016, USA. *E-mail:* thehives@goldve.com. *Website:* www.thehivesbroadcastingservice.com.

CARLTON, Larry; American musician (guitar) and composer; b. 2 March 1948, Torance, Calif.; m. Michele Pillar 1987; one s. *Career:* fmr Musical Dir, Mrs Alphabet (children's TV show); performed with Crusaders 1971–76; signed with Warner Bros. Records 1977; session musician with artists including Sammy Davis, Jr, Herb Alpert, Quincy Jones, Paul Anka, Michael Jackson, John Lennon, Jerry Garcia, Dolly Parton, Linda Ronstadt and Steely Dan; arranger, producer for Barbra Streisand, Joan Baez and Larry Gatlin; toured with jazz superband Stanley Clarke And Friends; collaborations with guitarist Lee Ritenour as Larry & Lee; fmr mem. Fourplay. *Recordings include:* albums: Larry and Lee, No Substitutions: Live in Osaka 2001 (with Steve Lukather) (Grammy Award for Best Pop International Album 2002), Take Your Pick 2010 (with Tak Matsumoto); solo albums: With A Little Help From My Friends 1968, Singing/Playing 1973, Larry Carlton 1978, Mr. 335 Live In Japan 1979, Strikes Twice 1980, Eight Times Up 1982, Friends 1983, Alone/But Never Alone 1985, Discovery 1986, Last Nite 1987, On Solid Ground 1989, Christmas at My House 1989, Collection 1990, Kid Gloves 1992, Renegade Gentlemen 1993, Gift 1996, Fingerprints 2000, Deep Into It 2001, Sapphire Blue 2003, The Very Best of Larry Carlton 2005, Fire Wire 2006, Plays the Sound of Philadelphia 2011. *Television includes:* Hill Street Blues (theme) (Grammy Award for Best Pop Instrumental Performance 1981). *Film:* Against All Odds (theme). *Honours:* Grammy Award for Best Pop Instrumental Performance (for Minute by Minute) 1987. *Website:* www.larrycarlton.com.

CARLTON, Vanessa Lee; American singer, songwriter and pianist; b. 16 Aug. 1980, Milford, Pa; m. John McCauley; one d. *Education:* American School of Ballet, New York. *Recordings include:* albums: Be Not Nobody 2002, Harmonium 2004, Heroes and Thieves 2007, Rabbits on the Run 2011, Liberman 2015. *Current Management:* c/o Brick Wall Management, 39 West 32nd Street, Suite 1403, New York, 10001, USA. *Telephone:* (212) 501-0748. *Fax:* (212) 202-4582. *E-mail:* vcmgmt@brickwallmgmt.com. *Website:* www.brickwallmgmt.com; www.vanessacarlton.com.

CARMEN, Eric; American singer and songwriter; b. 11 Aug. 1949, Cleveland, OH. *Education:* Cleveland Institute of Music. *Career:* singer in various groups, Cleveland 1960s; lead singer, The Choir 1968, renamed Raspberries 1971–75; solo artist 1975–80, 1985–. *Recordings include:* albums: with The Raspberries: The Raspberries, 1971; Fresh, 1972; Side 3, 1973; Starting Over, 1975; solo: Eric Carmen, 1975; Boats Against the Current, 1977; Change of Heart, 1978; Tonight You're Mine, 1980; Eric Carmen, 1985; The Best of Eric Carmen, 1988; Winter Dreams, 1998; Someone That You Loved Before, 1998; All By Myself (compilation), 2000, I Was Born to Love You 2000. *E-mail:* raspbernie@ericcarmen.com. *Website:* www.ericcarmen.com.

CARMICHAEL, Anita; British musician (saxophone, alto) and singer; b. 17 Sept. 1964, Upminster, Essex, England; m. Michael Tanousis 1993; one s. *Education:* Guildhall School of Music. *Career:* tours with The Communards, Jonathan Butler, Fay Weldon, Imagination, M-People; numerous TV and radio broadcasts, concerts and festival appearances; mem. Musicians' Union, PRS, MCPS. *Recordings include:* Live At The Premises (EP) 1993, The Unadulterated 1994, Plays Dinner Jazz (EP) 1995, Saxotronix 1995, Lipstick On My Reed 1996, Today 1997, Anita Carmichael 1999. *Honours:* Wire magazine Newcomer of the Year 1987.

CARMICHAEL, Jesse; American musician (keyboards); b. 2 April 1979, Boulder, Colo. *Career:* mem., Kara's Flowers, later renamed Maroon 5 1997–. *Recordings include:* albums: with Maroon 5: Songs About Jane 2002, It Won't Be Soon Before Long 2007, Hands All Over 2010, V 2014. *Honours:* with Maroon 5: Grammy Awards for Best New Artist 2004, for Best Pop Performance by a Duo or Group with Vocals (for Makes me Wonder) 2008, Billboard Music Award for Top Hot 100 Artist 2013, People's Choice Award for Favorite Band 2013, American Music Award for Favorite Adult Contemporary Artist 2013. *Current Management:* c/o Career Artist Management, 1100 Glendon Avenue, Suite 1100, New York, NY 90024, USA. *Telephone:* (310) 776-7640. *Fax:* (310) 776-7659. *Website:* camanagement.com; www.maroon5.com.

CARMICHAEL, Jim; British musician (drums), songwriter and producer; b. 21 Feb. 1971, Sevenoaks, Kent. *Education:* Berklee College of Music, Boston, USA. *Career:* principal percussionist in winning orchestra at National Festival For Youth 1988; drummer/producer K-Creative, Izit, Freak Power, Barry Adamson, Les Rhythmes Digitales, Every Day People (EDP), Ski Oakenfull, Freeland, Gwen McCrae, Zoot Woman. *Recordings include:* with K-Creative: QED, 1992; with Izit: The Whole Affair, 1993; Imaginary Man, 1995; with Freak Power: Drive Thru Booty, 1994; More of Everything for Everybody, 1996; Carmichael's Crunchy Nut Loops, 1997; Mandalay: Empathy, 1998; with EDP: Sweet Music, 2001. *Address:* Flat 2, 3 College Terrace, Brighton, BN2 2EE, England. *Telephone:* (7973) 176088 (office). *Fax:* (7970) 703043 (office). *E-mail:* decoy.productions@ntlworld.com.

CARNEIRO, (Fernando) Nando; Brazilian musician (guitar, piano); b. 26 June 1953, Belo Horizonte; m. Nora Kholki 1997; two s. *Career:* mem. A Barca Do Sol; recordings with singers Olivia Byington and Beth Goulart; world tours with E Gismonti 1986, 1990, 1991, 1993, 1994, 1995, 1996. *Compositions include:* soundtrack: Kiss of the Spider Woman (co-writer). *Recordings include:* A Barca do Sol 1974, Durante o Verão 1976, Pirata 1979, Violão 1983, Mantra Brasil 1985, Topázio 1985, Catavento 1998. *Honours:* Fiat Prize, Os Povos Da Floresta 1989.

CARNES, Kim; American singer and songwriter; b. 20 July 1945, Los Angeles, CA; m. Dave Ellington. *Career:* mem., New Christy Minstrels 1960s; solo artist; songwriter, with husband Dave Ellington. *Compositions include:* songs recorded by artists including Frank Sinatra; Barbra Streisand; Kenny Rogers. *Recordings include:* albums: Rest On Me, 1972; Kim Carnes, 1975; Sailin', 1976; St Vincent's Court, 1979; Romance Dance, 1980; Mistaken Identity, 1981; Voyeur, 1982; Cafe Racers, 1983; Lighthouse, 1986; View From The House, 1988; Gypsy Honeymoon – The Best Of, 1993; Crazy In The Night, 1990; Back To Back, 1998; Mistaken Identity Collection; King Biscuit Flower Hour, 1998; Sweet Love Song of My Soul, 1999, Chasin' Wild Trains 2004. *Address:* c/o Andy Kerr, Prime Source Entertainment Group, 2829 Dogwood Place, Nashville, TN 37204, USA. *Telephone:* (615) 269-8500 ext 12. *E-mail:* akerr@primesourceproductions.com. *Website:* www.primesourceproductions.com; www.kimcarnes.com.

CARNEY, Patrick J.; American musician (drums, bass guitar) and producer; b. 15 April 1980, Akron, Ohio; s. of Jim Carney and Mary Stormer. *Career:* Founder-mem. The Black Keys 2001–; f. Audio Eagle Records 2005–10; formed side project Drummer 2009; also producer for groups including Beaten Awake, Houseguest, Churchbuilder. *Recordings include:* albums: with The Black Keys: The Big Come Up 2002, Thickfreakness 2003, Rubber Factory 2004, Magic Potion 2007, Attack & Release 2008, Blakroc (collaboration with Damon Dash and several rap artists) 2009, Brothers (Grammy Awards for Best Alternative Music Album and Best Recording Package 2010) 2010, El Camino (Grammy Award for Best Rock Album 2013) 2011, Turn Blue 2014; with Drummer: Feel Good Together 2009. *Honours:* Grammy Award for Best Rock Performance by a Duo or Group with Vocals 2011, Best Rock Performance, for Best Rock Song (Lonely Boy) 2013, BRIT Award for Best Int. Group 2014. *Address:* c/o Nonesuch Records, Warner Music Group, 75 Rockefeller Plaza, New York, NY 10019, USA (office). *E-mail:* info@nonesuch.com (office). *Website:* www.theblackkeys.com (home).

CARONE, Anthony; Canadian keyboard player. *Education:* McMaster Univ. *Career:* mem. Arkells 2011–; toured USA with The Maine and Lydia 2012; toured Europe with Billy Talent and Anti-Flag 2012; support act for Tragically Hip on Canadian tour 2013. *Recordings:* albums: with Arkells: Michigan Left 2011. *Honours:* Juno Award for New Group of the Year 2012. *Current Management:* c/o Eggplant Entertainment Inc., 11 Davies Avenue, Suite 303, Toronto, ON M4M 2A9; Adam Countryman and Jack Ross, The Agency Group Ltd, 2 Berkeley Street, Suite 202, Toronto, ON M5A 4J5, Canada. *Telephone:* (416) 368-5599 (Agency Group). *Fax:* (416) 368-4655 (Agency Group). *E-mail:* info@eggplantent.com; adamcountryman@theagencygroup.com; jackross@theagencygroup.com. *Website:* www.eggplantent.com; www.theagencygroup.com; www.arkells.ca.

CARPENTER, Mary Chapin, BA; American country, folk singer, musician (guitar) and songwriter; b. 21 Feb. 1958, Princeton, NJ; m. Timmy Smith. *Education:* Brown Univ. *Career:* winner of numerous local music competitions; solo recording artist 1986–; has written songs for a variety of artists; conducted fundraising concerts for elimination of land mines. *Recordings include:* albums: Home Town Girl 1987, State of The Heart 1989, Shooting Straight In The Dark 1990, Come On Come On 1992, Stones In The Road (Grammy Award for Best Country Album 1995) 1994, A Place In The World 1996, Party Doll and Other Favourites 1999, Time Sex Love 2001, Between Here and Gone 2004, The Calling 2007, Come Darkness, Come Light: Twelve Songs of Christmas 2008, The Age of Miracles 2010, Songs from the Movies 2014; also appears on recordings by: Joan Baez, Roseanne Cash, The Chieftains, Shawn Colvin, Indigo Girls, Patty Loveless, Dolly Parton, The Rankin Family, Ricky Skaggs, Dusty Springfield, Pam Tillis, Trisha Yearwood. *Honours:* five Washington Area Music Awards, CMA Vocalist of the Year 1992, Grammy Awards for Best Female Country Vocal Performance 1992, 1993, 1994, 1995, Country Music Award for Female Vocalist of the Year 1993; inducted into Nashville Songwriters Hall of Fame 2012. *Current Management:* c/o Cathy Kerr Management, 7715 Sunset Boulevard, Suite 100, Los Angeles, CA 90046, USA. *E-mail:* cathy@cathykerr.com. *Website:* www.marychapincarpenter.com.

CARPENTER, Richard Lynn; American singer, composer, arranger and musician (piano); b. 15 Oct. 1946, New Haven, Conn.; m. Mary Rudolph 1984; five c. *Education:* California State Univ. *Career:* f. The Richard Carpenter trio (with sister Karen and Wes Jacobs) 1965; mem. Spectrum (Karen Carpenter, John Bettis, Leslie Johnston, Gary Sims and Danny Woodhams) 1967; Founder mem. Carpenters 1969–83 (until sister Karen Carpenter's death 1983); mem. The American Soc. of Composers, Authors and Publishers, Nat. Acad. of Recording Arts and Sciences. *Recordings include:* albums: with Carpenters: Offering (aka Ticket To Ride) 1969, Close To You 1970, Carpenters 1971, A Song For You 1972, Now and Then 1973, Horizon 1975, A Kind of Hush 1976, Live At The Palladium 1977, Passage 1977, The Singles 1974–78, Christmas Portrait 1978, Made In America 1981, Voice of The Heart 1983, Yesterday Once More 1984, An Old Fashioned Christmas 1985, Lovelines 1989; solo: Time 1987, Richard Carpenter: Pianist, Arranger, Composer 1998. *Honours:* Group of Year 1971, three Grammy Awards, American Music Award 1973; star in the Hollywood Walk of Fame. *Address:* PO Box 3787, Thousand Oaks, CA 91359-0787, USA. *Website:* www.richardandkarencarpenter.com.

CARPENTER, Stephen; American musician (guitar). *Career:* Founder mem., Deftones 1988–. *Recordings include:* albums: Adrenaline 1995, Around the Fur 1997, Live (EP) 1999, White Pony 2000, Back To School 2001, Deftones 2003, More Maximum Deftones 2003, Saturday Night Wrist 2006, Diamond Eyes 2010. *Honours:* Kerrang! Classic Songwriter Award 2007. *Website:* www.deftones.com.

CARR, Andy; musician (bass guitar, guitar), singer and songwriter; b. 6 Dec. 1967, Kirkcaldy, Fife, Scotland. *Education:* Fife Coll. of Further and Higher Education. *Career:* lead singer and bass guitar, Summerfield Blues 1988–96, with live sessions and radio broadcasts; mem. PRS, Musicians' Union. *Recordings:* with Summerfield Blues: Devil and The Freightman, Let's Scare The Posh People (EP) and Little Miss Behavin'. *Honours:* Scottish Blues Band of the Year 1993–94. *Address:* 192 Glasgow Road, Perth, Scotland. *Website:* www.myspace.com/summerfieldbluesband.

CARR, Budd, BA, MA; American music supervisor; b. 5 Sept. 1945, Jersey City, New Jersey; m. Jeanne, 4 Oct. 1970, two s., one d. *Education:* University of Illinois. *Career:* Began as music agent for CMA; Acts handled include: James Taylor; Bob Seger; Blind Faith; Carole King; Crosby Stills and Nash; Moved to IFA, acts handled: Eric Clapton Comeback Tour; Queen; Jefferson Starship; Stephen Stills; Left agency, signed band Kansas; Became personal manager, started management company, 1980; Joined forces with Wil Sharpe in Carr/Sharpe Entertainment Services, 1990; Clients include: Slaughter; Boxing Gandhis; The Buddah Heads; Eric Gale's Band; John Wetton; After 25 films as a music supervisor, joined Joel Sill, Windswept Pacific Entertainment, whose catalogue includes: John Mellencamp; Rod Stewart; Willie Nelson; Numerous hits songs of 50s, 60s, 70s. *Films:* credits as music supervisor or executive music supervisor include: The Terminator, 1984; Return of The Living Dead, 1985; Music supervisor: Salvador, 1986; Platoon, 1986; Wall Street, 1987; Talk Radio, 1988; Alien Nation, 1988; Born On The Fourth of July, 1989; Executive Music Producer: The Doors, 1991; JFK: 1991; Heaven and Earth, 1993; Natural Born Killers, 1994; Copycat, 1995; Nixon, 1995; Twister, 1996; Speed 2, 1997; I Know What You Did Last Summer, 1997; Stigmata, 1999, Any Given Sunday 1999, Whipped 2000, Beautiful 2000, Enemy at the Gates 2001, The Score 2001, Rock Star 2001, Life or Something Like It 2002, Hotel Rwanda 2004, W 2008, Nothing Like the Holidays 2008, The Crazies 2010. *Television:* credits as music supervisor: Californication 2007–, Eastwick 2009–10. *Current Management:* Gorfaine/Schwartz Agency, 4111 W. Alameda Avenue, Suite 509, Burbank, CA 91505, USA. *Telephone:* (818) 260-8500. *Website:* www.gsamusic.com.

CARR, Martin, (Brave Captain); British musician (guitar) and songwriter; b. 29 Nov. 1968, Thurso, Scotland. *Career:* mem. The Boo Radleys 1989–99; solo artist as Brave Captain 2002–. *Compositions include:* Lazarus 1993, Wake Up Boo 1994, Ride the Tiger 1995. *Recordings include:* albums: with The Boo Radleys: Ichabod and I 1989, Everything's Alright Forever 1992, Giant Steps 1993, Learning To Walk 1994, Sharks Patrol These Waters 1995, Wake Up 1995, C'mon Kids 1996; with Eggman: First Fruits 1996, King Size 1998; solo: Advertisements For Myself 2002, All Watched Over by Machines of Loving Grace 2004, Distractions 2006, Ye Gods (and little fishes) 2009. *Honours:* NME Brat Award for Best Album 1994, Select Magazine Best Album of the Year 1994, Liverpool Echo Album of the Year 1995. *Website:* www.bravecaptain.co.uk; www.martin-carr.com.

CARR, Vikki; American singer; b. (Florencia Bisenta de Casillas Martinez Cardona, 19 July 1940, El Paso, Tex.; d. of Carlos Cardona and Florencia Cardona. *Education:* Rosemead High School. *Career:* soloist with Pepe Callahan Mexican-Irish band; appeared at Royal Command Performance 1967, Inaugural Celebration, Kennedy Music Center 1973; host Mrs America Pageant 1981–87, Mrs World Pageant 1984–87, Hispanic World Vision 1989, 1990; numerous TV appearances; toured military bases in Viet Nam; f. Vikki Carr Scholarship Foundation 1971. *Stage appearances include:* South Pacific, The Unsinkable Molly Brown, I'm Getting My Act Together and Taking It on the Road. *Television appearance:* Mod Squad 1972. *Recordings include:* albums: Disculpame, Total, Ni Princesa, Cosas del Amor (Grammy Award for Best Latin Pop Album) 1991, Reta Manda Y Provoca 1998, Memorias Memorias 1999, Vikki Carr Christmas Album 2000, Viva La Vida 2012, Frente a Frente 2015. *Honours:* Los Angeles Times Woman of the Year 1970, Grammy Award for Best Mexican-American Performance 1985, YWCA Silver Achievement Award 1989, Nosotros Humanitarian and Golden Eagle Awards 1981, 1989, Hispanic Heritage Award 1996, Hispanic Heritage Award, La Prensa 2001, Trefoil Award, San Antonio Girl Scouts of America 2002, Medallion of Excellence Award, Congressional Hispanic Caucus Inst. 2011. *Address:* PO Box 780968, San Antonio, TX 78278, USA. *E-mail:* dannmosstv@aol.com. *Website:* www.vikkicarr.com.

CARRACK, Paul; British singer, songwriter and musician (keyboards, guitar); b. 22 April 1951, Sheffield, Yorks., England; s. of the late Ben Carrack and Joan Carrack; m.; four c. *Education:* Myers Grove Comprehensive, Sheffield. *Career:* fmr mem. Ace; mem. Squeeze 1980–81, Mike and The Mechanics 1986–; numerous concerts; solo artist 1980–; collaborations with Nick Lowe, Carlene Carter, John Hiatt, Phil Manzanera, The Pretenders, Roxy Music, Elvis Costello, The Undertones, The Smiths, Eric Clapton, Elton John, Roger Waters, Ringo Starr, BB King, Eagles. *Recordings include:* albums: with Squeeze: East Side Story 1981; with Mike and The Mechanics: Mike and The Mechanics 1986, The Living Years 1988, Word Of Mouth 1991, Beggar On A Beach Of Gold 1995, Hits 1996; solo: The Nightbirds 1980, Suburban Voodoo 1982, One Good Reason 1987, Ace Mechanic 1987, Carrack Collection 1988, Groove Approved 1989, Carrackter Reference 1991, Blue Views 1996, Beautiful World 1997, Satisfy My Soul 2000, Groovin' 2001, It Ain't Over 2003, The Story So Far 2006, I Know that Name 2008, A Different Hat 2010. *E-mail:* management@carrack.biz. *Address:* PO Box 450, Rickmansworth, Herts., WD3 5YX, England (office). *Telephone:* (114) 258-0338 (home). *E-mail:* paul@carrack.biz (home). *Website:* www.carrack-uk.com.

CARRASCO, Joe 'King'; American musician (guitar), vocalist and songwriter; b. (Joe Teutsch), 6 Dec. 1953, Dumas, Tex.; m. (divorced); one s. *Education:* Univ. of Texas. *Career:* f. bands Joe King Carrasco and El Molino in 1970s; solo artist 1978–; Founder mem., The Crowns 1980–; mem., The American Soc. of Composers, Authors and Publishers; f. Viva Perros (non-profit group). *Recordings include:* albums: with Joe King Carrasco and El Molino: Tex-Mex Rock & Roll (LP) 1979; with Joe King Carrasco and The Crowns: Party Safari 1981, Joe King Carrasco and The Crowns 1981, Synapse Gap 1982, Party Weekend 1983, Bordertown 1985, Bandido Rock 1987, Royal Loyal & Live 1990, Dia de los Muertos 1993, Hot Sun 1999, Hay Te Guacho Cucaracho 2001, El Rey 2008, Concierto Para Los Perros 2011, Tattoo Laredo 2011, Vamos A Get Down 2011, Que Wow 2012. *Honours:* inducted into Texas Music Hall of Fame, Austin Music Hall of Fame; Lifetime Achievement Award, Texas Music Acad. 2012. *E-mail:* joeking@joeking.com. *Website:* www.joeking.com.

CARRIÉ, Patrice; French musician (bass guitar). *Career:* mem., Rinôcérôse 1994–. *Recordings include:* albums: Retrospective 1998, Installation Sonore 1999, Music Kills Me 2002, Schizophonia 2005, Rinôcérôse 2006, Futurinô 2009. *Current Management:* P Pole Agency, 1 bis rue de Verdun, 34000 Montpellier, France. *Telephone:* (4) 67 12 81 70. *E-mail:* pascal@pi-pole.com. *Website:* www.pi-pole.com. *Address:* c/o Manuel Perez, Universal Music, 20 rue de Fossés St. Jacques, 75235 Paris, cedex 05, France. *E-mail:* Manuel.Perez@umusic.com; rinocerose@hotmail.fr. *Website:* www.universalmusic.fr; www.rinocerose.com.

CARRINGTON, Terri Lyne; American musician (drums), songwriter, singer and producer; *Professor of Percussion, Berklee College of Music;* b. 4 Aug. 1965, Medford, Mass; d. of Solomon Matthew Carrington and Judith Anne Carrington. *Education:* Berklee Coll. of Music, Boston. *Career:* original house drummer, Arsenio Hall Show; toured with Al Jarreau, Herbie Hancock, David Sanborn, Joe Sample, Stan Getz, Wayne Shorter, Stan Getz, Cassandra Wilson; Prof. of Percussion, Berklee Coll. 2005–; also Artistic Dir, Summer Jazz Workshop; mem. NARAS. *Compositions include:* Reach For Your Dreams, for 1996 Olympics; Josa Lee, for Dianne Reeves; Whatcha Gonna Do, Patrice Rushen. *Recordings include:* albums as a leader: Real Life Story, More to Say: Real Life Story, Next Gen 2009, The Mosaic Project (Grammy Award for Best Jazz Vocal Album 2012) 2011, Money Jungle: Provocative in Blue (Grammy Award for Best Jazz Instrumental Album 2013) 2014; solo:

Jazz Is A Spirit 2002. *Honours:* Dr hc (Berklee Coll.) 2003; Boston Music Award 1989, 1990. *Address:* PO Box 80393, Stoneham, MA 02180, USA. *Telephone:* (818) 569-5479. *E-mail:* TLCdrum@aol.com. *Website:* www .terrilynecarrington.com.

CARROLL, Dina; British singer and songwriter; b. (Geraldine Carroll), 21 Aug. 1968, Cambridge, England; m. John Cooper. *Career:* lead singer, Quartz, 1990; solo artist 1992–; tours and concerts. *Compositions:* co-writer with producer Nigel Lowis. *Recordings include:* albums: So Close 1993, Only Human 1996, Very Best Of 2001, The Collection 2004. *Honours:* BRIT Award for Best Female Artist 1994, Mercury Music Prize 1993, three International Dance Awards 1994, Great Britain Variety Award, Best Performing Artist, Silver Clef Award, Best Newcomer 1994.

CARRON-SMITH, Patricia, (Pat Spoons); Welsh singer, musician and teacher; b. (Patricia Carron Harvey), 3 April 1952, Llantrisant, Wales; d. of Cyril Ainsley Harvey and Elsie Reavley. *Career:* mem. Welsh traditional music groups, Swansea Jack 1977–78, Calennig 1978–2000, Calennig Dance Band 1978–, duo with Ned Clamp 2001–; numerous TV appearances; mem. Equity, Musicians' Union, Performing Right Soc., PPL, CDdWC, COTC. *Recordings include:* with Swansea Jack: The Seven Wonders 1978; with Calennig: Songs and Tunes From Wales 1980, You Can Take A White Horse Anywhere 1983, Dyddiau Gwynion Ionawr 1985, Dwr Glan 1990, Trade Winds 1994, A Gower Garland 2000, Live in Wanaka New Zealand 1999. *Television:* Gavin and Stacey (BBC), Grandpa in My Pocket (CBeebies). *Address:* 1 Ty Clwyta Cottages, Cross Inn, Llantrisant, Rhondda Cynon Taf, CF72 8AZ, Wales (home). *Telephone:* (1443) 226892 (office). *E-mail:* pat .spoons@virgin.net (office). *Website:* www.folkwales.org.uk (office); www .myspace.com/patsmithnedclamp.

CARSTEA, Elena; Romanian singer, songwriter and musician (guitar); b. 26 Feb. 1963, Agnita, Sibiu. *Career:* television shows include: Golden Orpheus 1993, Stars Duel 1993, Mamaia Festival, Five O'Clock Tea, Golden Stag; radio and TV concerts; mem. Radio Contact. *Recordings include:* Your Eyes (Public Prize for Composition) 1988, Tomorrow, Some Day 1990, Ballad For Sandra 1994. *Honours:* Cultural Merit in the Rank of Knight; Best Vocal Soloist of the Year Award 1994. *Address:* 61 Buzesti Street A6, Third Floor, Apartment 18, Sector 1, Bucharest, Romania.

CARTER, Carlene; American country singer and songwriter; b. (Rebecca Carlene Smith), 26 Sept. 1955, Nashville, Tenn.; d. of Carl Smith and June Carter; m. 1st Joe Simpkins (divorced); one d.; m. 2nd Jack Routh (divorced); one s.; m. 3rd Nick Lowe (divorced); m. 4th Joseph Breen 2006. *Education:* studied piano, and guitar with Carl Perkins. *Career:* solo country artist 1974–; mem. The Carter Sisters 1987. *Recordings include:* albums: Carlene Carter 1978, Two Sides to Every Woman 1979, Musical Shapes 1980, Blue Nun 1981, C'est Bon 1983, I Fell In Love 1990, Little Love Letters 1993, Little Acts of Treason 1995, Hindsight 20/20 1996, Stronger 2008. *Compositions include:* Easy From Now On, Appalachian Eyes, Guardian Angel, I Fell in Love, Stronger, Takes One to Know Me. *Film appearance include:* Too Drunk to Remember. *Theatre appearances include:* Pump Boys and Dinettes (London) 1985, Wildwood Rose 2006. *Current Management:* c/o Cathy Gurley, Gurley and Co., PO Box 150657, Nashville, TN 37215, USA. *Telephone:* (615) 269-0474. *Fax:* (615) 297-8755. *E-mail:* cathy@gurleybiz.com. *Website:* www .gurleybiz.com.

CARTER, Deana; American singer, songwriter and musician (guitar); b. 4 Jan. 1964, Nashville, Tenn. *Career:* British tour support to Jimmy Nail 1995; recording artist, extensive tours of USA and Canada; mem. Country Music Asscn (CMA), American Soc. of Composers, Authors and Publrs (ASCAP). *Recordings include:* albums: Did I Shave My Legs For This? (quadruple Platinum disc) 1995, Everything's Gonna Be Alright (Gold disc) 1998, Father Christmas (with Fred Carter Jr) 2001, I'm Just a Girl 2003, The Story of My Life 2005, The Chain 2007; singles: Strawberry Wine (CMA Single of the Year) 1997. *Honours:* Orville H. Gibson Award, Best Country Guitarist 1999. *Current Management:* c/o Warner/Chappell Music Limited, The Warner Building, 28 Kensington Church Street, London, W8 4EP, England. *Telephone:* (20) 7938-0000. *Fax:* (20) 7368-2777. *E-mail:* info@Deana.com. *Website:* deana.com.

CARTER, Derrick, (Sound Patrol, Tone Theory, Oneiro, The Unknown); American producer, remixer and DJ; b. 21 Oct. 1969, Chicago. *Career:* started to DJ, aged 9; worked for Curtis Jones' Cajual label; first release 1987; first break with Symbols and Instruments 1989; Co-founder, Classic Records (with Luke Solomon) 1996–; world-wide DJ; club residency at The End, London; collaborations with Mark Farina, Chris Nazuka, Basement Jaxx, Cajmere. *Recordings include:* albums: Sweetened – No Lemon (as Sound Patrol) 1995, The Future Sound of Chicago 1996, The Many Shades of Cajual 1996, The Cosmic Disco 1997, Pagan Offering 1998, Derrick L. Carter Presents: About Now… 2001, Squaredancing In A Roundhouse 2002, Choice 2003, Sessions 2005, Fabric 56 2010. *Address:* c/o Om Records, 2360 Third Street, San Francisco, CA 94107, USA. *E-mail:* info@on-records.com. *Website:* om-records .com; www.derrickcarter.com.

CARTER, James; American jazz musician (saxophone, clarinet, flute); b. 3 Jan. 1969, Detroit, Mich. *Career:* played and toured with Wynton Marsalis in 1986, aged 17; mem. Lester Bowie's New York Organ Ensemble 1988–99; performed with Lincoln Center Jazz Orchestra, the late Julius Hemphill, the late Ronald Shannon Jackson, Charles Mingus Big Band, Kathleen Battle,

Aretha Franklin, David Murray, Art Ensemble of Chicago, Ginger Baker, Sonny Rollins; mem. Heaven on Earth 2009. *Film:* Kansas City (portraying saxophonist Ben Webster) 1996. *Recordings include:* solo: Fat Man and the Hard Blues 1991, JC On The Set 1992, Jurassic Classics 1994, The Real Quietstorm 1995, Conversin' With The Elders 1996, In Carterian Fashion 1998, and Chasin' The Gypsy 2000, Layin' In The Cut 2000, Gardenias For Lady Day 2003, Live at Baker's Keyboard Lounge 2004, Out of Nowhere 2005, Gold Sounds 2005, Present Tense 2008, Caribbean Rhapsody 2011, At the Crossroads 2011, For Now 2011; with others: Heaven on Earth 2008. *Honours:* Dr Alaine Locke Award 2004. *Current Management:* c/o American International Artists, Inc., 356 Pine Valley Road, Hoosick Falls, NY 12090, USA. *Telephone:* (518) 686-0972. *Fax:* (518) 686-1960. *E-mail:* cynthia@aiartists .com. *Website:* www.aiartists.com; jamescarterlive.com.

CARTER, Kent; American musician (piano, cello, bassoon, bass); b. 12 June 1939, Hanover, New Hampshire; m. 1981; four s. *Education:* Berklee Coll. of Music, Boston. *Career:* participated in October Revolution, New York, early 1960s; performed with Jazz Composers Guild Orchestra; toured, recorded with artists including Paul Bley, Carla Bley, Michael Mantler, Steve Lacy, Don Cherry, Gato Barbieri, Alan Silva, Mal Waldron, Michael Smith, Bobby Bradford, Max Roach, Enrico Rava, Roswell Rudd, Derek Bailey, John Stevens, Trevor Watts, Steve McCall 1964–; mem., co-founder Tok Trio, including tours, Europe and Japan; mem. Steve Lacy Quintet, including tour, USA 1970–81; performed at many major European jazz festivals; founder, leader, chamber group Kent Carter String Trio, with Carlos Zingaro, Francois Dreno; collaboration with Michala Marcus (dance) in productions including Dance Music Image 1975–; f. new Kent Carter String Trio 2004–, concerts in Germany and France; fmr teacher, Ecole des Beaux Arts, Angouleme; played with Poitou-Charentes Symphony. *Compositions include:* Collaboration with choreographer Jean Pomares in ballet Paysages Avec Couple. *Recordings include:* Beauvais Cathedral, Kent Carter Solo with Claude Bernard, Suspensions, La Contrebasse, The Willisau Suites 1999, The Juillaguet Collection, Intersections 2006. *Films include:* Vanishing Traces, Batalha, Metemorphs de plants, Memoires de Charente, Corinne et Jeannot, Le Film File, A Treat. *Address:* Riviere, 16320 Juillaguet, France (home).

CARTER, Mel; American singer; b. 22 April 1939, Cincinnati, OH. *Education:* Cincinnati Conservatory of Music. *Career:* leading soloist and Asst Dir Greater Cincinnati Youth and Young Adult Choral Union; numerous live appearances include: Ciro's, with Dinah Washington; The Crescendo, with Bessie Griffin's Gospel Pearls; Guest on Ed Sullivan Show; Opened at The Flamingo, Las Vegas, with Damita Jo; headlined nightclubs across USA, Canada; films include: Prime Time, No Way Out; television appearances and tours. *Recordings include:* albums: When A Boy Falls In Love, My Heart Sings, Hold Me, Thrill Me, Kiss Me, Enter Laughing, Easy Listening, Be My Love, This Is My Life, Willing, Live In Hollywood, The Best Of Mel Carter. *Honours:* LA Weekly La Wee Award. *Website:* www.mel-carter.com.

CARTER, Nickolas (Nick) Gene; American singer, musician (drums), songwriter, dancer and actor; b. 28 Jan. 1980, Jamestown, NY; brother of Aaron Carter. *Career:* acted in commercials on TV; mem., Backstreet Boys 1993–; numerous tours and television appearances; started his own record label Kaotic. *Recordings include:* albums: with Backstreet Boys: Backstreet Boys 1996, Live in Concert 1998, Backstreet's Back 1998, Millennium 1999, Black And Blue 2000, Greatest Hits Chapter 1 2001, Never Gone 2005, Unbreakable 2007, This Is Us 2009, In a World Like This 2013; solo: Now Or Never 2002, I'm Taking Off 2011; others: Beautiful Lie (with Jennifer Paige) 2009. *Films appearances:* The Pendant (also directed) 2010, Kill Speed 2010, This is the End 2013. *Television:* House of Carters 2006. *Honours:* for Backstreet Boys: Billboard Music Awards for Best Group, Best Adult Contemporary Group 1998, Album of the Year, Artist of the Year 1999, MTV Music Video Award for Best Group Video 1998, MTV European Music Awards for Best Pop Act 1997, Best Group 1999, World Music Awards for Best-Selling Pop Group 1999, 2000, Best-Selling R&B Group 1999, 2000, Best-Selling Dance Group 1999, 2000, Best American Group 2000, American Music Awards for Favorite Pop/Rock Band, Duo or Group 2000, 2001. *Current Management:* Wright Entertainment Group (WEG Music), PO Box 590009, Orlando, FL 32859, USA. *Website:* www.backstreetboys.com; www.nickcarter .net.

CARTER, Regina, BMus; American jazz violinist, bandleader and academic; *Artist-in-Residence, Oakland University;* b. Detroit, Mich.; d. of Dan Carter and Grace Williamson Carter; m. Alvester Garnett 2004. *Education:* Cass Tech. High School, Center for Creative Studies, New England Conservatory of Music, Oakland Univ. *Career:* fmrly violinist, youth division, Detroit Symphony Orchestra; taught strings in USA and Germany; violinist, pop-jazz quintet Straight Ahead 1987–91; mem. String Trio of New York 1993–96; solo career 1995–, later formed own quintet; toured with Wynton Marsalis 1997; teacher at numerous colls including Berklee College of Music; Artist-in-Residence, Oakland Univ. 2007–; numerous collaborative recordings and appearances including with Mary J. Blige, James Carter, Aretha Franklin, Mark Helias, Lauryn Hill, Lena Horne, Joe Jackson, Oliver Lake, Carmen Lundy, Dolly Parton, Simon Rattle, Max Roach, Elliott Sharp, Steve Turre, Cassandra Wilson. *Recordings include:* albums: with Straight Ahead: Look Straight Ahead 1991, Body and Soul 1993; with String Trio of New York: Intermobility 1992, Octagon 1992, Blues…? 1993, An Outside Job 1994; solo: Regina Carter 1995, Something for Grace 1997, Rhythms of the Heart 1999, Motor City Moments 2000, Freefall (with Kenny Barron) 2001, Paganini:

After a Dream 2003, I'll Be Seeing You: A Sentimental Journey 2006, Reverse Thread 2010, Southern Comfort 2014; other appearances include: Loopin' the Cool, Mark Helias 1995, Xenocodex, Elliott Sharp 1996, Lotus Flower, Chasin' the Gypsy 2000. *Honours:* MacArthur Fellow Program Grant 2006, Jazz Journalists Asscn Awards for Violinist of the Year 2010, 2012, for Violinist/Violist/Cellist of the Year 2013, 2014, 2015. *Current Management:* c/o Darryl Pitt, Depth of Field Management, 1501 Broadway, Suite 1304, New York, NY 10036, USA. *Telephone:* (212) 302-9200. *Fax:* (212) 382-1639. *E-mail:* hello@dof3.com. *Address:* Oakland University Music, 2200 North Squirrel Road, Rochester, MI 48309-4401, USA (office). *Telephone:* (248) 370-2100 (office). *Website:* wwwp.oakland.edu/mtd (office); www.reginacarter.com.

CARTER, Roland M., MA; American composer and teacher; *Ruth S. Holmberg Professor of Music, University of Tennessee at Chattanooga*; b. 4 May 1942, Chattanooga, Tenn. *Education:* Howard High School, Hampton Univ. New York Univ., Catholic Univ. of America, Washington, DC, Aspen Choral Inst., Colo. *Career:* Asst Dir, accompanist and arranger, Crusader Male Chorus of Hampton 1962–79, Dir 1980–89; Asst Dir, Choir Dirs and Organists Guild of the Hampton Univ. Ministers Conference 1963–79, Dir 1980–89; Dir Peninsula Youth Symphony, Hampton 1974–80; Founder and Chief Exec. Mar-Vel Publishers, Chattanooga 1978–; accompanist and coach for Marilyn Thompson 1982–; Dir, Chattanooga Choral Soc. for the Preservation of Negro Spirituals 1989–; Dir of Music, First Baptist Church, Chattanooga 1992; teacher, Summer Music Inst. for High School Students, Hampton Univ. 1964–69, Dir 1966–69; Dir of Choral Music, Hampton Univ. 1965–88, Chair 1986–89; mem. Music Dept Faculty, Univ. of Tenn. at Chattanooga 1989–, Dept Head 1989–95, currently Ruth S. Holmberg Prof. of Music; mem. Nat. Asscn of Negro Musicians Inc. *Compositions include:* A Hampton Portrait: Prologue 1968, Hold Fast to Dreams 1978, You Must Have That True Religion 1982, No Room in the Inn 1988, Psalm 23 1988, Anniversary Hymn 1988, How Beautiful Are the Feet 1989, I Dream A World 1994. *Honours:* Hon. mem. Morehouse Glee Club 2004; Hampton Univ. Lindback Award for Distinguished Teaching 1982, Coll. of Arts and Sciences, Univ. of Tenn. at Chattanooga Excellence in Service Award 1992, Hon. DMus (Shaw Univ.); MacLellan Foundation Fellowship, Chattanooga 1965–66, Nat. Asscn of Negro Musicians Distinguished Musician Award 1974, Musician of the Year (Eastern Region) 1981, Black Music Caucus of MENC Nat. Award 1994, Tennessee Gov.'s Arts Award 2003. *Address:* Department of Music, 308 Fine Arts, Dept 1451, 615 McCallie Avenue, Chattanooga, TN 37403, USA (office). *Telephone:* (423) 425-4609 (office). *Fax:* (423) 425-4603 (office). *E-mail:* Roland-Carter@utc.edu (office). *Website:* www.utc.edu/Academic/Music/staff/roland-carter (office); www.rolandcarter.com.

CARTER, Ronald, BMus, MusM; American jazz musician (bass) and educator; b. 4 May 1937, Ferndale, MI; m. Janet Hosbrouck 1958; two s. *Education:* Eastman School of Music, Manhattan School of Music. *Career:* bass player for Chico Hamilton Quintet, Don Ellis, Cannonball Adderley, Thelonious Monk, Eric Dolphy, Miles Davis Quintet 1963–68, Wynton Marsalis; formed own quartet 1975; also prolific freelance musician for numerous artists; fmr Artistic Dir, Thelonius Monk Inst. of Jazz Studies; mem. music faculty, City Coll. of New York, currently Distinguished Prof. Emer.; mem, Jazz Musicians' Asscn. *Recordings:* over 2000 recordings; albums include: Out Front 1966, Uptown Conversation 1970, Blues Farm 1973, All Blues 1974, Magic 1975, Spanish Blue 1975, Anything Goes 1975, Yellow and Green 1976, Pastels 1977, Song For You 1977, Parade 1979, New York Slick 1980, Patrao 1980, Heart and Soul 1982, Etudes 1983, Live At Village West 1984, All Alone 1989, Friends 1993, Jazz, My Romance 1994, Mr Bow-Tie 1996, Brandenburg Concerto 1998, The Bass and I 1997, So What 1999, Orfeu 1999, When Skies are Grey 2001, Holiday in Rio 2001, Stardust 2002, The Golden Striker 2003, Eight Plus 2003, Live at The Village Vanguard 2006, Ron Carter's Great Big Band 2011; also on numerous recordings by: Roy Ayers, Gato Barbieri, Chet Baker, George Benson, Kenny Burrell, Billy Cobham, Chick Corea, Larry Coryell, Miles Davis, Art Farmer, Roberta Flack, Aretha Franklin, The Four Tops, Red Garland, Stan Getz, the Great Jazz Trio, Jim Hall, Herbie Hancock, Coleman Hawkins, Joe Henderson, Freddie Hubbard, Milt Jackson, Bob James, Antonio Carlos Jobim, Billy Joel, Quincy Jones, Hubert Laws, Michael Legrand, Manhattan Transfer, Houston Person, Diana Ross, Tom Rush, Horace Silver, Wayne Shorter, Paul Simon, Grace Slick, Jimmy Smith, McCoy Turner, Stanley Turrentine, VSOP. *Publications:* author of books on jazz and classical bass. *Honours:* Dr hc (New England Conservatory of Music), (Manhattan School of Music); Downbeat Critics Award, International Jazz Bassist of Year 1965, Readers Poll Winner 1973–75, 1983, Detroit Free Press, Jazz Bassist of Decade 1966, Japan All-Star Jazz Poll Winner 1969–70, Grammy Awards for Best Jazz Instrument Group (with the Miles Davis Tribute Band) 1993, for Best Jazz Instrumental Composition (for Call Sheet Blues) 1998, Hutchinson Award, Eastman School of Music 2002. *Current Management:* c/o Joanne Jimenez, The Bridge Agency, 35 Clark Street, Suite A5, Brooklyn, NY 11201, USA. *Telephone:* (718) 522-5107. *Fax:* (718) 522-3067. *E-mail:* joanne@roncarter.net. *E-mail:* info@roncarter.net (office). *Website:* www.roncarter.net.

CARTHY, Eliza Amy Forbes, MBE; British folk singer, songwriter, musician (violin), broadcaster and music producer; *Vice-President, English Folk Dance and Song Society*; b. 23 Aug. 1975, Scarborough, N Yorks., England; d. of Martin Carthy and Norma Waterson; two d. *Career:* sang with Watersons, Cambridge Festival 1988; with Waterdaughters, Vancouver Folk Music Festival 1989; numerous tours, TV appearances; headlined Sidmouth Folk Festival 1999; appeared mainstage Glastonbury Festival 2000; played for former US President Bill Clinton 2003; currently Vice-Pres., English Folk Dance and Song Soc.; mem., Waterson:Carthy, Imagined Village; also solo artist; mem., Musicians' Union, Performing Right Soc., PRS for Music. *Compositions:* By Then, The Wrong Favour, Time in the Sun, Peggy, Accordion Song 1998, Russia 1998, Red Rice 1998, Fallen Leaves 1998. *Radio:* Secombe on Sunday 1993, co-host, Mark Radcliffe (BBC Radio 2) 2003–06, Vaughan-Willams special 2006, various others. *Television:* Later… with Jools Holland (BBC Two) 1996–2008, special concert from Union Chapel (BBC Four) 2003, Cambridge Folk Festival coverage (co-presenter with Mark Radcliffe) (BBC Four) 2003, My Music (BBC Four) 2008. *Recordings include:* albums: Eliza Carthy and Nancy Kerr 1993, Waterson:Carthy 1994, Heat, Light and Sound 1995, Norma Waterson 1996, Common Tongue 1997, Eliza Carthy and the Kings of Calicutt 1997, Red Rice (solo) 1998, Angels and Cigarettes 2000, On Reflection (with Nancy Kerr, compilation) 2002, Anglicana (solo) (Best Album, BBC Radio 2 Folk Awards 2003) 2002, The Definitive Collection (solo compilation) 2003, A Dark Light (with Waterson:Carthy) 2002, Rough Music (solo) 2004, Holy Heathens and The Old Green Man (with Waterson:Carthy) 2006, Dreams of Breathing Underwater (solo) 2008, Gift (with Norma Waterson) 2010, Neptune (solo) 2011, Wayward Daughter (solo) 2013; guest on albums by Jools Holland and his Big Band, Rogue's Gallery, Paul Weller, Billy Bragg (solo and with Wilco), Patrick Wolf, David Rotheray. *Honours:* numerous BBC Radio 2 Folk Awards, including Best Group and Best Traditional Track (Waterson:Carthy) 2000, Folk Singer of the Year 2003, Best Traditional Track 2003, Paul Hamlyn Award 2012. *Current Management:* c/o Scarlet Music Services, Southview, 68 Siltside, Gosberton Risegate, Spalding, Lincs., PE11 4ET, England. *Telephone:* (1775) 841750. *E-mail:* liz@scarletrecording.co.uk. *Website:* www.scarletmusicservices.co.uk; www.eliza-carthy.com.

CARTHY, Martin, MBE; British folk singer and musician (guitar); b. 21 May 1940, Hatfield, Herts.; m. Norma Waterson; one s. one d. (Eliza Carthy). *Career:* mem. skiffle group, The Thameside Four; solo folk artist 1963–; resident musician, Troubadour folk club, London; mem. Three City Four; regular recordings, tours with Dave Swarbrick; mem. Steeleye Span 1969–72, Brass Monkey, The Watersons, Waterson:Carthy, Keith Hancock Band. *Recordings include:* albums: Martin Carthy 1965, Second Album 1966, Byker Hill 1967, But Two Came By (with Dave Swarbrick) 1968, Prince Heathen (with Dave Swarbrick) 1969, Landfall 1971, This Is Martin Carthy 1972, Sweet Wivelsfield 1974, Shearwater 1975, Crown of Horn 1976, Because It's There 1979, Out Of The Cut 1982, Right Of Passage 1989, Life and Limb (with Dave Swarbrick) 1990, Skin and Bone (with Dave Swarbrick) 1992, Kershaw Sessions 1995, Signs Of Life 1999, Both Ears And The Tail 2001, Straws in the Wind (with Dave Swarbrick) 2006, Holy Heathens and The Old Green Man (as Waterson:Carthy) 2006. *Honours:* BBC Folk Award for Folk Singer of the Year, for Best Traditional Track 2005. *Current Management:* Moneypenny, The Stables, Westwood House, North Dalton, Driffield, North Humberside, YO25 9XA, England. *Website:* www.watersoncarthy.com.

CARTWRIGHT, Deirdre Josephine; British musician (guitar), composer, author and teacher; b. 27 July 1956, London; one d. *Career:* guitar presenter of both series of BBC TV's Rockschool, shown world-wide; toured 17 countries with guest stars, national tours with own group Deirdre Cartwright Group 1994–95; Arts Council tour with her eight-piece band 1996; concerts in Germany and Switzerland 1996–97; Arts Council-funded comm. 1996; Co-operates weekly jazz club Blow the Fuse at Vortex, North London; presents new record releases for Jazz Notes, Radio 3; mem. Advisory Panel, Jazz Services; mem. Musicians' Union, PRS. *Recordings include:* with The Guest Stars: The Guest Stars, Out At Night, Live In Berlin, One Night Stands, Precious Things 2002, Dr Quantum Leaps 2005, Tune Up Turn On Stretch Out 2008, as featured artist, jazz compilation, debut with The Deirdre Cartwright Group, Play, second solo CD with Steve Lodder, Annie Whitehead 1998. *Publications include:* Rockschool Books, Rock Guitar Method, The Rockschool Sessions, The Rockfile, The Interactive Guitar Bible 2007. *Honours:* Arts Council Composition Award 1991.

CARTY, John; Irish musician (fiddle, banjo, flute); b. 7 Jan. 1962, London, England; s. of John P. Carty and Margaret Carty (née Folan); m. Maureen Brennan 1987; one s. one d. *Education:* studied traditional Irish music with Brendan Mulkere. *Career:* moved to Ireland 1991; multi-instrumentalist playing fiddle, banjo and flute; formed dance band At the Racket 1997; mem. Patrick Street 2007–; also performs with various musicians and bands including Matt Molloy, Arty McGlynn, Chieftains, John Carty Fesival Band, Leitrim Equation 3, De Danaan; performs at various festivals in Europe, North America and Australasia. *Recordings include:* albums: The Cat that Ate the Candle 1994, Last Night's Fun 1996, with At the Racket: At the Racket 1997, Mirth Making Heroes 2001; Yeah That's All It Is (with Arty McGlynn) 2000, At It Again 2003, Pathway to the Well 2008, It's Not Racket Science 2008, I Will if I Can 2009, Meadbh (The Crimson Path) 2010, At Complete Ease 2011, Leitrim Equation 3 (with Seamus Begley and Dónal Lunny) 2012, The Good Mixer (with Henry Benagh, Marcus Hernon and Noel O'Grady) 2015. *Honours:* TG4 Traditional Musician of the Year 2003. *Current Management:* c/o Racket Management, Knockroe, Boyle, Co. Roscommon, Ireland. *Telephone:* (71) 9668063. *E-mail:* info@johncartymusic.com. *Website:* www.johncartymusic.com.

CARVALHO, Beth; Brazilian singer, musician (guitar) and composer; b. (Elizabeth Santos Leal de Carvalho), 5 May 1946, Rio de Janeiro; d. of João

Francisco Leal de Carvalho and Maria Nair Santos Leal de Carvalho; m. Edson de Souza Barbosa 1979, one d. *Career:* solo artist 1969–. *Recordings include:* albums: Andança 1969, Canto Por Um Novo Dia 1973, Pra Seu Governo 1974, Pandeiro e Viola 1975, Mundo Melhor 1976, Nos Botequins da Vida 1977, De Pé No Chão 1978, Beth Carvalho no Pagode 1979, Sentimento Brasileiro 1980, Na fonte 1981, Traço de União 1982, Suor no Rosto 1983, Coração Feliz 1984, Das Bençãos Que Virão Com os Novos Amanhãs 1985, Beth 1986, Beth Carvalho Ao Vivo (Montreux) 1987, Alma do Brasil 1988, Saudades da Guanabara 1989, Intérprete 1991, Ao Vivo no Olympia – Som Livre 1991, Pérolas – 25 Anos de Samba 1992, Canta o Samba de São Paulo 1993, Brasileira da Gema 1996, Pérolas do Pagode 1998, Pagode de Mesa Ao Vivo 1999, Pagode de Mesa Ao Vivo 2 2000, Nome Sagrado – Beth Carvalho Canta Nelson Cavaquinho 2001, Canta Cartola 2003, A Madrinha do Samba – Ao Vivo 2004, 40 anos de Carreira – Ao Vivo no Theatro Municipal, Vol.2 2006, 40 anos de Carreira – Ao Vivo no Theatro Municipal, Vol.1 2006, Canta o samba da bahia 2008, Nosso Samba Tá na Rua 2011. *Address:* Caixa Postal 16.210, 22221-971 Rio de Janeiro, RJ, Brazil. *E-mail:* contato@bethcarvalho .com.br. *Website:* www.bethcarvalho.com.br.

CASABLANCAS, Julian; American singer and songwriter; b. 23 Aug. 1978, New York, NY; s. of Jeanette Christiansen and John Casablancas; m. Juliet Joslin 2005; one s. *Education:* L'Institut Le Rosey, Switzerland, Dwight School, New York. *Career:* mem. The Strokes 1998–; toured with The Sick Six 2009–2010; collaborated with various musicians (Danger Mouse, Sparklehorse, Daft Punk); f. Cult Records 2009. *Recordings include:* albums: with The Strokes: Is This It (NME Award for Album of the Year) 2001, Room on Fire 2003, First Impressions of Earth 2006; solo: Phrazes for the Young 2009. *Honours:* NME Awards for Band of the Year, Best New Act 2001, for Best International Band 2006, BRIT Award for Best International Newcomer 2002. *Current Management:* William Morris Endeavor Entertainment, Centre Point, 103 New Oxford Street, London, WC1A 1DD, England. *E-mail:* richard@cultrecords.com. *Website:* www.cultrecords.com; www.thestrokes .com; www.juliancasablancas.com.

CASADY, Bianca; American singer and musician (percussion); b. Hawaii; sister of Sierra Casady. *Career:* mem., CocoRosie 2004–; toured across Europe, USA; collaborated with numerous artists and bands, including Robert Wilson, Rajasthan Roots. *Recordings include:* albums: La Maison De Mon Rêve 2004, Noah's Ark 2005, The Adventures of Ghosthorse & Stillborn 2007, Grey Oceans 2010, Tales of a Grass Widow 2013. *E-mail:* mary@transistorinc.com. *Website:* www.transistorinc.com.

CASADY, John (Jack); American musician (bass); b. 13 April 1944, Washington DC. *Education:* Montgomery College, Maryland. *Career:* member, The Triumphs; member, Jefferson Airplane 1966–72, 1992; also member, side project, Hot Tuna 1968–; member, Kantner Balin Casady (KBC) Band 1985–88, 1992–; member, Moonalice 2007–; performances include Berkeley Folk Festival 1966, Monterey Jazz Festival 1966, Monterey Pop Festival 1967, Newport Pop Festival 1968, Isle of Wight Festival 1968, Atlantic City Pop Festival 1969, Woodstock Music and Art Fair 1969, Altamont Speedway, with Rolling Stones 1969, Bath Festival 1970. *Recordings:* albums: with Jefferson Airplane: Jefferson Airplane Takes Off 1966, After Bathing At Baxter's 1968, Crown of Creation 1968, Volunteers 1969, Blows Against The Empire 1970, Bark 1970, Jefferson Airplane 1989, Jefferson Airplane Loves You 1992; with Hot Tuna: Hot Tuna 1970, First Pull Up, Then Pull Down 1971, Burgers 1972, The Phosphorescent Rat 1974, America's Choice 1975, Yellow Fever 1975, Hopkorv 1976, Double Dose 1977, The Last Interview? 1978, Final Vinyl 1979, Splashdown 1984, Pair A Dice Found 1990, Live At Sweetwater 1992, Splashdown Trio 1997, Best Of 1998, And Furthermore 1999; with KBC Band: KBC Band 1986; with Jefferson Starship: Deep Space 1995, Windows of Heaven 1999, Ignition 2001; solo: Dream Factor 2003; guest musician: If Only I Could Remember My Name, David Crosby 1972. *Current Management:* Fur Peace Management, 39495 St Clair Road, Pomeroy, OH 45769, USA. *Telephone:* (740) 992-2575. *E-mail:* fpman@earthlink.net. *Website:* www .jackcasady.com (home).

CASADY, Sierra; American singer and musician (guitar, flute); b. 11 June 1980, Iowa; sister of Bianca Casady. *Education:* Conservatoire de Paris. *Career:* moved to New York 1998; moved to France 2000; Founder mem. CocoRosie 2004–; collaborated with numerous other artists (Rajasthan Roots, The Royal Concertgebouw Orchestra); curated and produced the CocoRosie project 2012. *Recordings include:* albums: with CocoRosie: La Maison De Mon Rêve 2004, Beautiful Boyz 2004 (EP), Noah's Ark 2005, The Adventures of Ghosthorse & Stillborn 2007, God Has a Voice, She Speaks Through Me 2008, Coconuts, Plenty of Junk Food 2009 (EP), Grey Oceans 2010, Tales of a Grass Widow 2013. *Address:* c/o Sub Pop Records, 2013 Fourth Avenue, Third Floor, Seattle, WA 98121, USA. *E-mail:* info@subpop.com. *Website:* www.subpop .com.

CASALS, Emmanuel; French sound engineer and producer; *CEO, Lucie-Music Ltd;* b. 9 May 1970. *Education:* Univ. of Nantes, Univ. of Brest. *Career:* sound engineer for Cesaria Evora, Gotan Project, Matmatah, The Silencers, Denez Prigent, Murray Head, Calvin Russel; CEO LucieMusic Ltd., also engineer and Dir La Chapelle and Gam Recording Studios, Belgium. *Recordings:* albums: as producer: Denez Prigent, Philmarie, The Silencers, Olli and the Bollywood Orchestra. *Address:* LucieMusic Ltd, La Chapelle Studios, 7 rue du Bac, 4950 Waimes, Belgium (office). *Telephone:* (8) 744-60-78

(office). *Fax:* (2) 802-26-89-6 (office). *E-mail:* info@lachapellestudios.com (office). *Website:* www.lachapellestudios.com (office).

CASE, Neko Richelle, BFA; American singer, songwriter and musician (guitar, piano, percussion); b. 8 Sept. 1970, Alexandria, Va; d. of James Bamford Case and Diana Mary Dubbs. *Education:* Emily Carr Inst. of Art and Design, Canada. *Career:* raised in Mass, Vt, Ore., Wash.; fmr drummer for punk rock or country music groups including Del Logs, Propanes, Weasels, Cub, Maow; moved to Vancouver, BC, Canada 1994–98; leader of own group, Neko Case and Her Boyfriends 1996–2001; relocated to Seattle, Wash., USA 1998–99; mem., New Pornographers 1998–; relocated to Chicago 1999–; Founder-mem. (with Carolyn Mark), Corn Sisters 1999–; solo artist 2001–; numerous collaborations including Andrew Bird, Camera Obscura, Jakob Dylan, Fran Healy, Laura Veirs, Peter Wolf. *Recordings:* albums: with Cub: Betti-Cola 1993; with Maow: Unforgiving Sounds of Maow 1996; solo: The Virginian (as Neko Case and Her Boyfriends) 1997, Furnace Room Lullaby (as Neko Case and Her Boyfriends) 2000, Blacklisted 2002, The Tigers Have Spoken 2004, Fox Confessor Brings the Flood 2006, Middle Cyclone 2009, The Worse Things Get, The Harder I Fight, The Harder I Fight, The More I Love You 2013; with Corn Sisters: The Other Women 2000; with New Pornographers: Mass Romantic 2000, Electric Version 2003, Twin Cinema 2005, Challengers 2007, Together 2010. *Honours:* Plug Independent Music Award for Female Artist of the Year 2006. *Address:* c/o Anti Records, 2798 Sunset Boulevard, Los Angeles, CA 99026, USA (office). *Telephone:* (213) 413-7353 (office). *E-mail:* info@anti.com (office); general@nekocase.com. *Website:* www .anti.com (office); nekocase.com.

CASEY, Harry Wayne; American musician (keyboards), singer, producer and arranger; b. 31 Jan. 1951, Hialeah, Fla. *Career:* Founder-mem. (as KC), KC and the Sunshine Band 1973; writer, arranger, producer, KC and the Sunshine Band; George McCrae; career interrupted by severe injuries in car crash 1982. *Recordings include:* albums: Do It Good 1974, KC and The Sunshine Band 1975, The Sound of Sunshine 1975, Part Three 1976, Who Do Ya Love 1978, Do You Wanna Go To Party 1979, Space Cadet 1981, Greatest Hits 1980, The Painter 1981, All In A Night's Work 1983, KC Ten 1983, The Best Of 1990, Oh Yeah! 1993, I'll Be There for You 2001, Yummy 2007. *Current Management:* c/o Bill Sammeth, Bill Sammeth Organization, 755 Baywood Drive, Los Angeles, CA 94954, USA. *Telephone:* (310) 275-6193. *E-mail:* sunshine@kcsbonline.com (office). *Website:* www.kcsbonline.com.

CASEY, Howard (Howie) William; British musician (saxophones) and teacher; b. 12 July 1937, Liverpool, England; s. of Tom Casey and Stella Casey; m. Sheila Casey 1980 (died 2012); one d. *Education:* Army Band, Kings Regt, Liverpool. *Career:* f. band The Seniors 1959; mem. Derry and Seniors 1960–62; mem. Kingsize Taylor and the Dominoes 1963; recording, live concerts with Paul McCartney, Wings (Over The World) 1975–76, played on Band on the Run, Wings at the Speed of Sound, Wings over America, Back to the Egg, Rockestra 1980, The Who, played on Tommy, Quadrophenia, ABC, Chuck Berry, Jimmy Ruffin, Cliff Richard, Lee Dorsey, PAL (Paice, Ashton, Lord), Roy Young Band, Marc Bolan, The Slobs, Les Humphries Singers, Present Band, Beatles with Wings 2015; mem. PRS, Musicians' Union, PPL. *Film soundtracks:* performed on Tommy, Zee & Co, Les Jeunes Loups. *Recordings include:* albums: with Wings: Band On The Run 1973, Wings At The Speed of Sound 1976, Back To The Egg 1979, Wings Over America, Rockestra; with ABC, Marc Bolan, PAL, Gilbert O'Sullivan, Cliff Richard, Elkie Brooks, Ashton, Gardner, Dyke, The Who; with Howie Casey and the Seniors: Twist at the Top 1962, The Sound Of '65 1965, There's A Bond Between U 1966. *Address:* 109 Yarmouth Road, Poole, Dorset, BH12 1LY, England. *E-mail:* sheilahowey@aol.com. *Website:* www.beatleswithwings.com; www.howiecasey .com.

CASEY, Karan; Irish singer; b. 5 April 1968, Waterford. *Career:* began performing in Waterford; moved to Dublin 1987; relocated to New York 1993; joined Solas; solo artist 1997–; involved with Africans in America TV documentary. *Recordings include:* with Solas: Solas 1996, Sunny Spells and Scattered Showers 1997, The Words That Remain 1998; solo: Songlines 1997, Fused (with Mike McGoldrick) 2000, The Seal Maiden 2000, The Winds Begin To Sing 2001, Chasing the Sun 2005, Ships in the Forest 2008. *Honours:* three NAIRD/AFIM indie awards with Solas, Grammy Award for Best New Age Album 2000. *Address:* c/o Crow Valley Music Ltd, Coome, Glenville, Co. Cork, Ireland (office). *E-mail:* info@crowvalleymusic.com (office); info@karancasey .com (office). *Website:* www.karancasey.com.

CASEY, Paddy; Irish singer, songwriter and musician; b. Dublin. *Career:* began career as teenage busker in Dublin and Galway; solo artist 1999–; concert appearances include Heineken Green Energy Festival 2005, support act on U2's Vertigo tour. *Recordings include:* albums: Amen (So Be It) (Best Debut Album, Hot Press Irish Music Awards) 1999, Living 2004, Addicted to Company Pt I 2007. *Honours:* Best Irish Male, Meteor Irish Music Awards 2004, 2005. *Current Management:* c/o Principle Management, 30–32 Sir John Rogersons Quay, Dublin 2, Ireland. *Website:* www.paddycasey.ie.

CASH, Bobby, (The Indian Cowboy); Indian country singer and musician (guitar); b. (Bal Kishore Das Loiwal), 13 Feb. 1961, Clement Town, near Dehradun; m. Angelina Cash; two c. *Career:* played at various venues in New Delhi; played at the Tamworth Country Music Festival, Australia 2003, as the subject of a documentary. *Television:* The Indian Cowboy... One in a Billion (documentary, Ovation Channel, ABC) 2003. *Recordings:* albums: Cowboy At Heart 2003, Phoenix To El Paso 2004, State of my Heart 2006; singles: Baby So

Are You 2003. *Current Management:* c/o Gobsmacked Television Pty Ltd, 1 Nothcote Street, St Leonards, Willoughby, NSW 2065, Australia. *E-mail:* cbromley@bigpond.net.au. *E-mail:* contactus@bobbycash.org (office). *Website:* www.bobbycash.org.

CASH, Roseanne; American singer and songwriter; b. 24 May 1955, Memphis, Tenn.; d. of the late Johnny Cash; m. 1st Rodney Crowell 1979 (divorced), three d.; m. 2nd John Leventhal, one s. one step-d. *Education:* Vanderbilt Univ., Lee Strasberg's Inst., Los Angeles. *Career:* worked for three years with her father's road show; worked with Rodney Crowell, Nashville; recording artist 1979–; collaborations include Mary Chapin Carpenter, Marc Cohn, Vince Gill, John Hiatt, Lyle Lovett, Carly Simon. *Recordings include:* albums: Roseanne Cash 1978, Right Or Wrong 1979, Seven Year Ache 1981, Somewhere In The Stars 1982, Rhythm and Romance 1985, King's Record Shop 1988, Hits 1979–89 1989, Interiors 1990, The Wheel 1993, Retrospective 1995, 10 Song Demo 1996, What Kinda Girl (live) 1999, Rules of Travel 2003, Black Cadillac 2006, The List 2009, The River and the Thread (Grammy Award for Best Americana Album 2015, Americana Music Asscn Album of the Year) 2014. *Publications include:* Bodies of Water (short stories) 1996, Penelope Jane (children's book) 2000, Composed: A Memoir 2010. *Honours:* Grammy Awards for Best Female Country Vocal Performance 1985, for Best American Roots Performance and Best American Roots Song (both for A Feather's Not a Bird) 2015, Billboard Award for Top Single Artist 1988. *Current Management:* c/o Danny Kahn, Cross Road Management, 45 West 11th Street, Suite 7B, New York, NY 10011, USA. *Telephone:* (212) 807-1509. *Fax:* (718) 504-7899. *E-mail:* dkahn@crossroadmanagement.com. *Website:* www.rosannecash.com.

CASH, Tommy; American musician (rhythm guitar); b. 5 April 1940, Dyess, Ark.; m. 1st Barbara Wisenbaker 1961; one s. one d.; m. 2nd Pamela Dyer 1978. *Career:* has appeared on all major country music television shows, many network television programmes; radio announcer, 1959–64, including: American Forces Network, Germany 1959–62; music publisher 1965–; professional entertainer 1965–; songwriter, songs recorded by Conway Twitty, Kitty Wells, Faron Young, Jean Sheppard, Johnny Cash, Loretta Lynn; music published by Tomcat Music; mem. BMI, American Fed. of Musicians (AFofM), Nashville, American Fed. of Television and Radio Artists (AFTRA), Nashville, Nat. Asscn of Realtors, ROPE Inc. *Recordings include:* albums: Here Comes Tommy Cash 1966, Country Cousins 1966, Your Loving Takes the Leaving Out of Me 1969, Six White Horses 1970, Rise and Shine 1970, Cash Country 1971, American Way of Life 1971, Only a Stone 1975, New Spirit 1978, All Around Cowboy 1984, Let an Old Racehorse Run 1992, Tommy Cash Sings Gospel, Tommy Cash Classics, All I Care About, A Musical Tribute: My Brother, Johnny Cash 2004, Winners 2006, Fade to Black 2008. *Honours:* two BMI Awards for Songwriting 1965, 1975, Music City News Most Promising Vocalist 1970. *Address:* c/o Marcy Cash, The Tommy Cash Company, PO Box 1230, Hendersonville, TN 37077, USA (office). *Telephone:* (615) 419-9021. *E-mail:* info@tommycash.com (office). *Website:* www.tommycash.com.

CASILLAS VON UCKERMANN, Christopher Alexander Luis; Mexican singer and actor; b. 21 Oct. 1986, Mexico City. *Career:* actor; mem. RBD 2004–09, now solo artist and actor. *Television include:* El Diario de Daniela, Amigos por Siempre, Aventuras en el Tiempo, Rebelde (series) 2004, RBD: La Familia (series) 2007, Verano de Amor 2009, Kdabra 2010. *Recordings include:* albums: Rebelde 2004, Nuestro Amor 2005, Celestial (Billboard Latin Music Award for Latin Pop Album of the Year by a Duo or Group 2007) 2006, Rebels (in English) 2006, Empezar Desde Cero 2007, Somos 2010. *Honours:* Billboard Latin Music Award for Top Latin Albums Artist of the Year, for Latin Tour of the Year 2007, some 24 Premios Juventud, Billboard Latin Music 'Tu Mundo' Award 2008.

CASSIDY, David; American actor, singer, songwriter and musician (guitar); b. 12 April 1950, New York, NY; s. of the late Jack Cassidy and Evelyn Ward; m. 1st Sue Shifrin; one c.; m. 2nd Meryl-Ann Tanz (divorced); m. 3rd Kay Lenz (divorced). *Career:* actor, The Partridge Family television series; lead singer, Partridge Family recordings; solo artist 1971–; actor, Joseph and the Amazing Technicolour Dreamcoat; lead role in musical, Time 1987. *Recordings include:* albums: Cherish 1972, Could It Be Forever 1972, Rock Me Baby 1972, Dreams Are Nothin' More 1973, Cassidy Live 1974, The Higher They Climb 1975, Greatest Hits 1977, Romance 1985, His Greatest Hits, Live 1986; Didn't You Used To Be... 1992, Old Trick, New Dog 1998, Then and Now 2001, A Touch of Blue 2005. *Films include:* as actor: The Night The City Screamed 1980, The Spirit of '76 1990, Popstar 2005. *Television includes:* The Survivors 1969, Ironside 1969, Adam-12 1970, The Mod Squad 1970, A Chance To Live 1978, Parade of Stars 1983, Instant Karma 1990, Ruby & The Rockits 2009. *Play:* Time in London 1987. *Publications include:* C'mon Get Happy: Fear And Loathing On The Partridge Family Bus 1994, Could It Be Forever? My Story 2007. *Honours:* Golden Globe Award. *Website:* www.davidcassidy.com.

CASTAÑEDA, Edmar; Colombian jazz musician (harp), bandleader and composer; b. 31 March 1978, Bogotá; s. of Pavelid Castañedas. *Education:* Five Towns Coll. *Career:* moved to USA 1994; Founder and bandleader Edmar Castañeda Trio; mem. Andrea Tierra Quartet; numerous collaborations including Candy Butchers, Simón Diaz, Lila Downs, Wynton Marsalis, Chico O'Farrill, John Patitucci, Arturo Romay, Marta Topferova, Samuel Torres, Yerba Buena. *Recordings:* albums: Cuarto de Colores 2006, Entre Cuardos 2009, Double Portion 2012. *Honours:* Jazz Journalists Asscn Jazz Award for Player of Instruments Rare in Jazz of the Year 2013. *Current Management:* c/o

Chris DiGirolamo, Two for the Show Media, 5750 Aldrich Lane, Mattituck, NY 11952-3719, USA. *Telephone:* (631) 298-7823. *E-mail:* chris@twofortheshowmedia.com. *Website:* www.twofortheshowmedia.com; www.edmarcastaneda.com.

CASTLE, Pete, Cert Educ.; British folk singer, musician (guitar), storyteller and writer; b. 25 Feb. 1947, Ashford, Kent; s. of Roy and Pamela Castle; m. Sue Brown 1967; one s. one d. *Education:* Maidstone Tech. High School, Bretton Hall Coll. of Educ. *Career:* organizer of Luton Folk Festival 1976–78; solo artist, working at clubs, festivals, in schools and on community projects 1978–; presenter, Chiltern Radio Folk Show 1981–87; collaboration with Aroti Biswas 1987; Mountsorrel Community Play 1993; launched the occasional band Popeluc 1994; Ed., Facts & Fiction Storytelling Magazine 1999–; mem. Musicians' Union, Performing Right Soc., Mechanical-Copyright Protection Soc., Soc. for Storytelling. *Recordings include:* Bedfordshire Folk Songs 1981, Rambling Robin 1982, Punk's Delight 1985, One Morning By Chance 1989, Cottage By the Shore 1992, Two Tongues One Voice 1994, Keys of Canterbury 1994, Maramures Et Cetera 1994, Falsewaters 1995, Blue Dor 1996, Mearcstapa 1999, The Jenny & the Frame & the Mule 2000, Outlandish Knight 2004, Tapping at the Blind 2004, Poor Old Horse 2008, Oyster Girls & Hovelling Boys 2009. *Publication:* Derbyshire Folk Tales 2010. *Address:* 42 Mill Street, Belper, Derbyshire, DE56 1DT, England (home). *E-mail:* steel.carpet@tiscali.co.uk (office). *Website:* www.petecastle.co.uk.

CATER, Pete; British musician (drums), bandleader and teacher; b. 8 Feb. 1963, Lichfield, Staffordshire, England. *Career:* Tour world-wide, with Elaine Delmar in Thank You Mr Gershwin; Played with Arturo Sandoval Quintet; Pete Cater Big Band; Sheena Davis Group; Spike Robinson Group; Rickey Woodard Quartet; Charlie Byrd Trio; Gene Bertoncinni Trio; Freelance session player with: BBC; ITV; Channel 4; BBC Big Band; NYJO; A Ross; Val Doonican; Dave Willetts; S Maughan; Herb Miller Orchestra; mem. Faculty mem., Musicians' Institute, London; concerts and tours world-wide. *Recordings include:* Upswing, with Pete Cater Big Band; Playing With Fire, with Pete Cater Big Band. *Honours:* Outstanding Drummer, BBC Radio 2 Nat. Big Band Competition 1980, 1991, Best Big Band, British Jazz Awards 2000. *Website:* www.petecaterbigband.com.

CATLEY, Bob; British singer; b. 11 Sept. 1947, Aldershot, Hants. *Career:* Founder-mem. and lead singer of rock group Magnum 1972–; tours and concerts worldwide. *Recordings include:* albums: Kingdom of Madness 1978, Magnum II 1979, Marauder 1980, Chase The Dragon 1982, The Eleventh Hour 1983, On A Storyteller's Night 1985, Vigilante 1986, Wings of Heaven 1988, Goodnight LA 1990, The Spirit 1991, Rock Art 1994, Stronghold 1997, Archive 2000, Middle Earth 2001, Breath of Life 2002, Spirit of Man 2006, Immortal 2008, The Flying Opera 2011. *Current Management:* c/o Annie Minion, PO Box 5251, Derby, DE73 8YX, England. *E-mail:* annie@bobcatley.com. *Website:* www.bobcatley.com.

CATLEY, Marc, British; singer, songwriter, musician (guitar) and satirist; b. 3 Nov. 1959, Birmingham. *Education:* Univ. of Liverpool , London Bible Coll. *Career:* religious satire with band The Flaming Methodists 1991–; television and radio appearances; formed progressive rock band, Paley's Watch 1993; mem. MCPS, PRS, BAC&S, Musicians' Union. *Recordings include:* albums: with Geoff Mann: The Off The End of The Pier Show 1991, Fine Difference 1992, with Paley's Watch: November 1994; solo: Peel of Hope 1991, Make The Tea 1992, Hot Air For Jesus 1993, No Tomorrow 1994. *Address:* 236 Sebert Road, Forest Gate, London, E7 0NP, England.

CATO, Andy; British musician (electronics, trombone, bass), DJ and producer; b. 1972, Yorks., England. *Education:* Univ. of Oxford. *Career:* began playing trombone in a colliery brass band; played as a jazz soloist; with Tom Findlay, established club nights in London and began collaborating on various musical projects 1994–; adopted Groove Armada name 1996–. *Recordings include:* albums: Northern Star 1998, Vertigo 1999, Back To Mine (mix album compiled by Groove Armada) 2000, Goodbye Country (Hello Nightclub) 2001, Another Late Night (mix album compiled by Groove Armada) 2003, Lovebox 2003, Soundboy Rock 2007, Black Light 2010. *Honours:* fmr Young Jazz Musician of the Year. *Current Management:* c/o Amy Thomson, ATM Artists, 55 Kentish Town Road, London, NW1 8NX, England. *E-mail:* info@groove-armada.com (office). *Website:* www.groovearmada.com (office).

CATO, Pauline, BA, PGCE; British musician (Northumbrian pipes); b. 14 Dec. 1968, Ashington, Northumberland, England. *Education:* Univ. of Sheffield, studied Northumbrian pipes with Richard Butler. *Career:* mem. Border Spirit 1988–90; solo artist 1990–94; performed in Cullercoats Tommy (opera), with Northern Sinfonia Orchestra 1993; full-time musician 1993–; also in duo with fiddler Tom McConville 1995–2006; TV and radio broadcasts; apptd Piper to Mayor of Gateshead 1989; AHRB Research Fellow in Creative and Performing Arts, Univ. of Sheffield 2002–05; mem. Pipes of Four Nations group with Mick O'Brien, Barnaby Brown, Francois Lazaravitch, Javier Sainz, Bill Taylor 2007–12. *Recordings include:* Hindley Steel, with Border Spirit 1988; solo albums: The Wansbeck Piper 1992, Changing Tides 1994; various recordings as session musician: By Land and Sea, with Tom McConville 1996, The Surprise, with Tom McConville, Chris Newman and Maggie Boyle 1999, The Great Northern Roadshow, with Tom McConville and Terry Docherty 2003, New Tyne Bridge 2005 with Phil Cunningham, Ciaran Boyle, Christine Hanson and Dave Wood. *Publication:* Pauline Cato's Northumbrian Choice (with recordings) 1997. *Honours:* Hon. mem. Northumbrian Pipers Soc. for

Services to Piping; Daily Telegraph Folk Album of the Year 1996, 1999. *Website:* www.tomcatmusic.com (office).

CATTO, Jamie; British musician, producer, singer and songwriter; b. 14 Aug. 1968, London. *Career:* began as singer/songwriter; mem. Big Truth Band; mem. Faithless 1996–99; worked as producer, art dir, video dir for Cheeky Records; travelled around world with Duncan Bridgeman recording music, vocals and interviews for One Giant Leap project; collaborated with artists including Asha Bohsle, Baaba Maal, Michael Franti, Michael Stipe, Robbie Williams; album accompanied by film produced and directed by Bridgeman and Catto; f. Spacious Music 2003. *Recordings include:* albums: with Faithless: Reverence 1996, Sunday 8pm 1998, with One Giant Leap: One Giant Leap 2001; singles: with Faithless: Insomnia 1996, Salva Mea 1996, Don't Leave 1996, God Is A DJ 1998; with One Giant Leap: Braided Hair 2001, My Culture 2001, What About Me? (Grand Jury Prize 2011) 2009, And She Moves 2010. *Address:* c/o Palm Pictures, 601 West 26th Street, 11th Floor, New York, NY 10001, USA. *E-mail:* info@1giantleap.tv. *Website:* www.1giantleap.tv.

CAUDEL, Stephen; British composer and musician (guitar); b. (Stephen Paul Caudle), 29 June 1955, Sheffield, Yorks., England; m. Shelagh Quinn 1983; one s. *Education:* City of Leeds Coll. of Music. *Career:* numerous TV and radio broadcasts; concert tours in UK and overseas; mem. Performing Right Soc., Mechanical-Copyright Protection Soc., Musicians' Union. *Compositions include:* Wine Dark Sea (rock symphony, world premiere, London 1983), Edel Rhapsody, for Wagner Tuba and Orchestra (world premiere, Carlisle 1993), The Earth In Turquoise; numerous compositions for film and TV. *Recordings include:* albums: Wine Dark Sea, Bow of Burning Gold, Impromptu Romance, The Earth In Turquoise, Scaramouche. *Address:* 24 Front Street, Brampton, Cumbria, CA8 1NT, England (office). *E-mail:* admin@stephencaudel.com (office). *Website:* www.stephencaudel.com.

CAUSTIC WINDOW (see James, Richard David)

CAUTY, James (Jimmy) Francis, (Rockman Rock); British programmer, musician (guitar), producer and DJ; b. 19 Dec. 1956, Devon; m. 1st Cressida Cauty; two c.; m. 2nd Alannah Currie (2011). *Career:* mem. Angels 1-5 1981–82, Brilliant 1984–86; DJ in chill out room, Heaven club, London; f. KLF Communications with Bill Drummond 1987–92; mem. The Justified Ancients of Mu Mu 1987–88, 1990–91, The Timelords 1988, Disco 2000 1988, The KLF 1988–92, The Orb 1989–90, Space 1990, The K-Foundation 1992–97; fmr mem. AAA (aka Triple-A, Advanced Acoustic Armorments); mem. The One World Orchestra 1995, The Scourge of the Earth 1999, Solid Gold Chartbusters 1999; f. record co., Crapola Records early 2000s; remixes include Pet Shop Boys, Depeche Mode, Atomizer, Black Dog, Blue Pearl, Marilyn Manson. *Art:* painted 'Lord of the Rings' (later sold by Athena) 1973. *Recordings include:* albums: with Brilliant: Kiss The Lips of Life 1986; as The JAMS: 1987 (What The Fuck Is Going On?) 1987, Who Killed The JAMS 1988, Shag Times 1989; as The KLF: The White Room 1991, Mu (compilation) 1991, This Is What The KLF Is About I (singles collection) 1992, This Is What The KLF Is About II (singles collection) 1992; contributed to The 'What Time Is Love' Story 1989; as The One World Orchestra: War Child: Help 1995; as Space: Space 1990; with The Orb: Adventures Beyond The Ultraworld 1991, U.F. Orb (compilation) 2000; singles: with Brilliant: Soul Murder 1984, Wait For It 1984, It's A Man's Man's Man's World 1985, Love Is War 1986, Somebody 1986, The End of the World 1986; as The Justified Ancients of Mu Mu: All You Need Is Love 1987; as The JAMS: Whitney Joins The JAMs 1987, 1987 (The JAMS 45 Edits) 1987, Downtown 1987, It's Grim Up North 1990; as The KLF: Burn The Bastards 1988, What Time Is Love? 1988, 3am Eternal 1989, Kylie Said To Jason 1989, Last Train To Trancentral 1990, What Time Is Love? (Live At Trancentral) 1990, 3am Eternal (Live At The SSL) 1991, Last Train To Trancentral (Live From The Lost Continent) 1991, America: What Time Is Love? 1991, Justified & Ancient (with Tammy Wynette) 1991, 3am Eternal (with Extreme Noise Terror) 1992; as Disco 2000: I Gotta CD 1987, One Love Nation 1988, Uptight (Everything's Alright) 1989; as The Timelords: Doctorin' The Tardis 1988; with The Orb: A Huge Ever-Pulsating Brain Which Rules From The Centre Of The Ultraworld 1989, Little Fluffy Clouds 1990; as K-Foundation: K Foundation Presents The Red Army Choir Performing: K. Cera Cera (War Is Over If You Want It) 1993; as 2K; Fuck The Millennium 1997. *Film:* Waiting 1990. *Publication:* The Manual: How to Have a Number One Hit the Easy Way (with Bill Drummond) 1989.

CAVALCANTI DE ARAGÃO, Monique, BA; Brazilian composer, musician (piano) and arranger; b. 10 Nov. 1960, Rio de Janeiro; m. David Ganc; one s. *Education:* Univ. of Rio de Janeiro. *Career:* solo artist; teacher of singing, Universidade do Rio de Janeiro 1999–2001; numerous television and radio appearances; mem. AMAR (RJ). *Recordings include:* albums: Monique Aragão 1991, Canoas 1993, Ventos do Brasil 1995, Os Olhos de Cristal 1997, Marcas de Expressão 1999, Suíte do Rio 2004; original soundtracks for theatre, films, ballet. *Publications include:* Coral Hoje 1989, O Melhor de Ernesto Nazareth 1997, Seis Estudos para a Mão Esquerda 1997. *Honours:* winner, Alcina Navarro competition 1970, Liddy Mignone competition 1973, Lúcia Branco competition 1976, Sharp Prize 1992.

CAVALERA, Max; American (b. Brazilian) rock musician (guitar, percussion) and singer; b. 4 Aug. 1969, Belo Horizonte, Brazil; m. Gloria Cavalera 1993, four s. one d. *Career:* mem. Brazilian heavy rock group, Sepultura 1984–97; side project, Nailbomb 1994–95; formed new band, Soulfly 1997–, Cavalera Conspiracy (with brother Igor Cavalera) 2007–; mem. American Soc.

of Composers, Authors and Publishers; Nat. Wildlife Org.; Co-founder Iggy Diabetes Fund. *Recordings include:* albums: with Sepultura: Morbid Visions 1985, Schizophrenia 1988, Beneath The Remains 1989, Arise 1991, Chaos AD 1993, Roots 1996, Nativity In Black (Black Sabbath tribute), Virus 100 (Dead Kennedys tribute), Tales From The Crypt (soundtrack), The Roots of Sepultura 1996, Blood-Rooted 1997, Under a Play Grey Sky 2002; with Nailbomb: Point Blank 1994, Proud To Commit Commercial Suicide 1995; with Soulfly: Soulfly 1998, Primitive 2000, 3 2002, Prophecy 2004, Dark Ages 2005, Conquer 2008, Omen 2010, Enslaved 2012, Savages 2013; with Cavalera Conspiracy: Inflikted 1996, Blunt Force Trauma 2011. *Television:* as writer: Metal Evolution (Episode 1) 2011. *Publication:* My Bloody Roots: From Sepultura to Soulfly and Beyond (autobiography) 2013. *Address:* Soulfly, PO Box 55147, Phoenix, AZ 85078, USA (office). *Website:* www.soulfly.com; www.cavaleraconspiracy.com.

CAVALERI, Nathan Michael; Australian musician (guitar); b. 18 June 1982, Camden, NSW. *Education:* St Gregory's Coll., Campbelltown, NSW, Australia. *Career:* played at San Francisco Blues Festival with Albert Collins 1992; toured with B. B. King, special guest 1995; 25th Birthday for Guitar Player magazine; Kennedy Lifetime Achievement Awards, honouring B. B. King 1995; Out In The Green Festival, Zurich 1995; tours with Jimmy Barnes of Diesel, Australia; mem. SAG. *Recordings include:* albums: Jammin' With the Cats (five co-written songs) 1994, Nathan (six co-written songs). *Honours:* Young Variety Award, Variety Club Australia 1993, BMW Jazz and Blues Best New Talent Award 1993, Young Australian Achiever Award 1994. *Address:* 2512 Zorada Drive, Los Angeles, CA 90046, USA.

CAVALLO, Robert (Rob) Siers, BA; American record producer, musician (guitar, bass guitar, keyboards) and record company executive; *Chairman, Warner Music Group;* b. 21 March 1963, Washington, DC. *Education:* Univ. of Southern California, Dick Grove School of Music. *Career:* fmrly worked at Complex Recording Studios; A&R Rep., Warner Bros. Records 1987–94, signed acts including Goo Goo Dolls 1989, Green Day 1993, Sr Vice-Pres. of A&R, Warner Bros./Reprise Records 1994–98; A&R Sr Vice-Pres., Hollywood Records 1998–2002; rejoined Warner Music Group 2002–09, Chief Creative Officer 2009–, Chair. 2010–; Co-founder and Pres., Level 7 Artists 2006; record producer for many acts including Eric Clapton, Phil Collins, Fleetwood Mac, Goo Goo Dolls, Green Day, Jewel, Kid Rock, Dave Matthews Band, Alanis Morissette, My Chemical Romance, Paramore, Shinedown, Sixpence None the Richer. *Films:* producer for soundtracks including: City of Angels 1998, Runaway Bride 1999, Tarzan 1999, Rent 2005, Twilight 2008. *Recordings include:* albums: as producer: Dookie, Green Day 1994, Insomniac, Green Day 1995, Nimrod, Green Day 1997, Dizzy Up the Girl, Goo Goo Dolls 1998, Gutterflower, Goo Goo Dolls 2002, Testify, Phil Collins 2002, Say You Will, Fleetwood Mac 2003, American Idiot, Green Day (Grammy Award for Best Rock Album 2005) 2004, The Black Parade, My Chemical Romance 2006, Let Love In, Goo Goo Dolls 2006, The Best Damn Thing, Avril Lavigne 2007, Brand New Eyes, Paramore 2009, Danger Days: The True Lives of the Fabulous Killjoys, My Chemical Romance 2010, ¡Uno!, Green Day 2012, ¡Dos!, Green Day 2012, ¡Trés!, Green Day 2012, Magnetic, Goo Goo Dolls 2013, All That Echoes, Josh Groban 2013. *Honours:* Grammy Awards for Producer of the Year 1998, 1999, for Record of the Year (for Boulevard of Broken Dreams, Green Day) 2005. *Address:* c/o Warner Music Group, 75 Rockefeller Plaza, New York, NY 10019, USA (office). *Telephone:* (212) 275-2000 (office). *Fax:* (212) 757-3985 (office). *Website:* www.wmg.com (office).

CAVE, Nicholas (Nick) Edward; Australian singer, songwriter and actor; b. 22 Sept. 1957, Warracknabeal, Victoria; m. Susie Bick. *Education:* Caulfield Grammar School, Melbourne, Caulfield Inst. of Technology. *Career:* founder mem. The Boys Next Door 1977–80; mem. Birthday Party 1980–83; founder mem. Nick Cave & The Bad Seeds 1983–; mem. Grinderman 2006–. *Films:* Die Stadt 1983, Wings of Desire 1987, Ghosts... of the Civil Dead (also writer) 1988, Johnny Suede 1991, Rhinoceros Hunting in Budapest 1997, The Proposition (writer) 2006. *Recordings:* albums: with The Birthday Party: The Birthday Party 1980, Prayers On Fire 1981, Junkyard 1982, It's Still Living 1985; with Nick Cave & The Bad Seeds: From Her To Eternity 1984, The Firstborn Is Dead 1985, Kicking Against The Pricks 1986, Your Funeral... My Trial 1986, Tender Prey 1988, Ghosts... Of The Civil Dead 1989, The Good Son 1990, Henry's Dream 1992, Live Seeds 1993, Let Love In 1994, Murder Ballads 1996, The Boatman's Call 1997, And The Ass Saw The Angel 1999, The Secret Life Of The Love Song/The Flesh Made Word 1999, No More Shall We Part 2001, Nocturama 2003, Abbatoir Blues/The Lyre Of Orpheus 2004, B-Sides And Rarities 2004, The Proposition (OST, with Warren Ellis) 2005, The Assassination of Jesse James by the Coward Robert Ford (with Warren Ellis) 2007, Dig!!! Lazarus, Dig!!! 2008, White Lunar (with Warren Ellis) 2009, Push the Sky Away (with Warren Ellis, Ivor Novello Award for Best Album Award for songwriting 2014) 2013; with Grinderman: Grinderman 2007, Grinderman 2 2010. *Publications include:* And The Ass Saw The Angel (novel) 1989, King Ink (collection of lyrics and verse) 1988, King Ink II 1997, The Death of Bunny Munro (novel) 2009, The Sick Bag Song 2015. *Honours:* Q Award for Classic Songwriter 2005. *Website:* nickcave.com; www.grinderman.com.

CAZES, Henrique; Brazilian musician (cavaquinho, acoustic guitar, banjo), producer and arranger; b. 2 Feb. 1959, Rio de Janeiro; s. of Marcel Cazes; m. Maria A. C. L. Fernandes, two s. *Education:* studied with Ian Guest. *Career:* worked with Radames Gnatelli, seven years; tours as cavaquinho soloist: Japan, 1985–90; USA, 1988, 1990; Europe, 1993; Founder-mem. Orchestra Brazilian Strings; Founder and Dir Brasília Orchestra; Carrefour Mondial de la Guitare, Martinique; mem. Brazilian Asscn of Arrangers and Conductors. *Recordings include:* Henrique Cazes 1988, Henrique Cazes – Tocando Waldir Azevado 1990, Henrique Cazes – Waldir Azevado, Pixinguinha, Hermeto and Cia 1992, Cristina Buarque e Henrique Cazes Sem Tostao 1994, Henrique Cazes and The Guitar Family – Since The Choro Is Choro 1995, Also appears on: Deixa Clarear 1996, Rhythm and Romance 1998. *Television:* India: A Love Story 2009. *Publication:* Escola Moderna de Cavaquinho (text book). *Honours:* Sharp Awards 1991, 1992, 1995, Number One Cavaquinho of the World, Japan 1990. *Address:* Paulo Barreto, No. 25/802 Botafogo, 22280-010 Rio de Janeiro, RJ, Brazil. *Website:* www.henriquecazes.com.br.

CEBERANO, Kate; Australian singer, songwriter and actress; b. 17 Nov. 1966, Melbourne; m. Lee Rogers; one d. *Career:* mem. I'm Talking 1983–87; fmr mem. The Models; solo artist 1987–; performed role of Mary Magdalene in Jesus Christ Superstar 1992; performed with West Australian Symphony Orchestra 2005; Victorian Amb., Nat. Breast Cancer Foundation; Artistic Dir, Adelaide Cabaret Festival 2012–13. *Recordings include:* albums: with I'm Talking: Bear Witness 1986; with The Models: Out of Mind, Out of Sight 1985, Barbados; solo: Kate Ceberano and Her Septet 1987, You've Always Got The Blues 1988, Brave 1989, Like Now 1990, Think About It 1991, Jesus Christ Superstar Cast Album 1992, Kate and Friends 1994, Blue Box 1996, Pash 1997, True Romantic: The Best Of Kate Ceberano 1999, The Girl Can Help It 2003, 19 Days In New York 2004, Live with the West Australian Symphony Orchestra 2006, Nine Lime Avenue 2007, So Much Beauty 2008, Bittersweet 2009, Dallas and Kate 2009, Merry Christmas 2010, Kensal Road 2013. *Television:* Kate Ceberano and Friends 1993–94, X-Factor (judge) 2005, Dancing With Stars 2007. *Films include:* Arguing the Toss of a Cat 1989, Garbo 1990, Dust Off the Wings 1996, Molokai: The Story of Father Damien 2002. *Honours:* Best Female Vocalist, Countdown Awards 1985, Best Female Artist, Australian Record Industry Asscn (ARIA) Awards 1985, 1988, 1989, Highest Selling Australian Single, ARIA Awards 1989, Contemporary Concert Performer of the Year, Female Rock Performer of the Year and Jazz Performer of the Year, MO Awards 1990, Favourite Female Singer, People's Choice Awards 1992, 1993, 1994, Outstanding Achievement in the Arts in Asia, Business Asia Awards 1999. *Current Management:* c/o Ralph Carr Management, Lennox House, 229 Lennox Street, PO Box 2319, Richmond, Vic. 3121, Australia. *E-mail:* richard@ralphcarr.com. *Website:* www.kateceberano.com.

CECA; Serbian singer; b. (Svetlana Raznatovic), 14 June 1973, Prokuplje; m. Zeljko Raznatovic 1995 (died 2000); two c. *Career:* solo artist, singing modern Serbian folk music; first record deal at 14 years old; concert, Red Star Stadium, Belgrade, 2002; under house arrest 2011–. *Recordings include:* Albums: Cvetak Zanovetak 1988, Ludo Srce 1989, To Miki 1990, Babaroga 1991, Sta Je To U Tvojim Venama 1993, Ja Još Spavam U Tvojoj Majici 1994, Fatalna Ljubav 1995, Emotivna Luda 1996, Maskarada 1998, Album 2000 2000, Decenija 2001, Jedna Je... 2001, Idealno Loša 2006, Ljubav Živi 2011.

CECCARELLI, Andre; French musician (drums); b. 5 Jan. 1946, Nice; m. Marcelle Ritling 1968, one s. *Education:* Music Academy of France. *Career:* mem. Les Chats Suavages 1961; worked with Aime Barelli, Monte Carlo 1964; played with Rocky Roberts and the Piranas 1966–68; freelance musician 1968–; worked with artists including: Brian Auger, Tania Maria, Tina Turner, Michel Legrand, Bireli Lagrene, Mike Stern, Tom Harle; mem. SACEM, ADAMI, SPEDIDAM. *Recordings include:* with Ceccarelli Trio: Hat Snatcher, Three Around The Floor, with Dee Dee Bridgewater: Keeping Traditions, Love and Peace, with Tina Turner: Love Explosion, with Tania Maria: Live In Copenhagen, with M. Portal: Turbulence, with Bireli Lagrene and Joey De Francesco: Devils Avenue Blues 2006, with Elisabeth Kontomanou, Enrico Pieranunzi, Hein Van De Geyn: Golden Land 2007, with Sylvain Beuf and Julian Oliver Mazzariello: Sweet Peopled 2008, with Pierre Alain Goualch and Diego Imbert: The Rooster and the Pendulum 2009. *Honours:* Chevalier, Ordre des Arts et des Lettres 2005; Django D'Or, Best Jazz Group 1993; Victoire de la Musique, Best Jazz Album 1993, Aigle D'Argent, Nice, Grand Prize for Lifetime Achievement SACEM Jazz 1998. *Address:* 22 rue Ernest Revillon, 77630 Barbizon, France. *Website:* www.andrececcarelli.com.

CECH, Christoph; Austrian composer, arranger and musician (keyboards, orchestral percussion); *Professor of Jazz Composition, Anton Bruckner Private University for Music, Drama, and Dance*; b. 29 June 1960, Vienna; four s. one d. *Education:* Technical Univ., Vienna, Vienna Conservatory. *Career:* jazz fairy tale, F.F. Company and Co. (co-composer with Christian Mühlbacher) 1987; TV production (ORF) 1993; Concerto No. 1 for piano and orchestra, radio production (ORF) 1993; Aus allen Blüten Bitternis, Opera, Chamber Opera Vienna 1996; Triple Concerto, Musikverein Vienna 1999; Orfeo, Neue Oper Wien 2005; MISSA, Tiroler Festspiele Erl 2008; Totentanz Fragmente, Bruckner Hall, Linz 2011; numerous tours with different ensembles; Conductor/Leader, Max Brand Ensemble for Contemporary Music Austria; teacher, harmonics and counterpoint, Univ. of Music, Vienna 1998–2004; Head of Inst. JIM for Jazz and Improvised Music, Anton Bruckner Private Univ., Linz 1999–2014, now Prof. of Jazz Composition. *Compositions include:* Chamber Opera, Die Befreiung Des Modulors, State Theatre Schwerin, Germany 1988, Protophantasm, Concerto Grosso for big band and orchestra; Opera, Aus Allen Blüten Bitternis, Chamber Opera, Vienna 1996, B.A.C.H. Kantate, Dom St Pölten 1997, Requiem 1998, Bruckner Festival, Linz 1998, Cantata das lied der lieder 1999, Triple Concerto, Musikvereins Hall, Vienna 1999, Nachklang-Nachtklang, Konzerthaus, Vienna 2000, Linea Nova, ISCM-World Music Days, Ljubljana 2003, Mosaik 1 & 2, Konzerthaus, Vienna 2003, IO for orchestra, Brucknerhaus, Linz 2004, Orfeo, Neue Oper Wien 2005

MISSA, Tiroler Festspiele Erl 2008, Die Unnunnerierte, Brucknertage St.Florian 2010, Totentanz Fragmente, Osterklang Krems 2010, Bruckner Hall, Linz 2011. *Recordings:* with Nouvelle Cuisine Big Band: Flambée 1988, 1989, Elephant Terrine 1990, Phrygian Flight 1994, Ultimate Sentences 1997, Live at Porgy & Bess 2002, gDoon 2008, Swing 2012; with Striped Roses: Bonsai Beat 1990, Insection 1994, Tulpen 1997, Solo: Mondautos 1993; with Mondautos Trio: Euroblues 1999; with Jubilo Elf: Missing Link 1991, live at Porgy & Bess 2010; with Camerata Obscura, Batpulse 1997; in duo with Bertl Mütter, Lobgesang 1997, Requiem 1998; with JANUS Ensemble: Janus 1 – things 2000, Janus 2 – Spielmann Lieder 2000, Janus 3 – Correctness 2003; with Trio ZaVoCC: on tour 2010, Daham 2014; with Blechimperium: Blechimperium plays Bilder meiner Ausstellung 2011; with Heginger-Herbert-Cech: Springlink 2014. *Publications:* Keyboard 1–4 1991, Spiel dich fit, Etudes for Piano 2001. *Honours:* Stipendium for Composition, City of Vienna 1987, 1995, First Prize, Kunstpreis Leibnitz, Austria 1994, State Stipendium, Austrian Repub. 1995, Austro Mechana Publicity Prize 1997, First Prize, Kompositionspreis, Stadt Ternitz 2003, Lower Austrian Honoration Prize for Music 2004, 2013. *Address:* Mühlweg 10, 4242 Hagenberg im Mühlkreis, Austria (home). *E-mail:* c.cech@bruckneruni.at (office). *Website:* www.christoph-cech.com.

CECH, Vladimír, DipEng; Czech music and theatre journalist; b. 22 March 1944, Brno; m. Alena Benešová-Čechová 1975; one s. *Education:* Brno Univ. of Tech., Masaryk Univ. *Career:* regular programmes on music and theatre, Radio Brno and Radio Prague; writer and broadcaster, public playbacks of classical and pop music. *Publications:* contrib. to Brno, Prague, Vienna newspapers, including RT-Rovnost, Opus Musicum, Hospodářské noviny; radio broadcasts on music life in Czech Repub. and Austria. *Honours:* Czech Music Foundation Prize 1984–90. *Address:* Drobného 16, 602 00 Brno, Czech Republic (home). *Telephone:* (54) 5573721 (home). *E-mail:* babel@volny.cz (office).

CE'CILE; Jamaican reggae singer; b. (Cecile Charlton), 24 Feb. 1977. *Career:* fmr choir girl; fmr Gen. Man. Celestial Sounds studio, Kingston. *Recordings:* album: Bad Gyal 2004, Waiting 2009, Worth It 2009, Jamaicanization 2011. *Website:* www.cecileflava.com.

CEPEDA, Andrés; Colombian singer, songwriter and producer; b. 7 July 1973, Bogotá. *Education:* Universidad Javeriana. *Career:* lead singer, Poligamia 1990–98; solo career 1999–. *Recordings:* albums: with Poligamia: Una canción 1993, Vueltas y Vueltas 1995, Promotal 500 m.g 1996, Buenas Gracias Muchas Noches 1998; solo: Sé morir 1999, El carpintero 2001, Siempre queda una cancion 2002, Cancion rota 2003, Para Amarte Mejor 2006, Pop Latino 2007, Día tras día 2009, Lo Mejor Que Hay En Mi Vida (Latin Grammy Award for Best Traditional Pop Vocal Album 2013) 2013. *Honours:* Premios Nuestra Tierra Awards for Artist of the Year, Producer of the Year, Pop Performance of the Year, Best Pop Artist and Best Song 2010. *Address:* c/o FM Discos, Calle 74 No. 11–81 8° Edificio Milenuim, Bogotá, Colombia (office). *E-mail:* informacion@fmdiscos.com.co (office). *Website:* www.andrescepeda .com.co.

CEREZO, Gilberto; Mexican musician (guitarist) and singer. *Career:* Founder-mem. electro-pop band Kinky 1998–. *Recordings include:* albums: Kinky 2002, Atlas 2003, Reina 2006. *Soundtracks include:* Robbery Homicide Division 2002, Thirteen 2003, Man on Fire 2004. *Television:* Clase 406 2002. *Address:* c/o Sonic360 Records, 33 Riding House Street, London, W1 7DZ, England. *Website:* www.sonic360.com/kinky.

CERMAK, Johann Leopold (Zappa); Austrian musician (guitar, drums, percussion, harmonica) and singer; b. 7 July 1949, Heidenreichstein; m. Erika Cermak. *Career:* began as Blues Zappa 1974–76; Founder mem., Bluespumpm 1975; parallel project with Fritz Glatzl as Blues Zappa and Pumpm Fritz (also with Johannes Müller); tours around Europe, radio and television broadcasts; mem. AKM, AUME, LSG. *Recordings include:* albums: with Bluespumpm: Bluespumpm 1979, Edlau 1980, Village 1981, Live With Friends 1985, The 5th Ten Years Jubilee 1987, Live At Utopia 1988, Birthday 1991, Live In Vienna 1992, Living Loving Riding 1994, You Got It 1995, 20 Years Party 1995, Dirty Dozen, Live: The Wolfpack Tapes, Dirty Thirty: Open Hearts 2006, Zappa & The Wild Irish Lasses 2006; with Blues Zappa: Gitarrero 1985, Blue Balance 1987, Glaskar 1987. *Honours:* Silbenes Ehrenzeichen 1992. *Address:* Kindergartenstrasse 182, 3872 Amaliendorf, Austria (office). *Telephone:* (2) 862-524-10 (office). *E-mail:* office@bluespumpm.at (office). *Website:* www.bluespumpm.at.

CESAR, Chico; Brazilian composer and musician (guitar); b. (Francesco Cesar Goncalves), 26 Jan. 1964, Catole do Rocha, Paraiba. *Career:* fmr copy-ed. and reporter, Sao Paulo; composer of over 300 songs, recorded by Daniela Mercury, Elba Ramalho, Maria Bethania and others; composer for TV show, O Rei do Gado; collaborations include Ray Lema, Da Lata, The Fabulous Troubadours. *Films include:* Musiques Rebelles Americas 2004, Paraíba meu Amor 2007. *Recordings include:* albums: Aos Vivos 1995, Cuscuz Clã 1996, Beleza Mano 1997, Mama Mundi 2000, Chico Cesar 2000, Respeitem Meus Cabelos, Brancos 2002, De uns Tempos pra cá 2005, Francisco, forró y frevo 2008. *Telephone:* (1) 8153956 (Austria). *Fax:* (1) 8153956 (Austria). *E-mail:* constanze@uol.com.br. *Website:* www.agenciaprodutora.com.br. *Address:* Avenida Professor Alfonso Bovero, 430 cj 11, Sumaré, São Paulo, SP 01254-000, Brazil. *Telephone:* (11) 3673-0165 (also fax). *E-mail:* chicoces@uol.com.br. *Website:* www.chicocesar.com.br.

CESTER, Christopher; Australian rock musician (drums); b. 16 Sept. 1981, Melbourne. *Career:* formed rock band Jet with his brother Nic and Cameron Muncey 2001–, drummer and backing vocalist; toured as support act with the Rolling Stones, Australia 2003; toured USA with other Australian bands The Vines and The Living End 2004; tours of USA, UK, Europe, Japan, Australia 2006–07. *Recordings include:* albums: Get Born 2003, Shine On 2006, Shaka Rock 2009. *Address:* c/o Atlantic Records, 1290 Avenue of the Americas, New York, NY 10104, USA.

CESTER, Nic; Australian singer, songwriter and rock musician (guitar); b. 6 July 1979, Melbourne. *Career:* formed rock band Jet with his brother Chris and Cameron Muncey 2001–, lead singer, songwriter and rhythm guitarist; toured as support act with the Rolling Stones, Australia 2003; toured USA with other Australian bands The Vines and The Living End 2004; tours of USA, UK, Europe, Japan, Australia 2006–07; also Founder mem. The Wrights supergroup. *Recordings include:* albums: Get Born 2003, Rare Tracks 2004, Shine On 2006, Shaka Rock 2009. *Address:* c/o Atlantic Records, 1290 Avenue of the Americas, New York, NY 10104, USA (office).

CETERA, Peter; American singer and musician (bass); b. 13 Sept. 1944, Chicago, Ill.; m. 1st Janice Cetera (divorced); m. 2nd Diane Nini (divorced). *Career:* bassist, The Exceptions; mem. Chicago (fmrly Big Thing, Chicago Transit Authority) 1967–85; solo artist 1985–; regular worldwide tours, concerts and festival appearances. *Compositions include:* Wishin' You Were Here, Baby What A Big Surprise, Hard To Say I'm Sorry (co-writer with David Foster), You're The Inspiration (co-writer with David Foster). *Recordings include:* albums: with Chicago: Chicago Transit Authority 1969, Chicago II 1970, Chicago III 1971, Chicago At Carnegie Hall 1971, Chicago V 1972, Chicago VI 1973, Chicago VII 1974, Chicago VIII 1975, Chicago X 1976, Chicago XI 1980, Hot Streets 1978, Chicago 13 1979, Chicago XIV 1980, Chicago 16 1982, Chicago 17 1984, Chicago 18 1987, Chicago 19 1988, Chicago 21 1991; solo: Peter Cetera 1981, Solitude/Solitaire 1986, One More Story 1988, World Falling Down 1992, One Clear Voice 1995, Another Perfect World 2001, You Just Gotta Love Christmas 2004. *Honours:* Grammy Award 1977, American Music Award 1977. *Website:* www.petercetera.com.

CETINIC, Meri; Croatian singer, musician (piano) and composer; b. 15 June 1953, Split; one d. *Education:* Music high school Josip Hatze Split Music Acad. Split. *Career:* mem. Croatian Composer's Soc. *Recordings include:* albums: The Sea, Meri 1979, I'm A Woman 1980, By The Way, Road Dust, Ace, Golden Dreams, Meri (6), Look For Me 1988, Why Do I Love You 1992, Journeys 1998, A Bit of Sea in the Palm of My Hand (Porin Award 2002), Faithful heart, Tiramola, Allow me. *Honours:* Singer of the Year 1981–82. *E-mail:* mericetinic@mericetinic.com. *Website:* www.mericetinic.com.

CHABRIER, Jean-Claude Charbonnier dit, (Chabrier), DMed, DMus, PhD (Mus); French orientalist and musicologist (retd); *Founder, Owner and Manager, Centre pour l'Histoire, la Recherche, l'Illustration, la Sauvegarde des Traditions de l'Orient Spirituel (CHRISTOS)*; b. (Jean-Claude Charbonnier), 10 Nov. 1931, Neuilly-sur-Seine; s. of Jules Charbonnier; one s. one d. *Education:* Faculté de médecine de Paris, Paris VII Univ., Institut nat. des langues et civilisations orientales, Sorbonne-nouvelle Univ., Paris-Sorbonne Univ. *Career:* fmr researcher, CNRS, Paris; fmr Prof. of Music Analysis, Sorbonne nouvelle, Paris-Sorbonne 1989–2005; mem. Soc. française d'analyse musicale, Int. Musicology Soc., Soc. for Music Theory, Int. Council for Traditional Musics, Soc. for Ethnomusicology, Euro-Seminar for Ethnomusicology, UNESCO Conseil Int. de la Danse, Inst. de la Maison de Bourbon, Comité scientifique du Musée de la Corse; Founder, Owner and Man. Centre pour l'Histoire, la Recherche, l'Illustration, la Sauvegarde des Traditions de l'Orient Spirituel (CHRISTOS); mem. Soc. des Explorateurs français. *Achievement:* owner of 80,000 photographs and 500 recordings and videos about Christians of South-East Europe and the Middle-East. *Films:* De la Seine à la Caspienne: Paris–Teheran Car Rally 1957, Du Danube au Gange: Paris–Calcutta Car Rally 1960, Le Turabdin en Turquie: monastères et villages syriaques orthodoxes 2010, Chrétiens d'Urumîyé en Iran 2010. *Compositions:* ten Arabesques albums. *Radio:* numerous broadcasts. *Recordings:* ten Arabesques recital albums, Prélude dans le mode oriental Ràst en sol 1973, anthology of oriental recitals 1974–84. *Publications:* Arabesques – Analysis of Traditional Music: Identification, Representation, Paris Arabesques (two vols) 1996 (new edn 2012), Un demi-siècle d'agonie des chrétiens du moyen-orient 2010, Souvenirs d'un enfant de Neuilly 2012; contrib. of more than 200 reviews. *Honours:* Winner, Paris–Calcutta car rally 1960, ten-times Winner, Grand Prix, Acad. du disque français 1975, Acad. Charles Cros 1980, Winner, Paris–Arbil–Tabriz car rally 2005–10, Winner, Paris–Teheran–Mosul–Paris car and cultural rally 2012. *Address:* 213 avenue de Versailles, 75016 Paris, France. *Telephone:* 1-46-51-26-99. *E-mail:* jean.claude.cha@aliceadsl.fr (home). *Website:* www.christos.fr; www.arabesques.eu.

CHAD, Dominic Brian; British musician (guitar); b. 5 June 1972, Cheltenham, Gloucestershire. *Career:* Founder-mem. Grey Lantern, later renamed Mansun 1995–2003; numerous TV and live appearances. *Recordings include:* albums: Attack Of The Grey Lantern 1996, Desperate Icons 1997, Legacy 1998, Six 1998, Little Kix 2000, Electric Man 2000, Kleptomania 2004.

CHADIMA, Mikoláš; Czech composer, musician (saxophone, guitar), singer and publicist; b. 9 Sept. 1952, Cheb; s. of Jiri Chadima and Marie Chadimová; m. Marta Gotthard-Zelinkova; one d. *Education:* Čakovice Music School, Karel Velebny Jazz School, Prague. *Career:* printer Svoboda Graphics Co. 1968–74; labourer Geodesy state enterprise 1975–77; postman Czechoslovak Post Office 1977; clerk for Printing Dept, Nat. Tech. Museum, Prague 1977, 1988–89; printer and graphic designer 1979–88, labourer, Military Bldgs-Metro 1977–78; composer and musician 1990–; mem. of bands Purple Fleas/Yellow Defect 1970–72, Inrou 1972–74, Elektrobus 1975–76, Old Teenagers/Classic Rock and Roll Band 1976–83, Extempore 1977–81, Kilhets 1980–81, MCH Band 1982–, Richter and Chadima 2002–; numerous guest appearances; collaborations with Pavel Richter, Pavel Turnovsky, Otakar 'Jopa' Pistora, Nemec Martin, Chris Cutler, Nick Hobbs, Tim Hodkinson, Fred Frith, Pavel Fajt, Peter Binder, Fröhlich Tomás, Ales Charvát, Gulliani Fred, Marc Sense; live performances and festival appearances; activist, Jazzova sekce (Jazz Section) 1978–89; mem. Cttee for Protection of Frantisek Stárek 1988; founder mem. SAI (Union of Authors and Peformers) 1989–; mem. OSA, INTER-GRAM, Unijazz; mem. bd of admin for Czech Music Fund Foundation 2000–06. *Compositions:* The City, We Are Well and We Feel Fine, Es Reut Mich F…, Exodus. *Recordings include:* with Elektrobus: Nedefinitivní 1976, with Extempore Band: Milá 4 viselců 1977, Ebonitový samotář 1978, Dům č.p.112/34 1978, Zabíjačka 1979, Velkoměsto I. / The City I 1979, Velkoměsto II. / The City II 1982, with MCH Band: Krokodlak 1982, Jsme zdrávi a daří se nám dobře 1983, MCH Band's Feeling Fine 1983, 198Four Well?! 1984, Gorleben 1986, Es reut mich f… 1988, Gib Acht!!! 1993, Karneval / Carnival 1999, Tagesnotizen (with J. Fuchs) 2002, Live (20 let) 2003, with Kilhets: Koncert č.6 tancovačka v hotelu Tichý 1983, Koncert č.4-elektrický 1983, Koncert č.3 & 5 1983, Koncert č.2 & 7 1983; solo: Pseudemokritos 1996, Transparent People/Pruhlední lidé (with Fajt) 1998, Inrou 2004. *Films include:* music for Sestricky/Nurses 1980, Povídání o smrti (Talking of Death) 1995. *Plays:* music for Sestricky/Nurses 1990. *Television:* Concert for Charter 77 1990, Kanafas 1994, Big Beat 1995–96, MCH Band Na Chmelnici 1998, Mezi proudy – Crescendo (Between Currents – Crescendo) 2002. *Publications include:* Exempore – Cerná kniha (Extempore: The Black Book) 1980, Od rekvalifikací k Nové vlne se starym obsahem (From Retraining to the New Wave with Old Content) 1985; contrib. columns to Salon magazine 1997–; contrib. to various anthologies 1979–. *Honours:* first place Jazz Bulletin (with Extempore Band) 1981, Best Group of the Year 1981, All Stars – Jazz Bulletin 1981, Nadace ceský hudebni fond Album of the Year 1991, Zlutá motork Golden Motorbike Award 1998, Black Point Prize 1998. *Current Management:* Agentura AMP, Romek Hanzlík, Jindřišská 5, 110 00 Prague 1, Czech Republic. *Telephone:* (222) 240 932. *Fax:* (222) 247 473. *E-mail:* amp@atlas.cz. *Website:* www.rock-jazz.cz. *Address:* c/o Black Point Music, Vacínova 5, 180 00 Prague 8, Czech Republic. *Website:* www.mchband.cz.

CHADWICK, James Manfred; British jazz musician (guitar) and academic; b. 16 Oct. 1966, Lusaka, Zimbabwe; m. 31 March 1995. *Education:* Shiplake Coll., Henley-on-Thames, Welsh Coll. of Music and Drama. *Career:* mem. Enrico Quartet performing at three venues in Italy in 1994; various appearances throughout Britain including tour of Northern England 1995; mem. Musicians' Union. *Recordings:* In The Bag, with James Chadwick Quartet 1992.

CHADWICK, Mark; British singer, musician (guitar) and songwriter. *Career:* Founder mem., The Levellers 1988–; also solo artist. *Recordings include:* albums: with The Levellers: Weapon Called The Word 1990, Levelling The Land 1991, See Nothing, Hear Nothing, Do Something 1993, Levellers 1993, Zeitgeist 1995, Mouth To Mouth 1997, Dog Train 1997, One Way of Life: The Very Best of The Levellers 1998, Bozos 1998, Too Real 1998, Subway Songs 1999, Happy Birthday Revolution 2000, Special Brew 2000, Hello Pig 2000, Green Blade Rising 2002, Come On 2002, Truth & Lies 2005, Make You Happy 2005, Levelling the Land 2007, Letters from the Underground 2008, Going Underground 2008, Static on the Airwaves 2012, Special Brew 2013, Levelling the Land Live 2013, Chaos Theory Live; solo: All the Pieces 2010. *Publications:* The White Book (directory of action groups). *Address:* The Levellers, PO Box 29, Winkleigh, Devon, EX19 8WE, England. *E-mail:* info@levellers.co.uk; info@dmfmusic.co.uk; otf@levellers.co.uk (office). *Website:* www.levellers.co.uk.

CHAIREZ, Carlos; Mexican musician (guitarist). *Career:* founder mem. electro-pop band, Kinky 1998–. *Recordings include:* albums: Kinky 2002, Atlas 2003, Reina 2006. *Address:* c/o Sonic360 Records, 33 Riding House Street, London, W1 7DZ, England. *Website:* www.sonic360.com/kinky.

CHAKRABARTY, Kaushiki, BA, MA; Indian singer; b. 1980, Kolkata; d. of Pandit Ajoy and Chandna Chakrabarty; m. Partha Desikan. *Education:* Calcutta Univ., Sangeet Research Acad., Shrutinandan School of Music, studied with Gnan Prakash Ghosh and her father. *Career:* performs khayal and thumri forms of Hindustani music; has performed in USA, Canada and Europe; performed QEH, London 2005; contributed to film soundtrack, Deepa Mehta's Water; participated in numerous concerts including Dover Lane Music Conf., ITC Sangeet Sammelans, Spring Festival of Music (Calif.), Parampara Programme (Los Angeles). *Recordings include:* albums: Footsteps 1998, Journey Begins 2002, Pure 2004, The Spiritual Realisation 2005, Kaushiki 2007, Live at Saptak Festival 2008. *Honours:* Jadu Bhatta 1995, Outstanding Young Person 2000, BBC World Music Award for Asia/Pacific 2005. *Address:* Daffodil Greens, Flat # B3A, 17 Chandi Ghosh Road, Tollygunge, Kolkata 700 040, India (office). *Telephone:* (33) 32973311 (home); 9830107 868 (mobile). *E-mail:* contact@kaushiki.net (home); kaushiki.music@gmail.com (home); kaushiki_music@yahoo.com (home). *Website:* www.kaushiki.net.

CHAKROBARTY, Mridul Kanti, BMus, MMus, PhD; Bangladeshi singer and musician; *Professor, Department of Music, Dhaka University*; b. 1955, Sunamganj; s. of the late Manoranjan Chakrobarty and of Dipali Chakrobarty. *Career:* enlisted artist, Radio Bangladesh, Dhaka; regular artist on Bangladesh TV; currently Prof. of Music, Dhaka Univ.; Life Mem. Nat. Acad. (Bangla Acad.); mem. Int. Council for Traditional Music. *Compositions:* sources of Rabindranath Tagore songs in western folk music, modifier and developer of folk instrumental Dotara: Surasree. *Recordings:* Tagore Songs: Odhora Madhura, Songs of Hason Raja, Surasree, Folk Instrumental. *Publications:* Hason Raja: His Mystic Songs 1992, Evolution and Development of Bengali Music 1993, Sangit Sanglap (research articles on music) 1994, Ganer Jhorna Tolay (research articles on Tagore songs and folk songs) 1997, Folk Music 1999, Hajar Bochorer Bangla Gan (Evolution of Bengali Music) 2005; ed.: Pancho Giti Kobir Gan 2000, Bhasha O Desher Gan 2005. *Honours:* Yuv '77, India, Loknath Award 1998, Hrishija Artist Group 2009, Nat. Ind. Award 2011. *Address:* Department of Theatre and Music, University of Dhaka, Dhaka 1000 (office); 46 B House Tutor Quarters, Jagannath Hall, University of Dhaka, Dhaka 1000, Bangladesh (home). *Telephone:* (2) 9661920 (office); (2) 8652225 (home). *Fax:* (2) 8615583 (office). *E-mail:* duregstr@bangla .net. *Website:* www.univdhaka.edu.

CHALMERS, Thomas; British musician (saxophone, clarinet, flute); b. 4 Dec. 1930, Glasgow, Scotland; m. Jeanette D McGhee, 21 Dec. 1950; three s. one d. *Education:* tutored by mem. of BBC S V Orchestra. *Career:* played with military band 1949–54, Ken Stevens Orchestra 1960–66, Tommy Sampson Orchestra 1970–86; mem. of Fat Sam's Band, Edinburgh 1986–96; freelance musician with Bobby Wishart groups and Strathclyde Youth Jazz Orchestra; mem. Musicians' Union. *Recordings:* with Fat Sam's Band: Boogie On Down, Jive On Down, Ring Dem Bells, Fat Sam's Band Live At.

CHAMBERLIN, Jimmy; American musician (drums); b. 10 June 1964, Joliet, Ill. *Education:* Northern Illinois Univ. *Career:* mem., Smashing Pumpkins 1988–95, 1998–2000, 2006–09; Founder mem. This 2009 (renamed Skysaw 2010–2012); mem., The Last Hard Men; solo artist as 'Jimmy Chamberlin Complex' 2004–. *Recordings include:* albums: with Smashing Pumpkins: Gish 1991, The Peel Sessions 1992, Siamese Dream 1993, Pisces Iscariot 1994, Mellon Collie and the Infinite Sadness 1995, MACHINA/The Machines of God 2000, Machina II: The Friends and Enemies of Modern Music 2000, Earphoria 2002, Zeitgeist 2007, Teargarden by Kaleidyscope 2009; with The Last Hard Men: The Last Hard Men 1998; with Skysaw: Great Civilisations 2010; solo: Life Begins Again 2005.

CHAMBERS, Guy; British producer, songwriter and musician (keyboards); b. 12 Jan. 1963, Hammersmith, London; m. Emma Chambers. *Education:* Guildhall School of Music and Drama. *Career:* mem., The Waterboys 1985–86, World Party 1986–91, The Lemon Trees 1992; co-songwriter and producer for Robbie Williams 1997–2002, 2007–; collaborations with artists, including Jimmy Nail, Cathy Dennis, Frances Ruffelle, Tom Jones, Holly Johnson, Julian Cope, Brian McFadden, Annie Lennox, Jamie Cullum, Kylie Minogue, Jesse James, Kerli, Kelis, Tina Turner, Beverley Knight, Maverick Sabre, Rufus Wainwright; mem. Musicians' Union, PRS. *Compositions include:* co-writer of songs for Robbie Williams: Lazy Days 1996, South of The Border 1997, Angels (BRIT Award for Best Single 1999, Ivor Novello Award for Songwriter of the Year 1999) 1997, Let Me Entertain You 1998, Millennium 1998, No Regrets 1998, Strong 1999, She's The One 1999, Rock DJ (BRIT Award for Best Single 2001) 2000, Kids (duet with Kylie Minogue) 2000, Supreme 2000, Let Love Be Your Energy 2001, Eternity/The Road To Mandalay 2001, Reality Killed the Video Star 2009, Swings Both Ways 2013, and all songs on albums Life Thru A Lens 1997, I've Been Expecting You 1998, Sing When You're Winning 2000; co-writer of songs on Kylie Minogue album Your Disco Needs You 2000, Don't Forget Who You Are (with Miles Kane) 2013, The Shocking Miss Emerald (with Caro Emerald) 2013. *Recordings include:* albums: with World Party: Private Revolution 1986, Goodbye Jumbo 1990; with Lemon Trees: Open Book 1993; solo: The Isis Project 2005. *Current Management:* c/o Dylan Chambers, Sleeper Music, Block 2, 6 Erskine Road, Primrose Hill, London, NW3 3AJ, England. *Telephone:* (20) 7580-3995. *Fax:* (20) 7900-6244. *E-mail:* dylan@sleepermusic.co.uk. *Website:* www .guychambers.com.

CHAMBERS, Jacqueline (Jackie) Diane, (JAX); British musician (guitar); b. 27 March 1964, Bradford, Yorks., England; d. of Colin Chambers and Sylvia Chambers. *Education:* Pudsey Grammar School. *Career:* lead guitarist, Girlschool 1999–; lead guitarist, Blitzkrieg 2008–. *Recordings include:* albums: with Girlschool: 21st Anniversary: Not That Innocent 2002, Second Wave 2003, Believe 2004, Emergency/London 2005, Race with the Devil, Auld Lang Syne, Legacy 2008, Hit and Run Revisited 2011, Fear and Control 2011, Guilty As Sin 2015. *Current Management:* c/o Crash Bang Management, Av. Bento Goncalves 31-8B, 2910-433 Setúbal, Portugal. *Telephone:* (265) 572297. *E-mail:* tommymorriello@gmail.com. *Website:* www.cbbm.dk. *E-mail:* girlschool@hotmail.com. *Website:* www.girlschool.co.uk.

CHAMBERS, Martin Dale; British musician (drums); b. 4 Sept. 1951, Hereford, England; one s. one d. *Education:* Hereford Coll. of Art. *Career:* drummer, Pretenders 1979–85, 1994–. *Recordings:* albums: Pretenders 1980, Pretenders II 1981, Learning To Crawl 1984, The Singles 1987, Last of The Independents 1994, The Isle of View 1995, Viva El Amor 1999, Loose Screw 2002, Break Up the Concrete 2009; other work include: Paul McCartney, Pete Townshend, Roger Daltrey. *Address:* c/o Shangri-La Music, 2202 Main Street,

Santa Monica, CA 90405, USA (office). *E-mail:* info@shangrilamusic.com (office). *Website:* www.shangrilamusic.com (office); www.thepretenders.com.

CHAMBERS, Wendy Mae, BA, MA; American composer and musician; b. 24 Jan. 1953; m. Rajesh Karki. *Education:* Barnard Coll., State Univ. of New York. *Career:* mem. American Music Center, American Composer Forum. *Compositions:* 4 CDs, Symphony of The Universe, A Mass For Mass Trombones. *Honours:* NEA Grant 1983, 1986, American Composers Forum Comm. 1998, CAPS Grant. *Telephone:* (609) 661-8399. *E-mail:* wendymae@ wendymae.com. *Website:* www.wendymae.com.

CHAMPION, Will; British musician (drums) and songwriter; b. 21 July 1977, Southampton, Hants., England. *Education:* University Coll., London. *Career:* mem. Coldplay 1998–. *Recordings include:* albums: Parachutes (BRIT Award for Best Album 2001, Grammy Award for Best Alternative Album 2002) 2000, A Rush Of Blood To The Head (BRIT Award for Best British Album 2003, NME Award for Best Album 2003) 2002, X&Y (MasterCard British Album, BRIT Awards 2006, Juno Award for Int. Album of the Year 2006) 2005, Viva la Vida (Grammy Award for Best Rock Album 2009) 2008, Mylo Xyloto (Billboard Music Award for Top Rock Album 2012) 2011, Ghost Stories (Billboard Music Award for Top Rock Album 2015) 2014, A Head Full of Dreams 2015. *Honours:* BRIT Awards for Best British Group 2001, 2003, 2012, for Best British Single (for Speed of Sound) 2006, for Best Live Act 2014, MTV Europe Music Awards for Best UK and Ireland Act 2002, for Best Song (for Speed of Sound) 2005, for Best Rock Act 2015, Billboard Music Awards for Group of the Year 2002, for Top Rock Artist 2012, for Top Alternative Artist 2012, Ivor Novello Awards for Songwriters of the Year 2003, for Best Selling British Song (for Viva la Vida) 2009, Grammy Awards for Record of the Year (for Clocks) 2004, for Best Rock Vocal Performance by a Duo or Group (for In My Place) 2004, for Song of the Year 2009, for Best Pop Performance by a Duo or Group (both for Viva la Vida) 2009, Q Awards for Best Act in the World 2005, 2011, Digital Music People's Choice Award for best official site, for Best Digital Music Community (for Coldplay.com) 2005, American Music Award for Favorite Alternative Music Artist 2005, Echo Award for Best Int. Group, Germany 2006, ASCAP Award for Song of the Year (for Speed of Sound) 2006, World Music Award for Best Rock Act 2008. *Address:* c/o Dave Holmes, 3-D Management, 1901 Main Street, #3000, Los Angeles, CA 90405, USA. *Telephone:* (310) 314-1390. *Website:* www.coldplay.com.

CHAN, Agnes, PhD; Japanese singer and academic; b. 20 Aug. 1955, Hong Kong; m. Tsutomu Kaneko 1985; three c. *Education:* Sophia Univ., Univ. of Toronto, Canada, Stanford Univ., USA. *Career:* debut single Circle Game released in Hong Kong 1969; Japan debut single Hinagesi no Hana released 1972; performed charity concerts for Cambodia in Hong Kong and Japan 1980, Beijing 1985; Lecturer, Shinshui and Reitaku Univs 1986; Lecturer on Cross-Cultural Communication, Nagoya Women's Cultural Coll. 1993–97, Prof. 1997–; Asst Prof., Mejiro Univ. 1994–97, Prof. 1997–; Prof., Kyouei Univ. 2001; Amb. of Japan Cttee, UNICEF 1998–, travelled to Vietnam, Cambodia, Thailand, Sudan and Philippines on issues of child prostitution and child soldiers; lobbied the law against child prostitution and won its passage in the diet 1999; named Amb. of Hong Kong and Japan 2001; cr. new clothing line called Dear Agnes 1990; opened Chan's Boutique, Odaiba, Tokyo 2001; mem. Bd of Dirs, Wild Bird Asscn of Japan, Children's Dream Foundation, Children's Earth Club, Blue Sky Foundation, Kaijo Hoan Tomo no Kai; mem. Bd of Trustees, Day of Peace of Tokyo, Yokohama Museum, Sung Kei Ling Foundation, Japan and China Goodwill Asscn; TV talk show personality; regular contribs to newspapers and magazines; makes over 100 concert performances and speech tours throughout Japan each year. *Television:* Agnes' Music Salon 2006, Kitajima Wink Heart 2007. *Radio:* Agnes' Sunny Side Up, City Snapshot. *Albums include:* more than 100 albums in several different languages. *Publications include:* My Chinese Dishes 1983, Be Peaceful With Songs 1984, We All Are the People Who Live on the Earth 1984, Neo Woman 1993, Mama You Don't Need To Be a Doctor 1994, Hong Kong Guide 1997, The Road Winds Uphill All The Way (co-author) 1999, Positive Child Care 2001, Perfection Couple, Ring of Cullet 2002, This Road Leads to the Hill 2003, Cheers to the World! 2004, The Right Track – To People Who Live For the Future 2005, What the Marriage Life Is? (co-author), Agnes' Style Aging 2006. *Honours:* Hong Kong Top Ten Singers Award 1971, Japan Records Grand Prize 1973, New Artist Award 1973, Shinjuku Music Award 1973, Best New Artist Award 1974, Golden Arrow Award 1974, Japan Cable Music Award 1974, Int. Year of Youth Award (for essay on world peace) 1984, S. J. Grand Prize Winner, Asscn of Women Working in Broadcasting 1986, Asscn of Japanese Journalists Special Award 1986, Galaxy Award 1986, Most Popular Name of the Year Award 1988, Best Eye Wear Award 1997; numerous gold and platinum discs. *Address:* Japan Committee for UNICEF, UNICEF House, 4-6-12 Takanawa, Minato-ku, Tokyo 108-8607, Japan (office). *Telephone:* (3) 5789-2032 (office); (3) 5789-2011 (office). *E-mail:* unicefjc@unicef.or .jp (office). *Website:* www.unicef.or.jp (office); www.agneschan.gr.jp.

CHANA, Shan; British musician (drums, percussion, latin, timpani); b. 4 March 1969, Plymouth, Devon, England. *Education:* London Coll. of Music. *Career:* mem. Musicians' Union. *Stage appearances:* Crazy For You (Prince Edward Theatre), Grease (Dominion Theatre), Sunset Boulevard (Adelphi Theatre), She Loves Me (Savoy Theatre), Fame (Cambridge Theatre). *Recordings include:* Fame (original cast album), Himalaya Dawn (with Kuljit Bhamra) 2006. *Honours:* Henry Bromley Derry Music Performance Prize 1990.

CHANDLER, Gene; American singer and songwriter; b. (Eugene D. Dixon), 6 July 1940, Chicago, Ill. *Career:* lead singer, Gene Chandler and The Dukays; solo artist. *Recordings include:* albums: The Duke of Earl 1962, Just Be True 1964, Live At The Regal 1965, The Girl Don't Care 1967, Gene Chandler 1967, There Was A Time 1968, The Two Sides of Gene Chandler 1969, Gene and Jerry: One on One (with Jerry Butler) 1970, The Gene Chandler Groovy Situation 1970, Get Down 1978, When You're Number One 1979, 80 1980, Soul Master 1995, The Soul Of 1996. *Honours:* inducted to Grammy Hall of Fame, Producer of the Year, Nat. Asscn of TV and Radio Announcers, Rhythm and Blues Foundation's Pioneer Award. *Address:* 8829 South Bishop, Chicago, IL 60620, USA (home). *Telephone:* (773) 651-2020 (office). *Fax:* (708) 283-3959 (office). *E-mail:* earlduke1@aol.com (office). *Website:* www.genechandler.com.

CHANDLER, Kerri, (Gate-Ah, Paper Mache); American producer, remixer and DJ; b. East Orange, NJ. *Career:* started DJ career aged 13; started producing in the late '80s; set up own label, Express Records; debut single Superlover/Get It Off released by Atlantic Records 1991; Founder Madhouse, Sfere Records; collaborations with Jerome Sydenham, Dee Dee Brave, Dennis Ferrer, Arnold Jarvis, Byron Stingily, Femi Kuti, Shawn Christopher, Ultra Nate, Ce Ce Rogers. *Recordings include:* albums: A Basement, Redlight and a Feeling 1992, Inspiration 1994, Hemisphere 1996, Kaoz on King Street 1997, Kaoz Theory 1998, Trionisphere 2003, Coast 2 Coast 2007, Computer Games 2008; singles: Superlover/Get It Off 1991, The Shelter (as Gate-Ah) 1992, Inspiration (with Arnold Jarvis) 1994, Ionosphere EP 1995, See Line Woman (with The Songstress) 1998, My Old Friend 1999. *Address:* Simply Cool Music (office). *Telephone:* (212) 673-1535 (office). *E-mail:* robwunderman@mac.com (office). *Website:* www.simplycoolmusic.com; www.kerrichandler.com.

CHANDRA, Sheila; British singer, songwriter and author; b. 14 April 1965, London, England. *Education:* Italia Conti Theatre School, London. *Career:* began collaboration with Steve Coe, forming Monsoon 1981–82; solo artist, working with Coe as producer and co-writer; Asian-influenced world fusion. *Television:* Grange Hill (children's programme). *Film music:* Breath Of Life, featured in Lord of the Rings: The Two Towers 2003. *Recordings include:* albums: with Monsoon: Third Eye 1982; solo: Out On My Own 1984, Quiet 1984, Nada Brahma 1985, The Struggle 1985, Roots And Wings 1990, Weaving My Ancestors' Voices 1992, The Zen Kiss 1994, ABoneCroneDrone 1996, Moonsung 1999, This Sentence Is True (The Previous Sentence Is False) 2001, The Indipop Retrospective 2003. *Publication:* Banish Clutter Forever 2010. *E-mail:* sheila@sheilachandra.com. *Website:* www.sheilachandra.com.

CHANG, Hui-mei, (A-mei); Taiwanese singer; b. 9 Aug. 1972. *Career:* winner, Five Lights Singing Contest (TV talent show) 1994. *Recordings include:* albums: Jie Mei 1996, Holding Hands 1998, Can I Hold You Lover? 1999, Regardless 2001, Fever 2002, Brave 2003, Maybe Tomorrow 2004, I Want Happiness 2006, Star 2007, Amit (Golden Melody Award 2010) 2009, R U Watching? 2011. *Honours:* Taiwan Channel V Music Award for Best Newcomer 1997, Golden Melody Award for Best Female Artist 2002, World Peace Music Award (Greater China Region) 2004, MTV Asia Favourite Music Artist Award (Taiwan) 2004, China Central Television (CCTV) and Channel V Award for Most Popular Female Singer 2004, Beijing Pop Music Award 2011. *Address:* c/o EMI Music Taiwan, Suite 1, 7/F, World Builidng 126, Sector 4, Nanjing E. Road, Taipei 105, Taiwan. *E-mail:* taiwan@emimusicpub.com. *Website:* www.emimusic.com.tw.

CHANG WANG, Sylvia Ai-Chia; American filmmaker, actress and singer; b. 22 July 1953, Chiayi, Repub. of China (Taiwan); d. of Chang Wen Cheung and Emily Wei; m. Billy Wang 1991; one s. *Education:* Int. School of the Sacred Heart, Taipei. *Career:* TV presenter and producer 1970; actress 1971–, now also film producer and dir. *Films include:* actress in: Long hu jin hu (The Tattooed Dragon) 1973, Shi qi shi qi shi ba 1974, Slaughter in San Francisco 1974, Men li men wai (The Story of Four Girls) 1975, Xing yu 1976, Wen nuan zai qiu tian (Warmth in Autumn) 1976, Qiu chan 1976, Mei hua (Victory) 1976, Luo ye piao piao 1976, The Longest Bridge 1976, Lang hua 1976, Bi yun tian 1976, Bian se de tai yang 1976, Zuo ri chong chong 1977, Taibei liu shi liu 1977, Shan liang de ri zi (The Golden Age) 1977, Qing se shan mai 1977, Jin yu liang yuan gong lou meng (The Dream of the Red Chamber) 1977, Gui ma gu ye zi (The Lady Killer) 1977, Ai qing wo zhao dao le 1977, Ai de zei quan (A Pirate of Love) 1977, Bo sai xi yang qing (Mitra) 1977, Ma feng nu 1979, Fung gip (The Secret) 1979, Shan-chung ch'uan-ch'i (Legend of the Mountain) 1979, Xue jian leng ying bao 1980, Mo li hua (White Jasmine) 1980, Jin zhi yu ye (The Imperious Princess) 1980, Zhong shen da shi 1981, Tian xia yi da xiao (The Funniest Movie) 1981, Kong zhong wu shi 1981, Da, i xiao jiang jun 1981, Zuijia Paidang (Aces Go Places) 1982, Ye jing hun (He Lives by Night) 1982, Wo de ye ye (My Grandfather) 1982, Wo de ye ye (My Grandfather) 1982, Da sao ba (Crazy Romance) 1982, Attack Force Z 1982, Zuijia paidang daxian shentong (Aces Go Places II) 1983, Tai shang tai xia (Cabaret of the Streets) 1983, Haitan de yitian (That Day, on the Beach) 1983, Guangyinde gushi (In Our Time) 1983, Cabaret Tears 1983, Shanghai zhi ye (Shanghai Blues) 1984, Gao liang di li da mai shou (The Story in Sorghum Field) 1984, Da xiao jiang jun (Funny Face) 1984, Da xiao bu liang (Double Trouble) 1984, Zuijia paidang zhi nuhuang miling (Aces Go Places III: Our Man From Bond Street) 1984, Zhui xiang nian de ji jie (My Favourite Season) 1985, Robby the Rascal (video) (voice) 1985, Jasmine House, My Grandpa (Taiwan Golden House Award), Zuijia paidang zhi qianli jiu chaipo (You Never Die Twice) 1986, Zui jia fu xing (Lucky Stars Go Places) 1986, Zui ai (Passion) (Best Actress, Hong Kong Film Festival) 1986, Hoi seung fa (The Flower Floating on the Sea) 1986, Tian ci liang yuan (Heavenly Fate) 1987, Qi nian zhi yang (Seven Year's Itch) 1987, Huang-se gushi (The Game They Call Sex) 1987, Dai jian de xiao hai (Kidnapped) 1987, Ku jia tian xia (King of Stanley Market) 1988, Gai tung aap gong (Chicken and Duck Talk) 1988, Soursweet 1988, You jian A Lang (All About Ah-Long) 1989, Ren zai Niu Yue (Full Moon in New York) 1989, Liang ge you qi jiang (Two Painters) 1989, Ji xing gong zhao (The Fun, the Luck, and the Tycoon) 1989, Ba liang jin (Eight Tales of Gold) (Best Actress, Hong Kong Film Festival) 1989, Chun qiu cha shi (My Mother's Tea House) 1990, Miao jie huang hou (Queen of Temple Street) (Best Actress, Hong Kong Film Festival) 1990, Sha sha jia jia zhan qi lai (Sisters of the World Unite) (also producer) 1991, Bao feng shao nian (A Rascal's Tale) 1991, Ti dao bao (Lucky Encounter) 1992, Shuang long hui (Brother vs. Brother) 1992, Huan ying 1993, San tung gui shut doi (Conjugal Affair) 1994, Xin buliao qing (Endless Love) (uncredited) 1994, Yin shi nan nu (Eat Drink Man Woman) 1994, Wo yao huo xia qu (I Want to Go on Living) 1995, Killer Lady 1995, The Fragile Heart (TV) 1996, Xiao Qian (A Chinese Ghost Story: The Tsui Hark Animation) (voice) 1997, Paternity and Perplexity (Best Actress, Asian Film Festival, Taiwan Golden House Award), Le violon rouge (The Red Violin) 1998, Xin dong (Tempting Heart) 1999, Dei gau tin cheung (Forever and Ever) 2001, 20:30:40 2004, Hainan ji fan (Rice Rhapsody) 2004; directed: Passion (Taiwan Golden House Award), Once Upon a Time 1978, My Way 1981, The Game They Call Sex 1987, Mary From Beijing 1991, Conjugal Affairs 1993, Siao Yu (Best Picture, Best Screenplay, Best Actress, Best Production Design, Best Sound Effects awards, Asian Pacific Film Festival), Tonight Nobody Goes Home 1996, Tempting Heart 1999, Princess D 2001 (writer, dir and producer), 20:30:40 2004, Hainan ji fan 2004, American Fusion 2005, Wu Qingyuan 2006, Sun yat fai lok (screenplay) 2007, Yat kor ho ba ba (screenplay and dir) 2008. *Recordings:* seven albums. *Address:* 17 Homantin Hill Road, Apt 1A Canbury Court, Kowloon, Hong Kong Special Administrative Region, People's Republic of China. *Telephone:* 27613975. *Fax:* 27157098.

CHANGMIN; South Korean singer and rapper; b. (Lee Changmin), 1 May 1986. *Education:* Dongee Bangsong Univ. *Career:* mem. 2AM 2008–, live debut 2010; has also recorded with 8eight, Lee Hyun. *Recordings:* with 2AM: Saint o'Clock 2010; other 2AM appearances include: Personal Preference (soundtrack) 2010, Listen Up!: The Official 2010 FIFA World Cup Album 2010, Acoustic (soundtrack) 2010. *Honours:* Mnet Asian Music Award for Best Vocal Performance by a Group 2011. *Address:* c/o JYP Entertainment, JYP Center, 41, 79-gil Apgujeong-ro, Gangnam-gu, Seoul, South Korea (office). *Telephone:* (2) 3438-2300 (office). *Fax:* (2) 3442-7020 (office); (2) 3438-2330 (office). *E-mail:* publicity@jype.com (office). *Website:* www.jype.com (office); 2am.ibighit.com.

CHANTRE, Teofilo; Cabo Verde/French singer, musician (guitar) and composer; b. (Almeida Chantre Teofilo Sousa), 1963, São Nicolau, Cabo Verde; s. of Vitorino Chantre and Suzana Almeida Noro. *Career:* moved to France aged 13; songwriter for Cesaria Evora; solo artist 1993–. *Recordings include:* albums: Terra et Cretcheu 1993, Di Alma 1997, Rodatempo 2000, Live à la Maroquinerie Paris 2001 2002, Azulando 2004, Viaja 2007, Metissage 2011; other: Alma Morna, Allem Disso, Lua Desencantada. *Honours:* Chevalier des Arts et des Lettres 2002. *Current Management:* 3D FAMILY, 50 rue Servan, 75011 Paris, France. *Telephone:* 1-40-09-64-66 (office). *Fax:* 1-40-09-15-39 (office). *E-mail:* info@3dfamily.org (office). *Website:* www .3dfamily.org (office). *Address:* c/o Lusafrica, 115 rue Lamarck, 75018 Paris, France (office). *Telephone:* 1-53-11-19-00 (office). *E-mail:* tchantre@orange.fr (office); lusafrica@lusafrica.com (office). *Website:* www.lusafrica.com (office); www.teofilo-chantre.com (home).

CHANYEOL; South Korean rapper and singer; b. (Park Chanyeol), 27 Nov. 1992, Seoul. *Education:* Hyundai Chungun High School, Dong-gu, Ulsan. *Career:* fmr mem., school bands Heavy Noise, Seiren; mem., K-pop boy band Exo 2012–; mem. sub-group Exo-K 2012–; debut single 2012; numerous TV and live appearances. *Television:* EXO's Showtime 2013–, Royal Villa (guest star) 2013. *Recordings:* albums: Mama 2012, XOXO (Mnet Asian Music Award for Album of the Year 2013) 2013. *Honours:* numerous awards including: for Exo: Mnet Asian Music Award for Best New Asian Artist/Group 2012, MTV Europe Music Award for Best Japan/Korea Act 2013, MelOn Music Award for Song of the Year (for Growl) 2013; for Exo-K: Golden Disk Newcomer Award 2012. *Address:* c/o SM Entertainment, 521 Apgujeong 2-dong, Gangnam-gu, Seoul, South Korea (office). *Telephone:* (2) 6240-9800 (office). *Website:* www .smtown.com (office); exo.smtown.com (home).

CHAO, Manu; French singer and songwriter; b. (José-Manuel Thomas Arthur Chao), 26 June 1961, Paris; one s. *Career:* as teenager played in various bands, including Les Hot Pants; formed Mano Negra 1987, band split 1993; first single earned group contract with Virgin; toured Latin America; moved to Spain 1995; formed 10-mem. Radio Bemba Sound System; spent next few years recording in South and Central America; King of Bongo recording featured on soundtrack to Madonna's The Next Big Thing film; British tour 2002; producer for Amadou and Mariam, Akli D. *Recordings include:* with Mano Negra: Patchanka 1988, Puta's Fever 1989, King Of The Bongo 1991, Hell Of Patchinko 1992, Casa Babylon 1994; solo: Clandestino 1998, Próxima Estación: Esperanza 2001, Sibérie m'était contée 2004, La Radiolina 2007, Estación México 2008, Baionarena 2009. *Honours:* BBC Radio 3 World Music Innovator award 2002, Latin Grammy Award for Best Alternative Song (for Me Llaman Calle) 2007. *Current Management:* c/o Management Corida, 120 boulevard Rochechouard, 75018 Paris, France. *Fax:* (1) 42-23-67-04. *Website:* www.manuchao.net.

CHAOS AD (see Jenkinson, Tom)

CHAPIN, Tom; American singer, songwriter, musician (guitar, banjo, autoharp) and actor; b. (Thomas Forbes), 13 March 1945, Charlotte, NC; m. Bonnie Chapin 1976; two d. one step-s. one step-d. *Education:* State Univ. of New York, Plattsburgh. *Career:* numerous concerts, mainly in N America; mem. AFofM, SAG, AFTRA, NARAS, NAS. *Television:* host Make A Wish (ABC) (Peabody Award 1972, Emmy Award 1975) 1971–76, host Nat. Geographic Explorer (TBS) 1986–89. *Theatre:* Pump Boys and Dinettes (Broadway) 1983. *Recordings:* albums: for children: Family Tree 1988, Moonboat 1989, Mother Earth 1990, Billy The Squid 1992, Zag Zig 1994, Just For Kids 1996, Around the World and Back Again 1996, In My Hometown 1998, This Pretty Planet 2000, Great Big Fun For The Very Little One 2001, Making Good Noise 2003, Some Assembly Required 2005, Give Peas a Chance 2011; for adults: Life Is Like That 1974, In The City of Mercy 1982, Let Me Back Into Your Life 1986, So Nice To Come Home 1994, Join The Jubilee 1996, Doing Our Job (with John McCutcheon) 1997, Common Ground 2001, The Turning of the Tide 2006, Let the Bad Times Roll 2009, Broadsides (with John Forster) 2010. *Publications:* Sing A Whale Song (juvenile story book). *Honours:* Harry Chapin Award for Contribution to Humanity, NACA 1990. *Address:* c/o Sundance Music, 100 Cedar Street, Suite B-19, Dobbs Ferry, NY 10522, USA (office). *Telephone:* (914) 674-0247 (office). *E-mail:* info@ tomchapin.com. *Website:* www.tomchapin.com.

CHAPLIN, Tom; British singer; b. 8 March 1979, Battle, East Sussex, England. *Career:* Founder-mem. Keane 1997–. *Recordings include:* album: Hopes and Fears (Best Album, Q Awards 2004, BRIT Award for Best British Album 2005) 2004, Under the Iron Sea 2006, Perfect Symmetry 2008, Night Train (mini-album) 2010, Strangeland 2012. *Honours:* Best Int. Band, Premios Onda, Spain 2004, BRIT Award for Best British Breakthrough Act 2005, Songwriter of the Year (with Tim Rice Oxley), Ivor Novello Awards 2005, Band of the Year, GQ Awards 2006. *Current Management:* c/o Everybody's, 53 Corsica Street, London, N5 1JT, England. *Telephone:* (20) 3227-0420. *Fax:* (20) 3227-0420. *E-mail:* info@everybody-s.com. *Website:* www .everybody-s.com; www.keanemusic.com.

CHAPMAN, Mike; Australian songwriter; b. 15 April 1947, Queensland. *Career:* mem. Tangerine Peel; songwriting partnership with Nicky Chinn; producer for Blondie hits; Co-founder (with Nicky Chinn) Dreamland (label) 1979–81. *Compositions include:* hits include: Kiss You All Over, Exile 1978, Hot Child In The City, Nick Gilder 1979, Mickey, Toni Basil 1982; composed other hits for Sweet, Gary Glitter, Mud, Suzi Quatro, Smokie, Patti Smith, Lita Ford, Lisa Douglass, Sarah Jeanette. *Recordings include:* as producer: with Blondie: Heart of Glass 1979, Sunday Girl 1979, Atomic 1980, The Tide Is High 1980, Rapture 1981, with The Knack: My Sharona 1979; also produced for Patti Smith, Lita Ford, Blondie, Pat Benatar, Lisa Douglass, Sarah Jeanette.

CHAPMAN, Tom Louis; French/British musician (bass, guitar, keyboards), songwriter and record producer; b. 15 May 1972, Chevreuse, France. *Career:* mem. Bad Lieutenant 2008–11; bass guitarist, New Order 2011–; Founder-mem. Rubberbear 2013–. *Recordings include:* albums: with Bad Lieutenant: Never Cry Another Tear 2009; with New Order: Music Complete 2015. *Honours:* with New Order: Q Outstanding Contrib. to Music Award 2015. *Website:* www.neworder.com.

CHAPMAN, Tracy; American singer and songwriter; b. 30 March 1964, Cleveland, Ohio. *Education:* Tufts Univ. *Recordings include:* albums: Tracy Chapman 1988, Crossroads 1989, Matters of the Heart 1992, New Beginning 1995, Telling Stories 2000, Collection (compilation) 2001, Let It Rain 2002, Where You Live 2005, Our Bright Future 2008. *Honours:* Hon. DFA (Tufts Univ.) 2004; Grammy Award for Best New Artist, Best Female Pop Vocal Performance and Best Contemporary Folk Performance 1989, Grammy Award for Best Rock Song (for Give Me One Reason) 1996, IFPI Platinum Europe Music Awards 2002. *Website:* www.tracychapman.com.

CHAR; Japanese singer and rock guitarist; b. (Takenaka Hisato), 16 June 1955, Tokyo; s. *Career:* began taking classical music piano lessons age seven; began playing the guitar age eight; formed first band with friends at school age 11; formed underground music band Smoky Medicine 1973; launched solo career with release of self-titled debut album 1976; formed blues-rock-fusion power band JL&C (renamed Pink Cloud) with Johnny Yoshinaga and Kabe Shogi 1979, disbanded 1994; later formed bands Psychedelix 1991 and Baho (acoustin duo); performs with son who raps in English 1998–. *Recordings include:* albums: Char 1976, Have a Win 1977, Thrill 1978, U.S.J. 1981, The Best of Char 1982, Moon Child 1982, Play Back Series 1987, Psych 1987, Psych II 1988, When I Wake Up in the Morning 1989, Black Shoes 1989, Flash Back Memories 1991, Days Went By 1988–1993 1993, Mustang 1995, Character 1996, Char e Doya Collection 1999, All Around Me 1999, Char Psyche 2000, Char Played With and Without 2000, Bamboo Shoots 2001, Sacred Hills 2002, You Set Me Free 2003, Amano Jack 2005, Flying Toys 2007.

CHARA; Japanese singer; b. (Miwa Watabiki), 13 Jan. 1968, Kawaguchi-shi, Saitama Co.; m. Tadanobu Asano (q.v.) 1994 (divorced 2009); one d. one s. *Career:* began taking piano lessons aged four; signed contract with Epic/Sony Records 1990; first performance debut at Quattro Club, Tokyo 1991; released debut single Heaven and debut album Sweet 1991; TV commercials for Suntory, Shiseido and Marui 1990s; formed Mean Machine duo (with Yuki) 2001–05. *Films:* Swallowtail Butterfly (Best Actress Award, Japanese Acad.

Awards) 1996. *Recordings include:* albums: Sweet 1991, Soul Kiss 1992, Violet Blue 1993, Happy Toy 1994, Baby, Baby, Baby XXX 1995, Yen Town Band (soundtrack album for film Swallowtail Butterfly) 1996, Junior Sweet 1997, Strange Fruits 1999, Mood 2000, Caramel Milk 2000, Cream (with Mean Machine) 2001, Madrigal 2001, Yokae Mae 2003, Sweet 2004, A Scenery Like Me 2004, Something Blue 2005, Union 2007, Sugar Hunter 2007, Honey 2008, Kiss 2008, Carol 2009, Dark Candy 2011, Cocoon 2012, Jewel 2013, Secret Garden 2015. *Website:* www.charaweb.net.

CHARICE; Philippine singer and actress; b. (Charmaine Clarice Relucio Pempengco), 10 May 1992, Laguna. *Career:* appeared on TV talent show Little Big Star in Philippines (placed third) 2005; appeared on TV talent show Star King, S Korea 2007; US concert debut 2008; collaborations with Andrea Bocelli, Celine Dion, David Foster. *Television:* Little Big Star (finalist) 2005, Star King 2007, Glee (cast member) 2010-11, Charice: Home for Valentine's (musical special) 2011; numerous guest appearances. *Films:* Alvin and the Chipmunks: The Squeakquel 2009. *Recordings:* albums: My Inspiration 2009, Charice 2010, Infinity 2011. *Honours:* appointed Operation Smile's Smile Amb. 2010; numerous awards including ALIW Awards for Best Female Artist and Best Female Recording Artist, Philippines 2008, for Best Major Concert (Female Category) 2011, for Entertainer of the Year 2011, MYX Music Special Citation Award, Philippines 2009, Awit Awards for Best Selling Album of the Year 2009, for Best Inspirational or Religious Song 2010, Box Office Entertainment Awards for Outstanding Global Achievement 2010, for Female Concert Performer of the Year 2011. *Current Management:* Marc Johnston, Align Entertainment Group LLC, 200 West 54th Street, 11th Floor, New York, NY 10019, USA. *Telephone:* (212) 333-2524. *E-mail:* marc@aligneg.com. *Website:* www.aligneg.com; www.charicemusic.com.

CHARLES, Debbie; British singer and songwriter; b. 9 Aug. 1966, London. *Career:* backing vocalist with Fine Young Cannibals, Al Green, Bob Geldof, Gabrielle, Alison Moyet, Lighthouse Family; mem. of capella sextet Mint Juleps; mem. The Matinee Idles; mem. PRS.

CHARLESON, William (Bill), MA, GRSM, ARCM; British educator, composer, arranger and musician (saxophone); b. 20 June 1940, Oldham, Lancs.; m. Diane Margaret Fox 1965; one s. one d. *Education:* Royal Manchester Coll. of Music, Univ. of York. *Career:* appearances with Ken Mackintosh and Orchestra, BBC Northern Dance Orchestra, BBC Northern Symphony Orchestra, Hallé Orchestra, Royal Liverpool Philharmonic Orchestra; theatre and cabaret work, accompanying British and American artists; radio and TV broadcasts; consultancy, Open Univ.; Leader, Manhattan Sound Big Band; mem. Performing Right Soc. *Compositions include:* jazz compositions for Nat. Youth Jazz Orchestra, brass band arrangements. *Recordings include:* Tucker – A Man and his Dream (film soundtrack, with Joe Jackson); Library music, composed and performed for studio and music. *Publications include:* Jazz Sax 1 (with J. R. Brown); contrib. of articles to Crescendo International, British Education Music Journal. *Honours:* YTV/MU Peter Knight Award 1989, BBC Rehearsal Band Competition Arranging Prize 1989. *Address:* 144 Sunnybank Road, Mirfield, WF14 0JQ, England (home). *Telephone:* (1924) 493413 (home). *E-mail:* billcharleson@btinternet.com.

CHARLTON, Michael Anthony, (Mad Dog Santini), BA; British musician (drums, percussion, keyboards); b. 27 Feb. 1964, South Shields, Tyne and Wear; one d. *Education:* Univ. of Northumbria, Newcastle. *Career:* mem. PRS, Musicians' Union, Equity. *Recordings:* No More War, Is That It, Smooth Funk, Scratch It, Addicted, Devils In Heaven. *Address:* 55 Marsden Lane, South Shields, Tyne and Wear, England.

CHARMASSON, Rémi; French musician (guitar) and composer; b. 3 May 1961, Avignon. *Education:* Baccalaureate, Philosophy; Gold Medal in Jazz, Avignon Conservatory. *Recordings include:* Cinoche, with André Jaume, Rémi Charmasson, Claude Tchamitchian 1989, Piazza Di Luna, with André Jaume, Rémi Charmasson, Jean-Marc Montera, Fredy Studer, Claude Tchamitchian, Tavagna singers 1989, FollyFun Music Magic, with Charles Tyler, Rémi Charmasson, Jean Pierre Jullian, Bernard Santacruz, Christian Zagaria 1990, Caminanado, duo with Claude Tchamitchian 1990, A Scream For Charles Tyler, with Rémi Charmasson, Dennis Charles, Bernard Santacruz; Casa Blu, with Thierry Maucci; Nemo, trio with F Studer, Jenny Clarke; 10 records in 5 years 1993, Merapi, with André Jaume, Rémi Charmasson 1995, Iliade, with André Jaume, Rémi Charmasson, Christian Gorelli, Hakim Hamadouche, Bernard Gueit 1997, L'Ombre De La Pluie, with Rémi Charmasson, Claude Tchamitchian, Jean-Pierre Jullian 2002, Fly Baby, Fly !, Rémi Charmasson, Drew Gress, André Jaume, Tom Rainey 2013; current recordings with André Jaume, Charlie Mariano Quintet, A Jaume and Groupes de Gamelans Indonésiens, A Soler and Larry Schneider,. *Honours:* Diapason D' Or from music newspaper Diapason. *Current Management:* Association pour le Jazz et la Musique Improvisée, La Manutention 4, rue escaliers, Ste Anne, 84000 Avignon, France. *Telephone:* 4-90-31-84-89 (home).

CHASE, Brian Nathaniel; American musician (drums); b. 12 Feb. 1979. *Education:* Oberlin Coll., New York Univ. *Career:* mem. rock band Yeah Yeah Yeahs 2000–. *Recordings include:* albums: Fever To Tell 2002, Show Your Bones 2006, It's Blitz! 2009, The Shape of Sound (with Seth Misterka) 2010, Mosquito 2013. *E-mail:* yeahyeahyeahsctc@hotmail.com. *Website:* www .yeahyeahyeahs.com. *E-mail:* bc@chasebrian.com. *Website:* chasebrian.com.

CHASE, Katharine Ann, BA; American singer, songwriter and musician (bass and rhythm guitars); b. 29 April 1963, Ridgecrest, Calif. *Education:*

Univ. of California, Los Angeles. *Career:* solo appearances with Hootie and the Blowfish; Mary Lou Lord; Exene Cervankova, Elliot Smith; Co-founder Spanking Violets 1992; Founder Katharine Chase Band 1994; Co-founder Kindness 1999; mem. BMI, NARAS. *Compositions:* Cake, The Blasters, Southern Culture On The Skids, Tripping Daisy. *Recordings include:* albums: solo: Loverman 1994; with the band: Spanking Violets 1994, The Truth 1995, The Truth 1997; with Kindness: Welcome To Planet Excellent. *Honours:* 12 Gold Medals, Regional Texas State Flute Competitions 1980–86.

CHASEZ, Joshua Scott (J.C.); American singer, songwriter and actor; b. 8 Aug. 1976, Washington, DC. *Career:* fmr presenter, The Mickey Mouse Club (television); worked as singer/songwriter in Los Angeles and Nashville; mem. vocal quintet, *NSYNC 1995–; solo artist, songwriter, actor and producer 2004–. *Television:* judge on America's Best Dance Crew (MTV) 2008–. *Films:* as actor: Killer Movie 2008, 21 and a Wake-Up 2009. *Recordings include:* albums: with *NSYNC: *NSYNC 1998, Home For The Holidays 1998, The Winter Album 1998, No Strings Attached 2000, Celebrity 2001; solo: Schizophrenic 2004. *Honours:* presented with keys to City of Orlando 2000, American Music Award for Favorite Pop/Rock Band, Duo or Group 2002. *Address:* c/o MTV, Viacom, 1515 Broadway, New York, NY 10036 (office); c/o Wright Entertainment Group, PO Box 590009, Orlando, FL 32859-0009, USA (office). *Telephone:* (212) 258-8000 (office). *Fax:* (212) 258-6175 (office). *Website:* www.mtv.com (office); www.wegmusic.com (office); www.nsync.com.

CHASSAGNE, Régine; Canadian singer, songwriter and musician (keyboards, accordion, xylophone, drums); b. Haiti; m. Win Butler. *Career:* founder mem., Arcade Fire 2003–. *Recordings include:* albums: Funeral 2004, Neon Bible (Juno Award for Alternative Album of the Year 2008) 2007, The Suburbs (Grammy Award for Album of the Year 2011) 2010, Reflektor (Juno Awards for Album of the Year and Alternative Album of the Year 2014) 2013. *Address:* Quest Management, 1D–36 Warple Way, London, W3 0DY, England. *Telephone:* (20) 8749-0088. *Fax:* (20) 8749-0080. *E-mail:* info@quest-management.com. *Website:* www.quest-management.com; www.arcadefire.com.

CHATER, Robbie; Australian musician. *Career:* Founder-mem. punk band, later electronic music collective, The Avalanches 1997–. *Recordings include:* album: Since I Left You 2000. *Address:* c/o Modular Records, PO Box 1666, Darlinghurst, NSW 1300, Australia. *Website:* www.theavalanches.com.

CHATTO, Grace Elizabeth; British musician (cello), singer and songwriter; b. 1985, London, England. *Education:* Westminster School, Jesus Coll., Cambridge. *Career:* formerly cellist in string quartet at Univ. of Cambridge (with Milan Neil Amin-Smith); Founder-mem. Clean Bandit 2009–; released debut single A+E 2012; toured UK with Disclosure 2013; released single Rather Be (with Jess Glynne) 2013; numerous collaborations with other artists including Noonie Bao, Sharna Bass, Gorgon City, Love Ssega, Kandaka Moore and Nikki Cislyn, Stylo G. *Recordings:* albums: with Clean Bandit: New Eyes 2014. *Honours:* Grammy Award for Best Dance Recording (for Rather Be) 2015. *Current Management:* c/o Machine Management, Studio 16, London Fields Studios, 11–17 Exmouth Place, London, E8 3RW, England. *Telephone:* (20) 7923-3502. *E-mail:* info@machinemanagement.co.uk. *Website:* machinemanagement.co.uk; cleanbandit.co.uk.

CHAUDAGNE, Remy; French composer and musician (electric bass); b. 26 Aug. 1959, Melun; m. Cora 1994; one s. *Career:* tours of France, India, Indonesia, Viet Nam, Philippines, Cambodia, Sudan; performances with: David Liebman, Scott Henderson, F. Corneloup, Claude Barthelemy, Andy Sheppard. *Compositions:* music for short films, theatre, saxophone quartet, Creation with jazz orchestra (24 musicians) or classical (13 musicians). *Recordings include:* seven albums as leader, including last in trio with Peter Erskine and Andy Sheppard: 3 Colors. *Honours:* First Prize, Villembourne Festiva. *Address:* 4B rue de la Convention, 94270 Kremlin Bicêtre, France. *E-mail:* remy@remychaudagne.com. *Website:* www.remychaudagne.com.

CHAUHAN, Mohit, MSc; Indian singer; b. 11 March 1966, Himachal Pradesh. *Education:* Dharamshala Coll. *Career:* fmr mem. band Silk Route, now solo artist; playback singer in numerous films. *Recordings include:* albums: Boondhein (with Silk Route) 1998, Pehchan (with Silk Route) 2000, Kalaam — Poetry of Dr A. P. J. Abdul Kalam 2008, Fitoor 2009, Aao Sai 2011. *Films include:* as playback singer: Road 2002, Main Madhuri Dixit Banna Chahti Hoon 2003, Let's Enjoy 2004, Main, Meri Patni Aur Woh 2005, Rang De Basanti 2006, Jab We Met 2007, Kismat Konnection 2008, Ugly Aur Pagli 2008, Welcome to Sajjanpur 2008, Fashion 2008, Delhi-6 (Filmfare Award 2010) 2009, Let's Dance 2009, New York 2009, Sikandar 2009, Love Aaj Kal 2009, Kaminey 2009, Tum Mile 2009, Well Done Abba 2010, Badmaash Company 2010, Rajneeti 2010, Once Upon A Time In Mumbai (Zee Cine Award 2011, Global Indian Films And Television Award 2011) 2010, Lafangey Parindey 2010, Aashayein 2010, Dil Toh Baccha Hai Ji 2011, Tanu Weds Manu 2011, Dum Maaro Dum 2011, Kucch Luv Jaisaa 2011, Zindagi Na Milegi Dobara 2011, Aarakshan 2011, Rockstar (Filmfare Award 2012) 2011; as actor: Dhoom:2 2006, Chak De India! 2007, Dil Kabaddi 2008, Detective Naani 2009, Prince 2010, Life Express 2010. *Current Management:* c/o Parikrama Inc., E-27 NEB Valley, PO Box I.G.N.O.U, Sainik Farms, New Delhi 110 068, India. *Website:* www.mohitchauhan.in.

CHAUHAN, Sunidhi; Indian singer; b. 14 Aug. 1983, New Delhi. *Career:* lead singer in Little Wonders Troupe (formed by composer Kalyanji); playback singer in numerous films; numerous collaborations including with Enrique Iglesias; fmr judge, Indian Idol 5. *Recordings include:* albums: Aira Gaira Nathu Khaira, Euphoria 2011. *Films include:* as actor: Ehsaas-A Feeling 2001; as playback singer: Shastra 1996, Mast 1999, Jaanwar 1999, Joru Ka Ghulam 2000, Bichhoo 2000, Ajnabee 2001, Humraaz 2002, Zindagi Khoobsoorat Hai 2002, Zindagi Khoobsoorat Hai 2002, Escape from Taliban 2003, Armaan 2003, Chameli (Star Screen Award for Best Playback Singer – Female 2004) 2004, Main Hoon Na 2004, Madhoshi 2004, Dhoom (Best Female Playback Singer, Int. Indian Film Acad. 2005, Zee Cine Award for Best Female Playback Singer 2005) 2004, Ho Jaata Hai Pyaar 2005, Kaal 2005, Bluffmaster! 2005, Omkara (Filmfare Award for Best Playback Singer 2006, Star Screen Award for Best Playback Singer - Female 2007, Best Female Playback Singer, Int. Indian Film Acad. 2007) 2005, Chup Chup Ke 2006, Dor 2006, Namastey London 2007, Thoda Pyaar Thoda Magic 2008, Tees Maar Khan (Apsara Award for Best Female Playback Singer 2011, Global Indian Film Award for Best Female Playback Singer 2011, Filmfare Award for Best Playback Singer 2011) 2010, Teen Patti 2010, Once Upon a Time in Mumbai 2010, Rascals 2011, Murder 2 2011, Dum Maaro Dum 2011, Kucch Luv Jaisaa 2011, Rascals 2011, The Dirty Picture 2011. *Honours:* Chevrolet Global Indian Music Award, R.D. Burman Award for Most Promising Newcomer, Filmfare Awards 2001.

CHAUHAN, Vijay; Indian musician (dholki); s. of Sulochana Shamrao Chauhan. *Career:* toured with Gurdass Mann; participant, Zakir Hussain and The Masters of Percussion 2002–; regular performer for film score composers. *Recordings include:* albums: Zakir Hussain and the Rhythm Experience 1992. *Address:* c/o Moment Records, 237 Crescent Road, San Anselmo, CA 94960, USA (office). *E-mail:* moment237@aol.com (office). *Website:* www.momentrecords.com; nh7.in.

CHAULK, (Lloyd) Wayne, BCom; Canadian composer, arranger, musician and producer; b. 10 June 1950, Corner Brook, Newfoundland; m. Denise Chaulk 1975; one d. *Career:* CBC television features 1993; over 20 radio interviews 1992–93; music featured on international airlines, world-wide; music played on over 4,000 US premises and on over 400 radio stations; over 200 original compositions and 18 CDs produced; mem. Soc. of Composers, Authors and Music Publrs). *Recordings include:* albums: Dreamer's Themes 1991, New Directions and Christmas Keyboards 1992, No Regrets 1993, The Christmas to Remember 1996, Nature's Splendour 1996, Journey Home 1997. *Honours:* Billboard Certificate of Achievement: Your Love Is My Song 1992, Best Light Rock (Pop) Artist On Record, Aria 1994, 1995; albums rated among best instrumentals, Adult Contemporary Music Research Group, USA 1993–94. *Website:* waynechaulk.ca.

CHAURASIA, Pandit Hariprasad; Indian singer and musician (flute, bansuri); b. 1 July 1938, Allahabad; m. Anuradha Chaurasia. *Education:* trained with Pandit Rajaram and Pandit Bholanath. *Career:* fmr mem. AIR, Cuttack, Orissa; numerous collaborations, including Jan Garbarek, John McLaughlin, Padma Talwalkar, Amjad Ali Khan, Pandit Jasraj, Shahid Parvez, Rajan Sajan Mishra, Mallikarjun Mansur, Shruti Sadolikar, Pandit Bhimsen Joshi; currently Artistic Leader, Northern Indian Classical Music programme, Rotterdam Music Conservatory. *Recordings include:* albums: Call of the Valley (with Shivkumar Sharma and Brij Bhushan Kabra) 1967, Krishnadhwani 60 1978, Making Music (with Zakir Hussain) 1986, Morning to Midnight Ragas 1987, Call of the Valley 1988, Now 1989, Immortal Series 1990, Megh Malhar 1991, Night Ragas 1992, Daylight Ragas 1993, Thumri: The Music of Love 1994, In a Mellow Mood 1994, Possession 1994, Music Of The Rivers (vols 1 and 2) 1994, Flying Beyond: Improvisations On Bamboo Flute 1995, Written on the Wind 1995, Maestro's Choice 1995, Great Jugalbandis 1995, Ragas Lalit/Sindhi Bhairavi 1996, Elements: Wind 1996, Immortal Essence 1997, Bustan Abraham: Fanar (with Zakir Hussain) 1997, Ragas Durgawati/Mishra Shiv 1998, Living Legend of Bansuri Live (vol. 1) 1999, Rasdhara (with Pandit Shivkumar Sharma) 1999, Murali Prasadam 1999, Daylight Ragas 1999, Meditative Romance 1999, Raga Jait 1999, Raga Bageshri 1999, Hare Krishna (In Praise Of Janmashtami) 1999, Remember Shakti (with John McLaughlin) 1999, The Valley Recalls (vol. 1, with Pandit Shivkumar Sharma) 2000, Krishna's Flute 2001, Krishna's Charm 2001, Adi Anant 2001, Music Without Boundaries (with Larry Coryell) 2002, Healing Music For Ayurveda 2003, Being Still (with Kenneth Lauber) 2003, Flute, Rag Bhimpalasi 2003, Flute, Raga Darbari Kanada, Dh 2003, Sounds of Silence 2003, Salvation 2003, Flute, Rag Kaunsi Kanhra 2003, Flute, Rag Lalit 2003, Flute, Rag Ahir Bhairav 2003, Power and Grace (vols 1 and 2) 2004, Flute Deity 2004, Shikhar 2004, Hariprasad Chaurasia & His Divine 2005, Guru Shishya 2006, Music for Yog 2007, Sangeet Sartaj-Hariprasad Chaurasia 2009. *Honours:* Officier, Orde van Oranje-Nassau (Netherlands), Ordres des Arts et Lettres 2009; Dr hc (North Orissa Univ.) 2008, (Indian Inst. of Tech., Kharagpur) 2011, (Utkal Univ.) 2011; Sangeet Natak Acad. Nat. Award 1984, Padma Bhushan 1992, Konarak Samman 1992, Yash Bharati Sanman 1994, Padma Vibhushan 2000, Hafiz Ali Khan Award 2000, Dinanath Mangeshkar Award 2000, Akshaya Sanman 2009, Nat. Eminence Award Visakha Music and Dance Acad. Vizag 2009, Sangeet Natak Acad. Fellowship Award 2012. *Address:* Vrindaban Gurukul Juhu Versova Link Road Andheri (W), Mumbai 400 053, India (home). *Telephone:* (22) 26212121 (home). *E-mail:* info@hariprasadchaurasia.com. *Website:* www.hariprasadchaurasia.com.

CHAUTEMPS, Jean-Louis; French musician (saxophone) and composer; b. 6 Aug. 1931, Paris; m. (divorced); one s. one d. *Career:* mem. Claude Bolling Orchestra 1952; also played with Sidney Bechet, Django Reinhardt, Zoot Sims, Lester Young, Bobby Jaspar, Albert Ayler, Roy Eldridge, Don Byas;

European tour with Chet Baker; three years as saxophone player, musical arranger, Kurt Edelhagen Orchestra, Cologne, Germany; played Paris jazz clubs early 1960s; played with Kenny Clarke, Martial Solal, Slide Hampton, Eddy Louiss, René Urtreger, Johnny Griffin, Dexter Gordon, Daniel Humair; composer for films; teacher, improvisation; worked with the Ensemble InterContemporain, extensive tours of USA with Musique Vivante early 1970s; leader of jazz workshop, Univ. of Paris (Sorbonne) 1975; Founder, Rhizome 1976; concerts, tours including with Dizzy Gillespie; world premiere, Périples for solo saxophone, by Paul Méfano; soloist, leader, Albert Mangelsdorff band two years; mem., Martial Solal Big Band; works for classical and avant garde orchestras; works with computers and synthesizers; played at Guggenheim Museum, New York with Quatuor de Saxophones 1987; three jazz concerts, Opéra-Bastille 1992; also with Ensemble Contrechamps 1994; Musical Dir, The Threepenny Opera, Théâtre Nat. de Chaillot 1995; fmr Vice-Pres., Assafra. *Film appearances (as musician):* Nous irons tous au paradis 1977, La Scarlatine 1983, The Frog Prince 1984. *Compositions for film include:* Les Coeurs Verts, L'Ombre de la Pomme, also music for theatre and television. *Recordings include:* album: Chautemps 1988. *Honours:* Chevalier, Ordre des Arts et des Lettres, Ordre Nat. du Mérite; Prix du Jazz SACEM. *Current Management:* 95 rue de Vaugirard, 75006 Paris, France. *Telephone:* 1-45-48-99-71. *E-mail:* jlchautemps@free.fr.

CHÁVEZ GARZA, (José) Christian; Mexican singer and actor; b. 7 Aug. 1983, Reynosa, Tamaulipas. *Career:* actor; mem. RDB 2004–. *Television include:* Clase 406 2002, Rebelde (series) 2004, RBD: La Familia (series) 2007. *Recordings include:* albums: Rebelde 2004, Nuestro Amor 2005, Celestial (Billboard Latin Music Award for Latin Pop Album of the Year by a Duo or Group 2007) 2006, Rebels (in English) 2006, Empezar Desde Cero 2007, Transparent Soul 2010, Esencial 2012. *Honours:* Billboard Latin Music Award for Top Latin Albums Artist of the Year, for Latin Tour of the Year 2007, some 24 Premios Juventud, Billboard Latin Music 'Tu Mundo' Award 2008. *Address:* c/o EMI Latin, 404 Washington Avenue, Suite 700, Miami Beach, FL 33139, USA. *Website:* www.emimusiclatam.com.

CHAYANNE; Puerto Rican singer, actor and dancer; b. (Elmer Figueroa Alce), 28 June 1968. *Career:* first group Los Chicos; moved to Mexico to start a solo career, aged 17; solo artist 1986–; named UN Special Amb. for Immigration 1992. *Film and television appearances:* Dance With Me 1998, Linda Sara 1994, Los Chicos en Conexion Caribe, Las Divorciadas (miniseries), Provócame (telenovela) 2001. *Recordings include:* albums: Es Mi Nombre 1984, Sangre Latina 1986, Chayanne 1989, Tiempo De Vals 1990, Provócame 1992, Influencas 1994, Volver A Nacer 1996, Atado A To Amor 1998, Simplemente 2000, Grandes Éxitos 2002, Sincero 2003, Desde Siempre 2005, Cautivo 2005, Mi Tiempo 2007, No Hay Imposibles 2010, A Solas Con Chayanne 2012. *Honours:* MTV Award, Best International Video, Este Ritmo Se Baila Asi 1989. *Current Management:* c/o Richard De La Font Agency, 4845 South Sheridan Road, Tulsa, OK 74145, USA. *Telephone:* (918) 665-6200. *Website:* delafont.com; www.chayanne.net.

CHEB FAUDEL (see Faudel)

CHEB KHALED (see Khaled)

CHEB MAMI (see Mami)

CHECKER, Chubby; American singer; b. (Ernest Evans), 3 Oct. 1941, South Carolina. *Career:* numerous television appearances; featured in films: Twist Around The Clock 1961; Don't Knock The Twist 1962; numerous worldwide tours; featured artist, Dick Clark's Caravan of Stars 1961. *Recordings include:* albums: Twist With Chubby Checker 1960, It's Pony Time 1961, All The Hits (For Your Dancin' Party) 1961, For Twisters Only 1962, Your Twist Party 1962, Bobby Rydell/Chubby Checker 1962, For Teen Twisters Only 1962, Twistin' Round The World 1962, Don't Knock The Twist (film soundtrack) 1962, Limbo Party 1963, Chubby Checker's Biggest Hits 1963, Let's Limbo Some More 1963, Beach Party 1963, Chubby Checker In Person 1963, Chubby Checker's Greatest Hits 1973, The Change Has Come 1982, Still Twistin' 1986, In Deutschland 1988, Mister Twist 1988. *Honours:* Grammy Award for Best Rock and Roll Recording (for Let's Twist Again) 1961. *Current Management:* Mary Parisi, Twisted Entertainment, 320 Fayette Street, 2nd Floor, Conshohocken, PA 19428, USA. *E-mail:* twisted2@erols.com; mparisi@thelasttwist.com. *Website:* www.chubbychecker.com.

CHEN; South Korean singer; b. (Kim Jong-dae), 21 Sept. 1992, Silheung, Gyeonggi-do. *Career:* mem. K-pop boy band Exo 2011–; mem. sub-group Exo-M 2012–; debut single 2012; numerous TV and live appearances. *Television:* EXO's Showtime 2013–. *Recordings:* albums: Mama 2012, XOXO (Mnet Asian Music Award for Album of the Year 2013) 2013. *Honours:* numerous awards including: for Exo: Mnet Asian Music Award for Best New Asian Artist/Group 2012, MTV Europe Music Award for Best Japan/Korea Act 2013, MelOn Music Award for Song of the Year (for Growl) 2013; for Exo-M: Top Chinese Music Award for Most Popular Group 2013. *Address:* c/o SM Entertainment, 521 Apgujeong 2-dong, Gangnam-gu, Seoul, South Korea (office). *Telephone:* (2) 6240-9800 (office). *Website:* www.smtown.com (office); exo.smtown.com (home).

CHEN, Tania, MMus; British musician (piano). *Education:* Royal Coll. of Music, studied with Stephen Coombs, Artur Pizarro, John Tilbury, Goldsmiths Coll., Univ. of London. *Career:* performances in England, Europe and Japan; composed music for piano, electronic sounds and voice. *Recordings include:* Cornelius Cardew with Apartment House, Earle Brown Graphic Compositions with Dal Niente 2002, Cornelius Cardew Piano Sonatas 1, 2, 3, Michael Parsons Piano Music, Alan Hovhaness, Terry Riley, Lou Harrison—Piano Music. *Honours:* Shelley Scholarship in Performing Arts, Masterclasses with Mstislav Rostropovich. *E-mail:* thebeatexperience@yahoo.com; tania@minuet.freeserve.co.uk. *Website:* www.taniapiano.com.

CHENEOUR, (Ian) Paul; British musician (flute); b. 19 April 1952, Southsea, Hampshire. *Education:* Guildhall School of Music and Drama with Prof. Rainer Schielein. *Career:* mem. Dutch Jazz Quintet, France; leader, own 7 piece group The Cornish Connection; leader, jazz fusion quartet, Cheneour 1983–; leader, The Aeona Flute Quartet 1991–; leader, Impromptu 1993; Owner, Red Gold Music 1994–; Flute teacher, Kent Music 2006–; freelance musician for films, radios and documentaries; numerous tours in UK, Europe, Middle East, North America, Canada, Greece, Turkey 1997; masterclasses in Improvisation and Composition, and flute playing; New Duo, Paul Cheneour and Dilly Meah, flutes and tabla, 1997; mem. Musicians' Union, PRS, MCPS, PPL. *Recordings include:* albums: Inner Landscapes, Deep Reflections, Looking Glass, Winds of Change, Winds of Space, Dance in the Fire, Between Silence, Simply Breathe, Blue Perfection, Yoga, Spirit of the Nile, Across the Border, Contained, Out of Town, Feng Shui, Healing Flutes by the Ocean, Astral Planes, The Time Has Come 1952, Sweet Kafka, This Being Human, 49 Times, 7 Changes, Inner Silence, The Devil is an Idiot, Sound Sketches, Sound Sculptures, Space and Time, Zen Bicycle. *Telephone:* (1304) 826526 (office). *E-mail:* paul@redgoldmusic.com (office). *Website:* www.redgoldmusic.com.

CHENEVIER, Guigou, BA; French musician (percussion) and composer; b. 21 Nov. 1955, La Tronche; two s. *Career:* concerts worldwide, tours with Etron Fou Leloublan 1973–86; drummer, composer, with Les Batteries, Octavo, Encore Plus Grande, Volapék, 1986–95, Les Figures, collaboration with Maguy Marin 1996; f. collective Dupon et ses Fantômes (with Étron Fou Leloublan, Camizole, Grand Gouia, Nouvel Asile Culturel) 1976. *Recordings include:* Demesure Révolutionnaire, Les Batteries; Reedition, Etron Fou Leloublan 1991; Des Pieds et des Mains, Octavo 1992; Le Diapason du Père Ubu 1993; Le Feu du Tigre, Volapék 1995; Slang 1997; Les Rumeurs de la Ville 1998, Body Parts (with Nick Didkovsky) 2000, Le Batteur Est Le Meilleur Ami Du Musicien 2003. *Address:* 3A Maison IV de Chiffre, 26 rue des Teinturiers, 84000 Avignon, France. *E-mail:* cuneiway@aol.com. *Website:* www.cuneiformrecords.com.

CHENG, Sau Man (Sammi) (Twinnie); Hong Kong singer; b. 19 Aug. 1972. *Education:* Tang Shui Kin Victoria Technical School. *Career:* honoured at seventh Hong Kong Amateur Singing Contest 1998; solo artist 1995–. *Film appearances include:* Needing You 2000, Fighting for Love 2001, Magic Kitchen 2004, Everlasting Regret 2005, Lady Cop & Papa Crook 2008, Romancing in Thin Air 2012. *Recordings include:* albums: Sammi 1990, Holiday 1991, Never Too Late 1992, Happy Maze, Big Revenge 1993, Ten Commandments, Time Place People, Sammi 1994, After, It's About Time, Can't Let You Go 1995, Never Want To Let You Go, Worth It, Passion, Sammi X Live 1996, Waiting For You, Our Theme Song, Life's Language, Sammi Star Show 97, Feel So Good 1998, Listen To Sammi, I Deserved, Really Love You, Arigatou, Loving Deeply, Love Stories, I Concert 1999, To Love, Ladies First, Mei Fei Seik Mo, Love Is. . ., Taipei Concert 2000, 2001, Complete, Shocking Pink 2001, Love Mi World Tour 2009–11. *Honours:* Asian CCTV-MTV Music Award for Best Female Artist 2000, Singapore Golden Hits Award for Most Popular Female Artist 2001. *E-mail:* sammi@warnermusic.com.tw.

CHER; American singer and actress; b. (Cherilyn Lapierre Sarkisian), 20 May 1946, El Centro, Calif.; d. of John Sarkisian and Georgina Holt; m. 1st Sonny Bono 1964 (divorced 1975, died 1998); one d.; m. 2nd Gregg Allman 1975 (divorced); one s. *Career:* formed singing duo Sonny & Cher with Sonny Bono 1964–74, with TV series; solo artist 1964–, with own TV variety series and night club act. *Theatre:* Come Back to the Five and Dime, Jimmy Dean, Jimmy Dean. *Television:* Sonny & Cher Comedy Hour (CBS) 1971–74, Cher (CBS) 1975–76, Sonny & Cher Show (CBS) 1976–77. *Films:* Chastity 1969, Come Back To The Five and Dime, Jimmy Dean Jimmy Dean 1982, Silkwood 1983, Mask (Cannes Film Festival Best Actress Award) 1985, The Witches of Eastwick 1987, Suspect 1987, Moonstruck (Acad. Award for Best Actress 1988) 1987, Mermaids 1989, Club Rhino 1990, Faithful 1996, If These Walls Could Talk 1996, Nine 1996, Tea with Mussolini 1999, Stuck on You 2003. *Recordings include:* albums: as Sonny & Cher: Baby Don't Go 1965, Look At Us 1965, The Wondrous World Of Sonny & Cher 1966, Good Times 1967, In Case You're In Love 1967, Sonny & Cher Live 1971, All I Ever Need Is You 1972, Live In Las Vegas 1974, Mama Was A Rock 'N' Roll Singer 1974; solo: All I Really Want To Do 1965, Cher 1966, The Sonny Side Of Cher 1966, With Love 1967, Backstage 1968, 3614 Jackson Highway 1969, Cher 1971, Gypsies Tramps and Thieves 1971, Foxy Lady 1972, Half Breed 1973, Bittersweet White Light 1974, Dark Lady 1974, Stars 1975, I'd Rather Believe In You 1976, Cherished 1977, Two The Hard Way 1977, This Is Cher 1978, Take Me Home 1979, Prisoner 1982, I Paralyze 1984, Cher 1987, Heart Of Stone 1989, Outrageous 1989, Love Hurts 1991, It's A Man's World 1995, Believe 1998, Black Rose 1999, Not.Com.mercial 2000, Holdin' Out For Love 2001, Believe 2001, Living Proof 2001, Live: The Farewell Tour 2003. Closer to the Truth 2013; singles: as Sonny & Cher: I Got You Babe 1975, Baby Don't Go 1965, Just You 1965, But You're Mine 1965, What Now My Love 1966, Little Man 1966, The Beat Goes On 1967, All I Ever Need Is You 1971, A Cowboy's Work Is Never Done 1972; solo: All I Really Want To Do 1965, Bang Bang 1966, Gypsies Tramps And Thieves 1971, The Way Of Love 1972, Half Breed 1973,

Dark Lady 1974, Take Me Home 1979, Dead Ringer For Love (duet with Meatloaf) 1982, I Found Someone 1987, We All Sleep Alone 1988, After All (duet with Peter Cetera, for film Chances Are) 1989, If I Could Turn Back Time 1989, Jesse James 1989, Heart of Stone 1990, The Shoop Shoop Song (for film Mermaids) 1990, Love And Understanding 1991, Save Up All Your Tears 1991, Oh No Not My Baby 1992, Love Can Build A Bridge (with Neneh Cherry and Chrissie Hynde) 1995, Walking In Memphis 1995, One By One 1996, Paradise Is Here 1996, Believe (Grammy Award for Best Dance Recording 2000) 1998, Strong Enough 1999, All Or Nothing 1999, Dov'e l'Amore 1999, The Music's No Good Without You 2001, Alive Again 2002, A Different Kind Of Love 2002, When The Money's Gone 2003. *Honours:* VH1 First Music Award for achievements within the music industry 2005, Lifetime Achievement Award, Glamour Women of the Year Awards 2010. *Current Management:* ICM, 10250 Constellation Boulevard, Beverly Hills, CA 90067, USA. *Website:* www.cher.com.

CHERNEY, Ed; American producer and music engineer. *Career:* apprentice engineer, Chicago 1976; 5.1 surround sound mixer; Co-Music Dir DH1 Studios 2002; Founder-mem. Music Producers Guild of America (now Producers' and Engineers' Wing of The Recording Acad.); worked with Jann Arden, B-52's, Buddy Guy, Jackson Browne, Eric Clapton, Sonia Dada, Bob Dylan, Goo Goo Dolls, Hootie & the Blowfish, Iggy Pop, Billy Joel, Bette Midler, Keb Mo, Roy Orbison, Bonnie Raitt, Leon Russell, Bob Seger, Steely Dan, The Rolling Stones. *Honours:* three Grammy Awards, Primetime Emmy Award for Outstanding Sound Mixing for a Limited Series or a Movie (for Bessie) 2015. *Address:* Studio Ed, @ The Village, 1616 Butler Avenue, Los Angeles, CA 90025, USA. *Telephone:* (310) 478-8227 (office). *E-mail:* ed@edcherney.com (office). *Website:* edcherney.com.

CHERONE, Gary; American singer and songwriter; b. 24 July 1961, Malden, Mass. *Career:* fmr mem. Dream; singer funk/rock group, Extreme 1985–96; worldwide appearances and tours; lead singer Van Halen 1997–99; f. Tribe of Judah (band). *Recordings include:* albums: with Extreme: Extreme 1989, Extreme II – Pornograffiti 1991, III Sides To Every Story 1992, Waiting for the Punchline 1994, Running Gag 1998, Accidental Collision 1998, The Best of Extreme – An Accidental Collocation of Atoms? 2000, Exit Elvis 2002, Need I Say More 2005, Saudades de Rock 2008, Hurtsmile 2011; with Van Halen: 3 1998. *Honours:* Boston Music Awards for Act of the Year, for Outstanding Rock Single (for Hole-Hearted), for Outstanding Pop Single, for Outstanding Singer/Songwriter (for More Than Words) 1992. *Website:* www.cherone.com.

CHERRY, Eagle Eye; American/Swedish musician, singer and songwriter; b. 7 May 1969, Skåne. *Education:* New York School of the Performing Arts. *Career:* played drums in band for his father, Don Cherry; worked as model and acted in several US TV shows; wrote and performed debut album including duet with half-sister, Titiyo and remixed by Cameron McVey. *Recordings include:* albums: Desireless 1998, Living In The Present Future 2000, Present | Future 2001, Sub Rosa 2003, Live and Kicking 2007, Can't Get Enough 2012. *Address:* c/o The Umbrella Group, 425 West 23rd Street, Suite 1BB, New York, NY 10001, USA. *Telephone:* (212) 785-1133. *E-mail:* info@umbrella -group.com. *Website:* www.umbrella-group.com; www.eagle-eye-cherry.com.

CHERRY, Neneh; Swedish singer and songwriter; b. (Neneh Mariana Karlsson), 10 March 1964, Stockholm; step-d. of the late Don Cherry; m. 1st Bruce Smith; m. 2nd Cameron McVey; three d. *Career:* mem. punk band The Cherries, New Age Steppers, The Thing 2011–; singer, Rip Rig and Panic 1981, later Float-Up CP; backing vocalist for the Slits and The The; solo artist 1989–2006; f. new band CirKus 2006; collaborated with Tricky and Youssou N'Dour, Kleerup 2008, RocketNumberNine 2013; co-host Neneh and Andi Dish It Up, BBC. *Recordings include:* albums: with Rip Rig and Panic: God 1981, I Am Cold 1982, Attitude 1983; solo: Raw Like Sushi 1989, Homebrew 1992, Man 1997, Blank Project 2014; singles: solo: Buffalo Stance 1988, Manchild 1989, Kisses On The Wind 1989, I've Got You Under My Skin 1990, Money Love 1992, 7 Seconds (with Youssou N'Dour) 1994, Trouble Man 1995, Love Can Build A Bridge (with Chrissie Hynde and Cher) 1995, Woman 1996, Buddy X (with Dreem Team) 1999; with CirKus: Laylow 2006, Medicine 2009; with The Thing: The Cherry Thing 2012. *Current Management:* c/o The Umbrella Group, 425 West 23rd Street, Suite 1BB, New York, NY 10011, USA. *Telephone:* (212) 785-1133. *E-mail:* info@umbrella-group.com. *E-mail:* info@cirkustent.com. *Website:* www.cirkustent.com.

CHESCOE, Laurie; musician (drums); b. 18 April 1933, London, England; m. Sylviane Yanou Chescoe 1960, one s. one d. *Career:* Teddy Layton Band 1957, Monty Sunshine 1960, Dick Charlesworth 1964, Bruce Turner 1965, Bob Wallis 1966, Alan Elsdon 1976 (14 years), Midnite Follies Orchestra 1978, Alex Welsh Band 1979; formed own band, Laurie Chescoe's Good Time Jazz 1990, leader, Reunion Band 1990–; performed at all major festivals, television and radio; mem. Musicians' Union. *Recordings include:* albums: two with Midnite Follies, three with Keith Nicholls, 78s with Eric Allendale New Orleans Knights, Teddy Layton Band, albums with own band, six albums with Benny Walters, Ralph Sutton. *Address:* 10 Southfield Gardens, Twickenham TW1 4SZ, England.

CHESNEY, Kenneth (Kenny) Arnold; American country singer and songwriter; b. 26 March 1968, Knoxville, Tenn.; s. of David Chesney and Karen Chandler; m. Renée Zellweger 2005 (annulled 2005). *Education:* Gibbs High School, East Tennessee State Univ. *Career:* fmr resident performer, The Turf, Nashville. *Tours:* Greatest Hits Tour (with Lee Ann Womack) 2001, No Shoes, No Shirt, No Problems Tour (with Montgomery Gentry, Jamie O'Neal

and Phil Vassar) 2002, Margaritas N' Senorita's Tour (with Deana Carter, Sara Evans and Keith Urban) 2003, Guitars, Tiki Bars and a Whole Lotta Love Tour (with Rascal Flatts, Dierks Bentley and Keith Urban) 2004, Somewhere in the Sun Tour (with Gretchen Wilson, Uncle Kracker, and Pat Green) 2005, The Road & The Radio Tour (with Dierks Bentley, Big & Rich, Carrie Underwood and Gretchen Wilson) 2006, Flip-Flop Summer Tour (with Brooks & Dunn, Sugarland, Sara Evans and Pat Green) 2007, The Poets & Pirates Tour (with Keith Urban, LeAnn Rimes, Gary Allan, Luke Bryan and Sammy Hagar) 2008, Sun City Carnival Tour (with Miranda Lambert, Sugarland, Lady Antebellum and Montgomery Gentry) 2009, 2010 With a Two Tour 2010, Goin' Coastal Tour (with Zac Brown Band, Uncle Kracker and Billy Currington) 2011, Brothers of the Sun Tour (with Tim McGraw, Grace Potter and the Nocturnals and Jake Owen) 2012. *Television:* Live by Request: Kenny Chesney 2004. *Recordings include:* albums: In My Wildest Dreams 1993, All I Need to Know 1995, Me and You 1996, I Will Stand 1997, Everywhere We Go 1999, No Shirt, No Shoes, No Problem 2002, All I Want for Christmas is a Real Good Tan 2003, When the Sun Goes Down 2004, Be As You Are (Songs from an Old Blue Chair) 2005, The Road and the Radio 2005, Just Who I Am: Poets & Pirates 2007, Lucky Old Son 2008, Hemingway's Whiskey 2010, Welcome to the Fishbowl 2012, Life on a Rock 2013, The Big Revival 2014; compilations: Greatest Hits 2000, Live: Live Those Songs Again 2006, Super Hits 2008, Greatest Hits II 2009. *Honours:* CMA Award for Entertainer of the Year 2004, 2006, 2007, 2008, American Music Award for Favorite Performer 2005, ACM Award for Best Entertainer 2005, 2006, 2007, Billboard Award for Country Songs Artist of the Year 2006, 50th Anniversary Milestone Award, Acad. of Country Music 2015. *Address:* c/o Columbia Nashville, Sony BMG Entertainment, 550 Madison Avenue, New York, NY 10022, USA. *Website:* www.sonymusicnashville.com; www.kennychesney .com.

CHESNUTT, Mark Nelson; American country singer and musician (guitar, drums); b. 6 Sept. 1963, Beaumont, Tex.; s. of Bob Chesnutt. *Career:* played with father's band around Beaumont region before pursuing solo career aged 15; residency with the house band at Cutter's Bar; recorded for several ind. labels in mid—1980s, signing with MCA Records 1990; numerous live appearances and tours with own New South Band. *Recordings include:* albums: Too Cold at Home 1990, Longnecks and Short Stories 1992, Almost Goodbye 1993, What a Way to Live 1994, Wings 1995, Greatest Hits 1996, Thank God for Believers 1997, I Don't Want to Miss a Thing 1999, Lost in the Feeling 2000, Mark Chesnutt 2002, Savin' the Honky Tonk 2004, Heard it in a Love Song 2005, Rollin' With the Flow 2008, Outlaw 2010. *Honours:* CMA Horizon Award 1993, CMA Vocal Event of the Year 1993. *Current Management:* c/o Richard De La Font Agency Inc., 4845 S Sheridan Road, Suite 505, Tulsa, OK 74145-5719, USA. *Website:* delafont.com. *E-mail:* mike@ markchesnutt.com. *Website:* www.markchesnutt.com.

CHESTER, Ilan; Venezuelan singer, composer and musician (keyboards); b. (Ilan Czenstochouski Schaechter), 30 July 1952, Tel-Aviv, Israel; m. Mercedes Mayorca. *Career:* performed in local bands as a child; fmr mem. various rock and pop bands; solo artist 1983–. *Recordings:* albums: Por Principio 1979, Canciones de Todos las Días 1983, Amistad 1984, Ilan Chester 1985, Al Pie de la Letra 1987, Opus # 10 1990, Un Mundo Mejor 1992, Terciopelo 1994, Cancionero Del Amor Venezolano 1998, Bhakti 1998, Ofrenda Para Un Niño 1999, Sinfonico 2000, Cancionero Del Amor Venezolano II 2000, Corazón Navideño 2001, Ilan Canta Onda Nueva 2002, Cancionero Del Amor Puertorriqueño 2003, Así 2004, Cancionero Del Amor Venezolano III 2007, Tesoros de la Música Venezolana (Latin Grammy Award for Best Folk Album 2010) 2009. *Telephone:* (212) 335-0546 (office). *E-mail:* mercimayorca@mac .com (office). *Website:* www.ilanchester.com.

CHESTER, Johnny; Australian broadcaster, singer/songwriter, band-leader, playwright and television producer; *General Manager, Johnny Chester Music (Australia) HomeSpun Records;* b. (John Howard Chester), 26 Dec. 1941, North Fitzroy; s. of the late John Chester and Norma Chester; m. Larraine 1964; three d. *Education:* Preston Tech. Coll. *Career:* Teen Scene (ABC TV) 1964–65, Country Road ABC TV 1977–78; DJ, Radio 3U2, Melbourne 1966–69; Presenter, Radio Australia 1989–91; recording artist 1961–; toured Australia and New Zealand with The Beatles 1964, Australia with Roy Orbison 1961, The Everly Brothers 1961, Kenny Rogers 1984, Johnny Cash 1986, Tammy Wynette 1992, Freddy Fender 1995, Charley Pride 2001; led various groups including Johnny Chester and The Chessmen, Johnny Chester and Jigsaw, Johnny Chester and Hotspur; Gen. Man. Johnny Chester Music (Australia) HomeSpun Records; mem. APRA, AMCOS. *Compositions include:* The Hokey Pokey 1961, Shy Away 1962, Summertime Blues 1962, Wild and Warm 1963, Come On Everybody 1963, The Best of Ches! 1964, Johnny Chester's Greatest Hits 1965, When will I be Loved 1965, Heaven Help the Man 1968, Green Green 1969, If Only I Could Leave You 1970, Glory Glory 1971, Shame and Scandal in the Family 1971, Midnight Bus 1972, World Greatest Mum 1973, Let's Build a Love Together 1973, My Kind of Woman 1974, My Special Angel 1974, Highway 31, Lord I'd Forgotten, Sally on Sunday 1975, My China Doll 1976, Country Salute 1978, I Love You So Rebecca 1979, All on Your Own 1980, Love in the Meantime 1981, You Bring Out the Devil in Me 1982, Country Girl 1983, Side by Side 1985, My Sweet Janie 1986, So Far So Good 1987, Among My Souvenirs 1988, Waiting for the Lightning 1992, Songmaker 1995, Listen 1997, Get a Little Dirt on Your Hands 2005, Memories that linger 2009. *Plays:* Rebound – The Musical (writer), The Pub (writer). *Recordings include:* What You Hear is What You

Get (album) 2011, My heart 2013, Alone 2014. *Radio:* announcer: Melbourne Radio Station 3UZ 1966–75, Radio Australia (worldwide broadcast) 1989–91. *Publication:* Johnny Chester Songbook. *Honours:* Golden Guitar for Best Selling Track, Australia Country Awards 1975, Male Vocalist of the Yea, Australia Country Awards 1981, 1982, 1983, Australian Songmaker Award 1994. *Address:* c/o HomeSpun Records, PO Box 2150, Rosebud, VIC, 3939 Australia. *E-mail:* chess@johnnychester.com. *Website:* www.johnnychester .com.

CHEUNG, Jacky; Chinese singer, songwriter and actor; b. 10 July 1961, Hong Kong; m. May Lo Mei-mei; two d. *Career:* fmr reservation officer, Cathay Pacific Airline; considered one of 'Four Heavenly Kings' of Cantopop; apptd Amb. End Child Sexual Abuse Foundation 2009. *Recordings include:* more than 70 albums including Uncontrolled Passion 1991, True Love Expression 1992, Sparks of Love 1992, The Goodbye Kiss 1993, Me and You 1993, Born to be Wild 1994, Jacky Live Performance (Best Selling Cantonese Album Award, Hong Kong IFPI Awards) 2005, Life is Like a Dream, Private Corner 2010. *Films include:* as actor: The Eighth Happiness 1988, As Tears Go By (Hong Kong Film Award) 1988, Swordsman (Golden Horse Award) 1990, Days of Being Wild 1990, Ashes of Time 1994, Meltdown 1995, July Rhapsody 2002, Perhaps Love 2005, Bodyguards and Assassins 2009, Hot Summer Days 2010, Crossing Hennessy 2010; as singer: Perhaps Love (Hong Kong Film Award 2005). *Honours:* Asia-Pacific Most Popular Male Singer, Jade Solid Gold Best Ten Music Award 1994, 1997, 1998, Billboard Music Award as most popular singer in Asia 1994, Most Popular Male Artist, Jade Solid Gold Best Ten Music Award 1996, Monte Carlo World Music Award as the world's best-selling Chinese artist 1996, named one of 10 Outstanding Young Persons of the World by Junior Chamber International 1999, Radio Television Hong Kong (RTHK) Golden Needle Award 2000. *Current Management:* c/o Fun Entertainment Ltd, Room 3202, Tower A Southmark, 11 Yip Hing Street, Wong Chuk Hang, Hong Kong Special Administrative Region, People's Republic of China. *Telephone:* 28668282. *Fax:* 28662662. *E-mail:* fun@fun.corp.com.hk. *Website:* www.jackycheung.hk.

CHEVALLIER, D.; French musician (electric and acoustic guitar) and composer; b. 13 Jan. 1969, Ris Orangis. *Education:* Conservatoire National de Région de Paris. *Career:* concerts Rome, Berlin, New York, Rochester, Hartford, Richmond, Prague (EBU big band), Paris Jazz Festival, Nord Jazz Festival (Germany), Festival of Montpellier, Festival of Assier, Souillac, Ramatuelle and Montréal Jazz Festival 1996; mem. SACEM, SPEDIDAM. *Recordings include:* Migration, with Daniel Humoir, Yves Robert; Nilxa: State of Grace; Terre Nova: Danses.

CHIARELLI, Robert C.; American mixer and remix producer; *CEO, Final Mix Inc.*; b. 13 Jan. 1963. *Education:* Univ. of Miami, Fla. *Career:* producer and/or Mixer for numerous recordings including Will Smith, The Temptations, Madonna, Janet Jackson, K-Ci and JoJo, Christina Aguilera, Jennifer Paige, The Corrs, Boyz II Men; CEO Metro Beat Records 1993–96; formed 3.6 Records 1997; currently CEO Final Mix Inc.; fmr Dir The Great Leap Foundation; mem. American Fed. of Musicians, Nat. Acad. of Recording Arts and Sciences. *Recordings include:* albums: as producer: Lethal Injection 1993, 24 Hour, 365, 7 Day a Week Job 1997, The Remedy 1997, Against da Grain 1999, Willennium 1999, Music From and Inspired by Shaft 2000, Leap of Faith 2002, Twisted Angel 2002, From the Inside 2002, Metamorphosis 2003, Soulful 2003, Style 2003, Real Life 2004, You Made Me 2004, Are You Feelin' Me 2005, Best Fiction 2008, Bring Back the Love 2009, The Road... 2011, Hello Fear 2011, Hurtlovebox 2011, Go Get It 2012. *Publication:* The Electric Bass Bible: Volume 1 Dexterity Exercises 2009. *E-mail:* kwame@kkmc.co.uk; mmavrolas@yahoo.com. *E-mail:* rob@finalmix.com. *Website:* www.finalmix .com.

CHIASSON, Warren; Canadian jazz musician (vibraphone, piano) and composer; b. 17 April 1934, Cheticamp, Nova Scotia. *Education:* St Francis Xavier Univ., Antigonish, Nova Scotia; jazz with Lenny Tristano, George Russell. *Career:* mem. George Shearing Quintet 1959–61, 1972–74; played clubs, concerts, tours with Chet Baker, Tal Farlow, Roberta Flack 1975–82; Broadway show, Hair (composed the percussion) 1968–72; mem. American Soc. of Composers, Authors and Publrs (ASCAP), Recording Musicians of America, Nat. Acad. of Recording Arts and Sciences (NARAS). *Compositions include:* Ultramarine, Bossa Nova Scotia, Bedouin, Hazel Eyes, Bravel; Festival. *Recordings include:* as leader: Good Vibes For Kurt Weill, Point Counterpoint, Quartessence; with George Shearing Quartet: Satin Brass, Satin Affair, San Francisco Scene, The Very Best 2005; with B. B. King: Blues and Jazz (Grammy Award 1984); others: Point Counterpoint 1988, Comin' Alive 1988, Soft Whyte 1994, Put Some Style in It 1998, Quartessence 2007. *Publication:* The Contemporary Vibraphonist. *Honours:* named as One of the Top Six Outstanding Jazz Vibraphonists over the last half-century, New York Times 19989. *E-mail:* warrenvibes@msn.com (office). *Website:* www .warrenchiasson.com.

CHIAVOLA, Kathy, BM, MM; American artist, singer and musician (guitar); b. 7 March 1952, Chicago, IL. *Education:* Oberlin Conservatory, Indiana Conservatory. *Career:* sang opera professionally; moved to Nashville, 1980; toured with The Doug Dillard Band, Vassar Clements, The Country Gazette; formed The Lucky Dogs; toured Eastern Europe with Douglas and Mark O'Connor, USIA tour: The Nashville Masters; UK debut tour, 1993; recorded with: Garth Brooks; Emmylou Harris; Vince Gill; Kathy Mattea; Ricky Skaggs; mem. IBMA; AFofM; AFTRA; NARAS. *Recordings include:* albums:

Labor of Love, 1990, The Harvest, 1995, From Where I Stand... A Personal Tribute 2001, Somehow 2007. *Honours:* Nammie Award for Backup Vocalist of the Year 1995. *Address:* PO Box 90629, Nashville, TN 37209, USA. *E-mail:* kcsing1@aol.com. *Website:* www.kathychiavola.com.

CHILD, Desmond; American songwriter, producer and musician (keyboards); b. (John Charles Barrett), 28 Oct. 1953, Miami, Fla. *Career:* formed Desmond Child and Rouge 1973; concentrated on songwriting in 1980s. *Compositions include:* hit songs include: You Give Love A Bad Name, Bon Jovi 1986, Livin' On A Prayer, Bon Jovi 1986, I Was Made For Loving You, Kiss 1979, Dude Looks Like a Lady and Angel, Aerosmith 1987, Livin' La Vida Loca, Ricky Martin 1999, Who Let The Dogs Out, Baha Men 2001, Because You Live, Jesse McCartney 2004, I Live for the Day, Lindsay Lohan 2005, Waking Up in Vegas, Katy Perry 2008, Brokenpromiseland, Fast Cars, Happy Now, Learn to Love, Bon Jovi 2009, Trainwrecks, Weezer 2010, Rock Angels, Porcelain Black 2012, Another Last Goodbye, Aerosmith 2012; other songs for: Cher, Michael Bolton, Alice Cooper, Jimmy Barnes, Boyzone, Hanson, Robbie Williams, Joss Stone, Kelly Clarkson, The Scorpions, Hilary Duff, Meatloaf, Ace Young, The Rasmus, Katy Perry, Sebastian Bach, Lindsay Lohan, Jonas Brothers, Carrie Underwood, Alejandra Guzman, Leanne Rimes, Sisqo, Amanda Marshall. *Recordings include:* albums: with Desmond Child and Rouge: Desmond Child and Rouge 1978, Runners In The Night 1979; solo: Discipline 1991, Songs without Words 1997. *Honours:* several Grammy Awards, inducted into Songwriters Hall of Fame 2008. *Current Management:* c/o Deston Entertainment, PO Box 210249, Nashville, TN 37221, USA. *Website:* www.desmondchild.com.

CHILDERS, Elsie T.; American studio owner and songwriter; b. 26 Sept. 1924, Henderson, KY; d. of Enoch Bradshaw Arbuckle and Lola Pearl Trust Arbuckle; two s. *Education:* Midway Coll. *Career:* Owner and Man. Trusty Tuneshop Recording Studio 1992–; pianist and soloist for Johnson Island Baptist Church 1950–; various radio and cable TV performances; Deputy Dir IBC, ABI; mem. CMA, CMOA, Rotary Club (fmr Sec.). *Compositions:* 380 songs published, more than 100 recorded, artists include Jennifer Nelson 1991, Barry Russell 1998, Jeremy Scott Busby 2000, 2003. *Publications:* Instant Knowhow 1971, Trusty International Newsletter 1978–98. *Honours:* Country Music Orgs of America Song of the Year, Record Label Promoter of the Year, Artist Promoter of the Year, CD of the Year, Record Label of the Year 2000. *Address:* Trusty Tuneshop Recording Studio, 8771 Rose Creek Road, Nebo, KY 42441, USA. *Telephone:* (270) 249-3194 (office). *E-mail:* etrusty@vci .net. *Website:* www.vci.net/~trusty.

CHILDISH, Billy; British singer, songwriter, musician (guitar), writer and poet and painter; b. (Stephen Hamper), 1 Dec. 1959, Chatham, Kent, England; m. Julie Childish; one c. *Career:* mem. various bands, including Pop Rivets, the Milkshakes, Thee Mighty Caesars, the Delmonas, Thee Headcoats, the Natural Born Lovers, The Buff Medways, The Musicians of the British Empire. *Recordings include:* albums: I Remember, I've Got Everything Indeed, Laughing Gravy, Plump Prizes and Little Gems, The 1982 Cassettes, Which Dead Donkey Daddy?, Talkin' Bout Milkshakes, Acropolis Now, In Tweed We Trust, Ypres 1917 Overture 1987, Play: Capt'n Calypso's Hoodoo Party 1988, Poems of Laughter and Violence 1988, Long Legged Baby 1989, I Am the Billy Childish 1991, The Original Chatham Jack 1992, At the Bridge 1993, Live in the Netherlands 1993, Hunger at the Moon 1994, Live 1994, Devil in the Flesh 1998, The Cheeky Cheese 1999, In Blood 1999, I Am the Object of Your Desire 2000, Steady the Buffs 2002, Here Come the Fleece 2002, Medways 2003, Medway Wheelers 2005, Heavens Journey (with The Chatham Singers) 2005, Punk Rock at the British Legion Hall 2007, Thatcher's Children 2008, Juju Claudius 2009, Archive From 1959 – The Billy Childish Story 2009, Poets of England 2010. *Publications:* Poems from the Barrier Block 1984, Monks Without God 1986, Companions in a Death Boat 1987, To the Quick 1988, Girl in the Tree 1988, Maverick Verse 1988, Admissions to Strangers 1989, Death of a Wood 1989, The Silence of Words (short stories) 1989, The Deathly Flight of Angels 1990, Like a God I Love All Things 1990, Child's Death Letter 1990, The Hart Rises 1991, Poems of Laughter and Violence: Selected Poetry 1981–86 1992, Poems to Break the Harts of Impossible Princesses 1994, Days With a Hart Like a Dog 1994, Big Hart and Balls 1995, Messerschmitt Pilot's Severed Hand 1996, My Fault (novel) 1996, Billy Childish and his Famous Headcoat 1997, Notebooks of a Naked Youth (novel) 1997, I'd Rather You Lied: Selected Poems 1980–1998 1999, Chatham Town Welcomes Desperate Men (poems) 2001, Chatham's Burning 2004, Knite of the Sad Face 2004, Sex Crimes of the Futcher 2005, My Fault 2005, The Idiocy of Idears 2007, Bombs, Buggery and Buddhism or Diaries of a Mock Human (Part one) 2010. *Address:* c/o Hangman Books, 11 Boundary Road, Chatham, Kent, ME4 6TS, England. *Website:* www .billychildish.com.

CHILDS, Robert Alexander; British musician (guitar, steel guitar), singer, songwriter and music journalist; b. 23 April 1961, London. *Career:* mem. of country band, Greta and The Stray Shots; concerts, festival and television appearances, radio broadcasts; mem. PRS. *Recordings include:* albums: Live 1987, Above and Beyond 1990, Livewire 1991, Playtime 1993; Inclusion of track: I Didn't Mean To Do It, on Declaration of Independence, The Best of British Country 1994. *Publications include:* contrib.: articles to Making Music, Country Music Gazette, International Country Music News. *Address:* 40 Fielding Way, Hutton, CM13 1JN, England.

CHILDS, William (Billy) Edward; American composer and musician (piano); b. 8 March 1957, Los Angeles; m. Holly Hamilton 1991; one s. *Education:* Univ. of Southern California. *Career:* played with Freddie Hubbard 1978–84, with J J Johnson 1977; also played with Allan Holdsworth, Dianne Reeves, Branford Marsalis, Bobby Hutcherson; played twice as leader, North Sea Jazz Festival, Monterey Jazz Festival; Guggenheim Fellow 2009. *Compositions:* Two performed by Los Angeles Philharmonic, One for Akron Symphony Orchestra, One (strings, bass, rhythm section), performed at Monterey Jazz Festival, part of commission series; One at Grenoble Jazz Festival. *Recordings include:* albums: Take For Example This 1988, Twilight Is Upon Us 1989, His April Touch 1991, Portrait of a Player 1993, I've Known Rivers 1995, The Child Within 1996, Skim Coat 1999, Bedtime Stories 2000, Lyric-Jazz/Chamber Music Vol. 1 2005, Autumn: In Moving Pictures 2010. *Honours:* Composition Department Award, Univ. of Southern California, Chamber Music America composer's grant 2003, three Grammy awards, two for best instrumental composition for Into the Light from Lyric and The Path Among The Trees from Autumn: In Moving Pictures 2011 and one for best arrangement accompanying a vocalist 2009. *Address:* Billy Childs, PO Box 94416, Pasadena, CA 91109, USA. *Website:* www.billychilds.com.

CHILTON, John; British musician (trumpet), arranger, bandleader and writer; b. 16 July 1932, London. *Career:* leader of own band during mid-1950s; mem. and arranger, Bruce Turner Jump Band 1958–63; played with Alex Welsh and Mike Daniels during early 1960s; co-leader, Feetwarmers during late 1960s; bandleader 1974–; musical dir for George Melly 1974–2003; tours, recordings, broadcasts as George Melly and John Chilton's Feetwarmers 1974–2003; writer and researcher into jazz history. *Recordings include:* Nuts 1972, Son of Nuts 1973, It's George 1974, Making Whoopee 1982, Best of Live 1995, Anything Goes 1996, Goodtime George, The Ultimate Melly 2006. *Publications include:* Who's Who of Jazz: Storyville to Swing Street, Louis – The Louis Armstrong Story, Who's Who of British Jazz, Billie's Blues (biog.); historical accounts of the Jenkins Orphanage bands, McKinney's Cotton Pickers, The Bob Crosby Bobcats; biographies of: Sidney Bechet, Coleman Hawkins, Louis Jordan, Henry 'Red' Allen, Roy Eldridge.

CHINAI, Alisha; Indian playback singer; b. (Sujata Chinai), 18 March 1965; m. Rajesh Jahveri. *Career:* playback singer in numerous films; collaborations with Anand-Milind, Divya Bharati, Juhi Chawla, Madhuri Dixit, Shankar Ehsaan Loy, Remo Fernandes, Kishore Kumar, Anu Malik, Mandakini, Nadeem-Shravan, Smita Patil, Pritam, Himesh Reshammiya, Rajesh Roshan, Sridevi. *Films include:* numerous credits as playback singer including: Dance Dance 1987, Mr India 1987, Jalwa 1987, Tridev 1989, Khiladi 1992, Vijaypath 1994, Zaalim 1994, Main Khiladi Tu Anari 1994, Khuddar 1994, Bambai Ka Babu 1994, Raja Hindustani 1996, Insaaf 1997, Keemat 1998, Mujhse Dosti Karoge 2002, Bollywood/Hollywood 2002, Ishq Vishk 2003, Murder 2004, Plan 2004, Fida 2004, Dobara 2004, Karam 2005, Bunty Aur Babli 2005, No Entry 2005, Chandramukhi 2005, Don 2006, Dhoom 2 2006, Kya Love Story Hai 2007, Jhoom Barabar Jhoom 2007, Namastey London 2007, Love Story 2050 2008, Kalyug 2009, Ajab Prem Ki Ghazab Kahani 2009, Kambakkht Ishq 2009, Prince 2010. *Television:* Indian Idol 3 (as judge) 2007, Star ya Rockstar (judge) 2011. *Recordings include:* albums: Jaadoo 1985, Madonna 1989, Kamasutra 1994, Made in India 1995, Om – The Inner Voice 1998, Om Antratma 1998, Thakshak 1999, Shut Up n Kiss Me 2007. *Honours:* Filmfare Award for Best Female Playback (for Kajra Re) 2005, International Billboard Award, Freddie Mercury Award for Artistic Excellence. *Website:* www.alishachinai.com.

CHISHOLM, Melanie (Mel) Jayne, (Melanie C); British singer; b. 12 Jan. 1976, Liverpool; d. of Joan Chisholm; one d. with Tom Starr. *Career:* mem. Touch, later renamed The Spice Girls 1993–2001, as 'Sporty Spice', reunion tour 2007–08; solo artist 1999–. *Plays include:* Blood Brothers, London 2009, Jesus Christ Superstar 2012–13. *Film appearances:* Spiceworld: The Movie 1997, Keith Lemon: The Film 2012. *Recordings include:* albums: with The Spice Girls: Spice 1996, Spiceworld 1997, Forever 2000, Greatest Hits 2007; solo: Northern Star 1999, Reason 2003, Let's Love 2004, Beautiful Intentions 2005, This Time 2007, The Sea 2011, Stages 2012; other: The Night (EP). *Honours:* two Ivor Novello songwriting awards 1997, Smash Hits Award for Best Band 1997, BRIT Award for Best Single (for Wannabe) 1997, BRIT Award for Best Video (for Say You'll Be There) 1997, for Best Performance of the last 30 years 2010, three American Music Awards 1998, Special BRIT Award for Int. Sales 1998, Best Int. Female Artist, German Radio Awards 2005, Best World Artist, Eska Music Awards 2006. *Current Management:* c/o Solo Music Agency, 53-55 Fulham High Street, London, SW6 3JJ, England. *Telephone:* (20) 7384-6644. *Website:* www.solo.uk.com; www.melaniec.net; www.northern-star.co.uk.

CHITHRA, K. S.; Indian playback singer; b. (Krishnan Nair Shantakumari Chithra), 27 July 1963, Thiruvananthapuram, Kerala; d. of the late Krishnan Nair; m. Vijayashankar; one d. (deceased). *Education:* Univ. of Kerala. *Career:* trained in Carnatic music with Dr. K. Omanakutty; playback singer for many Malayalam and Tamil musicians 1979–; has sung for numerous composers and music directors including A.R. Rahman, Rajesh Roshan, Anu Malik, Ilayaraja, G. Deverajan, M.S. Viswanathan, K.V. Mahadevan, Ouseppachan, Deva, Vidyasagar, Bharadhwaj, Chakravarthy. *Films include:* playback singer for numerous titles including: Nokkethadhoorathu Kannum Nattu 1984, Poove Poochudava 1985, Nakhakshathangal 1986, Vaishali 1988, Mazhavilkavadi 1989, Our Vadakkan Veeragatha 1989, Innale 1990, Seetharamaiah Gari Manavaralu 1991, Parinayam 1994, Devaraagam 1996,

Minsara Kanavu 1997, Virasat 1997, Theerthadanam 2001, Autograph 2004, Varsham 2004, Nottam 2006, Thirakkatha 2008, Pazhassi Raja 2009. *Television:* Idea Star Singer, Airtel Super Singer Junior. *Recordings include:* albums: with Voodoo Rapper: Ragga Ragga 1993, My Tribute 2006. *Honours:* Dr hc (Sathyabama Univ.); Kerala State Film Awards for Best Playback Singer 1985, 1986, 1987, 1988, 1989, 1990, 1991, 1992, 1993, 1994, 1995, 1999, 2001, 2002, 2005, Nat. Film Awards for Best Female Playback Singer 1986, 1987, 1989, 1996, 1997, 2004, Tamil Nadu State Film Awards for Best Female Playback Singer 1988, 1990, 1995, 2004, Nandi Awards (Andhra Pradesh State Film Awards) for Best Female Playback Singer 1990, 1991, 1992, 1993, 1996, 1998, 1999, 2004, 2009, Karnataka State Film Awards for Best Female Playback Singer 1997, 2001, 2005, Tamil Nadu Government Kalaimamani Award 1997, Star Screen Award for Best Female Playback 1998, Asianet Film Awards for Best Female Playback 1999, 2000, 2003, 2005, 2007, 2009, Mathrubhumi Film Awards for Best Female Playback 1999, 2000, 2001, 2002, 2003, 2008, 2011, Global Malayalee Council in London Lifetime Achievement Award 2003, Filmfare Awards South for Best Female Playback Singer 2004, 2006, 2008, 2009, Swaralaya Yesudas Award 2004, Bollywood Movie Award for Best Female Playback Singer 2004, Padma Shri Award 2005, Jai Hind Film Award for Best Female Playback Singer 2010, Radio Mirchi Listeners Choice Award 2010, Swaralaya-Eenam Award for Decade's Best Talent in Malayalam Music 2010, South Scope Film Award for Best Female Singer 2011, Lata Mangeshkar Award 2011, Thikkruissy Award for Best Female Playback Singer 2012. *Website:* www.audiotracsonline.com (office).

CHIWESHE, Stella Rambisai; Zimbabwean singer; b. 8 July 1946, Harare; m. 1st; two d.; m. 2nd Peter Reich 1988. *Career:* mem. Nat. Dance Co. of Zimbabwe as Mbira soloist, actress and dancer 1981–84; solo tours in Germany, Great Britain and Italy 1984; tour through Germany 1985, European tours 1988, 1995, 1996, 1997, 1999, 2000, 2004, 2005, 2006, tour of USA, Netherlands, Germany and Italy 1998; appeared at Global Interchange Conf., New York 1999; directed music theatre performance of Chiedza – Light, in Cologne 1999; workshop session for Dimensions Theatre Oakland, USA 2000; mem. GEMA. *Compositions include:* Kasahwa, Chaa!, Nsuzu Chamakuwende, Mapere. *Recordings include:* Chisi 1990, Kumusha 1991, Shungu 1994, Tapera 1998, Talking Mbira 2002, Double Check 2006. *Honours:* Billboard Music Award 1993, Zimbabwe Silver Jubilee Award for Outstanding Contribution to the Music Industry 2005. *E-mail:* tipire@yahoo.co.uk (office). *Website:* www.stellachiweshe.com.

CHO, Kyu-chan; South Korean singer and songwriter; b. 13 Jan. 1971, Seoul. *Recordings include:* albums: Shadow That a New Wind Blows (with Kim Jung Ryeol and Lee Joon) 1990, Even the Warm Coffee 1993, Adam and Eve Bit the Apple 1995, The Third Season 1996, The Fourth Wind 1997, Cho Kyu-chan Vol. 5 1999, Cho Kyu-chan Vol. 6: Sea Ice 2001, Thank You (For Saving My Life) 2001, Rainbow 2002, Cho Kyu-chan Vol. 7: Single Note 2003, Cho Kyu-chan Vol. 8: Guitology 2005. *Honours:* Yoo Jae Ha music contest Grand Prize 1989. *Address:* c/o EMI Music Publishing Korea, 6/F Haecheon Building 69–13, Samsung-1 dong, Gangnam-gu, Seoul 135-870, Republic of Korea. *E-mail:* korea@emimusicpub.com. *Website:* www.emimusicpub.com.

CHOLET, Jean-Christophe, DipMus; French musician (piano), composer and arranger; b. 11 May 1962, Böhl, Germany; m. (divorced); one s. one d. *Career:* mem. Union of Jazz Musicians. *Recordings include:* with Odéjy: Osti Natologie, Suite Alpestre; with Mathias Rüegg and Michel Portal: Third Dream. *Honours:* First Prize, Soloist, Composition and Orchestra, Int. Festival of Jazz, La Défense, Paris. *Current Management:* c/o Caroline Quatrehomme, 98 rue Abbé Pasty, 45130 Baulou, France. *Telephone:* 6-13-08-17-52. *E-mail:* caroline.quatrehomme@caraba.fr. *Website:* www.caraba.fr. *Address:* 295 Chemin de la Motte, 45200 Paulcourt, France. *Telephone:* 2-38-98-16-33. *E-mail:* jccholet@club-internet.fr. *Website:* www.jeanchristophecholet.com.

CHOU, Jay; Taiwanese singer, songwriter, musician (cello, piano, guitar, Jue Shigu) and actor; b. 18 Jan. 1979, Taipei. *Education:* Tamkang Middle School. *Career:* mixes rap and R&B with traditional Chinese elements; plays piano, guitar, cello, jazz drums; numerous tours of Asia; concerts in USA 2004, 2007, 2010; has written songs for other artists and directed pop videos; f. record co., JVR Music 2007–. *Recordings include:* albums: Jay 2000, Fantasy (five Golden Melody Awards) 2001, Eight Dimensions 2002, Yeh Hui Mei 2003, Common Jasmine Orange 2004, November's Chopin 2005, Still Fantasy 2006, On the Run 2007, Capricorn 2008, Dragon Rider 2009, The Era 2010. *Films:* actor: Hidden Track 2003, Initial D (Golden Horse Award for Best Newcomer, Hong Kong Film Award for Best Newcomer) 2005, Curse of the Golden Flower 2006, Secret (Shanghai Int. Film Festival for Most Popular Actor, Golden Horse Award for Outstanding Movie of the Year, Best Original Film Song, and Best Visual Effect) 2007, Kung Fu Dunk 2008, Treasure Hunter 2009, The Green Hornet (first Hollywood movie) 2010. *Television:* Pandamen 2010, Mr. J Channel (talk show) 2010. *Honours:* numerous music awards. *Address:* JVR Music Ltd, 451 Changchun Road, 11th Floor, Taipei, Taiwan (office). *E-mail:* jvrservice@jvrmusic.com (office). *Website:* www.jvrmusic.com (office); www.jay2u.com; www.facebook.com/jay.

CHOWDHURY, Boyan; British musician (guitar); b. 19 Dec. 1979. *Career:* Founder-mem. (lead guitarist) The Zutons 2002–07; formed new band The Gravity Trap 2007; mem. The Venus Fury. *Recordings include:* albums: Who Killed... The Zutons? 2004, Tired of Hanging Around 2006.

CHOWTA, Sandeep; Indian film composer and musician; b. Ghana. *Career:* raised in Nigeria and Bangalore; currently based in Chennai, India; fmr mem. Pulse; long-time collaborator with Ramgopal Varma; Head of Columbia Records India, Mumbai 2008–. *Films include:* soundtracks: Ninne Pelladatha 1996, Insaaf 1997, Dus 1997, Satya 1998, Vaastav 1999, Mast 1999, Shool 1999, Prema Katha 1999, Kaun 1999, Jungle 2000, Dhadkan 2000, Asoka 2001, Company 2002, Yeh Kaisi Mohabbat 2002, Jaani Dushman: Ek Anokhi Kahani 2002, Bollywood/Hollywood 2002, Road 2002, Durga 2002, Dum 2003, Boom 2003, Samay: When Time Strikes 2003, Ranga 2004, Super 2005, Sri 2005, Sandwich 2006, Bujjigaadu: Made in Chennai 2008, Mukhbiir 2008, Saleem 2009, Josh 2009, Kedi 2010: produced: Dead End 2003. *Recordings include:* albums: Mitti: Songs of the Soil 2003, Now That's Sandeep Chowta 2003. *Honours:* Filmfare Award 1999, 2001. *Address:* Yatra Studio, Midas Chambers, Link Road, Andheri West, Mumbai, India (office). *E-mail:* yatra2006@gmail.com (office). *Website:* www.sandeepchowta.com.

CHRIS, Jo; Cameroonian musician (piano); b. 12 Nov. 1960, Balengou; m. Ngandjeu Iavre 1984; one s. three d. *Career:* Prof. of Music, Lycee de Newbell; mem. Socimada. *Compositions include:* 17 published songs, arranged by Billy Mussango. *Address:* c/o Billy Mussango, PO Box 8363, Yaounde, Cameroon.

CHRISSY BOY; British musician (guitar, keyboards); b. (Christopher Foreman), 8 Aug. 1958, London; m. 1st 1976; one s.; m. 2nd 1992; one s. *Career:* founder mem., Madness 1976–86, 1992– (sporadically); numerous TV appearances; became The Madness 1988; formed group, The Nutty Boys 1990; mem. PRS, VPL, Musicians' Union. *Recordings include:* albums: with Madness: One Step Beyond 1979, Absolutely 1980, 7 1981, Complete Madness 1982, The Rise and Fall 1982, Madness 1983, Keep Moving 1984, Mad Not Mad 1985, Peel Sessions 1986, Utter Madness 1986, The Madness 1988, Divine Madness 1992, Madstock (live) 1993, Wonderful 1999, The Dangermen Sessions, Vol. 1 2005, The Liberty of Norton Folgate 2009, Oui Oui Si Si Ja Ja Da Da 2012; with Nutty Boys: Crunch! 1990. *Honours:* Ivor Novello Award (for Our House). *Current Management:* Hannah Management, Fulham Palace, London, SW6 6EA, England. *Telephone:* (20) 7758-1494. *E-mail:* management@madness.co.uk. *E-mail:* info@madness.co.uk (office). *Website:* www.madness.co.uk; www.crunch.uk.com.

CHRISTENSEN, Nikolaj; Danish singer and actor; b. 19 Feb. 1966, Copenhagen. *Career:* films: Christian, dir Gabrial Axel, Hjerter I Slor, Jesper W Nielsen; mem. DJBFA. *Recordings include:* Piloter 1990, Jimmy and Vicky 1991, Hen Over Jorden 1994, Vi Er På Vej 1996, Hvis Du Skal Med 1997, Selvantaendt 2006. *Honours:* Grammy Award for Best New Artist 1990.

CHRISTENSEN, Shawn; American singer, songwriter and musician (guitar). *Education:* Pratt Inst. of the Arts, NY. *Career:* mem. and lead singer, Stellastarr 2000–. *Recordings include:* albums: Stellastarr 2003, Harmonies for the Haunted 2005, Civilized 2009. *Current Management:* c/o Plus One Music, 242 Wythe Avenue, Studio 6, Brooklyn, New York, NY 11211, USA. *Telephone:* (718) 599-3740. *Fax:* (718) 599-0998. *E-mail:* jonnykaps@plusonemusic.net. *Address:* c/o Sony BMG, 550 Madison Avenue, New York, NY 10022, USA. *E-mail:* band@stellastarr.com. *Website:* www.stellastarr.com.

CHRISTENSEN, Søren; Danish musician (drums); b. 6 June 1963, Copenhagen. *Education:* Public Music School, Berklee Coll. of Music, Boston, USA, studied in Copenhagen. *Career:* appearances in major festivals throughout Scandinavia; many broadcasts on nat. TV and radio; appearance in film The Naked Trees. *Recordings include:* with EV's Youth Big Band 1984, 1985, Hens Winther, The Planets, Claus Waidtlow, Claustrophobia. *Honours:* Grammy Award (for The Planets) 1995. *Address:* Nyelandsvej 7, U T H, 2000 Frederiksburg, Denmark.

CHRISTI, Ellen, BA; American singer, composer, arranger and producer; b. 7 March 1958, Chicago, Ill. *Education:* studied with Jaki Byard, Virginia Davidson and Galli Campi. *Career:* solo jazz singer 1975–; f. Network Records; co-f. New York City Artists' Collective. *Compositions include:* I'm A Fan (of Every Man), Japanese Twilight, Midnight Moon, Senza Parole, Open Your Eyes, Anna Speaks. *Recordings include:* Star of Destiny 1987, Senza Parole (with Art Studio) 1989, Dreamers (with Claudio Lodati) 1990, Piece of Rock (with Fiorenzo Sordini) 1992, Better World (with Lisa Sokolov and Illustrio) 1992, Instant Reality 1995, Vocal Desires (with Claudio Lodati) 1996, Reconstruction of Sound (with Mauro Orselli) 1996, The Blues for Allah Project (with Joe Gallant) 1998, Aliens' Talk 1998, Terrapin Station (with Joe Gallant) 1999, Song Cycle (with William Parker) 2001, A Deeper Season than Reason (with Jurg Solothurnmann) 2001, Deep Beats 2001. *E-mail:* ellen@ellenchristi.com (home). *Website:* www.ellenchristi.com.

CHRISTIAN, Garry; British singer; b. 27 Feb. 1955, Liverpool; s. of Gladstone Christian and Ada Christian; partner Emma Roberts. *Career:* mem. The Christians 1984–95, re-formed 2000; numerous live appearances, tours. *Recordings include:* albums: The Christians 1987, Colour 1990, Happy in Hell 1992, The Best of The Christians 1993, Prodigal Sons 2003, Soul from Liverpool 2009, Speed of Life 2012; solo: Your Cool Mystery 1997. *Telephone:* 07951738748. *E-mail:* emma@thechristianslive.co.uk. *Website:* www.thechristianslive.co.uk (home). *E-mail:* emma@emmarobertspr.com (office).

CHRISTIAN, James John; American singer, songwriter, musician (guitar, drums, keyboards) and record producer; b. Milford, Conn. *Career:* lead singer, LA Rocks; lead singer, House of Lords, also fmrly with Jasper Wrath, Eyes; world tours, opened for acts including Ozzy Osbourne, Queensryche, Cheap Trick, Scorpions, Tesla; producer, writer, solo musician; lead singer, tour of Japan with Pata (lead guitarist with Japanese band X) 1993; opened own recording studio, Bodeo Rodeo Records. *Compositions include:* Les Ideos Noires, platinum hit single for Julie Masse; songs for group, Alias. *Recordings include:* albums: with Eyes: We're in it Together 1978; with House of Lords: House of Lords 1988, Sahara 1990, Demons Down 1992, The Power and the Myth 2004, World Upside Down 2006, Come to my Kingdom 2008; solo: Rude Awakening 1995, Meet the Man 2004, Lay It All On Me 2013, Precious Metal 2014. *Current Management:* c/o Wim van der Bij, No Nonsense Booking and Management, Reijerskoop 12A, Boskoop, The Netherlands. *Telephone:* (50) 9215281. *E-mail:* info@nononsense-bookings.com. *Website:* www.nononsense-bookings.com; www.jameschristianmusic.com.

CHRISTIAN, Rick; British singer, songwriter and musician (6- and 12-string guitars); b. (Derek Watson), 22 Sept. 1951, Romford, Essex, England; m. Gillian Mary Moore 1981. *Career:* professional musician since 1987; many radio appearances include Capital, LBC, BBC and ind. local radio stations, including Essex, Suffolk, Kent, Bedford, Shropshire and Newcastle; festivals include South Downs, Broadstairs, Walton, and numerous smaller festivals; co-presenter, Essex Folk, BBC Essex 1986–94; organizer, Maldon Folk Club and Maldon Folk Festival (now both ceased); supported artists including Jim Couza, Fred Wedlock, Harvey Andrews; played charity event alongside Griff Rhys Jones, Wrabness, Essex 1990; tours, Denmark 1994, 1995, Arizona USA 1999, 2000, 2002, 2004, 2006, 2008, 2010, 2012, 2014; numerous concerts for the Council for Music in Hospitals 1995–; folk column writer, Maldon & Burnham Standard –2008; reviewer, EFN Magazine, Tradition Magazine; mem. Musicians' Union, Performing Right Soc., Mechanical-Copyright Protection Soc. Alliance, PPL, Essex Folk Asscn. *Recordings include:* albums: Reason Enough 1983 (re-released 2006), Looking For Signs 1990, The Open Road 1996, These Things Happen 1996, Loose Association 2004, It's About Time 2014. *Publications include:* major contrib. to Guinness Who's Who of Folk Music, Guinness Encyclopaedia of Popular Music. *Website:* www.rickchristian.co.uk.

CHRISTIAN, Russell; British singer; b. 8 July 1956, Liverpool. *Career:* mem. The Christians 1984–95; numerous live appearances and European tours. *Recordings include:* albums: The Christians 1987, Colour 1990, Happy In Hell 1992, The Best of The Christians 1993.

CHRISTIANE, Kelvin, DPLM; British jazz musician (saxophones, flute, clarinet, keyboards, percussion) and composer; b. (Kelvin Howard Wigger), 16 March 1958, Watford, Herts., England; s. of Don Wigger and Marjorie Wigger; divorced; one s. *Education:* Watford School of Music, City of Leeds Coll. of Music. *Career:* television appearances, Blue Mercedes, Afrique, Chris Evans; toured Europe and India with Afrique 1980, The Flyers 1981–84; toured with the Bernard 'Pretty' Purdie band 1998; Pucho and the Latin Soul Bros; played Nice and Montauban Festivals, France, Brecon and Swanage, Strawberry Hill Festivals, UK; played with Pete King, Gilad Atzmon, Alan Barnes, Roland Perrins' Blue Planet Orchestra; composes and arranges for his Allstar Big Band and hosts Twickenham Jazz Club; Head of Jazz, Hampton School 2005–07. *Recordings include:* Albums: with Kelvin Christiane Band: Awakening 1992, Soho 1993, Great Spirit 1994, Salute the Sun 1997, Tribute to Roland Kirk 1998, Piper at the Pearly Gates, Parisian Summer, Pleiadian Tales, Wigger. *Radio:* several tracks featured on Humphrey Lyttleton's Best of Jazz (BBC Radio 3). *Telephone:* (20) 8286-3242 (home). *E-mail:* kc@kcmusic.co.uk (office). *Website:* www.kcmusic.co.uk (office).

CHRISTIDES, Konstantinos (Kostas), BMus, DipMus; Greek composer and musician (piano); b. 30 April 1973, Thessaloniki. *Education:* Macedonian Conservatoire, Thessaloniki, London Coll. of Music, UK, Univ. of Southern California, USA. *Career:* fmr scoring asst to Christopher Young; mem. Soc. of Composers and Lyricists, USA, American Musicians' Union. *Compositions for film include:* Puzzle Box (short), The Footsteps of Apostle John (short), Measure for Measure 1997, Olympic Fanfare 1998, Out of the Ruins 1998, Waiting on the Lost 2001, The Moment After 2002, The Drone Virus 2004, Morphine 2005, Blackberries 2005, 29 Reasons to Run (Bare Bones Int. Festival Award 2006) 2006, Dark Ride 2006, Eduart (Greek State Film Awards 2006) 2006. *Honours:* Henry Purcell Prize for Composers 1996, Wilfred Joseph's Prize for Composers 1997, Sir Malcolm Arnold President's Award 1997, Univ. of Southern California Int. Students' Award 1998. *Telephone:* (323) 7191484. *E-mail:* info@limelightagency.com. *Website:* www.limelightagency.com; www.kostaschristides.com.

CHRISTIE, Lou; American singer, songwriter and producer; b. (Lugee Alfredo Giovanni Sacco), 19 Feb. 1943, Glenwillard, PA; m. Francesca Winfield 1971; one s. one d. *Education:* studied music with Joliann Williams, Lennie Martin. *Career:* leader, The Crewnecks 1957–58, The Classics 1959–60, Lugee and the Lions 1961–62; backing singer, Marcy Jo 1961; solo artist 1962–; numerous concerts and tours, television appearances. *Film soundtrack contributions:* Mondo Trasho 1969, Rain Man 1988, Dutch 1990, A Home of Our Own 1993, Barcelona 1994, Before Sunrise 1995, Burnzy's Last Call 1995, Waiting for Guffman 1996, Nick and Jane 1997, The Last Days of Disco 1998. *Recordings:* The Gypsy Cried 1962, Two Faces Have I 1963, Have I Sinned 1964, Lightnin' Strikes 1965, Rhapsody In The Rain 1966, Painter 1966, Wild Life's In Season 1966, Don't Stop Me 1967, Genesis and The Third Verse 1968, I'm Gonna Make You Mine 1969, Beyond The Blue Horizon 1973, Guardian Angels 1981, Enlightnin'ment 1988, Glory River: The Buddah Years, 1968–72 1992, Beyond The Blue Horizon: More of the Best of Lou Christie 1994, Pledging My Love 1997, The Complete Co and Ce/Roulette

Recordings 1998, Beyond the Blue Horizon/Hey You Cajun 1998, Lou Christie Strikes Again 1999, Egyptian Shumba (compilation) 2001, Paint America Love 2008, Summer in Malibu 2009. *Honours:* BMI Citation 1966, BMI Award 1994. *Current Management:* Dick Fox Entertainment, 1650 Broadway, New York, NY 10019, USA. *Telephone:* (212) 582-9072. *E-mail:* foxentco@aol.com. *Website:* www.lou-christie.com.

CHRISTOPHERSEN, Nicolaj Strøyer; Danish musician (guitar). *Career:* mem. Diefenbach 1999–; band started own label, Display Records. *Recordings include:* albums: Diefenbach 2001, Run Trip Fall 2003, Make Your Mind (EP) 2004, Re-Make Your Mind (EP) 2005, Set And Drift 2005.

CHUCK D, BFA; American rap artist; b. (Carlton Ridenhour), 1 Aug. 1960, Long Island, NY; m. Gaye Theresa Johnson. *Education:* Adelphi Univ. *Career:* Super Special Mix Show, radio WBAU 1982; own mobile DJ and concert promotion co., Spectrum City; Founder mem. rap group, Public Enemy 1982–; Man. and Promoter, The Entourage (hip hop venue), Long Island, New York 1986; Founder, Offda Books, Under the Radar Publishing 2003. *Recordings include:* albums: with Public Enemy: Yo! Bum Rush The Show 1987, It Takes A Nation of Millions To Hold Us Back 1988, Fear of a Black Planet 1990, Apocalypse 91... The Enemy Strikes Black (Soul Train Music Award for Best Rap Album 1992) 1991, Greatest Misses 1992, Muse Sick-n-Hour Mess Age 1994, He Got Game (film soundtrack) 1998, There's a Poison Goin' On... 1999, Revolverlution 2002, Rebirth of a Nation 2005, New Whirl Odor 2005, How you Sell a Soul to a Soulless People who Sold their Soul??? 2007, Most of My Heroes Still Don't Appear on No Stamp 2012, The Evil Empire of Everything 2012, Man Plans God Laughs 2015; solo: No 1996, The Autobiography of Mistachuck 1996, The Black in Man 2014. *Publications include:* Public Enemy (autobiography) 1994, Fight the Power: Rap, Race and Reality (non-fiction, with Yusuf Jah) 1997. *Honours:* MOBO Award for Outstanding Contrib. to Black Music 2005, inducted into Rock and Roll Hall of Fame 2013. *E-mail:* Mistachuck@rapstation.com (office). *Website:* www.rapstation.com; www.publicenemy.com.

CHURCH, Charlotte; British singer and songwriter; b. 21 Feb. 1986, Llandaff, Cardiff; m. Gavin Henson (divorced 2010); one s. one d. *Education:* Howell's School, Llandaff. *Career:* singer of opera, musical hits, folk songs and contemporary songs; numerous live concerts, television and radio appearances; Patron, The Topsy Foundation, UK 2007. *Recordings include:* albums: Voice of an Angel 1998, Charlotte Church 1999, Dream a Dream 2000, Enchantment 2001, Prelude: The Best of Charlotte Church 2002, Tissues and Issues 2005, Back to Scratch 2010. *Film:* as actor: I'll Be There 2003. *Television includes:* presenter The Charlotte Church Show 2007. *Publication includes:* Voice of an Angel (My Life So Far) 2005, Keep Smiling (memoir) 2007. *Honours:* British Artist Of The Year, Classical BRIT Awards 2000, Woman Of The Year, GQ Award 2005, Solo Artist of the Year, Glamour Awards 2006, Best Female Newcomer, British Comedy Awards 2006, Readers Favourite TV Personality, Glamour Awards 2007. *Website:* charlottechurchmusic.com.

CHURCH, (Kenneth) Eric; American singer, songwriter and musician (guitar, piano, banjo); b. 3 May 1977, Granite Falls, NC; m. Katherine Blasingame 2008; one s. *Education:* South Caldwell High School, Appalachian State Univ. *Career:* relocated to Nashville; became songwriter for Terri Clark and Dean Miller; signed to Capitol Records 2005; released debut album 2006; first appearance on Grand Ole Opry 2006; toured with Brad Paisley, Miranda Lambert, Jason Aldean, Josh Kelley, Toby Keith, Rascal Flatts; collaborated with Jason Aldean and Luke Bryan 2012. *Recordings include:* albums: Sinners Like Me 2006, Carolina 2009, Chief (Country Music Asscn Award for Album of the Year 2012, Acad. of Country Music Award for Album of the Year 2013) 2011, The Outsiders 2014, Mr Misunderstood 2015. *Honours:* Acad. of Country Music Award for Top New Solo Vocalist 2011, for Vocal Event of the Year (with Jason Aldean and Luke Bryan for 'The Only Way I Know') 2013, for Musical Event of the Year (with Keith Urban for 'Raise 'Em Up') 2015. *Current Management:* c/o John Peets, Q Prime Management, 131 South 11th Street, Nashville, TN 37206, USA. *E-mail:* admin@qprime.com. *Website:* www.qprime.com; www.capitolnashville.com (office); www.emimusic.com (office); www.EricChurch.com.

CHURCH, Joseph, BA, MM, DA; music director, conductor, composer, academic and arranger and musician; b. 25 Nov. 1957, New York, USA; one d. *Education:* Swarthmore Coll., Univ. of Illinois, New York Univ. *Career:* Music Dir, Conductor, including nat. tour, Little Shop of Horrors 1984–86; Radio City Music Hall Christmas special 1988–89; Promenade Theatre, Catch Me If I Fall 1990; Giuseppe Verdi Soc. Chorus and Orchestra, Italy 1991; St James Theatre, Broadway, The Who's Tommy 1992–95; La Jolla Playhouse, California 1995–97; Music Dir, Conductor, The Lion King, New Amsterdam Theatre; Music Supervisor, The Lion King, London, Japan, Toronto; Assoc. Conductor, In the Heights 1997–2005; Assoc. Conductor, Richard Rodgers Theater 2008–11; Adjunct Prof. of Music, New York Univ. School of Education 1998–; numerous TV appearances; mem. ASCAP, American Music Center, Coll. Music Soc. *Compositions:* Les Fables, Sonata for two pianos, Vibrachrome, Mock Opera, Soggiorno, Duo for violin and viola. *Publications:* Music Direction for the Stage: A View from the Podium 2015. *Honours:* Drama Logue Award, two ASCAP Composition Awards. *Address:* 305 West 98th Street, Apt 3E N, New York, New York, NY 10025, USA. *Website:* www.churchmuse.com.

CHURCHLEY, Richard Allen, BA, MA, PhD; British musician (accordion, guitar, mandolin), songwriter and singer; b. 13 Nov. 1952, Birmingham,

England; m. Prue Dobell 1975; two s. *Education:* Univs of Reading and Birmingham. *Career:* appearances with various bands on folk and acoustic music circuits, including Harry-Ca-Nab, Peaky Blinders, Barker's Knee, Mind Your Own Business, O'Cajunal Playboys, Brandy Wine Bridge, Accordion2Us, Jolly Boys, Pat's On The Fiddle; also solo work; broadcasts on local radio and BBC Radio 2; mem. Musicians' Union. *Compositions:* various folk songs. *Recordings include:* Mega-Maggot (Harry-Ca-Nab) 1990, Good Times (O'Cajunal Playboys) 2000. *Address:* 1293 Evesham Road, Astwood Bank, Redditch, B96 6AY, England (home). *Telephone:* (1527) 892361 (home). *E-mail:* rachurchley@totalise.co.uk. *Website:* www.churchley.org.uk.

CIARA; American singer, songwriter and actress; b. (Ciara Princess Harris), 25 Oct. 1985, Austin, Tex.; d. of Carlton Harris and Jackie Harris. *Education:* Riverdale High School. *Career:* fmr mem. teenage girl group Hearsay; fmrly songwriter for artists including Fantasia Barrino; signed as artist to LaFace Records 2002; toured with Gwen Stefani, Bow Wow, Chris Brown, Rihanna, T.I.; co-headlined tour with Jay-Z 2009; opening act for Britney Spears' Circus tour 2009; numerous collaborations on record including Petey Pablo, Missy Elliott, Ludacris, Chamillionaire, Field Mob, Tiffany Evans, Young Jeezy, Justin Timberlake, Nelly, Enrique Iglesias, Pitbull, 2 Chainz. *Films:* as actress: All You've Got 2006, That's My Boy 2012. *Television:* as actress: The Game 2013. *Recordings:* albums: Goodies 2004, Ciara: the Evolution 2006, Fantasy Ride 2009, Basic Instinct 2010, Ciara 2013. *Honours:* numerous including: ASCAP Pop Music Awards for Most Performed Songs (for Goodies) 2005, (for Goodies, 1, 2 Step, Oh) 2006, (for Like You, So What) 2007, ASCAP Rhythm & Soul Music Awards for Award Winning R&B/Hip-Hop Song (for Goodies) 2005, (for 1, 2 Step, Like You, Oh) 2006, BET Award for Best Collaboration (for 1, 2 Step) 2005, MTV Video Awards for Best Dance Video and Best Hip-Hop Video (both for Lose Control) 2005, Soul Train Music Awards for Best R&B/Soul Single: Female 2005, for Best R&B/Soul or Rap New Artist 2005, for Sammy Davis Junior Female Entertainer of the Year 2005, for Best R&B/Soul or Rap Dance Cut (for Lose Control) 2006, for Best Dance Performance (for Ride) 2010, Teen Choice Awards for Choice Music Make-Out Song (for Oh) 2005, for Choice Music R&B/Hip Hop Track (for 1, 2 Step) 2005, for Best Hook-Up Song (for Love Sex Magic) 2009. *Address:* c/o Epic Records, Sony Music Entertainment, 550 Madison Avenue, Room 2316, New York, NY 10022, USA (office). *Telephone:* (212) 833-8000 (office). *Fax:* (212) 833-5828 (office). *Website:* www.sonymusic.com (office); onlyciara.com.

CIÁRÁN, Cian; Welsh musician (keyboards) and singer; b. 16 June 1976, Bangor. *Career:* mem., Super Furry Animals 1993–; recorded two EPs on indie label, then obtained major indie label deal; Label Man. SomBom and Strangetown Records; numerous tours in the UK and abroad. *Recordings include:* albums: with Super Furry Animals: Fuzzy Logic 1996, Radiator 1997, Out Spaced 1998, Guerrilla 1999, Mwng 2000, Rings Around The World 2001, Phantom Power 2003, Phantom Phorce 2004, Love Kraft 2005, Hey Venus 2007, Dark Days/Light Years 2009, Outside In 2012, They are Nothing Without Us 2013. *E-mail:* info@superfurry.com (office). *Website:* www.superfurry.com; www.sombom.eu.

CIBELLE; Brazilian singer, songwriter and producer; b. (Cibelle Cavalli), 1978, São Paulo. *Education:* Marcelo Tupinambá Conservatory. *Career:* main vocalist in São Paulo Confessions 1999; signed to Belgian record label Crammed Discs 2003. *Recordings include:* albums: Cibelle 2003, The Shine of Dried Electric Leaves 2006, Las Vênus Resort Palace Hotel 2010. *Current Management:* c/o Crammed Discs, 43 rue Général Patton, 1050 Brussels, Belgium. *E-mail:* crammed@crammed.be (office). *Website:* www.crammed.be (office); www.cibelle.net.

CINGL, Pavel; Czech musician (violin); b. 1962, Teplice; m. Katerina Cingl 1989, two s. *Education:* Conservatory of Jaroslav Jezek, Prague. *Career:* support to Alan Stivell in Prague; tours of Germany, Austria, France, Netherlands, Belgium, Denmark; regular Czech television and radio appearances; currently mem. Phil Shoenfelt and Southern Cross. *Recordings include:* 16 albums with Czech bands. *Website:* www.philshoenfelt.com.

CÍSAŘ, Miroslav; Czech composer and conductor; b. 2 Dec. 1929, Prague; two s. *Education:* Music Conservatory, Charles Univ., Prague. *Career:* mem. Symphonic Orchestra; conductor of brass bands and folk groups; arranger; numerous broadcasts on Radio Prague; mem. Co. of Brass Music, Group Composers, Czech Repub. *Recordings:* 40 albums. *Publications:* Compositions published. *Honours:* winner of radio competition, Winner, Compositions for Children and Sportsmen. *Address:* Branická 65/46, Braník, 147 00 Prague 4, Czech Republic (home). *Telephone:* (732) 424137 (home).

CISSOKHO, Malang; Senegalese musician (kora, guitar, bass guitar, percussion), singer and songwriter; b. 27 May 1962, Thies; m. Pirjo Saastamoinen, 24 Nov. 1989, one s. *Education:* Traditional Musical Education of Mandinko Griot. *Career:* performed at Kaustinen Folk Music Festival 1988, 1989, 1995; Jyvaskyla Summer Festival 1989; Pori Jazz Festival 1989, 1996; Joensuu Festival 1994, 1996; Ruisrock 1996; mem. Finnish Musician Asscn. *Compositions include:* Mun-Mun 1982, Warale 1985, Yendi 1985, Touba 1985, Foroya 1997, Kano 1997, Alimaton Salia 1990. *Recordings include:* Solo albums: Lotus 1990, Foroya 1997, Dialia 1997; Contrib.: Super Etoile II de Dakar: Náteel Weerwi, Piirpanke: Tuku Tuku; Kristian Blak: Addeq; Rinne Radio: Rok; The Cool Sheiks: Serve Cool, Trance Planet Vol. 3; J Karjalainen and Electric Sauna: Electric Sauna; Piirpauke: Metamorphosis. *Honours:* Emma Award 1996. *Address:* Haapalahdenkatu 5 G44, 00300 Helsinki, Finland.

CISSOKO, Issa; Senegalese musician (tenor saxophone). *Career:* mem. Orchestra Baobab 1970–85, originally at Club Baobab to 1977, then Jandeer Club, Balafon Club to 1978, time in Paris, then at Ngalam Club to 1985; Orchestra Baobab re-formed 2001–, resident at Just 4U Club, Dakar. *Recordings include:* albums: M'Beugene 1972, Hommage à Lay M'Boop 1974, Orchestre Baobab '75 1975, Guy Gu Rey Gi 1975, Senegaal Sunugaal 1975, Visage du Sénégal 1975, Aduna Jarul Naawoo 1975, N'Deleng N'Deleng 1977, Une Nuit Aun Jandeer 1978, Baobab à Paris Vols 1 and 2 1978, Gouygui Dou Daanou 1979, Mohamadou Bamba 1980, Sibou Odia 1980, Ken Dou Werente (re-released as Pirate's Choice 2001) 1982, On Verra Ça: The 1978 Paris Sessions 1992, Bamba 1993, Specialist in All Styles (BBC Radio 3 Awards for World Music Critic's Award for Album of the Year 2003) 2002, A Night at Club Baobab 2006, Made in Dakar 2007. *Honours:* BBC Radio 3 Awards for World Music, Africa Region 2003. *Address:* c/o World Circuit Records, First Floor, Shoreditch Stables, 138 Kingsland Road, London, E2 8DY, England (office). *E-mail:* post@worldcircuit.co.uk (office). *Website:* www .worldcircuit.co.uk (office); www.orchestrabaobab.com.

CL; South Korean singer and rapper; b. (Chae-rin Lee), 26 Feb. 1991, Seoul. *Career:* recorded with Uhm Jung Hwa 2008; mem. 2NE1 2009–; other collaborations include Big Bang, YMGA, G-Dragon featuring Teddy Park. *Film:* Girlfriends 2009. *Television includes:* 2NE1 TV 2009–11; also appearances on Style 2009, Inkigayo (SBS) 2009–11, M! Countdown (Mnet) 2009–11, Music Bank (KBS) 2009–11, Project Runway Career 2011. *Recordings:* albums: with 2NE1: To Anyone (Melon Music Award for Album of the Year 2010, Mnet Asian Music Award for Album of the Year 2010, Korean Music Award for Best Dance and Electronic Album 2011) 2010, Crush 2014. *Honours:* numerous awards for 2NE1 including: Asia Song Festival Asian Newcomer's Award 2009, Melon Music Awards for New Artist and Top 10 2009, for Top 10 2010, Mnet 20's Choice Awards for Hot New Star 2009, Hot CF Star 2009 and Hot Online Song 2009, Mnet Asian Music Awards for Best New Female Artist 2009, for Music Portal Award 2009, for Song of the Year 2009, for Best Music Video 2009, 2010, for Best Female Group 2010, for Artist of the Year 2010, Rhythmer Awards for R&B Artist of the Year and Rookie of the Year 2009 Style Icon Best Female Singer Awards 2009, 2010, MTV Daum Music Fest Award for Artist of the Year 2011, MYX Music Favorite K-pop Video Award 2011; also numerous Cyworld Digital Music Awards including Top Selling Artist Award 2009, Newcomer of the Year 2010, Bonsang Award 2010, Artist of the Year Award 2010, Song of the Year 2010. *Address:* c/o YG Entertainment, 397–5 YG Building, Hapjeong-Dong, Mapo-Gu, Seoul, 109-819, South Korea (office). *Telephone:* (2) 3143-1105 (office). *Fax:* (2) 544-1546 (office). *E-mail:* web@ygmail.net (office). *Website:* eng.ygfamily.com/main/main.html (office); www.yg-2ne1.com.

CLAIR, Mark, (Mark Mac, Cold Mission); British producer, remixer and DJ; b. London. *Career:* mem. 4hero, Manix, Jacob's Optical Stairway; Co-founder, Reinforced Records 1990; collaborations with Jill Scott, Ursula Rucker, Terry Callier. *Recordings include:* albums: with 4hero: In Rough Territory 1991, Parallel Universe 1995, Two Pages 1998, Creating Patterns 2001, Play With the Changes 2007; with Jacob's Optical Stairway: Jacob's Optical Stairway 1996.

CLAPTON, Eric Patrick, CBE; British musician (guitar), singer and songwriter; b. (Eric Patrick Clapp), 30 March 1945, Ripley, Surrey; m. 1st Patti Harrison (née Boyd) 1979 (divorced 1988); one s. (deceased) by Lori Delsanto one d.; m. 2nd Melia McEnery 2002; three c. *Career:* guitarist with Roosters 1963, Yardbirds 1963–65, John Mayall's Bluesbreakers 1965–66, Cream 1966–68, Blind Faith 1969, Derek and the Dominoes 1970, Delaney and Bonnie 1970–72; solo artist 1972–; Dir Clouds House 1993; mem. Bd of Dirs Chemical Dependency Centre 1994–99; f. Crossroads Center 1998. *Film appearances:* Tommy 1974, Blues Brothers 2000 1998. *Recordings include:* albums: Disraeli Gears 1967, Wheels of Fire 1968, Goodbye Cream 1969, Blind Faith 1969, Layla 1970, Eric Clapton 1970, Concert For Bangladesh 1971, Eric Clapton's Rainbow Concert 1973, 461 Ocean Boulevard 1974, There's One In Every Crowd 1975, E. C. Was Here 1975, No Reason To Cry 1976, Slowhand 1977, Backless 1978, Just One Night 1980, Another Ticket 1981, Money and Cigarettes 1983, Behind The Sun 1985, August 1986, Homeboy 1989, Journeyman 1989, 24 Nights 1991, Rush 1992, Unplugged 1992, From The Cradle 1994, Crossroads 2 1996, Live In Montreux 1997, Pilgrim 1998, Riding With The King (with B. B. King) (Grammy Award for Best Traditional Blues Album 2001) 2000, Reptile (Grammy Award for Best Pop Instrumental Performance 2002) 2001, One More Car One More Rider 2002, Me And Mr Johnson 2004, Sessions For Robert J. 2004, Back Home 2005, The Road to Escondido (with J. J. Cale; Grammy Award for Best Contemporary Blues Album 2008) 2006, Clapton 2010, Old Sock 2013, The Breeze 2014. *Publication:* Eric Clapton: The Autobiography 2007. *Honours:* Silver Clef Award for Outstanding contrib. to British Music 1983, six Grammy Awards 1993, Grammy Award for Best Rock Performance by Duo or Group (for The Calling, with Santana) 2000, Grammy Award for Best Male Pop Vocalist 1996, Grammy Lifetime Achievement Award 2006; inducted into Rock and Roll Hall of Fame 2000. *Address:* c/o Michael Eaton, Bushbranch Ltd, 36 Old Church Street, London, SW3 5BY, England. *Website:* www.ericclapton.com.

CLARIN, Bjorn A. F.; Swedish songwriter, composer, producer and scriptwriter; b. 15 Dec. 1936; m. Marianne 1958; two s. two d. *Career:* over 500 appearances, mostly in children's programmes. *Compositions include:* more than 60 songs with lyrics by Harry Martinson. *Recordings include:* 25 albums of popular Swedish music. *Honours:* Fred Winter Scholarship, Swedish Scholarship of Music, Cultural Nobility of Lerum Community 2004. *Address:* Hampakersvagen 14, 43 339 Lerum, Sweden.

CLARK, Anne; British poet, songwriter and musician (piano, violin, viola); b. 14 May 1960, London. *Career:* tours of Europe, North America; Co-Ed., Paul Weller's Riot Stories; mem. PRS, MCPS, GVL. *Recordings include:* The Sitting Room 1982, Changing Places 1983, Hopeless Cases 1987, Unstill Life 1991, Notes Taken, Traces Left 2004, The Smallest Acts of Kindness 2008; live album: Psychometry 2000. *Publications include:* Hard Lines, Notes Taken, Traces Left. *E-mail:* officialanneclark@gmail.com. *Website:* www .anneclarkofficial.com.

CLARK, Brandy Lynn; American country music singer, songwriter and musician (guitar, piano); b. 1977, Morton, Wash. *Education:* Central Washington Univ., Belmont Univ. *Career:* relocated to Nashville 1998; fmrly worked for Leadership Music; songwriter for numerous artists 2005–; opening act on tour for Sheryl Crow 2012, for Jennifer Nettles 2014. *Compositions:* numerous songs for other artists including The Band Perry (Better Dig Two), Wade Bowen, Craig Campbell, Sheryl Crow, Sarah Darling, Rebecca Lynn Howard, Toby Keith, Miranda Lambert (Mama's Broken Heart, Two Rings Shy), Buffy Lawson, Reba McEntire, Craig Morgan, Kacey Musgraves (Follow Your Arrow), David Nail, Guy Penrod, LeAnn Rimes, Mica Roberts, Darius Rucker, Ray Scott, Ashton Shepherd, Joanna Smith, Pam Tillis and Lorrie Morgan, Keith Urban, Gretchen Wilson. *Recordings:* album: 12 Stories 2013. *Honours:* CMA Award for Song of the Year (for Follow Your Arrow, by Kacey Musgraves) 2014. *E-mail:* Emilie@smackmgmt.com. *Website:* www .brandyclarkmusic.com.

CLARK, Elbernita 'Twinkie'; American gospel singer, musician (B3 Hammond organ) and songwriter; b. 15 Nov. 1954, Detroit, Mich.; d. of the late Dr Mattie Moss Clark; sister of Dorinda Clark Cole, Jacky Clark Chisholm and Karen Clark Sheard. *Education:* Howard Univ. *Career:* mem. Clark Sisters 1970–89; solo artist 1990–; co-f. Clark Conservatory of Music, Detroit 1979; minister in Church of God in Christ. *Recordings include:* albums: with Clark Sisters: Jesus Has a Lot to Give 1973, Dr Mattie Moss Clark presents The Clark Sisters 1974, Unworthy 1976, Count it All Joy 1978, New Dimensions of Christmas Carols 1978, He Gave Me Nothing to Lose (But All to Gain) 1979, Is My Living in Vain 1980, You Brought the Sunshine 1981, Sincerely 1982, Heart and Soul 1986, Conqueror 1988, Bringing it Back Home 1989, Live – One Last Time (Grammy Award for Best Traditional Gospel Album 2008) 2007, The Clark Sisters Definitive Gospel Collection 2008, A Clark Family Christmas 2009; solo: Praise Belongs To God 1979, Ye Shall Receive Power 1981, Comin' Home 1982, Masterpiece 1984, FAMU Gospel Choir 1996, Live in Charlotte 2002, Home Once Again… Live in Detroit 2004, Praise and Worship 2006, With Humility 2011, Live and Unplugged 2013. *Honours:* inducted in Int. Gospel Music Hall of Fame 1999, Stellar Award for Most Notable Achievement 2007, Grammy Award for Best Gospel Performance 2008. *Address:* The Clark Sisters, 19161 Schaefer Highway, Suite 202, Detroit, MI 48235, USA. *Telephone:* (313) 342-7496. *Fax:* (313) 342-8204. *Website:* theclarksisters.net.

CLARK, Graeme; British musician (bass); b. 15 April 1966, Glasgow, Scotland. *Career:* mem. Wet Wet Wet 1982–. *Recordings include:* albums: Popped In Souled Out 1987, Sgt Pepper Knew My Father 1988, The Memphis Sessions 1988, High On The Happy Side 1992, Wet Wet Wet Live At The Royal Albert Hall 1993, End of Part One (Their Greatest Hits) 1993, Picture This 1995, 10 1997, Timeless 2007. *Honours:* BRIT Award for Best British Newcomer 1988. *Current Management:* c/o No Half Measures Limited, 1st Floor, 5 Eagle Street, Glasgow, G4 9XA, Scotland. *Telephone:* (141) 331-9888. *Fax:* (141) 331-9889. *E-mail:* info@nohalfmeasures.com. *Website:* www .nohalfmeasures.com. *Address:* www.graemeclark.co.uk. *Website:* www .wetwetwet.co.uk.

CLARK, Guy; American singer and songwriter; b. 6 Nov. 1941, Rockport, Tex. *Career:* fmr photographer; solo artist; collaboration with artists, including Emmylou Harris, Rodney Crowell, Steve Earle, Jerry Jeff Walker, Hoyt Axton, Waylon Jennings, Don Everly, Gordon Payne, K.T. Oslin, Rosanne Cash, Vince Gill; numerous concerts and festival appearances. *Compositions include:* LA Freeway, Jerry Jeff Walker; Desperados Waiting For A Train, Tom Rush; Texas 1947, Johnny Cash; The Last Gunfighter Ballad; Virginia's Real; Heartbroke, Ricky Skaggs; Co-writer with Rodney Crowell: The Partner Nobody Chose; She's Crazy For Leavin'. *Recordings include:* albums: Old No. 1 1975, Texas Cookin' 1976, Guy Clark 1978, South Coast of Texas 1981, Better Days 1983, Old Friends 1988, Boats to Build 1992, Dublin Blues 1995, Craftsman (compilation) 1995, The Essential Guy Clark (compilation) 1997, Keepers (live) 1997, Cold Dog Soup 1999, The Dark 2002, Workbench Songs 2006, Somedays the Song Writes You 2009, Songs and Stories 2011, My Favorite Picture of You (Grammy Award for Best Folk Album 2014) 2013. *Honours:* American Music Asscn Lifetime Achievement Award in Songwriting 2005. *Current Management:* c/o Mr Keith Case, Keith Case & Associates, 1025 17th Avenue South, Floor 2, Nashville, TN 37212, USA. *Telephone:* (615) 327-4646. *Fax:* (615) 327-4949. *E-mail:* keith@keithcase.com. *Website:* www .keithcase.com; www.guyclark.com; www.dualtone.com.

CLARK, Petula, CBE; British singer and actress; b. (Sally Olwen), 15 Nov. 1932, Epsom, Surrey; d. of Leslie Norman Clarke and Doris Olwen; m. Claude Wolff 1961; one s. two d. *Career:* started career as child singer entertaining troops during Second World War; early appearances in films under contract to Rank Organization; made numerous recordings and television appearances in both England and France; success of single Downtown started career in USA; currently Patron Art-Therapie Foundation. *Compositions include:* Petula Clark Sings 1956, A Date with Pet 1956, You Are My Lucky Star 1957, Tête à Tête avec Petula Clark 1961, In Other Words 1962, Le Soleil dans les Yeux 1963, Hello Paris 1964, Le James Dean 1964, Downtown 1965, The International Hits 1965, My Love 1966, Just Say Goodbye 1966, I Couldn't Live Without Your Love 1966, The Many Faces of Petula Clark 1967, These Are My Songs 1967, The Other Man's Grass Is Always Greener 1967, Just Pet 1969, Memphis 1970, Today 1971, La Chanson de Marie Madeleine 1972, Come on Home 1974, Live in London 1974, Just Petula 1975, Destiny 1978, Portrait of a Song Stylist 1991, Treasures 1992, Where the Heart Is 1998, Sign of the Times 2001, The Ultimate Collection 2002, In Her Own Write 2007, Then & Now: The Very Best of Petula Clark 2008, Lost in You 2013. *Films include:* Medal for the General 1944, Murder in Reverse 1945, London Town 1946, Strawberry Roan 1947, Here Come the Huggets, Vice Versa, Easy Money 1948, Don't Ever Leave Me 1949, Vote for Huggett 1949, The Huggetts Abroad, Dance Hall, The Romantic Age 1950, White Corridors, Madame Louise 1951, Made in Heaven 1952, The Card 1952, The Runaway Bus 1954, My Gay Dog 1954, The Happiness of Three Women 1955, Track the Man Down 1956, That Woman Opposite 1957, Calling All Cats 1958, Daggers Drawn 1964, Finian's Rainbow 1968, Goodbye Mr Chips 1969, Dame dans l'auto avec des lunettes et un fusil 1970, Drôle De Zèbres 1977, Second Star to the Right 1980, Twin Town 1997, Billy's Hollywood Screen Kiss 1998, Girl Interrupted 1999, The Yards 2000, How To Kill Your Neighbour's Dog 2002. *Stage appearances:* Sound of Music 1981, Someone Like You (also wrote) 1989, Blood Brothers (Broadway) 1993, Sunset Boulevard 1995–96; nat. tour 1994–95, Sunset Boulevard 1995, 1996, New York 1998, US tour 1998–2000, London 2000. *Honours:* two Grammy Awards, Francis Carco Prize 1962, Grand Prix de la Chanson 1964, Radio Caroline Bell Award 1965, Radio Luxembourg Golden Lion Award 1965, Fry's Shooting Star Award 1965, Cash Box Award 1966, Hon. Citizen Award, Greater Reno Chamber of Commerce 1965, Int. Award 1966, Midem Int. Award 1967, Médaille de Vermeil de Paris 1970, Waldorf Astoria Award 1975, Achievement in Arts Award 1994, Grammy Hall of Fame Award 2003, Gold Badge Award 2003, Heritage Foundation Pres.'s Award 2004. *Current Management:* John Ashby, John Ashby Associates, PO Box 288, Woking, Surrey, GU22 0YN, England. *Telephone:* (14) 8379-9686. *Fax:* (14) 8379-9687. *Address:* Art-Therapie Foundation, 11 Rue de Beaumont, 1206 Geneva, (office). *Telephone:* 227890540 (office). *Fax:* 227890551 (office). *E-mail:* info@arttherapie.org (office). *Website:* www.arttherapie.org (office); www.petulaclark.net.

CLARK, Roy Linwood; American singer, songwriter and musician (guitar, banjo, mandolin); b. 15 April 1933, Meherrin, VA. *Career:* winner, National Banjo Championship, aged 16; Former professional boxer; radio broadcasts, television appearances; host of show, early 60s; actor, The Beverly Hillbillies; host, television series Swingin' Country; co-host, Hee Haw, CBS, 1969–; lead guitarist, Wanda Jackson; film appearances include: Uphill All The Way, 1986; Member, Grand Ole Opry, 1987–; later involvement in ranching, publishing, advertising, property. *Recordings include:* albums: The Lightning Fingers of Roy Clark 1962, The Tip of My Fingers 1963, Happy To Be Unhappy 1964, Guitar Spectacular 1965, Sings Lonesome Love Ballads 1966, Stringin' Along With The Blues 1966, Roy Clark 1966, Live 1967, Do You Believe This Roy Clark 1968, In The Mood 1968, Urban, Suburban 1968, Yesterday When I Was Young 1969, The Everlovin' Soul of Roy Clark 1969, The Other Side of Roy Clark 1970, I Never Picked Cotton 1970, The Magnificent Sanctuary Band 1971, The Incredible Roy Clark 1971, Roy Clark Country! 1972, Family Album 1973, Superpicker 1973, Come Live With Me 1973, Family and Friends 1974, The Entertainer 1974, Roy Clark 1974, So Much To Remember 1975, Heart To Heart 1975, In Concert 1976, Hookin' It 1977, My Music and Me 1977, Labour of Love 1978, Makin' Music 1979, Back to the Country 1980, Last Word in Jesus Is Us 1981, Turned Loose 1982, Rockin' in the Country 1986, Great Picks and New Tricks 1993, Play Hank Williams (with Joe Pass) 1994, My Favorite Hymns 1995. *Honours:* CMA Award for Instrumentalist of the Year 1977, 1978, 1980. *Address:* Julia Staines, Roy Clark Productions Inc., 3325 South Norwood, Tulsa, OK 74135, USA. *Telephone:* (918) 663-7986. *Website:* www.royclark.org.

CLARK, Terri; Canadian country music singer, songwriter and musician (guitar); b. 5 Aug. 1968, Montréal; m. 1st Ted Stevenson 1991 (divorced 1996); m. 2nd Greg Kaczor (divorced 2007). *Career:* numerous tours and TV and live performances; mem. American Fed. of Musicians, Broadcast Music Inc., Country Music Asscn, Acad. of Country Music. *Recordings include:* albums: Terri Clark 1995, Just the Same 1996, How I Feel 1998, Fearless 2000, Pain To Kill 2003, Life Goes On 2005, The Long Way Home 2009, Roots and Wings 2011. *Honours:* Billboard Music Award for Top New Female Artist 1995, Big Country Award for Best Female Vocalist 1997, Canadian Country Music Award for Top Entertainer 2001, 2002, 2003, 2004, for Female Artist of the Year 2005. *Address:* c/o Spalding Entertainment, 54 Music Square East, Suite 200, Nashville, TN 37203, USA. *E-mail:* info@terriclark.com. *Website:* www.terriclark.com.

CLARK, W. C.; American singer, songwriter and musician (guitar); b. 16 Nov. 1939, Austin, TX; one s. one d. *Career:* Toured with Joe Tex Band, 1960s; Member, Southern Feeling, with Angela Strehli, Denny Freeman; Worked on Triple Threat Revue, with Stevie Ray Vaughan, Lou Ann Barton, Mike Kindred; Support tours to B. B. King; Bobby Bland; Also performed with Albert Collins; Buddy Guy; Johnny Taylor; Lowell Fulsom; Joe Turner; Lou Rawls; Brooks Benton; Freddie King; Alvin Bishop; George Thorogood; James Brown; Matt Murphy; Jimmy Vaughan; Clarence Holliman; Carol Fran; Appeared on Austin City Limits, 1990; mem, BMI. *Compositions:* Cold Shot, co-author; Standing Here at the Crossroads. *Recordings include:* albums: Something For Everybody 1987, Heart of Gold 1994, Texas Soul 1996, Lover's Plea 1998, From Austin with Soul 2002, Deep in the Heart 2004, Were You There? 2011. *Honours:* Austin Chronicle Music Awards: Best Blues Band, Best Soul Band; Inducted into Texas Music Hall of Fame, 1990; W C Handy Award, Best Blues/Soul Album, 1997; W C Handy Award for first time cotaegory: Artist Most Deserving Wider Recognition, 1999. *Current Management:* Vicky Gay Moerbe, Crossfire Productions, 304 Braeswood Road, Austin, TX 78704, USA. *Telephone:* (512) 442-5678. *E-mail:* vicky@wcclark.com. *Website:* www.crossfireproductions.net. *E-mail:* wc@wcclark.com (home). *Website:* www.wcclark.com (home).

CLARK CHISHOLM, Jacky; American gospel singer; b. 1948, Detroit, Mich.; d. of the late Dr Mattie Moss Clark; sister of Dorinda Clark Cole, Elbernita Clark and Karen Clark Sheard; m. Glynn Chisholm; three c. *Career:* mem. Clark Sisters 1970–; solo artist 2005–; co-f. Clark Conservatory of Music, Detroit 1979; evangelist, Greater Emmanuel Institutional Church of God in Christ, Detroit; apptd Dir, Youth Choir for the Church of God in Christ, Inc. National Music Department; Spokesperson, American Diabetes Asscn; instructor for American Red Cross for ten years. *Recordings include:* albums: with Clark Sisters: Jesus Has a Lot to Give 1973, Dr Mattie Moss Clark presents The Clark Sisters 1974, Unworthy 1976, Count it All Joy 1978, New Dimensions of Christmas Carols 1978, He Gave Me Nothing to Lose (But All to Gain) 1979, Is My Living in Vain 1980, You Brought the Sunshine 1981, Sincerely 1982, Heart and Soul 1986, Conqueror 1988, Bringing it Back Home 1989, Miracle 1994, Live – One Last Time (Grammy Award for Best Traditional Gospel Album 2008) 2007, The Clark Sisters Definitive Gospel Collection 2008, A Clark Family Christmas 2009; solo: Expectancy 2005. *Honours:* Stellar Award for Most Notable Achievement 2007, Grammy Award for Best Gospel Performance 2008. *Address:* c/o The Clark Sisters Ministries, 19161 Schaefer Highway, Suite 202, Detroit, MI 48235, USA. *Telephone:* (313) 342-7496. *Fax:* (313) 342-8204. *Website:* www.theclarksisters.net.

CLARK COLE, Dorinda; American gospel singer; b. 19 Oct. 1957, Detroit, Mich.; d. of the late Dr Mattie Moss Clark; sister of Elbernita Clark, Jacky Clark Chisholm and Karen Clark Sheard; m. Greg Cole. *Career:* mem. Clark Sisters 1970–; solo artist 2002–; Pres. First Ecclesiastical Southwest Jurisdiction No. 1 of the Church of God in Christ (COGIC), Vice-Pres. COGIC Int. Music Dept; Founder and CEO Lifeline Productions; mem. and Admin. Greater Emmanuel Institutional Church of God; co-f. The Bloom Collection (with Mr Song). *Recordings include:* albums: with Clark Sisters: Jesus Has a Lot to Give 1973, Dr Mattie Moss Clark presents The Clark Sisters 1974, Unworthy 1976, Count it All Joy 1978, New Dimensions of Christmas Carols 1978, He Gave Me Nothing to Lose (But All to Gain) 1979, Is My Living in Vain 1980, You Brought the Sunshine 1981, Sincerely 1982, Heart and Soul 1986, Conqueror 1988, Bringing it Back Home 1989, Miracle 1994, Live – One Last Time (Grammy Award for Best Traditional Gospel Album 2008) 2007, The Clark Sisters Definitive Gospel Collection 2008, A Clark Family Christmas 2009; solo: Dorinda Clark Cole 2002, The Rose of Gospel 2005, Take it Back 2008, I Survived 2011. *Television includes:* Dorinda Show, Celebrate on the Road. *Radio:* Serving Up Soul. *Honours:* Hon. DTheol; Hon. DD (Mount Carmel Theological Seminary, Fresno, Calif.) 2004; Soul Train Lady of Soul Award for Best Female Gospel Artist 2002, Stellar Award for Most Notable Achievement 2007, Grammy Award for Best Gospel Performance 2008. *Address:* c/o Harvestime Ministries, 19161 Schaefer Hwy, Suite 204, Detroit, MI 48235, USA (office). *Telephone:* (866) 744-7664 (office). *E-mail:* thedorindashow@aol.com. *Website:* www.dorindaclarkcole.net; www.theclarksisters.com.

CLARK SHEARD, Karen; American gospel singer; b. 15 Nov. 1960, Detroit, Mich.; d. of the late Dr Mattie Moss Clark; sister of Dorinda Clark Cole, Elbernita Clark and Jacky Clark Chisholm; m. Rev. J. Drew Sheard; one s. one d. *Career:* mem. Clark Sisters 1970–97, 2007–; solo artist 1997–. *Recordings include:* albums: with Clark Sisters: Jesus Has a Lot to Give 1973, Dr Mattie Moss Clark presents The Clark Sisters 1974, Unworthy 1976, Count it All Joy 1978, New Dimensions of Christmas Carols 1978, He Gave Me Nothing to Lose (But All to Gain) 1979, Is My Living in Vain 1980, You Brought the Sunshine 1981, Sincerely 1982, Heart and Soul 1986, Conqueror 1988, Bringing it Back Home 1989, Miracle 1994, Live – One Last Time (Grammy Award for Best Traditional Gospel Album 2008) 2007, The Clark Sisters Definitive Gospel Collection 2008, A Clark Family Christmas 2009, The Ultimate Collection 2011; solo: Finally Karen 1997, Second Chance 2002, The Heavens Are Telling 2003, It's Not Over 2006, All in One 2010. *Plays include:* Church Girl 2011–12, For Richer Or Poorer 2012. *Honours:* Stellar Award for Most Notable Achievement 2007, Grammy Awards for Best Gospel Performance (for Blessed & Highly Favored) 2008, (for Wait on the Lord) 2010. *Address:* c/o The Clark Sisters Ministries, 19161 Schaefer Highway, Suite 202, Detroit, MI 48235, USA. *Telephone:* (313) 342-7496. *Fax:* (313) 342-8204. *Website:* www.theclarksisters.net; www.karewrecords.com.

CLARKE, Dave, (Pig City, Directional Force); British producer, remixer, sound engineer, radio presenter and DJ; b. 1968, Brighton, England. *Career:* co-founder, Magnetic North; recorded for: Bush/Deconstruction, Skint Records, XL, R&S, Strangefruit, K7, News, Icrunch, React; world-wide DJ; remixes include DJ Hel, DJ Rush, Chemical Brothers, Gary Numan, New

Order, Felix da Housecat, Mirwais, Leftfield, Death in Vegas, Adam Clayton & Larry Mullen (Mission Impossible), Underworld, Depeche Mode, Moby, Laurent Garnier, Green Velvet, Fatboy Slim, Fischerspooner; mem. PRS. *Recordings include:* albums: Archive 1 1995, Devil's Advocate 2003, Remixes and Rarities 2006; singles include: I Like John 1989, Parameter 1990, Red 1 1993, Red 2 1994, Red 3, Southside 1995, No One's Driving 1996, Shake Your Booty 1997, The Compass 2001, The Wolf 2002; compilations: Electro Boogie 1997, Electro Boogie 1998, Fuse Presents 1999, World Service 2001. *Honours:* Best Remix, Q Magazine 1997, Muzik Award, Best Essential Mix 2000, Best Int. DJ, Outsoon Magazine, Belgium/France 2001, 2002, Best Album, BBM 2001, Best Compilation, Danceclub, Portugal 2001. *Current Management:* Martje Kremers, Decked Out. *Telephone:* (20) 7400-4500. *E-mail:* martje@decked-out.co.uk. *Website:* www.daveclarke.com.

CLARKE, David Roger, BSc, MSc, FCIM; British musician (guitar, keyboards), singer, songwriter and record company owner; b. 28 Jan. 1948, Essex, England; m. 1st Patricia Clarke 1966 (deceased 2004); one s. one d.; m. Christina Clarke 2007. *Education:* piano tuition. *Career:* joined Sapphires aged 13 1961, band renamed Blue Angels 1963; with Noel Redding Band 1971–75; also worked with Tim Rose, Jimmy McCulloch, Shut Up Frank, members of The Kinks, The Animals, The Beach Boys; major US, European tours, TV appearances; joined RN, active service in Falkland Islands War, on HMS Fearless, retired as Commdr 1979–92; f. Mouse Records 1993; tours to USA, Canada, Sweden, Norway, Germany, Holland, France, New Zealand; currently mem. Kast Off Kinks with Mick Avory, John Dalton, Ian Gibbons; mem. PRS, MCPS, PPL, PAMRA, Inst. of Man. *Recordings include:* albums: as Dave Carlsen: Pale Horse 1974; with Noel Redding Band: three albums 1975–76; as Frigate: album 1981; with Jimmy McCulloch and White Line: album 1994; as Dream Machine: album 1995; as Kast off Kinks (with Mick Avory, John Dalton, John Gosling): album 2001; singles: two singles as Danny Clyve and the Blue Angels 1964; as Chester Baynes: lead vocals on hit single 1972; as producer: Hit Me With Music, by Gaylords 1974; with Noel Redding Band: two singles 1975–76; with Jimmy McCulloch and White Line: two singles 1976; as Shut Up Frank (with members of The Kinks, The Animals, Jimi Hendrix Experience): four releases 1993–97. *Website:* www.kastoffkinks .co.uk; www.mouserecords.kastoffkinks.co.uk.

CLARKE, 'Fast' Eddie; British rock musician (guitar); b. 5 Oct. 1950, Isleworth, Middlesex. *Career:* fmr mem. Continuous Performance; fmr mem. blues band, Curtis Knight; mem. heavy rock group, Motörhead 1976–82; Founder-mem. Fastway 1982–. *Recordings include:* albums: with Motörhead: Motörhead 1977, Overkill 1979, Bomber 1979, Ace of Spades 1980, No Sleep 'Til Hammersmith 1981, Iron Fist 1982, No Class 2001; with Fastway: Fastway 1983, All Fired Up 1984, Waiting For The Roar 1986, The World Waits For You 1986, Trick Or Treat 1987, On Target 1988, Bad Bad Girls 1989; solo: It Ain't Over Till It's Over 1994, Steal The Show 2010, Eat Dog Eat 2011. *E-mail:* stevegoldby@fasteddieclarke.com. *Website:* www .fasteddieclarke.com.

CLARKE, John Cooper; British performance poet; b. 25 Jan. 1949, Salford, Lancs., England; m. Evie Clarke; one d. *Career:* fmr laboratory technician, Salford Tech. Coll.; first single release for Rabid Records 1977; UK tour with band Be-Bop Deluxe 1978; backed by group Invisible Girls; numerous tours and live appearances; collaborations include Plan B, Reverend and the Makers; contributed words to Arctic Monkeys song I Wanna Be Yours 2013. *Film appearances include:* Urgh! A Music War (documentary) 1982, John Cooper Clarke – Ten Years in an Open Necked Shirt (documentary) 1982, Control 2007, Ill Manors 2012, South of the Border 2013. *Recordings:* albums: Disguise in Love 1978, Snap, Crackle & Bop 1980, Zip Style Method 1982. *Publication:* Ten Years in an Open Necked Shirt 1981. *Honours:* Dr hc (Univ. of Salford) 2013; Q Magazine Poet Laureate Award 2013. *Current Management:* c/o Edge Street Live, 44 Edge Street, Northern Quarter, Manchester, M4 1HN, England. *Telephone:* (161) 834-4312. *E-mail:* enquiries@edgestreetlive.com. *Website:* www.edgestreetlive.com; www.johncooperclarke.com.

CLARKE, Kim Annette, BA; American musician (acoustic bass, electric upright, electric bass guitar), composer and educator; b. 14 Nov. 1954, New York. *Education:* City Univ. of New York, Long Island Univ., Barry Harris Workshop. *Career:* fmr mem., Barry Harris Jazz Cultural Theatre house band; long tour collaboration with trombonist Joseph Bowie and his band, Defunkt from 1981; mem., Joe Henderson Quartet 1986–87; touring throughout Europe; tours with Nat. Black Theatre, Yusef Lateef Quartet, Teri Thornton Trio, Bertha Hope Trio, Robert Palmer, Kit McClure Big Band, Rachel Z Trio, Bigfood, Wallace Roney and Cindy Blackman Quartet, Oliver Lake and Jump Up, James Blood Ulmer Experience, Jack McDuff Quartet, Rodney Kendricks Quartet; collaborations with poets Ntozake Shange and Trazana Beverly, dancers Tina Pratt and Roxanne Butterfly, and rap artist and actress Queen Latifah; Co-founder (with Rob Scheps) MAGNETS! 1997; co-produced 'Lady Got Chops' Women's Month Jazz Festival 2003–05. *Recordings include:* with Defunkt: Defunkt 1980, Thermonuclear Sweat 1982; with MAGNETS!: MAGNETS! Live at the Earshot Jazz Festival; numerous other recordings. *Honours:* NEA Jazz Study Fellowship three times, New York State Assembly Certificate of Merit 2008, EAA Satchmo Music Award 2008. *E-mail:* k8ladybass@yahoo.com. *Website:* www.kimclarke.8m.com; www.ladygotchops .com; www.magnets.8m.net.

CLARKE, Kory; American rock singer and songwriter. *Career:* singer and lyricist of heavy rock group, Warrior Soul 1988–95; mem., Space Age Playboys, Trouble 2008–; tours and concerts, festival appearances. *Recordings include:* albums: with Warrior Soul: Last Decade, Dead Century 1990, Drugs, God and The New Republic 1991, Salutations from the Ghetto Nation 1992, Chill Pill 1993, Space Age Playboys 1994, Odds and Ends 1996, New Age Underground 1998, Live in London 1999, Destroy the War Machine 2009; solo: Opium Hotel 2003, Opium Hotel II 2011. *Website:* www.koryclarke.com.

CLARKE, Paul Frazer; British songwriter, producer and musician (keyboards, drums, guitar); b. 25 Sept. 1962. *Education:* Wyggeston Queen Elizabeth I Coll., Leicester. *Career:* recording artist, British tours 1987; with November One, London's Burning (LWT film/series) 1988; writer, Warner Chappell 1987–91; co-writes with/for Glenn Nightingale, Angie Brown, Rick Astley; numerous television appearances; Director, Fast Floor Multimedia Ltd; Writer, MCA 1996–98; Film/TV Writer 1998–; mem. PRS, MCPS. *Recordings include:* albums: Deja Vu, Magna Charta, Quest For Intelligence, Fast Floor, Purveyors of the New Groove, Earl Grey, The Eternal Dream, Fast Floor.

CLARKE, Sharon D.; British actress and singer; b. 28 May 1965, London. *Career:* played The Voice of Audrey II in The Little Shop of Horrors, London Bubble Theatre, Leicester Haymarket; The Singing Detective, Dennis Potter, BBC TV; 6 appearances, Top of the Pops, with Nomad; guest presenter DJ, Saturday Morning Mayhem; Sunset Radio, Manchester; Princess of Wales Birthright Charity Trust; lead vocalist, Royal Albert Hall; lead vocalist, Stonewall Concert, Royal Albert Hall, 1995; played opposite Chaka Khan, Mama I Want To Sing, Mama Winter, Cambridge Theatre, London; role of Rafiki, The Lion King, Lyceum Theatre 2000–02; originated role of Killer Queen, We Will Rock You, Dominion Theatre 2002–04; mem. Equity. *Plays:* The Amen Corner (Olivier Award for Best Actress in a Supporting Role) 2014. *Recordings include:* I Wanna Give You (Devotion), Nomad, Happiness, Serious Rope. *Honours:* What's On Stage Award for Best Support 2002. *Current Management:* c/o Sandra Boyce Management, 125 Dynevor Road, London, N16 0TA, England. *Telephone:* (20) 7923-0606. *Fax:* (20) 7241-2313. *Website:* www.sandraboyce.com.

CLARKE, Simon C., BA; British arranger and musician (flutes, piccolo, saxophones); b. 9 May 1955, Sheffield, South Yorkshire; m. Helen Sykes 1988. *Education:* York Univ. *Career:* tours with artists, including Pete Townshend's Deep End, The Who, The Waterboys, Eric Clapton, Africa Express; session work with Blur, The Beautiful South, China Crisis, Communards, Etienne Daho, Deacon Blue, Dodgy, Dubstar, Terence Trent D'Arby, Gabrielle, David Gray, Geri Halliwell, Groove Armada, Jamiroquai, Tom Jones, Primal Scream, Chris Rea, The Rolling Stones, The Spice Girls, Suede, Spiritualized, Rachid Taha, Pete Townshend, Rufus Wainwright; mem. Kick Horns 1983–. *Recordings include:* album: The Other Foot. *Address:* 2 Firbank Road, London SE15 2DD, England (office). *Telephone:* (20) 8693-5991 (office). *E-mail:* simon@kickhorns.com (office). *Website:* www.kickhorns.com (office).

CLARKE, Stanley, DMus; American jazz musician (bass); b. 30 June 1951, Philadelphia, Pa; s. of Marvin Clarke and Blanche Bundy; m. Sofia Clarke; two s. one d. *Education:* Philadelphia Musical Acad. *Career:* mem. various funk groups; played jazz with Horace Silver, Joe Henderson, Pharoah Sanders, Chick Corea and Return To Forever Band; partnership with George Duke; mem. S.M.V., The Stanley Clarke Band, Clarke Duke Project. *Recordings include:* albums: solo: Children of Forever 1973, Stanley Clarke 1974, Journey To Love 1975, School Days 1976, Modern Man 1978, I Wanna Play For You 1979, Rocks Pebbles and Sand 1980, Let Me Know You 1982, Time Exposure 1984, Find Out 1985, Hideaway 1986, Shieldstone 1987, If This Bass Could Only Talk 1988, East River Drive 1993, At the Movies 1995, Bass-ic Collection 1997, To the Bass 2003, Jazz in the Garden 2009, The Stanley Clarke Band (with Hiromi) (Grammy Award for Best Contemporary Jazz Album 2011) 2010; with Pharoah Sanders: Black Unity 1972; with George Duke: The Clarke/Duke Project 1981, The Clarke/Duke Project II 1983, 3 1990; with Return To Forever: Return To Forever 1972; with Aziza Mustafa Zadeh: Dance of Fire 1995; with Al DiMeola, Jean-Luc Ponty: The Rite of Strings 1996, Portrait Stanley Clarke 2000; with S.M.V.: Thunder 2009; with Chick Corea and Lenny White: Forever (Grammy Award for Best Jazz Instrumental Album 2012) 2011, The Stanley Clarke Band UP 2014, D-Stringz 2015. *Film includes:* The Transporter 2002. *Films:* The Best Man Holiday 2013. *Honours:* Miles Davis Award, Playboy Jazz Man of the Year, Bass Player Magazine's Lifetime Achievement Award. *E-mail:* management@stanleyclarke.com. *Website:* www.stanleyclarke.com.

CLARKE, Vince; British musician (keyboards, synthesizers) and songwriter; b. 3 July 1960, Basildon, Essex. *Career:* mem., No Romance In China, Depeche Mode 1980–81, Yazoo (with Alison Moyet) 1982–83, Erasure 1985–; numerous UK and Int. tours, TV appearances. *Recordings include:* albums: with Depeche Mode: Speak and Spell 1981; with Yazoo: Upstairs At Eric's 1982, You And Me Both 1983, Reconnected Live 2011; with Erasure: Wonderland 1986, The Circus 1987, The Two-Ring Circus 1987, The Innocents 1988, Wild! 1989, Chorus 1991, Pop!—The First 20 Hits 1992, I Say I Say I Say 1994, Erasure 1995, Cowboy 1997, Rain (EP) 1997, Loveboat 2000, Other People's Songs 2003, Nightbird 2005, Union Street 2006, Light at the End of the World 2007, In Your Room 2008, Innocents 2009, Erasure Club (EP) 2009, Tomorrow's World 2011, Snow Globe 2013; with Martyn Ware: The Clarke And Ware Experiment 2000, Pretentious 2000; The Mind in the Trees 1998,

Swimmer 2000, Spectrum Pursuit Vehicle 2001, Family Fantastic 2007. *Honours:* BRIT Awards for Best British Newcomer (Yazoo) 1983, Best British Group (Erasure) 1989, Ivor Novello Awards for Most Performed Work (for Blue Savannah) 1991, for Outstanding Song Collection 2009. *Address:* c/o Erasure Information Service, 1 Albion Place, London, W6 0QT, England (office). *E-mail:* info@mute.co.uk. *Website:* www.mute.com (office); www.erasureinfo.com; www.vinceclarkemusic.com.

CLARKIN, Tony; British musician (guitar) and songwriter; b. 24 Nov. 1946. *Career:* Founder-mem. and guitarist rock group Magnum 1972–; regular tours include support tours with Judas Priest, Whitesnake, Blue Oyster Cult, Def Leppard. *Recordings include:* albums: Kingdom of Madness 1978, Magnum II 1979, Marauder 1980, Chase The Dragon 1982, The Eleventh Hour 1983, On A Storyteller's Night 1985, Vigilante 1986, Wings of Heaven 1988, Goodnight LA 1990, The Spirit 1991, Rock Art 1994, Stronghold 1997, Archive 2000, On the 13th Day 2012; numerous compilation albums; singles include: Kingdom of Madness 1978, Just Like An Arrow 1985, On A Storyteller's Night 1985, Midnight 1986, Days of No Trust 1988, Start Talking Love 1988, It Must Have Been Love 1988, Rocking Chair 1990. *Address:* Annie Minion, P.O. Box 5251, Derby, DE73 1YX, England. *E-mail:* annie@magnumonline.co.uk. *Website:* www.magnumonline.co.uk.

CLARKSON, Alison Moira; British songwriter, rap artist and singer; b. 6 March 1970, London; m. Paul Toogood. *Career:* mem. rap group She-Rockers, duo Hit 'n' Run; solo artist as 'Betty Boo' from 1989–92; songwriter for artists, including Girl Thing, Louise, Tweenies 2000–; Founder-mem., WigWam 2006–. *Compositions include:* Pure and Simple (for Hear'Say, co-writer). *Recordings include:* albums: Boomania 1990, Grrr… It's Betty Boo! 1992, Doin' the Do: The Best of Betty Boo 1999. *Honours:* BRIT Award for Best British Breakthrough Act 1991, Ivor Novello Award for Best Selling Single (for Pure and Simple) 2001. *Current Management:* c/o Big Life Management, 67–69 Chalton Street, London, NW1 1HY, England. *E-mail:* reception@ biglifemanagement.com. *Website:* www.biglifemanagement.co.uk.

CLARKSON, Ian Christopher; British musician (trumpet) and singer; b. 7 May 1964, Ormskirk; m. Grazia Bevilacqua 1993. *Career:* Founder-mem. Aces of Rhythm, renamed The Emperors of Rhythm, renamed The Jive Aces 1989–; numerous television appearances; concerts include the Royal Albert Hall, Theatre Royal, Apollo Theatre, Harlem, Hollywood Palladium, Cotton Club and The Derby, Los Angeles, many European tours; 25 city tour of US swing clubs and tribute to Louis Prima guest starring trombone player James 'Little Red' Blount. *Recordings include:* albums: Our Kinda' Jive 1996, Bolt from the Blue 1997, Planet Jive 1999, Life is a Game 2004, White Cliffs of Dover 2005, Dance All Night 2005, Recipe for Rhythm 2008, King of the Swingers: A Salute To Louis Prima 2012. *Address:* The Jive Aces, Saint Hill Manor, East Grinstead, RH19 4JY, England (office). *Telephone:* (1342) 300075 (office). *E-mail:* band@jiveaces.com (office). *Website:* www.jiveaces.com.

CLARKSON, Kelly Brianne; American singer and songwriter; b. 24 April 1982, Fort Worth, Tex.; m. Brandon Blackstock 2013; one d. *Career:* winner TV competition, American Idol: The Search for a Superstar (Fox TV) 2002; solo artist 2002–. *Recordings include:* albums: Thankful 2003, Breakaway (Grammy Award for Best Pop Vocal Album 2006) 2004, My December 2007, All I Ever Wanted 2009, Stronger (Grammy Award for Best Pop Vocal Album 2013) 2011, Greatest Hits: Chapter One 2012, Wrapped in Red 2013, Piece by Piece 2015. *Films appearances:* Issues 101 2002, From Justin to Kelly 2003. *Television:* Who Do You Think You Are? (documentary series) 2010. *Honours:* American Music Award for Favorite Adult Contemporary Artist 2005, 2006, for Favorite Pop/Rock Female 2006, Grammy Award for Best Female Pop Vocal Performance (for Since U Been Gone) 2006, Acad. of Country Music Award for Single Record of the Year (with Jason Aldean for Don't You Wanna Stay) 2012, for Vocal Event of the Year (with Jason Aldean for Don't You Wanna Stay) 2012. *Current Management:* c/o Narvel Blackstock, Starstruck Entertainment, 40 Music Square West, Nashville, TN 37203, USA. *Telephone:* (615) 259-5400. *Fax:* (615) 259-5401. *Website:* www.starstruckstudios.com; www.kellyclarkson.com.

CLASTRIER, Valentin; French musician; b. 14 Feb. 1947, Nice. *Career:* guitar player with Jacques Brel 1968–69, with Ricet Barrier 1975–82; composer for Hurdy Gurdy (acoustic, electro-acoustic) 1970–; Hurdy Gurdy teacher in training course. *Recordings include:* Vielle à Roue de l'Imaginaire 1984, Esprit de la Nuit 1986, Grands Maîtres de la Vielle à Roue 1988, Hérésie 1992, Le Bûcher des Silences 1994, Palude 1995, Hurdy-Gurdy from Land of Cathars 1997. *Publications include:* Anthology For Hurdy Gurdy, 1985. *Honours:* Chevalier dans L'Ordre des Arts et des Lettres, Grand Prix de l'Académie Charles Cros, Grand Prix Audiovisuel de l'Europe. *Telephone:* 2-48-58-00-19. *Website:* www.valentinclastrier.com.

CLAUSELL, Deborah (Debbie) Deloris, BA; American/French Creole musician (guitar), songwriter, watercolour artist, author and poet; b. 16 July 1951, Mobile, Ala; d. of Stephen J. Clausell and Estelle Clausell. *Education:* Univ. of South Alabama, Mobile, Univ. of Mobile, Ala. *Career:* numerous TV appearances; mem. Mount Vernon Ladies' Asscn, Nat. Trust for Historic Preservation, US Border Control, Civil War Preservation Trust, Democratic Nat. Cttee, Republican Nat. Cttee, Air Force Asscn, Wounded Warrior Project, USO, AOPA, MLB Insiders Club. *Art:* Jesus and Mary, Mount Rushmore, Marilyn Monroe, Twin Towers, Monticello, Rain Bows, Hallelujah, Praising His Holy Light (1st Prize Ribbons). *Films:* Class Wars, Different Affair. *Compositions:* The Fewest Words I Need To Say, Major John

Pelham, Willing Willie, He Is, Father, September 11 2001 (Editor's Choice Award). *Recordings include:* Strong Feeling of Love, Success In Christ, Angels, The Happier I Am In Thee The Greater I Am, Life, September 11 2001. *Publications:* The Encyclopedia of Living Artists, Contemporary Art. *Honours:* American Order of Merit; several Fine Arts prizes, Gold Stars and Eagle Letters from Pres. George W. Bush 2006, 2007, 2008, Genius Laureate Award. *Address:* 5859 North Reams Drive, Mobile, AL 36608, USA (home). *Telephone:* (251) 341-1217 (office).

CLAUSEN, Thomas; Danish composer and musician (piano, keyboards); b. 5 Oct. 1949, Copenhagen; m. 1st Pi Sveistrup (divorced); two d.; m. 2nd Tove Bornhift (divorced 2001) 1999. *Education:* Royal Conservatory, Copenhagen. *Career:* musician for Dexter Gordon, Palle Mikkelborg, Ben Webster, Jan Garbarek; leader of own groups 1978–, including Mirror quartet; own trio, with NHOP 1980–83; trio with Mads Vinding and Alex Riel 1987–1996, with Jesper Lundgaard & Peter Danemo 2001–03, with TC Brazilian Quartet 1997–, with Thomas Fonnesbæk & Karsten Bagge; quartet with Tomas Franck, Jesper Lundgaard and Billy Hart; mem., KODA, NCB, DJFBA, Danish Arts Foundation. *Compositions include:* Prism 1975, Sonata for Oboe, Cello, Harp 1989, Woods and Lakes 1993, Danish Weather 1996. *Recordings include:* Mirror 1979, Rain 1980, The Shadow of Bill Evans 1985, She Touched Me 1988, Piano Music 1989, Café Noir 1990, Flowers and Trees 1991, Psalm 1995, Turn Out the Stars 1998, Follow the Moon 1999, Prelude to a Kiss 2001, Danske Sange 2002, My Favorite Things 2002, Balacobaco 2003, Back to Basics 2007, After the Carnival 2007, Even Closer 2009, Sol 2012, Morning…Dreaming… 2013, Blue Rain 2015. *Honours:* Radio Jazz Prize 1988, Ben Webster Prize 1989, JASA Prize 1990, Danish Grammy 1991, Fanfare Prize 1992. *Telephone:* 27-29-40-94. *E-mail:* denise@thigpen.dk. *Address:* Thomas Clausen, Stenpilstræde 5, Søsum 3670 Veksø Sj, Denmark. *Telephone:* 44-48-06-02. *E-mail:* mail@thomasclausen.com. *Website:* www .thomasclausen.com.

CLAXTON, Andrew, MMus, GRSM, ARAM, LRAM, ARCM, PGCE; British composer, instrumentalist (keyboards, low brass), teacher (piano, composition) and piano-broker; *Principal, Oxford School of Music;* b. 22 Jan. 1950, London, England; m.; three s. (one deceased). *Education:* Nat. Youth Orchestra of Great Britain, Royal Acad. of Music, London, Bretton Hall Coll., Univ. of Reading. *Career:* multi-instrumentalist, City of Oxford Orchestra 1974–2000, Dead Can Dance 1987–93, Meltdown 1997–2001; Dir Peacock Epoch 1985–92; Musical Dir, Gintare 1998–99; apptd Prin., Oxford School of Music 2002; fmr mem. Performing Right Soc., Int. Piano Teachers Group. *Film includes:* Silent Spaces 1998. *Compositions include:* Six 1996, Spires and Spirits 1997, it was…it is…it will be 2001. *Plays:* three professional pantomimes 1980–82, Elements 1988, Fall of The House of Usher 1992. *Television:* Liar 1995, The Big Sleazy 1996, Drug Raped 1998, Silent Spaces 1998, Inside Polygamy 1999, The Forbidden Journey 1999. *Recordings include:* Cobwebs and Cogwheels 2003; collaborations: Dead Can Dance albums: Within The Realm of a Dying Sun 1987, Toward The Within 1994, The Mirror Pool 1995, Dead Can Dance 1981–98 (compilation) 2001. *Publication:* Tuba Technique 1986. *Honours:* winner, Oxford Town Hall Centenary Composers Competition 1997, Finalist, Best Re-Recorded Music Category, British TV Advertising Craft Awards 1998. *Telephone:* (1865) 430409 (office). *E-mail:* principal@oxfordschoolofmusic.org.uk (office). *Website:* www.oxfordschoolofmusic.org.uk (office).

CLAYDERMAN, Richard Philippe Pages; French musician (piano) and composer; b. 28 Dec. 1953, Paris. *Education:* Paris Conservatory. *Career:* fmr bank clerk; became successful performer and recording artist; played with French pop stars including Johnny Halliday, Michel Sardou; numerous television appearances; concerts include Japan, Brazil, Australia. *Recordings include:* Albums: Ballade Pour Adeline (The Love Song) 1981, Dreaming (Traumereien) 1981, Dreaming (Traumereien) 3 1981, Richard Clayderman 1982, A Comme Amour 1982, Lettre A Ma Mere 1982, Musiques De L'Amour 1982, The Music Of Richard Clayderman 1983, A Pleyel 1983, Marriage Of Love 1984, The Music Of Love 1984, Christmas 1984, The Classic Touch (with Royal Philharmonic) 1985, Hollywood And Broadway 1986, Songs Of Love 1987, A Little Night Music 1988, Eleana 1988, The Love Songs Of Andrew Lloyd Webber 1989, Together At Last 1991, A Little Romance 1994, Romance Of… 1995, Christmas Album 1998, Con Amor 2000, Amor Latino 2000, Concerto For You 2001, Mysterious Eternity 2002, Romantic Moments 2005. *Current Management:* c/o Richard De La Font Agency, Inc, 4845 South Sheridan Road, Tulsa, OK 74145, USA. *Telephone:* (918) 665-6200. *Website:* www.delafont.com; www.clayderman.co.uk.

CLAYSON, Alan Robert Gordon, BA (Hons); British composer, writer, musician (keyboards, guitar), singer and record producer; b. 3 May 1951, Dover, Kent, England; s. of Gordon Clayson and Rosemary Clayson; m. Inese Pommers 1979; two s. one d. *Education:* Farnborough Tech. Coll., Univ. of Reading. *Career:* mem. Turnpike 1971–74, Billy and the Conquerors 1972–75, Average Joe and the Men in the Street 1974–75; viola player, Portsmouth Sinfonia 1975; mem. Clayson and The Argonauts 1975–86, 2005–; toured UK, Europe; BBC Radio in Concert show 1977; solo performer 1985–; USA debut 1992; worked with Wreckless Eric, Twinkle, Screaming Lord Sutch, Dave Berry, Dick Taylor (Rolling Stones/Pretty Things), Jim McCarty (Yardbirds/ Renaissance), Mungo Jerry; Clayson Sings Chanson presentation 2011–; mem. Performing Right Soc., PPL. *Exhibition:* Rising Sun Arts Centre, Reading 2012. *Compositions include:* Moonlight Skater (with Jim McCarty for Dave Berry, Jane Relf and Stairway's Raindreaming album), Sol Nova 1985,

The Landlocked Sailor (for Poacher's Pocket) 1992, Man of the Moment 1995, Angelette 1997, The Last Show on Earth 2002, Heedless Child 2003, Celestial City 2004, One More Day 2005, Cressida 2006, The Refugees 2007, The Old Dover Road 2008, Geronimo 2009, Martian Afternoon 2009, Long-Awaited One 2010, Lone Cloud 2012, The Local Mister Strange 2013, This Time Tomorrow 2014, Rendezvous 2015 and others. *Radio:* scripted and hosted Death Discs (BBC Radio 2) 1996. *Recordings include:* albums: with The Argonauts: What A Difference A Decade Made 1985, Sunset on a Legend (retrospective) 2005, Aetheria: Alan Clayson and the Argonauts In Concert (DVD) 2009; solo: Soirée 1997, One Dover Soul 2012. *Publications include:* Call Up The Groups! The Golden Age of British Beat 1985, Back in the High Life – A Biography of Steve Winwood 1988, Only the Lonely – The Life and Artistic Legacy of Roy Orbison 1989, The Quiet One – A Life of George Harrison 1990, Ringo Starr – Straight Man or Joker 1991, Death Discs 1992, Backbeat (with Pauline Sutcliffe) 1994, Aspects of Elvis (co-ed. with Spencer Leigh) 1994, Beat Merchants 1995, Jacques Brel 1996, Hamburg: The Cradle of British Rock 1997, Serge Gainsbourg: View from the Exterior 1998, The Troggs File: The Official Story of Rock's Wild Things (with Jacqueline Ryan) 1999, Edgard Varese 2002, The Yardbirds 2002, Brian Jones 2003, Woman: The Incredible Story of Yoko Ono (with Robb Johnson and Barb Jungr) 2004, Charlie Watts 2004, Keith Richards 2004, Mick Jagger 2005, Instant Party 2005, Led Zeppelin: The Origin Of The Species 2006, The Rolling Stones: The Origin Of The Species 2007, Beggars Banquet 2008, Jacques Brel: La Vie Boheme 2010; contrib. to Record Collector, The Guardian, The Times, The Sunday Times, Goldmine, Medieval World, The Independent, Folk Roots, Daily Telegraph, Country Music People, Mojo, The Beat Goes On, The Beat, Drummer, Gold, The 'Schoolkids' Oz, Rock 'N' Reel, Guitar & Bass, Hello, Ink, Ugly Things, Daily Mail, Vintage Rock, Discoveries, Rhythm. *Website:* www .alanclayson.com.

CLAYTON, Adam Charles; British musician (bass guitar); b. 13 March 1960, Chinnor, Oxon., England; s. of Brian Clayton and Jo Clayton. *Education:* Castle Park School, Dalkey, St Columba's, Rathfarnham, Mount Temple Comprehensive School, Dublin. *Career:* family moved to Malahide, Co. Dublin 1965; Founder-mem. Feedback 1976, renamed The Hype, finally renamed U2 1978–; numerous concerts, including Live Aid Wembley 1985, Self Aid Dublin, A Conspiracy of Hope (Amnesty International Tour) 1986, Smile Jamaica (hurricane relief fundraiser) 1988, Very Special Arts Festival, White House, Washington, DC 1988; numerous tours world-wide. *Film:* Rattle and Hum 1988. *Recordings include:* albums: Boy 1980, October 1981, War 1983, Under a Blood Red Sky 1983, The Unforgettable Fire 1984, Wide Awake In America 1985, The Joshua Tree (Grammy Award for Album of the Year, Best Rock Performance by a Duo or Group with Vocal) 1987, Rattle and Hum 1988, Achtung Baby (Grammy Award for Best Rock Performance by a Duo or Group with Vocal 1992) 1991, Zooropa (Grammy Award for Best Alternative Music Album) 1993, Passengers (film soundtrack with Brian Eno) 1995, Pop 1997, The Best Of 1980–90 1998, All That You Can't Leave Behind (Grammy Award for Best Rock Album 2001) 2000, The Best Of 1990–2000 2002, How To Dismantle An Atomic Bomb (Meteor Ireland Music Award for Best Irish Album 2006, Grammy Awards for Album of the Year, for Best Rock Album 2006) 2004, No Line on the Horizon 2009, Songs of Innocence 2014. *Honours:* 22 Grammy Awards with U2, including Album of the Year and Best Rock Performance by a Duo or Group with Vocal (for The Joshua Tree) 1987, Grammy Awards for Best Rock Performance by a Duo or Group with Vocal (for Desire) and Best Performance Video, short form (for Where the Streets Have No Name) 1988, BRIT Awards for Best Int. Act 1988–90, 1992, 1998, 2001, Best Live Act 1993, Outstanding Contribution to the British Music Industry 2001, JUNO Award 1992, World Music Award 1992, Grammy Award for Best Rock Vocal by a Duo or Group (for Achtung Baby) 1992, Grammy Award for Best Alternative Music Album (for Zooropa) 1993, Grammy Award for Best Music Video, long form (for Zoo TV Live from Sydney) 1994, Grammy Award for Song of the Year, Record of the Year, Best Rock Performance by a Duo or Group with Vocal (all for Beautiful Day) 2000, Grammy Awards for Best Pop Performance by a Duo or Group with Vocal (for Stuck In A Moment You Can't Get Out Of), for Record of the Year (for Walk On), for Best Rock Performance by a Duo or Group with Vocal (for Elevation), for Rock Album of the Year (All That You Can't Leave Behind) 2001, American Music Award for Favorite Internet Artist of the Year 2002, Ivor Novello Award for Best Song Musically and Lyrically (for Walk On) 2002, Golden Globe for Best Original Song (for The Hands That Built America, from film Gangs of New York) 2003, Grammy Awards for Best Rock Performance by a Duo or Group with Vocal, Best Rock Song, Best Short Form Music Video (all for Vertigo) 2004, TED Prize 2004, Nordoff-Robbins Silver Clef Award for lifetime achievement 2005, Q Award for Best Live Act 2005, Digital Music Award for Favourite Download Single (for Vertigo) 2005, Meteor Ireland Music Award for Best Irish Band, Best Live Performance 2006, Grammy Awards for Song of the Year, for Best Rock Performance by a Duo or Group with Vocal (both for Sometimes You Can't Make it on Your Own), for Best Rock Song (for City of Blinding Lights), for Album of the Year and Best Rock Album of the Year (both for How to Dismantle an Atomic Bomb) 2006, Golden Globe Award for Best Original Song, Motion Picture (Ordinary Love in Mandela: Long Walk to Freedom) 2014; Portuguese Order of Liberty 2005; Ambassadors of Conscience Award, Amnesty International 2006. *Current Management:* c/o Principle Management, 30–32 Sir John Rogersons Quay, Dublin 2, Ireland. *E-mail:* candida@ numb.ie. *Website:* www.u2.com.

CLAYTON, Gerald, BA; American jazz pianist; b. 11 May 1984, Utrecht, Netherlands; s. of John Clayton. *Education:* Los Angeles County High School for the Arts, Univ. of Southern California Thornton School of Music. *Career:* studied classical piano with Linda Buck; studied jazz piano and composition with Donald Vega, Kenny Barron, Billy Childs, Shelly Berg; mem. The Clayton Brothers (relocated to New York 2006; toured with Roy Hargrove Quintet 2006–07; mem. Clayton-Hamilton Jazz Orchestra; f. Gerald Clayton Trio 2008–; numerous recording credits including Ambrose Akinmusire, Terri Lyne Carrington, Robert Gambarini, Roy Hargrove, Diana Krall, Melissa Morgan, Teedra Moses, Dick Oatts & Terell Stafford Quintet, Bobby Rodriguez, Kendrick Scott, Laura Welland. *Recordings:* with Clayton Brothers: Back in the Swing of Things 2005, Brother to Brother 2008; solo: Two-Shade 2009, Bond: The Paris Sessions 2011, Life Forum 2013. *Honours:* Los Angeles Jazz Soc. Shelly Manne Award 2002. *Current Management:* Addeo Music International, 37 West 26th Street, Suite 315, New York, NY 10010, USA. *Telephone:* (212) 260-2921. *E-mail:* info@theAMIagency.com. *Website:* www.theAMIagency.com. *Address:* c/o Concord Jazz Records, Concord Music Group Inc., 100 North Crescent Drive, Beverly Hills, CA 90210, USA (office). *Telephone:* (800) 385-4253. *Website:* www2.concordmusicgroup .com; www.geraldclayton.com; www.myspace.com/geraldclayton.

CLAYTON-THOMAS, David Thomsett; Canadian singer; b. (David Henry Thomsett), 13 Sept. 1941, Surrey, England; s. of Fred Thomsett and Freda Thomsett. *Career:* fmr mem., The Shays, The Bossmen; singer, Blood Sweat and Tears 1969–72, 1975–2004; performances include: Newport Jazz Festival 1969, Atlanta Pop Festival 1969, US State Dept sponsored tour, Eastern Europe 1970, US tour 1992, Le Festival Les Heros Sont Immortals, Calais, France, two reunion concerts, New York. *Recordings include:* albums: with Blood Sweat and Tears: Blood, Sweat and Tears (five Grammy Awards) 1969, Blood, Sweat and Tears 3 1970, The Owl and the Pussycat 1970, B, S and T – 4 1971, New City 1975, More than Ever 1976, Brand New Day 1977, Nuclear Blues 1980, Found Treasures 1990, What Goes Up! 1995, You've Made Me So Very Happy (compilation) 2001; solo: David Clayton-Thomas 1972, Tequila Sunrise 1972, Harmony Junction 1974, Clayton 1977, Blue Plate Special 1997, The Christmas Album 2001, Aurora 2005, The Evergreens 2007, Soul Ballads 2010. *Publication:* Blood Sweat and Tears 2010. *Honours:* inducted into Canadian Music Hall of Fame 1996, received star on Canada's Walk Of Fame 2010. *Current Management:* c/o A440 Entertainment, 3500 de Maisonneuve West. Suite 800, Montreal, PQ H3Z 3C1, Canada. *Telephone:* (514) 738-2140. *E-mail:* info@a440entertainment.com. *Website:* www.a440entertainment .com; www.davidclaytonthomas.com.

CLEGG, Jonathan (Johnny), (Le Zoulou Blanc), OBE; South African singer, composer and anti-apartheid activist; b. 7 June 1953, Bacup, Lancs., England; one s. *Education:* Wits Univ., South Africa. *Career:* moved to South Africa 1959; mem. of duo, Johnny and Sipho (with Sipho Mchunu) 1972; f. sextet Juluka 1976–85; tours of UK, Europe and USA; leader, Savuka 1986. *Recordings include:* albums: with Juluka: World Network 9 (Duo Juluka/ Ladysmith Black Mambazo, released 1992) 1977, Universal Men 1979, African Litany 1981, Ulshule Bemvelo 1982, Scatterlings of Africa 1982, Work For All 1983, Stand Your Ground 1984, Musa Ukungilandela 1984, The International Tracks 1984, The Hope Concerts 1985, Crocodile Love/Ya Vuka Inkunzi 1997; with Savuka: Savuka 1987, Third World Child 1987, Shadow Man 1987, Freedom 1989, Cruel, Crazy Beautiful World 1989, Heat, Dust and Dreams 1993, In My African Dreams 1994, Anthology 2000; solo: Johnny Clegg Third World Child 1985, Le Rock Zoulou de Johnny Clegg & Sipho Mchunu 1988, New World Survivor 2002, Heart of the Dancer 2006, One Life 2006, Human 2010. *Honours:* Chevalier des Arts et des Lettres 1991, Order of Ikhamanga 2012; Dr hc (Univ. of the Witwatersrand) 2007, (CUNY) 2011; Hon. DHumLitt (Dartmouth Coll.) 2012; Hon. DMus (Univ. of KwaZulu-Natal) 2013. *Current Management:* c/o Roddy Quin, Salt Management, PO Box 1964, Parklands, Gauteng, Johannesburg 2121, South Africa. *Telephone:* (11) 4823550. *E-mail:* real@realsa.co.za. *Website:* www.saltmanagement.co .za; www.johnnyclegg.com.

CLEMENTINE (see Slater, Luke)

CLEVELAND, Ashley Alexander; American singer, musician (guitar) and songwriter; b. 2 Feb. 1957, Knoxville, Tenn.; m. Kenny Greenberg 1991, one s. two d. *Education:* Univ. of Tennessee, Knoxville. *Career:* featured on television series The Road; performed on televised Dove Awards 1993; mem. John Hiatt's band 1990–; appearances in clubs, theatres and festivals; mem. Nat. Acad. of Recording Arts and Sciences, GMA, CMA. *Recordings include:* albums: Big Town 1991, Bus Named Desire 1993, Lesson of Love 1995, You Are There (Grammy Award) 1998, Second Skin 2002, Men and Angels Say 2005, Before the Daylight's Shot (Grammy Award for Best Rock or Rap Gospel Album 2008) 2006. *Honours:* Nashville Area Music Award, Best Contemporary Christian Album 1995, Grammy Award, Best Contemporary Rock Album, Lesson of Love 1996. *Current Management:* c/o Street Level Artists Agency, P.O. Box 34560, North Kansas City, MO 64116, USA. *Telephone:* (877) 740-7007. *E-mail:* streetlevel@streetlevelagency.com. *Website:* www .streetlevelagency.com; www.ashleycleveland.com.

CLIFF, Jimmy; Jamaican reggae singer and composer; b. (James Chambers), 1 April 1948, St Catherine; one s. *Education:* Kingston Tech. School. *Career:* singer, songwriter 1960s–; backing vocalist, London 1963; tours world-wide; concerts include Montreux Jazz Festival 1980, World Music Festival, Jamaica 1982, Rock In Rio II, Brazil 1991, Worlds Beat Reggae Festival, Portland, USA

1992; formed own record label, Cliff Records 1989, own production co. Cliff Sounds and Films 1990. *Films include:* The Harder They Come 1972, Bongo Man 1980, Club Paradise 1986. *Compositions include:* You Can Get It If You Really Want (recorded by Desmond Dekker), Let Your Yeah Be Yeah (recorded by The Pioneers), Trapped (recorded by Bruce Springsteen). *Recordings include:* albums: Hard Road 1967, Jimmy Cliff 1969, Can't Get Enough 1969, Wonderful World 1970, Another Cycle 1971, The Harder They Come 1972, Struggling Man 1974, Follow My Mind 1975, Give Thanx 1978, I Am The Living 1980, Give The People What They Want 1981, Special 1982, The Power and The Glory 1983, Cliff Hanger 1985, Hanging Fire 1988, Images 1990, Breakout 1992, 100% Pure Reggae 1997, Shout for Freedom 1999, Humanitarian 1999, Live And In The Studio 2000, Wanted (compilation) 2000, Best of Jimmy Cliff 2001, Fantastic Plastic People 2002, Sunshine in the Music 2003, Black Magic 2005, Rebirth (Grammy Award for Best Reggae Album 2013) 2012. *Honours:* Grammy Award, Best Reggae Recording 1985, MOBO Award for contrib. to Urban Music 2002, inducted into Rock and Roll Hall of Fame 2010. *E-mail:* sunpowerproductions3@yahoo.fr. *Website:* www .jimmycliff.com.

CLIFFORD, (Brisley) Grieg; British musician (drums); b. 31 Aug. 1971, Gillingham, Kent. *Career:* drummer with Hit 'n' Run, hard rock band 1989–94; tours in Britain, Europe; member, If 6 Was 9 (three–piece rock band) 1995; many sessions, studio and live work, for many Rock/Funk bands, notably Suicide Ride; sessions by singer Mark Lehman; live sessions for Suicide Ride offshoot band, Creed; mem. Musicians' Union. *Recordings include:* with Hit 'n' Run: Hit 'n' Run 1992, Suicide Ride session recordings, 1994; with If 6 Was 9: Out of The Fire, Silent Nights, Your Heart Somebody 1995; solo: Funky Rock Drum Loops.

CLIFFORD, Michael Gordon; Australian guitarist and singer; b. 20 Nov. 1995, s. of Daryl Clifford and Karen Clifford. *Education:* Norwest Christian Coll. *Career:* mem. 5 Seconds of Summer 2011–; released debut EP Unplugged 2012; supported One Direction on worldwide tours 2013, 2014; signed to Capitol label 2013. *Recordings:* albums: 5 Seconds of Summer 2014, Sounds Good Feels Good 2015. *Honours:* Billboard Mid-Year Music Breakout Star Award 2014, Kerrang! Best Int. Newcomer Award 2014, MTV Award for Favorite Breakthrough Band 2014, MTV Europe Music Award for Best Australian Act 2014, 2015, MTV Video Music Award for Best Lyric Video 2014, for Song of Summer 2015, Teen Choice Awards for Breakout Group and Music Group 2014. *Current Management:* c/o Modest Management, Matrix Complex, 91 Peterborough Road, London, SW6 3BU, England. *E-mail:* info@ modestmanagement.com. *Website:* www.modestmanagement.com; www.5sos .com.

CLIFTON, Bill, BA, MBA; American singer, musician (guitar, autoharp) and producer; *CEO, Elf Records and Mendota Music;* b. (William August Marburg), 5 April 1931, Riderwood, Md; s. of Francis Glauber Marburg and Mary Robbins Hocking; m. Trijntje B. Labrie 1978; four s. six d. *Education:* Univ. of Virginia. *Career:* extensive work in radio late 1940s to mid 1950s; recordings 1953–; organized first all-bluegrass festival, Luray, Virginia 4 July 1961; founding dir, Newport Folk Festival; compere, weekly BBC programme, Cellar Full of Folk; Founder and CEO Elf Records 1981–, Mendota Music 1991–; Life mem. Int. Bluegrass Music Asscn; mem. Birthplace of Country Music Alliance, Int. Bluegrass Music Museum, European Bluegrass Music Asscn, Int. Bluegrass Music Hall of Fame. *Compositions:* Little White-Washed Chimney, Mary Dear, Where The Rainbow Finds Its End, Happy Days (instrumental). *Recordings include:* albums: Bill Clifton: The Early Years, Autoharp Centennial Celebration, Where The Rainbow Finds Its End, River of Memories, Around The World To Poor Valley (eight vols), Alive (with Red Rector), Playing Where the Grass is Greener (live), Grassroots to Bluegrass (video) 1999, Mountain Laurel 2005. *Publications:* Bill Clifton's 150 Old-time Folk and Gospel Songs 1955. *Honours:* Int. Bluegrass Music Asscn Award of Merit 1992, Preservation Hall of Greats, Soc. for the Preservation of Bluegrass Music of America 1993, Inductee, Int. Bluegrass Music Asscn Hall of Fame 2008. *Address:* PO Box 69, Mendota, VA 24270, USA (office). *Telephone:* (276) 669-6996 (office). *Fax:* (276) 669-0996 (office). *E-mail:* billcliftonrecords@gmail .com (office).

CLINTON, George; American singer and bandleader; b. 22 July 1941, Kannapolis, NC; one s. *Career:* Founder and leader, The Parliaments in 1950's, changed name to Funkadelic 1969, also performed and recorded as Parliament; solo artist 1982–; Owner, Bridgeport Music; regular worldwide concerts and tours; formed record label, The 2005–. *Recordings include:* albums: with The Parliaments: I Wanna Testify 1967, Osmium 1970, Up for the Down Stroke 1974, Chocolate City 1975, Clones of Dr Funkenstein 1976, Mothership Connection 1976, Funkentelechy Vs The Placebo Syndrome 1977, Get Down & Boogie 1977, Live Earth Tour 1977, Motor Booty Affair 1978, Gloryhallastoopid (Pin The Tale On The Funky) 1979, Trombipulation 1980; with Funkadelic: Funkadelic 1970, Free Your Mind... And Your Ass Will Follow 1970, Maggot Brain 1971, America Eats Its Young 1972, Cosmic Slop 1973, Standing On The Verge of Getting It On 1974, Let's Take It to the Stage 1975, Hardcore Jollies 1976, Tales of Kidd Funkadelic 1976, One Nation Under A Groove 1978, Uncle Jam Wants You 1979, The Electric Spanking of War Babies 1981; solo: Computer Games 1982, You Shouldn't Nuf Bit, Fish! 1983, Some of My Best Jokes Are Friends 1985, R&B Skeletons In The Closet 1986, Mothership Connection 1986, The Cinderella Theory 1989, Hey Man... Smell My Finger 1993, Go Fer Yer Funk 1995, P is the Funk 1995, Plush Funk 1995, Testing Positive 4 The Funk 1995, A Fifth of Funk 1995, The Awesome

Power of a Fully Operation Mothership 1996, Live & Kickin' 1997, Dope Dogs 1998, Six Degrees of P-Funk 2003, How Late Do You Have 2BB4UR Absent 2006, George Clinton and His Gangsters of Love 2008. *Honours:* Hon. DMus (Berklee Coll. of Music) 2012, Lifetime Achievement Award, Nat. Asscn for Advancement of Colored People, Vanguard Award, Oxfam America 2013. *E-mail:* unclejam@georgeclinton.com (office). *Website:* www.georgeclinton .com.

CLIVILLÉS, Robert; American DJ and producer; b. 1964, New York. *Education:* coll. *Career:* mem. of production team (with the late David Cole), C + C Music Factory 1989–95, 2010–; mem. Robi Rob's Club World 1996; mem. MVP; club DJ, performances worldwide and solo artist 1995–; collaborations with Mariah Carey, Aretha Franklin, Ultra Nate. *Recordings include:* albums: with C + C Music Factory: Gonna Make You Sweat 1990, Greatest Remixes Vol. 1, Anything Goes 1994; with Robi Rob's Club World: Robi Rob's Club World 1996; with MVP: Stagga Lee Presents MVP 2003, Hip Hop, Clubs, Girls and Life Volume 1 2006. *Website:* www.myspace.com/robertclivilles.

CLOUT, Tony; British arranger, copyist, composer and musician (bass guitar, guitar); b. 25 Feb. 1945, Danbury Palace, Chelmsford, England; m. Julia Anne Lamprell, 15 Aug. 1977, four s., two d. *Career:* guitar with Paul Raven (Gary Glitter), 1960; with The Transatlantics, 1965–69; recorded six singles; television appearances include: 5 O'Clock Club; Thank Your Lucky Stars; BBC Light Programme, Easy Beat; Saturday Club; Bank Holiday Specials with The Beatles; with The Ross Mitchell Band, 1972; with The Ray McVay Band, 1975–83; Television, radio, records, touring, society functions include Prince Charles' 30th Birthday at Buckingham Palace; Musical Director, Circus Tavern cabaret club, Essex, 1983–93; British tour with Michael Barrymore, Stutz Bear Cats, Roly Polys, 1985; Arranger, copyist, West End Shows: Blood Brothers; Only The Lonely; Good Rockin' Tonite; Provincial Shows: Harry's Web; Thank You For The Music; Shows for BBC Radio 2, artists including: Charles Augins; Warren Mitchell; Chas 'n' Dave; Marti Caine; Bobby Crush; John Inman; Marti Webb and Elaine Paige tours; mem, British Music Writers' Council; PaMRA. *Compositions:* La Concordia; Paso Doble De Cadiz; Spring's the Time, 1996. *Recordings:* Singles: Many Things From Your Window; Don't Fight It; Run For Your Life; Albums: Ray McVay dance albums; Pan Pipe Moods; Chas 'n' Dave's Street Party albums.

CLOVER, Val; British singer, songwriter, model and actress; b. (Valerie Ann Cope), 17 Sept. 1952, Liverpool, England. *Career:* mem. female trio, The Cherolees 1968; lead singer, The Wheels of Fortune 1969–70; mem. Justine 1970; solo artist 1976–, doing session and voice-over work; numerous TV, film and music videos as actress; rock/pop reviewer for Disability Times; mem. PRS, MCPS, NCB, BAC&S, Equity. *Compositions include:* as co-writer: Don't Make My White Christmas Blue, Iris Williams 1982, Oikotie Sydameen; Tahtikaaren Taa, Aikakone 1995, Children of the Sea (English lyricist, Estonian entry in Eurovision Song Contest) 1998. *Recordings include:* album: Justine 1970. *Television:* Life of Shakespeare 1978, Bust 1987, Blakes 7 1980, Doctor Who 1980, Nancy Astor 1982, BBC 2 Playhouse 1982, The Bill 1984. *Website:* www.valclover.co.uk.

CMIRAL, Elia; Czech composer; b. 1 Oct. 1950; m.; two s. *Education:* Prague Conservatory of Music. *Career:* mem. ASCAP. *Compositions include:* for tv: Rosenholm 1991, Kopplingen 1992, Macklean 1993, Nash Bridges 1996, The Rats 2002, The Reading Room 2005, Blackbeard 2006, While the Children Sleep 2006; for computer game: The Last Express 1997; for film: På liv och död 1986, Super Freak 1988, En Hundsaga 1988, Apartment Zero 1989, Sökarna 1993, Cesta Peklem 1995, Somebody is Waiting 1996, Sunsets by Candlelight 1997, Babies for Babies 1997, Visions of America 1998, Ronin 1998, The Wishing Tree 1999, The Decadent Visitor 1999, Stigmata 1999, Six Pack 2000, Battlefield Earth 2000, Bones 2001, They 2002, Son of Satan 2003, Wrong Turn 2003, Species III 2004, Iowa 2005, The Mechanik 2005, Pulse 2006, Tooth and Nail 2007, Missionary Man 2007, Splinter 2008, Forget Me Not 2009, The Killing Jar 2010, Habermann 2010, Rites of Passage 2011. *E-mail:* elia@eliacmiral.com. *Website:* www.eliacmiral.com.

COATES, Bruce Brian Gilbert, BA, MA; British musician (saxophones), writer and lecturer; *Senior Lecturer in Music, Newman University College, Birmingham;* b. 3 July 1972, Birmingham, England; s. of Andrew Coates and Elizabeth Coates; m. Claire Coates; one s. one d. *Education:* De Montfort Univ., Leicester. *Career:* performance of Burdocks by Christian Wolff (with Zo Sosinka, Christian Wolff, Dave Smith), 25th Anniversary Concert of the Scratch Orchestra, ICA 1994; formed trio, Lusus Naturae (with Jamie Smith and Zo Sosinka) 1996; Strand Leader – Music (part-time), School of Educ., Univ. of Birmingham 1999–2008, also Head of Performing and Visual Arts; trio with John Edwards and David Ryan 2001–; Co-founder Birmingham Improvisers Orchestra with Michael Hurley 2006–, commissioned by Birmingham Jazz 2007; Sr Lecturer in Music, Newman Univ. Coll., Birmingham 2008–; has also worked and recorded with a variety of improvising musicians in UK and internationally, including Lol Coxhill, Paul Dunmall, John Edwards, Jonny Marks, Tony Marsh, Tony Oxley, Simon Picard, Paul Rogers and Mark Sanders, as well as occasionally working with pop/folk group Misterlee; tour of England with John Edwards and David Ryan 2003, 2007; Jazz Services tours of England 2003, 2007, 2008; other perform-ances include Djanogly Concert Hall, Univ. of Nottingham (with Jamie Smith and Cercle) 1997, Studio des Islettes, Paris (with Peter Corser) 2003, St Cyprians Church, London (with John Edwards, Sarah Nicholls and David Ryan) 2004, Birmingham Improvisers Orchestra 2006–, The Blackberry

Project and Blackberry Orchestra, Paris 2006, The Mount Fuji Doom Jazz Corporation, Amsterdam 2007, trio with Chris Hobbs and Virginia Anderson, Groningen 2007, Sym-Bio (with Lol Coxhill, Paul Dunmall, Mike Hurley, Mark Sanders and Walt Shaw), Derby 2007, duo with Han-Earl Park, Lewis Gluckmann Gallery, Cork, Ireland 2007, tour of England with SCHH (Christopher Hobbs, Mike Hurley, Walt Shaw) 2008, Mutt with Jonny Marks and Walt Shaw, Coventry 2009, Derby 2013, BIO Migrations, Coventry 2010, Derby 2011, Disaster Box with BIO and Juxtavoices (conductor), Magna, Rotherham 2012, C-Melody Three with Dunmall, Mike Fletcher, Trevor Lines and Miles Levin, Birmingham 2013, CHA with Chris Hobbs and Virginia Anderson, Manchester 2013; A, B & C with Lee Allatson and Stewart Brackley 2014; Trio with John Edwards and Mark Sanders. *Compositions include:* Solos and Accompaniments, with Lusus Naturae, for improvisers, commission 1996, Sym-Bio, commision for Derby Jazz 2007. *Recordings include:* Sound Score/ Tape Collage for She Ain't Jumping Off That Bridge (touring physical theatre piece), Conscious Opera Association, premiered Birmingham Dance Centre 1994, Lusus Naturae-View 1999, 19 Years Later (with Paul Dunmall) 2003, Live at the Old Library (with Paul Dunmall, Phil Gibbs and Hilary Jeffrey) 2005, 'Round Teatime (with Chris Hobbs and Jamie Smith) 2005, MisterLee is not a Lifestyle Sandwich 2006, In Lubenham (with Jamie Smith) 2006, Doomjazz Future Corpses! 2007, Murmurations (with Christopher Hobbs, Mike Hurley, Walt Shaw) 2007, Paul Dunmall/Paul Rogers (Bruce Coates conductor and bells) Repercussions 2009, io 0.0.1 beta – Human Machine Improvisations (with Han-earl Park and Franziska Shroeder) 2011, Realization Trio and Quartet with Paul Dunmall/Nick Jurd and Jim Bashford recorded by the BBC 2013. *Address:* 22 Ashmore Road, Cotteridge, Birmingham, B30 2HA, England (home). *Telephone:* (121) 624-7672 (home). *E-mail:* brucecoates@googlemail.com. *Website:* www.myspace.com/brucecoates (home).

COBAIN, Garry; British musician; b. 1967, Bedford. *Career:* projects include Semi Real, Yage, Metropolis, Art Science Technology, Mental Cube, Candese, Intelligent Communication and Smart Systems; mem. Future Sound of London, The Amorphous Androgynous. *Recordings include:* albums under various guises: Lifeforms 1994, Urbmix: Flammable Liquid 1994, Far-Out Son Of Lung And The Ramblings Of A Madman 1995, ISDN 1995, Dead Cities 1996, Accelerator 1996, Tales Of Ephidrina 2001, Papua New Guinea: Translations 2002, The Isness 2002, Alice In Ultraland 2005, Teachings from the Electronic Brain 2006. *Address:* c/o Harvest/EMI, 27 Wrights Lane, London, W8 5SW, England. *E-mail:* info@fsoldigital.com. *Website:* www .fsoldigital.com.

COBBI, Daniel; French musician (piano) and jazz composer; b. 3 May 1953, Paris; one d. *Recordings include:* Music For The Blue Bar 1980, Eighteen Surprises For Christmas 1981, Ayanamsa 1982, Dilation 1985, For Camille 1995. *Honours:* First Command in France of the Culture Ministère 1982.

COBHAM, William (Billy) Emmanuel, Jr; musician (drums); b. 16 May 1944, Panama; m. Marcia Ann McCarthy; one s. one d. *Education:* High School of Music and Arts, New York. *Career:* musician with: Billy Taylor's New York Jazz Sextet 1967, Dreams, with Michael and Randy Brecker 1969, Miles Davis 1971, John McLaughlin's Mahavishnu Orchestra 1972; Founder-mem. Spectrum 1975–; currently teacher, Billy Cobham School of Drums, ArtistWorks Drum Acad.; own television series, Billy Cobham's World of Rhythm. *Recordings include:* albums: Spectrum 1973, Total Eclipse 1974, Crosswinds 1974, Shabazz 1975, A Funky Thide of Sings 1975, Life and Times 1976, Live In Europe 1976, Magic 1977, Inner Conflicts 1978, Simplicity of Expression 1978, BC 1979, The Best Of 1980, Flight Time 1982, Observatory 1982, Smokin' 1983, Warning 1985, Powerplay 1986, Picture This 1987, Best Of 1986, Stratus 1988, Billy's Best Hits 1988, By Design 1992, Rudiments – The Billy Cobham Anthology 2001, Drum 'N' Voice 2004, Art of Three, Billy Cobham Culture Mix, Billy Cobham's Culture Mix - Colours, The Art of Five, Drum 'N' Voice 2 2005; with Horace Silver: Serenade To A Soul Sister; with Miles Davis: Directions, Big Fun, Live Evil, Tribute To Jack Johnson, Circle In The Round, On The Cover; with John McLaughlin and Mahavishnu Orchestra: My Goals Beyond, The Inner Mounting Flame, Birds of Fire, Love Devotion and Surrender, Between Nothingness and Surrender, Electric Guitarist; with Ron Carter: Blues Farm, All Blues, Spanish Blue, Yellow and Green; with Asere: De Cuba y De Panama; also featured on albums by: George Benson, Stanley Clarke, McCoy Tyner, Grover Washington, Larry Coryell, Milt Jackson. *Address:* ArtistWorks Inc, 68 Coombs Street, Building C1, Napa, CA 94559, USA (office). *Telephone:* (800) 326-5596 (office). *Website:* www.billycobham.com; www.artistworksdrumacademy.com (office).

COBRIN, Spencer James; British musician (drums, piano); b. 31 Jan. 1969, Paddington, London. *Education:* private lessons, trumpet, drums, piano. *Career:* played London club circuit 1986–91; int. tours as drummer with Morrissey 1991–98; TV performances include: Tonight Show with Johnny Carson; Saturday Night Live, MTV, Tonight Show with Jay Leno, Later With Jools Holland; mem. Musicians' Union, Elva Snow. *Recordings include:* albums: with Morrissey: Your Arsenal 1992, Southpaw Grammar 1995, Maladjusted 1997; videos: Live In Dallas; Malady Lingers On (compilation). *Publications include:* Featured in: Morrissey Shot, by Linder Sterling.

COCCIANTE, Richard (Riccardo); Italian composer, singer, musician (piano) and arranger; b. Saigon, Viet Nam; m. Catherine Boutet; one s. *Career:* composer, solo artist 1972–; world-wide TV, radio appearances; tour venues include Gran Teatro La Fenice, Venice 1988, Sporting Club, Monaco 1988,

1990, 1995, Teatro dell'opera Caracalla, Rome 1991, Vina del Mar Festival, Chile 1994, Olympia, Paris 1994, 1996, Zenith, Paris 1994, Taj Mahal, Atlantic City 1995, Teatro Sistina, Rome 1988, 1993, 1995, 1997, Théâtre St Denis, Montréal 1994, 1996, Stadsschouwberg, Amsterdam 1995, Vienna Rathaus 1997; collaborated with producers, including Paul Buckmaster, Humberto Gatica, Ennio Morricone, James Newton-Howard, Vangelis; participated in album World War II, interpreting Michelle with London Symphony Orchestra; concert, Christmas In Vienna (with Plácido Domingo, Sarah Brightman and Helmut Lotti) 1997. *Compositions include:* Notre Dame de Paris (musical, Felix Award for Album of the Year, Canada) 1998–99, 2000 (Hymne pour la ville de Lyon) commissioned by Raymonde Barre, Mayor of Lyon, to celebrate the new millennium, Le Petit Prince (musical) 2007. *Recordings include:* albums: (in Italian) Mu 1972, Poesia 1973, Anima 1974, L'alba 1975, Concerto per Margherita 1976, Riccardo Cocciante: A Mano A Mano 1978, ...E Io Canto 1979, Cervo a Primavera 1981, Cocciante (Celeste Nostalgia) 1982, Sincerità 1983, Il Mare dei Papaveri 1985, La Grande Avventura 1987, Se Stiamo Insieme 1991, Eventi e Mutamenti 1993, Un Uomo Felice 1994, Innamorato 1997, Tutti I Miei Sogni 2006, Sulle Labbra E Nel Pensiero 2013; in French: Atlanti 1973, Quand un Amour 1974, Concerto pour Marguerite 1978, Je Chante 1979, Au Clair de tes Silences 1980, Vieille 1982, Sincérité 1983, L'Homme qui vole 1986, Empreinte 1993, L'Instant Présent 1995, La Compilation Italienne 1997, La Compilation Beue 2000; 10 albums in Spanish; three albums in English; film soundtracks: Roma Bene 1971, Tandem 1987, Storia di una capinera 1994, Toy Story 1996, Astérix et Obélix contre César 1999; international hit singles: Bella Senz' Anima (Italy)/ Bella Sin Alma (Spain, Latin America) 1973, Quand un Amour (France, Belgium, Canada) 1974, Margherita (Italy)/Marguerite (France, Belgium, Canada)/Margarita (Spain, Latin America) 1976–78, Coup de Soleil (France, Belgium) 1980, Cervo a Primavera (Italy)/Yo Renascere (Spain, Latin America) 1980, Sincérité (France) / Sincerità (Italy, Holland) / Sinceridad (Spain, Latin America)/ Sincerity (USA) 1983, Questione di Feeling (duet with Mina, Italy)/Question de Feeling (duet with Fabienne Thiebeault, France, Belgium, Canada)/Cuestion de Feeling (duet with Melissa, Spain, Latin America) 1985–86, Se Stiamo Insieme (Italy, Belgium, Holland, Brazil) 1991, Pour Elle (France)/Per Lei (Italy, Brazil)/I'd Fly (Italy, France, Belgium, Holland)/Por Ella (Latin America)/Voorbij (Holland) 1993–95, Il ricordo di un istante (Italy, France, Belgium, Canada, Holland), Belle, Le Temps des Cathédrales, Vivre (excerpts from musical Notre Dame de Paris, France, Belgium, Canada) 1998–99, Songs 2005, Tutti i Miei Sogni 2006, Giulietta & Romeo 2007. *Honours:* Grande Ufficiale della Repubblica Italiana (Italy) 1999; Rose d'Or Award (Greece) 1981, Rino Gaetano Award (Italy) 1982, Telegatto (Italy) 1991, Médaille de la Ville de Paris (France) 1998, Victoire de la Musique Award (France) for Song of the Year 1999, for Show of the Year 1999, World Music Award (Monaco) for Best-selling French Artist/Group 1999, Rolf Marbot Award (France) for Song of the Year 1999, Felix Awards (Canada) for Song of the Year 1999, for Show of the Year 1999, for Best-selling Album 1999, for Album of the Year 1999. *E-mail:* riccardo.cocciante@coccianteclub.it (office). *Website:* www.coccianteclub.it.

COCKBURN, Bruce, OC; Canadian singer and songwriter; b. 27 May 1945; one d. *Career:* singer, songwriter, reflecting Christian beliefs and environmental issues. *Recordings include:* albums: Bruce Cockburn 1970, High Winds White Sky 1971, Sunwheel Dance 1972, Night Vision 1973, Hand Dancing 1974, Salt, Sun and Time 1974, Joy Will Find A Way 1975, Further Adventures 1976, In The Falling Dark 1976, Circles In The Stream 1977, Dancing In The Dragon's Jaws 1979, Humans 1980, Resume 1981, Inner City Front 1981, Stealing Fire 1984, World of Wonders 1984, Trouble With Normal 1985, Rumours of Glory 1986, Waiting For A Miracle 1987, Big Circumstance 1989, Live 1990, Nothing But A Burning Light 1991, Christmas 1993, Dart to the Heart 1994, Charity of Night 1997, Breakfast In New Orleans 1999, Anything Anytime Anywhere 2002, Speechless 2005, Life Short Call Now 2006, Small Source of Comfort 2011. *Current Management:* c/o Bernie Finkelstein, The Finkelstein Management Company, 2384 Yonge Street, PO Box 1206, Toronto, ON M4P 3E5, Canada. *Telephone:* (416) 596-8696. *E-mail:* Bernie@finkelsteinmanagement.com. *Website:* www.finkelsteinmanagement .com; brucecockburn.com.

COCKER, Jarvis Branson, BA; British singer and songwriter; b. 19 Sept. 1963, Sheffield, S Yorks. *Education:* St Martin's Coll. of Art and Design. *Career:* lead singer, Pulp (fmrly named Arabacus Pulp) 1981–; dir of videos for Pulp, Aphex Twin, Tindersticks; solo artist 2006–; Artistic Dir, Meltdown Festival, Southbank Centre, London 2007. *Compositions for film:* Do You Remember the First Time? 1994, Wild Side 1995, Harry Potter and the Goblet of Fire 2005. *Recordings include:* albums: with Pulp: It 1983, Freaks 1986, Separations 1992, His 'n' Hers 1994, Different Class 1995, This is Hardcore 1998, We Love Life 2001; solo: Jarvis 2006, Further Complications 2009. *Radio:* Jarvis Cocker's Sunday Service (BBC 6Music) 2010–. *Film appearance:* Harry Potter and the Goblet of Fire 2005. *Honours:* Dr hc (Sheffield Hallam) 2009; Mercury Music Prize 1995, BRIT Award 1996. *Current Management:* Rough Trade Management, 66 Golborne Road, London, W10 5PS, England. *Telephone:* (20) 8960-9888. *Fax:* (20) 8968-6715. *Website:* www .roughtraderecords.com; www.pulponline.com; www.jarviscocker.net.

COCKRELL, Zachary Riley; American rock musician (bass guitar) and songwriter; b. 20 Feb. 1989, Athens, Ala. *Education:* East Limestone High School, Athens, Ala. *Career:* Founder-mem., The Shakes, renamed Alabama Shakes 2009–; debut EP released 2011; first major tour 2011; many live tours and festival appearances; numerous TV appearances. *Recordings:* albums: with Alabama Shakes: Boys & Girls 2012, Sound & Color (Grammy Award for Best Alternative Music Album 2016) 2015. *Honours:* Americana Music Honors and Awards Award for Emerging Artist of the Year 2012, Grammy Awards for Best Rock Performance and Best Rock Song (both for Don't Wanna Fight) 2016. *Current Management:* c/o Kevin Morris and Christine Stauder, Red Light Management, 44 Wall Street, 22nd Floor, New York, NY 10005, USA. *Telephone:* (646) 292-7400. *Fax:* (646) 292-7450. *Website:* www .redlightmanagement.com; www.alabamashakes.com (home).

CODLING, Neil John; British musician (keyboards, synthesizers); b. 5 Dec. 1973, Stratford-upon-Avon. *Career:* mem. Suede 1996–2001, 2010–; numerous tours and television appearances; festival dates in UK and Europe. *Recordings include:* albums: with Suede: Coming Up 1996, Sci-Fi Lullabies 1997, Head Music 1999, Bloodsports 2013, Night Thoughts 2016; singles: Trash 1996, Filmstar 1996, Lazy 1996, Beautiful Ones 1996, Electricity 1999, She's In Fashion 1999, Everything Will Flow 1999, Can't Get Enough 1999. *Honours:* with Suede: Q Icon Award 2013. *Current Management:* Quietus Management Limited, 13 Bramley Road, 2nd Floor Phoenix Brewery, London, W10 6SP, England. *Telephone:* (20) 3220-0310. *Website:* www .quietusmanagement.co.uk; www.suede.co.uk.

COE, Anthony (Tony) George; British jazz musician (saxophones, clarinet) and composer; b. 29 Nov. 1934. *Career:* worked with many ensembles led by musicians, including Joe Daniels, Humphrey Lyttelton, John Dankworth, Clarke-Boland Big Band, John Picard, Derek Bailey, Mike Gibbs, Stan Getz, Dizzy Gillespie, Bob Brookmeyer, Stan Tracey; leader of many groups, including Axel and Coe, Wheeler and Coe (with Kenny Wheeler); toured Europe with United Jazz and Rock Ensemble; recorded with Bob Moses and Norma Winstone; collaborated with Henry Mancini as the soloist on early Pink Panther film soundtracks 1970s; other contribs to soundtracks include Superman II, Victor Victoria; performed under Pierre Boulez and worked with Matrix (small ensemble formed by clarinettist Alan Hacker); appearances on pop and rock albums by artists, including CCS, Caravan, Spencer Davis Group, Georgie Fame, The Hollies, Joe Jackson. *Compositions include:* film scores: Mer De Chine, Camomile, Peau de Pêche; works recorded by Matrix, Danish Radio Big Band, Metropole Orchestra, Skymasters; wrote Zeitgeist (orchestral work fusing jazz and rock elements with techniques from European art music) 1975. *Recordings include:* albums: Some Other Autumn 1971, Nutty On Willisau (with Tony Oxley) 1983, Canterbury Song 1989, Les Voix d'Itxassou 1990, Les Sources Bleues 1991, Captain Coe's Famous Racearound 1996, Tournée du Chat 1996, Days of Wine and Roses 1997, Ruby 1998, Mainly Mancini 2000, British-American Blue 2000, Dreams 2001, Blue Jersey 2003, Coe Existence 2003, Love Walked In 2008. *Honours:* Hon. DMus (Univ. of Kent) 1995; Danish Jazzpar Prize, BT British Jazz Award in Clarinet 1997. *Website:* www.tonycoe.co.uk.

COFFEY, Catherine (Cath) Muthomi; British singer; b. 1965, Kenya. *Career:* mem. Stereo MCs 1990–; numerous live performances with extended band and extra vocalists; also solo artist. *Recordings include:* albums: with Stereo MCs: Supernatural 1990, Connected (BRIT Award for Best British Album 1994) 1992, Stereo MCs 1993, Deep Down and Dirty 2001, Paradise 2005, Double Bubble 2008; solo: Mind The Gap 1997. *Honours:* BRIT Award for Best British Group 1994. *Current Management:* c/o Anglo Management, Fulham Palace, Bishops Avenue, SW6 6EA, London, England. *Telephone:* (20) 7384-7373. *Fax:* (20) 7384-7375. *E-mail:* paul@anglomanagement.co.uk. *Website:* www.anglomanagement.co.uk. *E-mail:* info@stereomcs.com. *Website:* www.stereomcs.com.

COGHILL, Jon; Australian musician (drums); b. 26 Aug. 1971. *Education:* Univ. of Queensland. *Career:* joined Brisbane-based rock group Powderfinger 1992; many Australian tours/festival appearances, also world-wide tours. *Recordings include:* albums: Parables For Wooden Ears 1994, Double Allergic 1996, Internationalist 1998, Odyssey Number Five 2000, Vulture Street 2003, Dream Days at the Hotel Existence 2007, Golden Rule 2009. *Honours:* ARIA Awards: Album of the Year; Song of the Year, Best Rock Album; Best Cover Artwork 1999. *Current Management:* c/o Secret Service Artist Management, PO Box 401, Fortitude Valley, Brisbane, QLD 4006, Australia. *Telephone:* (7) 3854-1488. *Fax:* (7) 3854-0655. *E-mail:* general@secret-service.com.au. *Website:* www.secret-service.com.au; www.powderfinger.com.

COHEN, Anat; Israeli jazz musician (clarinet, saxophones) and bandleader; b. 1975, Tel-Aviv. *Education:* Jaffa Conservatory, Thelma Yelin High School for the Arts, Berklee Coll. of Music, USA. *Career:* played tenor saxophone in Israeli Air Force Band (as part of mil. service) 1993–95; relocated to USA 1996; tenor saxophonist with Alex Alvea's Mango Blue, Pablo Ablanedo, Leonardo Cioglia, Fernando Brandao during late 1990s; fmr mem. Sherrie Maricle's Diva Jazz Orchestra, New York; fmr mem. David Ostwald's Gully Low Jazz Band; Founder-mem. (with brothers Yuval and Avishai) 3 Cohens sextet 2003–; several albums as bandleader 2005–; numerous collaborators as clarinetist and tenor saxophonist including Francisco Mela, Duduka Da Fonseca's Quintet, the Jason Lindner Big Band, Waverly Seven, Aquiles Báez, Gilfema, Howard Alden, Wycliffe Gordon. *Recordings:* albums: with 3 Cohens: One 2003, Braid 2007, Family 2011; as bandleader: Place & Time 2005, Poetica 2007, Notes from the Village 2008, Clarinetwork 2010, Claroscuro 2012, Luminosa 2015; with the Choro Ensemble: Choro Ensemble 2005, Nosso Tempo 2007; with the Anzic Orchestra: Noir 2007. *Honours:* Jazz Journalists Asscn Awards for Up and Coming Artist 2007, for Clarinetist of the Year 2007,

2008, 2009, 2010, 2011, 2012, 2013, 2014, 2015, for Multi-Reeds Player of the Year 2012, 2013, 2015, ASCAP Jazz Wall of Fame Prize 2009, BNP Foundation Paul Acket Award 2013. *Current Management:* c/o International Music Network, 278 Main Street, Gloucester, MA 01930, USA. *Telephone:* (978) 283-2883. *Fax:* (978) 283-2330. *E-mail:* info@imnworld.com. *Website:* www.imnworld.com; www.anzicrecords.com (office); anatcohen.com.

COHEN, Leonard, CC, BA; Canadian singer, songwriter and poet; b. 21 Sept. 1934, Montreal; s. of Nathan B. Cohen and Masha Klinitsky; two c. *Education:* McGill Univ. *Career:* f. country-and-western band, The Buckskin Boys 1951; initially wrote poetry; moved to New York early 1960s; as a songwriter, over 2,000 renditions of his songs have been recorded; limited edition artwork first displayed to public 2005, lithograph prints have achieved widespread critical acclaim and nearly 600 limited edition prints had been sold by 2010. *Recordings include:* albums: The Songs of Leonard Cohen 1968, Songs From A Room 1969, Songs of Love and Hate 1971, Live Songs 1973, New Skin For the Old Ceremony 1974, Greatest Hits 1975, The Best of Leonard Cohen 1976, Death of a Ladies' Man 1977, Recent Songs 1979, Various Positions 1985, I'm Your Man 1988, The Future 1992, Cohen Live 1994, More Best Of 1997, Live Songs 1998, Ten New Songs 2001, Field Commander Cohen 2001, The Essential Leonard Cohen 2002, Dear Heather 2004, Old Ideas 2012, Popular Problems (Juno Award for Album of the Year 2015) 2014. *Film:* Leonard Cohen I'm Your Man 2006. *Publications include:* poetry: Let Us Compare Mythologies (McGill Literary Award) 1956, The Spice-Box of Earth 1961, Flowers for Hitler 1964, Beautiful Losers 1966, Parasites of Heaven 1966, Selected Poems 1956–1968 1968, The Energy of Slaves 1972, Death of a Ladies' Man 1978, Book of Mercy (Canadian Authors' Asscn Literary Award) 1984, Stranger Music: Selected Poems and Songs 1993, Book of Longing 2006; other: The Favourite Game (novel) (Quebec Literary Prize) 1963. *Honours:* Dr hc (Dalhousie Univ.) 1970, (McGill Univ.) 1992; Grand Officer, Nat. Order of Quebec 2008; numerous awards including William Harold Moon Award (Recording Rights Org. of Canada) 1984, Juno Hall of Fame 1991, Gov. Gen.'s Performing Arts Award 1993, Canadian Songwriters' Hall of Fame 2006, Rock and Roll Hall of Fame 2008, Grammy Award for Album of the Year on Herbie Hancock's River: the Joni Letters 2008, Grammy Lifetime Achievement Award 2010, Prince of Asturias Award 2011, Glenn Gould Prize 2011, PEN New England Excellence in Lyrics Award 2012, Prix Denise-Pelletier 2012, Juno Award for Artist of the Year 2013. *Current Management:* 9300 Wilshire Boulevard, Suite 200, Beverly Hills, CA 90212, USA.

COHEN, Lyor; American music company executive; *Founder, 300 Entertainment;* b. 3 Oct. 1959, New York. *Education:* Univ. of Miami. *Career:* financial officer, Bank Leumi; Hip-Hop Performance Promoter, Mix Club, Los Angeles; joined Rush Entertainment 1985, later Partner; Pres. and CEO Island Def Jam Records 1988–2004; Vice-Chair. and CEO US and UK Recorded Music, Warner Music Group 2004–12; founder 300 Entertainment record label 2013–. *Website:* 300ent.com.

COHEN SOLAL, Philippe; French songwriter, producer, musician, film score composer and DJ; b. 13 May 1961, Issy les Moulineaux. *Career:* musical supervisor, collaborations with film dirs; Owner Ya Basta! Records; mem. Boyz From Brazil (with Christoph H. Muller); founder-mem. Gotan Project 1999–; tours worldwide, live performances mixing videos; collaborations with many tango musicians; project $olal presents The Moonshine Sessions, recorded with Bluegrass and Country musicians in Nashville. *Recordings include:* albums: with Gotan Project: La Revancha del Tango 2001, Inspiración – Espiración (DJ set) 2004, Lunático 2006, Tango 3.0 2010; solo: $olal presents The Moonshine Sessions 2007, La Revancha en Cumbia 2011. *Honours:* BBC Radio 3 Best Newcomer Award 2003, Victoires de la Musique Best Electronic Album Award 2003, BBC Radio 3 World Music Award (Club Global) 2007. *E-mail:* park@globalnet.co.uk. *Address:* Ya Basta! Records, 4 rue Martel, 75010 Paris, France (office). *Telephone:* 1-55-33-16-00 (office). *Fax:* 1-55-33-16-01 (office). *E-mail:* info@yabastarecords.com (office). *Website:* www .gotanproject.com (office).

COKELL, Joseph; British record company executive; b. 1957. *Education:* Peckham Manor School, London. *Career:* fmr Dir in Marketing and Sales, BMG Records, Universal, Warner Brothers; fmr Man. Dir, Castle Music; CEO Sanctuary Records Group (excluding N America) 2000–04; CEO Sanctuary Recorded Music Worldwide 2004–06; Man. Dir, Pinnacle Records 2008; Dir of Business Devt, Cooking Vinyl/Essential Music and Marketing 2009–10. *Address:* 14–15 Swainson Road, London, W3 7XB, England.

COLBERT, Laurence John; British musician (drums); b. 27 June 1970, Kingston, Surrey. *Career:* mem. Ride 1988–96, 2014–, Animal House 1999; also drummer, The Jesus and Mary Chain; concerts include Royal Albert Hall, Reading Festival, Glastonbury; television includes The Word, Top of the Pops, BBC Radio 1 sessions: John Peel, Mark Goodier; mem. PRS. *Recordings include:* albums: with Ride: Nowhere 1990, Going Blank Again 1992, Carnival of Light 1994, Live Light 1995, Tarantula 1996; with Animal House: Ready To Receive 2000. *Website:* www.ridemusic.net.

COLBURN, Richard; British musician (drums, percussion); b. 25 July 1970. *Career:* mem., Belle & Sebastian 1996–; collaborations with Snow Patrol, Hefner; mem. project, The Reindeer Section 2001–; mem. project, Tired Pony 2009–. *Recordings include:* albums: with Belle & Sebastian: Tigermilk 1996, If You're Feeling Sinister 1996, The Boy With The Arab Strap 1998, Fold Your Hands Child, You Walk Like A Peasant 2000, Storytelling 2002, Dear Catastrophe Waitress 2003, The Life Pursuit 2006, Write About Love 2010,

Girls in Peacetime Want to Dance 2015; with The Reindeer Section: Y'all Get Scared Now, Ya Hear! 2001, Son Of Evil Reindeer 2002; with Tired Pony: The Place we Ran From 2010. *Honours:* BRIT Award for Best Newcomer 1999, Q Magazine Spirit of Independence 2013. *Current Management:* Banchory Management, PO Box 25074, Glasgow, G3 8TT, Scotland. *Telephone:* (141) 204-2269. *E-mail:* banchoryman@gmail.com. *Website:* www.belleandsebastian .com; www.tiredpony.com.

COLBY, Mark Steven, MusB, MusM; American musician (saxophone) and academic; b. 18 March 1949, Brooklyn, New York; m. 1st Janet McIntyre (divorced); m. 2nd Mary Deacon; one s., three d. *Education:* Univ. of Miami. *Career:* musician with: Maynard Ferguson 1975–77, Bob James 1977–83; freelance musician 1980–; has performed as soloist with Milwaukee Symphony, Miami Philharmonic; teacher of jazz saxophone, De Paul Univ., Chicago 1983–; clinic musician for Selmer and Sugal Mouthpieces 1987–. *Recordings include:* solo albums: Serpentine Fire 1978, One Good Turn 1979, Mango Tango (with Frank Caruso) 1990, Playground 1991, Reunion with Vince Maggio 1999, Heart of the City (with Frank Caruso) 2002, Tenor Reference 2004, I Didn't Have Wings 2004, Speaking of Stan: A Tribute to Stan Getz 2005, Reflections 2008, Yesterday's Gardenias. *Recordings include:* with Bill Wyman: Monkey Grip 1974, Stone Alone 1976, Destively Bonaroo, Doctor John 1974, Real Life Ain't This Way, Jay Ferguson 1979, Cat In The Hat, Bobby Caldwell 1980, Marbles, Software 1981; with Maynard Ferguson: Primal Scream, Conquistador, New Vintage; with Bob James: All Around the Town, Hands Down. *Film appearance:* Public Enemies 2009. *Address:* DePaul School of Music, 804 West Belden Avenue, Chicago, IL 60614-3296, USA (office). *Telephone:* (773) 325-4384 (office). *E-mail:* mark.colby@sbcglobal.net (office). *Website:* music.depaul.edu (office).

COLD MISSION (see Clair, Mark)

COLDWELL, Terence (Terry) Mark; British singer; b. 21 July 1974, Islington, London. *Career:* mem. East 17 1992–; numerous television and live appearances. *Recordings include:* albums: Walthamstow 1993, Steam 1994, Up All Night 1996, Around the World – The Journey So Far 1996, Resurrection 1998; singles: House of Love 1992, Deep 1993, West End Girls 1993, It's Alright 1993, Around The World 1994, Steam 1994, Stay Another Day 1994, Let It Rain 1995, Thunder 1995, Do U Still 1996, If You Ever (with Gabrielle) 1996, Hey Child 1997, Each Time 1998, Betcha Can't Wait 1999, Dark Light 2012. *Current Management:* c/o Mission Control Artists Agency, 50 City Business Centre, Lower Road, Rotherhithe, London, SE16 2XB, England. *Telephone:* (20) 7252-3001. *E-mail:* agents@missioncontrol.net. *Website:* www.missioncontrol.org; www.east17official.com.

COLE, Brian John (B. J.); British musician (pedal steel guitar) and producer; b. 17 June 1946, London. *Career:* musician, country music circuit, London 1964–; Founder-mem., pedal steel guitar player, Cochise; f. Cow Pie Records; Founder-mem., producer, Hank Wangford Band; session musician and solo artist; leader of own group Transparent Music Ensemble; replacement guitarist for the Verve 1998–99. *Recordings include:* albums: solo: New Hovering Dog 1973, Transparent Music 1989, The Heart of The Moment 1995, Into the Blue, Stop The Panic (with Luke Vibert) 2000, Trouble in Paradise 2004, Into the Blue (with Emily Burridge); as session musician: Tiny Dancer, Elton John 1970, Wide Eyed and Legless, Andy Fairweather-Low 1975, No Regrets, Walker Brothers 1976, City To City, Gerry Rafferty 1978, Everything Must Change, Paul Young 1984, Silver Moon, David Sylvian 1986, Diet of Strange Places, k d lang 1987, Montagne D'Or, The Orb 1995, Possibly Maybe, Björk 1995; with Hank Wangford: Hank Wangford 1980, Live 1982; other recordings with: Kiki Dee, Steve Marriott, Johnny Nash, Deacon Blue, Level 42, Danny Thompson, Alan Parsons Project, Shakin' Stevens, Beautiful South, John Cale, Echobelly, Dot Allison, Richard Ashcroft, Pet Shop Boys, Eliza Carthy, REM, David McAlmont, Robbie Williams, Spiritualized. *Current Management:* Mark Vernon, Firebrand Management, Chester House, Fulham Green, 81–83 Fulham High Street, London, SW6 3JA, England. *E-mail:* bj@ bjcole.co.uk. *Website:* www.bjcole.co.uk.

COLE, Gardner; American singer, musician (keyboards, drums, guitar), songwriter and producer; b. 7 Feb. 1962, Flint, Mich. *Education:* Berklee Coll. of Music. *Career:* drummer with ABC; keyboard player with A-Ha on Grammy Awards; toured as opening act for Toni Tony Tone 1991; mem. American Fed. of TV and Radio Artists, Screen Actors Guild. *Compositions include:* 60 songs recorded by various artists including Amy Grant, Al Jarreau, Tom Jones, Chaka Khan, Madonna, Michael McDonald, Brenda Russell, Vonda Shepard, 3T, Jody Watley, Jane Wiedlin, Ofra Haza, Tiffany, Howard Hewitt, Stephen Dante, Bill Chaplin, Nick Kamen, Nile Rodgers, Tamia Akado, Byron Lee, Donna Delory, Peter Murphy. *Recordings include:* two solo albums 1988, 1991. *Honours:* BMI Million-Air Award, three BMI Pop Awards, one Juno Award, Sixty- three Platinum Album Awards, Six Platinum Video Awards. *E-mail:* gcole@gardnercole.com. *Website:* www.gardnercole.com.

COLE, Holly; Canadian singer; b. 25 Nov. 1963, Halifax, Nova Scotia. *Education:* studied classical piano as a child. *Career:* sang in a big band in early 1980's; formed own trio (with David Piltch and Aaron Davis) 1985; regularly tours Canada, USA, Japan and Europe. *Recordings include:* Girl Talk 1990, Blame It On My Youth 1991, Don't Smoke In Bed 1993, Temptation 1995, It Happened One Night 1996, Dark Dear Heart 1997, Romantically Helpless 2000, Baby It's Cold Outside 2001, Shade 2003, Holly Cole 2007, Steal The Night: Live at the Glenn Gould Studio 2012, Night 2012. *Current Management:* c/o W. Tom Berry, Alert Music Inc., 51 Hillsview Avenue,

Toronto, ON M6P 1J4, Canada. *E-mail:* tom@alertmusic.com. *Website:* www .alertmusic.com; www.hollycole.com.

COLE, Jermaine Lamarr, (J. Cole); American rapper, songwriter and record producer; b. 28 Jan. 1985, Frankfurt, Germany. *Education:* Terry Sanford High School, Fayetteville, NC, St John's Univ. *Career:* raised in Fayetteville, NC, USA; mem., Bomm Sheltuh 2000–01; teenage rapper, as Therapist 2002; solo career, as J. Cole 2007–; collaborators include Jay Z, Wale, Mos Def, Hi-Tek, B.o.B, Miguel, DJ Khaled, Kendrick Lamar, Missy Elliott, TLC, Young Chris; support act to Drake and Tinie Tempah on UK tours 2011; support act to Rihanna on int. tour 2011. *Recordings:* mixtapes: The Come Up 2007, The Warm Up 2009, Friday Night Lights (BET Hip Hop Award for Best Mixtape 2011) 2010; albums: Cole World: The Sideline Story 2011, Born Sinner 2013, 2014 Forest Hills Drive (BET Hip Hop Award for Album of the Year 2015, Billboard Music Award for Top Rap Album 2015) 2014. *Honours:* BET Hip Hop Awards for Impact Track (for Crooked Smile, featuring TLC) 2013, for Best Live Performer 2015. *Current Management:* c/o Julius Garcia or Wayne Barrow, ByStorm Entertainment, 550 Madison Avenue, 10th Floor, New York, NY 10022, USA. *Telephone:* (646) 450-4042. *Website:* www.bystorm-ent.com; www.jcolemusic.com (home).

COLE, Lionel Frederick (Freddy), BMus, MMus; American musician (piano), singer and composer; b. 5 Oct. 1931, Chicago, Ill.; s. of Edward Cole and Paulina Nancy Cole; younger brother of Nat 'King' Cole; m. Margaret Cole. *Education:* Roosevelt Inst., Chicago, Juilliard School of Music, New York, New England Conservatory. *Career:* recording artist performing with numerous jazz musicians 1952–; int. festivals, hotels, resorts, nightclubs, performing arts centres and others in USA (including Lincoln Center, Kennedy Center), Japan, Asia, Europe, South Africa. *Film:* The Cole Nobody Knows 2002. *Recordings include:* albums: I'm Not My Brother, I'm Me 1990, A Circle of Love 1993, I Want a Smile for Christmas 1994, Always 1995, I'm Crazy but I'm in Love 1997, To the Ends of the Earth 1997, Love Makes the Changes 1998, Le Grand Freddy Sings The Music of Michel Legrand 2000, This is the Life 2000, Merry Go Round 2000, Rio de Janeiro Blue 2001, In the Name of Love 2002, This Love of Mine 2005, Because of You 2006, Music Maestro Please 2007, The Dreamer in Me 2009, Freddy Cole Sings Mr B 2010, Talk to Me 2011, This and That 2013; contrib. to All My Tomorrows, Grover Washington Jr 1994. *Honours:* Hon. DMus (New England Conservatory) 2012. *Current Management:* 2055 Center Ave PHA, Fort Lee, NJ 07024, USA. *Telephone:* (201) 947-0961. *Fax:* (201) 947-0962. *E-mail:* suzi@suzireynolds .com. *Website:* www.freddycole.com.

COLE, Lloyd; British singer and songwriter; b. 31 Jan. 1961, Buxton, Derbyshire. *Career:* leader, Lloyd Cole and The Commotions 1984–88; solo artist 1989–. *Recordings include:* albums: with the Commotions: Rattlesnakes 1984, Easy Pieces 1985, Mainstream 1987; solo: Lloyd Cole 1989, Don't Get Weird On Me Babe 1991, Bad Vibes 1993, Love Story 1995, Antidepressant 2006, Broken Record 2010. *Current Management:* c/o Deb Bernadini, Tony Margherita Management, 116 Pleasant Street, Easthampton, MA 01027, USA. *Telephone:* (413) 529-2830. *E-mail:* deb@dbmpr.com; info@tmmchi.com. *Website:* tmmchi.com. *E-mail:* lloydweblog@gmail.com. *Website:* www .lloydcole.com.

COLE, M. J.; British producer, musician (keyboards) and remixer; b. (Matthew James Colman), 24 Sept. 1973, London. *Education:* Royal Coll. of Music. *Career:* competitor in BBC Young Musician of the Year; became engineer at SOUR studios in London; set up Prolific Records 1998; collaborations with Elisabeth Troy, Jason Kaye; remixed: Incognito, Jill Scott, Nitin Sawhney, Masters At Work. *Recordings include:* albums: Sincere 2000, Back To Mine (compilation) 2002, Cut to the Chase 2003; singles: Sincere 1998, Crazy Love 2000, Hold On To Me 2000. *Address:* Prolific Recordings, Flat 19, 1-10 Summers Street, London, EC1R 5BD, England (office). *Website:* www.prolificrecordings.com (office).

COLE, Pamela, BA; Canadian musician (bass guitar, acoustic guitar); b. 1 Jan. 1959, Edmonton, Alberta; one s. one d. *Career:* mem. of country band, Quickdraw; numerous live and TV performances; mem. Soc. of Composers, Authors and Music Publrs of Canada, American Soc. of Composers, Authors and Publrs, ARIA, NCMO 1994. *Recordings include:* Change of Heart, Just A Guess, Winning Was The Only Thing, Weekend Cowboy, Next To Nothing, An Angel Told Me So. *Honours:* Alberta Music Project Award 1992, winner, 960 CFAC Country Showdown, with band Headin' West.

COLE, Paula; American singer and songwriter; b. 1970. *Education:* Berklee College of Music. *Career:* singer, Peter Gabriel's Secret World Tour, 1993–94; solo artist 1996–. *Recordings:* albums: Harbinger 1994, This Fire 1996, Amen 1999; This Fire 1997, Amen 1999, Courage 2007, Ithaca 2010. *Current Management:* The Colomby Group, 2110 Main Street, Suite 302, Santa Monica, CA 90405, USA. *Telephone:* (310) 399-8881. *Fax:* (310) 392-1323. *E-mail:* info@thecolombygroup.com. *Website:* www.thecolombygroup.com. *E-mail:* thelessonsinlife@aol.com. *Website:* www.paulacole.com.

COLEMAN, George Edward; American musician (saxophones); b. 8 March 1935, Memphis, TN; m. 1st Gloria Bell 1959 (divorced); one s. one d.; m. 2nd Carol Hollister 1985. *Education:* private music lessons. *Career:* played with B. B. King Blues Band 1952–53, Max Roach Quintet 1958–59, Miles Davis Quintet 1963–64, Lionel Hampton 1965–66, Lee Morgan Quintet 1969, Elvin Jones Quartet 1970, George Coleman Quartet and Octet 1971–; NYU 1984; New School 1987; LI Univ. 1987; Consultant, Lenox Jazz School, MA 1988.

Film: The Preacher's Wife 1996. *Compositions:* 5/4 Thing, You Mean So Much To Me, Blondies Waltz, Amsterdam After Dark, Music in Free Jack. *Recordings:* albums: Revival 1976, Playing Changes 1988, Manhattan Panorama 1989, My Horns of Plenty 1991, Live At Yoshi's 1992, I Could Write a Book: The Music of Richard Rodgers 1998, Danger High Voltage 2000; with Miles Davis: My Funny Valentine 1965; with Cedar Walton: Eastern Rebellion 1976; Duo, with Tete Montelui: Meditation 1977. *Honours:* Int. Jazz Critics Poll 1958, Record World Magazine Artist of the Year 1969, Knight of Mark Twain 1972, Beale Street Asscn AWD Contribution to Music 1977, Tip of the Derby Awards 1978, 1979, Jazz Audience Award 1979, Good Note Jazz Award 1985, Key to City of Memphis 1991, NEA grants 1975, 1985, Jazz Foundation of America Lifetime Achievement Award 1996, Concertgebouw Jazz Award 2002. *Current Management:* Maurice Montoya Music Agency, 1133 Broadway, Suite #1605, New York, NY 10010, USA. *Telephone:* (212) 229-9160. *Fax:* (212) 229-9168. *E-mail:* mauricemontoya@earthlink.net. *Website:* georgecoleman .com.

COLEMAN, Jeremy (Jaz); New Zealand (b. British) singer, musician (keyboards) and composer; b. 26 Feb. 1960, Cheltenham, Gloucestershire, England. *Career:* Founder-mem. rock band, Killing Joke 1978–; numerous tours worldwide, TV and radio broadcasts; Composer-in-Residence, Auckland Philharmonia Orchestra 1992; arranged Nigel Kennedy's Riders On The Storm, The Doors Concerto 2000; fmr Composer-in-Residence, Prague Symphony Orchestra; Producer, East Meets East 2003; collaboration with Hinewehi Mohu on Oceania 2000; formed record label, Malicious Damage. *Compositions include:* one symphony. *Recordings include:* albums: with Killing Joke: Killing Joke 1980, What's This For? 1981, Revelations 1982, Fire Dances 1983, Night Time 1985, Brighter Than A Thousand Suns 1986, Extremities, Dirt and Various Repressed Emotions 1990, Pandemonium 1994, Democracy 1996, The Unperverted Pantomime 2003, Killing Joke 2003, XYV Gathering: Let Us Prey 2005, Hosannas from the Basements of Hell 2006, Absolute Dissent 2010, MMXII 2012; solo: Outside the Gate (with Anne Dudley) 1988, Songs from the Victorious City 1998. *Current Management:* c/o Christian Bernhardt, The Agency Group Limited, 142 West 57th Street, Sixth Floor, New York, NY 10019, USA. *Telephone:* (212) 581-3100. *Fax:* (212) 581-0015. *E-mail:* ChristianBernhardt@theagencygroup.com. *Website:* www .theagencygroup.com. *Address:* c/o Malicious Damage, 41 Charteris Road, London, NW6 7EY, England. *E-mail:* info@maliciousdamage.co.uk. *Website:* www.maliciousdamage.biz; www.killingjoke.com.

COLEMAN, Lisa Annette; American musician (piano, keyboards), composer, producer and songwriter; b. 17 Aug. 1960, Los Angeles, Calif. *Career:* keyboard player in Prince's band 1980, toured and recorded extensively, featured in film Purple Rain; formed duo, Wendy and Lisa (with Wendy Melvoin); numerous TV appearances in Europe and the USA; collaborations include Seal, Joni Mitchell, kd lang, MeShell NdegeOcello, Victoria Williams, Neil Finn. *Recordings include:* albums: Wendy and Lisa 1987, Fruit At The Bottom 1988, Eroica 1990, Re-Mix-in-a-Carnation 1991, Are You My Baby 1996, Girl Bros 1998, Always in My Dreams 2000, White Flags of Winter Chimneys 2008, Snapshots 2011. *Television includes:* Nurse Jackie (Emmy Award for Outstanding Original Main Title 2010) 2010. *Website:* www .thelisacoleman.com; www.wendyandlisa.com.

COLEMAN, Steven Douglas (Steve); American musician (alto saxophone), composer, producer and computer programmer; *President, M-Base Concepts;* b. 20 Sept. 1956, Chicago, IL; s. of Earl and Wilma Coleman; m. Ana Patricia Magalhaes Santos. *Education:* Wesleyan Univ., Bloomington, Chicago Music Coll. *Career:* moved to New York 1978; toured and recorded with numerous artists; formed Steve Coleman and Five Elements 1981–, Steve Coleman and Metrics 1993–, Steve Coleman and The Mystic Rhythm Society 1994–, Steve Coleman and The Council of Balance 1997–; founder mem., M-Base collective; faculty mem., Banff School of Fine Arts 1985–89, Artistic Head 1990–91; faculty mem., Stanford Jazz Workshop 1995–96; Assoc. Prof., Univ. of California at Berkeley 2000–02; Pres., record cos, Time Lord Records, C & M Music Productions Inc., and music publishers, M-Base Concepts, Goemon Publishing Co. *Film:* Elements of One 2004. *Commissions:* Rameses Interactive Computer Music Program (Ircam) for L'Institut de Recherche et de Coordination Acoustique/Musique 1999, Chicago World Music Festival commission for Field Museum & Jazz Institute of Chicago 2000, American Composers Orchestra commission 2007. *Recordings include:* albums: Motherland Pulse 1985, Rhythm In Mind 1992, Invisible Paths: First Scattering 2007; with Five Elements: On The Edge Of Tomorrow 1986, World Expansion 1987, Sine Die 1988, Rhythm People 1990, Black Science 1991, Drop Kick 1992, The Tao of Mad Phat 1993, Def Trance Beat 1994, Curves Of Life 1995, The Opening Of The Way 1998, The Sonic Language Of Myth 1999, The Ascension To Light 2000, Resistance Is Futile 2002, Alternate Dimensions Series I 2002, On The Rising Of The 64 Paths 2003, Lucidarium 2004, Weaving Symbolics 2006, Harvesting Semblances and Affinities 2010; with Metrics: A Tale of 3 Cities 1994, The Way Of The Cipher 1995; with The Mystic Rhythm Society: Myths, Modes and Means 1995, The Sign And The Seal 1996; with The Council of Balance: Genesis 1998. *Honours:* NEA grant for composition 1995, Lila Wallace-Reader's Digest Fund 1996, Arts International grant for research/concert in Senegal 1997, CalArts/Alpert Award in the Arts 2000. *Current Management:* Sooya Arts, PO Box 87, Tappan, NY 10983-0087, USA. *Telephone:* (646) 233-1370 (office). *Fax:* (646) 698-4822 (office). *E-mail:* management@sooyaarts.com (office). *Website:* www.sooyaarts.com (office). *Address:* M-Base Concepts, PO Box 114, Allentown, PA 18105-0114, USA

(office). *Telephone:* (212) 602-4386 (office). *E-mail:* info1@m-base.com (office). *Website:* www.m-base.com (office).

COLINET, Paul Marie Marcel; composer (classical and folk music) and musician (violin, viola d'amore, viola, cello, mandolin, sarangi, lyra, diatonic accordion); b. 27 Jan. 1954, Elisabethville, Belgian Congo; m. Segers Yvonna 1982. *Career:* fmr piano tuner; composer of orchestra, viola and chamber music; mem. Société d'Auteurs Belge–Belgische Auteurs Maatschappij (SABAM). *Compositions include:* two mandolin concertos, one viola concerto, four suites, for mandolin solo, 48 diatonic dances for diatonic accordion, chamber music and some compositions for folk instruments, including bagpipes, hurdy-gurdy and lyra. *Publications include:* 37 own editions of own compositions. *Honours:* First Prize, Instrument Building, Viola d'amore 1995. *Address:* Blvd E Bockstael 294, 1020 Brussels, Belgium.

COLLAZO, Steven André; American recording engineer, arranger, composer, artist and producer and musician (keyboards); *Proprietor, Dumb Yank Productions;* b. 24 Jan. 1960, Brooklyn, NY; s. of Inocencio Collazo and Lillian Arnille Lopez. *Career:* formed nine-piece band in high school; performed throughout USA and recorded around NYC; now based in Basingstoke, England, performing solo and with well-known 70s/80s groups; proprietor, Dumb Yank Productions (music production and recording studio), Salisbury; currently Man. Dir, lead vocalist and Musical Dir of 70s/80s recording group Odyssey. *Publications:* Sound on Sound 1997. *Address:* 75 Winterthur Way, Victory Hill, Basingstoke, Hampshire RG21 7UB, England (office). *Telephone:* (1256) 330345 (office). *E-mail:* steven.collazo@dumbyank.co.uk (home). *Website:* www.stevencollazo.co.uk.

COLLEN, Philip (Phil) Kenneth; British rock musician (guitar) and singer; b. 8 Dec. 1957, London; m. 1st Jacqueline (divorced); m. 2nd Anita (divorced 2010); two c.; m. 3rd Helen L. Simmons 2010. *Career:* fmr mem. Dumb Blondes, Lucy, Tush; mem. Girl 1979–82; mem. Def Leppard 1982–; numerous concerts and tours worldwide, festival appearances. *Recordings include:* albums: with Girl: Sheer Greed 1980, Wasted Youth 1982, Live At The Marquee 2001; with Def Leppard: Pyromania 1983, Hysteria 1987, Adrenalize 1992, Retro Active 1993, Vault 1980–95 1995, Slang 1996, Euphoria 1999, X 2002, Yeah 2006, Songs from the Sparkle Lounge 2008, Mirrorball: Live And More 2011, Def Leppard 2015. *Television include:* Behind the Music (documentary series, VH1) 1998, Storytellers (documentary, VH1), Hysteria: The Def Leppard Story (documentary, VH1), Ultimate Albums (documentary, VH1). *Honours:* American Music Awards for Favorite Heavy Metal Album, for Favorite Heavy Metal Artist 1989. *Current Management:* c/o Primary Wave Music, 116 East 16th Street, 9th Floor, New York, NY 10003, USA. *E-mail:* info@primarywave.com. *Website:* www.defleppard.com; www.philcollenpc1 .com.

COLLIE, (John Maxwell) Max; Australian musician (trombone); b. 21 Feb. 1931, Melbourne; m. (divorced); four s. one d. *Career:* band leader, Melbourne Max Collie Jazz Bandits 1948, Max Collie Jazz Kings 1952; moved to England; mem. Melbourne New Orleans Jazz Band 1962, London City Stompers 1963; Founder, Max Collie Rhythm Aces 1966; played at festivals, concerts and theatres in UK, Ireland, Germany, France, Spain, Denmark, Belgium, Holland, Switzerland, Austria, Norway, Sweden, Poland, Yugoslavia, USA, Canada, Finland, Japan; several radio and television appearances; mem. Musicians' Union, MCPS, PRS, PPL. *Recordings include:* Battle of Trafalgar 1973, World Champions of Jazz 1976, New Orleans Mardi Gras 1984, Latest and Greatest 1993, On Tour in the USA, Live in Stuttgart 1998, Hot Jazz Celebration 2001, Live Storckshof-Dortmund 2004. *Honours:* winner World Championship of Jazz 1975. *Address:* Max Collie Rhythm Aces, 26 Wendover Road, Bromley, BR2 9JX, England. *Telephone:* (20) 8460-1139. *Fax:* (20) 8466-7005. *E-mail:* amber_collie@hotmail.com. *Website:* www.maxcollie.co.uk.

COLLIER, Pat; British record producer; b. 20 Oct. 1951, London; m. Jill Collier; one s. two d. *Career:* mem. The Wonder Stuff, Kingmaker, The Soft Boys, The Vibrators, New Model Army. *Recordings include:* albums: with The Wonder Stuff: Hup! 1989, Construction for the Modern Idiot 1993; with Kingmaker: Sleepwalking 1993, Bloodshot and Fancy Free: The Best of and The Rest of Kingmaker 1997; with Morcheeba: Head up High 2013; with Carly Rae Jepsen: Kiss 2012; with The Lucy Show: Remembrances 2012; with New Model Army: No Rest for the Wicked 1985, Impurity 1990, Lost Songs 2002, Great Expectations 2003, Anthology 2011; with The Method Actors: Rhythms of You 1981, This Is Still It 2010; with Miles Hunt: 5 Songs 2000, Not an Exit 2007, Catching More Than We Miss 2009; with The Vibrators: Pure Mania 1977, Batteries Included 1980, Alaska 127 1984, We Vibrate: The Best of the Vibrators 1997, Public Enemy Number 1 1999, The BBC Punk Sessions 2000; with The House of Love: The House of Love 1988, Best of The House of Love 1998, Days Run Away 2005; with The Soft Boys: Underwater Moonlight 1980, Side Three 2002, Nextdoorland 2002.

COLLIER, Tom, BA, MusB; American musician (drums, vibraphone), bandleader and academic; *Director of Percussion Studies, University of Washington;* b. 30 June 1948, Puyallup, Wash.; m. Cheryl Zilbert 1970; two d. *Education:* Univ. of Washington. *Career:* jazz vibraphonist, duo Collier and Dean 1966–; mem. Northwest Jazz Quintet 1972–80; timpanist, Northwest Chamber Orchestra 1972–73, Los Angeles Repertoire Orchestra 1976; vibraphonist, Los Angeles Contempo Four 1975–77; freelance musician for various artists (1975–90) including Bud Shank, Barbra Streisand, Ry Cooder, Sammy Davis Jr, Olivia Newton-John, Natalie Cole, Johnny Mathis, Diane Schuur, Earl Hines, The Beach Boys, Jermaine Jackson; Lecturer Univ. of

Washington 1980–2000, then Prof., later Dir of Percussion Studies; mem. American Soc. of Composers, Authors and Publishers, Percussive Arts Soc. *Recordings include:* with Barry Zweig: Desert Vision 1978; with The Northwest Jazz Quintet: Journey Without Maps 1979; with Howard Roberts: Turning to Spring 1981, Illusion 1988, Pacific Aire 1990, Tin Pan Vibes 1995, Mallet Jazz 2004; with Collier and Dean: Whistling Midgets 1981, Duets 2005, Gary Herbig Montana Shooting Star 2005, Desert Vision, Mallet Fantastique 2010, Tom Collier Plays Haydn, Mozart, Telemann, and Others 2012, Sleek Buick 2014, Tom Collier: Alone In The Studio 2015. *Publication:* Jazz Improvistion and Ear Training 1983, History Of Jazz Lecture Notes and Listening Examples 2013. *Honours:* Adelaide D. Currie Cole Endowed Professorship in the UW School Of Music 2011–13; Univ. Of Washington Educational Outreach Award for Teaching Service 2000, Univ. Of Washington Royalty Research Fund Grant 2014; Outstanding Service Award, National Asscn of Jazz Educators 1980. *Address:* School of Music, University of Washington, PO Box 353450, Seattle, WA 98195-3450, USA (office). *Telephone:* (206) 420-7671 (office). *E-mail:* tomcollier@tomcolliervibes.com; mallets@u.washington.edu. *Website:* www.tomcolliervibes.com; www.music .washington.edu.

COLLIGNON, Médéric; French jazz and blues musician (trumpet, bugle) and singer; b. 6 July 1970, Villers-Semeuse, Ardennes. *Education:* Conservatoire de Charleville-Mézières, Centre musical et créatif de Nancy. *Career:* started playing trumpet 1977; moved to Paris 1997; joined the 'Chief Inspector' music collective, playing in groups Collectif Slang, Lunfardo, Camisetas. *Recordings include:* albums: Slanguistic 2003, Lunfardo 2005, Addict 2006, Camisetas 2007, Shangri-Tunkashi-La 2010. *Honours:* Django Reinhardt Prize, Académie du Jazz 2009.

COLLING, Jonathon; British programmer, engineer and record producer; b. 28 May 1968. *Career:* record producer, Rumour Records/X-Clusive; all types of dance music, including: house, Euro, jungle; also jingles for radio/television and radio idents for BBC and local radio; mem. Musicians' Union, PRS. *Recordings include:* Rhythm Nation 1993, Inner State 1993, Prohibition Groove 1994, Music Is My Life; remixes for X-clusive Records, under name of Proof.

COLLINS, William (Bootsy); American musician (bass); *President, Bootzilla Productions Inc.*; b. 26 Oct. 1951, Cincinnati, OH. *Career:* mem. James Brown's backing group, The JBs 1969–71; mem. George Clinton's Parliament/Funkadelic 1972–; also leader of own groups, Bootsy's Rubber Band, Bootzilla Orchestra; producer, Icandi, D-Jizzle, Halo. *Recordings include:* albums: with Parliament/Funkadelic: America Eats Its Young 1972, Cosmic Slop 1973, Up For The Down Stroke 1974, Standing On The Verge Of Getting It On 1974, Chocolate City 1975, Let's Take It To The Stage 1975, Mothership Connection 1976, The Clones Of Dr Funkenstein 1976, Parliament Live 1977, Funkentelechy v. The Placebo Syndrome 1977, One Nation Under A Groove 1978, Motor Booty Affair 1978, Underjam 1979, Gloryhallastoopid (Pin The Tale On The Funky) 1979, Trombipulation 1980, The Electric Spanking Of War Babies 1981, Computer Games 1982, Dope Dogs 1994; solo: Stretchin' Out 1976, Ahh... The Name Is Bootsy Baby 1977, Player Of The Year 1978, Keepin' Dah Funk Alive 4 1995 1995, Fresh Outta P University 1997, Glory B – Da Funk's On Me 2001, Play With Bootsy 2002, Christmas is 4 Ever 2006, The Official Boot-Legged-Bootsy-CD 2009, Tha Funk Capital of the World 2011; with Science Faxtion: Living on Another Frequency 2008. *Honours:* Grammy Award (with Fatboy Slim, for Weapon of Choice) 2002. *Address:* c/o Bootzilla Productions, PO Box 44158, Cincinnati, OH 45244, USA (office). *Telephone:* (513) 528-3404 (office). *Fax:* (513) 528-7227 (office). *E-mail:* bootsy@zoomtown .com (office). *Website:* www.bootsycollins.com.

COLLINS, Charlie; British musician (saxophone, clarinet, flute, synthesizer), composer and producer; b. 26 Sept. 1952, Sheffield, South Yorkshire, England. *Career:* mem. of jazz, improvised and mixed media groups 1969–, Clock DVA 1979–81, The Box 1981–85, The Bone Orchestra 1985–88; Company Week 1988; Arts Council Tours, 1988, 1990, 1992; Left Hand Right Hand 1992–; solo and production work. *Recordings include:* with Clock DVA: Thirst, White Souls In Black Suits, All recordings with The Box; with Hornweb: Sixteen; with Martin Archer: Wild Pathway Favourites, Telecottage, Left Hand Right Hand, Shockheaded Peters, Ideals of Freedom, Arts Council Funded Composer 1990.

COLLINS, Cody; American singer and musician (guitar); b. Pace, Fla. *Career:* fmr mem. McAlyster; lead singer country music group Lonestar 2007. *Recordings include:* album: My Christmas List 2007, Party Heard Around the World 2010. *Address:* c/o BNA Records, Sony BMG, 1400 18th Avenue, South Nashville, TN 37212, USA. *Website:* www.lonestarnow.com.

COLLINS, Edwyn; British singer, musician (guitar) and producer; b. 23 Aug. 1959, Edinburgh, Scotland; m. Grace Maxwell; one s. *Career:* Founder and lead singer, Orange Juice (formerly Nu-Sonics) 1977–84; solo artist 1985–; Owner of a recording studio; worked as record producer with numerous artists, including Vic Godard, The Proclaimers, The Cribs, A House, Space, Robert Foster, Little Barrie. *Recordings include:* albums: with Orange Juice: You Can't Hide Your Love Forever 1982, Rip It Up 1982, Texas Fever 1984, Orange Juice 1984, The Esteemed Orange Juice 1992, Ostrich Churchyard 1992, The Heather's On Fire 1993; solo: Hope and Despair 1989, Hell Bent On Compromise 1990, Gorgeous George 1995, I'm Not Following You 1997, Doctor Syntax 2002, Home Again 2007, Losing Sleep 2010, Understated 2013.

Honours: Ivor Novello Inspiration Award 2009. *Website:* www.edwyncollins .com.

COLLINS, John; Australian musician (bass guitar); b. 27 April 1970. *Career:* worked as book salesman; joined Brisbane-based rock group Powderfinger 1992; numerous Australian tours/festival appearances, also world-wide tours. *Recordings include:* albums: Parables For Wooden Ears 1994, Double Allergic 1996, Internationalist 1998, Odyssey Number Five 2000, Vulture Street 2003, Dream Days at the Hotel Existence 2007, Footprints. *Honours:* ARIA Awards: Album of the Year, Song of the Year, Best Rock Album, Best Cover Artwork, 1999. *Current Management:* c/o Secret Service Artist Management, PO Box 401, Fortitude Valley, 4006 QLD, Australia. *Website:* www.powderfinger.com.

COLLINS, Judy Marjorie; American singer and songwriter; b. 1 May 1939, Seattle, Wash.; d. of Charles T. Collins and Marjorie Collins; m. 1st Peter A. Taylor 1958 (divorced 1965); one s. (deceased); m. 2nd Louis Nelson 1996. *Education:* MacMurray Coll. *Career:* trained as classical pianist; began folk singing career in clubs in Central City and Denver 1959; full-time career at Gate of Horn Club, Chicago and Gerde's Club, New York; signed to Elektra Records 1961; has performed concerts at major concert halls around the world; numerous radio and TV appearances. *Albums include:* A Maid of Constant Sorrow 1961, Golden Apples of the Sun 1962, Judy Collins #3 1963, The Judy Collins Concert 1964, Judy Collins' Fifth Album 1965, In My Life 1966, Wildflowers 1967, Who Knows Where the Time Goes 1968, Whales and Nightingales 1970, True Stories and Other Dreams 1973, Judith 1975, Bread & Roses 1976, Hard Times for Lovers 1979, Running for my Life 1980, Times of Our Lives 1982, Home Again 1984, Trust Your Heart 1987, The Stars of Christmas 1988, Sanity and Grace 1989, Baby's Morningtime 1990, Judy Sings Dylan 1993, Shameless 1995, Christmas at the Biltmore Estate 1996, Forever 1997, Both Sides Now 1998, All on a Wintry Night 2000, Judy Collins Sings Leonard Cohen: Democracy 2004, Portrait of an American Girl 2005, Paradise 2010, Bohemian 2011, Live from the Metropolitan Museum of Art at the Temple of Dendur 2012, Live at the Metropolitan Museum of Art: Celebrating 50 Years of Timeless Music 2012, Live in San Diego 2012. *Publications include:* Trust Your Heart (autobiography) 1987, Sanity and Grace 2003. *Honours:* Dr hc (Pratt Inst.) 2009; Grammy Award for Best Song (for Send in the Clowns) 1975, Silver Medal, Atlanta Film Festival, Blue Ribbon Award, American Film Festival, Spirit of Americana Free Speech Award, First Amendment Center/American Music Asscn 2005, Survivor Award, American Foundation for Suicide Prevention 2000. *Address:* c/o Wildflower Records, PO Box 1296, New York, NY 10025, USA (office). *E-mail:* wfrecords@aol.com (office). *Website:* www.judycollins.com.

COLLINS, Mark; British musician (guitar); b. Aug. 1965. *Career:* mem., The Charlatans 1992–; numerous tours, festivals, television and radio appearances. *Recordings include:* albums: Between 10th And 11th 1992, Up To Our Hips 1995, The Charlatans 1995, Tellin' Stories 1997, Us And Us Only 1999, Songs From The Other Side 2000, Wonderland 2001, Live It Like You Love It 2002, Up At The Lake 2004, Simpatico 2006, You Cross My Path 2008, Who We Touch 2010, Modern Nature 2015. *Current Management:* Big Life Management, 67–69 Chalton Street, London, NW1 1HY, England. *Telephone:* (20) 7554-2100. *Fax:* (20) 7554-2101. *E-mail:* tim@biglifemanagement.com. *Website:* www.biglifemanagement.com. *Address:* The Charlatans, PO Box 134, Sandbach, Cheshire CW11 1AE, England (office). *E-mail:* info@ thecharlatans.net (office). *Website:* www.thecharlatans.net.

COLLINS, Michael (Mike) Edmond, BSc, MSc; British recording engineer, producer, songwriter and musician (guitar); b. 25 July 1949, Manchester, England; s. of Dr Luke Joseph Collins and Patricia Mary Collins. *Education:* private tuition in guitar and keyboards with Oliver Hunt. *Career:* guitarist, songwriter with jazz-funk band, Light of the World; songwriter, producer, Chappell Music 1982–83; Dick James Music 1984–85; session musician on various music TV shows 1985–86; MIDI programmer for records and films 1987–99; guitarist, composer, recording engineer/producer 2000–; Music Tech. Consultant 2000–; mem. PRS-for-Music, PPL, Musicians' Union. *Recordings:* Still Haven't Found What I'm Looking For. *Films:* Wuthering Heights, Little Buddha. *Television includes:* Top of the Pops 1984–86, Soul Train/Solid Soul/Razzmatazz 1984–86. *Publications:* contribs to magazines including Pro Sound News Europe, Future Music, MacWorld, Sound On Sound, Jazzwise; writes books for Focal Press: Pro Tools for Music Production 2002, 2004, 2009, 2011, Audio Plug-ins and Virtual Instruments 2003, Choosing and Using Music and Audio Software 2004. *Address:* Flat 1C, 28 Pellatt Grove, Wood Green, London, N22 5PL, England (office). *Telephone:* (20) 8888-5318 (office). *E-mail:* mike@mikecollinsmusic.com. *Website:* www .mikecollinsmusic.com.

COLLINS, Philip (Phil), LVO; British singer, songwriter, musician (drums) and producer; b. 30 Jan. 1951, Hounslow, London; s. of Greville Collins and June Collins; m. 1st 1976 (divorced); one s. one d.; m. 2nd Jill Tavelman 1984 (divorced 1995); one d.; m. 3rd Orianne Cevey 1999 (divorced); two s. *Education:* Barbara Speake Stage School. *Career:* fmr child actor, appearing as Artful Dodger in London production of Oliver Twist; fmr mem. various music groups, including The Real Thing, The Freehold, Hickory, Flaming Youth 1967–70; mem. rock group, Genesis, as drummer 1970–96, as lead singer 1975–96, 2006–; mem. Brand X 1975–; solo artist 1981–; record producer for various artists including John Martyn, Frida, Eric Clapton, Adam Ant, Philip Bailey, The Four Tops, Stephen Bishop; Trustee Prince of Wales Trust 1983–; f. Little Dreams Foundation 2000. *Films include:* as actor:

Calamity the Cow 1967, Buster 1988, Hook 1991, Frauds 1993, Balto (voice) 1995, The Jungle Book 2 (voice) 2003; as composer and performer: Tarzan 1999. *Recordings include:* albums: with Genesis: From Genesis To Revelation 1969, Trespass 1970, Nursery Cryme 1971, Foxtrot 1972, Genesis Live 1973, Selling England By The Pound 1973, The Lamb Lies Down On Broadway 1974, A Trick Of The Tail 1976, Seconds Out 1977, Wind And Wuthering 1977, And Then There Were Three 1978, Duke 1980, Abacab 1981, Three Sides Live 1982, Genesis 1983, Invisible Touch 1986, We Can't Dance 1991, The Way We Walk: The Shorts 1992, The Way We Walk: The Longs 1993, Calling All Stations 1997, Turn It On Again 1999, Archive 1967–75 1999, Archive 1976–92 2001; with Brand X: Unorthodox Behaviour, Moroccan Roll 1977, Livestock 1977, Product 1979, Do They Hurt? 1980, Is There Anything About? 1982, Xtrax 1986, The Plot Thins 1992, Brand X Featuring Phil Collins 1996, Live At The Roxy 1996, Missing Period 1997, A History 1976–80 1997, The X-Files 1999; solo: Face Value 1981, Hello, I Must Be Going! 1982, No Jacket Required 1985, 12"ers 1987, ...But Seriously 1989, Serious Hits... Live! 1990, Both Sides 1993, Dance Into The Light 1996, ...Hits! 1998, A Hot Night In Paris 1999, Tarzan 1999, Testify 2002, Love Songs: A Complication Old And New 2004, The Platinum Collection 2004, Going Back 2010. *Publications include:* Genesis: Chapter and Verse (with other band mems) 2007, The Alamo and Beyond: A Collector's Journey 2012. *Honours:* Hon. DFA (Fairleigh Dickinson Univ.) 1987; Hon. DMus (Berklee Coll. of Music) 1991; Hon. DHist (McMurry Univ.) 2012, Grammy Awards (seven), Ivor Novello Awards (six), BRIT Awards (four), Variety Club of Great Britain Awards (two), Silver Clef Awards (two), Elvis Awards, Golden Globe Award for Best Original Song (two, for Two Hearts, from film Buster and You'll Be in My Heart, from film Tarzan), Acad. Award (for You'll be in My Heart, from film Tarzan) 1999, American Music Award for Favorite Adult Contemporary Artist 2000. *Current Management:* Hit and Run Music, 30 Ives Street, London, SW3 2ND, England. *E-mail:* info@genesis-music.com. *Website:* www.philcollins.co.uk; www.genesis-music.com.

COLMAN, Stuart; British record producer, broadcaster and journalist; b. 19 Dec. 1944, Harrowgate, West Yorkshire; m. Janet Colman 1973; one s. two d. *Career:* producer for Jeff Beck, The Big Town Playboys, Billy Swan, Cliff Richard, Phil Everly, Duane Eddy, Shakin' Stevens, The Crickets, The Jordanaires, Little Richard, The Shadows, Gary Glitter, Billy Fury, Kim Wilde, The Hank Wangford Band, Rich Sharp; presenter BBC Radio 2, BBC Radio London, Capital Gold 1999; freelance journalist; mem. Musicians' Union, Country Music Asscn, Nashville. *Publication:* They Kept On Rockin'. *Honours:* Music Week Award for Top Singles Producer 1981.

COLÓN ZAYAS, Edwin; Puerto Rican musician (cuatro Puertorriqueño, guitar) and composer; b. 27 Oct. 1965, Orocovis. *Career:* solo musician and composer. *Recordings include:* albums: El cuatro... más allá de lo imaginable 1988, Siguiendo hacia lo infinito 1989, 100 Años con Don Felo 1990, En Vivo desde el Teatro Tapia 1991, Este es tu taller campesino 1991, Bien Jíbaro!: Country Music of PR 1992, 100% Puertorriqueño 1992, El cuatro y la danza Puertorriqueña 1993, Descarga 1993, Morel... en tiempo de cuatro 1995, Víctor Manuel Reyes en un taller campesino: típico romántico y diferente 1997, La hora de tu partida 1999, Navidad con el taller campesino 2000, Homenaje a los maestros del cuatro, vol. 1: Maso Rivera 2001, Amanecer Tiplero 2002, Homenaje a los maestros del cuatro, vol. 2 2003, Reafirmacion 2007. *Honours:* Premio Nacional del Cuatro Puertorriqueño 1982, Medalla de la Cultura del Instituto de Cultura Puertorriqueña 1982, Premio Tu Música de Mejor Grabación Instrumental del Año 1996. *Address:* Apdo 771, Isabela, PR 00662, USA (office). *E-mail:* elcuatro@edwincolonzayas.com (office). *Website:* www.edwincolonzayas.com.

COLTER, Jessi; American singer, musician (piano) and songwriter; b. (Mirriam Johnson), 25 May 1947, Phoenix, Ariz.; m. 1st Duane Eddy 1963 (divorced 1968); m. 2nd Waylon Jennings 1969; one d. *Career:* church pianist, aged 11; solo artist, also performed with Waylon Jennings in late 1960s and 1970s. *Compositions include:* No Sign of The Living (recorded by Dottie West), You Hung The Moon, Storms Never Last, Jennifer, co-writer (with Waylon Jennings), I'm Not Lisa. *Recordings include:* albums: solo: A Country Star Is Born 1970, I'm Jessi Colter 1975, Jessi 1976, Diamond In The Rough 1976, Mirriam 1977, That's The Way A Cowboy Rock 'n' Rolls 1978, Ridin' Shotgun 1982, Rock 'n' Roll Lullaby 1984, Just for Kids 1994, Out of the Ashes 2006; with Waylon Jennings: Wanted–The Outlaws (with Willie Nelson) 1975, White Mansions 1978, Leather and Lace 1981, Right for the Time 1996, Closing in on the Fire 1998; film soundtrack: The Pursuit of D B Cooper 1982. *Website:* www.officialjessicolter.com.

COLTRANE, Chi; American singer, songwriter, producer and musician (multi-instrumentalist); b. 16 Nov. 1952, Racine, Wis. *Education:* studied in Los Angeles and Las Vegas. *Career:* numerous tours, TV appearances; headlined with The Who; Rod Stewert, The Eagles, Stevie Wonder, Gary Brooker (Procol Harum), Barry McGuire, Jennifer Rush, Nina; mem. AARC, AFTRA, AFM, ASCAP, SUISA, Sound Exchange. *Compositions include:* Thunder and Lightning, Go Like Elijah, You Were My Friend, Wheel of Life, Who Ever Told You, Ooh Baby, I'm Gonna Make You Love Me. *Recordings include:* Chi Coltrane 1972, Let It Ride 1973, Special Chi Coltrane 1975, Best of Chi Coltrane 1975, Road To Tomorrow 1977, Silk and Steel 1981, Ready To Roll 1983, Chi Coltrane Live 1982, The Message 1986, Golden Classics 1996, Oh Holy Night 2009, The Best of 1982 2009, Essential Chi Coltrane – Yesterday, Today & Forever 2010, The Comeback Concert – Live in Vienna 2011. *Films:* Beaches, Spiritual Warriors. *Television:* Chi Coltrane with the Edmonton Symphony Orchestra, Rock Meets Classic with the Kiel Philharmonics Orchestra 2012, With Tony Uthoff & the Big Band, and many other shows. *Honours:* Gold Hammer, Silver Hammer, Best Female Artist: Germany, Switzerland, Austria, Netherlands. *Current Management:* c/o Kit Bramwell, Bramwell Management, 2322 Canyon Drive, Hollywood, CA 90068, USA. *Telephone:* (213) 379-0449. *E-mail:* bramwell.management@gmail.com. *Address:* PO Box 663, Hollywood, CA 90078-0663, USA (office). *Telephone:* (323) 304-9786 (office). *E-mail:* chicoltrane@yahoo.com (office). *Website:* www.chicoltrane.com.

COLVIN, Shawn; American country singer, songwriter and musician (guitar); b. 10 Jan. 1956, Vermillion, SDak. *Education:* guitar lessons from age 10. *Career:* 15 years as bar musician; joined bands Dixie Diesels, Buddy Miller band (later Shawn Colvin Band) 1980. *Recordings include:* albums: Steady On (Grammy Award for Best Contemporary Folk Album) 1989, Fat City 1992, Cover Girl 1994, Live 88 1995, A Few Small Repairs (Grammy Award for Record of the Year) 1996, Holiday Songs and Lullabies 1998, Whole New You 2001, Polaroids: A Greatest Hits Collection 2004, These Four Walls 2006, Shawn Colvin 2009, All Fall Down 2012. *Publication:* Diamond in the Rough 2012. *Honours:* Grammy Award for Song of the Year (for Steady On) 1990, for Record of the Year (for Sunny Came Home) 1997. *Current Management:* c/o Vector Management, PO Box 120479, Nashville, TN 37203, USA. *Telephone:* (615) 269-6600. *E-mail:* info@vectormgmt.com. *Website:* www.vectormgmt.com; www.shawncolvin.com.

COMBELLE, Philippe Alix François; French musician (drums); b. 14 July 1939, Paris; s. of Alix Combelle; m. Françoise Ruiz 1964; one s. one d. *Education:* lessons in piano, saxophone, drums, tabla. *Career:* jazz concerts and clubs in Europe, USA, UK, Japan, Africa, Russia, Turkey, Thailand, India, Viet Nam, Israel, Martinique, Guadaloupe, Syria, Jordan, Yemen Oman; teacher, Marly Conservatory of Music, International Music School, Paris; mem. Société des auteurs, compositeurs et éditeurs de musique (SACEM). *Recordings include:* recorded with Don Byas, Sonny Criss, Memphis Slim, Willie Dixon, Christian Escoudé, Toots Thielemans, Cat Anderson, Barclay, Buck Clayton, Buddy De Franco, Jimmy Gourley, Marc Johnson, Lavelle, OMD with Ray Brown, Eddie Harris, Guy Lafitte, Alix Combelle, Jimmy Gourley, Rene Mailhes, Bernard Maury Trio, Pierre Michelot, Daniel Colin. *E-mail:* fifi@philippecombelle.com (office). *Website:* www.philippecombelle.com.

COMBS, Sean John, (Diddy); American rap artist, record producer, fashion designer and business executive; *Chairman and CEO, Bad Boy Worldwide Entertainment Group*; b. 4 Nov. 1969, Harlem, New York; s. of Melvin Combs and Janice Combs; fmr pnr Misa Hylton-Brim; one s.; fmr pnr Kim Porter; two s. twin d. *Education:* Mount Saint Michael High School, Bronx, Howard Univ. *Career:* early positions at Uptown Records (R&B label) 1990–93; talent spotter for artists such as Jodeci and Mary J. Blige; producer for Ma$e, Sting, MC Lyte, Faith Evans, The Lox, Mariah Carey, Aretha Franklin, 112, Notorious BIG, Jennifer Lopez, Britney Spears, Jay-Z, Rick Ross; f. Bad Boy Entertainment record label 1994 (now a part of Bad Boy Worldwide Entertainment Group); remixed and reworked songs by artists including Jackson 5, Sting, Goldie, Trent Reznor and The Police; co-producer (with Jimmy Page) of soundtrack to film Godzilla; soundtrack to approx. 50 films; launched fashion collection under name Sean John 1998, opened flagship store in Manhattan 2002; known as Puff Daddy until 2001, when he changed his pseudonym to P Diddy, then Diddy 2005–; producer of MTV's Making the Band; launched fragrances Unforgiveable 2006, I Am King 2009. *Play:* A Raisin in the Sun (actor) 2004. *Films:* Bad Boy's 10th Anniversary..., The Hits (video) 2004, The Notorious B.I.G.: Ready to Die – The Remaster (video short) 2004, Notorious 2009, Undefeated (documentary) (Academy Award for Best Documentary Feature 2012) 2011. *Television includes:* Making the Band 2 (series) 2002, Borrow My Crew (documentary) 2005, Making the Band 3 (series) 2005, P. Diddy Presents the Bad Boys of Comedy (series documentary) 2005, Celebrity Cooking Showdown (mini-series) 2006, The Making of 'Press Play' (film) 2006, Diddy Makes an Album (film) 2006, Making the Band 4 (series) 2007, Taquita & Kaui (series) 2007, A Raisin in the Sun (film) 2008, If I Were King: Sean John Internship by Design (documentary) 2008, Daddy's Girls (series) 2009, Run's House (series documentary) 2005–09, Making His Band (series) 2009, StarMaker (series) (exec. producer) 2009, (co-exec. producer) 2009, I Want to Work for Diddy (series) 2008–10, Nicki Minaj: My Time Now (documentary) 2010. *Recordings include:* albums: No Way Out (Grammy Award for Best Rap Album 1998) 1997, Forever 1999, The Saga Continues... 2001, We Invented the Remix 2002, Maximum Puff Daddy 2003, Press Play 2006, Last Train to Paris (with Dirty Money) 2010. *Honours:* Grammy Award for Best Rap Performance by a Duo or Group for I'll Be Missing You, with Faith Evans 1998, for Shake Ya Tailfeather 2004, Council of Fashion Designers of America menswear designer of the year award 2004. *Address:* Bad Boy Worldwide Entertainment Group, 1710 Broadway, New York, NY 10019, USA (office). *Telephone:* (212) 381-1540 (office). *Fax:* (212) 381-1599 (office). *Website:* www.seanjohn.com; www.badboyonline.com.

COMMERFORD, Tim; American musician (bass guitar); b. 1968, Irvine, CA. *Career:* mem., Rage Against the Machine 1991–2000, re-formed 2007–; supports causes such as Fairness and Accuracy in Reporting, Rock for Choice and Refuse and Resist; numerous tours and live appearances; founder mem., Audioslave 2002–07; guest collaborator with Puscifer 2007. *Recordings include:* albums: with Rage Against the Machine: Rage Against The Machine 1992, Evil Empire 1996, The Battle Of Los Angeles 1998, Renegades 2000,

Live And Rare 2002; with Audioslave: Audioslave 2002, Out Of Exile 2005, Revelations 2006. *Address:* c/o Sony BMG, 550 Madison Avenue, New York, NY 10022, USA. *Website:* www.ratm.com; www.audioslave.com.

COMMON, (Common Sense); American rap artist, actor and writer; b. (Lonnie Lynn Jr), Chicago. *Career:* fmr Gap model; started recording as 'Common Sense', releasing debut album in 1992; collaborations with Bilal, Slum Village, D'Angelo, Chantay Savage. *Recordings:* albums: Can I Borrow A Dollar 1992, Resurrection 1994, One Day It'll All Make Sense 1997, Like Water For Chocolate 2000, Electric Circus 2003, Be 2005, Finding Forever 2007, Universal Mind Control 2008, The Dreamer/The Believer 2011, Nobody's Smiling 2014. *Films:* Smokin' Aces 2006, American Gangster 2007, The Night Watchman 2008, Wanted 2008, Terminator Salvation 2009, Date Night 2010, Happy Feet Two 2011, LUV 2012, Now You See Me 2013, Selma 2014. *Publications:* One Day It'll All Make Sense (autobiography), I Like You but I Love Me (children's book). *Honours:* Grammy Awards for Best Rap Performance by a Duo of Group (for Southside, with Kanye West) 2008, for Best Song Written for Visual Media (for Glory, with John Legend) 2016, Golden Globe for Best Original Song - Motion Picture (for Glory) 2015. *Address:* Common for the People, c/o Senseless Music, PO Box 511533, Milwaukee, WI 53203-0261, USA (office). *E-mail:* common@ officialcommonsite.com (office). *Website:* www.common-music.com.

CONCINA, Roberto, (Robert Miles); Italian composer, DJ, producer and arranger; *Director, Salt Records Ltd*; b. (Roberto Concina), 3 Nov. 1969, Fleurier, Switzerland. *Career:* Dir, Salt Records Ltd, London. *Recordings include:* albums: Dreamland 1996, Children 1996, 23 AM 1997, In The Mix 1997, Organik 2001, Miles_Gurtu (with Trilok Gurtu) 2004, Thirteen 2011. *Honours:* BRIT Award for Best Int. Newcomer 1997, World Music Award for Best Male Newcomer of the Year 1997, numerous platinum and gold records for sales in excess of 14 million records. *E-mail:* info@saltrecords.com (office). *Website:* www.robert-miles.com (home).

CONGREAVE, Edwin Thomas; British musician (keyboards) and songwriter; b. 9 June 1984, Leeds. *Career:* mem. Foals 2006–. *Recordings:* albums: with Foals: Antidotes 2008, Total Life Forever 2010, Holy Fire 2013, What Went Down 2015. *Honours:* with Foals: NME Awards for Best Track (for Spanish Sahara) 2011, (for Inhaler) 2013, Q Magazine Awards for Best Live Act 2013, for Best Act in the World Today 2015. *Current Management:* c/o Steve Matthews, Q Prime Management, 729 Seventh Avenue, #1600, New York, NY 10019, USA. *Telephone:* (212) 302-9790. *E-mail:* info@qprime.com. *Website:* www.qprime.com; www.foals.co.uk.

CONLEY, Earl Thomas; American country singer, songwriter and musician; b. 17 Oct. 1941, Portsmouth, OH. *Recordings include:* albums: Blue Pearl 1980, Fire and Smoke 1981, Somewhere Between Right and Wrong 1982, Don't Make It Easy For Me 1983, Treadin' Water 1984, Greatest Hits 1985, Too Many Times 1986, The Heart of It All 1988, Yours Truly 1991, Perpetual Motion 1998, Should've Been Over by Now 2003. *Current Management:* c/o Buddy Lee Attractions, 38 Music Square East, Suite 300, Nashville, TN 37203, USA. *Telephone:* (615) 244-4336. *Website:* www.buddyleeattractions .com; www.earlthomasconley.com.

CONNEFF, Kevin; Irish musician; b. 8 Jan. 1945, Donore, Louth Co. *Career:* bodhrán player and vocalist, The Chieftains 1976–. *Recordings include:* albums: with The Chieftains: Chieftains 8 1978, Boil The Breakfast Early/ Chieftains 9 1980, Chieftains 10 1981, The Chieftains In China 1984, Ballad Of The Irish Horse 1985, Celtic Wedding 1987, The Chieftains In Ireland (with James Galway) 1987, Year Of The French 1988, Irish Heartbeat (with Van Morrison) 1988, A Chieftains Celebration 1989, Chieftains Collection 1989, The Celtic Connection – James Galway And The Chieftains 1990, Bells Of Dublin 1991, An Irish Evening 1992, Another Country 1992, The Celtic Harp (with Belfast Harp Orchestra) 1993, The Long Black Veil 1995, Santiago 1996, Tears of Stone 1999, Water From The Well 2000, Down The Old Plank Road: The Nashville Sessions 2002, The Wide World Over: A 40 Year Celebration 2002, San Patricio 2010; solo: The Week before Easter 1988; other: Prosperous (with Christy Moore). *Film:* The Water Horse 2007. *Television includes:* An Irish Evening: Live at the Grand Opera House, Belfast 1991, Kelly 2002, A Capitol Fourth 2003, Legends 2008. *Current Management:* c/o Macklam Feldman Management, 200–1505 West 2nd Avenue, Vancouver, BC V6H 3Y4, Canada. *Telephone:* (604) 734-5945. *E-mail:* info@mfmgt.com. *Website:* www .mfmgt.com; www.thechieftains.com.

CONNICK, Harry, Jr; American jazz musician (piano), singer and actor; b. 11 Sept. 1967, New Orleans, La; m. Jill Goodacre 1994. *Education:* New Orleans Center for the Creative Arts, Hunter Coll. and Manhattan School of Music; studied with Ellis Marsalis. *Films include:* Memphis Belle 1990, Little Man Tate 1991, Copycat 1995, Independence Day 1996, Excess Baggage 1997, Action League Now!! (voice) 1997, Hope Floats 1998, The Iron Giant (voice) 1999, Wayward Son 1999, My Dog Skip (voice) 2000, The Simian Line 2000, Life Without Dick 2001, Basic 2003, Mickey 2004, The Happy Elf (voice) 2005, Bug 2006, P.S. I Love You 2007, New in Town 2009, Dolphin Tale 2009, When Angels Sing 2011. *Television includes:* South Pacific 2001, Will & Grace (series) 2002–06, Law & Order 2012. *Theatre:* Thou Shalt Not (composer, Broadway) 2001, The Pajama Game (actor, Broadway) 2005. *Recordings include:* albums: 11 1978, Harry Connick Jr 1987, 20 1988, When Harry Met Sally (Grammy Award for Male Jazz Vocal Performance 1990) 1989, Lofty's Roach Soufflé 1990, We Are In Love 1990, Blue Light, Red Light 1991, 25 1992, When My Heart Finds Christmas 1993, Imagination 1994, She 1994, Whisper

Your Name 1995, Star Turtle 1995, All Of Me 1996, To See You 1997, Come By Me 1999, 30 2001, Songs I Heard 2001, Other Hours: Connick On Piano, Vol. I 2003, Harry For The Holidays 2003, Only You 2004, Occasion 2005, Harry on Broadway, Act 1 2006, Oh, My Nola 2007, Chanson de Vieux Carré 2007, What a Night! A Christmas Album 2008, Your Songs 2009, In Concert on Broadway 2011, Music from the Happy Elf 2011, Smokey Mary 2013; contrib. music for films Memphis Belle 1990, Little Man Tate 1991. *Current Management:* Wilkins Management Inc., 323 Broadway, Cambridge, MA 02139, USA. *Telephone:* (617) 354-2736. *E-mail:* info@wilkinsmanagement.com. *E-mail:* info@harryconnickjr.com (office). *Website:* www.hconnickjr.com.

CONNOLLY, Nathan; British musician (guitar) and backing singer; b. 20 Jan. 1981, Belfast, NI. *Career:* mem. Snow Patrol 2002–. *Recordings include:* albums: Final Straw (Meteor Ireland Music Award for Best Irish Album 2005, Ivor Novello Award for Best Album 2005) 2004, Eyes Open (Meteor Ireland Music Award for Best Irish Album 2007) 2006, A Hundred Million Suns 2008, Fallen Empires 2011. *Honours:* Meteor Ireland Music Award for Best Irish Band 2005, 2007, for Most Downloaded Song and Best Live Performance 2007. *E-mail:* info@snowpatrol.com. *Website:* www.snowpatrol.com.

CONNOR, Sarah; German singer; b. 13 June 1980, Delmenhorst; m. Marc Terenzi 2005; one s. one d. *Career:* collaborations include TQ, Wyclef Jean, Naturally Seven, Natural. *Recordings include:* albums: Green Eyed Soul 2001, Unbelievable 2002, Key To My Soul 2003, Naughty But Nice 2005, Sexy as Hell 2008, Under My Skin 2008, Real Love 2010. *Film:* Robots (voice) 2005. *Honours:* Echo Award for Female Nat. Rock/Pop Artist 2002, World Music Award for Most Successful German Artist Abroad, USA 2004, World Of Music Award 2008. *Address:* c/o X-cell Records GmbH & Co. KG, Wittelsbacherstr. 18, 10707 Berlin, Germany. *E-mail:* info@x-cell.de (office). *Website:* www .sarah-connor.com.

CONNOR-CRAWFORD, Geraldine Roxanne; British musician; b. 22 March 1952, London; d. of Edric Eselus Connor and Pearl Cynthia Connor (née Nunez); m. Thorma Anthony Crawford 1989. *Education:* Diego Martin Secondary School, Trinidad, Camden School for Girls, London, Valsayn Teacher Training Coll., Trinidad and Royal Coll. of Music, London. *Career:* Head, Dept of Music, Queen's Royal Coll., Trinidad and Tobago 1976–84; Educ. Supervisor and Registrar Brent Black Music Co-operative, London 1984–87; apptd Chair. Steelband Asscn of Great Britain 1987, apptd Lecturer in Extra-Mural Musical Studies Univ. of the West Indies 1987; apptd Dir Nat. Steelband Music Co. Ltd 1988; Lecturer and Co-ordinator, Indo/Afro-Caribbean Music Tutorials, Best Village Folk Programme 1989; apptd Sr Lecturer of Afro-Caribbean Music Studies, City of Leeds Coll. of Music 1990; apptd Sr Lecturer in Music, Univ. of Leeds, seconded as Assoc. Producer West Yorkshire Playhouse 2002–03; Presenter, Trinidad and Tobago TV Co. Ltd, TV series Learn to Make Music 1984; Consultant to Birmingham Task Force, Music Survey (UK) 1987, CARIFESTA V 1989; has sung backing vocals for Bob Marley, Tom Jones, Judith Durham and Jimmy Cliff. *Recordings with:* Jimmy Cliff, Wilma Reading, Judith Durham, Tom Jones, Gene Lawrence, Sound Revolution, Reggae Sunsplash, Millie Jackson. *Musicals composed/ directed include:* Ah, Pan for Christmas 1983, From Coffee Beans to Disinfectant 1986, O Babylon 1988, Ebony Eyes 1991, A Jamaican Airman Foresees His Death 1991, Hiphopera 1991, The Man Who Lit Up The World 1991, Afro-Goth 1991, Pot Pourri 1991, Yaa Asantewaa with Adzido Pan African Dance Ensemble, Carnival Messiah, West Yorkshire Playhouse 1999, 2002.

CONROY, Patricia; Canadian songwriter and singer; b. 30 Jan. 1957, Montréal. *Career:* numerous television appearances; mem. American Fed. of Musicians (AFM). *Recordings include:* albums: Blue Angel 1990, Bad Day For Trains (Canadian Country Music Asscn Award for Album of the Year 1993) 1992, You Can't Resist 1994, Wild As the Wind 1998, Talking to Myself 2007. *Honours:* Canadian Country Music Asscn Female Vocalist of the Year 1994, Canadian Country Music Asscn Ind. Female Artist of the Year 2006. *Website:* www.oreillyinternational.com; www.patriciaconroy.net.

CONSTANTIN, François; French musician (percussion, drums); b. 2 Dec. 1961, Paris; m. Catia Carvalho da Silva 1986; two d. *Education:* Normal School of Music, Paris. *Career:* jazz performances with Lavel, Arturo Sandoval, Francis Lockwood, Veronique Sanson, France Gall, Elsa, Louis Chedid, Johnny Hallyday, Patrick Bruel, Jean-Patrick Capdeviel, Michel Sardoux, Fabian; f. record label. *Recordings include:* Shah Shah persan, Mon manege à moi, Les 400 coups, Ma ptite rime, Lettre à Virginia, Ma gigolette, Feets too Big, Caravane, Bain, amour, etc., Aimez-vous Liszt?.

CONSTANTINOU, Chris, (Chris de Niro); British musician (bass guitar, guitar, flute), singer and actor; b. 20 July 1957, London, England. *Career:* fmr mem. punk band, The Drill and Hollywood Exiles 1976; mem. Adam and the Ants (as Chris de Niro) 1981–86; several world tours, television appearances; formed S.F.Go; formed band and songwriting partnership with Annabella Lwin; singer/writer in own band, Jackie On Assid; formed band with Marco Pirroni, The Wolfmen 2007–; film appearances include Touch (BBC 2), Play Dead, Shopping; mem. PRS, MCPS, Equity, Musicians' Union, American Fed. of Television and Radio Artists, Performing Artists Media Rights Asscn. *Recordings include:* with The Drill and Hollywood Exiles: Drill; with Adam and the Ants: Dirk Wears White Sox, Kings of the Wild Frontier, Prince Charming; with The Wolfmen: Modernity Killed Every Night 2008. *E-mail:* chrisconstantinou1@gmail.com; info@thewolfmen.net. *Website:* www .thewolfmen.net; chrisconstantinou.com.

CONTE, Luis; Cuban musician (percussion); b. 16 Nov. 1954, Santiago. *Career:* emigrated from Cuba to Madrid, Spain at age 15 then moved to Hollywood, Calif. playing guitar in numerous local rock bands; took up drums while attending Los Angeles City Coll.; has played with numerous musicians from many different musical genres; featured musician for James Taylor's US Tour 2011. *Recordings include:* La Cocina Caliente 1987, Black Forest 1990, Cuban Dreams 2000, A Coat of Many Colours 2006, Marimbula 2007, En Casa de Luis 2011; with Gordon Goodwin's Big Phat Band: Life In The Bubble (Grammy Award for Best Large Jazz Ensemble Album 2015) 2014. *Film:* The Lost City 2008. *Honours:* Percussionist of the Year, Drum Magazine 2007, 2008, 2009, Percussionist of the Year, Modern Drummer 2009, 2010, Studio Percussionist of the Year Award, Drum Magazine 2007, 2008, 2009. *Current Management:* BFM Jazz, 12650 Riverside Drive, 203 Valley Village, Los Angeles, CA 91607, USA. *Telephone:* (818) 762-0191. *Fax:* (818) 762-1652. *E-mail:* info@bfmjazz.com. *Website:* www.bfmjazz.com. . *Website:* www .luisconte.com.

CONTE, Paolo; Italian singer, musician (piano, guitar, vibraphone), songwriter and composer; b. 6 Jan. 1937, Asti. *Education:* Univ. of Parma. *Career:* began career as jazz musician in various bands; recorded The Italian Way to Swing with the Paolo Conte Quartet 1962; began composing songs in 1960s; songs recorded by artists, including Patty Pravo, Enzo Jannacci, Johnny Hallyday, Shirley Bassey; solo artist 1974–. *Compositions include:* La Coppia piu' Bella Del Mondo. *Recordings include:* albums: The Italian Way To Swing 1962, Paolo Conte 1974, Gelato Al Limon 1979, Paris Milonga 1981, Appunti Di Viaggio 1982, Concerti 1985, Come Di 1986, Aguaplano 1987, Live 1988, Collezione 1988, A Macchina 1990, Boogie 1990, Wanda, stai seria con la faccia ma però 1992, Tournée 1993, Una Faccia In Prestito 1995, The Best of Paolo Conte 1996, Tournée 2 1998, Razmataz 2000, Elegia 2004, Wonderful 2006, Psiche 2008, Nelson 2010, Gong-oh 2011. *Current Management:* c/o Concerto Management, Via Massarenti 208, 40138, Bologna, Italy. *Telephone:* (13) 47278. *E-mail:* info@concerto.net. *Website:* www.concerto.net; www .paoloconte.it.

CONTE, Steve; American musician (guitar) and singer. *Career:* mem. and lead singer, The Company of Wolves, The Contes; mem., New York Dolls 2004–. *Recordings include:* albums: with Company of Wolves: Company of Wolves 1990, Shakers and Tambourines 1998, Steryl Spycase 2001; with Crown Jewels: Spitshine 1996, Linoleum 1998, Bubble and Squeak 2000; with The Contes: Bleed Together 2003; with New York Dolls: One Day it Will Please Us to Remember Even This 2006, Cause I Sez So 2009; with Steve Conte & The Crazy Truth: Steve Conte & The Crazy Truth 2009; other: with Michael Monroe: Another Night In The Sun - Live in Helsinki 2010, Sensory Overdrive 2011; solo: The Steve Conte NYC Album 2013. *Website:* www .nydolls.org; www.thecontes.com; www.steveconteandthecrazytruth.com.

CONWAY, John; American musician (keyboards). *Education:* Vassar Coll. *Career:* Founder mem., The Bravery 2003–. *Recordings include:* albums: The Bravery 2005, The Sun and the Moon 2007, Stir the Blood 2009. *E-mail:* petegalli@cybercom.net. *Website:* www.thebravery.com.

CONWAY, James Anthony (Tony); American entertainment company executive; *President, Conway Entertainment Group*; b. 3 Aug. 1953, Louisville, KY; m. Nancy Schaefer 1976; one s. one d. *Education:* Northwood Coll., Southern IN, West Baden, IN. *Career:* opened first talent agency, Lexington, Kentucky; moved to Nashville; agent for Buddy Lee Attractions, Inc. 1975, Pres. 1987–98, CEO and Co-Owner 1998–2009; Founder and Pres. Conway Entertainment Group 2010–; over 30 clients include: Willie Nelson; Emmylou Harris; Ricky Van Shelton; Clay Walker; Mark Chestnutt; Waylon Jennings; Lorrie Morgan; handled special event department in offices in Nashville, Kansas City, Los Angeles; Director Services of Main Stage Production Enterprises Inc, producing major events, festivals, state fairs, North America; Exec. Producer, CMA Music Festival Nashwille, Tenn. 2000–11, BAMA Jam Enterprise, Ala 2010–11, Show Me Music Festival Springfield Md 2011, Co-promotor, Farm Aid Concert, Champaigne, Ill.; first agent in Nashville to develop new breed of country acts; artists signed include: George Strait; Mary Chapin Carpenter; Patty Loveless; Garth Brooks; John Anderson; Sawyer Brown; Talent Co-ordinator, FarmAid Concerts, Illinois, Texas; Co-ordinated, booked, Highwayman I and II tours, with Willie Nelson, Waylon Jennings, Johnny Cash, Kris Kristofferson; handles international tours for all clients. *Honours:* CMA Agent of the Year (twice), SRO Convention 1990, 1991, Country Agent of the Year, Performance Magazine Readers Poll, 1992, 1993, Hubert Long Lifetime Achievement Award, Pollstar Tour of the Year, Courmil Tom Park Award. *Address:* Conway Entertainment Group, 1625 Broadway, Suite 500, Nashville, TN 37203, USA (office). *Telephone:* (615) 724-1818 (office). *E-mail:* info@conwayent.com (office); tonyc@conwayent.com (office). *Website:* www.conwayent.com (office).

COODER, Ryland (Ry) Peter; American musician (guitar, slide guitar) and composer; b. 15 March 1947, Los Angeles, CA. *Career:* mem., Jackie DeShannon's backing group, aged 17; mem., The Rising Sons 1965–66, Captain Beefheart & The Magic Band 1967; session guitar work included Everly Brothers, Paul Revere and The Raiders, Randy Newman, The Rolling Stones; solo recording artist 1970–; formed Little Village (with Nick Lowe, John Hiatt, Jim Keltner) 1991; film music writer 1980s–; established Buena Vista Social Club project 1996. *Film soundtracks include:* Pacific Vibrations 1970, The Long Riders 1980, Southern Comfort 1981, The Border 1982, Streets of Fire 1984, Paris, Texas 1984, Alamo Bay 1985, Brewster's Millions 1985, Crossroads 1986, Blue City 1986, Tales from the Crypt (episode The Man Who Was Death) 1989, Johnny Handsome 1989, Trespass 1992, Geronimo 1993, Last Man Standing 1996, The End of Violence 1997, Primary Colors 1998, Homegrown 1998, A Civil Action 1998, One Hour Photo 2002, Chávez Ravine: A Los Angeles Story 2003, My Blueberry Nights 2008. *Recordings include:* albums: Ry Cooder 1970, Into The Purple Valley 1971, Boomer's Story 1972, Paradise And Lunch 1974, Chicken Skin Music 1976, Show Time 1976, Jazz 1978, Bop Till You Drop 1979, Borderline 1980, Ry Cooder Live 1980, The Slide Area 1982, Why Don't You Try Me Tonight? 1986, Get Rhythm 1987, Pecos Bill (with Robin Williams) 1988, A Meeting By The River (with V. M. Bhatt) 1993, Talking Timbuktu (with Ali Farka Toure) (Grammy Award for Best World Music Recording) 1994, Music By Ry Cooder 1995, Buena Vista Social Club 1997, The Gabby Pahinui Hawaiian Band and Ry Cooder Vol. 1 2000, Mambo Sinuendo 2003, Chávez Ravine 2005, My Name is Buddy 2007, I, Flathead 2008; with Little Village: Little Village 1992. *Honours:* Grammy Award for Best Recording for Children 1989, BBC Radio 3 Award for World Music (Americas) 2006. *Address:* c/o World Circuit Records, 138 Kingsland Road, London, E2 8DY, England (office). *Telephone:* (20) 7749-3222 (office). *Fax:* (20) 7749-3232 (office). *E-mail:* post@worldcircuit.co.uk (office). *Website:* www.worldcircuit.co.uk (office).

COOK, Barbara; American singer and actress; b. 25 Oct. 1927, Atlanta, Ga; d. of Charles Bunyan and Nell Cook (née Harwell); m. David LeGrant 1952 (divorced 1965); one s. *Career:* Broadway debut as the ingenue lead in the musical Flahooley 1951; came to prominence after starring in Candide 1956 and The Music Man 1957; continued performing mostly in theatre until mid-1970s; then began a second career as a cabaret and concert singer; recognized as one of the "premier interpreters" of musical theatre songs and standards, especially those of Stephen Sondheim; numerous recordings. *Broadway productions:* Flahooley 1951, Oklahoma! 1953, Carousel 1954, 1957, Plain and Fancy (Theatre World Award 1955) 1956, Candide 1957, The Music Man (Tony Award for Best Featured Actress in a Musical 1958) 1961, The Gay Life 1962, She Loves Me 1964, Something More! 1964, Any Wednesday 1966, Little Murders 1967, The Grass Harp 1971, Enemies 1972, Barbara Cook: A Concert for the Theatre (Drama Desk Award Outstanding One Person Show 1987) 1987, Angela Lansbury – A Celebration (benefit) 1996, Mostly Sondheim 2002, Something Good 2002, Barbara Cook's Broadway! 2004, Children and Art (benefit) 2005, Sondheim on Sondheim 2010. *Films include:* Thumbelina (voice) 1994. *Television includes:* Studio One (series) 1950, Armstrong Circle Theatre (series) – Mr. Bemiss Takes a Trip 1952, Golden Windows (series) 1954, Producers' Showcase (series) – Bloomer Girl 1956, The Yeomen of the Guard (film) 1957, Kraft Television Theatre (series) (Kelly 1950, The Man Who Couldn't Say No 1957), Hallmark Hall of Fame (series) – The Yeoman of the Guard 1957, Alfred Hitchcock Presents (series) – A Little Sleep 1957, Hansel and Gretel (film) 1958, The Chevy Show (series) – O'Halloran's Luck 1961, The Dinah Shore Chevy Show (series) – O'Halloran's Luck 1961, Play of the Week (series) – In a Garden 1961, The United States Steel Hour (series) – The Go-Between 1962. *Music includes* solo: Songs of Perfect Propriety 1958, Barbara Cook Sings 'From the Heart' (The Best of Rodgers & Hart) 1959, At Carnegie Hall 1975, As Of Today 1977, It's Better With a Band 1981, The Disney Album 1988, Dorothy Fields: Close as Pages in a Book 1993, Live from London 1994, Oscar Winners: The Lyrics of Oscar Hammerstein II 1997, All I Ask of You 1999, The Champion Season: A Salute to Gower Champion 1999, Have Yourself a Merry Little Christmas 2000, Sings Mostly Sondheim: Live at Carnegie Hall 2001, Count Your Blessings 2003, Barbara Cook's Broadway! 2004, Tribute 2005, Barbara Cook at The Met 2006, No One Is Alone 2007, Rainbow Round My Shoulder 2008; albums: Cheek to Cheek: Cook & Feinstein 2011, You Make Me Feel So Young: Live at Feinstein's 2011, Loverman 2012; cast and studio cast recordings: Flahooley 1951, Plain and Fancy 1955, Candide 1956, The Music Man (Grammy Award for Best Original Cast Album) 1957, Hansel and Gretel (TV soundtrack) 1958, The Gay Life 1961, Show Boat (studio cast) 1962, She Loves Me (Grammy Award for Best Score From An Original Cast Show Album) 1963, The King and I (studio cast) 1964, Show Boat (Lincoln Center cast) 1966, The Grass Harp 1971, The Grass Grows Green 1972, Follies in Concert 1985, The Secret Garden (world premiere recording) 1986, Carousel (studio cast) 1987, Thumbelina (motion picture soundtrack) 1994, Lucky in the Rain 2000, Sondheim on Sondheim 2010; compilations: The Broadway Years: Till There Was You 1995, Legends of Broadway – Barbara Cook 2006, The Essential Barbara Cook Collection 2009. *Honours:* Honoree, 34th Annual Kennedy Center Honors 2011. *Current Management:* c/o Jeff Berger Management, 301 West 53rd Street, Suite 10J, New York, NY 10019, USA. *Telephone:* (212) 586-4978. *Fax:* (212) 247-2724. *E-mail:* jeffnooyawkagent@yahoo.com. *E-mail:* barbara@barbaracook.com. *Website:* www.barbaracook.com.

COOK, Clay; American singer, songwriter and musician (guitar, organ, mandolin); b. Atlanta, Ga. *Education:* Berklee Coll. of Music. *Career:* has recorded and toured with John Mayer, Sugarland, The Marshall Tucker Band, Shawn Mullins; owns The Small Room Studio, Inman Park, Ga; mem. Zac Brown Band 2009–. *Compositions include:* songs performed by John Mayer including No Such Thing, Comfortable, Neon, by The Marshall Tucker Band. *Recordings:* albums: solo: The Year I Grew Up 2008, On Mountain Time 2009; with Zac Brown Band: You Get What You Give 2010. *Honours:* Acad. of Country Music Award for Top New Vocal Duo or Group 2009, for Vocal Event of the Year (for As She's Walking Away, featuring Alan Jackson) 2011, Grammy Award for Best New Artist 2010, CMA New Artist of the Year 2010. *Current Management:* ROAR, 9701 Wilshire Boulevard, Eighth Floor, Beverly

Hills, CA 90212, USA. *Telephone:* (310) 586-8222. *E-mail:* zbb@roar.la. *Website:* www.roar.la. *E-mail:* clay@zacbrownband.com (office). *Website:* www.claycook.com; www.zacbrownband.com.

COOK, David Lynn, MBA, MMus, DMus, PhD; American singer, charity spokesman and model; b. 11 Nov. 1965, Pascagula, MS. *Career:* mem., The Cook Family Singers; David L. Cook and the Trinidetts; performs religious songs; performed at White House for Ronald Reagan, 1986; appearances in: Japan; Israel; England; Russia; Netherlands; People's Republic of China; Australia; television appearances; mem. GMA; NARAS; CMA; AMARA; SAG; SESAC. *Recordings include:* albums: Come Follow Me 1985, Personal Feelings 1986, In the Middle of It All 1997, Split Personality 1999, Wind of Change 2002, Have You Ever 2006. *Honours:* 3 Manitoba Awards; AMAAA Male Vocalist of Year, 1986–87; AMAAA Composer of Year, 1987–90; ABG Rising Star Award, 1989; numerous Robi Awards, 1986–90; Gospel Music Humanitarian Award, ARAMA, 1995; Sacred Music USA Award, Contemporary Christian Artist of the Year, 1996. *Address:* 1336 Cheshire Avenue, Charlotte, NC 28208, USA. *E-mail:* david@davidlcook.com. *Website:* www.davidlcook.com.

COOK, Jamie Robert; British musician (rhythm guitar); b. 8 July 1985, Sheffield. *Education:* Stockbridge High School, Sheffield. *Career:* founder mem., Arctic Monkeys 2002–. *Recordings include:* albums: with Arctic Monkeys: Five Minutes with the Arctic Monkeys (EP) 2005, Whatever People Say I Am, That's What I'm Not (Mercury Music Prize 2006, Q Award for Best Album 2006, Meteor Ireland Music Award for Best Int. Album 2007, BRIT Award for Best British Album 2007, NME Award for Best Album 2007, Ivor Novello Award for Best Album 2007) 2006, Favourite Worst Nightmare (BRIT Award for Best British Album 2008) 2007, Humbug 2009, Suck It and See (MOJO Award for Best Album 2011) 2011, AM 2013. *Honours:* with Arctic Monkeys: BRIT Awards for Best British Breakthrough Artist 2006, for Best British Group 2007, 2008, NME Awards for Best British Band 2006, 2008, for Best Track (for I Bet You Look Good on the Dancefloor) 2006, (for Flourescent Adolescent) 2008, for Best Music DVD (for Scummy Man) 2007, (for Arctic Monkeys at the Apollo) 2009, for Best Live Band 2010, 2012, Q Magazine Awards for People's Choice 2006, for Best Act in the World Today 2007, for Best Live Act 2009, for Best Track (for Do I Wanna Know?) 2013. *Current Management:* Press Here Publicity, 138 West 25th Street, Seventh Floor, New York, NY 10001, USA. *E-mail:* info@pressherepublicity.com. *Website:* www.pressherepublicity.com. *E-mail:* arctic.monkeys@gmail.com. *Website:* www.arcticmonkeys.com.

COOK, Jeff; American singer and musician (guitar, keyboards, fiddle, bass guitar, banjo, mandolin); b. 27 Aug. 1949, Fort Payne, AL; m. Lisa Williams 1995. *Education:* Gadsden State Community College. *Career:* founder mem., country music group, Young Country, 1969, renamed Wild Country, 1972, renamed Alabama, 1977–2003, 2011–; founder mem. Cook & Glenn, Allstar Goodtime Band (AGB); owner, Cook Sound Studio. *Recordings include:* albums: with Alabama: Alabama, 1980; My Home's In Alabama, 1980; Feels So Right, 1981; Stars, 1982; Mountain Music, 1982; The Closer You Get, 1983; Roll On, 1984; 40 Hour Week, 1985; Alabama Christmas, 1985; The Touch, 1986; Just Us, 1987; Live, 1988; Tennessee Christmas, 1989; Southern Star, 1989; Pass It On Down, 1990; American Pride, 1992; Gonna Have A Party... Live, 1993; Cheap Seats, 1993; In The Beginning, 1994; In Pictures, 1995; From The Archives Vol. 1, 1996; Christmas Vol. 2, 1996; Live at Ebbets Field, 1997; Dancin' On The Boulevard, 1997; Twentieth Century, 1999; Alabama For The Record, 2000; When It All Goes South, 2001; Christmas, 2002; with the AGB: 2 Rock 4 Country 2003, Just Pickin' 2008, Ashes Won't Burn 2009, Shaken... Not Stirred 2010. *Honours:* Country Music Asscn Awards, 1981–84; Acad. of Country Music Awards, incl. Artist of the Decade, 1989; American Music Awards, incl. Award of Merit, 2003; Grammy Awards, for Mountain Music, 1983, for The Closer You Get, 1984; BMI President's Award, 2000; Billboard Awards. *E-mail:* JeffCook-AGB@hotmail.com. *Website:* www.wildcountry.com; www.jeffcook-agb.com; www.thealabamaband.com.

COOK, Kyle; American musician (guitar) and songwriter; b. 29 Aug. 1975, Frankfort, Ind.; m. Sabrina; two d. *Education:* Atlanta Inst. of Music. *Career:* studied classical violin before taking up guitar; guitarist and backing vocalist, Matchbox Twenty 1996–; co-writer on several Matchbox Twenty songs, numerous tours worldwide; currently also guitarist and vocalist for band The New Left. *Recordings include:* with Matchbox Twenty: albums: Yourself or Someone Like You 1996, Mad Season 2000, More Than You Think You Are 2002, Exile on Mainstream 2007, North 2012; with The New Left: Let Go (EP). *Address:* c/o Richard De La Font Agency, 4845 South Sheridan Road, Tulsa, OK 74145, USA. *Telephone:* (918) 665-6200. *Website:* delafont.com; www.matchboxtwenty.com.

COOK, Norman, (Fatboy Slim); British musician (guitar), record producer and DJ; b. (Quentin Cook), 31 July 1963, Bromley; m. Zoë Ball 1999; one s. one d. *Education:* Reigate Coll. *Career:* mem., The Housemartins 1985–88; worked with Billy Bragg 1989; formed Beats International 1990–92, Freakpower (with Ashley Slater) 1994–98, The Beautiful South (with Dave Hemingway); released records under guises of Pizzaman 1993, Mighty Dub Katz 1993, Fatboy Slim 1995–, BPA 2009–; numerous DJ sets, festival appearances; producer for band Blur; f. Brighton Port Authority project 2008. *Recordings include:* albums: with The Housemartins: London 0 Hull 4 1986, The People Who Grinned Themselves to Death 1987, Now That's What I Call Quite Good (double album) 1988; with Beats International: Excursion on the Version; with

Freakpower: Drive Thru Booty 1994; as Fatboy Slim: Better Living Through Chemistry 1996, On the Floor at the Boutique 1997, Let's Hear It 1998, You've Come A Long Way Baby 1998, Halfway Between The Gutter and The Stars 2000, A Break From The Norm (mix album) 2001, Palookaville 2004, The Greatest Hits – Why Try Harder? 2006, Here Lies Love (with David Byrne) 2010; as BPA: I Think We're Gonna Need a Bigger Boat 2009, The Legend Returns 2010. *Honours:* BRIT Award for Best British Dance Act 1999, 2001, MTV Award for Best Cinematography, for Best Direction, for Breakthrough Video, for Best Editing in a Video (for Weapon of Choice) 2001, Grammy Award for Best Short Form Music Video (for Weapon of Choice) 2002, PRS Outstanding Contribution to British Music Award 2007, Ivor Novello Award for Outstanding Contribution to British Music 2007. *Address:* c/o Skint Records, PO Box 174, Brighton, BN1 4BA, England. *E-mail:* mail@skint.net. *Website:* fatboyslim.net.

COOK, Paul; British musician (drums); b. 20 July 1956, London, England. *Career:* drummer, UK punk group, The Sex Pistols 1975–78; performances include first gig, St Martin's School of Art, London 1975, Screen On The Green Special, London 1976, 100 Club punk rock festival 1976, Anarchy In The UK Tour 1976; tours, Europe 1977, USA 1978; plays dates with Johnny Thunders 1978; mem. band, The Professionals 1979; Sex Pistols reunion concert 1996; collaborations with Edwyn Collins 1992–97. *Recordings:* albums: Never Mind The Bollocks – Here's The Sex Pistols 1977, The Great Rock 'n' Roll Swindle 1979, Some Product – Carry On Sex Pistols 1979, Flogging A Dead Horse 1980, Kiss This 1992, Jubilee 2002; singles: God Save The Queen 1977, Pretty Vacant 1977, Holidays In The Sun 1977, Something Else 1979, Silly Thing 1979, C'mon Everybody 1979, The Great Rock 'n' Roll Swindle 1979; with Steve Jones and Ronnie Biggs: No One Is Innocent (A Punk Prayer By Ronnie Biggs) 1978.

COOKE, Mick; British musician (trumpet, guitar); b. 15 Dec. 1973. *Career:* mem. Hardbody during mid-1990s, Amphetameanies; mem. Belle & Sebastian 1996–; collaborations with Mojave 3, Ex-Cathedra; mem. project, The Reindeer Section 2001–. *Recordings include:* albums: with Belle & Sebastian: The Boy With The Arab Strap 1998, Fold Your Hands Child, You Walk Like A Peasant 2000, Storytelling 2002, Dear Catastrophe Waitress 2003, Push Barman to Open Old Wounds 2005, The Life Pursuit 2006, The Monkeys are Breaking Out the Zoo (Colours Are Brighter) 2006, Write About Love 2010, The Third Eye Centre 2013; with The Reindeer Section: Y'all Get Scared Now, Ya Hear! 2001, Son Of Evil Reindeer 2002; with Amphetameanies: Make Another World 2004. *Play:* Cannibal Women of Mars. *Honours:* BRIT Award for Best Newcomer 1999. *Current Management:* c/o Red Light Management, Unit 4, 16 The Paintworks, Bath Road, Bristol, BS4 3EH, England. *E-mail:* james.sandom@redlightmanagement.com. *Website:* redlightmanagement.com; www.belleandsebastian.com; www.toomanycookes.co.uk. *Website:* www.belleandsebastian.com; www.toomanycookes.co.uk.

COOKE, Paul Anthony, BA, PGCE; British musician (drums, piano), singer, songwriter, manager and producer; *Manager, Paul Cooke Music and Diamond Life Records;* b. (Paul Cook), 18 Dec. 1961, Hull, England; s. of Anthony Cook and Mavis Cook; m. Susan Lesley Jarvis 1991; two s. one d. *Education:* Hull Univ., 2000, Lincoln Univ., Hull College, Beverley College. *Career:* drummer, Pride 1981–82; founder mem., drummer, Sade 1982–84; tours: Danceteria, New York City, East Coast, Philadelphia 1982; U4, Vienna 1983; television and radio appearances include: Switch 1983, Loose Talk 1983, Top of the Pops 1984, Radio 1, Peter Powell Sessions 1983; singer, songwriter, man., Esposito 1985–86, Papa Divine 1987–88; songwriter, prod., MBDK 1989–90; solo artist 1991–93; singer, songwriter, prod., P Eye Eye 1994; exec. prod. for Rolan Bolan 2004–; major concerts include: Esposito, Royal Albert Hall, 1986; Papa Divine, Brighton Pavillion 1987; business ventures: P. R. Clarke Management, PSP Productions, IVI Records Ltd, IVI Management, 88interactive.com, Cybertech Support Services Ltd, IAPC (Int. Asscn of Professional Creators), DigitalDomain.org, PCM (PaulCookeMusic), Diamond Life Entertainment Ltd, Diamond Life Records, PCM2U Ltd; artist man. for Esposito, Papa Divine, MBDK, Buff Meaba, Proud, P Eye Eye, Brave, MMJ; mem., PRS, MCPS, MU, PAMRA (mem. of board 2003–), PPL, ASCAP. *Compositions:* co-writer, Smooth Operator and Your Love Is King, Sade, 1984. *Recordings:* albums: with Sade: Diamond Life 1984, Best of Sade 1994; with P Eye Eye: EMIT2295 1995, Beyond Control 2000, 21st Century Data Flood 2005 Scarborough Warning 2008, The Best of P Eye Eye 2009; singles: Smooth Operator, Sade 1984; Your Love is King, Sade 1984; Snakebite, Sade 1984; Message In A Melody, Esposito 1986; You Don't Have To Say You Love Me, Paul Cooke 1991; Love, Paul Cooke 1991; Emma, Paul Cooke 1991; Lost At Sea, P Eye Eye 1994; Rivers of Tears, Paul Cooke 2002. *Art Exhibition:* Interactive Tour of the Cabala, Hull School of Art & Design, 2000. *Film:* as exec. music producer: Bye Bye Fidel. *Publications:* The Sade Story 2008, Eden 12 2008. *Honours:* BPI Award; Triple Platinum record, Diamond Life, 1984. *Current Management:* Diamond Life Records, PCM (Paul Cooke Music), PCM2U, 6 Cheyne Walk, Hornsea, North Humberside HU18 1BX, England. *Telephone:* (1964) 536193 (office). *Fax:* (1964) 536193 (office). *E-mail:* paulcookemusic@hotmail.com (office). info@diamondliferecordings.co.uk (office). *Website:* www.paulcookemusic.co.uk; www.diamondliferecordings.co.uk.

COOL, Tre; American musician (drums, percussion); b. (Frank Edwin Wright III), 9 Dec. 1972, Willits, CA; m. 1st Lisea (divorced); one d.; m. 2nd Claudia 2000. *Career:* mem., Green Day 1992–; numerous tours and television appearances; side projects include Pinhead Gunpowder, Screeching Weasel,

The Network and Foxboro Hot Tubs. *Recordings include:* albums: with Green Day: 39/Smooth 1990, Kerplunk 1991, Dookie 1994, Insomniac 1994, Nimrod 1997, Warning 2000, International Superhits (compilation) 2001, Shenanigans 2002, American Idiot (Grammy Award for Best Rock Album 2005, MTV Europe Music Award for Best Album 2005, American Music Award for Favorite Pop/Rock Album 2005, BRIT Award for Best Int. Album 2006) 2004; with The Network: Money Money 2020 2003, 21st Century Breakdown (Grammy Award for Best Rock Album 2010) 2009, ¡Uno! 2012, ¡Dos! 2012, ¡Tres! 2012; with Foxboro Hot Tubs: Stop Drop and Roll!!! 2008. *Honours:* Australian MTV Awards for Best Group 2005, for Best Rock Video (for American Idiot) 2005, MTV Award for Best Rock Video, Best Group Video (both for Boulevard of Broken Dreams), Best Group, MTV Viewer's Choice Award 2005, Kerrang! Awards for Best Band on the Planet, Best Live Act 2005, NME Award for Best Video (for American Idiot) 2005, MTV Europe Music Awards for Best Rock Act 2005, 2009, 2013, Billboard 200 Album Group of the Year 2005, Billboard Music Awards for Pop Group of the Year, for Hot 100 Group of the Year, for Rock Artist of the Year, for Rock Song of the Year (for Boulevard of Broken Dreams), for Modern Rock Artist of the Year 2005, Grammy Award for Record of the Year (for Boulevard of Broken Dreams) 2006, BRIT Award for Best Int. Group 2006, ASCAP Awards for Creative Voice, and for Song of the Year (for Boulevard of Broken Dreams) 2006, American Music Award for Favorite Rock Artist 2009. *E-mail:* info@greenday .com (office). *Website:* www.greenday.com.

COOLIDGE, Rita; American singer; b. 1 May 1944, Nashville, TN; m. Kris Kristofferson 1973 (divorced 1979). *Career:* radio commercials with sister, Memphis, TN; session singer with artistes incl. Eric Clapton, Stephen Stills, mid-1960s; tours with Delaney and Bonnie; Leon Russell; solo artist 1970–; British tour with Kris Kristofferson, including Royal Albert Hall, 1978; music for UNICEF concert, New York 1979. *Recordings include:* albums: Rita Coolidge, 1971; Nice Feelin', 1971; Lady's Not For Sale, 1972; Fall Into Spring, 1974; It's Only Love, 1975; Anytime Anywhere, 1977; Love Me Again, 1978; Satisfied, 1979; Heartbreak Radio, 1981; Never Let You Go, 1983; Inside The Fire, 1988; Cherokee, 1995; Out of the Blues, 1996; Walela, native American recording, 1997; with Kris Kristofferson: Full Moon, 1974; Breakaway, 1975; Natural Act, 1979; Thinkin' About You, 1998, And So is Love 2005. *Honours:* Grammy Award for Best Country Duo/Group Vocal Performance (with Kris Kristofferson) 1974, 1975. *Current Management:* c/o Axis Artist Management Inc., 9715 Belmar Avenue, Northridge, CA 91324, USA. *Telephone:* (818) 998-2595. *Fax:* (818) 998-2875. *E-mail:* staff@axismanagement.com. *Website:* www .axismanagement.com; www.ritacoolidge.com.

COOLIO; American rap artist, singer, producer and actor; b. (Artis Ivey Jr), 1 Aug. 1963, Compton, Calif.; five c. *Career:* rapper from age 15; former fireman; joined briefly WC and The Maad Circle 1991; began solo rap career 1994; signed by Tommy Boy Records 1994; collaborations include 40 Thevz, Red Hot Org.; began own record label, Crowbar 1997. *Recordings include:* albums: It Takes A Thief 1994, Gangsta's Paradise 1995, My Soul 1997, Fantastic Voyage – Greatest Hits 2001, El Cool Magnifico 2003, The Return of the Gangsta 2006, Steal Hear 2008, From the Bottom 2 the Top 2009; guest appearances: with WC and The Maad Circle, Ain't A Damn Thang Changed (vocalist) 1991, Quincy Jones, Q's Jook Joint 1994, Clueless 1995, Phat Beach 1996, George Clinton, Greatest Funkin' Hits (vocals) 1996, Forty Thevz, Honor Among Thevz 1997, 17 Reasons (producer) 1998, Coolio's Crowbar Records Presents 1999. *Publication:* Cookin' with Coolio: 5 Star Meals at a 1 Star Price 2009. *Honours:* MTV Video Music Award for Best Rap Video, for Best Video from a Film (for Gangsta's Paradise) 1994, International Dance Music Award, Best Rap 12 Single 1996, American Music Award for Favorite Rap Artist 1996, Grammy Award for Best Rap Solo Performance (for Gangsta's Paradise) 1996. *Website:* www.coolio.com.

COOMBES, Gareth (Gaz); British singer and musician (guitar); b. 8 March 1976, Oxford; brother of Rob Coombes; m.; one c. *Career:* lead singer, The Jennifers –1992, Supergrass 1993–2010; Founder mem. The Hot Rats 2009–; numerous concerts and festival appearances. *Recordings include:* albums: with Supergrass: I Should Coco 1995, Bag O Grass (compilation) 1996, In It For The Money 1997, Supergrass 1999, B-Side Trax (compilation) 2000, Life On Other Planets 2002, Road To Rouen 2005, Diamond Hoo Ha 2008; with The Hot Rats: Turn Ons 2010; solo: Here Come the Bombs 2012, Matador 2015. *Honours:* Q Award for Best New Act 1995, BRIT Award for Best British Newcomer 1996. *Current Management:* c/o Courtyard Management, 21 The Nursery, Sutton Courtenay, Abingdon, Oxfordshire, OX14 4UA, England. *Telephone:* (1235) 845800. *E-mail:* chris@cyard.com. *Website:* www .gazcoombes.com; www.hotrats.net.

COOMBES, Robert (Rob); British musician (keyboards); b. 27 April 1972, Oxford; brother of Gaz Coombes. *Career:* toured with Supergrass from 1995, became official mem. 2002–10; numerous tours, festival dates and TV appearances. *Recordings include:* albums: Life On Other Planets 2002, Road To Rouen 2005, Diamond Hoo Ha 2008. *Current Management:* c/o Courtyard Management, 21 The Nursery, Sutton Courtenay, Abingdon, Oxfordshire OX14 4UA, England. *E-mail:* kate@cyard.com. *Website:* www.supergrass.com.

COOMBS-ROBERTS, Kris; British musician (guitar). *Career:* mem. rock band, Funeral for a Friend 2001–. *Recordings include:* albums: Casually Dressed & Deep in Conversation 2003, Hours 2005, Tales Don't Tell Themselves 2007, Memory and Humanity 2008, Welcome Home Armageddon 2011. *Honours:* Kerrang! Award for Best British Band 2006. *Current*

Management: c/o Good Fight Entertainment, 33 Imlaystown Road, Cream Ridge, NJ 08514, USA. *E-mail:* info@goodfightentertainment.com. *Website:* www.goodfightmusic.com. *E-mail:* contact@funeralforafriend.com.br. *Website:* www.ffaf.co.uk; www.funeralforafriend.com.br.

COONEY, Steve; Australian musician (guitar, bass, didgeridoo) and songwriter; b. 1953, Melbourne; m. Sinéad O'Connor 2010 (divorced 2011). *Career:* started playing music aged 17; fmr mem. Bushwackers, Red Gum, Fruitcake; moved to Ireland 1981; mem. Stockton's Wing; long-term musical partnership with Séamus Begley, as Begley & Cooney; other collaborations include Sharon Shannon, Altan, Martin Hayes, Mary Black, Kirsty MacColl; est. FACE with Laoise Kelly; mem. band Éiníní. *Recordings include:* albums: Meiteal (with Seamus Begley) 1997, Rabhlai Rabhlai 1998; solo: Rhapsody and Rascality 2012. *Honours:* Nat. Entertainment Award for Most Popular Traditional Act (with Séamus Begley), Ireland 1997.

COOPER, Alice; American singer; b. (Vincent Damon Furnier), 4 Feb. 1948, Detroit; s. of the late Mick Furnier and of Ella Furnier; m. Sheryl Goddard; one s. two d. *Education:* Cortez High School, Phoenix, Ariz. *Career:* mem. of band Alice Cooper, adopted this name after band split; first to stage theatrical rock concert tours; among first to film conceptual rock promotional videos (pre-MTV); considered among originators and greatest hard rock artists; host on Virgin Radio Classic Rock 2005–; mem. BMI, NARAS, SAG, AFTRA, AFofM. *Film appearances:* Sextette 1978, Sgt. Pepper's Lonely Hearts Club Band 1978, Leviatán 1984, Prince of Darkness 1987, Freddy's Dead: The Final Nightmare 1991, The Attic Expeditions 2001, Suck 2009, Dark Shadows 2012, Bigfoot 2012, Skum Rocks! 2013. *Recordings include:* with band Alice Cooper: Pretties For You 1969, Live At The Whisky 1969, Easy Action 1970, Love It To Death 1971, Killer 1971, School's Out 1972, Billion Dollar Babies 1973, Muscle of Love 1973, Alice Cooper's Greatest Hits 1974; solo: Welcome To My Nightmare 1975, Alice Cooper Goes To Hell 1976, Lace And Whiskey 1977, Alice Cooper Show (live) 1977, From The Inside 1978, Flush The Fashion 1980, Special Forces 1981, Zipper Catches The Skin 1982, Dada 1982, Constrictor 1986, Raise Your Fist And Yell 1987, Trash 1989, Prince Of Darkness 1989, Hey Stoopid 1991, The Last Temptation 1994, Fistful Of Alice (live) 1997, He's Back 1997, Science Fiction 2000, Brutal Planet 2000, Alice Cooper Live 2001, Take 2 2001, Dragontown 2001, Eyes Of Alice Cooper 2003, Hell Is 2003, Dirty Diamonds 2005, Along Came a Spider 2008, Welcome to My Nightmare 2 2011. *Honours:* Foundations Forum Lifetime Achievement Award 1994, inducted into Rock and Roll Hall of Fame 2011. *Current Management:* Alive Enterprises, PO Box 5542, Beverly Hills, CA 90211, USA. *Website:* www.alicecooper.com.

COOPER, Giles Richard; British singer, songwriter and musician (guitar, bass guitar, keyboards); b. 6 Oct. 1968, Amersham, Buckinghamshire. *Career:* numerous concerts; mem. various bands, including Kindred Spirit, Misbeat, Splinter; mem. Musicians' Union, International Songwriters' Asscn, Guild of International Songwriters and Composers. *Recordings include:* Painted Sun, That Was The Year That Was, Fly Away, Don't Play Those Games, Minds Eye.

COOPER, Neil; musician (drums). *Career:* mem. rock group Therapy? 2002–; owner of label, Sumo Recordings. *Recordings include:* albums: High Anxiety 2003, Never Apologise Never Explain 2004, One Cure Fits All 2006, Crooked Timber 2009, We're Here To The End 2010, A Brief Crack Of Light 2012. *E-mail:* churchofnoise@therapyquestionmark.co.uk. *Website:* www .therapyquestionmark.co.uk.

COOTE, Anthony William John; British musician (guitar, bass guitar) and singer; b. 29 March 1961, Hilderborough, Kent. *Education:* Canterbury Coll. *Career:* with Ruby Blue: major tours of UK, television appearances and festivals; with Rebecca Pidgeon, recording and touring in USA; Animals That Swim, recording, touring UK, Europe; tours with Bjorn Again; mem. Musicians' Union. *Recordings include:* Ruby Blue: Down From Above, Virginia Astley: All Shall Be Well, Rebecca Pidgeon: The Raven, Animals That Swim: Workshy; Singles: Ruby Blue: So Unlike Me, Because, Bloomsbury Blue, Stand Together, The Quiet Mind, Primitive Man, Can It Be, John Martyn: Deny This Love, Animals That Swim: Madame Yevonde, Pink Carnations, Animals that Swim: I Was the King, I Really Was the King, Rebecca Didgeon: New York Girls Club, Cinerama: Va Va Voom, Bjorn Again Live at the Albert Hall, Holiday Suite, Cinerama: Disco Volante 2000, This Is Cinerama 2000; with Richard Wilson: Archipelago 2006; Videos: Ruby Blue: The Quiet Mind, Primitive Man, Animals That Swim: Madame Yevonde. *Telephone:* (18) 4329-8778. *E-mail:* anthonycoote@hotmail.com. *Website:* www .anthonycoote.co.uk.

COPANI, Ignacio Anibal; Argentine musician (guitar, piano), composer and singer; b. 25 Oct. 1959, Buenos Aires; m. Nora Krichmar 1981; three d. *Career:* concerts at theatres throughout Argentina, including Opera Theatre, Luna Park, Excursionistas Football Stadium; tours: Argentina; Uruguay; Chile; Colombia; numerous radio, TV programmes; own two-hour daily radio programme; apptd Cultural Amb. Party of La Costa 2007; mem. Sociedad Argentina de Autores y Compositores de Música (composers), Sindicato Argentino de Musicos (musicians). *Recordings include:* Ignacio Copani 1988, Ya Vendram Temps Mejores 1989, Copani 1994, Copani Completo 1992, Afectos Especiales 1993, Puerto 1994, Salvese Quien Pued'a 1995, Compromiso 1995, Dos en Uno 1997, Rivertidísimo 1997, Lo mejor 2005, Teatro Ópera en vivo 2006, Yo nunca me metí en política 2011. *Honours:* Ace 1994, Winner, Previsario 1993, Konex 1995. *Address:* 1605 Lavalle Street, 4, 8, Buenos Aires, Argentina. *E-mail:* copani@sinectis.com.ar. *Website:* www.copani.com.ar.

COPE, Julian David; British singer, musician (guitar, bass), songwriter, author and antiquary and poet; b. 21 Oct. 1957, Bargoed, Wales; m. Dorian; two d. *Career:* Founder-mem., Crucial Three 1977–78; lead singer, The Teardrop Explodes 1978–82; numerous live concerts, festival appearances; solo artist 1983–; f. Head Heritage 1997. *Recordings include:* albums: with The Teardrop Explodes: Kilimanjaro 1980, Wilder 1981, Everybody Wants To Shag The Teardrop Explodes 1990, The Greatest Hit (compilation) 2001; solo: World Shut Your Mouth 1984, Fried 1984, St Julian 1987, My Nation Underground 1988, Skellington 1990, Peggy Suicide 1991, Jehovah Kill 1992, Floored Genius 1992, 20 Mothers 1995, Ritey 1997, Leper Skin 1999, Citizen Cain'd 2005, Dark Orgasm 2005, You Gotta Problem With Me 2007, Black Sheep 2008, The Unruly Imagination 2009, The Jehovacoat Demos 2011, Psychedelic Revolution 2012, Revolutionary Suicide 2013. *Publications include:* Head On (autobiog., Vol. 1) 1991, Krautrocksampler (guide to German music 1968–95) 1995, The Modern Antiquarian 1996, Repossessed (autobiog., Vol. 2) 1999, Japrocksampler: How The Post-War Japanese Blew Their Minds On Rock 'n' Roll 2007, Copendium: A Guide to the Musical Underground 2012, One Three One: A Time-Shifting Gnostic Hooligan Road Novel 2014. *Address:* Head Heritage Ltd, The Stables, Yatesbury Manor, Yatesbury, SN11 8YE, England (office). *E-mail:* info@headheritage.co.uk (office). *Website:* www.headheritage.co.uk (office).

COPELAND, Shemekia; American blues, gospel and R&B singer; b. 10 April 1979, Harlem, New York City; d. of Johnny Copeland. *Education:* Teaneck High School, New Jersey. *Career:* fmr opening act for father Johnny Copeland; signed to Alligator Records 1998; signed to Telarc Records 2009; appearances at numerous blues festivals worldwide; collaborators include Ruth Brown, Steve Cropper, Dr John, Marc Ribot. *Films:* Three to Tango 1999. *Recordings include:* albums: Turn the Heat Up! 1998, Wicked (Blues Music Award for Blues Album of the Year 2001) 2000, Talking to Strangers (Blues Music Awards for Blues Album of the Year 2003, for Contemporary Blues Album of the Year 2003) 2002, The Soul Truth 2005, Never Going Back 2009, 33 1/3 2012. *Honours:* Living Blues Critics' Awards for Best Blues Artist (Female) 2001, for Most Outstanding Blues Singer 2012, Living Blues Readers' Poll Awards for Female Artist of the Year 2001, for Best Blues Artist (Female) 2002, for Best Female Blues Singer 2003, for Female Blues Artist of the Year 2006, 2010, Downbeat Magazine's Critics' Poll for Blues Artist: Talent Deserving Wider Recognition 2001, for Rising Star – Blues Artist 2005, 2009, Blues Music Awards for Blues Song of the Year (for It's 2AM) 2001, for Contemporary Blues Female Artist of the Year 2001, 2002, 2003, Blues Blast Music Award for Best Female Blues Artist 2010, Chicago Blues Festival's Queen of the Blues Honor 2011. *Current Management:* c/o John Hahn Management Inc., 12 West 72nd Street, Apt 2-A, New York, NY 10023, USA. *E-mail:* jhahn4@gmail.com. *Address:* c/o Kelly Johanns-DiCillo, Telarc International Corporation, 23307 Commerce Park Road, Cleveland, OH 44122, USA (office). *Telephone:* (206) 636-3507 (office). *Website:* www.telarc.com (office); www.shemekiacopeland.com.

COPELAND, Stewart; musician (drums, percussion), singer and composer; b. 16 July 1952, Alexandria, Egypt. *Career:* fmr mem., Curved Air; mem. of rock group, The Police 1977–86, re-formed to tour 2007–; numerous worldwide tours, television and radio broadcasts with The Police; founder, Animal Logic (with Deborah Holland, Stanley Clarke) 1989. *Compositions:* film scores: numerous including Rumble Fish, Wall Street, Talk Radio, Hidden Agenda, First Power, Men At Work, Lovewrecked 2005; ballet: King Lear (for San Francisco Ballet) 1982; opera: Holy Blood and Crescent Moon (for Cleveland Opera) 1989. *Recordings include:* albums: with The Police: Outlandos D'Amour 1978, Regatta De Blanc 1979, Zenyatta Mondatta 1980, Ghost In The Machine 1981, Synchronicity 1983; solo: The Equalizer and Other Cliff Hangers 1988, Noah's Ark 1990, Leopard Son 1996, Four Days In September 1998, Simpatico 2000. *Publication:* Strange Things Happen: A Life with the Police, Polo and Pygmies 2009. *Honours:* Chevalier, Ordre des Arts et des Lettres 2007; Grammy Awards with The Police. *Current Management:* The Derek Power Company and Kahn Power Pictures, 818 North Doheny Drive, 1003, Los Angeles, CA 90069, USA. *Telephone:* (310) 550-0770. *Fax:* (310) 550-6292. *E-mail:* iampower007@gmail.com. *Website:* www.music4film.com. *E-mail:* giovanni@stewartcopeland.net. *Website:* www.stewartcopeland.net.

COPLAND, Clive Rowan; British musician (guitar); b. 6 June 1956, Hampton Court, Richmond upon Thames, England; m. Linda Copland; two s. *Education:* studied with Andre Edmonds, Kevin Stacey, John Mizaroli. *Career:* mem. soul band, The Strutters 1974; later worked with Ray Shields Orchestra, Herb Miller Orchestra; now freelance musician; recording sessions with Hurricane Smith, John Miller, Cliff Longhurst Jazz Knights, Chris Smith Jr, Five Star Swing; mem. Asscn of Motion Picture Sound. *Recordings include:* played on film soundtrack to Yanks, four albums with Herb Miller. *Honours:* BAFTA Award for Best Sound (for Colditz TV film). *Address:* 116 Mortlake Road, Kew, Richmond, Surrey, TW9 4AR, England (home). *Telephone:* (20) 8876-3728 (home). *E-mail:* clive.copland@gmail.com.

COPPEL, Michael Henry, BL, BCom; Australian concert promoter; *President and CEO, Live Nation Entertainment*; b. 1 Oct. 1949, Melbourne; m. Michelle Coppel 1981; one s. three d. *Education:* Melbourne Univ. *Career:* concerts promoted include AC/DC, Tori Amos, Biohazard, Björk, Michael Bolton, Garth Brooks, The Cardigans, Catatonia, Joe Cocker, The Corrs, Elvis Costello, The Cranberries, Sheryl Crow, Céline Dion, Ben Elton, Eurythmics, The Fugees, Garbage, Green Day, Herbie Hancock, Emmylou Harris, Hole, Whitney Houston, Natalie Imbruglia, Janet Jackson, Jamiroquai, B. B. King, Korn, M People, Reba McEntire, Marilyn Manson, Massive Attack, Metallica, Alanis Morissette, Oasis, Pantera, Pet Shop Boys, Placebo, Public Enemy, LeAnn Rimes, Salt 'n' Pepa, Simply Red, Slayer, Smashing Pumpkins, Tina Turner, U2, UB40, Violent Femmes, Victoria Wood, and numerous festivals; Exec. Councillor, EIEA; Pres. and CEO Live Nation Entertainment, Australia 2012–. *Honours:* Australian Concert Promoter of the Year 1993, 1994. *Address:* Live Nation Entertainment, PO Box 4142, East Richmond, Victoria, 3121, Australia (office). *Telephone:* (3) 8632-2500 (office). *Fax:* (3) 8632-2511 (office). *E-mail:* info@livenation.com.au (office); mcpinfo@coppel.com.au. *Website:* www.livenation.com.au (office); www.coppel.com.au.

COPPIN, Johnny; British singer, songwriter, musician (guitar, piano) and anthologist; b. 5 April 1946, South Woodford, London; pnr Katharine Nelson; one s. *Education:* Gloucester Coll. of Art and Design. *Career:* lead singer and songwriter, Decameron 1969–76; solo performer 1976–; numerous European festivals, concert tours, TV and radio broadcasts; Musical Dir and Composer, The Festival Players Theatre Co. 1991–; Hon. Pres., Glosfolk 2008–; mem. BAC&S, Equity, PRS, MCPS. *Play:* Songs on Lonely Roads – The Story of Ivor Gurney (with David Goodland) 1990. *Radio:* presenter/producer: Folk Roots (BBC Radio Gloucestershire); various UK nat. and local radio programmes including A Cotswold Christmas, A Slice of Apple on BBC Radio 2. *Recordings include:* four albums with Decameron; solo albums: Roll On Dreamer 1978, No Going Back 1979, Get Lucky 1982, Forest and Vale and High Blue Hill 1983, Line of Blue 1985, English Morning 1987, Edge of Day, with Laurie Lee 1989, West Country Christmas 1990, Songs on Lonely Roads (Story of Ivor Gurney) 1990, Force of The River 1993, A Country Christmas 1995, The Shakespeare Songs 1997, A Journey 1999, Keep the Flame 2004, The Winding Stair 2005, Breaking the Silence 2007. *Publications include:* Forest and Vale and High Blue Hill 1991, Between the Severn and the Wye 1993, A Country Christmas 1996. *Honours:* Hon. Fellow, Cheltenham and Gloucester Coll. of Higher Educ. (now Univ. of Gloucestershire) 1997. *Current Management:* CTM, Stroud, GL5 2LS, England. *Telephone:* (1453) 757376. *E-mail:* ctm@crispinthomas.orangehome.co.uk. *Website:* www.ctmuk.com. *Address:* Red Sky Records, PO Box 27, Stroud, Gloucestershire GL6 0YQ, England (office). *Telephone:* (1453) 885088 (office). *Fax:* (1453) 885088 (office). *E-mail:* johnny@johnnycoppin.co.uk (office). *Website:* www.johnnycoppin.co.uk.

CORBEIL, Olivier; Canadian musician (bass) and singer. *Career:* mem. The Stills 2000–11. *Recordings include:* albums: Logic Will Break Your Heart 2003, Without Feathers 2005, Oceans Will Rise (Juno Award for Best Alternative Album of the Year 2009) 2008. *Honours:* Juno Award for Best New Group of the Year 2009. *Current Management:* c/o Agency Olivier Corbeil 5130, Saint Hubert, Montreal, PQ H2L 2Y3, Canada. *Telephone:* (514) 848-9330. *Fax:* (514) 848-7269. *E-mail:* info@agenceoc.com. *Website:* www.agenceoc.com.

CORBI, Rafel; Spanish (Catalan) broadcaster; *Managing Director, Radio Palafrugell*; b. 30 July 1966, Palafrugell, Girona; m. 1st Mariona Viella 1987 (divorced), one s. one d.; m. 2nd Rosa Llenas 2002. *Career:* worked in radio since age of 16; worked for various Catalan newspapers; featured in all major country music magazines world-wide; Man. Dir RPEM-FM 1991–; Pres. European Country Music Asscn 1996–2012; Founder Spanish Acad. of Country Music; Host, Country Club Radio syndicated show 1987–; fmr mem. CMA, Nashville, CCMA, etc. *Honours:* Radio Personality of the Year 1994, 1997, 1998, Nashville Award, Country Music's European Man of the Year, Airplay International 1998, numerous American Eagle Awards, Country Music Asscn of America, Palafrugell City Man of The Year 2015. *Address:* C/ de la Estrella, Palafrugell 17200, Girona, Catalonia, Spain (office). *E-mail:* rafelcorbi@yahoo.es (office). *Website:* www.rafelcorbi.com.

CORDERO, Jorge Luis; Cuban singer, composer and bandleader; b. 12 May 1952, Holguin; m. Anne Nielsen Cordero 1976; one s. one d. *Career:* bandleader, Los Gran Daneses; concerts, tours include: Germany, Cuba, Poland, Sweden, Norway, Spain, Calle 8 Festival (Miami) 1992; television and radio, USA 1993–; mem. DMF, DJBFA. *Recordings include:* Que Vida 1975, Salsa Na'ma 1981, Diferente 1988, Rompiendo el Hielo 1994, Del Morte y Tropical 1996, Al Tiempo 1999. *Address:* Mondrupsvej 8, 8260 Viby, Denmark. *E-mail:* cuba@salsa.dk. *Website:* www.cordero.dk.

CORDIER, Thierry; French writer, composer and jazz musician (guitar, keyboards); b. 29 May 1963, Mont Saint Martin; m. Joëlle Cordier 1989; two d. *Career:* recorded with Charles Baudelaire 1986; concerts in France, Luxembourg, Belgium; television and radio broadcasts; mem. Société des auteurs, compositeurs et éditeurs de musique (SACEM), ADAMI. *Recordings include:* albums: Correspondances, Tableau Noir, Charles Baudelaire 1986, Human, Garcon d'Café, Compilat, Coup d'Pauce '95, Noirs et Couleurs, 1./kri/, Selected Recordings 2002, Mon Intérieur 2008. *Address:* 7 rue de la Chappelle, 54400 Longwy, France. *Telephone:* 3-82-25-67-86 (office). *E-mail:* 1poisson@wanadoo.fr. *Website:* www.thierrycordier.com.

COREA, Chick; American musician (piano) and composer; b. (Armando Corea), 12 June 1941, Chelsea, Mass; m. Gayle Moran; one s. one d. *Education:* Juilliard School of Music. *Career:* pianist with artists, including Mongo Santamaria 1962, Blue Mitchell 1965, Stan Getz 1966–68, Miles Davis 1969–71, Sarah Vaughan 1970; Founder mem., leader, pianist with group, Return To Forever 1971–; Founder The Elektric Band 1986–. *Recordings include:* Piano Improvisations 1 and 2, Leprechaun, My Spanish Heart, Mad Hatter, Delphi 1, 2 and 3, Light As A Feather, Romantic Warrior, Hymn of The Seventh Galaxy, Music Magic, Voyage (with Steve Kujala) 1984, The Chick

Corea Akoustic Band 1989, Elektric Band Inside Out 1990, Chick Corea Akoustic Band Alive! 1991, Elektric Band Beneath The Mask 1991, Time Warp 1995, Remembering Bud Powell 1997, Native Sense 1997, Standards 2000, Past Present and Futures 2001, Elektric Band: To The Stars 2004, The Ultimate Adventure (Grammy Awards for Best Jazz Instrumental Album, Individual or Group, for Best Instrumental Arrangement 2007) 2006, The Enchantment (with Béla Fleck) (Latin Grammy Award for Best Instrumental Album) 2007, The New Crystal Silence (with Gary Burton) (Grammy Award for Best Jazz Instrumental Album 2009) 2008, Five Peace Band—Live (with John McLaughlin Five Peace Band) (Grammy Award for Best Jazz Instrumental Album 2010) 2009, Forever (with Stanley Clarke and Lenny White) (Grammy Award for Best Jazz Instrumental Album 2012) 2011, Orvieto 2011, Further Explorations 2012, The Continents 2012, Hot House 2012, The Mothership Returns 2012, Mozart Goes Dancing (with Gary Burton) (Grammy Award for Best Instrumental Composition 2013) 2012, The Vigil (with Hadrien Feraud, Marcus Gilmore, Tim Garland and Charles Altura) 2013, Trilogy (Grammy Award for Best Jazz Instrumental Album 2015) 2013. *Honours:* Dr hc (Norwegian Univ. of Science and Technology) 2010; numerous magazine awards from Downbeat, Keyboard Magazine; Jazz Life Musician of World, Jazz Forum Music Poll 1974, Best Electric Jazz group 1990, Best Acoustic Pianist 1990, Top Jazz Pianist 1990, many Grammy Awards including Best Improvised Jazz Solo (for 500 Miles High) 2012, Best Instrumental Composition (for Mozart Goes Dancing), Best Improvised Jazz Solo (with Gary Burton) (for Hot House) 2013, Best Improvised Jazz Solo (for Fingerprints) 2015, Jazz Journalists' Asscn Award for Keyboard Player of the Year 2015. *Current Management:* Chick Corea Productions Inc., 411 Cleveland Street, No. 215, Clearwater, FL 33755, USA. *Telephone:* (727) 446-8100. *E-mail:* writein@chickcorea.com. *Website:* www.chickcorea.com.

CORGAN, William (Billy) Patrick; American singer, songwriter and musician (multi-instrumentalist); b. 17 March 1967, Elk Grove, Chicago, IL; m. Christine Fabian 1994 (divorced 1997). *Career:* lead singer, Smashing Pumpkins 1989–2000, 2006–; numerous concerts, television and radio appearances; joined New Order as additional guitarist 2001; founder mem., Zwan 2001; solo artist 2002–. *Recordings include:* albums: with Smashing Pumpkins: Gish 1991, The Peel Sessions 1992, Siamese Dream 1993, Pisces Iscariot 1994, Mellon Collie and the Infinite Sadness 1995, The Aeroplane Flies High 1996, Adore 1998, MACHINA/The Machines of God 2000, Machina II: The Friends and Enemies of Modern Music 2000, Earphoria 2002, Zeitgeist 2007, Oceania 2012; with Zwan: Mary Star Of The Sea 2003; solo: TheFutureEmbrace 2005. *Publication:* Blinking with Fists (poems) 2004. *Website:* www.billycorgan.com; www.smashingpumpkins.com.

CORMIER, John Paul; Canadian musician (fiddle, guitar, banjo, mandolin, resophonic guitar, bass, piano), singer and songwriter; b. 23 Jan. 1969, London, Ont.; m. Hilda Chiasson 1994. *Career:* regular guest on Up Home Tonight (ATV); studio, stage and session work with Travis Tritt, Waylon Jennings, Marty Stuart, Carl Perkins and Steve Warner; major Folk and Celtic festivals including: Tonder Festival, Denmark; Celtic Connections, Scotland; Celtic Colours; touring extensively in Canada and USA; mem., AFofM, SOCAN, CMRRA. *Compositions:* Another Morning; Highland Dream; The Island; Gone; Kelly's Mountain; Long For The Sea. *Recordings:* Out of the Blue, 1986; North Wind, 1989; The Fiddle Album, 1990; The Gift, 1992; When January Comes, 1993; Lord of the Dance, 1993; Return to the Cape, 1995; Another Morning, 1997. *Honours:* Canadian Open Guitar Champion, 1986; Maritime Fiddle Champion, 1995; East Coast Music Award Winner, Roots/Traditional Vocal Artist of the Year, 1998. *Address:* J.P. Cormier School of Strings, 276 Charlotte Street, Sydney, NS B1P 1C6, Canada. *E-mail:* contact@jp-cormier.com. *Website:* www.jp-cormier.com.

CORNEILLE; Canadian/Rwandan R & B singer and songwriter; b. 24 March 1977, Fribourg, Germany. *Education:* Concordia Univ. *Career:* mem. of an R & B group in Rwanda 1993; moves to Germany, then Canada; mem. R & B group, O.N.E. 1997–2001; solo artist 2001–; named UNICEF Goodwill Amb. *Recordings:* albums: Parce qu'on vient de loin 2002, Les Marchants des Rêves 2005, The Birth of Cornelius 2008. *Honours:* Felix Award for Best Male Artist 2004, Award for Best Int. Singer-Songwriter, SOCAN. *Address:* c/o Déjà Musique, 391 Laurier Ouest, Montreal, QC H2V 2K3, Canada (office). *Website:* www.dejamusique.com (office); www.corneille.ca.

CORNELIUS; Japanese musician, composer, producer and remixer; b. (Keigo Oyamada), 27 Jan. 1969, Setagaya-ku, Tokyo. *Career:* collaborations with artists, including Nigo; remixer and producer. for numerous artists, including Beck, Bloc Party, Blur, Manic Street Preachers, Money Mark, Sting. *Recordings include:* albums: The First Question Award 1994, 69/96 1995, 96/69 1996, Fantasma 1997, CM/FM 1999, Point 2002. *E-mail:* info@cornelius-sound.com. *Website:* www.cornelius-sound.com.

CORNELIUS, Claes; Danish A&R manager, publisher and musician (guitar, keyboards); b. 14 May 1949, Copenhagen; one s. *Education:* Universita Internazionale dell'Arte, Italy. *Career:* professional musician 1959–; Man., Edition Wilhelm Hansen 1973–77; A&R and Publishing Man., Mega Records/Megasong Publishing 1983–2002; Man. Sing A Song Publishing 1982–; Publishing Man., Laid Back Management 2006–. *Honours:* Shared Critics Prize for production in Italy. *Address:* Stenosgade 9, 1616 Copenhagen, Denmark (home). *E-mail:* john@laidback.dk. *Website:* www.laidback.dk.

CORNELIUS, Helen Lorene; American singer and songwriter; b. 6 Dec. 1941, Hannibal, MO; m. Jerry Garren 1981, two s. one d. *Career:* songwriter,

1970–; recording artist, 1975–80; television appearances; stage performances: Annie Get Your Gun, US touring production, 1984; mem. BMI, AFTRA, CMA, National Asscn of Songwriters, West Coast Academy of Country Music. *Recordings include:* albums: Helen Cornelius 1975, Encore 2011; with Jim Ed Brown: I Don't Want to Have to Marry You 1976, Born Believer 1977, I'll Never Be Free 1978, You Don't Bring Me Flowers 1979, One Man, One Woman 1980 Born Believer; I Don't Want To Have To Marry You. *Honours:* CMA Vocal Duo of the Year 1977. *E-mail:* helen@helencornelius.net. *Website:* www.helencornelius.net.

CORNELL, Chris; American singer, songwriter and musician (guitar); b. 20 July 1964; m. 1st Susan Silver (divorced 2004); one d.; m. 2nd Vicky Karayiannis; one s., one d. *Career:* mem. heavy rock group, Soundgarden 1984–97, 2010–; numerous concerts, tours, festival appearances; mem. tribute group, Temple of the Dog 1991; solo artist 1997–; Founder-mem., Audioslave 2002–07; mem. Nat. Acad. of Recording Arts and Sciences. *Film music:* recorded theme tune to James Bond: Casino Royale, 'You Know My Name' 2006. *Recordings include:* albums: with Soundgarden: Ultramega OK 1989, Louder Than Love 1989, Badmotorfinger 1991, Superunknown 1994, Down On The Upside 1996, King Animal 2012; with Temple of the Dog: Temple Of The Dog 1991; solo: Euphoria Morning 1999, Carry On 2007, Scream 2008, Songbook 2011, Higher Truth 2015; with Audioslave: Audioslave 2002, Out Of Exile 2005, Revelations 2006. *Honours:* two Grammy Awards (with Soundgarden) 1995. *Current Management:* c/o Amy Decker, Lafitte Management Group, Maverick Management. *E-mail:* amy@maverick.com. *Website:* www.maverick.com; www.chriscornell.com; www.soundgardenworld.com.

CORNER, Chris; British singer, musician (guitar), songwriter and producer; b. 23 Jan. 1974. *Career:* various musical projects, with Liam Howe, first band 1990, F.R.I.S.K. 1992, Line Of Flight 1993; Founding mem., Sneaker Pimps 1995–; numerous festivals and concerts; band founded Splinter Recordings 1999; project I Am X 2003–. *Recordings include:* with Sneaker Pimps: Becoming X 1996, Splinter 1999, Bloodsport 2002; singles: with Line Of Flight: World As A Cone (EP) 1993; with Sneaker Pimps: 6 Underground (EP) 1996, Roll On 1996, Tesko Suicide 1996, Spin Spin Sugar 1997, Post Modern Sleaze 1997, 6 Underground 1998, Low Five 1999, Ten To Twenty 1999, Sick 2002. *Current Management:* c/o Reza Davoudi, Nineteen95 Artist Management, Adalbertstrasse 91, 10999 Berlin, Germany. *E-mail:* reza@nineteen95.com. *Website:* www.nineteen95.com; www.iamx.eu.

CORNWELL, Hugh; British singer and musician (guitar); b. 28 Aug. 1949, London. *Education:* Bristol Univ., Lund Univ. *Career:* fmr science teacher; Founder-mem. rock group, Stranglers 1976–90; tours of Europe, UK, Canada, USA; solo artist 1991–; worked with Roger Cook and Andy West as Cornwell, Cook and West 1992. *Recordings include:* albums: with Stranglers: Rattus Norvegicus 1977, No More Heroes 1978, Black and White 1978, Live (X Cert) 1979, The Raven 1979, Themeninblack 1981, La Folie 1982, The Collection 1982, Feline 1983, Aural Sculpture 1984, Dreamtime 1986, All Live and All of the Night 1988, 10 1990; solo: Nosferatu 1979, Wolf 1988, Wired 1993, Black Hair, Black Eyes, Black Suit 1999, First Bus to Babylon 1999, Hi-Fi 2000, Footprints in the Desert 2002, In the Dock 2003, Beyond Elysian Fields 2004, Hooverdam 2008, New Songs for King Kong 2010; with Cornwell, Cook and West: C C W 1992. *Publications include:* A Multitude of Sins: The Stranglers, Golden Brown and Strange Little Girl 2004, Window on the World 2011. *Honours:* Ivor Novello Award for Most Performed Work (for Golden Brown) 1983. *E-mail:* info@hughcornwell.com. *Website:* www.hughcornwell.com.

CORONADO, Gilles; French musician (guitar) and composer; b. 26 Oct. 1966, Avignon. *Career:* mem. various bands (jazz, funk, rock), South of France; moved to Paris 1991; mem. HASK collective (musicians' asscn, Paris); Founder-mem. and leader quartet, Urban Mood; played various festivals in Germany, Belgium, Portugal, France; collaborator with dance performances 1993–; teacher; mem. Société des auteurs, compositeurs et éditeurs de musique. *Recordings include:* albums: Gilles Coronado Solo 2001, Golden Retriever (with F. Poulet) 2005.

CORR, Andrea Jane; Irish singer, musician (tin whistle) and actress; b. 17 May 1974, Dundalk, Louth Co.; m. Brett Desmond 2009; one d. *Career:* mem., The Corrs 1991–2005, 2015–; numerous TV appearances, live shows and festival appearances; solo artist 2007–. *Film appearances:* The Commitments 1991, Evita 1996, Quest for Camelot (voice) 1998, The Boys from County Clare 2003, The Bridge 2005, Broken Thread 2006, Pictures 2009. *Plays include:* Dancing at Lughnasa (Old Vic theatre, London) 2009, Jane Eyre 2010. *Recordings include:* albums: with The Corrs: Forgiven, Not Forgotten 1996, Corrs Live 1998, Talk on Corners 1998, MTV Corrs Unplugged 1999, In Blue 2000, VH-1 Presents The Corrs: Live in Dublin 2002, Borrowed Heaven 2004, Home 2005, White Light 2015; solo: Ten Feet High 2007, Lifelines 2011. *Honours:* BRIT Award for Best Int. Group 1999; Hon. MBE 2005. *Website:* www.andreacorr.com; www.thecorrswebsite.com.

CORR, Caroline; Irish musician (drums, bodhran); b. 17 March 1973, Dundalk; m. Frank Woods; three c. *Career:* mem. The Corrs 1991–2005, 2015–; numerous TV appearances, live shows and festival appearances. *Recordings include:* albums: Forgiven, Not Forgotten 1996, Corrs Live 1998, Talk On Corners 1998, MTV Corrs Unplugged 1999, In Blue 2000, VH-1 Presents the Corrs: Live in Dublin 2002, Borrowed Heaven 2004, Home 2005, Dreams: The Ultimate Corrs Collection 2007, White Light 2015. *Honours:* Hon. MBE 2005; BRIT Award for Best Int. Group 1999. *E-mail:* grabow@grabow.biz. *Website:* www.thecorrswebsite.com.

CORR, (James Steven) Jim; Irish musician (guitar, keyboards); b. 31 July 1968, Dundalk, Co. Louth. *Career:* mem. The Corrs 1991–2005, 2015–; numerous TV appearances, live shows and festival appearances. *Recordings include:* albums: Forgiven, Not Forgotten 1996, Corrs Live 1998, Talk On Corners 1998, MTV Corrs Unplugged 1999, In Blue 2000, VH-1 Presents the Corrs: Live in Dublin 2002, Borrowed Heaven 2004, Home 2005, Dreams–The Ultimate Corrs Collection 2007, Mum of the Year 2009, White Light 2015. *Honours:* Hon. MBE 2005; BRIT Award for Best Int. Group 1999. *E-mail:* grabow@grabow.biz. *Website:* www.thecorrswebsite.com.

CORR, Sharon; Irish musician (violin) and singer; b. 24 March 1970, Dundalk, Louth Co.; m. Robert Gavin Bonnar 2001; two c. *Career:* mem., The Corrs 1991–2005, 2015–; solo artist 2010–; numerous TV appearances, live shows and festival appearances. *Recordings include:* albums: with The Corrs: Forgiven, Not Forgotten 1996, Corrs Live 1998, Talk On Corners 1998, MTV Corrs Unplugged 1999, In Blue 2000, VH-1 Presents the Corrs: Live in Dublin 2002, Borrowed Heaven 2004, Home 2005, White Light 2015; solo: Dream of You 2010, The Same Sun 2013. *Honours:* BRIT Award for Best Int. Group 1999; Hon. MBE 2005. *Website:* www.thecorrswebsite.com; www.sharoncorr.com.

CORRIGAN, Briana; Irish singer; b. 30 May 1965. *Career:* mem. The Beautiful South 1989–93; solo artist 1993–. *Recordings include:* albums: with The Beautiful South: Welcome To The Beautiful South 1989, Choke 1990, 0898 1992; solo: When Your Arms Wrap Around Me 1996, Redbird 2012. *Current Management:* c/o AMA Music Agency, The Gate Lodge, Fitzpatrick's Castle, Killiney, Ireland. *Telephone:* (8) 6250-4795. *Website:* www.amamusicagency.ie. *E-mail:* redbirdandanchor@gmail.com. *Website:* www.brianacorrigan.com.

CORSBY, Dave; British composer, arranger and musician (saxophones, flute, clarinet, keyboards); b. (David Roger Corsby), 29 June 1938, Hounslow, Middx, England; s. of Arthur Gilbert Corsby and Doris Rose Corsby; m. Jill Corsby 1992. *Career:* Founder-mem. Cave Jazz Club, Ramsgate, Kent 1955; Co-organizer Thanet Jazz Festival 1982, 1983; baritone saxophonist, John Burch Octet; radio, TV, film and recording sessions; appeared at Dunkirk Jazzopale 1994, Hot Club of Lyon 1995, Arts Council tour with John Burch Octet 1994–95, Canterbury Festival 1998, Ramsgate Spring Festival 1999; bandleader, Doctor Crotchet's Good Time Jazz, Dave Corsby Quartet (modern jazz group), Brass Tacks Jazz Sextet, Mission Impossible Big Band; business ventures include Carpe Diem Arts, Carpe Diem Music, Lincoln Studios; mem. Musicians' Union, Performing Rights Soc., Art Pepper Soc. *Compositions include:* The Subterraneans, Rajans Banquet, Samuel Pepys Jazz Suite, Tale of Two Cities Jazz Suite (Arts Council Commission), Seven Deadly Sins (jazz musical), The Endeavour Experience (film score) 1994, Cinque Ports Jazz Suite (Sandwich Festival commission) 1997, Time and Tide Suite 2001, Medway Jazz Suite 2001, Spirits by Night 2004. *Recordings include:* Tale of Two Cities Jazz Suite, Samuel Pepys Jazz Suite, The Seven Deadly Sins, Roll Call, Just the Two of Us, Second Thoughts, Nuggets. *Telephone:* (1843) 841501 (home). *E-mail:* dave@davecorsby.com. *Website:* www.davecorsby.com.

CORSO, Terence (Terry); American musician (guitar); b. 28 Nov. 1971, Riverside, Calif. *Education:* learned drums and guitar at band workshop programme sponsored by local music store. *Career:* played with local bands Sinister Fiend, Brother Vibe, Wallop; mem., Alien Ant Farm 1996–2003, 2008–; released self-financed ind. LP 1999; signed to Papa Roach's New Noize label; second album released in conjunction with DreamWorks Records label 2001; mem. Powerman 5000 2005–07. *Recordings include:* albums: with Alien Ant Farm: Greatest Hits (LA Music Award, Best Independent Album) 1999, ANThology 2001, truANT 2003; with Powerman 5000: Destroy What You Enjoy 2006. *Address:* c/o Primary Wave Music Publishing, 116 East, 16th Street, 9th Floor, New York, NY 10003, USA. *Telephone:* (212) 661-6990. *Fax:* (212) 661-8890. *Website:* www.primarywavemusic.com; www.alienantfarm.com.

CORTES, Garðar Thór; Icelandic singer (tenor); b. 2 May 1979, Reykjavík; s. of Garðar Cortes and Krystyna Cortes. *Education:* attended singing school in Reykjavik, Hochschule Vienna, RAM, London, pvt. studies with Andrei Orlowitz in Copenhagen. *Career:* child actor in tv series Nonni and Manni; lived and worked in Denmark for five years; Raoul in Phantom of the Opera, London 1999; has performed roles including José in Carmen Negra, the Italian Tenor in Der Rosenkavalier, Ferrando in Così fan tutte, Rinuccio in Gianni Schicchi, Conte Alberto in L'occasione fa il ladro, Duke of Mantua in Rigoletto; appearances with English Touring Opera, Icelandic Opera, Nordfjord Opera, Norway, Co-Opera Ireland, Nordurop Opera, Rossini Festival, Germany; concert appearances have included Mendelssohn's Elijah, Carnegie Hall, New York, Bach's Mass in B Minor, St Nicolas, Dvořák's Requiem, Verdi's Requiem, Handel's Messiah, Puccini's Missa di Gloria, Rossini's Petite Messe Solennelle and Stabat Mater, Saint-Saëns' Christmas Oratorio and Les Noces; appeared as Passarino in The Phantom of the Opera, Royal Albert Hall, London 2011; appeared as Alfredo in La Traviata, Harpa concert hall, Reykjavik 2014. *Recordings:* albums: Cortes 2007, When You Say You Love Me 2008, Ísland 2011, Rossini: L'occasione fa il ladro 2012. *Play:* L'occasione fa il ladro 2012. *Address:* Believer Music, Bankastraeti 11, Reykjavík 101, Iceland (home). *E-mail:* einar@believer.is (office). *Website:* www.believer.is.

CORTEZ, Alberto; Argentine singer and composer; b. (José Alberto García Gallo), 11 March 1940, Rancul; m. Renee Govaerts 1964. *Education:* Chopin Conservatory, Mendoza. *Career:* solo artist; numerous live performances; mem. SGAE (Spain). *Recordings include:* albums: Welcome to the Latin Club 1961, Mr Sucu Sucu 1963, Boleros 1965, Poemas y canciones Vol. 1 1967, Alberto Cortez canta a Atahualpa Yupanqui 1968, Poemas y canciones Vol. 2 1968, El compositor, el cantante 1969, Distancia 1970, No soy de aquí 1971, Equipaje 1972, Ni poco... ni demasiado 1973, Como el ave solitaria 1974, A mis amigos 1975, Soy un charlatán de feria 1976, Pensares y sentires 1977, En Vivo desde Madrid 1978, A partir de mañana 1979, Castillos en el aire 1980, Como el primer día 1983, Gardel... como yo te siento 1984, En Vivo 1985, Entre líneas 1985, Sueños y quimeras 1986, Como la marea 1987, Almafuerte 1989, Coincidencias 1990, Si vieras que fácil 1991, Aromas 1993, Lo Cortez no quita lo Cabral Vol. 1 1994, Lo Cortez no quita lo Cabral Vol. 2 1995, A todo corazón 1996, Testimonio 1997, Cortezías y cabralidades Vol. 1 1998, Cortezías y cabralidades Vol. 2 1998, Fe 1998, Marcha mundial 1998, En un rincón del alma 2001, Estela Raval & Alberto Cortez tour 2002 en vivo 2002, Después del amor 2003, Alberto Cortez sinfónico 2004, Identidad 2005. *Current Management:* Pitokes sl, Crossing Adelfas, 3 Montepríncipe, 28668 Madrid, Spain. *Telephone:* 34606956879 (mobile). *E-mail:* danielfrega@gmail.com. *Website:* www.albertocortez.com.

CORYELL, Larry; American musician (guitar), composer and Lorenz Ven Delinder III; b. 2 April 1943, Galveston,; m. 2nd Tracey Piergross; two s. two d. *Education:* Univ. of Washington, studied with Jerry Gray, Leon Bolotine, New York City. *Career:* jazz guitarist 1966–; musician with Chico Hamilton 1966, Gary Burton 1967; Founder of fusion band Free Spirits; Leader, Eleventh House 1969; touring solo guitarist, also in duos with Philip Catherine, Alphonse Mouzon, Steve Kahn, Emily Remier. *Recordings:* albums include: Out of Sight and Sound 1967, Lady Coryell 1968, Spaces 1969, Introducing The 11th House 1974, The Restful Mind 1975, Aspects 1976, Basics 1976, The Lion and The Ram 1977, Standing Ovation 1978, Bolero 1981, Comin' Home 1984, A Quiet Day In Spring 1984, Equipoise 1986, The Dragon Gate 1989, Twelve Frets To The Octave 1991, Fallen Angel 1993, Dynamics 1994, I'll Be Over You 1994, Sketches of Coryell 1996, Spaces Revisited 1997, Major Jazz Minor Blues 1998, Cause and Effect 1998, Monk, Trane, Miles and Me 1999, Private Concert (live) 1999, At Montreux (with The 11th House) 2000, Barefoot Boy 2000, Inner Urge 2001, Tricycles 2004, Electric 2005, Traffic 2006, Larry Coryell with the Wide Hive Players 2011, Montgomery 2011, Duality 2011, Wide Hive Records 2012–14, world premiere of War & Peace, the Opera in Ljubljana, Slovenia 2014; also recordings with Michael Urbaniak, Chet Baker, Gary Burton, Sonny Rollins and Laurindo Almeida. *E-mail:* lcjazzfusion@yahoo.com; traceyland@yahoo.com. *Website:* www.larrycoryell.net.

COSGROVE, Mike; American musician (drums); b. 7 Nov. 1975, Long Beach, Calif. *Career:* played with local bands Out of Order, Wallop, Brother Vibe, Tyemus; mem. Alien Ant Farm 1996–, self-financed ind. LP 1999, signed to Papa Roach's New Noize label, second album released in conjunction with DreamWorks Records label 2001. *Recordings include:* albums: Greatest Hits (Los Angeles Music Award, Best Ind. Album) 1999, ANThology 2001, Truant 2003, Up In The Attic 2006. *Address:* c/o Primary Wave Music Publishing, 116 East, 16th Street, 9th Floor, New York, NY 10003, USA. *Telephone:* (212) 661-6990. *Fax:* (212) 661-8890. *Website:* www.primarywavemusic.com; www.alienantfarm.com.

COSMOS (see Middleton, Tom)

COSTA, Antony Daniel; British singer; b. 23 June 1981, Edgware, Middlesex. *Career:* mem. band Blue 2001–05, reformed 2009–; solo artist 2005–. *Stage:* Blood Brothers 2006–07, Boogie Nights 2007. *Recordings include:* albums: with Blue: All Rise 2001, One Love 2002, Guilty 2003; solo: Heart Full of Soul 2006. *Honours:* Smash Hits Awards for Best Newcomer 2001, Best Live Act, Best UK Band 2002, Interactive Music Award for Artist of the Year 2002, BRIT Award for Best British Newcomer 2002, NRJ Music Award for Best Int. Group (France) 2005.

COSTA, Gal; Brazilian singer; b. (Maria da Graça Costa Pena Burgos), 26 Sept. 1945, Salvador, Bahia. *Career:* solo artist, part of tropicália movement; tours internationally, many TV appearances. *Recordings include:* albums: Maria da Graça 1965, Domingo (with Caetano Veloso) 1967, Gal Costa 1969, Gal 1969, LeGal 1970, Fa-Tal- 1971, India 1973, Temporada de verão 1974, Cantar 1974, Gal canta Caymmi 1976, Doces Bárbaros 1976, Caras & Bocas 1977, Água viva 1978, Gal tropical 1979, Aquarela do Brasil 1980, Fantasia 1981, Minha voz 1982, Baby 1983, Gabriela (film soundtrack) 1983, Profana 1984, Bem Bom 1985, Lua de mel como o diabo gosta 1987, Rio revisited 1987, Plural 1990, Gal 1992, O sorriso do gato de Alice 1993, Mina d'agua do meu canto 1995, Tieta do Agreste 1996, Acústico 1997, Aquele frevo axé 1998, Gal Costa canta Tom Jobim 1999, De tantos amores 2001, Gal bossa tropical 2002, Todas as coisas e eu 2004, Hoje 2005, Ao Vivo 2007, Recanto 2012. *Honours:* Shell Prize 1984. *Telephone:* (11) 2361-3604. *E-mail:* baraka.gal@terra.com.br; ana.torres@barakaproducoes.com.br. *Website:* www.galcosta.com.br.

COSTA, Manuel (Manecas) Leal Emidio; Guinea-Bissau musician (guitar), singer, songwriter and producer; b. 1967, Cacheu. *Career:* formed Africa Libre (with brother, Nelson) 1976; moved to Lisbon, Portugal 1990; worked with Waldemar Bastos, Bana, Paulinho Vieira, Sushelela Rahman and others; Goodwill Amb. UNICEF. *Recordings include:* albums: Fundo di matu 2002, Paraiso Di Gumbe 2003. *Address:* c/o Sasa Music, Cecil Sharp House 2, Regent's Park Road, London, NW1 7AY, England. *Telephone:* (20) 7359-9232.

Fax: (20) 7359-9233 (office). *E-mail:* rab@sasa.demon.co.uk. *Website:* www
.sasamusic.com.

COSTELLO, Elvis; British singer and songwriter; b. (Declan Patrick
Aloysius McManus), 25 Aug. 1954, London, England; s. of Ross McManus
and Lillian McManus (née Costello); m. 1st Mary Costello 1974; one s.; m. 2nd
Cait O'Riordan 1986 (divorced 2003); m. 3rd Diana Krall 2003; twin s. *Career:*
fmr mem. Flip City; formed Elvis Costello and the Attractions 1977; Dir South
Bank Meltdown 1995. *Films include:* Americathon 1979, No Surrender 1985,
Straight to Hell 1987, Prison Song 2001, De-Lovely 2004. *Television includes:*
Scully (Granada TV for Channel 4) 1984, The Juliet Letters 1993, presenter,
Spectacle: Elvis Costello With... (Sundance Channel) 2008–. *Recordings
include:* albums: My Aim Is True 1977, This Year's Model 1978, Armed Forces
1979, Get Happy 1980, Trust 1980, Almost Blue 1981, Taking Liberties 1982,
Imperial Bedroom 1982, Punch The Clock 1983, Goodbye Cruel World 1984,
The Best Of 1985, Blood and Chocolate 1986, King of America 1986, Spike
1989, Mighty Like A Rose 1991, The Juliet Letters (with the Brodsky Quartet)
1993, Brutal Youth (with Steve Nieve, Pete Thomas, Bruce Thomas and Nick
Lowe) 1994, The Very Best of Elvis Costello and The Attractions 1995, Kojak
Variety 1995, Deep Dead Blue, Live At Meltdown (with Bill Frisell) 1995, All
This Useless Beauty 1996, Extreme Honey 1997, Terror and Magnificence
1997, Painted From Memory (Grammy Award 1999) 1998, The Sweetest
Punch: The Songs of Costello 1999, Best of Elvis Costello 1999, For The Stars
(with Anne-Sofie von Otter) 2001, When I Was Cruel 2002, North 2003, My
Flame Burns Blue 2006, The River in Reverse (with Allen Toussaint) 2006,
Momofuku 2008, Secret, Profane and Sugarcane 2009, National Ransom 2010,
Wise Up Ghost 2013. *Publication:* Unfaithful Music & Disappearing Ink
(autobiography) 2015. *Honours:* Hon. DMus, (New England Conservatory)
2013; BAFTA Award for Best Original Television Music (for G.B.H.) 1992,
MTV Video Award for Best Male Video 1989, Rolling Stone Award for Best
Songwriter 1990, two Ivor Novello Awards, Nordoff-Robbins Silver Clef
Award, ASCAP Founders Award 2003. *Current Management:* c/o Darrell
Gilmour, Macklam Feldman Management, Suite 200, 1505 West 2nd Avenue,
Vancouver, V6H 3Y4, Canada. *Telephone:* (604) 630-3199. *E-mail:* gilmour@
mfmgt.com; info@mfmgt.com. *Website:* www.mfmgt.com; www.elviscostello
.com.

COTTLE, Laurence; British musician (bass guitar); b. 16 Dec. 1961,
Swansea, Wales; m. Alison Hooper 1994; one s. one d. *Career:* played most
jazz festivals with Jim Mullen; tours with Laurence Cottle Quintet include
USA, Cuba, Germany, France, Spain, Italy; collaborations include: Eric
Clapton, Labi Siffre, James Taylor Quartet, Jason Rebello, Hue and Cry, Seal,
Tom Jones, Rhythm and Blues (with Mark Feltham); currently touring with
Laurence Cottle Big Band; mem. Bill Bruford's Earthworks 2004–06; mem.
Musicians' Union. *Recordings include:* solo album: Five Seasons; with
Laurence Cottle Quintet: Live 1995. *Address:* 52 Highfield Way, Rickmans-
worth, WD3 7PR, England. *Website:* laurencecottle.com.

COULAIS, Bruno; French composer; b. 13 Jan. 1954, Paris. *Compositions for
film and TV:* Nuit féline 1978, México mágico 1979, Quidam (TV) 1984,
Meurtres pour mémoire (TV) 1985, Bel ragazzo 1986, Lien de parenté 1986,
Qui trop embrasse... 1986, La Femme secrète 1986, Les demoiselles de
Concarneau (episode in TV series, L'Heure Simenon) 1987, Adieu Christine
(TV series) 1989, Juliette en toutes lettres (TV series) 1989, Zanzibar 1989, Le
Lien du sang (TV) 1990, La Campagne de Cicéron 1990, Peinture fraîche 1991,
Le Jour des rois 1991, Piège pour femme seule (TV) 1991, Ma soeur, mon
amour 1992, Les Équilibristes 1992, Odyssée bidon (TV) 1992, Le Retour de
Casanova 1992, Le Petit prince a dit 1992, Vieille canaille 1992, La Place du
père (TV) 1992, Siméon 1992, Flight from Justice (TV) 1993, L'Instit (TV
series) 1993, Le Juge est une femme (TV series) 1993, Le Fils du requin 1993,
L'Ange et le génie - Correspondances Paris-Berlin 1994, Der Grüne Heinrich
1994, Cognacq-Jay (TV) 1994, Mort d'un gardien de la paix (TV) 1994, La
Colline aux mille enfants (TV) 1994, Waati 1995, Le Blanc à lunettes (TV)
1995, Un si bel orage (TV) 1995, Des mots qui déchirent (TV) 1995, L'Enfant
des rues (TV) 1995, La Rivière Espérance (mini TV series) 1995, Adultère,
mode d'emploi 1995, Le Nid tombé de l'oiseau (TV) 1995, Embrasse-moi vite!
(TV) 1995, Coeur de cible (TV) 1996, Sixième classique (TV) 1996,
Microcosmos: Le peuple de l'herbe 1996, Une fille à papas (TV) 1996, L'Orange
de Noël (TV) 1996, J'ai rendez-vous avec vous (TV) 1996, Vice vertu et vice
versa (TV) 1997, Victor (TV) 1997, La Mère de nos enfants (TV) 1997, La Belle
vie (mini TV series) 1997, Pardaillan (TV) 1997, La Famille Sapajou (TV)
1997, Jeunesse 1997, L'Amour dans le désordre (TV) 1997, Les Héritiers (TV)
1997, Combat de fauves 1997, Flammen im Paradies 1997, Le Dernier été (TV)
1997, Mireille et Vincent (TV) 1997, Deux flics (TV series) 1998, Don Juan
1998, Serial Lover 1998, Déjà mort 1998, Préférence 1998, Le Comte de Monte
Cristo (mini TV series) 1998, L'Enfant des terres blondes (TV) 1998, Das
Mädchen aus der Fremde 1999, Belle maman 1999, Véga (TV series) 1999,
Himalaya - l'enfance d'un chef 1999, Balzac (TV) 1999, Un dérangement
considérable 1999, La Débandade 1999, Épouse-moi 2000, Scènes de crimes
2000, Le Libertin 2000, Comme un aimant 2000, Jacqueline dans ma vitrine
2000, Les Fleurs d'Harrison 2000, Les Rivières pourpres 2000, Le Blanc et le
rouge (TV) 2000, Zaïde, un petit air de vengeance (TV) 2001, Faut pas rêver
(TV series) 2001, Belphégor - Le fantôme du Louvre 2001, De l'amour 2001, Un
aller simple 2001, Origine océan - 4 milliards d'années sous les mers 2001,
Vidocq 2001, Le Peuple migrateur 2001, Les Ailes de la nature (TV) 2002, Les
Tombales 2002, Drengen der ville gøre det umulige 2002, Toute une histoire
2003, Les Parents terribles (TV) 2003, Les Choristes 2004, Agents secrets

2004, Genesis 2004, Milady (TV) 2004, Brice de Nice 2005, Sometimes in April
(TV) 2005, Je préfère qu'on reste amis 2005, Les Rois maudits 2005, Gaspard
le bandit (TV) 2006, La Planète blanche 2006, L'Affaire Villemin (TV) 2006,
Truands 2007, René Bousquet ou Le grand arrangement (TV) 2007, Hellphone
2007, Ulzhan 2007, Max & Co 2007, Le Deuxième souffle 2007, Les Femmes de
l'Ombre 2008, MR 73 2008, Villa Amalia 2009, Brendan and the Secret of Kells
2009, Coraline 2009. *Other compositions include:* Mémoires d'un cabotin for
nine pianos 1985. *Current Management:* Marsh, Best and Associates, 9150
Wilshire Boulevard, Suite 220, Beverly Hills, CA 90212-3429, USA. *Telephone:* (310) 285-0303. *Fax:* (310) 285-0218. *E-mail:* info@marshbest.com.
Website: www.sandramarsh.com.

COULIBALY, Cheikhou (Cheikh); Senegalese singer, songwriter and
musician (guitar); b. 1961, Kaolack. *Education:* Dakar Conservatory. *Career:*
trained in law; mem. Pape & Cheikh 1997–; signed to Jololi label 1999.
Recordings include: albums: with Pape & Cheikh: Yakaar 2001, Mariama
2002. *Address:* c/o Real World Records, Box Mill, Mill Lane, Box, SN13 8PL,
England. *Telephone:* (1225) 743188. *Fax:* (1225) 743787. *Website:* www
.realworldrecords.com.

COUNT DUBULAH, (Dub Colossus, Tax D, Kid Ouzo); British musician
(guitar, bass guitar), programmer and producer; b. (Nicholas Plato Page).
Career: Founder-mem., TransGlobal Underground collective 1992–99; mem.
Temple of Sound 1999–. *Recordings include:* albums: with TransGlobal
Underground: Dream Of 100 Nations 1993, International Times 1994,
Interplanetary Meltdown 1995, Psychic Karaoke 1996, Innernation Vol. 2
1998, Rejoice Rejoice 1998; with Temple of Sound: Black Orchid 1998, People's
Colony No. 1 (with Rizwan-Muazzam Qawwali) 2001, First Edition 2002,
Shout At The Devil (with Jah Wobble) 2002, Gold Of The Sun Live 2004,
Globalhead 2007. *Current Management:* c/o Steven Machat, Namaste, 59
Maiden Lane, 27th Floor, New York, NY 10038, USA. *E-mail:* management@
templeofsound.org.uk; smachat@gmail.com. *E-mail:* countdubulah@
templeofsound.org.uk (office). *Website:* www.nickpagesongs.com.

COUPLAND, Gary, MBE; British musician (accordion, keyboards); b. 27
March 1964, Dumfries, Scotland; m. Karen Chaisson Sept. 1987; 3 d.
Education: Dumfries Acad., Napier Coll., Edinburgh, Scotland. *Career:*
Musical Dir with The Singing Kettle, Scotland's Theatre Box Office Record
Breakers, London Palladium and Sadler's Wells; 4 series for Children's BBC
TV; folk musician at Cambridge Folk Festival, Stage 1 1992; mem. Musicians'
Union, Equity. *Recordings include:* Appears on Ian Hardie, Ecosse: A Breath
of Scotland 1994, Brian McNeill, No Gods 1996, Holding Up Half the Sky,
Holding Up Half the Sky 1997. *Honours:* BAFTA, Scotland, Best Children's
TV Show. *Address:* The Singing Kettle, Post House, 26 Main Street,
Kingskettle, KY15 7PN, Scotland (office). *E-mail:* info@singingkettle.com
(office); gary@themusicman.co.uk. *Website:* www.themusicman.co.uk; www
.singingkettle.com (office).

COURTOIS, Vincent; French musician; b. 21 March 1968, Paris; m. Muriel
1990, one s. *Career:* played with: Michel Petrucciani, Niels Lan Doky; Tour
with Michel Petrucciani, 1994–95; Founder Wat 2010. *Recordings include:*
Cello News, Pleine Lune, Pendulum Quartet; appears on Cheb Khaled, N'ssi
N'ssi 1993, Sahra 1996, Philippe Eidel, Mammas 1997, Imuhar 1999, What Do
You Mean By Silence 2006, Avion The Man with Ze Jam Afane 2008, The
Unexpected 2010. *Honours:* Chevalier of the Ordre des Arts et des Lettres
2010. *Telephone:* 6-01-95-59-91. *E-mail:* contact@lacompagniedelimprevu
.com. *Website:* violoncelle.free.fr.

COUSENS, Peter William Light, BDramArts, JD; Australian singer, actor,
film director, producer and academic; *Adjunct Associate Professor, School of
Creative and Performing Arts, Central Queensland University;* b. 2 Nov. 1955,
Tamworth, NSW; s. of the late William Light Cousens and Marjorie Joyce
Graham; m. Suzanne Hazel Roylance 1984; three d. *Education:* The Armidale
School Australia, Gordonstoun School, UK, St Paul's Coll., Univ. of Sydney,
Nat. Inst. of Dramatic Art, Univ. of New South Wales, Univ. of New England.
Career: Asst Sub-Warden, St Paul's Coll., Univ. of Sydney 1982–83; CEO and
Artistic Dir, Kookaburra: The Nat. Musical Theatre Co. 2006–08; Adjunct
Assoc. Prof., School of Creative and Performing Arts, Central Queensland
Univ. 2012–; Dir, Mateur Holdings Pty Ltd 1985–; Dir, Ginger Meggs Musical
2012–; Visiting Fellow, Univ. of Wollongong; Artist-in-Residence, Australian
Inst. of Music May–Nov. 2009; Amb. White Ribbon Campaign; Chair. and
CEO Production One Inc. 2012–; Patron Nat. Asscn for Prevention of Child
Abuse and Neglect 1995–99. *Stage appearances include:* musicals: Camelot
with Richard Harris (Mordred) 1983, Sweeney Todd (Anthony) 1986, Blood
Brothers with Russel Crowe, Chrissie Amphlett (Eddie) 1987, The Mikado
(with Australia Opera) 1986, Les Miserables (Marius) 1989–91, Aspects of
Love (Alex) 1992, Phantom of the Opera (in Sydney, as Raoul) 1993–94, Miss
Saigon (Chris) 1995–96, West Side Story (Tony) 1996, Phantom of the Opera
(in London) 1997, Showboat (Ravenal) 1998, Sweeney Todd (Tobias) 2002,
Company (Bobby) 2000, The Convict's Opera (UK tour, Out of Joint Co.) 2009.
Plays include: Sydney Theatre Co.: Macbeth, Nicholas Nickleby, Measure for
Measure; Chicago, Chinchilla, The Convict's Opera, Griffin The Falls; Philip
Street Theatre: Whose Life is it Anyway; The Queensland Theatre Co.:
Camille, Breaker Morant, You Never Can Tell, The Sentimental Bloke;
Melbourne Theatre Co.: Marian Street, London Assurance, Fanny; Sydney
Dance Co.: Tivoli; Out of Joint Co., UK: The Convict's Opera; Darlinghurst
Theatre: The Paris Letter. *Producer:* Victoriana 1984–89, Pippin 2007,
Company 2007, Tell Me on a Sunday 2008, Little Women 2008: I Love You

Your Perfect Now Change 2008, Up Close and Musical 2007–08, The Noel Coward Letters 2008, Songs for a New World 2008, The Launch Concert (Sydney) 2006, Gala Concert (Melbourne) 2008, Crusade 2010. *Films directed include:* Carry Me Home 2014. *Television includes:* Cliffy, Phryne Fisher, Return to Eden, The Sullivans, Carson's Law, The Young Doctors, Son and Daughters, The Timeless Land, Under Capricorn, Break a Leg (TV series) 2004, An Audience with Stephen Sondheim (TV event on stage with ABC and Foxtel) 2007. *Recordings include:* albums: Corner of the Sky 1994, From a Distance 1996, Miss Saigon (int. symphonic recording) 1996, A Life on Earth 2002, A Musical Christmas 2005, Peter Cousens Collection 2008. *Honours:* Variety Club of Australia Heart Award 1996, Glug Award for Services to Theatre 2009. *E-mail:* pwlcoz@gmail.com (office). *Current Management:* c/o Ambrose Artist Management, PO Box 38, St Pauls, Sydney, NSW 2031, Australia. *E-mail:* jayne@ambrosemanagement.com (office). *Address:* Central Queensland University, School of Creative and Performing Arts, 108 Lonsdale Street, Melbourne, Vic. 3000, Australia (office). *Telephone:* (2) 8383-9051 (office). *Website:* www.carrymehomemovie.com (office); www .productiononeinc.com (office); www.petercousens.com.

COUSIN, Andy; British musician (bass guitar) and singer; b. 28 March 1963, Huddersfield. *Career:* mem., All About Eve 1988–, The Mission 1995, Pink and Black, Sex Gang Children; Founder mem., The Lucy Nation. *Recordings include:* albums: with All About Eve: All About Eve 1988, Wild Hearted woman 1988, Martha's Harbor 1988, Scarlet And Other Stories 1989, Touched By Jesus 1991, Ultraviolet 1992, Seeing Stars 1997, Fairy Light Nights Vol. 1 2000, Fairy Light Nights Vol. 2 2001, Live and Electric At The Union Chapel 2002, Live At Brixton 2003, Iceland 2003, Cinemasonic 2003, Acoustic Nights 2003, Keepsakes 2006, The Mission: Neverland 1995, Blue 1996, Aural Delight 2002, God is a Bullet 2007, Dum Dum Bullets 2010, The Brightest Light 2013; with Mice: Because I Can 1996; with The Lucy Nation: On 1999. *E-mail:* info@sexgangchildren.com. *Website:* themissionuk.com; www .sexgangchildren.com.

COVACI, Nicolae (Nicu); Romanian musician (six string and 12-string guitar) and singer; b. 19 April 1947, Timisoara; m. 1st 1976 (divorced 1978); m. 2nd 1980 (divorced 1989). *Education:* Acad. of Arts. *Career:* mem. Transsylvania Phoenix 1962–; played at Nat. Student Festival, Iasi 1968, Nat. Student Festival, Bucharest 1969–71, Sopot Festival Poland 1973; mem. GEMA, OCMR. *Recordings include:* with Transsylvania Phoenix: Vremuri 1968, Floarea Stincilor 1969, Cei Ce Ne-Au Dat Nume 1972, Mesteroul Manole 1973, Mugur De Fluier 1974, Cantafabule 1975, Transsylvania 1981, Symphoenix 1992, Evergreens 1993, Aniversare 35 1997, Ora-hora 1999, In umbra marelui URSS 2000, Baba Novak 2005. *Honours:* first prize, Nat. Student Festival, Iasi 1968, Awards for: Composition and Creativity, Bucharest 1969–71, Originality, Bratislawskalyra, Czechoslovakia 1973. *E-mail:* office.phoenix@ yahoo.com (office); nicucovaci_phoenix@yahoo.com. *Website:* www .transsylvania-phoenix.net; www.covaci.de.

COVERDALE, David; British singer and songwriter; b. 22 Sept. 1949, Saltburn-by-the-Sea, Cleveland; m. Tawny Kitaen 1989. *Career:* lead singer rock group, Deep Purple 1974–76; Founder-mem. and lead singer heavy rock group, Whitesnake 1977–91, 1994–; solo artist 1991–; mem. Coverdale/Page (with Jimmy Page) 1993; numerous int. tours, concerts and festival appearances. *Recordings include:* albums: with Deep Purple: Burn 1974, Stormbringer 1974, Come Taste The Band 1975; with Whitesnake: Whitesnake 1977, Northwinds 1978, Trouble 1979, Ready An' Willing 1980, Come An' Get It 1981, Saints 'N' Sinners 1982, Slide It In 1984, Whitesnake 1987, Slip of The Tongue 1989, Restless Heart 1997, Good to Be Bad 2008, Forevermore 2011, The Purple Album 2015; with Coverdale/Page: Coverdale/Page 1993; solo: Into The Light 2000. *Current Management:* c/o International Talent Booking, First Floor, Ariel House, 74a Charlotte Street, London, W1T 4QJ, England. *Telephone:* (20) 7637-6979. *Fax:* (20) 7637-6978. *E-mail:* mail@itb.co.uk. *E-mail:* pooralbert@whitesnake.com. *Website:* www.whitesnake.com; www .davidcoverdale.com.

COWELL, Sir Harry Edmund, Kt; British artist manager; *Managing Director, Mission Entertainment Group Ltd;* b. 4 Sept. 1960, Dorking, Surrey; m. Anita Harriet 1995; one d. *Career:* Man. Partner of Simon Napier-Bell; Man. Dir A&R Rive Droite Music 2000–06; f. Private and Confidential Group Ltd 2005; Founder and Man. Dir, Mission Publishing Ltd and Mission Recordings Ltd (now Mission Entertainment Group Ltd) 2009–; clients have included Yardbirds, Japan, Marc Bolan, Wham!, Asia, Ultravox. *Address:* Mission Entertainment Group Ltd, Fairlight Mews, 15 St Johns Road, Kingston-Upon-Thames, KT1 4AN, England (office). *Telephone:* (20) 8977-0632 (office). *Fax:* (87) 0770-8669 (office). *E-mail:* info@missionlimited.com (office). *Website:* www.missionlimited.com (office).

COWELL, Simon Phillip; British television personality, television executive, record company executive and A&R consultant; b. 7 Oct. 1959, Lambeth, London; s. of the late Eric Cowell and of Julie Brett (née Josie Dalglish). *Education:* Dover Coll., Windsor Technical Coll., St Columba's Coll., St Albans. *Career:* brought up in Elstree, Herts.; worked for EMI Music Publishing 1977–82; Founder Fanfare Records (with Iain Burton) 1982–89; A&R Consultant, BMG Records 1989; screen debut on TV series Sale of the Century 1990; Founder and Co-Owner S Records 2001; first made a TV appearance on Pop Idol 2001, then on American Idol 2002; f. Syco record label (subsidiary of Sony BMG) 2002, artists include Westlife, Five, Robson & Jerome, Zig & Zag, Girl Thing, Will Young, Gareth Gates, Six, Il Divo, Steve

Brookstein, Shayne Ward, Journey South, Paul Potts, Ray Quinn, Leona Lewis, Olly Murs, Rebecca Ferguson, Cher Lloyd, Susan Boyle, Little Mix, One Direction. *Films:* as producer: One Chance 2013, Pudsey the Dog: the Movie 2014. *Television includes:* writer, producer and judge, Pop Idol (ITV) 2001–02, American Idol: The Search for a Superstar (Fox TV) 2002–10, Cupid 2003, The X Factor (ITV) 2004–10, 2013–, (producer) 2011–13, The Xtra Factor 2004–, America's Got Talent 2006–, Celebrity Duets 2006, American Inventor 2006–07, Grease Is the Word (ITV) 2007, Britain's Got Talent (ITV) (BAFTA Award for Best Entertainment Programme 2010) 2007– , Britain's Got More Talent 2007–, Rock Rivals (ITV drama) 2008, Piers Morgan's Life Stories (special episodes) 2010–, Red or Black (ITV) 2011–13, The X Factor USA 2011–13. *Honours:* Record Exec. of the Year 1998, 1999, A & R Man. of the Year 1999, Variety Club Showbusiness Personality of the Year 2005, BAFTA Special Award 2010, listed by New Statesman at No. 41 amongst The World's 50 Most Influential Figures 2010.

COWEN, Jeanine M.; American composer and musician (percussion); b. 4 April 1965, Bettendorf, Ia; m. Sara Whitman 1991; three c. *Education:* Northwestern Univ., Berklee Coll. of Music. *Career:* film work as composer: Home Before Dark 1997, Intermezzo 1998, Sporting Dog 1999, Killing the Badge 1999, A Far Distant Place 2000, Killing Cinderella 2000, My Father's Love 2001, Sandy 'Spin' Slade: Beyond Basketball 2001, Breaking Up Really Sucks 2001, The Gay Marriage Thing 2005; mem. International Alliance for Women in Music, American Soc. of Composers, Authors and Publrs, SCL, WIFVNE. *Telephone:* (617) 332-2970. *Website:* www.jmcmusicinc.com.

COX, Carl; British DJ, producer and remixer; b. 29 July 1962, Manchester, England; m. Rachel Cox (née Turner) 1994. *Career:* DJ 1980–; Sunrise Rave 1989; afterwards known as '3 Deck Wizard'; signed album deal with Perfecto/ BMG 1991; resident at UK House/Techno clubs, including Cream (Liverpool), Final Frontier (London); also DJ in Germany; tours to Australia, USA, Japan, France, Switzerland, Austria, Ibiza (Spain); started Ultimate Music Management 1993; f. MMR record label 1994; f. Intec record label 1998–2006, renamed Intec Digital 2010–; mem. Musicians' Union. *Film appearance:* Human Traffic 1998. *Recordings include:* albums: At the End of the Cliche 1998, Phuture 2000 1999, Second Sign 2005, Carl Cox at Space 2005, Carl Cox and Friends at Space 2007, Dance Valley 2008–Carl Cox Live 2008, Main Stage Madness 2009, Carl Cox 24/7 2009, Carl Cox at Space–The Revolution Continues 2010, Black Rock Desert 2010, All Roads Lead to Dancefloor 2011, Carl Cox at Stage–The Revolution Recruits 2012, Pure Intec 2 2013, Carl Cox at Space–The Part Unites 2013. *Honours:* DJ Magazine No. 1 Rave DJ 1992, Stepping Out Top UK DJ 1992, 1993, DJ of the Year, Int. Dance Awards 1994, 1995, Frontpage Magazine Top Overseas DJ, Germany 1994, Ibiza DJ Award for Best Ibiza Club Night 2006. *Current Management:* Safehouse Management, Reverb House, Bennett Street, London, W4 2AH, England. *Telephone:* (20) 8743-4000. *Fax:* (20) 8743-4021. *E-mail:* lynn@safehousemanagement .com. *Website:* www.safehousemanagement.com. *Address:* 49 Highlands Road, Horsham, RH13 5LS, England (home). *Website:* www.carlcox.com.

COX, Deborah; Canadian singer and songwriter; b. 13 July 1974; m. Lascelles Stephens; three c. *Education:* Performing Arts School. *Career:* singer on commercials and local club circuit, Toronto age 12; R&B singer; songwriting partnership with Lascelles Stephens; tour with Céline Dion; concerts in Europe, Japan, Asia. *Recordings include:* albums: Deborah Cox (Juno Award 1996) 1995, One Wish (Juno Award 1999) 1998, The Morning After 2002, Destination Moon 2007, The Promise 2008. *Website:* www .deborahcox.com.

COX, Peter; British singer, songwriter and musician (guitar, keyboards); b. 17 Nov. 1955, Kingston, Surrey. *Career:* songwriting partnership with Richard Drummie, ATV Music, EMI Music; founder mem. of duo, Go West 1982–; solo artist 1997–. *Compositions include:* One Way Street (for film soundtrack Rocky IV). *Recordings include:* albums: with Go West: Go West 1985, Bangs and Crashes 1986, Dancing On The Couch 1987, Indian Summer 1992, Aces and Kings 1993, futurenow 2008, 3D 2010; solo: Peter Cox 1997, Desert Blooms 2004, Motor City Music 2006, The S1 Sessions 2010, Riding The Blinds 2013. *Honours:* (with Go West) BPI Best Newcomer Award 1986. *Current Management:* c/o John Glover, Blueprint Management, PO Box 593, Woking, Surrey GU23 7YF, England. *Telephone:* (1483) 715336. *E-mail:* john@blueprint-management.com. *Website:* www.blueprint-management .com; www.gowest.org.uk; www.peter-cox.org.

COXON, Graham Leslie; British musician (guitar, saxophone, drums) and singer; b. 12 March 1969, Rinteln, West Germany. *Education:* North Essex School of Art, Goldsmiths Coll., London. *Career:* mem. Blur –2002, 2007–; extensive tours and festival appearances; solo artist 1998–. *Recordings include:* albums: with Blur: Leisure 1991, Modern Life Is Rubbish 1993, Parklife (Best Album, Q Awards 1994, Best Album, Best Single, Best British Video, BRIT Awards 1995, Best Album, NME Awards 1995) 1994, The Great Escape (Best Album, Q Awards 1995) 1995, Blur 1997, 13 1999, The Best of Blur 2000, Think Tank (Best Album, Q Awards 2003, Best Album, South Bank Show Awards 2003) 2003, Midlife 2009, The Magic Whip 2015; solo: The Sky Is Too High 1998, The Golden D 2000, Crow Sit On Blood Tree 2001, The Kiss Of Morning 2002, Happiness In Magazines 2004, Love Travels at Illegal Speeds 2006, The Spinning Top 2009, A+E 2012. *Honours:* with Blur: BRIT Awards for Best Single, Best Video, Best Album, Best Band 1995, for Outstanding Contrib. to Music 2012, Best Alternative Band, Smash Hits Awards 1994, Best Band and Best Live Act, NME Awards 1995, Best Act in the World Today, Q

Awards 1999, Best Band, Best Single (Tender), NME Awards 2000, NME Award for Best Live Event (Blur at Hyde Park) 2010. *Current Management:* c/o Eleven Management, Suite B, Park House, 206–208 Latimer Road, London, W10 6QY, England. *Telephone:* (20) 8749-1177. *E-mail:* info@ elevenmgmt.com. *Website:* www.elevenmgmt.com; www.blur.co.uk; www .grahamcoxon.co.uk.

COYLE, Nadine; British singer; b. (Nadine Elizabeth Louise Coyle), 15 June 1985, Derry, Northern Ireland; d. of Niall Coyle and Lillian Coyle. *Education:* Thornhill Coll., Derry. *Career:* successful contestant in Irish reality TV show Popstars 2001, forced to withdraw from winning group for being under age limit; mem. Girls Aloud, pop group created from winning contestants on UK reality tv show Popstars: The Rivals 2002–13; also solo artist 2010–; f. Black Pen Records record label. *Compositions include:* co-writer of songs including 100 Different Ways, Why Do It. *Recordings include:* albums: with Girls Aloud: Sound of the Underground 2003, What Will the Neighbours Say? 2004, Chemistry 2005, Tangled Up 2007, Out of Control 2008; solo: Insatiable 2010. *Television includes:* Popstars: Ireland 2001, RI:SE 2002, Greasemania 2003, Girls Aloud: Home Truths 2005, Ghost Hunting with Girls Aloud 2006, Girls Aloud: Off the Record 2006, The Passions of Girls Aloud 2008, Girls Aloud: Ten Years at the Top 2012, Pop Life, I'm in a Girl Group! 2013. *Films include:* Surfing with William 1999, St Trinian's 2007, St Trinian's 2: The Legend of Fritton's Gold 2008. *Publication:* Dreams that Glitter: Our Story 2008. *Honours:* Best Single, Disney Channel Awards 2003, Popjustice Music Prize 2003, 2005, 2006, BRIT Award for Best British Single (for The Promise) 2009. *Current Management:* Shaw Thing Management, Unit 12A, Utopia Village, 7 Chalcot Road, London, NW1 8LH, England. *Telephone:* (20) 7722-6161. *Fax:* (20) 7722-9661. *E-mail:* info@shawthingmanagement.com. *Website:* www .shawthingmanagement.com; www.girlsaloud.com.

COYNE, Wayne Michael; American singer, songwriter, musician (guitar) and actor; b. 13 Jan. 1961, Pittsburgh, Pa; s. of Thomas Coyne and Dolores Jackson; m. Michelle Martin. *Education:* Classen School of Advanced Studies, Oklahoma City. *Career:* founder mem. The Flaming Lips 1983–; music teacher, Acad. of Contemporary Music, Univ. of Central Oklahoma 2009–; numerous side projects and collaborations with The Chemical Brothers, Thievery Corporation, Faultline, Danger Mouse & Sparklehorse. *Films:* as actor and director: Christmas on Mars 2008; other appearances: Fearless Freaks (documentary on band) 2005; soundtrack contributions: The Sponge-Bob SquarePants Movie 2004, Spider-Man 3 2007, Good Luck Chuck 2007, Mr Magorium's Wonder Emporium 2007. *Recordings:* albums with The Flaming Lips: Hear It Is 1986, Oh My Gawd!!! 1987, Telepathic Surgery 1989, In a Priest Driven Ambulance 1990, Hit to Death in the Future Head 1992, Transmissions from the Satellite Heart 1993, Clouds Taste Metallic 1995, Zaireeka 1997, The Soft Bulletin 1999, Yoshimi Battles the Pink Robots 2002, At War with the Mystics 2006 (Grammy Award for Best Engineered Album, Non-Classical 2007), Embryonic 2009; with Stardeath and White Dwarfs: The Flaming Lips and Stardeath and White Dwarfs with Henry Rollins and Peaches Doing Dark Side of the Moon 2010. *Honours:* Grammy Award for Best Rock Instrumental Performance 2002, 2006. *Current Management:* c/o Scott Booker, Hellfire Enterprises Limited, 1208 Chowning Avenue, Edmond, OK 73034, USA. *Telephone:* (405) 715-0600. *Fax:* (405) 715-0632. *E-mail:* SDBMKTG@hellfireltdcom. *Website:* www.hellfireltd.com. *Address:* c/o Warner Bros. Records Inc., 3300 Warner Boulevard, Burbank, CA 91505, USA (office). *Website:* www.theflaminglips.com.

COZENS, Chris; British programmer and musician (keyboards); b. 3 June 1959; m. Mel 1988; one d. *Education:* City of Leeds Coll. of Music. *Career:* composed and performed music for new production: The Rise and Fall of The City of Mahogany, by Brecht; spent year in Canada, with own band, Long Distanz; returned to UK, joined Johnny Mars Band; worked as arranger, orchestrator, session keyboard player for John Parr, Cozy Powell, Jan Akkerman, Barry Humphries, Graham Bonnet, Harry Nilsson, Francis Rossi, Demis Roussos, Jon English; producer Terry Britten; programmer, musician, recording of Paris, rock opera by Jon English and Dave Mackay, with London Symphony Orchestra, Royal Philharmonic Orchestra 1989; toured Australia, MD for Jon English; co-writer, two Australian television series, including All Together Now; collaborated with Alan Parker, Dave Mackay, on incidental music for scores; writer, portfolio of library music; worked with Alan Attfield on Facades (musical); produced, recorded series of albums for Telstar Records under name Project D; credits include: films and television: What's Eating Gilbert Grape?; Wild Justice; To Be The Best; Voice of The Heart; Red Fox; Van Der Valk; Minder, by Alan Parker; 99 To 1, by Mike Gibbs; Coasting, West Beach, Making Out, by Dave Mackay; Bullseye, John Du Prez; composer, incidental music, Children's Ward 1994; Bridge To The Past 1994; music for documentary, Burning Rubber; mem. PRS, MCPS. *Recordings include:* album: Synthesiser Greats 1994, Lights Camera Action 2001. *Current Management:* c/o Eaton Music Limited, 39 Lower Richmond Road, London, SW15 1ET, England. *Telephone:* (20) 8788-4557. *Website:* www.eatonmusic .com; www.chriscozens.com.

COZENS, Spencer James, BMus; British musician (piano, keyboards), composer and producer; b. 11 Feb. 1965, Weston-Super-Mare. *Education:* East Notts Music School, Newark Technical Coll., Goldsmiths Coll. *Career:* tours with Julia Fordham, Joan Armatrading 2001–; producing, touring with John Martyn 1990–; writer, producer, albums with Miles Bould (percussion) as Peoplespeak, also with Jacqui McShee (vocals), Gerry Conway (drums); writer, musician with Carol Decker; toured with Jacqui McShee's Pentangle;

mem. PRS, MCPS, PAMRA. *Recordings include:* albums: with John Martyn: Cooltide (producer, musician), And (producer, musician), No Little Boy (co-producer, musician), Couldn't Love You More (musician), The Church with One Bell (musician); with Steps Ahead: Yin Yang; with Jacqui McShee's Pentangle: Passé Avant (writer, producer, musician); albums by Peoplespeak and About Thyme (as producer, writer, musician), Miten, David Hughes: 50 Yards of David Hughes (musician). *E-mail:* spen@spencercozens.com (office). *Website:* www.spencercozens.com.

CRACKNELL, Sarah Jane; British singer; b. 12 April 1967, Chelmsford, Essex; d. of Derek Cracknell and Julie Samuel; m. Martin Kelly 2004; two s. *Education:* Italia Conti Stage School, Drama Studio, Tona De Brett. *Career:* lead singer, Saint Etienne 1991–; mem., LoveCut dB; numerous television appearances, concerts, tours; also solo artist 1997–; mem. Equity. *Recordings include:* albums: with Saint Etienne: Foxbase Alpha 1991, So Tough 1993, Tiger Bay 1994, Continental 1997, Good Humor 1998, The Misadventures of Saint Etienne (soundtrack) 1999, Sound of Water 2000, Finisterre 2002, Tales From Turnpike House 2005, Words and Music by Saint Etienne 2012; solo: Lipslide 1997, Red Kite 2015; singles with LoveCut dB, Mark Brown and as Cola Boy. *Films:* Finisterre 2002, What Have You Done Today Mervyn Day 2005, This is Tomorrow 2007. *Current Management:* c/o Martin Kelly, Heavenly Management, 221 Portobello Road, London, W11 1LU, England. *Telephone:* (20) 7494-2998. *Fax:* (20) 7437-3317. *E-mail:* martin@ heavenlymanagement.com. *Website:* www.sainteetienne.com (home).

CRADDOCK, William (Billy) Wayne 'Crash'; American singer; b. 16 June 1939, Greensboro, NC, USA. *Career:* talent shows from age 10; rock/country recording artist 1957–. *Recordings include:* albums: I'm Tore Up 1964, Knock Three Times 1971, You Better Move On 1972, Still Thinkin' About You 1975, Crash (with Janie Fricke) 1976, Changes 1980, Back On Track 1989, Boom Boom Baby 1992, Crash's Smashes 1996, Christmas Favorites 2006. *Honours:* Cashbox Award for New Find of the Year 1972. *Current Management:* c/o Great American Talent, PO Box 2476, Hendersonville, TN 37077, USA. *Telephone:* (615) 452-7878. *E-mail:* info@gtalent.com. *Website:* www.gtalent .com. *Address:* c/o Ace Productions, PO Box 292725, Nashville, TN 37229-2725, USA.

CRADOCK, Steve; British musician (guitar, keyboards); b. 22 Aug. 1969, Birmingham. *Career:* fmr mem. The Boys, The Fanatics; Founder-mem. Ocean Colour Scene 1989–; joined Paul Weller's tour 1993, and subsequent backing band; numerous TV appearances, radio broadcasts and tours. *Recordings include:* albums: Ocean Colour Scene 1992, Moseley Shoals 1996, B-Sides, Seasides and Freerides 1997, Marchin' Already 1997, One From The Modern 1999, Mechanical Wonder 2001, Songs For The Front Row (compilation) 2001, Anthology 2003, North Atlantic Drift 2003, Marchin' Melody 2004, On The Leyline 2007, The Collection 2007; solo: The Kundalini Target 2009, Peace City West 2011. *Current Management:* c/o Asgard Promotions Ltd, 125 Parkway, London, NW1 7PS, England. *Address:* Ocean Colour Scene Music, PO Box 3424, Warwick, CV34 6XS, England (office). *E-mail:* info@ocsmusic.com (office). *Website:* www.oceancolourscene.com (office); www.stevecradock.com.

CRAIG, Carl, (Paperclip People, 69, BFC, Psyche, Innerzone Orchestra, Tres Demented); American producer, remixer and DJ; b. 22 May 1969, Detroit, Mich. *Career:* protégé of Derrick May; Founder, Planet-E Recordings; organizer Detroit Electronic Music Festival 2000–03; remixed LCD Sound-system, Friendly Fires, Theo Parrish, Junior Boys, Maurizio, Tori Amos, Gus Gus, Incognito, Caribou, Tom Trago; collaboration with Derrick May. *Recordings include:* albums: Landcruising 1995, DJ-Kicks 1996, More Songs About Food and Revolutionary Art 1997, The Secret Tapes of Dr Eich (as Paperclip People) 1997, House Party 013: A Planet E Mix 1999, Programmed (as Innerzone Orchestra) 2000, Abstract Funk Theory 2001, Onsumotha-sheeat 2001, The Workout 2002, The Detroit Experiment 2002, Darkness 2007, The Album Formerly Known As 2007, Sessions 2008, DJ Kicks, Carl Craig Presents Masterpiece. *Address:* Planet E Communications, PO Box 27218, Detroit, MI 27218, USA. *Telephone:* (313) 874-8729 (office). *Fax:* (313) 874-8732 (office). *E-mail:* james@paramountartists.com. *Website:* www.planet -e.net (home); www.carlcraig.net.

CRAIG, David Mark, BA; British musician (guitar) and songwriter; *Guitarist, Zyna Hel;* b. (David Mark McCarty), 4 April 1969, Leeds, West Yorks., England; s. of Ron Franklin; m. Debra Craig; two s. *Education:* St Mary's Coll., Twickenham, Univ. of Sunderland, Newcastle Coll., Univ. of Northumbria. *Career:* guitarist with Drill 1990–91, 2008–09; mem. The Sojourners 1994–99; recorded solo material as Scrumpcha; guitarist with NEU2 and Owasis; currently guitarist with Zyna Hel working on new material; mem. Musicians' Union. *Compositions:* Blue Sky. *Television:* Elements (ITV) 1990. *Recordings:* with Drill: Skin Down 1991. *Telephone:* (191) 420-2388 (home). *E-mail:* davdeb .craig@blueyonder.co.uk (home).

CRAIG, Jay; British musician (baritone saxophone); b. 15 Oct. 1958, Bellshill, Scotland. *Education:* Napier Coll., Edinburgh, Berklee Coll. of Music, Boston, USA. *Career:* mem., Nat. Youth Jazz Orchestra 1976–81, Tommy Sampson Orchestra Glasgow 1979–82, Buddy Rich Band 1984–87, BBC Big Band 1992–; Performances with: Frank Sinatra, Tony Bennett, Sarah Vaughan, Jack Jones, Natalie Cole, Shirley Bassey, Vic Damone, Buddy Greco, Al Martino, Anita O'Day, Syd Lawrence Orchestra, BBC Scottish Radio Orchestra, Various West End shows. *Recordings include:* 4 NYJO albums; with Buddy Rich: Live on King Street, San Francisco 1985,

Live In Leonberg 1986; session work with: Terrorvision, Wet Wet Wet, George Martin. *E-mail:* thebandleader@jaycraigorchestra.com.

CRAIG, Mikey; British musician (bass); b. 15 Feb. 1960, London; m. 1st Cleo Scott; two c.; m. 2nd Lilli Craig; three c. *Career:* Founder-mem. In Praise of Lemmings, renamed Sex Gang Children, then Culture Club 1981–87, 1998–2002; numerous TV appearances and live dates; worked as record producer. *Recordings include:* albums: Kissing To Be Clever 1982, Colour By Numbers 1983, Waking Up With The House On Fire 1984, From Luxury To Heartache 1986, Don't Mind If I Do 1999, 12 Mixes Plus 2003; singles: Do You Really Want To Hurt Me 1982, Time (Clock of the Heart) 1982, Church Of The Poisoned Mind 1983, Victims 1983, It's A Miracle 1983, Karma Chameleon (BRIT Award for Best-Selling British Single 1984) 1983, The War Song 1984, The Medal Song 1984, Move Away 1986, I Just Wanna Be Loved 1998, Your Kisses Are Charity 1999, Cold Shoulder 1999. *Honours:* BRIT Awards for Best British Newcomer 1983, Best British Group 1984. *E-mail:* cultureclub@music3w.com. *Website:* www.culture-club.co.uk.

CRANITCH, Matt, BE, BMus, PhD; Irish traditional musician (fiddle), ethnomusicologist and lecturer; b. 27 March 1948, Cork; m. Liz MacNamara 1973; two s. *Education:* Univ. Coll. Cork, Univ. of Limerick. *Career:* numerous concert performances as soloist, and with Na Filí, Any Old Time, Sliabh Notes, Jackie Daly; festival appearances include Armagh, Basel, Belfast, Brest, Cambridge, Catskills, Chicago, Clifden, Cologne, Copenhagen, Cork, Cornwall, Dallas, Derry, Dingle, Dublin, Ennis, Exeter, Killarney, Kilkenny, Galway, Inverness, Lenzburg, London, Loughborough, Milwaukee, Montreal, New York, Newcastle-on-Tyne, Newfoundland, Norwich, Nyon, Orkney, Paris, Penzance, Quimper, Rome, Rotterdam, Shetland, Sligo, Swansea, Turin, Vienna; numerous radio and TV broadcasts; lectures, workshops, master classes in Ireland and abroad; music consultant, TG4 (Irish language TV station); Adviser, Irish Arts Council 2006–13; research work ongoing in aspects of Irish traditional fiddle music; Govt of Ireland Sr Research Scholar 2002–03; Dir and Chair. Cork Arts Fest 1993–98; Lecturer, Univ. Coll. Cork; mem. Bd Irish Traditional Music Archive 2006–10; mem. Folk Music Soc. of Ireland, Irish Music Rights Org. *Recordings include:* with Dave Hennessy and Mick Daly: Any Old Time 1982, Phoenix 1987, Crossing 1995, Solo: Éistigh Seal 1984, Take A Bow 1992, Give It Shtick 1996; with Dónal Murphy and Tommy O'Sullivan: Sliabh Notes 1995, Gleanntán 1999, Along Blackwater's Banks 2002; with Jackie Daly: The Living Stream 2010, Rolling On 2014. *Publications include:* The Irish Fiddle Book 1988, Irish Session Tunes: The Red Book 2000, Irish Fiddle Tunes 2013; contribs on Irish traditional music in several books; academic and conf. publs. *Honours:* Univ. Coll. Cork Hall of Fame Award 2003. *Address:* Kerry Pike, Co. Cork, Ireland. *Telephone:* 87-6782418 (mobile). *E-mail:* mcranitch@eircom.net. *Website:* www.mattcranitch.com.

CRAVEN, Beverley; British singer, songwriter and musician (piano); b. 28 June 1963, Sri Lanka; m. Colin Campsie 1994 (divorced 2011); three d. *Career:* toured with soul singer Bobby Womack and other musicians; solo artist 1990–. *Recordings include:* albums: Beverley Craven 1990, Love Scenes 1993, Mixed Emotions 1999, The Very Best of Beverley Craven 2004, Legends 2005, Close to Home 2009, Promise Me: The Best of Beverley Craven 2011. *Honours:* BRIT Award for Best British Newcomer 1992. *Address:* PO Box 1380, Beaconsfield, Hertfordshire, HP9 9AJ, England (office). *E-mail:* rlnoble24@hotmail.com (office). *Website:* www.beverleycraven.com.

CRAWFORD, Michael, CBE, OBE; British actor and singer; b. (Michael Dumbell-Smith), 19 Jan. 1942, Salisbury, Wilts. *Education:* St Michael's Coll., Bexley, Oakfield School, Dulwich. *Career:* actor 1955–; films for Children's Film Foundation; hundreds of radio broadcasts; appeared in original productions of Noyes Fludde and Let's Make an Opera by Benjamin Britten; has toured in UK, USA and Australia. *Stage roles include:* Travelling Light 1965, The Anniversary 1966, No Sex Please, We're British 1971, Billy 1974, Same Time, Next Year 1976, Flowers for Algernon 1979, Barnum (Olivier Award for Best Actor in a Musical) 1981–83, 1984–86, Phantom of the Opera, London (Olivier Award for Best Actor in a Musical) 1986–87, Broadway (Tony Award for Best Actor in a Musical, Drama Desk Award for Outstanding Actor in a Musical, Outer Critics Circle Award for Best Actor in a Musical) 1988, Los Angeles 1989, The Music of Andrew Lloyd Webber (concert tour), USA, Australia, UK 1991–92, EFX, Las Vegas 1995–96, Dance of the Vampires (Broadway) 2002–03, The Woman in White (Outstanding Stage Performance Award, Variety Club of GB, Best Supporting Actor in a Musical, Theatregoers Choice Award voted by on-line readers of WhatsonStage.com) 2004–05, The Wizard of (BroadwayWorld UK Award for Best Featured Actor in a Musical) 2011–12. *Films include:* Soap Box Derby 1950, Blow Your Own Trumpet 1954, Two Living One Dead 1962, The War Lover 1963, Two Left Feet 1963, The Knack 1965, A Funny Thing Happened on the Way to the Forum 1966, The Jokers 1966, How I Won the War 1967, Hello Dolly 1969, The Games 1969, Hello Goodbye 1970, Alice's Adventures in Wonderland 1972, Condorman 1981, Barnum 1986, Once Upon a Forest (voice) 1993, David Foster's Christmas Album 1993, Tony Palmer's Film About The Fantastic World of Michael Crawford 1996, My Favorite Broadway: The Love Songs 2001, The Ghosts of Christmas Eve 2001, WALL-E (archive footage from the film version of Hello Dolly!) 2008. *Television includes:* Sir Francis Drake (series) 1962, Some Mothers Do 'Ave 'Em (several series) 1973–78, Chalk and Cheese (series) 1979, Sorry (play) 1979, Barnum (film) 1986, Coronation Street 1998. *Publication:* Parcel Arrived Safely: Tied with String (autobiog.) 2000. *Honours:* Los Angeles Drama Critics Circle Award for Distinguished

Achievement in Theatre (Lead Performance) 1990, named Showbusiness Personality of the Year by the Variety Club of GB, voted No. 17 in the 100 Greatest Britons poll sponsored by the BBC 2002. *Current Management:* c/o Knight Ayton Management, 35 Great James Street, London, WC1N 3HB, England. *Telephone:* (20) 7831-4400. *Fax:* (20) 7831-4455. *E-mail:* info@knightayton.co.uk. *Website:* www.knightayton.co.uk.

CRAWFORD, (Randall Hugh) Randy; American publisher, cartoonist and musician (guitar); b. 16 Jan. 1953, Grand Rapids, Mich. *Career:* wrote and acted in stage play Time Capsule; wrote play Good Old Spot, performed at Grand Rapids Arts Fair; mem. BMG Music Service 1986–. *Compositions include:* Autumn, Bothered, Sick, Black Velvet Elvis, Children of the Night. *Recordings include:* produced cassette box cover art, Acid Orangutan, CD cover art, Bloodsucking Mosquitos, producer, Crooked Foot Live, assembled compilations, Glove Box Sampler, Bad Exampler Sampler, Black Paper Packages. *Publications include:* issues on numerous magazines, comic strip artist, The Three Pals. *Honours:* Student Award, Haiku 1971.

CRAWFORD, (Veronica) Randy; American singer; b. 18 Feb. 1952, Macon, Ga. *Career:* singer 1967–; appearances include: World Jazz Asscn tribute concert to Cannonball Adderley 1968, Montreux Jazz Festival 1982, two concerts with London Symphony Orchestra, Barbican Centre, London 1988. *Recordings include:* albums: Everything Must Change 1976, Miss Randy Crawford 1977, Raw Silk 1979, Now We May Begin 1980, Secret Combination 1981, Windsong 1982, Nightline 1983, Casino Nights (with Al Jarreau) 1983, Miss Randy Crawford – The Greatest Hits 1984, Abstract Emotions 1986, The Love Songs 1987, Rich and Poor 1989, The Very Best Of 1993, Don't Say It's Over 1993, Naked and True 1995, Every Kind of Mood – Randy Randi Randee 1998, Play Mode 2001, Permanent 2001, Feeling Good (with Joe Sample) 2006, No Regrets (with Joe Sample) 2008, Live 2012; singles include: Street Life (with The Crusaders) 1979, One Day I'll Fly Away 1980, You Might Need Somebody 1981, Rainy Night In Georgia 1981, Almaz (own composition) 1987, Knockin' On Heaven's Door, used in film soundtrack Lethal Weapon 2 1989; guest vocalist on albums: Please Don't Touch, Steve Hackett 1977, Marching In The Streets, Harvey Mason 1978, Street Life, The Crusaders 1979, Hard To Hold, Rick Springfield 1984, Lethal Weapon 2 1989, Best of Smooth Jazz 1997, Jackie Brown, Music from the Motion Picture Soundtrack 1997, Funky Jazz Party 1998, Crusaders, Priceless Jazz 1998, Classic Gold Vol. 2: The Love Song 1999, Barry Williams, Return of Johnny Bravo 1999; guest vocalist on single, Diamante, Zucchero 1992. *Honours:* BRIT Award for Best Female Artist 1982. *Current Management:* c/o Patrick Rains & Associates, 1255 Fifth Avenue, #7K, New York, NY 10029, USA. *E-mail:* pra@prarecords.com. *Website:* www.prarecords.com.

CRAWFORD, Stephanie, BA; American singer, songwriter, artist and educator; b. 30 Aug. 1942, Detroit, Mich. *Education:* Wayne State Univ., , studied with Barry Harris and Frank Foster in New York. *Career:* played clubs and festivals including Crest Jazz Festival, Aix-En-Provence Jazz Festival; Prof. of Jazz Vocals, Centre d'Informations Musicales and Institut d'Art, Culture et Perception, Paris 1989–96. *Film:* La Vie en Rouge 1995. *Recordings include:* The Art of Romance 1990, A Time For Love 1991, The Gift 1992, The Real Thing 2008. *Honours:* Django D'Or for Best Int. Jazz Vocalist 1993, Best Singer Award, East Bay Express 2009. *E-mail:* stephaniecrwfd@yahoo.com (office). *Website:* stephaniecrawfordjazz.com; www.mirabilevisu.org.

CRAY, Robert William; American blues musician (guitar), singer and songwriter; b. 1 Aug. 1953, Columbus, Ga; m. Sue Turner-Cray. *Career:* began playing guitar aged 12; mem., Albert Collins' band 1973–75; formed Robert Cray Band 1974–; numerous live appearances, tours and festival appearances. *Film appearances:* Animal House, Hail! Hail! Rock and Roll. *Compositions include:* songs covered by other artists, include Bad Influence (Eric Clapton), Old Love (co-writer with Eric Clapton), Phone Booth (Albert King), Playin' With My Friends (B. B. King). *Recordings include:* albums: Who's Been Talking 1978, Bad Influence 1983, False Accusations 1985, Showdown! 1985, Strong Persuader 1986, Don't Be Afraid of The Dark 1988, Midnight Stroll 1990, I Was Warned 1992, Shame and A Sin 1993, Some Rainy Morning 1995, Sweet Potato Pie 1997, In Concert (live) 1999, Take Your Shoes Off 1999, Heavy Picks 1999, Shoulda Been Home 2001, Time Will Tell 2003, Twenty 2005, Live From Across the Pond 2007, This Time 2009, Cookin' in Mobile 2010, Nothin But Love 2012, In My Soul 2014. *Honours:* Nat. Blues Awards 1983, 1986, Nat. Asscn of Ind. Record Distribution Award for Best Blues Album 1985, Grammy Awards 1985, 1986, 1988, 1999, numerous W. C. Handy Awards 1984–, including Best Male Blues Artist, Vocalist of the Year, Single of the Year, Band of the Year, Song of the Year, Best Contemporary Blues Album 1987, numerous magazine awards from Billboard, Downbeat, Rolling Stone, Esquire, Living Blues; inducted to Blues Hall of Fame 2011. *Current Management:* c/o Chad Jensen, The Fitzgerald-Hartley Company, 34 North Palm Street, Suite 100, Ventura, CA 93001, USA. *Telephone:* (805) 641-6441. *Fax:* (805) 641-6444. *Website:* www.fitzhart.com; www.robertcray.com.

CRAYMER, Judy, MBE; British theatre and film producer; *CEO, Littlestar Services Ltd;* b. 1957, London. *Education:* Guildhall School of Music. *Career:* began career as stage man., including original London production of Cats; Man. Dir Three Nights 1984; worked in TV; Co-founder (with Benny Andersson, Björn Ulvaeus and Richard East) Littlestar Services Ltd 1996, currently CEO; Exec. Producer Chess; currently Founding Muse, Modern Muse Project; lead Producer Mamma Mia! 1999–. *Films include:* Mamma Mia!

(producer) 1998. *Publication:* Mamma Mia! How Can I Resist You! (with Benny Andersson and Björn Ulvaeus) 2006. *Honours:* Woman of the Year Award 2002, Women in Film ITV Achievement of the Year Award 2008, Breast Cancer Research Foundation Humanitarian Award 2010. *Address:* Littlestar Services Ltd, 32-33 St. James's Place, London SW1A 1NR, England (office). *E-mail:* littlestar@littlestarservices.com (office). *Website:* www .littlestarservices.com (office); www.judycraymer.com.

CREASEY, Jason M.; British record producer, remixer, composer, arranger and musician; b. 23 July 1969, Andover, Hampshire. *Career:* f. Hitsound (music composition and production co.); extensive work in areas of writing, arranging, producing for various artists; music to film; keyboards and drum programming; most recent productions in partnership with Hamish Hutchison (also known as remix duo Hiss and Hum for Absolute Basic Productions); mem. Performing Right Soc., Mechanical-Copyright Protection Soc., Musicians' Union. *Recordings include:* producer (including arranging) for: Chesney Hawkes, Big Fun, Glen Goldsmith, Think 2wice (including writing), Deni Lew (additional production only); remixer for PJ and Duncan, Love City Groove, Jack 'n' Chill, Chesney Hawkes. *E-mail:* info@hitsound.co.uk. *Website:* www .hitsound.co.uk.

CRÈME, Lol; British musician (guitar), singer, songwriter, producer and film director; b. 19 Sept. 1947, Manchester. *Career:* Founder-mem., guitarist, songwriter, Hotlegs 1970–71; 10cc 1972–76; numerous festival appearances, tours of UK, USA; Producer, songwriter, mem. Godley and Creme (with Kevin Godley) 1976–; debut feature film, Howling At The Moon 1988; film dir, The Lunatic 1992; mem. Art of Noise 1998–; mem. The Producers 2007–. *Recordings include:* Albums: with Hotlegs: Thinks: School Stinks 1970, with 10cc: 10cc 1973, Sheet Music 1974, The Original Soundtrack 1975, How Dare You? 1976; with Godley and Creme (mostly self-written and produced): Consequences 1977, L 1978, Music From Consequences 1979, Freeze Frame 1979, Ismism 1981, Birds of Prey 1983, The History Mix Vol. 1 1985, The Changing Faces of 10cc and Godley and Creme 1987, Goodbye Blue Sky 1988, Images 1994; with Art of Noise: The Seduction of Claude Debussy 1999; with The Producers: Studio 1 2007; other session work includes: Tina Turner, Rod Stewart, Producer, Long Distant Romancer, Mickey Jupp 1981; Dir of videos including: Every Breath You Take, The Police, Rockit, Herbie Hancock, Feel The Love, 10cc, Relax, Frankie Goes To Hollywood, Two Tribes, Frankie Goes To Hollywood. *Honours:* Ivor Novello Awards: Best Beat Song, Rubber Bullets 1974, Most Performed British Work, Best Pop Song, Int. Hit of the Year, I'm Not In Love 1976, 5 MTV Music Video Awards, Rockit 1984, MTV Video Vanguard Award (shared) 1985. *Address:* www.theartofnoiseonline.com.

CRETU, Michael; Romanian musician (keyboards), arranger, producer and composer; b. 18 May 1957, Bucharest; m. Sandra Lauer 1988 (divorced). *Education:* Piano Lyzeum No. 2, Bucharest, Acad. of Music, Frankfurt. *Career:* studio musician 1978–; writer, producer, musician for artists, including Moti Special, Mike Oldfield, Sylvie Vartan, Sandra 1985–; Founder-mem. Enigma 1990–; writer, arranger of tracks for soundtrack to film, Sliver. *Recordings include:* albums: solo: Legionare 1983; with Enigma: MCMXC AD 1990, The Cross of Changes 1993, Le Roi Est Mort, Vive Le Roi! 1996, Screen Behind The Mirror 2000, Love, Sensuality and Devotion (compilation) 2001, A Posteriori 2006, Seven Lives Many Faces 2008; six albums with Sandra. *Current Management:* c/o Crocodile Music Management GmbH, Oelmüllerstraße 2a, 82166 Gräfelfing, Germany. *Telephone:* (89) 89809830. *Fax:* (89) 89809844. *E-mail:* thuernau@crocodile-music.de. *Website:* www.crocodile-music.de; www.enigmaspace.com.

CRISS, Peter; American musician (drums), singer and songwriter; b. (Peter Crisscoula), 20 Dec. 1947, Brooklyn, New York. *Career:* Founder-mem. rock group Kiss 1973–80, 1995–2004; numerous tours and live appearances; solo artist 1980–82; mem. Balls of Fire. *Recordings include:* albums: with Kiss: Kiss 1974, Hotter Than Hell 1974, Dressed To Kill 1975, Alive 1975, Destroyer 1976, The Originals 1976, Rock and Roll Over 1976, Kiss Alive II 1977, Love Gun 1977, Double Platinum 1978, Dynasty 1979, MTV Unplugged 1996, Psycho Circus 1998, Kiss Symphony: Alive IV 2003; solo: Peter Criss 1978, Out of Control 1980, Let Me Rock You 1982, Criss Cat #1 1994, One for All 2007. *Honours:* inducted into Modern Drummer's Drum Hall Of Fame 2012. *Address:* c/o Josselyne Herman & Associates, 345 East 56th Street, #3B, New York, NY 10022, USA. *Telephone:* (212) 355-3033. *Fax:* (212) 937-5270. *E-mail:* j@jhamanagement.com. *Website:* www.jhamanagement.com; www .petercriss.net.

CRISWELL, Kim; American singer and actress; b. 19 July 1957, Hampton, Va. *Education:* Univ. of Cincinnati Coll., Conservatory of Music. *Career:* began Broadway career in early 1980s. *Plays include:* musicals include: The First 1981, Nine 1982, Baby 1983, Three Musketeers 1983, Cats 1985–86, Stardust 1986, The Threepenny Opera 1989, Annie Get Your Gun 1992, Dames at Sea 1996, The Slow Drag 1997, Of Thee I Sing 1998, Anything Goes 2002, Call Me Madam 2004, Into the Woods 2006, Candide 2006, The Sound of Music 2009, Hysteria 2011. *Recordings include:* solo albums: The Human Cry 1993, The Lorelei 1994, Back To Before 1999; cast recordings: Baby 1983, Anything Goes 1988, Fifty Million Frenchmen 1991, Annie Get Your Gun 1990, Miss Saigon 1994, Annie 1995, Guys & Dolls 1995, On The Town 1996, The Pajama Game 1996, Elegies For Angels Punks And Raging Queens 2001, Man Of La Mancha 2001, Something To Dance About 2004.

CRO; German rapper, singer, songwriter, musician (piano, guitar) and record producer and designer; b. (Carlo Waibel), 31 Jan. 1990. *Education:* Realschule auf dem Galgenberg, Aalen. *Career:* trained as media designer; worked as cartoonist for Stuttgarter Zeitung; debut releases as recording artist 2009; f. own clothing label VIOVIO 2010–; signed to Chimperator Productions record label 2011; competitor in Bundesvision Song Contest 2012; several national and international tours. *Recordings include:* mixtapes: Trash 2009, Meine Musik 2011; album: Raop 2012. *Honours:* 1LIVE Krone Award for Best Single (for Easy) 2012, Bambi Pop National Award 2012. *Address:* Chimperator Productions, Bennigsenstr. 2, 12159 Berlin (office); VIOVIO, Herzogstrasse 4, 70176 Stuttgart, Germany (office). *Fax:* (30) 28473440 (Berlin) (office). *E-mail:* kontakt@chimperator.de (office); info@thisisviovio.com (office). *Website:* www .chimperator.de (office); www.thisisviovio.com (office); www.cromusik.info.

CROISILLE, Nicole; French singer and actress; b. 9 Oct. 1936, Neuilly-Sur-Seine. *Career:* tour with mime artist, Marcel Marceau; lead role, musical, L'Apprenti Fakir; released first record 1961; worked in USA with Lester Wilson, Lalo Schifrin; performed across France at Olympia, Paris, Theatre des Champs-Elysées, Paris, Bataclan, Paris, Casino de Paris; lead role, Un Homme et une Femme (A Man and a Woman) 1966, Hello Dolly, Thèatre du Chatelet, Paris 1992–93; appearances in Canada, Latin America, Poland, Morocco; mem., Soc. of Authors, Composers and Editors of Music, France. *Film appearances:* Erotissimo 1969, Underground 1970, There Were Days ...and Moons 1990, Les Misérables 1995, The Golded Cage 2013. *Television appearances:* Loin de Rueil 1961, Quelques pas dans les nuages 1963, Un Enfant dans la ville 1971, Musidora 1973, Impressions d'Afrique 1977, Chouette, chat, chien 1980, Les uns et les autres 1981, La Bella Anglaise 1988–90, Loin des Yeix 1996, Deux Mamans pour Noël 1998, Un Homme à la Maison 2000, Psy d'urgence 2000, Ville mon rêve 2001, Le Temps Perdu 2001, Maigret 2002, Menteur! Menteuse! 2004, Dolmen 2005, Un Viol 2009, Beauté Fatale 2009, Le juge est une femme 2013. *Recordings include:* albums: Nicole Croisille 1961, Nous les Amoureux 1963, Climats 1970, Ses Grands Succès 1973–74, Partir 1974, Femme 1974, Si l'on pouvait choisir sa vie 1976, La Femme et l'Enfant 1977, C'est ma vie 1978, Le coeur au garde-a-vous 1980, Le Coeur funambule 1981, Jazzville 1987, Ses Plus Bells Chansons 1988, Black et Blanche 1990, Super Croisille 1992, Ume Femme 1997, De vous à moi 2003, Nougaro, le Jazz et moi 2006, Tu me Manques 2008, Bossa d'hiver 2009, Croisille 2011. *Honours:* Chevalier, Ordre des Arts et des Lettres. *Current Management:* c/o Agence Parallaxe, 11 rue Delambre, 75014 Paris, France. *Telephone:* 1-44-10-73-13. *Fax:* 1-44-10-73-10. *E-mail:* info@agenceparallaxe .com. *Website:* www.agenceparallaxe.com.

CROKER, Brendan; British musician (guitar); b. 15 Aug. 1953, Bradford, Yorkshire, England. *Career:* formed duo, Nev and Norris, with fellow guitarist Steve Phillips; formed own band, the 5 O'Clock Shadows in early 1980s; mem. Notting Hillbillies (with Mark Knopfler, Guy Fletcher, Steve Phillips) 1990; British tour 1990. *Recordings include:* albums: Close Shave 1986, Brendan Croker and The 5 O'Clock Shadows 1989, The Great Indoors 1992, The Kershaw Sessions 1996, Not Just A Hillbilly 2000, Life Is Almost Wonderful; with the Notting Hillbillies: Missing... Presumed Having a Good Time 1990; Guest musician, Ancient Heart, Tanita Tikaram; Singles: That's The Way All My Money Goes 1986. *Current Management:* Adastra, The Stables, Westwood House, Main Street, North Dalton, Driffield, YO25 9XA, England. *Telephone:* (1377) 217662. *Website:* www.adastra-music.co.uk; www.brendancroker.com.

CROMPHOUT, Francis, BA; Belgian singer, songwriter and musician (saxophone, keyboards); b. 24 Oct. 1947, Antwerp; m. Alejandra Anfossi 1994; two d. *Education:* Ghent State Univ., Ghent Music Conservatory, Brussels Univ. *Career:* several performances in jazz, blues and Latin music; creator and performer, En Avian La Zizique, song programme around Boris Vian; founder and leader, Cuisine Cajun and Café con Leche; songwriter, Cuisine Cajun, Café con Leche and Catherine Delasalle; concerts in the Netherlands, Germany, Belgium, France, Peru; broadcasts on VRT Radio and RTBF TV; mem. Soc. d'Auteurs Belge – Belgische Auteurs Maatschappij (SABAM), Belgian Asscn of Authors and Composers. *Compositions include:* Allons au Fais-Do-Do, Le Grand Dérangement, Cofé Bon Dieu, Démarche, (Pigalle), Tango del laberinto, Tango de cuna, Limatango, Insen-satez (Kamikazekuit), Condor, De nacht betrapt, Zeepbel, Para que te sientas feliz. *Recordings include:* Le Grand Dérangement 1996. *Publications include:* Als un pas vernielde stad (poems) 1978, El Susto 2007, Les plus beaux 2014. *Honours:* Chevalier, Ordre des Palmes académiques; Premio Internacional Mosaico de Narración Breve. *Current Management:* c/o Berkenhof 7, 9050 Ghent, Belgium. *Telephone:* (9) 2311591 (home). *Fax:* (7) 9119697 (office). *E-mail:* franciscromphout@gmail.com. *Website:* franciscromphout.unblog.fr.

CRONIN, Kevin; American singer and songwriter; b. 6 Oct. 1951, Evanston, IL. *Career:* lead singer of rock group, REO Speedwagon 1972, 1976–; solo artiste 1973–76; regular US and international concerts. *Compositions include:* Keep On Loving You; Can't Fight This Feeling; Hard To Believe, for Home Front Trust (for families of Gulf War casualties). *Recordings include:* albums: with REO Speedwagon: REO TWO 1972, REO 1976, REO Speedwagon Live/ You Get What You Play For 1977, You Can Tune a Piano But You Can't Tuna Fish 1978, Nine Lives 1979, A Decade of Rock 'n' Roll 1970–80 1980, Hi Infidelity 1981, Good Trouble 1982, Wheels are Turning 1984, Best Foot Forward 1985, Life as We Know It 1987, The Earth, a Small Man, his Dog and a Chicken 1990, A Second Decade of Rock 'n' Roll 1981–91 1991, Building the Bridge 1996, Ballads 1999, Live Plus 2001, Find Your Own Way Home 2007, Not So Silent Night... Christmas with REO Speedwagon 2009. *Website:* www .speedwagon.com; www.kevincronin.com.

CROOK, Jenny, BA; British musician (non-pedal harp) and singer; b. 16 Jan. 1971, Bath, Avon. *Education:* Middlesex Univ. *Career:* folk clubs, television appearances and radio broadcasts, festival appearances; mem. Madigan; session musician and recording artist; mem. of duo, Jenny Crook and Henry Sears; mem. of duo, Cythara (with Maclaine Colston) 1991–95; mem. Musicians' Union, PRS, Performing Artists Media Rights Asscn (PAMRA), Clarsach Soc. *Recordings include:* Evolving Tradition, Cythara 1992, Pluckin' Hammered 1995, Uncorked 1997, Merry-Go-Round 2011. *E-mail:* info@jennifercrook.com. *Website:* www.jennycrook.com.

CROPPER, Steve; American musician (guitar), songwriter and producer; b. 21 Oct. 1941, Dora, Mo. *Career:* Founder mem., Booker T. and the MG's, The Mar-Keys, Blues Brothers; engineer, Stax Records; producer for Jeff Beck, Mitch Ryder, Joe Louis Walker; session musician for artists including Otis Redding, Wilson Pickett and Rod Stewart; Owner, Insomnia Studio; started his own label Play It, Steve! Records 1998. *Compositions include:* Sittin' on the Dock of the Bay, Crop Dustin', Give 'em What They Want, In the Midnight Hour. *Recordings include:* with Booker T: Green Onions 1962, Soul Dressing 1965, Sweet Potato, And Now... Booker T and the MG's 1966, Hip Hug-Her 1967, Doin' Our Thing 1968, Soul Limbo 1968, Uptight 1968, McLemore Avenue 1970, Melting Pot 1971; solo: Steve Cropper: With a Little Help from My Friends 1971, Playin' My Thang 1981, Night After Night 1982, Jammed Together (Albert King and Pops Staples) 1991, This Is Steve Cropper & His Friends 2007, Nudge It Up A Notch (with Felix Cavaliere) 2008, Midnight Flyer 2010, Dedicated: A Salute To The 5 Royales 2011. *Films include:* The Blues Brothers 1980, Satisfaction 1988, Blues Brothers 2000 1999. *E-mail:* info@playitsteve.com. *Website:* www.playitsteve.com.

CROSBY, David; American singer and musician (guitar); b. (David van Cortland), 14 Aug. 1941, Los Angeles, Calif.; s. of Floyd Crosby; m. Jan Dance 1987. *Career:* mem. Les Baxter's Balladeers, The Byrds 1964–67, Crosby Stills and Nash 1968–, later Crosby Stills Nash and Young; Founder mem. CPR; numerous live performances, festival appearances; collaborations include Jeff Bridges, Jackson Browne, Phil Collins, Bob Dylan, Art Garfunkel, Carole King, Joni Mitchell, Stevie Nicks, Neil Young. *Film appearance:* No Nukes 1980. *Television appearances:* guest, Roseanne (ABC) 1992, The Simpsons (Fox) 1993. *Recordings include:* albums: with the Byrds: Mr Tambourine Man 1965, Turn! Turn! Turn! 1965, Fifth Dimension 1966, Younger Than Yesterday 1967; with Crosby Stills and Nash: Crosby Stills and Nash 1969, Déja Vu 1970, 4-Way Street 1971, So Far 1974, Daylight Again 1982, Looking Forward 1999; with Graham Nash: Graham Nash/David Crosby 1972, Wind On The Water 1975, Whistling Down The Wire 1976, Crosby/Nash Live 1977, The Best Of 1978, Another Stoney Evening 1998; solo: If Only I Could Remember My Name 1971, Oh Yes I Can 1989, Thousand Roads 1993, Now It's All Coming Back To Me 1995, King Biscuit Flower Hour 1996, Live 2000, Voyage Box Set 2006, Croz 2014; with CPR: CPR 1998, Just Like Gravity 2001. *Publications include:* Long Time Gone (with Carl Gottlieb) 1988, Stand Up and Be Counted 2000, Since Then (with Carl Gottlieb) 2006. *Honours:* Grammy Award for Best New Artist (with Crosby Stills and Nash) 1970, Best Int. Group, Melody Maker Poll 1971, MusiCares Man of the Year, Nat. Acad. of Recording Arts and Sciences 1991. *Current Management:* c/o Michael Jensen, Jensen Communications, Suite 220, 709 East Colorado Boulevard, Pasadena, CA 91101, USA. *Telephone:* (626) 585-9575. *Fax:* (626) 564-8920. *E-mail:* info@jensencom.com. *Website:* www.jensencom.com; www.davidcrosby.com; www.csny.com.

CROSS, Christopher; American musician (guitar), singer and songwriter; b. (Christopher Geppert), 3 May 1951, San Antonio, TX. *Career:* mem. of rock group, Flash; support for various acts; formed band for own compositions 1975; solo artist 1978–; own publishing co., Pop 'n' Roll 1978. *Compositions include:* co-writer (with Burt Bacharach, Carole Bayer Sager, Peter Allen): Arthur's Theme (Best That You Can Do), for film Arthur 1981. *Recordings include:* albums: Christopher Cross, 1980; Another Page, 1983; Every Turn of The World, 1985; Back of My Mind, 1988; Rendezvous, 1992; Window, 1995; Walking in Avalon, 1998; Red Room, 2000, A Christopher Cross Christmas 2007, The Café Carlyle Sessions 2008, Christmas Time is Here 2010, Dr Faith 2011. *Honours:* Grammy Award for Album of the Year, for Best New Artist, for Record of the Year, Song of the Year and Best Arrangement (all for Sailing) 1981, Academy Award for Best Song from a Film (for Arthur's Theme) 1982. *Website:* www.christophercross.com.

CROW, Bill; American musician (bass, tuba); b. 27 Dec. 1927, Othello, Wash.; m. Aileen Armstrong 1965, one s. *Career:* bassist for various artists, including Stan Getz, Claude Thorhill, Marian McPartland, Gerry Mulligan, Zoot Sims, Bob Brookmeyer, Clark Terry, Benny Goodman, Walter Norris, Peter Duchin; musician, Broadway shows 1975–89; mem. American Fed. of Musicians (AFofM). *Recordings include:* two albums with Bill Crow Quartet. *Publications include:* author: Jazz Anecdotes 1990, From Birdland to Broadway 1992; contrib. to The Jazz Review, Jazz Letter, Oxford Companion to Jazz. *Website:* www.billcrowbass.com.

CROW, Sheryl; American singer, songwriter and musician (guitar); b. 11 Feb. 1962, Kennett, Mo.; two adopted s. *Education:* Univ. of Missouri. *Career:* trained as classical pianist; worked as music teacher and part-time bar singer; fmr backing singer to Rod Stewart, Eric Clapton, Don Henley, Michael Jackson, Joe Cocker; solo artist mid-1980s–. *Film appearance:* De-Lovely 2004. *Recordings include:* albums: Tuesday Night Music Club (three Grammy Awards 1995) 1993, Sheryl Crow 1996, The Globe Sessions 1999, Sheryl Crow

and Friends: Live in Central Park 1999, C'mon C'mon 2002, Sheryl Crow: Live At Budokan 2003, Wildflower 2005, Hits and Rarities 2007, Detours 2008, 100 Miles from Memphis 2010, Feels Like Home 2013. *Honours:* BRIT Award for Best Int. Female Artist 1997, American Music Awards for Best Female Pop/ Rock Artist 2003, 2004. *Current Management:* c/o Stephen Weintraub. *E-mail:* wmgmt@aol.com (office). *Address:* c/o A&M Records, 2220 Colorado Avenue, Santa Monica, CA 90404, USA (office). *E-mail:* sheryl@sherylcrow.com (office). *Website:* www.sherylcrow.com.

CROWELL, Rodney; American country singer, songwriter, musician (guitar) and producer; b. 7 Aug. 1950, Houston, Tex.; m. 1st Rosanne Cash 1979; four d.; m. 2nd Claudia Church 1998. *Career:* mem., songwriter, Emmylou Harris' Hot Band 1974–79; worked with Willie Nelson, Ry Cooder, Jim Keltner; solo artist and with own band 1978–; producer on recordings for Guy Clark, Albert Lee, Carl Perkins, Jerry Lee Lewis, Bobby Bare, Roseanne Cash, Lari White, Brady Seals, Beth Nielsen Chapman, Chely Wright; mem. CMA, Nashville Songwriters' Asscn, Nat. Acad. of Recording Arts and Sciences. *Compositions include:* songs for Emmylou Harris include: Bluebird Wine 1974, Till I Gain Control Again 1975, I Ain't Living Long Like This 1979, Leaving Louisiana in the Broad Daylight 1979; 250 versions of own compositions recorded by artists, including Willie Nelson, Foghat, Bob Seger, The Dirt Band, Waylon Jennings, George Jones. *Recordings include:* albums: Ain't Living Long Like This 1978, But What Will The Neighbours Think 1980, Rodney Crowell 1981, Street Language 1986, Diamonds and Dirt 1988, The Rodney Crowell Collection 1989, Keys To The Highway 1989, Life Is Messy 1992, Jewel of The South 1995, Soul Searchin' 1995, The Houston Kid 2001, Fate's Right Hand 2003, The Notorious Cherry Bombs 2004, The Outsider 2005, Sex and Gasoline 2008, KIN: Songs by Rodney Crowell and Mary Karr 2012, Old Yellow Moon (with Emmylou Harris) (Grammy Award for Best Americana Album 2014) 2013. *Publication:* Chinaberry Sidewalks: A Memoir 2011. *Honours:* Grammy Award for Best Country Song (for After All This Time) 1990, Americana Award for Lifetime Achievement in Songwriting 2006. *Current Management:* c/o Vector Management, PO Box 120479, Nashville, TN 37212, USA. *E-mail:* jtalley@vectormgmt.com. *Website:* www.rodneycrowell .com.

CRUCIAL BANKIE; Saint Christopher and Nevis musician (guitar, keyboard) and singer; b. (Ian Veira), 23 Nov. 1965, St Kitts; one s. *Career:* Bunny Wailer First Antigua Show; numerous radio broadcasts; Reggae Sunsplash, with Sagittarius Band 1986, Stud Band 1988; performed with Leroy Horsemouth Wallace, Jose Whale, Brigadier Jerry, Buju Banton, Legendary Bunny Wailer; mem. American Society of Composers, Authors and Publrs. *Recordings include:* Just A Sting 1986, Sweet Reggae Muzik 1993, Shakedown 2004; film soundtrack: Uptown. *Publication:* The New Music of Reviews. *Website:* www.crucialbankie.com.

CRUZ, Taio; British singer, rapper, songwriter and producer; b. (Jacob Taio Cruz), 23 April 1983, London. *Education:* Bilton Grange School. *Career:* songwriter for RedZone Entertainment from 2002, co-writer or producer for numerous artists including Will Young, JLS, David Guetta, McFly, Tinchy Stryder, The Wanted, The Saturdays, Justin Bieber, Jennifer Lopez; Founder and CEO Rokstarr Music London (later Rokstarr Entertainment Division) 2006–; solo recording career 2006–; recordings include collaborations with Busta Rhymes, Sugababes, Kylie Minogue, Tinchy Stryder, Luciana. *Recordings:* albums: solo: Departure (Ascap Vanguard Award for Recognition of Album 2008) 2008, Rokstarr 2009, TY.O 2011. *Honours:* BRIT Award for Best British Song 2004, Billboard Awards for Top Hot 100 Song, Top Digital Song, Top Pop Song 2011, MuchMusic Video Award for Most Watched Video 2011. *Address:* c/o Universal Music, 364–366 Kensington High Street, London, W14 8NS, England. *E-mail:* info@rokstarr.com. *Website:* www.rokstarr.com; www .taiocruzmusic.co.uk.

CUBA, Alex; Cuban/Canadian singer, songwriter and musician (bass guitar); b. 1974, Artemisa. *Career:* began career performing with his brother as The Puentes Brothers; solo artist, performing with the Alex Cuba Band 2005–; f. own record label, Caracol Records; collaboration with Nelly Furtado. *Recordings:* albums: with The Puentes Brothers: Morumba Cubana 2001; solo: Humo de Tabaco (Juno Award for Best World Music Album 2006) 2004, Agua del Pozo (Juno Award for Best World Music Album 2008) 2007, Alex Cuba 2009, Static in the System 2012, Healer (Latin Grammy Award for Best Singer-Songwriter Album 2015) 2015. *Honours:* Latin Grammy Award for Best New Artist 2010. *Telephone:* (416) 457-4900 (office). *E-mail:* andres@cuto.ca (office); sarah@caracolrecords.ca (office). *Website:* www.alexcuba.com.

CUBER, Ronnie; American musician (baritone saxophone); b. (Ronald Edward Cuber), 25 Dec. 1941, Brooklyn, New York; m. Roberta Arnold. *Education:* Brooklyn Conservatory of Music. *Career:* five years with Saturday Night Live Show Band; currently musician with Ronnie Cuber Band, Ronnie Cuber - Toninho Horta Band; numerous TV appearances and radio broadcasts including Late Show with David Letterman, two Jazz-in-Concert programmes for DRS Swiss Television; played at every major jazz festival in Europe, USA and Japan; masterclasses and clinics; mem. AFM. *Film:* Borgia Stick. *Recordings include:* over 300 pop/jazz/rock recordings including Cuber Libre! 1976, The Eleventh Day of Aquarius 1978, New York Jazz 1981, Passion Fruit 1985, Two Brothers King 1985, Pin Point 1985, Live at Blue Note 1986, Cubism 1992, The Scene is Clean 1993, Airplay 1994, In a New York Minute 1996, Three Baritone Saxophone Band 1998, Love for Sale 1998, Ronnie 2009, Ronnie Cuber Band Live at JazzFest Berlin 2013, Ronnie Cuber Cuber Libre

2016. *Honours:* Downbeat Magazine Wider Recognition. *Address:* 58 Samantha Circle, Westhampton, NY 11977, USA (office). *Telephone:* (631) 998-0320 (office). *E-mail:* arnoldmusic@optonline.net (office). *Website:* www .ronniecubermusic.com (office).

CUBIC U (see Utada, Hikaru)

CUGNY, Laurent, BA; French bandleader, arranger, musician (piano) and academic; *Professor, Université Paris-Sorbonne;* b. 14 April 1955, La Garenne-Colombes; m.; two c. *Education:* Université Paris X-Nanterre, Université Paris-Panthéon-Sorbonne (Paris 1). *Career:* Founder Lumière Big Band 1979; European tour, Lumière and Gil Evans 1987; Dir Orchestre Nat. de Jazz (ONJ), 1994–97; European tour, ONJ and Lucky Peterson 1995; Prof. of Music and Musicology, Univ. of Paris-Sorbonne 2006–; Dir, Gil Evans Paris Workshop 2014–. *Recordings include:* with Lumière and Gil Evans: Rhythm-A-Ning 1988, Golden Hair 1989; with Lumière: Santander 1991, Dromesko 1993; with ONJ: Yesternow 1994; with Abbey Lincoln: A Turtle's Dream 1995; with Orchestra National de Jazz: Reminiscing (Prix Boris Vian 1996) 1995, In Tempo 1995, Merci, Merci, Merci 1996, A Personal Landscape 2001. *Publications include:* Las Vegas Tango – Une Vie De Gil Evans 1989, Electrique Miles Davis 1993, Analyser le jazz 2009, Une Histoire du Jazz en France, Vol. 1, Du milieu du XIXe siècle à 1929 2014. *Honours:* Officier des Arts et des Lettres; Dr hc (Paris-Sorbonne) 2001; Jazz Acad. Django Reinhardt Award 1991, Acad. Charles-Cros Award 1991. *Address:* Université Paris-Sorbonne, 2 rue Francis de Croisset , 75018 Paris, France (office). *Telephone:* 6-07-75-13-09 (mobile). *E-mail:* laurent.cugny@paris-sorbonne.fr. *Website:* laurentcugny.org (office).

CUI JIAN; South Korean singer and musician (guitar, trumpet); b. 2 Aug. 1961, Beijing, People's Repub. of China. *Career:* fmr classical trumpeter; mem. Beijing Symphony Orchestra 1981–86; mem. ADO. *Recordings include:* albums: Vagabond's Return 1986, Rock 'n' Roll On The New Long March 1987, Nothing To My Name 1989, Solution 1991, Balls Under The Red Flag 1994, Power Of The Powerless 1998, The Village Attacks The City 2004, Show You Colour 2005. *Films include:* Beijing Bastards 1996, Roots and Branches 2003, The Sun Also Rises 2007, Dooman River 2010, The Blue Bone 2012. *E-mail:* dongximusic@sina.com. *Website:* www.cuijian.com.

CUILLERIER, Philippe 'Doudou'; French musician (guitar) and lyricist; b. 5 Sept. 1961, Versailles. *Education:* saxophone and guitar lessons with Eric Boell, Frederic Sylvestre. *Career:* guitar teacher 1983–; backing guitarist with Angelo Debarre; Romane, Rodolphe Raffalli, Patrick Saussois, Latcho Drom, Bireli Lagrene, Babik Reinhardt; lead guitarist, vocalist with Fernando Jazz Gang; Doudou Swing, Echoes of Friends; magazine journalist French Guitare 1998–2000. *Recordings include:* with Romane and Tchavolo Schmitt: Alors... voilà; with Romane: Quintet, Ombre, Samois sur Seine, Acoustic Spirit, Ombre: Complete Romane, Vol. 3; with Romane and Frédéric Manoukian Orchestra; with Romane and Babik Reinhardt: New Quintet du Hot Club de France; with Angelo Debarre: Caprice; with Rodolphe Raffalli: Hommage à Brassens, Gypsy Swing Guitars; with Latcho Drom: Live 2001; with Patrick Saussois and Alma Sinti: Le chemin des forains; with Doudou Swing: Doudou a Feu Doux. *Address:* 2 Ruelle des Poulies, 78490 Montfort-l'Amaury; Daniel Martin, 8 allée du Parc des Vallergues 06400 Cannes, France. *Telephone:* (6) 20-46-84-78. *E-mail:* philippe.cuillerier@club-internet.fr. *Website:* www .doudouswing.com; www.popswingandfire.com.

CULLIMORE, Stan; British musician (bass); b. (Ian Peter Cullimore), 6 April 1962, Hull; m. Amelia Cullimore 1988; two s. two d. *Education:* Univ. of Hull. *Career:* mem. The Housemartins 1984–88; Owner, Cucumber Street; 1985–; numerous TV appearances, live performances; author of children's books 1993–, also scripts for children's TV; Head, Creative Devt, CINAR 1999–2002; writer, script ed. and consultant 2002–09; co-writer, producer and presenter The Bopps 2009–12. *Recordings include:* albums: London 0 Hull 4 1986, The People Who Grinned Themselves To Death 1987, Now That's What I Call Quite Good 1988. *Publications include:* over 80 children's books including The Turtle Who Danced With A Crane, Spider Boy, Long Live The Boy King, Where's Blinky?. *Website:* www.stancullimore.com.

CULLUM, Jamie; British musician (piano) and singer; b. 20 Aug. 1979, Essex, England; m. Sophie Dahl 2010. *Education:* Univ. of Reading. *Career:* began playing piano aged eight years; played in bars and clubs in London and Paris in his late teens; financed, recorded and distributed first album; weekly show on digital radio station The Jazz 2007–08, BBC Radio 2 2010–. *Recordings:* albums: Heard It All Before 2000, Pointless Nostalgic 2002, Twentysomething 2003, Catching Tales 2005, The Pursuit 2009, Momentum 2013, Interlude 2014. *Honours:* BBC Jazz Awards Rising Star of the Year 2003, Radio 2 Artist of the Year 2005, Ronnie Scott Award for UK Male Singer 2007. *Current Management:* Air Management, Unit 27, The Quadrangle, 49 Atalanta Street, London, SW6 6TU, England. *Telephone:* (20) 7386-1600. *E-mail:* info@airmtm.com. *Website:* www.airmtm.com; www.jamiecullum .com.

CUMMINGS, Burton, OC; Canadian singer and songwriter; b. 31 Dec. 1947, Winnipeg, Man. *Career:* lead singer band The Guess Who 1965–75 (disbanded), reunited in 1984, 2000; performs with touring band The Carpet Frogs; has done occasional shows with Randy Bachman as The Bachman-Cummings Band; Co-owner Salisbury House restaurant chain. *Recordings include:* albums with Guess Who: Shakin' All Over 1965, Hey Ho (What You Do To Me) 1965, It's Time 1966, Wheatfield Soul 1968, Canned Wheat 1969,

American Woman 1970, Share the Land 1970, So Long, Bannatyne 1971, Rockin' 1972, Live at the Paramount 1972, Wild One 1972, #10 1973, Artificial Paradise 1973, Road Food 1974, Flavours 1975, Power in the Music 1975; solo albums: Burton Cummings 1976, My Own Way to Rock 1977, Dream of a Child 1978, Woman Love 1980, Sweet Sweet 1981, Heart 1984, Plus Signs 1990, Up Close and Alone 1996, Above the Ground 2008. *Film:* as actor: Melanie 1982. *Publication:* The Writings of B.L. Cummings 2010. *Honours:* Dr hc (Brandon Univ.). *Address:* c/o Lorne Saifer, 11564 Dona Pepita Place, Studio City, CA 91604, USA. *Website:* www.burtoncummings.net (home).

CUMMINGS, David Alexander; British musician (guitar) and screenwriter; b. 26 Nov. 1958. *Education:* Univ. of East Anglia. *Career:* mem. The Higsons 1980–81, Lloyd Cole & The Commotions 1987, Del Amitri 1987–95; writer for TV and film comedy 1994–, collaborators include Harry Enfield, Paul Whitehouse and Alexei Sayle. *Recordings include:* with Del Amitri: albums: Waking Hours 1989, Change Everything 1992, Twisted 1995, Hatful Of Rain: The Best Of 1998; singles: Always The Last To Know 1992, Be My Downfall 1992, Just Like A Man 1992, When You Were Young 1993, Here And Now 1995, Driving With The Brakes On 1995, Roll To Me 1995, Tell Her This 1995. *Writing for film:* The Last Seduction II 1999, Kevin and Perry Go Large 2000. *Radio:* Rockton Manor Studios (BBC) 2009. *Writing for television:* The Fast Show (BBC) 1994–2000, Harry Enfield & Chums (Tiger Aspect/BBC) (jt winner, Writers' Guild of GB Award 1997) 1994–98, Alexei Sayle's Merry-Go-Round (BBC) 1998, Happiness (BBC) 2001–03, Spine Chillers: Goths (BBC) 2003, Death Metal Chronicles (BBC) 2005, Parents of the Band (BBC) 2009. *Publication includes:* The Fast Show Book (with Paul Whitehouse and Charlie Higson) 1996. *Current Management:* c/o Independent Talent Group, 40 Whitfield Street, London, W1T 2RH, England. *Telephone:* (20) 7636-6565. *Website:* www.independenttalent.com.

CUNLIFFE, William (Bill), MMus; American composer, arranger and jazz pianist; b. 26 June 1956, Andover, Mass. *Education:* Duke Univ., Eastman School of Music. *Career:* taught at Central State Univ., Wilberforce; debut with Buddy Rich Big Band; performed with Frank Sinatra, Joe Henderson, Freddie Hubbard, Benny Golson and James Moody; f. own trio, mem. Joe LaBarbera Quintet and plays with flautist Holly Hofmann; also plays with his big band, Latin Band Imaginación, and classical-jazz ensemble Trimotif; composer of big band, chamber, orchestral and choral music; works performed by orchestras including Cincinnati Pops, Illinois Philharmonic, Reading Symphony and Manhattan School of Music; teaches at Vail Jazz Workshop and Skidmore Jazz Inst.; Assoc. Prof. of Music and Distinguished Faculty Mem., Coll. of the Arts, Calif. State Univ., Fullerton; Composer-in-Residence, All Saints Episcopal Church, Pasadena, Calif. *Compositions include:* To Ruth for jazz piano trio and orchestra, Fourth Stream... La Banda, concerto for trumpet and orchestra (premiered at Alice Tully Hall, New York and Verizon Hall, Philadelphia), Overture, Waltz and Rondo for jazz piano, trumpet and chamber orchestra, Symphony #1 Hearts Reaching Upward, tuba and saxophone concertos, Fantasy for jazz piano trio and orchestra, Ballade for trumpet and wind ensemble. *Music for film:* The Northern Kingdom 2009, Split Ends 2009, Janet's Class 2010, On the Shoulders of Giants (documentary about jazz and basketball in 1930s Harlem) 2011. *Recordings include:* A Rare Connection 1994, Satisfaction 1999, Romantic Fantasy 1999, How My Heart Sings 2003, Partners in Crime (with Jim Herschman and Jeff Hamilton) 2005, Imaginación 2005, The Blues and the Abstract Truth, Take 2 2008, Transformation 2008, Resonance Big Band Plays Tribute to Oscar Peterson 2009, Nostalgia in Corcovado 2009, Fourth Stream...La Banda 2010, Concerto for Tuba and Orchestra 2011, That Time of Year 2011, Overture, Waltz and Rondo for jazz piano, trumpet and chamber orchestra 2012, Concerto for Tuba and Orchestra 2012, Bill Cunliffe Trio: River Edge, New Jersey 2013; in duo with Holly Hofmann: Just Duet, Vol. 2 2003, Three's Company 2010. *Publications:* Jazz Keyboard Toolbox, Max Blues Keyboard 2004, Jazz Inventions for Keyboard 2005, Uniquely Familiar: Standards for Advanced Solo Piano 2010, Uniquely Christmas 2012. *Honours:* Thelonious Monk Int. Jazz Piano Award 1989, Grammy Award for Best Instrumental Arrangement (for West Side Medley), Los Angeles Jazz Soc. Composer/Arranger Award 2010. *Address:* c/o Azica Records, 1645 Eddy Road, Cleveland, OH 44112, USA. *Telephone:* (216) 681-0778. *Fax:* (216) 851-9813. *E-mail:* billcunliffe@me.com (office). *Website:* www.billcunliffe.com (office).

CUNNAH, Peter; British singer, songwriter and musician (guitar); b. 30 Aug. 1966, Belfast, Northern Ireland. *Education:* York Street Art Coll., Univ. of Ulster. *Career:* singer, songwriter with D:Ream 1992–97; tours and concerts, festival appearances; songwriter for bands, A1 and Steps 1998–2001; Founder-mem. Shane. *Recordings include:* albums: with D:Ream: D:Ream On Vol. 1 1993, World 1995. *Honours:* IDA Best Dance Act 1993. *Website:* d-ream.co.uk.

CUNNINGHAM, Abe; American musician (drums). *Career:* Founder mem., Deftones 1988–. *Recordings include:* albums: Adrenaline 1995, Around the Fur 1997, Live (EP) 1999, White Pony 2000, Back To School 2001, Deftones 2003, More Maximum Deftones 2003, Saturday Night Wrist 2006, Diamond Eyes 2010. *Honours:* Kerrang! Classic Songwriter Award 2007. *Website:* www .deftones.com.

CUNNINGHAM, Déirdre Mary Gerradine; Irish singer, songwriter and musician (acoustic guitar); b. 31 May 1956, Sutton, Surrey, England; m. Liam Cunningham 1977; one s. *Career:* tours of Europe, Japan, Singapore and The Philippines; radio broadcasts and television appearances; mem. IASC, ISA,

IMRO, MCPS. *Recordings include:* albums: City of Tribes 1996, Sunny Days, Cry From the Heart 1998, Song of the River. *Address:* KRL, PO Box 5577, Newton Mearns, Glasgow, G77 9BH, Scotland.

CUNNINGHAM, Jeremy; British musician (bass guitar) and artist; b. Sussex. *Career:* Founder mem. The Levellers 1988–; numerous concerts and festival appearances. *Recordings include:* albums: Weapon Called The Word 1990, Levelling The Land 1991, See Nothing, Hear Nothing, Do Something 1993, Levellers 1993, Zeitgeist 1995, Mouth To Mouth 1997, Special Brew 2000, Hello Pig 2000, Green Blade Rising 2002, Truth & Lies 2005, Letters from the Underground 2008, Live at the Royal Albert Hall 2009, Chaos Theory Live 2011, Headlights, White Lines, Black Tar Rivers - Best Live 2012, Static On The Airwaves 2012, Chaos Theory Live 2013. *Address:* 51 Queen Street, Exeter, EX4 3SR, England. *E-mail:* info@dmfmusic.co.uk. *Website:* www.dmfmusic.co.uk. *Address:* The Levellers, PO Box 29, Winkleigh, EX19 8WE, England. *Telephone:* (1273) 608887. *E-mail:* info@levellers.co.uk. *Website:* www.levellers.co.uk (home).

CUNNINGHAM, Phil; British musician (guitar, keyboards); b. 7 Dec. 1974. *Career:* mem., Marion 1993–99, New Order 2001–, Bad Lieutenant 2007–; collaborations with Jaime Harding. *Recordings include:* albums: with Marion: Toys for Boys 1995, This World and Body 1996, The Program 1998, Alive in Manchester 2012; with New Order: Get Ready 2001, In Session (live) 2004, Waiting For The Sirens' Call 2005, Lost Sirens 2013, Music Complete 2015; with Bad Lieutenant: Never Cry Another Tear 2009. *Honours:* Ivor Novello Award for Outstanding Song Collection 2006, Q Outstanding Contribution to Music Award 2015. *Current Management:* c/o Jayne Houghton, Excess Press, 11 Old Steine, Brighton BN1 1EJ, England. *Website:* www.badlieutenant.net; www.neworder.com.

CUNNINGHAM, Philip Martin, MBE; British composer, musician (accordion), music director and producer; b. 27 Jan. 1960, Edinburgh, Scotland; m. Donna Macrae 1982; one m. *Career:* tours of UK, Europe and USA; formed duo with Aly Bain; mem. Musicians' Union. *Television and radio:* Music Dir, Talla A' Bhaile (four series over four years for BBC Scotland); Music Dir, presenter, Hogmanay Live (BBC) 1991–94; co-presenter, Live From The Lemon Tree (weekly radio series for BBC). *Compositions:* music for Bill Bryden theatre productions, The Ship and The Big Picnic, Orchestral Suite 1996, compositions used for film soundtrack Last of the Mohicans. *Recordings include:* solo: Airs & Graces 1984, Palomino Waltz 1989; with Aly Bain: The Pearl 1995, The Ruby 1997, Another Gem 2000, Spring The Summer Long 2003, Roads Not Travelled 2006, Portrait 2010, Five and Twenty 2012; with Connie Dover: If Ever I Return 1997, The Border of Heaven 2000; with Kris Drever: Mark the Hard Earth 2010. *Honours:* Hon. Citizen, Reading, Pa, USA; BBC Radio 2 Folk Award for Best Duo (with Phil Cunningham) 2005. *Current Management:* c/o Chris Wade, Adastra, 2 Star Row, North Dalton, Driffield, YO25 9UX, England. *Telephone:* (13) 7721-7662. *E-mail:* chris@adastra-music.co.uk. *Website:* www.adastra-music.co.uk; www.philcunningham.com.

CUNNINGHAM, Tom; British musician (drums); b. 22 June 1965, Glasgow, Scotland. *Career:* mem. Wet Wet Wet 1982–97, 2004–; formed The Sleeping Giants 1999; numerous performances and tours. *Recordings include:* albums: Popped In Souled Out 1987, Sgt Pepper Knew My Father 1988, The Memphis Sessions 1988, Holding Back The River 1989, High On The Happy Side 1992, Wet Wet Wet Live At The Royal Albert Hall, 1993, End of Part One (Greatest Hits) 1993, Picture This 1995, 10 1997, Timeless 2007, City of Soul 2011. *Honours:* BRIT Award for Best British Newcomer 1988. *Current Management:* c/o No Half Measures Limited, 1st Floor, 5 Eagle Street, Glasgow, G4 9XA, Scotland. *Telephone:* (141) 353-8822. *Fax:* (141) 353-8823. *E-mail:* info@nohalfmeasures.com. *Website:* www.nohalfmeasures.com; www.wetwetwet.co.uk.

CUOMO, Rivers; American singer, songwriter and musician (guitar); b. 13 July 1970, New York; m. Kyoto Ito 2006; one d. *Education:* Harvard Univ. *Career:* Founder mem., lead singer and songwriter, Weezer 1992–; also solo artist; mem. Avant Garde (renamed Zoom). *Recordings include:* albums with Weezer: Weezer (blue album) 1994, Pinkerton 1996, Meet The Deedles 1998, Weezer (green album) 2001, Maladroit 2002, Make Believe 2005, Weezer 2008, Raditude 2009, Hurley 2010; solo: Alone: The Home Recordings of Rivers Cuomo 992-2025 2007, Alone II: The Home Recordings of Rivers Cuomo 2008, Not Alone: Rivers Cuomo and Friends 2009, Alone III: The Pinkerton Years 2011; collaborations: Spirit (with Hitomi) 2011, Scott and Rivers (with Scott Murphy) 2013. *Address:* Laffitte Management Group, 1100 Glendon Avenue 2000, Los Angeles, CA, 90024-3524; c/o Karl Koch, PO Box 733, Derby, NY 14047, USA (office). *E-mail:* karl@weezer.net (office). *Website:* www.weezer.com.

CURNIN, Cy; British singer; b. (Cyril John Curnin), 12 Dec. 1957, Wimbledon; m. Peri Curnin 1985; two d. *Education:* Wimbledon Coll., London. *Career:* singer with Fixx; USA tours throughout 1980s; TV appearances; mem. PRS, ASCAP. *Recordings include:* albums: Shuttered Room 1981, Reach The Beach 1983, Phantoms 1984, Walkabout 1986, Calm Animals 1988, Ink 1990, King Biscuit Flower Hour 1996, Real Time Stood Still 1997, Elemental 1998, 1011 Woodland 1999, Beautiful Friction 2012; solo: Mayfly 2005, The Returning Sun 2007, Solar Minimum 2009, The Horse's Mouth 2012. *Address:* c/o Hypertension–the art of music, Studio Hamburg, Building T, 80 22039 Hamburg, Germany. *Telephone:* (49) 40476993. *Fax:* (49) 40478383. *E-mail:* info@hypertension-music.de. *Website:* www.hypertension-music.de; www.cycurnin.com; www.thefixx.com.

CURRIE, Justin; British singer, songwriter and musician (bass guitar, acoustic guitar, piano); b. 11 Dec. 1964, Glasgow; s. of John Semple Currie and Barbara Margaret Kirkwood. *Education:* Jordanhill Coll. School, Glasgow, Univ. of Glasgow. *Career:* Founding mem. and lead singer, Del Amitri 1981–; solo artist 2007–; numerous projects and collaborations. *Recordings include:* albums with Del Amitri: Del Amitri 1985, Waking Hours 1989, Change Everything 1992, Twisted 1995, Some Other Sucker's Parade 1997, Hatful Of Rain/Lousy With Love 1998, Can You Do Me Good? 2002; solo album: What Is Love For 2007, The Great War 2010, Lower Reaches 2013. *Current Management:* JPR Management Ltd., 10 Hansard Mews, London W14 8BJ, England. *Telephone:* (20) 7460-3527. *E-mail:* info@jprmanagement.co.uk. *Website:* www.jprmanagement.co.uk; www.justincurrie.com.

CURTIS, Brandon; American singer and musician (keyboards, bass guitar). *Career:* mem. Secret Machines 2000–. *Recordings include:* albums: Now Here Is Nowhere 2004, Ten Silver Drops 2006, Secret Machines 2008, Nonsense In the Dark 2009, Empros 2011, Ghostory 2012. *Address:* c/o Andrew Skikne, The Agency Group Limited, 142 West 57th Street, Sixth Floor, New York, NY 10019, USA. *Telephone:* (212) 581-3100. *Fax:* (212) 581-0015. *E-mail:* AndrewSkikne@theagencygroup.com. *Website:* www.theagencygroup.com; www.thesecretmachines.com.

CURTIS, Catie, BA; American singer and songwriter; b. 22 May 1965, Saco, Me; m. Liz Marshall; two d. *Education:* Brown University. *Career:* performances at clubs in USA, Lilith Fair and other festivals; theatre tour with Mary Chapin Carpenter 1998–99; mem. American Fed. of TV and Radio Artists. *Recordings include:* Dandelion 1989, Years to Hours 1991, Truth From Lies 1996, Catie Curtis (GLAMA Album of the Year 1998) 1997, A Crash Course in Roses 1999, My Shirt Looks Good On You 2001, Acoustic Valentine 2002, Dreaming in Romance Languages 2004, Long Night Moon 2006, Sweet Life 2008, Hello, Stranger 2009, Stretch Limousine on Fire 2009, A Catie Curtis Christmas 2012. *Honours:* GLAMA Award for Best Song (for Radical 1996, for What's the Matter 2000), Song of the Year, Boston Music Awards (for Kiss That Counted) 2002, Grand Prize, Int. Songwriting Competition (for People Look Around) 2005. *Current Management:* Tim Bernett, Deep Blue Arts, Studio City, CA 90068, USA. *Telephone:* (818) 907-8300. *E-mail:* info@bernett.us. *E-mail:* Catie@CatieCurtis.com. *Website:* www.catiecurtis.com.

CURTIS, Sonny; American songwriter and musician (guitar); b. 9 May 1937, Meadow, Tex. *Education:* Valley Conservatory of Music, Los Angeles, Sherman School of Music, Los Angeles. *Career:* mem. Buddy Holly and The Three Tunes 1956, left band, rejoined (now called The Crickets) 1958; toured as guitarist for Slim Whitman 1957; mem. The Everly Brothers 1959, solo artiste and songwriter, 1965–; numerous solo tours; songs recorded by: Eddy Arnold, Chet Atkins, Bobby Fuller Four, Rosanne Cash, Glen Campbell, The Clash, Perry Como, Rita Coolidge, Bing Crosby, Sammy Davis Jr, Val Doonican, Everly Brothers, Bobby Goldsboro, Waylon Jennings, Buddy Knox, Kris Kristofferson, Gary Lewis and The Playboys, Matchbox, Anne Murray, Sam Neely, Lou Reed, Johnny Rodriguez, Leo Sayer, Bobby Vee, Keith Whitley, Andy Williams, Hank Williams Jr. *Recordings include:* Albums: Beatle Hits, Flamenco Style 1964, The First Of Sonny Curtis 1968, The Sonny Curtis Style 1969, Sonny Curtis 1979, Love Is All Around 1980, Rollin' 1981, Spectrum 1987, Ready, Able And Willing 1988, No Stranger To The Rain 1990. *Compositions include:* A Fool Never Learns, Destiny's Child, Gypsy Man, I Fought The Law, I'm No Stranger To The Rain, Love Is All Around (theme song to the Mary Tyler Moore Show) 1970, More Than I Can Say, Rock Around With Ollie Vee, The Real Buddy Holly Story, The Straight Life, Walk Right Back, When You Ask About Love, Where Will The Words Come From. *Honours:* BMI Pop Awards, for Walk Right Back, 1961, for I Fought The Law, 1964, for The Straight Life, 1968, for More Than I Can Say 1980, for I'm No Stranger To The Rain, 1989; CMA Single of the Year, for I'm No Stranger To The Rain, 1989; inducted, Nashville Songwriters' Asscn, Songwriters Hall of Fame 1991, BMI Motion Picture and Television Award, for Evening Shade 1992, inducted into Music City Walk of Fame 2007, inducted into The Musicians Hall Of Fame 2009, inducted into The Rock and Roll Hall Of Fame 2012. *E-mail:* music@sonnycurtis.com. *Website:* sonnycurtis.com.

CURTIS, Wesley, (Mac Curtis); American singer, songwriter and musician (guitar); b. 16 Jan. 1939, Fort Worth, Tex.; m. Peggy Curtis 1967; three s. *Education:* Army Information and Broadcasting School, Anthony School of Real Estate, Moorpark Community Coll. Real Estates Course, Moorpark, CA, Licensed Real Estate Associate California. *Career:* recorded for King Records 1956; guest, Big D. Jambouree and Nat. Radio Show 1956; co-star, Alan Freed Rock 'n' Roll Revue, New York 1956; toured as Rock 'n' Roll Rockabilly –1960; country music DJ, Dallas radio station; recorded country for Epic and GRT Dj Atlanta, Nashville, La 1971; mem. American Soc. of Composers, Authors and Publrs (ASCAP). *Compositions:* I'd Run a Mile for Lynn Anderson, Give Us One More Chance. *Recordings:* The King Original Rockabilly Masters, Blue Jean Heart, The Rollin' Rock series of three albums, Rollin' Rock Singles, Rollin' Rock Switzerland, Rockabilly Ready (with The Rimshots). *Publications:* contrib. to Goldmine Magazine (Vol. 9, Issue 10) 1983, We Wanna Boogie 1988. *Honours:* Country Survey News Golden Ear Award 1969, ASCAP Chartbuster Award 1972, Class of 1957 Distinguished Alumnus 2010. *Current Management:* Rock 'n' Roll Enterprises, 21 Grove Terrace, Penarth, Vale of Glamorgan, CF64 2NG, South Wales. *Telephone:* (29) 2070-4279. *Fax:* (29) 2070-9989. *E-mail:* barrettrocknroll@ntlworld.com. *Address:* 529 Springcreek Road, Weatherford, TX 76087, USA (office). *Telephone:* (817) 996-0142 (office). *E-mail:* maccurtisbillyblog@gmail.com (office).

CURTOLA, (Robert Allen) Bobby, OC; Canadian singer and songwriter; b. 14 April 1943, Thunder Bay, Ont.; m. Ava 1975; two s. *Career:* co-host, After Four, TV series 1965–66; own TV series on CTV, Shake, Rock and Roll; guest on numerous national and regional talk and variety specials in Canada and USA; headlined in Las Vegas for many years; Rock 'n' Roll Blast 1999; mem. Alliance of Canadian Cinema, Television and Radio Artists, ARIA, American Fed. of Musicians, CARAS, Soc. of Composers, Authors and Music Publrs of Canada. *Composition:* The Real Thing 1966. *Recordings include:* singles: Fortune Teller, Aladdin, 3 Rows Over, Corrina, Songman 1973, Drivin' Down a Phantom Road 1990, Playin' the Shadows of Glory 1990; albums: Hitch-Hiker 1961, Changes 1970, Curtola 1971, Christmas Flashback Album 1992, Gotta Get Used to Being Country 1993, Turn the Radio Up 1998. *Honours:* Star on Italian Walk of Fame 2011, Diamond Jubilee Medal 2012; winner, Jingle Award for North America, Things Go Better with Coke, Canada's First RPM Top Male Vocalist Juno Award 1965, inducted into Canadian Music Industry Hall of Fame 1996. *Address:* c/o Entertainment Music Group, 2255B Queen Street, East Suite 132, Toronto, ON M4E 1G3, Canada. *Telephone:* (416) 686-9231. *E-mail:* chris@curtola.com. *Website:* entertainmentmusicgroup.ca. *E-mail:* fanmail@curtola.com. *Website:* www .curtola.com.

CUSSON, Michel; Canadian musician (guitar) and composer; b. 22 Jan. 1957, Drummondville, Quebec; m. Michelle Alie; two d. *Education:* CEGEP, Drumondville, McGill Univ., Berklee Coll. of Music, Boston, USA. *Career:* composed soundtrack for Omertà, La loi du silence, television series, 1996, 1997, 1998; composed soundtrack for films: La Comtesse de Baton Rouge (Amdré Forcier) 1997, and L'Automne Sauvage (Gabriel Pelletier) 1992; numerous themes for Canadian television shows; music themes for advertising campaigns; created jazz-world beat group Michel Cusson and the Wild Unit in 1991 and jazz-fusion group UZEB in 1976. *Recordings include:* two albums with Michel Cusson and the Wild Unit; 10 albums with UZEB. *Honours:* Felix Awards 1983, twice 1984, 1987, 1990, twice 1992, Gemeaux Awards 1989, 1996, Socan Awards 1990, 1993, 1995, 1996, Music Plus Award 1991, Oscar Peterson Trophy 1991. *E-mail:* info@michelcusson.com. *Website:* www.michelcusson.com.

CUSTER, Beth, MMus; American composer, musician (clarinets, piano), singer and teacher; b. (Elizabeth Jane Custer), 25 Feb. 1958, South Bend, Ind.; d. of the late William Custer and of Jean Huffman; partner Federico Cusigch. *Education:* Crane School of Music, State Univ. of New York, Potsdam, San Francisco State Univ.; studied clarinet with Rosario Mazzeo, Suzanne Stephens, Else Ludewig-Verderh, Don Carroll, James Pyne, Frank Wangler, Marlene Pauley. *Career:* composer/performer for TV, film, dance and theatre; leader Beth Custer Ensemble, Clarinet Thing; created soundtracks for independent films by Koohan Paik, Cathy Lee Crane, Melinda Stone, Will Zavala; resident composer, Joe Goode Performance Group 1992–2008; commissions from Left Coast Chamber Ensemble, Bernie Weiner, Overtone Industries, Earplay, Campo Santo Theatre, City Winds, Kronos Quartet; collaborated with MacArthur Fellow Trimpin; Propr BC Records; f. groups Club Foot Orchestra, Trance Mission, Eighty Mile Beach; Adjunct Prof. of Composition, Mills Coll. 2006–09; mem. BMI, AMC, ACF, Musicians Union Local 6. *Film soundtracks:* for Cathy Lee Crane: The Unoccupied Zone, Not For Nuthin', White City, Sketches After Halle, Red Helicopters; for Koohan Paik: Virtue, New Freedom; for Kwan & Iger: A Wok In Progress; for Melinda Stone: The California Tour, Visionary Environments; for Will Zavala: Grass; for George Spies: This Is The Life; for Peter McCandless: Pool of Thanatos; for Georgina Jahner: Women's Rites; for Karina Epperlein: I Won't Be Sad in This Life; for Craig Baldwin: Specters of the Spectrum. *Silent film soundtracks:* for Club Foot Orchestra: Buster Keaton's Sherlock Jr., Metropolis, Pandora's Box. *Compositions for theatre:* musicals (with writer Octavio Solis): The Ballad of Pancho and Lucy, Terracoma, Lethe, June In A Box; plays: California Shakespeare Company: Hamlet, Winter's Tale; Campo Santo Theatre: Hurricane, Language of Angels; Magic Theater: Kingfish; Berkeley Repertory Theater: A Practical Guide to the Night Sky; San Diego Repertory Theater: Hamlet, Happy Birthday Kim Hunter 2013. *Recordings include:* with Eighty Mile Beach: Inclement Weather, Arboleda de Manzanitas, There Are No Right Angles Found In Nature; solo: The Shirt I Slept In, In The Broken Fields Where I Lie; with Trance Mission: Head Light, Meanwhile…, Trance Mission; with Club Foot Orchestra: Buster Keaton's Sherlock Jr, Metropolis, Nosferatu, The Cabinet of Dr Caligari, Kidnapped, Wild Beasts; with Connie Champagne: La Strada; with Beth Custer Ensemble: Dona Luz 30 Besos (with City of Tribes) 2000, Vinculum Symphony 2000, Respect as a Religion 2005;

with Clarinet Thing: Agony Pipes and Misery Sticks 2005. *Telephone:* (510) 848-3864 (office). *Fax:* (510) 848-3972 (office). *E-mail:* artists@hanswendl.com (office). *Website:* hanswendl.com (office). *E-mail:* bethcuster@bethcuster.com (office). *Website:* www.bethcuster.com (office).

CUT CHEMIST; American producer and remixer; b. (Lucas MacFadden). *Career:* fmr mem., Unity Committee; mem., Jurassic 5 1993–2007; numerous live performances; also mem., Ozomatli. *Recordings include:* albums: with Jurassic 5: Jurassic 5 (EP) 1997, Quality Control 2000, Power in Numbers 2002, Feedback 2006; solo: Live at the Future Primitive Sound Session 1997, The Litmus Test 2004, The Audience is Listening 2006. Sound of the Police 2010; with DJ Shadow: Hard Sell Encore 2006; with Keb Darge: Lost & Found: Rockabilly & Jump Blues 2007. *Current Management:* William Morris Endeavour, 9601 Wilshire Boulevard, Beverly Hills, CA 90212, USA. *Website:* www.cutchemist.com.

CYPORYN, Dennis; American musician (banjo) and composer; b. 1 Feb. 1942, Detroit, Michigan; 1 s., 1 d. *Education:* Music Composition, Oakland University; Private theory lessons. *Career:* Dennis Cyporyn Band; Composes own music for band; Showcased at Detroit Music Awards, Motor City Music Awards; Won Best Instrumentalist 2 years, also Group Deserving Wider Recognition and Best Folk Group; Currently with Lonesome and Blue, bluegrass band; mem. IBMA; MCMA. *Recordings:* albums: Nashville Alley 1991, I Must be Dreaming 1992, Deja Vu Debut 1994, Duet to Quintet 1997, Out of the Blue 1998. *Publications:* The Bluegrass Song Book, 1972. *Honours:* 5 Awards.

CYRKA, Jan Josef; British musician (guitar) and composer; b. 31 Oct. 1963, Halifax, West Yorkshire. *Career:* mem., Max and the Broadway Metal Choir 1984; recording engineer, E-Zee Studios 1985; mem., Zodiac Mindwarp and the Love Reaction 1986–89; solo artist 1989–; session musician, television commercials; partner, Take It For Granted PR Co.; mem. Musicians' Union, Performing Rights Soc., Mechanical-Copyright Protection Soc., BMI. *Recordings include:* Max and The Metal Choir, 1985; Tattooed Beat Messiah, Zodiac Mindwarp, 1987; solo albums: Beyond The Common Ground, 1992; Spirit, 1993; Prickly Pear, 1997. *Website:* www.jancyrka.com.

CYRUS, Billy Ray; American country singer; b. 25 Aug. 1961, Flatwoods, KY. *Career:* formed own group, Sly Dog 1983; solo artist 1992–. *Recordings include:* albums: Some Gave All 1992, It Won't Be The Last 1993, Storm in the Heartland 1994, Trail of Tears 1996, Shot Full of Love 1998, Southern Rain 2000, Time Flies 2003, The Other Side 2003, Wanna Be Your Joe 2006, Home at Last 2007, Back to Tennessee 2009, I'm American 2011. *Address:* 818 18th Avenue S, Nashville, TN 37203, USA. *E-mail:* BRCSpirit@aol.com. *Website:* www.billyraycyrus.com.

CYRUS, Miley, (Hannah Montana); American singer and actress; b. (Destiny Hope Cyrus), 23 Nov. 1992, Franklin, Tenn.; d. of Billy Ray Cyrus and Leticia Cyrus. *Television includes:* The Suite Life of Zack and Cody 2006, Hannah Montana 2006–10, High School Musical 2 2007. *Films:* Bolt 2008, Hannah Montana: The Movie 2009, LOL 2012. *Recordings include:* albums: as Hannah Montana: Hannah Montana 2006, Hannah Montana 2: Meet Miley Cyrus 2007, Hannah Montana: The Movie 2009, Forever 2010; as Miley Cyrus: Breakout 2008, The Time of Our Lives 2009, Can't be Tamed 2010, Bangerz 2013, Miley Cyrus & Her Dead Petz 2015. *Honours:* Teen Choice Awards for Best TV Actress Comedy 2007, 2008, for Best Female Artist 2008, Kids' Choice Awards for Favorite Female Singer 2008, for Favorite TV Actress 2008, Australian Kids' Choice Award for Favorite Int. Singer 2008, for Favorite Int. TV Star 2008, MTV Europe Music Award for Best Video (for Wrecking Ball) 2013, Billboard Music Awards for Top Streaming Artist 2014, for Top Streaming Song (Video) (for Wrecking Ball) 2014, iHeartRadio Music Award for Best Lyrics (for Wrecking Ball) 2014, MTV Video Music Award for Video of the Year (for Wrecking Ball) 2014. *Current Management:* c/o Red Light Management, 321 East Main Street, Charlottesville, VA 22902, USA. *Telephone:* (434) 244-7200. *Website:* redlightmanagement.com; www .mileycyrus.com.

CZ; Belgian singer, musician (guitar) and composer; b. 25 June 1969, Charleroi. *Career:* solo artist, as Candy Stripe 1989–92, as Bloodminded 1992–; mem. Société d'Auteurs Belge–Belgische Auteurs Maatschappij, Brussels, Ciney Music Session, Arts Agency. *Recordings include:* albums: as Candy Stripe: As Above So Below 1990; as Bloodminded: Hypocrisy 1993, Demons for Tea 1996, Bloodyminded 1998. *Address:* 91 rue Jean Friot, 6180 Courcelles, Belgium.

D

D, Brenda; British singer and actress; b. 30 Dec. 1936, Surrey, England; m. Jerry Haymes 1961; one s. one d. *Education:* finishing school, schools of modelling. *Career:* film and television actress; appearances include original Robin Hood series; opened in England with Fess Parker as Davy Crockett; toured USA and Europe; first British female singer to perform country music on BBC; first British female country singer to perform at Grand Ole Opry; semi-retired 2000; mem., Screen Actors' Guild, Arts and Entertainments Council. *Recordings include:* singles: Will You Still Love Me Tomorrow, Little Bitty Tear, Love You More Than I Can Say, Just Enough To Keep Me Hanging On, Where Do You Go?, Welcome Home. *Honours:* CMA International Award, Art and Entertainment Council Award for Female Vocalist, A&E Film Actress Award. *Current Management:* Umpire Entertainment Enterprizes, 1507 Scenic Drive, Longview, TX 75604, USA. *Telephone:* (903) 759-0300. *Fax:* (903) 234-2944. *E-mail:* packnmail2@cablelynx.com.

D, Mike; American rap artist and musician (drums); b. (Michael Diamond), 20 Nov. 1965, New York. *Career:* Founder-mem. rap/rock group, Beastie Boys 1981–; numerous tours and festival appearances. *Films include:* Over Exposed 1984, Krush Groove 1985, Tougher Than Leather 1988. *Recordings include:* albums: Licensed To Ill 1986, Paul's Boutique 1989, Check Your Head 1992, Ill Communication 1994, Root Down 1995, The In Sound From Way Out 1996, Hello Nasty 1998, Sounds Of Science 1999, To The 5 Boroughs 2004, The Mix-Up (Grammy Award for Best Pop Instrumental Album 2008) 2007, Shrek Forever After 2010, Stop Us If You've Heard This One Before! 2012. *Address:* Gold Mountain Entertainment, 3575 Cahuenga Boulevard W, Suite 450, Los Angeles, CA 90068; c/o Capitol Records, 1750 North Vine, Hollywood, CA 90028, USA. *Website:* www.beastieboys.com.

D, N'Dango; Senegalese hip-hop artist; b. (Mamadou Lamine Seck). *Career:* mem., Daara J 1997–. *Recordings include:* albums: Daara J 1998, Xalima 1999, Boomerang 2003, School of Life 2010. *Honours:* BBC Radio 3 World Music Award for Best African Act 2004. *Current Management:* Traffixmusic, 130 Avenue Pasteur, 93170 Bagnolet, France. *Telephone:* 1-48-51-30-81. *E-mail:* emilie@traffixmusic.com. *Website:* www.traffixmusic.com; www.wrasserecords.com.

D DOUBLE E; British MC. *Career:* fmr mem. N.A.S.T.Y. (Natural Artistic Sound Touching You) Crew –2004, 'grime' music genre; own label, Braindead Entertainment. *Current Management:* c/o Xtreme Talent Artist Agency, PO Box 1034, Morden, SM4 6QX, England. *Telephone:* (844) 873-1988. *Fax:* (844) 873-1987. *E-mail:* info@xtremetalent.co.uk. *Website:* www.xtremetalent.co.uk.

D.O.; South Korean singer; b. (Do Kyung Soo), 12 Jan. 1993, Goyang, Gyeonggi Prov. *Career:* trainee at SM Entertainment 2010–12; mem., K-pop boy band Exo 2012–; mem. sub-group Exo-K 2012–; debut single 2012; numerous TV and live appearances. *Television:* EXO's Showtime 2013–. *Recordings:* albums: Mama 2012, XOXO (Mnet Asian Music Award for Album of the Year 2013) 2013. *Honours:* numerous awards including: for Exo: Mnet Asian Music Award for Best New Asian Artist/Group 2012, MTV Europe Music Award for Best Japan/Korea Act 2013, MelOn Music Award for Song of the Year (for Growl) 2013; for Exo-K: Golden Disk Newcomer Award 2012. *Address:* c/o SM Entertainment, 521 Apgujeong 2-dong, Gangnam-gu, Seoul, South Korea (office). *Telephone:* (2) 6240-9800 (office). *Website:* www.smtown.com (office); exo.smtown.com (home).

DA COSTA, Paulinho; Brazilian musician (percussion); b. 31 May 1948, Rio de Janeiro. *Career:* moved to USA 1973; mem. Sergio Mendes' group 1973–77; performed with jazz artists, including Dizzy Gillespie, Joe Pass, Milt Jackson, Freddie Hubbard, Herbie Hancock; freelance musician 1977–, playing on recordings by almost 400 artists. *Recordings include:* solo albums: Agora 1976, Happy People 1979, Sunrise 1984, Breakdown 1987, Real Love 1991. *Honours:* Nat. Acad. of Recording Arts and Sciences Most Valuable Player Award (three times), and Musician Emer. Award. *E-mail:* vibem@paulinho.com. *Website:* www.paulinho.com.

DA MATA, Vanessa; Brazilian singer and songwriter; b. (Vanessa Sigiane da Mata Ferreira), 10 Feb. 1976, Alto Garças. *Career:* performed with reggae group Shalla-Ball, São Paulo 1992; backing vocalist on Brazilian tour for Black Uhuru 1995; mem. group Mafuá 1996; wrote songs with Chico César, Ana Carolina; wrote songs for Maria Bethânia, Caetano Veloso, Daniela Mercury; duet with Ben Harper 2007, Seu Jorge and Alamaz 2011. *Recordings:* albums: Vanessa da Mata 2002, Essa Boneca Tem Manual 2004, Sim (Latin Grammy Award for Best Contemporary Brazilian Pop Album 2007) 2007, Bicicletas, Bolos e Outras alegrias 2010. *Honours:* Multishow Brazilian Music Awards for Best Song 2008, 2008 (jtly with Ben Harper) *Address:* Sony Music Brasil, c/o Sony Music Entertainment, 550 Madison Avenue, 23rd Floor, New York, NY 10022-3211, USA (office). *Telephone:* (21) 2559-5200 (Brazil) (office). *Website:* www.sonymusic.com (office); www.vanessadamata.com.br.

DA ONE WAY (see Ig Culture)

DA SILVA, Rui, (Doctor J, 4 Elements, Teimoso); Portuguese producer, remixer and DJ; b. 25 April 1968, Lisbon. *Career:* began DJ career in Lisbon as mem. of Underground Sound of Lisbon; Signed to Tribal Records; Relocated to London, 2000; Collaborations: Terry Farley, Chris Coco, DJ Vibe; f. Kismet Records; mem. MCPS/PRS. *Recordings include:* albums: with Underground Sound of Lisbon: Etno City 2001; solo: Produced and Remixed 2002, Praying Mantis 2006; singles: So Get Up 1994, Are You Looking For Me 1998; solo: Touch Me (with Cassandra Fox) 2000. *Honours:* Muzik Award, Best Single (for Touch Me) 2001. *E-mail:* info@madame-management.com. *Website:* madame-management.com. *E-mail:* ruipacheco@aol.com.

DADAWA; Chinese singer; b. (Zhu Zheqin), 1974, Guangzhou, Guangdong Prov. *Career:* solo artist, New Age music since 1992; debut concerts in Midem Asia, Hong Kong 1995, London Showcase 1995; named UNDP China Nat. Goodwill Amb. 2009. *Recordings:* albums: Yellow Children 1992, Sister Drum 1995, Voices from the Sky 1997, Seven Days 2006, Main Title Theme (main title theme of Taiwan's anime MAZU) 2007, Moonrise 2014; also provided her voice for tracks on He Xuntian's albums Paramita 2002 and Tathagata 2008; guest on one track of Jonathan Elias's Prayer Cycle: Path to Zero 2011. *Achievements include:* first Chinese singer to sell over a million CDs in China; first Chinese singer to receive an international release since the 1940s. *Address:* c/o Kiigo, HUGO Media Group Inc., PO Box 450890, Cleveland, OH 44145, USA (office). *E-mail:* info@hugomedia.com (office).

DADDY ASH (see Beedle, Ashley)

DADDY FREDDY; Jamaican rap artist; b. (Samuel Small), Kingston. *Career:* solo artist; numerous television appearances, radio broadcasts; mem. PRS. *Recordings include:* albums: Ragamuffin Hip Hop, Ragga House, Pain Killa, Stress, Raggamuffin Soldier 1992, The Big One 1994, Greatest Hits 1996, Old School New School 2000, Hardcore 2004. *E-mail:* pr@daddyfreddy.com.

DADDY G; British singer; b. (Grant Marshall), 18 Dec. 1959, Bristol. *Career:* mem. collective The Wild Bunch; Founder mem. Massive Attack 1987–; collaborations with Shara Nelson, Tricky, Horace Andy, Madonna, Tracey Thorn (Everything But The Girl), Liz Fraser (Cocteau Twins). *Recordings include:* albums: with Massive Attack: Blue Lines 1991, Protection 1994, No Protection: Massive Attack vs Mad Professor 1995, Mezzanine 1998, 100th Window 2003, Danny the Dog 2004, Collected 2006, Heligoland 2010; solo: Daddy G DJ Kicks 2004. *Honours:* BRIT Award for Best British Dance Act 1996, Ivor Novello Award for Outstanding Contrib. to British Music 2009. *Website:* www.massiveattack.com.

DADDY YANKEE; Puerto Rican rapper; b. (Raymond Ayala), 3 Feb. 1977, Rio Piedras, San Juan; m.; three c. *Career:* began professional career in duo with Nicky Jam; Co-owner El Cartel Records; concert tours throughout Latin America and USA; collaborations on own material with Akon, Nicole Scherzinger, Hector El Father, Will.i.am and Fergie of The Black Eyed Peas, Snoop Dogg, Jazzee Pha, Don Omar; introduced own clothing line, DY 2006; Founder Fundación Corazón Guerrero (charitable org.). *Recordings include:* albums: No Mercy 1994, El Yankee 2 1996, El Cartel 1998, El Cartel II 2001, El Cangri.com 2002, Los Homerun-es 2003, Barrio Fino 2004, The Kings of New York 2004, Ahora te Toca al Cangri! Live 2005, Barrio Fino en Directo 2005, Tormenta Tropical, Vol. 1 2006, El Cartel: The Big Boss 2007, Talento de Barrio 2008, Mundial 2010, Prestige 2012, El Imperio Nazza: King Daddy Edition 2013. *Film scores include:* Vampiros 2004, Talento de Barrio 2007. *Honours:* Reggaeton Album of the Year, Latin Billboard Awards 2005, Latin Grammy Award for Best Urban Music 2005, MTV Video Music Award for Best Latino Artist 2013. *Current Management:* El Cartel Records, 601 Calle Del Parque, San Juan, Puerto Rico. *Telephone:* (787) 999-0711 (office). *Fax:* (787) 999-0714 (office). *E-mail:* cartelrecordsdy@gmail.com (office). *E-mail:* info@daddyyankee.com (office). *Website:* www.daddyyankee.com.

DADSWELL, Melvyn John, BA; musician (saxophone) and academic; b. 8 Jan. 1946, Uckfield, Sussex, England; m. He Feng Qin 1990, two s. two d. *Education:* Exeter Univ. *Career:* began playing jazz 1959; teacher of jazz harmony, rhythm to undergraduate music students (privately); many club concerts and British tours; three recordings Devon Air Jazz; occasional session work; various festival appearances; schooled Red Army Orchestra in jazz 1990–91; mem. Musicians' Union. *Address:* Five Poplars, Ford Farm, Chudleigh-Knighton, Newton Abbot, TQ13 0ET, England.

DAESUNG; South Korean singer and actor; b. (Kang Daesung), 26 April 1989, Itaewon. *Education:* Kyeongln High School, Kyunghee Univ. *Career:* mem. Big Bang 2006–; solo career 2008–. *Recordings:* albums: with Big Bang: Bigbang Vol 1 2007, Remember 2008, Number 1 2008, Big Bang 2009, Big Bang 2 2011, Alive 2012. *Film:* Sammy's Adventure: The Secret Passage 2010. *Stage:* Cats (Korean production) 2008. *Television includes:* Family Outing 2008–10, Night After Night (presenter) 2010–, Running Man 2011, What's Up (drama) (forthcoming). *Honours:* Mnet KM Music Festival Awards for Best Male Group 2007, 2008, 2012, for Song of the Year 2007, for Digital Music 2008, for Artist of the Year 2008, for Guardian Angel Worldwide Performer 2012, Golden Disk Bonsang Award 2007, Mnet Music Portal Award 2008, Seoul Music Awards for Digital Music 2008, for Bonsang 2008, 2009, for Best Album 2009, for Popular Mobile 2009, Nickelodeon Korea Kids' Choice Best Male Artists Award 2008, 2009, Hiwon Award 2009, Korea PD Best Singer Award 2009, Best Hits Song Festival Gold Artist Award 2009, Japan

Cable Broadcasting Best Newcomer Award 2009, Ministry of Culture, Sports and Tourism Artist of the Year 2009, Japan Record Awards for New Artist and Best New Artist 2009, Gold Award 2010, Japanese Grand Prix du Disque for Best Newcomer 2010, Japan Gold Disc Awards for Best Five New Artists and Best New Artist 2010, MTV Video Music Awards Japan for Best New Artist Video and Best Pop Video 2010. *Address:* c/o YG Entertainment, 397–5 YG Building, Hapjeong-Dong, Mapo-Gu, Seoul 109-819, South Korea (office). *Telephone:* (2) 3143-1105 (office). *Fax:* (2) 544-1546 (office). *E-mail:* web@ ygmail.net (office). *Website:* eng.ygfamily.com/main/main.html (office); www .ybigbang.com (home); www.ybigbang.jp (home).

DAGARA, Hamouka; Nigerian musician. *Career:* appearances on television, shows in West Africa; mem. Gominak, Somair, Sonichar, Socs of Air Mines, Palais Congrés. *Recordings include:* album: Bakandarnia. *Honours:* first prize Music Competition, Niger 1990, third prize competition in Niger 1992, 20th Place, Africa Palmaress 1997.

DAGNELL, John Richard; British music promoter, record company executive and music publisher; b. 2 Aug. 1956, Oxford, England; m. Nicola Dagnell 1983; one s. one d. *Career:* promoted various concert tours and albums by Maddy Prior, The Carnival Band, Gilbert O'Sullivan, Steeleye Span, Pentangle, Davey Arthur, Guitar Orchestra, Wild Willy Barrett, Kathryn Tickell, Lindisfarne, Keltic Fusion, Abbie Lathe, Katik Doherty, Gerard Kenny and Kirsty McGhee; mem. PRS, ILA, PPL. *Address:* PO Box 651, Oxford, OX2 9RB, England (office). *Telephone:* (1865) 241717 (office). *E-mail:* info@parkpromotions.com (office). *Website:* www.parkrecords.com (office).

DAHLKE, Kurt, (Pyrolator); German musician and producer; b. 29 April 1958, Düsseldorf. *Career:* fmr mem. Der Plan; Founder-mem. Bombay1 2001–. *Recordings include:* albums: The Identity Thing 2001, Me Like You 2003, Strobl 2005, Handbuch für die Welt 2007, Glücksmaschinen 2010. *Address:* c/o Grönland Records, 9–10 Domingo Street, London, EC1Y 0TA, England. *E-mail:* thebear@groenland.com.

DAHO, Etienne Warren; French singer, songwriter and producer; b. 14 Jan. 1957, Oran, Algeria. *Career:* producer for Robert Farel, Max Valentins, Dani, Bill Pritchard, Les Valentins, Sylvie Vartan, Lio, Jacno, Brigitte Fontaine; songwriter for Francoise Hardy, Daniel Darc, Guesh Patti, Sylvie Vartan; collaborations include Arthur Baker, Saint Etienne, Chris Isaak, Jacques Dutronc, Astrud Gilberto, Vanessa Daou, Charlotte Gainsbourg; organised Urgence compilation in aid of AIDS charities 1992. *Films include:* Désordre 1986, Jeux d'Artifice 1987. *Recordings include:* albums: Mythomane 1981, La Notte La Notte 1984, Pop Satori 1986, ED Collection 1987, Pour nos vies martiennes 1988, Live ED 1989, Paris Ailleurs 1991, Daholympia 1994, Reserection 1995, Eden 1996, Corps et Armes 2000, Reevolution 2003, L'Invitation (Victoire de la Musique for Best Pop/Rock Album 2008) 2007, Daho Pleyel Paris 2009. *Publication:* Superstar et ermite (with Jérôme Soligny) 1986. *Honours:* European Video Award 1987. *Address:* c/o Virgin France, 11 place des Vosges, 75004 Paris, France. *Website:* www.etiennedaho .com.

DALE, Colin; British producer, remixer and DJ; b. 14 April 1963, London. *Career:* started as a soul/disco DJ on London pirate station, Kiss in the '80s; stayed with licensed Kiss FM, presenting weekly Abstrakt Dance show –2000; moved to internet station Groovetech 2001–; founder, Abstrakt Dance Records; collaborations include Gareth Oxby, Haris Custovic, Access 58, Affie Yusseff. *Recordings include:* singles: Upstate Feeling (with Civil Attack) 1996, Make You High (with Kleer) 2001. *Address:* Abstrakt Dance Records, 78 Mount Nod Road, Streatham Hill, London SW16 2LJ, England. *E-mail:* colindale@groovetech.com.

DALE, Mick; British musician (keyboards, percussion); b. 22 March 1968. *Career:* mem. Embrace 1996–; headline tours and TV appearances. *Recordings include:* albums: The Good Will Out 1998, Drawn From Memory 2000, If You've Never Been 2001, Fireworks (Singles 1997–2002) 2002, Out Of Nothing 2004, This New Day 2006. *Current Management:* c/o Tony Perrin, Coalition Management, Studio 2, 3A Brackenbury Road, London, W6 0BE, England. *Telephone:* (20) 8743-1000. *E-mail:* tp@coalitiongroup.co.uk. *Website:* www.coalitionmanagement.co.uk.

DALEMO, Carl; Swedish musician (bass guitar, keyboards); b. 9 Dec. 1980, Lidköping. *Career:* fmr mem. rock band Spiral Stairs; mem. Razorlight 2002. *Recordings include:* albums: Up All Night 2004, Razorlight 2006, Slipway Fires 2008. *Television:* The Mighty Boosh. *Address:* Vertigo Records, Mercury Music Group, 364–366 Kensington High Street, London, W14 8NS, England. *E-mail:* vertigo@umusic.com. *Website:* www.vertigorecords.co.uk.

DALEY, Paul; British producer, musician (percussion), remixer and DJ; b. 23 Dec. 1962, Margate, Kent, England. *Career:* fmr mem., A Man Called Adam; co-founder, Hard Hands Records (with Neil Barnes); world-wide DJ; mem., Leftfield 1995–2002; collaborations with A Man Called Adam, Afrika Bambaataa, Roots Manuva, John Lydon. *Recordings include:* albums with Leftfield: Leftism 1995, Rhythm and Stealth 1999, A Final Hit 2005. *Current Management:* c/o James Whiting, Coda Agency, 229 Shoreditch High Street, London, E1 6PJ, England. *Telephone:* (20) 7456-8888. *E-mail:* james@ codaagency.com. *Website:* www.codaagency.com.

DALGLEISH, Louise (Lou), BA; British singer, songwriter and musician (piano); b. 19 Oct. 1967, Birmingham. *Career:* professional dancer, theatre, film, including Steven Spielberg's Indiana Jones and the Temple of Doom;

singer-songwriter, including headline residencies at Ronnie Scott's, Birmingham; support act to Wet Wet Wet, NEC, Birmingham, Bryan Ferry, Dutch tour, Guestings, Brian Kennedy; founder mem., My Darling Clementine; nat. television performances include BBC and ITV (UK), Belgium; festival appearances SXSW Austin, Texas, USA, Lowlands, Waterpop, Valkos, Netherlands, Phoenix, England; mem. Equity, Musicians' Union. *Recordings include:* singles: Orange Plane 1995, Sold Out 1995, Charlie Girl 1996; album: Lou Dalgleish 1995; live album, solo acoustic at Ronnie Scott's 1997, Calmer 1999; backing vocals on: The Good Sons, Happiness 2001; with My Darling Clementine: The Reconciliaton 2013. *Website:* mydarlingclementinemusic.co .uk.

DALLIN, Sara Elizabeth; British singer; b. 17 Dec. 1961, Bristol, Somerset. *Education:* London School of Fashion. *Career:* mem., Bananarama 1981–; numerous concerts, television and radio performances. *Recordings include:* albums: Deep Sea Skiving 1983, Bananarama 1984, True Confessions 1986, Wow! 1987, Pop Life 1991, Please Yourself 1993, Ultraviolet 1996, Exotica 2001, I Found Love 2002, Drama 2005, Viva 2009, 30 Years of Bananarama 2012. *Compositions include:* Last Thing On My Mind (Steps) (co-writer) 1998, Baby It's Christmas (co-writer) 2010. *Current Management:* c/o ASM Damage Ltd, Unit 3, City Business Centre, Saint Olav's Court, Lower Road, London, SE16 2XB, England. *E-mail:* agent@bananarama.co.uk. *Website:* www .bananarama.co.uk.

DALLIO, Patricia; French musician (keyboard, sensors) and composer; *Artistic Director, cie sound track;* b. 3 Nov. 1958, Chaumont. *Career:* tours throughout Europe with Art Zoyd; concerts in Berlin, Milan, New York; performances at the London, Hong Kong, Adelaide, Mexico, Stockholm and Yokohama Festivals; live shows and films include Nosferatu, Faust; Häxan Composer, Dance theatre, videos; mem. Soundtrack (Composer Asscn); realizes and creates concerts and performances for keyboards, electronic and sensors with duet called YéP, with Yukari Bertocchi-Hamada; performances with Catriona Morrison; video performance with Mathieu Sanchez; numerous solo improvisation experiences with poetry and authors; currently Artistic Dir, cie sound track. *Exhibitions include:* La teneur de l'air, Stabat Mater Furiosa, Dans la nuit la plus claire jamais rêvée, Extra Ball – installation with a pin ball, Micro-concerts 'tous en scène', 'sons en auterus', Le Mystère des Oréadess, Eau Forte, Les instantanés. *Dance:* Le parvis des ondes for two musicians and a dancer. *Film:* La petite pousse – Chaïtance conversat. *Recordings include:* Procession, Champs de Mars, La Ronce N'est Pas Le Pire, D'où vient l'eau des puits, Barbe Bleue, Que personne ne bouge, L'encre des voix secrètes, Dans la nuit la plus claire jamais rêvée (Coup de coeur, Acad. Charles de Cros), Le mystère des oréades. *Honours:* Coup de coeur, Acad. Charles Cros. *Current Management:* c/o 8 bis rue Decomble, 52000 Chaumont, France. *Telephone:* (3) 25-32-24-29 (office); 6-86-41-70-19 (mobile). *E-mail:* contact@ciesoundtrack.com (office); contact@patriciadallio .com. *Website:* www.ciesoundtrack.com (office); www.patriciadallio.com.

DALSETH, Laila; Norwegian jazz singer; b. 6 Nov. 1940, Bergen; m. Totti Bergh 1963, two d. *Career:* solo jazz artist; television and radio appearances in Scandinavia; Germany; Yugoslavia; England; Scotland; concerts include Playboy Jazz Festival; Nice Jazz Festival; Sacramento Jazz Festival; Caribbean Jazz Cruises; Copenhagen Jazz Festival; Molde Jazz Festival; Jakarta Jazz Festival; own group with saxophonist (husband) Totti Bergh. *Recordings include:* Laila Dalseth/Wild Bill Davidson 1974; with Bengt Hallberg, Arne Domnerus: Glad There Is You 1978; with Louis Stewart: Daydreams 1984; with Red Mitchell Quartet: Time For Love 1986; with Al Cohn: Travelin' Light 1987; Woman's Intuition 1995; with Milt Hinton, Derek Smith, B Rosengarden, B Pizarelli: The Judge and I 1992; with Joe Cohn, Totti Bergh: Remember 1995; with Philip Catherine, Egil Kapstad: A Woman's Intuition 1995; One of a Kind 2000. *Honours:* Spellemannspris (Norwegian Grammy).

DALTON, Lacy J.; American country singer; b. (Jill Byrem), 13 Oct. 1946, Bloomsburg, Pa; m. 1st John Croston 1971 (died 1974); one s.; m. 2nd Aaron Anderson (divorced 2005). *Career:* club singer in California for 12 years; singer, psychedelic group Office, under name Jill Croston; solo artist 1979–; worked with Earl Scruggs, George Jones and Bobby Bare. *Recordings:* albums: as Jill Croston: Jill Croston 1978; as Lacy J Dalton: Lacy J Dalton 1979, Hard Times 1980, Takin' It Easy 1981, 16th Avenue 1982, Dream Baby 1983, Greatest Hits 1983, Can't Run Away From Your Heart 1985, I Love Country 1986, Blue Eyed Blues 1987, Survivor 1989, Lacy J 1990, Crazy Love 1991, Chains On The Wind 1992, Somethin Special 1995, Wild Horse Crossing 1999, The Last Wild Place 2004, The Last Wild Place Anthology 2006, Here's to Hank 2010. *Address:* Lacy J. Dalton Productions, 11625 US Highway 50, Stagecoach, NV 89429-8415, USA (office). *Telephone:* (775) 690-9894 (office). *Fax:* (775) 847-4705 (office). *E-mail:* bob@lacyjdalton.com. *Website:* www .lacyjdalton.com (home).

DALTREY, David Joseph, ALCM; British session musician (guitar, bass guitar, piano), tutor, composer and producer; b. 30 Dec. 1951, London, England. *Education:* Mid-Hertfordshire Coll., Guildhall School of Music and Drama, London Coll. of Music, studied with Rogers Covey-Crump, Ike Isaacs and Jimmy Page. *Career:* worked for BBC; numerous compositions and recordings for various artists; session musician, composer and producer; currently tutor, Guildhall Guitar Studio; mem., Musicians' Union, ISM, AES, Radio Acad., ISCE, APRS. *Recordings include:* Tales of Justine, Albert/ Monday Morning 1967, Joseph and the Amazing Technicolour Dreamcoat (lead vocalist and guitarist) 1969, 1971, Petals from a Sunflower 1998, The Wayfarer 2004.

DALTREY, Roger Harry, CBE; British singer and actor; b. 1 March 1944, Hammersmith, London, England; m. Heather Daltrey; two d. two s. (one by previous m.). *Career:* mem. rock group, The Detours, renamed The Who 1964–84 (various reunion tours and recordings); numerous festival appearances and tours; solo artist 1984–. *Films include:* Tommy 1974, Lisztomania 1975, The Legacy 1979, McVicar 1980, Threepenny Opera 1989. *Recordings include:* albums: with The Who: My Generation 1965, A Quick One 1966, Happy Jack 1967, The Who Sell Out 1967, Magic Bus 1968, Tommy 1969, Live At Leeds 1970, Who's Next 1971, Meaty Beefy Big And Bouncy 1971, Quadrophenia 1973, The Who By Numbers 1975, The Story Of The Who 1976, Who Are You 1978, The Kids Are Alright (live) 1979, Face Dances 1981, Hooligans 1982, It's Hard 1982, Once Upon A Time 1983, Who's Last (live) 1984, Two's Missing 1987, Joined Together (live) 1990, Live At The Isle Of Wight Festival 1970 1996, The BBC Sessions 2000, Moonlighting 2005, Endless Wire 2006; solo: Daltrey 1973, Ride A Rock Horse 1975, One Of The Boys 1977, If Parting Should Be Painless 1984, Under A Raging Moon 1985, I Can't Wait To See The Movie 1987, Rocks In The Head 1992, McVicar 1996, Martyrs And Madmen 1997, Anthology 2002; with Wilko Johnson: Going Back Home 2014. *Honours:* Gold Ticket Madison Square Garden 1979, Ivor Novello Award for Outstanding Contribution to British Music 1982, BRIT Award for Outstanding Contribution to British Music 1988, Q Legend Award 2006, South Bank Show Award for Lifetime Achievement 2007, Kennedy Center Honor 2008. *Current Management:* c/o Trinifold Management Ltd, 12 Oval Road, London, NW1 7DH, England. *Telephone:* (20) 7419-4300. *Fax:* (20) 7419-4325. *E-mail:* trinuk@globalnet.co.uk. *Website:* www.thewho.com.

DAMBRY, Stephane; French singer; b. 7 March 1959, Barentin. *Education:* teacher training. *Career:* lead singer, Little Big Band 1987–97; solo artist 1991–. *Recordings include:* albums: solo: Talk To The Mirror 1991, The Fatal Glass of Beer 1994, The Welsh Rare Beat 1994, Le Bour de le Serre 2001, En attendant l'hiver 2007; with Little Big Band: Hey! Doc 1994. *Address:* L'Echo du kazoo, 14 impasse Murizon, 76500 Elbeuf, France (office). *Telephone:* 2-35-77-45-32. *E-mail:* contact@stephanedambry.com (office). *Website:* www .stephanedambry.com.

DAMEN, Paul; Dutch musician (drums); b. 26 Jan. *Career:* Mid 80s Leading Dutch Top 40 Band accompanying major Dutch Artists, 1989; Toured in Holland, The Trammps; Jimmy Bo Horne; Dutch Group, Haitai; numerous jingles and commercials (studio) for: Mercedes; SAAB; General Motors; L'Oreal Cosmetics; TV appearances with Gloria Estefan; Toured with popular Dutch Artist Rob Janszen; Toured with International Artist, C. B. Milton, 1995; National Studio/Session Drummer, currently. *Recordings:* Promo; Endorser for Remo, Drums and Drumheads. *Current Management:* De Otter and De Vries, Entertainment Productions BC, Hertogin Juliana Singel 34 055, Netherlands. *Address:* Hogehofstraat 26, 5366 CC Megen, Netherlands. *Website:* www.pauldamen.nl (home).

DAMINESCU, Adrian; Romanian musician (cello, piano, guitar, bass guitar) and singer; b. 2 Oct. 1956, Timisoara; m. Francis Susan Walker 1990 (divorced). *Education:* Acad. of Music. *Career:* concerts, tours and recitals; television and radio broadcasts. *Compositions include:* Romania, You're Still Beautiful, Looking In My Teacup, Stop, Pleading For Michael Jackson, I Miss My Home, Final Day, Praying For Mercy, Midnight. *Recordings include:* I Will Love You (Eu Te Voi Iubi), Pieces of Me (Bucati Din Mine). *Honours:* Great Prize, Bucharest Festival, 1986; Most Beautiful Voice of the Festival, Bratislava, 1986; 3 times Great Prize winner as singer Mamaia Nat. Festival, 1986–88, Second Prize, Golden Orpheus Festival, Bulgaria 1988, 3 Mamaia Nat. Festival Awards as composer: First 1989, Third 1991, Second 1992. *Address:* Constanta 8700, 45 Gen Manu Street, Romania. *Telephone:* 0723305439 (mobile). *Website:* www.adriandaminescu.com.

DAMMERS, Gerald (Jerry) Dankin; British musician (keyboards); b. 22 May 1954, Coventry, Warwicks., England; s. of Horace Dammers. *Career:* founded 2 Tone Records 1970s; founder mem., Coventry Automatics 1977, renamed Coventry Specials, then Special AKA, then the Specials 1979–84, 1996; numerous tours and live appearances; designer, record label 2-Tone, marketed by Chrysalis Records 1979; f. The Spatial AKA Orchestra 2006. *Recordings include:* albums: The Specials 1979, More Specials 1980, Today's Specials 1996, Guilty 'Til Proved Innocent! 1998, Skinhead Girl 2000, Conquering Ruler 2001. *Film:* Dance Craze 1981. *Honours:* Grand Companion of O. R. Tambo (Silver), South Africa 2014; Dr hc (Coventry Univ.) 2006; Q Merit Award, Q Magazine 2000, Ivor Novello Inspiration Award 2014. *Website:* www.jerrydammers.com.

DAMONE, Vic; American singer and actor; b. (Vito Farinola), 12 June 1928, Brooklyn, NY; m. 1st Judy Rawlins; one s. three d; m. 4th Diahann Carroll; m. 5th Rena Rowan Damone. *Career:* winner Arthur Godfrey's Talent Scouts, CBS 1946; singer, La Martinique nightclub, New York; solo artist 1947–2001; regular concert tours, UK, USA and Australia 1980s–2001. *Films:* Rich, Young and Pretty 1951, The Strip 1951, Hell to Eternity, Athena 1954, Deep in my Heart 1954, Hit the Deck 1955, Kismet 1955, Crash Boat. *Television and radio:* Saturday Night Serenade (radio show, CBS) late 1940s, own television series 1956–57. *Recordings include:* albums: Vic Damone 1950, Christmas Favorites 1950, Rich Young and Pretty (soundtrack) 1951, April in Paris 1952, Vocals by Vic 1952, Take Me in Your Arms 1952, Deep in my Heart (soundtrack) 1955, That Towering Feeling 1956, The Stingiest Man In The World (soundtrack) 1956, Affair to Remember 1957, Yours for a Song 1957, The Gift of Love (soundtrack) 1958, Closer Than A Kiss 1959, Angela Mia 1959, This Game of Love 1959, On The Swingin' Side 1961, Linger Awhile With Vic Damone 1962, Strange Enchantment 1962, The Lively Ones 1962, My Baby Loves To Swing 1963, The Liveliest 1963, On The Street Where You Live 1964, You Were Only Fooling 1965, Stay With Me 1976, Young and Lively 1980, Make Someone Happy 1981, Christmas With Vic Damone 1984, Damone Type of Thing 1984, On the South Side of Chicago 1984, Eternally 1989, Let's Face the Music and Sing 1991, Glory of Love 1992, Feelings 1993, On the Street 1995. *Publications:* Recipes for Lovers (recipe book), Singing Was the Easy Part (with David Chanoff) 2009. *E-mail:* vic@vicdamone.com. *Website:* www.vicdamone.com.

DAMRON, Dick; Canadian singer. *Career:* Starday Studios, recording country rockabilly records with Tommy Hill, 1961; teamed up with Producer Joe Bob Barnhill, Soldier of Fortune Album, 1971. *Recordings include:* Countrified 1971, Susan Flowers, Jesus It's Me Again, Still Countrified, Dick Damron: The Anthology. *Honours:* four Times Top Canadian Country Singer; Best Country Record of 1977; Top Canadian Songwriter; Artist of the Year; Country Gospel Album of the Year, 1996; 7 Times Winner, Outstanding Contribution to Canadian Music; 2 Times Winner, Province of Alberta Award; Country Music Man of the Year; 5 Texas Proud Awards, inducted into International Country Music Hall of Fame 2001.

DANA; Irish singer; b. (Rosemary Brown), 30 Aug. 1951; m. Damien Scallon; two s. two d. *Career:* winner, Eurovision Song Contest, with All Kinds of Everything 1970; solo singer 1970–; elected to represent Connacht-Ulster constituency as MEP 1999–2004; f. DS Music Productions 2004. *Recordings include:* albums: All Kinds of Everything 1970, World of Dana 1975, Have A Nice Day 1977, Love Songs and Fairy Tales 1977, The Girl Is Back 1979, Everything Is Beautiful 1980, Totally Yours 1982, Magic 1982, Let There Be Love 1985, Please Tell Him I Said Hello 1984, If I Give my Heart to You 1985, In the Palm of His Hand 1987, No Greater Love 1987, The Gift of Love 1989, Dana's Ireland 1991, The Rosary 1991, Lady of Knock 1992, Hail Holy Queen 1993, Say Yes 1993, The Healing Rosary 1995, Humble Myself 1997, Forever Christmas 1997, Heavenly Portrait 1997, Stations of the Cross 1998, Perfect Gift 2004, In Memory of Me 2005, Little Baby 2006, Totus Tuus 2006, Good Morning Jesus! 2007, Thing Called Love 2007. *Television appearances include:* A Day with Dana 1974, I Believe in Music 1977, Wake Up Sunday 1979, The All Ireland Talent Show (judge) 2009. *Publication:* All Kinds of Everything (autobiography) 2008. *Honours:* Dr hc (Stonehill Coll.); San Benedetto Award 2004, Mother Teresa Award 2005. *Address:* DS Music Productions European Office, Drumhoney House, Gortatleva, Claregalway, Co. Galway, Ireland (office). *E-mail:* info@danaofficial.com. *Website:* danaofficial.com (office).

DANDO, Evan; American singer, musician (guitar) and songwriter; b. 4 March 1967. *Career:* founder mem., the Lemonheads 1986–97, 2006–; solo artist 2002–; numerous worldwide concert tours; collaborations with The Blake Babies, Kirsty MacColl, Juliana Hatfield, Godstar. *Recordings include:* albums: with The Lemonheads: Hate Your Friends 1987, Creator 1988, Create Your Friends 1989, Lick 1988, Lovey 1990, It's A Shame About Ray 1992, Come On Feel The Lemonheads 1993, Car Button Cloth 1996, The Best of the Lemonheads The Atlantic Years 1998, The Lemonheads 2006, Varshons 2009; solo: Live at the Brattle Theatre/Griffith Sunset (EP) 2002, Baby I'm Bored 2003. *Honours:* Boston Music Awards for Outstanding Modern Rock Act, Single of the Year 1993. *Address:* c/o Vagrant Records, 2118 Wilshire Blvd, #361, Santa Monica, CA 90403, USA. *E-mail:* editor@evandando.co.uk. *Website:* www.evandando.co.uk; www.thelemonheads.net.

D'ANGELO; American singer, songwriter, musician (multi-instrumentalist) and producer; b. (Michael Archer), 11 Feb. 1974, Richmond, Virginia. *Career:* recording artist 1992–. *Compositions include:* co-writer, producer, U Will Know, Black Men United. *Recordings include:* albums: Brown Sugar 1995, Live at the Jazz Cafe 1998, Voodoo (Grammy Awards for Best R&B Male Vocal Performance and Best R&B Album 2001) 2000, Black Messiah (Grammy Award for Best R&B Album 2016) 2014. *Honours:* three times winner, Harlem Apollo Talent Contest, Grammy Award for Best R&B Song (for Really Love) 2016. *Website:* www.blackmessiah.co.

DANGER MOUSE; American producer; b. (Brian Joseph Burton), White Plains, NY. *Career:* produced electronica/trip hop music as Pelican City while living in Athens, Ga; moved to London, England, signed recording contract under pseudonym Danger Mouse with Lex Records; gained notoriety with The Grey Album, an unofficial release which mixed vocal samples from Jay Z's Black Album with samples from The Beatles White Album; mem. Gnarls Barkley (with Cee-Lo Green) 2005–; mem. DANGER DOOM with MF Doom; Founding mem., Broken Bells 2009–; production credits include Gorillaz, Prince Po, The Good, the Bad and the Queen, The Shortwave Set, The Rapture, Sparklehorse. *Recordings include:* albums: as Danger Mouse: Ghetto Pop Life 2003, The Grey Album 2004, Dark Night of the Soul (with Sparklehorse) 2009, Rome 2011; with DANGERDOOM: The Mouse and the Mask 2003; with Gnarls Barkley: St Elsewhere 2006, The Odd Couple 2008; with Broken Bells: Broken Bells 2010; as producer: Gorillaz, Demon Days 2005, The Rapture, Pieces of the People We Love (two tracks) 2006, Sparklehorse, Dreamt for Light Years in the Belly of a Mountain 2006, The Good, the Bad and the Queen 2007, The Black Keys, El Camino 2011, Norah Jones, Little Broken Hearts 2012, Portugal, The Man, Evil Friends 2013.

Honours: Grammy Awards for Best Urban/Alternative Performance (Craze) 2006, Best Alternative Music Album (St. Elsewhere) 2007, Producer of the Year Non-Classical 2011, Best Rock Song (Lonely Boy) 2012, Best Rock Album (El Camino) 2013, Wired Rave Award 2005, Rolling Stone Magazine Best Producer in Rock 2008, Music Producers Guild International Producer of the Year 2013. *Address:* c/o Downtown Records, 73 Spring Street, Suite 504, New York, NY 10012, USA. *Telephone:* (212) 625-2980. *Fax:* (212) 625-2987. *Website:* downtownrecords.com; www.gnarlsbarkley.com; www.brokenbells .com; www.dangermousesite.com.

DANGEROUS, Chris; Swedish musician (drums); b. 12 June 1978. *Career:* mem. The Hives 1993–. *Recordings include:* albums: Barely Legal 1997, Veni Vidi Vicious 2000, Your New Favourite Band (compilation) 2001, Tyrannosaurus Lives 2004, The Black and White Album 2007, Lex Hives 2012. *Honours:* NME Award for Best Int. Band 2003. *Address:* The Hives, Regnbågsvägen 46, 737 43 Fagersta, Sweden (office). *E-mail:* hives@ innocent.com (office). *Website:* www.thehivesbroadcastingservice.com (office).

DANIELS, Bob; American musician (banjo); b. (Robert T. Hahn), 2 March 1959, Milwaukee, Wis.; m. Denise Blank; one s. two d. *Career:* professional musician for 20 years; played in bands including The Nashville Cats, The Nashtown Ramblers, Backroads, Johnny Rodriguez Backup Band; played with artists including Charley Collins, Bashful Brother Oswald, Earl Scruggs, Jethro Burns, Duane Stuermer, Jack Grassel, Warren Wiegratz, Infamous Ramblin' Rick Trudell, Grand Old Opry; Broadway production 1979; Assoc. songwriter for BMI; composes for other singers, commercials, theatre; mem. AFofM. *Recordings include:* albums: Bob Daniels and A Milwaukee All-Star Pot Pourri 1990, Bob Daniels, Rick Trudell, Best Banjo 1995, Bob Daniels, Rick Trudell, Rough Cuts 1995, Best Banjo 1995. *Honours:* rated by HFR as one of top 5 improvisational 5-string banjo players.

DANIELS, Charlie; American country singer, songwriter and musician (multi-instrumentalist); b. 28 Oct. 1937, Wilmington, North Carolina. *Career:* played guitar from age 15; founder bluegrass band, The Misty Mountain Boys, changed name to The Jaguars 1959; regular session work, Nashville 1960–; partnership with Earl Scruggs; formed Charlie Daniels Band 1970–; started Volunteer Jam (became annual event) 1974–. *Film music:* featured on soundtrack to Urban Cowboy, recorded film theme to Stroker Ace. *Compositions include:* It Hurts Me (recorded by Elvis Presley) 1964. *Recordings include:* albums: To John, Grease and Wolfman 1970, Charlie Daniels 1970, Honey In The Rock 1973, Way Down Yonder 1974, Fire On The Mountain 1975, Nightrider 1975, Teach Yourself Rock Guitar 1976, Saddletramp 1976, High Lonesome 1976, Midnight Wind 1977, Million Miles Reflections 1979, Full Moon 1980, Windows 1982, A Decade of Hits 1983, Me and The Boys 1985, Powder Keg 1987, Renegade 1991, Same Ol' Me 1995, By the Light of the Moon 1997, Tailgate Party 1999, Road Dogs 2000, How Sweet the Sound 2002, Redneck Fiddlin' Man 2002, Songs from the Longleaf Pines 2005, Deuces 2007, Joy to the World 2009, Land That I Love 2011. *Publication:* book of short stories 1986. *Honours:* Spirit of Americana Free Speech Award 2006. *Current Management:* c/o Agency for the Performing Arts, 405 South Beverly Drive, Beverly Hills, CA 90212, USA. *Telephone:* (310) 888-4200. *Fax:* (310) 888-4242. *Website:* www.apa-agency.com; www.charliedaniels.com.

DANIELS, Luke; British musician (button accordion); b. 18 Nov. 1973, Reading, England. *Career:* accordion player with Scarp, fmrly with De Danann; major concerts include St Chartier Festival, Philadelphia Festival of Folk Music, Theatre de Ville, Paris; accordionist with Riverdance; composer for English Nat. Opera; mem. Musicians' Union. *Compositions include:* Musette À Térésa, The Snoring Barber, Wednesday's Tune, Gallowstree Sonata, The King of Prussia, This Love, Breath Without a Sigh. *Recordings include:* Tarantella 1994, Scarp 1995, Across The Waters, Reeltime (compilation), Lost Music of the Gaels, Secret Sessions; features on: Kissing Fishes, Broderick 2000, Broad Street Ballads, Ray Hearne 2001, Cara Dillon, Cara Dillon 2001. *Honours:* Young Tradition Award, Folk Musician of the Year, BBC Radio 2 1992. *Address:* Wren Records Ireland, 6 Elton Court, Sandycove, Ireland. *Website:* www.wren.ie.

DANKO, Harold, BME; American musician (piano), composer and academic; *Professor, Eastman School of Music;* b. 13 June 1947, Sharon, Pa. *Education:* Dana School of Music, Youngstown State Univ., Ohio, additional studies at Juilliard School of Music, New York. *Career:* Leader, Composer and Arranger, Harold Danko Trio 1966–, Harold Danko Quartet 1974–; tours, concerts and recordings 1972–; pianist with various artistes, including Woody Herman, Chet Baker, Thad Jones and Mel Lewis, Lee Konitz, Gerry Mulligan; festival appearances include JVC, Rochester, New Haven and Clearwater, USA, Montreal, Canada, Metz, TBB and Fort Napoleon, France, Torino, Marca and Riva, Italy, Gouvy, Belgium and North Sea Jazz Festival, Netherlands; featured artist, Rochester Int. Jazz Festival, Meet the Artist series, Lincoln Center and Performing Arts Soc. series, JFK Center; concert series, Manhattan School of Music, New York funded by Nat. Endowment for the Arts fellowship; Pres. Aaychdee Music; Founder Jazz Haven (jazz soc.); Music Educator, Manhattan School of Music, New York, Hartt School of Music, Hartford, Connecticut and Neighborhood Music School, New Haven; Prof., Eastman School of Music, Rochester, NY; recordings as leader with Inner City, Dreamstreet, SunnySide and SteepleChase labels; mem. American Fed. of Musicians, American Soc. of Composers, Authors and Publrs (ASCAP). *Compositions include:* Tidal Breeze, Next Age, New Autumn, Alone But Not Forgotten, Ink and Water Suite, To Start Again, Blue Swedish Wildflower,

Sizzle; music for theatre and TV. *Recordings:* Coincidence 1979, Mirth Song 1982, Shorter By Two 1983, Alone But Not Forgotten 1985, The First Love Song 1988, Next Age 1993, After The Rain 1994, New Autumn 1995, The Feeling of Jazz 1996, Tidal Breeze 1997, This Isn't Maybe 1999, Stable Mates 2000, Three of Four 2000, Nightscapes 2001, Prestigious: A Tribute to Eric Dolphy 2001, Fantasy Exit 2002, Trillix 2004, Hinesight 2005, Oatts & Perry 2006, Times Remembered 2007. *Publications:* The Illustrated Keyboard Series 1982, Jazz Concepts for Keyboard (Brazil) (video). *Honours:* awards from ASCAP and Nat. Asscn of Concert and Cabaret Acts, Outstanding Service to Jazz Educ. Award, Int. Asscn of Jazz Educators, Distinguished Alumni Award, Youngstown State Univ., Fellowship, Nat. Endowment for the Arts 1995. *Address:* Eastman School of Music, University of Rochester, 26 Gibbs Street, Rochester, NY 14604, USA (office). *Telephone:* (585) 274-1449 (office). *E-mail:* hdanko@esm.rochester.edu (office). *Website:* www.esm .rochester.edu (office).

DANKWORTH, Alexander (Alec) William; British musician (double bass, acoustic bass guitar); b. 14 May 1960, London, England; s. of John Dankworth and Dame Cleo Laine; brother of Jacqui Dankworth. *Education:* Berklee Coll. of Music, Boston, USA. *Career:* played clarinet before taking up double bass; worked and toured internationally with parents 1981–91; during this period also worked with Tommy Chase, Dave O'Higgins, Tommy Smith, Jean Toussaint, Buddy De Franco, Nigel Kennedy, Stephane Grappelli, Michael Garrick; began long asscn with Clark Tracey and Pizza Express Modern Jazz Sextet, late 1980s; accompanied many visiting American jazz musicians; toured Europe and South Africa with Abdullah Ibrahim 1993; played in the Dankworth Generation Band; toured and recorded with Van Morrison and Georgie Fame, mid-1990s, and Dave Brubeck 1999; collaborations with Julian Joseph, Martin Taylor, Pete King, Pat Crumley, Tommy Smith, Guy Barker. *Recordings include:* albums: We've Been Expecting You (Clark Tracey Quintet) 1992, Nebuchadnezzar (with John Dankworth) 1994, Rhythm Changes (with John Dankworth) 1995, If You're Passing By (Alex Dankworth Trio), Spanish Accents 2008; features on: Bartók – Solo Violin Sonata/ Ellington – Mainly Black, Nigel Kennedy 1986, What Goes Around, Jean Toussaint 1992, Spirit of Django, Martin Taylor 1994, How Long Has This Been Going On, Van Morrison and Georgie Fame 1995, Into The Blue, Guy Barker 1995, Beasts of Scotland, Tommy Smith 1996, The Healing Game, Van Morrison 1997, Gold, Martin Taylor 1997, Brubeck's Back, Dave Brubeck 1999, Deep Water Drop Off, Sin É 1999. *Address:* Ravenscroft, Ibstone, HP14 3XY, England (office). *E-mail:* alecd@alecdankworth.com (office). *Website:* www.alecdankworth.com.

DANKWORTH, Jacqueline (Jacqui) Caryl; British singer and actress; b. 5 Feb. 1963, d. of John Dankworth and Dame Cleo Laine; sister of Alec Dankworth. *Career:* acted with the RSC; stage appearances in London's West End include Sophisticated Ladies (Ellington revue), Into The Woods (Stephen Sondheim), Les Liaisons Dangereuses; formed Alec and Jacqui Dankworth Quartet 1993; fmr mem. ensemble Field of Blue; f. The Passion, harmony group 2001; also solo artist. *Recordings include:* albums: with Field of Blue: Field of Blue 1996, Still 2000; with James Pearson: For All We Know 2000; with The Passion: One Good Reason 2002; solo: As the Sun Shines Down on Me 2003, Detour Ahead 2004, Back to You 2009, It Happens Quietly 2011. *Film appearances include:* Shoreditch 2003, Les Misérables 2012. *Website:* www.jacquidankworth.com.

DANNENBERG, Roger, BSEE, MSCE, PhD; American composer and musician (trumpet); *Associate Research Professor, School of Computer Science, Carnegie Mellon University;* b. 9 March 1955, Houston, Tex.; m. Frances Dannenberg; one s. *Education:* Rice Univ., Carnegie Mellon Univ., studied trumpet with Nelson Hatt, Frank Tripani, Anthony Pasquarelli, composition with Paul Cooper. *Career:* played trumpet with George Gee Orchestra, Apollo Theatre 1986; Greenwich Village Jazz Festival 1988; trumpet, composer, Nitely News, World Affairs Conference 1996; In Transit, Guanajuato 1997; Assoc. Research Prof., School of Computer Science, Carnegie Mellon Univ. 1999–; mem. Bd of Dirs ICMA, Pittsburgh New Music Ensemble; mem. Int. Computer Music Asscn. *Television:* Stuck with Each Other (NBC TV film) 1989. *Compositions include:* Ritual of The Science Makers 1990, Nitely News 1992, The Words Are Simple 1994, Aura 1998, Resound! Fanfares for Trumpet and Computer 2002, The Watercourse Way 2003, Feedback 2005, Archimedes 2006, Origin, Direction, Location 2006, Critical Point 2007, Patterns 2009, Concerto for Two Trumpets 2010. *Publications include:* Multimedia Interface Design 1992, Combining Instrument and Performance Models For High Quality Music Synthesis 1998 and numerous others. *Address:* School of Computer Science, Carnegie Mellon University, Pittsburgh, PA 15213, USA (office). *Telephone:* (412) 268-3827 (office). *Fax:* (412) 268-5576 (office). *Website:* www.cs.cmu.edu/~rbd (office).

DANTER, John, MA; British musician and composer; b. 3 Sept. 1946, Birmingham, England; one s. *Education:* Reading Univ. *Career:* toured as guitarist with various groups, Germany, Turkey, Greece, USA, 1960s and 70s; session work on 'Jingles', 1970s; Writing songs 1980s–90s; commissioned music for production companies and songwriting for the American country market; mem. PRS, The Lute Soc., West Bromwich Albion Supporters Club. *Compositions include:* Have You Ever Been In Love, Making Your Mind Up, The Perfect Kiss, Started So Well, Another Beautiful Guy, Daddy Said. *Recordings include:* about 1500 television and radio jingles. *Publication:* Sound As Inspiration-Study In Improvisation. *Honours:* Eurovision Song Contest Winner 1981, Ivor Novello Award 1983.

DANTZLER, Russ; American artist agent, artist manager and record producer; b. 5 Dec. 1951, Ainsworth, Neb. *Education:* Univ. of Nebraska. *Career:* began Hot Jazz Man. and Production as hobby, to preserve the Swing tradition 1974; Hot Jazz became full-time career, New York City 1989; clients include: Claude 'Fiddler' Williams, Earl May, Red Richards, Benny Waters, Al Grey, The Duke's Men with Arthur Baron, Carrie Smith, Bross Townsend, Norris Turney, Ken Peplowski, Bill 'Mr Honkey Tonk' Doggett; contracting work for the Smithsonian Jazz Oral History Dept, and Jazz Foundation of America; mem. Jazz Journalists Asscn, Kansas City Jazz Ambs, American Fed. of Jazz Socs, Duke Ellington Soc, New York Chapter, Nat. Jazz Service Org. *Recordings include:* Produced: Claude Williams, Live At J's, Vols 1 and 2 1993, Swingtime In New York, with Claude Williams, Sir Roland Hanna, Bill Easley, Earl May, Joe Ascione 1995. *Publications include:* Columnist, Jam/Jazz Ambs Magazine (Kansas City), Scrapple From The Apple 1993–. *Address:* Hot Jazz, 328 W 43rd Street, Suite 4F, New York, NY 10036, USA.

DANZIG, Glenn; American rock singer; b. (Glen Anzalone), 23 June 1955, Lodi, New Jersey. *Career:* singer, US punk groups, The Misfits, Samhain; Founder-mem. and singer Danzig 1987–. *Recordings include:* albums: with the Misfits: Beware 1979, Walk Among Us 1982, Static Age 1995, Collection II 1995, Box Set 1996; with Danzig: Danzig 1988, Danzig II – Lucifage 1990, Danzig III – How The Gods Kill 1992, Danzig 4 1994, Blackacidevil 1996, Satan's Child 1999, Live On The Black Hand Side 2001, Danzig 777: I Luciferi 2002, Circle of Snakes 2004, Deth Red Sabaoth 2010. *Address:* c/o Richard De La Font Agency, 4845 South Sheridan Road, Tulsa, OK 74145, USA. *Telephone:* (918) 665-6200. *Website:* www.delafont.com; www.danzig-verotik .com.

DAO, Lang; Chinese folk singer, songwriter and musician (keyboards); b. (Luo Lin), Luoquan Township, Zizhong County, Sichuan Province; m. 1st (divorced); m. 2nd Zhu; two d. *Career:* sings in Mandarin. *Recordings include:* albums: Love Songs from the Western Regions 2001, Songs from the Great Desert 2001, Daolang 2004. *Address:* c/o Universal Music Hong Kong, Hong Kong Special Administrative Region, People's Republic of China. *Website:* www.umg.com.hk.

DAOUD, Rageh, BMus; Egyptian composer, musician (piano) and teacher; b. 23 Nov. 1954, Cairo. *Education:* Cairo Conservatoire, Vienna Acad. of Music. *Career:* composer 1978–; teacher and Research Asst, Cairo Conservatoire 1978–81, apptd Assoc. Prof. of Composition 1988, Head, Composition and Conducting Dept 2008–; apptd conductor, Hanager Center Chamber Orchestra, Egyptian Ministry of Culture 1993; Pres. Nat. Cttee, Int. Music Council. *Compositions include:* Egyptian Glimpse for orchestra 1978, Sonata for piano 1978, Lied for soprano and piano 1978, Four Pieces for string orchestra 1981, Fugue for string orchestra 1981, Fantasy for harp, cello and percussion 1982, Four Dances for string quartet 1982, Fantasy for woodwinds and string orchestra 1983, Lied for alto and piano 1984, Takassim for clarinet and orchestra 1984, Quartet for flute, oboe, clarinet and bassoon 1985, Quartet for woodwinds 1985, Der neue Ankommende lied for alto, bass clarinet and vibraphone 1986, Meditation for string orchestra 1986, Portrait No. 1 for string orchestra 1986, Trio for piano, violin and cello 1987, Three Pictures for oboe and piano 1987, Three Children's Pictures for two pianos 1987, Portrait No. 2 for string orchestra 1987, Rhapsody for string orchestra 1988, Nocturne for cello and piano 1989, Nocturne for piano 1989, Requiem for choir and orchestra 1990, Thirty Songs for children and small orchestra 1991, Suite for alto flute solo 1992, Suite for flute and piano 1992, Rhapsody for flute, violin and orchestra 1992, Passacaglia for lute, organ and string orchestra 1993. *Honours:* Ministry of Culture Artistic Creation Prize 1990, Alexandria Film Festival Prize 1991, Film Critics Asscn Prize 1992. *Address:* Committee of Music, Opera and Ballet, Supreme Council of Culture, El Gabalia Street, Opera House, El Gezira, Cairo, Egypt. *Telephone:* (1) 4161141; (2) 5613451. *Fax:* (2) 5877545. *E-mail:* ragehdaoud@hotmail.com; contact@ragehdaoud .com. *Website:* www.ragehdaoud.com.

DAPOGNY, James; American academic, jazz musician (piano) and bandleader; b. 3 Sept. 1940, Illinois. *Education:* University of Illinois. *Career:* Prof. of Music, University of Michigan, 1966–; Jazz Pianist, Leader, James Dapogny's Chicago Jazz Band, 1975–; touring, recording, radio and television broadcasts. *Compositions:* West of The Mississippi; Santa Passed My House By This Christmas; Shortstory; Lobogo; Miles From Home. *Recordings:* Laughing At Life 1992, Original Jelly Roll Blues 1993, Hot Club Stomp 1995, On The Road 1995, Whatcha Gonna Swing Tonight 1999. *Address:* 1154 Olden Road, Ann Arbor, MI 48103, USA.

DARA; South Korean singer, dancer, actor and model; b. (Park Sandara), 12 Nov. 1984, Busan. *Career:* worked in entertainment industry in the Philippines 2004–07; came to prominence competing in TV's Star Circle Quest (ABS-CBN), finished first runner-up 2004; released several solo EPs and singles 2004–06; attended acting workshops in South Korea 2005; signed contract with YG Entertainment 2007; mem. 2NE1 2009–. *Recordings:* albums: with 2NE1: To Anyone (Melon Music Award for Album of the Year 2010, Mnet Asian Music Award for Album of the Year 2010, Korean Music Award for Best Dance and Electronic Album 2011) 2010, Crush 2014; other credits include: Heartbreaker, G-Dragon 2009. *Films:* as actor: Volta 2004, Bcuz of U (PMPC Star Award for Movies for Best New Actress 2005) 2004, Can This Be Love 2005, D'Lucky Ones 2006, Super Noypi 2007, Girlfriends 2009. *Television includes:* Star Circle Quest 2004, My Name is Sandara Park (documentary) 2004, Gudtaym (entertainment series) 2006, 2NE1 TV

2009–11; guest acting roles in: Krystala 2004, Komiks 2006, Abt Ur Luv 2006–07, Crazy for You (drama serial) 2006, O-Ha! (sitcom) 2006, Maalaala Mo Kaya 2009, The Return of Iljimae (drama series) 2009, 2NE1 TV 2009–11; also appearances with 2NE1 on Inkigayo (SBS) 2009–11, M! Countdown (Mnet) 2009–11, Music Bank 2009–11. *Honours:* numerous awards for 2NE1 including: Asia Song Festival Asian Newcomer's Award 2009, Melon Music Awards for New Artist and Top 10 2009, for Top 10 2010, Mnet 20's Choice Awards for Hot New Star 2009, Hot CF Star 2009 and Hot Online Song 2009, Mnet Asian Music Awards for Best New Female Artist 2009, for Music Portal Award 2009, for Song of the Year 2009, for Best Music Video 2009, 2010, for Best Female Group 2010, for Artist of the Year 2010, Rhythmer Awards for R&B Artist of the Year and Rookie of the Year 2009, Style Icon Best Female Singer Awards 2009, 2010, MTV Daum Music Fest Award for Artist of the Year 2011, MYX Music Favorite K-pop Video Award 2011; also numerous Cyworld Digital Music Awards including Top Selling Artist Award 2009, Newcomer of the Year 2010, Bonsang Award 2010, Artist of the Year Award 2010, Song of the Year 2010. *Address:* c/o YG Entertainment, 397–5 YG Building, Hapjeong-Dong, Mapo-Gu, Seoul 109-819, South Korea (office). *Telephone:* (2) 3143-1105 (office). *Fax:* (2) 544-1546 (office). *E-mail:* web@ ygmail.net (office). *Website:* eng.ygfamily.com/main/main.html (office); www .yg-2ne1.com (home).

DARATISTA, Inul, (Ainur Rokhimah); Indonesian singer; b. 21 Jan. 1979, Kejapanan, Gempol, East Java. *Career:* began performing career as rock singer aged 12; singer of 'dangdut' pop (blend of Indian, Malay and Arab music); performed on Warung Tojedo TV programme 2003; Indonesian Muslim Council issued edict against her for style of dancing; also criticized by other dangdut singers for corrupting the genre; owns chain of karaoke clubs in Indonesia. *Recordings include:* Kenapa Harus Inul, Two in One, Surabaya, Kepiye Mas, Cinta Suci, Mandarin, Pacar Asli, Embah Dukun, Tarling Koplo Mbah Dukun, De Bronnen van de Liefde 2000, Goyang Inul 2003, Separuh Nafas 2004, Too Phat-Rebirth Into Reality 2005, Mau Dong 2006, Ash-Sholaatu 2006, Rasain Lho 2008, Buaya Buntung 2012, Religius 2013.

D'ARBY, Terence Trent, (Sananda Maitreya); American singer, songwriter and producer; b. 15 March 1962, New York; m. Francesca Maitreya 2003. *Education:* Univ. of Central Florida. *Career:* lead singer German band, Touch 1980–86; joined The Bojangels 1986; solo artist 1986–; f. Sananda Records 2001; legally changed name to Sananda Maitreya 2001; numerous concerts and tours, television appearances. *Recordings include:* albums: Introducing The Hardline According To... (Grammy Award for Best R&B Vocal Performance) 1987, Neither Fish Nor Flesh 1989, Symphony Or Damn – The Tension Inside The Sweetness 1993, Vibrator 1995, Wildcard 2001, Angels and Vampires 2004, Angels and Vampires Volume II 2006, Nigor Mortis 2009, The Sphinx 2011, Return to Zooathalon 2013. *Television and film appearances include:* Heimat II: A Chronicle of a Generation (TV series) 1993, Shake, Rattle and Roll: An American Love Story (TV mini-series) 1999, Clubland (film) 1999, Static Shock (TV series) 2000. *Honours:* BRIT Award for Best International Newcomer 1988, Grammy Award for Best Vocal Performance by Duo or Group (with Booker T and the MG's) 1995. *E-mail:* info@ sanandamaitreya.com. *Website:* www.sanandamaitreya.com.

D'ARCY, Deck; French musician (bass guitar) and songwriter; b. (Frederic Moulin-Vidal), 1977, Versailles. *Education:* Lycée Hoche, Versailles. *Career:* mem. Phoenix 1997–. *Recordings:* albums: United 2000, Alphabetical 2004, It's Never Been Like That 2006, Wolfgang Amadeus Phoenix (Grammy Award for Best Alternative Album 2010) 2009, Bankrupt! 2013. *Address:* c/o Glassnote Music, 770 Lexington Avenue, New York, NY 10065, USA (office). *E-mail:* info@glassnotemusic.com (office). *Website:* www.glassnotemusic.com (office); www.wearephoenix.com.

D'ARCY, Doug, BA; British music executive; b. 23 Feb. 1946, Hull, Yorks., England; m. Catherine Williams 1974; one s. one d. *Education:* Hull Grammar School, Univ. of Manchester. *Career:* booking agent and manager, Ellis-Wright Agency 1968, later became Chrysalis Records, Man. Dir Chrysalis Records 1970–85, Pres. 1985–89; Founder and Man. Dir Dedicated Records (jt venture with BMG) 1990–98; Founder, Owner, music consultant, management and investment co. Songlines 1998–; Founding Bd mem. Asscn of Ind. Music (Chair. Training, Educ. and Mentoring Cttee). *Telephone:* (7770) 653255 (mobile) (office). *E-mail:* songlines@dougdarcy.com (office). *Website:* www.dougdarcy.com.

DARLING, David, BMus, MMus; American cellist and producer; b. 3 March 1941, Elkhart, Ind.; two d. *Education:* Indiana State Univ., Berklee Coll. of Music. *Career:* f. jazz ensemble at university; elementary and secondary school orchestra and band conductor, Evansville, Ind. 1966–69; faculty cellist, coll. orchestra conductor and music educ. teacher, Western Kentucky Univ. 1969–70; mem. Paul Winter Consort, Nashville 1970–87; fmr asst prin. cellist, Nashville Symphony Orchestra; co-f. Music for People (non-profit org.) 1986. *Films:* contrib. to soundtracks including Until the End of the World 1991, Nouvelle Vague 1996, For Ever Mozart 1996, Heat 1997, Mostly Martha 2001, Metaphors 2003, Salim Baba 2008. *Recordings:* albums: with Paul Winter Consort: Road 1970, Icarus 1972, Turtle Island 1978, Common Ground 1978; solo: Journal October 1980, Cycles 1981, Cello 1992, Dark Wood 1993, Cello Blue (Association for Independent Music AFIM Indie Award) 2001, The Tao of Cello 2003, Prayer for Compassion (Grammy Award for Best New Age Album 2010) 2009; numerous collaborations including: with Terje Rypdal: Eos 1984,

Skywards 1996; with Michael Jones: Amber 1987; with Radhika Miller: Origins 1988, Gems of Grace 1990, Blossoms in the Snow 1994, Arabesque 1996, Heaven 2003, Dancing Light 2008; with Peter Kater: Homage 1989, Migration 1992; with Sidsel Endreson: Exile 1993; with Ketil Bjørnstad, Terje Rypdal and Jon Christensen: The Sea 1995, The Sea II 1998; with Wind Over the Earth and Mickey Houlihan: Eight String Religion 1993, River Notes 2002, Refuge 2002; with Pierre Favre: Window Steps 1996; with Ketil Bjørnstad: The River 1996, Epigraphs 2000; with The Adagio Ensemble: Musical Massage–Balance 2000, Musical Massage–In Tune 2001, Open Window 2004; with Barry Lopez: River Notes 2002; with the Wulu Bunun: Mudanin Kata 2004; with Eric Roberts: In a Silent Place 2007; with Julie Weber: The Darling Conversations 2007; with Eve Kodiak: The Return of Desire: Improvisations 2008; with Chungliang Al Huang: The Tao of Poetry 2008; with Dakota Suite: The End of Trying 2009; with Jacqueline Tschabold Bhuyan: Reflections on Life's Journey 2009; other appearances: Old Friends, New Friends, Ralph Towner 1979; as producer: Keys to the Inside, Jane Buttars 1999, Tranzdanze, Monica Robelotto 2001 (also cellist), Like a River Through Me, Susan Rosati 2001, The Open Door to Everything, Chad Hardin 2001, Nightingale, Sarah Swersey 2002, Coming Home, Patricia Mulholland 2005, Passages Through Light, Mary Azima Jackson 2006, Seasons of the Soul, Karen Olson 2007, Dark Heart, Suzann Kole 2008. *Publications include:* as contributor: Open Ears: Musical Adventures for a New Generation 1995. *Honours:* Board of Directors of Young Audiences Inc Award for Artist of the Year 1995. *Address:* David Darling Productions, PO Box 397, 187 Sherbrook Drive, Goshen, CT 06756, USA (office). *Telephone:* (860) 491-0215 (office). *Fax:* (860) 491-4513 (office). *E-mail:* david@daviddarling.com (office). *Website:* www.daviddarling.com.

DARLING, Helen, BA; American singer and songwriter; b. 5 May, Baton Rouge, LA; m. Dennis Darling. *Education:* University of Texas, Austin. *Career:* jingle singer, Chicago; demo singer, Nashville; singer on Garth Brooks' The Red Strokes; co-writer with: Bob DiPiero; John Scott Sherill; Karen Staley; Chuck Jones; Michael Omartian. *Compositions include:* co-written with Tena Clark, Gary Prim: When The Butterflies Have Flown Away. *Recordings include:* albums: Helen Darling, 1995, Who Am I Tonight? 2003, Circus Town 2011. *E-mail:* helendarling@hotmail.com. *Website:* www.helendarlingmusic.com.

DARLINGTON, Jay; British musician (keyboards); b. 3 May 1969, Sidcup, England. *Career:* mem. The Kays, renamed Kula Shaker 1995–; numerous live tours and TV appearances; many festival appearances. *Recordings include:* Albums: K (No. 1, UK) 1996, Peasants Pigs and Astronauts 1999, Strangefolk 2007, Dig Out Your Soul 2008, Don't Hear It… Fear It! 2012. *Honours:* BRIT Award, Best British Newcomer 1997. *E-mail:* maurice@baconempire.com. *Address:* Kula Shaker, StrangeF.O.L.K LLP, 19 Portland Place, London, W1B 1PX, England (office). *E-mail:* kulashakerofficial@googlemail.com (office). *Website:* www.kulashakermusic.com (office).

DARYA, Farhad; Afghan singer, songwriter, composer and musician (rubab); b. 22 Sept. 1962, Gozargaah; m. Sultana Emam; one s. *Education:* Polytechnic Inst., Kabul, Univ. of Kabul. *Career:* formed band, Goroh-e-Baran 1983, which became the official orchestra for Afghan Radio and Television; songwriter and composer under the pseudonym Abr; Adjunct Prof. of Classical Music, Faculty of Fine Art, Univ. of Kabul 1985; exiled, left Afghanistan for the Czech Republic, Germany, France, USA; solo artist, singing in many regional Afghan languages and playing traditional Afghan instruments; concerts worldwide. *Recordings include:* albums: Rahe Rafta 1981, Afghan Folk Music 1982, Zaro jane 1982, Baran 1983, Ghazal 1985, Bolbole Awara 1986, Mazdeegar 1988, Bazme Ghazal 1988, Mehrabaani 1989, Begum Jan 1991–92, Afghanistan 1995, Shakar 1997, In Foreign Land 1999, Qabila-e-Ashiq 2000, Golom Golom 2001, Gularoos 2001, Salaam Afghanistan 2004, HA! 2008, Yahoo 2008. *Honours:* Youth Magazine & Radio Afghanistan, Best Singer 1990, Int. Musical Enterprises, Inc, (for Best Performer of the Year) 1995, Star of the Contemporary Music of Afghanistan 1996, BBC World Service, Favourite Singer 1998, A.Y.C British Columbia & Aina-e-Afghan TV, Best Singer 1999, Nedaa-e-Watan TV & Radio, Best Singer of Afghanistan 2000, 2001, Human Rights Award 2007, Peace Building Award 2011. *Telephone:* (50) 5300754. *E-mail:* haroon@mysticrock.de. *Address:* 43050 Pemberton Square, Suite 120, #150 South Riding, VA 20152, USA. *E-mail:* management@farhaddarya.info. *Website:* www.farhaddarya.info.

DAS, Aniruddha, (Dr Das); British musician (bass guitar) and producer; b. London. *Career:* Founder-mem. Asian Dub Foundation 1993–2005; ind. bassist, producer, remixer 2005–, works with Emergency Bass Sound System, Visionary Underground. *Recordings include:* albums: Concious (EP) 1994, Facts and Fictions 1995, R.A.F.I. 1997, Rafi's Revenge 1998, Conscious Party 1998, Community Music 2000, Enemy of the Enemy 2003, Bangin' On The Walls 2003, Tank 2005, Wonderland 2006: as Dr Das: Emergency Basslines 2006, Preparing 4 War 2008. *Honours:* BBC Asian Award for Music 1998.

DAS NEVES, Wilson; Brazilian musician (percussion), singer and composer; b. 1936, Rio de Janeiro. *Education:* studied with Edgar Nunes Rocca, Joaquim Naegele, Darcy Barbosa, Moacir Santos. *Career:* played with Orquestra de Permínio Gonçalves 1957, Orquestra Ubirajara Silva 1959; mem. Orquestra Rádio Nacional 1962–63, Orquestra Sinfônica do Teatro Municipal do Rio de Janeiro 1963–64; mem. Os Ipanemas 1964–; also played with Globo and Excelsior TV orchestras; collaborations with Roberto Carlos, Chico Buarque, Eumir Deodato, Elizeth Cardoso, Clara Nunes, Elza Soares, Elis Regina, Beth

Carvalho, Tom Jobim. *Recordings include:* albums: with Os Ipanemas: Os Ipanemas 1966, The Return of the Ipanemas 2001, Afro Bossa 2003, Samba is our Gift 2006, Call of the Gods 2008, Que Beleza 2010; solo: Juventude 2000 1968, Som Quente é o Das Neves 1969, Samba-Tropi: Até aí Morreu Neves 1970, O som sagrado de Wilson das Neves 1997, Pra Gente Fazer Mais Um Samba 2010, Pra Gente Fazer um Samba 2011. *Address:* c/o Far Out Recordings, Unit 217, The Saga Centre, 326 Kensal Road, London, W10 5BZ, England. *E-mail:* info@faroutrecordings.com. *Website:* www.faroutrecordings.com.

DAUGHTRY, Christopher (Chris) Adam; American singer, songwriter and musician (guitar); b. 26 Dec. 1979, Roanoke Rapids, North Carolina; s. of Pete Daughtry and Sandra Daughtry; m. Deanna Robertson 2000; one s. one d. one step-d. one adopted s. *Career:* competitor on American Idol 2006; Founder mem. and lead singer Daughtry 2006–; songwriter for other acts including 12 Stones, Kris Allen, Allison Iraheta, Day of Fire, Colton Dixon. *Recordings include:* albums: with Daughtry: Daughtry (American Music Award for Best Pop/Rock Album 2007, Top Billboard 200 Album 2007) 2006, Leave this Town 2009, Break the Spell 2011, Baptized 2013; with Cadence: All Eyes on You 1999; with Absent Element: Uprooted 2005. *Honours:* American Music Awards for Breakthrough Artist, Best Adult Contemporary Artist 2007, People Choice Award for Best Rock Song (for Home) 2007, Billboard Music Awards for Top Artists (Pop Duo or Group), Top New Artist, Top Comprehensive Artist, Hot 100 Artists (Duo or Group), and Hot Adult Top 40 Artist 2007, World Music Awards for World's Best-Selling Rock Group of 2007, for World's Best-Selling New Artist of 2007. *Current Management:* c/o 19 Entertainment, 8560 West Sunset Blvd, 9th Floor, West Hollywood, Los Angeles, CA 90069, USA. *E-mail:* inquiries@19entertainment.com. *Website:* www.daughtryofficial.com.

DAURAT, Jean-Sebastien; French musician (guitar); b. 11 Feb. 1961, Neuilly Sur Seine; two s. *Education:* art school. *Career:* played with H. Leonard, Corine Marchand, Maria Glen, Marion Montgomery, Erchy Lawson; own group, Jazz Oil Quintet; plays in numerous clubs, Paris (int. pop, rock, funk, jazz, Latin jazz); bass player on stage for Amarande Story, theatre production; on tour each year in South of France; mem. Société des auteurs, compositeurs et éditeurs de musique (SACEM). *Recordings include:* On Ne Discute Pas 1997, On ne Panique pas 1998, Jazz Oil Spirit 1999, Un Jour, le lendemain 1999.

DAVENPORT, Bob; British singer; b. 31 May 1932, Newcastle upon Tyne, England. *Education:* St Martins Coll. of Art, London. *Career:* mem., Bob Davenport and The Rakes; solo folk artist; appeared at Newport Folk Festival with Joan Baez, Phil Ochs, Bob Dylan, Tom Paxton 1963; guest on Pete Seeger's Central Park and Tanglewood concerts 1967; mem. Equity. *Recordings include:* Wor Geordie 1960, The Iron Muse 1963, Farewell Nancy 1964, Northumbrian Minstrelcy 1964, Bob Davenport and The Rakes 1965, Bob Davenport 1971, Bob Davenport and The Marsden Rattlers 1971, Pal of My Cradle Days 1974, Down The Long Road 1975, Postcards Home 1977, The Common Stone 2004; with The Rakes 1977, The Good Old Way – British Folk Music Today 1980, Will's Barn 1990, From The Humber To The Tweed 1991, The Red-Haired Lad 1998; with Roger Digby: Send Your Best Men Forward 2001, Wait Till The Work Comes Round 2002; guest on albums by David Essex, Mike Harding, Watersons, Flowers and Frolics (Reformed Characters album) 2000. *Television:* Cvitanovich's Road To Wigan Pier (documentary, Thames TV). *Address:* 14 Calthorpe Street, London, WC1X 0JS, England (home). *E-mail:* bob.davenport@lineone.net (home).

DAVERNE, Gary Michiel, ONZM, DipEd, FTCL, LRSM; New Zealand music director, composer, conductor, music producer and fmr schoolteacher; *Music Director Emeritus, Auckland Symphony Orchestra;* b. 26 Jan. 1939, Takapuna, Auckland, North Island; s. of Ron Daverne and Mollie Daverne; m. Sophia Yang. *Education:* Univ. of Auckland, Auckland Teachers Coll., Trinity Coll. of Music, UK. *Career:* grew up as a rock 'n' roll musician, playing piano and saxophone in New Zealand rock groups; teacher of econs and accountancy 1962–77; began career as a record producer early 1960s, produced more than 40 albums, several hit single records and one platinum and two gold albums; leading musical arranger and dir for Television New Zealand 1970s; now an int. composer and orchestral conductor, having conducted many of the world's major orchestras; Composer in Schools 1978–79; Pres. Composers' Asscn, New Zealand 1979; Founder, Music Dir and Conductor, Auckland Symphony Orchestra 1975–2010, Music Dir Emer. 2010–; Dir of Music, Waitangi Day celebrations 1975; Music Dir Mil. Searchlight Tattoo, New Plymouth 1997; Music Dir/Arranger, Man of Sorrows rock musical 1973; Music Dir for premiere of Jewish oratorio, Hear! O Israel by Cormac O'Duffy, celebrating Israel's 50th nat. birthday. *Compositions include:* recorded more than 100 pop songs, seven children's musicals, operettas, songs for children, three rock operas, concert accordion music, more than 500 TV and radio jingles, film soundtracks; many symphonic works for orchestra (recorded by New Zealand Symphony Orchestra, Moravian Philharmonic), including Rhapsody for Accordion and Orchestra, Gallipoli: Rhapsody for Trumpet and Orchestra. *Recordings include:* ten CDs of original music. *Honours:* Rotary Int. Paul Harris Fellow, Variety Artists Club of New Zealand Scroll of Honour 2000, Confed. Internationale des Accordéonistes Honoured Friend of the Accordion Award 2009, Companion of North Shore City Award 2010, Benny Award, Variety Artist Club of New Zealand 2010. *Address:* 48 Shelly Beach Road, Herne Bay, Auckland 1011, New Zealand (home). *Telephone:* (9) 378-6932 (office). *Fax:* (9) 378-6932 (office). *E-mail:* daverne@ihug.co.nz. *Website:* www.garydaverne.gen.nz.

DAVEY, Cathy; Irish singer, songwriter and musician; b. Wicklow. *Career:* solo artist 2003–. *Recordings include:* albums: Something Ilk 2004, Tales of Silversleeve 2007. *Honours:* Meteor Award for Best Irish Female 2008. *Website:* www.cathydavey.ie.

DAVEY, Rick, BA; British music publisher, record label executive and producer; b. 11 Jan. 1952, Devon. *Education:* Univ. of London. *Career:* jazz/blues musician, saxophone and keyboards from age 15; music consultant, Tomorrow's World, BBC; artist man. for Silver Bullet; tour man. for Big Youth/Alton Ellis; studio man. Machelle Alexander; acts and labels controlled include: Custers Last Stand Records (Kissing The Pink), Black Cat Records (Jungle/Reggae), Flowsound Ltd publish Zion Train, Terence McKenna (Shamen), KOTOT, Dennis Alcapone; tour man. Black Uhuru, Mindlink, Justin Hinds, Jonny Osbourne; mem. PRS, MCPS. *Recordings include:* New Era, on Face film with Damon Albarn (Blur), Bible and the Gun, Devon Russell, UTE, Black Cat, Tassoulla.

DAVEY, Shaun; Irish composer; b. 1948, Holywood, Co. Down; m. Rita Connolly. *Education:* Trinity Coll., Dublin, Courtauld Inst. of Fine Art, London. *Compositions include:* music for stage: Fair Maid of the West 1987, The Lion, The Witch and The Wardrobe 1998–2002, Pericles 2002, The Tempest 1993, King Lear 1993, A Winter's Tale 1993 (all for Royal Shakespeare Co.), Observe the Sons of Ulster Marching towards the Somme (Abbey Theatre, Dublin) 1992, The Well of the Saints 1993, The Steward of Christendom (Royal Court Theatre, London) 1996, James Joyce's The Dead (USA) (New York Drama Critics Circle Award for Best Musical) 1999, Lady from the Sea (Almeida Theatre, London) 2003, Skellig (Young Vic, London) 2003; music for film: The Tailor of Panama, Waking Ned, Twelfth Night; music for TV: Ballykissangel (series) (TRIC Award for Best Signature Theme), The Hanging Gale (series) (Ivor Novello Award), David Copperfield (feature film); documentaries: The Spice Islands Voyage, In Search of Moby Dick, In Search of Robinson Crusoe; other: music for Dublin Special Olympics 2003. *Recordings include:* concert works: The Brendan Voyage 1980, The Pilgrim, Granuaile, The Relief of Derry Symphony. *Address:* Tara Music, Basement, 18 Upper Mount Street, Dublin, 2, Ireland. *Fax:* (1) 6787873. *Website:* www .taramusic.com; www.shaundavey.com.

DAVID, Craig Ashley; British singer and songwriter; b. 5 May 1981, Southampton, England. *Education:* Southampton City Coll. *Career:* worked as club DJ and pirate radio presenter before meeting with local musician (and Artful Dodger mem.) Mark Hill; provided vocals for Artful Dodger duo; solo artist 1999–. *Recordings include:* albums: Born To Do It 2000, Slicker Than Your Average 2002, The Story Goes 2005, Trust Me 2007, Signed Sealed Delivered 2010. *Honours:* Hon. DMus, Southampton Solent Univ. 2008; MOBO Awards for Best Newcomer, Best R&B Act, Best UK Single 2001, Urban Music Award for Outstanding Achievement 2005. *Current Management:* CLM Entertainment, RB Building, Portobello Dock, 557 Harrow Road, London, W10 4RH, England. *Telephone:* (20) 8206-6500. *E-mail:* info@clm -entertainment.com. *Website:* clm-entertainment.com; www.craigdavid.com.

DAVIDO; Nigerian singer, rapper, songwriter and record producer; b. (David Adedeji Adeleke), 21 Nov. 1992, Atlanta, Ga, USA; s. of Chief Deji Adeleke and Vero Adeleke. *Education:* British Int. School, Lagos, Oakwood Univ., USA, Babcock Univ., Ogun State. *Career:* released debut recording Back When 2011; numerous collaborations including Mafikizolo, Mi Casa, Lola Rae, Sarkodie, Diamond Platnumz, Tiwa Savage. *Recordings:* album: Omo Baba Olowo 2012. *Honours:* Nigeria Entertainment Award for Best New Act of the Year 2012, for Best Collaboration 2012, 2014, for Hottest Single 2012, 2014, for Best Pop/R&B Artiste 2013, for Male Artist of the Year 2014, Kora Best Newcomer Award 2014, BET Best Int. Act: Africa Award 2014, African Musik Magazine Awards for Best Male West Africa 2014, for Artist of the Year 2014, MTV Africa Music Awards for Best Male Artist 2014, 2015, for Artist of the Year 2014. *Current Management:* c/o Kamal Ajiboye, Twenty20 Media, 6A Wole Ariyo, Lekki Phase 1, Lagos, Nigeria. *Telephone:* 7066642805. *E-mail:* booking@twenty20media.com.ng. *Website:* twenty20media.com.ng; iamdavido .com.

DAVIDS, Brent Michael, MMus; American musician (quartz crystal flutes); b. 4 June 1959, Madison, WI. *Career:* appearance on Sunday Morning with the Kronos Quartet, CBS, feature on Sunday Morning, 1997; performed with Kronos Quartet at Brooklyn Academy of Music, Lincoln Center Out-of-Doors, 1996, 1999; performed with Joffrey Ballet, 1998–99; performed with New Mexico Symphony Orchestra, 1999; mem. American Composers Forum; American Music Center; Society of Composers Inc; ATLATL. *Compositions:* Pauwau, for New Mexico Symphony Orchestra; Moon of the Falling Leaves for Joffrey Ballet; Singing Woods; Turtle People, and Native American National Anthem, for Kronos Quartet; Night Chant, for Chanticleer, Trumpeting the Stone 2006. *Recordings:* albums: Ni-Tcang 1992. *Honours:* ASCAP, 1989; International Music Festival, 1990; NEA grant, 1994; Rockefeller Fellowship, 1998; Sundance Institute Composer Fellowship, 1998. *Address:* Blue Butterfly Group, 1043 Grand Avenue, Suite 280, St. Paul, MN 55105, USA. *Telephone:* (651) 778-9611. *Website:* www.mnartists.org.

DAVIES, Bruce William; British musician, singer, songwriter and broadcaster; b. 25 Nov. 1955, Kirkcaldy, Fife, Scotland; s. of George Davies and Williamina Davies (née Knight); m. 3rd Sandra Davies 2004; three s.

Education: Royal Scottish Acad. of Music and Drama. *Career:* with folk duo Beggar's Mantle 1983–90; solo artist 1990–; TV appearances on BBC, Scottish, Border, Grampian, Ulster, various US channels; performances mainly in UK, but also in, Europe, Africa, USA, Canada; fmr presenter of weekly radio shows; host/singer, Jamie's Scottish Evening (Scotland's longest running variety show). *Recordings include:* albums: Livin' to Love, Lovin' to Live 2005, Then and Now 2008, Hand Picked 2010, Till A' The Seas Gang Dry 2011, plus 15 other solo albums no longer available; four albums with Beggars Mantle 1980s; produced/arranged and/or played on albums by Harvey Andrews, McCalmans, Scottish Tourist Board, Nell Hannah, Bill (Belinda) Jones and others. *Honours:* winner, Edinburgh Folk Club Songwriting Competition 1995. *Current Management:* c/o Rothes Recordings, PO Box 7, Glenrothes, Fife KY6 1YG, Scotland. *E-mail:* brucedavies@iname.com. *Website:* www .brucedavies.com.

DAVIES, Gareth; British musician (bass guitar). *Career:* mem. rock band, Funeral for a Friend 2001–08. *Recordings include:* albums: Casually Dressed & Deep in Conversation 2003, Hours 2005, Tales Don't Tell Themselves 2007, Memory and Humanity 2008. *Honours:* Kerrang! Award for Best British Band 2006. *Website:* www.ffaf.co.uk.

DAVIES, Mark John, BA; British musician (keyboards), singer, record producer and remixer; b. 19 Nov. 1969, Ampthill, Bedfordshire. *Education:* Univ. of East Anglia. *Career:* keyboards, vocals with Messiah 1990–; numerous television appearances, concerts; mem. Musicians' Union. *Recordings include:* album: 21st Century Jesus 1994; singles include: There Is No Law 1991, Temple of Dreams 1992, I Feel Love 1992, Thunderdome 1994, Creator, with Ian Astbury, Peace and Tranquility, 20,000 Hardcore Members 1990, Law of The Night, Marc Almond.

DAVIES, Matt; British singer and songwriter. *Career:* mem. and lead singer of rock band, Funeral for a Friend 2001–; side project, The Secret Show 2007–. *Recordings include:* albums: with Funeral for a Friend: Casually Dressed & Deep in Conversation 2003, Hours 2005, Tales Don't Tell Themselves 2007, Memory and Humanity 2008, Welcome Home Armageddon 2011, Conduit 2013; with The Secret Show: Impressionist Road Map of the West 2007. *Honours:* Kerrang! Award for Best British Band 2006. *Current Management:* c/o Raw Power Management, Bridle House, 36 Bridle Lane, London, W1F 9BZ, England. *Telephone:* (845) 331-3300. *Fax:* (845) 331-3500. *E-mail:* info@ rawpowermanagement.com. *Website:* rawpowermanagement.com; www .funeralforafriend.com.

DAVIES, Neol Edward; songwriter, musician (guitar) and guitar teacher; b. 26 April 1952, Coventry, England. *Career:* Founder, 2 Tone Records with The Specials; Founder-mem. The Selecter; tours of USA, Europe, Japan; mem. Selecter Instrumental (8-piece instrumental ska band); television and radio broadcasts; mem. MU. *Recordings include:* The Selecter 1979, On My Radio 1979, Three Minute Hero 1980, Too Much Pressure 1980, Missing Words 1980, The Whisper 1980, Celebrate The Bullet 1981, Selecter Greatest Hits 1996, Cruel Britannia 2000. *Address:* 35 Dillotford Avenue, Coventry, CV3 5DR, England.

DAVIES, Patricia Gail; American country singer, songwriter, musician and producer; *Record Executive, Little Chickadee Productions*; b. 5 June 1948, Broken Bow, Okla; m. 3rd Robert Victor Price; one s. *Education:* South Kitsap High School, Port Orchard, Wash. *Career:* own touring band featuring husband and son; featured in TV specials, The Women of Country and Lost Highway (BBC documentary); toured with Neil Young, Willie Nelson, Carl Perkins, Glen Campbell, Don Williams, Roger Miller; formed country-rock band, Wild Choir; Staff Producer, Liberty Records 1991, developed new acts including Mandy Barnett, Niki Dean; Founder Little Chickadee Records 1995; Country Music Int. Amb. 2009–. *Compositions include:* Bucket to the South, for Ava Barber 1977, Someone Is Looking For Someone Like You, Grandma's Song; music for Amy Merrill's play Cigarettes and Whiskey. *Recordings include:* albums: Gail Davies 1978, The Game 1980, I'll Be There 1980, Giving Herself Away 1982, Where Is A Woman To Go 1984, Pretty Words 1989, The Other Side of Love 1990, The Best of Gail Davies 1991, Gail Davies' Greatest Hits 1998, Live and Unplugged At The Station Inn (voted one of 10 Best Albums of 2001 by the Nashville Scene and New York Times) 2001, The Songwriter Sessions 2003, Unsung Hero: A Tribute to the Music of Ron Davies 2013; singles: No Love Have I, Someone Is Looking For Someone Like You, Blue Heartache, Like Strangers, Good Lovin' Man, It's A Lovely Lovely World (with Emmylou Harris), Round the Clock Lovin', Grandma's Song, Blue Heartache, Singing the Blues, Hold On, You Turn Me On I'm a Radio, You're A Hard Dog To Keep Under The Porch, Boys Like You, Break Away, Jagged Edge of a Broken Heart, Unwed Fathers (featuring Dolly Parton). *Publication:* The Last of the Outlaws (autobiography) 2011. *Honours:* Best New Female Vocalist, DJs of America, IBMA award for duet on Ralph Stanley's Clinch Mountain Sweethearts 2002. *Address:* Little Chickadee Productions, PO Box 120545, Nashville, TN 37212-0545, USA (office). *E-mail:* LCPStudio@Juno .com (office). *Website:* www.gaildavies.com.

DAVIES, Peter Max Crofts, BA; British luthier, instrument designer and musician (guitar, sonome); *Inventor, Designer, The Shape of Music*; b. 30 Nov. 1950, Salisbury, Wilts., England; s. of David Davies and Ilse Muller; m. Patricia Anne 1981, one s. one d. *Education:* Wimbledon School of Art. *Career:* invented Melodic Table musical note pattern and its use in new isomorphic keyboard instrument, 'Sonome' 1983; guitar technician to various artists 1987–2004; R&D consultant to Goodfellow Guitars 1985–87, to Patrick Eggle

Guitars 1993–95; consultant for care and preservation of Jimi Hendrix's Black Stratocaster guitar; initiated design of new MIDI musical interface based on Melodic Table; Inventor, Designer, 'Shape Of Music'; est. manufacture of Sonome models, 'Chameleon' and 'Gecko' 2004–; Sonome instruments used by keyboardist Dino Soldo for Lionel Richie and Leonard Cohen world tours 2008–10, NASA scientist Kelly Snooks for research programme 2009, featured in Bohlen-Pierce Symposium, Boston, USA 2010 and in use by Microtonal composers X. J. Scott and Carlo Serafini 2009–; currently collaborating with Caesar Glebbeek on new book, Jimi Hendrix: The Definitive Guide to His Guitars and Gear 1969–1970. *Publications:* contrib. to The Inner World of Jimi Hendrix by Monika Dannemann 1995, contrib. of information and images to biographical publ. Until We Meet Again: The Last Weeks of Jimi Hendrix by Caesar Glebbeek 2011, contrib. of Sonome photograph and music sample to World Explorers Coursework 2 2013. *Address:* The Shape of Music, 6 Pleasant Row, Woodford, Kettering, Northants., NN14 4HP, England (office). *Telephone:* (1832) 733214 (office). *E-mail:* info@theshapeofmusic.com (office); info@dreamguitarservices.co.uk (office). *Website:* www .theshapeofmusic.com (office); www.dreamguitarservices.co.uk (office).

DAVIES, Ray, CBE; British singer, songwriter, musician (guitar) and producer; b. 21 June 1944, Muswell Hill, London, England; m. 1st Rasa Didztpetris 1964; two d.; m. 2nd Yvonne; one d. with Chrissie Hynde. *Education:* Hornsey Art Coll., Croydon Coll. of Art. *Career:* Founder, Ray Davies Quartet aged 16, later renamed The Ravens; group became The Kinks 1963–; numerous concerts and tours world-wide, festival appearances; solo artist. *Film and television appearances include:* The Long Distance Piano Player (TV) 1970, Return to Waterloo 1985, Absolute Beginners 1986. *Recordings include:* albums: with The Kinks: Kinks 1964, Kinda Kinks 1965, Kinkdom 1965, Kinks-Size 1965, The Kink Kontroversy 1965, You Really Got Me 1965, Face to Face 1966, Something Else 1967, The Village Green Preservation Society 1968, Arthur (Or the Decline and Fall of the British Empire) 1969, Lola vs the Powerman & the Money-Go-Round Pt 1 1970, Percy (OST) 1971, Muswell Hillbillies 1971, Everybody's in Show-Biz 1972, Preservation: Act 1 1973, The Great Lost Kinks Album 1973, Preservation: Act 2 1974, The Kinks Present a Soap Opera 1975, The Kinks Present Schoolboys in Disgrace 1975, Sleepwalker 1977, Misfits 1978, Low Budget 1979, One for the Road 1980, Glamour 1981, Give the People What They Want 1981, State of Confusion 1983, Word of Mouth 1984, Think Visual 1987, Road 1988, UK Jive 1989, Phobia 1993, To the Bone 1994, The Early Years 1994, It's the Kinks 1999, Something Else by the Kinks 2000, BBC Sessions 1964–77 2001; solo: Return to Waterloo 1985, The Storyteller 1998, Other People's Lives 2006, Working Man's Café 2007, The Kinks Choral Collection 2009, See My Friends 2010. *Honours:* inducted into Rock and Roll Hall of Fame 1990, Ivor Novello Award for Special Contribution to Music 1990, Q Award for Classic Song (for Waterloo Sunset) 2005, BMI Icon Award 2006. *Current Management:* c/o The Agency Group Ltd, 361-373 City Road, London, EC1V 1PQ, England. *E-mail:* info@raydavies.info. *Website:* www.raydavies.info.

DAVIES, Rhodri John, BMus, MA, PGCTCM; British musician (harp), improviser, composer and artist; b. 19 Dec. 1971, Aberystwyth, Wales. *Education:* Univ. of Sheffield, Trinity Coll. of Music, London, Univ. of Huddersfield. *Career:* harpist, London 1995–2007, Newcastle-upon-Tyne 2007–15, Swansea/Abertawe 2015–; worked with Derek Bailey, Steve Beresford, Angharad Davies, Richard Dawson, Evan Parker, David Toop, Kahimi Karie, John Zorn, Jim O'Rourke, Ben Patterson, Philip Corner, Christian Wolff, Otomo Yoshihide, John Butcher, Sachiko M, Eliane Radigue. *Compositions:* Trem 2001, Perdereau 2004, Camber 2004, Over Shadows 2006, Five Knots 2008, Room Harp 2010, Dry Ice Harp 2010, Cut and Burn 2010, Wound Response 2012, An Air Swept Clean of All Distance 2014, Richard Dawson: Nothing Important 2014, Jenny Hval: Apocalypse, Girl 2015. *Recordings:* Murray The Hump – Songs of Ignorance 2001, Cinematic Orchestra – Every Day 2002, Bent – Ariels 2004, The Magic Numbers – Anima Sola 2005, Kahimi Karie – Nunki 2006, The Magic Numbers – Those the Brokes 2006, Cinematic Orchestra – Live at the Royal Albert Hall 2008, Dawson-Davies: Hen Ogledd 2013,. *Honours:* Foundation for Contemporary Arts Award 2012. *Telephone:* (191) 491-1459 (office); 7946-423627 (mobile) (office). *E-mail:* rhodrijd@yahoo.co.uk (office). *Website:* www.rhodridavies .com.

DAVIES, Saul; British musician (guitar, violin, percussion) and singer; b. 28 June 1965, England. *Career:* mem., James 1990–2002, re-formed 2007–; numerous tours, festivals dates and TV appearances; band manager 2002–. *Recordings include:* albums: Gold Mother 1990, Seven 1992, Laid 1993, Wah Wah 1994, Whiplash 1997, The Best Of James 1998, Millionaires 1999, B-Sides Ultra 2001, Pleased To Meet You 2001, Getting Away With It 2002, Hey Ma 2008, The Night Before 2010, The Morning After 2010, La Petite Mort 2014. *Address:* c/o Mercury Records, 364–366 Kensington High Street, London W14 8NS, England (office). *Website:* www.wearejames.com.

DAVIS, Anthony Curtis, BA; American composer, improviser and academic; *Professor of Music, University of California at San Diego;* b. 20 Feb. 1951, Paterson, NJ; s. of Charles T. Davis and Jeanne C. Davis; m. Cynthia Aaronson-Davis; two s. *Education:* Yale Univ. *Career:* appearances in USA and abroad as jazz pianist and Dir of Episteme, giving performances of improvised music 1970s; Co-founder Advent 1973; pianist in Leo Smith's New Delta Ahkri Band 1974–77; played in New York with violinist Leroy Jenkins 1977–79 and other mems of Advancement of Creative Musicians; taught music and Afro-American studies, Yale Univ. 1982–92, Visiting Composer

1990, 1993, 1996; Sr Fellow, Soc. for the Humanities, Cornell Univ. 1987; Visiting Lecturer in Afro-American Studies, Harvard Univ. 1992–96; Prof. of Music, Univ. of California at San Diego 1998–. *Plays:* Angels in America (on Broadway) 1993–94, King Lear (Yale Rep) 2004. *Compositions include:* Piano Concerto Wayang V 1984, Opera X: The Life and Times of Malcolm X (premiered at New York City Opera) 1986, Notes from the Underground for Orchestra 1988, Under the Double Moon (premiered at Opera Theater of St Louis) 1989, Tania (opera) 1992, Amistad, opera (premiered by Lyric Opera of Chicago) 1997, Jacob's Ladder, for orchestra 1997, Wakonda's Dream, opera (for Opera Omaha) 2007, Lilith, opera (premiered at Univ. of Calif. at San Diego) 2009, Lear on the 2nd Floor (opera) 2013. *Recordings:* Of Blues and Dreams 1978, Hidden Voices 1979, Under the Double Moon 1982. *Honours:* American Acad. of Arts and Letters Award 1996, Guggenheim Fellowship 2006. *Telephone:* (212) 765-9564 (office). *Address:* Department of Music, University of California at San Diego, CPMC 232, 9500 Gilman Drive, La Jolla, CA 92093, USA (office). *Telephone:* (858) 822-2543 (office). *E-mail:* adavis@ucsd.edu (office). *Website:* music.ucsd.edu (office).

DAVIS, Chip; American songwriter and composer; b. (Louis Davis Jr), Ohio; m. Trisha Davis; three c. *Education:* Univ. of Michigan. *Career:* new age music composer; composed first piece aged four; played percussion, Univ. of Michigan Marching Band; advertising jingle composer, Omaha, leading to record contract; Founder-mem. Mannheim Steamroller; created American Gramaphone record label; compositions used extensively on TV and radio, including: The Today Show, The Rush Limbaugh Show. *Compositions include:* Convoy (as C. W. McCall), Fresh Aire (series of albums) 1–8, music for television documentary, Saving The Wildlife, Ambience series. *Recordings include:* albums: Fresh Aire series, I–VIII 1983–2000 (Grammy Award for Best New Age Recording for Fresh Aire VII 1990), numerous Christmas and Halloween celebration recordings. *Honours:* Country Music Writer of the Year 1976. *Address:* Mannheim Steamroller, 9130 Mormon Bridge Road, Omaha, NE 68152, USA (office). *Telephone:* (402) 457-4341 (office). *Fax:* (402) 457-4332 (office). *Website:* www.amgram.com; www.mannheimsteamroller.com (office).

DAVIS, Clive; American music company executive and producer; *Chief Creative Officer, Sony BMG Worldwide;* b. 4 April 1932, New York. *Education:* New York Univ., Harvard Law School. *Career:* lawyer CBS 1960, Vice-Pres. and Gen. Man. 1966; with Columbia Records –1973, joined Bell Records 1974, founder Arista Records 1975, later Pres.; Founder, Chair. and CEO J Records (Jt project with RCA Music Group) 2000–08; Chair. and CEO RCA Music Group 2000–08; Chair. and CEO BMG North America 2000–08; Chief Creative Officer Sony BMG Worldwide 2008–; producer for Dido, Aretha Franklin, Sarah McLachlan, Whitney Houston, Billy Joel, Janis Joplin, Alicia Keys, Carlos Santana, Patti Smith and Bruce Springsteen. *Publications:* Clive – Inside the Record Business (autobiography) 1974, The Soundtrack of My Life (autobiography) 2013. *Honours:* Grammy Trustees Award 2000, Grammy President's Merit Award 2009. *Address:* Sony BMG, 550 Madison Avenue, New York, NY 10022-3211, USA (office). *Telephone:* (212) 833-8000 (office). *Website:* www.clivedavis.com.

DAVIS, Copeland, BFA; American pop and jazz musician (piano); b. 16 Aug. 1950, Orlando, Fla; m. Mary Birt Norman 1987. *Education:* Florida Atlantic Univ., Seminole State Coll. *Career:* arranger for The Fifth Dimension; conductor for Barbara McNair; arranger, guest artist, Florida Symphonic Pops Orchestra, Florida Sunshine Pops Orchestra, Space Coast Pops Orchestra, Indian River Pops Orchestra; Artist-in-Residence, Oxbridge Acad. of the Palm Beaches; numerous TV appearances; mem. BMI. *Recordings include:* albums: Smouldering Secrets 1975, Endangered Species 2002. *Honours:* Las Vegas Entertainers Hall of Fame, Las Vegas, Nev. *Current Management:* c/o Mary DeLater, Entertainment Consultants, Port Salerno, FL 34992, USA. *Telephone:* (772) 287-2515. *E-mail:* copeland@copelanddavis.com. *Website:* www.copelanddavis.com.

DAVIS, Don; American composer and conductor; b. 4 Feb. 1957, Anaheim, Calif.; m. Megan Davis; two c. *Education:* Univ. of California, Los Angeles. *Career:* mem. BMI, American Fed. of Music, Nat. Acad. of Recording Arts and Sciences, Acad. of Motion Picture Arts and Sciences, American Music Centre, Opera America, Hispanics for Los Angeles Opera, American Composers Forum, Amercian Civil Liberties Union, Center for Contemporary Opera, Amnesty Int., Sierra Club, MoveOn.org, Act Now to Stop War and End Racism, Progressive Democrats of America, UCLA Alumini Asscn. *Compositions include:* for television: Hart to Hart 1979, Sledge Hammer! 1986, Matlock 1986, Beauty and the Beast 1987, Star Trek: The Next Generation 1987, Bluegrass 1988, A Stoning in Fulham County 1988, Quiet Victory: The Charlie Wedemeyer Story 1988, Home Fires Burning 1989, Tiny Toon Adventures 1990, Running Against Time 1990, Lies Before Kisses 1991, My Life and Times 1991, A Little Piece of Heaven 1991, Notorious 1992, Capitol Critters 1992, Woman with a Past 1992, Murder of Innocence 1993, SeaQuest DSV 1993, Leave of Absence 1994, In the Best of Families: Marriage, Pride & Madness 1994, Sleep, Baby, Sleep 1995, Pandora's Clock 1996, For Love Alone: The Ivana Trump Story 1996, The Perfect Daughter 1996, The Beast 1996, In the Lake of the Woods 1996, The Third Twin 1997, House of Frankenstein 1997, Invasion 1997, A Match Made in Heaven 1997, The Alibi 1997, Not In This Town 1997, Life of the Party: The Pamela Harriman Story 1998, The Lake 1998, In the Company of Spies 1999, Race for Time 2000, MK Ultra 2000, Personally Yours 2000, Murder in Greenwich 2002, Space Odyssey: Voyage to the Planets 2004; for film: Hyperspace 1985, Blackout 1988, Spud 1991, Session Man 1993, When a Man Loves a Woman (additional music) 1994, Warriors of Virtue 1996, The Lesser Evil 1997, Bound 1997, Weapons of Mass Distraction 1997, Route 9 1998, Universal Soldier: The Return 1999, The Matrix 1999, House on Haunted Hill 1999, Turbulence II: Fear of Flying 1999, Antitrust 2001, Long Time Dead 2001, Valentine 2001, The Unsaid 2001, Jurassic Park III 2001, Behind Enemy Lines 2001, Long Time Dead 2002, Ballistic: Eck vs. Sever 2002, The Animatrix 2003, The Matrix Reloaded 2003, The Matrix Revolutions 2003, Mighty Times: The Children's March 2004, The Marine 2006, Ten Inch Hero 2007, The Good Life 2007; chamber music: Chronym I 1977, Trio 1978, 12 Poems for Jonathon David Wolf 1978, Chamber Concerto 1978, Timbral Spectra 1979, Chamber Variations 1979, Chronym II 1980, Chamber Symphony 1981, Chronym III 1981, Bleeding Particles 1983, Harsh 1988, Bleak 1989, The Eye and the Pyramid 1990, Going On 1992, Green Light 1992, What is the Silence 1993, Afterimages 1994, Of the Illuminated 1995, Flurry 1996, No Exit 1996, The Enchanted Place Suite, Pain 1998, Illicit Felicity 1999, Critical Mass 2000, Wandering 2002, A Lunatic Air 2002, Río de Sangre 2005. *Honours:* Emmy Awards, Beauty and the Beast, SeaQuest DSV. *Current Management:* c/o Randy Gerson, Fortress Talent Management, 23632 Calabasas Road, Suite 204, Calabasas, CA 91302, USA. *Telephone:* (818) 858-0020. *Website:* www .dondavis.net.

DAVIS, Eddy Ray; American composer, conductor and musician; b. 26 Sept. 1940, Greenhill, Ind. *Education:* Purdue Univ., Univ. of Chicago , Cosmopolitan Conservatory, Chicago School of Music. *Career:* numerous TV and live appearances, festivals worldwide; records and tours with Woody Allen; tours with George Segal; tours, recordings with Leon Redbone and Tom Waits; Musical Dir, Best of Spike Jones, Makin Whoopee, Warren G, Jazz Leggs; mem. New York Soc. for the Preservation of Illegitimate Music, The Bunk Project, The New York Banjo Ensemble. *Compositions include:* Penny Candy, Play For Me A Love Song, Now I'm Blue. *Recordings include:* soundtracks: Radio Days, Fried Green Tomatoes (with Patti Labelle), Sophie's Choice. *Publication:* The Theory Behind Chord Symbols.

DAVIS, Jean; French musician (drums, vibraphone, percussion); b. 2 March 1956, Suresnes, Paris; m. Cynthia Stone, March 1985; one s. one d. *Education:* Conservatoire de Montreux, Paris; Berklee Coll. of Music, Boston, USA. *Career:* drummer, vibraphone player, in clubs: New Morning, Hot Brass, Freelance percussionist playing with: Modulations, (contemporary music ensemble of composer Philippe Durville), Les Primitifs Du Futur, Big bands; Paris opera: Die Soldaten de Zimmerman; Television appearances: Stravinsky's Histoire du Soldat, with the Campagnol theatre troupe (FR3) (France 2); played with rock group Au Bonheur des Dames 1997; studio sessions with various artists; advertising jingles and cartoon theme tunes; plays with the Broadway Musical Co., tour of Japan 1998. *Recordings:* albums with: Les Primitifs Du Futur, The François Fichu Jazz Gang; Cordes Et Lames: Accordion Madness, Paris Scat, Au Bonheur des Dames Paris Musette 3. *Publications include:* 10 ètudes De Vibraphone Jazz (Salabert), Asscn Française de Percussion.

DAVIS, Jeremy Clayton; American songwriter and musician (bass guitar); b. 8 Feb. 1984, North Little Rock, Ark.; m. Kathryn Camsey 2011. *Career:* fmr mem. The Factory; Founder-mem. Paramore 2004–15, signed to Fueled by Ramen Records 2004. *Recordings:* albums: with Paramore: All We Know is Falling 2005, Riot! 2007, Brand New Eyes (Kerrang! Best Album Award 2010) 2009, Paramore 2013. *Honours:* with Paramore: Kerrang! Best New Band Award 2006, MTV Europe Music Award for Best Alternative Act 2010, NME Best Int. Band Award 2010, People's Choice Favorite Rock Band Award 2010, 2011. *Current Management:* Fly South Music Group, 189 South Orange Avenue, #1100, Orlando, FL 32801, USA. *Telephone:* (407) 841-6169. *Fax:* (407) 650-2664. *E-mail:* info@flysouthmusic.com. *Website:* www.flysouthmusic .com. *Address:* c/o Fueled by Ramen Records, PO Box 1803, Tampa, FL 33601, USA (office). *Website:* www.fueledbyramen.com (office); www.paramore.net.

DAVIS, Jonathan Houseman; American singer and musician (guitar, percussion, bagpipes); b. 18 Jan. 1970, Bakersfield, Calif.; m. 1st Renée Pérez 1998 (divorced 2000); one s. ; m. 2nd Devon Davis 2003. *Career:* fmr mem., SexArt; mem., KoRn 1992–; numerous tours and live appearances; Founder, Elementree record label. *Film scores include:* Queen of the Damned 2002, songs for numerous other films. *Film appearances include:* The Lucky Strike 2000, Queen of the Damned 2002, Seeing Other People 2004. *Recordings include:* albums: with Korn: KoRn 1994, Life Is Peachy 1996, Follow The Leader 1998, Issues 1999, Untouchables 2002, Take A Look In The Mirror 2003, See You On The Other Side 2005, Untitled 2007, Korn III: Remember Who You Are 2010, The Path of Totality 2011, The Paradigm Shift 2013; with Killbot: Sound Surgery 2012. *Current Management:* International Talent Booking, First Floor, Ariel House, 74a Charlotte Street, London, W1T 4QJ, England. *Website:* www.korn.com.

DAVIS, Linda Kaye; American singer; b. 26 Nov. 1962, Carthage, TX; m. Lang Jeffrey Scott 1984, two d. *Career:* solo artist; mem. ASCAP; CMA; ACM; AFTRA. *Recordings include:* albums: In a Different Light 1991, Linda Davis 1992, Shoot For The Moon 1994, Some Things Are Meant to Be 1996, I'm Yours 1998, I Have Arrived 2004, Young at Heart 2007. *Honours:* CMA Award 1993; Music City News/TNN Award, 1993; Grammy Award 1993. *Current Management:* Linda Davis Inc., PO Box 767, Hermitage, TN 37076, USA. *E-mail:* info@lindadavis.com. *Website:* www.lindadavis.com.

DAVIS, Mac; American singer and songwriter; b. (Scott Davis), 21 Jan. 1942, Lubbock, TX; m. Lise Kristen Gerard 1983, three s. *Education:* Emory

University, Georgia State College. *Career:* Man., Metric Music, 1966–68; solo artist 1969–; television and film performer, 1978–; screen performances include: North Dallas Forty, 1979; Cheaper To Keep Her, 1980; The Sting II, 1983. *Recordings include:* albums: Mac Davis, 1973; Baby Don't Get Hooked On Me, 1973; Forever Lovers, 1978; Thunder In The Afternoon, 1978; Midnight Crazy, 1981; Texas In My Rear View Window, 1981; Soft Talk, 1984; 20 Golden Greats, 1984; Till I Made It With You, 1986; I Sing the Hits, 1995; The Best of Mac Davis, 2000. *Current Management:* c/o Richard De La Font Agency, 4845 South Sheridan Road, #505, Tulsa, OK 74145-5719, USA. *Telephone:* (918) 665-6200. *Website:* www.delafont.com.

DAVIS, Richard, MusB; American musician (bass guitar), teacher and composer; *Professor of Bass (European Classical and Jazz), Jazz History, and Combo Improvisation, University of Wisconsin-Madison;* b. 15 April 1930, Chicago, Ill.; three c. *Education:* Vanderbrook Coll. of Music, Manhattan School of Music. *Career:* band leader, own quartet 1980–; performed at: Berkeley Jazz Festival, New Orleans Jazz Heritage Festival, Fletcher Henderson Memorial Concert, international tours with Elvin Jones, Lalo Schrifin, McCoy Tyner, Sun Ra, Archie Shepp, Don Cherry; joined Univ. of Wisconsin-Madison 1977, currently Prof. of Bass (European Classical and Jazz), Jazz History, and Combo Improvisation; Owner, Sympatico Music Publications Inc.; Founder-Pres., Richard Davis Foundation for Young Bassists 1993–, Retention Action Project (RAP) Inc., Everybody Listens and Talks; mem. International Composers Soc., International Soc. of Bassists, ASCAP, NARAS, Nat. String Artists, American Jazz Foundation, Screen Actors Guild, Nat. Asscn of Jazz Educators. *Recordings include:* albums: with Richard Davis Quartet: With Understanding 1975, Epistrophy 1981, Way Out West 1981, Harvest 1988, As One, One for Frederick 1989, Live at Sweet Basil 1990, The Bassist – Homage To Diversity 2001; other recordings with numerous artistes including Janis Ian, Herbie Mann, Van Morrison, Freddie Hubbard, Bo Diddley, Laura Nyro, Melissa Manchester, George Benson, Quincy Jones, Judy Collins, Elvin Jones, Charlie Mingus, Bonnie Raitt, Jimmy Smith, Bruce Springsteen, Loudon Wainwright III, Paul Simon, Carly Simon, Manhattan Transfer. *Publications include:* The Bass Tradition (with M.C. Gridley) 1984, Jazz Styles 1985; contrib. to numerous journals. *Honours:* Hon. doctorates in Musical Arts and Humane Letters; Downbeat International Critics Poll, Best Bassist 1967–74, Manfred E. Swarsensky Humanitarian Award, Rotary Club of Madison 2000, Wisconsin Gov.'s Award in Support of the Arts 2001, Urban League of Greater Madison Whitney M. Young Jr Award 2002, Madison Magazine Best of Madison Diversity Award 2002, Jazz Masters Award 2014. *Address:* School of Music, University of Wisconsin-Madison, 4415 Humanities Building, 455 North Park Street, Madison, WI 53706-1483 (office); 902 West Shore Drive, Madison, WI 53715, USA (home). *Telephone:* (608) 263-1911 (office); (608) 255-6666 (home); (608) 692-0378 (mobile). *Fax:* (608) 255-5524 (home). *E-mail:* rdavis1@wisc.edu (office). *Website:* www.music.wisc.edu (office); www.richarddavis.org.

DAVIS, Rob; musician (guitar) and songwriter; b. 1 Oct. 1947. *Career:* mem. Mud 1966–late 1970s; mem. Darts late 1970s–early 1980s; collaborations with Paul Oakenfold 1988; now a songwriter, with songs recorded by Sonique, Samantha Mumba, Shaznay Lewis, Fragma, Spiller, Kylie Minogue, Grace, Silicone Soul. *Compositions include:* Can't Get You Out Of My Head (with Cathy Dennis, recorded by Kylie Minogue) 2001, Toca's Miracle (recorded by Fragma) 2001, Groovejet (If This Ain't Love) (recorded by Spiller) 2001, Come Into My World (with Cathy Dennis, recorded by Kylie Minogue) 2004. *Honours:* Ivor Novello Awards for Most Performed Work, for Int. Hit of the Year (all for Can't Get You Out Of My Head) 2002, Grammy Award for Best Dance Recording (for Come Into My World) 2004. *Address:* c/o Universal Music Publishing Group, 2440 Sepulveda Blvd, Suite 100, Los Angeles, CA 90064-1712, USA.

DAVIS, Spencer; British musician (guitar); b. 17 July 1941, Swansea, Wales. *Education:* Birmingham Univ. *Career:* Founder, Spencer Davis Group 1963–69; solo artist and duo with Peter Jameson, 1971; record co. exec. Island Records; played in Blues Reunion 1988; re-formed Spencer Davis Group 1990; film appearances: The Ghost Goes Gear 1966, Here We Go Round The Mulberry Bush 1967; collaborations include: Keith Moon, Todd Rundgren, Paul Williams, Country Joe McDonald. *Recordings include:* albums: with The Spencer Davis Group: Their First LP 1965, The Second Album 1966, Autumn 66 1966, Gimme Some Lovin' 1967, I'm A Man 1967; solo albums: It's Been So Long, Mousetrap, Crossfire 1984; singles include: with the Spencer Davis Group: I Can't Stand It 1964, Strong Love 1965, Keep On Running (No. 1, UK) 1966, Somebody Help Me (No. 1, UK) 1966, When I Come Home 1966, Gimme Some Lovin 1966, I'm A Man 1967, Mr Second Class 1968. *Honours:* Carl Alan Award, Most Outstanding Group 1966. *Address:* c/o Talent Consultants International, Ltd (TCI), 105 Shad Row, 2nd Floor, Piermont, NY 10968, USA. *Telephone:* (845) 359-4609. *E-mail:* postmaster@tciartists.com. *Website:* www .spencer-davis-group.com.

DAVIS, Teresa Jane; British singer and musician; b. Leeds. *Education:* Wakefield Performing Arts Coll., Leeds Coll. of Music. *Career:* lead vocalist, Shiva, album and live concerts including Phoenix 1996, Tribal Gathering 1996, Northern Exposure 1996; featured artist on single, Brilliant Feeling, Full Monty All Stars; backing vocalist, D:ream; two UK headlining tours; one Australian headlining tour; various television appearances, including EastEnders (BBC 1), The Bill (ITV 1) 1991; backing singer for Gary Numan, two tours 1993; backing vocalist for Lisa Stansfield, ABC; played Frida in Bjorn Again, int. tours 1997–98; mem. Equity, Musicians' Union, PAMRA. *Record-*

ings include: solo: The Great Escape 1995; lead and backing vocals for Sonic R (Sega game) 1997, Blur, P. J. Proby/Marc Almond; others: Sigue Sigue Sputnik, Bjorn Again Live At The Royal Albert Hall 1998. *Website:* www.tjdavis.co.uk.

DAVISON, Peter; American composer, orchestrator, conductor and arranger; b. 26 Oct. 1948, Los Angeles, California; m. Iris Pell, 21 Sept. 1984, 1 d. *Education:* BA, MA, Music Composition, California State University, Northridge; Film Scoring Workshops, Earle Hagan, BMI; Fred Karlin, ASCAP; Travel to Bali to study Gamelan music. *Career:* Composed/arranged television series and documentaries, including: Seaquest; Batman – The Animated Series; John Denver Tour Special; Films; Interactive media; Commercials including: Hilton Hotels; India; videos; mem, SCL (Society of Composers and Lyricists); ASMA (American Society Music Arrangers); IFP/West; IDA (International Documentary Asscn). *Recordings:* As composer, arranger, producer, artist: Music on the Way 1980, Glide 1981, Star Gazer 1982, Forest 1982, Mountain 1983, Traces 1985, Winds of Space, 1987, Focal Point 1996, Adagio: Music for Meditation 1999, Adagio For Yoga (soundtrack) 2000, Adagio: Music For Relaxation 2000, Adagio: Music for Tai Chi 2000, Adagio: Music for Massage 2000, Adagio: Music for Healing 2000, Adagio: Classical Music for Yoga 2000, Vitality 2003, Solace 2005, Exhale 2005, Comfort 2005, Future, Present, Past 2010, Possibility 2011, Release 2011. *E-mail:* music@peterdavison.com. *Website:* www.peterdavison.com.

DAWSON, Mary A., BS; American songwriter, music publisher and broadcaster; *President, CQK Music Group;* b. 6 April 1944, Chicago, Ill.; m. David L. Dawson 1966; two s. two d. *Education:* Univ. of Wisconsin. *Career:* Music Publisher, Pres., CQK Music Group; host of nationally syndicated radio programme, I Write the Songs (also available online); columnist for four online magazines on songwriting; mem. Music Women Int., ASCAP. *Composition:* Recovery and Renewal. *Recording:* The Serenity Songs Project: Twelve Steps to Freedom. *Publication:* How to Get Somewhere in the Music Business from Nowhere with Nothing 2007. *Address:* c/o CQK Music Group/I Write the Songs, 2221 Justin Road, Suite 119–142, Flower Mound, TX 75028, USA (office). *Telephone:* (972) 317-2760 (office). *Fax:* (972) 317-4737 (office). *E-mail:* info@cqkmusic.com (office). *Website:* www.iwritethesongs.com; www.cqkmusic.com; www.fromnowherewithnothing.com.

DAWUNI, Rocky; Ghanaian singer; b. 1969, s. of Koyatu Dawuni and Asibi Dawuni; m. Carry Dawuni. *Education:* Univ. of Ghana. *Career:* f. Rocky Dawuni Independence Splash (annual music festival); apptd Goodwill Amb. for Tourism, Ministry of Tourism 2011; mem. Bd of Advisors Jammin Java Corpn 2011–; often referred to as 'Ghana's Bob Marley'. *Recordings include:* The Movement 1996, Crusade 1998, In Ghana (Reggae Song of the Year, Ghana Music Awards 2000) 1999, Awakening 2001, Book of Changes 2005, Hymns for the Rebel Soul 2010, Sun is Shining 2010, Branches of the Same Tree 2015. *Honours:* Best African Artist, Int. Reggae and World Music Awards 2011. *Current Management:* c/o Cary Sullivan, PO Box 1510, Pacific Palisades, CA 90272, USA. *Telephone:* (310) 663-7227. *E-mail:* afrofunke@yahoo.com. *Website:* www.rockydawuni.com.

DAY, Doris; American actress and singer; b. (Doris Mary Anne von Kappelhoff), 3 April 1924, Cincinnati, Ohio; d. of Frederick Wilhelm and Alma Sophia von Kappelhoff; m. 1st Al Jorden 1941 (divorced 1943); one s.; m. 2nd George Weidler 1946 (divorced 1949); m. 3rd Marty Melcher 1951 (died 1968); m. 4th Barry Comden 1976 (divorced 1981). *Career:* professional dancing appearances, Doherty and Kappelhoff, Glendale, Calif.; singer, Karlin's Karnival, radio station WCPO; singer with bands, Barney Rapp, Bob Crosby, Fred Waring, Les Brown; singer and leading lady, Bob Hope radio show (NBC) 1948–50; f. Doris Day Animal Foundation 1998; Founder and Pres. Doris Day Animal League. *Achievements include:* oldest artist to achieve a UK Top 10 hit album featuring new material (My Heart), entering at No. 9 Sept. 2011. *Recordings:* albums: You're My Thrill 1949, Tea for Two 1950, Lullaby of Broadway 1951, On Moonlight Bay 1951, I'll See You in My Dreams 1951, By the Light of the Silvery Moon 1953, Young Man with a Horn 1954, Day Dreams 1955, Day in Hollywood 1955, Young at Heart 1955, Love Me or Leave Me 1955, Most Happy Fella 1956, Day by Day 1957, Hooray for Hollywood Vols I and II 1959, Cuttin' Capers 1959, Day by Night 1959, Boys and Girls Together 1959, Hot Canaries 1959, Lights Cameras Action 1959, Listen to Day 1960, Show Time 1960, What Every Girl Should Know 1960, I Have Dreamed 1961, Bright and Shiny 1961, You'll Never Walk Alone 1962, Duet 1962, The Best of Doris Day 2002, My Heart (compilation of previously unreleased recordings produced by her son, Terry Melcher, prior to his death in 2004) 2011; singles: Day by Day 1949, Sugarbush 1952, Secret Love 1954, The Black Hills of Dakota 1954, If I Give My Heart to You 1954, Ready Willing and Able 1955, Whatever Will Be Will Be (Que Sera Sera) 1956, Move Over Darling 1964. *Films include:* Romance on the High Seas 1948, My Dream is Yours 1949, Young Man with a Horn 1950, Tea for Two 1950, West Point Story 1950, Lullaby of Broadway 1951, On Moonlight Bay 1951, I'll See You in My Dreams 1951, April in Paris 1952, By the Light of the Silvery Moon 1953, Calamity Jane 1953, Lucky Me 1954, Yankee Doodle Girl 1954, Love Me or Leave Me 1955, The Pajama Game 1957, Teacher's Pet 1958, The Tunnel of Love 1958, It Happened to Jane 1959, Pillow Talk 1959, Please Don't Eat the Daisies 1960, Midnight Lace 1960, Lover Come Back 1962, That Touch of Mink 1962, Jumbo 1962, The Thrill of It All 1963, Send Me No Flowers 1964, Do Not Disturb 1965, The Glass Bottom Boat 1966, Caprice 1967, The Ballad of Josie 1968, Where Were You When the Lights Went Out? 1968, With Six You Get Egg Roll 1968, Sleeping Dogs, Hearts and Souls 1993, That's

Entertainment III 1994. *Television includes:* Doris Day Show (CBS) 1952–53, 1968–72, The Governor & J.J. (series) 1970, The Pet Set 1972, Doris Day and Friends 1985–86, Doris Day's Best 1985–86. *Publication:* Doris Day: Her Own Story (autobiog., with A. E. Hotchner) 1975. *Honours:* Laurel Award, Leading New Female Personality in Motion Picture Industry 1950, Top Audience Attractor 1962, American Comedy Lifetime Achievement Award 1991, Grammy Award for Lifetime Achievement 2008. *Address:* c/o Doris Day Animal Foundation, 8033 Sunset Boulevard, Suite 845, Los Angeles, CA 90046, USA. *Website:* www.dorisday.com.

D'BANJ, (D'Koko Master); Nigerian singer, songwriter and musician (harmonica); b. (Dapo Daniel Oyebanjo), 1980, Zaria, Kaduna State. *Career:* solo artist 2005–. *Recordings include:* albums: No Long Thing 2005, Run Down Funk U Up 2006, The Entertainer 2008; compilation albums: Curriculum Vitae 2007, DKM (D'King's Men). *Honours:* Kora Award for Most Promising Male Artist 2005, Hip-Hop World Award for Revelation of the Year 2006, Nigerian Music Award for Artist of the Year, Channel O Music Award for Best Newcomer 2006, Hip-Hop World Award for Song of the Year 2007, Global Excellence Award for Artist of the Year 2007, City People Award for Artist of the Year 2007, Ghana Music Award for African Artist of the Year 2007, Amen Award for Artist of the Year, Song of the Year 2007, MTV Europe Music Award for Best African Act 2007, MTV Africa Music Award for Artist of the Year 2008, 2009, African Music Award for Best Collaboration (with Mo Hit Star) 2009. *E-mail:* contactus@dbanjrecords.com (office). *Website:* www.dbanjrecords.com.

DE BETHMANN, Pierre; French musician (piano); b. 21 April 1965, Boulogne Billancourt; m. Christel Hua 1990, two c. *Education:* Paris Graduate School of Man., Berklee Coll. of Music. *Career:* man. consultant, 1990–94; professional musician, 1994–; mem. of four groups, including PRYSM, trio with Christophe Wallemme and Benjamin Henocq 1994; numerous gigs in most Parisian clubs, various international festivals; numerous radio and television appearances with PRYSM; occasionally played with: Vincent Herring, Rick Margitza, Willie Williams, Vanessa Rubin, Sylvain Beuf, Philip Catherine, George Brown, Jean-Loup Longnon, François Jeauneau, François Théberge, Aldo Romano; mem. Société des auteurs, compositeurs et éditeurs de musique (SACEM), UMJ (Union des Musiciens de Jazz). *Recordings include:* PRYSM 1995, Oté ancestor 1991, Cubic 2009, Five 2011, GB 2012. *Honours:* First Prize, La Defense Nat. Jazz Contest 1994. *Telephone:* (6) 18-42-44-76. *E-mail:* pascal@g-steps.com. *Address:* 16 Cité de Trévise, 75009 Paris, France. *Website:* www.pierredebethmann.com.

DE BORST, Dolf; New Zealand singer and musician (bass guitar); b. Cambridge. *Career:* Founder-mem. Trinket 1996, renamed The Datsuns 1997–; own label, Hell Squad Records. *Recordings include:* albums: The Datsuns 2002, Outta Sight Outta Mind 2004, Smoke & Mirrors 2006, Head Stunts 2008, Death Rattle Boogie 2012. *Current Management:* c/o Tom Dalton, Thunderbird Management, PO Box 60496, Titirangi, Waitakere 0642, New Zealand. *Telephone:* (9) 836-3232. *E-mail:* tom@thunderbirdmanagement.com. *Website:* www.thunderbirdmanagement.com. *E-mail:* enquiries@thedatsuns.com. *Website:* www.thedatsuns.com.

DE BURGH, Chris; British singer and songwriter; b. (Christopher John Davison), 15 Oct. 1948, Argentina; m. Diane Patricia Morley; two s. one d. *Education:* Trinity Coll. Dublin. *Career:* solo artist 1974–; numerous concerts world-wide; first Western artist to perform in Iran since the Islamic Revolution 2008. *Recordings include:* albums: Far Beyond These Castle Walls 1975, Spanish Train And Other Stories 1975, At The End Of A Perfect Day 1977, Crusader 1979, Eastern Wind 1980, Best Moves 1981, The Getaway 1982, Man On The Line 1984, Into The Light 1986, Flying Colours 1988, High On Emotion – Live From Dublin 1990, Power Of Ten 1992, This Way Up 1994, Beautiful Dreams 1995, The Love Songs 1997, Quiet Revolution 1999, Notes From Planet Earth 2001, Timing Is Everything 2002, The Road to Freedom 2004, The Storyman 2006, Now and Then 2008, Footsteps 2009, Home 2012. *Honours:* ASCAP Awards 1985, 1987, 1988, 1990, 1991, 1997, IRMA Awards (Ireland) 1985–90, Beroliner Award (Germany), BAMBI Award (Germany), Midem Trophy (France). *Current Management:* Ferryman Productions, 754 Fulham Road, London, SW6 5SH, England. *Telephone:* (20) 7731-7074. *Fax:* (20) 7736-8605. *E-mail:* info@ferrymanproductions.com (office); ktmuk@dircon.co.uk (office). *Website:* www.cdeb.com.

DE DAVRICHEWY, Irakli; French jazz musician (trumpet) and bandleader; b. 1 Feb. 1940, Paris; m.; two d. one s. *Education:* studied violin, piano. *Career:* leader of numerous own groups, including On the Steps of Armstrong's Hot Five, Dickerson, Big Band, currently the All Stars with the Irakli Louis Ambs; as soloist on stage with or accompanying Barney Bigard, Trummy Young, Arvell Shaw, Claude Hopkins, Buddy Tate, Al Grey, Harry Edison, Cat Anderson, Jimmy Forrest, Eddie Vinson, Dorothy Donnegan, Lionel Hampton, Sam Woodyard, Vic Dickenson, Joe Muranyi, Peanuts Hucko, Moustache, Claude Luter, Geo Daly, Claude Bolling; tours to France, Netherlands, Germany, Sweden, Switzerland; jazz festivals in Antibes, Juan-Les-Pins, Breda, Rome, Nice, Andernos, Montauban, Vienna, Bayonne, Palermo, New Orleans (2001, for the 100th anniversary of Louis Armstrong's birth); concerts include the first part of the Louis Armstrong concert, Palais des Sports, Paris 1965, also inauguration ceremony of Louis Armstrong Square, Paris; television broadcasts for Jean-Christophe Averty, with Claude Bolling, Victoria Spivey, Edith Wilson, and interviews. *Recordings include:* numerous albums, recent ones include: Say It With A Kiss (with the Irakli Louis Ambs) 2000,

Keep On Jumpin' (with The Tuxedo Big Band) 2001, I Gotta Right To Sing Blues (with the Irakli Louis Ambs) 2002. *Publications include:* Louis Armstrong: complete and chronological, Masters of Jazz for Media 7, Le Jazz, for Encyclopédie Clartés. *Honours:* Jazz Hot Awards 1959, 1964, Antibes Award 1960, Jazz Magazine Award 1960, Académie du Jazz Award 1972, Hot Club de France Award 2001. *Address:* 10 avenue Fleury, 92700 Colombes, France. *Telephone:* 1-47-81-24-59 (home). *Fax:* 1-47-81-24-59 (home).

DE GREGORI, Francesco; Italian singer and songwriter; b. 4 April 1951, Rome. *Career:* journalist 1992–96. *Recordings include:* albums: Theorius Campus 1970, Alice non lo sa 1973, Francesco de Gregori 1974, Rimmel 1975, Buffalo Bill 1976, De Gregori 1978, Banana Republic 1979, Viva L'Italia 1979, Titanic 1982, La donna cannone 1983, Scacchi e tarocchi 1985, Terra di Nessuno 1987, Miramare 17.4.89 1989, Catcher in the Sky 1990, Musica leggera 1990, Niente da capire 1990, Canzoni d'Amore 1992, Il bandito e il campione 1993, Bootleg 1994, Prendere e lasciare 1996, La valigia dell'attore 1997, Amore Nel Pomerigio 2001, Fuoco amico 2002, Il fischio del vapore (with Giovanna Marini) 2003, Mix 2004, Pezzi 2005, Calypsos 2006, Per Brevità chiamato artista 2008. *Address:* c/o BMG Ricordi SpA, Via Benigno Crespi 19, 20159 Milan, Italy. *E-mail:* promozione.ricordi.italy@umusic.com (office). *Website:* www.ricordi.it.

DE GROOTE, Geeraard Albert; Belgian songwriter, musician (saxophones, guitar, bass) and singer; b. 3 Sept. 1958, Blankenberge; s. of Jean-Pierre de Groote and Erna Naudts. *Education:* School of Econs, Acad. of Music, Bruges, Jazz Studio, Antwerp, Jazz Acad., Knokke-Heist. *Career:* studio recordings and TV appearances with various Belgian artists and bands; TV appearances and concerts with Tom Robinson; Belgian concerts Tony O'Malley, with bluesband Hideaway, accompanied Jimmy Morello, Studebaker John, Phil Guy, Johnny Basset. *Recordings:* with Hideaway, Soul Spirit, Billy Goat Riders, Cly-An, Blond, Rhythm Deep, various Belgian artists. *Address:* Westmoere 50, B 8490 Snellegem, Belgium (home). *Telephone:* (50) 81-23-03 (home). *E-mail:* geeraarddg@hotmail.com (home). *Website:* www.hideaway20 .be.

DE HOMEM-CHRISTO, Guy-Manuel; French DJ; b. 2 Aug. 1974, Paris. *Career:* fmr mem. Darling; Co-founder, Daft Punk 1992–. *Film:* Tron: Legacy (score) 2010. *Recordings include:* albums: Homework 1996, Discovery 2001, Alive 1997 2001, Human After All 2005, Musique Vol. 1 1993–2005 2006, Alive 2007 (Grammy Award for Best Electronic/Dance Album 2009) 2007, Random Access Memories (Grammy Awards for Album of the Year 2014, for Best Dance/Electronica Album 2014, Billboard Music Award for Top Dance/ Electronic Album 2014) 2013. *Honours:* Grammy Award for Best Dance Recording (for Harder Better Faster Stronger) 2009, Grammy Awards for Record of the Year, for Best Pop Duo/Group Performance (both for Get Lucky) 2014, Billboard Music Award for Top Dance/Electronic Artist 2014. *Current Management:* Primary Talent International, The Primary Building, 10-11 Jockey's Fields, London, WC1R 4BN, England. *Telephone:* (20) 7400-4500. *Fax:* (20) 7400-4501. *E-mail:* PeterE@primary.uk.com. *Website:* www.primary .uk.com; www.daftpunk.com.

DE ITAMARACÁ, Lia; Brazilian singer and songwriter; b. (Maria Madalena Correio do Nascimento), 12 Jan. 1944, Itamaracá. *Career:* singing cirandas (dance song set to distinctive percussive rhythm with mostly rurally-themed lyrics) from age 11; her composition (with Teca Calazans) 'Esta ciranda quem me deu foi Lia' became well known all over Brazil; solo artist 1977–, performing shows all over Brazil. *Recordings include:* albums: (debut) 1977, Eu Sou Lia 2000. *Address:* c/o Ciranda Productions, Iran Gomes & Regina del Papa, Rua Lagoa dos Gatos n.511, Janga-Paulista-PE 53437 Olinda PE, Brazil.

DE JOHNETTE, Jack; American jazz musician (piano, drums), bandleader and composer; b. 4 Aug. 1942, Chicago; m. Lydia DeJohnette 1968; two d. *Education:* Chicago Conservatory of Music. *Career:* performed and recorded with John Coltrane, Thelonious Monk, Miles Davis, Stan Getz, Bill Evans, Herbie Hancock, Betty Carter; currently with Keith Jarrett Trio, Pat Metheny, Gateway Trio with Dave Holland and John Abercrombie, also leads own group. *Compositions:* Silver Hollow. *Recordings include:* albums: DeJohnette Complex 1969, Have you Heard? 1970, Compost: Take off your body 1971, Sorcery 1974, Cosmic Chicken 1975, Untitled 1976, Pictures 1977, New Rags 1977, Tin Can Alley 1981, Inflation Blues 1983, Piano Album 1985, Zebra 1986, Earthwalk 1991, Music For The Fifth World 1993, New Directions 1994, Works 1994, Album Album 1994, Audio-Visualscapes 1994, Special Edition 1994, Dancing with Night Spirits 1996, Oneness 1997, Irresistible Forces 1998, Parallel Realities 1998, Invisible Nature, Music from the Hearts of the Masters 2005, The Elephant sleeps but still Remembers, Peace Time (Grammy Award for Best New Age Album 2009), The Ripple Effect, Music in the Key of Om, Golden Beams, Music We Are 2009, Sound Travels 2012. *Honours:* Hon. DMus (Berklee Coll. of Music) 1990; Grand Prix Du Disque, Academy of Jazz, Paris 1978, NEA Fellow 1978, CAPS Composers Grantee 1980, winner, Downbeat Readers Poll, 13 consecutive years, numerous drum magazine awards; Swing Journal Video Award, NEA Jazz Masters Award 2012. *Current Management:* c/o Jane Chun, Now Forward Music/Kindred Rhythm, PO Box 1942, Radio City Station, New York, NY 10101, USA. *Telephone:* (212) 764-4609. *E-mail:* jane@kindredrhythm.com; nfm109@gmail .com. *Website:* www.kindredrhythm.com; www.jackdejohnette.com (home).

DE LA CRUZ, James; Australian musician (keyboards). *Career:* mem. electronic music collective Avalanches 1998–. *Recordings include:* album:

Since I Left You 2000. *Address:* c/o Modular Records, PO Box 1666, Darlinghurst, NSW 1300, Australia. *Website:* www.theavalanches.com.

DE LA ROCHA, Zack; American singer; b. 12 Jan. 1970, Long Beach, CA. *Career:* fmr mem. early bands, Headstance, Farside and Inside Out; mem., Rage Against the Machine 1991–2000, re-formed 2007–; mem. One Day as a Lion 2008–; involved in various causes such as Fairness and Accuracy in Reporting, Rock for Choice and Refuse and Resist; numerous tours, festival appearances. *Recordings include:* with Rage Against the Machine: Rage Against The Machine 1992, Evil Empire 1996, The Battle Of Los Angeles 1998, Renegades 2000, Live and Rare 2002. *Honours:* Grammy Award for Best Hard Rock Performance (for Guerrilla Radio) 2001. *Website:* www.ratm.com; www.onedayasalion.org.

DE MAEYER, Marc; Belgian musician (keyboard), author/composer, producer and vocal coach; *Director, Studio E;* b. 23 April 1966, Willebroek; one d. *Education:* Acad. of Music, Mechelen. *Career:* keyboards and backing in hard rock band Rubicon; keyboards and vocals in Flemish pop band, Van Gogh; writing for Bert, Thanii, Yasmine and Barbara Dex; TV appearances include Tien om te zien, BRT, Man bijt Hond; radio includes VRT, VTM, RSJ; Owner and Dir, Studio E. *Compositions include:* Elsje, Jij Bent Voor Mij, Icecubes and Diamonds, Shadow King, Moonlite, Avalanche, Redemption. *Radio:* Een uurtje rock met Marc Barock. *Recordings include:* Alles Draait Om Haar, Clearwater, Vers Bloed, Prime Mover, Colours of Life (compilation) 2006, Ocura Geheugenkoor 2013. *Publications include:* Alles Draait om Haar 1994, Stop Breaking My Heart 2006, You Won't Be Alone 2006, Ocura Geheugenkoor 2013. *Address:* Heufstraat 49, 3350 Overhespen, Belgium (office). *E-mail:* info@studio-e.be (office). *Website:* www.studio-e.be (office).

DE MARCOS GONZÁLEZ (CÁRDENAS), Juan; Cuban musician (tres, guitar), singer, composer, arranger and bandleader; b. 1954, Havana. *Education:* Univ., Agronomic Science Inst. *Career:* formed Sierra Maestra, styled on the traditional Cuban septeto group 1978–97; dir, arranger and conductor for Afro-Cuban All Stars 1997–; consultant, co-ordinator, conductor and musician, Ry Cooder's Buena Vista Social Club project; collaborations with Rubén Gonzaléz, Ibrahim Ferrer, Compay Segundo, Omara Portuonda, Eliades Ochoa, Barbarito Torres, Guajiro Mirabel; formed production co. in Cuba, Ahora. *Film:* Buena Vista Social Club (documentary) 1996. *Recordings include:* albums: with Sierra Maestra: Son Highlights From Cuba 1993, ¡Dundunbanza! 1994, Con Sabor A Cuba 1995, El Guanajo Relleno 1995, Criolla Garabali 1996, Tibiri Tabara 1998, Coco Mai Mai 1998, Rumberos De La Havana 1999, Viaje A La Semilla 2001, Rumbero Soy 2002; with Buena Vista Social Club: Buena Vista Social Club 1997; with Afro-Cuban All Stars: A Toda Cuba Le Gusta 1997, Distinto Diferente 1999, Live In Japan 2004, Absolutely Live 2011; solo: Step Forward 2005. *Current Management:* c/o Sasa Music, Cecil Sharp House, 2 Regent's Park Road, London, NW1 7AY, England. *E-mail:* rab@sasa.demon.co.uk. *Website:* www.sasamusic.com.

DE MARTINI, Jimmy; American singer and musician (violin); b. 1976; m. *Education:* Wheeler High School, Marietta, Ga. *Career:* mem. Dave Matthews Cover Band 2001–; founding mem. Zac Brown Band 2002–. *Recordings:* albums: Far From Einstyne 2004, Home Grown 2005, The Foundation 2008, You Get What You Give 2010. *Honours:* Acad. of Country Music Award for Top New Vocal Duo or Group 2009, for Vocal Event of the Year (for As She's Walking Away, featuring Alan Jackson) 2011, Grammy Award for Best New Artist 2010, CMA New Artist of the Year 2010. *Current Management:* ROAR, 9701 Wilshire Boulevard, Eighth Floor, Beverly Hills, CA 90212, USA. *Telephone:* (310) 586-8222. *E-mail:* zbb@roar.la. *Website:* www.roar.la. *E-mail:* jimmy@zacbrownband.com (office). *Website:* www.zacbrownband.com.

DE MARTINO, Jules; British musician (drums, guitar, piano) and songwriter; b. London. *Career:* fmr mem. Eskiimo; mem. The Ting Tings 2006–. *Recordings include:* album: We Started Nothing (Ivor Novello Award for Best Album 2009) 2008, Sounds from Nowheresville 2012. *Honours:* MTV Video Music Award for Best Video (for Shut Up and Let Me Go) 2008. *Website:* www .thetingtings.com.

DE MASURE, Geoffrey; French musician (trombone); b. 16 May 1969, Tourcoing. *Education:* musical study in Avignon 1984–89, with André Jaume in Paris 1989, in New York and at Banff, Canada, with Steve Coleman, Robin and Kevin Eubanks, Marvin Smith, Kenny Wheeler and Rufus Reid. *Career:* Founder, Tribu; appearances at La Défense, Concours de jazz d'Etréchy 1996, Orchestre Nat. de Jazz 1997; appearances with Tribu at Centre Culturel Jean Cocteau, Etréchy, Centre Culturel de Marines, théâtre de Vanves, festival de Radio France de Montpellier, Jazz Club d'Auxerre, Cave Dimière à Argentueil; mem. Union Musicians Jazz (UMJ). *Recordings include:* with Orchestre Nat. de Jazz: A plus tard 1992, Monk, Mingus, Ellington 1993, Bouquet final 1994; Quoi De Neuf Docteur: A l'envers 1995, 51 degrees below 1996.

DE MESMAY, Benoit; French composer and musician (piano); b. 10 Oct. 1961, Algeria. *Career:* European jazz festivals with Gil Evans, Orchestre Nat. de Jazz, Elizabeth Caumont, John Scofield, Lucky Peterson. *Recordings include:* two albums with Elizabeth Caumont; three albums with Laurent Cugny, Gil Evans.

DE REEDER, Pierre; American singer, songwriter, musician (bass guitar) and engineer; b. 1973, San Diego, Calif.; m. Melissa Litz 2006; two d. *Education:* La Jolia High School, San Diego. *Career:* founder mem. Rilo Kiley 1998–; solo artist 2008–; mem. The SqueeGees 2010–; contributed artwork releases by artists including Kozo, Ras Command, Skin to Skin, Slowdeck, Omnimotion, Bluetech, Johnathan Rice; recording engineer for artists including Eleni Mandell, Sia. *Recordings:* albums: with Rilo Kiley: Take Offs and Landings 2001, The Execution of All Things 2002, More Adventurous 2004, Under the Blacklight 2007, solo: The Way That It Was 2008; with The SqueeGees: Meet the SqueeGees 2010; also appeared on: I'm Having Fun Now, Jenny and Johnny 2010. *Current Management:* c/o Jessica Massa, Press Here Publicity, 138 West 25th Street, 9th Floor, New York, NY 10001, USA. *Telephone:* (212) 246-2640. *Fax:* (212) 582-6513. *E-mail:* jessica@ pressherepublicity.com. *Website:* www.pressherepublicity.com. *Address:* c/o Brant Weil, Warner Bros. Records Inc., 3300 Warner Boulevard, Burbank, CA 91505-4694, USA (office). *E-mail:* brant.weil@wbr.com (office). *Website:* www .warnerbrosrecords.com (office); www.pierredereeder.com; www.rilokiley .com.

DE ROCCO, Andrea, (Pupillo); Italian alternative DJ, dub master, producer and musician (accordion); b. 30 Sept. 1973, Nardo' (LE). *Career:* mem. Negramaro 2002–15. *Recordings include:* albums: Negramaro 2003, 000577 2004, Mentre Tutto Scorre 2005, La Finestra 2007, Casa 69 2010, Una Storia Semplice 2012, Natural Core – Natural Works And Electronic Frames 2014, La rivoluzione Sta Arrivando 2015. *Honours:* MTV Europe Music Award Best Italian Act 2005. *E-mail:* management@negramaro.com (office). *Website:* www .negramaro.com.

DE RYCKE, Herman; Belgian musician (double bass); b. 20 Aug. 1960, Oudenaarde; m. Maes Riet 1989; two s. *Education:* Solfège. *Career:* mem. pop groups Klepper 1976–77, Penthouse 1979–83, Allan Fawn and The State of the Art 1984, Kandahar 1983–86, The Peter Band Band 1986; mem. contemporary jazz group Work 4 1987–89; mem. gipsy music groups Kalinka Zigeunertrio 1991, Kallai 2001; television appearance, Villatempo (BAT) 1986; mem. Société d'Auteurs Belge–Belgische Auteurs Maatschappij (SABAM). *Composition:* Blue Ballad. *Recordings include:* albums: with Penthouse: Neighbour Fool; with Kalinka: Jalousie; with Kallai: Komm Tzigane; singles: with Penthouse: Neighbour Fool; with Peter Pan Band: Light My Fire. *Honours:* Winner, Humo's Rock Rally 1986. *Address:* Hoogmeers 9, 9031 Gent, Belgium.

DE SCHOOLMEESTER, Beverley; British songwriter, poet, musician (bass guitar, piano) and singer; b. 4 May 1962. *Education:* Nat. Diploma Business Studies. *Career:* solo artist as jazz fusion singer 1991–; bass player, backing vocalist for The Dolls; numerous television, radio broadcasts, tours of UK, France, Germany, The Netherlands, Sweden, Italy, Turkey, Singapore, Indonesia, Ireland; mem. Musicians' Union, London Acad. of Music. *Recordings include:* album: The Dolls: No Shame; solo: over 30 tracks written. *Publications include:* various poetry in magazines and local press. *Address:* 16 Battle Street, Reading, RG1 7NU, England.

DE SMET, Francis; Belgian music supervisor and musician (keyboards); b. 3 Dec. 1962, Bruges. *Education:* Conservatory of Bruges, Royal Conservatory of Brussels, Academia Chigichiana. *Career:* Producer, Transatlantic Films, Brussels 1992–; US Patent 7,287,021 B2, Oct. 23, 2007: Human Search Assistants; EYE-D Project. *Films:* The Sexual Life of the Belgians (producer, film soundtrack) 1993, Camping Cosmos 1995. *Current Management:* c/o BVBA INTERNETV, Generaal Lemanlaan 151, 8310, Bruges, Belgium. *Website:* www.transatlanticfilms.be.

DE SOUTEIRO, Arnaldo; Brazilian record producer, journalist, publicist and educator; b. 23 June 1963, Rio de Janeiro; m. Ithamara Koorax 1990. *Education:* studied with Delza Agricola. *Career:* Founder and Pres. Jazz Station Records 1991; jazz critic, Tribune da Imprensa 1979; Brazilian Corresp., Keyboard Magazine 1986–95; produced TV specials for Globo and Manchete networks, including Joao Gilberto and Antonio Carlos Jobim, Dizzy Gillespie, Tony Bennett, Airto, Flora Purim and Chuck Mangione; Assoc. mem. International Asscn of Jazz Educators. *Recordings include:* as producer: albums for Luiz Bonfá, The Bonfá Magic, Dom um Romao, Rhythm Traveller, Ithamara Koorax, Serenade in Blue, Joao Gilberto, Ao Vivo/Live in Rio, Thiago de Mello, Amazon, Deodato, Inútil Paisagem; also produced acclaimed compilation series for Brazilian Horizons and A Trip To Brazil; produced sessions featuring Herbie Hancock, Yana Purim, Steve Swallow, Antonio Carlos Jobim, Ron Carter, Sadao Watanabe, Larry Coryell and Gonzalo Rubalcaba. *Honours:* Hon. mem. International Acad. of Music.

DE VIS, Alain; Belgian musician (trumpet, flugelhorn), composer and arranger; b. 6 Sept. 1953, Brussels; m. Nanga Marie-Jeanne 1984, four s. one d. *Education:* studied in Nivelles. *Career:* mem. of small commercial bands 1975, jazz bands and big bands 1979, salsa and Brazilian bands 1979–; concerts with Fania All Stars, Brasil Tropical, Salsa de Hoy, Dynamita Salsa, Bem Brasil; mem. Société d'Auteurs Belge–Belgische Auteurs Maatschappij (SABAM). *Recordings include:* album: Act Big Band. *Address:* 46 rue du Chaufour, 611 Courcelles, Belgium (home). *Telephone:* (496) 21-53-69 (home). *E-mail:* alaindevis@yahoo.fr (home).

DE VITA, Franco; Venezuelan singer and songwriter; b. 23 Jan. 1954, Caracas. *Career:* Founder-mem. Icaro 1982; solo artist 1984–; signed to Sony Music 1988; toured USA as co-headliner with Ricardo Montaner 2004; collaborator with Wisin & Yandel 2007; songwriter for Ricky Martin, Chayanne. *Recordings:* albums: with Icaro: Icaro 1982; solo: Franco de Vita 1984, Fantasia 1986, Al Norte del Sur 1988, Extranjero 1990, Isto é America 1993, Straniero 1993, Voces a mi Alrededor 1993, Fuera de Este Mundo 1996,

Nada Es Igual 1999, Segundas partes también son buenas 2002, Stop 2004, Simplemente La Verdad 2008. *Honours:* MTV Video Music Award for Most Popular Single 1990. *Current Management:* Alegria Producciones, 2900 Glades Circle, Suite 1100, Weston, FL 33327, USA. *Telephone:* (954) 349-0090; (954) 389-3350; (212) 335-4969 (Venezuela). *Fax:* (954) 389-3316. *E-mail:* info@alegriacorp.com. *Website:* www.alegriacorp.com; www .francodevita.com.

DE VORE, David; American producer and engineer; b. 27 March 1943, Hilo, Hawaii; m. Janine 1976; one d. *Education:* studied engineering and architecture at coll. *Career:* producer, engineer for Fleetwood Mac, Grateful Dead, Santana, Elton John, REO Speedwagon, Ringo Starr, Russ Ballard, Foreigner, Survivor.

DE VRIES, Marius; British producer, remixer, songwriter, musician (keyboards) and programmer and arranger; b. 21 Oct. 1961, London; m. Felicity 1989; one s. one d. *Education:* Peterhouse Coll., Cambridge, St Paul's Cathedral Choir School, Bedford School. *Career:* two world tours with Blow Monkeys; Musical Dir for artists, including Rick Astley, Neneh Cherry; music supervisor for film production, The Avengers 1997–98; worked with artists, including Madonna, Björk, Massive Attack, Annie Lennox, U2, Robbie Robertson, Neil Finn, Melanie C, Josh Groban, Rufus Wainwright; mem. PRS, Musicians' Union. *Film scores include:* Baz Luhrmann's Romeo and Juliet (co-composer and co-producer) 1996, Eye of the Beholder 1999, Moulin Rouge! 2001, Easy Virtue 2008, Kick-Ass 2010, King Kong 2013. *Honours:* World Soundtrack Awards (for Moulin Rouge!) 2001, IF Award for Best Music (for Moulin Rouge!) 2001, BAFTA Award (for Moulin Rouge!) 2002. *Current Management:* Gorfaine/Schwartz Agency, Inc. Talent Agency, 4111 West Alameda Avenue, Suite 509, Burbank, CA 91505, USA. *Telephone:* (818) 260-8500. *Website:* www.gsamusic.com.

DEACON, John; British musician (bass guitar); b. 19 Aug. 1951, Leicester, England. *Education:* studied electronics. *Career:* mem. rock group Queen 1971–91; numerous tours and festival appearances. *Recordings include:* albums: with Queen: Queen 1973, Queen II 1974, Sheer Heart Attack 1974, A Night At The Opera 1975, A Day At The Races 1976, Good Old Fashioned 1977, News Of The World 1977, Jazz 1978, Live Killers 1979, The Game 1980, Flash Gordon (soundtrack) 1981, Hot Space 1982, The Works 1984, A Kind of Magic 1986, The Miracle 1989, Stone Cold Crazy 1991, Innuendo 1991. *Honours:* Ivor Novello Award (for Best Selling British Record) 1976, Britannia Award (for Best British Pop Single 1952–77) 1977, Gold Ticket Madison Square Gardens 1977, American Music Award (for Favorite Single) 1981, Nordoff-Robbins Music Therapy Centre Silver Clef Award 1984, Ivor Novello Award (for Outstanding Contrib. to British Music) 1987, BRIT Awards (for Outstanding Contrib. to British Music) 1990, (for Best British Single) 1991, Q Classic Song Award (for Bohemian Rhapsody) 2015. *Current Management:* c/o Queen Productions Limited, PO Box 141, West Horsley, KT24 9AJ, England. *Website:* www.queenonline.com.

DEADMAU5; Canadian DJ, record producer and musician; b. (Joel Thomas Zimmerman), 5 Jan. 1981, Niagara Falls, Ont.; s. of Rodney Thomas Zimmerman and Nancy Johnson. *Career:* f. mau5trap record label; issued debut recordings 2005; numerous collaborations including Kaskade, Rob Swire, Gerard Way; numerous live appearances. *Recordings include:* albums: Get Scraped 2005, Vexillology 2006, Random Album Title (Juno Award for Dance Recording of the Year 2009) 2008, For Lack of a Better Name (Juno Award for Dance Recording of the Year 2010) 2009, 4x4=12 2010, Album Title Goes Here 2012, while(1<2) 2014. *Honours:* Juno Award for Dance Recording of the Year (for All You Ever Want) 2008, Beatport Music Awards for Best Electro House Artist 2008, 2009, for Best Progressive House Artist 2008, 2009, for Best Single (for Not Exactly) 2008, International Dance Music Awards for Best Canadian DJ 2010, for Best Artist 2010, for Best Electro Track (for Ghosts 'n' Stuff 2010). *Current Management:* c/o Three Six Zero Group, 1411 Broadway, 39th Floor, New York, NY 10018, USA. *E-mail:* contact@tszgrp .com. *Website:* www.tszgrp.com; www.deadmaus5.com.

DEAKIN, Fred, MA; British DJ, musician and designer; b. 2 Dec. 1964, London; s. of Nicholas Deakin and Rose Donaldson; m. Natalie Hunter; one step-s. *Education:* Univ. of Edinburgh, Central Saint Martin's School of Art. *Career:* designer and illustrator; Founder mem., Lemon Jelly 1997–; Founder and Dir Airside design co. 1998–; visiting tutor Central Saint Martin's School of Art, London 1999–. *Recordings include:* albums: with Lemon Jelly: LemonJelly.ky 2000, Lost Horizons 2002, '64–'95 2005, The Triptych 2007, Nu Balearica 2008; with Robin Jones: To the Victor the Spoils! 2011. *Animation film:* '64–'95 (DVD) 2005. *Exhibition:* Insyde, Walker Gallery, Liverpool 2006. *Honours:* CAD Best CD Sleeve Award 2003, Design Week Best in Show Prize 2007, European Design Best CD Packaging 2008. *Address:* Airside, 339 Upper Street, London, N1 0PB, England (office). *Telephone:* (20) 7354-9912 (office). *Website:* www.airside.co.uk (office).

DEAL, Kim; American musician (bass, guitar), singer and songwriter; b. 10 June 1961, Dayton, Ohio; m. John Murphy (divorced 1988). *Career:* mem. the Pixies (originally billed as Mrs John Murphy) 1986–93, 2004–13; recorded demo, The Purple Tape 1987; formed The Breeders 1990–; formed The Amps 1995. *Recordings include:* albums: with the Pixies: Come On Pilgrim (EP) 1987, Surfer Rosa 1988, Doolittle 1989, Bossanova 1990, Trompe Le Monde 1991, Death To The Pixies 1987–1991 1997, Live At The BBC 1998, Complete B-Sides 2001, Pixies (DVD) 2004, Wave of Mutilation: The Best of the Pixies 2004; with The Breeders: Pod 1990, Safari (EP) 1992, Last Splash 1993, Title

TK 2002, Mountain Battles 2008; with The Amps: Pacer 1995. *Current Management:* c/o William Morris Agency, 1325 Avenue of the Americas, New York, NY 10019, USA. *Telephone:* (212) 586-5100. *Fax:* (212) 246-3583. *Address:* c/o 4AD Limited, 17–19 Alma Road, London, SW18 1AA, England (office). *E-mail:* kimdealmusic@yahoo.com (home). *Website:* www .kimdealmusic.com (home).

DEAN, Rob; British musician (guitar). *Career:* Founder-mem. Japan 1974–81. *Recordings include:* albums: Adolescent Sex 1978, Obscure Alternatives 1978, Quiet Life 1979, Gentlemen Take Polaroids 1980, Tin Drum 1981.

DeANGELIS, Mike; Canadian guitarist; b. Guelph; m. Fern DeAngelis. *Education:* McMaster Univ. *Career:* Founder mem. Charlemagne, formed in Hamilton, Ont. 2006, renamed Arkells 2008–; signed to Dine Alone Records 2006; released debut EP Deadlines 2007; opening act for Matt Mayes & El Torpedo on Canadian tour 2008; toured with Waking Eyes on Canadian tour 2009; toured USA with The Maine and Lydia 2012; toured Europe with Billy Talent and Anti-Flag 2012; support act for Tragically Hip on Canadian tour 2013. *Recordings:* albums: with Arkells: Jackson Square 2008, Michigan Left 2011, High Noon (Juno Award for Rock Album of the Year 2015) 2014. *Honours:* 102.1 The Edge CASBY Award 2009, Juno Awards for New Group of the Year 2010, for Group of the Year 2012, 2015. *Current Management:* c/o Tom Sarig, Kari Dexter and Christine Carson, ECG Management; Adam Countryman and Jack Ross, The Agency Group Ltd, 2 Berkeley Street, Suite 202, Toronto, ON M5A 4J5, Canada. *Telephone:* (416) 368-5599 (Agency Group). *Fax:* (416) 368-4655 (Agency Group). *E-mail:* info@ecgnyc.com; kari@ecgnyc.com; christine@ecgnyc.com; adamcountryman@theagencygroup.com; jackross@theagencygroup.com. *Website:* www.theagencygroup.com; www .arkells.ca.

DEARNLEY, Mark; British producer, engineer and musician (keyboards); b. 12 Aug. 1957, Barnet. *Education:* Southampton University. *Career:* engineer credits include AC/DC, Circus of Power, The English Beat, Joan Armatrading, Def Leppard, Paul McCartney; producer credits include The Dogs D'Amour, Steve Jones, Mother Love Bone, The Quireboys, Loudness, Bang Tango, Die Cheerleader, Owen Paul, The Wild Family, Scream 2, South Park, American Pie. *E-mail:* info@dearnley.com (office). *Website:* www.dearnley.com.

DEBNEY, John; American composer; b. 18 Aug. 1956, Burbank, Calif. *Education:* Loyola Univ. *Career:* mem. American Soc. of Composers, Authors and Publrs (ASCAP). *Compositions for television include:* Star Trek: The Next Generation 1987, A Pup Named Scooby-Doo 1988, Trenchcoat in Paradise 1989, The Young Riders (Emmy Award) 1989, The Face of Fear 1990, Still Not Quite Human 1992, Sunstroke 1992, Praying Mantis 1993, SeaQuest DSV (Emmy Award) 1993, Class of '61 1993, For Love and Glory 1993, Kansas 1995, Doctor Who 1996, The Pretender 1996, The Cape 1996, Running Mates 2000, Christmas Rush (theme) 2002. *Compositions for film include:* The Wild Pair 1987, Seven Hours to Judgment 1988, Not Since Casanova 1988, The Further Adventures of Tennessee Buck 1988, Jetsons: The Movie 1990, The Halloween Tree 1993, Hocus Pocus 1993, White Fang II: Myth of the White Wolf 1994, Gunmen 1994, Little Giants 1994, Sudden Death 1995, Runaway Brain 1995, Chameleon 1995, Houseguest 1995, Cutthroat Island 1995, Getting Away with Murder 1996, Carpool 1996, The Relic 1997, Liar Liar 1997, I Know What You Did Last Summer 1997, Paulie 1998, I'll Be Home for Christmas 1998, My Favourite Martian 1999, Lost & Found 1999, Inspector Gadget 1999, Dick 1999, The Adventures of Elmo in Grouchland 1999, End of Days 1999, Komodo 1999, Michael Jordan to the Max 2000, Relative Values 2000, The Replacements 2000, The Emperor's New Groove 2000, See Spot Run 2001, Spy Kids 2001, Heartbreakers 2001, Cats and Dogs 2001, The Princess Diaries 2001, Jimmy Neutron: Boy Genius 2002, The Scorpion King 2002, Snow Dogs 2002, Dragonfly 2002, Hobbs End 2002, Spy Kids 2: Island of Lost Dreams 2002, Swimfan 2002, The Tuxedo 2002, The Hot Chick 2002, Most 2003, Bruce Almighty 2003, Elf 2003, Looney Tunes: Back in Action (additional music) 2003, That's a Wrap 2004, Tag Along with Will Ferrell 2004, Santa Mania 2004, Lights, Camera, Puffin! 2004, Kids on Christmas 2004, How They Made the North Pole 2004, Film School for Kids 2004, Deck the Halls 2004, Christmas in Tinseltown 2004, Welcome to Mooseport 2004, The Passion of the Christ 2004, The Whole Ten Yards 2004, Raising Helen 2004, Spider-Man 2 (additional music) 2004, The Princess Diaries 2: Royal Engagement 2004, Christmas with the Kranks 2004, Lucky 13 2005, The Pacifier 2005, Sin City 2005, Duma 2005, The Adventures of Shark Boy and Lava Girl in 3-D 2005, Dreamer: Inspired by a True Story 2005, Chicken Little 2005, Zathura 2005, Cheaper by the Dozen 2 2005, Idlewild 2006, Barnyard 2006, The Ant Bully 2006, Yankee Irving 2006, Evan Almighty 2007, Meet Dave 2008, Swing Vote 2008, The Three Stooges 2012. *Honours:* ASCAP Henry Mancini Award 2005. *Current Management:* c/o Kraft-Engel Management, 15233 Ventura Blvd, Suite 200, Sherman Oaks, CA 91403, USA. *Telephone:* (818) 380-1918. *E-mail:* info@Kraft-Engel.com. *Website:* www .kraft-engel.com; www.johndebney.com.

DeBOER, Brent; American musician (drums). *Career:* mem. The Dandy Warhols 1999–. *Film appearance:* Dig! 2005. *Recordings include:* albums: Thirteen Tales From Urban Bohemia 2000, Welcome To The Monkey House 2003, The Black Album/Come On Feel The Dandy Warhols 2004, Odditorium Or Warlords Of Mars 2005, Earth to the Dandy Warhols 2008, The Farmer 2010, This Machine 2012. *E-mail:* lee@dandywarhols.com. *Address:* The Dandy Warhols, P. O. Box 6836, Portland, OR 97228, USA (office). *E-mail:* brent@dandywarhols.com. *Website:* www.dandywarhols.com (office).

DE BORG, Jerry Simon; British musician (guitar), songwriter and singer; b. 30 Oct. 1963, London, England. *Education:* Harrow Coll. of Art. *Career:* mem. Jesus Jones 1986–; numerous radio and TV broadcasts. *Recordings include:* albums: Liquidizer 1989, Doubt 1991, Perverse 1993, Already 1997, London 2001, Ultimate L.A. Guns 2002. *Honours:* MTV Award for Best New Band 1991. *Address:* c/o 30 Ives Street, London, SW3 2ND, England.

DEDE, Mercan; Turkish/Canadian musician (ney flute, percussion), producer and fmr DJ; b. (Akin Alical), 1966, Turkey. *Education:* Concordia Coll., Montréal. *Career:* worked as DJ under pseudonym Arkin Allen; changed name to Mercan Dede 1987; formed The Mercan Dede Ensemble 1997; producer for Golden Horn and Metropolis Records; composer and musical dir, Seyahatname, Turkish Nat. Modern Dance Troupe 2001; works with Orman Sehir (Jungle City) modern dance performance troupe; collaborations with Secret Tribe; live performer with Kani Karaca and Ihsan Ozgen, Peter Murphy, Natacha Atlas, Mich Geber, Omar Sosa, Maharaja (fmrly Musafir), Shams Brothers, Groove Ala Turca; has performed at numerous live events. *Recordings include:* albums: solo: Sufi Dreams 1987, Breath 2006; with The Mercan Dede Ensemble: Journeys of a Dervish 1999, Seyahatname 2003, Sufi Traveller 2004, Su' 2005, Nefes 2007, 800 2007, Dünya/Earth 2013; with Secret Tribe: Nar 2002. *Current Management:* c/o Heart Factory, Ö. Alper Altun, Resitpasa Mah. Tuncay Artun Cad. Number 16/4, Sariyer, Istanbul, Turkey. *Telephone:* (90) 5323331444. *Fax:* (90) 2122772132. *E-mail:* alper@mercandede.com. *Website:* www.heartfactory.net. *E-mail:* mercandede@mercandede.com. *Website:* www.mercandede.com.

DEDIC, Srdan; Croatian composer, arranger and musician (piano); b. 13 July 1965, Zagreb. *Education:* Zagreb Acad. of Music, Université des Sciences Humaines de Strasbourg, Sweelinck Conservatorium, Amsterdam. *Career:* participated at Gaudeamus Festival (Amsterdam), International Rostrum of Composers (Paris), Music Biennale, Zagreb; performed solo from own; mem. Croatian Composers Soc. *Compositions include:* Mouvemente Concertante, with Zagreb Philharmonic, 9 orchestral performances, Over 50 performances in Europe, America, Australia, writing music for television, theatres, films. *Compositions include:* Snake Charmer (bass clarinet solo) 1986, Beat On (for orchestra) 1988, Canzona (cello, guitar) 1988, Calix (symphonic poem) 1990, At The Party 1990, Concerto (for cello and chamber orchestra), 12 compositions recorded for Croatian Radio, Supercussion album includes composition: At The Party. *Publication:* Composing Using Music Software (brochure). *Honours:* First Prize, UNESCO – International Rostrum of Composers, Paris 1988, Award, student orchestral works, Music Biennale Zagreb 1989, winner, Composition Contest, 29th annual Contemporary Music Festival, Indiana State Univ. 1995. *Address:* Hugo de Grootplein 12, 1052 KW Amsterdam, The Netherlands.

DEE, Brian; British musician (piano) and songwriter; b. 21 March 1936, London; m. 1966 (divorced 1982); one s. one d. *Career:* jazz pianist late 1950s–; session musician and accompanist; extensive BBC radio with trio and many bands; pianist with Ted Heath Orchestra, Kenny Baker Dozen, Laurie Johnson; performed at numerous concerts and festivals; mem. PRS, Musicians' Union, BACSA, MCPS, Performing Artists Media Rights Asscn (PAMRA). *Compositions include:* background music. *Recordings include:* featured on numerous recordings, including own self-penned jazz albums. *Address:* 130 Sheering Mill Lane, Sawbridgeworth, CM21 9ND, England. *Telephone:* (1279) 723320.

DEE, Kiki; British singer; b. (Pauline Matthews), 6 March 1947, Bradford, England. *Career:* leader, Kiki Dee band; Recording artist 1964–; first white artist signed to Tamla-Motown; cabaret singer, Europe and South Africa; appearances, London musicals: Pump Boys and Dinettes 1984; Blood Brothers 1989; solo acoustic tour with guitarist Carmelo Uggeri, support to Jools Holland, UK 1995. *Recordings include:* Albums: I'm Kiki Dee 1968, Great Expectations 1971, Loving and Free 1973, I've Got The Music In Me 1974, Kiki Dee 1977, Stay With Me 1979, Perfect Timing 1982, Angel Eyes 1987, Almost Naked 1995, Where Rivers Meet 1998, The Walk of Faith 2005, Cage the Songbird 2008, The Best of Kiki Dee 2009; singles include: I'm Gonna Run Away From You, Running Out of Fools, Amoureuse 1973, I've Got The Music In Me 1974, How Glad I Am 1975, Don't Go Breaking My Heart, duet with Elton John (No. 1, UK and USA) 1976, Star 1981, True Love, duet with Elton John (No. 2, UK) 1993. *Current Management:* c/o Whatever Artists Management Ltd, PO Box 72301, London, NW7 0HG, England. *Telephone:* (20) 8349-0920. *E-mail:* RLNoble24@hotmail.com. *Website:* www.wamshow.biz. *E-mail:* info@kikiandcarmelo.com. *Website:* www.kikiandcarmelo.com; www.kikidee .com.

DEGAS, Jorge; Brazilian musician (bass); b. 5 July 1953, Rio De Janeiro; m. Stenia Degas; four s. one d. *Education:* Autodidact. *Career:* Festival of Art and Black Culture, Nigeria, 1977; Festival of Cascais, Portugal, 1978; Show, Celebration of Independence, Angola 1979; Festival in Montreaux, Nyon 1982; Rock in Rio 1983; Festival in Avante, Portugal 1984; Festival Free Jazz, Brazil 1985; Show, Pao De Acuca, Rio 1986; Show, Olympia de Paris 1988; Festival, Jazz in the Garden, Berlin 1989; Festival, Jazz in July, Berlin 1990; Copenhagen Jazzhouse Feat 1991; Midtfyns Festival, Denmark 1993; Copenhagen Jazz Festival 1994; Baixo Brasil, Bass Festival 1996; mem. The Danish Music Asscn. *Compositions include:* Music to Film, Paraiba Mulher Macho, Bom Burges, Dona Beija. *Recordings include:* M Resende and Index,

Uniao, Muxima, Quarteto Negro, Ready for Changes, Violeiro, Xiame, Shadow of My Soul, Cantar a Vida. *Website:* www.jorgedegas.dk.

DEGIORGIO, Kirk, (As One, Future Past, Esoterik); British producer, remixer and DJ; b. 1967, London. *Career:* worked in Reckless Records shop in London; travelled to Detroit, became inspired by Derrick May and Juan Atkins to make music; on return to London started producing; founder A.R.T, Op-Art Records; released tracks by artists including Carl Craig, Black Dog; also recorded albums for Mo' Wax and Ubiquity Records; collaborations with Jamie Odell, Ian O'Brien, Dan Keeling; remixed Alien, Newcleus, 4 Hero; mem. PRS. *Recordings include:* Check One 1996, Synthesis 1998, Two Worlds 2001; as As One: Reflections 1994, Planetary Folklore 1997, 21st Century Soul 2001, Out of the Darkness 2004, Elegant Systems 2005, Planetary Folklore 2 2006. *E-mail:* silv.rossetti@btinternet.com (office).

DEGRYSE, Fabien; Belgian musician (guitar), composer and teacher; b. 6 Nov. 1960, Brussels; m. Guns Colette 1985; two s. two d. *Education:* Berklee Coll. of Music, Boston, USA. *Career:* played with Zar 1985–87, including tour in Canada and Belgium; played with Quadruplex 1985–92; concerts with PH Catherine and Toots Thielemans; played with Panta Rhei including recording of three albums and numerous concerts and festivals 1994–97, in Europe and Africa; still plays with L'Ame Des Poètes including recording of four albums and numerous concerts and festivals, and broadcasting in Europe, Africa, Canada and Asia; also plays with own trio (with Bruno Castellucci and Bart Denolf), including concerts in Belgium, France, Tunisia, Lettonia, Taiwan; teaches jazz guitar, Conservatory of Brussels, Belgium; masterclasses. *Recordings:* Quadruplex 1990, Medor Sadness 1992, Hommage à René Thomas 1997, Fabien Degryse Jazz 2001, The Heart of the Acoustic Guitar (with Castellucci and Denolf) 2007. *Publications:* L'Improvisation Jazz par les arpèges 1999. *Current Management:* c/o JPR Production, Chemin des Meules 2, 08600 Rancennes, France. *Telephone:* 6-75-46-65-95 (mobile). *E-mail:* rolotjpr@wanadoo.fr. *Website:* www.jpr-production.org; www.fabiendegryse .com.

DEL FRA, Riccardo; Italian musician (double bass) and composer; b. 20 Feb. 1956, Rome. *Education:* studied Sociology; double bass, Conservatorio di Frosinone, Private music studies. *Career:* mem. RAI TV Orchestra; played with pianist Enrico Pieranunzi; freelance backing musician, touring with artists in Italy including: Slide Hampton, Art Farmer, Kai Winding; played with Chet Baker, trio and quartet (nine years partnership, 12 albums, radio, television and films, tours of Europe and Japan); freelance work with Johnny Griffin, Toots Thielemans (tours of USA and Japan), Bob Brookmeyer; also played with Art Blakey and the Jazz Messengers, Kenny Wheeler, Paul Motian, Sonny Stitt, James Moody, Clifford Jordan, Joe Diorio (tours of Italy). *Compositions include:* Silent Call (for jazz quartet and string orchestra), Inner Galaxy (for tenor sax, double bass and four cellos), Aux Fontaines Du Temple (for jazz septet, flutes, harp and string orchestra), Volo sul Lago (for symphonic orchestra and jazz septet) 1996. *Recordings include:* A Sip Of Your Touch; 12 with Chet Baker include: Chet Sings Again, Mr B, At The Capolinea; Paris Suite (with Bob Brookmeyer), Voulouz Loar (duet with Annie Ebrel); also recorded with Dominique Pifarely, Jacques Pellen. *Honours:* Chevalier de l'Ordre des Arts et des Lettres 2003. *E-mail:* r.delfra@free.fr. *Website:* www.riccardodelfra.net.

DEL NAJA, Robert (see 3-D)

DEL REAL, Emmanuel; Mexican musician (keyboards, guitar), programmer and singer. *Career:* Founder-mem. Café Tacvba 1989–; contrib. to film soundtracks, including Y tu mamá también, Vivir Mata, Amores Perros; collaborations with artists, including Celso Piña, El Gran Silencio, Inspector, Kronos Quartet, Ofelia Medina, David Byrne. *Recordings include:* albums: Café Tacuba 1992, Re 1994, Avalancha de Éxitos (EP) 1996, Reves/YoSoy (Latin Grammy Award for best rock album) 1999, Tiempo Transcurrido 2001, Vale Callampa (EP) 2002, Cuatro Caminos (Latin Grammy Award for best alternative music album 2004) 2003, SiNo 2007, Fontana Bella 2007, El Objeto Antes Llamado Disco 2012. *Honours:* Latin Grammy Awards for Best Rock Song (for Esta Vez) 2008, for Best Alternative Song (for Volver a Comenzar) 2008. *Address:* Universal Music Latino, 1425 Collins Avenue, Miami Beach, FL 33139, USA. *Telephone:* (305) 604-1380. *Fax:* (305) 604-1343 (office). *Website:* www.universalmusica.com; www.cafetacuba.com.mx.

DEL REY, Lana; American singer and songwriter; b. (Elizabeth Woolridge Grant), 21 June 1985, New York, NY; d. of Robert Grant. *Education:* Kent School, Conn., Fordham Univ. *Career:* early releases issued under name of Lizzy Grant; signed to Stranger Records 2011; signed to Next Model Management 2012. *Recordings include:* albums: Lana Del Rey AKA Lizzy Grant 2010, Born to Die 2012, Ultraviolence 2014, Honeymoon 2015. *Honours:* Q Awards Next Big Thing 2011, BRIT Award for Best Int. Breakthrough Act 2012, MTV Europe Music Award for Best Alternative 2012, 2015. *Current Management:* c/o Next Model Management, 15 Watts Street, 6th Floor, New York, NY 10013, USA. *Telephone:* (212) 925-5100. *Fax:* (212) 925-5931. *Website:* www.nextmodels.com; www.lanadelrey.com.

DELAFONS, Jonny, (L. B. Dope); British musician (drums) and producer. *Career:* mem. Alabama 3 (band known as A3 in USA). *Recordings include:* albums: with Alabama 3: Exile on Coldharbour Lane 1997, La Peste 2000, Power In The Blood 2002, The Last Train To Mashville 2003, Outlaw 2005, M.O.R. 2007, Revolver Soul 2010, There Will Be Peace in the Valley When We Get the Keys to the Mansion on the Hill 2011, Shoplifting 4 Jesus 2011; other:

Robert Love, Ghost Flight 2006, DJD Presents Hydraulic Dogs (co-producer); remix: Paul Hartnoll featuring Robert Smith, Please. *Website:* www.alabama3 .co.uk.

DELAKIAN, Michel Horen; French musician (trumpet) and composer; b. 6 Nov. 1957, Saint Etienne; m. Isabelle 1982; one s. one d. *Education:* Conservatoire de Musique, St Etienne. *Career:* mem. Claude Bolling Big Band 1982–; also played with Martial Solal 1983–85, Orchestre Nat. de Jazz 1986–89, orchestres de Jean-Loup Longnon 1988–93, Laurent Cugny 1989–92, Michel Legrand 1994–95, Sacha Distel et les Collegiens 1994–95, Jazz 'n Spirituals 1997–, Organic Jungle 1997–; co-leader own quartet 1990–; numerous television appearances, tours; mem. Société des auteurs, compositeurs et éditeurs de musique (SACEM), ADAMI, SPEDIDAM. *Recordings include:* with Claude Bolling Big Band: Bolling plays Ellington 1986; with Orchestre Nat. De Jazz: 1986, 1987; solo: Biarritz 1991; also recorded with Stéphane Grappelli. *Honours:* Prix Sidney Bechet, Académie du Jazz 1987. *E-mail:* md@micheldelakian.com. *Website:* www.micheldelakian.com.

DELANEY, Brian; American musician (drums). *Career:* mem. New York Dolls 2004–. *Recordings include:* album: One Day It Will Please Us to Remember Even This 2006, Cause I Sez So 2009. *Address:* c/o Roadrunner Records, 902 Broadway, Eighth Floor, New York, NY 10010, USA. *E-mail:* roadrunner@roadrunnerrecords.com. *Website:* www.nydolls.org (office).

DELANEY, Lawrence (Larry); Canadian newspaper editor and publisher; *Editor, Country Music News;* b. 30 Aug. 1942, Eastview, Ont.; m. Joanne Bonell 1964; one s. one d. *Career:* Co-founder, Ed. and Publr Country Music News, Canada's nat. music newspaper 1980–, providing int. exposure and profile for Canadian country music artists and industry; mem. Canadian Country Music Asscn, CMA, CPPA. *Honours:* received CCMA Country Music Person of the Year citation 11 times, inducted into Canadian Country Music Hall of Fame 1989, Ottawa Valley Country Music Hall of Fame 1993, CCMA Hall of Honour 1996. *Address:* Country Music News, PO Box 7323, Vanier Terminal, Ottawa, ON K1L 8E4, Canada (office). *E-mail:* larry@ countrymusicnews.ca (office). *Website:* www.countrymusicnews.ca (office).

DeLAUGHTER, Tim; American singer and musician (guitar); b. TX. *Career:* mem. and lead singer, Tripping Daisy 1991–99; founder mem., musical dir and lead singer of choral and instrumental pop group, The Polyphonic Spree 2000–; numerous live festival performances. *Recordings:* albums: with Tripping Daisy: Bill 1992, I Am An Elastic Firecracker 1995, Jesus Hits Like The Atom Bomb 1998, Tripping Daisy 2000; with The Polyphonic Spree: The Beginning Stages Of... 2002, Together We're Heavy 2004, The Fragile Army 2007. *Current Management:* Good Management, 617 N Good Latimer, Dallas, TX 75204, USA. *Telephone:* (214) 752-4663. *E-mail:* management@ thepolyphonicspree.com. *Website:* www.goodrecords.com. *E-mail:* Polyspreemgmt@gmail.com. *Website:* www.thepolyphonicspree.com.

DELGADO, Frank; American DJ. *Career:* mem., Deftones 1997–. *Recordings include:* albums: Around the Fur 1997, Live (EP) 1999, White Pony 2000, Back To School 2001, Deftones 2003, More Maximum Deftones 2003, Saturday Night Wrist 2006, Diamond Eyes 2010, Koi No Yokan 2012. *Honours:* Kerrang! Classic Songwriter Award 2007. *Current Management:* Velvet Hammer Management, 9911 West Pico Blvd, Suite 350, Los Angeles, CA 90035-2703, USA. *Telephone:* (310) 657-6161. *Website:* velvethammer.net; www.deftones.com.

DeLONGE, Thomas (Tom) Matthew; American singer and musician (guitar); b. 13 Dec. 1975, San Diego, Calif.; m. Jennifer Jenkins 2001. *Career:* Founder mem., Blink-182 1993–2005; numerous TV appearances and concerts worldwide; mem., Box Car Racer 2001–; Founder mem., Angels & Airwaves 2005–. *Recordings include:* albums: with Blink-182: Fly Swatter 1993, Buddah 1994, Cheshire Cat 1994, Dude Ranch 1997, Enema Of The State 1999, The Mark, Tom And Travis Show (The Enema Strikes Back) 2000, Take Off Your Pants And Jacket 2001, Blink-182 2003, Neighborhoods 2011; with Box Car Racer: Box Car Racer 2002, There Is 2002; with Angels & Airwaves: We Don't Need to Whisper 2006, I-Empire 2007, Love 2010, Love: Part 2 2011. *Current Management:* c/o International Talent Booking, First Floor, Ariel House, 74a Charlotte Street, London, W1T 4QJ, England. *Telephone:* (20) 7637-6979. *Fax:* (20) 7637-6978. *E-mail:* info@itb.co.uk. *Website:* www.itb.co .uk; www.blink182.com; www.angelsandairwaves.com.

DELS, Anita (see Doth, Anita)

DELSON, Brad; American musician (guitar); b. 1 Dec. 1977, Agoura, CA. *Education:* Univ. of California at Los Angeles. *Career:* mem., The Pricks, Relative Degree; founding mem., Xero 1996, renamed Hybrid Theory, later renamed Linkin Park 1999–; numerous int. concerts. *Recordings include:* albums: Hybrid Theory (Rock Bear Awards for Best Int. Album 2001) 2000, Reanimation 2002, In The End: Live & Rare 2002, Meteora 2003, Live in Texas 2003, Collision Course (with Jay-Z) 2004, Minutes to Midnight 2007, A Thousand Suns 2010, Living Things 2012, The Hunting Party 2014. *Honours:* Billboard Award for Best Modern Rock Artist 2001, Rock Bear Award for Best Int. Band 2001, Kerrang! Award for Best Int. Newcomer 2001, Rolling Stone Award for Best Hard Rock/Metal Band 2001, World Music Awards for Best Selling Rock Group 2002, 2003, 2007, MTV Awards for Best Group, Best Hard Rock 2002, MTV Europe Awards for Best Rock Act 2004, 2011, 2012, 2014, for Best World Stage Performance 2009, 2013, for Best Live Act 2010, Grammy Award for Best Rap/Sung Collaboration (for Numb/Encore, with Jay-Z) 2006, MTV Europe Music Award for Best Band 2007, American Music Awards for

Favorite Alternative Rock Music Artist 2007, 2008, 2012. *Current Management:* Andy Gould Management, 8484 Wilshire Boulevard, Suite 425, Beverly Hills, CA 90211, USA. *Website:* www.linkinpark.com.

DELTA HOUSE OF FUNK (see Beedle, Ashley)

DELVAUX, Floch, (Floch); Belgian singer, musician (guitar, bass) and songwriter; b. (Jean-Louis Delvaux), 26 Jan. 1968, Brussels. *Education:* classical music lessons, Brussels. *Career:* guitarist and songwriter, Brain Damage and Death 1986–89; singer and songwriter, Brain Damage and Death 1989–92; singer, guitarist and songwriter, Goyasnada 1990–98; singer, guitarist and songwriter, K-Oz Office 1994–; guitarist, 26 Tears; solo projects: Machine 26, Serial Joker. *Compositions include:* several songs with Goyasnada, some released on several compilation albums; Dreamland 1992. *Recordings include:* albums: 1986–92 (with Brain Damage and Death) 1993, Rage Rage Rage (with K-Oz Office) 1996, Death 2000 (with K-Oz Office) 1999, Let's Split Up It's Safer (with 26 Tears) 2008. *Address:* 52 rue Emile Claus, Boite 1, 1050 Brussels, Belgium. *E-mail:* totalfmr@hotmail.com.

DEMARCUS, Jay; American singer, songwriter, actor, musician (guitar, bass guitar, keyboards, mandolin) and producer; b. (Stanley Wayne DeMarcus, Jr), 26 April 1971, Columbus, Ohio; m. Allison Alderson DeMarcus 2004; one s. one d. *Education:* Tree of Life High School, Lee Univ., Cleveland, Tenn. *Career:* Founding mem. Rascal Flatts 1999–. *Films include:* The Emperor's Last Groove, Cars, Hannah Montana: The Movie, Rascal Flatts: Changed, Saving Santa. *Television includes:* American Idol, CSI: Crime Scene Investigation, The Oprah Winfrey Show, CMT Insider, Dancing with the Stars, Ellen: The Ellen DeGeneres Show, Yes, Dear, The Tonight Show with Jay Leno, Live with Regis and Kelly, Late Night with Jimmy Fallon, Late Night with David Letterman, The Today Show, Good Morning America, The View, The Voice, Chelsea Lately, Hannity, CMA Country Christmas, CMT Artist of the Year host, Late Night with Conan O'Brien, Jimmy Kimmel Live, Boston Pops Concert, CBS Home for the Holidays, Late Late Show with Craig Ferguson, CBS This Morning, To Appomattox (pre-production), Live with Kelly and Michael, Blue Collar TV, CMT Making the Video: Rascal Flatts Feels Like Today, Academy of Country Music Preshow, CMT Total Release: Most Wanted Live Tour, Backstory: Rascal Flatts. *Recordings include:* albums: Rascal Flatts 2000, Melt 2002, Feels Like Today 2004, Me and My Gang 2006, Still Feels Good 2007, Unstoppable 2009; produced: Chicago XXX 2004, James Otto: Sunset Man 2007, Jessica Andrews 2009. *Honours:* CMA Horizon Awards 2002, CMA Awards for Best Vocal Group 2003, 2004, 2005, 2006, 2007, 2008, ACM Awards for Best New Vocal Group 2001, for Best Vocal Group 2002, 2003, 2004, 2005, 2006, 2007, 2008, 2009, and for Song of the Year (for I'm Movin' On), ASCAP Vocal Group of the Year 2004, American Music Awards for Favourite Country Band, Duo or Group 2006, 2007, 2008, 2009, CMT Group Music Video of the Year Award 2003, 2004, 2005, 2006, 2007, 2008, Radio Music Award Country Song of the Year for 'God Bless Broken Road' 2005, People's Choice Award for Favourite Remake for 'Life is a Highway' 2007, People's Choice Award for Favourite Song from a Movie for 'Life is a Highway' 2007, People's Choice Award for Favourite Group 2008, People's Choice Award for Favourite Country Song (for 'Stand') 2008, inducted into Music City Walk of Fame 2010, Artist of the Decade, Acad. of Country Music Awards 2010, Tony Martell Lifetime Entertainment Achievement Award 2011, CMT Music Award, Collaborative Video of the Year with Justin Bieber 2011, inducted as mem. Grand Ole Opry, received a star on the Hollywood Walk of Fame 2012. *Current Management:* c/o William Morris Agency, 1600 Division Street, Suite 300, Nashville, TN 37203, USA. *Website:* www.wma.com; www.rascalflatts.com.

DEML, Marcus; German musician (guitar), producer and songwriter; b. 9 Aug. 1967, Prague, Czechoslovakia. *Education:* Guitar Inst. of Tech., Los Angeles. *Career:* formed own band Quest 1983; worked on Earth Nation project with Ralf Hildenbeutel 1993–95; session musician 1993–2005; Founder-mem. Errorhead 1995–; f. own record label, EGP-Records 2004; worldwide tours; project appearances on MTV; festival appearances; mem. GEMA, GVL. *Recordings include:* albums: with Earth Nation: Thoughts in Past Future 1994; with Errorhead: Errorhead 1998, Errorrhythm, Modern Hippie 2008, Organic Pill 2012; appearances on numerous albums, including for Rödelheim Hartreim Projekt, Kingdom Come, Lotto King Karl. *Website:* www .errorhead.net.

DEMPSEY, Damien; Irish singer and songwriter; b. Donaghmede, Dublin. *Education:* Ballyfermot Rock School. *Career:* has toured as support act to Sinéad O'Connor, Bob Dylan, Morrissey as well as headline tours in Ireland, UK, USA. *Recordings include:* albums: The Contender (EP) 1995, They Don't Teach This Shit In School 2000, Seize the Day 2003, Shots 2005, Live at the Olympia 2006, Sing All Our Cares Away 2006, The Rocky Road 2008. *Honours:* Meteor Ireland Music Award for Best Irish Male 2006, 2007. *Current Management:* c/o Jim Fleming, Fleming Artists, 543 North Main Street, Ann Arbor, MI 48104, USA. *Website:* www.flemingartists.com; www .damiendempsey.com.

DEMPSEY, Gaylene Katharan; Canadian writer and editor; b. 1 Aug. 1960, Winnipeg, Man. *Education:* Red River Coll. *Career:* Ed. monthly entertainment paper, Circuit 1989–; Ed.-in-Chief monthly entertainment paper, The Insider 1990–; Ed. Jazz Winnipeg Festival Programme 1990–; volunteer, Winnipeg Folk Festival 1990–; Exec. Dir Manitoba Audio Recording Industry Assen 1991–; represents Manitoba Music Industry from songwriters to labels; freelance work; currently Urban Missionary, Hood Mom Missions; mem.

FACTOR Nat. Advisory Bd, Artspace (exec. mem.). *Recordings:* albums: One Found Worthy, Deeper: Live from the Prayer Room. *Publications include:* contributed several articles to SOCAN Words and Music, Grafitti Magazine. *Honours:* Music Industry Exec. of the Year, Prairie Music Awards 1999. *Address:* 242 Spence Street, Winnipeg, MB R3C 1Y4, Canada (home). *Telephone:* (204) 786-2191 (home). *E-mail:* gaylenedempsey@yahoo.ca (office).

DEMPSEY, Paul; Australian singer, songwriter and musician (guitar); b. 25 May 1976; m. Stephanie Ashworth. *Career:* Founder, Fish of the Day 1994–, later renamed Something For Kate; formed Scared of Horses solo side project 1997–98. *Recordings include:* albums: Elsewhere For Eight Minutes 1997, An Empty Flight (solo as Scared of Horses) 1998, Beautiful Sharks 1999, QandA With Dean Martin (compilation) 2000, Echolalia 2001, The Official Fiction 2003, Phantom Limbs 2004, Desert Lights 2006, The Murmur Years 2007, Live at the Corner 2008, Leave Your Soul to Science 2012. *Honours:* Australian Music Industry Critics Award for Album of the Year 2000, Australian Live Music Award for Best Live Act 2000, JJJ Listeners' Poll Award for Best Album 2001. *Address:* PO Box 2235, Prahran, Vic. 3181, Australia (office). *E-mail:* paul@somethingforkate.com (office). *Website:* www .somethingforkate.com (office).

DEMUS, Chaka; Jamaican rap artist; b. (John Taylor), 1965, West Kingston. *Career:* billed as Nicodemus Jr on various sound systems, including Supreme and Jammy's; changed name to Chaka Demus 1985, solo artist 1985–91; rapper in duo, Chaka Demus and Pliers 1991–. *Recordings include:* albums: solo: Everybody Loves the Chaka 1988, The Original Chaka 1989, Unstoppable 1996, Ruff and Tuff 1997, DJ Spirit 2008, Second Coming 2013; with Chaka Demus and Pliers: Gal Wine 1992, Ruff This Year 1992, Chaka Demus and Pliers 1992, Tease Me 1993, Help Them Lord 2001, Back Off the Wall 2007, So Proud 2008; with Shabba Ranks: Rough and Rugged 1987. *Current Management:* c/o monkeybizmanagement. *Telephone:* (7940) 550153. *E-mail:* info@monkeybizmanagement.com. *Website:* www.monkeybizmanagement .com.

DENCH, Ian; British musician (guitar) and songwriter; b. 7 Aug. 1964. *Career:* mem. EMF 1989–96; later joined band Whistler. *Recordings include:* Albums: Schubert Dip 1991, Stigma 1992; Cha Cha Cha 1995, Best of EMF 2001; Singles: Unbelieveable 1990, I Believe 1991, Children, 1991, Lies 1991, They're Here 1992, It's You 1992, Perfect Day 1995, I'm A Believer (with Vic Reeves and Bob Mortimer) 1995, Afro King 1995, Guitarist on Dido, Here With Me 2000, Miracle Hits 2002, My Way 2009. *Website:* www.emf-theband.com.

DENGLER, Carlos; American musician (bass guitar, keyboards) and DJ. *Education:* New York Univ. *Career:* mem., Interpol 1998–2010. *Recordings include:* albums: Turn On The Bright Lights 2002, Antics 2004, Our Love to Admire 2007. *Website:* www.carlosdengler.com.

DENIO, Amy Eliott, BA; American composer, vocalist and multi-instrumentalist (saxophone, guitar, bass, accordion, clarinet); b. 9 June 1961, Boston, MA. *Education:* Hampshire Coll., Amherst, MA, Jazz India Vocal Inst., Mumbai, India. *Career:* performed in USA, Asia, South America, East and Central Europe 1977–; co-founder, The Entropics, performances in Canada and the USA 1985–87; co-founder, Tone Dogs, tours in USA and Europe 1987–91; played bass on soundtrack and acted in film, Shredder Orpheus 1988; co-founder, Billy Tipton Memorial Saxophone Quartet, tours in USA and Europe 1988–; Founder, Spoot Music (publishing co and record label) 1990; singer with Curlew, tours in USA 1990–93; Music Dir, Sit Still 1992–93; included in John Cage Exhibit, Venice Biennale 1993; co-founder, Nudes/Pale Nudes, tours in USA, Canada, Brazil and Europe 1994–99, Swiss TV performance 1999; co-founder, FoMoFlo, tours in USA and Japan 1995–97; played accordion and sang with The Four Accordionists of the Apocalypse tour, Europe 1998; Music Dir for David Dorfman Dance: Skydown 1997, To Lie Tenderly 2000; composed and sang for Die Knodel, tours in Seattle and Europe 1998; Music Dir for Lorenzo Pickle (clown) 1998–; plays saxophone and clarinet and sings with Kultur Shock, tours in Spain and USA 1999–; played accordion, alto saxophone and sang with Zu, tours in Italy 2000–; co-founder, Quintetto alla Busara, tours in Europe 2001–04; Music Dir for UMO Ensemble 2001; played bass and sang with Danny Barnes, tours in USA 2002–04; radio performances in Europe and USA 1995–; played accordion, alto sax and clarinet with Die Resonanz 2006–09; co-founder, Ama Trio 2005–; composer for Pat Graney, Saxhouse, Tattoo, Vivian Girls, House of Mind, Girl Gods 1992–; mem. ASCAP. *Compositions include:* For Jeff Bickford Dance: I & I 1990, Twilight & the Grove 1997, Into the Tumbling Ocean 1997; For Pat Graney Dance: Sax House 1991, Tattoo 2000; Bus Horn Concerto 1992; For Run/Remain Ensemble: Sit Still 1992, The Sherman Preludes 1994; Windows (music for Peter Vogt film) 1993; Tempesta: An Urban RAPsody (with poet Luis Rodriguez) 1994; The Seattle Sound (commissioned by RAI 3, Italian nat. radio) 1994; Green Fish Symphonette (for Berkley Symphony) 1995; For David Dorfman Dance: Approaching No Calm 1995, Skydown 1997, To Lie Tenderly 2000; Le Serve (The Maids, soundtrack for Jean Genet play) 1997; False Prophets or Just Dang Good Guessers (for Shaking Ray Levi Soc.) 1997; Non Lo So, Polo (for Die Knoedel, Austrian chamber octet) 1998; five compositions for Relache Ensemble 1999–2000; Brother Fox (commissioned by New York Festival of Song) 2001; TASOGARE (Twilight), for Yoko Murao Dance 2001; AcchorDREAM, for Henry Art Gallery installation 2001; Synchrony in Estrus (soundtrack for Thomas Edward film) 2001; White Girls, for KT Niehoff/D9 Dance 2002; Surveillance, for Victor Hugo House installation 2002; Against Ending (for Victoria Marks Dance) 2002; The Other One (for Aiko Kinoshita Dance) 2002. *Recordings include:* 45 CD releases including: with Tone Dogs: Ankety Low Day 1989, Early Middle Years 1991, Birthing Chair Blues 1991, Tongues 1993; Curlew with Amy Denio: A Beautiful Western Saddle 1993; Billy Tipton Memorial Saxophone Quartet: Saxhouse 1993, Make It Funky God 1994, Box 1996, Wise to the Heat (with Pale Nudes) 1996, Vanishing Point 1996, Soul Come Home 1998; FoMoFlo: Slug and Firearms 1997, No 11 1997; Amy Denio: More Spoot 1997; with The Science Group: …a mere coincidence… 1999; Die Knoedel: Non Lo So, Polo 1999; Greatest Hits 1999; Tattoo (with Pat Graney Dance Co) 2000, The Memphis Years (with George Cartwright) 2000, Danubians 2000, Belle Confusion (with Francisco Lopez) 2000, Les Voix Vulgaires 2001, Quintetto alla Busara 2002, To Lie Tenderly, with Petunia 2002, Chickenhawks Ought Not 2002, Vivian Girls (with Martin Hayes) 2004, Soul Come Home (with Pale Nudes) 2004, The Gospel Record (with Derek Bailey and Dennis Palmer) 2005, Venerdi' Santo (with Francesco Calandrino) 2006, sub-Rosa 2008; with the Tiptons: Tsunami 2004, Surrounded by Horns 2004, Drive 2005; with the Tiptons Sax Quartet: Laws of Motion 2008, Strange Flower 2010. *Honours:* Seattle Arts Commission Individual Artist Award for Composition 1990; Artist Trust Artist Fellowship 1996; Best Animated Film Award, New York Underground Film Festival 1997; Bessie Award for Composition, New York Dance and Performance Award 1997; ASCAP Special Awards 1996–2001; Civitella Ranieri Artist Fellowship, Italy 2003, Artist Trust Fellowship, Ireland 2007, Seattle Jazz Hall of Fame 2015. *E-mail:* amy@amydenio.com. *Website:* www.amydenio.com.

DENNARD, David Brooks; American record company executive and musician (bass guitar, guitar, resophonic guitar, harmonica); b. 5 July 1950, Dallas, TX; m. Mary Anna Austin 1980; two d. *Education:* Colorado Coll., Stanford and Univ. of Texas at Austin. *Career:* CBS/Epic Records recording artist with Gary Myrick and The Figures; Pres., owner, Dragon Street Records Inc. 1989–; Dir of A&R, Crystal Clear Sound; Dir, Steve Records, Dallas; mem., Texas Music Asscn Dallas, Cable Access of Dallas Inc., Documentary Arts (bd mem.); performs in The Novas, re-formed 1960s rock group. *Recordings:* with Gary Myrick and the Figures: two albums, two singles, seven videos; recent releases by Ronnie Dawson, Gene Summers, Scott Whitaker, Buck Jones, Centromatic, Meredith Louise Miller and Pump'n Ethyl; Gene Vincent and His Blue Caps, The Lost Dallas Sessions, 1957–58; Johnny Dollar, Mr Action Packed; Groovey Joe Poovey—Greatest Grooves; various artists: The Big 'D' Jamboree Live!; The Gals of the Big 'D' Jamboree; The Guys of the Big 'D' Jamboree. *Honours:* Dallas Society of Visual Communications Award of Excellence 1987, two Silver Microphone Awards 1987, Crystal Award 1988, Steve Records Topaz Award for Best Record Co. 1997, Team Networking Inc. Networker of the Year 2006. *Address:* Dragon Street Records Inc., PO Box 670714, Dallas, TX 75367-0714, USA (office). *Telephone:* (972) 934-2234 (also fax) (office). *E-mail:* daviddennard@mac.net (home); dragonst@flash.net (office); daviddennard@yahoo.com (home). *Website:* www.dragonstreet.com (office); web.mac.com/daviddennard/iWeb/Site/Home.html; www.thenovas.net.

DENNEHY, Timothy Christopher; Irish teacher, broadcaster and singer; b. 29 Dec. 1952, Cahersiveen; m. Máirín 1976; two s. *Career:* numerous radio appearances, local, nat., including own programme on Clare FM: Cuaird An Domhnaigh (Keep in Touch); television programmes dealing with Irish traditional music; f. Góilin Traditional Singers Club (with Donall de Barra) 1979; mem. IMRO, Cumann Cheoltíre Eireann. *Recordings include:* A Thimbleful of Song, Farewell to Miltown Malbay 1997, The Blue Green Door 2002, Old Boots And Flying Sandals 2007. *Address:* Sceilig Records, 2 Cluain Liag Ard, Ennis Road, Miltown Malbay, Ireland. *Telephone:* (7) 3148158. *E-mail:* tim@sceilig.com. *Website:* www.sceilig.com.

DENNERLEIN, Barbara; German jazz musician and composer; *Head, Bebab Records;* b. 25 Sept. 1964, Munich; d. of Hans Dennerlein and Waltraud Dennerlein. *Education:* Ernst-Mach Gymnasium, Haar. *Career:* began playing organ 1975; first concerts 1977, first played in clubs 1979; professional musician and composer 1983–, appearances, concerts and recordings worldwide including jazz clubs in New York, London, Tokyo, festivals in USA, Canada, Europe and radio and TV recordings; f. group Bebab; jazz performances on church, Hammond and concert organs, Germany 1985–; Producer Bebab Records (own record label) 1985–; Publr Bebab/Newtone Edn; Jazz Amb., Deutsche Jazz Fed. 2003; Cultural Amb., Regensburg 2004. *Recordings include:* Jazz Live 1983, Orgelspiele 1984, Bebab 1985, Days of Wine and Roses 1986, Tribute to Charlie 1986, From the Roots Up 1987, Straight Ahead 1988, Barbara Dennerlein Plays Classics 1988, Live on Tour 1989, Barbara Dennerlein Duo 1990, Hot Stuff 1990, Mozart No End and The Paradise Band 1991, Solo 1992, That's Me 1992, Barbara Dennerlein Solo 1992, Barbara Dennerlein B3 1993, Take Off (Jazz Award 1997) 1996, Junkanoo (Jazz Award) 1996, Orgelspiele 1999, Barbara Dennerlein Plays Classics 1999, Outhipped 1999, Love Letters 2001, Spiritual Movement No. 1 2002, In a Silent Mood 2003, It's Magic 2005, Change of Pace 2007, Spiritual Movement No. 2 2008, Bebabaloo 2010. *Television includes:* guest appearances on over 30 European programmes, has hosted her own tv specials. *Radio includes:* own radio shows for Deutschland Radio Berlin, Deutschland Funk Köln 2000–03, guest appearances on numerous shows including Pete Fallico's Doodlin' Lounge, KUSP radio, Santa Cruz, USA. *Honours:* Deutsche Schallplattenkritik Award 1985, 1986, 1995, Downbeat Critics' Poll No. 1 (Hammond B3 organ) 1990, 1991, 1993, 1996, 1998, No 1, German Jazz Charts 1995, Lithuanian Jazz Award for Best Performance 2003, Jazz Award, Rio de Janeiro 2007. *Address:* Bebab Records, Andreas-Wagner-Str. 39A, 85640 Putzbrunn, Germany (office). *Telephone:* (89) 95820305 (office). *Fax:* (89) 9582307 (office). *E-mail:* BarbaraDennerlein@bebab.com (office). *Website:* www.barbaradennerlein.com.

DENNIS, Cathy; British singer and songwriter; b. 25 March 1970, Norfolk. *Career:* featured singer, D-Mob 1989–90; numerous tours and TV appearances; solo artist, songwriter, producer 1990–; songs recorded by artists, including Hear'Say, Ronan Keating, Spice Girls, S Club 7/S Club/S Club 8, Will Young, Rachel Stevens, Kylie Minogue, Kelly Clarkson, Janet Jackson, Gareth Gates, Enrique Iglesias, Celine Dion, Charlotte Church, Britney Spears. *Compositions include:* Natural (S Club 7) 1999, Reach (S Club 7) 2000, Never Had A Dream Come True (S Club 7) 2000, Can't Get You Out of My Head (Kylie Minogue) (Ivor Novello Awards for Most Performed Work, Dance Award, Int. Hit of the Year 2002) 2001, Have You Ever (S Club 7) 2001, Anything Is Possible (Will Young) (Ivor Novello Award) 2002, Showdown (Britney Spears) 2003, Measure of a Man (Clay Aiken) 2003, Toxic (Britney Spears) 2004, About You Now (Sugababes) 2007, I Kissed a Girl (Katy Perry) 2008, Once (Diana Vickers) 2010. *Recordings include:* albums: Move To This 1991, Into The Skyline 1993, Am I The Kinda Girl? 1996, The Irresistible Cathy Dennis 2000; singles: C'Mon and Get My Love (with D-Mob) 1989, That's The Way of the World (with D-Mob) 1990, Touch Me (All Night Long) 1991, Just Another Dream 1991, Too Many Walls 1991, Everybody Move 1991, You Lied To Me 1991, Irresistible 1992, Falling 1993, Why (with D-Mob) 1994, West End Pad 1996, Waterloo Sunset 1997, When Dreams Turned to Dust 1997. *Honours:* Hon. DMus, Univ. of East Anglia 2012; Billboard Award for Best New Female Artist 2001, World Music Award for Best Int. Newcomer, Capital Radio Award for Best Female Artist, SE Asia Award for Top New Artist, Best Song of the Year, Grammy Award for Best Dance Song (for Come Into My World) 2004, seven ASCAP Awards. *Current Management:* c/o Simon Fuller, 19 Management Ltd, Unit 32, Ransomes Dock, 35–37 Parkgate Road, London, SW11 4NP, England.

DENNIS, Jon; British singer, musician (guitar) and songwriter; b. 27 May 1965, Lewisham, London. *Education:* Univ. of Leicester. *Career:* lead singer and guitarist, Blab Happy 1987–93, Slinky 1994; tours and live appearances; mem. Musicians' Union. *Recordings include:* albums: with Blab Happy: Boat 1991, Smothered 1993.

DENSMORE, John; American musician (drums), writer and theatre producer; b. 1 Dec. 1944, Santa Monica, Calif. *Education:* Santa Monica City Coll. *Career:* mem. Psychedelic Rangers 1965; mem. The Doors 1966–72; numerous live performances, festival appearances; with surviving mems of The Doors, played Rock and Roll Hall of Fame, Cleveland 1993, The Doors VH1 appearance 2001, The Doors reunion tour 2002–03; Co-founder, The Doors Music Co., Bright Midnight Records 1997; mem. The Butts Band 1972–75; session, solo work 1972; Founder mem. Tribaljazz; mem. Bess Snyder and Co. *Films include:* The Doors Are Open (documentary) 1968, Feast of Friends (documentary) 1969, appearances in Get Crazy, Dudes, The Doors. *Plays include:* Skins (writer and actor) 1984, Band Dreams and Bebop (actor) 1988, The King of Jazz (adaptor, actor) 1989. *Recordings include:* albums: with The Doors: The Doors 1967, Strange Days 1967, Waiting For The Sun 1968, Morrison Hotel 1970, Absolutely Live 1970, LA Woman 1971, Other Voices 1971, Weird Scenes Inside The Gold Mine 1972, Full Circle 1972, Live At The Hollywood Bowl 1987, Greatest Hits 1996; with Tribaljazz: Tribaljazz 2006. *Publications include:* Riders On The Storm–My Life With Jim Morrison and The Doors 1990. *Honours:* LA Weekly Theater Award for Music, inducted into Rock and Roll Hall of Fame 2001. *E-mail:* info@tribaljazzlive.com (office). *Website:* www.thedoors.com; www.tribaljazzlive.com; www.johndensmore.com.

DENTERS, Esmée; Dutch singer and songwriter; b. 1988, Arnhem. *Career:* after posting videos of her performances on YouTube, Denters came to the attention of Justin Timberlake, who signed her to a recording contract on his label, Tennman Records 2008; professional solo artist 2008–. *Recordings:* album: Outta Here 2009. *Honours:* TMF Award for Best Female Artist 2009, 2010, MTV Europe Music Award for Best Dutch and Belgian Act 2009. *E-mail:* info@tennmanrecords.com (office). *Website:* www.tennmanrecords.com (office); esmeeworld.com.

DENZLER, Bertrand; Swiss musician (tenor saxophone); b. 27 Oct. 1963, Geneva. *Education:* Zurich Conservatory, Switzerland. *Career:* concerts, tours and recordings in Europe and South America with musicians including Barry Guy, Mark Sanders, Benoit Delbecq, Hélène Labarrière, Norbert Pfammatter, Christophe Marguet, Hasse Poulsen, Ninh Le Quan, Sophie Agnel; festival appearances in Willisau, Cologne, Le Mans, Paris, Grenoble, Zurich, Berne, Lausanne, Neuchatel, Fribourg; appearances at Swiss New Jazz Festival 1998; leader, own ensemble, Bertrand Denzler Cluster; live or studio recordings for nat. broadcasting corpns throughout Europe; mem. Swiss Musicians' Syndicate. *Compositions include:* some 70 compositions played or recorded with various ensembles; numerous compositions for film, theatre and documentary. *Recordings include:* albums: appeared on Folies 1992, Dervis Mustafa 1993, Minor Works 1994, Now 1996, Y? 1999, Animal Language 1999, Ouverture Facile 1999, Les Correspondances 2000, Ub/Abu 2001, 02/2000 2000, Tentacles 2003, Asymétries 2003, Hoop Whoop 2003, Momentum 3 2002, Hoib 2004, Metz 2004, Stralau 2005, vasistas 2005, Three Dances 2005, Propagations 2007, Tenor 2010, Horns 2015, Heretofore 2015, Morph 2015. *E-mail:* denzler@club-internet.fr. *Website:* bdenzler.free.fr.

DEQUIDT, Loïc; French jazz musician (piano, percussion) and composer; b. 1 May 1973, Arras. *Education:* Conservatoire Nat. Supérieur de Musique de Paris, studied in Italy with E. Rava, F. D'Andrea, E. Pieranunzi. *Career:* Leader of The Opposite, Loïc Dequidt, Loïc Dequidt Quartet. *Honours:* Prix TB du Conservatoire Nat. Supérieur de Musique de Paris. *Address:* Spexarev. 6B, 224 71 Lund, Sweden (home). *E-mail:* mail@loicdequidt.com (home). *Website:* www.loicdequidt.com; www.theopposite.se.

DERRINGER, Rick; American musician (guitar) and producer; b. (Richard Zehringer), 5 Aug. 1947, Fort Recovery, O. *Career:* mem. The McCoys 1965–69; mem. Johnny Winter and Edgar Winter groups; solo artist 1974–; leader own group, Derringer Band 1976–83; session musician. *Recordings include:* albums: solo: All American Boy 1974, Spring Fever 1975, Derringer 1976, Sweet Evil 1977, If You Weren't So Romantic 1978, Guitars and Women 1979, Face To Face 1980, Rick Derringer 1981, Good Dirty Fun 1983, Back to the Blues 1993, Electra Blues 1994, Required Rocking 1996, Blues Deluxe 1998, Jackhammer Blues 2000; with Edgar Winter: White Trash 1971, Road Work 1972, They Only Come Out At Night 1973, Shock Treatment 1974, Jasmine Nightdream 1975, With Rick Derringer 1975; with Johnny Winter: Johnny Winter and Rick Derringer 1971, Johnny Winter Live 1971, Still Alive and Well 1973, Saints and Sinners 1974, John Dawson Winter III 1974, The Johnny Winter Story 1980; lead guitar solo, Eat It, Weird Al Yankovic (parody of Michael Jackson's Beat It) 1984; also featured on albums by Air Supply, Donald Fagen, Dan Hartman, Cyndi Lauper, Bette Midler, Meat Loaf, Mason Ruffner, Todd Rundgren, Steely Dan, Bonnie Tyler, Rosie Vela. *Website:* www.rickderringer.com.

DERUDDER, Peter; Belgian musician (concert flute, uillean pipes, whistle, fiddle, bodhran); b. 8 Jan. 1969, Wervik; m. Peggy Denorme; two s. *Education:* obtained highest honours in music theory, concert flute, music history, music harmony and chamber music. *Career:* mem. The Swigshift 1987–; festival appearances 1990–; regional radio and TV broadcasts; mem. Volksmuziekfederatie. *Film:* Stille Waters 2002. *Recordings include:* albums: Tales From the Great Whiskey Book 1996, Witness of a Celtic Past 1998, The Swigshift and Friends 2001, Walking Home 2008. *Honours:* hon. certificate for second place in nat. competition for young soloists, State Medal for concert flute and chamber music 1988. *Address:* Ten Brielensesteenweg 25, 8940 Wervik, Belgium (office). *Telephone:* (5) 631-26-78 (office). *E-mail:* peter.derudder@skynet.be (office); info@swigshift.com (office). *Website:* www.swigshift.com; www.peterderudder.com.

DESANDRE-NAVARRE, Xavier, BSc; French musician (drums, percussion) and composer; b. 11 Oct. 1961, Paris; m. Susan Mouget 1992; one d. *Career:* has worked with Gil Evans, Youn Sun Nah, Tania Maria, Niels Lan Doky, David Sanborn, Randy Brecker, Gino Vanelli, Orchestre National de Jazz, Les Rita Mitsouko, Michel Portal, Manu Dibango, Lars Danielsson, Julia Migenes; solo performances, United Nations Of Groove. *Composition:* Zoom. *Films:* The Professional (dir Luc Besson), Manolete (dir M. Mejies), Goldman (dir C. Blanc). *Recordings include:* with Gil Evans: The Complete Recordings, Golden Hair, Rythm A Ning; Niels Lan Doky: Asian Sessions, The Story Of Earth & Water 2010; with Caecilie Norby: Queen of Bad Excuses, First Conversation; with Lars Danielsson: Melange Bleu, Libera Me, Northern Lights; solo: Zoom. *Address:* 95 avenue Jean Lolive, 93500 Pantin, France. *E-mail:* xavier.desandre@free.fr. *Website:* xavier.desandre.free.fr.

DESEO, Csaba; Hungarian musician (violin, viola) and composer; b. 15 Feb. 1939, Budapest; m. Katalin Szony; one s. *Education:* Bartók Conservatory, Budapest (Violin Teacher's Diploma). *Career:* mem. Hungarian Nat. Philharmonic Orchestra 1966–2000; jazz soloist, Combo Leader, four own LPs, six CDs 1964–; mem. Hungarian Jazz Fed., Hungarian Composers' Union. *Publications:* jazz articles in Hungarian newspapers. *Honours:* Gold Cross of Merit of the Repub. of Hungary. *Address:* Bercsenyi U 36, 1117 Budapest, Hungary. *E-mail:* deseocsaba@freemail.hu.

DESMARAIS, Lorraine, BMus, MMus; Canadian jazz musician (piano), composer and arranger; *Professor of Jazz Piano, St Laurent College, Montreal*; b. 15 Aug. 1956, Montréal, Québec. *Education:* Acad. Internationale d'été de Nice, France, studied stage with Pierre Barbizet, École Vincent D'Indy, Univ. of Sherbrooke, McGill Univ., studied Combo jazz – Armas Maiste, Montreal Univ. of Montreal, studied musical arranging with Richard Ferland, studied jazz piano with Kenny Barron in New York. *Career:* int. festivals: Piano aux Jacobins (China), Piano aux Jacobins de Toulouse (France), Philippines Int. Jazz Festival, Festival Ciclo de Jazz (Spain), March of Jazz, Fla (USA), Festival Int. de Jazz de St-Louis du Sénégal, Cork Guinness Jazz Festival (Ireland), Tron Jazz Club (Scotland), Birdland Jazz Club, New York (USA), Festival de Radio France et Montpellier (Languedoc-Roussillon), Festival OFF Juan-les Pins (France), Club de Jazz Le Travers (Belgium), Festival de Jazz Århus (Denmark), Parc Floral (Paris), Women in Jazz, Kennedy Center, Washington, DC (USA), Epinal, Strasbourg, Nancy, Contrexéville (France), Club de Jazz, Café des Anges, Strasbourg (France), Festival Int. Jazz Days (Moscow) Festival de Caën Printemps Québécois (France), Club Le Méridien de Singapour (Asia) Festival Int. de Jazz de Jakarta (Indonesia), Puerta-Real de Manille (Philippines) Jazz Club Le Petit Opportun, Paris (France), Festival Int. de Jazz de Jacksonville, Fla (USA), Clubs Cappriccio and Greenmayer, Fla (USA), Festival Int. de Jazz de Zurich (Switzerland), Ella's Goru Club, Tenn. (USA)/Blue Note Jazz Club, New York, Scullers Club, Boston; Canadian festivals: Festival Int. de Jazz de Montréal, Festi Jazz de Rimouski; tours in major cities in Québec and New Brunswick; tours of festivals and Canadian cities: Ottawa, Toronto, Calgary, Edmonton, Banff, Red Deer, Canmore, Lethbridge, Victoria, Vancouver, Yukon, Saskatoon, etc.; artistic collaborations: Montreal Jazz Big Band, Dir Philippe Hudon 1998, Orchestre Symphonique de l'Université de Montréal, Dir Jean-François Rivest 2002, Orquesta Sinfonica de Galicia, Spain, Dir Alvaro Albiach 2003, Orchestre Métropolitain du Grand Montréal, Dir Yannick Nézet-Séguin 2003, Symphonie Halifax, Dir Simon Leclerc 2003, Université de Montréal Big Band, Dir Ron Di Lauro 2003, VEJI Vancouver Jazz Improvisation Ensemble, Dir Hugh Fraser 2003, Orchestre Symphonique de Laval, Dir Jean-François Rivest 2005, Orchestre Symphonique de Montréal, Dir David Coleman 2006, Sherbrooke Université Big Band, Dir Michel Lambert 2006, Lorraine Desmarais Big Band 2007, Orchestre Symphonique de Québec, Dir Airat Ichmouratov 2007, Orchestre Symphonique de Montréal, Dir Simon Leclerc 2010, DIVA Big Band, New York (American tour), Dir Sherrie Maricle; currently Prof. of Jazz Piano, St Laurent Coll., Montreal; mem. SOCAN, SODRAC, Guilde des Musiciens du Québec. *Compositions:* film scores for Nat. Film Board of Canada, Sonata for flute and piano 1995, XIII Theme and Variations 2008. *Recordings include:* albums: Trio Lorraine Desmarais (Félix Award for the Jazz Album of the Year 1985) 1985, Andiamo – Trio Lorraine Desmarais 1986, Pianissimo 1987, Vision (SOCAN Composer's Award for Best Jazz Album 1991) 1991, Lorraine Desmarais 1995, Lorraine Desmarais Quartette with Tiger Okoshi (video) 1996, Bleu Silence 1999, Love – Trio Lorraine Desmarais 2002, Jazz pour Noël – Jazz for Christmas (Felix Award for Best Jazz Album 2006) 2005, Live Club Soda 2007, Lorraine Desmarais Big Band (Felix Award from Asscn québécoise de l'industrie du disque (ADISQ) for Best Jazz Album 2009) 2009, Couleurs de Lune 2012; as guest pianist on these albums: Diva Big Band – I Believe In You 1999, Five Play – On The Brink 1999, Jim Corcoran: Entre tout et moi 2000, Lost In The Stars with Guido Basso (Juno Award 2004) 2003, Alain Caron: Conversations 2007, Montréal Variations 2007, Berceuses pour Philou 2008, Martin Deschamps: Le piano et la voix 2008; as composer on these albums: L. Daoust, L. Bessette 'Rhythm 'n' Flute' (Sonata for flute and piano) 1996, Oliver Jones 'Just In Time' 1998. *Publication:* Sonata pour Flûte et Piano. *Honours:* mem., Order of Canada 2013; Dr hc (Université du Québec à Montréal) 2011; Yamaha Award, Festival Int. de Jazz de Montréal 1984, Great American Jazz Competition Award, Fla 1986, Oscar Peterson Award, Festival Int. de Jazz de Montréal 2002, Creation Award, Conseil des arts et des lettres du Québec 2004, Arts et Culture Prize, Gala Femmes de mérite 2005, Opus Prize 'Elles Jazzent' Jazz Concert of the Year 2005, Keyboard Performance Award, Arts Foundation Ontario 2007, André Gagnon Composers Award, Soc. professionnelle des auteurs et des compositeurs du Québec 2007, Gérard Hébert Award from Festival de Jazz de Québec 2011, Prix Coq d'Arts 2012. *Current Management:* c/o Danielle Lefebvre, Agence d'artistes Danielle Lefebvre, 1035, des Écoliers, Trois-Rivières, QC G9B 7W1, Canada. *Telephone:* (819) 377-2608. *Fax:* (819) 377-2608. *E-mail:* Danielle@agencedlefebvre.com. *Website:* www.agencedlefebvre.com. *Telephone:* (450) 963-1669 (home). *E-mail:* lorrainedesmarais@videotron.ca (home). *Website:* www.lorrainedesmarais.com.

DESMOND, Denis Anthony; Irish promoter, artist manager and musician (piano, keyboards); b. 4 July 1950, Cork. *Career:* owner MCD Productions; performer on RTE Radio and TV, at Cork Opera House and many other venues; mem. IFMandAP. *Address:* MCD Productions, 7 Park Road, Dun Laoghaire, Ireland (office). *Website:* www.mcd.ie (office).

DESPLAT, Alexandre; French film score composer; b. 23 Aug. 1961, Paris. *Education:* Conservatoire Nat. Supérieur de Musique, Paris with Claude Ballif, studied orchestration with Jack Hayes in Los Angeles. *Career:* has conducted London Symphony Orchestra, Royal Philharmonic Orchestra, Czech Philharmonic; gives master-classes at Univ. of Paris (Sorbonne) and Royal Coll. of Music, London. *Film scores include:* Ki lo sa? 1985, V.O. 1987, Rossignol de mes amours 1991, Family Express 1991, The Weaker Sexes! 1992, In the Name of the Father and Son 1992, Lapse of Memory 1992, Papa veut pas que je t'épouse 1992, J'aime pas qu'on m'aime 1993, Jour de fauche 1993, Le Paradis absolument 1993, Le Tronc 1993, The Hour of the Pig 1993, See How They Fall 1994, Innocent Lies 1995, Le Fils de Paul 1995, Les Milles 1995, Marie-Louise ou la permission 1995, Quand je serai grand, mon père il sera policier 1995, Those Were the Days 1995, A Self-Made Hero 1996, D'amour et d'eau salée 1996, Death in Therapy 1996, L'Enfer vert 1996, Le Cri de la soie 1996, Love, etc. 1996, Lucky Punch 1996, La Voisine 1997, Sous les pieds des femmes 1997, Un Petit grain de folie 1997, Atilano, presidente 1998, Half a Chance 1998, La Femme du cosmonaute 1998, Restons groupés 1998, The Revergers' Comedies 1998, Une Minute de silence 1998, Brigade spéciale 1999, A Monkey's Tale 1999, C'est pas ma faute 1999, Empty Days 1999, Juliette 1999, Les Ritaliens 1999, Monsieur Naphtali 1999, N'oublie pas que tu m'aimes 1999, Petits nuages d'ete 1999, Retour à Fonteyne 1999, Toni 1999, Filligoggin 2000, Amazone 2000, The Luzhin Defence 2000, Vive nous! 2000, A Hell of a Day 2001, Bad Genres 2001, Barnie's Minor Annoyances 2001, Campagnes 2001, Doors of Glory 2001, Home Sweet Home 2001, Read My Lips 2001, 11'09"01: September 11 2002, Madame Sans-Gêne 2002, Michel Audiard et le mystère du triangle des Bermudes 2002, Sauveur Giordano: Noces de papier 2002, Tous les chagrins se ressemblent 2002, Une Autre femme 2002, Eager Bodies 2003, Girl with a Pearl Earring 2003, Laughter and Punishment 2003, Le Pacte du silence 2003, Les Baisers des autres 2003, Stormy Weather 2003, Tristan 2003, Virus au paradis 2003, Birth 2004, De battre mon coeur s'est arrêté (The Beat That My Heart Skipped) (Silver Bear, Berlin) 2005, Casanova 2005, Hostage 2005, Une aventure 2005, Syriana 2005, The Upside of Anger 2005, The Queen 2006, Firewall 2006, The Valet 2006, The Alibi

2006, La Doublure 2006, Quand j'etais chanteur 2006, The Painted Veil (Golden Globe for Best Original Score 2007) 2006, Michou d'Auber 2007, Ségo et Sarko sont dans un bateau... (documentary) 2007, L'Ennemni intime 2007, Lust, Caution 2007, Mr Magorium's Wonder Emporium 2007, The Golden Compass 2007, Afterwards 2008, Largo Winch 2008, The Curious Case of Benjamin Button 2008, Chéri 2009, Coco Before Chanel 2009, A Prophet 2009, The Army of Crime 2009, Julie & Julia 2009, Fantastic Mr. Fox 2009, New Moon 2009, The Ghost 2010, 'Tamara Drewe' 2010, The King's Speech (BAFTA Award for Best Original Music 2011, Grammy Award for Best Score Soundtrack For Visual Media 2012) 2010, Harry Potter and the Deathly Hallows: Part 1 2010, The Burma Conspiracy 2011, A Better Life 2011, The Tree of Life 2011, La fille du puisatier 2011, Harry Potter and the Deathly Hallows: Part 2 2011, The Ides of March 2011, Carnage 2011, Extremely Loud & Incredibly Close 2011, My Way 2012, Moonrise Kingdom 2012, Rust and Bone 2012, Reality 2012, Renoir 2012, Argo 2012, Rise of the Guardians 2012, Zero Dark Thirty 2012, Venus in Fur 2013, Zulu 2013, Marius 2013, Fanny 2013, Philomena 2013, The Monuments Men 2014, The Grand Budapest Hotel (BAFTA Award for Best Original Music 2015, Grammy Award for Best Score Soundtrack for Visual Media 2015) 2014, Godzilla 2014, Suite française 2014, The Imitation Game 2014, The Danish Girl 2015, Suffragette 2015. *Composition for TV*: The Special Relationship (film) 2010. *Current Management:* c/o Robert Urband & Associates Inc., 8981 Sunset Blvd, Suite 311, West Hollywood, CA 90069-1842, USA. *Telephone:* (310) 858-3000. *Fax:* (310) 858-3002. *E-mail:* CP@teamurband.com.

DES'REE; British singer and songwriter; b. (Des'ree Weekes), 30 Nov. 1968, London, England. *Career:* solo artist 1992–; contributed music to films: Clockers, Set It Off, Romeo & Juliet; Numerous television appearances and live shows. *Recordings:* albums: Mind Adventures 1992, I Ain't Movin' 1994, Supernatural 1998, Endangered Species 2000, Dream Soldier 2003; singles: Feel So High 1992, Mind Adventures 1992, Why Should I Love You 1992, You Gotta Be 1994, I Ain't Movin' 1994, Little Child 1994, Life 1998, What's Your Sign 1998, It's OK 2003; contributed to Delicate, Terence Trent D'Arby 1993, Ain't No Sunshine, Ladysmith Black Mambazo 1993, Plenty Lovin', Steve Winwood, Fire, Babyface. *Honours:* BMI Award, Ivor Novello Songwriting Award, World Music Award.

DESSNER, Aaron; American musician (bass guitar); b. Ohio. *Career:* mem., The National 1999–. *Recordings include:* albums: The National 2001, Sad Songs for Dirty Lovers 2003, Alligator 2005, Boxer 2007, High Violet 2010, Trouble Will Find Me 2013; numerous other collaborations. *Film and television scores include:* A Skin, A Night 2008, Last Minutes with Oden 2009, Big Sur 2013, Other Voices (TV series). *Current Management:* c/o Dawn Berger, Post Hoc Management, 310 7th Street, Suite 146, Brooklyn, NY 11215-7208, USA. *Telephone:* (718) 369-4544. *Fax:* (718) 369-4559. *E-mail:* dawn@posthocmanagement.com. *Website:* www.posthocmanagement.com. *E-mail:* info@americanmary.com. *Website:* www.americanmary.com.

DESSNER, Bryce; American musician (guitar); b. Ohio. *Career:* mem., The National 1999–. *Compositions include:* Memorial 2006, Quintets 2007, Propolis 2008, Lincoln Shuffle 2009, O Shut Your Eyes Against the Wind 2010, Tenebre 2010, To The Sea 2011, Lachrimae 2012, Little Blue Something 2012, Murder Ballades 2013. *Recordings include:* albums: The National 2001, Sad Songs for Dirty Lovers 2003, Alligator 2005, Boxer 2007, Dark Was the Night 2009, High Violet 2010, Trouble Will Find Me 2013; numerous collaborations with various artists. *Film score:* Turn the River 2007. *Current Management:* c/o Dawn Berger, Post Hoc Management, 310 7th Street, Brooklyn, NY 11215-7208, USA. *Telephone:* (718) 369-4544. *Fax:* (718) 369-4559. *E-mail:* dawn@posthocmanagement.com. *Website:* www.posthocmanagement.com. *E-mail:* info@americanmary.com. *Website:* www.americanmary.com; www.brycedessner.com.

DESTAGNOL, Yann, (Yann Destal); French musician (drums, keyboards), producer and singer; b. 14 July 1978, Paris. *Education:* American School of Modern Music, Paris. *Career:* fmrly drummer in several rock bands; Founder-mem. Modjo 1998–; Co-founder Modjo Music label; also solo artist (as Yann Destal). *Recordings include:* albums: with Modjo: Modjo 2001; solo: The Great Blue Scar 2004. *E-mail:* matt@modjo.com. *E-mail:* mail@modjo.com. *Website:* www.modjo.com.

DESTAL, Yann (see Yann Destagnol)

DESTRUCTION, Dr Matt; Swedish musician (bass guitar); b. 1978. *Career:* mem., The Hives 1993–. *Recordings:* albums: Barely Legal 1997, Veni Vidi Vicious 2000, Your New Favourite Band (compilation) 2001, Tyrannosaurus Lives 2004, The Black and White Album 2007, Lex Hives 2012. *Honours:* NME Award for Best Int. Band 2003. *Address:* The Hives, Regnbågsvägen 46, 737 43 Fagersta, Sweden. *E-mail:* hives@innocent.com. *Website:* www.hives.nu.

DETMER, Markus; German DJ, record label owner and journalist. *Career:* Founder, electronic music label, Staubgold 1998–; DJ as The Staubgolds (with Tim Tetzner) 2003–, with various residencies and festival appearances. *Address:* Staubgold, Danziger Strasse 16, 10435 Berlin, Germany (office). *Telephone:* (30) 2935-1189 (office). *Fax:* (30) 2935-1060 (office). *E-mail:* info@staubgold.com (office). *Website:* www.staubgold.com.

DETROIT, Marcella; singer, songwriter and musician (keyboards, guitar, harmonica); b. (Marcy Levy), 21 June 1959, Detroit, MI, USA. *Career:* mem., Shakespears Sister 1988–93; solo artist 1993–; numerous concerts, television and radio performances; collaborations with Elton John, Hall and Oates.

Recordings: Albums: with Shakespears Sister: Sacred Heart, 1989; Hormonally Yours, 1992; Solo: Jewel, 1994; Feeler, 1996; Abfab Songs, 1999; Dancing Madly Sideways, 2000, The Upside of Being Down 2005. Singles: with Shakespears Sister: You're History, 1989; Break My Heart, 1990; Goodbye Cruel World, 1991; Hello (Turn Your Radio On), 1992; Stay (No. 1, UK), 1992; I Don't Care, 1992; My 16th Apology (EP), 1993; I Can Drive, 1996; Solo: Ain't Nothing Like The Real, 1994; I'm No Angel, 1994; I Believe, 1994; Perfect World, 1995; I Hate You, 1996; Flower, 1997. *Compositions:* Co-writer, Lay Down Sally, Eric Clapton, 1977; with Siobhan Fahey: all tracks on album, Hormonally Yours, 1992. *Honours:* BRIT Award, Best Video, Stay, 1993; Ivor Novello Award, Outstanding Contemporary Song Collection, Hormonally Yours, 1993. *Address:* c/o i1 Media LLC, 449 South Beverly Drive, Beverly Hills, CA 90212, USA (office). *Telephone:* (310) 553-5866 (office). *Fax:* (866) 308-2942 (office). *E-mail:* info@i1media.com (office); info@marcelladetroit.com (home). *Website:* www.i1media.com (office); www.marcelladetroit.com (home).

DEVENDORF, Bryan; American musician (drums); b. Ohio. *Career:* mem., The National 1999–. *Recordings include:* albums: The National 2001, Sad Songs for Dirty Lovers 2003, Alligator 2005, Boxer 2007, High Violet 2010, Trouble Will Find Me 2013. *Current Management:* c/o Dawn Berger, Post Hoc Management, 310 7th Street, Brooklyn, NY 11215-7208, USA. *Telephone:* (718) 369-4544. *Fax:* (718) 369-4559. *E-mail:* dawn@posthocmanagement.com. *Website:* www.posthocmanagement.com. *E-mail:* info@americanmary.com. *Website:* www.americanmary.com.

DEVENDORF, Scott; American musician (guitar); b. Ohio. *Career:* mem., The National 1999–. *Recordings include:* albums: The National 2001, Sad Songs for Dirty Lovers 2003, Alligator 2005, Boxer 2007, High Violet 2010, Trouble Will Find Me 2013. *Current Management:* c/o Dawn Berger, Post Hoc Management, 310 7th Street, Brooklyn, NY 11215-7208, USA. *Telephone:* (718) 369-4544. *Fax:* (718) 369-4559. *E-mail:* dawn@posthocmanagement.com. *Website:* www.posthocmanagement.com. *E-mail:* info@americanmary.com. *Website:* www.americanmary.com.

DEVEREUX, Pete; British producer, remixer and DJ; b. 1972, Southampton, Hampshire, England. *Education:* Brunel Univ. *Career:* played violin in Southampton Youth Orchestra; Founder-mem. Artful Dodger (with Mark Hill) 1996–2001; Co-founder, (with Hill); solo production career 2001; collaborations include Craig David, Dreem Teem, Romina Johnson, Liberty; remixed Sisqo, Gabrielle. *Recordings include:* album: It's All About The Stragglers 2001. *Honours:* Ivor Novello Dance Award (for Re-Rewind) 2000, (for Woman Trouble) 2001.

DEVIC, Lino; Croatian musician (fretless bass, piano); b. 10 May 1954, Zagreb; m. (divorced); two s. one d. *Career:* many jazz festivals in former Yugoslavia and Germany; studio works in France, 1976; toured Germany with Trini Lopez; plays with fusion trio. *Compositions include:* Boulevard Barbes; Blue Duck. *Recordings:* Drazen Boic Trio: Mirno Itiho (Peaceful and Quiet); LD Experience. *Honours:* at jazz festivals: Ingolstadt, Germany; Ljubljana; Zagreb; Maribor. *Current Management:* A Zaie 39, Panton, Zagreb, Croatia. *Address:* N Grskovica 58, Zagreb, Croatia.

DEVINE, Frank Thomas; British songwriter and musician (drums, guitar, mandolin); b. 24 Nov. 1946, Dundee, Scotland; m. Jacqueline Harper; one s. one d. *Education:* Moseley School of Art, Birmingham Coll. of Art. *Career:* tour of England with Jimmy Cliff; weekly appearances at Marquee, London; played with Blues Hounds and Mike Burney; television appearance: Ready Steady Go (with the Alpines); currently songwriter and plays guitar and mandolin; mem. Musicians' Union. *Recordings include:* limited edition album with Steve Winwood and Dave Mason (prior to formation of Traffic).

DEVLIN, Adam; British musician (guitar) and songwriter; b. 17 Sept. 1969, Hounslow, Middlesex, England. *Career:* Founder-mem., The Bluetones 1994–2011; numerous tours, festivals, television and radio appearances. *Recordings include:* albums: Expecting To Fly 1996, Return To The Last Chance Saloon 1998, Science And Nature 2000, The Singles 1995–2002 2002, The Bluetones 2006, A New Athens 2010. *Address:* c/o Cooking Vinyl, 10 Allied Way, London, W3 0RQ, England. *E-mail:* info@cookingvinyl.com.

DEXTEXTER, Even; musician (keyboards, bass, drums) and programmer; b. 7 April 1971, Ellorio, Vizcaya, Spain. *Education:* Conservatoire of Logrono, La Rioja, Spain. *Career:* mem. Dexterter 1994–; tours and TV appearances; mem. Musicians' Union. *Address:* 70 Princes Square, London, W2 4NY, England.

DEYHIM, Sussan; Iranian singer, composer and performance artist; b. Tehran. *Education:* Pars Nat. Ballet, Maurice Bejart's School of Performing Arts. *Career:* performer, Bejart's Ballet of the XX Century; moved to USA 1980–; collaborations with Mickey Hart, Jerry Garcia, Peter Gabriel, Jaron Lanier, Brian Eno, Jah Wobble, Branford Marsalis, Peter Seherer, Naut Humon, DJ Spooky. *Theatre includes:* The Tibetan Book of the Dead, La Scala in Milan, A Midsummer Night's Dream, Nijinski (English Theatre Group, in S America and Italy). *Recordings include:* albums: Azaxattra: Desert Equations (with Richard Horowitz) 1981, Desert Equations (with Richard Horowitz) 1995, Majoun (with Richard Horowitz) 1997, Turbulent (with Shirin Neshat) 1998, Madman Of God (with Divine Love Songs of the Persian Sufi Masters) 2000, Shy Angels (with Bill Laswell) 2002, City of Leaves 2011. *Current Management:* c/o Lara Lavi, WIDEawake Entertainment Group Inc., 62 Riverview Gardens, Toronto, ON M6S 4ES, Canada. *Telephone:* (647) 299-0737. *E-mail:* sussan@sussandeyhim.com. *Website:* www.sussandeyhim.com.

DI BATTISTA, Stefano; Italian musician (saxophone); b. 14 Feb. 1969, Rome. *Career:* began playing saxophone aged 13 years; proficient on alto and soprano instruments; protégé of Massimo Urbani; worked as backing musician for pop artists; developed asscn with trumpeter Flavio Boltro; duo popular at Calvi Jazz Festival 1992–; relocated to Paris; joined Aldo Romano's Prosodie group 1994; collaborated with Nat Adderley, Elvin Jones, Michel Petrucciani; released first album as leader 1997. *Recordings include:* albums: Volare 1997, A Prima Vista 1998, Stefano Di Battista 2001, Round About Roma 2003. *Current Management:* c/o B. H. Hopper Management, Elvirastrasse 25, 80636 Munich, Germany. *Telephone:* (89) 1226970. *Fax:* (89) 12249779. *E-mail:* hopper@hopper-management.com. *Website:* www.hopper-management.com.

DI LEVA, Thomas; Swedish singer, songwriter and musician (guitar, keyboards); b. 23 Oct. 1963, Gavle. *Career:* 11 major tours 1986–97; several major northern television and radio programmes. *Plays include:* The City of Mahagonny, by Bertolt Brecht, Gavle Folktheatre 1987, Hamlet in Hamlet, Gavle Folktheatre 1990. *Film appearances include:* Tomorrow, Tomorrow, Tomorrow 1989, Kenny Starfighter 1997. *Compositions include:* all work self-penned. *Recordings include:* Marginal Cirkus 1982, På Ett Fat 1985, Pussel 1986, Flashback #2 1986, Vem Ska Jag Tro På? 1987, Rymdblomma 1989, Noll 1991, Naked Number One 1993, Love Is The Heart 1995, Jag Är Du 1997, I Am You 1997, För Sverige I Rymden 1999, Älska 2000, Tiden Faller 2004, Free Life 2005, Själens Krigare Samlade Sånger 1980–2005, Hoppets Röst 2006, Mantra Miracles 2006, Lovestar 2010, Hjärtat Vinner Alltid 2011, Vi har bara varandra-Di Levas klassiker 2012. *Honours:* Swedish Grammy Award for Best Artist of 1988. *Current Management:* c/o United Stage Artist AB, PO Box 110 29, 100 61 Stockholm, Sweden. *Telephone:* (70) 440-41-23. *E-mail:* lisse@unitedstage.se. *Website:* www.unitedstage.se; www.dileva.nu.

DI MATTEO, Luis; Uruguayan composer; b. 10 May 1934, Montevideo; m.; one s. one d. *Education:* studied composition and Bandoneon. *Career:* Bandoneon player in orchestras in Montevideo, Uruguay, and in Buenos Aires, Argentina, Astor Piazzolla's orchestra; Composer and Arranger, Bandoneonista; regular TV appearances; First European concerts 1983, and regular concert tours 1983–; cooperation with Uljanowsk Chamber Orchestra, Russia 1990; European concert tour with string quartet 1997–98; AGADU, Uruguay. *Compositions include:* A Sugerencia Club 1965, A Sugerencia del Club 1969, Estudio Para Tres 1971, Tango en Blue Jeans 1975, Proceso 1976, Monologando 1979, Rumbo al Cenit 1981, Latitud 55 1983, Tango Contemporáneo 1984, Le Dernier Tango 1985, Tango 1987, Mil Clores 1987, Por Dentro De Mi 1988, Concierto para contrabaio y orchestra 1989, Del Nuevo Ciclo 1991, Escribo Para Los Angeles 1996, Un dia de mi vida 1997. *Recordings include:* Tango Contemporaneo 1984, Le Dernier Tango 1985, Por Dentro De Mi 1988, Del Nuevo Ciclo 1991, Escribo Para Los Angeles 1997, Um Dia De Mi Vida 1998, Tango and Beyond 2004, Grout 2005, Iceberg 2010. *Publications include:* First edition of compositions published with Tonos in Germany 1998. *Current Management:* c/o JARO Medien GmbH, Bismarckstrasse 43, 28203 Bremen, Germany. *E-mail:* infomail@jaro.de. *Website:* www.jaro.de.

DI MEOLA, Al; American jazz musician (guitar) and composer; b. 22 July 1954, Jersey City, New Jersey. *Education:* studied with Robert Aslanian, Berklee Coll. of Music. *Career:* musician with Barry Miles; mem., Chick Corea's Return To Forever 1974–76; solo guitarist, composer, 1976–; tours as solo artist; also toured with acoustic trio (with John McLaughlin and Paco de Lucia); leader, Al DiMeola Project (musicians include Airto Moreiro) 1985–. *Recordings include:* albums include: with Return To Forever: Where Have I Known You Before 1974, No Mystery 1975, Romantic Warrior 1976, Returns 2009; solo: Land of Midnight Sun 1976, Elegant Gypsy 1977, Casino 1978, Splendido Hotel 1979, Electric Rendevous 1982, Tour de Force Live 1982, Scenario 1983, Cielo e Terra 1983, Soaring Through A Dream 1985, Tiramu Su 1988, World Sinfonia 1990, Heart of The Immigrants 1993, Kiss My Axe 1993, Orange and Blue 1994, The Essence of Al DiMeola 1994, The Infinite Desire 1998, Christmas Winter Nights 1999, World Sinfonia III 2000, Flesh on Flesh 2002, Vocal Rendezvous 2006, Consequence of Chaos 2006, Diabolic Inventions and Seductions 2006, La Melodia 2008, Pursuit of Radical Rhapsody 2011; with John McLaughlin and Paco de Lucia: Friday Night In San Francisco 1980, Passion, Grace and Fire 1983; with Aziza Mustafa Zadeh: Dance of Fire 1995; with Jean-Luc Ponty, Stanley Clarke: The Rite of Strings 1996. *Film:* Morocco Fantasia 2011. *Current Management:* c/o Bob Zievers, ICM Talent, 730 Fifth Avenue, New York, NY 10019, USA. *E-mail:* info@aldimeola.com. *Website:* www.aldimeola.com.

DIAB, Amr, BA; Egyptian singer and composer; b. (Amr Abd-Albaset Abd-Alaziz Diab), 11 Oct. 1961, Port Said; s. of Abdul Basset Diab; m. 1st Sherine Rida 1989 (divorced 1992); one d.; m. 2nd Zinah Ashour; twin s. one d. *Education:* Cairo Acad. of Art. *Career:* sang national anthem, Biladi, Biladi, on Egyptian radio when six years old; recorded his first song, El Zamn 1983; tours world-wide; represented Egypt at the Fifth Olympic African Tournament concert 1990; holds annual spring concert (The Carnival) at American Univ. in Cairo; held six concerts in USA and oneconcert in Toronto, Canada 2011; collaborations with Khaled, Stuart Crichton (founder of Progressive House), Frank Von Dem Bottlenberg, Jorg Evers, Shazz (Didier Delesalle), Klubbheads (Koen Groeneveld and Addy van der Zwan), Phunk Phorce (Leon and Matthew Roberts), Rhythm Masters (Robert Bruce Chetcuti and Steve McGuinness), Pete Beachill, Simon Gardner, Andy Greenwood, Kevan Gallagher, Jon Bishop, Juan Cerro, Angela Dimitriou; appeared in several

Pepsi commercials, including with Pink, Beyoncé and Britney Spears; composer of geel music; known as the Father of Mediterranean Music. *Film appearances:* Al Sagenatan 1988, El Afareet 1990, Ice Cream fi Glim 1992, Dehk, we leab we gad we hob (Laughter, Games, Seriousness and Love) 1993. *Film soundtracks:* O Clone (TV series) 2001, The Dancer Upstairs (performer, Awadouni) 2002, Yadon ilaheyya (performer, Wala Ala Baloh) 2002, The Dictator (performer, Wala Ala Baloh) 2012. *Recordings include:* albums: Ya Tareeq 1983, Ghanny Men Albak 1984, Hala Hala 1986, Khalseen 1987, Mayya! 1988, Shawa'na 1989, Matkhafesh (Platinum disc) 1990, Habibe (Platinum disc) 1991, Ice Cream Fi Gleem (soundtrack) 1992, Ayamna (Platinum disc) 1992, Ya Omrena (Platinum disc) 1993, We Yloumouny (nine awards 1995) 1994, Nour El Ain (Platinum disc) 1996, Awedony 1998, The Best of Amr Diab 1999, Amarain 1999, Tamaly Maak 2000, Aktar Wahed Beyhebak 2001, Allem Alby 2003, Leily Nahary 2004, Kammel Kalamak 2005, El Leila De 2007, Wayah 2009, Aslaha Betefre' 2010, Banadeek Ta'ala 2011. *Honours:* Arabic Festival Awards, Best Video, Best Song, Artist of the Year 1997, Artist of the Year 2002, World Music Awards, Best Selling Middle Eastern Artist 1998, 2002, 2007, 2009, African Music Awards for Artist of the Year, Song of the Year (for Wayah), for Video of the Year (for Wayah) 2009, Big Apple Music Award 2009, Life Achievements Awards: Best Singer of The Year 2009, Best Male Act, African Music Awards 2010, ranked by Arabian Business amongst the Power 500: The Worlds's Most Influential Arabs (43rd) 2012. *Address:* c/o EMI Music Arabia FZ LLC, Dubai Media City, United Arab Emirates (office). *Telephone:* (4) 8818225 (office). *Fax:* (4) 8818226 (office). *E-mail:* info@amrdiab.net (office). *Website:* www.amrdiab.net (office).

DIABATÉ, Fode Lassana; Guinean musician (balafon); b. 1971, Conakry. *Career:* relocated to Mali; protégé of Kélétigui Diabaté; albums by Salif Keita, Bassekou Kouyate, Kasse Mady Diabaté; long-time mem. of Toumani Diabaté's Symmetric Orchestra; mem. AfroCubism project 2010–. *Recordings:* albums: with Symmetric Orchestra: Boulevard de l'Independance 2006; with AfroCubism: AfroCubism 2010; has also appeared on: Kulanjan, Taj Mahal and Toumani Diabaté 1999, Malicool, Roswell Rudd 2002, Passage, Stefan Rigert 2003, Bamanankan, Lassina Coulibaly 2005, Segu Blue, Bassekou Kouyate 2007, Syliphone Years, Keletigui et ses Tambourinis 2009. *Address:* c/o World Circuit Records, 138 Kingsland Road, London, E2 8DY, England (office). *E-mail:* post@worldcircuit.co.uk (office). *Website:* www.worldcircuit.co.uk (office).

DIABATÉ, Kassé-Mady; Malian singer and musician; b. 1949, Kangaba. *Career:* family associated with Mali's 'Manding griot' music tradition; mem., Super Mande, Las Maravillas de Mali, National Badema du Mali 1970s; moved to Paris 1980s, returned to Mali 1998; mem. AfroCubism project 2010–. *Recordings include:* albums: Fode 1989, Kela Tradition 1990, Kassi Kassé 2003, Manden Djeli Kan 2009, AfroCubism (with AfroCubism) 2010, Kassi Kasse 2010; also appeared on Songhai 2 by Toumani Diabaté 1995, Kulanjan by Taj Mahal, Toumani Diabaté and Bassekou Kouyate 1998, Boulevard de l'Indépendence by Toumani Diabaté's Symmetric Orchestra 2006. *Address:* c/o World Circuit Records, First Floor, Shoreditch Stables, 138 Kingsland Road, Bethnal Green, London, E2 8DY, England. *Telephone:* (20) 7749-3222. *Fax:* (20) 7749-3232. *E-mail:* post@worldcircuit.co.uk (office). *Website:* www.worldcircuit.co.uk.

DIABATÉ, Sékou Bembeya; Guinean musician (guitar) and arranger; b. 1944, Thiero; m. Djanka Diabaté. *Career:* mem., Bembeya Jazz 1961–; solo artist 1985–. *Recordings include:* albums: with Bembeya Jazz: Regard sur le passe 1970, Dix ans de succés 1971, Authenticit 73: Parade Africaine 1973, Le défi 1976, La continuité 1977, Bembeya 2002; solo: Montagne 1985, Digné 1987, Concorde Gaye (with Djanka Diabaté) 1990, Diata 1993, Diamond Fingers 1996, Samba Gaye (with Djanka Diabaté) 1997, Guitar Fo 2004. *Address:* c/o World Village Music, 1117 Chestnut Street, Burbank, CA 91506, USA.

DIABATÉ, Toumani; Malian musician (kora) and composer; b. 10 Aug. 1965, Bamako; s. of the late Sidiki Diabaté and Nene Koita. *Career:* recorded first ever solo kora album, Kaira; collaborations with Kandia Kouyate, Ketama, Danny Thompson, Ballake Sissoko, Taj Mahal, Damon Albarn, Habib Koite, Keletigui Diabaté, Bela Fleck, Salif Keita; founder, Symmetric Orchestra; mem. AfroCubism project 2010–; solo and group tours in USA and Europe. *Recordings include:* albums: Kaira 1988, Songhai (with Ketama) 1989, Shake the World (including Habib Koite) 1991, Songhai 2 1995, Djelika (with Danny Thompson and Keletigui Diabaté) 1995, New Ancient Strings (with Ballake Sissoko) 1999, Kulanjan (with Taj Mahal) (Froots Best Album 1999) 1999, Jarabi-The Best of the Master of the Kora 2003, In the Heart of the Moon (with Ali Farka Touré) (Grammy Award for Best Traditional World Music Album 2006) 2005, Symmetric Orchestra 2006, The Mandé Variations 2008, Ali and Toumani (with Ali Farka Touré) 2010, AfroCubism (with AfroCubism) 2010, A Curva da Cintura 2011, Toumani & Sidiki (with his son Sidiki Diabaté Junior) 2014. *Honours:* Zyriab des Virtuoses Award (UNESCO) 2004. *Address:* c/o World Circuit Records, First Floor, Shoreditch Stables, 138 Kingsland Road, Bethnal Green, London, E2 8DY, England (office). *Telephone:* (20) 7749-3222. *Fax:* (20) 7749-3232. *E-mail:* post@worldcircuit.co.uk. *Website:* www.worldcircuit.co.uk; www.toumani-diabate.com.

DIAMANDIS, Marina Lambrini, (Marina and the Diamonds); British singer, songwriter and musician (keyboards, piano); b. 10 Oct. 1985, Brynmawr, Wales. *Education:* Haberdashers' School for Girls, Monmouth, St Catherine's British Embassy School, Greece, Univ. of East London. *Career:*

independently released first EP Mermaid vs Sailor 2007; signed to 679 Recordings 2008; first int. headlining tour 2010–11; supported Katy Perry and Coldplay on int. tours 2011–12. *Recordings:* albums: as Marina and the Diamonds: The Family Jewels 2010, Electra Heart 2012, Froot 2015. *Honours:* MTV Europe Music Award for Best UK & Irish Act 2010, Virgin Media Music Award for Best Newcomer 2010, Attitude Best Music Award 2012. *Current Management:* c/o Select Model Management, 27–35 Mortimer Street, London, W1T 3JG, England. *Telephone:* (20) 7299-1300. *Fax:* (20) 7299-1322. *Website:* www.selectmodel.com; marinaandthediamonds.com.

DIAMOND, Neil Leslie; American singer and composer; b. 24 Jan. 1941, Brooklyn, NY; m. 2nd Marcia Murphey 1975; two c. (and two c. from previous m.); m. 3rd Katie McNeil 2012. *Education:* New York Univ. *Career:* fmr songwriter for publishing co.; numerous tours world-wide, television and radio broadcasts; mem. SESAC. *Film scores:* Jonathan Livingston Seagull (Grammy Award) 1973, Every Which Way But Loose 1978, The Jazz Singer 1980; songs for numerous other films. *Film appearance:* The Jazz Singer 1980. *Recordings include:* albums: The Feel of Neil Diamond 1966, Just For You 1967, Velvet Gloves and Spit 1968, Brother Love's Travelling Salvation Show 1969, Touching You Touching Me 1969, Tap Root Manuscript 1970, Shilo 1970, Gold (live) 1970, Stones 1971, Hot August Night (live) 1972, Moods 1972, Serenade 1974, Beautiful Noise 1976, Love At The Greek (live) 1977, I'm Glad You're Here With Me Tonight 1977, Carmelita's Eyes 1978, You Don't Bring Me Flowers 1978, September Morn 1979, Voices Of Vista: Show # 200 1979, On The Way To The Sky 1981, Heartlight 1982, Song Sung Blue 1982, Primitive 1984, Headed For The Future 1986, Hot August Night II (live) 1987, The Best Years Of Our Lives 1989, Lovescape 1991, The Christmas Album 1992, Up On the Roof: Songs From The Brill Building 1993, The Christmas Album Vol. II 1994, Live In America 1994, Tennessee Moon 1996, Live In Concert 1997, The Movie Album: As Time Goes By 1998, Three Chord Opera 2001, 12 Songs 2005, Home Before Dark 2008, A Cherry Cherry Christmas 2009, Dreams 2010, Melody Road 2014. *Honours:* inducted into Songwriters Hall of Fame 1984, Rock and Roll Hall of Fame 2011, Honoree, Annual Kennedy Center Honors 2011, Billboard Icon Award 2011, Billboard Legend of Live Award 2012. *Website:* www.neildiamond.com.

DIAMOND PLATNUMZ, (Diamond); Tanzanian singer, songwriter and musician (guitar, piano, drums); b. (Nasibu Abdul Juma), 2 Oct. 1989, Dar es Salaam; pnr Zarinah Hassan; one d.; *Honours:* numerous awards, including Tanzanian Music Awards for Best Upcoming Artist 2010, for Best Song 2010, 2014, for Best R&B Song 2010, for Best Male Artist 2012, 2013, 2014, for Best Song Writer 2012, for Best Music Video 2012, 2014, for Best Male Writer 2014, for Best Male Entertainer of the Year 2014, for Best Afro Pop Song 2014, 2015, for Best Zouk/Rhumba Song 2015, Future Africa Prize in Entertainment 2014, Channel O Music Video Awards for Most Gifted Newcomer, Most Gifted East and Most Gifted Afro Pop Artist 2014, HiPipo Music Award for East Africa Superhit (for Number One) 2015, MTV Africa Music Award for Best Live Act 2015, MTV Europe Music Award for Best African Act 2015. *E-mail:* diamondplatnumz@gmail.com. *Website:* www.thisisdiamond.com.

DIAMONDS, Lex (see Raekwon)

DIAM'S; French rap artist; b. (Mélanie Marie Ghisla Georgiades), 30 July 1980, *Recordings include:* albums: Premier mandat 1999, Brut de femme (Les Victoires de la Musique Rap/Hip-Hop Album of the Year 2004) 2003, Ma vie/Mon live 2004, Dans ma Bulle 2006. *Honours:* MTV Europe Music Award for Best French Act 2006. *Address:* c/o Hostile Records, EMI Music France, 24 place des Vosges, 75004 Paris, France. *Website:* www.diams-lesite.com.

DIAS, Sérgio; Brazilian singer and musician (guitar); b. (Sérgio Dias Baptista), 1 Dec. 1951, São Paulo. *Career:* formed psychedelic rock band Os Mutantes with his brother Arnaldo and Rita Lee 1966, the band played an important role in the Tropicalia movt, remained only constant mem. of band through many changes to line-up until band finally split up in 1978; recorded several solo albums; joined a re-formed Os Mutantes for several concerts 2006; collaborated with British DJ JD Twitch for Trocabrahma project 2007. *Recordings include:* albums: with Os Mutantes: Os Mutantes 1968, Mutantes 1969, A Divina Comédia ou Ando Meio Desligado 1970, Jardim Elétrico 1971, Mutantes e Seus Cometas no País do Baurets 1972, Tudo Foi Feito Pelo Sol 1974, Mutantes Ao Vivo 1976, O A e o Z (recorded 1973) 1992, Tecnicolor (recorded 1970) 2000, Mutantes Ao Vivo: Barbican Theatre, Londres 2006, Haih or Amortecedor 2009, Fool Metal Jack 2013; solo albums: Sérgio Dias 1980, Mato Grosso (with Phil Manzanera) 1990, Mind Over Matter 1991, Song of the Leopard 1997, Estação da Luz 2000, Jazz Mania Live 2003, We Are the Lilies 2011. *Current Management:* Malab, rua Cristina, 1213, Santo Antônio, 30330-130, Belo Horizonte, MG, Brazil. *Telephone:* (31) 2532-8201. *E-mail:* malab@malab.com.br. *Website:* www.malab.com.br; www.osmutantes.com.br; www.sergiodias.com.br.

DIAS BAPTISTA, Arnaldo; Brazilian singer, songwriter and musician (bass, keyboards); b. 6 July 1948, São Paulo. *Career:* played in band The Wooden Faces as teenager, also played in bands including Six Sided Rockers and O'Seis; formed psychedelic rock band Os Mutantes with brother Sérgio Dias and Rita Lee 1966, the band played an important role in the Tropicalia movt, left Os Mutantes after releasing six albums 1973; embarked on solo career, joined re-formed Os Mutantes for several concerts 2006–07; collaborated with British DJ JD Twitch for Trocabrahma project 2007; left Os Mutantes to concentrate on solo work 2007; entered fine arts market through Emma Thomas Gallery 2010, solo exhibitions Lentes Magnéticas 2012, Exorealismo 2014; back on stage on solo concert playing piano and singing 2011–. *Recordings include:* with Os Mutantes: albums: Os Mutantes 1968, Mutantes 1969, A Divina Comédia ou Ando Meio Desligado 1970, Jardim Elétrico 1971, Mutantes e Seus Cometas no País do Baurets 1972, Tudo Foi Feito Pelo Sol 1974, Tecnicolor (recorded 1970) 2000, Mutantes Ao Vivo: Barbican Theatre, Londres 2006; solo albums: Lóki 1974, Singin' Alone 1982, Disco Voador 1987, Let it Bed 2004; with Patrulha do Espaço: Elo Perdido (recorded 1977) 1988, Faremos uma Noitada Excelente (recorded 1978) 1988. *E-mail:* arnaldobaptista9@gmail.com. *Website:* www.arnaldobaptista.com.br.

DIBANGO, Manu; Cameroonian musician (saxophone, piano); b. 12 Dec. 1934, Douala. *Education:* piano lessons. *Career:* moved to Paris 1949, then Brussels, Belgium 1956; residency at Black Angels Club, Brussels; joined band led by Joseph Kabsele, African Jazz 1960, played with African Jazz in Zaire –1963; returned to Cameroon to form own band 1963–65; studio musician, Paris 1965; backed musicians, including Peter Gabriel, Sinead O'Connor, Angélique Kidjo, Geoffrey Oryema, Ray Lema, Touré Kunda; solo artist 1968–; Pres., Francophone Diffusion; apptd UNESCO Artist for Peace 2004. *Compositions include:* commissioned by President Ahidjo to write song for Africa Cup football match 1971. *Recordings include:* albums: Manu Dibango 1968, Saxy-Party 1969, O Boso 1971, Soma Loba 1971, Soul Makossa 1972, African Voodoo 1972, Africadelic 1973, Blue Elephant 1973, Makossa Man 1974, African Funk 1974, Makossa Music 1975, African Rhythm Machine 1975, Super Kumba 1976, Manu 76 1976, Afrovision 1976, Big Blow 1978, A L'Olympia 1978, Ceddo 1978, Gone Clear 1979, Ambassador 1981, Waka Juju 1982, Deliverence 1983, Sweet and Soft 1983, Melodies Africaines vols 1 and 2 1983, Deadline 1984, Electric Africa 1985, Afrijazzy 1986, Negropolitains Vol. 1 1989, Polysonik 1991, Bao Bao 1992, Negropolitains Vol. 2 1992, Wakafrika 1994, Lamastabastani 1996, Sax & Spirituals 1996, Manu Safari 1998, Mboa' Su 1999, From Africa 2003, Voyage Anthologique 2004, Essential Recordings 2006, Lion of Africa 2007, Anthology 2009, Soft and Sweet 2010, Choc'n'Soul 2010, Past Present Future 2011, Ballad Emotion 2011, Africa Boogie 2013, Akoko Party 2013, Lagos Go Slow 2013, Balade en Saxo 2013. *Publications:* Trois Kilos de Café (autobiography) 1990. *Honours:* Grammy Award for Best R&B Instrumental Performance of the Year 1973, Ronnie Scott Award for Services to Jazz 2007. *Current Management:* c/o Global Mix Media Limited, PO Box 4702, Henley on Thames, RG9 9AA, England. *E-mail:* claire@manudibango.net. *Website:* www.manudibango.net.

DIBLASI, Toni; Australian musician. *Career:* mem. electronic music collective, The Avalanches 1997–. *Recordings include:* album: Since I Left You 2000. *Address:* c/o Modular Records, PO Box 1666, Darlinghurst, NSW 1300, Australia. *Website:* www.theavalanches.com.

DICK, Arthur, BSc; British musician (guitar), writer and arranger; b. 4 Aug. 1954, Dundee, Scotland. *Education:* Univ. of Liverpool. *Career:* numerous sessions as guitarist; recorded sessions for numerous artists including: Cliff Richard, Paul McCartney, Cilla Black, Barbara Dickson, Berni Flint, Susan Maughan; formed Tracks Music for production of TV and radio soundtracks 1986; Lecturer, Goldsmith's Coll., Univ. London, currently guitar teacher; mem. PRS, Musicians' Union. *Address:* Department of Music, Goldsmiths College, University of London, New Cross, London, SE14 6NW, England (office). *Telephone:* (20) 7919-7203 (office). *E-mail:* a.dick@gold.ac.uk (office). *Website:* www.gold.ac.uk (office).

DICKERSON, Roger Donald, BA, MM; American composer, musician (piano and double bass) and academic; b. 24 Aug. 1934, New Orleans, LA. *Education:* Dillard Univ., New Orleans, Ind. Univ. at Bloomington, Akademie für Musik und Darstellende Kunst, Vienna, Austria. *Career:* grew up playing jazz and blues in New Orleans; toured with Joe Turner and Guitar Slim 1951–54; mil. service in US Army, based in Ark. and Heidelberg, Germany 1957–59; played double bass with Fort Smith Symphony Orchestra 1957; composer, arranger for US Army in Europe Headquarters Co. Band, Heidelberg 1957–59; performed extensively in French Quarter of New Orleans 1962–; composed for New Orleans Symphony and others 1962–; Program Assoc. and Consultant in Humanities, Inst. for Services to Educ., Washington, DC 1979; private teacher of composition and piano 1962–; Adjunct Prof., Xavier Univ. of La, New Orleans 1979–82; Adjunct Prof., Southern Univ., New Orleans 1979–85; Assoc. Prof. and Co-ordinator of Music, Div. of Fine Arts 1985–; Lecturer in Music, Dillard Univ., New Orleans 1986–; co-f., Creative Arts Alliance of New Orleans (CAANO) 1975; Mayor's Task Force on Arts Policy for the City of New Orleans 1978; Mayor's Advisory Bd Arts and Cultural Affairs for the City of New Orleans 1979; La State Div. of the Arts Grant Cttee 1981; panellist La State Arts Council 1981–, Nat. Endowment for the Arts 1984–; mem. ASCAP. *Compositions include:* Prekussion for percussion 1954, Variations for woodwind trio 1955, Fair Dillard for chorus 1955, Sonatina for piano 1956, Chorale Prelude (Das neugeborne Kindelein) for organ 1956, String Quartet 1956, Music I Heard (vocal) 1956, Music for string trio 1957, Concert Overture for orchestra 1957, Essay for band 1958, Fugue 'n Blues for jazz ensemble 1959, Movement for trumpet and piano 1960, The Negro Speaks of Rivers (vocal) 1961, Quintet for wind instruments 1961, Ten Concert Pieces for beginning string players 1973, A Musical Service for Louis (A Requiem for Louis Armstrong) 1973, Orpheus an' His Slide Trombone for orchestra 1974–75, New Orleans Concerto 1976, Psalm 49 for chorus 1979, African-American Celebration for chorus 1984. *Honours:* Dr hc (Inst. for Minority Nationalities, People's Repub. of China) 1990; Dave Frank Award 1955, American Music Center Award 1972, 1975, New Orleans Bicentennial Comm. Certificate 1977, Citation of Achievement and Key to the City of New Orleans 1977, New

Orleans Recreation Dept Louis Armstrong Cultural Devt Fund Memorial Award 1977, Masons Enterprises of New Orleans Outstanding Musicianship Award 1977, City Council of New Orleans Special Commendation 1978, Univ. New Orleans Marcus-Christian Award 1979. *Address:* c/o ASCAP, ASCAP Building, One Lincoln Plaza, New York, NY 10023, USA (office).

DICKINSON, (Paul) Bruce, BA; British singer, writer and air pilot; b. 7 Aug. 1958, Worksop, Nottinghamshire, England. *Education:* Queen Mary Coll., London. *Career:* fmr mem., Speed, Shots, Samson 1980; lead singer heavy metal band, Iron Maiden 1981–93, 1999–; pilot for various charter airline cos., including Astraeus; host for music programmes for 6Music (BBC Digital radio station). *Film screenplay:* Chemical Wedding 2008. *Recordings include:* albums: with Samson: Head On 1980, Shock Tactics 1981; with Iron Maiden: The Number of the Beast 1982, Piece of Mind 1983, Powerslave 1984, Somewhere in Time 1986, Seventh Son of a Seventh Son 1988, No Prayer for the Dying 1990, Fear of the Dark 1992, Brave New World 2000, Dance of Death 2003, It's a Matter of Life and Death 2006, Flight 666 2009, The Final Frontier 2010, The Book of Souls 2015; solo: Tattooed Millionaire 1990, Balls To Picasso 1994, Alive In Studio A 1995, Skunkworks 1996, Accident of Birth 1997, Chemical Wedding 1998, Scream For Me Brazil 1999, Rock In Rio 2002, Tyranny of Souls 2005. *Film appearance:* Chemical Wedding (co-author, soundtrack) 2008. *Publications include:* novels: The Adventures of Lord Iffy Boatrace 1990, The Missionary Position 1992. *Honours:* Hon. DMus, Queen Mary Coll.; Ivor Novello Award 2000, BRIT Award for Best British Live Act 2009. *Current Management:* c/o Phantom Music Management, Bridle House, 36 Bridle Lane, London, W1F 9BZ, England. *Telephone:* (845) 331-3300. *Fax:* (845) 331-3500. *Website:* www.phantom-music.com; www.screamforme.com; www.ironmaiden.com.

DICKINSON, Luther Andrews; American rock guitarist and singer; b. 18 Jan. 1973, Memphis, Tenn.; s. of Jim Dickinson and Mary Lindsay. *Career:* formed North Mississippi Allstars with Jim Dickinson 1996–; guitarist with Black Crowes 2007–; many other recording credits including with John Hiatt, South Memphis String Band, DDT, Willy DeVille. *Recordings include:* albums: with North Mississippi Allstars: Shake Hands with Shorty 2000, 51 Phantom 2001, Polaris 2003, Electric Blue Watermelon 2005, Hernando 2008, Do It Like We Used to Do 2009, Keys to the Kingdom 2011, I'm Just Dead, I'm Not Gone 2012; with Jim Dickinson: Free Beer Tomorrow 2002, Jungle Jim and the Voodoo Tiger 2006; with John Hiatt: Master of Disaster 2005, Same Old Man 2008; with The Black Crowes: Warpaint 2008, Before the Frost... Until the Freeze 2009, Croweology 2010; with the Sons of Mudboy: Onward and Upward 2009; with the South Memphis String Band: Home Sweet Home 2010, Old Times There 2012; with Mato Nanji and David Hidalgo: 3 Skulls and the Truth 2012; solo: Hambone's Meditations 2012; other credits include: Some of My Best Friends are Blues, DDT 1994, Horse of a Different Color, Willy DeVille 1999, The Tri-Tone Fascination, Shawn Lane 1999, The Word, The Word 2001, Go On Now, You Can't Stay Here, The Wandering 2012, Candy Store Kid, Ian Siegal and the Mississippi Mudbloods 2012. *Current Management:* c/o Chris Tetzeli and Ryan Kingsbury, Red Light Management, 124 12th Avenue South, #600, Nashville, TN 37203, USA. *Telephone:* (303) 565-5690; (615) 279-3784. *E-mail:* nma@redlightmanagement.com. *Website:* www.redlightmanagement.com; www.blackcrowes.com; www.myspace.com/theblackcrowes; www.nmallstars.com.

DICKSON, Barbara, OBE; British singer and actress; b. 27 Sept. 1947, Dunfermline; d. of the late Alastair H. W. Dickson and of Ruth Dickson (née Malley); m. Oliver F. Cookson 1984; three s. *Education:* Woodmill High School, Dunfermline. *Career:* signed recording contract with Robert Stigwood Org. 1975, with CBS Records 1978. *Musicals include:* John, Paul, George, Ringo and Bert 1974, Blood Brothers 1983. *Recordings include:* singles: Answer Me 1976, Another Suitcase in Another Hall 1977, Caravans 1980, January February 1980, I Know Him So Well (with Elaine Paige) (UK No 1) 1985; albums: All For a Song 1982, Tell Me It's Not True 1983, Heartbeats 1984, Barbara Dickson Song Book 1985, Gold 1985, The Right Moment 1986, Coming Alive Again 1989, Don't Think Twice It's Alright 1992, Parcel of Rogues 1994, Dark End of The Street 1996, The 7 Ages of Woman 1998, For the Record 2002, Full Circle 2004, Nothing's Going to Change My World 2006, Time and Tide 2008, Barbara Dickson in Concert 2009, Words Unspoken 2011, To Each and Everyone 2013. *Honours:* Hon. Fellow, John Moores Univ. 2005; Scot of the Year, Soc. of West End Theatre Award (SWET–Best Actress in a Musical), Liverpool Echo Arts and Entertainment Awards Best Actress in Theatre 1997, Variety Club Showbusiness Awards Best Actress In A Musical 1999, Laurence Olivier Awards Best Actress In A Musical 2000, Platinum, Gold and Silver Discs for album sales. *Address:* The Coach House, Swinhope Hall, Swinhope, Lincolnshire LN8 6HT, England. *Telephone:* (1303) 850828. *Fax:* (1303) 244174. *Website:* www.barbaradickson.net.

DICKSON, Sean; British singer, songwriter, producer and musician (guitar, omnichord); b. 21 March 1967, Bellshill, Scotland. *Career:* singer, songwriter, guitarist, producer for The Soup Dragons 1986–94, The High Fidelity 1995–; worldwide tours; mem. The High Fidelity; runs own record label, Plastique Recordings; mem. PRS, Musicians' Union. *Recordings include:* albums: with The Soup Dragons: This Is Our Art 1988, Lovegod 1990, Hotwired 1992, Hydrophonic 1994; with The High Fidelity: Demonstration 2000.

DICO, Tina; Danish singer; b. (Tina Dickow), 1977, Århus. *Education:* Danish Royal Coll. of Music, Århus. *Career:* featured vocalist with Zero 7; solo career 2001–. *Recordings include:* albums: with Zero 7: When It Falls 2004;

solo: Fuel 2001, Notes 2003, In the Red 2005, Count to Ten 2008, A Beginning, A Detour, an Open Ending 2009, The Road to Gävle 2009, Welcome Back Colour 2010, Where Do You Go to Disappear? 2012. *Honours:* Singer of the Year, Danish Music Awards 2006. *Current Management:* Northern Lights Management, 1 North Grove, London, N6 4SH, England. *E-mail:* jonathan@northernlightsmgt.co.uk. *Website:* www.northernlightsmgt.co.uk; www.tinadico.com.

DIDDY (see COMBS, Sean)

DIDO; British singer, musician (piano, violin) and songwriter; b. (Dido Florian Cloud de Bounevialle Armstrong), 25 Dec. 1971, London, England; sister of Rollo Armstrong. *Education:* Guildhall School of Music, London. *Career:* toured UK with classical music ensemble before joining pop groups aged 16; toured with brother Rollo's band, Faithless; signed solo deal with Arista Records, New York. *Recordings include:* albums: No Angel (BRIT Award for Best Album 2002) 1999, Life for Rent 2003, Safe Trip Home 2008, Girl Who Got Away 2013; singles: The Highbury Fields (EP) 1999, Here With Me 2001, Thank You 2001, Hunter 2001, All You Want 2002, Life for Rent 2003, White Flag (BRIT Award for Best British single 2004) 2003. *Honours:* BRIT Award for Best Female Solo Artist 2002, 2004, Ivor Novello Songwriter of the Year Award 2002, BAMBI Award for Best Int. Pop Act 2003, ASCAP Award for Songwriter of the Year 2008. *Website:* www.didomusic.com.

DIEGO 'EL CIGALA'; Spanish flamenco singer; b. (Diego Ramón Jiménez Salazar), 27 Dec. 1968, Madrid. *Career:* solo artist 1994–; collaborations include Vicente Amigo, Paco de Lucia, Niño Josele, Bebo Valdés. *Recordings include:* albums: Undebel 1998, Entre vareta y canasta 2000, Corren tiempos de alegría 2001, Picasso en mis ojos 2006, Dos lágrimas 2008, Cigala & Tango 2010. *Telephone:* (62) 9487513. *E-mail:* contratacion@elcigala.com. *Address:* c/o Sony BMG Music SA, Avenida de los Madronos 27, 28043 Madrid, Spain. *Website:* www.elcigala.com.

DIESEL, (Yellow Sox); British producer, remixer and DJ; b. (Darren House), 8 Feb. 1966, Hayes, London. *Career:* started DJ career with partner, Rocky (Darren Rock); mem. Ballistic Brothers; Founder-mem. X-Press 2 1993–; mem. MCPS/PRS. *Recordings include:* albums: Ballistic Brothers vs The Eccentric Afros 1995, London Hooligan Soul (with Ballistic Brothers) 1995, My First Acid House (with Problem Kids) 2001; with X-Press 2: Muzikizum 2002, Makeshift Feelgood 2006, The House Of X-Press 2 2012. *Honours:* Muzik Award for Best Producer (with X-Press 2) 2001. *Address:* c/o Skint Records, 73A Middle Street, Brighton, BN1 1AL, England.

DIF, René; Danish singer; b. 17 Oct. 1967, Fredriksberg. *Career:* formed Joyspeed, renamed Aqua; numerous TV and live appearances. *Recordings include:* albums: Aquarium, 1997; Bubble Mix, 1998. *Website:* www.renedif.com.

DIFFIE, Joe Logan; American country singer, songwriter and musician (guitar, bass guitar, drums); b. 28 Dec. 1958, Tulsa, OK. *Career:* mem. high school gospel group, Genesis II and rock group, Blitz; joined gospel group, Higher Purpose and local bluegrass outfit, Special Edition; initial country performances with aunt, Dawn Anita and sister, Monica; moved to Nashville and worked for Gibson Guitars; staff songwriter at Forest Hills Music with occasional backing vocals and demo work for publishers; debut Opry appearance 1990; mem. Grand Ole Opry 1993. *Recordings include:* albums: A Thousand Winding Roads 1990, Regular Joe 1992, Honky Tonk Attitude 1993, Third Rock From The Sun 1994, Life's So Funny 1995, Twice Upon a Time 1997, A Night to Remember 1999, In Another World 2001, Tougher than Nails 2004, Homecoming: the Bluegrass Album 2010. *Honours:* Billboard Award for Top Singles Artist 1991, Cash Box Male Artist of the Year 1991, BMI Award (for There Goes My Heart Again) 1990. *Current Management:* c/o Big Show Music Company, 818 18th Avenue South, Nashville, TN 37203, USA. *Telephone:* (615) 730-5490. *E-mail:* info@bigshowmusicco.com. *Website:* www.bigshowmusicco.com; www.joediffie.com.

DIFFORD, Chris; British singer, musician (guitar) and songwriter; b. 4 Nov. 1954, Greenwich, London, England. *Career:* writing partnership with Glenn Tilbrook 1973–; Founder mem., Squeeze 1974–98, 2007–; numerous festival appearances and tours; worked with Helen Shapiro, Paul Young, Jools Holland, Aimee Mann, Joe Cocker, Mark Knopfler. *Compositions include:* Labelled with Love (songs for musical) 1983, lyrics for Marti Pellow album, Smile 2001. *Recordings include:* albums: with Squeeze: Squeeze 1978, Cool For Cats 1979, Argy Bargy 1980, East Side Story 1981, Sweets From A Stranger 1982, Cosi Fan Tutti Frutti 1985, Babylon And On 1987, Frank 1989, A Round And A Bout 1990, Play 1991, Some Fantastic Place 1993, Ridiculous 1995, Domino 1998, Live At Royal Albert Hall 1999, Essential Squeeze 2007, Spot the Difference 2010; with Glenn Tilbrook: Difford and Tilbrook 1984; solo: I Didn't Get Where I Am 2002, The Last Temptation of Chris 2008, Cashmere If You Can 2011. *Current Management:* c/o Suzanne Hunt, Stress Management, PO Box 27947, London, SE7 8WN, England. *Telephone:* (20) 8269-0352. *Fax:* (20) 8269-0353. *E-mail:* suzanne@quixoticrecords.com. *Website:* www.quixoticrecords.com. *E-mail:* whome@chrisdifford.com. *Website:* www.squeezeofficial.com; www.chrisdifford.com.

DiFRANCO, Ani; American folk singer and songwriter; b. 23 Sept. 1970, Buffalo, NY. *Career:* owner, Righteous Babe Records. *Recordings include:* albums: Ani DiFranco 1989, Not So Soft 1991, Imperfectly 1992, Puddle Dive 1993, Out Of Range 1994, Not A Pretty Girl 1995, Dilate 1996, Living In Clip (live) 1997, Little Plastic Castle 1998, Women In (E)motion 1998, Up Up Up

Up Up Up 1999, Fellow Workers 1999, To The Teeth 1999, Revelling: Reckoning 2001, So Much Shouting, So Much Laughter (live) 2002, Evolve 2003, Educated Guess 2004, Knuckle Down 2005, Reprieve 2006, Canon 2007, Red Letter Year 2008, ¿Which Side Are You On? 2012. *Current Management:* c/o Tracy Mann, MG Limited, 355 W 52nd Street, Sixth Floor, New York, NY 10019, USA. *Telephone:* (212) 956-3906. *Fax:* (212) 262-0814. *E-mail:* tmann@ mglimited.com. *Address:* c/o Righteous Babe Records, PO Box 95, Ellicott Station, Buffalo, NY 14205-0095, USA. *Telephone:* (716) 852-8020. *Fax:* (716) 852-2741. *E-mail:* info@righteousbabe.com. *Website:* www.righteousbabe.com.

DIGBY, Roger, BA, MA; British teacher and musician (concertina); b. 19 April 1949, Colchester, Essex, England; m. Sian Chatterton; two s. *Education:* Bristol Univ., Carlton Univ., Ottawa, Canada. *Career:* Leader, Anglo concertina player, Flowers and Frolics; venues include The Albert Hall, South Bank, Italian Alps; seven years as co-organizer, acoustic music venue The Empress of Russia, Islington; mem. Musicians' Union, EFDSS, International Concertina Asscn. *Recordings include:* Albums: Bees On Horseback, Sold Out, Wait Till The Work Comes Round (with Bob Davenport). *Publications:* numerous reviews. *E-mail:* rdigby@hoppits.demon.co.uk.

DIGITAL, Bobby (see RZA)

DIGWEED, John; British producer, remixer and DJ; b. 3 April 1967, Hastings, East Sussex, England. *Career:* began DJ career in Hastings at his own Bedrock events, early '90s; formed highly successful DJ partnership with Sasha, leading to a residency at Twilo in New York; released several successful mix compilations with Sasha, including Renaissance, Northern Exposure; Founder, Bedrock Records; mem. Bedrock with production partner Nick Muir, with monthly event at Heaven club, London; remixed Sasha, Danny Tenaglia, Farley and Heller, The Orb, New Order; mem. MCPS/PRS. *Radio include:* presenter, Transitiions programme, Kiss100. *Recordings include:* albums: Beautiful Strange 2001, Bedrock 10 Past, Present and Future 2008, Structures 2010, Bedrock 14 2012; numerous compilations. *Current Management:* c/o Safehouse Management, Reverb House, Bennett Street, London W4 2AH, England. *Telephone:* (20) 8743-4000. *Fax:* (20) 8743-4021. *Website:* www.safehousemanagement.com. *E-mail:* bedrockinfo@mac .com. *Website:* www.johndigweed.com.

DIKA, Nick; Canadian bass guitarist. *Education:* McMaster Univ. *Career:* Founder mem. Charlemagne, formed in Hamilton, Ont. 2006, renamed Arkells 2008–; signed to Dine Alone Records 2006; released debut EP Deadlines 2007; opening act for Matt Mayes & El Torpedo on Canadian tour 2008; toured with Waking Eyes on Canadian tour 2009; toured USA with The Maine and Lydia 2012; toured Europe with Billy Talent and Anti-Flag 2012; support act for Tragically Hip on Canadian tour 2013. *Recordings:* albums: with Arkells: Jackson Square 2008, Michigan Left 2011, High Noon (Juno Award for Album of the Year 2015) 2014. *Honours:* 102.1 The Edge CASBY Award 2009, Juno Awards for New Group of the Year 2010, for Group of the Year 2012, 2015. *Current Management:* c/o Tom Sarig, Kari Dexter and Christine Carson, ECG Management; Adam Countryman and Jack Ross, The Agency Group Ltd, 2 Berkeley Street, Suite 202, Toronto, ON M5A 4J5, Canada. *Telephone:* (416) 368-5599 (Agency Group). *Fax:* (416) 368-4655 (Agency Group). *E-mail:* tom@ecgnyc.com; kari@ecgnyc.com; christine@ ecgnyc.com; adamcountryman@theagencygroup.com; jackross@ theagencygroup.com. *Website:* www.theagencygroup.com; www.arkells.ca.

DILLARD, Rodney; American singer and musician (guitar); b. 18 May 1942, East St Louis, IL. *Career:* formed bluegrass group, The Dillards (with brother Doug) 1962–; side project, Dillard-Hartford-Dillard (with brother Doug and John Hartford). *Recordings include:* albums: Back Porch Bluegrass 1963, The Dillards Live! Almost! 1964, Pickin' and Fiddlin' 1965, Wheatstraw Suite 1969, Copperfields 1970, Roots and Branches 1972, Tribute To The American Duck 1973, The Dillards Versus The Incredible LA Time Machine 1977, Mountain Rock 1978, Decade Waltz 1979, Homecoming and Family Reunion 1979, I'll Fly Away 1988, Let It Fly 1991, Take Me Along for the Ride 1992, First Time Live 1999; with Dillard-Hartford-Dillard: Dillard Hartford Dillard 1977, Glitter Grass from the Nashwood Hollyville Strings 1977, Permanent Wave 1980; solo: At Silver Dollar City 1985; with the Dillard Band: Don't Wait for the Hearse to Take You to Church 2010. *Current Management:* Randy Campbell, Superior Communications Co. Talent., 340 South Columbus Blvd, Tucson, AZ 85711-4138, USA. *E-mail:* Campbellsuperior@aol.com. *Website:* www.the-dillards.com.

DILLON, Cara; British singer and songwriter; b. 1975, Dungiven, Co. Derry, Northern Ireland; m. Sam Lakeman. *Career:* fmr mem., Oige; mem., Equation 1995; formed writing partnership with Sam Lakeman, working as a duo. *Recordings include:* albums: Cara Dillon 2001, Sweet Liberty 2003, After the Morning 2006, Hill of Thieves 2009, A Thousand Hearts 2014. *Honours:* All-Ireland Traditional Singing trophy 1989, BBC Radio 2 Folk Award for Best Traditional Track (for Black is the Colour), Horizon Award 2002, Big Buzz Magazine Award-Best Traditional Act 2003, Meteor Music Awards-Best Irish Female 2004, 2007, Indie Acoustic Project Best Celtic Album of 2006 (After The Morning) 2007, Spiral Earth Awards (Best Female Singer, Best Traditional Song) 2010. *Current Management:* Unique Gravity, PO Box 114, Chesterfield, Derbyshire, S40 3YU, England. *Telephone:* (1246) 567712. *Fax:* (1246) 567713. *E-mail:* mark@uniquegravity.co.uk. *Website:* www .uniquegravity.co.uk; www.caradillon.co.uk.

DIMOND, David, BSc; British musician (saxophone, clarinet, flute), composer and woodwind teacher; b. 23 Nov. 1964, Barking, Essex, England; m. Merete Juul-Dimond; one s. *Education:* one year post-diploma, saxophone, Guildhall School of Music and Drama. *Career:* performed in ensembles from duos to big bands, including Duojazz, Jim Mullen Quintet, Caliban, Superjazz, NYJO; venues include Ronnie Scott's, 606 Club, Royal Albert Hall, Royal Festival Hall, Barbican; festivals include Soho Jazz Festival, Edinburgh Festival, London Jazz Festival. *Recordings include:* with numerous jazz ensembles and the BBC, as well as for archive music and jingles. *Publication:* article for International Journal on Acoustics. *Address:* 18 Osborne Road, Dagenham, RM9 5BB, England. *E-mail:* daviddimond_musician@yahoo.co .uk.

DION, Céline, CC, OQ; Canadian singer; b. (Marie Claudette Céline Dion), 30 March 1968, Charlemagne, Québec; d. of Adhémar Dion and Thérèse Tanguay; m. René Angélil 1994 (died 2016); three s. *Career:* recording artist 1981–; winner, Eurovision song contest, Dublin 1988; performed anthem The Power of the Dream at opening ceremony of Olympic Games, Atlanta 1996; Las Vegas show, A New Day 2002–07, Celine 2011–14; Taking Chances World Tour 2008–09. *Recordings include:* albums: Tellement J'ai d'Amour, Incognito, Unison 1990, Dion chante Plamondon 1991, Céline Dion 1991, The Colour of My Love 1993, Les Premières Années 1994, Des Mots Qui Sonnent 1995, Power of Love 1995, The French Album 1995, D'Eux 1995, Falling into You 1996, Live à Paris 1996, Let's Talk About Love 1997, A l'Olympia 1998, Chansons en Or 1998, Céline Dion Vol. 2 1998, S'il Suffisait d'Aimer 1998, These Are Special Times (Grammy and Juno Awards 1999) 1998, Amour 1998, Au Coeur du Stade 1999, Tout en Amour 2002, All The Way – A Decade of Song 1999, A New Day Has Come 2002, One Heart 2003, 1 Fille & 4 Types 2003, Miracle 2004, Taking Chances 2007, My Love: Essential collection 2008, Taking Chances World Tour – The Concert 2010, Tournée mondiale Taking Chances: Le spectacle 2010, Sans attendre 2012, Loved Me Back to Life 2013. *Publications include:* Celine 1997, My Story, My Dreams 2001, Miracle (with Anne Geddes) 2004, For Keeps 2006. *Honours:* Medal of Arts (France) 1996, Légion d'honneur 2008; Dr hc (Laval Univ.) 2008; numerous awards including Gala de L'ADISQ Awards (Quebec) for Pop Album of the Year 1983, for Best Selling Record 1984, 1985, for Best Selling Single 1985, for Pop Song of the Year 1985, 1988, for Female Artist of Year 1983–85, 1988, for Discovery of the Year 1983, for Best Québec Artist Outside Québec 1983, 1988, Journal de Québec Trophy 1985, Spectrel Video Award for Best Stage Performance 1988, Juno Awards for Female Vocalist of the Year 1991–94, 1997, 1999, for Album of the Year 1991, 1995, 1999, for Single of the Year 1993, Acad. Award for Best Song Written for a Motion Picture or TV (for Beauty and The Beast duet with Peabo Bryson) 1992, Grammy Award (for Beauty and the Beast) 1993, (for My Heart Will Go On, from film Titanic) 1999, American Music Award for Best Adult Contemporary Artist 2003, World Music Diamond Award 2004. *Current Management:* Les Productions Feeling, 2540 boul Daniel-Johnson, Bureau 755, Laval, PQ H7T 2S3, Canada. *Telephone:* (450) 978-9555. *Fax:* (450) 978-1055. *E-mail:* info@feelingprod.com. *Website:* www.celinedion.com.

DIOP, Wasis; Senegalese composer, singer and musician (guitar); b. 1950, Dakar. *Career:* toured France with jazz band, West African Cosmos late 1980s; worked with record producer Lee Perry in Jamaica, 1989; worked with Amina Annabi, France 1990 (song for her, C'est Le Dernier Qui a Raison, won the Eurovision Song Contest 1991); toured Japan with saxophonist, Tasuaki Shimizu; solo career began with his composition of the soundtrack for film, Hyenes, directed by his brother, Djibril Diop Mambety. *Recordings include:* albums: Hyenes 1992, No Sant 1995, Toxu, 1998, Judu Bek 2008. *Website:* www.wrasserecords.com.

DIPLO; American record producer, DJ, rapper and songwriter; b. (Thomas Wesley Pentz), 10 Nov. 1978, Tupelo, Miss. *Education:* Univ. of Central Florida, Temple Univ. *Career:* fmr schoolteacher in Philadelphia; held DJ gigs with Low Budget in Philadephia; recorded several mixtapes with Low Budget, M.I.A., Santigold, La Roux; toured with M.I.A. 2005; produced collaborations with Shakira, Bruno Mars, No Doubt, Snoop Dogg, Robyn; record producer, Beyoncé, Rolo Tomassi, Nicola Roberts, Usher, Marina & the Diamonds, Madonna; f. Mad Decent record label 2005–; Founder mem. (with Switch), Major Lazer project 2009–; collaborated with Skrillex as Jack Ü 2013–. *Films:* as producer and director: Favela on Blast (documentary) 2009. *Recordings include:* albums: solo: Sound and Fury 2002, Florida 2004, Decent Work for Decent Pay 2009; with Major Lazer: Guns Don't Kill People... Lazers Do 2009, Free the Universe 2013; with Skrillex: Diplo and Skrillex Present Jack Ü (Grammy Award for Best Dance/Electronic Album 2016) 2015; many mixtapes. *Honours:* American Music Award for Collaboration of the Year (for Where Are Ü Now?, with Skrillex and Justin Bieber) 2015, Grammy Award for Best Dance Recording (for Where Are Ü Now?) 2016. *Address:* c/o Mad Decent Records, Downtown Music, 465 Broadway, 3rd Floor, New York, NY 10013, USA (office). *Telephone:* (212) 625-2980 (office). *Fax:* (212) 625-2987 (office). *E-mail:* info@downtownmusic.com (office). *Website:* www .downtownmusic.com (office); www.maddecent.com; www.majorlazer.com.

DIRECTIONAL FORCE (see Clarke, Dave)

DIRNT, Mike; American musician (bass guitar) and backing singer; b. (Michael Pritchard), 4 May 1972, Berkeley, CA; m. Anastasia (divorced); one d. *Career:* founding mem., Sweet Children, renamed Green Day 1989–; numerous tours and television appearances; side projects include Pinhead Gunpowder, Screeching Weasel, The Network and Foxboro Hot Tubs.

Recordings include: albums: with Green Day: 39/Smooth 1990, Kerplunk 1991, Dookie 1994, Insomniac 1994, Nimrod 1997, Warning 2000, International Superhits (compilation) 2001, Shenanigans 2002, American Idiot (Grammy Award for Best Rock Album 2005, MTV Europe Music Award for Best Album 2005, American Music Award for Favorite Pop/Rock Album 2005, BRIT Award for Best Int. Album 2006) 2004, 21st Century Breakdown (Grammy Award for Best Rock Album 2010) 2009, ¡Uno! 2012, ¡Dos! 2012, ¡Tres! 2012; with The Network: Money Money 2020 2003; with Foxboro Hot Tubs: Stop Drop and Roll!!! 2008. *Honours:* Australian MTV Awards for Best Group 2005, for Best Rock Video (for American Idiot) 2005, MTV Award for Best Rock Video, Best Group Video (both for Boulevard of Broken Dreams), Best Group, MTV Viewer's Choice Award 2005, Kerrang! Awards for Best Band on the Planet, Best Live Act 2005, NME Award for Best Video (for American Idiot) 2005, MTV Europe Music Awards for Best Rock Act 2005, 2009, 2013, Billboard 200 Album Group of the Year 2005, Billboard Music Awards for Pop Group of the Year, for Hot 100 Group of the Year, for Rock Artist of the Year, for Rock Song of the Year (for Boulevard of Broken Dreams), for Modern Rock Artist of the Year 2005, Grammy Award for Record of the Year (for Boulevard of Broken Dreams) 2006, BRIT Award for Best Int. Group 2006, ASCAP Awards for Creative Voice, and for Song of the Year (for Boulevard of Broken Dreams) 2006, American Music Award for Favorite Rock Artist 2009. *E-mail:* info@greenday.com (office). *Website:* www.greenday.com.

DIRTY PIK; Belgian singer and musician (guitar); b. 1 Sept. 1961, Tielt; one s. two d. *Career:* mem. Machine Head 1980–82; Founder-mem. The Dirty Scums 1981–, The Dirty Numbers 1986, The Thirsty Scums 1998–; mem. Game Over 1998–2001; Founder-mem. Freddy & the D'oghz 2013–. *Recordings include:* albums: Dirty Songs 1985, Full Speed Ahead! 1987, 5th Anniversary Gig 1988, The Booze And The Chicks 1989, The Early Years 1990, If The Barkeepers Are United, The Scums Will Never Be Divided 1992, The Pils Sessions 1996, Setting New Standards To Stupidity 1996, Santa Clauz Has Come! 1997, Proud To Be A Punk 1999, Something Else 1999, Dirtier Than You'll Ever Be (compilation) 2000, Insert New Coin (with Game Over) 2000, R.A.M.O.N.E.S. 2002, Funerally Dressed (compilation) 2003, Black Leather, Knee-Hole Pants (with The Thirsty Scums) 2004, The First 25 Yearz (two-CD compilation) 2006, Live & Dirty (two CDs) 2007, Local Punk Heroes Vol. 1 (two-CD compilation) 2007, Made to Last 2011; singles: The Martens 1986, 'Rit'n zat te skit'n bacht'n d'hoage 1988, Really High 1993, Bob de Brouwer 2014, In Love Again 2015. *Address:* The Dirty Scums, Kapelleweg 10, 8700 Tielt, Belgium. *E-mail:* thedirtyscums@yahoo.com. *Website:* www.thedirtyscums.com.

DISTLER, John Edward (Jed), BA; American composer, concert pianist, artistic director, writer and curator and radio host; *Artistic Director, ComposersCollaborative Inc.;* b. 8 Dec. 1956, Newark, New Jersey; m. Célia Cooke 1984. *Education:* Sarah Lawrence Coll., composition with Andrew Thomas, piano with Stanley Lock and William Komaiko. *Career:* Artistic Dir, ComposersCollaborative Inc, a non-profit presenting organization for new music 1987–; Faculty mem. Sarah Lawrence Coll. 1978–2002; mem. American Fed. of Musicians (Local 802), American Music Center, ASCAP; Artist-in-Residence, WWFM.org, The Classical Network; host of Between the Keys. *Compositions include:* The Death of Lottie Shapiro, Calypso for Piano, Diva Demento, Three Landscapes for Peter Wyer, Sonata for Violin and Piano and Toy Piano, Assault on Pepper, String Quartet No 1 (Mr Softee Variations), Loose Changes, The Gold Standard. *Recordings include:* Three Landscapes for Peter Wyer, Margaret Leng Tan; arrangements and transcriptions for Conversations with Bill Evans, Reflections on Duke Ellington, with Jean-Yves Thibaudet, Eleven Art Tatum Transcripts, with Steven Mayer. *Publications include:* transcription books: Art Tatum: Jazz Master, Bill Evans 4; contributing writer for Gramophone magazine, Classicstoday.com, Steinway Artist. *Honours:* with ComposersCollaborative: Grants and Awards, Meet the Composer, The Virgil Thomson Foundation, The Aaron Copland Fund for Music, Foundation for Hellenic Culture. *Address:* ComposersCollaborative Inc., 210 Riverside Drive, 11G, New York, NY 10025-6883, USA (office). *Telephone:* (212) 663-1967 (office). *E-mail:* jdistler@composerscollab.org (office); info@composerscollab.org (office). *Website:* www.composerscollab.org (office).

DITCHAM, Martin Russell; British musician (percussion, drums); b. 22 Feb. 1951, Ilford, Essex, England. *Education:* studied trumpet, violin, recorder, percussion, at school. *Career:* world tours with Sade, Chris Rea, Live Aid, Everything But The Girl, USA tour; mem. Musicians' Union, PRS. *Recordings include:* all four Sade albums; all Chris Rea albums since 1985; Undercover, Rolling Stones; Ross, Diana Ross; Duets, Elton John; 3 albums with Talk Talk; two albums with Manic Street Preachers; Nik Kershaw, Mike and The Mechanics, Jimmy Nail, The Sundays, Heather Small, Tanita Tikaram, The Waterboys, Tina Turner, Jeff Beck, Brian May, Robert Palmer, Engelbert Humperdinck; international recordings with: Patricia Kaas (France), Westernhagen (Germany), Takanaka (Japan), Presuntas Implicados (Spain), Miki Imai (Japan), Amaral (Spain). *Honours:* BPI, ASCAP Awards for Sade, Sweetest Taboo (one of most played songs of year). *Address:* 10 Glyn Mansions, Kensington Olympia, London W14 8XH, England.

DITTO, Beth; American singer and songwriter; b. 19 Feb. 1981, Judsonia, Ark. *Career:* lead vocalist with band Gossip 1999–; collaborated on recordings with Calvin Harris. *Recordings include:* albums: That's Not What I Heard 2001, Movement 2003, Undead in NYC 2003, Standing in the Way of Control 2006, Music for Men 2009, A Joyful Noise 2012. *Honours:* NME Cool List 2006,

Glamour Awards International Artist of the Year 2008. *Address:* Music With A Twist, POB 1998, Radio City Station, New York, NY 10101, USA. *Website:* www.gossipyouth.com.

DIXGÅRD, Björn; Swedish musician (guitar) and singer; b. 8 May 1981. *Career:* Founder mem., Butler 1995; Founder mem., Mando Diao 1999–; joined Caligola (music project) 2008. *Recordings include:* albums: with Mando Diao: Bring 'Em In 2002, Hurricane Bar 2005, Ode to Ochrasy 2006, Never Seen the Light of Day 2007, Give Me Fire 2009, Infruset 2012; with Caligola: Back To Earth 2012, Back To Earth-Resurrection 2012. *Current Management:* Flagstone Management, Götabergsgatan 2, 411 34 Gothenburg, Sweden. *Telephone:* (3) 170-175-20. *Fax:* (3) 170-175-30. *E-mail:* info@flagstone.se. *Website:* www.flagstone.se; www.mandodiao.com.

DIXIT, Raghu; Indian singer and composer. *Education:* Univ. of Mysore. *Career:* professionally qualified as Indian classical dancer; f. Raghu Dixit Project; composer of music for radio, television and film. *Films:* as musical dir and composer: Psycho 2008, Quick Gun Murugan 2009, Just Math Mathalli 2009, Superman 2010. *Recordings:* albums: Raghu Dixit 2008. *Honours:* SFM Kalaa Award for Favourite Singer 2009. *E-mail:* paul@jenral.com. *Website:* www.jenral.com. *Address:* The Raghu Dixit Project, 159 8th Street, Bank Avenue, Banaswadi, Bangalore 560 043, India (office). *Telephone:* 990516145 (office). *E-mail:* music@raghudixit.com (office). *Website:* raghudixit.com.

DIXON, Alesha; British singer and songwriter; b. 7 Oct. 1978, Welwyn Garden City, England; m. Michael Harvey, Jr. 2005 (divorced 2006). *Career:* Founder-mem. Mis-Teeq 2001–05; numerous live appearances; solo artist 2005–. *Recordings include:* albums: with Mis-Teeq: Lickin' On Both Sides 2001, Eyecandy 2003; solo: Fired Up 2006, The Alesha Show 2008, The Entertainer 2010. *Television:* Strictly Come Dancing (judge) 2009–11. *Honours:* UK Garage Award for Best Artist 2001, MOBO Award for Best Garage Act 2002. *Website:* www.aleshadixon.com.

DIYICI, Senem; Turkish singer; b. 30 March 1953, Istanbul; m. Alain Blesing 1989; two d. *Education:* Istanbul Music Acad. *Career:* joined children's choir in Istanbul; formed several groups; performs about 100 shows throughout world annually; mem. SACEM, ADATI, SPEDIDAM. *Recordings include:* Nar Haniti 1970, Hatimeyva 1976, Casino No. 1 1979, Anatoliv 1986, Takalar 1989, Geste 1993, Divan 1995, Jell me Trabizan. *E-mail:* association.ritournelle @ gmail.com. *E-mail:* senem.diyici@free.fr. *Website:* www.senemdiyici.com.

DIZZEE RASCAL; British singer; b. (Dylan Mills), 1985, London, England. *Career:* began performing in early teens; emerged via unlicensed radio in London; collaborated with Basement Jaxx; f. record label, Dirtee Stank 2005–; performed in opening ceremony of London Olympics.2012. *Recordings include:* albums: Boy In Da Corner (Mercury Music Prize) 2003, Showtime 2004, Maths + English 2007, Tongue n' Cheek 2009, The Fifth 2013. *Television:* Must Be The Music (judge) 2010. *Honours:* NME Award for Innovation 2004, MOBO Awards for Best UK Male 2007, 2008, for Best Hip-Hop Artist 2008, Urban Music Awards (Best Male) 2009, BRIT Award for Best British Male Solo Artist 2010, BET Award for Best International Act 2010. *Current Management:* c/o Primary Talent Ltd, 11 Jockey's Fields, London, WC1R 4BN, England. *Telephone:* (20) 7400-4500. *E-mail:* info@dirteestank.com. *Website:* www.dirteestank.com; www.dizzeerascal.co.uk.

DJ TUKUTZ; South Korean hip hop DJ, songwriter and record producer; b. (Kim Jung-sik), 19 Nov. 1981, Seoul. *Career:* Founder mem., hip hop group Epik High 2003–; co-f. Map the Soul record label 2009; military service 2009–11. *Recordings include:* albums: with Epik High: Map of the Human Soul 2003, High Society 2004, Swan Songs 2005, Remapping the Human Soul (Mnet KM Music Festival Award for Album of the Year 2007) 2007, Pieces Part One 2008, (e) 2009, Epilogue 2010, 99 2012. *Honours:* Golden Disk Awards for Best Hip-Hop Artist 2005, 2009, for Bonsang (Fan) 2007, KBS Music Award for Best Hip-Hop Artist 2005, SBS Music Award for Best Hip Hop Artist 2006, Mnet KM Music Festival Awards for Best Hip-Hop Artist 2005, 2008, for Bonsang (Fan) 2007, Seoul Music Award for Bonsang (Fan) 2008, Mnet Asian Music Award for Best Rap Performance (for UP) 2012. *Address:* c/o YG Entertainment, 397-5 YG Building, 5th Floor, Hapjeong-Dong, Mapo-Gu, Seoul, 121886, South Korea (office). *Website:* www.mapthesoul.com; www.vg-epikhigh.com.

DJ FLEX; Panamanian singer; b. (Félix Danilo Gómez), 26 Aug. 1979; m. Osiris Vega 2008 (divorced 2011). *Career:* solo artist 1997–; known as 'Nigga' in Latin America, as DJ Flex, or Flex in USA. *Recordings include:* album: Te Quiero 2007, Vives En Mi 2012. *Honours:* Latin Grammy Award for Best Urban Song (for Te Quiero) 2008. *Current Management:* c/o Richard De La Font Agency, 4845 South Sheridan Road, Tulsa, OK 74145, USA. *Telephone:* (918) 665-6200. *Website:* delafont.com. *Address:* EMI Televisa Music, 404 Washington Avenue, Suite 700, Miami Beach, FL 33139, USA. *E-mail:* contacto@emilatin.com. *Website:* www.emitelevisa.com.

DJ SNAKE; French DJ, rapper and record producer; b. (William Grigahcine), 13 June 1986, Paris. *Career:* producer for tracks on Lady Gaga's Born This Way and ARTPOP albums 2011, 2013; remixed tracks by numerous artists including AlunaGeorge, Kanye West, Junior Senior, Bruno Mars, Skrillex and Diplo, Calvin Harris and Disciples; numerous collaborations including: Turn Down for What (with Lil Jon) 2013, Get Low (with Dillon Francis) 2014, You Know You Like It (with AlunaGeorge) 2014, Lean On (with Major Lazer and MØ) 2015, Middle (with Bipolar Sunshine) 2015. *Honours:* Billboard Music

Award for Top Dance/Electronic Song (for Turn Down for What) 2015. *E-mail:* steve@guess-agency.com. *Website:* www.djsnake.fr.

DJAVAN; Brazilian singer, musician (guitar) and songwriter; b. (Djavan Caetano Viana), 27 Jan. 1949, Maceió, Alagoas. *Career:* started own band, LSD, playing Beatles covers in local venues, aged 16; moved to Rio de Janeiro 1973; hired to sing TV soap opera themes between regular night club appearance; composition Abertura placed second in TV Globo's festival of same name 1975; signed to CBS and began recording in USA 1982; returned to roots and Rio 1986. *Recordings include:* Albums include: A Voz E O Violao 1976, Djavan 1979, Alumbramento 1980, Seduzir 1981, Luz 1982, Lilas 1984, Meu Lado 1986, Nao E Azul Mas E Mar 1987, Oceano 1989, Coisa De Acendar 1992, Novena 1994, Malasia 1996, O Bicho Solto 1998, Ao Vivo 1999, Milagreiro 2001, Para Siempre 2002, Vaidade 2004, Na pista, etc 2006, Matizes 2007, Ária 2010, Ária ao Vivo 2011, Rua dos Amores 2012. *Honours:* Latin Grammy, Best Brazilian Song, Acelerou 2000. *Website:* www.djavan .com.br.

DJINDJI, Dilon; Mozambican singer, songwriter and musician (guitar); b. (Venancio de Conceicao Dilone Jinge), 14 Aug. 1927, Marracuene. *Career:* started playing home-made guitar 1939; formed first group Estrela de Marracuene (Star of Marracuene) 1960; first recording for local radio broadcast 1964; mem. Mabulu 1998–, first int. appearance with Mabulu 2001. *Recordings include:* with Mabulu: Karimbo 2000, Soul Marrabenta 2001; solo: Dilon 2002.

D.M.C. (see Darryl McDaniels)

DMX, (DMX The Great, Dark Man X); American rap artist and producer; b. (Earl Simmons), 18 Dec. 1970, Baltimore, Md. *Career:* became a DJ in the local projects; released debut single after winning Source magazine's Unsigned Hype Award 1991; collaborations with Ja Rule, Jayo Felony, Ice Cube, Jay-Z, Eve, Limp Bizkit; own film co., Bloodline Films. *Film appearances include:* Belly 1998, Romeo Must Die 2000, Boricua's Bond 2000, Exit Wounds 2001, Cradle 2 the Grave 2003, Never Die Alone 2004, Last Hour 2006, The Bleeding 2009, King Dog 2013, Blame It on the Hustle 2013. *Recordings include:* albums: It's Dark and Hell Is Hot 1998, Flesh of My Flesh, Blood of My Blood 1998, . . . And Then There Was X 1999, The Great Depression 2001, The DMX Files 2002, Grand Champ 2003, Here We Go Again 2005, Year of the Dog Again 2006, Undisputed 2012. *Honours:* Source Award for Artist of the Year 1999, American Music Award for Favorite Rap/Hip Hop Artist 2000.

DOBBIS, Rick, BS; American music industry executive. *Education:* Syracuse Univ. *Career:* Exec. Vice-Pres. RCA Records late 1980s; Pres. PolyGram Label Group 1990–94; Pres. PolyGram Europe 1994–98; Exec. Vice-Pres. Sony Music International 1998–99, Pres. Sony Music International 1999–2004; currently owner, Rick Dobbis Org. 2006–; Co-founder, myKaZootv 2011–; mem. Int. Fed. for the Phonographic Industry (IFPI). *Website:* mykazootv.com.

DOBES, Pavel; Czech songwriter, singer and musician (guitar); b. 22 March 1949, Frydek-Mistek; s. of Lubomír Dobeš and Vlasta Dobešová; m.; six s. three d. *Education:* traditional school of art. *Career:* songs regularly broadcasted by private and nat. radio stations; some 100 concerts a year, at home and outside Czech Republic; mem. OSA, Intergram, SAI. *Recordings include:* Skupinové foto, Zátiši s červy, Zpátky do trenek, Pavel Dobeš Live, Něco o Americe, Průzkumný let, K svátku, Banány. *Publications include:* Něco o Americe, Gibraltar. *E-mail:* paveldobes@paveldobes.cz. *Website:* www .paveldobes cz.

DOCTOR J (see Da Silva, Rui)

DOCTOR ROCKIT (see Herbert, Matthew)

DODA; Polish singer and songwriter; b. (Dorota Rabczewska), 15 Feb. 1984, Ciechanów; d. of Paweł Rabczewski and Wanda Rabczewska; m. Radoslaw Majdan 2005 (divorced 2008). *Career:* fmr teenage athletics champion; embarked on singing career, coached by Elzbieta Zapendowska; fmr lead singer, Virgin 2000–07; solo artist 2007–. *Film:* Asterix and the Vikings (voice only) 2006. *Recordings:* albums: with Virgin: Virgin 2002, Bimbo 2004, Ficca 2005; solo: Diamond Bitch 2007, The Seven Temptations 2010. *Honours:* with Virgin: National Festival of Polish Song in Opole Superjedynka Award for Best Pop CD 2006; solo: VIVA Comet Awards for Artist of the Year 2007, 2008, Image of the Year 2007, 2008, Music Video of the Year 2007, 2008, 2010, Artist of the Decade 2010, and Song of the Decade 2010, VIVA Comet Chart Award 2008; MTV Europe Music Award for Best Polish Act 2007, 2009, Nat. Festival of Polish Song in Opole Superjedynka Award for Best Artist 2008. *Address:* c/o Universal Music Poland, Gdanska 27/31, 01-633, Warsaw, Poland (office). *E-mail:* jarekburdek@wp.pl (office); universal@universalmusic.pl (office); doda@doda.net.pl (office). *Website:* www.doda.net.pl.

DOHERTY, Ged; British music industry executive; *Chair, BPI and BRIT Awards Limited;* b. Manchester. *Career:* began career as booking agent, later becoming artist man. for Paul Young and Alison Moyet; Head of Int. Marketing, Sony Music, New York 1992–96; Man. Dir, Columbia Records, UK 1996–99; Man. Dir, Arista, BMG 1999–2001, Pres. Music Division Sony BMG Music Entertainment (following merger) 2001–06, Chair. and CEO 2006–11; Chair. Brit Awards Cttee 2007–10; Co-founder, Raindog Films 2011–; Chair., BPI and BRIT Awards Ltd 2015–. *Address:* BRIT Awards Limited, BPI, Riverside Building, County Hall, Westminster Bridge Road, London, SE1 7JA, England (office). *E-mail:* britswebmaster@bpi.co.uk. *Website:* www.brits.co.uk.

DOHERTY, Pete; British singer and songwriter; b. 12 March 1979, Hexham, Northumberland; s. of Jacqueline Michels and Peter John Doherty; one s. (with Lisa Moorish) one d. (with Lindi Hingston). *Career:* son of an army officer, was brought up in various barracks around Britain and in Northern Ireland, Germany and Cyprus; travelled to Russia as winner of British Council poetry competition aged 16; moved to London, formed band The Libertines with Carl Barât, performed numerous short-notice 'guerilla gigs' in small venues and pvt. homes; sentenced to six months imprisonment for burglary of Barât's flat, released after two months; expelled from band 2004; formed new band Babyshambles 2004; collaborations with Wolfman, Client, Littl'ans, The Streets; fashion model, Roberto Cavalli's advertising campaign 2007–08; reformed The Libertines 2014–. *Recordings include:* with The Libertines: albums: Up The Bracket 2002, The Libertines 2004, Anthems for Doomed Youth 2015; with Babyshambles: albums: Down in Albion 2005, Shotter's Nation 2007, Sequel to the Prequel 2013; solo: Grace/Wastelands 2009. *Film appearance:* Confession of a Child of the Century 2012. *Publication:* The Books of Albion: The Collected Writings of Peter Doherty 2007. *Honours:* Shockwave NME Awards Hero of the Year 2008, Best Solo Artist 2009, Q Award for Best Track (for Gunga Din) 2015. *Current Management:* c/o Adrian Hunter and Andy Boyd, Lazy Eye Management Ltd, 26–28 Goodall Street, Walsall WS1 1QL, England. *E-mail:* lazy-eye@hotmail.co.uk. *Website:* www.babyshambles.net; www.thelibertines.com.

DOKKEN, Don; American rock singer; b. 29 June 1953. *Career:* backing singer, Scorpions (recordings unreleased) 1982; founder and lead singer of rock group, Dokken 1978–89, 1993–; solo artist 1989–; worldwide concerts. *Recordings include:* albums: with Dokken: Breaking The Chains 1983, Tooth and Nail 1984, Under Lock and Key 1985, Back For The Attack 1987, Beast From The East 1988, Dysfunctional 1995, One Live Night 1995, Shadowlife 1997, Erase The Slate 1999, Live From The Sun 2000, Long Way Home 2002, Hell to Pay 2004, Lightning Strikes Again 2008; solo: Up From The Ashes 1990. *Website:* www.dokkencentral.com.

DOKY, Christian (Chris) Minh; Danish musician (bass), composer and producer; b. 7 Feb. 1969, Glostrup; brother of Niels Lan Doky. *Education:* studied with Orsted Pedersen. *Career:* mem. The Doky Brothers (with brother, Niels) 1995–97; solo artist and prod. 1997–; mem. of the bands of artists, including Bill Evans, Ryuichi Sakamoto, Trilok Gurtu, David Sanborn; worked with John Abercrombie, Bob Berg; composer for film and television. *Film and television soundtracks include:* This is Denmark 1996, Kronprins Frederik Pts 1 and 2 1998, Prinsesse Alexandra 2001, Henning Larsen 2003, Life in Denmark Pts 1–6 2003, Kongehuset Pts 1–10 2003, Vejret på TV2 2003–05, Kronprinsesse Mary 2004. *Recordings include:* albums: solo: Appreciation 1989, The Sequel 1990, Letters 1991, Minh 1998, Listen Up! 2000, Cinematique 2002, The Nomad Diaries 2006, A Jazz Life 2008; with the Doky Brothers: The Doky Brothers 1995, The Doky Brothers 2 1996, Listen Up! 2000, Nomad Diaries 2006, Scenes from a dream! 2010. *Publications include:* Minh – On Bass 1998, Jazz Kitchen 2001. *Honours:* Simon Spies Prisen for Artist of the Year 1992, Double Platinum Award 2012. *E-mail:* office@m1prod.net. *Website:* www.doky.com.

DOKY, Niels Lan; Danish composer, producer and jazz musician (piano); b. 3 Oct. 1963, Copenhagen; brother of Chris Minh Doky; m. Valentine Farlot 1989; one s. one d. *Education:* Berklee Coll. of Music, Boston, USA. *Career:* fmrly solo artist in New York; now mem. The Doky Brothers (with brother, Chris) 1995–97; solo artist 1997–; has played and recorded with artists, including Jack DeJohnette, David Sanborn, Ray Brown, Joe Henderson, John Scofield, Marcus Miller, Clark Terry, Tom Harrell, Charlie Haden, Gary Peacock; mem. DJBFA, NCB, KODA. *Recordings include:* albums: solo: Here or There 1986, The Target 1986, The Truth: Live at Montmartre 1987, Daybreak 1988, Close Encounter Vol. 1 1989, Close Encounter Vol. 2 1989, Dreams 1989, Friendship 1990, The Toronto Concert 1991, Paris By Night (live) 1992, An Evening of Standards 1992, Manhattan Portrait 1993, Misty Dawn 1994, Niels Lan Doky 1998, Asian Session 1999, Café en plein air 2001, Casa Dolce Casa 2002, Spain 2002, The Look of Love 2003, The Russian Album 2007, Return to Denmark 2010, Human Behavior 2011; with The Doky Brothers: The Doky Brothers 1995, The Doky Brothers 2 1996. *Honours:* Oscar Peterson Jazz Masters Award 1983, Boston Jazz Soc. Achievement Award 1983, Count Basie Award 1984, Hoistebro Musikpris 1987, Carlsberg Hof Legat 1988, Simon Spies Musikpris 1993, Kraks Blå Bog 1996–, Midi Magazine Årets Bob Award for keyboardist of the year 1997, Fermaten Live Award for Best Jazz Concert of the Year 1999, Royal Award, Denmark 2001. *E-mail:* nielslandoky@gmail .com. *Website:* www.nielslandoky.com.

DOLBY, Thomas; musician (synthesizers), singer, songwriter, programmer and producer; b. (Thomas Morgan Robertson), 14 Oct. 1958, Cairo, Egypt; m. Kathleen Beller; three c. *Education:* studied meteorology. *Career:* built own synthesizers and PA system; sound engineer, various groups; Co-founder, Camera Club 1979; musician with Lene Lovich 1980; solo recording artist 1981–; musician with David Bowie, Live Aid, Wembley 1985. *Compositions include:* New Toy, Lene Lovich; film scores include: Howard – A New Breed of Hero. *Recordings include:* albums: The Golden Age of Wireless 1982, The Flat Earth 1985, Aliens Ate My Buick 1988, Astronauts and Heretics 1992, Gate to the Mind's Eye 1994, Hyperactive 1999, A Map of the Floating City 2011; singles: Urges, Europa and The Pirate Twins 1981, Windpower 1982, She Blinded Me With Science 1983, Hyperactive 1984, Close But No Cigar 1992; contrib. for recordings by: Foreigner, Joan Armatrading, M, Stevie Wonder, Grace Jones, Howard Jones, Herbie Hancock, Ofra Haza, Robyn Hitchcock,

Belinda Carlisle, Dusty Springfield; record producer for artists including Joni Mitchell, Prefab Sprout. *Current Management:* c/o Conqueroo, 11271 Ventura Boulevard, Suite 522, Studio City, CA 91604, USA. *Telephone:* (323) 656-1600. *E-mail:* cary@conqueroo.com. *Website:* www.conqueroo.com; www.thomasdolby.com.

DOLENZ, (George) Michael (Mickey), Jr; American musician (drums), singer, actor, producer and writer; b. 8 March 1945, Tarzana, Los Angeles; m. 1st Samantha Juste 1968 (divorced); m. 2nd Trina Dow 1977 (divorced); m. 3rd Donna Quinter. *Education:* Valley Coll., Los Angeles Technical Inst. *Career:* child actor, television series, Circus Boy 1956–58; other acting roles in Peyton Place, Route 66, Mr Novak; as musician: mem. The One Nighters, The Missing Links, The Monkees 1966–70, 1985–91; actor, Monkees TV series 1966–68; other television includes 33 1/3 Revolutions Per Monkee TV Special, NBC; film appearance, Head; stage performances include Remains To Be Seen 1970, The Point 1978; solo artist 1971–72; Broadway production of Grease 1994; mem. Dolenz Jones Boyce and Hart 1975–76; also television director, producer 1977–85; voiceovers for My 3 Sons, Scooby Doo, Adam 12, Devlin; Monkees reunion concert, 1997; musical version of Aida 2003. *Recordings include:* albums: The Monkees 1966, More of The Monkees 1967, Headquarters 1967, Pisces, Aquarius, Capricorn and Jones, The Birds, The Bees and The Monkees 1968, Head 1969, The Monkees Greatest Hits 1969, The Monkees Present 1969, Instant Replay 1969, Changes 1970, Then and Now 1986, Pool It! 1987, Listen to the Band 1991, Greatest Hits 1995, Music Box 2001; hit singles: Last Train To Clarksville 1966, I'm A Believer 1966, I'm Not Your Steppin' Stone 1967, A Little Bit Me, A Little Bit You 1967, Alternate Title 1967, Daydream Believer 1967, Valleri 1968, Tear Drop City 1969. *Publications include:* I'm A Beliver: My Life of Monkees, Music and Madness (autobiography), with Mark Bego. *Honours:* NARM Awards, Best Selling Group and Album 1967, Emmy, Outstanding Comedy Series 1967, three BMI Awards 1968, Monkees Day, Atlanta 1986, Star on Hollywood Walk of Fame 1989. *Current Management:* c/o Michelle Grant, Grant Management, 1158 26th Street, Santa Monica, CA 90403, USA. *Telephone:* (310) 586-1166. *Website:* www.mickydolenz.com.

DOLLIMORE, Kris; musician (guitar) and producer. *Career:* mem. Del Amitri 1997–2002. *Recordings include:* albums: Hatful Of Rain/Lousy With Love 1998, Can You Do Me Good? 2002.

DOLMAYAN, John Hovig; American musician (drums); b. 15 July 1973, Lebanon. *Career:* moved to USA; mem. System of a Down 1996–; Founder-mem. Scars on Broadway 2006–. *Recordings include:* albums: with System of a Down: System Of A Down 1998, Toxicity 2001, Maximum 2002, Steal This Album! 2002, Mezmerize 2005, Hypnotize 2005, Vicinity of Obscenity 2006; with Scars on Broadway: Scars on Broadway 2008. *Honours:* MTV Europe Music Award for Best Alternative 2005, Grammy Award for Best Hard Rock Performance (for B.Y.O.B.) 2006. *Current Management:* c/o Velvet Hammer, 9911 W. Pico Boulevard, 350W, Los Angeles, CA 90035, USA. *Telephone:* (310) 657-6161. *Fax:* (310) 657-0310. *Website:* www.velvethammer.net; www.systemofadown.com; www.scarsonbroadway.com.

DOMBASLE, Arielle, Baccalauréat; French (b. American) actress and singer; b. (Arielle Sonnery De Fromental), 27 April 1958, Norwich, Conn., USA; m. Bernard-Henri Lévy. *Education:* Lyceo Franco-Mexicano, Mexico City, Conservatoire de Musique Paris. *Career:* spent childhood in Mexico; debut in film Perceval le Gallois (Dir Eric Rohmer) 1978; singer in Spanish, English and French, four albums recorded; Writer and Dir Chassé-croisé 1982 and Les pyramides bleues 1988; performer in production L'as-tu revue, Opéra-Comique 1991, La Toujours Belle et la Toute Petite Bête 2003. *Films include:* Perceval le Gallois 1978, Tess 1979, Justocoeur 1980, Les fruits de la passion 1981, Le beau mariage 1982, La belle captive 1983, Pauline à la plage 1983, La nuit porte jarretelles 1985, Flagrant désir 1985, The Boss' Wife 1986, Jeux d'artifices 1987, Try This One for Size 1989, El sueño de mono loco 1990, Lola Zipper 1991, Zwischensaison 1992, Villa mauresque 1992, La vie crevée 1992, L'Absence 1993, L'Arbre, le maire et la médiathèque 1993, Miroslava 1993 (Prize, New York Film Festival 1993), Grand bonheur 1993, Un indien dans la ville 1994, Fado majeur et mineur 1994, Mecánicas celestes 1995, Un bruit qui rend fou 1995, Raging Angels 1995, Les deux papas et la maman 1996, Trois vies et une seule mort 1996, Soyons amis 1996, Le jour et la nuit 1997, Jeunesse 1997, J'en suis! 1997, Les amis de Ninon 1997, Que la lumière soit 1998, Hors jeu 1998, L'Ennui 1998, Bo Ba Bu 1998, Astérix et Obélix contre Cesar 1999, Le temps retrouvé 1999, C'est pas ma faute 1999, Les infortunes de la beauté 1999, Le Libertin 2000, Vatel 2000, Amazone 2000, 30 ans 2000, Gamer 2001, Les âmes fortes 2001, Deux 2002, Lovely Rita, sainte patronne des cas désespérés 2003, Albert est méchant 2004, Le genre humain: Les parisiens 2004, Quand je serai star 2004, Le courage d'aimer 2005, Nouvelle chance 2006, Gradiva 2006, Sagan 2008, La possibilité d'une île 2008, Hitler in Hollywood 2010. *Recordings include:* albums: Cantate 78 1978, Amour Symphonique 1990, Liberta 2000, Extase 2002, C'est si bon 2006, Amor Amor 2007, Où tu veux 2007, Glamour à Mort 2009, Extra-Terrestre 2009, Woman, just a woman 2009. *Honours:* Légion d'honneur 2007; Ours d'Argent, Berlin 1983, Prix d'Interpretation Actrice, Festival de Cabourg 1993. *Address:* c/o Agence Adequat, Laurent Gregoire, 80 rue d'Amsterdam, 75009 Paris, France (office). *Telephone:* 1-42-80-00-42 (office); 6-28-29-32-93. *Fax:* 1-42-80-00-43 (office). *E-mail:* agence@agence-adequat.com (office); laurence.roblin@gmail.com. *Website:* www.arielle-dombasle.net.

DOMINIQUE, Carl-Axel Martinelli; Swedish pianist and composer; b. 1 Sept. 1939, Upplands Bälinge; m. Monica Dominique; three s. *Education:* Royal Acad. of Music, Stockholm, Juilliard School of Music, New York with Martin Canin, Swedish Film School; studied Oliver Messiaen's piano works with the composer. *Career:* concert pianist debut 1966; soloist in Swedish symphony orchestras 1968–; mem. jazz fusion group Solar Plexus 1971–75; mem. piano four hands duo with Monica Dominique; composer for theatre productions, films and TV shows; mem. Monica Dominique Quintet 2002–; mem. Swedish Composers of Popular Music, Royal Swedish Acad. of Music 2009–. *Compositions:* 31 Songs from Aniara, You Are Summer (Swedish entry in Eurovision Song Contest 1973); music for television, film, theatre; songs and orchestral works. *Recordings:* Blinded (LP), Alkan-Satie-Ives-Dominique (LP); Olivier Messiaen: Vingt Régards Sur L'Enfant Jésus (2CD), Complete Bird Music for piano solo (3CD), Harawi (LP with Dorothy Dorow 1980, CD with Annika Skoglund 2010); with Monica Dominique: One Grand Piano – Four Hands 1996, Fingers Unlimited (CD) 2011. *Television:* Med på noterna. *Film:* Badarna (soundtrack). *Publication:* We Play Together (with Monica Dominique). *Honours:* Pro Patria Great Gold Medal for Civil Merits 2003; Sångfågeln 1973, Expressen Musical Prize 1984, Royal Swedish Acad. of Music Medal for Music 2008. *Address:* Dominique Musik AB, Edition Dominique, Dominique Records, Apelvägen 21, 141 46 Huddinge (office); Apelvägen 21, 141 46 Huddinge, Sweden (home). *Telephone:* (8) 711-18-13 (home). *Fax:* (8) 774-27-60 (home). *E-mail:* info@dominiquemusik.se (office); carl.axel@dominiquemusik.se (home). *Website:* www.dominiquemusik.se (home).

DOMINIQUE, Monica; Swedish musician (piano), singer, arranger and composer; b. (Monica Danielsson), 20 July 1940, Västerås; m. Carl-Axel Dominique; three s. *Education:* Royal Acad. of Music, Stockholm. *Career:* jazz pianist, cabaret artist, actress; joined vocal group Gals and Pals 1967; mem. jazz fusion group Solar Plexus 1970–75; bandleader, Mitt i Strömmen, TV programme 1983–84; formed Monica Dominique Quintet 2002; mem. piano four hands duo with Carl-Axel Dominique; has performed with Toots Thielemans, Carla Bley, Steve Swallow, Wolfgang Puschnig, Arne Domnérus, Putte Wickman; mem. Swedish Composers of Popular Music, Swedish Jazz Acad., Swedish Jazz Musicians. *Films:* Repmånad, Monopol. *Compositions include:* Tillägnan, You Are Summer; for big band: Swedish Love in Southern Bronx, Inside The Rainbow; for choir: No Man Is An Island, Oh, What a Wonderful World; musicals: ODA, Jösses Flickor, Sopoperan Underbarnet; children's musical: Mr God, This Is Anna. *Recordings:* with Monica Dominique Quintet: Bird Woman 2003; with Monica Zetterlund: Monica-Monica 2009; with Carl-Axel Dominique: En Flygel Fyra Händer 1996; with Carol Rogers: So Nice 1997: with Monica Nielsen: Säg vad ni vill 2004, Boa; with Palle Danielsson: Togetherness 2012. *Television:* Mitt i strömmen, Gäster med gester. *Publications:* We Play Together (with C.-A. Dominique). *Honours:* Pro Patria Great Gold Medal for Civil Merits 2003; Sångfågeln (for You Are Summer, Swedish entry in Eurovision Song Contest) 1973, Expressen Musical Prize 1994, Evert Taube Award 1994, Royal Swedish Acad. of Music Medal for Music. *Current Management:* Dominique Musik AB, Edition Dominique, Dominique Records, Apelvägen 21, 141 46 Huddinge, Sweden. *Telephone:* (8) 711-18-13. *Fax:* (8) 774-27-60. *E-mail:* info@dominiquemusik.se. *Website:* www.dominiquemusik.se.

DOMINO, Fats; American blues singer; b. (Antoine Domino), 26 Feb. 1928, New Orleans, La. *Career:* fmr factory worker; began singing career in local clubs. *Television:* Treme (guest appearance) 2012. *Singles include:* The Fat Man, Goin' Home, Going To The River, Please Don't Leave Me, Don't You Know, Ain't That A Shame, Bo Weevil, I'm In Love Again, My Blue Heaven, Blueberry Hill, Walking to New Orleans, My Girl Josephine, Let The Four Winds Blow, Red Sails In The Sunset. *Recordings include:* albums: Here Comes Fats Domino 1963, Southland USA 1965, Fats Domino 1966, Trouble in Mind, Fats is Back 1968, Sleeping on the Job 1978, The Fat Man 1995, Live at Gilleys 1999, Live! Collector's Edition 2000. *Honours:* Hall of Fame Grammy Award 1997, Lifetime Achievement Grammy Award 1997, Nat. Medal of Arts 1998, inducted into Louisiana Music Hall of Fame 2007.

DOMM, Mario; Mexican singer, songwriter, musician (guitar, bass guitar, drums, keyboards) and record producer; b. (Mario Alberto Dominguez Zarzar), 22 Jan. 1977, Torreón, Coahuila. *Career:* mem. of rock band Dulce Ana 1993; released debut solo album 2002; Founder-mem. Camila (with Samo Parra and Pablo Hurtado) 2006–; songwriter and producer for artists including Reyli Barba, Alejandro Fernández, Alejandra Guzmán, Edel Juárez, Kalimba, Magneto, OV7, Paulina Rubio, Sin Bandera, Thalia, Yuridia. *Recordings:* albums: solo: Mexi-Funk-Music 2002; with Camila: Todo Cambío 2006, Dejarte de amar (Latin Grammy Award for Best Pop Vocal Album by a Group 2010, Premios Oye! for Album of the Year 2010, for Album of the Year by Group 2010, Premio Lo Nuestro for Album of the Year 2010) 2010, Elypse (Latin Grammy Award for Best Contemporary Pop Vocal Album 2014) 2014. *Honours:* Latin Grammy Awards for Record of the Year, for Song of the Year (both for Mientes) 2010, Premio Lo Nuestro Award for Song of the Year (for Mientes) 2011, Premios Juventud for Best Ballad (for Aléjate de Mi) 2011. *Address:* c/o Sony Music Latin, Sony Music Entertainment, 550 Madison Avenue, New York, NY 10022, USA (office). *Website:* www.sonymusiclatin.com (office); www.camila.tv/home.

DONAGHY, Siobhan; British singer; b. London, England. *Career:* founder mem., Sugababes 1998–2001; solo artist 2001–; starred in musical Rent, London 2007. *Recordings include:* albums: with Sugababes: One Touch 2000; solo: Revolution in Me 2003, Ghosts 2007. *Current Management:* CMO Management International Ltd, Studio 2.6, Shepherds East, Richmond Way,

London, W14 0DQ, England. *Telephone:* (20) 7316-6969. *Fax:* (20) 7316-6970. *E-mail:* reception@cmomanagement.co.uk; CMOinfo@cmomanagement.co .uk. *Website:* www.cmomanagement.co.uk; www.siobhandonaghy.co.uk.

DONAHUE, Jonathan; American singer, songwriter and musician (guitar); b. 6 May 1966. *Career:* Founder-mem. experimental rock group Mercury Rev, Buffalo, New York, mid-1980s; also guitarist with The Flaming Lips 1989–91; Mercury Rev began as composers of soundtracks for experimental films, made first recordings at State Univ. of New York; sound has gradually developed from a very experimental and psychedelic style to a more melodic approach; festival appearances in USA, Europe and Far East 2007; experimental side-project, Harmony Rockets. *Recordings include:* albums: with: Mercury Rev: Yerself Is Steam 1991, Boces 1993, See You on the Other Side 1995, Deserter's Songs (NME Magazine Album of the Year) 1998, All Is Dream 2001, The Secret Migration 2005, The Essential Mercury Rev: Stillness Breathes 1991–2006, Back to Mine compilation 2006, Hello Blackbird (soundtrack to film Bye Bye Blackbird) 2006, Snowflake Midnight 2008, The Light in You 2015; with The Flaming Lips: In a Priest Driven Ambulance 1990, Hit to Death in the Future Head 1992; with Harmony Rockets: Paralyzed Mind of the Archangel Void 1995, I've Got a Golden Ticket 1997. *Current Management:* c/o James Alderman, Free Trade Agency, 15 Timber Yard, Drysdale Street, London, N1 6ND, England. *Telephone:* (20) 7655-6900. *Fax:* (20) 3700-3355. *E-mail:* info@freetradeagency.co.uk. *Website:* freetradeagency.co.uk. *E-mail:* info@mercuryrev.com. *Website:* www.mercuryrev.com.

DONALD, Howard; British singer and DJ; b. (Howard Paul Donald), 28 April 1968, Droylsden, Manchester; m. Katie Halil 2015; one d. with Victoria Piddington; one d. with Marie-Christine Musswessels. *Career:* mem. all-male vocal group Take That 1990–96, 2006–; numerous TV appearances, tours and concerts; solo artist 1996–; house music DJ, as DJ HD. *Recordings include:* albums: Take That And Party 1992, Everything Changes 1993, Nobody Else 1995, Beautiful World 2006, The Circus 2008, Progress 2010, III 2014. *Honours:* (for Patience) 2007, (for Shine) 2008, for Best British Live Act 2008, for Best British Group 2011, Q Idol Award (with Take That) 2006. *Telephone:* (20) 8747-4534. *E-mail:* jonathan@10management.com. *Website:* www .takethat.com.

DONALDSON, John; British composer and musician (piano); b. 29 June 1954, London; m. Agotha Coffey; two s. one d. *Education:* Anglia Univ. *Career:* composes film and production music; US broadcasts with Eddie Henderson, Richie Cole, Jeff Ballard; BBC with Septpiece, Dick Pearce Quartet, Ben Castle; film, Painted Lady; European and US festivals include San Francisco, San Sebastian, Bath, London, Appleby, Malta; mem. PRS, Musicians' Union. *Compositions include:* Cakes and Wine, Medjugorje, Carneo, Django's Dilemma, Mirror Image, HRD, Plain Song, Balance. *Recordings include:* Septpiece, Sing The Line, Meeting In Brooklyn. *Honours:* winner (piano category) British Jazz Awards 2006. *E-mail:* mail@johndonaldson.org. *Website:* www.johndonaldson.org.

DONALDSON, Louis (Lou); American jazz musician (alto saxophone); b. 1 Nov. 1926, Badin, North Carolina; m. Maker Donaldson 1950; two d. *Education:* North Carolina Agricultural and Technical State Univ. *Career:* played in Navy band 1945; moved to New York 1950; played with numerous notable musicians including Charlie Parker, Sonny Stitt, Bud Powell, Milt Jackson, Philly Joe Jones, Horace Silver, Clifford Brown; mem. Art Blakey's Jazz Messengers; toured extensively in Europe and Japan. *Recordings include:* albums: Blues Walk, Alligator Boogaloo, New Faces, New Sounds, A Night at Birdland, Her 'Tis Midnight Creeper, Hot Dog, Sassy Soul Strut, Forgotten Man, Birdseed, Caracas, Sweet Papa Lou, Sentimental Journey, Relaxing at Sea: Live on the QE2; with Jimmy Smith: The Sermon, Cool Blues, Rockin' the Boat; with Gene Ammons: All Star Sessions; numerous collaborations with various artists. *Honours:* Charlie Parker Memorial Medal. *Current Management:* c/o Joel Chriss and Co., 60 East 8th Street, Suite 32 N, New York, NY 10003, USA. *Telephone:* (212) 353-0855. *Fax:* (212) 353-0094. *E-mail:* info@jchriss.com. *Website:* www.jchriss.com; www.loudonaldson.com.

DONATELLI, Denise; American jazz singer; b. Allentown, Pa; d. of Americo Donatelli and Gloria Donatelli. *Career:* studied classical piano as a child; fmrly worked at Turner Broadcasting Network, Atlanta, Ga; began professionally performing in Atlanta and Los Angeles, Calif.; headlining act, Jazz at Lincoln Center, New York; numerous live appearances; numerous collaborations including Bill Cunliffe, Geoffrey Keezer Quartet. *Recordings:* albums: In the Company of Friends 2005, What Lies Within 2008, When Lights Are Low 2010, Soul Shadows 2012, Find a Heart 2015. *Honours:* Los Angeles Jazz Soc. Jazz Vocalist Award 2012. *Current Management:* c/o Mary Ann Topper, The Jazz Tree, 648 Broadway, New York, NY 10012, USA. *Telephone:* (212) 475-0415. *Fax:* (212) 475-0502. *E-mail:* maryann@thejazztree.com. *Website:* www .thejazztree.com; denisedonatelli.com.

DONATO, João; Brazilian musician (piano, accordion), songwriter and bandleader; b. (João Donato de Oliveira Neto), 17 Aug. 1934, Rio Branco, Acre; s. of João Donato; m. Ivone Belem 2001; three c. *Education:* Colégio Lafayette, Rio de Janeiro. *Career:* began professional career 1949; collaborations with Altamiro Carrilho, Ernesto Nazareth; fmr mem. Fafá Lemos' band; f. Donato e Seu Conjunto, Donato Triom Os Namorados; also performs and records as solo artist; has lived in Brazil and USA. *Compositions include:* Minha Saudade 1958, Mambinho 1958. *Recordings:* albums: Chá Dançante 1956, Muito à vontade 1962, A Bossa Muito Moderna de João Donato e seu Trio 1963, Piano of Joao Donato: The New Sound of Brazil 1965, Donato/Deodato 1969, A Bad

Donato 1970, Quem é Quem 1973, Lugar Comum 1986, Coisas tão simples 1996, Café com Pão (with Eloir de Moraes) 1997, Só Danço Samba 1999, Songbook: João Donato, Vol. 1 1999, Songbook: João Donato, Vol. 2 1999, Songbook: João Donato, Vol. 3 1999, Amazonas 2000, Brazilian Time 2001, The Frog 2001, Remando na Raia 2001, Ê Lalá Lay-ê 2001, Managarroba 2002, Emílio Santiago encontra João Donato (Premio Tim 2004) 2003, Wanda Sá com João Donato 2003, João Donato reencontra Maria Tita 2006, Dois panos para manga 2006, O Piano de João Donato 2007, Uma tarde com Bud Shank e João Donato 2007, Donato Tropical 2008, Os Bossa Nova 2008, Sambolero (Latin Grammy Award for Best Jazz Album) 2010. *Honours:* Ordem do Mérito Cultural 2004; Shell Music Award 2000. *E-mail:* joaodonato@uol.com.br (office). *Website:* www.joaodonato.com.br.

DONELIAN, Armen, BA; American pianist, composer, bandleader, author and educator; *Adjunct Professor, New School University;* b. 1950, New York; s. of Khatchik Donelian and Lillian Donelian; of Armenian descent. *Education:* Westchester Conservatory of Music, Columbia Univ., pvt. study with Carl Bamberger (conducting), Ludmila Ulehla (harmonic analysis), Richard Beirach (jazz piano), Harold Seletsky (Schoenberg harmony and counterpoint). *Career:* bandleader and solo concert artist throughout North and South America, Europe, Middle East and Far East; performed with Sonny Rollins, Chet Baker, Mongo Santamaria, Billy Harper, Lionel Hampton, Paquito D'Rivera, Joe Williams Night Ark, Datevik Hovanesian and other jazz masters in festivals, concerts, clubs, TV and radio worldwide 1975–; Adjunct Prof., New School Univ., New York, William Paterson Univ., New Jersey; Sunnyside recording artist; Co-founder Hudson Jazzworks, Inc. (non-profit educational org.). *Compositions include:* more than 90 compositions recorded by various artists, published arrangements include Metropolitan Madness, Harem Girl, Stargazer. *Recordings include:* 13 albums, including Stargazer, A Reverie, Secrets, The Wayfarer, Trio '87, Wave, Mystic Heights, Full Moon Music, Quartet Language, All or Nothing at All, Oasis, Leapfrog, Sayat-Nova: Songs Of My Ancestors. *Publications include:* Training the Ear, Vol. I 1992, Vol. II 2005, Rutgers Annual Review of Jazz Studies 1994–95, Downbeat 1997–98, Keyboard 1997, Whole Notes 2011. *Honours:* six Jazz Performance Fellowships, Nat. Endowment for the Arts 1984, 1987, 1990, 1992, 1994, 1996, Fulbright Scholar Award 2002, Fulbright Sr Specialist, Armenia 2003, Finland 2004, Switzerland 2005, Sweden 2006, Greece 2009. *Address:* Donelian Music Co. and Hudson Jazzworks, Inc., 338 Kipp Road, Hudson, NY 12534, USA (office). *Telephone:* (518) 822-1640 (office). *Fax:* (518) 822-1640 (office). *E-mail:* armen.donelian@gmail.com (home); doneliaa@newschool.edu (office). *Website:* www.armendonelian.com (office); www.newschool.edu/jazz (office).

DONELLY, Tanya; American singer, songwriter and musician (guitar); b. 14 July 1966, Newport, Rhode Island; m. Dean Fisher 1996; one d. *Career:* Founder mem., Throwing Muses 1985–91; mem., The Breeders 1989–92; Founder mem., Belly 1992–96; solo artist 1996–; numerous TV appearances, tours. *Recordings include:* with Throwing Muses: Throwing Muses 1986, House Tornado 1988, Hunkpapa 1989, The Real Ramona 1991; with The Breeders: Pod 1990, Safari (EP) 1992; with Belly: Star 1993, King 1995; solo: Lovesongs for Underdogs 1997, Beautysleep 2002, Whiskey Tango Ghosts 2004, This Hungry Life 2006, Beautysleep and Lovesongs Demos 2006. *Address:* c/o Eleven Thirty Records, 449A Trollingwood Road, Haw River, NC 27258, USA. *Telephone:* (877) 733-3931. *Fax:* (336) 578-7388. *Website:* eleventhirtyrecords.com; www.tanyadonelly.com.

DONNELLY, Johnny; Irish musician (drums); b. 14 Feb. 1972, Dublin. *Career:* mem. The Saw Doctors 1989–96; drummer on Rise Tour with Mike Peters in the UK 1992; other tours and TV and radio broadcasts; mem. Performing Right Soc., Musicians' Union. *Recordings include:* albums with The Saw Doctors: If This Is Rock and Roll, I Want My Old Job Back 1991, All The Way From Tuam 1992, Same Oul' Town 1996. *Address:* The Parks, Ower, Headford, Co. Galway, Ireland (home). *Telephone:* (9) 1565705 (home). *Fax:* (9) 1569761 (home). *E-mail:* johnny@arcana.ie (office). *Website:* www.arcana.ie (office).

DONNELLY, Kerr; British singer, songwriter, entertainer and musician (guitar); b. 1 May 1964, Lanarkshire, Scotland; m. Lynn Fullwood; one s. two d. *Career:* mem. Legend 1978, Tennessee Flash Cats 1982, Crazy Wolf 1982, Kerr Donnelly Band 1987–; set up KDML record label; mem. Int. Songwriters' Asscn, Performing Rights Soc. *Television:* Lucky Chance (soundtrack, USA). *Film:* music soundtracks: Dust, Junkie. *Compositions include:* more than 500 songs, including Country Boy, One Burger One Coke, That's Life, Sneakin 'n' Cheatin, Rattlesnake Rock, The Day The Clown Cried, It's Him Again, Kissin At Christmas, House of Pain, I Cannot Bear to See You Cry, Sometimes Ghostly Guitar, Rockin into Christmas, Sign Up and numerous others. *Recordings include:* albums: No Help Needed 1987, EPs and Early Days, Haunted Heart 1992, Rough Cuts, Country Roots 1995, The Singles And Album Picks 1997, Guess Who? 1998, As The Curtain Falls 20/21 1999, That's Right 2001, Kerr Thru' The Years 2002, The Day The Clown Cried 2003, Hot Off The Press 2004, The Collection 2004, Its Him Again 2005, The Horror of it All 2005, Introducing - Kerr Donnelly Band 2007, Rock 2009, What You Hear is What you Get 2011, In The Spotlight 2012, Halloween 2012 Rockin Into Christmas 2012, Applause from the Crowd 2013 Tipe of My Tongue 2014; singles: As The Curtain Falls 1999, A Little Unfair, If I Knew Then What I Know Now 2000, Homewrecker 2000, Heartache Heartache 2001, Reckless And Lonely, A Haunted House On Broken Hearted Hill 2001, The Day the Clown Cried, Rockin into Christmas 2002, Hurt Talkin (USA release),

Partying in the Doghouse, Keeper of the Key to My Heart 2003, Valentine Card 2004, Don't Fool a Fool 2004. *Honours:* Best British Male Artist 2003. *Website:* www.kerr-donnelly.countrymusic.co.uk.

DONOHOE, David; British musician (trombone) and bandleader; b. 22 May 1940, Ashton-Under-Lyme, Lancashire, England; m. Victoria Hancock 1962; two s. two d. *Education:* Regional Coll. of Art, Manchester. *Career:* New Orleans-style jazz musician; concert with Woody Allen (actor, clarinet player), New Orleans Festival 1971; radio and television broadcasts; tour of USA with International Band 1977; appearances at Ascona Festa, New Orleans Music; Switzerland; tours of Switzerland with bands from New Orleans; mem. Musicians' Union. *Recordings include:* 14 albums (seven solo). *Address:* 2 Church Road, Uppermill, Oldham, OL3 6BH, England.

DONOVAN; British folk singer and songwriter; b. (Donovan Leitch), 10 Feb. 1946, Maryhill, Glasgow, Scotland; m. Linda Lawrence 1970; one s. two d. *Career:* numerous tours and live appearances worldwide. *Compositions include:* own recorded songs; songs for film If It's Tuesday It Must Be Belgium 1969, The Pied Piper 1971; film score for Brother Sun, Sister Moon 1972. *Recordings include:* albums: What's Bin Did and What's Bin Hid 1965, Catch The Wind 1965, Fairy Tale 1965, Sunshine Superman 1966, The Real Donovan 1966, Mellow Yellow 1967, Universal Soldier 1967, A Gift From A Flower To A Garden 1968, Like It Is, Was and Evermore Shall Be 1968, Donovan In Concert 1968, Barabajagal 1969, Open Road 1970, Donovan P. Leitch 1970, HMS Donovan 1971, Cosmic Wheels 1973, Essence To Essence 1974, 7-Tease 1974, Slow Down World 1976, Donovan 1977, Neutronica 1980, Love Is The Only Feeling 1980, Lady of the Stars 1983, Rising 1990, Troubadour-The Definitive Collection 1964–76 1993, Island of Circles 1991, Live in Concert 1992, Originals 1995, Sutras 1996, The Pied Piper 2002, Beat Cafe 2004, Ritual Groove 2010, The Sensual Donovan 2012, Shadows of Blue 2013. *Publication:* Hurdy Gurdy Man (autobiography) 2005. *Honours:* Officier, Ordre des Arts et des Lettres 2009; Hon. DLitt, Univ. of Hertfordshire 2003; Lifetime Achievement Award, BBC Radio Folk Awards 2011. *E-mail:* info@donovan.ie. *Website:* www.donovan.ie.

DONOVAN, Ida M.; French songwriter and musician; b. 6 Sept. 1948, Canada; m. Edwin Donovan; one s. four d. *Career:* mem. country gospel group; actress in theatre and film; mem. Canadian County Music Assocn, Songwriters' Asscn of Canada. *Films include:* Something About Love 1988, Le Musée de Margaret 1995, La Fille de New Waterford 1999. *Address:* 211 Macintyre Lane, Glace Bay, NS B1A 4S1, Canada. *Telephone:* (902) 849-4274.

DONOVAN, Jason Sean; Australian actor and singer; b. 1 June 1968, Melbourne, Vic.; s. of Terence Donovan and Susan Menlove. *Career:* appeared on Australian hit soap Neighbours, then went on to have solo music career with concert tours world-wide; has appeared in numerous stage shows in the UK and Australia; UK tour 2007. *Television:* Skyways (Network 7, Australia) 1979, I Can Jump Puddles (Australian Broadcasting Corpn) 1979, Neighbours (series) 1985–89, Heroes 1988, Shadows of the Heart 1990, I'm a Celebrity… Get Me Out of Here! (ITV) 2006, Echo Beach (ITV) 2008. *Theatre:* Joseph and the Amazing Technicolor Dreamcoat, as Joseph (London Palladium) 1991–92, Rocky Horror Picture Show (West End, London), Chitty Chitty Bang Bang, as Caractacus Potts (London Palladium) 2004–05, Sweeney Todd (UK tour) 2006, Priscilla Queen of the Desert: The Musical (West End, London) 2009, War of the Worlds (European tour) 2010. *Recordings include:* albums: Ten Good Reasons 1989, Between The Lines 1990, Joseph and The Amazing Technicolour Dreamcoat 1991, Greatest Hits 1991, Let It Be Me 2008, Soundtrack of the 80s 2010; singles: Nothing Can Divide Us 1988, Especially For You (duet with Kylie Minogue) 1988, Too Many Broken Hearts 1989, Sealed With A Kiss 1989, Everyday 1989, Hang On To Your Love 1990, Another Night 1990, Rhythm Of The Rain 1990, Doing Fine 1990, Any Dream Will Do 1991, Happy Together 1991, Dream 1991, RSVP 1991, Rough Diamonds 1994. *Publication:* Real: My Story 2007. *Honours:* recipient of numerous show business awards. *Current Management:* Bright Artist Management, First Floor, 50 Great Portland Street, London, W1W 7ND, England. *Telephone:* (20) 7631-4638. *E-mail:* info@brightartistmanagement.com. *Website:* www .brightartistmanagement.com; jasondonovan.com.

DONY; Bulgarian singer, musician (bass), songwriter and arranger. *Career:* mem. Atlas, Bulgaria 1987–93; formed Dony and Momchil 1993–; numerous tours, Bulgaria, include Sofia Nat. Theatre (unplugged with Nat. Philharmony) 1995. *Recordings include:* with Atlas: Doll; with Dony and Momchil: CD Albums: The Album! 1993, The Second One 1994.

DR DOOOM (see Kool Keith)

DORAN, Brian John; British singer, songwriter and musician (guitar, flute); b. 2 March 1965, Croydon, Surrey, England; m. Jane Kendrick 1994. *Career:* lead singer, Orchid Waltz 1983–86; played all over England; formed acoustic duo, Richard III (with Lee Collinson); solo acoustic world tour 1990–91; solo and session work; branch cttee mem. Musicians' Union. *Recordings include:* albums: Orchid Waltz, Acoustics 1991. *E-mail:* brian@ briandoran.com.

DORE, Michael, GGSM, PGCE; British singer, musician (piano) and teacher; b. Grimsby, Lincs., England. *Education:* Guildhall School of Music and Drama, London. *Career:* mem. Swingle Singers, Synergy Vocals, Singcircle, Electric Phoenix, Chameleon; concert soloist with BBC Radio 2, Royal Philharmonic Orchestra, BBC Concert Orchestra, Berlin Philharmonic Orchestra, Chicago Symphony, Bochum Symphony, New York Philharmonic, Boston Symphony, St Louis Symphony, Stavanger Symphony, Orchestre Nationale de Lyon, Philharmonique de Monte Carlo, Canadian Brass, London Symphony Orchestra, Los Angeles Philharmonic, Swedish National Radio, Royal Variety Performances, Music of Andrew Lloyd Webber, Jesus Christ Superstar (Peter), Magic of the Musicals, Rogers and Hammerstein at the Barbican; worked for Royal National Theatre, RSC, Nederlands Dans Theater; West End credits include Cats, Starlight Express, Grease; debuts at Carnegie Hall (New York), Royal Albert Hall Proms 1994; vocal coach for Sky TV Musicals series; mem., British Actors Equity, Musicians' Union. *Recordings:* albums: solo: Simply… Michael Dore; with Royal Philharmonic Orchestra: Here Come The Classics, Vol. 5: Christmas, Here Come The Classics: Vol. 7: The Musicals; with BBC Concert Orchestra: West Side Story 1993, Crazy For Gershwin, Let's Face The Music (tribute to Fred Astaire), Hits Of Broadway, Love And Romance, Passion (original London cast), Wonderful Town (with Simon Rattle), Every Song Has Its Play (with Gilbert O'Sullivan, manager); with Berio: Sinfonia, Canticum; Nigel Hess' Shakespeare Music, Chameleon. *Current Management:* World Showcase Promotions, 48 Shadeland Court, Cambridge, ON N1T 1V2, Canada. *Telephone:* (519) 624-9176. *Fax:* (519) 624-5334. *E-mail:* cheryl-wspromotions@rogers .com. *Address:* c/o Brett Records, PO Box 36210, London SE19 1YR, England (office). *Telephone:* (7973) 386658 (office). *E-mail:* brettrecords@aol.com (office). *Website:* www.michaeldore.com.

DORGE, Pierre; Danish composer, conductor and musician (guitar); b. 28 Feb. 1946, Frederiksberg; m. Irene Becker 1985. *Education:* Music, KDAS, Coll. of Copenhagen. *Career:* formed own group, Copenhagen Jazz Quintet 1960; formed New Jungle Orchestra, 1980; recorded with: Niels-Henning Orsted Petersen, John Tchicai, Svend Asmussen, Marilyn Mazur, Johnny Dyani; tours: Europe, USA, Canada, Indonesia, Ghana, USSR, Australasia. *Composition:* Symphony in C 1994. *Recordings include:* with New Jungle Orchestra: Pierre Dorge and New Jungle Orchestra 1982, Brikama 1984, Even The Moon Is Dancing 1985, Johnny Lives 1987, Different Places – Different Bananas 1989, Peer Gynt 1989, Live in Chicago 1991, David Murray and the Jazzbar Prize 1992, Karawane 1993, Polar Jungle Orchestra 1994, Absurd Bird 1995, Music from the Danish Jungle 1996, China Jungle 1997, Giraf 1999, Swinging Europe 1999. *Honours:* Grants, Danish Arts Council, JASA Prize 1985. *E-mail:* pierre@newjungleorchestra.com. *Website:* www .newjungleorchestra.com.

DORNEY, Tim; British musician (keyboards); b. 30 March 1965, Ascot, Berkshire, England. *Career:* fmr mem. Flowered Up, formed Republica; Numerous TV appearances and festival dates; contributed track Are Friends Electric for Gary Numan tribute album 1997. *Recordings include:* with Flowered Up: Singles: It's On 1990, Phobia 1990, Take It 1991, Weekender 1992; Albums: A Life With Brian 1991; with Republica: Singles: Out of This World 1994, Bloke 1994, Ready to Go 1996, Drop Dead Gorgeous 1996, From the Rush Hour With Love 1998; Albums: Republica 1996, Speed Ballads 1998. *Website:* www.republica.com.

DORONJGA, Sinisa; Croatian musician, singer, entertainer and actor; b. 15 March 1942, Zagreb; m. Bosiljka Kello 1969; one s. one d. *Education:* secondary music school. *Career:* singer and musician, Bijele Strijele 1961; world tour 1968–69; producer, composer, songwriter, arranger, Suzy record label; television entertainer; mem. Croatian Musicians' Union. *Recordings include:* album: Domestic Songs 1979, seven albums 1979–95. *Publication:* Dosel Je Sv Martin (book and video). *Honours:* Croatian Govt and Croatan Music AID Awards. *Address:* Siget 18 b/v, 10020 Zagreb, Croatia.

DOROUGH, Howard Dwaine (Howie D.); American singer; b. 22 Aug. 1973, Orlando, Fla. *Career:* acted in community theatre; mem., Backstreet Boys 1993–; numerous tours and television appearances. *Recordings include:* albums: with Backstreet Boys: Backstreet Boys 1996, Live in Concert 1998, Backstreet's Back 1998, Millennium 1999, Black And Blue 2000, Greatest Hits Chapter 1 2001, Never Gone 2005, Unbreakable 2007, This Is Us 2009, In a World Like This 2013; solo: Back to Me 2011. *Honours:* for Backstreet Boys: Billboard Music Awards for Best Group, Best Adult Contemporary Group 1998, Album of the Year, Artist of the Year 1999, MTV Music Video Award for Best Group Video 1998, MTV European Music Awards for Best Pop Act 1997, Best Group 1999, World Music Awards for Best-Selling Pop Group 1999, 2000, Best-Selling R&B Group 1999, 2000, Best-Selling Dance Group 1999, 2000, Best American Group 2000, American Music Awards for Favorite Pop/Rock Band, Duo or Group 2000, 2001. *Current Management:* Wright Entertainment Group (WEG Music), PO Box 590009, Orlando, FL 32859, USA. *Website:* www .wegmusic.com; www.backstreetboys.com.

DORSET, Ray; British musician (guitar, blues harp), singer and songwriter; b. 21 March 1946, Ashford, England; s. of Walter Edward and Nellie Dorset; m. *Career:* began career as singer/songwriter with The Good Earth; Founder-mem. Mungo Jerry 1970–; numerous live appearances, festivals; fmr mem. Katmandu 1986, The Insiders. *Compositions include:* In the Summertime, Feels Like I'm In Love, Kelly Marie 1980. *Recordings include:* albums: with Mungo Jerry: Mungo Jerry 1970, Electronically Tested 1971, You Don't Have To Be In The Army To Fight In The War 1971, Boot Power 1972, Golden Hour 1974, Long Legged Woman 1974, Impala Saga 1976, Lovin' In The Alleys, Fightin' In The Streets 1977, File 1977, Ray Dorset and Mungo Jerry 1978, Six Aside 1979, Together Again 1981, Snakebite 1990, The Early Years 1992, Old Shoes, New Jeans 1997, Candy Dreams 2001; with Mungo Jerry Blues Band: Adults Only 2003; solo: Cold Blue Excursion 1972; with Katmandu: A Case for the Blues 1986. *Honours:* ASCAP Award 1970, two Ivor Novello Awards 1970, Golden Gondolar 1971, PRS Iconic Award 2005, Sony/ATV Award 2005. *E-mail:* jimmystrings1@gmail.com. *Address:* Easyplay GmbH, Werrestrasse 53, 32049 Herford, Germany. *Telephone:* (5) 22198280 (office). *Fax:* (5) 221982811 (office). *E-mail:* mp@easyplay.de (office). *Website:* www .mungojerry.com.

DORUZKA, David, BMus; Czech musician, composer and educator; b. 25 Jan. 1980, Prague. *Education:* Berklee Coll. of Music, Thelonious Monk Inst. Jazz Colony. *Career:* band leader, David Doruzka Trio and David Doruzka Quartet; performances with George Mraz, Josefine Lindstrand, Aga Zaryan, Iva Bittová, Christian McBride, Django Bates, Tiger Okoshi, Rodney Green, Orrin Evans, Kenwood Dennard; performances and tours in USA, Czech Repub., Slovakia, Poland, Sweden, Denmark, Germany, Switzerland, France, Netherlands, Spain, Portugal; mem. Czech Jazz Soc. *Compositions:* Forgotten Time (on You Know What I Mean) 1997, Was This The Last Time (on Czech Radio) 1996, 12 + 3/4, Ups and Downs, Sincerely (on Czech Radio) 1998. *Recordings:* with Jorge Rossy, Phil Wilson, Greg Hopkins, Don Grusin; with Karel Ruzicka, Jr: You Know What I Mean 1997; with Jaromir Honzak: Earth Life 1998; solo: Hidden Paths 2004, Silently Dawning 2008. *Honours:* Czech Jazz Soc. Best Talent of the Year 1994, Berklee Coll. of Music Jimi Hendrix Awards 2000, 2001, Wayne Shorter Award 2000, John LaPorta Award 2000, Herb Pomeroy Award 2001. *E-mail:* ddoruzka@gmail.com (home). *Website:* www .daviddoruzka.com (home).

DOS SANTOS, Feliciano, MA; Mozambican musician; *Director, Estamos NGO;* b. 9 June 1964, Niassa; m. Berta Monica Polela. *Career:* Founder-mem. Massukos 1992–, popular group who use their music to raise awareness about sanitation, water and HIV/AIDS issues; Founder-mem., Dir and Trustee, Estamos NGO 1996–. *Recordings include:* albums: Kuimba kwa Massuko (prizewinner, Cannes Water Symposium), Bumping 2008, Nhimbo za Kwato 2013. *Honours:* Goldman Environmental Prize 2008, Nat. Geographic Emerging Explorer 2010, Grassroots Champion of Sanitation 2010, Best environment community educator 2014. *Address:* Estamos, Avenida Samora Machel, CP 174, Niassa, Mozambique (home). *Telephone:* 27121242 (office). *Fax:* 27120318 (office). *E-mail:* felicianos@tdm.co.mz (office); estamos@tdm.co.mz (office). *Website:* www.massukos.com (home); www.estamos.org.mz (home).

DOST, Andrew; American musician (bass guitar, keyboards, drums); b. 10 April 1983. *Career:* fmr mem. Anathallo 2003–06; solo career 2006–08; Founder mem. fun. 2008–; toured with Jack's Mannequin 2008, 2010; support act for Vedera, Paramore, Panic at the Disco; first single release 2009; collaborations include Janelle Monáe (We Are Young). *Recordings:* with Anathallo: Floating World 2006; solo: Columbus 2008; with fun.: Aim and Ignite 2009, Some Nights 2012. *Honours:* with fun.: Teen Choice Awards for Choice Rock Group 2012, for Choice Single by a Group (for We Are Young) 2012, Billboard Music Award for Top Rock Artist 2013. *Address:* Fueled by Ramen Records, Warner Music Group, 75 Rockefeller Plaza, New York, NY 10019, USA (office). *Telephone:* (212) 275-2000 (office). *Website:* www.wmg .com (office); www.fueledbyramen.com (office); www.ournameisfun.com; www .andrewdost.com.

DOTH, Anita; Dutch singer; b. 28 Dec. 1971, Amsterdam. *Career:* singer, 2 Unlimited 1990–96, 2010–; solo artist 1996–2010. *Radio:* presenter, Anita & Friends. *Television:* presenter, Welcome 2 the Pleasurezone. *Recordings include:* albums: with 2 Unlimited: Get Ready 1992, No Limits 1993, Real Things 1994, Hits Unlimited 1995; solo: Reality 2006. *E-mail:* info@ unlimitedways.com. *Website:* www.anitadoth.com.

DOUCET, Michael Louis, BS; American cajun musician (fiddle, guitar, bass, mandolin, piano); b. 14 Feb. 1951, LaFayette, Louisiana; m. Sharon Lee Arms 1951; two s. one d. *Education:* Louisiana State Univ. *Career:* mem. band Coteau –1977; formed Beausoleil 1975–; projects with Savoy-Doucet band and solo work; performed at Jimmy Carter's inaugural gala 1977; world-wide tours with Beausoleil, including Carnegie Hall, New York 1982, Great American Music Hall, San Francisco 1988; numerous television and radio appearances including Austin City Limits, Today Show, Conan O'Brien, Good Morning, Prairie Home Companion. *Recordings:* albums: with Beausoleil: The Spirit of Cajun Music 1976, Parlez Nous au Boire 1984, Louisiana Cajun Music 1984, Zydeco Gris Gris 1985, Allons a Lafayette 1986, Bayou Boogie 1986, Hot Chili Mama 1988, Cajun Experience 1988, Bayou Cadillac 1989, Cajun Jam Session 1989, Deja Vu 1990, J'ai été au bal 1990, Cajun Conga 1991, Rainbow Sign 1992, Bayou Deluxe 1993, La Danse de la Vie 1993, L'Echo 1994, Arc de Triomphe Two-Step 1997, L'Amour ou la Folie 1997, Cajunization 1999, Looking Back Tomorrow 2001, Gitane Cajun 2004, Live at the 2008 New Orleans Jazz Festival (Grammy Award for Best Zydeco or Cajun Music Album 2009) 2008; with Savoy-Doucet: Home Music with Spirits 1981, Two Step d'Amede 1989, Sam's Big Rooster 2000; solo: Christmas Bayou 1986, Cajun Brew 1988, Beau Solo 1990, Le Hoogie Boogie 1991, Mad Reel and Belizire The Cajun 1994, From Now On 2008. *Honours:* Master Folk Musician, Louisiana, Nat. Endowment for the Arts Grant 1975, First Clifton Chenier Award 1990, Grammy Award 1998. *Current Management:* The Rosebud Agency, PO Box 170429, San Francisco, CA 94117, USA. *Telephone:* (415) 386-3456. *Fax:* (415) 386-0599. *E-mail:* info@rosebudus.com. *Website:* www.rosebudus.com.

DOUCETTE, Paul John; American musician (drums, guitar); b. 22 Aug. 1972, Pittsburgh, Pa; m. Moon Zappa 2002; one d. *Career:* mem. Tabitha's Secret 1993–96; drummer for Matchbox Twenty 1996–2007, rhythm guitarist 2007–, numerous tours worldwide; solo project, The Break and Repair

Method. *Recordings include:* albums: Yourself or Someone Like You 1996, Mad Season 2000, More Than You Think You Are 2002, Exile on Mainstream 2007, North 2012. *Honours:* Best Composer Award, Rhode Island Film Festival. *Address:* Atlantic Records, 1290 Avenue of the Americas, New York, NY 10104, USA (office). *Website:* www.matchboxtwenty.com.

DOUDELLE, Jacques; French musician (soprano and tenor saxophones) and bandleader; b. 4 July 1949, Paris. *Career:* formed Jacques Doudelle Jazz Orchestra, Festival du Marais, Paris 1975–; numerous appearances across France include: Casino de Paris, Marciac Jazz Festival (3 times), Sidney Bechet Night 1993, 1994, festivals in Italy, Belgium, Switzerland, Germany, Greece, Turkey; Television: Accords Parfaits, with Pierre Petit, Jazz 6, with Philippe Adler, Sacrée Soirée, with Jean-Pierre Foucault; Pres. Sidney Bechet Acad. *Compositions include:* T'Exagères, Moulin à Légumes, Détournement de Mineur, Coeur de Perles; Film music: Des Enfants Gâtés, Félicité. *Recordings include:* 5 albums 1978–95; recordings with Roger Guerin, Jean Lou Longnon, Fabrice Eulry, Sidney Bechet Jr. *Honours:* Laureate, Concours Nat. de Jazz de la Défense 1986.

DOUGANS, Brian; British musician; b. 1968, Glasgow, Scotland. *Career:* solo artist as Humanoid, releasing Stakker Humanoid 1988; projects include Semi Real, Yage, Metropolis, Art Science Technology, Mental Cube, Candese, Intelligent Communication and Smart Systems; mem. Future Sound of London, The Amorphous Androgynous. *Recordings include:* albums under various guises: Lifeforms 1994, Urbmix: Flammable Liquid 1994, Far-Out Son Of Lung And The Ramblings Of A Madman 1995, ISDN 1995, Dead Cities 1996, Accelerator 1996, Tales Of Ephidrina 2001, Papua New Guinea: Translations 2002, The Isness 2002, Alice In Ultraland 2005, Teachings from the Electronic Brain 2006.

DOUGLAS, Jack; American producer, recording engineer and songwriter; b. New York; two s. two d. *Education:* Studio of Audio Engineering, New York. *Career:* janitor, Asst Engineer, Engineer, Producer, Record Plant Studio; Independent Producer; Producer, The Sopranos (TV series); Instructor Sound Arts Dept, Studio Etiquette and Psychology, Expression Center for New Media; worked with Aerosmith, Blue Oyster Cult, David Bowie, Cheap Trick, Alice Cooper, Bob Dylan, Gypsy Queen, Mick Jagger, The Knack, John Lennon, New York Dolls, Yoko Ono, Lou Reed, Slash, Patti Smith, The Who, Michael Monroe Band, Supertramp, Slash's Snakepit. *Honours:* Grammy Award for Album of the Year (for John Lennon and Yoko Ono's Double Fantasy) 1981. *Current Management:* c/o Sound Arts Department, Expression Center for New Media, 6601 Shellmound Street, Emeryville, CA 94608, USA. *Telephone:* (845) 353-9691. *Website:* www.expression.edu.

DOUGLAS, Gerald (Jerry) Calvin; American musician (guitar, slide guitar, resophonic guitar, dobro) and producer; b. 28 May 1956, Warren, OH. *Career:* began playing with his father's band; became session musician; played with artists, including Joan Baez, Garth Brooks, Glen Campbell, Ray Charles, Steve Earle, Emmylou Harris, Faith Hill, Waylon Jennings, Alison Krauss, Lyle Lovett, Reba McEntire, Mark O'Connor, Paul Simon, Ricky Skaggs, James Taylor. *Recordings include:* solo albums: Fluxology 1979, Fluxedo 1982, Under The Wire 1986, Changing Chanels 1987, Everything Is Going To Work Out Fine 1987, Plant Early 1989, Slide Rule 1992, Yonder (with Peter Rowan) 1996, Restless On The Farm 1998, Lookout For Hope 2002, The Best Kept Secret 2005, Best of the Sugar Hill Years 2007, Glide 2008, Jerry Christmas 2009, Get Low 2010. *Honours:* five Grammy Awards, ACM Musician of the Year 2002, CMA Musician of the Year 2002, CMA Award for Musician of the Year 2005, 2007. *Current Management:* D.J. McLachlan, McLachlan Management, 2821 Bransford Avenue, Nashville, TN 37204, USA. *Telephone:* (615) 292-0099. *Fax:* (615) 385-4013. *E-mail:* DJMGT@aol.com. *Address:* POB 58034, Nashville, TN 37205, USA (office). *E-mail:* info@ jerrydouglas.com. *Website:* www.jerrydouglas.com.

DOUGLAS, Lesley, BA; British broadcasting executive and music industry executive; *Director of Programming and Business Development, Universal Music UK;* b. 7 June 1963, Newcastle upon Tyne; m. Nick Scripps; one s. one d. *Education:* Univ. of Manchester. *Career:* joined BBC as Production Asst Research Dept, then BBC Radio 2 1985–2007, Production Asst David Jacobs Show 1985, Promotions Asst 1986–88, Producer Music Dept 1988–90 (programmes including Gloria Hunniford, David Jacobs, Ken Bruce, Brian Matthew's Round Midnight), Promotions Producer 1990–93, Ed. BBC Radio 2 Presentation and Planning 1993–97, Man. Ed. BBC Radio 2 1997–2000, Head of Programmes BBC Radio 2 2000–03, Controller BBC Radio 2, BBC 6 Music 2004–07, Controller, BBC Popular Music (working across TV, radio and online productions) 2007–08 (resgnd); Dir of Programming and Business Devt, Universal Music UK 2008–; Fellow, Radio Acad.; Chair. Radio Festival Steering Cttee (twice). *Address:* Universal Music UK, 364–366 Kensington High Street, London, W14 8NS, England (office). *Telephone:* (20) 7471-5000 (office). *Fax:* (20) 7471-5001 (office). *E-mail:* lesley.douglas@umusic.com (office). *Website:* www.umusic.com (office).

DOUGLAS, Robert James Elliot; British musician (guitar, banjo); b. 13 May 1942, Gifford, East Lothian, Scotland; m. Margaret Douglas; one s. *Career:* Clyde Valley Stompers 1960–61; It's All Happening, with Tommy Steele and On the Beat, Norman Wisdom; Aley Welsh Band 1963–82; Newport Jazz Festival 1966; freelance 1982–; working with Keith Smith, Dave Shepherd, Digby Fairweather; mem. Musicians' Union Pamra. *Recordings include:* complete Discography with Pamra, All Aley Welsh LPs, 2 CDs with Great British Jazz Band, 2 CDs recorded in Namburg with Vaché, Brother/

178

Bob Haggart, various LPs accompanying American Stars. *Honours:* British Jazz Award (Guitar) 1992.

DOUMBIA, Ko Kan Ko Sata; Malian singer. *Career:* one of Mali's few female ngoni players, sings and plays in the Wassoulou music tradition; collaborated with Damon Albarn on the album Mali Music; performed at Barbican Hall, London. *Recordings include:* appears on albums: Mali Music 2002, Mali Lolo! Stars of Mali 2003.

DOUMBIA, Mariam; Malian singer and musician; m. Amadou Bagayoko; three c. *Education:* Inst. for Young Blind People. *Career:* mem. duo, Amadou & Mariam. *Recordings include:* albums: Vols 1–5 (five albums on cassette), Sou ni tilé 1998, Se te djon ye (reissue on CD of first two cassette recordings) 1999, Tje ni Mousso 1999, Wati 2002, Dimanche à Bamako (Victoires de la Musique Award 2004, BBC Radio 3 Award for World Music Album of the Year 2006) 2004, Welcome to Mali 2008, The Magic Couple 2009, Folila 2012. *Honours:* BBC Radio 3 Award for World Music (Africa) 2006. *Website:* www.amadou -mariam.com.

DOWNES, Geoffrey (Geoff); British musician (keyboards), songwriter and producer; b. 25 Aug. 1952, Stockport, Greater Manchester. *Education:* Stockport Grammar School, City of Leeds Coll. of Music. *Career:* fmr session musician and composer of jingles; record producer; mem. The Buggles 1977–80, first single Video Killed the Radio Star later became first video played on MTV; mem. Rock band Yes 1980–81, 2010–; mem. Rock band Asia 1982–; solo artist, New Dance Orchestra, Wetton/Downes ICON; mem. Performing Right Soc., Musicians' Union, British Acad. of Songwriters, Composers and Authors, Mechanical-Copyright Protection Soc., PPL. *Recordings include:* albums: with The Buggles: The Plastic Age 1980, Adventures In Modern Recording 1982; with Yes: Drama 1980, Fly from Here 2011, Heaven & Earth 2014; with Asia: Asia 1982, Alpha 1983, Astra 1985, Then And Now 1990, Live In Moscow 1991, Aqua 1992, Aria 1994, Arena 1995, Archiva 1996, Anthology 1998, Aura 2001, Silent Nation 2004, Phoenix 2008, Omega 2010, XXX 2012; solo/with New Dance Orchestra: The Light Program 1987, Vox Humana 1993, Evolution 1995, The World Service 2000, Shadows And Reflections 2002, The Collection 2003, Live at St. Cyprian's 2003, Electronica 2010; with ICON: Icon 2005, Rubicon 2007, Icon 3 2009, Heat of the Rising Sun 2012; numerous other collaborations with various artists. *Honours:* with The Buggles: NME Award 1980, Deutsche Gramaphon Award 1980; with Asia: Billboard, Cashbox and Circus Magazine awards 1982, FM Magazine Award 1983, Ampex Gold Reel 1979, 1980, 1986, Keyboard Magazine Awards 1980, 1982, 1983, ASCAP Best Rock Song 1982, 1983. *Current Management:* c/o Martin Darvill, QEDG Management, PO Box 6249, Leighton Buzzard, Beds., LU7 0GE, England. *E-mail:* asiageof@yahoo.com. *Website:* www.geoffdownes .com.

DOWNEY, Brian; Irish musician (drums); b. 27 Jan. 1951, Dublin. *Career:* Founder-mem. drummer, rock group Thin Lizzy 1969–83, 2010–; mem. Grand Slam (with Thin Lizzy's Phil Lynott) 1984; regular UK and int. appearances with Thin Lizzy include: Reading Festival 1974, 1975, 1983, Great British Music Festival, London 1975, World Series of Rock, Cleveland 1983, Monsters of Rock European tour 1983. *Recordings include:* with Thin Lizzy: Hit singles: Whiskey In The Jar 1973, Wild One 1975, The Boys Are Back In Town 1976, Don't Believe A Word 1977, Dancin' In The Moonlight 1977, Rosalie 1978, Waiting For An Alibi 1979, Sarah 1979, Killer On The Loose 1980, Cold Sweat 1982; Albums: Thin Lizzy 1971, Shades of a Blue Orphanage 1972, Vagabonds of The Western World 1972, Nightlife 1974, Fighting 1975, Jailbreak 1976, Johnny The Fox 1976, Bad Reputation 1977, Live and Dangerous 1978, Black Rose (A Rock Legend) 1979, Chinatown 1980, The Adventures of Thin Lizzy 1981, Renegade 1981, Thunder and Lightning 1983, Dedication–The Very Best of Thin Lizzy 1991, Wild One 1996, All the Way from Dublin 1999, Close as You Get 2007. *Website:* www.thinlizzyband.com.

DOWNIE, Gordon; Canadian musician (acoustic guitar) and singer; b. 6 Feb. 1964, Kingston, Ont. *Education:* Queen's Univ., Kingston. *Career:* mem. The Tragically Hip 1983–. *Recordings include:* albums: with The Tragically Hip: Up to Here 1989, Road Apples 1991, Fully Completely 1992, Day for Night 1994, Trouble at the Henhouse 1996, Live Between Us 1997, Phantom Power 1998, Music @ Work 2000, In Violet Light 2002, In Between Revolution 2004, World Container 2006; solo: Coke Machine Glow 2001, Battle of the Nudes 2003, The Grand Bounce 2011. *Honours:* inducted into Canadian Music Hall of Fame 2005. *Address:* The Tragically Hip, PO Box 98130, 970 Queen Street East, Toronto, ON M4M 1J0, Canada. *E-mail:* Gord@gorddownie.com. *Website:* gorddownie.com; www.thehip.com.

DOWNING, Paul Scott; British composer and musician (bass guitar); b. 4 March 1966, London. *Education:* Leeds Coll. of Music, Guildhall School of Music and Drama. *Career:* worked with Martha Reeves, Mark Murphy, Jimmy Ruffin, Cayenne, Coup D'Etat, Anne Clark, John Etheridge, Vile Bodies, Evalution, Victoria Newton, Eva Abraham, Peter Byrne; mem. Musicians' Union, PRS, MCPS, PAMRA. *Compositions include:* Flight Through Sunlit Clouds, Elegy For A Lost Summer, So Quiet Here, Come In, At Midnight, Summer Night In Paris, Beetles Party. *Recordings include:* The Law Is An Anagram of Wealth, Elegy For A Lost Summer, Flight Through Cloudless Skies, Live 'n' Hot At Ronnie Scott's. *Honours:* Licentiate of The Guildhall School of Music and Drama. *Website:* pauldowningmusic.co.uk.

DOWNING, Will; American singer; b. 29 Nov. 1963, Brooklyn, NY; one s. two d. *Education:* Virginia Union Univ. *Recordings include:* albums: Will Downing 1988, Come Together as One 1989, A Dream Fulfilled 1991, Love's the Place to Be 1993, Moods 1995, Inivitation Only 1997, Pleasures of the Night 1998, All The Man You Need 2000, Sensual Journey 2002, Emotions 2003, Christmas, Love and You 2004, Soul Symphony 2005, After Tonight 2007, Classique 2009, Lust, Love & Lies 2010. *Current Management:* Kyle Newport, WD Productions. *Telephone:* (510) 834-0908. *E-mail:* kylebap@aol.com. *Address:* PO Box 7272, Somerset, NJ 08875, USA. *Website:* www.willdowning.com.

DOWNS, (Ana) Lila; Mexican singer and songwriter; b. 19 Sept. 1968, Tlaxiaco; d. of Allen Downs and Anastasia Sanchez; m. Paul Cohen. *Education:* Escuela de Bellas Artes, Oaxaca and Univ. of Minnesota, USA. *Recordings include:* albums: Tree Of Life 2000, La Linea 2001, La Sandunga 2003, Una Sangre (Latin Grammy Award for Best Folk Album) 2004, La Cantina 2006, Shake Away 2008, Lila Downs y La Misteriosa en Paris-Live a FIP 2010, Pecados y Milagros 2011, Canciones Pa' Todo el Año 2012, Raiz (with Nina Pastori and Soledad) (Latin Grammy Award for Best Traditional Folk Album 2014) 2014, Balas y Chocolate (Latin Grammy Award for Best Folk Album 2015) 2015. *Films include:* Frida 2003, Fados 2007. *E-mail:* paul@ liladowns.com (office). *Address:* POB 332, New York, NY 10002, USA. *E-mail:* liladowns@gmail.com. *Website:* www.liladowns.com.

DOY, Carl William, ONZM; musician (piano), arranger, composer and producer; b. 6 May 1947, Camberley, Surrey; m. Kathleen Mary Doy 1973; two s. *Education:* Royal Coll. of Music with Herbert Howells, Eric Harrison. *Career:* Musical Dir, Ocean Monarch cruise ship 1971–73; moved to New Zealand 1973; staff arranger at TVNZ for 15 years; resident pianist, New Zealand Today and Saturday Live; arranged, recorded with Dame Kiri Te Kanawa; played for Shirley Bassey, Gladys Knight and The Pips, Bob Hope, Rolf Harris, Dick Emery, The Four Aces, Del Shannon, B. B. King, Shirley Bassey; mem. APRA. *Recordings include:* albums: Piano By Candlelight 1995, Moonlight Piano 1995, The Music of Frank Sinatra, Quiet Nights, The Music of Nat King Cole, The Music of Barbra Streisand, The Music of the Beatles, The Classics, The Music of Burt Bacharach, Together, The Music of Christmas, Espresso Guitar. *Honours:* Artistic Award World Song Festival, Los Angeles 1984, Grand Prix, Pacific Song Contest (for Nothing But Dreams) 1979. *E-mail:* carl@carldoy.com. *Website:* www.carldoy.com.

DOYLE, Candida; British musician (keyboards); b. 25 Aug. 1963, Belfast, Northern Ireland. *Career:* mem. Pulp 1984–2002, 2011–13; numerous tours, television appearances and festival dates; contrib. to film soundtrack, Mission Impossible 1996. *Recordings include:* albums: Freaks 1987, Separations 1992, His 'N' Hers 1994, Different Class 1995, This Is Hardcore 1998, We Love Life 2001, Hits 2002. singles: Little Girl (With Blue Eyes) 1985, Countdown 1991, OU 1992, Babies 1992, Razzmatazz 1993, Lipgloss 1993, Do You Remember The First Time? 1994, Help The Aged 1997, This Is Hardcore 1998, A Little Soul 1998, Party Hard 1998, The Trees/Sunrise 2001, Bad Cover Version 2002. *Honours:* Mercury Music Prize 1995, BRIT Award 1996.

DOYLE, Patrick; British composer, musician and actor; b. 6 April 1953, Uddington, Scotland. *Education:* Royal Scottish Acad. of Music and Drama. *Career:* mem. ASCAP. *Compositions:* for film: Look Back in Anger (TV) 1989, Henry V 1989, Shipwrecked 1990, Dead Again 1991, Into the West 1992, Indochine 1992, Needful Things 1993, Carlito's Way 1993, Much Ado About Nothing 1993, Exit to Eden 1994, Mary Shelley's Frankenstein 1994, Une Femme française 1995, A Little Princess 1995, Sense and Sensibility 1995, Mrs Winterbourne 1996, Hamlet 1996, Donnie Brasco 1997, Great Expectations 1998, Quest for Camelot 1998, Love's Labour's Lost 1999, East West 2000, Bridget Jones' Diary 2001, Gosford Park 2002, Killing Me Softly 2002, El Misterio Galíndez 2003, Calendar Girls 2003, Secondhand Lions 2003, Nouvelle-France 2004, Jekyll + Hyde 2005, Man to Man 2005, Le Voyage de Lomama 2005, Wah-Wah 2005, Nanny McPhee 2005, Harry Potter and the Goblet of Fire 2005, Sir Billi the Vet 2006, As You Like It 2006, Eragon 2006, The Last Legion 2007, Nim's Island 2008, Igor 2008, Brave 2012. *Honours:* ASCAP Award 2006. *Current Management:* Air-Edel, 1416 N La Brea Avenue, Los Angeles, CA 90028, USA.

DOYLE, Teresa, BA; Canadian singer; b. 26 Jan. 1951, Prince Edward Island; m. Brett Bunston; one s. *Education:* Univ. of Prince Edward Island, McGill Conservatory of Music. *Career:* performed at festivals and concerts in Japan, Canada, the USA and UK; mem. American Fed. of Musicians. *Recordings include:* Prince Edward Isle, Adieu, Forerunner, Stowaway, Songs for Lute and Voice, Dance to Your Daddy, If Fish Could Sing 2004, Orrachan 2006. *Honours:* East Coast Music Award for Children's Album of the Year. *Address:* RR #3, Belfast, PEI C0A 1A0, Canada. *Telephone:* (902) 838-2973. *Fax:* (902) 838-0610. *E-mail:* teresa@teresadoyle.com. *Website:* www .teresadoyle.com.

DOZIER, Lamont; American composer, record producer, songwriter and academic; *Artist-in-Residence of Popular Music, Thornton School of Music, University of Southern California;* b. 16 June 1941, Detroit, Mich.; m. Barbara Dozier; three c. *Career:* Motown artist with group, The Romeos 1956–67; mem. songwriting and production team Holland/Dozier/Holland (with Eddie and Brian Holland) 1963–73; Co-founder, Invictus and Hot Wax Records 1967; resumed solo recording career 1972–; Founder, Megaphone Records 1983–; worked with artists as co-writer/producer, including Marvin Gaye, Martha and The Vandellas, The Supremes, The Isley Brothers, The Four Tops, The Miracles, Kim Weston, Aretha Franklin, Al Wilson, Freda Payne; currently Artist-in-Residence of Popular Music, Thornton School of Music, Univ. of Southern California. *Recordings include:* albums: Out Here On My Own 1973, Black

Bach 1974, Love and Beauty 1975, Right There 1976, Peddlin' Music On The Side 1977, Bittersweet 1979, Working On You 1981, Lamont 1982, Bigger Than Life 1983, Inside Seduction 1991, Going Back To My Roots 2000, Reflections Of... 2004, Ain't Got No Stop Button 2006. *Honours:* three Grammy Awards, three BMI Awards for Songwriter of the Year, Broadcast Music Icon Award 2003, mem. Rock and Roll Hall of Fame, Songwriter's Hall of Fame, 2007 Thornton Legacy Award, University of Southern California Thornton School of Music 2007, Johnny Mercer Award for Lifetime Achievement, Songwriter's Hall of Fame 2009. *Address:* Department of Popular Music, USC Thornton School of Music, 840 West 34th Street, LPB 118, Los Angeles, CA 90089-0851, USA (office). *Telephone:* (213) 740-3224 (office). *E-mail:* popularmusic@thornton.usc.edu (office). *Website:* www.lamontdozier.com.

DRAGON, Daryl; American musician (keyboards) and songwriter; b. 27 Aug. 1942, Los Angeles, CA; m. Toni Tennille 1974. *Career:* keyboard player and co-writer, The Beach Boys stage band; mem., Natalie Cole's Malibu Music Men; mem. of duo, Captain & Tennille 1972–; numerous tours and live appearances; musical variety show, Captain & Tennille (ABC TV) 1976; runs Rambo recording studio 1979–. *Recordings include:* albums: The Secret of Christmas 1974, Love Will Keep Us Together 1975, Song of Joy 1976, Come in from the Rain 1977, Dream 1978, Make Your Move 1980, Keeping Our Love Warm, Twenty Years of Romance 1995, Size 14 1997, Tennille Sings Big Band 1998, Incurably Romantic 2001, More Than Dancing... Much More 2002. *Honours:* Grammy Award for Record of the Year (for Love Will Keep Us Together) 1976, Juno Award for Best Int. Single (for Love Will Keep Us Together) 1976. *E-mail:* NAAProd@aol.com (office); tonianddarylcontact@gmail.com (home). *Website:* www.captainandtennille.net.

DRAKE; Canadian rapper, singer, songwriter and actor; b. (Aubrey Drake Graham), 24 Oct. 1986, Toronto, Ont.; s. of Dennis Graham and Sandi Sher. *Education:* Forest Hill Collegiate Inst., Vaughan Road Acad. *Career:* released several mixtapes; signed recording contract with Lil Wayne's Young Money Entertainment 2009; first EP release So Far Gone 2009; toured with Lil Wayne on America's Most Wanted rap tour 2009; released debut album 2010; featured as part of Young Artists for Haiti musicians collective 2010; songwriter for several other artists including Jamie Foxx, Alicia Keys; toured Club Paradise worldwide 2012 (most successful hip-hop tour of the year); numerous collaborations including Kanye West, Lil Wayne, Jay-Z, Trey Songz, Nicki Minaj, Rihanna, Rick Ross. *Television:* as actor: Degrassi: The Next Generation (as Jimmy Brooks) (Young Artist Award for Best Ensemble in a TV Series (Comedy or Drama) 2002, Teen Choice Summer Series Award 2005, Teen Choice Summer TV Show 2007) 2001–09, Blue Murder 2001, Soul Food 2002, Conviction (TV movie) 2002, Best Friend's Date 2005, The Border 2008, Being Erica 2009, Sophie 2009, Degrassi Takes Manhattan (TV movie) 2010. *Films:* Charlie Bartlett 2008, Breakaway 2011, Ice Age: Continental Drift 2012. *Recordings:* mixtapes: Room for Improvement 2006, Comeback Season 2007, So Far Gone (Juno Award for Rap Recording of the Year 2009) 2009; albums: Thank Me Later 2010, Take Care (Juno Award for Rap Recording of the Year 2012, Grammy Award for Best Rap Album 2013) 2011, Nothing Was the Same 2013, If You're Reading This, It's Too Late 2015. *Honours:* numerous including: BET Hip Hop Awards for Track of the Year 2009, for Rookie of the Year 2009, for MVP of the Year 2010, for Best Hip-Hop Song 2012, GQ Award for Man of the Year 2010, ASCAP Awards for Most Performed Songs (Best I Ever Had, Every Girl) 2010, (Forever) 2011, (I'm On One) 2012, (What's My Name?) 2012, BET Award for Best Male Hip-Hop Artist 2010, 2012, Juno Award for Rap Recording of the Year 2010, Soul Train Music Award for Record of the Year 2010, for Best Hip-Hop Song 2011, Songwriters Hall of Fame Hal David Starlight Award 2011, BMI Urban Music Award for Songwriter of the Year 2012, MTV Video Music Award for Best Hip-Hop Video 2012, Much Music Video Award for Hip Hop Video of the Year (for Worst Behavior) 2014, Much Music Video Award for Int. Video of the Year by a Canadian (featuring Majid Jordan for Hold On, We're Going Home) 2014. *Website:* www.youngmoney.com; www.drakeofficial.com.

DRAMINSKY HOJMARK, Jakob; Danish composer and musician (bass clarinet, sopranino saxophone); b. 18 Nov. 1959, Copenhagen. *Education:* Copenhagen Univ., composition and instrumental studies with Pierre Dorge, Copenhagen, Wolfgang Fuchs, Berlin and Gabriel Brncic, Barcelona, electro-acoustic workshops in DIEM, IRCAM and PHONOS. *Career:* musician and composer 1977–; woodwind instrumentalist 1986–; residencies in London, Berlin, Barcelona, Tokyo. *Compositions include:* Stjerneham I Stadier 1990, Timbre-Timber 1991, Travesias 1991, Darving for Good-Wood 1991, Canefloat 1992, aN eMPTY sPACE? V1 v2 2000, Sangfortælling #10/20 2001. *Recordings include:* At the Gallery, 9 collected chamber works; Memory, En landsoldats dagbog, Dreamjingles. *Honours:* grants from Nat. Danish Art Foundation. *Address:* MultiSounds, Apdo 34006, 08080 Barcelona, Spain. *E-mail:* kontor@multisounds.dk. *Website:* www.multisounds.dk.

DRAPER, Paul Edward; British singer and songwriter; b. 26 Sept. 1972, Chester, Cheshire. *Education:* Wrexham Art Coll. *Career:* Founder-mem. Grey Lantern, later renamed Mansun 1995–2003; numerous TV and live appearances. *Recordings include:* albums: Attack Of The Grey Lantern 1996, Desperate Icons 1997, Legacy 1998, Six 1998, Little Kix 2000, Electric Man 2000, Kleptomania 2004.

DRAVS, Markus; German record producer, engineer and programmer. *Career:* worked for producers in UK including Clive Langer and Alan

Winstanley, Gary Langan; worked in collaboration on records by Brian Eno 1992–; engineer, remixer and mixer on many records for Depeche Mode, 808 State, The Grid, James, Björk and others 1992–; producer for albums by Arcade Fire, Coldplay, Mumford and Sons. *Recordings include:* albums: as producer, mixer and musician: with Brian Eno: Nerve Net 1992, Ali Click 1992; as producer: Merz, Merz 2007, Viva la Vida, Coldplay 2008, Wall of Arms, The Maccabees 2009, Sigh No More, Mumford and Sons (BRIT Award for Best British Album 2011) 2009, The Suburbs, Arcade Fire (BRIT Award for Best International Album 2011, Grammy Award for Album of the Year 2011) 2010, Mylo Xyloto, Coldplay 2011, Babel, Mumford and Sons (Grammy Award for Album of the Year 2013) 2012. *Address:* c/o Casa-D Productions Limited, Kobalt Music Group, 4 Valentine Place, London, SE1 8QH, England (office). *E-mail:* info@kobaltmusic.com (office). *Website:* www.kobaltmusic.com (office); www.markusdravs.com.

DR. DRE; American rap artist, hip-hop producer and record producer; b. (Andre Romelle Young), 18 Feb. 1965, Compton, Los Angeles, Calif.; s. of Theodore Young and Verna Young; one s. with Lisa Johnson. *Education:* Centennial High School, Compton, Fremont High School. *Career:* mem. World Class Wreckin' Cru; mem. NWA 1980s; worked with Snoop Dogg, Warren G., Ice Cube, Eminem; Co-founder Death Row Records 1992–96; producer, numerous acts, including Blackstreet and Foxy Brown; Founder, Producer, Aftermath label 1996–, sold to Interscope Records 2001; soundtrack to numerous films. *Films:* A Cool Like That Christmas (TV film) (voice) 1993, Murder Was the Case: The Movie (video short) 1995, Set It Off 1996, Whiteboyz 1999, 25 Large (TV film) (voice) 1999, Training Day 2001, The Wash 2001, 50 Cent: Bulletproof (video game) 2005. *Recordings include:* albums: The Chronic 1992, Concrete Roots 1994, First Round Knock Out 1996, Back N Tha Day 1996, Dr. Dre Presents the Aftermath 1996, 2001 1999, Dr. Dre 2001, Chronicle: Best of the Works 2002, Chronicles: Death Row Classics 2006; singles include: Kush (ft. Snoop Dogg and Akon) 2010, I Need a Doctor (ft. Eminem & Skylar Grey) 2011, The Recipe 2012. *Honours:* Grammy Award for Best Rap Solo Performance (for Let Me Ride), Grammy Award for Best Rap Performance by a Duo or Group (for Crack a Bottle with Eminem and 50 Cent) 2010. *Address:* c/o Interscope Records, 2220 Colorado Avenue, Santa Monica, CA 90404, USA. *Website:* www.drdre.com.

DREIJER, Olof; Swedish DJ; b. 1981, brother of Karin Dreijer Anderssen. *Career:* mem., The Knife 1999–. *Recordings include:* albums: The Knife 2001, Deep Cuts 2003, Hannah Med H Soundtrack 2003, Silent Shout 2006, Tomorrow, In a Year 2010, Tomorrow, In a Year 2010, Shaking the Habitual 2013. *Honours:* Grammis Award for Best Pop Group 2003, Artist of the Year, Pop Album of the Year, Songwriters of the Year, Pop Producers of the Year, Pop Group of the Year 2007, Scandinavian Alternative Music Awards for Song of the Year 2004, Album of the Year 2007, Swedish National Radio P3 Gold (Group of the Year, Dance of the Year) 2006. *Current Management:* c/o D.E.F. Management, 51 Lonsdale Road, Queens Park, London, NW6 6RA, England. *Telephone:* (20) 7328-2922. *E-mail:* info@d-e-f.com. *Website:* www.d-e-f.com; www.theknife.net.

DREIJER ANDERSSEN, Karin; Swedish singer; b. 1975, sister of Olof Dreijer. *Career:* mem., The Knife 1999–; collaborated with Röyksopp 2005; solo artist; performing as Fever Ray 2008–. *Recordings include:* albums: with The Knife: The Knife 2001, Deep Cuts 2003, Hannah Med H Soundtrack 2003, Silent Shout 2006, Tomorrow, In a Year 2010, Shaking the Habitual 2013; as Fever Ray: Fever Ray 2009, Live in Luleå 2009. *Honours:* Grammis Award for Best Pop Group 2003, Artist of the Year, Pop Album of the Year, Songwriters of the Year, Pop Producers of the Year, Pop Group of the Year 2007, Scandinavian Alternative Music Awards for Song of the Year 2004, Album of the Year 2007, Swedish National Radio P3 Gold for Group of the Year, Dance of the Year 2006. *Current Management:* c/o D.E.F. Management, 51 Lonsdale Road, Queens Park, London, NW6 6RA, England. *Telephone:* (20) 7328-2922. *E-mail:* info@d-e-f.com. *Website:* www.d-e-f.com; www.theknife.net; feverray.com.

DREVER, Ivan Cursiter; British singer, songwriter and musician (guitar); b. 10 June 1956, Orkney, Scotland; two s. two d. *Career:* solo/duo work for six years; joined Wolfstone 1991; toured America, Canada, Spain, Denmark, Germany and Far East; formed Ivan Drever Band; numerous appearances with band; mem. MCPS, PRS. *Recordings include:* with Wolfstone: Unleashed 1991, Chase 1992, Year of the Dog 1994, Half Tail 1996, Pick of the Litter 1997, This Strange Place 1998; solo albums: Homeland 1989, Four Walls 1996, Notes from an Island 2010, Bless The Wind 2011, Keep On Keeping On 2012; three duo albums with Knowe O'Deil. *E-mail:* ivandreverwebsite@yahoo.co.uk. *Website:* www.ivandrever.co.uk.

DREVER, Kris John Robert; British folk singer, songwriter and musician (guitar); b. 1978, Orkney Islands, Scotland; s. of Ivan Drever. *Career:* moved to Edinburgh 1995; mem. folk trio Fine Friday 2000–05; Founder-mem. Session A9; Founder-mem. Lau 2005–, collaborations with Karine Polwart, Adem; solo act 2006–; recordings and tours with numerous artists including Roddy Woomble, John McCusker, Eddi Reader, Julie Fowlis, Kate Rusby, Idlewild, Heidi Talbot, Duncan Chisholm, Eamonn Coyne. *Recordings:* albums: with Fine Friday: Gone Dancing 2002, Mowing the Machair 2005; solo: Black Water 2006, Mark the Hard Earth 2010; with Lau: Lightweights and Gentlemen 2007, Arc Light, 2009, Race the Loser 2012; with Eamonn Coyne: Honk Toot Suite 2007, Storymap 2013; with Roddy Woomble and John McCusker: Before the Ruin 2008. *Honours:* BBC Radio 2 Folk Horizon Award for Best Newcomer

2007, with Lau: BBC Radio 2 Folk Awards for Best Band 2008, 2009, 2010, for Best Group 2013, Scottish Traditional Music Award for Best Live Act 2009. *E-mail:* tomreveal@mac.com. *Website:* www.revealrecords.co.uk. *E-mail:* management@krisdrever.com. *Website:* www.lau-music.co.uk; www .krisdrever.com.

DREW, Kevin; Canadian singer, songwriter and musician; b. 9 Sept. 1976, Toronto; m. Jo-ann Goldsmith (divorced). *Education:* Etobicoke School of the Arts. *Career:* mem. K.C. Accidental 1998–2000; founder mem. Broken Social Scene 1999–. *Films:* as writer and director: The Water 2008. *Recordings:* albums: with K.C. Accidental: Captured Anthems for an Empty Bathtub 1998, Anthems for the Could've Bin Pills 2000; with Broken Social Scene: Feel Good Lost 2001, You Forgot It in People (Juno Award for Alternative Album of the Year 2003) 2002, Bee Hives 2003, Broken Social Scene (Juno Award for Alternative Album of the Year 2006) 2005, Forgiveness Rock Record 2010, Lo-Fi for the Dividing Nights 2010; solo: Spirit If 2007; other contributions: Red Hot Organization, Dark Was the Night 2009. *Current Management:* Canvas Media, 460 Richmond Street West, Suite 402, Toronto, ON M5V 1Y1, Canada. *Telephone:* (416) 203-2217. *Fax:* (416) 203-2209. *E-mail:* press@canvasmedia .ca. *Website:* www.canvasmedia.ca. *E-mail:* raiseyourhands@arts-crafts.ca (office). *Website:* www.arts-crafts.ca (office); www.brokensocialscene.ca.

DREWETT, Steve; singer, songwriter and musician (guitar); b. 29 Oct. 1954, Islington, London. *Career:* solo artist; formed Newtown Neurotics 1979; mem. Musicians' Union. *Recordings include:* albums: Beggars Can Be Choosers 1983, Repercussions 1985, Kickstarting A Backfiring Nation 1986, Is Your Washroom Breeding Bolsheviks 1988, 45 Revolutions Per Minute 1990. *Website:* www.neurotics.org.uk.

DREXLER, Jorge; Uruguayan singer and songwriter; b. (Jorge Abner Drexler Prada), 21 Sept. 1964, Montevideo; m. Ana Laan (divorced 2005); pnr Leonor Watling; one s. *Career:* studied medicine and qualified as an ear, nose and throat specialist; singer and songwriter 1989–. *Film:* The Motorcycle Diaries (composed and performed song Al Otro Lado del Rio) 2004. *Recordings:* albums: La luz que sabe robar 1992, Radar 1994, Vaivén 1996, Llueve 1998, Frontera 1999, Sea 2001, Eco 2004, 12 Segundos de Oscuridad 2006, La edad del cielo 2007, Cara B 2008, Amar la trama 2010, Bailar en la cueva (Latin Grammy Award for Best Singer-Songwriter Album 2014) 2014. *Honours:* Acad. Award for Best Original Song 2004, Latin Grammy Award for Record of the Year (for Universos Paralelos, with Ana Tijoux) 2014. *Current Management:* Morgan Britos S.L., Calle Princesa 3 duplicado, Oficina 1331, 26008 Madrid, Spain. *Telephone:* (91) 5411732. *Fax:* (91) 5413291. *E-mail:* contraction@morganbritos.net. *Website:* www.morganbritos.com; www.jorgedrexler.com.

D'RIVERA, Paquito; Cuban musician (saxophone, clarinet), band leader, composer and arranger; b. 4 June 1948, Havana. *Career:* Founding mem. Orquestra Cubana de Musica Moderna; fmr mem. Cuban Nat. Symphony Orchestra; Founding mem. Irakere; performs with Paquito d'Rivera Ensemble and the Caribbean Jazz Project; conducts Dizzy Gillespie's UN Orchestra; guest soloist, jazz, classical, Latin/Caribbean music concerts and albums; Artistic Dir, New Jersey Chamber Music Soc.; Artist-in-Residence, New Jersey Performing Arts Center; Artistic Dir Festival International de Jazz en al Tambo, Uruguay; Composer-in-Residence, Caramoor Center for Music and the Arts with Orchestra of St Luke's 2007–08; mem. Bd of Dirs Chamber Music America. *Compositions include:* The New York Suite for saxophone quartet 1989, Aires Tropicales for woodwind quintet 1994, five Pieces for brass quintet 1997, Rivers, a Poetic Suite 1998, Adagio 1999, Panamericana Suite 2000, Fiddle Dreams 2002, Gran Danzón 2002, Kites 2005, The Chaser 2006, Three Poems from the New World 2006, Conversations with Cachao 2007. *Recordings include:* albums: Irakere (Grammy Award for Best Latin Recording 1979) 1978–79, Havana Jam 1979, Paquito - Blowin' 1981, Mariel 1982, The Young Lions 1983, Why Not! 1984, Expolosion 1985, Manhattan Burn 1987, Celebration 1988, Tico Tico 1989, Return to Ipanema 1989, Reunion 1991, Havana Cafe 1991, Who's Smokin' 1992, La Habana-Rio Conexión 1992, Paquito D'Rivera presents 40 Years of Cuban Jam Sessions 1993, Messidor's Finest 1996, Portraits of Cuba (Grammy Award for Best Jazz Performance 1996) 1996, Chamber Music from the South 1997, Pixinguinha 100 Años 1997, Baksa for Winds 1997, 100 Years of Latin Love Songs 1998, Habanera 1999, Cubarama 1999, Tropicana Nights (Latin Grammy Award for Best Latin Jazz Album 2000) 1999, Quintet Live at the Blue Note (Latin Grammy Award for Best Latin Jazz Album 2001) 2000, The Clarinetist, Vol. 1 2001, Historia del Soldado (Latin Grammy Award for Best Classical Album 2003) 2002, Brazilian Dreams (Latin Grammy Award for Best Latin Jazz Album 2003) 2002, Riberas (Latin Grammy Award for Best Classical Album 2005) 2004, Musica para los Amigos 2006, Funk Tango (Grammy Award for Best Latin Jazz Album 2008) 2007, Panamericana Suite (Grammy Award for Latin Jazz Album 2011) 2010, Song for Maura (Grammy Award for Best Latin Jazz Album 2013, Latin Grammy Award for Best Latin Jazz Album 2014) 2013, Jazz Meets the Classics (Latin Grammy Award for Best Latin Jazz Album 2015) 2015. *Publications include:* Music Minus Me instructional tapes, Lessons with the Greats, Jamey Aebersold: Play-along, Vol. 77, My Sax Life 1999, Oh, La Habana (novel). *Honours:* Hon. Diploma (Universidad de Alcalá de Henares, Spain), Hon. DMus (Berklee School of Music) 2003, Dr hc (State Univ. of New York at Old Westbury) 2012; Carnegie Hall Lifetime Achievement Award for Contribution to Latin Music, Grammy Award for Best Instrumental Composition (for Merengue) 2004, Nat. Medal for the Arts 2005, named Jazz Master, Nat. Endowment for the Arts 2005, Living Jazz Legend

Award, Kennedy Center 2007, John Simon Guggenheim Fellowship in Music Composition 2007. *Current Management:* Greenbug Productions Ltd. and Havana New York Music, PO Box 4899, Weehawken, NJ 07086, USA. *Telephone:* (201) 295-3176. *Fax:* (201) 869-4242. *E-mail:* brendafeliciano@msn .com. *Website:* www.paquitodrivera.com.

DROGE, Peter; American singer and songwriter; b. 11 March 1969, Eugene, Ore. *Career:* tours supporting Tom Petty, Melissa Etheridge, Sheryl Crow, Neil Young; mem. ASCAP. *Recordings include:* albums: Necktie Second 1994, Find a Door 1996, Spacey and Shakin' 1998, Skywatching 2003, Under the Waves 2006. *Address:* 417 Denny Way, Suite 200, Seattle, WA 98109, USA. *E-mail:* info@droge.com. *Website:* www.droge.com.

DROSSOS, Petros; Greek sound engineer and producer; b. 11 June 1966, Athens. *Career:* tape operator in several Parisian studios in 1986; Asst Engineer, Polysound Studios, Athens, Greece 1987; in-house engineer, Davout Studios, Paris, France 1988–91; freelance engineer, music, television, post-production 1991–. *Recordings include:* engineer, producer: single: with Mano Negra: King Kong Five; albums: Raggabuzzin (French Reggae Compilation); with Rosemary's Babies: Lutte De Classe; engineer: with Mano Negra: Live à la Cigale (TV programme tracks); with Hector Zazou and Les Polyphonies Corses, Ghetto Youth Progress (French Ragga Hip Hop Compilation), IAM, Red, Black and Green (maxi-single).

DROZD, Steven Gregory; American musician (guitar, drums), songwriter and singer; b. 11 June 1969, Houston, Tex.; s. of Vernon Drozd; m. Becky Stokesberry; one s. one d. *Education:* Eisenhower High School, Lawton, Okla. *Career:* fmr mem. The Defect Files; fmr mem. Janis 18; mem. The Flaming Lips 1991–; founder mem. side project, The Paris Gun; other appearances with Elliott Smith, Jay Farrar, Steve Burns, Cake, Maynard James Keenan. *Films:* as actor: Christmas on Mars 2008; other appearances: Fearless Freaks (documentary on band) 2005; soundtrack contributions: The SpongeBob SquarePants Movie 2004, Spider-Man 3 2007, Good Luck Chuck 2007, Mr Magorium's Wonder Emporium 2007. *Recordings:* albums: with The Flaming Lips: Hit to Death in the Future Head 1992, Transmissions from the Satellite Heart 1993, Clouds Taste Metallic 1995, Zaireeka 1997, The Soft Bulletin 1999, Yoshmi Battles the Pink Robots 2002, At War with the Mystics 2006 (Grammy Award for Best Engineered Album, Non-Classical 2007), Embryonic 2009; with Stardeath and White Dwarfs: The Flaming Lips and Stardeath and White Dwarfs with Henry Rollins and Peaches Doing Dark Side of the Moon 2010. *Honours:* Grammy Award for Best Rock Instrumental Performance 2002, 2006. *Current Management:* c/o Scott Booker, Hellfire Enterprises Limited, 1208 Chowning Avenue, Edmond, OK 73034, USA. *Telephone:* (405) 715-0600. *Fax:* (405) 715-0632. *E-mail:* SDBMKTG@hellfireltdcom. *Website:* www.hellfireltd.com. *Address:* c/o Warner Bros. Records Inc., 3300 Warner Boulevard, Burbank, CA 91505, USA (office). *Website:* www.theflaminglips .com.

DRU NASTY (see Sisqó)

DRUMMIE, Richard; British singer, musician (guitar, keyboards) and songwriter. *Career:* songwriting partnership with Peter Cox, ATV Music; Founder mem. of duo, Go West 1982–. *Recordings include:* albums: with Go West: Go West 1985, Bangs and Crashes 1986, Dancing On The Couch 1987, Indian Summer 1992, Aces and Kings 1993, futurenow 2008, 3D Part 1 2010, 3D Part 2 2011, 3D Part 3 2013. *Current Management:* c/o John Glover, Blueprint Management, PO Box 593, Woking, Surrey GU23 7YF, England. *Telephone:* (1483) 715336. *Fax:* (1483) 757490. *E-mail:* john@blueprint -management.com. *Website:* www.blueprint-management.com; www.gowest .org.uk.

DRUMMOND, Bill, (Tenzing Scot Brown, King Boy D, Time Boy); British musician and visual artist; b. (William Ernest Drummond), 29 April 1953, South Africa; s. of Jack Drummond and Rosalind Drummond; six c. *Career:* fmr fisherman, set designer, carpenter, trawlerman; mem. Big In Japan 1977; founder, Zoo Records and Zoo Publishing (with David Balfe); man., producer Teardrop Explodes, Echo and The Bunnymen; A&R consultant, WEA Records 1985; formed KLF Communications (with Jimmy Cauty) 1987–92; various recordings as JAMS 1987–88, Disco 2000 1989–91, Timelords 1988, KLF 1989–92, Justified Ancients of Mu Mu 1991–92, 2K 1997; DMC European Convention, Amsterdam 1990; own studios, Transcentral 1988. *Recordings include:* albums: as The JAMS: 1987 (What The Fuck Is Going On?) 1987; as The KLF: The 'What Time Is Love' Story 1989, Chill Out 1990, The White Room 1991, Mu (compilation) 1991, This Is What The KLF Is About I (singles boxed set) 1992, This Is What The KLF Is About II (singles boxed set) 1992; as Space: Space 1990; solo: Bill Drummond–The Man 1986, Time For A Change 1989 and numerous others. *Publications include:* The Manual, How to Have a Number One the Easy Way 1988, Bad Wisdom (with Mark Manning) 1996, 45 2000, How To Be An Artist 2002, The Wild Highway (with Mark Manning) 2005, 17 2008, Man Makes Bed 2011, Man Shines Shoes 2011, Ragworts 2012, 100 2012. *Honours:* BRIT Award for Best British Group, KLF (co-winners with Simply Red) 1992. *E-mail:* admin@penkilnburn.com (office). *Website:* www .penkiln-burn.com.

DRYDEN, Kesi, BSc (Hons); British songwriter, musician and record producer; b. 1986. *Education:* Leeds Metropolitan Univ. *Career:* Founder-mem. Rudimental 2010–; released debut single Deep in the Valley 2011; collaborations with MC Shantie, Adiyam, MNEK and Syron, John Newman, Alex Clare, Angel Haze, Ella Eyre, Emeli Sandé, Nas, Foxes. *Recordings:* album: with

Rudimental: Home (MOBO Award for Best Album 2013) 2013. *Current Management:* c/o Coda Music Agency LLP, CODA House, 56 Compton Street, Clerkenwell, London, EC1V 0ET, England. *Telephone:* (20) 7017-2500. *Fax:* (20) 7017-2555. *Website:* www.codaagency.com; www.rudimental.co.uk.

DU PEIXE, Jorge; Brazilian singer and musician (percussion). *Career:* mem. mangue beat band, Nação Zumbi with Lúcio Maia 1997–. *Recordings include:* albums: CSNZ 1998, Rádio SAMBA 2000, Nação Zumbi 2002, Futura 2005, Fome de Tudo 2007. *Honours:* São Paulo Asscn of Art Critics Award for Best Group (Nação Zumbi) 2005. *Website:* www.nacaozumbi.com.br.

DUBFIRE; Iranian/American producer, remixer and DJ; b. (Ali Shirazinia), 19 April 1971, Iran. *Career:* formed Deep Dish and founded Deep Dish/Yoshitoshi Records with partner, Sharam 1992; collaborations with Danny Tenaglia, John Selway, Everything But the Girl; remixed Madonna, De'Lacy, Billie Ray Martin, Joi Cardwell, Dusted, Sven Vath, The Shamen, Eddie Amador. *Recordings include:* albums: Junk Science 1998, George Is On 2005. *Honours:* Grammy Award for Remixer of the Year 2001. *Current Management:* c/o The Bullitt Agency, 3207a M Street, NW, Washington, DC 20007, USA. *Telephone:* (202) 338-8040. *Fax:* (202) 338-8343. *E-mail:* info@bullittbookings.com. *Website:* www.bullittbookings.com; www.dubfire.com; www.deepdish.com.

DUBOWSKY, Jack Curtis, MMus; American composer, arranger, record producer, musician (guitar, bass, piano) and singer; b. 1965, Conn. *Education:* Univ. of California, San Francisco Conservatory of Music. *Career:* recording technician with Metallica, Live Shit box set 1994; actor with Sick and Twisted Players, San Francisco; producer on: Glen Meadmore, Hot Horny and Born-Again 1998, Virgin Whore Complex, Succumb 1998, Winsome Griffles, Meet the Griffles 2007, Jack Curtis Dubowsky Ensemble I 2008; works for chorus performed by San Francisco Choral Artists, Lesbian/Gay Chorus of San Francisco; chamber works performed by various ensembles; music for theatre and dance; orchestral music performed by Castro Valley Chamber Orchestra; mem. BMI. *Compositions include:* chamber music: Nisus et Euryale 2000, Fallout 2000, Exploration 2000, Mystery 2000, Cupid and Psyche Dance No. 1 2001, Nicholas Contretaz 2001, Ranbir Prelude 2002, NYC Dilemma No. 1 2002, Watching the Rain 2003, Due North 2004, Brass Quintet No. 1 2004, Andromaque: Six Bongatelles 2005, Bassoon Concerto No. 1 2005, Marimba Study 1 2008; choral music: Double Nut 1999, Twilight in Technicolor 2000, Lynching Song 2000, Sing We and Chant It 2001, Psalm 13 2002, The Vanishing Line 2003, Big Feet 2004, Dan's Big Hands 2005, Our Room 2006, Melvin the Elf 2006, Magic Snow 2006, Silent Holy Hanukah Bush 2006, Your New Stupid Boyfriend 2006, Such a Nice Brisket 2007, Quaker Peace Testimony 2007; orchestral music: Kursk 2000, Oreste: Que Vois-Je 2001, Orchestra Piece No. 3 2004, Armin 2005, Bassoon Concerto No. 1 2005, Quaker Peace Testimony 2007, Eisenhower Farewell Address 2008. *Film and television soundtracks include:* Under One Roof 2002, Born in a Barn 2004, Lookalike (TV) 2004, That Man: Peter Berlin 2005, Can't Buy Me Love 2006, Rock Haven 2007, Redwoods 2009; shorts: Quality Orange 2000, State Title 2002–04, A Passion to Love 2002, Smile 2003, NYC Dilemma 2006. *Recordings include:* Diazepam Nights 1989, Helot Revolt 1992, Fallout 1990, Duchampians 1991, produced Glen Meadmore's songs for film Hustler White 1996. *Address:* De Stijl Records. *Telephone:* (646) 567-6315. *E-mail:* info@destijlmusic.com. *Website:* www.destijlmusic.com.

DUCAS, George, BA; American artist, singer, songwriter and musician (guitar); b. 1 Aug. 1966, Texas City, TX. *Education:* Vanderbilt Univ., Nashville, TN. *Career:* moved to Nashville, 1991; began songwriting and playing local clubs; numerous television appearances; mem. ASCAP, County Music Asscn. *Recordings include:* albums: George Ducas, 1995; Where I Stand, 1997. *Website:* www.myspace.com/georgeducas; www.georgeducas.com.

DUCHARME, Annette Marie-Jeanne Thérèse, BA; Canadian singer, songwriter and musician (guitar, bass, piano, keyboards); b. 23 Feb. , Windsor. *Career:* appeared, Peter Czowski show modelling for Evelyn Roth 1977; sang, played keyboards Grade 8 Concert, St Mary's Acad.; as lead singer, writer, bass player, toured with Bowers/Ducharme Trio 1980–81; keyboards, tour with John Lee Hooker 1982–83; opened for Richard Marx with own band, cross-Canada tour, 1989; own band, opening tour for Larry Gowan 1994; sang at Kumbaya Benefits 1993, 1994; sang at: Grey Cup Half-time Show, with Tom Cochrane 1994; mem. SOCAN. *Compositions include:* Sinking Like A Sunset, recorded by Tom Cochrane. *Recordings include:* Bowers/Ducharme 1981, Blue Girl 1988–89, Mad Mad World 1992, Sanctuary 1994, Ragged Ass Road 1995, Flowers In The Concrete 1995, Don't Argue with Her 1996, Mythos 1998. *Honours:* (West Coast) Caras Award for Most Promising New Artist 1985, CMPA Award for number 1 Rock Song of the Year 1993, SOCAN Award for Pop Song of the Year 1993, Last two for: Sinking Like A Sunset. *Address:* 1669 E, 13th Avenue, Vancouver, BC V5N 2B7, Canada.

DUCHEMIN, Philippe, Diplôme d'Etat de Jazz; French jazz musician (piano); b. 2 Jan. 1957, Toulouse. *Education:* self-taught. *Career:* played with Kenny Clarke, Lionel Hampton, Ray Brown, Joe Newman, Benny Powell, Scott Hamilton, Bob Wilber, Deborah Brown, Wild Bill Davis, Frank Wess, Ted Curson, Duffy Jackson, Alvin Queen; toured Europe with many French and American musicians 1985–; performed at jazz festivals with own trio throughout Europe, N Africa, Middle East, also concerts in Washington DC and St Petersburg, tours of Senegal, Burkina Faso, Romania, Jordan 2005, Brazil 2009, Australia. *Films:* Chignon d'Olga, Femme décibel. *Recordings*

include: Middle Jazz Quartet 1980, Hommage à Count Basie 1985, François Guin Et Les Four Bones 1987; with Philippe Duchemin Trio: Alizés 1990; Live! 1992, Three Pieces 1994, Trio with Dominque Vernhes 1995; with Paris Barcelona: Swing Connection 1990; Hard Swing 1991, Wild Cat 1992, Frank Wess Meets The Paris Barcelona 1992, Three Colors 1998, For Oscar 2004, The Best of a Jazz Pianist 2005, On The New Jersey Road 2006, Dualite 2008, Massilia 2010, Swing & Strings 2012. *Honours:* 1er Prix, Concours int. de jazz de Montauban édition 2011. *Address:* 42 rue de la Madeleine, 72000 Le Mans, France. *Telephone:* (2) 43-77-11-36. *E-mail:* duchemin@noos.fr. *Website:* www.philippeduchemin.com.

DUDLEY, Anne, BMus MMus, FRCM; British musician (keyboards), arranger, producer and composer; b. 7 May 1956. *Education:* Royal Coll. of Music, King's Coll. *Career:* pianist, Playschool (BBC TV); Founder mem. Art of Noise 1984–90, 1999–2000; solo artist, composer, producer, arranger 1990–; written with and arranged for artists, including ABC, A-Ha, Jeff Beck, Boyzone, Cher, Lloyd Cole, Phil Collins, Des'ree, Frankie Goes To Hollywood, Elton John, Tom Jones, Annie Lennox, Lord of the Dance, Paul McCartney, Malcolm McLaren, Moist, Jimmy Nail, The Opera Babes, Pet Shop Boys, Pulp, Rush, S Club 7, Seal, The Spice Girls, Rod Stewart, The The, Travis, Tina Turner, Wham, Will Young; Composer-in-Residence, BBC Concert Orchestra 2001–04. *Film themes and scores:* Perfect Creature, Tristan and Isolde, Bright Young Things, A Man Apart, Lucky Break, Buster, Hiding Out, Wilt, Silence Like Glass, The Pope Must Die, The Crying Game, Knight Moves, The Miracle Maker, Felidae, When Saturday Comes, The Grotesque, The Sadness of Sex, Hollow Reed, The Full Monty (Acad. Award for Best Original Score, musical or comedy 1998, BRIT Award 1998), American History X, Pushing Tin, Monkey Bone, The Human Body, The Gathering, Tristan + Isolde. *Television themes and scores:* Jeeves and Wooster, Anna Lee, Crime Traveller, Kavanagh QC, The Key, The Perfect Blue, Donovan Quick, The Tenth Kingdom; tv commercials for Volvo, Vauxhall Astra, Reebok, Guinness. *Other compositions include:* Music and Silence (orchestral score, Celebration Concert, Royal Festival Hall) 2002, Club Classical 2 (Brixton Acad., London) 2003. *Recordings include:* albums: with The Art of Noise: (Who's Afraid Of) The Art of Noise 1984, In Visible Silence 1986, Daft 1987, In No Sense? Nonsense! 1987, The Best of The Art of Noise 1988, The Ambient Collection 1990, The Seduction of Claude Debussy 1999; solo: Songs From The Victorious City (with Jaz Coleman) 1990, Ancient and Modern 1995, A Different Light 2002, Seriously Chilled 2003; singles: with The Art of Noise: Into Battle 1983, Beat Box 1984, Close To The Edit 1985, Peter Gunn (with Duane Eddy) (Grammy Award for Best Rock Instrumental Performance 1987) 1986, Paranoimia 1986, Kiss (with Tom Jones) 1988, Art of Love 1990, Minarets and Memories 1990, Ziggarats of Cinnamon 1991. *Current Management:* c/o COOL Music Ltd, 1A Fishers Lane, Chiswick, London, W4 1RX, England. *Telephone:* (20) 8995-7766. *Fax:* (20) 8987-8996. *E-mail:* enquiries@coolmusicltd.com. *Website:* www.coolmusicltd.com; www.annedudley.co.uk.

DUFF, Hilary Ann; American singer and actor; b. 28 Sept. 1987, Houston, Tex.; d. of Bob and Susan Duff; one s. *Career:* Int. Spokesperson, 'Kids With A Cause' charity 2004. *Television:* True Women 1997, The Soul Collector 1999, Lizzie McGuire 2001-02, other appearances include: Chicago Hope 2000, George Lopez 2003, 2005, American Dreams 2003, Frasier (voice) 2004, Joan of Arcadia 2005, Ghost Whisperer 2009, Law & Order: SVU 2009, Gossip Girl 2009, Community 2010, Raising Hope 2013, Two and a Half Men 2013, Younger (lead role) 2015. *Films:* Casper Meets Wendy 1998, Human Nature 2001, Cadet Kelly 2002, Agent Cody Banks 2003, The Lizzie McGuire Movie 2003, Cheaper By the Dozen 2003, A Cinderella Story 2004, Agent Cody Banks 2: Destination London 2004, In Search of Santa (voice) 2004, The Perfect Man 2005, Cheaper By the Dozen 2 2005, Material Girls 2006, Foodfight! (voice) 2006, Outward Blonde 2006, War Inc. 2008, What Goes Up 2009, Stay Cool 2009, According to Greta 2009, Bloodworth 2011, She Wants Me 2012, Foodfight! 2012, Wings 2013, Wings: Sky Force Heroes 2014, Flock of Dudes 2015. *Recordings include:* albums: Metamorphosis 2003, Hilary Duff 2004, Most Wanted 2005, Dignity 2007, Breathe In, Breathe Out 2015. *Publications:* Elixir 2010, Devoted 2011, True 2013. *Honours:* Young Artist Award for Best Performance in a TV Movie or Pilot (Supporting Young Actress) 1999, Kids' Choice Award for Favorite Female Singer 2004, World Music Award for Best New Female Artist 2004. *Address:* c/o RCA Records, RCA Music Group, 550 Madison Avenue, #6, New York, 10022, USA (office). *Telephone:* (212) 930-8000 (office). *Website:* www.rcarecords.com (office); www.hilaryduff.com (home).

DUFFIN, Graeme Ian; British musician (guitar); b. 28 Feb. 1956, Glasgow; m. Pamela Duffin 1978; one s. one d. *Education:* HNC, Medical Laboratory Science (Biochemistry), piano training. *Career:* mem. folk group New Celeste 1977–80; unofficial mem. Wet Wet Wet 1985–; major tours in UK, Europe, USA, Far East and Australia; co-f. The Foundry Music Lab. *Recordings:* albums: Popped In Souled Out 1987, The Memphis Sessions 1988, Holding Back The River 1989, High On The Happy Side 1991, End of Part One (Greatest Hits) 1993, Picture This 1995, 10 1997, Best of British Folk Rock. *Honours:* BRIT Award for Best Newcomers 1987. *Address:* The Foundry Music Lab, Unit 2, Flemington Industrial Park, Craigneuk Street, Motherwell, ML1 2NT, Scotland (office). *Telephone:* (1698) 268833 (office). *Fax:* (1698) 268860 (office). *E-mail:* graeme@foundrymusiclab.com (office). *Website:* www.foundrymusiclab.com.

DUFFY; British singer, songwriter and actress; b. (Amy Ann Duffy), 1984, Nefyn, Wales; d. of John Duffy and Joyce Duffy (née Williams). *Career:* solo artist 2007–. *Films:* Patagonia 2010. *Recordings include:* album: Rockferry (Grammy Award for Best Pop Vocal Album 2009, BRIT Award for Best British Album 2009) 2008, Endlessly 2010. *Honours:* MOJO Award for Song of the Year (for Mercy) 2008, Q Award for Best Breakthrough Act 2008, BRIT Awards for Best British Breakthrough Act, for Best British Female Solo Artist 2009, Ivor Novello/PRS Award for Most Performed Work (for Mercy) 2009. *Website:* www.iamduffy.com.

DUFFY, Billy; British musician (guitar); b. 12 May 1959, Manchester, England. *Career:* guitarist, Theatre of Hate; The Cult (fmrly Southern Death Cult and Death Cult) 1983–; world-wide tours; concerts with: Bauhaus, Billy Idol, Big Country, Metallica, Guns N' Roses, Lenny Kravitz; concerts include: Futurama Festival, Leeds 1983, A Gathering of The Tribes, USA 1990, Cult In The Park '92 Festival, Finsbury Park, London 1992, Guns N' Roses concert, Milton Keynes 1993. *Recordings include:* albums: Southern Death Cult 1983, Dreamtime 1984, Love 1985, Electric 1987, Sonic Temple 1989, Ceremony 1991, Pure Cult 1993, The Cult 1994, Ghost Dance 1996, High Octane Cult 1996, Cream 1996, Forever Mod 1998, Ten Years After 1998, Celebrity Deathmatch 1999, Zen Mafia 1999, Beyond Good and Evil 2001, Born Into This 2007, City Of Fire 2009, Choice of Weapon 2012. *Current Management:* c/o Tom Vitorino Management Inc., 11606 Vimy Road, Granada Hills, CA 91344, USA. *Telephone:* (818) 368-9060. *Fax:* (818) 368-9061. *Website:* www.billyduffy.com.

DUFFY, Keith Peter Thomas John; Irish singer, music manager and actor; b. 1 Oct. 1974, Dublin; m. Lisa Smith; one s. *Career:* mem., Boyzone 1993–2001, 2007–; co-man. band, Broken Hill 2002–. *Television:* presenter FBi (BBC) 2000, presenter The Race (ITV 2) 2001, participated in Celebrity Big Brother (Channel 4) 2001, actor Coronation Street (ITV 1) 2002–05. *Film appearance:* The Gift 2001. *Recordings include:* albums: Said And Done 1995, A Different Beat 1996, Where We Belong 1998, By Request 1999, Back Again... No Matter What 2008, Brother 2010. *Current Management:* Lisa Richard Agency, 108 Upper Leeson Street, Dublin 4, Ireland. *Telephone:* (1) 6375000. *Fax:* (1) 6671256. *E-mail:* info@lisarichards.ie. *Website:* www.lisarichards.ie. *E-mail:* keith@officialkeithduffy.com. *Website:* www.officialkeithduffy.com.

DUFFY, Martin; British musician (keyboards); b. Birmingham. *Career:* mem. Primal Scream 1984–; session work with Felt, Beth Orton, Dr John, Charlatans, Shack; numerous tours and festival appearances. *Recordings include:* albums: Sonic Flower Groove 1987, Primal Scream 1989, Screamadelica (Mercury Music Prize 1992) 1991, Give Out But Don't Give Up 1994, Vanishing Point 1997, EchoDek 1997, Xtrmntr 2000, Evil Heat 2002, Dirty Hits 2003, Shoot Speed (More Dirty Hits) 2004, Riot City Blues 2006, Beautiful Future 2008, More Light 2013. *Honours:* Q Groundbreaker Award 2006, NME Godlike Genius Award 2007. *Current Management:* c/o G. R. Management Ltd, 974 Pollockshaws Road, Glasgow, G41 2HA, Scotland. *Telephone:* (141) 632-1111. *Website:* www.primalscream.net.

DUFFY, Paul; British musician (bass guitar, saxophone); b. Hoylake, Wirral, England. *Education:* Hilbre High School, Hoylake. *Career:* Founder mem., The Coral 1996–. *Recordings include:* albums: The Coral 2002, Magic and Medicine 2003, Secret Kiss 2003, Nightfreak and the Sons of Becker 2004, The Invisible Invasion 2005, Roots and Echoes 2007, The Singles Collection 2008, Butterfly House 2010.

DUFORT, Denise; British musician (drums). *Career:* mem. heavy metal band Girlschool 1978–89; supported Motörhead on their Overkill tour; numerous tours, TV performances and hit singles; further collaborations with Motörhead; tours in Canada and USA; tour of Russia, supporting Black Sabbath; formed band Strangegirls, with Toyah, Kim McAuliffe and Enid Williams; Girlschool re-formed 1992–. *Recordings include:* albums: Demolition 1980, Hit 'N' Run 1981, Screaming Blue Murder 1982, Play Dirty 1983, Running Wild 1995, Nightmare At Maple Cross 1986, Take A Bite 1988, Girlschool 1992, Live 1995, Race With The Devil (Live) 1998, Live On The King Biscuit Flower Hour 1998, Can't Keep A Good Girl Down 1999, Very Best Of Remastered 2002, 21st Anniversary: Not That Innocent 2002, Second Wave 2003, Believe 2004, Emergency/London 2005, Legacy 2008, Hit and Run Revisited 2011. *E-mail:* girlschool@hotmail.com. *Website:* www.girlschool.co.uk.

DUJMIC, Ratko; Croatian musician (piano, violin, electronic keyboards); b. 7 Aug. 1954, Zagreb; m. Snjezana Simek-Dujmic 1990; one s. *Education:* Music Acad. *Career:* four solo television shows; world tours include Sydney Opera House, Australia; mem. Union of Professional Musicians, Soc. of Composers, Croatia. *Compositions include:* one film score; about 800 works, many compositions for children, TV series and theatre. *Recordings include:* around 90 audio and video recordings. *Honours:* fourth and sixth places 1987, 1988, winner 1989 Eurovision Song Contest. *Address:* LL Maksimirsko Naselje I/V, 41000 Zagreb, Croatia.

DUKES, Rebecca W. (Becky), BA; American singer, musician (piano) and songwriter; b. 21 Nov. 1934, Durham; m. Charles A. Dukes Jr 1955; two s. one d. *Education:* Duke Univ.; studied singing with Todd Duncan. *Career:* numerous stage and piano performances including Kennedy Center, Normandie Farm Lounge, Dulles Holiday Inn, The Castle, Thompson's Restaurant, Ocean City, Capitol Hill Club, Post Office Pavilion, Chateau de la Gesse, Decorator's Show House for Nat. Symphony Orchestra, Strathmore Mansion, numerous hotels; feature artist for Philharmonic sponsored concert; per-

formed with USA Navy Band commemorating 200 years of balloon flight in America; two cable specials 1990s; Pres., R.W. DukesMusic Inc.; mem. ASCAP, NARAS, NSAI, SAW. *Compositions include:* over 100 individual compositions recorded. *Recordings include:* Alive 1992, Rainbow 1994, Borrow the Sun 1995, Almost Country 1999, Rhapsody of Moods 2000. *Publications include:* poetry published in several editions, 1992–94. *Honours:* Hon. degree in Fine Arts; ASCAP Awards for Pop Writing 1994–2007, numerous awards, Mid-Atlantic Song Contest 1984–92, American Women Composers' Song Contest Award, Billboard Award, For the Children of the World 1996. *Address:* 7111 Pony Trail, Hyattsville, MD 20782, USA (home). *Telephone:* (301) 277-5514 (home). *Fax:* (301) 927-4073 (home). *E-mail:* bd@beckydukesmusic.com (office). *Website:* www.beckydukesmusic.com.

DULFER, Candy; Dutch musician (saxophone); b. 19 Sept. 1969, Amsterdam. *Career:* first recording with father Hans Dulfer, aged 11; Founder, jazz-funk group Funky Stuff, aged 15; played with Madonna, Prince, Van Morrison, Aretha Franklin, Pink Floyd, Dave Stewart. *Recordings include:* albums with Funky Stuff; solo albums: Saxuality 1991, Sax-A-Go-Go 1994, Big Girl 1996, For the Love of You 1997, What Does it Take 1999, Girls Night Out 2001, Right in My Soul 2003, Funked Up & Chilled Out 2009, Crazy 2011. *Honours:* Golden Harp for outstanding contributions to music in the Netherlands 2008. *E-mail:* management@candydulfer.nl. *Website:* www.candydulfer.nl.

DUMBRECK, Allan M., BSc; British music lecturer and musician (keyboards); *Senior Lecturer / Subject Leader Commercial Music, University of the West of Scotland;* b. 11 March 1961, Edinburgh, Scotland; partner Deidre Kelly; two s. *Education:* Univ. of Edinburgh. *Career:* keyboard player, Big Dish 1986–87, Horse 1988–89; Lecturer, Jewel and Esk Valley Coll. 1986–91, North Glasgow Coll. 1991–98, Univ. of Westminster 1998–99, James Watt Coll. 1999–2001; Sr Lecturer/ Subject Leader Commercial Music, Univ. of the West of Scotland (fmrly Paisley Univ.) 2001–; started working with Ariadne Publications 1998–, apptd CEO Ariadne Interactive 2006; est. HND Music, Performance and Promotion, NGM Records 1993, NGM Publishing 1994; Chair. Sound Advice 2002; mem. PRS. *Recordings include:* The Same Sky, Horse 1990, Rifferama, Thrum 1994. *Publications include:* Music Education Directory (ed. and compiler) 1996–. *Address:* School of Creative Industries, University of the West of Scotland, Ayr Campus, University Avenue, Ayr, KA8 0SX, Scotland (office). *E-mail:* allan.dumbreck@uws.ac.uk (office). *Website:* www.uws.ac.uk (office).

DUMONT, Tom; American musician (guitar); b. 11 Jan. 1968, Los Angeles, CA. *Education:* Orange Coast Coll. *Career:* mem., No Doubt 1988–. *Recordings:* albums: No Doubt 1992, Beacon Street Collection 1994, Tragic Kingdom 1995, Return Of Saturn 2000, Rock Steady 2001, Everything In Time 2004, Push and Shove 2012; singles: Just A Girl 1995, Don't Speak 1997, New 1999, Ex-Girlfriend 2000, Simple Kind Of Life 2000, Bathwater 2000, Hey Baby 2001, Hella Good 2002, Tour (EP) 2002, Underneath It All (Grammy Award for best performance by a duo or group with vocal 2004) 2002. *Address:* c/o Interscope Records, 2220 Colorado Ave, Santa Monica, CA 90404, USA. *Website:* www.nodoubt.com; www.tomdumont.com.

DUNBAR, (Lowell Fillmore) Sly; Jamaican reggae musician (drums) and producer; b. 10 May 1952, Kingston. *Career:* played with The Upsetter, Skin Flesh and Bones, The Revolutionaries; mem. house band, Channel One label; mem. rhythm partnership, Sly and Robbie (with Robbie Shakespeare) 1975–; co-f. record label, Taxi 1980; prolific session musician with numerous artists, including Peter Tosh, Bunny Wailer, Black Uhuru, Grace Jones, Bob Dylan, Ian Dury, Joan Armatrading, Buju Banton, Beenie Man, Dennis Brown, Jimmy Cliff, Mikey Dread, Gregory Isaacs, King Tubby, The Mighty Diamonds, Sugar Minott, U-Roy; tours with Black Uhuru. *Recordings include:* albums: solo: Simple Sly Man 1978, Sly Wicked and Slick 1979, Sly-Go-Ville 1982; with Sly and Robbie: Sly and Robbie Present Taxi 1981, A Dub Extravaganza 1984, Language Barrier 1985, Sly and Robbie Meet King Tubby 1985, The Sound of Taxi Vol. 1, Vol. 2 1986, Rhythm Killers 1987, Taxi Fare 1987, Uhuru In Dub 1987, The Summit 1988, Hardcore Dub 1989, Silent Assassin 1990, Remember Precious Times 1993, Mambo Taxi 1997, Hail Up Taxi 2 1998, Taxi Christmas 1998, Fatigue Chic 1999, Massive 1999, Dub Fire 2000, In Good Company 2001, Version Born 2004, Inspiration Information Vol. 1 2008.

DUNCAN, Zélia; Brazilian singer and musician; b. 28 Oct. 1964, Niterói. *Career:* fmr backing vocalist for singer José Augusto, and DJ for Rádio Fluminense; successful career in Brazil as singer-songwriter 1990–; released debut album Outra Luz 1990, recorded track on Dorival Caymmi songbook album 1992, toured Japan and Europe and played concerts in New York 1997; joined re-formed Os Mutantes as vocalist 2006; left band to concentrate on solo work 2007. *Recordings include:* albums: Outra Luz 1990, Zélia Duncan 1994, Intimidade 1996, Acesso 1998, Sortimento 2001, Sortimento Vivo 2002, Eu me Transformo em outras 2004, Pré-pós-tudo-Bossa-Band 2005, Pelo Sabor do Gesto 2009, Tudo Esclarecido 2012; with Os Mutantes: Mutantes Ao Vivo: Barbican Theatre, Londres 2006. *Honours:* APCA prize for Best Singer 1996. *Current Management:* Malab, rua Cristina, 1213, Santo Antônio, 30330-130, Belo Horizonte, MG, Brazil. *E-mail:* malab@malab.com.br. *Website:* www.malab.com.br; www2.uol.com.br/zeliaduncan.

DUNCKEL, Jean-Benoît, (Darkel); French producer and musician (keyboards); b. Versailles. *Education:* Conservatoire, Paris. *Career:* fmr mem., Orange; formed duo, Air 1995–; collaborations with Jean Jacques Perrey,

Francoise Hardy, Alex Gopher, Gordon Tracks; solo project as Darkel 2006–. *Recordings include:* albums: with Air: Moon Safari 1997, The Virgin Suicides (film soundtrack) 1999, Premiers Symptoms (compilation) 1999, 10,000 Hz Legend 2001, City Reading (backing music to Alessandro Baricco's novel, City) 2003, Talkie Walkie 2004, Pocket Symphony 2007, Love 2 2009, Le voyage dans la lune 2012; as Darkel: Darkel 2006. *Address:* c/o EMI Music France, 118 rue de Mont-Cenis, 75891 Paris, France (office). *E-mail:* reponse@emi-music.fr (office). *Website:* www.aircheology.com.

DUNDAS, (Tobias James) Toby; Australian drummer and songwriter. *Education:* Wesley Coll., Melbourne. *Career:* mem. The Temper Trap 2005–; released debut EP The Temper Trap 2006; group relocated to London 2008; released debut album 2009; int. tours. *Recordings:* albums: with The Temper Trap: Conditions 2009, The Temper Trap (ARIA Music Award for Best Rock Album 2012) 2012. *Honours:* with The Temper Trap: ARIA Music Awards for Best Group 2010, 2012, for Most Popular Australian Single (for Sweet Disposition) 2010. *Current Management:* c/o Lunatic Entertainment, Level 1, 490 Crown Street, Surry Hills, NSW 2010, Australia. *E-mail:* info@lunaticentertainment.com. *Website:* www.lunaticentertainment.com. *Address:* c/o Liberation Music, 9 Dundas Lane, Albert Park, Vic. 3206, Australia (office). *E-mail:* info@liberationmusic.net (office). *Website:* www.liberationmusic.net (office); www.thetempertrap.com.

DUNHAM, Aubrey, BA; American singer, blues musician (saxophone), writer, arranger and producer; b. Houston, Tex. *Education:* Texas Southern Univ. *Career:* tours, performances with artists including Wilton Felder, Johnny Clyde Copeland, The O'Jays, The Temptations, Roy Head, Hank Crawford; Leader, own bands, Aubrey Dunham and The Party Machine, Bluesdog, The Saxist; f. A.D. Records 1982; mem. Houston Blues Soc. *Recordings include:* albums: with Aubrey Dunham and The Party Machine: Now I'm Singing The Blues 1994; Aubrey Dunham: The Saxist 1988, I Feel Your Love (A Special Tribute to Johnny Clyde Copeland) 1999, For Lovers Only 2003. *Address:* A.D. Records and Productions, PO Box 8402, Houston, TX 77288, USA (office). *Telephone:* (713) 675-7802 (office). *Fax:* (713) 675-7802 (office). *E-mail:* aubrey@bluesdog.com (office); bluesdogs@juno.com (home). *Website:* www.bluesdog.com (office).

DUNKELMAN, Stephan; Belgian composer; b. 7 May 1956, Brussels; m.; one s. one d. *Education:* Conservatoire Royal de Musique, Brussels. *Career:* mem. SACEM, SACD, ACSR, CEC. *Compositions for dance:* duet piece by Olga de Soto 1997, En Jeu 1998; solo piece by Fernando Martin 1999, In Spite of Wishing and Wanting 1999, Motion Pictures 2002, Sans Queues ni Têtes 2002, Aphorismes Géométriques 2004. *Recordings include:* Acousnatica, Electro-clip Bis, En Jeu, Métamorphoses 2000, Rhizomes, Scorched Lips, I Hate Electronics, Winner Takes All. *Honours:* Stockholm Electronic Arts Award for Metharcana 1998. *E-mail:* stephan.dunkelman@gmail.com. *Website:* www.stephandunkelman.com.

DUNLOP, Andy; British musician (guitar); b. 16 March 1972, Scotland. *Career:* mem. Travis 1997–; numerous tours, festivals and television appearances. *Recordings include:* albums: Good Feeling 1997, The Man Who 1999, The Invisible Band 2001, 12 Memories 2003, The Boy With No Name 2007, Ode to J. Smith 2008. *Honours:* Q Magazine Award for Best Single 1999, Select Magazine Award for Album of the Year 1999, BRIT Awards for Best British Group 2000, 2002, Best British Album 2000. *Current Management:* c/o Wildlife Entertainment, Unit F, 21 Heathmans Road, London SW6 4TJ, England. *Telephone:* (20) 7371-7008. *Fax:* (20) 7371-7708. *E-mail:* info@wildlife-entertainment.com. *Website:* www.wildlife-entertainment.com; www.travisonline.com.

DUNLOP, Blair; British folk singer and musician (guitar); b. 11 Feb. 1992, Chesterfield, Derbyshire; s. of Ashley Hutchings. *Education:* Repton School, Derbyshire. *Career:* fmr actor as teenager; released debut solo EPs 2010, 2011; support act for Fairport Convention, Cara Dillon, Georgie Fame; succeeded father Ashley Hutchings as leader of Albion Band 2011–. *Film:* as actor: Charlie and the Chocolate Factory 2005. *Television:* as actor: Rocket Man 2005. *Recordings:* with the Albion Band: The Vice of the People 2012; solo: Blight and Blossom 2012. *Honours:* BBC Radio 2 Folk Horizon Award 2013. *Current Management:* c/o John Hart Music, Unit 14, No. 1 Mill, The Wharf, Shardlow, Derby, DE72 2GH, England. *Telephone:* (1332) 793497. *E-mail:* johnhartmusic@mac.com. *E-mail:* band@thealbionband.com. *Website:* www.thealbionband.com; blairdunlop.com.

DUNMALL, Paul Norman; British musician (saxophones, bass clarinet, woodwind, bagpipes); b. 6 May 1953, London. *Education:* Blackheath Conservatoire. *Career:* tours, Europe with Marsupilami 1970–71, USA with Blue Aquarius 1972–74, USA/Europe tour with Johnny Guitar Watson; Founder-mem. Spirit Level 1979, Tenor Tonic 1985; joined London Jazz Composers Orchestra 1989; co-f. Mujician 1990; est. record label, Duns Limited Edition 2000; mem. PRS, MCPS. *Recordings include:* Soliloquy 1986, The Journey (Mujician) 1990, Poem about the Hero (Mujician) 1994, Early October (British Saxophone Quartet) 1995, Desire and Liberation (Paul Dunmall Octet) 1996, Colours Fulfilled (Mujician) 1997, Shooters Hill (Paul Dunmall Sextet) 1998, Solo Bagpipes 1999, The Great Divide (Paul Dunmall Octet) 2000, Skirting the River Road: Songs and Settings of Whitman Blake and Vaughan Robin Williamson 2001, Spacetime (Mujician) 2001, Bridging: The Great Divide Live (Paul Dunmall Octet) 2002, I Wish You Peace (Paul Dunmall Moksha Big Band) 2003, Love, Warmth and Compassion (Paul Dunmall Quartet) 2004, There's No Going Back Now (Mujician) 2005, Music

on Two Pianos (with Philip Gibbs) 2006, Intervention (with Neil McGovern) 2012; numerous collaborations with various artists. *Honours:* Best Soloist, Dunkirk Jazz Festival 1979. *Telephone:* (1886) 832046 (office). *E-mail:* dunmallpaul@gmail.com (office). *Website:* www.pauldunmall.com.

DUNN, Gary Michael; British musician (guitar); b. 7 March 1960, Sunderland. *Education:* Leeds Metropolitan Univ. *Career:* joined band The Daintees 1986; tours of Europe and USA, including Glastonbury Festival, Reading Festival; appearances at major concert halls including Dominion Theatre, Sadler's Wells, Town and Country Club; TV and radio appearances; currently with Aaron Bayley Band; Visiting Lecturer, City of Sunderland Coll. Shiney Row Centre, Houghton-le-Spring; mem. Musicians' Union, PRS, MCPS. *Recordings include:* albums with: Martin Stephenson and the Dainties: Boat To Bolivia, Gladsome Humour and Blue, Salutation Road and The Boys Heart. *Website:* www.aaronbayleyband.co.uk.

DUNN, Holly S., BS; American singer, songwriter and artist; b. 22 Aug. 1957, San Antonio, Tex. *Education:* Abilene Christian Univ. *Career:* solo artist 1985–; hosted morning radio shows, WWWW in Detroit 1997, Opry Backstage on TNN 2000–01; appeared on numerous country music specials and award shows; mem. AFTRA, AFM, NARAS. *Compositions include:* Daddy's Hands, You Really Had Me Going, Love Someone Like Me, Are You Ever Gonna Love Me, Only When I Love, Strangers Again. *Recordings include:* albums: Holly Dunn 1986, Cornerstone 1987, Across The Rio Grande 1988, The Blue Rose of Texas 1989, Heart Full of Love 1990, Milestones 1991, Getting It Dunn 1992, Life and Love and All The Stages 1996, Leave One Bridge Standing 1997, Full Circle 2003. *Honours:* Acad. of Country Music Award 1986, Country Music Foundation Horizon Award. *Address:* PO Box 1203, Salado, TX 76571, USA. *E-mail:* admin@hollydunn.com. *Website:* www.hollydunn.com.

DUNN, Ronnie Gene; American country singer, producer and songwriter; b. 1 June 1953, Coleman, Tex. *Career:* mem., duo Brooks & Dunn (with Kix Brooks) 1988–2010. *Compositions include:* Boot Scootin' Boogie, Brand New Man, Darned If I Don't-Danged If I Do, Hard Workin' Man, He's Got You, Honky Tonk Truth, I Can't Get Over You, I'll Never Forgive My Heart, A Man This Lonely, Little Miss Honky Tonk, My Next Broken Heart, Neon Moon, You'll Always Be Loved By Me, She's Not The Cheatin' Kind, She Used To Be Mine, That Ain't No Way To Go, We'll Burn That Bridge, Whiskey Under The Bridge, You're Gonna Miss Me When I'm Gone. *Recordings include:* albums as Brooks & Dunn: Brand New Man 1991, Hard Workin' Man 1993, Waitin' On Sundown 1994, Borderline 1996, If You See Her 1998, Tight Rope 1999, Steers and Stripes 2001, It Won't Be Christmas Without You 2002, Red Dirt Road 2003, Hillbilly Deluxe 2005, Cowboy Town 2007; solo: Ronnie Dunn 2011. *Honours:* CMA Vocal Duo of the Year 1993–98, 2004, 2005, 2006, ACM Awards for Best Vocal Duo 2004, 2005, 2006, 2007, 2010, for Song of the Year (for Believe) 2006, four American Music Awards for Favorite Country Band, including 2005, CMA Award for Single of the Year, Song of the Year (jtly), Music Video of the Year (all for Believe) 2006, 50th Anniversary Milestone Award, Acad. of Country Music (with Kix Brooks) 2015. *Address:* c/o Little Will-E Records, 16th Avenue, Nashville, TN 37212, USA (office). *Website:* www.littlewill-erecords.com.

DUPONT, Hubert; French jazz musician (contrebass) and composer; b. 5 May 1959, Versailles; m. 1990; one s. *Career:* played with Steve Lacy, Glenn Ferris, Mathieu Michel, Harold Land, Robin Eubanks, Stefano Di Battista, Noël Akchoté, George Brown, Tommy Smith, Steve Potts, Laurent De Wilde, Le Marmite Infernale (ARFI), Mathias Rüegg, Paolo Fresu, Benoit Delbecq, Guillaume Orti, Hervé Samb, Rudresh Mahanthappa, Yvan Robilliard, Chander Sardjoe, Brice Wassy, Naïssam Jalal, Nelson Veras, Youssef Hbeisch; mem. Collectif HASK, Union des Musiciens de Jazz (UMJ). *Recordings:* A L'Envers 1994, Altissimo 1995, Pression 1995, Sérénade 1997, Jellyfishing 1999, Jyväskylä 2001, Ultraboles (solo) 2005, Spider's Dance 2007, The Bay Window 2007, Sawadu 2010, Jasmim 2013. *Address:* Ultrabolic, 15 rue Kléber, 93100 Montreuil, France. *Telephone:* 1-48-59-39-74. *E-mail:* hubert@ultrabolic.com. *Website:* www.ultrabolic.com; www.hubertdupont.com.

DUPRI, Jermaine (JD); American producer, singer and songwriter; *President, Island Records Urban Music;* b. 23 Sept. 1973, Atlanta, GA. *Career:* performed with Diana Ross aged nine years; toured USA as teenager; began producing aged 14; f. So So Def Recordings 1989; produced first platinum album (Totally Krossed Out, by Kriss Kross) 1991; Producer and Head of urban music division, Virgin Records 2005–06; Pres. of urban division, Island Records Urban Music 2007–; has worked with artists, including Aaliyah, Mariah Carey, Run DMC, TLC, Usher, Alicia Keys, Janet Jackson, Jay-Z, Aretha Franklin, Xscape, Da Brat, Bow Wow, Snoop Dogg, Monica. *Recordings include:* albums: Life in 1472 1998, Instructions 2001. *Honours:* Grammy Award 2006, Quincy Jones Award for Outstanding Career Achievement, Soul Train Awards 2007. *Current Management:* Artistic Control Management, 685 Lambert Drive NE, Atlanta, GA 30324, USA. *Telephone:* (404) 733-5511 (office). *Fax:* (404) 733-5512 (office). *Website:* www.jermainedupri.com.

DURAL, Stanley 'Buckwheat', Jr; American musician (zydeco, accordion); b. 14 Nov. 1947, Lafayette, La; m. Bernite Dural. *Career:* professional musician from age 9; formed Buckwheat and the Hitchikers 1970s; joined 'father of zydeco' Clifton Chenier 1978–80; formed Buckwheat Zydeco 1979–; signed to Island Records 1987 (first zydeco artist on major record label). *Recordings include:* albums: Turning Point 1983, Waitin' For My Ya Ya 1985,

On a Night Like This 1987, Taking it Home 1988, Where There's Smoke, there's Fire 1990, On Track 1992, Choo Choo Boogaloo 1994, Five Card Stud 1994, Trouble 1999, Jackpot 2005, Lay Your Burden Down (Grammy Award for Best Zydeco or Cajun Music Album 2010) 2009, Let The Good Times Roll: Essential Recordings 2009; also recorded with artists including Eric Clapton, Willie Nelson, Dwight Yoakam, Keith Richards. *E-mail:* zydecobuck@aol.com. *Website:* www.buckwheatzydeco.com.

DURHAM, Judith, AM, AMusA; Australian singer, songwriter and musician (piano, tambourine); b. 3 July 1943, Melbourne; m. Ron Edgeworth 1969 (died 1994). *Education:* Royal Melbourne Inst. of Tech., Melbourne Univ. with Ronald Farren Price. *Career:* lead singer of folk pop group, The Seekers –1968; numerous live concerts, TV appearances; solo artist 1967–; patron, Motor Neurone Disease Asscn. *Compositions include:* Australia Land of Today, Gotta Be Rainbows (musical), Colours of My Life, One World Love, Calling Me Home, It's Hard to Leave. *Recordings include:* albums: with The Seekers: Future Road 1997, seven other albums; solo: Mona Lisas 1996, Hot Jazz Duo 2001, Onto Your Dream 2000, Epiphany 2011, Colours of My Life 2011, The Australian Cities Suite 2012. *Honours:* Australian of the Year (with The Seekers) 1967. *Current Management:* c/o Greg Thomas, Musicoast Pty Limited, PO Box 555, Melbourne, Vic. 3141, Australia. *Fax:* (1) 3525-0344. *E-mail:* musicoast@musicoast.com. *Website:* www.judithdurham.com.

DURITZ, Adam; American singer and musician (piano); b. 1 Aug. 1964, Baltimore, MD. *Career:* formed acoustic duo with David Bryson, joined by others to form Counting Crows 1993–; numerous tours and live appearances. *Recordings include:* albums: August & Everything After 1993, Recovering the Satellites 1996, Across a Wire: Live in New York 1998, This Desert Life 1999, Hard Candy 2002, Saturday Nights and Sunday Mornings 2008, Underwater Sunshine 2012, Somewhere Under Wonderland 2014. *Current Management:* International Talent Booking, First Floor, Ariel House, 74a Charlotte Street, London, W1T 4QJ, England. *Telephone:* (20) 7637-6979. *Fax:* (20) 7637-6978. *E-mail:* mail@itb.co.uk. *Website:* www.countingcrows.com.

DURRANT, Clare Joanne Mary, (Ireti), BMus; British musician (keyboards, percussion, violin, guitar) and singer; b. 2 Dec. 1962, Southport. *Education:* Lancaster Univ., Salford Univ. Coll. with John Hammond, Tommy Odueso, Wadada, Clare Hogan-Taylor. *Career:* fmr keyboard player for Suns of Arqa (as Ireti); concerts include Womad Festival, Phoenix Festival, Hit The North, BBC Radio session; set up Ireti Percussion workshops; formed Otherworld 1992; Lecturer, Lowestoft Coll. 2000–05; composer and sound designer. *Recordings include:* albums: with Otherworld: Messages; also tracks on compilations; with Suns of Arqa as Ireti: Hey Jagunath; Bhoopali (track part of BBC Radio 5 session Hit The North). *Website:* soundcloud.com/dreamtime -music-1.

DURRANT, Richard; British musician (guitar, mandolin, banjo, double bass, bodhran); b. 2 Nov. 1962, Brighton; m. Louise Durrant; two d. one s. *Education:* Royal Coll. of Music. *Career:* debut, Purcell Room, London 1986; prolific concert guitarist and recording artist; composer of concert and television music; mem. PRS, MCPS, MU. *Compositions include:* Acoustic Rain, A Lowland Cinderella, The Rucenitsa Quartet; Exploring the Deep, The Early Learning Sonata. *Recordings include:* Guitar Latina, The Music of Mario Castelnuovo-Tedesco, Pandora, Soul Providence 2005. *E-mail:* marketing@richard-durrant.com. *Website:* www.richard-durrant.com.

DURST, (William Frederick) Fred; American singer, record company executive, producer and film director; b. 20 Aug. 1970, Gastonia, North Carolina; m. 1990 (divorced); one s. one d. *Career:* Sr Vice-Pres. of A&R, Interscope Records; Founder and Owner, Flawless Records; Founder mem., Limp Bizkit 1994–; solo artist 2001–. *Recordings include:* albums: Three Dollar Bill Y'All 1997, Significant Other 1999, Chocolate Starfish And The Hotdog Flavored Water 2000, New Old Songs 2001, Bipolar 2003, Results May Vary 2003, The Unquestionable Truth (Part 1) 2005, Gold Cobra 2010. *Films directed include:* The Education of Charlie Banks 2007, The Longshots 2008. *Honours:* American Music Award for Favorite Alternative Artist 2002. *Current Management:* c/o Peter Katsis, The Firm, 9100 Wilshire Blvd, Beverly Hills, CA 90212, USA. *Website:* www.limpbizkit.com.

DUTIRO, Chartwell, MMus; Zimbabwean singer, musician (mbira, saxophone, hosho) and songwriter; b. 26 Dec. 1957, Bindura. *Education:* School of Oriental and African Studies, Univ. of London. *Career:* played mbira in traditional ceremonies from early teens; mem. Rhodesia Prison Band, Thomas Mapfumo's Blacks Unlimited 1988–94; formed Spirit Talk Mbira; f. Mhararano (first UK Mbira Acad.) 2012; teaches mbira, singing and percussion at SOAS. *Recordings include:* albums: with Thomas Mapfumo: Zimbabwe – Mozambique 1988, Chamunorwa 1990; with Spirit Talk Mbira: Ndonga Mahwe – Return As Spirit 1997, Nhimbe 1998, Dzoro 1999, Voices of Ancestors 2000. *E-mail:* rachel@ingoma.co.uk. *Address:* 43 Tudor Road, Newton Abbot, Devon, TQ12 1HT; Mhararano Mbira Academy, Dartington Space, Dartington Hall, Totnes, TQ9 6EL, England (office). *Telephone:* (16) 2632-4988. *E-mail:* info@chartwelldutiro.com; info@mbira-academy.org.uk (office). *Website:* chartwelldutiro.com; mbira-academy.org.uk (office).

DUTOT, Pierre; French musician (trumpet) and trumpet teacher; b. 11 June 1946, Caen; m. Catherine Groult 1975, one s. two d. *Education:* Conservatoire National Supérieur de Musique, Paris. *Career:* solo trumpeter, National Orchestra of Lyon; Prof., CNSM Lyon and CNR Bordeaux; solo concert artist; tutor, international masterclasses; mem. of numerous ensembles, including

Hexagone, Trompolis, Polygone, Jericho. *Recordings include:* 10 solo albums, recordings with Hexagone, Trompolis, Polygone. *E-mail:* academies@expomed .org. *Address:* Domaine des Cerisiers, 105 Chemin du Soyard, 69126 Brindas-Lyon, France. *Website:* www.cnsmd-lyon.fr.

DUVALL, William; American singer, songwriter and musician (guitar); b. 6 Sept. 1967, Atlanta, Ga. *Career:* founding mem. Comes with the Fall 1999–; mem. Alice in Chains 2002–. *Recordings include:* albums: with Comes With the Fall: Comes With the Fall 2000, The Year is One 2001, The Reckoning 2006, Beyond the Last Light 2007; with Alice in Chains: Black Gives Way to Blue 2009. *Current Management:* Velvet Hammer Management, 9014 Melrose Avenue, West Hollywood, CA 90069, USA. *Telephone:* (310) 657-6161. *Fax:* (310) 657-0310. *Website:* www.velvethammer.net. *E-mail:* contact@ comeswiththefall.com (office). *Website:* www.comeswiththefall.com; www .aliceinchains.com.

DUVIVIER, Jérôme; French jazz singer; b. 9 Oct. 1965, St Cloud. *Education:* studied with Stephanie Crawford, Michelle Hendricks. *Career:* concerts in jazz clubs, including Le Sunset, Le Petit Journal Montparnasse; currently jazz vocal teacher at Conservatoire de Lyon, Voix sur Rhône (school he founded in 1999); mem. Jazz on the Blocks (French Jazz Singers' Asscn). *Recordings include:* Un Effet Boeuf, L'Ennui, Courtoisies, Epilogue. *Honours:* Prix de la SACEM, Crest Festival. *E-mail:* voixsurrhone@free.fr. *Website:* voixsurrhone .free.fr.

DVORAK, Jim, BMus; American/British musician (trumpet), composer and teacher; b. 16 Dec. 1948, Brooklyn, New York. *Education:* Eastman School of Music. *Career:* regular int. jazz festivals and concert tours; collaborations with South African musicians, including Brotherhood of Breath, District Six, Zila 1970s–80s; also played with Dreamtime, In Cahoots, Dedication Orchestra, Ian Shaw, Leanne Carrol, Jacqui Dankworth, poet John Fry, Annabel Lamb, Research, Harry Moscoe, Elton Dean, Joe Gallivan, Mama Quartetto, Gland, Stanislav Sojka, Gasoline Band, Eric Mingus, Wally Brill, Maeirando; leader of own band, Bardo State Orchestra; workshop leader with Community Music, London; mem. PRS, Composers' Guild. *Compositions include:* score for jazz drama Animal Farm 1979, score for Kosh Theatre Company's production, The Jago (co-writer) 1983. *Honours:* Greater London Arts Young Jazz Musician's Award 1976. *Address:* 43B Mulkern Road, London, N19 3HQ, England (home). *Telephone:* (20) 7281-1153 (home).

DVORSKY, Petr, (Mr PD); Czech musician (double bass); b. 29 June 1966; m. Madla Vyhnánková. *Education:* Technical Coll. Motol, Prague, Jaroslav Jezek Conservatory, private studies with Vaclav Fuka, Jan Kment and Jiri Valenta. *Career:* Festival Pragues Spring 1994, Brecon Jazz Festival 1996, Festival Liege, Belgium 1998; Dir Summer Jazz Workshop, Prague 2004–05; mem. Radio Prague Bigband 2002–, Miriam Bayle Band, Elena Suchankova & Jocose Jazz, Vibe Fantasy of Radek Krampl, Infinite Q, James Harries, Emil Viklický, Petr Dvorský Trio, Adam Tvrdý Trio, Czech Radio Bigband; mem. Cttee., Int. Prague Summer Jazz Workshop 2005–06. *Recordings:* The Four: Space and Rhythm; Stever Houben, Buhemia After Dark; Roman Pokorny, Jazz Perception; Najponk Trio, Autumn In New York; Jaroslav Jakobovic/ Randy Brecker: Jazz at the Castle. *Honours:* First Prize, Int. Jazz Festival, Karlovy Vary 1990, Third Prize, Jazz Jr Competition, Kraków, Poland 1992, named by The Czech Jazz Soc. as a Talent of the Year 2001, 2002, 2003. *Address:* 120 00 Prague 2, Czech Republic. *Telephone:* 603-289172 (mobile). *E-mail:* dvorsky@volny.cz. *Website:* www.petrdvorsky.cz.

DVORZAK, Zlatko; Croatian musician (piano), composer, conductor, arranger and teacher; b. 5 March 1939, Zagreb; m. Gordana Dvorzak; Oct. 1970; one s. one d. *Education:* Zagreb Musical Acad. *Career:* tours of Poland, Bulgaria, Russia, Hungary, Austria, Germany 1961–76; played and recorded with: Ernie Wilkins, Clark Terry, Art Farmer, Albert Mangelsdorff, Kai Winding, John Lewis, Bosco Petrovic, Stan Getz, Bud Shank, Al Porcino, Lee Harper, Sal Nistico, Gianni Basso, Ozren Depolo, Dusko Gojkovic, Johnny Griffin; also performed music for radio and television; mem. Croatian Composers' Soc., Orchestras Soc., Jazz Club, Zagreb. *Compositions include:* Revue, Amoroso, Clarinetorama, Black Street, All That Swing, Discopathia, Fender Express, Mr Hammond, Trumpet Swing, Jazz Concertino for String Quartet and Jazz Sextet, Croatian Folk Motives. *Recordings include:* with BP Convention Big Band: Blue Sunset, 1975, Green Lobster Dream 1978, Josipa Lisac and BP Convention 1975, Croatian Big Band 1977. *Honours:* First Prize, Contest for Young Pianists, Croatia 1958, Best Arrangement, Belgrade Pop Festival 1971.

DWANE, Edward James Milton (Ted); British songwriter and musician (string bass, drums, guitar); b. 15 Aug. 1984. *Education:* Univ. of West of England. *Career:* Founder-mem. Mumford & Sons 2007–, first EP release 2008, toured as support group to Laura Marling 2009, performed with Bob Dylan at Grammy Awards 2011. *Film:* Wuthering Heights (two songs for soundtrack) 2011. *Recordings:* albums: Sigh No More (Q Best New Act Award 2010, BRIT Award for British Album of the Year 2011, Billboard Music Awards for Top Rock Album and Top Alternative Album 2011) 2009, Babel (Grammy Award for Album of the Year 2013, Billboard Music Award for Top Rock Album 2013) 2012, Wilder Mind 2015; featured on: I Speak Because I Can, Laura Marling 2010, See My Friends, Ray Davies 2010. *Honours:* Australian Recording Industry Asscn Most Popular Int. Artist Award 2010, Billboard Music Award for Top Alternative Artist 2011, BRIT Award for Best British Group 2013, Ivor Novello Award for Int. Achievement (with Mumford & Sons) 2014. *Current Management:* c/o Everybody's Management, 53 Corsica Street, Highbury, London, N5 1JT, England. *Telephone:* (20) 3227-0420. *Fax:*

(20) 7226-2166. *E-mail:* info@everybody-s.com. *Website:* www.everybody-s .com; www.mumfordandsons.com.

DWECK, Sydney Stevan; American musician; b. 28 Dec. 1926, New York, NY; Divorced, 2 s. *Education:* AA, honours, Los Angeles Valley College, 1966; BA, honours, California State University at Northridge, 1968; PhD, University of Southern California, 1977. *Career:* Freelance drummer and percussionist, Broadway shows including Hello Dolly, Fiddler on the Roof, Kismet, Pajama Game; Film soundtracks include: Double Trouble, The Swinger, Made in Paris; Percussionist, TV Specials including Bob Hope, Lucille Ball, Perry Como, Fred Astaire, Perry Mason, Liberace; Albums include Stan Kenton, Freddy Martin, Jack Jones; Musical Director, artists including Debbie Reynolds, Carol Channing, Liza Minnelli, Jane Russell; Command performances for Royal Family of Monaco, England, Presidents Kennedy, Johnson, Nixon, Bush, Reagan; mem, American Federation of Musicians; Masonic lodge. *Compositions:* Scores, Altoon's Dance, 1965; Danny Thomas Show. *E-mail:* stevandweck@juno.com. *Website:* www.our-site.net/dweck.

DYE, Taylor Elizabeth; American country music singer, songwriter and guitarist; b. 18 Sept. 1995, Ada, Okla. *Career:* formed duo Sweet Aliana with Madison Marlow, renamed Maddie & Tae and relocated to Nashville. *Recordings:* album: with Maddie and Tae: Start Here 2015. *Honours:* ASCAP Country Music Award for Most Performed Song (for Girl in a Country Song) 2015, Country Music Asscn Award for Video of the Year (for Girl in a Country Song) 2015. *Address:* c/o Dot Records, Big Machine Label Group, 1219 16th Avenue South, Nashville, TN 37212, USA (office). *E-mail:* mail@bigmachine .us (office). *Website:* www.bigmachinelabelgroup.com (office); www .maddieandtae.com.

DYENS, Roland; French musician (guitar) and composer (classic-fusion style); b. 19 Oct. 1955, Tunis, Tunisia; m. Claire Fischbein 1986, one s. one d. *Education:* Ecole Normale de Musique de Paris. *Career:* concert artist playing throughout world; Guitar festivals include: Nice, Cannes, Paris, Festival du Marais (Paris), Aix En Provence, Radio France Festival, Montpellier, Midem, Printemps de Bourges, Musicora, Carrefour Mondial De La Guitare (Martinique), Liège (Belgium), Arvika (Sweden), Tichy (Poland), Estergom (Hungary), Marktoberdorf (Germany), Classical Guitar Festival of Great Britain; tours: Middle East, Indonesia, Scandinavia, Poland, Brazil; numerous television and radio shows; composer and arranger; teacher; mem. of juries of international contests including Montélimar, Geneva, Fort de France, Bari; mem. SACEM; ADAMI. *Compositions include:* Works for guitar solo, two octets, Concerto Métis (for guitar and string orchestra), Concerto En Si (for guitar and ensemble of 21 guitars). *Recordings include:* Heitor Villa-Lobos Preludes and Roland Dyens works, Hommage à Brassens with the Enesco Quartet and Roland Dyens works, Ao Vivo (jazz trio), Suite Populaire Brésilienne, Heitor Villa-Lobos (concerto for guitar and string orchestra), French Songs Vols 1 and 2, Concerto En Si (for guitar and ensemble of 21 guitars), Night and Day, Sor & Giuliani, Rodrigo: Concierto de Aranjuez; Dyens: Concerto métis. *Honours:* Grand Prix du Disque, Academie Charles-Cros. *Current Management:* Michele Libraro, Via Vito Sansonetti 64, 74017 Mottola, Italy. *Telephone:* (99) 8867361. *Fax:* (99) 8867361. *E-mail:* info@ mfmanagement.net. *Website:* www.mfmanagement.net; www.rolanddyens .com.

DYLAN, Bob; American composer, musician (guitar, piano, harmonica, autoharp) and singer; b. (Robert Allen Zimmerman), 24 May 1941, Duluth, Minn.; m. Sara Lowndes (divorced 1978); four c. one adopted d. *Education:* Univ. of Minnesota. *Career:* best known for composition and interpretation of pop, country and folk music; performer, numerous tours and concerts; devised and popularized folk-rock 1965; performed with The Band; f. new group The Traveling Wilburys 1988; host, Theme Time Radio Hour with Your Host Bob Dylan (XM Satellite Radio) 2006–; mem. American Acad. of Arts and Letters 2013–. *Films appearances:* Eat the Document, Pat Garrett and Billy the Kid, Renaldo and Clara (also directed), Hearts of Fire 1986, Concert for Bangladesh, Masked and Anonymous 2003. *Radio:* presenter weekly music programme (Deep Tracks Channel, XM) 2006–. *Recordings include:* albums: The Freewheelin' Bob Dylan 1964, Bringing It All Back Home 1965, Highway 61 Revisited 1965, Blonde On Blonde 1966, John Wesley Harding 1968, Nashville Skyline 1969, Self Portrait 1970, New Morning 1970, Planet Waves (with The Band) 1974, Before The Flood 1974, Blood On The Tracks (with The Band) 1975, Hard Rain 1976, Desire 1976, Street Legal 1978, Slow Train Coming 1979, Infidels 1983, Empire Burlesque 1985, Knocked out Loaded 1986, Down in the Groove 1988, Traveling Wilburys (with Traveling Wilburys) 1988, Dylan and the Dead (with Grateful Dead) 1989, Oh Mercy 1989, Under The Red Sky 1990 (Vol. 3) (with Traveling Wilburys) 1990, The Bootleg Series 1990, Good as I Been to You 1992, World Gone Wrong 1993,

Unplugged 1995, Time Out of Mind (Grammy Award 1998) 1997, Love and Theft 2001, Modern Times (Grammy Award for Best Contemporary Folk/ Americana Album 2007) 2006, Together Through Life 2009, Christmas in the Heart 2009, Tempest 2012, The Bootleg Series (Vol. 10): Another Self Portrait 2013, Bootleg Series Vol. 11): The Basement Tapes Complete 2014, Shadows in the Night 2015. *Publications include:* Tarantula 1966, Writings and Drawings 1973, The Songs of Bob Dylan 1966–1975 1976, Lyrics 1962–1985 1986, Drawn Blank 1994, Highway 61 Revisited (interactive CD-ROM), Chronicles: Volume One (memoir) (Quill Book Award for Best Biography or Memoir 2005) 2004, Lyrics 1962–2001 2005, Dylan's Inspirations 2006. *Honours:* Commdr, Ordre des Arts et des Lettres 1990, Chevalier, Legion d'honneur 2013; Hon. DMus (Princeton Univ.) 1970, (Univ. of St Andrews) 2004; Tom Paine Award 1963, Dorothy and Lillian Gish Prize 1997, Polar Music Prize 2000, Acad. Award for Best Theme Song (for Things Have Changed, from The Wonder Boys) 2002, Grammy Award for Best Solo Rock Vocal Performance (for Someday Baby) 2007, Premio Príncipe de Asturias 2007, Pulitzer Prize Special Citation 2008, Nat. Medal of Arts 2009, Presidential Medal of Freedom 2012, MusiCare Person of the Year 2015. *Current Management:* c/o Jeff Rosen, PO Box 870, Cooper Station, New York, NY 10276, USA. *Website:* www.bobdylan.com.

DYLAN, Jakob Abraham; American singer, songwriter and musician (guitar); b. 9 Dec. 1969, New York; s. of Bob Dylan and Sara Lowndes; m. Paige; three c. *Career:* mem., The Wallflowers 1990–; solo artist 2008–. *Recordings include:* albums: with The Wallflowers: The Wallflowers 1992, Bringing Down The Horse 1996, (Breach) 2000, Red Letter Days 2002, Rebel, Sweetheart 2005, Glad All Over 2012; solo: Seeing Things 2008, Women and Country 2010. *Honours:* Hon. DLitt, Idaho State Univ. 2011; Grammy Award for Best Rock Vocal Group 1997. *Current Management:* c/o Hard8 Management, 1000 Main Street, Suite 203, Nashville, TN 37206, USA. *Telephone:* (615) 262-3433. *Fax:* (615) 938-7275. *Website:* www.hard8mgt.com; www .thewallflowers.com; www.jakobdylan.com.

MS DYNAMITE; British singer; b. (Niomi McLean-Daley), 26 April 1981, London, England; partner Dwayne Seaforth; one s. *Education:* Acland Burghley School. *Career:* rap artist and MC; collaborations with Eminem, So Solid Crew; human rights and anti-war campaigner; UK tour 2002. *Recordings include:* albums: A Little Deeper (Mercury Music Prize) 2002, A Little Darker 2003, Judgement Days 2005. *Honours:* MOBO Awards, Best UK Act, Best Single, Best Newcomer 2002; BRIT Awards, Best British Female, Best British Urban Artist 2003, Emma multi-cultural award for Best British Music Act 2003. *Address:* c/o Richard Dawes, Polydor (UK), 72 Black Lion Lane, London, W6 9BE, England. *E-mail:* msdynamite@deadlymedia.co.uk. *Website:* www.msdynamite.co.uk.

DYNNESEN, Lise Kruuse; Danish musician (piano, keyboards) and composer (church organ, piano); b. 24 Dec. 1956, Copenhagen. *Education:* Royal Danish Acad. of Music. *Career:* freelance musician, composer, experimental, rhythmic music scene 1978–; bands include: Primi Band with Marilyn Mazur 1982–85, Salsanama 1988–91; mem. The Soc. of Danish Jazz Beat Folk Authors (DJBFA). *Compositions include:* Sleigh Song – Or Minea's Tale, for organ 1994. *Honours:* Scholarships from: The Art Foundation of The Danish State, The Royal Danish Acad. of Music, DJBFA. *E-mail:* ld@risbjergkirke.dk.

DÝRASON, Orri Páll; Icelandic musician (drums). *Career:* mem., Sigur Rós 2000–; numerous tours. *Recordings include:* albums: ( ) 2002, Takk... 2005, Hvarf-Heim 2007, Með Suð I Eyrum Við Spilum Endalaust 2008, Valtari 2012; DVD: Heima 2007. *Honours:* Shortlist Music Prize 2001. *Address:* c/o Smekkleysa Records, PO Box 1263, 121 Reykjavík, Iceland (office). *Website:* www.sigur-ros.com.

DYSON, John; British musician (keyboards, guitar) and music producer; b. 11 March 1948, Sheffield. *Career:* formed Wavestar (electronic music), with Dave Ward-Hunt 1983; record label folded and band split 1989; formed UK label Surreal to Real with partner/director Anthony Thrasher; mem. PRS, MU. *Recordings include:* with Wavestar: Mind Journey, Live at UKE, Moonwind, Zenith, Out of Time; solo: Evolution 1990, Aquarelle 1991, Different Values 1994, Beyond the Gates 1995, Silverbird 1995, Darklight 2009; Wavestar albums re-released on own label. *Honours:* Best Newcomer, Radio E M Show, Germany 1991. *Website:* www.johndysonmusic.com.

DZIERZANOWSKI, Udo; musician (guitar); b. 23 June 1964. *Education:* Guitar Craft, 1987. *Career:* International Touring, Europa String Choir; CD, The Starving Moon; Appearance on John Schaeffa's New Sounds Programme, New York; Local and National Radio, England, Italy and Germany. *Recordings:* The Starving Moon, 1995; Real Promo Demo, 1998. *E-mail:* info@ europastringchoir.com. *Website:* www.europastringchoir.com.

E

EALES, Geoff, MMus, PhD, LRAM; British pianist and composer; b. S Wales; s. of Horace Eales. *Education:* Cardiff Univ. *Career:* joined Joe Loss band 1977; pianist, BBC Big Band 1978–1982; worked with conductors, composers and singers including Henry Mancini, Andrew Lloyd Webber, Adelaide Hall, Tammy Wynette, Shirley Bassey, Andy Williams, Kiri Te Kanawa and Jose Carreras; performed at jazz clubs worldwide including the Blue Note Clubs in Osaka and Fukuoka, New York's Birdland, the Jazz Bakery in Los Angeles, Louisville's Jazz Factory and London's Ronnie Scott's; founder, Geoff Eales Trio 2000–, Worldwind band 2007–. *Stage work:* The Hot Shoe Show (musical assoc. and principal arranger). *Television:* Ellis Island (US mini series, tech. musical advisor) 1984. *Recordings include:* Mountains of Fire 1999, Red Letter Days 2001, Synergy 2004, Jazz Piano Legends 2007, Epicentre 2007; with Geoff Eales Trio: Facing the Muse 2002, The Homecoming 2006. *E-mail:* geoffreyeales@btinternet.com (office). *Website:* www.geoffeales.com.

EARL SIXTEEN; Jamaican songwriter, singer and record producer; b. (Earl Daley), 9 May 1958, Kingston; two s. *Career:* producer for L. Perry, Mikey Dread, Derrick Harriott, Neil Frazer, Douglas; soundtrack of Judge Dredd with Leftfield; concerts and tours; mem. Performing Rights Soc., Musicians' Union, MCPS. *Compositions include:* Love is a Feeling (Studio One), Release the Pressure. *Recordings include:* solo albums: Reggae Sound 1981, Julia 1982, Songs For A Reason 1983, Songs Of Love And Hardship 1984, Babylon Walls 1992, Steppin' Out 1997, Wondrous Works 1997, Feel the Fire 2000, Cyber Roots 2001, Cyber Roots Reggae 2002, Live With No More Babylon: Mash Up The Dance 2004, Jah Messingers 2008, The Fittest 2011. *E-mail:* earl16@btopenworld.com (home).

EARLE, Steve; American singer, songwriter and musician (guitar); b. 17 Jan. 1955, Fort Monroe, Va; s. of Jack Earle and Barbara Earle; m. 1st Sandy Earle; m. 2nd Cynthia Earle; m. 3rd Carol-Ann Earle; m. 4th and 6th Lou-Anne Earle; m. 5th Teresa Ensenat; m. 7th Allison Moorer. *Career:* moved to Nashville, where became bar room musician, staff writer for the publisher, Sunbury Dunbar, and songwriter; solo artist with own backing band, The Dukes 1982–. *Film and television appearances include:* Nashville 1975, The Wire (TV series) 2002, Slacker Uprising 2008, Leaves of Grass 2009, Treme (TV series) 2010. *Recordings include:* albums: Pink and Black (EP) 1982, Guitar Town 1986, Early Tracks 1987, Exit O 1987, Copperhead Road 1988, The Hard Way 1990, Shut Up And Die Like An Aviator 1991, Train A Comin' 1995, Fearless Heart 1996, I Feel Alright 1996, Angry Young Man 1996, El Corazón 1997, The Mountain 1999, Transcendental Blues 2000, Together At The Bluebird Cafe 2001, Sidetracks 2002, Jerusalem 2002, Just An American Boy 2003, The Revolution Starts… Now 2004, Live From Austin TX 2004, Washington Square Serenade (Grammy Award for Best Contemporary Folk/Americana Album 2008) 2007, Townes (Grammy Award for Best Contemporary Folk Album 2010) 2009, I'll Never Get Out of This World Alive 2011, The Low Highway 2013. *Publication:* Doghouse Roses (short stories) 2001. *Honours:* BBC Radio 2 Folk Award for Lifetime Achievement 2004. *Current Management:* c/o GoldVE, 260 West 35th Street, 13th Floor, New York, NY 10001, USA. *Telephone:* (212) 741-2400. *Fax:* (212) 741-4871. *E-mail:* info@goldve.com. *Website:* www.goldve.com; www.steveearle.com.

EASTON, Sheena; British singer and actress; b. (Sheena Shirley Orr), 27 April 1959, Bellshill, Scotland; m. 1st Rob Light 1985; m. 2nd Tim Delarm 1997; two c. *Education:* Royal Scottish Acad. of Music and Drama. *Career:* singer Glasgow club circuit 1979; career launched by appearance on TV show, The Big Time (BBC 1) 1980; solo recording artist 1980–; numerous concerts and worldwide tours, TV appearances. *Stage appearances include:* Man of La Mancha (Chicago, then Broadway) 1991–92, The Colors of Christmas 2001. *Television appearances include:* Miami Vice (series) 1987–88, Body Bags 1993, The Highlander 1993, The Adventure of Brisco County Jr 1993, TekWar 1995, Gargoyles 1995–96, Outer Limits 1996, Road Rovers 1996, All Dogs go to Heaven 1996–97, Duckman 1997, Chicken Soup for the Soul 1999, The Legend of Tarzan 2001, Young Blades 2005, Phineas and Ferb (series) 2009. *Recordings include:* albums: Take My Time 1981, You Could Have Been With Me 1981, Madness, Money And Music 1982, Best Kept Secret 1983, A Private Heaven 1985, Do You 1985, The Lover In Me 1989, The Collection 1989, What Comes Naturally 1991, No Strings 1993, My Cherie 1995, Body And Soul 1997, Freedom 2000, Fabulous 2000. *Honours:* Grammy Award for Best New Artist 1981, for Best Mexican/American Performance (with Luis Miguel) 1985, Emmy Award (for Sheena Easton… Act 1) 1983. *Current Management:* c/o Susan Holder, 21255 Burbank Blvd, #320, Woodland Hills, CA 91367, USA. *Telephone:* (323) 229-5209. *E-mail:* sholder@isp.com. *Website:* www.sheenaeaston.com.

EASY MO'T' (see Moten, Frank, Jr)

EATON, Christopher; singer, songwriter and musician (keyboards); b. 16 Sept. 1958, Dudley, West Midlands, England; m. Abby Scott 2009. *Education:* studied piano. *Career:* songwriter for Cliff Richard, Janet Jackson, Amy Grant, Sheena Easton, Patti Austin, Michael Ball, CeCe Winans, Sheila Walsh; solo artist with contemporary Christian and pop music; mem. Musicians' Union, Equity. *Recordings include:* solo albums: Vision 1986, Wonderful World 1995, What Kind of Love 1998, Dare to Dream 2008. *Honours:* Christian Song of the Year (for Breath of Heaven), USA 1993.

Current Management: c/o Stuart Ongley, SGO Ltd, PO Box 2015, Salisbury, SP2 7WU, England. *E-mail:* stuart@sgomusic.com. *Website:* www.sgomusic .com; www.chriseaton.co.uk (home).

EATON, Nigel; British musician (hurdy-gurdy); b. 3 Jan. 1966, Southampton, Hampshire. *Education:* Guildhall School of Music. *Career:* mem. Blowzabella 1985–90, Ancient Beatbox 1990, Whirling Pope Joan 1993–, Robert Plant and Jimmy Page 1995–; also with Howard Skempton: Hurdygurdy Concerto; Bournemouth Sinfonietta 1994; BBC Welsh Symphony 1992; Aldeburgh Festival with Scottish Chamber Orchestra; video: Snub TV 1989, VHI 1995. *Film work includes:* Aliens, Friends, Harnessing Peacocks, Mansfield Park 1999, The Hunchback of Notre Dame 1999. *Recordings include:* albums: with Blowzabella: The Blowzabella Wall of Sound 1986, The B to A of Blowzabella 1987, A Richer Dust 1988, Vanilla 1990; Panic at the Cafe (with Andy Cutting) 1993, Spin, Whirling Pope Joan (with Julie Murphy) 1994, No Quarter: Jimmy Page and Robert Plant Unledded-Page and Plant 1995; solo: Music of the Hurdy-Gurdy 1987, Pandemonium 2002.

EAVIS, Michael, CBE; British farmer and event manager; *Organizer and Host, Glastonbury Festival. Career:* founder, Pilton Festival 1970, renamed Glastonbury Fayre 1971, later Glastonbury Festival; created The Glastonbury Phonographic Soc. label 2006–. *Honours:* Hon. DArts (Bath) 2004, Hon. MA (Bristol) 2006; Virtual Festivals Awards for best major festival, best innovative festival 2004. *Address:* Worthy Farm, Pilton, Shepton Mallet, Somerset, BA4 4BY, England. *E-mail:* worthy@glastonburyfestivals.co.uk. *Website:* www.glastonburyfestivals.co.uk.

ECKERT, Vojtech; Czech musician (multi-instrumentalist); b. 27 Jan. 1956, Slovakia; m. Iva Hanusova 1997. *Education:* Charles Univ.; studied with Karel Velebny. *Career:* leader of many groups since age 15; established top Czech jazz trio in Prague 1983; mem. Czech Jazz Soc. *Compositions:* CD Blues, A First Piece, Humoresque From Phillips' Hill, Hammond Intermezzo, Blues for Unknown Queen. *Recordings include:* albums: recordings with Eva Olmerová and Eva Pilarová 1986, with Eva Olmerová and Jitka Vrbová 1986, Magic Violin (with Csaba Deseo) 1995; solo: Meditation 2002, Memories 2003, Ježek ve foyeru 2008. *Publications:* contrib. regular articles on jazz criticism and education in monthly periodical, Muzikus 1992–95. *Address:* Budečská 16, 120 00 Prague, Czech Republic (office). *E-mail:* vojtech@eckert .cz (office). *Website:* www.eckert.cz.

E-DANCER (see Saunderson, Kevin)

EDDY, Duane; American musician (guitar), songwriter and producer; b. 26 April 1938, Corning, New York; m. Miriam Johnson 1961. *Career:* bandleader, The Rebels 1958; numerous tours and live appearances. *Film appearances include:* Because They're Young 1960, The Savage Seven 1967, Kona Coast 1967. *Recordings include:* albums: Have Twangy Guitar Will Travel 1959, Especially For You 1959, The Twang's The Thang 1960, Songs of Our Heritage 1960, A Million Dollar's Worth of Twang 1961, Girls Girls Girls 1961, Twistin' and Twangin' 1962, Twangy Guitar – Silky Strings 1962, Dance With The Guitar Man 1963, Twanging Up A Storm 1963, Lonely Guitar 1963, Duane Eddy 1986, Twang Twang 1993, Ghostrider 1996, Duane Eddy – The Heroes Collection 2011, Road Trip 2011; as producer: Star Spangled Springer, Phil Everly 1973; singles include: Moving 'n' Groovin' 1958, Rebel Rouser 1958, Ramrod 1958, Cannonball 1959, The Lonely One 1959, Yep! 1959, Peter Gunn Theme 1959, Forty Miles of Bad Road 1959, Some Kinda Earthquake 1959, Kommotion 1960, Because They're Young 1960, Bonnie Come Back 1960, Pepe 1961, Theme From Dixie 1961, Ring of Fire 1961, Caravan 1961, The Ballad of Paladin (theme for television series Have Gun Will Travel) 1962, Dance With The Guitar Man 1962, Boss Guitar 1963, Play Me Like You Play Your Guitar 1975, Peter Gunn, with Art of Noise 1986; other recordings include session work with Phil Everly, Foreigner, Waylon Jennings, Kenny Rogers, Marty Stuart. *Honours:* NME Top Readers Poll Winner, World Musical Personality 1960, Grammy Award for Best Rock Instrumental Performance 1986. *E-mail:* scott.steele@emimusic.com. *Website:* www.duane-eddy.com.

EDE, Terence (Terry) Frederick; British musician (saxophones, clarinets, flute); b. London, England; m. 2nd Marilyn Wingrove 2010; one s. one d. *Education:* private tuition on piano. *Career:* professional freelance player 1962–; performs with own quartet; tours include Englebert Humperdinck, Jimmy Witherspoon, Larry Williams, Johnnie Ray; well-known teacher both at various schools and privately; mem. Musicians' Union, Asscn of British Jazz Musicians. *Address:* 7 Church Farm Lane, Cheam, Surrey, SM3 8PT, England (home). *Telephone:* (20) 8643-2784 (home). *E-mail:* terry@terryede.com. *Website:* www.terryede.com.

EDELMAN, Randy; American composer; b. 10 June 1947, Patterson, New Jersey. *Education:* Univ. of Cincinnati. *Career:* orchestrator for James Brown; staff writer, CBS; singer-songwriter; mem. Broadcast Music Inc. *Compositions for television:* Blood Sport 1973, Snatched 1973, Ryan's Four 1983, A Doctor's Story 1984, MacGyver 1985, Dennis the Menace 1987, The Adventures of Brisco County Jr 1993, Citizen X 1995. *Compositions for film:* Outside In 1972, Executive Action 1973, The Chipmunk Adventure 1987, Feds 1988, Twins 1988, Troop Beverly Hills 1989, Ghostbusters II 1989, Quick Change 1990, Come See the Paradise 1990, Kindergarten Cop 1990, V. I. Warshawski

1991, Drop Dead Fred 1991, Eyes of an Angel 1991, The Distinguished Gentleman 1992, My Cousin Vinny 1992, Beethoven 1992, The Last of the Mohicans 1992, Gettysburg 1993, Dragon: The Bruce Lee Story 1993, Beethoven's 2nd 1993, Pontiac Moon 1994, Greedy 1994, Angels in the Outfield 1994, The Mask 1994, Billy Madison 1995, Tall Tale 1995, While You Were Sleeping 1995, The Indian in the Cupboard 1995, The Big Green 1995, Down Periscope 1996, Diabolique 1996, The Quest 1996, Dragonheart 1996, Daylight 1996, Anaconda 1997, Gone Fishin' 1997, Leave It to Beaver 1997, For Richer or Poorer 1997, Six Days Seven Nights 1998, Edtv 1999, The Hunley 1999, The Skulls 2000, The Whole Nine Yards 2000, Shanghai Noon 2000, Passion of Mind 2000, Head Over Heels 2001, xXx 2002, 27 Dresses 2008. *Current Management:* c/o Amos Newman, WME, 9601 Wilshire Blvd, Beverly Hills, CA 90201, USA. *Website:* www.randyedelman.com.

EDER, Linda; American singer; b. 3 Feb. 1961, Tucson, Ariz.; m. Frank Wildhorn. *Career:* mem. of duo, Paul and Linda 1980–87; solo artist 1990–; worked with pianist, Jeremy Roberts; appeared in musicals, Jekyll and Hyde 1990, Svengali 1991. *Recordings include:* albums: Linda Eder 1990, Highlights from Jekyll and Hyde 1990, The Complete Work Jekyll and Hyde: The Gothic Music Thriller 1994, And So Much More 1994, The Scarlet Pimpernel 1995, It's Time 1997, It's No Secret Anymore 1999, Christmas Stays the Same 2000, Gold 2002, Storybook 2003, Broadway, My Way 2003, By Myself: The Songs of Judy Garland 2005, The Other Side of Me 2008, Soundtrack 2009, Now 2011, Christmas Where You Are 2013. *Current Management:* c/o Ronni Hart, Hart Management, 1900 Avenue Of The Stars, Suite 1800, Los Angeles, CA 90067, USA. *Telephone:* (310) 385-0905. *Fax:* (310) 385-0908. *E-mail:* rhart@hartmgmt.com. *Website:* www.lindaeder.com.

THE EDGE; Irish musician (guitar) and songwriter; b. (David Howell Evans), 8 Aug. 1961, Barking, Essex, England. *Education:* Mount Temple School. *Career:* founder mem. and guitarist, the Feedback 1976, renamed the Hype, finally renamed U2 1978–; major concerts include Live Aid Wembley 1985, Self Aid Dublin, A Conspiracy of Hope (Amnesty Int. Tour) 1986, Smile Jamaica (hurricane relief fundraiser) 1988, Very Special Arts Festival, White House, Washington, DC 1988; numerous tours world-wide. *Plays include:* Spider-Man: Turn Off The Dark (music and lyrics by Bono and The Edge), Broadway, New York 2011–14. *Films include:* Rattle and Hum 1988. *Recordings include:* albums: Boy 1980, October 1981, War 1983, Under a Blood Red Sky 1983, The Unforgettable Fire 1984, Wide Awake In America 1985, The Joshua Tree (Grammy Award for Album of the Year, Best Rock Performance by a Duo or Group with Vocal) 1987, Rattle and Hum 1988, Achtung Baby (Grammy Award for Best Rock Performance by a Duo or Group with Vocal 1992) 1991, Zooropa (Grammy Award for Best Alternative Music Album) 1993, Passengers (film soundtrack with Brian Eno) 1995, Pop 1997, The Best Of 1980–90 1998, All That You Can't Leave Behind (Grammy Award for Best Rock Album 2001) 2000, The Best Of 1990–2000 2002, How To Dismantle An Atomic Bomb (Meteor Ireland Music Award for Best Irish Album 2006, Grammy Awards for Album of the Year, for Best Rock Album 2006) 2004, No Line on the Horizon 2009, Songs of Innocence 2014; solo: Captive 1987. *Honours:* Order of Liberty (Portugal) 2005; U2 have won 22 Grammy awards including Album of the Year and Best Rock Performance by a Duo or Group with Vocal (for The Joshua Tree) 1987, Grammy awards for Best Rock Performance by a Duo or Group with Vocal (for Desire) and Best Performance Video, short form (for Where the Streets Have No Name) 1988, BRIT Awards for Best Int. Act 1988–90, 1992, 1998, 2001, Best Live Act 1993, Outstanding Contribution to the British Music Industry 2001, JUNO Award 1992, World Music Award 1992, Grammy Award for Best Rock Vocal by a Duo or Group (for Achtung Baby) 1992, Grammy Award for Best Alternative Music Album (for Zooropa) 1993, Grammy Award for Best Music Video, long form (for Zoo TV Live from Sydney) 1994, Grammy Award for Song of the Year, Record of the Year, Best Rock Performance by a Duo or Group with Vocal (all for Beautiful Day) 2000, Grammy Awards for Best Pop Performance by a Duo or Group with Vocal (for Stuck In A Moment You Can't Get Out Of), for Record of the Year (for Walk On), for Best Rock Performance by a Duo or Group with Vocal (for Elevation), for Rock Album of the Year (All That You Can't Leave Behind) 2001, American Music Award for Favorite Internet Artist of the Year 2002, Ivor Novello Award for Best Song Musically and Lyrically (for Walk On) 2002, Golden Globe for Best Original Song (for The Hands That Built America, from film Gangs of New York) 2003, Grammy Awards for Best Rock Performance by a Duo or Group with Vocal, Best Rock Song, Best Short Form Music Video (all for Vertigo) 2004, TED Prize 2004, Nordoff-Robbins Silver Clef Award for lifetime achievement 2005, Q Award for Best Live Act 2005, Digital Music Award for Favourite Download Single (for Vertigo) 2005, Meteor Ireland Music Award for Best Irish Band, Best Live Performance 2006, Grammy Awards for Song of the Year, for Best Rock Performance by a Duo or Group with Vocal (both for Sometimes You Can't Make it on Your Own), for Best Rock Song (for City of Blinding Lights), for Album of the Year and Best Rock Album of the Year (both for How to Dismantle an Atomic Bomb) 2006, Golden Globe Award for Best Original Song (Ordinary Love in Mandela: Long Walk to Freedom) 2014, Ambs of Conscience Award, Amnesty International 2006, Palm Springs Film Festival Sonny Bono Visionary Award 2014. *Current Management:* c/o Principle Management, 30–32 Sir John Rogersons Quay, Dublin 2, Ireland. *E-mail:* nadine@numb.ie. *Website:* www.u2.com.

EDMAN, Eric; Swedish musician (drums). *Career:* mem., Shout Out Louds 2001–. *Recordings include:* albums: 100° (EP) 2003, Oh, Sweetheart (EP) 2004, Howl Howl Gaff Gaff 2005, Very Loud (EP) 2005, Our Ill Wills 2007,

Work 2010, Optica 2013. *Current Management:* c/o Filip Wilén, Bud Fox Management, Saturnusgatan 13, 224 57 Lund, Sweden. *Telephone:* (46) 13-81-20. *E-mail:* filip@budfox.se. *Website:* www.budfox.se; www.shoutoutlouds .com.

EDMUNDS, Dave; British singer, musician (guitar) and record producer; b. 15 April 1944, Cardiff, Wales. *Career:* fmr mem. 99ers, The Raiders, The Image; mem., Love Sculpture 1968–69; solo artist 1969–77, 1981–; Founder mem., Rockpile 1977–81; record producer 1969–; built own Rockfield Recording Studios 1969; numerous tours, concerts, festival appearances, television broadcasts; film appearance Stardust 1974. *Recordings include:* albums: with Love Sculpture: Blues Helping 1968, Forms and Feeling 1969; with Rockpile: Tracks On Wax 1978, Repeat When Necessary 1979, Seconds of Pleasure 1980; solo: Rockpile 1972, Subtle As A Flying Mallet 1975, Get It 1977, Tracks On Wax 1978, Twangin' 1981, The Best of Dave Edmunds 1982, DE7 1982, Information 1983, Riff Raff 1984, Closer To The Flame 1990, I Hear You Rockin' 1993, Plugged In 1994, Musical Fantasies 1999, A Pile of Rock (live) 2001, The Many Sides of Dave Edmunds 2008; singles include: with Love Sculpture: Sabre Dance 1968; solo: I Hear You Knocking 1970, Baby I Love You 1973, Born To Be With You 1973, I Knew The Bride 1977, Girls Talk 1979, Queen of Hearts 1979, Singin' The Blues 1980, The Race Is On 1981; contributor, I Fell In Love, Carlene Carter 1990; producer for artists including Brinsley Schwartz, The Flamin'' Groovies, Shakin' Stevens, Stray Cats, Nick Lowe, Fabulous Thunderbirds, Everly Brothers, Status Quo, k d lang; music for film soundtracks Porky's Revenge, Planes, Trains and Automobiles. *Address:* c/o Universal Music, 364–366 Kensington High Street, London W14 8NS, England (office).

EDRISSI, Tahir al-; Moroccan singer and musician (sintir, percussion). *Career:* left Morocco for London 1980s; founder mem. band, MoMo (Music of Moroccan Origin); act's fusion of North African Gnawa music with western-style drum kit, samples and contemporary dance styles (including house and garage) described as 'Dar'; popular live band. *Recordings:* album: The Birth Of Dar 2001.

EDWARDS, Chris David; British musician (guitar, bass guitar); b. 20 Dec. 1980, Leicester, England. *Education:* Countesthorpe Community Coll. *Career:* mem., Kasabian 1999–. *Recordings include:* albums: Kasabian 2004, Empire 2006, West Ryder Pauper Lunatic Asylum (Q Award for Best Album 2009, NME Award for Best Album 2010) 2009, Velociraptor! 2011, 48:13 2014. *Honours:* NME Awards for Best Live Act 2007, for Best British Band 2012, Q Awards for Best Act in the World Today 2010, 2014, for Best Live Act 2014, BRIT Award for Best British Group 2010, MOJO Award for Song of the Year 2010. *Current Management:* c/o John Coyne, The Family Entertainment. *E-mail:* coyne@thefamilyent.com. *Address:* c/o Columbia Records, 9 Derry Street, London, W8 5HY, England (office). *Website:* www.kasabian.co.uk.

EDWARDS, Dave, CertEd, DipEd, Cert in Counselling; British musician (steel pan, guitar) and fmr music teacher; *Co-ordinator, Steelbands North Project;* b. 9 Aug. 1948, Shrewsbury, England; m. Andrea 1978; one s. *Education:* Shoreditch Coll. of Educ., Wolverhampton Polytechnic, Northumbria Univ. *Career:* Scandinavian tour with Razzle Dazzle Gatemouth Spasm String Band 1973; mem. and Musical Dir Pan L Beaters Steel Band 1992–96; mem. Steel Spirit Steel Band 1999–2001; numerous local radio broadcasts; freelance tutor and workshop leader; Musical Dir North Tyneside Steelband 1991–2014; Events, Tuition, Publs Co-ordinator, Steelbands North Project 2001–; Facilitator, Steel Pan Squad, Music Leader North East 2004–11; teacher, GCSE Music and Music Appreciation; helped organize three nat. steelband festivals 1994–96; established Dave Edwards Award 2014; mem. Bd Sound Sense (nat. org. for community music) 2000–10; mem. Musicians' Union, Nat. Union of Teachers 1994–; Trustee Tynemouth Coll. 1999–2005, N Tyneside Carers' Centre 2000–10. *Compositions include:* Steelband: Sunshine, Geordie Calypso, several other steelband compositions and arrangements. *Recordings include:* North Tyneside Steelband: On Broadway, Take Off Your Shoes and Hum, ...bring a smile to your ears. *Publications:* Steelpan booklet 1991 (revised 2005). *Honours:* Certificate of Merit, N Tyneside Steel Band, Nat. Steelband Festival 1991, Nat. Festival Music for Youth 2003, 2004, 2005, 2008, Schools Prom, Royal Albert Hall 2003, 2008. *Address:* Aynuck's Lodge, 20 Glendale Avenue, Whitley Bay, Tyne and Wear, NE26 1RX, England (home). *Telephone:* (7753) 604281 (mobile) (office). *E-mail:* dave@steelbandsnorth.org.uk (office). *Website:* www.northtynesidesteelband.org.uk (office).

EDWARDS, Don; American singer, songwriter and musician (acoustic guitar, banjo, mandolin); b. 20 March 1939, Boonton, NJ; m. Kathy Jean Davis 1978, two d. *Career:* started as actor, singer, stuntman, Six Flags Over Texas, 1961; solo artist 1964–; part-owner, White Elephant Saloon, Fort Worth, TX; tours of USA, Canada, UK, New Zealand, Europe; performs solo, with cowboy band, horse, cowboy poet Waddie Mitchell as The Bard and The Balladeer; as The Cowboy Jubilee; musicologist, author on Western and traditional cowboy music; educational services to universities; appearances with Fort Worth, Las Vegas and Colorado Springs symphony orchestras; mem. AFTRA. *Recordings include:* Happy Cowboy 1980; America's Singing Cowboy; Songs of The Cowboy; Guitars and Saddle Songs 1987, Desert Nights and Cowtown Blues 1990, Songs of The Trail 1992, Goin' Back to Texas 1993, The Bard and the Balladeer (with Waddie Mitchell) 1994, West of Yesterday 1996, Saddle Songs 1997, My Hero, Gene Autry 1998, The Bard and The Balladeer (with Waddie Mitchell); Prairie Portrait, 2000; Kin To The Wind

2001, High Lonesome Cowboy (with Peter Rowen) 2004, Moonlight and Skies 2006, Heaven on Horseback 2009, American 2010. *Publications:* Classic Cowboy Songs; book/tape anthologies: Songs of the Cowboy; Guitars and Saddle Songs. *Honours:* Cowboy Hall of Fame Western Heritage Wrangler Award for Outstanding Traditional Music 1992, Western Heritage Wrangler Awards 1992, 1996. *Address:* PO Box 9188, Colorado Springs, CO 80932, USA. *Website:* www.donedwardsmusic.com.

EDWARDS, Janet, (Narin Gylman), Diploma, ARCM, LTCL DipEd; British singer and musician (piano); b. Huddersfield, Yorkshire; m 1st; two s.; m 2nd. *Education:* Univ. of Huddersfield, studied piano with Dr Michael Kruszynski, studied conducting with Harry Rabinowitz. *Career:* piano and song recitals 1974–; performed with artists including those from Royal Opera House, ENO soloists; performances in Italy, France, Germany, UK; devised, performed own shows: Sounds Entertaining; I Say I Play; Munich, London, other British halls; solo work, classical, popular, theatre, jazz music, in Europe, Scandinavia, Middle East; accompanist, Asst musical Dir, Royal Gala Performance of works by Stephen Sondheim, Theatre Royal Drury Lane; voice coach, Royal Acad. of Music early 1980s; masterclass group sessions working with professionals and non-professionals 1989–; played Anna in Girls Were Made To Love and Kiss (West End, London) 1994; also runs professional seminar in auditioning techniques, workshops and seminars for the general public; began one-woman show, 'S' Wonderful, 'S' Marvellous, in theatres and venues in the UK, 1997–; London shows including Pizza on the Park, performing own songs and recording 1999–2005; coached professional singers and produced album work with artists 2007; worked on further modern/jazz development of her own piano and vocals in France; returned to live full time in London late 2013. *Films:* Aria (vocal work with Sir John Hurt) (Palm d'Or, Cannes Film Festival) 1989, City (as music supervisor). *Recordings include:* Songs Without Words 2000, Moving Emotions (piano) 2002, Back to Base (composer as Narin Gylman) 2014; several performances in France 2008–14. *Radio:* UK Radio, BBC radio 2014, LBC, Talk Radio, Radio Europe, BBC Radio 3. *Publications:* Choosing to Heal – Surviving the Breast Cancer System 2007. *E-mail:* info@naringylman.com (home); music@janetedwards.co.uk. *Website:* www.janetedwards.co.uk; www.naringylman.com (home).

EDWARDS, Kathleen Margaret; Canadian singer, songwriter, arranger and musician (guitar); b. 11 July 1978, Ottawa, Ont.; d. of Leonard Edwards; m. Colin Cripps. *Education:* studied classical violin as a child. *Recordings include:* albums: Failer 2003, Live from the Bowery Ballroom 2003, Back to Me 2005, Asking for Flowers 2008, Voyageur 2012. *Honours:* co-winner (with John Roderick) Echo Songwriting Prize (English version, for A Soft Place to Land) 2012. *Current Management:* c/o Jack Ross, The Agency Group, 2 Berkeley Street, Suite 202, Toronto, ON M5A 4J5, USA. *Telephone:* (416) 368-5599. *Fax:* (416) 368-4655. *E-mail:* jackross@theagencygroup.com. *Website:* www.theagencygroup.com. *E-mail:* info@kathleenedwards.com. *Website:* www.kathleenedwards.com.

EDWARDS, Richard (Richie) Benjamin; British musician (bass guitar); b. 25 Sept. 1974, Lichfield. *Career:* fmr mem., Onion Trump, and guitar technician for The Darkness; mem., The Darkness 2005–06, Stone Gods 2007–. *Recordings include:* albums: with The Darkness: One Way Ticket To Hell... And Back 2005; with Stone Gods: Silver Spoons and Broken Bones 2008, Burn the Witch (EP) 2008. *Honours:* Smash Hits Award for Best Rock Act 2005. *E-mail:* syd@syddavey.com. *Address:* c/o Pias UK Ltd, 1 Bevington Path, London, SE1 3PW, England. *Telephone:* (20) 7471-2700. *Fax:* (20) 7471-2706. *Website:* www.pias.com.

EDWARDS, Simon, (Sir Eddie Real); British musician (percussion). *Career:* mem. Alabama 3 (known as A3 in USA); solo work as Sir Eddie Real & The Realistics. *Recordings include:* albums: with Alabama 3: Exile on Coldharbour Lane 1997, La Peste 2000, Power In The Blood 2002, The Last Train To Mashville 2003, Outlaw 2005, M.O.R. 2007, Revolver Soul 2010, There Will Be Peace in the Valley... When We Get the Keys to the Mansion on the Hill 2011, Shoplifting 4 Jesus 2011; solo: Where's the Monkey EP 1999. *Website:* www.alabama3.co.uk.

EDWARDS, Skye; British singer. *Career:* Founder-mem., Morcheeba 1995–2003, 2010–; solo artist 2004–. *Recordings include:* albums: with Morcheeba: Who Can You Trust? 1996, Big Calm 1998, Fragments of Freedom 2000, Charango 2002, The Antidote 2005, Blood Like Lemonade 2010, Head Up High 2013; solo: Mind How You Go 2006, Keeping Secrets 2009, Back To Now 2012. *Current Management:* c/o CMO Management, 11 Westbourne Studios, 242 Acklam Road, London, W10 5JJ, England. *Telephone:* (20) 3735-5632. *E-mail:* info@blueraincoatmusic.com. *Website:* www.cmomanagement.co.uk; www.morcheeba.co.uk; www.skyewards.co.uk.

EDWARDS, Terry David, BA (Hons); British musician (saxophones, trumpet, guitar, piano, Hammond organ, flute); *Managing Director, Sartorial Records;* b. 10 Aug. 1960, Hornchurch, Essex, England; s. of Cliff Edwards and Doreen Edwards. *Education:* Univ. of East Anglia. *Career:* Founder-mem. The Higsons 1980–86; Co-founder (with Mark Bedford), Butterfield 8 1988–; solo artist with and without The Scapegoats 1991–; mem. Gallon Drunk, Near Jazz Experience, Big Sexy Noise 2009–12; session player with Madness, The Blockheads, Big Star 'Third' (conductor, woodwind), Hot Chip, Erika Stucky, Franz Ferdinand, Joby Talbot, Jimi Tenor, Lydia Lunch, PJ Harvey, Spleen, Jesus and Mary Chain, The Duke Spirit, Tom Waits and Robert Wilson (The Black Rider), Jerry Dammers' Spatial AKA, Faust, Lush, Julian Cope, JJ Stone, Nick Cave, The Brood, Drugstore, Frank and Walters, Tindersticks,

Billy Bragg, Robyn Hitchcock, Micko Westmoreland, Keziah Jones, Dopesmugglaz, Delakota, Boo Radleys, 18 Wheeler, The Creatures, Siouxsie Sioux, Spiritualized, Scott 4, Strangelove, Anthony Moore, David Holmes, Jack, Serious Drinking, Dept S, Test Department, Moonshake, Farmers Boys, Bikini Beach, Wire, Snuff, Repair Man, David Coulter, Sarah-Jane Morris, Glen Matlock, Anjali, Stuart A. Staples, Clayhill, Nitwood, Pauline Taylor, Tuner, Dot Allison, Proclaimers, Jack Penate, Salt Peter, Duncan Brown, Darren Hayman, Elbow, Dirty Pretty Things, Paul Weller, Jeremie Kisling, Bonzer, The Dash, Rain Dogs Revisited project (featuring St Vincent, Erika Stucky, Arthur H, Steve Nieve, Stef Kamil, Camille O'Sullivan, Seb Rochford, Dave Okumu, Tom Herbert, Thomas Bloch), Cold Specks, Kiria Lepink; performances at Yoko Ono's Meltdown and with Beck on the Song Reader project; currently Man. Dir Sartorial Records; Assoc. mem. Performing Right Soc.; mem. Performing Right Soc., Soc. for the Promotion of New Music, Musicians' Union. *Films:* performer with Tindersticks in festival presentations of Claire Denis's film works. *Compositions:* Pump for symphony orchestra 1998, music for Dan Rhodes' short story The Carolingian Period 2001. *Dance:* Rialto (cello & piano score), commissioned and choreographed by Charles Linehan 1998. *Film:* Dora Suarez 1993. *Radio:* John Peel Sessions with The Higsons 1981–84, also solo and with the Scapegoats 1993–99, Jesus & Mary Chain 1997, Tindersticks 1993–95. *Television:* appearances on Later with Jools Holland – Gallon Drunk 1993, Tindersticks 1994, Robyn Hitchcock 2009, Jerry Dammers' Spatial AKA 2010, Cold Specks 2011, Lee Thompson's Ska Orchestra 2013, Franz Ferdinand 2013; several appearances with Madness, including Parkinson. *Recordings include:* albums: Blow (with Butterfield 8) 1988, Plays, Salutes, and Executes 1993, No Fish is Too Weird for Her Aquarium 1994, I Was Dora Suarez (with Derek Raymond and James Johnston) 1994, My Wife Doesn't Understand Me 1995, I Didn't Get Where I Am Today 1997, Large Door 1998, Birth of The Scapegoats 1998, Yesterday's Zeitgeist 1999, Ontogeny (No Fish Is Too Weird For Her Aquarium, Vol. II) 2000, 681 At The Southbank/Plays, Salutes & Executes 2002, Butterfield 8 2003, Memory & Madness (with Lydia Lunch) 2003, Queer Street (No Fish... Vol. III) 2004, terryedwards 2005, Readymade/Sartorial Sampler 2007, Clichés 2010, All Ready for the 25th? – Wishing You a Sartorial Christmas 2012, Live at Indo (Near Jazz Experience) 2012, Acoustic Parts I and II (Near Jazz Experience). *Publications:* Madness' One Step Beyond (part of Continuum/Bloomsbury's 33⅓ series) 2009. *Address:* PO Box 30608, London, E1 1TS, England (office). *Telephone:* 7803-905467 (mobile). *E-mail:* sartorial@terryedwards.co.uk (office). *Website:* www.terryedwards.co.uk; sartorialrecords.greedbag.com.

EDWINS, Myron; American singer, musician (bass guitar, keyboards) and producer; b. 4 Jan. 1958, Washington, PA. *Career:* solo artist 1989–; tours, TV appearances; lead singer and keyboardist for R&B group, Movin'. *Recordings:* Do You Love Me 1990, Do You Like The Way I Do It 1991, Love Is 1993, Let Me Entertain You 1994, The Best Thing To Do 1994, I'll See You Again, Myron Edwins 1995. *Address:* Myron Edwins Productions, PO Box 8442, Pittsburg, CA 94565-8442, USA. *Website:* www.myronedwins.com.

EGAN, Kian John Francis; Irish singer; b. 29 April 1980, Sligo. *Career:* mem., Westlife 1999–; numerous tours, festivals and television appearances. *Recordings include:* albums with Westlife: Westlife 1999, Coast to Coast 2000, World of Our Own 2001, Unbreakable - The Greatest Hits 2002, Turnaround 2003, Face To Face 2005, The Love Album 2006, Back Home 2007, Where We Are 2009, Gravity 2010. *Honours:* BRIT Awards for Best Pop Act 2001, 2002, Meteor Ireland Music Award for Best Irish Pop Act 2005, 2006, 2007. *Current Management:* c/o Louis Walsh Management, 24 Courtney House, Appian Way, Dublin 6, Ireland. *Telephone:* (1) 668 0309. *Fax:* (1) 668 0721. *Website:* www.westlife.com.

EICHER, Manfred; German record company executive, producer and composer; *President, ECM Records;* b. 1943. *Education:* Acad. of Music, Berlin. *Career:* f. ECM Records (Edition of Contemporary Music), Munich 1969, currently Pres.; label dedicated to high-quality recordings of jazz, avant-garde and world music; released over 1000 records, of which Eicher has produced over 300, artists include Keith Jarrett, Jan Garbarek, Chick Corea, Gary Burton, Jack DeJohnette, Dave Holland, Pat Metheny, Ralph Towner, Terje Rypdal, Art Ensemble of Chicago; established ECM New Series for European classical music 1984, released recordings of compositions by composers including Steve Reich, Arvo Pärt, John Adams, Meredith Monk, Pérotin. *Films:* Holozän Man in the Holocene (co-writer, co-dir 1992. *Film soundtracks* producer: Eloge de l'Amour, The Old Place, Forever Mozart, JLG, Hélas Pour Moi, Allemagne Neuf Zéro, Nouvelle Vague, Histoires du Cinéma, Eternity And A Day, Ulysses' Gaze, The Suspended Step of the Stork, Journey to Hope, Mostly Martha, War Photographer; composer: Kedma 2002. *Honours:* Commdr, Royal Order of the Polar Star, Sweden 1999, Order of the Cross of St Mary's Land (V Class), Estonia 1999, Commdr, Royal Order of Merit, Norway 2001; Hon. DLitt (Brighton, UK) 2000; German Record Critics Award 1986, Music Prize of the City of Munich 1998, Grammy Award for Classical Producer of the Year 2002. *Address:* ECM Records, Postfach 600 331, 81203, Munich, Germany (office). *Telephone:* (89) 851048 (office). *Fax:* (89) 8545652 (office). *E-mail:* ecm@ecmrecords.com (office). *Website:* www.ecmrecords.com (office).

EICHER, Stephan; Swiss singer and songwriter; b. 17 Aug. 1960, Berne. *Career:* mem. Noise Boys 1977–79, Grauzone 1979–81; solo artist 1981–. *Recordings include:* albums: with Noise Boys: Noise Boys 1980; with Grauzone: Grauzone 1980; solo: Souvenir 1982, Les Chanson Bleues 1983, I Tell This Night 1985, Silence 1987, My Place 1989, Engelberg 1991,

Carcassonne 1993, Non Ci Badar, Guarda e Passa 1994, 1000 Vies 1996, Louanges 1999, Hotel *S 2001, Taxi Europa 2003, Tour Taxi Europa 2004, Eldorado 2007, L'Envolée 2012. *Address:* c/o Universal Music France, 20 rue Fossés St Jacques, 75005 Paris, France (office). *Website:* www.stephaneicher.com.

EINARSDOTTER, Elise, DipMus; Swedish musician (piano) and composer; b. 11 July 1955; m. Olle Steinholtz; one d. *Education:* Berklee Coll. of Music, USA, Royal Acad. of Music, Stockholm. *Career:* leader, Elise Einarsdotter Ensemble 1984–; composer of music to lyrics; writer for choir and orchestra; tours in Scandinavia, Italy, USA, Sweden, Norway, France, Belgium, Holland, England, Ethiopia, Australia and India; mem. Swedish Acad. of Jazz, NYA IDUN. *Compositions:* My Heart, Alexandrinen, Sphinx Acre, Ljus Dagg Grönska, I Live in Music, Summer Night, Glöd, Snövind och Sommarbris. *Recordings include:* albums: Sacred Hearts 1984, Secrets of Living 1989, Senses 1993, Rosenäng 1996, Sketches of Roses 1998, Green Walk, Slow Talk 1998, Summer Night 2001, Shimmer 2006, Snövind & Summer Breeze 2007, Hymne à l'amour 2008, So Shimmering 2010. *Publications:* Rosenäng, Sju Sånger. *Honours:* numerous grants and awards, Lo-Kulturpris 1993, Stockholm City Award of Honour 1998. *Address:* c/o Mistral Music, Bandyvägen 47, 129 49 Hagersten, Sweden. *E-mail:* elise.einarsdotter@telia.com. *Website:* www.mistralmusic.com.

EINARSSON, Noi Steinn; Icelandic musician (drums). *Career:* mem., Leaves 2004–. *Recordings include:* albums: Breathe 2002, The Angela Test 2005.

EINZIGER, Michael (Mike) Aaron; American musician (guitar); b. 21 June 1976, Los Angeles, Calif. *Career:* Founder-mem., Incubus 1991–; tours and live appearances, produced albums for Agent Sparks, Jason Schwartzman. *Recordings include:* albums: Fungus Amongus 1995, S.C.I.E.N.C.E. 1997, Make Yourself 1999, Morning View 2001, A Crow Left of the Murder 2004, Light Grenades 2006, Monuments and Melodies 2009, If Not Now, When? 2011, HQ Live 2012. *Honours:* Billboard Award for Modern Rock Single of the Year 2001. *Address:* c/o Epic Records, 550 Madison Avenue, New York, NY 10022, USA (office). *Website:* www.enjoyincubus.com.

EITZEL, Mark; American singer and songwriter; b. 30 Jan. 1959, Walnut Creek, Calif. *Career:* fmr mem., Naked Skinnies; Founder mem., lead singer American Music Club 1983–96, 2003–; simultaneous solo artist. *Recordings include:* albums with American Music Club: The Restless Stranger 1986, Engine 1987, California 1988, United Kingdom 1990, Everclear 1991, Mercury 1993, San Francisco 1994, Love Songs for Patriots 2004; solo: Songs of Love: Live at the Borderline 1991, 60 Watt Silver Lining 1996, Lover's Leap USA 1997, West 1997, Caught in a Trap and I Can't Back Out 'Cause I Love You Too Much, Baby 1998, Live on WFMU NYC 2001, Superhitsinternational 2001, The Invisible Man 2001, Music for Courage and Confidence 2002, The Ugly American 2003, Candy Ass 2005, The Golden Age 2008. *Website:* www.americanmusicclub.com.

EK, Daniel; Swedish technologist and music industry executive; *Co-founder and CEO, Spotify AB*; b. 21 Feb. 1983, Stockholm. *Career:* held sr roles at Tradera (auction co. subsequently acquired by Ebay); f. Advertigo (online advertising co.) 2004, subsequently acquired by TradeDoubler 2006; Chief Tech. Officer, Stardoll (fashion and entertainment community for tweens) 2005–06; Co-founder and CEO uTorrent 2006; Co-founder (with Martin Lorentzon) and CEO Spotify AB, Stockholm 2006, launched music streaming service Spotify 2008. *Address:* Spotify USA Inc., 45 West 18th Street, 7th Floor, New York, NY 10011, USA (office); Spotify AB, 4, Birger Jarlsgatan 61, 113 56 Stockholm, Sweden (office). *Telephone:* (347) 485-6083 (NY) (office). *E-mail:* office@spotify.com (office). *Website:* www.spotify.com (office).

EKBERG, Ulf 'Buddha'; Swedish producer, songwriter and singer; b. 6 Dec. 1970. *Career:* mem., Ace of Base 1990–. *Recordings include:* albums: Happy Nation 1993, The Bridge 1995, Flowers/Cruel Summer 1998, Da Capo 2002, 90's 2004, Classic Remixes 2008, Poptastic! 2011. *Current Management:* c/o Orlando John, Urbania Group Ltd, Box 3184, 103 63 Stockholm, Sweden. *Telephone:* (8) 609-00-15. *E-mail:* info@urbaniagroup.com. *Website:* www.urbaniagroup.com; www.aceofbase.com.

EL BAMBINO, Tito; Puerto Rican singer and songwriter; b. (Efraín Fines Nevarez), 5 Oct. 1981. *Career:* recorded first song on CD compilation, aged 12; mem. duet, Héctor & Tito –2004; solo reggaeton artist 2005–; has recorded with Latin American singers including José Feliciano, Victor Manuelle, Giovanni Hidalgo; f. On Fire Music record label. *Recordings include:* albums: as Hector & Tito: Violencia Musical 1998, Nuevo Milenio 2000, Lo De Antes 2001, A La Reconquista 2002, La Historia Live 2003; solo: Top of the Line 2006, It's My Time 2007, El Patrón 2009, Invencible 2011, Invicto 2012. *Honours:* Billboard Latin Award and Tu Musica Award 2003. *E-mail:* manejo@titoelbambinoelpatron.com. *Website:* www.titoelbambinoonline.com.

EL CANI, Juanlu; Spanish musician (bass guitar); b. Barcelona. *Career:* has lived in Spain, USA, Brazil; fmr mem. numerous bands including Magiaanimal, El Fantástico Hombre Bala, Mesmalva, La Burbuja, Umanawé, Otneim Kham, Flamencorro; Founder mem. Ojos de Brujo (with Ramón Giménez) 1990–2004, a group which fuses gypsy and flamenco music with Latin American, punk, hip hop, reggae and electronic influences; nicknamed 'el metralleta' (the submachine-gun); set up own label La Fábrica de Colores 2001; several tours in Europe, Latin America and USA; Founder mem. and leader Calima 2004–, an eleven-piece band featuring musicians from Spain,

Cuba, Venezuela, Bulgaria. *Recordings include:* albums: with Ojos de Brujo: Vengue 1999, Barí 2002, Barí: Remezclas de la Casa 2005; with Calima: Azul 2007. *Honours:* World Music Award for Europe, BBC Radio 3 2004. *Address:* EMI Music Spain, Calle Alcalá 44, 28014 Madrid, Spain (office).

EL GUINCHO; Spanish producer and musician; b. (Pablo Díaz-Reixa), 17 Nov. 1983, Las Palmas, Gran Canaria. *Career:* based in Barcelona; fmr composer for films and TV advertisements; mem. Coconot 2005–; solo artist 2007–, music incorporates elements of Tropicália, Afrobeat, pop and rock and roll. *Recordings include:* albums: with Coconot: Novo Tropicalismo Errado 2005, Cosa Astral 2008; solo: Folías 2007, Alegranza! 2008, Pop Negro 2010, Piratas de Sudamerica (EP) 2010. *E-mail:* discotecaoceano@gmail.com. *Website:* www.elguincho.com.

ELASTIC CHAKRA (see BT)

ELDREDGE, Brett Ryan; American country music singer, guitarist and songwriter; b. 23 March 1986, Paris, Ill. *Education:* Elmhurst Coll., Middle Tennessee State Univ. *Career:* songwriter for Gary Allan, Trace Adkins; collaborated with other songwriters including Bill Anderson; signed to Atlantic Records as solo artist 2010; opening act on tour for Taylor Swift, Brad Paisley, Keith Urban, Billy Currington. *Recordings:* album: Bring You Back 2013. *Honours:* Country Music Asscn Award for New Artist of the Year 2014. *Address:* c/o Atlantic Nashville, 20 Music Square East, Nashville, TN 37203, USA (office). *Website:* www.warnermusicnashville.com (office); www.bretteldredge.com.

ELDRITCH, Andrew; British singer; b. (Andrew Taylor), 15 May 1959, Ely, Cambridgeshire. *Education:* Univ. of Oxford. *Career:* Founder mem., The Sisters of Mercy 1980–85, 1987– (performed as The Sisterhood 1986); numerous int. tours, concerts. *Recordings include:* albums: First And Last And Always 1985, Gift (EP, as The Sisterhood) 1986, Floodland 1988, Vision Thing 1990, Enter The Sisters 1991, Some Girls Wander By Mistake 1992, A Slight Case Of Overbombing 1993; singles: Alice 1982, The Reptile House 1983, Temple Of Love 1983, Body And Soul 1984, Walk Away 1984, This Corrosion 1987, Dominion 1988, Lucretia My Reflection 1988, Doctor Jeep 1990, More 1990, When You Don't See Me 1991, Under The Gun 1993. *Website:* www.the-sisters-of-mercy.com.

ELEPHANT MAN; Jamaican singer; b. (O'Neil Bryan), 11 Sept. 1975, Seaview Gardens. *Career:* mem., Scare Dem Crew 1995–2000; solo artist 2000–; collaboration with Mr Vegas on songs, Jump Jump, What's Up, Ain't No Way, Dainty; collaboration with Harry Toddler for song, War War War. *Recordings include:* albums: with Scare Dem Crew: Scare Dem Crew The Album 1999, Scared From The Crypt 1999; solo: Comin' 4 You! 2000, Log On 2001, Higher Level 2002, Good 2 Go 2003, Let's Get Physical 2008, Dance & Sweep 2011. *Address:* c/o Bad Boy Records, 1710 Broadway, New York, NY 10019, USA (office). *Website:* www.badboyonline.com (office).

ELFMAN, Danny; American film music composer and musician (guitar); b. 29 May 1953, Amarillo, Tex.; m. Bridget Fonda 2003. *Career:* lead singer, rhythm guitarist and songwriter eight-piece rock band, Oingo Bongo 1974–95; numerous songs and scores for films, TV programmes and computer games. *Music for film:* Forbidden Zone 1980, Fast Times at Ridgemont High 1982, Bachelor Party 1984, Surf II 1984, Beverly Hills Cop 1984, Weird Science 1985, Pee-Wee's Big Adventure 1985, Wisdom 1986, Something Wild 1986, Back to School 1986, Summer School 1987, Hot to Trot 1988, Big Top Pee-Wee 1988, Beetlejuice 1988, Midnight Run 1988, Scrooged 1988, 1989, Ghostbusters II 1989, Dick Tracy 1990, Nightbreed 1990, Darkman 1990, Edward Scissorhands 1990, Pure Luck 1991, Batman Returns 1992, Article 99 1992, Army of Darkness 1993, Sommersby 1993, The Nightmare Before Christmas (Saturn Award for Best Music 1993) 1993, Black Beauty 1994, Dolores Claiborne 1995, To Die For 1995, Dead Presidents 1995, Mission: Impossible 1996, The Frighteners 1996, Freeway 1996, Extreme Measures 1996, Mars Attacks! (Saturn Award for Best Music 1996) 1996, Men In Black (Saturn Award for Best Music 1997) 1997, Flubber 1997, Good Will Hunting 1997, Scream 2 1997, A Simple Plan 1998, A Civil Action 1998, My Favorite Martian 1999, Instinct 1999, Anywhere But Here 1999, Sleepy Hollow (Saturn Award for Best Music 1999) 1999, The Family Man 2000, Proof of Life 2000, Spy Kids 2001, Planet of the Apes 2001, Heartbreakers 2001, Mazer World 2001, Novocaine 2001, Spider-Man (Saturn Award for Best Music 2002) 2002, Men in Black II 2002, Red Dragon 2002, Chicago 2002, Hulk 2003, Big Fish 2003, Spider-Man 2 2004, Charlie and the Chocolate Factory 2005, Charlotte's Web 2006, Spider-Man 3 2007, Hellboy II: The Golden Army 2008, Wanted 2008, Standard Operating Procedure 2008, Milk 2008, Notorious 2009, Terminator Salvation 2009, Taking Woodstock 2009, The Wolf Man 2009, Men in Black III 2012, Dark Shadows 2012, Promised Land 2012, Hitchcock 2012, Oz the Great and Powerful 2013, Epic 2013, Mr Peabody & Sherman 2014, The Unknown Known 2014, Fifty Shades of Grey 2015. *Music for television:* Amazing Stories 1985, Alfred Hitchcock Presents 1985, Fast Times 1986, Sledge Hammer! 1986, Pee-Wee's Playhouse 1986, Tales from the Crypt 1989, The Simpsons 1989, Beetlejuice 1989, The Flash 1990, Batman 1992, Family Dog 1993, Weird Science 1994, Perversions of Science 1997, Dilbert 1999, Desperate Housewives (Emmy Award for Outstanding Main Title Theme Music 2005) 2004. *Recordings:* albums with Oingo Boingo: Only A Lad 1981, Nothing To Fear 1982, Good For Your Soul 1983, Dead Man's Party 1985, Boingo 1986, Skeletons In The Closet 1989, Dark At The End Of The Tunnel 1990, Article 99 1992. *Honours:* Grammy Award for Best Instrumental Composition (for The Batman Theme) 1990, Frederick Loewe Award for Film Composing 2004,

Hollywood Film Festival Composer of the Year 2008. *Current Management:* c/o Kraft-Engel Management, 15233 Ventura Boulevard, Suite 200, Sherman Oaks, CA 91403, USA. *Telephone:* (818) 380-1918. *E-mail:* info@Kraft-Engel .com. *Website:* www.Kraft-Engel.com.

ELI, Mike; American country music singer, songwriter and guitarist; b. 5 April 1981, Tornball, Tex.; m. Kacey Eli 2010; one d. *Education:* Univ. of North Texas. *Career:* formed Eli & Young duo with James Young, late 1990s; Founder-mem. Eli Young Band 2000–. *Recordings:* albums: with Eli Young Band: Eli Young Band 2002, Level 2005, Jet Black & Jealous 2008, Life at Best 2011, 10,000 Towns 2014. *Honours:* Acad. of Country Music Award for Song of the Year 2012, MusicRow Breakthrough Artist Award 2012. *Current Management:* c/o George Couri, Triple 8 Management, 5524 West Highway 290, Austin, TX 78735, USA. *Telephone:* (512) 444-7600. *Fax:* (512) 444-7601. *Website:* www.eliyoungband.com.

ELIS, Hefin, BA; British composer, arranger, musician (piano, guitar, bass guitar) and producer; b. 4 June 1950, Port Talbot, Wales; s. of Robert Ellis and Pegi Llwyd Ellis (née Roberts); m. Marian Thomas 1981; two d. *Education:* Univ. Coll. of Wales, Aberystwyth. *Career:* Founder-mem. Welsh-language rock band, Edward H. Dafis; recording engineer, producer, Sain Records; TV and radio producer, Bryn Gellyg Cyf; mem. Performing Right Soc., Musicians' Union. *Recordings include:* Ysbryd Y Nos, I'r Gad. *Address:* Bryn Gellyg, 22 Lon Ddewi, Caernarfon, Gwynedd, Wales (office). *Telephone:* (1248) 676458 (office). *E-mail:* hefinelis@hotmail.co.uk (office).

ELISA; Italian singer; b. (Elisa Toffoli), 19 Dec. 1977, Monfalcone. *Recordings include:* albums: Pipes And Flowers (Best First Album, Premio Italiano Della Musica) 1997, Asile's World 2000, Then Comes The Sun 2001, Elisa 2002, Lotus 2003, Pearl Days 2004, Caterpillar 2007, Dancing 2008, Heart 2009, Ivy 2010, Steppin' on Water 2012; singles: Sleeping In Your Hand 1997, Labyrinth 1997, A Feast For Me 1998, Cure Me 1998, The Gift 2000, Happiness Is Home 2000, Asile's World 2000, Luce (Tramonti A Nord Est) (Best Single, Premio Italiano Della Musica) 2001, Heaven Out Of Hell (Best Single, Italian Music Awards) 2001, Rainbow 2002, Dancing 2002, Almeno Tu Nell'Universo 2003, Broken 2003. *Honours:* Best Italian Artist, MTV Music Awards 2001, Overall Prize, San Remo Festival 2001, Best Female Artist, Italian Music Awards 2001, Best Female Artist, Premio Italiano Della Musica 2001. *Current Management:* c/o Asile Management, via Aquileia 1/B, 37074 Monfalcone, Italy. *Telephone:* (481) 481525. *E-mail:* elena.toffoli@asile.it. *Website:* www .asile.it; www.elisatoffoli.com.

ELISSA; Lebanese singer; b. (Elissa Khoury), 27 Oct. 1972, Deir al-Ahmar; d. of Zakaria Khoury and Youmna Suud. *Education:* Lebanese Univ. *Career:* discovered on TV show Studio El Fan 1992; acted in theatre groups Chansonnier Wassim Tabbara, Theatre de 10 Heures; musical collaborations include Ragheb Alameh, Gerard Ferrer, Chris De Burgh, Cheb Mami, Fadl Shaker, Emrah. *Recordings include:* albums: Baddy Doub 1999, W'akherta 2000, Aayshalak 2002, Ahla Dounya 2004, Bastanek 2006, Ayami Bik 2007, Tsadaq Bmein 2009, As'ad Wahda 2012, Halet HOB 2014. *Honours:* Murex d'Or Award for Best Female Artist 2002, 2005, 2013, Arab Music Award for Best Video 2004, World Music Award for Best-selling Middle East and N Africa Artist 2005, 2006, 2010, Middle East Music Award for Best Female Arab Artist 2008, BIAF Award for Lifetime Achievement 2014. *Address:* c/o Rotana Records, Rotana Cafe, building 5th Floor, Down Town, Beirut, Lebanon. *E-mail:* amin@elissalb.com (office). *Website:* www.elissalb.com.

ELLING, Kurt; American singer and composer; b. 2 Nov. 1967, Chicago; s. of Henry Elling and Martha Elling; m. Jennifer Carney 1996; one d. *Education:* Gustavus Adolphus Coll., Univ. of Chicago Divinity School. *Career:* numerous collaborations including David Amram, Bob Belden, Joanne Brackeen, Oscar Brown Jr, Billy Corgan, Orbert Davis, George Freeman, Buddy Guy, Jon Hendricks, Charlie Hunter, Randy Bachman, Bob Mintzer, Rex Richardson, Bob Sheppard; apptd Nat. Trustee for Nat. Acad. of Recording Arts and Sciences 1999, Vice-Chair. 2003; Artist-in-Residence, Monterey Jazz Festival 2006. *Stage performances:* Tribute to Allen Ginsberg 1998, This Is Our Music, These Are Our People (millennial celebrations in Chicago) 1999–2000, LA/CHI/NY 2001, Four Brothers 2002, Leaves of Grass (composed by Fred Hersch) 2004, Red Man/Black Man (collaboration with John Clayton) 2006. *Recordings:* albums: Close Your Eyes 1995, The Messenger (Académie du Jazz, Paris Prix Billie Holiday 1997, Chicago Music Award for Record of the Year 1997) 1997, This Time It's Love 1998, Flirting with Twilight 2001, Man in the Air 2003, Dedicated to You (Grammy Award for Best Jazz Vocal Album 2010) 2009, The Gate 2011. *Honours:* numerous awards including JazzTimes Readers Poll Award for Male Vocalist of the Year 1998, 2000, 2001, 2002, 2008, DownBeat Critics Poll Winner for Male Vocalist of the Year 2000, 2001, 2002, 2003, 2004, 2005, 2006, 2007, 2008, 2009, 2010, Jazz Journalists Asscn (JJA) Award for Male Singer of the Year 2000, 2002, 2006, 2007, 2009, 2010, JazzWeek Award for Vocalist of the Year 2006, Nightlife Award for Outstanding Jazz Vocalist 2010, JJA Jazz Award 2011. *Current Management:* Depth of Field Management, 1501 Broadway, New York, NY 10036, USA. *Telephone:* (212) 302-9200. *Fax:* (212) 382-1639. *E-mail:* hello@dof3.com. *Address:* Concord Music Group, 100 North Crescent Drive, G Level, Beverly Hills, CA 90210, USA (office). *E-mail:* julie.porter@concordmusicgroup.com (office). *Website:* www.concordmusicgroup.com (office); www.kurtelling.com.

ELLIOTT, Anthony (Tony); British songwriter and musician (bass guitar, guitar, piano/keyboard); b. 18 Dec. 1963, Liverpool. *Education:* qualifications in sound eng. *Career:* mem. of various bands, Sebastian's Men 1982–85;

various appearances on UK national/regional radio, including Radio 1 John Peel session; 16 Tambourines 1986–90; signed to Arista Records/BMG Publishing; various British tours supporting Wet Wet Wet, Hue and Cry and Squeeze; numerous appearances on regional/national TV and radio (including Radio 1 sessions); The Tambourines 1990–93; European dates, including Barcelona Olympic Festival; numerous headlining tours, shared billing with Echo and the Bunnymen, The River City People and The Real People; Catapult 1996–99; British tour and various appearances; Alto Music Productions (TV and radio advertisements) 1999–2001; songwriting partnership with Elliott Davis 1999–; production, songwriting with Catapult Enterprises 2001–; music venture The Somnambulists 2002–; acoustic event Catacoustic 2003–. *Recordings include:* with Sebastian's Men: Horizon, 1984; with 16 Tambourines: Singles: If I Should Stay, 1989; How Green Is Your Valley, 1990; Album: How Green Is Your Valley, 1990; with The Tambourines: She Blows My Mind EP; You're So Beautiful, 1992; 5 Miles Wide, featured track on Unearthed compilation, 2001; with Catapult: Everybody Gets There In The End, featured track on Tramspotting compilation, 1998.

ELLIOTT, Chris; British musician (piano, keyboards), songwriter and arranger; b. 5 Aug. 1966, Lidlington, England; m. Kerry, 24 June 1995, 1 d., Georgette. *Education:* Dartington College of Arts; Goldsmiths College, London. *Career:* Played piano and keyboards with Anne Clark 1993–96; Performer, writer and arranger with Bruce Woolley and the Radio Science Orchestra, 1994–; performed with Paul McCartney, George Michael, Elvis Costello, Sinead O'Connor, Marianne Faithfull, The Pretenders, Tom Jones, Neil Finn, Johnny Marr, 1999; Anne Clark, 2000; played piano for The Pretenders, TFI Friday and Later with Jools Holland, 1999; mem, Musicians' Union; Performing Right Society. *Recordings:* Ambient Orchestral, Chappell, 1996; Memories of the Future, Radio Science Orchestra, 1997; Storm (from the film 'The Avengers') for Grace Jones and the Radio Science Orchestra, 1999; Reverb, Radio Science Orchestra, 1999; Different Roads, Joe Cocker, Piano, 1999; Orchestral Arrangements: I Wish You Love, (from the film 'Eye of the Beholder'); Chrissie Hynde, 1998; Storm, Grace Jones and Radio Science Orchestra, 1998; Live and Let Die, Geri Halliwell, 1999; Film and TV: Century, Nagano Olympic Theme, 1998; The Second World War in Colour, 1999; Churchill's Secret Army, 1999; Moulin Rouge (Orchestration) 2000. *Honours:* Ivor Novello Scholarship, Dartington International Summer School, 1992.

ELLIOTT, Joseph (Joe) Thomas; British singer; b. 1 Aug. 1959, Sheffield; m. Kristine Elliott. *Career:* mem. Atomic Mass, band renamed Def Leppard 1977–; numerous concerts and tours worldwide, festival appearances. *Recordings include:* albums: The Def Leppard EP 1978, On Through the Night 1980, High 'n' Dry 1981, Pyromania 1983, Hysteria 1987, Adrenalize 1992, Retro Active 1993, Vault 1980–95 1995, Slang 1996, Euphoria 1999, X 2002, Yeah 2006, Songs from the Sparkle Lounge 2008, Pour Some Sugar on Me 2012, Def Leppard 2015. *Television:* Behind the Music (documentary series, VH1) 1998, Storytellers (documentary, VH1), Hysteria: The Def Leppard Story (documentary, VH1), Ultimate Albums (documentary, VH1). *Honours:* American Music Awards for Favourite Heavy Metal Album, for Favourite Heavy Metal Artist 1989. *Address:* c/o Primary Wave Music, 116 East 16th Street, 9th Floor, New York, NY 10003, USA. *E-mail:* info@ primarywave.com. *Website:* www.defleppard.com; www.joeelliott.com.

ELLIOTT, Missy 'Misdemeanour'; American rapper, singer and record producer; b. 1 July 1971, Portsmouth, Va. *Career:* joined vocal group, Sista, obtained record deal; began collaborating with Tim Mosley on singles with Aaliyah; guest rapper on various releases; obtained solo record deal; CEO Goldmind Inc. production co. 1996–, signed numerous successful acts; began releasing solo records as vocalist and rapper; supervised and guest on soundtrack of film, Why Do Fools Fall in Love 1998; live appearances include Lilith Fair travelling festival, 1998; started own lipstick line with Iman Bowie's cosmetics line. *Recordings include:* albums: Supa Dupa Fly 1997, Da Real World 1999, Miss E. . . So Addictive 2001, Under Construction 2002, This is Not a Test! 2003, The Cookbook 2005, Respect M.E. 2006, Block Party 2008. *Honours:* five Soul Train Lady of Soul Awards, Grammy Awards for Best Rap Solo Performance 2001, Best Female Rap Solo Performance 2002, MTV Video of the Year 2003, American Music Award for Favorite Rap/Hip-Hop Female 2003, Grammy Award for Best Female Rap Solo Performance (for Work It) 2004, MTV Video Award for Best Hip Hop Video, for Best Dance Video 2005, Lady of Soul Award for Best R&B/Soul Video (for Lose Control) 2005, American Music Award for Favorite Female Rap/Hip-Hop Artist 2005, BET Award for Best Female Hip Hop Artist 2006. *Address:* c/o Elektra Records, 75 Rockefeller Plaza, New York, NY 10019, USA. *Website:* www.missy-elliott .com.

ELLIS, Robert (Bobby); Jamaican musician (trumpet); b. 2 July 1932, Kingston; four s. three d. *Education:* Alpha Boys' School. *Career:* played with Tony Brown Band, Val Bennett, Luther Williams; joined The Mighty Vikings 1962; played with The Soul Brothers, Lyn Taitt and The Jetts, Billy Vernon, Lance Helwell, The Wailers, Bob Marley and The Wailers (Peace Concert, Jackson 5, Stevie Wonder), Jimmy Cliff (BBC Concert), Toots and The Maytals, Brent Dowe, John Holt, Dennis Brown, The Two Ton Machine, Burning Spear (including Sunsplash Tour), Bunny Wailer (Music City Hall, Madison Square Garden); mem. JFM. *Compositions include:* Sweet Meat, Up Park Camp, Stormy Weather, Diseases, Michigan and Smiley 1983–84; songs: Shaka, Pep-Up, Jiheje Chant, Cutlass, Sounds of Reggae, Three Finger Jack,

Doreth. *Recordings include:* solo album: Shaka; all albums with Burning Spear.

ELLIS, Glyn, (Wayne Fontana); British entertainer; b. 28 Oct. 1945, Manchester, Lancashire. *Education:* Spurley Hey Secondary Modern School, Gorton, Manchester. *Career:* Founder-mem. Velfins Skiffle Group, The Jets, The Mindbenders 1963–65; solo artist 1965–; numerous tours, festival appearances; resident songwriter, Chappell music publishers 1970–79; touring with Solid Silver 60s Show, Reelin' 'n' Rockin' USA, Canada, Australia, Germany; f. Fontana Music Promotions. *Recordings include:* albums: Wayne Fontana and The Mindbenders 1965, Eric, Rick, Wayne and Bob 1966, Wayne One 1966. *Address:* Fontana Music Promotions, New Park, Park Lane, Maplehurst, Horsham, West Sussex, RH13 6LL, England (home). *Telephone:* (7775) 284676 (office). *E-mail:* fontanauk@aol.com (office). *Website:* www.waynefontana.com (office).

ELLIS, John Stewart Maxwell, MBE; British teacher; *Founder/Director, Doncaster Youth Jazz Association;* b. 22 Feb. 1945, Lower Slaughter, Gloucestershire; m. Mary Ellis; one s. one d. *Education:* RMSM Kneller Hall, Bretton Hall Coll. *Career:* mem. armed forces 1960–72; brass teacher 1972–77; founder and Dir of Music, Doncaster Youth Jazz Assn 1973– (preparing young musicians for modern profession); performance tours to Russia, Germany, Poland, Sweden, France, USA; mem., Doncaster Jazz Orchestra (first UK band to appear at jazz festivals in Montreux 1979, Nice 1981); numerous TV and radio broadcasts; band masterclasses and workshops; jazz panel adjudicator (home and abroad); fmr Head of Music Dept, Northcliffe School; fmr mem. Int. Asscn of Jazz Educators; Hon. Life Mem. Musicians' Union, NUT. *Recordings include:* albums Live From Montreux, France…, Here Again, A Celebration, A Concert For Friends, You're Nobody Till Somebody Loves You (second place Jazz Journal Int. Record of the Year 1988), Just For Phil. *Honours:* Freeman of the Borough, Doncaster MBC 2000; European Curriculum Award 1992, BBC Big Band of the Year 1994, seven NFMY Outstanding Performance Awards 1977–87. *Address:* The Northern Jazz Centre, Beckett Road, Doncaster, DN2 4AA, England (office). *Telephone:* (1302) 320002 (office). *E-mail:* admin@dyja.info (office). *Website:* www.dyja.info (office).

ELLIS, Paul David, BA; British composer, arranger, producer, musician (keyboards) and programmer; b. 27 April 1956, Manchester; m. Yasuko Fukuoka 1993. *Education:* studied fine art in Sunderland. *Career:* tours with Hot Chocolate in Germany, UK 1983, Middle East 1984, 1985, Australia 1986; British tour with Alison Moyet 1984; tours with Billy Ocean in UK, USA 1986, 1988, Japan 1986; Japanese tour with Epo 1988; software consultant, Yamaha R & D Centre, London 1990–; mem. Musicians' Union. *Recordings include:* player, arranger, two Top 10 albums with Koji Tamaki (Japanese artist); producer, tours, album, Epo 1988; many UK sessions 1981–90. *Address:* 55D Stapleton Hall Road, London N4 3QF, England.

ELLIS-BEXTOR, Sophie; British singer; b. 10 April 1979, d. of Robin Bextor and Janet Ellis; m. Richard Jones; two s. *Education:* Godolphin and Latimer School, Hammersmith, London. *Career:* fronted group, theaudience; solo artist 2001–. *Recordings include:* albums: with theaudience: theaudience 1998; solo: Read My Lips 2002, Shoot from the Hip 2003, Trip the Light Fantastic 2007, Make a Scene 2011, Wanderlust 2014. *Current Management:* c/o Derek MacKillop, Wallace Productions, 9 Grafton Mews, London, W1T 5HZ, England. *Telephone:* (20) 7387-8269. *E-mail:* derek@wallaceproductions.co.uk. *Website:* www.sophieellisbextor.net.

ELOFSSON, Jörgen Kjell; Swedish songwriter; b. 14 Jan. 1962, Ängelholm. *Career:* full-time songwriter 1994–; collaborated with David Kreuger and Per Magnusson 1998–; f. record label Planet Six 2005; co-f. Perfect Storm Music Group AB 2010–; songwriter for numerous int. artists including Carola, Agnes, Aikakone, Jessica Andersson, Kelly Clarkson, Darin, Celine Dion, Eclipse, Emilia, Paloma Faith, Gareth Gates, Geri Halliwell, Leona Lewis, Jamie Meyer, Jennifer Rush, Saturdays, Marie Serneholt, Björn Skifs, Britney Spears, Steps, Lucy Street, Twill, Westlife, Will Young. *Compositions include:* numerous int. hit songs including: Angels Brought Me Here, Anyone of Us (Stupid Mistake), Evergreen, A Moment Like This, That's My Goal, What You've Done to Me, Stronger (What Doesn't Kill You), (You Drive Me) Crazy, Unbreakable, My Love, Fool Again, If I Let You Go. *E-mail:* robin@forefront-music.com. *Address:* c/o Frank Bonn, Perfect Storm Music Group AB, PO Box 5712, 114 87 Stockholm, Sweden (office). *Telephone:* (8) 7010900 (office). *E-mail:* info@perfectstormmusicgroup.com (office). *Website:* www.perfectstormmusicgroup.com (office); www.jorgenelofsson.com.

ELSDON, Alan Robert; musician (trumpet), bandleader, jazz singer and music critic; b. 15 Oct. 1934, Chiswick, London, England; m. June Patricia Elsdon 1960; two s. *Education:* private tuition with Tommy McQuater, Freddie Staff and Phil Parker. *Career:* joined C. Y. Laurie's Band, aged 19 and Graham Stewart 7, recorded with both groups; moved to Terry Lightfoot's Band 1959–61; formed own group 1961; backed many visiting US musicians, including Edmond Hall, Albert Nicholas, Bud Freeman, Wingy Mannone, Warren Vache, Kenny Daverne and Marti Grosz; broadcasts include Easy Beat Saturday Club, Jazz Club; played guest slots over Europe and Middle East, including Germany, Belgium, Holland, Hong Kong; played in Westminster Abbey at Philip Larkin's funeral; retired owing to ill health. *Recordings:* Keepers of the Flame, Hotter Than That, The Alan Elsdon All Star Jazz Band. *Address:* 29 Dorchester Road, Northolt, Middlesex UB5 4PA, England. *Telephone:* (20) 8422-1055.

ELSNER, Jürgen, DrPhil habil.; German musicologist and academic; b. 22 April 1932, Finsterwalde, Brandenburg. *Education:* studied music theory, musicology, Arabic. *Career:* Asst, then Sr Asst, Humboldt Univ., Berlin 1958–64, 1968–70, Karl Marx Univ., Leipzig 1964–68; Lecturer in Ethnomusicology, Humboldt Univ. 1970, Chair in Ethnomusicology 1975–96; mem. Int. Council for Traditional Music, Soc. for Ethnomusicology, Int. Hanns-Eisler-Gesellschaft. *Publications:* Zur vokalsolistischen Vortragsweise der Kampfmusik Hanns Eislers 1971, Der Begriff des maqām in Agypten in neuerer Zeit 1973, Nordafrika 1983, Curt Sachs, Die Musik der Alten Welt (ed.) 1968, Nathan Notowicz: Gespräche mit Hanns Eisler und Gerhart Eisler 1971, Sozialistische Musikkultur, Traditionen, Probleme, Perspektiven Vol. 1 1974–77, Vol. 2 1983, Maqām, Rāga, Zeilenmelodik 1989, Beiträge zur traditionellen Musik 1990, Studies in Ethnomusicology 1–4 1991–93, Regionale maqām-Traditionen in Geschichte und Gegenwart 1992, The Structure and Idea of Maqām, Historical Approaches 1997, Nachdenken über Ernst Busch 2000, Ernst Busch: Schauspieler und Sänger 2003, Dichtung und Wahrheit – Die Legendenbildung um Ernst Busch (with C. Schramm) 2006, Maqām Traditions of Turkic Peoples 2006, Intercultural Comparison of Maqām and Related Phenomena 2008, Muqām in and outside of Xinjiang/China 2009, many articles on maqām and music of Algeria and Yemen. *Honours:* Hanns Eisler Prize 1971. *E-mail:* elsnermw@web.de (office).

ELSON, Karen; British model, singer, songwriter and musician (guitar); b. 14 Jan. 1979, Bolton; m. Jack White 2005 (divorced 2013); one s. one d. *Career:* started modelling career in London aged 15, then in Tokyo, Japan, signed up with Boss Agency, Manchester; appeared in Italian Vogue Jan. 1997; joined agencies Ford Models, New York and Models 1, London; appearances in American Vogue, Harper's Bazaar; signed contract with Chanel cosmetics; provided additional vocals for song by Robert Plant, Last Time I Saw Her; currently mem. The Citizens Band (cabaret group), New York, also solo singer. *Recording:* album: The Ghost Who Walks 2010. *Honours:* Best Female Model of the Year Award 2000, British Fashion Award for Best Model 2005. *Address:* c/o Women Management New York, 199 Lafayette Street, 7th Floor, New York, NY 10012, USA. *E-mail:* info@thecitizensband.net. *Website:* www.karenelson.com; www.thecitizensband.com.

ELY, Joe; American singer, songwriter and musician (guitar); b. 9 Feb. 1947, Amarillo, Tex.; m. Sharon Thompson 1983; one d. *Career:* numerous concert tours, TV appearances; mem. The Flatlanders 1972–73, 1998–; mem. ASCAP, BMI, NARAS. *Recordings include:* albums: solo: Joe Ely 1977, Honky Tonk Masquerade 1978, Down On The Drag 1979, Live Shots 1980, Musta Notta Gotta Lotta 1981, Hi Res 1983, Lord Of The Highway 1987, Dig All Night 1988, Live At Liberty Lunch 1989, Love And Danger 1992, Letter To Laredo 1995, Twistin' In The Wind 1998, Live At Antone's 2000, From Lubbock To Laredo: Best Of 2002, Happy Songs from Rattlesnake Gulch 2007, Silver City 2007, Live Cactus! 2008, Live Chicago 1987! 2009, Satisfied At Last 2011; with The Flatlanders: Live at the One Knite 1972, Now Again 2002, Wheels of Fortune 2004, Hills and Valleys 2009, The Odessa Tapes 2012. *Current Management:* c/o David Whitehead, Maine Road Management, 195 Chrystie Street, Suite 901 F, New York, NY 10002, USA. *Telephone:* (212) 979-9004. *Fax:* (212) 979-0985. *E-mail:* mailbox@maineroadmanagement.com. *Website:* www.maineroadmanagement.com; theflatlanders.com; www.ely.com.

EMERALD, Caro; Dutch singer; b. (Caroline Esmeralda van der Leeuw), 26 April 1981, Amsterdam. *Education:* Amsterdam Conservatory of Music. *Career:* mem. close harmony vocal group Les Elles, Philharmonic Funk Foundation; singing teacher at Babette Labeij School. *Recordings:* album: Deleted Scenes from the Cutting Room Floor (3FM Award for Best Album 2011) 2010, The Shocking Miss Emerald 2013. *Honours:* numerous awards in the Netherlands including: 3FM Awards for Serious Talent 2010, for Best Female Singer 2011, Schaal van Rigter Award 2010, De Eerste Prijs 2010, Edison Award for Best Female Singer 2010, MTV Europe Music Award for Best Dutch and Belgian Act 2010, European Border Breakers Award 2011, 3FM Mega Award 2010, Popprijs 2010, Buma Silver Harp (Zilveren Harp) for Best New Artist and Best Song 2010, Best Song of the Year 2010, TMF Award for Best Female Artist 2011. *Address:* Grandmono Records, PO Box 51210, Amsterdam, EE 1007, Netherlands (office). *Telephone:* (20) 4276755 (office). *E-mail:* info@grandmono.com (office). *Website:* www.grandmono.com (office); www.caroemerald.com.

EMERICK, Geoff; British engineer and producer; b. 1946. *Career:* second engineer, then engineer, Abbey Road Studios, EMI 1966; engineer, Apple Records; has worked with America, Badfinger, The Beatles, Jeff Beck, Cilla Black, Elvis Costello, Tim Hardin, Paul McCartney, Manfred Mann, Matt Monro, Nazareth, Split Enz, Supertramp, Robin Trower, Wings, The Zombies. *Publication:* Here, There and Everywhere: My Life Recording the Music of the Beatles (auto-biog.) 2006. *Honours:* Insect Award, Distinguished Engineers Audio Federation Awards 1978, Inductee, Technical Excellence & Creativity Hall of Fame 2002, four Grammy Awards.

EMERSON, Darren Paul; British DJ, remixer and producer; b. 30 June 1971, Hornchurch, Essex. *Career:* DJ around London early 1990s; mem., Lemon Interrupt 1992; Founder-mem., Underworld 1992–2000; solo DJ career 2000–; Co-founder Effective Records 1992; Founder, Underwater Records 1994; remixer for artists, including Bjork, The Chemical Brothers, Depeche Mode, Dreadzone, Everything But The Girl, Fatboy Slim, Fire Island, Front 242, Gat Decor, Gus Gus, Leftfield, Massive Attack, One Dove, Orbital, P Diddy, Shakespears Sister, Saint Etienne, Simply Red, U2, William Orbit.

Recordings include: albums: with Underworld: Dubnobasswithmyheadman 1993, Second Toughest In The Infants 1996, Beaucoup Fish 1999, Everything Everything 2000, Anthology 1992–2002 (compilation) 2002; solo: Cream Separates 1997, Global Underground: Uruguay 2000, Global Underground: Singapore 2001, Summer Love 2001: DJ Emerson & D. Dreyer 2001, Episode 1 (with Tim Deluxe) 2002, H2O 2002, Underwater Episode 3 2004, Bouncer 2005, H2O (EP) 2005, Underwater Episode 5 2006, Crashjack 2008, Global Underground: Bogotá 2009; singles: with Lemon Interrupt: Dirty/Minneapolis 1992, Bigmouth/Eclipse 1992; with Underworld: Mmm... Skyscraper I Love You 1993, Spikee/Dogmark Go Woof 1993, Dark And Long 1994, Born Slippy 1995, Pearl's Girl 1996, Push Upstairs 1999, Jumbo 1999, King Of Snake 1999, Bruce Lee 1999, Moaner 1999, Gracelands 2010. *Current Management:* Elite Music Management, PO Box 3261, East Sussex, Brighton, BN2 4WA, England. *Telephone:* (1273) 554022. *Fax:* (1273) 566123. *E-mail:* hq@elitemm .co.uk. *Website:* www.elitemm.co.uk; www.darrenemerson.com.

EMERSON, Grant; American bass guitarist. *Education:* Univ. of North Carolina at Wilmington. *Career:* fmr mem. Debonzo Brothers 2008–10; mem. Delta Rae 2010–; first EP released 2010; signed to Sire Records 2011; debut album 2012; numerous live performances; support act for Edwin McCain and Hanson. *Recordings include:* album: with Delta Rae: Carry the Fire 2012. *Current Management:* c/o Jordan Burger, Fleming Artists, 543 North Main Street, Ann Arbor, MI 48104, USA. *Telephone:* (734) 995-9066. *Fax:* (734) 662-6502. *E-mail:* Jordan@flemingartists.com; deltaraemgmt@gmail.com. *Website:* www.flemingartists.com; www.deltarae.com.

EMERSON, Keith; British musician (keyboards) and composer; b. 2 Nov. 1944, Todmorden, West Yorkshire. *Career:* member, The T-Bones, The Nice 1967–70, Emerson Lake and Palmer (ELP) 1970–; solo artiste; also recorded as: Emerson Lake and Powell (with Cozy Powell) 1985–86; 3 1988; performances include: Isle of Wight Festival 1970, Mar-Y-Sol Festival, Puerto Rico 1972. *Films:* Pictures at an Exhibition 1973. *Recordings:* albums include: Emerson Lake and Palmer 1970, Tarkus (No. 1, UK) 1971, Pictures At An Exhibition 1971, Trilogy 1972, Brain Salad Surgery 1974, Welcome Back My Friends... 1974, Works 1977, Works Vol. Two 1977, Love Beach 1978, Emerson Lake and Palmer In Concert 1979, The Best of Emerson Lake and Palmer 1979, Emerson Lake and Powell 1986, To The Power of Three 1988, Black Moon 1992, The Atlantic Years 1992, Live At The Royal Albert Hall 1992, Return of the Manticore 1993, ELP Live In Poland 2001; solo: Inferno 1980, Nighthawks 1981, Best Revenge 1985, Murder Rock 1986, Harmageddon 1987, The Christmas Album 1988, Changing States 1995, Emerson Plays Emerson 2002, Keith Emerson Band 2008, The Three Fates Project 2012; singles include: Fanfare for the Common Man 1977; solo: Honky Tonk Train Blues 1976. *Website:* www.keithemerson.com.

EMILIO; American tejano and country music singer; b. (Emilio Navaira), 23 Aug. 1962, San Antonio, Tex.; m. Cindy Casias 1986; two s. *Education:* Southwest Texas State Univ., San Marcos. *Career:* toured with David Lee Garza 1985–88; founder own group, Rio 1989–, later solo artist; numerous live performances; mem. Tejanos for Children Foundation. *Recordings include:* albums: Emilio y Rio 1989, Sensaciones 1990, Shoot It 1991, Unsung Highways 1992, Emilio Live 1992, Southern Exposure 1993, Sound Life 1994, Life Is Good 1995, Quedate 1996, It's on the House 1997, A Mi Gente 1997, El Rey del Rodeo 2000, Lo Dice Tu Mirada 2001, Acuérdate 2002, Entre Amigos 2003, La Historia 2004, De Nuevo (Latin Grammy Award for Best Tejano Album 2008) 2007. *Honours:* Tejano Music Award for Male Vocalist of the Year four times, Album of the Year six times, Male Entertainer of the Year seven times. *Current Management:* c/o Joe Casias, Universal Latin Agency, 3798 East FM 476, Poteet, TX 78065, USA. *Telephone:* (830) 480-2470. *Fax:* (830) 742-8212. *E-mail:* jcasias@universalatin.com.

EMINEM, (Slim Shady); American rap artist and musician; b. (Marshall Bruce Mathers III), 17 Oct. 1972, St Joseph, Mo.; m. Kim Mathers (divorced); one d. *Career:* moved to Detroit aged 12; dropped out of high school to join local rap groups Basement Productions, D12; released debut album The Infinite on ind. label FBT; after releasing Slim Shady EP, made guest appearances with Kid Rock and Shabbam Shadeeq, leading to deal with Dr Dre's Aftermath Records; collaborations with artists, including Dr Dre, D12, Missy Elliott, Dido; Founder and Owner Slim Shady record label 1999–, Eight Mile Style publishing co.; f. Marshall Mathers Foundation (charity). *Film:* 8 Mile 2002. *Recordings include:* albums: The Infinite 1997, The Slim Shady LP 1999, The Marshall Mathers LP (MTV Award for Best Album) 2000, The Eminem Show (MTV Award for Best Album 2002, Grammy Award for Best Rap Album, BRIT Award for Best Int. Album, American Music Awards for Best Pop/Rock Album, Best Hip Hop/R&B Album 2003) 2002, Eminem Is Back 2004, Encore 2004, Curtain Call 2005, Eminem Presents The Re Up 2006, Relapse (Grammy Award for Best Rap Album 2010) 2009, Relapse 2 2009, Recovery (Grammy Award for Best Rap Album 2011) 2010, The Marshall Mathers LP 2 (Billboard Music Award for Top Rap Album 2014, Grammy Award for Best Rap Album 2015) 2013. *Publications:* Angry Blonde 2000, The Way I Am (auto-biog.) 2008. *Honours:* MTV Annual American Music Awards Best Hip Hop Artist 2000, 2002, three Grammy Awards 2001, Best Pop/Rock Male Artist 2002, MTV Europe Music Awards for Best Male Act 2002, 2009, for Best Hip Hop Act 2002, 2013, for Global Icon 2013, BRIT Award for Best Int. Male Solo Artist 2003, 2005, American Music Awards for Best Male Pop/Rock Artist, Best Male Hip Hop/R&B Artist 2003, Acad. Award for Best Music (for Lose Yourself, from film 8 Mile) 2004, Grammy Award for Best Male Rap Solo Performance (for Lose Yourself) 2004, Grammy Award for Best Rap Song (for Lose Yourself)

2004, Grammy Award for Best Rap Performance by a Duo or Group (for Crack a Bottle with Dr Dre and 50 Cent) 2010, Grammy Award for Best Rap Solo Performance (for Not Afraid) 2011, Echo Award for Best Int. Hip Hop Artist, Germany 2005, Smash Hits Award for Best Hip-Hop Act 2005, American Music Award for Favorite Male Rap/Hip-Hop Artist 2005, 2006, Billboard Music Award for Top Rap Artist 2014, Grammy Award for Best Rap/Sung Collaboration (with Rihanna for The Monster) 2015. *Current Management:* c/o Paul Rosenberg, Goliath Artists, 151 Lafayette Street, New York, NY 10013, USA. *Telephone:* (212) 324-2410. *Fax:* (212) 324-2415. *E-mail:* howard@goliath -management.com. *Website:* goliath-management.com; www.shadyrecords .com; www.eminem.com.

EMMETT, Rik; Canadian musician (guitar) and singer; b. Toronto. *Career:* Founder mem. of rock group, Triumph 1975–88; later worked with Lee Aaron. *Recordings include:* albums: Triumph 1976, Rock 'n' Roll Machine 1977, Just A Game 1979, Progressions of Power 1980, Allied Forces 1981, Never Surrender 1982, Thunder Seven 1984, Stages 1985, The Sport of Kings 1985, Surveillance 1987, Classics 1989, Absolutely 1990, Spiral Notebook 1996, Raw Quartet 1999, Live At Berklee 2000, The Best of Rik Emmett 2002, Handiwork 2002, Good Faith 2003, One Night in Cinci 2005, Live at 10 Gigs 2005, Strung-Out Troubadours, Live at Hugh's Room 2007, Liberty Manifesto 2007, Push & Pull 2009, Trifecta 2009, Recovery Room 9 2011, Then Again 2012, Marco's Secret Songbook 2012. *Honours:* Toronto Music Award 1987. *Address:* c/o Darcy Gregoire, The Agency Group Ltd, 2 Berkeley Street, Suite 202, Toronto, ON M5A 4J5, Canada. *Telephone:* (416) 368-5599. *Fax:* (416) 368-4655. *E-mail:* darcygregoire@theagencygroup.com. *Website:* www .theagencygroup.com; www.rikemmett.com.

ENDICOTT, Sam; American musician (guitar) and singer; b. Washington, DC. *Education:* Vassar Coll. *Career:* Founder-mem. and lead singer, The Bravery 2003–. *Recordings include:* albums: Unconditional (EP) 2004, The Bravery 2005, The Sun and the Moon 2007, Stir the Blood 2009. *E-mail:* petegalli@cybercom.net. *Website:* www.thebravery.com.

ENDRESEN, Sidsel Margrethe, BA; Norwegian singer, composer and lyricist; b. 19 June 1952, Trondheim. *Education:* Univ. of Oslo, private music teachers. *Career:* singer, poet, composer 1981–; toured Scandinavia and Europe; various radio and TV broadcasts; composed music for various theatre and dance productions, Norway; worked with many Norwegian and int. jazz musicians; fronted numerous groups; mem. Norwegian Jazz Federation, Norwegian Popular Composers. *Recordings include:* Jivetalking, 1981; Polarities, 1982; City Visions, 1984; Stories, 1985; Pigs And Poetry, 1987; So I Write, 1990; Exile, 1994; Nightsong, 1994; Duplex Ride, 1998; Out Here: In There (with Bugge Wesseltoft), 2002, The Rest is Rumors 2002, Merriwinkle 2003, One 2006, Point - Live Remixed Vol. 1 2008. *Honours:* Norwegian Grammy 1981, 1985, 1998, Radka Toneff Memorial Prize 1993, State Cultural Scholarship 1995–98. *Current Management:* c/o Kjell Kalleklev Management AS, Georgernes Verft 12, 5011, Bergen, Norway. *Telephone:* 47-55-55-76-37. *Fax:* 47-55-55-76-31. *E-mail:* kjell@kalleklev.no. *Website:* www.sidselendresen .com.

ENEVOLD, Per, MMus, CandPhil; Danish choral conductor; b. 4 Aug. 1943, Copenhagen; m. Margrete Enevold; three d. *Education:* Univ. of Copenhagen, Royal Danish Conservatoire of Music, studied under conductors Poul Jørgensen, Copenhagen, Eric Ericson, Stockholm and Arvid Jansons, Leningrad. *Career:* Artistic Dir, Chamber Choir Trinitatis Kantori 1993–; Founder and Conductor Copenhagen Chamber Choir, Camerata 1965–85; Cantor, Copenhagen Cathedral, Vor Frue Kirke 1983–90; Conductor Copenhagen Boys' Choir 1984–91; Conductor Danish Nat. Radio Choir 1985–88; Visiting Prof., Music Dept, St Olaf Coll., Northfield, Minn., USA 1991; Cantor, Trinitatis Kirke, Copenhagen 1997–2013; mem. Danish Conductors' Asscn. *Recordings include:* numerous albums with Trinitatis Kantori, Camerata, Copenhagen Boys' Choir, Danish Radio Choir. *Honours:* The Gladsaxe Award 1976, First Prize, Bela Bartok Competition, Debrecen, Hungary 1978, The Mogens Wöldlike Award 1982, First Prize, European Broadcasting Union Competition, for Let the Peoples Sing 1999. *Address:* Strandvejen 61, 2th, 2100 Copenhagen, Denmark (office). *Telephone:* 39-27-39-26 (office). *E-mail:* perenevold@gmail.com (office). *Website:* www .perenevold.dk.

ENGDAHL, Elisabeth; Swedish musician and composer; b. 17 Dec. 1956, Karlskrona; m. Thomas Gustafsson, 2 d. *Education:* Swedish Acad. of Music. *Career:* orchestral leader and performing musician in a small big band and lady band, 1987–93; orchestral leader, performing house band pianist, television show, Good Morning Sweden, 1989–90; performing saxophonist, in charge of musical arrangement of a Swedish Talk Show, 1993–95; concert performances in Shanghai, People's Republic of China, 1994; mem. Swedish Popular Music Composers, Swedens Media Composers. *Compositions include:* Musical Score, Kurt Olsson - The Movie About My Life As Myself, 1989; The Love Project Jazz Opera, 1996. *Recordings include:* Musical Arrangements of three records with Kurt Olsson's Lady Band, 1987, 1988, 1990.

ENGEL, Soren Peter Bjarne; Danish musician (guitar, bass guitar); b. 6 April 1947, Copenhagen; m. Anne Grethe, 9 May 1991, 1 s. *Career:* television appearances in France; Germany; Sweden; Finland; Norway; Denmark; European tours with Bo Diddley; Link Wray; Sonny Terry; Brownie McGee; Delta Cross Band; mem. Danish Artists' Union. *Recordings include:* with Delta Cross Band: No Overdubs, 1979; Rave On, 1980; Up Front, 1981; Slide,

1984; Through Times, 1991; with C V Jorgensen: Tidens Tein, 1980; Vinden Vender, 1982.

ENGLAND, Ty; American singer and musician (guitar); b. 5 Dec. 1963, Oklahoma City; m. Shanna Burns England, three s. one d. *Education:* Oklahoma State Univ., Central State Univ. *Career:* harmony singer and acoustic guitarist for Garth Brooks six years; solo artist 1995–. *Recordings include:* albums: Ty England 1995, Two Ways to Fall 1996, Highways and Dancehalls 1999, Alive and Well and Livin' the Dream 2007. *Address:* 1111 17th Avenue South, Nashville, TN 37212, USA. *Website:* www.tyenglandmusic.com.

ENGLISH, Michael; American singer. *Career:* toured with The Singing Americans; joined The Goodmans; joined Gospel Group with Legend Bill Gaither; solo artist 1994–; mem. The Gaither Vocal Band 1995. *Recordings include:* Michael English 1991, Hope 1993, Healing 1995, Freedom 1996, Gospel 1998, Heaven To Earth 2000, A Michael English Christmas 2003, In Christ Alone 2006, The Prodigal Comes Home 2008, Greatly Blessed 2010, Some People Change 2012. *Publication:* The Prodigal Comes Home: My Story of Failure and God's Story of Redemption 2007. *Honours:* six Dove Awards including Artist of the Year and Best Male Vocalist 1994, for Best Southern Gospel Recorded Song of the Year. *Address:* c/o DayStar Promotions, PO Box 150207, Tulsa, OK 74115, USA. *E-mail:* michael@michaelenglishmusic.com (office); kevinstevens5@gmail.com. *Website:* www.michaelenglishmusic.com.

ENGLISH, Tom; British musician (drums). *Career:* Founder-mem., Maxïmo Park 2001–. *Recordings include:* albums: A Certain Trigger 2005, Our Earthly Pleasures 2007, Quicken the Heart 2009, The National Health 2012, Too Much Information 2014. *Current Management:* Prolifica Management, Unit 1, 32 Caxton Road, London, W12 8AJ, England. *Telephone:* (20) 8740-9920. *Fax:* (20) 8740-2976. *E-mail:* info@prolifica.co.uk. *Website:* www.prolificamanagement.co.uk; www.maximopark.com.

ENGLUND, Sverker, BA, PhD; Swedish ethnomusicologist; b. 26 Nov. 1968, Stockholm. *Education:* Stockholm Univ. *Career:* mem. Int. Council for Traditional Music. *Publications include:* De sista ljuva åren: upptäcktsresor i oldranders musikaliska landshap, 1996; Srigfinnare i pensionarsland, 1998; Det Gemensamma Minners Melodier, in Pigga pensionärer och populärkultur, 1998. *Address:* c/o M. Eklund, Torkel Knutssonsg 33 IV, 11849 Stockholm, Sweden.

ENGLUNDH, Peter; Danish musician (drums, keyboards), singer and songwriter; b. 4 Feb. 1950; m. Hanne Jakobsen 1974; one s. one d. *Education:* Danish music school. *Career:* mem. Scool Band 1960, Doctor Phill 1967, several dance bands 1971, Golden Diamond 1980, Grethe Ingmann and Sunset 1984, A/S Rockkompagniet 1985, 1998, Hit the Hay 1996; mem. KODA, NBC, DMF. *Recordings include:* Ann Mari 1975, Habet Er Gront 1977, A/S Rockkompagniet Songs 1985–98, Nikki Hokey 1982, Mooreen 1982. *Address:* Lysholm Alle 64, 4690 Haslev, Denmark. *E-mail:* info@strike.dk (office). *Website:* www.strike.dk (office).

ENO, Brian Peter George St John Baptiste de la Salle; British composer, artist, keyboard player and producer; b. 15 May 1948, Woodbridge, Suffolk; s. of the late William Arnold Eno and of Maria Alphonsine Eno (née Buslot); m. 1st Sarah Grenville 1967; one d.; m. 2nd Anthea Norman-Taylor 1988; two c. *Education:* St Mary's Convent, St Joseph's Coll., Ipswich School of Art, Winchester Coll. of Art. *Career:* Founder-mem. Roxy Music 1971–73; worked with guitarist Robert Fripp 1975–76; invented 'ambient music' 1975; Visiting Prof., RCA 1995–; Hon. Prof. of New Media, Berlin Univ. of Art 1998–; f. Long Now Foundation 1996; mem. PRS, BAC&S. *Exhibitions include:* over 75 exhbns of video, light and sound artworks world-wide. *Recordings include:* albums: Here Come The Warm Jets 1974, Taking Tiger Mountain (By Strategy) 1974, Another Green World 1975, Discreet Music 1975, Before and After Science 1977, Music For Films 1978, Ambient 1: Music For Airports 1978, After the Heat 1978, My Life in the Bush of Ghosts (with David Byrne) 1981, Ambient 3: Day of Radiance 1981, Empty Landscapes 1981, Ambient 4: On Land 1982, Music For Films Vol. 2 1983, Apollo: Atmospheres and Soundtracks 1983, Begegnungen 1984, Thursday Afternoon 1985, Begegnungen II 1985, Music For Films Vol. 3 1988, Wrong Way Up 1990, Nerve Net 1992, The Shutov Assembly 1992, Neroli 1993, Headcandy 1994, Spinner 1995, The Drop 1997, Extracts from Music for White Cube 1997, Kite Stories 1999, I Dormienti 1999, Music for Onmyo-Ji 2000, Music for Civic Recovery Center 2000, Drawn From Life 2001, January 07003: Bell Studies for The Clock 2003, Another Day on Earth 2005; with Robert Fripp: No Pussyfooting 1975, Evening Star 1976, The Equatorial Stars 2004, The Cotswold Gnomes 2006, Beyond Even 1992–2006 2007, Everything that Happens will Happen Today (with David Byrne) 2008, Small Craft on a Milk Sea 2010, Lux 2012, Someday World (with Karl Hyde) 2014; numerous albums as producer, co-producer, collaborations, guest appearances on albums, and remixes including: U2, Coldplay, Paul Simon, David Bowie, David Byrne. *Publications include:* A Year with Swollen Appendices 1995, The Margin: A Canongate Diary for 2007 (ed.). *Honours:* Hon. DTech (Plymouth) 1995; Dr hc, Royal Coll. of Art 2007; Q Magazine Award for Best Producer (with others) 1993, BRIT Awards for Best Producer 1994, 1996, Inspiration Award (with David Bowie) 1995, Grammy Awards for Producer of Best Record of the Year 2000, 2009. *Current Management:* c/o Shakedown Records Ltd, Regent House, 1 Pratt Mews, London, NW1 0AD, England. *Telephone:* (19082) 70546. *E-mail:* orders@shakedownrecords.com. *Website:* www.enoshop.co.uk (office).

ENRIQUE, Luis; Nicaraguan singer and songwriter; b. (Luis Enrique Mejía López), 28 Sept. 1962, Somoto. *Career:* solo salsa singer 1980s–; immigrated to USA 1978. *Recordings include:* Amor de Media Noche 1987, Amor y Alegria 1988, Mi mundo 1989, Luces del Alma 1990, Los Principes de la Salsa 1990, Una historia diferente 1991, Dilema 1993, Brillante 1994, Luis Enrique 1994, Brillantes 1994, Genesis 1996, Amiga 1999, Timbalaye 1999, Evolución 2000, Transparente 2002, Dentro Y Fuera 2007, Ciclos (Latin Grammy Award for Best Salsa Album 2009, Grammy Award for Best Tropical Latin Album 2010) 2009, Soy y Sere 2011. *Honours:* Latin Grammy Award for Best Tropical Song (for Yo No Sé Mañana) 2009. *E-mail:* neme@luisenriquemusic.com. *Website:* luisenriquemusic.com.

ENTHOVEN, David John; British company director and artist manager; *Managing Director, IE Music;* b. 5 July 1944, Windsor, Berkshire; m. twice; one s. one step-s. one d. one step-d. *Career:* f. EG Group of Companies 1969; signed King Crimson, T Rex, Emerson Lake and Palmer, Roxy Music, Bryan Ferry; f. IE Music Ltd 1988, currently Man. Dir; Artist Man. for Robbie Williams, Sia, Craig Armstrong, The Casuals, Sweet Chap, Archive. *Address:* IE Music Ltd, 111 Frithville Gardens, London, W12 7JG, England (office). *Telephone:* (20) 8600-3400 (office). *Fax:* (20) 8600-3401 (office). *E-mail:* info@iemusic.co.uk (office). *Website:* www.iemusic.co.uk (office).

ENYA; Irish singer, composer and musician (piano); b. (Eithne Ní Bhraonáin), 17 May 1961, Gweedore, Co. Donegal; d. of Leon Ó Braonáin and Máire Bean Uí Bhraonáin. *Career:* keyboard and background vocals with family group, Clannad (traditional Irish music) 1980–82; formed Aigle Music (with producer and sound engineer Nicky Ryan and man. and lyricist Roma Ryan) 1982; performed at the Queen's 50th Wedding Anniversary, birthday celebrations of King Gustav of Sweden and privately for Pope John Paul II; numerous other live appearances, including the Acad. Awards 2002. *Recordings include* albums: with Clannad: Crann Ull 1980, Fuaim 1982; as Enya: Enya 1987, Watermark (IFPI Platinum European Award) 1988, Shepherd Moons (IFPI Platinum European Award, Grammy Award, Billboard Music Award, NARM Best-Selling Album Award) 1991, The Celts 1992, The Memory of Trees (Grammy Award) 1995, Paint the Sky with Stars (Japanese Grand Prix Album of the Year) 1997, A Day Without Rain (Grammy Award, Japanese Grand Prix Album of the Year) 2000, Amarantine (Grammy Award for Best New Age Album 2007) 2005, And Winter Came 2008, Dark Sky Island 2015. *Honours:* Dr hc (Nat. Univ. of Ireland, Galway) 2007, (Univ. of Ulster) 2007; Ivor Novello Int. Achievement Award 1998, six World Music Awards including Best-Selling Artist in the World 2001, Japanese Grand Prix Award for New Artist of the Year, Hot Press Best Irish Solo Artist, Academy of Achievement of America Golden Plate Award, Billboard Artist Award, Echo Award (for Only Time), BMI Special Citation of Achievement (for Only Time, for Orinoco Flow, I Don't Wanna Know), Las Vegas Film Critics' Soc. Award for Best Original Song (for May It Be), Phoenix Film Critics' Award for Best Original Song (for May It Be), Broadcast Film Critics' Award for Best Song (for May It Be). *Address:* Treesdale, Church Road, Killiney, Co. Dublin, Ireland (office). *Website:* www.enya.com.

EOIN, Marcus, MA; British musician and producer; b. 21 July 1971, Stirling, Scotland; s. of John Eoin and Samantha Eoin; m. Chen Ziyi; three c. *Education:* School of Int. Relations, Univ. of St Andrews. *Career:* mem. Boards of Canada 1995–. *Radio:* John Peel Session (BBC Radio 1) July 1998. *Recordings include:* albums: Twoism 1995, Music Has The Right To Children 1998, Geogaddi 2002, The Campfire Headphase 2005, Tomorrow's Harvest 2013; EPs: Hi Scores 1996, In A Beautiful Place Out In The Country 2000, Trans Canada Highway 2006. *Address:* Hexagon Sun, PO Box 28607, Edinburgh, EH14 7YA, Scotland (office). *Website:* www.boardsofcanada.com.

EPPLE, Kat, BA; American musician (flute) and composer; b. 21 Aug. 1952, d. of Mark Epple and Erma Smalley. *Education:* Univ. of South Florida. *Career:* concerts at the Guggenheim Museum, New York, Bilbao, Spain, with symphony orchestras Nat. Gallery, Washington, DC, Metropolitan Museum of Art, New York, Hollywood Palace, Los Angeles, Palazzo dei Diamanti, Italy; concert tour of Russia; travelled to People's Repub. of China, Africa, Russia, Europe, Japan, Mexico, Brazil, Costa Rica, Peru and the Caribbean to collect flutes which she incorporates into compositions; live performances with Parson's Dance Co; also recording engineer and producer for TV and film soundtracks, Kat Epple Music Production; Artist Amb., Worldwide Peace Marker Project; mem. BMI, Alliance of the Arts of Lee County, New Arts Festival. *Compositions include:* television soundtracks for National Geographic, CNN, PBS-Nova, Carl Sagan, Guiding Light, Another World, CNN, Travel Channel, History Channel, Discovery Channel, Metropolitan Museum of Art, NASA. *Film:* Captive Island (music dir) 1995. *Recordings include:* Dragon Wings 1978, Whispered Visions 1979, Sound Trek 1980, Aqua Regia 1981, Valley of the Birds 1982, Nocturne 1983, Lights of the Ivory Plains 1985, Catspaw 1986, Dreamspun 1988, Manatee Dreams 1990, White Crow 1997, Azure Pieces of Life 2004, Works in Progress 2005, Mystic Moods 2006, From Wind and Earth 2007, Serenity Hideaway 2009. *Honours:* Emmy Awards for Music for TV, 1978, 1982, 1983, 1985, 1989, 1998, Angel of the Arts 2005, 2009. *Address:* Kat Epple Music Productions, North Fort Myers, FL 33903, USA (office). *Telephone:* (239) 997-0323. *E-mail:* kat@katepple.com (office). *Website:* www.katepple.com.

EPWORTH, Paul, (Phones, Epic Man, Echo Channel); British producer, remixer, musician and songwriter; b. London. *Career:* worked as sound engineer, Air Studios, The Strongroom, Chiswick Reach, London; fmr in-house producer/engineer, 93 Feet East music venue, London; producer, 679 Recordings; remixes under the names Phones and Echo Channel, records own music under name Epic Man; Founder Good and Evil Records 2006–; has produced for numerous artists including Adele, Coldplay, U2, Florence and the Machine, Bruno Mars, Lana Del Rey, Paul McCartney, John Legend, FKA twigs, The Rapture, Plan B, Kano, Bloc Party, Futureheads, Maxïmo Park, The Rakes, White Rose Movement, Wolf and Cub, Sons and Daughters, Death from Above 1979; remixed artists, including The Streets, Shaznay Lewis, The Music, Lomax, Goldfrapp, Annie, Tom Vek, U2, The Kills, Gang of Four, Simian Mobile Disco, The Others. *Recordings include:* solo single: Epic Man's More is Enough (featuring Plan B) 2006; 21 (by Adele, Grammy Award for Producer of the Year 2012 and Grammy Award for Album of the Year 2012) 2011, Grammy Award for Song of the Year and Record of the Year (for Rolling in the Deep by Adele) 2012, 25 (by Adele) 2015. *Honours:* Music Producers Guild Award for Producer of the Year 2010, Academy Award for Best Original Song (with Adele) (Skyfall) 2013, BRIT Award for British Producer of the Year 2015. *Address:* c/o Empire Artist Management, 36 Uxbridge Street, Notting Hill, London, W8 7TN, England. *E-mail:* info@empire-management.co.uk. *Website:* www.paulepworth.com.

ERGATOUDIS, George; British radio producer and broadcasting executive; *Head of Music, BBC Radio One. Career:* co-founder and ed., Babel music fanzine, while at univ.; co-founder and co-ed., Signs magazine, Sheffield; trainee producer, BBC Radio One 1989, worked with DJs Alan Freeman, Dave Lee Travis and Simon Bates, produced programme Last Night a DJ Saved My Life: A History of the Remix; Club Promotions Man., 4th & Broadway/Island Records 1990; freelance producer, BBC Radio One 1990–91; Sr Producer, Kiss 100 FM 1991–97; Producer, BBC Radio One (Jo Whiley and Simon Mayo shows) 1997, Music Man. BBC 1Xtra 2002–05, Head of Music, BBC Radio One 2005–16. *Honours:* Sony Gold Award (for the Steve Jackson Breakfast Show, Kiss 100 FM). *Address:* BBC Radio One, London, W1N 4DJ, England (office). *Website:* www.bbc.co.uk/radio1.

ERGUNER, Kudsi; Turkish musician (ney), composer, musicologist and teacher; b. 4 Feb. 1952, Diyarbakir; s. of Ulvi Erguner; brother of Süleyman Erguner. *Career:* mem. Istanbul Radio Orchestra 1969; concert and festival appearances worldwide; researched for Peter Brook's film Meetings With Remarkable Men 1967, film Mahabharata 1988; moved to France to study architecture and musicology 1975; f. Mevlana Inst. of Sufi Music 1981; founder (with brothers) Erguner School of Music; f. Fasl group, later renamed Kudsi Erguner Ensemble 1988; worked with Peter Gabriel on soundtrack to film The Last Temptation of Christ 1988; composed music for ballet, Neva by Carolyn Carlson 1991; composed music for ballet, Le Voyage Nocturne by Maurice Béjart 1997. *Recordings include:* albums: The Mystic Flutes Of Sufi 1988, The Mahabharata 1990, Turquie Musique Soufi (with Süleyman Erguner) 1991, Oriental Dreams (with Mahmoud Tébrizizadeh), Gazel (with others), L'orient De L'occident 1994, Kudsi Erguner 1995, Psaumes De Yunus Emre 1996, Tatyos Efendi, Chemins (with Derya Turkan), Le Concert De Nanterre (with others) 1998, Ottomania (with others) 1999, Ottomania Kudsi Erguner Sufi-Jazz-Project, Islam Blues 2001, Nazım Hikmet 2002, Gazing Point 2003, No Matter 2008.

ERGUNER, Süleyman, PhD; Turkish musician (ney), conductor and teacher; s. of Ulvi Erguner; brother of Kudsi Erguner. *Education:* Marmara Univ. *Career:* Co-founder (with brothers) Erguner School of Music; taught ney, Istanbul Univ. Conservatory 1980–81; ney player, Istanbul State Radio and Television 1981; leader, Istanbul Mevlevi Ensemble 1995; Faculty mem., Istanbul Univ. Turkish Music Conservatory; conductor, Classical Turkish Music Chorus and the Mystic Music Ensemble, Istanbul State Radio and Television; numerous solo concerts 1975–; Artistic Dir, Women's Ensemble of Istanbul; Founder, Erguner Ensemble Instrumental-Choeur Musique Turque, Erguner Dervishes Tourneurs, Erguner Musique Ottoman, Harem Ensemble of Istanbul Women. *Recordings include:* albums: Süleyman-Kudsi Erguner 1987, Mevlana Dervishes Music 1987, Mevlana Beyati Ayini ve Acemaéiran Ayini, Mevlana Beste-i Kadim Pencügah Mevlevi Ayini 1988, Mevlana Instrumantal Mevlevi Music: Hicaz Mevlevi 1988, Sufi Music of Turkey 1990, Fasl Musique De L'Empire Ottoman 1990, Ilahiler Sufi Music Istanbul Sema Grubu Mutrip Heyeti 1990, Sharki 1991, Gazel 1991, Ottoman Music Chants du Harem 1994, Süleyman Erguner Ney Improvisations 1994, Süleyman Erguner, Lawrence Butch Morris: Conduction 25–26 1995, Tatyos Efendi 1996, Les Dervishes de Turquie: Musique Sufi, Aárá Daáá Efsanesi & Tayfun 1997, Mevlana Whirling Dervishes III Selamlar 1999, Mevlana Whirling Dervishes: Peérev 1999, Ney Ile Tasavvuftan Seçmeler 1999, Rumi 2000, Ney Improvisations: Sah Ney 2001. *Honours:* Turkish Writers' Committee Award for Best Artist 1997. *E-mail:* suleyman@erguner.com. *Website:* www.erguner.com.

ERICSON, Peter R.; Swedish composer, producer, musician (guitar) and singer; b. 2 July 1950, Uppsala; m. Nina 1975; two s. one d. *Education:* St Martins Coll., Lancaster, England. *Career:* mem. Mobben 1970s; solo artist 1980s–; television, radio appearances and regular tours; currently writing music for major film. *Compositions:* music for major Swedish artists including Monica Zetterlund, Cornelis Vreeswijk. *Recordings:* four albums with Mobben, six solo albums, many albums as producer. *Current Management:* Hawk Records, Scandinavian Songs Music Group, Box 109, 18212 Danderyd, Sweden. *E-mail:* peterrericson@yahoo.se (home). *Website:* www.peterrericson .com.

ERIKSON, Doug (Duke); American musician (guitar, bass guitar, keyboards). *Career:* fmr guitarist and singer, Spooner, Firetown; worked with Nine Inch Nails, L7, U2; mem., Garbage 1994–; numerous tours, festivals, TV and radio appearances. *Recordings include:* albums: Garbage 1995, Version 2.0 1998, Beautifulgarbage 2001, Androgyny 2003, Bleed Like Me 2005, Absolute Garbage 2007, Not Your Kind of People 2012. *Film music:* The World is Not Enough (theme to James Bond: The World is Not Enough) 1999. *Current Management:* Free Trade Agency, 20–22 Curtain Road, London, EC2A 3NF, England. *Telephone:* (20) 7655-6900. *Fax:* (20) 7655-6909. *E-mail:* info@freetradeagency.co.uk. *Website:* www.freetradeagency.co.uk; www .garbage.com.

ERIKSSON, Maria; Swedish musician (guitar). *Career:* mem. The Concretes 1999–; band founded label, Licking Fingers. *Recordings include:* albums: Boyoubetterunow 2000, The Concretes 2003, Layourbattleaxedown 2005, In Colour 2006, Hey Trouble 2007, WYWH 2010. *Current Management:* c/o EC1 Music Agency, 1 Cowcross Street, London, EC1M 6DR, England. *E-mail:* theconcretes@theconcretes.com. *Website:* www.theconcretes.com.

ERNA, Salvatore (Sully) Paul; American singer; b. 7 Feb. 1968, Lawrence, Mass. *Career:* fmr drummer, Stripmind; singer, Godsmack 1995–; solo artist 1996–; numerous tours, live appearances. *Recordings include:* albums: with Godsmack: Godsmack 1998, Awake 2000, Faceless 2003, Godsmack IV 2004, The Oracle 2010, Live and Inspired 2012, 1000hp; solo: Avalon 2010. *Honours:* Boston Music Award for Act of the Year 2000, 2001, Billboard Award for Rock Artist of the Year 2001. *E-mail:* info@sullyerna.com. *Website:* www.godsmack .com; www.sullyerna.com.

ESCALLE, Jean-Louis; French jazz musician (drums); b. 3 March 1954, Aurimont, Gers; m. Marie-Jeanne Escalle 1982, one s. two d. *Education:* Toulouse Conservatory. *Career:* jazz sideman, with regional and national jazz musicians in the south of France. *Recordings include:* four albums with regional musicians: J. M. Pilc, R. Calleja, Ch. Brun.

ESCOVEDO, Alejandro; American singer, songwriter, musician (guitar) and arranger; b. 1951, San Antonio, TX; m. 1st (deceased); m. 2nd (deceased). *Career:* mem. The Nuns 1977–79; mem. of bands, Rank and File, True Believers –1987; solo artist 1992–; tours with his band, Buick MacKane, and Alejandro Escovedo Orchestra. *Recordings include:* albums: with The Nuns: The Nuns 1980; solo: Gravity 1992, Hard Road 1994, Thirteen Years 1994, With These Hands 1996, Buick MacKane: The Pawn Shop Years 1997, More Miles Than Money: Live 1994–96 1998, Bourbonitis Blues 1999, A Man Under The Influence (Austin Music Award for Best Album) 2001, By The Hand Of The Father 2002, The Boxing Mirror 2006, Real Animal 2008, Street Songs of Love 2010. *Music for film:* Man from Plains 2007. *Honours:* Austin Music Award for Musician of the Year 1993, Americana Award for Lifetime Achievement in Performance 2006. *Address:* c/o Jan Stabile, Jon Landau Management, 158 Rowayton Ave, Rowayton, CT 06853, USA. *Telephone:* (203) 854-0528. *E-mail:* jstabile@jonlandau.net. *Website:* www.alejandroescovedo .com.

ESOTERIK (see Degiorgio, Kirk)

ESPINOZA SAVIÑÓN, Dulce María; Mexican singer and actress; b. 6 Dec. 1985, Mexico City. *Career:* actress from childhood; fmr mem. Jeans; mem. RDB 2004–. *Television includes:* Plaza Sésamo, El Club de Gaby, Discovery Kids, Retrato de Familia 1995, Alondra 1995, El Vuelo del Aguila 1996, Huracán 1998, DKDA Sueños de Juventud 1999, Primer Amor... a mil por hora 2000, Locura de Amor 2000, Siempre te Amaré 2000, Clase 406 (series) 2002, Rebelde (series) 2004, RBD: La Familia (series) 2007, Verano de Amor 2009, Miss XV 2012, Mentir Para Vivir 2013. *Films include:* Quimera, Inesperado Amor, Desilusiones 1997, Juguito de Ciruela 1997, Bienvenida al Clan 2000, El Agente 00-P2 2007, ¿Alguien Ha Visto A Lupita? 2011, Quiero Ser Fiel 2013. *Recordings include:* albums: Rebelde 2004, Nuestro Amor 2005, Celestial (Billboard Latin Music Award for Latin Pop Album of the Year by a Duo or Group 2007) 2006, Rebels (in English) 2006, Empezar Desde Cero 2007, Extranjera 2010, Extranjera Primera Parte (EP) 2010, Extranjera Segunda Parte (EP) 2011. *Honours:* Billboard Latin Music Award for Top Latin Albums Artist of the Year, for Latin Tour of the Year 2007, some 24 Premios Juventud, Billboard Latin Music 'Tu Mundo' Award 2008. *Address:* c/o EMI Latin, 404 Washington Avenue, Suite 700, Miami Beach, FL 33139, USA. *Telephone:* (305) 674-7529. *Website:* www.emimusic.com.mx (office).

ESSEX, David, OBE; British singer, actor and composer; b. (David Albert Cook), 23 July 1947, London; s. of Albert Cook and Doris Cook (née Kemp); m. Maureen Neale Neal 1971; one s. one d. *Education:* Shipman Secondary School, E London. *Career:* started in music industry 1965; TV debut on Five O'Clock Club; has since made numerous TV appearances in UK, Europe and USA, including own BBC series 1977, The River BBC1 Series 1988; appeared on stage in repertory and later in Godspell 1971, Evita 1978, Childe Byron, Mutiny! (also wrote music) 1985, with Sir Peter Hall's Co. in She Stoops to Conquer tour and Queen's Theatre, London 1993–94; wrote score for Russian All Stars Co.'s Beauty and the Beast 1995–96; first concert tour of UK 1974, subsequent tours 1975 (including Europe, USA and Australia), 1976, 1977, 1978, 1979 (including Europe and USA), 1980, 1987, 1988, 1989/90 (World Tour); Amb. for Voluntary Service Overseas 1990–92; Pres. Stanstead Park Cricket Club. *Films include:* Assault, All Coppers Are . . . 1971, That'll Be The Day (Variety Club Award) 1973, Stardust 1974, Silver Dream Racer 1979, Shogun Mayeda 1991. *Albums include:* Rock On 1974, All the Fun of the Fair

1975, Out on the Street 1976, Gold and Ivory 1977, Imperial Wizard 1979, Hot Love 1980, Be Bop the Future 1981, Stage Struck 1982, The Whisper 1983, This One's For You 1984 (all solo); Under Different Skies (album of musicians from developing countries); War of the Worlds (with Jeff Wayne, Richard Burton and others), From Alpha to Omega (with Cat Stevens) 1978, Silver Dream Racer (film soundtrack: composer/producer) 1979, Centre Stage 1986, Touching the Ghost 1989, David Essex Greatest Hits 1991, Cover Shot 1993, Back to Back 1994, Living in England 1995, A Night at the Movies 1997, The Very Best of David Essex 1998, I Still Believe 1999, Thank You 2000, Wonderful 2001, Forever 2002, Sunset 2003, It's Gonna Be Alright 2004, Greatest Hits 2006, Beautiful Day 2006, Happily Ever After 2007, All the Fun of the Fair 2008, Unplugged 2009, Reflections 2013. *Publication:* A Charmed Life 2003. *Honours:* numerous gold and silver discs for LP and single records in Europe and USA; voted Best Male Singer and Outstanding Music Personality in Daily Mirror poll 1976; Variety Club of GB Award for Show Business Personality of the Year (joint) 1978 ASCAP Award 1989, BASCA Award for Composer 1994. *Address:* David Essex Management, PO Box 390, Billingshurst, West Sussex, RH14 4BE, England. *Website:* www.davidessex.com.

ESSIET, Chief Udoh; Nigerian musician (African percussion), singer, composer and bandleader; b. 21 Nov. 1959, Ikot Ekpene; m. Sherry Margolin; one s. *Career:* in Nigeria until 1983; performed traditional native music, Highlife music, with Dr Victor Olaiya, Rex Williams, Rex Lawson, Juju (Sunny Ade); performed Afrobeat music with Fela Anikulapo Kuti 1978–83; based in Paris 1983–; founded Ghetto Blaster, first part for Fela, James Brown 1984, Mory Kante, Salif Keita; formed Afrobeat Blaster, tours in Europe 1989–; mem. Société des auteurs, compositeurs et éditeurs de musique (SACEM), Société de perception et de distribution des droits des artistes-interprètes (SPEDIDAM), ADAMI. *Film:* Ghetto Blaster 1983. *Recordings include:* with Ghetto Blaster: Preacher Man 1984, People 1986; with Salif Keita: Soro; with Sixun, Fela Anikulapo Kuti: ITT, Unknown Soldier, Coffin For Head of State, Authority Stealing, 2000 Black (with Roy Ayers); with Afrobeat Blaster: No Condition Is Permanent 1991; solo: Time for Highlife 1999, Highlife Crossing 2006, Many Things 2008. *Honours:* Chief of African Feeling, Amsterdam 1986. *E-mail:* udoh@chiefudoh.com. *Website:* www.chiefudoh.com.

ESSING, John Leo Thomas; Swedish musician (guitar, synthesizer, percussion); b. 15 Aug. 1964, Stockholm. *Career:* mem., bob hund 1991–; numerous concerts in Scandinavia, including Roskilde, Lollipop, Ruisrock, Quartfestivalen and Hultsfred festivals; mem. Svenska Tonsättares Internationella Musikbyrå, SAMI. *Recordings include:* bob hund 1993, Edvin Medvind, 7 1994, I Stället för Musik: förvirring 1996, Omslag: Martin Kann 1996, Düsseldorf 3:53 1996, Ett fall och en lösning 1997, Nu är det väl revolution på gång? 1998, Jag rear ut min själ! Allt skal bort!!! 1998, Helgen V.48 1999, Sover aldrig 1999, Stenåldem kan börja 2001, Ingenting 2002. *Honours:* Swedish Grammy Awards for Best Live Act 1994, Best Lyrics 1996. *Website:* www.bobhund.nu.

ESTEFAN, Gloria Maria; American singer and songwriter; b. 1 Sept. 1957, Havana, Cuba; d. of Jose Fajardo and Gloria García; m. Emilio Estefan 1979; one s. one d. *Education:* Univ. of Miami. *Career:* went to USA 1959; f. Gloria Estefan Foundation 1997. *Recordings include:* albums: Primitive Love 1986, Let it Loose 1987, Anything For You 1988, Cuts Both Ways 1989, Coming Out of the Dark 1991, Greatest Hits 1992, Mi Terra 1993, Hold Me, Thrill Me, Kiss Me 1994, Destiny 1996, Gloria! 1998, Santo Santo 1999, Alma Caribeño: Caribbean Soul 2000, Greatest Hits: Vol. 2 2001, Unwrapped 2003, 90 Millas (Latin Grammy Award for Best Traditional Tropical Album 2008) 2007, Miss Little Havana 2011, The Standards 2013. *Honours:* hon. law degree (Barry Univ., Miami) 2002, Hon. DMus (Berklee Coll. of Music, Boston) 2007; American Music Award 1987, Billboard Latin Music Award for Best Female Tropical Airplay Track (for Tu Fotografía) 2005, Latin Grammy Award for Best Tropical Song (for Pintame de Colores) 2008, Billboard Spirit of Hope Award 2011, Presidential Medal of Freedom 2015. *Address:* Estefan Enterprises Inc., 420 Jefferson Avenue, Miami Beach, FL 33139, USA. *Telephone:* (305) 695-7000. *Website:* www.estefan.com; www.gloriaestefan.com.

ESTELLE; British vocalist, songwriter and producer; b. (Estelle Swaray), 18 Jan. 1980, London. *Career:* f. ind. record label Stellar Ents; collaborations with Faithless, DJ Skitz, 57th Dynasty, Social Misfits, Against The Grain, 3SL, Blak Twang, DJ Dynamite, Ben Watt, Natasha Bedingfield, Band Aid 2004; first signing to John Legend's Homeschool record label. *Recordings:* albums: The 18th Day 2004, Shine 2008, All of Me 2012, True Romance 2015. *Honours:* Best Female Artist, UK Hip Hop Awards (three times), MOBO Awards for Best Newcomer 2004, for Best UK Female 2008, for Best Song (for American Boy) 2008, Grammy Award for Best Rap/Sung Collaboration (for American Boy with Kanye West) 2009. *Current Management:* Empire Artist Management, 36 Uxbridge Street, London, W8 7TN, England. *Telephone:* (20) 7221-1133. *Fax:* (20) 7243-1585. *E-mail:* info@empire-management.co.uk. *Website:* www.empire-management.co.uk; www.estellemusic.com; www.john-legend.net/homeschool.

ESTER, Pauline; French singer; b. 18 Dec. 1963, Toulouse. *Career:* tours worldwide, television and radio broadcasts; mem. SACEM. *Recordings include:* albums: Le Monde Est Fou 1990, Je L'Autre Côté 1992, Best Of 2007. *Honours:* France International 1991, Trophy Radio, SACEM: Best Song of Year 1991, Best New Artist 1992. *Address:* c/o Studio Belleville, 53 rue de

Belleville, 75019 Paris, France. *Telephone:* 1-40-40-79-12. *E-mail:* paul@studiobelleville.com. *Website:* www.paulinester.com.

ESTRIN, Mitchell Stewart, BA, MMus; American performer and educator; *Professor of Clarinet, University of Florida*; b. 23 Dec. 1956, New York; one s. *Education:* Juilliard School. *Career:* clarinetist, New York Philharmonic 1979–99; Prof. of Clarinet, Univ. of Florida 1999–; Educ. and Creative Devt Man., Buffet Crampon USA, Inc. 2005–13; Vandoren Performing Artist and Buffet Clarinet Artist; mem. American Fed. of Musicians, Recording Musicians of America, MENC, Int. Clarinet Asscn. *Recordings include:* Clarinet Choir Classics, Wind in the Reeds, Clarinet Thunder, The Shadows of October, New York Philharmonic, Amadeus Ensemble, Motion Picture Soundtracks. *Television appearances:* Phil Donahue Show, Live From Lincoln Center, Late Show With David Letterman. *Publications:* Vandoren Etude and Exercise Book for Clarinet, Weber Concertino. *Honours:* Naumburg Scholarship, Sudler Foundation Award, Outstanding Young Men In America. *Address:* University of Florida, College of Fine Arts, School of Music, PO Box 117900, Gainesville, FL 32611-7900, USA (office). *Telephone:* (352) 273-3177 (home). *E-mail:* mestrin@ufl.edu (office). *Website:* www.arts.ufl.edu/music/clarinet (office).

ETHERIDGE, John M. G., BA; British musician (guitar); b. 12 Jan. 1948, London, England; one s. one d. *Education:* Univ. of Essex. *Career:* mem. Soft Machine 1975–79, reformed as Soft Machine Legacy 2006, Stéphane Grappelli 1976–81; numerous solo tours and appearances; Music Dir for Bertice Reading 1985–90; European tour with Birelli Lagrene, Vic Juris 1989, with Dick Heckstall-Smith (saxophone); mem. Danny Thompson's Whatever 1989–93; own quartet 1990–; mem. Andy Summers Duo 1993–, Nigel Kennedy Group 1993–; duo with John Williams 2006–; own groups Sweet Chorus (a tribute to Grappelli), Zappatistas (music of Frank Zappa), Blue Spirits Trio (contemporary organ blues); collaborations include with Billy Cobham, Mike Gibbs, Steve Swallow, Hawkwind, Arild Andersen, John Marshall. *Films:* Hear My Song, Little Voice, Long Way Down. *Recordings include:* albums with Soft Machine: Softs, Alive and Well, Triple Echo; with Stéphane Grappelli: At The Winery, Live At Carnegie Hall; with Stéphane Grappelli and Yehudi Menuhin: Tea For Two, Strictly For The Birds; with Nigel Kennedy: Kafka 1996, Kennedy Experience 1999; with own quartet: Second Vision 1981, Sweet Chorus: Tribute to Stéphane Grappelli 1999; with Vic Juris: Bohemia 1989; with Dick Heckstall-Smith: Obsession Fees 1990; with Danny Thompson: Elemental 1991; with Andy Summers: Invisible Threads 1993; with Wolf: Saturation Point 2001; with Soft Machine Legacy: Steam 2006; solo: Ash 1994, Sweet Chorus 1998, Chasing Shadows 2001, I Didn't Know 2004, In House (with Arild Andersen and John Marshall) 2007, Break Even (with Liane Carroll) 2008, Small Hotel (with Chris Garrick) 2009, Live Adventures (Soft Machine Legacy), Men on Wire (with Chris Garrick) 2010, When the World Stops for Snow (with Chris Garrick) 2013, Burden of Proof (Soft Machine Legacy) 2013. *Radio:* regular contrib. to BBC Radio 3 jazz programmes. *Television:* appearances with Stephane Grappelli and contrib. to Imagine series on Guitar. *E-mail:* johnetheridgewww@me.com (office). *Website:* www.johnetheridge.com.

ETHERIDGE, Melissa Lou; American singer, songwriter and musician (guitar); b. 29 May 1961, Leavenworth, Kan.; two c. (with Julie Cypher); twin c. (with Tammy Lynn Michaels). *Education:* Berklee Coll. of Music. *Career:* solo artist 1988–. *Recordings include:* albums: Melissa Etheridge 1988, Brave and Crazy 1989, Never Enough 1992, Yes I Am 1993, Your Little Secret 1995, Breakdown 1999, Skin 2001, Lucky 2004, Greatest Hits: The Road Less Traveled 2005, The Awakening 2007, Fearless Love 2010, Icon 2011, 4th Street Feeling 2012. *Film and television appearances:* Teresa's Tattoo 1994, The Sissy Duckling (TV film) 1999, King of the Hill (voice to TV series, episode 'Phish and Wildlife') 2004. *Publication:* The Truth Is: My Life in Love and Music (autobiography) 2002. *Honours:* Hon. DMus (Berklee Coll. of Music) 2006; Grammy Award for Best Female Rock Vocal Performance (for Ain't It Heavy) 1992, (for Come To My Window) 1994, Acad. Award for Best Original Song (for I Need to Wake Up in An Inconvenient Truth) 2007. *Current Management:* Jerry Lembo Entertainment Group, 96 Linwood Plaza, Suite 470, Fort Lee, NJ 07024-3701, USA. *Telephone:* (201) 482-4100. *E-mail:* jerry@lemboentertainment.com. *Website:* www.lemboentertainment.com; www.melissaetheridge.com.

EUBA, Akin, PhD; Nigerian composer, musician (piano) and lecturer; *Andrew W. Mellon Professor of Music, University of Pittsburgh*; b. 28 April 1935, Lagos; one s. one d. *Education:* CMS Grammar School, Lagos, Trinity Coll. of Music, London, England, Univ. of Calif., Los Angeles, and Univ. of Ghana, Legon. *Career:* Sr Programme Asst, Nigerian Broadcasting Corpn 1957–60; Head of Music and Music Research 1960–65; performer, numerous recitals in Europe, USA, Africa; organizer, numerous concerts of African music at home and abroad; lecturer in Africa and abroad 1966–; teacher, Univ. of Lagos 1966–68, Univ. of Ife 1968–77; Dir Center for Cultural Studies, Univ. of Lagos 1978–81; Dir Elekoto Music Centre, Lagos 1981–86; Research Scholar, Univ. of Bayreuth, Germany 1986–91; Dir Centre for Intercultural Music Arts, London 1988–; Hon. Visiting Prof., Dept of Music, City Univ., London 1993–96; Andrew W. Mellon Prof., Univ. of Pittsburgh, PA, USA 1997–; Overseas Fellow, Churchill Coll., Cambridge 2000–01; composer-in-residence, Ensemble Noir, Toronto, Canada 2003; World Music Scholar-in-Residence, Azusa Pacific Univ. 2004; Dir, Centre for Intercultural Musicology, Churchill Coll., Cambridge 2006–. *Compositions include:* Introduction and allegro 1956, String Quartet 1957, Two Yoruba Folk Songs 1959, The Wanderer for cello

1960, Igi nla so 1963, Five Pieces for English Horn and Piano 1963, Dance to the Rising Sun for chamber orchestra 1963, Three Songs for voice, piano and Iyalu drum 1963, Four Pieces 1964, Four Pictures from Oyo Calabashes for piano 1964, Impressions from an Akwete Cloth for piano 1964, Saturday Night at the Caban Bamboo for piano 1964, Tortoise and the Speaking Cloth (dramatic music) 1964, Abiku I (incidental music, for Iya–Abiku) 1965, Four Pieces for African Orchestra 1966, Legend 1966, Olurounbi: A Symphonic Study on a Yoruba Legend 1967, Wind Quartet 1967, Abiku II 1968, The Fall of the Scales 1970, Dirges 1970, Chaka (opera) 1970, The Laughing Tree 1970, Scenes from Traditional Life for piano 1970, Music for violin, horn, piano and percussion 1970, Ice Cubes for string orchestra 1970, Six Yoruba Folk Songs 1975, Two Tortoise Folk Tales in Yoruba 1975, FESTAC 77 1977, Black Bethlehem (opera) 1979, West African Universities Games Anthem 1981, Two Songs for orchestra with chorus 1983, Bethlehem (opera) 1984, Time Passes By 1985, Seven Modern African Poems 1987, Two Modern African Poems 1987, Wakar Duru: Studies in African Pianism Nos 1–3 1987, Themes from Chaka No. 1 1996, Orunmila's Voices 2002, Study in African Jazz No. 3 2002, Themes from Chaka 2 2003, Below Rusumo Falls 2003. *Honours:* first prize in piano performance Nigerian Festival of the Arts 1950–52, Fed. Govt of Nigeria Scholarship 1952–57, Rockefeller Foundation fellowship for study at Univ. of Calif., Los Angeles 1962–64. *Address:* Room 204, Music Building, Department of Music, University of Pittsburgh, Pittsburgh, PA 15260, USA (office). *E-mail:* aeuba@pitt.edu (office). *Website:* www.pitt.edu/~musicdpt (office).

EUBANKS, Robin; American jazz musician (trombone); b. 25 May 1955, Philadelphia, Pennsylvania. *Career:* Played in bands on Broadway; Appeared in film: Cotton Club; Member, Duke Ellington and Cab Calloway bands; plays with own bands EB3 and Mental Images; Played on Motown Television special; Played with: Art Blakey; Abdullah Ibrahim; Marvin 'Smitty' Smith; Geri Allen; Dave Holland; Wynton and Branford Marsalis; Steve Coleman; Regular tours: USA; Europe; Japan. *Recordings:* Different Perspectives 1988, Dedication 1989, Karma 1990, Mental Images 1994, Flashback on M-Base 1994, Wake Up Call 1997, 4:JJ/Slide/Curtis and Al 1998, Get 2 It 2001; with Dave Holland: The Razor's Edge 1987, Points of View 1998, Not for Nothin' 2001, What Goes Around 2002, Critical Mass 2006, Pass it On 2008, Pathways 2010; musician on: Art Blakey: Live At Montreux and Northsea 1980, Art Blakey, Not Yet 1988, I Get a Kick out of Bu 1988, Steve Coleman, World Expansion 1987, Sine Die 1992, Marvin 'Smitty' Smith, Keeper of The Drums 1987, Geri Allen: Open On All Sides in the Middle 1987; Mark Helias: The Current Set 1987, Herb Robertson, Shades of Bud Powell 1988, Branford Marsalis, Scenes In The City 1984. *E-mail:* AMSala@aol.com. *Website:* www .amsartists.com. *E-mail:* robineubanks@robineubanks.com. *Website:* www .robineubanks.com.

EURIPIDES, Georganopoulos, ARCM; Greek composer, producer and musician (keyboards); b. 12 Dec. 1961, Thessaloniki; m. Dr Agnes Leotsakos 1992; one s. *Education:* Royal Coll. of Music. *Career:* writing music for tv and video productions; Dir Optimus Int. Ltd (music production company); composition, production work in UK, France, Germany, Malta, Greece, Poland; mem. BAC&S, Musicians' Union, Performing Rights Soc., Mechanical-Copyright Protection Soc.

EUROBOY; Norwegian musician (guitar); b. (Knut Schreiner). *Career:* mem. glam-punk band, Turbonegro 1988–98, 2002–; side projects include The Vikings; Founder mem. and lead singer, Euroboys. *Recordings include:* albums: Turboloid 1990, Hot Cars and Spent Contraceptives 1992, Helta Skelta 1993, Never is Forever 1994, Ass Cobra 1996, Apocalypse Dudes 1998, Scandinavian Leather 2003, Party Animals 2005, Retox 2007. *Honours:* MTV Europe Music Award for Best Norwegian Act 2005.

EVANS, David Rhys, (Dan Evans), BSc (Hons); British musician (dulcimer, guitar, vocals); b. 26 May 1956, Middlesbrough, Teesside, England; m. Mary Collins 1995. *Education:* Durham Univ. *Career:* has performed all over UK and undertaken 15 int. tours, most often to USA; leading dulcimer player in UK. *Recordings include:* Sampler (cassette) 1988, Guardian Spirit 1993, Spirit Dancing 1997, Autumn Dance 2002, Let It Be Me 2010, Au Vieux Moulin 2014. *Publications:* contrib. to Dulcimer Players News magazine (USA), Nonsuch Dulcimer Newsletter (UK); numerous tech. articles in UK music press; several headline articles in nat. press on his singing course and voice-coaching process. *Telephone:* (1234) 241976 (office). *E-mail:* dan@english-dulcimer.com (office). *Website:* www.english-dulcimer.com (office).

EVANS, David (see (The) Edge)

EVANS, Faith; American singer, songwriter and arranger; b. 10 June 1973, Lakeland, Fla; m. 1st Christopher Wallace (Notorious BIG) 1994 (died 1997); one s. one d. (by previous relationship); m. 2nd Todd Russaw; one c. *Career:* started as backing singer for Mary J. Blige and Color Me Badd; released debut solo single, You Used To Love Me 1995; performed on tribute single to murdered rapper husband, I'll Be Missing You 1997; collaborations with Puff Daddy, Whitney Houston, Eric Benet, DMX. *Films include:* Turn It Up 2000, The Fighting Temptations 2003. *Recordings include:* albums: Faith (Lady of Soul Award for Best Female R & B/Soul Album 1996) 1995, Keep The Faith 1998, Faithfully 2002, The First Lady 2005, A Faithful Christmas 2005, Something About Faith 2010, R & B Divas 2012. *Publications:* Keep the Faith: A Memoir (African American Literary Award 2009) 2008. *Honours:* Grammy Award for Best Rap Performance (I'll Be Missing You) 1998, MTV Video Music Awards for Best R & B Video (I'll Be Missing You) 1997, Soul Train Award for Outstanding Music Video (I'll Be Missing You) 1998. *Current Management:* c/o

Emancipated Talented Management and Consulting, 344 Grove Street, Suite 21, Jersey City, NJ 07302, USA. *Telephone:* 888 479-9993. *Fax:* 501 621-7372. *E-mail:* info@emancipatedtalent.com. *Website:* www.emancipatedtalent.com; www.faithevansmusic.com.

EVANS, Lee, BA, MA, EdD; American composer and musician (piano); *Professor of Music, Performing Arts Department, Dyson College of Arts and Sciences, Pace University, New York;* b. 7 Jan. 1933, New York; m. Kelly Welles. *Education:* New York Univ., Columbia Univ. *Career:* worked as music coordinator and music dir with various artists including Carol Channing, Tom Jones; Cat Stevens; Engelbert Humperdinck; Gilbert O'Sullivan; Prof., Five Towns Coll., Seaford, L.I 1977–78, currently Prof. of Music, Dyson Coll. of Arts and Sciences, Pace Univ. 1989–; Pres., Piano Plus Inc. 1973–; Leader, Lee Evans Trio 1966–73; featured pianist, TV specials, The Gershwin Years; performed at two White House Command Performances for Pres. Lyndon B Johnson; mem. ASCAP, AFofM, Jazz Education Network. *Publications include:* series of jazz keyboard books; author and composer of over 100 music books in the US, former Soviet Union, Japan; numerous music magazine articles in Clavier, Piano Guild Notes, JAZZed Magazine, The California Music Teachers and others; contribs to journals. *Honours:* Hon. DMus (Five Towns Coll.). *Address:* Dyson College of Arts and Sciences, Department of Performing Arts, Pace University, One Pace Plaza W205b, New York, NY 10038, USA (office). *Telephone:* (212) 346-1 (office). *E-mail:* leeevansjazz@ yahoo.com. *Website:* www.pace.edu/dyson (office). *E-mail:* levans@pace.edu (office). *Website:* www.leeevansjazz.com.

EVANS, Sara; American country singer; b. 2 May 1971, Booneville, Mo.; m. Craig Schelske. *Career:* first performed on mandolin aged four as part of a family act, The Evans Family Band, playing local PTA meetings and bluegrass festivals; group became the Sara Evans Band; switched to country music and played in various groups; first regular performances at the Country Stampede, Columbia, Mo.; worked as waitress and wrote songs on first trip to Nashville 1991; played country club venues for three years as Sara Evans and North Santiam; returned to Nashville, singing demos for Tree Publishing 1995; solo artist 1997–; teamed up with Martina McBride and Reba McEntire for first all-female country music tour, Country Divas 2001. *Recordings include:* albums: Three Chords And The Truth 1997, No Place That Far 1998, Born To Fly 2000, Restless 2003, Real Fine Place 2005, Stronger 2011, Playlist: The Very Best of Sara Evans 2013. *Publication:* The Sweet By and By (novel) (with Rachel Hauck) 2009. *Honours:* ACM Award for Top Female Vocalist 2006. *Current Management:* c/o William Morris Endeavor Entertainment, 1325 6th Avenue, New York, NY 10019, USA. *Telephone:* (212) 586-5100. *Website:* www.wma.com; www.saraevans.com.

EVE, (Eve of Destruction); American rap artist and MC; b. (Eve Jihan Jeffers), 10 Nov. 1978, Philadelphia, Pa. *Career:* signed to Aftermath, signed to Ruff Ryders label; guest vocalist and solo artist. *Film appearances:* XXX 2002, The Woodsman (Black Reel Award for Best Actress 2005) 2004, Barbershop (contrib. to soundtrack) 2002, Flashbacks of a Fool (actor) 2008, Whip It 2009, 4.3.2.1 2010. *Television appearances:* Third Watch 1999, Spider-Man 2003, One on One 2004, Eve 2003–06, Numb3rs 2005, Glee 2009, Double Exposure 2010, Whitney 2012, Single Ladies 2011–12. *Recordings include:* albums: Ruff Ryders' First Lady (Best R & B/Soul Female Solo Album of the Year) 1999, Scorpion 2001, Eve-olution 2002, Here I Am 2008. *Honours:* MTV Video Music Award for Best Female Video with Gwen Stefani (Let Me Blow Ya Mind) 2001, Grammy Award for Best Rap/Sung Collaboration with Gwen Stefani (Let Me Blow Ya Mind) 2002, NAACP Image Awards for Outstanding New Artist 2000, Black Entertainment Television (BET) Awards for Best Female Hip-Hop Artist 2001. *Current Management:* c/o Tenth Street Entertainment, 38 West 21st Street, Suite 300, New York, NY 10010, USA. *Telephone:* (212) 334-3160. *E-mail:* info@10thst.com. *Website:* www.10thst .com; www.eve-360.com.

EVELYN, George; British DJ and musician; b. 15 Jan. 1970. *Education:* high school. *Career:* promoter, Funky Mule and The Headz Club, Leeds; DJ under name of E.A.S.E. (Experimental Sample Expert), Leeds; founder mem., Nightmares on Wax 1988–; mem. PRS. *Recordings include:* albums: A Word Of Science 1991, Smoker's Delight 1995, Carboot Soul 1999, DJ Kicks 2000, Mind Elevation 2002, Late Night Tales 2003, In A Space Outta Sound 2006, Thought So... 2008, Coming Home 2009, Feelin' Good 2013, N.O.W. is the Time 2014. *Website:* www.nightmaresonwax.com.

EVEN, François; French musician (bass guitar); b. 4 Jan. 1972. *Career:* mem. Superbus 1998–. *Recordings include:* albums: Aéromusical 2002, Pop'N'Gum 2004, Wow 2006, Lova Lova 2009, Sunset 2012. *Honours:* MTV Europe Music Award Best French Act 2005. *Address:* c/o Universal Music France, 16–20 rue des Fossés-Saint-Jacques, 75005 Paris, Cédex 05, France (office). *Website:* www.superbus.com.fr.

EVERETT, Dajon; British musician (percussion, keyboards). *Career:* mem., Gomez 2000–; numerous concerts, festival, radio and television appearances. *Recordings include:* albums: Abandoned Shopping Trolley Hotline 2000, In Our Gun 2002, Out West: Live at the Fillmore 2005, How We Operate 2006, A New Tide 2009, Whatever's on Your Mind 2011. *Current Management:* c/o Jason Colton, Red Light Management, 321 East Main Street, Suite 500 Charlottesville, VA 22902, USA. *Telephone:* (434) 245-4900. *Fax:* (434) 245-4933. *E-mail:* info@redlightmanagement.com; gomez@redlightmanagement .com. *Website:* www.redlightmanagement.com. *E-mail:* gomez@ gomeztheband.com. *Website:* www.gomez.co.uk.

EVERLY, Isaac Donald (Don); American singer, musician (guitar) and songwriter; b. 1 Feb. 1937, Brownie, KY; m. Adela Everly 1997. *Career:* mem., The Everly Brothers 1955–73, 1983–; solo artist 1973–83; numerous live performances, tours; collaborations with Albert Lee, Emmylou Harris. *Television:* Everly Brothers Show (ABC TV) 1970. *Recordings include:* albums: with The Everly Brothers: The Everly Brothers – They're Off and Running! 1958, Songs Our Daddy Taught Us 1958, It's Everly Time! 1960, The Fabulous Style of The Everly Brothers 1960, A Date With The Everly Brothers 1961, Instant Party 1962, Gone Gone Gone 1965, Rock 'n' Soul 1965, In Our Image 1966, Two Yanks In England 1966, The Everly Brothers Sing 1967, The Everly Brothers Show 1970, Stories We Could Tell 1972, Pass the Chicken and Listen 1973, Walk Right Back With… 1975, Living Legends 1977, Love Hurts 1983, The Reunion Concert 1984, Born Yesterday 1986, Some Hearts 1989, Heartaches and Harmonies 1994, Craftsmen 1995, Heroes of Country Music 1996, Brothers in Rhythm 1998, Devoted To You 2000; solo: Don Everly 1971, Sunset Towers 1974, Brother Jukebox 1977. *Honours:* Grammy Award for Lifetime Achievement 1997. *Current Management:* International Creative Management, 8942 Wilshire Blvd, Beverly Hills, CA 90211, USA.

EVERS, Jörg; German composer, producer, arranger and musician (guitar); b. 21 June 1950, Bayreuth; m. 1st Anna Maria 1981; one s. one d.; m. 2nd Susan Evers 2005; one d. *Education:* Uni München, Richard Strauss Konservatorium München. *Career:* tours in Europe with Embryo, Amon Düül II, Peter Maffay, Pack; Vice-Pres. Deutscher Kkomponistenverband 2004–06; Bd mem. GEMA, Pres. 2009–12. *Recordings include:* Claudja Barry: Boogie Woogie Dancin' Shoes, Sylvie Vartan: Disco Queen, Claudja Barry: Down and Counting, Die Jungen Tenöre, Montell Jordan: Get It On Tonite; television: Herzblatt; advertising: McDonalds, Odol, Maggi, Burger King, Löwenbräu, Wrigley's, Reebok, Esso. *Honours:* Best Composer's Award Ninth Tokyo Music Festival 1980, New York Clio Award 1991, two ASCAP awards 2001. *Address:* PO Box 1122, 85765 Unterföhring, Munich, Germany.

EWANJE EPEE, Charles, BEcons, DipMus; French (b. Cameroon) musician (guitar, flute), singer, composer and editor; *Editor, Harmonia Mundi;* b. 19 Dec. 1937, Douala; m. Michelle Lissandre 1973; three s. five d. *Career:* dance band musician 1960–72; classical guitar teacher 1972–76; African classical guitarist 1977–; currently leader of the Charles Ewanjé Group; various appearances on Cameroon and French TV including CRTV, MBC, Mosaïque; frequent performances on Africa Radio, RFI, MBC, Radio Douala, CRTV; ed. for Harmonia Mundi. *Compositions include:* Makala ma mbasi, African Strings for Luther King, Munyenge mwe o mboa, Earthly Paradise, Longe lasu, Sunga mba, O si topo, Noix de coco, Mboa'ngo, Ya, Ye mba ndutu, Bambambe, Le vrai trésor, Se mba nu, Ewanje Engingilaye, Patrice Lumumba, O si taka a Simon, Sese na sese, Munia, Savannah, Njowasowa, Never Too Late, A Kwedi, Ongele, O'i Ma Bwa Nyolo, Timba'Mboa, Esokesoke, Berceuse à Morgane, Black Blood. *Concerts include:* Merveilleuses cordes africaines (UNESCO), Africa Mama Festival (Utrecht), Palais des Congrès (Paris), Bayreuth Univ., ONCPB Douala, Cinéma Concorde (Douala), Douala (Cameroon). *Recording:* En avant les Lions (A Bana). *Publications include:* African music classical guitar parts: African Strings, Earthly Paradise, Let's Dance Like Yesterday, Berceuse à Morgane, Esok'am, Ya, Munia, Enfants d'Afrique, Ye Mba Ndutu. *Honours:* Esok'am – Earthly Paradise; first composition prize Guitar Word Thoroughfare 1982, International Radio France Discovery Award 1983. *Address:* 35 rue Savier, 92240 Malakoff,

France. *Telephone:* (9) 82-44-78-54; 6-66-72-12-27 (mobile). *E-mail:* ewanjeepee@yahoo.fr.

EWEN, Jade Almerie Louise; British singer; b. 24 Jan. 1988, Plaistow, London. *Education:* Sylvia Young Theatre School, London. *Career:* rep. UK at Eurovision Song Contest, performing Andrew Lloyd Webber's It's My Time 2009; mem. Sugababes 2009–. *Television:* Out There 2003–04, Eurovision: Your Country Needs You, 2010. *Recordings:* albums: with Sugababes: Sweet 7 2010. *Current Management:* Crown Music Management, 91 Peterborough Road, London SW6 3BU, England. *Telephone:* (20) 7371-5444. *Fax:* (20) 7371-5454. *E-mail:* info@crownmusic.co.uk. *Website:* www.crownmusic.co.uk. *Address:* c/o Island Records Group, 22 St Peters Square, Hammersmith, London, W6 9NW, England (office). *Website:* www.sugababes.com; www .jadeewen.com.

EWING, Thomas (Tom) D., BA, BS; American musician (guitar) and singer; b. 1 Sept. 1946, Columbus, Ohio; m. Margaret Avren (divorced) 1967; two s. one d. *Education:* Ohio State Univ. *Career:* mem. Earl Taylor and the Stoney Mountain Boys 1974–77, Bill Monroe and his Blue Grass Boys 1986–96, David Davis and the Warrior River Boys 1996–97, 1999–2001, Jim and Jesse and the Virginia Boys 1998; tours of USA, Europe, Japan; numerous live and television performances; columnist, Bluegrass Unlimited magazine 1994–2008. *Film appearance:* High Lonesome. *Recordings include:* albums: with Earl Taylor: Body and Soul 1976; with Bill Monroe: Bluegrass '87 1987, Southern Flavour 1988, 50 Years at Grand Ole Opry 1989, Cryin' Holy Unto The Lord 1991; solo: Take Me Home 1989, Lookin' Out A Window 1990, It's Good To Be Home 1993, Sacred Place 2008, A Bill Monroe Tribute (with Frank Wakefield) 2011. *Publication:* The Bill Monroe Reader (ed.) 2000.

EYDMANN, Stuart Anthony, DipArt, PhD; British musician (fiddle, concertina) and ethnomusicologist; b. 1 May 1953, Dunfermline, Fife, Scotland; m. Mairin Downes 1991, one s. one d. *Education:* Glasgow School of Art, Open Univ. *Career:* performer in various Scottish traditional music groups 1972–79; mem. Whistlebinkies 1980–; composer, Scottish Circus, including collaborations with John Cage; worked with Scottish Chamber Orchestra, Scottish Ballet, Royal Scottish Nat. Orchestra, Yehudi Menuhin in works by Edward McGuire; various film scores; Edinburgh Int. Festival and Festival Fringe; sessions with The Cutting Crew; tours to Sweden, France, People's Republic of China, Hong Kong, The Netherlands; engaged in ethnomusicological research 1985–; Fellow Soc. of Antiquarians of Scotland; mem. Musicians' Union, Traditional Music and Song Asscn of Scotland. *Recordings include:* as performer, co-writer, co-producer: The Whistlebinkies 3, 1980; The Whistlebinkies 4, 1982; The Whistlebinkies, 1985; The Whistlebinkies Anniversary, 1991; The Whistlebinkies Inner Sound, 1991; Wanton Fling, 1996. *Honours:* The Glenfiddich Living Scotland Award 1984. *Address:* 41 Hamilton Drive, Glasgow G12 8DW, Scotland. *Website:* www.scotchmusic.com.

EYRE, Simon James; British musician (guitar, bass, vocals); b. 30 Nov. 1964, Sheffield. *Career:* concert tours with Elaine Paige, The Style Council, Womack and Womack, Jimmy Ruffin; TV appearances with Randy Crawford, Jim Diamond, Sister Sledge, Second Image and Lenny Henry; mem. Musicians' Union; Assoc. mem., Performing Rights Soc. *Recordings include:* with Robert Palmer, Shara Nelson, Errol Brown; also with The Lighthouse Family, album: Ocean Drive (Quadruple Platinum Award). *Website:* www.myspace .com/eyreguitar.

F

F, Adam; British producer, remixer and DJ; b. (Adam Fenton), 8 Feb. 1972, Liverpool. *Career:* started career in a funk band; produced drum and bass for Lucky Spin Records, London; worked with US rappers, producing hip hop 2000; collaborations with Redman, M.O.P., Everything But The Girl, David Bowie, The Pet Shop Boys, Destiny's Child, Missy Elliott; Founder and Co-owner, Breakbeat Kaos record label; Founder Malpractice 2006. *Recordings include:* albums: Colours (MOBO Award for Best Album) 1997, Kaos 2001, Stadium Drum and Bass 2008, Shut the Lights Off 2010; singles: Circles 1995, F-Jam 1996, Metropolis 1996, Music In My Mind 1998, Smash Sumthin' (with Redman) 2001, Stand Clear (with M.O.P.) 2001.

FABBRI, Franco, PhD; Brazilian musician and musicologist; *Aggregate Professor of Popular Music, University of Turin, Italy*; b. 7 Sept. 1949, Sao Paulo. *Education:* State Univ. of Milan, Conservatory Giuseppe Verdi, Milan, Univ. of Gothenburg, Sweden, Univ. of Huddersfield, UK. *Career:* mem., experimental rock group, Stormy Six/Macchina Maccheronica 1965–82; Freelance writer and lecturer 1983–85; consultant to musical institutions in Milan: Musica Nel Nostro Tempo; G Ricordi and Co. (publrs); Chair. Int. Assocn for the Study of Popular Music 1985–87, 2005–07; Aggregate Prof. of Popular Music, Univ. of Turin, Italy. *Recordings include:* 9 albums with group Stormy Six; Domestic Flights 1983, Tempo Rubato 1983, La Casa Parlante 1984, Luci 2009, various soundtracks and stage music. *Radio:* Presenter of Radio Tre Suite, RAI, Italy 1997–2013. *Publications include:* La Musica In Mano, 1978; Elettronica e Musica, 1984; La Musica Che Si Consuma, 1985; What Is Popular Music? (ed) 1985, Compositore 1986, Il suono in cui viviamo 1996, Album bianco 2001, L'ascolto tabù 2005, Routledge Global Popular Music Series (ed.) 2011, Made in Italy: Studies in Popular Music (ed.) 2014. *E-mail:* prof.fabbri@gmail.com. *Website:* www.francofabbri.net.

FABER, Shane, BMus; American producer, songwriter, midi expert, musician (guitar, keyboards) and systems engineer; b. 23 Dec. 1953, Gainesville, Fla; s. of Shepard M. Faber and Maryann Faber; m. Elizabeth Burkland 1994. *Education:* Univ. of Miami, Florida. *Career:* mem., Bad Sneakers 1979–86; recording engineer for De La Soul, A Tribe Called Quest, Queen Latifah, Brand Nubians, Biz Markie, Omar, China Black; producer for Digable Planets 1991; musical supervisor film, Double Platinum 1999; computer consultant and software expert 2003–; currently Senior Altiris Engineer, JeepJazz Media Solutions. *Compositions include:* Shine On; Ladies First 1989, Turtle Power 1990, Degrees Of Motion 1992, Turtle Jam 1993. *Recordings include:* producer/mixer of albums: Reachin', Digable Planets; debut album, Bass Is Base; singles: Cool Like Dat, Turtle Power (from Teenage Mutant Ninja Turtles soundtrack), Digital Flavor on the Sonic Frontier, by JeepJazz Project. *Publications include:* three books on Client Management and Asset Management Suite software. *Address:* JeepJazz Music, 8 Graham Terrace, Montclair, NJ 07042, USA (office). *Telephone:* (973) 222-5737 (office). *E-mail:* jeepjazz@ hotmail.com (office). *Website:* www.jeepjazz.com.

FABIANO, Roberta Mary, BA; American musician (guitar), singer and composer; b. 25 June 1952, New York. *Education:* Berklee College of Music, Boston. *Career:* guitarist and composer, Lester Lanin and Peter Duchin Orchestras 1983–84, Doc Pomus 1984–; songwriter for Count Basie Band; performed with Cleo Laine, Melissa Manchester, Al B Sure!, Debbie Gibson, Carol Channing, Gloria Loring, Julia Budd; mem. AFofM, Songwriters' Guild, AFTRA. *Recordings include:* Working Girl (film soundtrack) 1988; solo: 11:11 2000. *Honours:* American Song Festival Award 1982, New York Songwriters Showcase Award 1984, New York State Senate Achievement Award 1984. *E-mail:* rfabian1@optonline.net. *Website:* www.robertafabiano.com.

FABRY, Anne; Belgian musician (drums, piano, keyboards); b. 13 Aug. 1950, Uccle; m. (divorced); two s. *Education:* Conservatoire Royal de Musique de Bruxelles et de Liège. *Recordings include:* Drava, Vent, Deux, Trio, Eva (film score). *Address:* 163 Avenue Brugmann, Boite 4, 1190 Brussels, Belgium.

FACCINI, Piers Damian Gabrielli; British singer and songwriter; b. 1970, London, England. *Career:* Founder-mem. of group Charley Marlowe 1997–2001; solo performer 2001–; numerous collaborations with musicians and singers including Francesca Beard, Ben Harper, Ibrahim Maalouf, Seb Martel, Busi Mhlongo, Vincent Ségal, Ballake Sissoko, Patrick Watson. *Recordings:* albums: with Charley Marlowe: This Could Be You 2000; solo: Leave No Trace 2004, The Streets of London 2005, Tearing Sky 2006, Two Grains of Sand 2009, My Wilderness 2011, Between Dogs and Wolves 2013, Songs of Times Lost (with Vincent Ségal) 2014. *E-mail:* talktobeatingdrum@ gmail.com (office). *Website:* www.beatingdrumrecords.com (office); www .piersfaccini.com.

FAGAN, James; Australian singer, musician (bouzouki, mandolin, tin whistle, clarinet, guitar, piano) and composer; b. 27 Jan. 1972, s. of Bob Fagan and Margaret Fagan. *Career:* fmrly recorded and toured as part of trio with Nancy and Sandra Kerr; mem. duo with Nancy Kerr. *Recordings include:* albums with Nancy Kerr: Starry Gazy Pie 1997, Steely Water 1999, Scalene (also with Sandra Kerr) 1999, Between The Dark And Light 2002, Strands of Gold 2005, Station House 2008, Twice Reflected Sun 2010; with The Fagans: Turning Fine 2004, Milk and Honey Land 2009. *Honours:* BBC Horizon Award for Best New Act (with Nancy Kerr) 2000, BBC Radio 2 Folk Award for Best Duo (with Nancy Kerr) 2003. *Current Management:* c/o Emerging Music,

Sarahs Cottage, Horn's Cross, Bideford, EX39 5DW, England. *Telephone:* (1237) 451933. *Fax:* (1237) 451931. *E-mail:* ken@emergingmusic.co.uk. *Website:* www.kerrfagan.com.

FAGEN, Donald; American singer and musician (keyboards); b. 10 Jan. 1948, Passaic, NJ. *Career:* mem., Steely Dan 1972–81, re-formed 1990s; solo artist 1981–; tours worldwide; organized New York Rock and Soul Revue, New York 1990, 1991; Music Ed. for film magazine, Premiere 1988. *Recordings include:* albums: with Steely Dan: Can't Buy A Thrill 1973, Countdown To Ecstacy 1973, Pretzel Logic 1974, Katy Lied 1975, The Royal Scam 1976, Aja 1977, Metal Leg 1980, Gaucho 1981, Steely Dan Gold 1982, Reelin' In The Years 1985, Do It Again 1987, Remastered – The Very Best of Steely Dan 1993, Citizen Steely Dan – 1972–80 1993, Alive In America 1995, Two Against Nature 2000, Everything Must Go 2003; solo: The Nightfly 1982, Kamakiriad 1993, Morph The Cat 2006, Sunken Condos 2012. *Honours:* Grammy Award for Best-Engineered Non-Classical Recording (for Aja) 1978, Q Inspiration Award 1993, four Grammy Awards, including Album of the Year (for Two Against Nature) 2001. *Current Management:* HK Management, 8900 Wilshire Blvd, Suite 300, Beverly Hills, CA 90211, USA. *Website:* www.donaldfagen .com; www.steelydan.com.

FAHEY, Siobhan; British singer, DJ and songwriter; b. 10 Sept. 1958, Dublin, Ireland; d. of Joseph Fahey and Helen Fahey; m. Dave Stewart 1987. *Career:* fmr press officer, Decca Records; mem., Bananarama 1981–88, 1998–; mem., Shakespears Sister 1988–93; numerous concerts, television and radio performances; solo artist and DJ 1993–. *Recordings include:* albums: with Bananarama: Deep Sea Skiving 1983, Bananarama 1984, True Confessions 1986, Wow! 1987, Drama 2005; with Shakespears Sister: Sacred Heart 1989, Hormonally Yours 1992, #3 2004, Songs From The Red Room 2009, Cosmic Dancer 2011; solo: Bitter Pill 2003. *Honours:* BRIT Award for Best Video (for Stay) 1993, Ivor Novello Award for Outstanding Contemporary Song Collection (for Hormonally Yours) 1993. *E-mail:* agent@bananarama.co.uk. *Website:* www.bananarama.co.uk; www.shakespearssister.co.uk.

FAIRBAIRN, Keith; British musician (percussion); b. 14 Jan. 1963, Horsham, Surrey, England. *Education:* Guildhall School of Music. *Career:* has worked with Shirley Bassey, Mike Oldfield, Lulu, Judie Tzuke, Madeline Bell, Vic Damone, Dionne Warwick, Joe Longthorne, Madonna, Tom Jones; numerous television shows for BBC, LWT, Granada; mem, Musicians' Union. *Recordings:* Andrew Lloyd Webber, Jim Steinman, Nick Heyward, Shirley Bassey, Madeline Bell, Joe Longthorne, Evita, Cats, Whistle Down the Wind; numerous films, shows, library music. *Honours:* AGSM. *Address:* Spirit of the Drum, 83 Main Road, Long Hanborough, Oxfordshire OX29 8JX, England. *E-mail:* kfairbairn@mac.com.

FAIRCHILD, Karen Renee; American country music singer and songwriter; b. 28 Sept. 1969, Gary, Ind.; m. Jimi Westbrook 2006; one s. *Education:* Samford Univ. *Career:* raised in Marietta, Ga; met and sang with Kimberly Schlapman (then Kimberly Bramlett) at univ. in late 1980s; singer with Christian vocal group Truth 1990s; mem. of duo KarenLeigh (with Leigh Cappillino) 1990s; Founder-mem. Little Big Town (with Kimberly Bramlett and Jimi Westbrook) 1998, appeared at Grand Old Opry 1999; toured with Keith Urban 2006, Sugarland and Jake Owen 2007, Martina McBride 2007–08, George Strait 2008, Carrie Underwood 2009, Sugarland 2010, Rascal Flatts 2012; numerous collaborations including Ashley Monroe, John Mellencamp, Collin Raye. *Recordings:* albums: with Little Big Town: Little Big Town 2002, The Road to Here 2005, A Place to Land 2007, The Reason Why 2010, Tornado 2012, Pain Killer 2014. *Honours:* Acad. of Country Music Awards for Top New Vocal Duo/Group 2007, for Top Vocal Group 2013, for Music Video of the Year (for Tornado) 2013, for Vocal Group of the Year 2014, Country Music Asscn Awards for Vocal Group of the Year 2012, 2013, 2014, 2015, for Single of the Year (for Pontoon) 2012, for Single and Song of the Year (both for Girl Crush) 2015, American Country Award for Music Video of the Year: Group or Collaboration (for Pontoon) 2012, Daytime Emmy Award for Outstanding Original Song (for Good Afternoon) 2013, Grammy Awards for Best Country Duo/Group Performance (for Pontoon) 2013, (for Girl Crush) 2016, for Best Country Song (for Girl Crush) 2016. *Current Management:* c/o Sandbox Entertainment, 54 Music Square East, Nashville, TN 37203, USA. *E-mail:* info@sandboxmgmt.com. *Website:* sandboxmgmt.com. *Address:* c/o Capitol Records Nashville, Universal Music Group, 401 Commerce Street, Suite 1100, Nashville, TN 37219, USA (office). *Telephone:* (615) 269-2000 (home). *Fax:* (615) 269-2023 (office). *Website:* umgnashville.com (office); littlebigtown.com.

FAIRUZ; Lebanese singer; b. (Nuhad Haddad), 21 Nov. 1935, Jabal Alarz; d. of Wadi Haddad and Liza Alboustani; m. Assi al-Rahbani 1954; two s. three d. *Education:* St Joseph School for Girls and Nat. Conservatory of Music, Beirut. *Career:* also known as Fayrouz; started singing as mem. of chorus, then lead soloist, Lebanese Radio Station; early collaborations with brothers, Assi and Mansour al-Rahbani; first live appearance, the Baalbeck Int. Festival at Temple of Jupiter 1957; concerts and tours world-wide, including in USA, Canada, the Middle East, across Europe and in Mexico, Brazil, Argentina and Australia; has performed in numerous venues including the Royal Albert Hall, London 1962, Carnegie Hall, New York 1971, London Palladium 1978,

L'Olympia de Paris 1979, Royal Festival Hall, London 1986, Shrine Auditorium, Los Angeles 1971, 1981, 2003, John F. Kennedy Center for the Performing Arts, Washington, DC 1981, 1987, amongst many others. *Films:* Biya al-Khawatim 1965, Safarbarlek 1966, Bint al-Harass 1967. *Recordings include:* over 80 album recordings include A Christmas Album, The Very Best of Fayrouz 1977, Fairuz sings Gibran, The Lady and the Legend 2005, Fayrouz: Live in Dubai 2008, Eh… fi amal 2010. *Honours:* Order of Merit 1962, Order of Cedars 1963, Order of Merit, First Class (Syria) 1967, Legion of Honour (Lebanon) 1970, Gold Medal of Honour (Jordan) 1975, Commdr, Ordre des Arts et des Lettres 1988, Chevalier, Légion d'honneur 1998; Dr hc (American Univ. of Beirut) 2005; Baalbeck Int. Festival Cavalier Medal 1957, Jerusalem Award 1997, named by Arabian Business amongst its Power 100: The World's Most Influential Arabs (77th) 2010, amongst its Power 500: The World's Most Influential Arabs (29th) 2012. *Website:* www.fairouz.com.

FAIRWEATHER-LOW, Andy; British singer and musician (guitar); b. 2 Aug. 1948, Ystrad Mynach, Hengoed, Wales. *Career:* mem. The Taffbeats, The Sect Maniacs; Founder mem. Amen Corner 1966–69; numerous live performances; solo artist and session musician; mem. Eric Clapton's backing band 1990s. *Film appearance:* Scream and Scream Again 1969. *Recordings include:* albums: with Amen Corner: Round Amen Corner 1968, Explosive Company 1969; solo: Beginning From An End 1971, Spider Jivin' 1974, La Booga Rooga 1975, Be Bop 'N' Holla 1976;, Mega-Shebang 1980, Sweet Soulful Music 2006, Lively 2012; with Eric Clapton: Unplugged 1992, From The Cradle 1994, Pilgrim 1996, Reptile 2001. *Website:* www.andyfairweatherlow.com.

FAITH, Paloma; British singer, songwriter and actress; b. Paloma Faith Blomfield, Hackney, London. *Education:* Northern School of Contemporary Dance, Central St Martin's Coll. of Art and Design, London. *Career:* recorded duet It's Christmas (And I Hate You) with Josh Weller 2008; debut single (Stone Cold Sober) 2009; recorded theme song to film 4.3.2.1 2010; live and festival appearances including Cheltenham Jazz Festival 2010, iTunes Festival 2010, BRIT Awards 2011; live solo tours 2010, 2012–13; Artist-in-Residence, Cheltenham Jazz Festival 2012; other collaborations include Basement Jaxx, MF Doom, Ghostface Killah. *Television:* Mayo 2006, HolbyBlue 2007, Coming Up 2010, Blandings 2013, The Voice UK 2016–. *Films:* St Trinian's 2007, The Imaginarium of Doctor Parnassus 2009, Dread 2009. *Recordings:* albums: Do You Want the Truth or Something Beautiful? 2009, Fall to Grace 2012, A Perfect Contradiction 2014. *Honours:* BRIT Award for British Female Solo Artist 2015. *Current Management:* c/o Innis Ferguson, Artist Manager, Lateral Management. *E-mail:* innis@lateralmgmt.com. *Website:* www.lateralmgmt.com. *Address:* c/o RCA Records, Sony Music Entertainment, 9 Derry Street, London, W8 5HY, England (office). *Website:* www.palomafaith.com.

FAITHFULL, Marianne; British singer; b. 29 Dec. 1946, Ormskirk, Lancs.; d. of Glynn Faithfull and Eva Faithfull; m. 1st John Dunbar; one s.; m. 2nd Ben Brierley; m. 3rd Giorgio della Terza. *Career:* made first recording (As Tears Go By) aged 17. *Films:* I'll Never Forget Whatsisname 1967, Girl on a Motorcycle 1968, Hamlet 1969, Lucifer Rising 1972, Ghost Story 1974, Assault on Agathon 1975, When Pigs Fly 1993, The Turn of the Screw 1994, Shopping 1994, Moondance 1995, Crimetime 1996, Intimacy 2001, Far From China 2001, Alone in the Dark 2003, A Letter to True 2003, Nord-Plage 2004, Paris, je t'aime 2006, Marie Antoinette 2006, Irina Palm 2007. *Television:* Anna 1967, The Door of Opportunity 1970, The Stronger 1971. *Stage appearances:* Three Sisters (London) 1967, Seven Deadly Sins (St Ann's Cathedral, New York) 1990, The Threepenny Opera (Gate Theatre, Dublin) 1992. *Recordings include:* albums: Come My Way 1965, Marianne Faithfull 1965, Go Away From My World 1966, North Country Maid 1966, Faithfull Forever 1966, Love in a Mist 1967, Dreaming My Dreams 1977, Faithless (with the Grease Band) 1978, Broken English 1979, Dangerous Acquaintances 1981, A Child's Adventure 1983, Summer Nights 1984, Music for the Millions 1985, Strange Weather 1987, Rich Kid Blues 1988, Blazing Away 1990, A Secret Life 1995, 20th Century Blues 1997, The Seven Deadly Sins 1998, Vagabond Ways 1999, Stranger On Earth 2001, Kissin' Time 2002, Before the Poison 2004, Easy Come Easy Go 2009, Sparrows Will Sing 2014. *Publications:* Faithfull (autobiog.) 1994, Marianne Faithfull Diaries 2002. *Honours:* Commdr, Ordre des Arts et des Lettres 2011. *E-mail:* assistante@mac.com (office). *Website:* www.mariannefaithfull.org.uk.

FAIUMU, Chris, (DJ Fitchie); New Zealand musician (electronics). *Career:* band leader of reggae and soul group, Fat Freddy's Drop. *Recordings include:* albums: Live at the Matterhorn 2001, Based on a True Story 2005, Dr Boondigga and the Big BW 2009, Live at Roundhouse London 2010, Blackbird 2013. *Honours:* New Zealand Music Award for Best Group 2005. *Address:* The Drop Ltd, PO Box 14-723, Kilbirnie, Wellington 6241, New Zealand (office). *Telephone:* (4) 934-3767 (office). *E-mail:* freddy@fatfreddysdrop.com (office). *Website:* www.fatfreddysdrop.com.

FAKANAS, Yiorgos, DipEcons; Greek musician (bass), composer, arranger and writer; *Founder and Artistic Director, Art Music School;* b. 18 July 1961, Athens; m. Nicoletta Pitsikali 1992; one d. *Education:* Univ. of Athens. *Career:* participated in historic recording of Manos Hadjidakis' (composer of Oscar-winning score for famous Never on Sunday 'Lilipoupolis' 1980; has taken part in numerous recordings by other composers, totalling more than 700 albums; formed group Iskra (became first jazz-fusion group in Greece); participated in Eurojazz orchestra as the only Greek representative, touring all of Europe; as leader, worked with numerous Greek and foreign musicians, including Dave

Weckl, Mike Stern, Wallace Roney, Lenny White, Brett Garsed, Bob Franceschini and many others; has given many concerts playing his own music and conducting some of the largest Greek orchestras (Radio-Television Orchestra, Greek Radio Big Band, Nat. Orchestra of Greek Music as well as many int. ensembles and orchestras) at Athens Concert Hall-Megaron, Lycabettus Theatre, Herodion and Pallas Concert Hall; composer and performer of music for films and theatre; f. Art Music School 'Y.V. Fakanas' 1997, Supervisor and Artistic Dir, Contemporary Music Dept, teaches electric bass and contemporary theory, more than 600 bass players have studied with him; f. Athina Live (club situated in the Art Music School), organizes concerts featuring many famous musicians; own ensemble gives frequent concerts and collaborates with musicians including Mike Stern, Frank Gambale, Anthony Jackson, Dave Weckl, Alex Acuna, Bireli Lagrene, Dennis Chambers, Horacio El Negro, Greg Howe, Eric Marienthal, Lew Soloff, Brett Garsed, Otmaro Ruiz, Barry Finerty, Tony Lakatos, Scott Kinsey, Jeff Richman, Bob Franceschini and many others; Publr Jazz Fusion Mood magazine; most recent recording contains music specially composed for Anthony Jackson. *Recordings:* with Iskra: A New Day 1986, Parastasis 1990; solo albums: Horizon 1989, Amorosa 1991, Stand-Art 1995, Cantabile 2003, Echoes 2004, Domino 2007, Interspirit 2009, Maestro (dedicated to Greek conductor Dimitri Mitropoulos, featuring Alex Acuna and Bireli Lagrene) 2011, Acrobat (featuring Dennis Chambers) 2011. *Publications:* educational books: 17 books on electric bass performance and music theory, including For The Bass (Vol. I, II), Scales of Modern Music, Jazz Harmony, Modern Counterpoint, Melody I, Melody II, Structure of Instruments, Modern Arrangement. *Honours:* Hon. mem. Greek Radio and TV's Jazz Orchestra. *Address:* Yiorgos Fakanas Art Music School, 3 Possidonos Avenue, 18344 Moschato, Athens, Greece (office). *Telephone:* (210) 4813605 (office). *E-mail:* fakanasg@otenet.gr (office). *Website:* www.fakanas.gr.

FAKOLY, Tiken Jah; Côte d'Ivoirian singer; b. 23 June 1968, Odienné. *Career:* began singing career in local cinema; first concerts in France 1998; exiled in Mali 2002–. *Recordings include:* albums: Les Djelys 1993, Missiri 1994, Mangercratie 1996, Cours D'Histoire 1999, Le Caméléon 2000, Françafrique (Victoires de la Musique Award for Best Reggae/Ragga/World Album) 2002, Coup de gueule 2004, L'Africain 2007, Le Caméléon 2008, African Revolution 2010, Listen To The Banned 2010. *Address:* c/o Universal Music France, 20–22 rue des Fossés Saint Jacques, 75005 Paris, France (office). *Telephone:* (0) 6-13-07-19-32 (office). *E-mail:* solouma@free.fr (office). *Website:* tikenjahfakoly.artiste.universalmusic.fr (office).

FALCONER, Earl; British musician (bass guitar) and singer; b. 23 Jan. 1959. *Education:* Road School of Art. *Career:* fmr plasterer; mem. reggae group UB40 1978–; numerous concerts, tours. *Recordings include:* albums: Signing Off 1980, Present Arms 1981, The Singles Album 1982, UB44 1982, Labour of Love 1983, Live 1983, More UB40 Music 1983, Geffery Morgan 1984, Baggariddim 1985, Little Baggaridim 1985, UB40 File 1985, Rat In The Kitchen 1986, CCCP: Live In Moscow 1987, UB40 1988, Labour of Love II 1990, Promises and Lies 1993, Anansi 1995, Guns In The Ghetto 1997, Labour of Love III 1998, Presents The Dancehall Album 1998, Homegrown 2003, Who You Fighting For? 2005, TwentyFourSeven 2008. *Address:* DEP International Ltd, PO Box 117, Birmingham, B5 5RG, England (office). *E-mail:* info@ub40 .co.uk (office). *Website:* www.ub40.co.uk.

FALL, Papa Amadou, (Pape); Senegalese singer, musician (guitar) and songwriter; b. 1965. *Education:* Dakar Conservatory. *Career:* fmrly apprentice tailor; fmr mem. acoustic group, Santamuma; mem., Pape and Cheikh 1997–; signed to Youssou N'Dour's Jololi label 1999. *Recordings include:* albums: with Pape and Cheikh: Yakaar 2001, Mariama 2002. *Current Management:* c/o Isabelle Lémann, 15 bis, rue Jean-Jacques Rousseau, 94200 Ivry-sur-Seine, France. *Telephone:* 1-46-58-11-04. *Fax:* 1-46-58-11-45. *E-mail:* salammbo@wanadoo.fr. *Address:* c/o Real World Records, Box Mill, Mill Lane, Box, Corsham, Wiltshire SN13 8PL, England (office). *Telephone:* (1225) 743188 (office). *Fax:* (1225) 743787 (office). *Website:* www.realworldrecords .com (office).

FALLON, Peter Sean; British record producer and songwriter; b. 3 June 1968, Reigate, Surrey. *Education:* piano from age of six. *Career:* signed to Big One Records aged 18 1986; UK club promo tour, signed to Swanyard Records 1990; performed at Cesmé 91 Festival in Turkey; signed with EMI Records and Publishing 1993; signed with 1st Avenue Management 1998; signed with BMG Music 2000; numerous UK and worldwide TV appearances; mem. PRS, BAC&S, ASCAP. *Television:* Top of the Pops (BBC), Pebble Mill, This Morning (ITV), New Zealand Channel 14, Good Morning America. *Recordings include:* with Twin Beat: Let's Pick Up The Pieces 1988; with Fallon: Get On The Move 1990; with Technotronic: Get Up Remix 1991; with Stevie Wonder: You Never Lose Remix 1991; as writer, producer: with David Hasselhoff: If I Could Only Say Goodbye 1993, Tighter and Tighter 1993; with Dannii Minogue: Love and Affection 1994; with PM Factor: Substitute 1999; with Janet and Jason: The Only Way Is Up 2001; with Alex Smart: This Is Me 2004; as writer: with Céline Dion: Don't Turn Away From Me; with Groove U: Step By Step; with Dannii Minogue: The 1995 Sessions 2010; numerous scores for film, TV and radio. *Address:* c/o Broadhill Recording Studios, Ockley Lane, Keymer, Hassocks, BN6 8PA, England.

FÄLTSKOG, Agnetha Åse; Swedish singer and actress; b. 5 April 1950, Jönköping; m. 1st Björn Ulvæus 1971 (divorced 1979); m. 2nd Tomas Sonnenfeld 1990 (divorced 1993). *Career:* solo recording artist aged 17;

actress, Jesus Christ Superstar, Sweden; mem. pop group ABBA 1972–82; winner, Eurovision Song Contest 1974; world-wide tours; concerts include Royal Performance, Stockholm 1976, Royal Albert Hall, London 1977, UNICEF concert, New York 1979, Wembley Arena 1979; reunion with ABBA, Swedish TV This Is Your Life 1986; solo artist 1982–90, 2004–. *Films:* ABBA: The Movie 1977, Nöjesmaskinen 1982, Rakenstam 1983. *Recordings:* albums: with ABBA: Ring Ring 1973, Waterloo 1974, ABBA 1975, Greatest Hits 1976, Arrival 1976, The Album 1978, Voulez-Vous 1979, Greatest Hits Vol. 2 1979, Super Trouper 1980, The Visitors 1981, The Singles: The First Ten Years 1982, Thank You For The Music 1983, Absolute Abba 1988, Abba Gold 1992, More Abba Gold 1993, Forever Gold 1998, The Definitive Collection 2001; solo: Eleven Women In One Building 1975, Wrap Your Arms Around Me 1983, Eyes of a Woman 1985, I Stand Alone 1987, My Colouring Book 2004, A 2013; singles include: with Abba: Ring Ring 1973, Waterloo 1974, Mamma Mia 1975, Dancing Queen 1976, Fernando 1976, Money Money Money 1976, Knowing Me Knowing You 1977, The Name Of The Game 1977, Take A Chance On Me 1978, Summer Night City 1978, Chiquitita 1979, Does Your Mother Know? 1979, Angel Eyes/Voulez-Vous 1979, Gimme Gimme Gimme (A Man After Midnight) 1979, I Have A Dream 1979, The Winner Takes It All 1980, Super Trouper 1980, On and On and On 1981, Lay All Your Love On Me 1981, One Of Us 1981, When All Is Said and Done 1982, Head Over Heels 1982, The Day Before You Came 1982, Under Attack 1982, Thank You For The Music 1983; solo: I Was So In Love, The Heat Is On, Can't Shake You Loose, I Wasn't The One (Who Said Goodbye), If I Thought You'd Ever Change Your Mind 2004, My Colouring Book 2004, My Very Best 2008. *Publications:* As I Am (autobiography) 1997. *Honours:* World Music Award, Best Selling Swedish Artist 1993. *Address:* Universal Music Sweden, Banérgatan 16, 102 44 Stockholm, Sweden (office). *Telephone:* (8) 629-53-00 (office). *E-mail:* info .se@umusic.com (office). *Website:* www.universalmusic.se; www.abbasite.com; www.agnetha.com.

FAME, Georgie; British singer and musician (keyboards); b. (Clive Powell), 26 Sept. 1943, Leigh, Lancashire. *Career:* mem. Billy Fury's backing group, The Blue Flames 1961, then independent band as Georgie Fame and the Blue Flames 1961–63; tours, concerts and television appearances, festivals; founder, Georgie Fame Band 1966; concerts as leader of various groups and ensembles; plays on jazz circuit. *Recordings include:* albums: Rhythm and Blues At The Flamingo 1963, Fame At Last 1964, Sound Venture 1966, Hall of Fame 1967, Two Faces of Fame 1967, The Third Face of Fame 1968, Seventh Son 1969, Fame and Price, Price and Fame Together 1971, All Me Own Work 1972, Georgie Fame 1974, That's What Friends Are For 1978, Georgie Fame Right Now 1979, Closing The Gap 1980, Hoagland, with Annie Ross 1981, In Goodman's Land 1983, My Favourite Songs 1984, No Worries 1988, Georgie Fame – The First 30 Years 1989, Cool Cat Blues 1991, Three Line Whip 1995, Blues and Me 1996, Walking Wounded 1999, Name Droppin' 1999, Poet In New York 2001, Charlestons 2003, Anthology 2003, Tone-Wheels 'A' Turnin' 2009, Lost in a Lover's Dream 2012, Can't Take My Eyes Off You 2012.

FANFANT, Thierry; French musician (bass guitar); b. 27 March 1964, Paris. *Career:* Olympia, with Michel Pugain 1993; Casino de Paris 1995; France Follies, La Rochelle 1994, 1995, 1996; France Follies, Montréal; Pantemps de Bourges 1990, 1991, 1995; Festival Jazz, Nice 1994; Petit Journal, 1997. *Compositions include:* Don d'organe, Ernest et firmin, Pausove Muen. *Recordings include:* With: Enzo-Enzo, Michel Fugain, Maria Glen, Tuluo De Piscopo, Hajime Mizoguehi, Shukichi Kina, Beethova Obas, Mario Canonge, Taratata, Tery Boise. *Honours:* Success Prize of the Year 1994. *E-mail:* thifan@noos.fr. *Website:* www.thierryfanfant.com.

FANNING, Bernard; Australian singer and musician (guitar, keyboards); b. 15 Aug. 1969. *Education:* Univ. of Queensland. *Career:* joined Brisbane-based rock group, Powderfinger 1992; numerous Australian tours and festival appearances; worldwide tours. *Recordings include:* Powderfinger albums: Parables For Wooden Ears 1994, Double Allergic 1996, Internationalist 1998, Odyssey Number Five 2000, Vulture Street 2003, Dream Days at the Hotel Existence 2007, Golden Rule 2009, Powderfinger Sunsets The Farewell Tour (DVD) 2010; Solo Album: Tea & Sympathy 2005. *Honours:* 17 ARIA Awards (Powderfinger), three APRA Awards (Powderfinger). *Current Management:* Secret Service Artist Management, PO Box 401, Fortitude Valley, 4006 QLD, Australia. *Telephone:* (7) 3854-1488. *Fax:* (7) 3854-0655. *E-mail:* general@ secret-service.com.au. *Website:* www.secret-service.com.au; www .powderfinger.com; www.bernardfanning.com.

FANNING, Shawn; American computer programmer and internet entrepreneur; *CEO, Airtime;* b. 1980, Harwich, Mass. *Career:* founder of peer-to-peer file-sharing platform, Napster 1999, sold, after numerous legal actions against the co. 2002; founder of co. developing a fully-legal files-haring platform, SNOCAP 2003–08, founder and CEO Rupture 2007–09, co-founder Path 2010–11, co-founder and CEO Airtime 2011–.

FANTASIA; American singer and actor; b. 30 June 1984, High Point, NC; d. of Joseph Barrino and Diane Barrino; one d. *Education:* Andrews High School, High Point, NC. *Career:* winner American Idol 2004; signed to J Records 2004 (RCA Records 2011–); opening act on Kanye West tour 2005; performed at Grammy Awards 2006; first solo concert tour in 2010; numerous collaborations including Aretha Franklin, Patti LaBelle, Yolanda Adams, Faith Evans, Lil' Mo, Coko, Jennifer Hudson, Charlie Wilson. *Recordings:* albums: Free Yourself 2005, Fantasia 2006, Back to Me 2010. *Films:* Life is Not a Fairy Tale (TV film) 2006, Mahalia! 2012, For My Girls: The Clark Sisters 2012.

Television: American Idol (winner) 2004, Fantasia for Real 2010–; as actor: American Dreams 2004, The Simpsons (guest voice) 2005. *Stage:* The Color Purple, Broadway (Theatre World Award 2007, Broadway.com Favorite Female Replacement Award 2007) 2007, Soul Kitten's Cabaret 2010. *Publication:* Life is Not a Fairy Tale (autobiography) 2005. *Honours:* Billboard Music Awards for Top Selling Single of the Year and Top Selling R&B/Hip-Hop Single of the Year 2004, for Outstanding Duo or Group (with Jennifer Hudson) 2009, Billboard American Urban Radio Networks Award for Top R&B/Hip-Hop Single 2005, NAACP Image Award for Outstanding Female Artist 2005, for Outstanding Song 2011, ASCAP Rhythm and Soul Awards for Most Performed Song 2006, Groovevolt Music Award for Best New Artist 2006, Greensboro Sit-ins Org Founder's Appreciation Award 2008, Barbados Music Int. Award of Excellence 2010, Grammy Award for Best Female R&B Vocal Performance 2011, NAACP Theater Distinguished Honoree Award 2011. *Current Management:* c/o BD Management, 16605 Pleasant Colony Drive, Upper Marlboro, MD 20774, USA. *Telephone:* (202) 905-4994. *Fax:* (301) 218-8871. *E-mail:* info@bdmanagement.net. *Website:* www .bdmanagement.net; www.fantasiaofficial.com.

FARGO, Donna; American country singer and songwriter; b. (Yvonne Vaughn), 10 Nov. 1945, Mount Airy, NC; m. Stan Silver. *Career:* solo artist 1969–; numerous television, stage and festival appearances. *Recordings include:* albums: The Happiest Girl in the Whole USA 1972, My Second Album 1973, All About a Feeling 1973, Miss Donna Fargo 1974, Whatever I Say Means I Love You 1975, On the Move 1976, Fargo Country 1977, Shame on Me 1977, Dark-Eyed Lady 1978, Just for You 1979, Fargo 1980, Brotherly Love 1981, Encore 1984, Winners 1986, Country Sweethearts 1996. *Publications:* Trust in Yourself 1997, To the Love of My Life 2001. *Honours:* Billboard Award for Best New Female Country Artist 1972, NARM Best Selling Country Artist 1972–73, ACM Top Female Vocalist 1972–73, Robert J. Burton Award for Most Performed Country Song 1972–73, C & W Record of the Year on Jukeboxes 1973, Grammy Award for Best Female Country Performer (for Funny Face) 1973. *Current Management:* c/o Stan Silver, Prima-Donna Entertainment Corpn, PO Box 150527, Nashville, TN 37215, USA. *E-mail:* StanSilver9999@comcast.net. *E-mail:* DonnaFargo@comcast.net.

FARIS, Myriam; Lebanese singer and dancer; b. 3 May 1983. *Education:* Nat. Conservatory of Music. *Career:* won first prize Lebanese Song Festival (aged 16), Studio el-Fan 2000; solo artist 2000–. *Recordings include:* The Album 2003, Nadini 2005, Bet'oul Eih 2008, Min Oyouni 2011. *Film:* Silina 2009. *Address:* EMI Music Arabia, PO Box 16003, Dubai, United Arab Emirates. *Telephone:* (4) 8818212. *Fax:* (4) 8818218. *E-mail:* info@ emimusicarabia.com. *Website:* www.emimusicarabia.com; www.myriamfares .com.

FARLEY, Terry; British producer, remixer and DJ; b. 13 June 1959, London. *Career:* Co-founder Boy's Own fanzine (with Andrew Weatherall and Cymon Eccles), Boy's Own Records (later Junior Boy's Own, now Junior Recordings); promoter/DJ at Boy's Own events; remixed (with Pete Heller) Ultra Nate, Primal Scream, Janet Jackson, Happy Mondays; mem. Bocca Juniors, Fire Island, Roach Motel; Co-founder Faith Fanzine 1999; collaborations with Pete Heller, Andrew Weatherall, Rui Da Silva. *Recordings include:* singles: Raise (with Bocca Juniors) 1990, In Your Bones (with Fire Island) 1992, There But For The Grace of God (with Fire Island) 1994, Ultra Flava (with Pete Heller) 1995, The Rising Sun (with Pete Heller) 1999. *Website:* www.faithfanzine.com.

FARNEJAD, Sharareh (Sherry), BSc; Iranian musician (guitar), backing singer and songwriter; b. 1975, Tehran. *Education:* Azad Univ. *Career:* mem., The Arian Band (the first officially sanctioned mixed-gender pop band in Iran); professional photographer. *Recordings include:* albums: Sunflower, And But Love!, Till Eternity, Without You With You 2008, Farewell 2015. *Play:* Beyond the Mirrors. *Current Management:* c/o Mr Mohsen Rajabpour, Taraneh Sharghee Cultural & Artistic Co., Apt No. 26, Seventh Floor, Suite 22, Second Alley, Shahnazari Street, Mohseni Square, Mirdamad Avenue, Tehran 1547914415, Iran. *Telephone:* (21) 22223670. *Fax:* (21) 22906211. *Website:* www.arianmusic.com.

FARNELL, Thomas, DipEd; British musician (drums); b. 24 Aug. 1947, Birmingham; m. 1968; one s. two d. *Career:* toured USA extensively with Savoy Brown; worked and recorded with artists, including Fairport Convention, Raymond Froggatt; mem. Musicians' Union.

FARNHAM, John Peter, AO; Australian (b. British) singer and entertainer; b. 1 July 1949, Essex, UK; m. Jillian Farnham 1973; two s. *Education:* Lyndale High School. *Career:* settled in Australia 1959; apprenticed as plumber; lead singer for Strings Unlimited 1965; began recording 1967; television appearances including nature series Survival with Johnny Farnham for ABC; f. John Farnham Band 1978; lead singer for Little River Band 1982–85. *Recordings include:* Sadie the Cleaning Lady 1967 (3 Gold Records), Friday Kind of Monday 1968, Rose Coloured Glasses 1968, One 1969, Raindrops Keep Falling on My Head 1969, Comic Conversation 1970, Rock Me Baby 1972, Don't You Know It's Magic 1973, Everything is Out of Season 1973, Uncovered 1980, The Net 1982, Playing to Win 1984, Whispering Jack (ARIA Awards for Highest Selling Album 1987, for Best Adult Contemporary Album 1987) 1986, Age of Reason (ARIA Award for Highest Selling Album 1989) 1989, Chain Reaction (ARIA Award for Highest Selling Album 1991) 1990, Full House 1991, Jesus Christ Superstar: The Album 1992, Then Again (ARIA Award for Highest Selling Album 1994) 1992, Romeo's Heart (ARIA Award for Best Adult Contemporary Album 1996) 1996, Anthology Series I, II and III 1997, 33⅓

2001, The Last Time (ARIA Award for Best Adult Contemporary Album 2003) 2002, I Remember When I was Young 2005, Jack 2010, The Acoustic Chapel Sessions 2011. *Honours:* 12 Gold Record Awards; ARIA Awards for Best Male Artist 1987, 1988, 1991, for Highest Selling Single (for You're the Voice) 1987, for Outstanding Achievement Award 1988, for Song of the Year 1991, Hall of Fame Award 2003, Australian of the Year, Bicentennial 1998. *Website:* www .johnfarnham.com.au.

FARQUARSON, William (Will); British musician (bass guitar, guitar, percussion); b. 22 Sept. 1983. *Career:* Founder-mem. Bastille 2010–; released debut single 2011; signed to Virgin Records 2011. *Recordings:* album: with Bastille: Bad Blood 2013. *Honours:* BRIT Award for British Breakthrough Act 2014. *Address:* c/o Virgin EMI Records, Universal Music Group, 364–366 Kensington High Street, London, W14 8NS, England (office). *Telephone:* (20) 7471-5000 (office). *E-mail:* contact@virginemirecords.com (office). *Website:* www.virginemirecords.com (office); bastillebastille.com.

FARRAR, Jay; American singer, songwriter and musician (guitar); b. 1967, Belleville, Ill. *Career:* fmr mem., The Primitives; mem., Uncle Tupelo 1987–94; mem., Son Volt 1994–; composed music for film, The Slaughter Rule 2003; Founder, Act/Resist Records 2003, re-launched as Transmit Sound Records 2004–. *Recordings include:* albums: with Uncle Tupelo: No Depression 1990, Still Feel Gone 1991, March 16-20 1992 1992, Anodyne 1993, Songs From Uncle Tupelo 89/93: An Anthology 1994; with Son Volt: Trace 1995, Straightaways 1997, Wide Swing Tremolo 1998, O Kemah and the Melody of Riot 2005, The Search 2007, American Central Dust 2009; solo: Sebastopol 2001, Terroir Blues 2003, ThirdShiftGrottoSlack, Stone Steel and Bright Lights, One Fast Move Or I'm Gone: Kerouac's Big Sur (with Benjamin Gibbard) 2009, New Multitudes 2012. *Current Management:* c/o Sharon Agnello, Steel Toe Management, PO Box 3165, Jersey City, NJ 07303, USA. *Telephone:* (201) 963-6030. *Fax:* (201) 963-6530. *E-mail:* info@steeltoemgmt .com. *Website:* www.steeltoemgmt.com; www.jayfarrar.net.

FARRELL, David (Dave) Michael, (Phoenix); American bass guitarist, keyboard player and singer; b. 8 Feb. 1977, Plymouth, Mass; m. Linsey Farrell 2002; three c. *Education:* Mission Viejo High School, Calif., Univ. of California, Los Angeles. *Career:* fmr mem. punk/ska group Tasty Snax; mem. Xero, with Mike Shinoda, Rob Bourdon, Brad Delson 1996–98; later joined all three in Linkin Park as full-time mem. 2000–; band collaborations include Busta Rhymes, Jay-Z. *Recordings:* albums: with Linkin Park: Meteora 2003, Minutes to Midnight 2007, A Thousand Suns 2010, Living Things 2012, The Hunting Party 2014. *Honours:* numerous including: World Music Awards for Best Selling Rock Group 2002, 2003, 2007, MTV Europe Music Awards for Best Hard Rock 2002, for Best Group 2002, for Best Rock 2004, 2011, 2012, 2014, for Best Band 2007, for Best World Stage Performance 2009, 2013, for Best Live Act 2010, Kerrang! Awards for Best Int. Band 2003, for Classic Songwriter 2009, American Music Awards for Favorite Alternative Artist 2003, 2004, 2007, for Favorite Alternative Rock Artist 2008, 2012, Grammy Award for Best Rap/Sung Collaboration (with Jay-Z) 2006. *Current Management:* Andy Gould Management, 8484 Wilshire Boulevard, Suite 425, Beverly Hills, CA 90211, USA. *Website:* www.linkinpark.com.

FARRELL, Perry; American singer; b. (Perry Bernstein), 29 March 1959, New York. *Career:* mem. Jane's Addiction 1984–91, 1999–2004, 2008–; originator, Lollapalooza rock festival; formed Porno for Pyros 1993–98; collaboration on soundtrack for Howard Stern film, Private Parts 1997; established Insect World record label; formed new act The Satellite Party 2005–. *Recordings include:* albums: with Jane's Addiction: Jane's Addiction 1987, Nothing's Shocking 1988, Ritual do lo Habitual 1990, Strays 2003, Up from the Catacombs 2006, A Cabinet of Curiosities 2009, The Great Escape Artist 2011; with Porno for Pyros: Porno for Pyros 1993, Good God's Urge 1996; solo: Rev 1999, Song Yet To Be Sung 2001; with The Satellite Party: Ultra Payloaded 2007. *Website:* www.janesaddiction.com.

FARRENDEN, Shaun; British musician (didjeridu); b. 17 April 1962, Bishopstoke. *Career:* concerts include: Glastonbury Festival; Glastonbury Assembly Rooms; mem, Musicians' Union. *Recordings include:* albums: Earth Songs, 1992; Double Spiral, 1994; Yidaki, 1996; With Global: Shamanka; Gig na Gig; guest musician, Welcome To The Cali, Ron Kavana and the Bucks; television music for Channel 4. *Publications include:* Earth Vibrations, An Introduction To The Didjeridu.

FARRINGTON, Clive; British singer and musician (bass guitar, keyboards, programming, drums, percussion); b. 25 Sept. 1957, Altrincham, Manchester. *Education:* studied civil engineering. *Career:* singer and bass guitarist, When in Rome 1985–90; remixed Diesel track Man Alive, Australia 1994, Chill Factor track One Touch, Australia; writer, producer, Underground Circus on tracks Wrapped Around Your Finger, Crazy, Tree Without A Shadow; remix for Bing Abrahams track One Touch; worked with John McGeoch on project Blue, as vocalist, programmer, producer; mem. Musicians' Union, Performing Rights Soc. (assoc. mem.). *Recordings include:* album: When in Rome 1988.

FARRISS, Andrew; Australian musician (keyboard, guitar), songwriter and producer; b. 27 March 1959, Perth; m. Shelley Banks; three c. *Career:* Founder mem. The Farriss Brothers 1977, renamed INXS 1979–; various side projects and contributions to other bands, including long-standing collaborations with Jenny Morris 1986–, Yothu Yindi 1994–. *Recordings include:* albums: INXS 1980, Underneath The Colours 1981, Shabooh Shoobah 1982, The Swing 1984, Listen Like Thieves 1985, Kick 1987, X 1990, Live Baby Live 1991, Welcome

To Wherever You Are 1992, Full Moon Dirty Hearts 1993, Elegantly Wasted 1997, Switch 2006, Original Sin 2010. *Honours:* Brit Award for Best Int. Group 1991, World Music Award for Outstanding Contribution To The Music Industry 1992. *E-mail:* info@inxs.com. *Website:* www.inxs.com.

FARRISS, Jonathon (Jon) James; Australian musician (drums, percussion) and producer; b. 10 Aug. 1961, Perth. *Career:* founder mem. The Farriss Brothers 1977, renamed INXS 1979–; producer for numerous artists 1985–. *Recordings include:* albums: INXS 1980, Underneath The Colours 1981, Shabooh Shoobah 1982, The Swing 1984, Listen Like Thieves 1985, Kick 1987, X 1990, Live Baby Live 1991, Welcome To Wherever You Are 1992, Full Moon Dirty Hearts 1993, Elegantly Wasted 1997, Switch 2006, Original Sin 2010. *Honours:* Brit Award for Best Int. Group 1991, World Music Award for Outstanding Contribution to Music Industry 1992. *E-mail:* info@inxs.com. *Website:* www.inxs.com.

FARRISS, Tim; Australian musician (guitar), songwriter and producer; b. 16 Aug. 1957, Perth; m. Buffy; two s. *Career:* fmr mem. Guiness; founder mem. The Farriss Brothers 1977, renamed INXS 1979–. *Recordings include:* albums: INXS 1980, Underneath The Colours 1981, Shabooh Shoobah 1982, The Swing 1984, Listen Like Thieves 1985, Kick 1987, X 1990, Live Baby Live 1991, Welcome To Wherever You Are 1992, Full Moon Dirty Hearts 1993, Elegantly Wasted 1997, Switch 2006, Original Sin 2010. *Honours:* Brit Award for Best Int. Group 1991, World Music Award for Outstanding Contribution to Music Industry 1992. *E-mail:* info@inxs.com. *Website:* www.inxs.com.

FARROW, Andrew McGregor, BA; music manager and A & R consultant; b. 24 July 1964, Hamilton, Bermuda. *Education:* Sheffield Polytechnic. *Career:* vocalist, Living Dead, 1980–82; established AMF Music 1987; partner Far North Music 1988; proprietor (renamed) Northern Music Company. *Address:* Northern Music Company, 1st & 2nd Floor, 5A Victoria Road, Saltaire, Shipley, BD18 3LA, England. *Telephone:* (1274) 306361 (office). *Fax:* (1274) 593546 (office). *E-mail:* andy@northernmusic.co.uk; info@northernmusic.co .uk (office). *Website:* www.northernmusic.co.uk (office).

FAST; American musician (keyboards, bass, trumpet, harmonica) and programmer; b. (Brian Leiser), 29 March. *Career:* founder mem., Fun Lovin' Criminals 1993–; numerous tours, festivals and TV appearances. *Recordings include:* albums: Fun Lovin' Criminals 1995, Come Find Yourself 1996, 100% Colombian 1998, Mimosa—The Lounge Album 1999, Loco 2001, Welcome To Poppy's 2003, Livin' In The City 2005, Remixed: Progressions into Trance 2008, It Would Be Easier If 2010, Classic Fantastic 2010. *Current Management:* c/o Sidewinder Management Limited, 10 Cambridge Mews, Brighton and Hove, BN3 3EZ, England. *Telephone:* (1273) 774460. *E-mail:* sdw@ sidewindermgmt.com. *Website:* www.sidewindermgmt.com.

FAST FORWARD, BFA, MFA; British composer, artist and culinarian; b. 24 March 1954, Whitley Bay, England; m. Lucienne Vidah 1993. *Education:* Ashington Tech. Coll., Jacob Kramer Art Coll., Leeds, Newcastle upon Tyne Polytechnic, Center for Contemporary Music, Mills Coll., Oakland, Calif., USA. *Career:* performances and concerts include Whitney Museum of American Art, New York, Lincoln Center, New York, Nat. Gallery, Hamburger Bahnhof, Berlin, Museum of Modern Art, Montreal, Canada, Merkin Concert Hall, New York, Walker Art Center, Minneapolis, Norrlands Opera, Umeå, Sweden, Kunsthal, Bergen, Norway, Soundpocket, Hong Kong, Roulette Intermedium, New York, Shaffy Theatre, Rosa Kube, Oslo, Amsterdam, Tenjin Barca Festival, Osaka, Japan, Studio 200, Tokyo, Time of Music Festival, Finland, New Music America Festival, Philadelphia; guest musician, Merce Cunningham Dance Co 1994–2009; producer of his own music and also musical events; curated The Accident, nine evenings of performance, with Wooster Group; composed and performed music for dance companies and theatre performances; mem. American Soc. of Composers, Authors and Publrs (ASCAP). *Compositions include:* Red Raw Steel Drum 1985, The Dream State 1988, Machine Guns 1988, Rollerball 1990, Waterball 1990, Flip Flop 1990, Simultaneous Music 1995, Feeding Frenzy 1995, 186 1998, Questionnaire 1999, Raw Footage 1999, No Fly Zone 1999, Signal to Noise 2001, Houston We Have a Problem 2001, Tomology 2001, Distance.-Dancerun.2 2003, Feeding Frenzy 2006, 44 Instructions 2008, Musique a la Mode (solo) 2008, (for quartet) 2009. *Recordings:* Same Same, Panhandling, The Caffeine Effect, %, Rotorblade, Zeitenwechsel, Apollo and Marsyas, Musique Submergides, Red Raw Steel Drum, Bye Bye Love. *Publications:* contrib. to Arcana IV (ed by John Zorn) 2009. *Honours:* New York State Council on the Arts Commissions 1986, 1992, DAAD Fellowship, Berlin 1988, 1998, Meet the Composer Fellowship, New York Foundation for the Arts 1989, Asian Cultural Council Fellowship, New York 1997, UMAMI Festival commission 2008, DAAD commission 2009. *Current Management:* c/o Bent Out of Shape Productions, 224 East Seventh Street No. 17, New York, NY 10009, USA. *Telephone:* (917) 558-7425 (office). *E-mail:* whoswho@ mrfastforward.com (office); europa@mrfastforward.com. *Website:* mrfastforward.com.

FATBOY SLIM (see Cook, Norman)

FATONE, Joseph (Joey) Anthony, Jr; American singer; b. 28 Jan. 1977, Brooklyn, New York; m. Kelly Baldwin 2004; two d. *Career:* father sang in New York doo-wop group The Orions; relocated to Orlando aged 12; mem., *NSYNC vocal quintet 1995–2002; signed to BMG Ariola Munich 1997; first headline US tour 1998. *Television include:* presenter: The Singing Office 2007, Singing Bee 2007–, Entertainment Tonight 2007–10, Dancing with the Stars

2007, My Family Recipe Rocks 2011. *Recordings include:* albums: *NSYNC 1998, Home For The Holidays 1998, The Winter Album 1998, No Strings Attached 2000, Celebrity 2001. *Films include:* On the Line 2001, Longshot 2001, My Big Fat Greek Wedding 2002, The Cooler 2003, Homie Spumoni 2006, Red Riding Hood 2007, Inkubus 2011, Mancation 2012. *Honours:* American Music Award, Favorite Pop/Rock Band, Duo or Group 2002. *Current Management:* c/o WME, 9601 Wilshire Blvd, Beverly Hills, CA 90210, USA. *Telephone:* (310) 285-9000. *Fax:* (310) 285-9010. *Website:* www.wma.com.

FAUDEL, Cheb; French singer and songwriter; b. (Faudel Bellula), 6 June 1978, Mantes la Jolie. *Career:* formed the Rai Stars (Les Étoiles du Raï) 1990, aged 12; performed at local parties and weddings; within three years was opening for MC Solaar and Cheb Khaled; featured in two French TV shows: Saga Cities, Les Enfants du Raï 1995; participated in Festival du Printemps de Bourges 1996; tours internationally. *Recordings include:* Baida 1998, Samra 2001, 1 2 3 Soleils (with Khaled and Rachid Taha) 2001, Un Autre Soleil 2003, Mundial Corrida 2006, Bled Memory 2010, I Love You More 2011. *Film include:* The Beating of the Wings of the Butterfly 2000. *Honours:* Victoires de la Musique Award 1999. *Website:* www.faudel.net.

FAULKNER, Newton; British singer, songwriter and musician (guitar); b. (Sam Newton Battenberg Faulkner), 11 Jan. 1985, Reigate, Surrey; s. of Keith Faulkner and Sally Battenberg. *Education:* Hawthorns School, Italia Conti Acad. of Theatre Arts, Acad. of Contemporary Music. *Career:* fmr mem. Half a Guy; solo career 2005–; released debut solo album 2007; numerous tours and festivals including Glastonbury, V Festival, Connect Music Festival, Lollapalooza, Isle of Wight Festival, BBC Radio 1's Big Weekend, T in the Park, Latitude Festival. *Recordings:* albums: Hand Built by Robots 2007, Rebuilt by Humans 2009, Write It on Your Skin 2012, Studio Zoo 2013, Human Love 2015. *Current Management:* c/o OMG-Music. *E-mail:* info@omg-music.com. *Website:* www.omg-music.com; www.newtonfaulkner.com.

FAXON, Roger, BA; American entertainment business executive; *Chairman, MirriAd. Education:* Johns Hopkins Univ. *Career:* fmrly Sr Staff mem. US Congress; COO LUCASFILM Ltd 1980–84; Founding Pnr The Mount Company 1984–86; worked at Tri-Star and Columbia Pictures 1986–90, rising to Sr Exec. Vice-Pres. Columbia Pictures Entertainment; fmrly COO Sotheby's North and South America, CEO Sotheby's Europe, Man. Dir Sotheby's –1994; Sr Vice-Pres. of Business Devt and Strategy EMI Music 1994–99, Exec. Vice-Pres. and Chief Financial Officer EMI Music Publishing 1999–2002, Chief Financial Officer EMI Group PLC 2002–05, Bd mem. 2002–05, 2006–, Pres. and COO EMI Music Publishing 2005–06, Jt CEO 2006–07, Chair. and CEO 2007–10, CEO EMI Music Group 2010–12; Chair., MirriAd 2013–; mem. Bd of Dirs ASCAP. *Address:* MirriAd, 624 Hampton Drive, Venice, CA 90291, USA (office). *Telephone:* (310) 392-2828 (office). *E-mail:* press@mirriad.com. *Website:* www.mirriad.com (office).

FAY, Johnny; Canadian musician (drums); b. 30 April 1966, Ontario. *Career:* mem. The Tragically Hip 1983–. *Recordings include:* albums: Up to Here 1989, Road Apples 1991, Fully Completely 1992, Day for Night 1994, Trouble at the Henhouse 1996, Live Between Us 1997, Phantom Power 1998, Music @ Work 2000, In Violet Light 2002, In Between Revolution 2004, World Container 2006, We are the Same 2009, Now for Plan A 2012. *Honours:* inducted into the Canadian Music Hall of Fame 2005. *Address:* c/o Universal Music, 2450 Victoria Park Avenue, Suite 1, Toronto, ON M2J 5H3, Canada (office). *Website:* www.thehip.com.

FAYROUZ (see Fairuz)

FEATHER, Lorraine; American jazz singer, lyricist and songwriter; b. (Billie Jane Lee Lorraine Feather), 10 Sept. 1948, New York; d. of Leonard Feather and Jane Feather; m. Tony Morales. *Education:* Los Angeles City Coll. *Career:* fmr backing singer, Petula Clark, Grand Funk Railroad; solo career 1978–; mem. and lyricist, vocal trio Swing, renamed Full Swing 1981–89; song lyricist for numerous artists including Patti Austin, David Benoit, Djavan, Phyllis Hyman, Cleo Laine, Kenny Rankin, Diane Schuur; numerous session credits as singer or backing singer including Michael Feinstein, Eric Marienthal, Bette Midler, Terry Trotter. *Films:* as song lyricist: MGM Sing-Alongs 1997, The Jungle Book 2 2003, The Princess Diaries 2: Royal Engagement 2004, Pooh's Heffalump Halloween Movie 2005, My Little Pony (series) 2005–09. *Television:* as song lyricist: All Dogs Go to Heaven: The Series 1996–98, The Lionhearts 1998. *Recordings:* albums: solo: Sweet Lorraine 1978, The Body Remembers 1997, New York City Drag 2001, Cafe Society 2003, Such Sweet Thunder: Music of the Duke Ellington Orchestra 2004, Dooji Wooji 2005, Language 2008, Ages 2010, Tales of the Unusual 2012, Fourteen 2012, Attachments 2013; with Swing: The Good Times Are Back 1982; with Full Swing: In Full Swing 1987, The End of the Sky 1989. *Current Management:* c/o Jim Wadsworth Productions Agency, 7916 Woodpointe Court, Sarasota, FL 34238-2946; c/o Maggie Rodford, Air-Edel Associates Ltd, 9100 Wilshire Blvd, Suite 350E, Beverly Hills, CA 90212, USA. *Telephone:* (941) 924-8452 (Sarasota); (310) 802-7655 (Beverly Hills). *Fax:* (206) 339-4461 (Sarasota). *E-mail:* jwadsworth@aol.com; MRodford@air-edel.co.uk. *Website:* jwpjazz.com; www.air-edel.co.uk; www.lorrainefeather.com (home).

FEEHAN, David; New Zealand singer, songwriter, producer and singing teacher; b. 9 Oct. 1948, Wellington; m. Shelley Catherine Melody; three s. *Education:* New Zealand Opera Co. *Career:* EMI session vocalist 1964–70; lead singer band, Tapestry 1970–78; lead singer, Rodger Fox Big Band

1974–87; concerts at Ronnie Scott's, London, Montreux Jazz Festival, Switzerland, Hong Kong, Singapore, New York, Poland, Los Angeles, Sydney, Vancouver; leader of David Feehan Band 1988–; Vocal Tutor, Whitireia Community Polytechnic 1990–97; Professtional Studies and Vocal Tutor, Univ. Conservatorium of Music, Wellington 1997–; appearances on all major New Zealand TV shows and concerts. *Stage appearance:* played Jesus in Jesus Christ Superstar 1983. *Recordings include:* with Tapestry: It's Wrong 1973; with Rodger Fox Big Band: Timepiece 1978, New York Tapes 1981, Heavy Company 1984; solo: Ballade 1986, DF 1993; appearances on over 20 other albums. *Address:* 27 Mortimer Terrace, Aro Valley, Wellington, New Zealand (home).

FEEHILY, Mark Michael Patrick; Irish singer; b. 28 May 1980, Sligo. *Career:* mem., Westlife 1999–; numerous tours, festivals and television appearances. *Recordings include:* albums: Westlife 1999, Coast to Coast 2000, World of Our Own 2001, Unbreakable – The Greatest Hits 2002, Turnaround 2003, Face To Face 2005, The Love Album 2006, Back Home 2007, Where We Are 2009, Gravity 2010. *Honours:* BRIT Awards for Best Pop Act 2001, 2002, Meteor Ireland Music Award for Best Irish Pop Act 2005, 2006, 2007, 2010, MTV Battle of the Boybands Ultimate Boyband of All Time 2012. *Current Management:* Louis Walsh Management, 24 Courtney House, Appian Way, Dublin 6, Ireland. *Telephone:* (1) 668 0309. *Fax:* (1) 668 0721. *Website:* www.westlife.com.

FEHLING, Annika; Swedish singer, songwriter and actress; b. 25 Oct. 1962, Gothenburg; m.; one d. *Education:* Univ. of Lund, Theatre Art School of Skara, State School of Theatre, Malmo, studied singing and piano, and arranging and composing in Stockholm. *Career:* Founder and producer SFM Living Room club for singer-songwriters, Visby, Sweden; Co-founder Listening Room Int. Songwriters' Retreat; numerous tours in USA, Germany, Switzerland, England, Ireland, Denmark, Sweden, Czech Republic; concerts with Visby Big Band in Norway, Poland, Rhodes; composes music for theatre; Mére Ubu in King Ubu, musical; solo-singer, Duke Ellington's Sacred Concert; participated in films, Women on the Roof, Petri Tears; participated in Sweden Song Contest, televised 1998; rep. Sweden at EXPO 2000 in Hannover; f. Singer-Songwriters of Sweden; co-f. Slow Food Music 2003; mem. STIM, SKAP. *Compositions include:* A Woman's Jazz; music for M. H. Caspers exhbn, From the Inside; music for plays Lille Hamlett, Offelia kom igen, Häxxxorna, Witches. *Recordings include:* albums: solo: Jazz Fehlings 1996, Alskar Du? (Do You Love) 1997, Fehling & Hillered Live 2001, Åkessonger 2002; with Ruediger Kebe: Anchor 2003, Orange 2004, Happy on the Red 2005; with Dana Cooper: Visby Texas 2007. *Television includes:* Go'kväll (SVT), Gomorron (TV4). *Publication:* The Real Swede 1997. *Honours:* STIM, Sweden's ASCAP Prize 1992, 1996, 1999, 2004, State Art Prize, Art Council 1993, 1994, 1999, 2001, 2003, 2004, 2007, SKAP Prize 1997, Swedish Arts Council Cultural Exchange grant 2005, 2006, 2007, Gotland Market and Export Asscn Prize 2007. *Current Management:* Arne Söderquist, SFM, Strandg 22 II, 62156 Visby, Sweden. *Telephone:* (708) 467203. *E-mail:* annika@annikafehling.com. *Website:* www.annikafehling.com.

FEIGIN, Leo; record company executive; b. 1 Feb. 1938, Leningrad, USSR; m. Lora Feigin Denisenko; one s. *Education:* Institute of Physical Culture and Sports, Leningrad, Pedagogical Institute. *Career:* broadcaster, World Service, BBC 1974–92; producer, presenter weekly new music programme 1974–98; proprietor, Leo Records 1979–; mem. Performing Rights Soc., Mechanical-Copyright Protection Soc. *Recordings:* over 400 albums. *Television:* New Music from Russia (documentary). *Publications:* Russian Jazz 1985. *Address:* Leo Records, 16 Woodland Avenue, Kingskerswell, Newton Abbot TQ12 5BB, England (office). *Telephone:* (1803) 872167 (office). *Website:* www.leorecords.com (office).

FEINSTEIN, Michael Jay; American singer, musician (piano), actor and musicologist; b. 7 Sept. 1956, Columbus, OH. *Career:* archivist, Ira Gershwin 1977–83; asst to Harry Warren 1979–81; hotel residencies in USA 1984–89; accompanist for artists, including Liza Minnelli, Estelle Reiner, Rose Marie, Jessie Matthews, Rosemary Clooney 1991–; Dir, Popular Music Series, Lincoln Center, New York 2009–; numerous concerts, tours, television appearances; mem. ASCAP. *Compositions include:* film score and songs for Get Bruce 1997. *Recordings include:* albums: Michael Feinstein Sings Irving Berlin 1987, Isn't It Romantic 1987, Over There – Songs of War and Peace 1989, The MGM Album 1989, Burton Lane Song Book, Vol. I 1990, Vol. II 1992, Jule Styne Song Book 1991, Pure Imagination 1991, Forever 1993, Jerry Herman Song Book 1994, Hugh Martin Song Book 1995, Such Sweet Sorrow 1995, Nice Work If You Can Get It 1996, Nobody But You 1998, Feinstein sings Gershwin 1998, Big City Rhythms 1999, Romance on Film, Romance on Broadway 2000, Michael Feinstein With The Israel Philharmonic Orchestra 2002, Livingston and Evans Songbook 2002, Only One Life: The Songs of Jimmy Webb 2003, Hopeless Romantics (with George Shearing) 2005, The Sinatra Project 2005. *Publications:* Ira Gershwin Song Book (ed.), Nice Work If You Can Get It (autobiog.) 1995; contrib. to Washington Post, New York Times. *Honours:* DFA (California State Univ. at Los Angeles) 1997; three Golden Laurel Awards, San Francisco Council for Entertainment, NYC Seal of Approval 1987, Drama Desk Award 1988, Outer Critics Circle Award 1988. *Current Management:* c/o Andrew Leff, Morey Management, 1100 Glendon Avenue, Suite 1100, Los Angeles, CA 90024, USA. *Telephone:* (310) 205-6100. *Fax:* (310) 205-6199. *E-mail:* aleff@moreymanagement.com. *Website:* www.moreymanagement.com. *Address:* The Pure Feinstein Fan Club, PO Box 6342, Orange, CA 92863, USA (office). *Website:* www.michaelfeinstein.com.

FEIST; Canadian singer, songwriter and musician (guitar); b. (Leslie Feist), 13 Feb. 1976, Amherst, Nova Scotia; d. of Harold Feist. *Career:* formed band Placebo as a teenager; guitarist with By Divine Right 1998–2001; also solo artist 1999–; numerous tours and recordings with Gonzales and Peaches; mem. indie rock supergroup Broken Social Scene 2001–; extensive tours of N America, Europe, Asia, Australia 2004–; has collaborated on recordings with Kings of Convenience, Wilco, Beck, Jane Birkin, Jason Collett, Apostle of Hustle, Mocky, Teki Latex; guest vocalist, Paris, je t'aime film soundtrack. *Recordings:* albums: with By Divine Right: Bless This Mess 1999; with Broken Social Scene: You Forgot It in People (Juno Award for Alternative Album of the Year 2003) 2002, Bee Hives 2004, Broken Social Scene (Juno Award for Alternative Album of the Year 2006) 2005; solo: Monarch (Lay Your Jewelled Head Down) 1999, Let It Die (Juno Award for Alternative Album of the Year 2005) 2004, Open Season 2006, The Reminder (Shortlist Music Prize 2008, Juno Awards for Album of the Year 2008, for Pop Album of the Year 2008) 2007, Metals 2011. *Honours:* Juno Awards for New Artist of the Year 2005, for Artist of the Year 2008, for Single of the Year (for 1234) 2008, for Songwriter of the Year 2008. *Address:* Arts & Crafts Records, 460 Richmond Street West, #402, Toronto, ON M5V 1Y1, Canada (office). *E-mail:* raiseyourhands@arts-crafts.ca (office). *Website:* www.arts-crafts.ca (office); www.cherrytreerecords.com (office); www.listentofeist.com.

FELDMAN, Samuel (Sam) Leon; Canadian entertainment company executive; b. 14 March 1949, Shanghai, People's Republic of China; one s. two d. *Career:* Pres., S. L. Feldman and Assocs, a div. of A & F Music Ltd, co-owned with partner Bruce Allen; partner in Macklam Feldman Management, clients include The Chieftains, Diana Krall, Norah Jones, Elvis Costello, James Taylor, Melody Gardot, Ry Cooder, Pink Martini, Susan Tedeschi; Pres., Big Pictures Entertainment Inc. (film and TV production company). *Honours:* Walt Grealis Special Achievement Award (Industry Builder), Canadian Acad. of Recording Arts & Sciences, Juno Awards 1998, SOCAN Special Achievement Award 2005. *Address:* S.L. Feldman and Associates, 200-1505 West 2nd Avenue, Vancouver, BC V6H 3Y4, Canada (office). *Telephone:* (604) 734-5945 (office). *Fax:* (604) 732-0922 (office). *E-mail:* feldman@slfa.com (office). *Website:* www.feldman-agency.com (office).

FELICIANO, José; Puerto Rican/American singer and musician (guitar, bass, drums, piano, percussion); b. 10 Sept. 1945, Lares, Puerto Rico. *Career:* moved to New York as child; performer of English and Latin music; recorded albums in Argentina, Mexico, Venezuela, Italy, USA, Austria; television show throughout South America; sang and composed theme music to TV series Chico and The Man; recording artist, classical guitar music, English pop, Spanish-language and jazz recordings. *Recordings include:* El Sentimiento 1966, La Copa Rota 1966, Sombra 1967, El Fantastico! 1967, Mas Éxitos de José 1967, Felicidades Con Lo Mejor de José Feliciano 1968, Sin Luz 1968, En Mi Soledad-No Llores 1968, José Feliciano Dos Cruces 1971, José Feliciano January 71 1971, José Feliciano Canta Otra 1971, Escenas De Amor 1982, Me Enamoré 1983, Como Tú Quieres 1984, Ya Soy Tuyo 1985, Te Amaré 1986, Tu Immenso Amor 1987, Niña 1990, Latin Street '92 1992, Americano 1996, Señor Bolero 1998, Señor Bolero 2 2001, Guitarra Mia Tribute 2003, A México, Con Amor 2005, José Feliciano y Amigos 2006, Señor Bachata (Grammy Award for Best Tropical Latin Album 2009) 2007, Con Mexico en el Corazón 2008, José Feliciano en vivo 2009, The Genius of José Feliciano, Vol.2 2011, Alma Rebelde 2012, The King: Jose Feliciano Tribute to Elvis Presley 2012. *Honours:* Hon. DHumLitt (Sacred Heart Univ.) 2001; Grammy Awards for Best New Artist 1968, for Best Male Contemporary Pop Vocal (for Light My Fire) 1968, for Best Latin Pop Performance (for Me Enamore) 1984, (for Lelolai) 1986, (for Cielito Lindo) 1989, (for Porque Te Tengo Que Dividar?) 1990, for Best Tropical Latin Album (Señor Bachata) 2008, Billboard Magazine Lifetime Achievement Award 1996, ASCAP Golden Note Award. *Current Management:* c/o Clip Productions, Helmuth Schaerf, Vienna, Austria. *Telephone:* (2) 566-57-09. *Fax:* (2) 566-47-85. *E-mail:* clip@inode.at. *Website:* www.josefeliciano.com.

FELIX DA HOUSECAT, (Sharkimaxx, Thee Maddkatt Courtship, Aphro-head, Thee Maddkatt Chronicles); American producer, remixer and DJ; b. (Felix Stallings Jr), 1971, Detroit, MI. *Career:* based in Chicago; started producing house tracks with DJ Pierre; Pierre's Phantasy Club classic Phantasy Girl released 1986; founder, Radikal Fear, Clashbackk, Thee Black Label; recorded tracks for numerous labels, including Strictly Rhythm, Soma, Guerilla, FFRR; collaborations with DJ Pierre, Miss Kittin, Mark Bell, Harrison Crump, K. Alexi. *Recordings include:* albums: By Dawn's Early Light 1994, Metropolis Present Day? Thee Album! 1995, Clashback Compilation Mix 1997, Transmissions Vol. 2 1997, I Know Electrikboy 1999, Kittenz And Thee Glitz (Muzik Award for Best Album) 2001, Excursions 2002, Rocketmann! 2002, A Bugged Out Mix 2003, Devin Dazzle & The Neon Fever 2004, Virgo Blaktro & the Movie Disco 2007, He Was King 2009, Son of Analogue 2011. *Address:* Nettwerk Productions, 1650 W. 2nd Avenue, Vancouver, BC V6J 4R3, Canada. *Website:* www.nettwerk.com; www.myspace.com/felixdahousecat.

FELL, Simon Howard; British musician (double bass) and composer; b. 13 Jan. 1959, Dewsbury, West Yorkshire; m. Jo Fell 1982. *Education:* Fitzwilliam Coll., Univ. of Cambridge; double bass with Peter Leah. *Career:* f. Bruce's Fingers record label 1983; mem. Performing Rights Soc., Mechanical-Copyright Protection Soc., Musicians' Union. *Compositions include:* Compilation I 1985, Compilation II 1990, Four slices of Zappa 1992, Music for 10(0) 1993, LeoSuite 1996, Icons 1997, Cubism 1998, Composition N 30 1998,

Papers 1998, Three Mondrians 1999, Thirteen New Inventions 2005, The Ragging Of Time 2014. *Recordings include:* The Coming of Kazar 1985, Compilation I 1985, Free Nelson 1986, Pride and Prejudice 1987, Two Steps to Easier Breathing 1988, The House in Paris 1989, L'huile sur le feu 1989, Five on Genius 1989, Termite One 1989, Termite Two 1989, Laid Back Leisure Spots 1990, Millions of Wishes Come True in Plastic Film 1990, Compilation II 1990, Songs About Housework 1990, M.M. 1990, Odeon's Dropout Piece 1990, Maz 1991, Bogey's 1991, foom! foom! 1992, Rear Quarters 1992, The Horrors of Darmstadt 1993, Start Moving Earbuds 1993, Music for 10(0) 1995, Frankenstein 1996, Composition No 30 1998, Registered Firm 1998, Pure Water Construction 1998, Ghost Notes 1998, Company in Marseille 1999, Trees 2000, Thirteen Rectangles 2001, The Soc. of the Spectacle 2003, Four Compositions 2004, Composition No. 62 2005, Positions & Descriptions 2007, The Necessary and the Possible 2009, Two Falls & A Submission 2011, Frank and Max 2011. *Publications include:* Report on the Composition of Improvised Music Nos 1–4 1993, 1994, 1997, 1998. *Address:* 29 Teillet, 23400 St Dizier-Leyrenne, France (home). *E-mail:* info@brucesfingers.com. *Website:* www.brucesfingers.co.uk.

FELLOUÉ, Guillermo; French musician (bugle, trumpet); b. 10 Feb. 1932, Havana, Cuba; m. Rosana Felloué 1969. *Education:* music conservatory. *Career:* professional from age 13; first trumpet and soloist with leading Cuban singers including Arsenio Rodriguez and Benny More; soloist with Perez Prado; tours of Europe and Japan with Havana Cuban Boys of Armando Orefiche; first trumpet and soloist with the Rosana and Guil Afro-Cuban jazz show, two tours Japan; arrived in Paris aged 19, played at Moulin Rouge, Casino de Cannes; first trumpet soloist, Big Band from Bourdeaux-Aquitane; worked at casino Sporting Club, Monte-Carlo for seven years; first trumpet and soloist, Bekummernis of Luc Le Masne; tours with singer Ellie Medeiros in Japan; USA, Canada; Co-Dir Los Salseros. *Recordings include:* with Arseño Rodriguez Conjunto Colonial: Cuba; three albums with Bekumernis de Luc Le Masne; album with Ellie Medeiros; album Los Salseros; live album with Africando 2007. *Address:* 20 rue de Rungis, 75013 Paris, France. *Telephone:* 6-16-68-17-72 (office); 1-45-80-02-24 (home).

FELTHAM, Mark; British musician (harmonica) and composer; b. 20 Oct. 1955, Bermondsey, London, England; s. of Leonard Feltham and Georgina Feltham. *Education:* South East London Tech. School, Greenwich. *Career:* Founder-mem. Nine Below Zero 1977–82, 1991–92, 2001–; harmonica player with Rory Gallagher for 11 years; varied studio and touring work, including Georgie Fame 1984, Godley and Creme (harmonica album) 1986, New Model Army, Deacon Blue 1988, Texas 1988, The The 1989–91, Talk Talk 1989–92, Joan Armatrading 1992, Annie Lennox 1995, Oasis, Zucchero 1999–2000, Tom Jones, The Christians, Rory Gallagher, Dido, Joe Cocker, Lightning Seeds, Godley and Crème, The Everly Brothers, Roy Harper, New Model Army, Will Young, Paul Young, Michael Ball, Ocean Colour Scene, KLF, Engelbert Humperdinck, Errol Brown, George Michael, Roger Daltrey, Mark Owen, Robbie Williams, Gabrielle, Karl Jenkins; mem. Musicians' Union. *Recordings include:* albums: with Nine Below Zero: Packed Fair and Square 1979, Live At The Marquee 1980, Don't Point Your Finger 1981, Chilled 2002, Hats Off 2005, Both Sides of Nine Below Zero 2008, It's Never Too Late! 2009; with Glenn Tilbrook: The Co-Operative 2011; with Godley and Creme: Goodbye Blue Sky 1986. *Current Management:* c/o 45 rpm Records, IMEX House, VIP Trading Estate, Anchor & Hope Lane, Charlton, London, SE7 7TE, England. *Website:* www.ninebelowzero.com.

FELTON, Timothy (Tim); British musician (guitar) and producer; b. Birmingham. *Career:* Founder mem. Broadcast 1995–2005; signed recording contract with Duophonic label 1996, moved to Warp Records 1997. *Recordings include:* albums: Work and Non Work 1997, The Noise Made By People 2000, HAHA Sound 2003, Tender Buttons 2005, The Future Crayon 2006.

FELTS, Narvel; American country and rockabilly singer and musician (guitar); b. 11 Nov. 1938, Keiser, Arkansas; m. Loretta Stanfield Felts 1962, 1 s., deceased, 1 d. *Career:* high school talent contest aged 17, Bernie, Missouri; one of original rockabillies, career lasting over 43 years; one of the major country artists of the '70s; mem. American Federation of Musicians; Reunion of Professional Entertainers. *Compositions:* Three Thousand Miles; Lonely Hours; Red Hair and Green Eyes; Four Seasons of Life; Foggy Misty Morning; When We Were Together; Away. *Recordings:* albums: Drift Away 1973, When Your Good Love Was Mine 1974, Narvel Felts 1975, Narvel the Marvel 1976, Doin' What I Feel 1976, The Touch of Felts 1977, Narvel 1977, Inside Love 1978, One Run for the Roses 1979, Teens Way 1987, Radio Rockabillies 1988, More Radio Rockabillies (with Jerry Mercer) 2003. *Honours:* Single of the Year, Billboard and Cashbox, 1975; 10 ASCAP Awards, 1973, 1974, 1977, 1979; ASCAP Artist of the Year, 1977; Rockabilly Hall of Fame, 1997. *Current Management:* Joe Taylor Artist Agency, 2802 Columbine Pl., Nashville, TN 37204, USA. *E-mail:* harold_boner@yahoo.com. *Address:* 2005 Narvel Felts Avenue, Malden, MO 63863, USA (home). *Website:* www.mkoc.com/NarvelFelts (home).

FENGER, Søs; Danish singer and songwriter; b. (Charlotte Fenger), 2 Dec. 1961, Copenhagen; one s. *Education:* studied piano, guitar and singing. *Career:* toured with pop band, News early 1980s; soul band (with brother), Love Construction 1986–89; solo artist 1989–; toured with Doky Brothers and Adam Nussbaum; recorded with Toots Thielemanns and Randy Brecker; contributor to several Scandinavian albums. *Recordings include:* Vinterdage 1983, On Holiday 1992, Et Kys Herfra 1994, Camouflage 1996, Gamle flammer 1997, Søs 2000, Beverly Way 2002, Nøglen til Paradis 2004, Vuggeviser 2007, Stjernenat 2009, Nogle gange er man så heldig, at man ikke nsår at tænke sig om 2011. *Honours:* Female Singer of the Year 1986, 1990, 2003, Grammy Awards, Spies Fondet's Music Award 1993. *Current Management:* Annetta Elmo Management, Travbanen, Traverbanevej 10, 2920 Charlottenlund, Denmark. *Telephone:* 70-20-12-02; 20-73-10-55. *E-mail:* annetta@annetta.dk. *Website:* www.annetta.dk; www.sosfenger.dk.

FENNESZ, Christian; Austrian musician (guitar/laptop); b. 25 Dec. 1962. *Career:* mem. Maische late 1980s–92; collaborations include Peter 'Pita' Rehberg, Ryuichi Sakamoto, Fenn O'Berg, Mark Fell. *Recordings include:* albums: solo: Hotel Paral.lel 1997, Plays 1999, Music for an Isolation Tank 1999, Plus Forty Seven Degrees 56'37" Minus Sixteen Degrees 51'08" 2000, Endless Summer 2000, Live at Revolver, Melbourne 2000, Field Recordings 1995–2002 2002, Venice 2004, Cendre 2007, Szampler 2010, Seven Stars 10" (EP) 2011; with Ryuichi Sakamoto: Black Sea 2009; with Fenn O'Berg: The Magic Sound of Fenn O'Berg 1999, The Return of Fenn O'Berg 2002, In Stereo 2010; soundtracks include: Beyond the Ocean 1999, Gelbe Kirschen 2000, Blue Moon 2002, AUN: The Beginning and the End of All Things 2012. *Address:* c/o Touch, 13 Osward Road, London, SW17 7SS, England. *E-mail:* touch@touch33.net. *Website:* www.touch33.net; www.fennesz.com.

FENTON, George; British composer and musician (guitar); b. 19 Oct. 1950, London, England. *Compositions for television:* Hitting Town 1974, Out 1978, Rain on the Roof 1980, The History Man 1981, Bergerac (theme) 1981, Fox 1981, A Woman of No Importance 1982, Saigon: Year of the Cat 1983, An Englishman Abroad 1983, East of Ipswich 1987, Talking Heads 1987, 102 Boulevard Haussmann 1991, China: Beyond the Clouds 1994, Talking Heads 2 1998, Planet Earth (Classical BRIT Award for Soundtrack Composer of the Year 2007, Primetime Emmy for Outstanding Music Composition 2007) 2006, Earth 2007, Frozen Planet 2011. *Compositions for film:* Private Road 1971, Bloody Kids 1979, Hussy 1980, Gandhi 1982, Runners 1983, The Company of Wolves 1984, Billy the Kid and the Green Baize Vampire 1985, Clockwise 1986, Walter and June 1986, 84 Charing Cross Road 1986, Cry French 1987, White Mischief 1987, High Spirits 1988, A Handful of Dust 1988, The Dressmaker 1988, Dangerous Liaisons 1988, We're No Angels 1989, Memphis Belle 1990, White Palace 1990, The Long Walk Home 1990, The Fisher King 1991, Hero 1992, Final Analysis 1992, Groundhog Day 1993, Shadowlands 1993, Born Yesterday 1993, China Moon 1994, Ladybird Ladybird 1994, The Madness of King George (adaptations) 1994, Mixed Nuts 1994, Land and Freedom 1995, The Viking Sagas 1995, Mary Reilly 1996, Heaven's Prisoners 1996, Multiplicity 1996, Carla's Song 1996, The Crucible 1996, In Love and War 1996, The Woodlanders 1998, Dangerous Beauty 1998, The Object of My Affection 1998, My Name is Joe 1998, Ever After 1998, Living Out Loud 1998, You've Got Mail 1998, Entropy 1999, Grey Owl 1999, Anna and the King 1999, Bread and Roses 2000, Center Stage 2000, Lucky Numbers 2000, Last Holiday 2005, The History Boys 2006, Fool's Gold 2008, The Angels' Share 2012, Byzantium 2012. *Honours:* Ivor Novello Acad. Fellowship 2007.

FENWICK, Raymond (Ray) John; British musician (guitar) and producer; b. 18 July 1946, Romford, Essex. *Career:* mem. The Syndicats 1965, Marty Wilde 1965, The Tee Set 1966, After Tea 1968, The Spencer Davis Group 1968–72, Fancy 1974, The Ian Gillan Band 1977, Forcefield 1984–92, Johnny Mars Band 1990, Steve Howe's Remedy 1994; numerous concert tours; mem. Performing Rights Soc., Mechanical Copyright Protection Soc., Repro. *Recordings include:* albums: After Tea 1968, Magpie (TV theme music) 1970s, Bo Diddley sessions 1972; with The Ian Gillan Band: Live At The Budokan 1978, Child In Time 1976, Clear Air Turbulence 1977, Scarubus 1977, What I Did on My Vacation 1986, Rockfield Mines 1997, Live at the Rainbow 1998; solo: Keep America Beautiful – Get A Haircut 1997, Riding The Rock Machine (compilation) 1997. *Website:* www.rayfenwick.com.

FERAL (see Brann, Chris)

FERGIE; American singer and songwriter; b. (Stacy Ann Ferguson), 27 March 1975, Los Angeles, Calif.; m. Josh Duhamel 2009; one s. *Career:* starred in children's TV programme Kids Incorporated 1984–89; mem. Wild Orchid 1992–2002; mem. Black Eyed Peas 2003–; simultaneous solo artist 2006–. *Recordings include:* albums: with Black Eyed Peas: Elephunk (NRJ Music Award for Best Int. Album, France 2005) 2003, Monkey Business (Juno Award for Int. Album of the Year 2006, American Music Award for Favorite Rap/Hip-Hop Album 2006) 2005, The E.N.D. (Grammy Award for Best Pop Vocal Album 2010) 2009, The Beginning 2010; solo: The Dutchess 2006. *Films include:* Monster in the Closet 1987, Outside Ozona 1998, Be Cool 2005, Poseidon 2006, Grindhouse 2007, Planet Terror 2007, Nine 2009, Madagascar: Escape 2 Africa (voice) 2008, Arthur and the Revenge of Maltazard (voice) 2009, Marmaduke (voice) 2010. *Honours:* MTV Europe Award for Best Pop Act 2004, 2005, Australian MTV Awards for Best R&B Video, for Sexiest Video (both for Hey Mama) 2005, American Music Award for Favorite Pop/Rock Band, Duo or Group 2005, 2009, for Favorite Rap/Hip-Hop Band, Duo or Group 2005, 2006, 2009, for Favorite Pop/Rock Female Artist 2007, Grammy Award for Best Rap Performance by a Duo or Group (for Don't Phunk with My Heart) 2006, for Best Pop Performance by a Duo or Group with Vocal (for My Humps) 2007, (for I Gotta Feeling) 2010, for Best Rap/Sung Collaboration (for All Of The Lights) 2012, for Best Rap Song (for All Of The Lights) (jtly) 2012, MOBO Award for Best Group 2006, MTV Video Music Award for Best Female Artist 2007. *Website:* www.fergie.com; www.blackeyedpeas.com.

FERGUSON, James Warner, MM; American musician (bass) and singer; b. 10 Dec. 1950, Jefferson City, Mo.; m. Antonia F. Ferguson; one d. *Education:* Univ. of South Carolina. *Career:* staff bassist, The American Popular Singer, NPR; staff bassist, Main St Jazz Festival, PBS; staff singer, Country Music Asscn Awards; mem. Screen Actors Guild, American Fed. of TV and Radio Artists, American Fed. of Musicians. *Compositions include:* Not Just Another Pretty Bass. *Recordings include:* The Messiah – A Soulful Celebration, Together At Last, Great Hits of the Past, Shadowlands, Three Good Reasons, Cheek to Cheek, River of Love, First Christmas, Our Love Is Here To Stay, Not Just Another Pretty Bass 1999, Deep Summer Music 2000, Cedar and Silver 2004. *Honours:* Music Dept Alumnus of the Year, Univ. of South Carolina 1997. *Address:* Jim Ferguson Music, 210 Mayfair Road, Nashville, TN 37205, USA (office). *E-mail:* jim@jimfergusonmusic.com (office). *Website:* jimfergusonmusic.com (office).

FERGUSON, Neil; British producer, engineer and musician (guitar, keyboards); b. 6 Dec. 1954, Castleford, Yorkshire; m. Helen Mary Ferguson 1976; one s. one d. *Career:* records produced, engineered for Black Lace, Chumbawamba, Smokie, Credit To The Nation, Chris Norman, Nick Berry; currently mem. of Chumbawamba; mem. Musicians' Union, PRS. *Recordings include:* Chumbawamba albums: Tubthumper 1997, Amnesia 1997, Top of the World 1998, Uneasy Listening 1999, Readymades 2002, Revengers Tragedy Soundtrack 2003, Un 2004, A Singsong and a Scrap 2005, The Boy Bands Have Won 2008, ABCDEFG 2010, Big Society! 2012; other: Agadoo, Teenage Sensation, Heartbeat (television theme music), Tacky Love Song, by Credit To The Nation 1998; backing vocals on This Is The Voice, by The Oyster Band 1999, Live at Antone's 2011, Dark River: Songs of the Civil War Era: Interpretations by Austin's Finest Musicians 2011. *Address:* 185 Highgate, Bradford, BD9 5PU, England (home). *Telephone:* (1274) 482327 (home). *E-mail:* fergie.neil@virgin.net (home).

FERIANTO, Djaduk; Indonesian composer and musician; b. 19 July 1964, Java; s. of Bagong Kussudiardja; brother of Butet Kertaredjasa. *Career:* Founder and leader of group Kua Etnika 1996–; f. Padepokan Seni Bagong K Foundation. *Films* as composer: Clowns of the City 1993, Leaf on a Pillow 1998, Untuk Rena 2005, Drupadi 2008, Sarinah 2011, Soegija 2012, Gending Sriwijaya 2013; as actor: Sherina's Adventure 2000, Cewek saweran 2011. *Compositions include:* Kompi Susu (Milk Brigade), Brigade Mailing (Thieves' Brigade). *Recordings include:* albums: Orkes Sumpeg Nang Ning Nong 1997, Ritus Swara 2000, Parodi Iklan 2000, Komedi Putar 2002, Janji Palsu 2003, Maling Budiman 2006, Dia Sumber Gembiraku 2006, Pata Java. *Honours:* UNESCO Grand Prize 2000. *Address:* c/o Padepokan Seni Bagong K Foundation, Jogjakarta, Indonesia.

FERNANDEZ, Julio; American musician (guitar); b. 29 Aug. 1954, Havana, Cuba. *Career:* moved to USA 1961; mem., jazz band Spyro Gyra 1984–. *Recordings include:* Alternating Currents 1985, Breakout 1986, Stories Without Words 1987, Rites of Summer 1988, Three Wishes 1992, Dreams Beyond Control 1993, Love & Other Obsessions 1995, Heart of the Night 1996, 20/20 1997, Road Scholars 1998, Got the Magic 1999, In Modern Times 2001, Original Cinema 2003, The Deep End 2004, Wrapped in a Dream 2006, Good to Go-Go 2007, Down the Wire 2009, A Foreign Affair 2011, The Rhinebeck Sessions 2013. *Honours:* George Benson Lifetime Achievement Award (for Spyro Gyra) 2007. *Current Management:* c/o Phil Brennan, Crosseyed Bear Productions, 270 Olympic Avenue, Buffalo, NY 14215-3258, USA. *Telephone:* (716) 831-1511. *E-mail:* phil@philbrennan.com. *Website:* www.spyrogyra.com.

FERNÁNDEZ (GOMEZ), Vicente; Mexican singer; b. 17 Feb. 1940, Huentitlán del Alto, Jalisco; m. María del Refugio Abarca Villaseñor 1963; three s. *Career:* worked as street serenader; appeared on TV show La Calandria Musical; has appeared in numerous films and TV shows. *Recordings include:* albums: A Pesar De Todo, Volver Volver, Es La Diferencia, Mexicano En La México, Vicente Fernández, De Un Rancho A Otro, Hoy Platique Con Mi Gallo, Vicente Fernández, Tesoros Musicales, El Cuatrero, Por Tu Maldito Amor, Canta A America Latina, Corridos, La Muerte De Un Gallero, Arriba Huentitlán, Personalidad, Gusta Usted?, Lástima Que Seas Ajena, Mi Amigo El Tordillo, El Tapatio, La Voz Que Usted Esperaba, Mexicanísimo, Motivos Del Alma, Ni En Defensa Propia, Línea Mexicanísimo, Camino Inseguro, Aunque Me Duela El Alma, El Charro Mexicano, Estatua De Márfil, Entre El Amor Y Yo, De Que Manera Te Olvido, Joyas Rancheras, Mujeres Divinas, A Tu Salud, Lobo Herido, El Mayor De Los Potrillos 2001, La Peor De Mis Locuras 2003, En Vivo Juntos Por Unltima Vez (with Alejandro Fernández) 2003, Se Mi Hizo Tarde La Vida 2003, Mis Duetos 2005, Sus Corridos Consentidos 2005, La Tragedia del Vaquero 2006, Para Siempre (Latin Grammy Award for Best Ranchero Album 2008) 2007, Primera Fila (Latin Grammy Award for Best Ranchero Album 2009) 2008, Neccessito de Tí (Grammy Award for Best Regional Mexican Album 2010, Latin Grammy Award for Best Ranchero Album 2010) 2009, Un Mexicano en la México 2010, El Hombre Que Más Te Amó 2010, Otra Vez 2011, Los 2 Vicentes 2012, Hoy 2013, Mano A Mano – Tangos A La Manera De Vicente Fernández (Grammy Award for Best Regional Mexican Music Album including Tejano 2015) 2014. *Honours:* Latin Grammy for Best Ranchero Album 2002, Billboard Latin Music Award for Best Latin Tour 2005, Lo Nuestro Award for Regional Mexican Male Artist 2008, Lifetime Achievement Award 2008, Ranchera Performance (2010, 2013). *Address:* c/o Sony BMG Music Entertainment, 550 Madison Avenue, New York, 10022-3211, USA.

FERNANDEZ-VERSINI, Cheryl; British singer; b. (Cheryl Ann Tweedy), 30 June 1983, Newcastle upon Tyne, England; m. 1st Ashley Cole 2006 (divorced 2010); m. 2nd Jean-Bernard Fernandez-Versini 2014. *Career:* mem. Girls Aloud, pop group created from winning contestants on reality tv show Popstars: The Rivals 2002–13; found guilty of assault but cleared of racially aggravated assault, fined and sentenced to community service 2003; judge, The X Factor, ITV 2008–10, 2014–; judge, The X Factor USA 2011; picture has appeared on covers of British Vogue, Elle and Harper's Bazaar magazines 2009; became the new face of cosmetic co. L'Oréal 2009; est. The Cheryl Cole Foundation (charity) 2011. *Achievement:* climbed Mount Kilimanjaro in Tanzania with Kimberley Walsh and other celebrities in aid of Comic Relief 2009. *Compositions:* co-writer of songs including Big Brother, History, Crazy Fool. *Recordings:* albums: with Girls Aloud: Sound of the Underground 2003, What Will the Neighbours Say? 2004, Chemistry 2005, Tangled Up 2007, Out of Control 2008; solo: Three Words 2009, Messy Little Raindrops 2010, A Million Lights 2012, Only Human 2014. *Television:* Girls Aloud: Off the Record 2006. *Films include:* St Trinian's 2007. *Publications:* contributed to book Dreams that Glitter – Our Story (autobiog. with her Girls Aloud bandmates) 2008, Through My Eyes 2010, Cheryl: My Story (autobiog.) 2012. *Honours:* Best Single, Disney Channel Awards 2003, Popjustice Music Prize 2003, 2005, 2006, BRIT Awards for Best British Single (for The Promise) 2009, named #1 Sexiest Woman in the World, FHM 100 Sexiest Women in the World 2009, 2010, Best Dressed, Glamour Women of the Year Awards 2009, 2010, BT Digital Music Awards for Best Female Artist 2010, for Best Single (for Fight for This Love) 2010, Musician Of The Year, Elle Style Awards 2011. *Current Management:* c/o Modest Management, Matrix Complex, 91 Peterborough Road, London, SW6 3BU, England. *Telephone:* (20) 7384-6410. *E-mail:* info@modestmanagement.com. *Website:* www.modestmanagement.com; www.girlsaloud.co.uk; www.cherylofficial.com.

FERREIRA, Zacarías; Dominican Republic singer. b. Cibao, Canca Arriba. *Recordings include:* albums: Nova Mía, Me Libere 1997, Adiós 2001, El Triste 2004, El Amor Vencera 2004, 12 Exitos 2006, La Historia de Voz de la Ternura 2006, Dime Que Faltó 2007, Historia de Un Ídolo 2008, Te Dejo Libre 2009, Lo Mejor de lo Mejor: Solamente Éxitos. . .2010, Tú y Nadie Más 2011.

FERRERA, Stephen, BMus, MM; American producer, songwriter, musician and record executive; *Executive Vice-President of A&R, Columbia Records;* b. 26 Dec. 1959, Boston, Massachusetts. *Education:* New England Conservatory of Music, Juilliard School of Music. *Career:* as producer, songwriter, arranger, musical director, musician, worked with: Bob Dylan, Billy Joel, Chaka Khan, Eurythmics, Suzanne Vega, Julian Cope, Shakespears Sister, Holly Cole, Shawn Colvin, Tom Jones, Mica Paris, Womack and Womack, Dave Stewart; fmr Head of A&R and producer, The Echo Label; fmr Head of A&R and staff producer, Jazz and Classics, Capitol Records; Sr Vice-Pres. of A&R and Staff Producer, RCA Music Group 2000–08; Exec. Vice-Pres. of A&R, Island and Mercury Records 2008–11; Exec. Vice-Pres. Columbia Records 2011–; mem. Musicians' Union, NARAS, ASCAP. *Address:* Columbia Records, 550 Madison Avenue, 24th Floor, New York, NY 10022, USA (office). *Website:* www.columbiarecords.com (office).

FERRO, Andrea; Italian singer. *Career:* mem. metal band, Lacuna Coil 1994–. *Recordings include:* albums: In a Reverie 1999, Unleashed Memories 2001, Comalies 2002, Karmacode 2006, Shallow Life 2009, Dark Adrenaline 2012. *Honours:* Female Metal Voices Fest Award for Best Album (Dark Adrenaline) 2012. *Current Management:* Riot Rock Management, 639 Dupont Street, Unit 216, Toronto, ON M6G 1Z4, Canada. *E-mail:* info@riotrock.com. *Website:* www.riotrock.com; www.lacunacoil.it.

FERRO, Tiziano; Italian singer, songwriter and producer; b. 21 Feb. 1980, Latina. *Career:* solo artist 2001–; moved to UK 2005. *Recordings:* albums: Rosso Relativo 2001, 111 Centoundici 2003, Nessuno è Solo 2006, Alla Mia Età (Wind Music Award 2009) 2008. *Honours:* MTV Europe Music Award for Best Italian Act 2004. *Address:* c/o EMI Italia S.R.L., Via Turati n° 5, Bresso, 20091 Milan, Italy (office). *E-mail:* infotf@tizianoferro.com (home). *Website:* www.emiitalia.it (office); www.tizianoferro.com.

FERRONE, Stephen; British musician (drums); b. 25 April 1950, Brighton, West Sussex; one s., one d. *Education:* Nice Conservatory of Music, France. *Career:* played with: Brian Auger, Average White Band, Eric Clapton, Duran Duran, Tom Petty and The Heartbreakers, Chaka Khan, Jeffery Osborne, George Benson, Anita Baker, Chris Botti, David Bowie, Sophie B Hawkins, Al Jarreau, Scritti Politti, Steve Winwood, Paul Young, Tribute To Buddy Rich; mem., ASCAP. *Recordings include:* with Average White Band: Cut The Cake, Soul Searching, Person To Person; others: Journeyman-Unplugged (with Eric Clapton), I Feel For You (with Chaka Khan), Secret Story, Pat Metheny, Wildflowers (with Tom Petty), The Live Anthology 2009 Stay With Me Tonight (with Jeffery Osborne), , I'm Your Baby Tonight (with Whitney Houston), The Black and White Years 2008; black n white album (with John Jones) 2009, Slash; Dove Comincia il Sole (with Pooh) 2010, I Feel Like Playing (with Ronnie Wood) 2010. *E-mail:* info@drumrollmediamusic.com. *Website:* drumrollmediamusic.com.

FERRY, Bryan, CBE; British singer and songwriter; b. 26 Sept. 1945, Washington, Co. Durham, England; s. of the late Frederick Charles Ferry and Mary Ann Ferry (née Armstrong); m. 1st Lucy Margaret Mary Helmore 1982 (divorced 2003); three s. one d.; m. 2nd Amanda Sheppard 2012. *Education:* Newcastle Univ. *Career:* formed Roxy Music 1971; official debut, Lincoln Festival 1972; first US concerts 1972; first British and European tours 1973.

Recordings include: albums: with Roxy Music: Roxy Music 1972, For Your Pleasure 1973 (Grand Prix du Disque, Golden Rose Festival, Montreux 1973), Stranded 1973, Country Life 1974, Siren 1975, Viva Roxy Music 1976, Manifesto 1979, Flesh & Blood 1980, Avalon 1982, The Atlantic Years 1983, Street Life – 20 Great Hits 1986; solo: These Foolish Things 1973, Another Time Another Place 1974, Let's Stick Together 1976, In Your Mind 1977, The Bride Stripped Bare 1978, Boys And Girls 1985, Bete Noire 1987, The Ultimate Collection 1988, Taxi 1993, Mamouna 1995, Bryan Ferry and Roxy Music Video Collection 1996, Frantic 2002, Dylanesque 2007, Olympia 2010, Avonmore 2014. *Honours:* Ivor Novello Award for Outstanding Contrib. to British Music 2003, BMI Icon Award 2008. *Current Management:* c/o Alistair Norbury, Studio One, Avonmore Place, London, W14 8RY, England. *E-mail:* info@denejesmond.co.uk. *E-mail:* info@bryanferry.com (office). *Website:* www.bryanferry.com.

FERSEN, Thomas; French singer and musician (guitar); b. (François Louis Gontard), 4 Jan. 1963, Paris. *Career:* fmr mem. of several bands, including UU, Figure of Fun; solo artist 1993–. *Recordings include:* albums: Le Bal Des Oiseaux 1993, Les Ronds De Carotte 1995, Le Jour Du Poisson 1997, Quatre 1999, Triplex 2001, Pièce Montée Des Grands Jours 2003, Le Pavillon des Fous 2005, Trois Petits Tours 2008, Je suis au paradis 2011. *Honours:* Victoires de la Musique Award for Best Newcomer of the Year, Radio France Prix Talent 1994. *Current Management:* c/o Tôt ou Tard, 113 rue St-Maur, 75011 Paris, France. *Telephone:* 1-55-28-85-85. *Fax:* 1-55-28-34-35. *E-mail:* info@totoutard.net. *Website:* www.totoutard.com.

FETTY WAP; American rapper, singer and songwriter; b. (Willie Maxwell II), 7 June 1991, Paterson, New Jersey. *Career:* released debut single Trap Queen 2014. *Recordings:* mixtapes: Fetty Wap: The Mixtape 2015; albums: Fetty Wap 2015. *Honours:* MC100 Award for Most-Played Video of the Year (for Trap Queen) 2015, MTV Video Music Award for Artist to Watch 2015, BET Hip Hop Who Blew Up Award 2015. *Address:* RGF Productions, 300 Entertainment, Atlantic Records, Warner Music Group, Paramount Plaza, 1633 Broadway, New York, NY 10019, USA (office). *E-mail:* info@threehundred.biz (office). *Website:* 300ent.com (office); www.wmg.com (office); www.fettywap.com.

FEW, Robert (Bobby); American musician (piano) and composer; b. 21 Oct. 1935, Cleveland, OH; m. 1972; one s. two d. *Education:* Cleveland Inst. of Music. *Career:* played vibraphone with Bob Cunningham; played with Hyawatha Edmonson, Dick Shelton; mem., Bill Dixon's Free Jazz Workshop 1958; worked with Frank Wright, Booker Ervin; formed own trio; pianist, Musical Dir, three major tours with Brook Benton; accompanist, Frank Foster; Roland Kirk; formed group Center of the World; collaboration with Alan Silva's Celestial Communication Orchestra; mem., Steve Lacy's Sextet, tours USA 1980–; several solo piano tv appearances, Paris; live concerts, television and radio, France, Japan, Italy, Spain, Morocco; mem. SACEM. *Recordings include:* albums: solo: Few Coming Thru, More Or Less Few, Continental Jazz Express, Mysteries; with own trio: Bobby Few Trio; with Steve Lacy: The Owl, The Flame, Dreams, Prospectus, Songs, Ballets, Momentum, Brion Gysin Songs, Condor, Live At The Sweet Basil In New York; with Center of the World: Center of the World, Last Polka in Nancy, Solo and Duets, Uhuru Na Umoja (with Art Taylor); with Albert Ayler: Reevaluations, Music is the Healing Force, Last Album; with Archie Shepp: Coral Rock, Peachin' Can, The In-Between (Booker Erwin), Traffic (Noah Howard), Egyptian Oasis (Talib Kibwe), Indians (Sunny Murray), El Saxofon (Hans Dulfer), What Else is New (Mike Ellis), Secrets from the Sun (Joe Lee Wilson), Diom Futa (Jo Maka), Flowers Around Cleveland (David Murray) 1995. *Address:* 42 rue Deguingand, 92300 Levallois, France (home). *E-mail:* ahbobmusic@hotmail.com (home). *Website:* www.bobbyfew.com (home).

FIASCO, Lupe; American rap artist, songwriter and producer; b. (Wasalu Muhammad Jaco), 16 Feb. 1982, Chicago, Ill. *Career:* fmr mem. Da Pak; Co-founder and Vice-Pres. 1st & 15th Entertainment 2004, CEO 2006–; solo artist (with band 1500 or Nothin') 2004–; Founder mem. Child Rebel Soldier 2007–. *Recordings include:* albums: Food & Liquor 2006, The Cool 2007, Lasers 2011, Food & Liquor II 2012. *Honours:* AOL Music Award 2006, Grammy Award for Best Urban/Alternative Performance (for Daydreamin' with Jill Scott) 2008. *Address:* c/o Atlantic Records, 1290 Avenue of the Americas, New York, NY 10019, USA (office). *E-mail:* 1stand15th@gmail.com. *Website:* www.lupefiasco.com.

FIDRI, Ladislav; Croatian musician (trumpet), arranger and conductor; b. 30 May 1940, Osijek; m. Mia Fidri 1961, one s. *Education:* Teachers' Coll. of Music. *Career:* soloist, Radio-Television Big Band, Zagreb, Croatia; mem. HRT Big Band, now mem. Zagreb Jazz Art Quartet; mem. Gerry Mulligan's Int. Big Band, Europe; also played with Clark Terry Big Band; several times mem. EBU Big Bands in Europe; played, recorded with: Lucky Thompson; Stan Getz; Johnny Griffin; Sou Nistico; Leo Wright; Art Farmer; Albert Mangelsdorf; Kai Winding; Buddy DeFranco; Maynard Ferguson; mem. Croatian Musicians' Union. *Publications include:* Jazz Greetings from the East, Blue Sunset, Nuages. *Address:* Vitasovićeva Square 6, 10000 Zagreb, Croatia.

50 CENT; American rapper, actor and entrepreneur; b. (Curtis Jackson), 6 July 1976, Queens, NY. *Career:* signed to JMJ recording label 1996, to Columbia 1998; survived attempts on his life in 1999 and 2000; already recorded album (Power Of The Dollar) remained unreleased when Columbia terminated contract; f. G Unit collective; signed to labels owned by Eminem and Dr Dre. *Films include:* Get Rich or Die Tryin' 2005, Home of the Brave

2006, The Ski Mask Way 2008, Righteous Kill 2008. *Recordings include:* albums: Get Rich or Die Tryin' (Source Hip-Hop Music Award for Album of the Year, MOBO Award for Hip-Hop Album of the Year, American Music Award) 2003, The Massacre (American Music Award for Favorite Rap/Hip-Hop Album, Billboard Music Award for Album of the Year) 2005, Get Rich or Die Trying 2005, Curtis 2007, Before I Self Destruct 2009, Animal Ambition 2014, Street King Immortal 2014. *Publication:* From Pieces to Weight: Once Upon a Time in Southside Queens (autobiog., with Kris X) 2005, The 50th Law 2009. *Honours:* Billboard Music Awards for Top Rapper, Top Artist 2003, MOBO Awards for Best Hip-Hop Act 2003, for Single of the Year (for In Da Club) 2003, American Music Award for Favourite Hip-hop Artist 2003, Source Hip-Hop Music Award for Single of the Year by a Male Artist (for In Da Club) 2003, BRIT Award for Best Int. Breakthrough Artist 2004, Billboard Music Awards for Artist of the Year, for Hot 100 Artist of the Year, for R&B/Hip-Hop Artist of the Year, for Rap Artist of the Year 2005, ASCAP Songwriter of the Year 2006, Grammy Award for Best Rap Performance by a Duo or Group (for Crack a Bottle with Eminem and Dr Dre) 2010. *Current Management:* c/o Chris Lighty, Violator Management, 36 W. 25th Street, 11th Floor, New York, NY 10010, USA. *Website:* www.violator.com; www.50cent.com.

FIGES, Kevin John; British jazz, classical musician (saxophone, flute) and composer; b. 29 Aug. 1964, Portsmouth. *Education:* Hons Degree, Masters Degree, Electrical and Electronic Engineering; Diploma, Classical Saxophone (Guildhall School Music). *Career:* performed in own jazz quartet in all major venues across UK; appeared on Radio 2 Jazz Parade and on Radio 4; writes own material for quartet; performed with contemporary jazz orchestra Ultrasound; formed 4 Sided Triangle band 2012–; mem. Musicians' Union. *Compositions include:* Bacon Madras, 1997, HP Source 1997. *Recordings include:* Dishy 1997, Critical Moment 1999, Circular Motion 2008, Hometime 2011, 4 Sided Triangle 2012. *Honours:* South West Touring Awards 1994, Jazz Services Touring Award 1997. *E-mail:* kevinfiges@blueyonder.co.uk. *Website:* www.kevinfiges.co.uk.

FILAN, Shane Steven; Irish singer; b. 5 July 1979, Sligo; m. Gillian Walsh 2003. *Career:* mem., Westlife 1999–; numerous tours, festivals and television appearances. *Recordings include:* albums: Westlife 1999, Coast to Coast 2000, World of Our Own 2001, Unbreakable – The Greatest Hits 2002, Turnaround 2003, Face To Face 2005, The Love Album 2006, Back Home 2007, Where We Are 2009, Gravity 2010; solo: You and Me 2013. *Honours:* BRIT Awards for Best Pop Act 2001, 2002, Meteor Ireland Music Award for Best Irish Pop Act 2005, 2006, 2007, 2008, 2009, 2010, MTV Battle of the Boybands Ultimate Boyband of All Time 2012. *Current Management:* Louis Walsh Management, 24 Courtney House, Appian Way, Dublin 6, Ireland. *Telephone:* (1) 668 0309. *Fax:* (1) 668 0721. *Website:* www.westlife.com.

FILEK, Michal; Czech musician (jazz double bass), music producer and singer; *Senior Manager, Media Marketing Agency Prague;* b. 22 April 1964, Pardubice; one d. *Education:* Jaroslav Jezek's Conservatory, Prague, summer courses in Frydland, double bass, Music Instruments school in Kraslice, band leader licence from 1984, Kraslice, Warwick Music Equipment courses of music and instruments, State certificate director for state admin. *Career:* double bass player, music instruments designer, jazz singer, teacher of music and composer; Metropolitan Jazz Band bass player; Jordi Torrens band player; band leader, OSA, Intergram; Sr Man. Media Marketing Agency Prague; Dir School of Music. *Recordings include:* Twin Q and Elena 1995, Metropolitan Jazz Band 1996, Everybody's Looking for Wonders, Lenka Filipova 1998, Dum Doobie Doobie Band 2002, Evergreen Swingtet 2003, Patrola 2003, numerous others. *Honours:* Jazz Club Sydney Medal, Warwick Music Instruments Prize for Manager 2006. *Address:* Media Marketing Agency Prague, Nevanova 1054, 16300 Prague 6, Czech Republic (office). *Telephone:* 605-440073 (mobile). *E-mail:* michal.filek@c-mail.cz (office). *Website:* www.mma-prague.com/en/michal-filek-rhythm-n-jazz (office); www .warwick.de (office); www.7-de.cz (office); michal-filek.byl.cz.

FILKINS, Zachary (Zach) Douglas; American guitarist, singer and songwriter; b. 15 Sept. 1978, Colo; m. Lindsay Filkins; one s. *Education:* Colo Springs Christian High School. *Career:* fmr model for Maximum Talent Agency; fmr mem. This Beautiful Mess (with Ryan Tedder); Founder mem. (with Ryan Tedder) Republic 2002–, renamed OneRepublic; support act to many artists including Bon Jovi, P!nk, Maroon 5; collaborated with Timbaland on track Apologize 2008. *Recordings:* albums: with OneRepublic: Dreaming Out Loud 2007, Waking Up 2009, Native 2013; other appearances: Echo, Leona Lewis 2009, Shock Value II, Timbaland 2009. *Honours:* with OneRepublic: Teen Choice Music Award for Rock Track (for Stop and Stare) 2008, MTV Asia Award for Best Hook Up (for Apologize – with Timbaland) 2008, ESKA Music Award (Poland) for Band of the Year (Int.) 2010. *Address:* c/o Patriot Records, Interscope Records, 1755 Broadway, New York, NY 10019, USA (office). *Website:* www.patriotrecords.com (office); www.onerepublic.net.

FILT, Anni Martensen; Danish singer and songwriter; b. 23 Nov. 1955, Thorsted; m. Klaus Filt 1977. *Career:* lead singer, Anni and the Countrysun 1989–92, Savannah Rose Band 1992–; television host 1991–93; mem. Danish Artists' Union. *Recordings include:* Show Me The Way To Nashville 1989, Tall Dark Stranger 1991, Giving It All 1993, Savannah Rose Band 1995, Dream Catcher 1997, Cloud Walker 1999. *E-mail:* filt@post9.tele.dk. *Website:* www .annifilt.dk.

FINCH, Catrin; British harpist and composer; b. 1980, Llanon, Ceredigion, Wales; m. Hywel Wigley 2003. *Education:* Purcell School, Royal Acad. of

Music. *Career:* performed at BBC proms aged 11, while mem. of Nat. Youth Orchestra; Royal Harpist to HRH, the Prince of Wales 2000–04; has performed in concerts with Bryn Terfel and Sinfonia Cymru in Dublin and Birmingham, English Chamber Orchestra, London Acad. Symphony Orchestra, RPO, Acad. of St Martin-in-the-Fields, London Mozart Players, Nat. Polish Radio Symphony Orchestra, BBC Nat. Orchestra of Wales, Manchester Camerata Orchestra, European Union Chamber Orchestra, Peoria Symphony, Canton Symphony, Cedar Rapids Symphony Orchestra, North Carolina Symphony Orchestra, Yakima Symphony Orchestra, Boston Pops, Charlotte Symphony; has given recitals at Wigmore Hall, Carnegie Hall, Young Concert Artists Series, New York and Boston; formed the Catrin Finch Band 2005–, debut performance Koh Samui Festival, Thailand 2005. *Recordings include:* Little Angels, Harp Recital 2000, Carnaval de Venise 2001, From Coast to Coast 2002, Crossing the Stone 2003, The Harpist 2004, Unexpected Songs 2006, String Theory 2008, Bach: Goldberg Variations 2009, Drift Away 2010, Clychau Dibon (with Seckou Keita) 2013, Lullabies 2013, Tides 2015. *Honours:* Hon. Fellowship, Royal Welsh Coll. of Music and Drama 2005, Univ. of Wales 2006; Royal Overseas League Music Competition Marisa Robles Harp Prize, London 1999, first prize Lily Laskine Int. Harp Competition, France 1999, winner Young Concert Artists Int. Auditions 2000, Princeton Univ. Concerts Prize 2000, Echo Klassik Award for Best Crossover Artist in Germany 2004. *Current Management:* c/o Hazard Chase Limited, 25 City Road, Cambridge, CB1 1DP, England. *Telephone:* (1223) 312400. *Fax:* (1223) 460827. *E-mail:* info@hazardchase.co.uk. *Website:* www.hazardchase .co.uk; www.catrinfinch.com.

FINDLAY, Tom; British DJ, producer and musician (electronics); b. 1972, Cambridge. *Career:* with Andy Cato, est. club nights and began collaborating on musical projects 1994–; adopted Groove Armada name 1996–; Co-founder www.TuneTribe.com (music download site). *Recordings include:* albums: Northern Star 1998, Vertigo 1999, Back To Mine (mix album compiled by Groove Armada) 2000, Goodbye Country (Hello Nightclub) 2001, Another Late Night (mix album compiled by Groove Armada) 2003, Lovebox 2003, Soundboy Rock 2007, Black Light 2010. *Address:* ATM Artists, 55 Kentish Town Road, Camden Town, London, NW1 8NX, England. *E-mail:* Amy@atmartists.com. *Website:* www.groovearmada.com.

FINER, Jem, BA; British musician (banjo, saxophone, hurdy gurdy); b. Stoke on Trent; m. Marcia Farquhar 1983; two d. *Education:* Keele Univ. *Career:* mem. Pogues 1981–96, 2004–; composer of experimental electronic music, film music, sound art, industrial country and western 1994–; f. band The Heironymous Monk Octet 1996–; Artist-in-Residence, Dept of Astrophysics, Univ. of Oxford 2003–05; mem. Performing Rights Soc. *Films include:* Straight to Hell 1986, French Connection IV. *Music installation:* Score for a Hole in the Ground (New Music Award to realize project 2005) to go on display 2006. *Recordings include:* albums: with Pogues: Red Roses For Me 1984, Rum Sodomy & The Lash 1985, If I Should Fall From Grace With God 1987, Peace And Love 1989, Hell's Ditch 1990, Waiting For Herb 1993, Pogue Mahone 1996; singles: with Pogues: A Pair Of Brown Eyes 1985, Poguetry In Motion 1986, Sally MacLennane 1985, Dirty Old Town 1985, Haunted 1986, A Fairytale Of New York (with Kirsty MacColl) 1987, The Irish Rover (with the Dubliners) 1987, Fiesta 1988, Yeah Yeah Yeah Yeah Yeah 1988, Misty Morning, Albert Bridge 1989, Summer In Siam 1989, Jack's Heroes 1990, Once Upon A Time 1993, Tuesday Morning 1993, How Come 1995. *Publications include:* three essays on Autodestruction 1998–99, Plot 1999. *Honours:* J. F. Sloane Golden Acad. Award, Long Duration Music 1990–99. *Current Management:* c/o Brontone Ltd, 361–373 City Road, 2nd Floor, London, EC1V 1PQ, England. *Telephone:* (20) 7278-7123. *Fax:* (20) 7837-1415. *E-mail:* enquiries@a-addis.co.uk. *Website:* www.brontone.com; www.pogues.com.

FINGERS, Rollie (see Inspectah Deck)

FINLAY, Neil Murray; New Zealand musician (electric and acoustic guitar, harmonica); b. 25 Dec. 1955, Hamilton; s. of Reg Finlay and Joyce Finlay; m. Crissi; two d. *Education:* studied photography. *Career:* harmonica player with Brownie McGhee, tours throughout NZ; guest appearances at folk festivals throughout NZ; appeared with Champion Jack Dupree, Billy Joe Shaver; session work with Al Hunter, Topp Twins, Patsy Rigger; played support for Buddy Guy, Robert Jr Lockwood, John Hammond Jr, John Cephus, Phill Wiggins, Carey Bell, Steve Young; mem. Devonport Folk Club; currently technician, School of Design, Unitec. *Photography exhibitions:* Sacred Soil (Solilquay Studio, Mt Eden), Solaris (Matakana Pictures). *Recordings:* albums: Jumping The Tracks (solo), Stop and Listen (with Peter Parnham). *Publication:* Sacred Soil – Stories and Images from the New Zealand Land Wars 1998. *Address:* c/o Unitec, Building 003, Room 1006, Carrington Road, Mount Albert, Auckland (office); 271 Henderson Valley Road, Henderson, Auckland, New Zealand (home). *Telephone:* (9) 815-4321 (office). *E-mail:* nfinlay@unitec.ac.nz (office).

FINN, Neil, OBE; New Zealand singer, musician (guitar) and songwriter; b. 27 May 1958, Te Awamutu; brother of Tim Finn. *Career:* mem., Split Enz 1977–85; Founder-mem., Crowded House 1985–96, re-formed 2007–; formed duo, The Finn Brothers 1995–; int. concerts and TV appearances. *Recordings include:* albums: with Split Enz: Frenzy 1978, True Colours 1979, Beginning Of The Enz 1980, Waita 1981, Time And Tide 1982, Conflicting Emotions 1984, See Ya Round 1985, History Never Repeats Itself – The Best Of Split Enz 1993; with Crowded House: Crowded House 1986, Temple of Low Men 1988, Woodface 1991, Together Alone 1993, Seductive and Emotional 1994,

Unplugged in the Byrdhouse 1995, Recurring Dream 1996, Originals 1998, Farewell to the World 2006, Time on Earth 2007, Intriguer 2010; as The Finn Brothers: Finn 1995, Everyone Is Here 2004, Everyone Is Here Special Edition 2005; solo: Try Whistling This 1998, Encore! 1999, One Nil 2001, 7 Worlds Collide 2001, The Sun Came Out 2009, Going Your Way (with Paul Kelly) 2013, Dizzy Heights 2014. *Honours:* Q Awards for Best Live Act (with Crowded House) 1992, Best Songwriter 1993, BRIT Award for Int. Group of the Year (with Crowded House) 1994. *Current Management:* c/o Mike Bradshaw, Meniscus Media, PO Box 136-150, Parnell, Auckland, New Zealand. *E-mail:* info@neilfinn.com. *Website:* neilfinn.com; www .crowdedhouse.com.

FINN, Tim, OBE; New Zealand singer, musician (piano, guitar, drums) and songwriter; b. 25 June 1952, Te Awamutu; brother of Neil Finn. *Education:* Auckland Univ. *Career:* Founder mem. Split Enz 1972–85; solo artist 1983–86, 1992–; mem. Crowded House 1991; mem. ALT (with Andy White and Liam O'Maonlai) 1994; formed duo, The Finn Brothers 1995–; int. concerts and TV appearances. *Recordings include:* albums: with Split Enz: Frenzy 1978, True Colours 1979, Beginning Of The Enz 1980, Waita 1981, Time And Tide 1982, Conflicting Emotions 1984, See Ya Round 1985, History Never Repeats Itself – The Best of Split Enz 1993; solo: Escapade 1983, Big Canoe 1985, Tim Finn 1989, Before and After 1993, Say it is So 2000, Feeding the gods 2001, Imaginary Kingdom 2006, North, South, East, West... Anthology 2009, The View Is Worth The Climb 2011; with Crowded House: Woodface 1991, Farewell to the World 2006; with ALT: Altitude 1994; as The Finn Brothers: Finn 1995, Everyone Is Here 2004. *Current Management:* c/o Stephen Wade, Select Music, PO Box 316, St Peters, NSW 2044, Australia. *Telephone:* (2) 8577-6977. *Fax:* (2) 8577-6999. *Website:* www.selectmusic.com.au. *E-mail:* management@timfinn.com. *Website:* www.timfinn.com.

FIRESTAR, (Angel Simmons), BSc; German/American composer and musician (harp, flute); b. (Frances Louise Wennes), 18 Oct. 1958, Iserlohn, Germany; m. David Andrew Simmons; one s. *Education:* Royal Conservatory of Music. *Career:* 42 years of performance live on TV in Canada; various programmes, CBC composing soundtracks for film and TV; performing live on radio; mem. Pacific Music Industry Asscn, Soc. of Composers, Authors and Music Publrs of Canada, ASCAP. *Recordings include:* albums: Heavenly Angels, Crescent Moon, Angel and the Canadian Celtic Cowboy. *Honours:* EBE Award for Best Musical Score (for StarDreams soundtrack) 2002. *Address:* 15263 Hesperian Blvd, Site #20, San Leandro, CA 94578, USA (office). *Telephone:* (510) 278-7835 (office). *E-mail:* music@angeltheharpist .com. *Website:* www.Angeltheharpist.com; www.myspace.com/angelfirestar.

FIRTH, Steven; British musician (bass); b. 1 Feb. 1968. *Career:* mem., Embrace 1996–; headline tours and TV appearances. *Recordings include:* albums: The Good Will Out 1998, Drawn From Memory 2000, If You've Never Been 2001, Fireworks (Singles 1997–2002) 2002, Out Of Nothing 2004, This New Day 2006.

FISH; British singer and lyricist; b. (Derek William Dick), 25 April 1958, Edinburgh, Dalkeith, Scotland. *Career:* fmr mem. Stone Dome; lead singer, lyricist progressive rock group, Marillion 1981–88; regular tours, festival appearances; solo artist 1988–f. Chocolate Frog Record Co. 2005–. *Recordings include:* albums: with Marillion: Script For A Jester's Tear 1983, Fugazi 1984, Real To Reel 1985, Misplaced Childhood 1985, Brief Encounter 1986, Clutching At Straws 1987, B-Sides Themselves 1988, Anorak In The UK Live 2002; solo: Vigil In A Wilderness Of Mirrors 1990, Internal Exile 1991, Songs From The Mirror 1993, Yin 1995, Yang 1995, Sunsets On Empire 1997, Raingods With Zippos 1999, Fellini Days 2001, Field of Crows 2004, 13th Star 2007. *Address:* Chocolate Frog Record Company Ltd., 6th Floor, New Baltic House, 65 Fenchurch Street, London, EC3M 4BE, England (office). *Website:* www.fishheadsclub.com; fish-thecompany.com.

FISHER, Dan; British musician (guitar); b. 8 Oct. 1979. *Career:* mem., The Cooper Temple Clause late 1998–2007. *Recordings include:* albums: See This Through And Leave 2002, Kick Up The Fire And Let The Flames Break Loose 2003, Make This Your Own 2007.

FISHER, Edward (Eddie) Ray; American musician (drums, percussion) and songwriter; b. 17 Dec. 1973. *Career:* raised in Mission Viejo, Calif.; mem. OneRepublic 2005–; support act to many artists including Bon Jovi, P!nk, Maroon 5; collaborated with Timbaland on track Apologize 2008; drummer with The Violet Burning. *Recordings:* albums: with OneRepublic: Dreaming Out Loud 2007, Waking Up 2009, Native 2013; other appearances: Echo, Leona Lewis 2009, Shock Value II, Timbaland 2009. *Honours:* with OneRepublic: Teen Choice Music Award for Rock Track (for Stop and Stare) 2008, MTV Asia Award for Best Hook Up (for Apologize – with Timbaland) 2008, ESKA Music Award (Poland) for Band of the Year (Int.) 2010. *Address:* c/o Patriot Records, Interscope Records, 1755 Broadway, New York, NY 10019, USA (office). *Website:* www.patriotrecords.com (office); www.onerepublic.net.

FISHER, Morgan; British musician (keyboards) and photographer; b. 1 Jan. 1950, London; m. Aki Kuniyasu 1987. *Education:* Hendon County Grammar School. *Career:* mem. rock/soul band, Love Affair 1968–70; leader progressive rock band, Morgan 1971–72; mem. rock band, Mott The Hoople 1973–76; solo artist 1977–; producer 1977–; Founder, experimental music label Pipe Records 1977–81; keyboard player rock band, Queen 1982; mem. Phonographic Performance Ltd, Performing Rights Soc., Nat. Acad. of Recording Arts and Sciences, Performing Artists Media Rights Asscn. *Exhibitions include:* NTT

Gallery, Tokyo 1990, Superdeluxe Gallery, Tokyo 2007. *Compositions include:* electronic music for Inst. of Contemporary Art, London 1971; numerous film and television soundtracks. *Recordings include:* albums: Miniatures 1980, Ivories 1985, Echoes of Lennon 1990, Inside Satie 1997, Peace In The Heart Of The City 1999, Water Music 2000, Claws 2001, Hybrid Kids 2003, Neverless 2005, Look at Life 2006, Seasons 2006. *Publication:* Far East Tour Diary 1995. *Address:* 2-9-7 Narita-Higashi, Suginami-ku, Tokyo 166-0015, Japan (home). *E-mail:* morgan@gol.com (home). *Website:* www.morgan-fisher.com.

FISHKIN, Paul E.; American record company executive; b. 29 April 1943, Philadelphia, Pennsylvania; m. Janis Beckerman 1982, one s. one d. *Education:* BSc Pharmacy (Phila College, Pharmacy and Science). *Career:* co-owner, Bearsville Records, with Albert Grossman 1971–79; established careers of Todd Rundgren; Foghat; Paul Butterfield; Jesse Winchester; founder, Modern Records with Danny Goldberg 1979; signed and established solo careers of Stevie Nicks and Natalie Cole; mem, RIAA. *Address:* 8295 Sunset Blvd, Los Angeles, CA 90046, USA.

FITZGERALD, DanDan; Irish recording engineer, producer, live engineer and mastering engineer; b. 14 Dec. 1955, Cork. *Education:* Electronic Technical Inst. of Acoustics (Diploma). *Career:* Assoc. mem. Inst. of Acoustics; mem. Audio Engineering Soc. *Recordings include:* No Frontiers by Mary Black, A Different Shore by Nightnoise, Horse with a Heart by Altan, Celts Rise Again 1990, Good People All 1993, Best of Altan 1997, Winter's Tale 1998. *E-mail:* soundsound@eircom.net (home). *Website:* www.irishacoustics.com; www.soundsound.ie.

FITZGIBBON, Martin William, (Fitz); British musician (drums) and singer; b. 11 May 1950, West Drayton, Middx, England; m. Frances Trussell 1981. *Education:* Nat. Youth Jazz Asscn, private tuition and self taught. *Career:* appearances include original production, The Rocky Horror Show, London 1973; BBC radio and TV; concerts, tours, throughout UK, Europe and USA; currently playing with The Jigantics, ColvinQuarmby, Sons of The Delta Blues Band, FolkLaw and The NY Band; mem. Musicians' Union. *Recordings:* The Rocky Horror Show, original London cast; five albums with ColvinQuarmby including CQV 2012; other albums include: The Jigantics, Sons Of The Delta. *Current Management:* c/o BWM Promo. *Telephone:* 7535-621615 (mobile). *Address:* c/o Nibley House, Blakeney, Glos., GL15 4AR, England.

FIX, Michael Josef; Australian musician (guitar), composer, performer, record producer and musical director; b. 23 Sept. 1959, Wollongong, NSW; s. of Hans Fix and Ann Fix; m. Susan Jarvis; four s. *Education:* diploma of teaching. *Career:* guitarist, East 1977–81, with Reg Lindsay 1982–83, with Bushwackers 1984; guitarist and bass guitarist, Sydney band Hat Trick 1984–90; lead guitarist, Graeme Connors' Prodigal Sons Band 1991–95; career as solo performer 1994–; tours throughout Europe, SE Asia, Japan 2004–; composer of music for TV and radio; mem. APRA, AMCOS. *Recordings:* albums: Tantalise 1992, Fingerpaintings 1993, The Heart Has Reasons 1996, Transfixed 2000, Sunday Morning 2001, Web of Dreams 2003, Something's Cooking 2005, Rewind 2007, ClassicFix 2009; singles: Bush Bash 1994, Breakup Breakdown 1997, Promise 1998, Walkin' the Walk 1999, Reach Out (with Rose Carleo) 2008, Play like Michael Fix 2010. *Plays:* as musical dir: Nadia's Wish (children's musical) 2010. *Publication:* Noted! (songbook). *Honours:* winner, Instrumental of the Year Category (Golden Guitar) 1999, 2000, 2003, CMAA Awards, Instrumental of the Year Finalist 1994–2000, QRA award (Best Instrumental Album) 2001, TIARA award 2002, Victorian CM award 2003, 2008, Queensland CM award 2010. *E-mail:* Arvid.Enge@t -online.de (office). *Address:* c/o Fret Music, PO Box 1194, Sunnybank Hills, Qld 4109, Australia. *E-mail:* info@michaelfix.com. *Website:* www.michaelfix .com.

FIXX-IT; rap artist, dancer and composer; b. (Guam Elmzoom), 1 July 1970, Paramaribo, Suriname; one s. *Education:* private dance training. *Career:* Founder, Twenty 4 Seven 1988; three European major hits; solo career 1990–; male rapper, Cappella 1994–95, mem. Anti-Cappella –1998; mem. FNV Kunstenbond. *Recordings include:* with Twenty 4 Seven: I Can't Stand It 1990; with Anti-Cappella: Move Your Body.

FKA twigs; British singer, songwriter, musician (keyboards, drums) and record producer; b. (Tahliah Debrett Barnett), 16 Jan. 1988, Glos., England. *Education:* St Edward's School, Cheltenham. *Career:* fmr backup dancer in music videos for artists including Ed Sheeran, Jessie J, Plan B, Kylie Minogue; released solo debut EP 2012; first int. tour 2014. *Recordings:* album: LP1 2014. *Honours:* UK Music Video Awards for Best Video Artist and Best Alternative Video (for Papi Pacify) 2014, MOBO Award for Best Video (for Pendulum) 2015, South Bank Sky Arts Award for Best Pop Artist 2015, AIM Ind. Music Award for Ind. Track of the Year (for Two Weeks) 2015. *E-mail:* info@mc1r.co. *Address:* c/o Young Turks Records, Beggars Group UK, 17–19 Alma Road, London, SW18 1AA, England (office). *Website:* fkatwi.gs (home).

FLACK, Roberta, BA; American singer; b. 10 Feb. 1937, Black Mountain, North Carolina; m. Stephen Novosel 1966 (divorced 1972). *Career:* teacher, music and English literature 1959–67; solo artist 1968–; numerous live appearances. *Compositions:* (with Jesse Jackson, Joel Dorn) Go Up Moses; television theme song Valerie. *Recordings include:* albums: First Take 1970, Chapter Two 1970, Quiet Fire 1972, Killing Me Softly 1973, Feel Like Makin' Love 1974, Blue Lights In The Basement 1978, Roberta Flack 1978, Roberta Flack Featuring Donny Hathaway 1980, Live and More 1981, The Best of

Roberta Flack 1981, I'm The One 1982, Born To Love 1983, Hits and History 1984, Roberta Flack's Greatest Hits 1984, Roberta Flack 1985, Oasis 1989, Roberta 1995, Christmas Album 1997, Holiday 2003. *Honours:* Grammy Award for Best Record 1972, 1973, for Best Pop Vocal Duo 1972, for Best Female Pop Vocal 1973;Roberta Flack Human Kindness Day, Washington, DC 1972. *Website:* www.robertaflack.com.

FLAHERTY, Nicholas Simon; British singer and songwriter; b. 18 Feb. 1967, Brewood, Staffordshire, England. *Education:* Shifnal School, Shropshire. *Career:* singer, Voodoo Sioux 1991–; solo artist 1998–; various tours, radio and television broadcasts; 20th anniversary tour with Voodoo Sioux 2011; mem. Musicians' Union, PRS, MCPS. *Recordings include:* albums: Skrape (with Voodoo Sioux) 1995, Indian Summer 2003. *Publication:* Indian Summer – Lyrics and Poetry 2003, Short Story Book of Horror 2011, Last Exit (novel). *Address:* 10 Victoria Court, Victoria Rd, Shifnal, Shropshire, TF11 8AF, England (home). *Telephone:* (7968) 682503 (home). *E-mail:* nicktheflaherty@hotmail.com (home).

FLANAGAN, Kevin Edward, MA; American musician (saxophones, flute, clarinet) and composer; b. 25 Feb. 1954, Lowell, Massachusetts. *Education:* Goldsmiths, London and Anglia Polytechnic Univ., Cambridge, England. *Career:* worked as jazz musician around New England, USA, before moving to UK in mid-1980s; played London jazz scene and did session work in late 1980s–early 1990s; teacher of saxophone and lecturer in jazz, Anglia Polytechnic Univ., Cambridge; formed Flanagan-Ingham Quartet (with vocalist and pianist Chris Ingham, double bassist Andy Brown and drummer Russ Morgan), recording and playing live; mem. Riprap Quartet. *Recordings include:* with Flanagan/Ingham Quartet: Zanzibar 1995, Textile Lunch 1999. *E-mail:* kflanagan@btinternet.com; riprap@kevinflanagan.net. *Website:* www .flanaganingham.f9.co.uk.

FLANZER, Richard; American manager, television producer and concert promoter; b. Feb. 1951, New York; m. Janice Rothman 1990; two s. one d. *Education:* Boston Univ. *Career:* clients have included Roger Daltrey, Manhattan Transfer, Jackson Browne, Dr John; numerous productions, including Florida Sunfest 1977, Roger Daltrey and Friends, Carnegie Hall, New York 1994, A Day In The Country, Rose Bowl, Pasadena, Calif. and numerous live/broadcast events for Walt Disney Co.; Man. Partner, Electric Lady Studios 1989–94; Pres. Safe Concerts, New York 2006–; consultant to Jimi Hendrix Estate; fmr Chair., Nat. Music Critics Asscn; mem. ASCAP.

FLASKETT, Peter; British guitar teacher and musician (guitar, bass guitar); *Guitarist, The Gumbo Flyers;* b. 9 July 1950, Woking, Surrey, England; m. Patsy Poley 1983. *Education:* London Coll. of Furniture and Music 1968–70. *Career:* worked with Long John Baldry, Screaming Lord Sutch, Tex Withers, Savoy Brown, Jim McCarty (of the Yardbirds); recorded and toured extensively with Emile Ford and The Checkmates, The Ramrods, The Flying Tigers; 30 years teaching guitar; 20 years repairing guitars; guitarist, The Gumbo Flyers 2011–; mem. Inst. of Musical Instrument Technology; Musicians' Union. *Recordings:* numerous recordings with Emile Ford; extensive session work on guitar and bass guitar. *Address:* 23 Bridge, St Columb Major, Cornwall, England (home). *Telephone:* (1637) 880646 (home).

FLAVELL, Roger Barry; British musician (bass guitar) and singer; b. 10 Feb. 1946, Ruislip; m. Annie Conlon 1971; two d. *Career:* Magic Roundabout 1966–68; Sessions 1969; Geno Washington's Ram Jam Band 1970; Tommy Hunt Ban, 1971–72; Christie 1973–74; Tommy Hunt Band 1975; Lonnie Donegan Band, Johnny Wakelin and Kinshasha Band 1976; Sessions 1977–78; band leader, top cabaret venue 1978–88; Byron Band (ex Uriah Heep) 1982; Sessions 1989–95; mem. Performing Rights Soc., British Acad. of Songwriters, Composers and Authors. *Compositions include:* music for television: The Animates, co-written with Vic Elmes; 2 songs for From Out of The East album 1999. *Recordings include:* Albums: Judd (with Kris Ife), Live At Wigan Casino, A Sign of The Times (with Tommy Hunt), On The Rocks (with Byron Band), Only One (with Joe Longthorne), Hold Fast (with Roger Flavell), Soul Reddy and Otis Remembered, Otis Redding Tribute Show (with Christie) 2003–04.

FLAVOR FLAV; American rap artist; b. (William Drayton), 16 March 1959, Roosevelt, Long Island; seven c. *Career:* mem. rap group, Public Enemy 1984–; MC, The Entourage (hip hop venue), Long Island, New York 1986; solo artist 1993–; numerous collaborations and guest appearances on recordings by Anthrax, De La Soul, George Clinton, Heavy D, Ice Cube, Madonna, Paris, Snoop Dogg. *Recordings include:* albums: with Public Enemy: Yo! Bum Rush The Show 1987, It Takes A Nation of Millions To Hold Us Back 1988, Fear of a Black Planet 1990, Apocalypse 91... The Enemy Strikes Black (Soul Train Music Award for Best Rap Album 1992) 1991, Greatest Misses 1992, Muse Sick-n-Hour Mess Age 1994, He Got Game (film soundtrack) 1998, There's a Poison Goin' On... 1999, Revolverlution 2002, Rebirth of a Nation 2005, New Whirl Odor 2005, How you Sell Soul to a Soulless People who Sold their Soul ??? 2007, The Evil Empire of Everything 2012, Man Plans God Laughs 2015; solo: Flavor Flav 1993, Hollywood 2006. *Honours:* MOBO Award for Outstanding Contribution to Black Music 2005. *E-mail:* Mistachuck@ rapstation.com (office). *Website:* www.publicenemy.com.

FLEA; American (b. Australian) musician (bass guitar); b. (Michael Balzary), 16 Oct. 1962, Melbourne, Australia. *Career:* first trumpet, Los Angeles Jr Philharmonic; Founding mem., Anthem, later renamed Red Hot Chili Peppers 1983–; trumpet player, Trulio Disgracias 1988; Founder, punk band Hate,

playing Hollywood clubs 1988; mem., Atoms for Peace 2009–; numerous tours, festivals and television appearances. *Film appearances include:* The Decline of Western Civilization 1991, Suburbia 1991, Motorama 1992. *Recordings include:* albums: The Red Hot Chili Peppers 1984, Freaky Styley 1985, The Uplift Mofo Party Plan 1987, Mother's Milk 1989, Blood Sugar Sex Magik 1991, One Hot Minute 1995, Californication 1999, By The Way 2002, Live In Hyde Park 2004, Stadium Arcadium (MTV Europe Music Award for Best Album) 2006, I'm With You 2011. *Honours:* MTV Music Video Award 1992, Rolling Stone Readers' Poll Winner for Best Bassist 1993, American Music Award for Favorite Alternative Artist 2000, MTV Awards for Best Live Act, Best Rock 2002, American Music Award for Favorite Pop/Rock Band 2006, for Favorite Alternative Music Artist 2006, Grammy Award for Best Rock Performance by a Duo or Group with Vocal (for Dani California) 2007. *Current Management:* c/o Goetz, Lindy Management Ltd, 12338 Linda Flora Drive, Ojai, CA 93023, USA. *Telephone:* (805) 649-2526. *Website:* www .redhotchilipeppers.com; atomsforpeace.info.

FLECK, Béla; American musician (banjo), singer and composer; b. 10 July 1958, New York, NY. *Education:* New York High School of Music and Art, studied with Tony Trishka, Erik Darling, Mark Horowitz. *Career:* banjo player, composer 1976–; played with Tasty Licks 1976–79, Spectrum 1979–81, New Grass Revival 1982–91; Founder-mem. Béla Fleck and The Flecktones 1989–; concerts, tours and television appearances. *Recordings include:* albums: Crossing the Tracks 1980, Natural Bridge 1982, Deviation 1984, Daybreak 1987, Inroads 1987, Places 1988, Béla Fleck and The Flecktones 1990, Flight of the Cosmic Hippo 1992, UFO TOFU 1993, Tales from the Acoustic Planet 1994, Outbound 2000, Perpetual Motion 2001, Live at the Quick 2002, Little Worlds 2003, Music for Two 2004, The Hidden Land (Grammy Award for Best Contemporary Jazz Album 2007) 2006, The Enchantment (with Chick Corea; Latin Grammy Award for Best Instrumental Album 2007) 2007, Jingle All the Way (Grammy Award for Best Pop Instrumental Album 2009) 2008, Throw Down Your Heart: Tales from the Acoustic Planet Vol. 3, Africa Sessions (Grammy Award for Best Contemporary World Music Album 2010) 2009, Rocket Science 2011, Béla Fleck and Abigail Washburn (Grammy Award for Best Folk Album 2016) 2015. *Honours:* Frets Readers' Poll Winner for Top Banjo Player many times, Grammy Award for Best Pop Instrumental Performance (for Throw Down Your Heart) 2010, Grammy Award for Best Instrumental Composition (with Howard Levy) (for Life In Eleven) 2012. *Current Management:* Ted Kurland Associates, 173 Brighton Avenue, Allston, MA 02134, USA. *Telephone:* (617) 254-0007. *Fax:* (617) 782-3577. *E-mail:* agents@tedkurland.com. *Website:* www.tedkurland .com; www.belafleck.com; www.flecktones.com.

FLEETWOOD, Mick; British musician (drums); b. 24 June 1942, London; m. 1st Jenny Boyd; m. 2nd Sara Recor 1988; two d. *Career:* mem., the Bluesbreakers 1967; Founder-mem., Fleetwood Mac 1967–; numerous tours, concerts and television appearances; solo artist 1978–; Founder-mem. band, Zoo 1992; Owner Fleetwoods club, Los Angeles 1991–; Owner TallMan Records, subsidiary of Sanctuary Records; established the Mick Fleetwood Band 2004–; Founder Island Rumours Band 2007–. *Recordings include:* albums: with Fleetwood Mac: Peter Green's Fleetwood Mac 1968, Mr Wonderful 1968, English Rose 1969, Then Play On 1969, Kiln House 1970, Future Games 1971, Bare Trees 1971, Penguin 1973, Mystery To Me 1973, Heroes Are Hard to Find 1974, Fleetwood Mac 1975, Rumours (Billboard Award for Album of the Year 1977, American Music Award for Favorite Pop/ Rock Album 1978, Grammy Award for Album of the Year 1978) 1977, Tusk 1978, Fleetwood Mac Live 1980, Mirage 1982, Tango In The Night 1987, Behind The Mask 1990, Time 1995, The Dance 1997, Say You Will 2003, Pious Bird Of Good Omen 2004; solo: The Visitor 1981, I'm Not Me 1983; with the Mick Fleetwood Band: Something Big 2004, Blue Again! 2008. *Publication:* My Life and Times in Fleetwood Mac 1990. *Honours:* American Music Award for Favorite Band 1978, BRIT Award for Outstanding Contribution 1998. *Current Management:* c/o Jonathon Todd, Sabre Entertainment, 5737 Kanan Road, Suite 237, Agoura Hills, CA 91301, USA. *Telephone:* (310) 929-0771. *E-mail:* info@SabreEntertainment.net. *Website:* www.mickfleetwoodblues .com; www.mickfleetwood.com.

FLEMING, Kye; American songwriter and publisher; b. 9 Oct. 1951, Pennsacola, FL. *Education:* college. *Career:* pres. of publishing companies, including Dream Catcher Music, Gila Monster Music, Painted Pony Music; mem. NSAI, CMA, BMI; songs recorded by numerous artists including Suzy Bogguss, Joe Cocker, Crystal Gayle, Vince Gill, Amy Grant, Janis Ian, The Judds, Kathy Mattea, Bette Midler, Willie Nelson, Tina Turner. *Compositions:* Co-wrote: Smokey Mountain Rain; Give Me Wings; I Was Country When Country Wasn't Cool; Nobody; Some People's Lives; Years; Sleeping Single In A Double Bed; Roll On Mississippi; Walk The Line, Kennedy-Rose. *Recordings include:* with James Galway, Wayward Wind, 1982; with Marti Jones, Used Guitars, 1988. *Honours:* 43 BMI Awards, three-time BMI Songwriter of the Year, NSAI Songwriter of the Year, CMA Triple Play Award.

FLETCHER, Andrew John; British musician (keyboards); b. 8 July 1961, Nottingham, England; m. Grainne Mullan 1993; one s. one d. *Career:* Founder-mem., Depeche Mode 1980–. *Recordings include:* albums: Speak and Spell 1981, A Broken Frame 1982, Construction Time Again 1983, Some Great Reward 1984, The Singles 81–85 1985, Black Celebration 1986, Music For The Masses 1987, 101 1989, Violator 1990, Songs Of Faith & Devotion 1993, Ultra 1997, The Singles 86–98 1998, Dream On 2001, Exciter 2001,

Playing the Angel 2005, Sounds of the Universe 2009, Delta Machine 2013, Should Be Higher 2013. *Honours:* BRIT Award (for Enjoy the Silence) 1991, MTV Europe Music Award for Best Group 2006. *Current Management:* Sensible Events Ltd, 90–96 Brewery Road, London, N7 9NT, England. *Telephone:* (20) 7700-9900. *Fax:* (20) 7700-4802. *Website:* www.depechemode .com.

FLETCHER, Tim; Canadian singer and musician (guitar); b. 1978. *Career:* mem. and lead singer, The Stills 2000–. *Recordings include:* albums: Logic Will Break Your Heart 2003, Without Feathers 2005, Oceans Will Rise (Juno Award for Best Alternative Album of the Year 2009) 2008. *Honours:* Juno Award for Best New Group of the Year 2009. *Address:* c/o Arts&Crafts, 460 Richmond Street West, Suite 402, Toronto, ON M5V 1Y1, Canada. *Website:* www.arts-crafts.ca/thestills.

FLETCHER, Tom; British musician (guitar) and singer; b. 17 July 1985, Harrow. *Career:* Founder mem., McFly 2004–. *Recordings include:* albums: Room on the Third Floor (Smash Hits Award for Best Album 2005) 2004, Wonderland 2005, Motion in the Ocean 2006, Radio:Active 2008, Above the Noise 2010. *Honours:* BRIT Award for Best Pop Act 2005, Smash Hits Awards for Smash Hits Star of the Year, for Best UK Band, for Best Video (for That Girl) 2005. *Website:* www.mcflyofficial.com.

FLICK, Vic, DipMus, LRAM; British musician (guitar) and composer; b. 14 May 1937, Worcester Park, Surrey, England; m. Judith Mary 1960, one s. one d. *Education:* Royal Acad. of Music. *Career:* mem. PRS, ASCAP. *Film scores:* Beat Girl 1960, The Cool Mikado 1962, Dr No 1962, From Russia with Love 1963, Goldfinger 1964, Thunderball 1965, The Ipcress File 1965, The Quiller Memorandum 1966, You Only Live Twice 1967, Midnight Cowboy 1969, On Her Majesty's Secret Service 1969, Diamonds Are Forever 1971, The Dove 1974, The Return of the Pink Panther 1975, Autobiography of a Princess 1975, Hullabaloo Over Georgie and Bonnie's Pictures 1978, The Europeans 1979, Quartet 1981, License to Kill 1989, The Scroll 1992, Wilson Chance 2005. *Television scores include:* Danger Man, The Avengers, The Prisoner, The Ethnic and Archaeological History of Saudi Arabia, Echoes: The Story of an Island, The Year of Sir Ivor, Kingfisher: Secret Splendor of the Brook, Conquest of Light, Facets of Glass, The Chaser, Saudi Arabia: Myth or Miracle, Happy Christmas, HGTV, The Oprah Winfrey Show, Americas Funniest Videos. *Recordings include:* Poor Me (Adam Faith) 1960, Hit and Miss (John Barry) 1960, Walk Don't Run (John Barry Seven) 1960, As Long As He Needs Me (Shirley Bassey) 1960, Are You Sure (Allisons) 1961, Theme for a Dream (Cliff Richard) 1961, Moon River (Danny Williams) 1961, Well, I Ask You (Eden Kane) 1961, Don't Treat Me Like a Child (Helen Shapiro) 1961, You Don't Know (Helen Shapiro) 1961, Remember Me (John Leyton) 1961, Wild Wind (John Leyton) 1961, Portrait of My Love (Matt Monro) 1961, My Kind of Girl (Matt Monro) 1961, Sailor (Petula Clark) 1961, I Only Want to Be with You (Dusty Springfield) 1963, Confessin' (Frank Ifield) 1963, Just Like Eddie (Heinz) 1963, Dance On (Kathy Kirby) 1963, Trains & Boats & Planes (Burt Bacharach) 1964, Anyone Who Had a Heart (Cilla Black) 1964, The Cryin' Game (Dave Berry) 1964, Have I the Right (Honeycombs) 1964, The Wedding (Julie Rogers) 1964, Shout! (Lulu) 1964, Hold Me (P.J. Proby) 1964, World Without Love (Peter and Gordon) 1964, Downtown (Petula Clark) 1964, Girl Don't Come (Sandie Shaw) 1964, It's Not Unusual (Tom Jones) 1964, What's New Pussycat (Tom Jones) 1965, Make It Easy on Yourself (Walker Brothers) 1965, Alfie (Cilla Black) 1966, Black is Black (Los Bravos) 1966, Green Green Grass of Home (Tom Jones) 1966, Sun Ain't Gonna Shine Anymore (Walker Brothers) 1966, Release Me (Englebert Humperdinck) 1967, The Last Waltz (Englebert Humperdinck) 1967, Puppet on a String (Sandie Shaw) 1967, Joanna (Scott Walker) 1968, Delilah (Tom Jones) 1968, Je t'aime (Jane Birkin) 1969, All Kinds of Everything (Dana) 1970, Alone Again (Gilbert O'Sullivan) 1972. *Website:* www.vicflick.com.

FLINT, Keith; British singer; b. 17 Sept. 1969. *Career:* mem., The Prodigy 1990–; mem., band Flint 2003–. *Recordings include:* albums: with The Prodigy: Experience 1992, Music for the Jilted Generation 1994, The Fat of the Land (MTV Music Award for Best Album) 1997, The Dirtchamber Sessions 1999, Always Outnumbered, Never Outgunned 2004, Their Law: The Singles 1990–2005 2005, Invaders Must Die 2009, The Day is My Enemy 2015; with Flint: Device #1 2003. *Honours:* BRIT Awards for Best British Dance Act 1997, 1998, five MTV Music Awards including for Best Live Band, Best Dance Band, Q Award for Innovation in Sound 2005, Kerrang! Spirit of Independence Award 2006. *Website:* www.theprodigy.com.

FLOOD; British record producer and engineer; b. (Mark Ellis), 16 Aug. 1960, London, England. *Education:* St Olave's Grammar School, Orpington. *Career:* fmr recording engineer, Marcus Studios, Trident Studios 1980s; production and engineering work with Some Bizarre and Mute record labels 1982–87; mem. one-off recording project Node 1995; Co-founder (with Alan Moulder) Assault & Battery studio complex 2008–; production or engineering work with numerous artists including Barry Adamson, a-Ha, Marc Almond, Nick Cave and the Bad Seeds, The Charlatans, Curve, Depeche Mode, Editors, Erasure, Karima Francis, Glasvegas, Goldfrapp, PJ Harvey, The Hours, Tom Jones, The Music, New Order, Nine Inch Nails, Nitzer Ebb, Gary Numan, Nine Inch Nails, Orbital, The Pains of Being Pure at Heart, Placebo, Pop Will Eat Itself, Sigur Rós, Soulwax, Thirty Seconds to Mars, U2, Warpaint; many production collaborations with Alan Moulder including Foals, Tom Jones, The Killers, Smashing Pumpkins. *Films:* State of Play (co-producer of score, with Alex Heffes) 2009. *Honours:* BRIT Award/Music Producers Guild Award for Best

British Producer (with Alan Moulder) 2014. *Address:* Assault & Battery 1, Miloco Studios, 1 Maybury Gardens, London, NW10 2NB, England (office). *Telephone:* (20) 7232-0008 (office). *Website:* www.miloco.co.uk (office).

FLOREK, Jaki; British singer and lyricist; b. Bradford; two s. one d. *Education:* Cardiff Coll. of Art. *Career:* tours with Shattered Dolls and Adam's Family; Ed. Feedback Music magazine; mem. Performing Rights Soc., Musicians' Union. *Recordings include:* album with Adam's Family: Disease 1995. *Publications include:* Adam's Family: The Scouse Phenomenon vol. 1 and 2, contrib. stories in anthologies. *Address:* PO Box 67, Runcorn, Cheshire, WA7 4NL, England.

FLORES, Rosario; Spanish singer and actress; b. 4 Nov. 1963, Madrid; d. of Antonio González and Lola Flores; partner Pedro Lazaga; one s., one d. (from previous relationship). *Career:* solo artist 1984–. *Film and television appearances include:* El taxi de los conflictos 1969, Al fin solos, pero... 1977, Colegas 1982, Moraleja 1984, Proceso a Mariana Pineda (TV series) 1984, Delirios de amor 1986, Calé 1987, Diario de invierno 1988, Entreacte 1989, El mejor de los tiempos 1989, Brigada central 1989, La intrusa 1990, Contra el viento 1990, Danzón 1991, Chatarra 1991, La mujer de tu vida 2: La mujer duende 1992, Hable con ella 2002, Filles perdues, cheveux gras 2002, Soy gitano 2003. *Recordings include:* albums: Vuela una Noche 1984, De Ley 1992, Siento 1994, Mucho por Vivir 1996, Jugar a la Locura 1999, Muchas Flores (Latin Grammy Award for Best Female Pop Album) 2001, De Mil Colores (Latin Grammy Award for Best Female Pop Album) 2003, Contigo Me Voy 2006, Parte de Mí 2008, Cuéntame 2009, Mientras Me Quede Corazon: Grandes Exitos, Grandes Versiones 2010, Raskatriski 2011. *Address:* c/o Universal Music Group Latin Entertainment, 1425 Collins Avenue, Miami Beach, FL 33139, USA. *Telephone:* (305) 604-1300. *Website:* www.rosarioflores.info.

FLOWERS, Brandon Richard; American singer, songwriter and musician (keyboards); b. 21 June 1981, Las Vegas, Nev. *Career:* fmr mem., Blush Response; founder mem., The Killers 2002–; also solo artist 2010–. *Recordings include:* albums: with The Killers: Hot Fuss 2004, Sam's Town (BRIT Award for Best Int. Album 2007) 2006, Sawdust 2007, Day and Age 2008, Battle Born 2012; solo: Flamingo 2010, The Desired Effect 2015. *Honours:* NME Award for Best Int. Band 2005, for Best Video 2007, MTV Video Award for Best New Artist 2005, MTV Europe Music Award for Best Rock Act 2006, BRIT Award for Best Int. Group 2007, ASCAP Vanguard Award 2010. *E-mail:* lauren .schneider@umusic.com. *Website:* www.thekillersmusic.com; www .brandonflowersmusic.com.

FLOWERS, Herbie; British musician (bass guitar, double bass, tuba); b. 19 May 1938, London; m. Ann Flowers 1959; one s. one d. *Education:* RAF School of Music. *Career:* played tuba in RAF 1955–63; played double bass, Fender bass, London theatre, club, studio circuit; joined Blue Mink 1970; worked for David Bowie, tour of USA 1974; mem. T-Rex for two years; played on recordings with Elton John, David Essex, Paul McCartney, Al Kooper, Nilsson, Tom Jones, Tiny Tim, Dusty Springfield, Henry Mancini, George Harrison, Ringo Starr; formed Sky with John Williams; performances with Gary Potter, David Jones, Tina May; lectures, Fun With Music, East Sussex Co. Council. *Recordings include:* albums: with Lou Reed: Transformer 1972; with David Essex: Rock On 1973, Imperial Wizard 1973; with David Bowie: Diamond Dogs, David Live 1974, Another Face 1981, Rare 1982, Changesbowie 1990, BBC Sessions 2000; with Elton John: Tumbleweed Connection 1970, Madman Across the Water 1971, A Single Man 1978, To Be Continued... 1990; with Paul McCartney: Broad Street 1984; with Mike Hatchard: The Business 1998; with Sky: Sky 1979, Box Set 1994, Best of Sky 1995, Squared 1998, Anthology 2004. *Address:* 15 High Street, Ditchling, East Sussex BN6 8SY, England (home).

FLOYD, Eddie; American singer, producer and composer; b. 25 June 1937, Montgomery, Ala; six s. two d. *Education:* Wayne State Univ. School of Music, Detroit. *Career:* Founder mem. The Falcons 1954–62; solo artist 1962–; guest singer, The Original Blues Brothers Band, Booker T and the MG's; Pres. Floyd Entertainment Group Inc.; mem. Broadcast Music Inc. (BMI). *Compositions include:* Songs for Otis Redding, Wilson Pickett, and Sam and Dave, including 634–5789, Ninety-Nine and A Half (Just Won't Do), You Don't Know What You Mean To Me, Knock On Wood. *Recordings include:* albums: with The Falcons: You're So Fine, I Found A Love; solo: Knock On Wood 1967, Looking Back 1968, I've Never Found A Girl 1969, Rare Stamps 1969, You've Got To Have Eddie 1969, California Girl 1970, Down To Earth 1971, Baby Lay Your Head Down 1973, Soul Street 1974, Experience 1978, Flashback 1988, Gotta Make a Comeback 1999, To the Bone 2002, Eddie Loves You So 2008; with the Blues Brothers Band: Live In Montreux, The Red White and Blues, California Girl. *Honours:* Governors Award/Memphis Blues Foundation Inductee, Tennessee, Hon. Lt Col, Alabama, Pres. Bush Performance Award, Alabama Hall of Fame Inductee, NAACP BMI 1 Million Performances Award, Knock On Wood, BMI Award. *Telephone:* (334) 613-6296. *E-mail:* govfloyd@bellsouth .net. *Website:* www.eddiefloyd.com.

FLÜR, Wolfgang; German musician (percussion, electronic percussion); b. 17 July 1947, Düsseldorf. *Career:* mem. Kraftwerk 1973–88; pioneer of electronic percussion (believed to be first performer to use an electronic drum kit in a live performance); Founder mem. Yamo 1992–; collaborated with Mouse on Mars 1995. *Recordings include:* albums: with Kraftwerk: Autobahn 1974, Radio-Activity 1975, Trans-Europe Express 1977, The Man-Machine 1978, Computer World 1981, Electric Café 1986; with Yamo: Time Pie 1997. *Publication:* Kraftwerk: I Was A Robot 1999.

FLYNN, Matt; American musician (guitar); b. 23 May 1970, Woodstock, New York; m.; two c. *Career:* fmrly played with The B-52's and Gavin DeGraw; mem. Maroon 5 2006–. *Recordings include:* albums: with Maroon 5: It Won't Be Soon Before Long (Billboard Music Award for Top Digital Album 2007) 2007, Hands All Over 2010, Overexposed 2012, V 2014. *Honours:* with Maroon 5: Grammy Awards for Best Pop Performance by a Duo or Group with Vocals (for Makes Me Wonder) 2008, American Music Awards for Favorite Pop/Rock Band/Duo/Group 2011, 2012, for Favorite Adult Contemporary Artist 2013, Billboard Music Award for Top Hot 100 Artist 2013, People's Choice Award for Favorite Band 2013. *Address:* c/o Career Artist Management, 1100 Glendon Avenue, Suite 1100, New York, NY 90024, USA. *Telephone:* (310) 776-7640. *Fax:* (310) 776-7659. *Website:* camanagement.com; www.maroon5.com.

FOCONE, Patrice; French musician (guitar); b. 7 Aug. 1971. *Career:* mem. Superbus 1998–. *Recordings include:* albums: Aéromusical 2002, Pop'N'Gum 2004, Wow 2006, Lova Lova 2009, Happy Busday 2010, Sunset 2012. *Honours:* MTV Europe Music Award Best French Act 2005. *Address:* c/o Universal Music France, 16–20 rue des Fossés-Saint-Jacques, 75005 Paris, Cédex 05, France (office). *Website:* www.superbus.com.fr.

FOGARINO, Sam; American musician (drums). *Career:* mem., Interpol 2000–. *Recordings include:* albums: Turn On The Bright Lights 2002, Antics 2004, Our Love to Admire 2007, Interpol 2010. *E-mail:* info@3Dmgmt.com. *E-mail:* info@interpolny.com. *Website:* www.interpolnyc.com.

FOGELKLOU, Carl-Johan; Swedish musician (bass guitar); b. 15 Aug. 1980. *Career:* mem., Mando Diao 1999–. *Recordings include:* albums: Bring 'Em In 2002, Hurricane Bar 2005, Ode to Ochrasy 2006, Never Seen the Light of Day 2007, Give Me Fire 2009, Infruset 2012, Infruset Guld 2013. *Current Management:* Flagstone Management, Götabergsgatan 2, 411 34 Gothenburg, Sweden. *Telephone:* (3) 170-175-20. *Fax:* (3) 170-175-30. *E-mail:* info@flagstone.se. *Website:* www.flagstone.se; www.mandodiao.com.

FOGERTY, John Cameron; American singer, composer, songwriter and musician (guitar); b. 28 May 1945, Berkeley, Calif. *Career:* mem. Blue Velvets, renamed the Golliwogs 1959–67, then renamed Creedence Clearwater Revival 1967–71; solo artist 1972–. *Recordings include:* albums: with Creedence Clearwater Revival: Creedence Clearwater Revival 1968, Bayou Country 1969, Green River 1969, Willie and The Poor Boys 1969, Cosmo's Factory 1970, Pendulum 1970, Mardi Gras 1972, Live In Europe 1973, Live At The Royal Albert Hall 1980; solo: The Blue Ridge Rangers 1973, John Fogerty 1975, Centerfield 1985, Eye of a Zombie 1986, Premonition 1998, Blue Moon Swamp 2004, Deja Vu All Over Again 2004, The Long Road Home 2005, Revival 2007, The Blue Ridge Rangers Rides Again 2009, Wrote a Song For Everyone 2013. *Address:* c/o Verve Music Group Inc., 1755 Broadway, 3rd Floor, New York, NY 10019, USA. *Telephone:* (212) 331-2000. *Fax:* (212) 331-2064. *E-mail:* contact@vervemusicgroup.com. *Website:* www.vervemusicgroup.com; www.johnfogerty.com.

FOGG, Heath Allen; American musician (guitar) and songwriter; b. Ala. *Career:* Founder-mem., The Shakes, renamed Alabama Shakes 2009–; debut EP released 2011; first major tour 2011; numerous live tours and festival appearances; numerous TV appearances. *Recordings:* albums: with Alabama Shakes: Boys & Girls 2012, Sound & Color (Grammy Award for Best Alternative Music Album 2016) 2015. *Honours:* Americana Music Honors and Awards Award for Emerging Artist of the Year 2012, Grammy Awards for Best Rock Performance and Best Rock Song (both for Don't Wanna Fight) 2016. *Current Management:* c/o Kevin Morris and Christine Stauder, Red Light Management, 44 Wall Street, 22nd Floor, New York, NY 10005, USA. *Telephone:* (646) 292-7400. *Fax:* (646) 292-7450. *Website:* www.redlightmanagement.com; www.alabamashakes.com (home).

FOLDS, Ben(jamin Scott); American singer, songwriter and musician (percussion, piano, bass guitar); b. 12 Sept. 1966, Winston-Salem, NC; m. 1st Anna Goodman 1987 (divorced 1992); m. 2nd Kate Rosen 1996 (divorced 1997); m. 3rd Frally Hynes 1999 (divorced 2007); two c.; m. 4th Fleur 2007. *Career:* mem. Ben Folds Five 1993–2000, 2011–; solo artist 1988–; mem. The Bens 2003–. *Television:* The Sing-Off (as mentor) 2009–13. *Recordings include:* albums: with Ben Folds Five: Ben Folds Five 1995, Whatever and Ever Amen 1997, Naked Baby Photos 1998, The Unauthorised Biography of Reinhold Messner 1999, The Sound of the Life of the Mind 2012; solo: Rockin' the Suburbs 2001, Songs for Silverman 2005, Supersunnyspeedgraphic 2006, Way to Normal 2008, Ben Folds Presents: University A Cappella 2009, Lonely Avenue (with Nick Hornby) 2010, So There 2015. *Current Management:* c/o All Good Factory, 30 Music Square West, Nashville, TN 37203, USA. *E-mail:* info@allgoodfactory.com. *Website:* allgoodfactory.com (office); www.benfolds.com; www.benfoldsfive.com.

FOLLETT, Marie-Claire; British singer, songwriter, actress, dancer and TV presenter, property developer and entrepreneur; b. 11 May 1975, Cardiff, Wales; d. of Ken Follett and Mary Follett; m. Andy Marshall; two c. *Education:* Brooklands Coll., Acad. of Live and Recorded Arts. *Career:* numerous radio broadcasts and TV appearances; concerts include Earls Court, Birmingham NEC, Rock Legends Int. tour 2003–04; bands include Subway, Nemesis, Abba Vision, Pop Tease, Funhouse, Fortune Cookies, Anti Social; Tina Turner support; mem. Musicians' Union, Equity, SAG-AFRA. *Plays:* Taming of the Shrew, Romeo and Juliet, Twelfth Night, Road, Dick Whittington, Don Juan Comes Back from the War, One Step Beyond. *Films:* A Guide for the Divorced Child. *Recordings:* Somnambu, Spreadeagle, Sky TV; A Guide For The Divorced Child, Jann Turner (film soundtrack); singles: Cry; Indestructable; Get Into Love, with Antisocial, Rock Legends Tour, Abba Vision Tour. *Television:* Tornado Alley, Jane the Virgin, commercials for Aerial, Saturday Times, The Sun newspaper, Domainnames.com, Black and Decker. *Address:* 7865 Summer Day Drive, Corona, CA 92883, USA (home). *E-mail:* kissmecoco@me.com (office). *Website:* www.marie-clairefollett.com; www.theabbashow.com.

FOLLOWILL, Caleb; American singer and musician (rhythm guitar); b. Memphis, Tenn.; m. Lily Aldridge 2011; one d. *Career:* settled in Nashville, Tenn. 1998; Founder-mem. Kings of Leon (with brothers Nathan and Jared, and cousin Matthew) 2000–. *Recordings include:* albums: Holy Roller Novocaine (EP) 2003, Youth & Young Manhood 2003, Aha Shake Heartbreak 2004, Because of the Times 2007, Only by the Night (BRIT Award for Best Int. Album 2009, Juno Award for Int. Album of the Year 2010) 2008, Come Around Sundown 2010, Mechanical Bull 2013. *Honours:* Grammy Awards for Best Rock Performance by a Duo or Group (for Sex on Fire) 2009, for Best Rock Performance by a Duo or Group with Vocals (for Use Somebody) 2010, for Record of the Year (for Use Somebody) 2010, for Best Rock Song (for Use Somebody) 2010, BRIT Award for Best Int. Group 2009. *Current Management:* c/o Vector Management, 1607 17th Avenue South, Nashville, TN 37212, USA. *Telephone:* (615) 269-6600. *Fax:* (615) 269-6002. *E-mail:* britti@vectormgmt.com. *Website:* www.kingsofleon.com.

FOLLOWILL, Jared; American musician (bass guitar); b. Memphis, Tenn.; m. Martha Patterson 2012. *Career:* settled in Nashville, Tenn. 1998; Founder-mem. Kings of Leon (with brothers Caleb and Nathan, and cousin Matthew) 2000–. *Recordings include:* albums: Holy Roller Novocaine (EP) 2003, Youth & Young Manhood 2003, Aha Shake Heartbreak 2004, Because of the Times 2007 Only by the Night (BRIT Award for Best Int. Album 2009, Juno Award for Int. Album of the Year 2010) 2008, Come Around Sundown 2010, Mechanical Bull 2013. *Honours:* Grammy Awards for Best Rock Performance by a Duo or Group (for Sex on Fire) 2009, for Best Rock Performance by a Duo or Group with Vocals (for Use Somebody) 2010, for Record of the Year (for Use Somebody) 2010, for Best Rock Song (for Use Somebody) 2010, BRIT Award for Best Int. Group 2009. *Current Management:* c/o Vector Management, 1607 17th Avenue South, Nashville, TN 37212, USA. *Telephone:* (615) 269-6600. *Fax:* (615) 269-6002. *E-mail:* britti@vectormgmt.com. *Website:* www.kingsofleon.com.

FOLLOWILL, Matthew; American musician (guitar); b. Okla. *Career:* settled in Nashville, Tenn. 1998; Founder-mem. Kings of Leon (with cousins Caleb, Nathan and Jared) 2000–. *Recordings include:* albums: Holy Roller Novocaine (EP) 2003, Youth & Young Manhood 2003, Aha Shake Heartbreak 2004, Because of the Times 2007, Only by the Night (BRIT Award for Best Int. Album 2009, Juno Award for Int. Album of the Year 2010) 2008, Come Around Sundown 2010, Mechanical Bull 2013. *Honours:* Grammy Awards for Best Rock Performance by a Duo or Group (for Sex on Fire) 2009, for Best Rock Performance by a Duo or Group with Vocals (for Use Somebody) 2010, for Record of the Year (for Use Somebody) 2010, for Best Rock Song (for Use Somebody) 2010, BRIT Award for Best Int. Group 2009. *Current Management:* c/o Vector Management, 1607 17th Avenue South, Nashville, TN 37212, USA. *Telephone:* (615) 269-6600. *Fax:* (615) 269-6002. *E-mail:* britti@vectormgmt.com. *Website:* www.kingsofleon.com.

FOLLOWILL, Nathan; American musician (drums); b. Okla. *Career:* settled in Nashville, Tenn. 1998; Founder-mem. Kings of Leon (with brothers Caleb and Jared, and cousin Matthew) 2000–. *Recordings include:* albums: Holy Roller Novocaine (EP) 2003, Youth & Young Manhood 2003, Aha Shake Heartbreak 2004, Because of the Times 2007, Only by the Night (BRIT Award for Best Int. Album 2009, Juno Award for Int. Album of the Year 2010) 2008, Come Around Sundown 2010, Mechanical Bull 2013. *Honours:* Grammy Awards for Best Rock Performance by a Duo or Group (for Sex on Fire) 2009, for Best Rock Performance by a Duo or Group with Vocals (for Use Somebody) 2010, for Record of the Year (for Use Somebody) 2010, for Best Rock Song (for Use Somebody) 2010, BRIT Award for Best Int. Group 2009. *Current Management:* c/o Vector Management, 1607 17th Avenue South, Nashville, TN 37212, USA. *Telephone:* (615) 269-6600. *Fax:* (615) 269-6002. *E-mail:* britti@vectormgmt.com. *Website:* www.kingsofleon.com.

FONSECA, (Juan Fernando); Colombian singer; b. 29 May 1979, Bogotá. *Career:* solo artist 2000–. *Recordings include:* albums: Fonseca 2002, Corazón (Nuestra Tierra Award for Album of the Year 2007, Billboard Latin Music Award for Best Tropical Album 2007) 2005, Gratitud (Shock Magazine Award for Album of the Year) 2008, Ilusión 2011 (Latin Grammy Award for Best Tropical Fusion Album) 2012, Fonseca Sinfónico (with National Symphony Orchestra of Colombia) (Latin Grammy Award for Best Traditional Pop Vocal Album 2014) 2014. *Honours:* Shock Magazine Award for Best Solo Male, for Best Radio Song (for Te Mando Flores) 2005, Latin Grammy Award for Best Tropical Song (for Te Mando Flores) 2006, MTV Latin Award for Best New Artist 2006, Shock Magazine Award for Artist of the Year, for Best Pop Artist, for Song of the Year (for Te Mando Flores), and for Best Tropical Pop Interpretation (for Te Mando Flores) 2007, Nuestra Tierra Award for Song of the Year (for Te Mando Flores), for Artist of the Year, for Best Interpretation, for Best Tropical Artist 2007, Lo Nuestro Award for Revelatory Artist of the Year 2007, Shock Magazine Award for Best Soundtrack Song (for Paraíso) 2008, Texas Award for Best Tropical Artist 2012. *Current Management:* c/o Sony Music Latin, 550 Madison Avenue, 23rd Floor, New York, NY 10022-

3211, USA. *E-mail:* anthony@cardonaentgroup.com; fonsecamanagement@ proyectonash.com. *Website:* www.sonymusiclatin.com; www.fonseca.net.

FONSECA, Celso; Brazilian singer, songwriter, musician (guitar) and producer; b. 15 Nov. 1956, Rio de Janeiro. *Career:* mem. Gilberto Gil's band 1981; producer, working for Vinicius Cantuaria 1986, and also Gilberto Gil, Daude, Virginia Rodrigues, Leo Gandelman, Gal Costa, Rosana, Adriana Maciel, Veronica Sabino, Zeca Baleiro; has also performed and recorded with other artists, including Chico Buarque, Djavan, Milton Nascimento, Caetano Veloso, Gal Costa, Elza Soares, Marisa Monte, Joao Bosco, Jorge Benjor, Leila Pinheiro, Simone. *Recordings include:* albums: Minha Cara 1986, Sorte 1994, O Som do Sim 1995, Paradiso 1997, Juventude 2001, Natural 2003, Rive Gauche Rio 2005, Polaroides 2006, Feriado 2007, Celso Fonseca ao vivo 2008, Página Central 2009, Voz e violão 2010, Liebe Paradiso 2011, No meu filme 2011. *Current Management:* c/o Alexandra Casazza, Trouble Worldwide, 2983 Folsom Street A, San Francisco, CA 94110, USA. *E-mail:* analins@ celsofonseca.com.br. *Website:* www.celsofonseca.com.br.

FONSECA, Roberto; Cuban musician (piano) and producer; b. 1975, Havana. *Education:* Instituto Superior de Arte. *Career:* first performed at Jazz Plaza Int. Festival, Havana aged 15; toured in Italy with singer Augusto Enriquez; formed group Temperamento with saxophonist Javier Zalba; joined Orquesta de Ibrahim Ferrer 2001, over 400 concerts performing with legends of Cuban music such as Cachaíto López, Guajiro Mirabal and Manuel Galbán; toured with Omara Portuondo 2002; pianist and producer with Ibrahim Ferrer's Mi sueño: A Bolero Songbook tour 2005; has produced albums for Asa Feeston, Mathew Stoneman, co-producer of posthumous Ibrahim Ferrer album 2007. *Recordings include:* with Temperamento: En el Comienzo 1998; solo: Tiene Que Ver 1999, No Limit 2000, Elengo 2001, Zamazu 2007, Akokan 2009, Live in Marciac 2010, Yo 2012. *Current Management:* Montuno Produciones y eventos, Plaza Doctor Letamendi, 08007 Barcelona, Spain. *Telephone:* (93) 3633600. *Fax:* (93) 3633450. *E-mail:* info@montuno.com. *Website:* www.montuno.com. *E-mail:* info@robertofonseca.com (office). *Website:* www.robertofonseca.com.

FONSI, Luis; Puerto Rican singer and songwriter; b. (Luís Alfonso Rodríguez López-Cepero), 15 April 1978, San Juan; Alfonso Rodriguez and Delia Rodriguez; m. Adamari Lopez 2006 (separated). *Education:* Florida State Univ. *Career:* sang at Nobel Peace Prize Concert 2009. *Recordings include:* albums: Eterno 2000, Amor Secreto 2002, Fight the Feeling 2002, Abrazar la Vida 2003, Paso a Paso 2005, Palabras del Silencio (Best Male Soloist in Spanish, Premios OYE 2009) 2008, Sexo y Más 2010, Tierra Firme 2011. *Honours:* Latin Grammy Awards for Song of the Year (for Aquí Estoy Yo) 2009, Premios OYE and ASCAP for Song of the Year (for No Me Doy Por Vencido) 2009, Premios lo Nuestro for Best Male Artist 2009. *Address:* c/o Universal Music Latino, 1425 Collins Avenue, Miami Beach, FL 33139, USA. *Telephone:* (305) 604-1300. *Fax:* (305) 604-1340. *Website:* www .universalmusica.com/luisfonsi/Home.

FONTAMILLAS, Jerome; American musician (keyboards) and producer. *Career:* mem., Mortal and Fold Zandura 1990s; mem., Switchfoot 2000–. *Recordings include:* albums: with Fold Zandura: Ultraforever 1997, King Planet 1999; with Switchfoot: The Beautiful Letdown 2003, Nothing is Sound 2005, Oh! Gravity 2006, Hello Hurricane 2009, Vice Verses 2011. *Current Management:* c/o Bruce Flohr, Red Light Management, 9200 Sunset Boulevard, Los Angeles, CA 90069, USA. *Telephone:* (424) 653-1701. *E-mail:* switchfoot@redlightmanagement.com. *Website:* www.redlightmanagement .com; www.switchfoot.com.

FOO, Sharin; Danish singer and musician (guitar). *Career:* Founder-mem., The Raveonettes 2002–. *Recordings include:* albums: Whip It On (EP) 2002, Chain Gang Of Love 2002, Pretty In Black 2005, Lust Lust Lust 2007, In and Out of Control 2009, Raven in the Grave 2011, Observator 2012. *Website:* www .theraveonettes.com.

FORBERT, Steve; American singer, songwriter and musician (guitar, harmonica); b. 15 Dec. 1954, Meridian, Miss. *Career:* solo artist 1977–; songwriter in Nashville during 1980s and 1990s; mem., The Rough Squirrels 1998–. *Recordings include:* albums: solo: Alive On Arrival 1978, Jackrabbit Slim 1979, Little Stevie Orbit 1980, Steve Forbert 1982, Streets Of This Town 1988, The American In Me 1992, Be Here Now: Solo Live 1994, Mission Of The Crossroad Palms 1995, In Concert 1982 1995, Rocking Horse Head 1996, Be Here Again Live Solo 1998 1998, Evergreen Boy 2000, Acoustic Live: The WFUV Concert 2000, Young Guitar Days 2001, More Young Guitar Days 2002, Any Old Time 2002, Just Like There's Nothin' To It 2004, Strange Names and New Sensations 2007, The Place and the Time 2009, Over With You 2012; with The Rough Squirrels: Here's Your Pizza 1998, Live At The Bottom Line 2001. *Address:* PO Box 8280, Des Moines, IA 50301, USA. *E-mail:* info@steveforbert.com (office). *Website:* www.steveforbert.com.

THE FORCE (see King Britt)

FORCIONE, Antonio; musician (guitar) and composer; b. 2 May 1960, Italy; one d. *Education:* studied in Italy. *Career:* tours world-wide tours as solo artist and with bands, Antonio Forcione Acoustic Band and Acoustic Mania, in theatres and major festivals; numerous radio and TV appearances; performed with Barney Kessel, Martin Taylor, Birelli Lagrene, Claudio Roditi and others; double bills with John McLaughlin, opened for Phil Collins, Barclay James Harvest, Zucchero, Jools Holland, Pino Daniele, Bobby McFerrin; masterclasses; composed music for TV, radio and documentaries; mem.

Musicians' Union, Performing Rights Soc. *Recordings include:* Albums: Light and Shade 1984, Eurotour 1986, Celebration 1987, Poema 1992, Acoustic Revenge 1993, Live Edinburgh Festival 1993, Dedicato 1996, Talking Hands 1997, Meet Me in London 1998, Ghetto Paradise 1998. *Current Management:* c/o Naim Label, Southampton Road, Salisbury, SP1 2LN, England. *E-mail:* info@naimlabel.com. *Website:* www.naimlabel.com. *E-mail:* info@ antonioforcione.com. *Website:* www.antonioforcione.com.

FORD, Baby, (Twig Bud, Solcyc); British producer, remixer and DJ; b. (Peter Ford), 1960, England. *Career:* started recording career as part of Acid House late 1980s; Co-founder techno labels, Trelik and Ifach Records; collaborations with Eon, Mark Broom. *Recordings include:* albums: Fordtrax 1988, Ooo The World of Baby Ford 1989, BFord 9 1992, Headphone Easyrider 1997, Basking In The Brakelights 2003, Birds 2007. *Website:* music.hyperreal.org/bford/ baby_ford.

FORD, Gerry; Irish country music entertainer, DJ, journalist, singer and songwriter and producer; b. 25 May 1943, Athlone, Co. Westmeath; m. Joan 1964; one s. *Career:* qualified baker, confectioner; served in Edinburgh City Police –1976; became professional entertainer, while broadcasting two country music programmes for Radio Forth, Edinburgh and performing in clubs; joined BBC Radio Scotland, country music presenter 1978–93; own series, BBC Radio 2, 1988–89, Clan FM (Glasgow Country); music reviewer, Country Music and Dance Scotland; emigrated to NSW, Australia 2009; Country DJ with 2SEA FM radio in Eden, NSW and still performing in that area. *Radio includes:* broadcasts with 2SEA FM, Eden, weekly three-hour programme, also broadcasts three-hour weekly radio programme with Sapphire FM in Pambula NSW, available on the web at www.sapphirefm.org, 10am Wednesdays. *Recordings include:* 17 albums, one video 1977–; seven duets with Jean Shepard. *Publications include:* various contribs to Country magazines. *Honours:* Hon. Citizen, Nashville, Tenn., Tenn. State, Tenn. Goodwill Amb., inducted into British Country Hall of Fame 2008; three Albums of the Year, BCMA 1986, BCM Radio Play Album of the Year 1991, Presenters Award 1993, 2005, UK Country Single of the Year 2004, 2005, British Country Hall of Fame 2008, Southern Country Awards Services to Country Award 2009, 21 appearances, Grand Ole Opry, Nashville, 35 awards as male vocalist and recording artiste, various country music clubs and magazines. *Address:* 14–26 Merimbola Street, Pambula, NSW 2549, Austra-lia. *Telephone:* (2) 6495-7149 (office). *E-mail:* gfordoz@gmail.com. *Website:* www.gerryford.co.uk.

FORD, Lita; British singer and musician (guitar); b. 23 Sept. 1959, London; m. Chris Holmes (divorced). *Career:* mem. of all-girl group, The Runaways 1976–79; solo artist 1980–. *Recordings include:* albums: with The Runaways: The Runaways 1976, Queens of Night 1977, And Now The Runaways 1979, Flamin' Schoolgirls 1980; solo: Out For Blood 1983, Dancin' On The Edge 1984, Lita 1988, Stiletto 1990, Dangerous Curves 1991, Black 1995, Wicked Wonderland 2009, Living Like a Runaway 2012. *Website:* www.litafordonline .com.

FORDE, Brinsley, MBE; British singer, musician (guitar) and actor; b. 16 Oct. 1953, Islington, North London, England. *Career:* child actor in Here Come the Double Deckers (BBC TV) 1970–71; Founder-mem. of reggae group Aswad 1975–; numerous live performances and festival appearances; musician and actor in films Leo the Last 1970, Please Sir! 1971, Diamonds Are Forever 1971, Babylon 1981; gained a UK No. 1 chart hit with Don't Turn Around 1988, followed by another top 20 chart hit, Give A Little Love; presenter, Soul Vibration (VH-1), BBC Radio 6. *Films:* The Magnificent Six and ½ (film series) 1967–69, Leo the Last 1970, Diamonds Are Forever (uncredited) 1971, Please Sir! 1971, Babylon 1981, Goodbye Charlie Bright 2001. *Television:* Here Come the Double Deckers! (series) 1970–71, Please Sir! (series) 1971, Villains (series) 1972, To Sir, with Love (film) 1974, The Georgian House (series) 1976, Black Silk (series) 1985. *Recordings include:* albums: Aswad 1976, Hulet 1979, New Chapter 1980, Not Satisfied 1982, Live and Direct 1983, Rebel Souls 1984, To The Top 1986, Distant Thunder 1988, Renaissance 1989, Too Wicked 1990, Live 1991, Roots Rocking 1997, Big Up 1997, Roots Revival 1999, Can't Stop Me Now 2013, Urban Jungle 2013. *Honours:* Reggae Industry Award for Best Group 1995. *E-mail:* brinsley.6music@bbc.co.uk. *Website:* myspace.com/ brinsleyforde.

FORDHAM, Julia; British singer, songwriter and musician (guitar); b. 10 Aug. 1962, Hampshire. *Career:* began performances of own material, folk music clubs aged 14–15; five years as backing vocalist; solo artist 1987–; mem. Musicians' Union, Equity. *Recordings include:* albums: Julia Fordham 1988, Porcelain 1989, Swept 1991, Falling Forward 1994, East West 1997, Julia Fordham Collection 1998, Concrete Love 2002, That's Life 2004, That's Live 2005, Songbook 2007, China Blue 2008, Unusual Suspects 2010. *Honours:* Silver Prize, Tokyo Music Festival 1989. *E-mail:* gonespinnin@earthlink.net. *Website:* www.juliafordham.com.

FOREMAN, Jon; American singer, songwriter and musician (guitar); b. 22 Oct. 1976. *Education:* Univ. of California, San Diego. *Career:* mem., Switch-foot 1997–; co-f. Fiction Family 2008–. *Recordings include:* albums: with Switchfoot: The Legend of Chin 1997, New Way to be Human 1999, Learning to Breathe 2000, The Beautiful Letdown 2003, Nothing is Sound 2005, Oh! Gravity 2006, Hello Hurricane 2009, Vice Verses 2011; with Fiction Family: Fiction Family 2009, Fiction Family Reunion 2013. *Current Management:* c/o Bruce Flohr, Red Light Management, 9200 Sunset Boulevard, Suite 1207, Los Angeles, CA 90069, USA. *E-mail:* switchfoot@redlightmanagement.com.

Website: www.redlightmanagement.com; www.jonforeman.com; www .switchfoot.com; www.fictionfamily.com.

FOREMAN, Tim; American musician (bass guitar) and songwriter; b. 15 Aug. 1978. *Education:* San Dieguito Acad. *Career:* mem., Switchfoot 1997–. *Recordings include:* albums: The Legend of Chin 1997, New Way to be Human 1999, Learning to Breathe 2000, The Beautiful Letdown 2003, Nothing is Sound 2005, Oh! Gravity 2006, Hello Hurricane 2009, Vice Verses 2011. *Current Management:* c/o Bruce Flohr, Red Light Management, 9200 Sunset Boulevard, Suite 1207, Los Angeles, CA 90069, USA. *Telephone:* (424) 653-1701. *E-mail:* switchfoot@redlightmanagement.com. *Website:* www .redlightmanagement.com; www.switchfoot.com.

FOREST, So'; Cameroonian singer, songwriter, musician (guitar) and programmer; b. Yaounde. *Career:* solo artist in Bikutsi Pop style of world music. *Recordings include:* album: Bikutsi Pop: The Songs Of So' Forest 2002.

FORRESTER, John; British musician (bouzouki, bass, acoustic guitar) and singer; b. 16 March 1969, Pembury, Kent. *Career:* mem. Killing The Rose 1986–87, The Colour Mary 1988–92, Pressgang 1992–94; solo artist 1993–; mem. WOB 1993–94, Sunspeak 1995, Nozzle 2000–, Silverlead 2002–; numerous tours, radio broadcasts; mem. Musicians' Union. *Recordings include:* albums: with Pressgang: Burning Boats 1994; with WOB: Can't Stay Long 1995, Straight On Til Morning 1998; solo: Scars and Memories 1993, Tales of Nothing 1997, All The Wrong Things 2000, Ne Me Quitte Pas, songs by Brel 1998; with Nozzle: Twisted Vision 2003. *E-mail:* info@forrester .uk.com. *Website:* www.forrester.uk.com.

FORRÓ, Daniel, AM, PhD; Czech composer, musician (keyboards, drums) and musicologist; b. 19 Feb. 1958, Jihlava. *Education:* Brno State Conservatory, Janacek Acad. of Music, Brno. *Career:* mem. rock groups 1978–84; own project of EA and computer music, Forrotronics 1983–; mem. drum group, Dama Dama; founder and owner, Museum of EMI 1989–; teacher, Janacek Acad. of Music 1991–2003, Head of Computer and Electronic Music Dept; Ed. and writer for music magazine, Muzikus 1991–2002; product specialist, Yamaha Europe Export Division, Hamburg 1991–2002, Czech and Slovak Korg Distributor MusicPark 2002; writer of a series of books on musitronics 1993–; Founder and Chair. Soc. for Microintervallic Music 1995; gives int. summer masterclasses at Janacek Acad. of Music 1996–, at nat. rock/pop/jazz music acad. 1998–; Founder and Chair. Soc. for Creative Improvisation 2001; moved to Kakamigahara, Japan 2003; mem. Soc. for EA Music, Soc. Q. *Compositions:* more than 1,100 in numerous styles. *Publications include:* MIDI—Communication in Music, Computers and Music, Home Recording, World of MIDI, Samplers, Analog and Analog-Digital Synthesizers, Historical EMI, Creative Improvisation, Microintervallic Music.

FORSMAN, Ingela 'Pling'; Swedish lyricist and record producer; b. 26 Aug. 1950, Stockholm; m. Lars 1990; one s. *Education:* Univ. of Stockholm. *Career:* fmr recording artist with girl group Bambis; tours in Sweden, Germany; lyricist 1971–; translated musicals into Swedish: Cats, Grease, Fame, Hair; also translated songs in films, including The Little Mermaid, Beauty and The Beast, Hymn for Swedish Hymnbook; written lyrics to over 1,000 songs; mem. STIM, NCB, SKAP. *Honours:* Swedish Song Contest (two first places), SKAP Award.

FORSTER, Robert; Australian singer, musician (guitar) and songwriter; b. 29 June 1957, Brisbane. *Education:* Queensland Univ. *Career:* Founder-mem., The Go-Betweens 1978–89, 2000–06; solo artist, also collaborating with Grant McLennan; regular columnist, The Monthly magazine 2005–. *Recordings include:* albums: with The Go-Betweens: Send Me A Lullaby 1981, Before Hollywood 1983, Spring Hill Fair 1984, Liberty Belle and the Black Diamond Express 1986, Tallulah 1987, 16 Lovers Lane 1988, The Friends Of Rachel Worth 2000, Bright Yellow Bright Orange 2003, Oceans Apart 2005, Intermission 2007; solo: Danger in the Past 1990, Calling From A Country Phone 1993, I Had A New York Girlfriend 1995, Warm Nights 1996, The Evangelist 2008. *Publications include:* The Go-Betweens (co-author) 2008, The 10 Rules of Rock and Roll: Collected Music Writings 2005–09 2009, numerous articles. *Honours:* Pascall Award for Critical Writing 2006. *Website:* www.robertforster.net.

FORTUNE, (Jason Dean) JD; Canadian singer and songwriter; b. (Jason Dean Bennison), 1 Sept. 1973, Mississauga, Ont. *Career:* fmr mem. various bands; winner of Rock Star: INXS (reality TV programme to find new INXS lead singer) 2005; mem. INXS 2005–11. *Recordings include:* album: Switch 2006, Original Sin 2010. *Website:* www.jdfortune.com.

FOSKETT, Charles A.; British musician (guitar, bass), composer and producer; b. 27 March 1949, Newcastle upon Tyne; m. Lauren Daniele Field 1990, one s. *Career:* started career in Newcastle, played alongside The Animals, 1960s; formed The Anti Heroin Project, 1985, 1986, 1987; worked with: Kim Wilde; Ringo Starr; Precious Wilson; John Cleese; Bonnie Tyler; Elkie Brooks; Daryl Pandy; Cliff Richard; Holly Johnson; Sheila Ferguson; Robin Gibb; Nik Kershaw; Hazel O'Connor; Founder, Veracruz Music International record production co.; mem. Performing Rights Soc., Equity. *Compositions include:* theme music, Strike Command, TV advertisement, 1996; theme music, ITV six-part series, 1997; theme music, High 5, Channel 4, 1997; New Age Jazz, ambient music for Midnight Music, film for TV, Los Angeles; compositions for: Sarah Jory, Joe Cocker; I Wanna Be There, Prudential Mexico '97. *Current Management:* c/o Mike Fisher Organisation

Ltd, Orbital House, 20 Eastern Road, Romford, Essex, RM1 3PJ, England. *Telephone:* (1708) 725-081.

FOSSATI, Ramon; Spanish musician (trombone, shells), composer, producer and arranger; b. 14 Sept. 1965, Barcelona. *Career:* Founder and Co-leader, Paris-Barcelona Swing Connection; played with Frank Wess, Teddy Edwards, Wild Bill Davis; performed at Jazz Vienne (France) 1993, Jazz Festival, Birmingham 1992–94, Terrassa, Spain 1993–95, Frankfurt 1995; currently performing and recording with quintet Five in Orbit and Ramon Fossati Glowing Trio. *Recordings include:* with the Paris-Barcelona Swing Connection: Hard Swing, Live In Barcelona; with Frank Wess: Frank Wess Meets The Paris-Barcelona Swing Connection; with Wild Bill Davis: Wild Cat; with Five in Orbit: Five in Orbit 2008, Freaks 2010; with Stromb: Island Stream 2014. *Telephone:* (60) 7169494. *E-mail:* info@ramonfossati.com. *Website:* www .ramonfossati.com.

FOSTER, Geoff; British recording engineer; b. 5 May 1965, Wimbledon, London, England; partner Dawn Tait; two d. *Education:* Marlborough Coll., Brunel Univ. *Career:* worked for Stones Mobile 1985, Cold Storage Studios 1986, Air Studios 1987, Chief Engineer 1994; mem. AMIEE. *Recordings include:* film scores include: High Rise, Victor Frankenstein, Woman In Gold, Man Down, Interstellar, Noah, Tron II, Home, Gone Girl, The Little Prince, Penguins of Madagascar, Terminator Genysis, The Great Gatsby, Filth, Sherlock Holmes: A Game of Shadows, The Dark Knight Rises, Inception, Despicable Me, Sherlock Holmes, The Dark Knight, Quantum of Solace, Casino Royale, Moon, Stargate, Stoker, Black Swan, The Wrestler, Restoration, Romeo and Juliet, Batman Begins, Madagascar, Mission Impossible II, The Da Vinci Code, Mighty Ducks 3, Don Juan de Marco, Last of the Dogmen, Meet Wally Sparks, Smilla's Sense of Snow, Photographing Fairies, Alien Love Triangle, Amy Foster, B. Monkey, Black Beauty, City of Angels, Moulin Rouge, Cousin Bette, Dreaming of Joseph Lees, Entrapment, About A Boy, Elizabeth: The Golden Age, The Last King of Scotland, Great Expectations, Jack and Sarah, James and the Giant Peach, Les Visiteurs, Gangs of New York, Loss of Sexual Innocence, Lost Souls, Mickey Blue Eyes, Midsummer Night's Dream, Peacemaker, Plunkett and Macleane, Pola X, Prince of Egypt, Purdita Durango, Ride with the Devil, Robinson Crusoe, Shadows of the Empire, Summer of Sam, The Avengers, The Beach, The Bone Collector, The Gold Diggers, The Last September, The Matchmaker, The Other Conquest, The Place of Lions, The Visitor, The War Zone, Tobacco Project, Tomorrow Never Dies, The World Is Not Enough, Tropical Island Hum, Une Femme Francaise, What Dreams May Come True, Wing Commander, Wings of a Dove, When A Man Loves A Woman; albums include with: David Gilmour, Gigi D'Alessio, George Martin, Martin Okasili, John Martyn, Michael Buble, Rumur, Il Divo, Westlife, Leona Lewis, Katherine Jenkins, Shirley Bassey, Crowded House, Debbie Harry, Hothouse Flowers, Jethro Tull, Grace Jones, Pulp, Roachford, Robert Palmer, Sting, The Pretenders, Paul Carrack, Radiohead, The The, Kula Shaker, David Essex, José Carreras, Vanessa-Mae, John Williams, Akin, Akira, Alisha's Attic, All Saints, Baby Bird, Bjork, Blur, Bone Muffin, Cast, Cilla Black, Dario G, David Cassidy, Petula Clark, David McAlmont, Debbie Gibson, Eliza Carthy, Elkie Brooks, Elton John, Fine Young Cannibals, Fredrick, Garbage, Gary Barlow, Gilbert O'Sullivan, Hombres G, Irene Barnes, Jimmy Nail, Joni Mitchell, Jo Hisaishi, Phil Collins, Leftfield, Lisa Stone, Madonna, Maestro Hattori, Mel C, Michael Ball, Michael Jackson, Michael Crawford, Mike Oldfield, Ofra Haza, Outfield, Paul Brady, Peter Cox, Phil Campbell, Rolph Harris, Rory McLeod, Sisters of Mercy, Stephen Duffy, Nigel Kennedy, Sugar Ray, The Pet Shop Boys, The Trash Can Sinatras, Tyrell Corporation, Virginia McNaughton, Yell, Eliza Carthy, Ute Lemper, Pulp, Sir Neville Marriner, Placido Domingo, Giselle Bendor, Jose Carreras, Kiri Te Kawana, John Adams. *Honours:* Grammy Award for Best Traditional Pop Vocal Album – Joni Mitchell's Both Sides Now 2000, Grammy Award: Best Score Soundtrack Album For Motion Picture, TV Or Other Visual Media – Ray 2005, for The Dark Knight 2008, BAFTA Award: Anthony Asquith Award for Film Music – Moulin Rouge, MPSE Best Sound Editing in a Feature Film - The Great Gatsby 2014. *E-mail:* engineer@ airstudios.com (home); management@airstudios.com (home). *Website:* www .air-management.co.uk (home).

FOUAD, Mohamed; Egyptian singer, composer and actor; b. (Mohamed Fouad abd al-Hamid Hassan), 20 Dec. 1961, Cairo. *Career:* fmr mem. Four M singing group; solo artist and actor. *Films include:* Amrica shika bika, El-kelb wa ma yaashaq, Ismailia Rayeh Gai, Rehlet hob, Howa fi eih, Ghawi hob. *Recordings include:* albums: Fe es-seka 1985, Hawed 1987, Khefet damo 1986, Yani, Esaali, Soltan zamani, Meshena 1992, Sheka beka, Habena 1993, Hairan 1996, Kamannana 1997, El-hob el-hakeki 1998, Albi wa Rohi w Omri 1999, El-alb et-tayeb 2000, Keber el-gharam 2001, Shareni 2003, Habebi ya 2005, Ghawy Hob 2006, Wala Nos Kelma 2007, Been Edeak 2010, Ghaly 2010, Besohola Keda 2010, Ben Edeik 2010, Ebn Balad 2010, Bashabeh 3alek 2011, Tameny 3alek 2011. *Website:* www.fo2sh.net.

FOUNTAIN, Peter (Pete); American clarinettist; b. 3 July 1930, New Orleans, LA; m. Beverly, 27 Oct. 1951, two s., one d. *Career:* Operator night club Pete Fountain's New Orleans; Member, Basin Street Six, 1949–54, Lawrence Walk Orchestra, 1957–60; Leader, own group; Appeared in (films), Pete Fountain Sextet, 1962, Pete's Place, 1966, The New Orleans Jazz Museum, 1967; Featured in: PBS spl, Dukes of Dixieland and Friends, 1980; Featured Guest with major orchestras throughout world; Co-author: A Closer Walk: The Pete Fountain Story, 1972; Appeared on Johnny Carson Show, 59 times; Performed for Papal visit, White House for Presidents Eisenhower,

Nixon, Ford and Reagan, 1987. *Recordings:* 85 albums including: Pete Fountain 1957, The Blues 1959, Bourbon Street 1961, New Orleans Scene 1961, Plenty of Pete 1962, Pete's Place 1964, Standing Room Only 1965, Those Were the Days 1968, Walking Through New Orleans 1968, Pete Fountain's Crescent City 1973, Dr Fountain's Magical Licorice Stick 1981, Basin Street Blues 1985, Swingin' Blues 1990, Do You Know What It Means to Miss New Orleans? 1991, New Orleans, Tennessee 1991, Something Misty 1991, High Society 1992, Pete's Beat 1992, Down on Rampart Street 1993, Cheek to Cheek 1993, Country 1994, Touch of Class 1995, Tradition Runs Deep 1998, Bourbon Street Magic 2005. *Honours:* 3 Gold Albums; 1 Gold Single (A Closer Walk). *Website:* www.petefountain.com.

4-BAR KILLER (see U-God)

4 ELEMENTS (see Da Silva, Rui)

FOUR TET (see Hebden, Kieran)

FOWLER, Simon; British singer and musician (guitar); b. 25 April 1965, Birmingham. *Career:* fmr mem. The Fanatics; Founder mem. Ocean Colour Scene 1989–; numerous TV appearances, radio broadcasts and tours. *Recordings include:* albums: Ocean Colour Scene 1992, Moseley Shoals 1996, B-Sides, Seasides and Freerides 1997, Marchin' Already 1997, One From The Modern 1999, Mechanical Wonder 2001, Songs For The Front Row (compilation) 2001, Anthology 2003, North Atlantic Drift 2003, Marchin' Melody 2004, On The Leyline 2007, The Collection 2007, Saturday 2010, 21 (compilation) 2010; solo: Merrymouth 2012. *Address:* The OCS Partnership, Unit 1, The Mill, Mill Lane, Little Shrewley, Hatton, Warwick, CV35 7HN, England (office). *E-mail:* info@ocsmusic.com (office). *Website:* www.oceancolourscene.com.

FOX, Donal Leonellis; American composer and jazz and classical musician (piano); b. 17 July 1952, Boston, Mass; m. Dr Karen L. Mapp. *Education:* New England Conservatory of Music, Berklee Coll. of Music, Berkshire Music Center, Tanglewood; piano with Jeanette Giguere and Margaret Chaloff, theory and counterpoint with Avram David, composition and harmony with T. J. Anderson, composition and orchestration with Gunther Schuller. *Career:* debut, premiere of Refutation and Hypothesis II for chamber orchestra, Festival of Contemporary Music at Tanglewood 1983; piano and improviser, world premiere of Oliver Lake's Movements Turns and Switches for violin and piano, Library of Congress, Washington, DC 1993; piano and improviser, world premiere, The Demon, Int. Ottawa Jazz Festival, Nat. Gallery of Canada 1995; piano and improviser, world premiere of Anthony Kelley's Africamerica for piano and orchestra 1999; piano and improviser, world premiere of T.J. Anderson's Fragments 2006; Composer-in-Residence, St Louis Symphony Orchestra 1991–92; publisher and writer, BMI 1993–; Pres., Leonellis Music 1994–, Harry Fox Agency Inc. 1996–; Artist-in-Residence, Tyrone Guthrie Centre, Northern Ireland 2003, Oberfäzer Künstlerhaus, Schwandorf, Germany 2004; Visiting Artist, Fusion Arts Exchange, US State Dept 2007; mem. Massachusetts Cultural Council (educational collaborative) 1984–. *Television includes:* Donal Fox and David Murray in Session 1993, The Fox/Troupe Project (PBS) 1993, Say Brother (WGBH) 1993, Donal Fox Plays T.J. Anderson Concerto (PBS) 2006. *Compositions include:* Refutation and Hypothesis I: a Treatise for piano solo 1981, Dialectics for two grand pianos 1988, Variants on a Theme by Monk for alto saxophone and piano 1990, Jazz Sets and Tone Rows for alto saxophone and piano 1990, Vamping with T. T. for bass clarinet and piano 1993, T-Cell Countdown for voice, piano and double bass 1993, River Town Packin House Blues, The Old People Speak of Death, Following the North Star Boogaloo for piano and poet 1993, Gone City: Ballet in Three Movements for clarinet, piano and double bass 1994, The Scream 1996, Toccata on Bach 2001, Hear de Lambs A-Cryin for baritone and orchestra 2005, Peace Out, My Brother for voice and piano 2006, Duetto II for clarinet and piano 2008, Star-Spangled Banner Fractured 2008. *Recordings include:* Boston Duets 1992, Videmus 1992, Ugly Beauty 1995, Donal Fox: Mellow Mood 1996, Donal Fox: Gone City 1997, Donal Fox Quartet: Scarlatti Jazz Suite Project 2008. *Honours:* American Acad. of Arts and Letters Award in Music 2008. *Address:* Leonellis Music, 14 Highland Park Avenue, Boston, MA 02119, USA (office). *Telephone:* (617) 821-0145 (office). *Fax:* (617) 427-6539 (office). *E-mail:* dfoxmu@aol.com. *Website:* www.leonellismusic.com (office).

FOX, Gavin; British musician (bass guitar); b. 6 March 1978. *Career:* mem., Idlewild 2002–07, Concerto for Constantine 2007–. *Recordings include:* albums: The Remote Part 2002, Warnings/Promises 2005, Make Another World 2007, Scottish Fiction: Best of Idlewild 2007.

FOX, George William; Canadian singer and songwriter; b. 23 March 1960, Cochrane, Alberta. *Career:* numerous TV appearances and live performances; mem. CARAS, NARAS, CMA, CCMA, ACTRA, AFofM. *Recordings include:* George Fox 1988, With All My Might 1989, Spice of Life 1991, Mustang Heart 1993, Time of My Life 1995, Survivor 1998, A George Fox Christmas 1999. *Honours:* Canadian Country Music Assscn Vista Rising Star 1989, Country Male Vocalist 1989–93, Juno Award for Country Male Vocalist of Year 1990, 1991, 1992, SOCAN Song of Year (for Clearly Canadian) 1993. *Current Management:* c/o Nick Meinema, The Agency Group, 2 Berkeley Street, Suite 202, Toronto, ON M5A 4J5, Canada. *E-mail:* trailofthefox@xplornet.com. *Website:* www.georgefox.com.

FOX, Simon; British retail executive; *Chief Executive, Trinity Mirror PLC;* m.; three c. *Career:* graduate trainee, Security Pacific Bank; worked at Boston

Consulting Group and Sandhurst Marketing PLC; founder office supplies retailer, Office World; joined Kingfisher 1998, held various posts, including CEO for Electricals, Man. Dir Comet (during de-merger with Kingfisher); fmr COO, Kesa Electricals PLC, with responsibility for Comet UK; Group Chief Exec., HMV Group PLC 2006–12; Chief Exec., Trinity Mirror PLC 2012–. *Address:* Trinity Mirror PLC, One Canada Square, Canary Wharf, London, E14 5AP, England (office). *Telephone:* (20) 7293-3000 (office). *Website:* www.trinitymirror.com (office).

FOXTON, Bruce; British musician (bass guitar); b. 1 Sept. 1955, Woking, Surrey. *Career:* Founder mem. The Jam 1972–82; solo artist 1984; mem. Stiff Little Fingers 1991–2006; Founder mem. From The Jam 2007–. *Recordings include:* albums: with The Jam: In the City 1977, This is the Modern World 1977, All Mod Cons 1978, Setting Sons 1979, Sound Affects 1980, The Gift 1982; solo: Touch Sensitive 1984, Back in the Room 2012; with Stiff Little Fingers: Flags and Emblems, Get a Life, Tinderbox, Guitar and Drum; with Paul Weller: Wake Up the Nation 2010. *Publication:* Our Story (autobiography of The Jam, with Rick Buckler) 1994. *Current Management:* c/o Rock Artist Management, Rothery House, Henthorn Road, Clitheroe, BB7 2LD, England. *E-mail:* rockartistmgmt@aol.com. *Website:* www.rockartistmanagement.com; www.brucefoxton.com.

FOXX, Jamie; American actor, comedian and singer; b. (Eric Marlon Bishop), 13 Dec. 1967, Terrell, Tex.; s. of Darrell Bishop and Louise Annette Talley Dixon; adopted and raised by his mother's adoptive parents, Mark Talley and Esther Marie Talley (née Nelson); two d. *Career:* began playing the piano aged five; made TV debut in comedy series In Living Color 1991; writer, performer, dir and producer on The Jamie Foxx Show 1996–2001; writer, performer and producer, two songs on Any Given Sunday film soundtrack 1999; tours: The Unpredictable Tour 2006, The Blame It Tour 2009. *Films include:* Toys 1992, The Truth About Cats and Dogs 1996, The Great White Hype 1996, Booty Call 1997, The Players Club 1998, Held Up 1999, Any Given Sunday 1999, Bait 2000, Date from Hell 2001, Ali 2001, Shade 2003, Redemption: The Stan Tookie Williams Story 2004, Breakin' All the Rules 2004, Collateral (BET Award for Best Supporting Actor) 2004, Ray (Best Actor in a Musical or Comedy, Golden Globe Awards 2005, Best Actor, Screen Actors Guild Awards 2005, Best Actor in a Leading Role, BAFTA Awards 2005, Best Actor, Acad. Awards 2005) 2004, Stealth 2005, Jarhead 2005, Miami Vice 2006, Dreamgirls 2006, The Kingdom 2007, The Soloist 2009, Law Abiding Citizen 2009, Valentine's Day 2010, Malice N Wonderland (video short) 2010, Due Date 2010, I'm Still Here 2010, Rio (voice) 2011, Horrible Bosses 2011, Django Unchained 2012, White House Down 2013, Rio 2 (voice) 2014, The Amazing Spider-Man 2 2014, Horrible Bosses 2 2014, Annie 2014. *Television includes:* In Living Colour 1991–94, C-Bear and Jamal (voice) 1996, The Jamie Foxx Show 1996–2001, Jamie Foxx: I Might Need Security (HBO Comedy Special) 2002. *Recordings include:* Peep This 1994, Unpredictable (Soul Train Award for Best R&B/Soul Album by a Male Artist 2007) 2005, Intuition 2008, Best Night of My Life 2010. *Honours:* Image Award for Best Musical Artist 2006, BET Award for Best Duet/Collaboration (for Gold Digger, with Kanye West) 2006, American Music Award for Favorite Male Soul/R&B Artist 2006, Grammy Award for Best R&B Performance by a Duo or Group with Vocals (for Blame It with T-Pain) 2010. *Address:* Foxxhole Productions, Inc., 15821 Ventura Boulevard 525, Encino, CA 91436, USA (office). *Telephone:* (310) 205-2800 (office). *Website:* www.jamiefoxxmusic.com.

FRAITES, Jeremiah Caleb; American folk rock, musician (drums, mandolin) and songwriter; b. 1985, Ramsey, NJ; s. of Kathleen Fraites. *Education:* Ramsey High School, William Paterson Univ. *Career:* Founder-mem. (with Wesley Schultz) Wesley Jeremiah, changed name to The Lumineers 2009–; released debut EP 2011; numerous tours. *Recording:* album: The Lumineers 2012. *Current Management:* c/o Christen Greene and David Meinert, Onto Entertainment, 2611 5th Avenue, Seattle, WA 98121-1517, USA. *Address:* c/o Dualtone Records, Dualtone Music Group, 203 North 11th Street, Suite B, Nashville, TN 37206, USA (office). *Telephone:* (615) 320-0620 (office). *Fax:* (615) 320-0692 (office). *E-mail:* info@dualtone.com (office); info@thelumineers.com. *Website:* www.dualtone.com (office); www.thelumineers.com.

FRAITURE, Nikolai; American musician (bass guitar); b. 13 Nov. 1979, New York. *Career:* mem., The Strokes 1998–; Founding-mem., Nickel Eye 2008–. *Recordings include:* albums: with The Strokes: Is This It (NME Award for Album of the Year) 2001, Room on Fire 2003, First Impressions of Earth 2006, Angles 2011, Comedown Machine 2013; with Nickel Eye: The Time of the Assassins 2009. *Honours:* NME Awards for Band of the Year, Best New Act 2001, for Best Int. Band 2006, BRIT Award for Best Int. Newcomer 2002. *Current Management:* Wiz Kid Management, 123 East Seventh Street, New York, NY 10001, USA. *Telephone:* (212) 473-3600. *Website:* www.thestrokes.com.

FRAME, Roddy; British singer, songwriter and musician (guitar); b. 29 Jan. 1964, East Kilbride, Scotland. *Career:* Founder mem., Aztec Camera 1980–96; numerous tours and live appearances; solo artist 1998–. *Recordings include:* albums: with Aztec Camera: High Land, Hard Rain 1983, Knife 1984, Love 1987, Stray 1990, Dreamland 1993, Frestonia 1995; solo: The North Star 1998, Surf 2002, Western Skies 2006, Live at Ronnie Scott's 2007, Live at The Blue Note, Osaka 2007, Seven Dials 2014. *E-mail:* info@redemption-records.com. *Website:* www.roddyframe.com.

FRAMPTON, Peter; British musician (guitar) and singer; b. 22 April 1950, Beckenham, Kent. *Career:* mem., The Herd; session musician, working with various artists; mem., Humble Pie 1969–71; solo artist 1971–; numerous live performances; formed new backing band, Escape 1990. *Film appearance:* Sgt Pepper's Lonely Hearts Club Band 1978. *Recordings include:* albums: with Humble Pie: As Safe As Yesterday Is 1969, Town and Country 1969, Humble Pie 1971, Rock On 1971, Performance—Rockin' the Fillmore 1972; solo: Wind of Change 1972, Frampton's Camel 1973, Somethin's Happening 1974, Frampton 1974, Frampton Comes Alive 1976, I'm In You 1977, Where Should I Be 1979, Breaking All the Rules 1981, The Art of Control 1982, Premonition 1983, Peter Frampton Classics 1987, New World 1988, When All the Pieces Fit 1989, Peter Frampton 1994, Peter Frampton Comes Alive II 1995, Love Taker 1995, Winds of Change 1998, A Day in the Sun 1999, Beat the Bootleggers 1999, Live In Detroit 2000, Now 2003, Fingerprints (Grammy Award for Best Pop Instrumental Album 2007) 2006, Thank You Mr Churchill 2010. *Current Management:* Vector Management, 113 East 55th Street, New York, NY 10022, USA. *Website:* www.vectormgmt.com. *E-mail:* info@frampton.com (office). *Website:* www.frampton.com.

FRANCE, Marie; French singer and actress; b. 9 Feb. 1946, Oran, Algeria. *Career:* moved to France 1963; collaborations with numerous artists, including Marc Almond. *Films include:* Les Intrigues de Sylvia Couski 1974, Barroco 1976, Le Jardin des Espérides 1982, Billy Ze Kick 1985, Les Keufs 1987, Belle maman 1999, DJ Le Défi 2002, Je vous hais petites filles 2008, L'orpheline avec en plus un bras en moins 2011, Le prolongement de moi 2012. *Plays include:* Maggie Moon 1975, La Barre 1977, Navire Night 1979, Détail sur la marche arrière 2000. *Recordings include:* albums: 39° de Fièvre 1981, Marie France 1997, Raretés 2006, Phantom featuring Marie France 2008, Marie France visite Bardot 2009. *E-mail:* patrick@lastcallrecords.com. *Website:* www.lastcallrecords.com.

FRANCE, Martin Perry; British musician (drums, percussion) and composer; b. 29 Feb. 1964, Rainham, Kent; s. of James Fisher France and Margaret Perry France. *Career:* session musician, with performances worldwide; worked with artists, including First House, Iain Ballamy, Cleveland Watkiss, Julian Argnelles, Django Bates, Loose Tubes, Human Chain, Mark Lockheart, Billy Jenkins, Eddie Parker, Buckley/Batchelor; regular performer with NDR radio orchestra, Hamburg; currently Prof. of Music, Royal Acad. of Music. *Current Management:* Orpheus Management. *Telephone:* (045) 8007433 (Italy). *E-mail:* orpheus@orpheusmanagement.it. *Website:* www .orpheusmanagement.it. *Address:* Royal Academy of Music, Marylebone Road, London, NW1 5HT, England.

FRANCE, Nicolas Michael; British musician (percussion, drums, piano); b. 30 March 1956, Standon, Hertfordshire; m. Billie (Susan Mary) Preston 1983, one s., two d. *Education:* Chorister, Ely Cathedral, Univ. of Cambridge. *Career:* worked with Tanita Tikaram, Bill Withers, Jaki Graham, Working Week, Mose Allison; recorded with Pete Townshend, Thomas Dolby, L Shankar; session player with artists including Phil Todd, Robbie Macintosh, Snake Davis, Laurence and Richard Cottle, Danny Cummings, Martin Ditcham; played with jazz artists including Loose Tubes, Ronnie Scott Quintet, John Taylor, Allan Holdsworth, Jim Mullen; concerts and tours include: tours with Loose Tubes 1983–86, three European tours, three festivals with Working Week 1984–87, two tours, UK, Europe 1988–89; tour, including Montreux and Nice festivals, with Heitor; three world tours with Tanita Tikaram 1990–95; mem. PRS. *Recordings include:* with Loose Tubes: Loose Tubes, Delightful Precipice 1983–85, The Way Through The Woods, Bronte Brothers 1993, Johnson, The Fat Lady Sings 1993; with The Working Week: Working Nights, Companeros, Fire In The Mountain, Rodrigo Bay from Absolute Beginners, Supergrass, Comic Strip Movie (film soundtrack) 1984–87; with Tanita Tikaram: Everybody's Angel, Eleven Kinds of Loneliness, Lovers In The City 1990–95.

FRANCES, Andrew, BA; American record company executive, producer and manager; b. 17 March 1950, New York City. *Education:* New York City High School of the Performing Arts, Northwestern Univ. *Career:* worked for labels MCA, RCA, Millennium, RSO, Sony Gold/MCA; f. own labels Chameleon/Elektra, North South/Atlantic; f. own management company Adwater and Stir; artists handled include David Bowie, Wang Chung, Ruth McCartney, Benny Mardones; currently Advisor, McCartney Multimedia Inc.; mem. Bd of Dirs, Elken Entertainment; mem. NARAS, CMA. *Address:* McCartney Multimedia Inc., 322 Culver Blvd, Suite 124, Playa Del Rey, CA 90293, USA. *E-mail:* andrew@mccartney.com. *Website:* www.mccartney.com.

FRANCIS, Connie; American singer and musician (accordion); b. (Concetta Rosa Maria Franconero), 12 Dec. 1938, Newark, NJ. *Career:* professional musician 1949–; winner, Arthur Godfrey Talent Show; recording artist 1955–; charity work for organizations, including UNICEF; entertained US troops, Viet Nam 1960s; retired from public performance 1970s, resumed performances 1981–. *Recordings include:* albums include: Who's Sorry Now? 1958, The Exciting Connie Francis 1959, My Thanks To You 1959, Italian Favourites 1960, Rock 'n' Roll Million Sellers 1960, Country and Western Golden Hits 1960, Sings Great Jewish Favorites 1961, Songs To A Swinging Band 1961, Never On Sunday 1961, Folk Song Favorites 1961, Do The Twist 1962, Second Hand Love and Other Hits 1962, Country Music Connie Style 1962, Modern Italian Hits 1963, In The Summer of His Years 1964, Great Country Favourites, with Hank Williams Jr 1964, A New Kind of Connie 1964, Connie Francis Sings For Mama 1965, Love Italian Style 1967, Happiness 1967, My Heart Cries For You 1967, Hawaii Connie 1968, Connie and Clyde 1968, The Wedding Cake 1969, Connie Francis Sings Great Country Hits, Vol.

2 1973, Sings The Big Band Hits 1977, I'm Me Again – Silver Anniversary Album 1981, Connie Francis and Peter Kraus, Vols 1 and 2 1984, Country Store 1988; various compilations including Star Power 2001, Ultimate EP Collection 2002; singles: Who's Sorry Now, Stupid Cupid, Everybody's Somebody's Fool, My Mind Has A Heart of Its Own, Don't Break The Heart That Loves You. *E-mail:* cf@conniefrancis.biz. *Website:* www.conniefrancis .com.

FRANCIS, Terry, (Love Panda); British producer, remixer and DJ; b. 1966, Leatherhead, Surrey. *Career:* began DJ career at Stern's Club; Co-founder, Wiggle Records and underground house night in London with Nathan Coles; compiler and mixer of Architecture series for Pagan Records; resident DJ at Fabric club in London; mem. 2 Smokin' Barrels, The Delinquents; collaborations: Nathan Coles; Housey Doingz. *Recordings include:* albums: Architecture Vols 1 and 2 (DJ-mixed compilations), Fabric 02 2002; singles: Dub Town 1997, Took From Me 1998, Breaking The Law EP (with The Delinquents) 1998, Smokey Rooms EP 1999, Strong Woman EP 2001. *Honours:* Muzik Award for Best New DJ 1997. *Address:* c/o Fabric, 77A Charterhouse Street, London EC1M 3HN, England (office). *Website:* www.fabriclondon.com (office).

FRANCOMBE, Mark; British musician (guitar, bass, keyboards); b. 4 Dec. 1963, Ongar, Essex, England. *Education:* Portsmouth Art Coll. *Career:* numerous tours of Europe and USA with the Cranes; also support tour with The Cure, USA and Europe, 1992; various radio and television appearances include: 2 sessions on John Peel show, BBC Radio 1; MTV; Snub TV, BBC. *Recordings include:* with The Cranes: Self Non Self, Wings of Joy, Forever Loved, Radio Oddyssey 1996, Population 4 1997. *Website:* www .markfrancombe.com.

FRANGLEN, Nick; British producer and musician; b. 1965. *Career:* fmr session musician, composer for film, television and advertisements; Founder-mem., Lemon Jelly 1997–; Founder-mem. Blacksand 2007–; producer for John Cale, Badly Drawn Boy, MD Nico. *Recordings include:* albums: with Lemon Jelly: LemonJelly.ky 2000, Lost Horizons 2002, '64–'95 2005, Make Things Right 2005, The Triptych 2007; with Blacksand: Barn 2008. *Address:* c/o Terra Artists Ltd, The Old Exchange, 234 South Church Road, , Southend-on-Sea, Essex, SS1 2EG, England. *Telephone:* (20) 8846-3737. *Fax:* (20) 8846-3738. *E-mail:* info@terraartists.com. *Website:* www.lemonjelly.ky.

FRANKIE J; Mexican singer, musician (piano), songwriter and record producer; b. (Francisco Javier Bautista, Jr), 7 Dec. 1975, Tijuana, Baja California. *Education:* Southwest Senior High School, San Diego, Calif., USA. *Career:* raised in San Diego, Calif., USA; first recordings issued as Frankie Boy 1997–99; mem. of group Kumbia Kings (as Cisco) 1999–2003; solo artist (as Frankie J) 2003–, several album releases in Spanish and English; collaborations with other artists including Baby Bash, Chamillionaire, Mannie Fresh, Pitbull, Omar Cruz; songwriter for JLS; Founder of own record label Soulsick Records; toured N America with Jennifer Lopez and Enrique Iglesias 2012. *Television:* RPM Miami 2011–. *Recordings:* albums: with Kumbia Kings: Amor, Familia Y Respeto 1999, Shhh! 2001, All Mixed Up 2002, 4 2003; solo: What's a Man to Do 2003, Frankie J 2003, The One 2005, Un Nuevo Dia 2006, Priceless 2006, Courage 2010, Faith, Hope y Amor 2013. *Address:* c/o Universal Music Latin Entertainment, Universal Music Group, 2220 Colorado Avenue, Santa Monica, CA 90401, USA (office). *Telephone:* (310) 865-5000 (office). *Website:* www.universalmusica.com/frankiej (office).

FRANKLIN, Aretha; American singer and songwriter; b. 25 March 1942, Memphis, Tenn.; d. of the late Rev. C. L. Franklin; m. 1st Ted White (divorced); m. 2nd Glynn Turman 1978 (divorced). *Career:* began singing in choir at New Bethel Baptist Church, Detroit, where her father was pastor. *Film appearances:* The Blues Brothers 1980, Blues Brothers 2000 1998. *Recordings include:* albums: The Great Aretha Franklin 1960, Aretha 1961, The Electrifying Aretha Franklin 1962, The Tender, the Moving, the Swinging Aretha Franklin 1962, Unforgettable: A Tribute to Dinah Washington 1964, The Gospel Sound Of Aretha Franklin 1964, Runnin' Out Of Fools 1965, Yeah!!! 1965, Soul Sister 1966, I Never Loved A Man (The Way I Loved You) 1967, Aretha Arrives 1967, Aretha: Lady Soul 1968, Aretha In Paris 1968, Aretha's Gold 1969, This Girl's in Love With You 1969, Spirit In The Dark 1970, Live At Fillmore West 1971, Young, Gifted And Black 1972, Amazing Grace 1972, Hey Now Hey (The Other Side Of The Sky) 1973, The First Twelve Sides 1973, Let Me In Your Life 1974, With Everything I Feel In Me 1974, You 1975, Sweet Passion 1977, Almighty Fire 1978, La Diva 1979, Aretha 1980, Love All The Hurt Away 1981, Jump To It 1982, Get It Right 1983, Who's Zoomin' Who? 1985, The First Lady Of Soul 1986, Aretha 1987, One Lord, One Faith, One Baptism 1988, Through The Storm 1989, What You See Is What You Sweat 1991, Jazz To Soul 1992, Queen Of Soul 1993, Aretha After Hours, Chain Of Fools 1993, Love Songs 1997, The Delta Meets Detroit 1998, A Rose Is Still A Rose 1998, You Grow Closer 1998, So Damn Happy 2003, Jewels in the Crown: All-Star Duets with the Queen 2007, Rare and Unreleased Recordings from the Golden Reign of the Queen of Soul 2007, A Woman Falling Out of Love 2008, This Christmas Aretha 2008, A Woman Falling Out of Love 2010. *Publication:* Aretha: From these Roots (with David Rib) 1999. *Honours:* numerous Grammy Awards, American Music Award 1984, NARAS Living Legend Award 1990, Rhythm and Blues Foundation Lifetime Achievement Award 1992, John F. Kennedy Center Award 1994; elected to Rock and Roll Hall of Fame (first woman) 1987, Lady of Soul Lena Horne Award for Outstanding Career Achievements 2005, Presidential Medal of Freedom 2005, Grammy Award for Best Traditional R&B Vocal Performance (for A House is Not a Home) 2006, United Negro Coll. Fund Award of Excellence 2006, inducted into Gospel Music Hall of Fame 2012, Icon Award, Billboard Women in Music 2014. *Address:* c/o Arista Records, 888 7th Avenue, New York, NY 10106, USA (office). *Telephone:* (212) 489-7400 (office). *Website:* www.jrecords.com (office).

FRANKLIN, Kirk; American singer, songwriter and record company executive; b. (Kirk Smith), 26 Jan. 1970, Fort Worth, Tex.; m.; one s. *Career:* Choir Dir Greater Strangers Rest Baptist Church, Fort Worth 1988; worked with Dallas-Fort Worth Mass Choir on albums I Will Not Let Nothing Separate Me 1991, Another Chance 1993; f. choir group The Family; f. record company Fo Yo Soul. *Film soundtrack contributions include:* My Life is in Your Hands (for Get on the Bus 1996), Joy (for The Preacher' Wife 1996). *Recordings include:* albums: with The Family: Kirk Franklin and The Family 1992, Christmas 1995, Watcha Lookin' 4 (Grammy Award for Best Contemporary Soul Gospel Album 1997) 1996; solo: God's Property from Kirk Franklin's Nu Nation (Grammy Award for Best Gospel Album by a choir or chorus 1998) 1997, The Nu Nation Project (Grammy Award for Best Contemporary Soul Gospel Album 1999) 1998, Kirk Franklin and the Family 2001, The Rebirth of Kirk Franklin 2002, Hero (Grammy Award for Best Contemporary R&B Gospel Album 2007) 2006, Songs from the Storm, Vol. 1 2006, The Fight of My Life (Grammy Award for Best Contemporary R&B Gospel Album 2009) 2007, Hello Fear (Grammy Award for Best Gospel Album 2012) 2011. *Publications include:* Church Boy: My Music and My Life (auto-biography) 1998, The Blueprint: A Plan for Living Above Life's Storms 2010. *Honours:* BET Award for Best Gospel Artist 2006, 2007, American Music Award for Favorite Contemporary Inspirational Artist 2006, Grammy Awards for Best Gospel Song (for Imagine Me) 2007, (for Help Me Believe) 2009, (for Hello Fear) 2012. *Current Management:* William Morris Agency, 1325 Avenue of the Americas, New York, NY 10019, USA. *Telephone:* (212) 586-5100. *Fax:* (212) 246-3583. *Website:* www.wma.com; www.kirkfranklin.us.

FRANOLIC, Drazen; Croatian musician (Arabian lute) and composer; b. 4 July 1961, Biograd; m. Vesna Gorse 1992. *Career:* mem. Franolic-Gorse Duo, Gorse-Franolic Trio, Tao; concerts worldwide; mem. Croatian Composers' Soc., Croatian Music Union, Amnesty International. *Recordings include:* with Vesna Gorse: Waterfalls 1986, New Era of Instrumental Music 1990, Wonderland 1990, Asgard Live 1993, Just A Music 1995; with Nimai Roy: Live in SC 2006, Live in Cabahia 2007, Live in Rijeka 2008; with Kamenko Culap: Cesma 2009, Bujrum 2012: solo: Molobadzi 2001, Live in Golubovec 2002. *Address:* Vankina 3/4, 41020 Zagreb, Croatia. *E-mail:* dfrancolic@ franolic-oud.com. *Website:* www.franolic-oud.com.

FRANZÉN, K. B. V. Hawkey; Swedish composer, singer, songwriter, artist and actor and musician (guitar, keyboard, accordion, tenor saxophone); b. 29 March 1946, Böda, Kalmarlän. *Career:* mem. Lea Riders Group 1962–68, Jason's Fleece 1970–71; solo performer, Theatremusic-composer and for radio and TV; film music, Dom Kallar Oss Mods (They Call Us Misfits); mem. Swedish Performing Rights Soc., Swedish Soc. of Popular Music Composers, Swedish Artists and Musicians Interest Org., Svenska Teaterförbundet, Swedish Actors Equity Asscn. *Recordings include:* Lea Riders Group 1989, Många Varv Kring Solen 1996, Stig Dagerman 2005. *Honours:* Stockholm City, Prize for Best Private Theatre Play 1969, Konstnärsnämnden, Arts Grants Cttee Scholarships 1971, 1975, 1985, 1986, 1989, 1990, 1992, 1993, 1996, 1997, 1998, 2003, 2004, STIM, Swedish Performing Rights Soc. 1995, 1997, Culture Prize of Ödeshög 2009. *Address:* Nygatan 5 nb, 599 31 Ödeshög, Sweden. *E-mail:* hawkey@telia.com. *Website:* www.hawkey.se.

FRANZETTI, Carlos; American composer and conductor; b. 1948, Buenos Aires, Argentina. *Education:* Conservatório Nacional de Buenos Aires, Juilliard School, New York. *Career:* jazz and classical composer; compositions performed at Teatro Colón, with Orquesta de la Plata, Boston Pops Orchestra, Nat. Symphony Orchestra, Washington, DC, St Louis Symphony, Brooklyn Philharmonic, Buffalo Philharmonic, Nat. Symphony of Mexico, Nat. Symphony of Argentina, Orquesta Filarmónica de Buenos Aires, Czech Nat. Symphony, City of Prague Philharmonic, Modus Chamber Orchestra, Janáček Philharmonic, Bratislava Radio Orchestra, orchestras in Mexico, Venezuela, Spain, Sweden, Norway and France. *Compositions include:* Gauchito and the Pony (children's opera), Concierto del Plata for guitar and chamber ensemble, Millennium Concerto for flute and orchestra, Piano Concerto No. 2, Sinfonia No. 1. *Recordings include:* Tropic of Capricorn 1993, Portraits of Cuba with Paquito d'Rivera (Latin Grammy Award for Best Latin Jazz Album) 1997, Remembrances 1999, Obsesión 1999, Tango Fatal (Latin Grammy Award for Best Tango Album) 2001, Tango Bar 2002, Poeta de Arrabal 2003, You Make Believe in Spring 2004, Reflexiones 2004, Promises Kept 2004, Corpus Evita: An Opera in Two Acts 2005, Carlos Franzetti and the Jazz Kamerata 2005, Songs for Lovers 2006, Graffiti 2007, Duets with Eddie Gomez (Latin Grammy Award for Best Instrumental Album) 2009, Mambo Tango 2009, Galaxy Dust, Alborada, Pierrot et Colombine. *Publication:* The Cuchifrito Circuit and Other Stories 2009. *Honours:* Yamaha Composers Award, Trofeu Laus, Spain, Clio Award, Pensario Award, Premio Konex, Argentina. *Address:* 14 Dartmouth Road, Cranford, NJ 07016, USA (office). *Telephone:* (908) 709-0937 (office). *Fax:* (908) 709-0938 (office). *E-mail:* yumba@aol.com. *Website:* www.carlosfranzetti.com.

FRASER, Brooke; New Zealand singer; b. 15 Dec. 1983, Wellington; d. of Bernie and Lynda Fraser. *Career:* fmr tv presenter; fmr writer and Ed., Soul Purpose Magazine; solo artist 2002–; currently based in Australia; worship leader and collaborator, Hillsong United series of worship albums; Amb. for charitable orgs World Vision, Opportunity Int. *Recordings:* albums: What To Do With Daylight 2003, Albertine 2007. *Honours:* Best Female Solo Artist and Breakthrough Artist of the Year, NZ Music Awards 2004, APRA Silver Scroll Award 2007. *Current Management:* CRS Music Management Ltd., Level 1, 2 Hakanoa Street, Grey Lynn, Auckland, New Zealand. *Telephone:* (9) 361-3967. *E-mail:* info@crsmanagement.co.nz. *Website:* www.crsmanagement.co.nz; www.brookefraser.com (home).

FRASER, Elizabeth; British singer; b. 29 Aug. 1963, Grangemouth, Scotland; one d. *Career:* founder mem., Cocteau Twins 1981–98; sang on collective projects with This Mortal Coil; collaboration with pianist Harold Budd; guest appearances with Ian McCulloch on Candleland album, with Future Sound of London on Lifeforms, with Massive Attack on Teardrop single and tracks on their Mezzanine album. *Recordings include:* albums: Garlands 1982, Head Over Heels 1983, Treasure 1984, The Pink Opaque 1985, Victorialand 1986, The Moon and the Melodies (with Harold Budd) 1986, Blue Bell Knoll 1988, Heaven or Las Vegas 1990, Four Calendar Café 1993, Milk and Kisses 1996, The BBC Sessions 1999, Stars and Topsoil (compilation) 2000. *E-mail:* michael@etherweave.com. *Website:* www.cocteautwins.com.

FRAZIER, Charles Stanton (Stan); American musician (drums); b. 23 April 1968. *Career:* fmr mem. local group, The Tories, renamed The Shrinky Dinx, signed to Atlantic Records and renamed Sugar Ray. *Recordings include:* albums: Lemonade and Brownies 1995, Floored 1997, 14–59 1999, Sugar Ray 2001, In Pursuit of Leisure 2003, Music for Cougars 2009. *Address:* PO Box 6188, Olympia, WA 98507, USA. *E-mail:* stan@sugarray.com. *Website:* www.sugarray.com.

FREDDY, Faada; Senegalese hip-hop artist and musician (guitar); b. (Abdou Fatha Seck). *Career:* mem., Daara J 1997–. *Recordings include:* albums: Daara J 1998, Xalima 1999, Boomerang 2003, School of Life 2010. *Honours:* BBC Radio 3 World Music Award for Best African Act 2004. *Current Management:* Traffixmusic, 130 avenue Pasteur, 93170 Bagnolet, France. *Telephone:* 1-48-51-30-81. *E-mail:* alice@traffixmusic.com. *Website:* www.traffixmusic.com; www.wrasserecords.com.

FREDERICKX, Jan, (JAN AG); Belgian singer, songwriter and musician (bass guitar, guitar); b. 30 Sept. 1971, Mol. *Education:* Music Acad., Geel. *Career:* mem. Agathocles 1985–; other projects include Jan Ag, Bloodred Bacteria, Etterbek, Fahrenheit AGX, The Gajna, Ulcerrhoea; also played in bands including Hellsaw, MSD, Extrem, Acoustic Grinder; concerts with Napalm Death, Extreme Noise Terror, The Varukers, Death, The Gathering, Doom, Kuolema, Anarchus, and others. *Recordings include:* with Agathocles: Theatric Symolisation of Life 1991, Black Clouds Determinate 1994, Razor Sharp Daggers 1995, Thanks for your Hostility 1996, Humarrogance 1997, To Serve… To Protect 1999, Superiority Overdose 2001, Mincer 2006, Grind is Protest 2008; EPs: Riek Boois 1988, Disgorge 1989, Violent Noise Attack 1990, Fascination Of Mutilation 1989, If This Is Cruel 1989–90, Blood 1990, Smegma 1990, Putrid Offal 1990, Cabbalic Gnosticism 1988, Morbid Organs Mutilation 1989–90, Agarchy 1991, Psycho 1989–90, Violent Headache 1992, Kompost 1993, Distrust and Abuse 1993, Nyctophobic 1993, Punisher 1993–94, Nasum 1990, Man Is The Bastard 1993, Patareni 1993, Audiorrea 1993, Social Genocide 1993, Carcass Grinder 1994, Plastic Grave 1994, Rot 1994, No Use… (Hatred) 1993, Unholy Grave 1996, Autoritar 1996, Back To 1987 1994, Preparation H 1996, Krush 1996, Mincemongers In Barna 1994, Excruciating Terror 1997, Shikabane 1997, Bad Acid Trip 1993, Bwf 1997, Smash The Brain 1993, Abstain 1997, D.I.E. 1997, Bloodsuckers 1998, PP7 Gaftzeb 1997, Black Army Jacket 1996, Grind Buto 1999, Abortion 1997–99, Monolith 1997, Looking For An Answer 1997, Embalming Theatre 1999, Disreanti………. 1999, Kontatto 2000, Worship 1999, Mitten Spider 1997, Sterbehilfe 1989-1999, Malignant Tumour 1997, Depressor 1998, Din Addict 1999, Urban Struggle 1998, Jan Ag 1998/2002, Godstomper 1989, Siviil Imurha 2003, Keep Mincing 1988, Les Baudoins Morts 2002, Gotcha 1998, The Mad Thrashers 2003, Front Beast 2003, Rot In Pieces 2003, Fat Ass Fuckers 2003, The Usual Suspects 2003, Kuolema 2003, The Gajna 1989/2002, Kadaverficker 2003, Bloodred Bacteria 2003, Mucus 1999, Permanent Death 1987, Fahrenheit AGX 1996/2005, Archagatus 1996, Sakatat 2002, Proud To Be Out 2002/2006, Self Made God 2002, Bestial Vomit 2007, Occult 1985, Gorgonized Dorks 1993, Desecrator 2003, Avulsion 2007, Heamophagus 2007, Repulsione 2007, Seven Minutes Of Nausea (split 7" EP) 2007, Fucked By The State (split 7" EP) 2007, Pos Split 2008, The Lettuce Vultures 2004, Hunt Hunters 1998, VRV 2007, Disleksick 2001, Tinner 2007, Minced In Piracicaba, Brazil, 2007 2007, Tsubo 2009, Insomnia Isterica 2009, Sissy Spacek 2009, Black September 2009, Painful Defloration 1997/1999, Semtex 10 1997, Thedead 1998, Violent Gorge 2008; double EPs: Live and Noisy 1997, Keep Mincing 1988, Hunt Hunters 1998, Peel Sessions 1997; LPs: Drudge 1989, Lunatic Invasion 1989–91, Cliché? 1992, Use Your Anger 1988–92, Averno 1992–93, Thanks For Your Hostility 1996, Vomit Fall 1996, Minced Alive 1992–93, Humarrogance 1997, Deadmocracy 1998, Disculpa 1999, Unholy Grave 1999, Mince Core 1989–98, Bomb Brussels 1996, Razor Sharp Daggers 1995, Live In Gierle/Keep Mincing 1988/1989, Superiority Overdose 2001, Depression 1997, Agatho-Grave 2002, Mincer 2005, Roger Moore 2006, Gorgonized Dorks 1993, Grind Is Protest 2008, Obey Their Rules 2007/2008, Cyanamid 1995, Matadores Del Libertad 2007, Abrir Las Puertas 2007, King Terror 2009, Black Clouds Determinate 1994, This Is Not A Threat, It's A Promise 2010; double LPs: Theatric Symbolisation of Life 1988–91, Black Clouds Determinate 1993–94; CDs: Theatric Symbolisation of Life 1988–91,

Black Clouds Determinate 1993–94, Averno 1992–93, Razor Sharp Daggers 1993–95, The LP's: 1989–1991 1989–91, Thanks for Your Hostility 1996, Agarchy/Use Your Anger 1991–92, Depression 1997, Humarrogance 1997, Humarrogance/The Dark Ages Revived 1997, Nuclear Devastation 1997, Scrawl/7 Mon 1997, Until It Bleeds 1994–97, Suppository 1998, Humarrogance/Live 1992–97, Irritate/Nyab 1997, Mince Core 1989–98, Comrades 1998, To Serve… To Protect 1999, Live In Leipzig, 1991 1991, Mince Core History 1989–1993 1989–93, CHC 1996, Din Addict 1999, Maligant Tumour/Abortion/Din Addict 1999, Bomb Brussels 1996, Mince Core History 1985–1990 1985–90, Until It Bleeds Again 1994–99, Axed Up Conformist 1997, Keep Mincing 1988, Superiority Overdose 2001, Ravage/Comrades 1998, Live In Gierle, 1989 1989, To Serve… To Protect/Leads To… 1999/2000, Unholy Grave 2002, Stomachal Corrosion 1998, Mincemania In Bulgaria 1989-2003, World Downfall 2003, Alive And Mincing 2000, Dios Hastio 2003, Siviil Imurha 2003, Superiority Overdose Live 2002 (DVD 2002), Mince Core History 1993–1996 1993–96, Fahrenheit AGX 2003/2005, Venereal Disease 1998, Mincer 2005, H 407 1997, Brutal Market 2002, Theatric Symbolisation Of Life And Live 1990/1991, Senseless Trip 1993, Drudge 1989, Ruido Grind 1991–2001, Depresy Mouse 2006, Intestinal Infection 2007, Saul Turteltaub 2007, Mince Core History 1996–1997 1996–97, Untamed 2006, Vanishing Act 2007, Torture Incident 2007, Noisebazooka 1994, Amoclen 2007, Slaughtergrave 2007, Dissected 2007, Armatura 2007, Cu Sujo 2007, Motherpig 2002, Jack/Mizar 2002, Crowd Control 2007, Dios Hastio/The Gajna 2003, Grind Is Protest 2008, Live In Arica, Chile 2007, I Hope You Suffer 2007, Grind Bashers 2007, Gatt 1995, Live In Gierle/Keep Mincing 1988/1989, Reds At The Mountains Of Death 2008, Generation Spasfon 2008, Vegativ 1993, Simbiose 2007, Peel Sessions 1997, Hierarchical Punishment/Forbidden Ideas 2007, Obey Their Rules 2007, This is Not a Threat, It's a Promise 2010, Cliché/Pressure 1992/1998, Mince Core History 1997–1999. *Radio:* (with Agathocles) BRT Session 1996, Peel Session (BBC Radio 1) 1997. *Television:* Rock Hard Brazil show (Agathocles) 2007. *E-mail:* mincemania@hotmail.com (office). *Website:* www.agathocles.com; www.myspace.com/agathocles.

FREDERIKSEN, Lars; American musician (guitar) and singer; b. 1972; m. Megan Frederiksen 1998. *Career:* mem., UK Subs, Cajones; Founder , Slip 1992; mem., Rancid; numerous live shows; mem., Lars Frederiksen and the Bastards. *Recordings include:* albums: with Rancid: Rancid 1993, Let's Go 1994, And Out Come The Wolves 1995, Life Won't Wait 1998, Rancid 2000, Indestructible 2003, Let the Dominoes Fall 2009; with Lars Frederiksen and the Bastards: Lars Frederiksen and the Bastards 2001, Viking 2004; with Tim Timebomb and Friends: Tim Timebomb and Friends 2012. *Address:* c/o HellCat Records, 2798 Sunset Blvd, Los Angeles, CA 90026, USA. *E-mail:* info@hell-cat.com. *Website:* www.hell-cat.com; www.rancidrancid.com.

FREDRIKSSON, Marie; Swedish singer; b. 29 May 1958; one d. *Career:* solo artist 1980s; Founder-mem., Roxette 1984–; numerous TV and radio broadcasts, live appearances world-wide. *Recordings include:* albums: Pearls Of Passion, 1986; Look Sharp!, 1988; Joyride, 1991; Tourism, 1992; Den Sjunde Vagen, 1992; Den Standiga Resa, 1993; Efter Stormen, 1993; Mammas Barn 1993; Crash! Boom! Bang!, 1994; Het Vind, 1995; Balades en Español, 1996; Have A Nice Day, 1999; Room Service, 2001, The Ballad Hits 2002, The Pop Hits 2002, The Rox Box 2006, Charm School 2011, Travelling 2012; solo: The Change 2004, Min bäste vän 2006, Tid för tystnad 2007, Nu 2012. *Honours:* Grammy Awards, MTV Awards, Medal of Achievement from King Carl XVI Gustaf of Sweden 2003. *Current Management:* c/o Dimberg Management, Ölandsgatan 42, 116 63 Stockholm, Sweden. *E-mail:* marie@dimberg.com. *Website:* www.dndmanagement.com; www.mariefredriksson.se; www.roxette.se.

FREELAND, Adam; British producer, remixer and DJ; b. 1974, London. *Career:* Founder Marine Parade Records, Friction club night (pioneering the Nu-Skool Breakbeat sound); world-wide DJ; remixed Pressure Drop, Aquasky, BT; mem. Tsunami One; collaborations with Kevin Beber. *Recordings include:* albums (DJ-mixed compilations): Coastal Breaks #1 1997, Coastal Breaks #2 1998, Tectonics 2000, On Tour 2001, FabricLive.16 2004, Global Underground 032: Mexico City 2007, Two Hours to Jupiter 2007; solo: Now and Them 2003, Cope 2010. *Address:* c/o Hope Management, The Paintworks, Unit 4.16, Bath Road, Bristol BS4 3EH, England (office). *E-mail:* steve@hopemanagement.com; lizzy@marineparade.net (office). *Website:* www.marineparade.co.uk; www.freeland.fm.

FREELON, (Chinyere) Nnenna; American jazz singer; b. 28 July 1954, Cambridge, Mass; m.; three c. *Education:* Simmons Coll. *Career:* fmrly worked in health services in Durham, North Carolina; performed with Ellis Marsalis; spokeswoman, Nat. Asscn of Partners in Educ. *Recordings include:* albums: Nnenna Freelon 1992, Heritage 1993, Listen 1994, Shaking Free 1996, Maiden Voyage 1998, Soulcall 2000, Tales Of Wonder 2002, Church: Songs Of Soul And Inspiration 2003, Blueprint of a Lady 2005, Better than Anything 2008, Home Free 2010, Christmas 2012. *Honours:* Eubie Blake Award, Billie Holiday Award. *Current Management:* c/o Ed Keane, Ed Keane Associates, 573 Pleasant Street, Winthrop, MA 02152, USA. *Telephone:* (617) 846-0067. *Fax:* (617) 846-1767. *E-mail:* info@edkeane.com. *Website:* www.edkeane.com; www.nnenna.com.

FREEMAN, Matt; American musician (bass) and singer; b. 1966, Albany, New York. *Career:* Founder-mem., Operation Ivy 1987; mem., MDC 1990; Founder-mem., Rancid. *Recordings include:* albums: Rancid 1993, Let's Go 1994, And Out Come The Wolves 1995, Life Won't Wait 1998, Rancid 2000,

Indestructible 2003, Let the Dominoes Fall 2009. *Address:* c/o HellCat Records, 2798 Sunset Blvd, Los Angeles, CA 90026, USA (office). *E-mail:* info@hell-cat.com. *Website:* www.hell-cat.com; www.rancidrancid.com.

FREHLEY, Paul Daniel (Ace); American musician (guitar); b. 22 April 1951, Bronx, New York. *Career:* mem. rock group, Kiss 1973–82; numerous tours worldwide; Founder, Frehley's Comet 1987–. *Recordings include:* albums: with Kiss: Kiss 1974, Dressed To Kill 1975, Alive! 1975, Destroyer 1976, The Originals 1976, Rock and Roll Over 1976, Kiss Alive II 1977, Love Gun 1977, Double Platinum 1978, Dynasty 1979, Kiss Unmasked 1980, Music From The Elder 1981, Killers 1982, Creatures of the Night 1982; solo: Ace Frehley 1978, Trouble Walking 1989, Anomaly 2009; with Frehley's Comet: Frehley's Comet 1987, Live + 1 1988, Second Sighting 1989, 12 Picks 1998, Loaded Deck 1998. *Current Management:* c/o Dave Frey, Red Light Management, 44 Wall Street, 22nd Floor, NY 10005 USA. *E-mail:* acefrehley@redlightmanagement.com. *Website:* www.redlightmanagement.com; www.acefrehley.com.

FRENGEL, Mike, BA, MA, PhD; American composer and guitarist; b. 20 Jan. 1972, Mountain View, California. *Education:* San Jose State Univ., Dartmouth Coll., City Univ., London, England. *Career:* participant as composer/performer in int. contemporary music festivals 1990–; early internet broadcast of electro-acoustic music at ArtNet Concert, San Jose State Univ. 1995; Assoc. Academic Specialist, Northeastern Univ.; mem American Composer's Forum (ACF),. Int. Computer Music Asscn (ICMA), Soc. for Electro-Acoustic Music in the United States (SEAMUS), Broadcast Music Inc (BMI); founder and board mem Electronic Arts Focus, London. *Compositions include:* Three Short Stories 1995, Rock Music 1996, Long Slender Heels 1998, Variations on an Already Complex Theme No 1 1998, Dropped On My Head, Upside Down 1999, And Then, Romina…2000, The Three Faces of Karen Black 2001, Slinky 2004, Hotbird 2010, Gesture Frames 2012. *Recordings:* ICMC'97 Hong Kong; CDCM Vol. 26; Sonic Circuits VII; Luigi Russolo, 2000, ICMC 2009. *Publications:* contribs to New Grove Dictionary of American Musicians 1999, The Oxford Handbook of Interactive Audio 2011, Encyclopedia of American Music and Culture 2011. *Honours:* Luigi Russolo Prize 2000. *Address:* Northeastern University Department of Music, 351 Ryder Hall, Boston, MA 02115, USA (office). *E-mail:* m.frengel@neu.edu (office). *Website:* www.mikefrengel.com.

FRESU, Paolo; Italian musician (trumpet, flugelhorn), arranger and composer; b. 10 Feb. 1961, Berchidda, Sardinia. *Education:* Conservatory of Music Cagliari, Sardinia, DAMS Faculty, Univ. of Bologna. *Career:* Prof., Siena Jazz Nat. Seminars 1985–; Jazz Univ. courses at Terni 1987–; winter courses at Siena and seminars in Nuoro 1989–; guest soloist at numerous innovative jazz recording projects; Artistic Dir, Time in Jazz Festival, Berchidda 1988–; Eurojazz Concorso Internazionale per Giovani Musicisti Europei', Oristano 1994, Jazz Seminary, Nuoro 1989–; performs contemporary, ancient, ethnic and world music; directs own quintet, also duos, trio, quartets and performs with several artists. *Dance:* Verdi Colline by Paolo Damiani, Rome 1984, A Mar Mediterraneo by Flavia Buccero-Movimentinactor, Pisa and Sassari 1993, Ogni donna una sera diversa by Giorgio Rossi/Sosta Palmizi with Furio Di Castri, Turin 1994, Anaglifo by Roberto Zappalà/Balletto di Sicilia, Messina 1996–97, Janas, Sassari 1997, composed for the Chamber Orchestra of Bologna, the Quartetto Internos, the singer Tomasella Calvisi and the choir Su Cuncordu 'e su Rosariu by Santu Lussurgiu for the ASMED with choreography by Enrica Palmieri and arrangement by Claudio Scannavini, Lacrime di vetro by Rita Spadola and Carla Onnis, Berchidda and Cagliari 2001, Casi e analogie with Giorgio Rossi/Sosta Palmizi and the trio PAF, Rome 2002, collaboration with Nathalie Cornille, Faches Thumesnil (France) 2002, Calais (France) 2003 and again in duo with Giorgio Rossi 2006–. *Live soundtracks:* La Fanciulla di Amalfi 1989, Silent Movie 1992, Fiere 1998 and others. *Compositions:* Verdi Colline 1984, A Mar Mediterraneo 1993, Ogni donna una sera diversa 1994, Anaglifo 1996, Janas 1997, Lacrime di vetro 2001, Casi e analogie 2002. *Recordings:* Ostinato 1985, Inner Voices 1986, Mämût 1987, Live in Montpellier 1988, Qvarto 1988, Opale 1989, Ossi di Seppia 1991, Maiakowski, il 13° Apostolo 1991, Ballads 1992, Urlo 1994, Ensalada Mistica 1994, Mythscapes 1995, Night on the City (Choc des choc Award, Jazzman 1995, named as one of the 100 CDs of the 20th century, Jazzman 2004) 1995, Contos 1995, 6 x 30 1996, Wanderlust 1997, Angel (Award of the French magazine Télérama) 1998, Condaghes (Trio Paolo Fresu-Erik Marchand-Jacques Pellen) (Choc Award, Le Monde de la Musique) 1998, Metamorfosi 1999, Shades of Chet 1999 (Musica Jazz Arrigo Polillo Award 2000), Berchidda 1999, Mélos (Choc des choc Award, Jazzman, Django d'Or for Best Int. Musician 2001) 2000, Fellini 2000, Night on the City 2001, Evening Song 2001, Sonos 'e Memoria (Choc Award, Le Monde de la Musique) 2001, Paolo Fresu Limited Edition (Award at Olympia of Paris) 2002, Kind of Porgy and Bess 2002, Here be Changes Made 2002, Scores! 2003, Live in Studio 2004, Ethnografie 2004, Morph 2004, Kosmopolites 2005, Te Lo Leggo Negli Occhi 2005, P.A.R.T.E. 2005, Incantamento 2006, Things 2006, Thinking 2006, Rosso, Verde, Giallo e Blu 2007, Mare Nostrum (with Richard Galliano and Jan Lundgren) 2007. *Film:* 365 (dir Roberto Minini-Meròt) 2013. *Radio:* Un certo discorso for RadioTre (RAI) with Orchestra of Bruno Tommaso 1982, Risultanze for the festival AudioBox-RadioTre, Matera 1990, production of the European Jazz Award for German Radio of Baden Baden 1992, Nordic Meeting 2000, Göteborg 2000, recordings for Italian Nat. Radio and several foreign radio stations (Che tempo che fa, Geo, Quark, Invasioni Barbariche, Il Caffè, Concerto di Natale 2008, Prix Italia 2008,

Primo maggio 2009, SuperQuark, Sostiene Bollani, L'Infedele etc.) 2003–. *Television:* produced Progetto Fauré for Swiss German TV, Zurich with the Treya Quartet 2002, Operazione Kebab directed by Enrico Carlesi for RaiTrade, recorded with Dhafer Youssef, Teo Ciavarella and Sonia Peana 2002. *Publications include:* The first 63 jazz compositions 1989, 49 compositions 1996, Paolo Fresu si racconta 1996, Paolo Fresu, un Sardegna il Jazz 2005. *Honours:* Hon. Citizen, City of Nuoro 2000, City of Junas (France) 2003, City of Sogliano 2006, City of Sogliano 2006, Mamuthones ad honorem Award from the City of Mamoiada (Italy) 2006; Hon. mem. Confraternita del Vermentino, Berchidda 2010; hon. degrees from Università la Bicocca, Milan 2013, Berklee School of Music, Boston, Perugia 2015; Award for Best New Talent of Italian Jazz, Musica Jazz magazine and RadioUno Jazz (RAI) 1984, Award form Radio Corriere TV magazine 1985, Award 'Città di Alassio' 1985, Award for Best Italian Musician, Best Band (Paolo Fresu Quintet) and Best Recording 'Live in Montpellier', Musica Jazz 1990, Acknowledgment from Pres. of Regional Bd of Sardinia for his artistic activities 1991, Award 'Bobby Jaspar', Académie du jazz magazine 1995, Award 'Concorso Golfo degli Angeli/Lyon', Cagliari 1995, Django d'Or for Best Jazz Musician 1996, Award 'Città di Ozieri' 1996, Award 'Accademia Mozart', Taranto 1996, Award 'Arrigo Polillo' (Musica Jazz) for Best Italian Recording 'Shades of Chet' for the French Django d'Or 2000, Award for Best Int. Musician, with Keith Jarrett and Charlie Haden 2000, Django d'Or for Best Musician 2002, Award 'Roma c'è' 2002, Award 'Banari Arte' 2003, Award 'Nastri d'Argento' for film soundtrack of L'Isola by Costanza Quatriglio 2004, Award 'Porto Rotondo' for his career 2005, Award 'Otocha', Santa Giusta (OR) 2007, Award 'Navicella d'argento', Castelsardo 2007, Award Cala di Volpe, Porto Cervo 2008, Award Manniron, Rome 2008, Award Chatwin, Genoa 2008, Award Mario/SconfinArt, Suzzara 2009, Candeliere d'oro, Sassari 2009, Award 'Roccella Jonica 30 anni', Roccella Jonica 2010, Award Maria Carta, Siligo (SS) 2010, China Awards 2010, Milan Award 2011, Amnesty International Award 2011, Ittiri Award 2011, Sorradile Award for Tuk Music, Faenza 2011, Award 'B.A. Film Festival' for film soundtrack of Il mio Domani by Marina Spada 2012, Tempio Pausania Award 2012, Opening Award, Olbia 2012, Iglesias Award 2012. *Current Management:* c/o Pannonica Music, 22/B Corso Italia, 39100 Bolzano, Italy. *Telephone:* (0471) 400193. *E-mail:* info@pannonica.it. *Website:* www.pannonica.it. *E-mail:* infopaolofresu@gmail.com (office). *Website:* www.paolofresu.it.

FRETWELL, Stephen; British singer and songwriter; b. 1981, Scunthorpe. *Career:* formed band Label; moved to Manchester to pursue solo career 2000; support act for Travis, Elbow, Athlete, Keane, KT Tunstall, Oasis. *Recordings include:* albums: Magpie 2004, Man on the Roof 2007. *Address:* c/o Fiction/Polydor, 72 Black Lion Lane, London W6 9BE, England (office). *Website:* www.stephenfretwell.com.

FREU, Jean-Philippe; French musician (guitar). *Career:* mem. Rinôçérôse 1994–. *Recordings include:* albums: Retrospective 1998, Installation Sonore 1999, Music Kills Me 2002, Schizophonia 2005, Rinôçérôse 2006, Futurinô 2009. *Current Management:* c/o Pascal Sanchez, P Pole Agency, 1 bis rue de verdun, 3400 Montpellier, France. *Telephone:* (4) 67 12 81 70. *Address:* c/o V2 France, 17 rue Bouchardon, 75010 Paris, France. *E-mail:* matthieu.couturier@v2music.com. *Website:* www.rinocerose.com.

FRICKE, Janie; American country singer; b. 19 Dec. 1947, South Whitley, Ind.; m. Jeff Steele. *Education:* Indiana Univ. *Career:* fmr session singer in Los Angeles; mem. Lea Jane Singers, Nashville; solo artist. *Recordings include:* albums: Singer of Songs 1978, Love Notes 1979, From the Heart 1980, I'll Need Someone to Hold me When I Cry 1981, Nice 'n' Easy (with Johnny Duncan) 1980, Sleeping with Your Memory 1981, It Ain't Easy 1982, Love Lies 1983, The First Word in Memory is Me 1984, Someone Else's Fire 1985, Black and White 1986, After Midnight 1987, Saddle the Wind 1988, Labor of Love 1989, Janie Fricke 1991, Crossroads 1992, Now and Then 1993, Bouncin' Back 2000, Tributes to My Heroes 2002, Roses and Lace 2008, Country Side of Bluegrass 2010. *E-mail:* shelley@entertainmentevolution.net. *Website:* www.entertainmentevolution.net. *Address:* c/o Janie Fricke Concerts, PO Box 798, Lancaster, TX 75146, USA (office). *Website:* www.janiefricke.com.

FRIDAY, Gavin; Irish singer and songwriter; b. (Fionán Hanvey), 8 Oct. 1959, Dublin. *Career:* Founding mem. The Virgin Prunes 1977–86; solo artist 1991–; film appearance in Breakfast on Pluto 2005. *Composition for film:* In the Name of the Father (co-writer), Angel Baby 1996, The Boxer 1997, In America 2003, Get Rich or Die Tryin' 2005. *Recordings include:* albums: with Virgin Prunes: If I Die I Die 1982, The Hidden Lie 1986, Sons Find Devils 1998; solo: Each Man Kills The Thing He Loves 1990, Adam and Eve 1992, Shag Tobacco 1995, Peter and the Wolf 2002, Catholic 2011. *E-mail:* contact@gavinfriday.com (office). *Website:* www.gavinfriday.com.

FRIDMANN, Dave; American producer and musician (bass guitar). *Career:* founding mem. and original bass player, experimental rock group Mercury Rev, Buffalo, New York in mid-1980s; Mercury Rev began as composers of soundtracks for experimental films, made first recordings at State Univ. of New York, Fredonia; retired from live performing to concentrate on studio production work 1993, continued to work on all Mercury Rev's studio recordings; co-producer on most albums by The Flaming Lips; set up Tarbox recording studio; producer or mix engineer on recordings by artists including Dan Berggren, Weezer, Saxon Shore, Ammonia, Ed Harcourt, Sparklehorse, Café Tacuba, Elf Power, Mogwai, Thursday, The Delgados, Low, Phantom Planet, Gemma Hayes, Dot Allison, Goldrush, Number Girl, Sleater-Kinney, Clap Your Hands Say Yeah, MGMT, Tapes 'n' Tapes, Tame Impala, OK Go, Neil Finn, The Vaccines. *Recordings include:* with Mercury Rev: Yerself Is Steam 1991, Boces 1993, See You on the Other Side 1995, Deserter's Songs (NME magazine Album of the Year) 1998, All Is Dream 2001, The Secret Migration 2005, Hello Blackbird (soundtrack to film Bye Bye Blackbird) 2006, Snowflake Midnight 2008; with The Flaming Lips: In a Priest Driven Ambulance 1990, Hit to Death in the Future Head 1992, Clouds Taste Metallic 1995, Zaireeka 1997, The Soft Bulletin 1999, Yoshimi Battles the Pink Robots 2002, At War with the Mystics 2006, Christmas on Mars 2008, Embryonic 2009. *Current Management:* c/o Breathing Protection, Inc., PO Box 1991, New York, NY 10013-0873, USA. *Telephone:* (917) 674-5514. *Fax:* (425) 790-7136. *Website:* www.breathingprotection.com; www.tarboxroadstudios.com (office); www.mercuryrev.net; www.davefridmann.com.

FRIED, Gerald, BS; American composer, conductor and musician (oboe); b. 13 Feb. 1928, New York, NY; three s. one d. *Education:* Juilliard School. *Career:* jazz saxophonist, New York 1945–51; Principal Oboe, English Horn, Dallas Symphony, Pittsburgh Symphony, New York Little Orchestra, Los Angeles Philharmonic 1948–59; composer, conductor, arranger on numerous motion pictures, TV and mini series, theatre works, operas and albums; mem. AMPAS; ASCAP; ATAS; SGA. *Compositions:* scores for motion pictures include: Birds Do It, Bees Do It; Whatever Happened to Aunt Alice; One Spy Too Many; One of Our Spies Is Missing; The Cabinet of Dr Caligari; A Cold Wind in August; Cast A Long Shadow; Machine Gun Kelly; Paths of Glory; The Killing; Blood Money; Fear and Desire; Animation: The Great Rights; Scores for numerous mini series and TV pilots and series including Flamingo Road; Roots; Police Woman; Star Trek; The Man from UNCLE; The Mouse That Roared; Gunsmoke; Rawhide; Symphonic suites for Roots; The Bell Jar; The Mystic Warrior; Time Travel for oboe and orchestra. *Recordings:* Vampire Circus; Return of Dracula; The five early Stanley Kubrick films; Star Trek Vol. 1; Roots 1978; More Music from The Man from UNCLE; The Cabinet of Dr Caligari; The Mystic Warrior; Sounds of the Night, with Johnny Mercer. *Honours:* Emmy Award 1977, UCLA Teacher of the Year Award 1992.

FRIED, Joshua, BA; American composer and performance artist; b. 8 July 1969, Los Angeles, Calif. *Education:* Cornell Univ. *Career:* pioneer of headphone-driven performance, musical shoes activated by electronics; remixed works by They Might Be Giants, Chaka Khan and Ofra Haza; work presented at New Music America, Israel Festival, ICC Tokyo, Café de la Danse, Lincoln Centre, Dutch Royal Palace, Knitting Factory, The Kitchen, Limelight, Irving Plaza, La MaMa Experimental Theatre; visiting composer, Yale Univ., Bucknell Univ. 1997. *Exhibition:* Group Sound Art Exhbn, Constriction, New York 1996. *Recordings:* New Live Dub 1985, Jimmy Because (My Name Is) (single) 1987, Hello The Band 1993, Insane (single) 1996. *Honours:* Nat. Endowment for Educ. Composers Fellowship 1994, New York Foundation for the Arts Fellowship 1995, American Composers Forum Comm. 1996, Rockefeller Foundation Residency 1997, Grand Prize, Danish Radio Competition in Sound 1997, MacDowell Colony Fellowship 1997, Yaddo Residency 1998, youngest composer in Schirmer Books' American Music in the 20th Century. *Address:* 277 North 7th Street, Apt 4R, Brooklyn, NY 11211, USA (office). *Website:* composer.home.acedsl.com; radiowonderland.com.

FRIEND, Simon; British singer and musician (guitar, mandolin, harmonica). *Career:* mem., The Levellers 1990–; numerous concerts, festival appearances. *Recordings include:* albums: Weapon Called The Word 1990, Levelling The Land 1991, See Nothing, Hear Nothing, Do Something 1993, Levellers 1993, Zeitgeist 1995, Mouth To Mouth 1997, Special Brew 2000, Hello Pig 2000, Green Blade Rising 2002, Truth & Lies 2005, Letters from the Underground 2008, Static on the Airwaves 2012. *Address:* c/o The Levellers, PO Box 29, Winkleigh, Devon, EX19 8WE, England. *E-mail:* info@levellers.co.uk. *Website:* www.levellers.co.uk.

FRIPP, Robert; British musician (guitar), composer and producer; b. 16 May 1946, Wimborne, Dorset; m. Toyah Willcox 1986. *Career:* mem. Ravens; The League of Gentlemen; Founder mem. Giles, Giles and Fripp, which became King Crimson, 1969–84; regular UK, Europe, US and Far East tours; collaborations with Brian Eno; solo recording artist 1979–; Founder, Guitar Craft guitar school, 1985; re-formed King Crimson, 1994–. *Recordings include:* albums: with Giles, Giles and Fripp: The Cheerful Insanity of Giles, Giles and Fripp 1968; with King Crimson: In The Court of The Crimson King 1969, In The Wake of Poseidon 1970, Lizard 1971, Earthbound 1972, Larks' Tongues In Aspic 1973, Starless and Bible Black 1974, Red 1974, USA 1975, Discipline 1981, Beat 1982, Three of a Perfect Pair 1984, Vrooom 1995, Thrak 1995, B'Boom 1995, THRaKaTTak 1996, Epitaph 1997, The Nightwatch 1997, Absent Lovers 1998, Live at the Marquee 1969 1998, Live at Jacksonville 1972 1998, The Beat Club Bremen 1972 1999, Cirkus 1999, Live at Cap D'Adge 1982 1999, On Broadway 1999, Live in Mexico City 1999, No Construkction 2000, Vrooom Vrooom 2001; with Brian Eno: No Pussyfooting 1975, Evening Star 1976, The Equatorial Stars 2004, The Cotswold Gnomes 2006, Beyond Even 1992–2006 2007; with The League of Gentlemen: The League of Gentlemen 1981, God Save The King 1985; solo albums: Exposure 1979, God Save The Queen/Under Heavy Manners 1980, Let The Power Fall 1981, Robert Fripp and The League of Crafty Guitarists 1986, Network 1987, Live II 1990, Show of Hands 1991, The Bridge Between 1995, Soundscapes – Live In Argentina 1995, A Blessing of Tears 1995, Radiophonics 1996, That Which Passes 1996, November Suite 1997, The Gates of Paradise 1997; with FFWD (Fripp, Fehlman, Weston, Dr Alex): FFWD 1994; with Andy Summers: I Advance Masked 1982, Bewitched 1984; with Toyah: Kneeling At The Shrine 1991, The Lady and The Tiger 1987; with David Sylvian: The First Day 1993,

218 www.worldwhoswho.com

Damage 1994; A Scarcity of Miracles: A King Crimson ProjeKct, (with Jakko Jakszyk and Mel Collins) 2011; contributor: albums by David Bowie, Peter Gabriel, Daryl Hall; producer: Gabriel, Hall, Roches; several experimental jazz releases. *Website:* www.king-crimson.com.

FRISCHMANN, Justine Elinor; British singer, musician (guitar) and songwriter; b. 16 Sept. 1969, Twickenham, London. *Career:* mem., Suede from late 1980s to 1991; Founder-mem., Elastica 1993–2001; toured extensively world-wide. *Television:* presenter, Dreamspaces (BBC3) 2003. *Recordings include:* albums: with Elastica: Elastica 1995, The Menace 2000, The BBC Sessions 2001; singles: with Suede: Be My God/Art; with Elastica: Stutter 1993, Connection 1994, Line Up 1994, Waking Up 1995, Car Song 1996, Elastica (EP) 1999, Mad Dog 2000. *Honours:* NME Readers Award for Best New Band 1994. *Current Management:* c/o CMO Management International Ltd, Fourth Floor, Phoenix Brewery, 13 Bramley Road, London, W10 6SP, England. *E-mail:* cmoinfo@cmomanagement.co.uk. *Website:* www .cmomanagement.co.uk.

FRISELL, Bill; American jazz musician (guitar) and composer; b. 18 March 1951, Baltimore, Md; one d. *Education:* Univ. of Northern Colorado, Berklee Coll. of Music. *Career:* played with numerous artists, including Eberhard Weber, Mike Gibbs, Jan Garbarek, Charlie Haden, Carla Bley, John Scofield; David Sylvian, Bono, Marianne Faithfull, Robin Holcomb, Gavin Bryars, Brian Eno, Daniel Lanois, Paul Simon, Van Dyke Parks, Vic Chesnutt, Elvis Costello, Suzanne Vega, Loudon Wainwright III, Ron Carter, Dave Douglas, Rinde Eckart, Wayne Horvitz, Ginger Baker, Rickie Lee Jones, Laurie Anderson, Vernon Reid, Ron Sexsmith, Caetano Veloso, Vinicius Cantuaria, Mark Ribot, Ron Carter, T-Bone Burnett, The Campbell Brothers, Chip Taylor & Carrie Rodriquez, Buddy Miller and Renée Fleming; fmr mem., Power Tools, John Zorn's Naked City, The Paul Bley Quintet, Paul Motian Trio; Music Dir, Century of Song Ruhr Triennale Arts Festival 2003–05. *Compositions include:* Tales from the Far Side (music to TV series). *Recordings include:* albums: In Line 1983, Theoretically (with Tim Berne) 1984, Rambler 1985, News For Lulu (with John Zorn, George Lewis) 1987, Strange Meeting (with Power Tools) 1987, Lookout For Hope 1988, Before We Were Born 1989, Is This You? 1990, Where In The World? 1991, More News For Lulu (with John Zorn, George Lewis) 1992, Grace Under Pressure (with John Scofield) 1992, Have A Little Faith 1993, Music From The Films of Buster Keaton 1995, Going Home Again (with Ginger Baker Trio) 1995, Deep Dead Blue: Live At Meltdown (with Elvis Costello) 1995, Quartet 1996, Nashville 1997, Gone, Just Like a Train 1998, Songs We Know 1998, The Sweetest Punch (with Elvis Costello) 1999, Good Dog, Happy Man 1999, Ghost Town 2000, Blues Dream 2001, Bill Frisell With Dave Holland and Elvin Jones 2001, Selected Recordings 2002, The Willies 2002, The Intercontinentals 2003, Unspeakable 2004, Petra Haden's Bill 2004, Richter 858 2005, East/West 2005, Bill Frisell, Ron Carter, Paul Motian 2005, Floratone 2007, History, Mystery 2007, All Hat 2008, Hemispheres (with Jim Hall) 2008, Disfarmer 2009, Beautiful Dreamers 2010, Lágrimas Mexicanas (with Vinicius Cantuária) 2011, Sign of Life: Music for 858 Quartet 2011, All We Are Saying... 2011, The Kentucky Derby Is Decadent and Depraved 2012, Window & Door 2012, Enfants Terribles: Live at the Blue Note 2012, Quiver 2012, Silent Comedy 2013, John Zorn: The Mysteries 2013, Big Sur 2013, Guitar in the Space Age! 2014. *Publication:* Bill Frisell: An Anthology. *Honours:* Harris Stanton Guitar Award, Downbeat Critics' Poll Guitarist of the Year 1998, Deutsche Schallplatten Preis 1998, 2005, Critics' Award for Best Guitarist, Industry Award for Best Guitarist 1998, Jazz Journalists' Asscn Award for Guitarist of the Year 2013, 2014. *Current Management:* c/o Phyllis Oyama, Songline/Tone Field Productions, 1649 Hopkins Street, Berkeley, CA 94707, USA. *Telephone:* (510) 528-1191. *Fax:* (510) 528-1193. *E-mail:* staff@songtone.com. *Website:* www.songtone .com; www.billfrisell.com.

FRISTORP, Göran; Swedish singer and musician (guitar); b. 26 May 1948, Skara; m. 1975; one d. *Education:* Music Conservatory, Gothenburg and Framnäs Coll., Ojebyn. *Career:* winner, European Song Contest with Claes af Geijerstam and the group Malta 1973; many television and radio appearances; mem. STIM, SKAP, GRAMO (Norway), SAMI. *Recordings include:* albums: Sympathy 1970, Malta 1973, Egna Låtar 1974, Sjunger Nils Ferlin 1975, Lyxlir 1975, Sjunger Gustav Fröding 1979, På mjuka vågor 1979, Fred är en hemlig sång 1981, Återsken 1983, Musik från Norge 1984, Göran Fristorp/ Martin Best 1984, Rinktning 1986, Psalmer 1989, Sjunger och spelar Taube 1990, Amabile 1991, Julsånger 1993, Songs for the Broken Hearted (with Lars Johansson) 1994, Flickan från fjärran 1996, Live (with Anna Lotta Larsson) 1997, Fullständigt 1999, Pie Jesu 2003, En Sommarkonsert 2004, Min Lyckas Hus 2008, From All of Us (with Anna-Lotta Larsson and Andreas Landegren) 2009. *Honours:* Evert Taube Prize 1997, Nils Ferlin Troubadour Prizedeolith 1998. *Address:* PO Box 37, 276 03 Skillinge, Sweden (office). *E-mail:* goran@ fristorp.se (office). *Website:* www.fristorp.se.

FRIZZELL, John; American composer; b. 1966, New York City. *Education:* Univ. of Southern California, Manhattan School of Music. *Career:* began career in chorus, Paris Opera Co., Metropolitan Opera Co.; mem. ASCAP. *Compositions include:* for television: VR.5 1995, It Was Him or Us 1995, Whose Daughter Is She? 1995, Crime of the Century 1996, Deadly Pursuits 1996, Possessed 2000, James Dean: An Invented Life 2001, The Goodbye Girl 2004, Karroll's Christmas 2004, Four Minutes 2005, A Liitle Thing Called Murder 2006, Moonlight 2007, Wisegal 2009, United States of Tara 2009, The Secret Circle 2011, The Following 2013; for film: Red Ribbon Blues 1995, Opposite Corners 1995, The Rich Man's Wife 1996, Beavis and Butt-head Do

America 1996, Undertow 1996, Dante's Peak 1997, The Empty Mirror 1997, Alien Resurrection 1997, Jane Austen's Mafia! 1998, I Still Know What You Did Last Summer 1998, Office Space 1999, The White River Kid 1999, The Empty Mirror 1999, Teaching Mrs Tingle 1999, Beautiful 2000, Lockdown 2000, Josie and the Pussycats 2001, 13 Ghosts 2001, Ghost Ship 2002, Scorched 2003, Gods and Generals 2003, Cradle 2: The Grave 2003, The Prize Winner of Defiance Ohio 2005, The Woods 2006, Stay Alive 2006, First Born 2006, Primeval 2007, The Reaping 2007, Henry Poole is Here 2008, From Mexico with Love 2009, Whiteout 2009, The Roommate 2011. *Current Management:* c/o First Artists Management, 4764 Park Granada, Suite 210, Calabasas, CA 91302, USA. *Telephone:* (817) 377-7750. *Fax:* (817) 377-7760.

FROSCH, Wolfgang; Austrian musician (bass) and backing singer; b. 2 July 1960, Knittelfeld; m. Maria 1989, one s. two d. *Career:* mem. Blues Pumpm 1978–, Giant Blonder 1988–94; tours, television and radio broadcasts throughout Europe; mem. AKM; AUME; LSG. *Recordings include:* albums: with Giant Blonder: Colours of Rock; with Blues Pumpm: Bluespumpm 1979, Edlau 1980, Village 1981, Live With Friends 1985, The 5th Ten Years Jubilee 1987, Live At Utopia 1988, Birthday 1991, Live In Vienna 1992, Living Loving Riding 1994, You Got It 1995, 20 Years Party 1995, Dirty Dozen 2000, The Wolfpack Tapes 2001, Dirty Thirty Open Hearts 2006, Folk Meets Blues 2007. *Honours:* Silbernes Ehrenzeicher 1992. *E-mail:* office@bluespumpm.at (office). *Website:* www.bluespumpm.at (office).

FROST, Jenny; British singer; b. 22 Feb. 1978, Liverpool. *Career:* represented UK in Eurovision Song Contest, 1999, as part of female vocal quintet Precious; mem. Atomic Kitten (replacing Kerry Katona) 2001–; appearance, Party at the Palace, Buckingham Palace Jubilee celebrations 2002; co-spearheaded MTV Asia Awards, Pan European Breakthrough with Whole Again single; guest at Celebrate South Africa Freedom Concert. *Recordings include:* albums: with Precious: Precious 2000; with Atomic Kitten: Right Now (reissue) 2001, Feels So Good 2002, Ladies' Night 2003, The Collection 2005. *Current Management:* c/o Money North Ltd, 85 Bold Street, Liverpool, L1 4HF, England. *Telephone:* (151) 709-1791. *Fax:* (151) 709-1895. *E-mail:* Kate@ MoneyNorth.co.uk. *Website:* www.moneymanagementuk.com/money-north .htm; www.jennyfrostofficial.com; www.atomickitten.com.

FROST, Per Christian; Danish musician (guitar, bass guitar) and singer; b. 30 Oct. 1954, Århus; s. of Jørgen Revsbach Frost and Anne Dorthea Hyldgaard-Jensen; m. Dorthe Th. Holtet 1987; two s. *Education:* art acad. *Career:* mem. Gnags 1974–96; tours to Europe, Africa, India, Cuba, Nicaragua; numerous television appearances; also solo artist, guest musician; mem. DMF, DJBFA, KODA. *Recordings include:* albums: with Gnags: Del af en ring, Det er Det, La' det gro, Er du hjemme i aften?, Burhøns, Intercity, Safari, X, Den blå hund, En underlig fisk, Plads til begejstring, Har de puttet noget i kaffen?, Me Swing King, Lygtemandens sang, Øjne på stilke, Gøsta Hammerfedt, 13 rigitige; solo: Ned Ad Gaden 1978, Old Friend's Back 1990, Breakin' Ice 1996, SeaSideSongs 1998, Frost 2007, When The Time Is Right 2011. *Honours:* Award of Honour, Danish Musicians Union 1988, IFPI Prize 1990, Ken Gudman Award 2005. *Address:* c/o RecArt Music, Dronningensgade 68, 1 Sal, 1420 Copenhagen K, Denmark (office). *Telephone:* 33-91-21-10. *E-mail:* kjeld.stefansen@umusic.com. *Website:* recart.dk (office); www.per-chr -frost.dk.

FROST, Soren; Danish musician (drums, percussion); b. 5 Feb. 1965, Århus. *Education:* Drummer Collective, 10 Week Certificate Program, New York City, 1988. *Career:* played Pop Rock, Jazz and Chorus Line, Sweet Charity Jesus Christ Superstar; worked with Lillian Boutte, Dr John, Bob Berg, Eliane Elias, Lee Konitz, Bob Brookmeyer, Thad Jones, Slide Hampton, Dee Dee Bridgewater; numerous TV and radio shows and tours of Japan, 1990, USSR, 1988, Thailand, 1991, USA, 1997; with Danish Radio Big Band 1990–. *Recordings include:* Lillian Boutte: The Jazz Book; The Danish Radio Orchestra: Fusion Symphony; Nikolaj Bentzon: Brotherhood; Jazzgroup 1990 with Bob Berg: Live in Denmark, My Sisters Garden. *Website:* www.dr .dk/Koncerthuset/dr-ensembler/dr-big-bandet.

FRUITBAT; British musician; b. (Leslie Carter), 12 Feb. 1958. *Career:* Founder mem. (with Jimbob), duo, Carter The Unstoppable Sex Machine (later billed as Carter USM) 1988–98, 2007–; Founder mem. Abdoujaparov 1998–; int. concerts including USA, Japan. *Recordings include:* albums: 101 Damnations 1990, 30 Something 1991, 1992 – The Love Album 1992, Post Historic Monsters 1994, Worry Bomb 1995, Straw Donkey 1996, A World Without Dave 1997, I Blame The Government 1998, Live 1999, Air Odeon Disco Pub (with Abdoujaparov) 2002, Cycle Riot History Gang (with Abdoujaparov) 2007; singles: Sheltered Life 1988, Sheriff Fatman 1989, Rubbish 1990, Anytime, Anyplace, Anywhere 1990, Bloodsports For All 1991, After The Watershed 1991, Only Living Boy In New Cross 1992, Lean On Me I Won't Fall Over 1993, Glam Rock Cops 1994, Let's Get Tattoos 1994, Young Offenders Mum 1995, Born On Fifth November 1995. *E-mail:* fruity@ carterusm.co.uk (office). *Website:* www.carterusm.co.uk; www.abdou.co.uk.

FRUSCIANTE, John; American musician (guitar); b. 5 March 1970, New York. *Career:* mem., Red Hot Chili Peppers 1988–92, 1998–2008; numerous tours, festivals and television appearances. *Recordings include:* albums: with Red Hot Chili Peppers: Mother's Milk 1989, Blood Sugar Sex Magik 1991, Californication 1999, By The Way 2002, Live In Hyde Park 2004, Stadium Arcadium (MTV Europe Music Award for Best Album) 2006; solo: Niandra Ladies And Usually Just A T-Shirt 1995, Smile From The Streets You Hold 1997, To Record Only Water For Ten Days 2001, Shadows Collide With People

2004, Curtains 2005, The Empyrean 2008, PBX Funicular Intaglio Zone 2012, Enclosure 2014. *Honours:* MTV Music Video Award 1992, American Music Award for Favorite Alternative Artist 2000, MTV Awards for Best Live Act, Best Rock 2002, American Music Award for Favorite Pop/Rock Band 2006, for Favorite Alternative Music Artist 2006, Grammy Award for Best Rock Performance by a Duo or Group with Vocal (for Dani California) 2007. *Current Management:* c/o Lindy Goetz Management, 12338 Linda Flora Drive, Ojai, CA 93023-9721, USA. *Telephone:* (805) 649-2526. *Website:* johnfrusciante.com.

FRY, Martin; British singer and producer; b. 9 March 1958, Manchester. *Education:* Sheffield Univ. *Career:* launched fanzine, Modern Drugs 1979; lead singer, ABC 1980–; UK and world tour 1982; featured in Julien Temple's film Man Trap 1983. *Recordings:* albums with ABC: The Lexicon of Love 1982, Beauty Stab 1983, How To Be A Zillionaire 1985, Alphabet City 1987, Up 1989, Absolutely 1990, Abracadabra 1991, Skyscraping 1997, Hello – An Introduction To ABC 2001, The Look of Love (The Very Best of ABC) 2001, Traffic 2008. *Honours:* Dr hc (Sheffield) 2012. *Current Management:* c/o Matt Glover, Blueprint Management, PO Box 593, Woking, Surrey GU23 7YF, England. *Telephone:* (1296) 624874. *E-mail:* matt@blueprint-management .com. *Website:* www.blueprint-management.com; www.abcmartinfry.com.

FRY, Tristan Frederick Allan; British musician (percussion, trumpet); b. 25 Oct. 1946, London; m. Dorothy E. Garland 1993. *Education:* Royal Acad. of Music with Peter Allen, many amateur orchestras and groups, London. *Career:* mem. London Philharmonic Orchestra at age of 17; Founder mem. ensembles, including Nash, Fires of London and the London Sinfonietta; drummer, Sky 1979–94, with concerts worldwide; played on soundtracks, including James Bond films, Pink Panther, Dr Who, Rolf Harris shows; timpanist, Acad. of St Martin in the Fields Orchestra; Co-Artistic Dir, London Pro Arte Percussion Ensemble; mem. Royal Soc. of Musicians. *Recordings include:* albums with Sky: Sky 1979, Sky 2 1980, Sky 3 1981, Westminster Abbey 1982, Sky 4: Forthcoming 1981, Sky Five Live 1983, Cadmium 1983, The Great Balloon Race 1985, Mozart 1987, various compilation albums. *Address:* London Pro Arte Percussion Ensemble, 90 Emmanuel Road, London, SW12 0HR, England (office). *Telephone:* (20) 8674 0619 (office). *E-mail:* office@ londonproarte.co.uk (office). *Website:* www.londonproarte.co.uk (office).

FRYAR, Chris; American musician (drums); b. 22 Nov. 1970, Birmingham, Ala. *Education:* North Texas State Univ. *Career:* collaborations with Ray Reach and Friends, Alabama Jazz Hall of Fame All-Stars, Oteil and the Peacemakers, Charles Neville, Victor Wooten, John Popper, Gravy; mem. Zac Brown Band 2006–. *Recordings:* albums: with Zac Brown Band: The Foundation 2008, You Get What You Give 2010. *Honours:* Acad. of Country Music Award for Top New Vocal Duo or Group 2009, for Vocal Event of the Year (for As She's Walking Away, featuring Alan Jackson) 2011, Grammy Award for Best New Artist 2010, CMA New Artist of the Year 2010. *Current Management:* ROAR, 9701 Wilshire Boulevard, Eighth Floor, Beverly Hills, CA 90212, USA. *Telephone:* (310) 586-8222. *E-mail:* zbb@roar.la. *Website:* www.roar.la. *E-mail:* chris@zacbrownband.com (office). *Website:* www.chrisfryar.com; www .zacbrownband.com.

FUGLER, Jonathan (Jon) Howard; British singer and producer; b. 13 Oct. 1962. *Career:* mem. Fluke 1988–; contributed remixes for Talk Talk, Björk, Simple Minds, Smashing Pumpkins, The Rolling Stones, Yello, New Order and others; toured with Sander Kleinenberg 2011. *Recordings include:* albums: The Techno Rose Of Blighty 1990, Out 1991, Six Wheels On My Wagon 1993, Oto 1995, Risotto 1997, Progressive History X (compilation) 2001, Puppy 2003; singles: Thumper 1989, Joni 1989, Philly 1990, Slid 1993, Electric Guitar 1993, Groovy Feeling 1993, Bubble 1994, The Peel Sessions 1994, Bullet 1995, Tosh 1995, Atom Bomb 1996, Absurd 1997, Squirt 1997, Pulse 2002, Hang Tough 2003, Switch 2003. *Address:* c/o One Little Indian Records, 34 Trinity Crescent, London, SW17 7AE, England (office).

FUJII, Sachiko; Japanese musician (drums). *Career:* Founder mem. The 5.6.7.8s 1986–; numerous live performances. *Film appearances:* Kill Bill Vol. 1 2003. *Recordings include:* albums: Can't Help It! 1991, The 5.6.7.8s 1994, Bomb The Twist 1995, Pin Heel Stomp 1997, Teenage Mojo Workout 2002, Bomb The Rocks: The Early Days Singles 1989–1996 2003, Best Hits Of The 5.6.7.8s 2003. *E-mail:* the5678s@fujiiya.com (office). *Website:* www.the5678s .net.

FUJIYAMA, Ronnie Yoshiko; Japanese musician (guitar). *Career:* Founder mem. The 5.6.7.8s 1986–; numerous live performances. *Film appearances:* Kill Bill Vol. 1 2003. *Recordings include:* albums: Can't Help It! 1991, The 5.6.7.8s 1994, Bomb The Twist 1995, Pin Heel Stomp 1997, Teenage Mojo Workout 2002, Bomb The Rocks: The Early Days Singles 1989–1996 2003, Best Hits Of The 5.6.7.8s 2003. *E-mail:* the5678s@fujiiya.com (office). *Website:* www .the5678s.net.

FUKUYAMA, Masaharu; Japanese singer, songwriter, musician (guitar), record producer and actor; b. 6 Feb. 1969, Nagasaki. *Career:* released first solo album 1990; formed group KOH+ with Kou Shibasaki 2008. *Recordings:* albums: solo: Dengon 1990, Lion 1991, Bros. 1991, Boots 1992, Calling 1993, On and On 1994, Sing a Song 1998, F 2001, 5 Nen Mono 2006, Zankyō 2009. *Films:* as actor: Hon no 5g 1988, Atlanta Boogie 1996, Suspect X 2008, Amalfi: Rewards of the Goddess 2009. *Television:* as actor: Ashita ga Aru Kara 1991, Ai wa Dōda 1992, Homework 1992, Hitotsu Yane no Shita 1993, Itsuka Mata Aeru 1995, Hitotsu Yane no Shita 2 1997, Meguri Ai 1998, Furuhata Ninzaburō 1999, Perfect Love 1999, Bijo ka Yajū 2003, Tengoku no Daisuke e

2003, Galileo (55th Television Drama Academy Best Actor Award 2008) 2007, Taiga drama Ryōmaden 2010. *Address:* c/o Universal Music LLC, 8-5-30 Akasaka, Minato-ku, Tokyo 107-8583, Japan (office). *Website:* www .fukuyamamasaharu.com.

FULKS, Robbie; American singer, songwriter and musician; b. 25 March 1963, Pennsylvania; m. Donna; three s. *Education:* Columbia Coll., New York. *Career:* appearances at Mountain Stage, Fresh Air NPR, World Cafe, Acoustic Cafe, Austin City Limits; cast mem., Woody Guthrie's American Song 1990–93; staff instructor, Old Town School of Folk Music, Chicago. *Recordings include:* albums: Country Love Songs 1996, South Mouth 1997, Let's Kill Saturday Night 1998, Couples in Trouble 2000, 13 Hillbilly Giants 2001, Georgia Hard 2005, Revenge! 2007, Happy 2010. *Website:* www.robbiefulks .com.

FULL; Japanese musician (bass guitar); b. Tokyo. *Career:* Founder mem. punk band, Nicotine 1994–; band formed its own record label, Sky Records 1997. *Recordings include:* albums: Royal Mellow Day 1996, ¡Hola Amigo! 1997, Pleeeeeeeez! Who Are You? 2000, Fitness Dayz 2001, Samurai Shot 2002, School Of Liberty 2003, Hey Dude! We Love the Beatles 2005, Desperado 2006, Carnival 2006, Sound from the Schizoid Core 2006, Probably the Best 2007. *E-mail:* nicotine@skyrecords.co.jp (office). *Website:* www.skyrecords.co .jp/nicotine.

FULLBRIGHT, John; American singer, songwriter and musician (guitar, piano, harmonica); b. 23 April 1988, Bearden, Okla. *Education:* Okemah High School. *Career:* fmr mem. Turnpike Troubadours; collaborator with Mike McClure 2007–08; solo career 2008–; released first live recording 2009; debut studio album 2012; numerous live appearances including SXSW, Woody Guthrie Folk Festival. *Recordings include:* album: Live at the Blue Door 2009, From the Ground Up 2012; other credits: did7, Mike McClure 2008. *Honours:* ASCAP Foundation Harold Adamson Lyric Award 2012. *Address:* c/o Greg Johnson, Blue Door Music, 2805 North McKinley, Oklahoma City, OK 73106, USA (office). *Telephone:* (405) 524-0738 (office). *E-mail:* bluedoorokc@gmail .com. *Website:* www.johnfullbrightmusic.com.

FULLER, Parmer, BA, MM, PhD; American composer, conductor, music director, musician (piano) and university professor; *Adjunct Professor, University of Southern California;* b. 15 July 1949, San Francisco, CA; m. Narcissa C. Vanderlip 1982, one d. *Education:* Harvard Univ., Indiana Univ., Univ. of California at Los Angeles. *Career:* composer, music for feature films including Daddy's Girl, Reflections on a Crime, Mortal Passions, Time Trackers, Spirit of the Eagle, Ulterior Motives; music for TV shows: The Morton Downey Jr Show, Distant Cousins, Easy Street, Dynasty, Family, Ronn Lucas Show, Monsters; miscellaneous compositions for educational films, interactive CDs; solo performances as pianist including shows for President Reagan, George Bush, Gerald Ford and Richard Nixon; Conductor, Young Musicians' Foundation Orchestra concerts; coached actor James Caan in conducting skills; appeared as self in Easy Street; Music Dir, San Diego Civic Light Opera 1994–; Adjunct Prof. Univ. of Southern California 2000–; mem, ASCAP, BMI, SCL, AFM. *Compositions include:* concert works: Spirit of the Eagle, Twice Upon a Time, A Child's Christmas in Wales, Alpine Wanderings; music comedy: director and conductor: High School Musical, Das Barbecü, Batboy, The Sound of Music, Music Man, Singin' in the Rain, Enchanted Cottage, Brigadoon, Once Upon This Mattress, Guys and Dolls, Hello Dolly!, Seven Brides for Seven Brothers, Camelot, Molly Brown, Crazy for You, Into The Woods, My Fair Lady, Sugar (Some Like It Hot), South Pacific, Peter Pan, Evita, Me and My Girl, The Wizard of Oz, A Chorus Line, 1776, Annie, My One and Only, Jekyll and Hyde, Company, Fiddler on the Roof, How to Succeed, The Scarlet Pimpernel, Hair, Little Shop of Horrors (twice), Lucky Stiff, Oklahoma, Grease, Pippin, Patience; other: Solferino (opera), 12 Songs and Incidental Music for Twelfth Night, Chalet Mirabel (music comedy), Stations (dance theatre); numerous arrangements, including works for Pavarotti and Jack Lemmon. *Publication:* Stations, a Los Angeles Holiday Story. *Honours:* Frank Sinatra Prizes, Henry Mancini Award, San Diego Critics Circle Craig Noel Awards 2004, 2007, Ovation Award Los Angeles for Best Music and Lyrics for a New Musical 2012. *Address:* 10374 Cheviot Drive, Los Angeles, CA 90064, USA (home).

FULLER, Simon; British music promoter, business executive and artist manager; m. Natalie Swanston 2008. *Career:* Founder and Dir 19 Group 1985–2005 (comprising 19 Brands, 19 Entertainment, 19 International Sports Management, 19 Management, 19 Merchandising, 19 Productions, 19 Recordings, 19 Songs, 19 Touring, 19 TV, Brilliant 19), sold to CFX 2005 (mem. Bd of Dirs 2005–); founder, XIX Entertainment 2010–; current or fmr man. of numerous artists, including Annie Lennox, Emma Bunton, Will Young, Gareth Gates, Kelly Clarkson, Paul Hardcastle (1985), Madonna, Cathy Dennis, Spice Girls (–1997), 21st Century Girls and S Club 7 (later S Club, including TV series and S Club Juniors); dir of numerous other cos. *Television includes:* creator of Popstars (ITV 1), Pop Idol (ITV 1), American Idol – The Search for a Superstar (Fox TV), Popstars – The Rivals (ITV 1). *Honours:* Hon. degree, (Univ. of Sussex) 2014; GQ Magazine Entrepreneur of the Year 2006, Music Managers Forum Peter Grant Award 2008, Producers Guild of America Music Visionary Award 2008, Anglo-American Cultural Award 2012. *Address:* XIX Management, Unit 33, Ransomes Dock, 35–37 Parkgate Road, London, SW11 4NP, England (office). *Telephone:* (20) 7801-1919 (office). *Fax:* (20) 7801-1920 (office). *E-mail:* info@xixentertainment.com (office). *Website:* xixentertainment.com.

FUNK DOCTA SPOCK (see Redman)

FUNK JUNKEEZ (see Sanchez, Roger)

FUNKEY; Belgian musician (synthesizer) and singer; b. 20 July 1961, Sint-Niklaas. *Career:* debut, keyboard player and singer, The Soap 1992, Oortcloud 1993; radio: several times on Bassta 1995–96, TV: Prettig Gestoord 1996; mem. SABAM, ZAMU. *Publications include:* Oortcloud: Raindances 1995, Colour Dot: Floating Atmospheres 1997. *Honours:* Studio Brussels' Candidate for Debut Rock Contest. *E-mail:* mail@funkey.be.

FUREY, Eddie; Irish musician (guitar, mandola, mandolin, harmonica, fiddle, bodhran) and singer; b. 23 Dec. 1944, Tipperary; m. Bibi; five c. *Career:* mem. duo (with brother, Finbar) 1960s; joined Clancy Brothers on US tour 1969; mem. Tam Linn; numerous live and festival appearances; mem. The Fureys and Davey Arthur 1980; mem. IMRO. *Recordings include:* albums: The Sound of The Fureys and Davey Arthur 1981, When You Were Sweet Sixteen 1982, Steal Away 1983, In Concert 1984, Golden Days 1984, At The End of The Perfect Day 1985, The First Leaves of Autumn 1986, The Fureys Finest 1987, The Fureys Collection 1989, The Scattering 1989, The Winds of Change 1992, Irish Folk Favourites 1994, Best of Irish Folk 1998, Essential Fureys 2001; with Finbar Furey: The Dawning of The Day 1970, Traditional Irish Pipe Music 1998. *Current Management:* c/o Joe McCadden Promotions, 19 Stockton Green, Castleknock, Dublin 15, Ireland. *Website:* www.thefureys .com.

FUREY, Finbar; Irish musician (uillean pipes, banjo, whistles, flute), singer and actor; b. 28 Sept. 1946, Dublin. *Career:* mem. duo (with Eddie Furey) 1960s; played clubs, radio work; joined Clancy Brothers for US tour 1969; mem. Tam Linn; numerous live and festival appearances; mem. The Fureys and Davey Arthur 1980–93; solo artist 1993–. *Films include:* Gangs of New York 2000, Adam and Paul 2004, Strength and Honour 2007, Paris Sexy (short) 2010. *Recordings include:* albums: The Cisco Special 1960, Songs of Woody Guthrie 1961, I Ain't Got No Home 1962, The Sound of The Fureys and Davey Arthur 1981, When You Were Sweet Sixteen 1982, Steal Away 1983, In Concert 1984, Golden Days 1984, At The End of a Perfect Day 1985, The First Leaves of Autumn 1986, The Fureys Finest 1987, The Fureys Collection 1989, The Scattering 1989, The Very Best Of 1991, The Winds of Change 1992, with Eddie Furey: The Dawning of The Day 1972; solo: Love Letters 1990, No Farewells, No Goodbyes 2007, Finbar Furey 2009, Colours 2011. *E-mail:* michael@gfdpromotions.com. *E-mail:* sheila@finbarfurey.com (office). *Website:* www.finbarfurey.com.

FUREY, George; Irish singer, musician (guitar, accordion, mandola, autoharp, whistles) and songwriter; b. 11 June 1951, Dublin; m. Mary Furey 1971; three s. three d. *Career:* mem. The Buskers 1972, later renamed The Furey Brothers; TV appearances in the UK and Ireland; mem. IMRO, Phonographic Performance Ltd. *Compositions include:* Evening Falls, 1979; Green Fields of France. *Recordings include:* albums: The Cisco Special 1960, Songs of Woody Guthrie 1961, I Ain't Got No Home 1962, The Sound of The Fureys and Davey Arthur 1981, When You Were Sweet Sixteen 1982, Steal Away 1983, In Concert 1984, Golden Days 1984, At The End of the Perfect Day 1985, The First Leaves of Autumn 1986, The Fureys Finest 1987, The Fureys Collection 1989, The Scattering 1989, The Winds of Change 1992, Through the Eyes of an Irishman 1997, The Fureys: 21 Years On This Year 1999, Essential Fureys 2001. *Current Management:* c/o Joe McCadden Promotions, 19 Stockton Green, Castleknock, Dublin 15, Ireland. *E-mail:* mccaddenjoe@ gmail.com. *Website:* www.thefureys.com.

FURIC LEIBOVICI, Stéphane, DipMus; French composer and musician (double bass); b. (Stéphane Furic), 15 July 1965, Paris; s. of Simon Salomon Leibovici and Zelia Leibovici; partner, Corinne Pautard; two s. from previous relationship. *Education:* Berklee Coll. of Music, USA, double bass studies with William H. Curtis, improvisation studies with John LaPorta. *Career:* concerts include int. jazz festivals, tours, radio and TV shows, recordings for series of albums releases (Europe, N America, Asia), as leader of ensemble including Chris Cheek, Patrick Goraguer, Lee Konitz, Chris Speed, Jim Black; mem. SACEM, BMI (as composer and publr); written pieces for Dag Gabrielsen, Robert Schumann, Lee Konitz. *Major compositions include:* Kishinev (suite for quartet) 1990, Dances (suite for septet) 1994, Penelope: her hands 2002, Les Nuits de la Chapoulie-Nocturnal 2004, Clair-Obscurs I–V 2004, Le Feuillage des Gestes 2004, Phongsaly 2004, Quatre Intermezzi 2004, Siddartha (A Music of Tranquillity) 2005, (...les Astres sont anciens mais la

nuit est nouvelle...) 2005, Vier Orchesterstücke 2005, Concertino for Piano 2005, Fragmente 2006, Erste Sinfonie 2007. *Recordings include:* Kishinev 1991, The Twitter-Machine 1993, Crossing Brooklyn Ferry 1995, Music for 3, vol. 1 2003, Phongsaly 2005, Starry Nights 2005. *Publication:* Downshifting— Capturing Music Performance. *Address:* Château de Fressanges, 87260 Vicq-sur-Breuilh, France (home). *Telephone:* 6-33-97-27-22 (home). *E-mail:* stephane.furic@gmail.com. *Website:* www.stephanefuric.com.

FURTADO, Nelly Kim; Canadian singer, musician (guitar, ukelele, trombone) and songwriter; b. 2 Dec. 1978, Victoria, BC; m. Demacio Castellon 2008. *Career:* trombonist in various jazz/marching/concert bands while at school; performed and recorded with trip-hop outfit, Nelstar aged 18; discovered at Toronto talent contest; relocated to Toronto to forge songwriting partnership with Gerald Eaton and Brian West of Canadian group, The Philosopher Kings; solo artist 2000–. *Recordings include:* albums: Whoa Nelly! 2000, Folklore 2003, Loose (MTV Europe Music Award for Best Album 2007, Juno Awards for Album of the Year and R&B Album of the Year 2007) 2006, Mi Plan (Latin Grammy Award for Best Female Pop Vocal Album 2010) 2009, The Spirit Indestructible 2012. *Honours:* numerous including: Juno Awards for Best New Solo Artist 2001, for Best Single (for I'm Like a Bird) 2001, for Best Songwriter 2001, for Best Producer 2001, for Single of the Year (for Powerless) 2002, for Single of the Year (for Promiscuous feat. Timbaland) 2007, for Artist of the Year 2007, ASCAP Pop Music Award 2002, Grammy Award for Best Female Pop Vocal Performance (for I'm Like a Bird) 2002, Billboard Award for Pop 100 Single of the Year (for Promiscuous) 2006, BRIT Award for Best Int. Female Solo Artist 2007, Cyprus Music Award for Best Canadian Artist 2012. *Current Management:* Chris Smith Management Inc., 21 Camden Street, Fifth Floor, Toronto, ON M5V 1V2, Canada. *Telephone:* (416) 362-7771. *Fax:* (416) 362-6648. *E-mail:* info@chrissmithmanagement.com. *Website:* www .chrissmithmanagement.com; www.nellyfurtado.com.

FURUHOLMEN, Magne (Mags); Norwegian musician (keyboards) and singer; b. 1 Nov. 1962, Manglerud, Oslo. *Career:* mem., a-ha 1982–94, 1999–2009, 2015–; mem., Timbersound; solo artist; numerous tours world-wide, television and radio broadcasts. *Recordings include:* albums: with a-ha: Hunting High And Low 1985, Scoundrel Days 1986, Stay On These Roads 1988, East Of The Sun West Of The Moon 1990, Memorial Beach 1992, Lifelines 2002, How Can I Sleep With Your Voice In My Head (live) 2003, Singles 1984–2004 2005, Analogue 2005, Foot of the Mountain 2009, a-ha 25 2010, Cast in Steel 2015; solo: Hermetic 1998, If You Can, Solve This Jumble 2012, Winter Days 2013. *Honours:* Kt, 1st Class, Royal Norwegian Order of St Olav 2012; eight MTV Music Video Awards (for Take On Me and The Sun Always Shines On TV) 1986, BMI Award for One Million Broadcast Performances (for Take On Me) 1991, World Music Award for Best Selling Norwegian Artist of the Year 1993. *Website:* www.a-ha.com.

FUSE (see Hawtin, Richie)

FUSE ODG; British rapper, singer and songwriter; b. (Nana Richard Abiona), 1988, Ghana. *Recordings:* Antenna (EP with Wyclef Jean) 2013, Azonto 2013, Million Pound Girl (Badder Than Bad) 2013. *Honours:* Urban Music Award for Best Afrobeats Artist 2012, MOBO Award for Best African Act 2013, Ghana Music Award for Afro Pop Song of the Year (for Antenna) 2013. *E-mail:* info@ fuseodg.com (home). *Website:* fuseodg.com (home).

FUTURE PAST (see Degiorgio, Kirk)

FYFFE, William John Angus; musician (piano) and music director; b. 18 Sept. 1927, Margate, Kent, England; s. of Will Fyffe; m. 1st Michelle Franks 1951; one s. one d.; m. 2nd Sue Addams 1968; one s. one d. *Education:* George Watson's Coll., Edinburgh. *Career:* joined Rank Organisation film studios 1948; moved to Chappells as song plugger; A&R, Decca Records; personal accompanist to artists, including Allan Jones, Josef Locke, Evelyn Laye, Frankie Vaughan, Petula Clark, Ronnie Hilton 1950s–70s; Sr MD, Triumph Productions; in concert act with Anthea Askey; numerous television and radio broadcasts, stage appearances; mem. PRS, BAC&S, Grand Order of Water Rats. *Compositions:* words and music for Glasgow Belongs To Me (working title); songs include: My September; With A Love Like Ours, The True Love I've Known, Bells Across the Snow, Such Beautiful Thoughts. *Address:* 153/ 155 Avonmouth Road, Bristol, BS11 9LW; Appletree Lodge, Golden Acre, Angmering-on-Sea, West Sussex BN16 1QP, England (home). *Telephone:* (117) 982-2540; (117) 982-2540 (office); (1903) 785782 (home). *E-mail:* willfyffejr@hotmail.co.uk.

G

G, Kenny; American musician (saxophone), composer and songwriter; b. (Kenneth Gorelick), 5 June 1956, Seattle, Wash. *Education:* Univ. of Washington. *Career:* European tour with Franklin High School Band 1974; musician with Barry White's Love Unlimited Orchestra 1976; backing musician for numerous artists, including Whitney Houston, Natalie Cole, Aretha Franklin, Toni Braxton, Peabo Bryson; fmr mem., Cold, Bold and Together; fmr mem. jazz fusion group, Jeff Lorber Fusion; solo artist 1981–; regular collaborations with Michael Bolton. *Recordings include:* albums: Kenny G 1982, G Force 1984, Gravity 1985, Duo Tones 1986, Silhouette 1988, Live 1989, Breathless 1992, Miracles: The Holiday Album 1994, The Moment 1996, Classics In The Key Of G 1999, Faith: A Holiday Album 1999, Paradise 2002, Wishes: A Holiday Album 2002, At Last… The Duets Album 2004, The Romance of Kenny G 2004, The Greatest Holiday Classics 2005, The Essential Kenny G 2006, I'm in the Mood for Love 2006, The Holiday Collection 2006, Rhythm and Romance 2008, Heart and Soul 2010, The Christmas Classic Album 2012, Namaste 2012. *Current Management:* c/o Concord Records, Concord Music Group, 23307 Commerce Park Road, Cleveland, OH 44122, USA. *Website:* www2.concordmusicgroup.com; www.kennyg.com.

G-DRAGON; South Korean singer, songwriter, rapper and producer; b. (Kwon Ji Yong), 18 Aug. 1988, Seoul. *Career:* mem. group Little Roora at age of eight; signed to YG Entertainment 2002; lead singer, Big Bang 2006–; collaborations with T.O.P., Lexy, CL, Taeyang, W-inds, Teddy Park, Flo Rida, Kush. *Recordings:* with Big Bang: Bigbang Vol 1 2007, Remember 2008, Number 1 2008, Big Bang 2009, Big Bang 2 2011, Alive 2012; solo: Heartbreaker (Mnet Asian Music Award for Album of the Year 2009, Melon Music Award for Album of the Year 2009) 2009, One of a Kind 2012; with T.O.P.: GD&TOP 2010. *Honours:* Mnet KM Music Festival Awards for Best Male Group 2007, 2008, 2012, for Song of the Year 2007, for Music Arrangement 2007, for Digital Music 2008, for Artist of the Year 2008, 2012, for Guardian Angel Worldwide Performer 2012, for Best Male Artist 2012, Golden Disk Bonsang Award 2007, Mnet Music Portal Award 2008, Seoul Music Awards for Digital Music 2008, for Bonsang 2008, 2009, for Best Album 2009, for Popular Mobile 2009, Nickelodeon Korea Kids' Choice Best Male Artists Award 2008, 2009, Hiwon Award 2009, Korea PD Best Singer Award 2009, Best Hits Song Festival Gold Artist Award 2009, Japan Cable Broadcasting Best Newcomer Award 2009, Ministry of Culture, Sports and Tourism Artist of the Year 2009, Japan Record Awards for New Artist and Best New Artist 2009, Gold Award 2010, Japanese Grand Prix du Disque for Best Newcomer 2010, Japan Gold Disc Awards for Best Five New Artists and Best New Artist 2010, MTV Video Music Awards Japan for Best New Artist Video, Best Collaboration Video and Best Pop Video 2010. *Address:* c/o YG Entertainment, 397–5 YG Building, Hapjeong-Dong, Mapo-Gu, Seoul 109-819, South Korea (office). *Telephone:* (2) 3143-1105 (office). *Fax:* (2) 544-1546 (office). *E-mail:* web@ygmail.net (office). *Website:* eng.ygfamily.com/main/main.html (office); www.ybigbang.com/gdragon.

GABRIEL, MA; Italian record producer, songwriter and playwright; b. (Gabriel J. Maciocia), 8 Oct. 1948, Providence, RI, USA. *Education:* Rhode Island Coll., Roben Williams Coll. *Career:* producer for Budweiser Girls Band, 18 albums; producer for Joey Welz, The Four Tops, Gloria Gaynor; Pres. Slack Entertainment Group, BMI; Vice-Pres. of Artist Devt, Canadian American Records; mem. ASCAP. *Films include:* Christmas Holiday on the Moon (writer and producer), Hearts of Bounty (screenplay and score). *Television include:* organiser Las Vegas Entertainment Hall of Fame Concert (nat. and worldwide network TV awards show). *Compositions include:* Elvis is Smiling 1989, You Don't Own Me 1989. *Recording:* The Fabulous Gabriel (collection of own songs). *Publications include:* Whisper Pines (novel), Hearts of Bounty (novel), Christmas Holiday on the Moon (play). *Honours:* Cashbox Magazine Single of Week 1988. *Website:* thefabulousgabriel.com.

GABRIEL, Ana; Mexican singer, songwriter, producer and actress; b. (María Guadalupe Araújo Yong), 10 Dec. 1958, Guamuchil, Sinaloa. *Career:* solo artist 1986–. *Television and film appearances include:* Wings (TV) 1993, The Nature of the Beast (film) 1995, Ned and Stacey (TV) 1995, Live Shot (TV) 1995, The Parent Hood (TV) 1997, Caroline in the City (TV) 1998, Melrose Place (TV) 1998, The Deep End of the Ocean (film) 1999, Malcolm in the Middle (TV) 2003, NYPD Blue (TV) 2003, ¡Ay, amor! (TV series) 2003. *Recordings include:* albums: Un estilo 1985, Pecado original 1987, Tierra de nadie 1988, Quién como tú 1989, En vivo 1990, Mi México (Billboard Latin Music Award for Mexican Album of the Year 1992) 1991, Silueta 1992, The Best 1992, Luna 1993, Ayer y hoy 1994, Joyas de dos siglos 1995, Vivencias 1996, Con un mismo corazón 1997, En la plaza de toros-México 1998, Soy como soy 1999, Eternamente 2000, Huelo a soledad 2002, Sagitario 2002, Dulce y salado 2003, Tradicional 2004, Historia de una reina 2005, Dos amores, un amante 2006, Con Sentimiento 2006, Best of Ana Gabriel 2006, Arpegios de amor 2007, Los Gabriel… Simplemente Amigos 2007, Los Gabriel: Cantan a México 2008, Renacer… Homenaje a Lucha Villa, En Altos de Chavón: El Concierto 2013, Un Mariachi en Altos de Chavón 2013. *Honours:* Billboard Latin Music Awards for Song of the Year (for Cosas del amor), Mexican Female Artist of the Year, Pop Female Artist of the Year 1992, Ritmo Latino Music Award for Female Pop Artist of the Year 2000, Billboard Latin Music Estrella Award 2002, Lo Nuestro Award for Best Regional/Mexican Female

Artist 1999, 2000, Lo Nuestro Award Excellence Award 2006. *Address:* c/o Hauser CIE Entertainment, 11003 Rooks Road, Whittier, CA 90601-1624, USA (office). *Website:* www.anagabriel.com.

GABRIEL, Gilles (Blacky); French musician (drums); b. 1 Nov. 1946, Clermont Ferrand; divorced; one s. one d. *Education:* Music High School, Nancy. *Career:* first professional appearance in cabaret, Nancy 1967; mem. dance orchestra 1967–; mem. big bands including Swing Orchestra; Leader, Myster Black (jazz) 1989–, Jaguars 1995, Pat and the Blue Wizards 1999–; mem. SLAM.

GABRIEL, Juan; Mexican singer and songwriter; b. (Alberto Aguilera Valadéz), 7 Jan. 1950, Parácuaro, Michoacán. *Recordings include:* albums: El alma joven (three vols) 1971–73, Juan Gabriel, Juan Gabriel con el Mariachi Vargas de Tecatitlán (two vols) 1974–76, A mi guitarra 1976, Te llegará mi olvido 1977, Siempre en mi mente 1978, ¡Espectacular! 1978, Mis ojos tristes 1979, Me gusta bailar contigo 1979, Recuerdos (two vols) 1980, Juan Gabriel con el Mariachi América de Jesús Rodríguez de Hijar 1980, Con tu amor 1981, Cosas de enamorados 1982, Todo 1983, Pensamientos 1986, Juan Gabriel en el Palacio de Bellas Artes (two vols) 1990, Gracias por esperar 1994, El México que se nos fue 1995, Aniversario, Juan Gabriel con la banda el Recodo 1996, Todo está bien 1999, Abrázame muy fuerte 2001, Por los siglos 2001, Inocente de ti 2003, La historia del divo 2006, Los Gabriel…Simplemente Amigos 2007, Los Gabriel…Cantan a México 2008, Los Gabriel…Para ti 2008, El Divo Canta a México 2008, Mis Canciones, Mis Amigos 2009, Juan Gabriel 2010. *Honours:* Latin Recording Acad. Person of the Year 2009. *Address:* c/o Ralph Hauser Management, 9701 Wilshire Blvd., Suite 1000, Beverly Hills, CA 90212, USA.

GABRIEL, Peter; British rock singer and songwriter; b. 13 Feb. 1950, Woking, Surrey; m. 1st Jill Gabriel; two d.; m. 2nd Meabh Flynn 2002; two s. *Education:* Charterhouse School. *Career:* Founde-mem., rock band Genesis 1966–75; solo artist 1975–; f. World of Music, Arts and Dance (WOMAD) featuring music from around the world 1982; f. Real World Group to develop interactive projects in arts and tech. 1985, Real World Studios 1986, Real World Records (world music record label) 1989, Real World Multimedia 1994; launched 'Witness' Human Rights Programme 1992; co-f. Europe digital music wholesaler OD2; co-f., with Brian Eno, the Magnificent Union of Digitally Downloading Artists (MUDDA) 2004; co-f., with Richard Branson, the Elders. org. 2000, launched by Nelson Mandela 2007. *Film scores:* Birdy 1985, Last Temptation of Christ 1989, Long Walk Home (from Rabbit-Proof Fence) 2002, Wall-E (two Grammy Awards 2009) 2008, A Year Ago in Winter 2008, Inside Job 2010, The Reluctant Fundamentalist 2012. *Recordings include:* albums: with Genesis: From Genesis To Revelation 1969, Foxtrot 1972, Genesis Live 1973, Selling England By The Pound 1973, Nursery Crime 1974, The Lamb Lies Down On Broadway 1974; solo: Peter Gabriel I 1977, II 1979, III 1980, IV 1982, Peter Gabriel Plays Live 1983, So 1986, Passion 1989, Shaking The Tree 1990, Us 1992, Revisited 1992, Secret World 1995, Come Home to Me Snow 1998, Ovo 2000, Up 2002, Hit 2003, Big Blue Ball 2008, Scratch My Back 2010, New Blood 2011, Live Blood 2012, Scratch My Back/And I'll Scratch Yours 2013, Courage 2013. *Publication:* Genesis: Chapter and Verse (with other band mems) 2007. *Honours:* Dr hc (City Univ.) 1991; Hon. MA (Univ. Coll., Salford) 1994; Hon. DMus (Bath) 1996; Ivor Novello Award for Outstanding Contribution to British Music 1983, Ivor Novello Award for Best Song (for Sledgehammer) 1987, BRIT Award for Best British Music Video (for Sledgehammer) 1987, for Best British Male Artist 1987, for Best Producer 1993, Grammy Awards for Best New Age Performance 1990, Best Short Form Video 1993, for Best Song Written for Motion Picture (for Down to Earth from Wall-E) 2009, for Best Instrumental Arrangement (for Define Dancing from Wall-E) 2009, Q Award for Lifetime Achievement 2006, Ivor Novello Lifetime Achievement Award 2007, BMI Icon 2007, Amb. of Conscience, Amnesty International 2008, Quadriga Award 2008, Time 100 Most Influential People Award 2008, Polar Music Prize 2009, inducted into Rock and Roll Hall of Fame (with Genesis) 2010, (as solo artist) 2014. *Address:* Real World Holdings Ltd, Box Mill, Mill Lane, Box, Wiltshire, SN13 8PL, England (office). *Telephone:* (1225) 740600 (office). *Website:* www.petergabriel.com; www.realworld.co.uk; www.realworldmultimedia.com; www.realworldrecords.com.

GABRIELLE; British singer and songwriter; b. (Louisa Gabrielle Bobb), 16 May 1970, Hackney, London. *Career:* solo recording artist 1993–; numerous tours and live performances. *Recordings include:* albums: Find Your Way 1993, Gabrielle 1996, Rise 2000, Dreams Can Come True: Greatest Hits Vol. 1 2001, Play To Win 2004; singles: Dreams 1993, I Wish 1994, Going Nowhere 1994, Because of You 1994, Forget About The World 1996, Give Me A Little More Time 1996, If You Really Cared 1996, If You Ever (with East 17) 1996, Walk On By 1997, Sunshine 1999, Rise 2000, When A Woman 2000, Should I Stay 2000, Out of Reach 2001, Don't Need The Sun To Shine (To Make Me Smile) 2001, Ten Years' Time 2004, Always 2007. *Honours:* BRIT Awards for Best Newcomer 1994, Best British Female Solo Artist 19977. *E-mail:* info@gabrielle.co.uk. *Website:* www.gabrielle.co.uk.

GAGE, Peter (Pete), BSc; British musician (guitar, keyboards), producer, arranger, programmer and engineer; b. 31 Aug. 1954, London; m. 1st Elkie Brooks; m. 2nd Ruby James 1996. *Education:* Eltham Coll., London, Univ. of Westminster, London. *Career:* Founder and leader, Geno Washington and the

Ram Jam Band; Founder, Dada and Vinegar Joe; Musical Dir for Elkie Brooks; production, engineering career commenced with debut LP for Joan Armatrading 1974. *Compositions include:* She's Lost You, Less Than Zero, Hazy Shade of Winter, Bangles, Black Smoke, Calumet 1972. *Recordings include:* with Vinegar Joe: Vinegar Joe 1972, Rock n' Roll Gypsies 1972, Six Star General 1973.

GAHAN, David (Dave); British singer and songwriter; b. 9 May 1962, Epping, England; m. 1st Joanne Fox 1985; one s.; m. 2nd Theresa Conroy 1992; m. 3rd Jennifer Skilas 1999; one d. *Career:* Founder-mem., Depeche Mode 1980–; mem. band Composition of Sound 1980; solo artist 2003–; songwriter for Soulsavers 2012. *Recordings include:* albums: with Depeche Mode: Speak and Spell 1981, A Broken Frame 1982, Construction Time Again 1983, Some Great Reward 1984, The Singles 81–85 1985, Black Celebration 1986, Music For The Masses 1987, 101 1989, Violator 1990, Songs Of Faith & Devotion 1993, Ultra 1997, The Singles 86–98 1998, Dream On 2001, Exciter 2001, Playing the Angel 2005, Sounds of the Universe 2009, Delta Machine 2013; with Soulsavers: The Light the Dead See 2012, Angels and Ghosts 2015; solo: Paper Monsters 2003, Hourglass 2007. *Honours:* BRIT Award (for Enjoy the Silence) 1991, MTV Europe Music Award for Best Group 2006. *Current Management:* Sensible Events Ltd, 90–96 Brewery Road, London, N7 9NT, England. *Telephone:* (20) 7700-9900. *Fax:* (20) 7700-7845. *Website:* www.depechemode.com; www.davegahan.com.

GAINSBOURG, Charlotte; French actress and singer; b. 22 July 1971, London, UK; d. of the late Serge Gainsbourg and of Jane Birkin (q.v.); partner Yvan Attal 1997; one s. *Career:* mem. Jury, 22nd American Film Festival, Deauville, 62nd Berlin Int. Film Festival 2012. *Film appearances include:* Paroles et musique 1984, La Tentation d'Isabelle 1985, L'Effrontée (An Impudent Girl, César Award) 1985, Charlotte Forever 1986, Le Petit amour 1987, Kung-Fu master 1987, A. V. sur J. B. 1987, La Petite voleuse 1989, Aux yeux du monde 1990, Il sole anche di notte 1990, Merci la vie 1991, Contre l'oubli 1991, Amoureuse 1992, The Cement Garden 1993, Grosse fatigue 1994, Jane Eyre 1995, Anna Oz 1996, Love, etc. 1996, The Intruder 1999, La Bûche 1999, Le Soleil le plus près 2000, Les Enfants des photos 2000, Passionnement 2000, Nuremberg 2000, Les Misérables 2000, Félix et Lola 2000, Ma femme est une actrice 2001, La Merveilleuse odyssée de l'idiot Tobaggan 2002, Embrassez qui vous voulez 2002, Anna M. 2002, 21 Grams 2003, Une Star internationale 2004, Ils se marièrent et eurent beaucoup d'enfants (...And They Lived Happily Ever After) 2004, L'Un reste, l'autre part 2005, Lemming 2005, La Science des Rêves (The Science of Sleep) 2006, Nuovomondo (The Golden Door) 2006, Prête-moi ta main 2006, I'm Not There 2007, The City of Your Final Destination 2007, Antichrist (Award for Best Actress, Cannes Film Festival) 2009, Persécution 2009, The Tree 2010, Melancholia 2011, Confession of a Child of the Century 2011. *Recordings include:* albums: Charlotte Forever 1986, Élastique, 5:55 2006, I.R.M. 2010, Stage Whisper 2011. *Current Management:* c/o Dominique Besnehard, Artémedia, 20 avenue Rapp, 75007 Paris, France. *Telephone:* 1-43-17-33-82. *E-mail:* d.besnehard@artemedia.fr. *Website:* www.charlottegainsbourg.com.

GALANIN, Sergey; Russian singer, songwriter and musician (guitar, bass guitar); b. 16 Nov. 1961, Moscow; m. Olga Galanina 1982; one s. *Education:* Railroad Coll. *Career:* mem. of various bands, including Redkaya Ptitsa, Gulliver, Brigada S, Brigadiry Ser'ga; regular tours in Russia, and appearances at festivals, concerts and festivals. *Recordings include:* All This Is Rock 'N' Roll (by Brigada S), Rivers (by Brigada S), I Adore Jazz (by Brigada S), Dog's Waitz (by Ser'ga) 1994, Ser'ga 1995.

GALLAGHER, Benny; British singer, songwriter and musician (guitar); b. Largs, Ayrshire, Scotland. *Career:* songwriting partnership with Graham Lyle 1960s–79; staff writer, Beatles publishing co., Apple 1966–69; mem., McGuinness Flint 1969–71; folk duo, Gallagher and Lyle 1972–80; also mem. band Slim Chance, The Manfreds 1992–99; solo artist 1980–; Founding Dir and Chair. Performing Artists Media Rights Asscn 1996–2002. *Compositions include:* A Heart In New York, Breakaway, A Heart In New York, Stay Young; The Fields of St Etienne, When I'm I'm Dead and Gone, Malt and Barley Blues, Heart On My Sleeve, I Wanna Stay With You, Every Little Teardrop, Mr Heartbreak's Here Instead, Breakaway, The Runaway, The Friendship Song, I'm Amazed, When I'm Dead and Gone, Keep the Candle Burnin', The First Leaves of Autumn. *Recordings include:* albums: with Gallagher and Lyle: Gallagher and Lyle 1972, Willie and The Lap Dog 1973, Seeds 1973, The Last Cowboy 1974, Breakway 1976, Love On The Airways 1977, Showdown 1978, Gone Crazy 1979, Lonesome No More 1979, Living on the Breadline 1980, Breakaway 1981, The Best of Gallagher & Lyle 1995, Live In Concert 1999, The River Sessions 2004; with Slim Chance: Anymore for Anymore; solo: On Stage, At The Edge Of The Wave. *E-mail:* onsongmusic@btopenworld.com. *Website:* www.bennygallagher.com.

GALLAGHER, Eve; British singer and actress; b. 12 Feb. 1956, Sunderland, England. *Education:* drama at college. *Career:* actress, singer, appeared in various West End productions, including Hair, Oh Calcutta; signed by, and co-writer with, Boy George, More Protein Records; began new music project Galacteve (electronica/rock); co-wrote album Stray with husband Yves Poli and producer Uli Heinzler; working on new material with Boy George 2012–13. *Recordings include:* album: Woman Can Have It 1995, Stray 2012; singles: Love Come Down 1991, Love Is a Master of Disguise 1995, Heartbreak 1996; features on: The Unrecoupable One Man Bandit, Boy George 1999, Take It or Leave It, by DJ Antoine 2001; remixes: Love Come Down 2013, You Can

Have It All 2013. *Honours:* Best Actress Award in Shakespeare for playing having played Queen Margaret in Richard III 1974. *Current Management:* c/o Action Artist Management, Förrlibuckstrasse 66, 8005 Zurich, Switzerland. *Telephone:* (1) 2725055. *Fax:* (1) 2726066. *E-mail:* info@evegallagher.com. *Website:* www.evegallagher.com.

GALLAGHER, Liam (William John Paul); British singer, musician (guitar, keyboards) and producer; b. 21 Sept. 1972, Burnage, Manchester; s. of Peggy Gallagher; brother of Noel Gallagher (q.v.); m. 1st Patsy Kensit 1997 (divorced 2000); one s.; one d. (with Lisa Moorish); m. 2nd Nicole Appleton; one s. *Education:* St Mark's High School, Didsbury, Manchester. *Career:* founder mem., Oasis 1991–2009; f. and recorded for Big Brother Records 2000–; founder mem., Beady Eye 2009–; numerous concert and festival appearances; regular tours UK, Europe and USA. *Recordings include:* albums: with Oasis: Definitely Maybe 1994, (What's The Story) Morning Glory? (BRIT Award for Best Album 1996) 1995, Be Here Now 1997, The Masterplan 1998, Standing On The Shoulder of Giants 2000, Familiar To Millions (live) 2001, Heathen Chemistry 2002, Don't Believe The Truth (Q Award for Best Album) 2005, Stop the Clocks 2006, Dig Out Your Soul 2008; with Beady Eye: Different Gear, Still Speeding 2011, BE 2013. *Honours:* Q Awards for Best New Act 1994, Best Live Act 1995, BRIT Awards for Best Newcomers 1995, Best Single, Best Video, Best British Group 1996, NME Awards for Best UK Band, Artist of the Year 2003, Q Award for Best Act in the World Today 2006, BRIT Award for Outstanding Contribution to Music 2007. *Current Management:* Ignition Management, 54 Linhope Street, London, NW1 6HL, England. *Telephone:* (20) 7298-6000. *Fax:* (20) 7258-0962. *E-mail:* mail@ignition-man.co.uk. *Website:* www.oasisinet.com.

GALLAGHER, Noel Thomas David; British singer, songwriter and musician (guitar); b. 29 May 1967, Burnage, Manchester; s. of Peggy Gallagher; brother of Liam Gallagher (q.v.); m. 1st Meg Matthews 1997 (divorced 2001); one d.; m. 2nd Sara MacDonald 2011; one s. *Career:* fmrly worked as guitar technician for Inspiral Carpets 1990–93; mem., Oasis 1991–2009; f. and recorded for Big Brother Records 2000–; mem., Noel Gallagher's High Flying Birds 2011–; numerous concert and festival appearances; regular tours UK, Europe and USA; numerous collaborations with other artists including Ian Brown, the Chemical Brothers, Goldie, Miles Kane, Paul Weller; founder Sour Mash Records 2001–; mem. Tailgunner. *Recordings include:* albums: Definitely Maybe 1994, (What's The Story) Morning Glory? (BRIT Award for Best Album 1996) 1995, Be Here Now 1997, The Masterplan 1998, Standing On The Shoulder of Giants 2000, Familiar To Millions (live) 2001, Heathen Chemistry 2002, Don't Believe The Truth (Q Award for Best Album) 2005, Stop the Clocks 2006, Dig Out Your Soul 2008; with Noel Gallagher's High Flying Birds: Noel Gallagher's High Flying Birds 2011, Chasing Yesterday (Q Best Album Award 2015) 2015. *Honours:* Q Awards for Best New Act 1994, Best Live Act 1995, BRIT Awards for Best Newcomers 1995, Best Single, Best Video, Best British Group 1996, Ivor Novello Award 1995, Music Week Award for Top Songwriter 1996, Grammy Award for Best Song (Wonderwall) 1996, NME Awards for Best UK Band, Artist of the Year 2003, Q Award for Best Act in the World Today 2006, BRIT Award for Outstanding Contribution to Music 2007. *Current Management:* Ignition Management, 54 Linhope Street, London, NW1 6HL, England. *Telephone:* (20) 7298-6000. *Fax:* (20) 7258-0962. *E-mail:* info@ignition.co.uk. *Website:* www.ignition.co.uk/management.php; www.oasisinet.com; www.noelgallagher.com.

GALLAGHER, Rob, (Rob Galliano, Earl Zinger); British singer and producer; b. 18 Oct. 1964, London. *Career:* Founder and mem. of Galliano 1988–96; solo career, recording as Earl Zinger; collaborations with Mick Talbot, Valerie Etienne, Ski Oakenfull; mem. Performing Right Soc. *Recordings include:* albums: In Pursuit of The 13th Note 1991, A Joyful Noise Unto The Creator 1992, The Plot Thickens 1994, 4our 1996, Put Your Phazers On Stun and Throw Your Health Food Skyward (as Earl Zinger) 2001; singles: Frederick Lies Still 1988, Prince of Peace, Skunk Funk 1992, Roofing Tiles 1996, Song 2 (as Earl Zinger) 2000.

GALLIANO, Richard; French accordionist, composer and arranger; b. 12 Dec. 1950, Le Cannet, Côte d'Azur; s. of Lucien Galliano (Italian-born accordion teacher). *Education:* studied with Claude Noel, studied harmony, counterpoint and trombone at Nice Conservatoire. *Career:* renowned for creating a fusion of jazz, classical and traditional styles of accordion music; began playing the accordion aged four; was introduced to jazz through discovery of music of Clifford Brown aged 14; became interested in Brazilian accordionists including Sivuca and Dominguinhos; discovered American jazz specialists (Tommy Gumina, Ernie Felice and Art Van Damme), and leading Italian players, Felice Fugazza, Volpi and Fancelli; moved away completely on traditional style of playing that dominated in France; moved to Paris 1973; composer, arranger and conductor with Claude Nougaro Orchestra 1973–76; played on numerous recordings by popular French artists, including Barbara, Serge Reggiani, Charles Aznavour and Juliette Gréco, and on film scores; played with, and improvised alongside, jazz musicians from all backgrounds, including Chet Baker (in Brazilian repertoire), Steve Potts, Jimmy Gourley, Toots Thielemanns, cellist Jean-Charles Capon (with whom he cut his first disc) and Ron Carter, with whom he paired up to make an album in 1990; returned to his roots, on advice of Astor Piazzolla, and traditional repertoire of Valses-Musette, Javas, Complaintes and Tangos 1991; travelled to USA to record New York Tango with George Mraz, Al Foster and Biréli Lagrène 1996; other collaborations have included Enrico Rava, Charlie Haden and Michel

Portal, accordionist Antonello Salis, Italy, and organist Eddy Louiss 2001; played in trio with Daniel Humair and Jean-François Jenny-Clarke 1993–98, returned to this format with a 'New York' rhythm, made up of Clarence Penn and Larry Grenadier 2004; one-off collaborations with Jan Garbarek, Martial Solal, Hermeto Pascoal and Anouar Brahem, Paolo Fresu and Jan Lundgren and Gary Burton, among others; presented own compositions, with chamber orchestra accompaniment, together with pieces by Astor Piazzolla 1999; played with Brussels Jazz Orchestra 2008; solo appearances at Paris Concert from the Châtelet 2009. *Recordings:* New Musette (with Aldo Romano, Pierre Michelot and Philip Catherine for Label bleu) (Django Reinhardt Prize for French Musician of the Year, Acad. du Jazz 1993) 1992, Spleen 1993, Viaggio 1993, Panamanhattan, Live, with Ron Carter (Classical and Jazz Award for Best Jazz Album 1996) 1994, Laurita 1995, New York Tango (with George Mraz, Al Foster and Biréli Lagrène) (Victoire de la Musique 1996) 1996, Blow Up (Victoire de la Musique 1997, Classical and Jazz Award for Best Jazz Album 1997) 1997, French Touch (with Wynton Marsalis) (Musica Jazz Award for Best Int. Jazz Album) 1998, Passatori 1999, Concerts Inédits 2000, Blues Sur Seine (with Jean-Charles Capon) 2001, Gallianissimo 2001, Face to Face (with Eddy Louiss) 2001, Piazolla Forever 2003, Concerts (with Michel Portal) 2004, Blue Hat (with Josephine Cronholm) 2005, Ruby My Dear 2005, Solo 2006, Luz Negra 2007, Mare Nostrum (with Paolo Fresu and Jan Lundgren) 2008, Love Day (with Gonzalo Rubalcaba, Charlie Haden and Mino Cinelu) 2009, Ten Years Ago (with Brussels Jazz Orchestra) 2008, Tribute to Billie Holliday and Edith Piaff with the Wynton Marsalis Quintet 2010, The JS Bach Project 2010, Tribute to Nino Rota 2011, Southern Exposure with Christian Howes 2012, Vivaldi Four Seasons 2013, Sentimentale 2014. *Publication:* co-author (with father Lucien) of accordion method (SACEM Prize for Best Pedagogical Work) 2009. *Honours:* Officier des Arts et des Lettres, Légion d'honneur. *Current Management:* c/o Jean Michel de Bie, Ginga Productions, Chaiseray, 72310 Vancé, France. *Telephone:* (2) 43-35-92-52. *Fax:* (2) 43-35-92-53. *E-mail:* ginga@wanadoo.fr; gingaproductions@yahoo.fr. *Website:* www.richardgalliano.com.

GAMBARINI, Roberta; Italian singer; b. 1972, Turin. *Career:* started music career in 1986; toured jazz clubs throughout Italy with French Hammond organ player Emmanuel Bex 1997; moved to USA 1998. *Recordings include:* albums: Easy to Love 2006, You Are There 2008, So in Love 2009. *Honours:* Female Jazz Vocalist of the Year, Jazz Journalists Awards 2010. *Address:* Amsterdam Jazz Agency B.V., PO Box 14649, 1001 LC Amsterdam, Netherlands. *Website:* www.robertagambarini.com.

GAMBLE, Kenneth; American songwriter and producer; b. 11 Aug. 1943, Philadelphia, Pa. *Career:* fmr singer with Kenny Gamble and The Romeos; Founder, Gamble Records; formed songwriting and production team with Leon Huff 1963–, Co-founder Philadelphia Int. Records (with Huff) 1971, signed and developed numerous artists, including Harold Melvin and The Bluenotes, The O'Jays, Lou Rawls, Billy Paul, Teddy Pendergrass, MFSB, The Jones Girls; style came to be known as 'The Philadelphia Sound'; fmr Chair., The Black Music Asscn, Clean Up The Ghetto Inc.; fmr partner publishing co., Mighty Three Music; Founder and Chair. of non-profit urban re-devt org., Universal Companies Inc.; Co-founder, The Philadelphia Music Foundation; Co-founder, Gamble-Huff Music; music instructor, Raising Horizons Quest Charter School; f. Universal Bluford Charter School. *Compositions include:* co-writer with Leon Huff of over 3,000 songs, including Wake Up Everybody (Harold Melvin and The Bluenotes), For the Love of Money (The O'Jays), You'll Never Find (Another Love Like Mine) (Lou Rawls), Me and Mrs Jones (Billy Paul), TSOP (The Sound of Philadelphia) (MFSB), Silly, Silly Fool (Dusty Springfield), Only the Strong Survive (Jerry Butler), Now That We Found Love (The O'Jays), When Will I See You Again (The Three Degrees). *Honours:* Grammy Award 1989, Grammy Award for Best R&B Song (for If You Don't Know Me By Now) 1990, Grammy Trustees Award 1999, Boyer Coll. Tribute Award 2004, inducted into Dance Music Hall of Fame (with Leon Huff) 2005, Ahmet Ertegün Award (with Leon Huff), inducted into Rock and Roll Hall of Fame 2008. *Address:* Gamble-Huff Music, 309 South Broad Street, Philadelphia, PA 19107, USA (office). *E-mail:* chuckgamble@gamble-huffmusic.com. *Website:* www.gamble-huffmusic.com.

GAMBLE, Patsy; British musician (saxophone) and teacher; b. (Patricia Margaret Gamble), 13 Sept. 1963, Stroud, Gloucestershire, England; d. of Patrick Gamble and Rosalie Gamble. *Career:* teacher, session musician 1990–; toured with The Patsy Gamble Band, The Little Big Horns, Eddie Martin, Eugene 'Hideaway' Bridges, Keith Thompson; worked with Dick Heckstall-Smith, Steve Winwood, Mick Jagger, Grand Drive, Muddy Manninen, Chris Farlowe; mem. Musicians' Union, PPL, PRS. *Recordings include:* various as session musician; album: After Sunset, Secret Soul, Skyline, Warsaw Nights. *E-mail:* info@patsygamble.co.uk. *Website:* www.patsygamble.co.uk.

THE GAME; American rap artist; b. (Jayceon Taylor), 27 Nov. 1979, Compton, Los Angeles, Calif.; one s. *Career:* rap artist 2001–; f. The Black Wall Street Records. *Recordings include:* albums: Chronicles 2004, Untold Story 2004, The Documentary 2005, West Coast Resurrection 2005, Untold Story Vol. 2 2005, Doctor's Advocate 2006, L.A.X 2008, The R.E.D. Album 2011, Jesus Piece 2012, OKE 2013. *Films include:* Waist Deep 2006, Belly 2: Millionaire Boyz Club 2006, Street Kings 2008, House Arrest 2012. *Honours:* World Music Award for Bestselling Male Artist 2005. *Website:* www.thisizgame.ning.com.

GANC, David, BA; Brazilian musician (flute and saxophone) and arranger; b. 24 May 1958, Rio de Janeiro; m. Monique C. Aragao; one s. *Education:* Federal Univ. of Rio de Janeiro with C. Noltzenlogel, Berklee Coll. of Music with Joe Viola and Gary Burton, studied with John Neschling. *Career:* session musician, recording and playing with artists, including Stevie Wonder, Gal Costa, Simone, Paulo Moura, Luiz Melodia, Nivaldo Ornelas, Elba Ramalho, Geraldo Azevedo, Monique Aragao, Emílio Santiago; recording musician at Globo TV; special radio programme with David Ganc Quartet at Radio Mec; played as guest saxophonist, Brazilian Symphony Orchestra. *Recordings include:* solo albums: Brazilian Ballads 1996, Caldo de Cana 2000, David Ganc & Quarteto de Cordas Guerra Peixe interpret Tom Jobim 2004, Pixinguinha + Benedito (with Mário Sève) 2005. *E-mail:* dganc@terra.com.br. *Website:* www.davidganc.com.

GANESH, V. Selva; Indian musician (percussion, kanjira); b. 28 Dec. 1966, Palakol, Andhra Pradesh; s. of T. H. Vikku Vinayakram. *Career:* first public performance aged ten; toured the world with Zakir Hussain and John McLaughlin as part of Remember Shakti; participant, The Masters of Percussion 2002; f. group dr jsm (with German songwriter Dr Joel and Carnatic singer Mahesh). *Compositions include:* (with Rikhi Ray) score for dance production, Pratirupa: The Mirror Image 1997, scores for Tamil movie Vennila Kabadi Kuzhu 2008, Kola Kolaya Mundhirika 2009, Drohi 2010, Nil Gavani Sellathey 2010, Kullanari Koottam 2011, Pilla Zamindar 2011, Shiva Manasulo Shruti 2012, Nirnayam (also producer) 2013, Rettai Vaalu 2013. *Recordings include:* album: Together (with T. H. Vikku Vinayakram and Shankar) 1997; played on film soundtracks: Kama Sutra: A Tale Of Love 1996, Monsoon Wedding 2002, Vanity Fair 2004, Water 2005, Turn On The Dreams 2005; solo: Soukha 2006. *Film:* Bodhai (dir) 2012. *Address:* 14/5, Parasu Street, Kilpauk, Chennai 600 010, India (home). *Telephone:* (44) 6444066 (home).

GANG RELATED (see Krust)

GANNON, Angela; British musician (percussion) and singer; sister of Sean Gannon. *Career:* mem., The Magic Numbers 2002–; collaborated with numerous artists and bands including Ed Harcourt, The Boxer Revolution, Duke Special, The Chemical Brothers. *Recordings include:* albums: The Magic Numbers 2005, Those The Brokes 2006, Undecided 2007, The Runaway 2010. *Current Management:* c/o Stephen Budd, SuperVision Management Group, 59–65 Worship Street, London, EC2A 2DU, England. *Telephone:* (20) 7688-9000. *Fax:* (20) 7688-8999. *E-mail:* info@supervisionmgt.com. *Website:* www.themagicnumbers.net.

GANNON, Oliver, BMus; Canadian jazz musician (guitar); b. 23 March 1943, Dublin; m. Patty Hervey 1979; one s. one d. *Education:* Univ. of Manitoba, Berklee Coll. of Music, USA. *Career:* has been active in Vancouver and Canadian jazz scenes since 1970s; performed at major jazz festivals in Europe and North Sea, America and fmr USSR; three Russian tours with tenor saxophonist Fraser MacPherson. *Recordings include:* (cellar live label) Oliver Gannon Quartet Live at The Cellar 2002, That's What 2004, Two Much Guitar 2006, Up a Step 2012, Easy Sailing 2014, Broadway 2015, Two Much More 2015; with Ian MacDougall: Three 1976, Rio 1988, The Warmth of the Horn 1996, Burning Down the House 2001, Nights In Vancouver 2003, In a Sentimental Mood 2005, The Ian McDougall 12tet - Live 2012, The Very Thought of You 2012; with Fraser MacPherson: Live At The Planetarium 1978, 2015, Live From Montreux 1979, Live at Puccini's 2012, I Didn't Know About You (JUNO Award for Best Jazz Album 1982) 1980, Indian Summer 1983, Honey and Spice 1987, Encore 1990, In The Tradition 1991, Someday You'll Be Sorry 1996; with Miles Black: Broadway 2015; also albums with Ross Tagart, George Robert, Pacific Salt and others; contrib. to Band-in-a-Box (music accompaniment program). *Honours:* JUNO Award for Best Jazz Album 1982, Jazz Guitarist of the Year, Canadian Jazz Awards 2003. *Address:* Oliver Gannon, 2781 McKenzie Avenue, Surrey, BC V4A 3H5, Canada (home). *Telephone:* (604) 535-4618 (home). *E-mail:* ogannon@shaw.ca. *Website:* www.olivergannon.com.

GANNON, Sean; British musician (drums); brother of Angela Gannon. *Career:* mem., The Magic Numbers 2002–. *Recordings include:* albums: The Magic Numbers 2005, Those The Brokes 2006, Undecided 2007, The Runaway 2010; others: The Beautiful Lie (with Ed Harcourt) 2006, Sounds Eclectic: The Covers Project. *Current Management:* c/o Stephen Budd, SuperVision Management Group, 59–65 Worship Street, London, EC2A 2DU, England. *Telephone:* (20) 7688-9000. *Fax:* (20) 7688-8999. *E-mail:* info@supervisionmgt.com. *Website:* www.themagicnumbers.net.

GARA, Jeremy; Canadian musician (drums, guitar) and singer; b. Ottawa. *Career:* fmr mem., Kepler, Weights and Measures; mem., Arcade Fire 2003–. *Recordings include:* albums: Funeral 2004, Neon Bible (Juno Award for Alternative Album of the Year 2008) 2007, The Suburbs (Grammy Award for Album of the Year 2011) 2010, Reflektor (Juno Awards for Album of the Year and Alternative Album of the Year 2014) 2013. *Address:* Quest Management, 1D–36 Warple Way, London, W3 0DY, England. *Telephone:* (20) 8749-0088. *Fax:* (20) 8749-0080. *E-mail:* info@quest-management.com. *Website:* www.quest-management.com; www.arcadefire.com.

GARBAREK, Anja; Norwegian singer, songwriter and composer; b. 24 July 1970, Oslo; d. of Jan Garbarek and Vigdis Garbarek; m. John Mallison; one c. *Career:* collaborations with Robert Wyatt, Mark Hollis, Satyricon, Rita Marcotulli, Wibutee, Steve Jansen, Gisli, Jan Garbarek; contributed music to Luc Besson's film, Angel-A 2005. *Recordings include:* albums: Velkommen Inn 1992, Balloon Mood 1996, Smiling and Waving (Spellemanns Prize 2001) 2001, Briefly Shaking 2006, Angel-A soundtrack 2006, Volcano (with Satyricon) 2002, Koine (with Rita Marcotillu) 2002, Sweet Mental (with Wibutee) 2006, Rock Bottom/Comicopera (with Robert Wyatt) 2010). *Honours:* Spellemanns Prize 2001. *Current Management:* c/o Live Nation, Sonja Henies plass 2, Oslo 0185, Norway. *Telephone:* 23-16-32-60. *E-mail:* christian@livenation.no; rune@livenation.no. *Website:* www.livenation.no; www.myspace.com/anjagarbarek; www.anjagarbarek.com.

GARBAREK, Jan; Norwegian musician (saxophone), songwriter and producer; b. 4 March 1947, Mysen. *Career:* mem. group with Jon Christensen, Arild Andersen, Terje Rypdal 1960s; played with Keith Jarrett's Belonging, Zakir Hussain, Paul Giger, David Darling, Ralph Towner 1970s; leader of own groups, featuring Bill Frisell, Eberhard Weber, Nana Vasconcelos 1980s–; also played with Don Cherry, George Russell. *Recordings include:* albums: The Esoteric Circle 1969, Works 1970, Afric Pepperbird 1970, Sart 1971, Triptykon 1972, Witchi-Tai-To (with Bobo Stenson) 1973, Red Lanta (with L. Shankar) 1973, Belonging (with Keith Jarrett) 1974, Luminescence (with Keith Jarrett) 1974, Dansere (with Bobo Stenson) 1975, Dis 1976, Places 1977, Photo With Blue Sky, White Cloud, Wires, Windows And A Red Roof 1978, Folk Songs (with Charlie Haden and Egberto Gismonti) 1979, Aftenland (with Kjell Johnsen) 1979, Eventyr 1980, Magico (with Charlie Haden and Egberto Gismonti) 1980, Paths, Prints 1981, Wayfarer 1983, It's OK To Listen To The Gray Voice 1984, Song For Everyone (with L. Shankar) 1985, To All Those Born With Wings 1986, Legend of The Seven Dreams 1988, I Took Up The Runes 1990, Star 1991, Rosensfole (with Agnes Buen Garnås) 1991, Madar (with Anouar Brahem) 1992, Twelve Moons 1992, Ragas And Sagas (with Ustad Fateh Ali Khan) 1992, Officium (with The Hilliard Ensemble) 1993, Visible World 1995, Rites 1999, Mnemosyne (with The Hilliard Ensemble) 1999, Monodia 2002, Universal Syncopations 2003, In Praise Of Dreams 2004, Neighbourhood 2006, Stages of a Long Journey 2007, Elixir 2007, Officium Novum (with The Hilliard Ensemble) 2010, Sleeper: Tokyo, April 16th, 1979 2012, Magico: Carta de Amor 2012, Eleni Karaindrou: Concert in Athens 2013. *Film:* Sounds and Silence 2009. *Address:* c/o ECM Records, Postfach 600 331, 81203 Munich, Germany (office). *E-mail:* ecm@ecmrecords.com (office). *Website:* www.ecmrecords.com (office); www.garbarek.com; www.soundsandsilence.ch.

GARBUTT, Vin; British folk musician (guitar, tin-whistle), singer, songwriter and humorist; b. South Bank, Middlesbrough; m. Pat Garbutt; four c. *Career:* musician, songwriter 1969–; live appearances worldwide, festivals include Cambridge, Edinburgh, Wath, Auckland, Fylde, Sidmouth Folk Week, Port Fairy (Australia), Blue Mountains (Australia). *Recordings include:* albums: The Valley Of Tees 1972, Young Tin Whistle Pest 1974, King Gooden 1976, Eston California 1978, Tossin' A Wobbler 1978, Little Innocents 1983, Shy Tot Pommy 1986, When The Tide Turns 1989, The South Banker Show 1991, The Bypass Syndrome 1992, Bandalised 1994, Plugged 1995, When The Tide Turns Again 1998, Word of Mouth 2001, The Vin Garbutt Songbook Vol. 1 2001, Persona... Grata 2006. *Publication:* The Vin Garbutt Song Book. *Honours:* Hon. MA (Teesside Univ.); BBC Radio 2 Folk Award for Best Live Act 2001. *Current Management:* c/o Home Roots Music, 52, Micklow Lane, Loftus, TS13 4JE, England. *E-mail:* vingarbutt@talktalk.net. *Website:* www.vingarbutt.com.

GARCIA, Dean; British musician; b. 3 May 1958, London; m. J. P. Fletcher; one s. one d. *Career:* tours with Eurythmics, Sinead O'Connor, Bryan Ferry; mem. own band Curve 1991–94, 1996–2005; Founder-mem. SPC ECO 2007–; Co-founder Xd Records 2011; mem. PRS, Musicians' Union, PAMRA. *Compositions include:* Chinese Burn 1998. *Recordings include:* albums: with Curve: Doppleganger 1992, Cuckoo 1993, Public Fruit, Come Clean 1998, Open Day At The Hate Fest 2001, Gift 2001; with The Eurythmics: Touch 1983, Be Yourself Tonight 1985; with Mick Jagger: Primitive Cool 1987, Lethal Weapon 1; with Gang of Four: Tattoo; with Ultrasound: Flying Saucer; with Recoil: Liquid 2000, Strange Hours 2000; with SPC ECO: 3-D 2009, Alternative Mixes and Remixes 2010, You Tell Me 2011, Dark Notes 2012. *Website:* www.spceco.com.

GARCIA, Kany; Puerto Rican singer, songwriter and musician (guitar, cello); b. (Encarnita Garcia de Jesus), 25 Sept. 1982, Toa Baja. *Education:* Escuela Libre de Música, Conservatorio de Música. *Career:* competed in TV series Objetivo Fama 2004; solo artist, debut recording 2007; international tours and TV appearances. *Television:* Objetivo Fama (contestant) 2004. *Recordings include:* albums: Cualquier Dia (Latin Grammy Award for Best Female Pop Vocal Album 2008) 2007, Boleto de Entrada 2009, Kany Garcia 2012. *Honours:* Latin Grammy Award for Best New Artist 2008. *Address:* c/o Sony Music España, Sony BMG Music Entertainment, Avda. de los Madroños 27, ES 28043 Madrid, Spain (office). *E-mail:* contacto@sonymusic.es (office). *Website:* www.sonymusic.es (office); www.kanygarcia.com.

GARCIA-FONS, Renaud; French musician (double bass) and composer; b. 24 Dec. 1962, Boulogne-Billancourt; s. of Pierre Garcia-Fons. *Education:* Paris Conservatory, studied with Jean-Pierre Logerot and François Rabbath. *Career:* began career playing jazz in Roger Guérin's band; mem. L'Orchestre de Contrebasses 1983–87; fmr mem. Orchestre National de Jazz under Claude Barthélémy; plays a customised five-stringed bass; regular concerts solo and with his trio in Europe, USA, Middle East; appearances include Knitting Factory, New York, Festival de la Côte d'Opale, Festival de Sully, Spoleto Festival, USA; performed concerts with Scottish Chamber Orchestra; studio and live collaborations with musicians including Jean-Louis Matinier, Michael Riessler, Nguyên Lê, Michel Godard, Gerardo Núñez, Kudsi Erguner, Dhafer Youssef, Cheb Mami, Sylvain Luc, Pedro Soler, Vincente Pradal, Carmen Linares, Sabrina Romero. *Recordings include:* albums: Légendes 1992, Alboreá 1995, Suite Andalouse (with Pedro Soler) 1995, Oriental Bass 1997, Fuera 1999, Navigatore 2002, Entremundo 2004, Arcoluz 2006, La Linea del Sur 2009, Acoustic Songs, Free Songs (with Gerard Marais), Suite Andalouse (with Pedro Soler), Jazzspaña 2 (with Gerardo Nuñez), Méditerranées 2011, Solo-The Marcevol Concert (ECHO Jazz Award 2013) 2012, Beyond The Double Bass 2013, Silk Moon (with Derya Turkan) 2014, Paseo a dos (with Dorantes) 2015. *Honours:* Int. Soc. of Bassists Award 2009. *Current Management:* Francois Peyratout, 31 Rue de la Haute Musse, Prefailles, 44770, France. *Telephone:* 6-20-76-10-10. *E-mail:* fr.peyratout@gmail.com. *Website:* www.nemomusic.com; www.renaudgarciafons.com.

GARDINER, Bobby; Irish musician (accordion) and teacher; b. 1939, Aughdarra, County Clare. *Career:* mem. Kilfenora Ceili Band, Malachy Sweeney Band 1950s; moved to New York 1961; made recordings and joined US Army; returned to Ireland 1970s; mem. Bru Boru; Departmental Tutor, niv. Coll., Cork. *Recordings include:* albums: Memories of Clare 1962, Bobby Gardiner At Home 1979, The Best of Bobby Gardiner 1982, The Master's Choice 1989, The Clare Shout 1998, The High Level 2010. *Honours:* Eigse Award, Comhaltas Ceoltori Eireann 2003. *Website:* www.bobbygardiner.com.

GARDINER, Boris Oliver Patrick; Jamaican singer and musician (bass, piano, guitar); b. 13 Jan. 1943, Kingston; m. (divorced); two s. two d. *Career:* lead singer, The Rhythm Aces 1960, Kes Chin and Souvenirs Band 1962; bassist and singer, Carlos Malcolm Afro-Jamaican Rhythm Band 1964; formed own band, The Boris Gardiner Happening 1968–82; numerous live performances, radio and TV broadcasts; mem. MCPS, PRS. *Recordings include:* albums: Is What's Happening 1995, I Want to Wake Up With You: The Best Of Boris Gardiner 2004. *Honours:* Swing Magazine Award for Best Vocalist 1972, Canadian Reggae Music Int. Award for Top Reggae Single (for I Wanna Wake Up With You) 1986.

GARDNER, Jeff; American musician (piano), composer and educator; b. (Jeffrey Dana Gardner), 23 Oct. 1953, New York, NY; s. of Edward Benjamin Gardner and Iljana Schreiber Gardner; m. Rosa Gardner. *Education:* Harvard Univ., studied music with Hall Overton, Nadia Boulanger, John Lewis, Jaki Byard, Don Friedman, Ivan Tcherepnin. *Career:* played in Brazil with Wayne Shorter, Hermeto Pascoal, Pat Metheny, Helen Merrill, Helio Delmiro, Monterey Jazz Festival, with Victor Assis Brasil, Clark Terry, Slide Hampton 1980; European tours with Steve Lacy and Eddie Harris; concerts with Gary Peacock, Freddie Hubbard; solo concerts for French television and radio; mem. piano quartet with Martial Solal, Paul Bley, Jaki Byard 1985; solo concert tour, Brazil 1992; tour of France with Rick Margitza 1995; also played with Kenny Wheeler, André Ceccarelli, Paulo Moura, Charlie Mariano, Etta Cameron; duo with Andrew Schloss, performed IRCAM, Paris, Germany; USA; worked with soprano S'Ange Susan Belling; concerts include October Jazz Festival, Saint Lucia, CMAC, Martinique, Paris Jazz Festival, Madajazzcar Festival, Antananarivo; tour of Japan, with Lisa Ono 1996; moved to Brazil 2002; mem. SACEM. *Recordings include:* Bop Top (with Alan Praskin, Dodo Sosoka, Peter Koorinek) 1992, California Daydream (with Kenny Wheeler, Hein van de Geyn, Andre Ceccarelli) 1992, Sky Dance (with Gilberto Gil, Carlos Malta, Nivaldo Ornellas) 1992, Noches Habaneras (with Anga, Maraca, Julio Barreto, Diego Valdez, Felipe Cabrera) 1998, The Music of Chance (with Rick Margitza, Ingrid Jensen, Drew Gress, Tony Jefferson) 1999, Street Angels 2001, Spirit Call 2001, Continuum (with Eddie Gomez and Billy Hart) 2002, Grace (with David Friesen) 2002, Agatha, Le rêve de la Forêt 2002, Abraços (with Carlos Balla, Alberto Continentino) 2004, Agatha, Everyday Miracles 2004, Second Home (with Rick Margitza) 2005, Alchemy (with Gary Peacock) 2006, The Music of Chance, Breath 2007, Lovelight 2009, Home is a River 2012. *Publications include:* Jazz Piano – Creative Concepts and Techniques 1997, Jazz Transcription (with Niels Lan Doky) 1997, Blues Book 2004, Sentimento Brasileiro 2004, Easy Jazz Preludes 2008, Shapes 2010. *E-mail:* jeffgardnerjazz@gmail.com. *Website:* www.jeffgardner.com.br.

GARFUNKEL, Arthur (Art), MA; American singer and actor; b. 5 Nov. 1941, Forest Hills, NY; m. 1st Linda Marie Grossman 1972 (divorced 1975); m. 2nd Kim Cermak 1988; one s. *Education:* Columbia Univ. *Career:* mem. singing duo Simon & Garfunkel (with Paul Simon) 1964–71; solo artist 1972–. *Films include:* Catch 22 1970, Carnal Knowledge 1971, Bad Timing 1980, Good To Go 1986, Boxing Helena 1993, 54 1998, The Rebound 2010. *Recordings include:* albums: as Simon & Garfunkel: Wednesday Morning 3am 1964, Sounds of Silence 1966, Parsley, Sage, Rosemary and Thyme 1966, The Graduate (film soundtrack) (two Grammy Awards) 1968, Bookends 1968, Bridge Over Troubled Water (six Grammy Awards 1971) 1970, Concert in Central Park (live) 1982, Early Simon & Garfunkel 1993, Old Friends 1997; solo: Angel Clare 1973, Breakaway 1975, Watermark 1977, Fate for Breakfast (Doubt for Dessert) 1979, Art Garfunkel 1979, Scissors Cut 1981, The Animals' Christmas 1986, Lefty 1988, Garfunkel 1989, Up Till Now 1993, Across America 1997, Songs from a Parent to a Child 1997, Everything Waits to be Noticed 2002, Some Enchanted Evening 2007. *Publication:* Still Water 1989. *Honours:* Britannia Award for Best International Pop LP and Single 1977, six Grammy Awards, inducted into Rock and Roll Hall of Fame (with Paul Simon) 1990. *Current Management:* Metropolitan Talent, Inc., 100 Fifth

Avenue, 11th Floor, New York, NY 10011, USA. *E-mail:* contact@artgarfunkel .com. *Website:* www.artgarfunkel.com.

GARG, Zubeen; Indian singer and actor; b. (Zubeen Borthakur), 18 Nov. 1972, Jorhat, Assam; s. of Mohan Borthakur and the late Ily Borthakur; m. Garima Garg. *Education:* Gauhati Univ. *Career:* first public performance when he played Tabla in 1992; plays dhols, guitar, dotora, mandolin, keyboard and various percussion instruments; sings in various Indian languages. *Recordings include:* more than 9,000 songs and 40 albums; albums: Anamika 1992, Meghor Boron, Mukti, Hiya mon, Shapoon, Xabda, Paakhi 2000, Snigdha Jonak, Shishu 2002, Maya, Chinaki Mon, Akou Hiya Mon, Niribili Godhuli, Lajuki Mon, Jantra 2004, Raang, Rangdhali, Zindagi 2007, Abujan Mon 2010, Bahi 2010. *Films include:* Tumi Mor Matho Mor (actor and dir) 2000, Dinabandhu (actor and co-producer) 2000, You Are Not My Julie (actor) 2011; as playback singer: Gaddar 1995, Fiza 2000, Kaante 2002, Ek Hasina Thi 2004, Gangster (Global Indian Film Award 2006) 2006, Strings-Bound By Faith 2006, Namastey London 2007, London Dreams 2009, Aashayein 2010, Dum Maaro Dum 2011.

GARLAND, Tim; British musician (saxophone) and composer; b. (Tim Garland-Waggett), 19 Oct. 1966, Ilford, Essex; m. Amanda Phillipa Cooper 1995. *Education:* West Kent Coll., Guildhall School of Music. *Career:* joined Ronnie Scott's Band aged 23; Founder mem. jazz/folk fusion band, Lammas (several British tours, radio broadcasts); mem. Chick Corea's Origin sextet 1999; mem. Acoustic Triangle 2000–; Founder mem. trio, Storms/Nocturnes; mem. Lighthouse Project; fmr Composer-in-Residence, Newcastle Univ.; mem. PRS, MCPS. *Compositions include:* Dance for Human Folk for big band (recorded by BBC Big Band). *Recordings include:* albums: Lammas (with Lammas), This Morning (with Lammas), The Broken Road 1995, Source Book 1997, Sea Changes 1999, Nebucadnezzar (with Dankworth Generation Band), Live At Ronnies, Enter the Fire (solo) 1996; with Acoustic Triangle: Resonance 2005, Three Dimensions 2008; Via (with Storms/Nocturnes) 2011; with Light House: If the Sea Replied 2005, Libra 2009, Simcock, Garland, Sirkis 2012. *Honours:* Soloist Award 1988, British Jazz Award for Best Ensemble 1993, BBC Composition Award 1995, BBC Jazz on 3 Innovation Award 2006, Grammy Award 2009. *Current Management:* c/o Air Artist Agency Ltd, Shepherd's Building - Unit G7, Rockley Road, London, W14 0DA, England. *E-mail:* tim@timgarland.com. *Website:* www.timgarland.com.

GARNER, Kate; British musician and photographer; *Owner, Gaato Ltd*; b. 9 July 1954, Wigan; m. David Turin. *Education:* Notre Dame High School, Wigan and Blackpool Coll. of Art. *Career:* freelance photographic asst 1977–80; formed pop group, Haysi Fantayzee 1981–84; freelance photographer working mainly on fashion, music and portraits 1988–; work has appeared in The Face, Vogue, Harpers; work also used by all major recording cos, Wmag, I.Dmag; Owner, production co. Gaato Ltd; sings backing for punk/ country artist Emit Bloc; currently preparing major exhbn for Victoria and Albert Museum for 2008. *Exhibitions:* retrospective exhbn at Painter's Gallery, London 2006, Identity Artists, Varnish Gallery, San Francisco 2007. *Television:* arts/music show for Midlands TV 1985. *Recordings include:* John Wayne is Big Leggy, Shiny Shiny, Battle Hymns for Children Singing 1981–84, PeopleTree Sessions 1996–98, Monsta 2005, Emit Bloch 2007, electronic/metal album with her husband David Turin for Little Indian. *Address:* 10 Denning Road, London, NW3 1SU, England (office). *Telephone:* (7974) 140750 (mobile) (office); (20) 7722-3668 (home). *E-mail:* gaatoltd3@ hotmail.com (office).

GARNIER, Laurent; French producer, remixer and DJ; b. 1 Feb. 1966, Boulogne Sur Seine. *Career:* trained as a chef; moved to London to work in French embassy; relocated to Manchester; DJ at the Hacienda club; Co-founder: F Communications record label; resident DJ at the Rex Club, Paris; remixed Reese Project, System 7. *Recordings include:* albums: A Shot In The Dark 1994, 30 (Victoire de la Musique Award) 1996, Unreasonable Behaviour 2000, Excess Luggage 2004, Retrospective 2006, Public Outburst (live album) 2007, Tales of a Kleptomaniac 2009, Suivront mille ans de calme 2010. *Address:* F Communications, 8 rue André Messager, 75018 Paris, France (office). *Telephone:* 1-47-70-78-08 (office). *Fax:* 1-47-70-76-06 (office). *E-mail:* info@fcom.fr (office). *Website:* www.fcom.fr; www.laurentgarnier.com.

GARRETT, Kenny; American musician; b. 9 Oct. 1960, Detroit, Mich. *Career:* mem., The Duke Ellington Orchestra 1978, The Mel Lewis Orchestra and the Dannie Richmond Quintet 1982; numerous concerts worldwide, extensive tours; worked with numerous artists including Art Blakey, Miles Davis, Marcus Miller, Woody Shaw. *Recordings include:* solo: Introducing Kenny Garrett 1984, Garrett 1988, Prisoner of Love 1989, African Exchange Student 1990, Black Hope 1992, Threshold 1994, Stars & Stripes Live 1995, Trilogy 1995, Pursuance: The Music of John Coltrane 1996, Songbook 1997, Simply Said 1999, Happy People 2002, Standard of Language 2003, Beyond the Wall 2006, Sketches of M.D. 2009, Seeds from the Underground 2012, Pushing the World Away 2013. *Honours:* Rolling Stone Hot Jazz Artist 1996, Down Beat Readers' Poll Alto Saxophonist of the Year 1996, Grammy Award for Best Jazz Instrumental Album (for Five Peace Band Live) 2010, Echo Award for Saxophonist of the Year 2012, Down Beat Readers Poll Alto Saxophonist of the Year 2012, 2013. *Current Management:* c/o The Management Ark, 116 Village Blvd, Suite 200, Princeton, NJ 08540, USA. *Telephone:* (609) 734-7403. *Website:* www.managementark.com. *E-mail:* info@ kennygarrett.com. *Website:* www.kennygarrett.com.

GARRETT, Malcolm, BA (Hons), FISTD, FRSA; British graphic designer; *Creative Director, Applied Information Group*; b. 2 June 1956, Northwich, Cheshire. *Education:* Univ., of Reading, Manchester Polytechnic. *Career:* f. Assorted Images Design Co. 1978, renamed Assorted Images Ltd 1983, Design Dir 1978–94; designed for artists such as Buzzcocks, Duran Duran, Culture Club and Simple Minds, and pioneered digital and interactive work with Peter Gabriel; f. AMX Digital Ltd 1994, joined Havas Advertising (re-named AMX Studios, then AMX) 1998, Chair. 1999–2001; Visiting Prof. Univ. of the Arts, London (fmrly London Inst.); Visiting Prof. in Interactive Communication, RCA 2001–04; currently Creative Dir Applied Information Group; mem. RDI Exec. Cttee 2006–, Eye Magazine Editorial Bd 2007–, FontShop Type Bd 2007–08; External Examiner, Manchester Metropolitan Univ. 2008–. *Exhibitions:* Malcolm Garrett: Ulterior Motifs (Design Museum, London, Parco Gallery, Tokyo, SVA Gallery, New York, Savannah Coll. of Art and Design, USA, Univ. of Salford); has work included in perm. collection of 20th Century Graphic Design at the Victoria and Albert Museum, London. *Publications:* Duran Duran: Their Story (with Kasper de Graaf) 1982, When Cameras go Crazy: Culture Club (with Kasper de Graaf) 1983, Duran Duran Unseen: Photographs by Paul Edmond (with Kasper de Graaf) 2005. *Honours:* Hon. MA (Salford Univ.) 1999, Hon. Dr of Design (Robert Gordon Univ.) 2005. *Address:* Applied Information Group, 26–27 Great Sutton Street, London, EC1V 0DS, England (office). *Telephone:* (20) 7017-8488 (office). *Fax:* (20) 7017-8489 (office). *E-mail:* mx@aiglondon.com (office). *Website:* www.aiglondon.com (office).

GARRETT, Peter Robert, AM, BA, LLB; Australian environmentalist, musician and politician; b. 16 April 1953, Wahroonga, NSW; s. of the late Peter Maxwell Garrett and Betty Garrett; m.; three d. *Education:* Barker Coll., Hornsby, Australian Nat. Univ., Univ. of New South Wales. *Career:* mem. Rock Island Line; lead singer, Midnight Oil 1973–2002; benefit concerts for Aboriginal Rights Asscn, Tibet Council, Rainforest Action Network, other orgs; Exxon Valdez oil spill protest concert 1990; ran for Australian Senate, Nuclear Disarmament Party 1984; Pres. Australian Conservation Foundation 1989–91, 1998–2004; mem. Bd Greenpeace International 1991–93; mem. Australian Labor Party 2004–; MP for Kingsford Smith 2004–13; Minister for the Environment, Heritage and the Arts 2007–10, for School Educ., Early Childhood and Youth 2010–13. *Recordings:* albums with Midnight Oil: Midnight Oil 1978, Head Injuries 1979, Bird Noises 1980, Place Without A Postcard 1981, Red Sails In The Sunset 1982, 10 9 8 7 6 5 4 3 2 1 1983, Diesel and Dust 1987, Blue Sky Mining 1990, Scream In Blue – Live 1992, Earth, Sun and Moon 1993, Breathe 1996, 20,000 Watt RSL – The Midnight Oil Collection 1997, Redneck Wonderland 1998, The Real Thing (live) 2000, Capricornia 2002, Best of Both Worlds 2004, Essential Oils 2012. *Publication:* Political Blues 1987. *Honours:* Officier des Arts et des Lettres 2009; Hon. DLitt (Univ. of NSW) 2001; four Australian Record Industry Asscn Awards 1991, Sony Music Crystal Globe Award 1991, Australia's Living Treasures Award, Nat. Trust of Australia 1999, Australian Humanitarian Foundation Award (Environment category) 2000, Leaders for a Living Planet Award, WWF Australia and International 2010. *Website:* www.petergarrett.com.au.

GARRETT, Siedah; American singer and songwriter; b. 24 June 1963, Los Angeles, Calif. *Career:* backing singer for numerous artists; mem. Brand New Heavies 1997–98; solo artist; contributed lyrics to Dreamgirls 2006, Rio 2011 soundtrack. *Recordings include:* solo: Kiss of Life 1991, K.I.S.S.I.N.G. 1991, Refuse to Be Loose 1991, Siedah 2004. *Honours:* Grammy Award for Best Song written for Motion Picture (for Love You I Do from Dreamgirls) 2008. *Address:* c/o Erik Nuri, E. Nuri Management, 2118 Wilshire Blvd, Suite 206, Santa Monica, CA 90403, USA. *E-mail:* info@siedah.com. *Website:* www.siedah.com.

GARRICK, Michael, BA, MBE; British composer, bandleader, musician (piano, organ), teacher and lyricist; *Leader, Jazz Academy*; b. Enfield, Middx, England; four s. two d. *Education:* Univ. Coll., London, Univ. of London, Berklee Coll. of Music, Boston, USA. *Career:* BBC broadcasts 1960–; Dir Poetry and Jazz in Concert 1961–69; Dir of Travelling Jazz Faculty, f. Wavendon jazz course; Dir Jazz Acad. vacation courses and record label; group leader of trio, sextet, big band ensembles; first jazz musician to give concerts on pipe organs at St Paul's Cathedral 1968, Royal Festival Hall 1969; numerous other performances; Guest Conductor European Community Youth Jazz Orchestra; Faculty, RAM 1985–98, Trinity Coll. of Music, Guildhall summer school; currently Leader Jazz Acad.; mem. Royal Soc. of Musicians, Asscn of British Jazz Musicians, Berkhamsted Jazz Soc. (Pres.). *Compositions include:* Jazz Praises 1967: Mr Smith's Apocalypse 1969, Judas Kiss 1971, The Hobbit Suite 1973, Heavenly Bodies 1977, Underground Streams 1979, Faces of Love 1980, Catechism 1981, Zodiac of Angels 1988 (symphony orchestra), Carioca Celebration 1983, New Flower of Europe 1981, The Stirring 1982, Romance of the Rose 1986 (Rhapsody for jazz violinist and orchestra), Hardy Country 1990, Garrick's Jazz Characters 1960–, The Royal Box 1993, Bovingdon Poppies 1993, A Diana Sonata 1997, Asha's Ear 1999, Peter Pan Jazzdance Suite 2002, Linda 2003, For Children: All God's Children, Tree of Dreams, What is Melody?, Norman Gnome and the Rhinoceros, Jazz Curries. *Recordings include:* Poetry and Jazz in Concert (four vols), October Woman, Promises, Black Marigolds, Heart is a Lotus, Home Stretch Blues, Troppo, You've Changed, Kronos, Cold Mountain, Anthem, Jazz Praises at St Paul's 1968, A Lady in Waiting 1993, Meteors Close at Hand 1994, Parting is Such 1996, For Love of Duke... and Ronnie 1998, Down on Your Knees 1999, The New Quartet 2001, Green and Pleasant Land 2002, Peter Pan Jazzdance Suite 2003, Big Band Harriott 2004, Children of Time 2005, Inspirations 2006, Yet

Another Spring 2006, Moonscape 2007, Lady of the Aurian Wood—A Magic Life of Duke 2009, Remembered Time 2010, Tone Poems 2010, Silhouette vinyl 2010. *Publications:* contrib. to Jazz Now, Times Educational Supplement, The Stage, Piano Magazine. *Honours:* Hon. ARAM; Whittingham Award 1997. *Address:* Jazz Academy Resources, 12 Castle Street, Berkhamsted, Herts., HP4 2BQ, England (office). *Telephone:* (1442) 864989 (office). *Fax:* (1442) 384493 (office). *E-mail:* mgarrick@rocketmail.com (office). *Website:* www.jazzacademy.co.uk (office); www.jazzscript.co.uk.

GARRIX, Martin; Dutch musician, DJ, composer and record producer; b. (Martijn Garritsen), 14 May 1996, Amstelveen. *Education:* Herman Brood Acad., Utrecht. *Career:* numerous collaborations including Christina Aguilera, Jay Hardway, Firebeatz, Dillon Francis, Afrojack, Hardwell, MOTi, Usher, Ed Sheeran, Tiesto, Avicii; debut solo release Animals 2013. *Honours:* MTV Europe Music Award for Best Electronic Artist 2015. *Current Management:* c/o Scooter Braun Projects, Worldwide Plaza, 825 Eighth Avenue, 28th Floor, New York, NY 10019, USA. *E-mail:* info@scooterbraun.com. *Website:* www.scooterbraun.com; martingarrix.com.

GARTSIDE, Green; British singer and songwriter; b. (Green Strohmeyer-Gartside), 22 June 1956, Cardiff, Wales. *Education:* Leeds Art School. *Career:* Ffounder mem. Scritti Politti 1977– (now as a solo artist); numerous concerts, tours and festival appearances. *Compositions include:* The Sweetest Girl 1981, The Perfect Way 1985, Love of a Lifetime (recorded by Chaka Khan) 1986, L Is For Lover (written with David Gamson, recorded by Al Jarreau) 1986. *Recordings include:* albums: Songs To Remember 1982, Cupid and Psyche 85 1985, Provision 1988, Anomie and Bonhomie 1999, White Bread, Black Beer 2006, Absolute 2011. *Address:* c/o Rough Trade Records, 66 Golborne Road, London, W10 5PS, England.

GARVEY, Guy Edward John; British singer, songwriter and musician (guitar); b. 6 March 1974, Bury, Lancs. *Career:* formed band Mr Soft with Mark Potter, Richard Jupp and Pete Turner 1990, renamed Soft and eventually renamed Elbow 1997–; numerous concerts and tours throughout UK, Europe and USA; played concerts in Cuba 2004, becoming first British band to perform outside Havana; headlined UKULA Bright Lights Festival, Toronto, Canada 2006; collaborations with Western Arms, J-Walk; radio presenter, BBC 6 Music, XFM Manchester; Co-founder and A&R Man. Skinny Dog Records; Patron, Mines Advisory Group, Manchester Craft and Design Centre; mem. British Acad. of Songwriters, Composers and Authors. *Recordings include:* albums: with Elbow: Asleep in the Back 2001, Cast of Thousands 2003, Leaders of the Free World 2005, The Seldom Seen Kid (Mercury Music Prize) 2008, Build a Rocket Boys! 2011, The Take Off and Landing of Everything 2014. *Recordings as producer:* with I am Kloot: Natural History album 2001, Sky at Night 2010, Let It All In 2013. *Honours:* Dr hc (Manchester Metropolitan Univ.) 2012; BRIT Award for Best British Group 2009, Ivor Novello Awards for Best Song Musically and Lyrically (for One Day Like This) 2009, for Best Contemporary Song (for Grounds for Divorce) 2009. *Current Management:* TRC Management, 23 New Mount Street, Manchester, Greater Manchester, M4 4DE, England. *Telephone:* (1619) 534091. *E-mail:* mail@trcmanagement.com. *Website:* www.trcmanagement.com; www.elbow.co.uk.

GARZA, Josh; American musician (drums). *Career:* mem. Secret Machines 2000–. *Recordings include:* albums: Now Here is Nowhere 2004, Ten Silver Drops 2006, Secret Machines 2008. *Address:* c/o World's Fair Records, 147 West 24th Street, 5th Floor, New York, NY 10011, USA (office).

GASPARYAN, Djivan; Armenian musician (duduk), singer and composer; b. 1928, Solag, nr Yerevan. *Career:* mem. Tatool Altounian Nat. Song and Dance Ensemble 1948; fmr soloist, Yerevan Philharmonic Orchestra; toured Europe, Asia, Middle East, USA; currently Prof., Yerevan Conservatory; musical collaborations with artists, including Lionel Richie, Peter Gabriel, The Kronos Quartet, LA Philharmonic Orchestra. *Recordings include:* albums: I Will Not Be Sad In This World 1989, Moon Shines At Night 1992, Ask Me No Questions 1994, Apricots From Eden 1996, The Art Of The Duduk 1998, Black Rock (with Michael Brook) 1998, Armenian Fantasies 2000, Fuad 2001, The Soul of Armenia 2008. *Honours:* UNESCO competitions gold medal 1959, 1962, 1973, 1980, People's Artist of Armenia 1973 (first winner) 1973, WOMEX Lifetime Achievement Award 2002. *Address:* c/o Run Productions, 44 Grand'rue, BP 34, 86470 Lavausseau, France (office); Yerevan State Conservatory, Sayat-Nova 1, Yerevan 375001, Armenia (office). *Website:* www.jivanduduk.com.

GATE-AH (see Chandler, Kerri)

GATICA, Humberto; Chilean/American producer; b. Rancagua, Chile. *Career:* Owner (with David Foster) 143 Records, Miami; has worked with Marc Anthony, Chicago, Andrés de León, Céline Dion, Gloria Estefan, Myriam Hernández, Michael Jackson, Alejandro Lerner, La Ley, Ricky Martin, Luis Miguel, Alejandro Sanz, Olga Tanon. *Honours:* five Grammy Awards for Best Engineered Recording (Non-Classical) 1984, 1987, for General Album of The Year 1996, for General Record of The Year 1998, for Best Latin Rock/ Alternative Album 2000, for Best Traditional Pop Vocal Album 2007. *Address:* Lionshare Studio, 8255 Beverly Blvd, #219, Los Angeles, CA 90048, USA.

GATLIN, Larry Wayne; American singer and songwriter; b. 2 May 1948, Seminole, TX; m. Janis Gail Moss 1969, one s. one d. *Career:* country singer, songwriter 1971–; mem., Gatlin Brothers; mem. CMA. *Recordings include:* albums: The Pilgrim 1973, Rain/Rainbow 1974, High Time 1975, Larry Gatlin with Family and Friends 1976, Love is Just a Game 1977, Oh Brother 1978,

Straight Ahead 1979, Help Yourself 1980, Not Guilty 1981, Sure Feels Like Love 1982, Houston To Denver 1984, Smile 1985, Partners 1986, Alive and Well 1987, Pure 'n Simple 1989, Cookin' Up a Storm 1990, Adiós 1992, Moments to Remember 1993, Cool Water 1994, In My Life 1998, Pilgrimage 2009. *Honours:* BMI Songwriter Award (for Delta Dirt) 1975, (for Broken Lady) 1976, ACM Award for Best Album, for Best Single, for Best Male Vocalist 1980. *Website:* gatlinbrothers.musiccitynetworks.com.

GATTO, Olivier; French musician (double bass), arranger and composer; b. 22 Jan. 1963, Manosque; m. Shekinah Rodz; one s. *Education:* Univ. of Sciences, Bordeaux, Berklee Coll. of Music, Boston, USA. *Career:* concerts with Joe Henderson, Billy Cobham, Ravi Coltrane, Roy Hargrove and Antonio Hart, Julian Joseph, Ernie Watts, Bill Evans, Benny Golson Vincent Herring, Mark Turner, Jerry Bergonzi; European tour with John Stubblefield, George Cables and Billy Hart. *Recordings include:* albums: Here and There 1993 with John Stubblefield, George Cables and Billy Cobham, Craig Bailey, Brooklyn 1999, Lydia Filipovic Nekada 2002, Paris Transilvania Express 2004. *Radio:* France Musique, Voice of America. *Address:* 19 rue Platon, 33185 Le Haillan, France (home). *Telephone:* 6-34-28-15-83 (office); 5-56-28-16-63 (home). *E-mail:* olga.jedan@orange.fr (office).

GAUDETTE, Claude; Canadian composer, producer and musician (keyboards); b. 15 Oct. 1959, Montréal. *Education:* Montréal Conservatory of Music, Dick Grove School of Music, Los Angeles, New York Recording Workshop. *Career:* Musical Director, France Joli, Yamaha International Song Festival 1985; keyboards, David Foster's Super Producer '94 Tour, Japan; mem. BMI, NARAS, SCL. *Recordings include:* producer, writer, musician on albums: The Colour of My Love, Céline Dion, Belinda, Belinda Carlisle, Everlasting, Good To Be Back, Natalie Cole, Slip of The Tongue, Whitesnake; also albums by Fiona, Michael Bolton, Peter Cetera, Earth Wind and Fire, Roberta Flack, Sergio Mendes, Eddie Money, Dionne Warwick, Kenny Loggins, Five Star, Little River Band, Smokey Robinson, Martika, Barry Manilow, George Benson, The Commodores, Céline Dion, Ricky Martin; singles: Mad About You, Belinda Carlisle, Wind Beneath My Wings, Bette Midler, Time of My Life, Bill Medley and Jennifer Warnes, Make Me Lose Control, Eric Carmen, I Live For Your Love, Pink Cadillac, Natalie Cole, Walk Away, Dionne Warwick; also singles by Sheena Easton, Kenny Loggins, Melissa Morgan, Ziggy Marley. *Address:* 4912 Stern Ave, Sherman Oaks, CA 91423, USA.

GAUL, Sven H.; Danish musician (drums) and broadcaster; b. 11 April 1953, Flensburg, Germany. *Education:* Univ. of Århus. *Career:* mem. rock band, Taurus 1974–80, pop-rock band, TV-2 1980–; host, television show, Lul, Lul, Rocken Gaar, 1989; mem. Danish Music Council 1991–, Danish Musicians' Union. *Recordings include:* with TV-2: Fantastiske Toyota 1981, Verden er Vidunderlig 1982, Beat 1983, Nutidens Unge 1984, Rigtige Maend 1985, En Dejlig Torsdag 1987, Naermest Lykkelig 1988, Vi Blir Alligevel Aldrig Voksne 1990, Slaraffenland 1991, Verdens Lykkeligste Mand 1994, Kys Bruden 1996, Yndlingsbabe 1998, Manden der onskede sig en havudsigt 1999, Amerika 2001, På kanten af småt braendbart 2002, De Første Kaerester På Månen 2005, For dig ku' jeg gøre alting 2007, Showtime 2011. *Honours:* Danish Grammy Award 1985. *Website:* www.tv-2.dk.

GAUTHIER, Marcel, BAC, DEC; Canadian arranger and publisher; b. 7 Nov. 1963, Iberville, Quebec; one s. one d. *Career:* arranger and copyist, Samedi de Rire, Demons du Midi, Country Centre-Ville, Double Etoiles, La Fureur, La Boite à Chansons, ADiSQ; mem. SOCAN. *Compositions include:* Il fait toujours beau quelque part, Radio theme, Radio Canada; Un pitbull chez les moules (big band); Desert (recorded by Robin Grenon); Stimulus (Robin Grenon). *Recordings include:* Stimulus (with Robin Grenon, harp); Dionne (with Jean-Marie Dionne); Carmen Bonifacio (keyboards); Claude Olivier (keyboards); Secret Lake (with Christian Vanderre).

GAUTHIER, Mary Veronica; American singer, musician (guitar) and songwriter; b. New Orleans, La. *Education:* Louisiana State Univ. *Career:* alternative country artist; opened an award-winning restaurant; plays many of the USA folk festivals, including Kerrville, Philadelphia, Newport. *Recordings include:* albums: Dixie Kitchen 1997, Drag Queens in Limousines 1999, Filth and Fire 2002, Mercy Now 2005, Between Daylight and Dark 2007, The Foundling 2010, The Foundling Alone 2011, Live at Blue Rock 2012. *Publications include:* numerous stories in anthologies. *Honours:* Gay and Lesbian American Music Award (GLAMA) for Country Artist of the Year 2000, New Artist of the Year, Americana Music Asscn. *Current Management:* c/o The Mark Spector Company, 1515 Broadway, 36th Floor, New York, NY 10036, USA. *Telephone:* (212) 277-7175. *Fax:* (212) 840-3256. *E-mail:* ms44post@aol.com. *E-mail:* marygoshay@mac.com (office). *Website:* www.marygauthier.com.

GAUTREY, Benedict; British singer; b. 9 Sept. 1979. *Career:* mem., The Cooper Temple Clause late 1998–2007. *Recordings include:* albums: See This Through And Leave 2002, Kick Up The Fire And Let The Flames Break Loose 2003, Make This Your Own 2007.

GAVIN, Frankie; Irish musician (fiddle, whistle, flute) and composer; b. 1956, Corrandulla, Galway Co., Ireland; m. Tracey Harris. *Career:* Founder-mem. De Danann (with Alec Finn) 1973–2003; formed group Frankie Gavin and The New De Dannan; collaborations include Rolling Stones, Yehudi Menuhin, Stéphane Grappelli, Earl Scruggs, Elvis Costello, Keith Richards. *Television includes:* appeared in series, Bringing It All Back Home 1992, wrote soundtrack for series, The Irish RM. *Recordings include:* albums include: with De Danann: De Danann 1976, The Star-Spangled Molly 1978, Selected Jigs, Reels and Songs 1978, The Mist Covered Mountain 1980, Star-Spangled Molly 1981, No Home is Real 1981, Song for Ireland 1983, Jacket of Batteries 1983, The Irish RM 1984, Anthem 1985, Ballroom 1987, Half Set in Harlem 1995, How the West was Won 1999, Welcome to the Hotel Connemara 2000, Jigs, Reels & Rock'n'Roll 2010; solo: Traditional Music of Ireland 1977, Croch Suas E 1983, Omós Do Joe Cooley 1986, Frankie Goes To Town 1989, An Irish Christmas 1992, Jigs and Jazz (with Stéphane Grappelli) 1993, Irlande 1994, Fierce Traditional 2001, Hibernian Rhapsody 2008. *Honours:* Hon. MA (Nat. Univ. of Ireland, Galway) 2009; winner, All Ireland Fiddle, All Ireland Flute competitions 1973, AIB Traditional Music Award 1996. *E-mail:* frankiegavin@aol.com.

GAYLE, Crystal; American country singer; b. (Brenda Gail Webb), 9 Jan. 1951, Paintsville, Kentucky; m. Vassilios (Bill) Gatzimos; one s. one d. *Career:* solo artist late 1960s–; numerous TV appearances, concerts; first US country artist to perform in People's Republic of China 1979. *Recordings include:* albums: Crystal Gayle 1975, Somebody Loves You 1975, Crystal 1976, We Must Believe In Magic 1977, I've Cried the Blue Right Out of My Eyes 1978, When I Dream 1978, We Should Be Together 1979, Miss The Mississippi 1979, Classic Crystal 1979, These Days 1980, Hollywood/Tennessee 1981, True Love 1982, One From The Heart (with Tom Waits) 1982, Cage The Songbird 1983, Nobody Wants To Be Alone 1985, Straight To The Heart 1986, A Crystal Christmas 1986, What If We Fall In Love (with Gary Morris) 1987, Nobody's Angel 1988, Ain't Gonna Worry 1990, Three Good Reasons 1992, Best Always 1993, Someday 1995, He is Beautiful 1997, Sings the Heart and Soul of Hoagy Carmichael 1999, In My Arms 2000, All My Tomorrows 2003, Live! An Evening with Crystal Gayle 2006. *Honours:* Female Vocalist of the Year, Academy of Country Music 1976, Grammy Awards for Beat Female Country Vocal Performance, Best Country Song; Female Vocalist of the Year, CMA. *Address:* Gayle Enterprises Inc., 51 Music Square East, Nashville, TN 37203, USA (office). *Telephone:* (615) 327-2651 (office). *Fax:* (615) 327-2657 (office). *E-mail:* info@crystalgayle.com (office). *Website:* www.crystalgayle.com.

GAYLE, Michelle; British singer, songwriter and actress; b. 2 Feb. 1971, London, England; m. Mark Bright (divorced 2007). *Career:* solo artist 1993–; numerous concerts and live appearances; collaborations with numerous artists. *Television includes:* Grange Hill, EastEnders 1990–93. *Theatre:* starred in Beauty and the Beast, West End, London. *Recordings include:* albums: Michelle Gayle 1995, Sensational 1997, Looking Up 2000. *Publication:* Pride and Premiership 2011.

GAYNOR, Gloria; American singer; b. 7 Sept. 1947, Newark, NJ. *Career:* singer with the Soul Satisfiers, 1960s; solo artist 1970s–. *Recordings include:* albums: Never Can Say Goodbye 1975, Experience Gloria Gaynor 1976, I've Got You 1976, Glorious 1977, Love Tracks 1979, I Have A Right 1979, Stories 1980, I Kinda Like Me 1981, Gloria Gaynor 1982, I Am Gloria Gaynor 1983, The Power of Gloria Gaynor 1986, Love Affair 1992, I'll Be There 1995, The Answer 1997, I Wish You Love 2002, The Album, 2002, Christmas Presence 2007. *E-mail:* webmaster@gloriagaynor.com. *Website:* www.gloriagaynor.com.

GAZE, Lee; Welsh musician (guitar); b. 21 May 1975. *Career:* mem. rock bands, Lostprophets 1997–2013, No Devotion 2014–. *Recordings include:* albums: thefakesoundofprogress 2000, Start Something 2004, Liberation Transmission (Kerrang! Award for Best Album 2006 and Pop Factory Award for Best Album 2006) 2006, The Betrayed 2010, Weapons 2012. *Honours:* NME Award for Best Metal Act 2002, Kerrang! Award for Best British Band 2006, 2007, for Classic Songwriter 2010, Pop Factory Award for Best Live Act 2001, 2006, for Best Welsh Act 2004–06. *Website:* www.nodevotion.com; www.wakeupmakeamove.com.

GEDDES, Chris; British musician (piano, keyboards); b. 2 Oct. 1975. *Career:* mem., Belle & Sebastian 1996–, V Twin 1999–, Golden Rodeo; collaborations with Arab Strap, Salako. *Recordings include:* albums: Tigermilk 1996, If You're Feeling Sinister 1996, The Boy With The Arab Strap 1998, Fold Your Hands Child, You Walk Like A Peasant 2000, Storytelling 2002, Dear Catastrophe Waitress 2003, The Life Pursuit 2006, Write About Love 2010, Girls in Peacetime Want to Dance 2015. *Honours:* BRIT Award for Best Newcomer 1999, Q Magazine Spirit of Independence Award 2013. *Current Management:* Banchory Management, PO Box 25074, Glasgow, G3 8TT, Scotland. *Telephone:* (141) 204-2269. *E-mail:* banchoryman@gmail.com. *Website:* www.belleandsebastian.com.

GEERS, Didier; Belgian musician (drums, percussion) and singer; b. 9 Sept. 1954, Ghent; m. Naima Barbro Johansson 1986; two s. one d. *Education:* Ghent Music Conservatoire, studied with Richard Boone. *Career:* session musician with Sammy Rimington Band, Waso Quintet, George Probert, Al Casey, Bill Dillard Earl Warren; Founder-mem. Didier Geers Jazz and Blues Band 1986–89; mem. Papa Bue's Viking Jazz Band for seven years; mem. of own trio, The DNA Band. *Honours:* Golden Mermaid Award, Ostende 1971. *Address:* Karl Nils väg 15–17, 290 11 Linderöd, Sweden.

GEFFEN, Aviv; Israeli singer, songwriter and musician (guitar); b. 10 May 1973, s. of Yonatan Geffen; m. 1st Elana Berkowitz 1996 (divorced 1998); m. 2nd Shani Friedan; one s. *Education:* Rimon School of Jazz and Contemporary Music. *Career:* began career performing in bands Hatauyot and Cats in the Piping; formed Blackfield with Steven Wilson 2001; collaborations with musicians including Keren Hachth, Rockfour, Porcupine Tree, Daniel

Salomon, Shachar Even-Tzur, Daniel Salomon, Ninette Tayeb. *Recordings include:* solo: Ze Rak Or Hayareach 1992, Ahshav Meunan 1993, Aviv Geffen III 1994, Shumakom 1995, HaMihtav 1996, Hayareach Malee 1997, Halulim 1998, Leyloth Levanim 1999, Yoman Masah 2000, Memento Mori 2002, Im Hazman 2006, Rak Shirey Ahava 2006, Aviv Geffen (first English album) 2009, Mosaic 2012; with Blackfield: Blackfield I 2004, Blackfield II 2007, Welcome to My DNA 2011. *Address:* Snapper Music, 1 Star Street, London, W2 1QD, England (office). *Telephone:* (20) 7563-5500 (office). *Fax:* (20) 7563-5566 (office). *E-mail:* mail@snappermusic.com (office); rk@avivarchive.co.il (office). *Website:* www.snappermusic.com (office); www.avivarchive.co.il; www.blackfield.org.

GEFFEN, David Lawrence; American film, recording and theatre executive; b. 21 Feb. 1943, Brooklyn, New York; s. of Abraham Geffen and Batya Geffen (née Volovskaya). *Education:* New Utrecht High School, Brooklyn, Univ. of Texas, Brooklyn Coll. *Career:* joined William Morris talent agency as mail clerk 1964, promoted to jr agent; launched new film studio with Steven Spielberg and Jeffrey Katzenberg; f. music publishing co. Tunafish Music, with Laura Nyro; joined Ashley Famous Agency, then apptd Exec. Vice-Pres. Creative Man. (now Int. Creative Man.) 1968; f. Asylum Records and Geffen-Roberts Man. Co. with Elliot Roberts 1970, sold Asylum to Warner Communications, but remained Pres. 1971, merged it with Elektra, signed Bob Dylan and Joni Mitchell, Vice-Chair. Warner Brothers Pictures 1975–76; taught business studies at Yale Univ.; f. Geffen Records, Pres. 1980, signed Elton John, John Lennon and Yoko Ono and many others, sold label to Music Corpn of America Inc. 1990; f. Geffen Film Co.; Co-Producer musical Dreamgirls 1981–85, Cats 1982, M. Butterfly 1986, Social Security, Chess 1990, Miss Saigon; f. DGC record label 1995; Co-founder and Prin. Dreamworks SKG 1994–2008. *Honours:* Ahmet Ertegun Award, inducted into Rock and Roll Hall of Fame 2010, President's Merit Award for Indelible Contrib. to the Music Industry, Nat. Acad. of Recording Arts and Sciences 2011.

GEILS, (John W.) J.; American musician (guitar); b. 20 Feb. 1946, New York. *Education:* Worcester Technical Coll. *Career:* mem. The Hallucinations; Founder mem. and guitarist, The J. Geils Blues Band 1968–85; numerous live appearances, tours, television appearances; owner, vintage and sports car shop 1992–96. *Recordings include:* albums: J Geils Band 1971, The Morning After 1971, Live 1971, Bloodshot 1973, Nightmares… 1974, Hotline 1975, Blow Your Face Out 1975, Monkey Island 1977, Sanctuary 1979, Love Stinks 1980, Freeze Frame 1982, Showtime! 1983, You're Getting Even While I'm Getting Odd 1984, Flashback 1987, The J Geils Band Anthology: A House-party 1993, Must of Got Lost 1995, The Best of The J Geils Band 1998, Fool's Paradise 1999; singles include: Looking For Love, Give It To Me, Must've Got Lost, Centrefold, Angel In Blue, Freeze Frame, I Do, Fright Night, title track for film Fright Night. *Honours:* Rolling Stone magazine Award for Most Promising New Band 1971.

GELB, Peter; American business executive, film and television producer and arts administrator; *General Manager, Metropolitan Opera;* b. 1953, s. of Arthur Gelb and Barbara Gelb; m. Keri-Lynn Wilson; two s. (from a previous m.). *Career:* fmr Man., Vladimir Horowitz; Pres. Sony Classical USA 1993–95, Pres. Sony Classical Int. Operations 1995–2005; Gen. Man. Metropolitan Opera, New York 2006–. *Honours:* Officier, Ordre des Arts et des Lettres 2010, Chevalier, Légion d'honneur 2013; Dr hc (Macaulay Honors Coll., CUNY) 2008; Emmy Award for Outstanding Classical Program in the Performing Arts 1987, 1990, 1991, Emmy Award for Outstanding Individual Achievement in Int. Programming 1991, Int. Documentary Asscn Award 1991, Grammy Award 2002, Diplomacy Award, Foreign Policy Asscn 2012, Sanford Prize, Yale School of Music 2013. *Address:* The Metropolitan Opera, Lincoln Center, New York, NY 10023, USA (office). *Telephone:* (212) 799-3100 (office). *Website:* www.metoperafamily.org (office).

GELDOF, Bob; Irish rock singer and songwriter; b. 5 Oct. 1954, Dublin; m. Paula Yates 1986 (divorced 1996, died 2000); three d. (one deceased). *Education:* Blackrock Coll. *Career:* worked in several casual jobs, including lorry driving, busking, teaching English, working in factory, etc., then journalist on pop music paper, Georgia Strait, Vancouver, Canada; later journalist for New Musical Express, Melody Maker; returned to Dublin and f. rock group, Boomtown Rats 1975–84; solo artist 1986–; organized recording of Do They Know It's Christmas? by Band Aid, raising money for African famine relief Nov. 1984, f. Band-Aid Trust (incorporating Live Aid, Band Aid, Sport Aid) to distribute proceeds 1984, Chair.; organized Live Aid concerts in Wembley Stadium, London and JFK Stadium, Philadelphia, USA with int. TV link-up by satellite 13 July 1985, raised £40 million for famine relief in Africa; f. Live Aid Foundation, USA; organized publ. of Live Aid book The Greatest Show on Earth 1985; Owner, Planet 24 (TV production co.) 1990–99; Co-founder and Dir (non-exec.) Ten Alps plc 2001–; mem. Africa Comm. 2004–; organized re-recordings of Do They Know It's Christmas?, raising money for African famine relief 2004, 2014; organized Live 8 concerts in London, Philadelphia, Paris, Rome and Berlin, with int. TV link-up by satellite, to highlight ongoing problem of global poverty and debt 2 July 2005, The Long Walk to Justice, Edinburgh, Scotland, to present leaders of G8 Summit at Gleneagles with plan to double aid, drop debt and make trade fair 6 July 2005; Patron, Exeter Entrepreneurs Society, Univ. of Exeter. *Film appearances include:* Pink Floyd – The Wall 1982, Number One 1985, Sketches of Frank Gehry 2006, Oh My God 2009. *Recordings include:* albums: with Boomtown Rats: The Boomtown Rats 1977, A Tonic For The Troops 1978, The Fine Art Of Surfacing 1979, Mondo Bongo 1981, V Deep 1982, In the Long

Grass 1984; solo: Deep In The Heart Of Nowhere 1986, The Vegetarians Of Love 1990, The Happy Club 1993, Sex Age And Death 2001, How to Compose Popular Songs That Will Sell 2011. *Publications include:* Is That It? (autobiog.) 1986, Geldof in Africa 2005. *Honours:* Freeman of Ypres 1986; Hon. KBE 1986, Elder of the Repub. of Tanzania; Dr hc (Ghent) 1986, (Univ. Coll. Dublin) 2005; Hon. DLit (London) 1987; Hon. DCL (Newcastle) 2007; Hon. MA (Univ. for the Creative Arts) 2010; Hon. DPhil (Ben-Gurion Univ. of the Negev) 2011; Order of Two Niles (Sudan), Order of Leopold II (Belgium), Irish Peace Prize, UN World Hunger Award, EEC Gold Medal, four Ivor Novello Awards, MTV Video Awards Special Recognition Trophy 1985, American Music Awards Special Award of Appreciation 1986, Third World Prize 1986, BRIT Award for Outstanding Contrib. to Music 2005, Golden Rose Charity Award (Switzerland) 2005, MTV Europe Free Your Mind Award 2005, Man of Peace Award 2005, Nichols-Chancellor's Medal, Vanderbilt Univ. 2008. *Current Management:* c/o Amanda Hon, PO Box 13995, London, W9 2FL, England. *Telephone:* (20) 7289-7331. *E-mail:* amanda.hon@dsl.pipex .com. *Address:* Ten Alps plc, 9 Savoy Street, London, WC2E 7HR, England. *Telephone:* (20) 7878-2484. *Website:* www.bobgeldof.com.

EL GÉNÉRAL; Tunisian rap artist; b. (Hamada Ben Amor), 7 Oct. 1989, Sfax. *Career:* studied pharmacy; began creating rap music 2009; subject to censorship under regime of Pres. Zine al-Abidine Ben Ali, banned from performing in concert, making CDs or being played on Tunisian radio stations; arrested by Tunisian police Dec. 2010. *Music:* Malesh? (Why?), Sidi Rais (Mr President), Rais Lebled (President of our Country) 2010, Tounes Lebled (Tunisia Our Country) 2010. *E-mail:* general.management@hotmail.com.

GENEST, Francis; French musician (percussion); b. 31 Dec. 1960, Paris. *Career:* performed at many festivals throughout Europe (France, Spain, Belgium, Italy), USA; several concerts for Radio France and the French Speaking Public Radios Community; Founder, El Tu Yo and La Comparsita street orchestra; mem. Union des Musiciens de Jazz, Paris. *Recordings include:* albums with the Cache-Cache Trio: L'Océane; Tandems. *Honours:* First prize, National Jazz Contest with Cache-Cache trio.

GENIUS (see GZA)

GENTRY, Bobbie; American singer, songwriter and musician (guitar); b. (Roberta Lee Streeter), 27 July 1944, Chicasaw County, Mississippi; m. 1st Bill Harrah; m. 2nd Jim Stafford. *Career:* solo artist 1967–; retired from performing to look after business interests. *Television:* The Bobbie Gentry Show (UK series) 1969. *Recordings include:* albums: Bobbie Gentry and Glen Campbell 1968, Local Gentry 1968, Touch 'Em With Love 1969, I'll Never Fall In Love Again 1970, Fancy 1970, Patchwork 1971, Sittin' Pretty/Tobacco Road 1971, Greatest Hits 1990, The Golden Classics 1998, Ode To Bobbie Gentry 2000, An American Quilt 1967–1974 2002.

GENTRY, Teddy Wayne; American musician (bass guitar), singer and songwriter; b. 22 Jan. 1952, Fort Payne, AL; m.; one d. one s. *Career:* founder mem. of country music group, Young Country 1969, renamed Wild Country 1972, renamed Alabama 1977–; record producer for artists including Emerson Drive, Collin Raye. *Recordings include:* albums: Alabama 1980, My Home's In Alabama 1980, Feels So Right 1981, Stars 1982, Mountain Music 1982, The Closer You Get 1983, Roll On 1984, 40 Hour Week 1985, Alabama Christmas 1985, The Touch 1986, Just Us 1987, Live 1988, Tennessee Christmas 1989, Southern Star 1989, Pass It On Down 1990, American Pride 1992, Gonna Have A Party… Live 1993, Cheap Seats 1993, In The Beginning 1994, In Pictures 1995, From The Archives Vol. 1 1996, Christmas Vol. 2 1996, Live at Ebbets Field 1997, Dancin' On The Boulevard 1997, Twentieth Century 1999, Alabama for the Record 2000, When It All Goes South 2001, Christmas 2002, Songs of Inspiration 2006, Songs of Inspiration II 2007. *Honours:* numerous CMA Awards 1981–84, ACM Awards, including Artist of the Decade 1989, American Music Awards, including Award of Merit 2003, Grammy Award (for Mountain Music) 1983, (for The Closer You Get) 1984, BMI President's Award 2000, numerous Billboard Awards. *Website:* www.wildcountry.com; www .thealabamaband.com.

GEORGE, Jimmy; American composer, producer, record label owner and publisher. *Career:* studio guitarist, played on many No 1 hits; produced many top recording artists; owner, recording studio; two vocal hits while at university; produced Mary Kaye Trio; performed, night clubs in Los Angeles, toured US with the Beach Boys; wrote and recorded with Jackie DeShannon, Dr John; played guitar on hits for Michael Jackson, the Jackson Five, Diana Ross, Marvin Gaye, Thelma Houston; performer, recording producer and musician for Etta James, Little Richard, Leon Russell, Chuck Berry, Ike and Tina Turner and Kenny Rogers; songs recorded by Carl Anderson, Nancy Sinatra, Bobby Womack, the Commodores, Smokey Robinson, Taylor Dayne, The Temptations and George Benson; performed in many major venues world-wide with Jimi Hendrix, Sly and the Family Stone, Crosby, Stills, Nash and Young, Janis Joplin; performed on TV commercials and programmes; toured as guitarist/bass player with Shaun Cassidy, Leif Garrett, Gary Lewis and the Playboys; mem. Musicians' Union, Los Angeles, American Federation of Television and Radio Artists, Nat. Acad. of Recording Arts and Sciences, Los Angeles World Affairs Council. *Compositions include:* Magic Man, Just To See Her, I Wonder Who She's Seeing Now, The Temptations, I'll Always Love You, Taylor Dayne, Real Thing; Love Remembers, George Benson, Everything Reminds Me of You, Commodores, A Night To Remember. *E-mail:* jimmy@ luvsongs.com. *Website:* luvsongs.com.

GEORGE, Sergio; American pianist, arranger and record producer; b. 23 May 1961, New York, NY. *Education:* City Coll. of New York. *Career:* mem. Conjunto Caché and Conjunto Clásico 1979; session work with many salsa artists 1980s; musical dir, Grupo Star 1987; mem. Grupo Baruc 1988; producer and musical dir Johnny & Ray 1988; arranger, producer and musical dir RMM Records & Video 1988–95; producer, Sir George Entertainment 1995; formed DLG 1995; producer, WEA Latina 1997; Co-founder, SGZ Entertainment (with George Zamora) 2004; Founder, Top Stop Music 2009–; collaborator with numerous Latin artists including Marc Anthony, Ricardo Arjona, Bacilos, Celia Cruz, La India, Jennifer Lopez, Victor Manuelle, Tito Nieves, Orquesta de la Luz, Prince Royce, Tito Puente, Jerry Rivera, Johnny Rivera, Gloria Trevi. *Recordings include:* as producer: The Classic, Tito Nieves 1988, Mascarada, Johnny & Ray 1988, 100th LP, Tito Puente 1991, Otra Nota, Marc Anthony 1993, Combinacion Perfecta, Familia RMM 1993, Todo A Su Tiempo, Marc Anthony 1995, El Cantante, Marc Anthony 2008, 3.0, Marc Anthony 2013; as main artist: Sergio George Presents Salsa Giants (Latin Grammy Award for Best Salsa Album 2014) 2014. *Honours:* Latin Grammy Awards for Producer of the Year 2008, 2011, 2014, for Producer of Record of the Year (for Marc Anthony's Vivir Mi Vida) 2014. *Address:* Top Stop Music, 101 SE 4th Avenue, Delray Beach, FL 33483, USA (office). *Telephone:* (561) 303-1629 (office). *Fax:* (561) 303-1649 (office). *Website:* www .topstopmusic.com (office).

GERALDO, Neil; American musician (guitar) and record producer; b. 29 Dec. 1955; m. Pat Benatar 1982. *Career:* guitarist, Derringer; John Waite; guitarist, record producer, Pat Benatar 1977–. *Recordings include:* albums: with Pat Benatar: Crimes of Passion 1980, Precious Time 1981, Get Nervous 1982, Get Nervous (producer) 1982, Live From Earth 1983, Tropico 1984, In The Heat of The Night 1985, Seven The Hard Way 1985, Best Shots 1987, Wide Awake in Dreamland 1988, True Love (producer) 1991, Gravity's Rainbow (co-producer) 1993, Innamorata 1997, Go 2003, Ultimate Collection 2008; also appears on Best of Steve Forbert 1993, Rock and Roll Hoochie Coo 1996, Yesterday Today Tomorrow 1997, Best of Rick Springfield 1999; singles include Heartbreaker, All Fired Up, Treat Me Right, Love Is A Battlefield, Hell Is For Children, Invincible, Hit Me With Your Best Shot, Sex As A Weapon, We Belong. *E-mail:* info@benatarstore.com (office). *Website:* www .benatar.com.

MR GERBIK (see Kool Keith)

GERIMON, Paul, DipMus; Belgian singer (bass); b. 14 Oct. 1954, Dinant. *Education:* St Paul's Coll. and Dinant's Royal Athenee, Opera Studio Brussels, Centre de Musique Baroque, Paris. *Career:* sings opera, standards, original songs, musicals, baroque and contemporary 1974–; first part of Kid Creole, with Allez Allez 1982; bass soloist, Opera Royal Wallonie 1983–86; TV and radio appearances, festivals; played part of Don Juan at theatre 1990; tricentenary of La Monnaie 1995; int. tour with R. Jacobs and Trisha Brown Co. 1998–99; The Phantom of the Opera 2000; mem. Union des Artistes, Brussels. *Recordings include:* M. Kolbe, 1989; DuMont, 1992; WOMA, 1992; Sodoma, 1993; L'Orfeo, 1995; Intra Muros, 1996; Allez Allez, 1997; Euridice, 1998; Don Giovanni, 1999. *Honours:* Académie du Disque Orphée d'or, Paris 1991. *Address:* Fedor asbl, rue Sax, 8, 5500 Dinant, Belgium. *E-mail:* pgerimon@hotmail.com. *Website:* www.paulgerimon.com.

GERONIMO, Sarah; Philippine singer, musician (piano) and actress; b. (Sarah Asher Tua Geronimo), 25 July 1988, Santa Cruz, Manila; d. of Delfin Geronimo and Divina Geronimo. *Education:* Dominican School, Manila. *Career:* fmr TV child star, later actress and performer in TV and film; competed in TV's Star for a Night singing competition 2002–03; numeroust albums and concerts. *Films include:* as actor: Sarah… Ang Munting Prinsesa 1995, Filipinas 2003, Captain Barbell 2003, Masikip Sa Dibdib 2004, Annie B. 2004, Lastikman: Unang Banat 2004, A Very Special Love 2008, You Changed My Life 2009, Hating Kapatid 2010, Catch Me, I'm in Love 2011, Won't Last a Day Without You 2011. *Television:* Pen Pen de Sarapen (children's series) 1992–94, Ang TV (children's series) 1995–96, Star for a Night (competitor) 2002–03, SOP 2003, ASAP 2004–, Sarah: the Teen Princess 2004, SCQ Reload: Kilig Ako 2005, Bitung Walang Ningning 2006, Your Song (cameos) 2006–09, Pangarap na Bituin 2007, Love Spell 2007, Maalaala Mo Kaya 2008, Hair is Your Moment 2010, 1DOL 2010, Sarah G. Live! 2012. *Recordings include:* albums: Popstar: A Dream Come True 2003, Sweet Sixteen 2004, Becoming 2006, Taking Flight 2007, Just Me 2008, Your Christmas Girl 2009, Music and Me 2010, One Heart (Awit Award for Best Selling Album of the Year 2012) 2011, Pure OPM Classics 2012. *Honours:* Aliw Awards for Most Promising Female Entertainer 2003, for Record Breaking Major Concert Act (Female) 2010, for Entertainer of the Year 2010, for Best Concert Collaboration 2011, for Best Female Major Concert of the Year 2012, Awit Awards for Best Performance by a New Female Recording Artist 2004, People's Choice Award 2010, Mnet Asian Music Award for Best Asian Artist (Philippines) 2006, many Myx Music Awards 2008, 2009, 2010, 2012, Radio Music Listeners Choice Award 2009, Star Awards for Female Pop Artist of the Year 2009, 2010, for Female Recording Artist of the Year 2011. *Address:* c/o VIVA Records, VIVA Entertainment Inc., 6th and 7th Floor, East Tower, Pse Center, Exchange Road, Ortigas Center, 1605, Pasig City, Philippines (office). *Telephone:* (2) 687-6181 (office). *Fax:* (2) 632-1849 (office). *E-mail:* feedback@viva.com.ph (office). *Website:* www.viva.com.ph (office); www.sarahgeronimo.com.

GERRITSEN, Rinus; Dutch singer and musician (bass); b. 9 Aug. 1946, The Hague. *Career:* Founder-mem. of rock group, Golden Earring 1961–; tours and live appearances; producer for numerous artists; numerous collaborations. *Recordings include:* albums: with Golden Earring: Just Earrings 1965, Winter Harvest 1966, Miracle Mirror 1968, On The Double 1969, Eight Miles High 1969, Golden Earring 1970, Seven Tears 1971, Together 1972, Moontan 1973, Switch 1975, To The Hilt 1976, Contraband 1976, Golden Earring Live 1977, Grab It For A Second 1978, No Promises, No Debts 1979, Prisoner Of The Night 1980, 2nd Live 1981, Cut 1982, N.E.W.S. 1984, Something Heavy Goin' Down 1984, The Hole 1986, Keeper Of The Flame 1989, The Complete Singles Collection 1975–91 1991, Bloody Buccaneers 1991, The Naked Truth 1992, Face It 1995, Lovesweat 1995, Naked II 1997, The Complete Naked Truth 1998, Paradise In Distress 1999, Last Blast Of The Century 2000, The Devil Made Us Do It 2000, Millbrook USA 2003, Naked III 2005, Live in Ahoy 2006, Tits 'N Ass 2012. *Current Management:* c/o Rob Gerritsen, Wingerd 38, 2496 VC The Hague, The Netherlands. *Telephone:* (15) 380-55-88. *Fax:* (15) 380-55-91. *E-mail:* daan@golden-earring.nl (office). *Website:* www.goldenearring.nl; www.rinus.golden-earring.nl.

GERS, Janick Robert; British musician (guitar); b. 27 Jan. 1957, Hartlepool, England. *Career:* fmr mem., White Spirit, Gillan, Gogmagog; mem. heavy metal band, Iron Maiden 1990–. *Recordings include:* albums: with White Spirit: White Spirit 1980; with Gillan: Double Trouble 1981, Magic 1982; with Gogmagog: I Will Be There 1985; with Iron Maiden: No Prayer for the Dying 1990, Fear of the Dark 1992, The X-Factor 1995, Virtual XI 1998, Brave New World 2000, Dance of Death 2003, A Matter of Life and Death 2006, Flight 666 2009, The Final Frontier 2010, The Book of Souls 2015. *Film appearance:* Maiden Heaven (documentary) 2010. *Honours:* Ivor Novello Award 2000, BRIT Award for Best British Live Act 2009. *Current Management:* c/o Phantom Music Managment Ltd, Bridle House 36 Bridle Lane, London, W1F 9BZ, England. *Telephone:* (845) 331-3300. *Fax:* (845) 331-3500. *Website:* www.phantom-music.com; www.ironmaiden.com.

GERUP, Martin; Danish singer, composer and musician (keyboards); b. 24 Feb. 1960, Himmelev Sogn; m. Dorte Schou 1995, one d. *Education:* Danish Conservatory of Jazz, Rock and Latin Music. *Career:* Roskilde Festival, with Dieters Lieder, 1988; Roskilde Festival, with Flying Fish, 1993; several radio and television shows; mem. Danish Jazz, Rock and Folk Authors. *Recordings include:* with Dieters Lieder: Jeg Ka' Lieder, 1983; Hvorflink Ka' Man Blive?, 1986; with Flying Fish: It's Almost Fairytime, 1993. *Address:* Østergade 21, 4000 Roskilde, Denmark. *Telephone:* 40920747. *E-mail:* Martin@gerup.dk. *Website:* www.gerup.dk.

GERVERS, Walter James Morrison; British musician (bass guitar) and songwriter; b. 21 Dec. 1983, Tunbridge Wells, Kent. *Education:* Abingdon School. *Career:* fmr mem. Face Meets Grill; Founder-mem. Foals 2005–. *Recordings:* albums: with Foals: Antidotes 2008, Total Life Forever 2010, Holy Fire 2013, What Went Down 2015. *Honours:* with Foals: NME Awards for Best Track (for Spanish Sahara) 2011, (for Inhaler) 2013, Q Magazine Awards for Best Live Act 2013, for Best Act in the World Today 2015. *Current Management:* c/o Steve Matthews, Q Prime Management, 729 Seventh Avenue, #1600, New York, NY 10019, USA. *Telephone:* (212) 302-9790. *E-mail:* info@qprime.com. *Website:* www.qprime.com; www.foals.co.uk.

GESSLE, Per; Swedish musician (guitar), singer and songwriter; b. 12 Jan. 1959, Halmstad. *Career:* mem., Gyllene Tider; Founder-mem., Roxette, with Marie Fredricksson, 1984–; numerous TV, radio and live appearances worldwide; Founder and Owner, music publishers, Jimmy Fun Music, Hip Happy, Tom Bone Music; Co-owner, Gessle Music, Happy Accident Music. *Recordings include:* Albums: Pearls of Passion 1986, Look Sharp! 1988, Joyride 1991, Tourism 1992, Den Sjunde Vagen 1993, Den Standiga Resa 1993, Efter Stormen 1993, Mammas Barn 1993, Crash! Boom! Bang! 1994, Het Vind 1995, Don't Bore Us, Get To The Chorus—Roxette's Greatest Hits 1995, Balades En Español 1996, Have a Nice Day 1999, Room Service 2001, Charm School 2011, Travelling 2012, The Per Gessle Archives 2014; singles include: The Look (No. 1, 23 countries) 1989, Listen To Your Heart (No. 1, USA) 1989, Dangerous 1989, Dressed For Success 1989, It Must Have Been Love (from film Pretty Woman, No. 1, USA) 1990, Joyride (No. 1, 19 countries) 1991, Fading Like a Flower (No. 2, USA) 1991, The Big L 1991, Spending my Time 1991, Church of Your Heart 1992, How Do You Do! 1992, Queen of Rain 1992, Almost Unreal (from film Super Mario Brothers) 1993, Sleeping in My Car 1995, You Don't Understand Me 1996, Wish I Could Fly 1999, Anyone 1999, Stars 1999. *Honours:* Grammy Awards; MTV Awards, Achievement medals from King Carl XVI Gustaf of Sweden 2003. *Current Management:* Dimberg Management, Ölandsgatan 42, 116 63 Stockholm, Sweden. *Telephone:* (8) 54-50-23-90. *E-mail:* office@dimberg.com. *Website:* www.gessle.com.

GEVAERT, Alan; Belgian musician (bass guitar). *Career:* fmr mem. Chris Withley & Arno; mem. dEUS 2004–. *Recordings include:* albums: Pocket Revolution 2005, Vantage Point 2008, Keep You Close 2011, Following Sea 2012. *Current Management:* c/o Christian Pierre, Musickness Bvba, Rozenlaan 57, 2970 'S Gravenwezel, Belgium. *Telephone:* (3) 285-34-05. *Fax:* (3) 254-01-25. *E-mail:* info@musickness.be. *Website:* www.musickness.be; www.deus.be.

GHIGLIONE, Bill; French composer, arranger, producer, music director and publisher; *Publisher / Producer / Composer, Léa & Bill Music*; b. 5 July 1947, Nice. *Education:* univ. diploma in literature, classical piano studies. *Career:* fmr musician (keyboard); tours with Eddy Mitchell 1976–77, Claude Nougaro 1977, Johnny Halliday 1978–80, Michel Polnareff, Japan (musical director) 1979, Maxime Le Forestier, Europe 1982–83; performer, theme music, TV series Dallas; producer, composer for Léa Ivanne; mem. Soc. des auteurs, compositeurs et éditeurs de musique (SACEM), Soc. civile des producteurs phonographiques. *Compositions include:* composer/writer with Léa Ivanne of single song Où sont les hommes by Patricia Kaas; Jonatan Cerrada's first album, composer/writer with Léa Ivanne of songs Rien ne me changera, Par amour, Regarde moi dans les yeux; Platinum Record for Roch Voisine's album Je te serai fidèle 2003, composer/writer with Léa Ivanne of songs Tant Pis, Je l'ai vu, On a tous une étoile; Gold Record for Roch Voisine's album Sauf si l'Amour 2005; composer/writer with Léa Ivanne of songs Une Femme, Apothéose, Quelque part; also composer/writer for Julio Iglesias' Je me sens bien chez vous; composer/writer for Chimène Badi 'Avec ou sans lui' 'Plus de devoirs que de droits'; composer/writer for Roch Voisine albums Confidences, Prends ton temps 2010, composer of Non Ho Maï on album Opéra Rouge by Vincent Niclo (Platinum Record) 2012, and others. *Recordings:* Dallas album 1981; with Lasya Victory: L'Age D'or 1989, Tout Ça Nous Fait Mal 1990, Le Messie Est De Retour 1991, Tout S'Arrange 1992, Mona 1993, Sound Design, television series Inventions of Life 3 1995, Léa Ivanne, A Prendre ou à Laisser 1999, Song of the Universal Exposition (Hanover) 2000, To Enlighten The World, by Léa Ivanne. *Honours:* Double Gold Record Award (for Dallas theme) 1982, Best French Record of Year (for Tout Ça Nous Fait Mal) 1990, Gold Records 2003/04: Patricia Kaas's album Sexe fort. *Address:* 43 rue de la Liberté, 93230 Romainville, France (office). *Fax:* 6-13-50-68-49 (mobile) (office). *E-mail:* leabillmusic@sfr.fr (office); billghiglione@sfr.fr (office). *Website:* myspace.com/billghiglione (office).

GHOSHAL, Shreya; Indian singer; b. 12 March 1984, Berhampore, West Bengal; d. of Biswajeet Ghoshal and Sarmistha Ghoshal. *Education:* SIES Coll. of Arts, Science and Commerce. *Career:* playback singer in numerous films; judge, Star Voice Of India-Chhote Ustaad with singer Kunal Ganjawala and composer Pritam; currently one of three judges on X Factor with Sonu Nigam and Sanjay Leela Bhansali. *Films include:* Devdas (Nat. Film Award for Best Female Playback Singer 2003, Zee Cine Award for Best Female Playback Singer 2003, Filmfare Award for the Best Female Playback Singer 2003, Filmfare R.D. Burman Award for Best Music Talent 2003, Sansui Award for Best Female Playback Singer 2003) 2000, Armaan 2003, Jism (Filmfare Award for Best Female Playback Singer 2004, Screen Award for Best Female Playback Singer 2004, IIFA Award for Best Female Playback Singer 2004) 2003, Dil Bechara Pyaar Ka Maara 2004, Krishna Cottage 2004, Phir Milenge 2004, Blackmail 2005, Zameer 2005, Paheli (Nat. Film Award for Best Female Playback Singer 2006) 2005, Parineeta (Zee-Cine Award for Best Female Playback Singer 2006, Screen Award for the Best Female Playback Singer 2006) 2005, Kasak 2005, Dehati Babu 2006, Jaane Hoga Kya, Honeymoon Travels Pvt. Ltd. 2007, Jab We Met (National Film Award for Best Female Playback Singer 2007) 2007, Antaheen (Nat. Film Award for Best Female Playback Singer 2008) 2007, Black & White 2008, Singh Is King (IIFA Award for Best Female Playback Singer 2009, Filmfare Award for the Best Female Playback Singer 2009, Apsara Film & Television Producers Guild Award for the Best Female Playback Singer 2008) 2008, Guru (Zee-Cine Award for Best Female Playback Singer 2008, Filmfare Award for the Best Female Playback Singer 2008, Screen Award for the Best Female Playback Singer 2008, Apsara Film & Television Producers Guild Award for the Best Female Playback Singer 2008) 2008, Banares (Kerala State Film Award for the Best Female Playback Singer 2009) 2009, Rab Ne Bana Di Jodi (Apsara Film & Television Producers Guild Award for the Best Female Playback Singer 2010) 2009, Tees Maar Khan 2010, I Hate Love Stories (Screen Award for the Best Female Playback Singer) 2010, When Harry Tries to Marry 2010, Singham 2011, Agathan (Best Female Playback Singer, Asianet Film Awards 2011) 2011, Dabangg 2 2012, Jab Tak Hai Jaan 2012, Aiyyaa 2012, Heroine 2012, Ishaqzaade 2012, Kahaani 2012, Ageepath 2012, Jolly LLB 2013, Aashiqui 2 (Life Ok Screen Award for Best Playback Singer (Female) 2014, IIFA Award for Best Playback Singer (Female) 2014) 2013, Raanjhaa 2013, Hasee to Phasee 2014, Bewakoofian 2014. *Honours:* winner All India Light Vocal Music Competition, New Delhi 1995, winner TVS SaReGaMa 1999, Best Female Playback Singer, ETV Bangla Film Awards 2005, Zee Astiva Award 2008, Mirchi Music Awards Female Vocalist of the year (Kannada) 2009, Star Anando Sera Bengali Award 2010, BIG Bangla Female Singer of the Year 2010, Swaralaya Yesudas Award 2011, Life Ok Screen Award for Best Playback Singer (Female) 2014. *E-mail:* contact@shreyaghoshal.com. *Website:* www.shreyaghoshal.com.

GHOST, Amanda; British singer, songwriter, musician (guitar) and music industry executive; b. (Amanda Louisa Gosein), 1974, London; m., one d. *Career:* songwriter, collaborations with artists, including Whitney Houston, Kylie Minogue, Beverley Knight, James Blunt, Beyoncé, Shakira, Mariah Carey, Liam Howlett, Boy George; producer of own labels, PLAN A Records, Outsiders; Pres., Epic Records, USA 2009–10; currently CEO record label Outsiders (jt venture with Universal Music Group). *Recordings include:* albums: Ghost Stories 2000, Singles and Remixes 2004, Blood on the Line 2008; as songwriter: You're Beautiful (for James Blunt), Beautiful Liar, Tattoo, wrote four songs for Beyoncé's album I am....Sasha Fierce, Colours (for Prodigy) 2009, Gypsy (for Shakira), Only the Horses 2011; as producer: Cadillac Records 2008, Magic Hour 2011, Old Tyme Religion 2011. *Honours:* three Ivor Novello Awards. *Current Management:* c/o Jeremy Pearce, Axis Management, 42 Ferry Road, Barnes, London, SW13 9PW, England. *Telephone:* (7768) 852216. *Fax:* (20) 8563-0290. *E-mail:* jeremy.pearce@axismanagement.net. *E-mail:* info@amanda-ghost.com (office). *Website:* www.amanda-ghost.com.

GHOSTFACE, (Tony Starks, Sun God); American hip-hop and rap artist; b. (Dennis Coles), 9 May 1970. *Career:* mem. Wu-Tang Clan 1993–; solo artist 1996–, as Ghostface Killah, later simply Ghostface; numerous guest appearances and film soundtrack contribs; f. Starks Enterprises. *Recordings include:* albums: with Wu-Tang Clan: Enter the Wu-Tang (36 Chambers) 1993, Wu-Tang Forever 1997, The W 2000, Iron Flag 2001, Disciples of the 36 Chambers 2004, The 8 Diagrams 2007; solo: Ironman 1996, Supreme Clientele 2000, Bulletproof Wallets 2001, The Pretty Toney Album 2004, Fishscale 2006, The Big Doe Rehab 2007, Ghostdini: The Wizard of Poetry in Emerald City 2009, Wu Massacre 2010, Apollo Kids 2010, Twelve Reasons to Die 2013; others: 718 (with Theodore Unit) 2004, Put it on the Line (Trife Da God) 2005, Sniperlite (with J Dilla and MF Doom) 2008, Wu Block (with Sheek Louch) 2012. *Films include:* Black and White 1999, Hunter Dawson 2002, Fade to Black 2004, Walk Hard: The Dewey Cox Story 2007, When in Rome 2010. *Address:* c/o Def Jam, 2220 Colorado Avenue, Santa Monica, CA 90404, USA (office). *Website:* www.wutangcorp.com.

GIACCHINO, Michael; American composer; b. 10 Oct. 1967, Riverside Township, NJ. *Education:* School of Visual Arts, New York, Juilliard School. *Career:* fmrly worked in publicity for Disney and Universal, New York; fmrly worked in feature film publicity dept, Disney Studios, Burbank; fmr asst producer, Disney Interactive. *Films:* as composer: Legal Deceit 1997, No Salida 1998, My Brother the Pig 1999, The Trouble with Lou 2001, Semper Fi 2001, Redemption of the Ghost 2002, Phenomenon II 2003, String of the Kite 2003 (Accolade Competition Award of Excellence 2003), Sin 2003, The Incredibles 2004 (World Soundtrack Award for Discovery of the Year 2005, ASCAP Film and Television Music Award for Top Box Office Film 2005, Annie Award for Music in an Animated Feature Production 2005, BMI Film and TV Award for Film Music 2005), The Muppets' Wizard of Oz 2005, Sky High 2005, The Family Stone 2005, Looking for Comedy in the Muslim World 2005, Mission: Impossible III 2006, Ratatouille (Grammy Award for Best Score Soundtrack Album for Motion Picture, Television or Other Visual Media 2007, Annie Award for Best Music in an Animated Feature Production 2008) 2007, Speed Racer 2008, Up (Golden Globe Award for Best Original Score – Motion Picture 2010, Grammy Award for Best Score Soundtrack Album for Motion Picture, Television or Other Visual Media 2010, Academy Award for Achievement in Music Written for Motion Pictures, Original Score 2010, BAFTA Film Award 2010) 2009, Checkmate 2009, Star Trek 2009, Land of the Lost 2009, Live With It 2010, Let Me In 2010, Mission: Impossible IV 2011, Super 8 2011, Monte Carlo 2011. *Television:* as composer: Alias 2001–06, Lost (BMI Film and TV Award for TV Music 2005, Emmy Award for Outstanding Music Composition for a Series 2005, ASCAP Film and Television Music Awards 2005, 2006) 2004–10, What About Brian 2006, Six Degrees 2006-07, Fringe 2008–10, Undercovers 2010. *Compositions for video games:* Gargoyles 1995, Donald Starring in Maui Mallard 1995, The Lost World: Jurassic Park 1997, Warpath: Jurassic Park 1999, Medal of Honor 1999, Muppet Monster Adventure 2000, Medal of Honor: Allied Assault 2002, Medal of Honor: Frontline 2002, Call of Duty 2003, Secret Weapons Over Normandy 2003, Alias 2004, Call of Duty: United Offensive 2004, Call of Duty: Finest Hour 2004, The Incredibles 2004, Black 2006, Medal of Honor: Airborne 2007, Turning Point: Fall of Liberty 2008, Fracture 2008, Up 2009; music for Disneyland Resort Paris rollercoaster Space Mountain: Mission 2 2005. *Honours:* Hon. Pres. Int. Film Music Conf. 2010. *Current Management:* c/o Gorfaine/Schwartz Agency, 4111 West Alameda Avenue, Suite 509, Burbank, CA 91505, USA. *Telephone:* (818) 260-8500. *Website:* www.gsamusic.com. *E-mail:* contact@michaelgiacchinomusic.com (office). *Website:* www .michaelgiacchinomusic.com.

GIANESINI, Laurent Gilbert, (Laurent Gianez); French jazz musician (tenor saxophone, flute, clarinet); b. 13 May 1942, Moyeuvre-Grande. *Education:* Metz Conservatory. *Career:* mem. various jazz groups, including Duo J. M. Albertucci-Gianez, Duo Denis Moog-Gianez, Ecaroh, Quartet Gianez (own compositions, Samba music); annual concert with Archie Shepp and Ted Curson; founder of 10-mem. New Orleans-style, Bix Band; founder 17-mem. swing/Basie/Ellington-style, Bix Big Band; mem. SACEM (Paris). *Recordings include:* albums: Car La Rouille N'Aura Pas Raison Du Jazz (with Duo Denis Moog-Gianez), Strasbourg Jazz Cession, Brindille, Backhome, Jazz At Home (with Duo J. M. Albertucci-Gianez). *Address:* 28 rue Paul Vaillant Couturier, 57300 Hagondange, France. *Telephone:* (3) 87-70-13-72; (6) 70-45-20-50.

GIANEZ, Laurent (see Gianesini, Laurent Gilbert)

GIBB, Barry Alan Crompton, CBE; British/American singer, songwriter and record producer; b. 1 Sept. 1946, Isle of Man; s. of Hughie Gibb and Barbara Gibb; m. Linda Gray 1970; five c. *Career:* emigrated to Australia 1958, returned to UK 1967; formed The Bee Gees (with brothers Robin, Maurice and Andy) 1958; started singing in nightclubs, Australia; numerous performances at major venues around the world. *Compositions include:* writer or co-writer, producer or co-producer of numerous songs for other artists including: Elvis Presley (Words), Cliff Richard (I Cannot Give You My Love), Sarah Vaughan (Run To Me), Al Green, Janis Joplin, Barbra Streisand (Guilty album), Diana Ross (Chain Reaction), Dionne Warwick (Heartbreaker), Dolly Parton and Kenny Rogers (Islands In The Stream), Ntrance (Staying Alive), Take That (How Deep Is Your Love), Boyzone (Words), Yvonne Elliman (If I Can't Have You). *Recordings include:* albums: with The Bee Gees: Bee Gees Sing and Play 14 Barry Gibb Songs 1965, Monday's Rain 1966, Bee Gees 1st 1967, Horizontal 1968, Idea 1968, Odessa 1969, Cucumber Castle 1970,

Marley Purt Drive 1970, Sound of Love 1970, Two Years On 1971, Melody (OST) 1971, Trafalgar 1971, To Whom It May Concern 1972, Life in a Tin Can 1973, Mr Natural 1974, Main Course 1975, Children of the World 1976, Here at Last... Bee Gees Live 1977, Saturday Night Fever (OST) 1977, Spirits Having Flown 1979, SWALK 1979, Living Eyes 1981, Staying Alive (OST) 1983, E.S.P. 1987, One 1989, High Civilization 1991, Size Isn't Everything 1993, Still Waters 1997, One Night Only 1998, This Is Where I Came In 2001, Harmonies Down Under 2002, Alone 2002, In the Beginning 2003, Merchants of Dream 2003, Bee Gees Number Ones 2004; solo: Now Voyager 1984, Hawks 1988. *Honours:* Hon. degree (Univ. of Manchester) 2004; seven Grammy awards, American Music Award for Int. Achievement 1997, BRIT Award for Outstanding Contribution to Music 1997, World Music Award for Lifetime Achievement 1997, Q Lifetime Achievement Award 2005, Ivor Novello Acad. Fellowship 2006, BMI Icon Award 2007, Freeman of the Borough of Douglas (Isle of Man) 2009. *Address:* c/o Crompton Songs, 5820 North Bay Road, Miami Beach, FL 33140, USA. *Telephone:* (305) 672-2390. *Fax:* (305) 531-8041. *E-mail:* middleear@earthlink.het. *Website:* www.barrygibb.com.

GIBBONS, Beth; British singer and songwriter; b. 4 Jan. 1965, Devon. *Career:* worked in an advertising agency in Bristol; lead singer, Portishead 1991–; worked with Paul 'Rustin' Man' Webb 2001–. *Film:* To Kill A Dead Man (short feature, also projected on MI5 building, London) 1995. *Recordings include:* albums: with Portishead: Dummy (Mercury Music Prize for Best Album) 1994, Herd Of Instinct 1995, Portishead 1997, PNYC (live) 1998, Glory Times 1998, Roseland, New York (DVD) 2002, Third 2008; solo: Out Of Season (with Paul Webb) 2001. *Honours:* NME Brat Award 1995. *Website:* www .portishead.co.uk.

GIBBONS, Billy; American musician (guitar); b. 4 March 1950, Houston, Tex. *Career:* fmr mem. Coachmen, name later changed to Moving Sidewalks – 1969; mem. ZZ Top 1970–; also collaborates with other artists, under name Justis Walkert. *Recordings include:* albums: with Moving Sidewalks: Flash 1968; with ZZ Top: ZZ Top's First Album 1970, Rio Grande Mud 1972, Tres Hombres 1973, Fandango 1975, Takin' Texas To The People 1976, Tejas 1976, Deguello 1979, El Loco 1981, Eliminator 1983, Afterburner 1985, Recycler 1990, Antenna 1994, Rhythmeen 1996, XXX 1999, Mescalero 2003, Eliminator 2008, La Futura 2012. *Honours:* Nordoff-Robbins Music Therapy Foundation Silver Clef Award 1992. *Address:* 2600 East Southlake Blvd, Suite 120-159, Southlake, TX 76092, USA. *Telephone:* (817) 756-9282. *E-mail:* custserv@ billygibbonsgear.com. *Website:* www.billygibbons.com. *E-mail:* info@zztop .com (office). *Website:* www.zztop.com.

GIBBONS, Ian Ronald; British musician (keyboards, accordion); b. 18 July 1952, Rochford, Essex; m. Amanda Gaskin 1985. *Career:* mem. The Kinks 1979–89, 1992–96; also worked with Sweet, Roger Chapman, The Crystals, The Shirelles, Dr Feelgood, Eddie and the Hotrods, Chris Farlowe, Kursaal Flyers, The Inmates; mem. Kast Off Kinks 2008–; mem. PRS. *Recordings:* all Kinks albums 1979–96. *Website:* www.kastoffkinks.co.uk.

GIBBONS, Steve; British singer, songwriter and musician (guitar). *Career:* Founder The Steve Gibbons Band 1971; tours and live appearances. *Recordings include:* albums: Short Stories 1971, Any Road Up 1976, Rolling On 1977, Caught in the Act 1977, Down in the Bunker 1978, Street Parade 1980, Saints and Sinners 1981, On The Loose 1986, From Birmingham to Memphis 1995, The Dylan Project 1998, Riding Out the Dark 2003, Double Live 2004, Chasing Tales 2008, Street Parade/Saints & Sinners 2012. *Website:* www .stevegibbonsband.com.

GIBERT, Alain; French musician (trombone), composer and arranger; b. 1 Jan. 1947, Langogne; m. Nadine Faure 1970; three s. *Career:* Co-founder ARFI (Asscn à la Recherche d'un Folklore Imaginaire); mem. various bands, including Marvelous Band, Marmite Infernale, Apollo, Bomonstre, Kif Kif; mem. SACEM, ARFI. *Compositions include:* Music for Louis Sclavis, Steve Waring. *Recordings include:* L'Age Du Cuivre, Apollo; trombonist, singer, Chariot d'Or; Pticado; as composer, arranger: Le Roi Demonte, L'Art de la Retraite Sonne. *Current Management:* c/o ARFI, 16 rue Pizay, 69202 Lyon Cedex 01, France. *Website:* www.arfi.org. *Address:* Coissard de Montmorin, 63160 Billom, France.

GIBSON, (Deborah Ann) Debbie; American singer, songwriter, musician (piano) and actress; b. 31 Aug. 1970, Brooklyn, New York. *Education:* private piano and voice lessons. *Career:* solo artist. *Stage appearances:* Eponine in Les Miserables (Broadway) 1992, Sandy in Grease (West End, London) and Rizzo in Grease (Broadway) 1994, Fanny Brice in Funny Girl (Broadway), Belle in Disney's Beauty and the Beast (Broadway), Gypsy Rose Lee in Gypsy (Paper Mill Playhouse), The Narrator in Joseph and the Amazing Technicolor Dreamcoat (US tour) 2000, Cinderella in Rodgers and Hammerstein's Cinderella 2001, Velma Kelly in Chicago (North Shore Theatre, Boston) 2002, (Lyric Theatre, Oklahoma City) 2003, Sally Bowles in Cabaret (Broadway) 2003, Marta in Company 2004, Anna Leonowens in The King and I (Thousand Oaks Civic Arts Plaza) 2008. *Composition:* Skirts (composer and lyricist of musical, produced on Broadway). *Recordings include:* albums: Out Of The Blue (New York Music Award for Debut Album of the Year 1989) 1987, Electric Youth 1989, Anything Is Possible 1990, Body Mind Soul 1993, Think With Your Heart 1995, Deborah 1996, MYOB 2001, Colored Lights: The Broadway Album 2003, Ms Vocalist 2010. *Honours:* New York Music Award for Debut Artist of the Year 1989, ASCAP Songwriter of the Year 1989, New York Music Award for Best Pop Female Vocalist 1990, New York Music Award for Song of the Year (for Lost in Your Eyes) 1990, New York Music Award for

Artist of the Year 1990, American Songwriter Award for Rock Producer of the Year 1990. *Current Management:* c/o Gibson Management, 300 Main Street #201, Huntington, NY 11743, USA. *E-mail:* info4debbiegibson@gmail.com. *Website:* www.debbiegibsonofficial.com.

GIBSON, Lee, BA; British singer; b. 5 March 1950, Watford, Hertfordshire; m. Gerry Boyce 1973; one d. *Career:* worked across Europe with UMO Danish Orchestra, Helsinki; Danish Radio Band, Copenhagen; Skymasters, Metropol Orchestra, Netherlands; television appearances, concerts, festivals; tours with Syd Lawrence Orchestra; Don Lusher Band; Big Band Specials, BBC Radio Band; guest appearances with Glenn Miller UK Orchestra; Herb Miller Band; singer, The Music of Andrew Lloyd Webber, concert for Prince and Princess of Wales at Expo '92, Seville; mem. Musicians' Union, Equity. *Film and television appearances include:* The Great Muppet Movie, Privates on Parade, Victor Victoria, Yentl, An American Tale, Willow, Benny Hill Show, Only Fools and Horses, Morecambe and Wise Show. *Recordings include:* chorale, One World One Peace, You Can See Forever, Never Let Me Go, also appears on: Music of Andrew Lloyd Webber 1988, Broadway Musicals 1991, Jesus Christ Superstar 1992, Swing Boogie 1999. *Publications:* contrib. music reviews to The Musician. *Honours:* Knikke Festival Singer's Prize. *E-mail:* kim@spmanagement.biz. *Website:* www.leegibson.co.uk.

GIERS, Samuel; Swedish musician (drums); b. 12 Feb. 1980. *Career:* mem. Mando Diao 1999–2011, Viktor and The Blood 2013–. *Recordings include:* albums: Bring 'Em In 2002, Hurricane Bar 2005, Ode to Ochrasy 2006, Never Seen the Light of Day 2007, Give Me Fire 2009. *Current Management:* c/o Flagstone Management, Götabergsgatan 2, 411 34 Gothenburg, Sweden. *Website:* www.viktorandtheblood.com.

GIFT, Roland; British singer, musician (saxophone) and actor; b. 28 May 1962, Birmingham. *Career:* musician and actor in Hull during 1980s; mem. Fine Young Cannibals 1984–; regular UK and US tours; solo artist. *Film appearances:* Tin Men 1987, Sammy and Rosie Get Laid 1987, Scandal 1989. *Stage appearance:* played Romeo, in Romeo and Juliet (UK rep tour) 1990. *Recordings include:* albums: with Fine Young Cannibals: Fine Young Cannibals, 1985; The Raw and The Cooked 1989; Beautiful Girls, 1996; Finest, 1996; solo: Roland Gift, 2002. *Honours:* BRIT Awards, Best British Group, Best British Album 1990.

GIGOT, Raquel; Belgian chromatic and diatonic accordions and composer; b. 9 Nov. 1965, Ottignies. *Career:* mem. Orion celtic music group; numerous radio and TV performances; studio musician recording with different artists. *Compositions:* Bully Wully Jig; Blue Room; Road to Bally Heighue; Rue Des Dunes; Lesidren; Mouse in the Kitchen. *Recordings include:* Blue Room, Restless Home, Leaving the World Behind, Histoires de Rue, Oceanides, About to Go, Strawberry Town. *Website:* www.orionceltic.com.

GIL, Gilberto; Brazilian politician, musician (guitar, accordion) and singer; b. (Gilberto Passos Gil Moreira), 26 June 1942, Salvador, Bahia State; s. of José Gil Moreira and Claudina Passos Gil Moreira. *Education:* Fed. Univ., Bahia. *Career:* began playing accordion aged eight; composed songs for TV advertisements in early 1960s; appeared in Nós Por Exemplo (show directed by Caetano Veloso) 1964; moved to São Paulo 1965; had first hit when Elis Regina recorded Louvação; participated in Tropicalia movt, sang protest songs that proved controversial with mil. dictatorship; imprisoned 1968; forced to leave Brazil on release and moved to UK; worked with groups such as Pink Floyd, Yes, Incredible String Band and Rod Stewart's band in London clubs; returned to Brazil in 1972; toured with Caetano Veloso, Gal Costa and Maria Bethânia; recorded album Nightingale in USA 1978; appearances at Montreux Jazz Festival; Pres. Fundação Gregorio de Matos, Salvador 1987; mem. Council of City Hall of Salvador 1988–92, Pres. Environmental Defence Cttee 1987; mem. Advisory Council Fundação Mata Virgem and Fundação Alerta Brasil Pantanal; Pres. Negro-Mestizo Reference Centre (CERNE); mem. Green Party 1989, later mem. Nat. Exec. Cttee; mem. Parl. for Salvador; Minister of Culture 2003–08 (resgnd); fmr Pres. Fundação Onda Azul (Blue Wave Foundation). *Recordings include:* albums: Louvação 1967, Gilberto Gil 1968, Tropicália ou Panis et Circensis 1968, Gilberto Gil 1969, Expresso 2222 1972, Barra 69 1972, Temporada de Verão 1974, Gilberto Gil ao Vivo 1974, Gil Jorge Ogum Zangô 1975, Refazenda 1975, Doces Bárbaros 1976, Refavela 1977, Refestança 1978, Antologia do Samba-Choro: Gilberto Gil e Germano Mathias 1978, Gilberto Gil ao Vivo em Montreux 1978, Nightingale 1978, Realce 1979, A Gente Precisa Ver o Luar 1981, Brasil: João Gilberto Gil, Caetano e Bethânia 1981, Um Banda Um 1982, Extra 1983, Quilombo 1984, Vamos Fugir (with The Wailers) 1984, Raça Humana 1984, Dia Dorim Noite Neon 1985, Gilberto Gil em Concerto 1987, Ao Vivo Em Tóquio 1987, Soy Loco por Ti, América 1987, O Eterno Deus Mu Dança 1989, Parabolicamará 1992, Tropicália 2 1993, Gilberto Gil Unplugged 1994, Quanta 1997, O sol de Oslo 1998, Ensaio Geral 1999, Cidade do Salvador 1999, O Viramundo 1999, Gilberto Gil – Satisfação 1999, Gil & Milton 2000, São João Vivo 2001, Kaya N'Gan Daya 2002, Eletracústico (Grammy Award for Best Contemporary World Music Album 2006) 2005, Gil Luminoso 2006, Banda Larga de Cordel 2008, BandaDois (Latin Grammy Award for Best Música Popular Brasileira Album 2010) 2009, Fé na Festa (Latin Grammy Award for Best Native Brazilian Roots Album) 2010, Concerto de cordas & máquinas de ritmo. *Honours:* Cruz da Ordem de Rio Branco, Chevalier, Ordre des Arts et des Lettres, Grand Officier, Légion d'honneur 2005; Shell and Sharp Prize 1990, UNESCO Artist for Peace 1999, Polar Music Prize 2004, 2005. *Current Management:* Gege Produções, Estrada de Gávea 135, 22451-260 Rio de

Janeiro, RJ, Brazil. *Telephone:* (21) 3323-1600. *Fax:* (21) 2239-9727. *E-mail:* atendimento@gege.com.br. *Website:* www.gege.com.br; www.gilbertogil.com .br.

GILBERT, Brantley Keith; American country music singer, songwriter and musician (guitar); b. 20 Jan. 1985, Jefferson, Ga. *Career:* songwriter for numerous artists including Colt Ford, Jason Aldean; toured with artists including Willie Nelson 2011, Toby Keith 2012; first solo headlining tour 2012. *Recordings:* albums: Modern Day Prodigal Son 2009, Halfway to Heaven 2010, Just As I Am (American Music Award for Favorite Country Album 2014) 2014. *Honours:* Acad. of Country Music Award for Top New Male Artist 2013. *Address:* c/o The Valory Music Company, Big Machine Label Group, 1219 16th Avenue South, Nashville, TN 37212, USA (office). *Telephone:* (615) 324-7777 (office). *E-mail:* mail@bigmachine.us (office). *Website:* bigmachinelabelgroup .com (office); brantleygilbert.com.

GILBERT, Gillian Lesley; British musician (keyboards, guitar); b. 27 Jan. 1961, Manchester; m. Stephen Morris 1993; two d. *Education:* Stockport Technical Coll. *Career:* fmr mem. all-female punk group, The Inadequates; mem. New Order 1980–98, 2011–, The Other Two 1991–; tours world-wide, concerts and festival appearances. *Television:* Celebration (documentary, BBC) 1982, Rock Around the Clock (BBC) 1985. *Recordings include:* albums: with New Order: Movement 1981, Power, Corruption & Lies 1983, Low-Life 1985, Brotherhood 1986, Substance 1987, Technique 1989, Republic 1993, Best of New Order 1994, Rest of New Order 1995, Music Complete 2015; with The Other Two: The Other Two and You 1994, Superhighways 1999. *Honours:* NME 'Godlike Genius' Award (with New Order) 2005, Q Outstanding Contribution to Music Award 2015. *Website:* www.neworder.com.

GILBERT, Paul; American musician (guitar); b. 6 Nov. 1966, Carbondale, Illinois. *Career:* guitarist, rock groups: Racer X, 1986–8, 1997–; Mr Big, 1989–96, 2009–; solo career 1998–. *Recordings:* albums: with Racer X: Street Lethal 1986, Second Heat 1987, Extreme Volume... Live 1988, Technical Difficulties 1999, Superheroes 2000, Snowball of Doom 2002, Getting Heavier 2002, Snowball of Doom 2 2007; with Mr Big: Mr Big 1989, Lean Into It 1991, Bump Ahead 1993, Hey Man 1996, What If... 2011; solo: King of Clubs 1998, Flying Dog 1999, Beehive Live 1999, Alligator Farm 2000, Burning Organ 2002, Raw Blues Power (with Jimi Kidd) 2002, Gilbert Hotel 2003, Space Ship One 2005, Get Out of My Yard 2006, Silence Followed by a Deafening Roar 2008, United States (with Freddie Nelson) 2009, Fuzz Universe 2010. *E-mail:* paulvsgodzilla@paulgilbert.com. *Website:* www.paulgilbert.com.

GILBERT, Simon; British musician (drums); b. 23 May 1965, Stratford-upon-Avon. *Career:* mem. Suede, 1991–2004, 2010–; mem. Futon 2005–; numerous concerts, festival and television appearances. *Recordings include:* albums: with Suede: Suede 1993, Dog Man Star 1994, Coming Up 1996, Sci-Fi Lullabies 1997, Head Music 1999, A New Morning 2002, Bloodsports 2013, Night Thoughts 2016; with Futon: Love Bites 2005, Give Me More! 2005, Pain Killer 2007. *Honours:* Mercury Music Prize 1993, Q Icon Award 2013. *Current Management:* Quietus Management Limited, 13 Bramley Road, 2nd Floor Phoenix Brewery, London, W10 6SP England. *Telephone:* (20) 3220-0310. *E-mail:* jordi23@mac.com. *Website:* www.quietusmanagement.com; www .suede.co.uk.

GILBERTO, Astrud; Brazilian singer; b. 30 March 1940, Bahia; m. João Gilberto (divorced). *Career:* singer, with João Gilberto on guitar and Stan Getz on saxophone; tours with Stan Getz; numerous collaborations. *Recordings include:* albums: Getz au Go Go 1964 (Grammy Award for Album of the Year 1965), The Astrud Gilberto Album 1965, The Shadow of Your Smile 1965, Haven't Got Anything Better To Do, 1968, Once Upon A Summertime 1971, The Girl From Ipanema 1977, Best Of 1982, The Essential Astrud Gilberto 1984, Look To The Rainbow 1986, Plus (with James Last) 1986, So and So 1988, Astrud Gilberto 1996, Live in New York 1999, Astrud Gilberto's Finest Hour 2001, Jungle 2002, Astrud Gilberto: Verve Ultimate Cool 2013. *Films include:* as singer: The Deadly Affair (Who Needs Forever) 1966; as actress: Get Yourself a College Girl 1964, The Hanged Man 1964. *Honours:* Latin Jazz USA Award for Lifetime Achievement 1992, elected to Int. Latin Music Hall of Fame 2002. *E-mail:* magya@astrudgilberto.com. *Website:* www.astrudgilberto .com.

GILBERTO, Bebel; Brazilian singer and songwriter; b. 12 May 1966, New York, USA; d. of João Gilberto and Miucha Gilberto. *Career:* made first appearance with mother and Stan Getz, Carnegie Hall 1975; appeared on children's TV in Brazil late 1970s; recorded vocals for various soundtracks 1980s; released solo EP 1989; returned to New York 1991; became influenced by dance club scene and started performing on club circuit; worked with musicians, including David Byrne, Arto Lindsay, Romero Lubambo; co-wrote club hit Technova (with Towa Tei) 1995; moved to London 1997; contributed vocals to Kenny G's recording of The Girl From Ipanema 1999; solo artist 2000–. *Recordings include:* albums: De Tarde, Vendo O Mar 1991, Tanto Tempo 2000, Bebel Gilberto 2004, Bebel Gilberto: Remixed 2005, Momento 2007, All in One 2009. *Honours:* Premio Sharp Award for Best Single (for Preciso Dize Que Te Amo) 1989. *E-mail:* contact@bebelgilberto.com. *Website:* www.bebelgilberto.com.

GILBERTO, João; Brazilian singer, songwriter and musician (guitar); b. 10 June 1931, Juazeiro, Bahia; m. 1st Astrud Gilberto; m. 2nd Miucha Gilberto; one d. Bebel Gilberto. *Career:* started playing guitar aged 14, on radio in Salvador by age 18; joined the radio station's band, Garotos da Lua and moved with them to Rio de Janeiro; left band to do live solo concerts in Porto Alegre; solo artist 1959–; relocated to USA 1961–80 (collaborations with Stan Getz during this period); continues to perform and record. *Compositions include:* Bim Bom; Ho-Ba La La; Minha Saudade; Abraco No Bonfa. *Recordings include:* albums: Quando Você Recordar/Amar é Bom 1951, Quando Ela Sai/Meia Luz 1952, Chega De Saudade 1959, O Amor O Sorriso E A Flor 1960, João Gilberto 1961, Getz/Gilberto 1963, Getz/Gilberto #2 1966, João Gilberto En Mexico 1970, João Gilberto 1973, Best of Two Worlds 1976, Amoroso 1977, João Gilberto Prado Pereira De Oliveira 1980, Brasil 1981, João Gilberto Live In Montreux 1986, João 1991, Eu Sei Que Vou Te Amar 1994, João – Voz E Violao 2000, Live at Umbria Jazz 2002, In Tokyo 2004, 20 Grandes Sucessos de João Gilberto 2009, The Very Best Of João Gilberto 2012, O Grande Encontro 2013. *Address:* c/o Universal Music Brasil, Avenida das Américas, 3500, Le Monde, Bloco 1, Loja A, Edificio Londres, Barra da Tijuca, Rio de Janeiro 22640-102, Brazil (office). *E-mail:* bookings@joaogilberto.com (office). *Website:* www.joaogilberto.com; www.joaogilberto.org.

GILKYSON, Eliza; American singer, musician (piano, guitar) and songwriter; b. 24 Aug. 1950, Hollywood, Calif.; m. Reavis Moore 1981, one s. one d. *Career:* tours with Ladysmith Black Mambazo, Dan Fogelberg, Arlo Guthrie, Andreas Vollenweider, Mary Chapin Carpenter; TV and film appearances; collaborated with numerous musicians including Lucy Kaplansky, Petula Clark, John Gorka, Conspirare, Tim Rush. *Compositions:* Rosie Strike Back, recorded by Roseanne Cash. *Recordings include:* albums: Eliza '69 1969, Love from the Heart 1979, Pilgrims 1987, Legends of Rainmaker 1988, Undressed 1994, Redemption Road 1996, Misfits 1999, Hard Times In Babylon 2000, Lost And Found 2002, Land of Milk and Honey 2004, RetroSpecto 2005, Paradise Hotel 2005, Your Town Tonight 2007, Beautiful World 2008, Red Horse (with John Gorka and Lucy Kaplansky) 2010, Roses at the End of Time 2011, The Nocturne Diaries 2014. *Honours:* inducted into Texas Music Hall of Fame 2003, three Austin Music Awards, four Folk Alliance Music Awards. *Telephone:* (512) 413-8461 (Val Denn Agency). *E-mail:* valdenn@valdenn .com. *Website:* www.valdenn.com; www.elizagilkyson.com.

GILL, Andy, BA; British musician (guitar), composer and producer; b. 1 Jan. 1957, Manchester. *Education:* Leeds Univ. *Career:* Founder-mem. Gang of Four 1977–83, 1987–97, 2004–; numerous TV appearances; as producer worked with artists including Red Hot Chilli Peppers, Busta Jones, The Balancing Act, The Most Beautiful Girl, Downey Mildew, Addie Brik, MCD, Inastella, The Morgans, Michael Hutchence, The Futureheads, Fight Like Apes, The Young Knives; mem. PRS. *Recordings include:* albums: with Gang of Four: Entertainment 1979, Solid Gold 1981, Songs of the Free 1982, Hard 1983, The Peel Sessions 1990, Mall 1991, Shrinkwrapped 1995, 100 Flowers Bloom 1998, Return the Gift 2005, At the Palace (live), Content 2011; solo: Dispossession 1987. *Current Management:* c/o Stephen Budd Music, 10 Greenland Street, Camden, London, NW1 0ND, England. *Telephone:* (70) 4040-9533. *E-mail:* andy@gillmusic.com. *Website:* www.gangoffour.co.uk; www.gillmusic.com.

GILL, Jonathan Benjamin (J.B.); British singer and songwriter; b. 7 Dec. 1986, Antigua. *Education:* Centre for Young Musicians, Croydon, Kings Coll., London. *Career:* mem. UFO 2006–08, changed group name to JLS (Jack the Lad Swing) 2008–13; competed in The X Factor (UK version) 2008, placed second; signed to Epic Records 2009; toured with Lemar 2009; debut single Beat Again released 2009; debut album released 2009; first headline tour 2010; recorded single Love You More for Children in Need charity 2010; collaborations include Tinie Tempah, Dev; recorded Sport Relief charity single Proud 2012; performed at Diamond Jubilee concert, outside Buckingham Palace 2012; patron for Rays of Sunshine Children's Charity. *Television:* JLS Revealed (special) 2009. *Film:* JLS: Eyes Wide Open 3D (concert film and documentary) 2011. *Recordings:* albums: with JLS: JLS (MOBO Award for Best Album 2010) 2009, Outta This World 2010, Jukebox 2011, Evolution 2012. *Publications:* Our Story So Far 2009, Just Between Us: Our Private Diary 2010. *Honours:* with UFO: Urban Music Award for Best Unsigned Act 2007; with JLS: MOBO Awards for Best UK Newcomer 2009, for Best Song (for Beat Again) 2009, for Best UK Act 2010, BBC Switch Live Award for Outstanding Artist 2009, BRIT Awards for British Breakthrough 2010, for Best British Single (for Beat Again) 2010, BT Digital Music Awards for Best Group 2010, 2011, for Best Video (for Everybody in Love) 2010, (for Eyes Wide Shut) 2011, (for Do You Feel What I Feel?) 2012, Urban Music Awards for Best Group 2010, for Best R&B Act 2010. *Current Management:* c/o Modest! Management, The Matrix Complex, 91 Peterborough Road, London, SW6 3BU, England. *E-mail:* info@modestmanagement.com. *Website:* www .modestmanagement.com; www.jlsofficial.com.

GILL, Janis; American singer and musician (guitar); b. 1 March 1955, Torrance, Calif.; m. 1st Vince Gill 1980 (divorced 1998); one d.; m. 2nd Roy Cummins 2000. *Career:* mem. of duo, Sweethearts of the Rodeo (with sister Kristine Arnold); winner of Wrangler Country Showcase 1985. *Recordings include:* Sweethearts Of The Rodeo 1986, One Time One Night 1988, Buffalo Zone 1990, Sisters 1992, Rodeo Waltz 1993, Beautiful Lies 1996, Restless 2012. *Honours:* CMA Vocal Duo of the Year (nine times), Music City News Best Vocal Duo, TNN Viewers' Choice Award for Favourite Group, NAIRD Award for Best Country Album 1994. *Address:* c/o Tony Conway, Ontourage Management, 1625 Broadway, Suite 500, Nashville, TN 37203, USA. *Website:* www.SweetHeartsOfTheRodeo.com.

GILL, Vincent (Vince) Grant; American country singer, musician (guitar) and songwriter; b. 5 April 1957, Norman, Okla; m. 1st Janis Oliver 1980 (divorced 1998); one d.; m. 2nd Amy Grant 2000; one d. *Career:* fmr mem. Mountain Smoke; mem. Bluegrass Alliance 1975–79, Pure Prairie League 1979–81, Rodney Crowell's band, The Cherry Bombs 1982; solo artist 1983–. *Recordings include:* albums: with Pure Prairie League: Can't Hold Back 1979, Firin' Up 1980, Something in the Night 1981; solo: Turn Me Loose 1983, The Things That Matter 1984, Vince Gill 1985, The Way Back Home 1987, When I Call Your Name 1989, Pocket Full of Gold 1991, I Never Knew Lonely 1992, I Still Believe In You 1992, Let There Be Peace on Earth 1993, When Love Finds You 1994, The Key 1998, Let's Make Sure We Say Goodbye 2000, These Days (Grammy Award for Best Country Album 2008) 2006, Guitar Slinger 2011. *Honours:* 20 Grammy Awards, CMA Single of the Year (with Patti Loveless), CMA Male Vocalist of the Year 1991, 1992, Song of the Year (for Look At Us) 1992, inducted into Country Music Hall of Fame 2007, Hollywood Walk of Fame 2012. *Website:* www.vincegill.com.

GILLAN, Ian; British singer; b. 19 Aug. 1945, Hounslow, Middlesex, England; m. Bronwen 1984; one d. *Career:* fmr lead singer, Episode Six; mem., Deep Purple 1969–73, 1984–89, 1992–; Founder mem., Gillan 1974–82; fmr mem., Black Sabbath; Founder mem., Gillan and Glover (with Roger Glover) 1988; mem., The Javelins; numerous tours world-wide, TV and radio broadcasts. *Recordings include:* albums: with Episode Six: Here There and Everywhere 1966; with Deep Purple: Concerto For Group And Orchestra 1969, Deep Purple In Rock 1970, Fireball 1971, Machine Head 1972, Who Do We Think We Are? 1973, Perfect Strangers 1985, Fireworks 1985, The House Of Blue Light 1987, The Battle Rages On 1992, Perpendicular 1996, Abandon 1998, Butterfly Ball Wizards Convention 1998, Child In Time 1998, Under The Gun 2001, Bananas 2003, Deep Purple And Friends 2003, Total Abandon 2004, Rapture of the Deep 2005, numerous live albums; with Gillan: Child In Time 1976, Gillan 1978, Mr Universe 1979, Glory Road 1980, Future Shock 1981, Double Trouble 1981, Magic 1982; with Black Sabbath: Born Again 1983; with Gillan and Glover: Accidentally On Purpose 1988; solo: Naked Thunder 1990, Toolbox 1991, Dreamcatcher 1998; with The Javelins: Sole Agency and Representations 2001. *Current Management:* c/o Phil Banfield CODA Agency, 229 Shoreditch High Street, London, E1 6PJ, England. *E-mail:* info@deep-purple.com. *Website:* www.deep-purple.com.

GILLESPIE, Bobby; British singer and musician (drums); b. 22 June 1964, Scotland. *Career:* mem. drummer, Jesus & Mary Chain 1984–85; Founder mem. and lead singer, Primal Scream 1984–. *Recordings include:* albums: with Jesus & Mary Chain: Psychocandy 1985; with Primal Scream: Sonic Flower Groove 1987, Primal Scream 1989, Screamadelica (Mercury Music Prize 1992) 1991, Give Out But Don't Give Up 1994, Vanishing Point 1997, EchoDek 1997, Xtrmntr 2000, Evil Heat 2002, Dirty Hits 2003, Shoot Speed (More Dirty Hits) 2004, Riot City Blues 2006, Beautiful Future 2008, More Light 2013. *Honours:* Q Groundbreaker Award (with Primal Scream) 2006, NME Godlike Genius Award 2007. *Current Management:* G. R. Management Ltd, 974 Pollockshaws Road, Glasgow, G41 2HA, Scotland. *Telephone:* (141) 632-1111. *Website:* www.primalscream.net.

GILLESPIE, Dana; British singer and songwriter; b. 30 March 1949, *Recordings include:* albums: Foolish Seasons 1967, Box of Surprises 1968, Jesus Christ Superstar 1972, Weren't Born a Man 1973, Ain't Gonna Play No Fiddle, Mojo Blues Band 1974, Blue Job 1982, Solid Romance 1984, Below The Belt 1984, It Belongs To Me 1985, Move Your Body Close To Me 1986, I'm a Woman 1986, Hot News' 1987, Amor 1990, Blues It Up 1990, Where Blue Begins 1991, Boogie Woogie Nights 1991, Big Boy, with Joachim Palden 1992, Methods of Release 1993, Andy Warhol 1994, Blue One 1994, One to One 1995, Hot Stuff 1995, Have I Got Blues for You 1996, Mustique Blues Festivals 1996, Inner View 1996, Cherry Pie, with Big Jay McNeeley 1997, Jan Mustique Bluesfest 1997, Back to the Blues 1999, Experienced 2000, Staying Power 2003, These Blue Nights 2006, I Rest My Case 2010. *Honours:* voted Top British Female Blues Vocalist 1993, 1994, 1995, 1996. *E-mail:* info@ danagillespie.com. *Website:* www.dana-gillespie.com.

GILLESPIE, Lee; American musician (bass guitar). *Career:* Founder mem. The American Analog Set 1995–. *Recordings include:* albums: The Fun Of Watching Fireworks 1996, From Our Living Room To Yours 1997, The Golden Band 1999, Know By Heart 2001, Through The 1990s: Singles & Unreleased 2001, Updates 2002, Promise Of Love 2003, Set Free 2005. *E-mail:* requests@ amanset.com. *Website:* www.amanset.com.

GILLEY, Mickey Leroy; American country singer, musician (piano, guitar), songwriter and actor; b. 9 March 1936, Natchez, Miss. *Career:* local record success 1960s; solo artist 1974–; Owner, Gilley's night club, Pasadena, Tex. (with Sherwood Cryer) 1971–89; opened own theatre in Branson, Missouri in early 1990s; numerous TV appearances. *Recordings include:* albums: Lonely Wine 1964, Down the Line 1967, Room Full of Roses 1974, City Lights 1974, Movin' On 1975, Overnight Sensation 1975, Smokin' 1976, First Class 1977, Flyin' High 1978, The Songs We Made Love To 1978, Mickey Gilley 1979, That's All That Matters to Me 1980, Encore 1980, You Don't Know Me 1981, Christmas at Gilley's 1981, Put Your Dreams Away 1982, Fool for Your Love 1983, You Really Got a Hold on Me 1983, It Takes Believers 1984, Too Good to Stop Now 1984, I Feel Good About Loving You 1985, One and Only 1986, Back to the Basics 1987, Chasin' Rainbows 1989, I Saw the Light 1996. *Address:* Mickey Gilley Interests, PO Box 1242, Pasadena, TX 77501, USA (office).

Telephone: (281) 998-8480 (office). *Fax:* (281) 998-8733 (office). *E-mail:* mickey@gilleys.com (office). *Website:* www.gilleys.com (office).

GILLINGHAM, Charlie; American musician (keyboards); b. 12 Jan. 1960, Torrance, CA. *Career:* founder mem., Counting Crows 1993–; numerous tours and live appearances. *Recordings include:* albums: August & Everything After 1993, Recovering the Satellites 1996, Across a Wire: Live in New York 1998, This Desert Life 1999, Hard Candy 2002, Saturday Nights and Sunday Mornings 2008, Underwater Sunshine 2012, Somewhere Under Wonderland 2014. *Current Management:* International Talent Booking, First Floor, Ariel House, 74a Charlotte Street, London, W1T 4QJ, England. *Telephone:* (20) 7637-6979. *Fax:* (20) 7637-6978. *E-mail:* mail@itb.co.uk. *Website:* www .countingcrows.com.

GILLIS, Verna, PhD; American artist manager and record producer; b. 14 June 1942, New York; m. Brad Graves 1965. *Career:* Asst Prof. of Ethnomusicology, Brooklyn Coll. 1974–80, Carnegie Mellon Univ. 1988–90; Host, Radio Programme, WBAI 1975–83; Founder, Director, Soundscape Performance Space, New York City 1979–84; artist manager for Youssou N'dour, Yomo Toro, Salif Keita, Malouma Mint Maideh, Habib Faye, Ivan Rubenstein-Gillis, Roswell Rudd. *Honours:* Woman of the Year 1975. *E-mail:* soundscape@soundscapepresents.com. *Website:* www.vernagillis.com.

GILMORE, Marque, (the inna-most); American musician (acoustic and electronic drums) and producer; b. Cambridge, Mass. *Career:* Founder mem. Black Rock Coalition, New York; Founder live jungle/drum & bass ensemble, Drum-FM: Interactive Tribalistic Sessions project 1994–; frequent collaborations with Cheick Tidiane Seck 1996–; duo with tabla player, Aref Durvesh 1999–; mem. Katia Labèque Band 2001–; Co-founder Tribal Broadcast Recordings 2002–; tours worldwide, session work and collaborations with artists and producers, including Roy Ayers, Otis Blackwell, Steve Coleman, Toumani Diabate, David Gilmore, Graham Haynes, Keziah Jones, MeShell, Mica Paris, Susheela Ramen, Vernon Reid, Gonzalo Rubalcaba, Nitin Sawhney, Talvin Singh, State of Bengal, Sting, Joe Zawinul; producer for artists, including Aref Durvesh, Project 23, Steve Williamson. *Composition:* Millennium Migration 1999. *Recordings include:* albums: Creation Step (with Drum-FM) 2002, Unspoken (with Katia Labèque Band) 2003. *Honours:* Arts Council England New Music Commissions grant 1999. *E-mail:* lisaredoz@ onetel.net.uk.

GILMORE, Thea Eve; British singer, musician (guitar, keyboards) and songwriter; b. 25 Nov. 1979, Oxford; d. of Robert William Anthony Gilmore and Eileen Mary Joan Gilmore; m. Nigel John Stonier 2005; one s. *Recordings include:* albums: Burning Dorothy 1999, The Lipstick Conspiracies 2000, Rules For Jokers 2001, Avalanche 2003, Songs From The Gutter 2004, Loft Music 2004, Harpo's Ghost 2006, Liejacker 2008, Strange Communion 2009, Murphy's Heart 2010, John Wesley Harding 2011, Don't Stop Singing with Sandy Denny 2011, Regardless 2013. *Current Management:* c/o Paul Fenn, Asgard, 125 Parkway, London, NW1 7PS, England. *Telephone:* (20) 7387-5090. *Fax:* (20) 7387-8740. *E-mail:* paulfenn@asgard-uk.com. *Website:* www .asgard-uk.com. *E-mail:* shameless.records@btopenworld.com (office). *Website:* www.theagilmore.net.

GILMOUR, David, CBE; British singer, musician (guitar) and composer; b. 6 March 1946, Cambridge; m. Polly Samson 1994; eight c. *Career:* mem. Pink Floyd 1968–; numerous live performances, festival appearances; Exec. Producer for Kate Bush's album, The Kick Inside; solo artist. *Recordings include:* albums: with Pink Floyd: A Saucerful Of Secrets 1968, More (film soundtrack) 1969, Ummagumma 1969, Atom Heart Mother 1970, Relics 1971, Meddle 1971, Obscured By Clouds 1972, The Dark Side Of The Moon 1973, Wish You Were Here 1975, Animals 1977, The Wall 1979, The Final Cut 1983, A Momentary Lapse Of Reason 1987, The Delicate Sound Of Thunder 1988, Shine On (box set) 1992, The Division Bell 1994, Pulse 1995, Echoes: The Very Best Of Pink Floyd 2001, The Endless River 2014; solo: David Gilmour 1978, About Face 1984, Live In Concert 2002, On An Island 2006, Metallic Spheres (with The Orb) 2010, Rattle That Lock 2015. *Honours:* Nordoff-Robbins Music Therapy Silver Clef Award 1980, MTV Music Video Award 1988, Ivor Novello Award for Outstanding Contribution to British Music 1992, Q Award for Best Live Act 1994, Grammy Award for Producer in Best Instrumental Performance (for Marooned), Polar Music Prize 2008. *Current Management:* Steve O'Rourke, EMKA Productions Ltd, 43 Portland Road, Holland Park, London, W11 4LJ, England. *Website:* www.pinkfloyd.com/index2.php; www .davidgilmour.com; www.davidgilmourblog.com.

GILTRAP, Gordon; British musician (guitar); b. 6 April 1948, East Peckham, Tonbridge, Kent. *Career:* played college, folk club and university circuit; regular tours with Ric Sanders; duets with John Renbourn and Juan Martin; collaborations with Martin Taylor; contributor, Guitarist magazine. *Compositions include:* Heartsong, theme to Holiday programme, BBC TV, 1980s; Other television music for: Wish You Were Here; The Open University; Hold The Back Page, 1985. *Recordings include:* albums: Early Days 1968, Gordon Giltrap 1968, Portrait 1969, Testament of Time 1971, Giltrap 1973, Visionary 1976, Perilous Journey 1977, Fear of The Dark 1978, Performance 1980, The Peacock Party 1981, Live 1981, Airwaves 1982, Elegy 1987, A Midnight Clear 1988, Gordon Giltrap – Guitarist 1988, Mastercraftsman 1989, One To One, with Ric Sanders 1989, A Matter of Time, with Martin Taylor 1991, Live at the BBC 1995, Music for the Small Screen 1995, Live At Oxford 2000, compilations: The Very Best of Gordon Giltrap 1988, The Best of Gordon Giltrap – All The Hits Plus More 1991, Giltrap And Taylor 2002,

Under This Blue Sky 2002, Drifter 2004, Secret Valentine 2007, As It Happens 2009, From Brush and Stone 2009, Double Visions 2009, Shining Morn 2011, 4 Parts Guitar 2011, Ravens & Lullabies 2013. *Address:* c/o The Bucks Music Group Ltd, Onward House, 11 Uxbridge Street, London, W8 7TQ, England. *Telephone:* (20) 7221-4275. *E-mail:* info@bucksmusicgroup.co.uk. *Website:* www.bucksmusicgroup.com; www.giltrap.co.uk.

GIMENES, Raymond François; French arranger, conductor, producer, musician (guitar) and composer; b. 12 Dec. 1939, Fes, Morocco; m. Beatrice Belthoise 1987; two s. one d. *Career:* backing guitarist for Petula Clark, Dean Martin, Shirley Bassey; Musical Director for Sacha Distel, Henri Salvador, Charles Aznavour; solo guitarist for Paul Mauriat Orchestra, including US tour 1971, Japanese tours 1971, 1986, 1988, 1990; mem. SACEM, SPEDIDAM, ADAMI. *Recordings:* four albums as leader of Guitars Unlimited; as guitarist: Wings, Michael Colombier, Slide Hampton with Jazz Big Band, Hajime Mizoguchi, Dionne Warwick In Paris. *Publications:* Orchestration for Paganini's Sonata for Viola and Symphonic Orchestra.

GIMÉNEZ, Ramón; Spanish singer and musician (guitar); b. Barcelona; m.; one c. *Career:* worked with rumba band Los Xavis and flamenco co. Carmen Amaya; fmr breakdancer; Founder mem. (with Juanlu) Ojos de Brujo 1990 (later known as Lenacay), which fused gypsy and flamenco music with Latin American, punk, hip hop, reggae and electronic influences; nicknamed 'el metralleta' (the submachine-gun), set up own label La Fábrica de Colores 2001; several tours in Europe, Latin America and USA; collaborations with Nitin Sawhney, Asian Dub Foundation. *Recordings include:* albums: with Ojos de Brujo: Vengue 1999, Barí 2002, Barí: Remezclas de la Casa 2003, Techarí 2006, Aocaná 2009, Corriente vital 10 años 2010; with Lenacay: Ryma; other: Girando Barí (DVD) 2005. *Honours:* World Music Award for Europe, BBC Radio 3 2004. *Current Management:* c/o Entrelineas Management, Carrer of Arus 16, 08820 El Prat de Llobregat, Spain. *Telephone:* (93) 1756522. *E-mail:* martin@entrelineasent.com. *Website:* www.entrelineasent .com. *E-mail:* brujo10@ojosdebrujo.com. *Website:* www.lenacay.com; www .ojosdebrujo.com.

GINAPÉ, Viviane; French singer; b. 30 April 1955, Paris; m. Lionel Bouton 1988. *Education:* CNRBB, Supérieur. *Career:* singer with Urban Sax, Claude Bolling, Denis Badault, Yochk O'Seffer, François Mechali; own bands include Viviane Ginapé Quartet; duo with Eric Schultz. *Recordings include:* Fraction Sur Le Temp (with Urban Sax) 1989, Opéra Jazz François Mechali: L'Archipel 1995, Café (with Viviane Ginapé Quartet) 1999. *E-mail:* vivianeginape@free .fr; sylviecorossol@wanadoo.fr. *Website:* www.vivianeginape.com.

GINGER; British rock singer, songwriter and musician (guitar); b. (David Walls), 17 Dec. 1964, South Shields, Tyne and Wear. *Career:* fmr mem. of rock groups, The Quireboys, The Throbs, Clam Abuse, Supershit 666; Founder mem. The Wildhearts 1991–; numerous tours, festival appearances; solo artist 2001–. *Recordings include:* albums: with The Quireboys: A Bit of What You Fancy 1989; with The Wildhearts: Earth vs The Wildhearts 1993, Fishing for Luckies 1994, P H U Q 1995, Endless, Nameless 1997, The Wildhearts 2007, Stop Us If You've Heard This One Before, Vol. 1 2008, ¡Chutzpah! 2009, Mad, Bad and Dangerous to Know 2014; solo: Grevious Acoustic Behaviour: Live at the 12 Bar 2001, Valor Del Corazon 2005, Yoni 2007, Market Harbour 2008, 555% 2012, Albion 2013. *Website:* www.gingerwildheart.net; www .thewildhearts.com.

GINMAN, Lennart; Danish composer and musician (double bass); b. 2 March 1960, Copenhagen; s. of Måns Vidar Ginman and Elsa Margrethe Ginman; m. Lisbeth Maria Hansen 1987; two d. *Education:* studied in Copenhagen, New York. *Career:* began professional career around 1985; Founding mem. Sort Sol, Ginman de Luxe, GinmanBlachmanDahl; tours with Kenny Werner, Harry 'Sweet' Edison, Al Foster, Lee Konitz, Cæcilie Norby; collaborations with Jimmy Jørgensen, Kristina Stoltz, Tatsuki Oshima, Lisa Rosenmeier. *Compositions include:* soundtrack for Skjulte Spor TV series 2000–02; scores for The Snow Queen musical 2000, Fantasy of Boredom Dummies dance production 2001. *Recordings include:* with various artists: Twilight 1984, Beatin' Bop 1988, Love Boat 1989, 1991 1990, Scorpio Dance 1991, Rounds 1992, Lost Friends 1993, Back to Basics 1993, Gengio a lagio 1993, The Planets 1994, My Female Family 1994, Blachman introduces Standard Jazz and Rap 1994, Tales Details 1994, Caecilie Norby 1995, Four 1995, Crystal Ball 1995, Den Poppede Hone 1995, Shirtsville 1996, Raney 96 1996, My Corner of the Sky 1996, Ipsen/Markussen Jazz Code 1996, Dawn 1996, That's Life 1996, Will you make my soup hot and silver 1996, Burning Love 1997, Helt Kinesisk 1997, Part of a Circle 1997, Lad hele verden danse 1998, Ginman/Jørgensen 1998, Face the Music 1998, House of the Double Axe 1998, Symphonies Vol. 2 1998, Choo, Choo 1998, Time Problem 1998, 1,2,3,4 Testing 1998, Standards 1999, Charm school for pop singers 1999, Stairway to the Stars 1999, Charlie Butterfly 1999, Message from Bud 1999, Jazz and Poesi 2000, Snedronningen 2000, At the Circus 2000, If this is Cool 2000, Play 2001, In this Moment 2001, The Abyss 2001, Blue Train 2003, Domestika 2004, Dust in my Coffee 2004, Beautiful minor 2004, God Bless the Child 2004, GinmanBlachmanDahl 2004, We are Povo 2005, To the Long Lost 2006, Dicte and the Sugarbones 2006, Bebopish Rubbish Rabbit 2006, 1st sketches 2007, Happiness...is not included 2007, På kanten af virkeligheden 2007, Deep 2007. *Honours:* Composers Honour Award 1992, JASA Prize 1995, Producer of the Year, Album of the Year, Danish Grammy Awards 1999. *Address:* C. F. Richs Vej 80, 2000 Frederiksberg, Denmark (home). *Telephone:* 38-33-20-90 (office). *E-mail:* lennart@ginman.dk (office). *Website:* www.ginman.dk.

GINUWINE; American R&B singer, songwriter and actor; b. (Elgin Baylor Lumpkin), 15 Oct. 1970, Washington, DC; m. Tonya Lumpkin 2003. *Education:* Forestville High School, Forestville, Md, Prince George's Community Coll. *Career:* fmr backing singer for Danny Boy; released debut single 1996; numerous collaborations including P. Diddy, Brandy, Missy Elliott, Timbaland; Founder, Bag Entertainment label 2002, LoveSong International 2008; formed supergroup TGT with Tank and Tyrese 2007–. *Films:* Juwanna Mann 2002, Honey 2003. *Recordings:* albums: Ginuwine... The Bachelor 1996, 100% Ginuwine (Soul Train Music Award for R&B/Soul: Male Album 2000) 1999, The Life 2001, The Senior 2003, Back II Da Basics 2005, A Man's Thoughts 2009, Elgin 2011; with TGT: Three Kings 2013. *Address:* c/o Atlantic Records, Warner Music Group, 75 Rockefeller Plaza, New York, NY 10019, USA (office). *E-mail:* contact@atlanticrecords.com. *Website:* atlanticrecords.com (office); www.wmg.com (office); ginuwine.com.

GIOVANNETTI, Michel; French musician (guitar); b. 30 Nov. 1970. *Education:* Berklee Coll. of Music, Boston, USA. *Career:* mem. Superbus 1998–. *Recordings include:* albums: Aéromusical 2002, Pop'N'Gum 2004, Wow 2006, Lova Lova 2009, Sunset 2012. *Honours:* MTV Europe Music Award Best French Act 2005. *Address:* c/o Universal Music France, 16–20 rue des Fossés-Saint-Jacques, 75005 Paris, Cédex 05, France (office). *Website:* www.superbus .com.fr.

GIRARD, Keith; American editor; *Editor and Publisher, The Improper.* *Career:* fmr reporter, The Washington Post, Regardie's, Washingtonian magazine; Ed.-in-Chief, The Daily Record 1992–99, Investment News 1999–2003, Billboard magazine 2003–04; Ed. and Publisher, The Improper Online magazine 2006–. *Address:* TheImproper Network LLC, 4615 North Park Avenue, #103, Chevy Chase, MD 20850, USA (office). *Telephone:* (646) 246-4477 (office). *E-mail:* kgirard@theimproper.com (office). *Website:* www .theimproper.com (office).

GIROT, Pierre; French jazz musician (guitar); b. 11 May 1936, Neuilly; m. 30 June 1960, 2 d. *Education:* Academie de Guitare de Paris; Student of Henri Salavador. *Career:* accompanied Josephine Baker, Charles Trenet, worked with jazz artists: Trio Arvanitas; Guy Lafitte; Lou Bennett; Bill Coleman; Hal Singer; int. festivals include: Antibes Juan-les-Pins; Zurich; San Sebastian; Souillac; Marciac; Montpellier; Clermont-Ferrand; mem. SACEM; SPEDI-DAM. *Compositions include:* Flamenco Blues 1996, Melancoliquement Vôtre, Mister JC 1996, Birdy 1996. *Recordings include:* album: Jazz and Brazilian guitar with Quatuor Galilé. *Publications:* Festival 92, Birdy, Clin d'Oeil 1998. *Honours:* Third Prize, Festival of Juan-les-Pins 1960.

GISLI; Icelandic singer and musician (drums). *Career:* lives in Oslo, Norway. *Recordings include:* album: How About That? 2002, Build-Ups and Break-Downs 2007. *Address:* c/o EMI Group PLC, 27 Wrights Lane, London, W8 5SW, England. *Website:* www.gisli.co.uk.

GIUSSANI, Claudio D. C., BEng; British musician (keyboards, percussion, djembe), programmer, engineer and remixer; b. 19 Sept. 1969, London. *Education:* Univ. of Warwick. *Career:* formed band Urban Shakedown (making new breakbeat music), 1990; formed Union Jack (trance music), 1992, 93; regular tours, USA; Canada; Russia; Europe; mem. PRS; MCPS; PPL. *Recordings include:* With Urban Shakedown: Some Justice (Top 20 hit); Bass Shake; With Union Jack: Album: Two Full Moons and A Trout 1994, Red Herring 1995, Cockroach 1997, There Will Be No Armageddon, 2001, Pylon Pigs 2009, Retrospective 2011; productions include: Speed Limit 140 BPM, 1994; All Mixed Up, 1995; Dimensions in Ambience, 1996; Platipus Records Ultimate Dream, 1996; Journey into Ambient Groove, 1996; Quando Un Musicista, 1999. *Website:* www.platipus.com/artists/union-jack.

GJERSTAD, Frode; Norwegian musician (saxophone, clarinet); b. 24 March 1948, Stavanger; m. Judith Sorvik 1983; one s. one d. *Career:* Leader, Frode Gjerstad Trio, Circulasione Totale Orchestra and Calling Signals; has recorded with Kent Carter, Bobby Bradford, John Stevens, Johnny Dyani, Nick Stephens, Paul Rutherford, Derek Bailey, Billy Bang, Borah Bergman, William Parker, Rashid Bakr, Louis Moholo, Peter Brøtzmann, Willber Morris, Kevin Norton, Pheeroan akLaff, Hamid Drake, Sabir Mateen, Lol Coxhill, Han Bennink, Mark Sanders, John Edwards, Steve Hubback, Paul Hession, Lasse Marhaug, Terje Isungset, Nils Henrik Asheim, Anders Hana, Morten Johan Olsen, Amit Sen, Fred Lonberg-Holm, Michael Zerang, Steve Swell, Øyvind Storesund and Paal Nilssen-Love; own record label Circulasione Totale. *Recordings include:* with Detail: Backwards and Forwards 1983, Okhela 1984, Way It Goes/Dance of the Soul 1986, Ness 1987, Less More 1989–90, In Time Was 1990, Less More 1991, Last Detail – Live at the Cafe Sting 1996, First Detail 2000; with John Stevens: Sunshine 1996, Let's Just Keep On Playing 2005; with Circulasione Totale Orchestra: Accent 1989, Enten Eller 1993, Recycling Grieg 1996, Borealis 1998, Open Port 2008, Bandwith 2009; with William Parker: Seeing New York from the Ear 1996, Remember to Forget 1998, Ultima 1999; with Borah Bergman: Ikosa Mura 1998, Rivers in Time 2003; with Øyvind Storesund and Paal Nilssen-Love: The Blessing Light 2001, Sharp Knives Cut Deeper 2003, St Louis 2003, Mothers and Fathers 2006; with Peter Brøtzmann: Invisible Touch 1999, Soria Moria 2003; with Lasse Marhaug: TOU 2003, Red Edge 2004; with Derek Bailey: Hello Goodbye 2001, Nearly a D 2003; with Ultralyd: Shadows and Lights 2002, The Welsh Chapel 2002, Ultralyd 2004, No Definitive, The Longest Day, Born to Collapse 2004, Chromosome Gun 2005, This That and the Other 2005; with Calling Signals: Calling Signals 2005, Dreams in Dreams 2005, Theremite Club 2006, Antioch 2007, Calling Signals 2008, Bergen 2009,

Quiddity 2009, Han & Frode 2009, Reknes 2009, Gromka 2010, Sextet 2010, Soundgathering 2010, Tipple 2011. *Honours:* Jazz Musician of the Year 1997, The Buddy Prize, Norwegian Jazz Fed. 2008, Culture Prize, Stavanger 2009. *Address:* Circulasione Totale, Gandsveien 11, 4017 Stavanger, Norway. *E-mail:* frode.gjerstad@lyse.net. *Website:* www.frodegjerstad.com.

GLADWELL, Robert; British musician (guitar, bass) and journalist; b. 16 June 1950, Colchester; m. 1st (divorced); m. 2nd (divorced); four s. one d.; m. 3rd Julie Gladwell. *Education:* Martin Lukins School of Music. *Career:* session guitarist, clinician, worked for Gibson Guitars for 10 years; wrote Dr Robert column, Guitarist magazine 11 years; own guitar workshop building, customising guitars; toured extensively with Steve Harley and Cockney Rebel, Suzi Quatro, Rolling Stones; mem. Musicians' Union. *Recordings include:* with Twink: Mr Rainbow 1990; with Steve Harley: Yes You Can 1992, Christmas All Stars Album 1994, Poetic Justice 1996, Acoustic and Pure: Live 2002, Stranger Comes to Town 2010; with Suzi Quatro: Free The Butterfly 1995, What Goes Around 1996. *Publication:* Guitar Electronics and Customising 1995. *Address:* Dr Robert's Guitar Surgery 2, The Old Granary, Goldingham Farm, Bulmer, Sudbury, CO10 7ER, England. *E-mail:* guitarsurgery@aol.com. *Website:* www.robbiegladwell.com.

GLAMOUR GOLD (see Krust)

GLASSER, Adam, BA; South African musician (chromatic harmonica); b. 20 Sept. 1955, s. of Stanley Glasser and Mona Glasser; m. Vivien Roberts 1994; one d. *Education:* Univ. of Warwick. *Career:* has performed with Dudu Pukwana, Martha Reeves, Jimmy Witherspoon, Joe Zawinul, Eurythmics, Dominic Miller, Sting, The Manhattan Brothers, Hugh Masekela, Incognito; recorded harmonica for Howard Shore, Elliot Goldenthal, Debbie Wiseman, Mark Thomas, DJ Cleo, Simphiwe Dana, Rhythmic Elements; orchestral and theatre experience with BBC Concert Orchestra, Orchestra of the Welsh Nat. Opera, Royal Northern Sinfonia, Royal Nat. Theatre, Shakespeare's Globe; Patron Nat. Harmonica League. *Recordings include:* produced The Manhattan Brothers album 'Inyembezi' for EMI South Africa 2006; albums: Free at First (SAMA Award for Best Contemporary Jazz Album 2010), Mzansi 2012. *Honours:* winner, Peter Whittingham Award, Musicians' Benevolent Society 1997. *E-mail:* contactme@adamglassermusic.com. *Website:* www .adamglassermusic.com.

GLATZL, Friedrich; Austrian musician (guitar) and backing singer; b. 17 March 1956, Gmünd; m. Marianne Glatzl 1982; one s. one d. *Career:* Founder-mem. Giant Blonder 1972–83; mem. Blues Pumpm 1983–; TV, radio broadcasts, tours; mem. ALM, AUME, LSG. *Recordings include:* albums: with Giant Blonder: Giant Blonder; Rock and Blues 2; with Blues Pumpm: Live With Friends 1985, The 5th Ten Years Jubilee 1987, Live At Utopia 1988, Birthday 1991, Live In Vienna 1992, The 5th 1992, Living Loving Riding 1994. *Honours:* Silbernes Ehrenzeichen 1992; Third Best Blues Album Ö3, Rot-Weiss-Rote Critics Poll for Live In Vienna) 1992. *E-mail:* office@bluespumpm.at; bluespumpm@utanet.at. *Website:* www.bluespumpm.at.

GLEESON, David Sean; Australian singer; b. 3 June 1968, Newcastle. *Career:* mem. of local rock band, Aspect 1985; played with The Screaming Jets, 1989–; engineer on albums by Mariah Carey, Kenny G, Michael Bolton, Céline Dion, Jennifer Lopez, Linda Ronstadt, Savage Garden, Destiny's Child, Jessica Simpson. *Recordings include:* albums with The Screaming Jets: All For One 1991, Tear of Thought 1992, The Screaming Jets 1995, World Gone Crazy 1997, Scam 2000, Do Ya 2008, The Essential: Screaming Jets 2008. *Website:* www.thescreamingjets.com.au.

GLEN, Alan; British musician (harmonica, guitar); b. 21 Dec. 1951, Wuppertal, Germany; m. Jacqueline Lewis 1995; three s. *Career:* mem. Nine Below Zero 1991–95, Little Axe 1996–, Yardbirds 1998–2003, 2008–09, The Barcodes 1999–, Incredible Blues Puppies 2005–; performed with Eric Clapton, 'Slash', Steve Vai, John Mayall, Peter Green, Steve Lukather, Mick Taylor, 'Skunk' Baxter, Hubert Sumlin; with Nine Below Zero, tour of Spain, Scandinavia with Sting 1993, toured with and supported Eric Clapton, Royal Albert Hall 1994, ZZ Top, Brian May, The Kinks, Joe Cocker 1994, Alvin Lee 1994; played and recorded with Alannah Myles, Canadian tour 1994; played and recorded with Jeff Beck, Junior Delgado, Dub Syndicate, Dr Feelgood, Lee 'Scratch' Perry, Gordon Smith, Zoot Money, Alan Barnes, Art Themen, Jim Mullen, Gypie Mayo, Buddy Whittington, Nigel Price, Chris Youlden, Paul Jones, Pee Wee Ellis; performed at Hollywood House of Blues, Hilton Las Vegas, Royal Albert Hall (15 times), Wembley Arena, Sporting Lisbon Stadium, Montreux Jazz Festival, Nice Jazz Festival, Brecon Jazz Festival, Colne Blues Festival, Ronnie Scott's Club; regular music broadcasts on radio and TV in UK, Europe and USA; mem. British Acad. of Songwriters, Composers and Authors, Musicians' Union. *Compositions include:* Bad Town Blues, film soundtrack for Circuitry Man II, On a Blue Note, film soundtrack for The Riddle, Slide Ride, film soundtrack for B.B. King – Life of Riley, Another Kind of Love, It's Nothing New, Crazy Life, A Little Bit More, Tell Me The Truth, Blow Diddley, Be Cool, Fat Tuesday, The Purple Cat, No Time For You, I Don't Want Your Love, Smitty's Corner, Away from Here, Everything or Nothing, Halfway to Nowhere, Zip your Lip, The Snitch, Tuff Days, I Don't Get It, Don't Keep Me Waiting, T-Time, Motya. *Recordings include:* albums: with Nine Below Zero: Off The Hook 1993, Best of Nine Below Zero 1994, Hot Music For A Cold Night 1994, Ice Station Zebro 1995, Live in Europe 2011; with Dr Feelgood: On the Road Again 1996; with The Yardbirds: Birdland 2003, Birdland Live 2008; with The Barcodes: Keep Your Distance 2002, Independently Blue 2004, Friends Like These 2006, 'Live' for the BBC

2007, Be Cool 2013; with Daniel Smith: Dreamtime 2003, Chicken and Egg 2004, Highwire 2013; with Little Axe: Slow Fuse 1996, Hard Grind 2002, Stone Cold Ohio 2003, Champaigne and Grits 2004, Bought for a Dollar, Sold for a Dime 2010, If You Want Loyalty 2012, Little Axe Live 2013; with Junior Delgado: Reasons 2000, Dub Syndicate Acres of Space 2001; with Alan Glen & Roger Cotton: Born in Black and White 2004; with The Incredible Blues Puppies: Puppy Fat 2006, In the Doghouse 2008; with Gordon Smith: The Essential 2009, Live at Brooks Blues Bar 2013, Steve Morrison & Alan Glen Live 2013, Tim Hain Gold Reserve 2013, Alan Glen: Zip Your Lip 2014, Delta Ladies Refugee 2015; has performed on more than 50 albums with various artists. *Address:* 72 Woods Road, London, SE15 2SW, England. *E-mail:* glenalan9@aol.com. *Website:* www.thebarcodes.co.uk.

GLENNIE, James (Jim); British musician (bass guitar) and songwriter; b. 10 Oct. 1963, Manchester, England. *Career:* founder mem., James 1982–2001, re-formed 2007–; numerous tours, festival dates and TV appearances; producer 2002–. *Recordings include:* albums: Stutter 1986, Strip Mine 1988, One Man Clapping 1989, Gold Mother 1990, Seven 1992, Laid 1993, Wah Wah 1994, Whiplash 1997, The Best Of James 1998, Millionaires 1999, B-Sides Ultra 2001, Pleased To Meet You 2001, Getting Away With It 2002, Hey Ma 2008, The Night Before 2010, The Morning After 2010, La Petite Mort 2014. *Address:* c/o Mercury Records, 364–366 Kensington High Street, London W14 8NS, England (office). *Website:* www.wearejames.com.

GLENNIE-SMITH, Nicholas Hugh; British composer, musician (keyboards) and engineer; b. 3 Oct. 1951, Kingston-on-Thames, England; m. Janet 1974; two s. two d. *Education:* New Coll., Oxford, Trinity Coll., London. *Career:* tours with David Essex, Randy Edelman, Glen Campbell, Classic Rock, Roger Waters, The Wall, Berlin; recordings with Cliff Richard, Leo Sayer, Nik Kershaw, Tina Turner, The Adventures, Beltane Fire, Phil Collins, Paul McCartney, Roger Waters, Roger Daltrey, Katrina and The Waves, Five Star, Barbara Dickson; music for Puy du Fou, CineScenie (historical theme park), France; mem. American Soc. of Composers, Authors and Publrs (ASCAP), Performing Right Soc. *Film scores:* Two if by Sea 1995, The Rock 1996, Fire Down Below 1997, Home Alone 3 1997, The Man in the Iron Mask 1998, Lion King II: Simba's Pride 1998, Laura's Star (with Hans Zimmer) 2004, The Little Polar Bear-The Mysterious Island (with Hans Zimmer) 2005, A Sound of Thunder 2005, Children of Glory 2006, Secretariat 2010. *Television:* Max Q 1998, The Secret Adventures of Jules Verne 1999. *Current Management:* First Artists Management, 4764 Park Granada, Suite 210, Calabasas, CA 91302, USA. *Telephone:* (818) 377-7750. *Fax:* (818) 377-7760. *E-mail:* rjacobellis@firstartistsmgmt.com. *Website:* www.firstartistsmgmt .com.

GLOCKLER, Nigel Ian; British musician (drums, percussion); b. 24 Jan. 1953, Hove, Sussex. *Education:* Brighton Coll. *Career:* mem., The Associates 1980–82, Toyah 1980–81, Saxon 1981–87, 1989–; GTR 1987–88; tours, television and radio broadcasts; mem. PRS, MCPS, Musicians' Union. *Recordings include:* albums: with The Associates: The Affectionate Punch, Sulk; with Toyah: Anthem 1981; with Saxon: The Eagle Has Landed 1982, Power and The Glory 1983, Crusader 1984, Innocence is no Excuse 1985, Rock the Nations 1986, Solid Ball of Rock 1990, Forever Free 1992, Dogs of War 1995, Unleash the Beast 1997, The Inner Sanctum 2007, Into the Labyrinth 2009; with Asia: Aqua 1992; with Steve Howe: Turbulenz, Guitar Speak; with Tony Martin: Back Where I Belong; with Fastway: Bad Bad Girls. *Current Management:* c/o Thomas Jensen, ICS GmbH, Hauptstrasse 47, 24869 Dörpstedt, Germany. *E-mail:* management@saxon747.com. *Website:* www .saxon747.com; www.nigelglockler.com.

GLOJNARIC, Silvestar; Croatian composer, conductor and arranger; b. 2 Dec. 1936, Ladislavec; m. Ana Jurisic 1962; one s. one d. *Education:* Zagreb Music Academy. *Career:* tours, concerts, Zagreb Jazz Quartet, Europe; tours with Zagreb Radio Big Band, Europe including Russia; television, radio appearances with various orchestras as composer, arranger, conductor; most European jazz festivals; mem. Croatian Composers' Assen. *Recordings:* Zagreb Big Band with: Art Farmer, Slide Hampton, Stan Getz, J Griffin, SFB Big Band, Berlin, NDR Big Band, Hamburg, Ljubljana Big Band, John Lewis, A Mangelsdorf: Animal Dance, Buck Clayton, BJ Turner: Feel So Fine, Georgie Fame. *Honours:* President's Medal for Outstanding Contrib. to Croatian art and culture 2009, Porin Award for Best Jazz Performance. *Current Management:* Cvjetno Naselje 3, 10430 Samobar, Croatia. *Telephone:* (1) 3362750 (also fax) (home). *E-mail:* sglojnaric@gmail.com (home).

GLOSSOP, Mick; producer, engineer and mixer; b. Nottinghamshire, England; m. Elva Williamson; one d. *Career:* recording engineer in various studios in UK and Canada –1979; freelance record producer and engineer 1980–; producer for: Camel, Lloyd Cole, Pino Daniele, Ian Gillan, Van Morrison, No Guru, Revolver, The Ruts, The Skids, Suede, UFO, The Waterboys, The Wonder Stuff, Frank Zappa, Sebastopol, Phil Swill Odgers; mem. Music Producers Guild; designer and chief engineer Manor Studios and Town House; Visiting Prof., Leeds Coll. of Music 2009. *Honours:* Recording Engineer of the Year, Music Producers Guild 2010. *E-mail:* contact_mick@ mickglossop.com. *Website:* www.mickglossop.com.

GLOVER, Corey; American singer and actor; b. 6 Nov. 1964. *Career:* lead singer in funk rock group Living Colour 1985–95, 2000–, with tours, concerts and festival appearances; mem. Black Rock Coalition; singer for band Galactic. *Films include:* Platoon 1986, The Keeper 1995, Reunion 2001. *Recordings include:* albums: with Living Colour: Vivid 1988, Time's Up 1990,

Biscuits 1991, Stain 1993, Collideøscope 2003, The Chair in the Doorway 2009; solo: Sonic Adventure Remix 1998, Hymns 1998, Live at Wetland 1999, The Pledge 2012. *Honours:* Elvis Award for Best New Band, International Rock Awards 1989, MTV Award for Best New Artist, for Best Group Video, for Best Stage Performance 1989, Grammy Award for Best Hard Rock Performance (for Cult of Personality) 1990, (for Time's Up) 1991, Rolling Stone Critics Poll Winner of Best Band 1991. *E-mail:* coreyglover@hotmail.com (office). *Website:* www.livingcolourmusic.com.

GLOVER, Roger; British musician (bass), composer, record producer and songwriter; b. 30 Nov. 1945, Brecon, Powys, Wales. *Career:* fmr mem. The Madisons; mem. Episode Six 1966–69; mem. Deep Purple 1970–73, 1984–; Head of A&R, Purple Records 1973; record producer for numerous artists, including Nazareth, Status Quo, Judas Priest, Rory Gallagher, Rainbow, Elf, David Coverdale, Pretty Maids, Spencer Davis, Ian Gillan, Rupert Hine, Barbi Benton, Young and Moody; solo artist; mem. Rainbow 1979–84; mem. Gillan and Glover 1988; numerous concerts, festival appearances and tours worldwide. *Compositions include:* The Butterfly Ball 1974. *Recordings include:* albums: with Episode Six: Here There and Everywhere 1966; with Deep Purple: Deep Purple In Rock 1970, Fireball 1971, Machine Head 1972, Who Do We Think We Are? 1973, Perfect Strangers 1985, Fireworks 1985, The House Of Blue Light 1987, Slaves And Masters 1990, The Battle Rages On 1992, Perpendicular 1996, Abandon 1998, Butterfly Ball Wizards Convention 1998, Child In Time 1998, Under The Gun 2001, Bananas 2003, Deep Purple And Friends 2003, Total Abandon 2004, Rapture Of The Deep 2005, Live at Montreux 2006; solo: Butterfly Ball 1974, Elements 1978, Mask 1984, Snapshot 2002, If Life Was Easy 2011; with Rainbow: Down To Earth 1979, Difficult To Cure 1981, Straight Between The Eyes 1982, Bent Out of Shape 1983, Finyl Vinyl 1986; with Gillan and Glover: Accidentally On Purpose 1988. *Current Management:* The Agency Group Ltd, 361–373 City Road, London, EC1V 1PQ, England. *Telephone:* (20) 7278-3331. *Fax:* (20) 7837-4672. *E-mail:* agencylondon@theagencygroup.com. *Website:* www.theagencygroup .com. *E-mail:* info@deep-purple.com. *Website:* www.deeppurple.com; www .rogerglover.com.

GLUKOZA; Russian singer; b. (Natasha Ionova), 7 June 1986, Moscow; m. Alexander Chistyakov 2006. *Career:* music is promoted with computer-animated videos and an animated character based on her; concert performances throughout Russia and in Belarus, Ukraine, Kazakhstan, Central Asia, the Caucasus, UK and USA. *Recordings include:* albums: Nostra 2002, Moskva 2005, Trans-FORMA 2011. *Honours:* MTV/EMA Award for Best Russian Act 2003, MuzTV Award for Breakthrough of the Year 2004. *Current Management:* c/o ZYX Music Distribution Ltd, 795 Franklin Avenue, Franklin Lakes, NJ 07417, USA. *Website:* www.zyxmusic.com. *E-mail:* assistant@ glukoza.com. *Website:* www.glukoza.com.

GLYNNE, Jessica (Jess) Hannah; British singer and songwriter; b. 20 Oct. 1989, London, England. *Education:* Fortismere School. *Career:* worked in brand management –2013; signed to Atlantic Records 2013; collaborations as featured vocalist include My Love (with Route 94) 2013, Rather Be (with Clean Bandit) 2014; solo debut single Right Here 2014; numerous songwriting collaborations including Iggy Azelea, Little Mix, M.O., Rita Ora, Rudimental, Tinie Tempah. *Recordings:* album: I Cry When I Laugh 2015. *Honours:* Grammy Award for Best Dance Recording (with Clean Bandit, for Rather Be) 2015. *Current Management:* c/o UROK Management, 42 Great Titchfield Street, London, W1W 7PY, England. *Website:* www.urokmanagement.co.uk; www.jessglynne.co.uk.

GNATYUK, Mikola; Ukrainian singer; b. 14 Sept. 1952; one s. *Education:* Music Inst., Rovno. *Career:* numerous TV and radio appearances, concerts; mem. SVIATO. *Recordings include:* songs: Bazaban; Molinovoi Zvon; Belii Stavni 1994; Shas Rikog Pluve; Starenki; Gospodi, pomiluj. *Honours:* First Prize, Sopot Festival, Poland, Grand Prix Festival, Dresden. *Address:* Vasilkovskai 2A/126, 252040 Kiev, Ukraine.

GOBAC, Davor, (Dado); Croatian singer, composer and actor; b. Karlovac; m. Deana Pavic 1994; one s. *Career:* solo artist, with tour and concerts in Europe and North America, numerous TV and radio broadcasts; mem. Hrvatska Glalbena Vnija (Croatian Musicians Union); lead singer for rock group Psihomodo Pop. *Recordings include:* Godina Zmaja (Year of Dragon) 1988, Live In Amsterdam 1989, Sexy Magazin 1990, Tko Je Ubio Mickey Mousea (Who Killed Mickey Mouse) 1991, Skrebrne Svinje (Silver Pigs) 1993, 1994, Unplugged 1995, Sextasy 1997, Live in Maribor 1999, Debakl (Porin Award for Best Album of the Year) 2000, Tekucih 20 2003, Jeee! Jeee! Jeee! 2009, Ste Dobro? 2010. *Honours:* Croatian Film and Video Award, Oktavijan Miletic 1995. *Address:* Sljemeuska 27, 41211 Zapresic, Croatia (home). *Website:* www .psihomodopop.hr.

GODFREY, Paul; British musician and producer. *Career:* Founder-mem. Morcheeba 1995–; numerous collaborations; festival appearances. *Recordings include:* albums: Who Can You Trust? 1996, Big Calm 1998, Fragments of Freedom 2000, Charango 2002, The Antidote 2005, Deep Dive 2008, Blood Like Lemonade 2010, Head Up High 2013. *Current Management:* c/o CMO Management International Ltd, 11 Westborne Studios, 242 Acklam Road, London, W10 5JJ, England. *E-mail:* info@cmomanagement.co.uk. *Website:* www.cmomanagement.co.uk; www.morcheeba.co.uk.

GODFREY, Ross; British musician and producer. *Career:* Founder-mem. Morcheeba 1995–; has composed songs for numerous films. *Recordings*

include: albums: Who Can You Trust? 1996, Big Calm 1998, Fragments of Freedom 2000, Charango 2002, The Antidote 2005, Deep Dive 2008, Blood Like Lemonade 2010, 100 Hits: Summer 2010, Fantastic Songs 2011, Head Up High 2013, Beach Club 2013. *Current Management:* c/o CMO Management International Ltd, 11 Westborne Studios, 242 Acklam Road, London, W10 5JJ, England. *E-mail:* info@cmomanagement.co.uk. *Website:* www.cmomanagement.co.uk; www.morcheeba.co.uk.

GODIN, Nicolas; French producer and musician (keyboards); b. Versailles. *Education:* Conservatoire, Paris. *Career:* met Jean-Benoît Dunckel at Conservatoire, Paris and joined Dunckel's band Orange; after departure of Alex Gopher from band, formed duo Air 1995–; collaborations with Jean Jacques Perrey, Francoise Hardy, Alex Gopher, Gordon Tracks; remixed Depeche Mode, Neneh Cherry. *Recordings include:* albums: Moon Safari 1997, The Virgin Suicides (film soundtrack) 1999, Premiers Symptoms (compilation) 1999, 10,000 Hz Legend 2001, City Reading (backing music to Alessandro Baricco's novel, City) 2003, Talkie Walkie 2004, Pocket Symphony 2007, Love 2 2009, Le voyage dans la lune 2012. *Address:* c/o EMI Music France, 118 rue de Mont-Cenis, 75891 Paris, France (office). *E-mail:* reponse@emi-music.fr (office). *Website:* www.aircheology.com.

GODINHO, Sergio; Portuguese singer and songwriter; b. 31 Aug. 1945. *Career:* hundreds of live shows; film score writer; actor; occasional script writer; mem. SPA. *Compositions include:* O Primeiro Dia, Lisboa Que Amanhece, Com Um Brilhozinho Nos Olhos. *Recordings include:* albums: Os Sobreviventes 1971, Pré Histórias 1972, Á Quema Roupa 1974, De Pequenino se Torce o Destino 1976, Pano Crú 1978, Kilas, o Mau da Fita 1980, Campolide 1979, Canto da Boca 1980, Coincidências 1983, Salão de Festas 1984, Era uma Vez um Rapaz 1985, Na Vida Real 1987, Os Amigos de Gaspar 1988, Aos Amores 1989, Escritor de Canções 1990, Tinta Permanente 1993, Noites Passadas 1995, Domingo no Mundo 1997, Rivolitz 1998, Lupa 2000, Afinidades 2001, Biografias do Amor 2001, O Irmão do Meio 2003, Ligação Directa 2006, Nove e Meia no Maria Matos Ao Vivo 2008, Mútuo Consentimento 2011. *Publications:* book for children; play. *Honours:* several times Record of the Year and Artist of the Year. *Current Management:* Praça Das Flores Produção de Espectáculos Ltda, Rua Da Imprensa Nacional 36, 1250-126 Lisbon, Portugal. *Telephone:* (21) 3972389. *Fax:* (21) 3972430. *E-mail:* pflores@pflores.com. *Website:* www.pflores.com.

GODLEY, Kevin; British singer, musician (drums), songwriter, producer and music video director; b. 7 Oct. 1945, Manchester. *Career:* played in local bands including Group 17, The Sabres, The MockingBirds; Founder-mem. and drummer, 10cc 1972–76; producer and songwriter for duo Godley and Creme (with Lol Creme) 1976–; TV includes: One World One Voice, series of programmes, with contribs from artists including Sting, Peter Gabriel, Lou Reed, Chrissie Hynde, Stewart Copeland; feature film, Howling At The Moon 1988; Co-founder, environmental org. ARK; formed new band GG/06 (with Graham Gouldman). *Recordings include:* albums: with 10cc: Sheet Music 1974, Original Soundtrack 1975, Greatest Hits 1975, How Dare You? 1976, Meanwhile 1992, Mirror Mirror 1995, Greatest Hits 1998; with Godley and Creme (mostly self-written and produced): Consequences 1977, L 1978, Music From Consequences 1979, Freeze Frame 1979, Long Distant Romancer 1981, Ismism 1981, Birds of Prey 1983, The History Mix, Vol. 1 1985, The Changing Faces of 10cc and Godley and Creme 1987, Goodbye Blue Sky 1988; singles include: with 10cc: Donna 1972, Rubber Bullets 1973, The Dean and I 1973, Wall Street Shuffle 1974, Silly Love 1974, Life Is A Minestrone 1975, I'm Not In Love 1975, Art For Art's Sake 1975, I'm Mandy Fly Me 1976; with Godley and Creme: Under Your Thumb 1981, Wedding Bells 1981, Cry 1985; producer, albums including Long Distant Romancer, Mickey Jupp 1981, One World One Voice 1989; director, videos including: Every Breath You Take, The Police, Rockit, Herbie Hancock, Feel The Love, 10cc, Relax, Frankie Goes To Hollywood, Two Tribes, Frankie Goes To Hollywood, Kele Le Roc, Duran Duran, Black Crowes, Sting, Charlatans; dir of TV commercials, including Seafrance, PSE&G, Toshiba, Audi, Granda, Nissan. *Honours:* Ivor Novello Awards for Best Beat Song (for Rubber Bullets) 1974, for Most Performed British Song, Best Pop Song, International Hit of the Year (for I'm Not In Love) 1976, five MTV Video Awards (for Rockit) 1984, MTV Video Vanguard Award 1985. *Current Management:* c/o Smash Management, 141 Wardour Street, London, W1F 0UT, England. *E-mail:* lucy@smashmanagement.com. *Website:* www.smashmanagement.com. *E-mail:* downloads@gg06.co.uk. *Website:* www.gg06.co.uk.

GODRICH, Nigel Timothy; British producer, musician, arranger and engineer; b. 1971. *Education:* School of Audio Eng. *Career:* worked at Audio One Studios, Rak Studios; engineer for Tim Booth and Angelo Badalamenti, McAlmont and Butler, Ride, Siouxsie & The Banshees, Sparks; prod. for Beck, The Divine Comedy, Jason Falkner, The Flaming Lips, Paul McCartney, Pavement, Radiohead, Silver Sun, Travis; has collaborated with R.E.M., Neil Finn, Natalie Imbruglia, Hopper, Band Aid 20, U2, The Harvest Ministers; Air; co-founder, Shabang Studios; mem., Atoms for Peace 2009–. *Current Management:* c/o Carol Crabtree, Solar Management Ltd, 13 Rosemont Road, London, NW3 6NG, England. *Telephone:* (20) 7794-3388. *Fax:* (20) 7794-5588. *E-mail:* info@solarmanagement.co.uk. *Website:* www.solarmanagement.co.uk.

GOETHE-McGINN, Lisa, BMus, MM; American musician (flute) and academic; *Head of Wind and Percussion Department, Sherwood Conservatory of Music;* b. 31 Jan. 1965, St Louis, Mo.; m. Gregg McGinn 1996. *Education:* Millikin Univ., Univ. of Illinois, Univ. of North Texas. *Career:* Head of Wind and Percussion Dept, Sherwood Conservatory of Music, Columbia Coll., Chicago 2003–; performer and interpreter of contemporary music and free improvisation; performed at many festivals and music series in USA and abroad; mem., numerous new music ensembles in Chicago; has worked with composers including Helmut Lachenmann, Salvatore Martirano and Herbert Brün; performed at Museum of Contemporary Art, The Arts Club of Chicago Renaissance Society and others; mem. American Composers Forum, National Flute Asscn, Chicago Flute Club. *Address:* Wind and Percussion Faculty, Sherwood Conservatory of Music, 1312 South Michigan Avenue, Chicago, IL 60605, USA (office). *Telephone:* (312) 427-6267 (office). *Fax:* (312) 427-6677 (office). *E-mail:* info@sherwoodmusic.org (office). *Website:* www.colum.edu/sherwood_conservatory (office).

GOFFEY, Danny; British musician (drums); b. 7 Feb. 1974, Oxford; m. Pearl Lowe 2008. *Career:* mem. The Jennifers 1991–93; mem. Supergrass 1993–2010; Founding-mem. The Hot Rats 2009–; with Babyshambles 2010–; numerous concerts and festival appearances. *Recordings include:* albums: with Supergrass: I Should Coco 1995, Bag O Grass (compilation) 1996, In It For The Money 1997, Supergrass 1999, B-Side Trax (compilation) 2000, Life On Other Planets 2002, Road To Rouen 2005, Diamond Hoo Ha 2008; with The Hot Rats: Turn Ons 2010; with Babyshambles: Sequel to the Prequel 2013. *Honours:* Q Award for Best New Act 1995, BRIT Award for Best British Newcomer 1996. *Current Management:* Courtyard Management, 21 The Nursery, Sutton Courtenay, Abingdon, OX14 4UA, England. *Telephone:* (1235) 845800. *E-mail:* kate@cyard.com. *Website:* www.supergrass.com; babyshambles.net.

GOLBEY, Brian James; British musician (guitar, fiddle), singer and journalist; b. 5 Feb. 1939, Pycombe, Sussex; m. 1st 1969 (divorced); two s.; m. 2nd Sandi Stubbs 1980; one s. *Career:* formed band Cajun Moon (with Allan Taylor) 1975; mem. PRS. *Recordings include:* Virginia Waters 1972, Silver Haired Daddy of Mine 1973, Moments 1974, The American Album; with Cajun Moon: Cajun Moon 1976. *Film appearance:* The American Way. *Publications include:* regular columnist, Country Music People 1989–; essay for Aspects of Elvis 1994. *Honours:* Billboard Award, Record Mirror Award for Top UK Artist 1972, CMA Award for Top UK Soloist 1972, BCMA Cttee Award for long and continuing service to country music in Britain 1993.

GOLD, Nick; British producer and record company executive; *Managing Director, World Circuit Records. Career:* fmrly worked at Arts Worldwide; Founder and Man. Dir, World Circuit Records; producer for numerous artists, including Ali Farka Touré, Orlando 'Cachaito' Lopez, Buena Vista Social Club, Afro-Cuban All Stars, Ruben González, Orchestra Baobab, Omara Portuondo, Oumou Sangaré, Khalifa Ould Eide, Abdel Gadir Salim All-Stars, Afel Bocoum, Cheikh Lo, Andrew Hamilton, Radio Tarifa, Black Umfolosi, Jerry Boys, Ali Farka Toure. *Address:* World Circuit Records, 138 Kingsland Road, London, E2 8DY, England (office). *Telephone:* (20) 7749-3222 (office). *Fax:* (20) 7749-3232 (office). *E-mail:* post@worldcircuit.co.uk (office). *Website:* www.worldcircuit.co.uk (office).

GOLDBERG, Barry; American musician (piano) and songwriter; b. 25 Dec. 1942, Chicago, Illinois; m. Gail, 15 May 1971, 1 s. *Career:* Appeared at Newport Folk Festival with Bob Dylan, 1965; Played at Woodstock and Monterey pop festivals; Has written the score or contributed songs for films: Forrest Gump; Ruby; Flashback; Pow-Wow Highway; Dirty Dancing; Nobody's Fool; Adventures In Babysitting; Studio sessions with: Leonard Cohen; The Byrds; Mitch Ryder; The Ramones; Charlie Musselwhite; Additional associations with: Electric Flag; Bob Crewe; Jimi Hendrix; Gerry Goffin; Neil Young; Solomon Burke; Merry Clayton; Percy Sledge; mem, BMI, NARAS; AFofM. *Compositions:* I've Got To Use My Imagination, recorded by Gladys Knight, Joe Cocker and Bobby Blue Bland; It's Not The Spotlight, recorded by Rod Stewart; Sittin' In Circles, recorded by Steve Miller; Additional songs recorded by artists including: Tom Jones; B J Thomas; Manhattan Transfer; Ben E King; The Neville Brothers; Jeff Healey; The Persuasions; Carole King; Junior Walker; Sam Moore. *Recordings:* albums: Blowing My Mind 1966, There's No Hole in My Soul 1968, Two Jews Blues 1969, Street Man 1970, Ivar Avenue Reunion 1970, Barry Goldberg and Friends 1972, Blasts from My Past 1974, Barry Goldberg 1974, Stoned Again 2002, Chicago Blues Reunion 2006. *Honours:* Pioneer Award, BMI, USA. *E-mail:* cbr@chicagobluesreunion.com; info@barrygoldbergmusic.net. *Website:* www.chicagobluesreunion.com; www.barrygoldbergmusic.net.

GOLDEN ARMS (see U-God)

GOLDENTHAL, Elliot; American composer; b. 2 May 1954, New York. *Education:* Manhattan School of Music with John Corigliano. *Career:* freelance composer of theatre, film and choral music; collaborations with Yo-Yo Ma, Julie Taymor and Neil Jordan; mem. American Soc. of Composers, Authors and Publishers. *Compositions include:* Brass Quartet 1983, The Transposed Heads (musical after Thomas Mann) 1987, Pastime Variations for chamber orchestra 1988, Shadow lay Scherzo for orchestra 1988, Juan Darien, A Carnival Mass 1988, Fire Water Paper: A Vietnam Oratorio 1995, Concerto for trumpet and piano 1996, Othello (for San Francisco Ballet) 2003, , incidental music for A Midsummer Night's Dream, The Taming of the Shrew, The Tempest, Titus Andronicus. *Film scores:* Cocaine Cowboys 1979, Blank Generation 1980, Drugstore Cowboy 1989, Pet Cemetery 1989, Grand Isle 1991, Alien 3 1992, Demolition Man 1993, Interview with the Vampire 1994, Golden Gate 1994, Cobb 1994, Voices 1995, Batman Forever 1995, Heat 1995,

Michael Collins 1996, A Time to Kill 1996, Batman & Robin 1997, The Butcher Boy (Los Angeles Film Critics Asscn Award for Best Original Score) 1998, Sphere 1998, In Dreams 1998, Titus 1999, Final Fantasy: The Spirits Within 2001, Frida (Golden Globe for Best Score 2003, Acad. Award for Best Original Score) 2002, The Good Thief 2002, S.W.A.T. 2003, Across the Universe 2007, Public Enemies 2009, The Tempest 2009. *Television music:* Criminal Justice 1990, Fool's Fire 1992, Behind the Scenes (series) 1992, Roswell 1994. *Honours:* Stephen Sondheim Award in Music Theater, Arturo Toscanini Award. *Current Management:* Gorfaine/Schwartz Agency Inc., 4111 West Alameda Avenue, Suite 509, Burbank, CA 91505, USA. *Telephone:* (818) 260-8500. *Website:* www.gsamusic.com.

GOLDFRAPP, Alison, BFA; British singer, musician (keyboards) and composer; b. Enfield, Middlesex. *Education:* Middlesex Univ. *Career:* worked with Add N to (X), Howie B, Pete Briquette, Kelli Dayton, Bryan Ferry, Robert Fowler, Grant Fulton, Steve Musters, Rowen Oliver, Orbital, Kevin Petrie, Alice Retif, Patti Russo, Troy Stanton, Paul Anthony Taylor, Keith G. Thompson, Tricky, Martin Wheatley, David E. Williams; formed Goldfrapp with Will Gregory late 1990s–. *Recordings include:* albums: Felt Mountain 2000, Black Cherry 2003, Supernature 2005, Seventh Tree 2008, Head First 2010, Tales of Us 2013. *Current Management:* c/o Fascination Management, 1st Floor, 6 South Hill Park, London, NW3 2SB, England. *Telephone:* (20) 7586-6457. *E-mail:* info@fascinationmanagement.com. *Website:* www .fascinationmanagement.com; www.goldfrapp.co.uk.

GOLDIE; British music producer, artist and actor; b. (Clifford Price), 19 Sept. 1965, Wolverhampton. *Career:* producer, drum 'n' bass/jungle music. *Acting roles include:* The World Is Not Enough 1999, Snatch (film) 2000, The Price of Air (film) 2000, EastEnders (BBC 1) 2001–02, The Case (film) 2002. *Recordings include:* albums: Goldie Presents Metalheadz: Timeless 1995, Saturnz Return 1998, Incredible Sound of Drum 'N' Bass 2000, Malice in Wonderland 2007, Sine Tempus-The Soundtrack 2008, Memoirs of an Afterlife 2009. *Exhibitions include:* Love Over Gold 2007, Kids Are All Riot 2009, Athleticizm 2009, Lostribes 2013. *Website:* www.goldie.co.uk.

GOLDING, Lynval; British singer; b. 24 July 1951, Jamaica. *Career:* mem. The Specials 1977–84, 1996, 2008–; established own record label 2-Tone; numerous tours and TV appearances; Founder-mem. Fun Boy Three –1983; currently mem. The Stiff Upper Lips, Pama International; toured with The Beats. *Recordings include:* albums: with The Specials: The Specials 1979, More Specials 1980, In the Studio 1984, Today's Specials 1996, Guilty 'Til Proved Innocent! 1998, Skinhead Girl 2000, Conquering Ruler 2001, More... Or Less: The Specials Live 2012; with Fun Boy Three: Fun Boy Three 1982, Waiting 1983, The Best of Fun Boy Three 1984, Fun Boy Three: The Best of 1996, Really Saying Something: The Best of Fun Boy Three 1997; with Pama International: Love Filled Dub Band 2008, Highrise Campaign 2009, Pama Outernational 2009. *E-mail:* stiffupperlips@stiffupperlips.com (office). *Website:* www.stiffupperlips.com; www.thespecials.com.

GOLDMAN, Akita; Japanese musician (bass guitar). *Career:* mem. jazz band, Soil & "Pimp" Sessions 2001–. *Recordings include:* albums: Pimpin' (EP) 2004, Pimp Master 2005, Summer Goddess (EP) 2005, Pimp of the Year 2006, Pimpoint 2007, Planet Pimp 2008, 6 2009, Stoned Pirates Radio 2010, Magnetic Soil 2011, Circles 2013, "X" Chronicle of Soil & Pimp Sessions. *Current Management:* c/o Victor Entertainment Inc., Palacion Tower, 3-6-7 Kita-Aoyama, Minato-ku, Tokyo 107-0061, Japan. *E-mail:* soil@jvcmusic.co .jp. *Website:* www.jvcmusic.co.jp.

GOLDSBORO, Bobby; American musician (guitar), singer and songwriter; b. 18 Jan. 1941, Marianna, Fla. *Career:* guitarist with Roy Orbison 1960; solo artist 1964–; later, country artist during 1980s. *Recordings include:* hit singles include: See The Funny Little Clown 1964, Whenever He Holds You, Little Things, Voodoo Woman, It's Too Late, Blue Autumn, Honey 1968, Watching Scotty Grow, Summer (The First Time); albums include: The Bobby Goldsboro Album 1964, Honey 1968, Today 1969, Muddy Mississippi Line 1970, We Gotta Start Lovin' 1971, Come Back Home 1971, Goldsboro 1977, Roundup Saloon 1982, Easter Egg Mornin' 1993, The Best of Bobby Goldsboro 1996, The Greatest Hits 1999, Hello Summertime 2001; also numerous compilations. *Exhibitions include:* numerous art exhibitions. *Honours:* inducted into Alabama Music Hall of Fame 1999, eight gold records, 37 BMI Songwriter Awards, numerous other awards. *Current Management:* c/o Jim Stephany Management, 1021 Preston Drive, Nashville, TN 37206, USA. *Telephone:* (615) 228-5638 (office). *E-mail:* steph139@comcast.net (office). *E-mail:* bobby@bobbygoldsboro.com. *Website:* www.bobbygoldsboro.com.

GOLDSMITH, Harvey, CBE; British music promoter; b. 4 March 1946, London; s. of Sydney Goldsmith and Minnie Goldsmith; m. Diana Goldsmith 1971; one s. *Education:* Christ's Coll. and Brighton Coll. of Tech. *Career:* joined Big O Posters, Kensington Market 1966; organized open-air free concerts, Parliament Hill Fields 1968; in partnership with Michael Alfandary opened Round House, London 1968; organized 13 Garden Party concerts at Crystal Palace, London 1969; merged with John Smith Entertainment 1970–75; formed Harvey Goldsmith Entertainment promoting rock tours by Elton John, Rolling Stones etc.; in partnership with Ed Simons, rescued Hotel Television Network 1983; formed Allied Entertainment Group as public co. 1984–86, returned to pvt. ownership 1986; subsidiary Harvey Goldsmith Entertainment promotes some 250 concerts per year; formed Classical Productions with Mark McCormack, promoting shows at Earls Court including Pavarotti concert and productions of Aida 1988, Carmen 1989,

Tosca 1991; produced Bob Dylan Celebration, New York 1992, Mastercard Masters of Music (Hyde Park), The Eagles (Wembley), Three Tenors (Wembley), Lord of the Dance (world tour) 1996, Music for Montserrat (Royal Albert Hall), Boyzone (tour), Paul Weller (tour), Pavarotti (Manchester), Cirque du Soleil (Royal Albert Hall) 1997, Alegria (Royal Albert Hall), The Bee Gees (Wembley), Ozzfest (Milton Keynes Bowl), Paul Weller (Victoria Park) 1998; Chair. Nat. Music Day; Vice-Chair. Prince's Trust Bd; Vice-Pres. React 1989–; Trustee, Gret, Band Aid 1985–, Live Aid Foundation 1985–; Dir Pres.'s Club, London First, London Tourist Bd; Amb. for London Judges Award 1997; Chair. Ignition International 2006–; mem. Advisory Group Red Cross. *Honours:* Music Industry Trust Award 2006, Queen's Diamond Jubilee Award 2012. *Address:* Harvey Goldsmith Entertainments Ltd , 3rd Floor, 113 Great Portland Street, London, W1W 6QQ, England (office). *Telephone:* (20) 7224-1992 (office). *Fax:* (20) 7580-1853 (office). *Website:* www.harveygoldsmith.com.

GOLDSMITH, Timothy Simon; British musician (drums); b. 1 Dec. 1962, Hammersmith, London. *Career:* tours with Paul Brady, Tanita Tikaram, Nik Kershaw, Joan Armatrading, Jaki Graham; mem. Two Heroes, Musicians' Union. *Recordings include:* albums: Track Record 1983, Alf 1984, Go West 1985, I Refuse 1986, Bangs and Crashes 1986, Primitive Dance 1987, Spin Me Around 1989, About Love and Life 1990, All this Time 1982, Perfect World 1992, Songs and Crazy Dreams 1996, Mad with the World 1997, Nobody Knows 1999, The Messenger 1999, Live 2009 – Volume 1 2009, Live 2009 – Volume 2 2009. *E-mail:* infos-timgoldsmith@wanadoo.fr. *Website:* www .timgoldsmith.net.

GOLDSWORTHY, Tim; British producer, programmer and record label owner. *Career:* formed The DFA (Death From Above) production duo and record label (with James Murphy) 2002–, worked with Turing Machine, BS 2000, Zero Zero, The Rapture, David Holmes, Primal Scream, Radio 4, The Juan Maclean, Echoes, Gotham!, Massive Attack; co-f. Mo' Wax label with James Lavelle. *Recordings include:* album: as The DFA: Dance to the Underground 2003, DFA Compilation, Vol. 1 2003, DFA Compilation, Vol. 2 2004, DFA Holiday Remix 2005, The DFA Remixes – Chapter One 2006, The DFA Remixes – Chapter Two 2006. *Current Management:* c/o Elastic Artists Agency Ltd, Targetspace: Room 104, 1st Floor, 70 Saint Mary Axe, London, EC3A 8BE, England. *Telephone:* (20) 7336-8340. *Fax:* (20) 7608-1471. *E-mail:* info@elasticartists.net. *Website:* www.elasticartists.net. *E-mail:* dfaweb@ dfarecords.com. *Website:* www.dfarecords.com.

GOLIGHTLY, Holly; British singer and songwriter; b. 1966. *Career:* mem. Thee Headcoatees 1990–95; solo artist 1995–; mem. Holly Golightly and the Brokeoffs 2007–. *Recordings:* albums: with Thee Headcoatees: Kids Are All Square (also with Thee Headcoats) 1990, Girlsville 1991, Have Love Will Travel 1992, Ballad Of The Insolent Pup 1994, Live In London (also with Thee Headcoats) 1994, Sound Of The Baskervilles (also with Thee Headcoats) 1995, Bozstik Haze 1997, Punk Girls 1997, The Sisters Of Suave 1998, Taylor Meets Thee Headcoatees (with Woodie Taylor) 1998, Here Comes Cessation 1999, Live At The Boston Arms (EP) 1999; solo: The Good Things 1995, Laugh It Up 1996, Serial Girlfriend 1996, Painted On 1997, Laugh It All Up 1997, Up The Empire 1998, In Blood (with Billy Childish) 1999, God Don't Like It 2000, Live In America 2000, Desperate Little Town (with Dan Melchior) 2001, The Main Attraction 2001, Singles Round-Up 2001, ...Truly She Is None Other 2003, Down At Gina's At 3 2004, Slowly But Surely 2004; with Holly Golightly and the Brokeoffs: You Can't Buy a Gun When You're Crying 2007, Nobody Will Be There 2007, Dirt Don't Hurt (Ind. Music Award for Best Americana Album 2009) 2008, Medicine County 2010, No Help Coming 2011, Sunday Run Me Over 2012. *Current Management:* c/o Nancy Scibilia, Deep Blue Arts, 4440 Morse Avenue, Studio City, CA 91604, USA. *Telephone:* (310) 422-4990. *E-mail:* nancy@bernett.us. *Website:* www.hollygolightly.com.

GOLSON, Benny; American composer, musician (piano, saxophone), arranger and producer; b. 25 Jan. 1929, Philadelphia, PA. *Education:* Howard Univ. *Career:* arranged for and played saxophone with bands led by 'Bull Moose' Jackson 1951, Tadd Dameron 1953, Lionel Hampton 1953, Johnny Hodges 1954, Earl Bostic 1954–56, Dizzy Gillespie 1956–58, Art Blakey 1958–59; co-leader Jazztet (with Art Farmer) 1959–62; composer and prod. radio and TV commercials 1963–; prod., arranger and composer for numerous artists, including Miles Davis, Sammy Davis Jr, Ella Fitzgerald, Connie Francis, Dizzy Gillespie, Eartha Kitt, Lou Rawls, Max Roach, Diana Ross; wrote music for TV and film 1967–74; resumed performing career 1974–; artist-in-residence, William Paterson Coll. 1991–92; Lecturer, Conservatoire Nat. des Arts et Métiers, Paris, Eastman School of Music, Howard Univ., Jazz at Lincoln Center, Juilliard School of Music, Loyola Univ., New Orleans, LA, Manhattan School of Music, New York Univ., Stanford Univ. and others. *Compositions include:* (for jazz ensemble, unless otherwise stated) Blue Walk 1954, Strut 1954, Stablemates 1955, Step Lightly/Junior's Arrival 1956, Whisper Not 1956, Mesabi Chant 1956–58, Stand By 1956–58, Slightly Hep 1956–58, Domingo 1956–58, Out Of The Past 1957, B.G.'s Holiday 1957, Tip-Toeing 1957, Blues It 1957, Venetian Breeze 1957, Just By Myself 1957, Blues On Down 1957, Hassan's Dream 1957, Along Came Berry/Along Came Manon 1958, You're Not The Kind 1958, Little Karin 1958, The Blues March (March On) 1958, Cry A Blue Tear 1958, City Lights 1958, Blue Thoughts 1958, Killer Joe 1959, Tippin' On Thru 1959, Blues After Dark 1959, Minor Vamp 1959, Blues on my Mind 1959, My Blues House 1959, Jam for Bobbie 1959, Bob Hurd's Blues 1959, Blue Streak 1959, Park Avenue Petite 1960, Swing It 1961, Junction 1961, Impromptune 1961, A Swedish Villa 1965, Stockholm Sojourn 1964, Tryst 1968, Two Part Inventions for the Trumpet 1970, Outta Sight

1970, I'd Do It All With You 1977, Tomorrow, Paradise 1977, Easy All Day 1977, Timbale Rock 1977, Walkin' and Stalkin' 1977, Time's Past (This is for you, John) 1983, I'm Always Dancin' to the Music 1978, Happy I'm Happy 1979, Fair Weather 1983, Change of Heart 1983, Yesterday's Thoughts 1983, Jam the Avenue 1983, Moment to Moment 1983, No Dancin' 1985, Cool One 1985, Back to the City 1986, Vas Simeon 1986, Time Speaks 1986, Without Delay 1986, From Dream to Dream 1986, Up, Jump, Spring 1987, Gypsy Jingle-Jangle 1987, City Bound 1989, Thinking Mode 1991, Two Faces (for orchestra with soloists) 1991, Heartstrings 1992, One Day Forever (I Remember Miles) 1992, Uptown Afterburn 1992. *Film music contributed to:* Skifascination 1962, Ed's Next Move 1996. *Television music:* Room 222 1967–70, Run for Your Life 1967, It Takes a Thief 1967–68, Where It's At 1968, Mannix 1968, Ironside 1968, Mission: Impossible 1968–69, Mod Squad 1969, The Partridge Family 1971, M*A*S*H 1972, The Creative Spirit 1994. *Recordings include:* albums: solo: Modern Touch 1957, New York Scene 1957, Blues On Down 1957, Remembering Clifford 1958, The Other Side of Golson 1958, Benny Golson in Paris 1958, Groovin' With Golson 1959, Gone With Golson 1959, Gettin' With It 1959, Meet The Jazztet 1960, Reunion 1962, Turning Point 1962, Just Jazz! 1962, Pop + Jazz = Swing 1962, Turn In, Turn On To The Hippest Commercials of the Sixties 1967, Killer Joe 1977, I'm Always Dancin' To The Music 1978, One More Mem'ry 1981, Time Speaks 1982, Domingo 1991, I Remember Miles 1992, California Message 1995, Up Jumped Benny 1996, Walkin' 1997, Tenor Legacy 1998, That's Funky 2000, This Is For You, John 2000, One Day, Forever 2001, Terminal 1 2004, New Time, New 'Tet 2009; with Benny Golson Quartet: Free 1962, Benny Golson Quartet 1990, Up Jump Spring 1990. *Honours:* Dr hc (William Paterson Coll.) 1993; Down Beat Int. Jazz Poll New Star Composer Award 1952, Down Beat Int. Jazz Poll New Star Saxophonist Award 1952, 1953, Guggenheim Fellowship 1994, NEA American Jazz Masters Award 1996. *Address:* c/o Concord Records Inc., 270 N Canon Drive, Suite 1212, Beverly Hills, CA 90210, USA (office). *E-mail:* bennygolson@bennygolson.com (office). *Website:* www.bennygolson.com.

GOLT, Debbie, (DJ Debbie), BA (Hons); British consultant, music and arts management and broadcaster; *Director, Outerglobe.co.uk*; b. (Deborah Golt), 2 April 1952, London, England; d. of Sidney Golt CB and Jean Golt; two d. *Education:* Univ. of York; Postgraduate Diploma (masters equivalent), Applied Youth and Community Work, Manchester Polytechnic. *Career:* diverse career on alternative/ind. circuit; parallel career in arts, community and youth work and arts man.; ran sound system battles and concerts with Rock Against Racism 1977–80; managed major UK-based African Band, Taxi Pata Pata (first UK-based African band on BBC Radio 1 and with Arts Council support); f. Taxi Pata Pata African Arts; Co-Dir Nyrangongo Records 1985–90, Half The Sky women's music promotions (including first UK date for Oumou Sangare) 1990–94, Portobello Festival; Arts Officer RBKC 1990–2005; set up Eleventh Hour Arts; Co-Man. Frank Chickens 1994–98; set up Outerglobe.-co.uk 1997; Man. MoMo (Music of Moroccan Origin) 1997–2004, Weird MC 2002–05, Fusing Naked Beats/DJ Asif 2003–07, Moroccan Roll Convention 2005–07, Nsimba Foggis 2005–, Taxi Pata Pata 2005–, Mosi Conde 2009–, Yaaba Funk 2011–, Juwon Ogungbe 2011; adviser to many others, including Poetry Olympics 2005–09; Co-Curator City Showcase Roots & Flutes 2009–; Trainer, Women's Radio Group 2010–; Co-ordinator/Programmer World Music Portobello Festival 1994–98; Host, Year of the Artist residency, www.gaialive.com Internet radio 2000; Dir London Link Radio and Women's Radio Group; panellist, BBC Radio 1 Sound City, Umbrella, Modal, Women in Music/SOAS Symposia; contrib. to BBC Radio 1, BBC Radio 5, BBC London, W10FM, Modal FM; regular broadcaster, Resonance FM, London Link Radio, Women's Radio Group online, Purple Radio, Refugee Week Radio, Radio 1812, www.gaialive.com; fmr mem. Advisory Bd Modal; fmr Co. Sec. Leaparts; mem. Women in Music (Chair.), Sound Sense; Ed./Publr Topical 1992–94. *Contributions to publications:* Topical 1991–94, Worldbeat 1992–93, World Music Magazine 1993, Guardian, fROOTS, Straight No Chaser, Black Film Maker Magazine, Women in Music Now, Bubble Jam Delite 2003–04, Avant magazine, www.funk-me.com, www.griots.net, www.bubblejam.net, www.wah-magazine.com, WAH magazine, Music Week, Catch A Vibe, AfricanMusicansProfiles.com. *E-mail:* info@outerglobe.co.uk (office); outerglobe@yahoo.co.uk (office). *Website:* www.outerglobe.co.uk (office); www .african-essence.com (office).

GOMEZ, Selena Maria; American singer, actress and fashion designer; b. 22 July 1992, Grand Prairie, Tex.; d. of Ricardo Joel Gomez and Amanda Dawn Teefey (née Cornett). *Career:* performer and actress in TV and film 2002–; co-f. July Moon Productions 2008; signed with Hollywood record label 2008; fronted band Selena Gomez & the Scene 2008–12; launched Dream Out Loud clothing line 2010; apptd UNICEF Amb. 2009. *Television:* Barney and Friends 2002–04, Walker, Texas Ranger: Trial by Fire 2005, The Suite Life of Zack & Cody 2006, Hannah Montana 2007–08, Wizards of Waverly Place (ALMA Award for Special Achievement Comedy – Television – Actress 2009, Capricho Award for Best Int. TV Show 2010, Kids' Choice Awards for Favorite TV Star 2010, 2011, 2012, 2013) 2007–12, The Suite Life on Deck 2009. *Films:* as actress: Spy Kids 3-D: Game Over 2003, Another Cinderella Story 2008, Horton Hears a Who! (voice) 2008, Arthur and the Revenge of Maltazard 2009, Arthur 3: The War of the Two Worlds 2010, Ramona and Beezus 2010, Monte Carlo 2011, The Muppets 2011, Hotel Transylvania (voice) 2012, Spring Breakers 2013, Aftershock 2013, Getaway 2013, Behaving Badly 2014, Rudderless 2014, Hotel Transylvania 2 2015. *Recordings include:* albums: with Selena Gomez & the Scene: Kiss & Tell 2009, A Year Without Rain 2010,

When the Sun Goes Down 2011; solo: Stars Dance 2013, Revival 2015. *Honours:* numerous awards including: MTV Europe Music Award for Biggest Fans 2011, MTV Video Music Award for Best Pop Video (for Come & Get It) 2013, Much Music Video Award for Favorite Int. Artist 2014. *Current Management:* c/o Brian Teefey, LH7 Management, 10960 Wilshire Boulevard, 5th Floor, Los Angeles, CA 90024, USA. *E-mail:* brian@lh7management.com. *Website:* selenagomez.com.

GOMIS, Rudy; Senegalese singer and teacher; b. Casamance. *Career:* fmr mem. Star Band, Club Miami, Dakar to 1970; Founder-mem. Orchestra Baobab 1970–85, originally at Club Baobab to 1977, then Jandeer Club, Balafon Club to 1978, time in Paris, then at Ngalam Club to 1985; language teacher 1985–2001; Orchestra Baobab re-formed 2001–, resident at Just 4U Club, Dakar. *Recordings include:* albums: M'Beugene 1972, Hommage à Lay M'Boop 1974, Orchestra Baobab '75 1975, Guy Gu Rey Gi 1975, Senegaal Sunugaal 1975, Visage du Sénégal 1975, Aduna Jarul Naawoo 1975, N'Deleng N'Deleng 1977, Une Nuit Aun Jandeer 1978, Babab à Paris Vols 1 and 2 1978, Gouygui Dou Daanou 1979, Mohamadou Bamba 1980, Sibou Odia 1980, Ken Dou Werente (re-released as Pirate's Choice 2001) 1982, On Verra Ça: The 1978 Paris Sessions 1992, Bamba 1993, Specialist in All Styles (BBC Radio 3 Awards for World Music Critic's Award for Album of the Year 2003) 2002, A Night at Club Baobab 2006, Made in Dakar 2007, La Belle Epoque 2009, Laru Beya 2011. *Honours:* BBC Radio 3 Awards for World Music, Africa Region 2003. *Address:* c/o World Circuit Records, First Floor, Shoreditch Stables, 138 Kingsland Road, London, E2 8DY, England (office). *Website:* www .orchestrabaobab.com.

GONGORA, Omar; Mexican musician (drums); b. Monterrey. *Career:* mem. electro-pop band, Kinky 2000–. *Recordings include:* albums: Kinky 2002, Atlas 2003, Reina 2006, Sueño de la Maquina 2011. *Current Management:* c/o Sonic360 Records, PO Box 6451, London, W1A 6DL, England. *Telephone:* (20) 7636-3939. *Website:* www.sonic360.com/kinky; www.kinkymusic.com; www .gonbops.com.

GONZÁLEZ, Alejandro (Alex); Cuban/Colombian drummer, singer and songwriter; b. 24 Feb. 1969, Miami, Fla, USA. *Career:* mem. Mexican rock group Maná 1986–; group f. Salva Negra Foundation (financing and supporting projects to protect environment) 1995–; over 25 million records sold worldwide; numerous int. tours. *Recordings:* albums: with Maná: Falta Amor 1990, ¿Dónde Jugarán Los Niños? 1992, Cuando los Ángeles Lloran 1995, Sueños Líquidos (Grammy Award for Best Latin Rock/Alternative Performance 1999, Premio Lo Nuestro for Pop Album of the Year 1999) 1997, Maná MTV Unplugged (Ritmo Latino Music Award for Album of the Year 2000) 1999, Revolución de Amor (Billboard Latin Music Awards for Latin Rock Album of the Year 2003, for Latin Pop Album of the Year – Duo or Group 2003, Grammy Award for Best Latin Rock/Alternative Album 2003, Latin Grammy Award for Best Rock Album by a Duo or Group 2003, Premio Lo Nuestro for Rock Album of the Year 2003, Ritmo Latino Music Award for Album of the Year 2003) 2002, Amar es Combatir (Billboard Latin Music Award for Latin Rock/Alternative Album of the Year 2007, Grammy Award for Best Latin Rock/Alternative Album 2007, Premio Lo Nuestro for Rock Album of the Year 2007) 2007, Arde el Cielo (Billboard Latin Music Awards for Latin Pop Album of the Year – Duo or Group 2009, for Latin Rock/Alternative Album of the Year 2009) 2008, Drama y Luz (Latin Grammy Award for Best Rock Album 2011, Premio People en Español Award for Best Album 2011, Grammy Award for Best Latin Pop, Rock or Urban Album 2012, Premio Lo Nuestro Award for Rock/Alternative Award of the Year 2012) 2011, Cama Incendiada (Latin Grammy Award for Best Pop/Rock Album 2015) 2015; other contribs include: Supernatural, Santana 1999. *Honours:* appointed FAO Goodwill Amb. 2003; with Maná: Premios Lo Nuestro for Best Pop Group 1997, 1999, 2000, for Pop Song of the Year (for Mariposa Traicionera) 2004, for Rock Song of the Year (for Labios Compartidos) 2007, (for Bendita Tu Luz) 2008, for Rock Artist of the Year 2007, 2008, for Lifetime Achievement 2011, for Rock/Alternative Artist of the Year 2012, Ritmo Latino Music Award for Best Solo or Rock Group Artist 1999, Premios Oye! Special Social Prize to Music 2002, Award for Best Solo or Group Artist 2003, Mexican Public Commercial Award 2004, MasterTone Award (for Labios Compartidos) 2007, Latin Grammy Awards for Record of the Year 2000, for Best Rock Performance by a Duo or Group (both with Santana, for Corazón Espinado) 2000, for Best Pop Performance by a Duo or Group with Vocal (for Se Me Olvidó Otra Vez) 2000, Latin Grammy Special Award for Musical Accomplishments 2006, Billboard Latin Awards for Pop Airplay Song of the Year – Duo or Group (for Labios Compartidos) 2007, for Latin Tour of the Year 2008, for Hot Latin Song of the Year – Duo or Group (for Si No Te Hubieras Ido) 2009, for Latin Pop Airplay Song of the Year – Duo or Group (for Si No Te Hubieras Ido) 2009, for Latin Duet or Group Songs 2012, for Latin Duet or Group Album 2012, for Latin Pop Duet or Group of the Year Songs 2012, for Latin Pop Duet or Group of the Year Album 2012, Premio Juventud Supernova Award 2006, Premios Juventud for Favorite Rock Artist 2007, 2008, 2009, 2011, 2012, World Music Awards for World's Best Selling Latin Group 2007, for Best Selling Latin American Artist 2007, Los Premios 40 Principales for Best Concert/Tour 2007, 2011, Pan American Health Org. Champions of Health (for Salva Negra Foundation), World Health Day 2008, Premios Telehit for Best Int. Mexican Band 2011, Premio People en Español Award for Best Rock Artist or Group 2011, Premio Cadena Dial 2011, Premio Casandra Internacional 2012. *Address:* c/o Warner Music Mexico, SA de C.V. Leibnitz 32 Col., Nueva Anzures, México, DF 11590, Mexico (office).

Telephone: (55) 5279-3800 (office). *Website:* www.warnermusic.com.mx (office); www.mana.com.mx.

GONZALEZ, Jimmy; American/Mexican singer, musician (guitar), songwriter and producer; b. Brownsville, Tex. *Career:* co-f. Tejano band, Grupo Mazz 1978–98; f. Jimmy Gonzalez y Grupo Mazz 1999–. *Recordings include:* around 50 albums including: Siempre Humilde 2003, Quien Iva a Pensar 2003, Si Me Faltas Tu 2004, Para Mi Gente 2005, Mejor Que Nunca 2006, Mazz Cumbias2006, It's Christmazz 2006, Una Vez Mas (with Joe Lopez) 2007, Incomparable 2007, The Legend Continues... La Continuacion 2008, Eternamente 2009, Linea de Oro, Vol. 1 2009, Linea de Oro, Vol. 2 2009, Mi Vida Sin Tu Amor. *Honours:* seven Latin Grammy Awards for Best Tejano Album, Grammy Award for Best Tejano Album. *Address:* c/o Freddie Records, 5979 South Staples Street, Corpus Christi, TX 78413, USA. *Telephone:* (361) 992-8412. *Fax:* (361) 992-8428. *E-mail:* jimmyg@supermazz.com. *Website:* freddierecords.com; www.jimmygonzalezyelgrupomazz.com.

GONZÁLEZ, José; Swedish singer, songwriter and guitarist; b. 1978, Gothenburg. *Education:* Univ. of Gothenburg. *Career:* played in bands including Back Against the Wall, Renascence, Only if You Call Me Jonathan; performs in Junip with Tobias Winterkorn and Elias Araya; solo artist 2002–; tours in N and S America, Europe and Asia. *Recordings include:* solo: Veneer 2003, B-Sides Collected 2006, In Our Nature 2007; with Junip: Fields 2010. *Honours:* Grammy Award for Best New Artist 2004, Swedish Music Publishers Association Award for Best Swedish Songwriter of the Year, European Border Breaker Award 2006. *Current Management:* c/o Morgan Johansson, Moondog Entertainment, PO Box 24151, 104 51 Stockholm, Sweden. *Telephone:* (8) 578-679-00. *Fax:* (8) 578-679-30. *E-mail:* morgan@moondog.se; info@moondog.se. *Website:* www.moondog.se; www.jose-gonzalez.com.

GONZALEZ, Kenny, (Kenny Dope, The Bucketheads, Untouchables, Powerhouse, Swing Kids); American producer, remixer and DJ; b. 7 June 1970, Brooklyn, New York. *Career:* started producing for New York labels Strictly Rhythm, Nu Groove; formed Masters at Work with Louie Vega; duo also recorded as Nu Yorican Soul; f. Dope Wax label, Co-founder MAW Records; numerous studio projects including with The Bucketheads, Nuyorican Soul. *Recordings include:* albums: The Kenny Dope Project 1992, All in the Mind (as The Bucketheads) 1995, Supa-Dope Classics Volume 1 2001, Found Instrumentals 2001, Our Time Is Coming (as Masters At Work) 2002, Found Instrumentals Volume 2 2005; with Masters at Work: The Album 1993, The Essential KenLou House Mixes 1995, Nuyorican Soul 1997, The Remixes 1998, The Tenth Anniversary Collection- Part I 2000, Our Time is Coming 2001; solo: The Unreleased Project 1993, Hip Hop Forever 1998, Strange Games and Funky Things 2000, Disco Heat 2002, In the House 2003, Break Beats 2004, Brazilika 2004, Black Roots 2006, Kay-Dee, Vol. 2 2008. *Current Management:* c/o Kay-Dee Records, 1313 Paterson Plank Road, Secaucus, NJ 07094, USA. *E-mail:* info@kaydeerecords.com (office). *Website:* www.kaydeerecords.com (office); www.mawrecords.com (office).

GONZÁLEZ, Rodrigo; German musician (bass, vocals) and producer; b. (Rodrigo Andrés González Espindola), 19 May 1968, Valparaíso, Chile. *Career:* family fled Chile, granted asylum in Germany in 1970s; played with punk band Die Goldenen Zitronen; guitarist, The Rainbirds 1988–89; mem., Depp Jones 1988–93; mem. punk rock band, Die Ärzte 1993–; also played guitar with Abwärts 2004–; Co-owner, record co. Rodrec. *Recordings include:* Die Bestie in Menschengestalt 1993, Planet Punk 1995, Le Frisur 1996, 13 1998, Satanische Pferde 1999, Wir wollen nur deine Seele 1999, Runter mit den Spendierhosen, Unsichtbarer! 2000, Männer haben kein Gehirn 2001, 5, 6, 7, 8 - Bullenstaat 2001, Rock'n'Roll Realschule 2002, Geräusch 2003, Jazz ist anders 2007, Lied vom Scheitern 2008, Auch 2012, Die Nacht der Dämonen: Live 2013. *Current Management:* c/o Girke Management, Nymphenburgerstrasse 4, 10825 Berlin, Germany. *E-mail:* info@girkemanagement.de. *Address:* c/o Rodrec GbR, Wetzer & González GbR, Amandastrasse 28, 20357 Hamburg, Germany. *Telephone:* (40) 31797396. *Fax:* (40) 59455588. *E-mail:* info@rodrec.com. *Website:* www.rodrec.com; www.bademeister.com.

GOODACRE, Tony; British singer, entertainer and musician (guitar); b. 3 Feb. 1938, Leeds, Yorks., England; m. 1st Cherry 1960; one s. two d.; m. 2nd Sylvia 1974. *Education:* Roundhay Grammar School, Leeds. *Career:* first professional engagement 1956; first recording 1957; radio debut 1958; formed band Goodacre Country 1969; guest, The Arthur Smith Show (US TV show) 1973; first appearance, Grand Ole Opry, Nashville 1977; Wembley Festival 1982, 1983; started own music publishing co. Sylvantone Music 1983; promoted careers of Stu Page 1984–86, Jeannie Dee 1984–86, Sarah Jory 1987–88; toured Australia 1988, 1990, 1995, 2001, New Zealand 1988, 2001. *Recordings include:* albums: Roamin' Round In Nashville 1974, Grandma's Feather Bed 1975, Thanks To The Hanks 1976, Written In Britain 1977, The Best of Tony Goodacre 1978, Mr Country Music 1978, You've Made My Life Complete 1979, Recorded Live In Ilkley 1980, 25th Anniversary 1981, Red Roses 1983, Sylvantone Song Book, Vols 1 and 2 1984–85, The Tony Goodacre Collection 1986, Country Favourites 1988, Something Special 1989, Livin' On Livin' 1992, 40th Anniversary Album 1996, The Millennium Project 2000, Snow Covered 2004, Man in the Sky 2007, Completing the Collection 2008, The Country Side of Britain 2010, More Songs from the Geoff Ashford Songbook 2011, Sylvantone Singers & Songwriters 2011, The Chart Hits 2012, I Believe 2013, Sing Sing Sing 2013, Pure Nostalgia 2013, Country Classics Traditional Style 2014, 2015 Compilation Favourites 2015. *Honours:* Record Mirror Award 1973, three British Country Music Asscn Awards 1982–84,

Favourite Male Vocalist in Europe, Country Gazette (Dutch magazine) 1986, 18 Country Music Club Awards, Top Solo Artist, three Country Music Club Awards, Top Duo, with Sarah Jory 1987, British Country Music Lifetime Achievement Award 2007. *Address:* 11 Saunton Avenue, Rosedale, The Ings, Redcar, TS10 2RL, England (home). *Telephone:* (1642) 479898. *E-mail:* sylvantone@hotmail.com; tonygoodacre@hotmail.com. *Website:* www.tonygoodacre.com.

GOODIER, David Charles Gray, BEd (Hons); British musician (bass guitar, double bass); b. 11 July 1954, Salisbury, Wilts., England; s. of Cecil Gray Goodier and Cecilia Joy James (née Robson); m. Lynn Thompson; one s. two d. *Education:* St Luke's Coll., Univ. of Exeter. *Career:* worked in theatre pit bands, TV and radio sessions; club and festival appearances; appeared live or recorded with jazz musicians, including John Etheridge, Andy Sheppard, John Parricelli, Mark Lockheart, Gerard Presencer, Iain Ballamy, Ed Jones, Damon Brown, Pete King, Guy Barker, Dave De Fries, Tal Farlow, Art Farmer, Greg Abate, Michael Hashim, Slim Gaillard, Dick Morrissey, Don Rendell, Norma Winstone, Pee Wee Ellis; UK tour with Kwame Kwei-Armah's soul musical featuring Ruby Turner 2001; UK tour with soprano Lesley Garrett 2006; Musical Dir and Co-founder Bristol Jazz Workshop 1991–2001; bass tutor, Dartington Int. Summer School, Dartington Coll. of Arts, Exeter Univ.; int. tours and recording with flautist Ian Anderson 2002–; bass player Jethro Tull 2007–. *Recordings include:* John Parricelli, Mark Lockheart: Matheran, The Korgis: This World's For Everyone, Ian Anderson: Rupi's Dance, Ian Anderson Plays the Orchestral Jethro Tull, Thick As A Brick 2, Homo Erraticus.

GOODMAN, Joy Marie, BA; American country gospel singer and musician (woodwind); b. 19 Oct. 1948, Sharon, Pa; m. Harold L. Grim Jr; one s. one d. *Education:* Bob Jones Univ. *Career:* video with James Blackwood and numerous appearances with Blackwood Quartet; mem. Christian Country Music Asscn, Country Gospel Music Guild. *Recordings include:* album: Ashes To Gold 2000, Love is the Foundation 2006. *Honours:* Country Gospel Music Guild Golden Harp Award for Female Horizon Artist 2001.

GOODREM, Delta Lea; Australian singer, songwriter and actress; b. 9 Nov. 1984, Sydney; d. of Denis Goodrem and Lea Goodrem. *Recordings include:* albums: Innocent Eyes (ARIA Awards for Best New Artist, Best Pop Release, Highest Selling Album) 2003, Mistaken Identity 2004, Delta 2007. *Television:* Neighbours 2002–05; numerous guest appearances on other dramas. *Film:* Hating Alison Ashley 2005. *Honours:* ARIA Award for Best Female Artist 2003, ARIA Awards for Best New Artist, Single of the Year and Highest Selling Single (all for Born to Try) 2003, Channel V Australian Artist of the Year 2003, TV Week Logie Award for Most Popular New Female Talent 2003, MO Award for Australian Performer of the Year 2004, APRA Breakthrough Award 2004. *Address:* c/o Sony Music Australia, PO Box 88, Darlinghurst, NSW 2010, Australia. *Website:* www.deltagoodrem.com.

GOODRICK, Mick; American jazz musician (guitar). *Education:* BM Berklee College of Music. *Career:* Former faculty member, Berklee College of Music; Faculty member, Jazz Studies, New England Conservatory of Music; Performed and recorded with: Jack DeJohnette; Gary Burton; Paul Motian; Steve Gadd; Pat Metheny; Michael Brecker; Charlie Haden. *Recordings:* In Passing 1978, Biorhythms 1990, Cities 1993, Rare Birds 1993, Sunscreams 1993; two albums with Jack DeJohnette's Special Edition. *Publications:* Author, The Advancing Guitarist. *Address:* Mr Goodchord Publications, PO Box 320309, Boston, MA 02132, USA (office). *E-mail:* mrgoodchord@mrgoodchord.com (office). *Website:* www.mrgoodchord.com (office).

GOODRIDGE, Robin; British musician (drums); b. 10 Sept. 1966, Crawley, West Sussex; m. Ellie Goodridge; two c. *Career:* mem., Future Primitive, became Bush 1992–2002, 2010–; mem. Spear of Destiny 2006–08, Stone Gods 2008–10; numerous headlining tours, festival appearances. *Recordings include:* albums: with Bush: Sixteen Stone 1994, Razorblade Suitcase 1996, Deconstructed 1997, The Science of Things 1999, Golden State 2001, Zen X Four 2005, The Sea of Memories 2011; with Spear of Destiny: Imperial Prototype 2007; with Stone Gods: Silver Spoons & Broken Bones 2008. *Current Management:* Tami Thomsen c/o Kirtland Records, 3100 Main Street. Suite 347, Dallas, TX 75201, USA. *E-mail:* themgmtcompany@gmail.com. *Website:* www.kirtlandrecords.com; www.onesecondbush.com; www.bushofficial.com.

GOODWIN, Jimi; British singer, songwriter and musician (guitar, bass guitar); b. 28 May 1970, Manchester, England. *Career:* mem. dance-club music trio Sub Sub late 1980s, changed name to Doves 1998–; tours in UK and USA. *Recordings include:* albums: with Doves: Lost Souls 2000, The Last Broadcast 2002, Some Cities 2005, Kingdom of Rust 2009, The Best of Doves: The Places Between 2010; solo: Odludek 2014; other: Twisted Tenderness (with Bernard Sumner and Johnny Marr as Electronic) 1999, Global Underground: Bangkok 2009, Epic, Vol. 2 2011. *Address:* c/o Heavenly Recordings, 47 Frith Street, London, W1D 4SE, England (office). *E-mail:* info@heavenlyrecordings.com (office). *Website:* www.heavenlyrecordings.com; www.doves.net.

GOOGOOSH; Iranian singer and actress; b. (Faegheh Atashin), 1951, Tehran; m. 1st Mahmoud Ghorbani (divorced 1972); m. 2nd Behrouz Vosoughi (divorced 1976); m. 3rd Homayoun Mestaghi (divorced 1989); m. 4th Masoud Kimiai (divorced 2003); one s. *Career:* banned from performing in Iran 1979–; now based in Toronto, Canada. *Films include:* Bim va omid (Hope and Fear) 1960, Fereshteh farari (The Runaway Angel) 1961, Partgahe makhouf (Cliff of

Fear) 1963, Sheitune bala (The Naughty One) 1965, Panjereh (The Window) 1970, Bita (Sepas Award 1973) 1972, Nazanin 1976, Dar emtedad shab (Along the Night) 1978, Emsab aski mirizad (Tonight Someone Cries) 1979. *Recordings:* albums: Googoosh LIVE!, Do-Mahi, Kavir, Mosabeb, Do-Panjareh, Nimeh Gomshodeh Man, Behtarin Fasl-e-Tazeh, POL, Live in Concert, Ageh Bernooni, Kooh, Dar Emtedadeh Shab, Man-o-Gonjeshkhayeh Khaneh, Setareh, Mordab, Jadeh, Zartosht 2000, QQ Bang Bang 2003, Akharin Khabar (Last News) 2004, Manifest 2005, Shabe Sepid 2008, Hajme Sabz 2010. *Honours:* First Prize, Carthage Music Festival 1972, Special Cultural Medal of Tunisia 1973. *E-mail:* info@googoosh.com (home). *Website:* www.googoosh.com.

GORCE, Patrick; French musician (percussion); b. 23 May 1962, Algiers, Algeria; m. Odile; one s. one d. *Education:* L'Ecole Superieur de Batterie, Dante Agostini, Paris. *Career:* performed in Paris clubs, Zénith, Olympia, New Morning; played with Ghetto Blaster, Luis Antonio, Jean-Claude Borrelli, Richard Clayderman; teacher, drumming and traditional percussion; currently plays with flamenco group, Los Cabales; mem. SPEDIDAM. *Compositions:* Tambours de la Paix. *Recordings include:* African Vibration, Samy Samiamam, Clypso O'Samba, Ile Axe, Percussions of Latin America, Travel and See, Nomadic Activities. *Honours:* Titualire de la Bourse 'Lavoisier', Ministry of Foreign Affairs. *Current Management:* c/o Camille Abergel, 150 reu des Rabats, 92160 Antony, France. *Telephone:* 6-61-82-09-07. *E-mail:* tini_loscabales@hotmail.com (office). *Website:* tini.loscabales.free.fr.

GORDON, Iain, (Dobbie Blaze); New Zealand musician (keyboards). *Career:* mem. reggae and soul band, Fat Freddy's Drop. *Recordings include:* albums: Live at the Matterhorn 2001, Based on a True Story (New Zealand Music Award for Album of the Year) 2005, Dr Boondigga and the Big BW 2009, Live at Roundhouse 2010, Blackbird 2013. *Honours:* New Zealand Music Award for Best Group 2005. *Current Management:* c/o The Drop Ltd, PO Box 14-723, Kilbirnie, Wellington 6241, New Zealand. *Telephone:* (4) 934-3767. *E-mail:* freddy@fatfreddysdrop.com. *Website:* www.fatfreddysdrop.com.

GORDON, Kim; American artist, singer and musician (bass guitar); b. 28 April 1953, Rochester, NY; m. Thurston Moore (divorced 2013); one d. *Career:* Founder-mem., Sonic Youth 1981–2011, Ciccone Youth 1986–88, Free Kitten 1992–97, 2008–, Body/Head 2012–; collaborations with Ikue Mori, DJ Olive, William Winant, Lydia Lunch, Yoko Ono, Raymond Pettibon, Courtney Love, Chris Corsano. *Recordings include:* albums: with Sonic Youth: Sonic Youth 1982, Confusion is Sex 1983, Sonic Death 1984, Bad Moon Rising 1985, E.V.O.L. 1986, Sister 1987, Daydream Nation 1988, The Whitey Album 1989, Goo 1990, Dirty 1992, Experimental Jet Set, Trash and No Star 1994, Screaming Fields of Sonic Love 1995, Made in USA 1995, Washing Machine 1995, A Thousand Leaves 1998, SYR4: Goodbye 20th Century 1999, NYC Ghosts & Flowers 2000, Murray Street 2002, Sonic Nurse 2004, Rather Ripped 2006, The Destroyed Room: B-sides and Rarities 2006, The Eternal 2009; with Ciccone Youth: The Whitey Album 1989; with Free Kitten: Unboxed 1994, Nice Ass 1995, Sentimental Education 1997, Inherit 2008; with Body/Head: Coming Apart 2013. *Current Management:* c/o Michele Fleischli, Silva Artist Management, 722 Seward Street, Los Angeles, CA 90038-3504, USA. *Telephone:* (323) 856-8222. *E-mail:* mfleischli@sammusicbiz.com. *Website:* www.sammusicbiz.com; www.bodyheadmusic.com; www.sonicyouth.com.

GORDON, Lorraine; American jazz entrepreneur; m. 1st Alfred Lyons; m. 2nd Max Gordon (died 1990); two c. *Career:* Owner and Man. The Village Vanguard jazz club, New York 1990–. *Publication:* Alive at the Village Vanguard: My Life In and Out of Jazz Time 2006 (ASCAP Deems Taylor Award). *Honours:* Jazz at Lincoln Center Award for Lifetime Achievement 2002, Nat. Endowment for the Arts Jazz Masters Fellowship 2013. *Address:* The Village Vanguard, 178 Seventh Avenue South, New York, NY 10014, USA (office). *Telephone:* (212) 255-4037 (office). *Fax:* (212) 929 4589 (office). *E-mail:* email@villagevanguard.com (office). *Website:* www.villagevanguard.com (office).

GORDON, Noah Adrian, BEng; American singer, writer and musician (guitar, drums); b. 19 Sept. 1971, Pinckneyville, IL. *Career:* Charlie Daniels' Volunteer Jam, 1992; Nashville Now; Music City Tonight; Country Music Television; The Nashville Network; Nascar Country; Wal-Mart Country Music Across America Tour; TNN Wildhorse Saloon, 1994–95; founder mem. Phoenix 1999; mem. AFTRA; AFofM. *Recordings include:* albums: solo: I Need A Break 1995; other appearances: Christmas Time In Dixie, Charlie Daniels 1994–95. *Website:* www.myspace.com/noahgordonmusic.

GORDON, Robert; British music programmer; b. 4 Oct. 1966, Sheffield; 2 d. *Career:* mem., PRS, MCPS, PEMRA, PPL, Musicians' Union. *Compositions:* Track With No Name, The Forgemasters. *Recordings include:* House Arrest, Krush 1987, Wanted, Yazz 1988, Track with No Name, The Forgemasters, Rob Gordon Projects 1996, Ozooma 1996, Shiftwork, The Fall 1993, Remixed Pop Will Eat Itself, Art of Noise, Yellow Magic Orchestra, It's Now or Never 2007. *E-mail:* rob@fonstudios.com. *Website:* www.robgordonproductions.co.uk.

GORDON, William 'Flash'; American singer, songwriter, musician (bass, guitar) and actor; b. 16 March 1947, Miami, Florida; m. Mary Ellen Jesse. *Education:* United States Army Engineering School; Miami Dade Jr College. *Career:* played at Willie Nelson's Fourth of July Picnic, 1974, 1976; member: David Allan Coe band; toured with: Charlie Walker; Justin Tubb; Jan Howard; Bobby Lewis; various Grand Ole Opry stars; mem, BMI; Nashville

Publishers Network. *Compositions:* All You Ever Have To Do Is Touch Me, Charlie Rich; My Woman's Honky Tonkin' Me To Death, Mel Tillis; As Far As This Feeling Will Take Us, David Allan Coe; In The Arms of Cocaine, Hank Williams Jr (on gold-selling album); (She Won't Have A Thing To Do With) Nobody But Me, Alabama (on triple platinum-selling album). *Recordings:* albums: solo: Alternative Country 1992, Flash II 1995, Confessions of a Cowboy Singer 1999. *Current Management:* Georgia Boy Management, Box 265, Springfield, TN 37172, USA. *Address:* 4545 Mount Sharon Rd, Greenbrier, TN 37073, USA (home). *E-mail:* flashgordon327@charter.net (home). *Website:* www.flashgordonmusic.com (home).

GORDON, Wycliffe A.; American jazz musician (trombone, trumpet, tuba, didgeridoo), bandleader, composer, arranger and educator; *Faculty Member, Jazz Arts Program, Manhattan School of Music;* b. 29 May 1967, Waynesboro, Ga; s. of the late Lucius Gordon. *Education:* Butler High School, Augusta, Ga. *Career:* fmr mem. Wynton Marsalis Septet; fmr mem. Lincoln Center Jazz Orchestra; numerous recordings as bandleader and trombonist 1999–; Founder, Wycliffe Gordon Quartet; currently mem. US Statesmen of Jazz; Founder, Blues Back record label 2006–11; numerous recordings as sideman including with John Allred, Marcus Roberts, Maurice Hines, Eric Reed; performances with numerous artists including Tommy Flanagan, Dizzy Gillespie, Joe Henderson, Shirley Horn, Branford Marsalis; currently Faculty Mem., Jazz Arts Program, Manhattan School of Music. *Compositions include:* I Saw the Light (tribute to Muhammad Ali) 2004, Body and Soul (new score for silent film) 2008, Within Our Gates (new score for silent film) 2011, Apollo: Yesterday, Today and Tomorrow 2011, Beyond the Blackberry Patch 2012. *Recordings:* albums: as bandleader: Slidin' Home 1999, The Search 2000, The Gospel Truth 2000, What You Dealin' With 2001, United Soul Experience 2002, Dig This! 2003, In the Cross 2004, Cone's Coup 2006, This Rhythm on My Mind (with Jay Leonhart) 2006, Bloozbluzeblues 2007, Boss Bones 2009, Cone and T-Staff 2010, The Word 2011, Hello Pops – A Tribute to Louis Armstrong 2011, Dreams of New Orleans 2012, The Intimate Ellington/Ballads and Blues 2013; with Marcus Roberts: Deep in the Shed 1989; with Ron Westray: Bone Structure 1996; with Randy Sandke: The Music of Bob Haggart 2002; with John Allred: Head to Head 2002; with Eric Reed: We 2002, We 2 2007; with Maurice Hines: To Nat 'King' Cole with Love 2006. *Honours:* Dr hc (Univ. of Scranton) 2006; Jazz Journalists Asscn Critics Choice Award for Best Trombonist 2000, Jazz Journalists Asscn Awards for Trombonist of the Year 2001, 2002, 2006, 2007, 2008, 2011, 2012, 2013, ASCAP Concert Vanguard Award 2007. *Current Management:* c/o April Brumfield, Brumfield and Associates, 1430 Union City Road, Richmond, KY 40475, USA. *Telephone:* (859) 893-0621. *Fax:* (859) 972-0400. *E-mail:* april@brumfieldassociates.com. *Website:* www.brumfieldassociates.com. *Address:* Manhattan School of Music, 120 Claremont Avenue, New York, NY 10027, USA (office). *Telephone:* (212) 749-2802 (office). *E-mail:* coupdeconebiz@aol.com. *Website:* msmnyc.edu (office); www.wycliffegordon.com.

GORDY, Berry, Jr; American music industry executive and songwriter; b. 28 Nov. 1929, Detroit; s. of Berry Gordy, Sr and Bertha Fuller Gordy; m. 1st Thelma Coleman (divorced 1959); m. 2nd Raynoma Mayberry Liles (divorced 1964); m. 3rd Grace Eaton 1990 (divorced 1993); eight c. *Career:* owned record store in Detroit 1955; composer and ind. producer during late 1950s; Founder, Jobete Music 1958, Tamla Records 1959, Motown Record Corpn 1961–88; fmr Chair. The Gordy Co. *Films include:* Lady Sings The Blues (exec. producer) 1972, Mahogany (dir) 1975, The Last Dragon (exec. producer) 1985. *Play:* Motown: The Musical (co-producer) 2013. *Recordings include:* as composer/producer: Reet Petite (Jackie Wilson), Shop Around (The Miracles), Do You Love Me? (The Contours), Try It Baby (Marvin Gaye), Shotgun (Junior Walker and The All-Stars), I Want You Back and ABC (The Jackson 5), Compilation: The Music, The Magic, The Memories of Motown 1995. *Publication:* To Be Loved 1994 (autobiography). *Honours:* Dr hc (Michigan State Univ., Occidental Coll.); American Music Award, Outstanding Contrib. to Music Industry 1975, inducted into Rock and Roll Hall of Fame 1990, Michigan Rock and Roll Legends Hall of Fame 2009, NARAS Trustees Award 1991, Songwriters Hall of Fame Pioneer Award 2013. *Address:* Michael Lovesmith, West Grand Media LLC, 933 Cecina Way, Los Angeles, CA 90077, USA (office). *Telephone:* (818) 772-4443 (office). *Fax:* (818) 772-4454 (office). *E-mail:* mlovesmith@westgrandmedia.com (office). *Website:* www.westgrandmedia.com (office); www.berrygordy.com.

GORE, Martin Lee; British musician (keyboards, guitar), singer and songwriter; b. 23 July 1961, London; m. Suzanne Boisvert 1994 (divorced); three d. *Career:* Founder-mem., Depeche Mode 1980–; as prin. songwriter has written vast majority of songs recorded by the band 1982–; also solo artist. *Recordings include:* albums: with Depeche Mode: Speak and Spell 1981, A Broken Frame 1982, Construction Time Again 1983, Some Great Reward 1984, The Singles 81–85 1985, Black Celebration 1986, Music for the Masses 1987, 101 1989, Violator 1990, Songs of Faith & Devotion 1993, Ultra 1997, The Singles 86–98 1998, Dream On 2001, Exciter 2001, Playing the Angel 2005, Sounds of the Universe 2009, Delta Machine 2013; solo: Counterfeit 1989. *Honours:* BRIT Award (for Enjoy the Silence) 1991, Ivor Novello Award for Int. Achievement 1999, MTV Europe Music Award for Best Group 2006. *Current Management:* c/o Andrew Zweck, Sensible Events Ltd, Unit 6, Utopia Village, 7 Chalcot Road, London, NW1 8LH, England. *Telephone:* (20) 3468-9490. *E-mail:* andrew@sensibleevents.com. *Website:* www.sensibleevents.com; www.martingore.com; www.depechemode.com.

GORHAM, Scott; American rock musician (guitar); b. USA. *Career:* guitarist, pub circuit, with Fast Buck, early 1970s; guitarist, UK rock group Thin Lizzy, 1974–83; founder mem., 21 Guns, 1992; appearances with Thin Lizzy include: Reading Festival, 1974, 1975, 1983; Great British Music Festival, London, 1975; World Series of Rock, Cleveland, 1979; Monsters of Rock, European tour, 1983; reunion tribute to Phil Lynott, Self Aid concert, Dublin (with Bob Geldof), 1991. *Recordings:* Albums: with Thin Lizzy: Nightlife 1974, Fighting 1975, Jailbreak 1976, Johnny The Fox 1976, Bad Reputation 1977, Live And Dangerous 1978, Black Rose (A Rock Legend) 1979, Chinatown 1980, Adventures Of Thin Lizzy 1981, Renegade 1981, Thunder And Lightning 1983, Dedication – The Very Best Of Thin Lizzy 1991, Thin Lizzy Live 1992, Wild One 1996, One Night Only 2000; with Phenomena: Dream Runner 1987; with 21 Guns: Salute, 1992.

GÖRING, Brezel; German singer and musician (guitar, keyboard). *Career:* fmr project, Sigmund Freud Experience; Founder-mem., Stereo Total 1993–. *Recordings include:* albums: with Stereo Total: Oh Ah! 1995, Monokini 1997, Juke-Box Alarm 1999, My Melody 1999, Musique Automatique 2001, Do The Bambi 2005, Paris-Berlin 2007, No Controles 2009, Baby Ouh! 2010, Stereo Total: Cactus vs. Brezel 2012; solo: Bad News From The Stars. *Current Management:* c/o Wieland Kräme, Powerline Agency, Kastanienallee 29, 10435 Berlin, Germany. *Telephone:* (30) 47375290. *E-mail:* wk@powerline -agency.com. *Website:* www.powerline-agency.com. *E-mail:* stereototal@ stereototal.de. *Website:* www.stereototal.de.

GORMAN, Steve; American musician (drums); b. 17 Aug. 1965, Muskegon, Mich. *Education:* Western Kentucky Univ. *Career:* mem., Mary My Hope, Black Crowes 1987–2002, 2005–; concerts and festival appearances; played with Stereophonics for tour, following departure of their drummer Stuart Cable 2004; host, The Game 2012 (Nashville radio). *Recordings include:* albums: Shake Your Money Maker 1990, The Southern Harmony and Musical Companion 1992, Amorica 1994, Three Snakes and One Charm 1996, Sho Nuff: The Complete Black Crowes 1998, By Your Side 1999, Live at the Greek 2000, Tribute to A Work in Progress: Greatest Hits 1990–1999 2001, Lions 2001, Warpaint 2008, Before the Frost ...Until the Freeze 2009, Croweology 2010. *Honours:* Best New American Band, Best Male New Singer, Rolling Stone magazine 1991. *E-mail:* info@blackcrowes.com (office). *Website:* www .1025thegame.com; www.blackcrowes.com.

GORNA, Jarmila Xymena, MA; Polish composer, pianist, vocalist and sound engineer; b. 26 April 1967, Lodz. *Education:* Karol Szymanowski Acad. of Music. *Career:* numerous tv and radio broadcasts, concerts; mem. Musicians' Union. *Music for theatre:* composed music to Bram Stoker's Dracula, Bruntion Theatre Co. 1997, The Singularity Show, Albany Theatre, London 1998, Trojan Women, Cambridge Arts Theatre 1998, Elektra, Cambridge Arts Theatre 2001. *Film and television music:* composed music to TV documentary, Hidden Children 2001, sang on soundtrack to film, Luna Rossa 2001. *Compositions include:* Which Way?; Swansong; Always?; Dark Spell; The Swallow's Flight Dream; Tatra; Pebbles And Seagulls; Fairy Tale World; It's OK; Love Search; Until We Find It!; A Seal Upon Thy Heart; Approaching Your Insanity; My Hope; From There To Here; Closing, Silver Bird. *Recordings:* Hashgachah 2004, Furmanka. *Address:* Flat 4, 8 Clapton Terrace, London, E5 9BW, England (home). *E-mail:* info@jarmilagorna.com. *Website:* www.jarmilagorna.com.

GOROG, Chris; American b. Fontainebleau, France. *Education:* San Diego State Univ. *Career:* fmr Vice-Pres. Business Affairs, Motion Pictures and Television, Walt Disney Co.; fmr Pres. and CEO ITC Entertainment Group; fmr Pres. New Business Devt and Exec. Vice-Pres. Group Operations, Universal Studios Recreation Group; fmr Dir House of Blues, The Guitar Center; joined Roxio Inc. (owner of Napster) 2000; fmr Chair. and CEO Napster and Roxio Inc.; mem. Young Pres. Org., Acad. of Motion Picture Arts and Sciences. *Address:* gorog.net, 11434 Bellagio Road, Los Angeles, CA 90049, (office). *Telephone:* (310) 367-2510 (office). *E-mail:* info@gorog.net (office). *Website:* www.gorog.net (office).

GORR, Jon Carl; American composer and musician (keyboards); b. 26 Sept. 1958, Fredericksburg, Virginia. *Education:* Jazz Composition, Chatauqua Institute, 1975; BM, Jazz Composition, Berklee College of Music, 1980. *Career:* President, Massmedia, 1983–; Songwriter, Cortlem Production, 1983–88; Castle Music, 1984–87; Keyboard player for: I-Tones; Eek-A-Mouse; Mighty Diamonds; Horace Andy, 1980–88; Steve Recker, 1986–87; Bo Diddley, 1987–88; Keyboard player, Gladiators (Europe), 1988–89; Composer, television and film music; Film appearance: Day of The Dead, 1976; Television appearance: Spenser For Hire, 1987. *Recordings:* albums: It's No Lie 1985, Walk On By 1985, On The Right Track 1988. *Honours:* Boston Music Award, Best Reggae Band, 1987; Beat Magazine Readers Poll, Best Keyboard Player, 1987. *E-mail:* jon@jongorr.com.

GORRIE, Alan; Scottish singer, musician (bass, guitar, keyboards), composer and painter; *Band Leader and Administrator, Average Enterprises LLC*; b. 19 July 1946, Perth. *Education:* Perth Acad., Dundee Art Coll. *Career:* mem. The Vikings, Scotland 1964–67; mem. Scots of St James, London 1967–68; mem. Forever More, London 1969–71; Founder and bandleader, The Average White Band 1972–83, 1989–; mem. Daryl Hall Band and Hall and Oates 1993–94; int. performances, festival appearances and tours; mem. Performing Right Soc., American Soc. of Composers, Authors and Publrs (ASCAP), American Fed. of Television and Radio Artists. *Film scores:* Take Some Girls 1969, The Fast Kill 1971. *Recordings include:* albums: Show Your Hand 1973,

Average White Band 1974, Cut The Cake 1975, Soul Searching 1976, Person To Person 1977, Benny and Us 1977, Warmer Communications 1977, Atlantic Family Live at Montreux 1977, Feel No Fret 1979, Shine 1980, Vol. VIII 1980, Cupid's In Fashion 1982, Sleepless Nights (solo) 1985, Aftershock 1989, Soul Alone (with Daryl Hall) 1993, Soul Tattoo 1996, Face to Face 1997, Living in Colour 2003, Greatest & Latest 2005, Soul and The City 2006, Times Squared 2009. *Exhibitions:* First Look, Ramscale Gallery, New York 2009. *Honours:* ASCAP R&B Awards 1993, 1996, Nordoff-Robbins Lifetime Achievement Award 2000, First Prize (Painting), Summer Exhbn, Silvermine Arts Guild, Conn. *Current Management:* c/o Free Trade Agency, 20–22 Curtain Street, London, EC2A 3NQ, England; c/o The Agency Group Ltd, 1880 Century Park East, Suite 711, Los Angeles, CA 90067, USA. *Telephone:* (20) 7655-6900 (London); (310) 856-4477 (Los Angeles). *Fax:* (203) 966-6493 (USA). *Website:* www.averagewhiteband.com.

GOSS, Kieran John, LLB; British songwriter and singer; b. 18 May 1962, Newry, Northern Ireland. *Education:* Queen's Univ., Belfast. *Career:* numerous TV appearances, tours of Ireland, UK, Australia, New Zealand, USA; mem. Musicians' Union. *Recordings include:* Brand New Star, Frances Black and Kieran Goss, New Day 1995, Worse Than Pride 1998, Red Letter Day 2000. *Current Management:* c/o Cog Communications, Temple Lodge, Dromore West, Sligo, Ireland. *Website:* www.kierangoss.com.

GOSSARD, Stone; American musician (guitar); b. 20 July 1966, Seattle, Wash. *Career:* mem., Green River 1987–89, Mother Love Bone 1989, Pearl Jam 1990–, Temple of the Dog 1991; Founder-mem., Shame, later renamed Brad 1993–; numerous concerts and festival appearances; collaborations with Three Fish, Neil Young, Josh Freese, Meganut, Steve Turner, Caspar Babypants. *Recordings include:* albums: with Pearl Jam: Ten 1991, Vs. 1993, Vitalogy 1994, Merkin Ball 1995, No Code 1996, Yield 1998, Live on Two Legs 1998, Binaural 2000, Riot Act 2002, Pearl Jam 2006, Backspacer 2009, Lightning Bolt 2013; with Mother Love Bone: Shine (EP) 1989, Apple 1990; with Temple of the Dog: Temple Of The Dog 1992; with Brad: Shame 1993, Interiors 1997, Welcome To Discovery Park 2002, Brad vs Satchel 2005, Best Friends? 2010, United We Stand 2012; solo album: Bayleaf 2001, Moonlander 2013. *Honours:* American Music Awards for Favorite New Artist, Pop/Rock and Hard Rock categories 1993, Favorite Alternative Artist 1996, 1999, Favorite Heavy Metal/Hard Rock Artist 1996, Rolling Stone Readers Awards for Best New American Band, Best Video 1993. *Website:* www.bradcorporation .com; www.pearljam.com.

GOTO, Suguru; Japanese composer and multimedia artist. *Career:* uses innovative tech. in the creation and performance of his work, including computers, electronics and robots; based at L'Institut de Recherche et Coordination Acoustique/Musique (IRCAM), Paris 1996–; has worked at Electronic Music Studio, NHK Broadcasting Co., Tokyo, Electro-acoustic Studio, Tech. Univ. of Berlin, and STEIM Foundation, Amsterdam; technical creations have included the Superpolm (a virtual violin), the Bodysuit (using sensors attached to human body), and a robot ensemble; Composer-in-Residence, ACREQ and Montréal Conservatory, Canada 1998; has given solo recitals at ICC, Tokyo, Atheneum, Belfort, Pompidou Centre, France. *Compositions include:* VirtualAERI II, o.m.2-g.i.-p.p., RoboticMusic, CsO, Resonance II. *Honours:* Boston Symphony Orchestra Fellowship, Tanglewood Music Center Koussevitzky Prize, first prize Marzena Int. Composition Competition, Senate Admin for Cultural Affairs Berliner Kompositionauft-räge 1993, UNESCO IMC Int. Rostrum of Composers Prize. *Current Management:* c/o Le Studio Interactif, 7 rue des Beaux-Arts, Bordeaux 33800, France. *Telephone:* 5-56-33-49-10. *Fax:* 5-56-31-46-23. *E-mail:* lestudiointeractif@gmail.com. *E-mail:* sugurugoto@free.fr. *Website:* suguru .goto.free.fr.

GOTT, Karel; Czech singer; b. 14 July 1939, Plzeň; two d. *Education:* Prague Conservatory (studied under Prof. Karenin). *Career:* mem. Semafor Theatre, Prague 1963–65; mem. Apollo Theatre, Prague, 1965–67; freelance artist 1967–; numerous foreign tours; charity concerts with Eva Urbanová 1998; CD Rocky mého mládí (Rocks of my Youth) 1999; exhbn of paintings, Bratislava 1999; f. and Chair. Interpo Foundation 1993–96; concerts in Carnegie Hall, New York, Expo, Hanover, Kremlin Palace, Moscow 2000; charity concerts in Czech Repub. after 2002 floods. *Radio:* presenter monthly show Radio Impuls 2002–. *Film appearance:* Luck from Hell. *Recordings include:* Vánoce ve zlaté Praze 1969, 42 největších hitů 1991, Věci blízké mému srdci 1993, Zázrak vánoční 1995, Belcanto 1996, Duety s Lucií Bilou 1997, Miluj 1997, Svátek svátků 1998, Rocky mého mládí 1999, Originální nahrávky ze 70.let 2000, Originální nahrávky ze 80.let 2000, Originální nahrávky ze 90.let 2000, Pokaždé 2002, Gott & Vondaáčková 2003, Lásko má 2004, Můj strážný anděl 2004, K. Gott zpívá hity K. Svobody 2005, Jsou svátky 2006, Má pout' 2006, Každý má svůj sen 2007, Zlatá Kolekce 2007, Zmírám láskou 2008, Leben 2009, Oslava 70 narozenin 2009, Frohe Weihnacht 2010, Sentiment 2011, Dotek lásky 2012. *Publication:* Why Painting is Important for Me 2001. *Honours:* Golden Nightingale trophy (annual pop singer poll 1963–66, 1968–81, 1983, 1989–90, 1997–2001), MIDEM Prize, Cannes 1967, MIDEM Gold Record 1969, Polydor Gold Record 1970, Supraphon Gold Record 1972, 1973, 1979, 1980, 1996, Music Week Star of the Year 1974 (UK) 1975, Artist of Merit 1982, Gold Aerial 1983, radio station BRT (Belgium) 1984, Nat. Artist 1985, Polydor Golden Pin (Germany) 1986, Czech Nightingale Trophy 1996, 1997, 1999, 2001, 2002 (28 times in total), Czech TV Prize 1997, 1999, Platinum Record (for duets with Lucia Bílá) 1998 and many other awards. *Current Management:* GOJA spol. s r.o., Pod Prusekem 3, 102 00 Prague 10,

Czech Republic. *Telephone:* (2) 72658337. *Fax:* (2) 72659265. *E-mail:* goja@ goja.cz. *Website:* www.goja.cz. *Address:* Nad Bertramkou 18, 150 00 Prague 5, Czech Republic (home). *Website:* www.karelgott.com; www.karel-gott.de.

GOTT, Larry; British musician (guitar); b. 24 July 1957, England. *Career:* mem., James 1985–96, re-formed 2007–; numerous tours, festival dates and TV appearances; coll. teacher. *Recordings include:* albums: Stutter 1986, Strip Mine 1988, One Man Clapping 1989, Gold Mother 1990, Seven 1992, Laid 1993, Wah Wah 1994, Getting Away With It 2002, Hey Ma 2008, The Night Before 2010, The Morning After 2010, La Petite Mort 2014. *Address:* c/o Mercury Records, 364–366 Kensington High Street, London W14 8NS, England (office). *Website:* www.wearejames.com.

GOTT, Susan (Susi), BA; American musician (fiddle), singer and songwriter; b. 4 Sept. 1962, Asheville, NC; m. Christian Séguret, 30 Sept. 1990, one s., one d. *Career:* Performing, including The Smithsonian National Institute, 1977; The Kennedy Center, with Masters of Bluegrass, 1986; NPR's All Things Considered, 1982; Nashville Networks' Fire on the Mountain; The Knoxville World's Fair, 1982; Sacrée Soirée, Paris, with Hugues Aufray; mem., International Bluegrass Music Assn; Women in Bluegrass; SACEM. *Compositions:* Bound for New Orleans; Dancing Man; Hole in the Deep Blue Sea, with Christian Séguret. *Recordings:* CMH with Eddie Adcock and Talk of the Town; Cowbell Hollow; A Video Postcard of the Blue Ridge, with David Holt; Talking Feet, with Mike Seeger; Guitars, with Christian Séguret and Thierry Massoulore. *Honours:* Champion Fiddler, Fiddler's Grove, 1978, 1984; First Place Songwriter, Chris Austin Songwriting Contest, 1996. *Address:* AJL Productions, 1 rue du Pourtour, 45340 Auxy, France (office). *Telephone:* 80-54-89-72 (office). *E-mail:* sgseg@wanadoo.fr (home).

GOTTI, Irv; American music company executive and producer; *CEO, The Inc. Records;* b. (Irv Lorenzo), Hollis, Queens, New York; m. Debbie Gotti. *Career:* began music career as DJ Irv; fmr producer Island Def Jam Records, artistes produced include Ashanti, Charli Baltimore, Toni Braxton, DMX, Ja Rule, Jay-Z; currently CEO Murder Inc. Records, now known as The Inc. Records. *Recordings include:* Irv Gotti Presents. . . (series of albums). *Address:* c/o The Inc. Records, 2220 Colorado Avenue, Santa Monica, CA 90404, USA (office). *Website:* www.theincrecords.com (office).

GOTTLIEB, Gordon, BMus, MMus; American percussionist, conductor and composer; b. 23 Oct. 1948, Brooklyn, NY. *Education:* High School of Performing Arts, Juilliard School of Music, studied with James Wimer, Saul Goodman. *Career:* extensive performing with New York Philharmonic, including solo appearances 1974 and 1986; commissioning and performing new works for piano and percussion with brother Jay, active in contemporary music and has played with Contemporary Chamber Ensemble, Speculum Musicae, the Juilliard Ensemble, the Group for Contemporary Music and others; as conductor performed the New York premiere of Vesalii Icones by Peter Maxwell Davies and made his Carnegie Hall debut conducting William Walton's Facade with Anna Russell narrating 1981; conducted Histoire du Soldât of Stravinsky with L'Ensemble and Shaker Loops of John Adams at the Santa Fe Chamber Musical Festival 1986; performed with Stevie Wonder, Ray Charles, Patti LaBelle, Tony Bennett, Paula Abdul, Michael Bolton, Bette Midler, Sarah Vaughan, Quincy Jones, Al Jarreau, Paul Winter; mem. Percussive Arts Soc., NARAS, Recording Musicians' Asscn. *Compositions:* Graines gemellaires (improvisation 1), Traversées (improvisation 2) Saudades do Brasil, The River Speaker, Improvisations with Jay Gottlieb, Ritual Dancer, Fanfare (with Paul Winter), various jingles. *Recordings:* History, Michael Jackson; Kingdom of the Sun, film with Sting; Bulletproof Heart, with Grace Jones; A Secret Life, with Marianne Faithfull; Romulus Hunt, My Romance, with Carly Simon; Sostice Live!, Prayer for the Wild Things, with Paul Winter; Pete, Pete Seeger; many films and jingles; Bartók, Sonata for 2 Pianos; Histoire du Soldât, I Stravinsky; Two Against Nature, Steely Dan (four Grammy awards, including Album of the Year 2001); Everything Must Go, Steely Dan, 2003, Something to Be, Rob Thomas 2005, Morph the Cat, Donald Fagen 2006, Circus Money, Walter Becker 2008, Duets II, Tony Bennett 2011. *Publications:* The Percussion of Carnival, for Modern Percussionist magazine 1984, World Influences: Africa and South India 1985, contrib. three articles on studio playing 1985. *Honours:* Martha Baird Rockefeller grant 1980, four Grammy Awards (including for Paul Winters, Prayer for the Wild Things 1994, Pete Seeger, Pete), NARAS Most Valuable Player Award, New York Studios 1989, Meet the Composer grant 1989. *E-mail:* gorgot@earthlink.net.

GOTTWALD, Lukasz Sebastian (Luke), (Dr Luke); American songwriter, musician (guitar), record producer and record company executive; *Founder and Head, Kemosabe Records;* b. 26 Sept. 1973, Westerly, RI; s. of Janusz Jerzy Gottwald and Laura Gottwald. *Career:* lead guitarist for house band, Saturday Night Live (NBC-TV) 1997–2007; fmr session guitarist, numerous advertisements; fmr remixer for artists including KRS-One, Mos Def, Nappy Roots; record producer and songwriter 2004–; Co-founder and Owner, Kasz Money Publishing and Prescription Songs; Founder and head, Kemosabe Records 2011–. *Compositions:* numerous hit songs as writer or co-writer including: Since U Been Gone, Kelly Clarkson 2004, Who Knew, Pink 2006, Girlfriend, Avril Lavigne 2007, About You Now, Sugababes 2007, I Kissed a Girl, Katy Perry 2008, Circus, Britney Spears 2008, Right Round, Flo Rida 2009, My Life Would Suck Without You, Kelly Clarkson 2009, Party in the USA, Miley Cyrus 2009, California Gurls, Katy Perry 2010, Dynamite, Taio Cruz 2010, Take it Off, Kesha 2010, Hold It Against Me, Britney Spears 2011,

Part of Me, Katy Perry 2012, Price Tag, Jessie J 2012, Wrecking Ball, Miley Cyrus 2013, Roar, Katy Perry 2013. *Recordings:* albums: as artist: The Fighting Temptations 2003; as producer: numerous including: Breakaway, Kelly Clarkson 2004, I'm Not Dead, Pink 2005, The Best Damn Thing, Avril Lavigne 2007, One of the Boys, Katy Perry 2008, Circus, Britney Spears 2008, Animal, Kesha 2010, Teenage Dream, Katy Perry 2010, Cannibal, Kesha 2011, Femme Fatale, Britney Spears 2011, Who You Are, Jessie J 2011, TY.O, Taio Cruz 2011, Talk That Talk, Rihanna 2011, Warrior, Kesha 2012, Prism, Katy Perry 2013. *Honours:* ASCAP Awards for Songwriter of the Year 2010, 2011. *Address:* c/o Kemosabe Records, Sony Music Entertainment, 550 Madison Avenue, New York, NY 10022, USA (office). *Telephone:* (212) 833-8000 (office). *Website:* kemosabeonline.com (office); www.sonymusic.com (office).

GOUGH, Damon (see Badly Drawn Boy)

GOUGH, Orlando; British composer; b. 24 Aug. 1953, Brighton, England; m. Joanna Osborne, 2 Dec. 1989, two s. *Career:* Member of Bands: The Lost Jockey, 1978–82; Man Jumping, 1983–87; Founded the choir The Shout, 1998. *Compositions:* Hoovering the Beach, 1979; Buzz Buzz Buzz Went the Honeybee, 1980; Secret Gardens, 1981; New Tactics, 1982; Further and Further into the Night, 1984; Mozart At Palm Springs, 1983–84; Bosendorfer Waltzes, 1985; Weighing The Heart, 1986–87; Goes Without Saying, 1988; Mathematics of a Kiss, 1989; Savage Water, 1989; Currulao, 1989; Late, 1991; Lives of the Great Poisoners, 1991; Slow Walk, Fast Talk, 1992; The Air Shouts, 1992; Earth Bound, 1993; Saeta, 1993; The Empress, 1992–93; Escape at Sea, 1994; On the Rim of the World, 1994–97; Badenheim, 1995; People's Century, 1995–97; Sleeping with Audrey, 1996; Hotel, 1996–97; Room of Cooks, 1996–97; Room of Cooks, 1997; Axaxaxas Mlo, 1997; When We Stop Talking, 1998; The Shouting Fence, 1998; Why Do You Sing?, 1998; Corona, 1999; Pierrot: A Biography, 1999; Fortune Cookies 1999, A Ring A Lamp A Thing (British Composer Awards Stage Works category 2011) 2010. *Recordings:* Message From the Border, 1996; The Dancing Lawn, 1999. *Publications:* The Complete A Level Maths, 1987. *Address:* 12 Spencer Rise, London NW5 1AP, England. *Website:* www.theshout.org.

GOUIRAND, Gérard 'Doudou'; French musician (saxophone) and composer; b. 28 April 1940, Menton; m. Monica Adrian 1966; two s. one d. *Education:* university. *Career:* played at many festivals, tours worldwide. *Recordings include:* albums: Islands 1981, Mouvements Naturels 1983, Chanting and Dancing 1985, Forgotten Tales 1986, Space 1987, La Nuit de Wounded Knee 1990, Le Matin d'un Fauve 1994, Nino Rota/Fellini 1995, Passages 1999, Les Racines du ciel 2002, Boleros 2006. *Website:* doudou .gouirand.free.fr.

GOULD, Tony, BMus, MA, PhD; Australian musician (piano), composer and educator; b. 21 Feb. 1940, Melbourne. *Education:* Melbourne Univ., Monash Univ., LaTrobe Univ. *Career:* Lecturer, Univ. of Melbourne 1973–83; Head, Postgraduate Dept and Improvisation Dept, School of Music, Victorian Coll. of Arts, Melbourne; Chief Music Critic, Herald Sun; mem. Australia Council Music Fund. *Compositions include:* Concerto for Percussion, Violin, Viola Piano and Saxophone; Music for Narration of Dylan Thomas's Under Milk Wood; Music for various jazz ensembles. *Recordings include:* Gould Plus Gould, Best of Friends, Tony Gould Quartet, Chronicle, Lirill, Tin Roof For The Rain, At the End of the Day: A Ramble on Irish Melodies, The Very Thought of You. *Publications include:* contrib. New Grove Dictionary of Jazz, 1988, 1999, Oxford Companion to Australian Music, 1997. *Address:* PO Box 493, Elwood, Vic. 3184, Australia. *E-mail:* gould3184@gmail.com. *Website:* www.tonygould.com.

GOULDING, Elena Jane (Ellie); British singer, songwriter and musician; b. 30 Dec. 1986, Lyonshall, Herefords., England; d. of Arthur Goulding and Tracey Clark. *Education:* Lady Hawkins' School, Kington, Univ. of Kent. *Career:* signed to Polydor Records 2009; supported Little Boots on UK tour 2009; supported John Mayall on UK tour 2010; sang at wedding reception of Prince William and Kate Middleton 2011; songwriter for Gabrielle Climi, Diana Vickers; collaborated with Skrillex, Calvin Harris, Zedd, Jessie J, Tinie Tempah; performed at numerous festivals including iTunes, Glastonbury, V Festival, Isle of Wight Bestival, BBC Radio 1's Big Weekend, Lollapalooza. *Recordings:* albums: Lights 2010, Halcyon 2012, Delirium 2015. *Honours:* Winner, BBC Sound of 2010 Poll 2010, BRIT Awards Critics' Choice Award 2010, Glamour Magazine Award for Pandora Newcomer of the Year 2011, Q Magazine Best Solo Artist Award 2013. *Current Management:* c/o Turn First Artists, Grove Studios, Adie Road, London, W6 0PW, England. *Telephone:* (20) 8742-6700. *E-mail:* info@turnfirstartists.com. *Website:* www.turnfirstartists .com; www.elliegoulding.com.

GOULDMAN, Graham Keith; songwriter and musician (guitar, bass); b. 10 May 1946, Manchester; m. Gill Gouldman 1988; three s. (one by a previous m.) three d. (one by a previous m.). *Career:* many concert tours, TV and radio appearances as mem., 10cc; mem. Musicians' Union, PRS, Soc. of Distinguished Songwriters. *Compositions include:* for The Yardbirds: For Your Love; Heart Full of Soul; for The Hollies: Bus Stop; Look Thru Any Window; for Herman's Hermits: No Milk Today; co-wrote for 10cc: Rubber Bullets; Wall Street Shuffle; I'm Mandy Fly Me; Good Morning Judge; I'm Not In Love; Things We Do For Love; Dreadlock Holiday; co-wrote for Wax: Bridge To Your Heart; co-wrote Straight To Video, with Kirsty MacColl, 1999. *Recordings include:* 10cc hit singles: Donna 1972, Rubber Bullets (No. 1, UK) 1973, The Dean and I 1973, Wall Street Shuffle 1974, Silly Love, 1974, Life is a

Minestrone 1975, I'm Not in Love (No. 1, UK; No. 2, USA) 1975, Art for Art's Sake 1975, I'm Mandy Fly Me 1976, The Things We Do for Love 1976, Good Morning Judge 1977, Dreadlock Holiday (No. 1, UK) 1978, 10cc Alive 1995, Two from Ten 2000, Dressed to Kill 2002, Donna 2005; solo: Graham Gouldman Thing 1968, Animalolympics 1980, And Another Thing 2002, Love and Work 2012. *Honours:* Ivor Novello Awards (for Rubber Bullets, I'm Not In Love), BMI citations. *Website:* www.grahamgouldman.info.

GOUPY, Christian; French composer and musician (piano); b. 21 June 1962, Evreux. *Education:* Brevet de Technician Superieur Mechanique et Automatisme, American School of Modern Music, Conservatoire Int., Paris. *Career:* concerts in France with The Footprints Quintet and The Croco Jazz Big Band; pianist, Dagorno Restaurant, Paris; now working with the marching band, Les Pieds Mobiles (piano, saxophone and drums) playing jazz, funk and groove music; numerous compositions for saxophone (Quatuor de Saxophones de Paris). *Films:* 45 short films about India, Myanmar and diving. *Recordings:* Escale, Footprints Quintet; Oh Happy Day, Voce Vita Gospel Group; Next To, Croco Jazz Big Band, Impressions d'Inde, 25 courts metrages sur l'Inde; Voyages, Christian Goupy Piano Solo 2003, Voyages 2 (piano solo) 2010, Prise de vue – Montage – Musique Christian Goupy 2012. *Publications:* Quatuors de Saxs 1998, 2000. *Address:* 18 Impasse St Sébastien, 75011 Paris, France (office). *Telephone:* 1-43-38-71-04 (office). *E-mail:* chgfrance111@hotmail.com (home). *Website:* www.christiangoupy.com.

GOURDIKIAN, Herve; French musician (saxophones, piano); b. 31 Dec. 1966, Lyon; m. Olga Kroutolapova 1992; one d. *Education:* Berklee Coll. of Music, USA, French Conservatory, Lyon. *Career:* currently mem. Sidji Moon (with Laurent Cokelaere). *Recordings include:* with Liane Foly: Reve Orange, Cameleon, Lumières, Sweet Misery, Acoustique 1999, Entre Nous 2001, Fur et a Mesure: Best of Liane Foly 2003; with Nilda Fernandez, HMF, Mellow Man, Brigitte Fontaine, Mario Stanchen; with Sidji Moon: Nomades 2005, Kontrast 2010. *Current Management:* c/o Cristal Records, BP 138, 17005 La Rochelle Cedex 1, France. *E-mail:* celine@cristalprod.com. *Website:* www .sidjimoon.com.

GOURLEY, Sean; French jazz musician (guitar) and singer; b. 12 Dec. 1963, Paris; s. of Jimmy Gourley. *Education:* studied in the USA. *Career:* singer, musician and arranger for own band, playing bebop jazz, concerts, clubs; mem., Family Affair Band; numerous festival appearances; played with Barney Wilen, Stephanie Crawford, Kim Parker, with arrangers Onzy Mathews, Mundell Lowe. *Recordings include* with Stefan Patry: Bam Bam Bam 1996, with Manda Djinn: Back To Jazz 1997; with Jil Caplan: A Tribute to Antonio Carlos Jobim 1997; with Sanseverino: Le Tango Des Gens 2001, Les Sénégalaises 2004, Les Faux Talbins 2009, Honky Tonk 2013; with Jimmy Gourley: Straight Ahead Express 2004. *Address:* 26 boulevard Bessières, 75017 Paris, France (home). *Telephone:* 1-42-28-61-36 (home). *Website:* www .reverbnation.com/seangourley.

GOVERT, Eddy Van Mouffaert; Belgian accordionist, songwriter and producer; b. 15 Jan. 1949, Bruges; m. Anneke Van Thorre 1991; two d. *Education:* Muziek Conservatorium, Bruges. *Career:* band player 1964–70; singer and songwriter 1970–; solo as international accordion act Le Grand Julot 1973–; f. Jump Records and Music 1975; mem. SABAM, URADEX (Brussels), ZAMU (Brussels). *Recordings include:* with Paul Severs: Ik Ben Verliefd Op Jou 1971, Love 1972; with Ronald and Donald: Couac Couac 1974; with Ricky Gordon: Such A Night; with Margriet Hermans: Don Bosco; many top 10 hits 1975–81; as Eddy Govert: Te Kort Van Duur 1988; albums: Belgian Accordion Championship 1965, International 1 1991, International 2 1993, , Het Complete Overzicht 2010. *Honours:* Golden Lion Joepie 1974, Gold Record 1974, Cultuurprys Erpe-Mere 1996. *Current Management:* c/o Happy Melody VZW, Paul Gilsonstraat 31, 8200 Sint-Andries, Belgium. *Telephone:* (5) 031-63-80. *Fax:* (5) 031-52-35. *E-mail:* happy.melody@belgacom.net.

GRAAE, Silas; Danish musician (drums). *Career:* Founder-mem. Mew 1996–; the band formed record label, Evil Office 2000. *Recordings include:* albums: A Triumph For Man 1997, Half The World Is Watching Me 2000, Frengers (Danish Music Critics Award for Album of the Year) 2003, Mew And The Glass Handed Kites 2005, No More Stories 2009, Eggs Are Funny 2010. *Honours:* Danish Music Critics Award for Band of the Year 2003, MTV Europe Music Award for Best Danish Act 2005. *E-mail:* hq@evil-office.net (office). *Website:* www.evil-office.net (office); www.mewsite.com.

GRABOWSKI, Stephan C.; Danish musician (drums), singer, composer, producer and arranger; b. 18 Dec. 1964, Copenhagen; one d. *Education:* lessons with Hans Fagt, Hanne Bekow. *Career:* played with Lars H.U.G. 1987–93; solo artist 1994–; several nat. tours; several radio and TV appearances and gigs in France, Russia, Greenland; performances with Love Shop, Janes Rejoice, Goldfinger and special appearances with Peter Belli, Caroline Henderson, Thomas Di Leva, Elisabeth, Shirtsville, Nina Forsberg, Nanna; has also produced and arranged for numerous Danish artists; mem. Artisten, Danish Artist Union, DPA. *Compositions:* Girl in the Ghetto 1993, Crazy Restless Summer, Who Are You? 1996, Verden Fuld Af Frugt, Gaderne Hvisker 1997. *Recordings:* Glitter Angels 1993, Songs For Night Clubs 1996, Underligere End Kaerlighed 1997, Danmark Drømmer 1999, Kings for an Evening 2003, Bombay Feber 2009, Bad Boy Bollywood, with Republique Theatre 2011. *Honours:* grant, Nat. Arts Trust 1994, 1996, numerous Grammy Awards with Lars H.U.G. 1990–92. *Address:* Nørrebrogade 70, 1.th, 2200 Copenhagen N, Denmark (home). *E-mail:* stephangrabowski@ hotmail.com (office). *Website:* www.stephangrabowski.dk.

GRACIE, Charles (Charlie); American singer and musician (guitar); b. 14 May 1936, Philadelphia, PA; m. Joan D'Amato 1958; one s. one d. *Education:* tutored by father, Sam Gracie; studied guitar under professional teacher Anthony Panto. *Career:* Youthful Guitar Prodigy, Paul Whiteman TV Teen Show; played on radio commercials for the Sealtest, Big Top, CBS program; cut first record 1951 (age 15); first Rock & Roll star to emerge from Philadelphia, Pa; headlined The Alan Freed Show, Brooklyn Paramount 1957; Ed Sullivan Show; numerous appearances on American Bandstand TV; headlined the London Hippodrome and Palladium 1957 (first solo US rocker to tour UK), Yarmouth Rock Festival, England 1980s; continued annual tours of Europe including Italy, Germany, England, France, Finland; opened major US shows for, and recorded with, Van Morrison 2000; mem. ASCAP, BMI. *Films:* Jamboree 1958. *Compositions:* Fabulous, incl. on album, Run Devil Run, Paul McCartney 1999. *Recordings:* albums: Charlie Gracie – The Cameo Parkway Sessions 1979, Amazing Gracie 1982, Charlie Gracie – Live At The Stockton Globe 1957 1996, It's Fabulous – It's Charlie Gracie (compilation) 1996, I'm All Right 2001, Baby Doll 2012; singles include: Butterfly (Gold disc) 1957, Fabulous, I Love You So Much. *Current Management:* Paul Barrett, R & R Enterprises, 21 Grove Terrace, Penarth CF64 2NG, Wales. *Telephone:* (29) 2070-4279. *E-mail:* barrettrocknroll@ntlworld.com. *Address:* 820 Edmonds Avenue, Drexel Hill, PA 19026, USA (home). *Website:* www.charliegracie.com (home).

GRADY, John; American music company executive. *Career:* fmrly at Capitol Records, Arista Records, MCA Records and A&M Records; Sr Vice-Pres. Sales, Marketing and Promotion, Mercury Nashville and Lost Highway Records 1993–2002; Pres. DMZ Records 2002–03; Pres. and CEO Sony Nashville 2003–06; Partner, Redlight Management –2009; Head, Borman Management 2009–10; currently Partner, Crush Management Nashville; Pres. I.R.S. Nashville 2013–; fmr Chair. Acad. of Country Music; Trustee Country Music Hall of Fame. *Honours:* YP Nashville Impact Award 2013. *Address:* Crush Management Nashville, 1227 17th Avenue South, Unit 2, Nashville, TN 37212, USA (office). *E-mail:* info@crushmm.com (office). *Website:* www .crushmm.com/#nashville (office).

GRAESSER, Johann (Hanno) Peter, MA, DPhil; German violin teacher, publisher and music scientist; b. 26 Dec. 1961, Wehrda. *Education:* Music Coll., Dortmund, Univ. of Munich, Univ. of Giessen. *Publications include:* Jazz Violin 1991, Stéphane Grappelli's Violintechnik 1994, Der Jazzgeiger Stéphane Grappelli 1996, Stéphane Grappelli und die Musik des Quintette du Hot Club de France 1997, Electric Violins 1998.

GRAF, Bernd Heinrich, (Der Graf); German singer, songwriter and musician (keyboards). *Career:* Founder mem. Unheilig 1999–; released debut single Sage Ja! (Say Yes!) 1999, debut album 2001; numerous live tours including support slots with L'Ame Immortelle and Terminal Choice, and at festivals. *Recordings include:* albums: with Unheilig: Phosphor 2000, Frohes Fest 2002, Das 2. Gebot 2003, Zelluloid 2004, Moderne Zeiten 2006, Puppenspiel 2008, Grosse Freiheit (Diva Award for Album of the Year 2010, ECHO Award for Album of the Year 2010) 2010, Lichter der Stadt 2012. *Honours:* as Der Graf: Video Champions Award for Best Personality 2012; with Unheilig: Bambi Pop National Award 2010, Diva Awards for Artist of the Year 2010, for Best Single (for Geboren um zu Leben) 2010, ECHO Awards for Most Successful Production Team 2011, for Best National Rock/Alternative Group 2011, Swiss Music Award for Best Breakout Int. 2011, Rainbow Radio Band Award for National Band 2011, Comet Award for Best Song (for Geborem um zu Leben) 2011. *Address:* c/o Universal Music GmbH, Stralauer Allee 1, 10245 Berlin, Germany (office). *Website:* www.universalmusic.de (office); www.unheilig.com; www.myspace.com/Unheilig.

GRAHAM, Bruce Hebenton; Scottish musician (multi-instrumentalist), composer, author and entertainer; b. 9 Nov. 1941, Dundee; s. of Thomas Galloway Graham and Christina Hebenton; m. 1st Phyllis Elizabeth McFarlane 1963; one adopted d.; m. 2nd Sharon Belinda Maxim 1988. *Education:* pvt. tuition, Schillinger course in composition, studied with Henry Nelmes Forbes. *Career:* session musician; Musical Dir London recording, TV and film studios, West End Theatres; Founder Jingles Records and Jingles Music 1985; featured in cabaret, Old Tyme Music Halls, one-man keyboard concerts 1988; second one-man show based on comedy and piano style of Victor Borge; worked with Andy Williams, Rock Hudson, Juliet Prowse, Lulu, The Three Degrees, Sacha Distel, Bob Hope, Sir Harry Secombe, Faith Brown, Tommy Steele, Paul Daniels, Cleo Laine and John Dankworth, Matt Monro, Bruce Forsyth, Marti Webb, Richard Chamberlain, Vince Hill, Jimmy Shand, Jeff Wayne, Des O'Connor, Rolf Harris, Val Doonican, Anthony Newley, Helen Reddy, Wayne Sleep, David Hemmings, Michael Crawford, Lionel Blair, Gemma Craven, Toni Basil, Miss World TV Orchestra, Andrew Lloyd Webber, Phil Tate, Ray McVay, Johnny Howard, Ike Isaacs, Geoff Love; orchestras include Sydney Thompson's Old Tyme, Nat. Philharmonic, London Concert, BBC Radio, Scottish Radio, Northern Dance, London Palladium; own small groups; mem. Musicians' Union, Equity, British Music Writers' Council. *Compositions include:* nine symphonies, A Divertimenti for strings, Reverie for brass band, Brass Quintet No. 1, 15 Suites for large jazz orchestra, Tam O'Shanter (one-act ballet), Robbie (musical), Circus and Fair Suite, The Legend of Tutenkamun, Spanish Gold Suite for concert orchestra, Expressions (electronic suite), Impressions (electronic suite), Concertante (cycles) for violin, cello and strings, Guitar Concerto No. 1, Double Guitar Concertos Nos 1 and 2; more than 400 songs and shorter pieces, numerous comedy pieces for concert orchestra. *Publications:* Music and The Synthesizer 1969; contrib. of

244

magazine articles. *Address:* 25 Milton Road, Wallington, Surrey, SM6 9RP, England (home). *E-mail:* brucehgraham@blueyonder.co.uk (office). *Website:* www.brucegraham.org.uk; www.brucehebentongraham.co.uk.

GRAHAM, Edwin (Ed) James; British musician (drums); b. Great Yarmouth, Norfolk. *Career:* played in various bands; joined The Darkness 2000–06, 2011–; mem. Stone Gods 2007–08. *Recordings include:* albums: with The Darkness: I Believe In A Thing Called Love (EP) 2002, Permission To Land (Best Album, Kerrang! Awards, BRIT Award for Best British Album 2004) 2003, One Way Ticket To Hell... And Back 2005, Hot Cakes 2012; with Stone Gods: Silver Spoons and Broken Bones 2008. *Honours:* Kerrang! Award for Best Live Act 2003, The Observer Band of the Year 2003, BRIT Award for Best British Group, Best British Rock Act 2004, Ivor Novello Songwriters of the Year 2004, Smash Hits Award for Best Rock Act 2005. *Website:* www .theactualdarkness.com.

GRAHAM, Michael (Mikey) Christopher Charles; Irish singer and record producer; b. 15 Aug. 1972, Dublin; m. Karen Corradi 2004; one d. *Career:* mem., Boyzone 1993–2001, 2007–; solo artist 2001–; formed Mikey Graham Network. *Film appearance:* Hey Mr DJ 2005. *Recordings include:* albums: with Boyzone: Said and Done 1995, A Different Beat 1996, Where We Belong 1998, By Request 1999, Back Again... No Matter What 2008, Brother 2010, Menarche 2010; solo: Meet Me Half Way 2001. *Current Management:* c/o ASM Damage Ltd., Unit 3, City Business Centre, Saint Olav's Court, Lower Road, London SE16 2XB, England. *Telephone:* (20) 7740-1600. *Fax:* (20) 7252-2225. *E-mail:* tammy@asmdamadge.co.uk. *Website:* www.asmanagement.co.uk; boyzonenetwork.com.

GRAHAME, Alan; British musician (percussion); b. Cornwall, England; m. Dulcie Sawyer; one s., two d. *Career:* played with Ralph Sharon Sextet, London Jazz Club groups, Jerry Allen Trio; freelance studio percussionist; tours of UK and Europe with Tom Jones; Shirley Bassey, Perry Como, Englebert Humperdinck, Howard Keel, played with orchestras of Alec Gould, Ronnie Aldrich, Frank Chacksfield, Cy Payne, Colin Sell; mem. ISM, Musicians' Union. *Recordings include:* with Tom Jones, Shirley Bassey, Englebert Humperdinck, Matt Monro, Love Affair, White Plains, Brotherhood of Man, Casuals, 101 Strings, Dana, Lena Zavaroni, Rolf Harris, Frank Pourcell, Jack Emblow, David Essex, Mike Batt, Les Reed, Jeff Wayne, Bee Gees, Peters and Lee, Lena Martell; contributed to albums: Festivals Blues and Saunters 2000, Rumba 2001. *Publications include:* Articles in Percussion Press (drums, percussion). *E-mail:* alangrahame@btinternet.com. *Website:* alangrahamevibes.com.

GRAINGE, Lucian Charles, CBE; British music industry executive; *Chairman and CEO, Universal Music Group*; b. 1960, London; m.; three c. *Career:* song promoter April Music/CBS, later Head Creative Dept 1979–82; Dir and Gen. Man. RCA Music Publishing 1982–84; Dir of A&R MCA Records 1984–86; est. PolyGram Music Publishing UK office 1986–93; Gen. Man. A&R and business affairs, Polydor 1993–97, Man. Dir 1997–2001, following merger of Polygram and Universal promoted to Deputy Chair. Universal Music UK 2001, Chair. and CEO 2001–05, Chair. and CEO Universal Music Group Int. 2005–10, CEO Universal Music Group 2010–; Co-Chair. BRITS Cttee 2003–05; Dir BPI; bd mem. Int. Fed. of Phonographic Industry. *Honours:* Music Industry Trusts Award 2008, Humanitarian Award, Foundation for Ethnic Understanding 2013, SAG-AFTRA American Scene Award 2013, Salute to Industry Icons Award, Recording Acad. 2013. *Address:* Universal Music Group, 2220 Colorado Avenue, Santa Monica, CA 90404, USA (office). *Telephone:* (310) 865-4000 (office). *Website:* www.universalmusic.com (office).

GRAMM, Lou; American singer and songwriter; b. (Louis Grammatico), 2 May 1950, Rochester, NY. *Career:* lead singer, Black Sheep 1975, Foreigner 1976–90, 1992–; regular world-wide tours, concerts and festival appearances; founder mem., Shadow King 1990–91; also solo artist. *Recordings:* albums: with Black Sheep: Black Sheep 1975, Encouraging Words 1975; with Foreigner: Foreigner 1977, Double Vision 1978, Head Games 1979, 4 (No. 1, USA) 1981, Records 1983, Agent Provocateur (No. 1, UK) 1984, Inside Information 1987, The Very Best Of 1992, The Very Best... and Beyond 1992, Mr Moonlight 1994; solo albums: Ready Or Not, 1987; Foreigner in a Strange Land 1988, Long Hard Look 1989, Lou Gramm Band 2009; hit singles: with Foreigner: Feels Like The First Time 1977, Cold As Ice 1977, Long Way From Home 1978, Hot Blooded 1978, Double Vision 1978, Blue Morning Blue Day 1979, Head Games 1980, Urgent 1981, Juke Box Hero 1981, Waiting For A Girl Like You 1981, I Want To Know What Love Is (No. 1, USA) 1985, That Was Yesterday 1985, I Don't Want To Live Without You 1988; solo: Midnight Blue 1987, Just Between You and Me 1990; provided backing vocals for: Drivers Eyes, Ian McDonald, 1999. *Current Management:* Chris Hardin and Brendan Bourke, Hardin Entertainment, 2615 West Magnolia Boulevard, Suite 106, Burbank, CA 91505, USA. *Telephone:* (818) 557-7566. *Fax:* (818) 557-7298. *E-mail:* chris@hardinentertainment.com; brendan@hardinentertainment.com. *Website:* www.hardinentertainment.com. *Address:* c/o Dennis Katz, 845 Third Ave, New York, NY 10022, USA. *Website:* www.lou -gramm.com.

GRANAT, Endre; American musician (violin); b. 3 Aug. 1937; m. Mimi Granat 21 Aug. 1993; one s. *Education:* studied with Joseph Gingold and Jascha Heifetz. *Career:* tours of Europe, USA, South America, Asia; has served as Prof. of Violin at Royal Conservatory of Music, Sweden, Cleveland Inst. of Music, Univ. of Illinois, California State Univ. Northridge, Univ. of Southern California; prin. concertmaster for Hollywood film industry; mem.

AFofM. *Honours:* Ysaye Award, Grand Prix du Disque. *Website:* endregranat .com.

GRANDE, Ariana; American singer, songwriter and actress; b. 26 June 1993, Boca Raton, Fla; d. of Edward Butera and Joan Grande. *Education:* North Broward Preparatory School. *Career:* opening act on Justin Bieber's Believe tour 2013; headlined own tour The Listening Sessions 2013. *Plays:* as actress: 13 (Nat. Youth Theatre Asscn Award 2008) 2008, Cuba Libre 2012, A Snow White Christmas 2012. *Film:* as actress: Swindle 2013. *Television:* as actress: The Battery's Down 2009, VICTORiOUS (Hollywood Teen TV Award for Favorite Television Actress 2012) 2010–13, iCarly 2011, Winx Club 2011, Sam and Cat 2013–. *Recordings:* album: Yours Truly 2013, My Everything 2014. *Honours:* Billboard Mid-Year Music Award for Best Newcomer 2013, American Music Awards for New Artist of the Year 2013, for Favorite Female Artist 2015, iHeartRadio Young Influencer Award 2014, MTV Video Music Award for Best Pop Video (for Problem featuring Iggy Azalea) 2014, MTV Europe Music Awards for Best Pop Video (for Problem featuring Iggy Azalea) 2014, for Best Song (for Problem) 2014, for Best Female Artist 2014. *Current Management:* c/o Scooter Braun Management, Worldwide Plaza 825, 8th Avenue, 28th Floor, New York, NY 10019, USA. *E-mail:* info@scooterbraun .com. *Website:* scooterbraun.com; www.arianagrande.com.

GRANDMARNIER; French musician songwriter and record producer; b. (Jean-François Perrier). *Career:* Founder-mem. Yelle (with Julie Budet and Tepr) 2005–; released debut single Je veux le voir 2005; supported Mika on tour of France 2007; featured as MTV Artist of the Week, USA 2008; f. own record label, Recreation Center 2010; supported Katy Perry on UK tour 2011. *Recordings:* albums: Pop Up 2007, Safari Disco Club 2011, Complètement fou 2014. *E-mail:* yelle.mgmt@gmail.com. *Website:* www.yelle.fr.

GRANDMASTER FLASH; American DJ and rap artist; b. (Joseph Saddler), 1 Jan. 1958, Barbados. *Career:* mobile DJ, The Bronx, New York; formed Grandmaster Flash and the 3 MCs, the Furious Five 1977–83; solo artist 1985–. *Recordings include:* albums: with the Furious Five: The Message 1982, Greatest Messages 1984, The Greatest Hits 1993, Message from Beat Street: The Best of Grandmaster Flash, Melle Mel & the Furious Five 1994, The Adventures of Grandmaster Flash, Melle Mel & the Furious Five: More of the Best 1996, The Greatest Mixes 1997, Adventures on the Wheels of Steel 1999, The Showdown: The Sugarhill Gang vs. Grandmaster Flash & The Furious Five 1999, Essential Cuts 2005, Grandmaster Flash, Melle Mel and the Furious Five: The Definitive Groove Collection 2006, The Essential 2007, Kings of the Streets 2010; solo: They Said It Couldn't Be Done 1985, The Source 1986, Ba Dop Boom Bang 1987, On the Strength 1988, Greatest Hits 1992, Salsoul Jam 2000 1997, Adventures On The Wheels of Steel (compilation) 1999, The Official Adventures of Grandmaster Flash 2002, Mixing Bullets and Firing Joints 2003, The Bridge 2009. *Publication:* The Adventures of Grandmaster Flash (autobiography). *Honours:* Icon Award, BET, Lifetime Achievement Award, RIAA, Vamguard Award, inducted into Rock and Roll Hall of Fame 2007, Grammy Hall of Fame (The Message) 2012. *Address:* Grandmaster Flash Enterprises, 600 Johnson Avenue, Suite E-7, Bohemia, NY 11716, USA (office). *Telephone:* (347) 281-5567. *E-mail:* msparker@ grandmasterflash.com (office). *Website:* www.grandmasterflash.com.

GRANFELT, Ben Edward; Finnish musician (guitar) and songwriter; b. 16 June 1963, Helsinki; m. Nanna Granfelt, 14 Jan. 1997. *Recordings include:* Ben Granfelt: The Truth, Radio Friendly, Live, All I Want to Be 2001, The Past Experience 2004, Live Experience 2006, Sum of Memories 2006, Notes from the Road 2007, Kaleidoscope 2009, Melodic Relief 2012; with Guitar Slingers: Guitar Slingers: I, Song and Dance, That Little Something; with Leningrad Cowboys: We Cum From Brooklyn, Leningrad Cowboys Go Space, Let's Work Together, Russian Red Army Ensemble, Live in Prowinzz; with Gringos Locos: Raw Deal; Punch Rock; Gringos Locos; Ego, 2000. *Film appearances include:* Leningrad Cowboys Meet Moses 1994, Total Balalaika Show (documentary) 1994. *Honours:* Pro Musica Award, Gymnasiet Grankulla Samskola. *Address:* c/o Sprucefield Oy Ltd, Sinebrychoffinkatu 13 as.16, 00120 Helsinki, Finland. *Telephone:* (400) 383383. *E-mail:* sprucefield@bengranfelt.com. *Website:* www.bengranfelt.com.

GRANT, Allison Jean, BMus; Canadian actress, singer, director and choreographer; b. 23 Nov. 1958, Vancouver, BC; d. of Ian Van Felson and Antoinette Suzanne Grant. *Education:* Banff School of Fine Arts, Alberta, Univ. of Western Ontario, Morley Coll. and The Dance Centre, UK. *Career:* mem. Stratford Festival Acting Co. seven years; co-writer musical featuring Gilbert and Sullivan compositions; Resident Dir Showboat Festival five years; teacher, dir and choreographer, Opera Division, Univ. of Toronto; currently Artistic Dir Theatre Athena, Waterloo, Ont. *Stage appearances include:* Private Lives, Double Double, Sylvia, Much Ado About Nothing, Cats, The Drunkard, Desert Song, The Magic Flute, Heat, Brigadoon, Not Available in the Stores (premiere), Guys and Dolls, They're Playing Our Song, The Secret Garden (world premiere) (Dora Mavor Moore Award for best actress in a musical) 1986, Carousel (as Julie Jordan) 1991, The House of Martin Guerre (world premiere) 1993. *Television includes:* Iolanthe 1984, The Pirates of Penzance 1985. *Productions as Director:* A Meeting of Minds at Canstage, All Grown Up, Carmen (Opera Ontario), Cinderella (Canadian Opera Co.), Così fan tutte (Vancouver Opera), Die Zauberflöte, Double Double, Figaro, Figaro, Figaro (Vancouver Opera), L'Italiana in Algeri (L'Opéra de Montréal), Smokey Joe's Cafe (Stagewest Calgary), The Boyfriend (University of Toronto Opera School), The Long Weekend (Showboat Festival Theatre), The Pirates of Penzance (Canadian Children's Opera Chorus), This is a Changing World – A Noel Coward Revue, When the Reaper Calls, Don Giovanni, The Brothers Grimm, Private Lives, Bach at Leipzig. *Choreography:* Eugene Onegin, Queen of Spades, Dido and Aeneas (Canadian Opera Co.), Die Fledermaus (Vancouver Opera, Kentucky Opera, Opera Hamilton), Die Lustige Witwe (Hawaii Opera Theatre, Opera Hamilton, Edmonton Opera), La Fille du Régiment, Carmen (Opera Ontario), Le Nozze di Figaro (Opera Saskatchewan), Lullaby of Broadway, Pretty Woman, Roll Over Beethoven (Showboat Festival Theatre). *Honours:* Tyrone Guthrie Awards, Stratford, Ont. 1982, 1983, 1985. *Current Management:* Dean Artists Management, 204 St George Street, Toronto, Ont. M5R 2N5, Canada. *Telephone:* (416) 969-7300. *Fax:* (416) 969-7969. *E-mail:* deanarts@interlog.com. *Website:* www.deanartists.com.

GRANT, Amy Lee; American singer and songwriter; b. 25 Nov. 1960, Augusta, GA; m. 1st Gary W. Chapman 1982; one s. two d.; m. 2nd Vince Gill 2000. *Education:* Furman Univ. and Vanderbilt Univ. *Career:* contemporary Christian (later also pop) singer, songwriter; began solo career 1978–; tours and live appearances. *Compositions include:* Tender Tennessee Christmas (co-writer). *Recordings include:* albums: Amy Grant In Concert Vols I and II, Age To Age 1982, A Christmas Album 1983, Unguarded 1985, Lead Me On 1988, Heart in Motion 1991, Home for Christmas 1992, House of Love 1994, Behind the Eyes 1997, A Christmas to Remember 1999, A Special Wish 2001, Simple Things 2003, Rock of Ages... Hymns and Faith (Grammy Award for Best Southern, Country or Bluegrass Gospel Album 2006) 2005, The Christmas Collection 2008, Somewhere Down the Road 2010, How Mercy Looks From Here 2013. *Publications:* Amy Grant's Heart To Heart Bible Stories (book and cassette). *Honours:* St John's University Pax Christi 1994; numerous Grammy Awards, 17 Dove Awards, including Artist of the Year (four times). *Address:* Blanton/Harrell Entertainment, 2910 Poston Avenue, Nashville, TN 37203, USA. *E-mail:* management@amygrant.com. *Website:* www.amygrant.com.

GRANT, Edmond (Eddy) Montague; British singer, producer and musician (multi-instrumentalist); b. 5 March 1948, Plaisance, Guyana. *Career:* fmr mem., The Equals; f. own production company; solo artist 1977–; f. record label, Ice Records; own studio, The Coach House. *Recordings include:* albums: Message Man 1977, Walking On Sunshine 1979, Love In Exile 1980, Can't Get Enough 1981, Killer On The Rampage 1982, Going For Broke 1984, All The Hits 1984, File Under Rock 1988, The Best of Eddy Grant 1989, Barefoot Soldier 1990, Paintings of the Soul 1992, Soca Baptism 1994, I Don't Wanna Dance 1997, Eddy Grant's Greatest Hits 2001, Hearts and Diamonds 2001, The Road to Reparation 2008. *Address:* Ice Records Ltd, Bayley's Plantation, St Philip, Barbados (office). *Telephone:* (246) 423-6286 (office). *Fax:* (246) 423-5154 (office). *E-mail:* info@icerecords.com (office). *Website:* www.icerecords.com (office); www.eddygrant.com.

GRANT, Manson, HNC; British singer and musician (keyboards, trumpet, accordion); b. 9 April 1951, John O'Groats, Scotland. *Career:* mem. Dynamos Band 1970–; mem. Musicians' Union. *Recordings include:* 30 albums. *Current Management:* c/o Pan Records, Achnaclyth, Tannach, Wick, KW1 5SF, Scotland. *Telephone:* (1955) 602646. *E-mail:* robert@mansongrantandthedynamos.com. *Website:* www.mansongrantandthedynamos.com.

GRASSHOPPER; American musician (guitar); b. (Sean Mackowiak), 25 May 1967, New York. *Education:* State Univ. of New York, Buffalo. *Career:* founder mem. experimental rock group Mercury Rev, Buffalo, New York, mid-1980s; Mercury Rev began as composers of soundtracks for experimental films, made first recordings at State Univ. of New York, Fredonia; sound gradually developed from a very experimental and psychedelic style to a more melodic approach; festival appearances in USA, Europe and Far East 2007; experimental side-project, Harmony Rockets. *Recordings include:* albums: Yerself Is Steam 1991, Boces 1993, See You on the Other Side 1995, Deserter's Songs (NME magazine Album of the Year) 1998, All Is Dream 2001, The Secret Migration 2005, The Essential Mercury Rev: Stillness Breathes 1991–2006, Back to Mine compilation 2006, Hello Blackbird (soundtrack to film Bye Bye Blackbird) 2006, Snowflake Midnight 2008, The Light in You 2015. *Current Management:* c/o James Alderman, Free Trade Agency, 15 Timber Yard, Drysdale Street, London, N1 6ND, England. *Telephone:* (20) 3700-3377. *Fax:* (20) 3700-3355. *E-mail:* info@freetradeagency.co.uk. *Website:* www.freetradeagency.co.uk. *E-mail:* info@mercuryrev.com. *Website:* www.mercuryrev.com.

GRAY, David; British singer, songwriter and musician (multi-instrumentalist); b. 1970, Manchester; m. Olivia Rooney; two d. *Education:* Ysgol Dewi Sant, Univ. of Liverpool. *Career:* experimented in various punk bands prior to residence in London; recorded and released fourth album on self-owned IHT label; contributed tracks to and appeared in film, This Year's Love 1998; numerous concert, festival appearances and tours. *Recordings include:* albums: A Century Ends 1993, Flesh 1994, Sell, Sell, Sell 1996, White Ladder 1999, Lost Songs 95–98 2000, A New Day At Midnight 2002, Life In Slow Motion 2005, Draw the Line 2009, Foundling 2010. *Honours:* Ivor Novello Award for Best Song Lyrically and Musically (for Babylon) 2001. *Address:* IHT Records, Unit 2D, Clapham North Arts Centre, 26–32 Voltaire Road, London SW4 6DH, England (office). *Telephone:* (20) 7720-7411 (office). *Fax:* (20) 7720-8095 (office). *E-mail:* contact@ihtrecords.com (office). *Website:* www.davidgray.com.

GRAY, Howard; British (b. Australian) record engineer, producer and musician. *Career:* engineer for Steve Lillywhite; independent producer during

mid–1980s; recording artist with Apollo 440; numerous remixes/production credits; producer, mixer, recording engineer on Terence Trent D'Arby's Introducing The Hardline, Danny Wilson's Danny Wilson, The Cure's Head On The Door, UB40's Labour of Love, OMD's Sugar Tax, Scritti Politti's Cupid and Psyche '85, Tom Verlaine's Cover, Blue Pearl's Naked; recordings by Yazz, Mory Kanté, Geoffrey Williams, Kirsty MacColl, Genesis, U2, Duran Duran, Youssou N'Dour, Manic Street Preachers, Skunk Anansie, Siegman, Dust Junkys. *Recordings include:* albums with Apollo 440: Millennium Fever 1995, Electro Glide in Blue 1995, Gettin' High on Your Own Supply 1999, Ain't Talkin Bout Dub 2002, Dude Descending a Staircase 2003, The Future's What It Used to Be 2012. *Current Management:* c/o XL Talent, Reverb House, Bennett Street, London, W4 2AH, England. *Telephone:* (20) 8747-0660. *Fax:* (20) 8742-3749. *E-mail:* management@reverbxl.com. *Website:* www.apollo440.com.

GRAY, Macy; American R&B singer and songwriter; b. (Natalie McIntyre), 1969, Canton, Ohio; m. (divorced); three d. *Education:* classical piano training, Univ. of Southern California Film School. *Career:* fmr lyricist and session jazz singer; solo artist 1998–. *Film appearances:* Domino 2005, Lackawanna Blues 2005, Idlewild 2006, For Colored Girls 2010. *Recordings include:* albums: On How Life Is 1999, The Id 2001, The Trouble With Being Myself 2003, Big 2007, The Sellout 2010, Covered 2012, Talking Book 2012. *Honours:* BRIT Award for Best Int. Newcomer, Best Int. Female Artist 2000, Grammy Award for Best Female Pop Vocal Performance (for I Try) 2001. *Current Management:* William Morris Endeavor, 1325 Avenue of the Americas, New York, NY 10019, USA. *Telephone:* (212) 586-5100. *Fax:* (212) 246-3583. *Website:* www.wma.com; ; www.macygray.com.

GRAY, Rocky; American musician (drums). *Career:* mem. rock bands, Soul Embraced 1997–, Evanescence 2002–07, Mourningside 2004–, Living Sacrifice, We Are the Fallen; founder CrimeWave Records. *Recordings include:* albums: with Soul Embraced: For the Incomplete 2000, Immune 2003, Dead Alive 2008, Mythos 2011; with Evanescence: Origin 2002, Fallen 2003, Anywhere But Home (live) 2004, The Open Door 2006; with Living Sacrifice: In Memoriam 2005, Infinite Order 2010; with We Are the Fallen: Tear the World Down 2010. *Honours:* Grammy Award for Best New Artist 2003, Grammy Award for Best Hard Rock Performance (for Bring Me To Life) 2003. *Address:* c/o Wind-up Records, 72 Madison Avenue, New York, NY 10016, USA. *E-mail:* evanescence@winduprecords.com. *Website:* www.evanescence.com; www.wearethefallen.com.

GRAY, Tom; British musician (guitar, bass, keyboards, percussion) and singer; b. 1976, Southport, England. *Career:* Founder-mem., Gomez 1996–; numerous concerts, festival, radio and television appearances. *Recordings include:* albums: Bring It On 1998, Liquid Skin 1999, Abandoned Shopping Trolley Hotline 2000, In Our Gun 2002, Out West: Live at the Fillmore 2005, How We Operate 2006, A New Tide 2009, Whatever's on Your Mind 2011. *Honours:* Mercury Music Prize 1998. *Current Management:* c/o Jason Colton, Red Light Management, 321 East Main Street, Suite 500, Charlottesville, VA 22902, USA. *Telephone:* (434) 245-4900. *Fax:* (434) 245-4933. *E-mail:* gomez@redlightmanagement.com. *Website:* www.redlightmanagement.com. *E-mail:* gomez@gomeztheband.com. *Website:* www.gomeztheband.com.

GREBENSHCHIKOV, Boris Borisovich; Russian musician and singer; b. 27 Nov. 1953, Leningrad; s. of Boris A. Grebenshchikov and Ludmila Grebenshchikova; m.; one s. two d. *Education:* Leningrad Univ. *Career:* worked as a computer programmer 1977–80; lead singer and guitarist of rock group Akvarium 1975–; music for films and sound track albums includes Assa 1988, Black Rose 1990; tours and recordings in USA, Canada, Great Britain, all-Russia tour 1991 (110 concerts in 68 cities); performances at Royal Albert Hall, London 2007, 2008; artist as a painter has taken part in various art exhbns throughout fmr USSR. *Radio:* presenter, Aerostat. *Recordings include:* albums: with Akvarium: Akvarium (USSR) 1987, Radio Africa 1987, Equinox 1988, Radio Silence 1989, Russian Album 1992, Kostroma Mon Amour 1994, Navigator 1995, Snow Lion 1996, Hyperborea 1997, Lilith 1998, Psi 1999, Sister Chaos 2002, Fisherman's Song 2003, Zoom, Zoom, Zoom 2005, Careless Russian Rover 2006, White Horse 2008, Pushkinskaya 10 2009. *Art exhibition:* Russian Museum, Kyiv 2009. *Publications include:* Ivan and Danilo 1989, poetry and song lyrics, trans. of Indian and Tibetan religious works, three vols of Aerostat's Musical Encyclopedia. *Honours:* Medal for Services to the Fatherland 2003; Triumph Prize (for outstanding achievements in Russian culture) 1998. *Address:* 2 Marata Street, Apt. 3, 191025 St Petersburg, Russia. *Fax:* (812) 272-05-41. *E-mail:* bg@aquarium.ru. *Website:* www.aquarium.ru.

GRÉCO, Juliette; French actress and singer; b. 7 Feb. 1927, Montpellier; d. of Louis Gérard and Juliette Gréco; m. 1st Philippe Lemair; one d.; m. 2nd Michel Piccoli; m. 3rd Gérard Jouannest 1988. *Education:* acting with Solange Sicard, Pierre Dux and Béatrice Dussane. *Career:* performed at Tabou cabaret (with Raymond Quesneau, Roger Vadim, Boris Vian, Jean-Paul Sartre, etc.) 1946; numerous cabaret performances in France and abroad; concerts include shows at Olympia, Paris 1954, 1957, 1966, 1991, Théâtre Nat. de Paris (with Georges Brassens) 1966 and at the Odéon-Théâtre de l'Europe 1999. *Films include:* Aller et retour 1948, Orphée 1949, Au royaume des cieux 1949, Sans laisser d'adresse 1951, The Green Glove (scenes deleted) 1952, Saluti e baci 1953, Quand tu liras cette lettre 1953, Boum sur Paris 1954, 33 tours et puis s'en vont 1955, Eléna et les hommes 1956, La châtelaine du Liban 1956, L'homme et l'enfant 1956, The Sun Also Rises 1957, The Naked Earth 1958,

Les racines du ciel 1958, Whirlpool 1959, Drame dans un miroir 1960, The Big Gamble 1961, Maléfices 1962, Canzoni nel mondo 1963, L'amour à la mer 1963, Onkel Toms Hütte 1965, The Night of the Generals 1967, Le désordre à 20 ans 1967, Far West 1973, Lily, aime-moi 1975, Belphégor – Le fantôme du Louvre 2001, Jedermanns Fest 2002, An Education 2009. *Television appearances include:* Belphégor (mimi-series) 1965; numerous variety shows including Top à Juliette Gréco. *Songs include:* Si tu t'imagines… L'éternel féminin, Les feuilles mortes, Romance (Grand Prix du Disque) 1952, La valse brune, Si l'amour est un péché, Rêveuse et fragile, Toi que j'aime, Les pingouines, J'en tremble, Ta jalousie. *Publications include:* Jujube 1982, Un jour d'été et quelques nuits 1998. *Honours:* Chevalier, Ordre des Arts et des Lettres; Grand Prix Nat. de la Chanson 1990. *Address:* c/o Maurice Marouani, 37 rue Marbeuf, 75008 Paris, France.

GREEN, Al; American soul singer and songwriter; b. 13 April 1946, Forrest City, Ark. *Career:* founder, The Creations 1964; singer, Al Green and The Soul Mates; f. of his own record label Hot Line Music Journal, 1967; purchased his own church, The Full Gospel Tabernacle in Memphis, Tenn. in late 1970s, became pastor; left secular music 1980, returned 1993. *Recordings include:* albums: Al Green Gets Next To You 1971, Let's Stay Together 1972, I'm Still In Love With You 1972, Green Is Blues 1973, Call Me 1973, Livin' For You 1974, Al Green Explores Your Mind 1975, Al Green Is Love 1975, Full of Fire 1976, Have A Good Time 1977, Truth 'n' Time 1978, The Belle Album 1978, Cream of Al Green 1980, The Lord Will Make A Way 1980, Higher Plane 1982, Precious Lord 1983, I"ll Rise Again 1983, White Christmas 1983, Going Away 1986, Soul Survivor 1987, I Get Joy 1989, Al 1992, Love and Happiness 2001, I Can't Stop 2003, Everything's OK 2005, Lay it Down 2008. *Honours:* American Music Award, Favourite Soul/R&B Album 1974, Grand Prize, Tokyo Music Festival 1978, Al Green Day, Los Angeles 1978, Soul Train, Best Gospel Recording 1987, numerous Grammy awards include: Best Soul Gospel Performances 1982–85, 1988, 1990, Best Male Soul Performance 1987, Best R&B Performance by a Duo or Group (for Stay With Me with John Legend) 2009, Best Traditional R&B Vocal Performance (for You've Got All the Love I Need) 2009, Grammy Lifetime Achievement Award 2002, Kennedy Center Honor 2014. *Address:* Full Gospel Tabernacle, 787 Hale Road, Memphis, TN 38116, USA. *Telephone:* (901) 396-9192. *E-mail:* algreenmusic@hotmail.com; reverend@algreenmusic.com. *Website:* www.algreenmusic.com.

GREEN, Cee Lo; American vocalist, songwriter and producer; b. (Thomas DeCarlo Callaway), 30 May 1974, Atlanta, Ga; m. Christina Johnson (divorced); one s. one step-d. *Career:* fmr mem. Goodie Mob hip-hop group; released three solo albums which mix elements of hip hop, soul, gospel and funk; mem. Gnarls Barkley (with Danger Mouse) 2005–, first single, Crazy, was first song to reach No. 1 from download sales alone; collaborations with Jazzee Pha, Jack Splash (as Lovestink); guest vocalist on numerous recordings by artists including De La Soul, Kelis, Everlast, Common, Carlos Santana, Royce Da 5'9", Twista, OutKast, Rehab, Seeed, Black Eyed Peas, Danger Mouse & MF Doom, Musiq, Cunninlynguists, Diddy, Mad Skillz, Lil Kim, Erykah Badu, Heavy D, The Rapture, Brandy, Amerie; production credits include tracks by Pussycat Dolls, Brandy, Amerie, Backbone. *Recordings include:* albums: with Goodie Mobb: Soul Food 1995, Still Standing 1998, World Party 1999; with Dungeon Family: Even in Darkness 2001; solo: Cee-Lo Green and His Perfect Imperfections 2002, Cee-Lo Green… Is the Soul Machine 2004, The Lady Killer 2010, Cee Lo's Magic Moment 2012, Heart Blanche 2015; with Gnarls Barkley: St Elsewhere 2006, The Odd Couple 2008; with Love Stink: Jack Splash & Cee-Lo Are The Heart Attack. *Composition:* co-writer: Don't Cha by Pussycat Dolls. *Honours:* Grammy Award for Best Urban/Alternative Performance 2011, BRIT Award for Best Int. Male Solo Artist 2011, Grammy Awards for Best Traditional R&B Performance (with Melanie Fiona for Fool For You) 2012, for Best R&B Song (with Melanie Fiona and Jack Splash for Fool For You) 2012. *Current Management:* c/o Primary Wave Entertainment, 116 East 16th Street, 9th Floor, New York, NY 10003, USA. *Telephone:* (212) 661-6990. *Fax:* (212) 661-8890. *Website:* www .primarywave.com; www.gnarlsbarkley.com; www.jazzephaandceelo.com; www.ceelogreen.com.

GREEN, Earl Oliver; British singer; b. 11 Feb. 1945, Kingston, Jamaica; m. Valerie Jean 1973, one s. one d. *Career:* has performed at most major blues festivals in Europe, including Belgium Rhythm and Blues Festival, Nyon Festival, Lugano Festival, Switzerland, Diamond Awards, Antwerp; Founder-mem. Otis Grand and Dance Kings 1986; f. The Earl Green Band 1995; currently singer, Earl Green and The Right Time; mem. PRS, Musicians' Union. *Recordings include:* Always Hot, Otis Grand and The Dance Kings; Special Delivery, He Knows The Blues, Otis Grand, Feel The Fire 1996, Live at Bronte Blues Club 2011. *Website:* www.earlgrayband.co.uk; www .therighttime.co.uk.

GREEN, Edward, BA, MA, PhD; American composer, musician (keyboards) and academic; *Professor, Manhattan School of Music;* b. 12 Nov. 1951, Queens, NY; s. of Bernard Green and Dorothy Green; m. Carrie Wilson. *Education:* Oberlin Coll., New York Univ. *Career:* staff composer, Imagery Films 1980–, working with dir Ken Kimmelman, film scores include What Does a Person Deserve?, Hot Afternoons Have Been in Montana, and Thomas Comma; Musical Dir, Aesthetic Realism Theater Co. 1978–, productions include The Melody Persists, Ethics is a Force in American Song, Rock & Roll: The Opposites, Our Biggest Hopes; Prof., Manhattan School of Music, classes include Songwriting, Musical Theatre Composition, Film Scoring, World Music; Faculty, Aesthetic Realism Foundation, teaching The Opposites in Music class; presentations on Aesthetic Realism and music to conventions and meetings of Int. Asscn of Jazz Educators, European Soc. for the Cognitive Studies of Music, American Musicological Soc., American Soc. of Univ. Composers, Soc. for American Music, Soc. for Ethnomusicology; concerts with flautist Barbara Allen (played keyboards); Smithsonian Inst. sponsored lecture on the music of Duke Ellington, given widely in USA, Europe, South America; editorial columnist, US African Eye 1998–2004; Fulbright Sr Specialist in American Music, Council for Int. Exchange of Scholars; mem. Editorial Bd Int. Review of the Aesthetics and Sociology of Music; mem. American Soc. of Composers, Authors and Publrs (ASCAP). *Compositions:* Symphony for band, Sextet for piano and strings ('Riding with the Devil'), Piano Concertino, Chamber Symphony for guitars and flutes, brass quintet, Quartet for guitars, Shakespeare Songs, Constitutional Amendment, Overture in G, Trumpet Concerto, Zhou, for Pipa and Erhu, Sextet for saxophone and brass quartet, Saxophone Concerto, Music for Shakespeare, Overture for concert wind ensemble, Once Upon a Time (orchestral fantasy), Symphony for band, Sextet for piano and strings. *Films:* What Does a Person Deserve?, Hot Afternoons Have Been in Montana, Thomas Comma. *Publications:* The Press Boycott of Aesthetic Realism 1978, China and the West: the Birth of a New Music 2009, Cambridge Companion to Duke Ellington (ed.) 2014, China and the West – the Birth of a New Music (ed.); Guest Ed., Popular Music Studies, centenary issue on Bernard Herrmann; contrib. to more than 200 articles world-wide on music, social issues, aesthetic realism. *Honours:* Delius Award for Musical Composition 1985, First Prize, Julius Albert Composers' Competition 1996, First Prize, Zoltan Kodaly Composers' Competition 1996, African Music Hall of Fame 2002, Received Music Alive! grant, American Symphony Orchestra League 2004. *Address:* 208 East Broadway, Suite J1007, New York, NY 10002, USA (home). *Telephone:* (212) 529-7745 (office). *E-mail:* edgreenmusic@gmail.com (office). *Website:* www.edgreenmusic.org.

GREEN, Ian Michael; British musician (percussion, drums); b. 19 Nov. 1957, London, England; m. Carolyn Margaret Morris, 7 May 1994. *Education:* Kingsdale, 1968–74. *Career:* Musician with: Mike Oldfield, 1972–73; Druid, 1977–78; Catherine Howe; Randy Edelman; Lynsey De Paul; Sally Oldfield (Germany), 1978–79; Matt Monro (London), 1980–81; Michael Crawford, Barnum, TV and radio; Tony Britten; Sammy Davis Jr (Monte Carlo), 1988; Jerry Lee Lewis (Monte Carlo), 1991–92; mem, Musicians' Union; ISM. *Recordings* with artistes including: Michael Crawford; Mike Oldfield; Sally Oldfield; Anthony Newley; produced single: What Kind of Fool Am I?; Film and television: Lace 1 and 2; Lennon The Movie; Casualty; Head Over Heels; Shows: Barnum, 1981; Guys and Dolls, 1987; She Loves Me, 1994; The Snow Queen, 1995; Fame, 1995; Singing In The Rain; Stop The World.

GREEN, Martin; British folk musician (accordion, keyboards) and composer; b. East Anglia, England. *Career:* regular collaborator with Eliza Carthy 1998–2002; mem. folk trio Lau 2005–, collaborations with Karine Polwart, Adem; Founder, Martin Green Machine group; other collaborators include Linda Thompson, Joan Baez, Eliza Carthy, Kathryn Tickell, Joe Townsend, Becky Unthank, Be Good Tanyas. *Stage:* The Little World of Don Camillo (composed score with Colin Steele) 2004. *Compositions include:* Strange Attractors for folk trio and orchestra 2011, Accordophone for accordion and string quartet 2011. *Recordings include:* albums: with Eliza Carthy: Dinner 2001; with Joe Townsend: Return to the Woods 2005; with Lau: Lightweights and Gentlemen 2007, Arc Light 2009, Race the Loser 2012; with Martin Green Machine: First Sighting 2009. *Honours:* with Lau: BBC Radio 2 Folk Awards for Best Band 2008, 2009, 2010, for Best Group 2013, Scottish Traditional Music Award for Best Live Act 2009. *E-mail:* tomreveal@mac.com. *Website:* www.revealrecords.co.uk; www.lau-music.co.uk; www.martingreen.tv.

GREENAWAY, Roger, OBE; British songwriter and music publishing executive; *Executive Vice-President, International, ASCAP;* b. 23 Aug. 1938, Bristol. *Career:* fmr mem., The Kestrels; formed songwriting partnership with Roger Cook 1965–75; formed pop duo, David and Jonathan (with Roger Cook) 1965–68; gave up performing to concentrate on writing 1968; Chair., PRS 1983–86, fmr bd mem.; started working ASCAP London office 1994, currently Exec. Vice-Pres., Int. *Compositions include:* (with Roger Cook) Home Lovin' Man (Andy Williams), Blame it on the Pony Express (Johnny Johnson), Something Tells Me Something's Gonna Happen Tonight (Cilla Black), I've Got You On My Mind (White Plains), Long Cool Woman in a Black Dress (The Hollies), Green Grass (Gary Lewis), Something's Gotten Hold of My Heart (Gene Pitney), High and Dry (Cliff Richard), I'd Like to Teach the World to Sing (The New Seekers), You've Got Your Troubles, I've Got Mine (The Fortunes), Here Comes That Rainy Day Feeling Again (The Fortunes), Like Sister & Brother (The Drifters), Kissing in the Back Row of the Movies (The Drifters), Say You'll Stay Until Tomorrow (Tom Jones), Conversations (Cilla Black), Doctor's Orders (Sunny & Carol Douglas, USA), My Baby Loves Lovin' (White Plains). *Honours:* seven Ivor Novello awards (two for Songwriter of the Year). *Address:* ASCAP, 8 Cork Street, London, W1S 3LJ, England (office). *Website:* www.ascap.com.

GREENSLADE, Dave; composer and musician (keyboards); b. 18 Jan. 1943, Woking, Surrey, England; m. Jan Greenslade, two d. *Career:* keyboard player with Chris Farlowe's The Thunderbirds; worked with Geno Washington in the Ram Jam Band; founder mem., Colosseum –1971, re-formed 1994–; founder, Greenslade 1972; also solo project, Cactus Choir; wrote television score for BBC series, Gangsters; full-time composer; mem. Musicians' Union, PRS, MCPS. *Compositions:* worked on more than 35 drama series, single plays, films, stage plays; credits include: Kinsey, BBC TV; A Very Peculiar Practice,

BBC TV; Wipe Out, Granada TV; Tales of The Unexpected, Anglia TV; The Detective, BBC TV; Bratt Farrer, BBC TV; Bird of Prey, BBC TV; The Houseman's Tale, BBC TV; A Family Man, BBC TV; films: Artemis, BBC Films; Jekyll and Hyde, BBC films; Worked with novelist Terry Pratchett on recording project based on the DiscWorld fantasy novel series; Storms Behind the Breeze; The Playground; No Pleasin'; Wherever I Go; The Other Side of the Sky. *Recordings include:* Colosseum: Daughter of Time; Live; Valentyne Suite; Albums with Greenslade; Cactus Choir; Pentateuch, double album based on illustrations of Patrick Woodroffe; DiscWorld project, 1995; Large Afternoon, 2000; Live 1973–75, 2000. *Honours:* Premio Ondas TV Award at Barcelona Film Festival, Prix Italia at Palermo, Toyama Prize, Japan. *Address:* 16 Queens Road, Berkhamsted, Hertfordshire, HP4 3HU, England.

GREENWOOD, Colin Charles; British musician (bass guitar) and composer; b. 26 June 1969, Oxford, England; brother of Jonny Greenwood. *Education:* Univ. of Cambridge. *Career:* mem., On A Friday 1987, renamed Radiohead 1991–; numerous tours, festivals and TV appearances. *Recordings include:* albums: Pablo Honey 1993, The Bends 1995, OK Computer (Grammy Award for Best Alternative Music Performance) 1997, Kid A (Grammy Award for Best Alternative Music Album) 2000, Amnesiac 2001, I Might Be Wrong (live recordings) 2001, Hail To The Thief 2003, In Rainbows (Grammy Award for Best Alternative Music Album 2009) 2007, The King of Limbs 2011. *Honours:* Q Award for Best Act in the World Today 2001, 2002, 2003. *Current Management:* Courtyard Management, 21 The Nursery, Sutton Courtenay, Abingdon, Oxfordshire OX14 4UA, England. *Website:* www.radiohead.com.

GREENWOOD, Jonathan (Jonny) Richard Guy; British musician (guitar, piano, keyboards, synthesizer) and composer; b. 5 Nov. 1971, Oxford, England; brother of Colin Greenwood; m.; one c. *Career:* mem., On A Friday 1987, renamed Radiohead 1991–; numerous tours, festivals and TV appearances; composer-in-residence, BBC Concert Orchestra 2004–07. *Recordings include:* albums: with Radiohead: Pablo Honey 1993, The Bends 1995, OK Computer (Grammy Award for Best Alternative Music Performance) 1997, Kid A (Grammy Award for Best Alternative Music Album) 2000, Amnesiac 2001, I Might Be Wrong (live recordings) 2001, Hail To The Thief 2003, In Rainbows (Grammy Award for Best Alternative Music Album 2009) 2007, The King of Limbs 2011; solo: Bodysong (soundtrack) 2003, There Will Be Blood (soundtrack) (Ivor Novello Award for Best Original Film Score 2009) 2007. *Films:* scores for: Bodysong 2003, There Will Be Blood 2007, Norwegian Wood 2010, We Need to Talk about Kevin 2011, The Master 2012. *Honours:* with Radiohead: Q Award for Best Act in the World Today 2001, 2002, 2003, solo: BBC Radio 3 Listeners' Award, BBC British Composer Awards 2006. *Current Management:* Courtyard Management, 21 The Nursery, Sutton Courtenay, Abingdon, Oxfordshire OX14 4UA, England. *Website:* www.radiohead.com.

GREENWOOD, Lee Melvin; American country singer; b. 27 Oct. 1942, Southgate, CA; m. Melanie Cronk. *Recordings include:* albums: Inside and Out 1982, If There's Any Justice 1983, Somebody's Gonna Love You 1983, The Wind Beneath My Wings 1984, You've Got a Good Love Comin' 1985, Streamline 1985, Christmas is Christmas 1987, God Bless the USA 1990, Holdin' a Good Hand 1991, American Patriot 1992, Back to Back 1996, Wounded Heart 1998, Same River Different Bridge 2000, Have Yourself A Merry Little Christmas 2001, Stronger Than Time 2003, I Want to Be in Your World 2010, Icon 2011. *Honours:* CMA Male Vocalist of the Year 1983, 1984, ACM Male Vocalist of the Year 1984, Cash Box Choice Award 1984, Music City Award for Best Male Vocalist 1984, 1985. *Current Management:* Jerry Bentley, 1025 16th Avenue, South Nashville, TN 37212, USA. *E-mail:* leegreenwood@leegreenwood.com. *Website:* www.leegreenwood.com.

GREER, Joseph; Australian keyboard player, guitarist and songwriter. *Career:* became mem. The Temper Trap 2008–; group relocated to London 2008; released debut album 2009. *Recordings:* albums: with The Temper Trap: Conditions 2009, The Temper Trap (ARIA Music Award for Best Rock Album 2012) 2012. *Honours:* with The Temper Trap: ARIA Music Awards for Best Group 2010, 2012, for Most Popular Australian Single (for Sweet Disposition) 2010. *Current Management:* c/o Lunatic Entertainment, Level 1, 490 Crown Street, Surry Hills, NSW 2010, Australia. *E-mail:* info@lunaticentertainment .com. *Website:* www.lunaticentertainment.com. *Address:* c/o Liberation Music, 9 Dundas Lane, Albert Park, Vic. 3206, Australia (office). *E-mail:* info@ liberationmusic.net (office). *Website:* www.liberationmusic.net (office); www .thetempertrap.com.

GREGORY, Will; British composer, songwriter, musician (saxophones, oboe, fiddle) and arranger. *Career:* worked with Tori Amos, Apollo Saxophone Quartet, Jim Barr, Marc Bessant, John Cornick, Stephen Cottrell, Jenny Crook, The Cure, Clive Deamer, Jim Eanes, David Ferguson, Peter Gabriel, Chloë Goodchild, Stuart Gordon, Johnny Kalsi, Rowen Oliver, John Parish, Portishead, Hossam Ramzy, David Rhodes, Adrian Utley, B. Waghorn, Tim Wheater; formed Goldfrapp with Alison Goldfrapp during late 1990s. *Recordings include:* albums: Felt Mountain 2000, Black Cherry 2003, Supernature 2005, Seventh Tree 2008, Head First 2010, Tales of Us 2013. *Current Management:* c/o Fascination Management, 1st Floor, 6 South Hill Park, London, NW3 2SB, England. *Telephone:* (20) 7586-6457. *E-mail:* info@ fascinationmanagement.com. *Website:* www.fascinationmanagement.com; www.goldfrapp.co.uk.

GREGSON, Clive James; British musician, singer, songwriter and record producer; b. 4 Jan. 1955, Ashton-Under-Lyne, Lancs.; m. Nancy Ann Kirkland 1993. *Education:* Crewe and Alsager Coll. of Educ. *Career:* Founder Any

Trouble 1976–84, 2007–; mem. duo, Clive Gregson and Christine Collister 1985–92; mem., Richard Thompson Band 1987–92; solo artist 1992–; mem., The Blue Moon Orchestra 2005–; mem. PRS, BAC&S, EFDSS, Musicians' Union. *Recordings include:* with Any Trouble: Where Are All The Nice Girls 1980, Live At The Venue 1980, Wheels In Motion 1981, Any Trouble 1983, Wrong End of The Race 1984, Life in Reverse 2007; solo: Strange Persuasions 1985, Welcome To The Workhouse 1990, Carousel of Noise 1994, People and Places 1995, I Love this Town 1996, Happy Hour 1999, Comfort and Joy 2001, Long Story Short 2004; with Gregson and Collister: Home and Away 1986, Mischief 1987, A Change In The Weather 1989, Love Is A Strange Hotel 1990, The Last Word 1992; with Eddi Reader and Boo Hewerdine: Wonderful Lie/ Last Night I Dreamt That Somebody Loved Me/Who's Your Jailer Now? 1993. *Current Management:* c/o Andy Murray, 4 Tunes Ltd, PO Box 36534, London W4 3XE, England. *Telephone:* (20) 8442-7560. *Fax:* (20) 8442-7561. *E-mail:* andy@4-tunes.com. *Website:* www.4-tunes.com. *E-mail:* clivegregson@hotmail .com (office). *Website:* www.clivegregson.com.

GRESSWELL, Steve; British composer, producer, musician (keyboards) and programmer; b. 20 Jan. 1955, Reading, Berks.; m. Jacqui Gresswell 1993; one s. one d. *Career:* performed with Justin Canns 1971–76, Scorpio 1977–81, Steve Gresswell Band 1981–82, Dream 1982–84, Poiema 1984–85, After Dark 1985, Guardian Angel 1985–86; formed own label, Sumo Records, with recording studio 1988; video with SG Band: Just For You 1989, Robin Wilson Productions 1990, Coalition 1992–; mem. Musicians' Union, PRS, PPL, MCPS, BAC&S, BSWC, PAMRA. *Recordings include:* with Scorpio: Taking England By Storm 1977; with Oddjob: Express Yourself 1977; with Dream: Just For You 1982; with Poiema: two singles from play: Cross Purposes 1984; with After Dark: Call of The Wild 1985; album: Masked By Midnight 1985; with SG Band: Just For You (Official Record for Lockerbie Air Disaster Fund) 1989; producer, single for duo, Vincent 1989; composer, musician, engineer, producer, album for Czech rock guitarist Karel Espandr 1990; producer, composer, Robin Wilson Project single (fundraising for child with Cerebral Palsy) 1990, Steve Gresswell, Spirit of Freedom 1994, Coalition: Rise of the Coalition 1996, 1997, Steve Gresswell, Visions 1997; produced and arranged Brent Morley, Burn 1997.

GREY, Carola, MA; German musician (drums), composer and producer; b. 5 Aug. 1968, Munich. *Education:* studied classical piano. *Career:* performed and/or recorded with Mike Stern, Ravi Coltrane, Benny Green, Craig Handy and other jazz artists; drummer for New York–based all female gothic rock band, Maria Excommunikata Bandleader 1989–; performed at clubs and festivals in Europe, USA and Asia (Thailand International Jazz Festival 1996, Jakarta Jazz Festival 1995–96, Indian Music Festival, Chennai 1996); mem. Int. Drum Organization. *Recordings include:* albums: solo: Noisy Mama 1992, The Age of Illusions 1994, Girls Can't Hit 1996, Drum Attack 2007, Road to Goa 2013. *Address:* Noisy Mama Productions, Kiefernweg 18, 85604 Zorneding, Germany. *E-mail:* info@carolagrey.de. *Website:* www.carolagrey .de.

GREY, Skylar; American singer, songwriter and musician (guitar, keyboards); b. (Holly Brook Hafermann), 23 Feb. 1986, Mazomanie, Wis.; d. of Candace Kreitlow. *Career:* as child and teenager, fmr mem. of folk duo Generations with mother; moved to Los Angeles 2003; signed to Machine Shop Recordings under the name Holly Brook 2004; debut album 2006; opening act on tours by k. d. lang, Jamie Cullum, Daniel Powter; changed name to Skylar Grey 2010; collaborator on songs with producer Alex da Kid; guest singer on titles for Fort Minor, Lupe Fiasco, Kaskade, Diddy-Dirty Money, Eminem & Dr Dre, Zedd; sang at Grammy Awards 2011, World Peace Event, Washington DC 2011. *Compositions:* songs for other artists including: Love the Way You Lie (for Eminem and Rihanna), Coming Home (for Diddy-Dirty Money), Castle Walls (for T.I. and Christina Aguilera), I Need a Doctor (for Eminem and Dr Dre). *Recordings include:* albums: as Holly Brook: Like Blood Like Honey 2006; as Skylar Grey: Don't Look Down 2013; other credits: as Holly Brook: Finally Out of P.E., Brie Larson 2005, The Rising Tied, Fort Minor 2005, Whisper House, Duncan Sheik 2009, Butterflies and Elvis, Yohanna 2009; as Skylar Grey: Lasers, Lupe Fiasco 2011, Fire & Ice, Kaskade 2011, Welcome to: Our House, Slaughterhouse 2012, Don't Look Down 2013. *Current Management:* c/o William Morris Endeavor, 1325 Avenue of the Americas, New York, NY 10019, USA. *Address:* c/o Interscope Records, Universal Music Group, 1755 Broadway, New York, NY 10019, USA (office). *Website:* www .skylargreymusic.com.

GRIFF, Ray; Canadian artist, writer and musician (piano, guitar); b. 22 April 1940, Vancouver, BC; m. Trudy Griff. *Career:* Host, Goodtime Country, Ray Griff Show, Sun Parlour Country; mem., ASCAP, NSA, BMI, CMA, CCMA. *Compositions include:* has written over 2,000 songs, including Baby, Step Aside, The Morning After Baby Let Me Down, Darlin', It Couldn't Have Been Any Better, Canadian Pacific, Where Love Begins, After The Laughter, Who's Gonna Play This Old Piano, Better Move It On Home. *Recordings include:* over 550 including Baby, Better Move It On Home, Hold Me, Getting Back To Norma, You're Wearin' Me Down, After The Laughter, Where Love Begins, Step Aside, It Couldn't Have Been Any Better, Between This Time and The Next, Ray Griff & Friends: Honest to Goodness Amigos, There'll Always Be Christmas, Ray Griff: Through the Years, Vol. 1 & 2. *Honours:* seven BMI Citations for Songwriting and Publishing. *Website:* www.raygriff.com.

GRIFFIN, Albert Sidney (Sid), (Sid the Squid), BA; American musician, writer, broadcaster, DJ and record company executive; *Owner, Prima Records*

Limited; b. 18 Sept. 1955, Louisville, Ky; s. of Gus M. Griffin and Elizabeth S. Griffin ('Bunch'); m. 1st Kate St John 1993 (divorced); one d.; m. 2nd Dr Rhiannon Owen 2009. *Education:* Univ. of South Carolina, Univ. of Southern California. *Career:* played with The Frosties 1973–77, The Unclaimed 1979–82, The Long Ryders 1982–87, Western Electric 1999–2001; soloist and leader with The Coal Porters 1991–98, 2002–; released various singles, EPs and albums with these bands; Owner Prima Records Ltd; DJ, Mean Country 1035AM, BBC 6 Music Radio (resident musicologist for The Radcliffe & Maconie Show); Founder-mem. The Paisley Underground; mem. American Fed. of Musicians, Int. Bluegrass Music Asscn. *Films:* Gram Parsons, Fallen Angel (Warner Bros/BBC). *Radio:* Will the Circle Be Unbroken: The Story of the Carter Family (narrated by Dolly Parton) (BBC). *Recordings include:* albums: with the Long Ryders: 10-5-60 1983, Native Sons 1984, State of Our Union 1985, Two-Fisted Tales 1987, Metallic B.O. 1988, Anthology 1998, Three Minute Warnings: The Long Ryders Live In New York City 2004, The Best of the Long Ryders 2004, State of Our Reunion 2004; others: Danny and Dusty, The Lost Weekend 1986; with The Cole Porters: Rebels Without Applause 1991, The Coal Porters 1992, Land of Hope and Crosby 1994, Los London 1995, EP Roulette 1998, Gram Parsons Tribute Concert 1999, Western Electric 1999, Chris Hillman Tribute Concert 2001, How Dark This Earth Will Shine 2004, Turn the Water On, Boy 2008, Durango 2010, Find the One 2012; solo: Little Victories 1997, Sid Griffin: Worldwide Live, 1997–2002 2002, As Certain as Sunrise 2005. *Publications:* Bluegrass Guitar: Know the Players, Play the Music 2005, Million Dollar Bush: Bob Dylan, The Band and the Basement Tapes 2007, Shelter from the Storm: Bob Dylan's Rolling Thunder Review 2009; contrib. to Q, Mojo, BAM, and Country Music International magazines, The Guardian, Music Week, Variety, Uncut. *Honours:* Hon. mem. Athenaeum Literary Asscn; Lifetime Achievement Plaque, Premio Piero Ciampi Festival, Florence, Italy 2002. *Current Management:* c/o 830 Warren Avenue, Venice, CA 90291, USA. *Telephone:* (310) 399-7047. *E-mail:* danperloff@me.com. *Address:* PO Box 2539, London, NW3 6DF, England (office). *Telephone:* (20) 7794-4450 (office). *E-mail:* squidside@ blueyonder.co.uk (office). *Website:* www.sidgriffin.com.

GRIFFIN, Dan; Canadian keyboard player and record producer. *Education:* McMaster Univ. *Career:* Founder mem. Charlemagne, formed in Hamilton, Ont. 2006, renamed Arkells 2008–11; signed to Dine Alone Records 2006; released debut EP Deadlines 2007; opening act for Matt Mayes & El Torpedo on Canadian tour 2008; toured with Waking Eyes on Canadian tour 2009; enrolled at law school 2011–; mem. The Regrets 2012–. *Recordings:* albums: with Arkells: Jackson Square 2008, Michigan Left (also producer) 2011; solo: Leave Your Love 2012, Bordertown 2013. *Honours:* 102.1 The Edge CASBY Award 2009, Juno Awards for New Group of the Year 2010, for Group of the Year 2012. *Current Management:* Adam Countryman, The Agency Group Ltd, 2 Berkeley Street, Suite 202, Toronto, ON M5A 4J5, Canada. *Telephone:* (416) 368-5599 (Agency Group). *Fax:* (416) 368-4655 (Agency Group). *E-mail:* adamcountryman@theagencygroup.com. *Website:* www.theagencygroup.com. *E-mail:* dangriffinmusic@gmail.com. *Website:* dangriffin.ca.

GRIFFIN, Della; American jazz singer and musician (drums); b. 6 Dec. 1925, Newberry, South Carolina. *Career:* played clubs in New York, including The Blue Note, The Blue Book 1973–87; recorded first album aged 65. *Recordings include:* albums: I'll Get By 1990, Travelin' Light 1992, The Very Thought Of You 1998. *Address:* c/o Savant Records, Jazz Depot, 106 71st Street, New York, NY 10023, USA. *Website:* www.jazzdepot.com.

GRIFFIN, Richard (see Professor Griff)

GRIFFITH, Nanci; American singer, songwriter and musician (guitar); b. 6 July 1953, Seguin, Tex.; d. of Griff Griffith and Ruelene Griffith. *Career:* fmr schoolteacher. *Theatre:* Nanci Griffith on Broadway 1994. *Recordings include:* albums: There's A Light Beyond These Woods 1977, Once In A Very Blue Moon 1984, The Last Of The True Believers 1985, Poet In My Window 1986, Lone Star State of Mind 1987, Little Love Affairs 1988, One Fair Summer Evening 1988, Storms 1989, Late Night Grand Hotel 1991, The MCA Years – A Retrospective 1993, Other Voices, Other Rooms 1993 (Grammy Award for Best Folk Album 1994), Flyer 1994, Blue Roses from the Moons 1997, Revisited 1999, The Dust Bowl Symphony 1999, Clocks Without Hands 2001, Ruby's Torch 2006, The Loving Kind 2009, Intersection 2012. *Publications include:* Two Of A Kind Heart 1988. *Honours:* Folk Award for Lifetime Achievement, BBC Radio 2 2010. *Current Management:* Gold Mountain Entertainment, 11 Music Square East, Suite 103, Nashville, TN 37203, USA. *Telephone:* (615) 255-9000. *Website:* www.gmemusic.com; www.nancigriffith.com.

GRIFFITHS, Franny; British musician (keyboards) and songwriter; b. 1970. *Career:* mem., Space 1993–2005, 2011–; numerous tours and television appearances. *Recordings include:* singles: If It's Real 1993, Money 1995, Neighbourhood 1996, Female of the Species 1997, Me and You vs the World 1997, Dark Clouds 1997, Avenging Angels 1997, The Ballad of Tom Jones with Cerys Matthews 1998, Begin Again 1998, Bad Days 1998; albums: Spiders 1996, Remixes and B-Sides 1997, Tin Planet 1998, Greatest Hits 2001, Suburban Rock 'N' Roll 2004, Greatest Hits: Collectors Edition 2005; also collaborated with Tom Jones, Sunny Afternoon (on Reload album) 1999. *Website:* spacetheband.com.

GRIFFITHS, Marcia; Jamaican reggae singer; b. 1954, Kingston. *Career:* singer with Byron Lee and the Dragonaires, 1964–; studio singer for Studio One; mem., Bob and Marcia (with Bob Andy) 1969–74; mem., I-Threes, with

Rita Marley and Judy Mowatt; worked with the Wailers, and Bob Marley, – 1981; worked with numerous artists, including Owen Boyce, Free-I, Tony Gregory, Bob Marley, Judy Mowatt, Max Romeo, Sanchez, Martha Velez, Bunny Wailer. *Recordings include:* albums: The Original – At Studio One 1973, Sweet Bitter Love 1974, Young, Gifted And Black 1976, Naturally 1978, Steppin' 1979, Rock My Soul 1984, I Love Music 1986, Marcia 1988, Carousel 1990, Indomitable 1993, Put A Little Love In Your Heart: The Best Of... 1969–1974 1993, Truly 1998, Certified 1999, with the I-Threes: Many Are Called 1983, Beginning 1986, Dreamland 1996, Certified 1999, Shining Time 2005, Melody Life 2007, Marcia Griffiths & Friends 2012. *Website:* www .marciagriffiths.net.

GRIFFITHS, Ryan; Australian musician (acoustic guitar); b. 1978. *Career:* mem., The Vines 2002–; numerous tours and festival appearances. *Recordings include:* albums: Highly Evolved 2002, Winning Days 2004, Vision Valley 2006, Melodia 2008, Future Primitive 2011. *Honours:* ARIA Award for Breakthrough Artist Single (for Get Free) 2002, NME Award for Best Single (for Get Free) 2003. *Current Management:* Winterman and Goldstein Management, PO Box 1669, Potts Point, NSW 2011, Australia. *Website:* www .thevines.com.

GRIGOROV, Robert (Robo); Slovak singer, composer and producer; b. 25 Sept. 1964, Bratislava; s. of Božidar Jankov Grigorov and Elizabeth Grigorov; two d. *Career:* has written song lyrics co-operatively with K. Peteraj, L. Zeman, J. Žák, D. Mikletič, V. Krausz, B. Filan and in English with V. Cort; music for theatre: Eunuch 1985; music for films: Obycajny Den 1985, Most 1993; touring with own group, Midi 1982–; other bands: Presporok (folk and ethnic music) 1981, Ventil RG (reggae and ska) 1983; mem. SOZA, Slovenskyhudobny Fond, Lita. *Play:* Eunuch (theatre music for Andrej Bagar's theatre Nitra, directed by Jozef Bednarik). *Compositions:* Robo and Midi, 1985; Mohy, LP, 1986; Olohy, 1984; Cierny Kon, 1989; Chcemja Najst, 1985; Espresso Orient, 1987; Unplugged, 1994; Udychni Reggae, 1995; The Best of Chodci Sveta, 1997. *Films:* Fontána Pre Zuzanu 1 (actor and singer) 1986, Obycajny den; duets with M. Gombitovou: koncert našej lásky, Most. *Television:* Pa a pi (series) 1987, Documentary (STV) 1989, Vlastnymi slovami (documentary, STV) 1996, Obchod so stastim (series) 2008, Legends of Pop (RTVS) 2012. *Recordings:* LPs (Slovak): Robo Grigorov & midi 1987, Robo-midi-Nohy 1987, Noconi 1990, Narod kanibal 1990, Chybas mi 1992, Z extremu do ekstremu 1993, Unplugged 14 naj 1994, Vdychni Reggae 1995, Chodci sveta 1997, Sam 2000, Laska pivo anjel smutok 2001, Gold 2006, Balady 2006, Live 2007, Complete of 2008; LPs (English): Don't Punk Out 1987, I Stand By 'U' 1991; SPs: Posledný valčík pre Európu – Espresso Orient 1985, Úlohy – Primrznutá 1986, Vel'ký smútok malých miest 1986, Chcem t'a nájst' – Cierny kôň 1987, Bud'me si vzácni/Gott, birka, Grigorov, Březinová, Semelka 1991, Ona je Madona 1992, Zbohom zásadám – Láska, viera, nádej 1993, Happy Birthday/Elán, Grigorov, Lehotský, birka, Haščáková, Müller 1995, Malý Gavroch – Bonita Señorita 1996, Len ty 1999, Robo Grigorov & The Band, Bojuj, vstváj – Skús ma láska viest' 1998 etc.; compilations: Ze mi je luto 1987, Boom hits Vol. 1–Vol. 5 2005–07, Gold 2006 etc.; other compilations: Ja viem 1981, Superhity II 1989–2000, Ona je Madona 2002, Dvaja 2005, Kým ta mám 2006, Legalizuj 2006, Povedzme 2006, Povedzme 2007, Pocta Maja-kovskému 2007, Pocta Majakovskému 2007, Neviem, či viem 2008, Najrý-chlejší z rýchlych, Dvaja 2008, Pocta Majakovskému 2008, Naj Sk Hitov 2008, Povedzme 2008. *Honours:* Bratislavska Lyra 1984, 1985, 1986, Cena Hulobne'ho Fontu 1985, Diskoslavik 1984, Zlaty slavik radios 2004, Prize for most played song, SOZA 2005. *E-mail:* grigorovrobo@gmail.com.

GRILLO, Alex; French musician (vibraphone); b. 7 March 1956, Fiume-Veneto, Italy. *Career:* mem. SACEM, SACD, UMJ. *Recordings include:* A Table! 1985, Neuf Pour Neuf 1988, Mass For Choir and Organ, Music for theatre and ballet 1990, 1991,Vibraphone Alone 1993, Sweet Desdemone (rock jazz oratorio) 1995, Couples 1997, Triplett 2001, L'Amour tome 1 2002, Momento 2005, La musique de l'Afrique est en nous 2006, Katak2 Bertanggo. *Publications include:* C'est Tout Droit (suite for xylophone).

GRIMES, Ged; British musician (bass guitar, upright bass, percussion, keyboards, drums), composer and producer; *Director, Heist Records;* b. 28 March 1962, Dundee, Scotland; m. Patricia Colette Boyle 1991. *Career:* Founding mem. Danny Wilson 1983–90; tours: USA, UK, Japan; toured with Eddi Reader 1994–95; worked with Natalie Imbruglia, Lostboy AKA; Bassist with Deacon Blue 2007–10; mem. Simple Minds 2010–; radio and TV appearances: Montreux Rock Festival, Top of the Pops, Chart Show, The Late Show, Jools Holland Show, Radio 1 sessions; set up production co. Jack's Hoose Music 1997; currently producer and Dir, Heist Records; mem. Musicians' Union, Performing Right Soc., PPL. *Compositions:* music for computer games, including Earthworm Jim 3D, Amplitude, Enter The Matrix, Pop Idol, Rhythmic Star, Quarrel, Ben 10, Spongebob Squarepants. *Recordings:* hit single: Mary's Prayer 1987; albums: with Danny Wilson: Meet Danny Wilson 1987, Be-Bop Mop-Top 1988, Sweet Danny Wilson 1991; with Gary Clark: Ten Short Songs About Love 1993; contrib. to White Lillies Island, Natalie Imbruglia 2001; co-producer: Bel Canto, Eilidh Mackenzie, Simple Minds. *Honours:* Scottish Music Futures Award 2008. *Address:* c/o Jack's Hoose Music, The Radio Tay Building, 6 North Isla Street, Dundee, DD3 7JQ, Scotland (office). *E-mail:* studio@jackshoosemusic.com (office). *Website:* www .heistrecords.com (office).

GRIP, Erik, Cand. Architect; Danish singer, songwriter, composer and musician (guitar); b. 2 July 1947, Nykobing Falster; m. Joan Riboe; two s.

one d. *Career:* Gen. Sec., Danish Soc. for Jazz, Rock and Folk Composers (DJBFA) 1976–86; mem. Roskilde Co. Council 2000–06. *Recordings include:* 29 albums. *Honours:* Special Prize, Søren Gyldendal Foundation 1982, Award of Honour from his colleagues for his honest approach to folk singing 1986. *Address:* Stationsvej 23, 4320 Lejre, Denmark. *Website:* www.grip.dk.

GROBAN, Joshua (Josh) Winslow; American singer and songwriter; b. 27 Feb. 1981, Los Angeles, Calif. *Education:* Los Angeles Co. High School for the Arts. *Career:* solo artist 1997–; has performed or recorded with artists including Celine Dion, Barbra Streisand, Andrea Bocelli, Sarah Brightman, Imogen Heap; performed at Winter Olympics closing ceremony 2002, Nobel Peace Prize Concert, Sundance Film Festival; Amb., Nelson Mandela's Project 46664. *Recordings include:* Josh Groban 2001, Closer 2003, Awake 2006, Noël 2007, Illuminations 2010, All That Echoes 2013. *Honours:* Acad. Award (for Believe from soundtrack to Polar Express) 2005. *Website:* www.joshgroban .com.

GROCOTT, Stephen, BA (Hons); British composer, musician (guitar, mandolin, harmonium, flowerpots), vocalist and teacher; b. 21 Feb. 1953, London, England. *Education:* Univ. of Kent. *Career:* composer and performer, The Drones Quartet 1986–; music teacher 1990–; mem. PRS, Musicians' Union, Carl Orff Soc. *Compositions:* Playing With Fire (music for bonfire, pyrotechnics, quartet) 1991, The Toy Symphony (music for toys and instruments) 1992. *Recordings include:* Albums: with The Drones: The Drones 1992, Giant Bonsai 1994; with Rory McLeod: Angry Love 1996, Footsteps and Heartbeats 1996. *E-mail:* steve.grocott@btinternet.com (office). *Website:* www.dronesmusic.net (office).

GROHL, David (Dave); American musician (drums, guitar), singer and actor; b. 14 Jan. 1969, Warren, Ohio; m. 1st Jennifer Youngblood (divorced); m. 2nd Jordyn Blum; one d. *Career:* fmr mem. Freak Baby, later renamed Mission Impossible, and Fast 1980s; fmr mem. Dain Bramage; mem. Scream 1986–90; mem. Nirvana 1990–94; Founder-mem. Foo Fighters 1994–; side projects include Probot 2004, Them Crooked Vultures 2009–. *Recordings include:* albums: with Nirvana: Nevermind 1991, Incesticide 1993, In Utero 1993, Unplugged In New York 1994, From the Muddy Banks 1996, Hormoaning 1999; with Foo Fighters: Foo Fighters 1995, The Colour And The Shape 1997, There Is Nothing Left To Lose (Grammy Award for Best Rock Album 2001) 1999, One By One (Grammy Award for Best Rock Album 2003) 2002, In Your Honor 2005, Skin and Bones 2006, Echoes, Silence, Patience and Grace (Grammy Award for Best Rock Album 2008, BRIT Award for Best Int. Album 2008) 2007, Wasting Light (Grammy Award for Best Rock Album 2012) 2011, Sonic Highways 2014; with Probot: Probot 2004; with Them Crooked Vultures: Them Crooked Vultures 2009. *Films include:* Tenacious D in The Pick of Destiny 2006, The Muppets 2011, Back and Forth 2011. *Soundtracks include:* This Life 1997, Daria 2000, The Perfect Score 2004, Parashat Ha-Shavua 2008, Somewhere 2010. *Honours:* two MTV Video Music Awards (for Smells Like Teen Spirit) 1992, BRIT Award for Best Int. Newcomer (with Nirvana) 1993, Grammy Award for Best Short Form Music Video (for Learn To Fly) 2001, Grammy Awards for Best Hard Rock Performance (for All My Life) 2003, (for The Pretender) 2008, (for White Limo) 2012, Kerrang! Award for Best Single (for Best of You) 2005, Nordoff-Robbins Silver Clef Raymond Weil Int. Award 2006, BRIT Awards for Best Int. Group 2008, 2012, 2015, Grammy Award for Best Song (for Walk) 2012, Grammy Award for Best Rock Performance (for Walk) 2012, for Best Rock Song (for Cut Me Some Slack) 2014. *Current Management:* c/o Gold Mountain Entertainment, Suite 450, 3575 Cahunega Blvd West, Los Angeles, CA 90068, USA. *Website:* www.themcrookedvultures.com; www.foofighters.com.

GROOVEBOX (see Vega, Louie)

GROSZ, Martin Oliver; American musician (guitar); b. 28 Feb. 1930, Berlin, Germany; m. Rachel Whelan; two s. *Career:* professional musician 1948–; recorded under own name in 1950s; performed with Village Stompers, Dukes of Dixieland; Bandleader, New York Jazz repertory group, Soprano Summit 1975–76; mem., Musicians' Union. *Recordings include:* Hooray For Bix, Riverside '57 1975, Let Your Fingers Do The Walking (Guitar Duets) 1978, Swing It, Unsaturated Fats, Donaldson Redux, Just Imagine: The Music of DeSylva, Brown and Henderson, The Rhythm for Sale, Remembering Louis, Chasin' the Spots, Marty Grosz and His Hot Combination, Acoustic Heat: Jazz Guitar Duets, Hot Winds: The Classic Sessions, The James P. Johnson Songbook. *Publications include:* Writer on Jazz Guitars and Frank Teschemacher for Time/Life magazines. *Honours:* winner, Jazzology Guitar Poll 1986. *Website:* www.martygrosz.com.

GRUSIN, Dave; American composer, record producer and musician (piano, keyboards); b. 26 June 1934, Littleton, Colo. *Education:* Univ. of Colorado. *Career:* Dir of Music, Andy Williams Show 1959–66; as pianist, played with Art Pepper, Spike Robinson, Terry Gibbs, Benny Goodman, Thad Jones, Carmen McRae, Sarah Vaughan; arranger for Phoebe Snow, Peggy Lee, Barbra Streisand, Patti Austin, The Byrds, Grover Washington Jr, Al Jarreau, Donna Summer; Co-founder (with Larry Rosen) and Owner, GRP Records 1976–; solo pianist, also performs with brother Don Grusin, and jazz-fusion septet NY-LA Dream Band. *Compositions for film and television include:* Three Days of The Condor, The Graduate, Heaven Can Wait, On Golden Pond, Tootsie, Reds, The Little Drummer Girl, The Goonies, The Milago Beanfield War (Academy Award for Best Original Score 1988, Grammy Award for Best Arrangement on an Instrumental), The Fabulous Baker Boys (Grammy Award for Best Original Background Score 1989), Havana, The

Firm, Mulholland Falls, Random Hearts, Dinner With Friends, Even Money, Recount; also composed television themes, including St Elsewhere, Roots, The Girl from U.N.C.L.E. *Recordings include:* albums: solo: Candy 1961, The Many Moods of Dave Grusin 1962, Kaleidoscope 1964, Discovered Again 1976, One of a Kind 1977, Dave Grusin and the GRP All-Stars 1980, Out of The Shadows 1982, Mountain Dance 1983, The NY-LA Dream Band 1988, Cinemagic 1987, One of a Kind 1988, Migration 1989, Havana 1990, The Dave Grusin Collection 1991, The Gershwin Collection 1992, Homage To Duke 1993, The Orchestral Album 1994, Two for the Road 1996, Presents West Side Story 1997, Two Worlds 2000, Amparo 2008, An Evening with Dave Grusin 2010, One Night Only! 2011; with Lee Ritenour: Harlequin 1984; with Don Grusin: Sticks and Stones 1988; also recorded with Billy Joel, Paul Simon, Gerry Mulligan. *Honours:* Grammy Awards include for Best Instrumental Arrangement (for My Funny Valentine) 1989, for Best Arrangement on an Instrumental (for Bess You Is My Woman) 1991, for Best Instrumental Arrangement (for Mood Indigo) 1993, for Best Instrumental Arrangement (for Three Cowboy Songs) 1994. *Current Management:* c/o Kraft-Engel Management, 15233 Ventura Blvd, Suite 200, Sherman Oaks, CA 91403, USA. *Telephone:* (818) 380-1918. *E-mail:* info@Kraft-Engel.com. *Website:* www .kraft-engel.com.

GRUZ, Sergio, DE; Argentine/French musician (piano), composer and arranger; b. 17 Feb. 1968, Buenos Aires. *Education:* Univ. of Buenos Aires. *Recordings include:* Bernardo Baraj Quintet Argentina 1992, Tierra del Fuego France 1994, Sergio Gruz Trio France 1995, Misanthrope France 1997, Point de vue (Sergio Gruz Quintet) 1998, Intuitions (Damien Prud'homme Quartet) 2004, Ensemble (Sergio Gruz Trio) 2005, Eclipsis (Sylvain del Campo) 2007, Carrousel (Sergio Gruz Trio) 2008, Records et Gats (Japan), Onda Alpin, Karlheinz Miklin & Qinteto Argentina 2009, Ida (Ricardo Izquierdo Quartet) 2014, Free Tango (with Olivier Manoury) 2015, Hypnosis (Sergio Gruz Quartet) 2015. *Television:* music scores for many commercials for Musée Quai Branly, Paris. *E-mail:* yo@sergiogruz.com; sergruz@gmail.com. *Website:* www .sergiogruz.com.

GRYTT, Kajsa; Swedish singer, songwriter and musician (guitar); b. 20 June 1961, Stockholm; one s. *Career:* leader of punk group, Tant Strul 1981–85; mem. SKAP, Svenska Musiker Föbundet; mem. Aunt Fuzz 2008–. *Compositions include:* Amason, Dunkar varmt, Sucka Migren, Igen, Vand Digbort, Han Sager, Om Du Kunde Semig, Som Om Himlen; Revolution; Visa Horman Alskar. *Recordings include:* Tant Strul, Amason, Ojag Onskar Dig, Historier Fran En Vag, Den Andra Varuden, Kajsa Grytt, Revolution, Är Vi På Väg Hem? 2003, Historier Från Ett Kvinnofängelse 2006, En Kvinna under Påverkan 2011. *Honours:* Skap Stipendie 1981. *E-mail:* info@kajsagrytt.com. *Website:* www.kajsagrytt.com.

DJ GUAN (see Allstar Fresh)

GUBAIDULINA, Sofia Asgatovna; Russian (b. Tatar) composer; b. 24 Oct. 1931, Chistopol; d. of Asgat Gubaidulin and Fedossia Gubaidulina; m. Peter Meshchaninov; one d. *Education:* Kazan and Moscow Conservatories, pvt. studies with Nikolai Peiko, Vissarion Shebalin and Grigori Kogan. *Career:* first noticed abroad, Paris 1979; UK debut (Symphony in 12 Movements) 1987; freelance composer in Moscow 1963–91, in Germany 1991–. *Compositions include:* instrumental: Piano quintet 1957, Allegro rustico for flute and piano 1963, Five Etudes for harp, double bass and percussion 1965, Vivente non vivente for synthesizer 1970, Concordanza for chamber ensemble 1971, String Quartet No. 1 1971, Fairytale Poem 1971, Stufen (The Steps) 1971, Detto II for cello and ensemble 1972, Rumore e Silenzio for percussion and harpsichord 1974, Quattro for 2 trumpets and 2 trombones 1974, Concerto for bassoon and low strings 1975, Sonata for double bass and piano 1975, Light and Darkness for solo organ 1976, Dots, Lines and Zigzag for bass clarinet and piano 1976, Revue for orchestra and jazz band 1976, Duo-Sonata for 2 bassoons 1977, Quartet for 4 flutes 1977, Misterioso for 7 percussionists 1977, Te Salutant capriccio for large light orchestra 1978, Introitus concerto for piano and chamber orchestra 1978, Detto I sonata for organ and percussion 1978, De profundis for solo bayan 1978, Sounds of the Forest for flute and piano 1978, In Croce for cello and organ 1979, Jubilatio for 4 percussionists 1979, Offertorium concerto for violin and orchestra 1980, Garten von Freuden und Traurigkeiten for flute, harp and viola (speaker ad lib) 1980, Rejoice sonata for violin and cello 1981, Descensio for ensemble 1981, Seven Words for cello, bayan and strings 1982, In the Beginning there was Rhythm for 7 percussionists 1984, Et exspecto sonata for solo bayan 1985, Quasi Hoquetus for viola, bassoon, cello and piano 1985, Stimmen... vetummen..., symphony in 12 movements 1986, Answer without Question collage for 3 orchestras 1988, Pro et Contra for large orchestra 1989, Silenzio 5 pieces for bayan, violin and cello 1991, Even and Uneven for 7 percussionists 1991, Tatar dance for 2 double basses and bayan 1992, Dancer on a Tightrope for violin and piano 1993, Meditation on the Bach-Choral Vor deinen Thron tret ich hiermit for harpsichord, 2 violins, viola, cello and double bass 1993, Early in the Morning, Right Before Waking for 7 kotos 1993, The Festivities at Their Height for cello and orchestra 1993, Now Always Snow for chamber ensemble and chamber choir on poems of Gennady Aigi 1993, 2nd cello concerto 1994, In anticipation... for saxophone quartet and 6 percussion 1994, Zeitge-stalten symphony in 4 movements 1994, Quaternion for 4 cellos 1996, Galgenlieder à 3 15 pieces for mezzo, double bass and percussion 1996, Galgenlieder à 5 1996, Ritorno perpetuo for harpsichord 1997, Canticle of the Sun for cello, chamber chorus and 2 percussionists 1997, Im Schatten des Baumes for koto, bass-koto, cheng and orchestra 1998; vocal: Phacelia vocal cycle for soprano and orchestra 1956,

Night in Memphis cantata for mezzo-soprano, male chorus and chamber orchestra 1968, Rubaiyat 1969, Roses 5 romances for soprano and piano 1972, Counting Rhymes 5 children's songs 1973, Hour of the Soul for mezzo-soprano and large orchestra 1976, Perception for soprano, baritone and 7 string instruments 1981, Hommage à Marina Tsvetava, suite in 5 movements for chorus a cappella 1984, Hommage à T. S. Eliot for soprano and octet 1987, Witty Waltzing in the style of Johann Strauss for soprano and octet 1987, Two Songs on German Folk Poetry for soprano, flute, harpsichord and cello 1988, for piano and string quartet 1989, Jauchzt vor Gott for chorus and organ 1989, Aus dem Stundenbuch for cello, orchestra, male chorus and female speaker 1991, Johannes Passion 2000, Johannes Ostern 2001, Risonanza for chamber ensemble 2001, Reflections on the theme B-A-C-H 2002, Mirage: the Dancing Sun for eight violoncelli 2002, On the Edge of the Abyss for seven violoncelli and two waterphones 2002, The Rider on the White Horse for large orchestra and organ 2002, The Light of the END for large orchestra 2003, Under the Sign of Scorpio for bayan and large orchestra 2003, Verwandlung for trombone, saxophone quartet, cello, contra basso and tam-tam 2004, The Deceitful Face of Hope and Despair for flute and large orchestra 2005, Feast during a Plague for large orchestra 2006, Die Leier des Orpheus for violin, string orchestra and percussion 2006, Ravvedimento for cello and guitar quartet 2007, In Tempus Praesens for violin and orchestra 2007, Glorious Percussion concerto for percussion and orchestra 2008, Fachwerk concerto for bayan, percussion and strings 2009, Sotto voce for viola, double bass and two guitars 2010. *Honours:* Hon. DHumLitt (Univ. of Chicago) 2011; Great Distinguished Service Cross of the Order of Merit (FRG) 2002; numerous awards including Prix de Monaco 1987, Koussevitzky Int. Record Award 1989 and 1994, Premio Franco Abbiati 1991, Heidelberg Artists Prize 1991, Russian State Prize 1992, Premium Imperiale 1998, Léonie Sonning Music Prize 1999, Goethe Medal, City of Weimar 2001, Royal Swedish Acad. of Music Polar Prize 2002, Living Composer Prize, Cannes Classical Awards 2003, European Culture Prize 2005, Bach Prize, Hamburg 2007. *Address:* Ziegeleiweg 12, 25482 Appen, Germany (home). *Telephone:* (41) 2281875 (home).

GUBBAY, Raymond, CBE, FRSA; British music promoter; *Chairman, Raymond Gubbay Ltd*; b. 2 April 1946, London, England; s. of the late David Gubbay and Ida Gubbay; m. Johanna Quirke 1972 (divorced 1988); two d. *Education:* Univ. Coll. School, Hampstead. *Career:* concert promoter 1966–; Founder, Man. Dir and Chair. Raymond Gubbay Ltd 1966–; presents regular series of concerts at major London and regional concert halls including Royal Albert Hall, Royal Festival Hall, Barbican Centre, Symphony Hall Birmingham, Bridgewater Hall Manchester, Royal Concert Hall Glasgow and in Ireland, Belgium, Germany, Austria, Switzerland, Netherlands and Scandinavia; has presented productions of: (operas and operettas) The Ratepayer's Iolanthe 1984, Turandot 1991–92, La Bohème (centenary production) 1996, 2004, 2006, Carmen 1997, 2002, 2005, 2009, 2010, 2013, Madam Butterfly 1998, 2000, 2003, 2011, The Pirates of Penzance 1998–99, 2000, Tosca 1999, Aïda 2001, Cavalleria Rusticana and Pagliacci 2002; (ballets) Swan Lake 1997, 1999, 2002, 2004, 2007, 2010, 2013, Romeo and Juliet 1998, The Sleeping Beauty 2000; D'Oyly Carte Opera Co. seasons 2000–03, Follies 2003, On Your Toes 2004, Savoy Opera 2004, Showboat 2006, Carmen Jones 2007, Strictly Gershwin 2008, 2011, The King and I 2009, Aïda (new production) 2012; mem. Bd Royal Philharmonic Orchestra, Bd Govs Cen. School of Ballet. *Honours:* Hon. FRAM 1988, Hon. FTCL 2000, Gold Badge Award, British Acad. of Songwriters, Composers and Authors 2009. *Address:* Dickens House, 15 Tooks Court, London, EC4A 1QH, England (office). *Telephone:* (20) 7025-3750 (office). *E-mail:* info@raymondgubbay.co.uk (office). *Website:* www.raymondgubbay.co.uk (office).

GUDJONSSON, Arnar; Icelandic singer, songwriter and musician (guitar). *Career:* Founder-mem., Leaves 2001–. *Recordings include:* albums: Breathe 2002, The Angela Test 2005, We Are Shadows 2009. *E-mail:* leaves@leaves.is. *Website:* www.leaves.is.

GUERRA, Juan Luis; Dominican Republic singer and musician (guitar); b. 7 July 1956, Santo Domingo; m.; one s. *Education:* Conservatorio Nacional de Música, Santo Domingo, Univ. Autónoma de Santo Domingo, Berklee Coll. of Music, USA. *Career:* formed group 4.40 1984–; leading artist in Merengue style; f. charitable org. Fundación Juan Luis Guerra 1991–. *Recordings include:* albums: Soplando 1984, Mudanza Y Acarreo 1986, Mientras Más Lo Pienso... Tú 1987, Ojalá Que Llueva Café 1989, El Original 4.40 1990, Burbujas de Amor 1990, Bachata Rosa (Grammy Award for Best Tropical Latin Album) 1990, Bilirrubina 1991, Areito 1992, Fogaraté 1994, Ni Es Lo Mismo Ni Es Igual 1998, Para Ti (Billboard Latin Music Award for Best Male Tropical Album, for Best Latin Christian/Gospel Album 2005) 2004, La Llave de mi Corazón (Latin Grammy Awards for Album of the Year and Best Merengue Album 2007, Grammy Award for Best Tropical Latin Album 2008) 2007, A Son de Guerra (Latin Grammy Awards for Album of the Year, for Best Contemporary Tropical Album) 2010, Colección Cristiana 2012, Todo Tiene Su Hora (Latin Grammy Awards for Album of the Year, for Best Contemporary Tropical Album 2015) 2014. *Honours:* Hon. Prof., Univ. Autónoma de Santo Domingo; El Soberano de Casandra, Latin Grammy Awards for Best Merengue Performance, Best Tropical Song (for El Niagara En Bicicleta) 2000, for Record of the Year, Song of the Year and Best Tropical Song (for La Lleve de mi Corazón) 2007, Billboard Latin Music Spirit of Hope Award 2005, Latin Grammy Award for Best Tropical Song (for Bachata en Fukuoka) 2010. *Website:* www.juanluisguerra.com.

GUERREIRO, Katia, MD; Portuguese singer and medical doctor; b. 23 Feb. 1976, South Africa. *Education:* Universidade Nova de Lisboa. *Career:* moved to the Azores as a child, then to Lisbon; fmr singer in group, Os Charruas; solo fado singer 2000–; collaborations with Rui Veloso, João Braga, Bernardo Sassetti, Pedro Jóia, Maria Bethânia, Martinho da Vila, Ney Matogrosso, Zé Renato, Manecas Costa, among others; mem. European Cultural Parl. *Recordings:* albums: Fado Maior (Prémio José Alfonso) 2001, Nas Mãos do Fado 2003, Tudo ou Nada 2005, Fado 2008, Os Fados do Fado 2009. *Honours:* named as one of Portugal's 30 most important contributors to the arts and sciences, to celebrate 30th anniversary of the Portuguese revolution 2005, Female Personality of the Year 2005. *Address:* Rua de São João 17, 1° andar, 2645-303 Alcoitão, Portugal (office). *Telephone:* (21) 4604410 (office). *Fax:* (21) 4604419 (office). *E-mail:* bg@bgeventos.com (office); producao.katiaguerreiro@gmal.com (office). *Website:* katiaguerreiro.blogs.sapo.pt; www.katiaguerreiro.com.

GUETTA, David; French producer, DJ and promoter; b. 7 Nov. 1967, Paris; m. Cathy Guetta; one s. one d. *Career:* house music DJ, Radio Nova, Paris 1988–90; fmrly artistic manager, Le Palace nightclub, Paris; organised events in clubs in Paris and Ibiza; headline appearances world-wide in Europe, America, Australia, Japan, South America; collaborations with artists including Akon, Black Eyed Peas and Kelly Rowland. *Recordings:* Just a Little More Love 2002, Guetta Blaster 2004, Pop Life 2007, One Love 2009, Fuck Me I'm Famous (three mix vols) 2009, One More Love 2010, Nothing But the Beat 2011, Listen 2014. *Honours:* DJ Awards for Best Int. DJ and Best Ibiza Night (for Fuck Me I'm Famous) 2007, for Best House DJ 2008, Grammy Awards for Best Remixed Recording (for When Love Takes Over) 2010, (for Revolver) 2011, MTV Europe Music Award for Best Electronic 2012, Billboard Music Award for Top Electronic Dance Music Artist 2013. *Address:* c/o Ultra Records, 235 West 23rd Street, 6th Floor, New York, NY 10011, USA (office). *Telephone:* (212) 343-9429 (office). *E-mail:* info@ultrarecords.com (office). *Website:* www.ultrarecords.com (office); www.davidguetta.com.

GULBRANDSSEN, Arve; Norwegian musician (drums); b. 25 Sept. 1972, Namsois. *Education:* Univ. of Trondheim. *Career:* played in various jazz bands including Fotveita; Smaagnagerne; joined Hedge Hog, 1993; toured Europe 1994, 1995; mem., Norwegian Asscn of Musicians. *Recordings include:* Primal Gutter 1993, Mercury Red 1994, Mindless 1994, The Healing EP, Thorn Cord Wonder 1995, Party Terror Vol. 2 1996, Reverb No Hollowness 1998, The Smell of Fish Balls 1998, Øyvind Ryan - Gruppen 2003, Are Og Odin: Bæ To Da Bone 2004.

GULLEY, John Kenneth, (J. K. Gulley); Canadian singer, songwriter, producer and musician (guitar, mandolin); *Owner/Producer, Blue Gull Studio*; b. 11 Oct. 1954, Toronto; s. of Kenneth George Gulley and Marie Elizabeth McGowan; m. Tami Haskell Jennifer; four c. *Education:* EDHS High School. *Career:* 15 charted singles; tours across Canada, USA, Europe, Scandinavia; with Glen Campbell, Billie Jo Spears, Freddie Hart, Michelle Wright; Owner Gullco Music Group; Owner/Producer, Blue Gull Studio; TV appearances: Ronnie Prophet Show, CTV, John Cameron, CBC, Global Easy Country, NCN, CMT Video and Songwriters Café Special; studio sessions for John Cowan, Mati Haskell, John Landry, Jamie Warren, Gil Grand, Marty Robbins, Roy Clark and many others. *Recordings:* over 100 songs recorded and released, including Dusty Road 1978, Under Cover 1987, Blue Jeans Boy (SOCAN Song of the Year Award) 1990, If She Only Knew Me 1995. *Honours:* RPM Big Country Awards, CCMA Vista Rising Star Award 1986, SOCAN Award. *Current Management:* Gull-Trax Productions: Blue-Gull Studio. *Telephone:* (519) 514-0073. *E-mail:* info@jkgulley.com. *Website:* www.jkgulley.com.

GULZAR; Indian filmmaker, poet and lyricist; b. (Sampooran Singh Kalra), 18 Aug. 1936, Deena, Jhelum Dist (now in Pakistan); s. of Makhan Singh Kalra and Sujan Kaur; m. Rakhee Gulzar; one d. *Career:* came to Delhi following partition; started as poet and was associated with Progressive Writers Asscn; joined Bimal Roy Productions in 1961; first break as lyricist came when he wrote Mora Gora Ang Lai Lae for Bimal Roy's Bandini 1963; began writing for films for dirs Hrishikesh Mukherjee and Asit Sen; turned filmmaker with first film Mere Apne 1971; began partnership with Sanjeev Kumar. *Films directed:* Shriman Satyawadi (Asst Dir) 1960, Kabuliwala (Chief Asst Dir) 1961, Bandini (Asst Dir) 1963, Mere Apne 1971, Parichay 1972, Koshish 1972, Achanak 1973, Mausam (Nat. Award for Best Dir, Filmfare The Best Dir Award) 1975, Khushboo 1975, Aandhi (Storm) 1975, Kitaab (also Producer) 1977, Kinara (also Producer) 1977, Meera 1979, Sahira 1980, Namkeen 1982, Angoor 1982, Suniye 1984, Aika 1984, Ek Akar 1985, Ijaazat (Guest) 1987, Ghalib (TV) 1988, Libaas 1988, Lekin... (But...) 1990, Ustad Amjad Ali Khan 1990, Pandit Bhimsen Joshi 1992, Maachis 1996, Hu Tu Tu 1999. *Film roles include:* Jallianwalla Bagh 1979, Grihapravesh (The Housewarming) (as himself) 1979, Wajood (guest appearance as himself) 1998, Chachi 420 (uncredited cameo appearance during end credits) 1998, Raincoat (voice) 2004, Yuvraaj (special appearance) 2008. *Film dialogue or scripts:* Sangharsh 1968, Aashirwad (The Blessing) 1968, Khamoshi 1969, Anand 1970, Guddi (Darling Child) 1971, Mere Apne 1971, Koshish (Nat. Award for Best Screenplay) 1972, Bawarchi 1972, Namak Haraam (The Ungrateful) 1973, Achanak 1973, Mausam 1975, Khushboo 1975, Chupke Chupke 1975, Aandhi (Storm) 1975, Palkon Ki Chhaon Mein 1977, Meera 1979, Grihapravesh (The Housewarming) 1979, Khubsoorat (Beautiful) 1980, Basera 1981, Namkeen 1982, Angoor 1982, Masoom (Innocent) 1983, New Delhi Times 1986, Ek Pal (A Moment) 1986, Ijaazat (Guest) 1987, Mirza

Ghalib (TV) 1988, Lekin... (But...) 1990, Rudaal (The Mourner) 1993, Maachis 1996, Chachi 420 1998, Hu Tu Tu 1999, Saathiya 2002, Dus Kahaniya 2007. *Film song lyrics:* Swami Vivekananda 1955, Shriman Satyawadi 1960, Kabuliwala 1961, Prem Patra (Love Letter) 1962, Bandini 1963, Purnima 1965, Sannata 1966, Biwi Aur Makan 1966, Do Dooni Char 1968, Aashirwad (The Blessing) 1968, Rahgir 1969, Khamoshi 1969, Anand 1970, Guddi (Darling Child) 1971, Anubhav (Experience) 1971, Seema 1971, Mere Apne 1971, Parichay 1972, Koshish 1972, Doosri Seeta 1974, Chor Machaye Shor 1974, Mausam 1975, Khushboo 1975, Aandhi (Storm) 1975, Shaque 1976, Palkon Ki Chhaon Mein 1977, Kinara 1977, Gharaonda (The Nest) 1977, Ghar (Home) 1978, Meetha (Sweet and Sour) 1978, Devata 1978, Gol Maal (Hanky Panky) 1979, Ratnadeep (The Jewelled Lamp) 1979, Grihapravesh (The Housewarming) 1979, Sitara 1980, Thodisi Bewafaii 1980, Swayamvar 1980, Khubsoorat (Beautiful India) 1980, Garam 1981, Basera 1981, Namkeen 1982, Angoor 1982, Sadma 1983, Masoom (Innocent) 1983, Ghulami 1985, Jeeva 1986, Ek Pal (A Moment) 1986, Ijaazat (Guest) (Nat. Award for Best Lyricist) 1987, Libaas 1988, Lekin... (But...) 1990, Maya Memsaab (Maya: The Enchanting Illusion) 1992, Rudaali (The Mourner) 1993, Mammo 1994, Daayraa (The Square Circle, USA) 1996, Maachis 1996, Aastha (Aastha in the Prison of Spring) 1997, Satya 1998, Dil Se... (From the Heart, USA) 1998, Chachi 420 1998, Hu Tu Tu 1999, Khoobsurat 1999, Fiza 2000, Aks 2001, Asoka (Ashoka the Great, USA) 2001, Filhaal... 2002, Leela 2002, Lal Salaam (Red Salute) 2002, Dil Vil Pyar Vyar 2002, Makdee (The Web of the Witch) 2002, Saathiya 2002, Chupke Se 2003, Pinjar (The Cage) 2003, Jaan-E-Mann 2006, Guru 2007, Slumdog Millionaire (Jai Ho) (Academy Award for Best Original Song 2009, Grammy Award for Best Song Written for Motion Picture, Television or Other Visual Media 2010) 2008, Kaminey 2009, Veer 2010, Ishqiya 2010, Striker 2010, Raavan 2010, 7 Khoon Maaf 2011, Chala Mussaddi... Office Office 2011, Teen Thay Bhai 2011, Jab Tak Hai Jaan 2012, Do Paise Ki Dhoop, Chaar Aane Ki Baarish 2012, Kya Dilli Kya Lahore 2012, Matru Ki Bijlee Ka Mandola 2013, Ek Thi Daayan 2013, Shoebite 2013, Dedh Ishqiya 2014. *Publications include:* poetry: Jaanam 1962, Kuch Aur Nazme 1980, Chand Pukhraj Ka 1995, Triveni 2001, Dhuan 2001, Raat Pashmine Ki 2002, Raat Chand Aur Main 2004, Selected Poems 2008, Yaar Julaahe 2009, 100 Lyrics 2009, Selected Poems 2012; short stories: Raavi Paar 1999, Dhuaan (Sahitya Acad. Award 2003) 2001, Kharaashein 2003, Meelo Se Din 2013, Half a Rupee Stories 2013, My Favourite Stories: Boskys Panchatantra 2013; 12 books for children, including Ekta (Nat. Council for Educ. Research and Training Award 1989). *Honours:* Lifetime Hon. Fellowship, Indian Inst. of Advanced Studies 2001; five Nat. Film Awards, more than 17 Filmfare Awards, including seven for Best Lyricist, Filmfare Lifetime Achievement Award 2002, Padma Bhushan 2004, Dada Saheb Phalke Award 2013. *Address:* Boskiyana, Pali Hill, Bandra (W), Mumbai 400 050, India (home). *Telephone:* (22) 6498351 (home).

GUNDECHA, Ramakant, MMus, MCom; Indian musician; b. 24 Nov. 1962, Ujjain, Madhya Pradesh; m. Renu Ramakant; one s. *Career:* performed Dhrupad Music (vocal) with brother, Umakant, in major festivals in India and in Germany, Switzerland, UK, France, USA, Norway, Singapore, Hong Kong; mem., Multi Arts Complex, Bharat Bhavan, Bhopal; currently teaches at Dhrupad Sansthan, Bhopal; Nat. Fellowship 1987–89; Ustad Allauddin Khan Fellowship 1993. *Recordings include* Raga Komal Rishabh Asavari, Raga Bhairav, Raga Bageshri, Gurupath – Raga Faridi Todi, Gurupath – Raga Bhoopali, Raga Miyan Malhar, Dhrupad Mala (Vol. 1, 2, 3), Raga Kedar, Live at 19th Tokyo Festival, Raga Bilaskhani Todi, Raga Marwa, Raga Ahir Bhairav. *Honours:* Sanskriti Award 1994, Kumar Gandharva Award, Govt of MP 1998, Dagar Gharana Award, Mewar Foundation 2001. *Address:* Gundecha Brothers, 'Sundaram', 15, Lakeside Professor's Colony, Bhopal 462 002 (office); c/o Seher, 59 Jorbagh, 2nd Floor, New Delhi 110 003, India. *Telephone:* (755) 2660873 (Bhopal) (office). *Fax:* (755) 2660873 (Bhopal) (office). *E-mail:* gundechabrothers@gmail.com; gundecha@sancharnet.in; seherculture@hotmail.com. *Website:* www.dhrupad.org.

GUNDECHA, Umakant, MMus, MA; Indian musician; b. 8 May 1959, Ujjain, Madhya Pradesh; m. Aruna Umakant; one s., one d. *Career:* performed Dhrupad Music (vocal) with brother, Ramakant, at major festivals in India and in Germany, Switzerland, UK, France, USA, Norway, Singapore, Hong Kong; mem. Multi Arts Complex, Bharat, Bhavan, Bhopal; currently teaches at Dhrupad Sansthan, Bhopal; Nat. Fellow, 1987–89; Ustad Allauddin Khan Fellowship 1993. *Recordings include* Raga Komal Rishabh Asavari, Raga Bhairav, Raga Bageshri, Gurupath – Raga Faridi Todi, Gurupath – Raga Bhoopali, Raga Miyan Malhar, Dhrupad Mala (Vol. 1, 2, 3), Raga Kedar, Live at 19th Tokyo Festival, Raga Bilaskhani Todi, Raga Marwa, Raga Ahir Bhairav. *Honours:* Sanskriti Award 1994; Kumar Gandharva Award, Govt of MP 1998, Dagar Gharana Award, Mewar Foundation 2001. *Address:* Gundecha Brothers, 'Sundaram', 15, Lakeside Professor's Colony, Bhopal 462 002 (office); c/o Seher, 59 Jorbagh, 2nd Floor, New Delhi 110 003, India. *Telephone:* (755) 2660873 (Bhopal) (office). *Fax:* (755) 2660873 (Bhopal) (office). *E-mail:* gundechabrothers@gmail.com; gundecha@sancharnet.in; seherculture@hotmail.com. *Website:* www.dhrupad.org.

GUO, Yue; Chinese flautist and composer; b. 1958, Beijing; m. Clare Farrow. *Education:* Guildhall School of Music, UK. *Career:* plays traditional Chinese bamboo flute and silver flute; left China 1982; soloist 1990–; also performs with brother Guo Yi as Guo Brothers at int. festivals including WOMAD; performed bamboo flute concerto with BBC Concert Orchestra, WOMAD 1999; played on soundtrack of several films including The Killing Fields 1984,

The Last Emperor 1987; has worked with numerous musicians including Peter Gabriel and the Chieftains. *Recordings include:* Yuan (with Guo Yi and Guo Xan) 1990, Trisan (with Joji Hirota and Pol Brennan) 1992, Red Ribbon (with Joji Hirota) 1995, Music, Food and Love 2007. *Publications include:* Music, Food and Love (with Clare Farrow) 2006, Little Leap Forward 2008. *Address:* 76A Mount Ararat Road, Richmond, Surrey, TW10 6PN, England (office). *E-mail:* guoyue@mac.com (office).

GURD, Geoffrey Robert; British composer, songwriter and musician (guitar, keyboards); b. 24 Feb. 1951, Nottingham. *Education:* Manchester Univ., Univ. of California, Los Angeles, USA. *Career:* guitarist and singer, Crystal, The Sadista Sisters 1975–79; Musical Dir for various acts including The Flirtations, Ritz, Love Bandit; mem., The Twentieth Century Saints 1979–81; The Flying Fratellinis 1981–82; Chief Sound Engineer, Red Shop Studios, London 1982–85; mem., Design for Living 1985–86; mem., Richmond Gurd duo; started own production co. 1986; formed own publishing co., De Mix Music 1989; own record label, DiscoVery 1994; producer of corporate videos and commercials; writer, producer for artists, including Freddie McGregor, Lisa Stansfield, June Montana, Force MDs, Nick Kamen; songwriter for Gina Foster, Dina Carroll; mem. BAC&S, Performing Rights Soc., Musicians' Union, BMI. *Recordings include:* Travels Within (with Richmond Gurd duo) 1994.

GURTU, Trilok; Indian singer, musician (percussion), composer and producer; b. 30 Oct. 1951, Mumbai; s. of Shobha Gurtu. *Education:* Don Bosco High School, Mumbai. *Career:* played with prominent jazz musicians, including John McLaughlin, Ralph Towner, Pat Metheny, Larry Coryell, Jan Garbarek, Bill Evans, Nana Vasconcelos, Joe Zawinul; mem., Don Cherry's Band 1976–78, acoustic jazz-fusion group Oregon 1984–88; solo artist late 1980s–; later moved towards a fusion between Indian and African music, in collaboration with musicians such as Oumou Sangare, Angélique Kidjo, Salif Keita, Zap Mama's Sabine Kabongo. *Recordings include:* albums: with Oregon: Ecotopia 1987, 45th Parallel 1988; solo: Usfret 1987, Living Magic 1990, Similado 1990, Crazy Saints 1993, Believe 1994, Bad Habits Die Hard 1995, The Glimpse 1997, Kathak 1998, African Fantasy 2000, The Beat Of Love 2001, Remembrance 2002, Izzat: The Remix Album 2003, miles_gurtu (with Robert Miles) 2004, Broken Rhythms 2004, Farakala (with the Frikyiwa Family) 2006, Arkeology (with Arkè String Quartet) 2006, Twenty Years of Talking Tabla 2007, Massical 2009. *Honours:* Best Percussionist, Down Beat's Critics Poll 1994, 1995, 1996, 1999, 2000, 2001, 2002, Best Overall Percussionist, Drum Magazine 1999, Carlton TV Multicultural Music Award 2001. *Current Management:* c/o Graham Lawson, Mintaka Music Ltd, Furze Hill, Kilcoe, Skibbereen, West Cork, Ireland. *E-mail:* graham@mintakamusic.com. *Website:* www.mintakamusic.com; www.trilokgurtu.net (home).

GUSEV, Nikolai; Russian composer, songwriter, lyricist, musician (keyboards) and journalist; *Scientific Consultant, INKROM Ltd*; b. 12 May 1957, St Petersburg; m. Marina Guseva 1987; two d. *Education:* St Petersburg Electrical Eng Inst., St Petersburg Univ.; jazz piano, Music Coll.; composition, St Petersburg. *Career:* Founder-mem. alternative bands Strannye Igry and Avia; Russian tours and int. tours with Avia, toured UK, Germany, Netherlands, Italy, France, Belgium, Finland 1988–93; mem. band NOM, toured Russia, Switzerland, Austria, Germany, Italy, France 1996–; freelance journalist 1994–; Chief Ed. Nevsky TV Channel 2001–07; Scientific Consultant, INKROM Ltd 2007–; music project with DEREVO Theatre, Dresden, Germany (with Anton Adasinsky's Positive Band), tours in Russia, Germany; also performs experimental computer music; mem. Russian Authors Asscn, Russian Journalists Soc. *Compositions:* I Don't Like You (with Avia), St Petersburg region anthem 1997. *Recordings include:* albums with Strannye Igry: Red Wine 1984, Keep Your Eyes Open 1986; with Avia: Zudov 1987, Avia for Everybody 1989, Horray! 1991, The Songs About Love and Nature 1994; solo: Zdanov (soundtrack) 1995, No Mistakes! 1997; with NOM: Jir 1998, Extra Compact 2000, The Very Best Show 2001, The Album of Real Art 2003, More Powerful 2007, Above Everything 2009; solo: Fantomas (sountrack) 2008. *Honours:* Best Keyboard Player, St Petersburg Open Rock Festivals, 1985, 1987, 1988, 1990, 1992. *Website:* www.nomzhir.spb.ru.

GUSTAFSSON, Rigmor Elisabeth, MFA; Swedish singer, composer and teacher; b. 12 April 1968, Värmland. *Education:* Royal Coll. of Music, Stockholm, New School Jazz Program and Mannes School of Music, USA. *Career:* lived in New York 1993–96; formed The Rigmor Gustafsson Quintet 1994–; teacher, Mannes Coll. of Music 1995; teacher of jazz singing, Royal Acad. of Music, Stockholm 1996–2000, Royal Coll. of Music, Stockholm 1997. *Recordings include:* albums: with the Rigmor Gustafsson Quintet: In the Light of Day 1997, Plan #46 1998; solo: Live 2000, I Will Wait For You 2003, Close To You (with Jacky Terrasson Trio) 2004, On My Way to You 2006, Alone with You 2007, Calling You (with Radio String Quartet Vienna) 2010, The Signature Edition 6 2011. *Honours:* Jazz Award (Germany) 2004, Värmlänning 2009. *Current Management:* c/o Hilda Sandgren, MTA Production AB, Linnégatan 3, 11447 Stockholm, Sweden. *Telephone:* (8) 660-80-88. *Fax:* (8) 660-84-03. *E-mail:* hilda@mtaprod.se. *Website:* www.mtaprod.se; www.rigmorgustafsson.com.

GUTHRIE, Arlo; American folk singer and songwriter; b. 10 July 1947, Coney Island, NY; s. of Woody Guthrie. *Career:* appearances on folk circuit include Newport Folk Festival. *Recordings include:* albums: Alice's Restaurant, 1967; Arlo, 1968; Running Down The Road, 1969; Alice's Restaurant (soundtrack), 1969; Washington County, 1970; Hobo's Lullaby, 1972; Last of

The Brooklyn Cowboys, 1973; Arlo Guthrie, 1974; Together In Concert (with Pete Seeger), 1975; Amigo, 1976; Outlasting The Blues, 1979; Power of Love, 1981; Someday, 1986; Son of the Wind, 1992; Arlo Guthrie/Pete Seeger, More Together Again, 1994; Alice's Restaurant The Massacre Revisited, 1995; Mystic Journey, 1996, In Times Like These 2007, 32¢ Postage Due 2008, Tales from '69 2009. *Address:* c/o Rising Son Records, ClamZo's Court, 218 Beach Road, Washington, MA 01223, USA. *E-mail:* info@risingsonrecords.com. *Website:* www.risingsonrecords.com; www.arlo.net.

GUTHRIE, Robin; British musician (guitar, keyboards) and producer; b. 4 Jan. 1962, Grangemouth, Scotland; m.; one d. (with Elizabeth Fraser). *Career:* Founder-mem., Cocteau Twins 1981–98; mem., Violet Indiana 1999–; solo artist; worked with 4AD collective This Mortal Coil; collaboration with pianist Harold Budd; producer for numerous indie acts, including Lush, Ian McCulloch, Felt, Guy Chadwick; established own label Bella Union; contributed with band to Found Sound by Spooky 1996. *Recordings include:* albums: with Cocteau Twins: Garlands 1982, Head Over Heels 1983, Treasure 1984, The Pink Opaque 1985, Victorialand 1986, The Moon And The Melodies (with Harold Budd) 1986, Blue Bell Knoll 1988, Heaven Or Las Vegas 1990, Four Calendar Café 1993, Milk And Kisses 1996, The BBC Sessions 1999, Stars And Topsoil 2000; solo: Drifting 1999, Imperial 2003, Continental 2006, Waiting for Dawn 2006, Lumiere 2006, Argenta 2006, Everlasting 2006, 3:19 Bande Originale du Filme 2008, Carousel 2009, Emeralds 2011, Fortune 2012; with Violet Indiana: Roulette 2001, Casino 2002, Russian Doll 2004. *Website:* www.robinguthrie.com; www.cocteautwins.com.

GUTIÉRREZ MUÑOZ, Rafael; Spanish musician (guitar); b. 11 April 1960. *Career:* mem. Hombres G 1983–92, 2002–. *Films include:* Sufre mamón 1987, Suéltate el pelo 1988. *Recordings include:* Hombres G 1985, La cagaste... Burt Lancaster 1986, Estamos locos... ¿o qué? 1987, Agitar antes de usar 1988, Voy a pasármelo bien 1989, Esta es tu vida 1990, Historia del bikini 1992, Peligrosamente juntos 2004, Todo esto es muy extraño 2004, 10 2007, Desayuno Continental 2010, En la playa 2011. *Website:* www.hombres-g.com.

GUTJAHR, Michael; German manager, singer and songwriter; b. Mühlacker; m. Andrea Gutjahr 1990; one s. *Career:* fmr mem. Stromberger music group, ZDF Volkstumliche Hitparade, ARD Schlagerparade der Volksmusik, MDR, SWF television shows and radio interviews; mem. GEMA, IFPI, GVL. *Compositions include:* as lyricist and composer: Jeden Tag Nur Sonnenschein, Das Ist Unser Land, Menschen Helfen Menschen, Frage Nicht, Flieg Vogel Flieg. *Recordings include:* Mitdem Glück Per Du, Stromberger; five albums with Stromberger and others. *Honours:* SDR Golden 7 1993. *Address:* Aischbühlstrasse 28, 75443 Ötisheim, Germany. *E-mail:* michael.gutjahr@t-online.de.

GUY, Athol; Australian singer and musician (bass guitar); b. 5 Jan. 1940, Victoria. *Career:* Founder-mem. folk/pop group, The Seekers –1968, 1993–, worldwide concert tour 1964–68; elected to three successive terms in Victorian Parl. 1971–79; Exec. Dir Clemenger Group 1979–89; fmr Business Development Consultant, St George Bank; Patron, Kids Under Cover, Riding For the Disabled, Relay For Life; Trustee, Mount Macedon Memorial Cross. *Recordings include:* album: Future Road 1997. *Honours:* Queen's Silver Jubilee Medal, Australia's Centenary Medal. *Address:* The Seekers, PO Box 555, South Yarra, Vic 3141, Australia (office). *E-mail:* scbovey@ukonline.co.uk. *Website:* www.theseekers50th.com (office); atholguyandfriends.com.

GUY, George (Buddy); American blues musician (guitar); b. 30 July 1936, Lettsworth, La. *Career:* played with artists, including Slim Harpo, Lightnin' Slim; mem., Rufus Foreman Band; solo artist; mem. houseband, Chess Records, including sessions with Muddy Waters, Howlin' Wolf; musical partnership with Junior Wells; numerous live performances. *Recordings include:* albums: Blues From Big Bill's Copa Cobana 1963, A Man and The Blues 1968, This Is Buddy Guy 1968, Hold That Plane! 1972, I Was Walking Through The Woods 1974, Hot and Cool 1978, Got To Use Your House 1979,

Dollar Done Fell 1980, DJ Play My Blues 1982, The Original Blues Brothers – Live 1983, Ten Blue Fingers 1985, Live At The Checkerboard, Chicago 1979 1988, Breaking Out 1988, Damn Right I Got The Blues (with Eric Clapton, Jeff Beck, Mark Knopfler) (Grammy Award 1992) 1991, My Time After Awhile 1992, Feels Like Rain (Grammy Award 1994) 1993, American Bandstand, Vol. 2 1993, Slippin' In (Grammy Award 1996) 1994, I Cry 1995, Live! The Real Deal 1996, As Good As It Gets 1998, Heavy Love 1998, Last Time Around 1998, The Real Blues 1999, 20th Century Masters – The Millennium Collection 2000, Sweet Tea 2001, Blues Singer (Grammy Award 2004) 2003, Bring 'Em In 2006, Skin Deep 2008, Living Proof (Grammy Award 2011) 2010, Rhythm & Blues 2013, Born to Play Guitar (Grammy Award for Best Blues Album 2016) 2015; with Junior Wells: Buddy and The Juniors 1970, Buddy Guy and Junior Wells Play The Blues 1972, Drinkin' TNT and Smokin' Dynamite 1982, Alone and Acoustic 1991, Alive in Montreux 1992. *Publications:* When I Left Home: My Story (autobiography) 2012. *Honours:* numerous awards including 23 W.C. Handy Awards, Billboard Music Awards Century Award 1993, Nat. Medal of Arts 2003, Kennedy Center Honor 2012. *Address:* Annie Lawlor, GBG Enterprises, 700 South Wabash Avenue, Chicago, IL 60605, USA (office). *Telephone:* (312) 427-0962 (office). *Fax:* (312) 427-5922 (office). *E-mail:* annie@buddyguy.com (office). *Website:* www.buddyguy.com.

GUZMÁN PINAL, (Gabriela) Alejandra; Mexican singer and actress; b. 9 Feb. 1968, Mexico City; d. of Enrique Guzmán and Silvia Pinal; one d. *Career:* actress in stage musicals, TV and film; solo artist 1988–. *Recordings include:* albums: Bye Mamá 1988, Dame tu amor 1989, Eternamente bella 1990, Flor de Papel (ERES magazine album of the year) 1991, Libre 1993, Enorme 1994, Cambio de piel 1996, Algo natural 1999, Soy (Latin Grammy Award for Best Solo Vocal Album 2002) 2001, Lipstick 2004, Indeleble (Premio Oye! for Best Album) 2006, Fuerza 2007, Unico 2009, 20 Años de Exitos 2011. *Honours:* Premio Oye! for Best Female Pop Vocal 2006, Premios Juventud Best Rock Artist 2010. *Website:* www.aleguzman.com.

GWYNEDD, Peredur ap; British musician (guitar); b. Pontypool, Gwent. *Career:* fmr guitarist for Freak Power; guitarist in Natalie Imbruglia's band 1997–2006; mem. Pendulum 2006–; has also worked with Sophie Ellis Bextor, Mylène Farmer, Kim Wilde. *Television:* judge, Wawffactor, S4C 2003–05. *Recordings:* albums: with Pendulum: In Silico 2008, Immersion 2010; has also appeared on Drive Thru Booty, Freak Power 1994, Wyau, Pyst a Libertino, Datblygu 2004, Counting Down the Days, Natalie Imbruglia 2005, Avant que l'Ombre... A Bercy, Mylène Farmer 2006, Come Out and Play, Kim Wilde 2010. *Current Management:* c/o JHO Management, 1–5 Exchange Court, Maiden Lane, Covent Garden, London,, WC2R 0JU, England. *Telephone:* (20) 7420-4372. *Fax:* (20) 7420-4399. *E-mail:* jho@jhooakley.com. *Website:* www.jhooakley.com. *Address:* c/o Warner Bros. Records, Warner Music UK Limited, The Warner Building, 28 Kensington Church Street, London, W8 4EP, England (office). *Website:* www.warnerbrosrecords.co.uk (office); www.pendulum.com.

GYPSYMEN (see Terry, Todd)

GZA, (Genius, Justice, Maxi Million); American MC and rap artist; b. (Gary Grice), 22 Aug. 1966, Staten Island, NY. *Career:* mem., All in Together Now early 1980s; solo artist 1991–; founding mem., Wu-Tang Clan 1993–. *Films:* Coffee and Cigarettes 2003. *Recordings include:* albums: with Wu-Tang Clan: Enter The Wu-Tang (36 Chambers) 1993, Wu-Tang Forever 1997, The W 2000, Iron Flag 2001, Disciples Of The 36 Chambers: Chapter 1 (live) 2004, The 8 Diagrams 2007; solo: Words From The Genius 1990, Liquid Swords 1995, Beneath The Surface 1999, Legend Of The Liquid Sword 2002, GrandMasters (with DJ Muggs) 2005, Pro Tools 2008. *Address:* c/o Sony Music Entertainment, 550 Madison Avenue, New York, NY 10022-3211, USA. *Telephone:* (212) 833-8000. *Fax:* (212) 833-4270. *Website:* www.wutangcorp.com.

H

HACE, Jani; Slovenian musician (bass guitar). *Career:* mem. Siddharta. *Recordings include:* albums: Id 1999, Nord 2001, Silikon Delta 2002, Rh- 2003, Petrolea 2006, Maraton 2007. *Honours:* Viktor Award for Best Act 2003, 2004, 2006, for Special Achievement 2003, MTV Europe Music Award 2005. *Address:* Siddharta, PO Box 179, 1236 Trzin, Slovenia (office). *Telephone:* (4) 1382192 (office). *E-mail:* info@siddharta.net (office). *Website:* www .siddharta.net (office).

HACKE, Alexander; German musician (guitar, electronics); b. (Alexander von Borsig), 11 Oct. 1965, Berlin. *Career:* mem., Einstürzende Neubauten 1980–; solo artist. *Recordings include:* albums: with Einstürzende Neubauten: Kollaps 1981, Zeichnungen des Patienten O. T. 1983, Halber Mensch 1985, Fünf Auf der Nach Oben Offenen Richterskala 1987, Haus der Lüge 1989, Tabula Rasa 1993, Ende Neu 1996, Silence is Sexy 2000, Perpetuum Mobile 2004, Grundstück 2005; solo: Hiroshima 1982, Filmarbeiten 1992, Sanctuary 2005. *Website:* www.hacke.org.

HACKETT, Eric Dexter; American musician (keyboards); b. 13 April 1956, Los Angeles. *Education:* BMus, University of South California, 1977. *Career:* Keyboard player with: Diana Ross and the Supremes; Talk Back, Forward Motion; Scheme Payne; The Temptations; The Four Tops; Musical Dir Curtis Mayfield, 1977–83; Pres., Can't Hack It Music, 1978–; mem, NARAS; AFofM. *Recordings:* albums: numerous appearances including: If My Friends Can See Me Now, Linda Clifford 1978, Unforgettable, Leroy Hutson 1979, Let Me Be Your Woman, Linda Clifford 1979, I've Got Dreams, Michael Grimm 2011.

HACKETT, Steve; British musician (guitar); b. 12 Feb. 1950, London. *Career:* fmr mem., Quiet World; mem., Genesis 1971–77; concerts, festival appearances and tours; solo artist 1975–; mem., GTR 1986. *Recordings include:* albums: with Genesis: Nursery Cryme 1971, Foxtrot 1972, Genesis Live 1973, Selling England by the Pound 1973, The Lamb Lies Down on Broadway 1974, A Trick of the Tail 1976, Wind and Wuthering 1977, Seconds Out 1977; solo: Voyage of the Acolyte, Please Don't Touch, Spectral Mornings, Defector, Cured, Highly Strung, Bay of Kings, Till We Have Faces, Blues With A Feeling, Momentum 1988, Time Lapse 1992, Guitar Noir 1993, There are Many Sides to the Night 1995, Genesis Revisited 1996, A Midsummer Night's Dream 1997, Tokyo Tapes 1999, Darktown 1999, Sketches of Satie 2000, Feedback 86 2001; with GTR: GTR 1986. *Honours:* Ivor Novello Award 1979. *Address:* c/o Manor Cottage 23, The Street, Burgh, Norfolk, NR11 6TP, England. *E-mail:* info@hackettsongs.com. *Website:* www.hackettsongs.com.

HADAD, Astrid; Mexican singer and actress; b. 4 Jan. 1957, Quintana Roo, Yucata. *Education:* Centro Universitario de Teatro, Mexico City. *Plays include:* Nostalgia Arrabalera, Del Rancho a la Ciudad, La Occisa or Luz, Levántate y Lucha, Heavy Nopal, Pecadora, Sol y Sombra, Oh-diosas, Corazón sangrante, and La multimamada. *Films include:* Sólo con tu pareja. *Recordings include:* albums: Ay! (with Los Tarzanes) 1995. *E-mail:* astrid@ astridhadad.com (office). *Website:* www.astridhadad.com.

HADDAD, Diana; Lebanese singer; b. (Diana Joseph el-Haddad), 1 Oct. 1976, Bsalim; m. Suhail al-Abdool 1995 (divorced), two d. *Education:* Al-Feheheel Nat. School, Kuwait. *Career:* solo artist 1992–; apptd Amb. of Goodwill for Human Rights and Peace, Int. Human Rights Comm. 2011. *Recordings include:* albums: Saken 1996, Ahl el-eshig 1997, Ammanih 1997, Yammaya 1998, Shater 1999, Jahr al-habeeb 2000, Akhbar helwa 2001, Law Yesaloni 2002, Awal marra 2004, Diana 2006, Men Diana Illa 2008, Bent Osol 2011. *Honours:* Al-hilm al-Arabi Award for Song of the Year, UAE (for Saken) 1996, Emarat FM Song of the Year Award, UAE (for Ahel el-eshig) 1997, Al-Reyada wa Shgabab magazine Award for Best Arabic Female Singer, UAE 1997, The Golden Star, Egypt 1999, Shbeib Festival Star Award, Jordan 2000, Al-Reradeya newspaper Award for Best Arabic Female Singer, Saudi Arabia 2000, Zahrat al-Khaleej magazine Award for Best Arabic Female Singer, UAE 2001, Zahrat al-Khaleej magazine Award for Most Popular Arabic Female Singer, UAE 2002, Hureitay Award for Best Arabic Female Singer, Egypt 2002, Best Lebanese Artist 2008. *Current Management:* c/o Alam el-Phan, 4 Soliman El Halaby Street. Downtown, Cairo, Egypt. *Telephone:* (2) 25742418. *Fax:* (2) 25782155. *E-mail:* info@dianahaddadonline.com. *Website:* www .alamelphan.com; www.dianahaddad.me.

HADDAD, Sepehr; American musician (keyboards, guitar); b. Washington, DC. *Education:* Tehran Int. School, Univ. of California, Davis. *Career:* met Shahin Shahida while at school in Iran; returned to USA to attend univ.; performed in folk clubs in western USA; formed duo with Shahida, early 1990s–; also solo artist. *Recordings include:* albums: with Shahin and Sepehr: One Thousand and One Nights 1994, E 1995, Aria 1996, World Café 1998, East/West Highway (compilation album) 2000, Nostalgia 2002; solo: Summer in Beijing: One World, One Dream 2007. *Current Management:* c/o Higher Octave Music, 23852 Pacific Coast Highway, Suite 2C, Malibu, CA 90265, USA. *Website:* www.sepehrmusic.com.

HADDAWAY, Nester Alexander; German singer and dancer; b. 9 Jan. 1965, Tobago. *Career:* Founder-mem., Elegato; solo singer, dance music 1992–. *Recordings include:* albums: Haddaway: The Album 1993, The Drive 1995, Let's Do It Now 1999, My Face 2001, Love Makes 2002, Pop Splits 2005. *Current Management:* c/o YME Entertainment, 4568 Wildewood Drive,

Delray Beach, FL 33445, USA. *Website:* www.yme-entertainment.com; haddawaymusix.com.

HADIMOĞLU, Erkin, BMus; Turkish musician (violin, piano); b. 1972, Istanbul. *Education:* Marmara Univ., studied violin with Ernst Patkolo. *Career:* mem., Yeni Türkü 1992–. *Recordings include:* albums with Yeni Türkü (does not play on all): Yeni, Her Dem Yeni, Telli Telli Remixes, Süper Baba (film music), Ask Yeniden, Rumeli Konseri, Külhani Şarkilar, Vira Vira, Yeşilmişik?, Günebakan: Dünyanin Kapilari, Akdeniz Akdeniz. *E-mail:* erkin@yeniturku.com. *Website:* www.yeniturku.com.

HADJI-LAZARO, François; French singer and songwriter; b. 1956, Paris. *Career:* mem., Pigalle 1982–; Founder, Boucherie Productions 1986–2001; mem. Les Garçons Bouchers. *Recordings include:* with Pigalle: Pigalle 1986, Pigalle 2 1990, Pigallive 1992, Rire et Pleurer 1993, Francois Detexte Topor 1996, Alors 1997, Regards Affligés 2002; with Les Garçons Bouchers: Les Garçons Bouchers 1987, Tome 2 1988, Un concert 1989, On a Mal Veilli 1990, Vacarmélite 1992, Ecoute petit Frère 1995; solo: Rekapituleidoscope 1999, Recueil Frais et Disco 2003, Et si que..? 2003, Contre-Courant 2004, Aigre-Doux 2006. *Website:* www.pigallepigalle.fr.

HADJINEOPHYTOU, George Constantinou; British composer and musician (mandolin); b. 28 Oct. 1965, London; m. Eleni Hadjineophytou 1994. *Education:* Trinity Coll. of Music, London. *Career:* performances and compositions for BBC TV and radio, City of London Sinfonia, Royal Shakespeare Co., Shakespeare's Globe, Nat. Theatre. *Recordings include:* Psyche and Eros (animation), Channel 4; Grandmother's Hands (short film for TV), Under the Stars (film soundtrack). *Honours:* Isabelle Bond Gold Medal.

HADJOPOULOS, Sue, BA; American musician (percussion) and singer; b. 26 June 1953, New York. *Education:* Columbia University, Mannes College of Music. *Career:* professional percussionist, 1970–; founder mem. of female salsa group, Latin Fever; performed and recorded as freelance musician with Laurie Anderson; Mick Jones; Michael Monroe, They Might Be Giants; Laura Nyro; Teena Marie; percussionist for numerous commercials; mem. AFTRA; ASCAP; NARAS; AFofM; Percussive Arts Society; Recording Musicians Asscn. *Recordings include:* with Joe Jackson: Night and Day, 1982; Mike's Murder (soundtrack), 1983; Live 1980–86, 1988; Blaze of Glory, 1989; Laughter and Lust, 1991; Heaven and Hell, 1997; Night and Day II, 2000; with Simple Minds: Once Upon A Time, 1985; Live In The City of Light, 1987. *E-mail:* info@suehadjopoulos.com; osuesana@yahoo.com. *Website:* www .suehadjopoulos.com.

HADLEY, Anthony (Tony); British singer; b. 2 June 1960, Islington, London. *Career:* mem., Spandau Ballet 1979–90, 2009–; numerous live performances; solo artist 1997–. *Television appearance:* winner of programme Reborn in the USA (ITV) 2003. *Stage appearance:* played Billy Flynn in Chicago (West End, London) 2007. *Recordings include:* albums: with Spandau Ballet: Journeys to Glory 1981, Diamond 1982, True 1983, Parade 1984, The Singles Collection 1985, Through the Barricades 1986, Heart Like a Sky 1989, Once More 2009; solo: The State of Play 1992, Tony Hadley 1997, Obsession 2000, True Ballads 2003, Passing Strangers 2006, Live from Metropolis Studios 2013. *Publication:* To Cut a Long Story Short 2004. *Honours:* BRIT Awards, Sony Trophy for Technical Excellence 1984, Ivor Novello Award 2012. *Current Management:* c/o Steve Dagger, Reformation Publishing, 14 Lambton Place, London, W11 2SH, England. *Telephone:* (20) 7792-1040. *Fax:* (20) 7221-7625. *E-mail:* contact@daggerents.com. *Website:* www.reformationpublishing .co.uk. *E-mail:* marianne@tony-hadley.com. *Website:* www.spandauballet .com; www.tonyhadley.com.

HADZO, Davor Kodzoman; Croatian musician (guitar, bass guitar), songwriter, writer and singer; b. 27 Jan. 1967, Zagreb. *Career:* played biggest festivals in Croatia and Salata 1997, Ecstazy, Berlin 1990, Zoro, Leipzig, Germany 1993; mem. Patarene (Croatian punk band). *Television:* Underground Out of Yugoslavia (documentary) 1986. *Compositions:* Obrij me Majko Motornom Pilom, Fuck You All 1993, Pataren, Sank, Nema Vise. *Publications:* Croatian Pop/Rock Encyclopedia 1994, Patareni Tribute 1996, Patareni Buka, We Can't be Banned from Here 1991. *Honours:* Best Alternative Album (for Porin) 1993, Hladno Pivo Dzinovski 1994. *Current Management:* Jabukaton, B Trenka 9, 10000 Zagreb, Croatia. *Address:* Mandroviceva 5, 10000 Zagreb, Croatia. *E-mail:* patareni@hgu.hr. *Website:* www.inet.hr/patareni.

HAGAR, Sammy; American rock singer, musician (guitar) and songwriter; b. 13 Oct. 1947, Monterey, CA. *Career:* fmr mem. singer, Fabulous Castillas, Skinny, Justice Brothers, Dust Cloud; lead singer, Montrose 1973–75; solo artist 1975–87; project, HSAS (with Neal Schon, Kenny Aaronson and Michael Shrieve) 1984; lead singer of rock band, Van Halen 1985–96, 2004–06; US and int. tours, festival appearances; co-host, Westwood One radio show with Michael Anthony 1992; founder mem., Red Rocker, Chickenfoot. *Recordings include:* albums: with Montrose: Montrose 1973, Paper Money 1974; solo: Nine On a Scale of Ten 1976, Sammy Hagar Two 1977, Musical Chairs 1978, All Night Long-Live 1978, Street Machine 1979, Danger Zone 1979, Loud and Clear 1980, Standing Hampton 1982, Rematch 1982, Three Lock Box 1983, Live from London to Long Beach 1983, VOA 1983, Voice of America 1984, Looking Back 1987, Sammy Hagar 1987, Red 1993, Unboxed 1994, Marching to Mars 1997, Red Voodoo 1999, Ten Thirteen 2000, Cosmic Universal Fashion 2008; with HSAS: Through the Fire 1984; with Van Halen: 5150 1986, OU812 1988, For Unlawful Carnal Knowledge 1991, Right Here Right Now 1993, Balance 1995; with Red Rocker: Livin' it Up 2006; with Chickenfoot: Chickenfoot 2009, Chickenfoot III 2011. *Honours:* Grammy Award for Best Hard Rock Performance 1992, American Music Award for Favorite Album 1992, Bay Area Music Award for Outstanding Male Vocalist 1992, 1993, MTV Music Video Award 1992. *E-mail:* webmaster@redrocker.com. *Website:* www .redrocker.com.

HAGGARD, Merle; American singer and songwriter; b. 6 April 1937, Bakersfield, Calif. *Career:* accompanied Wynn Stewart 1960; founder-mem., The Strangers. *Recordings include:* albums: Just Between The Two of Us (with Bonnie Owens) 1966, Same Train A Different Time 1969, The Land of Many Churches (with Bonnie Owens, Carter Family) 1971, My Love Affair with Trains 1976, A Taste of Yesterday's Wine (with George Jones) 1982, Poncho and Lefty (with Willie Nelson) 1983, Heart to Heart (with Leona Williams) 1983, That's the Way Love Goes (Grammy Award for Best Country Vocal Performance, Male 1984) 1983, It's All in the Game 1984, Kern River 1985, Amber Waves of Grain 1985, Out Among the Stars 1986, A Friend in California 1986, Seashores of Old Mexico 1987, Chill Factor 1988, 5:01 Blues 1989, Blue Jungle 1990, If I Could Only Fly 2000, New Light Through Old Windows 2000, Cabin in the Hills 2001, Last of the Breed (with Willie Nelson and Ray Price) 2007, The Original Outlaw 2007, I Am What I Am 2010. *Publication:* Sing Me Back Home (autobiography, with Peggy Russell) 1981. *Honours:* BMI Icon Award 2006, Kennedy Center Honor 2010. *Address:* Haggard Inc., PO Box 536, Palo Cedro, CA 96073, USA (office). *E-mail:* merle@ merlehaggard.com (office). *Website:* www.merlehaggard.com.

HÄGGMAN, Ann-Mari Solveig, PhD; Finnish music organization executive; b. 19 Sept. 1941, Vasa, Finland; m. Lars-Eric Häggman 1964; one s. one d. *Career:* researcher and Head of Svenska litteratursällskapets Folkkultursarkiv; Asst Prof., Dept for Folklore, Helsinki Univ. 1993–95; Head of the Inst. of Finland-Swedish Traditional Music 1985–; mem. Word of Honour of the Finlands svenska spelmansförbund (League of Traditional Musicians); Bd mem. Swedish Literature Soc.; Pres., SFV Foundation for Adult Education and Culture 1998–; numerous folk music orgs. *Publications include:* Magdalena på källebro (The Ballad of Mary Magdalene's Conversion), dissertation 1992, Björn Aksdal & Ann-Mari Häggman: Den folkliga musiktraditionen 1997, Ann-Mari Häggman: Att förvalta en musiktradition 2004; numerous articles, albums and films about folk music in Finland. *E-mail:* ann-mari.haggman@sls.fi.

HAGUE, Melvyn (Mel) Ian; British singer, songwriter, musician (guitar) and novelist; b. 20 Jan. 1943, Whiston, S Yorks., England; s. of John Hague and Lois Hague; m. Ivy Walton 1966; one s. one d. *Education:* secondary schools in Rotherham and Toronto, Canada. *Career:* grew up in Canada 1951–61; played most UK concert venues, including Wembley Conf. Centre; all UK Country Music festivals; several European tours; appearances: BBC 2, most regional TV stations, including Country Club, Channel Islands; Nightride; WSM Nashville radio, TV; own record label, OGB Records; retired from music industry 2004, currently full-time novelist; mem. Performing Rights Soc. *Radio:* presenter, BBC Radio Sheffield 1976–86, South Yorkshire Radio 1991–92. *Television:* One in Four (BBC 2). *Recordings:* 17 albums 1974–2002. *Publications:* novels: To Hell With The Badge, Death on a Rope, Twisted River, The Grey Man (republished as Emporium of Death), The Black Bowl (short story published in Words magazine Christmas edn) 2009, The Dog (published in Winter Fiction by Author Essentials) 2012, Harvest (published on Kindle) 2012. *Honours:* Aria Guitars/Daily Mirror Golden Guitar Award, Top Country Entertainer, 1981 and several regional and club awards. *Address:* 37 Wroot Road, Finningley Village, Doncaster, S Yorks., DN9 3DR, England. *Telephone:* (1302) 771287; 7704-138182 (mobile). *E-mail:* mel .hague@talktalk.net. *Website:* www.melhaguebooksnmusic.co.uk.

HAGUE, Stephen; American music producer. *Career:* worked with: Ace of Base, Dicte, Dink, Dubstar, Extra Verv, Gregory Grey, Jaguar, James, Tom Jones, Manbreak, Manic Street Preachers, Maren Ord, New Order, Robert Palmer, Planet Claire, The Pogues, Pretenders, Robbie Williams. *Current Management:* Stephen Budd Management, 59-65 Worship Street, London, EC2A 2DU, England.

HAHN, Joseph (Joe); American DJ; b. 15 March 1977, Glendale, CA. *Education:* Pasadena Art Coll. of Design. *Career:* mem., Xero 1996, renamed Hybrid Theory, later renamed Linkin Park 1999–; numerous int. concerts. *Recordings include:* albums: Hybrid Theory (Rock Bear Awards for Best Int. Album 2001) 2000, Reanimation 2002, In The End: Live & Rare 2002, Meteora 2003, Live in Texas 2003, Collision Course (with Jay-Z) 2004, Minutes to Midnight 2007, A Thousand Suns 2010, Living Things 2012, The Hunting Party 2014. *Honours:* Billboard Award for Best Modern Rock Artist 2001, Rock Bear Award for Best Int. Band 2001, Kerrang! Award for Best Int. Newcomer 2001, Rolling Stone Award for Best Hard Rock/Metal Band 2001, World Music Awards for Best Selling Rock Group 2002, 2003, 2007, MTV Awards for Best Group, Best Hard Rock 2002, MTV Europe Awards for Best Rock Act 2004, 2011, 2012, 2014, for Best World Stage Performance 2009, 2013, for Best Live Act 2010, Grammy Award for Best Rap/Sung Collaboration (for Numb/Encore, with Jay-Z) 2006, MTV Europe Music Award for Best Band 2007, American Music Awards for Favorite Alternative Rock Music Artist 2007, 2008, 2012.

Current Management: Andy Gould Management, 8484 Wilshire Boulevard, Suite 425, Beverly Hills, CA 90211, USA. *Website:* www.linkinpark.com.

HAIM, Alana Mychal; American musician (keyboards, drums, guitar), singer and songwriter; b. 15 Dec. 1991, Calif.; d. of Mordechai Haim and Donna Haim. *Career:* Founder-mem. Haim (with sisters Este and Danielle) 2007–; released debut EP Forever 2012; support act for Mumford & Sons US tour 2012, for Florence and the Machine UK tour 2012; performed at many festivals including Glastonbury 2013, 2014; collaborator with Kid Cudi, Calvin Harris, A$AP Ferg, Stevie Nicks. *Recordings:* album: with Haim: Days Are Gone 2013. *Honours:* winner, BBC Sound of 2013, 2012, NME Best Int. Band Award 2014, NME Award for Best Band Blog or Twitter 2014. *Current Management:* c/o Roc Nation LLC, 9348 Civic Center Drive, Beverly Hills, CA 90210, USA. *Website:* rocnation.com; haimtheband.com.

HAIM, Danielle Sari; American musician (guitar), singer and songwriter; b. 16 Feb. 1989, Calif.; d. of Mordechai Haim and Donna Haim. *Career:* fmr touring band mem. with Jenny Lewis and Julian Casablancas; fmr mem. Valli Girls (with sister Este); fmr band mem. Scarlet Fever (backing group for Cee-Lo Green); Founder-mem. Haim (with sisters Este and Alana) 2007–; released debut EP Forever 2012; support act for Mumford & Sons US tour 2012, for Florence and the Machine UK tour 2012; performed at many festivals including Glastonbury 2013, 2014; collaborator with Kid Cudi, Calvin Harris, A$AP Ferg, Stevie Nicks. *Recordings:* album: with Haim: Days Are Gone 2013. *Honours:* winner, BBC Sound of 2013, 2012, NME Best Int. Band Award 2014. *Current Management:* c/o Roc Nation LLC, 9348 Civic Center Drive, Beverly Hills, CA 90210, USA. *Website:* rocnation.com; haimtheband.com.

HAIM, Este Arielle; American musician (bass guitar), singer and songwriter; b. 14 March 1986, Calif.; d. of Mordechai Haim and Donna Haim. *Education:* Univ. of California, Los Angeles. *Career:* fmr mem. Valli Girls (with sister Danielle); Founder-mem. Haim (with sisters Danielle and Alana) 2007–; released debut EP Forever 2012; support act for Mumford & Sons US tour 2012, for Florence and the Machine UK tour 2012; performed at many festivals including Glastonbury 2013, 2014; collaborator with Kid Cudi, Calvin Harris, A$AP Ferg, Stevie Nicks. *Recordings:* album: with Haim: Days Are Gone 2013. *Honours:* winner, BBC Sound of 2013, 2012, NME Best Int. Band Award 2014. *Current Management:* c/o Roc Nation LLC, 9348 Civic Center Drive, Beverly Hills, CA 90210, USA. *Website:* rocnation.com; haimtheband.com.

HAIMOVICI, Fabien-David; French musician (drums); b. 22 April 1968, Bordeaux. *Education:* Musicians' Inst., USA. *Career:* played with Bireli Lagrene; tours all over USA, Europe, Japan; tour with French artists Jacques Higelin, Nicole Croisille; tours in Japan, France; played with int. artists in France, including Lucky Peterson; played and recorded with Coke Tale (comprising Paris studio musicians). *Recordings include:* albums: I Muvrini (with I Muvrini) 2001, Intimidade (Tania Maria) 2005, Mrpain (with Francis Jocky) 2006, Transamericana (Pajaro Canzani) 2008. *Current Management:* 16 rue des cascades, 75020 Paris, France.

HAINES, Emily; Canadian singer, songwriter and musician (keyboards, guitar); b. 1974, New Delhi, India. *Education:* Etobicoke School of the Arts, Univ. of British Columbia, Concordia Univ. *Career:* Founder mem. Metric 1998–; also solo artist; collaborations with Broken Social Scene, Tiesto, Delerium, Jason Collett, KC Accidental, MSTRKRFT, Stars, The Stills, k-os, The Crystal Method, Todor Kobakov, Wavin' Flag. *Films:* soundtrack contributions: Scott Pilgrim vs the World 2010, The Twilight Saga: Eclipse 2010. *Recordings:* albums: with Metric: Old World Underground Where Are You Now 2003, Live it Out 2005, Grow Up and Blow Away 2007, Fantasies (Juno Award for Alternative Album of the Year 2010) 2009; solo: Cut in Half and Also Double 1996; with the Soft Skeleton: Knives Don't Have Your Back 2006. *Honours:* Juno Award for Group of the Year 2010. *Address:* c/o Last Gang Records, 171 East Liberty Street, Suite 330, Toronto, ON M6K 3P6, Canada (office). *Telephone:* (416) 534-3000 (office). *Fax:* (416) 534-3005 (office). *E-mail:* management@ilovemetric.com (office). *Website:* www.ilovemetric .com.

HAINES, Luke; British singer and songwriter; b. 7 Oct. 1967, Walton-on-Thames, Surrey. *Career:* mem., The Auteurs 1992–2003; mem., Black Box Recorder 1998–2000; solo artist 2001–. *Recordings include:* albums: with The Auteurs: New Wave 1993, Now I'm a Cowboy 1994, After Murder Park 1996, How I Learned to Love The Bootboys 1999, Das Capital 2003; with Black Box Recorder: England Made Me 1998, The Facts of Life 2000; solo: The Oliver Twist Manifesto 2001, Christie Malry's Own Double-Entry (soundtrack) 2001, Off My Rocker at the Art School Bop 2006, 21st Century Man 2009, Outsider/ In: The Collection 2012, Rock and Roll Animals 2013. *Publications:* Bad Vibes: Britpop and My Part in its Downfall 2009, Post Everything: Outsider Rock and Roll 2011. *E-mail:* info@lukehaines.co.uk. *Website:* www.lukehaines.co .uk.

HAJDOVSKA-TLUSTA, Katerina; Czech singer, musician (percussion) and songwriter; b. 27 Feb. 1953, Prague; m. Martin Tlusty 1982, two step-d. *Education:* Prague Charles Univ. *Recordings include:* albums: with Ester: To You, Jerusalem; with Alexander Hajdovsky, Ester: Shalom, Chaverim, 1998; with Chesed: Jewish Feasts in Songs; Jewish Songs Live, The Jewish Samovar 2000. *Current Management:* Rosa Ltd, Thákurova 3/676, 160 00 Prague 6, Czech Republic. *E-mail:* hajtl@volny.cz. *Website:* www.ester.euweb.cz; www .haj-tl.wz.cz.

HAJDOVSKY-POTAPOVIC, Alexandr 'Lesik'; Czech composer; b. 27 Feb. 1953, Prague; m. Miroslava Hajdovska-Vlková 1973; two s. *Career:* mem. of Czech TV and radio broadcasting groups FOK, folk rock, Svehlik, rock, Mazelé, rap, Extempore, rock/humour, Ester, Jewish traditional songs; mem. OSA. *Recordings include:* albums: Jizák, Lesik Hajdovsky: Uz horísvíce, Lesik Hajdovsky: Manzelé, Prague: Zizkov Kuplets, Svehlík: There's No Time, Ester: Shalom Chaverim, with Katerina Hajdovska-Tlusta 1998. *Honours:* Mlady svet – Bílá Vrána; Melodie magazine award, 1991. *Current Management:* Rosa Ltd, Thákurova 3/676, 160 00 Prague 6, Czech Republic. *E-mail:* info@rosamusic.cz. *Website:* www.ester.euweb.cz. *E-mail:* lesikovi@gmail.com. *Website:* www.manzele.xf.cz.

HAKALA, Aki-Markus; Finnish musician (drums); b. 28 Oct. 1979, Espoo; one d. *Career:* mem., The Rasmus 1999–. *Recordings include:* albums: Into 2001, Dead Letters 2003, Hide From The Sun 2005, Black Roses 2008, Best of the Rasmus: 2001–2009 2009. *Honours:* MTV Europe Music Award Best Finnish Act 2005. *Current Management:* c/o Seppo Vesterinen, Oy Hinterland Ltd, PO Box 201, 00121 Helsinki, Finland. *E-mail:* seppo@heartagram.com. *Website:* www.therasmus.com.

HAKMOUN, Hassan; Moroccan musician (sintir) and singer; b. 1963, Marrakech; m. Chikako Iwahori. *Career:* specialises in Gnawa style; began studying Gnawa music aged four; known as Master of Gnawa Music 1977; made US debut with Etian and Blanca Lee's Trio Gna and Nomadas group, New York 1987; mem. of group Magmouat Hakmoun 1989; Founder-mem. of group Zahar 1990; numerous collaborations including with Dee Dee Bridgewater, Don Cherry, Paula Cole, Peter Gabriel, The Kronos Quartet, David Sanborn; many live performances including at WOMAD festival, Woodstock 1994. *Films:* as composer and musician: The Past and the Present of Djemma El Fna 1995, Rendezvous in Samarkand 1999, Footsteps in Africa 2009; as performer: Jungle 2 Jungle 1997, Rollerball 2002. *Recordings:* albums: with Zahar: Zahar 1990; solo: Gift of the Gnawa (with Don Cherry and Adam Rudolph) 1992, Trance 1993, The Fire Within 1995, Black Mud Sound (with Cornelius Claudio Kreusch) 1995, Life Around the World 1998, The Gift (AFIM INDIE Award for Best Contemporary World Music Recording 2003) 2002, Spirit 2012, Unity 2014. *Current Management:* c/o Bill Smith, 1139 San Carlos Avenue, #310, San Carlos, CA 94070, USA. *Telephone:* (650) 595-2274. *Fax:* (650) 585-6810. *Website:* www.hassanhakmoun.com.

HALE, Keith; British songwriter, musician (keyboards) and record producer; b. 6 Nov. 1950, Hull; one d. *Education:* Dartington Coll. of Arts. *Career:* joined Comus to record To Keep From Crying for Virgin Records 1974; formed Blood Donor 1977; support to J. J. Burnel on Euroman Tour; mem. Hawkwind 1980, left with Ginger Baker and formed Ginger's Nutters, toured Europe 1981; mem. Toyah's band for Warrior Rock tour 1982; mem. PRS, MCPS, Musicians' Union. *Theatre:* Before the Storm, Animate Theatre 1990, Aquaphobic Sailor, Smart Arts 1993, A Matter of Style, Amsterdam Theatre School 1996. *Musical:* Wildest Dreams 2005. *Compositions:* It's A Mystery 1981. *Recordings include:* producer of Toyah's first album Sheep-Farming In Barnet; other albums include: Zones/Stonehenge, Hawkwind, Toyah on Tour 1983, Ginger Baker in Concert 1985, Toyah – Live and More 1998, Jasper Fish – Around the Room in 80 Days 1998, Night of the Long Knives 2000, Toyah: Warrior Rock 2005, Mayhem 2005; with Comus: Song to Comus 2005, Out of the Coma 2012. *Address:* 32 Bencurtis Park, West Wickham, Kent, BR4 9QG, England (home). *Current Management:* GEMS, Firs Cottage, 5 Firs Close, London, SE23 1BB, England. *Telephone:* (20) 8291-7052. *Fax:* (20) 8699-2279.

HALEY, Mark Jonathan; British musician (keyboards, guitar); b. 2 Feb. 1961, Portsmouth, Hants. *Education:* classical training in piano, guitar, trumpet. *Career:* Founder-mem. Haley Brothers 1976; various TV appearances; toured with Billy Fury 1982; joined The Monkees comeback tours 1986–89; mem., The Kinks 1989–93, The Chaps 1994–96; mem., The Rubettes 2000–; Founder-mem., Gorge 1997; mem. PRS, Musicians' Union (mem. Exec. Cttee), MCPS, BRIT Awards Voting Acad. *Recordings include:* with Haley Brothers: One Way Love Affair 1978; with The Monkees: That was Then, This is Now 1986; with The Kinks: Down All the Days 1991, Picture Book [Box Set] 2008; with The Chaps: The Collector 1995. *Publication:* Journeyman (online autobiography) 1999. *Honours:* Ivor Novello Award for Services to Music (with The Kinks).

HALFORD, Rob; British singer; b. 25 Aug. 1951, Birmingham. *Career:* lead singer, UK heavy rock group Judas Priest 1974–92, 2003–; numerous tours, concerts, festivals; Founder and lead singer, heavy rock group Fight 1991–; Founder Halford 1999–; appearance as stand-in singer for Black Sabbath, Pacific Amphitheatre, Calif. 1992. *Recordings include:* albums: with Judas Priest: Rocka Rolla 1974, Sad Wings of Destiny 1976, Sin After Sin 1977, Stained Class 1978, Killing Machine 1978, Hell Bent for Leather 1979, Unleashed in the East 1979, British Steel 1980, Point of Entry 1981, Screaming for Vengeance 1982, Defenders of the Faith 1984, Turbo 1986, Priest Live 1987, Ram It Down 1988, Painkiller 1990, Angel of Retribution 2005, Nostradamus 2008, Hell Bent for Leather/Defenders of the Faith 2012, Stained Class/Ram It Down 2013; with Fight: War of Words 1994, Mutations 1994, A Small Deadly Space 1995, K5 – The War of Words Demos 2007, Into the Pit 2008; solo: Resurrection 2000, Crucible 2002, Halford III: Winter Songs 2009, Halford IV: Made of Metal 2010. *Honours:* Grammy Award for Best Metal Performance (for Dissident Aggressor) 2010. *E-mail:* halfordrob@aol.com. *Website:* judaspriest.com.

HALL, Chris; British musician (accordion, drums), singer, artist agent, record company executive and journalist and broadcaster. *Career:* accordion player, vocalist with The Zydeco Brothers, Cajun Roosters, The Bearcats, Zydecomotion; tour organizer, US and UK agent, for Cajun and Zydeco; writer and co-partner, Cajun Users Manual; radio presenter, BBC Radio 2; club organizer, The Swamp Club; Man., Bearcat Records; recorded and appeared on TV with Paul McCartney; featured accordion player on McCartney's Run Devil Run album recorded at Abbey Road and also featuring Dave Gilmour (Pink Floyd), Ian Paice (Deep Purple), Mick Green (The Pirates) and Pete Wingfield. *Current Management:* c/o Swamp, PO Box 94, Derby, DE22 1XA, England. *E-mail:* chrishall@swampmusic.co.uk. *Website:* www.swampmusic.co.uk.

HALL, Daryl; American singer, musician (guitar) and songwriter; b. (Daryl Franklin Hohl), 11 Oct. 1948, Pottstown, Pa; m. 1st Bryna Lublin 1969 (divorced 1972); m. 2nd Amanda Aspinall; two step-d. *Education:* Temple Univ. *Career:* fmr mem., Kenny Gamble and The Romeos, Gulliver; session singer, Sigma Sounds Studios; backing singer, The Stylistics, The Delfonics; mem. duo, Hall and Oates 1969–; concerts worldwide. *Compositions:* many hit songs co-written with John Oates; other songs include Sara Smile, Wait For Me, Kiss On My List (co-written with Janna Allen), One On One, Did It In A Minute (co-written with Sara and Janna Allen), Foolish Pride, Everything Your Heart Desires, Swept Away, for Diana Ross; film theme, Ruthless People (co-written with Mick Jagger and Dave Stewart). *Recordings include:* albums: with Hall and Oates: Whole Oats 1972, Abandoned Luncheonette 1974, War Babies 1974, Daryl Hall and John Oates 1975, Bigger Than Both of Us 1976, No Goodbyes 1977, Beauty on a Back Street 1977, Livetime 1978, Along the Red Edge 1978, X-Static 1979, Voices 1980, Private Eyes 1981, H2O 1982, Rock n' Roll Soul, Part 1 1983, Big Bam Boom 1984, Live at the Apollo (With David Ruffin and Eddie Kendricks) 1985, Ooh Yeah! 1988, Change of Season 1990, Marigold Sky 1997, Behind the Music 2002, Do It for Love 2003, Our Kind of Soul 2004, Home for Christmas 2006, Do What You Want, Be What You Are 2009, The Atlantic Albums 2011, Angelina & Other Favorites 2012, Original Album Classics 2013; solo: Sacred Songs 1980, Three Hearts in the Happy Ending Machine 1986, Soul Alone 1993, Can't Stop Dreaming 1996, Best of the Ballads 2000, Laughing Down Crying 2011. *Honours:* American Music Awards for Favorite Pop/Rock Duo or Band 1983–85. *Current Management:* c/o Wolfson Entertainment Inc., 22201 Ventura Blvd, Suite 207, Woodland Hills, CA 91364, USA. *Telephone:* (818) 615-0499. *Fax:* (818) 615-0498. *E-mail:* info@wolfsonent.com. *Website:* www.wolfsonent.com. *E-mail:* admin@hallandoates.com. *Website:* www.hallandoates.com; www.livefromdarylshouse.com.

HALL, Gary Martin; British singer, songwriter and musician (guitar); b. 29 Nov. 1964, Ormskirk, Lancs. *Career:* mem., The Stormtroopers 1986–92; mem. PRS, MCPS. *Recordings include:* albums: Garage Heart, 1989; Wide Open To The World, 1991; What Goes Around, 1993; Twelve Strings and Tall Stories, 1996; Return to the Flame, 1998, That Old Brand New 2011, Winning Ways On Losing Streaks 2013. *Honours:* BCMA Rising Star Award 1995. *Website:* www.garyhallmusic.co.uk.

HALL, Graham Peter (GP); British artist, composer and musician (saxophone, bass, flamenco guitar, synthesizer, electric guitar); b. 15 July 1943, Hampton Hill; m. Päivi Annikki Vilkman 1987 (divorced); four s. two d. *Career:* mem. blues bands 1960s; resident musician 100 Club, London 1960s; toured Europe 1962–68; mem. Casey Jones and the Governors 1966–68, toured Europe; invented Industrial Sound-Sculptures (incorporating use of industrial objects with guitar to produce abstract layered sound); played and recorded with numerous jazz artists including Jeff Clyne, Paul Rutherford, Lol Coxhill, Lyn Dobson; mem PRS, MCPS. *Compositions:* Commissioned, Sea Sorrow (Isle of Lewis), 1997. *Recordings:* New Town Suite 1977, The Estates 1977, Manifestations 1979, Full Moon Over Madrid 1979, Colours 1986, The Collection 1986, Imaginary Seasons 1992, Eclectic Guitars 1995, Figments of Imagination 1996, Mouvements 1996, Mar-Del-Plata 1997, Marks on the Air 1998, Steel Storms 1998, Tender Spirits 1998, Each a Glimpse and Gone Forever 2000, Mercurial State 2002, Songs from the House Within 2003, Gothic Flamenco 2004, Pure 2007. *E-mail:* gphall@musician.org. *Website:* www.gphall.com.

HALL, Keith Robert; British musician (drums); b. 24 April 1951, Edgware, Middx, England; m. Titvi Ikäheimo. *Education:* studied with Joe Hodson, Frank King, Joe Morello. *Career:* professional musician 1966–; Founder-mem. Pickettywitch 1969–72; mem. Gerry and The Pacemakers 1973–77; Terry Lightfoot 1978–84; musicals: Hair Nat. Tour 1980, Godspell 1980, Joseph and The Amazing Technicolour Dreamcoat 1981, West Side Story 1982; as freelance musician, played with Kenny Ball, Maxine Daniels, Bertice Reading, Fiona Duncan, Jay McShan, Laverne Butler, Ritchie Cole 1984–; formed jazz-rock fusion band Storm Warning with Jill Jarman 1987; concerts include festivals throughout Europe; toured with Engelbert Humperdinck; performed and recorded with The June Harris Trio 1987–89 which also toured Scandinavia; worked with Tommy Whittle, Terry Lightfoot, Peter Ind, Januz Carmello, Al Gray, Spike Robinson, Mike Longo, John Etheridge, Dick Heckstall-Smith, Roy Williams, Hans Backenroth, Janne Lundgren, Alec Dankworth; moved to Helsinki 1990; regular drummer with Antti Sarpila Swing Band and with Grammy Award-winning pianist Marian Petrescu and his trio; also worked with UMO, Espoo Big Band, Pentti Lasanen, Severi Pyysalo, Karita Mattila, Kymi Sinfonietta, Jormas, Finnish Opera Big-Band; appearances at most Scandinavian music festivals, including the Pori Int.

Jazz Festival 1992–95, 1997–99 and on Finnish TV and radio; performed at Repub. of Finland's Pres.'s Independence Day gala party in Helsinki, with the Antti Sarpila Swing band 1999, 2009; toured USA, Europe, Australia, NZ, Romania, Turkey and TV recording at the Kremlin, Moscow with the Marian Petrescu Trio 2007; mem. Musicians' Union, Finnish Drummers' Asscn, Jazz Network, Finnish Musicians' Union, PPL, GRAMEX. *Radio:* presenter and producer, Playback, Helsinki Radio 2000–05. *Television:* Top of The Pops, Kenny Everett Show, Magpie, Lift Off, Golden Shot, We Want to Sing, Stars On Sunday, Australia (all channels), NZ, RTE (Ireland), RTF (Germany), Spain, Portugal, Italy. *Recordings:* with Pickettywitch: That Same Old Feeling 1970, Sad Old Kinda Movie 1970, Baby I Won't Let You Down 1970; with Gerry and The Pacemakers: Lovely Lady 1974; albums: with Pickettywitch: Pickettywitch 1970, with Spirit Level: Storm Warning 1988; over 25 albums with Antti Sarpila including Father, Son and Holy Swing 1993, Chrisse Schwindt Memorial Concert 1993, Live At Storyville 1994; with Claus Anderson: Chrisse Schwindt Memorial Concert 1993; with Swing Gentlemen: Swing Gentlemen's Ball 1995; with Love Messengers: She Said She Said 2010. *Address:* Rakuunantie 17 A 12, 00330 Helsinki, Finland (office). *Telephone:* (9) 488422 (office). *E-mail:* keith.hall@kolumbus.fi (office).

HALL, Martin; British music manager; *Managing Director, Hall Or Nothing*; b. 1962. *Career:* fmr journalist on various music magazines; Co-founder, Hall or Nothing PR, worked with The Pogues, The Stone Roses, Manic Street Preachers, Groove Armada, Ed Harcourt, Futureshock, Weekend Players, The Departure, Make Good Your Escape; joined Sanctuary Artist Man. 2003, Man. Dir Sanctuary Artist Man. UK 2006–07; currently Man. Dir Hall Or Nothing Man. *Address:* Hall or Nothing Management, James Grant Group Ltd, 94 Strand On The Green, Chiswick, London, W4 3NN, England (office). *Telephone:* (20) 8742-4950 (office). *E-mail:* office@hallornothing.co.uk (office). *Website:* www.hallornothing.co.uk (office).

HALL, Martin; Danish singer, composer and musician (multi-instrumentalist); b. 26 April 1963, Copenhagen. *Education:* Acad. of Piano and Music, Copenhagen and Royal Acad. of Fine Arts, Copenhagen. *Recordings include:* Avenues of Oblivion 1980, The Icecold Waters of The Egocentric Calculation 1981, For 1982, Ritual 1983, Apparently all the Same 1984, Free Force Structure 1984, Fusion 1985, Relief 1985, Warfare 1985, Treatment 1985, Cutting Through 1986, Beat of the Drum 1988, Presence 1988, Surreal Thing 1989, The Martin Hall Document 1989, Crush: The Point of No Return Soundtrack 1989, Prime Material, 1990, Imperfect 1990, Dreamworld 1990, Palladium 1990, The Rainbow Theatre 1990, Read Only Memory 1991, Sweet Mystery 1993, All the Way Down 1993, Strange Delight 1993, A Touch of Excellence 1993, Angel of the Night 1994, Phantasmagoria 1994, Random Hold 1996, Testcards 1989–95 1997, Performance 1997, Burning Sugar 1999, Elia 2001, Inskription 2003, Damage Control 2006, Hospital Cafeterias 2009, Phasewide Exit Signs 2013. *Publications include:* The World Days, 1996, Kommunikaze 2001, Infordementia 2008, The Last Romantic 2005, Kinoplex (Audiobook) 2010, Nostatic! 2012, Memo 2013. *Current Management:* Panoptikon/VME, Vesterbrogade 95 H, 1620 Copenhagen V, Denmark. *Telephone:* 33-21-01-35. *E-mail:* vme@vme-group.com. *Website:* www.vme-group.com. *E-mail:* info@martinhall.dk. *Website:* www.martinhall.com.

HALL, Terry; British singer; b. 19 March 1959, Coventry. *Career:* singer, The Special AKA (later as The Specials) 1977–81, 1996, 2008–; Founder mem. Fun Boy Three 1981–83; Founder mem. Colourfield 1983–88; mem. Terry, Blair and Anouchka 1989–90; mem. Vegas (with Dave Stewart) 1992; also solo artist. *Recordings include:* albums: with The Specials: The Specials 1979, More Specials 1980, Today's Specials 1996, Guilty 'Til Proved Innocent! 1998, Conquering Ruler 2001; with Fun Boy Three: Fun Boy Three 1982, Waiting 1983, Best Of. . . 1984; with Terry Blair and Anouchka: albums: Ultra-Modern Nursery Rhymes 1990; with Vegas: Vegas 1992; solo: Terry Hall – The Collection 1993, Home 1995, Laugh 1997, The Hour of Two Lights (with Mushtaq) 2003.

HALL, Thomas James, BA; American record producer and sound engineer; b. 19 May 1957, Longview, Washington. *Education:* East Washington Univ. *Career:* producer, sound engineer, Viacom Studios; Logic West Studios; London Bridge Studios; Triad Studios, 1982–. *Recordings include:* As producer/sound engineer: with Queensryche: Queensryche 1983, Mindcrime Live 1991, Promised Land 1994; with Kenny G: Kenny G Live 1990; other credits include albums by: Gail Swanson, Don Lamphere.

HALL, Tom T.; American songwriter, singer and writer; b. 25 May 1936, Olive Hill, Ky. *Career:* broadcaster, musician, WMOR radio station, Ky, with Kentucky Travellers, 1950s–60s; Leader, own touring band The Storytellers; novel writer and composer of children's songs. *Compositions include:* DJ For A Day, Jimmy C. Newman; Goodbye Sweetheart, Hello Vietnam, Johnny Wright; Mama Tell 'Em What We're Fighting For, Dave Dudley; Harper Valley PTA, Jeannie C Riley; I Can't Dance, Gram Parsons and Emmylou Harris; Margie's At The Lincoln Park Inn, Bobby Bare; A Week In The County Jail; Pinto The Wonder Horse Is Dead; I Miss A Lot of Trains; Old Dogs, Children and Watermelon Wine. *Recordings:* albums include: The Storyteller 1972, The Rhymer and Other Five and Dimers 1973, For The People In The Last Hard Town 1973, Country Is 1974, Songs of Fox Hollow 1974, Faster Horses 1976, The Magnificent Music Machine 1976, About Love 1977, New Train Same Rider 1978, Places I've Done Time 1978, Saturday Morning Songs 1979, Ol' T's In Town 1979, Soldier of Fortune 1980, The Storyteller and The Banjoman (with Earl Scruggs) 1982, In Concert 1983, World Class Country

1983, Everything From Jesus To Jack Daniels 1983, Natural Dreams 1984, Songs In A Seashell 1985, Country Songs For Kids 1988, Loves Lost and Found 1995, Songs from Sopchoppy 1996, Homegrown 1997, A Soldier of Fortune 1997, The Ultimate Collection 2000; features on: Write Your Story, Scott Burnett 2001. *Publications:* The Songwriter's Handbook, The Storyteller's Nashville, The Laughing Man of Woodmont Cove, Spring Hill (novel). *Honours:* Grammy Award (for Tom T. Hall's Greatest Hits). *Address:* Tom T. Hall Enterprises, PO Box 1246, Franklin, TN 37065, USA.

HALLAHAN, Patrick; American musician (drums). *Career:* mem., My Morning Jacket 2002–. *Recordings include:* albums: It Still Moves 2003, Early Recordings Chapter 1: The Sandworm Cometh 2004, Early Recordings Chapter 2: Learning 2004, Z 2005, Okronokos 2006, Evil Urges 2008, Circuital 2011. *Address:* c/o RCA Records, 1540 Broadway, New York, NY 10036, USA. *E-mail:* patrickhallahan@mymorningjacket.com. *Website:* www.mymorningjacket.com.

HALLAM, Nick; British producer and DJ; b. 11 June 1960, Nottingham. *Career:* Co-founder, Gee Street studio and record label; Founder-mem., Stereo MCs 1984–; numerous live performances with extended band and extra vocalists; remixed artists, including Jungle Brothers, U2, PM Dawn, Queen Latifah, Disposable Heroes of Hiphoprisy, Monie Love, Electronic, Madonna (Frozen); est. music publisher, Spirit Songs. *Recordings include:* albums: 33-45-78 1989, Supernatural 1990, Connected (BRIT Award for Best British Album 1994) 1992, Stereo MCs 1993, Deep Down and Dirty 2001, Paradise 2005, Double Bubble 2008, Emperor's Nightingale 2011. *Honours:* BRIT Award for Best British Group 1994. *E-mail:* info@stereomcs.com. *Website:* www.stereomcs.com.

HALLDÓRSSON, Björgvin Helgi, (Bo Halldorsson); Icelandic singer, songwriter and producer; *Owner and CEO, Tonaljos Music;* b. 16 April 1951, Hafnarfjordur; s. of Halldor Baldvinsson and Sigridur Thorleifsdottir; m. Ragnheidur B. Reynisdottir 1977; two s. one d. *Education:* piano with private tutor, Brauner, self taught on guitarr, plays harmonica. *Career:* began singing with Bendix band; formed band Ævintýri (Fairy Tale) with Sigurjón Sighvatsson and Arnar Sigurbjörnsson, performed in Laugardalshöllin arena 1969, left band and joined band Change for a short time, left to join band Hljómar which was reforming, band dissolved 1974; formed band Ðe lónlí blú boys and released several albums; worked with Gunnar Þórðarsson on two albums of children's ballads; band Brimkló revived 1976; teamed up with rock 'n' roll comedic brother duo Halli og Laddi in band HLH 1979; various appearances on stage, Little Shop of Horrors 1985, Evita 1997, Köldum klaka 1991, Eurovision Song Contest 1996; one of the first artists to popularize gospel music in Iceland; has also worked as a producer and musical director; can be heard on more than 500 recordings in Icelandic music history; has taken part in numerous song contests both in Iceland and abroad; has recorded approx. 900 songs; staged show at Broadway Club in Reykjavik to celebrate 35 years in the recording business 2005–; staged concerts at Sports Stadium in Reykjavik, with Icelandic Symphony Orchestra, Fostbrædur male choir, a rock band and several popular Icelandic singers 2006; three Christmas concerts (Jolagestir Björgvins) at Laugardal Sports Stadium, Reykjavík with Sigridur Beinteisdottir, Svala Bjorgvinsdottir, Helgi Bjornsson, Stefan Hilmarss, Eyjolfur Kristjansson, Fridrik Omar, Bjorgvin Franz, Ragnar Bjarnason, Edgar Smari and Bjarni Arason and others 2007; six Christmas shows at Reykjavik Stadium 2011; Owner and CEO Tonaljos Music; announcer, 365 Media; Sr Vice-Pres. FM Bylgjan radio, FM Stjarnan radio, Bíórásin (Icelandic movie channel); mem. APRS, STEF of Iceland, FTT (Iceland). *Plays:* Á Köldum klaka, Little Shop of Horrors, Evita. *Films:* Devils Island, Gullsandur, Odal fedranna. *Compositions:* Skyid, Riddari Gotunnar, Vertu ekki ad plata mig, I útvarpinu heyröi ég lag, Ennpá thessi asni, Undir blaum mana, and numerous others. *Recordings:* albums: Þó liði ár og öld 1969, Hljómar 74 1974, Einu sinni var 1976, Út um græna grundu 1977, Ég syng fyrir þig (I Sing for You) 1978, Dagar og Nætur (Days and Nights) with Ragnhildur Gísladóttir 1980, Á hverju kvöldi (Every Night) 1982, Björgvin 1986, Jólagestir 1987, Allir fá þá eitthvað fallegt 1989, Kom Heim (Come Home) 1993, Yrkjum Ísland 1994, Jólagestir Björgvins 3 1995, Núna 1995, Hærra til þín 1995, Alla leið heim 1997, Bestu jólalög Björgvins 1999, Um jólin 2000, Á hverju kvöldi 2000, Eftirlýstur 2001, Ég tala um þig 2002, Brúðarskórnir 2003, Duet 2003, Manstu það 2005, Ár og öld 2005, Björgvin 2006, Björgvin ásamt Sinfóníuhljómsveit Ísland 2006, Jólagestir 4 2007, Íslandslög 7 (Songs of Iceland 7) (series featuring popular singers in Iceland) 2007, Duet 2 2010. *Honours:* voted Pop Star of the Year 1969, Medal of Arts, Iceland, Perfomer of the Year Award 2006, OBE from Pres. of Iceland 2011, Lifetime Achievement Awards from radio and TV, Icelandic MBE Medal for contribution to music. *Address:* Tonaljos Music, PO Box 520, 220 Hafnarfjordur, Iceland (office). *Telephone:* 8929000 (office). *E-mail:* tonaljos@internet.is (office). *Website:* www.bo.is.

HALLIWELL, Geraldine (Geri) Estelle; British singer; b. 7 Aug. 1972, Watford; one d. *Career:* mem. (with Victoria Adams, Melanie Brown, Emma Bunton and Melanie Chisholm) Touch, later renamed The Spice Girls 1993–98, as 'Ginger Spice', reunion tour 2007–08; UN Goodwill Amb. 1998–; Prince's Trust Amb.; Patron Breast Cancer Care; solo artist 1998–. *Films include:* Spiceworld The Movie 1997, Fat Slags 2004. *Television appearances:* judge on Popstars – The Rivals (ITV 1) 2002, appearance in Sex and the City (HBO) 2003, Australia's Got Talent (series judge) 2013. *Recordings include:* albums: with The Spice Girls: Spice 1996, Spiceworld 1997, Greatest Hits 2007; solo: Schizophonic 1999, Scream If You Wanna Go Faster 2001, Passion

2005. *Publications include:* If Only (autobiography) 1999, Just for the Record (autobiography) 2002; Ugenia Lavender children's series: Ugenia Lavender 2008, Ugenia Lavender and the Terrible Tiger 2008, Ugenia Lavender and the Burning Pants 2008, Ugenia Lavender: Home Alone 2008, Ugenia Lavender and the Temple of Gloom 2008, Ugenia Lavender the One and Only 2008. *Honours:* two Ivor Novello songwriting awards 1997, Smash Hits Award for Best British Band 1997, BRIT Award for Best Single (for Wannabe, with The Spice Girls) 1997, BRIT Award for Best Video (for Say You'll Be There, with The Spice Girls) 1997, for Best Performance of the last 30 years 2010, three American Music Awards 1998, Special BRIT Award for Int. Sales 1998. *Current Management:* c/o Brontone Management, Delphian House, Riverside, Salford, Manchester, M3 5FS, England. *Telephone:* (161) 834-2308. *E-mail:* info@brontone.com. *Website:* www.brontone.com; gerihalliwell.com.

HALLSSON, Hallur; Icelandic musician (bass guitar). *Career:* Founder-mem., Leaves 2001–09. *Recordings include:* albums: Breathe 2002, The Angela Test 2005, We Are Shadow 2009. *E-mail:* leaves@leaves.is. *Website:* www.leaves.is.

HALLYDAY, Johnny; French singer, musician (guitar) and actor; b. (Jean-Philippe Smet), 15 June 1943, Paris; s. of Léon Smet; m. 1st Sylvie Vartan; one s.; m. 2nd Elisabeth Etienne; m. 3rd Adeline Blondiau; m. 4th Laetitia Boudou 1996; one c. with Nathalie Baye. *Career:* appeared on stage aged five; music hall tours with his cousin and her husband, American dancer Lee Halliday; numerous concerts. *Films include:* Les Diaboliques 1955, Les Parisiennes 1961, Un Coup dans l'aile 1963, D'où viens-tu, Johnny? 1964, A Tout casser 1968, Visa de censure 1968, Gli Specialisti 1970, Point de chute 1970, Malpertuis 1971, Pour une pomme 1972, L'Aventure, c'est l'aventure 1972, L'Animal 1977, Le Jour se lève et les conneries commencent 1981, Détective 1985, Conseil de famille 1986, Terminus 1987, The Iron Triangle 1989, La Gamine 1991, Pourquoi pas moi? 1999, Love Me 2000, L'Homme du train 2002, Crime Spree 2003, Les Rivières pourpres 2: Les anges de l'apocalypse 2004, Quartier VIP 2005, Jean-Philippe 2006, The Pink Panther 2 2009, Vengeance 2009. *Television:* David Lansky (series) 1989. *Recordings include:* albums: Retiens la nuit 1961, Whole Lotta Shakin' Goin' On 1962, Sings America's Rockin' Hits 1962, Les Bras en croix 1963, Da dou ron ron 1963, L'Idole des jeunes 1963, D'Où viens-tu Johnny? 1963, Le pénitencier 1964, Excuse-moi partenaire 1964, Noir c'est noir 1966, Je suis né dans la rue 1968, Que je t'aime 1969, Fils de personne 1971, Toute la musique que j'aime 1972, J'ai pleuré sur ma guitare 1973, Rock n' Roll Man 1974, Flagrant Delit 1975, Gabrielle 1975, Hamlet 1976, Johnny Hallyday Story: Palais des Sports 1976, J'ai oublié de vivre 1977, Le Bon temps du rock 'n' roll 1978, Ma gueule 1979, Pavillon de Paris 1979, Mon Amérique à moi 1981, Je suis victime de l'amour 1982, Signes extérieurs de richesse 1983, Nashville Blues 1984, Rock 'n' Roll Attitude 1985, Gang 1986, Mon p'tit loup 1988, Oh ma jolie Sarah 1988, La Peur 1988, Ses 32 premieres chansons 1988, Johnny à Bercy 1988, Mirador 1989, Ca ne change pas un homme 1991, Dans la chaleur de Bercy 1991, La Nuit Johnny 1993, Parc de Princes 1993, Deux étrangers 1993, Cheveux longs et idées courtes 1993, A tout casser 1993, Paroles d'hommes 1995, Rough Town 1996, Destination Vegas 1996, Aimer vivre 1997, Insolitudes 1997, Vie 1998, Stade de France 1998, Derrière l'amour 1998, Ce que je sais 1998, Sang pour sang 1999, Les rocks les plus terribles 1999, Ballades 1999, Solitude a deux 2000, Salut les copains 2000, Rock 'n' Slow 2000, Rock a Memphis 2000, Riviere ouvre ton lit 2000, Reve et amour 2000, Quelque part un aigle 2000, Pas facile 2000, La Generation perdue 2000, Chant 2000, Johnny 67 2000, Jeune homme 2000, Je t'aime, je t'aime, je t'aime 2000, Hollywood 2000, Halleluyah 2000, Entre Violence et Violon 2000, En V O 2000, En pieces detachees 2000, Country Folk Rock 2000, C'est la vie 2000, A Partir de maintenant 2000, La Terre promise 2000, À la vie, à la mort! 2002, Ma Vérité 2005, Le Cœur d'un homme 2007, Ça ne finira jamais 2008, Jamais seul 2011. *Publications include:* Johnny raconte Hallyday 1980, Johnny la forme (jtly) 1990, Déraciné (1943–1964) 1996. *Honours:* Chevalier, Légion d'honneur 1997, Officier, Ordre des Arts et des Lettres, Ordre de la Couronne (Belgium); Prix Cinématographique Jean-Gabin 2003. *Address:* c/o Camus and Camus Productions, 6 rue Daubigny, 75017 Paris, France. *Website:* www .johnnyhallyday.com.

HALSALL, Jennie; British media executive; b. 23 Jan. 1954, London. *Education:* Kilburn Polytechnic. *Career:* fmrly with Jacksons Advertising Agency, Cue Films Ltd, EMI Records, UK, David Geffen and Elliot Roberts Man., USA, Elektra Asylum Records, USA; formed own business, Jennie Halsall Consultants (media consultants) 1980. *Honours:* PR of the Year 1980. *Address:* Jennie Halsall Consultants, 87 Cardross Street, PO Box 22467, London W6 0DP, England (office). *Telephone:* (20) 8741-0003 (office). *Fax:* (20) 8846-9652 (office). *E-mail:* jhc@dircon.co.uk (office).

HALVORSON, Mary; American jazz guitarist and academic; b. Boston. *Education:* Wesleyan Univ., New School of Jazz and Contemporary Music. *Career:* has taught guitar and composition, New School of Jazz and Contemporary Music, School for Improvised Music, Banff Int. Workshop in Jazz and Creative Music; formed own trio with John Hébert and Ches Smith, and quintet with additional members Jonathan Finlayson and Jon Irabagon; formed chamber-jazz duo with violist Jessica Pavone; mem. avant-rock band People, Crackleknob, MAP, Thirteenth Assembly; active band member, Marc Ribot's Sun Ship, Tim Berne, Anthony Braxton, Taylor Ho Bynum, Tomas Fujiwara, Curtis Hasselbring, Ingrid Laubrock, Myra Melford, Tom Rainey, Matthew Welch; formed new quartet Reverse Blue 2011. *Recordings include:* with Mary Halvorson Trio: Dragon's Head 2008; with Mary Halvorson

Quintet: Saturn Sings 2010, Bending Bridges 2012; as part of MAP: Six Improvisations for Guitar, Bass and Drums 2003, Fever Dream 2010; with Trevor Dunn's Trio-Convulsant: Sister Phantom Owl Fish 2004; with Assif Tsahar's New York Underground Orchestra: Fragments 2004; with Jessica Pavone: Prairies 2005, On and Off 2007, Thin Air 2009, Departure of Reason 2011; with People: People 2005, Misbegotten Man 2007, 3XaWoman 2011; with Anthony Braxton 12+1tet: Compositions 2006; with MPTHREE: Sleeps Cells 2006; with Taylor Ho Bynum Sextet: The Middle Picture 2007, Apparent Distance 2011; with Weasel Walter: Opulence 2008; with Ches Smith, Jessica Pavone and Devin Hoff: Calling All Portraits 2008; with The Thirteenth Assembly: (un)sentimental 2009, Station Direct 2011; with Nate Wooley and Reuben Radding: Crackleknob 2009; with Tom Rainey Trio: Pool School 2010; with Christian Marclay: Graffiti Composition 2010; with Ches Smith & These Arches: Finally Out of My Hands 2010; with Tomas Fujiwara & the Hook Up; Actionspeak 2010; with Matthew Welch: Blarvuster 2010; with Weasel Walter and Peter Evans: Electric Fruit 2011, with Aych: As the Crow Flies 2012. *Honours:* DownBeat Critics Rising Star Guitar Award 2011, Village Voice New York's Best Guitarist Award 2011, Jazz Journalists' Asscn Award for Guitarist of the Year 2015. *Address:* c/o Scott Menhinick, Improvised Communications, PO Box 70964, Belmont, MA 02479, USA (office). *Telephone:* (781) 373-5825 (office). *E-mail:* scott@improvisedcommunications.com (office); info@maryhalvorson.com. *Website:* www.maryhalvorson.com.

HAMAKI, Mohamed Ibrahim el-; Egyptian singer; b. 4 Nov. 1975, Cairo. *Career:* solo artist 2003–. *Recordings include:* albums: Khallena n'eesh 2003, Khalas el-kalam 2006, Naweeha 2008, Kol lela 2009, Men Albi Baghani 2012. *Honours:* MTV Europe Music Awards for Best Arabia Act Award 2010. *Current Management:* c/o Delta Sound FZ-LLC, Office 96, 2nd Floor, DMC Building 2, Dubai Media City, PO Box 72280, Dubai, UAE. *Telephone:* (50) 640 3288. *E-mail:* enquire@deltasound.ae. *Website:* www.deltasound.ae; www .nogoumrecords.com.

HAMASAKI, Ayumi; Japanese singer, songwriter and musician (piano); b. 2 Oct. 1978, Fukuoka, Kyushu. *Career:* moved to Tokyo to act and model; relocated to New York, USA for vocal lessons 1997; numerous concert tours; launched own range of cellphones 2001. *Acting roles:* Twins Kyoshi (TV) 1993, Saiyuki (TV) 1994, Ladies Socho Saigo No Hi (film) 1995, Miseinen (TV) 1995, Gakko II (film) 1996, Tsuki ni Shizumu 2002, Distance Love 2007. *Recordings include:* albums: A Song For xx 1999, ayu mi x 1999, Love Appears 1999, Duty 2000, Best 2001, I Am... 2002, Rainbow 2002, Ballads 2003, Memorial Address 2003, My Story 2004, (Miss)understood 2006, Guilty 2008, Next Level 2009, Rock 'n' Roll Circus 2010, Party Queen 2012, Love Again 2013, Colours 2014, A One 2015. *Honours:* Japan Music Grandprix Award 2001, Japan Gold Disc Award for Artist of the Year 2001, World Music Award for Best Selling Japanese Artist 2001, 2005, MTV Asia Awards for Best Female Artist 2002. *Current Management:* c/o Avex Management Co. Ltd, Sumitomo Seimei Aoyama Building, 3-1-30 Minami-Aoyama, Minato-ku, Tokyo 107-0062, Japan. *Telephone:* (3) 5413-8792. *Website:* www.avexnet.or.jp/ayu.

HAMBE, Alf; Swedish composer, songwriter, writer, poet and artist and musician (piano, accordion and guitar); b. 24 Jan. 1931; m. Ulla; one s. one d. *Career:* first song collection Astronaut on Horseback 1962; full-time writer, composer from 1962; stage, TV and radio broadcasts; mem. Swedish Composers of Popular Music, Swedish Composers Int. Asscn, Swedish Authors' Asscn. *Compositions:* 15 collections of songs and poems. *Recordings include:* Alf Hambe in Molom; 20 Recordings with Songs From My Collections; Song in Molom; Scandinavian Songs with Alice and Svend, Ingeland 2005, I sommarn sena 2006. *Publications include:* Song in Molom; Another Song About the Forest of the Green Mist. *Honours:* Prize in the Memory of Ulf Peder Olrog 1975, Nils Ferlin Prize 1988, two Evert Taube Prizes 1990, Litteris et Artibus 2008, Dan Andersson Prize 2010. *Website:* www.dahlbergforlag.se/ hambe.

HAMELIN, Dave; Canadian singer, songwriter and musician (guitar, drums); b. 3 Oct. 1980. *Career:* mem. The Stills 2000–11. *Recordings include:* albums: Logic Will Break Your Heart 2003, Without Feathers 2005, Oceans Will Rise (Juno Award for Best Alternative Album of the Year 2009) 2008. *Honours:* Juno Award for Best New Group of the Year 2009. *Website:* www .arts-crafts.ca/thestills.

HAMILL, Andy; British musician (double bass, bass guitars); b. 25 March 1972, Glasgow, Scotland; m. Rebecca Hollweg. *Career:* session musician, many jazz, pop, drum and bass bands, including 4 Hero, Nitin Sawhney, Chris Bowden; co-production, musician, June Babies, two albums for Rebecca Hollweg; mem. Musicians' Union. *Recordings include:* solo album: Bee For Bass 2003. *E-mail:* info@andyhamill.com (office). *Website:* www.andyhamill .com.

HAMILTON; British musician (bass guitar) and singer; b. (Neil Hamilton Wilkinson), Cumbria. *Career:* Founder-mem., British Sea Power 2000–; the band runs Club Sea Power, a monthly variety show in Brighton, England; numerous live performances and festival appearances. *Recordings include:* albums: The Decline of British Sea Power 2003, Open Season 2005, Do You Like Rock Music? 2008, Man of Aran (film soundtrack) 2009, Valhalla Dancehall 2011, Machineries of Joy 2013, From the Sea to the Land Beyond 2013, Happiness 2014, Sea of Brass 2015. *Honours:* Time Out Award for Live Band of the Year 2004. *Current Management:* c/o David Taylor, British Sea Power, 95 Beaconsfield Road, Hastings, TN34 3TW, England. *E-mail:* bspmanagement@googlemail.com. *Website:* www.britishseapower.co.uk.

HAMILTON, Anthony Cornelius; American R&B singer, songwriter and record producer; b. 28 Jan. 1971, Charlotte, NC; m. Tarsha Hamilton; three s., three s. from a previous relationship. *Education:* South Mecklenburg High School, Charlotte, NC. *Career:* relocated to New York 1993; signed with Uptown Records; backing singer, D'Angelo tour 2000; collaborated with Nappy Roots on Po' Folks 2002; numerous contributions to recordings by artists including 2Pac, Sunshine Anderson, Elayna Boynton, Nick Cannon, Cru, Da Brat, Al Green, Buddy Guy, Ace Hood, Jadakiss, Nas, Nelly, The RH Factor, Busta Rhymes, Mark Ronson, Santana, Jill Scott, Angie Stone, Young Jeezy. *Recordings:* albums: XTC 1996, Comin' From Where I'm From 2003, Soulife 2005, Ain't Nobody Worryin' 2005, Southern Comfort 2007, The Point of It All 2008, Back to Love 2011. *Honours:* Vibe Music Next Award Winner 2004, Vibe Music Award for Best Collaboration 2004, BET J Cool Like Dat Award 2006, Grammy Award for Best Traditional R&B Vocal Performance (with Al Green; for You've Got the Love I Need) 2009. *Current Management:* c/o Creative Artists Agency, 162 Fifth Avenue, 6th Floor, New York, NY 10010, USA. *Website:* www.caatouring.com. *Address:* c/o Sony Music Entertainment, 550 Madison Avenue, Room 2316, New York, NY 10022, USA (office). *Website:* www.sonymusic.com (office); www.anthonyhamilton.com.

HAMILTON, Eamon; British singer and musician (guitar, keyboards, percussion); b. Canada; m. Koren Zailckas 2008. *Career:* fmr mem., British Sea Power; mem., Brakes 2002–; numerous live performances and festival appearances. *Recordings include:* albums: Give Blood 2005, The Beatific Visions 2006, Touchdown 2009. *E-mail:* brakes@brakesbrakesbrakes.com. *Website:* www.brakesbrakesbrakes.com.

HAMILTON, Frank; American musician and singer; b. 3 Aug. 1934, New York, NY; m. Mary Hamilton 1983. *Education:* Los Angeles City Coll. 1952, 1955, 1966; Roosevelt Univ., Chicago, 1960–61; Los Angeles Valley Coll., Van Nuys, 1963–64; Santa Monica City Coll., 1964–69; California Univ., Los Angeles, 1970, 1978; Santa Barbara City Coll., 1974; California Univ., Northridge, 1978; Georgia State Univ., 1984–87. *Career:* Co-founder Old Town School of Folk Music, Chicago 1957; house musician, Gate of Horn, Chicago 1958–62; Newport Folk Music Festival 1959; with folk music group, The Weavers, Carnegie Hall, Lincoln Center, Forest Hills Stadium 1963; concert with Pete Seeger, Abbott Hall, Marblehead, MA 1984; Meridian Folk Trio 1986–2000; mem. of duo Classic Jazz with symphony clarinetist, Bill Rappaport; mem. Chicago Historical Soc., Irish Arts of Atlanta, Hot Club of Atlanta (Founder). *Compositions:* with others: We Shall Overcome 1956; Survival 1965, The Surfers 1964, Baby, What I Mean 1965, I Feel It 1967. *Recordings:* A Folksinger's Folksinger, Frank Hamilton Sings Folksongs, Nonsuch, with Pete Seeger, The World of Frank and Valucha, Weavers Reunion at Vanguard Carnegie Hall, Folk Festival at Newport, Long Lonesome Home 1999, Goodnight Irene (Weavers compilation) 2000. *Publication:* Choosing a Guitar Teacher 1981. *Honours:* Composition Award, Los Angeles Valley Coll. 1963. *Address:* 852 Cinderella Court, Decatur, GA 30033, USA. *Telephone:* (404) 748-9247. *Fax:* (404) 748-9247. *E-mail:* songlines2@clear.net. *Website:* www.songlines.ws.

HAMILTON, Mark; British musician (bass guitar); b. 21 March 1977, Lisburn. *Career:* Founder-mem. Ash 1992–; numerous headline tours, UK festivals, TV appearances, worldwide tours. *Recordings include:* albums: Trailer 1994, 1977 1996, Live At the Wireless 1997, Nu-Clear Sounds 1998, Free All Angels 2001, Cosmic Debris 2002, Intergalactic Sonic 7"s: The Best of Ash 2002, Meltdown 2004, Twilight of the Innocents 2007. *Honours:* NME BRAT Award for Best Single (for Burn Baby Burn) 2002, Q Award for Best Single (for Burn Baby Burn) 2002, Ivor Novello Award for Best Contemporary Song (for Shining Light) 2002. *E-mail:* mark@ash-official.com. *Website:* www.ash-official.com.

HAMILTON, Natasha Maria; British singer; b. 17 July 1982, Kensington, Liverpool; m. Riad Erraji 2007 (divorced 2013); three s. *Career:* mem., Atomic Kitten 1999–; UK support tours 1999–2000; co-spearheaded MTV Asia Awards 2000; Pan-European breakthrough with Whole Again single; guest at Celebrate South Africa Freedom Concert, London 2001; appearance, Party at the Palace, Buckingham Palace Jubilee celebrations 2002. *Recordings include:* albums: Right Now 2000, Feels So Good 2002, Ladies' Night 2003, The Greatest Hits 2004, The Collection 2005; solo: Round and Round 2007. *Current Management:* c/o Leisa Maloney, Fire PR and Management, 21-23 Slater Street, Liverpool, L1 4BW, England. *Telephone:* (777) 335-1938. *E-mail:* lmaloney@fireprandmanagement.co.uk. *Website:* www.fireprandmanagement.co.uk; www.natashahamilton.biz; www.atomickitten.com.

HAMILTON, Page, MA; American musician (guitar); b. Eugene, Oregon. *Education:* Manhattan School of Music, New York. *Career:* fmr mem., Glenn Branca's Guitar Orchestra; mem., Band of Susans; founder mem., Helmet 1989–98, 2004–; founder mem. Gandhi; collaborations with David Bowie, Joe Henry, Ben Neill, Nine Inch Nails, Norma Jean, P.O.D., Therapy?; numerous live appearances. *Recordings include:* albums: with Band of Susans: Love Agenda 1989; with Helmet: Strap It On 1990, Meantime 1992, Betty 1994, Aftertaste 1997, Size Matters 2004, Monochrome 2006, Seeing Eye Dog 2010. *E-mail:* mailbox@maineroadmanagement.com. *Website:* www.maineroadmanagement.com; www.helmetmusic.com.

HAMILTON, Patrick, BMus; Belgian producer, musician (keyboards) and songwriter; *General Manager, The Globe Recording Studios & Bromo Music Publishing*; b. 16 March 1963, Bruges. *Education:* Royal Music School, Ghent.

Career: played with several well-known bands in Belgium; Owner and Gen. Man. The Globe Recording Studios and Bromo Music Publishing. *Compositions:* composed for Sandra Kim, Eurovision contest winner mid 1980s, also for 2 Lips, Partyzone, Monday Justice, Marisa, Kabouter Plop, Udo, Johnny Logan, Ingeborg, La Sakhra, Barry Mason. *Address:* The Globe Recording Studios, Stationsstraat 17, 8210 Loppem, Belgium (office). *E-mail:* info@the-globe.be (office). *Website:* www.the-globe.be (office).

HAMMARLUND, Jan; Swedish singer, songwriter, musician (guitar) and translator; b. 17 July 1951, Stockholm. *Career:* festival appearances, tours; mem. STIM, Svenska Teateförbundet, SKAP, Musikcentrum. *Recordings include:* albums: Tusentals Swarnor Over Chile 1974, Karlek Olh Sang 1981, Jan Hammarlund 1972–92, Tvars Over Garn 1995, Om Trädgårdsbevattning 1996, Alby-Bilbao 2000, Grässtrån och gatsten 2002, Roda Linjan 2007. *Honours:* SKAP Award 1978, STIM Award 1989, Konstnärsnämnden (artists' cttee) 1992–96, José Martí Award 1994. *E-mail:* post@janhammarlund.se. *Website:* janhammarlund.se.

HAMMEL, Joan, BA; American singer; b. Lake Forest, Ill. *Education:* Columbia Coll., Chicago, Coll. of Lake County. *Career:* toured the Caribbean; hosted the Midday Show, on radio; numerous commercials, TV and film work; fmr Pres. and Trustee Lake County Discovery Museum Friends; mem. Bd of Govs The Grammys, Chicago; mem. NARAS, NATAS. *Compositions:* Learn to Fly, Love Prevails, Run Like the Wind, The Gift, Give It to Me Straight, Timeless, See Ya. *Recordings include:* Oh Lady Di, Tribute To Princess Diana, Joanland 2005. *Honours:* Emmy Award, Best Children's Special 1987, ITVA Award, Best Health Care Video 1986, 1987, Nat. and Int. Vocal Competition Medals. *Current Management:* c/o Paxton Productions, PO Box 486, Grayslake, IL 60030, USA. *E-mail:* joan@joanhammel.com (office). *Website:* www.joanhammel.com.

HAMMER; American rap artist and dancer; *CEO, Alchemist Management*; b. (Stanley Kirk Burrell), 30 March 1962, Oakland, Calif. *Career:* mem., rap duo Holy Ghost Boys; Founder, Bustin Records; solo artist (originally as MC Hammer) 1987–; concerts include Please Hammer, Don't Hurt 'Em US tour 1990, US tour, with Vanilla Ice and En Vogue 1990, UK and Japan tours 1991, The Simple Truth (benefit concert for Kurdish refugees), Wembley 1991, Too Legit To Quit tour, with Boyz II Men 1992, USA Harvest Hunger Relief Concert 1992, Kiel Summer Jam 1992; Founder, man., production and video co., Roll-Wit-It Entertainment 1992; currently Pres., record label, FullBlast Digital Music Group; CEO Alchemist Management. *Television includes:* Hammer's MTV Birthday Bash 1992, Hammer From The Heart, CBS 1992, Hammerman Cartoon series, ABC 1991. *Recordings includes:* hit singles: U Can't Touch This 1990, Have You Seen Her? 1990, Pray 1990, Here Comes The Hammer, from Rocky V film soundtrack 1991, Yo! Sweetness 1991, Addams Groove, from Addams Family film soundtrack 1992, 2 Legit 2 Quit 1992, Do Not Pass Me By 1992, It's All Too Good 1994, Pumps and A Bump 1994, Don't Stop 1994, Going Up Yonder 1995, Sultry Funk 1995; albums: Feel My Power 1987, Please Hammer Don't Hurt 'Em 1990, Too Legit to Quit 1991, The Funky Headhunter 1994, Inside Out 1995, Family Affair 1998, Active Duty 2001, Full Blast 2003, Look Look Look 2006, DanceJamTheMusic 2009. *Honours:* several American Music Awards 1990–91, three Grammy Awards 1991, People's Choice Award 1991, BRIT Award for Best International Newcomer 1991, two Bammy Awards 1991, JUNO Award for International Artist of the Year 1991, three Rolling Stone Readers Poll Wins 1991, four Soul Train Awards, including Sammy Davis Jr Award 1991–92, four NARM Awards 1991, George and Ira Gershwin Award 2013. *Website:* www.mchammer.com; www.alchemistmma.com.

HAMMER, Jan; American (b. Czech) musician (keyboards), composer and producer; b. 17 April 1948, Prague, Czechoslovakia; s. of Jan Hammer Sr and Vlasta Pruchova; m. Ivona Reich; one s. one d. *Education:* Prague Acad. of Music and Arts, Berklee Coll. of Music. *Career:* moved to USA 1968; mem., John McLaughlin's Mahavishnu Orchestra 1971–73; Founder Jan Hammer Group 1975–80; Co-founder and mem. Jeff Beck/Jan Hammer Group 1976–77; freelance musician and bandleader 1973–2016; film and TV TV composer 1983–2016. *Compositions include:* film scores: A Night In Heaven 1983, Secret Admirer 1985; TV series soundtrack: Miami Vice 1984. *Recordings include:* singles: Sister Andrea 1973, Don't You Know 1977, Theme from Miami Vice 1985, Crockett's Theme 1987, Too Much to Lose 1989; solo albums: Maliny Maliny 1968, Like Children 1974, First Seven Days 1975, Timeless 1975, Oh Yeah 1976, Melodies 1977, Black Sheep 1978, Hammer 1979, Untold Passion 1981, Here To Stay 1982, Miami Vice 1985, The Early Years 1986, Escape from TV 1987, Snapshots 1989, Behind the Mind's Eye 1993, Drive 1994, Snapshots 1.2, 2000, Miami Vice The Complete Collection 2002, Cocaine Cowboys 2008; with John McLaughlin: Inner Mounting Flame 1971, Birds of Fire 1972, Between Nothingness and Eternity 1973, Love Devotion and Surrender 1973, The Lost Trident Sessions 1999; with Jeff Beck: Wired 1976, Live With The Jan Hammer Group 1977, There and Back 1980, Flash 1985, Who Else? 1999; with Al Di Meola: Elegant Gypsy 1977, Splendido Hotel 1979, Electric Rendezvous 1982, Tour de Force 1982, Scenario 1983; with John Abercrombie: Timeless 1975, Night 1984; other recordings with: Tommy Bolin, Stanley Clarke, Clarence Clemons, Billy Cobham, Jerry Goodman, Mick Jagger, Elvin Jones, Steve Lukather, Santana, Neal Schon, Jeremy Steig, Tony Williams, James (JY) Young. *Honours:* two Grammy Awards, inducted into Keyboard Hall of Fame. *Current Management:* c/o Elliott Sears, Elliott Sears Management, 7 Dunham Drive, New Fairfield, CT 06812, USA.

Telephone: (203) 746-8500. *Fax:* (203) 746-8638. *E-mail:* elliott@janhammer .com. *Website:* www.janhammer.com.

HAMMER, Joseph; American musician (drums) and composer; b. 7 June 1954, San Antonio, Tex.; m. Jacquelyn Henry 1983; one s. *Education:* Berklee Coll. of Music, Boston School of Electronic Music. *Career:* studio production 1975–85; co-production for Daniel Balavoine; tours, concerts, with Daniel Balavoine, France Gall, Jean-Michel Jarre; mem. Institut de Percussions Modernes. *Compositions include:* Summer Dreaming, Love of a Woman. *Recordings include:* with Daniel Balavoine, Jean-Michel Jarre, Jon Anderson, Mick Jagger, Peter Gabriel; Dynasty Suites 2003, I Love You, Please Love Me Too 2010. *Publications:* Trophee Sonor, 6–10 Drums. *E-mail:* thehammer@ josephhammer.com. *Website:* www.josephhammer.com.

HAMMETT, Kirk; American musician (guitar); b. 18 Nov. 1962, San Francisco, Calif.; m. 1st Rebecca Hammett (divorced 1990); m. 2nd Lani Hammett 1998; two s. *Career:* fmr mem. Exodus, Joe Satriani; mem. heavy rock group, Metallica 1983–; world-wide tours and concerts. *Films:* Some Kind Of Monster (Independent Spirit Award for Best Documentary 2005) 2004, Metallica Through The Never 2013. *Recordings include:* albums: Kill 'Em All 1983, Ride the Lightning 1984, Master of Puppets 1986, ...And Justice for All 1988, The Good, The Bad and The Live 1990, Metallica 1991, Load 1996, Reload 1997, Early Days 1997, S&M (live) 1999, St Anger 2003, Death Magnetic 2008; singles: Whiplash 1985, Garage Days Revisited 1987, Creeping Death 1990, Harvester of Sorrow 1988, One (Grammy Award for Best Heavy Metal Performance) 1989, Stone Cold Crazy (Grammy Award for Best Heavy Metal Performance) 1991, Jump in the Fire 1991, The Unforgiven (Grammy Award for Best Heavy Metal Performance 1992) 1991, Enter Sandman 1991, Nothing Else Matters 1992, Wherever I May Roam 1992, Sad But True 1992, Until It Sleeps 1996, Hero of the Day 1996, Mama Said 1996, King Nothing 1997, The Memory Remains 1997, Fuel 1998, Turn the Page 1998, Whisky in the Jar (Grammy Award for Best Hard Rock Performance 2000) 1999, Die Die My Darling 1999, No Leaf Clover 2000, I Disappear 2000, Call of the Ktulu (Grammy Award for Best Rock Instrumental Performance) 2001, St Anger 2003, Frantic 2003, Unnamed Feeling 2003, St. Anger 2003, Death Magnetic 2008. *Publication:* Too Much Horror Business 2012. *Honours:* American Music Award for Favorite Heavy Metal Artist (with Metallica) 1993, Grammy Award for Best Metal Performance (for My Apocalypse) 2009. *Current Management:* c/o Q-Prime Inc., 729 Seventh Avenue, 16th Floor, New York, NY 10019, USA. *Telephone:* (212) 302-9790. *Fax:* (212) 302-9589. *E-mail:* info@qprime.com. *Website:* www.metallica.com.

HAMMILL, Peter Joseph Andrew; British singer and musician (guitar, piano); b. 5 Nov. 1948, London. *Career:* Founder-mem., Van Der Graaf Generator 1967–72, 1975–78, 2004–; solo artist 1971–. *Recordings include:* albums: with Van Der Graaf Generator: Aerosol Grey Machine 1968, The Least We Can Do is Wave to Each Other 1969, H to He, Who Am the Only One 1970, Pawn Hearts 1971, Long Hello 1973, Godbluff 1975, Still Life 1976, World Record 1976, The Quiet Zone, the Pleasure Dome 1977, Reflection 1978, Vital (live) 1978, Time Vaults 1982, I Prophesy Disaster 1993, An Introduction 2000, The Box 2000, Present 2005, Real Time 2007, Trisector 2008, A Grounding in Numbers 2011, Alt 2012; solo: Fool's Mate 1971, Chameleon In the Shadow of Night 1972, The Silent Corner and the Empty Stage 1974, In Camera 1974, Nadir's Big Chance 1975, Over 1976, The Future Now 1978, Skeletons of Songs 1978, PH7 1979, A Black Box 1980, Sitting Targets 1981, Enter K 1982, Loops and Reels 1983, Patience 1983, The Love Songs 1984, The Margin + 1985, Skin 1986, And Close as This 1986, In a Foreign Town 1988, Out of Water 1989, Room Temperature 1990, The Fall of the House Of Usher 1991, Spur of the Moment 1991, Fireships 1991, The Noise 1992, The Storm 1993, The Calm 1993, There Goes the Daylight 1993, Roaring Forties 1994, Offensichtlich Goldfisch 1995, Sonix 1996, X My Heart 1996, Everyone You Hold 1997, This 1998, Typical 1999, The Appointed Hour 1999, None of the Above 2000, Unsung 2001, What Now? 2001, Margin + Live 2001, Clutch 2002, Thin Man Sings Ballads 2003, Incoherence 2004, Singularity 2006, Veracious 2006, Thin Air 2009, Consequences 2012. *Address:* Sofa Sound, Suite 109, 3 Edgar Buildings, George Street, Bath, BA1 2FJ, England (office). *E-mail:* contact@sofasound.com (office). *Website:* www.sofasound.com (office); www .peterhammill.com.

HAMMOND, Albert, Jr; American musician (guitar); b. 9 April 1980, Los Angeles, Calif.; s. of Albert Hammond Sr. *Career:* mem., The Strokes 1998–; also solo artist 2006–. *Recordings include:* albums: with The Strokes: Is This It (NME Award for Album of the Year) 2001, Room on Fire 2003, First Impressions of Earth 2006, Angles 2011, Comedown Machine 2013; solo: Yours to Keep 2006, Como te Llama? 2008. *Honours:* NME Awards for Band of the Year, Best New Act 2001, for Best Int. Band 2006, BRIT Award for Best Int. Newcomer 2002. *Current Management:* c/o Ryan Gentles, Wiz Kid Management, 123 East Seventh Street, New York, NY 10001, USA. *Telephone:* (212) 473-3600. *E-mail:* info@wizkidmanagement.com. *Website:* www.alberthammondjr.com; www.thestrokes.com.

HAMMOND, Albert, Sr, OBE; British songwriter, singer and producer; b. 18 May 1944, London; father of Albert Hammond Jr (mem. The Strokes). *Career:* brought up in Gibraltar; formed first band The Diamond Boys, Gibraltar 1960; performing in duo with Richard Cartwright 1963–65; mem. Los Cincos Ricardos 1965; mem. songwriting and performing team Hammond and Hazlewood (with Mike Hazlewood) 1965–74; mem. Family Dogg 1966–69; moved to USA 1971, pursued solo performing career; collaborated with lyricists Hal David, Carole Bayer-Sager 1970s; writing and recording songs for Spanish market 1978–81; writing and producing for Julio Iglesias mid-1980s; songs have been recorded by artists including The Carpenters, José Carreras, Johnny Cash, Joe Cocker, Chris de Burgh, Neil Diamond, Céline Dion, Art Garfunkel, The Hollies, Whitney Houston, Julio Iglesias, Elton John, Tom Jones, Barry Manilow, Johnny Mathis, Willie Nelson, Roy Orbison, Helen Reddy, José Luis Rodriguez, Diana Ross, Leo Sayer, Simply Red, Sonny and Cher, Starship, Steppenwolf, Tina Turner; production work with Julio Iglesias, Lani Hall, José Luis Rodriguez as well as producing own solo albums. *Compositions include:* writer or co-writer: It Never Rains in Southern California, To All the Girls I've Loved Before, Nothing's Gonna Stop Us Now, The Free Electric Band, The Air that I Breathe, Good Morning Freedom, When I Need You, Don't Turn Around, 99 Miles from LA, One Moment in Time (Emmy Award 1988), I Don't Wanna Live Without Your Love, Down by the River. *Recordings include:* solo albums: It Never Rains in Southern California 1972, The Free Electric Band 1973, Albert Hammond 1974, 99 Miles from LA 1975, Canta Sus Grandes Exitos En Español E Ingles 1976, My Spanish Album 1976, Mi Album De Recuerdos 1977, When I Need You 1977, Albert Louis Hammond 1978, Greatest Hits 1978, Al Otro Lado Del Sol 1979, Comprenderte 1981, Your World and My World 1981, Somewhere in America 1982, Hammond & West 1986, Revolution of the Heart 2005, Legend 2010, Legend II 2012; with Family Dogg: The View from Rowland's Head 1972. *Current Management:* c/o Lisa Dolan, R.J. Brenner & Co., Inc., 10100 Santa Monica Building, Suite 1050, Los Angeles, CA 90067, USA. *Telephone:* (310) 734-1235. *Fax:* (310) 734-1230. *E-mail:* lisa@rjbrennerco.com. *Website:* www .alberthammond.net.

HAMMOND, David Jonathan (Didz); British musician (bass guitar); b. 19 July 1981. *Career:* mem., The Cooper Temple Clause 2001–05; mem., Dirty Pretty Things 2005–. *Recordings include:* albums: with The Cooper Temple Clause: See This Through and Leave 2002, Kick Up the Fire and Let the Flames Break Loose 2003, Make This Your Own 2007; with Dirty Pretty Things: Waterloo to Anywhere 2006, Romance at Short Notice 2008. *Website:* www.coopertempleclause.co.uk.

HAMMOND, John Paul; American blues musician (guitar) and singer; b. 13 Nov. 1942, New York, NY. *Career:* began playing guitar aged 17; solo artist 1962–; British tours 1960s; worked with artists, including Duane Allman, J.J. Cale, John Lee Hooker, Robbie Robertson, Bill Wyman, Charles Brown, Charlie Musselwhite, Duke Robillard, Bob Dylan, Michelle Shocked; host and performer on television documentary The Search for Robert Johnson 1992. *Recordings include:* albums: John Hammond; Big City Blues; Country Blues; So Many Roads; Mirrors; I Can Tell; Sooner Or Later; Southern Fried; Source Point; I'm Satisfied; Triumvirate; Can't Beat The Kid; John Hammond Solo; Footwork; Hot Tracks; Mileage; Frogs For Snakes; John Hammond Live; John Hammond Live In Greece; Nobody But You; Got Love If You Want It; Trouble No More; Found True Love; Wicked Grin, 2001; Ready for Love 2003, Push Comes to Shove 2007. *Honours:* Grammy Award for Blues Explosion (with Stevie Ray Vaughan, Koko Taylor) 1985. *Current Management:* The Rosebud Agency, PO Box 170429, San Francisco, CA 94117, USA. *Telephone:* (415) 386-3456. *Fax:* (415) 386-0599. *E-mail:* info@rosebudus.com. *Website:* www .rosebudus.com/hammond.

HAMZA, Kawkab; Iraqi composer; b. 1 July 1944, Babylon; m. (divorced); one s., two d. *Education:* Fine Art Inst., Baghdad, Kiev Univ., USSR. *Career:* composed first song, 1966, moved to Syria, 1983, wrote four theatre plays, two TV series; moved to Detroit, Mich., composed for theatre; refugee in Denmark composing for theatre; returned to Iraq 2009; mem., Danish Society for Jazz, Rock, Folk Composers. *Compositions include:* more than seventy songs including Afish Borouj Al-Hinaya, Basateen Al-Banafsaj, Mahattat, Al-Qantara Bayida, Makateeb, Ya Toyour Al-Tayra; albums: Nehebbkum Wallah Nehebkum, New Babylon Music, Sar Alumur Mahetat.

HAN, Geng; Chinese singer, actor and dancer; b. 9 Feb. 1984, Mudanjiang, Heilongjiang. *Education:* Central Univ. for Nationalities, Beijing. *Career:* studied Chinese traditional dance; participant as representative of Nanai group, parade for China's 50-year anniversary 1999; auditioned for SM Entertainment agency 2001; cameo actor 2002; relocated to S Korea to work with SM Entertainment 2003; mem. boyband Super Junior 2005–08; leader Super Junior-M 2008–09; torch bearer at Beijing Olympics 2008; solo career 2010–; apptd Mainland China initiator, Love Life Charity Movement 2012. *Films:* as actor: Attack on the Pin-Up Boys 2007, The Founding of a Party 2011, My Kingdom 2011, The First President 2011. *Television:* as actor: numerous cameo appearances including: Rainbow Romance 2006, Stage of Youth 2009. *Recordings:* albums: with Super Junior: SuperJunior05 (Twins) 2005, Don't Don 2007; with Super Junior-M: Me 2008; solo: Geng Xin 2010, Hope in the Darkness 2012. *Honours:* numerous awards including: with Super Junior-M: Southeast Explosive Music Chart Award for Most Popular Group 2008, China Tencent Stars Award for Mainland's Best Group 2008, Music King Award for Asia's Most Popular New Group 2008, CCTV-MTV Music Award for Mainland's Best Group 2008, CCTV Chinese Entertainment Awards for Mainland's Best Album 2008, for Mainland's Most Popular Group 2008, China Digital Music Award for Most Downloaded Overseas Singer 2009; solo: for music: CCTV-MTV Music Awards for Mainland Most Popular Male Singer 2010, 2011, Meng Niu Award for Best Newcomer 2010, Meng Niu Future Star Festival Award for Children's Favourite Male Singer, Tencent Star Award for Male Singer of the Year 2010, China Power Fashion Award for Most Talented Male Singer of the Year 2011, Sina Network Award for Male

Singer of the Year 2011, Sprite Chinese Music Awards for Best Male Singer of the Year, Favourite Idol of the Year, Golden Melody of the Year 2011, Baidu Entertainment Hottest Award for Golden Song of the Year 2011, Eastern Billboard Annual Award for All-Round Entertainer of the Year 2011, for Golden Song of the Year 2011, Global Chinese Golden Chart Award for Most Popular Newcomer 2011, Meng Niu Music Billboard Awards for Most Popular Male Singer of the Year 2011, 2012, Channel V Music Award for Mainland Most Popular Male Singer 2011, Music Radio China Top Chart Awards for Most Popular Newcomer 2011, for Best Mainland All-Round Artist 2011, China Mobile Wireless Music Ceremony Awards for Artist of the Year 2012; for acting: Hua Ding PASSAT Award for Most Anticipated Mainland Chinese Actor 2011, New York Chinese Film Festival Award for Most Popular Asian Artist 2011, LUX Fashion Power Award for Actor of the Year 2012. *Website:* www.chinahangeng.com.

HANCOCK, Herbert (Herbie) Jeffrey, BA; American jazz pianist and composer; b. 12 April 1940, Chicago, Ill.; s. of Wayman Edward Hancock and Winnie Griffin; m. Gudrun Meixner 1968, one d. *Education:* Grinnell Coll., Roosevelt Univ., Manhattan School of Music, New School for Social Research. *Career:* Owner and Publr Hancock Music Co. 1962–; Founder Hancock and Joe Productions 1989–; Pres. Harlem Jazz Music Center, Inc.; Creative Chair for Jazz, Los Angeles Philharmonic Orchestra 2010–; has performed with Chicago Symphony Orchestra 1952, Coleman Hawkins, Chicago 1960, Donald Byrd 1960–63, Miles Davis Quintet 1963–68; recorded with Chick Corea; mem. Nat. Acad. of Recording Arts and Sciences, Jazz Musicians Assccn, Nat. Acad. of TV Arts and Sciences, Broadcast Music; apptd UNESCO Goodwill Ambassador 2011; Prof., UCLA Univ. 2013–. *Albums include:* Takin' Off 1963, Succotash 1964, Maiden Voyage 1965, Speak Like a Child 1968, Fat Albert Rotunda 1969, Mwandishi 1971, Crossings 1972, Sextant 1972, Headhunters 1973, Thrust 1974, The Best of Herbie Hancock 1974, Man-Child 1975, The Quintet 1977, V.S.O.P. 1977, Sunlight 1978, An Evening with Herbie Hancock and Chick Corea In Concert 1979, Feets Don't Fail Me Now 1979, Monster 1980, Greatest Hits 1980, Lite Me Up 1982, Future Shock 1983, Sound System 1984, Perfect Machine 1988, Jamming 1992, Cantaloupe Island 1994, A Tribute to Miles (Grammy Award for Best Jazz Instrumental Performance 1995) 1994, Dis Is Da Drum 1995, The New Standard 1996, Gershwin's World (Grammy Award for Best Jazz Instrumental Performance 1999) 1998, Night Walker 2000, Future 2 Future 2001, Directions in Music (with others) (Grammy Award for Best Jazz Instrumental Album 2003) 2002, River: The Joni Letters (Grammy Awards for Best Album and Best Contemporary Jazz Album 2008) 2007, The Imagine Project 2010; with Miles Davis Quartet: Miles in the Sky, Nefertiti, Sorcerer, ESP, Miles Davis In Concert (My Funny Valentine), A Silent Way, Jack Johnson, Seven Steps to Heaven); contrib. to Colour and Light – Jazz Sketches On Sondheim 1995. *Films:* composed film music for Blow Up 1966, The Spook Who Sat by the Door 1973, Death Wish 1974, A Soldier's Story 1984, Jo Jo Dancer, Your Life is Calling 1986, Action Jackson 1988, Colors 1988, Harlem Nights 1989, Livin' Large 1991; wrote score and appeared in film Round Midnight 1986 (Acad. Award Best Original Score 1986). *Publications include:* A Tribute to Miles 1994, Dis is Da Drum 1994, The New Standard 1996, I H with Wayne Shorter 1997, Gershwin's World 1998, Possibilities (co-author) 2014. *Honours:* numerous awards including Citation of Achievement, Broadcast Music, Inc. 1963, Jay Award, Jazz Magazine 1964, several awards from Black Music Magazine 1967–71, 5 MTV Awards, Grammy Award for Best Rhythm and Blues Instrumental Performance 1984, 1985, for Best Jazz Instrumental Composition 1988 (as co-composer), 1997, for Best Instrumental Arrangement Accompanying Vocals 1999, for Best Jazz Instrumental Solo 2003, 2005, for Best Improvised Jazz Solo 2011, for Best Pop Collaboration with Vocals 2011, Jazz Journalists' Assccn Lifetime Achievement in Jazz Award 2014. *Current Management:* c/o Melinda Murphy, Hancock Music Company, 1250 North Doheny Drive, Los Angeles, CA 90069, USA. *Telephone:* (310) 273-3321. *E-mail:* hhmusicco@ herbiehancock.com. *Website:* www.herbiehancock.com.

HANCOCK, Keith; British singer, songwriter, musician (diatonic accordion) and writer; b. 28 Oct. 1953, Manchester; m. Janet Karen Wood 1979 (divorced); two s. *Career:* mem., various English country dance bands; began writing 1984; toured Europe, Canada, New Zealand, Hong Kong, Australia; TV Ballads (BBC 2) 1995; Founder-mem., Keith Hancock's Famous Last Words 1996; mem. Musicians' Union, Equity. *Recordings include:* This World We Live In 1985, Madhouse 1988, Compassion 1992, Born Blue 1997; single: Absent Friends 2013. *Website:* www.keithhancock.co.uk.

HANCOCK, Robin Jonathon Coventry, BSc; British record producer and musician (guitar); b. Croydon, Surrey. *Education:* Univ. of Reading. *Recordings:* Seal, Seal 1991, Erotica, Madonna 1992, Cyberpunk, Billy Idol 1993; other recordings by Tina Turner, Simple Minds, Robert Miles.

HAND, Richard, ARAM; British musician (guitar); b. 27 Nov. 1960, Marsden, Yorks., England. *Education:* Royal Acad. of Music, London. *Career:* mem. English Guitar Quartet (tour of Israel), flute and guitar duo, The Light-fingered Gentry (tours of Germany, Holland, Egypt, Dubai, Brunei, Malaysia), guitar duo, Hand/Dupré (tours of Norway, Poland, India, Bangladesh, Sri Lanka, Philippines, Malaysia, Indonesia, Singapore, Hong Kong, USA, Turkey, Azerbaijan), Pro Arte Trio (tour of Sweden), Tetra Guitar Quartet (tour of Saudi Arabia, India); concerts in Wigmore Hall, St John's Smith Square, Purcell Room, Barbican and BBC Proms at Royal Albert Hall; numerous TV and radio broadcasts world-wide; has performed premieres of new works by Peter Dickinson, Tim Souster, Jonathon Lloyd, David Bedford,

Roger Steptoe, Michael Ball, Brian May, Judith Bingham, Wilfred Josephs; mem. Inc. Soc. of Musicians. *Recordings:* Carey Blyton: Complete Guitar Music, Lyric Pieces (Hand-Dupré Duo), Scenes from Childhood (with Pro Arte Guitar Trio), Summer Waves (with English Guitar Quartet), Carmen (with Tetra Quartet); world premieres of works by Edward Cowie, Malcolm Williamson, Peter Dickinson, David Bedford, Tim Souster. *Honours:* RAM Open Scholarship 1979, RAM Julian Bream Prize 1981, RAM String Players' Prize 1981, RAM John Munday Prize 1981. *Address:* 61 Balcombe Street, Marylebone, London, NW1 6HD, England. *E-mail:* info@richardhand.net. *Website:* www.richardhand.net.

HANDLEY, Edward Sampson; British programmer and producer; b. 1970. *Career:* mem., Black Dog Productions 1988–95, Plaid 1995–. *Films include:* as composer: Tekkonkinkreet 2006, Heaven's Door 2008. *Recordings include:* albums: with Black Dog Productions: Bytes 1993, Temple of Transparent Balls 1994, Spanners 1995, Parallel (compilation) 1995; with Plaid: Not For Threes 1997, Rest Proof Clockwork 1999, Trainer 2000, Double Figure 2001, Parts in the Post 2003, Spokes 2003, Greedy Baby (with Bob Jaroc) 2006, Heaven's Door 2009, Scintilli 2011. *Current Management:* c/o Warp Records, Spectrum House, 32–34 Gordon House Road, London, NW5 1LP, England. *E-mail:* editor@warp.net. *Website:* www.warp.net; www.plaid.co.uk.

HANDS, Guy, MA; British financier; *Chief Investment Officer, Terra Firma Capital Partners;* b. 27 Aug. 1959; m. Julia Hands; four c. *Education:* Mansfield Coll., Oxford. *Career:* joined Goldman Sachs Int. as bond trader 1982, Head of Eurobond Trading, then Head of Global Asset Structuring Group –1994; est. Prin. Finance Group, Nomura Int. 1994–2002; led spin-off and became CEO, Terra Firma Capital Partners (led takeover of EMI Group plc 2007, later Chair.) 2002–09, Chief Investment Officer and Group Chair. 2009–; Co-owner, Hand Picked Hotels; Pres. Access for Excellence campaign; mem. Univ. of Oxford Chancellor's Court of Benefactors; Bancroft Fellow, Mansfield Coll., Oxford; Fellow, Duke of Edinburgh's Award Scheme. *Honours:* World Econ. Forum Global Leader of Tomorrow 2000. *Address:* Terra Firma Capital Partners Ltd, 2 More London Riverside, London, SE1 2AP, England (office). *Telephone:* (20) 7015-9500 (office). *Website:* www .terrafirma.com (office).

HANNAN, Patrick Edward Dean (Patch); British musician (drums), sound engineer and tour manager; b. 4 March 1966, Lymington, Hants., England; s. of David Hannan and Sonia Hannan; partner Sarah Giles; one s. four d. *Career:* bands/artists toured with: TM/FOH: Midlake, Dirty Three, Newton Faulkner, David Sylvian, Ron Sexsmith, The Aliens, Reuben, Howling Bells, Laura Veirs, Ed Harcourt, The Veils, John Grant; TM/BL: The Dears, Mercury Rev, Sufjan Stevens, Ladytron, Jah Wobble; FOH: Steeleye Span, Maddy Prior, John Martyn, Barbara Dickson, The Long Ryders, Carnival band, Mediaeval Baebes; drummer: The Sundays, Theaudience (Sophie Ellis Bextor), Robyn Hitchcock, Departure Lounge, Arnold; companies/venues/festivals worked for: Centre Stage PA, Kinetic PA, Bella Union Records, Park Records, Rough Trade Records; other bands/artists worked for: drummer: Damien Wilson, Tim Keegan, Fire in the South, Star 69, Homer, Perry Rose (Belgium), Bennet, Quruli (Japan), Pmff (Outer Space); currently freelance sound engineer and tour manager for Newton Faulkner. *Recordings:* albums: with the Sundays: Reading Writing Arithmetic 1990, Blind 1992, Static and Silence 1997; with Perry Rose: Bright Ring of The Day 1995; with Arnold: Windsor Park 1997; Hillside 1998; with Tim Keegan: Long Distance Information 1998; with theaudience: theaudience 1998; with Robyn Hitchcock: Jewels for Sophia 1999; with Union Starr: Falling Apart Together 2012. *Honours:* Gold and Silver Discs, two Gold US Discs. *Address:* Bandwagon, 9 Broomacres, Fleet, Hants., GU52 7UU, England (office). *Telephone:* 7973-213353 (mobile). *E-mail:* patrickhannan@btinternet.com (home). *Website:* www.bwtouring.com.

HANNIBAL, Lars; Danish musician (lute, guitar); *Director, OUR Recordings;* b. 15 July 1951, Risskov; s. of Peder Knudsen and Margrethe Knudsen; m. Michala Petri 1992 (divorced 2010); two d. *Education:* Royal Danish Conservatory, Århus, studied lute with Toyohiko Satoh in The Hague, Netherlands. *Career:* classical guitarist and lutenist 1980–; toured as chamber musician throughout Europe, USA, Japan, Mexico, China, Taiwan, Korea, Middle East; worked with musicians and artists such as Michala Petri, Kim Sjøgren, Palle Mikkelborg, Niels-Henning, Ørsted Pedersen, Svend Asmussen, Chen Yue, Chen Yi, Yan Jiang, Ghita Nørby, Lone Hertz; f. OUR Recordings recording co. 2007; apptd Artistic Curator, Danish EXPO, Shanghai 2010; mem. VL4 (professional network for sr execs), Danish Man. Soc.; mem. IAMA. *Recordings include:* albums: with Duo Concertante: 10 albums (violin and guitar, including music by Giuliani, Paganini, Sarasate and Lalo and contemporary music); solo: Romance; with recorder player Michala Petri: Air, Souvenir, Kreisler Inspirations, Siesta, Café Vienna and Virtuoso Baroque; with trumpeter Michael Brydenfelt: Memory 1999; with actress Lone Hertz: Thomas Evangelium 2004; with Chinese bamboo flute player Chen Yue: Spirits –East Meets West 2007; with violin player Chen Yi: Melodies 2009. *Honours:* FTF Cultural Prize 1991, Anniversary Grant, Danish Soloist Union 1993, Deutscher Schallplattenpreis 2002, Danish Music Award for Best Classical Album 2006, ECHO Classical Award. *Address:* Duevej 12, 2th, 2000 Frederiksberg C, Denmark (home). *Telephone:* 40-15-05-77 (home). *E-mail:* hannibal@michalapetri.com. *Website:* www.ourrecordings .com (office); www.larshannibal.com.

HANNON, (Edward) Neil Anthony; Northern Irish songwriter, singer and musician (guitar); b. 7 Nov. 1970, Londonderry; m. Orla Little; one d. *Career:* Founder-mem., The Divine Comedy 1989–; numerous live appearances, TV and radio broadcasts. *Recordings include:* albums: Fanfare for the Comic Muse 1990, Liberation 1993, Promenade 1994, Casanova 1996, A Short Album About Love 1997, Fin de Siecle 1998, A Secret History (compilation) 1999, Regeneration 2001, Absent Friends 2004, Victory for the Comic Muse (Choice Music Prize for Irish Album of the Year) 2006, Bang Goes the Knighthood 2010. *Honours:* James Joyce Award, Literary and Historical Soc., Univ. Coll. Dublin 2005. *Current Management:* Divine Management, Top Floor, 9 Trinity Avenue, London, N2 0LX, England. *Telephone:* (20) 8922-9020 (office). *Fax:* (20) 8922-9021 (office). *E-mail:* info@divinemanagement.co.uk. *Website:* www.thedivinecomedy.com.

HANOT, Pierre; French singer, writer, composer and artist; b. 25 March 1952, Metz; m. Martine Bonici 1992; two d. *Career:* numerous concerts, live appearances, festivals 1975–; mem. Société des auteurs, compositeurs et éditeurs de musique (SACEM). *Recordings include:* Rock Derivé 1985, En un instant damnés 1995, Mosquée bleue 1996, On n'est pas des chiens 1997, Vu à la télé 2000. *Publications:* Rock'n Taules 2005, Men are Icebergs 2006, Serial Loser 2007, Nails fakir (prize Erckmann Chatrian) 2009, All armadillo 2012. *E-mail:* alcatrazprod@aol.com. *Website:* www.pierrehanot.com.

HANSARD, Glen; Irish singer, musician (guitar) and songwriter; b. 21 April 1970, Dublin. *Career:* busker on the streets of Dublin; Founder-mem., The Frames 1990–, The Swell Season 2005–11 (currently on hiatus); set up own label, Plateau Records; tours of USA and Europe with The Frames and solo. *Film appearances include:* The Commitments 1991, Once 2007. *Recordings include:* albums: with The Frames: Fitzcarraldo 1995, Dance the Devil 1999, For the Birds 2001, Breadcrumb Trail 2002, Set List 2003, Burn the Maps 2004, The Cost 2006, Another Love Song 2010; with The Swell Season: The Swell Season (with Marketa Irglova) 2007, Strict Joy 2009, Once (with Marketa Irglova) (WhatsOnStage Award for The Autograph Best Original Music 2014, Olivier Award for Outstanding Achievement in Music (for music and lyrics) 2014). *Current Management:* c/o Howard Greynolds, Overcoat Management, 2209 West North Avenue, Chicago, IL 60647-6084, USA. *Telephone:* (773) 238-2550. *E-mail:* info@overcoatmgmt.com. *Website:* www.overcoatmgmt.com; www.theframes.ie; www.glenhansardmusic.com.

HANSEN, Dinah Jane; American singer; b. 22 June 1997, Santa Ana, Calif.; d. of Gordon Hansen and Milika Hansen. *Career:* mem. Love You Like a Sister, renamed 1432, then renamed Fifth Harmony (or 5H) 2012–; contestants on US version of The X Factor (finished in third place) 2012; signed with Syco Music and Epic Records 2012; issued debut EP Better Together 2013; opening act on Cher Lloyd's I Wish tour 2013, on Demi Lovato's Neon Lights Tour 2014, on Austin Mahone's tour of North America and Brazil 2014; headlining act, MTV Artists to Watch concert 2014. *Television:* The X Factor (contestant on US series) 2012. *Recordings:* album: with Fifth Harmony: Reflection 2015. *Honours:* Teen Choice Single: Group Award 2014, MTV Video Music Artist to Watch Award 2014, MTV Europe Music Awards for Best North America Act, for Best US Act and for Best Worldwide Act 2014. *Address:* c/o Syco Music, Syco Entertainment, 9830 Wilshire Blvd, Beverly Hills, CA 90212, USA. *Website:* www.sycoentertainment.com; www.fifthharmonyofficial.com.

HANSEN, Jacob; Danish musician (guitar) and singer; b. 9 Nov. 1970. *Career:* toured and recorded with heavy metal band, Invocator 1986–95, 2000–, with Beyond Twilight 2004–; freelance producer and engineer 1993–; mem. KODA, GRAMEX. *Recordings include:* with Invocator: Excursion Demise 1991, Weave the Apocalypse 1993, Early Years 1994, Dying to Live 1994, Through the Flesh to the Soul 2003; with Beyond Twilight: Section X 2005, For the Love of Art and the Making 2006. *Address:* Oster Vedstedvej 140, 6760 Ribe, Denmark (office). *Telephone:* 40-59-15-80 (office). *E-mail:* info@jacobhansen.com (office). *Website:* www.jacobhansen.com (office).

HANSEN, Kai; German singer and rock musician (guitar); b. 17 Jan. 1963, Hamburg. *Career:* Founder-mem. German rock band Gentry, renamed Second Hell, 1978–84, renamed Helloween 1984–89, Gamma Ray 1989–, mem. Iron Savior 1997; numerous tours across Europe, live appearances and festivals. *Recordings include:* albums: with Helloween: Helloween 1985, Walls of Jericho 1985, Keeper of the Seven Keys Partt I 1987, Partt II 1988, The Best The Best The Rare 1989, Pumpkin Tracks 1989, Live in the UK 1989; with Gamma Ray: Heading for Tomorrow 1990, Sigh No More 1991, Insanity and Genius 1993, Land of the Free 1995, Alive '95 1996, Somewhere Out in Space 1997, The Karaoke Album 1997, Power Plant 1999, Blast from the Past 2000, No World Order 2001, Skeletons in the Closet 2003, Majestic 2005, Land of the Free 2 2007, Hell Yeah!: The Awesome Foursome Live in Montreal 2008, To the Metal! 2010, Skeletons & Majesties 2011, Skeletons & Majesties Live 2012; with Iron Saviour: Iron Saviour 1997, Unification 1998, Dark Assault 2001. *Current Management:* c/o All Access Management, Kieler Street 103-107, 25474 Bönningstedt, Germany. *Telephone:* (43) 28330. *Fax:* (43) 283323. *E-mail:* info@all-access.de. *Website:* www.all-access.de.

HANSON, Lloyd A.; Canadian musician (bass), producer and recording engineer; b. 1 Nov. 1964, Fredericton, New Brunswick. *Education:* Berklee Coll. of Music, USA. *Career:* played bass in many jazz, folk, experimental ensembles at major festivals including: Mama's and Papa's 1987; Harvest Jazz and Blues Festival, with Long John Baldry 1992; formed Thrash Peninsula 1993; mem. AFofM, Musicians' Union, SOCAN. *Recordings include:* with Thrash Peninsula: A Different Drummer, A D Shade Café, Thunder God's

Wife; with Brent Mason: Down to Heaven; with Ned Landry: Fiddling Champ. *Honours:* New Brunswick Arts Branch Creation Grant 1992. *Address:* Reel North Recording Studio, 741 McEvoy Street, , Fredericton, NB E3A 3B8, Canada. *Telephone:* (506) 450-3299. *Website:* www.reelnorth.ca.

HANSON, Simon; British musician (drums) and programmer; b. 3 Feb. 1964, Grantham, Lincs.; m. Kath Hanson 1994; two c. *Education:* Lincolnshire Youth Orchestra. *Career:* mem. Radio Science Orchestra; European tour with Energy Orchard; The Blessing; regular columnist, UK Rhythm Magazine 1994–; mem. Musicians' Union. *Current Management:* c/o Dermot Smyth, Fantastic Partners Ltd, 21 Montague Street, Bloomsbury, London, WC1B 5BH, England. *Telephone:* (20) 7436-3357. *E-mail:* info@fantastic-partners.com. *E-mail:* info@simonhanson.co.uk (office). *Website:* www.simonhanson.co.uk.

HANSSON, Martin; Swedish musician (bass guitar). *Career:* mem. The Concretes 1999–; band founded label, Licking Fingers. *Recordings include:* albums: Boyoubetterunow 2000, The Concretes 2003, Layourbattleaxedown 2005, In Colour 2006, Hey Trouble 2007. *Current Management:* c/o EC1 Music Agency, 1 Cowcross Street, London, EC1M 6DR, England. *Telephone:* (20) 7490-8990. *Fax:* (20) 7490-8987. *E-mail:* jack@ec1music.com. *E-mail:* theconcretessweden@gmail.com. *Website:* www.theconcretes.com.

HANZICK, Helene Hommel Brincker; Danish musician (bass guitar), songwriter and singer; b. 18 June 1958, Copenhagen; m. Poul F. Hanzick 1987. *Career:* singer, Mayflowers band 1980; solo artist, 1981–82; formed country duo, Twins with husband, playing in Denmark and in Norway, Sweden, Holland and Canary Islands; mem. Danish Musicians' Union. *Compositions include:* From Alaska to LA 1989, No Good Full-Time-Cheating, Good-For-Nothing Son-Of-A-Gun 1991 1996, Ten Days Together 1991; She'll Come Again 1991. *Recordings include:* albums: Champagne and Bourbon 1989; Days Together, 1991. *Honours:* Danish Championship in Country Music 1989.

HANZICK, Poul Fynbo; Danish musician (guitar) and singer; b. 22 May 1954, Mariager; m. Helene H. B. Hanzick 1987. *Career:* played in several dance and rock bands, 1969–82; formed the country duo, Twins (with wife Helene), playing in Denmark and in Norway, Sweden, Holland and Canary Islands; mem. Danish Musicians' Union. *Recordings include:* albums: Days Together 1991; Champagne and Bourbon 1989. *Honours:* winner, Danish Championship in Country Music 1989. *Address:* Poul Fynbo Hanzick Company, Nørre Snedevej 140, Rask Molle; Oesterbro 5, st. th, 8970, Havndal, Denmark. *Telephone:* 26-73-56-86; 52-40-22-05.

HAPPY-TOM; Norwegian musician (bass guitar); b. (Thomas Seltzer), 27 July 1969. *Career:* Founder-mem. glam-punk band, Turbonegro 1988–98, 2002–; side projects include The Vikings, SCUM. *Recordings include:* albums: Turboloid 1990, Hot Cars and Spent Contraceptives 1992, Helta Skelta 1993, Never is Forever 1994, Ass Cobra 1996, Apocalypse Dudes 1998, Scandinavian Leather 2003, Party Animals 2005, Retox 2007, Sexual Harassment 2012. *Honours:* MTV Europe Music Award for Best Norwegian Act 2005. *Current Management:* c/o Burning Heart Records, PO Box 441, 70148 Örebro, Sweden. *Telephone:* (1) 917-46-90. *Fax:* (1) 917-46-99. *Website:* www.burningheart.com; www.turbonegro.nu.

HARBO, Nils; Danish rock musician (guitar) and record producer; *Manager,* Techpoint; b. 12 May 1956, Nyborg; m. Ulla Rasmussen; three s. *Career:* musician 1978–; record producer for various artists 1990–; own projects have included Jimi Bikini, Jox, Palle Pirat, Mohavi; Owner Techpoint music studios; mem. KODA, NCB, DMF, DJBFA. *Compositions:* Fidt På Fyn 1991, Palle Pirat 1996, Out of Control 1997, Cant Let Go 1997, Killing Me 1999, Hjemme hos os 2003, Trolddom og Magi 2005, Give Me The Gun 2009. *Recording:* Palle Pirat. *Publications:* Improvisation 1981, Danish Music Yearbook (ed.) 1992–2009. *Address:* Techpoint Studio and Production Co., Birkebakken 8, 2500 Valby, Denmark (office). *E-mail:* info@techpoint.dk (office). *Website:* www.techpoint.dk (office).

HARCOURT, Ed; British singer, musician (multi-instrumentalist) and songwriter; b. 14 Aug. 1977, Lewes, England. *Career:* mem., Snug 1994, playing bass; trained as chef; solo artist 2000–. *Recordings include:* albums: with Snug: Snug 1997; solo: Maplewood 2000, Here Be Monsters 2001, From Every Sphere 2003, The Beautiful Lie 2006, Until Tomorrow Then 2007, Lustre 2010, Back Into The Woods 2013. *Current Management:* c/o Steve Nice, Nice Management, 2109 Cooley, PI, Pasadena, CA 91104, USA. *Telephone:* (626) 345-9794. *E-mail:* steve@mgmt.com. *Website:* www.nicemgmt.com; www.edharcourt.com.

HARCOURT, Stephen David; British musician (guitar) and sequencer; b. 30 Nov. 1973, Harlow, Essex. *Career:* Founder-mem. Collapsed Lung 1992–97, several tours of the UK and Ireland, festival appearances, radio and TV broadcasts, reunion gig 2010; solo artist as Jack Slack and Slackwagon; mem. Spoiler (with Lee Edwards), Aerobic Christians (with Donald Cummings); mem. Musicians' Union, PRS. *Compositions:* short film scores 1998. *Recordings include:* albums: with Collapsed Lung: Jackpot Goalie 1995, Cooler 1996.

HARDAKER, Sam; British producer and remixer; b. 1971, London. *Career:* started as studio engineer; began remixing with partner, Henry Binns, under the name Zero 7, later producing own material 1999–; collaborations with Sia Furler, Sophie Barker, Mozez; remixed Terry Callier, Radiohead, Lenny Kravitz, Lambchop, NERD; mem. PRS. *Recordings include:* albums: Simple

Things 2001, Another Late Night 2002, When It Falls 2004, The Garden 2006, Yeah Ghost 2009; singles: EP 1 1999, EP 2 2000, Destiny (featuring Sia and Sophie) 2001, I Have Seen (featuring Mozez) 2001, In the Waiting Line (featuring Sophie) 2001, Distractions (featuring Sia) 2002, Somersault 2004. *Honours:* Muzik Award for Best New Artist 2001. *Current Management:* Solar Management Ltd, Unit 10, Union Wharf, 23 Wenlock Road, London, N1 7SB, England. *Telephone:* (20) 7794-3388. *Fax:* (20) 7794-5588. *E-mail:* info@solarmanagement.co.uk. *Website:* www.solarmanagement.co.uk.

HARDCASTLE, Paul; British musician (keyboards), composer, mixer and record producer; b. 10 Dec. 1957, London. *Compositions:* The Wizard (used as Top of the Pops theme, BBC), 1986–91; Songwriter, composer for television, including: Themes to BBC series, Supersense and Lifesense; Founder, own record label Fast Forward. *Recordings:* Singles: 19 (No. 1, UK), 1985; Just For Money, 1985; Don't Waste My Time, with Carol Kenyon, 1986; The Wizard, 1986; Rainforest 90, 1991; Can't Stop Now, 1994; other recordings under pseudonym: Def Boys; Beeps International; Jazzmasters; Kiss The Sky (with Jaki Graham); albums: Hardcastle, 1996; Cover to Cover, 1997; First Light, 1997; Jazzmasters III, 1999; Jazzmasters: The Greatest Hits, 2000; P.H., 2001; producer for: LW5; Phil Lynott; Carol Kenyon; remixed: Third World; Ian Dury. *Website:* www.paulhardcastle.com.

HARDING, Abi; British musician (saxophone). *Career:* mem., The Zutons 2002–. *Recordings include:* albums: Who Killed... The Zutons? 2004, Tired of Hanging Around 2006, You Can Do Anything 2008.

HARDING, Michael (Mike), FRGS; British singer, musician (English concertina, banjo guitar), comedian, writer and broadcaster and actor; b. 23 Oct. 1944, Crumpsall, Manchester. *Education:* Univ. of Manchester. *Career:* played in skiffle and rock bands 1960s; after a variety of jobs, took a degree in educ. whilst working in folk clubs; began telling jokes to fill pauses as band tuned up during a gig with the Edison Spasm Band at Leeds Univ. 1967 and jokes and real-life storytelling became part of act; nat. exposure with UK hit single The Rochdale Cowboy 1975; in addition to folk music, has diversified into areas including travel writing, comedy writing, poetry, playwriting, short stories, photography; first acting role as Valdimir in Beckett's Waiting For Godot, Octagon Theatre, Bolton; presented show on BBC Radio 2 1998–2012; fmr Pres. The Ramblers, now Lifetime Vice-Pres.; launched Mike Harding Folk show 2013. *Radio:* presenter, radio programme Folk on 2, BBC Radio 2. *Recordings include:* albums: A Lancashire Lad 1972, Mrs 'Ardin's Kid 1975, The Rochdale Cowboy Rides Again, One Man Show 1976, Mike Harding's Back, Old Four Eyes Is Back 1977, Captain Paralytic and the Brown Ale Cowboys 1978, On the Touchline, Komic Kutz 1979, The Red Specs Album 1981, Take Your Finger Off It 1982, Rooted! 1983, Bombers' Moon 1984, Roll Over Cecil Sharp 1985, Foo Foo Shufflewick and Her Exotic Banana 1986, God's Own Drunk 1989, Plutonium Alley 1989, Footloose in the Himalaya (Outdoor Writers Guild Award 1991) 1990, Chinese Takeaway Blues 1992, The Bubbly Snot Monster 1994, Classic Tracks 1995. *Publications include:* Strange Lights Over Bexleyheath, A Guide to North Country Flies, The Connemara Cantos. *Honours:* Ralph Lewis Poetry Award, Univ. of Sussex, The Signal Award for Children's Poetry 1996. *Address:* The Mike Harding Folk Show, PO Box 92, Settle, BD24 5AG (office); c/o The Ramblers, 2nd Floor Camelford House, 87-90 Albert Embankment, London, SE1 7TW, England. *Website:* www.mikehardingfolkshow.com; www.mikeharding.co.uk.

HARDING, Paul, (El Hornet); Australian DJ and songwriter. *Career:* drum'n'bass DJ, Perth –2002; founder mem. Pendulum 2002–. *Recordings:* albums: with Pendulum: Hold Your Colour 2005, In Silico 2008, Immersion 2010. *Honours:* Knowledge Magazine Awards for Best Single and Best Breakthrough Producers 2003. *Current Management:* c/o JHO Management, 1–5 Exchange Court, Maiden Lane, Covent Garden, London, WC2R 0JU, England. *Telephone:* (20) 7420-4372. *Fax:* (20) 7420-4399. *E-mail:* jho@jhooakley.com. *Website:* www.jhooakley.com. *Address:* c/o Warner Bros. Records, Warner Music UK Limited, The Warner Building, 28 Kensington Church Street, London, W8 4EP, England (office). *Website:* www.warnerbrosrecords.co.uk (office); www.pendulum.com.

HARDING, Sarah Nicole; British singer and model; b. 17 Nov. 1981, Ascot. *Education:* Stockport Coll. *Career:* began career working in promotions team for nightclubs; fmr mem. Project G pop group; mem. Girls Aloud, pop group created from winning contestants on reality TV show Popstars: The Rivals 2002–13. *Recordings include:* albums: Sound of the Underground 2003, What Will the Neighbours Say? 2004, Chemistry 2005, Tangled Up 2007, Out of Control 2008. *Television:* Girls Aloud: Off the Record 2006. *Films:* St Trinian's 2007, Freefall 2009, Run for Your Wife 2013. *Honours:* Best Single, Disney Channel Awards 2003, Popjustice Music Prize 2003, 2005, 2006, BRIT Award for Best British Single (for The Promise) 2009. *Current Management:* c/o Shaw Thing Management, Unit 12A, Utopia Village, 7 Chalcot Road, London, NW1 8LH, England. *Telephone:* (20) 7722-6161. *Fax:* (20) 7722-9661. *E-mail:* info@shawthingmanagement.com. *Website:* www.shawthingmanagement.com; www.girlsaloud.co.uk.

HARDY, Françoise; French singer, writer and astrologer; b. 17 Jan. 1944, Paris; m. Jacques Dutronc 1981; one s. *Education:* Inst. La Bruyère, Faculté des Lettres de Paris. *Career:* solo recording artist 1962–; lyricist for musicians, including Diane Tell, Julien Clerc, Khalil Chahine, Guesch Patti and composer-arranger Alain Lubrano; also worked as model and actor; presents Horoscope RTL. *Films include:* Château en suède 1963, I Ragazzi dell'hully-gully 1964, Questo pazzo, pazzo mondo della canzone 1965, What's New, Pussycat 1965, Altissima pressione 1965, Une balle au coeur 1966, Europa canta 1966, Grand Prix 1966, Le Lapin de Noël (TV) 1967, Les Colombes 1972, Émilie Jolie (TV) 1980. *Recordings include:* albums: Françoise Hardy 1965, The Yeh-Yeh Girl from Paris 1965, Ma jeunesse fout le camp 1967, Comment te dire adieu 1968, Françoise Hardy en anglais 1969, Je vous aime 1969, Soleil 1970, La Question 1971, Et si je m'en vais avant toi 1972, Love Songs 1972, Message personnel 1973, Star 1977, J'écoute de la musique saoûle 1978, Gin Tonic 1980, Vingt ans vingt titres 1993, Blues 1995, Le Danger 1996, Maison ou j'ai grandi 1996, Clair obscur 2000, En Resume 2000, If You Listen 2000, Ce petit coeur 2004, Tant de Belle Choses 2005, Parenthèses 2006, La Pluie sans parapluie 2010, L'Amour fou 2012. Message personnel 2013. *Publications include:* Le Grand livre de la vierge (with B. Guenin), Entre les lignes, entre les signes (with Anne-Marie Simond) 1986, Françoise Hardy présente L'Astrologie universelle 1986, Notes secrètes (with E. Dumont) 1991, 35 Succès 1992, Les Rythmes du Zodiaque 2003, Le Désespoir des Singes et Autres Bagatelles 2008, Entre les lignes entre les signes 2009. *Current Management:* c/o VMA, 20 avenue Rapp, 75007 Paris; 13 rue Hallé, 75014 Paris, France. *E-mail:* info@vma.fr. *Website:* www.francoise-hardy.com.

HARDY, Robert (Bob); British musician (bass guitar). *Education:* Glasgow School of Art. *Career:* mem., Franz Ferdinand 2001–. *Recordings include:* albums: Franz Ferdinand (Mercury Music Prize 2004, NME Award for Best Album 2005, Meteor Award for Best Int. Album 2005) 2004, You Could Have It So Much Better 2005, Tonight: Franz Ferdinand 2009, Right Thoughts, Right Words, Right Action 2013. *Honours:* BRIT Awards for Best British Group, Best British Rock Act 2005, Meteor Award for Best Int. Band 2005, NME Award for Best Live Band 2006. *Website:* www.franzferdinand.co.uk.

HARGROVE, Roy Anthony; American jazz musician (trumpet); b. 16 Oct. 1969, Waco, Texas. *Education:* Booker T. Washington School for Visual and Performing Arts, Dallas, Berklee School of Music, Boston, New School Univ., New York. *Career:* toured Europe and Japan, playing with established jazz artists; formed own quintet and made debut solo record 1989; f. Roy Hargrove's Big Band 1995; formed The RH Factor 2003–; sideman for numerous other artists including: Cyrille Aimée, Roy Assaf, Erykah Badu, Ray Brown Trio, Jimmy Cobb Quartet, Steve Coleman, Common, D'Angelo, Roy Haynes, Shirley Horn, Eddie Khaimovich Quartet, Angelique Kidjo, John Mayer, Christian McBride, Jackie McLean, Marcus Miller, Oscar Peterson, Sonny Rollins, Jimmy Smith, Superblue, Bob Thiele Collective, Cedar Walton. *Recordings include:* albums: Diamond in the Rough 1989, Public Eye 1990, Tokyo Sessions (with Antonio Hart) 1992, The Vibe 1992, With the Tenors Of Our Time 1994, Family 1995, Damn! 1995, Parker's Mood: Tribute to Charlie Parker 1995, The Main Ingredient 1996, Angel Eyes 1996, Crisol: Habana 1997, Jazz 'Round Midnight 1998, I Remember Miles 1998, Moment to Moment 2000, Directions In Music (Celebrating Miles Davis and John Coltrane) 2002, Nothing Serious 2006, Earfood (with the Roy Hargrove Quintet) 2008, Emergence (with the Roy Hargrove Big Band) 2009; with the RH Factor: Hard Groove 2003, Distractions 2006. *E-mail:* contact@vervemusicgroup.com. *Website:* www.vervemusicgroup.com.

HARIHARAN, BSc, LLB; Indian singer; b. 3 April 1955, Mumbai; s. of the late Ananthasubramani Iyer ('H. A. S. Mani') and Shrimati Alamelu; m. Lalita 1994; two s. *Education:* SIES Coll., trained in Hindustani music with Ustad Ghulam Mustafa Khan. *Career:* signed by the late music dir Jaidev to sing for Hindi film Gaman following success in singing competition 1977; toured concert circuit and performed on TV for several serials, e.g. Junoon; recorded several successful ghazal albums for which he wrote the scores; sang in several Hindi movies such as Sahibaan, Lamhe, Raam Nagari, Dard Ke Rishte, Zamana, Sindoor, Rangeela, Bombay, Pardes, Traffic Signal, Muukhbir; debut singing in Tamil in film Roja 1993; sang more than 1000 Tamil songs. *Albums include:* Shamakhana, Horizon 1983, Sukoon 1983, Aabshar-e-Ghazal 1985, Reflections 1987, Dil Nasheen 1988, The Very Best of Hariharan (compilation) 1989, Hariharan In Concert 1989, Dil Ki Baat 1989, My Favourite Hits (compilation) 1990, Hazir 1992, Gulfam (Double Platinum) (Diva Award for Best Album of the Year 1994) 1994, Saptarishi 1995, Paigham 1995, Intoxicating Hariharan 1996, Qaraar 1996, Visaal 1996, Halka Nasha 1996, Jashn 1996, Colonial Cousins (first Indian act to be featured on MTV Unplugged, also won MTV Indian Viewers' Choice Award and US Billboard Award) 1996, Paigham 1997, Aathwan Sur – The Other Side of Naushad 1998, 2009, The Way We Do It 1998, Kaash (Screen Videocon Award for Best Non-film Album 2000) 2000, Aatma 2001, Swar Utsav 2001, Lahore Ke Rang Hari Ke Sang 2005, Dil Aisa Kisi Ne Mera Toda 2006, Waqt Par Bolna 2007, Lafzz... 2008, Nandagopalam 2013. *Films include:* Power of Women. *Honours:* All-India Sur Singaar Competition Prize 1977, UP State Award 1977, Best Male Playback Singer, Tamil Nadu State Govt Film Awards 1995, 2004, Nat. Award for Best Male Playback Singer 1998, 2009, Padma Shri 2004, Yesudas Award 2004, Dinanath Mangeshkar Award 2010, Kerala State Film Award for Best Singer 2011, Asianet Film Award for Best Male Playback Singer 2011, Filmfare South Award for Best Male Playback Singer 2011. *Current Management:* c/o Tarsame Mittal Talent Management, Bungalow no. 181, 1st Floor, Aram Nagar Part 2, Versova, Andheri (W), Mumbai 400 061, India. *Telephone:* (22) 26358498. *E-mail:* info@tmtalentmanagement.com. *Website:* www.tmtalentmanagement.com. *Address:* 101 (1st Floor), Legacy Tower, Powai Vihar Complex, Powai, Mumbai 400 076, India (home). *Telephone:* (22) 25701673 (office). *Fax:* (22) 25704619 (office). *E-mail:* singerhari@gmail.com (office). *Website:* www.singerhariharan.co (office).

HARJO, Joy, BA, MFA; American poet, musician, lyricist, writer and screenwriter and playwright; *Chair of Excellence, University of Tennessee, Knoxville;* b. 9 May 1951, Tulsa, Okla; d. of Allen W. Foster, Jr and Wynema Jewell Baker; m. Owen Sapulpa; one s. one d. *Education:* Inst. of American Indian Arts, Univ. of New Mexico, Univ. of Iowa. *Career:* Instructor, Inst. of American Indian Arts 1978–79, 1983–84, Santa Fe Community Coll. 1983–84; Lecturer, Arizona State Univ. 1980–81; Asst Prof., Univ. of Colorado at Boulder 1985–88; Assoc. Prof., Univ. of Arizona, Tucson 1988–90; Prof., Univ. of New Mexico 1991–97, Joseph M. Russo Prof. of Creative Writing 2005–09; Prof., UCLA 2001–; Prof., Univ. of Illinois, Urbana-Champaign 2013–16; Chair of Excellence, Univ. of Tennessee, Knoxville 2016–; Nat. Endowment for the Arts Creative Writing Fellowships 1978, 1992; Arizona Comm. on the Arts Poetry Fellowship 1989; Woodrow Wilson Fellowship 1993; Witter Bynner Poetry Fellowship 1994; mem. PEN (Advisory Bd), Nat. Council of the Arts, Univ. of Arizona Sun Tracks Series Bd; mem. Native Arts and Cultures Foundation, Founding mem. Bd of Trustees 2007–12. *Screenplay:* A Thousand Roads (signature film of the National Museum of the American Indian). *Compositions:* Letter From The End of The 20th Century, The Musician Who Became A Bear. *Recordings:* Letter From The End of The 20th Century, Eagle Song (video) 2002, Native Joy 2003, Native Joy for Real 2004, She Had Some Horses 2006, Winding Through the Milky Way 2008, Red Dreams 2010, A Trail Beyond Tears 2010. *Plays:* Wings of Night Sky, Wings of Night Morning 2007–09. *Publications:* The Last Song 1975, What Moon Drove Me To This? 1980, She Had Some Horses 1983, Secrets From the Center of the World (with Stephen Strom) 1989, In Mad Love and War 1990, Fishing 1992, The Woman Who Fell From the Sky 1994, Reinventing the Enemy's Language 1997, A Map to the Next World 2000, The Good Luck Cat 2000, How We Became Human 2002, For a Girl Becoming 2009, Soul Talk, Song Language, Conversations with Joy Harjo, with Tanaya Winder 2011, Crazy Brave (memoir) (PEN USA Literary Award in Creative Non-Fiction 2013) 2012, Conflict Resolution for Holy Beings (American Library Asscn Notable Book) 2015; contrib. to many anthologies, magazines and recordings. *Honours:* Dr hc (Benedictine Coll.) 1992, (St Mary In the Woods); Pushcart Prize in Poetry 1987, in Poetry Anthology 1990, American-Indian Distinguished Achievement in the Arts Award 1990, Before Columbus Foundation American Book Award 1991, New York Univ. Delmore Schwartz Memorial Award 1991, Mountains and Plains Booksellers Award for Best Book of Poetry 1991, Poetry Soc. of America William Carlos Williams Award 1991, Native Writers Circle of the Americas Lifetime Achievement Award 1995, Oklahoma Book Arts Awards 1995, State of New Mexico Gov.'s Award for Excellence in the Arts 1997, Lila Wallace-Reader's Digest Writers Award 1998–2000, Eagle Spirit Award, American Indian Film Festival 2005, Rasmusson US Artist Fellowship 2008, Native American Contemporary Award, New Mexico Music Awards 2007, 2008, Native American Music Award for Best Female Artist of the Year 2009, Indian Summer Music Award for Best Instrumental 2011, Artist of the Year Award, Mvskoke Women's Initiative 2011, inducted into Mvskoke Hall of Fame 2012, Guggenheim Creative Non-Fiction Fellowship 2014, Black Earth Inst. Award 2014, Oklahoma Writers Hall of Fame 2014, Wallace Stevens Award, Acad. of American Poets 2015. *Current Management:* c/o Mekko Productions Inc., 5223 S. 32nd W. Pl. Tulsa, OK 74107, USA. *E-mail:* joy.harjo@gmail.com (office). *Website:* www.joyharjo.com.

HARKET, Morten; Norwegian singer and songwriter; b. 14 Sept. 1959, Konigsberg. *Career:* fmr lead singer, Mercy, Laelia Anceps, Soldier Blue; mem. a-ha 1982–94, 1999–2009, 2015–; solo artist 1994–; numerous tours world-wide, TV and radio broadcasts. *Film:* Kamilla Og Tyven 1989. *Recordings include:* albums: with a-ha: Hunting High and Low 1985, Scoundrel Days 1986, Stay on These Roads 1988, East of the Sun West of the Moon 1990, Memorial Beach 1992, Lifelines 2002, How Can I Sleep With Your Voice in My Head (live) 2003, Singles 1984–2004 2005, Analogue 2005, Foot of the Mountain 2009, Cast in Steel 2015; solo: Poentenes Evangelium 1993, Wild Seed (Spellemannprisen for Best Album) 1995, Vogts Villa 1996, Letter from Egypt 2008, Out of My Hands 2012, Brother 2014. *Honours:* Order of St Olav 2012; eight MTV Music Video Awards (for Take On Me and The Sun Always Shines On TV) 1986, BMI Award for One Million Broadcast Performances (for Take On Me) 1991, World Music Award for Best Selling Norwegian Artist of the Year 1993, Spellemannprisen Award for Best Male Performer, Spellemann of the Year 2005. *Website:* www.a-ha.com; www.mortenharket.com.

HARLEY, Steve; British singer and songwriter; b. 27 Feb. 1951, London. *Career:* fmr journalist; Founder-mem., Cockney Rebel 1973–77, 1989–; solo artist 1978–88; presenter, Sounds of the 70s (BBC Radio 2) 1999–2008; Amb., Mines Advisory Group. *Recordings include:* albums: Human Menagerie 1973, The Best Years of Our Lives 1975, Timeless Flight 1976, Love's a Prima Donna 1976, Face to Face: A Live Recording 1977, Hobo with a Grin 1978, Candidate 1979, Greatest Hits 1988, Best of Steve Harley and Cockney Rebel 1992, Make Me Smile 1996, Stripped to Bare Bones 1999, Yes You Can 2000, Poetic Justice 2001, In Pursuit of Illusion 2000, The Quality of Mercy 2005, Stranger Comes to Town 2012. *Publication:* The Impression of Being Relaxed 2008. *Honours:* Gold Badge of Merit, British Acad. of Composers and Songwriters 2002. *Current Management:* c/o The Agency Group, 361-373 City Road, London, EC1V 1PQ, England. *Telephone:* (20) 7278-3331. *Fax:* (20) 7837-4672. *E-mail:* maloryholden@theagencygroup.com. *Website:* www.theagencygroup.com; www.steveharley.com.

HARMÁČEK, Václav; Czech musician (clarinet, saxophone, viola), recording director, editor and teacher; b. 6 Nov. 1952, Prague; m. (divorced); two d. *Education:* Charles Univ., Prague, Prague Conservatory. *Career:* appearance in numerous jazz festivals as mem. of various bands and orchestras, notably Prague Big Band, Original Prague Syncopated Orchestra, Causa Bibendi; several TV and radio appearances in various types of programmes, notably Causa Bibendi or the Reason for a Drink (Czech TV) 1994; currently teacher, Teplice Conservatory, Johannes Kepler Gymnasium, Prague, Harmcore jazz band, Causa Bibendi. *Recordings:* contrib. to albums of the orchestras: Prague Big Band 1974–78, Original Prague Syncopated Orchestra 1979–84, Causa Bibendi – Czech Swingharmonic Orchestra 1992, Blue World 1996, Prague Folklore Cymbalon Orchestra 1975–91. *Publication:* Small Encyclopaedia of Music (ed. and contrib.) 1983. *Address:* Studentská 2, 160 00 Prague 6, Czech Republic (office). *Telephone:* (2) 77270054 (home); (2) 45009963 (office). *E-mail:* phill.harmacek@centrum.cz (office). *Website:* www.causabibendi.cz; gjk.cz/harmcore.

HARMAN, James Gary; American bandleader, singer, songwriter, producer and musician (harmonica); b. 8 June 1946, Anniston, Ala; m. Ella Caroline Harman; two s. *Education:* Gulf Coast Coll., Univ. of Florida. *Career:* bandleader, Southern dance circuit 1962–; bandleader, house band Ash Grove Club, Los Angeles in 1970s; several songs used in TV shows. *Recordings include:* albums: B.Y.O. 1971, This Band Just Won't Behave 1972, Do Not Disturb 1991, Two Sides to Every Story 1993, Cards on the Table 1994, Black and White 1995, Extra Napkins 1997, Takin' Chances 1998, Mo'Na'Kins, Please! 2000, Lonesome Moon Trance 2003. *Address:* Icepick Productions, 5901 Warner Avenue, Suite 248, Huntington Beach, CA 92649, USA. *Telephone:* (714) 421-8366. *E-mail:* james@jamesharman.com. *Website:* www.jamesharman.com.

HARMER, Sarah; Canadian singer and songwriter; b. 12 Nov. 1970, Burlington, Ont. *Education:* Queen's Univ. *Career:* played with The Saddletramps while at univ.; Founder-mem. Weeping Tile –1998; solo artist 1999–; appeared as guest vocalist on albums by artists including Blue Rodeo, Great Big Sea, Rheostatics, Bruce Cockburn, Skydiggers, The Weakerthans, Great Lake Swimmers; Co-founder PERL (Protecting Escarpment Rural Land), org. which campaigns to protect the Niagara Escarpment. *Film:* Escarpment Blues 2006. *Recordings include:* albums: with Weeping Tile: Cold Snap 1996, Valentino 1997; solo: Songs for Clem 1999, You Were Here 2000, All of Our Names 2004, I'm a Mountain 2005, Oh, Little Fire 2010. *Publication:* The Last Stand: A Journey Through the Ancient Cliff-Face Forest of the Niagara Escarpment (jtly) 2007. *Current Management:* c/o Universal Music Canada Inc., 2450 Victoria Park Avenue Suite 1, Toronto, ON M2J 5H3, Canada. *Telephone:* (416) 718-4000. *E-mail:* info@sarahharmer.com. *Website:* umusic.ca/sarahharmer; www.sarahharmer.com.

HARNICK, Sheldon Mayer; American lyricist; b. 30 April 1924, Chicago; s. of Harry M. Harnick and Esther Harnick (née Kanter); m. 1st Mary Boatner 1950 (annulled 1957); m. 2nd Elaine May 1962 (divorced 1963); m. 3rd Margery Gray 1965; one s. one d. *Education:* Northwestern Univ. *Career:* wrote songs for univ. musicals; contrib. to revues: New Faces of 1952, Two's Company 1953, John Murray Anderson's Almanac 1954, The Shoestring Revue 1955, The Littlest Revue 1956, Shoestring '57 1957; with composer Jerry Bock wrote shows Body Beautiful 1958, Fiorello 1959 (Pulitzer Prize), Tenderloin 1960, Smiling the Boy Fell Dead (with David Baker) 1961, She Loves Me 1963, Fiddler on the Roof (Tony Award) 1964, The Apple Tree 1966, The Rothschilds 1970, Captain Jinks of the Horse Marines (opera, with Jack Beeson) 1975, Rex (with Richard Rodgers) 1976, Dr. Heidegger's Fountain of Youth (opera, with Jack Beeson) 1978, Gold (cantata, with Joe Raposo) 1980, trans.: The Merry Widow 1977, The Umbrellas of Cherbourg 1979, Carmen 1981, A Christmas Carol 1981 (musical; book and lyrics), Songs of the Auvergne 1982, A Wonderful Life 1986, The Appeasement of Aeolus 1990, Cyrano 1994.

HARPER, Ben; American singer, songwriter and musician (guitar); b. 28 Oct. 1969, Claremont, Calif.; m. 1st Joanna Harper 1996 (divorced 2001); one s. one d.; m. 2nd Laura Dern 2005 (divorced 2013); one s. one d. *Career:* solo artist 1992–, with supporting band, The Innocent Criminals 1997–; co-f. Relentless7 2005–. *Recordings include:* albums: solo: Pleasure and Pain 1992, Welcome To The Cruel World 1994, Fight for Your Mind 1995, The Will To Live 1997, The Innocent Criminals Live 1999, Burn To Shine 1999, Live From Mars 2001, Diamonds On The Inside 2003, There Will Be A Light (with Blind Boys of Alabama) (Best Traditional Soul Gospel Album 2005) 2004, Both Sides Of The Gun 2006, Lifeline 2007, Give Till It's Gone 2011, Get Up! (with Charlie Musselwhite) (Grammy Award for Best Blues Album 2014) 2013; with Relentless7: White Lies for Dark Times 2009. *Honours:* Grammy Award for Best Pop Instrumental Performance (for 11th Commandment) 2005. *Current Management:* c/o Red Light Management, 44 Wall Street, 22nd Floor, New York, NY 10005, USA. *E-mail:* benharper@redlightmanagement.com. *Website:* www.redlightmanagement.com; www.benharper.net.

HARPER, Billy R., BMus; American jazz saxophonist, flutist and bandleader; b. 17 Jan. 1943, Houston, Tex. *Education:* Evan E. Worthing High School, Univ. of North Texas. *Career:* formed first ensemble 1957; mem. Art Blakey's Messengers 1967–70; regular collaborator with Lee Morgan 1969–71, Thad Jones-Mel Lewis Big Band 1971–78, Max Roach 1971–79, Randy Weston 1972–; teacher and lecturer in saxophone and flute, Livingston Coll., Rutgers Univ. 1975; leader of own quintet 1979–; teacher, New School of Jazz and

Contemporary Music 1992–; numerous lectures and masterclasses world-wide 1993–; numerous credits as sideman musician including with Art Blakey, Donald Byrd, Charles Earland, Gil Evans, Jon Faddis, Sonny Fortune, Bobbi Humphrey, Thad Jones/Mel Lewis Orchestra, Mark Masters, Grachan Moncur III, Lee Morgan, Max Roach, Woody Shaw, Malachi Thompson, Charles Tolliver, McCoy Tyner. *Recordings include:* as bandleader: Capra Black 1973, Black Saint (Modern Jazz League of Tokyo Jazz Record of the Year 1976) 1975, Soran-Bushi, B.H. 1977, Trying to Make Heaven My Home 1979, Billy Harper Quintet in Europe 1979, The Awakening 1979, The Believer 1980, Destiny is Yours 1981, Somalia 1993, If Our Hearts Could Only See 1998, Soul of an Angel 2000, Blueprints of Jazz Vol 2 2009; with Randy Weston: Tanjah 1973, Carnival 1974, The Spirits of Our Ancestors 1991, Saga 1995, The Roots of the Blues (with Randy Weston) (Jazz Journalists Assn Award for Duo of the Year 2014) 2013. *Honours:* Nat. Endowment for the Arts Music Composition Grants 1970, 1973, 1974, Down Beat Int. Critics Award for Tenor Saxophone 1974, Swing Journal Int. Critics Award for Tenor Saxophone 1975. *Telephone:* (917) 555-1212. *E-mail:* billy@billyharper.com. *Website:* www.billyharper.com.

HARPER, Jon; British musician (drums); *Drum Tutor, Bristol Institute of Modern Music*; b. 15 Feb. 1978. *Career:* mem., The Cooper Temple Clause 1998–2007; currently Drum Tutor, Bristol Institute of Modern Music. *Recordings include:* albums: See This Through And Leave 2002, Kick Up The Fire And Let The Flames Break Loose 2003, Make This Your Own 2007. *Address:* Bristol Institute of Modern Music, 25 King Square, Bristol, BS2 8JN, England (office). *Telephone:* (1273) 626666 (office). *E-mail:* info@bimm.co.uk (office). *Website:* www.bimm.co.uk.

HARPER, Ray; American singer, entertainer and musician (guitar, fiddle, banjo); b. 6 Jan. 1961, Copperhill, TN. *Career:* Hamby Mt Music Park, Baldwin, Georgia; fmr mem., Carl Story's Rambling Mountaineers; mem. Drovers' Old Time Medicine Show 1992–; also worked with Bill Monroe, Larry Sparks and others; shows, festivals across USA with audiences up to 10,000; guest appearances on Rambling Mountain Bluegrass Radio Show WESC in Greenville; performed as Ray Harper and Friends; mem. International Bluegrass Music Assn, Bluegrass Music Assn of Georgia, South Carolina, North Carolina. *Recordings:* Ray Harper and Friends with Special Guest Carl Story, 1992; solo: What A Wonderful Saviour Is He, 1994; with Drovers' Old Time Medicine Show: It's Sunday in Prater's Creek 1995, Melissa's Waltz 1998, One More River 2001, Dreamland 2004. *Address:* c/o Wagon Wheel Productions, 308 North Fairplay Street, Seneca, SC 29678, USA. *Telephone:* (864) 650-3154. *E-mail:* Praterscreek@Bellsouth.net. *Website:* www.thedroversotms.com.

HARPER, Roy; British singer and songwriter; b. 12 June 1941, Manchester. *Career:* started career as poet/busker; played across Europe; many concert hall and festival appearances; residency, Les Cousins club, London; solo artist 1965–; f. Science Friction record label; has released c. 40 albums and 3 video recordings, with total sales of about 1 million. *Recordings include:* albums: The Sophisticated Beggar 1966, Come Out Fighting Genghis Smith 1967, Folkjokeopus 1969, Flat Baroque and Berserk 1970, Stormcock 1971, Lifemask 1973, Valentine 1974, Flashes From The Archives of Oblivion 1974, HQ (aka When An Old Cricketer Leaves The Crease) 1975, Bullinamingvase 1977, Harper 1970–75 1978, The Unknown Soldier 1980, Work of Heart 1981, Whatever Happened To Jugula 1985, Born In Captivity 1985, In Between Every Line 1986, Descendents of Smith/Garden of Uranium 1988, Loony On The Bus 1988, Once 1990, Burn the World 1990, Death Or Glory? 1992, Unhinged 1993, Commercial Breaks 1994, An Introduction to ....1994, The Dream Society 1998, The Green Man 2000, East of the Sun 2000, Hats Off! (compilation) 2001, Today is Yesterday 2002, Counter Culture 2005, Stormcock 2008, Man and Myth 2013. *Films:* Made 1973, Brokeback Cowboy 2008, The Magpie Index 2009. *Publication:* The Passions of Great Fortune 2003. *Honours:* MOJO Hero Award 2005, BBC Radio 2 Folk Award for Lifetime Achievement 2013. *Address:* c/o Science Friction Ltd, PO Box 2, Clonakilty, Co. Cork, Ireland (office). *E-mail:* info@royharper.co.uk (office). *Website:* www.royharper.co.uk (home).

HARRIGAN, Katie, BA; British musician (Celtic harp); b. 17 Sept. 1963, Irvine, Scotland. *Education:* Heriot Watt Univ., Coll. of Europe, Belgium, studied Clarsach (Celtic harp) with Sanchia Pielou. *Career:* Celtic harpist with Flumgummery 1981–83, Hamish Moore, including US tour 1985–86, Ceolbeg 1988–91; toured Canada and USA with Vale of Atholl Pipe Band 1988; periodically worked with Billy Ross; Life Mem. Clarsach Soc. *Recordings include:* Flumgummery One (with Flumgummery) 1982, Highland Mandolin (with Dagger Gordon) 1988, Not the Bunny Hop (with Ceolbeg) 1990, Celtic Connection (with KPM) 1994. *Honours:* Solo Clarsach Champion, Nat. MOD 1980, 1982, Edin. Music Festival 1981.

HARRIS, Calvin; British producer, DJ and singer; b. (Adam Wiles), 17 Jan. 1984, Dumfries, Scotland. *Career:* began recording electronic/pop demos, under Stouffer pseudonym 1999; signed as professional solo artist 2006–; collaborations with Dizzee Rascal, Kylie Minogue, Jamiroquai, Groove Armada, All Saints, CSS, Rihanna, Scissor Sisters, Cheryl Cole, Florence Welch, Ne-Yo. *Recordings:* albums: I Created Disco 2007, Ready for the Weekend 2009, 18 Months 2012, Motion 2014. *Honours:* Music Producers Guild Award for Best Remixer 2009, NME Awards for Best Dancefloor Filler (for Dance Wiv Me) 2009, for Dancefloor Anthem (for Sweet Nothing) 2012, International Dance Music Awards for Best R&B/Urban Dance Track (for We

Found Love) 2012, for Best Commercial/Pop Dance Track (for We Found Love) 2012, (for Sweet Nothing) 2013, Ivor Novello Award for Songwriter of the Year 2013, American Music Awards for Favorite Electronic Dance Music Artist 2014, 2015, MTV Europe Music Award for Best Electronic Act 2014, Billboard Music Award for Top Dance/Electronic Artist 2015. *Current Management:* c/o Mark Gillespie, Three Six Zero Group, A14 Jacks Place, 6 Corbet Place, London E1 6NN, England. *Telephone:* (20) 3051-7930. *Fax:* (20) 3004-1589. *E-mail:* mark.gillespie@threesixzerogroup.com. *Website:* www .threesixzerogroup.com. *Address:* c/o Columbia Records, 9 Derry Street, London W8 5HY, England (office). *Website:* www.calvinharris.co.uk.

HARRIS, Clifford Joseph 'Tip', (T.I.); American hip-hop artist, producer and actor; b. 25 Sept. 1980, Atlanta, GA; m. Tameka Cottle 2010. *Career:* solo artist, fmrly known as T.I.P., now known as T.I.; leader of group, P$C (Pimp Squad Click); formed Grand Hustle Records 2001, and film production company, Grand Hustle Films 2005; numerous collaborations including: Beenie Man, Jamie Foxx, Wyclef Jean, Swizz Beatz, Jay-Z, Kanye West, Lil Wayne, Rihanna, Justin Timberlake, Eminem, Robin Thicke and Pharrell Williams. *Film appearances:* ATL 2006, American Gangster 2007. *Recordings include:* albums: solo: I'm Serious 2001, Trap Muzik 2003, Urban Legend 2004, King (Billboard Award for Rap Album of the Year, for Rap Album Artist of the Year 2006) 2006, T.I. vs T.I.P. (American Music Award for Favorite Rap/ Hip-Hop Album 2007) 2007, Paper Trail 2008, King Uncaged 2010, No Mercy 2010, Trouble Man: Heavy is the Head 2012, Trouble Man II: He Who Wears the Crown 2013; with P$C: 25 to Life 2005. *Honours:* Billboard Award for Rap Artist of the Year, for Rap Songs Artist of the Year, for Videoclips Artist of the Year 2006, BET Award for Best Hip-Hop Artist 2007, American Music Award for Favorite Male Rap/Hip-Hop Artist 2007, Grammy Award for Best Rap/ Sung Collaboration (for My Love, with Justin Timberlake) 2007, for Best Rap Solo Performance (for What You Know) 2007, Billboard Music Awards for Top Hot 100 Song, for Top Digital Song, for Top Radio Song, for Top R&B Song (all for Blurred Lines, with Robin Thicke and Pharrell) 2014. *Current Management:* Grand Hustle, PMB 161, 541 Tenth Street, Atlanta, GA 30318, USA. *E-mail:* info@grandhustle.com. *Website:* www.grandhustle.com; www .trapmuzik.com.

HARRIS, Dale G., BA, MA, PhD; British musician (guitar and lute); b. 25 July 1968, West London. *Education:* Brooklands Coll., West London Inst., Brunel Univ., Canterbury Univ. *Career:* guitarist and arranger with Pretty Blue Gun; guitarist with The Lorne Gibson Trio 1993–; performed with Roland Chadwick and Sir Cliff Richard; currently Dir Cryptogram Records Ltd. *Recordings include:* albums: with Pretty Blue Gun: The Only Girl, Big Blue World; Espiritu De La Guitarra 2006, Dark Tales (with Jez Henderson) 2007, Reverie On A Hill 2008, The Music of Dale Harris: A Case of the Spanish Guitar 2013, From The Vaults (Vol. 1): Is There Life On Mars? 2013, From The Vaults (Vol. 2): Nowhere To Hide Here In The West 2013, From The Vaults (Vol. 3): Beyond Classical 2013. *Publications:* Cryptograms in the Music of Alban Berg 2004. *Honours:* The Larissa Lovelock Memorial Prize 1998. *Website:* www.dale -harris.com.

HARRIS, Emmylou; American singer; b. 2 April 1947, Birmingham, Ala; m. 1st Brian Ahern; m. 2nd Paul Kennerley 1985; two d. *Education:* Univ. of North Carolina. *Career:* singer 1967–, toured with Fallen Angels Band in USA and Europe; Pres. Country Music Foundation 1983–; Fellow, American Acad. of Arts and Sciences 2009–. *Recordings include:* albums: Gliding Bird 1969, Pieces of the Sky 1975, Elite Hotel 1976, Luxury Liner 1977, Quarter Moon in a Ten-Cent Town 1978, Blue Kentucky Girl 1979, Light of the Stable 1979, Roses In The Snow 1980, Evangeline 1981, Cimarron 1981, Last Date 1982, White Shoes 1983, The Ballad of Sally Rose 1985, Thirteen 1986, Trio (with Dolly Parton and Linda Ronstadt) (Acad. of Country Music Album of the Year 1988) 1987, Angel Band 1987, Bluebird 1989, Brand New Dance 1990, Duets (with Nash Ramblers) 1990, At The Ryman 1992, Cowgirl's Prayer 1993, Songs of the West 1994, Wrecking Ball 1995, Portraits 1996, Nashville 1996, Spyboy 1998, Red Dirt Girl 2000, Singin' with Emmylou Harris (vol. I) 2000, Anthology 2001, Stumble Into Grace 2003, All the Roadrunning (with Mark Knopfler) 2006, Neil Young Heart of Gold 2006, All I Intended to Be 2008, Hard Bargain 2011, Old Yellow Moon (with Rodney Crowell) (Grammy Award for Best Americana Album 2014) 2013. *Honours:* Grammy Awards 1976, 1977, 1980, 1981, 1984, 1987, 1992, 1996, Country Music Assn Female Vocalist of the Year 1980, Grammy Award for Best Female Country Vocal Performance (for The ion) 2006, Polar Music Prize 2015. *Current Management:* 1025 16th Ave South, Suite 202, Nashville, TN 37212-2328, USA.

HARRIS, Sam; American actor, singer and writer; b. 4 June 1961, Cushing, Okla. *Education:* Univ. of California, Los Angeles. *Stage appearances:* Grease (Broadway), Joseph and the Amazing Technicolour Dreamcoat (nat. tour), The Life (Broadway). *Compositions:* musicals: Hurry! Hurry! Hollywood!; Hard Copy; television sitcom, Down to Earth. *Recordings include:* albums: Sam Harris 1984, Sam-I-Am 1986, Standard Time 1994, Different Stages 1994, The Life (cast album), Grease (cast album), A Hollywood Christmas, A Gershwin Tribute, Best of the Motown Sessions, Revival 1999, On This Night 2000, Free 2008, Always 2008, Suitcase of Memories 2014. *Publication:* HAM: Slices of a Life 2014. *Honours:* Dramalogue Award (for Hard Copy and Different Hats). *Website:* www.samharris.com.

HARRIS, Sean; British singer and songwriter. *Career:* Founder-mem. rock group, Diamond Head 1977–85, 1991–2004, British tours, festival appearances; mem. Notorious 1990. *Compositions include:* In The Heat of The Night,

Am I Evil, Helpless, It's Electric. *Recordings include:* albums: with Diamond Head: Lightning to the Nations (remixed as Behold The Beginning) 1980, Canterbury 1983, Death and Progress 1993, To Heaven from Hell 1997, Diamond Nights 2000, The MCA Years 2009, Am I Evil?: The Best of Diamond Head 2013; with Notorious: Notorious 1990, Rising Up (mini-album) 1992, Radio Silence 2001. *Current Management:* Angel Air Records, St Edmunds Offices, Broad Road, Bacton, Stowmarket, IP14 4HP, England.

HARRIS, Simon Kenneth; British DJ and producer; b. 10 Sept. 1962, London. *Career:* record producer and remixer; production credits include Derek B, Ambassadors of Funk, Daddy Freddy; remix credits include Stone Roses, James Brown, Tony Toni Tone, Real Thing, DMB, Prince, Steve Silk Hurley, Joyce Sims; Founder Music of Life; mem. PRS, BMI. *Recordings include:* solo singles: Bad on the Mike 1987, Bass (How Low Can You Go) 1988, Here Comes that Sound 1988, Another Monsterjam 1989, Don't Stop the Music 1990. *Honours:* NME Rap Label of the Year 1988–89. *Website:* www.harrismix.com.

HARRIS, Stefon, BA, MA; American jazz musician (vibraphone, percussion, marimba) and bandleader; b. 23 March 1973, Albany, NY. *Education:* Albany High School, Manhattan School of Music. *Career:* fmr mem. Empire State Youth Orchestra; mem. Classical Jazz Quartet; Founder, Blackout project 2004; sideman for numerous artists including Kenny Barron, Ry Cooder, Lea DeLaria, Kurt Elling, Joe Henderson, Charlie Hunter, Diana Krall, Raul Midón, Jason Moran, Greg Osby, Courtney Pine, Joshua Redman, Janis Siegel, Terell Stafford, Steve Turre, Tim Warfield; mem. Exec. Bd of Dirs Chamber Music America. *Recordings:* albums: as bandleader: A Cloud of Red Dust (New York Jazz Award for Best Debut Recording 1999) 1998, Black Action Figure 1999, Kindred 2001, The Grand Unification Theory 2003, Evolution 2004, African Tarantella: Dances with Duke 2006, Urbanus 2009; with Classical Jazz Quartet: Tchaikovsky's Nutcracker 2001, Plays Bach 2002, Play Rachmaninov 2006, Play Tchaikovsky 2006, Christmas 2006; with Blackout: Evolution 2004; with David Sanchez and Christian Scott: Ninety Miles 2011. *Honours:* Lincoln Center Martin E. Segal Award, North Sea Jazz Int. Bird Award for Artist Deserving Wider Recognition 2002, Jazz Journalists Asscn Awards for Best Mallet Player 2000, 2001, 2002, 2003, 2004, 2005, 2013. *Current Management:* c/o Karen Kennedy, 24 Seven Artist Development, 6 Richmond Street, Newark, NJ 07103, USA. *Telephone:* (973) 230-3160. *Fax:* (973) 353-9477. *E-mail:* Karen@karenkennedy.net. *Website:* www.karenkennedy.net; www.stefonharris.com.

HARRIS, Steve; British musician (bass); b. 12 March 1957, Leytonstone, London. *Career:* fmr mem. pub band, Smiler; Founder-mem. heavy metal band, Iron Maiden 1975–; regular tours worldwide, concerts and festival appearances. *Recordings include:* albums: Iron Maiden 1980, Killers 1981, The Number of the Beast 1982, Piece of Mind 1983, Powerslave 1984, Somewhere in Time 1986, Seventh Son of a Seventh Son 1988, No Prayer for the Dying 1990, Fear of the Dark 1992, The X-Factor 1995, Virtual XI 1998, Brave New World 2000, Dance of Death 2003, It's a Matter of Life and Death 2006, Flight 666 2009, The Final Frontier 2010, The Book of Souls 2015. *Honours:* Ivor Novello Award 2000, BRIT Award for Best British Live Act 2009. *Current Management:* c/o Phantom Music Management, Ltd, Bridle House, 36 Bridle Lane, London, W1F 9BZ, England. *Telephone:* (845) 331-3300. *Fax:* (845) 331-3500. *Website:* www.phantom-music.com; www.steveharrisbritishlion.com; www.ironmaiden.com.

HARRISON, Gavin; British musician (drums, bass, keyboards) and composer; b. 28 May 1963, Harrow, London. *Career:* Founder mem., Dizrhythmia; worked with Level 42, Paul Young, Iggy Pop, Eros Ramazotti, Claudio Baglioni, Incognito. *Recordings include:* albums: with Sam Brown: Stop 1988; with Incognito: Inside Life, Always There. *Publications include:* Rhythmic Illusions Book; contrib. columns to Rhythm, Modern Drummer magazines. *Website:* www.gavharrison.com.

HARRISON, Orlando, (The Spirit of Love); British musician (keyboards). *Career:* mem. Alabama 3 (known as A3 in USA); also mem. Miasma and the Carousel of Headless Horses. *Recordings:* albums with Alabama 3: Exile on Coldharbour Lane 1997, La Peste 2000, Power in the Blood 2002, The Last Train to Nashville 2003, Outlaw 2005, M.O.R. 2007, Revolver Soul 2010; with Miasma and the Carousel of Headless Horses: Perils 2005. *Current Management:* c/o Paul Johannes, One Little Indian Records, 34 Trinity Crescent, London, SW17 7AE, England. *Telephone:* (20) 8772-7600. *E-mail:* info@indian.co.uk. *Website:* www.indian.co.uk; www.alabama3.co.uk.

HARRISON, Oscar; British musician (drums, keyboards); b. 15 April 1965, Birmingham. *Career:* fmr mem. jazz rock reggae band Echo Base; fmr mem. The Fanatics; Founder-mem. Ocean Colour Scene 1989–; numerous TV appearances, radio broadcasts and tours. *Recordings include:* albums: Ocean Colour Scene 1992, Moseley Shoals 1996, B-Sides, Seasides and Freerides 1997, Marchin' Already 1997, One from the Modern 1999, Mechanical Wonder 2001, Songs for the Front Row (compilation) 2001, Anthology 2003, North Atlantic Drift 2003, Marchin' Melody 2004, On the Leyline 2007, The Collection 2007, Saturday 2010, OCS 21 2010, Painting 2013. *Address:* The OCS Partnership, Unit 1, The Mill, Little Shrewley Hatton, Warwick, CV35 7HN, England. *E-mail:* info@ocsmusic.com. *Website:* www.oceancolourscene.com.

HARRY, Deborah (Debbie) Ann; American singer and actress; b. 1 July 1945, Miami, Fla; d. of Richard Smith and Catherine Harry (Peters).

Education: Centenary Coll. *Career:* singer and songwriter, rock group Blondie 1975–83, reformed 1997. *Singles include:* Heart of Glass, Call Me, Tide is High, Rapture. *Recordings:* albums: with Blondie: Blondie 1976, Plastic Letters 1977, Parallel Lines 1978, Eat to the Beat 1979, Autoamerican 1980, The Hunter 1982, Rapture 1994, No Exit 1999, Livid 2000, The Curse of Blondie 2003, Panic of Girls 2011, Ghosts of Download 2014; solo: Koo Koo 1981, Rockbird 1986, Def, Dumb and Blonde 1989, Debravation 1993, Virtuosity (with the Heads) 1995, Necessary Evil 2007. *Film appearances:* The Foreigner 1978, Unmade Beds 1980, Union City 1980, New York Beat Movie 1981, Videodrome 1983, Forever, Lulu 1987, Satisfaction 1988, Hairspray 1988, New York Stories 1989, Tales from the Darkside: The Movie 1990, Dead Beat 1994, Drop Dead Rock 1995, Heavy 1995, Cop Land 1997, Six Ways to Sunday 1997, Joe's Day 1998, Zoo 1999, Red Lipstick 2000, Deuces Wild 2000, Spun 2002, Try Seventeen 2002, My Life Without Me 2003, A Good Night to Die 2003, Tulse Luper Suitcases, Part 1: The Moab Story 2003, Patch 2005, I Remember You Now 2005, Elegy 2007. *Television appearances:* Saturday Night Live, The Muppet Show, Tales from the Darkside, Wiseguys. *Theatre:* Teaneck Tanzi, The Venus Flytrap. *Honours:* awarded Gold, Silver and Platinum records. *Current Management:* Tenth Street Entertainment, 700 San Vicente Boulevard, Suite G410, West Hollywood, CA 90069, USA. *Website:* www.blondie.net; www.deborahharry.com.

HARSCH, Eddie; Canadian musician (keyboards); b. 27 May 1957, Toronto. *Career:* joined James Cotton's band 1981–86; played with Albert Collins 1989–90; mem. The Black Crowes 1991–2006, Detroit Cobras 2002–05; currently mem. of jam band Bulldog, Siberia K.O. *Recordings include:* albums: Amorica 1994, Three Snakes and One Charm 1996, Sho Nuff: The Complete Black Crowes 1998, By Your Side 1999, Live at the Greek 2000, Tribute to A Work in Progress: Greatest Hits 1990–1999 2001, Lions 2001. *E-mail:* steve@backstageproductions.com. *Website:* www.siberiako.com.

HART, Angela Ruth; Australian singer and musician (guitar); b. 8 March 1972, Adelaide. *Career:* solo artist; singer with Frente. *Recordings include:* albums: Marvin the Album 1993, Ruby's Arm, Tom Waits Tribute 1995, Shape 1996; solo: Grounded Bird 2007, Eat My Shadow 2009. *Website:* www.ihartangie.net.

HART, Freddie; American country singer, songwriter and musician (guitar); b. (Frederick Segrest), 21 Dec. 1926, Loachapoka, Ala. *Career:* left school aged 12; joined US Marines at age 15 by lying about age; saw action in Guam and Iwo Jima; returning to Nashville, became roadie for Hank Williams Sr 1949; first song cut Every Little Thing Rolled Into One, George Morgan 1949; toured with Lefty Frizzell 1950–53; regular on Home Town Jubilee TV Show in Hollywood; composition, Loose Talk, a country chart hit for Carl Smith 1954; song subsequently recorded by others including Patsy Cline; signed to Columbia Records 1959; label debut, The Wall, was first of many Billboard chart entries until 1987; semi-retired, concentrating on business interests, running school for handicapped children; mem. Grand Ole Opry in early 1960s. *Recordings include:* albums: Easy Loving 1971, My Hang Up Is You 1972, Got the All Overs For You (All Over Me) 1972, Bless Your Heart 1972, Super Kind of Woman 1973, Trip To Heaven 1973, Freddie Hart's Greatest Hits 1975, The First Time 1976 The Pleasure's Been All Mine 1977, Only You 1978, My Lady 1979, A Sure Thing 1980. *Honours:* CMA Song of the Year (Easy Loving) 1971, 1972, Academy of Country Music Song of the Year (Easy Loving) 1971, ACM Award for Entertainer of the Year, Top Male Vocalist, Grammy Awards for Best Country Male Vocalist (Easy Loving) 1972. *Current Management:* c/o Musical World, 818 Western Avenue, Brattleboro, VT 05301, USA. *Telephone:* (802) 257-5789. *Fax:* (802) 257-5789. *E-mail:* harthunt@comcast.net. *Website:* www.musicalworld.com; www.mreasylovin.com.

HARTNOLL, Paul; British musician (keyboards); b. 19 May 1968, Dartford, Kent, England; brother of Phil Hartnoll. *Career:* fmr mem., Noddy and the Satellites; mem., Orbital (with brother) 1987–2004, 2009–; numerous live appearances at clubs and festivals, including Glastonbury Festival, Tribal Gathering, V Festival, Phoenix Festival, Royal Albert Hall, Brixton Acad.; collaborations with Metallica's Kirk Hammett and composer Michael Kamen; solo artist 2007–. *Film soundtracks:* contributions to Shopping 1994, The Saint 1996, Spawn 1997, Event Horizon 1997, xXx 2002, Octane 2003, Pusher 2012. *Recordings include:* albums: with Orbital: Untitled ('green album') 1991, Untitled ('brown album') 1992, Snivilisation 1994, In Sides 1996, The Middle Of Nowhere 1999, The Altogether 2001, Back To Mine (compilation of other artists' tracks) 2002, B-Sides (compilation) 2002, Work 1989–2002 2002, Blue Album 2004, Wonky 2012; solo: The Ideal Condition 2007. *Honours:* NME Award for Best Dance Act 1993, NME BRAT Award 1995, Dance Star Tiscali World Dance Music Award for Dance Star of the Year 2002. *Current Management:* Mondo Management, Unit 2D, Clapham North Arts Centre, 26–32 Voltaire Road, London, SW4 6DH, England. *Telephone:* (20) 7720-7411. *Fax:* (20) 7720-8095. *E-mail:* rob@intrecords.com. *Website:* www.loopz.co.uk; www.paulhartnoll.com; www.orbitalofficial.com.

HARTNOLL, Phil; British musician (keyboards); b. 9 Jan. 1964, Dartford, Kent, England; brother of Paul Hartnoll. *Career:* mem., Orbital (with brother) 1987–2004, 2009–; numerous live appearances at clubs and festivals, including Glastonbury Festival, Tribal Gathering, V Festival, Phoenix Festival, Royal Albert Hall, Brixton Acad. and others; collaborations with Metallica's Kirk Hammett and composer Michael Kamen; founder mem., Long Range 2005–. *Film soundtracks:* contribs to Shopping 1994, The Saint 1996, Spawn 1997, Event Horizon 1997, xXx 2002, Octane 2003, Pusher 2012. *Recordings* *include:* albums: with Orbital: Untitled ('green album') 1991, Untitled ('brown album') 1992, Snivilisation 1994, In Sides 1996, The Middle Of Nowhere 1999, The Altogether 2001, Back To Mine (compilation of other artists' tracks) 2002, B-Sides (compilation) 2002, Work 1989–2002 2002, Blue Album 2004, Wonky 2012, Pusher soundtrack 2012; with Long Range: Madness and Me 2007. *Honours:* NME Award for Best Dance Act 1993, NME BRAT Award 1995, Dance Star Tiscali World Dance Music Award for Dance Star of the Year 2002. *Current Management:* c/o Mondo Management, Suite 2, 92 Lots Road, , London, SW10 0QD, England. *Telephone:* (20) 7352-4844. *E-mail:* chris@ihtrecords.com. *Website:* www.mondo-management.com; www.philhartnoll.com; www.longrange.tv; www.orbitalofficial.com.

HARVEY, Brian Lee; British singer; b. 8 Aug. 1974, Edmonton, London. *Career:* mem. East 17 1992–97, 2006–10; numerous TV and live appearances. *Recordings include:* albums: with East 17: Walthamstow 1993, Steam 1994, Up All Night 1996, Around the World – The Journey So Far 1996, Resurrection 1998; solo: Solo 2002; singles: with East 17: House of Love 1992, Deep 1993, West End Girls 1993, It's Alright 1993, Around The World 1994, Steam 1994, Stay Another Day 1994, Let It Rain 1995, Thunder 1995, Do U Still 1996, If You Ever (with Gabrielle) 1996, Hey Child 1997, Each Time 1998, Betcha Can't Wait 1999. *Current Management:* c/o B&H Management, PO Box 1162, Bovingdon, Herts., HP1 9DE, England. *Telephone:* (1442) 832010. *Fax:* (1442) 834910. *E-mail:* simon@bandhmanagement.demon.co.uk.

HARVEY, Michael (Mick) John; Australian musician (drums, guitar), arranger and producer; b. 29 Aug. 1958, Rochester, Vic. *Career:* mem. Boys Next Door 1977–80; Founder-mem. The Birthday Party 1980–83; mem. Crime and the City Solution 1985–91; Founder-mem. Nick Cave & The Bad Seeds 1984–2009; producer for artists including Once Upon A Time, Anita Lane, The Cruel Sea, Congo Norvell, PJ Harvey; mem. APRA, PPCA, Performing Artists Media Rights Asscn. *Film scores:* Ghosts… of the Civil Dead 3 1989, Alta Marea & Vaterland 1993, To Have and To Hold (Aria Award for Best Soundtrack 1997) 1996, Chopper 2000, Australian Rules (Aria Award for Best Soundtrack 2003) 2002, Australian Rules 2003, Suburban Mayhem (AFI Award for Best Original Score) 2006, Deliver Us From Evil 2006. *Recordings include:* albums: with The Birthday Party: The Birthday Party 1980, Prayers on Fire 1981, Junkyard 1982, Drunk on the Pope's Blood 1982; with Nick Cave & The Bad Seeds: From Her to Eternity 1984, The Firstborn is Dead 1985, Kicking Against the Pricks 1986, Your Funeral… My Trial 1986, Tender Prey 1988, The Good Son 1990, Henry's Dream 1992, Live Seeds 1993, Let Love In 1994, Murder Ballads 1996, The Boatman's Call 1997, No More Shall We Part 2001, Nocturama 2003, Abattoir Blues/ The Lyre Of Orpheus 2005, Dig, Lazarus, Dig!!! 2008, Push the Sky Away 2013; solo: Intoxicated Man 1995, Pink Elephants 1997, And the Ass Saw the Angel – Readings and Music (with Nick Cave) 1999, One Man's Treasure 2005, Two of Diamonds 2007, Three Sisters Live at Bush Hall 2008, Sketches from the Book of the Dead 2011, Four Acts of Love 2013. *Website:* www.mickharvey.com.

HARVEY, Polly Jean (PJ), MBE; British singer, songwriter, musician (guitar, percussion, keyboards), writer and poet; b. 9 Oct. 1969, Yeovil, Somerset. *Career:* formed PJ Harvey trio 1991; solo artist 1993–; numerous TV appearances, concerts and festivals; collaborations with John Parish, Eric Drew Feldman, Pascal Comelade, Tricky, Nick Cave, Mick Harvey, Josh Homme, Sparklehorse, Marianne Faithfull; has exhibited sculpture. *Film:* The Book of Life 1998. *Recordings include:* albums: The Peel Sessions 1991–2004, Demonstration 1992, Dry 1992, Rid Of Me 1993, 4-Track Demos 1993, To Bring You My Love 1995, Dance Hall At Louse Point 1996, Is This Desire? 1998, Stories From The City, Stories From The Sea (Mercury Music Prize 2001) 2000, Uh Huh Her 2004, White Chalk 2007, A Woman A Man Walked By (with John Parish) 2009, Let England Shake (Mercury Music Prize 2011) 2011, The Hope Six Demolition Project 2016. *Publication:* The Hollow of the Hand 2015. *Honours:* Hon. DMus (Goldsmiths Univ.) 2014; Rolling Stone Awards for Best Songwriter, Best New Female Singer 1992, Artist of the Year 1995, South Bank Show Popular Music Award 2002, Meteor Award for Best Int. Female Artist 2005, NME Award for Outstanding Contribution to Music 2011. *Website:* www.pjharvey.net. *Current Management:* c/o Sumit Bothra, ATC Management, The Hat Factory, 166-168 Camden Street, London, NW1 9PT, England. *Telephone:* (20) 7323-2433. *E-mail:* sumit@atcmanagement.com. *Website:* www.atcmanagement.com.

HARVIE, Ian; British musician (guitar, mandolin, resophonic guitar), singer and producer; b. 19 May 1962, Glasgow, Scotland; m. Madeline Harvie; one s. *Education:* Glasgow School of Arts. *Career:* founding mem., Del Amitri 1981–; numerous tours, television and radio appearances. *Recordings:* albums: Del Amitri 1985, Waking Hours 1989, Change Everything 1992, Twisted 1995, Some Other Sucker's Parade 1997, Hatful Of Rain/Lousy With Love 1998, Can You Do Me Good? 2002. *Current Management:* JPR Management Ltd, PO Box 3062, Brighton, East Sussex, BN50 9EA, England. *Telephone:* (1273) 779944. *Fax:* (1273) 779967. *E-mail:* info@jprmanagement.co.uk. *Website:* www.jprmanagement.co.uk; www.delamitri.com.

HASLAM, Annie; British singer, songwriter and artist; b. Bolton, England; d. of George Haslam and Annie Haslam; m. Marc I. Hoffman 1991 (divorced). *Education:* art coll., opera training with Sybil Knight in London. *Career:* lead vocalist The Annie Haslam Band (previously Renaissance), with numerous concerts worldwide including Carnegie Hall, New York, Royal Albert Hall, London; mem. Equity. *Recordings include:* albums: with Renaissance: Prologue 1972, Ashes are Burning 1973, Turn of the Cards 1974, Scheherazade and Other Stories 1975, Live at Carnegie Hall 1976, Novella 1977, In the Beginning 1978, Song for All Seasons 1978, Azure d'Or 1979, Camera, Camera 1981, Timeline 1983, Tales of 1001 Nights Vols 1–2 1990, Tuscany 2000, In the Land of the Rising Sun 2001; solo: Annie in Wonderland 1977, Still Life (with Royal Philharmonic Orchestra) 1985, Annie Haslam 1989, Blessing in Disguise (with Annie Haslam's Renaissance) 1994, Live Under Brazilian Skies 1997, The Dawn of Ananda 2000, It Snows in Heaven Too 2001, One Enchanted Evening 2003, Woman Transcending 2007, Snowball 2009, Realms of Glory 2010, Turn of the Cards, Scheherazade and Other Stories 2011. *Exhibitions include:* Florence Biennale, Italy 1995, Image Makers Art Gallery, New Hope, Phila 2003. *Address:* The White Dove Organisation Inc., PO Box 1157, Doylestown, PA 18901, USA (office). *E-mail:* whtdoveorg@aol.com (office). *Website:* www.anniehaslam.com.

HASLAM, George, BSc, MSc, PhD; British jazz musician (baritone saxophone, tarogato, clarinet) and teacher; *Sole Proprietor, SLAM Productions*; b. 22 Feb. 1939, Preston, Lancs., England; m. Beryl Murphy 1960; four s. one d. *Education:* Kirkham Grammar School, Salford Univ., Manchester Univ., Univ. of Strathclyde; some private music tuition. *Career:* two albums on Spotlite, early 1980s; extensive work in Eastern Europe; tour of Mexico; Cervantino Festival, led first British jazz group to play in Cuba 1986; f. and Dir record label, SLAM 1989–; first British jazz musician to play in Argentina 1990; Founder Oxford Jazz Festival 1990; featured in Impressions of George Haslam (BBC Radio 3) 1993; several other broadcasts on BBC Radio 3 and on many radio and TV programmes world-wide; working in Ukraine, Russia and Finland 1996–, including first jazz concert in Odessa Opera House and first album of improvised music released in Ukraine; toured in Argentina, Canada, Cuba, Hong Kong, Mexico, USA, Belgium, Croatia, Czech Repub., Estonia, Finland, France, Germany, Hungary, Ireland, Italy, Latvia, Portugal, Russia, Serbia, Slovakia, Ukraine; leads blues and improvisation workshops and directs big band; worked with Mal Waldron 1994–2002; made first live concert by Internet between Koktebel Jazz Festival, Crimea, Ukraine and Oxford, UK 2006; f. Oxford Jazz Masters Series 2006; mem. Performing Right Soc., Mechanical-Copyright Protection Soc. *Radio:* specially recorded sessions for Jazz on 3, Jazz Today, Jazz in Britain and Impressions (BBC Radio 3) 1980s–. *Recordings include:* albums: Live In Hungary 1984, The Healing 1986; more than 40 CDs since 1989. *Honours:* Japanese Encyclopaedia of Jazz 19th All-time World Greatest Baritone Saxist. *Address:* 3 Thesiger Road, Abingdon, Oxon., OX14 2DX, England (home). *Telephone:* (1235) 529012 (home). *Website:* www.georgehaslam.com.

HASSALL, John Cory; British bass guitarist and songwriter; b. 17 Feb. 1981, London, England. *Education:* Highgate School, London. *Career:* mem. The Libertines 2001–04, 2014–; Founder-mem. Yeti 2004–09; Founder-mem. The April Rainers. *Recordings include:* albums: with The Libertines: Up the Bracket 2002, The Libertines 2004, Anthems for Doomed Youth 2015; with Yeti: The Legend of Yeti Gonzales 2008. *Honours:* Q Best Track Award (for Gunga Din) 2015. *Current Management:* c/o Various Artists Management, 17 Lonsdale Road, London, NW6 6RA, England. *Telephone:* (20) 7372-6075. *E-mail:* info@variousartistsmanagement.com. *Website:* www.variousartistsmanagement.com; www.thelibertines.com.

HASSAN, Norman; British musician (percussion, trombone) and singer; b. 26 Jan. 1958. *Career:* fmr carpet fitter; mem. reggae group UB40 1978–; numerous concerts, tours. *Recordings include:* albums: Signing Off 1980, Present Arms 1981, The Singles Album 1982, UB44 1982, Labour of Love 1983, Live 1983, More UB40 Music 1983, Geffery Morgan 1984, Baggariddim 1985, Little Baggariddim 1985, UB40 File 1985, Rat In The Kitchen 1986, CCCP: Live In Moscow 1987, UB40 1988, Labour of Love II 1990, Promises and Lies 1993, Anansi 1995, Guns In The Ghetto 1997, Labour of Love III 1998, Presents The Dancehall Album 1998, Homegrown 2003, Who You Fighting For? 2005, TwentyFourSeven 2008, Labour of Love IV 2010, All the Best 2012, Collected 2013, Getting Over the Storm 2013. *Current Management:* c/o Part Rock Management Ltd, 1 Conduit Street, London, W1S 2XA, England. *Telephone:* (20) 8207-1418. *E-mail:* stewartyoung@mindspring.com. *Address:* DEP International Ltd, PO Box 15345, Birmingham, B9 9GJ, England (office). *E-mail:* info@ub40.co.uk (office). *Website:* www.ub40.co.uk.

HASSELL, Jon, PhD; American musician (trumpet) and composer; b. 22 March 1937, Memphis, Tenn. *Education:* Eastman School of Music; also studied in Germany under Karlheinz Stockhausen. *Career:* trumpet performances on recordings of artists including Björk, Baaba Maal and Ibrahim Ferrer; sessions and collaborations with kd lang, Ry Cooder, Ronu Majumdar, Brian Eno and others; f. Maarifa Street 2005–, tours of Europe and USA; performed at first World of Music, Arts and Dance (WOMAD) Festival 1982. *Film scores:* Million Dollar Hotel (with Bono), Lurch, Zangezi. *Television theme music:* The Practice. *Recordings include:* Vernal Equinox 1977, Earthquake Islands 1978, Fourth World Vol. 1: Possible Musics (with Brian Eno) 1980, Fourth World Vol. 2: Dream Theory in Malaya 1981, ka-Darbari-Java/Magic Realism 1983, Power Spot 1986, The Surgeon Of The Nightsky Restores Dead Things By The Power Of Sound 1987, Flash of the Spirit 1988, City: Works of Fiction 1990, Voiceprint 1990, Dressing for Pleasure 1994, Personals 1994, Sulla Strada 1995, The Vertical Collection 1997, Fascinoma 1999, Maarifa Street/Magic Realism 2 2005, Last Night The Moon Came Dropping Its Clothes In The Street 2009. *Current Management:* c/o Franck Feret, Jazz Musiques Productions, 520 rue de la Ducque, 34730 Prades le Lez, France. *Telephone:* 4-67-59-74-97. *Fax:* 4-67-59-72-84. *E-mail:* jmp@jmp.fr; info@nyenmusic.com. *Website:* www.jmp.fr; www.jonhassell.com.

HASTINGS, Graham (G); British hip hop musician and songwriter; b. Edinburgh, Scotland. *Career:* fmr mem. 3 Style; mem. Young Fathers 2008–. *Recordings include:* albums: with Young Fathers: Inconceivable Child... Conceived 2009, Dead (Mercury Music Prize 2014) 2014, White Men Are Black Men Too 2015; mixtapes: Tape One 2011, Tape Two 2013. *Address:* Big Dada Records, Big Dada HQ, PO Box 4296, London, SE11 4WW, England (office). *E-mail:* info@bigdada.com (office); youngfathers@googlemail.com. *Website:* www.bigdada.com (office); www.young-fathers.com.

HATCH, Anthony Peter (Tony); British composer, arranger, music director and songwriter; b. 30 June 1939, Pinner, Middx, England; s. of Cyril Hatch and Eileen Hatch; m. Maggie Hatch; two s. four d. *Education:* London Choir School. *Career:* Band Coldstream Guards 1959–61; record producer, Pye Records 1961–71; producer for Petula Clark, Jackie Trent, The Searchers; musical dir, Carols In The Domain (Australia) 1984–94. *Recordings:* singles: Downtown, Call Me, I Know A Place, Where Are You Now, Joanna, Don't Sleep In The Subway, I Couldn't Live Without Your Love. *Musical:* The Card. *Films:* Travels with My Aunt, Sweeney II. *Television:* regular panellist, New Faces 1973–78; TV theme music for Neighbours, Crossroads, Emmerdale. *Publications:* So You Want To Be In The Music Business 1975. *Honours:* several Ivor Novello Awards, ASCAP Awards, BMI Awards. *Address:* Lyric Productions Ltd, Suite 11, Accurist House, 44 Baker Street, London, W1U 7AZ, England (office). *Telephone:* (20) 7224-2280 (office). *E-mail:* hatchtonyhatch@aol.com (office). *Website:* www.tonyhatch.com.

HATFIELD, Juliana; American singer and songwriter; b. 27 July 1967, Wiscasset, Me. *Education:* Berklee Coll. of Music. *Career:* Founder-mem. Blake Babies (with John Strohm) 1986–92, 1999–, Juliana Hatfield Three 1993–95; collaborations with The Lemonheads; solo artist 1995–; Founder-mem. Some Girls (with Freda Love and Heidi Gluck) 2005–, Minor Alps (with Matthew Caws) 2013; mem. American Fed. of Musicians; f. own record label Ye Olde Records 2005. *Recordings include:* albums: with The Blake Babies: Nicely Nicely 1987, Slow Learner 1989, Earwig 1990, Sunburn 1992, Innocence and Experience (compilation) 1993, God Bless The Blake Babies 2001; with The Juliana Hatfield Three: Become What You Are 1993, Only Everything 1995; solo: Hey Babe 1992, Forever Baby, Bed, Juliana's Pony – Total System Failure 2000, Beautiful Creature 2000, In Exile Deo 2004, Made in China 2005, The White Broken Line: Live Recordings 2006, How to Walk Away 2008, Peace and Love 2010, There's Always Another Girl 2011, Juliana Hatfield 2012, Wild Animals 2013; with Some Girls: Feel It 2003, Crushing Love 2006; with Minor Alps: Get There 2013. *Publication:* When I Grow Up 2008. *Address:* Ye Olde Records, PO Box 398110, Cambridge, MA 02139, USA. *E-mail:* yeolderecords@earthlink.net. *Website:* www.julianahatfield.com.

HATHERLEY, Charlotte Franklin; British musician (guitar, keyboards), singer and songwriter; b. 20 June 1979, London. *Career:* fmr mem. Night Nurse; mem. Ash 1997–2004, Client 2007, Bat for Lashes 2009; solo artist 2004–; started performing as Sylver Tongue 2012–. *Recordings include:* albums: with Ash: Nu-Clear Sounds 1998, Free All Angels 2001, Cosmic Debris 2002, Intergalactic Sonic 7"s: The Best of Ash 2002, Meltdown 2004; solo: Grey Will Fade 2004, The Deep Blue 2007, New Worlds 2009. *Honours:* NME BRAT Award for Best Single (for Burn Baby Burn) 2002, Q Award for Best Single (for Burn Baby Burn) 2002, Ivor Novello Award for Best Contemporary Song (for Shining Light) 2002. *Address:* c/o Out There Management Ltd, Strong Room, 120–124 Curtain Road, London, EC2A 3SQ, England. *E-mail:* outthere@outthere.co.uk. *Website:* www .charlotthatherley.com.

HAUG, Ian; Australian musician (guitar); b. 21 Feb. 1970, Tasmania. *Education:* Brisbane Univ. *Career:* mem. Brisbane-based rock group, Powderfinger 1989–2010; many Australian tours/festival appearances; also mem. of side-project group F.O.C and The Predators. *Recordings include:* albums: Parables For Wooden Ears 1994, Double Allergic 1996, Internationalist (ARIA Award for Album of the Year, for Song of the Year, for Best Rock Album, for Best Cover Artwork 1999) 1998, Odyssey Number Five (ARIA Award for Best Cover Art, Best Rock Album, Best Group, Album of the Year 2001) 2001, Vulture Street (ARIA Award for Best Cover Art, Best Rock Album, Best Group, Album of the Year 2003) 2003, Dream Days at the Hotel Existence 2007, Golden Rule 2009, Seven Deadly Spins 2009, Fingerprints & Footprints: The Ultimate Collection (1994-2011) 2011. *Current Management:* c/o Paul Piticco, Secret Service Artist Management, PO Box 401, Fortitude Valley, 4006 Queensland, Australia. *Telephone:* (7) 3854-1488. *Fax:* (7) 3854-0655. *E-mail:* general@secret-service.com.au. *Website:* www.secret-service.com.au; www.powderfinger.com.

HAUGEN, Tom Jackie; Norwegian songwriter, folk singer and musician (guitar); b. 29 Sept. 1961, Telemark; one d. *Career:* mem. Drangedal 1999; numerous tv appearances. *Recordings include:* Haeimomkring 1992, Bestefars Hevn 1993, Ingrid Bergman 1994, Rosmala Neger 1998; with Drangedal Rationalizing: Drangedal Rationalizing 2001, Taste and Deception 2003. *Honours:* This Year's Artist 1994, Language Prize 1995. *E-mail:* geirr@dippner.com. *Website:* www.dippner.com. *Address:* Tordalsun 52, 3750 Drangedal, Norway.

HAURAND, Ali; German musician (double bass) and teacher; b. 15 Nov. 1943, Viersen; m. 2004; one d. (from previous relationship). *Education:* studied classical music, Folkwangschool, Essen. *Career:* Founder-mem. and Leader George Maycock Trio 1967–79; Quintet with Philly Joe Jones 1968–69; International Jazz Quintet with Jon Eardly 1969–70; Third Eye 1970; European Jazz Quintet 1977; SOH Trio 1978–84; The Quarte 1982; Leader, European Jazz Ensemble 1976–; numerous tours and festivals in Europe, USA, Canada and Australia; numerous tv and radio appearances presenter German TV WDR for Jazz Series Round Midnight and Fullhouse 1991–; played with Charlie Mariano and Daniel Humair as Mariano-Haurand-Humair 1999; played pantomime and jazz with Milan Sládek; Art Dir Int. Jazz Rally, Dusseldorf 2003; Art Dir Int. Jazzfestival, Viersen 2003; mem. Jazz Union, Germany. *Recordings:* solo: Naked 1974, Vitamine A+D 1976, Ali Haurand and Friends 2005; with European Jazz Quintet: Live at Moers Festival 1977, European Jazz Quintet 1978, III 1982; with The Quartet: Dedications 1984, Relation 1985, Interchange 1986; with European Jazz Ensemble: Meets the Khan Family 1992, 25th Anniversary 2002; other credits including: Jon Eardly Quartet 1970, Brown Taste, Jan Huydts Trio 1970, Remembering, Jan Huydts Trio and Theo Lovendie 1970, George Maycock Trio, George Maycock Trio 1975, Third Eye, Third Eye 1976, Connection, Third Eye 1977, Contrasts, Lajos Dudas 1978, It's Blues Time, George Maycock Trio 1979, S.O.H., Skidmore/Oxley/Haurand 1979, Detour, Lajos Dudas 1980, Alpharian, Wilton Gaynair Quintet 1982, Relation, The Quartet 1984, Tomorrow is Here, Tony Oxley's Celebration Orchestra 1985, Urban Blues, Lajos Dudas 1993, Pulque, The Trio 1993, Bordertalk, Haurand/Stivin/van den Broeck 1995, Crossing Level, The Trio featuring Tony Levin 1997, Plays Bach, Lajos Dudas 2000, Just the Two of Us, Haurand/Stivin 2000, Schinderkarren mit Buffet, Haurand/Stivin/Dudek/Esser 2001, Frontier Traffic, Haurand/Humair/Mariano 2002, Ali Haurand and Friends 2005, Cascaden, Haurand/Dudek/Drews 2007, The Two of Us, Haurand/Stivin 2008, Old Wine New Bottled, Stivin/Haurand 2011. *Honours:* Chevalier de l'Ordre des Arts & Jazz et des Lettres 2005; winner European Jazz Poll, Jazz Forum, seven times as bass player and with European Jazz Ensemble. *E-mail:* ali -haurand@t-online.de. *Website:* www.alihaurand.de.

HAUTA-AHO, Teppo; Finnish composer and musician (bass); b. 27 May 1941. *Education:* Sibelius Acad., studied with Prof. Frantisek Posta. *Career:* bassist Helsinki Philharmonic 1965–72, Finnish Nat. Opera 1975–2000; played with numerous artists including Seppo Paakkunainen in early 1960s, Juhani Vilkki, Kaj Backlund Big Band, Pekka Pöyry Quartet, Tuohi Quartet; leader own group, Kalmisto-Klang; mem. Quintet Moderne 1980s–; also classical and chamber musician; performed at annual festivals in Kuhmo; now concentrating on composing; duos with singer/pianist Carita Holmström, pianist/composer Eero Ojanen, violinist/composer Phil Wachsmann; mem. Cecil Taylor European Quintet. *Compositions include:* Fantasy for trumpet and orchestra, Kadenza for contrabass (used as set piece in int. bass competitions) 1990–99. *Honours:* Royal Acad. Composer's Prize, Stockholm, winner EBU competition for jazz groups, Montreux (with Tuohi Quartet) 1971, first prize Reine Marie José competition, Geneva 1986, Int. Soc. of Bassists Recognition Award for composition 2003, British and Int. Bass Forum Award for Lifetime Achievement 2004. *Address:* Mechelininkatu 27 B, 00100 Helsinki, Finland.

HAVER, Greg; producer. *Career:* worked with: John Cale, Catatonia, Cosmic Rough Riders, Gorky's Zygotic Mynci, Manic Street Preachers, Super Furry Animals, Melanie C; has produced major label artists including Tribes of the City, The Feelers, Junica, Onirama, Gem, States of Emotion, Dusso and the Holy Smokes; music adviser, Arts Council of Wales; Musical Dir for launch of Welsh Assembly concert; spent several years as songwriter for EMI Music Publishing and London Music; f. Big Noise Recordings and Boobytrap record label (with DJ Huw Stephens); Producer, York Street Recording Studios, New Zealand; has delivered lectures at numerous schools, music clubs and confs. *Honours:* won numerous Best Producer at Welsh Music Awards, Contribution to the Music Industry, Pop Factory Awards. *Current Management:* c/o Stephen Budd Management, 59–65 Worship Street, London, EC2A 2DU, England. *Website:* www.record-producers.com/roster/greg-haver.

HAVET, Didier; French musician (tuba, bass trombone); b. 9 March 1964, Lille; m. 1994; one d. *Education:* Lille Conservatory, Paris Conservatory. *Career:* mem. Nat. Jazz Orchestra, France (ONJ) 1986–94; bass trombone player with Belmondo Big Band; toured Europe with Mingus Big Band of New York 1994; Paris and Nice Jazz Festival 1995; mem. Bloc-notes Quintet, Peru and Columbia 1995; regular work in traditional jazz and on his own project Dixieland; performed on numerous film soundtracks. *Recordings include:* five records with National Orchestra of Jazz, France; other recordings with: Michel Legrand, Claude Bolling, Julien Clerc, Jacques Higelin, Georges Moustaki, William Sheller; also appears on: Santander with Laurent Cugny, Golden Hair with Gil Evans, Danses with Terra Nova, Cyclades with Jean-Loup Longnon; 20 Ans de Jazz en France, Mingus Cuernavaca with Padovani/Cormann, Montgolfiere with Gianmaria Testa. *Address:* c/o Dixi Project, 4, avenue du drapeau, Colombes, 92700 Paris, France. *E-mail:* havet.didier@wanadoo.fr. *Website:* www.orchestredelalune.com.

HAVOC; American rap artist and producer; b. (Kejuan Waliek Muchita), Queensbridge, New York. *Education:* Graphic Arts High School, Manhattan, New York. *Career:* mem., Mobb Deep 1992–; solo artist 2007–. *Recordings include:* albums: with Mobb Deep: Juvenile Hell 1993, The Infamous Mobb Deep 1995, Hell On Earth 1996, Murda Muzik 1999, Infamy 2001, Free Agents 2003, Amerikaz Nightmare 2004, Blood Money 2006, The Infamous Mobb Deep 2014; solo: The Kush 2007, Hidden Files 2009, 13 2013. *Website:* www.theinfamousmobbdeep.com.

HAWK, Dane T. S. (see Høeg, Thorsten Sehested)

HAWKEN, Dominic; British musician (keyboards), songwriter, producer and remixer; b. 19 April 1967, Welwyn Garden City, Herts. *Education:* studied classical piano. *Career:* session keyboard player, performed with Joy Polloi, Kid Deluxe, Eric and the Good Good Feeling, late '80s–early '90's; writer and producer, various leading artists, 1994–; keyboard/remix credits include Shamen, Donna Summer, Malcolm McLaren, A Tribe Called Quest, Errol Brown, Kym Mazelle, Hammer, Mike Oldfield, Black Duck; writing/production credits include North and South, Alphaville, Shiona, Right Said Fred, Babe Instinct, Rey, David Fernandez; producer: Adam Masterson; mem. BAC&S, PRS, Musicians' Union; Founding Dir, Deluxe Corpn. *Compositions include:* co-writer East 17 tracks: Stay Another Day (Christmas No. 1, UK) 1994, Be There 1994, Let It All Go 1994, I Remember 1995, Don't You Feel So Good 1995, Someone To Love 1995; Ant and Dec tracks: Cloud 9 1997, Bound 1997. *Recordings include:* albums: on keyboards: Steam, East 17; as writer/keyboard player: Up All Night, East 17 1995, All Around the World, East 17 1996–97; as writer/producer: The Cult of Ant and Dec 1997; singles: as additional producer/remixer/keyboards: Don't Call Me Baby (No. 1, UK), Madison Avenue 2000, Prickly Heat (theme music, Sky TV) 2001, Double A side incl. Stay Another Day (No. 1, UK), Girls Aloud 2002; mixer and producer for various artistes including Part 3, Katia, Lamja, Machines, Hussey; writing for various projects including Atlantis; gen. TV adverts 2005–06. *Current Management:* The Deluxe Corpn, 13 Charnhill Crescent, Bristol, BS16 9JU, England. *E-mail:* info@del.co.uk. *Website:* www.del.co.uk.

HAWKINS, Daniel (Dan) Francis; British musician (guitar); b. 12 Dec. 1976, Chertsey, Surrey; brother of Justin Hawkins. *Career:* f. band Empire (with his brother Justin, and Frankie Poullain) playing guitar, band split 1999, reconstituted as The Darkness 2000–06, 2011–; mem. Stone Gods 2006–10. *Recordings include:* albums: with The Darkness: I Believe In A Thing Called Love (EP) 2002, Permission To Land (Best Album, Kerrang! Awards) 2003, One Way Ticket To Hell… And Back 2005, Hot Cakes 2012, Last of Our Kind 2015; with Stone Gods: Silver Spoons and Broken Bones 2008. *Honours:* Kerrang! Award for Best Live Act 2003, The Observer Band of the Year 2003, BRIT Award for Best British Group, Best British Rock Act 2004, Ivor Novello Songwriters of the Year 2004, Smash Hits Award for Best Rock Act 2005. *Website:* www.thedarkness.co.uk.

HAWKINS, Justin David; British singer and musician (guitar, keyboards); b. 17 March 1975, Chertsey, Surrey; brother of Dan Hawkins. *Education:* Univ. of Huddersfield. *Career:* f. band Empire (with his brother, Dan and Frankie Poullain) playing keyboards, band split 1999, reconstituted as The Darkness 2000–06, 2011–; founder mem. Hot Leg 2008–10. *Recordings include:* albums: with The Darkness: I Believe In A Thing Called Love (EP) 2002, Permission To Land (Kerrang! Award for Best Album 2003, BRIT Award for Best British Album 2004) 2003, One Way Ticket To Hell… And Back 2005, Hot Cakes 2012, Last of Our Kind 2015; with Hot Leg: Red Light Fever 2009. *Honours:* Kerrang! Award for Best Live Act 2003, for Best Live Act and Best British Band 2004, The Observer Band of the Year 2003, Metal Hammer 'Golden God' for Best Single 2003, for Best Video 2004, BRIT Awards for Best British Group, Best British Rock Act 2004, Ivor Novello Songwriters of the Year 2004, MTV Europe Music Award 2004, Smash Hits Award for Best Rock Act 2005, ASCAP Award 2005. *Website:* www.thedarkness.com.

HAWKINS, Taylor; American musician (drums); b. 16 Feb. 1972, Dallas, Tex.; m. Alison Hawkins; one s. *Career:* mem. Foo Fighters 1997–; side project, Coattail Riders 2004–. *Recordings include:* albums: with Foo Fighters: The Colour And The Shape 1997, There Is Nothing Left To Lose (Grammy Award for Best Rock Album 2001) 1999, One By One (Grammy Award for Best Rock Album 2003) 2002, In Your Honor 2005, Skin and Bones 2006, Echoes, Silence, Patience and Grace (Grammy Award for Best Rock Album 2008, BRIT Award for Best Int. Album 2008) 2007, Wasting Light (Grammy Award for Best Rock Album 2012) 2011, Sonic Highways 2014; solo/with Coattail Riders: Taylor Hawkins and the Coattail Riders 2006, Red Light Fever 2010. *Honours:* Grammy Award for Best Short Form Music Video (for Learn To Fly) 2001, Grammy Awards for Best Hard Rock Performance (for All My Life) 2003, (for The Pretender) 2008, (for White Limo) 2012, Kerrang! Award for Best Single (for Best of You) 2005, Nordoff-Robbins Silver Clef Raymond Weil Int. Award 2006, BRIT Awards for Best Int. Group 2008, 2012, 2015, Grammy Award for Best Rock Song (for Walk) 2012, Grammy Award for Best Rock Performance (for Walk) 2012. *Current Management:* Gold Mountain Entertainment, Suite 450, 3575 Cahunega Blvd West, Los Angeles, CA 90068, USA. *Address:* c/o RCA Records, 1540 Broadway, New York, NY 10036, USA. *Website:* www.foofighters.com; www.taylorhawkins.com.

HAWLEY, Richard; British musician (guitar) and producer; b. 17 Jan. 1967, Sheffield. *Career:* mem. The Longpigs 1994–2000; mem. Pulp 2001–02; session work for various artists; solo artist 2001–. *Recordings include:* albums: with The Longpigs: The Sun Is Often Out 1996, Mobile Home 1999; solo: Richard Hawley 2001, Late Night Final 2002, Lowedges 2003, Coles Corner (South Bank Show Award for Best Pop Album of the Year 2006) 2005, Lady's Bridge 2007, Truelove's Gutter 2009, Standing at the Sky's Edge 2012, Hollow Meadows 2015. *E-mail:* richard.hawley1@virgin.net (office). *Website:* www.richardhawley.co.uk.

HAWORTH, Bryn; Britsh musician (guitars, especially slide, mandolin) and singer; b. 29 July 1948, Blackburn; m. Sally Haworth 1973. *Career:* joined Fleur De Lys, Motown/soul band, house band for Atlantic Records, late 1960s;

went to California, toured USA in bands including: Jackie Lomax Band; Wolfgang; returned to England, 1973; signed to Island Records; numerous radio and television appearances include: Old Grey Whistle Test (BBC 2); tours of England, Europe, supporting artistes including: Traffic; Bad Company; Gallagher and Lyle; Fairport Convention; Worked with musicians including: Chris De Burgh; Marianne Faithfull; John Cale; Ian Matthews; Joan Armatrading; Gerry Rafferty; Cliff Richard (toured with as member of band); currently leader, Bryn Haworth Band, extensive tours, UK; notable exponent slide guitar. *Recordings include:* albums include: Let The Days Go By 1974, Sunny Side of The Street 1975, Grand Arrival 1978, Keep The Ball Rolling 1979, The Bryn Haworth Band Live 1993, One Way Ticket 2010, Time Out 2014; Gospel albums include: The Gap 1980, 12 Classics 1981, Pass It On 1984, Wings of The Morning 1984, Mountain Mover 1986, Keep the Faith 2005; with Gerry Rafferty: On A Wing and A Prayer, Over My Head 1995, Slide Don't Fret 1996, The Finer Things in Life 1997. *Publications include:* Bryn Haworth Song Book, Vol. One. *E-mail:* music@brynhaworth.com; brynuk@gmail.com. *Website:* www.brynhaworth.com.

HAWTIN, Richie, (Plastikman, Fuse); Canadian producer and DJ; b. 4 June 1970, Banbury, Oxon., England. *Career:* Co-founder Plus 8 Records (with John Aquaviva) 1990–; f. Minus record label 1998–; worldwide DJ; collaborations with Eddie Richards, Joey Beltram. *Recordings:* albums: as Fuse: Dimension Intrusion 1993; as Plastikman: Sheet One 1993, Musik 1994, Recycled Plastik 1994, Consumed 1998, Artifakts 1998; as Richie Hawtin: Decks, EFX and 909 (DJ mix album) 1999, DE9 – Closer To The Edit 2001, Closer 2003, DE9 Transitions 2005, DE9 Life: Electronic Adventures 2006, Minus Orange 1 Decks 2007. *Current Management:* c/o CAB Clonk Artist Booking GmbH, Gaudystrasse 26, 10437 Berlin, Germany. *E-mail:* katrin@clonk.com. *Website:* www.clonk.com. *Address:* Minus Multimedia GmbH, Eberswalderstrasse 26, 10437 Berlin, Germany (office). *Telephone:* (30) 40504033 (office). *Fax:* (30) 405040340 (office). *E-mail:* x@m-nus.com (office). *Website:* www.m-nus.com; www.richiehawtin.com; www.plastikman.com.

HAY, Barry; Dutch singer and musician (guitar, flute, saxophone); b. 16 Aug. 1948, India. *Career:* mem. Golden Earring 1966–; tours of Europe, Canada, USA; worked on project Barry Hay Flying V Formation 2012. *Recordings include:* albums: with Golden Earring: Just Earrings 1965, Winter Harvest 1966, Miracle Mirror 1968, On The Double 1969, Eight Miles High 1969, Golden Earring 1970, Seven Tears 1971, Together 1972, Moontan 1973, Switch 1975, To The Hilt 1976, Contraband 1976, Golden Earring Live 1977, Grab It For A Second 1978, No Promises, No Debts 1979, Prisoner Of The Night 1980, 2nd Live 1981, Cut 1982, N.E.W.S. 1984, Something Heavy Goin' Down 1984, The Hole 1986, Keeper Of The Flame 1989, The Complete Singles Collection 1975–91 1991, Bloody Buccaneers 1991, The Naked Truth 1992, Face It 1995, Lovesweat 1995, Naked II 1997, The Complete Naked Truth 1998, Paradise In Distress 1999, Last Blast Of The Century 2000, The Devil Made Us Do It 2000, Millbrook USA 2003, Naked III 2005, Tits 'n Ass 2012; solo: Only Parrots Frogs and Angels 1972, Victory of Bad Taste 1987, The Big Band Theory 2008. *Current Management:* c/o Barry Hay Flying V Formation, 1e Van der Kunstraat 286, 2521 AV The Hague, Netherlands. *Telephone:* (70) 3301000. *Fax:* (70) 3451034. *E-mail:* contact@atproductions.com. *Website:* www.atproductions.com. *E-mail:* daan@golden-earring.nl. *Website:* www.barryhaymusic.com; www.goldenearring.nl.

HAY, Roy; British musician (guitar, keyboards) and songwriter; b. 12 Aug. 1961, Southend-on-Sea, Essex. *Career:* fmr mem. Russian Bouquet; mem. Culture Club 1981–87, 1998–2002, 2011–; formed band This Way Up; numerous tv appearances and live tours; various solo projects; composer for TV including Fitz (ABC) 1996–97; also recorded with Paul Young, Jaki Graham, The Beach Boys; composed songs for numerous films. *Recordings include:* albums: with Culture Club: Kissing To Be Clever 1982, Colour By Numbers 1983, Waking Up With The House On Fire 1984, From Luxury To Heartache 1986, Don't Mind If I Do 1999, 12 Mixes Plus 2003, Remix Collection 2006, Essential 2011, Sight and Sound 2012, Icon 2013; with This Way Up: Feeling Good About It; singles: with Culture Club: Do You Really Want To Hurt Me 1982, Time (Clock of the Heart) 1982, Church Of The Poisoned Mind 1983, Victims 1983, It's A Miracle 1983, Karma Chameleon (BRIT Award for Best-Selling British Single 1984) 1983, The War Song 1984, The Medal Song 1984, Move Away 1986, I Just Wanna Be Loved 1998, Your Kisses Are Charity 1999, Cold Shoulder 1999. *Honours:* BRIT Awards for Best British Newcomer 1983, Best British Group 1984. *E-mail:* cultureclub@music3w.com (office). *Website:* www.culture-club.co.uk.

HAYES, Darren Stanley; Australian singer and songwriter; b. 8 May 1972, Brisbane; m. Colby Taylor (divorced); partner Richard Cullen. *Education:* Kelvin Grove Univ. *Career:* fmr mem. Red Edge; Founder-mem. Savage Garden 1996–2001; numerous live performances, including closing ceremony of Olympic Games, Sydney 2000; solo artist 2001–. *Recordings include:* albums: with Savage Garden: Savage Garden 1997, Affirmation 1999, Truly Madly Completely (compilation) 2005; solo: Spin 2002, The Tension and the Spark 2004, These Delicate Things We've Made 2007, Secret Codes and Battleships 2011. *Honours:* 10 ARIA Awards 1997, APRA Award for Songwriters of the Year 2000. *Current Management:* c/o Ms Wendy Laister, Magus Entertainment Inc., 33 Greene Street, #3W, New York, NY 10013, USA. *Telephone:* (212) 343-1577. *Fax:* (917) 591-8188. *E-mail:* info@magusentertainment.com. *Website:* www.magusentertainment.com; www.darrenhayes.com.

HAYES, Gemma; Irish singer and songwriter; b. 11 Aug. 1977, Tipperary. *Career:* numerous collaborations including with Counting Crows; solo artist 2001–. *Recordings include:* albums: Night On My Side 2002, The Roads Don't Love You 2005, The Hollow of Morning 2008, Let It Break 2011, Night and Day 2013, Bones + Longing 2014. *Honours:* Irish Tatler Woman of the Year Music Award 2003, Meteor Ireland Music Award for Best Irish Female Artist 2006. *Current Management:* c/o Collins Long Solicitors, 24 Pepper Street, London, SE1 0EB, England. *E-mail:* simonlong@collinslong.com. *Website:* www.collinslong.com; www.gemmahayes.com.

HAYES, Hunter Easton; American country music singer, songwriter and musician (guitar, keyboards); b. 9 Sept. 1991, Breaux Bridge, La; s. of Leo Hayes and Lynette Hayes. *Career:* fmr child actor and singer; songwriter based in Nashville for Rascal Flatts, Jewel, Owl City, Jay Sean in Nashville 2008–; as artist, signed to Atlantic Records Nashville 2010; opening act on tour for Taylor Swift 2011, Rascal Flatts 2012, Carrie Underwood 2012; first solo tour, Most Wanted Tour 2011; collaborations with other artists include Victoria Justice, Brad Paisley. *Films:* The Apostle 1997, Figure it Out 1998, My Dog Skip 2000, Charlie's War 2003. *Recordings:* albums: Through My Eyes 2000, Make a Wish 2001, Holidays with Hunter 2003, Honoring Our French Heritage 2006, Songs About Nothing 2008, Hunter Hayes 2011, Storyline 2014. *Honours:* Teen Choice Awards for Male Country Artist Award 2012, 2013, Country Music Assn Award for New Artist of the Year 2012, inducted into Louisiana Music Hall of Fame 2012, American Country Award for Single of the Year: New Artist (for Wanted) 2012, CMT Nationwide Insurance On Your Side Music Award 2013. *Current Management:* Darin Murphy, Creative Artists Agency, 401 Commerce Street, Penthouse, Nashville, TN 37219, USA. *Telephone:* (615) 383-8787. *Fax:* (615) 383-4937. *Website:* www.caatouring .com; www.hunterhayes.com.

HAYES, Martin O.; Irish musician (fiddle) and composer; *Artistic Director, Masters of Tradition Festival*; b. 13 Nov. 1961, Maghera, Co. Clare; s. of the late P.J. Hayes. *Career:* made recording debut 1990; mem. Tulla Céilí Band 1996–; regular collaborator with guitarist Dennis Cahill 1997–; Founder-mem. The Gloaming 2011–; currently Artistic Dir, Masters of Tradition Festival; numerous recording credits including albums with Kevin Burke, William Coulter, Alasdair Fraser, Natalie Haas, Helen Hayes, Laura MacKenzie, Mary MacNamara, Dean Magraw, Christy McNamara, Bruce Molsky, Peadar Ó Riada, Caoimhin Ó Raghallaigh, John Williams. *Recordings include:* albums: with P.J. Hayes and Mark Gregory: The Shores of Lough Graney 1990; solo: Martin Hayes 1992, Under the Moon 1995; with Tulla Céilí Band: A Celebration of 50 Years 1996, 60th Anniversary Celebration 2007; with Dennis Cahill: The Lonesome Touch 1997, Live in Seattle 1999, Welcome Here Again 2008; with Peadar Ó Riada and Caoimhin Ó Raghallaigh: Triúr Sa Draighean 2010, Triúr Aris 2012, Triúr Omós 2013; with Alasdair Fraser, Natalie Haas and Bruce Molsky: Highlander's Farewell 2011; with The Gloaming: The Gloaming 2014. *Honours:* six-times All Ireland Fiddle Champion during 1970s, Nat. Entertainment Award, BBC Radio 2 Folk Award for Instrumentalist of the Year 2000, TG4 Gradam Ceoil Musician of the Year 2008. *E-mail:* m@barquemgmt.com; martinhayesmgmt@gmail.com. *Website:* www.martinhayes.com; thegloaming.net.

HAYES, Peter; American singer and musician (guitar); b. 11 Feb. 1976, San Francisco, Calif. *Career:* Founding-mem. Black Rebel Motorcycle Club 1998–; also mem. The Brian Jonestown Massacre. *Recordings include:* albums: B.R.M.C. 2001, Take Them On Your Own 2003, Howl 2005, Baby 81 2007, Beat the Devil's Tattoo 2010, Specter at the Feast 2013; with The Brian Jonestown Massacre: Give It Back! 1997. *Film appearance:* DiG! 2004. *Address:* c/o Dan Russell, PO Box 197, Merrimac, MA 01860, USA (office). *Website:* www.blackrebelmotorcycleclub.com.

HAYES, (Tony) Wade; American country singer; b. 20 April 1969, Bethel Acres, Okla; s. of Don Hayes and Trisha Hayes. *Career:* began playing music initially on mandolin but switching to guitar, age 11; sang backing vocals in father's band Country Heritage; dropped out of school to pursue music career, returning to Nashville; played guitar on demos and wrote songs with producer Chick Rains who organized audition with Columbia's A&R dir Don Cook Hayes; signed to Columbia Records and Tree publishing; made progress throughout 1990s and into 2000s, charting regularly and touring extensively with own road band Wheel Hoss; f. duo McHayes (with Mark McClurg) 2003. *Compositions include:* I'm Still Dancin' With You, Old Enough To Know Better. *Recordings include:* albums: Old Enough To Know Better 1995, On A Good Night 1996, When The Wrong One Loves You Right 1998, Highways and Heartaches 2000, Place to Turn Around 2009. *Honours:* various awards including: ACM Top New Male Vocalist 1995, TNN/Music City News, Male Star of Tomorrow 1997. *Address:* c/o Mike Robertson Management, 1227 17th Avenue South, Nashville, TN 37212, USA. *E-mail:* mike@mrmmusic.com. *Website:* www.wadehayes-woww.com; www.wadehayes.com.

HAYLY, Sheldon (Shay); American rap artist; b. 18 Dec. 1972. *Career:* mem. N.E.R.D. (Nobody Ever Really Dies) 2001–, with Chad Hugo and Pharrell Williams; numerous stage, tv appearances. *Recordings include:* albums: In Search Of... 2001, Fly Or Die 2004, Seeing Sounds 2008, Nothing 2010. *Website:* www.n-e-r-d.com.

HAYNE, Michael Shane; British singer; b. 22 Nov. 1937, Plymouth; m. Heather Anne Tarry 1971; one s. one d. *Education:* Warren's Coll., Plymouth. *Career:* lead vocalist, R&B band The Betterdays 1963–66; tv appearances Westward TV, TSW; tours throughout UK 1991–. *Recordings include:* Here Tis, Cracking Up, Aw Shucks, Hush Your Mouth, Don't Want That, Honey What's Wrong, (all 1964–65), EP's: Howl of The Streets 1991, Down On The Waterfront 1992, Here Tis 1992, No Concessions 1993; also featured on compilation albums, Australia, France, USA.

HAYNES, Kevin; British jazz musician (saxophone, percussion); b. 5 Feb. 1965, Paddington, London; one s. *Education:* North London Coll. of Performing Arts, Kingsway Coll. *Career:* Founder Grupo Elega 1994; toured Europe with Nigerian musician Keziah Jones as percussionist and saxophone player 2002–03; mem. Musicians' Union. *Recordings include:* Albums: with Ed Jones: The Home Coming 1988; with Steve Williamson: Waltz For Grace 1989; with Courtney Pine: Bath Jazz Festival 1993; with Kevin Haynes Group: Eleggra 1994, Recording track for Bachology 1995; with Grupo Elega: Tomorrow's Path 1997. *E-mail:* haynes678@hotmail.com. *Website:* www.kevinhaynes.f9.co .uk.

HAYNES, Roy Owen; American jazz drummer, bandleader and composer; b. 13 July 1925, Roxbury, Mass. *Career:* made professional debut in Boston 1944; worked with Luis Russell 1945, Lester Young 1947–49; mem. Charlie Parker quintet 1949–52; active bandleader 1950s–; toured with Sarah Vaughan 1954–59; worked with Thelonious Monk 1959–60, Eric Dolphy 1960–61, Stan Getz 1961–65, John Coltrane Quartet 1963–65; numerous credits as sideman including: Kenny Burrell, Gary Burton, Alice Coltrane, John Coltrane, Chick Corea, Miles Davis, Art Farmer, Stan Getz, Stephane Grappelli, Wardell Gray, Milt Jackson, Roland Kirk, Jackie McLean, Bud Powell, Sonny Rollins, Archie Shepp, Sarah Vaughan, Randy Weston. *Recordings include:* albums: numerous including: as leader: Busman's Holiday 1954, Roy Haynes Sextet 1954, Jazz Abroad 1956, We Three 1958, Just Us 1960, Out of the Afternoon 1962, Cracklin' 1963, Cymbalism 1963, People 1964, Hip Ensemble 1971, Equipoise 1972, Senyah 1973, Jazz A Confronto Vol. 29 1976, Sugar Roy 1976, Vistalite 1977, Thank You Thank You 1977, True or False 1986, Homecoming 1992, When It's Haynes It Roars 1992, Praise 1998, The Roy Haynes Trio 2000, Roy Haynes 2000, Birds of a Feather 2001, Love Letters 2003, Fountain of Youth 2004, Whereas 2006, Roy-Alty 2011; with Pat Metheny: Te Vou! 1994. *Honours:* Down Beat Readers Poll Best Drummer Award 1996, inducted into Down Beat Magazine Hall of Fame 2004, Mid-Atlantic Arts Foundation's BNY Mellon Jazz Living Legacy Award, Washington DC 2010, Grammy Lifetime Achievement Award 2010, Jazz Journalists Assn Award for Best Drummer 2012. *Address:* c/o Disques Dreyfus, Francis Dreyfus Music, 26 avenue Kléber, 75016 Paris, France. *Website:* www.disquesdreyfus.com.

HAYNES, Warren Dale; American singer, songwriter, musician (guitar, slide guitar) and producer; b. 6 April 1960, Ashville, North Carolina. *Career:* performed with David Allan Coe 1980–84; studio musician 1984–87; mem. Dickey Betts Band 1987–89, Allman Bros Band 1989–, Gov't Mule 1994–; world-wide tours; mem. American Fed. of TV and Radio Artists, American Fed. of Musicians, Broadcast Music Inc.; f. Evil Teens Records. *Compositions include:* (co-writer) Two of a Kind (Workin' On A Full House) for Garth Brooks, True Gravity, A Kind of a Bird. *Recordings include:* albums: with Allman Bros Band: Seven Turns 1990, Shades of Two Worlds 1991, An Evening With... 1992, Where It All Begins 1994, Second Set 1995, Mycology 1998, Peakin' at the Beacon 2000, Hittin' the Note 2003, One Way Out 2004; solo: Tales of Ordinary Madness 1993, Live at Bonnaroo 2004, Man in Motion 2011, Live at the Moody Theater 2012; with Gov't Mule: Gov't Mule 1995, Dose 1998, Life Before Insanity 2000, Deep End Vol. 1 2001, Deep End Vol. 2 2002, Rising Low 2003, Deepest End 2003, Déjà Voodoo 2004, High and Mighty 2006, Mighty High 2007, Holy Haunted House 2007, By a Thread 2009, Mulennium 2010, Shout! 2013; also appears on: Language with Richard Leo Johnson 2000. *Current Management:* c/o Hard Head Management, PO Box 651, Village Station, New York, NY 10014, USA. *E-mail:* info@hardhead.com. *Website:* www.hardhead.com; www.warrenhaynes.net; www .allmanbrothersband.com; www.mule.net.

HAYWARD, (David) Justin; British singer and musician (guitar); b. 14 Oct. 1946, Swindon, Wiltshire. *Career:* mem. The Offbeats, Marty Wilde Trio; singer The Moody Blues 1967–74; 1978–; numerous festival and live appearances; opened own recording studio, London 1974; solo artist 1974–. *Recordings include:* albums: with the Moody Blues: Days of Future Passed 1967, In Search of The Lost Chord 1968, On the Threshold of a Dream 1969, To Our Children's Children's Children 1969, Caught Live + 5 1969, A Question of Balance 1970, Every Good Boy Deserves Favour 1971, Seventh Sojurn 1972, This is The Moody Blues 1974, Octave 1978, Out of this World 1979, Long Distance Voyager 1981, The Present 1983, Voices in the Sky 1985, The Other Side of Life 1986, Sur la mer 1988, Keys of the Kingdom 1991, Live at Red Rock 1993, Strange Times 1999, Live at the Royal Albert Hall 2000, Journey into Amazing Caves 2001; solo: Blue Jays (with John Lodge) 1975, Songwriter 1977, Night Flight 1980, Moving Mountains 1985, Classic Blue 1989, View from the Hill 1996, Live in San Juan Capistrano 1998, Strange Times 1999, Journey into Amazing Caves 2001, December 2003, War of the Worlds 2009, Spirits of the Western Sky 2013. *Honours:* Ivor Novello Award for Outstanding contrib. to British Music (with the Moody Blues) 1985, for Composer of the Year (for I Know You're Out There Somewhere) 1988, Golden Note Award for Lifetime Achievement, American Soc. of Composers, Authors and Publishers 2000, Golden Badge for Lifetime Achievement, British Acad. of Songwriters, Composers and Authors. *E-mail:* info@moodybluestoday.com. *Website:* www .moodybluestoday.com; www.justinhayward.com.

HAYWARD, Lawrence; British singer and songwriter; b. 12 Aug. 1961, Birmingham. *Career:* Founder band Felt 1979–89; mem. band Denim 1992–96; solo project Go-Kart Mozart 2000–. *Recordings include:* albums: with Felt: Crumbling the Antiseptic Beauty (EP) 1981, The Splendour of Fear (EP) 1984, The Strange Idols Pattern and Other Short Stories 1984, Ignite the Seven Cannons 1985, Forever Breathes the Lonely Word 1985, Ballad of the Band (EP) 1986, Let the Snakes Crinkle Their Heads 1986, Poem of the River (EP) 1987, The Final Resting of the Ark 1987, Pictorial Jackson Review 1988, Me and a Monkey on the Moon 1989, Here Are the Facts You Requested 2002, Stains on a Decade 2003; with Denim: Back in Denim 1992, Denim on Ice 1996, Novelty Rock 1997; as Go-Kart Mozart: Instant Wigwam and Igloo Mixture 2000, Tearing Up The Album Charts 2006, On the Hot Dog Streets 2012. *Address:* c/o Cherry Red Records, Power Road Studios, 114 Power Road, London, W4 5PY, England. *E-mail:* infonet@cherryred.co.uk. *Website:* www.cherryred.co.uk.

HAYWOOD, Dave Wesley; American musician (guitar, piano, mandolin), singer and songwriter; b. 5 July 1982, Augusta, Ga; s. of Van Haywood and Angie Haywood; m. Kelli Cashiola 2012. *Education:* Lakeside High School, Univ. of Georgia. *Career:* mem., country music group Lady Antebellum 2006–; performed at Grand Old Opry; songwriter for Luke Bryan, Miranda Lambert; songwriter and producer for Mary Bragg. *Recordings include:* albums: Lady Antebellum 2008, Need You Now (Grammy Award for Best Country Album 2011, Acad. of Country Music Award for Album of the Year 2011) 2010, Own the Night (Grammy Award for Best Country Album 2012) 2011, On This Winter's Night 2012, Golden 2013, 747 2014. *Honours:* numerous including: Acad. of Country Music Awards for Best New Group 2008, for Best Vocal Group 2010, for Best Single Record of the Year (for Need You Now) 2010, for Best Song of the Year (for Need You Now) 2010, for Top Vocal Group 2011, for Vocal Group of the Year 2012, Jim Reeves Int. Award 2013, Country Music Asscn Awards for New Artist of the Year 2008, for Single of the Year (for I Run to You) 2009, (for Need You Now) 2010, for Vocal Group of the Year 2009, 2010, for Int. Artist Achievement 2012, Grammy Award for Best Country Performance by a Duo or Group with Vocals (for I Run to You) 2010, Grammy Award for Record of the Year, Song of the Year, Best Performance by a Duo or Group (all for Need You Now) 2011, Billboard Music Award for Top Country Artist 2012, American Music Awards for Favorite Band, Duo or Group – Country 2012, 2013, American Country Awards for Duo/Group Artist of the Year 2012, 2013, for Single by a Duo/Group (for We Owned the Night) 2012, (for Downtown) 2013. *Address:* c/o Capitol Nashville Records, 3322 West End Avenue, 11th Floor, Nashville, TN 37203-1100, USA. *Telephone:* (615) 269-2000. *Fax:* (615) 269-2059. *E-mail:* support@ladyantebellum.com. *Website:* ladyantebellum.com.

HAZELL, Patrick James; American musician (piano, organ, harmonica, drums), singer and songwriter; b. 23 Sept. 1945, Burlington, Vt; m. Pamela Ann Cummings 1967; three s. one d. *Career:* professional musician 1960–; Founder-mem. Mother Blues Band 1968–70, Sound Pool 1972; mem. Rocket 88's; re-formed Mother Blues Band 1973–83, 1997–; solo performer 1983–; music instructor Washington High School 1987–95; concerts supporting Led Zeppelin, Jefferson Airplane, John Mayall, Robert Cray, Muddy Waters, John Lee Hooker, George Thorogood, Suzy Bogguss, Luther Allison, Asleep At The Wheel, Junior Walker; mem. Arts Midwest, Ia Arts Council, Touring Arts Team of Ia, Nat. Acad. of Performing Arts, Heartland Arts Fund (on artists' roster). *Recordings include:* albums: Band Music, Vol. 1 1975, Vol. 2 1978, Vol. 3 1980, Iowa Ear Music 1976, Vicksburg Vol. 1 1981, Vol. 2 1981, Christmas Visions 1982, Studios Solos 1985, The New Cool 1986, Solo Improvisations 1986, Patrick Hazell-Live! 1987, Blues Jam 1988, East of Midnight 1989, Nemo's Island 1989, Mystery Winds 1989, Santa Was Eating The Christmas Tree/Nicci and The Project 1989, Tuba and Piano Jam Session 1990, Blues on the Run 1995, Patrick Hazell and the Mother Blues Band, 1975–80 1996, In The Prairieland 1996, Dreamcatcher 1996, Blue Blood 1997, Soundtracks 1997, Cityscape Precipice 1997, Soul Changes 1999, Vicksburg 2000, Rollin' In The Moonlight 2003, Hawkeye Valley Bell Project 2003, Iowa Ear Music Revisited 2007, In the Prairie Land 2008. *Honours:* four Prairie Sun Awards, Best Rhythm and Blues Band, Iowa Blues Hall of Fame 2000, Iowa Music Asscn Rock and Roll Hall of Fame 2007. *Address:* Blue Rhythm Recordings, 220 East 17th Street, Washington, IA 52353, USA. *Telephone:* (319) 653-4370 (office). *E-mail:* pat@patrickhazell.com (office). *Website:* www.patrickhazell.com.

HEALY, Francis (Fran); British singer and musician (guitar); b. 23 July 1973, Scotland. *Career:* lead singer and songwriter, band Travis 1997–; numerous tours, festivals and TV appearances. *Recordings include:* albums: with Travis: Good Feeling 1997, The Man Who 1999, The Invisible Band 2001, 12 Memories 2003, The Boy With No Name 2007, Ode to J. Smith 2008, Where You Stand 2013; solo: Wreckorder 2010. *Honours:* Q Magazine Award for Best Single 1999, Select Magazine Award for Album of the Year 1999, BRIT Awards for Best British Group 2000 2002, Best British Album 2000. *Current Management:* MCT Management, 520 Eighth Avenue, Suite 2206, New York, NY 10018, USA. *Telephone:* (212) 563-0630. *E-mail:* mailbox@mctbold.com. *Website:* www.mctbold.com; www.travisonline.com; www.franhealy.com.

HEALY, Jeremy; British DJ, producer and musical director; b. 18 Jan. 1962, Woolwich, London; m. Patsy Kensit 2009. *Career:* formed band Haysi Fantayzee with Kate Garner, also songwriter and co-producer for E-Zee Possee, Bleachin, Seraphim Suite; int. club DJ; Musical Dir for fashion houses including Christian Dior/John Galliano, Tommy Hilfiger, Etro, Victoria's Secret, The Golden Age of Couture; launched recording project Seraphim Suite 2004; mem. PRS. *Recordings include:* albums: Mixmag Live 1995, House Collection Vol. 4 1996, British Anthems 1998, Ibiza The Closing Party 1999; singles: Stamp 1996, Argentina 1997; other recordings with Haysi Fantayzee: John Wayne Is Big Leggy 1982, Shiny Shiny 1983, Sabres of Paradise, Everything Starts With An 'E', E-Zee Possee 1989. *E-mail:* info@dexnfx.com. *Website:* www.dexnfx.com (office); www.jeremyhealy.com (home).

HEAP, Imogen Jennifer; British singer, songwriter and engineer; b. 9 Dec. 1977, Romford, Essex. *Education:* BRIT School of Performing Arts and Technology. *Career:* fmr mem. Acacia, Frou Frou (duo); now solo artist; live debut, Prince's Trust Concert, Hyde Park, London 1996; tours of Europe, N America. *Films include:* featured on film and TV soundtracks including The OC, Garden State, CSI, Shrek 2, Six Feet Under, The Chronicles of Narnia: The Lion, The Witch & The Wardrobe, Just Like Heaven, The Last Kiss. *Recordings include:* with Frou Frou: Details 2002; solo: iMegaphone 1998, Speak For Yourself 2005, Ellipse 2009, Sparks 2014. *Honours:* Grammy Award for Best Engineered Album (for Ellipse) 2010, Ivor Novello Award for Int. Achievement 2010. *Address:* c/o RCA Records, 550 Madison Avenue, New York, NY 10022, USA (office). *E-mail:* info@rcarecords.com (office). *Website:* www.rcarecords.com (office); www.imogenheap.com.

HEARD, Paul; British musician (keyboards, programming); b. 5 Oct. 1960, London. *Career:* fmr mem. Orange Juice; mem. M People 1990–; numerous live and tv appearances; composer for film and tv dramas. *Films include:* as composer: Secret Society 2000, The Bone Snatcher 2003, Clubbed 2009. *Television:* Ahead of the Class 2005. *Recordings include:* albums: with M People: Northern Soul 1992, Northern Soul Extended 1992, Elegant Slumming (Mercury Music Prize 1994) 1993, Bizarre Fruit 1994, Bizarre Fruit Vol. 2 1995, Fresco 1997, Testify 1999, 3 Originals 2003. *Honours:* BRIT Award for Best Dance Act 1994, 1995, Freedom of Manchester 1999. *Website:* www.m-people.com.

HEATH, Chris; British journalist and writer. *Career:* journalist, Jamming! 1984–85, Smash Hits 1984–89, The Guardian, The Face, The Daily Telegraph, The Sunday Telegraph, Empire, Rolling Stone, GQ; fmr Contributing Ed. Details magazine; official biographer, Pet Shop Boys, Robbie Williams. *Publications:* Pet Shop Boys, Literally 1990, Pet Shop Boys Vs America 1993, Feel: Robbie Williams 2004. *Address:* c/o Ebury Press, Random House, 20 Vauxhall Bridge Road, London, SW1V 2SA, England (office).

HEATH, Martin, BA; British record company executive; *CEO, Lizard King Records;* b. 12 March 1961, Sussex. *Career:* Man. Dir and Co-founder indie record label Rhythm King Records (with Adele Nozedar) 1988; Founder and CEO Lizard King Records 2002–, Digital Animal 2009–; Founder Renegade Software and Perfect World Programmes. *Address:* Lizard King Records, The Unit, 2 Manor Gardens, London, N7 6ER (office); Digital Animal, 26–27 Southampton Street, London, WC2E 7RS, England (office). *Telephone:* (20) 7561-6700 (office). *Fax:* (20) 7561-6701 (office). *E-mail:* info@lizardkingrecords.co.uk (office). *Website:* www.lizardkingrecords.net (office); www.digitalanimal.com (office).

HEATH, Rohan Vernon, BSc, MSc; British songwriter and musician (keyboards); b. 19 July 1964, Wembley, London. *Education:* Victoria Coll. of Music. *Career:* played keyboards with A Guy Called Gerald 1990–91, with Together 1991–92, with Eek A Mouse 1992–93; Leader, Urban Cookie Collective 1993–; tours include: USA, Canada, Australia, Japan, Singapore, UK, Europe, Israel, Lithuania, Turkey. *Compositions include:* co-wrote: Automatik (for A Guy Called Gerald). *Recordings include:* Urban Cookie Collective singles: The Key The Secret (No. 2, UK) 1993, Spend the Day, Feels Like Heaven, Sail Away; albums: with Urban Cookie Collective: High On A Happy Vibe 1994, Tales from the Magic Fountain 1995, Bring It On Home, Reggae Summer Splash, The Key, The Secret 2010; compilation: Very Best of The Urban Cookie Collective 2000. *Publications include:* The Phylogenetic Significance of The Ventral Nervous Chord In Carabid Beetles, Journal of Entomology. *Honours:* Perfect 10 Award, Best Live Act, Singapore 1994.

HEATHER, Charlie; British musician (drums). *Career:* Founder-mem. The Levellers 1988–; numerous concerts, festival appearances. *Recordings include:* albums: Weapon Called The Word 1990, Levelling The Land 1991, See Nothing, Hear Nothing, Do Something 1993, Levellers 1993, Zeitgeist 1995, Mouth To Mouth 1997, Special Brew 2000, Hello Pig 2000, Green Blade Rising 2002, Truth & Lies 2005, Letters from the Underground 2008, Static on the Airwaves 2012. *Honours:* Roots Award, BBC Radio 2 Folk Awards 2011. *Address:* The Levellers, PO Box 29, Winkleigh, Devon, EX19 8WE, England. *E-mail:* info@levellers.co.uk. *Website:* www.levellers.co.uk.

HEATLIE, Bob; British musician (keyboards, drums, saxophone, flute), producer and songwriter; b. 20 July 1946, Edinburgh, Scotland; m. Mary Jane Davie 1967; three s. *Education:* taught by his father, Thomas Heatlie. *Career:* mem. MCPS, PRS, BAC&S; composed music for numerous children's tv and documentaries. *Recordings include:* Aneka: Japanese Boy, Merry Christmas Everyone, Cry Just A Little Bit 1983, Breaking Up My Heart 1985, Woman (What Have You Done To Me) 1988; numerous tv theme tunes including The Fresh Beat Band, Franklin, The Curious Case of Santa Claus, Little Robots. *Honours:* two ASCAP Awards. *Address:* 39 Frogston Road, Edinburgh, EH10 7AH, Scotland (home). *Telephone:* (131) 445-3188 (home).

HEATON, Mike; British musician (drums); b. 18 Sept. 1968. *Career:* mem. Embrace 1996–; headline tours and TV appearances. *Recordings include:*

albums: The Good Will Out 1998, Drawn From Memory 2000, If You've Never Been 2001, Fireworks (Singles 1997–2002) 2002, Out Of Nothing 2004, This New Day 2006. *Current Management:* c/o Tony Perrin, Coalition Management, Studio 2, 3A Brackenbury Road, London, W6 0BE, England. *Telephone:* (20) 8743-1000. *E-mail:* tp@coalitiongroup.co.uk. *Website:* www.coalitionmanagement.co.uk.

HEATON, Paul David, (Biscuit Boy); British singer, songwriter and musician; b. 9 May 1962, Birkenhead, Merseyside. *Career:* lead singer The Housemartins 1983–88; Founder-mem. The Beautiful South 1989–2007; solo artist 2001–; duo with The Beautiful South's Jacqui Abbott 2014–. *Recordings include:* albums: with The Housemartins: London 0 Hull 4 1986, The People Who Grinned Themselves to Death 1987, Now That's What I Call Quite Good 1988; with The Beautiful South: Welcome To The Beautiful South 1989, Choke 1990, 0898 1992, Miaow 1994, Blue Is The Colour 1996, Quench 1998, Painting It Red 2000, Gaze 2002, Golddiggas, Headnodders & Pholk Songs 2004, Superbi 2006, Gold 2006, Soup 2007; solo: Fat Chance (as Biscuit Boy) 2001, Under the Influence 2004, The Cross Eyed Rambler 2008, Acid Country 2010; with Jacqui Abbott: What Have We Become? 2014, Wisdom, Laughter and Lines 2015. *Publications include:* contrib. to Introduction to Blades Business Crew, by Steve Cowans. *Honours:* BPI Award for Best Newcomers (with The Housemartins) 1987, BPI Award for Best Video (for A Little Time, The Beautiful South) 1991. *Current Management:* c/o SJM Concerts, St Matthews, Liverpool Road, Manchester, M3 4NQ, England. *Telephone:* (161) 907 3443. *Fax:* (161) 907 3446. *E-mail:* conrad@sjmconcerts.com. *Website:* paulheaton.co.uk.

HEBDEN, Kieran, (Four Tet); British musician; b. 1978, London. *Career:* mem. post-rock band Fridge 1995–; also solo artist (often as 'Four Tet') 1998–; various tours and appearances, including Venice Biennale arts festival, Italy 2003; f. record label Text Records. *Recordings include:* albums: with Fridge: Ceefax 1997, Semaphore 1998, EPH 1999, Happiness 2001, The Sun 2007; solo: Dialogue 1999, Pause 2001, As Serious As Your Life 2003, Rounds 2003, My Angel Rocks Back And Forth 2004, Everything Ecstatic 2005, The Exchange Sessions Vol. 1 (with Steve Reid) 2006, Remixes 2006, Tongues (with Steve Reid) 2007, Ringer 2008, NYC (with Steve Reid) 2008, There is Love in You 2010, Fabric Live.59 2011, Pink 2012, Beautiful Rewind 2013, Morning/Evening 2015. *Address:* c/o Domino Recording Company, PO Box 47029, London, SW18 1WD, England. *E-mail:* info@dominorecordco.com. *Website:* www.dominorecordco.com; www.fourtet.net.

HECKARD, Gary Davis, EdM, BM; composer; b. 15 March 1974, Los Angeles, CA, USA. *Education:* Teachers' College Columbia University, Manhattan School of Music, Berklee College of Music. *Career:* Composer in Residence, the Greenwich Village Orchestra; Member, Grussner Band, Toured World-wide, Radio Broadcasts on National Radios; mem, Compose NY; The American Music Center; BMI; BMI Classical. *Compositions include:* Triple Concerto for Jazz Orchestra, 1995; Three Months in Rotterdam, 1996; Two Pages in the New City, 1997; Continuation, 1997; . . . Fore, 1998; Untitled, 1998; Recollection, 1999. *Recordings:* Gary Davis Heckar – Improvisations.

HECTOR, Kevin Jon; British producer, musician (guitar) and electronic artist; b. 17 Jan. 1967, Nantwich, Cheshire. *Career:* session guitarist, 1983–87; London Club DJ, 1988–; dance producer, 1990–; Autocreation world tour, 1993, including live broadcast on Japan TV. *Compositions:* miscellaneous dance compositions. *Recordings:* Mettle, Autocreation.

HEDEGAARD, Svend; Danish musician and composer; b. 19 Dec. 1959, Sonderborg. *Education:* pvt. studies and several seminars in composition and orchestration; guitar and piano lessons. *Career:* guitarist in numerous rock, fusion and jazz bands 1975–2005; several major works for different classical ensembles and orchestras in Denmark 1986–2005; with Wind O Four, jazz fusion quartet 1991–96; mem. Danish Musicians' Union, Danish Jazz, Beat and Folk Music Composers, KODA. *Compositions include:* Maximal/Minimal 1991, Some Colours Remain, Some Remind 1991, Twins Turn 1996, Efter regnen saaes 1996, Sangenes Sang 1997, Via 1998, Via (guitar quartet) 2001, Northpoints (Corona guitar quartet) 2003. *Recordings include:* With Wind O Four, Jazz Quartet 1995, Voices 1997, CD including Via 2003, Sping-A-Spong (solo) 2003. *Honours:* Laurens Bogtman Fondens Haederslegat 1996, DJBFA, Arbejdslegat 1997. *Address:* Romersgade 23 2 tv, 1362 Copenhagen K, Denmark (home).

HEDGES, Mike; record producer. *Career:* engineer, Morgan Studios late 1970s–1980s; Founder Playground Studio 1980s; converted Chateau Rouge Motte, Normandy, into full residential studio 1990; moved to Wessex Studio, London 2002; producer for numerous artists including Siouxsie and The Banshees, Marc Almond, The Beautiful South, The Cure, McAlmont and Butler, Manic Street Preachers, Everything But The Girl, The Shamen, Bauhaus, Mighty Wah!, U2, Cooper Temple Clause, The Dentists, Dreamchaser. *Current Management:* c/o Jessica Norbury, 3Khz Management, 54 Pentney Road, London, SW20 0NY, England. *E-mail:* threekhz@hotmail.com.

HEGARTY, Antony; British singer, musician (piano) and songwriter; b. 1971, Chichester, West Sussex. *Education:* New York Univ. *Career:* moved to USA aged 10; Founder-mem. performance collective Blacklips 1992, performance group The Johnsons 1995– (later known as Antony and the Johnsons), Hercules and Love Affair 2007–; numerous collaborations including with Lou Reed, Brooks, CocoRosie, Matmos, Little Annie; Musical Dir The Life and Death of Marina Abramović 2011; curator Meltdown 2012. *Film appearances:*

Wild Side 2004, The Secret Life of Words 2005. *Recordings include:* albums: with Antony and the Johnsons: Antony and the Johnsons 2000, I Am A Bird Now (Mercury Music Prize) 2005, The Crying Light 2009, Swanlights 2010, Cut the World 2012, Del suo veloce volo 2013; with Hercules and Love Affair: Hercules and Love Affair 2008, Blue Songs 2011. *Exhibition includes:* numerous drawings and sculpture exhibitions. *Television includes:* Rapture 2000. *Honours:* New York Foundation for the Arts Fellowship 1995. *Website:* www.antonyandthejohnsons.com; herculesandloveaffair.com.

HEINILA, Kari Juhani; Finnish musician (saxophone, flute); b. 31 Oct. 1966, Kiukainen; m. Arja Mäkelä; two s. one d. *Education:* Sibelius Acad., Rauma Conservatory, Pori Conservatory. *Career:* saxophonist, UMO Jazz Orchestra 1987–93; jazz groups under own name 1987–; performed with numerous jazz artists including Billy Hart, Tim Hagans, Vince Mendoza, Anders Jormin and Wayne Krantz; performed with numerous bands including Espoo Big Band, EBU Big Band; Leader and flautist Albero chamber music quartet 2005–; Co-artistic Dir UMO 2010–; mem. Iro Haarla Sextet 2013; regular teacher, Sibelius Acad. Jazz Dept 1993–. *Compositions include:* Frozen Petals, Blue in the Distance, Crossings, Wavestar, Popp, Indigo, Passacaglia, Leitourgia. *Recordings include:* albums: solo: Tribus 2000, Antiqua 2003, Lill'Lisa 2004, Mosaique 2010, Stilleben 2010; with Espoo Big Band: Grand Mystery; with Jarmo Savolainen: Blue Dreams, True Image; with Edward Vesala: Lumi; with Umo Jazz Orchestra: Selected Standards; with Pekka Luukka: Splash of Colors; with Jukka Linkola: The Tentet; with Sonny Heinla: Tribus; with Von Hertzen Brothers: Approach 2006, Love Remains the Same 2008. *Honours:* BAT-Finland Composition Prize 1992, Pori Jazz Festival Artist of the Year 1995, Georgie Award, Finnish Jazz Fed. 2001. *Address:* Tontunmäentie 35, B19, 02200 Espoo, Finland (home).

HEINONEN, Eero Aleksi; Finnish musician (bass guitar) and backing singer; b. 27 Nov. 1979, Helsinki; m.; two d. *Career:* Founder-mem. The Rasmus 1994–; Founder-mem. Korpi Ensemble 1999–2004; f. rock band Ray and Stone 2003. *Recordings include:* albums: Peep 1996, Playboys (Emma Award) 1997, Hell Of A Tester 1998, Into 2001, Dead Letters 2003, Hide From The Sun 2005, Black Roses 2008, The Rasmus 2012. *Honours:* Emma Award for Best New Artist 1996, MTV Europe Music Award Best Finnish Act 2005. *Address:* c/o Seppo Vesterinen/Oy Hinterland Ltd., PO Box 201, 00121, Helsinki, Finland (office). *Website:* www.therasmus.com.

HELDERS, Matthew (Matt); British musician (drums) and DJ; b. 7 May 1986, Sheffield. *Education:* Stockbridge High School, Sheffield. *Career:* founder mem., Arctic Monkeys 2002–; mem. Mongrel 2008–09; remixer of tracks for acts including Duran Duran, Hives, Roots Manuva, We Are Scientists. *Recordings include:* albums: with Arctic Monkeys: Five Minutes with the Arctic Monkeys (EP) 2005, Whatever People Say I Am, That's What I'm Not (Mercury Music Prize 2006, Q Award for Best Album 2006, Meteor Ireland Music Award for Best Int. Album 2007, BRIT Award for Best British Album 2007, NME Award for Best Album 2007, Ivor Novello Award for Best Album 2007) 2006, Favourite Worst Nightmare (BRIT Award for Best British Album 2007) 2007, Humbug 2009, Suck It and See (MOJO Award for Best Album 2011) 2011, AM 2013; with Mongrel: Better Than Heavy 2009; solo: Late Night Tales: Matt Helders (compiler) 2008. *Honours:* with Arctic Monkeys: BRIT Awards for Best British Breakthrough Artist 2006, for Best British Group 2007, 2008, NME Awards for Best British Band 2006, 2008, for Best Track (for I Bet You Look Good on the Dancefloor) 2006, (for Flourescent Adolescent) 2008, for Best Music DVD (for Scummy Man) 2007, (for Arctic Monkeys at the Apollo) 2009, for Best Live Band 2010, 2012, Q Magazine Awards for People's Choice 2006, for Best Act in the World Today 2007, for Best Live Act 2009, for Best Track (for Do I Wanna Know?) 2013. *Current Management:* Press Here Publicity, 138 West 25th Street, Seventh Floor, New York, NY 10001, USA. *E-mail:* info@pressherepublicity.com. *Website:* www.pressherepublicity.com. *E-mail:* arctic.monkeys@gmail.com. *Website:* www.arcticmonkeys.com.

HELFER, Erwin, MusB, MusM; American blues and jazz musician (piano) and piano teacher; b. 20 Jan. 1936, Chicago, Illinois. *Education:* American Conservatory of Music, Northeastern Illinois Univ. *Career:* annual performances at Chicago Blues Festival; annual concert tours, Europe, Rolf Schubert Concertburo, Cologne, Germany; plays in local jazz and blues clubs, Chicago; college tours, USA; recording artist for Flying Fish, Steeple Chase, Red Beans, CMA, Sirens. *Recordings:* Erwin Helfer and Friends On The Sunny Side of The Street 1979, Erwin Helfer Plays Chicago Piano 1986, I'm Not Hungry But I Like to Eat Blies! 2001, Careless Love 2005; appears on: Voice of Blues, Angela Brown 2000. *Honours:* Critics Choice Award, Maybe I'll Cry, Downbeat Magazine 1983, Illinois Arts Council Grant 1986, Nelson Algren Award 2010, Tower Records Lifetime Achievement Award. *Address:* 2240 N. Magnolia Avenue, Chicago, IL 60614, USA (home). *Telephone:* (773) 472-4787 (home). *Website:* www.erwinhelferpiano.com.

HELL; German DJ and producer; b. (Helmut Josef Geier), 1962, Altenmarkt. *Career:* began DJ career in rural Bavaria; f. International Deejay Gigolos record label 1996; collaborated with Dave Clarke, Laurent Garnier, Jeff Mills, Gary Numan, P Diddy, Sven Väth. *Recordings include:* albums: Geteert und Gefedert 1994, Munich Machine 1998, NY Muscle 2003, Listen to the Hiss, Fun Boy, Teufelswerk 2009, Teufelswerk (House Remixes) 2011. *Honours:* German Dance Award for Best Compilation (for Electronic Body House Music) 2003. *Address:* International Deejay Gigolo Records, Rolandufer 13, 10179

Berlin, Germany (office). *E-mail:* andrea@gigolo-records.de. *Website:* www.djhell.com.

HELLER, (Franz) André; Austrian poet, writer, singer and theatre producer; b. 22 March 1947, Vienna. *Career:* actor 1965–67; Co-founder, Ö3 radio station 1967; recording artist 1968–83; Dir TV documentaries 1978–. *Albums include:* No. 1 1970, Platte 1971, Das war André Heller 1972, Neue Lieder 1973, A Musi Musi A 1974, Bei lebendigem Leib 1975, Abendland 1976, Basta 1978, Bitter und Süß 1978, Ausgerechnet Helle 1979, Heurige und gestrige Lieder (with Helmut Qualtinger) 1979, Verwunschen 1980, Stimmenhören 1983, Narrenlieder 1985, Liebeslieder 1989, Kritische Gesamtausgabe 1967–1991 1991, Ruf und Echo 2003, Bestheller 1967–2007 2008. *Publications include:* Die Ernte der Schlaflosigkeit in Wien 1976, Auf und davon: Erzähites 1979, Schlamassel 1993, Sitzt ana und glaubt er is zwa (with Helmut Qualtinger) 1993, Bilderleben. Öffentliches & Privates 2000, Als ich ein Hund War. Liebesgeschichten und weitere rätselhafte Vorfälle 2001, Mein Garten. Flora-Führer durch den Giardino Botanico Gardone 2001, Augenweide. Der Garten der Gärten 2003, Afrika! Afrika! Das magische Zirkusereignis vom Kontinent des Stauens 2005, Vienna Warhol Vienna 2005, Wie ich lernte, bei mir selbst Kind zu sein 2008, Wienereien oder ein absichtlicher Schicksalsnarr 2012. *Honours:* Culture Award 1993, Amadeus Austrian Music Award 2004. *E-mail:* contact@andreheller.com. *Website:* www.andreheller.com.

HELLER, Jana Louise Greenberg; singer, songwriter and musician (guitar, dulcimer, piano, celestaphone); b. 18 July 1948, California, USA; m. A. Gilhooley 1999. *Education:* Stephens College, Missouri, University of Southern California, USA; UCLA, Santa Monica City College. *Career:* solo work; bands: AAAHS; The Phantoms; concerts, folk music festivals: UK; USA; Poland; Radio: KPFK's Folkscene, Los Angeles, USA; Kroc, USA; Radio Poznan, Poland; BBC Radio 2 (We Stayed In With Jungr and Parker); GLR Radio; London Talkback Radio; BBC Radio Essex Folkscene; Kazu Radio, USA; Brian Willoughby's All Stars; mem. Musicians' Union, PRS. *Recordings:* Mad Waltzing, 1986; Twist and Turn, 1990; Laughing In Crime, 1995. *Honours:* American Song Festival, winner lyric division. *Address:* 2 Friars Close, Wilmslow, Cheshire SK9 5PP, England. *E-mail:* info@janaheller.com. *Website:* www.janaheller.com.

HELLER, Pete, (Stylus Trouble); British producer, remixer and DJ; b. 1965, London. *Education:* Univ. of Manchester. *Career:* mem. Boy's Own collective; remixed (with Terry Farley), Ultra Nate, Primal Scream, Janet Jackson, Happy Mondays; mem. Bocca Juniors, Fire Island, Roach Motel; collaborations with Terry Farley, Andrew Weatherall, Rui Da Silva; f. Phela record label 2005. *Recordings include:* singles: Raise (with Bocca Juniors) 1990, In Your Bones (with Fire Island) 1992, There But For The Grace of God (with Fire Island) 1994, Ultra Flava 1995, The Rising Sun (with Terry Farley) 1999, Big Love 1999, Sputnik One (as Stylus Trouble) 2001, Ultraflava Remixes 2008. *E-mail:* info@peteheller.com (office). *Website:* www.peteheller.com.

HELLQUIST, Mats; Swedish musician (bass, guitar); b. 15 May 1964, Stockholm; one s., two d. *Career:* mem. bob hund 1991–, Bergman Rock; fmr mem. Kitsch Mobile, Three Sterner, Gary Cooper Combo; numerous concerts in Scandinavia, including Roskilde, Lollipop, Ruisrock, Quartfestivalen and Hultsfred festivals; mem. Swedish Performing Rights Soc., SAMI. *Recordings include:* bob hund 1993, Edvin Medvind, 7 1994, I Stället för Musik: förvirring 1996, Omslag: Martin Kann 1996, Düsseldorf 3:53 1996, Ett fall och en lösning 1997, Nu är det väl revolution på gång? 1998, Jag rear ut min själ! Allt skal bort!!! 1998, Helgen V.48 1999, Sover aldrig 1999, Stenåldem kan börja 2001, Ingenting 2002, Folk Music for Folk Who Cannot Behave Like People 2009, The Overexposed Sanctum 2011, Sounds Billion 2012. *Honours:* Swedish Grammy Award for Best Live Act 1994, Best Lyrics 1996. *Website:* www.bobhund.nu.

HELLRIEGEL, Jan, BA; New Zealand musician (piano, guitar), singer, songwriter and actor; b. 2 Sept. 1967, Auckland. *Education:* Univ. of Otago. *Career:* mem. Cassandras Ears Band, Working With Walt; guest vocalist for numerous bands including Straitjacket Fits, The Verlaines, The Mutton Birds; worked on numerous projects including Project Runway; Man. Dir Blind Date Records 2009–; Partner, Aeroplane Music Services 2011–. *Recordings include:* solo albums: It's My Sin 1993, Tremble 1995, All Grown Up 2009, Kiwi Hit Disc 2010; with Cassandras Ears Band: Private Wasteland (EP) 1990, Your Estimation 1992 (EP), The Cassandra's Ears Story 2010; with Working With Walt: The Prophet 1984, 5 Sides (EP) 1990. *Honours:* Songwriter of the Year 1993, Most Promising Female Vocalist 1993. *Website:* www.janhellriegel.com.

HELMS, Mickey; American composer; b. 4 Sept. 1972, California, USA. *Education:* AA, De Anza College, 1992; BM, San Jose State University, 1997. *Career:* composer; mem, BMI; International Computer Music Association; Society of Electro-Acoustic Music in the United States; Society of Composers. *Compositions:* Whispering Modulations, 1996; Variations On A Theme By Chris Mann, 1996; Music For Tuba and Piano, 1998. *Recordings:* albums: Frog Peak Collaborations Project 1998, Music From Cream 1998. *Address:* 244 Corral Ave, Sunnyvale, CA 94086, USA. *E-mail:* mhelms2@aol.com. *Website:* www.sjsu.edu/depts/composersforum/composers/helms/index.html.

HELSON, Robert (Bob); British music (drums, percussion); *Drummer/Organizer, FringeFreeMusic;* b. 20 Aug. 1949, Bristol, England; s. of Donald Helson and Freda Helson; m. Christine Bridges. *Education:* drum lessons

with Geoff Smith. *Career:* drummer with Plasma early 1970s, Bullit 1974–90; appearances with Bullit include Bracknell Festival 1986, Le Mans Jazz Festival 1987; Will Menter's Wind and Fingers, appearing at Bristol Arnolfini and Dunkirk Jazz Festival 1976; with Both Hands Free 1976–82; with Community, appearing at Palais de Beaux Arts, Brussels and Arnolfini 1980–81; with Out Loud 1984–87; with Keith Tippett's Canoe 1984–85; Drummer/Organizer, FringeFreeMusic, performances with Phil Gibbs guitar, Mark Langford tenor saxophone and bass clarinet, Paul Anstey double bass. *Dance:* dance and percussion duet with dancer Beppie Blankert (Bristol Arnolfini) 1981. *Radio:* perfomances on BBC Radio 3's Jazz in Britain, with Both Hands Free 1979, Steve Mulligan Quartet 1983, 1984, Out Loud 1986, Bullit 1987. *Recordings include:* with Both Hands Free: Use From the Pocket 1978; solo: Noise Reduction 1979, Will Menter's Community 1981, The Foul Tempered Clatterer (percussion improvisations) 2008, Fringe Music CD with Mark Langford, Phil Gibbs and Paul Anstey. *Address:* Basement Flat, 34 Cornwallis Crescent, Clifton, Bristol, BS8 4PH, England. *E-mail:* bobhelson@yahoo.co.uk.

HEMINGWAY, Dave; British singer; b. 20 Sept. 1960, Hull, Humberside. *Career:* mem. (drummer), The Housemartins 1987–88; founder mem., The Beautiful South 1989–2007. *Recordings include:* albums: with The Housemartins: The People Who Grinned Themselves To Death 1987, Now That's What I Call Quite Good 1988; with The Beautiful South: Welcome To The Beautiful South 1989, Choke 1990, 0898 1992, Miaow 1994, Blue Is The Colour 1996, Quench 1998, Painting It Red 2000, Gaze 2002, Golddiggas, Headnodders & Pholk Songs 2004, Superbi 2006. *Current Management:* SJM Concerts, St Matthews, Liverpool Road, Manchester, M3 4NQ, England. *Telephone:* (161) 907-3443. *Fax:* (161) 907-3446.

HEMMINGS, Luke Robert; Australian singer and guitarist; b. 16 July 1996, Sydney, NSW. *Education:* Norwest Christian Coll. *Career:* mem. 5 Seconds of Summer 2011–; released debut EP Unplugged 2012; supported One Direction on worldwide tours 2013, 2014; signed to Capitol label 2013. *Recordings:* albums: 5 Seconds of Summer 2014, Sounds Good, Feels Good 2015. *Honours:* Billboard Mid-Year Music Breakout Star Award 2014, Kerrang! Best Int. Newcomer Award 2014, MTV Award for Favorite Breakthrough Band 2014, MTV Europe Music Award for Best Australian Act 2014, 2015, MTV Video Music Award for Best Lyric Video 2014, for Song of Summer 2015, Teen Choice Awards for Breakout Group and Music Group 2014. *Current Management:* c/o Modest Management, Matrix Complex, 91 Peterborough Road, London, SW6 3BU, England. *E-mail:* info@modestmanagement.com. *Website:* www.modestmanagement.com; www.5sos.com.

HEMMINGS, Paul; British musician (guitar, lap steel, mandolin). *Career:* fmr mem. the La's, The Onset, The Australians, Sensurround, Lightning Seeds, The Floatation Project; tours of the UK, Europe, the USA; mem. Musicians' Union, PRS; Partner, Viper Label. *Recordings include:* albums: Pool of Life (with The Onset) 1988, Timeless Melody (with The La's) 1990, Electric Mothers of Invention (with Neuro # Project) 1993, Pool of Life Revisited (with The Onset) 1994, The Future Played Backwards (with Otaku No Denki) 2003, Fierce Truth and Fortune (with Chris Elliot) 2007, Rogue State (with Mike Badger) 2011; with The Floatation Project: Sonic Stories 2005, Sounds from the Solar System 2006, Made out of Worldly Shapes 2011, Late Night Blue 2011. *Honours:* two BRIT Awards. *Address:* The Viper Label, PO Box 48, Liverpool, L17 7JE, England (office). *Telephone:* (151) 281-6893 (office). *Fax:* (151) 281-6893 (office). *E-mail:* theviperlabel@hotmail.co.uk (office). *Website:* www.the-viper-label.co.uk (office).

HENDERSON, Scott; American composer and musician (guitar); b. 26 Aug. 1954, West Palm Beach, FL. *Education:* Florida Atlantic University, Musicians' Institute. *Career:* touring, recording 1981–; worked for three years with Jean-Luc Ponty, one year with Chick Corea, four years with Joe Zawinul, ten years with Tribal Tech (co-leader with Gary Willis), five years with Scott Henderson trio. *Recordings include:* albums: with Tribal Tech: Spears 1985, Dr Hee 1987, Nomad 1990, Tribal Tech 1991, Illicit 1992, Face First 1993, Reality Check 1995, Primal Tracks, Thick 1999, Rocket Science 2000; solo: Dog Party 1994, Tore Down House 1997, Well to the Bone 2002, Scott Henderson Live! 2005; with Vital Tech Tones: Vital Tech Tones 1998, VTT2 2000; with Joe Zawinul: The Immigrants 1988, Black Water 1989; with Chick Corea: Elektrik Band 1986; with Jeff Berlin: Crossroads 1999; with Elvis Schoenberg and the Orchestre Surreal: Manic Voodoo Lady 2009. *Publications:* The Scott Henderson Guitar Book, Best of Scott Henderson, Scott Henderson Jazz Guitar Chord System. *Honours:* Guitar World magazine Best Jazz Guitarist 1990, Guitar Player magazine 1991, Guitar Player magazine Best Blues Album (for Dog Party) 1994. *Address:* 6044 Buena Vista, Los Angeles, CA 90042, USA (office). *Website:* www.scotthenderson.net (office).

HENDRICKS, Jon; American singer and lyricist; b. 16 Sept. 1921, Newark, Ohio. *Career:* sang on local radio in Toledo, Ohio; after serving in military during WWII, switched to jazz playing drums and writing songs; composition 'I Want You To Be My Baby' recorded by Louis Jordan 1952; made own first recordings in 1957 with the Dave Lambert Singers; teamed up with Lambert and Annie Ross 1957, forming vocal trio Lambert Hendricks and Ross; toured and recorded together (Ross replaced by Yolande Bevan 1962) –1964; moved to Europe 1965; returned as jazz critic for the San Francisco Chronicle during early 1970s; began teaching jazz; formed The Hendricks Family (with wife and two children); taught at California State Univ. and Univ. of California; Prof. of Jazz Studies, Univ. of Toledo 2000; mem. Kennedy Center Honors Cttee.

Compositions include: transformed instrumental solo parts of bebop jazz instrumentals by writing lyrics for classic works including: I Remember Clifford, Airgin, Centrepiece, Little Pony, Sing Joy Spring, Birdland. *Recordings include:* with Lambert Hendricks and Ross: Sing A Song of Basie, 1957, The Swingers, Sing Along With Basie 1958, The Hottest New Group In Jazz 1959, Lambert Hendricks and Ross Sing Ellington 1960, The Way-Out Voices of Lambert Hendricks and Ross 1961, The Real Ambassadors 1962; with Lambert Hendricks and Bevan: Live At Basin Street, At Newport '63, Havin' A Ball At The Village Gate 1963; solo: A Good Git-Together, New York New York 1959, Evolution of The Blues Song 1960, Fast Livin' Blues 1961, In Person At The Trident, Salute To Joao Gilberto 1963, Cloudburst 1972, Tell Me The Truth 1975, September Songs 1976, Love 1981, Freddie Freeloader 1990, In Person 1991, Boppin' At The Blue Note 1993, Birdmen and Birdsongs 2000. *Films appearances:* Jazz Is Our Religion 1971, Hommage a Cole Porter, People I Know 2002, No One But Me (documentary) 2012. *Television includes:* Somewhere to Lay My Weary Head (won Iris, Emmy and Peabody Award). *Honours:* Chevalier, Ordre nat. de la Legion d'Honneur 2004, won numerous awards, Grammy Award for Best Singer, Gov.'s Special Recognition Award, Univ. of Toledo; inducted into ASCAP Jazz Wall of Fame 2009.

HENDRICKS, Michele; American singer; b. 27 Sept. 1953, New York; m. Pierre Bornard 1992. *Education:* studied music at college. *Career:* appearances at North Sea Festival, Monterey Festival, Montréal Festival, Vienna, Pori, Marciac, Juan Les Pins, Nice, Crest, Mt Fuji; television appearances; has sung with: Jon Hendricks, Buddy Rich, Stan Getz, Count Basie, Benny Golson, Slide Hampton, George Benson, Al Jarreau, Bobby McFerrin, Roland Hannah, Herbie Hancock, Freddie Hubbard; faculty mem., Spoleto Vocal Jazz Workshop; mem. ASCAP, Shellrose Music (ASCAP). *Recordings include:* albums: solo: Carryin' On 1987, Keepin' Me Satisfied 1988, Me and My Shadow 1990; other appearances: Live At Ronnie Scott's With Buddy Rich; Live with Jon Hendricks and Company; The Peacocks with Stan Getz and Jimmy Rowles; Vocal Summit; Santa's Bag; Second Impression; Boppin' At The Blue Note; A Little Bit of Ella. *Address:* 182 rue Nationale, 75013 Paris, France.

HENDY, Jonathan (John) Darren; British singer; b. 26 March 1971, Barking, Essex; one d. *Career:* mem. East 17 1992–; numerous tv and live appearances. *Recordings include:* albums: Walthamstow 1993, Steam 1994, Up All Night 1996, Around the World – The Journey So Far 1996, Resurrection 1998, Dark Light 2012; singles: House of Love 1992, Deep 1993, West End Girls 1993, It's Alright 1993, Around The World 1994, Steam 1994, Stay Another Day 1994, Let It Rain 1995, Thunder 1995, Do U Still 1996, If You Ever (with Gabrielle) 1996, Hey Child 1997, Each Time 1998, Betcha Can't Wait 1999. *Current Management:* c/o Mission Control Artists Agency, Unit 3, City Business Centre, Saint Olav's Court, Lower Road, Rotherhithe, London, SE16 2XB, England. *Telephone:* (20) 7252-3001. *Fax:* (20) 7252-2225. *E-mail:* info@missioncontrol.net. *Website:* www .missioncontrol.net.

HENLEY, Don; American musician (drums), singer and songwriter; b. 22 July 1947, Linden, Tex. *Career:* mem. The Four Speeds 1963, Shiloh 1970; Founder-mem. The Eagles 1971–80, 1994–; solo artist 1982–; Founder-mem. Walden Woods Project; f. non-profit Caddo Lake Inst. 1993; co-f. Recording Artists Coalition 2000. *Recordings include:* albums: with The Eagles: The Eagles 1972, Desperado 1973, On The Border 1974, One Of These Nights 1975, Hotel California (Grammy Award for Record of the Year 1978, American Music Award for Favorite Pop/Rock Album 1977) 1976, The Long Run 1979, Hell Freezes Over 1994, Long Road out of Eden 2007, The Studio Albums 1972-1979 2013; solo: I Can't Stand Still 1982, Building The Perfect Beast 1984, The End Of Innocence 1989, Actual Miles: Henley's Greatest Hits 1995, Inside Job 2000, The Very Best of Don Henley 2009. *Honours:* Grammy Awards for Best Pop Vocal 1976, Best Rock Vocal 1986, for Best Country Performance by a Duo or Group with Vocals (for How Long) 2008, for Best Pop Instrumental Performance (for I Dreamed There Was No War) 2009, American Music Award 1981, MTV Music Video Awards 1985, 1990, Boston Music Awards Special Recognition 1992, Nordoff-Robbins Music Therapy Lifetime Achievement Award (with The Eagles) 2006. *Current Management:* c/o Irving Azoff, Revolution, 8900 Wilshire Blvd, Suite 200, Beverly Hills, CA 90211, USA. *Website:* www.donhenley.com.

HENNES, Peter Michael; American musician (guitar, bass) and educator; b. 25 Feb. 1954, Great Lakes, Illinois. *Education:* Wayne State University, 1972; University of Michigan, 1973–74; Professional diploma, Berklee College of Music, Boston, 1978. *Career:* Musician with numerous artistes including: Frank Sinatra; Liza Minnelli; Perry Como; Anthony Newley; Marvin Hamlisch; Musician, touring stage productions including: Grease; Evita; A Chorus Line; 42nd Street; La Cage Aux Folles; Instructor, Jazz Studies, Georgia State University School of Music, 1982–88; mem, AFofM. *Telephone:* (847) 756-2050. *E-mail:* peter@peterhennes.com. *Website:* www.peterhennes .com.

HENNING, Ann-Marie Elisabeth; Sweden jazz musician, composer and arranger; b. 2 Dec. 1952, Stockholm. *Education:* Royal Acad. of Music, Stockholm, Berkelee Coll. of Music, USA. *Career:* tours in Sweden and Europe with rock band NQB 1973–74; mem. jazz-rock group Wave Play 1978; Founder-mem. Blue Cluster 1987–92, Red Cluster 1992–2000, Bitches Brew 2000–05, Ann-Marie Henning Sextet featuring Gustavo Bergalli 2010–; pianist, Big Band Satin Dolls; Piano Lecturer, Jazz Dept, Kungl. Musikhögs-

kolan, Stockholm; mem. Swedish Composers' Org., Swedish Composers of Popular Music, Swedish Jazz Musicians' Org. *Compositions include:* April Light for Big Band, The Trees Are Listening, Waltz for Evert, The Rubber Jolly Boat, Going to Brazil, Morning Swim, Point of No Return, Mason Meets Mingus. *Recordings include:* Blue Cluster 1989, Les Misérables 1990, Tidal Dreams 1997. *Publication includes:* The Real Swede (co-author). *Address:* Västra Finnbodavägen 9B, 13172 Nacka, Sweden (office). *Telephone:* (70) 473-63-88 (office). *E-mail:* annmariehenning@tele2.se (office). *Website:* www .annmariehenning.se.

HENOCQ, Benjamin; French musician (drums), singer and songwriter; b. 1969. *Education:* Conservatoire du Centre de Paris, Ecole Agostini, IACP, studied with Daniel Humair, Paul Motian, Keith Copeland. *Career:* began studying music at age 4; first concert at age 12; has played with Jean-Christophe Beney Quartet, Jean-Christophe Cholet Quartet, David Patrois Quintet, Philippe Sellam Quintet, Les Standardistes (funk octet), Phantastique Orchestre Modulaire, Quoi de Neuf Docteur Big Band, KARTET; played in numerous clubs in Paris, festivals in France; played with Eric Le Lann, Stéphane Belmondo, Robin Eubanks, Glenn Ferris, Tommy Smith, Red Holloway, Rick Margitza, François Janneau, Lionel Belmondo, Sylvain Beuf, Geoffroy de Mazure, Peter Osborne, Olivier Ker-Ourio, Philip Catherine, Louis Winsberg, Harold Land, Laurent de Wilde, Franck Amsallem, Andy Emler, Denis Badault, Wayne Dockery, Henri Texier, Michel Benita, Patrice Caratini, Paul Breslin, Jean-Marc Thorès; teacher IACP 1986–88; Founder-mem. (with Pierre de Bethmann and Christophe Wallemme) PRYSM. *Recordings include:* Le Retour, Quoi de Neuf Docteur Big Band 1991, Hask, KARTET 1992, En Attendent La Pluie, Quoi de Neuf Docteur Big Band 1993, AL'Envers, Quoi de Neuf Docteur Big Band 1994, Pression, KARTET 1995, La Compil, Instant Charirés 1995, PRYSM, PRYSM 1995. *Honours:* First Prize, La Défense Nat. Jazz Contest 1994, Soloist Award, La Défense Nat. Jazz Contest 1994, Django d'Or 1998. *Website:* www.parafono.gr.

HENRIKSON, Richard Ralph, BS, MusM; American composer, lyricist and musician (violin); b. 27 Nov. 1948, Portland, OR. *Education:* Juilliard School of Music. *Career:* violinist, various orchestras and chamber ensembles 1970–; violinist, Barnum, Broadway 1980–82; Musical Dir, numerous stage productions, including Singing in the Rain, Sweet Charity, Me and My Girl, Fiddler on the Roof, Les Misérables 1991–; Musical Dir, violinist for numerous artists, including Tom Jones, Billy Ocean, George Benson, Freddie Jackson, Jeffrey Osborne, Stephanie Mills, Gregg Allman, Rick Wakeman, Paul Anka; mem. ASCAP, AFofM, NARAS, Recording Musicians of USA and Canada. *Recordings include:* albums with: Music Minus One, The Tango Project, Hampton String Quartet; violinist on film soundtracks: The Wiz; Silkwood, The Cotton Club, When Harry Met Sally, Do The Right Thing.

HENRY, Jay Edward; American recording engineer, producer, consultant and audio educator; b. 17 Feb. 1950, Brooklyn, NY. *Education:* Cabrillo Coll., San Francisco State Univ. *Career:* has worked with major recording artists and labels since 1980s; more than 80 gold and platinum albums and awards, work includes albums for Universal, MCA, Warner Bros., Columbia, CBS, Epic and Arista; has worked on projects with Prince, Living Colour, LL Cool J, Heavy-D, Teddy Riley, Shannon, Bell Biv Devoe and Public Enemy; work has consistently appeared in the top of the record charts (Top Pop 100, Hot Singles, R&B Albums and Singles) of Billboard Magazine; Voting mem. Nat. Acad. of Recording Arts and Sciences; Founding mem. Latin Acad. of Recording Arts and Sciences. *Recordings include:* albums include: with LL Cool J: Bigger and Deffer 1987, Walking With A Panther 1989; with Heavy D: Livin' Large 1987; with Public Enemy: It Takes A Nation of Millions 1987; with Run DMC: Tougher Than Leather 1988; with Defunkt: Defunkt In America 1988; with Living Colour: Vivid 1989; with Big Mountain: Things to Come 1999. *Honours:* including eight Top 10 albums, eight Top 10 singles, six No. 1 Albums, three No. 1 singles, 45 gold albums and singles, 20 platinum albums, three double platinum albums, three platinum singles, two triple platinum albums, one quadruple platinum album, three AMG Best in Genre Awards, seven AMG Best of Artist Awards, five Golden Reel Awards for Excellence in Recording, Int. Producer Award 1990, work has been inducted into the Rock & Roll Hall of Fame. *Address:* Performing Arts Department, Southwestern College, 900 Otay Lakes Road, Chula Vista, CA 91910, USA (office). *Telephone:* (616) 421-6700 (office). *E-mail:* studio@swccd.edu (office). *Website:* www.swccd.edu (office); www.recording-arts.org.

HENRY, Michael Anthony, (Milverson), ARCM, DipRCM; British composer, arranger, singer, musical director and clarinettist; b. 10 March 1963, London, England; s. of Vernon Henry and Millecent Butler. *Education:* Centre for Young Musicians, Royal Coll. of Music, London. *Career:* singer, songwriter with Buddy Curtess and The Grasshoppers 1985–89, with The Flying Pickets 1991–95, 2002–; singer, songwriter, co-producer with Cut 2 Taste 1994–99; vocalist, composer with 15-piece contemporary choir The Shout 1999–; singer songwriter with Casino 2005–09; Musical Dir, The Unity Project 2009–12; recorded vocals for Diana Ross, Robbie Williams, Chrissie Hynde, Billy Bragg, Michael Ball, José Carreras; live backing vocals for Cliff Richard 2000, Lesley Garrett 2004, Barry Manilow 2006, Michael Ball 2006, Chaka Khan 2007, Jamelia 2007, George Michael 2009; tours include support to Roy Orbison 1985, backing vocalist, Pet Shop Boys 1989; support to concerts with Beach Boys, Wembley 1986, Bo Diddley, Hammersmith Odeon 1987, Dr Feelgood 1987, Glastonbury main stage 1987, Ray Charles 1993, Michael Jackson tour 1997; radio and TV appearances include The Tube 1987, Saturday Live 1987, Ruby Wax 1988, Meltdown 1988, BBC 1 and Channel 4 schools workshops

1991–93, Cue The Music 1995; opera performances 1991–93; presenter, Young Musician of the Year 1992; judge, Choir of the Year 1993; sang role of Bluette, The Official Tribute to the Blues Brothers, London 2000–01; featured composer for opera Family Matters, Tête-à-Tête 2003, 2004; singer in Honda Choir for Honda Civic advertisement 2006; featured vocalist in Scott Walker's theatre-piece Drifting & Tilting 2008; Vocal Music Dir for Soyinka's Death & The King's Horseman (Nat. Theatre) 2009, Fela! (Nat. Theatre) 2010, Emperor and Galilean (Nat. Theatre) 2011; Music Dir for Feast (Young Vic) 2013; Asst Man. Dir on The Amen Corner (Nat. Theatre) 2014; Composer and Music Dir for Mr Burns (Almeida Theatre) 2014, Boi Boi Is Dead (West Yorkshire Playhouse) 2015; Deputy Music Dir and vocalist/percussionist on Merchant of Venice (Globe) 2015; Music Dir and performer on May Contain Food (Protein Dance, UK tour) 2015–16; mem. Musicians' Union, Performing Right Soc., Equity, PPL. *Compositions:* Wind Quartet No. 1, Say Ave For Me for saxophone and piano (performed on BBC Radio 3), Three Interludes for saxophone and piano, Birdwatching for clarinet quartet 1998, Stand for 16 voices (BBC Proms) 2006, Refractions for clarinet quartet and percussion 2006, The Rocket Symphony for 500 voices and fireworks (co-composer), for opening ceremony of Linz European Capital of Culture 2009, Moi-Mwah 2010, Circus Tricks (opera) for Tête a Tête 2012, Jilted 2012, Mr Burns (Act 3) 2014, Boi Boi Is Dead 2015. *Films:* vocals on soundtrack for Ray Charles biopic 2004, The Da Vinci Code 2006, RCVR 2011. *Recordings include:* Caravan, John Harle, all vocals 1990, Rain Song, Moodswings 1990, Real Love, Driza Bone 1991, The Warning, Flying Pickets 1993, 1994, backing vocals for Diana Ross, Robbie Williams, Michael Ball 2001, Next Generation (Live from Hamburg) 2003, Everyday 2004, Big Mouth 2008, Only Yule 2010; album: with Casino: That's The Way 2009. *Honours:* winner of composition prizes: Joseph Horowitz; Stanford, Cornelius Cardew, Time Out Magazine Best Live Act (with Buddy Curtess) 1986, 1987, (with The Shout) 2007. *E-mail:* milverson@ btinternet.com (office). *Website:* www.milversonmusic.com (office).

HENSHALL, Ruthie; British singer, actor and dancer; b. 1967, Bromley, Kent; m. Tim Howar; two c. *Education:* Laine Theatre Arts, Surrey. *Career:* joined British tour of A Chorus Line, followed by appearances in Cats, Miss Saigon, Children of Eden; spent a summer at the Chichester Festival Theatre; returned to West End, London, with subsequent appearances including Les Misérables, Crazy For You, She Loves Me, Peggy Sue Got Married, Chicago, Fosse, The Woman in White, Marguerite; joined New York cast of Chicago, leading to other Broadway roles, including Putting It Together, Ziegfeld Follies of 1939, The Vagina Monologues, The Other Woman 2006, Stairway to Paradise 2007, Marguerite, Chicago 2009, Blithe Spirit 2011, Side by Side by Sondheim 2012, Guys and Dolls 2012; US and UK TV credits include: Law and Order, Deadline, Mysteries of 71st Street, Get Back, Dancing on Ice (judge), The Case 2011, Wizards vs Aliens 2012. *Recordings include:* cast recordings: Children of Eden 1991, Crazy For You 1993, Godspell 1993 (studio cast), She Loves Me 1994, Divorce Me Darling 1997, Chicago 1998, Marguerite 2008; solo: Love Is Here To Stay 1994, Pilgrim 2001, Ruthie Henshall Sings Gershwin. *Publication:* So You Want to Be in Musicals? (with Daniel Bowling) 2012. *Honours:* Olivier Award for Best Actress in a Musical (for She Loves Me) 1994. *Current Management:* The Agency Group, 361-373 City Road, London, EC1V 1PQ, England. *Telephone:* (20) 7278-3331. *Fax:* (20) 7837-4672. *E-mail:* AngieRance@theagencygroup.com. *Website:* www.theagencygroup.com; www .ruthiehenshall.com.

HENSLEY, Ken; British musician (guitar, keyboards), singer, record producer and songwriter; b. 24 Aug. 1945, London. *Career:* mem. Kit and The Saracens, Jimmy Brown Sound, The Gods 1965–69, Head Machine 1969, Toe Fat 1969, Weed 1971, Shotgun 1980; mem. rock group Uriah Heep 1969–80, rock group Blackfoot 1981–84; Dir Artistic Relations St Louis Music Inc. 1987–2001. *Recordings include:* albums: with Uriah Heep: Very 'Eavy Very 'Umble 1970, Salisbury 1971, Look At Yourself 1971, Demons and Wizards 1972, Magician's Birthday 1972, Live 1973, Sweet Freedom 1973, Wonderworld 1974, Return To Fantasy 1975, Best Of 1975, High and Mighty 1976, Firefly 1977, Innocent Victim 1978, Fallen Angel 1978, Conquest 1980; with Blackfoot: Siogo 1983, Vertical Smiles 1984; with The Hensley Lawton: The Return 2001, Salisbury Live 2001; with W.A.S.P: The Headless Children 1989; with John Wetton: More Than Conquerors 2002, One Way Or Another 2002; solo: Proud Words On A Dusty Shelf 1973, Eager To Please 1975, Free Spirit 1980, From Time To Time 1994, A Glimpse Of Glory 1999, Running Blind 2002, The Last Dance 2003, Cold Autumn Sunday 2005, Inside The Mystery 2006, Love & Other Mysteries 2012, Live Tales 2013. *E-mail:* webmaster@ken -hensley.com. *Website:* www.ken-hensley.com.

HERBERT, Gwyneth; British jazz singer and songwriter; b. 1981, Wimbledon, London. *Education:* Durham Univ. *Career:* mem. Wasted Minds; formed jazz duo Black Coffee with guitarist Will Rutter; appeared at London Jazz Festival 2004; joined Buck Claton Legacy Band 2012. *Recordings include:* albums: First Songs 2003, Bittersweet And Blue 2004, Between Me and the Wardrobe 2007, All the Ghosts 2009, Clangers and Mash 2011, The Sea Cabinet 2013. *Honours:* Stiles and Drewe Song of the Year Award (for Lovely London Town) 2010. *Current Management:* c/o Peter Conway Management, 158 Westcombe Hill, Blackheath, London, SE3 7DH, England. *E-mail:* info@peterconwaymanagement.com. *Website:* www .peterconwaymanagement.com. *E-mail:* gwyneth.herbert@googlemail.com. *Website:* www.gwynethherbert.com.

HERBERT, Matthew, (Doctor Rockit, Herbert, Radio Boy, Wishmountain); British musician, producer and songwriter; *Creative Director, Radiophonic Workshop, Accidental Records*; b. 1971, Kent, England. *Education:* Univ. of Exeter. *Career:* classically trained pianist; began playing violin and piano aged four; sang in school choir and played with orchestras aged seven; while a theatre student at univ., built own home studio; experimented with wide range of sounds (electro-organic music) collected, sampled and processed from the house and home: washing machines, toasters and toothbrushes; first large public performance 1995; wrote a manifesto, 'Personal Contract for the Composition Of Music (PCCOM) (Incorporating the Manifesto of Mistakes)' with specific rules to define compositional methods 2000, manifesto prohibits use of any pre-recorded musical sources, as well as any synthetic sounds that imitate acoustic instruments, while accidental sounds or errors should influence the process of production; est. own record label Accidental; f. Matthew Herbert Big Band 2002–; recordings often feature Dani Siciliano on vocals; live shows, including Sonar in Barcelona, Montreux jazz festival, Roskilde Festival in Denmark; music increasingly political in recent years; produced 'Ruby Blue', debut solo album of Moloko singer Roisin Murphy 2005; 723 items sampled on album Scale 2006, including coffins, petrol pumps, meteorites, an RAF Tornado bomber, and a person being sick outside a banquet for a notorious London arms fair; has also produced and remixed artists including Björk, REM, John Cale, Roisin Murphy, Yoko Ono and Serge Gainsbourg; Creative Dir Radiophonic Workshop, Accidental Records; recent musical works included 'One Pig' following the whole life of a pig and 'The End Of Silence' made out of a five-second recording of a bomb being dropped by a Gaddafi war plane in Libya. *Play:* The Hush (Royal Nat. Theatre, London) 2013. *Film score:* Life In A Day. *Recordings include:* albums: Parts 1, 2 and 3 (as Herbert) 1996, 100 Lbs (as Herbert) 1996, The Music of Sound (as Doctor Rockit) 1996, Around the House (as Herbert) 1998, Wishmountain is Dead (as Wishmountain) 1998, Indoor Fireworks (as Doctor Rockit) 2000, Bodily Functions (as Herbert) 2001, Goodbye Swingtime (with Matthew Herbert Big Band) 2003, Plat du Jour 2004, Scale (as Herbert) 2006, Score (as Herbert) 2007, There's Me and There's You (with Matthew Herbert Big Band) 2008, Mahler Symphony X 2010, One Club 2010, One One 2010, Royal Wedding Part 2 2011, One Pig 2011, Tesco (as Wishmountain) 2012, Herbert Complete (as Herbert) 2013, The End Of Silence 2013. *Current Management:* c/o Solar Management, Unit 10, Union Wharf, 23 Wenlock Road, London, N1 7SB, England. *Telephone:* (20) 7794-3388. *E-mail:* gunther@solarmanagement.co .uk. *Website:* www.solarmanagement.co.uk. *Address:* c/o Accidental Records, Unit 10, Union Wharf, 23 Wenlock Road, London, N1 7SB, England (office). *Website:* www.accidentalrecords.com (office); www.matthewherbert.com.

HERMAN, Gerald (Jerry); American composer, lyricist and pianist; b. 10 July 1931, New York; s. of Harry Herman and Ruth Herman. *Education:* Parsons School of Design, Univ. of Miami. *Career:* made Broadway debut 1960. *Stage shows:* as composer: I Feel Wonderful 1954, Nightcap (also director) 1958, Parade (also dir) 1960, From A to Z 1960, Madame Aphrodite 1961, Milk and Honey 1961, Hello, Dolly! (won 10 Tony Awards including Best Composer and Lyricist) 1964, Mame 1966, Dear World 1969, Mack and Mabel 1974, The Grand Tour 1979, La Cage aux Folles (Tony Award for Best Musical) 1984 (Tony Award for Best Revival of a Musical 2004, 2010), Jerry's Girls 1985, An Evening with Jerry Herman (Theatre World Special Award 1999) 1998, Showtune 2003. *Television:* as composer: Hello, Dolly! 1969, Mame 1974, Mrs Santa Claus 1996. *Recordings:* albums: Hello, Jerry! 1965, The New Sound of Broadway 1965; cast recordings of songs: Milk and Honey 1961, Hello, Dolly! 1964 (film soundtrack 1969), Mame 1966, Dear World 1969, Mack and Mabel 1974, A Day in Hollywood, a Night in the Ukraine 1980, La Cage aux Folles 1983. *Honours:* Special Tony Award for Lifetime Achievement in the Theatre 2009, Kennedy Center Honor 2010. *Current Management:* William Morris Agency, 151 El Camino Drive, Beverly Hills, CA 90212-2775, USA. *Telephone:* (310) 285-9000. *E-mail:* jerry@jerryherman.com (office). *Website:* www.jerryherman.com.

HERMITAGE, Richard; British artist agent, manager and record company executive; *Managing Director, War Zones and Associates*; b. 20 Oct. 1955, London. *Career:* fmr agent for artists, including The Human League, Steel Pulse, ABC, INXS, UB40, Psychedelic Furs, Aswad, Daf, The Art of Noise, The Residents; agencies worked at include March Artists, TKA, Asgard, ITB, Fair Warning 1974–85; management for artists, including The Human League, Pale Saints, The Darling Buds, Slowdive, The Boo Radleys, Teenage Fanclub, Denim 1986–93; Gen. Man., record co. 4AD, 1994–95; currently Man. Dir, War Zones and Assocs man. agency. *Address:* War Zones and Associates, 33 Kersley Rd, London N16 0NT, England (office). *Telephone:* (20) 7249-2894 (office). *Fax:* (20) 7254-3729 (office). *E-mail:* wz33@aol.com (office).

HERNÁNDEZ, Eduardo; Mexican musician (accordion, saxophone, six-string bass) and singer; b. Rosa Morada, Sinaloa; brother of Jorge Hernández, Hernán Hernández, Luis Hernández, and cousin of Oscar Lara. *Career:* mem. Los Tigres del Norte (norteño-style band) 1971–. *Film:* La Misma Luna 2008. *Recordings include:* albums: Cuquita 1971, El Cheque 1972, Contrabando y Traición 1974, La Banda del Carro Rojo 1975, La Tumba del Mojado – Internacionalmente Norteños 1976, Pueblo Querido 1976, Vivan los Mojados 1977, Numero Ocho 1978, El Tahúr 1979, Plaza Garibaldi 1980, Un Día a la Vez 1981, Padre Nuestro – éxitos para siempre 1982, Carrera Contra la Muerte 1983, Jaula de Oro 1983, A ti Madrecita 1985, El Otro México 1986, Gracias América – Sin Fronteras (Grammy Award for Best Album (Regional Mexican Music Category) 1987) 1986, Idolos del Pueblo 1988, Corridos Prohibidos 1989, Triunfo Sólido – mi buena suerte 1989, Para Adoloridos 1990, Incansables! 1991, Con Sentimiento y Sabor – Tan Bonita 1992, Una Noche con los Tigres del Norte 1992, La Garra de... 1993, Los dos Plebes 1994, El Ejemplo 1995, Unidos Para Siempre 1996, Así como tú 1997, Jefe de Jefes 1997, Herencia de Familia 1999, De Paisano a Paisano 2000, Uniendo Fronteras 2001, La Reina del Sur 2002, Pacto de Sangre (Latin Grammy Award for Best Norteño Album) 2004, Directo al Corazón 2005, Historias que Contar (Grammy Award for Best Norteño Album 2007) 2006, Detalles y Emociones 2007, Raíces (Grammy Award for Best Norteño Album 2009) 2008, Tu Noche Con...El Tigres del Norte (Grammy Award for Best Norteño Album 2010) 2009, La Granja 2009, Los Tigres Del Norte and Friends (Grammy Award for Best Banda or Norteño Album 2012) 2011. *Honours:* Academia Nacional de la Música Mexicana Award 2003, Oye! Homenaje a la Trayectoria Artistica and Award for Best Norteño Group 2003, BMI Latin Award for Songwriting Icons 2007. *Address:* Los Tigres del Norte, 99 Almaden Blvd, Suite 333, San Jose, CA 95113, USA (office). *E-mail:* management@ lostigresdelnorte.com (office). *Website:* www.lostigresdelnorte.com (office).

HERNÁNDEZ, Hernán; Mexican musician (electric bass) and singer; b. Rosa Morada, Sinaloa; brother of Jorge Hernández, Eduardo Hernández, Luis Hernández, and cousin of Oscar Lara. *Career:* mem. Los Tigres del Norte (norteño-style band) 1971–. *Film:* La Misma Luna 2008. *Recordings include:* albums: Cuquita 1971, El Cheque 1972, Contrabando y Traición 1974, La Banda del Carro Rojo 1975, La Tumba del Mojado – Internacionalmente Norteños 1976, Pueblo Querido 1976, Vivan los Mojados 1977, Numero Ocho 1978, El Tahúr 1979, Plaza Garibaldi 1980, Un Día a la Vez 1981, Padre Nuestro – éxitos para siempre 1982, Carrera Contra la Muerte 1983, Jaula de Oro 1983, A ti Madrecita 1985, El Otro México 1986, Gracias América – Sin Fronteras (Grammy Award for Best Album (Regional Mexican Music Category) 1987) 1986, Idolos del Pueblo 1988, Corridos Prohibidos 1989, Triunfo Sólido – mi buena suerte 1989, Para Adoloridos 1990, Incansables! 1991, Con Sentimiento y Sabor – Tan Bonita 1992, Una Noche con los Tigres del Norte 1992, La Garra de... 1993, Los dos Plebes 1994, El Ejemplo 1995, Unidos Para Siempre 1996, Así como tú 1997, Jefe de Jefes 1997, Herencia de Familia 1999, De Paisano a Paisano 2000, Uniendo Fronteras 2001, La Reina del Sur 2002, Pacto de Sangre (Latin Grammy Award for Best Norteño Album) 2004, Directo al Corazón 2005, Historias que Contar (Grammy Award for Best Norteño Album 2007) 2006, Detalles y Emociones 2007, Raíces (Grammy Award for Best Norteño Album 2009) 2008, Tu Noche Con...El Tigres del Norte (Grammy Award for Best Norteño Album 2010) 2009, La Granja 2009, Los Tigres Del Norte and Friends (Grammy Award for Best Banda or Norteño Album 2012) 2011. *Honours:* Academia Nacional de la Música Mexicana Award 2003, Oye! Homenaje a la Trayectoria Artistica and Award for Best Norteño Group 2003, BMI Latin Award for Songwriting Icons 2007. *Address:* Los Tigres del Norte, 99 Almaden Blvd, Suite 333, San Jose, CA 95113, USA (office). *E-mail:* management@lostigresdelnorte.com (office). *Website:* www .lostigresdelnorte.com (office).

HERNÁNDEZ, Jorge; Mexican singer and musician (accordion); b. Rosa Morada, Sinaloa; brother of Hernán Hernández, Eduardo Hernández, Luis Hernández, and cousin of Oscar Lara. *Career:* mem. Los Tigres del Norte (norteño-style band) 1971–. *Film:* La Misma Luna 2008. *Recordings include:* albums: Cuquita 1971, El Cheque 1972, Contrabando y Traición 1974, La Banda del Carro Rojo 1975, La Tumba del Mojado – Internacionalmente Norteños 1976, Pueblo Querido 1976, Vivan los Mojados 1977, Numero Ocho 1978, El Tahúr 1979, Plaza Garibaldi 1980, Un Día a la Vez 1981, Padre Nuestro – éxitos para siempre 1982, Carrera Contra la Muerte 1983, Jaula de Oro 1983, A ti Madrecita 1985, El Otro México 1986, Gracias América – Sin Fronteras (Grammy Award for Best Album (Regional Mexican Music Category) 1987) 1986, Idolos del Pueblo 1988, Corridos Prohibidos 1989, Triunfo Sólido – mi buena suerte 1989, Para Adoloridos 1990, Incansables! 1991, Con Sentimiento y Sabor – Tan Bonita 1992, Una Noche con los Tigres del Norte 1992, La Garra de... 1993, Los dos Plebes 1994, El Ejemplo 1995, Unidos Para Siempre 1996, Así como tú 1997, Jefe de Jefes 1997, Herencia de Familia 1999, De Paisano a Paisano 2000, Uniendo Fronteras 2001, La Reina del Sur 2002, Pacto de Sangre (Latin Grammy Award for Best Norteño Album) 2004, Directo al Corazón 2005, Historias que Contar (Grammy Award for Best Norteño Album 2007) 2006, Detalles y Emociones 2007, Raíces (Grammy Award for Best Norteño Album 2009) 2008, Tu Noche Con...El Tigres del Norte (Grammy Award for Best Norteño Album 2010) 2009, La Granja 2009, Los Tigres Del Norte and Friends (Grammy Award for Best Banda or Norteño Album 2012) 2011. *Honours:* Academia Nacional de la Música Mexicana Award 2003, Oye! Homenaje a la Trayectoria Artistica and Award for Best Norteño Group 2003, BMI Latin Award for Songwriting Icons 2007. *Address:* Los Tigres del Norte, 99 Almaden Blvd, Suite 333, San Jose, CA 95113, USA (office). *E-mail:* management@lostigresdelnorte.com (office). *Website:* www .lostigresdelnorte.com (office).

HERNÁNDEZ, Luis; Mexican musician (six-string bass) and singer; b. Rosa Morada, Sinaloa; brother of Jorge Hernández, Hernán Hernández, Eduardo Hernández, and cousin of Oscar Lara. *Career:* mem. Los Tigres del Norte (norteño-style band) 1971–. *Film:* La Misma Luna 2008. *Recordings include:* albums: Cuquita 1971, El Cheque 1972, Contrabando y Traición 1974, La Banda del Carro Rojo 1975, La Tumba del Mojado – Internacionalmente Norteños 1976, Pueblo Querido 1976, Vivan los Mojados 1977, Numero Ocho 1978, El Tahúr 1979, Plaza Garibaldi 1980, Un Día a la Vez 1981, Padre Nuestro – éxitos para siempre 1982, Carrera Contra la Muerte 1983, Jaula de Oro 1983, A ti Madrecita 1985, El Otro México 1986, Gracias América – Sin Fronteras (Grammy Award for Best Album (Regional Mexican Music

Category) 1987) 1986, Idolos del Pueblo 1988, Corridos Prohibidos 1989, Triunfo Sólido – mi buena suerte 1989, Para Adoloridos 1990, Incansables! 1991, Con Sentimiento y Sabor – Tan Bonita 1992, Una Noche con los Tigres del Norte 1992, La Garra de... 1993, Los dos Plebes 1994, El Ejemplo 1995, Unidos Para Siempre 1996, Así como tú 1997, Jefe de Jefes 1997, Herencia de Familia 1999, De Paisano a Paisano 2000, Uniendo Fronteras 2001, La Reina del Sur 2002, Pacto de Sangre (Latin Grammy Award for Best Norteño Album) 2004, Directo al Corazón 2005, Historias que Contar (Grammy Award for Best Norteño Album 2007) 2006, Detalles y Emociones 2007, Raíces (Grammy Award for Best Norteño Album 2009) 2008, Tu Noche Con...El Tigres del Norte (Grammy Award for Best Norteño Album 2010) 2009, La Granja 2009, Los Tigres Del Norte and Friends (Grammy Award for Best Banda or Norteño Album 2012) 2011. *Honours:* Academia Nacional de la Música Mexicana Award 2003, Oye! Homenaje a la Trayectoria Artistica and Award for Best Norteño Group 2003, BMI Latin Award for Songwriting Icons 2007. *Address:* Los Tigres del Norte, 99 Almaden Blvd, Suite 333, San Jose, CA 95113, USA (office). *E-mail:* management@lostigresdelnorte.com (office). *Website:* www .lostigresdelnorte.com (office).

HERNANDEZ, Myriam; Chilean singer, songwriter and television presenter; b. (Myriam Raquel Hernández Navarro), 2 May 1967, Santiago; one s. *Career:* recording artist 1988–; f. School of Vocal Arts with Ricardo Álvarez 1992; collaborator with Paul Anka 1996, Los Nocheros 2004; host and participant, Viña del Mar Int. Song Festival 2002–06. *Recordings:* albums: Myriam Hernández (Asociación de Periodistas de Espectáculos de Chile Award for Best Record 1989) 1988, Dos 1990, Myriam Hernández III 1992, IV 1994, Todo el Amor 1998, + y Más 2000, Enamorándome 2007, Seducción 2011. *Film:* as actor: La frontera 1992. *Television includes:* as host: La noche del mundial 2006. *Honours:* Asociación de Periodistas de Espectáculos de Chile APES Award for Best Female Performer 1989, Recipient, Viña del Mar Int. Song Festival Antorcha and Gaviota de Plata Awards 1991, Viña del Mar Int. Song Festival Awards for Gaviota de Plata and Oro 2001. *Address:* c/o Universal Latino, Universal Music Group, 1755 Broadway, New York, NY 10019, USA (office). *Website:* www.myriamhernandez.cl.

HERNÁNDEZ, Saúl; Mexican singer, songwriter and musician (guitar); b. 15 Jan. 1964, Mexico City. *Career:* mem. Caifanes 1986–95; Founder–mem. and lead singer Jaguares 1995–. *Recordings include:* albums: with Caifanes: Caifanes 1988, El Diablito 1990, El Silencio 1992, Matenme Porque me Muero 1994, El Nervio del Volcan 1994; with Jaguares: El Equilibrio de los Jaguares 1996, Bajo de Azul de Tu Misterio 2001, Cuando la Sangre Galopa 2001, Cronicas de un Laberinto 2005, 45 (Grammy Award for Best Latin Rock of Alternative Album 2009, Latin Grammy Award for Best Rock Album by a Duo/ Group 2009) 2008, Remando 2011. *Honours:* Latin Grammy Award for Best Rock Song (for Entre tus Jardines) 2009. *Address:* c/o EMI Music Mexico, Rio Tigris 33, Cuauhtemoc, 06500 México, DF, Mexico. *Website:* www.jaguaresmx .com; www.emimusicmexico.com; www.saul-hernandez.com.

HERNDON, Mark Joel; American musician (drums); b. 11 May 1955, Springfield, MA; m., one d. *Career:* mem., country music group, Alabama, 1979–2008. *Recordings:* with Alabama: Alabama 1980, My Home's In Alabama 1980, Feels So Right 1981, Stars 1982, Mountain Music 1982, The Closer You Get 1983, Roll On 1984, 40 Hour Week 1985, Alabama Christmas 1985, The Touch 1986, Greatest Hits 1986, Just Us 1987, Live 1988, Tennessee Christmas 1989, Southern Star 1989, Pass It On Down 1990, Greatest Hits Vol. 2 1991, American Pride 1992, Gonna Have A Party... Live 1993, Cheap Seats 1993, In The Beginning 1994, In Pictures 1995, From The Archives Vol. 1 1996, Christmas Vol. 2 1996, Live at Ebbets Field 1997, Dancin' On The Boulevard 1997, Twentieth Century 1999, Alabama For The Record 2000, When It All Goes South 2001, Christmas 2002. *Honours:* numerous Country Music Asscn Awards, 1981–84; Numerous Acad. of Country Music Awards, incl. Artist of the Decade, 1989; Numerous American Music Awards, incl. Award of Merit, 2003; Grammy Awards, for Mountain Music, 1983, for The Closer You Get, 1984; BMI President's Award, 2000; Numerous Billboard Awards.

HERREN, (Guillermo) Scott, (Prefuse 73, Savath y Savalas, Piano Overlord, La Corrección, Ahmad Szabo); American hip-hop producer; b. Miami, Fla. *Career:* mem. Sons of the Morning, Risil and Diamond Watch Wrists; f. Eastern Developments Music (with Peter Rentz, Carolina Chaves, Ben Loiz, Carlos Niño and Paz Ochs). *Recordings include:* albums: as Delarosa and Asora: Sleep Method Suite 1997, Agony 2001; Savath y Savalas: Folk Songs for Trains and Honey 2000, The Rolls & Waves (EP) 2002, Apropat't 2004, Mañana (EP) 2004, Golden Pollen 2007, La Llama 2009; as Prefuse 73: Vocal Studies + Uprock Narratives 2001, One Word Extinguisher 2003, Extinguished: Outtakes (EP) 2003, Surrounded by Silence 2005, Security Screenings 2006, Preparations 2007, Interregnums 2007, Everything She Touched Turned Ampexian 2009, Meditation upon Meditations 2009, The Only She Chapters 2011; as Diamond Watch Wrists: Ice Capped at Both Ends 2009; as Ahmad Szabo: This Book is about Words 2003, Luck has a Million Meanings 2006. *Address:* 212 Prince Street, PMB 313, New York, NY 10012, USA (office). *Website:* www.prefuse73.com.

HERRERA RODRÍGUEZ, Alfonso; Mexican singer and actor; b. 28 Aug. 1983, Mexico City. *Education:* Edron Acad., Centro de Educación Artística. *Career:* actor; mem. RDB 2004–. *Recordings include:* albums: Rebelde 2004, Nuestro Amor 2005, Celestial (Billboard Latin Music Award for Latin Pop Album of the Year by a Duo or Group 2007) 2006, Rebels (in English) 2006,

Empezar Desde Cero 2007, Para Olvidarte De Mí 2009. *Television includes:* Clase 406 2002, Rebelde (series) 2004, RBD: La Familia (series) 2007, El Equipo 2011, El Diez 2011, Camaleones 2009. *Theatre includes:* Las Brujas de Salem 2001, Como Matar a un Ruiseñor 2001, Antigona 2001, The Pillowman 2008, Rain Man 2010, Nadando con Tiburones 2012. *Film includes:* Amarte Duele 2002, Volverte a Ver 2007, Venezzia 2009, Así es la Suerte 2011. *Honours:* Billboard Latin Music Award for Top Latin Albums Artist of the Year, for Latin Tour of the Year 2007, some 24 Premios Juventud, Billboard Latin Music 'Tu Mundo' Award 2008. *Address:* c/o EMI Latin, 404 Washington Avenue, Suite 700, Miami Beach, FL 33139, USA. *Website:* www.emimusic .com.mx; www.alfonsoherrerarodriguez.com.

HERRING, James (Jimmy); American musician (guitar); b. 1962, Fayetteville, North Carolina; m.; two c. *Education:* Berklee Coll. of Music, Guitar Inst. of Tech. *Career:* mem. Jazz Is Dead (project performing jazz interpretations of Grateful Dead songs) 1996–; Founder–mem. Col Bruce Hampton and The (renamed Aquarium Rescue Unit); toured with Allman Brothers 1998; joined Frogwings 1999; co-f. Project Z 2000; played with Phil Lesh and Friends, project of Grateful Dead bassist, Phil Lesh 2000; recruited to play with The Dead (as The Grateful Dead was renamed, following the death of guitarist Jerry Garcia) 2002–. *Recordings include:* albums: with Col. Bruce Hampton and Aquarium Rescue Unit: Col. Bruce Hampton And The Aquarium Rescue Unit 1992, Mirrors Of Embarrassment 1993, with Aquarium Rescue Unit: Eepeee 1994, In A Perfect World 1994, The Calling 1997; with Jazz Is Dead: Blue Light Rain 1998, Laughing Water 1999, Great Sky River 2001; with Lavitz/Heyward/Gradney: Endangered Species 2001; with Phil Lesh and Friends: There And Back Again 2002; with Project Z: Self Titled 2001, Lincoln Memorial 2005; with Widespread Panic: Free Somehow 2008, Dirty Side Down 2010; solo: Lifeboat 2008, Subject to Change Without Notice 2012. *Current Management:* c/o Abstract Logix, 103 Sarabande Drive, Cary, NC 27513, USA. *E-mail:* souvik@abstractlogix.com. *Website:* www.abstractlogix .com; www.jimmyherring.net.

HERSH, Kristin; American musician (guitar) and singer; b. 7 Aug. 1966, Atlanta, Ga; three s. *Career:* mem. Throwing Muses 1986–97; solo artist 1994–; mem. 50 Foot Wave 2003–; mem. American Fed. of Musicians; Cofounder non-profit open-source software project Cash Music. *Recordings include:* albums: with Throwing Muses: Throwing Muses 1986, House Tornado 1988, Hunkpapa 1990, The Real Ramona 1991, Red Heaven 1992, University 1995, Limbo 1996, Anthology 2011, Throwing Muses 2003, Purgatory/Paradise 2013; solo: Hips and Makers 1994, Strings (EP) 1994, Strange Angels 1998, Murder, Misery and Then Goodnight 1998, Sky Motel 1999, Sunny Border Blue 2001, The Grotto 2003, Learn to Sing Like a Star 2007, Speedbath 2008, Crooked 2010; with 50 Foot Wave: Golden Ocean 2005. *Publications include:* Toby Snax 2007, Rat Girl: A Memoir 2010, Crooked 2010, Paradoxical Undressing 2011, Purgatory/ Paradise 2013. *Address:* c/o Throwing Music Ltd, 520 Southview Drive, Athens, GA 30605, USA (office). *E-mail:* jesse@cashmusic.org. *Website:* www.kristinhersh.com; www .kristinhersh.cashmusic.org; www.throwingmuses.com.

HERZHAFT, Gerard; French blues musician, writer on music and writer on novels; b. 8 Nov. 1943, Meyzieu; m. Lise Briere de L'Isle 1967; one s. one d. *Education:* Sorbonne, Paris. *Career:* numerous radio broadcasts and TV shows; concerts: Blues Passion, Cognac, Thullins Festival, Café Campus (Montréal), Parthenay Blues, Doua De Jazz, Sathonay Blues Festival. *Compositions:* If It Wasn't for Muddy Waters, Rhone River is Rising, Old Bluesman From Texas, Redneck Blues, My Blues Will, Write, Gerard, Write 1998, A Full Bank Account 1998. *Recordings:* albums: with Herzhaft Blues: Never Been Plugged, Two Brothers And A Pick, Herzhaft Special 2000. *Publications include:* about 40 books, including Un long blues en la mineur 1986, Catfish Blues 1997, Des crocs dans la nuit 1998, A Chicago, un harmonica sanglote le blues 2000, Tupac amaru, la révolte des Incas 2002, La ballade de John Henry 2003, Le dernier chant de l'Inca 2006, Americana 2007. *Honours:* Grand Prix Littéraire de la Ville de Lyon 1986, Prix des Auteurs et Ecrivains Lyonnais 1987, Prix Soc. des Gens de Lettres 1995, Prix des Lyceens d'Île de France 1997, The Blues Foundation Keeping the Blues Award 2013. *Address:* 57 rue Florian, 69100 Villeurbanne, France (office). *Telephone:* (4) 72-33-45-89 (office). *E-mail:* gerardherz@yahoo.fr (home). *Website:* www .gerardherzhaft.com.

HESSION, Paul; British musician (drums); b. 19 Sept. 1956, Leeds; m. Cecilia Jane Charnley, 23 May 1987, one s., one d. *Career:* toured Mexico and Cuba with The Siger Band 1986; played in Derek Bailey's co. week in London (twice); duos with Alan Wilkinson on BBC Radio 3, sound symposium, St Johns, Newfoundland, Canada with Hession/Wilkinson/Fell; mem. Musicians' Union; performs with Leeds-based trio Unit of Resistance. *Recordings include:* albuma: The Real Case (with Hans-Peter Hiby) 1988, Playing with Tunes 1995, Improvability 2000, Acts of Love 2003, Do Easy 2010; with Hession/Wilkinson/Fell: Foom Foom 1992, The Horrors of Darmstadt 1994, Registered Firm 1998, Two Falls and a Submission 2011; with Mick Beck: Start Moving Earbuds; solo: St Johns 2000. *E-mail:* paul@softdrum.com; hessionoftheyard@gmail.com. *Website:* www.softdrum.com.

HETFIELD, James Alan; American singer and musician (guitar); b. 3 Aug. 1963, Downey City, CA; s. of Virgil Hetfield and Cynthia Hetfield. *Career:* fmr mem. Obsession, Leather Charm; mem. and lead singer heavy rock group, Metallica 1981–; world-wide tours and concert appearances. *Film:* Some Kind Of Monster (Independent Spirit Award for Best Documentary 2005) 2004.

Recordings include: albums: Kill 'Em All 1983, Ride The Lightning 1984, Master Of Puppets 1986, ...And Justice For All 1988, The Good, The Bad And The Live 1990, Metallica 1991, Load 1996, Reload 1997, Early Days 1997, S&M (live) 1999, St Anger 2003, Death Magnetic 2008; singles: Whiplash 1985, Garage Days Revisited 1987, Creeping Death 1990, Harvester Of Sorrow 1988, One (Grammy Award for Best Heavy Metal Performance) 1989, Stone Cold Crazy (Grammy Award for Best Heavy Metal Performance) 1991, Jump In The Fire 1991, The Unforgiven (Grammy Award for Best Heavy Metal Performance 1992) 1991, Enter Sandman 1991, Nothing Else Matters 1992, Wherever I May Roam 1992, Sad But True 1992, Until It Sleeps 1996, Hero Of The Day 1996, Mama Said 1996, King Nothing 1997, The Memory Remains 1997, Fuel 1998, Turn The Page 1998, Whisky In The Jar (Grammy Award for Best Hard Rock Performance 2000) 1999, Die Die My Darling 1999, No Leaf Clover 2000, I Disappear 2000, Call Of The Ktulu (Grammy Award for Best Rock Instrumental Performance) 2001, St Anger 2003, Death Magnetic 2008. *Honours:* American Music Award for Favorite Heavy Metal Artist (with Metallica) 1993, Grammy Award for Best Metal Performance (for My Apocalypse) 2009. *Current Management:* Q-Prime Inc., 729 Seventh Avenue, 16th Floor, New York, NY 10019, USA. *Telephone:* (212) 302-9790. *Fax:* (212) 302-9589. *Website:* www.metallica.com.

HEURLIN, Martin; Danish musician (guitar, bass, keyboards), singer and producer; b. 20 Nov. 1963, Frederiksberg; three s. *Career:* Founder-mem. rock band Sy-Daff; mem. KB Hallen 1980; played club circuit in Los Angeles 1986–88; worked with producer Soren Wolf; guitarist on Danish TV for Michael Penn, John Farnham, Anders Glenmark and Tomas Ledin 1990; mem. Pupil 1997–; mem. DJFBA. *Compositions include:* TV show theme, Set and Swet, Pupil, Frederik Jorgensen, major hit in Denmark 1997. *Recordings include:* soundtracks for many Danish television documentary programmes 1990–; albums with Sy-Daff 1982, Mr Man 1987, James Thomas 1991, Pupil 1997; solo album 1995, Super Glass Eyes 1999. *Publication includes:* Pupil: Superglasojne 1997. *Website:* www.djbfa.dk.

HEWAT, Corrina Dawn, BA; British singer, musician (harp, clarsach) and composer; b. 21 Dec. 1970, Edinburgh, Scotland; m. Dave Milligan. *Education:* Royal Scottish Acad. of Music and Drama, City of Leeds Coll. of Music. *Career:* mem. Bachué (with David Milligan) 1995–2006, Chantan 1996–99, Shine 1999–2003, Seannachie 1994–97; Founder and leader, band Unusual Suspects (with Dave Milligan) 2003–; mem. vocal harmony trio with Annie Grace and Karine Polwart; teacher and visiting tutor Balnain House, Home of Highland Music, Inverness and Fettes Coll., Edinburgh; tutor Newcastle Univ. and Royal Scottish Acad. of Music and Drama, Glasgow; worked with Lammas, Carol Kidd, Eric Bibb, Seannachie; commissions include Songs of Redshank, The Highland Festival 1997, Making the Connection, Celtic Connections Festival 1998, Photons In Vapour 2000; Owner, record label Big Bash Records; mem. Musicians' Union, Clarsach Soc., UKHA, PRS, MCPS, Performing Artists Media Rights Asscn. *Recordings include:* Bachué Café 1996, 1998, Primary Colours 1997, A Certain Smile 1999; with The Unusual Suspects: Harp I Do 2008, My Favourite Place. *E-mail:* info@corrinahewat.com. *Website:* www.corrinahewat.com.

HEWERDINE, Boo; British songwriter and producer; b. 1961. *Career:* worked as producer and songwriter for The Corrs, Rosalie Deighton, Nicky Love, Eddi Reader, Scarlet; worked as songwriter for Melanie C, Fever Pitch, Hepburn, Natalie Imbruglia, Brian Kennedy, Heather Small, Suggs, James Taylor, Twenty Four Seven; fmr mem. The Bible; solo artist 1992–. *Recordings include:* albums: with The Bible: Walking the Ghost Back Home 1986, Eureka 1988, Content 1988, The Bible 1989, Random Acts of Kindness 1995, Dodo 1999; with The Great Divide: Money and Time 2007; with State of the Union: State of the Union 2012; solo: Ignorance 1992, Baptist Hospital 1996, Thanksgiving 1999, A Live One 2002, Anon 2002, Harmonograph 2006, Toybox No. 2 2008, God Bless the Pretty Things 2009. *Current Management:* c/o Compass Records, 916 19th Avenue South, Nashville, TN 37212, USA. *Telephone:* (615) 320-7672. *Fax:* (615) 320-7378. *Address:* 55 Lynn Road, Ely, Cambs., CB6 1DD, England. *E-mail:* audrey@ripleymusic.co.uk. *Website:* www.boohewerdine.net; www.stateoftheunionmusic.com.

HEWITT, Steve; British musician (drums, percussion); b. 22 March 1971, England. *Career:* fmr mem., The Electric Crayons, Mystic Deckchairs; fmr mem., Breed, toured Germany; fmr mem., Boo Radleys, worked on their debut album and played numerous concerts; played with K-Klass, dance outfit; numerous contracts with session work and provided music for advertisements; mem., Placebo 1996–. *Recordings include:* albums: Without You I'm Nothing 1998, Black Market Music 2000, Sleeping With Ghosts 2003, Meds 2006, Battle for the Sun 2009. *Honours:* Kerrang! Classic Songwriter Award 2006, MTV Europe Music Award for Best Alternative Act 2009. *Current Management:* c/o Riverman Management, George House, Brecon Road, London W6 8PY, England. *Telephone:* (20) 7381-4000. *Fax:* (20) 7381-9666. *E-mail:* info@riverman.co.uk. *Website:* www.riverman.co.uk; www .placeboworld.co.uk.

HEWLETT, Jamie; British artist, animator and designer. *Education:* Northbrook Coll. *Career:* cr. comic strip Tank Girl (with Allan Martin); Owner, multimedia co. (design, animation and website), Zombie Flesh Eaters; Founder-mem. and Visual Dir of 'virtual band' Gorillaz 1998–, collaborated with numerous guest artists. *Opera includes:* designed set and costumes for Monkey: Journey To The West 2007. *Recordings include:* albums: Gorillaz 2001, G-Sides 2002, Laika Come Home 2002, Demon Days 2005, D-Sides 2007,

Plastic Beach 2010, The Fall 2011. *Publications include:* Gorillaz Rise of the Ogre 2006, Deadline comics and Tank Girl graphic novels. *Honours:* with Gorillaz: VMA Award for Best Breakthrough video 2001, Best Video, MTV Asia 2002; Q Awards for Best Video, for Best Producer 2005, Digital Music Award for Top Online Band, for Best Use of Digital Platforms 2005, MTV Europe Music Award for Best Group 2005, Grammy Award for Best Pop Collaboration with Vocals (for Feel Good Inc.) 2006, NME John Peel Music Innovation Award 2006, Ivor Novello Award for Songwriter of the Year 2006, Design Museum Designer of the Year (for Gorillaz website, animations, etc.) 2006, Webby Award for Artist of the Year (for Gorillaz.com) 2006; other: Jim Henson Award for Creativity 2005. *Current Management:* c/o CMO Management, Studio 2.6, Shepherds East, Richmond Way, London, W14 0DQ, England. *Telephone:* (20) 7316-6969. *E-mail:* reception@cmomanagement.co.uk. *Website:* www.gorillaz.com; www.jamiehewlett.com.

HEWSON, Paul (see BONO)

HEYWARD, Nick; British singer, musician (guitar) and songwriter; b. 20 May 1961, South London. *Career:* Founder-mem. Haircut One Hundred 1981–82; solo artist 1983–. *Recordings include:* albums: with Haircut 100: Pelican West 1982; solo: North of a Miracle 1983, Postcards From Home 1986, I Love You Avenue 1989, From Monday To Sunday 1993, Tangled 1995, The Apple Bed 1996, Pizza Tears, Open Sesame Seed 2001, The Mermaid and the Lighthouse Keeper 2006. *Website:* www.nickheyward.com.

HIATT, John; American singer, songwriter and musician (guitar); b. 20 Aug. 1952, Indianapolis, Ind. *Career:* mem. Four Fifths, The White Ducks, Joe Lynch and The Hangmen; songwriter with Tree Publishing, Nashville in early 1970s; signed a recording contract with Epic Records; solo artist 1974–, with backing group The Goners; musician for Sonny Terry, Brownie McGhee, Leon Redbone, Tom Waits, Roy Orbison; tours with Leo Kottke, Southside Johnny and the Astbury Jukes, Edie Brickell; mem. Ry Cooder's backing band 1981; Founder-mem. Little Village (with Ry Cooder, Nick Lowe, Jim Keltner) 1992. *Compositions include:* Thinking of You (Tracy Nelson), As Sure As I'm Sitting Here (Three Dog Night), Bring Back Your Love To Me (Earl Thomas Conley). *Recordings include:* albums: Hangin' Around The Observatory 1974, Overcoats 1974, Slug Line 1979, Two Bit Monsters 1980, All Of A Sudden 1982, Riding With The King 1983, Warming Up To The Ice Age 1985, Bring The Family 1987, Slow Turning 1988, Stolen Moments 1990, Perfectly Good Guitar 1993, Love Gets Strange 1993, Walk On 1995, Little Head 1997, Crossing Muddy Waters 2000, The Tiki Bar Is Open 2001, Beneath This Gruff Exterior 2003, Master of Disaster 2005, Same Old Man 2008, The Open Road 2010, Dirty Jeans and Mudslide Hymns 2011, Mystic Pinball 2012, My Kind of Town 2013; with Little Village: Little Village 1992. *Honours:* BMI Country Music Award (for Bring Back Your Love To Me) 1991, Nashville Music Award for Songwriter/Artist of the Year 2000, Lifetime Achievement Award for Songwriting, Americana Music Asscn 2008. *Current Management:* Vector Management, PO Box 120479, Nashville, TN 37212, USA. *E-mail:* info@vectormgmt.com. *Website:* www.johnhiatt.com.

HIBBERT, Frederick 'Toots'; Jamaican reggae singer and songwriter; b. 8 Dec. 1942, Clarendon. *Career:* lead singer of reggae group, The Maytals 1962–, later renamed Toots and The Maytals; numerous collaborations including with JJ Grey & Mofro, Red Hot Chili Peppers. *Film appearance:* The Harder They Come. *Recordings include:* albums: The Sensational, Never Grow Old, Sweet and Dandy, From The Roots, Monkey Man, Funky Kingston, In The Dark, Slatyam Stoot, Reggae Got Soul, Toots Live, Life Could Be A Dream, Toots in Memphis, Light Your Light, Jamaican Monkey Man 1999, World is Turning 2003, True Love 2004, Rhythm Kings 2005, Light Your Light 2007, Flip and Twist 2010; with Otis Redding: Otis! The Definitive Otis Redding 1993. *Honours:* winner (with The Maytals) Jamaican Festival Song Competition 1966, 1969, 1972, one Grammy Award. *E-mail:* mike@tootsandthemaytals.net. *Website:* www.tootsandthemaytals.net.

HICKS, Ivan, BA, BEd, MEd; Canadian musician (fiddle, guitar, mandolin); b. 6 July 1940, Upper Sackville, New Brunswick; m. Vivian Paulette Webb, 4 July 1970. *Career:* As teenager, formed The Golden Valley Boys; began teaching, Salisbury, New Brunswick 1964; formed danceband Marshwinds 1969–89; formed old-time and bluegrass band Ivan Hicks and Maritime Express 1979–; wrote; fiddle teacher; television appearances include Up Home Tonight (ATV) 1980s; host, weekly radio show, CFQM Moncton 1982–95; MC of Maritime Old-Time Fiddling Contest (CBC) 1985–; concerts: Canada, USA; entertainer, special occasions; organizer, promoter, concerts, tours; retired from teaching 1996; mem. Canadian Country Music Asscn; Dir, Maritime Fiddlers Asscn; Dir, National Oldtime Fiddlers Asscn; East Coast Music Asscn; Pres., Fiddles of the World Soc.; Dir, New Brunswick Country Music Hall of Fame; Dir, Music New Brunswick; associated with Fiddles on the Tobigue, Pilaster Rock, New Brunswick. *Compositions include:* Apohaqui; Gram Lee's Waltz; Jim, The Fiddle Maker; Marshwinds Waltz; Purple Violet Waltz; Riverview Jig; Maritime 40; Forever Friends; Memories of Father James Smith; Fiddler's Roast; The MacDonalds of Highfield; The Fiddler From Douro; Sussex Avenue Fiddlers Two Step. *Recordings:* The Life and Music of Ivan and Vivian Hicks (video); For You; Shingle The Roof; Old Time Christmas; Fiddlingly Yours; Swinging Fiddles; Purple Violet Fiddling; Friendly Fiddling The Maritime Way; Fiddling For Fun and Friends; The Strength of God's Hand 1997. *Publications:* Ivan Hicks Fiddle Tunes and Souvenirs; Ivan Hicks: Fifty Years of Fabulous Fiddle Music by Allison Mitcham 1996. *Honours:* Two-time winner, Maritime Fiddling Contest

1979–80; inducted into New Brunswick Country Music Hall of Fame, North American Fiddlers Hall of Fame 1990; recipient, Gov. Gen.'s Caring Canadian Award 1999; Hon. mem. Nova Scotia Country Music Hall of Fame 2004. *Address:* 1631 Hwy 112, Upper Coverdale, New Brunswick, E1J 1X9, Canada (home). *Telephone:* (506) 386-2996 (home). *E-mail:* ivan@ivanhicks.com (home). *Website:* www.ivanhicks.com (home).

HICKS, Jacqueline (Jacqui); British singer, musician (saxophone, flute, clarinet) and songwriter; b. 7 July 1966, Pontefract, West Yorkshire; m. Patrick Hartley. *Education:* Wakefield District Coll., City of Leeds Coll. of Music, Guildhall School of Music and Drama. *Career:* four years with Nat. Youth Jazz Orchestra; mem. Shakatak 1993–; also performed with John Dankworth, Dick Morrisey, Harry Becket, Don Lusher, Roger Odell, Matt Bianco, Paprika Soul, Hal David, John Cacavas, Duncan Lamont, Johnny Keating; supported George Benson 1993; own jazz/funk band, Jacqui Hicks Band; tours with Paul Lacey's Back To Basie Orchestra, John Critchinson Trio. *Recordings include:* albums: solo: Looking Forward, Looking Back 1990, Spellbound, 2000, With a Song in my Heart 2005; with Shakatak: Let the Piano Play 1997, View from the City 1998, Live at Ronnie Scott's 1998, Latin Trip, Blue Savannah 2003, Beautiful Day 2005, Emotionally Blue 2007, Afterglow 2009, Across the World 2011, Once Upon a Time 2013; with Macfarlane Group: Bright Lights Big City; with NYJO: Cooking With Gas; with Matt Bianco: Another Time Another Place, Gran Via, A Collection; with Paprika Soul: Into the Light. *Address:* c/o Colin Newman & Company, Regent House 1, Pratt Mews, London, NW1 0AD, England. *E-mail:* info@shakatak.com. *Website:* www.shakatak.com.

HIDAKA, Masahiro; Japanese music promoter and event manager; *President, Smash Corporation. Career:* Pres. and Co-founder Smash Corpn 1983; runs the annual Fuji Rock Festival 1997–, and the Asagiri Jam (on Mount Fuji). *Honours:* Hon. OBE (UK). *E-mail:* mail@smash-jpn.com (office). *Website:* www.smash-jpn.com (office).

HIDALGO, David; American musician (percussion, guitar, drums, accordion) and songwriter; b. 6 Oct. 1954, Los Angeles. *Career:* mem., Los Lobos 1973–; collaborated with Elvis Costello, Roy Orbison, Dolly Parton, Paul Simon and Tom Waits among others. *Recordings include:* albums: De Este De Los Angeles 1978, How Will The Wolf Survive 1984, By the Light of the Moon 1987, La Pistola y El Corazón 1988, The Neighborhood 1990, Kiko 1992, Colossal Head 1996, This Time 1999, Good Morning Aztlán 2002, The Ride 2004, The Town and the City 2006, Los Lobos Goes Disney 2009, Tin Can Trust 2010. *Current Management:* c/o Chris Tetzeli, Red Light Management, 321 East Main Street, Suite 500, Charlottesville, VA 22902, USA. *Telephone:* (434) 245-4900. *Fax:* (434) 245-4933. *E-mail:* info@redlightmanagement.com. *Website:* www.redlightmanagement.com; www.loslobos.org.

HIDALGO, Manolo; Peruvian musician (guitar). *Career:* Founder-mem. Libido 1996–; numerous live performances and festival appearances. *Recordings include:* albums: Libido 1998, Hembra 2000, Pop*Porn 2003, Libido Acústica 2004, Lo Último Que Hablé Ayer 2005, Bebe 2007, Un Día Nuevo 2009, Rarezas 2010. *Honours:* Latin American MTV Video Music Award for Best Artist 2002, 2003. *E-mail:* manolo@libidonet.com (office). *Website:* www.libidonet.com.

HIGGINS, Brian Thomas; British songwriter and producer; *Co-Founder and Head, Xenomania;* b. 1966. *Career:* began career as session musician; worked with Motiv8; co-wrote and co-produced hit songs including: All I Wanna Do for Dannii Minogue 1997, Believe for Cher 1998; worked for London Records; Co-founder and Head, Xenomania production co.; has written songs for Sugababes, New Order, Girls Aloud, Texas, The Wanted, The Saturdays, Pet Shop Boys; worked with Miranda Cooper. *Website:* www.xenomania.net.

HIGGINS, Missy; Australian singer, songwriter and actress; b. 19 Aug. 1983, Melbourne. *Recordings include:* album: The Sound of White 2005, On a Clear Night 2007, The Ol' Razzle Dazzle 2012, Spitfire (with LeAnn Rimes) 2013. *Film appearance:* Bran Nue Dae 2010. *Honours:* winner nine ARIA Awards including Best Pop Release (for Scar) 2004; numerous other awards. *E-mail:* mail@missyhiggins.com. *Website:* www.missyhiggins.com.

HIGHAM, Darrel; British musician (guitar, double bass), singer, songwriter and producer; b. 5 Jan. 1970, Bedford; m. Imelda May. *Career:* solo career as singer and guitarist with backing band The Enforcers; supported Chuck Berry 1995; played lead guitar for Rocky Burnette, Glen Glenn, Johnny Carroll, Vernon Taylor, Merrill E. Moore, Don and Dewey; toured USA 1992, fronting Eddie Cochran's original backing band The Kelly Four; worked in London's West End, lead guitar and singer, Elvis The Musical 1996; currently performs with Imelda May and Kat Men; mem. Musicians' Union. *Compositions include:* over 30 compositions released worldwide. *Recordings include:* solo albums: Mobile Corrosion (Nervous) 1995, Let's Rock Tonight (Fury) 1995, Rockin' At the Coconut Top (Crazy Love) 1996, The Cochran Connection (Rockstar) 1997, Darrel Higham and the Barnshakers (Gaofin') 1998, How To Dance The Bop 2000, Ghost of Love 2001, The Sweet Georgia Brown Sessions 2002, The Cochran Connection, Volume 2 2004, Midnight Commotion 2004, Crazy with Love 2006, Wild in Hollywood 2013; with Kat Men: The Kat Men 2006, The Kat Men Cometh 2013; three albums with Bob and the Bearcats; two albums with Johnny Bach and the Moonshine Boozers; one album with Dave Phillips; one album with Blue Devils as lead guitarist; six albums with Darrel Higham & The Enforcers. *Publication:* Don't Forget Me: The Eddie

Cochran Story (with Julie Mundy) 2000. *Current Management:* c/o The Sound Advice Group, 5 Berghem Mews, Blythe Road, London, W14 0HN, England. *Telephone:* (20) 7229-2219. *Fax:* (20) 7229-9870. *E-mail:* info@soundadvice.uk .com. *Website:* www.soundadvice.uk.com; www.katmen.co.uk; www .imeldamay.co.uk.

HIGHAM, Mike; programmer and music editor. *Career:* clients include The Art of Noise, Gary Barlow, Boyzone, Bobby Brown, Eric Clapton, Geri Halliwell, Whitney Houston, Public Demand, Seal, The Spice Girls, Rod Stewart, Tina Turner, Barry White; programmed music on films including Toys, Spice World, Elizabeth, King Arthur, Notting Hill, Clash of the Titans; numerous collaborations with producers and dirs including Tim Burton (on films Chocolate Factory and Dark Shadows), Paul Greengrass (on film Captain Phillips), Disney (on film Into the Woods) and others. *Honours:* Emmy Award for Outstanding Sound Editing (for nini-series Band of Brothers). *Address:* c/o Kraft-Engel Management, 15233 Ventura Blvd, Suite 200, Sherman Oaks, Los Angeles, CA 91403, USA. *E-mail:* info@Kraft-Engel.com. *Website:* www.kraft-engel.com.

HIJAZI, Amal; Lebanese singer; b. 20 Feb. 1978, Beirut; d. of Mahmoud Hijazi and Nadia Hijazi; one adopted d. *Career:* fmr model; solo artist 2000–. *Recordings include:* Akher Gharam 2001, Zaman 2002, Bedawwar a albi 2004, Baya al-ward 2006, Keef al-amar 2008, Waylak Min Allah 2010.

HILL, Beau, BA; American record producer and musician (keyboards, guitar); b. 25 Sept. 1952, Dallas, Tex. *Education:* Univ. of Colorado. *Career:* engineer at Applewood Studios 1971–74, Head Engineer 1974–78; mem. band Airborne 1978–80, Shanghai 1980–81; f. Control Management 1987–90; co-f. Interscope Records 1990; producer for Bob Dylan, Alice Cooper, Ratt, Sandy, Warrant, Winger, Europe, Prisoners in Paradise, Chaka Khan, Fiona, Roger Daltrey, John Miles, Gary Moore, Steve Stevens, Bad Brains, Venture, Track Fighter; mem. Nat. Acad. of Recording Arts and Sciences, Audio Eng Soc., Broadcast Music, Inc., American Soc. of Composers, Authors and Publishers. *Website:* beauhillproductions.com.

HILL, Dave; British musician (guitar); b. 4 April 1946, Fleet Castle, Devon; m. Jan Hill; three c. *Career:* fmr mem. The Vendors 1965; mem. rock group Slade (fmrly N'Betweens, Ambrose Slade) 1966– (later billed as Slade II); numerous live concerts, tours and festival appearances. *Film appearance:* Flame 1974. *Recordings include:* albums: Beginnings (as Ambrose Slade) 1969, Play It Loud 1970, Slade Alive 1972, Slayed 1973, Sladest 1973, Old New Borrowed Blue 1974, Slade In Flame (soundtrack) 1974, Nobody's Fool 1976, Slade Alive Vol. 2 1978, Return To Base 1979, Slade Smashes 1980, Till Deaf Do Us Part 1981, We'll Bring The House Down 1981, Slade On Stage 1982, The Amazing Kamikaze Syndrome 1983, Slade's Greats 1984, Rogue's Gallery 1985, Crackers 1985, You Boyz Make Big Noize 1987, Wall of Hits 1991, Keep On Rockin' 1996, Slade II 2001, Slayed? 2006. *Honours:* Hon. Fellow, (Univ. of Wolverhampton) 2002. *Website:* users.swing.be/amazingslade.

HILL, Joe Michael (Dusty); American musician (bass) and singer; b. 19 May 1949, Dallas, Tex. *Career:* Founder-mem. The Warlocks 1967, renamed The American Blues 1968; Founder-mem. ZZ Top 1970. *Recordings include:* albums: with The American Blues: American Blues Is Here 1967, The American Blues Do Their Thing 1969; with ZZ Top: ZZ Top's First Album 1970, Rio Grande Mud 1972, Tres Hombres 1973, Fandango 1975, Takin' Texas To The People 1976, Tejas 1976, Deguello 1979, El Loco 1981, Eliminator 1983, Afterburner 1985, Recycler 1990, Antenna 1994, Rhythmeen 1996, XXX 1999, Mescalero 2003, Eliminator 2008, ZZ Top: A Tribute from Friends 2011, La Futura 2012. *Honours:* Nordoff-Robbins Music Therapy Foundation Silver Clef Award 1992. *E-mail:* info@zztop.com. *Website:* www .zztop.com.

HILL, Faith; American country singer; b. (Audrey Faith Perry), 21 Sept. 1967, Jackson, MS; m. Tim McGraw 1996; two c. *Career:* moved to Nashville 1989; signed to Warner Bros Records 1992. *Recordings include:* albums: Take Me As I Am 1993, It Matters To Me 1995, Faith (aka Love Will Always Win) 1998, Breathe 1999, Cry 2002, Baby You Belong 2002, Fireflies 2005, Joy to the World 2008, Illusion 2012. *Honours:* Country Music Asscn Award (for It's Your Love) 1997, American Music Award for Favorite Female Country Artist 2002, 2006, Grammy Award for Best Country Collaboration with Vocals (for Like we Never Loved at All, with Tim McGraw) 2006. *Current Management:* Asgard Promotions Ltd, 125 Parkway, London, NW1 7PS, England. *Telephone:* (20) 7387-5090. *Fax:* (20) 7387-8740. *E-mail:* info@asgard-uk.com. *Address:* c/o Warner Bros Records Inc, 3300 Warner Blvd, Burbank, CA 91505, USA. *Website:* www.faithhill.com.

HILL, Lauryn; American singer, actress, songwriter and producer; b. 26 May 1975, South Orange, New Jersey. *Education:* Columbia Univ. *Career:* Founder-mem. Tranzlator Crew, renamed The Fugees 1987–; numerous TV and live appearances; solo artist 2000–. *Films include:* King of the Hill 1993, Sister Act 2: Back in the Habit 1993, Hav Plenty 1997, Restaurant 1998, Turn It Up 2000. *Television includes:* As the World Turns (series) 1991, Daddy's Girl (film) 1996. *Recordings include:* albums: with The Fugees: Blunted on Reality 1994, The Score 1996; solo: The Miseducation of Lauryn Hill (American Music Award for Favorite Album 2000) 1998, MTV Unplugged No. 2.0 2002. *Honours:* BRIT Award for Best Int. Group 1997, Grammy Awards for Album of the Year, Best New Artist, Best Female R&B Vocal Performance, Best R&B Song, Best R&B Album 1999, American Music Award for Favorite Soul/R&B Female Artist 2000. *Current Management:* William

Morris Endeavor Entertainment, 9601 Wilshire Blvd, Beverly Hills, CA 90212, USA. *Telephone:* (310) 859-4000. *Fax:* (310) 248-4440. *Website:* www .wma.com; www.lauryn-hill.com.

HILL, Mark; British producer, remixer and DJ; b. 22 Dec. 1972, Wales. *Education:* Univ. of Southampton. *Career:* played violin in Southampton Youth Orchestra; Founder-mem. Artful Dodger (with Pete Devereux) 1996–2001 (duo split, but records and produces under Artful Dodger name); Co-founder, Centric Records (with Devereux); collaborations include Craig David, Dreem Teem, Romina Johnson, Melanie Blatt; remixed Sisqo, Gabrielle; hosted dance music show on Voice FM Southampton 2011, 2013. *Recordings include:* album: Rewind 2000, It's All About The Stragglers 2001. *Honours:* Ivor Novello Dance Award (for Re-Rewind) 2000, (for Woman Trouble) 2001, Songwriter of the Year (with Craig David), Best Contemporary Song (for 7 Days, co-writer) 2001.

HILL, Warren; Canadian musician (alto, soprano saxophone); b. 15 April 1966. *Education:* Berklee Coll. of Music, USA. *Career:* Unforgettable tour supporting Natalie Cole; also supported Ray Charles, Air Supply, Four Play; worked with Mitch Malloy, Sheila E, Alex Acuna, Lenny Castro, Jeff Pocaro, Ricardo Silveira. *Recordings include:* Albums: Kiss Under The Moon 1982, Devotion 1993, Truth 1994, Shelter 1997, Life Thru Rose Coloured Glasses 1998, Love Life 2000, A Warren Hill Christmas 2002, PopJazz 2005, La Dolce Vita 2008; performed on: Restless Heart: Tell Me What You Dream; also The Passion Theme, from Body of Evidence soundtrack, Can't Get You Out of My Mind with Aswad and General Levy, Jazz at Midnight, Hot Summer Swing. *Address:* Michael Brotten, Infinity Artists Group, PO Box 303, Westminster, CO 80036-0303, USA. *E-mail:* info@warrenhill.com; info@popjazz.com. *Website:* www.warrenhill.com.

HILLE, Veda; Canadian singer, songwriter and musician (piano, guitar); b. 8 Nov. 1968, Vancouver, BC. *Recordings include:* albums: Songs about People and Buildings 1992, Path of a Body 1994, Spine 1996, Here is a Picture 1998, You Do Not Live in This World Alone 1999, Field Study 2001, Silver 2002, Escape Songs 2004, Return of the Kildeer 2005, This Riot Life 2008. *Current Management:* Gary Cristall, PO Box 21547, 1424 Commercial Drive, Vancouver, BC V5N 4A0, Canada. *Address:* PO Box 4763, VMPO, Vancouver, BC V6B 4A4, Canada (office). *E-mail:* veda@vedahille.com (office). *Website:* www.vedahille.com.

HILLERED, Eva Karin Maria; Swedish singer, songwriter, singing teacher and music therapist; b. 4 April 1958, Stockholm; m. Peter Ostman; one d. *Career:* backing singer for Bob Manning, Py Bäckman, Eva Dahlgren, Anne-Grete Preus, Marie Bergman; toured with Rock Runt Riket, Py Bäckman, Anne-Grete Preus, Eva Dahlgren, Rolf Wikström, Riksteaterns Cornelis-show; own shows in Stockholm; Co-founder Diva Records; Owner, label Hill Songs; f. Black Sheep Girls 2006; mem. STIM, SKAP. *Recordings include:* Inte Varför Utan Hur 1988, Stråets längd 1990, Jag Vet 1995, Öppningsskedet 1996, Live: Fehling & Hillered 2001, Hjärtats Röda Mening 2004, Life Line 2005, Hill Song 2007, Heaven and Hill 2011. *Plays include:* Cabaret: Min Bror Var Enda Barnet, Mosebacke, Stockholm 1991, En Kvinnas Bekännelser, Mosebacke 1992, Ballad På En Soptipp, Riksteatern 1993–95, Det Är Tufft Att Bli Hel – Jag Vet (tour) 1995–96. *Publication:* Lathund för låtskrivare 2009. *Address:* Tallkrogsvägen 26, 122 63, Enskede, Sweden (home). *E-mail:* info@ evahillered.se (home). *Website:* www.evahillered.se.

HILLMAN, Chris; American musician (guitar, bass guitar), singer and songwriter; b. 4 Dec. 1944, Los Angeles, Calif. *Career:* mem. Scottsville Squirrel Barkers, Golden State Boys, The Hillmen, The Byrds 1964–68; numerous live performances and festival appearances; mem. McGuinn Clark and Hillman (with Gene Clark and Roger McGuinn); Founder-mem. The Flying Burrito Brothers 1969; mem. Manassas, Southern Hillman Furay Band, Desert Rose Band, Chris Hillman & Herb Pedersen. *Recordings include:* albums: with The Byrds: Mr Tambourine Man 1965, Turn! Turn! Turn! 1966, Fifth Dimension 1966, Younger Than Yesterday 1967, Sweetheart Of The Rodeo 1968, The Byrds 1973; with The Flying Burrito Brothers: The Gilded Palace of Sin 1969, Last of the Red Hot Burritos 1972, Sleepless Nights 1976, Farther Along 1988, Out of the Blue 1996; with Manassas: Manassas 1972, Down The Road 1973, Pieces 2009; with Desert Rose Band: Desert Rose 1984, The Desert Rose Band 1987, Pages of Life 1990, A Dozen Roses 1991, Life Goes On 1999; solo and collaborations: Blue Grass Favorites (with The Scottsville Squirrel Barkers) 1963, Souther Hillman Furay Band (with Souther-Hillman-Furay Band) 1974, Slippin' Away 1976, McGuinn-Clark-Hillman (with Roger McGuinn and Gene Clark) 1979, City (with Roger McGuinn) 1980, Morning Sky 1982, Bakersfield Bound (with Herb Pedersen) 1996, Out of the Woodwork (with Herb Pedersen) 1997, Rice, Rice, Hillman & Pedersen (with Herb Pedersen) 1997, Like a Hurricane 1998, Running Wild (with Herb Pedersen) 2001, Way Out West (with Herb Pedersen) 2003, The Other Side 2006, Chris & Herb Live at Edwards Barn 2010. *Honours:* Americana Music Asscn Lifetime Achievement Award 2004. *Current Management:* New Frontier Touring, 1921 Broadway, Nashville, TN 37203, USA. *Telephone:* (615) 321-6152. *E-mail:* paullohr@newfrontiertouring.com. *Address:* c/o Bar None Music, Inc., PO Box 24610, Ventura, CA 93002-4610, USA (office). *Website:* www.chrishillman.com.

HINAWI, Mayada al-; Syrian singer. *Career:* popular singer who has released numerous albums, often with producer Muhsin Jabr; concerts and tours throughout the Arab world. *Recordings include:* We Betehlef Leih, Hekayet Hob, Ana Baashkak, Hobak Mayentehish, Awal Mashoftak, Habena,

Seedy Ana, Ana Moghrama, El Hal El Wahid, Thalg We Nar, Akher Zaman, Awel Wa Akher Habib, Aktar Men El Hob 1986, El Layaly 1987, We Law Ennak Beid Anni 1988, Gebt Kalb Meneen 1989, Amr El Hawa 1989, Ehlaw Omry 1990, Bayent Al Hob Alaya 1995, Ya Shouk 1996, Howa Mish Ana 1996, Matgarabnish 1997, Tobah 1999, Aerfo Ezaay 2004, Rige'na elba'dena (We are Back Together), The Exotic of Exotics 2009, Habena. *Honours:* Best Arab Singer, Ministry of Information and the Asscn of Singers, Morocco. *Website:* www.alamelphan.com.

HINCHLIFFE, Keith Phillip, BA, PhD; British musician (guitar), singer and teacher; b. 4 Jan. 1951, Glossop, Derbyshire, England. *Education:* Univs of Leicester and Hull. *Career:* several years, Folk and Blues club and concert circuit; mem. Albion Band 1991–92; extensive tuition and workshop experience; several appearances on BBC Radio and ITV; mem. Performing Right Soc., Musicians' Union, PPL. *Recordings:* albums: solo: Carolan's Dream 1994, Islands 1999, Red Scarf Smiler 2004, Ancient Music 2011; with The Albion Band: Captured 1994. *Publications:* guitar music books: Carolan's Dream 1995, O'Carolan for Everyone 1999, Islands 2007. *Address:* 23A Spring Hill, Sheffield, South Yorks., S10 1ET, England. *Telephone:* (114) 266-9896. *E-mail:* mail@keithhinchliffe.com. *Website:* www.keithhinchliffe.com.

HINCHLIFFE, Roger Redman, BA, MBA; American singer, composer, translator, teacher and editor; *Founder and CEO, A Man of His Words, E.T.C.;* b. 27 Dec. 1944, Springfield, Vt; s. of John H. Hinchliffe and Mary Elizabeth Redman Hinchliffe; m. Karen Soderberg 1995; one s. one d. *Education:* Bowdoin Coll., Johnson School at Cornell Univ., Univ. of Stockholm. *Career:* 11 tours of USA as solo vocalist, including 100 concerts in 20 states since 1988; numerous guest appearances on TV and radio in USA and Sweden; wrote and produced many musical productions for Swedish Nat. Radio; produced more than two dozen concert videos for TV; choral dir and teacher; Founder and CEO A Man of His Words (consultancy co.); mem. American Asscn of Sweden, Compact Disc Asscn, Choral Art Soc. of Portland, Maine; Asst Dir and Producer, Boy Singers of Maine; arranger/soloist, Cornell Sherwoods, Ithaca, NY. *Compositions:* more than 30 English translations and solo recordings of Sweden's greatest popular songs; 12 original compositions. *Recordings:* Cantalucha 1979, Festival Theme 1980, Sweden's Greatest 1988, Swedes on Love 1992, Master Olofs Choir 1994. *Publications include:* films translated from Swedish to English: Three Loves 1990, Greta Garbo 1994, Who Killed Olof Palme? 1995, Jerusalem 1996, Tattooed Widow 1997, Beginnings of Life 1998, numerous others. *Honours:* ten Festival Awards for Translations, Cannes, Montreux, 1986–98, named Sweden's Roving Amb. of Popular Music on nat. TV show 1997. *Address:* RogeRecords, 1221 Westbrook Street, Portland, ME 04102, USA (home); A Man of His Words, E.T.C., 1221 Westbrook Street, Portland, ME 04102, USA (office). *Telephone:* (207) 775-7501 (home); (207) 775-7504 (office). *Fax:* (207) 775-7502 (home); (207) 775-7502 (office). *E-mail:* roghinch@maine.rr.com (home); roger@amanofhiswords.com (office). *Website:* www.amanofhiswords.com (office).

HINDIRT, Mike; American musician (bass guitar). *Career:* mem., The Bravery 2003–. *Recordings include:* albums: Unconditional (EP) 2004, The Bravery 2005, The Sun and the Moon 2007, Stir the Blood 2009. *Address:* c/o Island Records, 364–366 Kensington High Street, London, W14 8NS, England.

HINDS, David; British singer, songwriter and musician (guitar); b. 15 June 1956, Birmingham. *Education:* Handsworth School, Birmingham. *Career:* Founder-mem., Steel Pulse 1975–; numerous TV appearances, world-wide tours. *Recordings include:* albums: Handsworth Revolution 1978, Tribute to the Martyrs 1979, Caught You (aka Reggae Fever) 1980, True Democracy 1982, Earth Crisis 1984, Reggae Refreshers 1985, Babylon the Bandit (Grammy Award) 1985, State of Emergency 1988, Victims 1991, Rastafari Centennial 1992, Smash Hits 1993, Vex 1994, Rastanthology 1996, Rage & Fury 1997, Sound System: The Island Anthology 1996, Living Legacy 1999, African Holocaust 2004. *Address:* c/o Richard Hermitage, Steel Plus Ltd, 33 Kersley Road, London, N16 0NT, England. *Telephone:* (121) 622-6857. *E-mail:* info@steel-pulse.com. *Website:* www.steel-pulse.com.

HINE, Rupert Neville; British record producer and musician (multi-instrumentalist); b. 21 Sept. 1947, Wimbledon; m. Natasha Hine; one s. *Career:* songwriter for Tina Turner, Stevie Nicks, Wilson Phillips, Robert Palmer, Dusty Springfield. *Recordings include:* albums: with Quantum Jump: Quantum Jump 1976, Barracuda 1977; solo albums: Pick up a Bone 1971, Unfinished Picture 1973, Immunity 1981, Waving Not Drowning 1982, Wildest Wish to Fly 1983, Deep End 1995; producer of over 100 albums for artists including Tina Turner, Bob Geldof, Rush, The Fixx, Howard Jones, Chris De Burgh, Stevie Nicks, Duncan Sheik; numerous film scores and television projects, including One World One Voice featuring: Peter Gabriel, Chrissie Hynde, Suzanne Vega, Lou Reed, Laurie Anderson, Dave Stewart, Sting.

HINKLER, Simon Thomas; British musician (guitar, keyboards), producer and programmer; b. 13 Nov. 1959, Sheffield; one s. *Career:* mem., Artery 1981–86, Pulp 1983–85; mem., The Mission 1986–90; worldwide tours, numerous television appearances; freelance programmer, producer 1994–; mem. Musicians' Union, PRS, PPL. *Recordings include:* albums: with Artery: Oceans 1982, Pulp-it 1983, Artery Live In Amsterdam 1985, The Flight Commander 1985; with Pulp: It 1983, Freaks 1986; with The Mission: God's Own Medicine 1986, The First Chapter 1987, Children 1988, Carved In Sand

1990; solo: Lose the Faith 2005. *Publication:* Names are for Tombstones Baby 1993. *E-mail:* info@simonhinkler.com. *Website:* www.simonhinkler.com.

HINTJENS, Arno; Belgian singer and musician; b. 21 May 1949, Ostend. *Career:* began performing while travelling through Europe during late 1960s; formed first band 1970; mem. Freckle Face 1972–74; formed Tjens Couter 1975–77; formed TC Matic with Jean-Marie Aerts 1980–86; began solo career; composed music for numerous films. *Recordings include:* albums: with Freckle Face: Freckle Face 1972; with Tjens Couter: Who Cares 1975, Plat Du Jour 1978; with TC Matic: TC Matic 1981, L'Apache 1982, Choco 1983, Ye Ye 1985; solo or as band leader: Arno 1986, Charlatan 1988, Ratata 1990, Charles Et Les Lulus 1991, Idiots Savants 1993, Water 1994, A La Française 1995, Give Me The Gift (compilation) 1997, Charles And The White Trash European Blues Connection 1998, Le European-Cowboy 1999, A Poil Commercial 1999, Le Best Of Arno (compilation) 2001, Charles Ernest 2002, Aux suivants 2003, Vers l'infini et au-delà! 2004, French Bazaar 2004, Chevalier des Zazous 2005, Arno 2005, Jus de Box 2007, Covers Cocktail 2008, Brussld 2010, Future Vintage 2012. *Current Management:* c/o Talent Sorcier, 56 Rue Notre Dame de Nazareth, 75003 Paris, France. *Telephone:* 1-44-59-99-00. *E-mail:* info@talentsorcier.com. *Website:* www.arno.be.

HIRAI, Ken; Japanese singer; b. 17 Jan. 1972, Osaka. *Career:* collaborations include Babyface, Stevie Wonder. *Recordings include:* albums: Un-balanced 1995, Stare At 1996, The Changing Same 2000, Gaining Through Losing 2001, KH Remixed-Up 1 2001, Life Is 2003, Ken's Bar 2003, Sentimental Lovers 2004, Fakin' Pop 2008, Japanese Singer 2011. *Honours:* RTHK Radio Award for Best New Japanese Act, Hong Kong, MTV Music Video Award for Best Male Artist Japan 2002. *Address:* c/o Sony Music Entertainment (Japan) Inc., 1–4 Ichigaya-Tamachi, Shinjuku-ku, Tokyo 162-8715, Japan. *Website:* www.sonymusic.co.jp/artist/KenHirai.

HIRO; Japanese musician; b. (Hiroyuki Igarashi), 1 June 1969. *Career:* fmr mem. Zoo; Founder-mem. J Soul Brothers, later renamed Exile, a 14-mem. band and dance group 1999–. *Recordings include:* albums: Our Style 2002, Styles of Beyond 2003, Exile Entertainment 2003, Asia 2006, Exile Evolution 2007, Exile Love (MTV Video Music Award Japan for Best Album 2008) 2007, Aisubeki Mirai e 2009, Negai no Tō 2011, Exile Japan/Solo 2012. *Honours:* MTV Video Music Awards Japan for Best Group Video 2007, 2009, for Best Video 2008, 2009, for Best Choreography 2009. *Address:* c/o Rhythm Zone Records, Avex Network, 3–1–30, Minami-Aoyama, Minato-ku, 107-0062 Tokyo, Japan. *E-mail:* sysadmin@avexnet.com. *Website:* www.exile.jp.

HIROMI, Go; Japanese singer and actor; b. (Hiromi Haratake), 18 Oct. 1955, Kasuya, Fukuoka; m. 1st Yurie Nitani (divorced); two d.; m. 2nd Nami Haratake. *Career:* professional debut 1971. *Television:* Shin-Hiraya Monogatari (NHK-TV) 1972, numerous acting appearances. *Films:* Saraba natsuno hikariyo 1976, Totsuzen arashi no youni 1977, Wani to oum to ottosei 1977, Daburu kuracchi 1978, Setouchi shonen yakyu dan 1984, Seijo densetsu 1985, Yari no gonza 1986, Komikku zasshi nanka iranai! 1986, Saraba itoshiki hito yo 1987, Maihime 1989, Samurai Cowboy 1993. *Recordings:* 58 solo albums include: Dandyism 1985, Hiromix 1991, Luna Llena 1993, The Goldsinger 1999, True Love Story 2000, Evolution 2005. *Honours:* Japan Records Newcomer Award 1972. *Address:* c/o Sony Music Entertainment (Japan) Inc., 1–4 Ichigaya-Tamachi, Shinjuku-ku, Tokyo 162-8715, Japan (office). *Website:* www.sonymusic.co.jp (office); www.hiromi-go.net.

HIROSE, Taka; Japanese musician (bass guitar); b. Tokyo. *Career:* mem. Feeder 1995–. *Recordings include:* albums: Polythene 1997, Yesterday Went Too Soon 1999, Echo Park 2001, Comfort In Sound 2002, Pushing The Senses 2005, Silent Cry 2008, Renegades 2010, Generation Freakshow 2012. *Address:* c/o Feeder Central, PO Box 2539, London, W1A 3HZ, England. *E-mail:* info@feederweb.com. *Website:* www.feederweb.com.

HIRST, Clare; British musician (saxophone), singer and composer; b. 13 Aug. 1959, Alston, Cumbria; m. Alan Barnes 1995; one s. *Career:* mem. of pop band, The Bellestars 1981–86; numerous live and television appearances. *Recordings include:* all Bellestars recordings; with The Communards: Don't Leave Me This Way 1986; with Luxuria: Unanswerable Lust 1988; with Clare Hirst Quartet: Tough and Tender 1995. *E-mail:* info@clarehirst.co.uk. *Website:* www.clarehirst.co.uk.

HIRST, Willie, LRAM, ARCM, LTCL; British bandleader, music director, arranger and musician (saxophone, clarinet, flute, recorder); *Partner, Maestro Music and Entertainment Agency;* b. 2 May 1941, Barnsley, South Yorks.; m. Hazel Irene Rainbow 1966; two s. *Education:* Huddersfield Coll. of Music, Bretton Hall Coll. *Career:* Lecturer in Instrumental Music, Bretton Hall Coll. and Leeds Coll. of Music; Partner with Hazel Hirst, Maestro Music and Entertainment Agency; Music Dir Wakefield Theatre Club, for 15 years; tours: Bobby Vee, Tony Christie, Marti Caine, Lionel Blair; concerts: Johnny Mathis, Tony Bennett, Buddy Greco, Victor Borge, Sacha Distel, Tommy Steele, Bruce Forsyth, Matt Monro, Drifters, Des O'Connor, Bob Monkhouse, Gladys Knight and the Pips; mem. Musicians' Union, Asscn of Teachers and Lecturers. *Address:* Belmont House, 32 Bell Lane, Ackworth, Pontefract, West Yorkshire, WF7 7JH, England. *Telephone:* (7760) 454269 (mobile) (office); (1977) 611107 (home).

HISASHI; Japanese musician (guitar); b. (Tonomura Hisashi), 2 Feb. 1972, Hakodate. *Career:* mem. pop/rock band, Glay, moved band to Tokyo 1990–; numerous live performances and tours, numerous radio broadcasts. *Recordings include:* albums: Hai to Daiyamondo 1994, Speed Pop 1995, BEAT out!

1996, Beloved (Nihon Record Grand Prize 1997) 1996, Review: Best of Glay 1997, Pure Soul (Nihon Record Best Album) 1998, Heavy Gauge 1999, Mirai Diary (film soundtrack) 2000, One Love 2001, Unity Roots & Family, Away 2002, The Frustrated 2004, Love is Beautiful 2007, Glay 2010, Justice 2013, Guilty 2013; singles: Rain 1994, Manatsuno Tobira 1994, Kanojo no Modern 1994, Freeze My Love 1995, Zutto Futari de 1995, Yes, Summerdays 1995, Ikiteju Tsuyosa 1995, Glorious 1996, Beloved (Japan Usen Broadcast Networks Gold Request Prize) 1996, Zutto Wasurenai (A Boy) 1996, Kuchibiru 1997, However (Nihon Record Excellent Work Award) 1997, Yuuwaku 1998, Soul Love 1998, Be With You 1998, Winter Again (Nihon Record Grand Prize) 1999, Kokodewanai, Dokokae 1999, Happiness 2000, Mermaid 2000, Tomadoi/ Special Thanks 2000, Missing You 2000, Global Communication 2001, Stay Tuned 2001, Hitohira no Jiyuu 2001, Way Of Difference 2002, Mata Kokode Aimashou 2002, Aitai Kimochi 2002, Beautiful Dreamer/Street Life 2003, Blue Jean 2004. *Honours:* Japan Usen Broadcast Networks Grand Prize 1997, 1999, Golden Arrow Music Prize 1998, Gold Disc Awards for Best Rock Artist of the Year, Best Music Video of the Year, Artist of the Year 1998, Gold Disc Awards for Song of The Year 1999, 2000, 2001, 2003, 2006. *Website:* www.glay.co.jp.

HITOMI; Japanese singer and musician (guitar); b. (Hitomi Furuya), 26 Jan. 1976, Tochigi; m. 2002; two c. *Career:* fmr model; solo artist 1995–. *Recordings include:* albums: Go to the Top 1995, By Myself 1996, Déjà vu 1997, Thermo Plastic 1999, Love Life 2000, Huma-Rhythm 2002, Self Portrait 2002, Traveler 2004, Love Concent 2006. *Address:* c/o Avex Inc., Sumitomo Seimei Aoyama Bldg, 3-1-30 Minami-Aoyama, Minato-ku, Tokyo 107-8577, Japan. *Website:* www.hitomilovelife.net.

HITOTO, Yo; Japanese singer; b. (Yan Yao), 20 Sept. 1976, Taipei, Taiwan. *Education:* Keio Univ. *Career:* J-pop style singer and songwriter; released debut single 2002; film acting debut 2004. *Recordings include:* albums: Tsukitenshin 2002, Hito-omoi 2004, & 2005, Bestyo 2006, Key 2008; singles: Morai naki (Sympathy Tears) 2002, Da-jia 2003, Kingyo Sukui 2003, Edo Polka 2003, Hanamizuki 2004, Kagefumi (JRA CM Theme Song) 2005, Kazaguruma 2005, Yubikiri 2005, Tsunaide Te 2007, Tadaima 2007, Ukeirete 2008, Hajimete (theme song for Gyoretsu no Dekiru Horitsu Sodanjo Cambodia Project, Nippon Television Network Corpn) 2008. *Films:* Coffee Jikou (Café Lumière) 2003, The Innocent Man in Love 2006, Rabu W Sotsugyô no uta: Songs for Tomorrow (TV film) 2008. *Address:* c/o Nippon Columbia Company Ltd, 4-14-14 Akasaka, Minato-ku, Tokyo 107-8011, Japan. *Website:* www.hitotoyo.ne.jp.

HITZ, Michael; Swiss singer and musician; b. 12 Oct. 1968, Baden. *Education:* studied acting, singing and phonetics. *Career:* church singing, nightclubs 1986; stage Cariete Polygon, Zurich 1989; radio show, Risiko, Seeperle, DRS Kultur 1992; tours Switzerland and Germany; worked with The Platters, Sina, Maja Brunner, musical Remember Me 1994; Talk Show, Bernard Theatre Zurich 1997–98; mem. Freunde Des Leedes, SUISA. *Recordings include:* Polygon, Clowns, Remember Me, Like A River Flows. *Address:* Thurwiesenstrasse 15, 8037 Zurich, Switzerland.

HNILIČKA, Jaromír; Czech composer and musician (trumpet); b. 11 Feb. 1932, Bratislava; m. (divorced); two d. *Education:* State Conservatory for Music. *Career:* composer and arranger 1953–; mem. Gustav Brom Big Band 1955–, currently leader; also f. jazz band Brno; mem. OSA. *Recording:* Missa Jazz 1968. *Honours:* Josef Blaha Prize, Ludek Hulan Prize, Composers' Asscn Prize. *Address:* Kupkova 22, 63800 Brno, Czech Republic.

HO, Fred Wei-Han Houn, BA; American composer, musician (baritone saxophone), writer and producer; b. 10 Aug. 1957, Palo Alto, Calif. *Education:* Harvard Univ. *Career:* Next Wave Festival, Brooklyn Academy of Music 1997, San Francisco Jazz Festival Herbst Theatre 1998; mem. ASCAP, American Composers Forum, American Music Center. *Compositions include:* Warrior Sisters (opera), Night Vision (opera), Journey Beyond the West: The New Adventure of Monkey, A Chinaman's Chance (opera). *Recordings include:* Warrior Sisters, Monkey: Part One and Part Two, Underground Railroad to My Heart, Tomorrow Is Now!, Turn Pain Into Power!. *Publications include:* Sounding Off!, Music as Subversion 1996, Womyn Warriors Calendar. *Honours:* Duke Ellington Distinguished Artist Lifetime Achievement Award 1988, National Endowment for the Arts Jazz Competition Fellowship 1992, Harvard Arts Medal 2009. *Address:* Big Red Media, 443 12th Street, Brooklyn, NY 11215, USA.

HOBBS, Paul Ernest Leonard; British musician (drums); b. 28 Dec. 1948, Burnt Oak, Edgware, Hendon, Middlesex; m. 1st Jane Pitkin 1975; m. 2nd Sylvia Picton 1987; two d. *Education:* tuition from Buddy Rich, Phil Seaman, James Blades, Sylvia Hobbs, Diana Clement, Brian Norman, Ron Watt. *Career:* mem., 'Twas Brillig 1964–65, Dr John and the Blues Preachers 1965–67, Dream Machine 1967–68, support to John Mayall's Blues Breakers 1967, Mahogany 1968–72, support to Peter Green's Fleetwood Mac/Status Quo 1968, Cochise 1980–82, T-Bone Boogie Band 1983–84, Pink 'N' Black 1984, The Anxious Brothers 1987–89, W. Arts et al 1990–99, Robert Bee Blues Corporation 1992–93, Danny White and The Shadds 1995–98, Ray Cave and Paul Hobbs (Sounds And Colour) 1998–99, Tigger and Paul 2001–04, Pat Hammond's Reflections 2004–; resident drummer, Gatsby's Nightclub, Chesham 1973–74. *Television and radio:* Utrecht Railway Museum performances for Jam (Dutch TV) 1970, 1971, Late Night Line-up with Marty Wilde (BBC) 1970–71, BBC Radio One Club. *Recordings include:* albums: Mahogany 1969, Mahogany with Marty Wilde 1970, Bring Back Rock 'N' Roll, Roy Powell

Combo 1971–72, Old Nick's Trainset 1972, Good Rockin' Now and Then (Marty Wilde) 1973, Kirsch 1973, Graunch 1973–74, Pale Lights 1973–76. *Honours:* Hon. mem. Musicians' Union. *Address:* Room 24, Symphony House, 43/45 Queen's Park Parade, Kingsthorpe, Northamptonshire, NH2 6LP, England (home). *Telephone:* (7939) 558775 (mobile).

HOBBS, Rebecca (Becky) Ann; American singer and songwriter; b. 24 Jan. 1950, Bartlesville, Okla; d. of William Harvey Hobbs and Geneva Clayton Hobbs; m. Frank Duane Sciacqua. *Education:* Tulsa Univ. *Career:* has performed in more than 40 countries; numerous live and TV performances; mem. Screen Actors Guild–American Fed. of Television and Radio Artists, American Fed. of Musicians, Nashville Songwriters Asscn International, Country Music Asscn, Daughters of the American Revolution. *Musical:* co-wrote Nanyehi-Beloved Woman of the Cherokee 2012. *Compositions:* co-wrote Angels Among Us (recorded by Alabama), co-wrote I Want To Know You Before We Make Love (recorded by Conway Twitty), co-wrote and recorded Jones On The Jukebox, wrote other songs recorded by George Jones, Loretta Lynn, Glen Campbell, Emmylou Harris, Helen Reddy, Shirley Bassey, Wanda Jackson and others. *Recordings include:* albums: All Keyed Up 1988, The Boots I Came to Town In 1993, From Oklahoma With Love 1998, Swedish Coffee & American Sugar 2000, Songs From the Road of Life 2004, Best of the Beckaroo 2006, Nanyehi-Beloved Woman of the Cherokee 2011. *Honours:* Citizen of the Cherokee Nation; Country Music Round-Up's Most Promising Int. Act 1989, Cashbox's Top Female Country Artist on Independent Label 1994. *Address:* c/o Beckaroo Music, PO Box 150272, Nashville, TN 37215, USA (office). *Telephone:* (615) 383-0041 (office). *E-mail:* beckaroomusic@comcast.net (office). *Website:* www.nanyehi.com; www.beckyhobbs.com.

HOBBS, Russel; American musician (drums, percussion). *Career:* animated mem. of virtual band, Gorillaz 1998– (see creator and Musical Dir Damon Albarn and creator and Visual Dir, Jamie Hewlett). *Website:* www.gorillaz.com.

HOBROUGH, Mark, BA; British record company executive and artist manager; b. 11 Sept. 1965, Cheshire. *Education:* Durham Univ. *Career:* with Spin Promotions Ltd, 1989; Man. Dir, Revolution Promotions and Lemon Records, 1991; Man. Dir, Revolution Promotions and Jealous Records; Man. of Sack and Darling Sugar Honey (Revolution Management), 1995, Founder, Swansfield Music 2010–. *E-mail:* mark@swansfieldmusic.com. *Website:* www.swansfieldmusic.com.

HOCHMAN, Larry; American composer and orchestrator; b. 21 Nov. 1953, New Jersey; m. Diane Hochman, one step-s., one step-d., one d. *Education:* Manhattan School of Music, 1972–75. *Career:* co-founder, with Larry Gates, Newfound Music Productions; mem, American Federation of Musicians; Pushcart Players. *Compositions include:* Steven Spielberg's Amazing Stories, 1986; Views of a Vanishing Frontier, 1987; Phantom of the Opera, 1990; In Memoriam, 1993; Dear America, 1993; American Portraits, 1996; The Very Last Butterfly, 1997; Music for the Movies, 1998; Hot Klezmer, 1998; Orchestrated: How Glory Goes, Audra McDonald, 2000. *Recordings:* One Man Band 1992, In Memoriam 1994. *Honours:* New Jersey Theatre Group Applause Award; Various CLIO Awards; ASCAP Award; Bistro Cabaret Award. *E-mail:* lh@larryhochman.net. *Website:* www.larryhochman.net.

HODES, Paul William, BA, JD; American consultant, attorney, record company executive, musician and producer; *President, Economic Innovation Institute and Action Fund;* b. 21 March 1951, New York, NY; m. Margaret A. Horstmann 1979; one s. one d. *Education:* Dartmouth Coll., Boston Coll. Law School. *Career:* Asst Attorney Gen., NH Criminal Justice Div.; Trial and Entertainment Attorney, Shaheen and Gordon PA, Concord, NH; cand. (Democrat) for US Congress 2004, 2006; US Representative, NH's 2nd Congressional Dist 2007–11; cand. (Democrat) for US Senate 2010; Pres. Econ. Innovation Inst. and Action Fund 2011–; Of Counsel, Shaheen & Gordon, P.A. 2012–; Man. mem. Big Road Music, LLC; mem. Bd of Dirs NJDC 2011–, ADL NE 2011–; Chair. Capitol Center for the Arts, 1990–96; mem. Bd Concord Community Music School, Children's Entertainment Asscn, New Hampshire Children's Alliance, Public Advisory Bd NH Inst. of Politics, Saint Anselm Coll. 2011–, Nat. Council on the Arts 2012–; Founding mem. Peggosus rock group; mem. American Soc. of Composers, Authors and Publrs (ASCAP), AFM local 374, NARAS. *Plays:* The People's House, The Edsel Was a Mistake. *Recordings:* Peggosus Jubilee! 1986, Peggosus Diggin' in the Dirt 1991, Peggo and Paul Patchwork Quilt 1996, Peggo and Paul Winter's Light 2000, Paul Hodes The People's House Musical 2000, Peggo and Paul Summer Nights 2003, Peggo and Paul Rock-A-Baby Band 2004, Peggo and Paul Bathtub Blues 2005, Paul Hodes Oscar Wilde Opera 2006. *Publications:* Peggo and Paul Rock-A-Baby Band 2004, Peggo and Paul Bathtub Blues 2005. *Honours:* ASCAP Awards, Parents Choice Honours 1987, 1996. *Address:* Shaheen and Gordon, PA, 107 Storrs Street, Concord, NH 03301, USA (office). *Telephone:* (603) 225-7262 (office). *E-mail:* paul.hodes@gmail.com (office). *Website:* www.economicinnovationinstitute.org (office).

HODGES, Charles (Chas) Nicholas; British musician (piano, guitar, bass), songwriter, singer and author; b. 28 Dec. 1943, Edmonton, London; m. Joan Adeline Findley 1966; two d. one s. *Education:* Higher Grade Senior School, Edmonton. *Career:* turned professional 1960; fmr mem. Mike Berry and the Outlaws, Cliff Bennett and the Rebel Rousers, Heads, Hands and Feet; mem. cockney duo, Chas & Dave (with Dave Peacock) 1960s–2009, 2013–; performing as solo artist, Chas and His Band 2009; worldwide tours, numerous radio, TV and live appearances; mem. Performing Right Soc., Mechanical-Copyright

Protection Soc., PPL. *Recordings include:* albums: with Chas & Dave: Oily Rags 1974, One Fing 'n' Anuvver 1975, Rockney 1978, Don't Give a Monkeys 1979, Mustn't Grumble 1981, Joblot 1982, Well Pleased 1984, Flying 1987, The EMI Years 2005, That's What Happens 2013; first solo album: Chas Hodges 2009. *Publications:* Chas Before Dave (autobiog.), All About Us (The Chas & Dave Story), Chas & His Rock 'n' Roll Allotment, The Adventures of Grapenut 2011. *Honours:* NME Bass Player of Year 1962. *Current Management:* c/o Barry Collings Entertainments Ltd, PO Box 1151, St Albans, AL1 9WB, England. *Telephone:* (1582) 792666. *E-mail:* barry-collings@btconnect.com. *Website:* www.barrycollings.co.uk. *Address:* PO Box 73, Stevenage, SG2 7JT, England (home). *Telephone:* (7831) 418031 (mobile). *Fax:* (1438) 880150 (home). *E-mail:* chasnhodges@yahoo.co.uk. *Website:* www.chasndave.com; www.chashodges.com.

HODGSON, Nick; British musician (drums) and songwriter. *Career:* Founder-mem., Runston Parva 1997, renamed Parva, renamed Kaiser Chiefs 2003–12. *Recordings include:* albums: Employment (Meteor Ireland Music Award for Best Int. Album 2006, NME Award for Best Album 2006, Ivor Novello Award for Best Album 2006) 2005, Yours Truly, Angry Mob 2007, Off With Their Heads 2008, The Future Is Medieval 2011, Souvenir: The Singles 2004–2012 2012. *Honours:* Meteor Ireland Music Award for Best Int. Group 2006, BRIT Awards for Best British Rock Act, Best British Live Act, Best British Group 2006, Nordoff-Robbins Silver Clef Award for Best Group 2006, Q Award for Best Video (for 'Ruby') 2007. *Current Management:* c/o SuperVision Management, Channelfly Group, 59–65 Worship Street, London, EC2A 2DU, England. *Telephone:* (20) 7688-9000. *Fax:* (20) 7688-8999.

HØEG, Thorsten Sehested, (Dane T. S. Hawk); Danish musician (saxophone), bandleader, composer, writer and entertainer; b. 6 Jan. 1957, Frederiksberg. *Education:* studied with saxophonist and composer, John Tchicai 1973–78, composer and arranger, Bob Brookmeyer 1997–99. *Career:* mem., John Tchicai and his Festival Band 1975–78, Sods/Sort Sol 1980–83; formed trio, Cockpit Music with percussionist Peter Ole Jørgensen (aka Pere Oliver Jørgens) and guitarist Søren Tarding 1978–; numerous concerts and tours in Denmark, Sweden, Switzerland, former Czechoslovakia and Yugoslavia; bandleader, Tapehead 1981–85, six- to nine-piece saxophone orchestra Somesax 1985–90; bandleader, 12-piece orchestra, Dane T. S. Hawk and his Great Mongo Dilmuns 1990–, and dectet Dane T. S. Hawk & The Locomotion Starsemble 2002–; numerous concerts, mostly in Denmark, including Copenhagen Jazz Festival, Venue Festival, Roskilde Festival, Århus Festuge and the jazz, rock and techno club circuit, also in Slovenia, Croatia, Expo 2000; solo entertainer 1980–, combining spoken word and saxophone, keyboard, turntable and taped music; tours in Denmark, Scandinavia, fmr Yugoslavia and Egypt; duo with sonic-programmer Troels Bech; mem. PEN, DJBFA, DSF. *Compositions include:* pieces for all groups of which a mem.; scores for Danish and French dance companies 1980's, The Royal Danish Theatre, Billedstofteatret, Denmarks Radio; The Sweet Devil On The Loose / I am 3 (for 75 musicians) 1994, SOAP (opera score, with libretti by poet Morti Vizki) 1995, Listen, No Heavy Breathing, Just Knock It Off (for percussion) 1997, I've Been Chopping Wood, That Makes Me A Hungry Man (piano concerto) 1998, Mista BB, You Pushed My Wall (for big band) 1999, Tromfoniske Maskinetter (for saxophone and percussion) 1999, 3 Betingelser For Liv (for octet) 1999, Millenniature (for string quartet) 2000, Hey Boys & Girls, We're Goin' To Pump You Up (for dectet) 2002, There Goes My Soul (for saxophone quartet) 2003, Dome Music (quintet) 2004. *Recordings include:* albums: with Cockpit Music: Transworlds Of Sounds 1981, Snow Lake City 1982, Salute For General Wasteland 1983, Stop/Go 1984, Hands Up 1989, The Great Dividing Range 1996, Tales From The North 1999, Solitude At Borderline 2003, This Does Not Look Like Our Town 2010; with Somesax: Flapper 1990; with Dane T. S. Hawk & His Great Mongo Dilmuns: Don't Hesitate (To Get Out There) 1996, Bøh (Music To An Imaginary Nordic Horror Tale) 1997, Death Disco 2000 (with remixes by Goodiepal) 1998, Dreamblues 2002, Dane T. S. Hawk & The Locomotion Starsemble: A General Broad View 2005; solo: Det Talte Ord & Raske Råberemser 2000, Danerlandet & Alt Det Andet 2004, Music to Hotel Proforma's The Sandchild 2007, Me my ear 2014. *Publications include:* books: Træer vinkler vandstråle i en kort forvintret sommer 1981, Amokoma 1982, Landskab ruller zone 1983, ½ så gammel som tiden 1987, Hotel Kontinental i likvidation 1990, Gutboy 1996, Ramt af jordens midte 1998, Verdens 25 bedste Jazzplader 2001, Samtid 2003; radio plays (music and words) for Denmarks Radio: Tilbud 1989, Som det er her i landet 1992, Damian Dagligdags Byrdefulde Brydningsår 1994, Dengang der fremtid til 2000; theatre plays: Alt Op Fra Grunden 1987, De Syv Dødssynder 1992, Saxo Vender Tilbage II 1997. *Honours:* several awards and grants for literature and music. *E-mail:* tshawk@mail.dk. *Website:* www.t.s.hoeg.dk.

HOFF, Jan Gunnar; Norwegian musician (piano), composer and educator; *Professor of Popular Music, Tromsø University*; b. 22 Oct. 1958, Bodø. *Education:* Trøndelag Music Conservatory, Norges musikkhøgskole, private classes with Harold Danko, Django Bates, Andy Laverne. *Career:* debut concert, Harstad Music Festival as solo artist 1992; concerts with Jan Gunnar Hoff Group, Vossajazz, Norway 1995, Molde Int. Jazz Festival 1996, (with Pat Metheny) 2001, Oris London Jazz Festival, Barbican 1996, Bergen Festival 1996, 1998, Stavanger Int. Jazz Festival 1998; collaborations with drummers, Kenwood Dennard 1999, Martin France 2000; Norwegian House concert, Paris 2000, La Maroquenerie club, Paris 2000; Vossajazz Festival, Norway with Maria Joao and others 2005; collaboration with Mike Stern 2006, Alex Acuna 2007–12; Mike Stern in Ukraine and Estonia 2007–08, with Alex Acuña in Stockholm, Zagreb and Rochester, New York 2009, Los Angeles 2010, Peru 2011; teacher of jazz, Tromsø Univ. 2003–, Prof. of Popular Music 2006–; Prof., Univ. of Agder (UiA), Kristiansand 2008–; Prof. of Popular Music, Univ. of Kristiansand 2011–; formed trio with Alex Acuña and Per Mathisen 2008–; Head of Bodø Jazz Open (jazz festival) 2011–; mem. NOPA (popular composers), Gramart (recording artists). *Recordings include:* Syklus 1993, Moving 1995, Crosslands 1998, Equilibrium 2001, In Town 2003, Meditatus (w/Bodø Domkor) 2007, Magma 2008, Jungle City 2009, Atmospheres 2011 Quiet Winter Night 2012, Barxeta 2012, Living 2013, Fly North 2014. *Honours:* The Stubö Prize 1997, Govt Grant 2000–01, Composer's Grant 2003–04, Edvard Grieg Prize 2005, Northern Lights Prize, Tromsø 2006, Buddy Prize, Norwegian Jazzfederation 2013. *Address:* Schyttesgt 14B, 8005 Bodø, Norway (home). *Telephone:* 90-55-32-36 (office). *E-mail:* jg@jangunnarhoff.no (office). *Website:* www.jangunnarhoff.no.

HOFFS, Susanna; American singer and musician (guitar); b. 17 Jan. 1959, Los Angeles, Calif. *Education:* Univ. of California, Berkeley. *Career:* Founder-mem. all-female group, The Bangles (originally Supersonic Bangs, then The Bangs) 1981–89; numerous tours and concerts; solo artist 1989–; re-formed The Bangles 2003–. *Film appearance:* The Allnighter 1986. *Recordings include:* albums: with The Bangles: The Bangles 1982, All Over The Place 1984, Different Light 1986, Everything 1988, Doll Revolution 2003, Sweetheart of the Sun 2011; solo: When You're A Boy 1991, Playback (with Tom Petty) 1995, Susanna Hoffs 1996, Under the Covers Vol. 1 (with Matthew Sweet, collection of other musicians' work) 2006, Under the Covers Vol. 2 1999, Under the Covers Vol. 3 2012, Someday 2012. *Current Management:* c/o William Morris Endeavor Entertainment, 9601 Wilshire Blvd, Beverly Hills, CA 90210, USA. *E-mail:* management@thebangles.com. *Website:* www.wmeentertainment.com; www.thebangles.com; www.susannahoffs.com.

HOFSTEIN, Francis, PhD; French psychoanalyst, writer and critic; b. 9 Oct. 1937, Thionville; m. Nicole Cerf; three s. *Education:* Conservatoire de Musique. *Career:* Ed. L'Ordinaire du psychanalyste 1973–78; Ed. La Pierre; mem. Acad. du Jazz, École Freudienne de Paris. *Exhibitions:* Le Siècle du jazz (MART, Rovereto, Musée du Quai Branly, Paris, CCCB, Barcelona) 2008–09, Django Reinhardt, Swing de Paris, Cité de la Musique 2012. *Publications:* Au Miroir Du Jazz 1985, Oakland Blues 1989, James Pichette Et Le Jazz (co-author) 1991, Body and Soul (co-author) 1991, Le Rhythm and Blues 1991, Black, Brown and Beige (co-author) 1992, Rencontre (co-author) 1994, Jazz: Suite Pour Sacha 1995, Blue Moon 1996, Muddy Waters (biog.) 1996, Bonsoir ma Jolie (co-author) 1998, Guide du Jazz (co-author) 1998, Noir Soleil (co-author) 1998, Demain (co-author) 1999, Braise (co-author) 2000, Le Poison de la Dépendance 2000, La Pulsion de Mort (co-author) 2004, Agharta (co-author) 2004, Gris (co-author) 2005, Ladybird (co-author) 2005, L'Amour du corps 2005; contribs to Dictionnaire du Jazz, Coulot: la peinture devant soi, Blues, les Incontournables; journals: Jazz Magazine, Soul Bag, Présence Africaine, Essaim, Le Bloc-notes de la Psychanalyse; Chief Ed. L'Art du Jazz 2009, 2011. *Honours:* Chevalier des Arts et des Lettres 2009. *Address:* 5 rue Ernest et Henri Rousselle, 75013 Paris, France. *Telephone:* 1-45-89-71-03. *E-mail:* franhof@wanadoo.fr.

HOGAN, Michael Gerard; Irish musician (bass guitar); b. 29 April 1973, Limerick. *Career:* founding mem., The Cranberry Saw Us, renamed The Cranberries, 1990–2003, 2009–; numerous headlining tours, festivals, radio and television appearances. *Recordings:* albums: Everybody Else Is Doing It, So Why Can't We? 1993, No Need To Argue 1994, To The Faithful Departed 1996, Bury The Hatchet 1999, Bury The Hatchet: The Complete Sessions 2000, Wake Up And Smell The Coffee 2001, Treasure Box 2002, Stars: The Best Of 1992–2002 2002, Roses 2012. *Current Management:* c/o Danny Goldberg, Gold Village Entertainment, 72 Madison Avenue, Eighth Floor, New York, NY 10016, USA. *Telephone:* (212) 741-2400. *Fax:* (212) 741-4871. *E-mail:* info@goldve.com. *Website:* www.goldve.com; www.cranberries.com.

HOGAN, Noel Anthony; Irish musician (guitar); b. 25 Dec. 1971, Limerick. *Career:* founding mem., The Cranberry Saw Us, renamed The Cranberries, 1990–2003, 2009–; numerous headlining tours, festivals, radio and television appearances; founder mem. Mono Band 2004–07. *Recordings:* albums: with The Cranberries: Everybody Else Is Doing It, So Why Can't We? 1993, No Need To Argue 1994, To The Faithful Departed 1996, Bury The Hatchet 1999, Bury The Hatchet: The Complete Sessions 2000, Wake Up And Smell The Coffee 2001, Treasure Box 2002, Stars: The Best Of 1992–2002 2002, Roses 2012; with Mono Band: Mono Band 2005. *Current Management:* c/o Danny Goldberg, Gold Village Entertainment, 72 Madison Avenue, Eighth Floor, New York, NY 10016, USA. *Telephone:* (212) 741-2400. *Fax:* (212) 741-4871. *E-mail:* info@goldve.com. *Website:* www.goldve.com. *Address:* The Cranberries, PO Box 180, Limerick, County Limerick, Ireland. *Website:* www.cranberries.com.

HOGARTH, Steve, (H); British musician, singer and songwriter; b. 14 May 1959, Kendal, Cumbria. *Career:* singer with groups The Europeans, How We Live; lead singer, progressive rock group Marillion 1989–; numerous tours; collaborations with The The, Julian Cope and Toni Childs; solo artist 1997–. *Recordings include:* albums: with The Europeans: Vocabulary 1982, Recurring Dreams 1984; with Marillion: Season's End 1989, Holidays In Eden 1991, Brave 1994, Afraid of Sunlight 1995, Made Again 1996, This Strange Engine 1997, Radiation 1998, Afraid of Sunlight 1999, Anorak In The UK Live 2002, Somewhere Else 2007; solo (as 'H'): Ice Cream Genius 1997, Live Spirit: Live Body 2002, H Natural Selection 2010, Not the Weapon But the Hand 2012.

E-mail: info@knowmoremanagement.com. *Address:* PO Box 252, Aylesbury, Buckinghamshire HP18 0YS, England. *Fax:* (1296) 770-839. *E-mail:* band@ marillion.com. *Website:* www.marillion.com; www.stevehogarth.com.

HÖGLUND, Kjell, BA; Swedish songwriter, artist and musician (guitar); b. 8 Dec. 1945, Östersund; partner Margaretha Granström. *Compositions include:* Witch-Trial, Smooth Water, Sea of Gennesaret, One Big Strong, One Gets Accustomed, The Last Battle. *Recordings include:* albums: Undran 1971, Blomstertid 1972, Häxprocess 1973, Baskervilles Hund 1974, Hjärtat sitter till vänster 1975, Dr Jekylls testamente 1979, Vägen mot Shangri-La 1980, Tidens tecken 1984, Hemlig kärlek 1986, Ormens år 1989, Höglund Forever 1992, Inkognito 1995, Kryptonit 2001, Pandoras Ask 2006. *Publications include:* Brända skepp (song book) 1987, Magnum Opus (novel) 1991, Det sicilianska sigillet (novel) 1997, Genomträngningen 1999, Den förbjudna boken 2000, Det snöar i Edens lustgård 2005, Ando-Random Haglund 2013. *E-mail:* lugnarevatten@gmail.com (office). *Website:* www.kjellhoglund.com.

HÖH, Volker; German guitarist and guitar teacher; *Guitar Teacher, Landesmusikgymnasium Rheinland-Pfalz, Montabaur;* b. 24 April 1959, Altenkirchen, Pfalz; m. Jutta Maria Höh 1980; two d. *Education:* Univ. Rheinland-Pfalz, Koblenz, Staatliche Hochschule für Musik, Westfalen-Lippe, Münster. *Career:* recitalist and soloist with orchestras; radio and TV engagements; performed in most major cities and festivals; guitar teacher, Landesmusikgymnasium Rheinland-Pfalz, Montabaur 1994–, Univ. of Rheinland-Pfalz, Koblenz 1998–2011; master-classes and workshops; jury -mem. at int. competitions and festivals; ed. of pedagogic and chamber music guitar literature; mem. EGTA, BDZ. *Recordings include:* solo: Cantos de Cuba, Danzas Fantásticas, Triops-Botschaft, Matthias Drude: Kammermusik, Zypern-Variationen, Gala d'Opera (Mozart, Rossini, Verdi on historic instruments), Dreams of Love (Romantic love songs), J. S. Bach: Ich ruf zu dir Herr Jesu Christ, Cenas Brasileiras: Villa-Lobos and Savio; duets: Calliope-Calls (with Christina Ascher), Annette Schlünz: Kammermusik, 7. und 8. Dresdner Tage der zeitgenössischen Musik; played on The Straits of Magellan (Turfan Ensemble), Fünf Stücke op. 10 (RSO Frankfurt), Zwei Suiten für Jazzorchester (RSO Frankfurt), Von Heute Auf Morgen (RSO Frankfurt), Die Jakobsleiter (RSO Frankfurt), Cristoforo Colombo (RSO Frankfurt), German composers for 1, 2, 3 and 4 guitars, Ein Tango für Gardel, Tango with music and text, with Raphaela Crossey. *Publications include:* contrib. of articles on guitar to music periodicals. *Honours:* stipends and scholarships from Kultusministerium Rheinland-Pfalz, Darmstädter Ferienkurse, Richard Wagner Verband, Deutscher Musikrat, Deutscher Orchesterwettbewerb (with guitar ensemble cantomano) 2000, 2004, 2008, 2012, 2016, Glücksspirale Prize 2013. *Address:* Taunusstrasse 14, 56410 Montabaur, Germany (office). *Telephone:* (2620) 9506667 (office). *E-mail:* volker.hoeh@t-online.de. *Website:* www.volker-hoeh.de.

HOIER, Svein; Norwegian musician (guitar, keyboard, drums); *Associate Professor Norwegian University of Science and Technology;* b. 18 Nov. 1970, Oslo. *Education:* Trondheim Univ. *Career:* started as drummer with Closet Queens; joined Hedge Hog, playing guitar, keyboard, sampler, 1994; toured Europe, 1994, 1995. *Recordings include:* with Closet Queens: Closet Queens 1993; with Hedge Hog: Mindless 1994, The Healing (EP) 1995, Thorn Cord Wonder 1995. *Films include:* Smoking, Svein (short films). *Honours:* Svein, Best Film, Trondheim Film Festival, 1995. *Address:* Department of Art and Media Studies, Norwegian University of Science and Technology, Høgskoleringen 1, 7491 Trondheim, Norway (home). *Telephone:* 73-59-64-52 (office). *E-mail:* svein.hoier@ntnu.no (office). *Website:* www.ntnu.edu (office).

HOLDER, Neville (Noddy), MBE; British singer, songwriter, musician (guitar), actor and radio presenter; b. 15 June 1950, Walsall, West Midlands. *Career:* fmr guitarist and backing vocalist, Steve Brett and The Mavericks; singer and guitarist, rock group Slade (formerly N'Betweens, Ambrose Slade) 1966–91, co-writer of Slade's songs with Jimmy Lea; numerous concert tours and festival appearances; occasional radio presenter, Piccadilly Radio (Manchester), Capital Gold (London), host, Noddy Holder's Party Crazee (radio) 2002–. *Film appearance:* Flame 1974. *Television appearances include:* The Grimleys (ITV 1) 1997–2001, I Love 1973 (BBC 2) 2000, Max and Paddy's Road to Nowhere (Channel 4) 2004. *Recordings include:* albums: Beginnings (as Ambrose Slade) 1969, Play It Loud 1970, Slade Alive 1972, Slayed 1973, Sladest 1973, Old New Borrowed Blue 1974, Slade In Flame (soundtrack) 1974, Nobody's Fool 1976, Slade Alive Vol. 2 1978, Return To Base 1979, Slade Smashes 1980, Till Deaf Do Us Part 1981, We'll Bring The House Down 1981, Slade On Stage 1982, The Amazing Kamikaze Syndrome 1983, Slade's Greats 1984, Rogue's Gallery 1985, Crackers 1985, You Boyz Make Big Noize 1987, Wall of Hits 1991, The Very Best of Slade 2006, Slade Anthology 2006, Flame Dud 2007. *Publications:* Who's Crazee Now (autobiography) 2000, The World According to Noddy 2014. *Honours:* awarded freedom of his home town of Walsall 2014; Hon. Fellow, Univ. of Wolverhampton 2002. *Current Management:* c/o Newman and Co., Regent House, 1 Pratt Mews, London, NW1 0AD, England. *Telephone:* (20) 7554-4840 (office). *E-mail:* clive@newman-and.co .uk. *Website:* www.noddyholder.com.

HOLE, (Christopher Charles) Maximilian (Max); British music industry executive; *Chairman and CEO, Universal Music Group International;* b. 26 May 1951, London, England; m. Jan Ravens 1999; three s. *Career:* began career in music industry as Co-founder (with Geoff Jukes) Gemini Artists (agency) 1972; Man., Artists and Repertoire Dept, Warner Music Group 1982–98, Man. Dir East West Records 1990; Sr Vice-Pres. for Marketing and

A&R, Universal Music Group International 1998–2004, Exec. Vice-Pres. 2004, also assumed responsibility for Universal's Asia/Pacific business, COO Universal Music Group International 2010–13, Chair. and CEO 2013–. *Address:* Universal Music Group International, 364–366 Kensington High Street, London, W14 8NS, England (office). *E-mail:* info@universalmusic.com (office). *Website:* www.universalmusic.com (office).

HOLIDAY, Doc, BMus; American record producer, recording artist and record company executive; b. (Edward Wohanka), 29 Jan. 1943, Newark, New Jersey; one s. two d. *Career:* worked at Sun Studios, Memphis, Sigma Sound Studios, Philadelphia, Virtue Studios, Philadelphia, Alpha Audio, Virginia, Acoustic Loop Studios, Alabama; fmr mem. JayWalkers; fmr Head of A&R, ABC Paramount Records; co-f. The Soul Set, later known as The Doc Holiday Band; 76 US Country No. 1 hits as record producer; retired from touring 1983; est. Power Plant Recording Studios 1983–; CEO Tug Boat International Records 1984–, Mega International Records 1987–; mem. BMI, ASCAP, SESAC. *Recordings include:* as recording artist: Expressway To Your Heart, Just My Imagination, Walkin' In Memphis; as producer: Cajun Baby, Hank Williams Jr, Louisiana Man, Doug Kershaw, Mr Jones, Big Al Downing. *Honours:* 36 Music Awards, two Grammy Awards, ICMA Producer of the Year 1993–95. *Address:* Doc Holiday's Power Plant Studios, 2708 Build America Drive, Hampton, VA 23666, USA (office). *Telephone:* (757) 827-8733 (office). *E-mail:* hithithit@aol.com. *Website:* www.1docholiday.com.

HOLLAND, Annabel (Annie); British musician (bass guitar); b. 26 Aug. 1965. *Career:* mem., Elastica 1992–95, 1999–2001; toured extensively worldwide. *Recordings include:* albums: Elastica 1995, The Menace 2000, The BBC Sessions 2001; singles: Stutter 1993, Connection 1994, Line Up 1994, Waking Up 1995, Mad Dog 2000, The Menace 2000. *Honours:* NME Readers Award for Best New Band 1994.

HOLLAND, Brian; American composer, songwriter and record producer; b. 15 Feb. 1941, Detroit, MI. *Career:* lead singer, the Satintones, 1950s; mem. of composition and production team, Holland/Dozier/Holland (with brother Eddie Holland and Lamont Dozier) 1963; co-founder, Invictus and Hot Wax record labels 1967–75. *Recordings include:* as co-writer, producer: with Marvin Gaye: Can I Get A Witness? 1963, You're A Wonderful One 1964, How Sweet It Is (To Be Loved By You) 1964, Little Darling 1966; with Martha and The Vandellas: Heatwave, Quicksand, Nowhere To Run, Jimmy Mack; with Diana Ross and the Supremes: Where Did Our Love Go 1964, Baby Love 1964, Come See About Me 1965, Stop! In The Name of Love 1965, Back In My Arms Again 1965, You Can't Hurry Love 1966, You Keep Me Hanging On 1966, Love Is Here and Now You're Gone 1967, The Happening 1967; with the Four Tops: Baby I Need Your Loving 1965, I Can't Help Myself 1965, (It's The) Same Old Song, 1965, Reach Out I'll Be There 1966, Bernadette 1967, Standing in the Shadows of Love 1967; with the Miracles: Mickey's Monkey, I'm The One You Need; with the Isley Brothers: This Old Heart of Mine 1966, I Guess I'll Always Love You 1966, Put Yourself In My Place 1969; other recordings with Aretha Franklin, Kim Weston, Freda Payne, Chairmen of the Board. *Honours:* BMI Icon Award 2003.

HOLLAND, Dave; British jazz musician (double bass, cello, bass guitar); b. 1 Oct. 1946, Wolverhampton, W Midlands, England. *Education:* Guildhall School of Music and Drama, London. *Career:* made professional debut 1963; regular musician at Ronnie Scott's club 1967–68; mem., Miles Davis band 1968–70; co-founder and mem., Circle 1970–71; mem., Stan Getz Quartet 1972–73; guest teacher, Creative Music Studio, Woodstock, NY 1972; worked with Anthony Braxton 1973–74, Sam Rivers 1973–81; founding mem., Gateway 1975–; formed Dave Holland Quintet 1982–87, 1997–, Dave Holland Trio 1988, Dave Holland Quartet 1988, 1994, Dave Holland Octet 2001, Dave Holland Big Band 2002, Overtone Quartet; toured with Jack DeJohnette's Parallel Realities 1990; mem., Herbie Hancock Trio 1992; Artistic Dir, summer jazz workshop, Banff School, AB, Canada 1983–90; Faculty mem., New England Conservatory of Music, Boston, MA 1987–90; collaborations with artists, including Jack DeJohnette's Parallel Realities, Herbie Hancock, John Surman, John McLaughlin, Evan Parker, Kenny Wheeler, John Taylor, Chris MacGregor, Thelonious Monk, Betty Carter, Hank Jones, Joe Henderson. *Recordings include:* albums: Conference of the Birds 1972, Dave Holland & Sam Rivers 1976, Volume 2 (with Sam Rivers) 1977, Emerald Tears 1977, Life Cycle 1981, Jumpin' In (with Dave Holland Quintet) 1984, Seeds Of Time (with Dave Holland Quintet) 1985, The Razor's Edge (with Dave Holland Quintet) 1987, Triplicate (with Dave Holland Trio) 1988, Extensions (with Dave Holland Quartet) 1989, Ones All 1993, Feed The Fire 1994, Homecoming (with Gateway) 1994, Dream Of The Elders (with Dave Holland Quartet) 1995, Points Of View (with Dave Holland Quintet) 1998, Prime Directive (with Dave Holland Quintet) 1999, Not For Nothin' (with Dave Holland Quintet) 2001, What Goes Around (with Dave Holland Big Band) 2002, Extended Play: Live At Birdland (with Dave Holland Quintet) 2003, Rarum X: Selected Recordings 2004, Overtime (with Dave Holland Big Band) (Grammy Award for Best Large Jazz Ensemble Album 2006) 2005, Music from Two Basses (with Barre Phillips) 2005, Critical Mass 2006, Pass It On 2008, Pathways 2010, Hands (with Pepe Habichuela) 2010, Prism 2013, The Art of Conversation (with Kenny Barron) (Jazz Journalists' Asscn Award for Record of the Year 2015) 2014. *Honours:* Dr hc (Berklee School of Music); Bell Atlantic Jazz Award, Jazz Journalists' Asscn Award for Trio or Duo of the Year 2015. *Current Management:* c/o Louise Holland, Vision Arts Management, 307 W 36th Street, New York, NY 10018, USA. *Telephone:* (845) 247-8969. *Fax:* (845)

247-8970. *E-mail:* louise@visionartsmgmt.com. *Website:* www .visionartsmgmt.com; www.daveholland.com.

HOLLAND, Dexter, PhD; American singer and musician (guitar); b. (Bryan Keith Holland), 29 Dec. 1966, Orange County, Calif.; m. Kristinia Luna; one d. *Education:* Univ. of Southern California. *Career:* fmr drummer; Founder-mem., Manic Subsidal 1984, renamed The Offspring 1986–; numerous live shows, festival appearances and tours; Co-owner, Nitro label; Owner, D-13 studios, Huntington Beach. *Recordings include:* albums: The Offspring 1989, Ignition 1992, Smash! 1994, Ixnay On The Hombre 1997, Americana 1998, Conspiracy Of One 2000, Splinter 2003, Greatest Hits 2005, Rise and Fall, Rage and Grace 2008, Days Go By 2012. *Honours:* Kerrang! Award for Classic Songwriter (with The Offspring) 2002. *E-mail:* info@offspring.com. *Website:* offspring.com.

HOLLAND, Edward (Eddie), Jr; American composer, songwriter and record producer; b. 30 Oct. 1939, Detroit, Mich. *Career:* fmr mem. Fideltones, mem. songwriting and production team Holland/Dozier/Holland (with Brian Holland and Lamont Dozier); co-writer, producer, numerous records by numerous Motown artists, including a dozen US number 1 hits 1963–68; split from Motown 1967; Co-founder, Invictus and Hot Wax record labels 1967–75. *Recordings include:* as co-producer, writer (with Marvin Gaye): Can I Get A Witness? 1963, You're A Wonderful One 1964, How Sweet It Is (To Be Loved By You) 1964, Little Darling 1966; with Martha and The Vandellas: Heatwave, Quicksand, Nowhere To Run, Jimmy Mack; with Diana Ross and the Supremes: Where Did Our Love Go 1964, Baby Love 1964, Come See About Me 1965, Stop! In The Name of Love 1965, Back In My Arms Again 1965, You Can't Hurry Love 1966, You Keep Me Hanging On 1966, Love Is Here and Now You're Gone 1967, The Happening 1967; with the Four Tops: Baby I Need Your Loving 1965, I Can't Help Myself 1965, (It's The) Same Old Song 1965, Reach Out I'll Be There 1966, Bernadette 1967, Standing In The Shadows of Love 1967; with the Miracles: Mickey's Monkey, I'm The One You Need; with the Isley Brothers: This Old Heart of Mine 1966, I Guess I'll Always Love You 1966, Put Yourself In My Place 1969; solo: Eddie Holland 1962; other recordings with Aretha Franklin, Kim Weston, Freda Payne, Chairmen of The Board. *Honours:* Broadcast Music Icon Award 2003.

HOLLAND, Julian (Jools) Miles, OBE; British musician (piano, keyboard) and broadcaster; b. 24 Jan. 1958, London; one s. two d.; m. Christabel McEwen 2005. *Education:* Invicta Sherington School, Shooters' Hill School. *Career:* pianist 1975–78; Founder-mem. Squeeze 1974–81, 1985–90; regular tours and concerts; formed The Jools Holland Big Band 1987, later renamed The Rhythm and Blues Orchestra 1991–. *Films:* Spiceworld: The Movie 1997, Milk (wrote score) 1999. *Radio:* presenter BBC Radio 2 1997–. *Television:* The Tube (presenter) 1982–87, Walking to New Orleans (writer, producer and presenter, documentary) 1985, The Groovy Fellas (actor and writer) 1988, Juke Box Jury (presenter) 1989–90, Saturday Night (co-presenter New York NBC music show with David Sanborn) 1989, The Happening 1990, Mr Roadrunner (writer and producer, film) 1991, Later with Jools Holland (presenter) 1992–, Hootenanny (presenter) 1993–, Don't Forget Your Toothbrush 1994–95, Name That Tune 1997, Beat Route (writer and producer, film) 1998, Jools Meets The Saint (writer and producer) 1999, Jools' History of the Piano 2002, Jools Holland: London Calling 2012. *Recordings include:* albums: with Squeeze: Squeeze 1978, Cool for Cats 1979, Argy Bargy 1980, East Side Story 1981, Cosi Fan Tutti Frutti 1985, Babylon and On 1987, Frank 1989, Tom Jones and Jools Holland 2004, Swinging the Blues, Dancing the Ska 2005; solo: A World of his Own 1990, Full Complement 1991, A–Z of the Piano 1992, Live Performance 1994, Solo Piano 1994, Sex and Jazz and Rock and Roll 1996, Lift the Lid 1997, Sunset Over London 1999, Hop the Wag 2000, Small World, Big Band – Friends 2001, Small World, Big Band Vol. 2 – More Friends 2002, Small World, Big Band Vol. 3 2003, Moving Out to the Country (with Rhythm & Blues Orchestra) 2006, The Informer 2008, Rocking Horse (with Rhythm & Blues Orchestra) 2010, The Golden Age of Song 2012, Sirens of Song 2014. *Publications:* Beat Route 1998, The Hand That Changed Its Mind 2004, Barefaced Lies and Boogie-Woogie Boasts (autobiog.) 2007. *Honours:* BBC Radio 2 Jazz Artist of the Year 2006. *Current Management:* One-Fifteen, 1 Globe House, Middle Lane Mews, London, N8 8PN, England. *Telephone:* (20) 8442-7560. *Fax:* (20) 8442-7561. *E-mail:* enquiries@onefifteen.com. *Website:* www.onefifteen.com. *Address:* Helicon Mountain Ltd, Helicon Mountain, Station Terrace Mews, London, SE3 7LP, England (office). *Telephone:* (20) 8858-0984 (office). *Fax:* (20) 8293-4555 (office). *E-mail:* contact@joolsholland .com (home). *Website:* www.joolsholland.com (home).

HÖLLJES, Brittany; American singer; s. of Christian Hölljes and Laurie Kramer Hölljes. *Education:* Univ. of California, Berkeley. *Career:* Founder mem. Delta Rae (with brothers Eric and Ian) 2009–; first EP released 2010; signed to Sire Records 2011; debut album 2012; numerous live performances; support act for Edwin McCain and Hanson. *Recordings include:* album: with Delta Rae: Carry the Fire 2012, After It All 2015. *Current Management:* c/o Jordan Burger, Fleming Artists, 543 North Main Street, Ann Arbor, MI 48104, USA. *E-mail:* Jordan@flemingartists.com; deltaraemgmt@gmail.com. *Address:* c/o Sire Records, Warner Bros. Records, Warner Music Group, 75 Rockefeller Plaza, New York, NY 10019, USA (office). *Website:* www.deltarae .com.

HÖLLJES, Eric Richard; American singer, songwriter and musician (piano, keyboards); b. Durham, North Carolina; s. of Christian Hölljes and

Laurie Kramer Hölljes. *Education:* Duke Univ. *Career:* fmr mem. (with brother Ian) Running Lights; Founder mem. Delta Rae (with brother Ian and sister Brittany) 2009–; first EP released 2010; signed to Sire Records 2011; debut album 2012; numerous live performances; support act for Edwin McCain and Hanson. *Recordings include:* album: with Delta Rae: Carry the Fire 2012, After It All 2015. *Current Management:* c/o Jordan Burger, Fleming Artists, 543 North Main Street, Ann Arbor, MI 48104, USA. *E-mail:* Jordan@flemingartists.com; deltaraemgmt@gmail.com. *Address:* c/o Sire Records, Warner Bros. Records, Warner Music Group, 75 Rockefeller Plaza, New York, NY 10019, USA (office). *Website:* www.deltarae.com.

HÖLLJES, Ian Christian; American singer, songwriter and musician (guitar); b. 1985, Durham, North Carolina; s. of Christian Hölljes and Laurie Kramer Hölljes. *Education:* Duke Univ. *Career:* fmr mem. (with brother Eric) Running Lights; Founder mem. Delta Rae (with brother Eric and sister Brittany) 2009–; first EP released 2010; signed to Sire Records 2011; debut album 2012; numerous live performances; support act for Edwin McCain and Hanson. *Recordings include:* album: with Delta Rae: Carry the Fire 2012, After It All 2015. *Current Management:* c/o Jordan Burger, Fleming Artists, 543 North Main Street, Ann Arbor, MI 48104, USA. *E-mail:* Jordan@flemingartists.com; deltaraemgmt@gmail.com. *Address:* c/o Sire Records, Warner Bros. Records, Warner Music Group, 75 Rockefeller Plaza, New York, NY 10019, USA (office). *Website:* www.deltarae.com.

HOLLOWAY, Laurence (Laurie), MBE; British musician (piano), composer and music director; b. 31 March 1938, Oldham, Lancs., England; s. of Marcus Holloway and Annie Gillespie Holloway; m. Marion Montgomery 1965 (died 2002); two d. *Education:* Oldham Grammar School. *Career:* touring dance band pianist 1950s, Cyril Stapleton Showband, Joe Daniels Hotshots 1950s, Cunard Line 1956–57; London Weekend Television, regular pianist 1967–80; Musical Dir, Engelbert Humperdinck 1970–75, Marion Montgomery, Judy Garland; played at studios in London 1975–85; now mainly charity work and Montgomery Holloway Music Trust. *Compositions include:* Instant Marriage (musical) 1963; numerous TV signature tunes, including Blind Date, Beadle's About. *Television:* Musical Dir: first three series of Strictly Come Dancing (BBC 1) 2004–05, Parkinson (BBC) for ten years. *Recordings include:* solo albums: Blue Skies, Showtime, Cumulus, About Time, Live at Abbey Road; also recorded with many artists including Kiri Te Kanawa, Marion Montgomery, Robert Farnon, Rolf Harris, Cleo Laine (Loesser Genius). *Publication:* Piano Studies. *Honours:* Gold Badge of Merit, British Acad. of Songwriters, Composers and Authors. *Address:* Elgin, Fishery Road, Bray, SL6 1UP, England.

HOLLWEG, Rebecca, BA (Hons); British singer and songwriter; b. 30 June 1964, London, England; d. of Alexander Hollweg and Geraldine Hollweg; m. Andy Hamill; one d. *Education:* Univ. of Oxford, Guildhall School of Music and Drama (Diploma Jazz and Studio Music), postgraduate jazz course. *Career:* venues include South Bank Centre, Borderline, Ronnie Scott's, Union Chapel, London, arts centres and theatres around the UK, festivals and gigs across Europe; support artist to Roger McGuinn of The Byrds 2001–02, to Paul Carrack 2003; Co-founder, with Andy Hamill, Emu Records; mem. Performing Right Soc., PPL, Musicians' Union. *Music soundtrack:* The Bitterest Pill. *Radio:* BBC Radio 2 sessions with Janice Long, Aled Jones, BBC Radio 4 sessions on Loose Ends, Woman's Hour, BBC 6 Music Tom Robinson Show, album airplay on BBC Radio 2 from Jamie Cullum, Janice Long, Jeremy Vine, Aled Jones, Eamon Holmes, Alex Lester. *Television:* The Ayala Show (Irish TV) 2015. *Recordings:* albums: The Demos 1999, June Babies 2001, Orange Roses 2008, Country Girl 2015. *Publication:* The Ball That Got Stuck in the Tree (children's story, illustrated by Jeb Loy Nichols) 2010. *E-mail:* info@rebeccahollweg.com. *Website:* www.rebeccahollweg.com.

HOLM, Georg (Goggi); Icelandic musician (bass guitar). *Career:* founder mem., Sigur Rós 1994–; numerous tours. *Recordings include:* albums: Von, Ágœtis Byrjun 2000, ( ) 2002, Takk... 2005, Hvarf-Heim 2007, Með Suð I Eyrum Við Spilum Endalaust 2008, Valtari 2012; DVD: Heima 2007. *Honours:* Shortlist Music Prize 2001. *Address:* c/o Smekkleysa Records, PO Box 1263, 121 Reykjavík, Iceland (office). *Website:* www.sigur-ros.com.

HOLMES, David; Northern Irish producer, remixer and DJ; b. 14 Feb. 1969, Belfast. *Career:* started as concert promoter in Belfast; began to DJ at own club night, Sugar Sweet, early 1990s; first recorded with Ashley Beedle as the Disco Evangelists 1992; remix work followed; signed to Go! Discs as solo artist; produces music for film soundtracks; collaborations include Ashley Beedle, Bobby Gillespie; remixed Saint Etienne, U2, Monkey Mafia, Manic Street Preachers; performs live with his band, The Free Association; co-founder, Canderblinks Film and Music (film production co.) 2006; mem. PRS. *Soundtracks:* for film: Resurrection Man 1998, Out Of Sight 1998, Three Chords and a Wardrobe 1998, Buffalo Soldiers 2001, Ocean's Eleven 2001, Analyze That 2002, Code 46 2003, Stander 2003, Ocean's Twelve 2004, Ocean's Thirteen 2007, Hunger 2009, Five Minutes of Heaven 2009, Perrier's Bounty 2010; for television: Supply & Demand 1997, Bag om Krøniken – en bebudet succes 2004; for computer game: Red Dead Redemption 2010. *Recordings include:* albums: This Film's Crap, Let's Slash The Seats 1995, Let's Get Killed 1997, Bow Down To The Exit Sign 2000, Come Get It, I Got It 2002, David Holmes Presents The Free Association 2002, Cherrystones: Hidden Charms 2004, The Holy Pictures 2008, The Dogs are Parading 2010. *Current Management:* Solar Management, 13 Rosemont Road, London, NW3 6NG, England. *Telephone:* (20) 7794-3388. *Fax:* (20) 7794-5588. *E-mail:* info@

solarmanagement.co.uk. *Website:* www.solarmanagement.co.uk; www
.davidholmesofficial.com.

HOLMES, Ian Johnstone; British musician; b. 11 March 1935, Dumfries,
Scotland; m. Margaret Bell 1958; two d. *Education:* accordion lessons with
Alex Carter. *Career:* appeared on TV in White Heather Club; recorded TV
shows in Germany; broadcast on BBC Radio Scotland 1958–, as soloist and
bandleader 1962–; appearances at accordion festivals at Vinstra, Norway,
Varberg and Ransäter, Sweden mem. MPS, PRS, Phonographic Performance,
PAMRA. *Compositions:* more than 450 tunes in various styles, especially
Scottish dance music, and also accordion tunes in Irish, French, Norwegian,
Swedish and Swiss styles. *Radio:* numerous broadcasts with band on BBC
Radio Scotland 1962–2011. *Recordings:* 19 albums, mostly of Scottish dance
music; recordings of music by the Beatles and Scandinavian and Swiss
accordion music; Sounds Scandinavian, Ian in Switzerland, The Button Box in
Scotland, Scottish Dance, Vol. 4. *Publications:* The Dumfries Collection of
Music by Ian Holmes, Vols 1, 2 and 3. *Honours:* Hon. mem. Bromolla
Accordion Orchestra (Sweden) 1987; All-Scotland Champion of Traditional
Music 1957, Scroll Award for Services to Music, Dumfries and Galloway
Council 2002, inaugurated into Scottish Traditional Music Hall of Fame 2014.
Address: 11 Averill Crescent, Rotchell, Dumfries, DG2 7RY, Scotland (home).
E-mail: marianmusic@btinternet.com.

HOLMSTROM, Peter Gustav; American musician (guitar). *Career:* Foun-
der-mem., The Dandy Warhols 1994–. *Film and television appearances
include:* Dig! 2005, MADtv (TV series) 2005. *Recordings include:* albums:
Dandys Rule OK 1995, Come Down 1998, Thirteen Tales From Urban
Bohemia 2000, Welcome To The Monkey House 2003, The Black Album/Come
On Feel The Dandy Warhols 2004, Odditorium Or Warlords Of Mars 2005,
Earth to the Dandy Warhols 2008, The Dandy Warhols are Sound 2009, This
Machine 2012. *Film compositions include:* Dig! 2005, Water Wings 2009.
Address: The Dandy Warhols, PO Box 6836, Portland, OR 97228, USA.
E-mail: gothman@dandywarhols.com. *Website:* www.dandywarhols.com.

HOLOFERNES, Judith; German singer and musician (guitar); b. 1976,
Berlin; m. Pola Roy. *Career:* mem., Wir sind Helden 2001–. *Recordings
include:* albums: Die Reklamation 2003, Von hier an blind 2005, Soundso
2007, Informationen Zu Touren und Anderen Einzelheiten 2008, Bring Mich
Nach Hause 2010, Tausend Wirre Worte: Lieblingslieder, 2002-2010 2011.
Honours: ECHO Award for Best National Group 2006. *Address:* Wir sind
Helden, Weidenallee 27, 20357 Hamburg, Germany. *E-mail:* gutentag
.wirsindhelden@com. *Website:* www.wirsindhelden.com.

HOLT, Courtney, BS; American music industry executive. *Education:*
Boston Univ. *Career:* began career as freelance producer and dir of music
videos and commercials; Dir, Video Production, Atlantic Records 1993–96;
Head of New Media, A&M Records 1996–98; Sr Vice-Pres. of New Media and
Strategic Marketing, Interscope, Geffen A&M/Universal Music 1998–2006;
Exec. Vice-Pres. of Digital Music, MTV Networks Music 2006–09; Pres.
MySpace Music 2009–11; COO Maker Studios 2011–. *Address:* 13428 Maxella
Avenue, Suite 525, Marina del Rey, CA 90292, USA (office). *Telephone:* (310)
606-2182 (office). *Website:* www.makerstudios.com (office).

HOLYFIELD, Wayland D., BA; American songwriter; b. 15 March 1942,
Mallettown, Ark.; m. Nancy Holyfield; three c. *Education:* Hendrix Coll., Univ.
of Arkansas. *Career:* moved to Nashville 1972; signed publishing contract with
Jack Clement, as songwriter 1973; signed publishing contract with Bill Hall
1974; sang Arkansas, You Run Deep In Me at President Bill Clinton's
inauguration 1993; songs recorded numerous artists; mem. Bd of Dirs ASCAP
1990–; fmr Chair. Nashville Songwriters Hall of Fame Foundation Bd.
Compositions include: Arkansas, You Run Deep In Me (adopted as official
state song of Ark.), Could I Have This Dance (with Bob House), Don't
Count The Rainy Days, Down In Tennessee, I'll Do It All Over Again, Nobody
Likes Sad Songs (with Bob McDill), Only Here For A Little While (with
Richard Leigh), Rednecks, White Socks And Blue Ribbon Beer (with Bob
McDill and Chuck Neese), She Reminded Me Of You, Some Broken Hearts
Never Mend, Till The Rivers All Run Dry, (Wish I Had A) Heart Of Stone,
You're My Best Friend. *Honours:* Nashville Songwriters Asscn International
Presidents Award 1979, ASCAP Country Writer of the Year (jtly) 1983,
inducted into Nashville Songwriters Hall of Fame 1992. *Address:* 178 January
Place, Smithville, TN 37166-5205, USA (home).

HOLZHAUER, Rudy; German music publisher and artist manager; b. 14
Dec. 1951, Hamburg. *Career:* live engineer and studio engineer; Owner,
Musikverlag Progressive GmbH; mem. GEMA, DMV, DKV. *Address:*
Musikverlag Progressive GmbH, Moorweidenstrasse 8, 20148 Hamburg,
Germany (office). *Telephone:* (40) 64250-46 (office). *Fax:* (40) 64259-99 (office).
E-mail: office@progressive-mv.de (office); barbara@progressive-mv.de.
Website: www.rudy-holzhauer.de.

DJ HOMICIDE; American musician (drum programming effects) and DJ; b.
(Craig Anthony Bullock), 17 Dec. 1970. *Career:* fmr radio presenter on Los
Angeles hip hop stations, K-DAY and The Beat; worked in studio on Sugar
Ray's Lemonade and Brownies album; joined group for live shows then became
full-time mem.; cameo in Fathers Day (film) 1997. *Recordings include:*
albums: with Sugar Ray: Lemonade and Brownies 1995, Floored 1997, 14–59
1999, Sugar Ray 2001, In Pursuit of Leisure 2003, Music for Cougars 2009.
Address: PO Box 6188, Olympia, WA 98507, USA. *E-mail:* djhomicide@
sugarray.com. *Website:* www.sugarray.com; djhomicide.com.

HOMME, Joshua (Josh) Michael, (Baby Duck, Carlo Von Sexron, J.Ho,
Ginger Elvis); American singer, songwriter, musician (guitar, drums) and
record producer; b. 17 May 1973, Joshua Tree, Calif.; m. Brody Dalle 2007; one
s., one d. *Career:* founder mem. and guitarist, Katzenjammer 1987, renamed
Sons of Kyuss 1990, renamed Kyuss 1991–95; touring guitarist, Screaming
Trees 1995–96; founder mem., Gamma Ray 1996, renamed Queens of the
Stone Age 1997–; founder, The Desert Sessions musical collective 1997–2004;
founder mem. and drummer (as 'Carlo von Sexron'), Eagles of Death Metal
1998–, support act to The Strokes 2006, debut US tour as headlining act 2006;
founder mem., Them Crooked Vultures (with Dave Grohl and John Paul
Jones) 2009–10; numerous other collaborations including Foo Fighters, Biffy
Clyro, PJ Harvey, The Strokes, Arctic Monkeys, Primal Scream, Trent
Reznor, Mondo Generator, Glen Campbell, Jack White. *Film compositions
include:* The Dangerous Lives of Altar Boys (with Nick Oliveri) 2002.
Television: as actor: Comedy Bang! Bang! 2014, Portlandia 2014, House of
Fools 2014, Toast of London 2014. *Radio:* as host: The Alligator Hour 2015–.
Recordings include: albums: with Kyuss: Wretch 1991, Blues for the Red Sun
1992, Welcome to Sky Valley 1994, ...And the Circus Leaves Town 1995; with
Queens of the Stone Age: Queens of the Stone Age 1998; Rated R 2000, Songs
for the Deaf 2002, Lullabies to Paralyze 2005, Era Vulgaris 2007, Like
Clockwork 2013; with Eagles of Death Metal: Peace, Love, Death Metal 2004,
Death by Sexy 2006, Heart On 2008, Zipper Down 2015; with Them Crooked
Vultures: Them Crooked Vultures 2009. *Honours:* with Them Crooked
Vultures: Grammy Award for Best Hard Rock Performance (for New Fang)
2011. *Current Management:* c/o The MGMT Company, 4240 Lankershim
Boulevard, North Hollywood, CA 91602, USA. *Telephone:* (818) 760-7657.
E-mail: themgmtcompany@gmail.com; inquiries@themgmtcompany.com.
Website: www.themgmtcompany.com; www.qotsa.com; www
.eaglesofdeathmetal.com.

HONK, Jivi; Austrian musician (guitar, piano), songwriter, music publisher
and producer; b. (Herbert Gebetsroither), 5 Oct. 1957, Linz ad Donau, Upper
Austria. *Education:* Franz Schubert Conservatory, Vienna. *Career:* mem. US
salsa and Latin band, Obote; tours of Germany and Netherlands; founder, Jivi
Honk and Band 1983–, with numerous concerts in and around Austria;
various solo projects include Jivi Honk and the Funkplanet, The Honk Rock
Project, Honk Instrumental Project 1990; TV appearances, radio broadcasts;
mem. AKM, Austro Mechana, LSG/Östig. *Recordings:* instrumentals: Love-
dancer, Space Me To The Stars 1988, Sunrider, Vienna Skyline, Moonrider,
Highway of Fame, Golden Days 1993, 1994; albums: as Jivi Honk: Got My
Style 1990, Sunrider 1993, Moonrider 1993, Golden Days 1994, Live At The
Garage 1995, Stardance 1999, The Definitive Collection 2006, Cosmic Funk
2010, Blue Land 2011, Maybe 2011, Nothing You Can Do 2015, But One Day
2015, Samba in the House 2015, Housemusic 2015, Radiohits 1 2015. *Address:*
Herbert Gebetsroither, www.honkmusic.com, Burgfriedstrasse 6, 3300
Amstetten, Austria (office). *Website:* www.jivihonk.com (office); www
.honkmusic.com (office); www.facebook.com/jivi.honk (home).

HOOD, Calum Thomas; Australian bass guitarist and singer; b. 25 Jan.
1996, s. of David Hood and Joy Hood. *Education:* Norwest Christian Coll.
Career: mem. 5 Seconds of Summer 2011–; released debut EP Unplugged
2012; supported One Direction on worldwide tours 2013, 2014; signed to
Capitol label 2013. *Recordings:* album: 5 Seconds of Summer 2014, Sounds
Good Feels Good 2015. *Honours:* Billboard Mid-Year Music Breakout Star
Award 2014, Kerrang! Best Int. Newcomer Award 2014, MTV Award for
Favorite Breakthrough Band 2014, MTV Europe Music Award for Best
Australian Act 2014, 2015, MTV Video Music Awards for Best Lyric Video
2014, for Song of Summer 2015, Teen Choice Awards for Breakout Group and
Music Group 2014. *Current Management:* c/o Modest Management, Matrix
Complex, 91 Peterborough Road, London, SW6 3BU, England. *E-mail:* info@
modestmanagement.com. *Website:* www.modestmanagement.com; www.5sos
.com.

HOOK, Peter; British musician (bass); b. 13 Feb. 1956, Salford, Lancs.
Career: mem., Joy Division 1977–80, New Order 1980–2007, Revenge
1989–96, Monaco 1996–; numerous tours worldwide, concerts and festival
appearances; leader of house band, The Mrs Merton Show (TV) 1994–95.
Recordings include: albums: with Joy Division: Unknown Pleasures 1979,
Closer 1980, Still 1981, The Peel Sessions 1988; with New Order: Movement
1981, Power, Corruption & Lies 1983, Low-Life 1985, Brotherhood 1986,
Substance 1987, Technique 1989, Republic 1993, Best of New Order 1994,
Rest of New Order 1995, Get Ready 2001, Back To Mine (compilation of other
artists' work) 2002, In Session (live) 2004, Waiting For The Sirens' Call 2005;
with Revenge: One True Passion 1990; with Monaco: Music For Pleasure
1997. *Film appearances include:* 24 Hour Party People 2002, Control 2007.
Publication: The Haçienda: How Not to Run a Club 2009. *Honours:* NME
'Godlike Genius' Award (with New Order) 2005, Q Legend Award (with Joy
Division) 2005, Ivor Novello Award for Outstanding Song Collection 2006.
E-mail: fletch@onelove-music.com. *Address:* Suite 169, Court Hill House, 60
Water Lane, Wilmslow, Cheshire, SK9 5AJ, England. *Website:* www
.peterhook.co.uk.

HOOKER, Jake; American songwriter, record producer and musician
(guitar); b. 5 March 1951, New York; m. 1994; one s. two d. *Career:* founder
mem., The Arrows 1974–78; f. Lorjake Music 1978–, Hook Entertainment
1980–, Hookmo Music/Dirty Feet Records 1997–, HTA 2002–, Edge Management 2005–07; mem. NARAS, BMI, AFofM. *Composition:* I Love Rock and
Roll. *Recordings:* I Love Rock and Roll, Destination Unknown (from film

soundtrack Top Gun), Sweetest Victory (from film soundtrack Rocky IV), Iron Eagle (from film soundtrack Iron Eagle); with Edgar Winter, Not a Kid Anymore 1994, Real Deal 1996; with Justin Trevino, Loud Music and Strong Wine 2000. *Publications:* The Arrows Biography. *Address:* Hook Entertainment, Rock Lodge, 26033 Mulholland Highway, Malibu, CA 91302, USA (office). *Telephone:* (818) 871-9696 (office). *E-mail:* hookent@earthlink.net (office). *Website:* www.hookent.com.

HOOPER, Nellee; British record producer and arranger. *Career:* mem., The Wild Bunch Crew; mem. mixing crew, Massive Attack; joined Soul II Soul, offering sound systems services to UK dance clubs 1985; residency, Africa Centre, Covent Garden, London; relocated to Fridge Club, Brixton 1988; opened two shops, London 1988; developed video and film co., fan club, talent agency, record co. 1990–; worked with U2, No Doubt. *Recordings include:* albums: with Soul II Soul: Club Classics Vol. I, 1989; Vol. II, A New Decade, 1990; Vol. III – Just Right, 1992; Singles include: Keep On Movin', 1989; Back To Life (However Do You Want Me), 1989; A Dream's A Dream, 1990; Missing You, with Kym Mazelle, 1990; Joy, 1992; Just Right, 1992; Move Me No Mountain, 1992; Wish, 1993; as producer: with Massive Attack: Unfinished Sympathy; Protection; with Madonna: Bedtime Stories, Something to Remember 1995; with Björk: Debut; Post; Universal James, James Brown, 1993; with Special Brew: Special Brew, 1996; with All Saints, All Saints, 1997; Best of Bond... James Bond, 1999; As arranger (with Jazzie B): Nothing Compares To U, Sinead O'Connor, 1990; contributor, Mad About The Mouse (Disney compilation), 1991. *Honours:* three American Music Awards 1990, four British DMC Dance Awards 1990, Grammy Award for Best R&B Instrumental Performance 1990, three Soul Train Awards 1990, BMI College Radio Award (for Back To Life) 1991, ASCAP Award (for Back To Life) 1991, BRIT Award for Best Producer 1995.

HOPE-EVANS, Peter John, MA; British composer, performer and musician (mouth organ, mouth bow, Jew's harp); b. 28 Sept. 1947, Brecon, Wales; m. Christine Frances Rich 1973. *Education:* lessons with Texas Slim, Maurice Blanchot, Edgar Fünf. *Recordings include:* New Bottles Old Medicine 1970; with Pete Townshend: Pete Townshend Live 1999; with Tears for Fears: Seeds of Love 1999; with Robbie McIntosh: Wide Screen, 2001, Cassette only series: Elgin Moveme(a)nts, Closer Than Breath (Itself), In The Sacred Cedars, Shadow of The Object; theatre: Up Your Ass Solanas 1992, The Tempest (RSC) 1995. *Publications include:* Harmonica Yoga 1990, Philosophising With A Harmonica (Back To Nietzsche) 1992. *E-mail:* info@peterhope-evans.co.uk. *Website:* www.peterhope-evans.co.uk.

HOPKINS, Elizabeth; American singer. *Career:* Founder mem. Delta Rae 2009–; first EP released 2010; signed to Sire Records 2011; debut album 2012; numerous live performances; support act for Edwin McCain and Hanson. *Recordings include:* album: with Delta Rae: Carry the Fire 2012, After It All 2015. *Current Management:* c/o Jordan Burger, Fleming Artists, 543 North Main Street, Ann Arbor, MI 48104, USA. *E-mail:* Jordan@flemingartists.com; deltraraemgmt@gmail.com. *Address:* c/o Sire Records, Warner Bros. Records, Warner Music Group, 75 Rockefeller Plaza, New York, NY 10019, USA (office). *Website:* www.deltarae.com.

HOPKINS, John Driskell; American singer and musician (bass guitar); b. 1971, Texas; s. of Ralph Hopkins and Joan Hopkins. *Education:* Gainesville High School, Ga. *Career:* fmr mem. Brighter Shade; fmr producer, 800 East Studios, Atlanta, Georgia; founding mem. Zac Brown Band 2002–. *Recordings:* albums: Far From Einstyne 2004, Home Grown 2005, The Foundation 2008, You Get What You Give 2010. *Honours:* Acad. of Country Music Award for Top New Vocal Duo or Group 2009, for Vocal Event of the Year (for As She's Walking Away, featuring Alan Jackson) 2011, Grammy Award for Best New Artist 2010, CMA New Artist of the Year 2010. *Current Management:* ROAR, 9701 Wilshire Boulevard, Eighth Floor, Beverly Hills, CA 90212, USA. *Telephone:* (310) 586-8222. *E-mail:* zbb@roar.la. *Website:* www.roar.la. *E-mail:* john@zacbrownband.com (office). *Website:* www.zacbrownband.com.

HOPKINS, Philip Nicholas, MA; British musician (percussion, chromatic harmonica); b. 5 Feb. 1962, Surrey; m. Barbara Mason 1993. *Education:* King's School, Canterbury, Univ. of Oxford. *Career:* concert tours of USA with Phil Coulter, Maura O'Connell, Liam Clancy, including Carnegie Hall, New York; played harmonica for film Fanny and Elvis; worked with Leon Redbone, Phil Coulter, Billy Connolly, The Dubliners, Rory Gallagher, Val Doonican; mem. Musicians' Union. *Stage appearances include:* Sweeney Todd (Nat. Theatre, London and European tour) 1993–94, A Little Night Music (Nat. Theatre, London) 1995, Lady in the Dark 1997, Oklahoma! 1998. *Television music sessions:* Next of Kin, Men of the World (BBC1) 1995, Roger Roger 1998. *Publications include:* contrib. articles to Modern Drummer magazine, USA.

HOPKINSON, Russell (Rusty) Keith; Australian musician (guitar, drums, percussion) and singer; b. 28 Jan. 1965, Fremantle. *Career:* fmr mem., Vicious Circle, Nursery Crimes; mem. rock band, You Am I 1993–; numerous worldwide tours; mem. Sneeze 1999–; Owner, Illustrious Artists label and Reverberation distribution co. *Recordings include:* albums: with You Am I: Sound As Ever 1993, Hi Fi Way 1995, Hourly, Daily 1996, # 4 Record 1998, What Rhymes With Cars And Girls 1999, ...Saturday Night, 'Round Ten 1999, Dress Me Slowly 2001, Deliverance 2002, Spit Polish 2005, Convicts 2007. *Honours:* ARIA Award for Best Alternative Release 1995, six Industry Awards 1996. *Current Management:* c/o Scott McKenzie, Premier Artists, Dundas La, Albert Park, Vic. 3206, Australia. *Telephone:* (3) 9699-9555. *E-mail:* scotty@premierartists.com.au. *Website:* www.premierartists.com.au.

HOPPUS, Markus (Mark) Allen; American musician (bass guitar); b. 15 March 1972, Ridgecrest, CA; m. Skye Everly 2001. *Career:* founder mem., Blink-182 1993–2005, 2009–; numerous TV appearances and concerts worldwide; founder mem., (+44) 2006–. *Film appearance:* American Pie 1999. *Recordings include:* albums: with Blink-182: Fly Swatter 1993, Buddah 1994, Cheshire Cat 1994, Dude Ranch 1997, Enema Of The State 1999, The Mark, Tom And Travis Show (The Enema Strikes Back) 2000, Take Off Your Pants And Jacket 2001, Blink-182 2003, Neighborhoods 2011; with (+44): When Your Heart Stops Beating 2006. *Current Management:* International Talent Booking, First Floor, Ariel House, 74a Charlotte Street, London, W1T 4QJ, England. *Telephone:* (20) 7637-6979. *Fax:* (20) 7637-6978. *E-mail:* info@itb.co.uk. *Website:* www.itb.co.uk; www.blink182.com; www.plusfortyfour.com.

HOPWOOD, Neil, (Fred Hopwood); British musician (drums, penny whistle, harmonica, concertina); b. (Neil Robert Hopwood), 22 Dec. 1948, Lichfield, Staffs., England; m. Beryl Agnes Nutt 1974; two s. *Education:* Uttoxeter and Burton Technical Coll. *Career:* mem. Dr Strangely Strange 1970–71, 1996, 2007–; TV appearances, John Peel session, BBC Radio 1; mem. Sutherland Brothers Band 1972; support tours, Free, Mott The Hoople, David Bowie; performance at Montreux Golden Rose Festival; TV appearances in Switzerland, Denmark, France; numerous radio and TV appearances 1987–2002; mem. R. Cajun and Zydeco Bros 1984–2001, Yeah Jazz 1989–94, Zydeco Hot Rods 1993–; formed Vice-Bishops' Blues Band 1997; session work for Paul McCartney 1998; formed Zydeco Brothers' Band 2004; mem. Performing Right Soc., Mechanical-Copyright Protection Soc., Performing Artists' Media Rights Asscn. *Recordings:* albums/singles: with Sutherland Brothers Band 1971, Leonard and Squires 1976, seven albums with R Cajun and the Zydeco Brothers 1984–2000, Yeah Jazz 1992, Vice-Bishops of Uttoxeter 1995, Big Red Kite 1996, The Vice-Bishops' Blues Band: House of Cards 2000, Songs from Biscuit Town 2000, Pete Oakley's CD Long Shadows 2002, The Vice-Bishops' Blues Band: Caught in the Crossfire 2004, Vice-Bishops of Uttoxeter: Airs & Disgraces 2005, Dr Strangely Strange: Halcyon Days 2007, Dr. Strangely Strange: Heavy Petting and Other Proclivities 2011. *Address:* Smalltown Music, 17 Colne Mount, Uttoxeter, Staffs., ST14 7QR, England (office). *E-mail:* fred@smalltownmusic.co.uk (office). *Website:* www.smalltownmusic.co.uk (office).

HORABIN, Gren; British senior lecturer (director of studies) and musician (alto and tenor saxophones, clarinet); b. 15 May 1939, Rainhill, Liverpool, England; m. Catherine Rawlinson, 28 Dec. 1968; one s. *Education:* Technical Teachers' Certificate; Private tuition, pianoforte, saxophone clarinet; Bandsman in Royal Air Force. *Career:* bands include: Leader (alto clarinet) Gren Horabin Combo, (alto saxophone) Band of The Royal Air Force Bridgnorth, Leader (saxophones, clarinet) Crescendo, (tenor clarinet) John Shepherd Combo, Leader (alto, tenor clarinet) 42nd Street Swing; performances include: jazz, dance gigs, various venues in Midlands with Pete King, Mick Large, Ricky Allan, Allan Billings, various small mainstream groups; productions include: Lady Audley's Secret, Dirty Work At The Crossroads, Hits From The Blitz, Concert Style In Jazz (with Duncan Swift, Geraint Ellis); creator, author, original Jazz Studies Units, BTEC National Diploma Level, Kidderminster Coll., Worcestershire; Sr Lecturer, Dir of Studies, Creative Arts and Community Studies, Kidderminster Coll., (retd); mem. Musicians' Union, Asscn of British Jazz Musicians. *Honours:* Skills Assessors and Verifiers Awards.

HORAN, Niall James; Irish singer; b. 13 Sept. 1993, Mullingar, Co. Westmeath; s. of Bobby Horan and Maura Gallagher. *Education:* Colaiste Mhuire School. *Career:* support act as solo artist for Lloyd Daniels; mem. One Direction 2010–; finished third in The X Factor (UK) 2010; signed to Syco Records 2010; participated in X Factor Live Tour 2011; released debut single 2011; debut album first by a British group to debut at #1 on USA Billboard 200 album chart 2011; numerous TV appearances and tours; group hiatus 2016–. *Recordings:* with One Direction: albums: Up All Night 2011, Take Me Home (American Music Award for Favorite Album 2013) 2012, Midnight Memories (American Music Award for Favorite Album 2014) 2013, Four 2014, Made in the A.M. 2015. *DVDs:* Up All Night: the Live Tour 2012. *Publications:* One Direction: Forever Young 2011, One Direction: The Official Annual 2012 2011, Dare to Dream: Life as One Direction 2011, Where We Are: Our Band, Our Story 2013, Who We Are: Our Official Autobiography 2014. *Honours:* numerous including: with One Direction: Bambi Pop Int. Award 2012, BBC Radio 1 Teen Awards for Best British Music Act 2012, for Best British Single 2012, 2013, 2014, 2015, for Best British Group 2013, 2015, BRIT Awards for Best British Single (What Makes You Beautiful) 2012, for BRITs Global Success 2013, for Best British Video (for You & I) 2015, JIM Awards (Flemish TV) for Best International Newcomer 2012, for Best Group 2013, for Best Pop 2013, MTV Europe Music Awards for Best New Act 2012, for Best UK & Ireland Act 2012, 2013, 2014, for Biggest Fans 2012, 2014, for Best Pop Act 2013, 2014, 2015, for Best Live Act 2014, for Best Worldwide Act (Europe North) 2014, MTV Video Music Awards Brazil Award for International Artist 2012, MTV Video Music Awards for Best New Artist 2012, for Best Pop Video and Most Share-Worthy Video (both What Makes You Beautiful) 2012, for Song of the Summer (for Best Song Ever) 2013, 4Music Video Honours Awards for Best Breakthrough and Best Group 2012, ARIA Music Awards for Best Int. Artist 2012, 2013, 2014, Billboard Music Awards for Top Duo/Group 2013, 2015, for Top New Artist 2013, for Top Pop Artist 2013, for Top Touring Artist 2015, American Music Awards for Favorite Band, Duo or Group 2013, 2014, 2015, for Artist of the Year 2014, 2015. *Current Management:* c/o Modest!

Management, The Matrix Complex, 91 Peterborough Road, London, SW6 3BU, England. *E-mail:* info@modestmanagement.com. *Website:* www .modestmanagement.com; www.onedirectionmusic.com.

HORN, Trevor, CBE; British record producer, singer and musician (double bass, bass guitar); b. 15 July 1949, Durham, England; m. Jill Sinclair (died 2014); one d. *Career:* session musician 1970s, joined house band at Hammersmith Palais, London; Founder-mem. The Buggles 1977–80, first single Video Killed the Radio Star later became first video played on MTV; mem., rock band Yes 1980–81, producer for Yes 1983; mem., The Art of Noise 1983–85, 1998–; independent record producer 1982–, working with ABC, Marc Almond, Belle & Sebastian, Tina Charles, Cher, Dollar, Frankie Goes to Hollywood, Genesis, Grace Jones, Tom Jones, Malcolm McLaren, Mike Oldfield, Pet Shop Boys, Propaganda, LeAnn Rimes, Seal, Simple Minds, Spandau Ballet, Rod Stewart, t.A.T.u., Tina Turner, Hans Zimmer; founder, ZTT Records 1983–; mem. The Producers 2007–. *Compositions include:* theme music for TV series, The Tube. *Recordings:* albums: with The Buggles: The Plastic Age 1980, Adventures In Modern Recording 1982; with Yes: Drama 1980; with The Art of Noise: (Who's Afraid Of?) The Art Of Noise! 1984, The Seduction Of Claude Debussy 1999, The Abduction Of The Noise of Noise 2003; with Robbie Williams & Gary Barlow: Shame 2010; singles: with Buggles: Video Killed The Radio Star 1979, The Plastic Age 1980, Clean Clean 1980, Elstree 1980, I Am A Camera 1981; with Yes: Owner of a Lonely Heart 1983; with The Art of Noise: Into Battle With The Art Of Noise 1983, Beatbox 1983, Close (To The Edit) 1984, The Art Of Noise Are Close-Up 1984, Moments In Love 1985, Dream On 1998, Metaforce 1999, Reduction 2000; with The Producers: Studio 1 2007; solo: The Closing Of The Year (theme from the film Toys) 1992. *Honours:* with Buggles: NME Award 1980, Deutsche Gramaphon Award 1980; solo: BRIT Awards for Best British Producer 1985, 1992, Q Award for Best Producer 1991, Ivor Novello/PRS Award for Outstanding Contrib. to British Music 2010. *Current Management:* c/o Mel Hoven, Head of Producer Management, Sarm Management, The Blue Building, 8–10 Basing Street, London, W11 1ET, England. *Telephone:* (20) 7229-1229. *Fax:* (20) 7221-9247. *E-mail:* mel@spz.com. *Telephone:* 7775-937494 (Ian Peel, mobile). *E-mail:* ian@letitbeep.com. *Website:* www.trevorhorn.com.

HORNSBY, Bruce Randall, BA; American musician (piano) and songwriter; b. 23 Nov. 1954, Richmond, Va; m. Kathy Lynn Yankovich 1983; two s. *Education:* Univ. of Miami. *Career:* played on over 100 albums for other artists including Bob Dylan, Grateful Dead, Bonnie Raitt, Don Henley, Bob Seger, Willie Nelson, Branford Marsalis, Chaka Khan, Squeeze, Robbie Robertson; written songs with Don Henley, Robbie Robertson, Leon Russell, Chaka Khan, Tupac Shakur, Lennie Meat; mem., ASCAP, AFofM. *Recordings include:* albums: The Way It Is 1986, Scenes From the Southside 1988, A Night On The Town 1990, Harbour Lights 1993, Hot House 1995, Spirit Trail 1998, Here Come The Noise Makers 2000, Big Swing Face 2002, Halcyon Days 2004, Ricky Skaggs and Bruce Hornsby 2007, Camp Meeting 2007, Levitate 2009, Bride of the Noisemakers 2011, Red Hook Summer [Music from the Original Motion Picture] 2012, Cluck Ol' Hen 2013. *Honours:* three Grammy Awards, eight times winner of Keyboard Magazine Readers Poll, Daytime Emmy Award for Outstanding Achievement in Music 1987–88, ASCAP Song of the Year (for The Way It Is) 1987, Elvis Award, International Rock Awards 1991. *E-mail:* marc.allan@redlightmanagement.com. *Address:* PO Box 3545, Williamsburg, VA 23187, USA (office). *Website:* www.brucehornsby.com.

HORVILLEUR, Emmanuel Javier; Argentine singer, songwriter and musician (guitar, bass guitar); b. 2 Jan. 1975, Buenos Aires; m. 1st Celeste Cid 2003 (divorced 2008), one s.; m. 2nd Macarena Paz 2013. *Career:* mem., group Pechugo (with Dante Spinetta) 1987–88; Founder-mem., Illya Kuryaki and the Valderramas (IKV) (with Dante Spinetta) 1990–2001, 2011–; solo artist 2001–; collaborations include Gustavo Cerati, Ana Cañas, Babasónicos, A-Tirador Láser, Los Látigos. *Recordings:* albums: with Illya Kuryaki and the Valderramas: Fabrico cuero 1991, Horno para calendar los mares 1993, Chaco 1995, Versus 1997, Leche 1999, Kuryakistan 2001, Chances 2012; solo: Música y delirio 2003, Mimosa 2004, Rocanrolero 2005, Mordisco (Gardel Award 2008) 2007, Amor en polvo 2010. *Honours:* Latin MTV Award for Best Latin Video of the Year (for Abarájame) 1996, Latin Grammy Award for Best Urban Song (for Ula Ula) 2013. *Address:* c/o Sony Music Argentina, Buenos Aires, Argentina (office). *E-mail:* contacto.argentina@sonymusic.com (office). *Website:* www .sonymusic.com.ar (office); www.emma-horvilleur.com; ikvoficial.com.

HOSEIN, Choque; British producer, singer and songwriter. *Career:* mem., Black Liner Star 1994–99; mem. Anglo-Asian duo, Sweet Blood 2005–. *Recordings include:* albums: with Black Liner Star: Yemen Cutta Collection 1998, Bengali Bantham Youth Experience 1999, Twelve Inch Confrontation Mix 2000; with Sweet Blood: Friendly Infidel 2005.

HOSNY, Tamer, BA; Egyptian singer, composer and actor; b. 16 Aug. 1977, Cairo; s. of Housni Sharif. *Education:* 6 October Univ. *Career:* fmr professional football player; solo artist 2000–; presenter, Tamer Hosny Generation (reality TV show) 2009. *Films include:* Halet hobb (Academy Award, Egypt 2004) 2004, Sayed el-atefy 2005, Omar wa Salma 2007, Captain Hima 2008, Noor Eieny 2010, Omar and Salma 3 2011. *Recordings include:* albums: Hobb 2004, Ennayah bethebbak 2006, Ya bent el-eih 2007, Al-gana fe byotna 2007, Arrab kaman 2008, Haeesh Hyati 2009, Ekhtart Sah 2010, Elly Gai Ahla 2011, Bahebak Enta 2013. *TV includes:* Adam 2011. *Honours:* numerous awards, including Best Song in 25 Years Award (for Oyounoh dar) 2003, Horeyaty magazine award 2005, DearGuest magazine award for Best Singer 2005,

2006, 2007, and for Best Video Clip 2006, Radio and TV Festival Award for Best Singer 2006, 2007, and for Best Song 2006, 2007, El Mogaz Award for Best Singer 2006, Arab Sounds Award Best Arab Singer 2009, African Music Award Best African Artist 2010. *E-mail:* tamer@tamerhosny.ws (office). *Website:* www.tamerhosny.ws.

HOTT NIKKELS (see Method Man)

HOTTE, Kevin Richard; Canadian musician (drums), composer, producer and photographer; b. 16 Nov. 1959, Port Colbourne, ON. *Education:* Niagara Coll. *Career:* owner, Audiocasters Music Productions; The Sound Kitchen Recording Studio; Creative Images Media; Creative Images, syndicated radio show about photography technique; performs with band, Kevin Richard; mem, SOCAN, ASCAP, CARAS. *Compositions:* various radio jingles, corporate video scores. *Recordings include:* albums: Windows, Inventing Fire, Illumination. *Address:* c/o Da Vinci's Notebook Records, 69 Rockwood Avenue, St Catharines, Ontario L2P 1EB, Canada (office). *E-mail:* kevin@kevinrichard .com (office). *Website:* www.kevinrichard.com (home).

HOUSTON, Cissy; American singer; b. (Emily Drinkard), 1933, Newark, NJ; one d. (Whitney Houston). *Career:* mem. family gospel group, Drinkard Singers; backing singers for numerous artists, including Wilson Pickett, Solomon Burke; singer, Sweet Inspirations 1967–70; prolific session singer. *Recordings:* albums: solo: Cissy Houston, 1977; Warning Danger, 1979; Step Aside For A Lady, 1980; Mama's Cooking, 1987; I'll Take Care of You, 1992; Face to Face, 1996; He Leadeth Me, 1997; with Whitney Houston: Whitney Houston 1985, Whitney 1987; with Aretha Franklin: Let Me Into Your Life 1974, Love All The Hurt Away 1981, Jump To It 1982; with Van Morrison: Moondance, 1970, No Sheets 1974; with Diana Ross: The Wiz (soundtrack) 1978, Diana's Duets 1982, Silk Electric 1982; with Paul Simon: Paul Simon 1972, Greatest Hits etc 1977; with Luther Vandross: Never Too Much 1981, Forever, For Always, For Love 1982, Busy Body 1983, The Night I Fell In Love 1985, Give Me The Reason 1987; other recordings with numerous artists, including Joe Cocker, Judy Collins, Kiki Dee, Jackie DeShannon, Gregg Allman, The Drifters, J. Geils Band, Chaka Khan, Don McLean, John Prine, Linda Ronstadt, Beyoncé.

HOUSTON, Thelma; American singer and actress; b. 7 May 1943, Leland, MS. *Career:* singer in gospel group, The Art Reynolds Singers late 1960s; solo artist 1969–. *Film appearances:* Death Scream, Norman. . . Is That You?, The Seventh Dwarf. *Recordings include:* albums: Sunshower 1969, Thelma Houston 1973, Anyway You Like It 1977, The Devil In Me 1978, Ready To Roll 1978, Ride To The Rainbow 1979, Breakwater Cat 1980, Never Gonna Be Another One 1981, I've Got The Music In Me 1981, Thelma Houston 1983, Qualifying Heats 1987, Throw You Down 1990, A Woman's Touch 2007. *Current Management:* J. Cast Productions, 2550 Greenvalley Road, Los Angeles, CA 90046-1438, USA. *E-mail:* jcast@castproductions.com. *Website:* www.thelmahouston.com.

HOVMAN, Klavs; Danish musician (double bass, bass) and teacher; *Associate Professor, Rhythmic Music Conservatory, Copenhagen;* b. 27 Oct. 1957, Århus; one s. one d. *Career:* mem. Savage Rose 1991–92; played with numerous jazz/rock bands; toured with Ernie Wilkins Almost Big Band, Horace Parlan, Toots Thielemans, Lee Konitz, Svend Asmussen; bassist with Etta Cameron's jazz and gospel groups 1980–; gospel concerts, Europe 1990s; mem. Marilyn Mazur's groups Future Song and Pulse Unit; Assoc. Prof., Rhythmic Music Conservatory, Copenhagen. *Compositions:* Music for New Music Orchestra, Copenhagen Jazz Festival Event. *Recordings:* albums: Baraban, Peter Danemo 1991, Månebarn, Savage Rose 1992, Marilyn Mazur's Future Song 1992, Echoez Of. . ., Harry Beckett and Pierre Dorge 1992, Being, Lotte Anker/Mette Peterson Quintet 1993, Savage Rose 25, Savage Rose 1993, Gospel Concert, Etta Cameron 1995, Circular Chant, Marilyn Mazur/Pulse Unit 1995. *E-mail:* mail@klavshovman.dk. *Website:* www.klavshovman.dk.

HOWARD, Brittany Amber; American rock singer, guitarist and songwriter; b. 1989, Athens, Ala. *Education:* East Limestone High School, Athens, Ala. *Career:* Founder-mem., The Shakes, renamed Alabama Shakes 2009–; debut EP released 2011; first major tour 2011; many live tours and festival appearances; numerous TV appearances. *Recordings:* albums: with Alabama Shakes: Boys & Girls 2012, Sound & Color (Grammy Award for Best Alternative Music Album 2016) 2015. *Honours:* Americana Music Honors and Awards Award for Emerging Artist of the Year 2012, Grammy Awards for Best Rock Performance and Best Rock Song (both for Don't Wanna Fight) 2016. *Current Management:* c/o Kevin Morris and Christine Stauder, Red Light Management, 44 Wall Street, 22nd Floor, New York, NY 10005, USA. *Telephone:* (646) 292-7400. *Fax:* (646) 292-7450. *Website:* www .redlightmanagement.com; www.alabamashakes.com (home).

HOWARD, Dominic James; British musician (drums); b. 7 Dec. 1977. *Career:* formed group Gothic Plague aged 13, group became Rocket Baby Dolls before finally settling on name Muse 1997–; released two 1,000-copy EPs on UK independent label, Dangerous; numerous festival appearances, broadcasts. *Recordings include:* albums: Showbiz 1999, Origin Of Symmetry 2001, Hullabaloo 2002, Absolution 2003, Time Is Running Out 2004, Black Holes and Revelations 2006, The Resistance (Grammy Award for Best Rock Album 2011) 2009, The 2nd Law 2012, Drones (Grammy Award for Best Rock Album 2016) 2015. *Honours:* NME Awards for Best New Band 2000, for Best Live Band 2005, 2008, 2009, for Best British Band 2007, 2010, 2011, Kerrang! Awards for Best British Band 2001, for Best British Live Act 2002, for Best

Live Act 2006, Q Awards for Innovation in Sound 2003, for Best Live Act 2004, 2006, 2007, for Best Act in the World Today 2009, 2012, MTV Europe Music Awards for Best Alternative Act 2004, 2006, for Best UK and Irish Act 2004, 2007, for Headliner 2007, BRIT Awards for Best Live Act 2005, 2007, American Music Award for Favorite Alternative Artist 2010, Ivor Novello Award for International Achievement 2011. *Website:* www.muse.mu.

HOWARD, James Newton; American composer; b. 9 June 1951, Los Angeles, CA. *Education:* Univ. of Southern California, Music Acad. of the West. *Career:* mem. ASCAP. *Compositions for television:* Go to the Light 1988, The Image 1990, Revealing Evidence: Stalking the Honolulu Strangler 1990, Somebody Has to Shoot the Picture 1990, Descending Angel 1990, A Private Matter 1992, ER 1994, From the Earth to the Moon 1998, Gideon's Crossing 2000. *Compositions for film:* Tough Guys 1986, Nobody's Fool 1986, Head Office 1986, Wildcats 1986, 8 Million Ways to Die 1986, Russkies 1987, Campus Man 1987, Five Corners 1987, Promised Land 1988, Off Limits 1988, Tap 1989, Some Girls 1989, Major League 1989, The Package 1989, Marked for Death 1990, Pretty Woman 1990, Coupe de Ville 1990, Flatliners 1990, Three Men and a Little Lady 1990, The Prince of Tides 1991, My Girl 1991, Grand Canyon 1991, Guilty by Suspicion 1991, King Ralph 1991, Dying Young 1991, The Man in the Moon 1991, Night and the City 1992, Glengarry Glen Ross 1992, American Heart 1992, Diggstown 1992, The Saint of Fort Washington 1993, Alive 1993, Falling Down 1993, Dave 1993, The Fugitive 1993, Intersection 1994, Wyatt Earp 1994, Junior 1994, Restoration 1995, Just Cause 1995, Outbreak 1995, French Kiss 1995, Waterworld 1995, Eye for an Eye 1996, The Juror 1996, Primal Fear 1996, The Trigger Effect 1996, The Rich Man's Wife (theme) 1996, Space Jam 1996, One Fine Day 1996, Dante's Peak (theme) 1997, Liar Liar (theme) 1997, Fathers' Day 1997, My Best Friend's Wedding 1997, The Devil's Advocate 1997, The Postman 1997, A Perfect Murder 1998, Snow Falling on Cedars 1999, Mumford 1999, Stir of Echoes 1999, Wing Commander 1999, Runaway Bride 1999, The Sixth Sense 1999, Wayward Son 1999, Dinosaur 2000, Unbreakable 2000, Vertical Limit 2000, Atlantis: The Lost Empire 2001, America's Sweethearts 2001, Signs 2002, Big Trouble 2002, Unconditional Love 2002, The Emperor's Club 2002, Treasure Planet 2002, Dreamcatcher 2003, Peter Pan 2003, Hidalgo 2004, The Village 2004, Collateral 2004, The Interpreter 2005, Freedomland 2005, R.V. 2006, Lady in the Water 2006, Blood Diamond 2006, The Lookout 2007, Michael Clayton 2007, The Water House 2007, I Am Legend 2007, The Great Debaters 2007, Charlie Wilson's War 2007, Mad Money 2007, The Happening 2008, The Dark Knight (Grammy Award for Best Soundtrack Album for Motion Picture 2009, Classical BRIT Award for Soundtrack of the Year 2009) 2008, The Hunger Games 2012, Snow White and the Huntsman 2012. *Current Management:* Gorfaine/Schwartz Agency Inc, 4111 West Alameda Avenue, Suite 509, Burbank, CA 91505, USA. *Telephone:* (818) 260-8500. *Website:* www.gsamusic.com.

HOWARD, John; British record company executive, singer, songwriter and musician (keyboards); b. 9 April 1953, Bury, Lancs. *Career:* solo artist 1973–; mem. Quiz (with Steve Levine and Graham Broad) 1981–83; Label Man. Conifer Records 1985; A&R Man. Pickwick Records 1986; Strategic Marketing Man. MCA Records 1993; A&R Dir Carlton Records 1995. *Recordings include:* albums: Kid In A Big World 1975, Technicolour Biography 1975, Can You Hear Me Ok? 1976, On Reflection 1993, Stormwatch 1996, The Dangerous Hours 2005, As I Was Saying 2005, Same Bed, Different Dreams 2007, Barefoot with Angels 2007, Navigate Home 2009, Exhibiting Tendencies 2011, You Shall Go to the Ball! 2012, Atmospheres & Soundscapes 2012, Storeys 2013. *E-mail:* j.howard@kidinabigworld.co.uk (office). *Website:* www.kidinabigworld.co.uk.

HOWE, Bob; Australian musician (guitars, harmonica), singer and composer; b. 1956, England. *Career:* cabaret artist and session musician; Musical Dir for Frank Ifield 1984–88, Guy Mitchell 1991; toured with many artists, including Lucky Starr, Slim Dusty; mem. Music Arrangers' Guild of Australia. *Theatre:* portrayed Paul McCartney in production of Lennon – The Musical 1986–87. *Compositions:* White Man's Blues, Some People Change, Last Cowboy Waltz, Celtic Bushman. *Radio:* Saturday night on ABC Radio as Big Bob from Bondi 2003–10. *Recordings:* contrib. to: John Chester Love in the Meantime; Waltzing Matilda, Diana Trask; Cross Country, Sarah Jory; The Fire Still Burns, Frank Ifield. *Publication:* Cowboys in Cyberspace 1997–. *Honours:* Southern Hemisphere Country Music Award for Most Popular Guitarist, Musician and Newcomer 1982, three times Variety Vocal/Instrumental Performer of the Year, Australian Entertainment 'MO' Awards, Musician of The Year, Australian Country Music People's Choice Awards 2007. *Address:* PO Box 7341, Bondi Beach, NSW 2026, Australia. *Website:* www.bobhowe.com.

HOWE, Brian; British singer; b. 22 July 1957, Portsmouth, Hants.; one s. one d. *Career:* mem., Ted Nugent Band; lead singer of rock group, Bad Company 1986–93; numerous tours, live and TV appearances; solo artist 1993–; mem. NARAS. *Recordings include:* albums: Penetrator (with Ted Nugent Band) 1984; with Bad Company: Fame and Fortune 1986, Dangerous Age 1988, Holy Water 1990, Here Comes Trouble 1992; solo: Tangled in Blue 1997, Diversity 2006, Circus Bar 2010. *Current Management:* c/o Artists International Management, 9850 Sandalfoot Boulevard, Suite 458, Boca Raton, FL 33428, USA. *Website:* www.brianhowe.com.

HOWE, Liam; British musician (keyboards), songwriter and producer; b. 29 Sept. *Career:* various musical projects with Chris Corner, first band 1990,

F.R.I.S.K. 1992, Line of Flight 1993; founding mem., Sneaker Pimps 1995–; numerous festivals and concerts; band founded Splinter Recordings 1999; producer for artists including Nerina Pallot, Marilyn Manson, Natalie Imbruglia, Clear Static. *Recordings:* albums: with Sneaker Pimps: Becoming X 1996, Splinter 1999, Bloodsport 2002; singles: with Line Of Flight: World As A Cone (EP) 1993; with Sneaker Pimps: 6 Underground (EP) 1996, Roll On 1996, Tesko Suicide 1996, Spin Spin Sugar 1997, Post Modern Sleaze 1997, 6 Underground 1998, Low Five 1999, Ten To Twenty 1999, Sick 2002. *Current Management:* This Much Talent Ltd, The Chapel, Everwood Court, Maybury Gardens, London NW10 2AF, England. *Telephone:* (20) 8208-5660. *Fax:* (20) 8459-2789. *E-mail:* contact@thismuchtalent.co.uk. *Website:* www.thismuchtalent.co.uk. *E-mail:* parmesanchic@aol.com. *Website:* www.sneakerpimps.com.

HOWE, Steve; British musician (guitar); b. 8 April 1947, London. *Career:* fmr mem., The Syndicats, The In Crowd, Tomorrow, Bodast; mem. progressive rock group, Yes 1970–81; formed group, Anderson Bruford Wakeman Howe 1989, then re-adopted the name Yes 1991–; solo artist 1975–; mem., GTR 1986–91; mem., Asia 1981–85, 1990–; numerous concerts, festivals and tours. *Recordings include:* albums: with Yes: Time And A Word 1970, The Yes Album 1971, Fragile 1971, Close To The Edge 1972, Yessongs 1973, Tales From The Topographic Oceans 1973, Relayer 1974, Yesterdays 1975, Going For The One 1977, Tormato 1978, Drama 1980, Yesshows 1980, Union 1991, Yesstory 1991, Symphonic Music Of Yes 1993, History Of The Future 1993, Talk 1994, An Evening Of Yes Music Plus 1994, Keys To Ascension 1996, Open Your Eyes 1997, Something's Coming 1998, The Ladder 1999, House Of Yes: Live From House Of Blues 2000, Magnification 2001, Keystudio 2001, Yestoday 2002, Yes Remixes 2003, Yes And Friends 2003, Re(Union) 2004, Fly from Here 2011, Heaven & Earth 2014; with Anderson Bruford Wakeman Howe: Anderson Bruford Wakeman Howe 1989, An Evening of Yes Music Plus 1993; with Asia: Asia 1982, Alpha 1983, Astra 1985, Aqua 1992, Aria 1994, Arena 1996, Rare 2000, Aura 2001, Alive In Hallowed Halls 2001, Dragon Attack 2003, Silent Nation 2004, Phoenix 2008, Omega 2010; with GTR: GTR 1986; solo: Beginnings 1975, The Steve Howe Album 1979, The Bodast Tapes 1981, Turbulence 1991, The Grand Scheme Of Things 1993, Mothballs 1994, Not Necessarily Acoustic 1994, Seraphim 1995, Voyagers 1995, Homebrew 1996, Quantum Guitar 1998, Pulling Strings 1999, Portraits Of Bob Dylan 1999, Homebrew 2 2000, Natural Timbre 2001, Guitar Player 2001, Guitar Plus 2001, Skyline 2002, Elements 2003, Spectrum 2005, Homebrew 3 2005, Motif 2008, Homebrew 4 2010, Time 2011, Homebrew 5 2013. *Honours:* Billboard Award for Best New Artist, Best Album (with Asia) 1982. *Current Management:* c/o Trudy Green, HK Management, 10866 Wilshire Blvd, Suite 200, Los Angeles, CA 90024, USA. *Telephone:* (310) 550-5254. *Fax:* (310) 550-5241. *E-mail:* trudydb@aol.com. *E-mail:* yes@yesworld.com. *Website:* www.yesworld.com; www.stevehowe.com.

HOWELL, Mark; American composer, performer and musician (guitar, trumpet); b. 11 July 1952; m. Stephanie Artz. *Education:* BA, University of Southern Mississippi; MA, SUNY, Stony Brook, NY. *Career:* Stop at Nothing, The Kitchen, 1987; Zero Pop, 1986–96; In Memory, 1989; Gt Schubertide, 1997; mem, BMI; Society for Ethnomusicology. *Compositions:* History of Magic, 1990; For A Birthday, 1996; To The Heart, 1997. *Recordings:* albums: North America, Moers 1986, Swimman (Better Than Death) 1987, All the Big Mystics 1987, Glows in the Dark 1987, Parts and Labor 1992, Quartets (with Fred Frith Guitar Quartet) 1994, Cuneiform 2002, Inconvenient Music 2007. *Publications:* Locronets: An Automatic Sketching Technique, The Improviser, 1989. *Address:* c/o Frog Peak Music, Box 1052, Lebanon, NH 03766, USA. *Telephone:* (603) 643-9037. *Fax:* (603) 643-9037. *E-mail:* fp@frogpeak.org. *Website:* www.frogpeak.org.

HOWELL-JONES, Richard; British actor, musician (drums, percussion) and singer; b. 1960, Altrincham, Cheshire, England; s. of Rev. David Howell-Jones and Marilyn Howell-Jones; one s. *Education:* Manchester Polytechnic (Diploma in Theatre). *Career:* drummer and vocalist with R&B band Flat Hedgehog 1981–83; theatre performance band Celebration of Joe 1984–85, Roy Woodward Big Band 1985–87, R&B band The Shades 1990–91, Feast of Life (Artistic Dir) Steel&Straw Theatre Co. 2008–09; Founder Northern Actors' Centre 1995; Devt Man., New Breed Theatre Co. 2003; mem. Musicians' Union, Equity (Br. Sec. and Treas., NW England Gen. 2008–12). *Theatre includes:* Dusty Pens, by Derek Martin 1997–2000, The Irish Giant, New Breed Theatre Co. (Production Man.) (Manchester Evening News Theatre Award for Best Fringe Production) 2003, The Rise & Demise of Kenneth Kennedy-Smythe, by Mike Heath (Studio Salford BIFTA Award for Best Actor) 2006, The Tempest, The Canterbury Tales, AWOL with Black Box Theatre Co. 2007, Dave & Jeff v the Crazed Corpse-Loving Consultant from Cardiothoracics, Our World is in Colour, with Steel & Straw 2008, OPOD 1,2 & 3 2011–12. *Films:* The Last Meeting 1996, Actors 2001, Best Little Whorehouse in Rochdale 2011. *Television:* King Lear (Channel 4) 1983, Dear Ladies (BBC) 1984. *Recordings:* Celebration of Joe, with Brian Roberts 1984, Feast of Life 2000. *Address:* 18 Wardle Road, Sale, Cheshire, M33 3DB, England (home). *E-mail:* richard@howell-jones.org.uk (office).

HOWIE; Japanese singer and musician (guitar); b. (Howie Sato), Tokyo. *Career:* Founder-mem. punk band, Nicotine 1994–; band formed its own record label, Sky Records 1997. *Recordings include:* albums: Royal Mellow Day 1996, ¡Hola Amigo! 1997, Will Kill You… (EP) 1998, Pleeeeeeez! Who Are You? 2000, Fitness Dayz 2001, Samurai Shot 2002, School Of Liberty 2003, Hey Dude! We Love the Beatles 2005, Desperado 2006, Carnival 2006,

Sound from the Schizoid Core 2006, Probably the Best 2007, Liberation 2007, Achromatic Ambitious 2007, Soundquake 2008. *Website:* skyrecords.net/nicotine.

HOWLETT, Liam, (The Prodigy, Liam Prodigy); British songwriter, musician (keyboards) and DJ; b. 21 Aug. 1971; m. Natalie Appleton; one s. *Career:* mem. The Prodigy 1990–; numerous festival and other live appearances, including Red Square, Glastonbury, V, Reading, Miami Music Festival. *Films:* music for Smokin Aces, Charlie's Angels, Tomb Raider. *Recordings include:* albums: Experience 1992, Music for the Jilted Generation 1994, The Fat of the Land (MTV Music Award for Best Album) 1997, The Dirtchamber Sessions 1999, Always Outnumbered, Never Outgunned 2004, Their Law: The Singles 1990–2005 2005, Invaders Must Die 2009, The Day is My Enemy 2015. *Honours:* BRIT Awards for Best British Dance Act 1997, 1998, five MTV Music Awards including for Best Live Band, Best Dance Band, Q Award for Innovation in Sound 2005, Kerrang! Spirit of Independence Award 2006. *Website:* www.theprodigy.com.

HOYDAL, Annika; Faroese singer, actress and songwriter; b. 19 Nov. 1945, Tórshavn, The Faroe Islands; d. of Karsten Hoydal and Marie Louise Hoydal; m. Klavs Lockwood 1994. *Education:* Statens Teaterskole, Copenhagen, Denmark. *Career:* The Faroe Islands 1966; mem. Harkalidid 1960s; freelance actress and singer throughout Scandinavia; mem. Dansk Artist Forbund, Danish Jazz Beat and Folk Music Composers' Org., Dansk Solist-Forbund, Skuespillerforeningen af 1879, Føroya Leikarafelag. *Compositions include:* Mit Eget Land, Min Krop, Hjemme, Drømmen, Bekendelse, Mørket, Lammet, Aldan, Dråben, Kasper, Til Dans, Tjipp, Munnur, Á Palli, Á Havi, Morgun, Snigil, Alt, Dulcinea, Hvalspýggja, Taraloppa, Ljós, Kópagenta, Dreymahav, Inn Móti Landi, Marmennil, Farin, Sjólátin, Nú Sigla…, Tid, Græsset Grønnes, Vigen, Barnetegning, Ratio, Avidus og Caritas, Forkynderen, Olympia, Mørket taler til den Blomstrende Busk, Digteren Einar Benediktssons Død, Stjerner mine Venner, Elvesuset, Prik, Prak, Prok, Tilegnelsen, Oratorium, Ein drongur gekk, Kvøldbøn, Nú vil eg, Útferd, Á nei, for hundan, Maria blída, Neytakonur, Eingilin, Steinstólpan, Mamman leggur lítlan, Snigla sorgarljód, Gáta, Tvær smáar grýlur, Nes og nes, Dreymur, Stavirnir, Bleytt er barnsins hjarta, Lítla kiska Lógvin, Tá títling, Lambid, Marra marra minni, Tvætlivísa, Kettan liggur í durunum deyd, Nátt, Lívi! Dýra undur, Tíðin. *Plays:* numerous. *Recordings include:* several albums with Harkalidid 1960s; solo: Til Børn og Vaksin 1975, Annika og Jógvan 1979, Mit Eget Land 1980, Spor í Sjónum 1983, Dulcinea 1991, Havid/The Ocean 1997, Stjerner Mine Venner 2000, Til Børnini hjá Børnunum 2005, Endurljós 2015. *Honours:* Melodi Grand Prix for Faroe Islands, Denmark 1979, The Faroese Cutural Prize of Honour 2015. *Address:* Admiralgade 22 2 tv, 1066 Copenhagen K, Denmark (home). *E-mail:* hoydal@mail.dk. *Website:* www.hoydal.dk.

HOZIER; Irish singer, guitarist and songwriter; b. (Andrew John Hozier-Byrne), 17 March 1990, Bray, Co. Wicklow. *Education:* Trinity Coll., Dublin. *Career:* mem. Anúna 2008–12; solo artist 2012–; released debut EP 2013. *Recordings:* albums: solo: Hozier (European Border Breakers Award for Album of the Year 2015) 2014. *Honours:* Billboard Music Award for Top Rock Artist 2015, for Top Rock Song (for Take Me to Church) 2015. *Address:* c/o Rubyworks, 6 Park Road, Dun Laoghaire, Co. Dublin, Ireland (office). *Telephone:* (1) 2841747 (office). *Fax:* (1) 2841767 (office). *E-mail:* info@rubyworks.com (office). *Website:* www.rubyworks.com (office); hozier.com.

HRADECKÝ, Emil; Czech teacher and composer; b. 25 Feb. 1953, Prague; m. Alexandra Hradecká 1978. *Education:* Prague Conservatory. *Career:* trained as pianist and composer; Dir Music School (LŠU), Prague; collaborates with children's choir Radost Praha; f. Hradecky music publ. firm 1990. *Compositions include:* vocal works: Love Songs (song cycle for tenor and piano), Up to the Mount Sněka's Top with a Gang of Hedgehogs (lyrics by J. Havel), Three Trivialities for Young Vocalists (choral cycle, lyrics by V. Fischer), The Menagerie (choral cycle, lyrics by V. Fischer), Boom, Boom Rat Tat (choral cycle, lyrics by V. Fischer), Love (series for female choir to words from folk poetry), Cosmic Songs (choral series, lyrics by V. Fischer), Three Choirs on Texts from the Bible (for Boy and Male Choir), A Little Song (lyrics by J. Havel), Cricket the Fiddler (lyrics by J. Balík), Bimbo the Elephant (lyrics by J. Havel), Little Nippers (lyrics by V. Fischer), The Upside Down Day (lyrics by J. Havel), A Spring Nosegay (lyrics by V. Fischer), Something for You, Mrs. Koubková (jazz), Lady and a Ford (lyrics by J. Havel, I Will Change (lyrics by J. Havel), How We Are Doing Sports (lyrics by J. Havel), Love Confession to a Meadow, Love Confession to a Rose (for mixed Choir, lyrics by V. Fischer), Fred Hubacek's Transformation (lyrics by J. Havel), Three Love Songs (folk poetry adaptations for girls choir, violin and Celtic harp); for wind orchestra: Fox-polka 1993, Sunny rag 1994, Swing-polka 1995. *Publications:* instructional literature and textbooks: Small Jazz Album – piano 2000, Dance for Guitar 1989, We're Playing the Piano According to Chordal Markings 1991, Jazz Pieces for Twenty Fingers 1992, Piano and Children (with D. Šimáčková) – piano lessons 1992; jazz winds: Jazz Studies for Piano 1993, Compositions on Two Pages – piano 1994, From Blues to Disco – keyboard and wind instruments 1998, S. Joplin The Easy Ragtimes – nine simplified ragtimes for piano arranged by E. Hradecký 2000, Dance Compositions for Four Hands 2002, Children's Carnival 2002, Jazz Flute, Clarinet and Trombone (plus CD) 2004; methodical aids on cassette and CD: Musical Instruments, Improvisations for musical movement studies, Musical Instruments (video), Musical Aids, Relaxation Music, Trades (with P. Jurkovič), Spring-Summer (with P. Jurkovič), Autumn-Winter (with P. Jurkovič), Cinderella (music fairytale) (video), The Sleeping Beauty (music fairytale) (video), The Humberto Circus (video); song books; Songbook for the Youngest 1987, The Three Magicians 1990, Songbook for Children's Pockets 1996. *Honours:* Musical Prize, Children's Choirs, Prague 1995, 1997. *Address:* Konselská 11, 180 00 Prague 8, Czech Republic. *E-mail:* emil.hrad@volny.cz. *Website:* www.emilhradecky.cz.

HUBBARD, Tyler Reed; American country music singer and songwriter; b. 31 Jan. 1987, Monroe, Ga; m. Hayley Stommel 2015. *Education:* Belmont Univ., Nashville, Tenn. *Career:* mem. of duo, Florida Georgia Line 2010–; released debut EP 2010; signed to Republic Nashville label 2011; support act to Luke Bryan on Dirt Road Diaries tour 2013. *Recordings:* albums: with Florida Georgia Line: Here's to the Good Times 2012, Anything Goes (American Music Award for Favorite Country Album 2015) 2014. *Honours:* Acad. of Country Music Awards for New Vocal Duo or Group of the Year 2013, for New Artist of the Year 2013, for Vocal Group of the Year 2014, CMT Music Awards for Duo Video of the Year (for Cruise) 2013, for Breakthrough Video of the Year (for Cruise) 2013, American Country Award for New Artist 2013, for Single of the Year (for Cruise) 2013, for New Artist Single of the Year (for Cruise) 2013, CMA Awards for Vocal Duo of the Year 2013, 2014, 2015, for Single of the Year 2013, American Music Awards for Single of the Year (for Cruise) 2013, for Favorite Country Duo or Group 2014, 2015, Billboard Music Awards for Top Country Song (for Cruise) (with Nelly) 2014, for Top Country Artist 2015. *Current Management:* Seth England and Kevin 'Chief' Zaruk, Big Loud Mountain Management, Suite 201, #1111, 16th Avenue South, Nashville, TN 37212, USA. *Website:* www.bigloudmountain.com. *Address:* c/o Republic Nashville Records, Big Machine Label Group, 1219 16th Avenue South, Nashville, TN 37212, USA (office). *E-mail:* mail@bigmachine.us (office). *Website:* www.bigmachinelabelgroup.com (office); floridageorgialine.com.

HUBLEY, Georgia; American musician (drums); b. New York City; m. Ira Kaplan. *Career:* formed band Yo La Tengo with husband Ira Kaplan, Hoboken, New Jersey 1984; frequent tours throughout USA and worldwide; collaborations with Yoko Ono, Jad Fair, Ray Davies, Robyn Hitchcock, Neil Innes, mems of Sun Ra Arkestra; composed soundtracks for several films. *Film soundtracks include:* The Sounds of the Sounds of Science 2001, Junebug 2005, Game 6 2005, Shortbus 2006, Old Joy 2006. *Recordings include:* albums: Ride the Tiger 1986, New Wave Hot Dogs 1987, President Yo La Tengo 1989, Fakebook 1990, May I Sing with Me 1992, Painful 1993, Electr-O-Pura 1995, I Can Hear the Heart Beating as One 1997, Strange But True (with Jad Fair) 1998, And Then Nothing Turned Itself Inside Out 2000, The Sounds of the Sounds of Science 2002, Summer Sun 2003, Prisoners Of Love: A Smattering Of Scintillating Senescent Songs, 1985–2003 2005, I Am Not Afraid of You and I Will Beat Your Ass 2006, Yo La Tengo Is Murdering the Classics 2006, Popular Songs 2009. *Address:* PO Box 6028, Hoboken, NJ 07030, USA (office). *E-mail:* info@yolatengo.com. *Website:* www.yolatengo.com.

HUCKNALL, Michael (Mick) James, BA; British singer and songwriter; b. 8 June 1960, Manchester; m. Gabriella Wesberry; one d. *Education:* Manchester Polytechnic. *Career:* fmrly with own punk band, Frantic Elevators 1979; founder mem. and lead singer, Simply Red 1984–2010, 2015–; numerous world tours; co-f. reggae music label, Blood and Fire 1992; mem. Govt Task Force on the Music Industry 1997–; founded record label, Simplyred.com 2003–; solo artist 2009–. *Recordings include:* albums: with Simply Red: Picture Book 1985, Early Years 1987, Men and Women 1987, A New Flame 1989, Stars 1991, Life 1995, Blue 1997, Love and the Russian Winter 1999, It's Only Love 2000, Home 2003, Simplified 2005, Stay 2007, Simply Red 25 2008, Songs of Love 2010; solo: Tribute to Bobby 2008, American Soul 2012. *Honours:* Hon. MSc (UMIST) 1997; BRIT Award for Best British Band 1991, 1992, Best Male Solo Artist 1992, Ivor Novello Songwriter of the Year Award 1992, MOBO Award for Outstanding Achievement 1997, Manchester Making it Happen Award 1998. *Current Management:* c/o Quietus Management, The Phoenix Brewery, 13 Bramley Road, London, W10 6SP, England. *E-mail:* info@quietusmanagement.com. *Website:* www.quietusmanagement.com. *E-mail:* info@simplyred.com (office). *Website:* www.simplyred.com; www.mickhucknall.com.

HUDSON, Jennifer Kate; American singer and actress; b. 12 Sept. 1981, Chicago; one s. *Education:* Dunbar Vocational Career Acad. *Career:* solo artist and actress 2003–; American Idol contestant 2004. *Television includes:* American Idol (contestant) 2004, Smash 2013. *Films:* Dreamgirls (Satellite Award for Best Actress in a Supporting Role 2006, NYFCC Award for Best Supporting Actress 2006, Screen Actors Guild Award for Outstanding Performance by a Female in a Supporting Role 2007, Image Award for Outstanding Supporting Actress in a Motion Picture 2007, Golden Globe for Best Performance by an Actress in a Supporting Role in a Motion Picture 2007, Critics Choice Award for Best Supporting Actress 2007, BET Award for Best Actress 2007, BAFTA Award for Best Actress in a Supporting Role 2007, Academy Award for Best Performance by an Actress in a Supporting Role 2007) 2006, Sex and the City 2008, Winged Creatures (aka Fragments) 2008, The Secret Life of Bees 2008, Winnie 2011, The Three Stooges 2012, The Inevitable Defeat of Mister and Pete 2013, Black Nativity 2013, Lullaby 2014. *Recordings include:* albums: Jennifer Hudson (Grammy Award for Best R&B Album 2009) 2008, I Remember Me 2011, JHUD 2014. *Honours:* Soul Train Sammy Davis Jr Award for Entertainer of the Year 2007. *Address:* Arista Records, 550 Madison Avenue, New York, NY 10022, USA (office). *Website:* www.jenniferhudsononline.com.

HUFF, Leon; American songwriter, producer and musician (piano); b. 8 April 1942, Camden, NJ; three d. one s. *Career:* fmr session musician in New York, worked with Phil Spector, The Ronettes, Carole King; fmr mem., The Dynaflows, later The Lavenders; solo songwriter, then formed prolific songwriting and production team with Kenneth Gamble 1963–, co-founder, Philadelphia Int. Records (with Gamble) 1971, signed and developed numerous artists, including Harold Melvin and The Bluenotes, The O'Jays, Lou Rawls, Billy Paul, Teddy Pendergrass, MFSB, The Jones Girls; style came to be known as 'The Philadelphia Sound'; co-founder and Vice-Chair., Gamble-Huff Music. *Compositions:* co-writer with Kenneth Gamble of over 3,000 songs, including Wake Up Everybody (Harold Melvin and The Bluenotes), For the Love of Money (The O'Jays), You'll Never Find (Another Love Like Mine) (Lou Rawls), Me and Mrs Jones (Billy Paul), TSOP (The Sound of Philadelphia) (MFSB), Silly, Silly Fool (Dusty Springfield), Only the Strong Survive (Jerry Butler), Now That We Found Love (The O'Jays), When Will I See You Again (The Three Degrees). *Honours:* Grammy Award 1989, Grammy Trustees' Award 1999. *Address:* Gamble-Huff Music, 309 South Broad Street, Philadelphia, PA 19107, USA (office). *E-mail:* chuckgamble@gamble-huffmusic.com. *Website:* www.gamble-huffmusic.com.

HUGHES, Christopher Merrick; British record producer and musician (drums); b. 3 March 1953; m. Elizabeth Hughes; two s. one d. *Career:* as producer worked with Adam & the Ants 1979–82, also worked with Adam Ant, The Associates, Lloyd Cole, Gay Dad, Gene, Howard Jones, Paul McCartney, Ric Ocasek, Robert Plant, Plastic Fantastic, Propaganda; as drummer worked with Enya, Howard Jones, Ric Ocasek; mem., Tears for Fears 1983–99. *Recordings include:* albums: with Tears for Fears: Hurting (also producer) 1983, Songs From The Big Chair (also producer) 1985, Seeds of Love 1989; solo: Shift 1994. *Honours:* Music Week Album Producer of the Year Award 1981. *Current Management:* c/o Carole Davies, Positive Producer Management, 4th Floor Studio, 16 Abbey Courtyard, Bath, Somerset BA1 1LY, England. *Telephone:* (1225) 31166. *Fax:* (1225) 482013. *E-mail:* carole@positiveproducermanagement.com. *Website:* www.chrishughesproducer.com. *E-mail:* chrishughes@helium.co.uk (office). *Website:* www.chrishughesproducer.com.

HUGHES, David Alan; British composer, musician (keyboards) and producer; b. 25 April 1960, Birkenhead; m. 1984; one s. one d. *Career:* world-wide tours, OMD and Thomas Lang; Founder-mem., electronic duo, Dalek 1; composer, film scores with composer John Murphy; numerous television appearances; mem. Musicians' Union, PRS, BAC&S. *Compositions include:* film scores: Il Paladini, CHUD, Hearts and Armour; film scores with John Murphy: Leon The Pig Farmer, Feast At Midnight, Solitaire For Two, Welcome To The Terrordome, Beyond Bedlam, Body Memories, Dinner In Purgatory, Destroying Angels, Proteus, Giving Tongue, Clockwork Mice; for television: White Men Are Cracking Up, All The President's Women, Funland 2005, Warplane 2006, Boy Meets Girl 2009.

HUGHES, James (Jimmy) William; British musician (drums, percussion) and backing singer; b. 18 May 1960, Liverpool, England; one d. *Education:* studied with Red Carter, Liverpool. *Career:* mem. Black, The Darling Buds 1990–93; numerous tours of USA, Japan and UK; numerous TV appearances, including Top of the Pops on BBC TV; numerous gigs and tours with Pete Wylie's Mighty Wah!; sessions with The Fourmost and Ian McNabb; played drums for Al Matthews and the late Isaac Hayes, Linda Gail Lewis 2004–05, 2010–13, Kevin Montgomery 2008, Tommy Allsop 2008–09, Gaz Gaskell 2013; mem. Musicians' Union. *Film:* played drums for Isaac Hayes' band in Soul Survivors. *Recordings:* albums: with Black: Wonderful Life (Gold Disc) 1987; with The Darling Buds: Crawdaddy 1990, Erotica 1992. *Address:* 247 Fernhill Road, Bootle, Merseyside, L20 0AQ, England. *Telephone:* (151) 476-2567. *E-mail:* jw.hughes@live.co.uk.

HUGHES, Jesse Everett, (The Devil, Boots Electric, J. Devil); American rock singer, songwriter and musician (guitar, bass guitar); b. 24 Sept. 1972, Greenville, South Carolina. *Education:* Greenville Tech. Coll. *Career:* raised in Calif.; Founder-mem. Eagles of Death Metal 1998–; support act to The Strokes 2006, debut US tour as headlining act 2006; solo career (as Boots Electric) 2011–; ordained as minister with Universal Life Church 2012. *Recordings include:* with Eagles of Death Metal: Peace, Love, Death Metal 2004, Death by Sexy 2006, Heart On 2008, Zipper Down 2015; solo: A Pair of Queens 2004, Honkey Kong (as Boots Electric) 2011; other: Volumes 3 & 4, The Desert Sessions 1998, Cruel & Delicious, Fatso Jetson 2002, Lullabies to Paralyze, Queens of the Stone Age 2005. *Current Management:* c/o The MGMT Company, 4220 Lankershim Boulevard, North Hollywood, CA 91602, USA. *Telephone:* (818) 760-7657. *E-mail:* themgmtcompany@gmail.com; inquiries@themgmtcompany.com. *Website:* www.themgmtcompany.com; www.eaglesofdeathmetal.com (office).

HUGHES, Richard; British musician (drums); b. 8 Sept. 1975, Battle, East Sussex. *Career:* Founder-mem. Keane 1997–. *Recordings include:* album: Hopes and Fears (Best Album, Q Awards 2004, BRIT Award for Best British Album 2005) 2004, Under the Iron Sea 2006, Perfect Symmetry 2008, Night Train (mini-album) 2010, Strangeland 2012, The Best of Keane 2013. *Honours:* Best Int. Band, Premios Onda, Spain 2004, BRIT Award for Best British Breakthrough Act 2005, Band of the Year, GQ Awards 2006. *Current Management:* c/o Adam Tudhope, Everybody's Management Ltd., 53 Corsica Street, London, N5 1JT, England. *Telephone:* (20) 3227-0420. *Fax:* (20) 7226-2166. *E-mail:* info@everybody-s.com. *Website:* www.everybody-s.com; www.keanemusic.com.

HUGO, Chad; American producer, remixer and musician; b. Virginia; m.; one c. *Career:* f. The Neptunes production duo with Pharrell Williams 2000–; co-f. recording act, N.E.R.D. (Nobody Ever Really Dies) 2001–, with Pharrell Williams and Shay Hayley; co-f. Star Trak Entertainment label; worked with Air, Mary J. Blige, Foxy Brown, Jay-Z, Kelis, Ludacris, Mystikal, Nelly, No Doubt, *NSYNC, Ol' Dirty Bastard, Britney Spears, Justin Timberlake, Usher. *Recordings include:* albums: with N.E.R.D.: In Search Of. . . 2001, Fly Or Die 2004, Seeing Sounds 2008, Nothing 2010; with The Neptunes: The Neptunes Present...Clones 2003. *Honours:* Source Award for Producer of the Year (The Neptunes) 2001, MOBO Award for Best Producer (The Neptunes) 2002. *Website:* www.n-e-r-d.com.

HULAN, Miroslav; Czech musician (guitar, mandolin); b. 23 April 1959, Brno; m. Drahomira Spidlikova 1981; two s. *Career:* mem. Poutnici 1980–; formed duo with Michal Hromcik 1995–; mem. Czech Bluegrass Music Asscn. *Recordings include:* albums: with Poutnici: Poutnici 1987, Wayfaring Strangers 1989, Chromi kone 1990, The Days of Auld Lang Syne 1991, Poutnici Live 1991, Je to v nas 1992, Pisne brnenskych kovboju 1994, Co uz je pryc 1997, Krajní meze 1998, Vzpomínky 1999, Pláč a smích 2003, Poutnici 2006 2006, Country vánoce 2013. *Publications include:* Guitar School for Beginners 1993, Guitar School for Advanced 1997. *Honours:* Best Non-American Bluegrass Recordings 1989, 1990. *Address:* Za branou 279, Slavkov u Brna, Jihomoravský, 684 01, Czech Republic. *E-mail:* polakaras@iol.cz. *Website:* www.poutnici.cz.

HULJIC, Tonci; Croatian composer, musician (keyboard) and producer; b. 29 Oct. 1961, Split; m. Vjekosava Huljic 1987; one s. one d. *Education:* High School of Music. *Career:* leader and composer, Magazin 1981–; numerous tours and television appearances, festival performances; Owner, record co., Tonika; co-f. Hush Music production co.; mem. Croatian Music Soc., Croatian Music Union (pres.), Croatian Composers' Asscn, Rotary Club. *Recordings include:* albums: with Magazin: Slatko Stanje 1982, Kokolo 1983, O la la 1984, Pisi mi 1985, Put putujem 1986, Magazin 1987, Besane noci 1988, Dobro Jutro 1989, Da mi je zaljubit u mene 1992, Najbolje godine 1993, Došlo vrijeme 1993, Simpatija 1994, Nebo boje moje ljubavi 1996, Da si ti ja 1998, Minus i plus 2000, S druge strane mjeseca 2002, Paaa...? 2004, Dama i car 2007, Bossa n' Magazin 2008; solo album: Waterland 2006. *Honours:* Composer of the Year 1988, 1989, 1994. *E-mail:* magazin@grupamagazin.com. *Website:* www.grupamagazin.com.

HUME, Daniel Benjamin (Dann); New Zealand musician (drums); b. 1 Sept. 1987, Feilding. *Career:* formed band Evermore with brothers Jon and Peter, winners Rockquest talent competition 2000; numerous tours of Australia and New Zealand. *Recordings:* albums: Dreams 2004, Real Life 2006, Truth of the World: Welcome to the Show 2009, Evermore 2010. *Honours:* Supernova Breakthrough Act (for Dreams), MTV Australia Awards 2005, Int. Achievement Award, NZ VMA Music Awards 2005, Best Popular Song (for It's Too Late), NZ APRA Silver Scroll Awards 2005, ARIA Channel V Oz Artist of the Year Award 2007, Single Of The Year (for Light Surrounding You) and Int. Achievement Award, NZ VMA Vodafone Music Awards 2007. *Address:* Evermore, PO Box 814, Potts Point, Sydney, NSW 1335, Australia (office). *E-mail:* rebekah@evermoreband.com (office). *Website:* www.evermoreband.com (office).

HUME, Jon Daniel; New Zealand singer and musician (guitar); b. 1 Sept. 1987, Australia. *Career:* formed band Evermore with brothers Peter and Dann, winners Rockquest talent competition 2000. *Recordings:* albums: Dreams 2004, Real Life 2006, Truth of the World: Welcome to the Show 2009, Evermore 2010. *Honours:* Supernova Breakthrough Act (for Dreams), MTV Australia Awards 2005, Int. Achievement Award, NZ VMA Music Awards 2005, Best Popular Song (for It's Too Late), NZ APRA Silver Scroll Awards 2005, ARIA Channel V Oz Artist of the Year Award 2007, Single Of The Year (for Light Surrounding You) and Int. Achievement Award, NZ VMA Vodafone Music Awards 2007. *Address:* Evermore, PO Box 814, Potts Point, Sydney, NSW 1335, Australia (office). *E-mail:* rebekah@evermoreband.com (office). *Website:* www.evermoreband.com (office).

HUME, Peter Elisha; New Zealand musician (bass guitar, keyboards); b. 4 Sept. 1985, Feilding. *Career:* formed band Evermore with brothers Jon and Dann, winners Rockquest talent competition 2000; numerous tours of Australia and New Zealand. *Recordings:* albums: Dreams 2004, Real Life 2006, Truth of the World: Welcome to the Show 2009, Evermore 2010. *Honours:* Supernova Breakthrough Act (for Dreams), MTV Australia Awards 2005, Int. Achievement Award, NZ VMA Music Awards 2005, Best Popular Song (for It's Too Late), NZ APRA Silver Scroll Awards 2005, ARIA Channel V Oz Artist of the Year Award 2007, Single Of The Year (for Light Surrounding You) and Int. Achievement Award, NZ VMA Vodafone Music Awards 2007. *Address:* Evermore, PO Box 814, Potts Point, Sydney, NSW 1335, Australia (office). *E-mail:* rebekah@evermoreband.com (office). *Website:* www.evermoreband.com (office).

HUMES, Marvin Richard James; British singer, rapper, songwriter and actor; b. 18 March 1985, Greenwich, London; m. Rochelle Wiseman 2012. *Career:* mem. VS 2004–05; mem. UFO 2006–08, changed group name to JLS (Jack the Lad Swing) 2008–13; competed in The X Factor (UK version) 2008, placed second; signed to Epic Records 2009; toured with Lemar 2009; debut single Beat Again released 2009; debut album released 2009; first headline tour 2010; recorded single Love You More for Children in Need charity 2010; collaborations include Tinie Tempah, Dev; recorded Sport Relief charity single Proud 2012; performed at Diamond Jubilee concert, outside Buckingham Palace 2012; patron for Childline charity. *Television:* K-Club 1999, Holby City (as actor) 2000–03; JLS Revealed (special) 2009, The Voice UK (as co-host) 2014–. *Film:* JLS: Eyes Wide Open 3D (concert film and documentary) 2011. *Recordings:* albums: with VS: All Kinds of Trouble 2004; with JLS: JLS (MOBO Award for Best Album 2010) 2009, Outta This World 2010, Jukebox 2011, Evolution 2012. *Publications:* Our Story So Far 2009, Just Between Us: Our Private Diary 2010. *Honours:* with UFO: Urban Music Award for Best Unsigned Act 2007; with JLS: MOBO Awards for Best UK Newcomer 2009, for Best Song (for Beat Again) 2009, for Best UK Act 2010, BBC Switch Live Award for Outstanding Artist 2009, BRIT Awards for British Breakthrough 2010, for Best British Single (for Beat Again) 2010, BT Digital Music Awards for Best Group 2010, 2011, for Best Video (for Everybody in Love) 2010, (for Eyes Wide Shut) 2011, (for Do You Feel What I Feel?) 2012, Urban Music Awards for Best Group 2010, for Best R&B Act 2010. *Current Management:* c/o Modest! Management, The Matrix Complex, 91 Peterborough Road, London, SW6 3BU, England. *E-mail:* info@modestmanagement.com. *Website:* www.modestmanagement.com; www.jlsofficial.com.

HUMPE, Annette; German singer, songwriter, musician (keyboards) and producer; b. 28 Oct. 1950, Hagen; one s. *Education:* Cologne Conservatory. *Career:* moved to Berlin 1974; Founder-mem. Neonbabies 1979–80, Ideal 1980–83; record producer 1983–97 for artists including DÖF, Palais Schaumburg, Rio Reiser, Heiner Pudelko; Founder-mem. of duo Humpe & Humpe 1985–87, Bamby 1995 (both with younger sister Inga Humpe); Founder-mem. Ich + Ich 2004–; also writer and producer for numerous artists including Udo Lindenberg, Die Prinzen, Lucilectric, Sin with Sebastian, Nena, Etwas, Band ohne Namen. *Recordings:* with Ideal: Ideal 1980, Der Ernst des Lebens 1981, Bi Nuu 1982; with Humpe & Humpe: Humpe & Humpe 1985, Swimming with Sharks 1987; solo: Solo 1990; with Bamby: Wall of Sugar 1995; with Ich + Ich: Ich + Ich 2005, Vom selben Stern 2007, Gute Reise 2009. *Honours:* solo: Honorary Award, ECHO Awards, Germany 2011; with Ich + Ich: Best National Rock/Pop Group, ECHO Awards 2009, 2011. *Current Management:* Artist Legend Management GmbH, Kurfürstendamm 186, 10707 Berlin, Germany. *E-mail:* ich-und-ich@artist-legend.de. *Website:* www.artist-legend.de. *Address:* Universal Music Deutschland, Universal Music Group, Stralauer Allee 1, 10245 Berlin, Germany (office). *Telephone:* (30) 52007-01 (office). *Fax:* (30) 52007-09 (office). *E-mail:* vorname.nachname@umusic.com (office). *Website:* www.universal-music.de (office); www.ich-und-ich.de.

HUMPERDINCK, Engelbert; British singer; b. (Arnold George Dorsey), 2 May 1936, Madras (now Chennai), India; s. of Mervyn Dorsey and Olive Dorsey; m. Patricia Healey 1963; four c. *Career:* family moved to Leicester, UK when he was ten; began learning the saxophone; originally billed as Gerry Dorsey, changed name late 1960s; regular concerts, USA and UK; best known for his No. 1 hits 'Release Me' and 'The Last Waltz', as well as 'After the Lovin' and 'A Man Without Love'; represented the UK in Eurovision Song Contest, Baku, Azerbaijan with the song 'Love Will Set You Free' (oldest male singer ever to participate in the contest) 2012. *Television:* Oh Boy (own series) 1950s, The Engelbert Humperdinck Show 1970. *Recordings include:* albums: Release Me 1967, The Last Waltz 1967, A Man Without Love 1968, Engelbert 1969, Engelbert Humperdinck 1969, We Made It Happen 1970, Another Time Another Place 1971, Live At The Riviera 1972, Greatest Hits 1974, Getting Sentimental 1975, Remember I Love You 1987, The Engelbert Humperdinck Collection 1987, Hello Out There 1992, Golden Love 1993, Ultimate 1993, King of Hearts 1993, Last Of The Romantics 1993, Back To Back (with Tom Jones) 1993, Love Unchained 1995, Lovely Way to Spend an Evening 1997, In the Still of the Night 1999, Let There Be Love 2005. *Publications:* Engelbert: What's in a Name? (autobiog., with Katie Wright) 2004. *Honours:* American Guild of Variety Artists Georgie Award for Best Singer 1978; Hon. DMus (Leicester) 2006. *Current Management:* c/o 3D Management, PO Box 16817, Beverly Hills, CA 90209-2817, USA. *E-mail:* info@engelbert.com. *Website:* www.engelbert.com.

HUNT, Brian George Edward; Belgian singer and musician; b. 7 June 1937; one s. *Education:* Clavissimo Music School, Antwerp. *Career:* mem. The Blue Tones 1960s; international country, folk, soft rock, ballad music; TV and radio in Belgium; support act to Steeleye Span and Frank Ifield; mem. Country Music Asscn. *Recordings include:* Louisa From Louisiana, Sing This Song With Me Tonight. *Honours:* Award, Assistant in the Promotion of Country Music Worldwide 1981. *Address:* Camille Huysmans Laan 118, 2020 Antwerp, Belgium (home). *Telephone:* (3) 236-59-46 (home). *E-mail:* marguerite.dufour@skynet.be.

HUNT, Sam Lowry; American country music singer, songwriter and musician (guitar, piano); b. 8 Dec. 1984, Cedartown, Ga; s. of Allen Hunt and Joan Hunt. *Education:* Middle Tenn. State Univ., Univ. of Alabama at Birmingham. *Career:* signed with MCA Nashville record label 2014; opening act, Lady Antebellum's Wheels Up tour 2015; first headlining tour 2015; released debut album 2014; songwriter for Kenny Chesney, Keith Urban, Billy Currington, Reba McEntire. *Recordings include:* albums: Montevallo 2014; mixtapes: Between the Pines 2015. *Honours:* American Music Award for New Artist of the Year 2015, Acad. of Country Music Award for New Artist of the Year 2015, ASCAP Country Music Award for Songwriter-Artist of the Year 2015, CMT Award for Breakthrough Video (for Leave the Night On) 2015.

E-mail: info@samhunt.com (home). *Website:* samhunt.bombplates.com (home).

HUNT, William Stephen, (Bill Hunt); British teacher and musician; b. 23 May 1947, Birmingham, England. *Education:* Birmingham School of Music. *Career:* performed with Birmingham band Breakthru', including their European Tour 1969; performed and recorded with Stourbridge-based band, Hannibal early 1970s; original mem. The Electric Light Orchestra (ELO), playing on first ELO tour of Italy; original mem. Wizzard, and Vincent Flat's Final Drive; co-writer with guitarist Dave Hill for Slade, with whom also recorded; tours with Raymond Froggatt, with whom also recorded. *Radio:* Raymond Froggatt. *Television:* Move, ELO, Wizzard, Raymond Froggatt. *Compositions:* The Carlsberg Special (Wizzard) and various others, including songs co-written with Dave Hill of Slade. *Recordings:* first album and single, ELO; first album and hit singles, Wizzard; various tracks, Slade and Slade II; Miles Hunt; featured on various ELO compilations. *Honours:* Hon. Treas. Don Arden Veterans' Asscn . *E-mail:* billhunt@9mb.co.uk (office). *Website:* www.tewkesbury-cottage.co.uk (office).

HUNT-TAYLOR, Amanda; American songwriter. *Career:* songwriter with Warner Chappell Music, 1991; songwriter with Bluewater Music, Nashville 1996; co-writer credits with: Rick Giles; Steve Bogard; John Scott Sherrill; Gene Nelson; Kent Robbins; Janis Ian; Rory Bourke; Director, AmandaRick Records, 1999–. *Compositions:* Your Love Amazes Me, recorded by John Berry; Tanya Tucker; Andy Childs; Joel Nova; All She Wants, recorded by Rena Gaile; No One Else Like You, recorded by Janis Ian; Able, recorded by Happy Goodmans; Wish I Could Wish On A Star, recorded by Mandy Barnett; A Fire In The Rain, recorded by Doug Supernaw; I Really Do Love You Lovin' Me, recorded by Lori Morgan; Wishing It All Away, recorded by Tanya Tucker. *Recordings:* albums: as backing or guest vocalist: Revenge, Janis Ian 1995, Celebration Day, Jay Turner 2001; solo: Only When I Breathe, 1999. *Honours:* For Your Love Amazes Me: SESAC Songwriter of the Year, 1994, SESAC Song of the Year, 1994; NSAI Achievement Award, 1995; Music City News Country Songwriters Award, Song of the Year, 1995; Song of the Year, 2nd Annual Country Radio Music Award Show, 1995; 2 NSAI Awards. *E-mail:* amandahunttaylor@yahoo.com. *Website:* amandahunttaylor.com; www.myspace.com/amandahunttaylor.

HUNTER, Ian; British singer; b. 3 June 1946, Shrewsbury, Salop. *Career:* singer, Mott the Hoople 1969–74, reformed for live performances 2009; solo artist 1975–; numerous live performances. *Recordings include:* albums: with Mott The Hoople: Mott The Hoople 1969, Mad Shadows 1970, Wild Life 1971, Brain Capers 1971, All the Young Dudes 1972, Rock 'n' Roll Queen 1972, The Hoople 1974, Mott The Hoople – Live 1974; solo: Ian Hunter 1975, All American Alien Boy 1976, Overnight Angels 1977, You're Never Alone With a Schizophrenic 1979, Shades of Ian Hunter 1979, Ian Hunter Live/Welcome to the Club 1980, Short Back and Sides 1981, All the Good Ones Are Taken 1983, YUIOrta 1990, Dirty Laundry 1995, Artful Dodger 1997, Welcome to the Club 1998, Missing in Action 2000, Rant 2001, Shrunken Heads 2007, Man Overboard 2009, When I'm President 2012. *Publication:* Diary of a Rock 'n' Roll Star. *Current Management:* c/o Gold Village Entertainment Inc., 260 West 35th Street, 13th Floor, New York, NY 10016, USA. *E-mail:* info@goldve.com. *Website:* www.goldve.com; www.mottthehoople.com; www.ianhunter.com.

HUNTER, James; British singer, musician (guitar, harmonica) and actor; b. 2 Oct. 1962, Colchester, Essex. *Career:* numerous television appearances and radio broadcasts; toured UK, Europe and USA as guest with Van Morrison R&B Revue; solo artist (fmrly as Howlin' Wilf) 1994–; mem. Musicians' Union, PRS, Equity. *Recordings include:* albums: Believe What I Say 1994, Kick It Around 2001, People Gonna Talk 2006, The Hard Way 2008, Minute by Minute 2013. *Current Management:* c/o Mr Matt Hanks, Shore Fire Media, 32 Court Street, Suite 1600, Brooklyn, NY 11201, USA. *Telephone:* (718) 522-7171. *Fax:* (718) 522-7242. *E-mail:* mhanks@shorefire.com; info@shorefire.com. *Website:* www.shorefire.com; www.jameshuntermusic.com.

HUNTER, Mark; British musician (keyboards); b. 5 Nov. 1968, England. *Career:* mem., James 1990–2001, re-formed 2007–; numerous tours, festival dates and TV appearances. *Recordings include:* albums: Gold Mother 1990, Seven 1992, Laid 1993, Wah Wah 1994, Whiplash 1997, The Best Of James 1998, Millionaires 1999, B-Sides Ultra 2001, Pleased To Meet You 2001, Getting Away With It 2002, Hey Ma 2008, The Night Before 2010, The Morning After 2010, La Petite Mort 2014. *Address:* c/o Mercury Records, 364–366 Kensington High Street, London W14 8NS, England (office). *Website:* www.wearejames.com.

HURLEY, Andy; American musician (drums); b. 31 May 1980, Milwaukee, Wis. *Education:* Univ. of Wisconsin-Milwaukee. *Career:* fmr mem. of bands including Project Rocket, Arma Angelus, Kill Pill, Racetraitor; joined Fall Out Boy 2003–; headline act, Nintendo Fusion Tour 2005, Black Clouds and Underdogs Tour 2005, Honda Civic Tour 2007, Young Wild Things Tour 2007; collaborations with Gym Class Heroes, Motion City Soundtrack. *Recordings include:* albums: From Under the Cork Tree 2005, Infinity on High 2007, Folie à Deux 2008, Save Rock and Roll 2013, American Beauty/American Psycho 2015. *Honours:* People's Choice Awards for Favorite Int. Group 2006, for Favorite Alternative Band 2014, Kerrang! Awards for Best Video (for Sugar, We're Going Down) 2006, (for This Ain't a Scene, It's an Arms Race) 2007, for Best Single (for The Phoenix) 2013, for Best Int. Band 2014, Teen Choice Awards for Best Rock Track and Best Single (for Dance, Dance) 2006, for Best

Single (for Thnks Fr Th Mmrs) 2007, MTV Video Music Awards for Viewers Choice 2007, for Best Group 2007, for Best Rock Video (for Uma Thurman) 2015, World Music Award for Best Alternative Act 2014, American Music Award for Favorite Alternative Rock Artist 2015. *Address:* c/o Island Records, 825 Eighth Avenue, New York, NY 10019, USA. *Website:* falloutboy.com.

HURLEY, Luke; New Zealand songwriter, musician (guitar) and performer; b. 31 Aug. 1957, Nyeri, Kenya; m. Jann Hurley 16 May 1992; one s., two d. *Career:* support act for Michelle Shocked and Marianne Faithfull in New Zealand; toured Europe,1998–99. *Compositions include:* Mona Lisa, Fait Accompli, Japanese Overdrive, Greenfields, Precious Time, Missing You, Hungry Gun Song, Information Station. *Recordings include:* albums: Policestate, Japanese Overdrive, Make Room, First Civilian, Alone in Her Field, Reha, Mona Lisa, High Risk, Brother Sun Sister Moon 2008. *Address:* 730 Sandringham Road Ext, Auckland, New Zealand. *E-mail:* luke@lukehurley.co .nz. *Website:* www.lukehurley.co.nz.

HURLEY, Steve 'Silk', (J. M. Silk, Jack Master Silk); American producer, remixer and DJ; b. 9 Nov. 1962, Chicago, Ill. *Career:* started as DJ in Chicago 1979; own show on local radio station WBMX; first release Music Is The Key (as JM Silk) 1985; Founder and CEO record label, Silk Entertainment 1997, production co., SilkMix.com; producer for Chantay Savage, Jamie Principle, Maurice Joshua, Keith Nunnally, Kym Sims, Ce Ce Peniston, Ann Nesby, Tene Williams, Tanya Blount, Rahsaan Patterson, Chaka Khan; remixed Michael Jackson, Janet Jackson, Mary J. Blige, Crystal Waters, Jennifer Lopez, Yolanda Adams, Kelly Rowland, Melanie B, Rahsaan Patterson, Madonna. *Recordings include:* Hold on to Your Dream 1987, Work It Out Compilation 1989. *Address:* Silk Entertainment Inc, 3011 West 183rd Street, Suite 302, Homewood, IL 60430, USA (office). *Telephone:* (708) 503-5002 (office). *Fax:* (708) 503-5007 (office).

HURTADO, Pablo; Mexican singer, musician (guitar, piano), songwriter and record producer; b. San Luis Potosí. *Education:* Academia de Música Fermatta. *Career:* raised in San Luis Potosi; Founder, Cypress Overdrive Studios; Founder-mem. Camila (with Mario Domm and Samo Parra) 2006–. *Recordings:* albums: with Camila: Todo Cambió 2006, Dejarte de Amar (Latin Grammy Award for Best Pop Album by a Duo or Group 2010, Premios Oye! for Album of the Year 2010, for Album of the Year by Group 2010, Premio Lo Nuestro for Album of the Year 2010) 2010, Elypse (Latin Grammy Award for Best Contemporary Pop Vocal Album 2014) 2014. *Honours:* Premio Lo Nuesto for Song of the Year (for Todo Cambió) 2008, Premio Lo Nuesto for Group of the Year 2008, two Latin Billbaord Awards 2008, Latin Grammy Awards for Record of the Year (for Mientes) 2010, for Song of the Year (for Mientes) 2010, Premios Juventud for Best Ballad (for Aléjate de Mi) 2011. *Address:* c/o Sony Music Entertainment Mexico, Horacio 1855, piso 2, Col. Los Morales Polanco, México 11510, Mexico. *Website:* www.camila.tv.

HUSBANDS, Simon Patrick; British musician (keyboards, guitar, bass guitar), songwriter and singer; b. 2 Feb. 1957, Nottingham; m. Janet Johnson 1994. *Education:* Newark-Sherwood Coll. *Career:* keyboard player, bass player, singer with band Blue Train; current solo projects include DIN and UXB; mem., PRS, Musicians' Union, BMI. *Recordings include:* album: The Business of Dreams (co-producer); singles: All I Need Is You , The Hardest Thing, The Business of Dreams. *Current Management:* c/o Gary Heller Management, 11692 Chenault Street, Suite 202, Los Angeles, CA 91411, USA. *Address:* 40 Millicent Road, West Bridgford, Nottingham, NG2 7PZ, England.

HUSEIN, Hasanefendić; Croatian musician (guitar) and songwriter; b. 30 Jan. 1954, Banja Luka; m. Viki Peric, 22 March 1980, one s., one d. *Education:* eight years music school, Zagreb. *Career:* 20 years with own band, Parni Valjek (Steam Roller); mem. HGU; HDS. *Recordings include:* 15 albums (most of them Platinum). *Honours:* 7 Porins (Croatian equivalent of Grammy), 1995. *Address:* c/o Zelengaj 67, 10000 Zagreb, Croatia.

HUSSAIN, Zakir; Indian musician (tabla), producer, actor and composer; b. 9 March 1951, Mumbai; s. of Ustad Alla Rakha Qureshi; m. Antonia Minnecola; two d. *Education:* St Michael's High School, St Xavier's Coll., Maharashtra. *Career:* plays with Ali Akbar Khan, Birju Maharaj, Ravi Shankar, Shivkumar Sharma; formed band Shanti with Aashish Khan 1970; formed band Shakti with John McLaughlin and L. Shankar 1975; first professional concert 1963; also formed percussion group, Rhythm Experience, Diga Rhythm Band, Making Music, Planet Drum with Mickey Hart, Tabla Beat Science, Sangam with Charles Lloyd and Eric Harland; f. Moment! Records 1992–; composed music for opening ceremony, Summer Olympic Games, Atlanta, USA 1996; Old Dominion Fellow, Humanities Council, Princeton Univ., Prof. of Indian classical music, Dept of Music 2005–06; Visiting Prof., Stanford Univ. 2007; commissioned by Indian Govt to compose anthem to celebrate 60 years of Indian independence 2007. *Films include:* soundtracks: Apocalypse Now 1979, Heat and Dust 1983, Miss Beatty's Children 1992, Little Buddha 1993, In Custody 1993, Saaz 1997, Gaach 1998, Zakir and his Friends 1998, Vaanaprastham 1999, Everybody Says I'm Fine 2001, The Mystic Masseur 2001, Mr and Mrs Iyer 2001, The Speaking Hand: Zakir Hussain and the Art of the Indian Drum 2003, One Dollar Curry 2004, The Way of Beauty 2006, Parzania 2005, For Real 2006, The Rhythm Devils Concert Experience 2008. *Recordings include:* albums: Making Music 1987, Planet Drum (with Mickey Hart) (Grammy Award for Best World Music Album) 1992, Tabla Duet (with Ustad Alla Rakha) 1988, Zakir Hussain And The Rhythm Experience 1991, Venu 1972 1991, Essence Of Rhythm 1998, Drums of India 2003, Raag Chandrakauns 2004, Sangam (with Charles Lloyd) 2006, Global Drum Project

(with Mickey Hart, Zakir Hussain, Sikiru Adepoju, Giovanni Hidalgo) 2007, The Melody of Rhythm - Triple Concerto and Music for Trio (with Béla Fleck, Edgar Meyer) 2009, Mysterium Tremendum (with Mickey Hart Band) 2012. *Honours:* Padma Shri 1988, Indo-American Award 1990, Sangeet Natak Akademi Award 1991, Nat. Heritage Fellowship, USA 1999, Padma Bhushan 2002, Kalidas Samman 2006, Grammy Award (best contemporary world music) 2009. *Current Management:* c/o Dean Shultz, IMG Artists, Carnegie Hall Tower, 152 West 57th Street, 5th Floor, New York, NY 10019, USA. *Telephone:* (212) 994-3500. *Fax:* (212) 994-3550. *E-mail:* dshultz@imgartists .com. *Website:* www.imgartists.com; www.zakirhussain.com.

HUSSENOT, Emmanuel; French jazz musician (trumpet, saxophone, recorder), singer and composer; b. 29 Sept. 1951, Saint Cloud; one d. *Career:* cornet player, French traditional band, Sharkey and Co.; composer, singer, trumpet, saxophone and recorder player, Orphéon Celesta 1980. *Recordings:* with Sharkey and Co. 1972–78; with Orphéon Celesta: Anoulanouba, Siphonnée Symphonie, La Préhistoire du Jazz, La vocalise en carton, De la fuite dans les idées. *Theatre:* creator of seven humorous musical reviews, Paris. *Honours:* Prix Sidney Bechet de l'Académie du Jazz 1990, Grand Prix du Festival d'Humour de Saint Gervais 1994. *Address:* 74 rue Alexandre Guilmant, 92190 Meudon, France (office). *Telephone:* (1) 46-26-49-17 (home); (1) 43-43-55-58 (office). *Fax:* (1) 46-26-49-17 (home); (1) 43-43-55-25 (office). *E-mail:* contact@orpheoncelesta.com (home); emmanuel.hussenot@9online.fr (home); infos@civp.net (office). *Website:* www.orpheoncelesta.com.

HUSSEY, Wayne; British musician (guitar) and singer; b. 26 May 1959. *Career:* mem. groups, Dead Or Alive, The Walkie Talkies; mem., The Sisters of Mercy 1983–86; numerous tours and concerts; Founder-mem., The Mission 1986–. *Recordings include:* albums: with The Sisters of Mercy: First And Last And Always 1985; with The Mission: God's Own Medicine 1986, The First Chapter 1987, Children 1988, Carved In Sand 1990, Masque 1991, Neverland 1995, Blue 1996, Ever After: Live 2000, Aura 2001, Aural Delight 2002, God is a Bullet 2007, Live and Last 2009, Dum-Dum Bullets 2010, The Brightest Light 2013; solo: Bare 2008. *Current Management:* c/o Flick Productions, PO Box 888, Penzance, Cornwall, TR20 8ZP, England. *Telephone:* (1736) 788798. *Fax:* (1736) 787898. *Website:* www.waynehussey.de.

HUTCHCRAFT, Theo David; British singer, songwriter and producer; b. 30 Aug. 1986, Stockton-on-Tees. *Education:* Darlington Coll., Univ. of Salford. *Career:* fmr mem. Bureau 2006–07, Daggers 2007–09; mem. Hurts 2009–; supported Scissor Sisters on UK tour 2010; recorded with Kylie Minogue 2010, first full European tour in 2011. *Recordings:* albums: Happiness (Fonogram Best Int. Album Award, Hungary 2011) 2010, Exile 2013, Surrender 2015. *Honours:* BAMBI Award for Best Int. Newcomer 2010, Musikexpress Best Int. Performer Style Award 2010, Bamby Shooting-Star Award, Germany 2010, NME Best New Band Award 2011, Best Int. Newcomer, ECHO Awards, Germany 2011. *Address:* RCA Records, RCA Label Group UK, 9 Derry Street, London, W8 5HY, England (office). *Telephone:* (20) 7361-8000 (office). *Website:* www.rca-records.co.uk (office); www.informationhurts.com.

HUTCHINGS, Ashley Stephen, MBE; British musician (bass guitar), songwriter, producer, dancer and scriptwriter and poet; b. 26 Jan. 1945, Southgate, Middx, England; m. 1971 (divorced 1978); one s. *Career:* Founder-mem. folk-rock groups, Fairport Convention 1967, Steeleye Span 1970–72, Albion Band 1972–2003, Rainbow Chasers 2004–; Music Dir, Nat. Theatre, London 1977–81; mem. Performing Right Soc., Mechanical-Copyright Protection Soc. *Recordings include:* albums: with Fairport Convention: Fairport Convention 1968, What We Did In Our Holidays 1969, Unhalfbricking 1969, Liege and Lief 1970; with Steeleye Span: Hark The Village Wait 1970, Please To See The King 1971, Ten Man Mop 1971; with The Albion Band: Battle of The Field 1976, Prospect Before Us 1977, Rise Up Like The Sun 1978, Light Shining 1984, The Wild Side of Town 1987, I Got New Shoes 1987, Give Me A Saddle I'll Trade You A Car 1989, 1990 1990, Acousticity 1993, Albion Heart 1995; solo: The Compleat Dancing Master 1974, Rattlebone & Ploughjack 1976, Kickin' Up The Sawdust 1977, By Gloucester Docks I Sat Down and Wept 1987, Twangin' N' A-Traddin' 1993, Birthday Bash (live) 1995, Sway With Me 1996, The Guv'nor 1999, Along The Downs 2000, Street Cries 2001, Burning Bright 2005; with Rainbow Chasers: Some Colours Fly 2005, Fortune Never Sleeps 2006, Chimes at Midnight 2014, Riot of Spring 2014. *Publications:* A Little Music (collection of folk songs, tunes and dances), Words, Words, Words (selection of song lyrics, poetry and album sleevenotes) 2014. *Honours:* BBC Radio 2 Folk Awards 'Good Tradition' Award 2006, Most Influential Folk Music Album of All Time (for Liege and Lief) 2006. *Address:* c/o Talking Elephant Records, 8 Martin Dene, Bexleyheath, Kent, DA6 8NA, England (office). *E-mail:* tigerhutch@hotmail.co.uk (office).

HUTCHINGS, Shabaka; British jazz musician (saxophone, clarinet) and composer; b. (Shabaka Akua Lumumba Kamau Hutchings), 1984, London. *Education:* Guildhall School of Music. *Career:* raised in Barbados 1990–2000; played in calypso bands, jazz groups, classical ensembles; fmr mem. Tomorrow's Warriors collective, Abraham Wilson Sextet, Jazz Jamaica; Founder-mem. and fmr frontman, Splay; mem. Courtney Pine's Jazz Warriors 2008; mem. Heliocentrics 2008; collaborated with Jerry Dammers' Spatial AKA Orchestra, Jack DeJohnette, Charlie Haden, Red Snapper; fmr mem. trio with Tony Marsh and Guillaume Viltard; worked with Tom Skinner in trio Zed-U 2007–, and with Seb Rochford in group Polar Bear; Founder-mem. Sons of Kemet (with Tom Skinner, Seb Rochford, Oren Marshall) 2011–, appearances at London Jazz Festival 2012, Cheltenham Jazz Festival 2012; other live appearances include work with John Butcher, Lol Coxhill, John Edwards, Louis Moholo, Evan Parker, Mark Sanders, Pat Thomas; performances with Julian Joseph, BBC Big Band, BBC National Orchestra of Wales; composer for BBC Concert Orchestra; commissioned to write music for clarinet and string quartet, Leasowes Bank Music Festival 2013. *Recordings:* with Zed-U: Night Time on the Middle Passage 2009; with Sons of Kemet: Burn 2013, Lest We Forget What We Came Here To Do 2015. *Honours:* BBC Radio 3's New Generation Jazz Artist 2010–12, Parliamentary Jazz Award for Jazz Musician of the Year 2013; with Sons of Kemet: MOBO Award for Jazz Act of the Year 2013. *Address:* c/o Simon Drake, Naim Jazz Records, Southampton Road, Salisbury, Wiltshire, SP1 2LN, England (office). *Telephone:* (1722) 426600 (office). *Fax:* (871) 230-1012 (office). *E-mail:* info@naimlabel.com (office); sonsofkemet@gmail.com. *Website:* www.naimlabel.com (office); sonsofkemet.com; www.shabakahutchings.com.

HUTCHINSON, Steff, BA, PGCE, MA; British singer and musician (guitar); b. 11 May 1964, Halton. *Education:* Portsmouth Polytechnic, City of Birmingham Polytechnic, De Montfort Univ. *Career:* solo singer and guitarist 1978–; mem., Dead After Dark 1991–99; mem., Firedaze; numerous television and radio broadcasts; mem. Musicians' Union. *Compositions include:* co-writer of all Dead After Dark and Firedaze songs. *Recordings include:* No Time To Waste (album) 1996; EPs: See 1998, Firedaze 1999, The Road 1999, My Turn 2000, Labyrinthinitis 2000, Coming Home 2004. *Address:* D Music, PO Box 213, Leamington Spa, Warwicks., CV31 1ZP, England (office). *Telephone:* (1926) 421830 (office). *E-mail:* info@dmusic.co.uk (office). *Website:* www.dmusic.co.uk (office).

HUTMAN, Olivier; French musician (piano), arranger and composer; b. 12 Nov. 1954, Boulogne. *Education:* PhD, Ethnology on Urban Music in Ghana; 10 years study, piano, National Conservatory of Music, St Maur. *Career:* Jazz performer, accompanist for pop singers; Founder, Moravigne, 1975; Member, Chute Libre, 1975–77; Founds own trio, 1983–84; Member Eric Lelann Quartet, 1984–88; Tours, festivals include: Singapore; Mumbai; Montréal; Prague; Tokyo, 1991, 1993; Newport, USA, 1993; Tahiti, 1995; Martinique, 1994, USA (Boston, San Francisco, Los Angeles), 1995; Antibes; Nimes; La Reunion; Montreux. *Compositions:* Composer, arranger in jazz, theatre, films: jingles, music for industrial films, TV documentaries, Long Range Films include: Mon Oncle, 1985; High Speed, 1987; Printemps Perdu, 1990; Ma Soeur Chinoise, 1994; Commissioned by International Musik Fetsival, Davos, to write suite performed by members of New York Philharmonia, 1993. *Recordings:* with: Moravagine; Chute Libre; J P Debarbat; G Ferris; Eric Lelann; Christian Escoude; Toots Thielemans; C Bellonzi; C Barthelemy; P Delletrz; J P L Labador; S Marc; G Acogny; Abus; Barney Wilen, 1992; A Brunet; M Barrot Quartet; R Galliano; Stephane Grappelli; Luigi Trussardi; Solo: Six Songs, 1984; The Man With The Broken Tooth, trio with Marc Bertaux, Tony Rabeson, 1987; Creole and African music recordings. *Honours:* Prix Boris Vian, French Academy of Jazz, for Best Record of the Year, 1983; 2nd European Keyboardist in Jazz, Hot Magazine, 1987; Awards for music for films: Mon Oncle, 1986; Printemps Perdu, 1990. *Address:* 36 rue de Fontanay, 94300 Vincennes, France.

HÜTTER, Ralf; German musician (electronics); b. 20 Aug. 1946, Krefeld. *Education:* Düsseldorf Conservatory. *Career:* met Florian Schneider while both were students in Düsseldorf, the two began collaborating on musical projects soon after, forming Organisation 1970; group reformed as Kraftwerk 1971–; left group briefly early 1972. *Recordings include:* albums: with Organisation: Tone Float 1970; with Kraftwerk: Kraftwerk 1 1971, Kraftwerk 2 1972, Ralf and Florian 1973, Autobahn 1974, Radio-Activity 1975, Trans-Europe Express 1977, The Man-Machine 1978, Computer World 1981, Electric Café 1986, Tour De France Soundtracks 2003, Minimum-Maximum 2005. *Address:* c/o Astralwerks Records, 104 West 29th Street, 4th Floor, New York, NY 10001, USA. *Website:* www.astralwerks.com; www.kraftwerk.com.

HUTTON, Mick; British jazz musician (double bass, piano, cuatro, steel drums, bass guitar, guitar, tuba drums, synthesizer, trumpet) and teacher; b. 5 June 1956, Chester; m., one s. *Education:* studied piano, organ and cello at school. *Career:* toured and recorded extensively with numerous artistes; fmr mem. Gordon Beck's Band, Bill Bruford's Earthworks, Jim Mullen's Quartet; mem., Humphrey Lyttelton Band; formed the Boat Rockers, Mick Hutton Group, Mick Hutton Quartet; appeared on over 40 jazz albums and over 200 radio broadcasts; played on the soundtrack of films, Absolute Beginners, Whore; taught jazz double-bass, Guildhall School of Music and Drama, Glamorgan Jazz Summer School; Visiting Examiner, Royal Northern Coll., Royal Coll. of Music, Trinity College; Prof., Trinity Coll.; runs numerous workshops in steel drums, trumpet; mem, Musicians' Union; PRS. *Compositions include:* See You PB; Souvenir; Arcadia; Ken Blake; Lister; Turing; HPT; Looga Barooga; Nowhere. *Recordings include:* Blue Glass, with John Taylor Trio; Busy Listening, with Steve Arguelles Band; Time Will Tell, with Tina May; Cantelina, with First House; Earthworks and Heavenly Bodies, with Bill Bruford's Earthworks; This Old Gang of Ours, with Humphrey Lyttelton; Morning Sunrise, with Barry Nathan Trio; 1 2 3, with Nick Purnell Group; Blues in the Night, with The Cast; Amazing Grace, with Martin Speake; Chris Biscoe Sextet; PyroTechnics, various artistes; Triple Exposure, with Mark Edwards; From the Heart, with Gary Husband Trio; Alternative Therapy, with Estelle Kokot; Trouble in Mind, with Humphrey Lyttelton and Elkie Brooks; Somewhere in the Hills, with Jim Mullen Quartet.

HÜTZ, Eugene; Ukrainian singer; b. 6 Sept. 1972, Kiev. *Career:* after years in refugee camps after Chernobyl disaster, moved to US 1986; leader, gypsy punk band Gogol Bordello 1999–. *Films include:* Kill Your Darlings (actor) 2004, Wristcutters – A Love Story (songs) 2004, Everything is Illuminated (actor) 2005, The Pied Piper of Hützovina (self, documentary) 2006, Filth and Wisdom 2008, Our School 2011. *Recordings include:* albums: Voi-La Intruder 1999, Multi Kontra Culti vs Irony 2002, East Infection 2005, Gypsy Punks 2005, Super Taranta! 2007, Trans-Continental Hustle 2010, Pura Vida Conspiracy 2013. *Current Management:* c/o Red Light Management, 321 East Main Street, Suite 500, Charlottesville, VA 22902, USA. *E-mail:* gogolbordello@redlightmanagement.com. *Website:* redlightmanagement.com. *E-mail:* gogolbordello@mac.com. *Website:* www.gogolbordello.com.

HVASS, Claus; Danish composer, producer and musician (guitar); b. 4 Feb. 1959; m. Birgitte Rode 1992; one s. *Recordings include:* with Johnny and The Cold Demons: Paraneuropa; with Walk The Walk: Walk The Walk, Feet On the Ground, Frog Dance; solo: Aquarium 1997, Onomatopoietikon 2000, Gæst 2004. *Honours:* Nat. Music Award 1991–95. *Address:* Kirkegaardsgade 3, 9000 Ålborg, Denmark. *E-mail:* hvass@events.dk. *Website:* www.claushvass.dk.

HWA, Jung Yong; South Korean singer, guitarist, rapper and actor; b. 22 June 1989, Seoul. *Career:* mem. CN Blue 2009–; solo artist 2011–. *Recordings:* albums: with CN Blue: Thank U 2010, First Step 2011, 392 2011. *Television includes:* CN Bluetory 2010, We Got Married 2010–11, Night After Night 2010–11; as actor: You're Beautiful 2009, Heartstrings 2011. *Honours:* solo: SBS Drama New Star Award 2009, MBC Entertainment Popularity Award 2010, SBS Entertainment Variety New Star Award 2010, Korea Drama Festival Popularity Award 2010; with CN Blue: Male Rookie Award, Mnet Asian Music Awards 2010, Golden Disk Bonsang Award 2010, Melon Music Awards for Best New Artist and 2010 TOP 2010, Seoul Music Award for Best Newcomer 2011. *Address:* c/o FNC Music, Mnet Media Building, Apgujeong-dong, Gangnam-gu, Seoul, South Korea (office). *Telephone:* 2517-5426 (office). *Fax:* 2518-5428 (office). *E-mail:* fncmusic1@naver.com (office). *Website:* www.fncmusic.com (office); cnblue.co.kr/cnblue/kor (home).

HYDE, Karl; British singer, musician (guitar), songwriter and producer; b. 10 May 1957, Worcester, England. *Education:* Univ. of Wales, Cardiff. *Career:* mem. The Screen Gems 1981–83, Freur 1983–86, Underworld 1986–, Lemon Interrupt 1992; remixer for artists, including Bjork, The Chemical Brothers, Depeche Mode, Dreadzone, Fire Island, Front 242, Gat Decor, Leftfield, Massive Attack, One Dove, Orbital, Shakespears Sister, Saint Etienne, U2, William Orbit. *Recordings include:* albums: with Freur: Doot Doot 1983, Get Us Out Of Here 1985; with Underworld: Underneath The Radar 1988, Change The Weather 1989, Dubnobasswithmyheadman 1993, Second Toughest In The Infants 1996, Beaucoup Fish 1999, Everything Everything 2000, A Hundred Days Off 2002, Anthology 1992–2002 (compilation) 2002, Back To Mine (selection of other artists' work) 2003, Oblivion with Bells 2007, Barking 2010; solo: Edgeland 2013, Someday World (with Brian Eno) 2014. *Publication:* Mmm... Skyscraper: A Typographical Journal of New York (with John Warwicker) 1995. *Current Management:* Jukes Productions Ltd, PO Box 13995, London, W9 2FL, England. *Telephone:* (20) 7286-9532. *Fax:* (20) 7286-4739. *E-mail:* jukes@easynet.co.uk. *Website:* www.jukesproductions.co.uk; www.underworldlive.com; www.karlhyde.com.

HYDE, Roger Erik, AB; American composer, record producer and writer; b. 3 June 1951, Hollywood, Calif. *Education:* Univ. of California, Los Angeles; studied history of jazz with Paul Tanner, composition with Gerald Strang, film scoring with David Raksin, production with Nik Venet. *Career:* Folk Scene radio concert 1970; series of Los Angeles salon concerts and readings 1975–76; Dir of Washoe Records, producer for Scatman Crothers 1980–81; Dir and Producer, Blue Planet Records 1985–; mem. AES. *Compositions include:* Our Hearts and Our Hands, Song Cycle 1979, Pittsburg; 2811, Symphony à Trois. *Recording:* Scatman Crothers and the Hollywood Radio Hooligans (producer). *Publications include:* novels: Famous Death, Weighing of Secret Burdens. *Address:* PO Box 91922, Los Angeles, CA 90009, USA.

HYDER, Ken; Scottish musician (drums), singer and composer; b. 29 June 1946, Dundee. *Education:* Harris Acad., Dundee, studied with John Stevens. *Career:* formed Celtic-Jazz band, Talisker; played and recorded with Celtic musicians, including Dick Gaughan, then with Tibetan monks, Russian musicians, duo with Tim Hodgkinson, South African musicians, Siberian shamans; mem. K-Space trio with Tim Hodgkinson and Gendos Chamzyryn, Shamfonk Rhythm Section, RealTime, Rituale Urbano, Hoots and Roots with Maggie Nicols; duos with Vladimir Miller and Raymond Macdonald; Edge with Maggie Nicols and Raymond Macdonald. *Recordings:* with Talisker: Dreaming of Glenisla, Land of Stone, The Last Battle, The White Light, Humanity with Talisker, Under The Influence, The Big Team, Fanfare For Tomorrow with Dick Gaughan, Shams, Bughan Interference with Tim Hodgkinson; The Goose with Hodgkinson, Ponomareva, Piping Hot with Dave Brooks, The Crux of The Catalogue with Tomas Lynch, Hot Sounds From The Arctic with Vladimir Rezitsky, The Ultimate Gift, Wheels within Wheels, Bardo State Orchestra, Urban Ritual, Ntshuks Bonga's Tshisa, Stillness in the Solovki, Northern Lights, We See Us in the Future with the Dynamix, Counting on Angels with Vladimir Miller, In the Stone, Ken Hyder with Maggie Nichols and Dave Brooks, Bear Bones, Going Up, Infinity and Black Sky with K-Space, In the Shaman's Pocket with RealTime, Raz3 with Raz3, Life and Death with Hoots and Roots, Ghost Time with z'ev and Andy

Knight. *Honours:* Order of the Red Banner, Angarsk. *Address:* 69 Ravenslea Road, Balham, London, SW12 8SL, England. *E-mail:* ken.hyder@gmail.com. *Website:* www.kenhyder.co.uk; www.myspace.com/kenhyderdrums.

HYELIM; South Korean singer, songwriter and actress; b. (Woo Hye Rim), 1 Sept. 1992, Seoul. *Career:* mem. Wonder Girls 2010–, first appeared on single 2 Different Tears 2010; toured USA and Canada with Wonder World Tour 2010; collaborated with Akon on single Like Money 2012; numerous festival appearances and tours. *Films:* The Last Godfather 2010, The Wonder Girls 2012. *Television:* Made in Wonder Girls 2010; numerous guest appearances. *Recordings:* album: Wonder World 2011. *Current Management:* c/o Creative Artists Agency, 162 5th Avenue, 6th Floor, New York, NY 10010, USA. *Address:* c/o JYP Entertainment, JYP Center, 123-50 Cheongdam-dong, Gangnam-gu, Seoul, South Korea (office). *Telephone:* (2) 3438-2300 (office). *Website:* www.jype.com (office); www.wondergirlsworld.com.

HYND, Richard; British musician (drums); b. 17 June 1965, Aberdeen, Scotland. *Career:* mem., Texas 1991–99; numerous tours and festivals; TV appearances. *Recordings include:* albums: Southside 1989, Mother's Heaven 1991, Rick's Road 1993, White on Blonde 1997, The Hush 1999.

HYNDE, Chrissie; American singer, songwriter and musician; b. 7 Sept. 1951, Akron, Ohio; one d. with Ray Davies; m. 1st Jim Kerr (divorced); one d.; m. 2nd Lucho Brieva 1999 (divorced 2002). *Career:* contrib. to New Musical Express; Co-founder Chrissie Hynde and the Pretenders 1978–, singer, songwriter and guitarist, new band formed 1983; tours in Britain, Europe and USA. *Singles include:* Stop Your Sobbing (debut) 1978, Kid 1979, Brass in Pocket 1979, I Go to Sleep 1982, Back on the Chain Gang 1982, Middle of the Road 1984, Thin Line Between Love and Hate, Don't Get Me Wrong 1986, Hymn to Her 1987, Night in my Veins 1994, I'll Stand By You 1994, Human 1999. *Albums include:* Pretenders (debut) 1980, Pretenders II 1981, Extended Play 1981, Learn to Crawl 1985, Get Close 1986, The Singles 1987, Packed! 1990, Last of the Independents 1994, The Isle of View 1995, Viva El Amor 1999, Loose Screw 2002, Break Up the Concrete 2009, Fidelity! (with JP Jones and the Fairground Boys) 2010; solo: Stockholm 2014. *Publication:* Reckless 2015. *Honours:* platinum and gold discs in USA; Ivor Novello Award for Outstanding Contrib. to British Music 1999; inducted into Rock & Roll Hall of Fame 2005; Q Award for Classic Songwriter 2013. *Current Management:* Quietus Management Limited, 13 Bramley Road, 2nd Floor Phoenix Brewery, London, W10 6SP, England. *Telephone:* (20) 3220-0310. *Website:* www.quietusmanagement.co.uk; www.chrissiehynde.com; www.pretenders.com.

HYNDMAN, Clint; Australian musician (drums); b. 24 Nov. 1975. *Career:* joined Fish of The Day group 1994; developed local following through pub/club gigs; group became Something For Kate; signed to Australian label Murmur; temporary hiatus to recruit new bassist 1997–98; band reformed and gradually broke nationally, then internationally with first USA/Japan tour 2000; big sell-out Australian shows, including Mythology and Echo-la-la-lia tours plus Powderfinger support slots 2001; group subject of JJJ radio station special 2001. *Recordings:* albums: Elsewhere For Eight Minutes 1997, Beautiful Sharks 1999, QandA With Dean Martin (compilation) 2000, Echolalia 2001, The Official Fiction 2003, Phantom Limbs 2004, Desert Lights 2006, The Murmur Years 2007, Leave Your Soul to Science 2012. *Honours:* Album of the Year, Australian Music Industry Critics Awards 2000, Best Live Act, Australian Live Music Awards 2000, Best Album, JJJ Listeners' Poll 2001. *Address:* PO Box 2235, Prahran, Vic. 3181, Australia (office). *E-mail:* clint@somethingforkate.com (office). *Website:* www.somethingforkate.com (office).

HYUK, Kang Min; South Korean musician (drums) and singer; b. 28 June 1991. *Career:* mem. CN Blue 2009–. *Film:* Acoustic 2010. *Recordings:* albums: with CN Blue: Thank U 2010, First Step 2011, 392 2011. *Honours:* Male Rookie Award, Mnet Asian Music Awards 2010, Golden Disk Bonsang Award 2010, Melon Music Awards for Best New Artist and 2010 TOP 2010, Seoul Music Award for Best Newcomer 2011. *Address:* c/o FNC Music, Mnet Media Building, Apgujeong-dong, Gangnam-gu, Seoul, South Korea (office). *Telephone:* 2517-5426 (office). *Fax:* 2518-5428 (office). *E-mail:* fncmusic1@naver.com (office). *Website:* www.fncmusic.com (office); cnblue.co.kr/cnblue/kor (home).

HYUN, Lee Jong; South Korean musician (guitar), songwriter and singer; b. 15 May 1990, Busan. *Career:* mem. CN Blue 2009–. *Recordings:* albums: with CN Blue: Thank U 2010, First Step 2011, 392 2011. *Film:* Acoustic 2010. *Television includes:* CN Bluetory 2010. *Honours:* Male Rookie Award, Mnet Asian Music Awards 2010, Golden Disk Bonsang Award 2010, Melon Music Awards for Best New Artist and 2010 TOP 2010, Seoul Music Award for Best Newcomer 2011. *Address:* c/o FNC Music, Mnet Media Building, Apgujeong-dong, Gangnam-gu, Seoul, South Korea (office). *Telephone:* 2517-5426 (office). *Fax:* 2518-5428 (office). *E-mail:* fncmusic1@naver.com (office). *Website:* www.fncmusic.com (office); cnblue.co.kr/cnblue/kor (home).

I

IAN, Janis; American singer, songwriter, musician, author and columnist and lecturer; *CEO, Rude Girl Group*; b. 7 April 1951, Bronx, New York; d. of Victor Fink and Pearl Fink; m. Patricia Snyder. *Career:* solo artist 1965–; debut hit single, "Society's Child", featured in Leonard Bernstein's TV special, Inside Pop – The Rock Revolution 1966; performances include Royal Festival Hall and Royal Albert Hall, London, Carnegie Hall and Philharmonic Hall, Sydney Opera House, Carre, Amsterdam; Founder and CEO Rude Girl Group (recording and music publishing group); masterclasses at New York Univ. and Stella Adler School. *Compositions include:* Society's Child 1966, Jesse (recorded by Roberta Flack), At Seventeen 1976, Fly Too High (co-writer with Giorgio Moroder, for film soundtrack Foxes) 1979, Tattoo, When Angels Cry, Some People's Lives (recorded by Bette Midler), other compositions recorded by artists including Dianne Schuur, Chet Atkins, Stan Getz, John Mellencamp, Hugh Masekela, Celine Dion. *Recordings include:* albums: Janis Ian 1967, A Song for All the Seasons of Your Mind 1968, The Secret Life of J. Eddy Fink 1969, Who Really Cares 1969, Present Company 1971, Stars 1974, Between The Lines 1975, Aftertones 1976, Miracle Row 1997, Janis Ian 1978, Night Rains 1979, Restless Eyes 1981, Breaking Silence 1993, Revenge 1995, Hunger 1997, The Bottom Line Encore 1999, God and The FBI 2000, Live: Working Without a Net 2003, Billie's Bones 2004, Folk is the New Black 2006, Best of Janis Ian-The Autobiography Collection 2008, The Essential Janis Ian 2010, Strictly Solo 2014. *Publications include:* Who Really Cares 1968 (poems) 2002, Stars: The Anthology (stories based on the songs of Janis Ian), The Tiny Mouse (children's book), Society's Child: My Autobiography (Grammy Award for Best Spoken Word Album 2013) 2008; monthly columnist for The Advocate and Performing Songwriter Magazine. *Honours:* three Grammy Awards, GLCCLA Award for Creative Integrity 1993, Fisk Univ. Award for Creative Excellence 1994, Audie Award 2013, two songs in Grammy Hall of Fame, honoured by Queen Beatrix of Holland for Extraordinary Contributions, honoured by Elton John Foundation. *Address:* PO Box 150099, Nashville, TN 37215, USA (office). *E-mail:* janis@janisian.com (office). *Website:* www .janisian.com. *E-mail:* manager@janisian.com. *Website:* www.thetinymouse .com.

IBOLD, Mark; American musician (bass); b. 1967, Cincinnati, Ohio. *Career:* mem., Pavement 1991–2000, reunited for live performances 2010; numerous headlining tours; mem. Sonic Youth 2006–. *Television appearance:* Space Ghost Coast to Coast (cartoon) 1997. *Recordings include:* albums: with Pavement: Slanted and Enchanted 1992, Crooked Rain, Crooked Rain 1994, Wowee Zowee 1995, Brighten the Corners 1997, Terror Twilight 1999, Crooked Rain, Crooked Rain (expanded edn) 2004, Brighten the Corners: Nicene Creedence Edition 2008, Quarantine the Past: The Best of Pavement 2010; with Sonic Youth: The Eternal 2009. *Current Management:* c/o Michele Fleischli, Silva Artist Management, 722 Seward Street, Los Angeles, CA 90038-3504, USA. *Telephone:* (323) 856-8222. *Fax:* (323) 856-8256. *E-mail:* info@sammusicbiz.com; mfleischli@sammusicbiz.com. *Website:* www .sammusicbiz.com; www.sonicyouth.com.

IBRAHIM, Abdullah; South African jazz musician (piano) and composer; b. (Adolphe Johannes Brand), 9 Oct. 1934, Cape Town; m. Sathima Bea Benjamin 1965. *Education:* studied piano from age seven. *Career:* became professional musician 1949; mem., The Jazz Epistles (with Hugh Masekela and Kippi Moeketsi); met Duke Ellington in the Africana Cafe, Zurich and recorded album with him 1963; appeared at the Newport Jazz Festival 1965, several appearances as Ellington's substitute with the Ellington Orchestra; collaborations with Elvin Jones, Don Cherry, Gato Barbieri, Max Roach; Munich Radio Philharmonic Orchestra toured with arrangements of his work 1998. *Recordings include:* albums: Duke Ellington Presents The Dollar Brand Trio 1963, Banyana - The Children of Africa 1976, Echoes from Africa 1979, Africa - Tears and Laughter 1979, African Marketplace 1980, African Dawn 1982, South Africa 1983, Water from an Ancient Well 1985, Round Midnight at the Montmartre 1988, Mindif 1988, African Sun 1988, Tintinyana 1988, Blues for a Hip King 1988, African Horns 1988, Voice of Africa 1988, African River 1989, No Fear, No Die 1990, Desert Flowers 1991, Mantra Mode 1991, Knysna Blue 1993, Yarona 1995, Cape Town Revisited 1997, Cape Town Flowers 1997, Made in South Africa Township 1998, Ekapa Lodumo 2001, African Symphony 2001, African Suite 2001, African Magic 2002, A Struggle for Love 2004, Senzo 2008, Bombella 2010. *Current Management:* Musikbuero Gert Pfankuch, Alter Fischbacher Weg 8a, 65817 Eppstein, Germany. *E-mail:* pfankuch@aol.com. *Website:* www.abdullahibrahim.co.za.

IBRAHIM, Zakaria; Egyptian singer and musician (percussion); b. Port Said. *Career:* Founder and leader of sufi music group, El Tanbura 1989–. *Recordings include:* albums: La Simsimiyya de Port Said 1999, Ahwa Qamar 2003, Between the Desert and the Sea 2006, Friends of Bamboute 2009. *Address:* El Mastaba Center for Egyptian Folk Music, 4 Sharia Sewequat, El Sabbaeen Sayyuda, Zainab, Cairo, Egypt (office). *E-mail:* info@eltanbura.com (office). *Website:* www.elmastaba.org (office).

ICE CUBE; American rap artist and actor; b. (O'Shea Jackson), 15 June 1969, Los Angeles. *Education:* Univ. of Phoenix. *Career:* formed duo (with Sir Jinx), CIA, then leader of group, HBO; founder mem., N.W.A. 1987–89; formed rap group, Da Lench Mob 1989–; simultaneous solo artist 1989–; collaborated with Public Enemy; began own corpn, producing work by protegée YoYo 1989–;

numerous tours; founder mem., Westside Connection 1996–; Founder Cube Vision Productions (film production co.). *Films:* Boyz n the Hood (actor) 1991, Trespass (actor) 1992, The Glass Shield (actor) 1994, Higher Learning (actor) 1995, Friday (actor, writer, exec. prod.) 1995, Dangerous Ground (actor, exec. prod.) 1997, Anaconda (actor) 1997, The Player's Club (actor, writer, exec. prod.) 1998, I Got the Hook Up (actor) 1998, Three Kings (actor) 1999, Thicker Than Water (actor) 1999, Next Friday (actor, writer, exec. prod.) 2000, Ghosts of Mars (actor) 2001, All About the Benjamins (actor, writer, exec. prod.) 2001, Barbershop (actor) 2002, Friday After Next (actor, writer, exec. prod.) 2002, Torque (actor) 2004, Barbershop 2: Back in Business (actor, exec. prod.) 2004, Are We There Yet? (actor, prod.) 2005–, xXx 2: The Next Level (actor) 2005, Are We Done Yet? (actor) 2007, First Sunday (prod.) 2008, The Longshots (prod.) 2008, The Janky Promoters (prod.) 2009, Lottery Ticket (prod.) 2010, 21 Jump Street (actor) 2012, Ride Along (actor) 2014, 22 Jump Street (actor) 2014, The Book of Life (voice actor) 2014. *Television:* as actor: Are We There Yet? 2010–13, Sean and Jake 2012–. *Recordings include:* albums: with N.W.A.: N.W.A. And The Posse 1987, Straight Outta Compton 1989; solo: AmeriKKKa's Most Wanted 1990, Death Certificate 1991, The Predator 1992, Lethal Injection 1993, Bootlegs And B Sides 1994, War And Peace 1998, War And Peace 2: The Peace Disc 2000, Greatest Hits 2001, Laugh Now, Cry Later 2006, Raw Footage 2008, I Am the West 2010; with da Lench Mob: Guerillas In Tha Mist 1992, Planet Of Da Apes 1994; with Westside Connection: Bow Down 1996. *Address:* Cube Vision Productions, 2900 West Olympic Blvd., Santa Monica CA 90404 (office); c/o Capitol Records, 1750 N Vine Street, Hollywood, CA 90028, USA (home). *Telephone:* (310) 255-7100 (Cube Vision) (office). *Fax:* (310) 255-7163 (Cube Vision) (office). *Website:* www.icecube.com.

ICE-T; American rap artist and actor; *Chairman and CEO, Final Level Productions;* b. (Tracey Marrow), 14 Feb. 1959, Newark, NJ; m. Darlene Ortiz; one c. *Career:* recording artist 1987–; mem., Body Count 1992–; world-wide tours, numerous television and film appearances; created Rhyme Syndicate Records early 1990s; currently Chair. and CEO, Final Level Productions, LLC; involved in two youth intervention programmes, Hands Across Watts and South Central Love. *Recordings include:* solo: The Pimp Penal Code, Sex, Money, Guns, Rhyme Pays 1987, Power 1988, The Iceberg 1989, O. G. Original Gangster 1991, Home Invasion 1993, VI: Return Of The Real 1996, Seventh Deadly Sin 1999, Ice-T Presents the Westside 2004, Gangsta Rap 2006; with Body Count: Body Count 1992, Born Dead 1994, Violent Demise, The Last Days 1997, Murder 4 Hire 2006, Manslaughter 2014. *Films:* Breakin' 1984, Breakin' 2: Electric Boogaloo 1984, New Jack City 1991, Ricochet 1991, Trespass 1992, Why Colors? 1992, Who's the Man? 1993, Surviving the Game 1994, Tank Girl 1995, Johnny Mnemonic 1995, Mean Guns 1997, The Deli 1997, Below Utopia 1997, Crazy Six 1998, Urban Menace 1999, Final Voyage 1999, Jacob Two Two Meets the Hooded Fang 1999, Corrupt 1999, The Wrecking Crew 1999, Sonic Impact 1999, Point Doom 1999, Judgment Day 1999, The Heist 1999, Frezno Smooth 1999, Stealth Fighter 2000, Leprechaun in the Hood 2000, Luck of the Draw 2000, The Alternate 2000, Sanity, Aiken's Artifact 2000, Guardian 2000, Gangland 2000, 3000 Miles to Graceland 2001, Deadly Rhapsody 2001, 'R Xmas 2001, Ticker 2001, Out Kold 2001, Ablaze 2001, Tara 2001, Stranded 2001, Kept 2001, Crime Partners 2000, Air Rage 2001, Tracks 2002, Pimpin' 101 2002, On the Edge 2002, Lexie 2004, Copy That 2006, Santorini Blue 2010. *Television:* Players (series) 1997, Exiled (film) 1998, Law & Order: Special Victims Unit (series) 2000–, The Disciples (film) 2000, Ice T's Rap School (series) 2006, The Magic 7 (voice) 2007. *Publications:* The Iceberg/Freedom of Speech... Just Watch What You Say 1989, The Ice Opinion 1994. *Honours:* Rolling Stone Readers' Poll Best Male Rapper 1992. *Address:* c/o Final Level Productions (office). *E-mail:* BodyCountIceT@gmail .com. *Website:* www.icet.com; www.finallevelprods.com.

IDIBIA, 2face; Nigerian singer and songwriter; b. (Innocent Ujah Idibia), Jos, Plateau State; s. of Micael Idibia and Rose Idibia. *Education:* Inst. of Man. Studies and Tech., Enugu. *Career:* moved to Lagos 1997; joined hip hop/R & B group Plantashun Boyz 1997, later launched solo career; performed concerts throughout Africa; collaborations with Wyclef Jean, Beenie Man, Kunle. *Recordings include:* solo albums: Face 2 Face 2004, Grass to Grace 2006, The Unstoppable 2008, The Unstoppable International Edition 2010, Away & Beyond 2012. *Honours:* Best African Artist, MTV Europe Awards, Lisbon, Portugal 2005, Best Male Video and Best African Video (for African Queen), Channel O Music Video Awards 2005, Revelation of the Year, KORA Awards 2005, Special Recognition Award, Hip Hop World Awards 2006, Special Recognition Award, Nigeria Breakthrough Artist of the Year, Nigeria Entertainment Awards 2006, Best African Act, MOBO Awards 2007. *Website:* kennisradio.com (office).

IDIR; Algerian singer, songwriter and poet; b. (Hamid Cheriet), 1955, Aït Lahcène, Kabylia. *Career:* sang on Radio Algiers 1973; served in Algerian army 1973–75; moved to France 1975, signed to Pathé-Marconi; organized and appeared in aid concert, Algerie, La Vie (Algeria, Life) 1995; collaborations with numerous artists, including Dan Ar Braz, Manu Chao, Frederic Galliano, Khaled, Orchestre National de Barbes, Geoffrey Oryema. *Recordings include:* albums: A Vava Inouva 1976, (second album) 1979, Identités 1999, Deux Rives Un Rêve 2002, Entre Scènes et terres 2005, La France des Couleurs 2007, Idir 2013. *Current Management:* c/o Blue Line Productions, BP 10021, 46600

Martel, France. *Telephone:* 5-65-27-15-15. *Website:* www.live-boutique.com/site/_blueline_.html; www.idir-officiel.fr.

IDOL, Billy; British singer, musician (guitar) and composer; b. (William Michael Albert Broad), 30 Nov. 1955, Stanmore, Middlesex. *Career:* lead singer and guitarist in punk group, Generation X 1976–81; solo artist 1981–; world-wide concert tours. *Recordings include:* albums: with Generation X: Generation X 1978, Valley Of The Dolls 1979, Kiss Me Deadly 1981, Live 1988, Sweet Revenge 1998; solo: Don't Stop, 1981, Billy Idol 1982, Rebel Yell 1984, Whiplash Smile 1986, Vital Idol 1987, Idol Songs 1988, Charmed Life 1990, Cyberpunk 1993, LA Woman 1993, Greatest Hits 2001, The Essential 2003, Devil's Playground 2005, Happy Holidays 2006; singles: with Generation X: Dancing With Myself 1981; solo: Don't Stop 1981, Hot In The City 1982, White Wedding 1983, Rebel Yell 1984, Eyes Without A Face 1984, Flesh For Fantasy 1984, Catch My Fall 1984, To Be A Lover 1986, Don't Need A Gun 1987, Sweet Sixteen 1987, Mony Mony 1987, Blue High 1990, Cradle of Love 1990, LA Woman 1990, Prodigal Blues 1991, Heroin 1993, Shock To The System 1993, Don't You Forget 2001. *Honours:* MTV Video Music Award for Best Video from a Film (Cradle of Love) 1990, BRIT Award for Best British Video 1991. *E-mail:* info@billyidol.net (office). *Website:* www.billyidol.net.

IERO, Frank; American musician (rhythm guitar); b. 31 Oct. 1981, New Jersey. *Education:* Rutgers Univ. *Career:* mem. rock band, My Chemical Romance 2001–. *Recordings include:* albums: I Brought You My Bullets, You Brought Me Your Love 2002, Three Cheers for Sweet Revenge 2004, The Black Parade 2006, Danger Days: The True Lives of the Fabulous Killjoys 2010. *Honours:* Kerrang! Award for Best Int. Band 2006, 2007, NME Award for Best Int. Band 2007. *Address:* c/o Warner Bros. Records Inc., 3300 Warner Blvd, PO Box 6868, Burbank, CA 91510, USA (office). *Telephone:* (818) 846-9090. *E-mail:* infomcr@mychemicalromance.com. *Website:* www.mychemicalromance.com.

IEUAN, Dafydd; British musician (drums); b. 1 March 1969, Bangor, Wales. *Career:* mem., Catatonia 1993–96; mem., Super Furry Animals 1996–; early releases on small indie label, then obtained major indie label deal; numerous tours in the UK and abroad, many festival appearances; mem. The Peth 2006–. *Recordings include:* albums: with Super Furry Animals: Fuzzy Logic 1996, Radiator 1997, Guerrilla 1999, Mwng 2000, Rings Around The World 2001, Phantom Power 2003, Love Kraft 2005, Hey Venus 2007, Dark Days/Light Years 2009; with The Peth: The Golden Mile 2008. *E-mail:* info@superfurry.com (office). *Website:* www.superfurry.com.

IF, Owen; British musician (drums); b. (Ian Frederick Rossiter), 20 March 1959, Newport, Wales. *Career:* mem., Stereo MCs 1990–; numerous live performances with extended band and extra vocalists. *Recordings include:* albums: Supernatural 1990, Connected (BRIT Award for Best British Album 1994) 1992, Stereo MCs 1993, Deep Down and Dirty 2001, Paradise 2005, Double Bubble 2008, Emperor's Nightingale 2011. *Honours:* BRIT Award for Best British Group 1994. *E-mail:* info@stereomcs.com. *Website:* www.stereomcs.com.

IG CULTURE, (Son of Scientist, Da One Way, Likwid Biskit); British producer, remixer and DJ; b. (Ian George Grant), 17 June 1965, London. *Career:* started production career as part of Dodge City Productions 1990; Founder, Main Squeeze label in late 1990s; co-promoter, The Co-Op club night in London with 4 Hero and Phil Asher; formed the New Sector Movements (NSM) collective 1997; collaborations with 4 Hero, Kaidi Tatham, Frank McComb, Julie Dexter, Dodge, Ronny Jordan; remixed 4 Hero, Noel McKoy, Luniz; mem. MCPS/PRS. *Recordings include:* albums: Steppin' Up and Out (with Dodge City Productions) 1993, Download This (as NSM) 2001, Turn It Up (as NSM) 2004, Zen Badizm 2008, Soulful Shanghai 2012; singles: As Long As We're Around (with Dodge City Productions) 1992, Unleash Your Love (with Dodge City Productions) 1993, Tings A Gwan 1993, My History (as NSM) 1997, No Tricks EP (as NSM) 2001, The Sun (as NSM) 2001, Turn It Up (as NSM) 2004.

IGLAUER, Bruce, BA; American record company executive; *President, Alligator Records;* b. 10 July 1947, Ann Arbor, Mich.; s. of John Iglauer and Harriett Iglauer; m. Jo Kolanda 1995. *Education:* Lawrence Univ., Appleton, Wis. *Career:* Founder and Pres. Alligator Records 1971–; released over 250 contemporary blues recordings; produced over 100 blues albums by artists, including Albert Collins, Koko Taylor, Johnny Winter, Roy Buchanan, Saffire, Michael Burks, Lil' Ed & The Blues Imperials; Co-founder Living Blues Magazine; Co-founder Nat. Asscn of Ind. Record Distributors and Mfrs; mem. Bd American Asscn for Ind. Music; Co-Dir Blues Community Foundation. *Honours:* Hon. DMus (Lawrence Univ.); mem. Blues Hall of Fame, Miki Granberg Award, Nat. Asscn of Recording Merchandisers, Chicagoan of the Year, Chicago Magazine 2001. *Address:* Alligator Records, PO Box 60234, Chicago, IL 60660, USA (office). *Telephone:* (773) 973-7736 (office). *E-mail:* info@allig.com (office). *Website:* www.alligator.com (office).

IGLESIAS, Enrique; Spanish singer and songwriter; b. 8 May 1975, Madrid; s. of Julio Iglesias. *Career:* sings in English and Spanish; numerous tours. *Recordings include:* albums: Enrique Iglesias 1995, Master Pistas 1997, Vivir 1997, Cosas Del Amor 1998, Enrique 1999, Escape 2001, Quizás 2002, 7 2003, Insomniac 2007, Euphoria 2010, Sex + Love (Billboard Music Award for Top Latin Album 2015) 2014; singles: Experiencia Religiosa, No Llores Por Mi, Bailamos 1999, Rhythm Divine 1999, Be With You 2000, Solo Me Importas Tu 2000, Sad Eyes 2000, Hero 2001, Don't Turn Off The Lights 2002, Love To See

You Cry 2002, Maybe 2002, Addicted 2003, Not In Love 2004. *Honours:* Grammy Award 1997, eight Premios Los Nuestro, Billboard Awards for Artist of the Year, Album of the Year 1997, ASCAP Award for Songwriter of the Year 1998, American Music Awards for Favorite Latin Artist 2002, 2008, 2014, 2015, Billboard Latin Music Award for Best Latin Dance Club Play Track (for Not In Love/No Es Amor) 2005, Top Latin Album (Euphoria) 2011, ASCAP Pop Award for Most Performed Song (Tonight I'm Lovin' You) 2012, MTV Europe Music Award for Best World Stage Performance 2014, Latin Grammy Awards for Song of the Year, for Best Urban Performance, for Best Urban Song (all for Bailando) 2014, for Best Urban Performance (for El Perdón, with Nicky Jam) 2015, Billboard Music Award for Top Latin Song (for Bailando) 2015. *Address:* c/o Republic Records, Universal Music Group, 2220 Colorado Avenue, Santa Monica, CA 90404, USA. *Telephone:* (310) 865-1000. *Website:* www.enriqueiglesias.com.

IGLESIAS (DE LA CUEVA), Julio José; Spanish singer and songwriter; b. 23 Sept. 1943, Madrid; m. 1st Isabel Preysler 1971 (divorced); one d. two s.; m. 2nd Miranda Rijnsburger 2010; three s. two d. *Education:* Univ. of Cambridge. *Career:* goalkeeper Real Madrid junior team; professional singer, songwriter 1968–; Eurovision Song Contest entrant 1970; English language releases 1981–; concerts and television appearances worldwide. *Compositions include:* La Vida Sigue Igual, Mi Amor, Yo Canto, Alguien El Alamo Al Camino, No Llores. *Recordings include:* albums: Soy 1973, El Amor 1975, A Mis 33 Años 1977, De Niña A Mujer 1981, 1100 Bel Air Lace 1984, Un Hombre Solo 1987, Starry Night 1990, La Carretera 1995, Tango 1996, Corazón Latino 1998, Noche De Cuatro Lunas 2000, Una Donna Puo Cambiar La Vita 2000, Ao Meu Brasil 2000, Divorcio 2003, Romantic Classics 2006; also appears on: Duets (with Frank Sinatra) 1993. *Publication:* Entre el Cielo y el Infierno (autobiog.) 1981. *Honours:* hon. mem. Spanish Foreign Legion; winner Spanish Song Festival, Benidorm 1968, Guinness Book of Records Diamond Disc Award (most records in most languages) 1983, Medaille de Vermeil de la Ville de Paris 1983, Grammy Award for Best Latin Pop Performance 1987, First and Most Popular Int. Artist of All Time, China 2013, Guinness World Reecords Award for Best-Selling Male Latin Artist 2013, inducted into Latin Songwriters Hall of Fame 2013. *Current Management:* Anchor Marketing, 1885 NE 149th Street, Suite G, North Miami, FL 33181, USA. *Website:* www.julioiglesias.com.

IGREC, Mario; Croatian musician (guitar), composer, arranger, guitar teacher and backing singer; b. 24 May 1959, Zagreb; m. Snjezana Drkulec Igrec 1986; three s. *Education:* Music Conservatory. *Career:* mem. of various groups, including Zagreb Jazz Portrait, Hot Club Zagreb, Steve Klink Quartet, Mario Igrec Quintet, Pentagon, Good Day, Ritmo Loco, Jazz Big Band HGZ, Big Festival Orchestra, Cubismo; live concerts and programmes for state television in Slovenia, Austria, Croatia; international jazz festivals, including Croatia, Slovenia, Germany, Hungary; mem. Croatian Music Union (HGU), Jazz Club, Zagreb. *Recordings include:* Moment Notice, Zagreb Jazz Portrait 1984; with Ritmo Loco: Baila Como Yo 1992, For A Love of One Woman 1995. *Honours:* Heineken Award for Jazz Band, Croatia 1995. *Address:* Ozaljska 93, 41000 Zagreb, Croatia. *E-mail:* hrvoje.rupcic@cubismo.com. *Website:* www.cubismo.com.

IHA, James; American musician (guitar) and composer; b. 26 March 1968, Elk Grove, IL. *Career:* mem., Smashing Pumpkins, 1989–2000; mem. A Perfect Circle 2004–; numerous headlining tours, television and radio appearances; launched Stratchie Records with D'Arcy Wretzky, 1997; contributed two tracks to soundtrack of film, Batman and Robin; guest appearances on recordings by: Melissa Auf der Maur, Isobel Campbell, Fountains of Wayne, Tinted Windows, Whiskeytown. *Recordings include:* albums: with The Smashing Pumpkins: Gish 1991, The Peel Sessions 1992, Siamese Dream 1993, Pisces Iscariot 1994, Mellon Collie and the Infinite Sadness 1995, The Aeroplane Flies High 1996, Adore 1998, MACHINA/The Machines of God 2000, Machina II: The Friends and Enemies of Modern Music 2000, Earphoria 2002; solo: Let It Come Down 1998, Luck (film soundtrack) 2003, Linda, Linda, Linda (film soundtrack) 2005, Kakera (film soundtrack) 2009; with A Perfect Circle: eMOTIVe 2004. *E-mail:* hello@jamesiha.com. *Website:* www.jamesiha.com; www.aperfectcircle.com.

ILLSLEY, John Edward, BA; British musician (bass) and oil painter; b. 24 June 1949, Leicester, England; s. of Wilfred Illsley and Florence Illsley; m. Stephanie Illsley; two s. two d. *Education:* Bromsgrove School, Worcs., Goldsmiths' Coll., London. *Career:* mem. Dire Straits 1977–88, 1991–95; numerous tours and TV appearances. *Exhibitions:* London, New York, Sydney, Singapore. *Recordings include:* albums: Dire Straits 1978, Communiqué 1979, Making Movies 1980, Love Over Gold 1982, Extendedanceplay 1983, Alchemy: Dire Straits Live 1984, Brothers In Arms 1985, Money For Nothing 1988, On Every Street 1991, On The Night 1993, Live at the BBC 1995, Sultans of Swing 1998, Live in Les Baux de Provence 2007, Beautiful You 2008, Streets of Heaven 2010, Live in London 2013, Testing the Water 2014, Long Shadows 2016. *Honours:* Honours Fellow, Goldsmiths' Coll. *E-mail:* info@johnillsley.com. *Website:* www.johnillsley.com.

IMBRUGLIA, Natalie; Australian singer, songwriter and actress; b. 4 Feb. 1975, New South Wales; m. Daniel Johns (divorced). *Career:* solo artist 1997–. *Recordings include:* albums: Left of The Middle 1997, White Lillies Island 2001, Counting Down the Days 2005, Glorious 2007, Come to Life 2010, Male 2015. *Films:* Johnny English 2003, Closed for Winter 2009, Underdogs 2013, Among Ravens 2014, Little Loopers 2015. *Television includes:* Neighbours (series) 1991–94, Legend of the Lost Tribe (film) 2002. *Honours:* BRIT Award for Best Int. Female, for Best Int. Newcomer 1999. *Current Management:* c/o Egg Management, The Studio, 16 Station Road, Sevenoaks, Kent, TN13 2XA, England. *Telephone:* (1732) 462554. *Fax:* (1732) 463565. *E-mail:* info@egg -management.com. *Website:* www.egg-management.com. *Address:* PO Box 55970, London, W11 9AN, England (office). *Website:* www.natalieimbruglia .com.

INABA, Kazuhiro, BA; Japanese musician (five-string banjo, guitar, fiddle); b. 12 June 1960, Osaka; m. Tomoe Mori 1994; one s. *Education:* Kansai Univ. *Career:* played with many artists from USA including: Butch Robbins, Larry Stephenson, The Lonesome River Band, Bill Clifton; interpreter Leon Russell, Japan Tour 1995; f. Kazuhiro Inaba Bluegrass Camp, Osaka 2012; mem., Musicians' Union Japan, International Bluegrass Music Asscn. *Recordings include:* albums: Shore to Shore 1986, Hard Times Come Again No More 1989, Goin' Across the Sea 1993, Dixie Dream 2000, Teardrop on a Rose 2003. *Publications include:* featured articles, Moonshiner magazine, Japan (Blue-grass Journal). *Address:* 4–2–16, Nishi-Tezukayama, Sumiyoshi, Osaka 558, Japan.

INAMDAR, Jayshree S.; Indian musician (tabla, harmonium), singer, actress and writer; b. 20 Sept. 1974, Kalyan. *Education:* Datapro Inst., Mumbai Univ., trained at All India Radio LDTH Channel. *Career:* fmr production asst, Doordarshan television service; fmr radio announcer and writer on various channels, AIR. *Television appearances include:* programme of Marathi songs (Gudi Padva festival), Marathi and Hindi TV serial; performed voiceovers for TV and radio. *Radio includes:* actress in numerous Marathi radio dramas, programme for Yuva Vani (Mumbai and Sangli Radio Centre), Lal Bahadur Shastrijj (documentary for All-India Radio). *Publica-tions include:* contrib. to poems to Pudhari newspaper. *Address:* Flat 205, Nav-Sundar Co-op Housing Society, Patharli, Kalyan Road, Dombivli (East) Taluka Kalyan, Thane 421 201, India (home). *Telephone:* (22) 2436601 (home).

INDERBERG, John Pål; Norwegian musician (saxophone) and academic; *Professor of Music, Music Conservatory, Trondheim;* b. 6 Aug. 1950, Steinkjer; m. Kirsten Oxaal 1976. *Education:* Univ. of Trondheim. *Career:* played with J. Eks, Bob Brookmeyer, Lee Konitz, Warne Marsh; EBU musician, soloist with Symphony Orchestra; duos with Henning Sommerro; Prof. of Music, Music Conservatory, Trondheim; mem. Norwegian Musicians' Federation. *Record-ings include:* albums: with Warne Marsh: Sax of a Kind 1987, For The Time Being 1988; with Siri's Svale Band: Blackbird 1990; with Lee Konitz: Steps Towards A Dream 1995, Baritone Landscape 2001, Live in Oslo 2007; with Poalo Fresu: Live at Sting 2007; with Steinar Raknes: Tangos, Ballads & More 2008; with Bjørn Alterhaug: Songlines 2009; with Espen Rud: Dobbeldans 2011, Løvsamleren 2012; solo: Baritone Landscape 2001, Sval Draum 2005. *Honours:* Norwegian Jazz Federation Buddy Award, Buddyprisen 1990, Gammlengprisen 2005, Lindemanprisen 2010. *Address:* Kjøpmannsgt 12, 7013 Trondheim, Norway (home). *Telephone:* 90834640 (home). *Fax:* 73597301 (home). *E-mail:* johnpalinderberg@gmail.com. *Website:* www .inderberg.com.

INEZ, Mike; American musician (bass); b. 14 May 1966, San Fernando, Calif. *Career:* mem. Alice in Chains 1993–; numerous tours and TV appearances including MTV Unplugged. *Recordings include:* albums: Jar of Flies 1994, Alice in Chains 1995, I Stay Away 1995, Unplugged 1996, Nothing Safe 1999, Music Bank 1999, Live 2000, Greatest Hits 2001, Black Gives Way to Blue 2009, The Devil Put Dinosaurs Here 2013. *Current Management:* Velvet Hammer Management, 9014 Melrose Avenue, West Hollywood, CA 90069, USA. *Telephone:* (310) 657-6161. *Fax:* (310) 657-0310. *E-mail:* info@ velvethammer.net. *Website:* www.velvethammer.net; www.aliceinchains .com.

INFINITI (see Atkins, Juan)

INGMAR; Belgian composer, musician (keyboards), singer, writer and translator; b. 31 Dec. 1970, Antwerp. *Education:* Jazz Studio, Antwerp. *Career:* secretary/translator –1998; several national radio appearances; several major stage live gigs (including one for His Majesty The Former King of Belgium); mem. SABAM, International Copyright Institute, Inter-national Writers and Artists Asscn. *Compositions include:* The Quest for Beauty and Truth Continues 1996, Ramifying Parallels on USA Import Music 1997. *Recordings include:* Insanity, Sister Sun, Amour Fatale, Exceptional, Solitude, The Quest, Beyond the Stars, The Dream. *Publications include:* The Quest on Club Excentrique 1996, Waiting… In These Skies (poem trilogy) 1997, Ramifying Parallels and Humanity 1997, 18 Poems and a Song (poetry book) 1999.

INGROSSO, Sebastian Carmine; Swedish DJ and record producer; b. 20 April 1983, Stockholm. *Career:* officially began releasing remixes 1999– under many aliases including Outfunk, Mode Hookers, The Sinners, General Moders, Fireflies, Buy Now (with Steve Angello); head of A&R for own label, Refune Records; collaborator with Axwell and Sebastian Ingrosso, formed Swedish House Mafia with both 2007–13; collaborations with other artists include Salem Al Fakir, David Guetta, Ryan Tedder, Tommy Trash; remixer and producer of many artists including Kylie Minogue, Usher, StoneBridge, Taio Cruz, Moby, Hard Fi, Justin Timberlake, Benny Benassi. *Films:* Take One (documentary) 2010. *Recordings:* albums: with Swedish House Mafia: Until One 2010, Until Now 2012. *Honours:* with Swedish House Mafia: MTV Europe Music Award for Best Swedish Act 2010, 2011. *Current Management:*

c/o ATM Artists, 55 Kentish Town Road, London, NW1 8NX, England. *E-mail:* amy@atmartists.com. *Website:* www.atmartists.com. *E-mail:* hello@refune .com (office). *Website:* www.refune.com (office); www.swedishhousemafia.com.

INNERSOUND (see McBean, Colin)

INNERZONE ORCHESTRA (see Craig, Carl)

INNES, Andrew; British musician (guitar). *Career:* mem., Primal Scream 1986–; numerous tours and festival appearances. *Recordings include:* albums: Sonic Flower Groove 1987, Primal Scream 1989, Screamadelica (Mercury Music Prize 1992) 1991, Give Out But Don't Give Up 1994, Vanishing Point 1997, EchoDek 1997, Xtrmntr 2000, Evil Heat 2002, Dirty Hits 2003, Shoot Speed (More Dirty Hits) 2004, Riot City Blues 2006, Beautiful Future 2008, Screamadelica Live 2011, Black to Comm: Recorded at the 2008 Meltdown Festival 2011, More Light 2013. *Honours:* Q Groundbreaker Award 2006, NME Godlike Genius Award 2007. *Current Management:* G. R. Management Ltd, 974 Pollockshaws Road, Glasgow, G41 2HA, Scotland. *Telephone:* (141) 632-1111. *Website:* www.primalscream.net.

INOUE, Yosui; Japanese singer and songwriter; b. 30 Aug. 1948, Fukuoka Prefecture. *Career:* co-f. For Life Records (with Yoshida Takuro) 1975; Founder-mem., The Nakayashi Group. *Radio:* appeared on radio show Shash Eleven (under stage name Andre Mandore) 1969. *Recordings include:* albums: Danzetsu 1972, Yosui Il Sentimental 1973, Inoue Yosui Live 1973, Kori no sekai 1973, White 1978, Every Night 1980, Lion and Pelican 1982, 9.5 1984, Re-view 1987, Negative 1987, Handsome Boy 1990, Under the Sun 1993, Golden Best 1999, Golden Bad 2000, United Cover 2001, Cassis 2002, Blue Selection 2002, Love Complex 2006, Double Drive 2007, Hikigatari Passion 2008. *Address:* c/o Sony Music Entertainment (Japan) Inc., 1–4 Ichigaya-Tamachi, Shinjuku-ku, Tokyo 162-8715, Japan. *Website:* www.y-inoue.com.

INSINNA, Robi, (Headman, Manhead); Swiss DJ, musician, producer and artist; b. 1972. *Career:* remixer for numerous artists, including Seelenluft, Coloursound, Trash Palace, Gina X, Panash, The Rapture, Radio 4, Franz Ferdinand, Mylo; co-f. Relish Records 2001–; solo projects as Headman, Manhead. *Recordings include:* albums: It Rough (as Headman) 2001, Relish 2002, Manhead 2005, ON (as Headman) 2006, Catch Me (as Headman) 2008. *E-mail:* martje@decked-out.co.uk (office). *Website:* www.headman.org (office).

INSPECTAH DECK, (Rollie Fingers, Rebel INS); American MC, rap artist and producer; b. (Jason Hunter), Brooklyn, NY. *Career:* mem., Wu-Tang Clan 1993–; solo artist 1999–. *Recordings include:* with Wu-Tang Clan: Enter The Wu-Tang (36 Chambers) 1993, Wu-Tang Forever 1997, The W 2000, Iron Flag 2001, Disciples Of The 36 Chambers: Chapter 1 (live) 2004, The 8 Diagrams 2007; solo: Uncontrolled Substance 1999, The Movement 2003, The Resident Patient 2006, Manifesto 2010. *Address:* c/o Sony Music Entertainment, 550 Madison Avenue, New York, NY 10022-3211, USA. *Telephone:* (212) 833-8000. *Fax:* (212) 833-4270. *Website:* www.wutangcorp .com.

IOMMI, Tony; British musician (guitar) and composer; b. 19 Feb. 1948, Birmingham. *Career:* guitarist, UK heavy rock group Black Sabbath 1967–. *Recordings include:* singles: Paranoid, Iron Man, War Pigs, Never Say Die; albums: with Black Sabbath: Black Sabbath 1969, Paranoid 1970, Master of Reality 1971, Vol. 4 1972, Sabbath Bloody Sabbath 1973, Sabotage 1975, Technical Ecstasy 1976, Never Say Die 1978, Heaven and Hell 1980, Mob Rules 1981, Live Evil 1983, Born Again 1983, Seventh Star 1983, The Eternal Idol 1987, Headless Cross 1990, Tyr 1990, Dehumanizer 1992, Forbidden 1995, Under Wheels of Confusion 1996, Reunion 1998, 13 2013; with Heaven & Hell: Live from Radio City Music Hall 2007, The Devil You Know 2009, Neon Nights: 30 Years of Heaven & Hell 2010; solo albums: Iommi 2000, Fused 2005. *Publication:* Iron Man: My Journey through Heaven and Hell with Black Sabbath (autobiography) 2011. *Honours:* Grammy Award for Best Metal Performance (for God Is Dead?) 2014, Gibson Les Paul Award 2015. *Current Management:* c/o Equator Music Ltd., Flat 17, Hereford Mansions, Hereford Road, London, W2 5BA, England. *Website:* www.equatormusic.com; www.iommi.com; www.blacksabbath.com.

IOVINE, Jimmy; American record company executive, record producer and film producer; *Chairman, Interscope Records;* b. 11 March 1953, Brooklyn, New York. *Career:* early career as recording engineer at Record Plant, New York 1973; worked as producer 1977–90, produced first album for Flame 1977, produced Patti Smith's Easter 1978; Co-founder Interscope Records 1989, Co-Chair. Interscope Geffen A&M Records, Chair. 2001–; Co-founder (with Doug Morris), Chair. and CEO Jimmy and Doug's Farm Club (project comprising a record label, website and cable TV show) 1999–; has worked with Dr Dre, Marilyn Manson, Stevie Nicks, Nine Inch Nails, No Doubt, 2Pac, Tom Petty, The Pretenders, Brian Setzer Orchestra, Patti Smith and U2. *Films produced include:* 8 Mile 2002, Get Rich or Die Tryin' 2005. *Honours:* Producer of the Year, Rolling Stone Magazine (twice). *Address:* Interscope Records, 2220 Colorado Avenue, Santa Monica, CA 90404, USA (office). *Website:* www .interscope.com (office); www.universalmusic.com (office).

IRABAGON, Jonathan (Jon); American musician (saxophone) and com-poser; b. Chicago. *Education:* Manhattan School of Music. *Career:* fmr mem. Juilliard Jazz Orchestra; leader, Tribute to Sonny Rollins; leader, Starship's Journey; co-leader Confluence, RIDD Quartet; mem. Mostly Other People Do the Killing; sideman in several groups including Jostein Gulbrandsen Quartet, Motel Project, Brandon Lee Group, Jon Lundbom's Big Five Chord,

Bryan and the Haggards, Tim Kuhl Group, Phil Mosberg Quartet; formed own quintet, Outright!; other collaborations with artists including Billy Joel, Wynton Marsalis, Bright Eyes, Tom Harrell, Tommy Iago, Joe Lovano, Dave Liebman, Deborah Gibson, John Abercrombie, Frank Wess, Wycliffe Gordon, Renee Fleming, Kenny Washington, Lou Reed, Jenny Lewis, Ron Sexsmith, Ken Vandermark. *Recordings:* albums: solo: Outright 2008, The Observer 2009, Foxy 2010; with Alex Smith, Mark Anderson and Andrew Bain: Confluence 2004; with Mostly Other People Do the Killing: Shamokin!!! 2007, This Is Our Moosic 2008, Forty Fort 2010; with Mike Pride: I Don't Hear Nothin' But the Blues 2009; has also appeared on: The New Balance, The Phil Mosberg Quartet 2001, Mozaic, Matt Geraghty Project 2003, Big Five Chord, Jon Lundbom 2004, All the Pretty Ponies, Jon Lundbom and Big Five Chord 2005, Mostly Other People Do The Killing, Moppa Elliott 2005, Smile, Dominick Farinacci 2005, Outside Scenic, Richie Miletic 2006, Dimensions, The Adam Czerepinski Sextet 2006, Twelve, Jostein Gulbrandsen 2007, The Hottest State (soundtrack), Jesse Harris 2007, Hardest Workin' Man in Christmas, Yulenog 3 2007, Ordination of the Globetrotting Conscripts, Talibam! 2007, From Within, Brandon Lee 2007, Fiction Avalanche, Ridd Quartet 2008, Atticus, Jesse Lewis 2008, King, Tim Kuhl 2009, Boogie in the Breeze Blocks, Talibam! 2009, Kaleidoscope, Jason Hainsworth Jazz Orchestra 2009, Sweet Sacrifice, Jason Liebman 2010, Blossom, Carl Maraghi 2010. *Honours:* winner, Thelonious Monk Int. Saxophone Competition 2008. *Address:* c/o Concord Music Group/Infinity Resources Inc., 900 North Rohlwing Road, Itasca, IL 60143, USA (office). *E-mail:* jon@jonirabagon.com (home). *Website:* www.concordmusicgroup.com (office); www.jonirabagon .com.

IRON LUNG (see Method Man)

IRONIK; British DJ and producer; b. (Michael Laurence), 18 Jan. 1988. *Career:* began career as DJ aged 13 at Twice as Nice events; signed as professional solo artist 2007–; collaborations with Roll Deep, Wiley, Chipmunk, Tinchy Stryder. *Recording:* album: No Point in Wasting Tears 2008. *Current Management:* Jonathan Lipman International Group, 7 Poland Street, London W1F 8PU, England. *Telephone:* (871) 221-0011. *E-mail:* neil@jonathanlipman.com. *Website:* www.jonathanlipman.com; www .myspace.com/djironik.

IRONS, Jack; American musician (drums); b. 18 July 1962, Los Angeles, CA. *Career:* founding mem., Anthym, later renamed What Is This? 1980–85; mem. Red Hot Chili Peppers 1983–88; mem. Eleven 1990–94; mem. Pearl Jam 1994–98; mem. Spinnerette 2007–; numerous tours and TV appearances; also appeared on numerous recordings by artists including Hole, Keith Levene, Michelle Shocked, Joe Strummer, Neil Young. *Recordings include:* albums: with What Is This?: What Is This? 1985; with Red Hot Chili Peppers: Freaky Styley 1985, The Uplift Mofo Party Plan 1987; with Eleven: Awake in a Dream 1991, Eleven 1993; with Pearl Jam: Vitalogy 1994, No Code 1996, Live on Two Legs 1998, Yield 1998; solo: Attention Dimension 2004, No Heads Are Better Than One 2010, Blue Manatee 2011; with Spinnerette: Spinnerette 2009. *Website:* www.jackirons.com.

IRVINE, Brian, MBE; Northern Irish jazz composer and conductor; b. 1965, Belfast. *Education:* Berklee Coll. of Music, USA and Univ. of Surrey, England. *Compositions:* Black Man Dance 1990, 280 Bells 1994, Ferragosto IV 1995, Wind Of The Wings Of Madness 1997, Our New House 1997, New York II 1997, I Dreamt I Dwelt In Marble Halls 1997, The Adventures Of Captain Weather And Magnet Man 1998, Bersudsky's Machines 1998, Thug! 1999, She Dreamt She Danced With Charlie 2000, Interrupting Cutler (Best New Work Award, BBC Jazz Awards 2003) 2000, Chaplin's Leg 2000, St George's Market 2002, And Pigs Might Fly 2003, The Tailor's Daughter (youth opera) (British Composer Award) 2006, Secret Cinema 2008, Junk Genius 2009, The Pied Piper 2009, Dumbworld 2009. *Recordings:* Stomach Remover 1993, Bersudsky's Machines 1999. *Address:* c/o Moving On Music, Weaverscourt, Belfast, Northern Ireland (office). *Telephone:* (28) 9188-8818 (office). *E-mail:* brian .irvine@btinternet.com (office). *Website:* www.brianirvine.co.uk (home).

IRWIN, Ashton; Australian drummer and singer; b. 7 July 1994, Hornsby, NSW; s. of Anne Marie Irwin. *Education:* Norwest Christian Coll. *Career:* mem. 5 Seconds of Summer 2011–; released debut EP Unplugged 2012; supported One Direction on worldwide tours 2013, 2014; signed to Capitol label 2013. *Recordings:* albums: 5 Seconds of Summer 2014, Sounds Good Feels Good 2015. *Honours:* Billboard Mid-Year Music Breakout Star Award 2014, Kerrang! Best Int. Newcomer Award 2014, MTV Award for Favorite Breakthrough Band 2014, MTV Europe Music Award for Best Australian Act 2014, 2015, MTV Video Music Awards for Best Lyric Video 2014, for Song of Summer 2015, Teen Choice Awards for Breakout Group and Music Group 2014. *Current Management:* c/o Modest Management, Matrix Complex, 91 Peterborough Road, London, SW6 3BU, England. *E-mail:* info@ modestmanagement.com. *Website:* www.modestmanagement.com; www.5sos .com.

ISAACS, Jason; British singer, songwriter and musician (guitar); b. 30 April 1968; m. Marion Isaacs. *Career:* with Dance Macabre 1985, The Promise 1994, Triggerfish 1996; solo artist 1996–. *Compositions include:* A Girl Called Jesus, Sigh, C-Life, Bike, Funky Chuny, Gun, Only A Northern Band, News, Hold It Down, Who Says I Can, Cornucopia. *Recordings include:* A Girl Called Jesus 1998. *Website:* www.jasonisaacs.co.uk.

ISAAK, Chris, BA; American singer, songwriter and actor; b. 26 June 1956, Stockton, Calif. *Education:* Univ. of the Pacific. *Career:* singer 1984–; extensive int. tours, festival appearances. *Films appearances include:* Married to the Mob 1988, Wild At Heart 1989, The Silence of the Lambs 1991, Twin Peaks: Fire Walk With Me 1992, Little Buddha 1993, Grace of My Heart 1996, That Thing You Do! 1996, Blue Ridge Fall 1999, A Dirty Shame 2004, The Informers 2009. *Television appearances include:* From the Earth to the Moon (mini-series) 1998, The Chris Isaak Show (series) 2001–04, The Chris Isaak Hour 2009. *Songs contributed to film and television:* Blue Velvet 1986, Married to the Mob 1988, Wild At Heart 1990, La Désenchantée 1990, True Romance 1993, Beautiful Girls 1996, Tin Cup 1996, The Late Late Show with Craig Kilborn (title song) 1999, Eyes Wide Shut 1999, The Family Man 2000. *Recordings include:* albums: Silvertone 1985, Chris Isaak 1987, Heart Shaped World 1989, Wicked Game 1991, San Francisco Days 1993, Forever Blue 1995, Baja Sessions 1996, Speak Of The Devil 1998, Wicked Ways Anthology 1998, Always Got Tonight 2002, Chris Isaak Christmas 2004, Mr Lucky 2009, Live at the Fillmore 2010, Beyond the Sun 2011. *Honours:* Int. Rock Award for Best Male Vocalist of the Year 1991, three MTV Music Video Awards (for Wicked Game) 1991. *Website:* www.chrisisaak.com.

ISHAM, Mark; American composer, producer, sound engineer and jazz musician (trumpet); b. 7 Sept. 1951, New York, NY; m. Donna Linson 1990. *Career:* mem., jazz ensemble, Group 87, The Rubisa Patrol, Sons of Champlin; mem. ASCAP. *Film scores:* Film scores include: Never Cry Wolf, 1983; Mrs Soffel, 1984; The Times of Harvey Milk, 1984; Country, 1984; Trouble in Mind, 1985; The Hitcher, 1986; Made in Heaven, 1987; Tibet, 1988; The Moderns, 1988; The Beast, 1988; Everybody Wins, 1990; Love at Large, 1990; Reversal of Fortune, 1990; Mortal Thoughts, 1991; Crooked Hearts, 1991; Point Break, 1991; A Midnight Clear, 1991; Little Man Tate, 1991; Billy Bathgate, 1991; Cool World, 1992; Of Mice and Men, 1992; The Public Eye, 1992; A River Runs Through It, 1992; Hidden Hawaii, 1993; Nowhere to Run, 1993; Fire in the Sky, 1993; Made in America, 1993; Short Cuts, 1993; Romeo is Bleeding, 1993; The Browning Version, 1994; Timecop, 1994; Thumbelina, 1994; Safe Passage, 1994; The Getaway, 1994; Quiz Show, 1994; Mrs Parker and the Vicious Circle, 1994; Nell, 1994; Miami Rhapsody, 1995; Losing Isaiah, 1995; The Net, 1995; Home for the Holidays, 1995; Waterworld (additional music), 1995; Last Dance, 1996; Fly Away Home, 1996; Night Falls on Manhattan, 1997; Afterglow, 1997; The Education of Little Tree, 1997; Kiss the Girls, 1997; The Gingerbread Man, 1998; Blade, 1998; Free Money, 1998; At First Sight, 1999; Varsity Blues, 1999; Breakfast of Champions, 1999; October Sky, 1999; Body Shots, 1999; Galapagos: The Enchanted Voyage, 1999; Rules of Engagement, 2000; Where the Money Is, 2000; Men of Honor, 2000; Save the Last Dance, 2001; Don't Say a Word, 2001; Hardball, 2002; Life as a House, 2002; The Majestic, 2002; Running Scared 2005, Eight Below 2005, The Black Dahlia 2006, Next 2007, The Mist 2007, Pride and Glory 2007, The Women 2008, The Express 2008, The Secret Life of Bees 2008. *Music for television:* Sketch Artist, 1992; Chicago Hope, 1994; Gotti, 1996; EZ Streets, 1996; Michael Hayes (theme), 1997; Nothing Sacred (theme), 1997; The Defenders: The Payback, 1997; The Defenders: Choice of Evils, 1998; From the Earth to the Moon, 1998; The Defenders: Taking the First, 1998; Family Law, 1999. *Recordings:* Solo: Vapor Drawings, 1983; Castalia, 1988; Mark Isham, 1991; Miles Remembered: The Silent Way Project, 1999; Blue Sun (with Charles Jankel), 1995; Deal It Out (with America); View From the Ground (with Van Morrison); Live at the Belfast Opera House; Into the Music; Inarticulate Speech of the Heart; Common One; Beautiful Vision (with Art Lande); Story of Baku; Eccentricities of Earl Dant; Rubisa Patrol; Desert Marauders; We Begin (with Group 87); Group 87; A Career In Dada Processing (with the Rolling Stones); Voodoo Lounge (with Bruce Springsteen); Human Touch (with Willie Nelson); Across the Borderline (with Toots Thielmans); Toots. *Honours:* Emmy Award, EZ Streets; American Music Award, Favourite Soundtrack, for Save the Last Dance, 2002.

ISHII, Ken; Japanese producer and remixer; b. 1970, Sapporo. *Career:* produced official opening and closing themes for Nagano Winter Olympics 1998; f. record label 70 Drums 2002. *Recordings include:* albums: Innerelements 1994, Jelly Tones 1995, Sleeping Madness 1999, Flatspin 2000, Future In Light 2002, Play, Pause and Play 2005, Sunriser 2006; singles: Garden On The Palm 1993, Pneuma 1993, Deep Sleep 1993, Tangled Notes 1994, Extra 1995, Overlap 1996, Game Over 1997, Circular Motion 1997, Stretch 1997, Echo Exit 1997, Misprogrammed Day 1999, Slapdish 2001, Flatspin 2001, Iceblink 2002, Auburnia 2003, Awakening 2003. *Honours:* DJ Award for Best Techno DJ 2004. *Address:* 70 Drums, 6-19-16-1001 Jingumae, Shibuyaku, Tokyo 150–0001, Japan (office). *E-mail:* info@musicmine.com (office). *Website:* www.kenishii.com.

ISLAM, Yusuf, (Cat Stevens); British singer, songwriter and producer; b. (Steven Demetre Georgiou), 21 July 1948, London; m. Fawzia Mubarik Ali 1979; two s. (one deceased) four d. *Career:* solo artist as Cat Stevens –1978, then as Yusuf Islam; extensive tours worldwide, numerous television appearances; mem. Musicians' Union; Founder and Chair. Small Kindness (charity); Founder and Chair. Islamia Schools Trust, f. Islamia Primary School, Islamia Girls' Secondary School, Brondesbury Coll. for Boys, London. *Recordings include:* albums: (as Cat Stevens) Matthew And Son 1967, New Masters 1967, World Of Cat Stevens 1970, Mona Bone Jakon 1970, Tea For The Tillerman 1970, Teaser And The Firecat 1971, Very Young and Early Songs 1971, Catch Bull At Four 1972, Foreigner 1973, Buddha And The Chocolate Box 1974, Saturnight (Live in Tokyo) 1974, View From The Top

1974, Numbers 1975, Greatest Hits 1975, Izitso 1977, Back To Earth 1978, Cat's Cradle 1978, Footsteps In The Dark 1984, Classics Vol. 24 – Cat Stevens 1989, Very Best of Cat Stevens 1990, (as Yusuf Islam) The Life Of The Last Prophet 1995, Prayers Of The Last Prophet 1999, I Have No Cannons That Roar 2000, A Is For Allah 2000, Majikat: Earth Tour 1976 2004, An Other Cup (Ivor Novello Award for Outstanding Song Collection 2007) 2006, Roadsinger 2009, Tell 'Em I'm Gone 2014. *Honours:* Dr hc (Univ. of Gloucestershire) 2005, (Univ. of Exeter) 2007; World Social Award 2003, Gorbachev Foundation Man for Peace Award 2004, ASCAP Award for Songwriter of the Year 2006, Mediterranean Prize for Peace 2007, Ivor Novello Award for Outstanding Song Collection 2007, inducted into Rock and Roll Hall of Fame 2014. *E-mail:* office@yusufislam.com (office). *Website:* www.yusufislam.com.

ISLEIFSSON, Arni; Icelandic musician; b. 18 Sept. 1927, Reykjavík; m. Kristin Axelsdottir; one s., three d. *Career:* mem., Jazzclub Egilsstadir; Egilsstadir Jazz Festival. *Address:* Hraunbar 122 110 Reykjavík, Iceland. *Website:* reykjavikjazz.is/arni-isleifsson.

ISLEY, Ernie; American musician (guitar, drums); b. 7 March 1952, Cincinnati, OH. *Career:* mem., The Isley Brothers, with brothers Rudolph, Ronald, O'Kelly, Marvin and cousin Chris Jasper, 1969–84; group billed as The Isley Brothers Featuring Ronald Isley, 1989–; mem., Isley, Jasper, Isley (with Marvin and Chris), 1984–. *Recordings:* albums: with The Isley Brothers: The Brothers Isley 1969, Live At Yankee Stadium 1969, Givin' It Back 1971, Brother Brother Brother 1972, The Isleys Live 1973, The Isleys' Greatest Hits 1973, Live It Up 1974, The Heat Is On 1975, Harvest For The World 1976, Go For Your Guns 1977, Forever Gold 1977, Showdown 1978, Winner Takes All 1979, Go All The Way 1980, Grand Slam 1981, Inside You 1981, The Real Deal 1982, Between The Sheets 1983, Eternal 2001, Greatest Hits, Vol. I 2002, Body Kiss 2003, Baby Makin' Music (Best Album by a Group, Soul Train Awards 2007) 2006, I'll be Home for Christmas 2007; with Isley Jasper Isley: Broadway's Closer To Sunset Boulevard 1985, Caravan of Love 1985, Masterpiece 1985, Different Drummer 1987, solo: High Wire 1990, Tracks of Life (with Marvin and Ronald) 1992, Beautiful Ballads 1994, Funky Family 1995, Mission to Please 1996, It's Your Thing: The Story of the Isley Brothers 1999, Love Songs 2001, Eternal 2001. *Address:* c/o Def Jam Recordings, 825 Eighth Avenue, New York, NY 10019, USA (office). *Website:* www.defjam.com (office).

ISLEY, Ronald, (Mr Biggs); American singer; b. 21 May 1941, Cincinnati, OH; m. Angela Winbush. *Career:* mem., gospel group, Isley Brothers, early 1950s; formed trio with Rudolph and O'Kelly, 1955; first British tour, 1964; formed T-Note record label, as prod. and writer, 1969; group joined by brothers Ernie, Marvin, and cousin Chris Jasper, 1969–84; group billed as The Isley Brothers Featuring Ronald Isley, 1989–; collaborations with: Quincy Jones, Nas, Lil' Kim, 112, Angela Winbush, Steve Harvey; Man. for The Johnson Sisters, 2001–. *Recordings:* albums: Twist and Shout 1959, This Old Heart of Mine 1966, It's Your Thing 1969, Givin' It Back 1971, Brother Brother Brother 1972, The Isleys Live 1973, The Isleys' Greatest Hits 1973, Live It Up 1974, The Heat Is On 1975, Harvest For The World 1976, Go For Your Guns 1977, Forever Gold 1977, Showdown 1978, Winner Takes All 1978, Go All The Way 1978, Grand Slam 1978, Inside You 1978, The Real Deal 1978, Between The Sheets 1978, Masterpiece 1985, Smooth Sailin' 1987, Spend The Night 1989, Tracks of Life (with Ernie and Marvin) 1983, Live 1993, Beautiful Ballads 1994, Funky Family 1995, Mission to Please 1996, It's Your Thing: The Story of the Isley Brothers 1999, Love Songs 2000, Eternal 2001, Greatest Hits, Vol. I 2002, Body Kiss 2003, Baby Makin' Music (Best Album by a Group, Soul Train Awards 2007) 2006, I'll be Home for Christmas 2007. *Honours:* Grammy Award, Best R&B Vocal Performance, It's Your Thing, 1969; inducted into Rock and Roll Hall of Fame, 1992; Soul Train Awards, Quincy Jones Award, 2001. *Address:* c/o Def Jam Recordings, 825 Eighth Avenue, New York, NY 10019, USA (office). *Website:* www.defjam.com (office).

ISLEY, Rudolph; American singer; b. 1 April 1939, Cincinnati, OH. *Career:* mem., Isley Brothers, gospel group, early 1950s; formed trio with brothers Ronald and O'Kelly, 1955; formed T-Neck record label, writing, producing, became vice-pres., 1969; group joined by brothers Ernie, Marvin, and cousin Chris Jasper, 1969–84; group billed as The Isley Brothers Featuring Ronald Isley, 1989–. *Recordings:* albums: Shout 1959, Twist and Shout 1962, This Old Heart of Mine 1966, It's Your Thing 1969, The Brothers 1969, Live At Yankee Stadium 1969, Brother Brother Brother 1972, The Isleys Live 1973, The Isleys' Greatest Hits 1973, Live It Up 1974, The Heat Is On 1975, Harvest For The World 1976, Go For Your Guns 1977, Showdown 1978, Winner Takes All 1978, Go All The Way 1978, Grand Slam 1981, Inside You 1981, The Real Deal 1982, Between The Sheets 1983, Smooth Sailin' 1987, The Isley Brothers Greatest Hits 1988, Spend The Night 1989, Love Songs 2000, Eternal 2001, Greatest Hits, Vol. I 2002, Baby Makin' Music (Best Album by a Group, Soul Train Awards 2007) 2006, I'll be Home for Christmas 2007. *Honours:* Grammy Award, Best R&B Vocal Performance, 1970; Gold Ticket, Madison Square Garden, New York, 1980; inducted into Rock and Roll Hall of Fame, 1992. *Address:* c/o Def Jam Recordings, 825 Eighth Avenue, New York, NY 10019, USA (office). *Website:* www.defjam.com (office).

IVE, Sir Jonathan (Jony), Kt, KBE, CBE, BA; British designer; *Chief Design Officer, Apple Inc.*; b. 1967, London; m. Heather Pegg; two s. *Education:* Newcastle Polytechnic. *Career:* Co-founder and Partner, Tangerine (design consultancy), London 1989; Designer, Apple Inc., Cupertino, Calif., USA 1992, Dir of Design 1996, then Vice-Pres. of Industrial Design, then Sr Vice-Pres. –2015, Chief Design Officer 2015–; designed the iMac 1998, iPod 2001, iPhone 2007, iPad 2010, Apple Watch 2015. *Honours:* Hon. Fellow, Royal Acad. of Engineering 2006; Dr hc (Northumbria Univ.) 2000, (Rhode Island School of Design) 2009, (Royal Coll. of Art) 2009; winner of design influence polls by Creative Review, the BBC and Q magazine; RSA student design awards 1988, 1989, RSA Medal for Design Achievement 1999, apptd RSA Designer for Industry 2003, Design Museum Designer of the Year 2003, RSA Benjamin Franklin Medal 2005, Pres.'s Medal, Royal Acad. of Eng 2005, Pres.'s Award, Design and Art Direction (D&AD) 2005. *Address:* Apple, 1 Infinite Loop, Cupertino, CA 95014, USA (office). *Telephone:* (408) 996-1010 (office). *Website:* www.apple.com (office).

IVINS, Michael Lee; American musician (bass guitar), songwriter and producer; b. 17 March 1963, Omaha, Neb.; m. Catherine Ivins 1998. *Education:* Classen High School, Oklahoma City. *Films:* Fearless Freaks (documentary on band) 2005; soundtrack contributions: The SpongeBob SquarePants Movie 2004, Spider-Man 3 2007, Good Luck Chuck 2007, Mr Magorium's Wonder Emporium 2007. *Recordings:* albums: with The Flaming Lips: Hear It Is 1986, Oh My Gawd!!! 1987, Telepathic Surgery 1989, In a Priest Driven Ambulance 1990, Hit to Death in the Future Head 1992, Transmissions from the Satellite Heart 1993, Clouds Taste Metallic 1995, Zaireeka 1997, The Soft Bulletin 1999, Yoshmi Battles the Pink Robots 2002, At War with the Mystics 2006 (Grammy Award for Best Engineered Album, Non-Classical 2007), Embryonic 2009; with Stardeath and White Dwarfs: The Flaming Lips and Stardeath and White Dwarfs with Henry Rollins and Peaches Doing Dark Side of the Moon 2010. *Honours:* Grammy Award for Best Rock Instrumental Performance 2002, 2006. *Current Management:* c/o Scott Booker, Hellfire Enterprises Limited, 1208 Chowning Avenue, Edmond, OK 73034, USA. *Telephone:* (405) 715-0600. *Fax:* (405) 715-0632. *E-mail:* SDBMKTG@hellfireltdcom. *Website:* www.hellfireltd.com. *Address:* c/o Warner Bros. Records Inc., 3300 Warner Boulevard, Burbank, CA 91505, USA (office). *Website:* www.theflaminglips.com.

IWAN, Dafydd, BArch; British politician, singer-composer and record company director; *Director, Sain (Recordiau) Cyf*; b. (Dafydd Iwan Jones), 24 Aug. 1943, Brynaman, Wales; s. of Rev. Gerallt Jones and Elizabeth Jane Jones; m. 1st Marion Thomas 1968 (divorced 1986); two s. one d.; m. 2nd Bethan Jones 1988; two s. *Education:* Aman Valley Grammar School, Ysgol Ty Tan Domen, Y Bala, Univ. Coll. of Wales, Aberystwyth and Welsh School of Architecture, Cardiff. *Career:* f. Sain (Recordiau) Cyf (now Wales' leading record co.) 1969, Man. Dir 1984–2006, currently Dir; f. Tai Gwynedd Housing Asscn 1971; Founder-Trustee, Nant Gwrtheyrn Language Centre 1975; Chair. Welsh Language Soc. 1968–71; parl. cand. 1974, 1983, 1984; Chair. Plaid Cymru (Nationalist Party of Wales) 1982–84, Vice-Pres. 1984–95, Pres. 2003–10; Plaid Cymru mem. of Gwynedd Unitary Authority 1995–2008; Chair. Planning and Economic Devt Cttee, Cyngor Gwynedd Council 1995–99, mem. Exec. Cttee responsible for Planning, Highways and Environment 1999–2003, Econ. Devt and Educ. 2003–08; Chair. Gwynedd Econ. Partnership 2008–; Trustee, Portmeirion Foundation, Carers Outreach, Plas Glyn-y-Weddw Gallery; nonconformist lay preacher; has promoted the Welsh language and culture for five decades. *Music:* composed, sung and recorded more than 250 songs; more than 40 albums and videos 1965–2010; numerous concert tours abroad. *Television:* Yma Mae Ngân, S4C (several series introducing own songs), documentaries on various countries. *Publications:* Dafydd Iwan (autobiog.) 1982, 100 O Ganeuon (collection of songs) 1983, Caneuon Dafydd Iwan (second collection of songs) 1991, Cân Dros Gymru (autobiog.) 2002, Dafydd Iwan: Bywyd mewn lluniau (A Life in Pictures) 2005. *Honours:* Hon. mem. Gorsedd of Bards for services to Welsh language; Hon. Fellow, Univs of Bangor and Aberystwyth for services to Welsh culture and Welsh music 1998; Hon. LLD (Univ. of Wales) 2004; Gold Disc for services to Welsh music. *Address:* Sain, Canolfan Sain, Llandwrog, Caernarfon, Gwynedd, LL54 5TG (office); Carrog, Rhos-Bach, Caeathro, Caernarfon, Gwynedd, LL55 2TF, Wales (home). *Telephone:* (1286) 676004 (home); 7984-202922 (mobile). *E-mail:* dafyddiwan@cymru1.net (home); dafydd@sainwales.com (office). *Website:* www.sainwales.com (office); www.dafyddiwan.com (home).

IYER, Vijay, MS, PhD; American jazz pianist and composer; b. (Vijay Srinivas Raghunathan), 26 Oct. 1971, Albany, NY; m. Christina Leslie; one d. *Education:* Yale Coll., Univ. of California, Berkeley. *Career:* as composer/performer/leader has performed concerts in USA (Library of Congress, Smithsonian Inst., Kennedy Center in Washington, DC, The Asia Soc., Merkin Hall, Zankel Hall, The Kitchen, Lincoln Center Festival in New York City, Brooklyn Acad. of Music) and Europe; festivals world-wide; comms for Chicago Jazz Festival, American Composers Orchestra, Silk Road Ensemble, Ethel, Imani Winds, Bang On a Can, Brentano String Quartet, So Percussion, Jennifer Koh, Matt Haimovitz, Brooklyn Rider; Artist-in-Residence, Metropolitan Museum of Art, SF Jazz, Ojai Festival; MacArthur fellow; Doris Duke Performing Artist; sideman or producer with numerous artists; Director of The Banff Centre's International Workshop in Jazz and Creative Music; Franklin D. and Florence Rosenblatt Prof. of the Arts, Dept of Music, Harvard Univ.; Faculty mem., New York Univ. and The New School Univ.; masterclasses and lectures in composition, improvisation, cognitive science, jazz studies and performance studies at California Inst. of the Arts, Columbia Univ., Manhattan School of Music, School for Improvisational Music. *Exhibition:* Release (audiovisual installation, in collaboration with filmmaker Bill Morrison) 2010. *Compositions include:* Three Episodes for Wind Quintet

1999, Mutations I-X for string quartet 2005 (recorded 2014), Interventions for orchestra 2007, Far From Over for quintet 2008, Dig the Say for Brooklyn Rider 2012, Playlist for an Extreme Occasion for the Silk Road Ensemble 2012, Radhe Radhe: Rites of Holi for International Contemporary Ensemble (ICE) 2013, Time Place Action and Mozart Effects for Brentano String Quartet 2014. *Theatre/dance score:* Betrothed 2007, score for 'Uneasy' – Karole Armitage Gone! Dance, premiered at Central Park Summerstage, New York 2011. *Film score:* Teza 2008. *Recordings:* with Vijay Iyer Quartet: Panoptic Modes 2001, Blood Sutra 2003, Reimagining 2005, Tragicomic 2008; with Vijay Iyer Trio: Historicity 2009, Accelerando 2012, Break Stuff 2015; with Mike Ladd: In What Language? 2004, Still Life with Commentator 2007, Holding It Down: The Veterans' Dream Project 2013; with Fieldwork: Your Life Flashes 2002, Simulated Progress 2005, Door 2008; with Rudresh Mahanthappa: Raw Materials 2006; solo: Solo 2010. *Publications:* contribs to Music Perception, Current Musicology, Journal of Consciousness Studies, Critical Studies in Improvisation, Journal for the Society of American Music, The Guardian, The Wire, JazzTimes, and the edited anthologies Uptown Conversation: The New Jazz Studies (Columbia University Press), Sound Unbound (MIT Press), and Arcana IV (Hips Road). *Honours:* commissioning grants from Rockefeller Foundation MAP Fund 2000, 2001, 2005, 2009, New York State Council on the Arts 2002, Creative Capital Foundation 2002, Mary Flagler Cary Charitable Trust 2002, 2004, American Composers Forum 2005, Chamber Music America 2005, Meet The Composer 2006, Jazz Inst. of Chicago 2008; CalArts Alpert Award in the Arts 2003, Fellowship in Music Composition from New York Foundation for the Arts 2006, Downbeat Magazine Int. Critics' Poll Rising Star Jazz Artist 2006, 2007, Rising Star Composer 2006, 2007, Rising Star Pianist 2009, Echo Award 2010, Jazz Journalists' Asscn Awards for Musician of the Year 2010, for Pianist of the Year 2013, Doris Duke Performing Artist Award 2012, Downbeat Magazine Artist of the Year and four other top awards 2012, Preis der Deutschen Schallplatten Kritik, MacArthur Fellow 2013, Downbeat Pianist of the Year 2014, Downbeat Artist of the Year 2015. *Current Management:* c/o Stephen Cohen, Music and Art Management, 9 West Walnut Street, Suite 2D, Asheville, NC 28801, USA. *Telephone:* (828) 225-5658. *Fax:* (888) 285-1412. *E-mail:* steve@musicandart.net. *Website:* www.musicandart .net; vijay-iyer.com (home).

IZAMBARD, Sébastien; French singer (tenor) and musician (guitar, piano); b. 7 March 1973. *Career:* mem., Il Divo 2003–. *Recordings include:* albums: Il Divo 2004, Ancora 2005, The Christmas Collection 2005, Siempre 2006, The Promise 2008. *Current Management:* c/o Becca Barr Management, 5th Floor, Dorland House, 14-16 Regent Street, London, SW1Y 4PH, England. *Website:* www.ildivo.com.

J

JA RULE; American rap artist; b. (Jeffrey Atkins), 29 Feb. 1976, Queens, New York; m. Aisha; three c. *Career:* began performing aged 16; first appeared on Mic Geronimo's Time To Build 1995; collaborations with Jay-Z, Blackstreet, So Plush, DJ Clue, Dru Hill, Jennifer Lopez. *Films include:* Turn It Up 2000, Backstage 2000, Da Hip Hop Witch 2000, The Fast and the Furious 2001, Crime Partners 2000 2001, Assault on Precinct 13 2004, Back in the Day 2005, Don't Fade Away 2010, The Cookout 2 2011, Once Upon a Time in Brooklyn 2013, I'm in Love with a Church Girl 2013. *Recordings include:* albums: Venni Vetti Vecci 1999, Rule 3:36 2001, Pain Is Love 2001, The Last Temptation 2003, Blood In My Eye 2003, R.U.L.E. 2004, The Mirror 2008, Pain Is Love 2012. *Honours:* MOBO Award for Best Hip Hop Artist 2002. *Address:* c/o The Inc. Records, Universal Records, 1755 Broadway, Floor 7, New York, NY 10019-3743, USA. *Website:* www.theincrecords.com; www.jarule.net.

JACKSON, Alan Eugene; American country singer and songwriter; b. 17 Oct. 1958, Newnan, GA; s. of Eugene Jackson and Ruth Jackson; m. Denise Jackson 1979; three d. *Career:* mem. ASCAP, NARAS, ACM, CMA. *Recordings include:* albums: Here in the Real World 1990, Don't Rock the Jukebox 1991, A Lot About Livin' 1992, Honky Tonk Christmas 1993, Who I Am 1994, Everything I Love 1996, High Mileage 1998, Under the Influence 1999, When Somebody Loves You 2000, Drive 2002, Let it be Christmas 2002, What I Do 2004, Precious Memories 2006, Like Red on a Rose 2006, Good Time 2008, Freight Train 2010, Thirty Miles West 2012, Precious Memories: Volume II (Billboard Music award for Top Christian Album 2014) 2013. *Honours:* numerous CMA Awards, including Entertainer of the Year 1995, Acad. of Country Music Awards for Male Artist of the Year 1995, for Record of the Year (for Five O'Clock Somewhere) 2004, for Vocal Event of the Year (for As She's Walking Away, with Zac Brown Band) 2011. *Website:* www.alanjackson.com.

JACKSON, Carl Eugene; American songwriter and musician (banjo); b. 18 Sept. 1953, Louisville, Mississippi. *Career:* Musician, Jim and Jesse; The Sullivan Family; Glen Campbell, 1972–84; Songwriter, Glen Campbell Publishing, 1984–87; Ricky Skaggs/Polygram Music Publishing, 1987–90; Famous Music Publishing, 1990–93; McSpadden Smith Music, 1993–96; Colonel Rebel Music, 1996–; mem. CMA; ACM, NARAS. *Compositions:* Letter To Home; Little Mountain Church House; Put Yourself In My Place; Breaking New Ground; Against The Grain; No Future In The Past; Fit For A King; Lonesome Dove. *Recordings:* albums: solo: Carl Jackson: Banjo Player 1973, Old Friends 1978, Mississippi Homecoming 1981, Song of the South 1982, 'Neath the Oaks in the Grove 1993; other credits include: Roll On, Alabama 1984, 13, Emmylou Harris 1987, Angel Band, Emmylou Harris 1987, Trio, Linda Ronstadt, Dolly Parton, Emmylou Harris 1987, Ropin' The Wind, Garth Brooks 1991, This Time, Dwight Yoakam 1993, Gone, Dwight Yoakam 1995, Sevens, Garth Brooks 1997, Down at the Fair, Quartette 2007, The Life of a Song, Joey + Rory 2008, Mountain Soul II, Patty Loveless 2009, Album #2, Joey + Rory 2010, Family Album, Buick Audra 2011. *Honours:* IBMA Song of the Year, Little Mountain Church House, 1990; Grammy for Best Bluegrass album, Spring Training, 1991; Dove Award for Best Southern Gospel Song, Where Shadows Never Fall, 1991. *Website:* www.carljackson.net.

JACKSON, David Nicholas George, MA, PGCE; British musician (saxophones, flute, whistles, Soundbeam) and teacher; b. 15 April 1947, Stamford, Lincs., England; s. of George John Stonewall Jackson and Yvonne Mary Jackson; m. Susan Elizabeth Jackson; one s. one d. *Education:* St Andrews Univ., Univ. of Surrey. *Career:* mem. Van Der Graaf Generator 1969–77, 2004–05; teacher 1980–92; saxophonist, Soundbeam consultant, David Jackson's Tonewall, an interactive performance with Soundbeams, Echo-Mirrors and Jellybean Eye 1990–; Man. Dir Concert for Parents, Eunice Kennedy Shriver Special Olympics, Dublin 2003, disability concerts in UK, Ireland, Norway, Italy, Germany; mem. Cross & Jackson (King Crimson/VdGG); frequent guest musician in Italy with Osanna (Naples), Alex Carpani Band, Aldo Taglipietra and many others; fmr Soundbeam Consultant, Meldreth Manor School; numerous TV appearances, workshops and festivals; mem. Performing Right Soc., Mechanical-Copyright Protection Soc., Sound Sense. *Recordings include:* albums with VdGG: The Least We Can Do Is Wave To Each Other 1969, H To He Who Is The Only One 1970, Pawn Hearts 1971, Long Hello (series) 1973, Godbluff 1975, Still Life 1976, World Record 1976, The Quiet Zone/The Pleasure Dome 1977, Reflection 1978, Vital (live) 1978, Tonewall Stands 1992, I Prophesy Disaster 1993, Fractal Bridge 1996, Beams and Bells 2001, Guastalla (DVD) 2002, Batteries Included 2003, A2Z Healthy Choices 2003, VdGG Present 2005, Celebration Concert (DVD) 2008, Osanna & David Jackson Prog Family 2009, Prog Exhibition (CD and DVD) 2011, Jaxon Faces The Jury 2012, etc. *Publications include:* Special Children 1994, Soundbeam Artistry 1995, Music on My Mind (SEN Magazine) 2009. *E-mail:* tonewall@btinternet.com (office). *Website:* www.jaxontonewall.com (office).

JACKSON, Eleanor (Elly) Kate; British singer, musician (keyboards), songwriter and record producer; b. 12 March 1988, London; d. of Kit Jackson and Trudie Goodwin. *Education:* Pimlico School, Sydenham High School, Royal Russell School. *Career:* formed Automan with Ben Langmaid 2006, became La Roux 2008–, supported Lily Allen on UK tour in 2009. *Recordings:* album: La Roux 2009, Trouble in Paradise 2014; also appears on My Beautiful Dark Twisted Fantasy, Kanye West 2010, Business Casual, Chromeo 2010,

Watch the Throne, Jay-Z and Kanye West 2011. *Honours:* O2 Silver Clef Best Newcomer Award 2009, Studio8 Int. Music Awards for Best Female Newcomer 2009, iTunes UK Music Award for Single of the Year 2009, NME Best Dancefloor Filler Award 2010, Int. Dance Music Awards for Best Dubstep/DNB/Jungle Track and Best Breakthrough Artist (Group) 2010, Grammy Award for Best Electronic/Dance Album 2011. *Address:* c/o Universal Music UK, 364–366 Kensington High Street, London, W14 8NS, England (office). *Website:* www.larouxonline.com; www.laroux.co.uk.

JACKSON, Jackie; American singer; b. (Sigmund Esco Jackson), 4 May 1951, Gary, Ind.; s. of Joseph W. Jackson and Katherine E. Jackson (née Scruse); two c. *Career:* Founder-mem. The Jackson Brothers, later renamed The Jackson 5 1962–76; numerous live and television appearances, concerts and tours; became solo artist and session musician. *Recordings include:* albums: with The Jackson 5: Diana Ross Presents The Jackson 5 1969, ABC 1970, Third Album 1970, The Jackson 5 Christmas Album 1970, Goin' Back To Indiana 1971, Maybe Tomorrow 1971, Lookin' Through The Windows 1972, Get It Together 1973, In Japan! (live) 1973, Skywriter 1973, Dancing Machine 1974, Moving Violation 1975, Joyful Jukebox Music 1976; with The Jacksons: The Jacksons 1976, Goin' Places 1977, Destiny 1978, Triumph 1980, The Jacksons Live 1981, Live 1982, Fliphits 1983, Victory 1984, 2300 Jackson Street 1989, Children of the Light 1993; solo: Jackie Jackson 1973, Be The One 1989, Are You With Me 2004. *Website:* www.jackiejackson5.com.

JACKSON, Janet Damita Jo; American singer and choreographer; b. 16 May 1966, Gary, Ind.; d. of Joseph Jackson and Katherine Jackson; m. 1st James DeBarge 1984 (annulled 1985); m. 2nd Rene Elizondo Jr 1991–2000; m. 3rd Wissam Al Mana 2012. *Education:* Valley Professional School. *Career:* singing debut at age seven with family singing group, The Jacksons; television actress 1977–81, appearing in series Good Times (CBS), Diff'rent Strokes, Fame, A New Kind of Family; solo recording artist 1982–; worldwide concerts and tours. *Recordings include:* albums: Janet Jackson 1982, Dream Street 1984, Control 1986, Janet Jackson's Rhythm Nation 1989, Rhythm Nation Compilation 1990, Janet 1993, Design of a Decade 1986–96 1995, The Velvet Rope 1997, All For You 2001, Damita Jo 2004, 20 Y.O. 2006, Discipline 2008, Unbreakable 2015. *Films include:* Poetic Justice 1993, Nutty Professor II: The Klumps 2000, Why Did I Get Married? 2007, Why Did I Get Married Too? 2010, For Colored Girls 2010. *TV includes:* The Jacksons 1976–77, Good Times 1977–79, A New Kind of Family 1979–80, Diff'rent Strokes 1980–84, Fame 1984–85. *Publication:* True You 2011. *Honours:* American Music Awards for Best Female Soul Singer (for Nasty), Best Female Soul Video (for What Have You Done For Me Lately?) and Best Pop Video (for When I Think of You) 1986, for Best Dance Artist, Best Female Pop Rock Artist and Best Female Soul R&B Artist 1991, for Favourite Pop/Rock Female Artist 2002, MTV Video Vanguard Award 1990, MTV Award for Best Female Video (for If) 1993, Starlight Foundation Humanitarian of the Year Award 1991, Grammy Award for Best R&B Song (for That's the Way Love Goes) 1993. *Current Management:* Jason Winters, Sterling/Winters Company, 10900 Wilshire Blvd, #15, Los Angeles, CA 90024, USA. *Telephone:* (310) 557-2700. *Website:* janetjackson.com.

JACKSON, Jermaine Lajuan; American singer, musician (bass guitar) and record producer; b. 11 Dec. 1954, Gary, Ind.; s. of Joseph W. Jackson and Katherine E. Jackson (née Scruse); m. 1st Hazel Gordy 1973; m. 2nd Alejandra Oaziaza 1995; seven c.; m. 3rd Halima Rashid. *Career:* Founder-mem. The Jackson Brothers, later renamed The Jackson 5 1962–76, briefly mem. The Jacksons 1984; simultaneous solo career 1972–; numerous live and television appearances, concerts and tours; moved into career development of artists, including Devo, Michael Lovesmith, Syreeta; formed own production co. and record label, WORK Records; worked with artists, including Whitney Houston. *Television:* The Jacksons – An American Dream (producer, series on ABC) 1992. *Recordings include:* albums: with The Jackson 5: Diana Ross Presents The Jackson 5 1969, ABC 1970, Third Album 1970, The Jackson 5 Christmas Album 1970, Goin' Back To Indiana 1971, Maybe Tomorrow 1971, Lookin' Through The Windows 1972, Get It Together 1973, In Japan! (live) 1973, Skywriter 1973, Dancing Machine 1974, Moving Violation 1975, Joyful Jukebox Music 1976; with The Jacksons: Victory 1984, 2300 Jackson Street 1989; solo: Jermaine 1972, Come Into My Life 1973, My Name Is Jermaine 1976, Feel The Fire 1977, Frontiers 1978, Let's Get Serious 1979, I Like Your Style 1981, Let Me Tickle Your Fancy 1982, Dynamite 1984, Jermaine Jackson 1984, Precious Moments 1986, Don't Take It Personal 1989, You Said 1992, Living Your Dream (with Al Walser) 2009, I Wish You L.O.V.E.: Jazz Standards 2013. *Address:* Jermaine L. Jackson Entertainment, PO Box 8608, Calabasas, CA 91372, USA (office). *Telephone:* (818) 436-2570 (office). *E-mail:* info@jermainejacksonentertainment.com. *Website:* jermainejacksonentertainment.com.

JACKSON, Joe; British singer and songwriter; b. 11 Aug. 1954, Burton-upon-Trent, Staffordshire, England. *Education:* Royal Coll. of Music, London. *Career:* played with Johnny Dankworth; mem. Nat. Youth Jazz Orchestra; Musical Dir Coffee and Cream 1977; solo artist 1978–; regular UK and int. tours, concerts; Founder, Joe Jackson Band. *Compositions for film include:* Mike's Murder 1983, Shijin No Ie (House of the Poet) 1985, Tucker 1988,

Recordings include: albums: Look Sharp! 1979, I'm The Man 1979, Beat Crazy 1980, Joe Jackson's Jumpin' Jive 1981, Night and Day 1982, Big World 1986, Will Power 1987, Live 1980/86 1988, Blaze of Glory 1988, Laughter and Lust 1990, Steppin' Out – The Best of Joe Jackson 1990, Night Music 1994, Heaven and Hell 1997, Symphony 1 (Grammy Award for Best Pop Instrumental Album 2001) 1999, Summer In The City 2000, Night and Day II 2001, Volume IV 2003, Rain 2008, Live Music: Europe 2010 2011, The Redettes 2011, The Duke 2012. *Publications include:* A Cure For Gravity (autobiography) 1999, The Smoking Issue (pamphlet) 2005, Smoke, Lies and the Nanny State (essay) 2007. *Current Management:* Big Hassle Management, 44 Wall Street, 22nd Floor, New York, NY 10005, USA. *Telephone:* (212) 619-1360. *Fax:* (212) 619-1669. *E-mail:* weinstein@bighassle.com. *Website:* www.bighassle.com; www.joejackson.com.

JACKSON, LaToya; American singer; b. 29 May 1956, Gary, Ind. *Career:* began as backing singer for family group, The Jacksons; solo artist 1979–; contrib. backing vocals to brother, Michael's Thriller album; numerous TV and live appearances. *Recordings include:* albums: LaToya Jackson 1980, My Special Love 1981, Heart Don't Lie 1984, Imagination 1986, LaToya 1988, You're Gonna Get Rocked 1988, No Relations 1991, From Nashville To You 1994, He's My Brother 1994, Bad Girl 1995, Be My Lover 1995, Moulin Rouge 2001, Startin' Over 2005. *Address:* c/o Ja-Tail Enterprises LLC, 8306 Wilshire Blvd, Suite 528, Beverly Hills, CA 90211, USA. *E-mail:* inquiries@jatail.com; info@latoyaonline.com. *Website:* www.latoyaonline.com.

JACKSON, Marlon; American singer and musician (guitar); b. 12 March 1957, Gary, Ind.; s. of Joseph W. Jackson and Katherine E. Jackson (née Scruse). *Career:* Founder-mem. The Jackson Brothers, later renamed The Jackson 5 1962–76, renamed The Jacksons 1976–84; numerous live and television appearances, concerts and tours; became solo artist and session musician. *Recordings include:* albums: with The Jackson 5: Diana Ross Presents The Jackson 5 1969, ABC 1970, Third Album 1970, The Jackson 5 Christmas Album 1970, Goin' Back To Indiana 1971, Maybe Tomorrow 1971, Lookin' Through The Windows 1972, Get It Together 1973, In Japan! (live) 1973, Skywriter 1973, Dancing Machine 1974, Moving Violation 1975, Joyful Jukebox Music 1976; with The Jacksons: The Jacksons 1976, Goin' Places 1977, Destiny 1978, Triumph 1980, The Jacksons Live 1981, Live 1982, Fliphits 1983, Victory 1984, 2300 Jackson Street 1989, Children of the Light 1993; solo: Baby Tonight 1987. *Film appearances include:* Student Confidential 1987, Nell 1994. *Current Management:* c/o Rick Barlowe, Sheridan Taylor Group, 14724 Ventura Blvd Penthouse, Sherman Oaks, CA 91403, USA. *Website:* www.thejacksons.com.

JACKSON, Millie; American singer; b. 15 July 1944, Thompson, GA. *Career:* professional singer 1964–; R&B singer, then country singer; collaborations with Isaac Hayes. *Recordings include:* albums: Millie Jackson 1972, It Hurts So Good 1973, Caught Up 1974, Soul Believer 1974, Still Caught Up 1975, Free and In Love 1976, Lovingly Yours 1977, Get It Out 'Cha System 1978, A Moment's Pleasure 1979, Live and Uncensored 1980, For Men Only 1980, Just A Lil' Bit Country 1981, Live and Outrageous 1982, Hard Times 1982, ESP (Extra Sexual Persuasion) 1984, An Imitation of Love 1986, The Tide Is Turning 1988, Will You Love Me Tom 1989, Back to the Shit 1989, Young Man Older Woman 1991, Check in the Mail 1994, Love Quake 1994, Rock 'N' Soul 1994, It's Over 1995, Breaking Up Somebody's Home 1996, Did You Think I Wouldn't Cry 1997, Not For Church Folk 2001, Soul for the Dancefloor 2008. *E-mail:* millie@weirdwreckuds.com. *Website:* www.weirdwreckuds.com.

JACKSON, Steven Randall (Randy); American singer and musician (percussion); b. 29 Oct. 1961, Gary, Ind.; s. of Joseph W. Jackson and Katherine E. Jackson (née Scruse); m.; three c. *Career:* mem. The Jacksons (renamed Jackson 5) 1976–84; numerous live and television appearances, concerts and tours; became session musician. *Recordings include:* albums: with The Jacksons: The Jacksons 1976, Goin' Places 1977, Destiny 1978, Triumph 1980, The Jacksons Live 1981, Live 1982, Fliphits 1983, Victory 1984, 2300 Jackson Street 1989, Children of the Light 1993; solo: Zucchero & the Randy Jackson Band 1985, Randy & Gypsys 1989, Randy Jackson's Music Club, Vol. 1 2008.

JACKSON, Steve; British sound engineer and mixer. *Recordings include:* Dire Straits: Brothers in Arms, Money For Nothing, Wet Wet Wet, Holding Back the River; Bryan Adams So Far So Good, Paul Young, Simply Red, Roachford, James Taylor Quartet, Tori Amos, Sting, Deacon Blue, Capercaillie, Cast, Whipping Boy, Mark Knopfler. *Honours:* Studio Master Award for Excellence (for Homelands by Steve Booker) 1990. *Website:* www.stevejacksonmusic.com.

JACKSON, Stevie; British singer, songwriter and musician (guitar); b. 16 Jan. 1969. *Career:* mem., Belle & Sebastian 1996–. *Recordings include:* albums: Tigermilk 1996, If You're Feeling Sinister 1996, The Boy With The Arab Strap 1998, Fold Your Hands Child, You Walk Like A Peasant 2000, Storytelling 2002, Dear Catastrophe Waitress 2003, The Life Pursuit 2006, Write About Love 2010, Girls in Peacetime Want to Dance 2015. *Honours:* BRIT Award for Best Newcomer 1999, Q Magazine Spirit of Independence Award 2013. *Current Management:* Banchory Management, PO Box 25074, Glasgow, G3 8TT, Scotland. *Telephone:* (141) 204-2269. *E-mail:* banchoryman@gmail.com. *Website:* www.belleandsebastian.com.

JACKSON, Stonewall; American country singer and musician (guitar); b. 6 Nov. 1932, Tabor City, NC. *Career:* mem., Grand Ole Opry 1956–; worked with Ernest Tubb; solo artist 1957–. *Recordings include:* albums: The Dynamic Stonewall Jackson 1959, Sadness In A Song 1962, I Love A Song 1963, Trouble and Me 1965, The Exciting Stonewall Jackson 1966, All's Fair In Love 'N' War 1966, Help Stamp Out Loneliness 1967, Stonewall Jackson Country 1967, The Great Old Songs 1968, Thoughts of a Lonely Man 1968, Nothing Takes The Place of Loving You 1968, I Pawned My Past Today 1969, The Old Country Church 1969, A Tribute To Hank Williams 1969, The Real Thing 1970, The Lonesome In Me 1970, Stonewall Jackson Recorded Live At The Grand Ole Opry 1971, Waterloo 1971, Me and You and A Dog Named Boo 1971, World of Stonewall Jackson 1972, Nashville 1974, Stonewall 1979, My Favorite Sin 1980, Stonewall Jackson 1982, Solid Stonewall 1982, Alive 1984, Up Against The Wall 1984, All the Best 1995, Classic Country 1998, Stonewall Jackson 1999, Hero Icon 2004.

JACKSON, Tito; American singer and musician (guitar); b. (Toriano Jackson), 15 Oct. 1953, Gary, Ind.; s. of Joseph W. Jackson and Katherine E. Jackson (née Scruse); three s. *Career:* Founder-mem. The Jackson Brothers, later renamed The Jackson 5 1962–76, renamed The Jacksons 1976–84; numerous live and television appearances, concerts and tours; became session musician. *Recordings include:* albums: with The Jackson 5: Diana Ross Presents The Jackson 5 1969, ABC 1970, Third Album 1970, The Jackson 5 Christmas Album 1970, Goin' Back to Indiana 1971, Maybe Tomorrow 1971, Lookin' Through The Windows 1972, Get It Together 1973, In Japan! (live) 1973, Skywriter 1973, Dancing Machine 1974, Moving Violation 1975, Joyful Jukebox Music 1976; with The Jacksons: The Jacksons 1976, Goin' Places 1977, Destiny 1978, Triumph 1980, The Jacksons Live 1981, Live 1982, Fliphits 1983, Victory 1984, 2300 Jackson Street 1989, Children of the Light 1993; solo: Season's Greetings from Tito Jackson 2009. *E-mail:* management@titojackson.com. *Website:* www.titojackson.com.

JACKSON, Trevor, (The Underdog); British producer and remixer; b. London. *Career:* f. Bite It!, design co. 1990–, Bite It! Recordings, record co. 1991–96, Output Recordings 1996–; producer for The Brotherhood, Brianchild, No Exit, Skull, Underdog, ENC, Dempsey, Playgroup, The Gossip; remixed Massive Attack, Sabres of Paradise, The Pharcyde, U2, Unkle. *Recordings include:* albums: Elementalz (with The Brotherhood) 1996, Playgroup (with Playgroup) 2001; singles: Alphabetical Response (with The Brotherhood) 1995, One Shot (with The Brotherhood) 1996, Punk Funk (with The Brotherhood) 1996, Make It Happen (with Playgroup) 2000, Number One (with Playgroup) 2001. *Address:* PO Box 16628, London, N1 7WE, England (office). *E-mail:* info@trevor-jackson.com (office). *Website:* www.trevor-jackson.

JACKSON, Wanda Lavonne; American singer and songwriter; b. 20 Oct. 1937, Maud, OK. *Career:* toured with Hank Thompson Band, Red Foley; solo artist 1956–; began recording Christian music 1970s. *Recordings include:* albums: Wanda Jackson 1958, Rockin' With Wanda 1960, There's A Party Goin' On 1961, Right Or Wrong 1961, Lovin' Country Style 1962, Wonderful Wanda 1962, Love Me Forever 1963, Two Sides of Wanda Jackson 1964, Blues in My Heart 1964, Sings Country Songs 1966, Reckless Love Affair 1967, You'll Always Have My Love 1967, Cream of the Crop 1968, The Happy Side Of 1969, Many Moods Of 1969, Country! 1970, Woman Lives For Love 1970, I've Gotta Sing 1971, I Wouldn't Want You Any Other Way 1972, Praise The Lord 1972, When It's Time To Fall In Love Again 1973, Country Keepsakes 1973, Now I Have Everything 1974, Rock 'N' Roll Away Your Blues 1984, Early Wanda Jackson 1986, Rockin' In The Country 1990, Tears Will Be the Chaser for Your Wine 1997, Queen of Rockabilly 2000, Wanda Rocks 2002, Heart Trouble 2003, Heartache 2004, I Remember Elvis 2006, Baby, Let's Play House 2010. *Website:* www.wandajackson.com.

JACOB, Julien Philippe Jacques; French composer, singer, songwriter, musician and poet; b. Benin. *Career:* moved to France aged four; fmr mem. Anaphase; performed at WOMAD festivals in USA, Australia, Singapore, New Zealand, UK, Spain, Gran Canarias, Italy 2000–04; concerts in Montréal, Canada and France. *Recordings include:* solo album: Shanti 2000, Cotonou 2005, Barham 2008. *E-mail:* evelyne.dano@free.fr. *Website:* www.julienjacob.com.

JACOBI, Gina; Swedish composer, singer and musician (keyboards); b. 12 Dec. 1962, Hammerdal; three d. *Education:* studied at univ. *Career:* dir of five projects including music, singing, theatre, choirs with young people; composed music for theatres, commercial videos; appearances on Swedish TV. *Recordings include:* albums: Bagateller Trifles 1985, Tid and Rum Time and Space 1986, Pa jakt efter solen, Haunting 1988, Ga som pa natar, Walking as Upon 1989, Gare Seretaye, The Kurdish Cassette 1996, Alla ar, Everybody In 1996, Jacobi's World 1998, Like Me 2005, Unlike Me 2007, Fragile 2009. *Honours:* Swedish Grammis Galan for Best Female Artist. *E-mail:* major.music@bredband.net. *Website:* ginajacobi.se.

JACOBS, Jon; engineer and mixer. *Recordings:* Engineered, Mixed, Produced: Tom Ribiero, album, 1990; The Slow Club, World of Wonders, album, 1990; Graham Parker, Burning Questions, album, 1992; Mary McLaughlin, Daughter of Lir, 1993; The Pretenders, 1992/93; Wendy James, singles, 1993; The Ya Ya's, See No Rain, single, 1993; Kenji Jammer, album mixed, 1993; Psychedelix, Psychedelix II, album mixed, 1993; Raw, 1993; Planet Claire, After the Fire, album mixed, 1993; Rynten Okazaki, album, 1994; Pacifists, album, 1994; Gota, album, 1994; Rynten Okazaki, album, soundtrack film, 1994; Psychedelix, 1995; Yuki Saito, album, 1995; Elio, Eat the Phikus, 1996; The Beatles, new singles, 1995–96; Elvis Costello, All This Useless Beauty,

1996; Paul McCartney: Flaming Pie, 1996; World Tonight, 1997; The Divine Comedy: Short Album about Love, 1997; Fin de Siecle, 1998; Certainty of Chance, 1999; Secret History: Best of Divine Comedy, 1999.

JACOBS, Judith (Judy) Kaye, BA; American singer; b. 27 Sept. 1957, Lumberton, North Carolina; m. James Eric Tuttle 1993; two c. *Education:* Lee Coll. *Career:* recording artist for New Vision Records; performed with Larnelle Harris, Carmen, Brooklyn Tabernacle Choir, Four Him. *Recordings include:* For Times Like These 1993, Once and For All 1995. *Honours:* Distinguished Music Performer as special guest with Brooklyn Tabernacle Choir. *Current Management:* c/o Jamie Tuttle, His Song Ministries Inc, 519 Urbane Road NE, Cleveland, TN 37312, USA. *Telephone:* (423) 559-0173. *Fax:* (423) 559-8599. *Website:* www.judyjacobs.com.

JACOBS, Laurie, BSc, LFHom, MBChB; British jazz promoter and musician (saxophone); b. 16 April 1950, London; m. Ann Cummings 1974; three s. *Education:* Univ. of Edinburgh, studied music with Leslie Evans. *Career:* founded Peterborough Jazz Club 1992; monthly presentations, best in British and American jazz; as musician played Dean Street, Pizza Express, Pizza-On-The-Park; appeared at Soho Jazz Festival; mem. Musicians' Union. *Recordings:* Midnight Voyage with John Turville (piano), Oli Hayhurst (double bass), Vincent Rusquet (drums). *Honours:* Peterborough City Leisure Award for Jazz Club 1996. *Address:* 38 Church Street, Werrington, Peterborough, Cambridgeshire PE4 6QE, England (home). *E-mail:* lauriejacobs_pjc@hotmail.com (home).

JACOBSEN, Bo; Danish musician (drums, alto saxophone), singer and consultant; b. 13 March 1945, Copenhagen; one s. one d. *Education:* studied architecture. *Career:* mem. Blue Sun 1969–75; Osiris (with Lone Kellermann), Nada 1977–83, Paul Ehlers Quartet 1985–88, Crescent 1988–89, Dream City 1991–98; numerous festival appearances, tours; started teaching in music schools 1996; played with Flower Pot Party at concerts and festivals across Denmark 1996–98; Founder-mem. Bo Jacobsen World Jazz Orchestra 1999; mem. of blues soul band, Soulshape 2002; mem. of orchestra, Dancing Moon 2002; Founder Beejaymusic man. co. and record label 2002; cultural consultant 2005–; formed new free jazz band Spirit 2010; mem. Danish Musicians' Union (Chair. 1998), DJFBA, KODA, Gramex, NCB. *Recordings include:* albums: with Blue Sun: Peace Be Unto You 1970, Festival 1970, Blue Sun 1971, Blue Sun 73 1973; with Povl Dissing: Mor Danmark and Niels Skousen: HRD 1976; with Nada: Nada 1 1978, Nada 2 1979, African Flower 1982; with Dream City: Do The Blues 1993, with Dream City: Syre 1996; with Bo Jacobsen's World Jazz Conspiracy: Thank You For Your Tips 2001; with Spirit: Spirit 2011, Free Spirit (Special Award for Most Hon. New Release 2013, NYC Jazz Record Magazine) 2013; solo: Sagarmatha Suite 1994–97. *Honours:* Cultural Prize, Norddjurs region 2006, 2008. *Address:* Emmelevkærvej 3, 8500 Grenaa, Denmark (office). *Telephone:* 22-41-77-01 (office). *E-mail:* beejaymusic@norddjursnet.dk (office); nytliv@norddjursnet.dk (office).

JACOBSEN, Sonia Michelle, BMus; Australian composer and musician; b. 5 Feb. 1967, Camden. *Education:* The New School, USA, Grenoble and Lyon Univs, France, Chambery Conservatory, France. *Career:* co-leader, composer, conductor, Mosaic Orchestra; composer, Musical Dir, No Strings Attached; leader, Melting Pot; mem. American Music Center. *Composition:* Tryzone Suite Melting Pot. *Recordings include:* Avalanche 1995, No Strings Attached 1997. *Address:* Sun Sounds, 210 Frick Court, Chapin, SC 29036-8362, USA (office); 183 Harbor Road, Colo Spring, Harbor, NY 11724, USA (home).

JACOBSSON, R(uth) Ewa M(aria); Swedish composer, visual artist and singer; *Composer and Visual Artist Freelance, Norwegian Society of Composers and Norwegian Association of Visual Artists;* b. 8 Dec. 1956, Uppsala; two s. *Education:* studied painting at Konstfack School of Arts and Handicraft, Stockholm, Royal Acad. of Fine Arts, Copenhagen, Denmark, studied classical piano with Kerstin Åberg in Uppsala and classical singing and theatre training in Sweden and Denmark. *Career:* Emerald Song (performance and exhbn), Skeppsholmskyrkan, Stockholm, Sweden 1985; Found Language (dance performance, sound and projected photos) in collaboration with choreographer Jody Oberfelder, BACA Downtown, New York, USA 1987; Die Menschmaschine (theatre and dance performance, sound, live sound and vocal), in collaboration with composer Morten Carlsen and theatre group Exment, Copenhagen 1988; Voix (concert), Malmö Art Museum 1989; Lingua (concert, performance), State Art Museum of Copenhagen 1993; Guldbukar (concert, sound and projected photos), Den Anden Opera, Copenhagen 1994; Interferens (sound composition) 1997, The Danish Radio; Ways of Red (concert, performance), Budapest Art Museum, Hungary 1998; Xfelt (sound installation and exhibition), Museum of Contemporary Art, Roskilde, Denmark 1998; Contemporary Lies I–IV (sound installation and exhbn) 1998–2004, De Overslag, Eindhoven, Netherlands; Combination of Truth (performance), Den Anden Opera, Copenhagen 2001; To Confirm a Real Room (performance), Nove Zamky, Slovakia 2002; Le Bonheur (sound installation and exhbn), Norwegian Museum for Watercraft, Odda, Norway 2007; A Liar's Map (sound installation and exhbn), Henie Onstad Art Centre, Norway 2008; The Happy Happy Leaves (sound and projected photos), Bergen Art Museum, Norway 2010; Teknikens Voodoo (live radio performance), Norwegian Asscn of New Music, Oslo 2010; comms from Norwegian Asscn of Composers. *Compositions:* Voix (tape, vocal, poem) 1989, Détour (solo performance, vocal, tape, 8mm film, poem) 1990, Delta for choir (words by Martin Sondergaard) 1991–92, Lingua (solo performance, tape, vocal, poem, photographic move-

ment) 1993, Guldbukar (tape, colour-slides) 1994, Anonymous (solo performance, vocal, tape, photo and objects) 1996, LOGR (solo performance, vocal, tape, objects, waterfountain Gefjon) 1996, Kongehoved (choir, tape, photo, words by Jens Bjorneboe) 1996, Cold Dews (tape, poem) 1996, No Title (installation with tape, poem, objects, twin pictures) 1998, Ways of Red (solo performance, vocal, tape, objects) 1998, Contemporary Lies I–IV (four installations with tape, text and objects) 1998–2004, Cimelice (installation with soundtape, objects, drawings, text) 2000, Combinations of Truth (solo performance with vocals, tape, poem, objects) 2001, To Confirm a Real Room (solo performance with vocals, tape, poem, objects, interaction with audience) 2002; Le Bonheur (sound installation with 2 sound pieces, objects, fragments of drawings, photo) 2007; A Liar's Map (sound installation with 4 sound pieces, objects, drawings, preparation of space) 2008; The Happy Happy Leaves (installation with seven songs for sound, vocal, projected photos and three sound objects) 2010, Jarring Sounds (for piano, sound composition, objects and projected photos) 2010–11. *Dance:* collaboration with Jody Oberfelder, New York City, theatre and dance group EXMENT, Copenhagen/Århus, Denmark. *Films:* Chrystal Pigs etc. (six 8mm films with sound composition transferred to DVD), Danish Film Workshop, Void (DVD installation for four screens). *Address:* Boegata 10, 0655 Oslo, Norway (office). *E-mail:* sopranotronic@hotmail.com (office). *Website:* www.komponist.no/medlemmer/131-jacobsson (office).

JACQUEMIN, André; British composer, sound designer, producer, musician (bass player) and music programmer; b. 16 Jan. 1952, Hampstead, London; m. 1988; one d. *Education:* APRS engineering course. *Career:* joined recording industry aged 17 as studio runner and started engineering after nine months to present date; record producer for Monty Python and produced every Python project from 1972; live performances; Co-owner, Redwood Studios 1975–; mem. Re-Pro Producers' Guild of Great Britain. *Compositions include:* cowriter: Every Sperm Is Sacred (Monty Python's Meaning of Life); The Brian Song (Monty Python's Life of Brian); six songs for Wind In The Willows, feature film; six songs for Mumbo Jumbo, feature film; score for The Big Freeze, Eric Sykes feature film; score for The Hound of the Baskervilles, feature film; A Christmas Adventure; Love Potion No. 9; Ezekiel; Rubbish King of the Jumble, network cartoon series; One Foot in the Grave; Plus many commercials and incidental music compositions. *Publications include:* Contrib. to Future Music, Sound On Sound, Home Studio Recording, Pro Sound News, Sound Engineer and Producer, Sound Int., Radio Month, Professional, Int. Musician. *Honours:* over 80 awards for sound productions in film and TV. *Address:* Redwood Studios, 20 Great Chapel Street, Westminster, London, W1F 8FW, England (office). *Telephone:* (20) 7287-3799 (office). *E-mail:* Andre@redwoodstudios.co.uk (office); andrestudios@yahoo.co.uk (office). *Website:* www.redwoodstudios.co.uk (office).

JAFET, Jean Marc; French musician (bass); b. 8 May 1956, Nice. *Education:* Conservatoire de Musique de Nice. *Career:* played with: Didier Lockwood, Toots Thielmans, Christian Escoude, Christian Vander (Magma), Trio Ceccarelli, Richard Galliano; own band Agora; mem. SACEM. *Recordings include:* Three albums with Trio Ceccarelli; three albums with Kalil Chahine, Brazilian Witch, Christian Escoude; solo: Agora 1996, Dolores 1999, Douceur Lunaire 2000, Mes Anges 2006, Live au Parc Floral. *Publications include:* Dolores, Hat's Snatcher, L'Arcange. *Honours:* For Hat's Snatchers, Trio Ceccarelli, Victoires Music 1994. *Address:* c/o Alexandre Lacombe, Just Looking Productions, 9, Rue de Capri, 75012 Paris, France. *E-mail:* alex@justlookingproductions.com; justalex@noos.fr. *Website:* www.justlookingproductions.com; alexandre.lacombe.free.fr.

JAFFE, Jerry, PhD; American artist manager; b. 12 Sept. 1946, New York, NY; m. Celeste Kringer 1983. *Education:* Columbia Univ., New York. *Career:* Man. for Joey McIntyre, Ann Marie Montade, Jesus and Mary Chain, Catherine, Course of Empire, Nancy Boy, Saint Etienne; Co-Man. (with Chris Morrison) for Dead Or Alive, Midge Ure, John Moore; US Head, Creation Records 1992–94; fmr Sr Vice-Pres. (Rock Div.) and Vice-Pres. Promotion and A&R, Polygram Records, USA; also in promotion, press and artist development, Management by Jaffe. *Address:* Management by Jaffe, 68 Ridgewood Avenue, Glen Ridge, NJ 07028, USA (office). *Telephone:* (917) 859-6836 (office). *E-mail:* jerjaff@aol.com (office).

JAGGER, Sir Michael (Mick) Philip, Kt, KBE; British singer, songwriter and actor; b. 26 July 1943, Dartford, Kent; s. of the late Joe Jagger and Eva Jagger; m. 1st Bianca Pérez Morena de Macías 1971 (divorced 1979); one d.; m. 2nd Jerry Hall 1990 (divorced 1999); two s. two d.; one d. by Marsha Hunt; one c. by Luciana Morad. *Education:* London School of Econs, Univ. of London. *Career:* began singing career with Little Boy Blue and the Blue Boys while at LSE; appeared in Blues Inc. at Ealing Blues Club, singer with Blues Inc. at London Marquee Club 1962; Founder-mem. and lead singer, Rolling Stones 1962–; wrote songs with Keith Richards under pseudonyms Nanker, Phelge until 1965, without pseudonyms 1965–; first own composition to reach No. 1 in UK charts The Last Time 1965; first major UK tour 1964; tours to USA, Europe; fmrly lived in France; solo career 1970–; mem., SuperHeavy supergroup 2009; Pres. LSE Students' Union 1994–. *Films:* Ned Kelly (actor) 1969, Performance (actor) 1969, Gimme Shelter (actor) 1972, Free Jack (actor) 1991, Freejack (actor) 1992, Bent (actor) 1996, Enigma (producer) 2001, Shine a Light 2007. *Recordings include:* albums: with The Rolling Stones: The Rolling Stones 1964, The Rolling Stones No. 2 1965, Out Of Our Heads 1965, Aftermath 1966, Between The Buttons 1967, Their Satanic Majesties Request 1967, Beggar's Banquet 1968, Let It Bleed 1969, Get Yer Ya-Ya's Out 1969,

Sticky Fingers 1971, Exile On Main Street 1972, Goat's Head Soup 1973, It's Only Rock And Roll 1974, Black And Blue 1976, Some Girls 1978, Emotional Rescue 1980, Tattoo You 1981, Still Life 1982, Undercover 1983, Dirty Work 1986, Steel Wheels 1989, Flashpoint 1991, Voodoo Lounge 1994, Stripped 1995, Bridges to Babylon 1997, Forty Licks 2002, Live Licks 2004, A Bigger Bang 2005; solo: She's The Boss 1985, Primitive Cool 1987, Wandering Spirit 1993, Goddess In The Doorway 2001, The Very Best of 2007; with SuperHeavy: SuperHeavy 2009. *Publication:* According to the Rolling Stones (autobiog., jtly) 2003. *Honours:* Nordoff-Robbins Silver Clef 1982, Grammy Lifetime Achievement Award 1986, Ivor Novello Award for Outstanding Contribution to British Music 1991, Golden Globe Award for Best Original Song (for Old Habits Die Hard, with Dave Stewart, for film Alfie) 2005. *Telephone:* (20) 8877-3100. *Fax:* (20) 8877-3077. *Website:* www.mickjagger .com.

JAGO, Nicholas (Nick); British musician (drums); b. 1976, Devon, England. *Career:* mem. Black Rebel Motorcycle Club 1998–2008. *Recordings include:* albums: B.R.M.C. 2001, Take Them On Your Own 2003, Howl 2005, Baby 81 2007. *Compositions include:* Playlist: Alternative 2008, Easy Come Easy Go 2008, The Twilight Saga: New Moon 2009, Alternative: 120 Original Hits 2009, 101 Indie Classics 2009, Epic Vol. 2 2011, Flaamingos 2013.

JAKATTA (see Lee, Dave)

JAL, Emmanuel; Sudanese singer, songwriter and rap artist; b. 1980, Tong; adopted s. of the late Emma McCune. *Career:* fmrly in military training camps in Ethiopia, then child soldier in Sudanese civil war; adopted and taken to Kenya by aid worker; rap artist in English, Arabic, Swahili, Dinka and his first language, Nuer; performed at Live 8: Africa Calling concert, Cornwall 2005, Greenbelt Festival, UK 2006; f. Gua Africa foundation; contributed to charity album, Help: A Day In The Life; spokesperson, Campaign to Stop the Use of Child Soldiers. *Recordings include:* album: Ceasefire (with Abdel Gadir Salim) 2005, War Child 2008, See Me Mama 2012. *Film appearances include:* War Child 2008, Africa United 2010. *Publication:* War Child: A Child Soldier's Story (memoirs) 2009. *E-mail:* mngmnt@emmanueljal.org; mngmnt@ emmanueljal.com. *Website:* www.emmanueljal.org.

JAM, Jimmy; American producer, composer and musician (keyboards); b. (James Harris III), 6 June 1959, Minneapolis, Minn. *Career:* founder mem., Flyte Tyme (with Terry Lewis) 1972, renamed Time 1981–83; Co-founder, Flyte Time Productions Inc. 1982–, built Flyte Tyme Studios, Minneapolis 1984–; Co-founder, Third Eye Imagery Inc. 1987–, the parent co. of Perspective Records 1989–, and Flyte Tyme Records 1997–; Co-founder, Flyte Tyme Tunes to publish songs written by the duo 1984–, Help The Bear Music Inc. (1989–) to publish songs written by BMI writers signed with them, New Perspective Publishing Inc. (1990–) to publish songs written by ASCAP writers signed with them, and Minneapolis Guys Music Inc. (1997–) to publish songs written by ASCAP writer James 'Big Jim' Wright and signed to them; Co-founder, Lewis & Harris Partnership real estate co. 1985–; involved with Int. Asscn of African American Music (IAAAM) 1990–; producer for artists, including Klymaxx, SOS Band, Patti Austin, Cheryl Lynn, Cherrelle, Janet Jackson, Mint Condition, Low Key, George Michael, Karyn White, Boyz II Men, Johnny Gill, Fine Young Cannibals, New Edition, Mariah Carey, Shaggy, Yolanda Adams, Chante Moore, Mary J. Blige, The Human League, The Isley Brothers. *Honours:* Grammy Award for Producer of the Year 1986, American Soc. of Composers and Publishers R&B Songwriting Awards 1989–94. *Website:* www.flytetyme.com.

JAMAL, Ahmad; American composer and pianist; b. 2 July 1930, Pittsburgh, Pa; (divorced); one d. *Education:* pvt. master-classes with Mary Cardwell Dawson and James Miller. *Career:* George Hudson Orchestra nat. tour 1949; mem. The Four Strings 1949; accompanist to The Caldwells 1950; trio The Three Strings 1950–; numerous concert tours, including with Philip Morris; exclusive Steinway artist 1960s–; appeared on film soundtracks of M*A*S*H 1970, Bridges of Madison County 1995; Duke Ellington Fellow, Yale Univ. *Television:* The Sound of Jazz 1962. *Compositions include:* six works for Asai Quartet 1994, New Rhumba, Ahmad's Blues, Night Mist Blues, Extensions, The Awakening, Excerpts From The Blues, Tranquility, Manhattan Reflections. *Recordings include:* Poinciana, But Not For Me (including Bridges of Madison County) 1995, Essence Part 1 (Django D'Or Award, Paris) 1996, Olympia 2000, Live in Baalbeck (DVD) 2003, After Fajr 2005, It's Magic 2008, A Quiet Time 2010, Blue Moon: The New York Session/The Paris Concert 2012, Saturday Morning 2013. *Honours:* Officier, Ordre des Arts et des Lettres 2007; NEA American Jazz Master, Pittsburgh Mellon Jazz Festival dedication 1994. *Current Management:* c/o Ellora Management, PO Box 755, 11 Brook Street, Lakeville, CT 06039, USA. *Telephone:* (860) 435-1305. *Fax:* (860) 435-9916. *E-mail:* elloramanagement@aol.com. *E-mail:* elloradesigns@aol.com. *Website:* www.ahmadjamal.net.

JAMELIA; British singer; b. (Jamelia Niela Davis), 11 Jan. 1981, Hands-worth, Birmingham, England; two c. *Television:* Loose Women (ITV) 2013–. *Recordings include:* albums: Drama 2000, Thank You (Urban Music Award for Best R&B Act 2005) 2003, Walk With Me 2006, Greatest Hits 2007. *Honours:* MOBO Award 2000, 2004, Q Award for Best Single (for See It In a Boy's Eyes) 2004, Urban Music Award for Best R & B Act 2005, 2007, Eska Award for Best Foreign Singer 2007. *Current Management:* c/o Roar Global, Roar House, 46 Charlotte Street, London, W1T 2GS, England. *Telephone:* (20) 7462-9060. *Website:* www.jamelia.com.

JAMES, (Stephen) Alexander (Alex); British musician (bass guitar); b. 21 Nov. 1968, Boscombe, Bournemouth, Dorset, England; s. of Jason James; m.; four s. *Education:* Goldsmiths Coll., London. *Career:* mem. Blur; extensive tours, festival appearances; Founder-mem. WigWam 2006–; has also played with temporary bands, Fat Les, Me Me Me, and Bad Lieutenant. *Radio:* a regular presenter of On Your Farm (BBC Radio 4). *Television:* represented The Idler on University Challenge: the Professionals (BBC 2) 2005, judge on show Mobile Acts Unsigned (Channel 4) 2007, panellist on Have I Got News for You (satirical news quiz, BBC 1) 2007, contestant in reality TV series, Maestro (BBC 2) 2008, Cocaine Diaries: Alex James in Colombia (documen-tary series premiered on BBC America in conjunction with BBC America Reveals programme) 2008, presented episode of Never Mind the Buzzcocks (BBC 2) 2009, participated in reality TV programme Popstar to Operastar (ITV 1) 2010, guest on Top Gear (BBC 1) 2012. *Recordings include:* albums: with Blur: Leisure 1991, Modern Life Is Rubbish 1993, Parklife (Best Album, Q Awards 1994, Best Album, Best Single, Best British Video, BRIT Awards 1995, Best Album, NME Awards 1995) 1994, The Great Escape (Best Album, Q Awards 1995) 1995, Blur 1997, 13 1999, The Best Of Blur 2000, Think Tank (Best Album, Q Awards 2003, Best Album, South Bank Show Awards 2003) 2003, Midlife 2009, The Magic Whip 2015; solo: Hanging Around, Me Me Me 1996, Vindaloo, Fat Les 1998, Naughty Christmas, Fat Les 1998, Jerusalem, Fat Les 2000. *Publication:* Bit of a Blur (autobiog.) 2007. *Honours:* Dr hc (Bournemouth) 2010; with Blur: BRIT Awards for Best Single, Best Video, Best Album, Best Band 1995, for Outstanding Contrib. to Music 2012, Best Alternative Band, Smash Hits Awards 1994, Best Band and Best Live Act, NME Awards 1995, Best Act in the World Today, Q Awards 1999, Best Band, Best Single (Tender), NME Awards 2000, NME Award for Best Live Event (Blur at Hyde Park) 2010. *Website:* www.blur.co.uk.

JAMES, Duncan Mathew; British singer; b. 7 April 1979, Salisbury, Wiltshire. *Career:* mem. band, Blue 2001–05; solo artist 2006–. *Plays include:* Chicago, London 2007, Legally Blonde The Musical, London 2010. *Recordings include:* albums: with Blue: All Rise 2001, One Love 2002, Guilty 2004; solo: Speed of Life 2003, Future Past 2006. *Honours:* Smash Hits Awards for Best Newcomer 2001, Best Live Act, Best UK Band 2002, Interactive Music Award for Artist of the Year 2002, BRIT Award for Best British Newcomer 2002, NRJ Music Award for Best Int. Group (France) 2005. *Current Management:* Merlin Elite Ltd, 36 Golden Square, London, W1F 9EE, England. *Telephone:* (20) 7259-1460. *E-mail:* info@merlinelite.co.uk. *Website:* www.merlinelite.co.uk.

JAMES, Jim; American singer, songwriter and musician (guitar). *Career:* founder mem., My Morning Jacket 1998–, Monsters of Folk 2004–. *Recordings include:* albums: with My Morning Jacket: The Tennessee Fire 1999, At Dawn 2001, It Still Moves 2003, Early Recordings Chapter 1: The Sandworm Cometh 2004, Early Recordings Chapter 2: Learning 2004, Z 2005, Okronokos 2006, Evil Urges 2008, Circuital 2011; with Monsters of Folk: Monsters of Folk 2009. *Address:* c/o RCA Records, 1540 Broadway, New York, NY 10036, USA (office). *E-mail:* jimjames@mymorningjacket.com (office); info@monstersoffolk .com (office). *Website:* www.mymorningjacket.com; monstersoffolk.com.

JAMES, Jynine; British singer, songwriter and actor; b. 30 March 1969, Wrexham, Clwyd, Wales; m. Tim Sanders. *Education:* Brigidine Convent, N Wales, Llandrillo Coll., LAMDA. *Career:* fmr photographic model; mem. Rhyl Operatics; mem. PAMRA, PRS. *Film appearances include:* Charlie and Chocolate Factory 2005, Vinyl 2013. *Recordings include:* albums: No Reason 1993, When I Dream 1993, Past Shadows 1999, Tonight (Alone At Christmas Time) 2001. *Current Management:* Edward Wyman Film Agency, 23 White Acre Close, Thornhill, Cardiff CF14 9DG, Wales. *Telephone:* (29) 2075-2351. *Fax:* (29) 2075-2444. *E-mail:* edward.wyman@btconnect.com; abergele@ hotmail.com; wymancasting@yahoo.co.uk. *Website:* www.wymancasting.co .uk.

JAMES, (Walter) Kevin Earl; American country singer and songwriter; b. 19 Aug. 1967, Greenville, Tex. *Education:* Texas A & M Univ. *Career:* mem. BMI, Press Club of Dallas, IFCO. *Compositions include:* Late to Breakfast, Generation Tex, First Sight Second Look, Jealous, Don't Answer That. *Recordings include:* albums: Wrapped in Hope, Generations; single: True Americans. *Address:* 2402 Beverly Drive, Greenville, TX 75402, USA.

JAMES, Mo; singer, musician (piano), radio producer and presenter; b. 16 March 1951, Darlington, England; m. Mike Jowett 1983; one s. one d. *Education:* Northumbria Studio of Music. *Career:* lead singer, White Knight 1968–70; solo artist; numerous concert appearances, tv appearances; leader, Mo James Soul Band 1984–90; solo artist 1990–; producer, presenter, regular talk shows on BBC Radio (N); mem. Musicians' Union, Asscn of Christians in Local Broadcasting. *Recordings include:* album: More Love (with Joe English) 1982. *Publications include:* music reviewer for Crossrhythms magazine.

JAMES, Richard David, (AFX, Aphex Twin, Caustic Window, Polygon Window, Powerpill); producer, remixer and DJ; b. 18 Aug. 1971, Ireland. *Career:* started producing tracks on custom-made equipment; solo artist, releasing under pseudonyms, including AFX, the Aphex Twin, Caustic Window, Polygon Window and Powerpill; collaborations with Mike Paradinas, Luke Vibert, LFO; remixed Baby Ford, Saint Etienne, Beck, Wagon Christ; owner, Rephlex label. *Recordings include:* albums: Selected Ambient Works 85–92 1993, Surfing On Sine Waves (as Polygon Window) 1993, Selected Ambient Works II 1994, I Care Because You Do 1995, Richard D. James LP 1996, Drukqs 2001, 26 Mixes For Cash 2003, Analord (series of EPs as AFX) 2005, Chosen Lords (as AFX) 2006, Caustic Window (as Caustic Window)

2014, Syro (Grammy Award for Best Dance/Electronic Album 2015) 2014. *Current Management:* c/o Tom Windish, The Windish Agency, 1658 North Milwaukee Avenue, #211, Chicago, IL 60647, USA.

JAMES, Sian, BMus; British folk singer, composer and musician (harp); b. 24 Dec. 1961, Wales; partner, Gwyn Jones; three s. *Education:* Caereinion High School, Bangor Univ. *Career:* various tours around folk festivals in Brittany, Galicia, Spain, Italy, USA, Canada, Japan, Ireland, Wales, England, Scotland 1980–; various theatre and TV productions; radio plays for BBC Radio Cymru; harp teacher; choir conductor, Parti Cut Lloi; mem. Equity, PRS, MCPS, PPL. *Television appearances include:* leading roles in dramas and films for S4C: Pengelli, Iechyd Da, Tylluan Wen (White Owl) 1999, own series on S4C. *Recordings include:* Cysgodion Karma (Shadows of Karma) 1990, Distaw (Silent) 1993, Gweini Tymor (Serving a Season) 1996, Di-Gwsg (Sleepless) 1997, Birdman, Pur (Pure) 2000, Y Ferch o Bedlam (The Girl from Bedlam) 2005, Henffych Well (Hail, choral folk album) 2005, Llythyrau Ellis Williams 2006, Hwiangerddi/Welsh Nursery rhymes 2007, Cymun (Communion) 2012. *Publication:* The Sky Over Wales (autobiography) 1998. *Honours:* Hon. Fellowship, Univ. of Wales (for contribs to music); Best Female Vocalist, Gwobrau Rap Awards, Radio Cymru 2000, Just Plain Folks Music Award for Best Celtic Song. *Current Management:* c/o BOS Records, PO Box 56, Welshpool, Powys, SY21 0WP, Wales. *Telephone:* (1938) 820359. *E-mail:* sian@sianjames.co.uk. *Website:* www.sianjames.co.uk.

JAMES, Sonny; American country musician (guitar, fiddle); b. (James Loden), 1 May 1929, Hackleburg, Ala. *Film appearances:* Second Fiddle to an Old Guitar, Nashville Rebel, Las Vegas Hillbillies, Hillbilly in a Haunted House. *Recordings include:* albums: Young Love 1962, Only the Lonely 1969, Empty Arms 1971, American Originals 1989, Young Love: The Classic Hits 1997, Sonny 1957 2000. *Website:* www.sonnyjames.com.

JAMES, Stafford Louis; American musician (double bass, piano) and composer; b. 24 April 1946, Evanston, Ill.; m. Claudine Decouttère 1992; one d. *Education:* Loop Coll., Chicago, Chicago Conservatory Coll., Mannes Coll. of Music, New York. *Career:* mem. Ukrainian Nat. Orchestra, Limberg 1991; Int. Congress of Viola D'amore, Europansches Musik Festival, Stuttgart 1988; WDR Radio, Köln, Germany 1989, 1992, 1994–97, 2001–02, Deutschland Radio, Berlin 2004; European tours with Stafford James Project (trio), Stafford James Special Project (quartet), Stafford James String Project 2006; Rossini Sketches; tours: Netherlands, France, Luxembourg, Germany, Italy, Austria, Spain, Switzerland, Belgium, India, Syria, Sudan, Egypt, Morocco 1984, Argentina, Peru, Chile, Uruguay, Mexico 1986; played with Art Blakey and The Jazz Messengers, Betty Carter, Jimmy Heath, Pharoah Sanders, Woody Shaw, Dexter Gordon, Joe Williams, Mingus Dynasty, Randy Weston, The Gounawas (from Morocco); teacher, double bass, UN Int. School, New York for five years, New School of Social Research, New York for two years, privately in Paris, France; mem. SACEM, BIMC; Thomastik-Infeld Sponsoree 2000. *Radio:* WDR Radio Cologne, Germany, Deutschland Radio Berlin, Radio France. *Television:* The Days and Nights of Molly Dodd 1987. *Compositions:* more than 150 pieces (many written for double bass as lead melodic voice), including Les Pyrénées à la Mer, Sonatina (duet for viola d'Amore/contrabass), That's What Dreams Are Made Of, Ethiopia Suite, Bertha Baptist, Game, Teotiuacan, Sashianova, Nighthawk, Blues in The Pockets, Des Alpes aux Carpates, Conspectus, Le Gecko, Au Cap Bénat, Changing World, Muguet, Rejuvenation, Sixth Sense, Kaleidoscope, Horizon, Us Together, Conscience, Mujiza, Meissa, Morning Dew, Metamorphosis, Bouncybernaughty, Rossini Sketches, Solériana, Tableau Madrilène. *Recordings:* albums: Stafford James Ensemble 1978; numerous other credits including: Music Is The Healing Force of The Universe, Albert Ayler 1969, Night of the Purple Moon, Sun Ra 1970, Juju Street Songs, Gary Bartz 1972, Homecoming, Dexter Gordon 1976, Welcome to Love, Pharoah Sanders 1991, Finest, Pharoah Sanders 2007; with Woody Shaw: Little Red's Fantasy Muse 1975, Rosewood 1977, For Sure! 1980, Night Music 1980, United 1981, Lotus Flower 1982, Time is Right 1983, Two More Pieces of the Puzzle 1998. *Honours:* grants from NEA, NYSCA, Gold Medal, Music, Karlstad, Sweden, Civitella Ranieri Foundation Fellowship 1998. *Current Management:* Communication United, Breitscheidstr. 131A 70176 Stuttgart, Germany. *Telephone:* (711) 633018-0. *Fax:* (711) 633018-18. *E-mail:* hb@cu-events.com. *Address:* 6 Quai des Célestins, 75004 Paris, France (home). *E-mail:* sjstaffordjamesmusic08@gmail.com (home). *Website:* www.staffordjames.com.

JAMES, Steve; British record producer; b. 19 Feb. 1954, London; three s. one d. *Career:* record producer and engineer, various projects, several years; early production work includes albums with Toyah; later credits include soundtrack The Rutles, Monty Python's The Life of Brian, featuring the single Always Look On The Bright Side of Life; worked with Angel City, Mental As Anything, The Screaming Jets in Australia 1988–93; returned to UK, worked with: Paul Young, Kiki Dee, Peter Skellern, Way of Thorns; mem. Producers' Guild. *Recordings include:* numerous as producer, co-producer, engineer including: albums: with Toyah: Sheep Farming In Barnet 1979, Toyah Toyah Toyah 1982; with Peter Skellern: Astaire 1980, The Continental 1981, Stardust Memories 1994; with Neil Innes: Off The Record 1981; with Ginger Baker: Nutters 1983; with Mental As Anything: Cyclone Raymonde 1989; with The Screaming Jets: All For One 1990, Tear of Thought 1991; with The Angels: Redback Fever 1992; with Kiki Dee: Best of Kiki Dee 1994; with Paul Young: Acoustic tracks 1994, Live tracks 1995; two tracks, animated version of Wind In The Willows, Kirsty MacColl and Tim Finn 1995; singles include: In The City, The Jam 1979, Something Else, The Sex Pistols 1979, Rock and Roll

Music, Mental As Anything 1988; other recordings with: Shirley Bassey 1976, Thin Lizzy 1977, Pat Travers 1977, Golden Earring 1978, Ryan Douglas 1993, Way of Thorns 1995, The Rutles (LP) 1996, The Teletubbies (LP) 1997, Oblivia and Cold Chisel 1998, Weta and H-Block 2000.

JAMIESON, Peter; British music executive; m. Jane Jamieson; three c. *Career:* fmr management trainee, EMI; fmr Man. Dir EMI Greece; fmr sr exec. EMI and BMG; worked extensively in Europe, Australasia and Far East; helped establish BMG Asia Pacific and MTV Asia; Founding Pres. MTV Asia 1995–97; Exec. Chair. British Phonographic Industry (BPI) 2002–07. *Address:* c/o British Phonographic Industry, Riverside Building, County Hall, Westminster Bridge Road, London, SE1 7JA, England.

JAMMER; British producer. *Career:* Owner, independent record label, Jahmek the World, with emerging 'grime' music genre; fmr mem. N.A.S.T.Y. (Natural Artistic Sound Touching You) Crew –2004. *Current Management:* c/o Xtreme Talent, PO Box 1034, Morden, Surrey, SM4 6QX, England. *Telephone:* (844) 873-1988. *E-mail:* info@xtremetalent.co.uk. *Website:* www.xtremetalent.co.uk.

JÁN, Hajnal, BMus; Slovak musician (piano, double bass, organ); b. 11 Dec. 1943, Košice; m. Maria Hajnalova, 14 Dec. 1968, one d. *Education:* Elementary Music School, Košice Conservatory, private music lessons. *Career:* f. Ján Hajnal Trio 1963–; performed with The Jazz Quartet, Košice Conservatory 1964–66; leader, military band 1967–69; mem. Tatra Singers 1973–79, Slovak Jazz Quintet 1977–83, Czechoslovak Radio Dance Orchestra 1980–83, Pavol Kozma's Esprit 1985–92, Jozef Šošoka's All Stars Trio 1993–, Tatra Quintet 2003–04, Classical and Jazz Art Duo (with Miloš Jurkovič) 2005; solo pianist 1983–; pianist and arranger, Slovak TV orchestra 1985–87; composer, Radio Bratislava Big Band 1990–94; participant of jazz festivals in Europe; piano performances in America, Asia, Europe; mem. Slovak Jazz Soc., Slovak Music Fond. *Compositions include:* Monk's Tatran Dream 1994, Mosebacke, Early Morning, Geneiro, Home made Blues, many others. *Recordings include:* Bratislava Jazz Days 1979, Slovak Jazz Mainstream 1994, Monk's Tatran Dream 1999, Pianoman 2002, Live in Prague 2003. *Honours:* winner, Czechoslovak Amateur Jazz Festival, Přerov 1967, First Prize, Slovak Music Competition for Composition (for Monk Tatran Dream) 1996.

JANDA, Dalibor; Czech singer, songwriter and musician; b. 21 March 1953, Hranice Na Morave; m. Jirina Jandova 1981; one s. one d. *Career:* singer in various rock bands 1969–79; professional singer 1981–. *Recordings include:* Hurricane 1985, Mc Kde Jsi 1987, Jen Ty Samotna A Ja 1989, Povidant Spisnickami 1990, Cose Ma'stat 1992, Zlaty Vyber 1994, Vlasce Nejsou Maty 1995, Krasne Silena 1996, 18 hitú o lásce 1998, Ty jsi můj benzin 2000, Hurikán koktejl 2001, Roky jako motýli 2003, Jeden den 2006, Páté poschodi 2007, Já se Priznám 2011. *Honours:* Decin Pop Festival Gold Award 1985, Gold Nightingale 1986, 1987, 1988. *Address:* c/o Hurricane Records, Kamenicka 39/303, 170 00 Prague 7, Czech Republic. *Telephone:* 604474435. *E-mail:* hurikan.rec@quick.cz. *Website:* www.daliborjanda.cz.

JANDA, Petr; Czech composer, musician (guitar) and singer; b. 2 May 1942, Prague; m. 1st Jana 1966; m. 2nd Martina 1992; one s. two d. *Education:* Conservatory Jaroslava Jezka, Prague, Conservatory Jaroslava, Jezka, Prague. *Career:* leader rock group, Olympic 1964–; mem. OSA. *Recordings include:* albums: with Olympic: Zelva 1968, Ptak Rosom'k 1969, Jedeme Jedeme 1971, Handful 1972, Olympic 4 1973, 12 nej 1976, Marathón 1978, Overhead 1978, Prazdniny Na Zemi 1980, Holidays on Earth 1980, Ulice 1981, Rokenrol 1982, Olympic v. Lucerně 1983, Akorát 1983, Laborator 1984, Kanagom 1985, Hidden in your Mind 1986, Bigbit 1986, 25 let 1987, Když ti sviti zelená 1988, O jé 1990, Jako za mlada 1992, Balady 1994, Dávno 1994, Vlak, co nikde nestavi 1995, Petr Hejduk 1995, Singly I-VII 1996–99, Brejle 1997, Ondráš podotýká 1997, Karavana 1999, Dám si te klonovat 2003, Stejskáni 2004: solo: Sólovka, Jednou Jo, Jednou Né 2008. *Honours:* Grammy Award 1993. *Current Management:* Bestia, Poupětova 3, 170 00 Prague 7, Czech Republic. *Telephone:* 220806802. *E-mail:* dagmara@bestia.cz. *Website:* www.bestia.cz/olympic.

JANIS, Conrad; American jazz musician (trombone), actor and film director; b. 11 Feb. 1928, New York; m. Maria Grimm 1987. *Career:* bandleader, Beverly Hills Unlisted Jazz Band, Tailgate Jazz Band; worked with Roy Eldridge, Henry Red Allen, Wild Bill Davison, Yank Lawson, Claude Hopkins, Coleman Hawkins, Panama Francis, Hot Lips Page, Herbie Hancock, Jimmy McPartland. *Films include:* Snafu 1945, Margie 1946, The Brasher Doubloon 1947, That Hagen Girl 1947, Beyond Glory 1948, Let's Rock 1958, Airport 1975 1974, The Happy Hooker 1975, The Duchess and the Dirtwater Fox 1976, Roseland 1977, The Buddy Holly Story 1978, Sonny Boy 1989, Mr. Saturday Night 1992, Crazy Hong Kong 1993, The Feminine Touch (also dir) 1994, The Cable Guy 1996, Bad Blood (also dir and producer) 2006, Maneater 2009, Bad Blood: The Hunger 2012. *Television includes:* numerous appearances including Bonino (series) 1953, Quark (series) 1977–78, Mork and Mindy (series) 1978–82. *Recordings include:* CJ and The Talegate Jazz Band 1950–58, Jammin' At Rudi's 1953; with Tony Parenti: A Night At Jimmy Ryan's 1972; with Conrad Janis and The Beverly Hills Unlisted Jazz Band: Way Down Yonder In Beverly Hills 1986, America 1987, This Joint Is Jumpin' (with Jack Lemmon, Bea Arthur, Dudley Moore) 1989; with Tom Kubis: At Last 1992. *Address:* 1920 South Beverly Glen, Suite 306, Los Angeles, CA 90025, USA. *Website:* www.conradjanis.com.

JANKE, Daniel Jacob, MA; Canadian composer, pianist and kora player; b. 8 Sept. 1957, Edmonton, Alberta; m. Susan Alton, two s., one d. *Career:* CBC Radio, Two New Hours; BBC, Kaleidoscope and Mixing It; Radio France, La Muse En Circuit; mem., Canadian Music Centre, Associate Composer. *Compositions include:* Commission, Music Canada 2000, 1999. *Recordings include:* Debut, 1984; Big Dance, 1989; In A Room, 1997; Not Too Dark, Longest Night Orchestra, 1999. *Honours:* Canada Council B Grant. *Website:* www.danieljanke.com.

JANNAH, Denise, BL; Dutch singer, songwriter, teacher and actress; b. (Denise Johanna Zeefuik), 5 Nov. 1956, Paramaribo, Suriname; d. of Karel August Zeefuik and Eleonore Antoinette Georgetine Zeefuik-Homoet. *Education:* Univ. of Utrecht, Conservatory of Hilversum. *Career:* moved to Netherlands mid-1970's; performances include he. North Sea Jazz Festival, The Hague, and with Carnegie Hall Jazz Orchestra, Dutch Jazz Orchestra, Rosenberg Trio, Jon Hendricks, Willem Breuker Kolletief, Rosenberg Trio, Orchestra of Royal Dutch Navy, Orchestra of Royal Dutch Air Force, Dutch Metropole Orchestra; established own band, Denise Jannah Quintet; numerous int. concerts, festival appearances and tours; vocal dir of theatrical productions, De Nieuw Amsterdam and Cosmic Theatre cos 1987–99; jazz teacher, Rotterdam Conservatory. *Musical theatre:* Night at the Cotton Club 1989–90, Joe, De Musical 1997, Ain't Misbehavin' 1998. *Television includes:* numerous guest appearances, including Grijpstra en De Gier 2005. *Film:* Jannah, New Lady in Jazz (documentary) 1996. *Recordings include:* albums: Take It From The Top 1991, A Heart Full Of Music (Edison Jazz Award) 1993, I Was Born in Love With You 1995, Different Colours 1996, The Madness Of Our Love 1999, Gedicht Gezongen 2004. *Honours:* third prize, Int. Lieder Festival 'Menschen und Meer', Rostock 1989, Golden Microphone Award, Nat. Jazz Vocal Contest, Breda 1991, first prize, Int. Golden Orpheus Festival, Burgas, Bulgaria 1992, Edison Jazz Award 1993, Edison Jazz Public Award 2000. *Address:* Jannah Music, Melissekade 217, 3544 CW Utrecht, The Netherlands (office). *Telephone:* (30) 2510855 (office). *E-mail:* info@denisejannah.com. *Website:* www.denisejannah.com.

JANOW, Steven Roy, AA, BMus, MBA; American composer and musician (classical/legit saxophone); b. 12 July 1973, Rhinebeck, NY; s. of Gordon Janow and Linda Janow. *Education:* State Univ. of New York, N Carolina School of the Arts, Univ. of Hartford, Marist Coll. *Career:* performances in New York City, upstate NY, local radio; mem. The American Soc. of Composers, Authors and Publrs (ASCAP). *Compositions:* Symphony, Symphony No. 2 for saxophone orchestra, Manifesto on Music, Untitled music for brass and saxophone band, String Quartet, Saxophone sonatas, quartets and sextets, etc. *Publication:* Manifesto on Music. *Honours:* ten ASCAP Awards 1998–2007, Univ. of Hartford Fellowship. *Address:* 69 Chestnut Street, Rhinebeck, NY 12572, USA (home). *Telephone:* (845) 876-3567 (office); (845) 663-4501 (mobile). *E-mail:* sjanow@hotmail.com (home). *Website:* www.home.earthlink.net/~janow.

JANSEN, Steve; British musician (drums); b. (Stephen Batt), 1 Dec. 1959, brother of David Sylvian. *Career:* Founder-mem., Japan 1974–83, The Dolphin Brothers (with Richard Barbieri) 1987, Rain Tree Crow (with mems of Japan) 1991, Nine Horses 2005–. *Recordings include:* albums: with Japan: Adolescent Sex 1978, Obscure Alternatives 1978, Quiet Life 1979, Gentlemen Take Polaroids 1980, Tin Drum 1981, Oil On Canvas 1983; with Richard Barbieri: Worlds In A Small Room 1986, Stories Across Borders 1991, Stone To Flesh 1995, Changing Hands 1998; with The Dolphin Brothers: Catch The Fall 1987; with Rain Tree Crow: Rain Tree Crow 1991; with Porcupine Tree: Signify 1997, Stupid Dream 1999; with Richard Barbieri and Mick Karn: Beginning to Melt 1994, Seed 1994, Playing in a Room with People 2001; with Richard Barbieri and N. Takemura: Changing Hands 1997; with Yukihiro Takahashi: Pulse 1999, Ism 1999; with Claudio Chianika: Kinoapparatom 2001; with Nine Horses: Snow Borne Sorrow 2005, Money for All 2007; solo: Slope 2007, Fifty Ain't What It's Cracked Up to Be 2010. *E-mail:* samadhisoundclient2@mac.com. *Website:* www.samadhisound.com; www.ninehorses.com; www.stevejansen.com.

JANZOONS, Klaas; Belgian musician (violin). *Career:* Founder-mem. dEUS 1991–. *Recordings include:* albums: Worst Case Scenario 1994, My Sister = My Clock 1995, In A Bar, Under The Sea 1997, The Ideal Crash 1999, Pocket Revolution 2005, Vantage Point 2008, Keep You Close 2011, Following Sea 2012. *Current Management:* c/o Christian Pierre, Musickness Bvba, Rozenlaan 57, 2970 Gravenwezel, Belgium. *E-mail:* christian.pierre@musickness.be. *Website:* www.musickness.be; www.deus.be.

JARDINE, Al; American musician (guitar) and singer; b. 3 Sept. 1942, Lima, OH. *Career:* mem. The Beach Boys 1961–62, 1963–; numerous tours and concerts, festival appearances; band est. Brother Records label 1967. *Recordings include:* albums: with the Beach Boys: Surfin' Safari 1962, Surfer Girl 1963, Little Deuce Coupe 1963, Shut Down Vol. 2, All Summer Long 1964, Christmas Album 1964, The Beach Boys Today! 1965, Summer Days (and Summer Nights) 1965, Beach Boys Party 1966, Pet Sounds 1966, Smiley Smile 1967, Wild Honey 1968, Friends 1968, 20/20 1969, Sunflower 1970, Surf's Up 1971, Carl and the Passions – So Tough 1972, Holland 1973, The Beach Boys in Concert 1973, Endless Summer 1974, 15 Big Ones 1976, The Beach Boys Love You 1977, M.I.U. 1978, LA (Light Album) 1979, Keepin' The Summer Alive 1980, The Beach Boys 1985, Still Cruisin' 1989, Two Rooms 1991, Summer in Paradise 1992, The Sounds of Summer – The Very Best of The Beach Boys 2003, That's Why God Made the Radio 2012; solo: A Postcard from California 2010. *Honours:* American Music Awards Special Award of Merit 1988, Grammy Lifetime Achievement Award 2001. *Current Management:* c/o Skyline Music Agency, 48 Prospect Street, Whitefield, NH 03598, USA. *Telephone:* (866) 531-2172. *Fax:* (866) 214-8562. *E-mail:* info@skylineonline.com. *Website:* www.skylineonline.com. *Address:* c/o Capitol Records, 1750 North Vine Street, Hollywood, CA 90028, USA. *Website:* www.thebeachboys.com; www.aljardine.com.

JARLETT, Dee, DipEd, Dip RSA; British singer and choir director; b. 28 Oct. 1951, Manchester, England; m. 1st John Jarlett 1977 (divorced 1997); two s. one d.; m. 2nd Scott Wood 1997. *Career:* mem. folk duo, Orion 1983–98; British tours of folk clubs; numerous radio appearances; played film music for Rosie The Great (HTV); mem. Sweet Soul Sisters 1987–99; mem. Naked Voices (Dir 1999–); Edinburgh Fringe 1997, 2001, 2002, 2003, 2005, 2007, Prague Fringe 2004, UK arts centres and theatres; Co-Dir (with Ali Orbaum) Gasworks Choir (150-strong community choir) 1997–; arranger of songs for a cappella choirs. *Recordings include:* with Orion: Jack Orion 1987, Chicken Soup 1989; with Sweet Soul Sisters: Live and Lovin' 1990, Freshly Squeezed 1995, Chemistry; with Naked Voices: Uncovered, Chambers Street, All Together, Gasworks Choir 1–10 (1997–2004). *Honours:* Edinburgh Fringe Festival Pick of the Fringe, Sell-Out Award 2003, Gilded Balloon Sell-Out Award 2005, 2007. *Address:* 27 Narroways Road, St Werburghs, Bristol, BS2 9XB, England. *Telephone:* (117) 941-1440. *Fax:* (117) 902-5680. *E-mail:* dee@deejarlett.co.uk; deejarlett@blueyonder.co.uk. *Website:* www.deejarlett.co.uk.

JARMUSCH, Jim; American film director and screenwriter; b. 22 Jan. 1953, Akron, OH. *Education:* Medill School of Journalism, Northwestern Univ., Colombia Coll. *Career:* teaching asst to Nicholas Ray at New York Univ. Graduate Film School 1976–79; has worked on several films as sound recordist, cameraman and actor; Founder-mem. band Sqürl. *Films include:* Permanent Vacation (writer, dir) 1980, You Are Not I (writer) 1981, The New World (dir) 1982, Stranger Than Paradise (writer, dir) (Camera d'Or Award, Cannes Film Festival 1984) 1983, Down By Law (writer, dir) 1986, Coffee and Cigarettes (short film, writer and dir) 1986, Mystery Train (writer, dir) 1989, Coffee and Cigarettes II (short film, writer and dir) 1989, Night on Earth (writer, dir) 1992, Coffee and Cigarettes III (short film, writer and dir) 1993, Dead Man (writer, dir) 1995, Year of the Horse (dir) 1997, Ghost Dog: The Way of the Samurai (writer, dir) 1999, Ten Minutes Older: The Trumpet (writer, dir) 2002, Coffee and Cigarettes (writer, dir) 2003, Broken Flowers 2005, The Limits of Control 2009, Only Lovers Left Alive 2013. *Music videos directed include:* The Lady Don't Mind (Talking Heads) 1985, Sightsee MC! (Big Audio Dynamite) 1987, It's Alright With Me (Tom Waits) 1991, I Don't Wanna Grow Up (Tom Waits) 1992, Dead Man Theme (Neil Young) 1995, Big Time (Neil Young and Crazy Horse) 1996. *Current Management:* c/o Bart Walker, ICM Partners, 730 Fifth Avenue, New York, NY 10019, USA.

JARRE, Jean Michel André, LèsL; French composer, musician (synthesizer, keyboard) and record producer; b. 24 Aug. 1948, Lyons; s. of Maurice Jarre and France Jarre (née Pejot); m. 2nd Charlotte Rampling 1978; m. 3rd Anne Parillaud 2005 (divorced); one s. and one d. from previous marriage. *Education:* Lycée Michelet, Université de la Sorbonne, Conservatoire de musique de Paris. *Career:* composer of electronic music 1968–; int. concerts include shows in China, Europe and USA; shows incorporate state-of-the-art sound and vision tech.; composer for ballet Aor and Opéra de Paris 1971; UNESCO Goodwill Amb. 1993–; spokesperson European Music Industry 1998–, Int. Fed. for Phonographic Industry 1998–2000. *Major live performances:* Place de la Concorde, Paris 1979 (record audience of one million); Peking, Shanghai 1981; Rendez-vous Houston (record audience of 1.3 million), Rendez-vous Lyons 1986; Destination Docklands, London 1988; Paris–La Défense: A City in Concert 1990 (2.5 million audience); Europe in Concert 1993; Hong Kong 1994; Eiffel Tower, Paris 1995 (one million audience); Moscow 1997 (record audience of 3.5 million); Electronic Night, Eiffel Tower, Paris 1998; Millennium Concert, Pyramids of Cairo (televised worldwide, estimated 2,000m. viewers) 1999; 2001 Rendez-vous in Space, Okinawa, Japan 2001; Akropolis Athens 2001; Aero, Aalborg, Denmark 2002; Forbidden City and Tiananmen Square, Beijing 2004; Gdansk Shipyard, Poland 2005. *Film scores:* Des Garçons et des filles 1968, Deserted Palace 1972, Les Granges brulees 1973, Die Hamburger Krankheit 1978, music and lyrics for numerous songs. *Recordings include:* albums: Oxygène 1976, Equinoxe 1978, Magnetic Fields 1980, The China Concerts (live) 1982, Zoolook (Grand Prix Académie du Disque 1985) 1984, Rendez-vous 1986, Cities in Concert: Houston/Lyons (live) 1987, Revolutions 1988, Jarre Live (Victoire de la Musique Best Instrumental Album 1986) 1989, Waiting for Cousteau 1990, Images (compilation) 1991, Chronologie 1993, Hong Kong (live) 1994, Oxygène 7–13 1997, Odyssey Through 02 (interactive) 1998, Metamorphoses 2000, Aero 2004, Téo & Téa 2007, Electronica 1: The Time Machine 2015. *Publications:* Concert d'Images 1989, Paris-la-Défense, une ville en concert 1990, Europe in Concert 1994, Paris-Tour Eiffel, Concert pour la Tolérance 1995, The Millennium Concert at the Great Pyramids of Egypt 2000, Akropolis 2001, Jean Michel Jarre à Pékin 2004. *Honours:* Soc. des auteurs, compositeurs et éditeurs de musique Gold Medal 1980, Grand Prix de l' Acad. Charles Cros 1985, IPFI Platinum Europe Award 1998, Eska Music Special Award 2007, MOJO Lifetime Achievement Award 2010, Grand Prix des Musiques Electroniques SACEM 2010, Q Innovation of Sound Award 2014; Officier, Ordre des Arts et des Lettres, Officer, Legion d'honneur 2011. *Current Management:* Fiona Commins, Aero Productions, 8 rue de Lévis, 75017 Paris, France. *Telephone:* (1) 44-90-91-70 (office). *Fax:* (1) 44-90-91-77 (office). *E-mail:* contact@aero-productions.com (office). *Website:* www.jeanmicheljarre.com.

JARREAU, Al, BS, MS; American singer; b. 12 March 1940, Milwaukee, Wis. *Education:* Ripon Coll., Univ. of Iowa. *Career:* solo artist 1975–. *Recordings include:* albums: We Got By 1975, Glow 1976, Look To The Rainbow (Grammy Award for Best Jazz Vocal) 1977, All Fly Home (Grammy Award for Best Jazz Vocal) 1978, This Time 1980, Breakin' Away (Grammy Awards for Best Pop Vocal, for Best Jazz Vocal) 1981, Jarreau 1983, High Crime 1984, Al Jarreau Live In London 1985, L Is For Lover 1986, Heart's Horizon 1988, Heaven And Earth (Grammy Award for Best R&B Male Vocal) 1992, Tenderness 1994, Best Of Al Jarreau 1996, Tomorrow Today 2000, Free Spirit 2002, One Note Samba 2002, All I Got 2002, Accentuate the Positive 2004, Love Songs 2008, Christmas 2008, Here I Am 2008, Live 2012. *Current Management:* c/o Joe Gordon, 1954 First Street, Suite 270, Highland Park, IL 60035, USA. *Telephone:* (847) 716-6336. *E-mail:* bzievers@icmpartners.com. *Website:* www.aljarreau.com.

JARRETT, Anita; British singer and songwriter; b. 8 Aug. 1964, London; one s. one d. *Career:* television and radio performances across Europe; mem., Yo Yo Honey 1990–92; mem. Musicians' Union. *Recordings include:* with Yo Yo Honey: Voodoo Soul album; Angel; Ghetto Blues; Rolling Stones remix: You Got Me Rocking, 1994; with Pressure Drop: Elusive, 1997; Vocal, Oakenfold Project.

JARRETT, Keith; American pianist and composer; b. 8 May 1945, Allentown, Pa. *Education:* Berklee School of Music. *Career:* gave first solo concert aged 7, followed by professional appearances; two-hour solo concert of own compositions 1962; led own trio in Boston; worked with Roland Kirk, Tony Scott and others in New York; joined Art Blakey 1965; toured Europe with Charles Lloyd 1966, with Miles Davis 1970–71; soloist and leader of own groups 1969–; Guggenheim Fellowship 1972. *Recordings include:* albums: Bach's Well-Tempered Klavier, Personal Mountains 1974, Luminessence 1974, Mysteries 1975, Changeless 1987, Nude Ants, The Cure 1990, Bye Bye Black 1991, At the Dear Head Inn 1992, Bridge of Light 1993, At the Blue Note 1994, La Scala 1995, Tokyo '96 1998, The Melody at Night With You 1999, Whisper Not 2000, Inside Out 2001, Always Let Me Go 2002, Selected Recordings 2002, Radiance 2005, The Carnegie Hall Concert 2006, Dmitri Shostakovich: 24 Preludes and Fugues 2006, Jasmine (with Charlie Haden) 2010. *Honours:* Prix du Prés. de la République 1991, Polar Prize, Royal Swedish Acad. of Music 2003, Léonie Sonning Music Prize 2004, Jazz Masters Award 2014; Officier, Ordre des Arts et des Lettres. *Current Management:* c/o Vincent Ryan, 135 West 16th Street, New York, NY 10011, USA.

JASMI, Hussein al-; United Arab Emirates singer; b. (Hussein Jasmi el Naqbi), 25 Aug. 1979. *Career:* performed with siblings in group Firqat El Khalij; signed with Rotana record label; performed at numerous int. festivals, including Salalah, Oman, Carthage, Tunisia 2006, Gulf Air Bahrain Grand Prix 2010. *Recordings include:* Hussain El Jasmi 2002, Hala Februair 2004, Hussain El Jasmi 2006, Ihtirit Aabar 2007, El Jasmi 2010, Bawada'ak, Wallah Mayiswa, Bahibik Wahachtiny, Bassbour Al Fourgakom, Into Kafo (You are Enough) 2010; theme music for TV shows Ba'ed Al Furaq (After Separating) 2008, Ahil Al Cairo (The People of Cairo) 2010. *Honours:* Al Mawaheb Prize, Dubai 1996, 6th Arab Radio and Television (ART) Award 2008. *Address:* PO Box 2788, Umm Hurair Road, Dubai, UAE. *Telephone:* (4) 3354440. *Fax:* (4) 3354448. *E-mail:* info@hussainaljassmi.com. *Website:* www.hussainaljassmi.com.

JASRAJ, Pandit, DMus; Indian musician; b. 28 Jan. 1930, Hissar, Haryana; s. of Pandit Motiram and Krishnabai; m. Madhura Pandit 1962; one s. one d. *Career:* studied under elder brother Maniram Pandit; belongs to Mewati Gharana (school of music); has conducted extensive research in Haveli Sangeet and presented the original Pure Haveli Sangeet with its devotional content intact; has est. an Ashram Motiram Sangeet Natale Acad. with main object of propagating Indian classical music by teaching students free of charge; mem. advisory bds of radio and TV. *Recordings include:* Invocation 1993, Inspiration 2000, Haveli Sangeet 2001, Maheshwara Mantra 2002, Darbar 2003, Soul Food 2005, Tapasya 2005, Miyan Tansen 2006, Upasana 2007, Baiju Bawra 2008, Khazana 2008, Raga Symphony 2009. *Works include:* compositions for opera, ballet and short films etc., including Kan Khani Sunyo Kare, Geet Govindam, Sur, Laya Aur Chhanda, Aath Prahar, Raga Bairagi, Raga Behag. *Publication:* Sangeet Saurabh. *Honours:* numerous awards and honours, including Rajiv Gandhi Award for professional excellence, Sangeet Natak Akademi Award 1987, Padma Bhushan 1990, Padma Vibhushan 2000, Yudhvir Memorial Award 2003, Swathi Sangeetha Puraskaram 2008, Bharat Muni Samman 2010 and Sangeet Martand. *Current Management:* c/o Art & Artistes (I) Pvt. Ltd, 307 Durga Chambers, Off Veera Desai Road, Andheri (West), Mumbai 400 053, India. *Telephone:* (22) 42727850. *Fax:* (22) 42727878. *E-mail:* panditjasraj@panditjasraj.com. *Website:* www.aaaind.in; www.panditjasraj.com.

JAUREGUI, Antonio; Peruvian musician (bass guitar). *Career:* Founder-mem., Libido 1996–; numerous live performances and festival appearances. *Recordings include:* albums: Libido 1998, Hembra 2000, Pop*Porn 2003, Libido Acústica 2004, Lo Último Que Hablé Ayer 2005, Un Día Nuevo 2009, Rarezas 2010. *Honours:* Latin American MTV Video Music Award for Best Artist 2002, 2003. *E-mail:* manager@libidonet.com. *E-mail:* antonio@libidonet.com. *Website:* www.libidonet.com.

JAUREGUI, Lauren Michelle; American singer; b. 27 June 1996, Miami, Fla; d. of Michael Jauregui and Clara Jauregui. *Career:* mem. Love You Like a Sister, renamed 1432, then renamed Fifth Harmony (or 5H) 2012–; contestants on US version of The X Factor (finished in third place) 2012; signed with Syco Music and Epic Records 2012; issued debut EP Better Together 2013; opening act on Cher Lloyd's I Wish tour 2013, on Demi Lovato's Neon Lights Tour 2014, on Austin Mahone's tour of North America and Brazil 2014; headlining act, MTV Artists to Watch concert 2014. *Television:* The X Factor (contestant on US series) 2012. *Recordings:* album: with Fifth Harmony: Reflection 2015. *Honours:* Teen Choice Single: Group Award 2014, MTV Video Music Artist to Watch Award 2014, MTV Europe Music Awards for Best North America Act, for Best US Act and for Best Worldwide Act 2014. *Address:* c/o Syco Music, Syco Entertainment, 9830 Wilshire Blvd, Beverly Hills, CA 90212, USA. *Website:* www.sycoentertainment.com; www.fifthharmonyofficial.com.

JAY, David (Dave) John, BA; British singer, songwriter and musician (guitar, keyboard); b. 13 Nov. 1971, Brentwood, Essex. *Career:* remix work with Vibe Alive Production for London Records and Atlantic Records, USA; solo and session work for Mr Exe, Wubble-U, Acorn Arts and various independent labels; mem. Musicians' Union. *Recordings include:* After The Dance Austin;,Ain't It Rough The Dave Jay Project, Dedicated To Love The Journeyman (5 track EP), House of Love East 17, Love Is Blind Echora, Spring Box (EP) Dilemma, Change the Style/Windows... Mighty Alliance, Spring Box Remix Matrix vs Dilemma, Taking It Back Stone Players featuring Soul Hooligan, Songs for Today's Attention Span 2007. *Website:* davejay.com.

JAY, Martin; British singer, musician (guitar), writer and producer; b. 27 July 1949, London, England; m. Lorraine Jay 1985; one s. *Career:* TV appearances on Top of the Pops with 5,000 Volts and Enigma; with Cockney Rebel, Yamaha Song Festival in Concert (LWT), Chile Song Festival, Never Mind the Buzzcocks, The One Show; produced Mike Nolan CD, Joe McElderry CD. *Recordings include:* with 5,000 Volts: Fly Away, I'm On Fire, Dr Kiss Kiss; Motion Man, Medleys with Enigma: Ain't No Stoppin', I Love Music, Back To The 60s, Tight Fit, Saturday Night Fever 'Megamix'. *Address:* 17 Brook Way, Chigwell, Essex, IG7 6AW, England (office). *Telephone:* (20) 8500-2849 (office). *E-mail:* info@martinjay.co.uk (office). *Website:* www.martinjay.co.uk.

JAY, Michael, (Michael Jay Margules); American songwriter and record producer; b. (Michael Jay Margules), 17 Dec. 1959, Chicago, Ill.; s. of Harold Margules and Elaine Margules. *Education:* Lincoln Coll., Illinois, Illinois State Univ. *Career:* A&R for Curtis Mayfield, Curtom Records, Chicago 1980; discovered Martika 1988; Owner Jambo Studios, Los Angeles; mem. NARAS, BAFTA, BMI. *Films:* Top Gun, Summer School, Superhero Movie. *Compositions:* Declaration of Love 1996, Bridge of Hope 1996. *Recordings:* Like Toy Soldiers, Eminem, Toy Soldiers, Martika, Cross My Heart, Patsy Kensit and Eighth Wonder, Hot Summer Nights, Gloria Estefan (Top Gun soundtrack), The World Still Turns, Kylie Minogue, I Wish The Phone Would Ring, Exposé, The Slightest Touch and If I Say Yes, Five Star; as writer and producer: Shining Through, recorded by Nancy Kerrigan, Olympic Silver Medallist ice-skater, Declaration of Love, Céline Dion, Bridge of Hope, Lara Fabian. *Honours:* AMPEX Golden Reel Awards, Silk and Steel and Martika, Grammy Award Album of the Year, Falling Into You, Céline Dion 1996. *Address:* Jambo Studios, 22647 Ventura Boulevard, #251, Woodland Hills, CA 91364, USA (office). *Telephone:* (818) 227-9669 (office). *E-mail:* jambomail@aol.com (office). *Website:* www.michaeljaymusic.com (office); www.facebook.com/michaeljay.songwriter.

JAY, Norman, MBE; British DJ, producer and remixer; b. 6 Nov. 1957, London, England; two s. *Career:* co-founder: Good Times sound system (with brother Joey); played at Notting Hill Carnival; set up pirate radio station Kiss FM with Gordon Mac; presented The Original Rare Groove Show; put on some of London's first warehouse parties with partner Judge Jules as Shake and Fingerpop, mid 1980s; resident DJ and promoter of High On Hope club, early '90s; presented weekly Giant 45 radio show on London Live; remixed: Azzido Da Bass; Montano vs Trumpetman. *Honours:* Blues and Soul Magazine Club DJ of the Year 1996–97. *E-mail:* dan@dustedworld.com (office). *Website:* www.dustedworld.com (office).

JAY, Robert; Dutch musician (guitar), producer, artist and singer; b. 15 Nov. 1967, Dieren. *Education:* Conservatory. *Career:* Schüttorf Open Air Concert; four television (nat.) shows; De 5 Uur show; Glamourland; Actor, television series; tour manager, clients include: Emmylou Harris, Freddy Fender, Chris Beckers, Ernie Watts, Randy Bernsen; performed in USA, Canada, Germany, Israel, Egypt, Spain, France; artists performed with: Hans Dulfer, Candy Dulfer, Jan Akkerman, Adje Vanderberg, Jasper Van't Hof, Joe Sample; writer for several pop journals; organizer, music festivals; mem. EMI Music/Publishing.

JAY SEAN; British singer, songwriter and producer; b. (Kamaljit Singh Jhooti), 26 March 1981, London. *Career:* pioneer of Bhangra/R&B fusion; began career as mem. Rishi Rich project; professional solo artist 2004–; f. own record label, Jayded Records 2006. *Recordings:* albums: Me Against Myself 2004, My Own Way 2008, All or Nothing 2009, Freeze Time 2011. *Honours:* 13 UK Asian Music Awards, Brit Asia Music Awards for Best UK Urban Act 2010, for Best Single (for Down) 2010.

JAY-Z; American rap artist and record producer; b. (Shawn Corey Carter), 4 Dec. 1969, Brooklyn, New York; m. Beyoncé Knowles 2008; one d. *Career:* Co-founder, Roc-A-Fella Records 1995–, later expanding to include Roc-A-Wear clothing line and film co. (purchased by Universal 2004); collaborations with Puff Daddy, Lil' Kim, Foxy Brown, Notorious BIG, Mary J. Blige, Mariah Carey, Timbaland; numerous live performances; Pres. Def Jam label 2005–08. *Film:* Streets Is Watching (writer and dir) 1998. *Recordings include:* albums: Reasonable Doubt 1996, In My Lifetime Vol. 1 1997, Vol. 2 Hard Knock Life (Grammy Award for Best Rap Album 2001) 1999, Vol. 3 Life And Times Of S. Carter 1999, The Dynasty—Roc La Familia 2000, The Blueprint (Soul Train Award for Album of the Year 2002) 2001, The Best Of Both Worlds (with R. Kelly) 2002, The Blueprint 2: The Gift And The Curse 2002, S Carter Collection 2002, The Black Album 2003, Collision Course (with Linkin Park) 2004, Kingdom Come 2006, American Gangster 2007, The Blueprint 3 (American Music Award for Favorite Rap/Hip Hop Album) 2009, Magna Carta Holy Grail 2013; with Kanye West: Watch the Throne 2011. *Publication:* Decoded 2010. *Honours:* MTV Video Music Award for Best Rap Video (for Can I Get A...) 1999, for Best Video from a Film (for Can I Get A...) 1999, Source Awards for Lyricist of the Year 1999, for Best Hip Hop Artist 2001, Billboard Music Award for Rap Artist of the Year 1999, MOBO Award for Best Int. Hip Hop Act 1999, Soul Train Award for Sammy Davis Jr Entertainer of the Year 2001, Grammy Awards for Best Rap Performance by Duo or Group (for Big Pimpin') 2001, (for Swagga Like Us with T.I) 2009, for Best Rap/Sung Collaboration (for Numb/Encore with Linkin Park) 2006, (for Run This Town with Rihanna and Kanye West) 2010, (for Empire State of Mind featuring Alicia Keys) 2011, (for Holy Grail, with Justin Timberlake) 2014, for Best Rap Solo Performance (for D.O.A.) 2010, for Best Rap Song (for Run This Town) 2010, for Best Rap Song (with Alicia Keys) (for Empire State of Mind) 2011, for Best Rap Song by Duo or Group (for On to the Next One featuring Swizz Beatz) 2011, for Rap Performance (for Otis with Kanye West) 2012, for Best Rap Performance, Rap Song (for N****s In Paris), Best Rap/Sung Collaboration (No Church In The Wild) 2013, for Best R&B Performance and R&B Song (both for Drunk in Love, with Beyoncé) 2015, MOBO Awards for Best Int. Male 2006, Best Hip-Hop Act 2008, Best Int. Act 2010, 2011, Michael Jackson Award for Best Video, Soul Train Awards (for Show Me What You Got) 2007, American Music Award for Favorite Rap/Hip Hop Artist 2009, BRIT Award for Best Int. Male Solo Artist 2010. *Address:* Roc-A-Fella Records, 825 Eighth Avenue, New York, NY 10019-7472, USA. *Website:* www.rocafella.com; www.jay-z.com.

JAYAKODY, Bathiya; Sri Lankan singer and rapper; b. 22 Dec. 1976. *Education:* Ananda Coll., Mary Anne David's School for Singing, Colombo. *Career:* mem. Bathiya & Santhush pop/rap duo (with Santhush Weeraman) 1998–, released several albums; achieved 25 number one singles in Sri Lanka, many live concerts; collaborated with Indian singers including Hariharan and Asha Bhosle, co-f. BNS Production Group; composed and performed official Sri Lankan cricket anthem. *Recordings include:* albums: with Bathiya & Santhush: Vasanthaye – A New Beginning 1998, Life 2000, Tharunaye 2002, Neththara 2005, Resvihidena 2007, Ayubowan 2007, Shaheena 2008, Lanka Matha 2009, Sara Sihina 2010. *Honours:* with Bathiya & Santhush: Azia Dauysy Music Festival in Kazakhstan Silver Award Winners 2001, Shanghai Music Festival Bronze Award Winners 2001, TYOP (Ten Young Outstanding Persons) Award for contribution to Culture and Arts 2002, Golden Clef Award for Best Fusion Band 2002, Male Icon Award, Colombo Hilton 2006. *Address:* c/o Saregama Digital, Saregama Records, 33 Jessore Road, Kolkata, 700028, India (office); c/o BNS Music, Colombo, Sri Lanka (office). *E-mail:* info@bnsmusic.com (office). *Website:* www.saregama.com/portal/pages/music.jsp (office); www.bnsmusic.com (office).

JAYSON, Mackie; American musician (drums). *Career:* fmr mem. Cromagnons, Bad Brains; mem. Fun Lovin' Criminals 1999–2003; mem. Madball 2008–; numerous tours, festivals and television appearances. *Recordings include:* with Fun Lovin' Criminals: Loco 2001, Welcome To Poppy's 2003, Livin' In The City 2005; with Bad Brains: Rise 1993. *E-mail:* righthandman2007@yahoo.com.

JAZZIE B, OBE; British musician, producer and songwriter; b. (Beresford Romeo), 16 Jan. 1963, London, England. *Career:* Founder-mem. Soul II Soul collective; launched fashion label and clothes shops; remixer/arranger for many artists, including Sinéad O'Connor, Fine Young Cannibals and The Family Stand; solo DJ and producer; numerous club appearances and appearances on TV and radio. *Recordings include:* albums: Club Classics Vol. I (Q Classic Album Award 2015) 1989, Vol. II A New Decade 1990, Vol. III Just Right 1992, Vol. IV The Classic Albums 1993, Vol. V Believe 1995, Time for Change 1997, Jazzie B Presents Soul II Soul at the Africa Centre 2004, Jazzie B Presents School Days: Life Changing Tracks from the Trojan Archives 2008, Masterpiece 2008. *Television:* Back 2 Life. *Honours:* listed among 100 Great Black Britons 2008, Ivor Novello Award 2008. *Address:* Soul II Soul, PO Box 67934, London, NW1W 8ZB, England (office). *Telephone:* (20) 7439-6060 (office). *E-mail:* press@soul2soul.co.uk (office). *Website:* www.soul2soul.co.uk (office).

DJ JAZZY JEFF; American b. (Jeffrey Townes), 22 Jan. 1965, Philadelphia, PA. *Career:* started as DJ 1970s; formed duo with Will Smith, as DJ Jazzy Jeff and the Fresh Prince; formed A Touch of Jazz Inc., collective of producers working on rap and R&B projects. *Recordings include:* albums: with the Fresh Prince: Rock the House 1986, He's the DJ, I'm the Rapper 1988; An In This Corner 1989, Homebase 1991, Code Red 1993; solo: The Magnificent 2002, The Return of the Magnificent 2007, He's the King... I'm the DJ 2009. *Honours:* Grammy Awards for Best Rap Performance (with Will Smith) 1988, 1991.

Address: c/o Rapster Records, 1 Devonport Mews, Devonport Road, London, W12 8NG, England (office). *E-mail:* sophie@deckstar.com. *Website:* www.djjazzyjeff.com.

JAZZY M; British producer, remixer and DJ; b. (Michael Schiniou), 5 Jan. 1962, Edmonton, London, England. *Career:* started as a mobile DJ in London; worked in Spin Off Records; landed job as a DJ on LWR Radio; presented The Jacking Zone, responsible for introducing house music to London on the airwaves; opened Vinyl Zone record shop on the King's Road, London; founder: Oh Zone Records, original label of Orbital's club hit Chime; resident DJ at Ministry of Sound club for 8 years; weekly show, The OhZone, Ministry of Sound Radio; collaborations with Julian Jonah, Mr Fingers; remixed Infinity and Duane Harden, Ramsey and Fen, Double 99; relaunched OhZone recordings 2011; tutor, The Ministry of Sound DJ Acad.; produces House Music programs for Kane FM. *Recordings include:* singles: Soft To Hard/Boom Ah! (as Klubzone 1), Forever On (as Zoogie) 1992, Be Yourself Be Free (as Sao Paulo) 1998, Jazzin' The Way You Know 2000. *Address:* c/o Ministry of Sound, 103 Gaunt Street, London SE1 6DP, England (office). *Website:* www.ministryofsound.com/radio; www.jazzym-official.co.uk.

JEAN, Wyclef; Haitian singer and rap artist; b. 17 Oct. 1972, Croix-des-Bouquets. *Career:* mem., Tranzlator Crew, renamed The Fugees 1987–; numerous television and live appearances; producer for Destiny's Child; solo artist 1997–; appointed Roving Amb. for Haiti by Pres. René Préval 2007. *Recordings include:* albums: with The Fugees: Blunted on Reality 1994, The Score 1996; solo: Presents The Carnival 1997, The Ecleftic: 2 Sides II A Book 2000, Masquerade 2002, The Preacher's Son 2003, Carnival 2004, Welcome To Haiti: Creole 101 2004, The Carnival 2 2007. *Honours:* BRIT Award for Best Int. Group 1997. *Address:* Miguel Baguer, Columbia Records, 515 Madison Avenue, New York, NY 10022, USA. *Website:* www.wyclef.com.

JEAN-MARIE, Alain Judes; French musician (piano); b. 29 Oct. 1945, Pointe-à-Pitre, Guadeloupe. *Career:* moved to Canada 1967–70, the Antilles 1970–73, Paris, France 1973–; concerts with Chet Baker, Art Farmer, Johnny Griffin, Hal Singer, Slide Hampton, Clark Terry, Sonny Scott, Lee Konitz, Maz Roach, Christian Escoudé, Dee Dee Bridgewater; recordings with Abbey Lincoln, Charles Tolliver. *Recordings include:* Piano Biguines 1969, Alain Jean-Marie Trio 1979, André Condouant Quartet 1981, La Note Bleue 1986, Latin Alley 1987, World is Falling Down 1990, The Scene is Clean 1991, Biguine Reflections 1992, Dreamtime 1992, Biguine Reflections II 1996, Clean and Class 1997, Fanny's Dream 1997, Afterblue 1999, Delirio and Biguine Reflections 2000, Lazy Afternoon 2000, Men Art Works 2002, Jazz Ka Philosophy 2002, That's What 2004, Tribute to le Petit Opportun 2005, Portrait in Black and White 2005, Live in Paris (with Ted Curson ensemble) 2006, Surrender to the Night (with Morena Fattorini, Vincent Ségal, Xavier Desandre Navarre and Roger Raspail) 2010, Biguine Reflections V-Tropical Blues 2013. *Honours:* Academie du Jazz Prix Django Reinhardt 1979. *Website:* www.alainjeanmarie.com.

JECZALIK, Jonathan Edward Stephen; British music director; b. 11 May 1955, Banbury, Oxfordshire; m. Joanna Louise Hill; two d. *Career:* programmer, Fairlight CMI; producer for Pet Shop Boys; Co-founder and member Art of Noise 1983 and Art of Silence; IT teacher, Oxford High School GDST; mem. Musicians' Union; collaborated with numerous artists and bands including Yes, Dollar, ABC, Kate Bush, Stephen Duffy. *Recordings include:* albums: Who's Afraid of The Art of Noise 1984, In Visible Silence 1986, In No Sense Nonsense 1987, Best of The Art of Noise 1988, Below The Waste 1989, The Ambient Collection 1990, The Seduction of Claude Debussy 1999; singles include: with Art of Noise: Into Battle EP 1983, Beatbox 1983, Close To The Edit 1984, Moments In Love 1985, Peter Gunn (Grammy Award) 1986, Paranoimia 1986, Dragnet 1988, Kiss, Art of Love, Instruments of Darkness, Shades of Paranoimia, Metaforce 1999; collaboration with Tom Jones 1988; producer of: Kiss Me, Opportunities, Pet Shop Boys 1985. *Honours:* Grammy Award for Best Rock Instrumental 1986.

JEFFERSON, Marshall; American producer, remixer and DJ; b. 19 Sept. 1959, Chicago, Ill. *Career:* started as record producer, Universal Recording Studios; produced own tracks with other Chicago house producers including Adonis mid-1980's; recorded for Chicago's Trax Records; formed group Virgo (with Vince Lawrence and Adonis); produced Ten City's debut album; remixed: The Pasadenas, Tom Jones, System 7, Kym Mazelle; Co-owner USB Records (with CeCe Rogers). *Recordings include:* albums: Virgo (with Virgo) 1989; singles: I've Lost Control (with Sleazy D), Move Your Body (The House Music Anthem) 1986, Open Our Eyes (with The Truth) 1988, Do You Know Who You Are (with Virgo) 1989, Tribal Gathering (with Universal Distribution) 1996, Mushrooms (with Noosa Heads) 1998, Everybody Dance (Clap Your Hands) (with DJ Pierre) 2001, My Salsoul: The Foundations of House 2005. *E-mail:* info@deejaybooking.com. *Website:* www.deejaybooking.com.

JEFFRIES, Peter John Martin; British composer, arranger, musician (piano) and music director; b. 1 March 1928, London; m. Pauline Lander 1955; one s. one d. *Education:* Eastman School of Music. *Career:* pianist, arranger Phil Tate Orchestra; arranger, musical director Philips Records, Pye Records, Decca Records; radio appearances include: own broadcasting orchestra, Breakfast Special, Radio 2 1967–72; accompanist for Kenny Lynch, Jimmy Tarbuck, Morecambe and Wise, Anne Shelton, Vera Lynn; mem. PRS, MCPS, BAC&S. *Compositions include:* 21 film scores 1966–80; co-arranger: If My Friends Could See Me Now, Cy Coleman.

JELAVIC, Matko, Dipl OECC; Croatian singer, composer and musician (drums); b. 29 March 1958, Split; m. 1982; two s. *Career:* drummer in rock band Metak; drummer in studios; singer and composer 1988–; mem. HGU (Croatian Music Union), DSH (Union of Composers). *Recordings include:* albums: Dobra Vecer Prijatelji 1988, Ljube Ljubavi 1989, Sretno Ti Bilo Andele 1990, Matko Jelavic Mix 1992, Moja Ljubavi 1993, Pianino 1995, Od Jubavi Bolujen 1996, Dueti 1997, Covjek Tvoj 1999, Pismo Moja Uzorita 2000, Tajna 2001, Duša Čista, Obična... 2004, Instrumentali 2005, O Lipi Splite Moj 2005, Zlatni Mix 2007, Prvoj rui Hrvatske 2009, Zlatna Kolekcija 2009. *Honours:* Winner, Split Festival 1988, Most Popular Song Award, Croatia 1988. *Address:* Dubrovacka 25, 21000 Split, Croatia (home). *Telephone:* (21) 539726 (office). *Fax:* (21) 539726 (office). *E-mail:* matko.jelavic@st.t-com.hr (home). *Website:* www.matkojelavic.com.

JENKINS, Delyth, BA; British musician (Celtic harp); b. (Delyth Evans), 28 May 1955, Oswestry, Shropshire, England; m. Nigel Jenkins 1982; two d. *Career:* mem. folk bands Cromlech 1978–82, Aberjaber 1982–; solo artist; toured UK, Europe. *Recordings include:* Gwlith Y Bore 1980, Igam Ogam 1982, Aberjaber 1985, Aber-Dau-Jaber 1988, Delta 1991, Aberjaber – The Perfect Bucket 1997, Ar Y Ffin 1998, Aros 2006, Llais 2012. *Publications include:* Del Y Delyn 1994. *Telephone:* (1792) 460150 (office). *E-mail:* contact@delyth-jenkins.co.uk (office); delythjenkins@btinternet.com. *Website:* www.delyth-jenkins.co.uk; www.dna-folk.co.uk.

JENKINS, Sir Karl William Pamp, Kt, CBE, DMus, ARAM, LRAM, FRAM; British composer, pianist and oboist; b. 17 Feb. 1944, Penclawdd, Wales. *Education:* Gowerton Grammar School, Univ. of Wales, Cardiff and Royal Acad. of Music, London. *Career:* initially resident jazz oboist at Ronnie Scott's; Co-founder Nucleus, then played in Soft Machine; currently composer and conductor; Pres. Friends of the Nat. Youth Orchestra of Wales, Penclawdd Brass Band; Patron Nat. Youth Choir of GB; Fellow, Royal Welsh Coll. of Music and Drama, Trinity Coll., Carmarthen, Swansea Inst. *Compositions include:* Palladio 1992–95, Adiemus I: Songs of Sanctuary 1994, Adiemus II: Cantata Mundi 1996, Eloise 1997, Adiemus III: Dances of Time 1998, The Armed Man: A Mass for Peace 1999, Y Celtiaid (film score) (BAFTA Cymru Award for Best Original Music Soundtrack) 2000, Dying to Dance (TV score) 2001, Over the Stone 2002, Pwy Ysgrifennodd Y Testament Newydd? (film score) (BAFTA Cymru Award for Best Original Music Soundtrack) 2003, In These Stones Horizons Sing 2003, Quirk 2005, River Queen (film score) 2005, The Peacemakers 2012, The Healer - A Cantata For St Luke 2014. *Recordings include:* Adiemus (Songs of the Sanctuary), Palladio (with Smith Quartet and London Philharmonic Orchestra) 1996, Imagined Oceans 1998, The Armed Man: A Mass for Peace (with Nat. Youth Choir of GB and London Philharmonic Orchestra) 2000, Requiem 2005, Quirk 2005, Kiri Sings Karl (with Kiri Te Kanawa) 2006, This Land of Ours 2007, Stella Natalis 2009, The Very Best of Karl Jenkins 2011, The Peacemakers 2012, Adiemus Colores 2013, Motets 2014, Still With The Music 2015. *Publication:* Still With The Music (autobiography) 2015. *Honours:* First Prize, Montreal Jazz Festival (with Nucleus), two D&AD awards for best advertising music, Classic FM Red F Award for outstanding service to classical music. *Address:* Karl Jenkins Music Ltd, 46 Poland Street, London, W1F 7NA, England (office). *Telephone:* (20) 7434-2225 (office). *Fax:* (20) 7494-4998 (office). *E-mail:* info@karljenkins.com (office). *Website:* www.karljenkins.com (office).

JENKINSON, Tom, (Squarepusher, Chaos AD); British musician and DJ; b. 1977. *Career:* solo artist and DJ; signed to Warp Records 1996; performances include Glastonbury Festival, UK, Mount Fuji Rock Festival, Japan, Ten Days of Techno, Belgium; video collaborations with Chris Cunningham. *Recordings include:* albums: as Chaos AD: Buzz Caner, Remixes; as Squarepusher: Feed Me Weird Things 1996, Hard Normal Daddy 1997, Burningn'n Tree 1997, Buzz Caner 1998, Music Is Rotten One Note 1998, Selection Sixteen 1999, Budakhan Mindphone 1999, Go Plastic 2001, Do You Know Squarepusher 2002, Ultravisitor 2004, Hello Everything 2006, Just a Souvenir 2008, Shobaleader One: d'Demonstrator 2010. *Address:* Warp Records, Spectrum House, 32–34 Gordon House Road, London NW5 1LP, England (office). *E-mail:* info@warprecords.com (office). *Website:* www.warp.net (office); squarepusher.net.

JENNER, Luke; American singer and musician (guitar); m. *Career:* Founder-mem. The Rapture 1998–. *Recordings include:* albums: Mirror 1999, Out Of The Races And Onto The Tracks 2001, Echoes 2003, Pieces of People We Love 2006, Tapes 2008, In the Grace of Your Love 2011. *Current Management:* Principle Management, 30–32 Sir John Rogerson's Quay, Dublin 2, Ireland. *Telephone:* (1) 6777330. *Fax:* (1) 6777276. *Website:* www.therapturemusic.com.

JENNINGS, John, (John Segs, Vince Segs, Frank Zappatista); British bass guitarist and songwriter; *Career:* bass guitarist, punk band The Ruts 1977–80, Ruts D.C. 1980–83, 2008–, Alabama 3 (as Frank Zappatista) 2000–07; played with numerous other artists including Edwyn Collins, Mad Professor, Aztec Camera, Mike Scott, Kirsty MacColl, Joe Strummer, Rat Scabies, Mick Jones, Splodgenessabounds, Tony Visconti, Vic Godard, Small Axe; production work with Ali Love 2007. *Recordings include:* albums: with The Ruts: The Crack 1979, Grin and Bear It 1980, In a Can 2000, Get Out of It!! 2006; with Ruts D.C.: Animal Now 1981, Rhythm Collision 1982, Rhythm Collision Vol. 2 2013; with Alabama 3: La Peste 2000, Power In The Blood 2002, The Last Train To Mashville 2003, Outlaw 2005, M.O.R. 2007, Revolver Soul 2010. *Website:* www.alabama3.co.uk.

JENSEN, Mark Russell; British composer, arranger, conductor and producer; *President, Zestzone;* b. 20 Nov. 1959, Eastbourne, England. *Education:* Eastbourne Coll., studied with Rodney Sadler, John Walker, MA. *Career:* arranger, conductor, record producer 1978–; recording artist 1985–; composer, arranger, conductor for film, TV, theatre 1992–; recorded as Spritzo Scaramanga –1993, as Mark Jensen 1994–; Pres. Zestzone; mem. Performing Right Soc., British Music Writers' Council, Musicians' Union, British Acad. of Songwriters, Composers and Authors, Asscn of Ind. Music. *Compositions:* film and television: The Papermen 1993, Angleterre Underground 1994, Caravan To Arcadia 1995, Monk Dawson (pilot) 1995, Famine 1998; theatre: Romeo and Juliet 1993, The Changeling 1994, The Tempest 1994, Hamlet 1995, The Way of Danger (ballet score) 1996, Monk Dawson (feature) 1997, Maestro 1999–2000, Perilous Night 2002. *Recordings:* albums: Monk Dawson (original soundtrack) 1998; as Mark Jensen: Zoom In... The Zest Zone 1999, The Naidax 2007; as producer: Life is for Living (Naidax) 2004, Brainwaves (Moddoo Wow'd) 2004. *Address:* Zestzone, PO Box 2936, Eastbourne, East Sussex, BN21 2XZ, England (office). *E-mail:* info@zestzone.net (office). *Website:* www.zestzone.net (office).

JENSEN, Soren Kjær; Danish musician (bass), composer and producer; b. 1 Dec. 1961, Århus; m. Turid N. Christensen 1995. *Education:* Univ. of Århus, New School for Social Science, USA. *Career:* teacher, Royal Conservatory of Music, Ålborg, Musik Projekt Århus; space invaders production for Multimedia; Lecturer in Anthropology of Music, Univ. of Århus; mem. KODA, NCB, Danish Musicians' Union. *Compositions include:* numerous works for TV, video, film, Planetaria, theme parks, CD-Roms and CD-I; producer and co-producer: Waaberi, New Dawn 1997, Maryam Mursal 1998. *Honours:* scholarships from Danish Music Council, Danish Arts Council, Danish Rock Council, Queen Margrethe and Prince Henriks Foundation, European Comm. Innovation Programme, Ministry for the Interior, Danish Cultural Foundation; Best CD-ROM in Scandinavia 1997, Industrial Design Award 1998.

JENSEN, Theis Eigil; Danish singer, musician (trumpet) and graphic designer (retd); b. 5 Aug. 1938, Copenhagen; s. of Eigil Jensen and Ingeborg Jensen (née Møller); m. 1st Lesley Celina Geen 1961 (divorced 1976); two c.; m. 2nd Ina Loendahl 1999. *Education:* art school. *Career:* mem. Louisiana Jazzband 1952–55, Henrik Johansen's Jazzband 1955–56, Adrian Bentzon's Jazzband 1956–63; Co-leader Theis/Nyegaard Jazzband 1963–98, Theis' Jazzband 1998–2010; tours and festivals in Europe, USA, Argentina, Brazil, Uruguay, Australia; radio and TV appearances in Scandinavia, S America and China. *Recordings:* Traditional Jazz 1964, Theis/Nyegaard Concert at Gothenburg 1969, Theis/Nyegaard Live At Montmartre 1972, Papa Bue's Viking Jazz Band Live At Vingården 1976, Jazztage Hanover 1977, Jazz For Hatz-Lovers 1979, Theis Jensen 1956–72 1980, Mand Mand 1980, Los Estudiantes Daneses En El Hot Club De Buenos Aires 1980, Gamle Er Unge, Der Er Blevet Aeldre 1981, The First 25 Years 1988, Jorgen Svare Meets Theis Jensen 1991, Jazz Event 1992, Theis-Nyegaard Jazzband, Tonight Live 1996, Papa Bue's Viking Jazzband Meets Theis Jensen 2003, Theis' Jazzband, All Of Me 2004, Songs to Remember 2005, Songs To Remember Too 2008. *Publications:* Historier Om Theis 1992, Love and Jazz 2002. *Honours:* Jazz Musician of the Year 1965. *Address:* Lovenborg Alle 11, 4420 Regstrup, Denmark. *Telephone:* 59-47-15-55. *E-mail:* tej@theisina.dk. *Website:* www.theisina.dk.

JEPSEN, Carly Rae; Canadian singer and songwriter; b. 21 Nov. 1985, Mission, BC. *Education:* Heritage Park Secondary School, Mission, Canadian Coll. of Performing Arts, Victoria. *Career:* achieved third place, Canadian Idol 2007; toured as part of Canadian Idol Top 3 concert tour; debut recording 2008; has toured Canada with Marianas Trench, Shiloh, The New Cities, Mission District; toured as part of the Shout It Out World Tour 2012; opening act for Justin Bieber tour in N America, France and UK 2012–13. *Recordings:* albums: Tug of War 2008, Kiss 2012, Emotion 2015. *Honours:* numerous awards including: Canadian Radio Music Award for Song of the Year (Tug of War) 2010, Teen Choice Awards for Breakout Artist 2012, for Summer Song 2012, Billboard's Rising Star 2012, Western Canadian Music Award for Pop Recording of the Year 2012, MTV Europe Music Awards for Best Song 2012, for Best Push Act 2012, American Music Award for Old Navy New Artist of the Year 2012, Billboard Music Awards for Top Pop Song 2013, for Top Digital Song 2013 (both for Call Me Maybe). *Current Management:* c/o Simkin Artist Management, #101–1001 Unit 165 West Broadway, Vancouver, BC V6H 4E4, Canada. *E-mail:* info@simkinartistmanagement.com. *Website:* www.simkinartistmanagement.com; www.604records.com (office); www.carlyraemusic.com.

JERBIC, Zeljko; Croatian record producer and teacher; b. 10 Oct. 1954, Koprivnica. *Education:* Acad. of Pedagogics, High School of Music. *Career:* mem. Croatian Musicians' Union. *Recordings include:* as music and executive producer: Damned Die Hard, Phonebox Vandals 1990, Foxxin, Messerschmitt 1990, Ikona, Lola V Stain 1990, 4 x 12, Borghesia 1991, Mansarda, Lola V Stain 1992, Asgard Live, Vesna Gorse and Drazen Franolic 1993, So Shine, Don't 1995, Ulje Je Na Vodi, Haustor 1995, KC Rock 98 1998.

JEREMÍAS; British/Venezuelan singer and songwriter; b. (Carlos Eduardo López Avila), 19 Sept. 1973, London, England. *Career:* solo artist 2006–; Owner Avila Records. *Recordings include:* album: Jeremías 2006, Ese Que Va Por Ahí 2006, Un Día Más En El Gran Circo 2007, Yo Te Amo 2013. *Address:* Universal Music Latino, 2220 Colorado Avenue, Santa Monica, CA 90404, USA (office).

JERKINS, Rodney, (Darkchild); American producer and songwriter; b. 1977, New Jersey. *Career:* began producing and writing songs aged 14 years; recorded gospel album aged 15 years; artists produced or performing songs include Aaliyah, Tatyana Ali, Mark Anthony, Backstreet Boys, Mary J. Blige, Brandy and Monica, Toni Braxton, Destiny's Child, Whitney Houston, Enrique Iglesias, Michael Jackson, Jennifer Lopez, Will Smith, Britney Spears; formed own production and promotion co., Darkchild Entertainment Inc. 1999–; Co-founder Music Mogul, Inc. (with Nicholas Longano, Ray Brown and Jonathan E. Eubanks) 2008; Exec. Producer Extreme Music 2009–. *Compositions include:* Honey (film soundtrack) 2003. *Recordings include:* On The Move 1994, Versatility 2006. *Music produced includes:* The Boy is Mine (with Brandy & Monica) 1998, Holler (with Spice Girls) 2000, Lose My Breath (with Destiny's Child) 2004, Scared of Lonely (with Beyonce) 2008, As Long As You Love Me (with Justin Bieber) 2012. *Honours:* MOBO Award for Best Producer 1998, Grammy Award for Best R&B Song (for Say My Name, performed by Destiny's Child) 2000, Grammy Award for Record of the Year (for Stay With Me, Darkchild Version, performed by Sam Smith) 2015. *Address:* Darkchild Entertainment Inc., POB 410, Pleasantville, NJ 08232-0410, USA (office). *E-mail:* info@darkchild.com. *Website:* www.darkchild.com (office).

JERROLF, Mats; Swedish composer and musician; b. 28 Aug. 1951, Stockholm. *Career:* appearances in various folk music programmes in radio; mem. SKAP, SAMI. *Compositions include:* Bekannelsen I Logen 1991, Adjo Till Stockholms Stad 1993, Krakemala Namdemanlard 1993, Förskingrarvisan 1995. *Recordings include:* Skanska Lasses Visor 1987, Flickan Fran Bellmansro 1988, Collage 1990, Haveri 1993, Namdemans Blandning 1995. *Publications include:* Birka 1981, Historisk Malarresa 1981. *Honours:* STIM Award 1991 1995 1997, Folk Music Foundation Award 1992, SKAP Award 1995, Nat. Artists Scholarship. *E-mail:* mats.jerrolf@musikarrangemang.com; mats.jerrolf@dataphone.se. *Website:* www.kulturpool.se/mats/engelsk.htm.

JERVIER, Paul Joseph; British musician (drums) and music producer; b. 21 Nov. 1966, London. *Career:* mem. Musicians' Union; Producer, P Jervier; mem. Phoenix Rose 2008–09. *Recordings include:* four UK No. 1 singles with Take That; other recordings for artists include: Yazz, Eternal, Kaos, Gabrielle, R Kelly, Danny Rampling.

JESSE, Graham; Australian musician (flute, saxophone) and composer; b. 19 Oct. 1955, Sydney, NSW; m. Peta Jesse 1986; one s. one d. *Education:* Sydney Conservatorium of Music, studied saxophone with Joe Allard and Dave Liebman, musical composition with Ludmilla Uhlehla, New York. *Career:* mem. Midday Show, live daily TV entertainment programme for 15 years; toured with Daly Wilson Big Band, Peter Allen, David Atkins; performed with Sydney Dance Co., James Morrison, Marcia Hines; mem. Australian Musicians' Union, Australasian Performing Right Asscn. *Compositions:* Reflections, In the Company of Women (Sydney Dance Co.), In The Flow. *Recordings:* as leader: Reflections 1996, In the Flow 2000; as co-leader: Blow!; as featured soloist: Tommy Emmanuel: Dare to Be Different, Up From Down Under, Gondwanaland; as featured soloist and composer: Pamela Knowles: Boites De Jazz, The Sydney All Star Big Band: Doin' Our Thing, Pyldriver; as co-writer and assoc. producer: Shimmer (Bonnie J. Jensen); as orchestrator: An Officer and a Gentleman (world premier, Sydney). *Honours:* Bicentennial Music Week Award for Most Outstanding Studio Musician (woodwinds), Musicians' Union. *Telephone:* (4) 1448-9614 (Australia) (office). *E-mail:* music@grahamjesse.com.au (home). *Website:* www.grahamjesse.com.au.

JESSEE, Darren; American drummer and songwriter; b. 8 April 1971. *Career:* mem. Ben Folds Five 1993–2000, 2011–; Founder mem. Hotel Lights 2004–. *Recordings:* albums: with Ben Folds Five: Ben Folds Five 1995, Whatever and Ever Amen 1997, Naked Baby Photos 1998, The Unauthorised Biography of Reinhold Messner 1999, The Sound of the Life of the Mind 2012; with Hotel Lights: Hotel Lights 2005, Goodnightgoodmorning 2006, Firecracker People 2008, Girl Graffiti 2011. *Address:* c/o Glenn Morrow or Mark Lipsitz, Bar/None Records, PO Box 1704, Hoboken, NJ 07030, USA (office). *Telephone:* (201) 770-9090 (office). *E-mail:* glenn@bar-none.com (office); info@hotellights.net. *Website:* www.benfoldsfive.com; www.hotellights.net.

JESSIE J; British singer and songwriter; b. (Jessica Ellen Cornish), 27 March 1988, Redbridge, Essex. *Education:* Mayfield High School, Colin's Performing Arts School, BRIT School. *Career:* joined girl group Soul Deep 2005; lyricist for artists including Chris Brown and Miley Cyrus; debut solo single released 2010; opening act on Katy Perry's North American tour 2011; house artist at MTV Europe Music Awards 2011; performed in front of Queen Elizabeth at Diamond Jubilee Concert, London 2012. *Stage:* Whistle Down the Wind, London 1999. *Recordings include:* albums: Who You Are (MOBO Best Album Award 2011) 2011, Alive 2013; also appears on: The Awakening, James Morrison 2011, Nothing But the Beat, David Guetta 2011. *Television:* coach on The Voice UK 2012–13. *Honours:* BBC Sound of 2011 Winner 2010, BRIT Award Critic's Choice 2011, BT Digital Music Awards for Best Newcomer, Best Female Artist and Best Song 2011, Capital FM Best Role Model in Pop Award 2011, Glamour Woman of Tomorrow Award 2011, MOBO Awards for Best Newcomer, Best UK Act and Best Song 2011, Q Award for Best Video 2011, Urban Music Award for Best Female Artist 2011. *Current Management:* c/o Crown Music Management, The Matrix Complex, 91 Peterborough Road, London, SW6 3BU, England. *Telephone:* (20) 7371-5444. *Fax:* (20) 7371-5454.

E-mail: info@crownmusic.co.uk. *Website:* www.crownmusic.co.uk; www.jessiejofficial.com.

JETT, Joan; American singer and musician (guitar); b. 22 Sept. 1960, Philadelphia, Pa. *Career:* mem. all-female group The Runaways 1976–79; solo artist with own backing band The Blackhearts 1979–. *Recordings include:* albums: with The Runaways: The Runaways 1976, Queens of Noise 1977, Live In Japan 1977; solo (with The Blackhearts): Bad Reputation 1980, I Love Rock 'N' Roll 1981, Album 1983, Glorious Results of a Misspent Youth 1984, Up Your Alley 1988, Good Music 1989, Hit List 1990, Notorious 1991, Pure and Simple 1994, Fetish 1999, Fit To Be Tied 2001, Sinner 2006, Unvarnished 2013. *Honours:* inducted into Long Island Music Hall of Fame 2006, Nanci Alexander Activist Award for her work for animal welfare 2012. *Current Management:* Blackheart Records Group, 636 Broadway, New York, NY 10012, USA. *Website:* www.joanjett.com.

JIM BOB; British musician and author; b. (James Morrison), 22 Nov. 1960. *Career:* Founder-mem. duo (with Fruitbat), Carter The Unstoppable Sex Machine (later known as Carter USM) 1987–98, 2007–; Founder-mem. Jim's Super Stereoworld 1998; extensive Int. tours and concerts; solo artist 2004–. *Recordings include:* albums: with Carter USM: 101 Damnations 1990, 30 Something 1991, 1992 – The Love Album 1992, Post Historic Monsters 1994, Worry Bomb 1995, Straw Donkey 1996, A World Without Dave 1997, I Blame The Government 1998, Live 1999; solo: J.R. 2001, Goodnight Jim Bob 2003, Angelstrike! 2004, School 2006, A Humpty Dumpty Thing 2007, Goffam 2009. *Publications include:* Storage Stories 2010, Goodnight Jim Bob 2012, Driving Jarvis Ham 2012, The Extra Ordinary Life of Frank Derrick, Age 81 2014. *Website:* www.jim-bob.co.uk; www.carterusm.co.uk.

JIMÉNEZ, (Leonardo) Flaco; American musician (accordion); b. 11 March 1939, San Antonio, TX; s. of Santiago Jiménez Sr. *Career:* fmr mem., Los Caporales, Los Carminantes; numerous collaborations, including Doug Sahm, Dr John, Ry Cooder, Peter Rowan, David Lindsey, Dwight Yoakam, Buck Owens, Linda Ronstadt, Emmylou Harris, Los Lobos, The Mavericks, John Hiatt, Bryan Ferry, The Clash, Stephen Hill, The Rolling Stones, Carlos Santana, The Chieftains, Jimmy Sturr, Willie Nelson, Bob Dylan, Ray Benson, Asleep at the Wheel, Alan Jackson, Abrahim Ferrer, Celso Piña, Rowwen Heze, Jaguares. *Film appearance:* Picking Up the Pieces 2000. *Recordings include:* albums: El Príncipe Del Acordeón 1977, Flaco Jiménez Y Su Conjunto 1978, Tex Mex Breakdown 1983, Ay Te Dejo en San Antonio y Más! 1986, Arriba El Norte 1988, Flaco's Amigos 1988, Entre Humo Y Botellas 1989, Said And Done 1990, San Antonio Soul 1991, Partners 1992, Un Mojado Sin Licencia 1993, Flaco Jiménez 1994, Melodias Inolvidables 1995, 15 Exitos 1995, Flaco's First 1995, Buena Suerte Señorita 1996, One Night At Joey's 1999, Sleepytown 2000, Polkas 2000, Ultimo Tornado 2001, Squeeze Box King 2003. *Honours:* Grammy Awards for Best Mexican-American Music Performance (for Ay Te Dejo en San Antonio) 1986, (for Soy de San Luis) 1991, (for Flaco Jimenez) 1996, (for Los Super Seven) 1999, for Best Tejano Music Performance (for Said and Done) 1999. *Address:* PO Box 241388, San Antonio, TX 78224, USA (office). *Telephone:* (210) 557-1292 (office). *E-mail:* info@flacojimenezmusic.com (office). *Website:* www.flacojimenezmusic.com.

JIMENEZ-OLARIAGA, Marcos Andres; Spanish jazz musician (piano); b. 25 April 1960, Madrid; one d. *Education:* Geneva CPM, also studied jazz piano with Michel Bastet, Kenny Werner. *Career:* moved to Geneva 1966; Founder-mem. Garbriela Bergallo Quartet 1995, Marcos Jimenez Trio; collaborations with Erik Truffaz, Maurice Magnoni, Mathieu Michel, Daniel Humair, Christine Python, Zizi Jeanmaire; numerous concerts. *Recordings include:* albums: Chris Cross (with Christine Python) 1993, After the Rain 2000, La Vie Zizi (with Zizi Jeanmaire), Song for the Trees, La Liberté est une Fleur (with Zizi Jeanmaire), I Thought About You 2008, Different 2008, Awakening 2013, Axium 2014, Streams 2015. *Honours:* Prix Spécial Kneiffel 1995, Sacem Prize (with Christine Python), Festival de Crest, France. *E-mail:* info@marcosjimenez.net (office). *Website:* www.marcosjimenez.net.

JIN, (The Emcee); American/Chinese rapper; b. (Jin Au-Yeung), 4 June 1982, Miami, Fla; m. Carol Au-Yeung 2011. *Career:* gained popularity as freestyle MC; after graduating from high school in Miami, moved to New York City 2001; won numerous freestyle rap contests in Miami and New York; entered and won numerous contests on 106 & Park show, BET (Black Entertainment Television); won Fight Klub freestyle rap contest; featured as character in NBA: Phenom video game; collaborations and guest appearances with Juggy D, Lee-Hom Wang; released album ABC with predominantly Cantonese lyrics 2007; now lives in Hong Kong. *Recordings include:* albums: The Rest Is History 2004, The Emcee's Properganda (as The Emcee) 2005, 100 Grand Jin 2006, I Promise 2006, ABC 2007, Rap Now 2010 2010, Charlie Sheen 2011, Homecoming 2011, CrazyLoveRidiculousFaith 2012. *Films include:* Jin: Making of a Rap Star 2003, 2 Fast 2 Furious 2003, No Sleep Til Shanghai 2007, Gallants 2010, Bruce Lee, My Brother 2010, Fast & Furious 6 2013. *Television includes:* as actor: Show Me the Happy 2010, Yes, Sir, Sorry, Sir! 2010, Lives of Omission 2011. *Website:* mcjin.com.

JIN, Mithra, (Choi Jin); South Korean hip hop musician, rapper and songwriter; b. 6 Jan. 1983, Goheung. *Career:* Founder mem. and MC, hip hop group Epik High 2003–; co-f. Map the Soul record label 2009; military service 2010–12. *Recordings include:* albums: with Epik High: Map of the Human Soul 2003, High Society 2004, Swan Songs 2005, Remapping the Human Soul (Mnet KM Music Festival Award for Album of the Year 2007) 2007, Pieces Part One 2008, (e) 2009, Epilogue 2010, 99 2012. *Honours:* Golden Disk

Awards for Best Hip-Hop Artist 2005, 2009, for Bonsang (Fan) 2007, KBS Music Award for Best Hip-Hop Artist 2005, SBS Music Award for Best Hip Hop Artist 2006, Mnet KM Music Festival Awards for Best Hip-Hop Artist 2005, 2008, for Bonsang (Fan) 2007, Seoul Music Award for Bonsang (Fan) 2008, Mnet Asian Music Award for Best Rap Performance (for UP) 2012. *Address:* c/o YG Entertainment, 397-5 YG Building, 5th Floor, Hapjeong-Dong, Mapo-Gu, Seoul, 121886, South Korea (office). *Website:* www .mapthesoul.com; www.vg-epikhigh.com.

JINWOON; South Korean singer and rapper; b. (Jung Jinwoon), 2 May 1991. *Education:* Daejin Univ. *Career:* mem. 2AM 2008–, live debut in 2010; has also recorded with May Doni, 8eight. *Recordings:* with 2AM: Saint o'Clock 2010; other 2AM appearances include Personal Preference (soundtrack) 2010, Listen Up!: The Official 2010 FIFA World Cup Album 2010, Acoustic (soundtrack) 2010; other appearances: Wax Unplugged, Wax 2009. *Honours:* Mnet Asian Music Award for Best Vocal Performance by a Group 2011. *Address:* c/o JYP Entertainment, JYP Center, 41, 79–gil Apgujeong-ro, Gangnam-gu, Seoul, South Korea (office). *Telephone:* (2) 3438-2300 (office). *Fax:* (2) 3438-2330 (office). *E-mail:* publicity@jype.com (office). *Website:* 2am .ibighit.com (office).

JIRO; Japanese musician (bass guitar); b. (Wayama Yoshihito), 17 Oct. 1972, Hakodate; m. *Career:* mem. pop/rock band Glay 1991–; bassist, The Predators; numerous live performances and tours, numerous radio broadcasts. *Recordings include:* albums: with Glay: Hai to Daiyamondo 1994, Speed Pop 1995, BEAT out! 1996, Beloved (Nihon Record Grand Prize 1997) 1996, Review: Best of Glay 1997, Pure Soul (Nihon Record Best Album) 1998, Heavy Gauge 1999, Mirai Diary (film soundtrack) 2000, One Love 2001, Unity Roots & Family, Away 2002, The Frustrated 2004, Love is Beautiful 2007, Glay 2010, Justice 2013, Guilty 2013; with The Predators: Hunting!! 2005, This World 2010, Monster in your head 2012; singles: Rain 1994, Manatsuno Tobira 1994, Kanojo no Modern 1994, Freeze My Love 1995, Zutto Futari de 1995, Yes, Summerdays 1995, Ikiteju Tsuyosa 1995, Glorious 1996, Beloved (Japan Usen Broadcast Networks Gold Request Prize) 1996, Zutto Wasurenai (A Boy) 1996, Kuchibiru 1997, However (Nihon Record Excellent Work Award) 1997, Yuuwaku 1998, Soul Love 1998, Be With You 1998, Winter Again (Nihon Record Grand Prize) 1999, Kokodewanai, Dokokae 1999, Happiness 2000, Mermaid 2000, Tomadoi/Special Thanks 2000, Missing You 2000, Global Communication 2001, Stay Tuned 2001, Hitohira no Jiyuu 2001, Way Of Difference 2002, Mata Kokode Aimashou 2002, Aitai Kimochi 2002, Beautiful Dreamer/Street Life 2003, Blue Jean 2004. *Honours:* Japan Usen Broadcast Networks Grand Prize 1997, 1999, Golden Arrow Music Prize 1998, Gold Disc Awards for Best Rock Artist of the Year, Best Music Video of the Year, Artist of the Year 1998. *Website:* www.glay.co.jp; www.thepredators.net.

JOAN, Marianne, BA, MFA; American singer; b. 12 March 1973, Jamestown, ND. *Education:* California Institute of the Arts, Peabody Conservatory, studied with Phyllis Bryn-Julson, Jacqueline Bobak and Irene Gubrud. *Career:* voice for Brigantia, recorded score by Clay Chaplin, Canadian Choreographer Anik Bouvrette; created new multimedia works with trio, Three Lanes Over, Los Angeles, 1999, and Digital Improvisation Ensemble, Los Angeles, 1998; soloist with Schola Antiqua, medieval music ensemble; mem. AES, ICMA.

JOBE, Badou; Gambian musician (bass guitar). *Career:* started career with Foyer band late 1950s; joined African Jazz; Founder-mem. Super Eagles 1968, name change to Ifang Bondi 1973; based in Holland 1984–. *Recordings include:* with The Super Eagles: Viva Super Eagles 1969, Senegambian Sensation; with Ifang Bondi: Saraba 1976, Mantra 1983, Sanjo 1989, Daraj 1994, Gis Gis 1998, Ifang Bondi Live 2001. *Honours:* EverGreen Award, Gambia 1997, Kora Award 1999. *E-mail:* mail@ifanbondi.demon.nl. *Website:* www.gambia.dk.

JOE; American singer and producer; b. (Joseph Thomas), 1972, Cuthbert, GA. *Career:* started singing in the choir of parents' Pentecostal Church, Alabama; worked in a gospel music store; played guitar at a local church; solo artist 1997–; collaborations with Brandy, Jay-Z, SWV, Big Punisher, Case, Mariah Carey. *Recordings include:* albums: Everything 1993, All That I Am 1997, My Name is Joe 2000, Better Days 2001, Joe... Joe Who? Joe Thomas 2007, Signature 2009, Home is the Essence of Christmas 2009, The Good, The Bad, The Sexy 2011. *Address:* c/o Kedar Entertainment, 21 West 39th Street, Sixth Floor, New York, NY 10018, USA (office). *Telephone:* (212) 391-1111 (office). *Fax:* (212) 391-1316 (office). *E-mail:* info@kedar.com (office). *Website:* www .kedar.com/joe.

JOEL, William (Billy) Martin; American singer, songwriter and musician (piano); b. 9 May 1949, Bronx, NY; s. of Howard Joel and Rosalind Nyman; m. 2nd Christie Brinkley 1985 (divorced 1994); one d.; m. 3rd Kate Lee 2004. *Career:* solo recording artist 1972–; first tour of USSR by American popular music artist 1987; numerous tours, live appearances world-wide. *Recordings include:* albums: Cold Spring Harbor 1971, Piano Man 1973, Streetlife Serenade 1974, Turnstiles 1976, The Stranger 1977, 52nd Street (Grammy Awards for Album of the Year, for Best Pop Vocal Performance) 1979, Glass Houses (Grammy Award for Best Pop Vocal Performance) 1980, Songs In The Attic 1981, The Nylon Curtain 1982, An Innocent Man 1983, Greatest Hits Volume I & II 1985, The Bridge 1986, Kohuept 1987, Storm Front 1989, River Of Dreams 1993, Greatest Hits Volume III 1997, 2000 Millennium Concert 2000, The Essential Billy Joel 2001, Fantasies and Delusions 2001, Movin Out 2002, My Lives 2005, 12 Gardens Live 2006, The Stranger 2008, The Hits

2010, She's Got A Way 2010, Piano Man 2011. *Publication:* Goodnight My Angel: A Lullabye (juvenile fiction) 2004. *Honours:* Dr hc (Fairfield Univ.) 1991, (Berklee Coll. of Music) 1993, (Manhattan School of Music) 2008, Hon. DHumLitt (Hofstra Univ.) 1997, Hon. DMus (Long Island Univ.) 2000, Hon. DFA (Syracuse University) 2006; Grammy Awards for Record of the Year (for Just the Way You Are) 1978, for Song of the Year (for Just the Way You Are) 1978, Grammy Legend Award 1990, ASCAP Founders' Award 1997, numerous American Music Awards, including American Music Award of Merit 1999, RIAA Diamond Award 1999, James Smithson Bicentennial Medal of Honor 2000. *Address:* c/o Columbia Records, Sony BMG Music, 550 Madison Avenue, New York, NY 10022-3211, USA (office). *Website:* www.sonybmg.com (office); www.billyjoel.com.

JOHANSEN, David, (Buster Poindexter); American singer, songwriter and actor; b. 9 Jan. 1950, Staten Island, New York; m. 1st Kate Simon 1983 (divorced), m. 2nd Mara Hennessey. *Career:* Founder-mem. New York Dolls 1971–75, re-formed 2004–; solo jazz and blues singer; numerous concerts and stage appearances. *Films include:* Candy Mountain 1988, Gandahar (voice) 1988, Married to the Mob 1988, Scrooged 1988, Let it Ride 1989, Tales from the Darkside: The Movie 1990, Freejack 1992, Desire and Hell at Sunset Motel 1992, Naked in New York 1993, Mr Nanny 1993, Car 54, Where Are You? 1994, Burnzy's Last Call 1995, Nick and Jane 1997, Cats Don't Dance (voice) 1997, The Deli 1997, 200 Cigarettes 1999, The Tic Code 1999, Campfire Stories 2001, God is on Their Side 2002, Crooked Lines 2003, Coda 2005. *Television includes:* appeared in episodes of Miami Vice 1985, The Equalizer 1987, The Adventures of Pete & Pete, Cupid 1998, Oz 2000, Deadline 2001, Teen Titans 2005. *Recordings include:* albums: with New York Dolls: New York Dolls 1973, Too Much Too Soon 1974, One Day it Will Please Us to Remember Even This 2006, Cause I Sez So 2009, Dancing Backward in High Heels 2011; solo: David Johansen 1977, In Style 1979, Here Comes the Night 1981, Live it Up 1982, Sweet Revenge 1984, Buster Poindexter 1987, David Johansen and the Harry Smiths 2000, Shaker 2002, The David Johansen Group Live 2004. *Address:* c/o Roadrunner Records, 902 Broadway, Eighth Floor, New York, NY 10010, USA (office). *E-mail:* roadrunner@roadrunnerrecords.com. *Website:* www.nydolls .org.

JOHANSEN, Per Oddvar Eide; Norwegian musician (drums, electronics); b. 1 March 1968, Oslo. *Education:* Music Gymnasium, Rud High School, Trondelag Music Conservatory of Music. *Career:* freelance drummer, mostly jazz and improvised music; has toured Norway and Europe with numerous artists and groups including: Airamero, Kenny Weeler, John Surman, Dave Holland, Karin Krog, Nils Petter Molvaer, Jon Christensen, Lee Konitz, Tore Brunborg, Vigleik Storaas, The Source, Close Erase; mem. Norwegian Jazz Fed., Norwegian Musical Union; teacher, Norges Musikkhøgskole; has conducted numerous workshops, schools and seminars. *Recordings include:* with Trond Bjertnes & Frode Barth: Egentlig 1994; with The Source: Olemanns kornett 1994, The Source & Different Cikadas 2002, The Source 2006; with Jan Erik Kongshaug: The Other World 1998, All These Years 2003; with Vigleik Storaas trio: Bilder 1995, Subsonic 2002, Epistel no 5 2012; with Close Erase: Close Erase 1995, Dance This 2002, R.I.P 2010; with Solveig Slettahjell: Slow Motion Orchestra 2001, Good Rain 2006, Tarpan seasons 2009; solo: Ferme Solus: This is My Music 2008, Solo At MIR - Blow Out! 2014. *Honours:* Spellemannsprisen in jazz (with Vigleik Storaas Trio) 1995, Spellemannsprisen in jazz (with Vigleik Storaas Trio) (for Andre Bilder) 1997, Spellemannsprisen in jazz (with Petter Wettre) (for The Only Way to Travel) 2000, Spellemannsprisen in jazz (with Solveig Slettahjell) (for Solveig Slettahjell) 2004, Spellemannprisen in jazz (with Hans Mathisen) (for Quiet Songs) 2005, received Preis Der Deutsche Schallplattenkritik (with Trygve Seims) (for Different Rivers) 2001. *E-mail:* peroddvar@peroddvar.no. *Website:* www.peroddvar.no.

JOHANSSON, Lars-Olof (Lasse); Swedish musician (keyboards, guitar); b. 23 Feb. 1973, Huskvarna. *Career:* mem. alternative rock band The Cardigans 1993–, country band Up The Mountain; numerous concert tours, festivals, TV and radio appearances; signed with Solid Air Records 2005; numerous collaborations. *Music for TV and film:* contributed tracks to films including Romeo and Juliet and A Life Less Ordinary, theme to 'Randall & Hopkirk Deceased' (BBC1, with David Arnold) 2000. *Recordings include:* albums: with The Cardigans: Emmerdale 1994, Life 1995, First Band On The Moon 1996, Other Side Of The Moon 1998, Gran Turismo 1998, Long Gone Before Daylight 2003, Super Extra Gravity 2005, Best Of 2008; numerous solo recordings. *Publications include:* Early Jazz For Fingerstyle Guitar 2003. *Honours:* Slitz Magazine Award for Best Band 1994, Swedish Government Export Prize 1997, BMI Award for Best Song 1997, Best Album 1998, Best Group 1996, 1998. *Current Management:* c/o Hagenburg Management, Kyrkogaten 31, 411 08 Gothenburg, Sweden. *Telephone:* (31) 339-95-90. *Fax:* (31) 13-95-09. *E-mail:* info@hagenburg.se. *Website:* www.hagenburg.se. *E-mail:* info@lassejohansson.se. *Website:* www.lassejohansson.se; www .cardigans.com.

JOHANSSON, Markku; Finnish conductor, arranger, composer and musician (trumpet, flugelhorn); *Conductor, Vantaa Pops Orchestra*; b. 22 March 1949, Lahti; one s. one d. *Education:* Music Conservatory, Lahti, Sibelius Acad., Helsinki, studied jazz in New York with Thad Jones and Lew Soloff. *Career:* radio, TV, recording artist, conductor, arranger, trumpet player; Conductor, UMO Jazz Orchestra 1992–93, Vantaa Pops Orchestra 1988–. *Recordings include:* with Vantaa Pops Orchestra: Finnish popular tunes 1992, Jealousy 1997, Christamas Memories 2002, Christmas Shine 2006, Stars and

Diamonds 2008; with Umo Jazz Orchestra: The song at the UMO 1991, Selected Standards 1993; with Nils Lindberg: Brass Galore 1994; with Lena Jansson: Lena Jansson 1995; with Thad Jones: Thad Jones, Mel Lewis and Umo 1995, Antti Sarpila Meets Markku Johansson 1996; solo: Sympathy 1970, Funny Tricks But Beautiful 1982, Echoes Blue 1986, Tenderly 1990, Exhorbitant 1994, Very Live at Groovy 2008. *Honours:* Yrjö Award for Musician of the Year 1993, Finnish Jazz Federation Georgie Award 1993, Kullervo Linna Foundation Award 1996, Finnish Musicians' Union Award 2002, Imatra Big Band Festival Jazz legend 2008; Knight (1st Class), Order of Lion of Finland 2004. *Current Management:* c/o MJ-Music Oy, Valajanraitti 1C, 18100 Heinola, Finland. *E-mail:* mj-music@phnet.fi.

JOHN, Sir Elton Hercules, Kt, CBE; British musician (piano), singer and songwriter; b. (Reginald Kenneth Dwight), 25 March 1947, Pinner, Middx; s. of Stanley Dwight and Sheila Eileen Dwight (née Harris); m. 1st Renata Blauel 1984 (divorced 1988); m. 2nd David Furnish 2014; two s. *Education:* Pinner County Grammar School, Royal Acad. of Music, London. *Career:* began piano lessons 1951; played piano in Northwood Hills Hotel bar 1964; mem. local group Bluesology 1961–67; worked for Mills Music Publrs; began writing songs with Bernie Taupin 1967; solo recording contract with DJM Records 1967; concerts in Los Angeles, USA 1970; formed Rocket Record Co. with Bernie Taupin 1973, first album released 1976; co-f. Rocket Music Entertainment Co.; f. publishing co. Big Pig Music 1974; frequent tours in UK, USA, Japan, Australia 1971–76; Vice-Pres. Nat. Youth Theatre of GB 1975–; first int. star to perform concerts in USSR 1979; produced records with Clive Franks for Kiki Dee, Blue, Davey Johnstone's China 1976–77; Chair. Watford Football Club 1976–90, 1997–, Life Pres. 1990–; fmr part-owner Los Angeles Aztecs of the North American Soccer League; occasional columnist, The Guardian; f. Elton John AIDS Foundation 1993; Rocket Pictures; Fellow, British Acad. of Composers and Songwriters 2004–; Trustee, Wallace Collection 1999–; Chair. The Old Vic Theatre Trust 2002–. *Stage productions:* The Lion King (musical) 2001, Billy Elliot (musical) 2004, Lestat (musical, with Bernie Taupin) 2006. *Soundtracks, scores and theatre albums:* Friends 1971, The Lion King 1994, Aida 1998, The Muse 1999, The Road to El Dorado 2000, Billy Elliot 2005, Lestat 2005, Gnomeo & Juliet (exec. producer) 2011. *Films include:* Born to Boogie 1972, Goodbye to Norma Jean 1973, Tommy 1975, To Russia with Elton 1980, The Rainbow 1989, The Lion King (music) 1994, Spice World (as himself) 1997, Desert Flower (producer) 1999, Women Talking Dirty (exec. producer) 1999, The Road to El Dorado (voice) 2000, Bob the Builder: A Christmas to Remember (video) (voice) 2001, The Country Bears (as himself) 2002, Tommy and Quadrophenia Live: The Who (video) 2005, It's a Boy Girl Thing (exec. producer) 2006, Elton John: Me, Myself & I (autobiog. as himself) 2007. *Television includes:* Zomercarroussel (mini-series) 1970, It's Cliff Richard (series) 1970, Russell Harty Plus (TV series) 1974, Great Performances (series) (exec. producer) – Elton John at the Royal Opera House 2003, Him and Us (film) (exec. producer) 2006, Spectacle: Elvis Costello with... (series) (exec. producer) 2008–10, David Bowie: The Story of Ziggy Stardust (film) 2012. *Recordings include:* albums: Empty Sky 1969, Elton John 1970, Tumbleweed Connection 1971, Friends (film soundtrack) 1971, 17-11-70 1971, Madman Across the Water 1972, Honky Chateau 1972, Don't Shoot Me, I'm Only the Piano Player 1973, Goodbye Yellow Brick Road 1973, Caribou 1974, Captain Fantastic and the Brown Dirt Cowboy 1975, Rock of the Westies 1975, Here and There 1976, Blue Moves 1976, A Single Man 1978, Victim of Love 1979, Lady Samantha 1980, 21 at 33 1980, The Fox 1981, Jump Up 1982, Too Low for Zero 1983, Breaking Hearts 1984, Ice on Fire 1985, Leather Jackets 1986, Reg Strikes Back 1988, Sleeping with the Past 1989, The One 1992, Made in England 1995, Love Songs 1995, The Big Picture 1997, Aida 1999, El Dorado 2000, Songs from the West Coast 2001, Peachtree Road 2004, The Captain and the Kid 2006, Rocket Man 2007, The Union (with Leon Russell) 2010, Good Morning To The Night (with Pnau) 2012, The Diving Board 2013, Wonderful Crazy Night 2016. *Honours:* Officier, Ordre des Arts et des Lettres 1993; Hon. mem. RAM 1997; Dr hc (RAM) 2002; Ivor Novello Awards (for Daniel) 1974, (for Don't Go Breaking My Heart, with Kiki Dee) 1977, (for Song for Guy) 1979, (for Nikita) 1986, (for Sacrifice) 1991, American Music Awards for Favorite Male Artist, Favorite Single 1977, Silver Clef Award 1979, BRIT Awards for Outstanding Contribution to British Music 1986, Best British Male Artist 1991, MTV Special Recognition Trophy 1987, Grammy Awards 1987, 1991, 1998, 2000, Grammy Lifetime Achievement Award 2000, Nat. Acad. of Popular Music Hitmaker Award 1989, Q Magazine Merit Award 1993, Acad. Award for Best Original Song (for Can You Feel the Love Tonight?) 1995, recipient of Kennedy Center Honors 2004, ranked by Billboard magazine as the most successful male solo artist on The Billboard Hot 100 Top All-Time Artists 2008, Brits Icon Award 2013. *Current Management:* c/o Rocket Music Management, 1 Blythe Road, London, W14 0HG, England. *Telephone:* (20) 7348-4800. *E-mail:* contact@rocketmusic.com. *Website:* www.rocketmusic.com; www.eltonjohn.com.

JOHN, Lee; British singer, songwriter, musician (keyboards), record producer and arranger and actor; b. 23 June 1957, Hackney, London. *Education:* Hewanoma Strolling Players, Anna Scher Stage School, World-wide Productions, USA. *Career:* lead singer, Imagination; backing vocalist major artists; numerous concert tours; mem. Musicians' Union, BAC&S, PRS, PPL. *Recordings include:* with Imagination: Body Talk 1981, Flashback 1981, In and Out of Love 1981, Just An Illusion 1982, Music and Lights 1982, In The Heat of The Night 1982, Changes 1982, Looking At Midnight 1983, Thank You My Love 1984, Instinctual 1988; albums include: Body Talk 1981, Scandalous 2000, The Best Of Imagination; solo: Let There Be Love (featured with Arthur

Baker), The Mighty Power of Love, Your Mind Your Body Your Soul 2000, Feel My Soul 2005, Let the Universe Set You Free 2008. *Honours:* Blues and Soul Award. *Current Management:* David Shepherd, Neil O'Brien Entertainment, 26 Eastcastle Street, London, W1W 8DQ, England. *E-mail:* david@neilobrienentertainment.com. *Website:* www.neilobrienentertainment.com. *E-mail:* leeejohn@hotmail.com. *Website:* www.leeejohn.com.

JOHNNY; Icelandic musician (bass guitar). *Career:* mem. rock band Mínus 1998–. *Recordings include:* albums: Hey Johnny! 1999, Jesus Christ Bobby 2001, Halldor Laxness 2004, The Great Northern Whalekill 2008, Demo 2009, Hard Feelings 2001, Minus 2013. *Address:* c/o Smekkleysa Records, PO Box 1263, 121 Reykjavík, Iceland.

JOHNNY BLAZE (see Method Man)

JOHNS, Ethan; British music producer, sound engineer and musician; b. 1969, s. of Glyn Johns. *Career:* producer who has worked with artists including Ryan Adams, Kings of Leon, Ray Lamontagne, Kevin Prosch, Rufus Wainwright, Howard Eliott Payne, Emmylou Harris, Crowded House, Laura Marling, Luthea Salom, and Crosby, Stills and Nash, amongst others; Founder Three Crows Music ind. record label; as musician has toured with numerous performers including Emmylou Harris, Ryan Adams, Ray LaMontagne and Tom Jones. *Recordings include:* producer: The Black Peppercorns, (Kevin Prosch) Tumbling Ground 1995, Brendan Benson, One Mississippi 1996, Chris Stills, 100 Year Thing 1998, Whiskeytown, Pneumonia, recorded 1999, released 2001, Ryan Adams, Heartbreaker 2000, Glen Phillips, Abulum 2000, Rufus Wainwright, Poses 2001, Ryan Adams, Gold 2001, Julianna Raye, Restless Night 2002, Tift Merritt, Bramble Rose 2002, Ryan Adams, Demolition 2002, The Jayhawks, Rainy Day Music 2003, Kings of Leon, Youth and Young Manhood 2003, Ours, Precious 2002, Leona Naess, Leona Naess 2003, Bernie Leadon, Mirror 2003, Kings of Leon, Aha Shake Heartbreak 2004, Ben Kweller, On My Way 2004, Ray LaMontagne, Trouble 2004, Nina Gordon, Even the Sunbeams (unreleased/2004 recorded), Ryan Adams, 29 2005, Dave Palmer, Romance 2006, Ray LaMontagne, Till the Sun Turns Black 2006, Gerling, 4 2006, Luther Russell, Repair 2007, Kings of Leon, Because of the Times 2007, Crowded House, Time On Earth 2007, Turin Brakes, Dark On Fire 2007, Sarabeth Tucek, Sarabeth Tucek 2007, Ray LaMontagne, Gossip in the Grain 2008, Howard Eliott Payne, Bright Light Ballads 2009, Paolo Nutini, Sunny Side Up 2009, Laura Marling, I Speak Because I Can 2010, Tom Jones, Praise & Blame 2010, Julianna Raye, Dominoes 2011, The Boxer Rebellion, The Cold Still 2011, Kaiser Chiefs, The Future Is Medieval (co-produced with Tony Visconti) 2011, Laura Marling, A Creature I Don't Know 2011, Once I Was an Eagle 2013; If Not Now Then When (solo album) 2012. *Honours:* BRIT Award for Best British Producer 2012. *Current Management:* c/o Jim Phelan or Jerimaya Grabher, GPS | Global Positioning Services, 3435 Ocean Park Blvd, Suite 107-191, Santa Monica, CA 90405, USA. *Telephone:* (310) 656-1350. *Fax:* (310) 656-1349. *E-mail:* JP@globalpositioningservices.net; JG@globalpositioningservices.net; JW@globalpositioningservices.net. *Website:* www.globalpositioningservices.net. *E-mail:* info@threecrowsmusic.com (office). *Website:* threecrowsmusic.com.

JOHNSON, Brian; British singer and lyricist; b. 5 Oct. 1947, Dunston, Gateshead. *Career:* lead singer UK rock band Geordie 1972–78; lead singer Australian heavy rock group AC/DC 1980–; numerous tours worldwide, festival appearances. *Recordings include:* albums: with Geordie: Hope You Like It 1973, Don't Be Fooled by the Name 1974, Save the World 1976, Brian Johnson and Geordie 1981; with AC/DC: Back in Black 1980, For Those About to Rock 1981, Flick of the Switch 1983, Fly on the Wall 1985, Who Made Who (soundtrack) 1986, Blow Up Your Video 1988, The Razor's Edge 1990, Ballbreaker 1995, Volts 1997, Private Parts 1997, Bonfire 1997, Stiff Upper Lip 2000, Satellite Blues 2001, Black Ice 2008, Rock or Bust 2014. *Honours:* inducted into the Rock and Roll Hall of Fame 2003, Grammy Award for Best Hard Rock Performance (for War Machine) 2010. *Current Management:* c/o AC/DC Management, Sony Music Entertainment, 550 Madison Avenue, New York, NY 10022-3211, USA. *Website:* www.acdc.com.

JOHNSON, Carolyn Dawn; Canadian country singer, songwriter and musician (guitar); b. 30 April 1970, Grande Prairie, Alberta; one d. *Career:* moved to Nashville 1995; employed as songwriter; joined Martina McBride's band 1999; signed recording contract 2000; numerous stage appearances and concerts. *Recordings include:* album: Room With A View 2001, Dress Rehearsal 2004, Love and Negotiation 2006, Love Rules 2010. *Honours:* Music Row Breakthrough Songwriter of the Year 2000, five awards, Canadian Country Music Awards 2001, Acad. of Country Music's Top New Female Vocalist 2002, American Music Award for Best New Country Artist 2003, Female Artist of the Year, Canadian Country Music Asscn 2006, 2007, 2012. *Website:* www.cdj.com.

JOHNSON, Derick; British musician (bass guitar); b. 7 June 1963, Manchester, England; two s. *Career:* started 52nd Street 1983–86; played with Swing Out Sister 1989–; four tours: Italy, Philippines, Spain, UK, Japan, America, Radio One sessions, Top of the Pops, Tube, The Word, Pebble Mill; mem. Musicians' Union. *Compositions include:* That's The Way It Goes; Low Down Dirty Business; Cool As Ice. *Recordings include:* album: Swing Out Sister, Get In Touch With Yourself, The Living Return 1994; with Telepath: Contact 2008, Crush 2011; with Doomsday Productions: Filthy 1999, Survival of the Siccest 2004, Northtown vs. Westside vs. Eastside 2005.

JOHNSON, Henry Joseph, Jr; American jazz guitarist, vocalist, composer, arranger and producer; *Instructor of Jazz Guitar Studies, Chicago College of Performing Arts, Roosevelt University*; b. 28 Jan. 1954, Chicago, Ill.; eldest s. of Henry Joseph Johnson and Murry L. Johnson. *Education:* Indiana Univ. Northwest. *Career:* African-American artist; guitarist for organist Jack McDuff 1976; singer, Donny Hathaway 1977; pianist, Ramsey Lewis 1979–82, 1985–; singer, Joe Williams 1985–; saxophonist, Stanley Turrentine 1995–; solo artist 1987–; performances include: all jazz festivals including Playboy Jazz Festival, JVC Jazz Festival, North Seas Jazz Festival; mem. Musicians' Union, American Fed. of TV and Radio Artists, Nat. Acad. of Recording Arts and Sciences. *Recordings include:* seven albums as solo artist: Downbeat: You're The One (awarded five stars, Billboard Top 100 List 1986, 1987, 1988) 1986, Future Excursions 1988, Never too Much 1990, New Beginnings 1993, Missing You 1994, An Evening at Sea 2000, Organic 2004. *Radio includes:* int. airplay on all major radio stations in UK, France, Germany, Austria, Canada, Japan, Norway, Sweden, Spain and Africa. *Television includes:* played main character in documentary filmed for Japanese TV, appeared on major programmes including Arsenio Hall, Joan Rivers, VH-1 and Live with the Boston Pops, composition used as background music in major network soap opera on ABC nation-wide. *Publications includes:* interviews and articles in major int. music magazines including DownBeat, Billboard, Cash Box, Coda, Guitar Player and Jazz Times. *Honours:* Life-Time Achievement Award, Duquesne Univ., Outstanding Achievement Award, City of Gary, Ind. *Address:* PO Box 10464, Chicago, IL 60610-0464, USA. *Telephone:* (312) 909-6373. *E-mail:* henry@henryjohnsonjazz.com. *Website:* www.henryjohnsonjazz.com.

JOHNSON, William (Holly); British singer, songwriter, writer, artist and actor; b. 9 Feb. 1960, Liverpool, England. *Career:* mem. Big in Japan; Founder-mem. Frankie Goes to Hollywood 1980–87; numerous live appearances, world tours, festival performances; solo artist 1987–; Owner, Pleasuredome record label. *Art exhibitions:* (paintings and sculptures) The House of Holly, Cork Street Gallery, London 1996, numerous exhibitions at Tate Liverpool, Royal Academy. *Recordings include:* albums: with Frankie Goes to Hollywood: Welcome to the Pleasuredome 1984, Liverpool 1986, Blast 1989, Hollelujah 1989, Dreams That Money Can't Buy 1991, Reload 1994, Maximum Joy 2000, Twelve Inches 2001, Frankie Said 2012; with Big in Japan: Brutality Religion and a Dance Beat 1977, From Y to Z and Never Again 1978, The Zoo: Uncaged 1978-1982 1990; solo: Soulstream 1999. *Publication:* A Bone in My Flute (autobiography) 1994. *Honours:* BRIT Award for Best British Single, for Best British Newcomer 1985, Ivor Novello Award for Best Contemporary Song (for Two Tribes) 1985. *Address:* Pleasuredome, PO Box 425, London, SW6 3TX, England. *Website:* www.hollyjohnson.com.

JOHNSON, Jack; American singer, songwriter and filmmaker; b. 18 May 1975, Hawaii; m. Kim Johnson; one s. *Education:* Univ. of California, Santa Barbara. *Career:* fmr professional surfer, career curtailed by serious accident; Co-founder The Moonshine Conspiracy film production co. (later renamed Woodshed Films) 1998; directed film about surfing Thicker than Water 2000; solo artist 2001–; Co-founder Brushfire Records 2002; collaborations with Black Eyed Peas, Handsome Boy Modeling School, G. Love & Special Sauce; Co-founder Kokua Hawaii Foundation (non-profit environmental org.) 2004. *Recordings include:* albums: Brushfire Fairytales 2001, On and On 2003, In Between Dreams 2005, Sleep Through the Static 2008, To the Sea 2010, From Here to Now to You 2013. *Film soundtracks:* contrib. to: Thicker than Water 2000, September Sessions 2002, Sprout 2005, A Brokedown Melody 2006; albums: Sing-A-Longs and Lullabies for the film Curious George 2006. *Honours:* Surfing's Music Artist of the Year, ESPN Action, Sports & Music Awards 2001, Best Int. Newcomer, BRIT Awards, UK 2006, Humanitarian Award, Billboard Touring Awards 2010, Nat. Conservation Achievement Award in Communications, Nat. Wildlife Foundation 2012. *Address:* Brushfire Records, c/o Universal Music Group, 1755 Broadway, New York, NY 10019, USA (office). *Website:* www.brushfirerecords.com (office); www.jackjohnsonmusic.com.

JOHNSON, Jamey Van; American country music singer, songwriter and musician (guitar); b. 14 July 1975, Enterprise, Ala. *Education:* Jeff Davis High School, Jacksonville State Univ. *Career:* served in 3rd Battalion 23rd Marines, US Marine Corps Reserve, became corporal; moved to Nashville 2000; signed to BNA Records 2005; support act on Kid Rock tour 2011; songwriter for Trace Adkins, Jessie James, George Strait, Joe Nichols, James Otto; released tribute album to Hank Cochran 2012, duetting with artists including Alison Krauss, Elvis Costello, Vince Gill, Merle Haggard, Willie Nelson, Ray Price, George Strait; other collaborators include Miranda Lambert, Sammy Kershaw, Blind Boys of Alabama, Randy Travis, George Jones. *Television:* Nashville 2007. *Recordings include:* albums: They Call Me Country 2002, The Dollar 2006, That Lonesome Song 2008, The Guitar Song 2010, Living for a Song: A Tribute to Hank Cochran 2012. *Honours:* Acad. of Country Music Song of the Year Awards (for Give it Away) 2007, (for In Color) 2009, Country Music Asscn Awards for Song of the Year (for Give it Away) 2007, (for In Color) 2009. *Address:* c/o Mercury Nashville Records, Universal Music Group Nashville, 401 Commerce Street, Nashville, TN 37219, USA (office). *Website:* www.umgnashville.com (office); www.jameyjohnson.com.

JOHNSON, John, (J. J.); British musician (drums, keyboards), singer and producer; b. 27 Oct. 1951, Newark, Notts.; partner Christine Robertson, two s. *Career:* drummer, Wayne County and The Electric Chairs 1976–80; mem. band Mystere Five; drums and vocals, Flying Lizards, Thomas Dolby, Skids, Nico, GBM; mem. Musicians' Union. *Recordings include:* with The Electric Chairs: The Electric Chairs (EP) 1977, Blatantly Offensive (EP) 1978; albums: The Electric Chairs 1977, Storm the Gates of Heaven 1978, Things Your Mother Never Told You 1979, Best of Jayne/Wayne County and the Electric Chairs 1982; eight singles including: Thunder When She Walks 1977, Trying to Get on the Radio 1978, Eddie and Sheena 1978, Waiting For the Marines 1979, Berlin 1979, So Many Ways 1979; with Mystere 5: singles include: Heart Rules the Head and No Message 1980; with The Flying Lizards: album: Fourth Wall 1981; singles: Lovers and Other Strangers, Jungle Line (EP), Thomas Dolby 1981; albums: Drama of Exile, Nico, Joy, The Skids 1981, Ten Thirty on a Summer's Night, Richard Jobson 1983; with GBM: album: Method in the Madness; with Neil Finn: One Nil 2001; Singles: Strange News, Diction and Fiction, Whistling in the Dark 1983–84.

JOHNSON, Laurence Reginald Ward (Laurie), MBE; British composer and bandleader; b. 7 Feb. 1927, Hampstead, London, England; m.; one d. *Education:* Royal Coll. of Music. *Career:* four years Nat. Service in the Coldstream Guards; taught at Royal College of Music; orchestral pieces broadcast by age 20; composer and arranger for Ted Heath Band and other bands and orchestras of 1950s; joined film industry 1955; formed own film production co. with Albert Fennell and Brian Clemens 1972; Co-owner, with Albert Fennell and John Hough, film production co. Gainsborough Pictures 1978–; Founder The London Big Band (25 British jazz and orchestral musicians) 1994. *Compositions include:* Lock Up Your Daughters (Ivor Novello Award) 1959,; Pieces of Eight, revue; The Four Musketeers, musical; scores for over 400 cinema and TV films including: Dr Strangelove, First Men In The Moon, The Avengers, The Professionals, The New Avengers; TV themes include: This Is Your Life, World In Action, Whicker's World. *Recordings include:* Synthesis (symphony), The Wind In the Willows (tone poem), Suite for Symphonic Band (RAF commission for 50th anniversary of Battle of Britain), The Conquistadors, Music for Royal occasions; numerous albums with own studio orchestra. *Honours:* various awards for music scores and record or film productions.

JOHNSON, Matt; British singer, songwriter, musician (guitar) and record producer; b. 15 Aug. 1961, East London. *Career:* mem. Road Star aged 11; recording engineer, London aged 15 1976; f. The The aged 17 1979; films include Infected (long-form video to accompany album) 1987, The The Versus The World 1991, From Dusk 'Til Dawn 1994. *Recordings include:* albums: Burning Blue Soul 1981, Soul Mining 1983, Infected (also film and book) 1986, Mind Bomb 1989, Dusk 1993, Solitude 1994, Hanky Panky 1995, Naked Self 2000; with Orang: Herd of Instinct 1995; with Shudder to Think: First Love Last Rites 1998; singles include: Controversial Subject 1981, Uncertain Smile 1982, Perfect 1983, This Is The Day 1983, Sweet Bird of Truth 1986, Heartland 1986, Infected 1986, Slow Train To Dawn 1987, Armageddon Days 1989, The Beat(en) Generation 1989, Gravitate To Me 1989, Shades of Blue, EP 1991, Dogs of Lust 1993, Slow Emotion Replay 1993, Love Is Stronger Than Death 1993, Dis-Infected EP 1994, I Saw The Light 1995. *Publications include:* Infected (lyrics and paintings) 1987. *Honours:* Best Long Form Video, Montreux Film and Music Festival, Infected 1988. *E-mail:* cally@thethe.com (office). *Website:* www.thethe.com.

JOHNSON, Ralph; American singer, musician (percussion) and producer; b. 4 July 1951, Los Angeles, Calif. *Career:* mem. Earth, Wind and Fire 1972–84, 1987–; live performances and tours include numerous special effects; leader of band, Audio Caviar 2005–. *Recordings include:* albums: Last Days And Time 1972, Head To The Sky 1973, Open Our Eyes 1974, That's The Way Of The World (soundtrack) (Grammy Award) 1975, Gratitude 1975, Spirit 1976, All 'N' All 1977, I Am 1979, Faces 1980, Raise! 1981, Secret Messages 1982, Powerlight 1983, Electric Universe 1983, Touch The World 1987, Heritage 1990, Millennium 1993, In The Name Of Love 1997, Take Two 2001, The Promise 2003, Avatar 2003, Illumination 2005, Now, Then & Forever 2013. *Honours:* American Music Award for Favorite Soul/Rhythm and Blues Band 1977, 1979, Grammy Award for Best R&B Vocal Performance (for All 'N' All) 1979, (for After The Love Has Gone) 1980, Best R&B Instrumental (for Boogie Wonderland) 1980, MTV Music Video Award 1985, Ivor Novello Award (for Easy Lover) 1986, Grammy Award for Best Gospel Performance 1987. *E-mail:* band@earthwindandfire.com (office). *Website:* www.earthwindandfire.com.

JOHNSON, Robb Jenner, BA, MA; British folk singer, songwriter and musician (guitar); b. 25 Dec. 1955, London, England; m. Meeta Kanabar 1992; two s. *Career:* performed in folk clubs 1975–80; mem. band, Grubstreet 1980–84; mem. agit-prop trio, Ministry of Humour 1984–86; solo, then duo with Pip Collings 1989–94; solo, Nicaragua TV, Managua Concert for the 10th anniversary of the Revolution 1989; Channel 4 documentary, Beyond the Maypole 1991; 25th Anniversary, Glastonbury Festival 1995; Passendael Peace Concert 1997; English Chanson at the Drill Hall Theatre, London, 2003; Folk Britannia Concert for BBC Four, Barbican, London 2006; Man. Dir Irregular Records; mem. Musicians' Union, Performing Right Soc. *Recordings include:* albums: Skewed Stewed and Awkward 1987, Small Town World 1989, Overnight 1991, Heart's Desire 1993, Lack of Jolly Ploughboy 1994, This Is The UK Talking 1994, The Night Cafe 1996, Gentlemen 1998, The Big Wheel 1999, Margaret Thatcher: My Part In Her Downfall 2000, 21st Century Blues 2001, Clockwork Music 2003, Tony Blair: My Part In His Downfall 2004, A Beginner's Guide 2005, Metro 2005, Saturday Night at the Fire Station 2006, All That Way For This 2007, Love & Death & Politics 2008, Margaret Thatcher: My Part in Her Downfall – Deluxe 2009, The Ghost of Love 2009, Man Walks into a Pub 2010, Some Recent Protest Songs 2011, Once Upon a

Time 2011, Happily Ever After 2012, Bring Down the Moon 2013, West Pier Serenade 2013, Gentle Men 2013. *Publications:* Words and Chords: A Robb Johnson Songbook 2000, Journeys Down Denbigh Rd (ed) 2002, Woman: The Incredible Life of Yoko Ono (with Alan Clayson and Barb Jungr) 2004, Gentle Men (book version) 2013. *Honours:* Northwest Songwriters' Competition 1980. *Address:* Irregular Records, PO Box 5143, Hove, East Sussex, BN52 9FT, England (office). *E-mail:* info@irregularrecords.co.uk (office). *Website:* www .robbjohnson.co.uk.

JOHNSON, Steven William; American musician (drums) and songwriter; b. Ala; two c. *Career:* Founder-mem., The Shakes, renamed Alabama Shakes 2009–; debut EP released 2011; first major tour 2011; many live tours and festival appearances; numerous TV appearances. *Recordings:* albums: with Alabama Shakes: Boys & Girls 2012, Sound & Color (Grammy Award for Best Alternative Music Album 2016) 2015. *Honours:* Americana Music Honors and Awards Award for Emerging Artist of the Year 2012, Grammy Awards for Best Rock Performance and Best Rock Song (both for Don't Wanna Fight) 2016. *Current Management:* c/o Kevin Morris and Christine Stauder, Red Light Management, 44 Wall Street, 22nd Floor, New York, NY 10005, USA. *Telephone:* (646) 292-7400. *Fax:* (646) 292-7450. *Website:* www .redlightmanagement.com; www.alabamashakes.com (home).

JOHNSON, Wilko, BA; British guitarist and songwriter; b. (John Peter Wilkinson), 12 July 1947, Canvey Island, Essex, England; m. Irene Knight (died 2004); two s. *Education:* Westcliff High School for Boys, Univ. of Newcastle upon Tyne. *Career:* fmr English teacher; Founder-mem. Dr Feelgood 1972–77; Founder-mem. Solid Senders 1977–78; Founder-mem. Wilko Johnson Band 1977–; guitarist with Ian Dury's Blockheads 1980; numerous collaborations and guest spots including with Mick Farren, Johnny Thunders, The Stranglers, Lew Lewis, Madness, Roger Daltrey. *Recordings include:* albums: with Dr Feelgood: Down by the Jetty 1975, Malpractice 1975, Stupidity 1976, Sneakin' Suspicion 1977; with Solid Senders: Solid Senders 1978; with Ian Dury and the Blockheads: Laughter 1980; solo: Ice on the Motorway 1981, Pull the Cover 1984, Call It What You Want 1987, Barbed Wire Blues 1988, Going Back Home 1998, Red Hot Rocking Blues 2005; with Roger Daltrey: Going Back Home 2014. *Television:* as actor: Game of Thrones 2011–12. *Publication:* Looking Back at Me (autobiography) 2012. *Honours:* Q Icon Award 2014. *Website:* wilkojohnson.com.

JOHNSTON, Ben Hamilton; British musician (drums, percussion), songwriter and singer; b. 25 April 1980, Kilmarnock, Scotland; m. Louise Johnston 2012; one s. *Career:* mem. Biffy Clyro late 1990s–, twin brother of group's James Johnston; group signed to Beggars Banquet Records 2001, numerous tours; drummer for live shows, Marmaduke Duke. *Recordings:* albums: with Biffy Clyro: Blackened Sky 2002, The Vertigo of Bliss 2003, Infinity Land 2004, Puzzle 2007, Only Revolutions 2009, Opposites (Kerrang! Award for Best Album 2013, Q Magazine Award for Best Album 2013) 2013. *Honours:* with Biffy Clyro: Kerrang! Awards for Best Music Video (for The Captain) 2010, for Classic Songwriter 2011, NME Awards for Best Music Video (for The Captain) 2010, for Best Live Band 2011, for Best British Band 2013, Q Magazine Award for Best Live Band 2011. *Address:* c/o 14th Floor Records, Warner Music UK Limited, The Warner Building, 28a Kensington Church Street, London, W8 4EP, England (office). *Telephone:* (20) 7368-2500 (office). *Fax:* (20) 7368-2770 (office). *Website:* www.14thfloorrecords.com (office); www .wmg.com (office); biffyclyro.com.

JOHNSTON, James Robert; British musician (bass guitar), songwriter and singer; b. 25 April 1980, Kilmarnock, Scotland. *Career:* Founder-mem. Biffy Clyro (initially called Screwfish) 1995–, twin brother of group's Ben Johnston; group signed to Beggars Banquet Records 2001, numerous tours; bass guitarist for live shows, Marmaduke Duke. *Recordings:* albums: with Biffy Clyro: Blackened Sky 2002, The Vertigo of Bliss 2003, Infinity Land 2004, Puzzle 2007, Only Revolutions 2009, Opposites (Kerrang! Award for Best Album 2013, Q Magazine Award for Best Album 2013) 2013. *Honours:* with Biffy Clyro: Kerrang! Awards for Best Music Video (for The Captain) 2010, for Classic Songwriter 2011, NME Awards for Best Music Video (for The Captain) 2010, for Best Live Band 2011, for Best British Band 2013, Q Magazine Award for Best Live Band 2011. *Address:* c/o 14th Floor Records, Warner Music UK Limited, The Warner Building, 28a Kensington Church Street, London, W8 4EP, England (office). *Telephone:* (20) 7368-2500 (office). *Fax:* (20) 7368-2770 (office). *Website:* www.14thfloorrecords.com (office); www.wmg.com (office); biffyclyro.com.

JOHNSTON, Jim, DipEd; Irish singer, songwriter and dancer; b. 20 Dec. 1954, Dundalk; m. Patricia Johnston 1981; one s. two d. *Education:* St Patrick's Training Coll., Drumcondra, Dublin, CCÉ, Dundalk, Matthews School of Irish Dance, studied traditional fiddle with Rose O'Connor. *Career:* tours with Dún Dealgan Cabaret, Comhaltas, Lá Lugh (traditional band); numerous festival performances, TV and radio broadcasts; Síbín Tna G 1998; supported: Mary Coughlan 1994, Mick Hanly 1994, Sonny Condell 1995, Don Baker 1995, Freddie White 1996, Something Happens, Drogheda 1998; mem. Irish Music Rights Org. *Recordings include:* albums: The Factories –They're All Closing Down 1986, Rian An Uaignis 1993, Politics of the Heart 1999, Ballads and Blues 2008. *Publications include:* Pléaráca Dhún Dealgan (The Humours of Dundalk: Collection of Folk Songs) 1985. *Honours:* Men's World Irish Dancing Champion 1975, 1977, 1979.

JOHNSTON, Timothy John; British musician (drums); b. 12 Nov. 1963, Newcastle upon Tyne, England. *Education:* Newcastle Coll. *Career:* toured extensively with Pauline Murray and The Storm including full tour supporting The Mission 1985–; TV and radio appearances with The Light Programme and Swing Palace 1987–94; regular appearances at nat. jazz festivals; toured with Deacon Jones and the Sinners 1994; performed in resident band Bourbon Street at Hilton, Park Lane, London 1995; mem. Musicians' Union. *Recordings include:* two albums with The Light Programme 1987, 1989; Album Storm Clouds 1989 and two singles This Thing Called Love and New Age with Pauline Murray; two albums with Swing Palace 1991, 1993.

JOLLY ROGER (see Richards, Eddie)

JONAS, Joe; American singer, musician (guitar, keyboard) and actor; b. (Joseph Adam Jonas), 15 Aug. 1989, Casa Grande, Ariz. *Career:* mem. Jonas Brothers (with brothers Kevin and Nick) 2005–. *Television appearances:* Hannah Montana 2007, Camp Rock 2008, Jonas 2009–, Jonas Brothers: The Journey (documentary) 2011. *Recordings include:* albums: It's About Time 2006, Jonas Brothers 2007, A Little Bit Longer 2008, Lines, Vines and Trying Times 2009; solo: Fast Life 2011. *Honours:* 11 Teen Choice Awards, Kids' Choice Awards for Best Music Group 2008, 2009, American Music Award for Best Breakthrough Artist 2008. *Current Management:* c/o Johnny Wright, Wright Entertainment Group, 7680 Universal Boulevard, Suite 500, Orlando, FL 32819-8998, USA. *Telephone:* (407) 826-9100. *Website:* www.wegmusic .com; www.jonasbrothers.com; www.joejonasmusic.com.

JONAS, Kevin; American singer, musician (guitar) and actor; b. (Paul Kevin Jonas II), 5 Nov. 1987, Teaneck, New Jersey; m. Danielle Deleasa 2009. *Career:* mem. Jonas Brothers (with brothers Joe and Nick) 2005–; numerous tours and concerts. *Television appearances:* Hannah Montana 2007, Camp Rock 2008, Jonas 2009, Married to Jonas 2012–. *Recordings include:* albums: It's About Time 2006, Jonas Brothers 2007, A Little Bit Longer 2008, Lines, Vines and Trying Times 2009, First Time (EP) 2013, Pom Poms (EP) 2013. *Honours:* 11 Teen Choice Awards, Kids' Choice Awards for Best Music Group 2008, 2009, American Music Award for Best Breakthrough Artist 2008. *Current Management:* c/o Johnny Wright, Wright Entertainment Group, 7680 Universal Boulevard, Suite 500, Orlando, FL 32819-8998, USA. *Telephone:* (407) 826-9100. *Website:* www.wegmusic.com. *Address:* c/o Hollywood Records, 500 South Buena Vista Street, Burbank, CA 91521, USA (office). *Website:* www.jonasbrothers.com; www.kevinjonasonline.com.

JONAS, Nick; American singer and actor; b. (Nicholas Jerry Jonas), 16 Sept. 1992, Dallas, Tex. *Career:* began career acting on Broadway, aged six; solo singer, signing record deal with Columbia Records 2004–; mem. Jonas Brothers (with brothers Joe and Kevin) 2005–; also sings as solo artist, with backing band the Administration 2009–. *Stage appearances:* A Christmas Carol 2000, Annie Get Your Gun 2001, Beauty and the Beast 2002, Les Misérables 2003. *Television appearances:* Hannah Montana 2007, Camp Rock 2008, Jonas 2009–. *Recordings include:* albums: with Jonas Brothers: It's About Time 2006, Jonas Brothers 2007, A Little Bit Longer 2008, Lines, Vines and Trying Times 2009; solo: Nicholas Jonas 2005, Who I Am (with the Administration) 2010. *Honours:* 11 Teen Choice Awards, Kids' Choice Awards for Best Music Group 2008, 2009, American Music Award for Best Breakthrough Artist 2008. *Current Management:* c/o Creative Artists Agency, 2000 Avenue of the Stars, Los Angeles, CA 90067, USA.

JONASSON, Jonas; Swedish musician (synthesizer, vocoder, melodica); b. 28 Aug. 1967, Angelholm, Sweden; m. Malin Jonasson-Sahlstedt 1992; two d. *Career:* mem., bob hund 1991–; numerous concerts in Scandinavia, including Roskilde, Lollipop, Ruisrock, Quartfestivalen and Hultsfred festivals; mem. STIM, SAMI. *Recordings:* bob hund 1993, Edvin Medvind, 7 1994, I Stället för Musik: förvirring 1996, Omslag: Martin Kann 1996, Düsseldorf 3:53 1996, Ett fall och en lösning 1997, Nu är det väl revolution på gång? 1998, Jag rear ut min själ! Allt skal bort!!! 1998, Helgen V.48 1999, Sover aldrig 1999, Stenåldem kan börja 2001, Ingenting 2002. *Honours:* Swedish Grammy Awards for Best Live Act 1994, Best Lyrics 1996. *Website:* www.bobhund.nu.

JONES, Belinda Helen (Bill); British singer, musician (accordion, piano, flute, whistle) and composer; b. 17 Aug. 1973, Codsall, Wolverhampton, England. *Education:* London City Univ. *Career:* folk musician; worked with accordionist Phil Cunningham; BBC Radio sessions for Folk on 2 and Andy Kershaw; Airplay on BBC nat. and local stations, and on many abroad; toured UK, USA, Japan, Spain, Netherlands, Germany and Belgium. *Recordings:* albums: Turn To Me 2000, Panchpuran 2001, Bits and Pieces 2001, Live at the Live 2002, Two Year Winter 2003, Faire Winds 2003. *Honours:* BBC Horizon Award for New Talent 2001. *Current Management:* Felicity Jones, 26 Druridge Avenue, Seaburn, Sunderland, SR6 0AD, England. *E-mail:* felicity@brickwallmusic.com. *Website:* www.brickwallmusic.com.

JONES, Bobby Louis, BS, BEd, MA, PhD; American gospel singer, television broadcaster and lecturer; *Presenter and Producer, The Bobby Jones Gospel Hour;* b. 1938, Henry, Tenn.; m. Ethel Williams Jones. *Education:* Tenn. State Univ. and Vanderbilt Univ., Nashville, Tenn. *Career:* teacher, elementary schools in Tenn. and Missouri; textbook consultant for educational publr; Instructor in Reading and Study Skills, Tenn. State Univ. 1974–86; began performing as gospel singer 1970s; Producer and Host Fun City 5 (children's programme), WTBF, Nashville; formed gospel group 'New Life' 1975; cr. first Black Expo, Nashville 1976; signed contract for first TV gospel show (Channel 4) 1976; Producer and Host The Bobby Jones Gospel Hour (BET) 1980–, Bobby Jones World (BET) 1978–84, Video Gospel (BET) 1986–, Bobby Jones Gospel Classics (Word Network) 2001–, Bobby Jones Presents (Word Network) 2001–,

Let's Talk Church (BET) 2002–, Bobby Jones Next Generation (The Gospel Channel) 2008–, radio programme The Bobby Jones Gospel Countdown (Sheridan Network); composed and acted in gospel opera 'Make a Joyful Noise' (Gabriel Award, Int. Film Festival Award) 1980; Instructor, Nova Southeastern Univ. 2007–; co-ordinator Exec. Int. Record Label Gospel Artists Retreat. *Recordings include:* New Life albums: Sooner or Later 1976, There Is Hope in This World 1978, Caught Up 1979, Tin Gladje 1981, Soul Set Free 1982, Come Together (Dove Award, Gospel Music Asscn) 1984, I'll Never Forget 1990, Bring It to Jesus 1993, Another Time 1996, Just Churchin' (featuring the Nashville Superchoir) 1998, Faith Unscripted 2007, The Ambassador 2007, Rejoice with Me! 2015; singles: I'm So Glad I'm Standing Here Today (with Barbara Mandrell, Grammy Award) 1984. *Television includes:* Sister Sister (film) 1982. *Plays:* Yes God is Real. *Radio:* The Bobby Jones Gospel Countdown, The Bobby Jones Gospel Radio Show. *Publication:* Touched by God: Stories of Nineteen Gospel Artists 1998, Make a Joyful Noise: My 25 Years in Gospel Music (autobiog.) 2000. *Honours:* Hon. PhD (Payne Theological Seminary, Wilberforce, Ohio) 1991; Commonwealth Award, Gospel Music Asscn 1990, 352 honours and awards housed at Indiana Univ. *Address:* c/o Humilitee, Gospel Fruits Inc. (office). *Telephone:* (866) 697-3161 (office). *E-mail:* gospelfruits@hotmail.com. *Website:* www.bobbyjonesgospel .com.

JONES, Booker T.; American musician (keyboards), songwriter and record producer; b. 12 Nov. 1944, Memphis, Tenn.; m. Priscilla Coolidge. *Career:* session musician, Memphis; leader, Booker T and The MGs (Memphis Group) 1962–71, 1977 (album reunion); concerts, tours and festival appearances; solo songwriter and vocalist 1971–; backing band for Neil Young's US tour 1993. *Compositions include:* film score: Up Tight 1969; songwriter, musician with Sam and Dave, Wilson Pickett, Otis Redding, Rufus Thomas. *Recordings include:* albums: Up Tight 1969, Booker T and Priscilla 1971, The Runaway 1972, Try and Love Again 1978; with the MGs: Green Onions 1964, Hip Hug-Her 1967, Back To Back 1967, Doin' Our Thing 1968, Soul Limbo 1968, The Booker T Set 1969, McLemore Avenue 1970, Melting Pot 1971, Union Extended 1976, Universal Language 1977, Potato Hole (Grammy Award for Best Pop Instrumental Album 2010) 2009, The Road from Memphis (Grammy Award for Best Pop Instrumental Album 2012) 2011. *Honours:* inducted into Rock and Roll Hall of Fame in 1992, Grammy Award for Lifetime Achievement 2007. *Current Management:* 525 Worldwide Music Co., PO Box 957, Salem, MA 01970, USA. *Telephone:* (888) 664-8145. *E-mail:* 525@525worldwide.com. *Website:* www.525worldwide.com. *E-mail:* BookerTJones@BookerT.com (office). *Website:* www.bookert.com.

JONES, Chris; American writer, composer and producer; *Executive Producer, Cocktailmusic Inc;* b. 10 Jan. 1963, Paris, France; m. 1st Anne Nbole; m. 2nd Salome Nga; m. 3rd Jackie Minlu; four d. *Education:* studied composition, musicology and copyright law. *Career:* concentrated on studio work and writing; Exec. Producer Cocktailmusic Inc; mem. ASCAP. *Compositions include:* Silent Lover, Till The Middle of The Night, Call Me, Hold On Me, Boys Come and Go, Lovin' Livin' Givin', Stay Around, Boogie Dancin' Shoes. *Recordings:* Call Me 1993, Till the Middle of the Night 1994, Lovin' Livin' Givin' 1995, The Beat Goes On 2001; singles: Stand By Me 2004, You Keep Me Hangin' On 2004, 2010-Till the Middle of theNight Trance version 2010, Best Trance Hits by Chris Jones 2010,You Make Me Feel 2011, Trance Pad 2011, You Should be Dancin' 2011, Time is Tight 2011. *Publications:* Surviving For Your Love; contrib. various musicological essays in professional journals. *Address:* 1600 Ocean Blvd, Boca Raton, Miami, FL 33432, USA (home). *Telephone:* (786) 623-5863 (office). *E-mail:* Jjones52@aol.com (office); joneschris53@hotmail.com (office). *Website:* www.cocktailmusic.com (office).

JONES, Chris Alan; British musician (drums, percussion); b. 18 Dec. 1966, Reading, England. *Education:* studied drums. *Career:* drummer, Mega City Four 1987–; world tours, TV appearances; mem. Musicians' Union. *Recordings include:* with Mega City Four: Tranzophobia 1989, Who Cares Wins 1990, Terribly Sorry Bob 1991, Sebastopol Road 1992, Magic Bullets 1993. *Address:* 5 Rother Road, Cove, Farnborough, Hampshire, GU14 9LP, England.

JONES, Daniel; Australian musician (multi-instrumentalist); b. 22 July 1973, Essex, England; m. Kathleen de Leon 2005; two c. *Education:* Shailer Park High, Logan City, Australia. *Career:* relocated to Brisbane, Australia as a child; worked as a printer and in a supermarket; fmr mem., Red Edge; Founder-mem., Savage Garden 1996–2001; numerous live performances, including closing ceremony of Olympic Games, Sydney 2000; Owner, production co. Meridien Musik 2001–. *Recordings include:* albums: Savage Garden 1997, Affirmation 1999, Truly Madly Completely (compilation) 2005; with Aneiki: Words in Place of Objects 2001. *Honours:* 10 ARIA Awards 1997, APRA Award for Songwriters of the Year 2000. *Address:* Meridien Musik, GPO Box 1501, Brisbane, Qld 4001, Australia. *Fax:* (7) 3488-6066.

JONES, Danny Alan David; British musician (guitar) and singer; b. 12 March 1986, Bolton. *Career:* Founder mem., McFly 2004–. *Recordings include:* albums: Room on the Third Floor (Smash Hits Award for Best Album 2005) 2004, Wonderland 2005, Motion in the Ocean 2006, Radio:Active 2008, Above the Noise 2010. *Honours:* BRIT Award for Best Pop Act 2005, Smash Hits Awards for Smash Hits Star of the Year, for Best UK Band, for Best Video (for That Girl) 2005. *Website:* www.mcflyofficial.com.

JONES, Donell; American singer; b. Chicago, IL. *Career:* influenced by gospel singer father; solo artist 1996–; written and produced tracks for Silk, Brownstone and Usher; contributed vocal arrangements to Madonna's Bedtime Stories album; collaborations with Guru, True Steppers, Lisa 'Left Eye' Lopes. *Recordings include:* albums: My Heart 1996, Where You Wanna Be 1999, Life Goes On 2002, Journey of a Gemini 2006, The Lost Files 2009, Lyrics 2010. *Honours:* American Music Award for Favorite New Artist 2001. *Website:* www.myspace.com/donelljones.

JONES, Dylan, OBE, BA (Hons); British journalist; *Editor-in-Chief, GQ magazine;* b. 1960; m. *Career:* Ed. Arena 1989–92; fmrly Ed. i-D magazine, Group Ed. Wagadon (publisher of Arena, The Face, etc.), Sr Ed. The Sunday Times, The Observer, Ed.-at-Large, The Sunday Times Magazine; has also worked for The Independent and The Guardian; currently Ed.-in-Chief, GQ; Chair. British Soc. of Magazine Eds; fmr Chair. Fashion Rocks; mem. Norman Mailer Asscn; Trustee, Hay Festival. *Publications include:* Jim Morrison: Dark Star 1991, Sex, Power and Travel: 10 Years of Arena (ed. and contrib.) 1996, Meaty, Beaty, Big and Bouncy: Classic Rock and Pop Writing from Elvis to Oasis 1996, Ultra Lounge: The Lexicon of Easy Listening 1997, iPod, Therefore I Am 2005, Mr Jones' Rules for the Modern Man 2006, Cameron on Cameron 2008, Heroes (with David Bailey) 2010, When Ziggy Played Guitar: David Bowie and Four Minutes that Shook the World 2012, The Biographical Dictionary of Popular Music 2012, From the Ground Up: U2 360° Tour Official Photobook 2012, The Eighties: One Day, One Decade 2013, Elvis Has Left the Building 2014. *Honours:* Hon. Prof. (Glasgow); 10 Magazine Ed. of the Year Awards 1993–2015. *Address:* GQ, Condé Nast Publications Ltd, Vogue House, Hanover Square, London, W1S 1JU, England (office). *Telephone:* (20) 7499-9080 (office). *Fax:* (20) 7495-1679 (office). *Website:* www.gq-magazine.co.uk (office).

JONES, Edgar (Ed) Francis, BA; British jazz musician (saxophone) and composer; b. 8 July 1961, Amersham, Buckinghamshire. *Education:* Middlesex Univ. *Career:* world-wide tours, TV and radio appearances with Us3, Incognito, Ed Jones Quartet/Quintet; Founder-mem., ED/GE (with Geoff Wilkinson) 2004–; mem. PRS, MCPS, Musicians' Union. *Recordings include:* albums: solo: Olé LA! 1988, The Home Coming 1989, Piper's Tales 1995, Out Here 1998, Seven Moments 2002; other: Hand on the Torch (with Us3) 1993, 100% and Rising (with Incognito), A View from the ED/GE (with Geoff Wilkinson) 2004, Schizophonic (with Us3) 2006, Eleven (with Incognito) 2006, Stop. Think. Run (with Us3) 2009.

JONES, Gordon Thomas; British musician (guitar) and record company executive; b. 21 Nov. 1947, Birkenhead, Merseyside, England; m. Jackie Jones 1984; one s. *Education:* art coll., Edinburgh, Scotland. *Career:* Founder Scottish folk band Silly Wizard; Founder and Partner Harbourtown Records, producing numerous albums; toured Europe and USA; guitarist with The Old Friends Band; mem. MCPS, PRS, PPC, EFDSS Nat. Council. *Recordings include:* albums: with Silly Wizard: Silly Wizard 1977, Caledonia's Hardy Sons 1978, So Many Partings 1979, Wild and Beautiful 1981, Kiss the Tears away 1983, Live in America 1985, Golden Golden 1985, A Glint of Silver 1987, Live Wizardry 1988. *Honours:* two MRS Awards as producer, Naird Award 1986. *Address:* PO Box 25, Ulverston, Cumbria, LA12 7UN, England. *Website:* www.harbourtownrecords.com.

JONES, Grace; American singer, model and actress; b. 19 May 1952, Spanishtown, Jamaica; d. of Robert Jones and Marjorie P. Jones; one s.; m. Atila Altaunbay 1996 (divorced). *Career:* moved to New York at age of 12; abandoned Spanish studies at Syracuse Univ. for first stage role, Phila; became fashion model in New York, then Paris; made first album, Portfolio, for Island Records 1977; debut as disco singer New York 1977; opened La Vie en Rose restaurant, New York 1987. *Films include:* Gordon's War 1973, Let's Make a Dirty Movie 1976, Colt 38 Special Squad 1976, Army of Lovers or Revolution of the Perverts (documentary) 1979, Deadly Vengeance 1981, Made in France (documentary) 1984, Conan the Destroyer 1984, A View to a Kill 1985, Vamp 1986, Straight to Hell 1987, Siesta 1987, Boomerang 1992, Cyber Bandits 1995, McCinsey's Island 1998, Palmer's Pick Up 1999, No Place Like Home 2006, Falco 2008, Chelsea on the Rocks 2008. *Television:* Stryx 1978, A One Man Show 1982, Pee-wee's Playhouse Christmas Special 1988, Beastmaster 1999, Wolf Girl 2001, Shaka Zulu: The Citadel 2001. *Recordings include:* albums: Portfolio 1977, Fame 1978, Muse 1979, Warm Leatherette 1980, Nightclubbing 1981, Living My Life 1982, Island Life 1985, Slave to the Rhythm 1985, Inside Story 1986, Bulletproof Heart 1989, Hurricane 2008, Icon 2013. *Publications:* I'll Never Write My Memoirs 2015. *Honours:* Q Idol Award 2008. *Current Management:* c/o CMO Management, 11 Westbourne Studios, 242 Acklam Road, London, W10 5JJ, England. *Telephone:* (20) 3735-5632. *E-mail:* info@blueraincoatmusic.com. *Website:* www.cmomanagement .co.uk.

JONES, (John) Howard; British songwriter, singer, musician (keyboards, computer) and record producer; b. 23 Feb. 1955, Southampton, Hampshire, England; m. Janet Lesley Smith 1978. *Education:* Royal Northern Coll. of Music, Manchester. *Career:* piano teacher; solo recording artist 1983–; tours include: US tour, support to Eurythmics 1984; British tour 1984, N America 1992; played at Live Aid, Wembley Stadium 1985; mem. American Soc. of Composers, Authors and Publishers, PRS, Sōka Gakkai Int.; Musical Dir, Glorious Life Chorus; Bd mem., Featured Artists Coalition. *Recordings include:* albums: Human's Lib 1984, The Twelve Inch Album 1984, Dream Into Action 1985, Action Replay 1986, One To One 1986, Cross That Line 1989, The Best of Howard Jones 1993, In The Running 1998, Greatest Hits, Working In The Backroom, Live Acoustic America 1996, Angels and Lovers 1997, People 1998, Pefawm 2000, Revolution of the Heart 2005, Ordinary Heroes

2009, Piano Solos for Friends and Loved Ones, vols 1, 2 2012; singles include: New Song 1983, What Is Love 1984, Hide and Seek 1984, Pearl In The Shell 1984, Like To Get To Know You Well 1984, Things Can Only Get Better 1985, Look Mama 1985, Life In One Day 1985, No One Is To Blame 1986, All I Want 1986, You Know I Love You… Don't You? 1986, Everlasting Love 1987, The Prisoner 1989, Lift Me Up 1992, What Is Love 1993, IGY 1993, Tomorrow Is Now 1998, Let the People Have Their Say 1999, Someone You Need 2000, Building Our Own Future 2006, Soon You'll Go 2009. *Contributions include:* Live-in World (Anti-Heroin Project charity album), 1986; Rubáiyát (Elektra's 40th Anniversary album), 1990. *Current Management:* c/o David and Joseph Stopps, FML Music Ltd., 33 Alexander Road, Aylesbury, Buckinghamshire, HP20 2NR, England. *Telephone:* (12) 9643-4731. *E-mail:* info@fmlmusic.com. *E-mail:* howard@howardjones.com. *Website:* www.howardjones.com.

JONES, John (Jack) Allen; American singer and actor; b. 14 Jan. 1938, Los Angeles, Calif. *Education:* studied singing at high school. *Career:* club singer 1957; solo artist 1962–; appearances with Jerry Lewis, Bob Hope; actor, TV: The Palace, Funny Face, Love Boat, Condominium, The Comeback; film appearance: Juke Box Rhythm; stage performance: Guys and Dolls, USA 1991; regular concert tours. *Recordings include:* albums: This Love of Mine 1959, Shall We Dance 1961, Lollipops and Roses 1961, I've Got a Lot of Livin' to Do 1961, Gift of Love 1962, Call Me Irresponsible 1963, She Loves Me 1963, Wives and Lovers 1963, Bewitched 1964, Where Love has Gone 1964, My Gift to You 1964, Dear Heart 1965, My Kind of Town 1965, There's Love and There's Love and There's Love 1965, For The In Crowd 1966, The Impossible Dream 1966, Jack Jones Sings 1966, Lady 1967, Our Song 1967, What the World Needs Now is Love! 1968, Without Her 1968, Curtain Time 1968, If You Ever Leave Me 1968, The Bliss of Mrs Blossom 1968, Jack Jones in Hollywood 1968, L.A. Break Down 1969, Where is Love? 1969, A Jack Jones Christmas 1969, A Time for Us 1970, Showcase 1970, Jack Jones Sings Michel Legrand 1971, A Song for You 1972, Bread Winners 1972, Together 1973, Harbour 1974, Write Me a Love Song, Charlie 1974, What I Did for Love 1975, The Full Life 1977, With One More Look at You 1977, Nobody Does It Better 1979, Don't Stop Now 1980, Sound of Applause 1982, I Am a Singer 1987, The Gershwin Album 1992, New Jack Swing 1997, Love Makes the Changes 2010, Love Ballad 2011. *Honours:* Grammy Awards: Lollipops and Roses 1962, Wives and Lovers 1964, Cash Box Award for Most Promising Vocalist 1962, 1963, Golden Globe Award for film theme (Kotch) 1967, Golden Palm Star, Palm Springs, Calif., Walk of Stars 2003. *Website:* www.jackjones.org.

JONES, John Paul; British musician (bass), producer, arranger and composer; b. (John Baldwin), 3 June 1946, Sidcup, Kent, England. *Career:* mem. rock group, Led Zeppelin 1968–80, re-formed for one-off performance 2007; numerous concerts and live appearances; also producer for artists, including Butthole Surfers, Stefan Grossman, Ben E. King, The Mission, John Renbourn; arranger for artists, including REM, Raging Slab; session musician; film score composer; mem. Them Crooked Vultures 2009–. *Recordings include:* albums: with Led Zeppelin: Led Zeppelin 1969, Led Zeppelin II 1969, Led Zeppelin III 1970, Led Zeppelin IV 1971, Houses Of The Holy 1973, Physical Graffiti 1975, Presence 1976, The Song Remains The Same (live) 1976, In Through The Out Door 1979, How The West Was Won 2003, Mothership 2007, Celebration Day (Grammy Award for Best Rock Album 2014) 2012; solo: Zooma 1999, Lovin' Up A Storm 2000, The Thunderthief 2001; with Them Crooked Vultures: Them Crooked Vultures 2009. *Honours:* Ivor Novello Award for Outstanding Contribution to British Music 1977, Q magazine Merit Award 1992, Grammy lifetime achievement award 2005, Royal Swedish Acad. of Music Polar Music Prize 2006, Kennedy Center Honor 2012. *Current Management:* The Agency Group Ltd, 361–373 City Road, London, EC1V 1PQ, England. *Telephone:* (20) 7278-3331. *Fax:* (20) 7837-4672. *E-mail:* agencylondon@theagencygroup.com. *Website:* www.ledzeppelin.com; www.themcrookedvultures.com.

JONES, Jonathan Bradley (Jon); American country music bass guitarist; m. Sarah Jones 2011; one s. *Education:* Univ. of North Texas. *Career:* mem. Eli Young Band 2002–. *Recordings:* albums: with Eli Young Band: Eli Young Band 2002, Level 2005, Jet Black & Jealous 2008, Life at Best 2011, 10,000 Towns 2014. *Honours:* Acad. of Country Music Award for Song of the Year 2012, MusicRow Breakthrough Artist Award 2012. *Current Management:* c/o George Couri, Triple 8 Management, 5524 West Highway 290, Austin, TX 78735, USA. *Telephone:* (512) 444-7600. *Fax:* (512) 444-7601. *Website:* www.eliyoungband.com.

JONES, Kelly; British singer, songwriter and musician (guitar); b. 3 June 1974, Aberdare, Wales; m. Jakki Healy 2013. *Career:* Founder-mem. Tragic Love Company 1991, renamed Stereophonics 1996–; numerous tours and festival appearances; solo artist 2007–. *Recordings include:* albums: with Stereophonics: Word Gets Around 1997, Performance and Cocktails 1999, Just Enough Education To Perform 2001, You Gotta Go There to Come Back 2003, Language.Sex.Violence.Other? 2005, Live From Dakota 2006, Pull the Pin 2007, Decade in the Sun 2008, Keep Calm and Carry On 2009, Graffiti on the Train 2013, Keep the Village Alive 2015; solo: Only the Names Have Been Changed 2007. *Honours:* BRIT Award for Best Newcomer 1998, Kerrang Awards for Best New Band 1998, Best Band, Best Album 1999, Q Awards for Best Live Act 1999, Best British Band 2000, BAFTA Cymru for Best Music Programme (for Stereophonics – Live at Morfa) 1999, Digital Music Award for Best Rock Artist 2005, Q Award for Classic Song (for 'Local Boy in the Photograph') 2007. *Current Management:* c/o Natalie Seymour, Nettwerk Management, 44 Chiswick Lane, London, W4 2JQ, England. *Telephone:* (20) 7456-9500 (office). *Fax:* (20) 7456-9501 (office). *E-mail:* natalie@nettwerk.com (office). *Website:* www.nettwerk.com. *E-mail:* info@stereophonics.com. *Website:* www.stereophonics.com.

JONES, Keziah; Nigerian musician (piano, guitar), singer and songwriter; b. (Olufemi Sanyaolu), 10 Jan. 1968, Lagos; m. 1st Akure Wall 1994 (separated 1996); m. 2nd Hauwa Mukan 2012. *Career:* brought up in the UK; busked in London and Paris, discovered while busking in the Paris Metro 1991; based in London and Brooklyn. *Recordings include:* albums: Blufunk Is A Fact! 1993, African Space Craft 1995, Liquid Sunshine 1999, Black Orpheus 2003, Nigerian Wood 2008, Captain Rugged 2013. *Website:* www.keziahjones.biz.

JONES, Mick; British musician (guitar, keyboards), songwriter and record producer; b. (Michael Leslie Jones), 27 Dec. 1944, Portsmouth. *Career:* musician with Nero and The Gladiators, Sylvie Vartan, Johnny Hallyday, Spooky Tooth, Leslie West; worked with Otis Redding, Jimi Hendrix, Jimmy Page and George Harrison; Founder-mem. rock group Foreigner 1976–; worldwide tours; producer for artists, including Van Halen, Bad Company, Billy Joel, Tina Arena. *Compositions:* Bad Love (recorded by Eric Clapton), Street Thunder 1984 Olympic Marathon theme, Dreamer (recorded by Ozzy Osbourne), numerous tracks for Foreigner, including Feels Like the First Time, I Want to Know What Love is, Urgent; with Lou Gramm: Juke Box Hero, Dirty White Boy, Waiting for a Girl Like You, That Was Yesterday. *Recordings include:* albums: with Foreigner: Foreigner 1977, Double Vision 1978, Head Games 1979, 4 1981, Records 1982, Agent Provocateur 1985, Inside Information 1988, Unusual Heat 1991, Mr Moonlight 1994, Can't Slow Down 2009, Acoustique 2011; solo: Mick Jones 1989. *Honours:* Grammy Award (for Bad Love) 1989, Ivor Novello Award (for The Flame Still Burns) 1998, inducted into Songwriters Hall of Fame 2013. *Address:* Somerset Songs Publishing Inc., 214 East 70th Street, New York, NY 10021, USA (office). *Telephone:* (212) 717-4473 (office). *E-mail:* IRSmusic@aol.com (office). *Website:* www.foreigneronline.com (office).

JONES, Mickey Wayne; American actor and musician (drums); b. 10 June 1941, Houston, Tex.; m. 1st Sandra Davis 1976; m. 2nd Phyllis Star 7 June 1980; one s. one d. *Education:* North Texas State Coll. *Career:* drummer for Trini Lopez 1957–64, Johnny Rivers 1964–66, Bob Dylan 1966–67, Kenny Rogers 1967–76, actor 1976–, film appearances include: Starman, National Lampoon's Vacation, Stir Crazy, Nadine, The Couch Trip; TV appearances include: V, M.A.S.H., The Incredible Hulk, The Colbys, T J Hooker; numerous other guest roles, commercials, theatre; mem. American Fed. of TV and Radio Artists; Screen Actors Guild, AFofM, AGVA, Screen Extras Guild. *Recordings include:* albums include: with Trini Lopez: Live At P J's; with Bob Dylan: Blonde On Blonde; with Johnny Rivers: Last Boogie In Paris; also for Jan and Dean, Kenny Rogers; singles include: with Johnny Rivers: Maybelline, Mountain of Love, Secret Agent Man; with Kenny Rogers and The First Edition: Just Dropped In to See What Condition My Condition Was In, Ruby, Don't Take Your Love to Town. *Publication:* That Would Be Me 2009. *Address:* c/o Shoestring Productions, PO Box 940321, Simi Valley, CA 93094-0321, USA. *E-mail:* mickeyjones@mickeyjones.com. *Website:* www.mickeyjones.com.

JONES, Nicolas (Nic) Paul; British singer, songwriter and musician (guitar, fiddle); b. 9 Jan. 1947, Orpington, Kent; m. Julia Seymour 1968; three c. *Career:* mem. the Halliard folk band 1964–68; solo artist 1969–; numerous session credits and guest appearances with artists including Richard Thompson, Dave & Toni Arthur, Gerry Hallom, Dave Burland, Steve Turner, Martin Wyndham-Read, Chris Foster, Tony Hall, Shirley Collins, June Tabor, Maddy Prior, Barbara Dickson; mem. Bandoggs 1978; seriously injured in road traffic accident 1982, returned to live performance 2010, 2012–; Founder-mem. Nic Jones Trio (with son Joseph and Belinda O'Hooley) 2012–13. *Recordings:* albums: with the Halliard: It's the Irish in Me 1967, The Halliard and Jon Raven 1967, Broadside Songs 2005, The Last Goodnight! 2005; solo: Ballads and Songs 1970, Nic Jones 1971, The Noah's Ark Trap 1977, From the Devil to a Stranger 1978, Penguin Eggs 1980. *Honours:* BBC Radio 2 Folk Awards for Good Tradition 2007, for Folk Singer of the Year 2013, English Folk Dance and Song Soc. Gold Badge 2012. *Address:* c/o Mollie Music, PO Box 189, Yelverton, Devon, PL19 1BA, England (office). *E-mail:* info@molliemusicrecords.co.uk (office). *Website:* nicjones.net.

JONES, Norah; American singer and pianist; b. (Geetali Norah Jones Shankar), 30 March 1979, New York, NY; d. of the late Ravi Shankar and Sue Jones. *Education:* Booker T. Washington High School for the Performing and Visual Arts, Dallas, North Texas Univ. *Career:* mem. Wax Poetic; formed band with Jesse Harris, Lee Alexander and Dan Rieser; solo artist 2001–; also mem. live band, The Little Willies. *Film appearances:* My Blueberry Nights 2007, Ted 2012. *Recordings include:* albums: solo: Come Away With Me (Grammy Awards for Album of the Year, Best Pop Vocal Album 2003) 2002, Feels Like Home 2004, Not Too Late 2007, The Fall 2009, Little Broken Hearts 2012; with The Little Willies: The Little Willies 2006. *Honours:* MOBO Award for Best Jazz Act 2002, VH1 Best Young Female Singer Award 2002, Grammy Awards for Best New Artist, for Record of the Year, for Best Female Pop Vocal Performance (both for Don't Know Why) 2003, BRIT Award for Int. Breakthrough Artist 2003, World Music Awards for Best Female Artist, Best Pop Female Artist 2004, Grammy Awards for Best Female Pop Vocal Performance (for Sunrise), for Record of the Year (for Here We Go Again, with Ray Charles) 2005. *Current Management:* Macklam Feldman Management, Suite 200, 1505 W Second Avenue, Vancouver, BC V6H 3Y4, Canada. *Address:*

c/o Blue Note Records, 304 Park Avenue S, Third Floor, New York, NY 10010, USA (office). *Website:* www.norahjones.com.

JONES, Paul; British singer, musician (harmonica), composer, actor and broadcaster; b. 24 Feb. 1942, Portsmouth, Hampshire, England; m. 1st Sheila MacLeod, two s.; m. 2nd Fiona Hendley 1984. *Education:* Edinburgh Acad., Jesus Coll., Oxford. *Career:* lead singer and harmonica player with Manfred Mann 1962–66; TV appearances, solo tours of UK, Australia, New Zealand and Europe 1966–; Founder-mem., singer and harmonica player, Blues Band 1979–; actor in films and TV; TV and radio presenter; mem. Musicians' Union, BACSA, Equity. *Theatre includes:* Conduct Unbecoming (London and New York), The Beggar's Opera, Guys and Dolls (Nat. Theatre, London), Kiss Me Kate (RSC). *Compositions include:* 54321 (Theme for Ready Steady Go); songs recorded by: Brian Poole and The Tremeloes; Helen Shapiro; Eric Clapton; Ten Years After; TV and film scores: Intimate Reflections, Fighting Back, The Wednesday Play. *Recordings include:* with Manfred Mann: The Five Faces of Manfred Mann 1964, Mann Made 1965, As Is 1966; Blues Band albums include: Bootleg 1980, Ready 1980, Itchy Feet 1981, 18 Years Old and Alive 1996, Paul Jones Collection Vols 1–3 1996–98, Green Stuff 2001, Thank You Brother Ray 2005, Few Short Lines 2011; solo: My Way 1966, Sings Privilege & Others 1967, Come into My Music Box 1969, Starting All Over Again 2009. *Honours:* British Blues Connection Award for Male Singer 1990, 1991, Scroll of Honour 1993. *Website:* www.thebluesband.net; www.pauljones.eu.

JONES, Quincy; American composer, arranger, conductor and musician (trumpet); b. 14 March 1933, Chicago; s. of Quincy Delight and Sarah Jones; m. 2nd Peggy Lipton; two d.; three c. by previous m.; one d. with Nastassja Kinski. *Education:* Seattle Univ., Berklee School of Music and Boston Conservatory. *Career:* musician and arranger, Lionel Hampton Orchestra 1950–53; arranger for orchestras and singers including Frank Sinatra, Dinah Washington, Count Basie, Sarah Vaughan and Peggy Lee; organizer and trumpeter, Dizzy Gillespie Orchestra, Dept of State tour of Near and Middle East and S. America 1956; Music Dir Barclay Disques, Paris; led own European tour 1960; Music Dir Mercury Records 1961, Vice-Pres. 1964; conductor of numerous film scores; composer, actor in film Blues for Trumpet and Koto; producer recordings of Off the Wall 1979 by Michael Jackson, Thriller 1982, Bad, videotape Portrait of An Album: Frank Sinatra with Quincy Jones and Orchestra 1986; composer The Oprah Winfrey Show 1989–; producer, Fresh Prince of Bel Air 1990–. *Recordings include:* albums: Body Heat 1974, The Dude 1981, Back on the Block 1989. *Publication:* The Complete Quincy Jones: My Journey and Passions 2008. *Honours:* Dr hc (Berklee Music Coll.) 1983; (Hebrew Univ.) 1993, (Clark Univ.) 1993; German Jazz Fed. Award, Edison Int. Award (Sweden), Downbeat Critics' Poll Award, Downbeat Readers' Poll Award, Billboard Trendsetters Award 1983, Martell Foundation Humanitarian Award 1986, Nat. Acad. of Songwriters Lifetime Achievement Award 1989, Jean Hersholt Humanitarian Award 1995, several Grammy Awards, Scopus Award, Producers' Guild of America Award 1999, World Econ. Forum Crystal Award 2000, Marian Anderson Award 2001, Nat. Foundation for Advancement in the Arts Ted Arison Prize 2001, Kennedy Center Honor 2001, BBC Jazz Lifetime Achievement Award 2006, Ivor Novello Special Int. Award 2007. *Current Management:* 10850 Wilshire Blvd, Suite 1200, Los Angeles, CA 90024; Quincy Jones Music Company, 6671 Sunset Blvd, #1574A, Los Angeles, CA 90028, USA. *Telephone:* (323) 957-6601. *Fax:* (323) 962-5231. *E-mail:* info@quincyjonesmusic.com. *Website:* www .quincyjonesmusic.com; www.quincyjones.com.

JONES, Richard; British musician (bass); b. 23 May 1974, Aberdare, Wales. *Career:* Founder-mem. Tragic Love Company 1991, renamed Stereophonics 1996–; numerous tours and festival appearances. *Recordings include:* albums: Word Gets Around 1997, Performance and Cocktails 1999, Just Enough Education To Perform 2001, You Gotta Go There to Come Back 2003, Language.Sex.Violence.Other? 2005, Live From Dakota 2006, Pull the Pin 2007, Keep Calm and Carry On 2009, Graffiti on the Train 2013, Keep the Village Alive 2015. *Honours:* BRIT Award for Best Newcomer 1998, Kerrang Awards for Best New Band 1998, Best Band, Best Album 1999, Q Awards for Best Live Act 1999, Best British Band 2000, BAFTA Cymru for Best Music Programme (for Stereophonics – Live at Morfa) 1999, Digital Music Award for Best Rock Artist 2005, Q Award for Classic Song (for 'Local Boy in the Photograph') 2007. *Current Management:* c/o Natalie Seymour, Nettwerk Management, 44 Chiswick Lane, London, W4 2JQ, England. *Telephone:* (20) 7456-9500. *Fax:* (20) 7456-9501. *E-mail:* natalie@nettwerk.com. *Website:* www .nettwerk.com. *E-mail:* info@stereophonics.com. *Website:* www.stereophonics .com.

JONES, Rickie Lee; American singer and songwriter; b. 8 Nov. 1954, Chicago, IL. *Career:* solo artist 1977–; numerous tours, TV appearances, benefit concerts. *Film and TV appearances:* Pinocchio and the Emperor of the Night (voice of the Fairy Godmother) 1987, Tricks (as Theresa) 2004, Tout le monde en parle (episode) 2004. *Compositions include:* Easy Money, The Last Chance, Texaco, Chuck E's in Love 1979. *Recordings include:* albums: Rickie Lee Jones 1979, Pirates 1981, Girl at her Volcano (EP) 1983, The Magazine 1984, Flying Cowboys 1989, Pop Pop 1991, Traffic from Paradise 1993, Naked Songs 1995, Ghostyhead 1997, It's Like This 2000, The Evening of My Best Day 2003, Rickie Lee Jones: Duchess of Coolsville 2005, The Sermon on Exposition Boulevard 2007, Balm in Gilead 2009. *Honours:* Grammy Award for Best New Artist 1979, Grammy Award for Best Jazz Vocal Performance (for Makin' Whoopee!) 1989, Premio Tenco, Italy 2001. *Current Management:* c/o Danny Goldberg, Gold Village Entertainment, 72 Madison Avenue, Eighth

Floor, New York, NY 10016, USA. *Telephone:* (212) 741-2400. *Fax:* (212) 741-4871. *E-mail:* dannyg2295@aol.com; info@goldve.com. *Website:* www.goldve .com. . *Website:* www.rickieleejones.com.

JONES, Rod; British musician (guitar), singer and songwriter; b. 3 Dec. 1976, Durban, South Africa. *Career:* Founder-mem. Idlewild 1995–, The Birthday Suit; co-creator of musical project The Fruit Tree Foundation; numerous stage performances; numerous collaborations with various artists. *Recordings include:* albums: with Idlewild: Captain 1998, Hope Is Important 1998, 100 Broken Windows 2001, The Remote Part 2002, Warnings/Promises 2005, Make Another World 2007, Scottish Fiction: Best of Idlewild 2007, Post Electric Blues 2009; with The Birthday Suit: The Eleventh Hour 2011, A Conversation Well Rehearsed 2012; with The Fruit Tree Foundation: First Edition 2011; solo: A Sentimental Education 2010, A Generation Innocence 2012. *Current Management:* c/o Steve Nice, Nice Management, 2109 Cooley Place, Pasadena, CA 91104-4111, USA. *Telephone:* (626) 345-9794. *E-mail:* steve@nicemgmt.com. *Website:* www.nicemgmt.com; www.idlewild.co.uk.

JONES, Sean, BMus, MMus; American musician (trumpet) and composer; b. 29 May 1978, Warren, Ohio. *Education:* Youngstown State Univ., Rutgers Univ., studied with Essotto Peligrini and Bill Fielder. *Career:* leader, Sean Jones sextet; lead trumpet, Lincoln Center Jazz Orchestra 2004–; Prof. of Jazz Studies, Duquesne Univ. 2005–; has performed with Chico O'Farrill Orchestra, Louis Armstrong Legacy Band, Chaka Khan, Patti LaBelle, India Arie, Kem, Me'Shell Ndegeocello, Heath Brothers Quintet, Stevie Wonder. *Recordings:* albums: Eternal Journey 2004, Gemini 2005, Roots 2006, Kaleidoscope 2007, The Search Within 2009; appearances on records by Nancy Wilson, Gerald Wilson, Charles Fambrough, Cleveland Jazz Orchestra, Int. Jazz Quintet, Paul Ferguson Big Band. *Current Management:* Addeo Music International, 37 West 26th Street, New York, NY 10010-1120, USA. *Telephone:* (212) 260-2921. *Fax:* (212) 260-8920. *E-mail:* info@theamiagency .com. *Website:* theamiagency.com. *E-mail:* sjonestrumpet@aol.com (office). *Website:* seanjonesmusic.com.

JONES, Sharon; American soul singer; b. (Sheron Lafaye Jones), 4 May 1956, Augusta, Ga. *Career:* worked in various jobs including prison guard, performed as an uncredited backing singer and at weddings and functions; discovered by producers from Desco record label when singing backing vocals at a Lee Fields recording session 1996, leading to regular appearances with Desco's house band The Soul Providers as part of Desco Super Soul Revue; recorded several singles for Desco; first int. tour with The Soul Providers 1999; after demise of Desco label began working with some of the same musicians as Sharon Jones and the Dap Kings; concerts and tours throughout USA, Canada, Europe, Australia; collaborations with Mark Ronson, Amy Winehouse. *Films include:* The Great Debaters (actress and singer) 2007. *Recordings include:* Dap Dippin' with Sharon Jones and the Dap-Kings 2001, Naturally 2005, 100 Days, 100 Nights 2007, I Learned the Hard Way 2010, Soul Time! 2011, Give the People What They Want 2014. *Current Management:* Lever and Beam, 325 West 38th Street, Suite 1101, New York, NY 10018, USA. *E-mail:* alex@leverandbeam.com. *Website:* www .leverandbeam.com. *Address:* c/o Daptone Records, 115 Troutman, Brooklyn, New York, NY 11206, USA (office). *E-mail:* info@daptonerecords.com (office). *Website:* www.daptonerecords.com (office); www.sharonjonesandthedapkings .com.

JONES, Simon; British musician (bass); b. 29 May 1972; m. Myra Jones; two s. *Career:* Founder-mem. Verve, later renamed The Verve 1989–99, 2007–09; numerous festival performances; Founding-mem. The Shining 2000–03. *Recordings include:* albums: with The Verve: A Storm in Heaven 1993, No Come Down 1994, A Northern Soul 1995, Urban Hymns (BRIT Award for Best British Album 1998, Q Award for Classic Album 2007) 1997, Forth 2008; with The Shining: True Skies 2002. *Honours:* BRIT Award for Best British Group (with The Verve) 1998.

JONES, Steve; British musician (guitar); b. 3 Sept. 1955, London, England. *Career:* guitarist in punk group, The Sex Pistols 1975–78, 1996–, first gig at St Martin's School of Art, London 1975; numerous live appearances, festivals and tours; reunion concert 1996; mem. Neurotic Outsiders. *Films include:* The Great Rock 'n' Roll Swindle 1979, The Filth and the Fury 2000, Played 2006, Cutlass 2007. *Television:* Californication 2013. *Recordings include:* albums: with The Sex Pistols: Never Mind The Bollocks – Here's The Sex Pistols 1977, The Great Rock 'n' Roll Swindle 1979, Some Product – Carry On Sex Pistols 1979, Flogging A Dead Horse 1980, Kiss This 1992, Jubilee 2002, Raw and Live 2004, Agents of Anarchy 2008; solo: Mercy 1987, Fire and Gasoline 1989; with Siouxsie and the Banshees: Kaleidoscope 1980; with Generation X: Perfect Hits 1975–81, 1986; with Si Kahn: I Have Seen Freedom 1991; with Buckcherry: Buckcherry 1999. *Address:* c/o Eclipse Entertainment, 100 Wilshire Blvd, Suite 1830, Santa Monica, CA 90028, USA. *Website:* www .sexpistolsofficial.com.

JONES, Steven; British singer and songwriter; b. 16 Sept. 1962. *Career:* mem. of theatre troupe, Dogs in Honey; writer of hundreds of pop songs, obtained music publishing deal; Founder-mem. Baby Bird 1995–2011; numerous TV appearances and live performances. *Recordings include:* albums: with Baby Bird: I Was Born A Man 1995, Bad Shave 1995, Fatherhood 1996, The Happiest Man Alive 1996, Ugly Beautiful 1996, Dying Happy 1997, Something's Going On 1998, Bugged 2000, Between My Ears There is Nothing But Music 2006, Ex-Maniac 2010, The Pleasures of Self Destruction 2011; solo: Stephen Jones 1985–2001 2001, Death of the

Neighbourhood 2008; as Black Reindeer: Music for the Film That Never Got Made and six more albums. *Publications include:* The Bad Book 2000, Travel Sickness 2000, Harry and Ida Swop Teeth 2003. *Website:* www.babybird.co.uk.

JONES, Sir Tom, Kt; British singer; b. (Thomas Jones Woodward), 7 June 1940, Pontypridd, Mid Glamorgan, S Wales; s. of Thomas Woodward and Freda Woodward (née Jones); m. Melinda Trenchard 1956; one s. *Career:* fmr bricklayer, factory worker; sang in clubs and dance halls billing himself as Tommy Scott, singing with the Senators and with self-formed group The Playboys; changed his name to Tom Jones, signed contract with Decca as solo artist 1963; first hit record It's Not Unusual 1965; toured USA 1965; appeared in Ed Sullivan Show at Copacabana, New York and in variety show This Is Tom Jones in UK and USA 1969; score for musical play Matador 1987; acted and sang in live performance of Dylan Thomas' Under Milk Wood 1992; performed in Amnesty International 40th Anniversary Special 2001, Pavarotti and Friends 2001, Prince's Trust Party in the Park 2001; mem. Screen Actors Guild, American Fed. of TV and Radio Artists, American Guild of Variety Artists. *Films:* The Jerky Boys – The Movie 1995, Mars Attacks! 1996, Agnes Browne 1999, The Emperor's New Groove (voice) 2000. *Television includes:* Beat Room, Top Gear, Thank Your Lucky Stars, Sunday Night at the London Palladium, The Right Time (series) 1992, The Voice 2012–15. *Albums:* Along Came Jones 1965, A-Tom-Ic Jones 1966, From The Great 1966, Green Green Grass Of Home 1966, Live At The Talk Of The Town 1967, Delilah 1968, Help Yourself 1968, Tom Jones Live In Las Vegas 1969, This Is Tom Jones 1969, Tom 1970, I Who Have Nothing 1970, Tom Jones Sings She's A Lady 1971, Tom Jones Live At Caesar's Palace, Las Vegas 1971, Close Up 1972, The Body And Soul Of Tom Jones 1973, Somethin' 'Bout You Baby I Like 1974, Memories Don't Leave Like People 1975, Say You'll Stay Until Tomorrow 1977, Rescue Me 1980, Darlin' 1981, Matador: The Musical Life Of El Cordorbes 1987, At This Moment 1989, After Dark 1989, Move Closer 1989, Carrying A Torch 1991, The Lead And How To Swing It 1994, Reload 1999, Mr Jones 2002, Reload 2 2002, 24 Hours 2008, Praise and Blame 2010, Spirit in the Room 2012, Long Lost Suitcase 2015. *Singles include:* It's Not Unusual 1965, What's New Pussycat 1965, Thunderball 1966, Green Green Grass of Home 1966, Detroit City 1967, Funny Familiar Forgotten Feelings 1967, I'll Never Fall In Love Again 1967, I'm Coming Home 1967, Delilah 1968, Help Yourself 1968, Love Me Tonight 1969, Without Love 1969, Daughter of Darkness 1970, I Who Have Nothing 1970, She's A Lady 1971, Till 1971, The Young New Mexican Puppeteer 1972, Can't Stop Loving You, Letter To Lucille 1973, Somethin' 'Bout You Baby I Like 1974, Say You Stay Until Tomorrow 1976, A Boy From Nowhere 1987, Kiss (with Art of Noise) 1988, All You Need Is Love 1993, If I Only Knew 1994, Burning Down The House (with The Cardigans) 1999, Baby It's Cold Outside (with Cerys Matthews) 1999, Mama Told Me Not To Come (with Stereophonics) 2000, Sex Bomb (with Mousse T) 2000, You Need Love Like I Do (with Heather Small) 2000, Tom Jones International 2002. *Publication:* The Fantasticks (screenplay) 2000. *Honours:* Hon. Fellow, Welsh Coll. of Music and Drama 1994; voted Britain's Most Popular Male Singer in Melody Maker Poll 1967, 1968, MTV Video Award 1988, BRIT Award for Best British Male Solo Artist 2000, Nordoff-Robbins Music Therapy Silver Clef Award 2001, Q Magazine Merit Prize 2002, BRIT Award for Outstanding Contrib. to Music 2003, Music Industry Trust Award for Outstanding Contrib. to Music 2010. *Current Management:* c/o Jennie Harris, Valley Music Ltd, Unit 6, Upper Culham Farm Barns, Upper Culham, Wargrave, Henley on Thames, Oxon., RG10 8NR, England. *Telephone:* (1491) 845840. *E-mail:* jennieharris@valleymusicuk.com. *Address:* Tom Jones Enterprises LLC, 1801 Avenue of the Stars, Suite 200, Los Angeles, CA 90067, USA (office). *Telephone:* (310) 552-0044 (office). *Fax:* (310) 552-0714 (office). *E-mail:* office@tomjones.com (office). *Website:* www.tomjones.com (office).

JONES, Tommy; British musician (drums), bandleader and music director; b. 5 Oct. 1926, Liverpool, England; m. Kathy Knight 1954; three s. one d. *Education:* studied drums with Max Abrams, Trinity Coll. of Music, London Coll. of Music. *Career:* played concerts, clubs, broadcasts with bands including Pete Pitterson Quintet, Cab Quaye Trio, Dill Jones Trio, Jack Butler (USA) Band, Leslie 'Jiver' Hutchinson Band, Bertie King Band, Dave (Jazz FM) Lee Trio, Tubby Hayes Band, Jimmy Deucher All-Stars, Acker Bilk Band, Major Holly and Rose Murphy (USA), Bruce Turner Band, Hutchinson/Henderson Band, Humphrey Lyttleton Band, Mike McKenzie Trio, Joe Harriot Quintet, Shake Keane Quintet, Sliderulers, Tommy Jones Trio, Tommy Eytle Trio, Malcolm Mitchell Trio; played with Just Jazz 1950–, Bernard Hilda Orchestra (Paris and Monte Carlo), Arthur Briggs (Paris and Geneva); venues include Royal Festival Hall 1953, 1954, 1956, Colony Club, London 1953–56, First Nat. Jazz Federation Jazz Today Concerts at Royal Festival Hall, Edinburgh Festival of Jazz 1958, Les Ambassadeurs Club 1960, residency at Lunchtime Jazz, Bishopsgate 1961, Bix's Club, San Francisco 1989, Hollywood Savoy Restaurant, Paris 1990, The Lion Lounge Jazz Club 1996, La Cigal jazz café, Paris, Studio 51 Jazz Club, Club 11 Jazz Club, Mapleton Jazz Club, Mayfair Hotel, London, Moss Empire Theatres, UK; Musical Dir, Clark Brothers' (USA) Dancers 1966–68. *Films include:* Blood Orange 1951, Rough and the Smooth 1958, Phoelix 1979. *Television includes:* Crane (series) 1956, BBC experimental colour transmission at Alexandra Palace 1957, The Jack Jackson Show, Mike McKenzie Trio, 6.5 Special (BBC) 1958, Danger Man (episode) 1960, Dark Pilgrimage 1963, Cable Jazz (producer and dir on Cable London) 1992, The House of Eliott 1991. *Radio includes:* Caribbean Carnival (series) 1955, Number Please 1955–56, BBC Jazz Club 1956, 1958, 1960, Jazz at the Marquee 1960, commercial for Smiths Crisps 1993. *Recordings include:* Jazz At Club Basie 1956, In My Condition (with Shake Keane Quintet) 1960,

With Shake Keane Quintet 1961. *Current Management:* Tuff Productions, 2A Middle Lane, London N8 8PN, England. *Telephone:* (20) 8342-9014.

JONES, Trevor, MA; British composer; b. 23 March 1949, Cape Town, South Africa. *Education:* Royal Acad. of Music, York Univ., Nat. Film School. *Compositions for television:* Joni Jones 1982, One of Ourselves 1983, Those Glory, Glory Days 1983, The Last Days of Pompeii 1984, Aderyn Papur… and Pigs Might Fly 1984, This Office Life 1984, The Last Place on Earth 1985, Dr Fischer of Geneva 1985, A Private Life 1988, Murder by Moonlight 1989, By Dawn's Early Light 1990, Chains of Gold 1991, Guns: A Day in the Death of America 1991, Death Train 1993, Gulliver's Travels 1996, Merlin 1998, Cleopatra 1999, Dinotopia 2002. *Compositions for film:* Brittania: The First of the Last 1979, Black Angel 1979, The Dollar Bottom 1980, Brothers and Sisters 1980, The Beneficiary 1980, The Appointment 1981, Excalibur 1981, The Sender 1982, The Dark Crystal 1982, Nate and Hayes 1983, Runaway Train 1985, From an Immigrant's Diary 1985, Labyrinth 1986, Angel Heart 1987, Sweet Lies 1988, Mississippi Burning 1988, Just Ask for Diamond 1988, Dominick and Eugene 1988, Sea of Love 1989, Bad Influence 1990, Arachnophobia 1990, True Colors, 1991, Criss Cross 1992, Freejack 1992, Blame It on the Bellboy 1992, The Last of the Mohicans 1992, In the Name of the Father 1993, Cliffhanger 1993, De Baby huilt 1994, Loch Ness 1995, Hideaway 1995, Kiss of Death 1995, Richard III 1995, Brassed Off 1996, Roseanna's Grave 1997, G.I. Jane 1997, Lawn Dogs 1997, The Mighty 1998, Desperate Measures 1998, Titanic Town 1998, Dark City 1998, Talk of Angels 1998, Notting Hill 1999, Thirteen Days 2000, Molly 2000, From Hell (with others) 2001, Crossroads 2002, The Long Run 2002, Stormbreaker 2006, Three and Out 2008. *Current Management:* c/o First Artists Management, 4764 Park Granada, Suite 210, Calbasas, CA 91302, USA. *E-mail:* fam-info@firstartistsmgmt.com. *Website:* www.firstartistsmgmt.com. *E-mail:* Info@trevorjonesfilmmusic.com. *Website:* www.trevorjonesfilmmusic.com.

JONZE, Spike; American film director, film producer, actor and screenwriter; b. (Adam Spiegel), 1969, Rockville, Md; s. of Arthur Spiegel III and Sandy Granzow; m. Sofia Coppola 1999 (divorced 2003). *Career:* fmr Ed. Freestylin', Go, BMX Action, Homeboy, Grand Royal magazines; f. Dirt magazine with Andy Jenkins and Mark Lewman 1991; began directing skating films and music videos. *Music videos as director:* California by Wax, Sure Shot by the Beastie Boys, Sabotage by the Beastie Boys, Drop by the Pharcyde, Cannonball by The Breeders, What's Up Fatlip? by Fatlip, Undone (The Sweater Song) by Weezer, Buddy Holly by Weezer (MTV Video Music Award for Best Direction 1995), Feel The Pain by Dinosaur Jr, If I Only Had A Brain by MC 900ft Jesus, Sky's The Limit by The Notorious B.I.G., Crush with Eyeliner by R.E.M., It's Oh So Quiet by Björk, Da Funk by Daft Punk, Praise You by Fatboy Slim, Weapon of Choice by Fatboy Slim, Elektrobank by The Chemical Brothers, Wonderboy by Tenacious D (as Spike Jones). *Films include:* Video Days (dir) 1991, Mi Vida Loca (actor) 1994, How They Get There (dir) 1997, The Game (actor) 1997, Amarillo by Morning (dir) 1998, Being John Malkovich (dir, actor) (New York Film Critics Circle Award for Best First Film, Broadcast Film Critics Asscn Breakthrough Performer, Online Film Critics Soc. Award for Best Debut) 1999, Three Kings (actor) 1999, Torrance Rises (dir, as Richard Coufey) 1999, Human Nature (producer) 2001, Adaptation (dir) (Berlin Film Festival Silver Bear 2003) 2002, Jackass: The Movie (writer, producer) 2002, Yeah Right! (dir, producer) 2003, Jackass Number Two (producer) 2006, Synecdoche, New York (producer) 2008, Where the Wild Things Are 2009, Her (Golden Globe Award for Best Screenplay, Motion Picture, Academy Award for Best Original Screenplay 2014) 2013. *Television includes:* Jackass (series writer and producer) 2000. *Current Management:* MJZ, 2201 Carmelina Avenue, Los Angeles, CA 90064, USA. *Telephone:* (310) 826-6200. *Fax:* (310) 826-6219.

JOOLZ; British singer, actress, dancer and presenter; b. 16 April 1966, London. *Career:* session work with artists including: Neneh Cherry, Neil Diamond, Danny Red, Soul II Soul; tours with Soul II Soul; appearances on children's shows; mem. R&B group Just Good Friends; supported Glen Jones, H. Town, Silk, Brandy, Keith Sweat; appeared on Count Prince Miller's Jamaican Independence TV special, cable TV special supporting Don Campbell; mem. Musicians' Union. *Recordings include:* Looking For An Answer 1993, The More I Try, Just Good Friends.

JORDAN, Cathy; Irish singer and musician (bodhran); b. 1 April 1969, Roscommon. *Career:* solo artist for five years, mainly based in Ireland; mem. Dervish 1990–, The Unwanted; int. tours and concerts. *Recordings include:* albums: with Dervish: Harmony Hill 1993, Playing With Fire 1995, At The End of The Day (Hot Press magazine Traditional Folk Album of the Year 1996) 1996, Live In Palma 1997, Midsummer's Night (Irish Times Best Traditional Album 1999) 1999, Decade (Irish Music magazine Best Compilation Album 2001) 2001, Spirit, Healing Heart; with The Unwanted: Music from the Atlantic Fringe 2010; solo: All the Way Home 2012. *Honours:* winner, Irish Music magazine Readers Poll for Best Overall Traditional Folk Band of the Year 1997. *E-mail:* whirling@oceanfree.net; blixstreet@aol.com. *Website:* www .dervish.ie; www.blixstreet.com.

JORDAN, Lorraine Marcella; Irish/Welsh singer, songwriter and musician (guitar, bouzouki); b. 22 Nov. 1965, Wales; d. of Tom Jordan and Margaret Jordan (née Golding). *Career:* singer, guitarist and bouzouki player in bands, Mooncoin and Malin Head; solo artist 1991–; toured Europe and Scandinavia extensively, performing in numerous major folk festivals; TV and radio broadcasts; leader of own band and solo performer; toured Australia and NZ with collaborative Celtic, Maori and Pacific project From Celtic Roots to Oceanic Soul-Planet Woman 2002–06; mem. Performing Right Soc., PPL; owner of independent record label Hazelville Music. *Recordings include:* Reeling In The Pacific, Inspiration 1991, 1993, Crazy Guessing Games 1994, This Big Feeling 2000, A Light Over There 2007. *Address:* Hazelville Music, 98 Hazelville Road, London, N19 3NA, England (office). *Telephone:* (20) 7281-6781 (office). *E-mail:* contact@lorrainejordan.net (office). *Website:* www .lorrainejordan.net; www.facebook.com/lorrainejordan.page.

JORDAN, Marc Wallace; Canadian musician (guitar, keyboards) and songwriter; b. 6 March 1948, New York, USA; m. Amy Sky 1989; one s. one d. *Education:* pvt. guitar and piano lessons. *Career:* mem. American Fed. of Television and Radio Artists, Alliance of Canadian Cinema, Television and Radio Artists, American Fed. of Musicians. *Compositions include:* songs recorded by Josh Groban, The Canadian Tenors, Diana Ross, Manhattan Transfer, Rod Stewart, Bette Midler, Joe Cocker, Chicago, Kansas, Natalie Cole, Amanda Marshall. *Recordings include:* albums: solo: Mannequin 1978, Blue Desert 1979, A Hole in the Wall 1983, Talking through Pictures 1987, C.O.W. 1990, Reckless Valentine 1993, Cool Jam Black Earth 1996, This is How Men Cry 1999, Living in Marina del Rey 2002, Make Believe Ballroom 2004, Crucifix In Dreamland 2010. *Honours:* numerous Juno Awards, Winner Smooth Jazz Male Vocalist of the Year. *Current Management:* c/o d | d Artist Management, 8721 Santa Monica Boulevard, Suite 918, West Hollywood, CA 90069, USA. *Telephone:* (213) 265-9087. *E-mail:* info@ddartistmanagement .com. *Website:* www.ddartistmanagement.com; www.marcjordan.com.

JORDAN, Stanley; American jazz musician (guitar, piano); b. 31 July 1959, Chicago, Ill. *Education:* Princeton Univ. *Career:* regular int. jazz festivals 1976–; musician with Dizzy Gillespie, Benny Carter, Dionne Warwick; solo recording artist 1982–; leading exponent of 'touch' technique. *Film:* Blind Date 1986. *Recordings:* albums: Touch Sensitive 1982, Magic Touch 1985, Standards 1986, Flying Home 1988, Cornucopia 1990, Stolen Moments 1991, Bolero 1994, Live in New York 1998, State of Nature 2008, Friends 2011. *Address:* 2370 West State Route 89A, Suite 11PMB518, Sedona, AZ 86336, USA (office). *Telephone:* (323) 274-7744 (office). *Fax:* (928) 255-1744 (office). *E-mail:* management@stanleyjordan.com (office); fanclub@stanleyjordan.com (office). *Website:* www.stanleyjordan.com.

JORGE, Seu; Brazilian singer, songwriter and actor; b. (Jorge Mário da Silva), 8 June 1970, Rio de Janeiro. *Career:* solo artist; founder mem., Seu Jorge and Almaz 2010–. *Films including:* Moro no Brasil, Cidade de Deus (City of God) 2002, The Life Aquatic with Steve Zissou 2004, Casa de Areia 2005, Elipsis 2006, The Escapist 2008, Sleepwalkers 2010, Reis e Ratos 2012, City of God– 10 Years Later 2012. *Recordings include:* albums: solo: Samba Esporte Fino 2001, Cru 2004, The Life Aquatic (OST) 2005, The Life Aquatic Studio Sessions Featuring... 2006, America Brasil (Latin Grammy Award for Best MPB Album) 2008; with Seu Jorge and Almaz: Seu Jorge and Almaz 2010, Músicas para Churrasco Vol. 1 2011. *E-mail:* marianajorge7@hotmail .com. *Website:* www.seujorgealmaz.com; www.seujorge.com.

JORGENS, Peter Ole; Danish musician (percussion, marimba, vibe); b. 20 April 1958, Sorgenfri; m. Reneé Paaschburg 1992. *Education:* classical percussion with Suzanne Ibstrup, improvisation with John Tchicai, percussion with Paul Motian. *Career:* played with John Tchicai's Festival Band 1975–78, Tchicai/Dorge Quartet 1976–77, Cockpit Music 1978–, Gronvirke 1982–83, Global Guaranty Orchestra 1983–, Clinch 1987–89, The Wild Mans Band 1990–, Dog God 1992–, Sweethearts in a Drugstore 1996, David Moss/ PO Jorgens Duo 1989–96, Ghost in the Machine 1989–; played solo concerts 1995, Knitting Factory, New York and 1997 at LEM Festival Barcelona, Gefion Calls 1996 with David Thomas (Pere Ubu), Jorgen Teler and Per Bull Acs, Two Midnight concerts in The Fountain, Gefion, Copenhagen; mem. SKREP (Danish Experimental Composers), DJBFA; Owner, Vejle Pianoma-gasin. *Compositions include:* Soil 1990, Metal 1–10 1992, Digital Metal 1994, Cambodia 1995, Black Box 1995, Springtime 1–15 1996, Somfoni 1996, The War Kitchen 1996, The Joy of Feeding Birds 1997, The Adventure of Hale Bob 1997, The Pearlbirds 2012. *Recordings include:* Dog God: Dog God 1993, Global Guaranty Orchestra, Musical Hair-Splitting in a Remote World 1993, Wiuf/Jorgens/DeRegt: Catchuptime 1994, Evan Parker/Ghost in the Machine 1995, Cockpit Music, The Great Dividing Range 1996, Dog God: God is Love 1997, PO Jorgens: The Technology of Touch 1997, Sweethearts in a Drugstore 1997. *Address:* PO Jorgens, Frydenlund, Humlebaekvej 56, 3480 Fredensborg, Denmark. *E-mail:* nwm@ninthworldmusic.com (office); olepeter@ hotmail.com (office). *Website:* www.vejlepiano.dk (office).

JORGENSEN, Carsten Valentin; Danish singer, musician (guitar), composer and poet; b. 9 May 1950, Lyngby; m. Anne Marie Albrectsen 1979. *Education:* art school. *Career:* f. own band C V Jorgensen 1974–; tours in Denmark, Sweden, Norway, Germany 1976–; Roskilde Festival; TV appearances include numerous C V Jorgensen specials 1980–94, Danish Live Aid 1985, Dylan and The Danes 1991, Leonard Cohen Talkshow 1992; performed in films Kloden Rocker 1978, Som Et Strejf 1992; lyricist/vocalist, film soundtracks for Mig and Charly 1978, Johnny Larsen 1979; mem. Nordic Copyright Bureau, KODA, Gramex, DJBFA. *Recordings include:* Storbyens Små Oaser 1977, Tidens Tern 1980, Lediggang Agogo 1982, Vennerne and Vejen 1985, Indian Summer 1988, Sjaelland 1994, Fraklip fra det fjerne 2002, Så live som muligt 2003, Det Ganske Lille Band 1977-1979 2011, Sange Fra Scenen 2012. *Honours:* Poetens Pris (Poets Award) 1989, two Danish Grammy

Awards for Songwriter of Year, Rock Album of Year 1991, Prize of Honour, DJBFA, two Danish State Art Foundation Awards 1993, 1994.

JORGENSEN, Per; Norwegian musician (trumpet, guitar, percussion) and singer; b. 9 Sept. 1952, Bergen; m. Else Vågen 1987; one d. *Career:* freelance musician for 20 years; played all major Scandinavian jazz festivals with different groups; tours, concerts in India, Japan, USA, Germany, Spain, France, Austria; numerous concerts recorded for TV and radio; jazz visits, teaching and working with Danish musicians, Copenhagen 1997. *Recordings include:* with Jokleba (trio): On and On 1991, Nu Jøk? 2012, Outland 2014; with Jokleba and the Magnetic North Orchestra: Further 1992, Magnetic Works 1993–2001 2012; with Anders Jormin: Jord; with Marilyn Mazur: Circular Chant; with Tamma (including Don Cherry and Ed Blackwell): Tamma; with David Murray: Jazzpar Prize 1991; with Jon Balke: Non-senstration 1992; with Michael Mantler: School of Understanding 1997; with Sjögren/Voust: The Thule Spirit 1997; with Jon Balke's Magnetic North Orchestra: Kyanos 2002, Diverted Travels 2004; with Fredrik Lundin Overdrive: Belly Up 2004; with Sjögren/Jorgensen Duo: Unspoken Songs 2005; with Miki 'n' Doye: Tuki 2006; with Terje Isungset: Two Moons 2007, Agbalagba Daada 2008. *Honours:* Vossajazz Prize 1990, Jazz Musician of the Year in Norway 1991, Norwegian Jazz Federation Buddy Statue 1996. *Address:* Lia 17, 5722 Dalekvam, Norway.

JORY, Sarah Elizabeth; British country singer and songwriter; b. 20 Nov. 1969, Reading, Berks. *Career:* concerts at London Palladium, toured with Eric Clapton, Glen Campbell and Charley Pride; numerous tv appearances and radio broadcasts; mem. Performing Rights Soc., Musicians' Union. *Recordings include:* Sarah On Steel 1984, Cross Country 1985, The Way To Survive 1987, No Time At All 1988, Deep In The Heart of Texas 1988, Dallas City Lights 1989, Especially For You 1990, Sarah's Dream 1990, New Horizons 1992, Web of Love 1994, Love With Attitude 1995, Kiss My Innocence 1998, Sarah Jory Band Live 2000. *Honours:* six British Country Music Awards, three European Awards. *Website:* www.sarahjory.co.uk.

JOSEI; Japanese musician (piano, keyboards). *Career:* mem. jazz band Soil & "Pimp" Sessions 2001–. *Recordings include:* albums: Pimpin' (EP) 2004, Pimp Master 2005, Summer Goddess (EP) 2005, Pimp of the Year 2006, PimPoint, Planet Pimp, 6, Magnetic Soil, Circles, X Chronicle of Soil and Pimp Sessions. *Address:* c/o Victor Entertainment Inc., Palacion Tower, 3-6-7 Kita-Aoyama, Minato-ku, Tokyo 107-0061, Japan (office). *E-mail:* soil@jvcmusic.co.jp. *Website:* www.soilpimp.com; www.jvcmusic.co.jp/soilpimp.

JOSEPH, David, CBE; British music industry executive; *Chairman and CEO, Universal Music UK. Career:* worked in advertising with computer games co. Sega; Head of Press Relations, RCA Records 1995–97, Head of Marketing 1997–98; joined Polydor Records, UK as Gen. Man. 1998, Jt Man. Dir 2002–06, Co-Pres. 2006–08, role expanded to Pres. Universal Music Operations 2006, giving him responsibility for Universal Classics & Jazz and TV production arm Globe Productions, Chair. and CEO, Universal Music UK 2008–; mem. Arts Council England 2013–, British Phonographic Council (fmr Chair.). *Address:* Universal Music UK, 364–366 Kensington High Street, London, W14 8NS, England (office). *Telephone:* (20) 7471-5000 (office). *Fax:* (20) 7471-5001 (office). *Website:* www.umusic.co.uk (office).

JOSEPH, Julian Rapheal Nathaniel, BMus; British musician (piano), bandleader, composer, arranger and broadcaster; b. 11 May 1966, London, England; s. of Nathaniel Howard Joseph and Ursula Joseph. *Education:* Berklee Coll. of Music, Boston, USA. *Career:* leading figure on the int. jazz scene since early 1990s; worldwide tours with his trio, Electric Band, and quartet, Forum Project band; has directed and performed with his All-Star Big Band at UK venues; premiered two operas, Bridgetower 2007, Shadowball 2010; has also est. himself as a jazz pioneer in the classical world; first jazz musician to be invited to give a series of all-acoustic concerts at London's Wigmore Hall; has recorded duets by Milhaud, Stravinsky and Poulenc with Brazilian pianist Marcelo Bratke, combining them with his own arrangements of music by Duke Ellington, Chick Corea and Bill Evans, and collaborated with concert violinist Viktoria Mullova on her fusion project, Through the Looking Glass; solo recitals of Bartók and Prokofiev sonatas, performed Gershwin's Piano Concerto in F and Rhapsody in Blue with several European symphony orchestras; Creative Dir Julian Joseph Jazz Acad.; Amb. for Youth Music; launched Jazz Syllabus for the Associated Bd of the Royal Schools of Music, including some of his own composition; mem. Performing Right Soc., Mechanical-Copyright Protection Soc., British Acad. of Songwriters, Composers and Authors; Patron World Heartbeat Music Acad., Band on the Wall, Manchester, Mayors Fund for Young Musicians, Jazz Devt Trust, Pembroke Music Acad., Firebird Trust. *Play:* Miles Davis and Juliette Greco. *Compositions include:* A Tale of a Vampire (film score), Winds of Change, The Brown Bomber 2012, Bridgetower, a fable of 1807 Opera, Shadowball Opera, Symphonic Stories, The Great Sage, major orchestral pieces and BBC comms, major big band and jazz orchestra works. *Radio:* Jazz Legends (weekly show, BBC Radio 3) 2000–07, This Sceptred Isle (BBC Radio 4), Jazz Line Up (BBC Radio 3) 2007–. *Television:* Jazz with Julian Joseph (two series, ITV), Jazzworld (Sky Artsworld). *Recordings include:* albums: The Language of Truth 1991, Reality 1993, Julian Joseph in Concert at the Wigmore Hall 1995, Universal Traveller 1996, Live at the Vortex 2012. *Honours:* Cultura Artistica (Hungary); Southern Comfort Award for Best Jazz Group, John Dankworth Award, Gold Badge Award for Outstanding Contrib. to British Music, Broadcaster of the Year, Parl. Jazz Awards 2006, Creative Industries

Luminary for London, Mayor of London. *Current Management:* c/o James Joseph Music Management, 85 Cicada Road, London, SW18 2PA, England. *Telephone:* (20) 8133-0849. *E-mail:* jj3@jamesjoseph.co.uk. *Address:* 85 Cicada Road, London, SW18 2PA, England (home). *Telephone:* (20) 8133-0847 (office). *E-mail:* jj3@jamesjoseph.co.uk (office). *Website:* www.julianjoseph.com.

JOUBRAN, Adnan; Palestinian musician (oud); b. 1985, Galilee, Nazareth; s. of Hatem Mbadaa Joubran and Ibtisam Hanna Joubran. *Career:* joined brothers Samir and Wissam to form Le Trio Joubran 2004–; repertoire consists of original compositions, improvisations and traditional tunes; also plays with Fattoumi-Lamoreux dance co. *Recordings include:* albums: with Trio Joubran: Randana 2005, Majâz 2007, A L'Ombre de Mots 2009, Le dernier vol 2009, AsFâr 2011, The First Ten Years 2013. *Honours:* Order of Merit and Excellence 2013; Arab Muhr, Dubai Int. Film Festival 2009, 2011, Int. Award of Palestine 2013. *Current Management:* c/o Nayla Abdul-Khalek, Commnprod International, 6 avenue de Versailles, 75016 Paris, France. *Telephone:* 6-11-17-51-75. *E-mail:* nayla@commnprod.com. *Website:* www .commnprod.com. *E-mail:* contact@letriojoubran.com (office). *Website:* www .letriojoubran.com.

JOUBRAN, Samir; Palestinian musician (oud); b. 1973, Nazareth; s. of Hatem Mbadaa Joubran and Ibtisam Hanna Joubran. *Education:* Inst. of Music, Nazareth, Mohamed Abdul Wahab Conservatory, Cairo, Egypt. *Career:* solo artist 1996–; began performing concerts with his brother Wissam 2003, joined by their younger brother Adnan, forming Le Trio Joubran 2004–; repertoire consists of original compositions, improvisations and traditional tunes. *Recordings include:* albums: solo: Taqaseem 1996, Sou'fahm 2001; with Trio Joubran: Tamaas 2003, Randana 2005, Majâz 2007, A L'Ombre de Mots 2009, Le dernier vol 2009, AsFâr 2011, The First Ten Years 2013. *Honours:* Order of Merit and Excellence 2013; Arab Muhr, Dubai Int. Film Festival 2009, 2011, Int. Award of Palestine 2013. *Current Management:* c/o Nayla Abdul-Khalek, Commnprod International, 6 avenue de Versailles, 75016 Paris, France. *Telephone:* 6-11-17-51-75. *E-mail:* nayla@commnprod.com. *Website:* www.commnprod.com. *E-mail:* contact@letriojoubran.com (office). *Website:* www.letriojoubran.com.

JOUBRAN, Wissam; Palestinian musician (oud, violin); b. 1983, Nazareth, Galilee; s. of Hatem Mbadaa Joubran and Ibtisam Hanna Joubran. *Education:* Nazareth Conservatory, Antonio Stradivari Inst., Cremona, Italy. *Career:* began career performing at local concerts in Palestine; began performing concerts with his brother Samir 2003, joined by their younger brother Adnan, forming Le Trio Joubran 2004–; repertoire consists of original compositions, improvisations and traditional tunes. *Recordings include:* albums: solo: Taqaseem 1996, Sou'fahm 2001; with Trio Joubran: Tamaas 2003, Randana 2005, Majâz 2007, A L'Ombre de Mots 2009, Le dernier vol 2009, AsFâr 2011. *Honours:* Arab Muhr, Dubai Int. Film Festival 2009, 2011. *Current Management:* c/o Nayla Abdul-Khalek, Commnprod International, 6 avenue de Versailles, 75016 Paris, France. *Telephone:* 6-11-17-51-75. *E-mail:* nayla@ commnprod.com. *Website:* www.commnprod.com. *E-mail:* contact@ letriojoubran.com (office). *Website:* www.letriojoubran.com; www .wissamjoubran.com.

JOURGENSEN, Allen (Al); Cuban singer and musician (guitar); b. 9 Oct. 1958, Havana; m. 1st Patty Marsh 1984–2002; one d.; m. 2nd Angelina Jourgensen. *Career:* Founder-mem. Ministry 1983–; numerous side projects, including Revolting Cocks, Lard (with Jello Biafra of Dead Kennedys), 1,000 Homo DJs (with Trent Reznor of Nine Inch Nails), Pigface (with Steve Albini, Jello Biafra, Chris Connelly and Dwayne Goettell); worked with Butthole Surfers' Gibby Haynes; numerous tours, collaborations. *Recordings include:* albums: With Sympathy 1983, Twitch 1985, Twelve Inch Singles 1981–84 1987, The Land of Rape and Honey 1988, The Mind is a Terrible Thing to Taste 1989, In Case You Didn't Feel Like Showing Up (live) 1990, Psalm 69: The Way To Succeed and the Way To Suck Eggs 1992, Filth Pig 1996, Dark Side of the Spoon 1999, Animositisomina 2003, Houses of the Molé 2004, Rio Grande Blood 2006, The Last Sucker 2007, Relapse 2012, From Beer to Eternity 2013; with Revolting Cocks: Big Sexy Land 1986, Beers, Steers and Queers 1990, Linger Ficken' Good 1993, Cocked and Loaded 2006, Sex-O Olympic-O 2009, Got Cock? 2010; with Lard: The Power of Lard 1989, Pure Chewing Satisfaction 1997, 70's Rock Must Die 2000.

JOVANOTTI; Italian singer, songwriter and rapper; b. (Lorenzo Cherubini), 27 Sept. 1966, Rome; m. Francesca Valiani 2008; one d. *Career:* solo career 1988–; numerous stage performances; has worked with numerous orgs including Amnesty Int., Make Poverty History. *Recordings include:* albums: Jovanotti for President 1988, La mia moto 1989, Giovani Jovanotti 1990, Una tribù che balla 1991, Lorenzo 1992, Lorenzo 1994, Lorenzo 90-95 1995, L'albero 1997, Capo Horn 1999, Il quinto mondo 2002, Buon Sangue 2005, Safari 2008, Ora 2011. *Current Management:* c/o Marco Sorrentino, Trident Management, Corso Europa 13, 20122 Milan, Italy. *Telephone:* (02) 760851. *Fax:* (02) 76085401. *E-mail:* info@tridentmanagement.it. *Website:* www .tridentmanagement.it. *E-mail:* info@soleluna.com (office). *Website:* www .soleluna.com.

JOYCE; Brazilian singer, musician (guitar, violin) and songwriter; b. (Joyce Silveiro Palhano de Jesus), 31 Jan. 1948, Rio de Janeiro; d. of Helge Arvid Johnston and Zemir Silveira Palhano de Jesus; m. 1st Nelson Angelo 1970 (divorced 1975); two d.; m. 2nd Tutty Moreno 2001; one d. *Education:* Pontífica Universidade Católica do Rio de Janeiro. *Career:* first recorded as part of vocal group 1964; solo debut 1968; mem. Sagrada Família musical group 1970, A

Tribo 1970–71; dropped out of the music business until invitation by Vinicius de Moraes to join him on international tour 1975; moved to New York City 1977; signed contract with EMI 1980; independent releases 1984–; 1990s brought a new audience when the 'drum 'n' bossa' style rejuventated interest in recordings; columnist, O Dia newspaper 1998–2000. *Television:* presenter, Cantos do Rio 1999–2000, 2002. *Recordings include:* albums include: Joyce 1968, Encontro Marcado 1969, Nelson Angelo E Joyce 1973, Passarinho Urbano 1976, Feminina 1980, Água e Luz 1981, Tardes Cariocas (Premio Chiquinha Gonzaga) 1981, Saudade do Futuro 1985, Wilson Batista: o Samba foi sua Glória 1986, Tom Jobim: Anos 60 1987, Negro Demais no Coração 1988, Music Inside 1990, Language and Love 1991, Revendo Amigos 1994, Delírios de Orfeu 1994, Sem Você 1995, Ilha Brasil 1996, Astronauta – Songs of Elis 1998, Hard Bossa 1999, Tudo Bonito 2000, Gafieira Moderna 2001, Bossa Duets 2003, Banda Maluca 2004, Rio-Bahia 2005, Samba-Jazz 2007, Joyce Ao Vivo 2008, Visions of Dawn 2009, Slow Music 2009, Aquarius 2010, Tudo 2012. *Publication:* Fotografei Você na Minha Rolleyflex 1997. *Honours:* Brazilian Int. Press Lifetime Achievement Award 2004. *E-mail:* memeca@zerenato.com .br (office). *Website:* www.joycemoreno.com.

JUANES; Colombian singer, songwriter and musician (guitar); b. (Juan Esteban Aristizábal Medellín), 9 Aug. 1972. *Career:* fmr mem., Ekhymosis; solo artist 2000–; collaborations include Nelly Furtado. *Recordings include:* albums: Fíjate Bien 2000, Un Dia Normal (Latin Grammy Award for Album of the Year, for Best Rock Solo Album 2003) 2002, Mi Sangre 2004, La Vida es un Ratico (Latin Grammy Awards for Album of the Year, for Best Male Pop Vocal Album 2008, Grammy Award for Best Latin Pop Album 2009) 2007, P.A.R.C.E. 2010, Juanes MTV Unplugged (Grammy Award for Best Latin Pop Album 2013) 2012, Loco de Amor (Latin Grammy Award for Album of the Year 2014) 2014. *Films include:* Bordertown (as himself) 2007. *Honours:* Latin Grammy Awards for Best New Artist 2001, for Record of the Year, Song of the Year, Best Rock Song 2003, Univision Premio Lo Nuestro Award, MTV Latin America Awards for Artist of the Year, for Best Rock Artist 2003, Latin Grammy Awards for Best Rock Song, for Best Music Video, and for Best Rock Solo Vocalist 2005, for Record of the Year, for Song of the Year (both for Me Enamora) 2008. *Address:* c/o Universal Music Latino, Universal Music Group, 2220 Colorado Avenue, Santa Monica, CA 90404, USA (office). *Website:* www .juanes.net.

JUB; British musician (double bass) and singer; b. (Molemo Maarohanye), Oxfordshire, England. *Education:* Guildhall School of Music, London. *Career:* bass player, Kreisler String Orchestra, English Nat. Opera, London Festival Ballet, London Contemporary Dance Theatre; mem. The Carnival Band 1985–; appearances include: Glasgow Cathedral, Birmingham Symphony Hall, Barbican Centre, arts centres and theatres; plays material from: Sweden, Croatia, USA, Bolivia, Spain, UK, France. *Recordings include:* Christmas Carols (with Maddy Prior).

JUDD, Harry Mark Christopher; British musician (drums); b. 23 Dec. 1985, Chelmsford. *Career:* founder mem., McFly 2004–. *Recordings include:* albums: Room on the Third Floor (Smash Hits Award for Best Album 2005) 2004, Wonderland 2005, Motion in the Ocean 2006, Radio:Active 2008, Above the Noise 2010. *Television includes:* Strictly Come Dancing (winner) 2011. *Honours:* BRIT Award for Best Pop Act 2005, Smash Hits Awards for Smash Hits Star of the Year, for Best UK Band, for Best Video (for That Girl) 2005. *Website:* www.mcflyofficial.com.

JUDD, Naomi Ellen; American singer, songwriter and writer; b. (Diana Ellen Judd), 1 Nov. 1946, Ashland, Ky; m. Larry Strickland 1989; two d. *Education:* RN degree. *Career:* mem. country music duo, The Judds (with daughter, Wynonna Judd) 1984–90. *Recordings include:* albums: The Judds 1984, Why Not Me? 1985, Rockin' With The Rhythm Of The Rain 1986, Heartland 1987, River Of Time 1989, Love Can Build A Bridge 1990, The Judds Reunion: Live 2000. *Film:* A Holiday Romance 1999. *Television:* Can You Duet 2008. *Publication:* Love Can Build a Bridge (with Wynonna Judd) 1993. *Honours:* seven Grammy Awards for Best Duet, four Acad. of Country Music Awards for Best Duet, three Country Music Asscn Awards for Best Vocal Duo. *Current Management:* c/o Hill Entertainment Group, 2200 21st Avenue South, Suite 401, Nashville, TN 37212, USA. *Telephone:* (615) 730-9151. *E-mail:* office@hillentgroup.com. *Website:* www.hillentgroup.com. *Address:* The Judd House, 325 Bridge Street, Franklin, TN 37064, USA. *Website:* www.naomijudd.com.

JUDD, Wynonna; American country singer and musician; b. 30 May 1963, Ashland, Ky; d. of Naomi Judd; one s., one d. *Career:* mem. country duo, The Judds (with mother, Naomi) 1984–90; solo artist, billed as Wynonna 1991–; Co-founder, booking agency Pro-Tours 1988–; guest vocalist on recordings by Huey Lewis, Kelly Price, Kenny Rogers, Brady Seals, Tammy Wynette. *Recordings include:* albums: with The Judds: The Judds 1984, Why Not Me? 1985, Rockin' With The Rhythm Of The Rain 1986, Heartland 1987, River Of Time 1989, Love Can Build A Bridge 1990, The Judds Reunion: Live 2000; solo: Wynonna 1992, Tell Me Why 1993, Revelations 1996, The Other Side 1997, New Day Dawning 2000, Music In High Places 2002, What The World Needs Now Is Love 2003, Her Story: Scenes from a Lifetime 2005, A Classic Christmas 2006, Sing: Chapter 1 2009. *Publication:* Love Can Build a Bridge (with Naomi Judd) 1993. *Honours:* seven Grammy Awards for Best Duet, four Acad. of Country Music Awards for Best Duet, three Country Music Asscn Awards for Best Vocal Duo, ACM Female Artist of the Year Award 1994.

Address: PO Box 128229, Nashville, TN 37212, USA. *E-mail:* wystaff@wynonna.com. *Website:* www.wynonna.com.

JUKS; Estonian musician (guitar). *Career:* mem. Tuberkuloited 1988–. *Recordings include:* albums: Klassiõhtu 1992, Lilleke rohus 1993, Religioon 1995, Õhtupimedas 1997, Seitseteist lillekest rohus 1999, D-Tuur, Vol. 6 1999, Kiirteel 2000, Wiimane 2001, Tuberkuloited unplugged 2001, Estraadialbum 2003, Põlevad väljad 2004, Mis sa teed 2007. *Current Management:* MMM Agentuur OÜ, Risti 2-21, 11624 Tallinn, Estonia. *E-mail:* mm@mmagentuur.ee. *Website:* www.mmagentuur.ee.

JULES, Gary; American singer and songwriter; b. (Gary Jules Aguirre, Jr), 1969, San Diego, Calif.; m. Greta Jules; one c. *Recordings include:* albums: Greetings From The Side 1998, Trading Snakeoil For Wolftickets 2003, Gary Jules 2006, Bird 2008. *Current Management:* c/o Jonathan Adelman, Little Big Man, 155 Avenue of the Americas, 6th Floor, New York, NY 10013, USA. *Telephone:* (646) 336-8520. *Fax:* (646) 336-8522. *E-mail:* info@garyjules.com (office). *Website:* www.garyjules.com.

JULES, Judge; British DJ, record producer, remixer and broadcaster; b. (Julius O'Riordan), 26 Oct. 1965, London, England; m. Amanda Judge; one s. one d. *Education:* London School of Econs. *Career:* remixed and produced over 20 top 30 singles, 1994–; mem. Musicians' Union. *Recordings include:* I Like To Move It Reel 2 Real, Doop Doop, Saturday Night T'empo, High on a Happy Vibe, I Put a Spell on You, Funky Groove, Down with the Underground, Pulsating Rhythms; Albums include: Clubbed 2001, Clubbed 2002 2002, Judgement Sundays 2003, Proven Worldwide 2006, Bring the Noise 2009, Follow the Sunrise 2011 2011. *Honours:* Best Club DJ, DJ Mag 1995, Best DJ, London Club Awards 1995, Best Radio DJ, Smirnoff Dance Star Awards 2000, 2001, Best Ibiza Trance DJ Award 2006. *Current Management:* c/o Integrity Artist Management Ltd, Studio 7, 6-8 Cole Street, London, SE1 4YH, England. *Telephone:* (20) 7407-4140. *Fax:* (20) 7407-5633. *Website:* www.integrityam.com; www.judgejules.net.

JUNGR, Barb, BSc, MMus; British singer, songwriter, musician (mandolin, harmonica) and cabaret artist; b. 9 May 1954, Rochdale, England. *Education:* Univ. of Leeds, Goldsmiths Coll. *Career:* television appearances with Julian Clary in all series of Sticky Moments, Terry and Julian; radio broadcasts: five series, We Stayed in with Jungr and Parker (BBC Radio 2); nat. tours with Alexei Sayle and Julian Clary; mem. PRS, PPL, MCPS, British Voice Asscn, Malawian Musicians' Asscn, British Forum Ethnomusicology, Centre Performance Research, Musicians' Union, Equity, ICTM, Women in Music, Jazz Singers' Network. *Compositions include:* television themes 1990–2000, theatre 1990–2000. *Recordings include:* 3 Courgettes, Barb, The Stroke, Jungr and Parker, Durga Rising (with Russel Churney and Kuljit Bhamra) 1997, Bare 1999, Chanson 2000, Every Grain Of Sand 2002, Waterloo Sunset 2003, Love me Tender 2005, Walking in the Sun 2006, Just Like a Woman –A Hymn to Nina 2008, The Men I Love: The New American Songbook 2010, Man in the Long Black Coat: Barb Jungr Sings Bob Dylan 2011, Stockport to Memphis 2012. *Honours:* Perrier Award 1987, Swansea Fringe Award 1988. *Address:* Linn Records, Glasgow Road, Waterfoor, Eaglesham, Glasgow, G76 0EQ, Scotland. *Telephone:* (141) 303-5027. *Fax:* (141) 303-5007. *E-mail:* info@linnrecords.co.uk. *Website:* www.linnrecords.com; www.barbjungr.com.

JUNKERA, Kepa; Spanish musician (trikitixa) and composer; b. (Kepa Junquera Urraza), 10 April 1965, Bilbao. *Career:* Basque folk musician; plays the trikitixa (Basque diatonic accordion); fmr mem., Oskorri, continues to guest on their albums and tours; collaborations with John Kirkpatrick and Riccardo Tesi (as the Trans-Europe Diatonic Project), with int. tours; collaborations with renowned Basque musicians and int. artists, including The Chieftains, Julio Pereira, Carlos Nuñez, Dulce Pontes, Andreas Vollenwaider; as composer, has combined jazz with own folk music and written pieces performed with Euskadi Symphony Orchestra. *Recordings:* albums: with Kepa Zabaleta eta Motriku: Infernuko Auspoa 1987, Triki Up 1990; solo: Trikitixa Zoom 1991, Trans-Europe Diatonic (with Riccardo Tesi and John Kirkpatrick) 1992, Kalejira Al-Buk 1994, Lau Eskutara (with Julio Pereira) 1995, Leonen Orroak (with Ibon Koteron) 1996, Bilbao 00–00h 1996, Maren 2001, K 2003, Athletic Bihotzez 2004, Hiri 2006, Etxea 2008, Fandango Probença Sessions (with Melonious Quartet) 2009, Kalea 2009, Fandango

Habana Sessions 2010 (with Rolando Luna) Herria 2010, Ultramarinos & Coloniales 2011. *Honours:* Young Contemporary Folk Musician Prize 1990, Latin Grammy Award 2004. *Current Management:* Kap, Hurtado de Amézaga, 27–10°, 48008 Bilbao, Spain. *Telephone:* (94) 4478840. *Fax:* (94) 4472239. *E-mail:* info@kap-produkzioak.com. *Website:* www.kap-produkzioak.com. *Address:* Calle Nueva 3, 48005 Bilbao, Spain (office). *Telephone:* (626) 661646 (office). *E-mail:* kepajunkera@gmail.com (office); infernukoauspoa@gmail.com (office). *Website:* www.kepajunkera.com.

JUPP, Richard Barry; British musician (drums) and songwriter. *Career:* formed band Mr Soft with Guy Garvey, Richard Jupp and Mark Potter 1990, renamed Soft and eventually renamed Elbow 1997–; numerous concerts and tours throughout UK, Europe and USA; played concerts in Cuba 2004, becoming first British band to perform outside Havana; headlined UKULA Bright Lights Festival, Toronto, Canada 2006. *Recordings include:* albums: Asleep in the Back 2001, Cast of Thousands 2003, Leaders of the Free World 2005, The Seldom Seen Kid (Mercury Music Prize) 2008, Build a Rocket Boys! 2011, The Take Off and Landing of Everything 2014. *Honours:* BRIT Award for Best British Group 2009, Ivor Novello Awards for Best Song Musically and Lyrically (for One Day Like This) 2009, for Best Contemporary Song (for Grounds for Divorce) 2009, South Bank Show Award 2009. *Current Management:* c/o TRC Management, 10c Whitworth Court, Manor Park, Manor Farm Road, Runcorn, Cheshire, WA7 1TE, England. *Telephone:* (1928) 571111. *E-mail:* mail@trcmanagement.com. *Website:* www.trcmanagement.com; www.elbow.co.uk.

JURICIC, Mladen, (Max Wilson); Croatian musician (guitar) and backing singer; b. 10 June 1958, Zagreb; m. Vanja Matujec 1988; one s. one d. *Education:* studied economy. *Career:* mem. Azra 1977–86, Le Cinema 1986–88, Vjestice 1989–99, Ziu Zao 1995, So! Mazgoon 1999, Gego I Picigin Band 2005; mem. HGU. *Recordings include:* with Film: Film 1, Live Kulusic, Zona Sumraka, Sva Cuda Svijeta, Signali U Nocí; with Le Cinema: Live Kulusic, Dorudak kod Trulog 2003; with Vjestice: Totalno Drukciji Od Drugih, Bez Tisine, Live In Schwarzwald, Djevojke U Ljetnim Haljinama Volim, Kradljivac scra; with So! Mazgoon: So! Mazgoon 1999, Umricu od Bonace 2001, Velegradele 2003, Otoce Volim Te 2005; with Gego I Picigin Band: Conon Jeto Non Je 2005, Kup! Prodoj! 2008. *Film:* Izgubljeno blago 1996. *Honours:* Porin for Best Alternative Music Album 1987. *Address:* Auzvinkl Tomisalavov trg 19, Zagreb, Croatia (office). *Telephone:* 14922275 (office). *E-mail:* m.jaricic@vip.hr (office).

JURIN, Michael; American musician (guitar). *Career:* mem., Stellastarr 2000–. *Recordings include:* albums: with Stellastarr: Stellastarr 2003, Harmonies for the Haunted 2005, Civilized 2009. *Current Management:* c/o Plus One Music, 242 Wythe Avenue, Studio 6, Brooklyn, New York, NY 11211, USA. *Telephone:* (718) 599-3740. *Fax:* (718) 599-0998. *E-mail:* jonnykaps@plusonemusic.net. *Address:* c/o Sony BMG, 550 Madison Avenue, New York, NY 10022, USA. *E-mail:* band@stellastarr.com. *Website:* www.stellastarr.com; www.myspace.com/michaeljurin.

JUSTICE (see GZA)

JXL (Junkie XL); Dutch musician and producer; b. (Tom Holkenborg), 8 Dec. 1967, Lichtenvoorde. *Career:* mem. Weekend at Waikiki 1986–88; Founder-mem., Nerve 1992–96; produced tracks for metal/industrial bands; began producing dance music; formed band Junkie XL 1997 (adopted name as soloist when the band broke up); collaborated with Sander Kleinenberg, The Prodigy, Sasha; composed music for films, advertisements and video games. *Recordings include:* albums: with Nerve: Cancer Of Choice, Blood And Gold; with/as Junkie XL/JXL: Saturday Teenage Kick 1998, Big Sounds Of The Drags 1999, Radio JXL 2002, Today 2006, Booming Back at You 2008, Darkspore 2011, Synthesized 2012. *Film compositions include:* The Delivery 2001, Resident Evil 2002, The Animatrix 2003, The Chronicles of Riddick: Dark Fury 2004, Domino 2005, Blind 2006, Siberia 2007, Johan1 2010, Megamind 2010, Bringing Up Bobby 2011, New Kids 2011, New Kids Turbo 2011, Madagascar 3 2012, The Dark Knight Rises 2012, Man of Steel 2013, Paranoia 2013, 300: Rise of an Empire 2014, Mad Max: Fury Road 2014. *E-mail:* jackie@junkiexl.com. *Website:* www.junkiexl.com.

K

K. WILL; South Korean singer, songwriter and actor; b. (Kim Hyung-soo), 30 Dec. 1981, Gwangiu. *Career:* vocal coach and trainee singer 2002–07; debut single 2006; debut solo album 2007; numerous collaborations including Lim Jeong-Hee, Uhm Jung-Hwa, 8Eight, Hye Mi, Suho, Navi, The Name, Zia; concerts in USA, Japan 2010–11. *Recordings include:* albums: Left Heart 2007, Miss, Miss and Miss 2009, The Third Album Part 1 2012. *Honours:* TV Writers Asscn Top Rookie Singer Award 2007, Repub. of Korea Entertainment Arts Award for Male Ballad Singer Award 2010, Golden Disk Award for Digital Music Bonsang (for My Heart Beating) 2011, Mnet Asian Music Award for Best Vocal Performance – Solo (for I Need You) 2012. *Address:* c/o Starship Entertainment, 2nd Floor, Seonho Building 577-92, Banpo-4dong, Seocho-gu, Seoul, South Korea (office). *E-mail:* starshipent@hanmail.net (office). *Website:* starship-ent.com/start (office).

KAAS, Patricia; French singer; b. 5 Dec. 1966, Stiring Wendel, nr Forbach. *Career:* tea-dance and night-club appearances aged 13; first single, Jalouse aged 17; first major success with Mademoiselle Chante le Blues; toured Viet Nam and Cambodia 1994; tours world-wide. *Recordings include:* albums: Mademoiselle Chante 1988, Scène de Vie 1990, Carnet de Scène (live) 1991, Je Te Dis Vous 1993, Tour de Charme (live) 1994, Café noir 1996, Dans Ma Chair 1997, Rendez-vous 1998, Le mot de passe 1999, Patricia Kaas Live 2000, Rien ne s'arrête 2001, Piano bar 2002, Sexe fort 2004, Toute la Musique 2005, Kabaret 2008, Kaas chante Piaf 2012. *Publications:* Patricia Kaas – Tour de Charme 1994. *Honours:* six Victoires de la Musique, two World Music Awards; de Gaulle-Adenauer Prize 2001, Goldene Europa Award for Best International Artist 2002, Zolotoy Gramophon Award for Best Song and International Artist 2008. *Current Management:* c/o Angela Di Corpo, GarberIMC, 1155 boulevard René-Lévesque Ouest, CIBC Tower, Suite 2500, Montreal, PQ H3B 2K4, Canada. *Telephone:* (514) 939-0100. *Fax:* (514) 875-8967. *E-mail:* angela@garberimc.com. *Website:* www.garberimc.com. *Address:* Attitude, 71 rue Robespierre, 93100 Montreuil, France. *Website:* www.patriciakaas.net; www .kabaretkaas.com/kabaret.

KAASINEN, Mari; Finnish singer; b. Rääkkylä, Karelia; sister of Sari Kaasinen. *Education:* Sibelius Acad. *Career:* Founder-mem. Värttinä 1983–; teacher of voice and kantele, Helsinki. *Music for theatre:* co-wrote score to stage musical, The Lord of the Rings (with A. R. Rahman) (Princess of Wales Theatre, Toronto) 2006. *Recordings include:* albums: Värttinä 1987, Musta Lindu 1989, Oi Dai 1990, Seleniko 1992, Aitara 1994, Kokko 1996, Vihma 1998, Ilmatar 2000, 6.12 2001, iki 2003, Miero 2006, 25 2007, Utu 2012. *Honours:* Kaustinen Folk Music Festival Band of the Year 1987, Arts Council of Finland State Prize for Merit in Music 1993, Finnish Nat. Group of IFPI Emma Award 1993. *Website:* www.varttina.com.

KAASINEN, Sari Johanna, MMus, DMus; Finnish singer, musician (kanteler) and record producer; b. 15 Sept. 1967, Rääkkylä; sister of Mari Kaasinen; m. Heikki Kemppainen 1991; three d. *Education:* Sibelius Acad., Helsinki. *Career:* Artistic Dir and lead singer, Värttinä 1983–96; Artistic Dir and lead singer, Sirmakka group 1994–97; solo artist 1996–; owner production co. Mipu Music Oy; teacher of music in Rääkkylä, Joensuu Music Inst., Central Karelian Music Inst., Central Karelian Civic Inst. 1983–; mem. Finnish State Music Art Cttee 1995–97; Artistic Dir, Kihaus Folk Music Festival 1991–; Man. Dir, Sari Kaasinen Ltd. *Recordings include:* albums: with Värttinä: Värttinä 1987, Musta Lindu 1989, Oi Dai 1991, Seleniko 1992, Aitara 1994, Kokko 1996; with Sirmakka: Sirmakka 1992, Tsihi Tsihi 1996; solo: Joko joulun alkaa saa (with Mari Kaasinen) 1997, Viisuja vintiltä 1998, Emo 1998, Joko joulun alkaa saa (with Otava-yhtye) 2001, Aika riemulle ruveta 2014; with Otawa: Reissunainen 2002, Sarin Joulu 2002, Mie kun 2006. *Honours:* Kaustinen Folk Music Festival Band of the Year (with Värttinä) 1987, Province of North Karelia Art Award 1992, Arts Council of Finland State Prize for Merit in Music (with Värttinä) 1993, Finnish Nat. Group of IFPI Emma Award (with Värttinä) 1993, Regional Council of North Karelia Innovator Award 1995, S.A. Tervo Kareliaani Award 1997, KVS Foundation Award 2000, Word in Culture Asscn Luonnotar Award 2001. *E-mail:* sari.kaasinen@sarikaasinen.com. *Website:* www.sarikaasinen.com.

KAEMPFERT, Marion; German producer, music publisher and author; b. (Marion Hanne-Lore Kaempfert), 28 Nov. 1946, Bremerhaven; d. of Bert Kaempfert; m. 1st Klaus Haake; two c.; m. 2nd Allan Botschinsky. *Education:* Jazz School, Lucerne, Switzerland, Hamburger Konservatorium, Hamburg, studied with Prof. Detlev Jürges. *Career:* Founder jazz label MA Music International 1985–; re-formed and produced Bert Kaempfert Orchestra, UK 1993–; Co-founder and Producer, First Brass ensemble, Duologue; Producer, Allan Botschinsky quartet, Allan Botschinsky quintet, Lee Konitz in Rio, Miguel Proença Brazilian Impressions; also producer for Marco Pereira Elegia, Thomas Clausen Piano Music, Jasper van't Hoff & Bob Malach, European Jazz Ensemble Live at the Philharmonic Cologne, The Bert Kaempfert Orchestra, dir Tony Fisher, Stefan Kaempfert: Kaempfert plays Kaempfert. *Films:* as music producer: Hamburg, Bilder einer Grossen Stadt 1989. *Television:* as music producer: Melodien, die man nie vergisst 1998–99, Sommermelodien 2000. *Publication:* Music Theory 1975. *Address:* Marion Kaempfert Music, Gartenstrasse 2, 6300 Zug (office); Bert Kaempfert Entertainment AG, Gartenstrasse 2, 6300 Zug, Switzerland (office). *Telephone:* (41) 7812100 (office). *Fax:* (41) 7472189 (office). *E-mail:* mkaempfert@

mac.com (office); mkaempfert@bertkaempfert.com (office). *Website:* www .mamusic.de (office); www.bertkaempfert.com (office).

KAERSAA, Morten; Danish composer, musician (piano) and singer; b. 26 Sept. 1957, Copenhagen; one s. *Career:* mem. of bands, Sneakers, Moonjam, Transition Trio. *Compositions:* Beat-Less 1992, Dance Floor 1992, Jazz House 1992, Salsa Olympia 1992, What Can I do Now 1992, Yellow Cab 1992, Una Bagatella 1997, Don't Hesitate 1997, House of the Rainbow 1997, Leave Me Like a Friend 1997, saxophonesong 1997, The Traveller 1997, Two Parrots 997, Wonder Why 1997, You're in My Heart 1997, O Vento 2000, On the Second Floor 2000. *Recordings include:* albums: with Moonjam: Songs for Saxophone Vols I & II, Sarai (musical), Bag De Bla Bjerge, Osten Fur Solen. *Current Management:* c/o Edition Wilhelm Hansen AS, Bornholmsgade 1, 1266 Copenhagen, Denmark. *E-mail:* ewh@ewh.dk. *Website:* www .musicsalesclassical.com. *Address:* Moonlab, Dampfaergevej 2 CD, 2100 Copenhagen, Denmark.

KAERSAA, Rasmus; Danish musician (bass); b. 29 Dec. 1960, Copenhagen; m. Annika Hueg, 25 June 1995; one s. *Career:* mem. Danse Orkestret; mem. Moonjam. *Compositions include:* Below the Yellow Moons, Kom Tilbage Nu (Come Back Now), with Jacob Andersen. *Recordings include:* albums with Moonjam: Songs for Saxophone, Saxophone Songs Vol. II, Xax Xonx; with Danse Orkestret: Danse Orkestret, Spred Vingerne Ud.

KAGADEEV, Andrei; Russian songwriter and musician; b. 9 July 1961, Moscow; m. Tatiana Kagadeeva, 2 March 1985, one d. *Education:* Technical Univ. of St Petersburg. *Career:* songwriter for band NOM. *Compositions include:* Films: Masters of the USSR or Ape's Snout 1994, Made In Europe (documentary) 1996. *Recordings include:* Albums: Brutto 1989, To Hell With It 1991, Superdisc 1992, Senka-Mosgas 1994, In the Name of Mind 1996, Ultracompact 1996, Live is Game 1996, Gire 1997, Extracompact 2000, 8 ye 2002, Russian Pig 2003, HOM 2005. *Honours:* . *Website:* www.nomzhir.spb.ru.

KAI; South Korean singer and rapper; b. (Kim Jong In), 14 Jan. 1994, Seoul. *Education:* School of Performing Arts, Seoul. *Career:* winner, 10th SM Youth Best Contest 2007; mem., K-pop boy band Exo 2012–; mem. sub-group Exo-K 2012–; debut single 2012; numerous TV and live appearances. *Television:* EXO's Showtime 2013–. *Recordings include:* albums: Mama 2012, XOXO (Mnet Asian Music Award for Album of the Year 2013) 2013. *Honours:* numerous awards including: for Exo: Mnet Asian Music Award for Best New Asian Artist/Group 2012, MTV Europe Music Award for Best Japan/Korea Act 2013, MelOn Music Award for Song of the Year (for Growl) 2013; for Exo-K: Golden Disk Newcomer Award 2012. *Address:* c/o SM Entertainment, 521 Apgujeong 2-dong, Gangnam-gu, Seoul, South Korea (office). *Telephone:* (2) 6240-9800 (office). *Website:* www.smtown.com (office); exo.smtown.com (home).

KAJDAN, Jean-Michel; French musician, songwriter and singer; b. 16 July 1954, Paris. *Career:* sideman, Didier Lockwood, Michel Jonasz, Eddy Mitchell, Lionel Richie, Eddy Louiss; The Big Blue (film); Subway (film); Taratata, (television with L Richie); Taratata (television with D E Mitchell); Montreux Jazz Festival (with Lassy Carlton), 1997; mem. SACEM; SPEDIDAM; ADAMI; SACD. *Compositions:* The Spy (D Lockwood Album); Spying Taranto; Song for LC. *Recordings:* Blue Scales; Blue Noise; Fasten Seat Belts; La Mouvellevie. *Address:* 1 rue du Général de Gaulle, 27500 Pont Audemer, France.

KAKA; Indonesian singer and musician (guitar, harmonica, drums); b. (Akhadi Wira Satriaji), 10 March 1974, Jakarta. *Career:* mem. Lovina 1988–89; joined Slank 1989–, band formed own record label and promotions co., Pulau Biru Productions and tabloid Koran Slank. *Recordings include:* albums: Suit…Suit…He…He… 1991, Kampungan 1992, Piss! 1993, Generasi Biru 1994, Minoritas 1995, Lagi Sedih 1996, Tujuh 1997, Mata Hati Reformasi 1998, 999 09 1999, Virus 2001, Satu Satu (Best Pop Rock Album, SCTV Music Awards 2003) 2003, Road to Peace 2004, Plur 2004, Slankissme 2006, Slow but Sure 2007, Anthem for the Broken Hearted 2008, Urustandur No. 18 2010, I Slank U The Album 2012, Slank Nggak Ada Matinya 2013, Indonesia Wow 2014. *Honours:* BASF Best Selling Album for 1990/1991 Award for Rock category, BASF Best Selling Album for 1991/1992 Award for Pop Rock category, BASF Best Selling Album for 1993/1994 Award for Rock/ Alternative category, BASF Best Selling Album for 1994/1995 for Rock category (Double Platinum Album Category), Best Song and Best Selling Album and Best Pop/Rock Band, Anugerah Musik Indonesia (AMI) Awards 1998, Best Rock Album, AMI Awards 1999, Best Video Clip Model and Best Video Clip Director, MTV Indonesia Music Awards 2002, Best Rock Song, AMI Awards 2002, World Peace Music Award 2003, MTV Asia Awards Nominator 2003, Best Rock Album, Best Rock Group, Best Rock Album Producer, AMI Awards 2003, Best Rock Album, Best Rock Song, AMI Awards 2004. *Website:* www.slank.com.

KALANIEMI, Maria Helena, MMus; Finnish musician and composer; b. 27 May 1964, Espoo; m. Olli Caris. *Education:* Sibelius Acad. *Career:* mem. various ensembles and side projects, including, Niekku, Helsinki Melodeon Ladies, Anna Kaisa Liedes Group, Ramunder, Vesa Matti Loiri Group 1983–; Gumbo Band 1999–; teacher, Sibelius Acad. (folk music dept); Leader and composer, Ensemble Aldargaz 1992–; mem. Accordion Tribe 1996–. *Compos-*

itions include: Hermannin Riili 1992, Lomasavel 1995, Iho 1995, Ahma 1998, Kaamos 1998, Kamppi 1998, Lovina 1998. *Recordings include:* Maria Kalaniemi 1992, Iho 1995, Accordion Tribe 1998, Ahma 1999, Bellow Poetry 2006, Vilda Rosor 2010, Åkerö 2011. *Honours:* Golden Accordion Competition 1983, Finnish Arts Award, Dept of Educ. 1996, three-year Composition grant 1997, Swede Vildrosen Prize 2004, Finnish Asscn of Musicians Award 2005. *E-mail:* maria.kalaniemi@gmail.com. *Website:* www.mariakalaniemi.com.

KALASZ, Juraj, DipEng; Slovak musician (double bass); b. 14 Nov. 1963, Bratislava; m. Dr Krausova Dagmar 1990; one s. *Education:* Slovak Techno-logical Univ., State Conservatory, Bratislava. *Career:* mem. Faculty, Slovak Technical Univ. 1983–89; mem. Esprit musical group 1986, John Hajnal Quintet 1987, Kellenberger Quartet 1988–89, Jazz Special 1992–, Czechoslo-vak Quintet 1993–94, Tutu 1993–94, Janusz Muniak's quartet 1995–96, Trio Shawna Loescher 1996–97, Peter Cardarelli Quartet 1998; f. own group, Just Jazz (tours in Denmark and Czech Republic) 1991–; mem. Slovak Jazz Soc. *Recordings include:* Monks Tatra Dream 1999, Angel Face 2002, Znovuzro-denie 2007. *Honours:* Prize for Outstanding Performance, Zilina Jazz Festival 1989.

KALIMOULLIN, Rashid; Russian composer; *Chairman, Union of Com-posers of the Russian Federation;* b. 6 May 1957, Zelenodolsk City, Tatarstan; m. 2nd Shreder Leyla; one s. one d. from previous m. *Education:* Kazan State Conservatoire. *Career:* Chair. Union of Composers of Repub. of Tatarstan 1989–; Sec. and Vice-Chair. Union of Composers of the Russian Fed. from 1995, now Chair.; mem. Public Chamber of Tatarstan Repub. *Compositions include:* Cuckoo's Cry (opera, libretto by I. Yuziev) 1989; symphonic works: Concerto for clarinet with orchestra 1985, Bulgary (poem) 1986, Silence and Tranquillity (vocal symphonic poem) 1987; chamber works: Quartet for wooden wind instruments 1981, About Silence (poem for voice and piano, lyrics by N. Arslanov) 1985, Sonata for cello solo No. 1 1986, About Happiness (poem for voice and two flutes, lyrics by R Mingalimov) 1989, Forgotten Prayer (fantasy for organ) 1992, Morning in Istanbul (fantasy for piano) 1993, Quartet No. 4 for two violins, viola and cello 1994, We Are Answerable to God for choir a capella 1995, Fantasy for Saxophone 1997, Head Into the Noose for violin and percussion (one performer) 1998, Poem about Kazan for mixed choir 1999, Windsor Wood for vocal quartet 1999, Dream about Sprout Rice (music for cello, percussions and tape-recorder) 2000, Chamber Symphony in four parts 2000, Poem-Fantasy for clarinet and violin 2000, Duo-Fantasy for two saxophones and soprano 2000, Sonata-Fantasy No. 2 for clarinet solo 2000, Train Frankfurt–Luxembourg for four saxophones 2002, Inside for a violin and accordion 2002, Quintet for clarinet and string quartet 2002, Sonata-Fantasy for French horn solo 2003, Concert-poem Legend About Kazan for the mixed chorus and orchestra 2004, Hawaii for chamber orchestra 2004, Night Wood for French horn, piano and percussion 2004, Awakening for a bass clarinet, piano and percussion 2004, Quartet for clarinet, violin, piano and percussion 2004, Concerto for piano and orchestra 2006. *Recordings:* Rashid Kalimoullin: Chamber Music 1989, Piano arrangements of songs by the Beatles: Hyper Beatles 1993, Chamber Works 1994, String Quartet No. 4 1996. *Honours:* First Prize, K.M. Veber Competition (Germany) 1987, Shostakovich Award (Russia) 1998, Honoured Worker of Arts of Russia 1996, Shostakovich Award (Russia) 1998, Nat. Artist of Tatarstan Repub., Prize of Govt of Russia 2005. *Address:* Union of Composers of the Republic of Tatarstan, 420111 Kazan, 10 Lobachevsky str., Tatarstan, Russian Feder-ation. *Telephone:* (843) 236-00-01. *Fax:* (843) 238-81-14. *E-mail:* skrt@list.ru. *Website:* www.rashidkalimullin.ru.

KAMAI, Allen; American musician (bass); b. 6 Dec. 1960, Marin County, California. *Education:* College of Marin. *Career:* Tours with: Oleta Adams; Sheena Easton; Wendy and Lisa; The Rainbirds; Michael Penn; Jude Cole; Ronnie Montrose; Extensive television and video performances in USA; Europe; Canada; Japan. *Recordings:* credits include: Sass Jordan, Curt Smith, Miki Howard, Jeanette Katt, Bronx-Style Bob, Pretty In Pink, The Rainbirds, Chanise Wilson, Wendy and Lisa, Kristian Vigard, Jim Chappell. *Honours:* Yamaha Soundcheck, Outstanding Bassist, 1987. *Address:* 14625 Dickens #207, Sherman Oaks, CA 91403, USA.

KAMINER, Wladimir; German writer, journalist and DJ; b. 1967, Moscow, USSR; m.; two c. *Career:* moved to Germany 1990; DJ, Russian Disco, Berlin. *Publications include:* Russendisko (short stories) 2000, Frische Goldjungs (ed.) 2001, Schönhauser Allee 2001, Militärmusik 2001, Die Reise nach Trulala 2002, Helden des Alltags (with Helmut Höge) 2002, Dschungelbuch 2003, Ich mache mit Sorgen, Mama 2004, Karaoke 2005, Küche totalitas: Das Kochbuch des Sozialismus 2006, Ich bin kein Berliner. Ein Reiseführer für faule Touristen 2007, Es gab keinen Sex im Sozialismus 2009, Meine kaukasische Schwiegermutter 2010, Meine Russischen Nachbarn 2011, Liebesgrüsse aus Deutschland 2011, Onkel Wanja kommt! 2012; contrib. to FAZ, taz and the Frankfurter Rundschau. *Address:* c/o Random House Ltd, 20 Vauxhall Bridge Road, London, SW1V 2SA, England. *Website:* www .wladimirkaminer.de; www.russendisko.de.

KANAL, Tony; musician (bass guitar); b. 27 Aug. 1970, Kingsbury, London, England. *Career:* mem., No Doubt 1987–. *Recordings:* albums: No Doubt 1992, Beacon Street Collection 1994, Tragic Kingdom 1995, Return Of Saturn 2000, Rock Steady 2001, Everything In Time 2004, Push and Shove 2012; singles: Just A Girl 1995, Don't Speak 1997, New 1999, Ex-Girlfriend 2000, Simple Kind Of Life 2000, Bathwater 2000, Hey Baby 2001, Hella Good 2002, Tour

(EP) 2002, Underneath It All (Grammy Award for Best Performance by a Duo or Group with vocal 2004) 2002. *Website:* www.nodoubt.com.

KANDA BONGO MAN; Democratic Republic of the Congo singer and songwriter; b. 1955, Inono. *Career:* started singing in Kinshasa 1973, one of key figures in devt of Congolese soukous music; mem. Orchestre Bella Mambo 1976; moved to Paris 1979, credited with introduction of kwassa kwassa dance rhythm; later Minister of Arts and Culture, Democratic Republic of Congo; Amb.-at-Large, United Congolese Party 2014–. *Recordings include:* Iyole 1981, Non Stop Non Stop 1985, Amour Fou 1985, Kwassa Kwassa 1989, Zing Zong 1991, Soukous in Central Park 1992, Francophonix 1995, Welcome to South Africa 1998, Sweet 1999, Best of Kanda Bongo Man 1999, Balobi 2001, Very Best of Kanda Bongo Man 2002, Swalati 2003, Soukous Time 2008, Non-Stop Feeling 2010.

KANE, Gregory; British singer, lyricist and composer; b. 11 Sept. 1966, Coatbridge, Strathclyde, Scotland; brother of Patrick Kane. *Education:* studied engineering. *Career:* Founder-mem., Hue and Cry late 1980s–; numerous concerts; composer for TV themes and musical scores. *Recordings include:* albums: Seduced and Abandoned 1987, Remote 1988, Bitter Suite 1989, Stars Crash Down 1991, Truth and Love 1992, Labours of Love 1993, Showtime! 1994, Piano and Voice 1995, Jazz Not Jazz 1999, Live '99 1999, Next Move 2000, The River Sessions, Vol. 1 2005, Open Soul 2008. *Website:* www.hueandcry.co.uk.

KANE, Patrick; British singer, musician (piano, keyboards), songwriter and journalist; b. 10 March 1964, Coatbridge, Strathclyde, Scotland; brother of Gregory Kane. *Career:* Founder-mem. Hue and Cry late 1980s–; composer for TV themes and musical scores; also journalist, The Guardian; radio presenter, Usual Suspects (BBC Radio Scotland); Rector, Glasgow Univ.; Founder, Artists for an Independent Scotland. *Recordings include:* albums: Seduced and Abandoned 1987, Remote 1988, Bitter Suite 1989, Stars Crash Down 1991, Truth and Love 1992, Labours of Love 1993, Showtime! 1994, Piano and Voice 1995, Jazz Not Jazz 1999, Live '99 1999, Next Move 2000, The River Sessions, Vol. 1 2005, Open Soul 2008, Revival 2009, Headin' for a Fall 2009, Hot Wire 2012. *Website:* www.hueandcry.co.uk.

KANE, Stephen (Stevie); British musician (bass, double bass); b. 13 April 1961. *Career:* mem. The Silencers 1992–. *Recordings include:* with The Silencers: Seconds of Pleasure 1993, So Be It 1995, Blood and Rain 1996, Receiving 1999, A Night of Electric Silence 2001, Come 2004, Real 2008. *E-mail:* silencersnews@yahoo.fr. *Website:* thesilencers.free.fr.

KANG, Minkyung; South Korean singer. *Career:* mem. K-pop duo Davichi 2008–. *Recordings include:* albums: with Davichi: Amaranth 2008, Davichi in Wonderland (Golden Disk Bonsang Award 2009) 2009, Innocence 2010, Love Delight 2011. *Honours:* with Davichi: Mnet Asian Music Awards for Best New Female Group 2008, for Best Group Vocal Performance (for Will Think of You) 2012, Golden Disk Award for Best Newcomer Artist 2008, Seoul Music Awards for Best New Artist 2009, for Bonsang (for 8282) 2010, Cyworld Digital Music Bonsang Award 2010, Gaon Chart K-Pop Bonsang Award 2012. *Website:* ccment.com; davichi.ccment.com.

KANNBERG, Scott; American musician (guitar) and singer; b. 1967, Stockton, CA. *Career:* Founder-mem. Pavement 1989–2000, reunited for live performances 2010; contrib. to Starlite Walker by the Silver Jews 1994; f. own label, Pray for Mojo 1998, later renamed Amazing Grease; Founder-mem. Preston School of Industry 2000–04; solo artist, performing as Spiral Stairs. *Television appearance:* Space Ghost Coast to Coast (cartoon) 1997. *Recordings include:* albums: with Pavement: Slanted and Enchanted 1992, Crooked Rain, Crooked Rain 1994, Wowee Zowee 1995, Brighten the Corners 1997, Terror Twilight 1999, Crooked Rain, Crooked Rain (expanded edn) 2004, Quarantine the Past: The Best of Pavement 2010; with Preston School of Industry: All This Sounds Gas 2001, Monsoon 2004; as Spiral Stairs: The Real Feel 2009. *E-mail:* spiralstairsmusic@gmail. *Website:* www.spiralstairsmusic.com.

KANO; British MC; b. (Kane Robinson), 21 May 1985, London. *Career:* mem. N.A.S.T.Y. (Natural Artistic Sound Touching You) Crew, with 'grime' music genre; solo artist. *Recordings include:* solo album: Home Sweet Home 2005, London Town 2007, 140 Grime Street 2008, Method to the Maadness 2010; singles: with N.A.S.T.Y. Crew: Good Ya Know, War Talk, Destruction; solo: Boys Love Girls, Lately, So Sure, Vice Versa. *Films include:* Rollin' with the Nines 2006, Point Blank 2007, Tower Block 2012. *Television:* Top Boy 2011–13. *Honours:* MOBO Award for Best UK Newcomer 2005. *Current Management:* c/o Xtreme Talent, PO Box 1034, Morden, Surrey SM4 6QX, England. *Telephone:* (844) 873-1988. *E-mail:* info@xtremetalent.co.uk. *Website:* www.xtremetalent.co.uk.

KANTARDZIJEV-MLINAC, Petko; Croatian composer, sound engineer, producer and musician (piano); b. 21 Oct. 1945, Sofia, Bulgaria; m. Mirjana 1971; one d. *Career:* musician 1961–69; Music Ed., TV Zagreb 1969; rehearser, Comedy Theatre, Zagreb: The Man From La Mancha, Fiddler On The Roof, Promises Promises 1969–71; radio-TV, Zagreb 1970–89; Music Producer, Suzy Record Co. 1971–72; sound engineer, Jugoton Record Co. 1974–76; Dir, Multimedia Youth Centre 1987–88; pianist 1990–; mem. Croatian Composers' Asscn, Croatian Artists' Asscn. *Compositions:* over 150 compositions and arrangements, pop, easy listening, classical. *Recordings include:* as sound engineer on more than 200 film soundtracks, animations, documentaries, TV series; 100 albums including by John Luis, Clark Terry, Sal Nistico, Art

Farmer. *Honours:* Best Soundtrack, Yugoslavia 1982, 1984, 1985, 1986, First P at festivals in Opatija 1968, Zagreb 1986.

KANTÉ, Mory; Guinean musician (kora), singer and composer; b. 29 March 1950, Albadaria, nr Kissidougou; s. of El Hadj Djelifode and Fatouma Kamissoko; partner Sira Kouyate. *Education:* studied in Mali. *Career:* guitarist and balafonist, later singer, Rail Band 1965–77; Founder-mem. 35-piece band, Les Milieus Branches 1977; solo artist late 1970s–, with tours of West Africa; moved to France 1984–89; appeared in Central Park and at Apollo Theater, Harlem 1990, at inauguration of the Grande Arche de la Défense, Paris 1991, and Pope's jubilee celebrations 2000; toured in Europe and Canada 1994, then toured worldwide including regular appearances at WOMAD, 15 European countries and South Africa 2002; apptd FAO Amb. 2001. *Films:* Black Mic Mac (contrib.) 1985, The Beach (soundtrack) 2000. *Recordings include:* albums: Courougnegne 1981, N'Diarabi 1982, À Paris 1984, 10 Cola Nuts 1986, Akwaba Beach 1987, Touma 1990, Nongo Village 1993, Tatebola 1996, Tamala – Le Voyageur 2001, Sabou 2004, La Guinéenne 2012. *Honours:* Voix d'Or (Nigeria) 1976, Griot d'Or (France) 1994, Radio Africa n°1 Prix Kilimandjaro (France) 1994. *E-mail:* management@morykante .com. *Website:* www.morykante.com.

KANTONEN, Seppo; Finnish musician (piano, keyboards); b. 13 Nov. 1963, Kivijärvi. *Education:* Sibelius Acad., Helsinki. *Career:* began career playing with Nono Söderberg and Otto Donner Treatment; pianist with UMO (New Music Orchestra); pianist with Eero Koivistoinen 1980s; leader, Klang trio 1990s; worked with numerous rock bands including Mustat Lasit 1980s; recorded as duo with Jarmo Savolainen; f. trio Tokka 2011. *Recordings include:* albums: Phases 1989, Pewit 1997, Pekka's Tube Factory 1999, Sometime Ago 1999, First Definition 1999, Loveship 2001, Helium 2001, A Tribute to Finnish Cinema 2001, Views 2001, Manuscript 2002, Utu 2002, Suhka 2003, X-Ray 2006, Paa-da-Pap 2007, Umo On Umo 2009, Clustrophy 2010, No Idling 2012, Supermusic! 2012, Kantonen-Herrala-Hassinen 2014. *Honours:* Yrjö Award, Finnish Jazz Federation 1985.

KAPHAN, Bruce Robert; American musician, producer, composer and engineer; b. 7 Jan. 1955, San Francisco, Calif.; m. Michele White 1987. *Career:* mem. American Music Club 1993–96; TV appearances with Jewel (Saturday Night Live and MTV Unplugged) 1997; European and US tours with David Byrne; mem. American Federation of Musicians. *Recordings include:* John Lee Hooker, Chill Out, The Black Crowes, Amorica, Chris Isaak, Forever Blue, with American Music Club: Mercury 1993, San Francisco 1994, Black Crowes, Three Snakes and One Charm, Love and Rockets, Sweet FA, Jellyfish, Spilt Milk, Red House Painters, Songs for a Blue Guitar, Francesco di Gregori, Premiere E Lasciare, Susanna Hoffs, Susanna Hoffs, Tara MacLean, Silence; Suzanne Little, Be Here Now; Mark Eitzel, 60 Watt Silver Lining, West, Up, REM, Legacy, Jewel; Solo album: Slider–Ambient Excursions For Pedal Steel Guitar 2001, Secular Steel 2004, Slider 2005, Living Death Valley 2009, Dirty Girl 2012, Bruce Kaphan Quartet 2012, Pelican Dreams, the Soundtrack Album 2014; film scores: Crank Calls 2002, Masked and Anonymous (adapted score) 2003. *Honours:* Award Winner, Northern California Film and Video Festival 2000. *E-mail:* bruce@brucekaphan.com. *Website:* www.brucekaphan .com.

KAPLAN, Ira; American singer, songwriter and musician (guitar); b. 7 Jan. 1957; m. Georgia Hubley. *Career:* formed band Yo La Tengo with wife Georgia Hubley, in Hoboken, NJ 1984; has performed in many styles including indie rock, acoustic, noise, experimental, punk; frequent tours throughout USA and worldwide; collaborations with Yoko Ono, Jad Fair, Ray Davies, Robyn Hitchcock, Neil Innes, mems Sun Ra Arkestra; composed soundtracks for several films; has written as music critic for publs including New York Rocker and Village Voice. *Film soundtracks:* The Sounds of the Sounds of Science 2001, Junebug 2005, Game 6 2005, Shortbus 2006, Old Joy 2006. *Recordings include:* albums: Ride the Tiger 1986, New Wave Hot Dogs 1987, President Yo La Tengo 1989, Fakebook 1990, May I Sing with Me 1992, Painful 1993, Electr-O-Pura 1995, I Can Hear the Heart Beating as One 1997, Strange But True (with Jad Fair) 1998, And Then Nothing Turned Itself Inside Out 2000, The Sounds of the Sounds of Science 2002, Summer Sun 2003, Prisoners Of Love: A Smattering Of Scintillating Senescent Songs, 1985–2003 2005, I Am Not Afraid of You and I Will Beat Your Ass 2006, Yo La Tengo Is Murdering the Classics 2006, Popular Songs 2009, Occupy This Album 2012, Nightmare Ending (with Eluvium) 2013, Fade 2013. *Address:* PO Box 6028, Hoboken, NJ 07030, USA (office). *E-mail:* info@yolatengo.com (office). *Website:* www .yolatengo.com (office).

KAPOOR, Kanika; Indian playback singer; b. 23 March 1978, Lucknow, Uttar Pradesh; m. Raj Chandok 1997 (divorced 2012); three c. *Career:* studied classical music with Ganesh Prasad Mishra 1990; released music video Jugni Ji, featuring Dr Zeus 2012; made Bollywood singing debut with song Baby Doll (featured in film Ragini MMS 2) 2014; toured North America with Shah Rukh Khan and Deepika Padukone 2014. *Films include:* as playback singer: Ragini MMS 2 2014, Happy New Year 2014, Roy 2015, Ek Paheli Leela 2015, All is Well 2015, Kis Kisko Pyaar Karoon 2015, Main Aur Charles 2015, Hate Story 3 2015, Diwale 2015. *Honours:* BIG Star Entertainment Award for Most Entertaining Singer (Female) 2014, Stardust Award for Best Playback Singer – Female 2014, Mirchi Music Number One Song of the Year Award 2014, Filmfare Award for Best Female Playback Singer 2015, Star Guild Award for Best Female Playback Singer 2015. *Current Management:* c/o Artist Management India, 84 Double Storey Basement, New Rajendra Nagar, New Delhi,

110 060, India. *Telephone:* (11) 45380809. *E-mail:* info@ artistmanagementindia.com. *Website:* artistmanagementindia.com.

KAPOOR, Steven (see Apache Indian)

KAPRANOS, Alex; British singer and musician (guitar); b. (Alexander Paul Kapranos Huntley), Almondsbury, Glos. *Career:* worked as a chef and waiter at various Glasgow restaurants; fmr mem. The Karelia; mem. Franz Ferdinand 2001–; has produced records for The Cribs, Citizens!; wrote food column Soundbites for the Guardian newspaper 2006. *Recordings include:* albums: with The Karelia: Divorce At High Noon 1997; with Franz Ferdinand: Franz Ferdinand (Mercury Music Prize 2004, NME Award for Best Album 2005, Meteor Award for Best Int. Album 2005) 2004, You Could Have It So Much Better... With Franz Ferdinand 2005, Tonight: Franz Ferdinand 2009, Right Thoughts, Right Words, Right Action 2013. *Publication:* Sound Bites 2006. *Honours:* BRIT Awards for Best British Group, Best British Rock Act 2005, Meteor Award for Best Int. Band 2005, NME Award for Best Live Band 2006. *Website:* www.franzferdinand.com.

KARAM, Fares; Lebanese singer; b. 1973, Jezzine. *Career:* winner Studio al-Phan 1996/97; solo artist 2002–. *Recordings include:* albums: Janen 2002, Aktar min rouhi 2003, Dakhilo 2004, Wa'adni 2005, Ya'borni 2007, Elhamdullah 2010, Fares Karam 2013. *Honours:* Sydney Cedars Club Award 1999, Art Lebanon Award 2002, An-nojoum production award, Australia 2003, Lions Int. Award 2005, Arms of Alberta 2005, Fifteenth Faces Concert Award 2005, Festival of Carthage Award 2006. *Website:* ar-ar.facebook.com/ FaresKaramOfficialPage.

KARAM, Najwa Nicola; Lebanese singer; b. 26 Feb. 1966, Zahle; d. of Karam Karam and Barbara Shaheen Karam. *Education:* Arabic Music Inst. *Career:* fmr teacher; winner of gold medal in TV show, Layali Lubnaan 1985; solo artist 1989–; live appearances include Orbit Festival, Jerash Festival (Jordan), Carthage Festival (Tunisia), Muscat Festival (Oman), Doha Festival (Qatar), Arab Communities Festival (Canada), Layali Dubai Festival (UAE), Tyre Festival (Lebanon), Al-Fatih Festival (Libya), Al-Zahra City Festival (Tunisia), Hala February Festival (Kuwait). *Recordings include:* albums: Ya habayeb 1989, Shams el-ghennieh 1992, Ana ma'akon 1993, Naghmet hob 1994, Ma bismahlak 1995, Hazi hilou 1996, Ma hada la hada 1997, Maghroumeh 1998, Rouh rouhi 1999, Oyoun qalbi 2000, Nedmaneh 2001, Tahamouni 2002, Saharni 2003, Shu mghaira 2004, Kibir al-hob 2005, Hayda haki (Mosaique FM Award for Album of the Year) 2007, Aam bemzah ma'ak 2008, Khallini Shoufak 2009, Hal Layle... Ma Fi Nom 2011. *Honours:* Hon. USA citizenship 1996, Key to the City of Chicago, USA 1996, Key to the City of Düsseldorf, Germany 1998, Lebanese Army Hon. Award 1999, Hon. Award, Australia 2003, Faraya City Award 2003, Zahle City Award 2004; Lebanese Broadcasting Asscn Best Artist of 1994, 1995, Murex D'Or for Best Arabic Artist 2001, Lions Club Award for Best Singer of Traditional Lebanese Song 2003, Sawt el-ghad Song of the Year (for Edhak lil donya), Australia 2003, (for Bhebak walaa) 2005, Award for Best Female Middle Eastern Singer, Canada 2007. . *Website:* www.najwakaram.com.

KARDINAL OFFISHALL; Canadian rapper and producer; b. (Jason Harrow), 12 May 1976, Scarborough, Ont. *Career:* began rapping aged 12; signed first publishing deal 1996. *Recordings include:* albums: Eye & I 1997, Quest for Fire: Firestarter 2001, Fire and Glory 2005, Not 4 Sale 2008, Allow Me to Re-Introduce Myself 2012; also appeared on recordings by Rascalz, Choclair. *Films:* Love, Sex and Eating the Bones 2003, My Baby's Daddy 2004, You Got Served: Beat the World 2011. *Television:* Drop the Beat 2000, After Hours 2001, Video on Trial 2005, Muchmusic VJ Search 2006. *Honours:* Juno Award for Single of the Year (for Dangerous) 2009, Juno Award for R & B/Soul Recording of the Year (for Can't Choose) 2014. *Current Management:* c/o Heavy Rotation LLC, 64 Fulton Street, Suite 1100, New York, NY 10038, USA. *E-mail:* bookkardinal@gmail.com. *Website:* www.kardinaloffishall.com.

KARGES, (Matthew) Murphy; American musician (bass guitar); b. 20 June 1967, Orange County, Calif.; m. Julie Holland-Karges; three s. *Career:* toured USA with Los Angeles punk group, The Weirdos 1990; mem. The Shrinky Dinx, later renamed Sugar Ray; numerous tours and TV appearances; f. Karges Media. *Film appearance:* cameo in Father's Day 1997. *Recordings include:* albums: Lemonade and Brownies 1995, Floored 1997, 14–59 1999, Sugar Ray 2001, In Pursuit of Leisure 2003, Music for Cougars 2009. *E-mail:* info@kargesmedia.com. *Website:* www.kargesmedia.com.

KARLOFF, Christopher; British musician (guitar, bass guitar, keyboards). *Education:* Countesthorpe Community Coll. *Career:* mem. Kasabian 1999–2006, Black Onassis (with Nick Forde) 2014–. *Recordings include:* albums with Kasabian: Kasabian 2004, Empire 2006; with Black Onassis: Desensitized 2013. *Honours:* NME Award for Best Live Act 2007, BRIT Award for Best British Group 2010. *Website:* blackonassis.com.

KARLSSON, Ulrik; Swedish musician (horns). *Career:* mem. The Concretes 1999–; band founded label, Licking Fingers. *Recordings include:* albums: Boyoubetterunow 2000, The Concretes 2003, Layourbattleaxedown 2005, In Colour 2006, Hey Trouble 2007, WYWH 2010. *E-mail:* theconcretessweden@ gmail.com. *Website:* www.theconcretes.com.

KARPOVA, Anastasia; Russian singer; b. 2 Nov. 1984, Balakovo. *Career:* fmr mem. Street Jazz ballet troupe; mem. Serebro 2009–, many hits in Russia; international hit with Mama Lover 2011. *Recordings:* with Serebro: albums: Mama Lover 2011. *Address:* c/o Monolit Records, Studio Monolit office,

Moscow, 117105, 4a Novodanilovskaya naberezhnaya, Russia (office). *Telephone:* (495) 5102255 (office). *E-mail:* pkmonolit@mail.ru (office). *Website:* www.pkmonolit.ru/english.php (office); www.serebro.su.

KÄRTSY; Finnish musician, composer, lyricist and singer; b. (Kari Hatakka), 17 Dec. 1967, Helsinki. *Career:* European tours 1993–97; Lead singer, Finnish rock band Waltari 1994; performed at Roskilde Festival, Denmark 1994, 1995; Ethno Meets Metal tour with Angelin Tytöt 1995; European tours 1995, 1996, 1997. *Recordings include:* Monk Punk 1991, Torcha! 1992, So Fine! 1994, Big Bang 1995, Yeah! Yeah! Die! Die! Death Metal Symphony in Deep C 1996, Space Avenue 1997, Decade 1998, Duty Freedom 2010, aWay 2014. *E-mail:* kartsy.official@gmail.com. *Website:* www.kartsy.com.

KARVONEN, (Jari-Pekka) Jartsa; Finnish musician (drums); b. 27 June 1955, Kuusamo. *Education:* Oulunkylä Inst. *Career:* played with Rovaniemi, Lapland; played with bands Blue Train, Jukka Syrenius Band, Tapiola Big Band; played with numerous artists including Jukka Linkola, Olli Ahvenlahti, Pentti Lahti, Mircea Stan; regular mem. UMO (New Music Orchestra) 1989. *Honours:* Musician of the Year 1989, Voted Best Drummer, Finnish Jazz Federation's magazine JazzIt Readers Poll 1989. *Address:* Paraistentie 11, 00280 Helsinki, Finland (home). *E-mail:* jartsa.karvonen@welho.com. *Website:* www.jartsa-karvonen.net.

KASHMARI, Sahar, DipMus; Iranian backing singer and actress; b. 1980, Tehran; sister of Sanaz Kashmari. *Career:* mem. The Arian Band (the first officially sanctioned mixed-gender pop band in Iran). *Theatre as actress:* Beyond the Mirror. *Television as actress:* The Adventures of Mr Somebody (series). *Recordings include:* albums: Sunflower, And But Love!, Till Eternity, Without You With You 2008. *Current Management:* c/o Mr Mohsen Rajabpour, Taraneh Sharghee Cultural & Artistic Co., Apt No. 26, Seventh Floor, Suite 22, Second Alley, Shahnazari Street, Mohseni Square, Mirdamad Avenue, Tehran 1547914415, Iran. *Telephone:* (21) 22223513. *Fax:* (21) 22223670 (office). *E-mail:* president@taranehsh.com.

KASHMARI, Sanaz; Iranian backing singer, actress and musician (percussion); b. 1983, Tehran; sister of Sahar Kashmari. *Career:* mem. The Arian Band (the first officially sanctioned mixed-gender pop band in Iran). *Films as actress:* Daftari az Aseman, Yek Boom-o-Do Havaa. *Theatre as actress:* Beyond the Mirror. *Television as actress:* New Year Holidays (series), Pahlavi's Cap (series). *Recordings include:* albums: Sunflower, And But Love!, Till Eternity, Without You With You 2008. *Current Management:* c/o Mr Mohsen Rajabpour, Taraneh Sharghee Cultural & Artistic Co., Apt No. 26, Seventh Floor, Suite 22, Second Alley, Shahnazari Street, Mohseni Square, Mirdamad Avenue, Tehran 1547914415, Iran. *Telephone:* (21) 22223513. *Fax:* (21) 22223670. *E-mail:* president@taranehsh.com.

KASPERSEN, Jan Per Sommerfeldt; Danish musician (piano), composer, arranger and bandleader; b. 22 April 1948, Copenhagen; one s. *Career:* musician, European jazz scene 1969–; bandleader, trios up to quintets, using name Space and Rhythm Jazz; mem. Danish Musicians' Union, Soc. of Danish Bandleaders, DJBFA Composers' Guild, ToneArt. *Recordings include:* Memories of Monk, Live At Sofie's Cellar, Heavy Smoke, Ballads and Cocktails, Special Occasion Band: Live In Copenhagen Jazz-House, Space and Rhythm Jazz, Joining Forces, Jan Kaspersen and the Danish Radio Jazz Orchestra: Live in Copenhagen Jazzhouse, Out of Sight, Katuaq Concert, More Ballads and Cocktails, Memo to the Moon, Mind Pictures, Blues for a Hip King, Public Piano, Happy as a Flower, Jiving in Kalamazoo, Black Rabbit Suite. *Honours:* DJBFA Jazz Composer Prize 1987, JASA Prize 1988, Danish Arts Foundation Lifelong Grant (as a composer) 1998, Be Bop Prize 2010, Ben Webster Prize 2012. *Address:* Gl. Kongevej 172A, 5. Sal, 1850 Copenhagen, Denmark (home). *Telephone:* 33-31-21-79 (office). *E-mail:* mail@jankaspersen.dk (office). *Website:* www.jankaspersen.dk.

KATERINE, Philippe; French singer, songwriter and actor; b. (Philippe Blanchard), 8 Dec. 1968, Vendée; two s. *Recordings include:* albums: Les mariages chinois 1991, Les mariages chinois et la relecture 1993, L'éducation anglaise 1994, Mes mauvaises fréquentations 1996, Les Créatures 1999, L'homme à trois mains 1999, 8ème ciel 2002, Robots après tout 2005, 100% VIP 2006, Katerine 2010, Magnum 2013; film soundtrack: Un home un vrai 2003. *Films include:* actor: Nom de code: Sacha 2000, La Vérité sur Charlie 2002; dir: Peau de Cochon 2004, Les Invisibles 2005, To Paint or Make Love 2005, Capitaine Achab 2007, Le Voyage aux Pyrénées 2008, Louise-Michel 2008, Les Regrets 2009, Gainsbourg 2010. *Publication includes:* Doublez votre mémoire 2007. *Website:* katerine.free.fr; www.katerine.net.

KATINA, Elena (Lena) Sergeevna; Russian singer; b. 4 Oct. 1984, Moscow; m. Sasho Kuzmanović. *Career:* mem. Neposedy –2000; mem. t.A.T.u. late 1990s–. *Recordings include:* albums: 200 km/h In The Wrong Lane 2002, Dvesti Po Vstrechiy 2002, Dangerous and Moving 2005, Happy Smiles 2008, This Is Who I Am 2014. *Current Management:* c/o Eric White, Star Technology, 127254 Moscow, Proezd Dobrolubova, 3, Russia. *E-mail:* katina@startech.me; info@tatu.ru (office). *Website:* www.lenakatina.com; www.tatu.ru.

KÄTKÄ, Ismo (Ippe) Paavo Matias; Finnish composer, producer and musician (drums, keyboards); b. 19 March 1948, Seinajoki; m. (divorced 1990); two s. *Career:* mem. several dance, pop, rock, jazz bands since 1965, including Starboys, Tangopojat, Yahoos, Kari Larne Group, Woodoo, Matthews, Kirka and Islanders, Royals, Pekka Pohjola Group, Veltto and Heru, Ippe Kätkä Band, Tampere Jazz Orchestra, Juice Leskinen, Dave Lindholm, Anssi

Tikanmäki Film Orchestra, Krakatau, Ismo Alanko, Galaxy (Senegal); int. tours with Pekka Pohjola Group 1980–82, Anssi Tikanmäki Film Orchestra 1989–93, Krakatau 1993–96, Galaxy 1993. *Recordings include:* albums: with Royals: Spring 76, Out, Live; with Pekka Pohjola Group: Kätkävaaran Lohikäärme; with Veltto and Heru: Tahdon; with Ippe Kätkä Band: Makumoka; with Juice: Minä, Sinä, Dave, Sissi, Sillalla; with A T Film Orchestra: Greed; with Krakatau: Matinale, with Ismo Alanko: Irti; Taiteilijaelämää; with Galaxy: Nobeel. *Honours:* Tampere City Creative Musician Award 1989, Critics' Poll Award for Best Group and Best Album of Year 1985, 1994, KOURA Award for the best radio programme 1997.

KATONA, Kerry Jane Elizabeth; British singer; b. 6 Sept. 1980, Warrington, England; m. Bryan McFadden 2002 (divorced 2006); two d. *Career:* mem., Atomic Kitten 1999–2001; numerous tours and concerts. *Television appearance:* I'm a Celebrity... Get me out of here (winner, gameshow on ITV) 2004. *Recordings include:* Albums: Right Now, 2000. Singles: Right Now, 1999; See Ya, 2000; I Want Your Love, 2000; Follow Me, 2000; Whole Again, 2001. *Address:* c/o Martin O'Shea, Bold Management Ltd., 85 Bold Street, Liverpool, L1 4HF, England. *Website:* www.kerrykatona.biz.

KAUKONEN, Jorma, BA; Russian/Finnish (American) musician (guitar, resophonic guitar, steel guitar); *Co-Owner, Fur Peace Ranch Music School;* b. 23 Dec. 1940, Washington, DC. *Education:* Santa Clara Univ., Antioch Coll., studied music with Ian Buchanan and Rev Gary Davis. *Career:* mem., The Triumphs, Jefferson Airplane 1966–72, side project Hot Tuna 1968–78, 1992–, Jefferson Airplane Reunion 1989–90; co-owner, Fur Peace Ranch Music School; numerous festival appearances. *Recordings include:* albums: Jefferson Airplane Takes Off 1966, After Bathing At Baxter's 1968, Crown of Creation 1968, Bless Its Pointed Little Head 1969, Volunteers 1969, Blows Against The Empire 1970, Long John Silver 1972, Flight Log (1966–76) 1977, Jefferson Airplane 1989, Jefferson Airplane Loves You 1992; with Hot Tuna: First Pull Up Then Pull Down 1971, Burgers 1972, The Phosphorescent Rat 1974, America's Choice 1975, Yellow Fever 1975, Hoppkorv 1976, Double Dose 1978, 2400 Fulton Street 1987; solo: Quah 1974, Jorma 1979, Barbeque King 1980, Magic 1985, Too Hot To Handle 1985, Embryonic Journey 1994, Magic Two 1995, Land of Heroes 1995, Jorma Kaukonen Christmas 1996, Too Many Years 1998, Blue Country Heart 2002, Stars in my Crown 2007, River of Time 2009. *Honours:* Antioch Coll. Lifetime Achievement Award 2004. *Current Management:* c/o Vanessa Lillian, Fur Peace Management, PO Box 389, Pomeroy, OH 45769, USA. *Telephone:* (740) 992-2575. *Fax:* (740) 992-9126. *E-mail:* fpman@earthlink.net. *Website:* www.furpeaceranch.com; www.jormakaukonen.com.

KAULITZ, Bill; German singer; b. 1 Sept. 1989, Leipzig; s. of Jörg W. Kaulitz and Simone Kaulitz. *Career:* mem. and lead singer of rock band, Tokio Hotel 2001–. *Recordings include:* solo album: Devilish 2001; with Tokio Hotel: Schrei 2005, Schrei: So Laut Du Kannst 2006, Zimmer 483 2007, Scream 2007, Humanoid 2009, Kings of Suburbia 2014. *Honours:* ECHO Award for Best Nat. Newcomer 2006, MTV Europe Music Awards for Best Int. Act 2007, for Best Headline Act 2008, for Best Group 2009. *Website:* www.tokiohotel.com.

KAULITZ, Tom; German musician (guitar); b. 1 Sept. 1989, Leipzig; s. of Jörg W. Kaulitz and Simone Kaulitz. *Career:* mem. rock band, Tokio Hotel 2001–. *Recordings include:* albums: Schrei 2005, Schrei: So Laut Du Kannst 2006, Zimmer 483 2007, Scream 2007, Humanoid 2009. *Honours:* ECHO Award for Best Nat. Newcomer 2006, MTV Europe Music Awards for Best Int. Act 2007, for Best Headline Act 2008, for Best Group 2009. *Website:* www.tokiohotel.com.

KAVANA, Ron; Irish musician, producer, arranger, songwriter and composer; b. Fermoy, Co. Cork. *Career:* fmr session musician, producer, arranger; worked with numerous artists including Charlie Watts, Richard Thompson, Paddy Moloney, The Pogues, Elvis Costello, Dr John, Clarence Henry, Doug Sahm, Big Jay McNeely; mem. various groups including Loudest Whisper, Panama Red, Chris Farlowe Band, Identity Kit, with guitarist Ed Deane, Juice On The Loose; in-house bandleader, producer for Ace Records; mem. various bands with Alexis Korner 1980s, Bees Make Honey; leader of own band Alias Ron Kavana; three support tours with The Pogues; other projects include: Home Fire, The Bucks; Founder-mem. and Dir of LILT (London Irish Live Trust); songwriter for films including: Ryan's Daughter, Sid and Nancy, Clash of The Ash, Hidden Agenda. *Compositions include:* co-writer (with The Pogues): Young Ned of The Hill, Every Man Is A King. *Recordings include:* albums: solo: Rollin' and Coasting, Home Fire; with Alias: Ron Kavana: Think Like A Hero 1989, Coming Days 1991, Galway To Graceland 1995, Irish Songs of Rebellion, Resistance and Reconciliation 2006, Irish Ways: Story of Ireland in Song, Music & Poetry 2007, 40 Favourite Folk Songs 2011; with Loudest Whisper: The Children of Lire; with Donovan, Liam Og O'Fynn, Philip Donnelly, RTE Chamber Orchestra: The Children of Lire (re-recorded) 1993; with The Bucks: Dancing To The Ceilidh Band 1995; with LILT: For The Children; guest musician with The Pogues: Sid and Nancy (soundtrack), Fall From Grace. *Honours:* Folk Roots Magazine Best Live Act in the World 1989–91.

KAVANAGH, Niamh; Irish singer; b. 13 Feb. 1968, Dublin; m. Paul Megahey; two s. *Education:* Bel canto school. *Career:* winner of Eurovision Song Contest 1993, also represented Ireland at Eurovision Song Contest 2010; now performs with Niamh Kavanagh and The Illegals; mem. Musicians' Union. *Recordings include:* albums: Flying Blind (solo) 1995, Together Alone (with Gerry Carney) 1998, Wonderdrug 2001; also sang on soundtrack of film

The Commitments 1991. *Honours:* Yamaha Int. Award of Excellence, Eurovision Song Contest Winner, In Your Eyes 1993. *Website:* www .facebook.com/ILLEGALSBAND.

KAY, Jason (Jay); British singer and songwriter; b. 30 Dec. 1969, Stretford, Manchester. *Education:* Oakham School, Rutland. *Career:* Founder and lead singer, Jamiroquai 1992–; numerous tours and TV appearances. *Recordings include:* albums: Emergency On Planet Earth 1993, The Return of the Space Cowboy 1994, Travelling Without Moving (four MTV Awards, Grammy Award 1997) 1996, Synkronized 1999, A Funk Odyssey 2001, Dynamite 2005, High Times: Singles 1992–2006 2006, Rock Dust Light Star 2010. *Current Management:* DWL, 2nd Floor, 53 Goodge Street, London, W1T 1TG, England. *E-mail:* info@dwl.uk.net. *Website:* www.jamiroquai.com.

KAY, Simon; British songwriter, producer and musician (keyboards); b. 1 May 1960, London; s. of Norman Kay. *Career:* fmr mem. Ultramarine, recorded and toured early 1990s and working with numerous artists, including Bjork, Orbital, Depeche Mode, The Orb; formed Exile (with Tim Ericson); worked on audio editor on several films, including Four Weddings and a Funeral, East is East, Simon Magus; Co-founder (with Michæl Jaffer) Sugarfree Films Ltd 2003; collaboration with Tricia Walsh-Smith; Co-founder (with Rory Flynn) Flynn Kay Songs. *Recordings include:* album with Ultramarine: United Kingdom. *E-mail:* simon@sugarfreefilms.com. *Website:* www.sugarfreefilms.com.

KAYE, Carol; American musician (electric bass guitar, guitar); b. 24 March 1935, Everett, Wash.; one s. two d. *Career:* teacher of guitar 1949–, electric bass 1969–; on the road, big band 1954–55; played bebop jazz, night clubs 1956–61; special records, studio guitarist 1957–66; studio electric bassist 1963–; invented 16th note bass recording styles; over 10,000 sessions; television credits, playing bass include M.A.S.H, Mission Impossible, Hawaii Five-O, The Brady Bunch, Soap; film credits, playing bass include Thomas Crown Affair, Heat of the Night, Valley of the Dolls, Shaft (theme); columnist, Bassics Magazine; mem. Musicians' Union. *Television:* First Lady of Bass TV (documentary). *Recordings include:* albums: Carol Kaye: Bass, Thumbs Up, Carol Kaye Guitars '65; credits on guitar include: Zippity Doo Dah, Batman Theme, Birds and Bees, The Beat Goes On, You've Lost That Lovin Feelin, La Bamba; credits on bass guitar include: Way We Were, Feelin' Alright, Good Vibrations, Help Me Rhonda, Wouldn't It Be Nice, Can't Help Myself, Heat of Night, I Don't Need No Doctor, Little Green Apples, Baby Love, River Deep Mountain High, Something Stupid, This is My Song, Mission Impossible, Pet Sounds, Smile. *Publications:* writer, composer of over 30 tutorials; How to Play the Electric Bass, Jazz Improvisation for Bass. *Honours:* Women in Music Award 2000, Lifetime Achievement Award, Duquesne Univ. Pittsburgh Jazz Soc. 2000, Los Angeles Composers–Arrangers Award 2004, Lifetime Achievement Award, Bass Player Magazine 2008. *Address:* 25852 McBean Parkway, Suite 200, Valencia, CA 91355, USA (office). *Telephone:* (661) 288-6551 (office). *E-mail:* carol@carolkaye.com. *Website:* www.carolkaye.com.

KAYE, Hereward Hilken Swain; British singer, songwriter and composer; *Musical Director, Rok Skool Limited;* b. 29 June 1953, Middlesbrough, Cleveland; m. Patricia Mary Lord 1974, three s. *Education:* drama Coll. *Career:* mem. The Flying Pickets; Founder and Musical Dir, Rok Skool Ltd 2009–; mem. PRS. *Compositions:* Moby Dick (Piccadilly Theatre) 1992, arranger and musical dir Return To the Forbidden Planet, composer and lyricist Hell Can Be Heaven (computer game, musical) 1996, composer and lyricist Underworld (musical, Seattle) 1998. *Recordings include:* with Flying Pickets: Blue Money 1996. *Honours:* . *Address:* Rok Skool Limited, 13 Brook Lane, Haywards Heath, RH16 1SF, England (office). *Website:* www .herewardkaye.com; www.sussex.rockschool.net (office).

KAZAN, Paul; British singer, musician (piano, violin), composer and producer; b. 9 April 1956, Taplow, Buckinghamshire, England; m. Montserrat Arruga 1994; one s. *Education:* Univ. of Bristol. *Career:* move to Spain 1976; session musician, arranger –1990; solo artist 1990–; mem. Spanish Soc. of Authors (SGAE). *Recordings include:* albums: Stay 1992, Miracle Street 1996.

KAZASSIAN, Hilda; Bulgarian singer, musician (keyboards, drums, percussion), composer and arranger; b. 1970, Sofia; d. of Vili Kazasyan. *Education:* Acad. of Popular Music, Sofia, studied percussion in the UK and Italy. *Career:* guest appearances at several jazz festivals; mem. Acoustic Version jazz combo; writes and arranges own compositions. *Recordings include:* albums: Cover Girl 1994, Why Not 1996, Zamulchi Zamulchi 2007, Jazz & Me 2014.

KAZDA, Jan; German musician (guitar, bass guitar), composer and producer; b. 3 Oct. 1958, Prague, Czech Republic; one s. *Career:* tours with KAZDA, Ginger Baker, Randy Brecker, Peter Brötzmann, Sonny Sharrock, Das Pferd; numerous festival appearances with own band. *Compositions:* composer, five albums with Das Pferd; five albums with KAZDA 1994–2007, four albums with singer Tom Mega 1988–92. *Recordings include:* Das Pferd, KAZDA, Tom Mega 1987–97, Why Is It Love? 2003, Short Tales from the Neigbourhood 2007, The Music Of Led Zeppelin (with Indigo Streichquartett) 2010; recorded with Ginger Baker, Harry Beckett, Randy Brecker, Marilyn Mazur, Ronnell Bey, Frank Wunsch, Nordwestdeutsche Philharmonique (classical orchestra), Therion, Covenant, Udo Lindenberg, Peter Kowald, Peter Brötzmann; music for films including King Ping, Jakobsflug, Leppel and Langsam. *Publications:* Funk It, E-bass studies, Leuverlag. *Address:*

Hergesellstrasse 11, 42285 Wuppertal, Germany. *E-mail:* mail@jankazda .de. *Website:* www.jankazda.de.

KEANE, Dolores; Irish singer and musician (flute); b. 1953, Caherlistrane, Co. Galway; m. 1st John Faulkner (divorced 1988); fmr partner Barry Farmer; two c. *Career:* first recording for Radio Eireann aged five; Founder-mem. De Danann 1975; collaborations with Planxty, The Chieftains; lead role in Dublin production of Brendan Behan's play, The Hostage; also appeared on stage in Dublin in The Playboy of the Western World; contributed to RTE/BBC TV production, Bringing It All Back Home 1992; tours internationally. *Recordings include:* albums: There Was A Maid 1978, Sail Og Rua 1983, Ballroom (De Danann) 1987, Dolores Keane 1988, Lion In A Cage 1989, Solid Ground 1994, The Best of Dolores Keane 1997, Night Owl 1998, How The West Was Won (De Danann) 1999, Tideland 2001, Where Have All the Flowers Gone? The Very Best of Dolores Keane 2003, Broken Hearted I'll Wander 2008; contrib. album A Woman's Heart 1992 with Eleanor McEvoy, Mary Black, others. *Honours:* Irish Music Magazine Award for Best Female Folk Performer, Best Folk album (for The Best of Dolores Keane) 1997.

KEANE, Seán; Irish singer and musician (fiddle); b. 12 July 1961, Co. Galway; m. Marie Keane; four c. *Education:* Dublin School of Music. *Career:* mem. Shegui 1970s, Reel Union 1980s, Arcady; Shaskeen, The Chieftains 1978–; solo artist 1994. *Recordings include:* albums: with Shegui: Around The World For Sport; with Reel Union: There Was A Maid; with Shaskeen: Atlantic Breeze; with the Keane family: Muintir Chathain; with The Chieftains: Chieftains 8 1978, Boil The Breakfast Early/Chieftains 9 1980, Chieftains 10 1981, The Chieftains In China 1984, Ballad Of The Irish Horse 1985, Celtic Wedding 1987, The Chieftains In Ireland (with James Galway) 1987, Year Of The French 1988, Irish Heartbeat (with Van Morrison) 1988, A Chieftains Celebration 1989, Chieftains Collection 1989, The Celtic Connection – James Galway And The Chieftains 1990, Bells Of Dublin 1991, An Irish Evening 1992, Another Country 1992, The Celtic Harp (with Belfast Harp Orchestra) 1993, The Long Black Veil 1995, Santiago 1996, Tears Of Stone 1999, Water From The Well 2000, Down The Old Plank Road: The Nashville Sessions 2002, The Wide World Over: A 40 Year Celebration 2002, San Patricio 2010, Voice of Ages 2012; solo: All Heart No Roses 1994, Turn A Phrase 1996, No Stranger 1998, The Man That I Am (featuring Nanci Griffith and an arrangement by Sir George Martin) 2000, Seánsongs 2002, Valley of the Heart 2005, You Got Gold 2006, The Irish Scattering 2008, Never Alone 2014. *Honours:* winner 13 All-Ireland titles, Irish Music Magazine Performer of the Year 1997–98, Best Male Folk Singer 1997–2001. *Current Management:* c/o Michelle Findlay, Macklam Feldman Management, 200–1505 West 2nd Avenue, Vancouver, BC V6H 3Y4, Canada. *Telephone:* (604) 630 3199. *E-mail:* findlay@mfmgt.com. *Website:* www.thechieftains.com; www.seankeanesinger .com.

KEAREY, Ian; British singer and musician (guitar, bass guitar, banjo, mandolin); b. 14 Oct. 1954, London, England; m. Rebekah Zoob 1986; one s. one d. *Education:* Univ. of Kent. *Career:* mem. Oyster Band 1976–88, Blue Aeroplanes 1983–; producer for Michelle Shocked, Bootfare; numerous TV and radio broadcasts; freelance session musician 1986–; mem. Heaven Factory 1990–; mem. Musicians' Union. *Recordings include:* albums: with Blue Aeroplanes: Bop Art 1984, Swagger 1990, Beatsongs 1991, Life Model 1993, Rough Music 1994, Cavaliers 2000, Altitude 2006, Friendloverplane 2 (Up in a Down World) 2007; with Oyster Band: Liberty Hall 1985, Step Outside 1986, Wide Blue Yonder 1987, Trawler 1995, Granite Years (compilation) 2000; with Gerard Langley: Siamese Boyfriends 1987; with Heidi Berry: Love 1991; with Leon Rosselson: Perspectives 1998, The World Turned Upside Down: Rosselsongs 1960–2010 2011. *Publications:* contrib. to Folk Roots magazine 1984–. *Honours:* Hon. BSc (Indian Inst. of Tech.) 1986; Freedom of the City of Bangor 1980. *Website:* www.theblueaeroplanes.com.

KEATING, Ronan; Irish singer, songwriter and actor; b. (Ronan Patrick John Keating), 3 March 1977, Dublin; s. of Gerry Keating and the late Marie Keating; m. 1st Yvonne Keating (divorced 2013); one s. two d.; m. 2nd Storm Uechtritz 2015. *Career:* mem. Boyzone 1993–2001, 2007–; solo artist 1999–; UN Goodwill Amb. Marie Keating Foundation. *Play:* Once 2015. *Television:* hosted Miss World Competition, Eurovision Song Contest and MTV Europe Awards; judge on X Factor in Australia for five seasons. *Recordings include:* albums: with Boyzone: Said and Done 1994, A Different Beat 1996, Where We Belong 1998, By Request 1999, Back Again… No Matter What 2008, Brother 2010, BZ20, From Dublin to Detroit 2014; solo: Ronan 2000, Destination 2002, Turn It On 2003, Bring You Home 2006, Songs for My Mother 2009, Winter Songs 2009, Duet 2010, When Ronan Met Burt 2011. *Publications include:* No Matter What 2000, Life is a Rollercoaster 2000. *Honours:* BMI European Song Writing Award, Ivor Novello Award. *Current Management:* c/o MP Music Services Ltd, 123 Winston Road, London, N16 9LL, England. *E-mail:* info@mpmusicservices.co.uk. *Website:* www .mpmusicservices.co.uk; boyzonenetwork.com; www.ronankeating.com.

KEELER, Patrick; American musician (drums); b. 6 Oct. 1975. *Career:* mem. The Greenhornes 1996–; mem. The Raconteurs 2006–. *Recordings include:* albums: with The Greenhornes: Gun For You 1999, The Greenhornes 2001, Dual Mono 2002, Four Stars 2010; with The Raconteurs: Broken Boy Soldiers 2006, Consolers of the Lonely 2008. *Current Management:* Monotone Management, 820 Seward Street, Hollywood, CA 90038, USA. *Telephone:* (323) 308-1818. *Fax:* (323) 308-1819. *Website:* www.theraconteurs.com.

KEELY, Conrad; American singer and musician (guitar); b. Ireland. *Career:* mem. and lead singer and You Will Know Us By The Trail Of Dead 1993–. *Recordings include:* albums: ...And You Will Know Us By The Trail of Dead 1998, Madonna 1999, Source Tags and Codes 2002, The Secret of Elena's Tomb 2003, Worlds Apart 2005, So Divided 2006, The Century of Self 2009, The Tao of the Dead 2011, Lost Songs 2012, IX 2014. *Current Management:* c/o Andy Farrow, Northern Music Co., 5A Victoria Road, Shipley, BD18 3LA, England. *Telephone:* (1274) 306361. *Fax:* (1274) 593546. *E-mail:* andy@northernmusic.co.uk. *E-mail:* merlin@trailofdead.com. *Website:* www.trailofdead.com; /www.conradkeely.com.

KEEREMAN, Peter, BMusEd; Belgian producer, composer and musician (piano); b. 21 Aug. 1968, Brugge. *Education:* studied in Ghent, Berklee Coll. of Music, USA. *Career:* concert tours with numerous Belgian artists; performances for BRT—Radio and TV; Owner PK Productions and recording studio; also performs with Trio Roland Keereman; mem. SABAM Author Organisation. *Compositions:* Everlasting Love and Revende Hemel (Intersong Primakera), Spaceflight/Snow Flakes, Crazy Comedy Capers (Parsifal). *Address:* PK Productions, Torhoutsesteenweg 296, 8210 Veldegem, Belgium (office). *Telephone:* (5) 081-69-99 (office). *Fax:* (5) 081-69-98 (office). *E-mail:* pk.productions@telenet.be (office). *Website:* pk-productions.net (office).

KEEZER, Geoffrey Graham; American jazz musician (pianist), composer and arranger; b. 20 Nov. 1970, Eau Claire, Wis.; s. of Ronald Keezer and Mary Keezer; m. Mayumi Tomokane 1995. *Education:* Berklee Coll. of Music. *Career:* pianist with Art Blakey and the Jazz Messengers 1989–90; pianist with Art Farmer 1991–95; leader of Geoff Keezer trio and quartet 1988; mem. Storms/Nocturnes trio; mem., BMI, AMRA. *Compositions:* numerous large and small ensemble pieces. *Recordings include:* as leader: Curveball 1989, Here and Now 1991, World Music 1991, Other Spheres 1992, All For One (with Art Blakey), The Key Players (with The Contemporary Piano Ensemble), Color and Light – Jazz Sketches On Sondheim, Some of My Best Friends... (with Ray Brown), Turn Up The Quiet 1998, Zero One 2000, Sublime, Falling Up, Wildcrafted, Yasukatsu Oshima with Geoffrey Keezer 2008, Via (Storms/Nocturnes) 2011, Signing 2012, Heart of the Piano 2013. *E-mail:* geoffreykeezer@gmail.com. *Website:* www.geoffreykeezer.com.

KEITA, Salif; Malian singer; b. 25 Aug. 1949, Djoliba. *Career:* began musical career in Bamako 1967; joined govt-sponsored group Super Rail Band; moved to Paris to begin solo career as a singer 1984; annual European tour including summer festivals; Founder-Chair. Salif Keita Global Foundation. *Recordings include:* albums: Soro 1987, Ko-Yan 1989, Destiny of a Noble Outcast 1991, Amen 1991, L'Enfant Lion 1992, Mansa of Mali 1994, Folon 1995, Rail Band 1996, Seydou Bathili 1997, Papa 1999, Sosie 2001, Compilation 1969–80 2001, Moffou 2002, Salif Keita: The Lost Album (with Kante Manfila) 2005, M'Bemba 2005, La Différence 2010, Talé 2012. *Honours:* Chevalier, Ordre des Arts et des Lettres, Chevalier, Order of the Nation (Mali), Nat. Order of Guinea 1977, Commdr, Nat. Order of Merit (Tunisia) 2014; Grammy Award. *Address:* Salif Keita Global Foundation Inc., 6900 Wisconsin Avenue, Unit 30306, Bethesda, MD 20824, USA (office). *Telephone:* (917) 397-6211 (office). *E-mail:* skgf@salifkeita.us (office). *Website:* www.salifkeita.net; www.salifkeita.us (office).

KEITH, (John) Larry; American musician (guitar, bass) and singer; b. 1 March 1955, Hendersonville, North Carolina; m. Denna O. Nix 1988; one s. two d. *Education:* Blue Ridge Community Coll. *Career:* WKIT-WHKP Radio Hendersonville, The Charlie Renfro Concerts 1980–84; appearances with: Carl Story and The Ramblin' Mountaineers, The Boys From Indiana, Jim and Jesse and the Virginia Boys, Bill Monroe and The Bluegrass Boys, Doyle Lawson and Quicksilver, Mac Wiseman, Dolly Parton's Premiere Bluegrass Band, Pigeon Forge, Tennessee 1984–88; founder mem. Lonesome Road Band 1995–; mem. IBMA, Bluegrass Music Asscns of North Carolina, South Carolina, Georgia. *Recordings include:* albums: First Time Around, On and On, Head Over Heels, Second Time Around, The Old Country Church, Travelin' Angel 2007. *Website:* www.lonesomeroadband.com.

KEITH, Toby; American country singer, songwriter and musician (guitar); b. (Toby Keith Covel), 8 July 1961, Oklahoma City, OK; m. Tricia Lucus; three c. *Career:* fmr mem. Easy Money. *Recordings include:* albums: Toby Keith 1993, Boomtown 1994, Blue Moon 1996, Dream Walkin' 1997, How Do You Like Me Now (ACM Award for Album of the Year 2000) 1999, Pull My Chain 2001, Unleashed 2002, Shock'n Y'all 2003, Honkytonk University 2005, White Trash with Money 2006, Big Dog Daddy 2007, Classic Christmas 2007, That Don't Make Me a Bad Boy 2008, American Ride 2009, Bullets in the Gun 2010, Clancy's Tavern 2011, Hope on the Rocks 2012, Drinks After Work 2013, 35 MPH Town 2015. *Films include:* as actor: Broken Bridges 2005, Beer for My Horses 2008. *Honours:* Dr hc (Villanova Univ.); S Oklahoma City Chamber of Commerce Native Son Award, ACM Award for Best Male Vocalist 2002, 2004, Album of the Year 2002, Entertainer of the Year 2003, 2004, Best Video 2004, American Music Award for Favorite Male Country Artist 2004, 2006, CMA Award for Music Video of the Year (for As Good As I Once Was) 2005, Billboard Music Awards for Country Artist of the Year, for Country Album Artist of the Year 2005, BMI Music Award for Country Song of the Year (for As Good As I Once Was), for Songwriter of the Year (jtly) 2006, American Country Award 2010, for Artist of the Decade 2011, AARP Inspire Award 2012, ACM Award for Video of the Year (for Red Solo Cup) 2012. *Current Management:* Innovative Artists, 1505 Tenth Street, Santa Monica, CA 90401, USA. *E-mail:* tobykeith@bubbleup.net (office). *Website:* www.tobykeith.com.

KEITHLEY, Joseph Edward; Canadian musician; b. Burnaby, BC; m. Laura Susan; two s. one d. *Career:* f. The Skulls 1977; mem. punk rock band D.O.A. 1978–2013, 2014–; Founder and Pres. Sudden Death Records 1978–; solo acoustic folk act. *Film appearances:* Terminal City, The Widower, American Hardcore 2006. *Recordings include:* with D.O.A.: Hardcore 81 1981, Bloodied but Unbowed 1984, Let's Wreck the Party 1985, The Dawning of a New Error 1985, True (North) Strong and Free 1987, Murder 1990, Last Scream of the Missing Neighbors 1990, Talk Minus Action Equals Zero 1991, 13 Flavors of Doom 1992, Moose Droppings 1993, Loggerheads 1993, The Black Spot 1995, The Lost Tapes 1998, Festival of Atheists 1998, Win the Battle 2002, War and Peace 2003, Live Free or Die 2004, Northern Avenger 2008, Kings of Punk, Hockey and Beer 2009, Talk-Action=0 2010, We Come In Peace 2012; solo: Beat Trash, Band of Rebels 2007. *Publications:* I Shithead, A Life in Punk 2003, Talk - Action = 0: An Illustrated History of D.O.A. 2011. *Address:* Sudden Death Records, Cascades, PO Box 43001, Burnaby, BC V5G 3H0, Canada (office). *Telephone:* (604) 777-6972 (office). *Fax:* (604) 777-6974 (office). *E-mail:* info@suddendeath.com (office). *Website:* www.suddendeath.com (office).

KELANI, Reem Yousef, BSc; Palestinian singer, musicologist, broadcaster and teacher; b. 7 Aug. 1963, Manchester, England; d. of Yousef Zaid Kelani and of the late Yusra Sharif Zu'bi; m. Christopher Somes-Charlton. *Education:* Kuwait Univ. *Career:* raised in Kuwait; fmr marine biologist; returned to UK 1989; est. The Miktab Ltd with Chris Somes-Charlton 2005; performer and researcher of Arabic music, has carried out research into traditional music in Palestine and in Lebanese refugee camps; workshops and lectures on Arabic and Palestinian music; performed jt concert with Kardes Turkuler, TIM Maslak, Istanbul 2014. *Radio:* Distant Chords (writer and presenter, BBC Radio 4) 2001–02, In Praise of God (presenter, BBC World Service), The Dance of the Seven Veils (writer and presenter, BBC Radio 4) 2007, Lullabies in the Arab World (contrib. in interview and songs) 2012. *Films:* The Unholy Land (series assoc. producer) 1998, Les Chebabs de Yarmouk (wrote and performed title music) 2013, The Brick 2013. *Recordings include:* Exile (BBC Jazz Award for Best CD) 2003, Sprinting Gazelle: Palestinian Songs from the Motherland and the Diaspora 2006, Celebrating Subversion – The Anti-Capitalist Roadshow 2012. *Address:* The Miktab Ltd, PO Box 31652, London, W11 2YF, England (office). *Telephone:* (7092) 811747 (office). *E-mail:* miktab@reemkelani.com (office). *Website:* www.reemkelani.com.

KELIS, (Thunderbitch); American singer; b. (Kelis Rogers), 21 Aug. 1979, Harlem, New York; m. Nas 2005 (divorced); one s. *Education:* La Guardia High School of Music and Art and the Performing Arts, New York. *Career:* started singing in Boys and Girls Choir of Harlem; collaborated with the Gravediggaz before joining girl group B.L.U.; began solo career working with The Neptunes production team; collaborations include Ol' Dirty Bastard, Busta Rhymes, Foxy Brown. *Recordings include:* albums: Kaleidoscope 2000, Wanderland 2001, Tasty 2003, Kelis Was Here 2006, Flesh Tone 2010, Food 2014. *Honours:* NME Award for Best R&B Artist 2001. *E-mail:* geoff.barnett@redlightmanagement.com; alexis.peluso@redlightmanagement.com. *Website:* www.redlightmanagement.com; www.iamkelis.com.

KELLERMAN, Wouter; South African flautist and composer; b. 20 Sept. 1961, Johannesburg. *Career:* began learning flute 1971; performed as soloist with Johannesburg Symphony Orchestra 1981; numerous live appearances including as opening act for Johnny Clegg's Down Under tour 2009, closing ceremony of Soccer World Cup 2010, 2010 Expo, Shanghai, China, Kennedy Center, Washington, DC 2012, 2015, Carnegie Hall, New York 2014, 2015. *Recordings include:* albums: Colour 2007, Two Voices (S African Music Award for Best Instrumental Album 2011) 2010, Half Moon (Vox Pop Independent Music Award for Best World Beat Album 2013) 2012, Mzansi 2013, Winds of Samsara (with Ricky Kej) (Grammy Award for Best New Age Album 2014, Zone Music Reporter Awards for Album of the Year 2015, for Best World Album 2015, S African Music Awards for Best Instrumental Album 2015, for Best Producer 2015, for Best Int. Achievement 2015) 2014, Love Language 2015. *Honours:* Perrenoud Foundation Prize, Vienna Int. Music Competition 1997. *Website:* wouterkellerman.com.

KELLEY, Brian; American country music singer and songwriter; b. 26 Aug. 1985, Ormond Beach, Fla; m. Brittney Marie Cole 2013. *Education:* Belmont Univ. *Career:* mem. of duo, Florida Georgia Line 2010–; released debut EP 2010; signed to Republic Nashville label 2011; support act to Luke Bryan on Dirt Road Diaries tour 2013. *Recordings:* albums: with Florida Georgia Line: Here's to the Good Times 2012, Anything Goes (American Music Award for Favorite Country Album 2015) 2014. *Honours:* Acad. of Country Music Awards for New Vocal Duo or Group of the Year 2013, for New Artist of the Year 2013, for Vocal Duo of the Year 2014, CMT Music Awards for Duo Video of the Year (for Cruise) 2013, for Breakthrough Video of the Year (for Cruise) 2013, American Country Award for New Artist 2013, for Single of the Year (for Cruise) 2013, for New Artist Single of the Year (for Cruise) 2013, CMA Awards for Vocal Duo of the Year 2013, 2014, 2015, for Single of the Year 2013, American Music Awards for Single of the Year (for Cruise) 2013, for Favorite Country Duo or Group 2014, 2015, Billboard Music Awards for Top Country Song (for Cruise) (with Nelly) 2014, for Top Country Artist 2015. *Current Management:* Seth England and Kevin 'Chief' Zaruk, Big Loud Mountain Management, Suite 201, #1111, 16th Avenue South, Nashville, TN 37212, USA. *Website:* www.bigloudmountain.com. *Address:* c/o Republic Nashville Records, Big Machine Label Group, 1219 16th Avenue South, Nashville, TN

37212, USA (office). *E-mail:* mail@bigmachine.us (office). *Website:* www
.bigmachinelabelgroup.com (office); floridageorgialine.com.

KELLEY, Charles Burgess; American singer and songwriter; b. 11 Sept.
1981, Augusta, Ga; m. Cassie McConnell 2009. *Education:* Lakeside High
School, Univ. of Georgia. *Career:* mem. teenage group (with siblings) Inside
Blue 1990s; mem., country music group Lady Antebellum 2006–; performed at
Grand Old Opry; songwriter for other artists including brother Josh Kelley,
Danny Gokey, Parachute, Luke Bryan, Miranda Lambert, Hunter Hayes.
Recordings include: albums: solo: 2 to 9s 2006; Lady Antebellum 2008, Need
You Now (Grammy Award for Best Country Album of the Year 2011, Acad. of
Country Music Award for Album of the Year 2011) 2010, Own the Night
(Grammy Award for Best Country Album 2012) 2011, On This Winter's Night
2012, Golden 2013, 747 2014. *Honours:* numerous including: Acad. of Country
Music Awards for Best New Group 2008, for Best Vocal Group 2010, for Best
Single Record of the Year (for Need You Now) 2010, for Best Song of the Year
(for Need You Now) 2010, for Top Vocal Group 2011, for Vocal Group of the
Year 2012, Jim Reeves Int. Award 2013, Country Music Asscn Awards for New
Artist of the Year 2008, for Single of the Year (for I Run to You) 2009, (for Need
You Now) 2010, for Vocal Group of the Year 2009, 2010, for Int. Artist
Achievement 2012, Grammy Award for Best Country Performance by a Duo or
Group with Vocals (for I Run to You) 2010, Grammy Award for Record of the
Year, Song of the Year, Best Performance by a Duo or Group (all for Need You
Now) 2011, Billboard Music Award for Top Country Artist 2012, American
Music Awards for Favorite Band, Duo or Group – Country 2012, 2013,
American Country Awards for Duo/Group Artist of the Year 2012, 2013, for
Single by a Duo/Group (for We Owned the Night) 2012, (for Downtown) 2013.
Address: c/o Capitol Nashville Records, 3322 West End Avenue, 11th Floor,
Nashville, TN 37203-1100, USA. *Telephone:* (615) 269-2000. *Fax:* (615) 269-
2059. *E-mail:* support@ladyantebellum.com. *Website:* www.ladyantebellum
.com.

KELLOCK, Brian, BMus (Hons); Scottish musician (piano); b. 1962, Edinburgh. *Education:* Univ. of Edinburgh. *Career:* played piano with a number of
leading British jazz figures; formed trio 1988; worked with trumpeter James
Morrison 1995–. *Recordings include:* albums: Something's Got To Give 1998,
The Crossing 2001, Live At Henry's (BBC Jazz Award for Best Album 2002)
2001, Symbiosis (with Tommy Smith) 2005, The Nine Mile Burn Sessions
2008, Love Still Wears A Smile 2013. *Honours:* BBC Jazz Award for Best
Instrumentalist 2003. *Current Management:* c/o Thick Skinned Productions,
19 Rutland Square, Edinburgh, EH1 2BB, England. *Telephone:* (1620) 861000.

KELLY, Jeff; American songwriter and musician (multi-instrumentalist); m.
Susanne. *Career:* Formed the Green Pajamas, 1984–; Also solo artiste.
Compositions include: Kim The Waitress, covered by Material Issue and
Sister Psychic. *Recordings:* albums: with The Green Pajamas: Summer of Lust
1984, 1990, Halloween 1984, Book of Hours 1987, November 1988, Ghosts of
Love 1990, In A Glass Darkly 2001, Northern Gothic 2002, Through Glass
Colored Roses 2003, Ten White Stones 2004, 21st Century Séance 2005, Night
Races into Anna 2006, Poison in the Russian Room 2009, Green Pajama
Country! 2011; solo: Baroquen Hearts 1985, Coffee In Nepal, 1987, 1991,
Portugal 1990, Twenty Five 1991, Private Electrical Storm 1992, Ash
Wednesday Rain 1995, Melancholy Sun 1999, Indiscretion 2001, For the
Swan in the Hallway 2004; Featured on compilations: Monkey Business, 1986;
Splat Sampler, 1988; Time Will Show The Wiser, 1989; The Fourth Adven-
ture, 1991. *E-mail:* joeross@seanet.com. *Website:* www.seapeace.org/bands/
greenpajamas.html.

KELLY, Jon; British record producer; three c. *Career:* producer for The
Beautiful South, Heather Nova, Tori Amos, Paul McCartney, Roddy Frame,
Prefab Sprout, Rosalie Deighton, Paul Heaton, Kate Bush, Chris Rea, Deacon
Blue, The Damned, The Levellers, New Model Army, The Bible, Jimmy Nail,
Mickey Harte, Paddy Casey, Melody Gardot. *Current Management:* Stephen
Budd Management, 10 Greenland Street, Camden, London, NW1 0ND,
England. *Telephone:* (70) 4040-9533. *E-mail:* enquiries@record-producers
.com. *Website:* www.record-producers.com.

KELLY, Judith (Jude) Pamela, CBE, OBE, BA; British theatre director;
Artistic Director, Southbank Centre; b. 24 March 1954, Liverpool, England; d.
of John Kelly and Ida Kelly; m. Michael Bird 1983; two s. (one deceased) one d.
Education: Calder High School, Liverpool and Univ. of Birmingham. *Career:*
freelance folk and jazz singer 1970–75; actress, Leicester Phoenix Theatre
1975–76; Founder Solent People's Theatre, Dir 1976–80; Artistic Dir
Battersea Arts Centre (BAC) 1980–85; Dir of Plays Nat. Theatre of Brent
1982–85; freelance dir 1985–88; Festival Dir York Festival and Mystery Plays
1988; Artistic Dir West Yorkshire Playhouse 1988–2002, Chief Exec.
1993–2002; Founder and Artistic Dir Metal community arts lab., London,
Liverpool, Bogotá, Colombia 2002–; Visiting Prof. of Drama, Leeds and
Kingston Univs; British Rep. on Culture for UNESCO 1997–; Chair. Common
Purpose Charitable Trust 1997–, Qualifications and Curriculum Authority
Advisory Group on the Arts 2001–03, Culture, Arts and Educ. Cttee, London
2012 Olympics; Artistic Dir Southbank Centre, London 2005–; Vice-Chair.
Nat. Advisory Cttee on Creative and Cultural Educ. 1998; mem. Council RSA
1998–, Ind. TV Comm. 1999–. *Productions include:* at West Yorkshire
Playhouse: The Merchant of Venice 1994, Beautification of Area Boy 1996,
The Seagull 1998, The Tempest 1998, Singin' in the Rain (Olivier Award for
Outstanding Musical Production 2001) 1999, 2000, Half A Sixpence 2000;
elsewhere: Sarcophagus (RSC) 1987, When We Were Married (Chichester

Festival Theatre, transferred to Savoy Theatre) 1996, Othello (Shakespeare
Theatre), Washington, DC 1997, The Elixir of Love (ENO) 1997, Johnson Over
Jordan, On the Town (ENO) 2005, The Importance of Being Earnest (Sydney
Opera House, Barbican London) 2005–06. *Honours:* Hon. Fellow, Dartington
Coll. of Arts, Cen. School of Speech and Drama; Hon. DLitt (Leeds Metropol-
itan) 1995, (Bradford) 1996, (Leeds) 2000, (York) 2001, (Open Univ.) 2001;
Woman of the Year, Yorks. 1996, 2002, Yorkshire TV Personality of the Year
2002, Dream Time Fellowship, NESTA 2003, named by The Independent
newspaper No. 8 in "Theatreland's top 100 players" 2006, assessed by
Woman's Hour (BBC Radio 4) as one of the 100 most powerful women in the
UK 2013. *Address:* Southbank Centre, Belvedere Road, London, SE1 8XX
(office); Metal, 198A Broadhurst Gardens, London, NW6 3AY, England.
Telephone: (20) 7921-0636 (office). *E-mail:* jude.kelly@southbankcentre.co.uk
(office). *Website:* www.southbankcentre.co.uk (office).

KELLY, Juliet, BSc, MA; British jazz singer; b. 6 May 1970, London.
Education: Guildhall School of Music and Drama. *Career:* part of a cappella
group, Darker Than Blue (formerly Jazz Voices); performed at Purcell Room,
South Bank, part of London Jazz Festival, 1994; festivals in Germany 1995,
Australia 1996; touring with Orphy Robinson, Phoenix Dance Co. Project,
across UK, including Sadler's Wells 1995; mem., Musicians' Union. *Recordings:* albums: Aphrodite's Child 2003, Delicious Chemistry 2005. *Website:*
www.julietkelly.com.

KELLY, Laoise; Irish musician (harp, fiddle); b. 1973, Westport, County
Mayo. *Education:* Maynooth, University Coll., Cork. *Career:* mem. Ciabh Rua,
age 15, Bumblebees 1996, harp teacher at UCC 1993; performed in: Bill
Whelan's Seville Suite 1993; Micheal O'Suilleabhain's Lumen, Eurovision
1995; Charlie Lennon's Famine Suite; toured USA and Australia 1997;
collaborations: Natalie MacMaster, The Chieftains, Tunde Jegede; Co-foun-
der: FACE (with Steve Cooney); teacher, DIT, Dublin; appearances in TV
series: River of Sound 1995, Sult 1996, Sin E E (with Liam O Maonlai),
Geantraí (with Matt Molloy) 1996. *Recordings include:* with Bumblebees:
Bumblebees 1996, Buzzin' 1999; solo: Just Harp 1999, Ceis 2010; with
Michelle O'Brien: The Wishing Well - Live at The Dock 2010. *Honours:* All-
Ireland titles 1989, 1991, 1992, Keadue O'Carolan Festival winner 1989,
Granard harp competitions 1989, 1990, 1992, Belfast Bicentennial Harp
Festival winner 1992. *E-mail:* contact@laoisekelly ie. *Website:* www
.laoisekelly.ie.

KELLY, Mark; Irish musician (keyboards) and producer; b. 9 April 1961,
Dublin. *Career:* fmr mem. Chemical Alice; keyboard player, progressive rock
group, Marillion 1981–; contrib. to albums by Altan; producer for artists,
including Jump, John Wesley. *Recordings include:* albums: Script For A
Jester's Tear 1983, Fugazi 1984, Real To Reel 1984, Misplaced Childhood
1985, Brief Encounter 1986, Clutching at Straws 1987, B-Sides Themselves
1988, The Thieving Magpie 1988, Season's End 1989, Holidays In Eden 1991,
A Singles Collection 1982–92 1992, Brave 1994, Afraid of Sunlight 1995, This
Strange Engine 1997, Radiation 1998, Marillion.com 1999, Anoraknophobia
2001, Made Again Live 2001, Anorak In The UK Live 2002, Somewhere Else
2007, Happiness is the Road 2008, Recital of the Script 2009, Less Is More
2009, Sounds That Can't Be Made 2012, A Sunday Night Above the Rain 2014.
E-mail: info@knowmoremanagement.com. *Address:* PO Box 252, Aylesbury,
Buckinghamshire, HP18 0YS, England. *E-mail:* band@marillion.com (office).
Website: www.marillion.com.

KELLY, Nancy; American jazz singer, musician and teacher; b. 12 Oct. 1950,
Rochester, New York. *Education:* Eastman School of Music, Univ. of
Rochester,. *Career:* performed with Benny Goodman Orchestra, Nelson
Riddle Orchestra, Houston Person, Joey DeFrancesco, Mark Murphy, Clayton
Cameron. *Recordings include:* albums: Live Jazz 1988, Singin' and Swingin'
1997, Born to Swing 2006, Well Alright 2009, B That Way 2014. *Current
Management:* c/o Joan Merrill, Saying it with Jazz, PMB 736, 15600 NE
Eighth Street, Suite B-1, Bellevue, WA 98008, USA. *Telephone:* (425) 653-
3036. *E-mail:* joan@sayingitwithjazz.com. *Website:* www.sayingitwithjazz
.com; www.nancykelly.com.

KELLY, Paul; British musician (guitar), songwriter and film director; b. 23
July 1962, Farnborough, Hampshire. *Career:* with groups East Village; Saint
Etienne; British tours 1988–90 with East Village; played with Saint Etienne
1992–; tours: UK, Europe, Japan, USA; festivals: Glastonbury, Roskilde,
Hultsfred. *Films include:* What Have You Done Today, Mervyn Day? (with St
Etienne) 2005, This Is Tomorrow 2007, Take Three Girls (The Dolly Mixture
Story) 2008, Lawrence Of Belgravia 2011, How We Used To Live 2014.
Television includes: Top of the Pops, The Beat, The Word, Later With Jools
Holland, Glastonbury 1994; BBC Radio 1 session with St Etienne 1994.
Recordings include: albums: with East Village: Drop Out, Hot Rod Hotel; with
Birdie: Some Dusty 1999, Triple Echo 2001. *Current Management:* c/o
Heavenly Films Limited, 221 Portobello Road, London, W11 1LU, England.
E-mail: martin@heavenlyfilms.net. *Website:* www.heavenlyfilms.net.

KELLY, Robert (R.); American producer, singer, musician and songwriter;
b. 8 Jan. 1969, Chicago, Ill. *Career:* began work with band Public Announcement 1992–; R&B producer, singer and multi-instrumentalist; wrote and
produced hits for Aaliyah, Mary J. Blige, Toni Braxton, The Isley Brothers,
Kelly Price and Janet Jackson; wrote You Are Not Alone, recorded by Michael
Jackson for HIStory album; produced soundtrack for film Lifers. *Recordings
include:* albums: Born into the 90s 1992, 12 Play 1993, R Kelly 1995, R 1998,
TP-2.com 2000, The Best Of Both Worlds (with Jay-Z) 2002, Chocolate Factory

2003, Happy People/U Saved Me 2004, The R in the R 'n' B Greatest Hits 2004, TP3 Reloaded 2005, Double Up 2007, Untitled 2009, Love Letters 2010, Write Me Back 2012, Black Panties 2013, The Buffet 2015. *Honours:* Grammy Awards for Best Male R&B Vocal Performance, Best R&B Song and Best Song Written For a Motion Picture, Television or Other Visual Media; Favourite Soul/R&B Male Artist 2000, Billboard R 'n' B/Hip Hop Awards for Top Artist, Songwriter, Producer, Male Artist 2004, Kora Award for Best Male Artist of the Africa-America Diaspora, Best Video of the Africa-America Diaspora 2004, American Music Award for Favorite Male Soul/R & B Artist 2005. *Website:* www.r-kelly.com.

KELLY, Roger, BA; British musician (guitar); b. 3 April 1953, Balby, Doncaster; m. Sabine Kirchner (divorced). *Career:* toured with Streetband (with Paul Young); appeared on Top of the Pops 1979; appeared Rock Palast, Germany with Starry-Eyed and Laughing; session work with Sandie Shaw in 1980s; teaching and transcription work, also production; mem. PRS. *Recordings include:* albums: Streetband: London 1979, Dilemma 1979; single: Toast (B Side of Hold On) 1979; co-wrote, produced all album, single material with Paul Young and co-mem. John Gifford.

KELLY, (Victoria) Tori; American singer, songwriter and record producer; b. 14 Dec. 1992, Wildomar, Calif. *Career:* participant in TV shows including America's Most Talented Kids 2004, American Idol 2010; released first EP 2012; signed to Capitol record label 2013; numerous collaborations including Professor Green, Pentatonix, Ed Sheeran. *Recordings:* album: Unbreakable Smile 2015. *Honours:* YouTube Music 50 Artists to Watch Award 2015, Billboard's Women in Music Breakthrough Artist Award 2015. *Current Management:* c/o Scooter Braun Management, Worldwide Plaza, 825 Eighth Avenue, 28th Floor, New York, NY 10019, USA. *E-mail:* info@scooterbraun .com. *Website:* www.scooterbraun.com; torikelly.com.

KELSEY, Peter R., BSc; British recording engineer, producer and re-recording mixer; *Re-recording Mixer, Smart Post Sound;* b. 25 Jan. 1949, Lincoln, England; m. Catherine Deguilly 1985; two d. *Education:* Imperial Coll. of Science and Tech., London. *Career:* est. Trident Studios, London 1972, Chief Engineer 1976, freelance engineer and re-recording mixer 1978; worked on recordings, including Goodbye Yellow Brick Road (Elton John), Heat Treatment (Graham Parker), Discreet Music (Brian Eno), Dialects (Zawinul), Sans Regrets (Veronique Sanson), Outside From The Redwoods (Kenny Loggins), Thinking Of You, Mandala, Heaven and Earth (all Kitaro), seven albums with Jean-Luc Ponty, including Tchokola, Mystical Adventures, No Absolute Time, Ward 1, Along The Way, When The Bough Breaks (both Bill Ward); moved to USA 1979, freelance engineer and producer of recordings, film and TV music; Re-recording Mixer, RH Factor, Smart Post Sound; re-recording mixer on shows Ally McBeal, Boston Legal, Harry's Law, My Name Is Earl, The Middle, Raising Hope; mem. Nat. Acad. of Recording Arts and Sciences, Acad. of Television Arts & Sciences, Cinema Audio Soc. *Films include:* Color of Night, Best of Best 2, Poison Ivy. *Television includes:* Thirtysomething, Picket Fences, Tekwar, Ally McBeal, The Brotherhood of Poland, Boston Public, Arrested Development, Medical Investigation, Cracking Up, Boston Legal, My Name is Earl, The Middle, Harry's Law, Breakout Kings. *Honours:* NME Engineering Award, Cafe Jacques 1976, three Emmy Awards (for sound mixing for Ally McBeal) 1998–2000, Emmy Award (for sound mixing for Boston Legal) 2006, Grammy Award (for Thinking of You). *E-mail:* prksound@gmail.com.

KEMANIS, Aina; American folk and jazz singer; b. 15 June 1952, Berkeley, Calif.; d. of Gunars Kemanis (refugee from Latvia), step-d. of John M. Swackhamer. *Career:* contemporary jazz with Barre Phillips 1979–82; sang in Eastern European women's chorus, Kitka 1987–88; toured Europe and Scandinavia with Marilyn Mazur 1988–2005; mem. Alex Cline Ensemble 1987–2001. *Recordings:* Journal Violone II 1979, The Lamp and the Star 1989, Future Song 1993, Montsalvat 1995, Small Labyrinths 1997, Sparks Fly Upward 1999, The Constant Flame 2001, Daylight Stories 2004. *Address:* PO Box 1460, Sebastopol, CA 95473, USA (home). *E-mail:* avlille@aol.com (home).

KEMP, Gary; British musician (guitar), songwriter and actor; b. 16 Oct. 1959, Islington, London; brother of Martin Kemp; m. 1st Sadie Frost (divorced 1995); one s.; m. 2nd Lauren Barber; three s. *Education:* Dame Alice Owen's School, Anna Scher Children's Theatre. *Career:* Founder-mem. Spandau Ballet (originally the Makers) 1979–90, 2009–; later solo artist. *Plays:* performed in Art, Pignight 2004, The Rubenstein Kiss 2005. *Films:* The Krays 1990, The Bodyguard 1992, Killing Zoe 1994, Dog Eat Dog 2001, American Daylight 2004, Poppies 2006, Voice from Afar 2007. *Television:* Murder in Mind 2003, Murder Investigation Team 2003, Casualty 2006. *Compositions:* all hit singles by Spandau Ballet. *Recordings include:* albums: with Spandau Ballet: Journeys To Glory 1981, Diamond 1982, True 1983, Parade 1984, The Singles Collection 1985, Through The Barricades 1986, Heart Like A Sky 1989, Once More 2009, True 2010, Parade 2010; solo: Little Bruises 1995, Your Splendid Light 2005. *Honours:* BRIT Award, Sony Trophy for Technical Excellence 1984, Ivor Novello Award for Outstanding Song Collection 2012. *Current Management:* c/o Steve Dagger, Reformation Publishing, 14 Lambton Place, London, W11 2SH, England. *Website:* www .spandauballet.com; www.garykemp.com.

KEMP, Martin; British musician; b. 10 Oct. 1961, Islington, London; brother of Gary Kemp; m. Shirlie Holliman 1988; one s. one d. *Education:* Anna Scher's Children's Theatre. *Career:* Founder-mem. Spandau Ballet (originally the Makers) 1979–90, 2009–. *Film appearances:* The Krays 1988, Waxwork II:

Lost in Time 1992, The Brides in the Bath 2003, The Best Years 2010, Jack Falls 2011, Crossmaglen 2012, Age of Kill 2015. *Television appearances:* Growing Rich 1991, EastEnders 1998–2002. *Recordings include:* albums: Journeys To Glory 1981, Diamond 1982, True 1983, Parade 1984, The Singles Collection 1985, Through The Barricades 1986, Heart Like A Sky 1989, Once More 2009. *Honours:* BRIT Award, Sony Trophy for Technical Excellence 1984. *Current Management:* c/o Steve Dagger, Reformation Publishing, 14 Lambton Place, London, W11 2SH, England. *E-mail:* contact@daggerents.com (office). *Website:* www.spandauballet.com.

KEMP, Steven; British musician (drums); b. 29 Dec. 1978, Lancaster. *Education:* Carnforth High School. *Career:* drummer with band Hard-Fi 2003–. *Recordings include:* albums: Stars of CCTV 2005, Once Upon a Time in the West 2007, Killer Sounds 2011; other: In Operation (DVD) 2006. *Current Management:* c/o Necessary Records, PO Box 28362, London SE20 7WH, England. *Telephone:* (7832) 141503. *E-mail:* info@necessaryrecords.com. *Website:* www.necessaryrecords.com; www.hard-fi.com (office).

KENJI, Endo; Japanese singer and songwriter; b. 1947, Hitachinaka. *Career:* started career as a folk singer in 1960s, later a rock singer. *Recordings include:* albums: Hontodayo 1969, Niyago 1970, Manzoku dekirukana (New Music magazine Japanese Rock Award), Fuufuu 2010, Eureka 2012, Ume/Saru 2013, The Background 2014. *Website:* www.kenjiendo.com.

KENNEDY, Brian; Northern Irish singer, musician (guitar) and songwriter; b. 12 Oct. 1966, Belfast. *Career:* toured internationally and recorded with Van Morrison's band, Blues and Soul World Review, also performed with The Corrs, Tina Turner, Joni Mitchell, Bob Dylan, Ray Charles, John Lee Hooker; solo artist 1990–; Broadway debut in Riverdance 2000; Irish rep. in Eurovision Song Contest 2006. *Recordings include:* albums: solo: The Great War of Words 1990, A Better Man 1996, Now That I Know What I Want 1999, Get On With Your Short Life 2001, On Song 2003, On Song 2 2005, Homebird 2006, Interpretations 2008. *Honours:* Hon. DLitt (Univ. of Ulster) 2006; IRMA for Best Irish Male Album, Hot Press/2 TV Award for Best Irish Male Artist, Meteor Award for Lifetime Achievement 2010. *E-mail:* jane@briankennedy.co .uk (office). *Website:* www.briankennedy.co.uk.

KENNEDY, John, OBE; British music industry executive; b. 10 Feb. 1953, London. *Education:* Univ. of Leicester. *Career:* mem. Business Affairs Dept, Phonogram 1978, Dir of Business Affairs 1979; then Dir of Business Affairs, CBS Records UK –1984; founding partner entertainment law firm, J. P. Kennedy & Co. 1984–96; CEO PolyGram UK 1996–98 (merged with Universal Music 1998), Chair. and CEO Universal Music UK 1998–2001, Pres. and COO Universal Music Int. 2001–04; bd mem. Int. Fed. for Phonographic Industry (IFPI) 2002–04, and Chair. European Regional Bd 2002–04, Chair. and CEO IFPI 2005–10; co-produced 10 Live 8 concerts worldwide 2005. *Honours:* Chevalier, Ordre des Arts et des Lettres.

KENNEDY, Nigel Paul, ARCM; British violinist; b. 28 Dec. 1956, Brighton; s. of John Kennedy and Scylla Stoner; m. Agnieska Kennedy; one s. *Education:* Yehudi Menuhin School, Juilliard School of Performing Arts, USA. *Career:* debut playing Mendelssohn's Violin Concerto at Royal Festival Hall with London Philharmonic Orchestra under Riccardo Muti 1977; subsequently chosen by BBC as subject of a five-year documentary on the devt of a soloist; other important debuts include with Berlin Philharmonic 1980, New York 1987; has made appearances at all leading UK festivals and in Europe at Stresa, Lucerne, Gstaad, Berlin and Lockenhaus; tours to Australia, Austria, Canada, Denmark, Germany, Hong Kong, India, Ireland, Italy, Japan, Republic of Korea, New Zealand, Norway, Poland, Spain, Switzerland, Turkey and USA; has given jazz concerts with Stephane Grappelli, including at Edinburgh Festival and Carnegie Hall; performs with his own jazz group; five-year sabbatical 1992–97; Artistic Dir Polish Chamber Orchestra 2002–; apptd Sr Vice-Pres. Aston Villa Football Club 1990. *Television:* Coming Along Nicely (BBC documentary on his early career) 1973–78. *Recordings include:* Strad Jazz 1984, Elgar Sonata with Peter Pettinger 1985, Elgar's Violin Concerto with the London Philharmonic and Vernon Handley (Gramophone magazine Record of the Year, BPI Award for Best Classical Album of the Year) 1985, Vivaldi's Four Seasons, Bartók Solo Sonata and Mainly Black (arrangement of Ellington's Black Brown and Beige Suite), Sibelius Violin Concerto with the City of Birmingham Symphony Orchestra conducted by Sir Simon Rattle, Walton's Violin Concerto with the Royal Philharmonic Orchestra and André Previn, Bruch and Mendelssohn concertos with the English Chamber Orchestra conducted by Jeffrey Tate, Kafka (Kennedy's compositions), Tchaikovsky's Chausson Poème with the London Philharmonic Orchestra 1988, Brahms Violin Concerto with the London Philharmonic under Klaus Tennstedt 1991, Beethoven Violin Concerto with the NDR-Sinfonieorchester and Klaus Tennstedt 1992, chamber works by Debussy and Ravel, Berg's Violin Concerto, Vaughan Williams' The Lark Ascending with Sir Simon Rattle and the CBSO, works by Fritz Kreisler 1998, The Kennedy Experience, chamber works by Bach, Ravel and Kodaly (with Lynn Harrell) 1999, Classic Kennedy with the English Chamber Orchestra 1999, Bach's Concerto for Two Violins in D Minor, Concerto for Oboe and Violin in D Minor and the A Minor and E Major violin concertos the Berlin Philharmonic 2000, Nigel Kennedy Plays Bach 2006, Inner Thoughts 2006, Blue Note Sessions 2006, Polish Spirit 2007, Beethoven and Mozart Violin Concertos 2008, A Very Nice Album 2008, Shhh! 2010. *Publication:* Always Playing 1991. *Honours:* Hon. DLitt (Bath) 1991; Golden Rose of Montreux 1990, Variety Club Showbusiness Personality of the Year 1991, BRIT Award for Outstanding Contribution to British Music

2000, Male Artist of the Year 2001, Echo Klassik Award for Instrumentalist of the Year 2008. *Address:* c/o John Stanley, Kennedy, 90–96 Brewery Road, London, N7 9NT, England. *Website:* www.nigel-kennedy.net.

KENNELL, Richard (Rick) W.; American musician (bass guitar) and record producer; b. 8 Nov. 1952, Fort Wayne, Indiana; m. Leah Marie Waybright 1976. *Education:* Indiana Univ., James Madison Univ. *Career:* Founder-mem. Happy the Man 1973–79, 2000–; mem. ASCAP, NARAS, AES. *Recordings include:* albums: Happy The Man: Happy The Man 1977, Crafty Hands 1978, Better Late 1983, Beginnings 1990, Retrospective, Happy The Man Live, Death's Crown 1999, The Muse Awakens 2004.

KENNEY, Ben; American musician (bass guitar). *Career:* mem. Incubus 2003–; side project, The Division Group. *Recordings include:* albums: A Crow Left of the Murder 2004, Light Grenades 2006, Monuments and Melodies 2009, If Not Now, When? 2011. *Website:* www.enjoyincubus.com.

KENNY, Andrew; American singer and musician (guitar). *Career:* mem. Electric Company –1994; Founder-mem. The American Analog Set 1995–; Founder-mem., The Wooden Birds 2008–. *Recordings include:* albums: with The American Analog Set: The Fun Of Watching Fireworks 1996, From Our Living Room To Yours 1997, The Golden Band 1999, Know By Heart 2001, Updates 2002, Through The 1990s: Singles & Unreleased 2001, Promise Of Love 2003, Set Free 2005; with The Wooden Birds: Magnolia 2009, Two Matchsticks 2011. *E-mail:* requests@amanset.com (home); thewoodenbirds@gmail.com (office). *Website:* www.amanset.com; www.thewoodenbirds.com.

KENNY DOPE (see Gonzalez, Kenny)

KENT, Andrew (Andy) Charles; New Zealand musician (bass guitar); b. 1971, Wellington. *Career:* mem. Australian rock band, You Am I 1991–; numerous worldwide tours. *Recordings include:* albums: Sound As Ever 1993, Hi Fi Way 1995, Hourly, Daily 1996, # 4 Record 1998, What Rhymes With Cars And Girls 1999, . . .Saturday Night, 'Round Ten 1999, Dress Me Slowly 2001, Deliverance 2002, Spit Polish 2005, Convicts 2007. *Honours:* ARIA Award for Best Alternative Release 1995, six Industry Awards 1996. *Current Management:* c/o Other Tongues, 23/94 Oxford Street, Darlinghurst, NSW 2010, Australia.

KENT, Jeffrey (Jeff) John William, BSc (Econ) (Hons), PGCE; English writer, musician (keyboards, percussion), singer, lecturer and campaigner; *Director,* *Witan Creations;* b. 28 July 1951, Stoke-on-Trent, Staffs., England; s. of Cyril Kent and Helen Kent; m. Rosalind Ann Downs 1987 (divorced 2010). *Education:* Univ. of London, Crewe Coll. of Educ. *Career:* freelance writer and ed. 1972–; songwriter and performing musician 1975–; lecturer in Humanities, various Staffordshire colls 1976–2010; guest speaker 1986–; Lecturer in Writing and Publishing, Stoke on Trent Coll. 1994–2010; performances include Dragon Fair 1984, Open Air Concert, Chamberlain Square, Birmingham 1984, Green Party Conf. concert 1987, Artists for the Planet concert 1989; appearance on BBC Midlands TV, launching album 1992; Only One World tour 2000; Lichfield Festival 2010–12; Co-ordinator, The Mercia Movement 1993–; Convener The Mercian Constitutional Convention 2001–03, The Acting Witan of Mercia 2003–; Br. Sec., Stoke on Trent Coll., Univ. and Coll. Union 2006–10. *Films:* Up the Vale! The Story of Port Vale FC (historical adviser) 1998, Millennium Documentary: Port Vale Football Club (historical adviser) 2000, Pictures from the Potteries (dir, screenplay, commentary and soundtrack composer) 2014. *Recordings include:* albums: Tales from the Land of the Afterglow Part 1, Part 2 1984, Port Vale Forever 1992, Only One World 2000; single: Butcher's Tale/Annie with the Dancing Eyes 1981. *Publications:* The Rise and Fall of Rock 1983, Principles of Open Learning 1987, Routes to Change: A Collection of Essays for Green Education (co-author) 1988, The Last Poet: The Story of Eric Burdon 1989, Back to Where We Once Belonged! 1989, The Valiants' Years: The Story of Port Vale 1990, Port Vale Tales 1991, Port Vale Forever 1992, 100 Walks in Staffordshire (co-author) 1992, The Port Vale Record 1879–1993 1993, Port Vale Personalities 1996, The Mercia Manifesto: A Blueprint for the Future Inspired by the Past (prin. author and ed.) 1997, Port Vale Grass Roots (ed.) 1997, The Potteries Derbies 1998, A Draft Constitution for Mercia (prin. author and ed.) 2001, The Mysterious Double Sunset 2001, The Constitution of Mercia (prin. author and ed.) 2003, A Potteries Past (ed.) 2010, What If There Had Been No Port in the Vale?: Startling Port Vale Stories! 2011, Stories From Stoke (ed.) 2012, Staffordshire's 1,000-Foot Peaks 2013, Peak Pictures 2014, Cheshire's 1,000-Foot Peaks 2015; contribs to Alsager Chronicle, Education Now, Eric Burdon Connection Newsletter, First Hearing, Hard Graft, NATFHE Journal, The Sentinel, TAG-mag, etc. *Address:* Cherry Tree House, 8 Nelson Crescent, Cotes Heath, via Stafford, Staffs., ST21 6ST, England (office). *Telephone:* (1782) 791673 (office). *E-mail:* witan@mail.com (office). *Website:* www.witancreations.com (office).

KENT, Rolfe, BSc; British composer; b. 18 April 1963, St Albans, Hertford-shire, England. *Education:* Univ. of Leeds. *Career:* taught psychology at Leeds Metropolitan Univ.; mem. PRS, AFofM, BMI. *Films include:* as composer: The Pitch 1993, Finding Interest 1994, Dead Connection 1994, Memory Lane 1995, Mercy 1995, Citizen Ruth 1996, The House of Yes 1997, Slums of Beverly Hills 1998, The Theory of Flight 1998, Don't Go Breaking my Heart 1999, Election 1999, Oxygen 1999, Silence Living in Houses 1999, Mexico City 2000, The Smoking Section 2000, Gun Shy 2000, Nurse Betty 2000, Happy Campers 2001, Someone Like You 2001, Town and Country 2001, Legally Blonde 2001, Kate and Leopold 2001, 40 Days and 40 Nights 2002, About Schmidt 2002,

Legally Blonde 2: Red, White and Blonde 2003, Freaky Friday 2003, Mean Girls 2004, Sideways 2004, The Last Shot 2004, The Lost Cause 2004, The Matador 2005, Wedding Crashers 2005, Thank You for Smoking 2005, Just Like Heaven 2005, Failure to Launch 2006, Sex and Death 101 2007, Reign Over Me 2007, The Hunting Party 2007, The Lucky Ones 2008. *Honours:* AICP (American Ind. Commercial Producers) Award, Best Music 1993. *Website:* www.rolfekent.com.

KENT, Stacey; American jazz singer and broadcaster; b. 27 March 1968, New York; m. Jim Tomlinson 1991. *Education:* Sarah Lawrence Coll., , Guildhall School of Music, UK. *Film appearance:* Richard III 1995. *Radio:* presenter: Jazz Line-Up (BBC Radio 3) 2000–04, Big Band Special (BBC Radio 2) 2001–04. *Recordings include:* albums: Stacey Kent Sings 1995, Close Your Eyes 1997, Love Is. . .The Tender Trap 1998, Let Yourself Go 1999, Dreamsville 2000, Brazilian Sketches (with Jim Tomlinson) 2001, In Love Again 2002, The Boy Next Door 2003, Shall We Dance 2004, The Lyric (with Jim Tomlinson) (BBC Jazz Award for Album of the Year) 2006, Breakfast on the Morning Train 2007, Raconte-Moi 2010, Dreamer In Concert 2011, The Changing Lights 2013. *Honours:* Ordre des Arts et des Lettres 2009; BT Jazz Award for Best Vocalist of the Year 1999, British Jazz Award 2001, BBC Jazz Award for Best Vocalist 2002. *Current Management:* c/o Kurland Associates, 173 Brighton Avenue, Boston, MA 02134-2003, USA. *Telephone:* (617) 254-0007. *Fax:* (617) 782-3577. *E-mail:* agents@thekurlandagency.com. *Website:* www.thekurlandagency.com; www.staceykent.com.

KENYON, Duncan; British studio owner and musician (bass guitar, guitar); b. 10 Dec. 1961, Wembley, Middlesex; m. 1991 (divorced 1993). *Career:* fmr mem., French Impression; toured with The Cool Notes; support to Rose Royce, Odyssey, Tell Him and New York Groove; mem. Hello 2002–; mem. PRS, Musicians' Union. *Recordings include:* albums: with Hello: Keeps Us Off the Streets 2007, Hello Again 2007. *E-mail:* info@helloband.co.uk (office). *Website:* www.helloband.co.uk.

KEREN ANN; Israeli/Dutch singer, songwriter, composer, producer and sound engineer and musician (guitar); b. (Keren Ann Zeidel), 10 March 1974, Caesarea, Israel. *Career:* based largely in Paris, Tel-Aviv and New York; has lived and recorded in France and New York for many years; mem. of band Lady & Bird with Barði Jóhannson, several composition projects including show with Icelandic Symphony Orchestra, Reykjavik with dir Daniel Kawka 2008, live performance recorded and post-produced by the band and released 2009; second show for Salle Pleyel, Paris with L'Orchestre Lamoureux directed by Christophe Mangou 2009; co-writer for many internationally acclaimed recordings including 'Chambre Avec Vue' written for Henri Salvador in 2000; song 'Beautiful Day' has been the sound of Skyteam' campaign; co-wrote and co-produced with Doriand the second album of singer/actress Emmanuelle Seigner released 2010. *Compositions:* various projects (with Barði Jóhannson) including show with the Icelandic Symphony Orchestra, Reykjavik 2008; sound design (with Tibo Javov) for European TV channel ARTE 2008; co-writer for The Isis Project (with Guy Chambers) 2004–05. *Music for film:* Deux Jours à Tuer 2008; original soundtrack for French feature film by dir Benoit Pétré starring Jane Birkin 2010. *Music for television:* series: Grey's Anatomy (song Not Going Anywhere), Skyteam Advertisement (song Beautiful Day), Six Feet Under (song Jardin d'hiver), Big Love (song L'onde Amere), The L Word (song Do What I Do/Lady & Bird), TGV advertisement (song Malmo Livs/Lady & Bird) 2005–07, H&M advertisement (song Lay Your Head Down) 2008. *Recordings include:* solo albums: La Biographie de Luka Philipsen 2000–01, Chambre Avec Vue/Henri Salvador 2000–01, La Disparition 2002, Not Going Anywhere 2003, Nolita 2005, Keren Ann 2007, Dingue (Emmanuelle Seigner/Doriand) 2010, Thelma, Louis & Chantal (original soundtrack) 2010, 101 2011; other: Lady & Bird (Lady & Bird band with Barði Jóhannson) 2003. *Address:* 18 rue de la Convention, 75015 Paris, France (office). *Telephone:* 1-40-71-32-00 (office). *Fax:* 1-40-71-61-80 (office). *E-mail:* sabrinalaas@free.fr (office); kerenann@kerenann.com. *Website:* www.kerenann.com.

KERMAN, Max, BA; Canadian singer and guitarist. *Education:* McMaster Univ. *Career:* Founder mem. Charlemagne, formed in Hamilton, Ont. 2006, renamed Arkells 2008–; signed to Dine Alone Records 2006; released debut EP Deadlines 2007; opening act for Matt Mayes & El Torpedo on Canadian tour 2008; toured with Waking Eyes on Canadian tour 2009; toured USA with The Maine and Lydia 2012; toured Europe with Billy Talent and Anti-Flag 2012; support act for Tragically Hip on Canadian tour 2013. *Recordings:* albums: with Arkells: Jackson Square 2008, Michigan Left 2011, High Noon (Juno Award for Rock Album of the Year 2015) 2014. *Honours:* 102.1 The Edge CASBY Award 2009, Juno Awards for New Group of the Year 2010, for Group of the Year 2012, 2015. *Current Management:* c/o Tom Sarig, Kari Dexter and Christine Carson, ECG Management; Adam Countryman and Jack Ross, The Agency Group Ltd, 2 Berkeley Street, Suite 202, Toronto, ON M5A 4J5, Canada. *Telephone:* (416) 368-5599 (Agency Group). *Fax:* (416) 368-4655 (Agency Group). *E-mail:* tom@ecgnyc.com; kari@ecgnyc.com; christine@ecgnyc.com; adamcountryman@theagencygroup.com; jackross@theagencygroup.com. *Website:* www.theagencygroup.com; www.arkells.ca.

KERNON, Neil Anthony; British record producer and sound engineer; b. 13 Sept. 1953, London; m. Kellie O'Neal 1991. *Career:* recording engineer, Trident Studios, UK 1971–75; Le Chateau d'Herouville, France 1975; Startling Studios, UK 1976–79; ind. producer, USA 1979–. *Recordings include:* as engineer, producer: albums with Hall and Oates: Voices 1980,

Private Eyes 1981, H2O 1982, Rock 'n' Soul Part 1 1983, Sign In Please, with Autograph 1984, Starting All over Again 1997, Soulful Sounds 1992, The Best of Hall and Oates 1997, The Ballads Collection 2001, The Essential Daryl Hall & John Oates 2005, Super Hits 2007, The Singles 2008, Super Hits, Vol. 2 2009, Do What You Want, Be What You Are: The Music of Daryl Hall & John Oates 2009, The Box Set Series 2014; with Dokken: Under Lock and Key 1985, Back For The Attack 1987, The Very Best of Dokken 1999, The Definitive Rock Collection 2009; with The Hixon: Truth Has Been Burned 2008. *Address:* Auslander, 1657 North Bell , Chicago, IL 60647, USA. *Telephone:* (773) 292-0964. *E-mail:* auslander@interaccess.com.

KERR, Jim; British singer; b. 9 July 1959, Glasgow, Scotland; m. 1st Chrissie Hynde 1984 (divorced); one d.; m. 2nd Patsy Kensit 1993 (divorced); one s. *Career:* Founder-mem. rock group, Simple Minds 1978–; world-wide tours and festival appearances. *Recordings include:* albums: Life In A Day 1979, Real To Real Cacophony 1980, Empires and Dance 1980, Sons and Fascinations 1981, Sister Feelings Call 1981, Celebration 1982, New Gold Dream 1982, Sparkle In The Rain 1984, Once Upon A Time 1985, Live In The City of Light 1987, Street Fighting Years 1989, Themes (four vols) 1990, Real Life 1991, Glittering Prize 81–92 1992, Good News From The Next World 1995, Neapolis 1998, Neon Lights 2001, Cry 2002, Black & White 2005, Graffiti Soul 2009, Big Music 2014; solo album: Lostboy! AKA Jim Kerr 2010. *Honours:* Q Award for Best Live Act 1991. *Website:* www.simpleminds.com.

KERR, Michael (Mike); British rock singer, songwriter and bass guitarist; b. Worthing, Sussex, England. *Career:* fmr mem. Flavour Country; Founder-mem. Royal Blood 2013–; released debut single Out of the Black 2013, supported Arctic Monkeys 2014, Foo Fighters 2015; performed at numerous music festivals including South by Southwest, Liverpool Sound City, Glastonbury Festival, T in the Park, Reading Festival. *Recordings:* album: Royal Blood 2014. *Honours:* Kerrang! Best British Newcomer 2015, BRIT Award for Best British Group 2015, Q Best Live Band Award 2015. *Current Management:* c/o Wildlife Entertainment, 21 Heathman's Road, London, SW6 4TJ, England. *Telephone:* (20) 7371-7008. *E-mail:* info@wildlife -entertainment.com. *Website:* www.wildlife-entertainment.com; www .royalbloodband.com.

KERR, Nancy; British folk singer, musician (violin, viola, cello, guitar, mandolin) and composer; b. 29 July 1975, England; d. of Sandra Kerr. *Career:* plays predominantly traditional material, both instrumental and songs; toured and recorded with Eliza Carthy, recorded and toured as part of trio with Sandra Kerr and James Fagan; mem. duo with James Fagan. *Recordings include:* albums: Eliza Carthy and Nancy Kerr (with Eliza Carthy) 1993, Shape of Scrape (with Eliza Carthy) 1995, Neat and Complete (with Sandra Kerr) 1996, Starry Gazy Pie (with James Fagan) 1997, Scalene (with Sandra Kerr and James Fagan) 1999, Steely Water (with James Fagan) 1999, On Reflection (with Eliza Carthy) 2002, Between The Dark And Light (with James Fagan) 2002, Strands of Gold (with James Fagan) 2005, Stiffs, Lovers, Holymen, Thieves (with Tim van Eyken band) 2006, Station House (with James Fagan and Robert Harbron) 2008, Milk and Honey Land (with The Fagans) 2009, Twice Reflected Sun (with James Fagan) 2010, Fifty Verses (with Melrose Quartet) 2013, Sweet Visitor 2014. *Honours:* BBC Horizon Award for Best New Act (with James Fagan) 2000, BBC Radio 2 Folk Award for Best Duo (with James Fagan) 2003. *Current Management:* Emerging Music, Sarah's Cottage, Horn's Cross, Bideford, EX39 5DW, England. *E-mail:* ken@emergingmusic.co.uk. *Website:* www.nancykerr.co.uk; www.kerrfagan .com.

KERR, Sandra; British folk singer, songwriter and musician (concertina, guitar, Appalachian dulcimer, autoharp); b. (Sandra Joan Faulkner), 14 Feb. 1942. *Education:* trained with the Critic's Group, with Ewan MacColl and Peggy Seeger. *Career:* co-writer and researcher of music for TV series, Bagpuss, and for programmes on BBC Children's Radio, including The Music Box, The Listening Corner; mem. female vocal group, Sisters Unlimited, performing close harmony renditions of contemporary and traditional songs exploring women's issues; recorded and toured with her daughter, Nancy Kerr, and James Fagan; leads numerous workshops, training programmes (including voice production, traditional singing style, concertina playing and teacher training in the use of song and dance); Dir folk choirs, Wercasfolk and VoiceMale; currently Lecturer, School of Arts and Cultures, Univ. of Newcastle upon Tyne. *Recordings include:* albums: John and Sandra 1969, Nuclear Power 1981, Supermum 1984, We Were There 1987, Neat and Complete (with Nancy Kerr) 1996, Scalene (with Nancy Kerr and James Fagan) 1999, Yellow Red and Gold 2000; with Sisters Unlimited: No Limits 1991, No Bed of Roses 1995. *Address:* School of Arts and Cultures, Armstrong Building, University of Newcastle, Newcastle upon Tyne, NE1 7RU, England (office). *Telephone:* (191) 443-4579 (office). *E-mail:* sandra.kerr@ncl.ac.uk (office). *Website:* www.ncl.ac.uk/sacs/staff/profile/s.j.kerr (office).

KERR, Tehimana, (Jetlag Johnson); New Zealand musician (guitar). *Career:* mem. Fat Freddy's Drop reggae and soul band. *Recordings include:* Fat Freddy's Drop: Live at the Matterhorn 2001, Based on a True Story (first ind. release to go Gold and debut at No. 1 on NZ Music Charts, Winner, Highest Selling Album, Wandering Eye Best Video, voted Worldwide Album of the Year at Radio 1 Gilles Peterson Worldwide Music Awards 2005) 2005, Ray Ray (Best Int. Music Video, New York Ind. Film and Video Festival) 2007, Dr Boondigga and the Big BW 2009. *Honours:* Best Live Act, B-Net NZ Music Awards 2004, NZ Music Award for Best Group 2005, Outstanding Achieve-

ment in the Field of Excellence, B-Net NZ Music Awards 2006, People's Choice Award, NZ Music Awards 2006, 'Male Fox', B-Net NZ Music Awards 2006. *Address:* The Drop Ltd, PO Box 14-723, Kilbirnie, Wellington 6241, New Zealand (office). *Telephone:* (4) 934-3767 (office). *E-mail:* freddy@ fatfreddysdrop.com (office). *Website:* www.fatfreddysdrop.com (office); www .fatfreddysdrop.tv (office).

KERSHAW, Martin John; British musician (guitar, banjo, bouzouki, mandolin, ukelele) and composer; b. 13 July 1944, Shipley, Yorkshire; m. (divorced), one d. *Education:* Bingley Grammar School. *Career:* mem. Manfred Mann; moved to London 1966; played with: John Dankworth Big Band, Jack Parnell Orchestra, James Last Orchestra; guitarist on all 120 Muppet Shows; toured with Sacha Distel; now runs his own digital record co.; mem. Musicians' Union, PRS. *Recordings include:* album: Acoustic Dreams 1998.

KERSHAW, Nicholas (Nik) David; British singer, musician (guitar) and songwriter; b. 1 March 1958, Bristol; m. Sheri. *Career:* Member, jazz-funk group Fusion; solo artiste, with backing band The Krew, 1983–. *Compositions include:* The One and Only Chesney Hawkes (No. 1, UK) 1991. *Recordings:* albums: Human Racing 1984, The Riddle 1984, Radio Musicola 1986, The Works 1990, The Collection 1991, Wouldn't It Be Good 1994, The Best of Nik Kershaw 1998, 15 Minutes 1999, The Essential 2000, To Be Frank 2001, You've Got to Laugh 2006, No Frills 2010, Ei8ht 2012; singles: I Won't Let The Sun Go Down On Me (No. 2, UK) 1984, Wouldn't It Be Good 1984, Somebody Loves You, 1999, Wounded, 2002. *Address:* c/o Eagle Records, Eagle House, 22 Armoury Way, Wandsworth, London, SW18 1EZ, England. *Website:* www .nikkershaw.net.

KERSHAW, Sammy; American country singer, songwriter, musician (guitar) and actor; b. (Samuel Cashat), 24 Feb. 1958, Abbeville, La; m. Lorrie Morgan 2001 (divorced 2007). *Career:* played in local bands, including Blackwater; DJ work; appeared in the film Fall Time 1995. *Recordings include:* albums: Don't Go Near The Water 1991, Haunted Heart 1993, Feelin' Good Train 1994, Politics, Religion and Her 1997, Labor of Love 1997, Maybe Not Tonight 1999, The Hits: Chapter One 1995, Coverin' The Hits 2000, The Hits: Chapter Two 2001, I Want my Money Back 2003, Honky Tonk Boots 2006, Better Than I Used to Be 2010, A Sammy Klaus Christmas 2012, All in the Same Boat 2013. *Honours:* inducted into Louisiana Music Hall of Fame 2008, Louisiana Songwriters Asscn Hall Of Fame 2010. *Current Management:* c/o Billy Holland, The Holland Group, Inc., 3212 West End Avenue/ Site 303, Nashville, Tenn. 37203, USA. *E-mail:* billywholland@yahoo.com. *Website:* www.sammykershaw.com.

KERSHAW, Steve P., BA (Hons), PhD; British musician (double bass, bass guitar); b. 17 March 1959, Bradford. *Education:* Univ. of Bristol, Bass Inst. of Technology, USA. *Career:* mem. British Youth Symphony Orchestra 1978–82, After Hours, False Idols, Then There Were Six, Claude Bottom and The Lion Tamers, The Honkin' Hep Cats, The Rascals of Rhythm, Stekpanna, The John Hoare 4, The Flat Back Four; mem. Musicians' Union, Int. Soc. of Bassists. *Recordings include:* with After Hours: All Over Town 1980; with False Idols: Ten Seconds To Midnight 1981, Centre of Attention 1985, Fine Blue Line 1987; with L'Orange, Si J'Etais Vous 1991; with The Honkin' Hep Cats: What's The Use? 1989; Honkin' 'n' Stompin' 1992, Rantin' Ravin' 'n' Misbehavin' 1994; with Stekpanna: Standin' Tall 1997, with The Steve Tayton Quartet and The Rolls Royce Brass Band, Dark To Light 1999; with Luis D'Agostino: Otros Caminos 1999, with The Flat Back Four, Dig-Dig. *Honours:* Outstanding Vocational Hons Award, GHS 1996, Outstanding Student of the Year Award, Fender 1996, Musicians Inst. *Address:* 5 Cardwell Crescent, Headington, Oxford, OX3 7QE, England. *Website:* www .stevekershaw.com.

KERWIN, Michael Thomas, BMus; Canadian producer and engineer; b. 19 Feb. 1970, Freiburg, Germany. *Education:* Humber Coll. *Career:* Founder, Newmarket Multimedia Recording Studio 1994; Co-founder, Limit Records Inc. 1995. *Recordings include:* producer, engineer: 30 Odd 6 1996, Beru's Nephew 1996, Stone Idols 1997; co-producer, engineer: Woodrow 1997, The Salads 1997, Engineer: Al Connelly 1996, Sarah Sloan 1997. *Address:* Limit Records, 17665 Leslie Street, Unit 5, Newmarket, ON L3Y 3E3, Canada (office). *Telephone:* (905) 895-1902 (office).

KE$HA; American singer, songwriter and rapper; b. (Kesha Rose Sebert), 1 March 1987, Los Angeles; d. of Pete Sebert. *Education:* Franklin High School, Brentwood High School, Nashville, Tenn. *Career:* signed to Kemosabe Entertainment 2005; backing vocalist for Paris Hilton, Britney Spears; appeared in video for Katy Perry's I Kissed a Girl; songwriter for The Veronicas, Britney Spears, Miley Cyrus; featured on Flo Rida's Right Round single 2009, also releases by Taio Cruz and 3OH!3; support act on Rihanna tour of N America 2010; first headlining world tour in 2011. *Recordings:* album: Animal 2010. *Honours:* Global Amb. for Animals, Humane Soc. 2011; MTV Europe Music Award for Best New Act 2010. *Address:* c/o RCA Records, Sony Music Entertainment, 550 Madison Avenue, Room 2356, New York, NY 10022, USA (office). *Website:* www.keshasparty.com.

KESSLER, Daniel; American musician (guitar) and backing singer; b. 25 Sept. 1974. *Education:* New York Univ. *Career:* Founder-mem. Interpol 1998–. *Recordings include:* albums: Turn on the Bright Lights 2002, Antics 2004, Our Love to Admire 2007, Interpol 2010, El Pintor 2014. *Publication:* Sarah Caldwell: The First Woman of Opera. *E-mail:* info@interpolny.com. *Website:* www.interpolnyc.com.

KEUNING, David; American musician (guitar); b. Las Vegas, NV. *Career:* founder mem., The Killers 2002–. *Recordings include:* albums: Hot Fuss 2004, Sam's Town (BRIT Award for Best Int. Album 2007) 2006, Sawdust 2007, Day and Age 2008, Battle Born 2012. *Honours:* NME Award for Best Int. Band 2005, for Best Video 2007, MTV Video Award for Best New Artist 2005, MTV Europe Music Award for Best Rock Act 2006, BRIT Award for Best Int. Group 2007, ASCAP Vanguard Award 2010. *E-mail:* lauren.schneider@umusic.com. *Website:* www.thekillersmusic.com.

KEVORKIAN, François; French producer, remixer, DJ and musician (drums); *President and Head of A&R, Wave Music, Wave Entertainment Group Inc.;* b. 10 Jan. 1954, Rodez. *Career:* drummer with various French bands before relocation to New York 1975; performed in nightclubs until finding work as DJ at New York New York; A&R work for disco label Prelude Records led to remix projects, firstly Musique's In the Bush; subsequently remixed: D-Train, Yazoo, Depeche Mode, The Cure; opened Axis Studios, New York 1987; Founder Wave Records 1994–, also Pres. and Head of A&R; resident DJ at Body and Soul club, New York. *Address:* Wave Music, 244 West 54th Street, Suite 800, New York, NY 10019, USA (office). *Telephone:* (212) 757-8466 (office). *Fax:* (212) 757-4684 (office). *E-mail:* info@wavemusic.com (office). *Website:* www.wavemusic.com (office); www.francois-k.com.

KEYS, Alicia; American singer, songwriter and musician (piano); b. (Alicia Augello Cook), 25 Jan. 1981, New York; m. Kasseem Dean (aka Swizz Beatz) 2010; one s. *Education:* Professional Performing Arts School, Manhattan. *Career:* classically trained pianist; solo artist; numerous live appearances, festivals; collaborations with Angie Stone, Jimmy Cozier, Jermaine Paul, Jack White, John Mayer, Jay-Z, Usher. *Recordings include:* albums: Songs In A Minor (Grammy Award for Best R&B Album 2001, MOBO Award for Best Album 2002) 2001, The Diary of Alicia Keys (Grammy Award for Best R&B Album 2005) 2003, Unplugged 2005, As I Am (American Music Awards for Best Album, Pop/Rock 2008, for Best Album, Soul/R&B 2008) 2007, The Element of Freedom 2009, Girl on Fire (Grammy Award for Best R&B Album 2014) 2012. *Films:* Smokin' Aces 2006, The Nanny Diaries 2007, The Secret Life of Bees 2008. *Honours:* numerous awards including: Grammy Awards for Best New Artist 2001, for Song of the Year, Best Female R&B Vocal Performance, Best R&B Song (all for Fallin') 2001, for Best R&B Song (for You Don't Know My Name) 2005, for Best Female R&B Vocal Performance (for No One) 2008, (for Superwoman) 2009, for Best Rap Song (with Jay-Z) (for Empire State of Mind) 2011, Billboard Music Awards for Female Artist of the Year 2001, 2004, for Female New Artist of the Year 2001, for New R&B/Hip-Hop Artist of the Year 2001, American Music Award Favorite New Artist, Pop/Rock, Favourite New Artist, Soul/R&B 2002, MTV Award Best R&B Act 2002, American Music Award for Best Female Soul/R&B Artist 2004, Source Hip Hop Music Award for Female Artist of the Year 2004, MTV Award for Best R&B Video 2005, Lady of Soul Award for Best R&B/Soul or Rap Song (for If I Ain't Got You) 2005, MTV Europe Music Award for Best R&B 2005, Image Awards for Top Female Musical Artist, for Best Song, for Best Video (for Unbreakable) 2006, World Music Award for Best R&B Act 2008. *Current Management:* William Morris Agency, 1325 Avenue of the Americas, New York, NY 10019, USA. *Telephone:* (212) 586-5100. *Fax:* (212) 246-3583. *Website:* www.wma.com; www.aliciakeys.net.

KHAHANI NAMIN, Amir Hossein, (Siamak Khahani); Iranian musician (violin), songwriter and actor; b. 1977, Tehran. *Education:* Azad Univ. *Career:* mem. The Arian Band (the first officially sanctioned mixed-gender pop band in Iran); simultaneous solo artist; violin teacher. *Film:* Santouri 2007. *Recordings include:* albums: Sunflower, And But Love!, Till Eternity, Without You With You 2008; solo: Palace of Dreams. *Current Management:* c/o Mr Mohsen Rajabpour, Taraneh Sharghee Cultural & Artistic Co., Apt No. 26, Seventh Floor, Suite 22, Second Alley, Shahnazari Street, Mohseni Square, Mirdamad Avenue, Tehran 1547914415, Iran. *Telephone:* (21) 22223513 (office). *Fax:* (21) 22223670 (office). *E-mail:* mohsenrajabpour@taranehsh.com (office). *Website:* www.taranehsh.com/en (office).

KHALADJ, Madjid; Iranian musician (percussion, tombak) and composer; b. 11 Nov. 1962, Ghazvin. *Education:* School of Fine Arts, France, , Traditional Acad. of Persian Art Music, Iran, School of Architecture Paris La Villette, France. *Career:* concerts and radio appearances: Grand Palais, Paris 1991, Barbad Symposium, Tadjikstan, with Master Shadjarian 1991, Grande Auditorium de Radio France, with Master Alizadeh 1992, 1994, Opéra de Lille 1992, Los Angeles Festival, USA, J Paul Getty Museum 1993, Théâtre de la Ville, Paris 1993, Théâtre de la Colline and Radio France, with Master Tala'i 1994; f. Ecole de Tombak, Paris 1996; taught in Musik Akademie der Stadt Basel, Switzerland for 15 years; mem. SACEM. *Recordings include:* Persian Classical Music 1992, Persian Art Music 1992, Iran-The Art of Tombak 1993, Music of Iran, Vols 1 and 2 1993, Iranian Music, Improvisations 1994, Persian Classical Music 1994, Los Angeles Festival 1995, Tombak and Percussion 1996, Anthology of Iranian Rhythms, Vol. 1 1997; Vol. 2 1999, Madjid Khaladj, Iranian Percussion 2001, Madjid Khaladj, Infinite Breath, Persian Art Percussion 2006, Madjid Khaladj, Selected Moments, Persian Art Percussion 2014. *E-mail:* ecole.de.tombak@gmail.com. *Website:* www .madjidkhaladj.net.

KHALED; Algerian singer, musician (keyboard, accordion) and songwriter; b. (Khaled Hadj Brahim), 29 Feb. 1960, Wahran. *Career:* mem. The Five Stars; first recording aged 14 as Cheb Khaled; first hit Trigue Al Lissi (The Way To School) 1975; lyrics censored in Algeria until 1983; performed at Bobigny Festival in France 1986, relocated to Paris 1990; first int. rai hit Didi 1992; collaborations with Chaba Zahouania, Rachid Taha and Faudel; apptd Goodwill Amb. of FAO 2003; performed at Opening Ceremony, World Cup (Fédération Internationale de Football Asscn) 2010. *Recordings include:* albums:Hada Raykoum 1985, Moule El Kouchi 1985, Rai King of Algeria 1985, Fuir Mais Ou? 1988, Khaled 1992, N'ssi N'ssi (César Award for Best Soundtrack) 1993, Sahra 1996, Kenza 1999, Les Monstres Sacrés du Rai, Ya Taleb (with Chaba Zahouania), Best Of The Early Years 2002, Ya Rayi 2004, Liberté 2009, C'est la vie (Kora Award for Best North African Singer 2012, Victoires de la Musique 2013, World Music Award 2013, Murex D'Or 2013, Rabab d'Or 2013) 2012. *Honours:* crowned 'King of Rai' at the first rai festival Oran 1985, BBC Radio 3 World Music Award for Middle East/North Africa region 2005, Antonio Carlos-Jobim Award, Montreal Int. Jazz Festival 2005, Empowering Award 2006, Mediterranean Prize for Creativity 2009, Big Apple Music Award 2009, NME Award 2009. *Address:* c/o AZ/Universal Music France, 20, rue des Fossés St-Jacques, 75005 Paris, France. *Website:* khaled -lesite.com.

KHALIFA, Wiz; American rapper, singer, songwriter and actor; b. (Cameron Jibril Thomaz), 8 Sept. 1987, Minot, North Dakota. *Education:* Taylor Allderdice High School, Pittsburgh. *Career:* adopted stage name 2004; debut mixtape 2005; debut album 2006; toured with Yelawolf 2010; numerous recordings; numerous cameos on other recordings including by MC, Wale, Rick Ross, Curren$y, Ski Beatz, Tinie Tempah, 50 Cent, Snoop Dogg. *Films:* as actor: Gangs of Roses 2: Next Generation 2012, Mac & Devin Go to High School 2012. *Recordings include:* albums: Show and Prove 2006, Deal or No Deal 2009, Rolling Papers 2011, O.N.I.F.C. 2012, Blacc Hollywood 2014; mixtapes: Prince of the City: Welcome to Pistolvania 2005, Grow Season 2007, Prince of the Season 2007, Star Power 2008, Flight School 2009, How Fly 2009, Burn After Rolling 2009, Kush and Orange Juice 2010. *Honours:* BET Award for Best New Artist 2011, Billboard Music Awards for Top New Artist 2012. *Address:* c/o Atlantic Records, 1290 Avenue of the Americas, New York, NY 10104, USA (office). *E-mail:* wizkhalifa.com@gmail.com. *Website:* www .wizkhalifa.com.

KHALIFE, Marcel; Lebanese musician (oud) and composer; b. 10 June 1950, Amchit, Mount Lebanon. *Education:* National Acad. of Music, Beirut. *Career:* Lecturer, Lebanese Nat. Higher Conservatory of Music, Beirut 1970–75; f. Al Mayadeen Ensemble 1976, extensive int. tours performing songs based on poetry by Mahmoud Darwish; co-f. Qatar Philharmonic Orchestra, Music Dir and resident composer 2008–; appearances at numerous int. festivals including Baalbeck, Beit Eddine (Lebanon), Antakya, Carthage, El Hamma-mat (Tunisia), Timgad (Algeria), Jarash (Jordan), Arles (France), Krems, Linz (Austria), Bremen (Germany), Re:Orient Club (Sweden), Pavia (Italy), world music festivals in San Francisco, New York, Cleveland (USA), Int. Festival of Carthage. *Compositions include:* The Symphony of Return, Sharq, Concerto Al Andalus (suite for oud and orchestra), Mouda'aba (Caress), Diwan Al Oud, Jadal Oud Duo, Oud Quartet, Al Samaa, Taqasimn (duo for oud and double bass), Sharq (choral symphonic composition), Arabian Concerto. *Recordings include:* more than 20 albums and DVDs including Promises of the Storm 1976, Rain Songs 1977, Where from Do I Enter the Homeland? 1978, Weddings 1979, At the Borders 1979, Stripped Bare 1980, Happiness 1981, The Bridge 1983, Collections – 3 Albums 1984, Dreamy Sunrise 1984, Ahmad Al Arabi 1984, Peace Be With You 1989, Ode to a Homeland 1990, Arabic Coffeepot 1995, Jadal Oud Duo 1996, Magic Carpet 1998, Concerto Al Andalus 2002, Caress 2004, Voyageur 2004, Taqasim 2007, Sharq 2007. *Publications:* Al Samaa 1981, Anthology of Studying the Oud 1982, Arabic Music-Theory and Practice 1984, Jadal Oud Duo 1996, OUD 1997, Andalusian Suite for Oud and Orchestra 2002. *Honours:* several awards including Jerusalem Medal, Beirut 1981, Palestine Award for Music 1999, named UNESCO Artist for Peace 2005, Charles Cros Award (world music category), Paris 2008, Intellectual Merit and Achievement Medal, Fez, Morocco 2008. *E-mail:* general@marcelkhalife.com (office). *Website:* www.marcelkhalife.com (office).

KHAN, Amjad Ali; Indian musician (sarod) and composer; b. (Masoom Ali Khan), 9 Oct. 1945, Gwalior, Madhya Pradesh; s. of the late Hafiz Ali Khan and Rahat Jahan Begum; m. Subhalakshmi Barooah 1976; two s. *Education:* Modern School, New Delhi. *Career:* numerous concert performances and festival appearances worldwide; mem. World Arts Council, Geneva; Founder-Pres. Ustad Hafiz Ali Khan Memorial Soc. (promotion of Indian classical music and dance); Visiting Prof., Univ. of York, UK 1995, Univ. of Pennsylvania, Univ. of New Mexico; apptd Nat. Amb. for UNICEF 1996. *Compositions include:* many ragas; music for Kathak ballets Shan E. Mughal, Shahajahan Ka Khwab, Ganesh; orchestral compositions Ekta Se Shanti, Ekta Ki Shakti, Tribute to Hong Kong (for Hong Kong Philharmonic Orchestra). *Radio includes:* promenade concert, BBC 1995. *Recordings include:* Tribute to Germany 1992, Inde Du Nord 1993, Sarod Ghar 1997, Evening Raga 2001, Amjad Ali Khan (with Amaan Ali Khan and Ayaan Ali Khan) 2002, Guftagoo 2002, Sadaayen 2002, Music from the 13th Century 2004, Ru Ba Ru 2005, Moksha 2005, Potrait of a Legend 2006, My Inspirations 2006, Romancing the Rains 2007, Breaking Barriers 2007, Yaara 2007, Remembering Mahatma Gandhi, Hope, Ancient Sounds (with Rahim AlHaj), Sarod Symphony 2010, Samaagam 2011, Everything is Everywhere 2011. *Publication:* My Father, Our Fraternity 2012. *Honours:* Hon. Citizen of Nashville, Tenn. 1997, of Houston, Tex. 1997, of Mass, of Atlanta, Georgia 2002, City of Tulsa, Okla, City of Albuquerque, New Mexico 2007; Commdr, Ordre des Arts et des Lettres 2003; Dr hc (Univ. of York) 1997, (Delhi Univ.)

1998, (Rabindra Bharati Univ.) 2007, (Jivaji Univ., Gwalior) 2002, (Vishva Bharati Univ.) 2001; Hon. DLitt, Jamia Milia Islamia Univ. 2007, North Bengal Univ. 2011, Jadavpur Univ. 2012; Sarod Samrat, Prayag Sangeet Samiti, Allahabad 1960, UNESCO Award 1970, Gandi UNESCO Medal, Int. Music Forum 1970, 1975, Padma Shri 1975, Special Honour, Sahitya Kala Parishad, Delhi 1977, Kala Ratna, Sangeet Kala Sangam, Bhopal 1980, Musician of Musicians, Bhartiya Vidhya Bhavan, Nagpur 1983, Amjad Ali Khan Day (Mass.) 1984, Shiromani Award 1986, Kala Saraswati, Andhra Ratna Andhra Pradesh Kalavedika 1987, Acad. Nat. Award (Tirupathi) 1987, Smitsmriti Award 1988, Raja Ram Mohan Roy Teacher's Award 1988, Sangit Natak Acad. Award 1989, Tansen Award, Nat. Cultural Org., New Delhi 1989, Vijaya Ratna Award, India Int. Friendship Soc., New Delhi 1990, Padma Bhusan 1991, Rajiv Gandhi Excellence Award 1992, Sarod Samrat 1993, Sangam Award 1993, Jawahar Lal Nehru Excellence Award 1994, Gandhi Medal, UNESCO 1995, Crystal Award, World Econ. Forum 1997, Padma Vibhushan 2001, Shankar Dev Award 2001, Fukuoka Cultural Grand Prize (Japan) 2004, USA-India Business Council 30th Anniversary Honour 2005, Medal of Honour, Tara Shevchenko Nat. Univ. of Kyiv, Ukraine 2009, Vivekananda National Award 2010, Banga Vibhusha Award 2011 Gulab Khan Award, Prem Nazir Int. Award 2012, Lifetime Achievement Award, Delhi Govt 2012, Rajiv Gandhi Sadbhavna Award 2012, NDTV Indian of the Year Award 2014. *Address:* 3 Sadhna Enclave, Panchsheel Park, New Delhi 110 017, India (home). *E-mail:* music@sarod.com. *Website:* www.sarod.com (office).

KHAN, Chaka; American singer; b. (Yvette Marie Stevens), 23 March 1953, Great Lakes, Ill.; m. 1st Hassan Khan (divorced 1971); m. 2nd Richard Holland (divorced 1980); m. 3rd Doug Rasheed (divorced 2004); one s. one d. *Career:* fmr mem. Afro-Arts theatre, Chicago; fmr mem. groups Shades of Black, Lock and Chain; mem. Rufus 1972–78, renamed Rufus & Chaka 1978–79; numerous live appearances; solo artist 1978–; Founder Chaka Khan Foundation. *Films include:* Night Shift (singer, Everlasting Love, as Rufus and Chaka Khan) 1982, Breakin' (aka Breakdance: The Movie) (singer, Ain't Nobody) 1984, Protocol (singer, I Feel For You) 1984, Krush Groove (singer, Can't Stop the Street) 1985, To Wong Foo Thanks for Everything, Julie Newmar (singer, Free Yourself) 1995, Waiting to Exhale (singer, My Funny Valentine) 1995, Set It Off (singer, Missing You) 1996, National Security (singer, It's All Good) 2003, Deliver Us from Eva (singer, Sweet Thing) 2003, Hollywood Homicide (singer, You Got the Love) 2003. *Television includes:* Beverly Hills, 90210 (series; singer, Time To Be Lovers) 1990, For Your Love (series; singer, title song) 1998. *Recordings include:* albums: with Rufus: Rufus 1973, Rags To Rufus 1974, Rufusized 1974, Rufus Featuring Chaka Khan 1975, Ask Rufus 1977, Street Player 1978, Numbers 1979, Masterjam 1979, Camouflage 1981, Party 'Til You're Broke 1981, Live. . . Stompin' At The Savoy 1983, Sweet Things: Greatest Hits 1993, The Very Best Of Rufus, Featuring Chaka Khan 1996; solo: Chaka 1978, Naughty 1980, Whatcha' Gonna Do For Me 1981, Chaka Khan 1982, I Feel For You 1984, Destiny 1986, CK 1988, I'm Every Woman 1989, It's My Party 1989, Life Is a Dance – The Remix Project 1989, Love You All My Lifetime 1992, The Woman I Am 1992, Epiphany 1996, Come 2 My House 1998, Classikhan 2004, Funk This (Grammy Award for Best R&B Album 2008) 2007. *Honours:* Grammy Awards for Best R&B Vocal Performance (for Chaka Khan) 1982, (for Ain't Nobody) 1983, (for I Feel For You) 1984, (for The Woman I Am) 1992, for Best Vocal Arrangement (for Be Bop Medley) 1984, for Best Traditional R&B Vocal Performance (for What's Going On) 2003, for Best R&B Performance by a Duo or a Group with Vocals (for Disrepectful with Mary J. Blige) 2008, Lena Horne Award 1998, MOBO Lifetime Achievement Award 2002, BET Lifetime Achievement Award 2006, Legends Award 2009, United Negro College Fund Award 2011. *Address:* Chaka Khan Foundation, 9100 Wilshire Blvd, Suite 450 East, Beverly Hills, CA 90212, USA (office). *Telephone:* (310) 285-5380 (office). *Fax:* (310) 247-1040 (office). *E-mail:* info@chakakhanfoundation.org (office). *Website:* www.chakakhanfoundation.org (office); www.chakakhan.com.

KHAN, Rahat Fateh Ali; Pakistani singer; b. 1974, Lyallpur (now Faisalabad); s. of Farrukh Fateh Ali Khan; nephew of the late Ustad Nusrat Fateh Ali Khan; m. Nida Rahat; one s. *Career:* sings Qawwali (devotional Sufi music), also ghazals and other light music; leader of Ustad Nusrat Fateh Ali Khan's group 1997–; fmr judge Chhote Ustaad 2. *Recordings include:* Mukh Tera Sohneya Sharab Nalon Changa Ae 1985, Gin Gin Taare Lang Gaiyaan Rattaan 1985, Dharti Dharti 2009, Hum Pakistan, Aman Ki Asha; albums: Tasveer, Cry For You, Rahat 2001, Charkha 2007, Nazrana-e-Aqeedat 2009, Koi Umeed 2009, Remembering Alama Iqbal 2010, Remembering Mirza Ghalib 2010, Kinna Sohna 2011, RFAK Sessions 2011. *Soundtracks include:* Dead Man Walking 1995, The Four Feathers 2002, Paap 2004, Love Aaj Kal (Star Screen Award 2010) 2009, London Dreams 2009, De Dana Dan 2009, Virsa 2010, Lahore 2010, I Hate Luv Storys 2010, Milenge Milenge 2010, Once Upon a Time in Mumbai 2010, Dabangg (BIG Star Entertainment Award 2010, Mirchi Music Award 2011, IIFA Award 2011) 2010, Anjaana Anjaani 2010, My Name Is Khan (Mirchi Music Award 2011) 2010, Ishqiya (Star Screen Award 2011, Filmfare Award 2011) 2010, Khamosh Raho 2011, Virsa 2010, Love Mein Gum 2011, Bhai Log 2011, Bodyguard 2011, Mere Brother Ki Dulhan 2011, Mausam 2011, Aazaan 2011. *Honours:* several Star Screen Awards and Filmfare Awards.

KHAN, Steve Harris, BA; American musician (guitar) and producer; b. 28 April 1947, Los Angeles, Calif. *Education:* Univ. of California, Los Angeles.

Career: mem. Elements from 1980s–90s; session musician with artists, including Ashford and Simpson, Patti Austin, George Benson, Michael and Randy Brecker, Billy Cobham, Judy Collins, Larry Coryell, Blood, Sweat and Tears, Luther Allison, Donald Fagen, Aretha Franklin, Billy Joel, Chaka Khan, Kenny Loggins, David Sanborn, Phoebe Snow, Steely Dan, Grover Washington, Bob James. *Recordings include:* solo albums: Tightrope 1977, The Blue Man 1978, Arrows 1979, Evidence, Best Of 1980; 1981, Blades 1982, Eyewitness 1983, Casa Loco 1983, Helping Hand 1987, Local Colour 1988, Public Access 1990, Let's Call This 1991, Crossing Bridges 1993, Got My Mental 1996, You Are Here 1998, The Green Field 2005, Borrowed Time 2007, The Suitcase 2008, Parting Shot 2011, Subtext 2014. *Publications include:* Wes Montgomery Guitar Folio 1978, Pat Martino Guitar Solos 1991, Steve Khan Song Book 1991. *Website:* www.stevekhan.com.

KHARISSOV, Ildar; Russian musicologist, ethnomusicologist and composer; b. 21 Jan. 1972, Yelabuga. *Education:* State Conservatoire of Kazan, Free Univ. of Berlin, Germany. *Career:* mem. Int. Council for Traditional Music, Gesellschaft für Musikforschung, Gesellschaft für Osteuropa-Förderung, Europäische Kulturwerkstatt. *Exhibition:* Ritmo di tre battute, Sinn und Raum, Bild und Erinnerung. *Musical works:* Rubai 1992, Cennär 2007, Kreml-Reichstag 2009, Orientreise 2010. *Publications:* contrib. of numerous papers on Tatar folk and popular music in academic journals. *Honours:* prize of the literary review Futurum Art 2007. *Address:* c/o FU Berlin, Schwendenerstr. 33, 14195 Berlin, Germany. *E-mail:* kirim@gmx.de.

KHER, Kailash; Indian singer and musician; b. 7 July 1973, Meerut. *Career:* started career in music and film in 2002; formed band Kailasa with Paresh Kamath and Naresh Kamath in 2005; fmr judge, Indian Idol; performed in more than 300 concerts world-wide. *Recordings include:* Kailasa, Jhoomo Re 2006, Chaandan Mein, Ya Rabba, Kailasa Rangeele. *Films include:* as actor: Mangal Pandey-The Rising 2005, Corporate 2006, Bhopal: A Prayer for Rain 2011; as playback singer: Hamra Se Biyah Karba 2003, Baaz: A Bird in Danger 2003, Khakee 2004, Dev 2004, Waqt: The Race Against Time 2005, Maja 2005, Dosti: Friends Forever 2005, Aap Ki Khatir 2006, Baabul 2006, Tumaku Paruni Ta Bhuli 2007, Welcome to Sajjanpur 2008, Delhi-6 2009, Kurbaan 2009, Allah Ke Banday 2010, Karthik Calling Karthik 2010, Bhindi Baazaar 2011, Azaan 2011; as music dir: Oye Lucky Lucky Oye, Dil Bole Hadippa, Sacred Evil 2006, Dasvidaniya 2008, Chandni Chowk To China 2009. *Current Management:* Promo Sapiens India, 201 Shalimar Morya Park, Andheri, Mumbai, 400 069, India. *Telephone:* (22) 42647442. *E-mail:* pakul@promosapiens.co.in. *Website:* www.kailashkher.com.

KHOVALYG, Kaigal-ool; Russian (Tuvan) singer. *Career:* mem. folk singing quartet, Huun-Huur-Tu 1992–; collaborations with the World Groove Band and Valkov Trio. *Recordings include:* albums: 60 Horses in My Herd 1993, The Orphan's Lament 1994, If I'd Been Born an Eagle 1997, Where Young Grass Grows 1999, Best Live 2001, More Live 2002, Huun-Huur-Tu & Malerija 2002, Spirits from Tuva 2003, Altai Sayan Tandy-Uula (with Samsonov) 2004, Eternal (with Carmen Rizzo) 2009, Ancestors Call 2010. *Current Management:* c/o Ulrich Balβ, JARO Record Company, Bismarckstr. 43, 28203 Bremen, Germany. *E-mail:* ub@jaro.de. *Website:* www.huunhuurtu.com.

KHOZA, Valanga; South African Singer, Songwriter and Musician (kalimba, guitar, marimbas, kora, mouthharp, m'bira, flute); b. 21 Dec. 1959, Tzaneen. *Education:* Univ. of South Africa, Pietersburg; BA, Business Accounting, Goshen Univ., Indiana, USA. *Career:* soloist, Hemisphere, five-piece a cappella and percussion band, Safika, eight-piece; toured Australia extensively; support act to Geoffrey Oryema, Lucky Dube, 1996, Ladysmith Black Mambazo, 1995, Soweto String Quartet, 1997; appearances at festivals all over Australia including Festival of Cultures, Sydney Opera House, Images of Africa, Festival Copenhagen, Denmark, six-week tour, 1996; ABC Music Deli Program (radio); Jaslyn Halls World Music; Live to air, Australian Broadcasting Commission. *Recordings:* Sebe. *Publications:* Gezani and the Tricky Baboon (children's book) 2003. *Current Management:* Booked Out, PO Box 380, South Yarra, Vic. 3141, Australia. *Telephone:* (3) 9824-0177. *Fax:* (3) 9824-0677. *Website:* www.bookedout.com.

KHUMALO, Sibongile, BMus, BA; South African singer; b. 24 Sept. 1957, Soweto, Johannesburg; d. of Khabi Mngoma. *Education:* Univ. of Zululand, Wits Univ. *Career:* fmr teacher, Univ. of Zululand, FUBA Acad., Madimba Inst. of African Music, Funda Centre; performed at Pres. Nelson Mandela's 75th Birthday 1993, and inauguration 1994; has performed with London Philharmonic Orchestra, Aviva Pelham, Nat. Symphony Orchestra, The Brodsky Quartet and others; Chair. Performers Org. of South Africa (POSA); Founding Chair. Asscn of South African Business Women in the Arts (SABWA); Musical Dir, Composer and Arranger, Africa Cup of Nations (AFCON) for opening and closing ceremonies 2013; mem. Bd of Dirs Southern African Music Rights Org. (SAMRO). *Recordings include:* albums: Ancient Evenings 1996, Live at the Market Theatre 1998, Immortal Secrets 2000, Quest 2002, Sibongile Khumalo 2006. *Honours:* Hon. DMus (Rhodes Univ., Grahamstown) 2008, Hon. Licentiate in Music (Univ. of South Africa) 2007, Dr hc (Univ. of South Africa) 2013, (Univ. of Zululand) 2013; Standard Bank Young Artist Award for Music 1993, FNB South African Music Awards for Best Female Vocal Performance, for Best Adult Contemporary Performance 1996, for Best Adult Contemporary Performance 1998, FNB Vita Award for Best Musical Performance of the Year 1999, Mzansi Magic Hon. Award 2011, Naledi Theatre Award with Lifetime Achievement Award 2013. *Current Management:* c/o Ayanda Khumalo, Magnolia Unlimited, PO Box 378,

Mondeor 2110, South Africa. *Telephone:* (83) 2751627. *E-mail:* info@ magnoliaunlimited.co.za; ayanda@magnoliaunlimited.co.za. *E-mail:* info@ magnoliaunlimited.co.za. *Website:* www.sibongilekhumalo.co.za.

KIANI, Hadiqa; Pakistani singer; b. 11 Aug. 1974, Rawalpindi; d. of Khawar Kiani; m. Syed Fareed Sarwary (divorced 2008); one s. (adopted). *Education:* Kinnaird Coll. *Career:* fmr host, Angan Angan Taray (children's TV music programme); UNDP Goodwill Amb. 2010–; works with Edhi Foundation. *Recordings include:* Mehr Ma 2006, Yeh Hum Naheen 2007; albums: Raaz 1995, Roshni 1998, Rung 2002, Rough Cut 2007, Aasmaan 2009. *Soundtracks include:* Sargam 1994, Bol 2010. *Honours:* NTM Award 1995, PTV Award 1995, PTV World Viewer's Choice Award 2000, Indus Music Award 2004, 2005, 2010, Tamgha-e-Imtiaz 2006, AAGTV Award 2009, TVONE Award 2009. *Current Management:* Ritz Entertainment, Office No. 210, Marine Point, (Above Dunkin Donuts), Schon Circle, Block No. 9, Clifton, Karachi, Pakistan. *Telephone:* 3008229669 (mobile). *E-mail:* email@ritzentertainment .com. *Website:* www.hadiqakiani.net (office).

KID COCO; Belgian singer, composer and musician (guitar, keyboards); b. (Marc Dierickx), 11 Nov. 1964, Ghent; m. Geena Lisa 1998 (divorced 2008); two s. *Career:* resident DJ, legendary Ghent disco Cirque Central; lead vocalist, The Dinky Toys 1981–94; solo artist 1995–, later known as Coco Jr; mem. SABAM/ZAMU. *Recordings include:* albums: with The Dinky Toys: The Colour of Sex 1992, Colourblind 1993, Keep Hope Alive 1994; solo: Acting Like a Glass Virgin 1998, Soul Rebel Salute 2006. *Honours:* ZAMU Award, Best Live Performer 1994. *Address:* c/o The Satisfactory, Deniesstraat 3, 2160 Wommelgem, Belgium. *Telephone:* (47) 586-69-20. *E-mail:* Cocojr@telenet.be. *Website:* www.cocojr.com.

KID CREOLE, (August Darnell), BA; American singer, songwriter, entertainer, playwright and director; *CEO, BrindisiReef Productions;* b. (Thomas Darnell Browder), 12 Aug. 1950, Bronx, NY; m. Eva Tudor-Jones; seven c. *Education:* Hofstra Univ., Stony Brook Univ. *Career:* Leader, Kid Creole and the Coconuts; worldwide tours over 15 years; Co-founder and mem. Dr Buzzard's Original Savannah Band for four years; CEO BrindisiReef Productions; mem. Broadcast Music, Inc., American Fed. of Television and Radio Artists. *Films include:* Against all Odds, Lambada the Forbidden Dance, Love Stinks, Be Kind Rewind, Something Wrong in Paradise, Le Grand Voyage. *Television:* numerous appearances with Savannah Band and with Kid Creole and the Coconuts, including Top of the Pops, Tony Orlando and Dawn, Mike Douglas, Dinah Shore, The Tonight Show, etc.. *Recordings:* albums include: Tropical Gangsters 1982, Fresh Fruit In Foreign Places 1982, Doppelganger 1983, Cre-ole 1984, Private Waters in the Great Divide 1990, Kiss Me Before the Light Changes 1995, To Travel Sideways 1995, Wonderful Thing 2000, Baby I'm Real 2000, Too Cool To Conga 2001, Going Places 2009, I Wake Up Screaming 2011; hit singles include: Cherchez la Femme, I'll Play the Fool 1976, Me No Pop I, with Coati Mundi 1981, I'm A Wonderful Thing, Baby 1982, Stool Pigeon 1982, Annie I'm Not Your Daddy 1982, Dear Addy 1982, There's Something Wrong In Paradise 1983, The Lifeboat Party 1983, The Sex of It 1990. *Honours:* BPI Best Int. Act 1982, numerous music awards, including Village Voice Best Pop Act 1981. *Address:* 315 South Beverly Drive, Suite 300, Beverly Hills, CA 90212, USA (office). *Telephone:* (310) 557-0661 (office). *E-mail:* brindisireef@hotmail.com (office); RRmgmt@aol.com (office). *Website:* www.kidcreoleandthecoconuts.com (office); www.kidcreole.com.

KID ROCK; American singer, songwriter and musician; b. (Robert James Ritchie), 17 Jan. 1971, Romeo, Mich.; m. Pamela Anderson 2006 (divorced 2006); one s. from previous relationship. *Career:* DJ and rap artist aged 17, later performing rock and country music; formed own label, Top Dog 1994; collaborations with Sheryl Crow, Insane Clown Posse, Lynyrd Skynyrd, Kenny Chesney, Hank Williams Jr. *Recordings include:* albums: Grits Sandwiches For Breakfast 1990, Polyfuse Method 1992, Fire It Up! 1994, Polyfuse Method Revisited 1997, Devil Without a Cause 1998, History of Rock 2000, Cocky 2001, Kid Rock 2003, Live Trucker 2006, Rock N Roll Jesus 2007, Born Free 2010, Rebel Soul 2012, First Kiss 2015. *Honours:* Billboard Music Video Award, American Music Award for Favorite Male Pop/Rock Artist, World Music Awards for Best Pop Male Artist 2008, for Best Pop/Rock Male Artist 2008. *Website:* www.kidrock.com.

KIDJO, Angélique; Benin singer and songwriter; b. 14 July 1960, Cotonou; d. of Frank Kidjo and Yvonne Kidjo; m. Jean Hébrail 1987; one d. *Education:* in Cotonou. *Career:* began performing in her mother's theatre co. aged six; joined Kidjo Brothers Band, Alafia, Pili Pili and later Parakou; moved to Paris, France 1983; solo artist 1986–; numerous tours and live appearances; collaborations with Carlos Santana, Manu Dibango, Branford Marsalis, Alicia Keys, Peter Gabriel, Joss Stone, Bono, John Legend; UNICEF Int. Goodwill Amb. 2002–; f. Batonga Foundation (non-profit org. which promotes education for girls) 2007. *Recordings include:* albums: Pretty 1980, Ninive, Ewa Kadjo 1985, Parakou 1989, Logozo 1991, Ayé 1994, Fifa 1996, Oremi 1998, Black Ivory Soul 2002, Oyaya! 2004, Djin Djin (Grammy Award for Best Contemporary World Music Album 2008) 2007, Oyo 2010, Spirit Rising 2012, Eve (Grammy Award for Best World Music Album 2015) 2014, Sings (Grammy Award for Best World Music Album 2016) 2015. *Publication:* Spirit Rising: My Life, My Music (autobiog.) 2014. *Honours:* Commdr, Ordre nat. du Mérite, 2008; Officier des Arts et des Lettres 2009; Hon. DMus (Berklee Coll.) 2010, (Yale Univ.) 2015; African Musician of the Year 1991, Best African Singer, Kora Awards 1997, MOBO Award for Best World Music Act 2002, Antonio Carlos Jobim Award 2007, NAACP Image Award for Outstanding World

Music Album 2008, Grammy Award for Best Contemporary World Music Album 2008, Medal of the Presidency of Italian Repub. 2008, Premio Tenco 2009, UN Champion of The Earth Award 2011, Prix Miroir des Musiques et Folklore du Monde, Quebec 2012, Trophée des Arts, Institut Français 2012, Keep A Child Alive Humanitarian Award 2012, Songlines Music Award 2013. *Current Management:* c/o Redlight Management, 44 Wall Street, 22nd Floor, New York, NY 10005, USA. *E-mail:* kevin@redlightmanagement.com. *Website:* www.kidjo.com.

KIEDIS, Anthony, (Antoine the Swan); American singer; b. 1 Sept. 1962, Grand Rapids, MI. *Career:* founding mem., Anthem, later renamed Red Hot Chili Peppers 1983–; numerous tours, festivals and television appearances. *Film appearance:* F.I.S.T. *Recordings include:* albums: with Red Hot Chili Peppers: The Red Hot Chili Peppers 1984, Freaky Styley 1985, The Uplift Mofo Party Plan 1987, Mother's Milk 1989, Blood Sugar Sex Magik 1991, One Hot Minute 1995, Californication 1999, By The Way 2002, Live In Hyde Park 2004, Stadium Arcadium (MTV Europe Music Award for Best Album) 2006, I'm with You 2011. *Publication:* Scar Tissue (autobiog.) 2004. *Honours:* MTV Music Video Award 1992, American Music Award for Favorite Alternative Artist 2000, 2006, MTV Awards for Best Live Act, Best Rock 2002, American Music Award for Favorite Pop/Rock Band 2006, for Favorite Alternative Music Artist 2006, Grammy Award for Best Rock Performance by a Duo or Group with Vocal (for Dani California) 2007. *Current Management:* Lindy Goetz Management, 11116 Aqua Vista, Suite 39, Studio City, CA 91602, USA. *Address:* c/o Rockinfreakapotamus, The Red Hot Chili Peppers Official Fan Club, PO Box 801, Rockford, MI 49341, USA. *Website:* www .redhotchilipeppers.com.

KIENLEIN, Kevin Dale; Canadian singer, songwriter, musician, entertainer and artist and photographer; b. 12 July 1960, Vernon, BC; s. of Ronald Dale Kienlein and Vivian Fay Ransom. *Education:* Vernon Sr Secondary School, Okanagan Coll. *Career:* first performances were playing organ at church and guitar at church coffeehouse; joined The BC Oldtime Fiddlers 1980, Velvet Rodeo Band 1989; formed duo Partnerz 1992; solo performer 1995–; joined String Loaded Bluegrass band for 1995–96; played at festivals, special events, benefits, concerts and private functions 1990s–; inspirational speaker promoting awareness of Organ & Tissue Donation registration and life journey with a congenital heart defect and subsequent transplant (mem. Toastmasters International—Kalamalka #4869, Charter mem. Okanagan Advanced Toastmasters #693235); mem. Soc. of Composers, Authors and Music Publrs of Canada (SOCAN), BC Oldtime Fiddlers, Nat. Oldtime Fiddlers Asscn, BC Country Music Asscn, Canadian Country Music Asscn, Pacific Music Industry Asscn; heart and double lung transplant recipient in Edmonton, AB 2010. *Exhibition:* Best Projected Pictorial Photo Central, Okanagan Photographic Soc. 2010. *Recordings:* two CDs of original songs/instrumentals; Fiddlers Rag (cassette), Heartbeats 1997, Wishing a Dream 2000. *Publications:* Wishing a Dream, 20 Oldtime Fiddle Tunes. *Honours:* numerous fiddle contest awards, Winner, Vernon BC Canada Centennial Song Competition 1992, Toastmaster of the Year, Kalamalka Toastmasters Club #4869, Vernon, BC 2006, First runner up for North Okanagan's Most Popular Entertainer, Okanagan Life Magazine 2009. *Address:* 3101-18 Avenue, Vernon, BC V1T 1C6, Canada (office). *Telephone:* (250) 545-8340 (office). *E-mail:* info@kevinkienlein.com (office). *Website:* www.kevinkienlein.com; www.lifeisthegig.com; www.lookingatyou.ca.

KIKABIDZE, Vakhtang Konstantinovich; Georgian actor, singer, composer and producer; b. 19 July 1938, Tbilisi; s. of Konstantin Kikabidze and Manana Bagrationi; m. Irene Kebadze 1964; one s. *Career:* soloist and leader of Georgian pop group Orera 1966–; film debut in 1967 with Meeting in the Hills; solo career 1988–. *Films include:* Meeting in the Hills 1967, Don't Grieve 1968, I'm a Detective 1969, The Stone of the First Water 1970, Pen-name Lukach, The Melodies of Verikysky Block 1973, Lost Expedition 1973, Completely Gone 1972, Mimino 1978, TASS is Authorized to Inform, Hi! Friend (TV film) 1981, To Your Health Dear (dir, scriptwriter, actor) 1983, Man and all the Others (scriptwriter, producer, actor) 1985, Fortuna (actor) 2000, Idiotocratia 2008, Yolki 2 2011, Lyubov s aktsentom 2012, Ded 005 2013. *Music:* albums: My Years, My Wealth 1994, Larisa Ivanovna Please! 1995, Letter to Friend 1996, Tango of Love 1999, Greatest Hits 2000, Luchshie pesni 2001, Grand Collection 2002, Moi good 2003, Stariki-pasboiniki 2004, Lyubownoye nastroyenie 2005. *Honours:* USSR State Prize 1978, People's Artist of Georgian SSR 1980, Order of Honour, special award (Georgia) 1994, Order of Konstantine (Russia) 1997, Order of St Nicholaus 1998, Golden Gramophone Prize 1998, Leonid Utesov Prize for Achievement in field of Music 2000.

KILBEY, Steve; Australian musician (guitar, keyboards), singer, songwriter, writer and artist; b. 13 Sept. 1954; two d. *Career:* Founder mem. The Church 1980–. *Recordings include:* albums: with The Church: Of Skins and Hearts 1980, The Blurred Crusade 1982, Séance 1983, Heyday 1986, Starfish 1988, Gold Afternoon Fix 1990, Priest=Aura 1992, Sometime Anywhere 1994, Magician Among the Spirits 1996, Hologram of Baal 1998, After Everything Now This 2002, Parallel Universe 2002, Forget Yourself 2003, El Momento Descuidado 2004, Uninvited, Like the Clouds 2006, El Momento Siguiente 2007, Untitled #2 2009, Further/Deeper 2014; solo: Unearthed 1986, Earthed 1987, The Slow Crack 1989, Remindlessness 1990, Narcosis 1997, Dabble 2001, Painkiller 2008, Art, Man + Technology 2009, Garage Sutra 2012, Addenda One 2012, Addenda Two 2012, The Idyllist 2013, Live at the Fly By Night Club 2013, Miscellanaea – Whispers in the Static 2014. *Publications* include: Earthed (fiction) 1986, Nineveh/The Ephemeron (poems) 1998. *Current Management:* c/o Keith Hagan, SKH Music, 15 Amherst Ln, Smithtown, New York, NY 11787-2346, USA. *E-mail:* khagan@skhmusic .com. *Website:* www.skhmusic.com/. *E-mail:* management@thechurchband .com. *Website:* www.thechurchband.com; www.stevekilbeyart.com.

KILDEA, Bobby; Irish musician (guitar, bass guitar). *Career:* fmr mem., V-Twin; mem., Belle & Sebastian 2001–. *Recordings include:* albums: Storytelling 2002, Dear Catastrophe Waitress 2003, The Life Pursuit 2006, Write About Love 2010, Girls in Peacetime Want to Dance 2015. *Honours:* Q Magazine Spirit of Independence Award 2013. *Current Management:* Banchory Management, PO Box 25074, Glasgow, G3 8TT, Scotland. *Telephone:* (141) 204-2269. *E-mail:* banchoryman@gmail.com. *Website:* www .belleandsebastian.com.

KILKELLY, Frank, BSc; Irish musician (acoustic guitar); b. 17 Sept. 1960. *Career:* regular touring in Europe, USA; has worked with singers and musicians including The Boys of the Lough, Christy O'Leary, Luke Daniels, Brendan Power, Alan Kelly. *Recordings include:* albums with: Luke Daniels, Tarantella 1994, Zumzeaux, Blazing Fiddles 1995, Kimbara Brothers, Now! 1995, Kimbara Brothers, Time To Leave 1995, Power and Kilkelly, Jig Jazz 1996, Simon Mayor, New Celtic Mandolin 1997, Simon Mayor, Mandolin Essentials 1997, Simon Mayor, New Celtic Mandolin 1998, Maggie Boyle, Gweebarra 1998, Pierre Schryer and Dermot Byrne 1999, with The Grappelli Trio: Gipsy Swing 2000. *Publications:* Accompanying Irish Music on Guitar 1999, Accompanying Irish Music on Guitar, Vol. 2 2014. *E-mail:* frank@ irishguitar.net. *Website:* www.irishguitar.net.

KILMORE, Chris; American DJ; b. 21 Jan. 1973, Pittsburgh, Pa. *Career:* mem. Incubus 1998–. *Recordings include:* albums: Make Yourself 1999, Morning View 2001, A Crow Left of the Murder 2004, Light Grenades 2006, Monuments and Melodies 2009, If Not Now, When? 2011, The Essential Incubus 2012. *Honours:* Billboard Award for Modern Rock Single of the Year 2001. *E-mail:* okaydawn@gmail.com. *Website:* www.enjoyincubus.com; www .djkilmore.com.

KIMBALL, Robert (Bobby) Toteaux; American singer; b. 29 March 1947, Vinton, LA. *Career:* lead singer, Toto 1978–84, 1998–2008; solo artist 1984–; mem., Far Corporation. *Recordings include:* albums: with Toto: Toto 1979, Hydra 1979, Turn Back 1981, Toto IV 1982, Isolation 1984, Past to Present 1990, Toto XX 1998, Mindfields 1999, Falling in Between 2006; solo: Rise Up 1996, All I Ever Needed 2000; with Jimi Jamison: Kimball/Jamison 2011. *Honours:* Grammy Award for Best Record, Best Album, Best Producer, Best Engineered Recording, Best Vocal Arrangement, Best Instrumental Arrangement (all with Toto) 1983. *Current Management:* Artists International Management, 9850 Sandalfoot Blvd, Suite 458, Boca Raton, FL 33428, USA. *Website:* www.bobbykimball.com.

KIMSEY, Chris; British producer and musician; b. 1951, Battersea, London. *Career:* worked with Ash, Bad Company, The Chieftains, Jimmy Cliff, The Cult, Deacon Blue, Duran Duran, ELP, Peter Frampton, Gipsy Kings, INXS, Killing Joke, Marillion, Proclaimers, Psychedelic Furs, The Rolling Stones, Ten Years After, Peter Tosh. *Website:* www.chriskimsey.com.

KIMURA, Takuya, (Kimutaku); Japanese singer and actor; b. 13 Nov. 1972, Tokyo; m. Kudo Shizuka 2000; two d. *Career:* mem. pop group, SMAP (Sports Music Assemble People) 1988–, has appeared with the band in numerous TV programmes, advertisements; also TV and film actor 1993–. *Films:* Shoot 1994, Kimi wo wasurenai 1995, Boku ga boku de aru tameni 1997, 2046 2004, Hauru no ugoku shiro (trans. as Howl's Moving Castle, voice) 2004, Buchi no Ichibun (trans. as Love and Honor) 2006, Hero 2007, I Come with the Rain 2008, Redline 2010, Space Battleship Yamato 2010. *Television:* Asunaro hakusho (series) 1993, Wakamono no subete (series) 1994, Long Vacation (series) 1996, Love Generation (series) 1996, Nemureru Mori (series) 1998, Oda Nobunaga (film) 1998, Beautiful Life (series) 2000, Chushingura 1/47 (film) 2001, Hero (series) 2001, Sora kara furu ichioku no hoshi (series) 2002, Good Luck! (series) 2003, Pride (series) 2004, Engine (series) 2005, Karei naru Ichikozu (series) 2007, Change (series) 2008, Mr. Brain 2009, Tsuki no Koibito aka Moon Lovers 2010, Priceless 2012, Ando Lloyd - A.I. Knows Love? 2013, Miyamoto Musashi 2014. *Recordings include:* albums: with SMAP: SMAP 001 1992, SMAP 002 1992, SMAP 003 1993, SMAP 004 1993, SMAP 005 1994, Sexy Six 1994, Gold Singer 1995, Tacomax 1996, SMAP 009 1996, Su 1997, Viva Amigos 2000, Birdman 1999, SMAP 014 2000, Ura SMAP 2001, Drink Smap! 2002, MIJ-SMAP 2003, Sample Bang! 2005, Pop Up! 2006, Super.-Modern.Artistic.Performance 2008; solo: The Songs of Kimura Takuya' Drama 2001. *Publications:* Kai-Ho-Ku Open Area 2003, Open Area 2 2011. *Website:* www.kimuratakuya.wordpress.com.

KINCAID, Jan; British musician (drums, keyboards); b. 17 May 1966, Ealing, London. *Career:* Founder-mem. The Brand New Heavies 1985–; obtained ind. label record deal; worked with several vocalists including Jaye Ella Ruth, N'Dea Davenport, Siedah Garrett and Carleen Anderson. *Recordings include:* Singles: Stay This Way 1991, Never Stop 1991, Dream Come True 1991, Spend Some Time 1994, Dream on Dreamer 1994, Mind Trips 1995, You've Got A Friend 1997, You Are the Universe 1997, Sometimes 1997, Shelter 1998, Saturday Nite 1999, Apparently Nothing 2000; Albums: The Brand New Heavies 1990, The Brand New Heavies 1992, Heavy Rhyme Experience 1992, Brother Sister 1994, Original Flava 1994, Excursions 1995, Shelter 1997, We Won't Stop 2003, Allaboutthefunk 2004, Get Used To It 2006,

Dunk Your Trunk 2011, Forward 2013, Sweet Freaks 2014. *Current Management:* c/o Larry Shields, The Agency Group, 1880 Century Park East, Suite 711, Los Angeles, CA 90067, USA. *E-mail:* larryshields@ theagencygroup.com. *Website:* www.thebrandnewheavies.net.

KINCH, Soweto, BA; British jazz musician (saxophone, piano, bass clarinet), composer and arranger; b. 1978, London, England; s. of Don Kinch and Yvette Harris. *Education:* Univ. of Oxford. *Career:* organized The Live Box music/ arts project, Birmingham 1999–2002; joined Tomorrow's Warriors 1999; collaborations with Jazz Jamaica, Nu-Troop, The Big Blue, Ernest Ranglin; composed for NITRO Black Theatre Co-operative 2001–, Nu Century Arts 2002, Dance Xchange (currently); formed The Soweto Kinch Trio 2001–, The Soweto Kinch Quartet 2002–. *Compositions for theatre:* Slamdunk 2001, It's Just A Name 2002. *Composition for film:* The Cat's Meow 2002. *Recordings include:* album: Conversations With The Unseen 2003, A Life in the Day of B19: Tales of the Towerblock 2006, War in a Rack 2009, The New Emancipation 2010. *Honours:* BBC Radio Jazz Rising Star Award 2002, White Foundation Int. Sax Competition Int. Young Saxophonist, Montreux Jazz Festival 2002, MOBO Award for Best Jazz Act 2003, 2007, BBC Jazz Awards for Best Instrumentalist, Best Band 2004. *Address:* Soweto Kinch Productions, PO Box 14341, Birmingham, B18 9DW, England (office). *E-mail:* contact@soweto-kinch.com (office). *Website:* soweto-kinch.com.

KING, Carole; American singer and songwriter; b. 9 Feb. 1942. *Career:* songwriter in partnership with Gerry Goffin; worked with artists, including Eric Clapton, Crosby and Nash, Branford Marsalis, David Sanborn; numerous concerts and tours; actress in theatre, including starring role, Mrs Johnstone, Broadway production Blood Brothers 1994; environmental activist for natural forest preservation; studied European traditional music; mem. AFTRA, AMPAS, NARAS, NAS, SAG, AFofM. *Compositions include:* hit songs include: Will You Love Me Tomorrow, Take Good Care of My Baby, Go Away Little Girl, The Locomotion, Up On The Roof, Chains, One Fine Day, Hey Girl, I Feel The Earth Move, Natural Woman, Smackwater Jack, You've Got A Friend, Now and Forever (For film, A League of Their Own), soundtrack, animated film, Really Rosie. *Recordings include:* albums: The City 1968, Writer 1970, Tapestry 1971, Rhymes and Reasons 1972, Music 1972, Fantasy 1973, Wrap Around Joy 1974, Thoroughbred 1975, Really Rosie 1975, Simple Things 1977, Welcome Home 1978, Greatest Hits 1978, Touch The Sky 1979, Pearls 1980, 1994, One To One 1982, Speeding Time 1983, City Streets 1989, For Our Children 1991, A League of Their Own 1992, 'Til Their Eyes Shine 1992, Colour of Your Dreams 1993, In Concert 1994, Time Gone By 1994, A Natural Woman 1994, Carnegie Hall Concert 1996, Goin' Back 1998, Love Makes The World 2001, Beautiful: The Carole King Musical (Grammy Award for Best Musical Theater Album 2015). *Publication:* A Natural Woman: A Memoir 2012. *Honours:* Dr hc (Berklee Coll. of Music) 2013; Nat. Acad. of Songwriters Lifetime Achievement Award 1988, Grammy Awards, inducted into Songwriters Hall of Fame 1987, Rock and Roll Hall of Fame (with Gerry Goffin) 1990, Mercer Award, Songwriters Hall of Fame 2002, Trustee Award, Recording Acad. 2004, Gershwin Prize for Popular Song, US Library of Congress 2013. *Current Management:* c/o Lorna Guess, Carole King Productions, 11684 Ventura Blvd, #273, Studio City, CA 91604, USA. *E-mail:* messages@ckmusic.com. *Website:* www.caroleking.com.

KING, Chad; American singer and songwriter; b. (Chad Vaccarino). *Career:* Founder-mem. A Great Big World 2011–; collaborated with Christina Aguilera on second version of song Say Something 2013. *Recordings:* albums: This is the New Year 2011; with A Great Big World: Is There Anybody Out There? 2013, When the Morning Comes 2015. *Honours:* Grammy Award for Best Pop Duo/Group Performance (for Say Something, with Christina Aguilera) 2015. *Current Management:* c/o Works Entertainment, 215 South La Cienega Boulevard, Suite 210, Beverly Hills, CA 90211, USA. *E-mail:* luke@worksentertainment.com. *Website:* worksentertainment.com; www .agreatbigworld.com.

KING, Eileen Maria Goretti; British singer; b. 6 Aug. 1959, Bandbridge, Co. Down, Northern Ireland; m. Joe Rafferty 1987. *Career:* numerous television and live apperances; has recorded in Nashville, The Fireside Studios, The Porter Wagoners Studio; mem. Equity. *Recordings include:* six albums. *Honours:* numerous music awards.

KING, Evelyn 'Champagne'; American singer; b. 1 July 1960, Bronx, NY. *Career:* soul/dance music singer, 1977–. *Recordings include:* albums: Smooth Talk 1977, Music Box 1979, Call On Me 1980, I'm In Love 1981, Get Loose 1982, Face To Face 1983, So Romantic 1984, A Long Time Coming 1985, Flirt 1988, The Girl Next Door 1989, I'll Keep a Light On 1995, Open Book 2007. *Address:* c/o Nationwide Entertainment Services, 2756 N Green Valley Parkway, Suite 449, Las Vegas, NV 89014-2100, USA. *Website:* www .evelynchampagneking.com.

KING, Joe; American musician (guitar) and singer. *Career:* founder mem., The Fray 2002–. *Recordings include:* albums: How to Save a Life (Billboard Award for Digital Album of the Year 2006) 2005, The Fray 2009. *Honours:* Billboard Award for Digital Album Artist of the Year, for Digital Songs Artist of the Year 2006. *Address:* c/o Sony BMG, 550 Madison Avenue, New York, NY 10022, USA. *E-mail:* fraymanagement@gmail.com. *Website:* www.thefray.net.

KING, Jonathan, MA; British singer, music journalist and television presenter; b. 6 Dec. 1944, London; s. of the late Jimmy King and Ailsa King. *Education:* Univ. of Cambridge. *Career:* occasional recording artist 1965–;

talent spotter for Decca Records (discovered Genesis, produced their first album); producer, Rocky Horror Picture Show 1984, Kylie Minogue, Eric Felton; launched UK Records 1972; newspaper and magazine columnist, radio and TV presenter, including own show Entertainment USA (BBC) 1980s; Founder weekly magazine The Tip Sheet 1993–2002; organizer for A Song for Europe (UK Eurovision Song Contest qualification show) 1995. *Recordings include:* albums: Or Then Again 1965, King Size King 1982, The Butterfly That Stamped 1989, The Many Faces of Jonathan King 1993, Earth to King 2007. *Films:* Vile Pervert: The Musical 2008, Me Me Me 2011, The Pink Marble Egg 2013. *Publications include:* 65: My Life So Far 2009, Beware the Monkey Man (as Rex Kenny) 2010, Death Flies, Missing Girls and Brigitte Bardot (as Kenneth George King) 2013, 70 FFFY 2014. *Honours:* Ivor Novello Award for Record of the Year (for trans. of Una Paloma Blanca) 1975, British Phonographic Industry Man of the Year Award 1997. *E-mail:* kingofhits@aol .com. *Website:* www.kingofhits.co.uk.

KING, Kanya, MBE, BA; British music events organizer; *Chief Executive Officer, MOBO Holdings Limited;* b. 12 Feb. 1961, d. of Christian King and Mary King. *Education:* S Kilburn High School, Paddington Coll. and Goldsmiths Coll., London. *Career:* fmrly worked in public relations; researcher for Carlton TV London 1992–95; celebrity booker, BBC Radio 2 1996; f. The Music of Black Origin (MOBO) Awards 1997, CEO MOBO Holdings Ltd 1996–; Patron, Horniman Museum; Founder mem. Net Women. *Address:* The MOBO Organisation Ltd, 29-33 Berners Street, London, W1T 3AB, England (office). *Fax:* (20) 7419-1600 (office). *Website:* www.mobo.com (office).

KING, Mark; British singer and musician (bass); b. 20 Oct. 1958, Cowes, Isle of Wight; m. 1st Pia King; m. 2nd Ria King; four c. *Career:* Founder-mem. Level 42 1980–; solo artist. *Recordings include:* albums: with Level 42: Level 42 1980, Strategy/The Early Tapes 1982, The Pursuit of Accidents 1983, Standing in the Light 1983, True Colours 1984, A Physical Presence 1985, World Machine 1985, Running in the Family 1987, Staring at the Sun 1988, Guaranteed 1991, Forever Now 1994, Retroglide 2006; solo: Influences 1984, One Man 1999, Trash 1999, Live on the Isle of Wight 2000, Ohne Filter Extra 2002. *Honours:* Making Music magazine poll Best Bass Player 1987. *Address:* Level 42, PO Box 23, Sandown, PO36 0QL, England. *Website:* www.level42 .com.

KING, Michael Weston; British singer, songwriter and musician (guitar, harmonica); b. 11 Nov. 1961, Derbyshire, England; m. 1st Ann Carter 1987 (divorced 2000); three s. one d.; m. 2nd Lou Dalgleish 2002. *Career:* lead singer and songwriter, Fragile Friends 1982–87; solo artist 1988, 1999–; guitarist, Gary Hall and The Stormtroopers 1989–93; lead singer, songwriter, The Good Sons 1993–2002; Co-founder (with wife Lou Dalgleish) country music duo My Darling Clementine; UK, European and American tours; TV appearances, radio broadcasts; numerous contribs and articles for The Independent newspaper, Country Music Int., Maverick, Get Rhythm. *Recordings include:* albums: with Fragile Friends: For Play; with The Stormtroopers: Wide Open To The World; with The Good Sons: Singing the Glory Down 1995, The King's Highway 1996, Wines, Lines and Valentines 1997, Angels in The End 1998, Happiness 2001; with My Darling Clementine: How Do You Plead? 2012, The Reconciliation? 2013; solo: God Shaped Hole 1999, Live...In Dinky Town 2002, A Decent Man 2003, Absent Friends 2004, Love's a Cover 2006, A New Kind of Loneliness 2007, Crawling Through The USA 2008, I Didn't Raise My Boy to be a Soldier 2010, Forget Me Nots 2010. *Publications include:* Beautiful Lies... The Songs of Michael Weston King, Twah! Publishing Cookin', The Folk Handbook. *Current Management:* c/o James Walker, Brighthelmstone Promotions, 28 Foundry Street, Brighton, BN1 4AT, England. *E-mail:* brighthelmstonepromotions@gmail.com. *Website:* www .brighthelmstonepromotions.co.uk. *E-mail:* info@michaelwestonking.com. *Website:* www.michaelwestonking.com; www.mydarlingclementinemusic.co .uk.

KING, Morgana; American jazz singer and actress; b. (Maria Grazia Morgana Messina), 4 June 1930, Pleasantville, New York; m. 1st Tony Fruscella (died 1969); m. 2nd Willie Dennis (divorced, died 1965); one c. *Career:* trained as opera singer but switched to jazz, c. 1955; recording career began with release of For You For Me Forever More 1956; worked the New York club circuit, late 1950s–early 1960s. *Films:* The Godfather 1972, The Godfather: Part II 1974, Nunzio 1978, A Time to Remember 1987, A Brooklyn State of Mind 1997. *Television:* Deadly Intentions 1985, All My Children 1993. *Recordings include:* albums: For You, For Me, Forever More 1956, Morgana King Sings The Blues 1958, The Greatest Songs Ever Swung 1959, Folk Songs a la King 1960, Let Me Love You 1960, A Taste of Honey 1964, Everybody Loves Saturday Night 1965, It's A Quiet Thing 1965, Miss Morgana King 1965, The End Of A Love Affair 1965, The Winter Of My Discontent 1965, Wild Is Love 1966, Gemini Changes 1967, I Know How It Feels To Be Lonely 1968, Cuore Di Mama 1972, New Beginnings 1973, Stretchin' Out 1977, Everything Must Change 1978, Higher Ground 1979, Portraits 1983, Simply Eloquent 1986, I Just Can't Stop Loving You 1990, Another Time Another Space 1992, This Is Always 1992, Looking Through The Eyes Of Love 1998, Tender Moments 2000.

KING, Peter; British musician (alto saxophone), composer and arranger; b. 11 Aug. 1941, Kingston. *Education:* Berrylands Coll., Kingston Grammar School. *Career:* played opening night, Ronnie Scott's Club, London 1959; played with numerous artists, including Bud Powell, Red Rodney, The Ray

Charles Orchestra, Lalo Schifrin, Philly Joe Jones and Elvin Jones; has worked with Tony Bennett, James Brown, Lauren Bacall and Marlene Dietrich amongst others; performed as musician and actor in Sir Peter Hall's revival of the Julian Barry play, Lenny, starring Eddie Izzard 1999; also known for his recorded work as featured soloist and Musical Dir/Arranger for the Charlie Watts Quintet and Tentet; toured with Benny Golson and his tribute band Roots 2000; has taught jazz masterclasses, run workshops and given lectures internationally; composer of jazz and classical music; TV appearances in UK and Europe. *Compositions:* classical music: Zyklon (opera in two acts, Libretto by Julian Barr, premiered in recital form as part of CUNY's Science and the Arts Series) 2004, Jazz Mass for jazz quintet and full cathedral choir 2006 (first performed at Newcastle Cathedral 2007). *Dance:* Solo Sax solo (on stage with female solo dancer and Royal Ballet Co.). *Films:* Blue Ice, The Talented Mr. Ripley, played on soundtrack for Mike Figgis film, Time Code. *Recordings include:* New Beginning 1982, East 34th Street 1983, Hi-Fly 1984, Brother Bernard 1988, Tamburello (Best CD of the Year Prize, BT British Jazz Awards 1995) 1994, Speed Trap 1996, Lush Life 1999, Footprints 2003, Janus 2006. *Radio:* Janus (commissioned by BBC Radio 3 for own jazz quartet and Lyric String Quartet); appearances in UK, USA and Europe. *Publications include:* Flying High: A Jazz Life and Beyond (autobiography) 2010; article in Science magazine on saxophone sound production 2009. *Honours:* Hon. DLitt (Roehampton Univ.) 2008; BBC Musician of the Year Award 2005, Life Time Achievement Award, Moscow Summer Festival 2005. *Address:* 15 Oakhill Place, London, SW15 2QN, England. *Website:* www .peterkingjazz.com.

KING, Stove; British musician (bass guitar); b. 8 Jan. 1974, Ellesmere Port, Merseyside. *Education:* Wrexham Art Coll. *Career:* Founder-mem. Grey Lantern, later renamed Mansun 1995–2003. *Recordings include:* albums: Attack Of The Grey Lantern 1996, Desperate Icons 1997, Legacy 1998, Six 1998, Little Kix 2000, Electric Man 2000, Kleptomania 2004, Legacy: The Best of Mansun 2006.

KING BRITT, (The Force, Oba Funke); American producer, remixer and DJ; b. (King James Britt), Philadelphia, Pa. *Career:* started as on-tour DJ for Philadelphia rap outfit Digable Planets; Co-founder, Ovum Records (with Josh Wink); formed Sylk 130 collective; debut album released on Ruffhouse/ Columbia 1998; residency at The End club, London, Sylk City, Philadelphia; Founder and CEO, Five Six Media production and record co.; collaborations with Josh Wink, Vikter Duplaix, Martin Fry, Alison Moyet; remixed: 4Hero, Donna Lewis, Tori Amos, Jazzanova, Macy Gray. *Recordings include:* albums: When The Funk Hits The Fan (with Sylk 130) 1998, Re-Members Only (with Sylk 130) 2001, Adventures in Lo-Fi 2002, Cosmo Afrique 2003, The Noca Dream Sequence 2006, King Britt Presents the Cosmic Lounge 2007, This Is King Britt 2007, Deep And Sexy 4 2009, The Intricate Beauty 2010; with Saturn Never Sleeps: Yesterday's Machine 2011; with Data Garden: The Bee and The Stamen 2012. *Website:* www.kingbritt.net.

KINGSBURY, Tim; Canadian musician (bass guitar, guitar) and singer. *Career:* fmr bass guitarist touring with band, Wolf Parade; fmr mem., New International Standards; founder mem., Arcade Fire 2003–. *Recordings include:* albums: Funeral 2004, Neon Bible (Juno Award for Alternative Album of the Year 2008) 2007, The Suburbs (Grammy Award for Album of the Year 2011) 2010, Reflektor (Juno Awards for Album of the Year and Alternative Album of the Year 2014) 2013. *Address:* Quest Management, 1D–36 Warple Way, London, W3 0DY, England. *Telephone:* (20) 8749-0088. *Fax:* (20) 8749-0080. *E-mail:* info@quest-management.com. *Website:* www .quest-management.com; www.arcadefire.com.

KINGSTON, Sean; Jamaican/American rapper; b. (Kisean Anderson), 3 Feb. 1990, Kingston. *Career:* moved to Florida, USA, aged six; began career performing in South Florida clubs; professional solo artist 2007–. *Recordings include:* albums: Sean Kingston 2007, Tomorrow 2009, Back 2 Life 2013. *Honours:* MOBO Award for Best Reggae Act 2007, Teen Choice Awards R&B (for Beautiful Girls) 2007. *Website:* www.seankingston.com.

KINNAIRD, Alison Margaret, MBE, MA; British musician (Scottish harp, clarsach); b. 30 April 1949, Edinburgh, Scotland; m. Robin Morton 1976; one s. one d. *Education:* Univ. of Edinburgh, studied Scottish harp with Jean Campbell. *Career:* freelance musician 1971–; concerts in Edinburgh, London, New York, San Francisco, Hawaii, Tokyo, Berlin; Presenter, The Music Show (Channel 4) 1995; mem. Scottish Arts Council Crafts Cttee 1993–96, Award Panel for Creative Scotland Award 2003–04; Life mem. The Clarsach Soc. *Recordings include:* The Harp Key 1978, The Harper's Gallery 1980, The Harper's Land 1983, Music In Trust I and II 1988, The Quiet Tradition 1989, Mactalla 1994; features on Gun Sireadh Gun Iarraidh, Christine Primrose 2001, The Silver String 2004. *Publications include:* The Harp Key, The Small Harp Tutor, Tree of Strings (with Keith Sanger). *Honours:* MTA Music Award 1983, Living Tradition Award 1995, Creative Scotland Award 2002, Glass Sellers Award 2004. *Current Management:* c/o Robin Morton, Shillinghill, Temple, Midlothian, EH23 4SH, Scotland. *Telephone:* (1875) 830328. *E-mail:* robin@templerecords.co.uk. *Website:* www.templerecords.co.uk; www .alisonkinnaird.com.

KINNEY, Sean; American musician (drums); b. 27 May 1966, Seattle, Washington. *Career:* mem. Alice in Chains; numerous tours and TV appearances including MTV Unplugged. *Recordings:* albums: Facelift 1990, Dirt 1992, Sap 1992, Jar of Flies 1994, Alice in Chains 1995, I Stay Away 1995, Unplugged 1996, Nothing Safe 1999, Music Bank 1999, Live 2000, Greatest

Hits 2001, Black Gives Way to Blue 2009. *Current Management:* Velvet Hammer Management, 9014 Melrose Avenue, West Hollywood, CA 90069, USA. *Telephone:* (310) 657-6161. *Fax:* (310) 657-0310. *Website:* www.velvethammer.net; www.aliceinchains.com.

KINSEY, Tony; British composer and musician (drums, piano); b. 11 Oct. 1927; m. Patricia Kinsey; one d. *Education:* Jazz Coll., New York with Bill West, Cozy Cole, Columbia Coll., Chicago with Bill Russo. *Career:* professional musician from age 18; joined John Dankworth, as drummer with Dankworth 7; drummer 1960s–70s, for visiting artists, including Oscar Peterson, Ella Fitzgerald, Lena Horne, Sarah Vaughan, Billie Holiday, Ben Webster, Clark Terry; Musical Dir, That's Life, BBC TV for three years; Founder, The Tony Kinsey Quintet. *Compositions include:* for films: Souvenir On The Bridge; for TV: That's Life, BBC, Castle of Adventure, TVS, The John Bird Show, BBC, The Londoners, BBC; A Tribute To Her Majesty, Colour, Four Seasons, Life At The Limit, Two's Company; over 100 commercials; classical: Pictures, Three Suites for string quartet, River Thames Suite, Alice Through the Looking Glass. *Honours:* NME Award for Small Group (Modern Jazz). *E-mail:* tony@tony-kinsey.co.uk. *Website:* www.tony-kinsey.co.uk.

KIPPER; British producer, arranger, writer and musician (guitar, keyboards); b. (Marc Eldridge), 19 March 1962, Frimley, Surrey. *Education:* jazz and classical training. *Career:* mem. One Nation; toured with: Jeff Beck, The Temptations, Ruby Turner, Curtis Stigers, Richard Marx; MD with Beijing Spring; three tours as guitarist for Gary Numan; mem. PRS. *Recordings include:* with One Nation: Strong Enough 1990, Big Life Big Tears 1991, Machine and Soul 1992; with Gary Numan: Machine and Soul 1992, Sacrifice 1994; with Beijing Spring: Guitars; with David Essex: Back 2 Back; with Sting: Brand New Day (Grammy Award for Best Pop Album) 2000, All This Time 2001, Sacred Love 2003, Songs from the Labyrinth 2006, 25 Years 2011; with Chris Botti: Night Sessions 2001, Let's Fall in Love 2008; also recorded with Curtis Stigers, Desperate Measures, Merlin, Titanic Town, Yasmin Levy, Esther Alexander, Clay Aikens. *Publications include:* The Complete Singer 1995. *E-mail:* web@kippermusic.co.uk. *Website:* www.kippermusic.co.uk.

KIRK, Nicholas Kenneth, BSc, FRMS; British musician (New Orleans jazz banjo) and electronics engineer; *Proprietor, P&P Electronics;* b. 27 Dec. 1945, Bradford, West Yorks., England; s. of Kenneth Earnest Kirk and Kathleen Brooksbank; m. Ruby Doreen Champion (divorced). *Education:* Univs of Wales, Southampton and Bradford. *Career:* appearances on radio and TV in Wales with Clive Evans' River City Stompers 1966–67; appeared at Keswick Jazz Festival, Bude Jazz Festival, Marsden Jazz Festival, and at jazz clubs and pubs in Yorks., Wales and S of England, with the Dennis Browne Creole Band; appeared at 100 Club in London with New Era Jazz Band; Propr, P&P Electronics; mem. Musicians' Union, New Orleans Wiggle Jazz Band; Fellow, Royal Microscopical Soc. *Composition:* Clouds. *Recordings:* with the Dennis Browne Creole Band: Float Me Down The River, City of a Million Dreams; CD with the Dennis Armstrong Jazz Band: Live at the Ritz; with the New Orleans Wiggle: Over the Waves; solo: In the Shadows of Clouds, Clouds from Yorkshire. *Television:* Disc a Dawn (BBC Wales) 1969. *Publications:* My Recollections 1990; author of British patent for apparatus for recording and replaying music (The Musical Arranger and Sequencer, sold to Waddingtons, now called Compute-a-Tune and Wizard). *Address:* 36 Kilpin Hill Lane, Staincliffe, nr Dewsbury, West Yorks., WF13 4BH, England. *Telephone:* (1924) 402931. *E-mail:* nickbanjokirk@tiscali.co.uk.

KIRKE, Simon Frederick; British musician (drums, guitar, piano) and songwriter; b. (Simon Frederick St George Kirke), 28 July 1949, London; s. of Vivian Kirke and Olive Kirke; m. Lorraine Dellal 1982; one s. three d. *Education:* Bishops Castle Grammar School. *Career:* mem. Black Cat Bones 1968; Founder-mem. Free 1968–73; Founder-mem. Bad Company 1973–83; mem. Musicians' Union. *Recordings include:* albums: with Champion Jack Dupree: When You Feel the Feelin' You Was Feeling 1968; with Free: Tons of Sobs 1968, Free 1969, Fire and Water 1970, Highway 1971, Live 1971, Free At Last 1972, Heartbreaker 1973, The Free Story 1973, Best of Free 1991, Walk in My Shadow: An Introduction to Free 1998; with Amazing Blondel: Blonde, 1973, Mulgrave Street 1974; with Bad Company: Bad Company 1974, Straight Shooter 1975, Run With the Pack 1976, Burning Sky 1977, Desolation Angels 1979, Rough Diamonds 1982, 10 From 6 1985, Fame and Fortune 1986, Dangerous Age 1988, Holy Water 1990, Here Comes Trouble 1992, Company of Strangers 1995, Stories Told & Untold 1996, Extended Versions 2011, Dangerous Age/Holy Water 2013; with John Wetton: Caught in the Crossfire 1980; with Wildlife: Wildlife 1983; with Mick Ralphs: Take This 1983; with Jim Colpody: Let the Thunder Die; also recorded with Jim Diamond, Snowy White, Bon Jovi, Ringo Starr; John Wetton; solo: Seven Rays of Hope 2005, Filling the Void 2011. *E-mail:* info@simonkirke.com. *Website:* www.officialsimonkirke.com.

KIRKOROV, Philip; Russian singer; b. (Filipp Bedrosovich Kirkorov), 30 April 1967, Bulgaria; m. Alla Pugacheva 1995 (divorced 2005); two c. *Career:* solo artist; UN Goodwill Amb. 2001. *Plays:* Chicago (Russian production) 2002–03. *Recordings include:* albums: Ti Ti Ti 1991, Takoy-syakoy 1992, Ya ne Rafael 1994, Primadonna 1995, Skazhi solncu: Da! 1995, Sinbad-Morehad 1996, Luchshee, lyubimoe I tol'ko dlya Vas 1998, Oy mama, shika dam! 1998, S lyubov'yu k edinstvennoy 1998, Kilimandzharo 2000, Chelofiliya 2000, Vchera, segodnya, zavtra (koncert v Kremle) 2001, Megamix 2002, Vlyublenniy I bezumno odinokiy 2002, Zhestokaya lyubov' 2002, Ti poverish? 2002, Ya za tebya umru 2002, Neznakomka 2003, Dueti 2003, Magico Amor 2004, Se

Thelo San Trelos (with Sakis Rouvas) 2005, For You 2007, Drugoy - 2 Edn 2011. *Television:* Starye pesni o glavnom 1996, Starye pesni o glavnom 2 1997, Starye pesni o glavnom 3 1998, Vechera na khutore bliz Dikanki 2001. *Honours:* Order of Francesc Skarina (Belarus) 2012; World Music Award for Best-Selling Russian Performer 1996, 1999, Distinguished Artist of the Russian Fed. 2001, ZD Awards for Singer of the Year 2011, Muz-TV for Artist of the Decade 2012. *Telephone:* (499) 146-55-55. *E-mail:* office@kirkorov.ru. *Website:* www.kirkorov.ru.

KIRKPATRICK, Christopher Allan, AA; American singer; b. 17 Oct. 1971, Clarion, Pa; m. Karly Skladany 2013. *Education:* Valencia Coll., Rollins Coll. *Career:* mem., *NSYNC vocal quintet 1995–2002; signed to BMG Ariola Munich 1997; first headline US tour 1998; appointed spokesman for Child Watch of North America; Owner FuMan Skeeto clothing firm, Nigels 11; f. Chris Kirkpatrick Foundation. *Recordings include:* albums: *NSYNC 1998, Home For The Holidays 1998, The Winter Album 1998, No Strings Attached 2000, Celebrity 2001. *Honours:* American Music Award, Favorite Pop/Rock Band, Duo or Group 2002. *Website:* www.chriskirkpatrickfoundation.com.

KIRKPATRICK, John Michael; British musician (melodeon, button accordion, anglo concertina); b. 8 Aug. 1947, Chiswick, London; m. Sue Harris (divorced); four s. *Career:* joined Hammersmith Morris Men in their second week 1959; took up the melodeon, button accordion and the anglo concertina whilst with them; mem. Albion Country Band, Magic Lantern, The Richard Thompson Band, Umps and Dumps, Steeleye Span, Brass Monkey, Trans-Europe Diatonique, Band of Hope; played with numerous ceilidh bands and made many albums with Sue Harris; collaborations include: Leon Rosselson, Roy Bailey, Martin Carthy, Ashley Hutchings, Sandy Denny, Ralph McTell, Gerry Rafferty; Founder, The Shropshire Bedlams morris team 1975; performed with The Albion Band for Nat. Theatre productions of Lark Rise and Candleford; also worked with The Victoria Theatre (later The New Victoria Theatre), North Staffordshire, The Orchard Theatre Touring Co., Devon; as songwriter, composer, choreographer and musical dir, has contributed to over sixty plays in the theatre and on radio. *Recordings include:* albums: Jump At The Sun 1972, The Compleat Dancing Master (with Ashley Hutchings) 1974, Plain Capers 1976, Going Spare 1978, Three in a Row (The English Melodeon) 1983, Blue Balloon 1987, Sheepskins 1988, Earthling 1994, Welcome to Hell (John Kirkpatrick Band) 1997, One Man and His Box 1998, Mazurka Berserker 2001, Orlando's Return 2003, Garrick's Delight 2003, The Duck Race 2004, Carolling and Crumpets 2006, Make no Bones 2007, The Dance of the Demon Daffodils 2009, God Speed the Plough 2011, Every Mortal Place 2012, The Complete John Kirkpatrick Band 2013; with Sue Harris: The Rose of Britain's Isle 1974, Among the many attractions at the show will be a Really High Class Band 1976, Shreds and Patches 1977, Facing the Music 1980, Stolen Ground 1989; with Junkera, Tesi and Kirkpatrick: Trans-Europe Diatonic 1993; with Brass Monkey: Brass Monkey 1983, See How it Runs 1986, Sound and Rumour 1998, Going and Staying 2001, Flame of Fire 2004; with Steeleye Span: Storm Force Ten, Live at Last 1978; with Albion Band: No Roses 1971, Battle of The Field 1976, Larkrise to Candleford 1979, BBC Sessions 1998; with Band of Hope: Rhythm and Reds 1994; features on: Richard Thompson albums: Henry The Human Fly 1972, Hand of Kindness 1983, Amnesia 1988, Rumour and Sigh 1991, Sweet Talker 1991, Mirror Blue 1994; Richard and Linda Thompson albums: I Want to See the Bright Lights Tonight 1974, Hokey Pokey 1974, First Light 1978, Sunnyvista 1979, The End of the Rainbow 2000; Martin Carthy albums: Because it's There 1979, Out of The Cut 1982, Right of Passage 1988; Leon Rosselson albums: That's Not The Way It's Got To Be (Roy Bailey and Leon Rosselson) 1975, Bringing in News from Nowhere 1986, I Didn't Mean It 1988; other featured appearances: Young Hunting, Tony Rose 1970, Roy Bailey 1971, Morris On 1972, Sandy, Sandy Denny 1972, Rave On 1974, Amaranth, Shirley Collins 1976, Julie Covington 1978, Slide Away the Screen, Ralph McTell 1979, Night Owl, Gerry Rafferty 1979, Still Pause, Maggie Holland 1983, Leaves from a Tree, Roy Bailey 1988, The Tenement Year, Pere Ubu 1988, Jali Roll, Dembo Konte and Kausu Kuyateh 1991, Reve De Siam, Dan Ar Braz 1992, Fanafody, Tarika Sammy 1992, Till The Grass O'Grew The Corn 1997, Wassail! 1997, The Garden of Love, Frankie Armstrong 1999. *Honours:* BBC Radio 2 Folk Award for Musician of the Year 2010. *Current Management:* c/o Sue Webster Music, 62 Windsor Avenue, St Johns, Worcester, WR2 5NB, England. *E-mail:* suewebstermusic@gmail.com. *Website:* johnkirkpatrick.co.uk.

KIRYA, Maurice; Ugandan singer, songwriter, musician (guitar, piano) and producer; b. 1984. *Career:* started singing professionally aged 15; fmr mem. u4ria; songwriter for Brenda Nanyonjo; runs monthly showcase The Maurice Kirya Experience; collaborations with numerous artists including AY, Moussa Diallo, Cecile Verny Quartet, Beniwe, First Love, Pragmo, Kaz Kasozi, Suzzanna Owiyo, Pauline Zongo, Thug Squad, Bataka Underground, Benon, Vamposs, Kawesa. *Recordings:* album: Misubbaawa 2009. *Honours:* Pearl of African Music Award for Best R&B Artist 2007, Radio France Int. Discovery Music Award 2010. *Website:* www.mauricekirya.org; www.myspace.com/mauricekirya.

KITARO; Japanese musician; b. (Takahashi Masanori), 4 Feb. 1953, Toyohashi. *Career:* self-taught electric guitar player; began music career during school studies; founding mem. rock band The Far East Family Band – 1976; abandoned rock for new age music and released first solo album Astral Voyage 1978; composed musical score for TV documentary series Silk Road 1980–85; signed with Geffen Records 1986; first live tour of N America leading to sales of two million albums in US 1987; featured as key artist and composer in Japan's Millennium celebration event; composed soundtrack for Chinese drama The Soong Sisters 2002; performs annual televised concerts from mountain location of his Japanese home and studio base in Nagano Pref. *Albums include:* Astral Voyage 1978, Millennia 1978, Ten Kai Astral Trip 1978, Full Moon Story 1979, Ki 1979, Oasis 1979, Silk Road Suite (Vols 1–4) 1980–83, Ten Huang 1980, Queen of Millennia 1982, India 1983, Tenjiku 1983, Tenku 1986, Silver Cloud 1986, Toward the West 1986, The Light of the Spirit 1987, Kojiki (Japan Gold Disc for Fusion Instrumental 1991) 1990, Kitaro Live in America 1991, Dream 1992, Mandala 1994, Peace on Earth 1996, Cirque Ingenieux 1998, Heaven and Earth 1997, Gaia 1998, Thinking of You (Grammy Award for Best New Age Album 2001) 1999, Ancient 2001, An Ancient Journey 2002, Mizuniinorite 2002, The Soong Sisters 2002, Sacred Journey of Ku-Kai 2003, Shikoku 88 Kasho 2004, Spiritual Garden 2006, Impressions Of The West Lake 2009, Final Call 2013. *Address:* c/o Domo Music Group Inc., 11340 West Olympic Boulevard, Suite 270, Los Angeles, CA 90064, USA (office). *Telephone:* (310) 966-4414 (office). *E-mail:* info@ domomusicgroup.com (office). *Website:* www.domomusicgroup.com/kitaro/ index.php (office).

KITCHEN, Elizabeth Jane, RNCM, PRNCM; British composer, arranger and musician (drums); b. 1 April 1959, Rochdale, England. *Education:* studied with James Blades, Gilbert Webster. *Career:* writes, arranges for television, including Playdays, Monster Cafe, Roundabout Stop, Dot Stop; worked on films and TV, including Life and Loves of a She Devil, King of The Ghetto; played with the Blues Band; in Blood Brothers; works with Chickenshed company; freelanced with the Hallé Orchestra, Royal Liverpool Philharmonic Orchestra, Northern Ballet, Opera North; written many theatre shows for Young Vic and Battersea Arts Centre, London; mem. Performing Right Soc., Mechanical-Copyright Protection Soc.

KITSCHIN, Fiona; Australian musician (bass guitar). *Career:* mem. The Drones 2001–. *Recordings include:* albums: Here Come the Lies 2002, Wait Long By the River & The Bodies of Your Enemies Will Float By (Australian Music Prize) 2005, The Miller's Daughter 2006, Gala Mill 2006, Havilah 2008, I See Seaweed 2013. *E-mail:* stacey@thedrones.com.au. *Website:* www .thedrones.com.au.

KJAER, Torben Edvard; Danish jazz musician (piano), composer, arranger and conductor; b. 26 Oct. 1946, Gentofte. *Education:* Inst. of Music and Science, Univ. of Copenhagen, studied with George Russell; Copenhagen Music Conservatory. *Career:* professional musician 1973–; pianist with Dexter Gordon, Dizzy Gillespie, Ben Webster, Clark Terry, Al Grey, Roy Eldridge, Red Mitchell, Milton Batiste, Rasheema; founder, own jazz quartet; Conductor, Danish Radio Jazz Group 1973–79, Danish Radio Light Orchestra 1979–88, Danish Radio Big Band, Royal Orchestra; orchestra leader, TV shows 1986–92; composer/arranger for numerous groups including Tritonius (Danish Gospel Choir) and Copenhagen Music Ensemble; arrangements include Candide (chamber version), Faust, Royal Theatre, Copenhagen; arranger, musicals including Guys and Dolls, My Fair Lady, Chicago, Kiss Me Kate; also music for TV, radio, film, theatre, cabaret, commercials. *Compositions include:* Mass of Peace 1976, Christmas Oratory 1981, Concerto Grosso 1983, David and Batseba 1985, Passion of Peace 2003, House of The Seven Virtues (opera) 2008. *Recordings include:* Whalesongs 1983, Jazz In Danish 1988, Tower At The End of The World 1988, Stolen Moments, Rasheema 1995. *Honours:* Danish State Fund of Art Awards, Best Popular Composer 1979. *Address:* Østerbrogade 54A 5, 2100 Copenhagen, Denmark (home). *Telephone:* 40-52-22-19 (home); 40-52-22-19 (mobile). *E-mail:* tk@ torbenkjaer.com. *Website:* www.torbenkjaer.com.

KJELLEMYR, Bjorn; Norwegian musician (acoustic and electric bass guitars); b. 4 Dec. 1950, Bamble; m. Mette Havrewold; two s. *Education:* Oslo Academy of Music. *Career:* mem. Erik Balke/Vidar Johansen quartet 1974–77, Christian Reim/Kalle Neumann quartet 1975–76, Per Høglend Qunitet 1976–77, Jon Balke Trio 1976–78, Busker Smoul 1977–78, Magni Wentzel Quintet 1978–79, Dag Arnesen trio 1978–80, Søbstad/Arnesen quartet 1979–80, Jon Eberson quartet 1980–81, Søyr 1980–83, Radio Big Band 1980–90, Thorgeir Stubø Quintet 1981–82, Lotus 1981–83, Susanne Fuhr quartet 1981–88, Knut Risnaes quartet 1982–85, Jazz Pønk ensemble 1982–85, Frode Alnaes/Nils Petter Molvaer quartet 1983–84, Dag Arnesen trio 1983–86, Terje Repdal and The Chase 1984–91, Sidsel Endresen/ Jon Eberson group 1985–90, Morten Halle/Jon Eberson quartet 1987–90, Stash 1989–92, Dag Arnesen Quintet 1990, Frode Gjerstad ensemble 1991–, Odd Riisnaes quartet 1995–, 1300 Oslo 1996–. *Recordings include:* appearances on albums: Amalgamation 1984, Bratislava Jazz Days 1985, Chaser 1985, Blue 1986, Etterlatte Sanger 1987, Bakchand Smash 1988, Blow 1989, Aurora Borealis 1989, Enough of that Jazz 1994, Electronique Noire 1997, Crosslands 1998, Domen 1998, Alene Huemme 2000, Dawn 2001, Bubbling 2001, Another Breeze 2003. *Honours:* Jazz Musician of the Year, Norway 1991, Buddy Award 1995.

KLAKEGG, Rune; Norwegian musician (piano) and composer; b. 19 April 1955, Skien; m. 2nd Gudrun Klakegg 2004; five c. *Education:* Univ. of Oslo. *Career:* freelance jazz musician, composer since late 1970s; appeared with groups Cutting Edge, Out To Lunch, Soyr, Rune Klakegg Trio; currently Leader of Scheen Jazzorkester; arranger, band leader, Van Morrison, Vossajazz 1988; mem. TONO, NOPA. *Recordings include:* Cutting Edge: CE 1982, Our Man In Paradise 1984, Duesenberg 1986, Out To Lunch: OTL 1988, Kullboksrytter 1995, Soyr: Vectors 1988, Bussene lengter hjem 1994, Med

Kjott og Kjarlighet 1997, R K Trio: Anaerobics 1992, Fuzzy Logic: FL 1996, Kraft Streets 1999, About to Kiss ein prince 2005, Sundslegen, herja og naken 2006, Lonely Woman 2010, Romantic Notions 2012, Scheen Jazz Orchestra 2009, Good Faith, Improper Coat 2013, Lush Life: 'ordinary things…' 2014; with Jan Olav Renvaag: Jazz på norsk 2015. *Honours:* NOPA Best Composition of the Year for Pamplemousse 1995. *Address:* Saudegata vest 39, 3716 Skien, Norway. *Telephone:* 95-15-74-25. *E-mail:* klakeggr@gmail.com. *Website:* www.runeklakegg.no.

KLASS, Myleene; British singer, pianist and television presenter; b. 6 April 1978, Norfolk; m. Graham Quinn 2011 (divorced 2013); two d. *Education:* Guildhall School of Music and Drama, Royal Acad. of Music. *Career:* made stage debut in Miss Saigon, London; winning participant on ITV series Popstars with band Hear'Say 2001; solo artist 2002–; owner of several fashion businesses and brands; Amb. for Save The Children 2012, Nat. Foundation for Youth Music. *Recordings include:* albums: with Hear'Say: Popstars 2001, Everybody 2001; solo: Moving On 2003, Myleene's Music for Romance 2007, Myleene's Music for Mothers 2008. *Radio:* presenter: Classic FM Weekend Breakfast Show, Friday Night is Music Night (BBC Radio 2) 2008. *Television:* presenter: cd:uk (ITV) 2005, Heaven and Earth Show (BBC 1) 2006, The Proms (BBC 1) 2006, The All Star Talent Show (Channel 5) 2006, The People's Quiz (BBC 1) 2007, The One Show (BBC 1) 2007, The Screening Room (CNN International) 2007, Saturday Night Divas (ITV1) 2007, The Classical Brits (ITV1) 2008–, Popstar to Operastar 2010–11, Loose Women (ITV) 2014–. *Film:* Igor (voice) 2008. *Publication:* My Bump and Me 2008. *Website:* www .myleeneklass.co.uk.

KLAŠTERKA, Željen; Croatian musician (guitar), composer, professor of classical guitar and television producer; *Head of Music Department, Croatian Radio and Television (HRT);* b. 24 Jan. 1958, Zagreb; m. Neda Urlicic 1995; one s. one d. *Education:* univ. grad.; 14 years, Faculty of Music, Univ. of Zagreb. *Career:* lead guitarist with Notturno, Ritmo Loco, Patchwork; studio musician; classical guitar duet with Milivoj Majdak, Stanko Selak Big Band (orchestra of Music Acad.); music ed., major TV show in Croatia: 7. NOC, Bravo; Head of Music Dept, Croatian Radio and TV (Hrvatska Radio-televizija—HRT); music producer and composer for many Croatian singers, including Tony Cetinski, Massimo Savić, Đani Stipaničev, Renata Sabljak, Antonija Šola, Žanamari Lalić, Danijela Pintarić, Davor Radolfi, Željko Kruslin-Kruska, Ivan Mikulić, Gelato Sisters, Luka Bulić, Mirko Svenda-Ziga, Vlatka Pokos, Miroslav Stanić-Jimmy; mem. HGU (Croatian Musicians' Union), HDS ZAMP (Croatian Composers' Soc., Collecting Soc.). *Recordings:* albums: with Ritmo Loco: Canto Latino; with Renata Sabljak: Hajde; with Patchwork: video of live concert of Zagreb Bienale 1994, Nek' Ti Bude Ljubav Sva (Love Forever And For All) in Eurovision Song Contest 1994, five video spots; more than 150 songs (pop and ethno-world music, music and jingles) for several shows on Croatian TV. *Honours:* First Prize, Croatian Nat. Song Contest (for Eurovision) 1994. *Address:* Davor 3, 10000 Zagreb, Croatia (home). *Telephone:* 99-6348012 (mobile) (office); 98-389087 (mobile) (office). *E-mail:* zeljen.klasterka@hrt.hr (home).

KLEIN, Guillermo; Argentine pianist, band leader and composer; b. 1969, Buenos Aires. *Education:* Berklee Coll. of Music, USA. *Career:* formed 17-piece Guillermo Klein Big Band, New York 1993; formed Los Guachos 1994; settled in Barcelona, Spain 2002; mem. jazz faculty, Musikene, Centro Superior de Música del País Vasco, San Sebastián. *Compositions:* Solar Return Suite for wind ensemble 2006. *Recordings:* albums: with Los Guachos: Los Guachos Vol 2 1999, Los Guachos III 2002, Los Filitros 2008; solo: Una Nave 2005, El Minotauro 2007, Domador de Huellas 2010. *Address:* c/o Sunnyside Communications, 348 West 38th Street, Suite 12B, New York, NY 10018, USA (office). *E-mail:* francois@sunnysiderecords.com (office). *Website:* www.sunnysiderecords.com (office).

KLEIN, Thomas, (SØLYST); German musician (drums) and designer; b. 24 Aug. 1968, Düsseldorf; m. Petra Bosch. *Career:* mem. electro-pop group, Kreidler 1994–. *Recordings include:* albums with Kreidler: Weekend 1996, Appearance and the Park 1998, Circles 2000, Kreidler 2000, Chicks on Speed/ Kreidler Sessions 2001, Eve Future 2002, Eve Future Recall 2006, Mosaik 2014 2009, Tank 2011, Den 2012; solo album (as Sølyst): Lead 2013. *Current Management:* c/o Bureau B, Stahltwiete 10, 22761 Hamburg, Germany. *Telephone:* (40) 88166662. *Fax:* (40) 88166622. *E-mail:* info@bureau-b.com. *Website:* www.bureau-b.com; www.ikreidler.de.

KLEINENBERG, Sander; Dutch DJ, producer and remixer; b. 29 Dec. 1971, The Hague. *Career:* DJ 1987–, with residencies in The Roxy, Amsterdam, Montréal, Pin-Up, Ibiza, Pacha, Ibiza, Arc, New York; est. own labels, Deal Recordings 1994, Little Mountain 2003–; remixed numerous artists, including Oliver Lieb, Junkie XL, Destiny's Child, Lamya, Justin Timberlake. *Recordings include:* album: Sander Kleinenberg Presents Melk 1998, Global Underground: NuBreed 4 2000, Next - Progressive 2001, Essential Mix 2002, Everybody mixed by Sander Kleinenberg 2003, This is Everybody Too! 2004, This is Everybody On Tour 2006, This is Sander Kleinenberg 2007, This is Sander Kleinenberg 2 2009, 5K 2010. *Honours:* European DJ of the Year (Winter Music Conference) 2006. *Current Management:* c/o MAK Management, Klingler GmbH Hötzendorfplatz 4 A, 6060 Hall, Austria. *E-mail:* anna@ mak-management.com. *Website:* www.mak-management.com; www .sanderkleinenberg.com.

KLEMMER, John; American musician (saxophones, flutes, clarinets, kalimba, piano, keyboards, synthesizers, percussion) and songwriter; b. 7

July 1956, Chicago. *Education:* Interlochen National Music Camp; Private studies, age 5 to mid 20s; Studied, classical saxophone, flute, clarinet; Jazz improvisation with Joseph Daly; Studied composition, arranging, conducting; Private studies, orchestration, film scoring with Albert Harris. *Career:* Tours with: George Benson; Herbie Hancock; Miles Davis; Weather Report; others; With Don Ellis Orchestra, USA, Europe, England; State Department tour of 11 countries of French West Africa with Oliver Nelson Septet, Impulse Artists on tour; Live Performances, concerts, clubs include: Shellys Manne Hole, The Light House, all major jazz and rock clubs, concert venues, USA; Carnegie Hall; Newport Jazz Festival; Antibes Jazz Festival; Montreux Jazz Festival; Television and radio include: Voice of America shows; Midnight Special; Rock Concert; Merv Griffin Show; At One With; Dial M for Music; Live at Tanglewood PBS Special; Kitty Hawk, featuring John Klemmer solo saxophone PBS Special; WWTW presents John Klemmer; Started own record company, Touch Records, 1999; mem, BMI; ASCAP; NARAS. *Compositions include:* Walk In Love, recorded by Manhattan Transfer, Acker Bilk; The Old Man's Tear; Last Summer's Spell, recorded by Don Ellis; Lost In Love, recorded by Freda Payne, 1975; The Beauty of Her Soul; Touch. *Recordings include:* Blow on Gold, 1969; Touch, 1975; Barefoot Ballet, 1976; Cry, solo saxophone, 1980; Hush, solo saxophone, 1981; Life, solo saxophone, 1981; Making Love Vol. 1, 1998. *Publications:* The Jazz Styles of John Klemmer. *Honours:* Down Beat Magazine International Jazz Critics Poll, Talent Deserving Wider Recognition, 1973. *Website:* www.johnklemmer.com.

KLUGH, Earl; American musician (guitar) and composer; b. 16 Sept. 1953, Detroit, Mich. *Career:* mem. George Benson Group, Chick Corea's Return To Forever; collaborations with numerous artists including George Duke, Stanley Clarke, Al Jarreau, Bob James, Chet Atkins, Patti Austin, Ravi Coltrane; performs as soloist, with his quartet, his electric band, his 'Little Big Band' and with renowned symphony orchestras; composer and songwriter on recordings by Aretha Franklin, Jamie Foxx, Roberta Flack, Mary J. Blige, Kenny Loggins, Al Jarreau. *Film performances:* How to Beat The High Cost of a Kind Living 1982, Marvin and Tige 1984, Just Between Friends 1985, Cool 1992. *Recordings include:* albums: solo: Earl Klugh 1976, Living Inside Your Love 1976, Finger Painting 1977, Magic in Your Eyes 1978, Heart String 1979, Dream Come True 1980, Late Night Guitar 1980, Crazy for You 1981, Low Ride 1983, Wishful Thinking 1984, Night Songs 1985, Soda Fountain Shuffle 1985, Life Stories (Edison Award 1987) 1986, Whispers and Promises 1989, Solo Guitar 1989, Trio Volume One 1991, Midnight in San Juan 1991, Trio Volume Two: Sounds and Visions 1993, Move 1994, Sudden Burst of Energy 1996, The Journey 1997, Peculiar Situation 1999, Naked Guitar 2005, The Spice of Life (Billboard and iTunes Bestselling Jazz Album) 2008, HandPicked 2013; with George Benson: Collaboration 1987; with Bob James: One On One (Grammy Award for Best Pop Instrumental Performance 1980) 1979, Two of a Kind 1982, Cool 1992; with Al Jarreau: This Time; with Jimmy Buffett: One Particular Harbour; with Jennifer Holliday: Say You Love Me; with McCoy Tyner: Inner Voices; with Flora Purim: Stories To Tell. *Honours:* Pittsburgh Post-Gazette Best Jazz Concert 2008. *Address:* PO Box 191766, Atlanta, GA 31119, USA. *E-mail:* info@earlklugh.com. *Website:* www.earlklugh.com.

K'NAAN; Somali/Canadian rapper, musician (keyboards, guitar) and poet; b. (Keinan Abdi Warsame), 1 Feb. 1978, Mogadishu, Somalia; s. of Marian Mohamed; two s. *Career:* left Somalia during civil war 1991, joined father in New York, USA, later moved to and settled in Rexdale, Ont., Canada; developed his skills as a rapper at numerous 'open mic' events; gave spoken word performance for UNHCR 1999; contributed to Youssou N'Dour's Building Bridges album 2001; performed at several UN events and the Montreal Jazz Festival; collaborated on recordings with Ba Cissoko, M-1; toured USA and Europe as support act for Damian Marley 2006; tours of Canada, Europe, UK, Australia 2007. *Recordings:* The Dusty Foot Philosopher (Juno Award for Rap Recording of the Year 2006) 2005, The Dusty Foot On The Road 2007, Troubadour 2009, The Messengers (with J. Period) 2010, Country, God or the Girl 2012. *Honours:* Rap Recording of the Year, Juno Awards for Artist of the Year 2010, for Songwriter of the Year 2010, Single of the Year 2011, winner, newcomer category, BBC Radio 3 World Music Awards 2007, MOBO African Artist of the Year Award 2010. *Address:* c/o A&M/Octone Records, 113 University Place, New York, NY 10003, USA (office). *Website:* www.knaanmusic.com.

KNAUER, Wolfram, PhD; German musicologist and institute director; *Director, Jazzinstitut Darmstadt*; b. 28 Jan. 1958, Kiel; s. of Prof. Dr Norbert Knauer and Gerlinde Knauer (née Theiner). *Education:* Kiel Univ. *Career:* Dir Jazzinstitut Darmstadt; teaching appointments at several major univs in Germany; Louis Armstrong Prof. of Jazz Studies, Columbia Univ., New York 2008; speaker at int. confs in Europe, USA; mem. Hessische Jazzakademie 1991–99, Int. Soc. for Jazz Research 1980–, Int. Advisory Bd Center for Black Music Research, Chicago 1999–, Int. Voting Panel Ertegun Jazz Hall of Fame at Jazz at Lincoln Center, New York 2003–10, Music Advisory Bd Goethe-Inst., Germany 2004–12, Bd Landesmusikrat Hessen 2006–09; mem. Editorial Bd, Univ. of Michigan Press, Ann Arbor jazz book series 2002–, Les Cahiers du Jazz, France 2004–08, Jazz Perspectives 2005–; mem. Bd Deutscher Musikrat 2007–10. *Publications include:* Zwischen Bebop und Free Jazz 1990, Jazz und Komposition 1992, Jazz in Europa 1994, Jazz in Deutschland 1996, Jazz und Sprache, Sprache und Jazz 1998, Duke Ellington und die Folgen 2000, Jazz und Gesellschaft: Sozialgeschichtliche Aspekte des Jazz 2002, improvisieren... 2004, Jazz Goes Pop Goes Jazz: Der Jazz und sein gespaltenes Verhältnis zur Popularmusik 2006, Begegnungen: The World Meets Jazz 2008, Louis Armstrong 2010, Albert Mangelsdorff: Tension/Spannung 2010, Jazz Schule Medien 2012, Jazz Debates/Jazzdebatten 2014, Charlie Parker 2014; trans from English into German, scholarly essays, many articles, interviews, concert, book and record reviews. *Honours:* Hessischer Jazzpreis 2002. *Address:* Jazzinstitut Darmstadt, Bessunger Strasse 88D, 64285 Darmstadt, Germany (office). *Telephone:* (6151) 963700 (office). *Fax:* (6151) 963744 (office). *E-mail:* knauer@jazzinstitut.de (office). *Website:* www.jazzinstitut.de (office).

KNAUS, Ulita; German jazz singer; b. 8 July 1969. *Education:* pvt. tuition with Nanni Byl, Music Conservatory, Hilversum, Netherlands. *Career:* lead singer with Latin big band Havana; concerts and recordings with Rolf Zielke's Blow up; launched solo career while based in Hamburg; recordings and concerts with Stefano di Battista, Herb Geller, Udo Lindenberg, Orange Blue, Fettes Brot, Joja Wendt, Nils Gessinger, Kenny Wheeler, HR-Big Band, JazzHaus Orchestra Hamburg, Avalon Casino Kings, Don Friedman, Roy Hargrove; fmr Lecturer, Musikhochschule Hamburg, Deutsches Schauspielhaus, Hamburg and Thalia Theater. *Recordings include:* with Havana: Rio Ara 1994, Colores del Amor 1998; with JazzHaus Orchestra Hamburg: JazzHaus Orchestra Hamburg 1999, Cosmopolitans 2003; with Avalon Casino Kings: Jumpin' 2002; solo: Cuisa 2002, So Lost Like Peace 2004, Sea Journey 2005, It's the City 2007, Tambor 2010, The Moon on My Doorstep 2014. *Honours:* Hamburg Jazz Award 2009. *E-mail:* info@ulitaknaus.com. *Website:* www.ulitaknaus.com.

KNIGHT, Beverley, MBE; British soul singer and songwriter; b. (Beverley Ann Smith), 22 March 1972, Wolverhampton. *Career:* collab. with artists including Take That, Prince, Carlos Santana, Chris Martin, Stevie Wonder; f. own label Hurricane Records 2009. *Television:* Just the Two of Us (BBC) 2001. *Radio:* as host: Beverley's Gospel Nights (BBC, four series). *Recordings include:* The B-Funk 1995, Prodigal Sista (Best Album, MOBO Awards 1999) 1998, Who I Am 2003, Affirmation 2004, Music City Soul 2007, 100% 2009. *Honours:* Hon. DMus (Wolverhampton); three MOBO awards, Lifetime Achievement Award, Urban Music Awards 2004. *Current Management:* c/o James Windle, DWL, 2nd Floor, 53 Goodge Street, London, W1T 1TG, England. *Telephone:* (20) 7436-5529. *Fax:* (20) 7436-5529. *E-mail:* james@dwl.uk.net. *Website:* www.dwl.uk.net; www.beverleyknight.com.

KNIGHT, Gavin; British musician (drums, percussion), writer, producer, programmer and arranger and remixer; b. 17 April 1966, Southampton, Hants., England. *Education:* studied music in Southampton with Antony Christmas, Albert Cooper. *Career:* drummer with The Shamen 1991–95; extensive world tours, including Europe, Scandinavia, USA, Australia and the Far East; headlined Glastonbury Festival; numerous TV appearances worldwide; drummer, Maroontown 1993–94; European shows and album recording; Urban Hype, live UK shows 1992; The Good Strawberries, live UK shows and TV 1994; played for Marc Almond show at the Royal Albert Hall, London, TV appearances and album recording 1995–98; with Victoria Wilson-James, European shows and TV appearances 1996–; Russian shows with Jam and Spoon 1997; drummer with Bang Bang Lulu 2006–; remixed, programmed various projects, including The Shamen; co-writer and Prod., single release, Urban Hype 1992; rhythm programming for album and single, Angelique Kidjo; assisted the Shamen on theme tune, The O-Zone, TV programme 1995; worked with P. J. Proby 1996; co-composer, TV programme for Meridian Television 1996; mem. dance production team, Universal State of Mind 1996; rhythm programming for commercial Release, Viva! 1996; mem. Musicians' Union, PAMRA. *Recordings:* co-writer The Feeling, with Urban Hype 1992, Inca – Syncronous 1994, The Ticket Men – Tunnel Vision 1994, Universal State of Mind – All Because of You 1997, Bang Bang Lulu – Ska Wars 2008, Bang Bang Lulu – Albert Road 2009.

KNIGHT, Gladys Maria; American singer; b. 28 May 1944, Atlanta, Ga; d. of Merald Knight and Elizabeth Knight (née Woods); m. 2nd Barry Hankerson 1974 (divorced 1979); one s. and two c. (from previous marriage). *Career:* tours with Morris Brown Choir 1950–53; formed Gladys Knight and The Pips 1953–89; mem. Lloyd Terry Jazz Ltd 1959–61; numerous tours and live appearances, TV and film appearances; solo artist 1989–. *Film and TV appearances:* Pipe Dreams 1976, Charlie & Co. (series) 1985, Desperado (TV film) 1987, An Enemy Among Us (TV film) 1987, Twenty Bucks 1993, Hollywood Homicide 2003, Unbeatable Harold 2005. *Recordings include:* albums: Letter Full of Tears 1961, Gladys Knight and The Pips 1964, Everybody Needs Love 1967, Feelin' Bluesy 1968, Silk & Soul 1968, Nitty Gritty 1969, All in a Knight's Work 1970, If I Were Your Woman 1971, Standing Ovation 1971, All I Need Is Time 1973, Imagination 1973, Help Me Make It Through The Night 1973, It Hurt Me So Bad 1973, Neither One Of Us 1973, Claudine (OST) 1974, I Feel A Song 1974, Knight Time 1974, 2nd Anniversary 1975, A Little Knight Music 1975, Bless This House 1976, Pipe Dreams 1976, Love Is Always On Your Mind 1977, Still Together 1977, Miss Gladys Knight 1978, The One And Only 1978, Gladys Knight 1979, Memories 1979, About Love 1980, Midnight Train To Georgia 1980, That Special Time of Year 1980, Teen Anguish 1981, Touch 1980, Visions 1983, Life 1985, All Our Love 1988, Christmas Album 1989, Good Woman 1991, Just For You 1994, Many Different Roads 1998, At Last 2000, Christmas Celebrations 2002, The Best Thing That Ever Happened To Me 2003, One Voice 2005, Before Me 2006, Where My Heart Belongs 2014. *Honours:* four Grammy Awards, American Music Awards 1984, 1988. *Current Management:* c/o WME, 9601 Wilshire Blvd, Beverly Hills, CA 90210, USA. *Telephone:* (310) 285-9000. *Fax:* (310) 285-9010. *Website:* www.wma.com; www.gladysknight.com.

KNIGHT, Holly; American songwriter, producer and musician (keyboards, piano); b. 24 Sept. 1956, New York, NY. *Education:* studied classical piano. *Career:* mem. Spider, Device; has written many songs and songs for film; mem. The American Soc. of Composers, Authors and Publrs (ASCAP), Songwriters' Guild. *Compositions include:* for Pat Benatar: Love Is A Battlefield (Grammy Award for Best Rock Vocal), Invincible, Sometimes The Good Guys Finish First; for Tina Turner: Better Be Good To Me (Grammy Award for Best Rock Vocal), One of The Living (Grammy Award for Best Rock Vocal), The Best, Ask Me How I Feel, Love Thing, Be Tender With Me Baby, You Can't Stop Me Loving You; for Heart: Never, All Eyes, There's The Girl, Tall Dark Handsome Stranger, I Love You, for Rod Stewart: Love Touch; for Aerosmith: Ragdoll; for John Waite: Change; for Patti Smyth: The Warrior; for Bon Jovi: Stick To Your Gunsi; for Cheap Trick: Space; for the Divinyls: Pleasure and Pain; for Hall and Oates: Soul Love; for Chaka Khan: Baby Me; for Lou Gramm: Just Between You and Me; for Bonnie Tyler: Hide Your Heart; for Kim Wilde: Turn It On; for Lita Ford: Stiletto; for Kiss: Hide Your Heart; for Aaron Neville: Try A Little Harder; for Patsy Kensit: It's Over When The Phone Stops Ringing; for Agnetha Falkstog: Wrap Your Arms Around Me; for Dusty Springfield: Time Waits For No-One; for Jimmy Barnes: Between Two Fires; for Ozzy Osbourne: Slow Burn; tracks for Spider, Device. *Recordings include:* albums: with Spider: Spider, Between The Lines; with Device: 22B3; solo: Holly Knight 1989, Heart Don't Fail me Now. *Current Management:* c/o Alia Fahlborg, Nettwerk Producer Management, 6525 Sunset Blvd, Eighth Floor, Hollywood, CA 90028, USA. *Telephone:* (323) 301-4200. *Fax:* (323) 301-4195. *E-mail:* alia@producermgmt.com. *Website:* www.nettwerk.com/producer; www.hollyknight.com.

KNIGHT, Larry (Fuzzy); American musician (bass), singer, songwriter, record producer and arranger; *President and CEO, Blowin' Smoke Records and Productions;* b. 21 Oct. 1944, St Louis, MO; s. of Frank and Flora Weisberg; m. Aleda Trabue 1974 (divorced 2003), one d. *Education:* St Louis Conservatory of Music, Missouri, Washington Univ., St Louis. *Career:* played with Albert King, Chuck Berry, Little Milton, Ike Turner 1964–69; Tim Rose, Delaney-Bonnie and Friends, Peter Kaukenon 1969–73; Albert Collins, Spirit 1971–80; The Urge 1985; bandleader, bassist and lead vocalist, Blowin' Smoke, R&B band 1994–2014; tours world-wide over 12 years; appeared on many US rock shows, also Old Grey Whistle Test, England; Rock Palace, Germany; performed at 40th anniversary of Woodstock, Golden Gate Park, San Francisco 2010; recorded over 26 albums; 1 live Spirit album produced by Miles Copeland, Rainbow Theatre, London; writes for Southland Blues magazine 2011–; owner, Pres. and CEO, Blowin' Smoke Productions 1995–, Pres., CEO and owner, Sky King Music Productions and Band 2010–; currently Pres. and CEO, Hailing Frequency Film/Video Productions; mem. NAMM, VSDA, Musicians' Union, ASCAP. *Recordings include:* Tim Rose, Delaney-Bonnie and Friends, 9 Spirit albums, Peter Kaukenon, Albert Collins, The Urge, Albert Lee, Kaptain Kopter and The Famous Twirlybirds, Randy California, Deborah Gibson; with Blowin' Smoke Rhythm and Blues Band: Beyond The Blues Horizon 1999, An Homage to Otis Redding 2012; with Spirit: Two Sides of the Rainbow 2012, with Sky King: Morose Tales from the Left Coast 2012. *Address:* 7438 Shoshone Avenue, Van Nuys, CA 91406-2340, USA. *Telephone:* (818) 881-9888. *Fax:* (818) 881-0555. *E-mail:* blowinsmokeband@ktb.net (office); fuzzy@ktb.net (home). *Website:* www.blowinsmokeband.com; www.myspace.com/larryfuzzyknight; www.skykingrockband.com.

KNIGHT, Suge; American record company executive; b. (Marion Hugh Knight Jr), 19 April 1965, Compton, Los Angeles, Calif.; s. of Maxine Knight and Marion Knight; m. Sheritha; one d. *Education:* Univ. of Nevada, Las Vegas. *Career:* fmr concert promoter; Co-founder and CEO Death Row Records 1992–2008; signed artists, including Dr Dre, Snoop Doggy Dogg, Tupac Shakur, Kurupt; arrested and charged with murder, attempted murder and hit-and-run 2015.

KNIGHTS, Olly; British singer and musician (guitar). *Career:* Founder-mem. Turin Brakes 1999–. *Recordings include:* albums: The Door (EP) 1999, The State of Things (EP) 2000, The Optimist 2001, Ether Song 2003, JackInABox 2005, Dark on Fire 2007, Outbursts 2010, The Optimist Live 2011, We Were Here 2013. *Current Management:* c/o Reservoir Media Management, Reverb House, Bennett Street, London, W4 2AH, England. *Website:* www.turinbrakes.com; www.ollyknights.etchshop.co.uk.

KNOPFLER, David; British musician (guitar); b. 27 Dec. 1952, Glasgow, Scotland; s. of Erwin Knopfler and Louisa Mary; brother of Mark Knopfler. *Education:* Bristol Polytechnic (now Univ. of Bristol). *Career:* fmr social worker; Founder-mem. Dire Straits 1977–80; solo artist 1980–. *Recordings include:* albums: with Dire Straits: Dire Straits 1978, Communiqué 1979; solo: Release 1983, Behind the Lines 1985, Cut the Wire 1987, Lips Against the Steel 1988, Giver 1994, Small Mercies 1994, Ship of Dreams 2005, Songs for the Siren 2006, Anthology: 1983–2008 2009; with Harry Bogdanovs: Acoustic 2011, Made in Germany (Live in Erfurt) 2013. *Publications include:* Bluffers Guide to the Rock Music Business 1996, Blood Stones and Rhythmic Beasts 2005. *Website:* www.knopfler.com.

KNOPFLER, Mark, OBE, BA; British musician (guitar), singer, songwriter and record producer; b. 12 Aug. 1949, Glasgow, Scotland; s. of late Erwin Knopfler and of Louisa Knopfler; brother of David Knopfler; m. Lourdes Salomone 1983; two s. *Education:* Leeds Univ. *Career:* fmr music journalist Yorkshire Evening Post; fmr mem. bands, Brewer's Droop, Cafe Racers; f.

mem., Dire Straits 1977–88, 1991–95; group toured world-wide; first-ever CD single, Brothers In Arms 1985; formed own ad hoc band, Notting Hillbillies 1989; solo artist 1984–, guest on numerous albums by other artists. *Film music composition:* Local Hero 1983, Cal 1984, Comfort and Joy 1984, Alchemy Live (television) 1984, The Princess Bride 1987, Last Exit to Brooklyn 1989, Tishina 1991, Wag the Dog 1998, Hooves of Fire (television) 1999, Metroland 1999, A Shot at Glory 2001, songs for numerous other films. *Recordings include:* albums: with Dire Straits: Dire Straits 1978, Communiqué 1979, Making Movies 1980, Love Over Gold 1982, Extendedanceplay 1983, Alchemy: Dire Straits Live 1984, Brothers In Arms (BPI Award for Best British Album 1987) 1985, Money For Nothing 1988, On Every Street 1991, On The Night 1993, Live at the BBC 1995, Sultans of Swing 1998; solo: Comfort and Joy 1984, Neck and Neck (with Chet Atkins) 1990, Golden Heart 1996, Sailing To Philadelphia 2000, The Ragpicker's Dream 2002, Shangri-La 2004, All the Roadrunning (with Emmylou Harris) 2006, Kill to get Crimson 2007, Get Lucky 2009, Privateering 2012, Tracker 2015; with Notting Hillbillies: Missing… Presumed Having a Good Time 1990. *Honours:* Hon. DMus (Newcastle) 1993, (Leeds) 1995, (Sunderland) 2007; BPI/BRIT Awards for Best British Group 1983, 1986, Ivor Novello Awards for Outstanding British Lyric 1983, Best Film Theme 1984, Outstanding Contribution to British Music 1989, Lifetime Achievement Award 2012, Nordoff-Robbins Silver Clef Award for Outstanding Services to British Music 1985, Grammy Awards for Best Rock Vocal Group 1986, for Best Country Performance (with Chet Atkins) 1986, 1991, for Best Surround Sound Album (for Brothers in Arms) 2006, Edison Award 2003, Music Producers Guild Award for Best Studio (British Grove Studios) 2009. *Current Management:* c/o Paul Crockford Management, Latimer House, 272 Latimer Road, London W10 6QY, England. *E-mail:* help@markknopfler.com. *Website:* www.markknopfler.com.

KNORR, Marianne; Danish folk singer, musician (guitar) and actress; b. 3 Feb. 1949, Copenhagen; m. Preben Friis 1989; two s. *Education:* Danish State Theatre School, studied voice with Jens Chr Schmidt. *Career:* appeared at Rimfaxe Theatre, Skagen Festival, Roskilde Festival, in radio concerts and on TV; concerts in Denmark, Norway, Sweden, Iceland and Greenland; worked in Rimfaxe Theatre 1974–82; mem. Danish Actors' Asscn, Danish Soc. of Jazz and Beat Authors. *Recordings include:* albums: Valmuer Og Jernbeton, Sa Laenge Fuglene Flyver, Sange Af Brecht, Sommerregn, Sangskatten: Samlede Værker, Vol. 2 (1980-1989) 2007, Jeg gir' dig min morgen 2000, I disse tider 2012. *E-mail:* knorr@mail.dk. *Website:* www.marianneknorr.dk.

KNOWLES, Beyoncé (see BEYONCÉ)

KNOX; British singer and musician (guitar, keyboards); b. (Ian Milroy Carnochan), 4 Sept. 1945, London. *Education:* Watford Grammar School. *Career:* lead singer, songwriter, The Vibrators 1976–2012; solo artist 1983; singer, songwriter, The Fallen Angels 1984–; mem. Urban Dogs; mem. PRS, MCPS. *Recordings include:* albums: with The Vibrators: Pure Mania 1977, V2 1978, Guilty 1982, Alaska 127 1984, Fifth Amendment 1985, Recharged 1988, Meltdown 1988, Vicious Circle 1989, Volume 10 1990, Power of Money 1993, Hunting for You 1994, French Lessons with Correction 1997, Buzzin' 1999, Noise Boys 2000, Energize 2002, Punk Rock Rarities 2003, Under the Radar 2009; solo: Plutonoum Express 1983, Thieving of The Well 2014; with The Fallen Angels: Fallen Angels 1984, In Loving Memory 1986, Wheel of Fortune 1989; with Urban Dogs: Urban Dogs 1983, No Pedigree 1985, Wipeout Beach 1998; with Die Toten Hosen: Baby, Baby; Troops of Tomorrow. *Publication:* The Vibrators: 21 Years Of Punk Maniat 1999. *E-mail:* knoximc@hotmail.com. *Website:* www.knox76.com.

KNOX, (Alexander John) Keith, BSc; British record company executive, record producer, music journalist and fmr electronic engineer; *Executive Producer, Silkheart Records;* b. 27 Nov. 1933, Belper, Derbyshire, England; s. of Norman Frederick Knox and Lillias Mary Knox (née Aitken); m. 1st Rita Knox (died 1998); m. 2nd Ingrid Knox; one s. one step-s. one step-d. *Education:* Univ. of Southampton, Brighton Coll. of Advanced Tech. *Career:* served with RAF 1955–57; electronic engineer, EMI 1957–59, Brush Clevite Company, Redifon Ltd 1962–64, Amplivox Ltd 1964–65, Transitron Electronic, Switzerland 1965–67, Transitron Electronic, Sweden 1967–72; freelance sound/record producer for various recording cos, including Caprice, Storyville, WEA-Metronome, Sonet (Universal Folk Sounds series) 1971–85; Co-founder and Exec. Producer, with Lars Olof Gustavsson, own jazz label, Silkheart Records, Sweden 1986–; artists on own label include Steve Lacy, Charles Gayle, David S. Ware, Dennis Gonzalez, Matthew Shipp, Booker T. Williams, Assif Tsahar, Jim Hobbs, Dennis Charles, Joel Futterman, Alvin Fielder, Rob Brown; Man. for music groups Sevda 1971–74, Music for Xaba 1972–73; marketing and liaison engineer, Sonab, Sweden 1972–74; ad agency copywriter, Andersson and Lembke (Sweden) 1974–75; support engineer, Royal Inst. of Tech. (KTH), Stockholm 1975–98. *Publications:* Jazz Amour Affair (The Lars Gullin Story) 1986; contrib. to jazz magazines and underground press, including Jazz Monthly, Jazz Forum (Int. Jazz Fed. magazine), Jazznews. *Address:* Silkheart Records, c/o Four Seasons VC AB, Sveavägen 17, 14th Hoov, 111 67 Stockholm, Sweden (office). *Telephone:* (8) 145420 (office). *Fax:* (8) 216995 (office). *E-mail:* info@silkheart.se (office); knoxkeithjazz@gmail.com (home). *Website:* www.silkheart.se (office).

KNUDSEN, Hans; Danish musician (piano), singer and songwriter; b. 7 Sept. 1950, Copenhagen. *Education:* Coll. of Education. *Career:* fmr teacher of music and biology 1975–80; professional musician 1980–; worked and toured with leading Danish jazz and blues artists 1980–83; mem. Lillian Boutté's band 1983–90; leader of own group, Hans Knudsen Jumpband 1990–. *Recordings include:* with Lillian Boutté: Music is My Life 1984; Let them Talk 1986; with Hans Knudsen Jumpband: So Long John 1995; Jump in Focus 1997, Caldonia 2008. *Honours:* Danish Blues Artist of the Year 2014. *Address:* Solnavej 84, 2860 Søborg, Copenhagen, Denmark. *Telephone:* 39-69-65-36. *E-mail:* hans.knudsen@youmail.dk. *Website:* www.henriksimonsen.dk.

KNUDSEN, Kenneth; Danish composer and musician (keyboard); b. 28 Sept. 1946, Copenhagen; m. Christine Heger 1987; one s. *Education:* architecture, Royal Danish Acad. of Fine Arts. *Career:* mem. of jazz/fusion groups Coronarias Dans 1969, Secret Oyster 1976, Anima 1979, Heart To Heart Trio 1986, Bombay Hotel 1988; special project with Jan Akkerman and Jon Hiseman 1982; numerous concerts and TV in Scandinavia, Europe, UK, Hong Kong and Japan; mem. Bd The Nordic Watercolour Museum, Skärhavn, Sweden; mem. Danish Composers' Soc. *Compositions:* film scores, ballet music for New Danish Dance Theatre and The Royal Danish Ballet, works for string quartet, cello, piano, choir and electronics, prizewinning advertisements for Carlsberg Breweries. *Recordings:* I Me Him 1989, Compacked 1989, Sounds and Silence 1994, Music For Eyes 1998, Light and Metal 1998, Black Diamond, Miniatures 2002, End of Silence 2009, May Be 2011; appeared on more than 100 records including Garland, Svend Asmussen and L. Subramaniam, It Could Happen To You, Jan Akkerman, Entrance, Heart To Heart, with Palle Mikkelborg, Pictures and Heart To Heart with Niels Henning Orsted Pedersen, Aura, Miles Davis, Anima, Kenneth Knudsen. *Honours:* Jazz Musician of the Year 1973, Niels Matthiasen Memorial Grant 1987, Danish Art Foundation Grant 1992–94, Lifelong Grant from the Danish Art Foundation 1998. *Address:* PO Box 51, 2840 Holte, Denmark (office). *E-mail:* mail@kenneth-knudsen.dk (office). *Website:* www.kenneth-knudsen .dk.

KNUDSEN, Marius Dahl, DMus; Danish musician (guitars, didgeridoo); b. 30 June 1947, Grinsted; m. Lise Jelsbech Knudsen 1979; two s. one d. *Career:* mem., Ostjydsk Musikforsyning 27 years; Danish show-band with numerous appearances on nat. TV and radio. *Stage appearances:* Rocky Horror Show (Arhus Teater), Return to the Forbidden Planet (Arhus Teater), Folk Og Rovere (Vejle Teater), Elverhoj (Dansk Spildtid), Annie Get Your Gun (Det Danske Teater/Odense Teater). *Recordings include:* Det Beskidte Dusin, Århus Syncopaterne. *Honours:* Arets Revykomponist 1996; hon. mem. Danish Musicians' Union. *Address:* Visbjerg Hegn 133, 8320 Marslet, Denmark. *E-mail:* mariusdahl@tele2adsl.dk.

KNUDSEN, Ole; Danish music teacher, multi-instrumentalist, singer and composer; b. 15 Sept. 1943, Koge. *Education:* Teacher Training Coll. *Career:* jazz drummer 1965–70; lead singer, guitarist, pianist, percussionist of jazz-rock group, Fujara 1970–76; leader, Arbejdersanggruppen 1976–82; freelance jazz-drummer, teacher 1982–; mem. Danish Jazz Musicians' Organization, Danish Jazz Beat Folk Music Authors. *Recordings include:* Fujara 1973, Nattevandring 1977, Jens Borges Fodselsdag (children's songs) 1979, Hvor Laenge Skal Vi Vente 1980, Det Handler Om Kaerlighed (solo) 1992. *Honours:* Danish Org. of Labour Culture Prize (with Arbejdersanggruppen) 1981.

KNUTSEN, Cecilie; Norwegian singer; b. 9 May 1967, Trondheim. *Education:* Conservatory of Music, Oslo, Conservatory of Music, Århus, Denmark, trained under Dr. William Riley. *Career:* solo artist; toured with Deepak Chopra, Louise Hay, Wayne Dyer and Stuart Wilde; mem. Gramart. *Recordings include:* Voice of the Feminine Spirit 1994, Violet 19 1996, Inner Harmony 1999, Let There Be Peace On Earth 2001, Best of Cecilia 2003, The Healing Voice 2006, Amazing Grace 2007. *E-mail:* arne@ceciliasings.com. *Website:* www.ceciliasings.com.

KOBZON, Iosif Davydovich, DPhil; Russian singer and politician; b. 11 Sept. 1937, Chasov Yar, Ukraine; m. Nelly Kobzon; one s. one d. *Education:* Moscow Gnessin Pedagogical Inst. of Music. *Career:* army service 1956–59, soloist, Ensemble of Dance and Song of Caucasian Mil. command 1957–59; soloist, All-Union Radio and TV Co. 1959–62; soloist, Moskonzert 1962–89; Artistic Dir and Chair. Vocal and Variety Show Faculty Gnessin Inst. (now Acad.) of Music 1989–, Prof. 1992; soloist and Artistic Dir Concert Co. Moskva; retd from concert activity 1997; Pres. Jt Stock Co. Moscovit 1990–97; USSR People's Deputy 1989–92; mem. State Duma (Parl.) 1997–98 (suspended membership), 1999–2003, re-elected (Yedinaya Rossiya faction) 2003–, Deputy Chair. Comm. on Culture 1999–2003, Chair. 2005–07. *Honours:* Order for Merit for the Fatherland 3rd Class 1997, 2nd Class 2002, 1st Class 2012, Order of Courage 2002, Order of Friendship 2003; People's Artist of USSR, Russia, Ukraine, Checheno-Ingushetia and Dagestan Autonomous Repub.; USSR State Prize 1984. *Address:* State Duma, 103265 Moscow, Okhotny ryad 1, Russia (office). *Telephone:* (495) 292-17-53 (office). *Fax:* (495) 292-73-85 (office). *Website:* www.iosifkobzon.ru (home).

KOENIG, Ezra Michael; American rock singer, songwriter and musician (guitar, piano); b. 8 April 1984, New York, NY; s. of Bobby Bass and Robin Koenig. *Education:* Glen Ridge High School, Columbia Univ. *Career:* fmr school teacher; Founder-mem. Vampire Weekend 2006–, signed to XL Recordings 2007; mem. other bands including Dirty Projectors, L'Homme Run, The Sophisticuffs; numerous festival appearances and tours. *Recordings:* albums with Vampire Weekend: Vampire Weekend 2008, Contra 2010, Modern Vampires of the City (Grammy Award for Best Alternative Music Album 2014) 2013. *Honours:* with Vampire Weekend: NME Award for Best New American Alternative/Indie Band 2008, Q Magazine Awards for Best Video (for Giving Up the Gun) 2011, for Best Act in the World Today 2013.

Current Management: c/o Ian Montone, Monotone, Inc., 820 Seward Street, Hollywood, CA 90038, USA. *Telephone:* (323) 308-1818. *Address:* c/o Kris Chen, XL Recordings, 304 Hudson Street, 7th Floor, New York, NY 10013, USA (office). *Telephone:* (212) 995-5882 (office). *E-mail:* krischen@ xlrecordings.com (office); vampireweekend@gmail.com (home). *Website:* www .xlrecordings.com (office); www.vampireweekend.com.

KOIKSON, Liisi; Estonian jazz singer and songwriter; b. 4 June 1983. *Education:* Kilingi Nõmme Secondary School, Georg Ots Music School. *Career:* debut TV appearance at age of eight. *Recordings include:* albums: The Gemini Diaries 2002, Liisi Koikson 2003, Maailma Kaunimad Jõululaulud 2003, Väike järv 2005, Väikeste asjade võlu 2007, Ettepoole 2010, Liisi Koikson ja Vaikne Esmaspäev 2012. *E-mail:* liisi@liisikoikson.ee. *Website:* www .liisikoikson.ee.

KOITÉ, Habib; Malian singer, musician (acoustic guitar, flute) and songwriter; b. 1958, Thiès, Senegal. *Education:* National Inst. of Arts, Bamako. *Career:* born to a griot family; music teacher at Nat. Inst. of Arts; sang and played on Toumani Diabate's Shake the World 1991; formed band, Bamada 1988–; became a regular on the European festival scene; toured USA with the Voices of Mali tour 2000. *Recordings include:* albums: Muso Ko 1994, Ma Ya 1998, Baro 2001, Fôly! 2003, Habib Koité & Bamada 2005, Afriki 2007, Acoustic Africa in Concert 2011, Brothers in Bamako 2012, Soô 2014. *Honours:* First Prize, Voxpole Festival in France 1991, Radio France Int. Discoveries Prize 1994, Kora Award for Best Artist – West Africa 2002. *Website:* www.habibkoite.com.

KOIVISTOINEN, Eero; Finnish composer and musician (tenor, soprano saxophone); b. 13 Jan. 1946. *Education:* Sibelius Acad., , Berklee Coll. of Music, USA. *Career:* leader of own quartet; performed at int. jazz competition, Montreux, Switzerland 1969, Newport Festival, USA; Founder, composer, arranger for UMO (New Music Orchestra) 1975–90, Artistic Dir 1996–98; leader, Dialog 1995–; est. PRO Records label 1983. *Compositions include:* Ballet, Mother Earth, 1979; Suite, Ultima Thule, 1981. *Recordings include:* 20 solo albums, later albums include Pictures in Three Colours (with John Scofield and Jack DeJohnette), Ultima Thule, UMO 1983, Dialog 1995, Timbila 2002, Suomalainen (Johanna Iivanainen) 2003, The Five Corners Quintet: Chasin' the Jazz Gone By (with Mark Murphy) 2005, Lennosta kii!! (with Johanna Iivanainen) 2007. *Honours:* first recipient, Yrjö (Georgie) Award, Finnish Jazz Fed. 1967, Best Jazz Ensemble, Montreux Festival 1969, Best Arranger, Nordring radio competition, Jersey 1981. *Current Management:* Lapinlahdenk 21 A 11, 00180 Helsinki, Finland. *E-mail:* eero .koivistoinen@kolumbus.fi. *Website:* www.eerokoivistoinen.com.

KOKKAS, Vassilios; Greek/German composer; b. 30 Sept. 1965, Athens, Greece. *Education:* Hochschule der Kunste, Berlin, Contemporary Conservatory of Athens. *Career:* Guest Lecturer, Hochschule der Kunste, Berlin 1997–98, Inst. for Research in Music and Acoustics, Athens 1999, Catholic Univ. of São Paulo 2004, Athens School of Fine Arts 2005; mem. German Soc. for Musical Rights, DEGEM. *Compositions include:* Four little pieces for flute and piano 1993, Narrations Tautologiques for 12 Saxophones 1994, Waiting for News 1994, Fowl, Fish, Beast was flown, was swum, was walked 1995, Aptontes Iptantai for piano, marimba, tomtoms and 5 bowed cymbals 1996, Agapi ston Kremno 1997, Bravo Juliett 1998, Amour Fou 1998, Astarte 2000. *Publications:* Navigation In Metamorphosis: Navigable Music 1996. *Honours:* Michelis Foundation grant 2001, 2002. *Address:* Trivonianou 69, 116 36 Athens, Greece (office). *Telephone:* (210) 7569133 (office). *Fax:* (210) 7569136 (office). *E-mail:* vassilios@kokkas.com (home).

KOLLOWRAT, Peter, MA; Austrian musician (guitar); b. 5 March 1967, Vienna; m. Birgit Kollowrat, 29 Oct. 1994. *Education:* Salzburger Musik-Schulwerk, Mozarteum, Salzburg, studied guitar with J. Clerch and Eliot Fisk, masterclasses with F. Bungartem, L. Brouwer, A. Pierri and S. Isbin. *Career:* soloist with Halleiner Chamber Orchestra; currently Teacher, Musikum Salzburg. *Recordings include:* Jason und die Argonauten!!: Live in Riff-Cafe 1996, CD with Eliot Fisk and Friends 1999. *Honours:* Premio di Musica Cesare Grigoletto 1997; Medal of the President of Italy 1997. *Address:* Salzburg Musikum, Black Street 49, 5020 Salzburg (office); Trautmannstrasse 6a 5020 Salzburg, Austria (home). *Telephone:* (662) 825-349 (home). *E-mail:* peter.kollowrat@musikum-salzburg.at (office). *Website:* www .musikum-salzburg.at (office); www.peterkollowrat.com.

KOMPPA, Kari Juhani; Finnish composer and musician (tenor saxophone); b. 5 Jan. 1939, Helsinki. *Career:* jazz session saxophonist, band leader, TV conductor/arranger, YLE/TV2, Tampere; founder, leader, writer, mem. Break Big Band, played Pori Festival 1970, 1972, 1982, 1984; writer for Radio (YLE) Jazz Orchestra, the UMO; founder, leader, composer, mem. Tampere Jazz Orchestra 1981–84; represented Finnish Broadcasting Co. (YLE), throughout Europe, including Nordring Festival, Belgium; teacher, big band leader, Tampere Conservatory of Music; European Broadcasting Union (EBU) Jazz Concert, Pori; saxophonist, writer for Ippe Kätkä Band 1980s; teacher, Sibelius Acad. Jazz Dept, Helsinki; withdrew from active public performance and teaching late 1980s, but still occasionally writing for UMO Jazz Orchestra and Radio (YLE); formed Zone (asscn of Finnish jazz composers) 1991–; jazz and electronic compositions for Zone; mem. Teosto RY, Elvis RY, Zone RY; Retrospective Concert of 1975–2007 works by Tampere Big Band and The Chamber Orchestra Prospero conducted by Juha Untala, Tampere Feb. 2008 (recorded for Alba); retrospective concert of 1972–2011 works by Pori Big Band and Pori Sinfonietta conducted by Juha Untala, Pori May 2011.

Recordings include: albums: Makumoka, Ippe Kätkä Band, Nordjazz Big 5, Umo Jazz Orchestra 1997, Zone: First Definition 1999, To The Stars: Music by Kari Komppa, Tampere Big Band and The Chamber Orchestra Prospero 2010; as arranger: Joy, Music of John Coltrane by Dave Liebman 1992, Utu by Eero Koivistoinen 2002. *Honours:* Winner (with Break Big Band), Finnish Big Band Championship 1973, Winner, EBU orchestral composition contest, Tethys 1981, Finnish Jazz Fed. Yrjö Award 1982, Arts Council of Finland grant 1982, 1984, 1986–88, Arts Council of Finland Extra Artist Pension 2005. *Address:* Kilterinrinne 10 C 67, 01600 Vantaa, Finland (home).

KONGSTED, Ole Dan; Danish musicologist, composer, church musician and jazz musician; *Senior Research Fellow, The Royal Library*; b. 22 Sept. 1943, Copenhagen; m. Ida Wieth-Knudsen 1967; one s. two d. *Education:* Univ. of Copenhagen. *Career:* holder of scholarship, Danish State 1976–80; freelance collaborator, Danish Radio 1976–; Conductor, Choir of the Jeunesses Musicales 1978–86; Asst Dir, Musikhistorisk Museum and Carl Claudius Samling, Copenhagen 1980–2000; Choirmaster and Organist, Church of the Sacred Heart, Copenhagen 1982–; Founder and Leader, Capella Hafniensis 1990–; holder of scholarship, Danish State/Royal Library 1994–2000; Sr Research Fellow, The Royal Library 2000–. *Compositions:* 71 opus numbers. *Recordings:* several recordings with Choir of the Jeunesses Musicales, with Ben Webster and Arnved Meyer Band, and Capella Hafniensis. *Publications:* E turri tibiis canere – Traek af taarnblaesningens historie, in Festskrift Johannes Simons (ed.) 1974, Census as Source Material for the History of Music 1976, Nils Schioerring: Musikkens Historie i Danmark (ed.) 1977–78, Music in Denmark at the Time of Christian IV 1988, Heinrich Schütz und die Musik in Dänemark zur Zeit Christians IV (co-ed.) 1989, Kronborg-Motetterne Tilegnet Frederik II og Dronning Sophie 1582, 1990, Kronborg-Brunnen und Kronborg-Motetten, Ein Notenfund des späten 16 Jahrhunderts aus Flensburg und seine Vorgeschichte 1991, Liber cantionum, I 1993, Royal Danish Water Music 1582 1994, Liber cantionum, II 1994, Liber cantionum, III 1996, Liber cantionum, IV 1996, Liber cantionum, V 1996, Liber cantionum, VI 1998, Liber cantionum, VII 1998, Gregorius Trehou in the Vatican Library 1998, Liber cantionum, VIII 1999, Liber cantionum, IX 2000, 10 Maria motetter, 10 Maria motets, Bernard Lewkovitch 2000, Dansk musik i 1000 år – syngespil og opera 2000, Motetter, Motets, Motetten, af Ludwig Senfl 2001, Liber cantionum, X 2001, Opusculum cantionum, 1571, Johannes Flamingus (floruit 1565–1573) 2002, Ps. 23: Herren er min hyrde, 14 kompositioner af danske komponister 2005, Motectorum quinque vocum Liber secundus (1591), Jan Tollius 2005, Lejlighedsværker, Gelegenheitswerke, Occasional works 2004, Jan Tollius 2005, 10 Maria motetter, 10 Maria motets, Bernard Lewkovitch 2005, Sacrarum cantionum (1601), Vincentius Bertholusius 2005, Liber primus motettorum (1581), Rinaldo del Mel 2005, Moduli trium vocum (1597), Jan Tollius 2005, Liber primus motectorum quinque vocum (1591), Jan Tollius 2005, Indspilning Musica nuptialis, Bartholomaeus Stockmann (co-ed.) 2005, Ars Baltica musicalis 2007, 12 korsatser 2008, 14 liturgiske kompositioner 2008, A due, musical essays in honour of John D. Bergsagel and Heinrich W. Schwab (co-ed. with assistance of Lisbeth Larsen, musikalische Aufsätze zu Ehren von John D. Bergsagel und Heinrich W. Schwab) 2008, Missa super doulce mémoire, necnon varii cantus, Mattheus le Maistre 2009. *Honours:* Organist and Kantor Otto Koebkes Mindelegat 1992. *Address:* The Royal Library, PO Box 2149, 1016 Copenhagen K, Denmark (office). *Telephone:* 40-31-93-23 (office). *E-mail:* ok@kb.dk (office).

KONISHI, Yasuharu; Japanese producer and composer; b. 3 Feb. 1959, Tokyo. *Career:* Founder-mem. Pizzicato Five 1979–2001; DJ 2001–. *Recordings include:* albums: Pizzicato Five in Action 1986, Couples 1987, Belissima! 1988, On Her Majesty's Request 1989, Soft Landing on the Moon 1990, Hi Guys! Let Me Teach You 1991, This Year's Model 1991, London Paris Tokyo 1991, Readymade Recordings 1991, Instant Replay 1993, Made in USA 1994, A Television's Workshop 1994, Five by Five 1994, Romantique 96 1995, The Sound of Music by Pizzicato Five 1995, Antique 96 1995, A Quiet Couple 1995, Great White Wonder 1996, Sister Freedom Tapes 1996, Combinaison Spaciale 1997, Happy End of the World 1997, Happy End of You 1998, Pizzicatomania! 1998, Playboy & Playgirl 1998, Darlin' of Discotheque 1999, Nonstop to Tokyo 1999, Overdose 1999, Perfect World 1999, Pizzicato Five TM 1999, Sweet Pizzicato Five 2000, Voyage a Tokyo 2000, Relax 2001, Bossa Nova 2001, 24 December 2001, Ca Et La Du Japon 2001, The Swingers Unlimited 2003.

KONITZ, Lee; American jazz musician (alto saxophone), bandleader and composer; b. 13 Oct. 1927, Chicago, Ill. *Career:* joined Teddy Powell Band 1945; worked with Jerry Wald 1945–47, Lennie Tristano 1946, Claude Thornhill 1947, Stan Getz 1949–50, Miles Davis 1948–50; debut recording as bandleader 1949; recordings with Stan Kenton 1950s; many live and recording collaborations as sideman including with Jakob Bro, Miles Davis, Gil Evans, Hal Galper, Stan Kenton, Warne Marsh Quartet, Charles Mingus, Rich Perry, Max Roach, Claude Thornhill, Lennie Tristano, Kenny Wheeler, Attila Zoller. *Recordings include:* as bandleader: With Tristano, Marsh and Bauer 1949–50, Subconscious-Lee 1949, Lee Konitz Featuring Miles Davis – The New Sounds 1951, Lee Konitz Plays with the Gerry Mulligan Quartet 1953, In Harvard Square 1954, Lee Konitz with Warne Marsh 1954, Inside Hi-Fi 1956, Tranquility 1957, The Real Lee Konitz 1957, Very Cool 1958, An Image: Lee Konitz with Strings 1958, Lee Konitz Meets Jimmy Guiffre 1959, You and Lee 1959, Motion 1961, Trio and Quartet 1965, Modern Jazz Compositions from Haiti 1966, The Lee Konitz Duets 1967, Impressive Rome 1968, European Episode 1968, Peacemeal 1969, Lee Konitz Sax Duets 1970, Spirits 1971, Jazz

à Juan 1974, Satori 1974, Lone-Lee 1974, I Concentrate on You 1974, Oleo 1975, Chicago 'n' All That Jazz 1975, Lee Konitz Meets Warne Marsh Again 1976, Figure and Spirit 1976, The Lee Konitz Quintet 1977, The Lee Konitz Nonet 1977, Tenorlee 1977, Pyramid 1977, Seasons Change 1979, Yes, Yes Nonet 1979, Heroes 1980, Anti-heroes 1980, Toot Sweet 1982, High Jingo 1982, Glad, Koonix! 1983, Dovetail 1983, Dedicated to Lee: Lee Konitz Plays the Music of Lars Gullin 1983, Art of the Duo 1983, Wild as Springtime 1984, Stereokonitz 1984, Ideal Scene 1986, Medium Rare 1986, The New York Album 1987, Blew 1988, Solitudes 1988, In Rio 1989, Konitz in Denmark 1989, Round and Round 1989, Zounds 1990, Once Upon a Line 1990, Lullaby of Birdland 1991, Jazz Nocturne 1992, Lunasea 1992, Frank-Lee Speaking 1992, Rhapsody 1993, So Many Stars 1993, Rhapsody II 1993, Swiss Kiss 1994, Haiku 1995, Move 1995, Free with Lee 1995, Alone Together 1996, Guarana 1996, Lee Konitz Meets Don Friedman 1996, It's You 1996, Out of Nowhere 1997, Dearly Beloved 1997, Body and Soul 1997, Tender Lee 1998, Another Shade of Blue 1999, Sound of Surprise 2000, Pride 2000, Some New Stuff 2001, Parallels 2001, BargaLee 2004, Inventions 2004, New Nonet 2005, Deep Lee 2008, Duos with Lee (with Dan Tepfer) 2009. *Honours:* Nat. Endowment for the Arts Jazz Master 2009, Jazz Journalists' Asscn Award for Alto Saxophonist of the Year 2014. *E-mail:* info@theAMIagency.com.

KONOPKA, Daniel Michael; American drummer and percussionist; b. 26 July 1974; m. Kristy Swailes 2007. *Career:* Founder-mem. Stanley's Joyful Noise 1997–98; mem. OK Go 1998–; signed to Capitol Records 2001; f own label for OK Go recordings, Paracadute Recordings 2010. *Recordings:* albums: with OK Go: OK Go 2002, Oh No 2004, Of the Blue Colour of the Sky 2010, Hungry Ghosts 2014. *Honours:* Grammy Award for Best Music Video 2007, UK Music Video Awards for Video of the Year and Best Rock Video 2010, CLIO Gold Award in Branded Entertainment 2013, MTV Video Music Award for Best Visual Effects 2014. *Address:* c/o Mike Rosenthal, Paracadute, 236 Hoyt Street, Suite 2, Brooklyn, New York, NY 11217, USA (office). *E-mail:* Rosenthal@paracadute.net (office); paracadute@okgo.net (office). *Website:* www.paracadute.net (office); www.okgo.net.

KOOL KEITH, (Rhythm X, Dr Octagon, Dr Dooom, Mr Gerbik, Ultra, Mr Nogatco); American rap artist and producer; b. (Keith Mathew Thornton), 19 Oct. 1966. *Career:* Founder and fmr mem. Ultramagnetic MCs 1987–93; solo artist 1993–, under several pseudonyms. *Recordings include:* albums: with Ultramagnetic MCs: Critical Beatdown 1988, Funk Your Head Up 1992, Four Horsemen 1993, Basement Tapes 1984–90 1994, New York What Is Funky 1996, Brooklyn To Brixton 1996, Mo Love's Basement Tapes 1996, B-Sides Companion 1997, Smack My Bitch Up 1998, The Best Kept Secret 2007; solo: as Dr Octagon: Dr Octagon (aka Dr Octagonecolygist) 1996, The Return of Dr Octagon 2006; as Ultra: Big Time/Pimp Fiction 1996; as Kool Keith: Erotic Man 1996, Sex Style 1997, Black Elvis/Lost in Space 1999, Matthew 2000, Spankmaster 2001, Lost Masters 2003, Presents Thee Undatakerz 2003, The Personal Album 2004, Official Kool Keith Space Tape 2004, Execution One 2005, Dr Octagon Part II 2005, Lost Masters Volume 2 2005, The Commi$$ioner 2006, DJ Junkaz Lou Selection 2006, The Commi$$ioner 2 2006, Ultra-Octa-Doom 2007, The Doctor is In 2011; with Godfather Don: Cenobites/Cenubites 1996; with Kutmasta Kurt Presents: Masters Of Illusion 2000, Diesel Truckers 2004, Sex Style: The Un-Released Archives 2009; with H-Bomb and Marc Live: Game 2002; with Nancy des Rose: White Label Mix Series Vol. 1 2004; with TomC3: Project Polaroid 2006; as Dr Dooom: First Come, First Served 1999, Dr Dooom 2 2008; with KHM: Game 2002; as Mr Nogatco: Nogatco Rd. 2006; with Tashan Dorrsett: Fidelity, Bravery, Integrity 2009, The Legend of Tashan Dorrsett 2011; with 54–71: Idea of a Master Piece 2009. *Website:* www.koolkeith.co.uk; www.ultrakeith.net.

KOOL SHEN; French rapper; b. (Bruno Lopes), 9 Feb. 1967, Saint-Denis. *Career:* mem. breakdance group Actuel Force during 1980s, travelled around France and Europe and won numerous competitions; co-founder hip hop group Suprême NTM with Joey Starr 1989, became one of the most successful ever French hip hop acts, their music was boycotted by all French radio stations due to controversial lyrics 1993–94; collaborated with US rapper Nas; Founder IV My People record label and production co. 1999–2005. *Recordings include:* albums: with NTM: Authentik 1991, 1993... J'Appuie Sur La Gâchette 1993, Paris Sous Les Bombes 1995, Suprême NTM 1998, Live (1991–1998) 2000, NTM Le Clash: BOSS Vs IV My People 2001; solo: Dernier round 2004, Live 2005, Crise de conscience 2009. *Films:* Qui paiera les dégâts? 1998, Old School 2000, Elie annonce Semoun 2000, The Dope 2003, Au petit matin 2005, J'reviens 2008, Abuse of Weakness 2013, Paris 2014. *Current Management:* c/o Cyril Cannizzo, Agence Agent Agitateur, 147 rue Saint Martin, 75003 Paris, France. *Telephone:* 1-47-23-05-46. *E-mail:* cyril@agentagitateur.com. *Website:* www.agentagitateur.com.

KOONIN, Brian; American musician (keyboards). *Career:* mem. New York Dolls 2004–06. *Recordings include:* album: One Day it Will Please Us to Remember Even This 2006, Cause I Sez So 2009.

KOOPER, Al; American musician (keyboards), producer, singer and songwriter; b. (Alan Peter Kuperschmidt), 5 Feb. 1944, Brooklyn, New York. *Career:* guitarist, The Royal Teens 1959; session musician with artists, including Tom Rush, Peter Paul and Mary, New York; mem. The Blues Project 1966–67; Founder-mem. Blood Sweat & Tears 1967–68; producer at Columbia Records; est. own record label, Sounds of the Earth (acts included Lynyrd Skynyrd); Founder, Sweet Magnolia 1970s. *Compositions include:* with Bobby Brass and Irwin Levine: This Diamond Ring, Gary Lewis and The Playboys; I

Must Be Seeing Things, Gene Pitney; The Water is Over My Head, The Rocking Berries. *Recordings include:* albums: with The Blues Project: Projections 1966, Live at Town Hall 1967; with Blood Sweat & Tears: The Child is Father to The Man 1968; solo: Super Session (with Mike Bloomfield and Stephen Stills) 1968, The Live Adventures of Al Kooper and Mike Bloomfield 1969, I Stand Alone 1969, You Never Know Who Your Friends Are 1969, Kooper Session 1970, Easy Does It 1970, Landlord 1971, New York City (You're A Woman) 1971, A Possible Projection of The Future 1972, Naked Songs 1973, Act Like Nothing's Wrong 1976, Four on the Floor 1979, Championship Wrestling 1982, Rekooperation 1994, Soul of a Man 1995, Black Coffee 2005, White Chocolate 2008. *Publication includes:* Backstage Passes and Backstabbing Bastards (memoir) 2008. *E-mail:* alfonts@aol.com. *Website:* www.alkooper.com.

KOOYMANS, George; Dutch singer and musician (guitar); b. 11 March 1948, The Hague. *Career:* Founder mem. rock group, Golden Earring 1961–; tours of Europe, Canada, USA. *Recordings include:* albums: with Golden Earring: Just Earrings 1965, Winter Harvest 1966, Miracle Mirror 1968, On the Double 1969, Eight Miles High 1969, Golden Earring 1970, Seven Tears 1971, Together 1972, Moontan 1973, Switch 1975, To the Hilt 1976, Contraband 1976, Golden Earring Live 1977, Grab It For a Second 1978, No Promises, No Debts 1979, Prisoner of the Night 1980, 2nd Live 1981, Cut 1982, N.E.W.S. 1984, Something Heavy Goin' Down 1984, The Hole 1986, Keeper of the Flame 1989, The Complete Singles Collection 1975–91 1991, Bloody Buccaneers 1991, The Naked Truth 1992, Face It 1995, Lovesweat 1995, Naked II 1997, The Complete Naked Truth 1998, Paradise in Distress 1999, Last Blast of the Century 2000, The Devil Made Us Do It 2000, Millbrook USA 2003, Naked III 2005, Live in Ahoy 2006, Tits 'N Ass 2012; solo: Jojo 1972, Solo 1987, On Location as Kooymans-Carillo (with Frank Carillo) 2010. *E-mail:* daan@golden-earring.nl. *Website:* www.goldenearring.nl.

KOPECKY, Ladislav; Czech songwriter, lyricist and musician; b. 8 April 1944, Prague; four d. *Education:* Charles Univ. *Career:* mem. various bands; more than 60 of his songs broadcast by Czech TV and radio; co-operation with singer and songwriter, Petr Ulrych; elected Pres., Asscn of Communication Agencies 1998; Managing Dir Createam 1999–; mem. OSA. *Compositions:* Pojdte Dal (Hana Ulrychova), Mec A Preslice, Ententyny, Bylinky, Nikola Suhaj the Robber (musical). *Recordings include:* albums: Mec A Preslice, Pojdte Dal, Ententyny, Bylinky; singles: Javory (Maple Tree), Jizda Kralu (Ride of the Kings), Trava (Grass), Kridla (Wings), Bylinky (Herbs), Kamen (Stone), Ententyny. *Honours:* Bratislavska Lyra Festival Silver Prize 1976, Golden Prize 1980, Decinska Kotva Festival Bronze Prize 1977, 1979. *Address:* Createam, Neklanova 11, 12800 Prague 2, Czech Republic (office). *Telephone:* (2) 24914961 (office). *Fax:* (2) 24914961 (office). *E-mail:* studio@createam.cz (office). *Website:* www.createam.cz (office).

KOPPEL, Anders; Danish composer and musician (organ, piano); b. 17 July 1947, Copenhagen; s. of the late Herman D. Koppel and Edel Vibeke Koppel; brother of Lone Koppel; m. Ulla Lemvigh-Müller 1969; one s. two d. *Career:* played the piano as a child and later clarinet, several TV and concert appearances; sang in Copenhagen Boys Choir; began playing the organ 1966; Co-founder rock group Savage Rose 1967, toured Europe and USA, performed at Newport Jazz Festival 1971; mem. trio Bazaar 1976–; active as a producer and studio musician 1974–80; since then has concentrated on composition and touring as a musician; also plays with his son, saxophone player Benjamin Koppel and musicians including Kenny Werner, Miroslav Vituos, Brian Blade; has hosted workshops in Salzburg, Vienna and Linz, Austria; mem. Danish Composers Asscn, Danish Artists Asscn. *Compositions:* music for 10 ballets, 200 films and plays, three musicals, one opera (Rebus), Piano Concerto, Percussion Concerto, four marimba concertos, two saxophone concertos, Bass Trombone Concerto, Flute/Harp Concerto, Saxophone and Piano Concerto, Violin and Saxophone Concerto, Tuba Concerto, Cello Concerto, Sinfonia Concertante for violin, viola, clarinet and bassoon, Doublebass Concerto, Concerto for violin and accordion, Viola Concerto, Bassoon Concerto, Concerto Piccolo for accordion, Concerto for recorder and saxophone, Triple Concerto for saxophone, cello and harp, Trio for saxophone, cello, piano, Trio for violin, cello, piano, Toccata for vibes, marimba and orchestra, three string quartets, Partita for chamber ensemble, Concertino for chamber ensemble, Passacaglia for chamber ensemble, Trio for violin, horn, piano, four pieces for two guitars, Sonata for recorder and guitar, Portrait for sextet, String Trio, Wind Quintet, Brass Quintet, Piano pieces, Piano Quintet, Mezzo Sax Quintet, Cello Quartet (Le Balajo); solo pieces for piano, clarinet and pipe organ. *Recordings:* nine albums with Bazaar; The Poetic Principle with Miroslav Vitous and Benjamin Koppel 2007, Everything is Subject to Change (with Benjamin Koppel and Kenny Werner) 2012, Breaking Borders (duo with Kenny Werner) 2013; own compositions: Works for saxophone and orchestra, Double Concertos, Concertos, String Quartets, Marimba Concertos, Double Triple Koppel. *Honours:* several awards and prizes, including Danish Prize for Best Film Score 1994, 1996, Wilhelm Hansen Prize, Danish State Art Foundation Lifetime Award. *Current Management:* c/o Edition Wilhelm Hansen AS, Bornholmsgade 1A, 1266 Copenhagen K, Denmark. *Telephone:* 33-11-78-88. *Fax:* 33-14-81-78. *E-mail:* ewh@ewh.dk. *Website:* www.ewh.dk. *Address:* Cæciliavej 70, 2500 Valby, Copenhagen, Denmark. *E-mail:* anders.h.koppel@gmail.com.

KOPPEL, Annisette; Danish singer and songwriter; b. (Annisette Hansen), 29 Aug. 1948, Copenhagen; m. Thomas Koppel 1971; two s. two d. *Career:* lead singer, The Savage Rose 1968–; mem. Danish Artists' Union, DJBFA, KODA, Gramex. *Stage appearance:* Bella Vita (title role and lyricist, musical drama,

with Thomas Koppel) 1997. *Compositions include:* numerous songs recorded by Savage Rose, lyrics for symphonic compositions by Thomas Koppel. *Recordings include:* albums: The Savage Rose 1968, In the Plain 1968, Travellin' 1969, Your Daily Gift 1971, Refugee 1971, Dødens Triumf 1972, Babylon 1972, Wild Child 1973, Solen var også din 1978, En vugge af stål 1982, Vi kaemper for at sejre 1984, Kejserens nye klaeder 1986, Sangen for Livet 1988, Ild og Frihed 1989, Gadens Dronning 1990, Månebarn 1992, Black Angel 1995, Tameless 1998, For Your Love 2001, Universal Daughter 2007, Love and Freedom 2012, Roots of the Wasteland 2014. *Honours:* Danish Film Acad. Award 1992, Danish Songwriters' Asscn Award of Honour 1995, Grammy Awards 1996, 1999. *Telephone:* 33-76-03-58. *E-mail:* karina.fenn@sonybmg.com. *Website:* www.thesavagerose.net.

KOPPES, Peter; Australian musician (guitar), singer and producer; b. 21 Nov. 1955. *Career:* Founder-mem. The Church 1980–91, 1997–; solo artist; Co-owner Immersion Records. *Recordings include:* albums: with The Church: Of Skins and Hearts 1980, The Blurred Crusade 1982, Séance 1983, Heyday 1986, Starfish 1988, Gold Afternoon Fix 1990, Hologram of Baal 1998, After Everything Now This 2002, Parallel Universe 2002, Forget Yourself 2003, El Momento Descuidado 2004, Uninvited, Like the Clouds 2006, El Momento Siguiente 2007, Untitled No. 23 2009, Further/Deeper 2014; solo: Manchild and Myth 1987, From the Well 1989, Love Era 1997, Simple Intent 2002, Misty Heights and Cloudy Memories 1987-2002 2007. *E-mail:* khagan@skhmusic.com. *Website:* www.skhmusic.com. *E-mail:* management@thechurchband.com. *Website:* www.thechurchband.com; www.peterkoppes.com.

KORB, Ron, (Longdi, Dragon Flute), BMus; Canadian musician (flute, keyboards) and singer; b. 7 Sept. 1961, Scarborough, Ont. *Education:* Univ. of Toronto and Royal Conservatory of Music. *Career:* mem. AFM, Soc. of Composers, Authors and Music Publrs of Canada (SOCAN). *Recordings:* Tear of The Sun 1990, Japanese Mysteries 1993, Flute Traveller 1994, Behind The Mask 1995, Celtic Dawn 1996, Mada Minu Tome E 1998, Taming the Dragon 1999, Celtic Heartland 2000, Celtic Quest 2001, Romancing the Dragon 2003, World of Ron Korb 2003, Ron Korb Live 2004, Ron Korb Live Collector's Edn (DVD) 2004, Rainforest Flute 2005, Seasons 2006, East West Road 2006, Longdi 2007, 2008 Native Earth 2009, Dragon Heart 2009, Once Upon A Time, The Oriental Angel vs Ron Korb (DVD) 2010, Europa 2012, Melody 2013, Asia Beauty 2015. *Honours:* Alexander Kinghorn Scholarship, Grand Prize Winner, Canadian Nat. Exhbn 1985, Best Original Composition, RTHK (Radio and Television Hong Kong) 1993, 2004, April Most Popular Foreign Artist, iRadio FM96.3 (Taiwan) 2010, Golden Maple Culture and Arts Awards – Artistic Achievement 2010, Best Instrumental Solo Performance, Excellence in Composition, Best Graphic Design, Album of the Year 2012, Best of Show, Best Instrumental Album, Best Instrumental Performance, Best Crossover World Music, Best Album Art/Graphics, Global Music Awards 2015. *Current Management:* c/o Mc-Ent Management, Workumstraat 7, 8244 EJ, Lelystad, The Netherlands. *Telephone:* (320) 241248. *E-mail:* info@whoisontour.org. *E-mail:* ronkorb@ronkorb.com (home); humbledragon@rogers.com (office). *Website:* www.ronkorb.com (office).

KORDEI, Normani; American singer; b. (Normani Kordei Hamilton), 31 May 1996, d. of Derrick Hamilton and Andrea Hamilton. *Career:* raised in Atlanta, Ga, New Orleans, La and Houston, Tex.; award-winning dancer and gymnast; recorded debut solo single 2009; mem. Love You Like a Sister, renamed 1432, then renamed Fifth Harmony (or 5H) 2012–; contestants on US version of The X Factor (finished in third place) 2012; signed with Syco Music and Epic Records 2012; issued debut EP Better Together 2013; opening act on Cher Lloyd's I Wish tour 2013, on Demi Lovato's Neon Lights Tour 2014, on Austin Mahone's tour of North America and Brazil 2014; headlining act, MTV Artists to Watch concert 2014. *Television:* The X Factor (contestant on US series) 2012. *Recordings:* album: with Fifth Harmony: Reflection 2015. *Honours:* Teen Choice Single: Group Award 2014, MTV Video Music Artist to Watch Award 2014, MTV Europe Music Awards for Best North America Act, for Best US Act and for Best Worldwide Act 2014. *Address:* c/o Syco Music, Syco Entertainment, 9830 Wilshire Blvd, Beverly Hills, CA 90212, USA. *Website:* www.sycoentertainment.com; www.fifthharmonyofficial.com.

KORJUS, Tapio; Finnish music manager; b. 18 June 1950, Pieksamaki; m. Eija Savolainen 1984; one d. *Education:* Tampere Univ. *Career:* f. Rockadillo Man. 1971, Rockadillo Records and Publishing 1982, Rockadillo Agency 1983, Zen Master Records and Publishing 1993, Finnish Music and Media Happening 1989; Chair. Bd, Indieco ry (Finnish Independent Labels Asscn); mem. Bd, ÄKT (Finnish IFPI), European Live Music Forum (ELMF), Independent Music Companies Asscn (IMPALA) 2009–; mem. Finnish Music Publishers' Asscn. *Address:* Rockadillo, Ilmarinkatu 12 A 2, 33500 Tampere, Finland (office). *Telephone:* (3) 2131260 (office). *Fax:* (3) 2131297 (office). *E-mail:* records@rockadillo.fi (office). *Website:* www.rockadillo.fi (office).

KÖROĞLU, Derya, BA, MA; Turkish singer, songwriter and musician (guitar, bağlama, percussion); b. 1955, Istanbul. *Education:* Ankara Fen Lisesi, Middle East Technical Univ. *Career:* founder mem. and lead singer, Yeni Türkü 1979–; concerts world-wide. *Recordings include:* albums with Yeni Türkü: "Yeni", Akdeniz Akdeniz 1983, Günebakan 1986, Dünyanin Kapilari 1987, Yeşilmişik? 1988, Vira Vira 1990, Rumeli Konseri 1991, Ask Yeniden 1992, Külhani Şarkilar 1994, Süper Baba (film music) 1995, Telli Telli (Remixes) 1996, Her Dem Yeni 1996, Koleksiyon 2003, Koleksiyon 2 2004, Koleksiyon 3 2006, Koleksiyon 4 2008, Şimdi ve Sonra 2012; solo:

Musikarium 1997. *E-mail:* derya@yeniturku.com. *Website:* www.yeniturku .com.

KOS, Lada; Croatian singer, writer, composer, arranger and musician (violin, guitar, piano); b. 12 Nov. 1944, Zagreb. *Education:* Musical Acad. for Violin. *Career:* solo concerts in Barcelona, Paris, Milan, Berlin, Frankfurt, Vienna; tours to Croatia, Russia, France, Italy, Germany, Austria, Slovenia; TV appearances on RAI, Moscow, St Petersburg, Tallinn among others, also on various TV series; mem. Croatian Composers' Soc. *Recordings include:* Zbog Ljubavi, Covjek Covjeku, Igracica Vjetrova; Music for the Theatre includes: B M Koltés, Roberto Zucco, S Sembera, Hodanje Prugom, E Kisevic, Macak u Trapericama, B Jelusic, Slava Voli Hranislava, V Parun, U Cast Darkerke Djevice Orleanske. *Honours:* numerous awards for best singer, writer, composer and arranger. *Address:* 41000 Zagreb, Menceticeva 26, Croatia.

KOSTER, Bo, (Christopher B. Honey, Bart Koozler); American musician (keyboards); b. Cleveland, Ohio. *Education:* Ohio Univ. *Career:* mem., My Morning Jacket 2004–. *Recordings include:* albums: Z 2005, Okronokos 2006, Evil Urges 2008, Circuital 2011. *Current Management:* Flatiron Management. *Telephone:* (212) 616-4787. *E-mail:* mike@flatironmgmt.com. *Address:* c/o RCA Records, 1540 Broadway, New York, NY 10036, USA (office). *E-mail:* bokoster@mymorningjacket.com (office). *Website:* www.mymorningjacket .com.

KOTCHE, Glenn; American musician (drums, percussion); b. 31 Dec. 1970, Chicago, Ill. *Education:* Univ. of Kentucky. *Career:* mem. Wilco 1999–; mem. Loose Fur 2002–, On Fillmore; also solo artist; other collaborations include Jim O'Rourke, Simon Joyner, Birddog; co-scored film Chelsea Walls 2001. *Recordings include:* albums: with Wilco: Yankee Hotel Foxtrot 2002, A Ghost is Born 2004, Sky Blue Sky 2007, Wilco (The Album) 2009, The Whole Love 2011, Star Wars 2015; with Loose Fur: Loose Fur 2002, Sleeps With Fishes 2003, Born Again in the USA 2006; with On Fillmore: On Fillmore 2003, Sleeps with Fishes 2004, Extended Vacation 2009; solo: Introducing Glenn Kotche 2002, Next 2004, Mobile 2006, Adventureland 2014, Fantasyland 2014. *Film:* I Am Trying To Break Your Heart 2002. *Current Management:* c/o Ben Levin, Tony Margherita Management, 116 Pleasant Street, Suite 245, Easthampton, MA 01027, USA. *Telephone:* (413) 529-2830. *E-mail:* info@ tmmchi.com. *Website:* www.tmmchi.com; www.glennkotche.com; www .wilcoworld.net.

KOTRUBENKO, Viktor; Czech composer and saxophonist; b. 3 May 1964; one d. *Education:* Coll. of Tech., School of Music, Prague. *Career:* mem. Asscn of Composers and Scientists, Music-ecological Asscn of the Czech Repub.; expert in IT and digital processing of multimedia and author's rights; Lecturer, Czech Tech. Univ. in Prague. *Compositions:* radio productions music: Mum, Dad, Sore Made; film music: Bohemian Ruby, The Light of Hope, Faul; music for TV serials: Rambles Round Bohemia and Moravia, Ecuador. *Recordings:* The Cat Crawls Through a Hole, Shadow, Virgin Eva, Virgin Bozena and a Little Dog Bobbie, Ballad About a Treefrog or When I Went Water A Little Garden, White Show, Attention Pothole, Accelerate. *Publications:* Secret of the Synthesizers. *Honours:* Prize, Saxophonist, Int. Jazz Festival, Prague 1971, Silver Tablet 1977, Appreciation for Composition 1977, The Golden Pip, Asscn of the Czech Advertising Agencies for the Sound Spot Citizen. *Address:* Cerchovska 6, 120 00 Prague 2, Czech Republic (home). *E-mail:* kotrubenko@znaleckyposudek.cz (home). *Website:* www.toleration.cz/ kotrubenko (office).

KOUBKOVÁ, Jana; Czech jazz singer and composer; b. 31 Oct. 1944, Prague; d. of Jaroslav Koubek and Hana Koubková; m. Jan. Kunst 1967 (divorced 1969). *Education:* People's Conservatory, Prague. *Career:* began singing with Czechoslovak Radio Children's Choir aged six 1950–57; Semafor Theatre 1975–76; Ludek Hulan Jazz Sanatorium 1975–79; Hot Tety and Hot Aunts Vocal Groups 1976–82; Co-founder Vokalíza (annual jazz, blues and rock festival) 1981; singer with various big bands since 1982; Teacher of Music, State Conservatory; regular TV and radio appearances. *Recordings include:* Horký dech Jany Koubkove 1982, Bosa 1985, Jazzperanto (co-author) 1988, Panta rhei 1989, Tenerife Blues 1995, Absolonie 1996, Madona z rosti 2002, Novinky 2014, Jazz? Oh, Yes! 2014. *Publications:* numerous articles on singing for Tvorba magazine, and writes rhythmical poetry. *Honours:* Best Vocal Performance Award, Prague Jazz Festival 1977, Melody Magazine Award for Artistic and Organizational Work 1985. *Address:* Karmelitská 23, 118 00 Prague 1, Czech Republic. *Telephone:* 2539272; 20-737350480 (mobile). *E-mail:* jana.koubkova@volny.cz. *Website:* www.janakoubkova.cz.

KOUYATE, Bassekou; Malian musician (ngoni); b. (Sekou Kouyate), 7 Aug. 1966, Garana; s. of the late Moustapha Kouyate and Yakare Damba; m. Amy Sacko 1995. *Education:* studied ngoni with his father in Garana. *Career:* player of griot music; sent to live with strict marabout (Muslim teacher and cleric) in Bamako aged 12, given job of shining shoes in the street; later returned home; took place of his father next his mother on tour in Burkina Faso aged 16; moved to Segu (capital of Segu region) to join guitar player Cheikh Oumar Diabate and his wife Nainy Diabate; began developing own techniques on ngoni; met singer and future wife, Amy Sacko (now lead singer in Ngoni ba) mid-1980s; left Segu and settled in Bamako; began playing on traditional sumu circuit (wedding parties held in the streets); met kora player, Toumani Diabate, and formed intention to advance their style of playing and to update ancient traditions by expanding scope of their instruments to accommodate elements of western harmony and jazz; began adding strings (up to seven in total) to ngoni to give wider melodic range; played concert with Nainy Diabate at Buffet de la Gare, Bamako 1985, began playing ngoni standing up, which many ngoni players soon copied; also experimented with different ways of plucking strings; Founding mem. Toumani Diabate's Symmetric Orchestra late 1980s, invited to play a concert at the French Cultural Centre; joined Symmetric Trio with Toumani Diabaté on kora and Keletigui Diabate on balafon; played at festival in Dranoute, Belgium 1990; made first trip to USA to participate in annual get-together of banjo players at Tennessee Banjo Inst., Cedars of Lebanon, Tenn. 1990; worked with Taj Mahal and Toumani Diabate on album Kulanjan 1999; produced with his wife several popular cassettes and were in constant demand on wedding circuit and on Mali TV; Co-founder, with Amy Sacko and singer Kasse Mady Diabate, group Samaguera 1995; played numerous tours in Europe and Japan; invited by Mali's "desert bluesman" Ali Farka Touré to play on his album Savane (released posthumously) 2005; formed own quartet, Ngoni ba 2006, toured extensively all over Europe, Africa and the Caribbean; Patron, Segu's Festival on the Niger 2009; mem. AfroCubism project 2010–. *Recordings include:* albums: Shake the Whole World (Symmetric Orchestra) 1990, Songhai 2 (in collaboration with Spanish new flamenco group, Ketama) 1994, Djelika 1995, Segu Blue (BBC Award for World Music Best Album 2008, BBC Award for World Music Best African Artist 2008) 2007, I Speak Fula 2009, AfroCubism (with AfroCubism) 2010, Jama ko 2013; has performed on albums by Bela Fleck, Youssou Ndour, Amadou and Mariam and others. *Honours:* Chevalier, Ordre nat. du Mali 2009; Tamani d'Or 2008. *Address:* c/o Outhere Records, Baaderstrasse 72, 80469 Munich, Germany. *Telephone:* (89) 23000975. *Fax:* (89) 23000976. *E-mail:* info@outhere.de. *Website:* www.outhere.de.

KOUYATE, Kandia; Malian singer and songwriter; b. 1958, Kita. *Education:* studied music with parents. *Career:* born into a griot family; mem. The Apollos, Bamako; moved to Abidjan and recorded first album 1980; formed own band, including Toumani Diabaté early 1980s. *Recordings include:* albums: Amary Dou presents Kandia Kouyate 1985, Project Dabia 1987, Kita Kan (including Ousmane Kouyate) 1999, Biriko 2002, Ngara 2009, Amary Daou (1981/1982) 2009.

KOZLOV, Alexey Semenovich; Russian composer, saxophone player and bandleader; b. 13 Oct. 1935, Moscow; m. 1st; one s.; m. 2nd Lyalya Adburakhmanovna Absalyamova. *Education:* Moscow Inst. of Architecture, Moscow Music Coll. *Career:* researcher, Inst. of Design 1963–76; started playing saxophone in youth clubs 1955; founder and leader of jazz quintet 1959, jazz band of café Molodezhnoye 1961–66; arranger and soloist orchestra VIO-66; teacher Moscow Experimental Studio of Jazz Music 1967–76; Founder and music Dir jazz-rock ensemble Arsenal 1973–, festivals and tours including Delhi and Bombay 1989, Woodstock 1990, Jazz Rally, Düsseldorf 1993, Carnegie Hall 1995, Bonn 1996, with Arsenal, Chamber Soloists of Moscow, the Shostakovich String Quartet, Ars Nova Trio; master classes in towns of Russia and Oklahoma City Univ. 1994; Gen.-Man. Jazz Div., Goskoncert 1995–97; mem. Musical Cttee under Pres. of Russia 1997–; Art Dir Radio Jazz, Moscow 2001–; author of TV programmes, All That Jazz, Improvisation; composer of jazz, film and theatre music. *Recordings include:* Lonely Dandy 2010, Third Wind 2012, Mindstream 2013, Reconciliation 2014. *Publications:* Rock: Roots and Development 1989, Memoirs—My 20th Century, He-Goat on the Saxophone 2000; numerous articles in music journals. *Honours:* Merited Artist of Russia; his ensemble Arsenal awarded Ovation Prize as the best jazz band in Russia 1995. *Address:* Shchepkin str. 25, Apt. 28, 129090 Moscow, Russia (home). *Telephone:* (495) 688-31-56 (home); (916) 183-88-82 (home). *E-mail:* askozlov@mtu-net.ru (home); askozlov1@jandex.ru (home). *Website:* www:musiclab.ru (office); www:arsenalband.com (office).

KOZLOWSKI, James John (Koz), BSc, MBA; American director of artist development; b. 7 Sept. 1949, Hartford, Conn.; m. Lula Shepard 1994. *Education:* Boston Univ. *Career:* managed retail outlet; started nationally syndicated radio programmes, Rock Around the World and Modern Music; Dir of Purchasing, import companies Peters International, Important Record Distributors; Label Dir, Production Man., Dir of Publicity, Dir of Creative Marketing, of Artist Management, for Relativity Records, Maze and Viceroy Music; Product Man. and Art Dir, Blue Storm Music; collaborations with Joe Satriani, John Lee Hooker. *Publications:* Writer for Creem; Trouser Press; King Biscuit Times; various freelance publs. *Address:* 230 East 44th Street, #5G, New York, NY 10017, USA.

KRAKAUER, David, MMus; American clarinettist; *Founder, Klezmer Madness!*; b. 1956, New York. *Education:* Juilliard School. *Career:* performances of classical chamber music, Eastern European Jewish klezmer music, and avant-garde improvisation; genre includes world music and jazz, rock, funk and hip-hop; began career as classical musician, veered towards klezmer 1980s; f. Klezmer Madness! ensemble 1990s; regular European tours, performances at festivals and jazz clubs and at Library of Congress, Stanford Lively Arts, San Francisco Performances, Hancher Auditorium, Symphony Space in New York; venues in Europe have included Venice Biennale, Krakow Jewish Culture Festival, BBC Proms, Saalfelden Jazz Festival, La Cigale, WOMEX, New Morning, Paris; has also appeared as guest soloist with ensembles including Tokyo String Quartet, Kronos Quartet, Emerson String Quartet, Orion String Quartet, Lark Quartet, Eiko and Koma, Orquesta Sinfonica de Barcelona, Brooklyn Philharmonic Orchestra; nine years with Aspen Wind Quintet; faculty mem. New School Univ.'s Mannes Coll. of Music, Manhattan School of Music, Bard Conservatory of Music. *Recordings:* klezmer albums: Klezmer Madness! 1995, Klezmer NY 1998, A New Hot One 2000, The Twelve Tribes

(Preis der Deutschen Schallplattenkritik in jazz category) 2001, David Krakauer Live in Krakow (with hip-hop artist Socalled) 2003, Bubbameises: Lies My Gramma Told Me (with Socalled) 2005; classical albums: The Dreams and Prayers of Isaac the Blind 1997, Klezmer Concertos and Encores 2003. *Current Management:* c/o Steven Saporta, Invasion Group, 34 E 32nd Street, Suite 100, New York, NY 10016, USA. *Telephone:* (212) 414-0505. *E-mail:* steven@invasiongroup.com. *Website:* www.davidkrakauer.com.

KRALL, Diana; Canadian singer, pianist and composer; b. 16 Nov. 1966, Nanaimo, BC; m. Elvis Costello 2003; twin s. *Education:* Berklee Coll., Boston. *Career:* began classical piano aged four; regular tours of North America, Britain, Europe and the Far East. *Film appearance:* De-Lovely 2004. *Recordings include:* albums: Steppin' Out 1993, Only Trust Your Heart 1994, All For You 1995, Love Scenes 1997, When I Look In Your Eyes (Grammy Award Best Jazz Vocal) 1999, The Look Of Love 2001, Heartdrops: Vince Benedetti Meets Diana Krall 2003, The Girl in the Other Room 2004, Christmas Songs 2005, From This Moment On (Juno Award for Vocal Jazz Album Of The Year 2007) 2006, The Very Best Of Diana Krall 2007, Quiet Nights 2009, Glad Rag Doll 2012, Wallflower 2015. *Current Management:* Macklam/Feldman Management, 1505 West Second Avenue, Suite 200, Vancouver, BC V6H 3Y4, Canada. *Telephone:* (604) 734-5945. *Fax:* (604) 732-0922. *E-mail:* management@mfmgt.com. *Website:* www.mfmgt.com; www .dianakrall.com.

KRAMER; American songwriter, record producer and record company executive; b. 30 Nov. 1958, New York, NY; m. Shannon 1982; one d. *Career:* f./performed in: Gong 1979, The Chadbournes 1980–82, The Fugs 1982–84, Shockabilly 1982–85, Butthole Surfers 1985, Half Japanese 1986–88, BALL 1987–90, Bongwater 1987–91, Ween 1990, Captain Howdy (with Penn Jillette) 1993–; Founder of three record labels: Shimmy-Disc 1987, Kokopop 1990, Strangelove 1994. *Recordings:* albums: with Shockabilly: Dawn of Shockabilly 1982, Vietnam 1984, Heaven 1985; with Bongwater: Double Bummer 1988, Too Much Sleep 1989, Power of Pussy 1991; solo: Guilt Trip 1992, Secret of Comedy 1994, Let Me Explain 1998, Songs from the Pink Death 1998, Greenberg Variations 2003; producer for: Palace Songs, New Radiant Storm Kings, Galaxie 500, White Zombie, King Missile, GWAR, Low, Urge Overkill (including track Girl You'll Be A Woman Soon, from Pulp Fiction soundtrack), Maureen Tucker, Daniel Johnston, Jon Spencer Blues Explosion, Dogbowl, John Zorn. *E-mail:* busterkeatons@gmail.com (home). *Website:* www.kramershimmy.com (home).

KRAMER, Billy J.; British singer and musician (guitar); b. (William Howard Ashton), 19 Aug. 1943, Bootle, Lancs. *Career:* guitarist, The Phantoms; singer, The Coasters, 1963; singer with backing group, The Dakotas, 1963–68; regular British tours and appearances at festivals; solo artist, with club tours 1968–. *Recordings include:* albums: Listen To Billy J Kramer, 1963; Little Children, 1964; Best of Billy J. Kramer and the Dakotas, 1993. *Honours:* Melody Maker Poll Winner for Best Newcomer 1963. *E-mail:* billy@ billyjkramer.com. *Website:* www.billyjkramer.com.

KRAMER, Eddie; British producer, engineer and musician (piano, cello, violin); b. South Africa. *Education:* South African Coll. of Music. *Career:* joined Pye Studios 1964; est. KPS Studios 1965, later part of Regent Sound; joined Olympic Sound Studios; joined Record Plant, New York 1968; Ind. Producer 1969–70; recorded Woodstock festival, later many live concerts and festivals; est. Electric Lady Studios, Dir of Engineering 1970–74; Producer for Kiss 1975–; Dir, The Making of Electric Ladyland (documentary film, BBC) 1997; est. Kramer Archives with Peter Kavanaugh, co. exhibiting and selling limited-edn photographs of artists; worked with: Ace Frehley, Alcatraz, Angel, Anthrax, Bad Company, The Beatles, Big Sugar, Havana Black, David Bowie, The Chrysalids, Petula Clark, Joe Cocker, Vince Converse, Sammy Davis Jr, Clayton Denwood, Derek and The Dominoes, Fair Verona, Fastway, Peter Frampton, The Gabe Dixon Band, Jimi Hendrix, Lena Horne, The Jewel Thieves, The Kinks, Kiss, Led Zeppelin, Loudness, John Mayall, Curtis Mayfield, Wilson Pickett, Raven, The Rolling Stones, Santana, Seven Sisters, Carly Simon, Traffic, Triumph, Robin Trower, Twisted Sister, Vanilla Fudge, Dionne Warwick, Whitesnake, Johnny Winter; mem. Advisory Bd of Dirs, Mars Music Stores. *Exhibition:* From the Other Side of the Glass, installed at the Rock and Roll Hall of Fame 2002. *Publications include:* Hendrix: Setting the Record Straight (with John McDermott), Jimi Hendrix Sessions (contributing ed.) 1995, Adventures in Modern Recording (video), From the Other Side of the Glass (photographs). *E-mail:* info@eddie-kramer.com; info@ eddiekramerarchives.com (office). *Website:* www.eddie-kramer.com; www .eddiekramerarchives.com (office).

KRAMER, Jana Rae; American country music singer and actress; b. 2 Dec. 1983, Detroit, Mich.; d. of Martin Kramer and Nora Kramer; m. 1st Michael Gambino 2004 (divorced); m. 2nd Johnathon Schaech 2010 (divorced). *Education:* Rochester Adams High School, Rochester, Mich. *Career:* numerous acting roles in films and TV series; made recording debut with single Why Ya Wanna 2012; supported Blake Shelton on tour 2012. *Films include:* as actress: Dead/Undead 2002, Click 2006, Prom Night 2008, Approaching Midnight 2008, Laid to Rest 2009, Spring Breakdown 2009, Heart of the Country 2012. *Television includes:* as actress: All My Children 2003, Friday Night Lights 2007, The 90210 2008–09, One Tree Hill 2009–12. *Recordings:* album: Jana Kramer 2012. *Honours:* Acad. of Country Music Award for Top New Female Artist 2013. *Address:* c/o Elektra Nashville, Warner Music Nashville, 20 Music Square East, Nashville, TN 37203, USA (office). *Telephone:* (615) 214-

1500 (office). *E-mail:* privacypolicy@wmg.com (office). *Website:* www .warnermusicnashville.com (office); www.janakramer.com.

KRAUSS, Alison; American country and bluegrass singer and musician (fiddle); b. 23 July 1971, Champaign, Ill.; m. Pat Bergeson (divorced 2001); one s. *Career:* singer, musician since age 14; lead singer with Union Station 1987–. *Recordings include:* albums: Different Strokes 1985, Too Late to Cry 1987, Two Highways (with Union Station) 1989, I've Got That Old Feeling (Grammy Award for Bluegrass Recording 1990, Int. Bluegrass Music Asscn Award for Album of the Year 1991) 1990, Every Time You Say Goodbye (with Union Station) (Grammy Award for Bluegrass Recording 1992, Int. Bluegrass Music Asscn Award for Album of the Year 1993) 1992, I Know Who Holds Tomorrow (with The Cox Family) (Grammy Award for Southern, Country or Bluegrass Gospel Album) 1994, Now That I've Found You: A Collection 1995, So Long So Wrong (with Union Station) (GAVIN Americana Album of the Year, Grammy Award for Best Bluegrass Album) 1997, Forget About It 1999, New Favorite (with Union Station) (Grammy Award for Best Bluegrass Album) 2001, Live (with Union Station) (Int. Bluegrass Music Asscn Awards Album of the Year, Grammy Award for Best Bluegrass Album 2003) 2002, Lonely Runs Both Ways (with Union Station) (Grammy Award for Best Country Album 2006) 2004, A Hundred Miles or More 2007, Raising Sand (with Robert Plant) (Grammy Awards for Album of the Year 2009, for Best Contemporary Folk/ Americana Album 2009) 2007, Paper Airplane (with Union Station) (Grammy Award for Best Bluegrass Album 2012) 2011. *Honours:* Int. Bluegrass Music Asscn Awards for Female Vocalist of the Year 1990, 1991, 1993, 1995, Country Music Television Award for Independent Video of the Year (for I've Got That Old Feeling) 1991, Entertainer of the Year 1991, 1995, Country Music Asscn Awards for Female Vocalist of the Year, Single of the Year (for When You Say Nothing At All), Vocal Event of the Year (for Somewhere In The Vicinity Of The Heart, with Shenandoah), and Horizon Award 1995, Grammy Award for Female Country Vocal Performance (for Baby, Now That I've Found You) 1995, Country Music Television Award for Rising Video Star of the Year 1995, GAVIN Americana Artist of the Year 1995, Great British Country Music Award for Int. Female Vocalist of the Year 1996, for Int. Bluegrass Band of the Year 1997, 1998, 1999, 2000, Grammy Awards for Best Country Performance by a Duo or Group (for Looking In The Eyes Of Love), for Best Country Instrumental Performance (for Little Liza Jane) 1997, Gospel Music Asscn Dove Award for Bluegrass Recorded Song of the Year (for Children of the Living God, with Fernando Ortega) 1998, Canadian Country Music Award for Vocal/Instrumental Collaboration (for Get Me Through December, with Natalie MacMaster) 2000, Int. Bluegrass Music Asscn Award for Gospel Recorded Event of the Year (for I'll Fly Away, with Gillian Welch) 2001, Grammy Award for Country Performance by a Duo or Group (for The Lucky One) 2001, Grammy Award for Best Country Instrumental Performance (for Cluck Old Hen) 2003, Country Music Asscn Award for Best Video and Music Event (for Whiskey Lullaby, with Brad Paisley) 2004, Grammy Awards for Best Country Performance by a Duo or Group with Vocal (for Restless, with Union Station), for Best Country Instrumental Performance (for Unionhouse Branch with Union Station) 2006, for Best Pop Collaboration with Vocals (for Gone Gone Gone with Robert Plant) 2008, (for Rich Woman with Robert Plant) 2009, for Record of the Year (for Please Read the Letter with Robert Plant) 2009, for Best Country Collaboration with Vocals (for Killing the Blues with Robert Plant) 2009, CMA Award for Musical Event of the Year (for Gone Gone Gone with Robert Plant) 2008. *Current Management:* c/o Borman Entertainment, 611 Commerce Street, Nashville, TN 37203, USA. *Telephone:* (615) 320-3000. *Address:* Union Station Land Inc., PO Box 121711, Nashville, TN 37212, USA. *E-mail:* support@alisonkrauss.com. *Website:* www.alisonkrauss.com.

KRAVITZ, Lenny; American singer, musician (piano, guitar), songwriter and producer; b. 26 May 1964, New York; m. Lisa Bonet (divorced). *Career:* actor, as teenager; mem. Calif. Boys Choir and Metropolitan Opera; solo artist 1989–; numerous tours world-wide, TV and live appearances; f. Kravitz Design, Miami 2005. *Recordings include:* albums: Let Love Rule 1989, Mama Said 1991, Are You Gonna Go My Way 1993, Circus 1995, 5 1998, Greatest Hits 2000, Lenny 2001, Baptism 2004, It Is Time For A Love Revolution 2008, Black and White America 2011, Strut 2014. *Honours:* Ordre des Arts et des Lettres 2011; BRIT Award for Best Int. Male 1994, Grammy Awards for Male Rock Vocal Performance 2000, 2001, American Music Award for Favorite Pop/ Rock Male Artist 2002. *Address:* Kravitz Design Inc, 13 Crosby Street, 5th Floor, New York, NY 10013, USA (office). *Telephone:* (212) 625-1644. *E-mail:* info@kravitzdesign.com. *Website:* www.kravitzdesign.com; www.lennykravitz .com.

KREMER, Andrew, BSc, MMus; British composer and musician; b. 8 Nov. 1966, s. of Jack Kremer and Audrey Kremer; m. Jaya Kremer; one s. *Education:* Univ. of Surrey. *Career:* composer of various film and TV scores; plays double bass, bass guitar, guitar, Hang drum, waterphone, percussion, tabla, sitar; Founder-mem. world fusion group, Zöhar; mem. Faculty, London Music School 1998–2000; Assoc. Tutor, Univ. of Surrey; mem. British Acad. of Songwriters (mem. exec. cttee), Composers and Authors, Producers and Composers of Applied Music. *Recordings include:* albums: with Zöhar: One. Three. Seven 2000, Do You Have Any Faith?; has performed on recordings by Terry Callier, Nitin Sawhney, Jocelyn Brown, Paul Schutze. *Honours:* World Music Peace Award 2003. *Address:* 3 Elm Gardens, London, N2 0TF, England. *Telephone:* (20) 8177-7025. *E-mail:* info@andrewkremer.com. *Website:* www .andrewkremer.com.

KREMER, Arthur; American musician (percussion, keyboards). *Education:* Pratt Inst. of the Arts, NY. *Career:* mem. Stellastarr 2000–; founder mem. Dear Comrade. *Recordings include:* albums: Stellastarr 2003, Harmonies for the Haunted 2005, Civilized 2009. *Current Management:* c/o Plus One Music, 242 Wythe Avenue, Studio 6, Brooklyn, New York, NY 11211, USA. *Telephone:* (718) 599-3740. *Fax:* (718) 599-0998. *E-mail:* jonnykaps@ plusonemusic.net. *Address:* c/o Sony BMG, 550 Madison Avenue, New York, NY 10022, USA. *E-mail:* band@stellastarr.com. *Website:* www.stellastarr.com.

KRIEF, Hervé; French musician (guitar), singer, composer and arranger; b. 3 Aug. 1965, Paris. *Career:* numerous concerts, France and abroad. *Recordings include:* albums: Paris Funk, SAEP 1988, Comme C'Est Bizarre, SAEP 1990, Live In Paris, Hervé Krief Big Band 1991, Barbés Blues, Hervé Krief Blues Trio 1992, La Dolce Vita, Hervé Krief Big Band 1994, Paris-Bruxelles, Hervé Krief Blues Trio 1995, Strong Love Affair 1996. *Address:* 29 rue Championnet, 75018 Paris, France. *Telephone:* 1-42-58-67-50. *E-mail:* assoquartz@orange.fr. *Website:* www.herve-krief.com.

KRIEGER, Robert (Robby) Alan; American musician (guitar); b. 8 Jan. 1946, Los Angeles, Calif. *Education:* UCLA. *Career:* mem. The Doors 1965–72, The Butts Band 1972–75; also formed Robby Krieger and Friends, Versions; Co-founder, The Doors Music Co., Bright Midnight Records 1997; with surviving mems of The Doors played Rock and Roll Hall of Fame, Cleveland 1993, The Doors VH1 appearance 2001, The Doors reunion tour 2002–03; toured as The Doors of the 21st Century 2002–05. *Films:* The Doors Are Open (documentary) 1968, Feats of Friends (documentary) 1969. *Recordings include:* albums: with The Doors: The Doors 1967, Strange Days 1967, Waiting For The Sun 1968, The Soft Parade 1969, Morrison Hotel 1970, LA Woman 1971, Other Voices 1971, Weird Scenes Inside The Gold Mine 1972, Full Circle 1972; with The Butts Band: The Butts Band 1974; solo: Robby Krieger and Friends 1977, Versions 1982, No Habla 1989, RKO Live 1995, Cinematix 2000, Singularity 2010. *Website:* www.robbykrieger.com.

KRIESEL, Gregory (Greg) David, BA; American musician (bass guitar); b. 20 Jan. 1965, Glendale, Calif.; m. Jane Costello; one s. *Education:* Long Beach State Univ., Calif. *Career:* founder mem., Manic Subsidal 1984, renamed The Offspring 1986–; numerous live shows, festival appearances and tours; co-owner, Nitro label. *Recordings include:* albums: The Offspring 1989, Ignition 1992, Smash! 1994, Ixnay On The Hombre 1997, Americana 1998, Conspiracy Of One 2000, Splinter 2003, Greatest Hits 2005, Rise and Fall, Rage and Grace 2008, Days Go By 2012. *Honours:* Kerrang! Award for Classic Songwriter (with The Offspring) 2002. *Address:* The Offspring, PO Box 3479, Huntington Beach, CA 92605-3479, USA (office). *Website:* www.offspring.com.

KRIS, Wu Yifan; Chinese/Canadian singer and rapper; b. (Kevin Li Jiaheng), 6 Nov. 1990, Guangzhou, Guangdong. *Education:* Sir Winston Churchill Secondary School, Vancouver, BC, Canada. *Career:* raised in Canada; trainee at SM Entertainment, S Korea 2008–12; mem. K-pop boy band Exo 2012–; mem. sub-group Exo-M 2012–; debut single 2012; numerous TV and live appearances. *Television:* EXO's Showtime 2013–. *Recordings:* albums: Mama 2012, XOXO (Mnet Asian Music Award for Album of the Year 2013) 2013. *Honours:* numerous awards including: for Exo: Mnet Asian Music Award for Best New Asian Artist/Group 2012, MTV Europe Music Award for Best Japan/ Korea Act 2013, MelOn Music Award for Song of the Year (for Growl) 2013; for Exo-M: Top Chinese Music Award for Most Popular Group 2013. *Address:* c/o SM Entertainment, 521 Apgujeong 2-dong, Gangnam-gu, Seoul, South Korea (office). *Telephone:* (2) 6240-9800 (office). *Website:* www.smtown.com (office); exo.smtown.com (home).

KRISHNAMURTI (SUBRAMANIAM), Kavita, BA (Hons); Indian singer; b. (Sharada Krishnamurthy), 25 Jan. 1958, Delhi; m. L. Subramaniam 1999. *Education:* St Xaviers Coll. *Career:* Indian film playback singer; first recording for a Bengali film song was done with Lata Mangeshkar; has sung more than 1,500 songs in Indian films in several languages; has recorded and performed with Indian classical violinist husband on several occasions; Founder-mem. Subramaniam Acad. of Performing Arts, Bangalore 2007, now mem. Advisory Bd; performed in concert halls including Royal Albert Hall, London, The Kennedy Center, Wash., DC, Madison Square Garden, The Lincoln Center, New York, Zhongshan Music Hall, Beijing, The Esplanade, Singapore, The Putra Jaya World Trade Centre, Kuala Lumpur, Gewandhaus Leipzigm. *Films:* first Hindi film under Laxmikant Pyarelal, Maang Bharo Sajna, followed by Pyar Jhukta Nahin, Mr India, Karma, Saudagar, Khuda Gawah, Chaalbaaz, 1942: A Love Story, Yaarana, Mohara, Mumbai, Saaz, Khamoshi, Pardesh, Bhairavi, Agnisakshi, Prem Agan, Kuch Kuch Hota Hai, Bade Miyan Chhote Miyan, Wajood. *Recordings include:* soundtracks include: Lovers 1983, Pyaar Jhukta Nahin 1984, Chaalbaaz 1989, Deewana Mujhsa Nahin, Khilaaf 1990, First Love Letter, Saudagar 1991, Ek Ladka Ek Ladki, Khiladi 1992, Aankhen, Boyfriend, Chandramukhi, Dalaal, Darr, Khalnayika, Phool, Sangram, Shreeman Aashique, Waqt Hamara Hai 1993, 1942: A Love Story (Film Fare Awards 1995), Bombay, Madhosh, Mohra 1994, Dhanwaan, Kartavya, Milan, Nazar Ke Saamne, Tu Chor Main Sipahi, Vaarana 1995, Agnisakshi, Chaahat, Dushmani, Jaan, Jeet, Khamoshi The Musical (Film Fare Awards 1997), Papa Kehte Hain, Rajkumar, Tere Mere Sapne, The Great Robbery 1996, Aar Ya Paar, Betaabi, Ishq, Judwaa, Koyla, Virasat 1997, Dil Se.., Jeans, Keemat, Kuch Kuch Hota Hai, Prem Aggan 1998, Dil Kya Kare, Dillagi, Hum Dil De Chuke Sanam (Lux Zee Cine Award 1999, Screen Videocon Award 1999), Hum Saath-Saath Hain, Khoobsurat, Mann, Shool, Taal, Vaastav 1999, Badal, Dil Hi Dil Mein, Hadh Kar Di Aapne,

Hera Pheri, Kya Kehna, Mela, Pukar 2000, Daman, Dil Chahta Hai, Pyaar Ishq Aur Mohabbat 2001; Solo albums: Koi Akela Kahan, Meera Ka Ram, Pop Time, Devotional Melodies. *Honours:* Film Fare Award (for Yaarana) 1996, Star Screen Award (for Khamoshi) 1997, Sansui Viewers Choice Award 1998, Stardust Millennium Award, Best Singer 2000, Bollywood Award 2000, Film Fare Award (with Shreya Ghoshal) (for Dola Re Dola) 2003, IIFA Award (with Shreya Ghoshal) (for Dola Re Dola) 2003, Padma Shri 2005, Yesudas Award 2008. *Address:* Subramaniam Academy of Performing Arts, #3, Postal Colony Layout, Sanjay Nagar, I Main, Bangalore 560 094, India (office). *Telephone:* (80) 23515622 (office). *E-mail:* sapa.bangalore@gmail.com (office). *Website:* www.sapaindia.com (office).

KRISTIANSEN, Morten; Norwegian musician (guitar) and singer; b. 4 April 1971, Trondheim. *Career:* Founder-mem. Hedge Hog 1989; several tours of Norway, Europe; mem. Norwegian Asscn of Musicians. *Recordings include:* albums: Erase 1992, Surprise 1992, Primal Gutter 1993, Mercury Red 1994, Mindless 1994, Thorn Cord Wonder 1995.

KRISTINA, Sonja, MA; British singer and musician (guitar, saxophone, flute, piano); b. 14 April 1949, Brentwood, Essex; m. 1st Malcolm Ross 1971; m. 2nd Stewart Copeland 1982 (divorced 1992); three s. *Career:* lead singer rock group, Curved Air; Chrissy, original London cast of musical Hair; several Fringe theatre projects, including Shona (directed by Claire Davidson); Pentameters Hampstead 1989; has performed on MASK with Marvin Ayres; mem. Equity, Musicians' Union, AOTOS. *Recordings include:* eight albums with Curved Air 1971–76, Lovechild 1990, Reborne 2000, Retrospective 2010, North Star 2014; Songs from the Acid Folk 1989, Sonja Kristina 1980, Harmonics of Love 1993, Cri de Coeur 2003, Mask-Healing Senses (DVD) 2005. *Honours:* Sounds Poll voted top female vocalist 1971. *Current Management:* c/o QEDG Management, Liscombe Park, Aylesbury, LU7 0GE, England. *E-mail:* qedg@qedg.co.uk. *Website:* www.qedg.co.uk; www.sonjakristina.com; www.mask.uk.net; www.curvedair.com.

KRISTOFFERSON, Kris, BA, PhD; American country singer, songwriter and actor; b. (Kris Carson), 22 June 1936, Brownsville, Tex.; m. 1st; one s. one d.; m. 2nd Rita Coolidge 1973 (divorced 1980); one d.; m. 3rd Lisa Meyers 1983; four s., one d. *Education:* Pomona Coll. and Univ. of Oxford, UK. *Career:* Capt. in US Army 1960–65; songwriter 1965–; solo recording artist 1969–; mem. of side project, The Highwaymen 1985; numerous concerts world-wide; actor 1972–. *Films include:* Cisco Pike 1972, Pat Garrett and Billy the Kid 1973, Blume in Love 1973, Bring Me the Head of Alfredo Garcia 1974, Alice Doesn't Live Here Anymore 1974, The Sailor Who Fell From Grace With The Sea 1976, A Star is Born 1976, Vigilante Force 1976, Semi-Tough 1977, Convoy 1978, Heaven's Gate 1981, Rollover 1981, Welcome Home 1989, Millennium 1989, A Soldier's Daughter Never Cries 1998, Blade 1 1998, Come Dance with Me 1999, Payback 1999, Limbo 1999, Joyriders 1999, Comanche 2000, Planet of the Apes 2001, Chelsea Walls 2001, Wooly Boys 2001, D-Tox 2002, Blade II 2002, Where the Red Fern Grows 2003, Blade III 2003, The Jacket, Lives of the Saints, Where the Red Fern Grows, Dreamer 2005, Gun (voice) 2005, The Wendell Baker Story 2005, Fast Food Nation 2006, Disappearances 2006, Requiem for Billy the Kid (voice) 2006, Room 10 2006, Crossing the Heart 2007, Jump Out Boys 2008, Powder Blue 2009, He's Just Not That Into You 2009, The Last Rites of Ransom Pride 2009, Bloodworth 2010, Dolphin Tale 2011, The Greening of Whitney Brown 2011, Joyful Noise 2012, Deadfall 2012, The Motel Life 2012, Angels Sing 2013, Dolphin Tale 2 2014. *Television appearances include:* Freedom Road (TV film) 1979, Amerika (series) 1987, Rip 1989, Sandino, Christmas in Connecticut 1992, Tad 1995. *Recordings include:* albums: Kristofferson 1970, The Silver-Tongued Devil and I 1971, Border Lord 1972, Jesus Was a Capricorn 1973, Full Moon (with Rita Coolidge) 1973, Spooky Lady's Sideshow 1974, Who's to Bless and Who's to Blame 1975, Breakaway (with Rita Coolidge) 1975, A Star Is Born (sound-track) 1977, Surreal Thing 1976, Songs of Kristofferson 1977, Easter Island 1978, Natural Act (with Rita Coolidge) 1979, Shake Hands With The Devil (with Rita Coolidge) 1979, Help Me Make It Through The Night 1980, To The Bone 1981, The Winning Hand 1983, Music From Songwriter (with Willie Nelson) 1984, Highwayman (with The Highwaymen) 1985, Repossessed 1986, Third World Warrior 1990, Highwaymen 2 (with The Highwaymen) 1992, A Moment of Forever 1995, The Austin Sessions 1999, Broken Freedom Song: Live from San Francisco 2003, Repossessed/Third World Warrior 2004, This Old Road 2006, Closer to the Bone 2009, Please Don't Tell Me How the Story Ends 2010, Feeling Mortal 2013. *Honours:* CMA Song of the Year (for Sunday Morning Coming Down) 1970, Grammy Awards for Best Country Song 1972, Best Country Vocal Performance (with Coolidge) 1973, 1976, Golden Globe for Best Actor 1976, ACM Single of the Year (for Highwayman, with The Highwaymen) 1986, two American Music Awards (with The Highwaymen) 1986, Americana Awards Free Speech Award 2003, Johnny Cash Visionary Award, CMT Music Awards 2007. *Current Management:* c/o Tamara Saviano, Ellis Creative. *Telephone:* (615) 400-0388. *E-mail:* tamara@tamarasaviano .com. *Website:* www.tamarasaviano.com. *Address:* c/o New West Records, 9215 West Olympic Boulevard, Beverly Hills, CA 90212, USA (office). *Website:* www.kriskristofferson.com.

KRIZIC, Davor; Croatian musician (trumpet, flugelhorn) and composer; b. 29 March 1966, Zagreb. *Education:* Musical High School, Zagreb; Univ. of Graz. *Career:* played with: Ernie Wilkins, Ed Thighpen, Bosko Petrovic, Jimmy Woody, David Liebmon; soloist, Croatian Radio-TV Big Band; played at Jazz Fair, Zagreb 1990, 1992–95, Ingolstadt Jazz Festival 1990, Springtime Jazz Feever 1995; numerous TV and radio appearances in Croatia; Greentown

Jazz Band German tour; Leader, Boilers Jazz Quartet, Zagreb; band mem. Cubismo; mem. Jazz Club, Zagreb, Croatian Music Union, Croatian Artistes' Soc. (ZUH). *Compositions:* Beleavin', Some Blues, Urony. *Recordings include:* Albums: with Miro Kadoic: Dry 1994; with Mia: Ne Ne Ker Se Ne Sme 1994; with Miljenko Prohaska: Opus 900 1994; with Boilers Jazz Quartet, Zagreb: Some blues 1997, Abstract lights 1999; with Boško Petrović: St. Miles Infirmary 2000; with Boilers All Stars: That's it (Discographic Award, Porin for Best Jazz Album 2004) 2003; with Cubismo: Cubismo 1997, Viva La Habana 1998, Motivo Cubano 2000, Junglesalsa 2002, Amigos 2004, Autobus Calypso 2007. *Honours:* Best Young Jazz Musician, Jazz Fair, Zagreb 1990, Discographic award for the best jazz composition (for To the lite) 1999. *E-mail:* davor.krizic@cubismo.com. *Website:* www.cubismo.com.

KROEGER, Chad; Canadian singer and musician (guitar); b. (Chad Robert Turton), 15 Nov. 1974, Hanna, Alberta; brother of Mike Kroeger; m. Avril Lavigne 2013. *Career:* lead singer rock band, Nickelback 1996–; extensive tours; collaboration with Santana 2002; Founder, 604 Records label. *Recordings include:* albums: Curb 1996, The State 1999, Silver Side Up (Juno Award for Best Rock Album 2002) 2001, The Long Road 2003, All The Right Reasons (Juno Award for Best Rock Album 2006, American Music Award for Favorite Pop/Rock Album 2006, Billboard Award for Rock Album of the Year 2006) 2005, Dark Horse (Juno Award for Album of the Year 2009) 2008, Here and Now 2011, No Fixed Address 2014. *Honours:* Juno Award for Best New Group 2001, Best Group, Best Single (for How You Remind Me) 2002, MuchMusic Video Award for Best Video (for Too Bad), Best Rock Video (for How You Remind Me) 2002, MTV Video Music Award for Best Video from a Film (for Hero, with Josey Scott) 2002, Juno Award for Best Group 2006, 2009, Billboard Award for Artist Duo/Group of the Year, for Hot 100 Artist Duo/Group of the Year 2006, American Music Award for Favorite Pop/Rock Band, Duo or Group 2007, Juno Fan Choice Award 2009. *Address:* 604 Records Inc., 12 3rd Avenue E, Vancouver, BC V5T 1C3, Canada (office). *Telephone:* (604) 879-7322 (office). *E-mail:* chad@gmail.com (office). *Website:* www.604records .com; www.nickelback.com.

KROEGER, Mike; Canadian musician (bass guitar); b. 25 June 1974, Hanna, Alberta; brother of Chad Kroeger; m. Angela Kroeger; two c. *Career:* mem. rock band, Nickelback 1996–. *Recordings include:* albums: Curb 1996, The State 1999, Silver Side Up (Juno Award for Best Rock Album 2002) 2001, The Long Road 2003, All The Right Reasons (Juno Award for Best Rock Album 2006, American Music Award for Favorite Pop/Rock Album 2006, Billboard Award for Rock Album of the Year 2006) 2005, Dark Horse (Juno Award for Album of the Year 2009) 2008, Here and Now 2011, No Fixed Address 2014. *Honours:* Juno Award for Best New Group 2001, Best Group, Best Single (for How You Remind Me) 2002, MuchMusic Video Award for Best Video (for Too Bad), Best Rock Video (for How You Remind Me) 2002, Juno Award for Best Group 2006, 2009, Billboard Award for Artist Duo/Group of the Year, for Hot 100 Artist Duo/Group of the Year 2006, American Music Award for Favorite Pop/Rock Band, Duo or Group 2007, Juno Fan Choice Award 2009. *Current Management:* c/o 604 Records Inc., 12 3rd Ave E, Vancouver, BC V5T 1C3, Canada. *Telephone:* (604) 879-7322. *E-mail:* chad@gmail.com. *Website:* www .604records.com; www.nickelback.com.

KROEGHER, Freddy; French singer, composer, musician (guitar, bass guitar), author and entertainer; *Director, Freddy Kroegher Studio;* b. 23 Sept. 1967, St-Etienne; m. Marie Kroegher; one d. *Education:* AIMRA Jazz School, Lyon, masterclass with Steve Vai, Greg Howe, Patrick Rondat, jazz workshop in Preyssac. *Career:* producer, Hacienda Records; distributor, Musidisc; Ed., Rondo Music, Universal; sang at Francofolies of La Rochelle Festival 1993, Festival of Young Creators, Tignes 1993, nat. FNAC Tour, special broadcast interview in France-Inter Radio; TV clip video (Killer); concerts and radio appearances; TV interviews, newspapers; as comedian/singer/composer: Les variations Goldberg, three-month run at Chaillot Theatre, Paris and French tour; TV cartoon music composer, 'Virelangues' Frederic Philibert; live sound engineer for Benighted (brutal-death core) during European tours, Hellfest (France), Summer Breeze, Was Soll Death Fest, Rock Area Festival (Germany), Obscene Extrem Festival (Czech Repub.), Neurotic Death Fest (Netherlands), Le GDL Metal Fest (Portugal), Le Metal Fest Open Air (Austria), Inferno Festival (Norway) etc.; producer of talents in own studio (Raphael Herrerias, Benighted, Le baron de Vezeline, Lioreiv, Heavylution etc.); guitar session musician and sideman for artists including Nilda Fernandez (French songwriter), Jimmy Oihid (Reggae-dub), Lapassenkoff (experimental funk), Michel Rouyre, Jean-Luc Lahaye, Nicoletta (French variety), Gilles Coquard (jazz), Heavylution (heavy-metal), Dandy Freaks (electro) and others; live participant with Mickey 3D (Mickaël Furnon), Michael Jones, Little Bob, Robert Lapassade, Gilles Coquard, André Verchuren, Jim Zeller, Louis Bertignac and others; opera rock composer/ writer, Le French Café with soprano Aurelie Baudet, Cecile Camatte and the Loire Maitrisien School; composer/conceptual artist, Guerrier (experimental show with acoustic music, dance, singing, theatre and martial arts). *Recordings include:* Freddy Kroegher: Le Meilleur 1993, Secoue Ton Seve 1995; compilations: Vol. 1, Rock à la MCC (DVD live with EP). *Publications:* contribs to Longueur d'ondes, Libération Lyon, le Progrès, Best, Hard Rock magazine. *Honours:* SACEM School bourse (for AIMRA Jazz School), Twice Best Rock Artist, Rhone-Alpes region, France 1990, 1991. *Address:* Le Moulin d'Anjou, Le Reynard, 42360 Cottance, France. *Telephone:* (4) 77-28-09-17; 6-75-05-28-60 (mobile). *E-mail:* stud.fk@gmail.com. *Website:* www.freddykroegher.wix .com.

KROG, Karin; Norwegian jazz singer; b. 15 May 1937, Oslo; d. of Eilif Krog and Ragnhild Krog; m. Johannes Bergh 1957 (died 2001); two d. *Education:* business school, studied music privately with Anne Brown, Ivo Knecevic. *Career:* mem. Kjell Karlsen Quartet, Frode Thingnaes Quintet and Egil Kapstad Trio; leader of own groups 1962–; worked with Don Ellis, Clare Fischer, Mikkel Flagstad, Einar Iversen, John Surman, Bengt Hallberg, Red Mitchell, Nils Lindberg, Warne Marsh, Richard Rodney Bennett; Founder and first Chair. Norwegian Jazz Forum 1965–66; numerous worldwide live radio and TV appearances, including jazz festivals; formed Meantime Records 1987; mem. Norwegian Musicians' Fed., Norwegian Soc. of Composers and Lyricists (NOPA), FONO. *Compositions include:* ballet music for Carolyn Carlson and Lario Ekson. *Recordings include:* By Myself 1964, Jazz Moments 1966, Joy 1968, Some Other Spring (with Dexter Gordon) 1970, Hi-Fly (with Archie Shepp) 1972, I Remember You (with Red Mitchell and Warne Marsh) 1980, Two of a Kind (with Beng Hallberg) 1981, Nordic Quartet (with John Surman, Terje Rypdal, Vigleik Storaas) 1995, Bluesand (with John Surman) 1999, Seagull (with Bergen Big Band) 2005, Together Again (with Steve Juhn) 2006, Cabin in the Sky (with Bengt Hallberg) 2011, In a Rag Bag (with Morten Gunnar Larsen) 2012, Songs About This & That 2013. *Publications:* Where Flamingos Fly 2002, Where You At 2003, Seagull 2005, Sweet Talker 2005. *Honours:* Royal Norwegian Order of St Olav 2004; Norwegian Jazz Foundation Buddy Award 1965, Spellemanns Prize 1974, 1999, Grammy Award, Norway 1974, European Jazz Fed. Award for Female Singer of the Year 1975, two Swing Journal Awards for Record of the Year, Japan 1970, 1978, Oslo Council Artist Award 1981, Radka Toneff Memorial Prize 1999, Anders Jahre Culture Prize 2007, The Ella Prize, several govt grants and scholarships. *Address:* Ørneveien 5, 1357 Bekkestua, Norway (office). *Telephone:* 67-12-55-09 (home). *E-mail:* karin@karinkrog.no (office). *Website:* www.karinkrog.no (office).

DJ KRUSH; Japanese DJ and producer; b. (Hideaki Ishi), 1962, Tokyo; m.; two d. *Career:* fmr mem. Krush Posse; numerous collaborations, including DJ Shadow, The Roots, Guru, C. L. Smooth, Shawn J. Period, Mos Def, DJ Cam, Galliano, Nas, Jhelisa, Omar, MC Solaar, DJ Spooky, Tunde Ayanyemi. *Recordings include:* albums: DJ Krush 1994, Bad Brothers (with Ronny Jordan) 1994, Strictly Turntablized 1994, Krush 1995, Meiso 1995, Milight 1997, Ki-Oku (with Toshinori Kondo) 1998, Holonic: The Self-Megamix 1998, Kakusei 1999, Code 4109 2000, Zen 2001, Shinsou 2002, Jaku 2004, Stepping Stones. *Address:* Es.U.Es Corporation, 4-12-4 Honcho, Nakano-ku, Tokyo 164-0012, Japan. *Telephone:* (3) 3381-4072. *E-mail:* krush@sus81.jp. *Website:* www.sus81.jp/djkrush.

KRUSPE, Richard Z.; German musician (guitar) and songwriter; b. 24 June 1967, Wittenburg; m. Caron Bernstein 1999 (divorced). *Career:* fmr mem., Orgasm Death Gimmicks; mem., Rammstein 1993–; the band has a reputation for theatrical live performances; mem. Emigrate 2005–; numerous European tours. *Recordings include:* albums: with Rammstein: Herzeleid 1995, Sehnsucht 1997, Live aus Berlin 1999, Mutter 2001, Reise, Reise 2004, Rosenrot 2005, Liebe ist für alle da 2009; with Emigrate: Emigrate 2007. *Honours:* MTV Europe Music Award for Best German Act 2005. *Current Management:* Pilgrim Management, Greifswalderstrasse 224, 10405 Berlin, Germany. *E-mail:* info@pilgrim-management.de. *Website:* www.pilgrim -management.de; www.rammstein.de; www.emigrate.eu.

DJ KRUST; (Gang Related, Glamour Gold); British producer, remixer and DJ; b. (Kirk Thompson), 1968, Bristol. *Career:* first releases on Ten Records, late 1980s; began releasing material with Roni Size on V Recordings and on Size's own Full Cycle Records; Co-founder, Reprazent (with Roni Size); released debut solo album 2000; Collaborations: Roni Size, DJ Die; remixed: Bjork, Moloko, DJ Rap, Nicolette. *Recordings include:* albums: New Forms (with Reprazent) (Mercury Music Prize) 1997, Coded Language 2000, In The Mode (with Reprazent) 2001, Hidden Knowledge 2006; singles: Deceivers 1993, Jazz Note 1994, Quiz Show 1995, Angles 1996, Genetic Manipulation 1997, Brown Paper Bag (with Reprazent) 1997, True Stories 1998, Decoded 2000.

KRZISNIK, Borut; Slovenian composer and musician (guitar); b. 7 Oct. 1961, Zagreb, Croatia. *Education:* Ljubljana Univ. *Career:* numerous works performed, including Love Song No. 1 with Symphonic Orchestra of Slovenian Philharmony, Questions with the Enzo Fabiani Quartet; festival appearances with own band Data Direct, Druga Godba 1993, Music of the 20th Century, Skopje 1994, Vorax, Vicenza 1994; collaborations with theatre dirs, including Gerald Thomas, Emil Hrvatin and Julie-Anne Robinson, and film dir Peter Greenaway. *Recordings include:* Currents of Time 1991; with Data Direct: La Dolce Vita 1995, The Stories from Magatrea 1999, Valse Brutal 2009, A life in Suitcase 2012, Sacre du Temps 2013, Lightening 2013. *Theatre:* collaboration with Emil Hrvatin: Camillo, Piccolo Teatro, Milan 1998; with Julie-Anne Robinson: Yard, Bush Theatre, London 1998; Two Gentlemen of Verona, Royal Nat. Theatre 1999; with Gerald Thomas: Nietzsche Contra Wagner, SESC, Sao Paulo 2000. *Films include:* Reitdiep Journeys (documentary) 2001, Grand Terp (installation, Groningen) 2001, Map to Paradise (installation, Ljubljana) 2001, Tulse Luper Suitcases trilogy (collaboration with Peter Greenaway) 2003–04. *Honours:* first prize Napoli Danza Festival, Il Coreografo Eletronico 1994. *E-mail:* borut.krzisnik@guest.arnes.si. *Website:* www2.arnes.si/~ksbkrzi/#target1.

KUBES, Stanislav, (Klasek); Czech musician (guitar) and songwriter; b. 4 March 1952, Prague; m. Marcela 1973. *Education:* Public School of Art.

Career: mem. The Wizards 1970, Eminence Group 1972, Benefit Group 1973, Respect Group 1974–75, JIFT Schelinger Group 1975–81, SLS Group 1981–85, ETC... Band 1985–2001; tour of Poland with Smokie 1977; support for Rolling Stones, Urban Jungle Tour, Prague 1990; mem. T4 blues rock group 2002–. *Compositions:* 20 titles published, including Jsem pry blazen jen 1978, Vanda a Zanda, LP and TV clip 1985, Za vodou 1997, Šedý pán 2005, Funny 2005, V prachu 2005. *Films:* Romance za korunu 1975, Parta hic 1976. *Recordings:* 35 singles, 1975–81; Hrr na ne! 1975, Nám se Líbí 1976, SL 1982, Coloured Dreams 1984, ETC... 1986, ETC... 4 1987, 20 deta duse 1989, Jen se smej 1994, ETC... Band, Unplugged Live 1996, Město z périn 1997. *Honours:* Hall of Glory, Radio Beat-Prague 2010. *E-mail:* B787@email.cz (office). *Website:* www.t4rock.cz.

KUBIŠOVÁ, Marta; Czech singer; b. 1 Nov. 1942, České Budějovice; d. of Jan Kubiš and Marta Kubišová; m. 1st Jan Němec 1969; m. 2nd Jan Moravec 1974; one d. *Education:* Grammar School, Poděbrady. *Career:* singer with Stop Theatre, Pardubice 1962–63, Alfa Theatre, Pilsen 1963–64, Rokoko Theatre, Prague 1964–68, Golden Kids Group 1968–70; Spokesperson of Charter 77 1977–78; banned from singing until 'Velvet Revolution' 1989; Ungelt Theatre, Prague. *Television:* presenter, Adventní koncerty (Czech TV) 1991–2012, Chcete mě?. *Honours:* Nat. Order of the Legion of Honour 2012; Golden Nightingale Award 1966, 1968, 1969, Thálie Award (Ungelt Theatre) 2002 and various other awards. *E-mail:* PR-MK@seznam.cz (office). *Website:* www.martakubisova.cz.

KUCERA, Josef Simon, (Saxophone Joe); Czech musician (saxophones, flute); b. 8 July 1943, Prague. *Career:* with Framus Five, soul band, Czechoslovakia 1967–68; in musical Hair 1969–70; with duo Jesse Ballard and Saxophone Joe 1972–74; sessions with Alexis Korner, London, Paradise Island Band, Berlin 1976; mem. Pete 'Wyoming' Bender Band 1980–90; Jazz Festival Karlovy Vary, Czech Republic 1990, 1993; Japan Tour with Marta Kubisova 1993; Artistic Dir Jazz Meeting Berlin 1997–2007; Initiator and Artistic Dir Europe Blues Train 2009–; mem. Rock and Pop Musikerverband. *Compositions:* Day Dream; Anyway; 1000 Reasons; Waltz for My Friends; Anotherway. *Recordings includes:* Control 1975, Crossroads 1982, Swindia 1984, Balance (solo album)1986, Triangle, Live 1997, Reifegerste Trio - Am I 2011, Talkin' to the Rain (with Jesse Ballard) 2003. *Address:* Koloniestr 28, 13359 Berlin, Germany. *Telephone:* (30) 4942106. *Website:* www.joe-kucera.com.

KUDERSKI, Jacek; Polish rock musician (bass guitar); b. 1970. *Career:* mem. rock band Myslovitz 1994–; first int. concerts, Sweden, Germany, USA 1998; numerous European festival appearances and support act for Iggy Pop and Simple Minds 2002; began releasing English-language versions of their music 2002; European tour and support act for Iggy Pop and The Corrs 2004; contributed to soundtracks for films Młode wilki ½ (Young Wolves ½), Duże zwierzę (The Big Animal), To my (That's us). *Recordings:* albums: Myslovitz 1995, Sun Machine 1996, Z rozmyślań przy śniadaniu 1997, Miłość w czasach popkultury 1999, Korova Milky Bar 2002, The Best Of 2003, Korova Milky Bar (English version) 2003, Skalary, mieczyki, neonki 2004, Happiness Is Easy 2006. *Honours:* Music Video of The Year 1998, Band of The Year and Rock Album of The Year 1999, Song of The Year and Video of The Year 2000, Album of The Year 2003, all Fryderyk awards; Polityka's Paszport award 1999, Best Polish Act, MTV Europe Music Awards 2002, 2003, Border Breakers European Breakthrough award (for Korova Milky Bar) 2005. *Current Management:* Maciej Pilarczyk, Chaos Management Group, ul. Karowa 31, 00-324 Warsaw, Poland. *E-mail:* m.pil@myslovitz.pl (office). *Website:* www.chaos.com.pl (office); www.myslovitz.pl.

KUDERSKI, Wojciech, (Lala); Polish musician (drums, percussion); b. 1972. *Career:* mem. rock band Myslovitz 1994–; first int. concerts, Sweden, Germany, USA 1998; numerous European festival appearances and support act for Iggy Pop and Simple Minds 2002; began releasing English-language versions of their music 2002; European tour and support act for Iggy Pop and The Corrs 2004; contributed to soundtracks for films Młode wilki ½ (Young Wolves ½), Duże zwierzę (The Big Animal), To my (That's us). *Recordings:* albums: Myslovitz 1995, Sun Machine 1996, Z rozmyślań przy śniadaniu 1997, Miłość w czasach popkultury 1999, Korova Milky Bar 2002, The Best Of 2003, Korova Milky Bar (English version) 2003, Skalary, mieczyki, neonki 2004, Happiness Is Easy 2006. *Honours:* Music Video of The Year 1998, Band of The Year and Rock Album of The Year 1999, Song of The Year and Video of The Year 2000, Album of The Year 2003, all Fryderyk awards; Polityka's Paszport award 1999, Best Polish Act, MTV Europe Music Awards 2002, 2003, Border Breakers European Breakthrough award (for Korova Milky Bar) 2005. *Current Management:* Maciej Pilarczyk, Chaos Management Group, ul. Karowa 31, 00-324 Warsaw, Poland. *E-mail:* m.pil@myslovitz.pl (office). *Website:* www.chaos.com.pl (office); www.myslovitz.pl.

KUJAHN, Lars Bo; Danish musician (drums); b. 22 June 1958, Copenhagen; s. of Gert Petersen and Maria Kujahn; m. Fatma Zidan Moamen Salla el Din. *Education:* attended Lectures in Rhythms, Istanbul Conservatory 1988, Cairo 1989, Casablanca 1992, Fanoon 1997. *Career:* played Jazz-Rock in Passengers, Milky Way 1979–86; played Gypsy Music in Svira 1982–87; Leader of Oriental Mood 1991; teacher, Oriental Percussion 1991–; mem. Danish Musicians' Union, Danish Rhythmic Composers Org. *Compositions include:* Raqsa Maghzebia 1992, Yallah Mustagbad 1992, Macera 1995, Hobb Harr 1995, Gediid 1995, Oriental Moods 1996, Ahman 1997, Mapsut 1997, 12 Ok 1997.

Recordings include: Travels 1994, Oriental Moods 1996, Oriental Garden 1996, Ax Kurdistaan 1996, Cölbanein 1998, Expoessive Mahala.

KUKIZ, Paweł; Polish singer, actor and politician; b. 24 June 1963, Paczków; m. Małgorzata Kukiz; three d. *Career:* as singer, genres include pop, rock, pop rock and punk rock, collaborations with CDN, Hak, Aya RL, Emigranci, Piersi, Maciej Maleńczuk and Jan Borysewicz; third-placed cand. in presidential election 2015. *Films include:* Jestem przeciw 1985, Girl Guide 1995, Billboard 1998, Matki, żony i kochanki II 1998, Poniedziałek 1998, Stacja PRL 1999–2000, Dzieci Jarocina 2000, Wtorek 2001, Czwarta władza 2004, S@motność w Sieci 2006. *Recordings include:* albums: Borysewicz & Kukiz (with Jan Borysewicz) 2003, Starsi panowie (with Maciej Maleńczuk) 2010, Siła i honor 2012, Zakazane piosenki 2014. *Address:* 50-134 Warsaw, Ul. Białoskórnicza 3/1, Poland. *E-mail:* kontakt@ruchjow.pl. *Website:* ruchjow.pl/#.

KUKKO, (Jyrki) Sakari; Finnish musician (flute, saxophone, keyboards), bandleader, composer and arranger; *Leader, Piirpauke;* b. 8 July 1953, Kajaani; m. 1st Marta Cecilia Renza Villanueva 1981 (divorced 1986); m. 2nd Sheila Jane Surban; one s. *Education:* Sibelius Acad., Helsinki, jazz with Edward Vesala, amongst others. *Career:* began as a street-singer early 1960s; two first prices in nat. singing contests 1965; Founder Piirpauke 1974–; Leader, Humbalax and Helle; concerts include: Festivals in Tbilisi, Mumbai, Zurich, Paris, London, Austin, Havana, Berlin, Leipzig, Zagreb, Sarajevo, Cannes, Barcelona, Molde, Izmir, Istanbul etc.; concerts and tours with Piirpauke in 30 different countries (four continents); also with Youssou N'Dour, El Hadji Faye, Baobab, Super Diamono, Gunter Chirstmann, Joonas Ahonen, Okay Temiz, Alameda, Aster Aweke & Sensation Band, Charlie Mariano, Thad Jones,Walter Bishop Jr, John McLaughlin, Zakhir Hussein, Apurba Mukherjee, Indrani Mukherjee, Iiro Rantala, Edward Vesala, Iro Haarla, Raoul Björkenheim, Olavi Louhivuori, Heikki Sarmanto, Mahmout Ahmed, EBB, RSO, HKO, Viktor Klimenko, Anneli Sari, Anu Komsi, David Schnitter, Partho Sarothy, Humbalax, Valo, Jazzoom, Baluji Shrivastav, Ivo Papasof, Amorphis, Kingston Wall, Polo Orti; TV and radio appearances world-wide. *Compositions:* for the Espoo Big Band: Moonlight Caravan, Finnish Characters. *Recordings:* 30 albums with Piirpauke; seven solo albums: Will of The Wisp 1979, Music For Espoo Big Band 1989, Virret 2001, Joulu 2003, Soi Kiitos 2010, Humbalax 2011, Valo 2013; with Sensation Band Ethiopia '76: Ethiopian Groove; features on: Am Universum, Amorphis 2001; hundreds of recordings as a side-man; music for films, theatre, dance etc. *Honours:* Yrjö Award, Finnish Jazz Fed. 1976, Special Emma 2014, amongst others. *Address:* Majavatie 10 as. 1, 00800 Helsinki; c/o Rockadillo, Kehräsaari A215, 33200 Tampere, Finland. *Telephone:* 40-5513717 (mobile); (10) 2712323 (Rockadillo). *E-mail:* jyrkisakarikukko@gmail.com; tapio@rockadillo.fi. *Website:* www.sakarikukko.com.

KULAS, Michael; Canadian musician (guitar, percussion) and backing singer. *Career:* mem., James 1997–2001; numerous tours, festival dates and television appearances; formed own band, Dead City Radio; composer for film and television. *Recordings include:* albums: with James: Whiplash 1997, The Best Of James 1998, Millionaires 1999, B-Sides Ultra 2001, Pleased To Meet You 2001, Getting Away With It 2002; solo: Mosquito 1995, Another Small Machine 2001. *E-mail:* contact@michaelkulas.com. *Website:* www.michaelkulas.com.

KULASH, Damian; American singer, musician (guitar, keyboards) and songwriter; b. (Damian Joseph Kulash Jr), 7 Oct. 1975, Washington, DC; m. Ambra Medda 2011. *Education:* St Albans School, Brown Univ. *Career:* Founder, Level Records 1994–96; mem. Calixto Chinchile 1996; Founder-mem. Stanley's Joyful Noise 1997–98; mem. OK Go 1998–; signed to Capitol Records 2001; f. own label for OK Go recordings, Paracadute Recordings 2010. *Recordings:* albums: with OK Go: OK Go 2002, Oh No 2004, Of the Blue Colour of the Sky 2010, Hungry Ghosts 2014. *Honours:* Grammy Award for Best Music Video 2007, UK Music Video Awards for Video of the Year and Best Rock Video 2010, CLIO Gold Award in Branded Entertainment 2013, MTV Video Music Award for Best Visual Effects 2014. *Address:* c/o Mike Rosenthal, Paracadute, 236 Hoyt Street, Suite 2, Brooklyn, New York, NY 11217, USA (office). *E-mail:* Rosenthal@paracadute.net (office); paracadute@okgo.net (office). *Website:* www.paracadute.net (office); www.okgo.net.

KULICK, Bruce; American musician (guitar); b. 12 Dec. 1953, Brooklyn, NY. *Career:* mem. various groups, including Blackjack, Goodrats, Union; mem. rock group, Kiss 1984–96; guitarist with Grand Funk Railroad 2001–; numerous live appearances, tours. *Recordings include:* albums: with Blackjack: Blackjack 1979, Worlds Apart 1980, with The Good Rats: Great American Music 1981; with Kiss: Asylum 1985, Crazy Nights 1987, Smashes Thrashes and Hits 1988, Hot in the Shade 1989, Revenge 1992, Kiss Alive III 1992, Carnival of Souls: The Final Session 1997; with Union: Union 1998, Live in the Galaxy 1999, The Blue Room 2000; with ESP: ESP 1999; solo: Audio Dog 2001, Transformer 2003, BK3 2010; numerous other credits include albums for: Michael Bolton, Michael Schenker, Billy Squier. *Current Management:* Entertainment Services Unlimited, Main Street Plaza 1000, Suite 303, Voorhees, NJ 08043, USA. *E-mail:* BruceKool@aol.com. *Website:* www.kulick.net.

KUND, Olav (Olku); Estonian musician. *Career:* mem., Tuberkuloited 1988–. *Recordings include:* albums: Klassiõhtu 1992, Lilleke rohus 1993, Religioon 1995, Õhtupimedas 1997, Seitseteist lillekest rohus 1999, D-Tuur, Vol. 6 1999, Kiirteel 2000, Wiimane 2001, Tuberkuloited unplugged 2001,

Estraadialbum 2003, Põlevad väljad 2004. *Current Management:* MMM Agentuur OÜ, Risti 2-21, 11624 Tallinn, Estonia. *E-mail:* mm@mmagentuur .ee. *Website:* www.mmagentuur.ee. *E-mail:* Olavkund@hotmail.com. *Website:* www.tuberkuloited.ee.

KUSSIN, Al, BA, MA (Econs); Canadian producer and musician (keyboards); *Owner, Kool Music, Slak Productions;* b. 24 Aug. 1952, Edmonton, Alberta; m. Lorraine Scott; one s. *Education:* Royal Conservatory of Music. *Career:* producer for artists, including Lorraine Scott, Céline Dion; Owner Kool Music, Slak Productions; supplies promotional music; mem. Soc. of Composers, Authors and Music Publrs of Canada (SOCAN), Canadian Institutional Research and Planning Asscn, Audio-Video Licensing Agency Inc., Canadian Acad. of Recording Arts and Sciences. *Recordings:* numerous platinum and gold records. *Address:* 9 Hector Avenue, Toronto, ON M6G 3G2, Canada (office). *Telephone:* (416) 533-3520 (office); (416) 533-3707 (office). *Fax:* (416) 533-3707 (office). *E-mail:* al@koolmusic.com (office); akussin@sympatico.ca (home). *Website:* www.koolmusic.com (office).

KUSTURICA, Emir; Bosnia and Herzegovina film director and musician (guitar); b. 24 Nov. 1954, Sarajevo. *Education:* FAMU School, Prague, Czechoslovakia. *Career:* teacher, Columbia Univ., New York, USA; mem. rock and roll band, No Smoking Orchestra 1986–; Chair. of Jury, Cannes Film Festival 2005. *Films include:* Do You Remember Dolly Bell? (Golden Lion Award, Venice) 1981, When Father Was Away On Business (Palme d'Or, Cannes 1984) 1984, Time of the Gypsies (Best Dir, Cannes) 1988, Arizona Dream (Special Jury Prize, Berlin) 1993, Underground (Palme d'Or, Cannes) 1995, Black Cat White Cat 1998, La Veuve de Saint-Pierre 2000, Super Eight Stories 2001, Life is a Miracle 2004, Maradona (documentary) 2008, L'Affaire Farewell 2009. *Recordings include:* albums with No Smoking Orchestra: Das ist Walter 1984, Dok cekaš sabah sa šejtanom 1985, Pozdrav iz zemlje Safari (Greetings from Safari Land) 1987, Male price o velikoj ljubavi (A Little Story of a Great Love) 1989, Ja nisam odavle 1997, Black Cat White Cat 1998, Unza Unza Time 2000, La Vie est un miracle (soundtrack to film) 2004. *Publications:* Smrt je neprovjerena glasina (Death is an Unverified Rumour) (autobiography) 2010, Sto jada (Hundred Pains) (novel) 2013. *Current Management:* c/o Rasta Films, Belgrade, Serbia. *Telephone:* (11) 308-64-60. *Fax:* (11) 308-64-61. *E-mail:* marie-christine.malbert@libertysurf.fr (office); office@thenosmokingorchestra.com. *Website:* www.kustu.com; thenosmokingorchestra.com.

KUTI, Femi Anikulapo; Nigerian musician (saxophone), singer and songwriter; b. 1962, Lagos; s. of the late Fela Kuti; m. Funke Kuti; one s. *Career:* musician in his father's band, The Egypt 80, specializing in Afrobeat music; performed at the Hollywood Bowl (as substitute for his father) 1985; formed own group Positive Force 1987; numerous concerts, TV and radio appearances; est. New Shrine open-air nightclub 2000. *Recordings include:* albums: No Cause for Alarm? (with the Positive Force) 1989, M.Y.O.B. 1991, Femi Kuti 1995, Wonder Wonder 1995, Shoki Shoki 1998, Fight to Win 2001, Africa Shrine 2004, Day by Day 2008, Africa for Africa 2010, No Place for My Dream 2013. *Publication:* AIDS in Africa (essay published by UNICEF in its Progress of Nations report) 2000. *Honours:* Kora Awards for Best Male Artist and Best West African Artist 1999, World Music Award for Best Selling African Artist 2000. *Current Management:* c/o LabelMaison, La Cile, 41 rue de la Duée, 75020 Paris, France. *Telephone:* 1-46-36-70-03. *Fax:* 1-44-24-04-67. *E-mail:* francis.kertekian@wanadoo.fr. *Website:* www.femikuti.tv. *Address:* c/o Wrasse Records, Wrasse House, The Drive, Tyrells Wood, Leatherhead, KT22 8QW, England. *Website:* www.wrasserecords.com.

KUTI, Seun; Nigerian singer, musician (saxophone) and record producer; b. (Oluseun Anikulapo Kuti), 11 Jan. 1983, s. of the late Fela Kuti; pnr Yetunde George Ademiluyi; one d. *Career:* lead singer of Egypt 80 (after death of Fela Kuti) 1997–; solo career 2008–; numerous international live appearances; collaborated with Calle 13 2010. *Recordings:* albums: Many Things 2008, From Africa with Fury: Rise 2011, A Long Way to the Beginning 2014. *Address:* c/o Knitting Factory Records, 281 North 7th Street, #2, Brooklyn, NY 11211, USA (office). *Telephone:* (347) 529-6628 (office). *E-mail:* info@ knittingfactoryrecords.com (office). *Website:* www.knittingfactoryrecords.com (office); myspace.com/seunkuti.

KUTZLE, Brent Michael; American musician (bass guitar, cello) and songwriter; b. 3 Aug. 1985, Newport Beach, Calif. *Education:* Sarah McGarvin School, Westminster, La Quinta High School, Westminster, California Baptist Univ., Vanguard Univ., Costa Mesa. *Career:* mem. OneRepublic 2007–; support act to many artists including Bon Jovi, P!nk, Maroon 5; collaborated with Timbaland on track Apologize 2008. *Recordings:* albums: with OneRepublic: Dreaming Out Loud 2007, Waking Up 2009, Native 2013; other appearances: Echo, Leona Lewis 2009, Shock Value II, Timbaland 2009. *Honours:* with OneRepublic: Teen Choice Music Award for Rock Track (for Stop and Stare) 2008, MTV Asia Award for Best Hook Up (for Apologize – with Timbaland) 2008, ESKA Music Award (Poland) for Band of the Year (Int.) 2010. *Address:* c/o Patriot Records, Interscope Records, 1755 Broadway, New York, NY 10019, USA (office). *Website:* www.patriotrecords.com (office); www .onerepublic.net.

KUVEZIN, Albert; Russian singer and musician (guitar, marinkhur); b. 27 Nov. 1965, Kyzyl, Tuva; m. Natalia Toka 1990; two d. *Education:* Kyzyl Musical Coll., folk instrument classes. *Career:* plays the marinkhur, an ethnic folk string instrument; mem., Yat-Kha; numerous festival appearances, tours. *Recordings include:* albums: Kahnparty, Yat-kha 1993, Yenisei Punk 1995,

Dalai Beldiri 1999, Aldyn Dashka 2000, Bootleg 2001, tuva.rock 2003, Recovers 2005. *Honours:* awards from Voice of Asia 1990, Wales Folk Fest 1992. *Current Management:* Dnotice Management Ltd, PO Box 33808, London, N8 9GY, England. *E-mail:* info@dnotice.net. *Website:* www.dnotice.net; www.yat -kha.com.

KUWATA, Keisuke; Japanese singer, musician (guitar, bass guitar, drums, keyboards), songwriter and film composer; b. 26 Feb. 1956, Chigasaki, Kanagawa; m. Yuko Hara 1982; two s. *Education:* Aoyama Gakuin Univ. *Career:* Founder mem. for group Southern All-Stars 1977–: fmr Founder mem. of own group the Kuwata Band; composed scores for films. *Films:* as composer: Aiko 16-sai 1983, as composer and director: Inamura Jane 1990. *Recordings include:* albums include: with Southern All-Stars: Atsui Munasawagi (Hot Uneasiness) 1978, 10 Numbers Carat 1979, Tiny Bubbles 1980, Stereo Sunny Youth 1981, Kirei (Beautiful) 1983, Go the Way of Stars 1984, Kamakura 1985, Southern All-Stars 1990, The Flower of Myriad Leaves Blooms in the World 1992, Midnight's Dandy 1993, Young Love 1996, Killer Street 2005; solo: Keisuke Kuwata 1988, The Sun of Solitude 1994, From Yesterday 2001, Rock and Roll Hero 2002, Top of the Pops 2002, Ashita Hareru Kana 2007, Musicman 2011; with Mr Children: Earth of Miracle 1995. *Current Management:* c/o Amuse Inc., 20-1 Sakuragaoka-cho, Shibuya-ku, Tokyo 150-8570, Japan. *Telephone:* (3) 5457-3333. *Website:* www.amuse.co.jp; www.sas-fan .net.

KWATEN, Kwame; British musician (keyboards) and artist manager. *Career:* mem., jazz funk quartet, D-Influence 1990–; support to Prince, Michael Jackson; tours, television appearances; D-Influence also production team for R&B music; Group owns Freakstreet label; runs KKM Management co. *Recordings:* albums: Good 4 We 1992, Prayer 4 Unity 1995, London 1997, D-Influence Presents D-Vas 2002. *Address:* c/o Dome Records Ltd, PO Box 3274, East Preston, Sussex BN16 9BD, England (office). *Website:* www .domerecords.co.uk (office).

KWATINETZ, Jeffrey; American producer and artist manager; *CEO, Prospect Park LLC;* b. Brooklyn, NY. *Education:* Harvard Law School. *Career:* founder, Q Management; Man., Gallin-Morey & Assocs; co-founder, CEO and Co-Chair., The Firm (artist management co.) 1997–2008; acquired film artists' agency, Artists Management Group 2002, represented music clients such as Mary J. Blige, The Dixie Chicks, Korn, Limp Bizkit, Linkin Park, actors and sports people, owns Pony sportswear co., Build-a-Bear Workshop, departments devoted to clothing, recording, animation, concerts, television and film production; co-founder and CEO, Prospect Park LLC production co. 2008–. *Address:* Prospect Park LLC, 2040 Century Park East, Suite 2550, Los Angeles, CA 90067, USA (office).

KWIATKOWSKI, Dawid; Polish singer and songwriter; b. 1 Jan. 1996, Gorzów Wielkopolski. *Television:* Dancing with the Stars: Taniec z gwiazdami (participant) 2014. *Recordings:* albums: 9893 2013, Pop & Roll 2014. *Honours:* Glam Awards for Fashionable Debut 2013, for Discovery of the Year 2013, Kid's Choice Award for Favourite Polish Artist 2014, Plejada Readers' Award 2014, MTV Europe Music Awards for Best Polish Act 2014, for Best Eastern European Act 2014. *Address:* c/o My Music Records, My Music Group, ul. Grunwaldzka 519 E, 62-064 Plewiska, Poland (office). *Telephone:* (61) 813-90-59 (office). *Fax:* (61) 810-35-39 (office). *E-mail:* secretariat@my-music.pl (office). *Website:* www.my-music.pl (office).

KWOK, Aaron, (Guo Fu Cheng, Kwok Fu Shing); Hong Kong singer and actor; b. 26 Oct. 1965. *Career:* joined Hong Kong TVB co. TV show for three years as professional dancer aged 16; transferred to TVB acting class aged 21; several small acting engagements before employing fmr coll. dir, Siu Mei, as man. for professional singing/acting career; live concerts and high profile film roles; records/performs in Cantonese and Mandarin languages. *Films include:* ParaPara Sakura 2001. *Recordings include:* albums (in Mandarin): No End Love 1990, Should I Leave Silently 1991, Who Can Tell Me 1991, Please Bring My Love Home 1992, Love You 1992, Aaron Kwok Loves You Deeply 1993, Leave You With All My Love 1993, Hard To Hold Back The Dreams 1993, End of The Dream 1994, Desire 1994, Lover For Life 1994, Here Is My Start 1995, Non Stop Wind 1995, Love Dove 1996, Sharing Love/Who Will Remember Me 1997, Devoted 1997, So Afraid 1999, Journey/Cheer 2000, Give You All My Love 2001; (in Cantonese): Hot Beat 1992, Without Your Love 1993, Merry Christmas 1993, Starting From Zero 1994, Wild City 1994, A Moment of Romantic II 1994, Iron Attraction 1994, AK-47 1994, You're Everything 1995, Tale of Purity 1995, Memorandum 1995, Most Exciting Empire 1996, Song In The Wind 1996, Love's Calling 1997, Generation Next 1997, The Best Remix 1998, Live In Concert '98 1999, Amazing Dream 2000, Wu Ji vs Wei Lai (EP) 2001, Memorandum 2001, Live On Stage In Concert (includes songs in Mandarin) 2001, Xin Tian Di (includes songs in Mandarin) 2001, Absolute 2001, Burning Flame 2002, The Power of Love 2002, In the Still of the Night 2003, Thematic 2005, My Nation 2006. *Address:* c/o Warner Music, 12/F, The Peninsula Office Tower, 18 Middle Road, TST Kowloon, Hong Kong. *Website:* www.aaronkwokonline.com.

KWON, Jo; South Korean singer, actor and musician (piano); b. 28 Aug. 1989, Suwon. *Education:* Kyunghee Univ. *Career:* discovered by Park Jin Young via SBS-TV variety show 99% Challenge Project 2001; lead singer, 2AM 2008–, live debut with 2AM in 2010; has also recorded with Baek Jiyoung, May Doni, Whale, Brown Eyed Girls, Wax, Lim Jeonghee, Lee Seung Hwan, Ga-in. *Television:* We Got Married 2009, Find It! Green Gold 2009, Family Outing 2 2010. *Recordings:* with 2AM: Saint o'Clock 2010; other 2AM appearances include: Personal Preference (soundtrack) 2010, Listen Up!: The Official 2010 FIFA World Cup Album 2010, Acoustic (soundtrack) 2010; other appearances: Sensibility, Baek Jiyoung 2008, 7 Teen, May Doni 2009, Wax Unplugged, Wax 2009, It Can't Be Real, Lim Jeonghee 2010. *Honours:* Mnet 20's Choice Award for Most Influential Artist (jtly) 2010, Mnet Asian Music Awards for Best Collaboration 2010, for Best Vocal Performance by a Group (with 2AM) 2011, MBC Entertainment Awards for Best Rookie, Best Couple and Special Award 2010, 3rd Korea Sharing Awards Ceremony Award 2010. *Address:* c/o JYP Entertainment, JYP Center, 41, 79-gil Apgujeong-ro, Gangnam-gu, Seoul, South Korea (office). *Telephone:* (2) 3438-2300 (office). *Fax:* (2) 3438-2330 (office). *E-mail:* publicity@jype.com (office). *Website:* 2am.ibighit.com (home).

KYRKJEBO, Sissel; Norwegian singer; b. 24 June 1969, Bergen. *Career:* singer 1985–; worldwide tours including Scandinavian concerts with Neil Sedaka 1991, Barcelona Cathedral, Christmas Concert in Vienna with Placido Domingo; musical ambassador, singer for Olympic Hymn, Winter Olympic Games, Norway 1994; theatre: Maria Von Trapp in The Sound of Music, Solveig in Peer Gynt; sang vocals on the soundtrack to the film Titanic; mem. GRAMO. *Recordings:* albums: Sissel 1986, Glade Jul 1987, Soria Moria 1989, Gift of Love 1992, Innerst I Sjelen (platinum disc) 1994, All Good Things 2001, My Heart 2003, Into Paradise 2006, Northern Lights 2007, Spirit of the Season with the Mormon Tabernacle Choir 2007; hit single: Fire In Your Heart (Olympic Hymn) with Placido Domingo. *Honours:* Norwegian Grammy for Artist of the Year 1986, 2006, H. C. Andersen Award. *Current Management:* c/o Barry Matheson, Continental Artist Management, Kr. Augusts Gate 10, 0164 Oslo, Norway. *Telephone:* 22-06-27-70. *Fax:* 22-06-27-71. *E-mail:* trude.bo@continentalmusic.net. *Website:* www.continentalmusic.net. *E-mail:* sissel@continentalmusic.net (office). *Website:* www.sissel.net.

L

LA CORRECCIÓN (see Herren, Scott)

LA MOMPOSINA, Totó; Colombian singer, dancer and teacher; b. (Sonia Bazanta Vides), Santa Cruz de Mompox. *Career:* cumbia singer, mixing traditional Colombian and Afro-Latin music 1960s–; performed on tours and in festivals including WOMAD tour across three continents. *Recordings include:* La Candela Viva 1993, Carmelina 1995, Pacantó 2000, La Bodega 2009. *Honours:* WOMEX Lifetime Achievement Award 2006. *Current Management:* Astar Music, 95 Penn Hill Road, Bath BA1 3RT, England. *Telephone:* (1224) 319944. *E-mail:* admin@astarmusic.co.uk. *Website:* www.astarmusic.co.uk. *E-mail:* cantadora@totolamomposina.com (office). *Website:* www.totolamomposina.com.

LA PORTE-PITICCO, Laurie Margaret; Canadian singer, songwriter and musician (rhythm guitar); b. 31 Aug. 1960, Sudbury, ON; m. Steve Piticco, one s. one d. *Career:* rhythm guitarist, singer, songwriter with South Mountain; television appearances, including band's own series for four years (CHRO TV); numerous concerts; mem. SOCAN, Canadian Country Music Asscn. *Recordings include:* South Mountain album: Where There's A Will. *Honours:* CCMA Vista Rising Star Award 1991. *Address:* PO Box 64, South Mountain, ON K0E 1W0, Canada. *E-mail:* llaportepiticco@sprint.ca.

LA SALLE, Denise; American singer, songwriter and publisher; b. 16 July 1941, Mississippi; m. James E. Wolfe 1977, one s. one d. *Career:* numerous tours and live appearances; co-owner, WFKX Radio Station (KIX96 FM) 1984–; owner, Denise La Salle's Chique Boutique and Wigs; co-owner, The Celebrity Club, Jackson, TN; formed own record label, Ordena Records 1999; founder mem. National Asscn for the Preservation of Blues (NAPOB); mem. BMI, NARAS. *Recordings include:* albums: Trapped By A Thing Called Love 1972, Doin' It Right 1972, On the Loose 1973, Here I Am Again 1975, Second Breath 1976, The Bitch Is Bad 1977, Under the Influence 1978, Shot of Love 1978, Unwrapped 1979, I'm So Hot 1980, Guaranteed 1981, A Lady in the Street 1983, Right Place Right Time 1984, Love Talkin' 1985, My Toot Toot 1985, Rain and Fire 1986, It's Lying Time Again 1987, Hittin' Where It Hurts 1989, Holdin' Hands with the Blues 1989, Still Trapped 1990, Love Me Right 1992, Still Bad 1995, Smokin' In Bed, 1997; God's Got My Back 1999, Down on Clinton 1999, This Real Woman 2000, There's No Separation 2001, Still the Queen 2002, Wanted 2004, Pay Before You Pump 2007, 24 Hour Woman 2010. *Publications:* America's Prodigal Son 1989, A Short Story About the Blues, How to be a Successful Songwriter (booklet). *Honours:* Jackie Award, Chicago 1974, BMI Award. *Address:* c/o Ordena Entertainment Inc., 17 Henderson Road, Jackson, TN 38305, USA. *Website:* www.myspace.com/msdeniselasalle.

LABARRIERE, Jacques; French composer, arranger and musician (piano); b. 29 Nov. 1956, Paris. *Education:* Licence de Musicologie; Prize for harmony, counterpoint. *Career:* Shows include: Gospel; Cats; Fantasticks; 42nd Street; Trouble in Tahiti; Radio-France broadcast: ACR de France Culture; Concerts: Jazz with Joe Lee Wilson; Anette Lowman; Eric Barret; Philippe Selam; Jean-Louis Mechali; Singers: C Combe; C Magny; Perone; mem. SACEM; SACD; ADAMI; SPEDIDAM; SCAM. *Recordings:* Cats; Tie Break, Second Set; Entre 3 and 5.

LABELLE, Patti; American singer and actress; b. (Patricia Holt), 24 May 1944, Philadelphia, PA. *Career:* founder mem., The Blue Belles 1961, renamed Labelle 1970–76; solo artist 1976–; numerous concerts, tours, television appearances. *Television:* Unnatural Causes (NBC) 1986, Motown 30 – What's Goin' On (CBS) 1990, Going Home To Gospel with Patti LaBelle 1991, Out All Night (sitcom, NBC) 1992. *Film:* A Soldier's Story 1984. *Recordings include:* albums: with LaBelle: LaBelle 1971, Gonna Take A Miracle 1971, Moonshadow 1972, Nightbirds 1974, Phoenix 1975, Chameleon 1976; solo: Patti LaBelle 1977, Tasty 1978, It's Alright With Me 1979, Released 1980, The Spirit's In It 1981, I'm In Love Again 1983, Patti 1985, Winner In You 1986, Be Yourself 1989, This Christmas 1990, Burnin' 1991, Live! 1992, Gems 1994, Flame 1997, When a Woman Loves 2000, Timeless Journey 2004, Classic Moments 2005, The Gospel According to Patti LaBelle 2006, Miss Patti's Christmas 2007. *Publication:* Don't Block the Blessings. *Honours:* Award of Merit, Philadelphia Art Alliance, 1986; Lifetime Achievement Award, CORE (Congress of Racial Equality), 1990; NAACP Entertainer of Year, 1992; American Music Award, Favourite Female R&B/Soul Artist, 1993; Star on Hollywood Walk of Fame, 1993. *Address:* Universal Records, 1755 Broadway, Floor 7, New York, NY 10019-3743, USA (office). *Telephone:* (212) 373-0600 (office). *E-mail:* info@pattilabelle.com. *Website:* www.universalrecords.com (office); www.pattilabelle.com.

LABÈQUE, Katia; French pianist; b. 3 March 1950, Bayonne; sister of Marielle Labèque. *Education:* Paris Conservatoire. *Career:* performs worldwide with sister, Marielle Labèque; appearances with the Berlin Philharmonic, Bayerischer Rundfunk, Boston Symphony, Chicago Symphony, Cleveland Orchestra, Leipzig Gewandhaus, London Symphony, London Philharmonia, Los Angeles Philharmonic, Filarmonia della Scala, Philadelphia Orchestra, Dresden Staatskapelle and Vienna Philharmonic; has played under direction of Bychkov, Davis, Dutoit, Mehta, Ozawa, Pappano, Rattle, Salonen, Slatkin and Tilson Thomas; festival performances at Berlin, Blossom, Hollywood Bowl, Lucerne, Ludwigsburg, Mostly Mozart New York, BBC Proms, Ravinia, Rheingau, Ruhr, Schleswig Holstein, Tanglewood,

Schubertiade in Schwarzenberg and Salzburg Easter Festival; formed new duo with Viktoria Mullova 2001, regular performances throughout Europe at Musikverein, Vienna, Musikhalle Hamburg, Philharmonie Munich, Schwetzinger Festspiele amongst numerous others; performances in 2005 season included recitals at Carnegie Hall, New York, Lucerne, Belgrade, Athens, Essen, throughout Italy as well as at Schubertiade Festival, Schwarzenberg; joined French saxophonist François Jeanneau's Paris Big Band Pandemonium; jazz collaborations with guitarist John McLaughlin; founder, Katia Labèque Band 2001–; first European tour with special guest Gonzalo Rubalcaba 2001; further concerts at Piano Festival Ruhr, Lucerne Festival, Easter Festival Salzburg and during opening ceremony of the new Konzerthaus in Dortmund; Katia Labèque Band and Orchestre Philharmonique de Montpellier performed première of a five-movt concerto (Spellbound by Dave Maric) for piano, keyboards, percussion and orchestra entitled 2004. *Recordings include:* Gershwin's Rhapsody in Blue and Concerto in F, recitals of Brahms, Liszt, Debussy, Ravel and Stravinsky, Rossini's Petite Messe (with the choir of King's College Cambridge), Bartók's Concerto for two pianos and orchestra, Symphonic Dances from West Side Story, España, Encores, Love of Colours, Visions de l'Amen (jtly), Little Girl Blue, Unspoken (with Katia Labèque Band) 2003, Ravel 2006, B for Bang 2007, Schubert/Mozart 2007, Stravinsky/Debussy 2007, De Fuego y De Agua 2008, Shape of My Heart 2009. *Current Management:* Abeille Musique, Usine Springcourt, 5 Passage Piver, 75011 Paris, France. *Telephone:* 1-49-26-97-77. *Fax:* 1-49-26-95-78. *E-mail:* benoitbuttner@abeillemusique.com. *Website:* www.abeillemusique.com. *E-mail:* info@labeque.com (office). *Website:* www.katialabeque.com; www.labeque.com.

LABÈQUE, Marielle; French pianist; b. 6 March 1952, Bayonne; sister of Katia Labèque; pnr Semyon Bychkov. *Education:* Paris Conservatoire. *Career:* performs worldwide with sister, Katia Labèque; appearances with the Berlin Philharmonic, Bayerischer Rundfunk, Boston Symphony, Chicago Symphony, Cleveland Orchestra, Leipzig Gewandhaus, London Symphony, London Philharmonia, Los Angeles Philharmonic, Filarmonia della Scala, Philadelphia Orchestra, Dresden Staatskapelle and Vienna Philharmonic; has played under direction of Bychkov, Davis, Dutoit, Mehta, Ozawa, Pappano, Rattle, Salonen, Slatkin and Tilson Thomas; festival performances at Berlin, Blossom, Hollywood Bowl, Lucerne, Ludwigsburg, Mostly Mozart New York, BBC Proms, Ravinia, Rheingau, Ruhr, Schleswig Holstein, Tanglewood, Schubertiade in Schwarzenberg and Salzburg Easter Festival; jazz collaborations with guitarist John McLaughlin. *Recordings include:* Gershwin's Rhapsody in Blue and Concerto in F, recitals of Brahms, Liszt, Debussy, Ravel and Stravinsky, Rossini's Petite Messe (with the choir of King's College Cambridge), Bartók's Concerto for two pianos and orchestra, Symphonic Dances from West Side Story, España, Encores, Love of Colours, Visions de l'Amen (jtly), Little Girl Blue, Unspoken (with Katia Labèque Band) 2003, Ravel 2006, B for Bang 2007, Schubert/Mozart 2007, Stravinsky/Debussy 2007, De Fuego y De Agua 2008. *Current Management:* Abeille Musique, Usine Springcourt, 5 Passage Piver, 75011 Paris, France. *Telephone:* 1-49-26-97-77. *Fax:* 1-49-26-95-78. *E-mail:* benoitbuttner@abeillemusique.com. *Website:* www.abeillemusique.com. *E-mail:* info@labeque.com (office). *Website:* www.labeque.com.

LADINSKY, Gary; American recording engineer; b. 2 May 1947, Los Angeles, California; two s. *Education:* BA, California State University, Northridge, 1970. *Career:* Recording engineer, Record Plant, Los Angeles, 1971–75; President, Gary Ladinsky Inc/Design FX Audio, 1979–; mem, NARAS; Audio Engineering Society; Society Professional Audio Recording Services, IATSE. *Recordings:* Engineer, albums by: Lynyrd Skynyrd; Van Morrison; Moody Blues; Cheap Trick; Donna Summer; George Benson; Manhattan Transfer; Mixer, film scores: Ferris Bueller's Day Off, 1987; Trains, Planes and Automoblies, 1987; Naked Gun, 1988. *Address:* Design FX Audio, PO Box 491087, Los Angeles, CA 90049, USA. *Telephone:* (818) 843-6555. *Website:* www.dfxaudio.com.

LADY GAGA; American singer and songwriter; b. (Stefani Joanne Angelina Germanotta), 28 March 1986, New York, NY; d. of Joseph Germanotta and Cynthia Germanotta (née Bissett). *Education:* Convent of the Sacred Heart School, New York, Tisch School of the Arts, New York Univ. *Career:* learned to play piano from age of four; wrote first piano ballad, aged 13; began performing in New York clubs, aged 14; began performing in rock music scene of New York City's Lower East Side 2003; signed with Streamline Records (imprint of Interscope Records); began solo professional singing career 2006–; has written songs for Britney Spears, the Pussycat Dolls; captured attention of Akon, who recognized her vocal abilities, and signed her to his own label, Kon Live Distribution; released her first fragrance, Lady Gaga Fame, in association with Coty, Inc. 2012; launched the Born This Way Foundation 2012. *Tours include:* The Fame Ball Tour 2009, The Monster Ball Tour 2009–11, The Born This Way Ball Tour 2012–13. *Recordings include:* albums: The Fame (Grammy Award for Best Electronic/Dance Album 2010, BRIT Award for Best Int. Album 2010) 2008, The Fame Monster (Grammy Award for Best Pop Vocal Album 2011) 2009, Born This Way (two MTV Video Music Awards 2011, MTV Europe Music Award for Best Song, 2011, MTV Europe Music Award for Best Video 2011) 2011, Artpop 2013, Cheek to Cheek (with Tony Bennett) (Grammy Award for Best Traditional Pop Vocal Album 2015) 2014. *Television includes:* American Horror Story: Hotel (Golden Globe Award for Best Actress – Miniseries or Television Film 2016) 2015–. *Honours:* ranked by Billboard the 73rd Artist of the 2000–10 decade, Billboard Rising Star Award 2009, Int. Dance Music Awards for Best Breakthrough Artist 2009, for Best Pop Dance Track (for Just Dance) 2009, MTV Europe Music Award for Best New Act 2009, MTV Video Music Award for Best New Artist 2009, Grammy Award for Best Dance Recording (for Poker Face) 2010, BRIT Awards for Best Int. Breakthrough Act 2010, for Best Int. Female Solo Artist 2010, eight MTV Video Music Awards 2010, named by TIME magazine in its annual TIME 100 list of the most influential people in the world 2010, ranked fourth by Forbes magazine on its list of the 100 Most Powerful and Influential Celebrities in the World 2010, also ranked as the second Most Powerful Musician in the World 2010, ranked by Forbes magazine amongst The World's 100 Most Powerful Women (seventh) 2010, (11th) 2011, (14th) 2012, (45th) 2013, (67th) 2014, Grammy Award for Best Female Pop Vocal Performance (for Bad Romance) 2011, MTV Europe Music Award for Best Female 2011, MTV Europe Music Award for Biggest Fans 2011. *Address:* c/o Interscope Records, 2220 Colorado Avenue, Santa Monica, CA 90404, USA. *Website:* www .ladygaga.com.

LADY SAW; Jamaican reggae artist; b. (Marion Hall), 1972, St Mary; three adopted c. *Career:* solo artist 1994–, as 'First Lady of Dancehall'; collaborations with Shabba Ranks, Shaggy, Beenie Man, No Doubt. *Recordings include:* albums: Lover Girl 1994, Give Me The Reason 1996, Passion 1997, 99 Ways 1998, Collection 1998, Raw: The Best Of Lady Saw 1999, Strip Tease 2004, Walk Out 2007. *Address:* c/o VP Records, 89-05 138th Street, Jamaica, New York, NY 11435, USA (office). *E-mail:* info@ladysaw.net (office). *Website:* www .vprecords.com; www.ladysaw.net.

LADY SOVEREIGN; British MC; b. London, England. *Career:* solo artist in 'grime' music genre. *Recordings include:* album: Public Warning 2005. *Address:* c/o Casual Records, Arch 62, 83 Rivington Street, London, EC2A 3AY, England (office). *E-mail:* info@casuallondon.com (office). *Website:* www .casual-london.com (office); www.ladysovereign.com.

LADYHAWKE; New Zealand singer, songwriter and musician (guitar, keyboards, percussion); b. (Phillipa Margaret Brown), 13 July 1979, Masterton, Wellington. *Education:* Chanel Coll. *Career:* mem. Two Lane Blacktop 2001–03; relocated to Australia 2004; Founder mem. (with Nick Littlemore) of rock band Teenager 2004–07; solo career (as Ladyhawke) 2007–; relocated to London 2007; released solo debut album 2008; several musical collaborations including Pnau, Tim Burgess, Junica. *Recordings:* albums: with Teenager: Thirteen 2006; solo: Ladyhawke (New Zealand Music Awards for Album of the Year 2009, for Best Dance/Electronica Album 2009, ARIA Music Award for Breakthrough Artist – Album) 2008, Anxiety 2012. *Honours:* New Zealand Music Awards for Single of the Year (for My Delirium) 2009, for Best Female Solo Artist 2009, for Breakthrough Artist of the Year 2009, for Int. Achievement Award 2009, ARIA Music Award for Breakthrough Artist – Single (for My Delirium) 2009. *Current Management:* c/o ie:music Management, 111 Frithville Gardens, London, W12 7JQ, England. *E-mail:* info@iemusic.co.uk. *Website:* www.iemusic.co.uk. *Address:* c/o Modular, PO Box 1666, Darlinghurst, NSW 1300, Australia (office). *E-mail:* info@ modularpeople.com (office). *Website:* www.modularpeople.com (office); www .ladyhawkemusic.com.

LAFFY, Stephen; British musician (drums), songwriter and producer; b. 29 May 1953, London; m. Lynn Heather 1994; two d. *Career:* performed at Glastonbury Festival, WOMAD, Notting Hill Carnival; overseas tours, television and radio; formed own band Rhythm Rising; Assoc. Lecturer in Music Practice, West Herts Coll.; mem, Musicians' Union, PRS, MCPS. *Recordings:* When 2000 Comes 1995, Don't Go Breaking Down, Carry On, Everybody Needs Someone. *E-mail:* webdrum1@mac.com (office). *Website:* www.stevelaffy.co.uk.

LAFOURCADE, Natalia; Mexican singer, songwriter, musician (piano, guitar) and record producer; b. (María Natalia Lafourcade Silva), 26 Feb. 1984, Mexico City; d. of Gastón Lafourcade. *Education:* Instituto Anglo Español. *Career:* sang in Mariachi group as child; mem. girl trio Twist 1998; solo career 2001–; fronted own band Natalia y La Forquetina 2005–06; numerous collaborations with other artists including Liquits, Reik, Control Machete, Los Daniels, Kalimba, Julieta Venegas; songwriter for Ximena Sariñana. *Recordings:* albums: Natalia Lafourcade 2003, Casa (as Natalia y La Forquetina) (Latin Grammy Award for Best Rock Album by Duo or Group with Vocal 2006) 2005, Las 4 Estaciones Del Amor 2008, Hu Hu Hu 2009, Mujer Divina, Homenaje a Agustin Lara (Latin Grammy Awards for Best Alternative Music Album 2013, for Best Long Form Music Video 2013) 2012, Hasta La Raíz (Latin Grammy Award for Best Alternative Music Album 2015, Grammy Award for Best Latin Rock, Urban or Alternative Album 2016) 2015. *Honours:* Latin Grammy Awards for Record of the Year, Song of the Year and Best Alternative Song (for Hasta La Raíz) 2015. *Current Management:* c/o Natalia LaFourcade Management. *Telephone:* (55) 5211-7973 (office). *E-mail:* info@natalialafourcade.mx. *E-mail:* natalialafourcadeyo@gmail.com. *Website:* nataliafourcadeyo.com.

LAGERBERG, Bengt Fredrik Arvid; Swedish musician (drums, bassoon, guitar, bass guitar, piano, trumpet, harmonica); b. 5 July 1973, Karolinska Sjukhuset, Stockholm. *Career:* fmr mem., Diver, Giraffe; mem., The Cardigans 1992–; numerous concert tours, festivals, television and radio appear-

ances. *Music for TV and film:* contributed tracks to films Romeo and Juliet and A Life Less Ordinary, theme to 'Randall & Hopkirk Deceased' (BBC1, with David Arnold) 2000. *Recordings include:* albums: Emmerdale 1994, Life 1995, First Band On The Moon 1996, Other Side Of The Moon 1998, Gran Turismo 1998, Long Gone Before Daylight 2003, Super Extra Gravity 2005. *Honours:* Slitz Magazine Award for Best Band 1994, Swedish Government Export Prize 1997, BMI Award for Best Song 1997, Best Album 1998, Best Group 1996, 1998. *Current Management:* Hagenburg Management, Kyrkogaten 31, 411 08 Gothenburg, Sweden. *Telephone:* (31) 339-95-90. *Fax:* (31) 13-95-09. *E-mail:* info@hagenburg.se. *Website:* www.hagenburg.se; www.cardigans.com.

LAGRÈNE, Biréli; French jazz musician (guitar) and singer; b. (Pierre Lagrène), 4 Sept. 1966, Soufflenheim, Alsace; m.; two c. *Education:* Berklee Coll. of Music, USA. *Career:* teenage performer with John McLaughlin, Al DiMeola, Paco de Lucia, Benny Carter, Larry Coryell, Stephane Grappelli, Paquito D'Rivera; later performed with Jack Bruce, Ginger Baker, toured Europe with Jaco Pastorius; founder mem., The Biréli Lagrène Ensemble, Gipsy Project; solo artist 1978–. *Recordings include:* albums: Routes To Django: Live At The Krokodil 1980, Biréli Swing '81 1981, Concert And Space (with Joseph Bowie) 1981, 15 1982, Down In Town 1983, Musique Tzigane/ Manouch 1984, Erster Tango 1985, A Tribute To Django Reinhardt 1985, Biréli Lagrène Ensemble Live Featuring Vic Juris 1985, Stuttgart Aria 1986, Zum Tratz 1986, Lagrène And Guests 1986, Foreign Affairs 1986, Inferno 1987, Biréli Lagrène 1988, Biréli & Jaco (with Jaco Pastorious) 1988, Highlights 1989, Acoustic Moments 1990, Standards 1992, Live In Marciac 1994, My Favorite Django 1995, Blue Eyes 1998, Duets (with Sylvain Luc) 2000, Front Page (with Dominique Di Piazza and Dennis Chambers) 2000, To Be Or Not To Be 2006; with Gipsy Project: Gipsy Project 2001, Gipsy Project And Friends 2002, The Complete Gipsy Project 2003, Move 2004, It's All Right With Me (also featuring Sara Lazarus) 2006; with WDR Big Band Köln: Djangology. *Honours:* Musicien français de jazz 2001. *Current Management:* Christian Pégand Productions, 19 rue Simart, 75018 Paris, France. *Telephone:* (1) 53-09-27-40 (office). *Fax:* (1) 53-09-27-49 (office). *E-mail:* info@ christianpegand.com (office). *Website:* www.christianpegand.com (office); www.lagrene.com.

LAHBIB, Lahcen; Moroccan singer and musician (percussion). *Career:* moved to London 1980s; founder mem., MoMo (Music of Moroccan Origin) 2000–, a fusion of North African Gnawa music with western-style drum kit, samples and contemporary dance styles (including house and garage) described as 'Dar'. *Recordings include:* album: The Birth of Dar 2001.

LAHTI, Pentti; Finnish musician (reeds, flutes, saxophones); b. 15 Aug. 1945. *Career:* mem., Eero Koivistoinen Octet, Mircea Stan Quartet early 1970s; mem., Jukka Linkola Octet; mem., UMO (New Music Orchestra); Finnish Broadcasting Co. tours to Oslo 1973; Laren Festival, Holland 1977; annual appearance, Pori Festival; mem., Wasama Quartet 1976–85; mem., Instinct 1985; mem. of trio, IN2á3 1990–. *Recordings include:* albums: solo: Ben Bay 1994, BaranBaran 2002, Music of Laszlo Süle 2004, Music of Markku Renko 2005. *Honours:* Finnish Jazz Federation Yrjö Award 1983. *Address:* UMO Jazz Orchestra, Katajanokanlaituri 5, 00160 Helsinki, Finland (office). *Telephone:* (45) 1290160 (office). *E-mail:* jazz@umo.fi (office). *Website:* www .umo.fi (office).

LAI, Leon; Chinese singer and actor; b. (Alexander Lai Chit), 11 Dec. 1966, Beijing; s. of Lai Xinsheng; m. Gaile Lai 2008; one c. *Education:* Kingsway Princeton Coll. *Career:* worked as salesperson for mobile phone co.; started career in music 1987; apptd UNICEF Goodwill Amb. 1994; f. A Music (East Asia Record Production Co. Ltd) with Peter Lam 2004. *Recordings include:* Leon, Meet in the Rain, Charged up 2002, Love until the End, A Happy Family, Really Wish to Be Like This Forever, It's Still You, Song of the Star, Never Give Up, Why Did I Let You Go?, Dawn 2004, A Story 2005, 4 In Love 2007. *Television:* The Breaking Point 1991. *Films include:* as actor: Comrades: Almost a Love Story 1996, Eighteen Springs (Golden Horse Film Festival Award, Hong Kong Film Award 1997), Everyday Is Valentine 2001, Seven Swords 2005, Moonlight in Tokyo 2005, Leaving Me, Loving You (Golden Deer Best Actor Award) 2005, The Matrimony 2007, A Melody Looking 2007 (also soundtrack) 2008, Forever Enthralled 2008, Bodyguards and Assassins 2009, Frozen 2010, Fire of Conscience 2010, White Vengeance 2011. *Honours:* Jade Solid Gold Top 10 Award 1990, RTHK Top 10 Gold Songs Award 1990, Most Popular Male Singer Award 1993, TVB Jade Solid Gold 1995, Hong Kong Film Award 1997, Medal of Honour 2003. *Address:* East Asia Record Production Co. Ltd, 1 Surrey Lane, Hong Kong Special Administrative Region, People's Republic of China (office). *Telephone:* 23397544 (office). *Fax:* 23046633 (office).

LAIDLAW, Raymond Joseph; musician (drums); b. 28 May 1948, Tynemouth, England; m. Lesley 1976, two s. *Education:* Newcastle Art Coll., Club A GoGo, Newcastle. *Career:* mem., Lindisfarne 1969–; studio owner, music publisher; mem. Musicians' Union. *Recordings incude:* albums: Nicely Out of Tune, 1970; Fog On The Tyne 1971; Dingly Dell, 1972; Finest Hour, 1975; Back and Fourth, 1978; On Tap, 1994; Buried Treasure Vol. 1, 2000. *Address:* Hi-level Recording, 18 Victoria Terrace, Whitley Bay, Tyne and Wear, England.

LAIDVEE, Meelis (Laits); Estonian musician (keyboards); b. 10 Jan. 1964, Pärnu; m. Eve Laidlee (Lublo) 1985; two d. *Education:* private lessons. *Career:* mem., Tuberkuloited 1988–. *Recordings include:* albums: Klassiõhtu 1992, Lilleke rohus 1993, Religioon 1995, Õhtupimedas 1997, Seitseteist lillekest rohus 1999, D-Tuur, Vol. 6 1999, Kiirteel 2000, Wiimane 2001, Tuberkuloited unplugged 2001, Estraadialbum 2003, Põlevad väljad 2004. *Current Management:* MMM Agentuur OÜ, Risti 2-21, 11624 Tallinn, Estonia. *E-mail:* mm@mmagentuur.ee. *Website:* www.mmagentuur.ee. *E-mail:* Laits@tuberkuloited.ee. *Website:* www.tuberkuloited.ee.

LAILA, Runa; Bangladeshi playback singer; b. 17 Nov. 1952, Sylhet; one d. *Career:* made debut at age of six; first recording for soundtrack of Pakistani film Jugnu 1964; numerous playback singing credits for films in Pakistan, India, Bangladesh; performer of Ghazal, pop and fusion music. *Films include:* singing contributor to many film soundtracks including: in Pakistan: Jugnu 1964, Hum Dono 1966, Commander 1968, Anjuman 1970, Man Ki Jeet 1972, Ehsaas 1972, Umrao Jan Ada 1972, Dilruba 1975; in India: Ek Se Badhkar Ek 1974, Agneepath 1990; in Bangladesh: Beder Meye Josna 1991. *Television:* Zia Mohyuddin Show 1972–74. *Recordings include:* albums: numerous including: Geet/Ghazals 1976, Runa in Pakistan 1980, Runa Sings Shahbaz Qalandar 1982, Runa Laila – Moods & Emotions 2008, Kala Sha Kala 2010. *Honours:* in Bangladesh: Independence Day Award, four Nat. Film Awards, Shelteck Award, Lux Channel I Lifetime Performance Award; in India: Saigal Award; in Pakistan: two Nigar Awards, Critics Award, two Graduate Awards, Nat. Council of Music Gold Medal.

LAINE, Dame Clementina (Cleo) Dinah, DBE; British singer; b. 28 Oct. 1927, Southall, Middx; m. 1st George Langridge 1947 (dissolved 1957); one s.; m. 2nd John Philip William Dankworth 1958 (died 2010); one s. one d. *Career:* joined Dankworth Orchestra 1953; lead role in Seven Deadly Sins, Edinburgh Festival and Sadler's Wells 1961; acting roles in Edinburgh Festival 1966, 1967; f. Wavendon Stables Performing Arts Centre (with John Dankworth) 1970; numerous appearances with symphony orchestras performing Façade (Walton) and other compositions; Julie in Showboat, Adelphi Theatre 1971; title role in Colette, Comedy Theatre 1980; Desiree in A Little Night Music, Mich. Opera House, USA 1983; The Mystery of Edwin Drood, Broadway, New York 1986; Into the Woods (US Nat. Tour) 1989; frequent tours and TV appearances, Europe, Australia and USA. *Film:* Last of the Blonde Bombshells 2000. *Recordings include:* albums: Smilin' Through (with Dudley Moore) 2005, I Hear Music 2007. *Publications:* Cleo: An Autobiography 1994, You Can Sing If You Want To 1997. *Honours:* Freedom of Worshipful Co. of Musicians 2002; Hon. MA (Open Univ.) 1975, Hon. DMus (Berklee School of Music) 1982, (York) 1993, (Cambridge) 2004, Hon. DA (Luton) 1994; Melody Maker and New Musical Express Top Girl Singer Awards 1956, Moscow Arts Theatre Award for acting role in Flesh to a Tiger 1958, top place in Int. Critics' Poll of American Jazz magazine Downbeat 1965,Woman of the Year (9th annual Golden Feather Awards) 1973, Edison Award 1974; Variety Club of GB Show Business Personality Award (with John Dankworth) 1977, TV Times Viewers' Award for Most Exciting Female Singer on TV 1978, Grammy Award for Best Jazz Vocalist-Female 1985, Best Actress in a Musical (Edwin Drood), Theatre World Award for Edwin Drood 1986, Nat. Asscn of Recording Merchandisers (NARM) Presidential Lifetime Achievement Award 1990, Vocalist of the Year (British Jazz Awards) 1990, Lifetime Achievement Award (USA) 1991, ISPA Distinguished Artists Award 1999, Back Stage Bob Harrington Lifetime Achievement Award (with John Dankworth) 2001, BBC British Jazz Awards Lifetime Achievement Award (with John Dankworth) 2002. *Address:* The Old Rectory, Wavendon, Milton Keynes, MK17 8LT, England (home). *Fax:* (1908) 584414 (home). *Website:* www.quarternotes.com (office).

LAINE, Reino, (Reiska Laine); Finnish musician (drums); b. 11 July 1946. *Career:* Played drums from age 16; Member, quartet with Pekka Pöyry, Montreux, 1968; Played with Eero Koivistoinen, winning group competition, Montreux, 1969; Also appeared at Newport Jazz Festival; Member, Seppo Paakunainen's Conjunto Baron, 1970s; Percussionist, numerous plays at Helsinki City Theatre; Played with major Finnish musicians, also artistes including: Dexter Gordon; Clifford Jordan; Charlie Mariano; Appeared with Juhani Aaltonen group, The Finnish Middle-Aged All Stars, Pori Festival, 1985; Mem. of board, Finnish Jazz Federation; Pop Musicians' Union; Mem. of government-appointed organizations; fmr Mem. of Parl. *Honours:* Yrjö Award, Finnish Jazz Federation, 1981.

LAING, Tony, (Toby Chang); New Zealand musician (trumpet). *Career:* mem. reggae and soul band, Fat Freddy's Drop. *Recordings include:* albums: Live at the Matterhorn 2001, Based on a True Story 2005, Dr Boondigga and the Big BW 2009. *Honours:* New Zealand Music Award for Best Group 2005. *Address:* The Drop Ltd, PO Box 14-723, Kilbirnie, Wellington 6241, New Zealand (office). *Telephone:* (4) 934-3767 (office). *E-mail:* freddy@fatfreddysdrop.com (office). *Website:* www.fatfreddysdrop.com.

LAIZEAU, François; French musician (drums); b. 19 Nov. 1955, Paris; one d. *Education:* Agostini School. *Career:* sideman for Tania Maria, Magma, Eddy Louiss, Michel Legrand, Toots Thielemans, Louis Sclavis, Michel Portal, Dominique Pifarely, Martial Solal, Kenny Wheeler, Claus Stotter; mem UMJ. *Recordings include:* albums with H Kaenzig and K Wheeler, Live At Fat Thursday, Michel Legrand, Eddy Louiss, Nuit Etoilée, three recordings with the National Jazz Orchestra, Magma, Retrospective Vol. 3, 1981, Joelle Ursull, Comme Dans Un Film December 1993, Jean-Loup Longnon, Cyclades 1996, 20 Ans de Jazz en France 1996. *E-mail:* laizeau@free.fr (office). *Website:* www.laizeau.com.

LAKATOS, Roby; Hungarian violinist; b. 1965, Budapest. *Education:* Béla Bartók Conservatory, Budapest. *Career:* made public debut on violin aged nine; resident with his ensemble at Restaurant Les Ateliers de La Grande Ille,

Brussels 1986–1996; performances at Schleswig-Holstein, Ludwigsburg and Helsinki festivals, at Acads Musicales de Saintes in New York Cen. Park, with Orchestre Nat. de Radio France and Dresden Philharmonic 1996, at Autumn Strings Music Festival, Prague 2003, at Genius of the Violin Festival, London Symphony Orchestra 2004; 'homecoming' concerts, Thalia Theatre, Budapest 1999; concerts with The Lakatos Sextet 2004–, included in cultural programme of Ireland's presidency of EU. *Recordings:* In Gypsy Style 1991, Alouette: König der Zigeunergeiger 1998, Lakatos Gold 1998–99, Post Phrasing: Lakatos Best 1998–99, Lakatos: Live from Budapest 1999, With Musical Friends 2001, Kinoshita Meets Lakatos 2002, As Time Goes By (film score from Le Grand Blonde) 2002, The Legend of the Toad 2004, Prokofiev 2004, Firedance 2005, Klezmer Karma 2006, Roby Lakatos with Musical Friends 2008. *Honours:* First Prize for Classical Violin, Béla Bartók Conservatory 1984. *Address:* Lakatos Productions, c/o Eric Sterckx, Bergstraat 127/2, 2220 Heist-op-den-Berg, Belgium (office). *Telephone:* (1) 524-88-96 (office). *Fax:* (1) 525-17-08 (office). *E-mail:* robylakatos@telenet.be (office). *Website:* www.robylakatos.com (office).

LAKE, Greg; British musician (bass) and singer; b. 10 Nov. 1948, Bournemouth, Dorset. *Career:* mem., The Gods 1968, King Crimson 1969–70, Emerson Lake and Palmer (ELP) 1970–78 (also as Emerson Lake and Powell 1985–86, 1992–), Asia 1983; numerous festival performances. *Recordings include:* albums: with King Crimson: In The Court of The Crimson King 1969, In The Wake of Poseidon 1970, Epitaph 1997, A Beginner's Guide To... (compilation) 2000; with ELP: Emerson Lake and Palmer 1971, Tarkus 1971, Pictures At An Exhibition 1971, Trilogy 1972, Brain Salad Surgery 1973, Welcome Back My Friends To The Show That Never Ends – Ladies and Gentlemen... Emerson Lake and Palmer 1974, Works, Vol. Two 1977, Love Beach 1978, Emerson Lake and Powell 1986, Black Moon 1992, Live At The Royal Albert Hall 1993, Return of The Manticore 1993, In The Hot Seat 1994, Then and Now 1998, The Sprocket Sessions 2003; solo: Greg Lake 1981, Manoeuvres 1983, In Concert on the King Biscuit Flower Hour 1996, From the Beginning – The Greg Lake Retrospective 1997, From the Underground II 2003, From Beginning 2005. *E-mail:* eileen@greglake.com (office). *Website:* www.greglake.com.

LAKE, Suzanne; American singer and actress; b. 26 June 1929, New Jersey; m. George A. de Vos. *Education:* studied opera at Juilliard, voice with Queena Mario, Joseph Florestano, acting with Claudia Franck, Yul Brynner, Larry Blyden, piano harmony and theory with Mayhew L. Lake. *Career:* Broadway and nat. tour as Tuptim, The King and I 1951–54; Broadway and nat. tour as Helen Chao, Flower Drum Song 1961–62; revival No No, Nanette 1964; featured in Leonard Bernstein's History of Musical Comedy (ABC TV); starred with Guy Lombardo, Desert Inn, Las Vegas and Tampa, performances throughout Caribbean and Canada 1963–72; Blossom Music Festival Concerts, USA and Asia Concerts 1970–92; teacher 1980–90; mem. Agma, Actors' Equity, Aftra, Agva. *Recordings:* The Soul of Chanson, Potpurri, Marieke, Broadway and Beyond; DVD: Leonard Bernstein's History of Musical Comedy. *Address:* 2835 Morley Drive, Oakland, CA 94611, USA.

LAKEMAN, Sean; British folk musician (guitar), songwriter and record producer; b. 1974, Devon, England; pnr Kathryn Roberts; two d. *Career:* formed duo with Tom McConville; mem. sibling trio Lakeman Brothers (with brothers Seth and Sam) –1994; Founder-mem. Equation, with brothers Seth and Sam Lakeman, and Kate Rusby and Kathryn Roberts 1995–; mem. duo with Kathryn Roberts 2003–; producer and touring guitarist for brother Seth Lakeman; numerous other production credits for artists including Rev Hammer, Show of Hands, Levellers, Carus Thompson. *Recordings:* albums: with Kate Rusby: Kate Rusby & Kathryn Roberts 1995; with Equation: Hazy Daze 1998, The Lucky Few 1999, First Name Terms 2002, Return to Me 2003; with Kathryn Roberts: 1 2003, 2 2004, Hidden People 2012. *Honours:* BBC Radio 2 Folk Music Award for Best Duo 2013. *Current Management:* c/o Matt Bartlett, Midnight Mango Limited, The Old Stables, Moorlinch, Bridgwater, Somerset, TA7 9DD, England. *Telephone:* (1458) 211117. *E-mail:* matt@midnightmango.co.uk. *Website:* www.midnightmango.co.uk; www.kathrynrobertsandseanlakeman.com.

LAKEMAN, Seth; British folk singer, songwriter and musician (fiddle, guitar); b. 26 March 1977, Yelverton, Devon. *Career:* performed with two brothers as The Lakeman Brothers, toured in Portugal with Kathryn Roberts and Kate Rusby 1994, after tour all five musicians formed band Equation 1995–2001; worked with brother Sam and his wife Cara Dillon on her solo recordings; released debut solo album 2002, successful UK tours 2005, 2006. *Recordings:* albums: solo: The Punch Bowl 2002, Kitty Jay 2004, Freedom Fields 2006, Poor Man's Heaven 2008, Hearts and Minds 2010; with The Lakeman Brothers: Three Piece Suite 1994; with Equation: Return To Me 1996, Hazy Daze 1998, The Lucky Few 1999; other: with Cara Dillon: Cara Dillon 2001, Sweet Liberty 2003, with Steve Knightley and Jenna Witts: Western Approaches 2004. *Honours:* Singer of the Year and Best Album awards, BBC Radio 2 Folk Awards 2007. *Current Management:* David Farrow, DMF Productions, Office 8, Gandy Street Chambers, 11 Gandy Street, Exeter EX4 3LS, England. *E-mail:* info@dmfmusic.co.uk. *Website:* www.dmfmusic.co.uk. *Address:* c/o Relentless Records, 43 Brook Green, London W6 7EF, England (office). *Telephone:* (20) 7605-5808 (office). *E-mail:* info@sethlakeman.co.uk (office). *Website:* www.relentless-records.net (office); www.sethlakeman.co.uk.

LALENDLE, Luvuyo; South African music educationist; b. 4 April 1964; m. Nomahlubl Tabitta Zulu, 1 s., 2 d. *Education:* Bachelor of Pedagogics, University of Fort Hare, South Africa, majored in Music Education and Pedagogics; BEd, University of Venda, South Africa; Master in Music Education, University of Iowa, USA. *Career:* Senior Lecturer, University of Venda, South Africa; Interview with Radio South Africa, Durban, 1989; Appearance on Zimbabwe National Television, 1994; mem, International Council for Traditional Music, Executive Board mem., 1997–. *Publications:* Music In and Out of School, Iowa Music Educators' Journal; Music Programmes in a Post-Apartheid South Africa. *Honours:* Ackerman's Scholarship, 1987; Atlas (USAID) Scholarship, 1998. *E-mail:* lalendle@msu.edu.

LAMAR, Kendrick, (K-Dot); American rapper and singer; b. (Kendrick Lamar Duckworth), 17 June 1987, Compton, Calif. *Education:* Centennial High School, Compton. *Career:* issued first mixtape (as K-Dot) 2003; toured with Game 2006–07, with Tech N9ne and Jay Rock 2010, Kanye West 2013; collaborations with many artists including Bun B, Busta Rhymes, Dr Dre, Drake, E-40, Game, Talib Kweli, Lil Wayne, Tech N9ne, Warren G, Young Jeezy, Snoop Dogg, Eminem, Taylor Swift. *Recordings include:* albums: Section.80 2011, good kid, m.A.A.d city (BET Hip Hop Award for Album of the Year 2013) 2012, To Pimp a Butterfly (Grammy Award for Best Rap Album 2016) 2015; mixtapes: Youngest Head Nigga in Charge (as K-Dot) 2003, Training Day 2005, C4 2009, Overly Dedicated 2010. *Honours:* BET Hip Hop Awards for Lyricist of the Year 2012, 2013, 2014, 2015, for Best Collaboration, Duo or Group 2013, for MVP of the Year 2013, BET Awards for Best New Artist 2013, for Best Male Hip-Hop Artist 2013, 2014, for Best Collaboration (for Problems) 2013, for Best Hip Hop Video and Impact Track (both for Alright) 2015, MOBO Award for Best Int. Act 2013, Grammy Awards for Best Rap Performance (for I) 2015, (for Alright) 2016, for Best Rap Song (for I) 2015, (for Alright) 2016, for Best Rap/Sung Collaboration (for These Walls, with Bilal, Anna Wise and Thundercat) 2016, Californian State Senate Generational Icon Award 2015, MTV Europe Music Award for Best Song (for Bad Blood, with Taylor Swift) 2015, MTV Video Music Awards for Best Collaboration and Video of the Year (both for Bad Blood) 2015. *Address:* c/o Top Dawg Entertainment, Interscope Records, Universal Music Group, 1755 Broadway, New York, NY 10019, USA (office). *E-mail:* tdebusiness@gmail.com (office). *Website:* www.topdawgmusic.com (office); www.kendricklamar.com.

LAMB, Andrew Martin, MA, DLitt, FIA; British writer and broadcaster; b. 23 Sept. 1942, Oldham, Lancs., England; s. of Harry Lamb and Winifred Lamb (née Emmott); m. Wendy Ann Davies 1970; one s. two d. *Education:* Manchester Grammar School, Corpus Christi Coll., Oxford. *Career:* noted authority on lighter forms of music theatre; extensive writings on wide range of musical topics, including opera, operetta, musical comedy and zarzuela; Life mem. Lancashire Co. Cricket Club. *Publications:* Jerome Kern in Edwardian London 1985, Gänzl's Book of the Musical Theatre (with Kurt Gänzl) 1988, Skaters' Waltz: The Story of the Waldteufels 1995, An Offenbach Family Album 1997, Shirley House to Trinity School 1999, 150 Years of Popular Musical Theatre 2000, Leslie Stuart: Composer of Florodora 2002, Fragson: The Triumphs and the Tragedy (with Julian Myerscough) 2004, The Merry Widow at 100 2005, A Life on the Ocean Wave: The Story of Henry Russell 2007, William Vincent Wallace, Composer, Virtuoso and Adventurer 2012; ed.: The Moulin Rouge 1990, Light Music from Austria 1992, Leslie Stuart: My Bohemian Life 2003; contrib. to Oxford Dictionary of National Biography, The New Grove Dictionary of Music and Musicians, The New Grove Dictionary of American Music, The New Grove Dictionary of Opera, Gramophone, Musical Times, Classic CD, American Music, Music and Letters, Wisden Cricket Monthly, Cricketer, Listener, Notes. *Address:* 1 Squirrel Wood, West Byfleet, Surrey, KT14 6PE, England. *Telephone:* (1932) 342566. *E-mail:* fullerswood@gmail.com.

LAMB, Paul; British musician (harmonica) and bandleader; b. 9 July 1955, Blyth, Northumberland, England; divorced; one s. *Career:* festivals in Europe and UK; formed the Blues Burglars with guitarist Johnny Whitehill early 1980s, eventually became Paul Lamb & the King Snakes; TV shows include Spender (UK), The Late Late Show (Ireland); other shows in Germany, Scandinavia, France, UK; radio appearances with BBC Radio 2, Jazz FM, Greater London Radio, radio stations around Europe, Paul Jones' BBC Radio 2 show 2011; concerts with Mark Knopfler; West End Show: A Slice of Saturday Night; mem. Musicians' Union, NHL, British Blues Connection, PRS. *Recordings:* with The Blues Burglars: Breakin In, John Henry Jumps In 1998, The Blue Album 1999, Blues Burglars Whoopin' 1999; with Paul Lamb and The King Snakes: Paul Lamb and the King Snakes 1990, Fine Condition 1995, She's a Killer 1996, Shifting Into Gear 1997, Harmonica Man, Take Your Time and Get It Right 2000, Paul Lamb and The King Snakes 2001, Live at the 100 Club 2001, I'm on a Roll 2005, Slice of Lamb 2007, Snakes and Ladders Live 2007, Mind Games 2010, The Games People Play 2012, Hole in the Wall 2014; compilation CDs and box sets: Cooking With The Blues, Blues Harp Boogie Music Club International, The Deluxe Blues Band, with Big Joe Louis, Otis Grand, Confessin' The Blues; session work includes Evil, Lucky Lopez Evans. *Publications:* Blues in Britain. *Honours:* First as team in World Harmonica Championships, Germany, Second as soloist 1975, voted Best UK Harmonica Player for five years, British and Blues Connection, inducted into British Blues Awards Hall of Fame 2008. *Current Management:* c/o Hazel, bluRobots Public Relations. *Telephone:* 7950-896381 (mobile). *E-mail:* bluroots@hotmail.co.uk. *E-mail:* paul@paullamb.com. *Website:* paullamb.com.

LAMB, Tracey; British musician (bass guitar). *Career:* mem., Rock Goddess; joined Girlschool 1987–89, 1992–2000; mem. Rock 'n' Roll Gypsies 2004–. *Recordings include:* albums: with Girlschool: Take A Bite 1988, Girlschool 1992, Live 1995, Race With The Devil (live) 1998, Live On The King Biscuit Flower Hour 1998, Can't Keep A Good Girl Down 1999, Very Best Of Remastered 2002, 21st Anniversary: Not That Innocent 2002.

LAMBERT, Adam Mitchel; American singer, songwriter and musician; b. 29 Jan. 1982, Indianapolis, Ind.; s. of Eber Lambert and Leila Mitchel. *Education:* Mount Carmel High School. *Career:* raised in San Diego, Calif.; sang and acted in musical theatre during teens and early adulthood with Starlight Theatre, Theatre Under the Stars, Pasadena Playhouse, Kodak Theatre; runner-up on TV's American Idol 2009; headline act on Glam Nation concert tour 2010; several live appearances as guest vocalist with Queen 2011–; many live performances, TV appearances. *Television:* American Idol (competitor; runner-up) 2009; numerous guest appearances. *Recordings include:* albums: For Your Entertainment (Fonogram Music Award Hungary for International Modern Pop/Rock Album of the Year 2011) 2009, Trespassing 2012, The Original High 2015. *Honours:* Teen Choice Award for Male Reality/Variety Star 2009, Young Hollywood Artist of the Year Award 2009, CMA Wild and Young Awards for Best International Male Singer 2010, for Best International Single (for Whataya Want From Me) 2010, numerous Flecking Records Awards including Entertainer of the Year 2010, Male Musician of the Year 2011, 2012, Male Star of the Year 2011, 2012, Song of the Year (for Never Close Our Eyes) 2012, BMI Award for Award-Winning Songs (for Whataya Want From Me) 2011, MTV O Music Awards for Must Follow Artist on Twitter 2011, 2012. *Current Management:* c/o Direct Management Group, Inc., 947 North La Cienega Blvd, Suite G, Los Angeles, CA 90069, USA. *E-mail:* info@directmanagement.com. *Website:* www.directmanagement.com. *Address:* c/o 19 Recordings, RCA Records, Sony Music Entertainment, 550 Madison Avenue, New York, NY 10022, USA (office). *Website:* www.rcarecords.com (office); www.adamofficial.com.

LAMBERT, David; British label head, club and radio DJ; b. 3 Dec. 1965, Wye, Kent, England. *Education:* BA Hons, Social Science, University of Westminster. *Career:* Helped launch Touch Magazine; Began as DJ, 1989; Performing throughout UK, Europe and Latin America; Founder (with Nick Halkes) and A&R, Positiva Dance Label at EMI, 1993–98; Label Head of AM:PM Records of Universal Island Records, 1998–; Started Saturday Night radio show on ILR station TFM (Stockton-on-Tees), 1999. *E-mail:* info@djdavelambert.com. *Website:* www.djdavelambert.com.

LAMBERT, Miranda Leigh; American singer, songwriter and musician (guitar); b. 10 Nov. 1983, Longview, Tex.; d. of Rick Lambert and Bev Lambert; m. Blake Shelton 2011 (divorced 2015). *Career:* began career by appearing on the Johnny High Country Music Review, Arlington, Tex. 1999; contestant on reality TV show Nashville Star 2003; professional solo artist 2003–; formed Pistol Annies with Ashley Monroe and Angaleena Presley 2011. *Recordings include:* albums: Kerosene 2005, Crazy Ex-Girlfriend (Acad. of Country Music Award for Album of the Year 2008) 2007, Revolution (Acad. of Country Music Award for Album of the Year 2010, CMA for Album of the Year 2010) 2009, Four the Record (Acad. of Country Music Award for Album of the Year 2012) 2011, Platinum (Country Music Asscn (CMA) Award for Album of the Year 2014, Grammy Award for Best Country Album 2015, Acad. of Country Music Award for Album of the Year 2015) 2014; with Pistol Annies: Hell on Heels 2011. *Honours:* Acad. of Country Music Awards for Top New Female Vocalist 2007, for Top Female Vocalist of the Year 2010, 2011, 2014, for Single Record of the Year, Song of the Year, Video of the Year (all for The House That Built Me) 2011, for Female Vocalist of the Year 2012, 2013, for Single of the Year, Single Record of the Year (both for Over You) 2013, for Single Record of the Year (for Mama's Broken Heart) 2014, for Song of the Year (with Blake Shelton for Over You) 2013, for Vocal Event of the Year (for We Were Us, with Keith Urban) 2014, for Song of the Year (for Automatic) 2015, Country Music Asscn (CMA) Awards for Female Vocalist of the Year 2010, 2012, 2013, 2014, 2015, for Song of the Year (for The House That Built Me) 2010, (for Over You) 2012, for Single of the Year (for Automatic) 2014, for Musical Event of the Year (for We Were Us, with Keith Urban) 2014, Grammy Award for Best Female Country Music Vocal Performance (for The House That Built Me) 2011, American Country Awards for Single by a Female Artist (for Over You) 2012, (for Mama's Broken Heart) 2013, for Most Played Female Radio Track 2013, CMT Performance of the Year (for Over You) 2013, Country Music Television Artist of the Year Award 2014, American Country Award for Artist of the Year: Female 2013, for Single of the Year: Female (for Mama's Broken Heart) 2013, 50th Anniversary Milestone Award, Acad. of Country Music 2015. *Current Management:* c/o William Morris Endeavor Entertainment, 1600 Division Street, Suite 300, Nashville, TN 37203, USA. *Telephone:* (615) 963-3000. *Fax:* (615) 963-3090. *Website:* www.wmeentertainment.com; www.mirandalambert.com.

LAMBERTH, Dag Ebbe Olaf, BA, MA, MMus; Swedish musician (piano), composer and writer; b. 13 May 1923, Mjölby; m. 1st Stina Lindblad-Rogers; m. 2nd Marion Brechbilder-Boecher; one s. two d. *Education:* Univs of Stockholm and Uppsala, Conservatory of Stockholm, private masterclasses. *Career:* early performances with Lamberth Family and also with brother, Arne Lamberth and Copenhagen; various radio recordings; mem. Int. Asscn of Swedish Composers (STIM), Swedish Composers of Popular Music (SKAP). *Compositions:* Jolly Party for symphony band and orchestra, Love in Monte Carlo, Christine Swedish Blonde, adaptation of poem by Per Lägerkvist for soloist and choir, Swedish translation of French waltz Pigalle. *Recordings:* Jolly Party, Love in Monte Carlo, Schwarze Ballade. *Honours:* Great Award of the Swedish State for Composers 1968. *Address:* Bellevuevägen 43 A, 217 72 Malmö, Sweden.

LAMBRECHT, Dimitri; Belgian producer and composer; b. 9 April 1967, Aalst. *Career:* mem., PLB System, performances in Belgium and France; touring mem., Natural Born Deejays 1989–. *Recordings:* Artificial Defence 1989, A Good Day 1996, Sonar Contact 1997, Deejay's Mind 1997, Today 1998, Airplay 1998. *E-mail:* booking@naturalborndeejays.com. *Website:* www .naturalborndeejays.com.

LAMEIGNÈRE, Christophe; French music executive; *Chairman and CEO, Sony BMG France. Career:* began career in artist management in early 1980s; joined EMI Music Publishing France 1984; joined Sony Music France as A & R Dir 1991, later Man.-Dir; founding Dir, Zomba Records France 1999; Man.-Dir, Music Division, BMG France 2003–04, Pres., BMG France 2004–05, Chair. and CEO 2005–; Pres., Les Victoires de la Musique 2002–. *Address:* Sony BMG Music Entertainment France, 20–26 rue Morel, 92111 Clichy, France (office). *E-mail:* contact@sonybmg.fr (office). *Website:* www.sonybmg.fr (office).

LAMMERS MEYER, Hermann; German musician (pedal steel guitar) and singer; b. 7 Dec. 1952, Aschendorf; m. Anke Barenborg 1988; one s. *Career:* worked with Clay Baker and the Texas Honky Band; success of Texas Country Road Show in USA followed by tours of Europe, including British tour 1981; writes and records own songs; tours with own band The Emsland Hillbillies, all over Europe, UK, USA; solo project The Honky Tonk Hearts performed for Germany on Euro Country Music Masters TV Show, Netherlands. *Recordings include:* albums: with Emsland Hillbillies: Texas Country Road Show, Vol. I 1979, Vol. II 1981, Texas Lone Star 1981; solo: Half My Heart's In Texas 1989, Above All The Starday Session, The End of Time, The Last Country Song (Album of the Year) 1998, I'd Like To Live It Again, with David Frizzell, Lois Johnson, Marion Möhring 2000, The Good Old Days 2004, Yesterday Once More 2006, 1961: A Love Song (European Country Music Asscn Album of the Year 2009) 2008; duets with: Norma Jean, Kitty Wells, Willie Nelson, Johnny Bush. *Honours:* Country Album of the Year, GACMA in Germany 1992, European Country Music Asscn Artist of the Year. *Current Management:* Desert Kid Records/E. L. Hillbillies Music, Drosselweg 15, 26871 Aschendorf, Germany. *Telephone:* (4962) 338. *Fax:* (4962) 338. *E-mail:* hermann.l.meyer@ freenet.de (home). *Website:* www.hermannlammersmeyer.com.

LAMOND, George; American singer; b. 25 Feb. 1967, Georgetown, Washington, DC; m. 1994. *Education:* New York High School of Art and Design. *Career:* numerous TV appearances; mem. NARAS. *Recordings include:* albums: Bad of The Heart 1990, In My Life 1992, Creo En Ti 1993, Entrega 1999, The Hits and More 1999, Que To Vas Remixes, GL 2001, Where Does That Leave Love 2005, Oye Mi Canto 2006. *Honours:* Winter Music Conference Best Dance 12" Award. *E-mail:* georgelamond@gmail.com. *Website:* www.georgelamondonline.com.

LAMOND, Mary Jane; Canadian Gaelic singer; b. 5 Nov. 1960, Kingston, ON. *Education:* Saint Francis Xavier Univ. *Career:* solo artist, with touring band; numerous live appearances; music programmer and consultant, Present Galaxie Celtic Channel; mem, SOCAN, CARAS, ECMA. *Recordings include:* albums: Bho Thir Nan Craobh 1994, Suas e! 1997, Làn Dùil 1999, Òrain Ghàidhlig (Gaelic Songs of Cape Breton) 2001, Stòras 2005. *Honours:* Much Music Award 1997, Global Groove Award 1997, ECMA Award for Best Single (for Sleepy Maggie) 1997, ECMA Roots/Traditional Solo Artist of the Year Award 2002, 2006, ECMA Female Artist of the Year 2006, Woman of Excellence Award 2007. *Current Management:* c/o Sheri Jones, Jones & Co., PO Box 25072, Halifax, NS B3M 4H4, Canada. *Telephone:* (902) 429-9005. *Fax:* (902) 457-1187. *E-mail:* sherijonesy@cs.com. *Website:* www .jonesandcoartistmanagement.com. *E-mail:* maryjane@maryjanelamond.com. *Website:* www.maryjanelamond.com.

LAMONT, Duncan; British musician (tenor saxophone, woodwinds) and composer; b. 4 July 1931, Greenock, Scotland; m. Bridget, 20 Feb. 1960, 2 s. *Education:* Private music study, Glasgow. *Career:* Started as jazz trumpet player, aged 14; Joined Kenny Graham Afro Cubist Band, age 20; Switched from trumpet to tenor saxophone, played with many Big bands; Studio Jazz player, accompanied major stars including: Frank Sinatra; Bing Crosby; Fred Astaire; Became composer, wrote several suites, success with songs, lyrics, performed by most major singers in England, USA; mem, PRS; ASCAP. *Compositions include:* Songs: Tomorrow's Standards; Best of Bossa Novas; Summer Sambas; I Told You So, recorded by Cleo Laine; Not You Again, recorded by Cleo Laine and George Shearing; Suites include: The Young Person's Guide To The Jazz Orchestra; Sherlock Holmes Suite (For City of London); The Carnival of The Animals; Cinderella; Children's television programmes: Mr Benn; King Rollo; Spot (the dog); Towser; Spot's Magical Xmas (for Disney Studios) 1995. *Publications:* Tomorrow's Standards. *Honours:* Tomorrow's Standards, The Music Retailers Asscn Annual Awards For Excellence, 1995; Best Song of Year, ASAC, USA: I Told You So, 1995. *Address:* c/o SFG Publications, Thornleigh, Ewell Road, Cheam, Surrey SM3 8AJ, England. *E-mail:* info@duncanlamont.com. *Website:* www.duncanlamont .com.

LAMONTAGNE, Ray; American singer and songwriter; b. (Raycharles LaMontagne), 18 June 1973, Nashua, New Hampshire. *Career:* recorded first demo 1999; discovered while playing support slots in a folk club in Maine. *Recordings:* albums: Trouble 2004, Till the Sun Turns Black 2006, Gossip in the Grain 2008, God Willin' & the Creek Don't Rise 2010, Supernova 2014. *Honours:* Album of the Year, Song of the Year, Best Male Singer/Songwriter, Boston Music Awards 2005, Best New Acoustic Rock Artist, XM Nation Awards 2005. *Current Management:* Michael McDonald, Mick Management, 35 Washington Street, Brooklyn, NY 11201, USA. *Telephone:* (212) 425-6425. *Fax:* (212) 422-6814. *E-mail:* info@mickmgmt.com. *Website:* mickmanagement .com. *E-mail:* info@raylamontagne.com (office). *Website:* www.raylamontagne .com.

LANDA, Omar; Mexican musician (drums, keyboards); b. 30 Nov. 1970, Morelia, Michoacan. *Education:* Conservatoria de Las Rosas en Morelia; Drum lessons with Abraham Calleros in Guadalajara. *Career:* Radio appearances in Mexico City, WFM Radio Station; Opening concerts for Caifanes and Maná; TV appearances playing live, Channel 2. *Compositions:* 13, 1992; Llananina, 1994; Musgosa Caja, 1994; Tierra, 1996; BaxLtTrt, 1998. *Recordings:* La Parca, 1994; BaxLtTrt, 1998; Pulso, 1999. *Honours:* Best Rock Group from Province, Nuestro Rock Awards, 1994, 1995, 1996. *Address:* La Privada a Gertrudis Boconegra No. 48, Morelia, Michoacan, Mexico. *Website:* www .omarlanda.com.

LANDER, Judd; British musician, actor, television producer and record company executive; *Director, Lander PR Ltd (UK);* b. (Judd Malcolm Andrew McNiven), 1 March 1948, Liverpool, England; m. 1st Janine de Wolfe 1987; two d.; m. 2nd Danielle; m. 3rd Sienna Tuesday. *Education:* Sherwoods Lane Secondary Modern. *Career:* mem. The Hideaways 1960s, The Selofane 1968; moved to London 1970s; session musician for bands Badfinger, Walker Brothers, Scaffold, Bay City Rollers, Nazareth, Madness, The The, ABC, Maxi Priest, Prefab Sprout, The Communards, Mike Oldfield, Dina Carroll, Tina Turner, Kirsty MacColl, Richard Ashcroft, Paul McCartney, Spice Girls; joined CBS Records 1974, London Records 1980s, Warner Bros 1990s; numerous performances include The Cavern (500 appearances), Liverpool, Kampuchea charity concert (with Paul McCartney) 1979; concerts include Wembley Stadium, Wembley Arena, Knebworth House, Reading Festival, London Palladium, Royal Albert Hall, Culture Club Tour 1998–99; currently Owner UK music public relations co., Lander PR and Music; mem. Groucho Club, BPI (British Recorded Music Industry) Ltd, Performing Right Soc., Mechanical-Copyright Protection Soc., Musicians' Union, Equity, British Acad. of Songwriters, Composers and Authors (BASCA). *Compositions:* Resting Rough (film score); Music for The Short Show (LWT). *Television:* appearances include Top of the Pops, The Tube, Old Grey Whistle Test, Wogan, Des O'Connor Show, MTV, Montreux Pop Festival, Later With Jools Holland, ITN News, BBC News, C5 News, The One Show, Sky News; Assoc. Producer, St Lucia Jazz Festival 1991, Floor Dir, BRIT Awards 1994–2013; Jerry Lee Lewis (documentary). *Recordings:* albums: Flowers In The Dirt, Paul McCartney 1989, Medusa, Annie Lennox 1995, Alone With Everybody, Richard Ashcroft 2000; singles: Church Of The Poisoned Mind, Karma Chameleon, Culture Club (lead harmonica lines), Say You'll Be There, Spice Girls 1996. *Honours:* BASCA Gold Award 1997, Gold Badge Award Winner/ Brit Awards TV & Classical Brit Awards (Floor Cam Dir) (30 shows). *Address:* Lander PR, Lander Music Group, Balfour House, 741 High Road, London, N12 0BP, England (office). *Telephone:* (20) 8446-8881 (office). *E-mail:* judd@ landerpr.com (office). *Website:* www.landerpr.com (office).

LANDERS, Paul H.; German musician (guitar); b. (Henry Hirsch), 9 Dec. 1964, Belarus; m. Nikki Landers 1984; one s. *Career:* mem. Feeling B 1983–93; mem. Rammstein 1993–; numerous European tours. *Recordings include:* albums: Herzeleid 1995, Sehnsucht 1997, Live aus Berlin 1999, Mutter 2001, Reise, Reise 2004, Rosenrot 2005, Liebe ist für alle da 2009. *Honours:* MTV Europe Music Award for Best German Act 2005. *Current Management:* Pilgrim Management, Greifswalderstrasse 224, 10405 Berlin, Germany. *E-mail:* info@pilgrim-management.de. *Website:* www.pilgrim-management .de; www.rammstein.de.

LANDESMAN, Rocco, DLit; American arts organization executive, business executive and fmr theatre producer; *Chair, National Endowment for the Arts;* b. 20 July 1947, St Louis, Mo.; m. Debby Landesman; three s. *Education:* Colby Coll., Univ. of Wisconsin, Madison, Yale School of Drama. *Career:* Asst Prof., Yale School of Drama 1973–77; f. private investment fund 1977; Pres., Jujamcyn, which owns and operates five Broadway theatres 1987–2009, owner 2005–; Chair, Nat. Endowment for the Arts 2009–; mem. numerous Bds, including Municipal Arts Soc., Times Square Alliance, The Actor's Fund, Educational Foundation of America. *Theatre includes:* as producer: Big River (Tony Award for Best Musical 1985), Angels in America: Millennium Approaches (Tony Award for Best Play 1993), Angels in America: Perestroika (Tony Award for Best Play 1994), and The Producers (Tony Award for Best Musical 2001). *Address:* National Endowment for the Arts, 1100 Pennsylvania Avenue NW, Washington, DC 20506, USA (office). *Telephone:* (202) 682-5414 (office). *Fax:* (202) 682-5639 (office). *E-mail:* chairman@arts.gov (office). *Website:* www.arts.gov (office).

LANDGREN, Nils Lennart, DipMus, BMus; Swedish musician (trombone), singer and composer; b. 15 Feb. 1956, Degerfors; m. Beatrice Jaras-Landgren 1979. *Education:* Univ. of Music, Arvika. *Career:* professional trombone player aged 19; fmr mem. Ball of Fire 1981–83; currently leader, Funk Unit; freelance work in Stockholm; recording and stage performance with major Swedish artists. *Stage musicals:* lead in Skål (Stockholm, two years), Villon

(Stockholm). *Compositions:* Red Horn, with Bruce Swedien, Ain't Nobody, recorded with Maceo Parker, Cheyenne, with Michael Ruff. *Recordings include:* solo: Planet Rock 1983, Streetfighter 1984, You Are My Number 1 1985, Miles From Duke 1987, Chapter Two 1 1987, Chapter Two 2 1989, Follow Your Heart 1989, Red Horn 1992, Gotland 1996, Ballads 1999, Layers of Light (with Esbjörn Svensson) 1999, Sentimental Journey 2002, Creole Love Call (with Joe Sample) 2005, Christmas with My Friends 2005, Christmas With My Friends II 2008; with Funk Unit: Paint It Blue 1996, 5000 Miles 1999, Funk da World 2001, Funky Abba 2004. *Honours:* two Swedish Grammy Awards, German Jazz Award 1997, Tore Ehrling Prize 2002. *Current Management:* Walter Brolund Inc., Rosersbergsv. 25, 19571 Rosersberg, Sweden. *E-mail:* w.b@telia.com. *E-mail:* info@nilslandgren.com (office). *Website:* www.nilslandgren.com.

LANE, David; Australian musician (guitar), singer and songwriter; b. Boronia, WA. *Career:* fmr mem., Odeon Sound; mem. rock band You Am I 1999–; mem. The Brides, later renamed The Twin Set 1999–; mem. The Pictures 2004–. *Recordings include:* albums: with You Am I: Sound As Ever 1993, Hi Fi Way 1995, Hourly, Daily 1996, # 4 Record 1998, What Rhymes With Cars And Girls 1999, ...Saturday Night, 'Round Ten 1999, Dress Me Slowly 2001, Deliverance 2002, Spit Polish 2005, Convicts 2007; with The Twin Set: What Rhymes With Cars and Girls? 1998; with The Pictures: Somethin' I Don't Know (EP), Singin' It Just To See (EP) 2005, Pieces Of Eight 2005. *Current Management:* c/o Scott McKenzie, Premier Artists, Dundas La, Albert Park, Vic. 3206, Australia. *Telephone:* (3) 9699-9555. *E-mail:* scotty@ premierartists.com.au. *Website:* www.premierartists.com.au. *E-mail:* management@youami.com.au. *Website:* www.youami.com.au.

LANE, Jamie, BA, MA Cantab.; British musician (drums), record producer, engineer and programmer; *Director, Britannia Row Studios;* b. 15 Sept. 1951, Kolkata, India; m. Katerina Koumi 1991; one d. *Education:* Magdalene Coll., Cambridge. *Career:* mem. The Movies 1976–80, Sniff 'n' The Tears 1980–82; session drummer 1982–; currently Tech. Dir, Britannia Row Studios; session drummer and record producer, working with Tina Turner, Van Morrison, Randy Newman, Mark Knopfler, 10cc, Michael Hutchence, Joan Armatrading, Ben E. King, Agnetha Fältskog, Diane Dufresne, Jean-Patrick Capdevielle; also producer for Microdisney, Railway Children, Pete Townshend, Paul Brady, Falco, Nick Kamen, Hot House, Jackie Quinn, Microgroove, Do Re Mi; mem. Musicians' Union. *Address:* Britannia Row Studios, 3 Bridge Studios, 318–326 Wandsworth Bridge Road, London, SW6 2TZ, England (office). *Telephone:* (20) 7371-5872 (office). *Fax:* (20) 7371-8641 (office). *E-mail:* jamie@britanniarowstudios.co.uk (office). *Website:* www.britanniarowstudios .co.uk (office).

LANE, Rick; British composer, producer, musician (keyboards, guitar, bass, percussion) and backing singer; b. 22 April 1953, London. *Education:* Guildhall Exhibition Scholar. *Career:* founder, Rent Boys, Private Lives; three tours with The Edgar Broughton Band; produces music for film, television, radio, commercials, corporate video, station idents and multimedia; mem, British Music Writers' Council, Society of Producers of Applied Music, Performing Rights Society, MCPS, BAC&S, Musicians' Union, Alliance of Composer Organisations, Asscn of Professional Composers, Composers Guild of Great Britain. *Recordings:* with Rent Boys: two singles, one album; with Private Lives: three singles, two albums; over 200 television, cinema, radio commercials, documentary and features for BBC, LWT, Granada, Anglia.

LANEGAN, Mark; American singer and songwriter; b. 25 Nov. 1964, Ellensburg, Wash. WA. *Career:* fmr mem. Screaming Trees 1983–2000; solo artist 1990–, with Mark Lanegan Band 2003–; mem. Queens of the Stone Age 2003–05; mem. The Gutter Twins 2005–. *Recordings include:* albums: with Screaming Trees: Clairvoyance 1986, Even if and Especially When 1987, Invisible Lantern 1988, Buzz Factory 1989, Uncle Anesthesia 1991, Sweet Oblivion 1992, Dust 1996; solo: The Winding Sheet 1990, Whiskey for the Holy Ghost 1994, Scraps at Midnight 1998, I'll Take Care of You 1999, Field Songs 2001, Bubblegum 2004, Ballad of the Broken Seas (with Isobel Campbell) 2005, Sunday at Dirt Devil (with Isobel Campbell) 2008, Hawk (with Isobel Campbell) 2010, Blues Funeral 2012; with Queens of the Stone Age: Lullabies to Paralyze 2005, Era Vulgaris 2007; with The Gutter Twins: Saturnalia 2007. *Address:* c/o Sub Pop Records, 2013 Fourth Avenue, Third Floor, Seattle, WA 98121, USA. *E-mail:* info@subpop.com. *Website:* www.subpop.com; www.qotsa .com.

LANG, Andy Lee; Austrian singer, entertainer and musician (piano); b. 26 July 1965, Vienna. *Education:* Commercial School. *Career:* piano player for Chuck Berry, European tour 1992–93; concerts with Jerry Lee Lewis, Wanda Jackson, Carl Perkins, The Magic Platters, Fats Domino; concerts, television and radio shows worldwide; mem. Austrian Composers' Asscn. *Recordings include:* Back To Rock 'n' Roll, 1990; Rockin' Piano Man, 1991; Back In Town, 1993; That's Entertainment Live, 1994; Rockin' Christmas, 1994. *Honours:* Golden Microphone 1991. *Address:* Simmerringer Haide 6/543, 1110 Vienna, Austria.

LANG, Kathryn Dawn (k.d.); Canadian singer and songwriter; b. 2 Nov. 1961, Consort, Alberta; d. of Adam Lang and Audrey L. Lang. *Career:* began playing guitar aged 10; formed band The Reclines in early 1980s, played N American clubs 1982–87; performed at closing ceremony, Winter Olympics, Calgary 1988, Winter Olympics, Vancouver 2010; performed with Sting, Bruce Springsteen, Peter Gabriel and Tracy Chapman in Amnesty Int. tour 1988; headline US tour 1992. *Film appearances:* Salmonberries 1991, Teresa's

Tattoo 1994, The Last Don 1997, Eye of the Beholder 1999; features on soundtrack to Dick Tracy. *Recordings include:* albums: A Truly Western Experience 1984, Angel With A Lariat 1987, Shadowland 1988, Absolute Torch And Twang 1989, Ingénue (Album of the Year 1993) 1992, Even Cowgirls Get The Blues (film soundtrack) 1993, All You Can Eat 1995, Drag 1997, Australian Tour 1997, Invincible Summer 2000, Live By Request 2001, A Wonderful World (with Tony Bennett; Grammy Award for Best Traditional Pop Vocal Album 2004) 2003, Hymns of the 49th Parallel 2004, Reintarnation 2006, Watershed 2008, Recollection 2010, Sing It Loud (with the Siss Boom Bang) 2011. *Honours:* Canadian Country Music Asscn Awards for Best Entertainer of Year 1989, Best Album of Year 1990, Grammy Awards for Best Country Vocal Collaboration 1989, for Best Female Country Vocal Performance 1990, for Best Female Pop Vocal Performance 1993, American Music Awards, Favourite New Artist 1992, Songwriter of the Year (with Ben Mink) 1993, BRIT Award for Best Int. Female 1995. *Current Management:* Direct Management Group, 947 North La Cienega Blvd, Suite G, Los Angeles, CA 90069, USA. *Telephone:* (310) 854-3535. *Fax:* (310) 854-0810. *E-mail:* info@ directmanagement.com. *Website:* directmanagement.com; www.kdlang.com.

LANG, Penny; Canadian folk singer, songwriter and musician (guitar); b. 15 July 1942, Montréal, QC; one s. *Education:* Sir George Williams Univ., Montréal. *Career:* numerous festivals, live performances; mem. SOCAN. *Recordings include:* YES!!, 1991; Live (solo), 1992; Carry On Children, 1993; Ain't Life Sweet, 1996; Penny Lang and Friends Live, 1998. *Honours:* several Canada Council Awards for touring, writing, recording, grant from Québec Ministère des Affaires Culturelles. *E-mail:* info@pennylang.com. *Website:* www.pennylang.com.

LANGBORN, Torbjorn; Swedish musician (piano) and composer; b. 17 May 1955, Stockholm; two d. *Education:* Adolf Fredrik Music School, Stockholm Univ., Royal Acad. of Music, Stockholm. *Career:* live performances, radio and television broadcasts throughout Sweden, Finland, Poland, Norway; freelance pianist in salsa, tango and jazz styles; teacher of improvisation, Afro-American and jazz theory; mem. STIM, SAMI, SKAP, Musicians' Union. *Recordings include:* Hot Salsa – Maldito Primitivo; Hot Salsa Meets Swedish Jazz; Torbjorn Langborn and his Feel Life Orchestra. *Address:* Hjalmar Söderbergs Väg 16 D 2tr, 112 52 Stockholm, Sweden.

LANGE, Barbara Rose; American ethnomusicologist; b. 14 Jan. 1955, Casper, New York. *Education:* PhD, Ethnomusicology, University of Washington, 1993. *Career:* Assistant Professor, Moores School of Music, University of Houston, 1996–, currently Associate Professor; mem. Society for Ethnomusicology; International Council for Traditional Music. *Publications:* Lakadalmas Rosk and the Rejection of Popular Culture in Post-Socialist Hungary, in Retuning Culture, 1996; Hungarian Romanian (Gypsy) Political Activism and the Development of Folkier Ensemble Music, 1997; What Was the Conquering Magic...: The Power of Discontuinity in Hungarian Gypsy Nota, in Ethnomusicology, 1997. *Honours:* IREX Exchange Fellowship, Hungary, 1990–91; Fulbright Graduate Grant, Hungary, 1990–91; Mellon Postdoctoral Fellow, Cornell University, 1995–96. *Address:* Moores School of Music, 120 School of Music Building, University of Houston, Houston, TX 77204-4017, USA. *E-mail:* rlange@mail.uh.edu. *Website:* www.uh.edu/class/ music/faculty-staff/lange_b/index.php.

LANGLOIS, Paul; Canadian musician (rhythm guitar). *Career:* mem., The Tragically Hip 1986–. *Recordings include:* albums: Up to Here 1989, Road Apples 1991, Fully Completely 1992, Day for Night 1994, Trouble at the Henhouse 1996, Live Between Us 1997, Phantom Power 1998, Music @ Work 2000, In Violet Light 2002, In Between Revolution 2004, World Container 2006. *Honours:* inducted into the Canadian Music Hall of Fame 2005. *Address:* c/o Universal Music, 2450 Victoria Park Avenue, Suite 1, Toronto, ON M2J 5H3, Canada. *Website:* www.thehip.com.

LANGMAID, Ben; British musician, songwriter and record producer; b. 31 Dec. 1969. *Career:* fmr mem. Atomic, Huff & Herb; mem. Huff & Puff 1996–2001, songwriter for Kubb 2005; Founder-mem. La Roux 2008–14, supported Lily Allen on UK tour in 2009. *Recordings:* albums: as songwriter: Mother, Kubb 2005; with La Roux: La Roux 2009, Trouble in Paradise 2014. *Honours:* O2 Silver Clef Best Newcomer Award 2009, Studio8 Int. Music Awards for Best Female Newcomer 2009, iTunes UK Music Award for Single of the Year 2009, NME Best Dancefloor Filler Award 2010, Int. Dance Music Awards for Best Dubstep/DNB/Jungle Track and Best Breakthrough Artist (Group) 2010, Grammy Award for Best Electronic/Dance Album 2011. *Address:* c/o Universal Music UK, 364–366 Kensington High Street, London, W14 8NS, England (office). *Telephone:* (20) 7471-5000 (office). *Website:* www .larouxonline.com; www.laroux.co.uk.

LANOIS, Daniel; Canadian producer and musician; b. 19 Sept. 1951, Hull, QC. *Career:* built recording studio at parental home with brother aged 19 years; became leading local producer; collaborated with Brian Eno; produced albums for Bob Dylan (Oh Mercy, Time Out Of Mind), Peter Gabriel (So, Us), Emmylou Harris, Luscious Jackson, Martha And The Muffins, U2 (The Unforgettable Fire and The Joshua Tree – jointly with Brian Eno – Achtung Baby, All That You Can't Leave Behind); composed music for film Sling Blade. *Recordings:* albums: Acadie 1989, For The Beauty Of Wynona 1993, Shine 2003, Belladonna 2005, Here Is What Is 2008, The Omni Series 2008. *Publication:* Soul Mining: A Musical Life 2010. *Honours:* Grammy Award for Producer of the Year 1992, Jack Richardson Producer of the Year, Juno

Awards 2009. *E-mail:* mjm65@mac.com (office); adam@redfloorrecords.com (office). *Website:* www.daniellanois.com.

LAPPALAINEN, Janne; Finnish arranger, composer and musician (wind and string instruments); *Audio-Visual Technician, Samediggi;* b. 21 April 1971, Rääkkylä. *Education:* studies in Sibelius Acad. *Career:* Founder-mem. Värttinä 1983–2008; also mem. Progmatics, Ottopasuuna, Punos, Irina Björklund's band, Riikka Timonen's band; currently audio-visual technician, Samediggi. *Music for theatre:* co-wrote score to stage musical, The Lord of the Rings (with A. R. Rahman) (Princess of Wales Theatre, Toronto) 2006. *Recordings include:* albums: Värttinä 1987, Musta Lindu 1989, Oi Dai 1990, Seleniko 1992, Aitara 1994, Kokko 1996, Vihma 1998, Ilmatar 2000, 6.12 2001, iki 2003, Miero 2006; with Progmatics: Vaarallinen lehmänkello 1996; with Ottopasuuna: Suokaasua 1996, Jouko Kyhälä & Saalas 2006, Ánnámáret Ensemble: Beallječiŋat 2011, Irina Björklund: Chanson D'Automne 2011; various guest appearances on albums, including with Pirnales, Maria Kalaniemi & Aldargaz, Petri Hakala, Angelin tytöt, Markku Lepistö, Ramunder. *Honours:* Kaustinen Folk Music Festival Band of the Year 1987, Arts Council of Finland State Prize for Merit in Music 1993, Finnish Nat. Group of IFPI Emma Award 1993.

LARA, Oscar; Mexican musician (drums); b. Rosa Morada, Sinaloa; cousin of Jorge Hernández, Hernán Hernández, Eduardo Hernández and Luis Hernández. *Career:* mem. Los Tigres del Norte (norteño-style band) 1971–. *Film:* La Misma Luna 2008. *Recordings include:* albums: Cuquita 1971, El Cheque 1972, Contrabando y Traición 1974, La Banda del Carro Rojo 1975, La Tumba del Mojado – Internacionalmente Norteños 1976, Pueblo Querido 1976, Vivan los Mojados 1977, Numero Ocho 1978, El Tahúr 1979, Plaza Garibaldi 1980, Un Día a la Vez 1981, Padre Nuestro – éxitos para siempre 1982, Carrera Contra la Muerte 1983, Jaula de Oro 1983, A ti Madrecita 1985, El Otro México 1986, Gracias América – Sin Fronteras (Grammy Award for Best Album (Regional Mexican Music Category) 1987) 1986, Idolos del Pueblo 1988, Corridos Prohibidos 1989, Triunfo Sólido – mi buena suerte 1989, Para Adoloridos 1990, Incansables! 1991, Con Sentimiento y Sabor – Tan Bonita 1992, Una Noche con los Tigres del Norte 1992, La Garra de... 1993, Los dos Plebes 1994, El Ejemplo 1995, Unidos Para Siempre 1996, Así como tú 1997, Jefe de Jefes 1997, Herencia de Familia 1999, De Paisano a Paisano 2000, Uniendo Fronteras 2001, La Reina del Sur 2002, Pacto de Sangre (Latin Grammy Award for Best Norteño Album) 2004, Directo al Corazón 2005, Historias que Contar (Grammy Award for Best Norteño Album 2007) 2006, Detalles y Emociones 2007, Raíces (Grammy Award for Best Norteño Album 2009) 2008, Tu Noche Con...El Tigres del Norte (Grammy Award for Best Norteño Album 2010) 2009, La Granja 2009, Los Tigres Del Norte and Friends (Grammy Award for Best Banda or Norteño Album 2012) 2011. *Honours:* Academia Nacional de la Música Mexicana Award 2003, Oye! Homenaje a la Trayectoria Artistica and Award for Best Norteño Group 2003, BMI Latin Award for Songwriting Icons 2007. *Address:* Los Tigres del Norte, 99 Almaden Blvd, Suite 333, San Jose, CA 95113, USA (office). *E-mail:* management@lostigresdelnorte.com (office). *Website:* www.lostigresdelnorte.com (office).

LARATTA, David Ottavio; French musician (bass, drums, trumpet); b. 19 April 1970, Saint Denis. *Education:* Arts and Letters (A3). *Career:* Guest musician, guest Youssou N'Dour, 1990; Francopholies, La Rochelle, France, 1992; Television show, TF1, 1992; 20th Anniversary, Sony France, 1993; National Concours Jazz in Paris, La Défense, with Used 2b Bop, 1995; Numerous concerts, shows, appearances, throughout France, with various bands; Marcel Sabiani Trio; Lewis Robinson, 1997; Léa loCicero, 1997; Divan du monde, with Cheick Tidiane Seck 'Tribute to Fela', 1997; Gino Williams, 1998; Caravana, Afro Cuban, Mars, 1998; mem, SPEDIDAM; SACEM.

LARSEN, Jens Kjaer; Danish rap artist, singer and songwriter; b. 30 May 1964, Copenhagen, Denmark; m. Camilla Palikaras 1997. *Career:* mem., Cut 'n' Move band, several television broadcasts, tours of Europe, Australia, USA and Asia. *Recordings include:* albums: Get Serious, Peace Love and Harmony, The Sounds of Now, Into the Zone. *Honours:* Silver Lion, Germany, four Grammy Awards, Denmark.

LARSEN, Jon; Norwegian musician (guitar), composer, record producer and artist; b. 7 Jan. 1959, Jar; m. Barbara Jahn 1994; two d. one step-d. *Education:* High School of Music. *Career:* full-time professional guitarist/composer with Hot Club de Norvège 1979–; worldwide touring since 1990; est. Django Festival 1980–, Hot Club Records 1982–, The Vintage Guitars Series 1989–, Zonic Entertainment 2006–; mem. Composers' Soc. of Norway (NOPA), Record Producers' Soc. of Norway (FONO). *Art exhibitions:* annually 1976–96, Retrospective Exhbns, Trondheim 2011, Aalesund 2011. *Films:* Symphonic Django 2008, Jon & Jimmy (Dutch Edison Award) 2009. *Recordings:* albums: with Hot Club de Norvege: String Swing 1981, Old, New, Borrowed and Blue 1982, Gloomy 1984, Swing de Paris 1986, La Roue Fleurie 1992, Swinging with Jimmy 1994, Portrait of Django 1995, Vertavo 1995, Hot Shots 1997, Moreno 1998, Presenting Ola and Jimmy 2000, Angelo is Back in Town 2001, White Night Stories 2002, Django's Tiger 2003, A Stranger in Town 2004, Hot Cats 2005, Django Music 2008; solo: Superstrings 1992, Guitaresque 1994, The Next Step 2003, Short Stories from Catalonia 2005, Strange News from Mars 2007, The Jimmy Carl Black Story 2008, Willie Nickerson's Egg 2009–11; produced more than 350 albums for Hot Club Records. *Publication:* Maler i solnedgang 2009. *Honours:* NOPA Composer of the Year 1994, Oslo Art Prize 2008, Kardemommestipendet 2009. *Address:* Hot Club Records, PO Box 5202, 0302 Oslo, Norway (office). *Telephone:* 22-50-19-78 (office). *E-mail:* jon.larsen@getmail.no (office). *Website:* www.hotclub.no (office).

LARSEN, Marit; Norwegian singer, songwriter and musician (guitar); b. 1 July 1983, Lørenskog. *Career:* mem. of teenage pop duo M2M with childhood friend Marion Raven –2002; solo artist 2004–. *Recordings:* albums: with M2M: Shades of Purple 2000, The Big Room 2001, The Day You Went Away: The Best of M2M 2003; solo: Under the Surface 2005. *Honours:* Best Norwegian Act, MTV Europe Music Awards 2006, Best Female Artist and Best Video, Spellemannprisen 2007. *Current Management:* Unit AS, Eliert Sundtsgate 14, 0259 Oslo, Norway. *Telephone:* 22-12-90-50. *Fax:* 22-12-90-51. *E-mail:* morten@unit.nu. *Website:* www.unit.nu; www.maritlarsen.com.

LARSSON, Anders; Swedish manager; b. 13 April 1958, Malmo. *Career:* own management co., United Stage Production AB, for Scandinavian artists, with some 30 artists in pop, jazz, blues, rock music; mem. of bd, Swedish Impressario Asscn, Swedish Publishers' Asscn. *Address:* United Stage Production AB, PO Box 9174, 200 39 Malmo, Sweden.

LASCELLES, Jeremy; artist manager; *CEO, Chrysalis Group Plc;* b. 14 Feb. 1955, London, England; one s. three d. *Career:* artist man. 1972–75; tour man. 1975–79; A&R Consultant, Virgin Records 1979–80, Dir of Marketing 1980–82, Dir of A&R 1982–88; Man. Dir Ten Records 1988–92, Offside Productions and Management 1993–94; Man. Dir Chrysalis Music 1994–2001, CEO Music Div., Chrysalis Group Plc 2001–07, CEO 2007–; Man. Dir The Echo Label 1998–2001, 2005–. *Address:* The Chrysalis Building, 13 Bramley Road, London, W10 6SP, England. *Telephone:* (20) 7465-1670. *Website:* www.chrysalis.com.

LASSEN, Nils; Danish composer; b. 10 March 1960; m. Sisse Lassen; one d. *Career:* composer for theatre and film, Danish television, including The Royal Theatre; mem. DJBFA. *Compositions:* Boy of 1000 Tears 1997, Riders of Depression 1997, No Lilacs, No Lillies, No More 1997. *Recordings:* composer of albums: for De Skrigende Halse: Testament for Ronni 1997; for Mr Sonic; My Stereo is my No. 1 1997, for Dreamtones; Lost in the Woods 1997, for El Lasso: Most of Us Prefer Not To Think 1997; for Nature: In a Gentle Mood 1996, Indoor/Outdoor 1998; for Bo Hr. Hansen: Idiot 2002; for Bulldozer: A State of Mind 2004; for 500 Feelings: Echoes in the Rain 2006, The Morning After 2008. *Website:* www.nilslassen.dk.

LASWELL, Bill; American musician (guitar, bass guitar), record company executive and record producer; b. 14 Feb. 1950, Salem, Ill. *Career:* leader, groups including Material, Curlew, Last Exit, Painkiller; founder, record labels OAO, Celluloid, Innerythmic; record producer for Herbie Hancock. *Recordings include:* albums: solo: Baselines 1984, Best of Bill Laswell 1985, Point Blank 1986, Low Life 1987, Hear No Evil 1988, Psychonavigation 1994, Axiom Ambient: Lost in the Translation 1994, Web 1995, Cymatic Scan 1995, Silent Recoil 1995, Bass Terror 1995, Dark Massive 1996, Oscillations 1996, Dub Meltdown 1997, Sacred System: Chapter Two 1997, City of Light 1997, Jazzonia 1998, Divination: Sacrifice 1998, Invisible Design 1999, Imaginary Cuba 1999, Lo Def Pressure 2000, Permutation 2000, Dub Chamber 3 2000, Radioaxiom, A Dub Transmission 2000, Filmtracks 2001, Points of Order 2001, ROIR Dub Sessions 2003, Aftermathematics Instrumental 2003, Hear No Evil 2006, Dub Terror Exhaust 2006; with Material: Temporary Music 1980, Third Power, Memory Serves, One Down; with Last Exit: The Noise of Trouble 1987; with Herbie Hancock: Future Shock, Perfect Machine 1988; with John Zorn and Eugene Chadbourne: The Parachute Years (7-disc set) 1997; also producer for numerous artists including Yoko Ono, Mick Jagger, Gil Scott-Heron, Nona Hendryx, Manu Dibango, PiL, Fela Kuti, Iggy Pop, Motörhead, Laurie Anderson, Afrika Bambaataa, Yellowman. *Address:* Innerythmic, 133 West 25th Street, Fifth Floor, New York, NY 10001, USA (office). *Telephone:* (212) 414-0505 (office). *Fax:* (212) 414-0525 (office). *E-mail:* info@innerhythmic.com (office). *Website:* www.innerhythmic.com (office).

LATHAM, (Anthony) John Heaton, BA, PhD; British musician and academic; b. 30 Oct. 1940, Wigan, England; m. Dawn Catherine Farleigh 1990. *Education:* Univ. of Birmingham. *Career:* debut, Wigan Jazz Club 1958; Penn-Latham Quintet, University of Birmingham 1961–63; Axiom Jazz Band, Swansea 1967–68; J. J.'s Rhythm Aces, Swansea Univ. 1982–84; Speakeasy Jazz Band, Swansea 1984–; John Latham's Jazztimers 1995–; live performances include Brecon Jazz Festival, Cork Jazz Festival, Birmingham Jazz Festival, BBC Wales, Llangollen Jazz Festival, Bude Jazz Festival, and clubs including Fritzel's, Gazebo, Bonaparte's Retreat; mem. Musicians' Union, Sandy Brown Soc. (sec. 1997–). *Recordings include:* Blanche Finlay with The Speakeasy Jazzband 1987, John Latham's Jazztimers, Sandy's Bar, Cardiff 1997, John Latham's Jazztimers 1998, Sandy and Co. 1998. *Publications:* Al Fairweather Discography 1994, Eurojazz Discographies No. 34, Stan Greig Discography 1995, Eurojazz Discography No. 42, Sandy Brown Discography 1997, Eurojazz Discography No. 5; contrib. to New Orleans Music Vol. 2 No. 1 1990, Jazz Journal International, Jan., Sept. 1993, June 1994, May 1996, British Jazz Times, Sept.–Oct. 1994, The Jazz Rag, March–April, Nov.–Dec. 1998, July–Aug. 1999.

LATIFA; Tunisian singer; b. (Latifa bint Alayah al-Arfaoui), 14 Feb. 1961, Manouba. *Education:* Arab Acad. of Music, Egypt. *Career:* solo artist 1985–. *Film:* Silence... We're Rolling 2001. *Recordings include:* albums: Andak shak? 1985, Ma laqtsh methalak – ma banamsh al-layl 1986, Ya hayati ana 1987, Meen yeqol? 1987, Dalleltni 1988, Akthar min roohi 1988, Ashan bahibbal 1989, Bil aql keda 1990, Waih waih 1990, Ad-donya betedh'hak leya 1992,

Hobbak hadi 1993, Ana ma atniseesh 1994, Wa akheeran 1995, Ma wahashtaksh? 1996, Al-ghinwa 1997, Taloomoni ad-donya 1998, Wadeh (aka Insha'allah) 1999, Ma etrohsh ba'ed 2003, Ma'alomat akeeda 2007, Fil kam yom illi fato 2008. *Honours:* Medal of Cultural Merit (Tunisia); World Music Award for best-selling artist in the Middle East and North Africa 2004. *Address:* c/o Rotana, Burj al-Ghazal, 11th Floor, al-Tabaris, Achrafieh, Beirut, Lebanon (office). *E-mail:* info@rotana.net (office). *Website:* www.rotana.net (home); www.latifaonline.net.

LATTIKAS, Urmas; Estonian composer, arranger, conductor and musician (piano); b. 17 Aug. 1960, Tapa, Estonia; m. Kaia, 22 Dec. 1993, 2 s. *Education:* Graduated as composer, Estonian Music Academy, 1977–86; Post-graduate studies, jazz composition, piano, Berklee College of Music, Boston, USA, 1990. *Career:* Performing artiste, founder, leader, own jazz group Urmas Lattikas Quintet; Arranger, jazz, pop, classical styles; Accompanist, numerous vocal and instrumental performances; Extensive club, concert appearances, numerous jazz events, Estonia and abroad; Recordings, appearances, radio and television; Urmas Lattikas Quintet represented Estonian jazz in European Jazz Night television programme; Conducted Estonian song, Eurovision Song Contest, 1994. *Compositions:* Symphonic, choral, chamber music, film scores; Music for single and album. *Recordings:* Single: In A Twilight Room; Album: Freedom To Love, Freedom To Lose. *Honours:* First Prize, U Naissoo composition contest, 1983, 1984; Levi Jaagup Award, Keyboard Player of the Year, 1990.

LAU, Andy; Hong Kong singer, actor, film producer and television presenter; b. (Liu Dehua), 27 Sept. 1961, Tai Po, Hong Kong; m. Carol Chu 2008; one d. *Education:* Band One Secondary School, Ho Lap Coll., San Po Kong, Kowloon, Ho Lap Coll., TVB Acad. *Career:* has performed in more than 160 films while maintaining a successful singing career; branded by the media as one of the 'Four Heavenly Kings' of Cantopop, along with Jacky Cheung, Aaron Kwok and Leon Lai 1990s; f. own film production co. Teamwork Motion Pictures Ltd (renamed Focus Group Holdings Ltd 2002); has own production house New Melody Production (renamed NMG 2000) 1992–; apptd Summer Paralympics Goodwill Amb. and sang theme song Flying with the Dream with Han Hong during Paralympics opening ceremony, Beijing 2008; involved with charity organizations Life Education Activity Program, Hong Kong Marrow Match Foundation, Ocean Park Conservation Foundation; f. Andy Lau Charity Foundation 1994. *Recordings include:* albums: I Only Know I Love You 1985, Would It Be Possible (RTHK Top 10 Gold Songs Award 1990) 1990, Long Distance Companion 2009, Unforgettable 2010. *Films include:* Tau ban no hoi 1982, On the Wrong Track 1983, Ga joi Heung Gong 1983, Shanghai 13 1984, Ting bu liao de ai 1984, Xia ri fu xing 1985, Fat ngoi ching 1985, Zui jia fu xing 1986, Mo fei cui 1986, Ying hung ho hon 1987, Gan dan xiang zhao 1987, Gong woo ching 1987, Zhong Guo zui hou yi ge tai jian 1988, Qun long duo bao 1988, Long zhi jia zu 1988, Lie ying ji hua 1988, Fa nei qing 1988, Jing zhuong zhui nu zi zhi er 1988, Zui jia sun you 1988, As Tears Go By 1988, In the Blood 1988, Zui jia sun you chuang qing guan 1988, Shen xing tai bao 1989, Zhi zun wu shang 1989, Sheng gang qi bing di san ji 1989, Ren hai gu hong 1989, Juen diu daai ngok 1989, Fu gui bing tuan 1989, Fa nei qing da jie ju 1989, Tong gen sheng 1989, Biao cheng 1989, Zui jie nan peng you 1989, Ao qi xiong ying 1989, Di yi jian 1989, Xiao xiao xiao jing cha 1989, China White 1989, God of Gamblers 1989, Lang zhi yi zu 1989, Stars & Roses 1989, No Risk, No Gain: Casino Raiders – The Sequel 1990, Zai zhan jiang hu 1990, Forbidden Imperial Tales (singing voice) 1990, Island of Fire 1990, A Moment of Romance 1990, Ma deng ru lai shen zhang 1990, Yi daam hung sam 1990, Yu zhong long 1990, A Home Too Far 1990, Days of Being Wild 1990, Tian zi men sheng 1991, Tricky Brains 1991, God of Gamblers II 1991, Zhong Huan ying xiong 1991, The Last Blood 1991, Casino Raiders II 1991, Wu hu jiang zhi jue lie (Jin pai wu hu jiang) 1991, Ji dao zhui zong 1991, Lee Rock 1991, Lee Rock II 1991, Saviour of the Soul 1991, Xia sheng 1992, Lee Rock III 1992, Fan dou ma liu 1992, Do sing dai hang san goh chuen kei 1992, Do sing daai hang II ji ji juen mo dik 1992, Hua! ying xiong 1992, Long teng si hai 1992, Ji Boy xiao zi zhi zhen jia wai long 1992, Chuan dao fang zi 1992, Miu kai sup yi siu 1992, Handsome Siblings 1992, Zhan shen chuan shuo 1993, Chao ji xue xiao ba wang 1993, Ji jun sam sap lok gai ji Tau tin wun yat 1993, Sat sau dik tung wah 1994, Dao jian xiao 1994, Tian chang di jiu 1994, The Legend of Drunken Master 1994, Tian yu di 1994, Yu long gong wu 1994, Jui kuen III 1994, Da mao xian jia 1995, Full Throttle 1995, A Moment of Romance III 1996, Ding Lik (as Andy T. W. Lau), San Seung Hoi taan 1996, ½ Chi tung chong 1996, Qi yi lu cheng zhi: Zhen xin ai sheng ming 1996, Tin dei hung sam 1997, Kau luen kei 1997, Island of Greed 1997, A True Mob Story 1998, Du xia 1999 1998, Ai qing meng huan hao 1999, Hei ma wang zi 1999, Du xia da zhan Lasi Weijiasi 1999, Running Out of Time 1999, Century of the Dragon 1999, Kuet chin chi gam ji din 2000, Needing You… 2000, A Fu (also producer) 2000, Love on a Diet 2001, Fulltime Killer (also producer) 2001, Oi gwan yue mung (also producer) 2001, Kap sze moon yat goh gei kooi 2002, Fat Choi Spirit 2002, Wai See Lee ji lam huet yan 2002, Infernal Affairs 2002, Love Under the Sun (short) 2003, Lou she oi sheung mao 2003, Running on Karma 2003, Mou gaan dou III: Jung gik mou gaan 2003, Golden Chicken 2 2003, Moh waan chue fong 2004, House of Flying Daggers 2004, Gong wu (also exec. producer) 2004, McDull, Prince de la bun (voice) 2004, Yesterday Once More 2004, A World Without Thieves 2004, Wait 'Til You're Older 2005, The Shoe Fairy (voice) (also exec. producer) 2005, All About Love (also exec. producer) 2005, I'll Call You (also exec. producer) 2006, My Mother Is a Belly Dancer (also producer) 2006, Battle of Wits 2006, Protégé 2007, Brothers 2007, The Warlords (as Dehua Liu) 2007, Three Kingdoms: Resurrection of the Dragon 2008, Yau lung hei fung 2009, The Founding of a Republic 2009, Future X-Cops 2010, Detective Dee: Mystery of the Phantom Flame 2010, Shaolin 2011, What Women Want (also exec. producer) 2011, Beginning of the Great Revival 2011, A Simple Life (also exec. producer) 2011; exec. producer: Made in Hong Kong 1997, Runaway Pistol (uncredited) 2002, Invisible Waves 2006, Gallants 2010; producer: Hui nin yin fa dak bit doh 1998, Crazy Stone 2006. *Television includes:* Choi wan kuk 1982, Sou hat yi (series) 1982, Return of the Condor Heroes (series) 1983, Lao dong (series) 1983, Luk ding gei (series) 1984, The Last Performance (series) 1985, Yang ka cheung (series) 1986, Hao men ye yan (presenter) 1991, Shin chou kyou ryo: Condor Hero (series) (title theme, singing voice) 2001. *Honours:* Hon. Fellow, Hongkong Acad. of Performing Arts; Medal of Honour (Hong Kong); Dr hc (Univ. of New Brunswick, Canada) 2010; Jade Solid Gold Top 10 Award, entered into Guinness World Records for Most Awards Won By A Cantopop Male Artist, Most Popular Male Artist 1990–92, 1994, 1999, 2004, Asia Pacific Most Popular Hong Kong Male Artist 1993, 1995–96, 2000–06, named of Ten Outstanding Young Persons of the World 1999, Honorary Award, Power Acad. Awards 2000, 2006, Performance Power Award, Power Acad. Awards 2001, 2005, Asian Filmmaker of the Year, Pusan Int. Film Festival 2006, Justice of Peace Award, Govt of Hong Kong Special Admin. Region 2008, World Outstanding Chinese Award 2010. *Address:* Focus Films, Focus Group Holdings Ltd, 9/F, Tower A, Billion Centre, 1 Wang Kwong Road, Kowloon Bay, Kowloon, Hong Kong Special Administrative Region, People's Republic of China (office). *Telephone:* 3120-3388 (office). *Fax:* 3120-3328 (office). *E-mail:* info@andylau.com (office). *Website:* www.focusgroup.cc (office); www.andylau.com/andylau/index.do.

LAUDERDALE, Jim; American singer, musician (guitar) and songwriter; b. 11 April 1957, Statesville, NC. *Career:* songwriter for other artists, including Patty Loveless, Dixie Chicks, Mark Chestnut, Vince Gill and George Strait; country and bluegrass solo artist 1989–. *Recordings include:* solo albums: Point of No Return 1989, Planet of Love 1991, Pretty Close to the Truth 1994, Every Second Counts 1995, Persimmons 1996, Whisper 1997, I Feel Like Singing Today 1998, Onward Through it All 1999, The Other Sessions 2001, The Hummingbirds 2002, Lost in the Lonesome Pines (with Ralph Stanley, Grammy Award for Bluegrass Album of the Year) 2002, Wait 'til Spring 2003, Headed for the Hills (Americana Award for Album of the Year) 2004, Bluegrass 2006, Country Super Hits Volume I 2006, The Bluegrass Diaries (Grammy Award for Bluegrass Album of the Year 2008) 2007, Honey Songs 2008. *Honours:* Americana Music Awards for Artist of the Year, Song of the Year 2002. *Address:* Nectar Management, PO Box 120957, Nashville, TN 37212, USA (office). *Telephone:* (615) 298-3224 (office). *E-mail:* marybeth@jimlauderdale.com (office). *Website:* www.jimlauderdale.com.

LAUDET, François; French musician (drums); b. 11 Nov. 1958, Paris. *Career:* big band jazz drummer; bandleader François Laudet Big Band; numerous appearances at festivals and on television; played with Count Basie Orchestra in European tour 1997; mem. Union des Musiciens de Jazz. *Recordings:* with Saxomania, Ellingtomania Ornicar Big Band, Super Swing Machine, François Laudet Big Band. *Honours:* Prix Sydney Bechet 1994. *Address:* 14 rue des Carrieres, 93230 Romainville, France.

LAUDET, Philippe; French composer, arranger and musician (trumpet, piano); b. 11 Dec. 1959, Nanterre; m. Catherine Laudet, 19 Dec. 1987, 1 s., 2 d. *Education:* Astrophysics, until age 28; Classical piano from age 6–16; Jazz piano from age 10; Jazz trumpet from age 15. *Career:* Leader, composer, Ornicar Big Band, 1980–95; Played all major jazz festivals in France: Paris; Nice; Salon de Provence; Marciac; Vienne; Trumpet soloist, Tuxedo Big Band, 1992–; Played in Marciac, Coutance, Spain; mem, SACEM; SPEDIDAM; UMJ. *Recordings:* with Ornicar Big Band: Mais où est Donc Ornicar?, 1984; Le Retour d'Ornicar, 1986; Jazz Cartoon, 1989; L'Incroyable Huck, 1991; 3 recordings with Tuxedo Big Band: Rhythm is our business, 1994; Siesta at the Fiesta, 1996; For Ella and Chick, 1998; Beautiful Love, Philippe Laudet Quartet, 1996. *Honours:* Winner, Concours National de la Defense, Paris, with Ornicar Big Band, 1982; Prizes from Academy of Jazz and Hot Club of France, with Tuxedo Big Band, 1994; Hot Club de France, for Siesta at the Fiesta, 1996.

LAUK, Tiit; Estonian musician (piano, keyboards); b. 9 Jan. 1948, Tartu; m. Eleonora Lauk, 22 Aug. 1952, 1 s. *Education:* Estonian Academy of Music; Pianist, leader, teacher, Jazz Education at Bob Brookmeyer's. *Career:* Over 35 years as pianist and leader, 15 years, piano and jazz teacher; 3 years as Producer, Musical Programmes, Estonian TV; Director, Estonian Jazz Foundation 1991–; Debut, Gintarine Triuba Festival, Lithuania, 1968; Numerous festivals, solo concerts in former USSR, Europe; Tours with famous Estonian opera singers in Sweden, Finland; Projects with Finnish, Swedish, British, Russian musicians; Numerous recordings, Estonian Radio, Estonian TV, 1972–; mem, International Asscn of Schools of Jazz. *Compositions:* Over 300 instrumental and vocal arrangements for jazz orchestra/band. *Recordings:* Numerous recordings since 1970 for Estonian Radio, Estonian Television; MC KohtumispaiK Jazzkaar, 1995; Pendel, 1997. *Publications:* By The Path of Estonian Light Music, Lithuania, 1987; Jazz Improvisation: Practical Course For Piano (I Bril), translation into Estonian; Several reviews in several publications in Estonia, Finland, France, Lithuania. *Honours:* Order of Nicola Rolin (France); Jazzclub du Vallage (France); Jazzclub of Tartu (Estonia). *Address:* c/o Lend Music, Koomne 33, 10617 Tallin, Estonia. *E-mail:* info@lendmusic.ee.

LAUPER, Cynthia (Cyndi) Anne Stephanie; American singer and songwriter; b. (Cynthia Ann Stephanie Lauper), 22 June 1953, New York; d. of Fred Lauper and Catrine Dominique; m. David Thornton 1991; one s. *Education:* Richmond Hill High School, NY. *Career:* took up playing the guitar and writing lyrics aged 12; performed as vocalist with various cover bands in New York mid-1970s; toured with Doc West's disco band, Flyer 1974–77; founder mem., Blue Angel 1978–79; solo artist 1983–; worldwide tours, numerous TV appearances; composed score for musical show Kinky Boots 2012. *Films:* The Goonies 1985, Vibes 1988, Mother Goose Rock 'n' Rhyme (TV) 1990, Paradise Paved 1990, Off and Running (aka Moon Over Miami) 1991, Life with Mikey 1993, Mrs Parker and the Vicious Circle 1994, The Opportunists 1999, Here and There 2009. *Stage:* as performer: The Threepenny Opera 2006; as composer: Kinky Boots (New York's Outer Critics Circle Awards for Best Musical 2013, for Best Score 2013, Tony Awards for Best Musical 2013, for Best Original Score 2013) 2012. *Recordings include:* albums: with Blue Angel: Blue Angel 1980; solo: She's So Unusual 1983, True Colors 1986, A Night To Remember 1989, Music Speaks Louder Than Words 1990, Hat Full Of Stars 1993, Twelve Deadly Cyns… and Then Some 1994, Sisters Of Avalon 1996, Merry Christmas… Have A Nice Life 1998, At Last 2003, Shine 2004, The Body Acoustic 2006, Bring Ya to the Brink 2008, Memphis Blues 2010. *Publications:* Cyndi Lauper: A Memoir (with Jancee Dunn) 2012. *Honours:* MTV Video Music Award for Best Female Video Performer 1984, American Video Award for Best Female Performer 1984, American Music Award for Favorite Female Artist, for Favorite Female Video Artist 1985, Grammy Award for Best New Artist 1985. *Current Management:* Hard To Handle Management, 640 Lee Road, Suite 106, Wayne, PA 19087, USA. *Website:* www.cyndilauper.com.

LAURENT, Mark Clive; New Zealand singer, songwriter, musician (electric guitar, acoustic guitar, harmonica, Rowan lute, bass, ukulele, percussion), sound engineer and writer and poet; b. 15 March 1954, Auckland; s. of Lyall Morris Laurent and Janet Frances Rogan; m. 1st Adrienne Lovegrove 1977; one s.; m. 2nd Brenda Liddiard 1990; one d. *Education:* De La Salle Coll., Manurewa High School, Univ. of Auckland. *Career:* solo, duo and band performer throughout NZ, Australia, UK 1968–; studio producer 1985–; major tours/gigs supporting Larry Norman 1984, Barry Maguire 1987, Larbanois Carrero 1989, Tom Russell 1991, Adrian Plass 1993, Thom Bresh 1995, Wishbone Ash 2000; major festivals include Sweetwaters 1985, Mainstage 1987, Jackey's Marsh, Tasmania 1990, Shelterbelt 1993, Auckland Folk Festival 1993–2016, Parachute 1994, 1995, Tahora 1989–2015, Wellington Folk Festival 1999–2014, New Spirit 1997–2003, Greenbelt, UK 2000, Gravesend World Music Festival 2000; mem. Australasian Performing Rights Asscn. *Film music:* music for soundtracks of Allie Eagle & Me 2004, On the Shoulders of Giants 2015. *Recordings include:* albums: Mark Laurent 1982, Kindness In A Strong City 1986, Songs For Our Friends 1989, Trust 1992, Heart Attack 1996, Tahora 21 (collaboration) 1997, Millennium Hippies 1998, Trebox 2000, Stations Of The Cross 2001, The Light And The Shadowland 2001, Waiting For Donald 2001, Journeys (compilation) 2002, Husk (soundtrack) 2003, Background (compilation) 2003, Spiritual Graffiti 2005, Under-Growth 2010, The Net 2013, This Is Not All There Is 2014, Here We Are Again 2015; contribs to numerous other artists' albums as songwriter, producer, musician, sound engineer. *Publications:* Perhaps (poetry) 1995, Throw Away the Stones (poetry) 2004, Rufus and the Rain (illustrated children's story) 2008, Snapshot of a Soul in Transit (poetry) 2010; numerous articles and reviews for music, arts, environmental and spiritual magazines. *Address:* Metropolis, 2002/1 Courthouse Lane, Auckland 1010, New Zealand (home). *Telephone:* (9) 972-1205 (office); 27-7114446 (mobile) (office). *E-mail:* mark@marklaurent.co.nz (office); markandbrenda@kiwilink.co.nz (home). *Website:* www.marklaurent.co.nz.

LAURITSEN, Jørgen; Danish conductor, composer, arranger and musician; b. 9 Aug. 1966, Svendborg; m. Pia Boysen. *Education:* MA, Music Theory, Conducting, Royal Danish Academy of Music, 1990; MA, Piano, Composition, Rhythmic Music Conservatory, Copenhagen, 1992. *Career:* All major musicals in Denmark for the last 5 years; Chess in concert with Elaine Paige, Tommy Korberg, 1997; Solo with Harolyn Blackwell, 1997; Live Symphonic with Lisa Nilsson, 1988; mem, Danish Society of Jazz, Rock and Folk Composers; Danish Conductors Asscn. *Compositions:* Sarajevo Butterfly; Dance of the Clogs; Songs in the Wind; Mixed Love; Intonation For The Wizard, Danish Radio Concert Orchestra, 1998. *Recordings:* Mixed Love; Les Miserables. *Honours:* Danish Ministry of Culture, 1991; Denmark-America Foundation, 1992. *Address:* 10 Kirsten Piilsvej, 2920 Charlottenlund, Denmark. *E-mail:* j@lauritsen.org. *Website:* www.lauritsen.org.

LAVELLE, Caroline; British musician (cello), singer and songwriter. *Career:* leader, all-female trio Electra Strings; group toured with Nigel Kennedy; as session musician played with Massive Attack, Peter Gabriel, Ride, The Fall; played on albums by Siouxsie and the Banshees, Del Amitri, Pale Saints, Voice of the Beehive, Bluetones, Massive Attack, Peter Gabriel, The Waterboys, Radiohead, Nigel Kennedy, Loreena McKennitt, Muse. *Recordings:* albums: Spirit 1995, Brilliant Midnight 2001, Brilliant Midnight 2.0 2002, A Distant Bell 2004. *Address:* PO Box 20078, London, NW2 3FA, England (office). *E-mail:* caroline@carolinelavelle.com (office). *Website:* www.carolinelavelle.com.

LAVELLE, James; British producer and DJ; *Founder and Managing Director, Mo' Wax Records;* b. 22 Feb. 1974, Oxford, England. *Career:* worked at Honest Jon's Record Shop, Ladbroke Grove; set up Mo' Wax Records aged 18 1992, Man. Dir 1992–; founder and Man. Dir Surrender All and Mo' Wax Arts; co-founder That's How It Is club night (with Gilles Peterson) at London's Bar Rumba; formed UNKLE with Kudo (Majorforce) and Tim Goldsworthy (D.F.A.); Resident DJ at Fabric in London, fmr Resident DJ at Blue Note, The Fridge, Bar Rumba, Scala, Gardening Club (all London); collaborations with DJ Shadow, Richard Ashcroft, Thom Yorke, Ian Brown, Josh Homme, Brian Eno, Jarvis Cocker, Will Malone, 3D, Howie B., Mike D., Slam; remixed Massive Attack, Metallica, DJ Shadow, Blur, Queens of the Stone Age, Beck, The Verve, Radiohead, Breakbeat Era, Howie B; mem. MCPS. *Recordings:* albums: with UNKLE: Psyence Fiction (with DJ Shadow) 1998, Never Never Land (with Richard File) 2003, James Lavelle: Romania # 26 (compilation) 2004, War Stories 2007, End Titles… Stories for Film 2008, End Title… Redux 2008, Where did the Night Fall 2010; singles: The Time Has Come 1994, Berry Meditation 1996, Rock On 1997, Rabbit In Your Headlights 1998, Be There 1999, An Eye for an Eye 2003, Reign 2004. *Current Management:* c/o Randy Reed, Red Light Management, 320 East Main Street, Charlottesville, VA 22902, USA. *Telephone:* (414) 245-4915. *E-mail:* randy@redlightmanagement.com. *Website:* www.redlightmanagement.com. *E-mail:* info@unkle.com (office). *Website:* unkle.com.

LAVIGNE, Avril R.; Canadian singer, songwriter, musician (guitar) and actress; b. 27 Sept. 1984, Napanee, ON; m. Deryck Whibley 2006 (divorced 2010). *Career:* f. Avril Lavigne Foundation 2010. *Recordings include:* albums: Let Go 2002, Under My Skin (Juno Award for Pop Album of the Year 2005) 2004, The Best Damn Thing 2007, Goodbye Lullaby 2011, Avril Lavigne 2013. *Film appearances:* Fast Food Nation 2006, The Flock 2007. *Honours:* NRJ Music Award for Best Int. Female, France 2005, Juno Award for Best Artist 2005, MTV Europe Music Awards for Best Solo Artist and Best Song (for Girlfriend) 2007. *Address:* Nettwerk Management, 1650 West Second Avenue, Vancouver, BC V6J 4R3, Canada. *Telephone:* (604) 654-2929. *Fax:* (604) 654-1993. *Website:* www.nettwerk.com; www.avrillavigne.com.

LAVIS, Gilson; British musician (drums, percussion) and songwriter; b. 27 June 1951, Bedford; m. Nicola Mercedes Keller 1993; one s. *Career:* fmr drummer with, The Bo Weavils, Headline News, Springfield Revival, Chris Rea; mem., Squeeze 1975–91; pick up drummer for Chuck Berry, Jerry Lee Lewis; cabaret drummer for artists, including Tommy Cooper, Bob Monkhouse, Lulu, Freddie Starr, David Frost, Engelbert Humperdinck; mem., Jools Holland and The Rhythm and Blues Orchestra 1991–; numerous concerts and tours. *Television:* house band drummer on Don't Forget Your Toothbrush (Channel 4), The Happening (BSB/Sky), Later with Jools Holland (BBC 2), Name That Tune (Channel 5). *Recordings include:* albums: with Squeeze: Squeeze 1978, Cool For Cats 1979, Argy Bargy 1980, East Side Story 1981, Sweets From A Stranger 1982, Cosi Fan Tutti Frutti 1985, Babylon And On 1987, Frank 1989, A Round And A Bout 1990, Play 1991; with Jools Holland and The Rhythm and Blues Orchestra: A World Of His Own 1990, The Full Compliment 1991, The A To Z Of The Piano 1992, Live Performance 1994, Sex And Jazz And Rock And Roll 1996, Lift The Lid 1997, Jools Holland The Best Of 1998, Jools Holland's Swing Album 2001, Small World Big Band 2001; solo: Drumbaba 1998. *Address:* c/o The Misty Moon Gallery, Ladywell Tavern, 80 Ladywell Road, London, SE13 7HS, England. *E-mail:* gilsonlavis@gilsonlavis.co.uk. *Website:* www.gilsonlavis.me.uk.

LAVOINE, Marc; French singer and actor; b. 6 Aug. 1962, Longjumeau, Essonne; m.; three c. *Career:* active since 1983; joined various rock bands and theatre companies; gained nat. prominence with release of Pour Une Biguine Avec Toi; appeared in numerous films and TV productions. *Films include:* Frankestein 90 1984, L'Enfer 1994, Fiesta 1995, Les menteurs 1996, Cantique de la racaille 1998, Le double de ma moitié 1999, Déception 2001, My Wife Is an Actress 2001, The Good Thief 2002, Blanche 2002, Le coeur des hommes 2003, Deception 2003, Les clefs de bagnole 2003, Toute la beauté du monde 2006, Arthur and the Minimoys (French version, voice) 2006, Le cœur des hommes 2 2007, Si c'était lui… 2007, Celle que j'aime 2009, Korkoro 2009, Les meilleurs amis du monde 2010, Arthur 3: The War of the Two Worlds (voice) 2010, Les tribulations d'une caissière 2011, Mains armées 2012, Quelques secondes de liberté (short) 2012, My Mummy is in America and She Met Buffalo Bill (voice) 2013, Le cœur des hommes 3 2013, La liste de mes envies 2014, Sous les jupes des filles 2014, The Grad Job 2014, Papa Was Not a Rolling Stone 2014, Take Me to the Water (short, voice) 2014. *Television includes:* Pause-café (series) 1981, Vice vertu et vice versa (film) 1996, The Judge Is a Woman (series) 1998, Evamag (series) 1999, Dans la gueule du loup (film) 2001, Crossing Lines (series) 2013. *Recordings:* albums: Marc Lavoine 1985, Le Parking Des Anges 1985, Fabriqué 1987, A La Cigale 1987, Live (live album) 1988, Les Amours Du Dimanche 1989, Paris 1991, Faux Rêveur 1993, Lavoine Matic 1996, Septième Ciel 1999, Marc Lavoine 2001, Olympia Deuxmilletrois (live) 2003, L'Heure D'été 2005, Les Duos de Marc 2008, Volume 10 2009, Je descends du singe 2012; singles include: Pour Une Biguine Avec Toi 1984, Elle A Les Yeux Revolvers 1985, Qu'est-ce Que T'es Belle (with Catherine Ringer) 1987, Paris 1992, L'Amour De 30 Secondes 1992, C'est Ça La France 1996, Petit À Petit Feu 1996, Les Hommes Sont Des Femmes Comme les Autres (with Princess Erika) 1997, Les Embouteillages 1997, J'habite En Jalousie 1998, Les Tournesols 1999, Fais Semblant 1999, J'écris Des Chansons 2000, Adieu Camille (with Julie Depardieu) 2000, Le Pont Mirabeau 2001, J'ai Tout Oublié (with Cristina Marocco) 2001, J'aurais Voulu 2002, Je Ne Veux Qu'elle (with Claire Keim) 2002, Dis-moi Que l'amour (with Bambou) 2003, Je Me Sens Si Seul 2005, Toi, Mon Amour 2005, Tu M'as Renversé 2006, J'espère (with Quynh Anh) 2006, J'ai Confiance En Toi/Me

Fido Di Te (with Jovanotti) 2007, Un Ami (with Florent Pagny) 2007, La Semaine Prochaine 2009, Reviens Mon Amour 2009, Rue Des Acacias 2010, Demande Moi 2010, Chère Amie 2013. *Address:* c/o Universal Music France, 20 rue des Fosses Saint Jacques, 75005 Paris, France (office).

LAWLER, Fergal Patrick; Irish musician (drums, percussion); b. 4 March 1971, Limerick. *Career:* mem., The Cranberry Saw Us, renamed The Cranberries 1990–2003, 2009–; numerous headlining tours, festivals, radio and television appearances. *Recordings:* albums: Everybody Else Is Doing It, So Why Can't We? 1993, No Need To Argue 1994, To The Faithful Departed 1996, Bury The Hatchet 1999, Bury The Hatchet: The Complete Sessions 2000, Wake Up And Smell The Coffee 2001, Treasure Box 2002, Stars: The Best Of 1992–2002 2002, Roses 2012. *Current Management:* c/o Danny Goldberg, Gold Village Entertainment, 72 Madison Avenue, Eighth Floor, New York, NY 10016, USA. *Telephone:* (212) 741-2400. *Fax:* (212) 741-4871. *E-mail:* info@goldve.com. *Website:* www.goldve.com; www.cranberries.com.

LAWLESS, Hugh James (Jim); British musician (tuned percussion); b. 18 Feb. 1935, Woolwich, London; m. Carole Ann 1968; three d. *Education:* HNC in Electronics; private piano lessons. *Career:* mem., The Eric Delaney Band 1960; worked at Hammersmith Palais, Lyceum Empire, Leicester Square 1963–65; freelance session player, records, television, broadcasts, films 1965; played jazz, Hollywood Bowl; various tours, including with George Shearing, Charlie Watts; recorded with LSO, Royal Philharmonic, Ted Heath, Jack Parnell, Stéphane Grappelli, Bob Parnow, Joe Loss, BBC Big Band, George Shearing, Henry Mancini, Mel Tormé, Peggy Lee, Lena Horne, Nelson Riddle, Kiri Te Kanawa, Lulu, The Beatles, Tom Jones; mem. Musicians' Union, PRS.

LAWRENCE, Andrew (Andy); British musician (trumpet), composer and singer; b. 2 Nov. 1954, Swindon, Wiltshire; three d. *Education:* trumpet lessons, brass band training. *Career:* professional on soul music scene 1972–; touring mem., Roy Pellett Jazzband 1973–78; settled W Berlin, Germany 1976–; freelance studio work, arranger, club work, concert and TV appearances; moved to Stuttgart 1983; Lecturer and instructor, Baden-Würtenberg Youth Jazz Orchestra 1984; numerous concert tours with Peanuts Hucko, Ben Waters, George Kelly; leader, Joe Schwarz Orchestra for five years; leader of own large and small ensembles; over 120 original compositions, some recorded. *Recordings:* 15 albums as featured soloist, one as leader.

LAWRENCE, Denise; British jazz singer and bandleader; *Leader, The Denise Lawrence Band*; b. (Denise Beal), 15 Feb. 1956, Hayes, Middx, England; m. Tony Lawrence 1985; two step-d. *Career:* singer, bandleader, The Denise Lawrence Band (fmrly Denise Lawrence and Storeyville Tickle) 1982–; also Denise Lawrence and her Trio (with husband, Tony Lawrence as pianist and Musical Dir) and Encore (a duo); most major jazz clubs, festivals, cruise liners, UK, Europe; compère, co-organizer of residential jazz festivals, in various hotels and holiday locations; appears in cabaret and theatres; particular interests are gospel music, hymns, spirituals; regular appearances on TV and radio, including ITV and Songs of Praise (BBC); mem. The Famous Five (jazz band formed from five top UK bandleaders in 2003); currently performs and organizes at residential jazz holidays around UK. *Films include:* Cottage for Sale (award-winning video), 25th Anniversary Concert (DVD recorded and released by Mediterranean Int. Television) 2011. *Recordings include:* albums: Let it Shine (Der Jazzfreund Award for Best New Jazz Recording of the Year), Can't Help Lovin' These Men of Mine, Hangin' Around 1997, Ain't that Good News 1997, I Guess There's an End to Everything 2000, Music Maestro Please 2002, Setting the Standards 2003, Encore 2005, Black Coffee (with John Hallam) 2008, Ballads 'n' Blues (with husband Tony on piano) 2011. *Honours:* UK Jazz Travel Award for Best Vocalist 1994. *Address:* 189 Loddon Bridge Road, Woodley, Reading, Berks., RG5 4BP, England (home). *Telephone:* (118) 969-0625 (home). *E-mail:* tony@jazzbreaks.freeserve.co.uk (office). *Website:* www.jazzbreaks.com.

LAWRENCE, Guy William; British electronic musician, songwriter and record producer; b. 25 May 1991, Reigate, Surrey, England. *Career:* Founder-mem. (with brother Howard Lawrence) of electronic duo Disclosure 2010–; debut release 2010; numerous live appearances in UK, Europe, USA and Canada; numerous collaborations including Aluna George, Eliza Doolittle, London Grammar, Sinead Harnett, Sasha Keable, Sam Smith; remixer of other artists including Janet Jackson & Nelly, Artful Dodger, Q-Tip, Jessie Ware, Everything Everything, Ralphi Rosario. *Recordings:* album: with Disclosure: Settle 2013, Caracal 2015. *E-mail:* sam@methodmusic.co.uk. *Website:* www.methodmusic.co.uk; www.pmrrecords.com; disclosureofficial.com.

LAWRENCE, Howard John; British electronic musician, songwriter and record producer; b. 11 May 1994, Reigate, Surrey, England. *Career:* Founder-mem. (with brother Guy Lawrence) of electronic duo Disclosure 2010–; debut release 2010; numerous live appearances in UK, Europe, USA and Canada; numerous collaborations including Aluna George, Eliza Doolittle, London Grammar, Sinead Harnett, Sasha Keable, Sam Smith; remixer of other artists including Janet Jackson & Nelly, Artful Dodger, Q-Tip, Jessie Ware, Everything Everything, Ralphi Rosario. *Recordings:* album: with Disclosure: Settle 2013, Caracal 2015. *E-mail:* sam@methodmusic.co.uk. *Website:* www.methodmusic.co.uk; www.pmrrecords.com; disclosureofficial.com.

LAWRENCE, Jack; American musician (bass guitar); m. Jo McCaughey 2009. *Career:* mem., the Greenhornes 1996–; mem., The Raconteurs 2006–, The Dead Weather 2009–. *Recordings include:* album: with The Greenhornes:

Gun For You 1999, The Greenhornes 2001, Dual Mono 2002, Four Stars 2010; with The Raconteurs: Broken Boy Soldiers 2006, Consolers of the Lonely 2008; with The Dead Weather: Horehound 2009, Sea of Cowards 2010. *Current Management:* Monotone Management, 820 Seward Street, Hollywood, CA 90038, USA. *Telephone:* (323) 308-1818 (office). *Fax:* (323) 308-1819 (office). *Website:* www.greenhornes.com; www.theraconteurs.com; www.thedeadweather.com.

LAWRENCE, Peter Raymond; producer, publisher and DJ; b. 29 Oct. 1957, Leamington Spa, England; one s. one d. *Career:* Man., Our Price Records; Sales Man., Making Waves Distribution –1986; owner, Cooking Vinyl Records 1986–, Global Headz; founder, The Big Chill; Prod. for Michelle Shocked, Texas Campfire Tapes. *Address:* Cooking Vinyl, PO Box 1845, London, W3 0ZA, England. *E-mail:* info@cookingvinyl.com. *Website:* www.cookingvinyl.com.

LAWRENCE, Rohn; American jazz musician (guitar) and singer; b. New Haven, CT. *Career:* played in New Haven funk bands, Good News, The Lift; performed with Marion Meadows, George Duke, Dianne Reeves, Jonathan Butler, Alex Bugñon, Freddie Jackson, Najee. *Recordings include:* albums: solo: Hanging On A String 1993, See Ya Around 1998; with Pieces of a Dream: Pieces 1997; with Will Downing: Invitation Only 1997, Christmas, Love and You 2008; with Jay Rowe: Jay Walking 1997; with Bread and Butter: Adventures of Bread and Butter 1998; with Boney James: Body Language 1999. *E-mail:* info@jazzateria.com. *Website:* www.jazzateria.com.

LAWRENCE, Steven, HNC (Elec. Eng); British musician (bouzouki, cittern, mandola, dulcimer, percussion), producer and composer; b. 29 Sept. 1961, Glasgow, Scotland. *Education:* Hillhead High School, Stow Coll. *Career:* appeared at Celtic Connections Festival, Glasgow 1993, 1994; mem. Iron Horse 1992–95; appearances include: Poland, Eygpt; tours of the Netherlands, Germany, Brittany; appeared at major European festivals; nat. radio and TV appearances in Scotland, Poland, Egypt and Sweden; since leaving Iron Horse has recorded and performed with Tannas, Anna Murray, Ross Kennedy, Canterach, Donnie Munro, Pete Seeger, Shane McGowan, Lena Martell, Sydney Devine, Carol Kidd; producing and arranging for many artists within traditional music; composer, theme and incidental music for videos and exhbns; mem. Canterach 1997–2007; rejoined Iron Horse to record final album 2003; mem. Red Hot Chilli Pipers 2008–; mem. Raintown 2012–; also touring and recording as duo with fiddle player Fiona Cuthill, cellist Wendy Weatherby; currently performing with acoustic roots act Rallion, as duo with Fiona Cuthill; has performed on more than 150 commercial releases; composed incidental and theme music for numerous media projects; Artistic Dir, Mugdock Music Festival 2011–13; mem. Musicians' Union, Performing Right Soc., PPL. *Recordings:* Doll's House, with Marylyn Middleton Pollock 1992; with Iron Horse: Thro' Water Earth and Stone (Best Folk Album Award) 1993, Five Hands High 1994, Voice of the Land, soundtrack to BBC Documentary The Gamekeeper 1995, The Wind Shall Blow for Evermore 2004; Celtic Dawn, with Whirligig 1995, Summer in Skye, with Blair Douglas 1996, Into Indigo, with Anne Murray 1996, Border Ballads, various artists 1998, Fyre and Sworde 1998, On The West Side 1999, The White Swan 1999, Canterach Canterach 2000; also appears on Calluna, Calluna 2000, John Wright, A Few Short Lines 2000, On The West Side, Donnie Munro 2000, Whirligig, First Frost 2001, Bram Taylor, Fragile Peace 2001, Angels from the Ashes, Blair Douglas 2004, Red Hot Chilli Pipers 2005, Songs From A Woman's Heart, Lena Martell 2005, Stand By Me, Lena Martell 2006, The Rose, Lena Martell 2007, Don't Blow Away, Craig Jeffrey 2008, Blast, The Red Hot Chilli Pipers (Triple Platinum Award for sales in Scotland 2009, UK Silver Award for sales in UK) 2008, Rallion 2009, One for Sorrow, Rallion 2009, Sark O' Snaw, Mick West 2010, Music for the Kilted Generation (Red Hot Chilli Pipers) 2010, Hope in Troubled Times (Raintown) 2011, Breathe (Red Hot Chilli Pipers) 2013, Writing on the Wall (Raintown) 2015; solo albums: Standing Alone 2002, The Hidden Gem 2007, The Broons Family Album (Gold Award) 2010, A Celtic Tapestry 2011, A Cruel Kindness, Fiona Cuthill 2011, Wanted, Kyle Warren 2011. *Honours:* Music Retailers' Asscn Award with Iron Horse 1993, Triple Platinum Award for Blast with Red Hot Chilli Pipers 2010, Best Live Act with Red Hot Chilli Pipers, Scottish Trad Music Awards 2010, Gold Award for The Red Hot Chilli Pipers Debut CD 2012, Producer of the Year, Scottish New Music Awards 2012, Folk Recording of the Year with Raintown, Scottish New Music Awards 2012, Record of the Year with Raintown, Scottish New Music Awards 2012, Duo of the Year with Raintown, British Country Music Awards 2013, Best New Band with Raintown, Scottish Variety Awards 2014, Country Artist of the Year 2014 with Raintown, UKCountryMusic.com, Entertainer of the Year with Raintown, British Country Music Awards 2014, Band of the Year with Raintown, British Country Music Awards 2015. *Current Management:* c/o KRL, PO Box 5577, Newton Mearns, Glasgow, G77 9BH, Scotland. *Telephone:* (141) 616-0900. *E-mail:* krl@krl.co.uk. *Website:* www.krl.co.uk. *Telephone:* (141) 330-2790 (office). *E-mail:* steven.lawrence@glasgow.ac.uk (office). *Website:* www.reverbnation.com/stevielawrence.

LAWRENCE, Tracy Lee; American country singer, songwriter and musician (guitar); *CEO, T.L.E. Inc.*; b. 27 Jan. 1968, Atlanta, Tex.; m. Becca Lawrence; two d. *Career:* solo artist 1991–; CEO T.L.E. Inc. *Recordings include:* albums: Sticks and Stones 1991, Alibis 1993, I See It Now 1994, Time Marches On 1996, The Coast Is Clear 1997, Lessons Learned 2000, Tracy Lawrence 2001, Strong 2004, Then and Now 2005, For the Love 2007, All Wrapped Up In Christmas 2007. *Honours:* CMA Award for Musical Event of the Year (with Tim McGraw and Kenny Chesney) 2007. *Current Management:* c/o William Morris Agency, 1600 Division Street, Suite 300, Nashville, TN 37203, USA. *Telephone:* (615) 963-3000. *Fax:* (615) 963-3091. *Website:* www .wma.com; www.tracylawrence.com.

LAWS, Hubert; American flautist; b. 10 Nov. 1939, Houston, Tex.; s. of Hubert Laws Sr and Miola Luverta Donahue. *Education:* Juilliard School. *Career:* mem. Jazz Crusaders 1954–60; studied classical flute at Juilliard School with Julius Baker; performed with Mongo Santamaria 1963–67; bandleader 1964–; mem. New York Metropolitan Opera Orchestra and New York Philharmonic Orchestra 1969–72; mem. New York Jazz Quartet 1970s; Founder and Dir Hulaws Music and Golden Flute Music (publishing cos); numerous credits as a session player on albums for Herbie Hancock, Quincy Jones, Paul McCartney, Stevie Wonder, Jaco Pastorius, Gil Scott-Heron, Aretha Franklin, Ella Fitzgerald, McCoy Tyner, Carly Simon and Lena Horne. *Recordings:* albums: solo: The Laws of Jazz/Flute By-Laws 1964, Crying Song 1969, Afro-Classic 1970, The Rite of Spring 1971, Wild Flower 1972, Morning Star 1972, Carnegie Hall 1973, In the Beginning 1974, Chicago Theme 1975, Romeo and Juliet 1976, Say it With Silence 1978, Land of Passion 1978, Family 1980, Hubert Laws and Earl Klugh: How to Beat the High Cost of Living 1980, Make it Last 1983, My Time Will Come 1990, Storm Then the Calm 1994, Hubert Laws Remembers the Unforgettable Nat 'King' Cole 1998, Baila Cinderella 2002, Moondance 2004, Hubert Laws Plays Bach for Barone and Baker 2005, Flute Adaptations of Rachmaninov and Barber 2009; as sideman: with Gary McFarland: America The Beautiful: An Account of Its Disappearance 1968; with Walter Wanderley: When It Was Done 1968, Moondreams 1969; with Quincy Jones: Walking in Space 1969; with George Benson: Tell It Like It Is 1969, The Other Side of Abby Road 1969, White Rabbit 1972, Good King Bad 1975, Pacific Fire 1983; with Ron Carter: Uptown Conversation 1970, Blues Farm 1973, Spanish Blue 1975; with Chick Corea: The Complete 'Is' Sessions 1969, Tap Step 1980; with Freddie Hubbard: First Light 1971, Skydive 1972; with Chet Baker: She Was Good to Me 1972, Studio Trieste 1982; with Randy Weston: Blue Moses 1972; with Grant Green: The Main Attraction 1976; with McCoy Tyner: Together 1978, La Levenda de la Hora 1981; with Alphonse Mouzon: Morning Sun 1981; with Stanley Turrentine: If I Could 1993. *Honours:* Nat. Endowment of the Arts Jazz Masters Lifetime Achievement Award 2011. *E-mail:* hubertlaws@hubertlaws .com (office). *Website:* www.hubertlaws.com.

LAY; Chinese singer; b. (Zhang Yixing), 7 Oct. 1991, Changsha, Hunan. *Career:* fmr child star; trainee, SM Entertainment 2008–12; mem. K-pop boy band Exo 2012–; mem. sub-group Exo-M 2012–; debut single 2012; numerous TV and live appearances. *Television:* Star Academy (participant) 2005, Yue Ce Yue Kai Xin 2005, Na Ke Bu Yi 2005, EXO's Showtime 2013–. *Recordings:* albums: Mama 2012, XOXO (Mnet Asian Music Award for Album of the Year 2013) 2013. *Honours:* numerous awards including: for Exo: Mnet Asian Music Award for Best New Asian Artist/Group 2012, MTV Europe Music Award for Best Japan/Korea Act 2013, MelOn Music Award for Song of the Year (for Growl) 2013; for Exo-M: Top Chinese Music Award for Most Popular Group 2013. *Address:* c/o SM Entertainment, 521 Apgujeong 2-dong, Gangnam-gu, Seoul, South Korea (office). *Telephone:* (2) 6240-9800 (office). *Website:* www .smtown.com (office); exo.smtown.com (home).

LAY, Edward; British musician (drums); b. 1982, Ipswich. *Education:* Staffordshire Univ. *Career:* Founder mem., Snowfield 2003, renamed Editors 2004–. *Recordings include:* albums: The Back Room 2005, An End Has a Start 2007, In This Light And On This Evening 2009. *Website:* www.editorsofficial .com.

LAYTON, Paul Martin; British entertainer and musician (bass guitar); b. 4 Aug. 1947, Beaconsfield, Buckinghamshire, England; m. Patricia Peters, 14 June 1981, 1 s., 1 d. *Education:* Hendon Music College. *Career:* Actor, films include: I Could Go On Singing, with Judy Garland; Television includes: Dixon of Dock Green; Emergency Ward 10, 1965–70; Vocalist, bass guitarist, The New Seekers, 1970–; Major world concert tours and television include: The White House for Nixon; Royal Command; Ed Sullivan; mem, Equity; Musicians' Union. *Compositions include:* Ride A Horse; Sweet Louise. *Recordings:* I'd Like To Teach The World To Sing; Never Ending Song of Love; Circles; You Won't Find Another Fool Like Me; I Get A Little Sentimental Over You; Look What They've Done To My Song Ma; Beg, Steal or Borrow (Eurovision 1972). *Honours:* Sun Award, Best Vocal Group.

LAZAREVITCH, Serge; French jazz musician (guitar) and educator; b. 18 Nov. 1957, St Germain En Laye. *Education:* Jazz diploma, Berklee College of Music, Boston, USA. *Career:* Concerts throughout Europe with various jazz bands; Member, Orchestre National de Jazz, 1989–91; Tours, Europe, Asia; Head of Jazz Department, Perpignan Conservatory; Clinics, France, Switzerland; Belgium; Germany; Italy; mem, UMJ (Union des Musiciens de Jazz). *Recordings:* CDs: (as leader) Cats Are Welcome, 1987; London Baby, 1989; Walk With A Lion, 1993; Many recordings as sideman. *Honours:* Choc of The Month, Record of the Year, in Jazz Man, for Walk With A Lion. *E-mail:* slazarev@free.fr.

LAZY HARRY, BA; Australian singer and songwriter; b. (Mark Stephens), 15 June 1947; m. Wendy; one s. one d. *Education:* Melbourne University. *Career:* fmr teacher; wrote and sang Proud to be Australian for Bicentenary 1988; tours of USA 1990–94, Germany 1995, Australia 1998; mem, Australian Performing Rights Assn. *Compositions:* Proud to be Australian, Edward Kelly, Riverboats Song, Weary Dunlop, Visiting Australia. *Recordings:* Big

Aussie Album, Lazy Harry Vol. II, My Country, Ned Kelly Story, Riverboats of Australia, Bound for Botany Bay, Bring Him Home, The Dog on the Tuckerbox, Spirit of Our Country, Australian Federation, Gold and Eureka, Best Aussie Camp Fire Songs,. *Publications:* Lazy Harry Song Book 1988. *Address:* PO Box 233, Beechworth, Vic. 3747, Australia (office). *Telephone:* (3) 5728-2817 (office). *Fax:* (3) 5728-2737 (office). *Website:* www .lazyharryaustralia.com.au.

LCD SOUNDSYSTEM (see Murphy, James)

LÊ, Nguyên, BPhil; French musician (guitar, bass), synthesizer programmer, composer and arranger; b. 14 Jan. 1959, Paris. *Career:* co-creator of multi-ethnic band, Ultramarine 1983–91; mem., Orchestre National de Jazz 1987; frequent guest soloist, WDR Big Band from 1993; concerts and tours throughout Europe, Martinique, Ile de la Réunion, Madagascar, Côte d'Ivoire, USA, Canada and North Africa; mem. numerous trios. *Recordings include:* albums: with Ultramarine: Programme Jungle 1985, Dé (Best World Music Album) 1989, Esimala 1991; with Orchestre National de Jazz: 88/89 1987, African Dream 1989; solo: Miracles 1989, Zanzibar 1992, Init 1993, Million Waves 1995, Tales From Viêt-Nam 1996, 3 Trios 1997, Maghreb & Friends 1998, Bakida 2000, Purple 2002, Walking On The Tiger's Tail 2005, Homescape 2006, Duos 2006. *Current Management:* Siegfried Loch, ACT Publishing, Postfach 14 03 99, 80453 Munich, Germany. *Telephone:* (89) 7294920. *Fax:* (89) 72949211. *E-mail:* info@actmusic.com. *Website:* www.act -music.com; www.nguyen-le.com.

LE BON, Simon; British singer and lyricist; b. 27 Oct. 1958, Bushey, Hertfordshire, England; m. Yasmin Parveneh 1985; three d. *Education:* Univ. of Birmingham. *Career:* singer, Dog Days; mem. and lead singer, Duran Duran 1979–, Arcadia 1985–86; numerous concerts and tours world-wide. *Recordings include:* albums: with Duran Duran: Duran Duran 1981, Rio 1982, Seven And The Ragged Tiger 1983, Arena 1984, Notorious 1986, Big Thing 1988, Liberty 1990, Duran Duran (The Wedding Album) 1993, Thank You 1995, Medazzaland 1997, Pop Trash 2000, online-only releases of Duran Duran recordings of live shows in Japan 2003, Astronaut 2004, Red Carpet Massacre 2007, All You Need is Now 2010, Paper Gods 2015; with Arcadia: So Red The Rose 1985. *Honours:* MTV Video Music Lifetime Achievement Award 2003, Q Magazine Lifetime Achievement Award 2003, BRIT Outstanding Contribution to Music Award 2004, Q Icon Award 2015, MTV Europe Music Video Visionary Award 2015. *Current Management:* c/o Ms Wendy Laister, Magus Entertainment Inc., 33 Greene Street, #3W, New York, NY 10013, USA. *Telephone:* (212) 343-1577. *Fax:* (212) 925-4007. *E-mail:* info@ magusentertainment.com. *Website:* www.magusentertainment.com; www .duranduran.com.

LE GENDRE, Dominique; musician (guitar) and composer; b. Trinidad. *Education:* Conservatoire Municipal de Paris XVII with Ramon de Herrera, Sorbonne Univ., Paris, Conservatoire Regional d'Orsay, Municipal de Paris VI. *Career:* various television, radio broadcasts, film appearances; mem. PRS, Musicians' Union. *Compositions:* music for television: The Healer, BBC1; B. D. Women (Channel 4); Synchro, ITV; Ragga Gyuls D'Bout, Carlton/Arts Council; Booker Prize '93, BBC2; Disabled Lives, BBC2; Kaiso For July (Channel 4); Films: Aliki Ou La Bague Engloutie; La Petite Valse; I Is A Long Memoried Woman; Theatre music includes: Measure For Measure, London Bubble Theatre; Orinoco, National Theatre Studio; Trapped In Time, Avon Touring Theatre Company; Love At A Loss, Wild Iris Theatre; When The Bough Breaks, Theatre Centre; BBC Radio includes: A Midsummer Night Dream; The Wizard of Oz; Edward II; Dance music for: The Burial of Miss Lady, Irie! Dance Company. *Recordings:* Romeo and Juliet, King John, Twelfth Night, All's Well That Ends Well, The Merchant of Venice, A Midsummer Night's Dream, The Taming of the Shrew. *Honours:* Best Performance Art Video (I Is A Long Memoried Woman), New York 1991. *Address:* 22 Ives Street, Chelsea, London, SW3 2ND, England.

LE MESSURIER, James; British musician (percussion), arranger and bandleader; b. 20 July 1958, Guernsey, Channel Islands; m. Flavia Chévez De La Cruz, 23 April 1994. *Education:* Bachelor of Music, Major in Professional Music, Berklee College of Music, Boston, USA. *Career:* Leader, percussionist, arranger, London-based Salsa group La Clave, 1986–; Numerous appearances clubs, festivals: UK; Eire; France; Italy; Holland; Germany; Switzerland; Featured on BBC Radio One, Andy Kershaw Show, 1994; Freelance percussionist, El Sonido de Londres, Alfredo Rodriguez, Orlando Watussi, Adalberto Santiago; mem, PRS; Musicians' Union.

LEA, Jimmy; British musician (bass, piano, violin), songwriter and record producer; b. 14 June 1952, Wolverhampton, England. *Career:* mem. rock group, Slade (formerly N'Betweens, Ambrose Slade) 1966–91; numerous concerts, tours and festival appearances; film appearance: Flame 1974; record prod. for rock group, Chrome Molly. *Compositions:* co-writer, all Slade's Top 20 singles, with Noddy Holder. *Recordings:* albums: Beginnings (as Ambrose Slade) 1969, Play It Loud 1970, Slade Alive 1972, Slayed 1973, Sladest 1973, Old New Borrowed Blue 1974, Slade In Flame (soundtrack) 1974, Nobody's Fool 1976, Slade Alive Vol. 2 1978, Return To Base 1979, Slade Smashes 1980, Till Deaf Do Us Part 1981, We'll Bring The House Down 1981, Slade On Stage 1982, The Amazing Kamikaze Syndrome 1983, Slade's Greats 1984, Rogue's Gallery 1985, Crackers 1985, You Boyz Make Big Noize 1987, Wall of Hits 1991; solo: Therapy 2007. *Honours:* Hon. Fellow, University of Wolverhampton 2002. *Website:* www.jimleamusic.com.

LEACH, Alan; British musician (drums); b. 1970, England. *Career:* mem., Shed Seven 1996–2003; numerous live dates, tours and television appearances; studio owner and drum teacher 2004–. *Recordings include:* albums: Change Giver 1996, A Maximum High 1996, Let It Ride 1998, Truth Be Told 2001.

LEBEUGLE, Patricia; French jazz musician (bass); b. 19 May 1963, Le Mans. *Career:* played with Walter Bishop, Bob Mover, Bobby Porcelli, Peter Ecklund, Mark Murphy, Ted Brown; European tours with many French and American musicians 1985–; jazz festivals throughout Europe with Philippe Duchemin Trio 1990–; tour, South Africa, with pianist Jack Van Poll; mem. Dany Doriz band; tours and CD with Scott Hamilton; CD with Christian Morin; concerts with Dany Doriz and Manu Di Bango. *Recordings include:* with Philippe Duchemin Trio: Alizés 1990, Live! 1992, Three Pieces 1994, Philippe Duchemin Trio with Dominique Vernhes 1995, Three Colors, with Philippe Duchemin 1998; with Marcel Azzola and Dany Doriz: Jazzola 1999; Philippe Duchemin with Magali Leon, Magali chante Ella 1999; with Dany Doriz Trio: On the New Jersey Road 2007; with Dany Doriz big band 2008. *Address:* Le Boulay, 72440 St Mars de Locquenay, France (home). *Telephone:* (2) 43-35-94-43 (office). *E-mail:* patlebeugle@orange.fr (home).

LECKIE, John William; British producer and recording engineer; *Owner, John Leckie Productions Limited;* b. 23 Oct. 1949, London, England; m. Christina Leckie; one d. *Education:* Quintin School, Ravensbourne Coll. of Art, Rajneesh Neo-Sannyas Commune. *Career:* tape operator and balance engineer, Abbey Road Studios 1970; session work includes George Harrison, John Lennon, Pink Floyd, Wings, Mott The Hoople, Roy Harper, various classical artists; freelance producer 1978–; has produced over 100 albums by various recording artists across different genres and has recorded in numerous countries world-wide; mem. Music Producers' Guild UK. *Recordings as producer and engineer:* albums: Sunburst Finish, Be-Bop Deluxe 1976, Modern Music, Be-Bop Deluxe, White Music, XTC 1978, Real Life, Magazine 1978, Life in a Day, Simple Minds 1979, Real To Real Cacophony, Simple Minds 1979, Go2, XTC 1979, Sound on Sound, Red Noise 1979, Empires and Dance, Simple Minds 1980, This Nation's Saving Grace, The Fall 1986, The Stone Roses, The Stone Roses 1989, Carnival Of Light, Ride 1994, The Bends, Radiohead 1995, K, Kula Shaker 1996, All Change, Cast 1997, Miles From Home, Cowboy Junkies 1997, Showbiz, Muse 1999, Anutha Zone, Dr John 2000, Origin of Symmetry, Muse 2001, Missing You (Mi Yeewnii), Baaba Maal 2001, Good Morning Aztlan, Los Lobos 2002, Longwave 2003, No CV, My Computer 2005, Waiting For Siren's Call, New Order 2006, Z, My Morning Jacket 2006, Kingdom of Rust, Doves 2007, 11:11, Rodrgio y Gabriela 2009, Butterfly House, The Coral 2010, Hedonism, Bellowhead 2010, Troubled Times, Cast 2011, Broadside, Bellowhead 2012, Inside Outside, Novastar 2014, Danger In The Club, Palma Violets 2015. *Honours:* Music Week Award for Best Producer 1996, Q Magazine Award for Best Producer 1996, BRIT Award for Best Producer 1997, Music Managers' Forum Award for Best Producer 2001, BASCA Gold Badge Award 2011, MPG Award for Best Album 2012. *Current Management:* c/o Safta Jaffery, SJP, 301 Fir Tree Road, Epsom, Surrey, KT17 3LF, England. *Telephone:* (20) 8780-3311. *Fax:* (20) 8785-9892. *E-mail:* safta@tastemusic.com. *Website:* www.sjpdodgy.co.uk.

LECOMPT, John; American musician (guitar). *Career:* mem. several bands including Mindrage, Kill System, Soul Embraced; mem. Evanescence 2002–07; founder mem. Mourningside; mem. We Are the Fallen 2009–. *Recordings include:* albums: with Mindrage: Sown in Weakness, Raised in Power 1998; with Evanescence: Origin 2002, Fallen 2003, Anywhere But Home (live) 2004, The Open Door 2006; with We Are the Fallen: Tear the World Down 2010. *Honours:* Grammy Award for Best New Artist 2003, Grammy Award for Best Hard Rock Performance (for Bring Me To Life) 2003. *Website:* www.wearethefallen.com.

LEDIN, Tomas Jonas Folke; Swedish artist, songwriter and producer; b. 25 Feb. 1952, Östersund; m. Marie Anderson 1982; two s. *Education:* Swedish Gymnasium, Uppsala University. *Career:* solo artist 1972–; tours of Sweden and Scandinavia 1980–, USA, with ABBA, Canada, Europe 1979, Japan 1980; initiated Rocktrain tour 1991; toured with the Rocktrain 1992–93; mem. SKAP (Swedish Composers' Society). *Recordings:* albums: Restless Mind 1972, Hjärtats Rytm 1973, Knivhuggarrock 1974, Nattan är Ung 1976, Tomas Ledin 1977, Fasten Seatbelts 1978, Tagen på bar gärning 1978, Ut på stan 1979, Looking for a Good Time 1980, Gränsiös 1982, The Human Touch 1982, Captured 1983, En Galen Kväll 1985, Down on Pleasure Avenue 1988, Ett Samlingsalbum 1990, Tillfalligheternas Spel 1990, Du Kan Lite På Mig 1993, T 1996, En hel del Ledin 1997, Sänger att älska till 1997, Djävulen & Ängeln 2000. *Honours:* two Grammy Awards 1991, Rockbjörn Award 1991, 1992, Mozart prize 1991, World Music Award 1992, represented Sweden, Eurovision Song Contest 1980, Platinum and Gold discs. *E-mail:* robbeuving@planet.nl (office). *Website:* www.tomasledin.net.

LEE, Albert; musician (guitar); b. 21 Dec. 1943, Leominster, Hertfordshire, England. *Career:* Guitarist, Chris Farlowe and The Thunderbirds, 1960s; In-demand session musician; Also member of Country Fever; Member, Poet and The One Man Band (with Chas Hodges of Chas 'n' Dave); Group became Heads Hands and Feet; Member, the Crickets; Emmylou Harris' Hot Band; Touring bands of Eric Clapton; Jackson Browne; Jerry Lee Lewis; Dave Edmunds; Concerts include: Everly Brothers Reunion, Royal Albert Hall, 1983. *Recordings:* Solo albums: Hiding, 1979; Albert Lee, 1983; Speechless, 1986; Gagged But Not Bound, 1987; Black Claw and Country Fever, 1991; In Full Flight, 1994; Country Legend, 1998; Con Sabor Latino, 2000; Other recordings: Albums with Eric Clapton: Just One Night, 1980; Another Ticket, 1981; Money and Cigarettes, 1983; with Joe Cocker: With A Little Help From My Friends, 1969; Stingray, 1976; with The Crickets: Bubblegum, Pop, Ballads and Boogie, 1973; Remnants, 1973; with Dave Edmunds: Repeat When Necessary, 1979; DE7, 1982; with Chris Farlowe: Chris Farlowe and The Thunderbirds, 1966; Stormy Monday, 1966; Out of The Blue, 1985; with Emmylou Harris: Luxury Liner, 1977; Quarter Moon In A Ten Cent Town, 1978; Blue Kentucky Girl, 1979; Christmas Album, 1979; Roses In The Snow, 1980; Evangeline, 1981; Cimarron, 1981; Ballad of Sally Rose, 1985; with Head Hands and Feet: Head Hands and Feet, 1971; Tracks, 1972; Old Soldiers Never Die, 1973; with Jimmy Page and John Paul Jones: No Introduction Necessary, 1984; Also recorded on albums with: Chas and Dave; Bobby Bare; Gary Brooker; Teresa Brewer; Guy Clark; Rodney Crowell; Bo Diddley; Lonnie Donegan; Don Everly; Everly Brothers; Nancy Griffith; Jerry Lee Lewis; Jon Lord; Steve Morse; Juice Newton; Dolly Parton; Ricky Skaggs; Shakin' Stevens. *E-mail:* info.hogansheroes@virgin.net. *Website:* www.albertlee.co.uk; www.albertleeandhogansheroes.com.

LEE, Alex; British musician (keyboards, guitar); b. 16 March 1970. *Career:* Mem., Strangelove; Joined Suede, 2001. *Recordings:* Album: A New Morning, 2002. Singles: Positivity, 2002; Obsessions, 2002. *Website:* uk.sonymusic.co.uk/suede

LEE, Amy Lynn; American singer and musician (piano); b. 13 Dec. 1981, Riverside, CA. *Education:* Pulaski Acad. *Career:* founder mem. rock band, Evanescence 1999–. *Recordings include:* albums: with Evanescence: Origin 2002, Fallen 2003, Anywhere But Home (live) 2004, The Open Door 2006, Evanescence 2011. *Honours:* Grammy Award for Best New Artist 2003, Grammy Award for Best Hard Rock Performance (for Bring Me To Life) 2003. *Address:* c/o Wind-up Records, 72 Madison Avenue, New York, NY 10016, USA. *E-mail:* evanescence@winduprecords.com. *Website:* www.evanescence.com.

LEE, Brenda, (Brenda Lee Tarpley); singer; b. 11 Dec. 1944, Lithonia, Georgia, USA. *Career:* solo artist 1950s–60s; actress, film The Two Little Bears. *Recordings:* Hit singles include: Sweet Nothin's, 1960; I'm Sorry (No. 1, USA), 1960; I Want To Be Wanted (No. 1, USA), 1960; Let's Jump The Broomstick, 1961; Speak To Me Pretty, 1962; One Step At A Time; Rockin' Around The Christmas Tree, 1962; Losing You, 1963; I Wonder, 1963; As Usual, 1963; Nobody Wins; Thanks A Lot, 1965; Too Many Rivers, 1965; Albums include: Grandma, What Great Songs You Sang, 1959; Brenda Lee, 1960; This Is Brenda, 1960; Emotions, 1961; All The Way, 1961; Sincerely, 1962; Brenda, That's All, 1962; The Show For Christmas Seals, 1962; All Alone Am I, 1963; Let Me Sing, 1963; By Request, 1964; Merry Christmas From Brenda Lee, 1964; Top Teen Hits, 1965; The Versatile Brenda Lee, 1965; Too Many Rivers, 1965; Bye Bye Blues, 1966; Coming On Strong, 1966; For The First Time (with Pete Fountain), 1968; Johnny One Time, 1969; The Brenda Lee Story, 1974; LA Sessions, 1977; Even Better, 1980; Little Miss Dynamite, 1980; 25th Anniversary, 1984; The Golden Decade, 1985; The Best of Brenda Lee, 1986; Love Songs, 1986; Brenda Lee, 1991; Rockin' Around, 1995; Jingle Bell Rock, 1995; Live Dynamite, 1997; Wiedersehn Ist Wunderschon, 1997; In the Mood for Love, 1998; Miss Dynamite Live, 2000; Guest singer, Shadowland, k d lang, 1988. *Current Management:* Brenda Lee Management, 2174 Carson Street, Nashville, TN 37211, USA.

LEE, Christopher James; British musician (trumpet, steel pan); b. 24 June 1961, Cheltenham, Gloucester; m. Lucy, 1 s., 1 d. *Career:* Founder Member, Pigbag, 1979; Toured Europe, America and Japan, 1980–83; Appeared on Top of the Pops, 1982–83; Radio sessions, John Peel, Kid Jensen, 1983–; Involved in Jazz and improvised musics, 1997–; mem, PRS; Musicians' Union; PAMRA. *Compositions:* The Shell Suite; The Arrow of Time; The Magician of Riga; On The Swing of a Prayer; Jakes Dance. *Recordings:* Papa's Got A Brand New Pigbag; Pigbag; The Shell Temple At Margate. *Honours:* Lottery award money to make recording with Sweet Thunder.

LEE, CoCo; American/Chinese (Hong Kong) singer; b. (Ferren Lee), 17 Jan. 1976, Hong Kong. *Education:* Univ. of Calif. at Irvine, USA. *Career:* moved to San Francisco, USA 1986; runner-up New Talent Singing Contest, Hong Kong, resulting in her first recording contract 1993; records and performs in Mandarin, Cantonese and English. *Stage appearance:* performed in The Phantom of the Opera (musical), China. *Films include:* Master of Everything 2004, voiced title role in Mandarin-language version of Disney's Mulan. *Recordings include:* albums: Love From Now On 1994, Promise Me 1994, Brave Enough To Love 1995, Woman In Love 1995, CoCo (Past Love) 1996, CoCo's Party 1996, Every Time I Think of You 1997, CoCo 1997, DiDaDi 1998, Sunny Day 1998, Just No Other Way 1999, True Lover, You and Me 2000, Promise 2001, D.IS.CoCo 2002, Just Want You 2006, East To West 2009, Illuminate 2013. *Honours:* Singapore Radio Music Award for Best New Artist and Best Love Song of the Year 2000, Yale Univ. Asian-American of 2000, Harvard Univ. Best Performer 2000, Best Mandarin Female Artist, Hong Kong 2001, MTV Chinese Award for Most Outstanding Female Artist of Asia 2001. *Website:* www.cocolee.net.

LEE, Crissy; musician (drums, percussion) and music teacher; b. 17 June 1943, Colchester, Essex, England. *Career:* mem., Ivy Benson Dance Band aged 17, tours worldwide; appeared with artists, including Dinah Washington, Frank Sinatra, Fats Domino, Caterina Valente, Tom Jones, Al Jarreau, Faith Brown, Marion Montgomery, Madeleine Bell; formed Crissy Lee Band;

Musical Dir for guests, including Roy Castle, Ken Dodd, Bob Monkhouse; launched and managed Koffee and Kreme duo; other musical projects include Beauty and the Beat (backing band for acts including The Supremes, Johnny Bristol, Sam Dees); formed Crissy Lee and her All-Female Orchestra (17-piece band); numerous television appearances; mem. Equity, Musicians' Union, Assen of British Jazz Musicians. *Recordings include:* The Beat Chics (EP), The Beat Chics: Skinny Mini/Now I Know. *Website:* www.crissylee.co.uk.

LEE, Dave, (Joey Negro, Raven Maize, Doug Willis, Z Factor, Sessomato, Akabu, Jakatta); British producer, remixer and DJ; b. 18 June 1964, Colchester, Essex. *Career:* Founder, Republic Records (one of the first UK house labels), Z Records; first British artist to record for New York label Nu-Groove; remixed: Sister Sledge, Lisa Stansfield, Pet Shop Boys, Diana Ross, M People; mem.: Sunburst Band, Hed Boys; collaborations with Mark Ryder, Taka Boom, Blaze. *Recordings include:* albums: Universe of Love (as Joey Negro) 1993, Get Down Tonight 1997, Here Come the Sunburst Band 2000, Can't Get High Without You (compilation) 2000, Visions 2002, Until the End of Time (as The Sunburst Band) 2004, Moving with the Shakers (as The Sunburst Band) 2008; singles: Get Acidic (with M-D-EMM) 1988, Forever Together (as Raven Maize) 1989, Do It Believe It (as Joey Negro) 1991, Do What You Feel (as Joey Negro) 1991, One Kiss (with Pacha) 1991, Enter Your Fantasy EP (as Joey Negro) 1992, Girls and Boys (with Hed Boys) 1994, Gotta Keep Pushin' (as Z Factor) 1998, Must Be the Music (with Taka Boom) 1999, Moody (as Sessomato) 2000, American Dream (as Jakatta) 2001, The Real Life (as Raven Maize) 2001, Visions (as Jakatta) 2002, Until the End of Time (as The Sunburst Band) 2004, Moving with the Shakers (as The Sunburst Band) 2008, The Phuture Ain't What It Used To Be (as Akabu) 2010, The Secret Life of Us (as The Sunburst Band) 2012. *Current Management:* Z Records, The Factory, 1 Coleridge Lane, London, N8 8EA, England. *Telephone:* (20) 8342-8948. *Fax:* (20) 8347-5930. *E-mail:* gordon@zrecords.ltd .uk; info@zrecords.ltd.uk. *Website:* www.zrecords.ltd.uk.

LEE, Geddy (Gary); Canadian musician (bass) and singer; b. 29 July 1953, Willowdale. *Career:* mem. of rock group, Rush 1969–; tours and live appearances. *Recordings include:* albums: Rush 1974, Fly By Night 1975, Caress of Steel 1975, 2112 1976, All the World's a Stage 1976, A Farewell to Kings 1977, Archives 1978, Hemispheres 1978, Permanent Waves 1980, Moving Pictures 1981, Exit... Stage Left 1981, Signals 1982, Grace Under Pressure 1984, Power Windows 1985, Hold Your Fire 1987, A Show of Hands 1988, Presto 1989, Chronicles 1990, Roll the Bones 1991, Counterparts 1993, Test for Echo 1996, Retrospective I 1997, Retrospective II 1997, Different Stages 1998, Vapor Trails 2002, The Spirit of Radio 2003, Rush in Rio 2003, Feedback 2004, R30 2005, Replay 2006, Snakes & Arrows 2007, Clockwork Angels 2012. *Honours:* Juno Awards for Most Promising Group 1975, Best Group 1978, 1979;Official Ambassadors of Music, Canadian Govt 1979. *E-mail:* info@rush.net. *Website:* www.rush.com.

LEE, Haeri; South Korean singer. *Career:* mem. K-pop duo Davichi 2008–. *Recordings include:* albums: with Davichi: Amaranth 2008, Davichi in Wonderland (Golden Disk Bonsang Award 2009) 2009, Innocence 2010, Love Delight 2011. *Honours:* with Davichi: Mnet Asian Music Awards for Best New Female Group 2008, for Best Group Vocal Performance (for Will Think of You) 2012, Golden Disk Award for Best Newcomer Artist 2008, Seoul Music Awards for Best New Artist 2009, for Bonsang (for 8282) 2010, Cyworld Digital Music Bonsang Award 2010, Gaon Chart K-Pop Bonsang Award 2012. *Website:* ccment.com; davichi.ccment.com.

LEE, Jack, BMus, BA; American conductor, voice coach, musician (piano) and music director; *Professor, Tisch School of the Arts;* b. 30 July 1929, Lakewood, OH; m. (divorced). *Education:* Baldwin-Wallace Coll. Conservatory of Music. *Career:* participated in the Mabel Mercer Music Foundation Noel Coward Evening, Carnegie Hall, Mabel Mercer Music Foundation Regina and Carmen Jones Revival; faculty mem., NY Univ. Teaching School; Prof. Tisch School of the Arts, New York 2004–; mem. The Players' Club, Tony Nominating Cttee. *Films:* Postcards from the Edge, Sweet Charity. *Theatre:* off-Broadway shows: Valmouth, Souvenir, York Theatre 2004–05; Broadway shows: Sweet Charity, Funny Girl, George M, Applause, No Strings, Billy, Peter Pan, Irene, My One and Only, Grand Hotel, My Fair Lady. *Recordings:* My One and Only, Grand Hotel, Sweet Charity, Irene. *Address:* 37 West 72nd Street, Apt 10 D, New York, NY 10023 (home); Tisch School of the Arts, 721 Broadway, New York, NY 10003, USA (office). *Telephone:* (212) 877-2308 (home). *Fax:* (212) 811-3453 (home). *E-mail:* masterjacklee@gmail.com (home).

LEE, Philip Robert; British musician (guitar); b. 8 April 1943, London; m. Doris Anna Zingerli 1964. *Career:* first bands John Williams Big Bands, Graham Collier Septet 1960s; Henry Lowther, Tony Coe 1970s; musician with singers Annie Ross, Marian Montgomery, Sylvia Sims, Norma Winstone; mem. fusion band, Gilgamesh; played for artists, including Benny Goodman 1980s; mem., Dardanelle 1990s; worked with Jessye Norman in London and Greece 1999; appeared in film, Eyes Wide Shut 1999; tour dates in London and Dublin with Rosemary Clooney and Michael Feinstein 2001; seasons with Michael Feinstein, Haymarket Theatre, London 2004, Shaw Theatre 2008, London Palladium 2009; concerts with London Jazz Orchestra 2009; annual tour dates with Jimmy Smith; mem. PRS, Musicians' Union. *Recordings:* Gilgamesh, with Gilgamesh; Another Fine Tune You've Got Me Into, with Gilgamesh; Twice Upon A Time, with Phil Lee and Jeff Clyne; Swingin' In London, with Dardanelle; Meteors Close At Hand, with Michael Garrick; Unity, with John Horler and Phil Lee; Multicolored Blue with The Strayhorn

Project 2004, Strayhorn collaboration with Ken Peplowski 2007, The Upper Manhattan Medical Group, remembering Billy Strayhorn. *Address:* 7C Thurlow Road, London, NW3 5PJ, England (office). *Telephone:* (20) 7794-2687 (office). *Fax:* (20) 7435-7816 (office).

LEE, Robert E.; British singer and musician (drums, guitar, bass, keyboards); b. (Robert Greehy), 30 May 1956, Leeds. *Education:* Roundhay Grammar School, Leeds. *Career:* session musician 1975–79; member, London Cowboys 1980–85; tours to Europe, Japan, USA, Scandinavia, UK, including two support tours with Johnny Thunders 1981, 1982; two support tours with Hanoi Rocks 1982, 1983; producer, session musician 1986–; world-wide television and radio appearances; full-time member of The Infidels; mem, PRC, PRS, MU, MCPS. *Compositions:* Long Time Lonely 1986; co-wrote Faithless and Blue. *Recordings:* albums: Animal Pleasure, Tall In The Saddle, Long Time Coming; Dead Or Alive; singles: Centrefold, Hook, Line and Sinker, Dance Crazy, Let's Get Crazy, Street Full of Soul, Faithless and Blue 1998, Infidels 2000. *Honours:* Best New British Band, Country Music International, Alternative Rock/Country Crossover.

LEE, Sara; British musician (bass guitar); b. 18 Aug. 1955, Hereford, England. *Career:* mem. League of Gentlemen 1980, Gang of Four; moved to New York 1984; toured With Thompson Twins, B 52's, Joan Osborne 1987–99. *Recordings include:* League of Gentlemen, Robyn Hitchcock: Gang of Four, Cosmic Thing, Good Stuff, Living In Clip, Little Plastic Castle, solo album: Make It Beautiful 2000.

LEE, Tommy; American musician (drums); b. (Thomas Lee Bass), 3 Oct. 1962, Athens, Greece; m. 1st Heather Locklear 1986 (divorced); m. 2nd Pamela Anderson 1995 (divorced); two s. *Career:* mem. groups, Suite 19, Christmas; founder mem. heavy rock group, Mötley Crüe 1981–99, reformed 2005–; worldwide concerts, tours and festivals; formed group, Methods of Mayhem 1999; solo artist 2002–. *Television:* Tommy Lee Goes to College (documentary series, NBC) 2005. *Recordings include:* albums: with Mötley Crüe: Too Fast For Love 1981, Shout At The Devil 1983, Theatre Of Pain 1985, Girls, Girls, Girls 1987, Dr Feelgood 1989, Decade of Decadence (American Music Award for Favorite Heavy Metal Album) 1991, Mötley Crüe 1994, Generation Swine 1997, Live: Entertainment Or Death 1999, Red, White & Crüe 2005, Saints of Los Angeles 2008; with Methods of Mayhem: Methods of Mayhem 1999, A Public Disservice Annoucement 2010; solo: Never A Dull Moment 2002, Tommyland: The Ride 2005. *Publications:* The Dirt: Confessions of the World's Most Notorious Rock Band (with Mötley Crüe) 2001, Tommyland (autobiog., with Anthony Bozza) 2004. *Honours:* Rolling Stone Best Heavy Metal Band 1991. *Website:* www.tommylee.tv; www.motley.com.

LEES, John; British singer and musician (guitar); b. 13 Jan. 1947, Oldham, Lancs. *Career:* mem. Barclay James Harvest (originally the Blues Keepers) 1967–; int. tours and concert appearances. *Recordings include:* albums: Barclay James Harvest 1970, Barclay James Harvest Live 1974, Time Honoured Ghosts 1975, Gone To Earth 1977, Harvest XII 1978, Eyes of The Universe 1980, Turn of The Tide 1981, Concert For The People 1981, Ring of Changes 1981, Face To Face 1987, Glasnost 1988, Welcome To The Show 1990, Alone We Fly 1990, The Harvest Years 1991, The Best of Barclay James Harvest 1992; solo: A Major Fancy 1977, Barclay James Harvest Through The Eyes of John Lees 1999. *E-mail:* jlwwbjh@aol.com. *Website:* www .barclayjamesharvest.com.

LEES, Simon (Buggy); British musician (guitar, drums), singer, songwriter and entertainer; b. 16 May 1970, Wolverhampton. *Education:* Wulfrun College. *Career:* formed Osprey 1986, Nitebreed 1990 (support band for The Mock Turtles); mem. Borderline 1990, The Red House Snakes 1990; formed Plain Jain 1993; mem. Tantrum 1994; solo artist 1995–; formed The Simon Lees Band 2000, Lost Souls 2000; mem. Ozzmosis 2000, Budgie 2003; radio appearances: The Reaper Rock Show, Freedom FM, Chester; Jenny Wilkes Show, BBC Radio WM 1999; mem, Musicians' Union. *Recordings:* Playing Truant, recorded live at London Music Show, Wembley Conference Centre 1994, My World 1998. *Publications:* contrib. to Guitarist magazine. *Honours:* Guitarist of the Year 1998. *E-mail:* simon@simonlees.co.uk (office). *Website:* www.simonlees.co.uk.

LEETCH, Russell; British musician (bass guitar); b. 1982, Solihull. *Education:* Staffordshire Univ. *Career:* Founder mem., Snowfield 2003, renamed Editors 2004–. *Recordings include:* albums: The Back Room 2005, An End Has a Start 2007, In This Light And On This Evening 2009. *Website:* www .editorsofficial.com.

LEFTWICH, Bradley Rush, BA, MA; American musician (traditional fiddle, banjo) and singer; b. 30 June 1953, Stillwater, OK; m. Linda Higginbotham 1982, one s. *Education:* Oberlin College, University of Chicago. *Career:* founder mem., Plank Road, 1975–77; toured with Linda Higginbotham as Leftwich and Higginbotham, 1981–, with the Humdingers, 1990s, and with Tom Sauber and Alice Gerrard as Tom, Brad and Alice, 1997–; stage appearances include: The White House, Philadelphia and Winnipeg folk festivals, Piccolo Spoleto, Charleston, Bele Chere, Asheville; radio broadcasts on Wheeling Jamboree, Renfro Valley Barn Dance, The Flea Market, Our Front Porch and on Danish national TV and radio; mem. of advisory bd Old-Time Herald magazine; mem. North American Folk Alliance. *Recordings include:* solo: Say Old Man 2000, Humdingers 2007, Been There Still, Carrying On The Tradition; Learn to Play Old-Time Fiddle, vols 1 and 2; Rounder Fiddle; A Moment in Time; No One To Bring Home Tonight; Banging and Sawing; Buffalo Gal; Southern Clawhammer Banjo; Vocal and Instrumental Blend; Plank Road Stringband. *Publications:* Bowing Workshop, series of columns in Old-Time Herald magazine; Reflections on Southern Appalachian Fiddling, article, 1995; Clawhammer Banjo, Round Peak Style, 1999. *Honours:* first place for fiddle, first place for band, Appalachian String Band Music Festival 1990. *E-mail:* brad@bradleftwich.net. *Website:* www .bradleftwich.net.

LEGEND, John, BA; American singer and musician (keyboards); b. (John Stephens), 28 Dec. 1978, Springfield, Ohio; m. Chrissy Teigen 2013. *Education:* Univ. of Pennsylvania. *Career:* fmr musical and choral dir, Bethal AME Church, Scranton, Pa; fmr man. consultant; collaborations with numerous artists, including Kanye West, Dilated Peoples, Alicia Keys, Janet Jackson, Talib Kweli, Jay-Z, Britney Spears, Eve, Common, Black Eyed Peas, Estelle; f. own record label, HomeSchool Records 2006–. *Recordings include:* albums: John Stephens 2000, Live at Jimmy's Uptown 2001, Live at S.O.B.'s 2003, Volume 1: Live at the Knitting Factory 2003, Solo Sessions 2004, Get Lifted (Grammy Award for Best R&B Album 2006) 2004, Once Again 2006, Evolver 2008, Wake Up! (with The Roots) (Grammy Award for Best R&B Album 2011) 2010, Love in the Future 2013. *Honours:* MOBO Award for Best R&B Act 2005, Grammy Awards for Best New Artist, for Best Male R&B Vocal Performance (for Ordinary People) 2006, Grammy Awards for Best Male R&B Vocal Performance (for Heaven) 2007, for Best R&B Song (for Shine) 2011, for Best Song Written for Visual Media (for Glory, with John Legend) 2016, Soul Train Award for Best Single by a Male (for Save Room) 2007, American Music Award for Favorite Soul/R&B Male Artist 2014, Golden Globe for Best Original Song – Motion Picture (with Common for Glory) 2015, Billboard Music Awards for Top Radio Song 2015, for Top Streaming Song (Audio) 2015. *Current Management:* c/o David Sonenberg, DAS Communications Ltd, 83 Riverside Drive, New York, NY 10024, USA. *E-mail:* DAS@johnlegend.com. *E-mail:* hollaatewe@gmail.com (office). *Website:* www.johnlegend.com.

LEGGETT, Andy, BA; British musician (saxophone, clarinet, guitar), songwriter and arranger; b. 31 March 1942, Much Wenlock, England; m. Teri Penfold 1975; two s. one d. *Education:* school orchestra, Univ. of Hull. *Career:* mem. of Alligator Jug Thumpers 1968, Pigsty Hill Light Orchestra 1970; duo with Pete Finch 1973; Avon Touring Theatre 1974; formed Sweet Substitute 1975, later became Musical Dir, writer and arranger for them; toured with Midnite Follies Orchestra, Pasadena Roof Orchestra, Syd Lawrence, Bob Kerr's Whoopee Band, Temperance Seven; playing clarinet and saxophone, Rod Mason's Hot Five 1996–; mem. PRS (assoc.), MCPS. *Compositions:* for Sweet Substitute: Tiger Blues, Dear Mr Berkeley, Sleepy Suzie, A Musical Christmas Card; for Henry's Bootblacks: Everyone's Got Horns, New Orleans Feels Like Home, Sugar Makes Your Teeth Fall Out; co-wrote songs for the play The Godmother, directed by Mel Smith; Music for film, Betjeman Revisited 1995. *Recording:* album: Shades of Bechet 2002, Shades of Bechet II 2005. *Address:* An der Blankstrasse 28, 41352 Korschenbroich, Germany (office). *Telephone:* (2161) 4022280 (office). *Fax:* (2161) 4022281 (office). *E-mail:* info@andyleggett.com (office). *Website:* www .andyleggett.com.

LEGRAND, Benjamin; French singer and musician (piano, drums); b. 16 Oct. 1962, Paris; one d. *Education:* studied piano, drums and singing in Paris. *Career:* numerous television broadcasts, live appearances, including Olympia Hall and Bobino Music Hall, Paris, tours to Japan, Tunisia, Belgium, Switzerland; concerts in Korea; EuroDisney concerts, Cannes Jazz Festival, Calvi Jazz Festival, Corsica; radio broadcasts; mem. SPEDIDAM, SACEM, ADAMI. *Recordings:* album with Michel Legrand Big Band, Chansons de Paris (album of French songs), record of jazz trio, participating in album of French songs with Michel Legrand and Natacha Atlas, album with Baden Powell and Phillipe Baden Powell. *Publications:* Letemps Qui Passe (poems), La Pensée Universalle. *Current Management:* Xavier Garnault, Arms Production, 7 rue de Surene, 75008 Paris, France. *Telephone:* 1-53-43-88-08. *Fax:* 1-40-07-02-21. *Address:* 14 Villa Molitor, 75016 Paris, France (home).

LEGRAND, Michel; French composer, musician (piano), conductor, singer and arranger; b. 24 Feb. 1932, Paris; m. Isabelle 1994, two s. two d. *Education:* Paris Conservatoire. *Career:* conducted, appeared with Pittsburgh Symphony Orchestra, the National Symphony Orchestra, Minnesota Orchestra, Buffalo Philharmonic, Symphony Orchestras of Vancouver, Montréal, Atlanta, Denver, New Orleans; collaborated with Maurice Chevalier, Miles Davis, Kiri Te Kanawa, Johnny Mathis, Neil Diamond, Sarah Vaughan, Stan Getz, Aretha Franklin, Jack Jones, James Galway, Ray Charles, Lena Horne, Barbra Streisand and numerous others; films: (with Miles Davis) Dingo, 1990; directed Cinq Jours En Juin 1989, Masque de Lune 1991; theatre productions, television appearances and film scores including Prêt-à-Porter 1994; mem. Songwriters' Guild, Dramatists' Guild, NARAS, Academy of Motion Arts and Sciences. *Compositions include:* Images, I Was Born In Love With You, I Will Wait For You, Love Makes The Changes, Noelle's Theme, On My Way To You, One At A Time, Once Upon A Summertime, Little Boy Lost, The Summer Knows, Summer Me, Winter Me, Watch What Happens, The Way He Makes Me Feel, What Are You Doing The Rest of Your Life?, The Windmills of Your Mind, You Must Believe In Spring; scored films include: The Thomas Crown Affair 1968, The Happy Ending 1969, Summer of '42 1971, Yentl 1982, Never Say Never Again 1983, Ready To Wear 1994, Madelaine 1997. *Recordings include:* Erik Satie By Michel Legrand, Four Piano Blues, Michel Plays Legrand, Paris Jazz Piano 2001. *Publication:* Michel Legrand Song Book. *Honours:* five Grammy Awards 1972–75, three Academy Awards (for Thomas

Crown Affair, Summer of '42, Yentl), Australian Film Institute Award (for Dingo) 1991. *E-mail:* grabow@grabow.biz. *Website:* www.grabow.biz.

LEHRER, Thomas (Tom) Andrew, BA, MA; American musician (piano), singer, songwriter, satirist and mathematician; b. 9 April 1928, New York. *Education:* Harvard Univ. *Career:* singer and satirical songwriter 1943–; part-time teacher of mathematics, Harvard Univ. 1947–51; theoretical physicist, Baird-Atomic Inc, Cambridge, Mass 1953–54; performer 1953–55, 1957–60, 1965–67; served in US Army 1955–57; Lecturer, Business Administration, Harvard Business School 1961, Education, Harvard Univ. 1963–66, Psychology, Wellesley Coll. 1966, Political Science, MIT 1962–71, Univ. of California at Santa Cruz 1972–2008; wrote for US edition of TV series That Was The Week That Was 1964–65; signed to Reprise Records 1965; wrote for TV series The Electric Company 1972; revue, Tomfoolery, based on his songs, adapted by Robin Ray and Cameron Mackintosh 1980; An Evening Wasted With Tom Lehrer (BBC Radio 2) 1998. *Recordings:* Songs By Tom Lehrer 1953, More Of Tom Lehrer 1959, An Evening Wasted With Tom Lehrer 1959, Tom Lehrer Revisited 1960, That Was The Year That Was 1965, Songs By Tom Lehrer (re-recording of first album) 1966, The Remains of Tom Lehrer 2000, The Tom Lehrer Collection 2010. *Publications:* Tom Lehrer Song Book 1954, Tom Lehrer's Second Song Book 1968, Too Many Songs by Tom Lehrer 1981; contrib. to Annals of Mathematical Statistics, Journal of Societies of Industrial and Applied Maths. *Address:* 11 Sparks Street, Cambridge, MA 02138, USA (home).

LEICK, Vagn, PhD; Danish composer and musician (piano); b. 13 April 1939, Lydersholm. *Education:* pvt. study in jazz improvisation and composition. *Career:* TV and radio appearances in Denmark, USA, France; mem. Danske Jazz, Beat og Folkemusik Autorer, Dansk Musiker Forbund. *Recordings:* Thing 1972, Twilight 1984, Jazz Digit 1996, Songscapes 1999, Third Encounter 2010. *Current Management:* c/o Orbit Productions, Borgergade 30, 5.-2 Copenhagen K, Denmark. *Website:* www.orbits.dk. *E-mail:* vagn@leick.dk (office).

LEIGH, Joy; American singer (country, southern gospel); b. 23 April 1964, Montgomery, West Virginia, USA; Divorced. *Education:* Associate degree, Nursing, West Virginia Institute of Technology. *Career:* performed on stage, Grand Ole Opry, Don Reed Talent Competition; showcase artiste, King Eagle Awards Show, Nashville, Tennessee; headlined Fayette County, West Virginia, Fair, 1994, 1995; performed at Boone County, West Virginia, Fair, 1994, 1995; Summerville, West Virginia's Suumerfest, 1994; Rotary Club of Montgomery, West Virginia, 1994, 1995; mem, Gospel Music Asscn, Nashville, Tennessee. *Recordings:* What's In It For Me?; Walk Away. *Honours:* Montgomery Rotary Festival Award; United Community Services Entertainment Award. *Current Management:* Claudia Johnson, Johnson and Johnson Music Group, PO Box 182 Cannelton, WV 25036, USA. *Address:* Joy Leigh Enterprises, PO Box 182, Cannelton, WV 25036, USA.

LEINER, Boris; Croatian musician (drums, percussion) and singer; b. 28 Jan. 1957, Cakovec; m. (divorced); one d. *Education:* Art Academy, Zagreb, Art University, Utrecht, The Netherlands. *Career:* drummer and singer of rock band, Azra 1977–87, Vjestice 1987–, Naturalna Mistika reggae band 1983–; mem. of Berlin Band, Love-Sister-Hope 1980–92; numerous tours and live appearances; mem. HGU (Croatian Musicians' Union), HZSU (Croatian Union of Independent Artists). *Recordings include:* Azra-Azra; Suncana Strana Ulice Azra; Ravno Do Dna-Azra Djevojke U Ljetnim Haljinama Volim, Vjestice; Kradljivci Srca Vjestice, Totalno Drukciji Od Drugih. *Honours:* three Porin Awards (with Cro Music) 1996, Kradljivci Srca Award for Best Album, Status Award for Best Drummer 1996. *Address:* Duzice 23, 1000 Zagreb, Croatia. *E-mail:* boris@borisleiner.com. *Website:* www.borisleiner.com.

LEITNER, George; Austrian artist manager and agent; b. 24 Nov. 1959, Vienna; m. Dr Brigitte Leitner-Friedrich 1991. *Education:* college in South Africa, university in Vienna. *Career:* founded Number One Music (with Andreas Eggar) 1977; founded George Leitner Productions 1980, representing artists, including James Brown, Kool and the Gang, Jimmy Cliff, Blood Sweat and Tears, VSOP, The Commodores, George Clinton. *Honours:* Mag, Rer Soc Ök. *Address:* GLP Artists Marketing, Hütteldorfstr 259, 1140 Vienna, Austria (office). *Telephone:* (1) 914-86-15 (office). *Fax:* (1) 911-16-61 (office). *E-mail:* gleitner@glp.at (office). *Website:* www.glp.at (office).

LEJEUNE, Philippe; French musician (piano); b. 6 Feb. 1954, Eu; m. Irene 1986. *Education:* Rouen and Reims Conservatoires. *Career:* appearances include Detroit Jazz Festival, Festival Radio France, Festival de Jazz de Montauban, Nuits Piano Jazz Lutetia, Paris, Cincinnati Queen City Blues Festival, Monterey Blues Festival, Caveau de la Huchette, Paris, MusicVillage, Brussels; mem. Asscn Jazz Vivant, Soc. des auteurs, compositeurs et éditeurs de musique (SACEM), SPEDIDAM, ADAMI. *Recordings:* albums: Piano Duet With Memphis Slim 1980, Live At Blue Moon 1990, Chicago Non Stop 1993, 100% Blues and Boogie Woogie 1996, Piano Groove 1999, Blues Inspiration 2003, Solo Piano 2005, Night Mist Blues 2008, Groovin' Blues 2012. *Current Management:* c/o Association Jazz Vivant, BP 82065, 31018 Toulouse, Cedex 2, France. *Telephone:* 6-89-34-03-46 (mobile). *E-mail:* philip .lejeune@yahoo.fr (office). *Website:* www.philippelejeune.com.

LEKMAN, Jens Martin; Swedish singer and songwriter; b. 6 Feb. 1981, Gothenburg. *Recordings include:* albums: When I Said I Wanted to Be Your Dog 2004, Night Falls Over Kortedala 2007; other recordings: Four Songs By Arthur Russell, Rocky Dennis' Farewell Song to the Blind Girl 2003, If You

Ever Need A Stranger (To Sing At Your Wedding) 2004, I Don't Know If She's Worth 900 Kronor 2004, A Sweet Summer's Night on Hammer Hill 2006, An Argument With Myself (EP) 2011. *Address:* c/o Secretly Canadian, 1499 West Second Street, Bloomington, IN 47403, USA. *E-mail:* Ben@Secretlycanadian .com. *Website:* www.jenslekman.com.

LEMA, Ray(mond); Democratic Republic of the Congo/French composer, arranger, producer, musician (guitar, piano) and singer; b. 30 March 1946. *Education:* Mikondo Seminary, Kinshasa, Collège Albert, Univ. of Lovanium, Kinshasa. *Career:* mem., Gérard Kazembe Orchestra mid-1960s; Musical Dir, Baby National 1968–69; mem., The Yes Boys 1970–72; Musical Dir, Zaire Nat. Ballet 1974–76, Ya Tupas 1977; worked for Rockefeller Foundation, USA 1979–81; moved to France 1981; f. Carma (Central Africa Rock Machine) 1982, Bwana Zoulou Gang 1988, African Jazz Trio 2006; collaborations with Stewart Copeland, Manu Dibango, We Were; toured as piano soloist 2003–, as African Jazz Trio 2006, Saka Saka Orchestra 2010–; also jazz concerts with Orquestra Sinfônica de São Paulo 2011– and Jazz Quintet 2013–. *Film soundtrack:* Black Mic Mac 1986. *Recordings include:* albums: Koteja 1980, Kinshasa–Washington DC–Paris 1983, Médecine (with Martin Meissonier) 1985, Nanga deef 1989, Gaia 1991, Euro African Suite (with Joachim Kühn) 1992, Tout Partout 1994, Green Light 1996, Bulgarian Voices (with Kirim Stefanov) 1997, Stoptime 1997, The Dream Of The Gazelle 1998, Safi (with Tyour Gnaoua) 2000, Mizila 2004, Paradox 2007, Ray Lema and Orquestra Sinfônica de São Paulo (DVD) 2011, Ray Lema Quintet V.S.N.P (Very Special New Production) 2013. *Honours:* Maracas d'Or 1978, Django d'Or 2003. *Address:* One Drop, 25 rue Trousseau, 75011 Paris, France. *Telephone:* 1-48-06-72-05. *E-mail:* one .drop@free.fr (office); raylema@raylema.com (office); raylema@free.fr (home). *Website:* www.raylema.com; www.ebl-laborie.com (office).

LEMAR; British singer; b. (Lemare Obika), 4 April 1978, Tottenham, London, England; pnr Charmaine Powell; one d. *Career:* solo artist 2001–; finalist, Fame Acad. TV competition (BBC 1) 2002–03; performed at Prince's Trust Urban Music Festival. *Film appearance:* De-Lovely 2004. *Recordings include:* albums: Dedicated 2003, Time To Grow (MOBO Award for Best Album 2005) 2004, The Truth About Love 2006, The Reason 2008. *Honours:* BRIT Award for Best British Urban Act 2004, Capital Award, MOBO Award for Best UK Act 2005, BRIT Award for Best British Urban Act 2006, MOBO Award for Best UK Male 2006. *Address:* c/o Sony BMG UK Ltd, 10 Great Marlborough Street, London, W1F 7LP, England (office). *Website:* www.lemar-online.com.

LEME, Ronaldo, (Dinho Leme); Brazilian musician (drums); b. 22 July 1949, Campo Grande. *Career:* joined psychedelic rock band Os Mutantes 1968, alongside artists like Caetano Veloso and Gilberto Gil the band played an important role in the Tropicalia movt, combining ideas from rock music and avant garde art with Brazilian musical styles, as well as experimenting with electronic instruments and modern production techniques; left band 1973; joined a re-formed Os Mutantes for several concerts including Barbican Centre, London and shows in New York, Los Angeles (with the Flaming Lips), San Francisco, Seattle, Denver, Chicago and Miami 2006; collaborated with British DJ JD Twitch for Trocabrahma project 2007. *Recordings:* Os Mutantes 1968, Mutantes 1969, A Divina Comédia ou Ando Meio Desligado 1970, Jardim Elétrico 1971, Mutantes e Seus Cometas no País do Baurets 1972, Tudo Foi Feito Pelo Sol 1974, Tecnicolor (recorded 1970) 2000, Mutantes Ao Vivo: Barbican Theatre, Londres 2006, Haih or Amortecedor 2009. *Current Management:* Malab, rua Cristina, 1213, Santo Antônio, 30330-130, Belo Horizonte, MG, Brazil. *E-mail:* malab@malab.com.br. *Website:* www.malab .com.br; www.osmutantes.com.br (office).

LEMPER, Ute; German singer, dancer and actress; b. 4 July 1963, Münster; pnr Todd Turkisher; three s. one d. *Education:* Dance Acad., Cologne, Max Reinhardt Seminary for Dramatic Art, Austria. *Career:* leading role in Viennese production of Cats 1983; appeared in Peter Pan, Berlin, Cabaret, Düsseldorf and Paris (recipient of Molière Award 1987), Chicago (Laurence Olivier Award) 1997–99 and in London and New York, Life's a Swindle tour 1999, Punishing Kiss tour 2000, The Last Tango in Berlin tour 2009; Die sieben Todsünden (Weill) at Covent Garden Festival, London 2000; collaborations with Michael Nyman, Paulo Coelho. *Recordings include:* Life is a Cabaret 1987, Ute Lemper Sings Kurt Weill 1988, (Vol. 2) 1993, The Threepenny Opera 1988, Mahagonny Songspiel 1989, Crimes of the Heart 1989, The Seven Deadly Sins 1990, Songbook (with Michael Nyman) 1992, Illusions 1992, Espace Indécent 1993, Portrait of Ute Lemper 1995, City of Strangers 1995, Berlin Cabaret Songs 1996, Nuits Étranges 1997, All that Jazz/The Best of Ute Lemper 1998, Punishing Kiss 2000, But One Day 2002, Blood and Feathers 2006, Between Yesterday and Tomorrow 2008, Paris Days/Berlin Nights (with Vogler String Quartet) 2012, Ute Lemper Sings Weill, Vol.2 2013, Punishing Kiss 2013, Forever: The Love Poems of Pablo Neruda 2013. *Television appearances include:* L'Affaire Dreyfus (Arte), Tales from the Crypt (HBO), Illusions (Granada) and The Look of Love (Gillian Lynne). *Film appearances include:* L'Autrichienne 1989, Moscou Parade 1992, Coupable d'Innocence 1993, Prêt à Porter 1995, Bogus 1996, Combat de Fauves, A River Made to Drown In, Appetite 1997. *Honours:* French Culture Prize 1993. *Current Management:* Dispeker Artists, 59 East 54th Street, Suite 81, New York, NY 10022, USA. *Telephone:* (212) 421-7678. *E-mail:* emmy@ dispeker.com. *Website:* www.utelemper.com.

LENA; German singer and songwriter; b. (Lena Meyer-Landrut), 23 May 1991, Hannover. *Education:* IGS Roderbruch Hannover School. *Career:* winner of TV talent show Unser Star für Oslo 2010; represented Germany

in Eurovision Song Contest 2010, 2011; first German tour 2011. *Recordings:* albums: My Cassette Player 2010, Good News 2011. *Honours:* Eurovision Song Contest Winner 2010, Goldene Henne Honor Amb. of Charm Award 2010, 1LIVE Krone Awards for Best Artist and Best Single 2010, Goldene Kamera Best Music Nat. Award 2011, ECHO Awards for Best Nat. Newcomer and Best Female Nat. Artist 2011, Comet Best Female Artist Award 2011, MTV Europe Music Awards for Best German Act and Best European Act 2011. *Current Management:* c/o Brainpool Management, Schanzenstrasse 22, 51063 Cologne, Germany. *Telephone:* (22) 16509-0. *Fax:* (22) 16509-3005. *E-mail:* musikmanagement@brainpool.de; info@brainpool.de. *Website:* www.brainpool .de; www.lena-meyer-landrut.com.

LENDING, Kenn; Danish musician (guitar), composer, songwriter and singer; b. 8 Feb. 1955, Copenhagen; m. Sanne Blomberg Lending. *Career:* mem. Himmelexpressen 1972–79, Survivors 1976–78, Blues Nite 1977–79; formed duo with American blues pianist and singer, Champion Jack Dupree 1979–92; formed Kenn Lending Blues Band 1980–, used as backing band by Jan Harrington, Lillian Boutté, Rose Hudson, Aron Burton, Louisiana Red, Champion Jack Dupree, Memphis Slim, Mickey Baker, Luther Allison, Bobby Rush; mem. Danish Musicians' Union, DJBFA, KODA. *Recordings include:* with Kenn Lending Blues Band: Live! 1981, I'm Coming Home 1983, Blues For People 1985, Steamin' Hot 1988, Diggin' The Blues 1990, Heartache Motel 1993, Game of Life 1995, Live at Skagen (with Lillian Boutté) 1999, Psychedelic Mind 2001, Still Payin' Dues 2005, Flying High 2011; with Champion Jack Dupree: An Evening With Champion Jack Dupree 1981, Still Fighting The Blues 1981, I Had That Dream 1982, Blues Is Freedom To All 1987, Back Home In New Orleans 1990, Forever and Ever 1991, One Last Time 1992, After All 1994; with Gospel United: Live Gospel United 1994, People Get Ready 1995; other: The Band, High on the Hog 1996, Portrait of Champion Jack Dupree 2000, Lending & LaCroix, Down Home Blues 2000; solo: The Acoustic Kenn Lending, Low Down Dog 2008. *Film:* Konge Kabale. *Honours:* Danish Blues Musician of the Year 1995, Copenhagen Blues Festival Jubilee Prize 2005. *Address:* Kenn Lending, Tørninglundvej 5, 6500 Vojens, Denmark (office). *Telephone:* 22-30-90-90 (home). *E-mail:* kenn .lending@gmail.com (home). *Website:* www.lending.dk.

LENDORPH, Jorn; Danish singer, songwriter and producer; b. 14 June 1966, Copenhagen. *Education:* Sct Annae Music College, Copenhagen's Boys' Choir. *Career:* played in Danish TV serial, Everyone Loves Debbie, composed background music and sung title song 1987; leading role in film An Abyss of Freedom, wrote one song which was released as single 1989; composed music for various short films and songs for own album; has sung in various TV shows, live concerts and on TV commercials; background singer, various releases including Sound of Seduction and Shirley, Sanne Graulund; currently songwriting in partnership with Elton Theander as Jor-El; mem, Danish Artists' Union. *Recordings:* album: Loosen Up 1996; title song to Danish version of Disney's Beauty and the Beast 1991; produced soundtrack for Danish film The Eighteenth 1997; produced Sanne Graulund's debut album, Better Get Some Dreams 1998.

LENGSTRAND, Gert O.; Swedish songwriter and publisher; b. 30 May 1942, Gothenburg; m. Jeanette 1987; one s. four d. *Career:* singer, pop group The Streaplers 1957–68; songwriter, record producer 1969–. *Compositions:* Hasta La Vista, Silvia 1974, Eloise, Arvingarna 1993. *Recordings:* Diggity Doggerty 1963, Rockin' Robin 1965, Mule Skinner Blues 1964. *Honours:* Ampex Golden Reel Award, Eloise, 1993.

LENGWINAT, Katrin; German musicologist; b. 10 Dec. 1960, Berlin; m. Eduardo Briceño, 16 April 1994, 1 s. *Education:* Bachelor degree; Dr phil, Musicology, Polish and German universities; Studied piano, guitar and folkharp. *Career:* Musicologist, Academy of Fine Arts, Berlin; Musicologist, Foundation of Ethnomusicology and Folklore, Caracas, Venezuela; Leader for Musicology, Free University of Berlin and Central University of Venezuela; Researcher of folk and popular music in Germany, Venezuela and Peru; mem, International Council for Traditional Music (ICTM). *Publications:* Arpa, Maraca y Buche, 1998; Joropo Central, 1998. *E-mail:* klengwinat@web.de.

LENGYEL, Peter M., BA, MM; American musician (piano), composer and arranger; b. 5 June 1946, New York; m. (divorced). *Education:* Glassboro St College, Indiana University. *Career:* Head of Jazz Studies, Eastfield College, Texas 1971–81; full time composer and arranger 1985–; clinician and judge for jazz bands, marching bands, concert bands, throughout the USA; teacher of jazz and conductor; President, P & D Jazz Publications; performances with Don Ellis, Bill Watrous, Clark Terry, Frank Rosolino; mem Texas Bandmasters; Patron mem., International Asscn of Jazz Educators. *Compositions:* over 400 works in various mediums. *Honours:* Award for Teaching Excellence, University of Texas at Arlington College of Liberal Arts Music Department 1983, 1984, 1985. *Address:* 4453 Wesley Way, Austell, GA 30106, USA (home). *Website:* panddjazz.com (office).

LENINE; Brazilian singer, musician (guitar) and songwriter; b. (Osvaldo Lenine Macedo Pimentel), Pernambuco. *Career:* mixes North Eastern-Brazilian grooves with pop music; collaborated with Gilberto Gil, Chico César, Djavan, Elba Ramalho; songs recorded by Dionne Warwick, Gilberto Gil, Danilo Caymmi, Sergio Mendes. *Recordings include:* albums: Baque Solto (with Lula Queiroga) 1983, Olha De Peixe (with Marcos Suzano) 1992, O Dia Em Que Faremos Contato 1997, Na Pressão 1999, Falange Canibal 2001, Incité 2004, Acústico MTV (Latin Grammy Award for Best Brazilian Contemporary Rock Album 2007) 2006, Labiata 2008. *Honours:* Sharp Prize for Best Song (for A Ponte with Lula Queiroga) 1998, Latin Grammy Award for Best Brazilian Song (for Martelo Bigorna) 2009. *Current Management:* Ciranda, Estrada Santa Marinha 5/105, Gávea, 22451-041, Rio de Janeiro, RJ, Brazil. *Telephone:* (21) 2540-5865. *E-mail:* contato@ciranda.inf.br. *Website:* www.ciranda.inf.br; www.lenine.com.br.

LENNEVALD, (John) Dhani; Swedish singer; b. 24 July 1984, Stockholm. *Education:* Gärdeskolan School, Stockholm. *Career:* mem., A*Teens 1998–2004. *Recordings include:* albums: The Abba Generation 1999, Teen Spirit 2001. *Honours:* Viva Music Award for Best Int. Newcomer 2000. *Website:* dhanimusic.com.

LENNI; British musician (saxophone) and singer; b. 17 April 1941, Staly-bridge, Cheshire; m. Irene Dale 1963; one s. *Career:* member, Gladiators, 1959; Corvettes, 1964; St Louis Union, 1965; Tony Christie's Band, 1968–70; Sad Cafe, 1979; Norman Beaker Band, 1986; Look Twice, 1987; Supercharge, 1990; Support tours with Carlos Santana; Toto; Otis Redding; Atlantic Star; Chuck Berry; American Bluesmen: Lowell Fulson; Phil Guy; Larry Garner; Louisianna Red; Johnny Mars; Rockin' Sydney; Also played for: Jack Bruce; Dave Dee; Kiki Dee; Vince Hill; Paul Jones; Lou Rawls; Lisa Stansfield; Alvin Stardust; Herbie Goins; Claire Moore; Gavin Sutherland; Victor Brox; Carl Wayne; When In Rome; mem, Musicians' Union; PAMRA; MENSA. *Recordings:* Sad Cafe (8 albums); Paul Jones R&B Show (3 albums); Norman Beaker Band (3 albums); Judy Boucher (2 albums); Also albums by Cannon and Ball; Magna Carta; Gilbert O'Sullivan; Eric Stewart; 10cc; Ruby Turner; Lurrie Bell; Louisiana Red; Featured on television themes and radio commercials. *Address:* 14A Moorside Road, Heaton Moor, Stockport, Cheshire SK4 4DT, England.

LENNON, Julian; British singer, songwriter and musician; b. 8 April 1963, Liverpool, England. *Career:* solo artist 1984–. *Recordings include:* albums: Valotte, 1984; The Secret Value of Daydreaming, 1986; Mr Jordan, 1989; Help Yourself, 1991; Photograph Smile, 1998. *Website:* www.julianlennon.com.

LENNOX, Annie, OBE, ARAM; British rock singer and lyricist; b. 25 Dec. 1954, Aberdeen, Scotland; d. of the late Thomas A. Lennox and of Dorothy Lennox (née Ferguson); m. 1st Rahda Raman 1984 (divorced); m. 2nd Uri Fruchtmann; one s. two d.; m. 3rd Mitch Besser 2012. *Education:* Aberdeen High School for Girls, Royal Acad. of Music. *Career:* Founder-mem. (with Dave Stewart q.v.) The Catch 1977, renamed The Tourists 1979–80, Eurythmics 1980–89, 1999–; numerous Eurythmics tours world-wide; solo artist 1988–. *Film:* Revolution 1985. *Recordings include:* albums: with The Tourists: The Tourists 1979, Reality Affect 1980, Luminous Basement 1980; with Eurythmics: In The Garden 1981, Sweet Dreams (Are Made of This) (Grammy Award for Best Video Album) 1982, Touch 1983, 1984 (For The Love of Big Brother) 1984, Be Yourself Tonight 1985, Revenge 1986, Savage 1987, We Too Are One 1989, Peace 1999, The Ultimate Collection 2005; solo: Diva (BPI Award for Best Album) 1992, Medusa 1995, Train In Vain 1995, Bare 2003, Songs of Mass Destruction 2007, A Christmas Cornucopia 2010, Nostalgia 2014. *Honours:* Dr hc (Royal Scottish Acad. of Music and Drama, Glasgow) 2006, (Berklee Coll. of Music) 2013; American Soc. of Composers Award, BPI Award for Best Female Vocalist 1982/83, 1987/88, 1989/90, 1992/93, Grammy Award for Best Female Performance (for Sweet Dreams) 1983, Ivor Novello Award for Best Pop Song (for Sweet Dreams, with Dave Stewart) 1983, MTV Music Award for Best New Artist Video (for Sweet Dreams (Are Made Of This)) 1984, Ivor Novello Award for Best Song (for It's Alright (Baby's Coming Back, with Dave Stewart) 1987, Ivor Novello Award for Best Song (for Why) 1992, BRIT Award for Best Female Solo Artist 1996, Grammy Award for Best Female Pop Vocals (for No More I Love You) 1996, BRIT Award for Outstanding Contrib. to Music 1999, Tartan Cleff Award 2001, Acad. Award for Best Song (for Into the West and Use Well the Days, from the film Lord of the Rings: The Two Towers) 2004, ASCAP Founders Award 2006, Woman of Peace Award, World Summit of Nobel Peace Prize Laureates 2009, Music Industry Trust Award 2013. *Current Management:* c/o 19 Management, 33 Ransomes Dock, 35–37 Parkgate Road, London, SW11 4NP, England. *Telephone:* (20) 7801-1919. *Fax:* (20) 7801-1920. *Website:* www.annielennox .co.uk; www.eurythmics.com.

LEON, (Robert) Craig; American/British producer, composer and arranger; *Director, Atlas Realisations;* b. 7 Jan. 1952, Miami, Fla, USA; m. Cassell Webb 1984. *Career:* mem. British Record Producers' Guild, BRIT Awards Nominating Cttee, Nat. Acad. of Recording Arts and Sciences, Grammy.com; Dir, Atlas Realisations. *Compositions include:* Izzy, Libera Me album 1998, Izzy, Ascolta 2000, Izzy, New Dawn 2002, Joshua Bell/Academy of St-Martin-in-the-Fields: The Romance of the Violin 2003, Julia Thornton, Harpistry 2003, Andreas Scholl and the Orpheus Chamber Orchestra: Wayfaring Stranger 2003, James Galway/London Symphony Orchestra: Wings of Song 2004, C.T.Griffes-C.Leon: Roman Sketches for Orchestra, recorded with the London Symphony Orchestra 2005, Natasha Marsh, Amour Recital album 2007, L. Bernstein-C. Leon Symphonic Dances from West Side Story, jazz version premiere performance with Evelyn Glennie (percussion) and the London Symphony Orchestra 2007, Maestro (film-score) 2007, Orbit, La Luna (TV soundtrack) 2009, Ophelie Gaillard: Dreams 2010, Bell'aria (TV soundtrack and CD) 2010. *Recordings include:* three albums as featured artist: Nommos (ballet score) 1981, Visiting 1982, Klub Anima Theatre score (premiered Bristol Old Vic theatre) 1993; one album in collaboration with Arthur Brown: Tape From Atoya 1981; five albums in collaboration with Cassell Webb: Llano 1985, Thief of Sadness 1987, Songs of a Stranger 1989, Conversations At

Dawn 1990, House of Dreams 1992; others as producer: Ramones 1976, Blondie 1977, Suicide 1977, Richard Hell 1977, Rodney Crowell 1980, Sir Douglas Quintet 1980, The Bangles 1983, The Roches 1983, Dr and the Medics 1986, The Pogues 1986, The Primitives 1986, Adult Net 1988, The Fall 1989–92, Jesus Jones 1990, New FADS 1992, Front 242 1993, Eugenius 1994, Angel Corpus Christi 1995, Martin Phillips and the Chills 1996, Mark Owen 1996, Cobalt 60 1996, Psyched Up Janis 1997, Blondie, No Exit 1998, Izzy 1998, Cinema Italiano, featuring Sting, Luciano Pavarotti, Lucio Dalla; James Galway's Wings Of Song (arranger) 2004, Charles T. Griffes' Roman Sketches (London Symphony Orchestra) (arranger) 2004, Midwinter (London Chamber Orchestra) (arranger) 2011, Early Electronic Works (composer and performer) 2014, The Anthology of Interplanetary Folk Music Vol. 1 (composer and performer) 2014, Bach to Moog (arranger, performer and conductor) 2015. *Radio:* numerous performances on BBC Radio 3 and Classic FM (UK), Radio Classique (France), Klassik Radio (Germany), NTS, Red Bull Radio, Boiler Room, etc. *Television:* Red Bull, Boiler Room in Concert, ARTE, and many others. *Honours:* Grammy Award 1976, Grammy Hall of Fame Award 2006. *Address:* Atlas Realisations Music, Trendalls Cottage, Beacons Bottom, Bucks., HP14 3XF, England. *Telephone:* (1494) 483121. *Fax:* (1494) 484303. *E-mail:* craig@craigleon.com (office). *Website:* www.craigleon.com; www .myspace.com/craigleon.

LEONG, Fish; Malaysian/Chinese singer; b. (Leong Chui Peng), 16 June 1978, Seremban, Malaysia; m. Tony Chao 2010. *Career:* started career as cover version singer at Hai Luo Music Cafe. *Recordings include:* Grown Up Overnight 1999, Courage 2000, Shining Star 2001, Sunrise 2002, Beautiful 2003, Wings Of Love 2004, Silk Road Of Love 2005, Kissing The Future Of Love 2006, j'Adore 2007, Today is Our Valentine's Day 2008, Fall in Love And Songs 2009, Don't Cry for Him Anymore 2009, What Love Songs Didn't Tell You 2010, I Love You Hereafter 2011. *Honours:* numerous awards including MTV Top 20 Favourite Female Vocalists 2002, Singapore Golden Hits Awards, Best Female Vocalist 2003, Singapore Golden Hits Awards, Regional (Malaysia) Most Popular Singer 2004, Singapore Golden Hits Awards, Regional (Malaysia) Most Popular Singer, Most Popular Female Singer 2005, HITO Radio Music Awards, Best Regional Singer (Malaysia) 2005, 5th Global Chinese Music Awards, Top 5 Female Vocalist 2005, TVBS Chinese Golden Chart Awards, Best Regional Female Singer 2006, Malaysian Outstanding Youth Award 2007, Top Chinese Music Chart Awards, Best Female Artist, Hong Kong & Taiwan 2007, 2008, Music Radio Chinese TOP Charts Awards, Most Popular Female Singer 2008, Singapore Hit Awards, Best Female Vocalist 2008.

LEOPOLD, Siniša; Croatian academic; b. 16 April 1957, Grubisno Polje; m. Ljiljana Leopold (Rogic) 1985; two s. *Education:* Academy of Music. *Career:* Chief Conductor, HRT Tambura Orchestra, 1985; Lecturer, Academy of Music, University of Zagreb, 1986–; Conductor, Ferdo Livadic Tambura Orchestra, Samobor, 1985; many compositions, arrangements for Tambura Orchestras; mem. Croatian Society of Composers; Croatian Folklore Society. *Publications:* Tambura School T 1992, Tambura Among Croatians 1995. *Honours:* Croatian Discography Award: Porin 1995. *Address:* Rapska 37A, 41000 Zagreb, Croatia.

LEPALLEC, Bernard, DPhil; French musician (saxophone); b. 20 Dec. 1951, Paris; two d. *Education:* Univ. of Paris (Sorbonne). *Career:* composer, saxophone player, improvised music; mem. jazz band, Ar Jazz; improvised concerts in France, Poland, Italy, Greece. *Music:* Shakespeare Project 2012. *Recordings include:* albums: Band Ar Jazz, Bissa Two, Gang Art Trois. *Address:* Venelle de Cosquelou, 22470 Plouezec, France (home). *Telephone:* 2-96-55-45-31 (home). *Fax:* 2-96-55-45-31 (home). *E-mail:* bernard.lepallec@ laposte.net (home). *Website:* www.ar-jaz.org.

LEPISTÖ, Markku; Finnish musician (accordion); b. Kuortane. *Education:* Sibelius Acad., Helsinki. *Career:* mem., Doina Klezmer 1997–, Värttinä 1998–; simultaneous solo artist. *Music for theatre:* co-wrote score to stage musical, The Lord of the Rings (with A. R. Rahman) (Princess of Wales Theatre, Toronto) 2006. *Recordings include:* albums: with Värttinä: Ilmatar 2000, 6.12 2001, iki 2003, Miero 2006; album with Petri Hakala 2001; solo: Silta 2001, Polku 2006; with Doina Klezmer: (albums) 2001, 2004. *Honours:* Composers' Grant, Ministry of Educ. 1998, 2000, 2003, 2008, Finland Prize (with Värttinä) 2005. *Current Management:* c/o Phillip Page, Hoedown Arts Oy, Neitsytpolku 9 F 81, 00140 Helsinki, Finland. *Telephone:* (50) 5692982. *Fax:* (9) 628950. *E-mail:* pap@hoedown.com. *Website:* www.hoedown.com; www.varttina.com; www.markkulepisto.com.

LEPOMME, Linda; Belgian actress, singer and artistic director; b. 16 March 1955, Lokeren, Flanders; d. of Willy Lepomme and Irma Hereman. *Education:* Higher Inst. of Dramatic Art, Antwerp. *Career:* mem. Teater Arena, Ghent – 1985; Rep. Belgium in Eurovision Song Contest 1985; Asst Artistic Dir of Musicals, Royal Ballet of Flanders, Musical Div. 1985–91, Artistic Dir 1989–. *Musicals:* Rocky Horror Picture Show, The Fantasticks, Chicago, Company, Grease, Side by Side by Sondheim, My Fair Lady, West Side Story, Dear Fox, The King and I. *Films include:* Zware jongens 1984, De leeuw van Vlaanderen 1985, Pauline and Paulette 2001. *Television includes:* Toch zonde dat 't een hoer is 1978, De paradijsvogels (series) 1980, De eerste sleutel 1980, TV-Touché (series) 1983, Levenslang 1984, De Leeuw van Vlaanderen 1985, Pauline and Paulette 2001. *Address:* Koninklijk Ballet van Vlaanderen, Kattendijkdok-Westkaai 16, 2000 Antwerpen (office); Miksebaan 254C/6,

2930 Brasschaat, Belgium. *E-mail:* balletvanvlaanderen@kbvv.be (office). *Website:* www.kbvv.be (office).

LERNER, Alejandro Federico; Argentine singer, musician (piano) and producer; b. 8 June 1957, Buenos Aires. *Education:* Universidad Católica Argentina. *Career:* musician supporting various bands and artists 1976–82; solo artist 1983–. *Recordings include:* albums: Alejandro Lerner y la Magia (with La Magia band) 1982, Todo a pulmón 1983, Lernertres 1984, Sus primeras canciones 1984, Conciertos 1985, Algo que decir 1987, Canciones 1988, Entrelíneas 1990, Amor infinito 1992, Permiso de volar 1994, La magia continúa 1995, Magic hotel 1997, Volver a empezar 1997, 20 años 1999, Si quieres saber quién soy 2000, Buen viaje 2003, Enojado 2007. *E-mail:* info@alejandrolerner.com.ar (office). *Website:* www.alejandrolerner.net.

LEROY, Christian; Belgian composer and musician (piano); b. 23 Nov. 1952; m. Nathalie Cuvelier, two s. *Education:* General electronic studies; Drum lessons. *Career:* Composed works for RTBF Programme 3; Works for theatre plays including Le Monde est Rond, Le Baiser de la Femme Araignée, Le Roi et le Cadavre, The Merchant of Venice; Works with Sandro Somaré, Bram Bogart, Miguel Berrocal; Lindströ m and others; Member of Métarythmes de l'Air musical group and Piano Kvartet, group of 4 pianists. *Compositions:* Le 37 Janvier, opera; Music for Dracula, film of Tod Browning; Music for Robert Flaherty's Nanouk the Eskimo; Images du Tarot, recorded. *Recordings:* Métarythmes de l'Air; Piano Duet with Fred Von Hove; Phagocyte; 33 Petits Tours; Le Temps Qui Passe; Les Chemins de Lumière; La Roue des Corps; Le Temps des Sabbats; The Merchant of Venice; Mystères d'un Théâtre et d'une Vie; Dracula et Nanouk l'Esquimau. *Honours:* Prix de Hainaut, 1982; Special Mention for Film Music, Caracas, 1983; Prix de la Presse, SPA Festival; Prix de la Pensée, Wallonne.

LESH, Philip (Phil) Chapman; American singer and musician (bass guitar); b. 15 March 1940, Berkeley, CA; m. Jill; two s. *Career:* fmrly jazz and classical trumpeter, studied under Luciano Berio; mem., The Warlocks 1965, renamed The Grateful Dead 1965–95; mem., The Other Ones 1999; founder mem., Phil and Friends 1999–; session work includes David Crosby, Graham Nash, Bob Weir, Mickey Hart, David Bromberg, Ned Lagin, The Rhythm Devils, The New Riders of the Purple Sage, The Rowan Brothers, Gov't Mule; founder Unbroken Chain Foundation promoting community service 1997–. *Recordings include:* albums: with The Grateful Dead: The Grateful Dead 1967, Anthem of the Sun 1968, Aoxomoxoa 1969, LiveDead 1969, Workingman's Dead 1970, American Beauty 1970, Grateful Dead (Skull and Roses) 1971, Europe '72 1972, History of the Grateful Dead Vol. 1 (Bear's Choice) 1973, Wake of the Flood 1973, Grateful Dead from the Mars Hotel 1974, Blues for Allah 1975, Steal Your Face 1976, Terrapin Station 1977, Shakedown Street 1978, Go to Heaven 1980, Reckoning 1981, Dead Set 1981, In the Dark 1987, Built to Last 1989, Without a Net 1990, Infrared Roses 1991; with Bob Dylan and the Grateful Dead: Dylan and the Dead 1988; with The Other Ones: The Strange Remain 1999; with Phil and Friends: Love Will See You Through (Highlights Vol. 1) 1999, There and Back Again 2002; solo: Searching for the Sound: My Life in the Grateful Dead 2005. *Publications:* Searching for the Sound (autobiog.) 2005. *Address:* c/o Unbroken Chain Foundation, PO Box 10188, San Rafael, CA 94912, USA (office). *Website:* www.phillesh.net.

LESKANICH, Katrina; American singer; b. 1960, Topeka, KS. *Career:* lead singer, Katrina and The Waves 1982–99; presenter, BBC Radio 2 1999–2000; solo career 1999–. *Recordings include:* albums: with Katrina and the Waves: Walking On Sunshine 1983, Katrina and The Waves 1984, Katrina and the Waves 2 1985, Waves 1986, Break of Hearts 1989, Pet the Tiger 1991, Edge of the Land 1993, Turnaround 1994, Anthology 1995, Walk on Water 1997; solo: Turn the Tide 2004, Katrina Leskanich 2006, Spiritualize 2011. *Honours:* Eurovision Song Contest winner (for Love Shine a Light) 1997. *E-mail:* kyboside@kybosidelimited.wanadoo.co.uk. *Website:* www.katrinaandthewaves.com; www.katrinasweb.com.

LESSARD, Stefan Kahil; American musician (bass guitar); b. 4 June 1974, Anaheim, CA. *Education:* Tandem Music School, Charlottesville. *Career:* fmr mem., Charlottesville-Albermarle Youth Orchestra; teamed up with Dave Matthews to assist with demo recording, on recommendation of music tutor John D'Earth 1990; mem., Dave Matthews Band 1991–; numerous tours and live appearances world-wide; first album released on group's own Bama Rags label. *Recordings:* albums: Remember Two Things 1993, Under The Table And Dreaming 1994, Crash 1996, Live At Red Rocks 8.15.95 1997, Before These Crowded Streets 1998, Listener Supported (live) 1999, Everyday 2001, Live In Chicago 12.19.98 2001, Live Trax, Vol. 1–12 2004–08, Busted Stuff 2002, Live At Folsom Field, Boulder, Colorado 2002, Central Park Concert 2003, The Gorge 2004, Stand Up 2005, Big Whiskey and the GrooGrux King 2009, Away from the World 2012. *Honours:* Grammy Awards for Best Rock Performance by a Duo or Group with Vocal 1997, VH-1 Awards for Favorite Group, Must Have Album, Song of the Year 2001. *E-mail:* fanmail@davematthewsband.com (office). *Website:* www.davematthewsband.com.

LESTARI, Dewi, (Dee); Indonesian novelist and singer; b. 20 Jan. 1976, Bandung; m. 1st Marcell Siahaan (divorced 2008); m. 2nd Reza Gunawan; two c. *Education:* Univ. of Parahyangan. *Career:* f. singing trio RSD (Rida, Sita, Dewi); f. Truedee Books 2001. *Recordings:* albums: with RSD: Antara Kita 1995, Bertiga 1997, Satu 1999; solo: Out of Shell 2006, Rectoverso 2008, Paper Boat 2012. *Publications include:* Supernova 1: Knight, Princess and The Shooting Star (novel) 2001, Supernova 2: Root 2002, Akar 2003, Supernova 3:

Lightning 2004, Supernova: petir 2005, Filosofi Kopi: Kumpulan Cerita and Prosa Satu Dekade 2006, Rectoverso 2008, Perahu Kertas 2009, Madre 2011, Supernova 4: Partikel 2012, Supernova 5: Waves 2014. *Honours:* Writer of the Year, Prestige Magazine 2008, Most Outstanding Woman 2009, Most Acknowledged Female Writer Award 2009. *E-mail:* truedeepustaka@gmail .com. *Website:* deelestari.com/id.

LESTER, Gregory; British musician (guitar) and songwriter; b. Brighton, England. *Education:* Studied classical guitar. *Career:* Session musician, composer, co-writer on albums by: Shola Ama, Camelle Hinds, Jeb Loy Nichols, Truce, Terminalhead, Lucid Source, Ultimate Kaos, The Collective, Love City Groove; Tours, recordings, radio, television appearances with: Julia Fordham, Des'ree, Danielle Gaha, John O'Kane, Joe Roberts, Sylvia Powell; Concerts incl.: with John O'Kane: support to Sting, Soul Cages tour, UK/European legs; with Des'ree: Summer festivals at Wembley Stadium, Old Trafford, Gateshead International; Tour of Japan; Jeb Loy Nichols, UK and US dates; Maggie Reilly, Polar Star featuring Cara Dillon; Radio and television appearances with: Kindred Spirit, 25th of May, Kim Appleby, Shania Twain; mem, PRS; MCPS Musicians' Union; Pamra. *Recordings:* Numerous sessions incl.: Adam F., Aco, Adeva, Atlantique, Azizi, Barry Adamson, Daniel Bedingfield, Caroline Bonnet, Blade, Cornelius, Danielle Dax, Des'ree, Definition of Sound, E-Type, Ace of Bass, Everything But the Girl, EYC, Dark Flower, Freaky Realistic, Love City Groove, Gangstarr, Camelle Hinds, Rodeo Jones, Karl Keaton, Lush Life, Lindy Layton, Alison Limerick, London Beat, James McMillan, Monie Love, Kylie Minogue, Jeb Loy Nichols, Nightcrawlers, Noriyuki Makahara, Osibisa, Peter Brown, Tconnection, Pop Will Eat Itself, Joe Roberts, Maria Rowe, Tom Robinson, Stex, Jimmy Somerville, Shola Ama, Shy FX & T Power, Sunscream, Spice Girls, Soundstation, Dave Stewart, Whitney Houston, Workshy, Worlds Apart, Keith Washington, Trumpet Thing, Tyrell Corporation; Live video: Porcelain—Live In Concert, Julia Fordham; Played on various television commercials; Played on film music incl.: My Boy (Channel 4); The Beat (theme music); Painted Lady (Granada TV); Ali G the Movie. *Honours:* BPI Awards: Platinum, three times, Spice Girls; Gold, Kylie Minogue, EBTG; Silver, Des'ree. *Website:* www.greglester.com.

DJ LETHAL; American musician (rhythm, sound effects) and DJ; b. (Leor DiMant), 18 Dec. 1972, Latvia. *Career:* mem., House of Pain 1992–96; mem., Limp Bizkit 1996–; various remixes and exec. production for other artists, including Sugar Ray, Rob Zombie. *Recordings:* albums: with House of Pain: House of Pain 1992, Same As It Ever Was 1994, Truth Crushed To Earth Shall Rise Again 1996; with Limp Bizkit: Three Dollar Bill Y'All 1997, Significant Other 1999, Chocolate Starfish And The Hotdog Flavored Water 2000, New Old Songs 2001, Bipolar 2003, Results May Vary 2003, The Unquestionable Truth (Part 1) 2005, Gold Cobra 2010. *Honours:* American Music Award for Favorite Alternative Artist 2002. *Current Management:* c/o Peter Katsis, The Firm, 9100 Wilshire Boulevard, Beverly Hills, CA 90212, USA. *Website:* www .limpbizkit.com.

LETO, Jared Joseph; American singer, songwriter, musician (guitar) and actor; b. 26 Dec. 1971, Bossier City, La; s. of Constance Leto. *Education:* Emerson Preparatory School, Washington, DC, Univ. of the Arts, Philadelphia, New York City School of Visual Arts. *Career:* TV and film actor 1992–; Founder-mem. 30 Seconds to Mars 1998–. *Recordings include:* with 30 Seconds to Mars: 30 Seconds to Mars 2002, A Beautiful Lie (MTV Asia Video Star Award 2008) 2005, This is War 2009, Love, Lust, Faith and Dreams 2013. *Films include:* How to Make an American Quilt 1995, The Last of the High Kings 1996, Switchback 1997, Prefontaine 1997, Basil 1998, Urban Legend 1998, The Thin Red Line 1998, Black and White 1999, Girl, Interrupted 1999, Fight Club 1999, American Psycho 2000, Sunset Strip 2000, Requiem for a Dream (Boston Society of Film Critics Award for Best Actor 2000, Stockholm Film Festival Award for Best Actor 2000) 2000, Highway 2002, Panic Room 2002, Phone Booth 2002, Alexander 2004, Lord of War 2005, Hubert Selby Jr.: It'll Be Better Tomorrow (documentary) 2005, Lonely Hearts 2006, Chapter 27 2007, Mr. Nobody (Puchon International Fantastic Film Festival Award for Best Performance 2009, Sitges Film Festival Award for Best Actor 2009) 2009, TT3D: Closer to the Edge (narrator for documentary) 2011, Dallas Buyers Club (Golden Globe Award for Best Supporting Actor in a Motion Picture, Screen Actors Guild Award for Outstanding Performance by a Male Actor in a Supporting Role, Academy Award for Best Supporting Actor 2014) 2013. *Television includes:* Camp Wilder (series) 1992, Almost Home (series) 1993, Rebel Highway (series) 1994, Cool and the Crazy (film) 1994, My So-Called Life (series) 1994. *Honours:* MTV2 Award at MTV Video Music Awards 2006, MTV Australia Video Music Awards for Best Rock Video and Video of the Year 2007, Kerrang! Awards for Best Int. Newcomer 2007, for Best Single 2007, 2008, 2011, for Best Int. Band 2008, 2010, 2011, TRL Award for Best New Artist 2007, Bandit Rock Award for Best Int. Breakthrough 2008, Los Premios MTV Award for Best Int. Rock Artist 2008, MTV Europe Music Rock Out Award 2008, MTV Europe Music Video Star Award 2008, MTV Video Music Award for Best Rock Video 2010, 2013, MTV Europe Music Award for Best Rock Act 2010, for Best Alternative Act 2013. *Website:* jaredleto.com/thisiswhoireallyam.

LETO, Shannon Christopher; American musician (drums); b. 9 March 1970, Bossier City, La. *Career:* occasional actor in TV and film during 1990s; founder-mem. 30 Seconds to Mars 1998–; mem. supergroup The Wondergirls 1999. *Recordings include:* with 30 Seconds to Mars: 30 Seconds to Mars 2002, A Beautiful Lie (MTV Asia Video Star Award 2008) 2005, This is War 2009,

Love, Lust, Faith and Dreams 2013. *Television:* as actor: My So-Called Life 1994. *Films include:* as actor: Prefontaine 1997, Highway 2002. *Honours:* MTV2 Award at MTV Video Music Awards 2006, MTV Australia Video Music Awards for Best Rock Video and Video of the Year 2007, Kerrang! Awards for Best International Newcomer 2007, for Best Single 2007, 2008, 2011, for Best International Band 2008, 2010, 2011, TRL Award for Best New Artist 2007, Bandit Rock Award for Best International Breakthrough 2008, Los Premios MTV Award for Best International Rock Artist 2008, MTV Asia Video Star Award 2008, MTV Europe Music Rock Out Award 2008, MTV Europe Music Video Star Award 2008, MTV Video Music Award for Best Rock Video 2010, 2013, MTV Europe Music Award for Best Rock Act 2010, for Best Alternative Act 2013. *Website:* www.thirtysecondstomars.com.

LEURS, Laurens; Belgian singer, songwriter and musician (guitar); *Head of Department PHL-Music, PHL University College;* b. 9 July 1965, Bree; m. Saskia Peeters 1994. *Education:* Univ. of Brussels, Acad. of Word and Music Maaseik, Belgium. *Career:* currently Head of Dept, PHL-Music, PHL Univ. Coll. *Recordings include:* albums: Ball and Chain 1989, Trigger Happy 1990, Major Panic 1993, Be My Star 1996, El Diablo 1998, So Far 2000, Bad Luck for Wilbur Brink 2010. *Address:* Koningin Astridlaan 37, 3680 Maaseik (home); PHL Music, Bootstraat 9, 3500 Hasselt, Belgium (office). *Website:* www.phl.be (office).

LEVAN, Christophe; French musician (contrabass, bass guitar); b. 29 Dec. 1959, Marseilles; 1 s. *Education:* Dental studies, Marseilles. *Career:* Concerts with: Michel Legrand; Michel Portal; Chet Baker; Sonny Stitt; Phil Woods; Peter King; Dee Dee Bridgewater; Nicole Croisille; Television and radio broadcasts include: Françaises Variétés et Jazz; Radio France; France Musique; mem, Syndicate des Musiciens; Membre de la Sacem, 1998. *Compositions:* Minou; Libreto; Swing Gome; Merci Glop; Waltz For Theo. *Recordings:* About 20 records include: Swinging Marilyn, Gerard Badini Swing Machine; Debussy Meets Mister Swing, Gerard Badini Big Band; Chassaguin Quartet; Johnny Griffin et Hervé Sellin' Sextet; Tribute To Jazz Michel Gaucher; Cannon Blues, Hervé Meschinet Quartet. *Honours:* Django D'Or, Hervé Meshinet Quartet, 1998; Victoires de la Musique, 1998. *Address:* c/o EMD, 92 rue Stanislas, 54000 Nancy, France. *E-mail:* jazz@labelemd.com. *Website:* labelemd.free.fr.

LEVANDER, Jan; Swedish composer and musician (saxophone, flute, clarinet); b. 29 March 1959, Stockholm; m. Malin Hülphers; one s. one d. *Education:* Stockholm Community Music Inst., Stockholm Music Conservatory. *Career:* led, wrote music for and played in own jazz groups, Kamel Kombo, Jan Levanders Oktett, Kung Lir; toured jazz clubs, festivals; musician, arranger, conductor in musicals and theatre music. *Compositions include:* Composer's Big Fun (with Ann–Sofi Soderqvist and Joakim Milder) 2006.

LEVI, Eric; French composer, musician (guitar) and producer; b. (Eric Jacques Levisalves), 23 Dec. 1955; two s. *Career:* founder mem., Shakin' Street 1977–81; moved to New York 1981; collaborations with Marianne Faithfull; soundtrack composer 1990s; founder mem., Era 1995. *Film scores include:* L'Opération Corned-beef 1990, Les Visiteurs 1993, La Vengeance d'une blonde 1994, Pourquoi maman est dans mon lit? 1994, Les Anges gardiens 1995, Ma femme me quitte 1995, Les Soeurs soleil 1997, Couloirs du temps: Les visiteurs 2 1998. *Recordings:* albums: with Shakin' Street: Vampire Rock 1978, Shakin' Street 1980; with Era: Ameno 1997, Era 1998, Erazistable 1999, Era Vol. 2 2001, The Mass 2003, Reborn 2008. *Address:* c/o Universal Music France, 20 rue des Fossés-Saint-Jacques, 75235 Paris 5, Cédex 0, France (office). *Website:* era-music.artistes.universalmusic.fr.

LEVIEV, Milcho; Bulgarian composer, musician (piano), arranger and conductor; b. 19 Dec. 1937, Plovdiv; m. Deborah Rothschild, 19 July 1990, 1 d. *Education:* Masters in Composition, Bulgarian State Conservatory, 1960. *Career:* Conductor, Bulgarian Radio and TV Pop Orchestra, 1962–66; Composer, Bulgarian Feature Film Studios, 1963–69; Arranger, Radio Frankfurt, 1970; Pianist, composer, arranger, Don Ellis Orchestra, Billy Cobham Band, Art Pepper Quartet; Music Director, Lanie Kazan Show; Co-leader, Free Flight quartet; Lecturer, University of Southern California; mem, AFofM; NARAS; BMI; GEMA. *Compositions:* Concerto For Jazz Combo and Strings; Music For Big Band and Symphony Orchestra; Sympho-Jazz Sketches; Orpheus Rhapsody for Piano and Orchestra; The Green House – Jazz Cantata; Film and Theatre Music. *Recordings:* Over 35 records under own name and over 50 records as a sideman; Blues For The Fisherman; Easter Parade; Live At Vartan Jazz; Anti Waltz. *Publications:* 8 Jazz Pieces, 1968; Milcho Leviev-Fake Book; 2 Songs For Jazz Choir, 1991. *Honours:* Dr hc (Music Acad., Plovdiv) 1995, (New Bulgarian Univ.) 1999. *E-mail:* minchev57@abv.bg. *E-mail:* mleviev@aol.com. *Website:* www.milcholeviev.net.

LEVIN, Michael David, BA, AM, PhD; American musician and composer; b. 29 May 1954, Syracuse, New York. *Education:* University of Illinois, University of Chicago, University of Illinois, Institute of Communications Research. *Career:* Performed and recorded with David Bromberg, Oscar Brown Jr, Barrett Deems, Hamid Drake, The Four Tops, Fireworks Jazz, Jerry Goodman, Charlie Musselwhite, Night on Earth, Jim Post, Bernard Purdie, Claudia Schmidt, Diane Schuur, The Supremes, The Temptations, Clark Terry, The Chicago Jazz Ensemble, The Illinois Philharmonic Orchestra, The Ethos Chamber Orchestra; Appearances at numerous jazz and pop festivals. *Recordings:* Over 50 Albums.

LEVINE, Adam; American singer and musician (guitarist); b. 18 March 1979, Los Angeles, CA. *Career:* mem and lead singer, Kara's Flowers, later renamed Maroon 5 1997–. *Recordings include:* albums: with Maroon 5: Songs About Jane 2002, It Won't Be Soon Before Long (Billboard Music Award for Top Digital Album 2007) 2007, Hands All Over 2010, Overexposed 2012, V 2014. *Honours:* with Maroon 5: Grammy Awards for Best New Artist 2004, for Best Pop Performance by a Duo or Group with Vocals (for Makes me Wonder) 2008, American Music Awards for Favorite Pop/Rock Band/Duo/Group 2011, 2012, for Favorite Adult Contemporary Artist 2013, Billboard Music Award for Top Hot 100 Artist 2013, People's Choice Award for Favorite Band 2013. *Address:* c/o Career Artist Management, 1100 Glendon Avenue, Suite 1100, New York, NY 90024, USA. *Telephone:* (310) 776-7640. *Fax:* (310) 776-7659. *Website:* camanagement.com; www.maroon5.com.

LEVINE, Steve; British producer and songwriter; *Chairman, Music Producers Guild.* *Career:* record producer 1975–; has worked with Alsou, The Beach Boys, The Beauties, Darren Berry, China Crisis, The Clash, The Creatures, Culture Club, The Honeyz, Louise, Ziggy Marley, Mis-Teeq, Motorhead, 911, Owen, Rozalla, Deniece Williams; Chair., Music Producers Guild 2009–. *Publications:* Hit Kit, The Art of Downloading Music. *Address:* Music Producers Guild, PO Box 32, Harrow HA2 7ZX, England (office). *Telephone:* (20) 8993-5504 (office). *Fax:* (20) 8992-1195 (office). *E-mail:* office@mpg.org.uk (office). *Website:* www.stevelevine.co.uk.

LEVITIN, Daniel J., AB, MSc, PhD; American cognitive psychologist, record producer, musician and journalist; *Associate Professor of Psychology, Behavioural Neuroscience and Music, McGill University;* b. 27 Dec. 1957, San Francisco, CA; s. of Lloyd A. Levitin and Sonia Wolff. *Education:* Stanford Univ., Univ. of Oregon. *Career:* Music Production Editor, REP Magazine 1989–92; Staff Writer, Billboard Magazine 1990–93; Director A&R, 415/Columbia Records 1984–89; Assoc. Prof. of Psychology, Behavioural Neuroscience and Music, Dept of Psychology, McGill Univ. 2000–, currently also FCAR Strategic Chair in Psychology, Bell Chair in Psychology of Electronic Communication, James McGill Chair in Psychology and Neuroscience and Assoc. Mem. Schulich School of Music, School of Computer Science, Faculty of Educ., School of the Environment; Assoc. Mem., Dept of Psychology, Univ. of Quebec at Montreal; mem. NARAS, AES. *Compositions:* First Strike, Now That You Are Gone, I Should've Told You, Anticipation, Here Come The Cops. *Radio:* The Sound of Musique, BBC Front Row, CBC Radio One Freestyle, Diane Rehm Show. *Recordings:* Heart Shaped World (Chris Isaak), Imaginoos (Blue Oyster Cult), Rockin' and Romance (Jonathan Richmond), Good News About Mental Health (The Afflicted). *Television:* Close To You: Remembering The Carpenters, BBC World News, MTV, Bravo! Arts & Minds, Jim Lehrer News Hour. *Films:* Architects of Victory, Good Will Hunting. *Publications:* The John Fogerty Interview, Liner notes for Stevie Wonder, Music, Cognition and Computerized Sounds, The Billboard Encyclopedia of Record Producers, This is Your Brain on Music: Understanding a Human Obsession 2007, The World in Six Songs: How the Musical Brain Created Human Nature 2008. *Honours:* Gold Medal for Best Soundtrack, Venice Film Festival 1986; 14 RIAA Gold or Platinum Records. *Address:* Department of Psychology, McGill University, 1205 Avenue Penfield, Montreal, QC H3A 1B1, Canada (office). *Telephone:* (514) 398-6080 (office). *Fax:* (514) 398-4896 (office). *E-mail:* daniel.levitin@mcgill.ca (office). *Website:* www.psych.mcgill.ca/levitin (office).

LEVOX, Gary; American musician and songwriter; b. 10 July 1970, Columbus, OH; two c. *Career:* founder mem., Rascal Flatts 1999–. *Recordings include:* albums: Rascal Flatts 2000, Melt 2002, Feels Like Today 2004, Me and My Gang 2006, Still Feels Good 2007, Unstoppable 2009. *Honours:* CMA Horizon Award 2002, CMA Awards for Best Vocal Group 2003, 2004, 2005, 2006, 2007, 2008, ACM Awards for Best New Vocal Group 2001, for Best Vocal Group 2002, 2003, 2004, 2005, 2006, 2007, 2008, 2009, and for Song of the Year (for I'm Movin' On), ASCAP Vocal Group of the Year 2004, American Music Award for Favorite Country Band, Duo or Group 2006, 2007, 2008, 2009, CMT Group Music Video of the Year Award 2003, 2004, 2005, 2006, 2007, 2008, Radio Music Award Country Song of the Year for "God Bless Broken Road" 2005, People's Choice Award for Favourite Remake for "Life is a Highway" 2007, People's Choice Award for Favourite Song from a Movie for "Life is a Highway" 2007. *Current Management:* William Morris Agency, 1600 Division Street, Suite 300, Nashville, TN 37203, USA. *Website:* www.wma.com; www.rascalflatts.com.

LEVY, Alain M., MBA; French record company executive; *Executive Chairman, Algean Group;* b. 19 Dec. 1946. *Education:* Ecole des Mines, Univ. of Pennsylvania, USA. *Career:* Asst to the Pres. CBS Int., New York 1972–73, Vice-Pres. Marketing for Europe, Paris 1973, Vice-Pres. of Creative Operations for Europe, also Man. CBS Italy 1978; Man. Dir CBS Disques, France 1979–84, CEO PolyGram France 1984–88, Exec. Vice-Pres. PolyGram Group, France and FRG 1988–90, Man. US Operations PolyGram Group 1990–98, Pres., CEO, mem. Bd Man. PolyGram USA 1991–98; mem. Group Man. Cttee Philips Electronics, majority shareholder PolyGram USA 1991–98; Chair. Bd EMI Group PLC 2001–07, Chair. and CEO EMI Recorded Music 2001–07; Sr Advisor to Banijay 2008–09; Exec. Chair., Algean Group 2013–; mem. advisory bd Film Business Academy 2006–. *Address:* c/o Algean Group, 19 Portland Place, London, W1B 1PX (office); c/o Film Business Academy, Cass Business School, 106 Bunhill Row, London, EC1Y 8TZ, England (office). *E-mail:* info@algeangroup.com (office). *Website:* www.algeangroup.com (office).

LEVY, Andrew; British musician (bass); b. 20 July 1966, Ealing, London, England. *Career:* founder mem. The Brand New Heavies; worked with numerous vocalists including Jaye Ella Ruth, N'Dea Davenport, Siedah Garrett and Carleen Anderson; numerous television appearances and live dates, including club dates. *Recordings:* Singles: Stay This Way, 1991; Never Stop, 1991; Dream Come True, 1991; Don't Let It Go To Your Head, 1992; Spend Some Time, 1994; Dream on Dreamer, 1994; Back To Love, 1994; Midnight At The Oasis, 1994; Mind Trips, 1995; Close To You, 1995; You've Got A Friend, 1997; You Are the Universe, 1997; Sometimes, 1997; Shelter, 1998; Albums: The Brand New Heavies, 1990; The Brand New Heavies, 1992; Heavy Rhyme Experience, 1992; Brother Sister, 1994; Original Flava, 1994; Excursions, 1995; Shelter, 1997. *Address:* c/o Delicious Vinyl, 6607 Sunset Boulevard, Los Angeles, CA 90028, USA. *E-mail:* dvinyl@deliciousvinyl.com. *Website:* deliciousvinyl.com.

LÉVY, Jean-Bernard; French business executive; *Chairman and CEO, EDF Group;* b. 18 March 1955. *Education:* École Polytechnique, École Nationale Supérieure des Télécommunications. *Career:* engineer with France Telecom 1978–86; Tech. Adviser to Minister for Postal Services and Telecommunications 1986–88; Gen. Man. Communication Satellites, Matra Marconi Space 1988–93; Chief of Staff to Minister for Industry, Postal Services, Telecommunications and Foreign Trade 1993–94; Chair. and CEO Matra Communication (Lagardère Group) 1995–98; Man. Partner, Corp. Finance, Oddo Pinatton (equities broker) 1998–2002; COO Vivendi Universal (now Vivendi) 2002–05, Chair. Man. Bd and CEO 2005–12 (resgnd); CEO, Thales Group 2012–14; CEO EDF Group 2014–; mem. Bd of Dirs, Société Générale, Institut Pasteur. *Honours:* Officier, Légion d'honneur, Ordre nat. du Mérite. *Address:* EDF Group, 22–30 avenue Wagram, 75382 Paris, Cedex 8, France (office). *Telephone:* 1-40-42-22-22 (office). *Fax:* 1-40-42-89-00 (office). *E-mail:* info@edf.fr (office). *Website:* www.edf.fr/groupe-edf (office).

LEVY, Rick, BA; American musician (guitar), songwriter and manager; *President, Rick Levy Management;* b. 1 Nov. 1949, Allentown, PA; m. (divorced); one s. *Education:* Univ. of Pennsylvania, Moravian Coll., Berklee Coll. of Music, Boston. *Career:* toured USA with Jay and The Techniques 1985–; Man., Jay and The Techniques; The Box Tops; performed at Rock 'n' Roll Hall of Fame, Sept. 1996; bandleader, Peter Noone and Herman's Hermits 2000–01; Pres., Rick Levy Management, Flying Governor Music, Luxury Records; mem. NARAS. *Compositions:* Rock Roots, History of American Pop Music. *Recordings:* Love's Just Not For Sale, Ricochet Waltz, The Limits, Songs About Girls, The Earley Daze 1965–68, The Main Course (Jay and The Techniques). *Honours:* Penna-Broadcasters Asscn, Rock Roots, Best Single, Children's Program 1992. *Address:* Rick Levy Management, 4250 A1A S, D-11 Street, Augustine, FL 32084, USA (office). *Telephone:* (904) 806-0817 (office). *Fax:* (904) 460-1226 (office). *E-mail:* rick@ricklevy.com (office). *Website:* www.ricklevy.com.

LEVY, Yasmin; Israeli singer and songwriter; b. 23 Dec. 1975, Jerusalem; d. of Itzhak Levy and Kochava Levy; m. Ishay Amir; one s. one d. *Career:* singer of Sephardic music; also sings Flamenco, Turkish music, Ladino, Persian music and combinations of them; festival appearances include WOMAD (six appearances around the world, including Singapore and UK), Spina, Forum Barcelona; has performed at New York's Carnegie Hall, Sydney Opera House and the Barbican, London; worldwide tour 2009–13; collaborations with Conche Buika, Omar Faruk Tekbilek, Enrico Macias, Yiannis Kotsiras, Eleni Vitaly, Natacha Atlas, Montse Kortes, Kubat, Ibrahim Tetlises and Maria Toledo. *Films:* Ladino 500 Years Young 2005, Music Mon Amour 2010. *Recordings:* Romance & Yasmin 2002, La Judería 2004, Live at the Tower of David, Jerusalem 2006, Mano Suave 2007, Sentir 2009, Libertad 2012, Tango 2014. *Publication:* Yasmin Levy Songbook 2011. *Honours:* Anna Lindh Euro-Mediterranean Foundation Award, Winner, USA Songwriter's Competition (World Music). *Current Management:* c/o Soho Artists, 18 Broadwick Street, London, W1F 8HS, England. *Telephone:* (20) 7434-0008. *Fax:* (20) 7434-0061. *E-mail:* paul@sohoartists.co.uk. *Website:* www.sohoartists.co.uk; www.yasminlevy.net.

LEWIN, Giles; British musician (fiddle, medieval bagpipes, recorders, shawm) and singer; b. Rayleigh, Essex, England. *Education:* Univ. of Cambridge. *Career:* mem., The Dufay Collective; plays with: The New London Consort; The Chuckerbutty Ocarina Quartet; Lost Jockey; Afterhours; Music Dir, The Medieval Players, tours worldwide; student of Egyptian Fiddle styles and culture; mem., The Carnival Band, 1984–; appearances include: Glasgow Cathedral; Birmingham Symphony Hall; Barbican Centre; numerous arts theatres and festivals; plays material from: Sweden; Croatia; USA; Bolivia; Spain; UK; France. *Website:* www.carnivalband.com.

LEWIS, Aaron; American singer; b. 13 April 1972; m. Vanessa. *Career:* fmr mem., The Geckoes; Founder mem., Staind 1995–. *Recordings include:* albums: Tormented 1996, Dysfunction 1999, Break The Cycle 2001, 14 Shades of Grey 2003, Chapter V 2005, The Illusion of Progress 2008. *Honours:* VH-1 'Your Song Kicked Ass But Was Played Too Damn Much' Award 2001. *Current Management:* c/o Ken Fermaglich, The Agency Group, 142 West 57th Street, Sixth Floor, New York, NY 10019, USA. *E-mail:* KenFermaglich@theagencygroup.com. *Website:* www.aaronlewismusic.com; www.staind.com.

LEWIS, Richard Keith (Cass); British musician (bass guitar); b. 1 Sept. 1960, London. *Career:* founder mem., Skunk Anansie 1994–2001, 2009–; numerous headlining tours, festival appearances, television and radio shows. *Recordings include:* albums: Paranoid and Sunburnt 1995, Stoosh 1996, Post Orgasmic Chill 1999, Smashes and Trashes 2009, Wonderlustre 2010. *Website:* www.skunkanansie.net.

LEWIS, David A. R.; British songwriter, composer and musician (guitar); b. 15 Feb. 1964, Morecambe, Lancashire; m. Andrea Lewis 1992. *Education:* J. L. Acad. *Career:* numerous television appearances, extensive touring throughout UK; mem. Musicians' Union. *Compositions include:* Independence Day, The Other Side, This Is England, Sunday, Revolution. *Recordings:* Jerusalem, Maralyn, Treason.

LEWIS, Donna; British singer and songwriter; b. Cardiff; one s. *Education:* Welsh Coll. of Music and Drama. *Career:* began performing in local bands to develop her singing and songwriting talents; worked solo (piano/vocal) in piano bars across UK and Europe 1990. *Film:* featured on soundtrack to 'Anastasia' (with the song At The Beginning). *Recordings include:* albums: Now In A Minute 1996, Blue Planet 1998, Be Still 2002, In The Pink 2006. *E-mail:* fanmail@donnalewis.com. *Website:* www.donnalewis.com.

LEWIS, George Emanuel, BA; American musician (trombone) and composer; *Edwin H. Case Professor of American Music, Columbia University;* b. 14 July 1952, Chicago, IL. *Education:* Walter Scott School, Chicago, Univ. of Chicago Laboratory School, Chicago, Yale Univ., School of the Asscn for the Advancement of Creative Musicians, Chicago. *Career:* played with Fred Anderson Sextet 1974–77; founder mem., quartet Quadrisect 1975–77; played with the Morris Ellis Orchestra 1976, Anthony Braxton Quartet, Duo and Big Band 1976–80, 1980–, Art Ensemble of Chicago 1977, Carla Bley Orchestra 1977, Sam Rivers Big Band 1977–78; Chair., Asscn for the Advancement of Creative Musicians 1975; duo concerts with Richard Teitelbaum 1977–; Music Curator, Kitchen Center for Video, Music, Dance and Performance, New York 1980–82; Lecturer, Royal Conservatory, The Hague, Netherlands 1985–86, School of the Art Inst., Chicago 1989–91, Simon Fraser Univ., BC, Canada 1993–95; Prof., Music Dept, Univ. of California at San Diego 1991–2004; Edwin H. Case Prof. of American Music, Columbia Univ. 2004–; taken part in numerous workshops; mem. New York Foundation on the Arts (bd of govs 1986), Roulette Intermedium, New York (bd mem. 1991–), Harvestworks/Pass, New York (bd mem. 1991–), American Music Center (bd mem. 1994–), Western Front, Vancouver, BC, Canada (hon. bd mem. 1996–), Spruce Street Forum, San Diego, CA (pres. of bd 1997–). *Compositions include:* Music for Trombone and Soprano Saxophone 1974. *Recordings include:* Solo Trombone Album 1976, George Lewis Solo Trombone Records 1977, Shadowgraph 1977, George Lewis/Douglas Ewart 1978, Homage to Charles Parker 1979, Jila-Save! Mon.: The Imaginary Suite 1979, Chicago Slow Dance 1981, Changing With The Times 1993, Voyager 1993, Conversations 1998, The Usual Turmoil and Other Duets 1998, Endless Shout 2000, The Shadowgraph Series 2003, Sequel 2006. *Honours:* NEA Fellowships 1976, 1979, 1989, 1990, 1992, Alpert Award in the Arts 1999, MacArthur Fellowship 2002. *Address:* Department of Music, Columbia University, 615 Dodge Hall, MC 1814, 2960 Broadway, New York, NY 10027, USA (office). *Telephone:* (212) 854-5837 (office). *E-mail:* gl2140@columbia.edu (office). *Website:* music.columbia.edu/people/bios/lewis-george (office).

LEWIS, Huey; American singer, songwriter, musician and actor; b. (Hugh Anthony Cregg III), 5 July 1950, New York, NY. *Career:* mem., Clover 1976–79; founder mem., Huey Lewis & The News 1979–; numerous tours and festival appearances. *Films:* Back to the Future 1985, Short Cuts 1993, Land of Milk and Honey 1996, Sphere 1998, Shadow of Doubt 1998, Dead Husbands (TV) 1998, Duets 2000, .com for Murder 2002, What Happens in Vegas 2008. *Theatre:* Chicago (as Billy Flynn, Broadway) 2005. *Recordings include:* albums: with Clover: Clover 1977, Love On The Wire 1977; with Huey Lewis & The News: Huey Lewis & The News 1980, Picture This 1982, Sports 1983, Fore! 1986, Small World 1988, Hard At Play 1991, Four Chords & Several Years Ago 1994, Plan B 2001, Live At 25 2005, Soulsville 2010. *Honours:* American Music Award for Favorite Single 1986, Favorite Band 1987, British Music Award for Best Int. Group 1986. *E-mail:* admin@hueylewis.com (office). *Website:* www.hueylewis.com.

LEWIS, Jennifer Diane (Jenny); American singer, songwriter and musician (keyboards, guitar, harmonica); b. 8 Jan. 1976, Las Vegas, Nev. *Career:* film and TV actor 1986–98; Founder mem. Rilo Kiley 1998–2011; also solo artist 2006–; mem. Jenny and Johnny (with Johnathan Rice); other collaborations include Cursive, Dritel, Elvis Costello, Brandon Flowers. *Films:* as actor: Trading Hearts 1988, Troop Beverly Hills 1989, The Wizard 1989, Big Girls Don't Cry... They Get Even 1992, Foxfire 1996, Little Boy Blue 1997, Pleasantville 1998, Don's Plum 2001. *Television:* as actor: TV movies: Suburban Beat 1985, Convicted 1986, Uncle Tom's Cabin 1987, A Place at the Table 1988, Who Gets the Friends? 1988, Baby M 1988, My Father, My Son 1988, A Friendship in Vienna 1988, Shannon's Deal 1989, Perry Mason: The Case of the Defiant Daughter 1990, Line of Fire: The Morris Dees Story 1991, Runaway Father 1991, Daddy 1991, Runaway Daughters 1994, Sweet Temptation 1996, Talk to Me 1996; TV series appearances: Life with Lucy 1986, The Golden Girls 1987, The Charmings 1987, Mr Belvedere 1988; Growing Pains 1988, Just the Ten of Us 1989, Roseanne 1989, Free Spirit 1989, Baywatch 1989, Shannon's Deal 1990–91, Brooklyn Bridge 1991–92, Murder She Wrote 1994, Get Real 1999, Once and Again 2000. *Recordings:* albums: with Rilo Kiley: Take Offs and Landings 2001, The Execution of All Things 2002, More Adventurous 2004, Under the Blacklight 2007, as Jenny Lewis and The Watson Twins: Rabbit Fur Coat 2006; solo: Acid Tongue 2008, The Voyager 2014; as Jenny and Johnny: I'm Having Fun Now 2010; has also performed on: Give Up, The Postal Service 2003, Ugly Organ, Cursive 2003, District Sleeps Alone Tonight, The Postal Service 2003, Album of the Year, The Good Life 2004, We Will Become Silhouettes, The Postal Service 2005, Awake is the New Sleep, Ben Lee 2005, Sun, Sun, Sun, The Elected 2006, Dumb Luck, Dritel 2007, Further North, Johnathan Rice 2007, Momofuku, Elvis Costello 2008, The Way That It Was, Pierre de Reeder 2008, Swim, The Whispertown 2000 2008, Flamingo, Brandon Flowers 2010. *Current Management:* c/o Jessica Massa, Press Here Publicity, 138 West 25th Street, 9th Floor, New York,, NY 10001, USA. *Telephone:* (212) 246-2640. *Fax:* (212) 582-6513. *E-mail:* jessica@pressherepublicity.com. *Website:* www.pressherepublicity.com. *Address:* c/o Brant Weil, Warner Bros. Records Inc., 3300 Warner Boulevard, Burbank, CA 91505-4694, USA (office). *E-mail:* brant.weil@wbr.com (office). *Website:* www.warnerbrosrecords.com (office); www.jennylewis.com; jennyandjohnnymusic.com; www.rilokiley.com.

LEWIS, Jerry Lee; American rock singer and musician (piano); b. 29 Sept. 1935, Ferriday, La; m. 6th Kerrie Lynn McCarver Lewis 1984 (divorced 2005); two s. (one deceased); one d.; m. 7th Judith Brown 2012. *Education:* Waxahachie Bible Inst., Texas. *Career:* numerous concert tours, festival appearances. *Films include:* Jamboree 1957, High School Confidential 1958, Be My Guest 1965. *Theatre includes:* Iago in Catch My Soul. *Recordings include:* albums: Jerry Lee Lewis 1957, Jerry Lee's Greatest 1961, Live At The Star Club 1965, The Greatest Live Show On Earth 1965, The Return Of Rock 1965, Whole Lotta Shakin' Goin' On 1965, Country Songs For City Folks 1965, By Request – More Greatest Live Show On Earth 1967, Breathless 1967, Together (with Linda Gail Lewis) 1970, Rockin' Rhythm And Blues 1971, Sunday Down South (with Johnny Cash) 1972, The Session (with Peter Frampton and Rory Gallagher) 1973, Jerry Lee Lewis 1979, When Two Worlds Collide 1980, My Fingers Do The Talking 1983, I Am What I Am 1984, Keep Your Hands Off It 1987, Don't Drop It 1988, Great Balls of Fire! (film soundtrack) 1989, Rocket 1990, Young Blood 1995, Keep Your Eyes Off Of It 2000, By Invitation Only 2000, Last Man Standing 2006, Mean Old Man 2010. *Current Management:* c/o Al Embry International, PO Box 206, Old Hickory, TN 37138, USA. *Telephone:* (615) 847-0123. *E-mail:* alembrymusic@aol.com. *Website:* alembryinternational.com. *Address:* The Lewis Ranch, Box 384, Nesbit, MS 38651, USA (office). *E-mail:* phoebemedia@aol.com (office). *Website:* www.jerryleelewis.com.

LEWIS, Juliette; American film actress and musician; b. 21 June 1973, Los Angeles, Calif.; d. of Geoffrey Lewis and Glenis Batley Lewis; m. Steve Berra 1999 (divorced 2003). *Career:* f. band Juliette & The Licks 2003–09. *Films include:* My Stepmother is an Alien 1988, Meet the Hollowheads 1989, National Lampoon's Christmas Vacation 1989, Cape Fear 1991, Crooked Hearts 1991, Husbands and Wives 1992, Kalifornia 1993, One Hot Summer, That Night 1993, What's Eating Gilbert Grape 1993, Romeo is Bleeding 1994, Natural Born Killers 1994, Mixed Nuts 1994, The Basketball Diaries 1995, Strange Days 1995, From Dusk Till Dawn 1996, The Evening Star 1996, The Audition, Full Tilt Boogie 1997, The Other Sister 1999, The 4th Floor 1999, Way of the Gun 2000, My Louisiana Sky 2001, Hysterical Blindness 2002, Enough 2002, Gaudi Afternoon 2003, Old School 2003, Cold Creek Manor 2003, Blueberry 2004, Starsky and Hutch 2004, Aurora Borealis 2005, Daltry Calhoun 2005, Lightfield's Home Videos 2006, The Darwin Awards 2006, Grilled 2006, Catch and Release 2006, Whip It! 2009, Sympathy for Delicious 2010, The Switch 2010, Conviction 2010, Due Date 2010, Hick 2011, August: Osage County 2013, Helion 2014, Kelly and Cal 2014. *Television appearances include:* Homefires (mini-series), I Married Dora 1988, Too Young To Die (movie) 1989, A Family For Joe 1990, The Firm (series) 2012, Secrets and Lies (series) 2015–, Wayward Pines (series) 2015. *Theatre:* Fool for Love (Apollo Theatre, London) 2006. *Recordings include:* albums: You're Speaking My Language 2005, Four on the Floor 2006, Terra Incognita 2009. *Honours:* Chicago Film Critics' Asscn Most Promising Actress 1991, NATO/ShoNest Female Star of Tomorrow 1993, Venice Film Festival Pasinetti Prize 1994. *Website:* www.juliettelewis.com; www.julietteandthelicks.com.

LEWIS, Laurie; American musician (fiddle, guitar, bass), singer and songwriter; b. 28 Sept. 1950, Long Beach, Calif. *Education:* traditional knowledge, skills passed on within folk/old time music community in oral tradition. *Career:* performing, touring nationally, internationally since early 1970s; TV appearances include Music City Tonight, The Grand Ole Opry, The American Music Show, Lonesome Pine Specials, PBS, Later with Jools, Prairie Home Companion, Mountain Stage, World Cafe; mem. The American Soc. of Composers, Authors and Publrs (ASCAP), Int. Bluegrass Music Asscn. *Recordings:* Restless Rambling Heart, Love Chooses You, Singing My Troubles Away, Together (with Kathy Kallick), True Stories, The Oak and The Laurel (with Tom Rozum), Earth and Sky: Songs of Laurie Lewis, Seeing Things, Blue Rose (with Cathy Fink, Marcy Marxer, Sally Van Meter, Molly Mason), Winter's Grace (with Tom Rozum) 1999, Laurie Lewis and her Bluegrass Pals 1999, Kristin's Story 2001, Guest House (with Tom Rozum) 2004, The Golden West (with the Right Hands) 2006, Blossoms 2010, Skippin' and Flyin' 2011, One Evening in May 2013. *Honours:* NAIRD Award for Best Country Album, IBMA Awards for Female Vocalist of the Year 1992, 1994, for Song of the Year 1994, FAR-West Lifetime Achievement Award 2011. *Address:* c/o Spruce and Maple Music, PO Box 9417, Berkeley, CA 94709–0417, USA. *E-mail:* laurie@laurielewis.com. *Website:* www.laurielewis.com.

LEWIS, Leona; British singer and songwriter; b. 3 April 1985, London; d. of Aural Josiah Lewis and Maria Lewis. *Education:* Sylvia Young Theatre School, The BRIT School. *Career:* TV X Factor contestant and winner 2006; solo artist 2007–. *Films:* Walking on Sunshine 2014. *Recordings include:* albums: Spirit (MOBO Award for Best Album 2008) 2007, Echo 2009, Glassheart 2012, Christmas, With Love 2013, Leona Lewis, I Am 2015. *Honours:* Ivor Novello Award for Best Selling British Single (for A Moment Like This) 2007, MTV Asia Award for Breakthrough Artist 2008, MOBO Award for Best Video (for Bleeding Love) 2008, World Music Awards for Best Pop Female Artist 2008, for Best New Artist 2008, for Best R'n'B Artist 2008. *Current Management:* c/o Red Light Management, Ground, 10–16 Scrutton Street, London, EC2A 4RU, England. *Telephone:* (20) 7737-4320. *Website:* redlightmanagement.com; www.leonalewismusic.co.uk.

LEWIS, Linda; British singer, songwriter and musician (guitar, piano); b. 27 Sept. 1953, London, England; m. Jim Cregan 1977 (divorced); one s. *Education:* Peggy O'Farrels Stage School. *Career:* solo artist; toured with Cat Stevens, Elton John and Richie Havens 1970s; numerous festival and television appearances; mem. PRS, Equity, PAMRA. *Recordings include:* albums: Say No More 1971, Lark 1972, Fathoms Deep 1973, Heart Strings 1974, Not a Little Girl Any More 1975, 2 Originals 1976, Woman Overboard 1977, Hacienda View 1979, A Tear and a Smile 1983, Second Nature 1995, Born Performer 1996, Whatever 1997, Kiss of Life 1999, Reprise Years 2002, Legends 2005. *Honours:* Saturday Scene British Pop Award 1975. *E-mail:* contact@lindalewis.co.uk. *Website:* www.lindalewis.co.uk.

LEWIS, Luke; American record company executive; CEO, *Lost Highway Records. Career:* Head of Mercury Nashville 1992–; founder, CEO, Lost Highway Records, as part of Universal Music Group 2001–; worked with Ryan Adams, Kim Richey, Shania Twain, Lucinda Williams. *Honours:* Grammy Award (with Bonnie Garner and Mary Martin) for Best Country Album (for Timeless: Hank Williams Tribute) 2001. *Address:* Lost Highway Records, Universal Music Group, 60 Music Square E, Nashville, TN 37203, USA (office). *Telephone:* (615) 524-7500 (office). *Fax:* (615) 524-7600 (office). *E-mail:* losthighwayfeedback@umusic.com (office). *Website:* www.losthighwayrecords.com (office).

LEWIS, Mike; Welsh musician (guitar). *Career:* mem. rock band, Lostprophets 1997–2013, No Devotion 2014–. *Recordings include:* albums: thefakesoundofprogress 2000, Start Something 2004, Liberation Transmission 2006, The Betrayed 2010, Permanence 2015. *Honours:* Kerrang! Award for Best British Band 2007. *Website:* www.nodevotion.com.

LEWIS, Pamela; American PR, marketing consultant, media executive and event planner; b. 23 Nov. 1958, Rhinebeck, New York. *Education:* BA, Wells College; Practitioner, Religious Science International; Leadership Music. *Career:* CEO, founder, PLA Media, Los Angeles, Nashville; NBC Specials: This Is Garth Brooks; This Is Garth Brooks Too; 7-year career as manager to Garth Brooks, including International World Tour, 1993–94; mem, Country Music Assccn; Academy of Country Music; Blair School of Music; Belmont School of Music. *Publications:* Dan Rivers Poetry Anthology; American Poetry Anthology. *Honours:* CMA Manager of Year, 1991; Pollstar Manager of the Year, 1991, 1992; Performance Manager of Year, 1993. *Address:* c/o PLA Media, 1303 16th Avenue South, Nashville, TN 37212, USA. *Telephone:* (615) 327-0100. *Fax:* (615) 320-1061. *E-mail:* info@plamedia.com. *Website:* www.plamedia.com.

LEWIS, Ramsey E., Jr; American musician (piano) and composer; b. 27 May 1935, Chicago, Illinois; m. Janet Tamillon 1990; five s. two d. (from previous marriage). *Education:* studied piano with Dorothy Mendelsohn, Chicago Musical College. *Career:* joined local jazz band, The Cleffs aged 15; f. The Ramsey Lewis Trio; performed, nightclubs, concerts, festivals, in USA, Canada, Western Europe, Japan, Mexico, The Caribbean 1957–; Artistic Dir, Ravinia Festival Jazz Series 1992–; Art Tatum Prof. of Jazz Studies, Roosevelt Univ. 1999–2001; co-f. LRSmedia (music entertainment co.) 2003–; began composing 2005–; est. Ramsey Lewis Foundation 2005–. *Radio:* presenter, The Ramsey Lewis Morning Show (WNUA-FM). *Compositions:* To Know Her (ballet) 2005, Muses and Amusements 2008, Proclamation of Hope: A Symphonic Poem 2009. *Recordings include:* albums: Ramsey Lewis and the Gentlemen of Swing 1956, Gentlemen of Jazz 1958, Lem Winchester with the Ramsey Lewis Trio 1958, Down to Earth 1959, Stretching Out 1960, More from the Soil 1961, Never on Sunday 1961, Sounds of Christmas 1961, Bossa Nova 1962, The Sound of Spring 1962, Pot Luck 1963, Barefoot Sunday Blues 1963, Bach to the Blues 1964, More Sounds of Christmas 1964, At the Bohemian Caverns 1964, Country Meets the Blues 1965, The In Crowd 1965, Wade in the Water 1966, The Movie Album 1966, Goin' Latin 1967, Dancing in the Street 1967, Up Pops Ramsey 1967, Maiden Voyage 1968, Mother Nature's Song 1968, Another Voyage 1969, The Piano Player 1969, Them Changes 1970, Back to the Roots 1971, Upendo Ni Pamoja 1972, Funky Serenity 1973, Solar Wind 1974, Sun Goddess 1974, Don't It Feel Good 1975, Salongo 1976, Love Notes 1977, Tequila Mockingbird 1977, Legacy 1978, Ramsey 1979, Routes 1980, Blues for the Night Owl 1981, Three Piece Suite 1981, Chance Encounter 1982, Les Fleurs 1983, Reunion 1983, The Two of Us 1984, Fantasy 1985, Keys to the City 1987, A Classic Encounter 1988, We Meet Again 1989, Urban Renewal 1989, Electric Collection 1991, Ivory Pyramid 1992, Sky Islands 1993, Urban Knights 1995, Between the Keys 1996, Dance of the Soul 1998, Appassionata 1999, Mean to Be 2002, Time Flies 2004, Ramsey Lewis Love Songs 2004, With One Voice (Stellar Award for Best Gospel Instrumental Album) 2005, Songs from the Heart: Ramsey plays Ramsey 2009. *Honours:* Dr hc (Depaul Univ.) 1993, (Univ. of Illinois) 1995, (Univ. of South Carolina)

2000, (St Xavier Univ.) 2001, (Loyola Univ.) 2008; three Grammy Awards 1965, 1966, 1973, White House State Dinner Performance 1995, Lifetime Achievement Award, Roosevelt Univ. 1996, Naras Award 2000, Nat. Endowment for the Arts Jazz Masters Award 2007. *Current Management:* c/o Jack Randall, Ted Kurland Agency, 173 Brighton Avenue, Boston, MA 02134, USA. *Telephone:* (617) 254-0007. *Fax:* (617) 782-3577. *E-mail:* jack@tedkurland .com. *Website:* www.tedkurland.com. *E-mail:* info@ramseylewis.com (office). *Website:* www.ramseylewis.com.

LEWIS, Ronald Chapman; musician (guitar), songwriter and music publisher; b. 20 Aug. 1950, Louisville, KY, USA; m. LaQuetta Wilson 1972, two s. *Education:* JCC Univ. School of Music, Louisville, KY. *Career:* BMI songwriter and publisher; cable TV host, music historian, Univ. of Louisville, Univ. Archives and Records Center. *Stage:* performed in The Abbey Road on the River show, Louisville. *Compositions:* When the Spirit of the Lord, Spraggie; songwriter for Tanita Gaines (on Another City Day album), for Women in Music DVD. *Recordings:* Spraggie, Hanlon Robinson, Swindell Brothers. *Honours:* Billboard Magazine Up-and-Coming Songwriter's Award. *Current Management:* Mr Wonderful Productions, 1730 Kennedy Road, Louisville, KY 40216, USA.

LEWIS, Ryan S.; American DJ, musician and record producer; b. 25 March 1988, Spokane, Wash. *Education:* Roosevelt High School, Seattle, Wash., Univ. of Washington. *Career:* fmr producer for rapper Symmetry; formed duo with rapper Macklemore 2008–; released own solo EP Instrumentals 2009. *Recordings include:* as producer: with Macklemore: The VS. EP 2009, The Heist (American Music Award for Best Album 2013, Grammy Award for Best Rap Album 2014) 2012. *Honours:* with Macklemore: BET Award for Best Group 2013, Billboard Music Awards for Rap Song of the Year (for Thrift Shop) 2013, (for Can't Hold Us) 2014, MTV Video Music Awards for Best Hip-Hop Video (for Can't Hold Us) 2013, for Best Video with a Message (for Same Love) 2013, for Best New Act 2013, mtvU Branching Out Woodie Award 2013, MuchMusic Video Award for Int. Video of the Year – Group (for Thrift Shop) 2013, Teen Choice Music Awards for Hip-Hop/Rap Artist 2013, for R&B/Hip-Hop Track (for Can't Hold Us) 2013, American Music Award for Favorite Rap/Hip-Hop Artist 2013, Grammy Awards for Best Rap Performance, for Best Rap Song (both for Thrift Shop) 2014, for Best New Artist 2014, MTV Europe Music Award for Best Video (for Downtown) 2015. *Current Management:* Zach Quillen, The Agency Group Ltd., 142 West 57th Street, 6th Floor, New York, NY 10019, USA. *Telephone:* (212) 581-3100. *Fax:* (212) 581-0015. *E-mail:* zachquillen@theagencygroup.com. *Website:* www.theagencygroup.com; www .macklemore.com.

LEWIS, Shaznay T.; British singer and songwriter; b. 14 Oct. 1977, England. *Career:* founder mem., female vocal group All Saints 1993–2001, 2006–; solo artist 2004–05. *Recordings include:* albums: with All Saints: All Saints 1997, Saints and Sinners 2000, Studio 1 2006; solo: Open 2004. *Honours:* BRIT Award for Best Single (for Never Ever) 1998. *Current Management:* c/o Fascination Management, 1st Floor, 6 South Hill Park, London, NW3 2SB, England. *Telephone:* (20) 7586-6457. *E-mail:* info@fascinationmanagement .com. *Website:* www.fascinationmanagement.com.

LEWIS, Terry; American producer, songwriter and musician (bass); b. 21 Nov. 1956, Omaha, Neb. *Career:* Founder mem., Flyte Tyme (with Jimmy Jam) 1972, renamed Time 1981–83; co-founder, Flyte Time Productions Inc. 1982–, built Flyte Tyme Studios, Minneapolis 1984–; co-founder, Third Eye Imagery Inc. 1987–, the parent co. of Perspective Records 1989–, and Flyte Tyme Records 1997–; co-founder, Flyte Tyme Tunes to publish songs written by the duo 1984–, Help The Bear Music Inc. (1989–) to publish songs written by BMI writers signed with them, New Perspective Publishing Inc. (1990–) to publish songs written by ASCAP writers signed with them, and Minneapolis Guys Music Inc. (1997–) to publish songs written by ASCAP writer James 'Big Jim' Wright and signed to them; co-founder, Lewis & Harris Partnership real estate co. 1985–; involved with International. Asscn of African American Music (IAAAM) 1990–; producer for artists, including Klymaxx, SOS Band, Patti Austin, Cheryl Lynn, Cherelle, Janet Jackson, Mint Condition, Low Key, George Michael, Karyn White, Boyz II Men, Johnny Gill, Fine Young Cannibals, New Edition, Mariah Carey, Shaggy, Yolanda Adams, Chante Moore, Mary J. Blige, The Human League, The Isley Brothers. *Honours:* Grammy Award for Producer of the Year 1986, American Soc. of Composers and Publishers R&B Songwriting Awards 1989–94. *Website:* www.flytetyme .com.

LEYERS, Jan; Belgian singer, musician (guitar, bass, keyboards) and composer; b. 16 May 1958, Antwerp. *Career:* mem. Soulsister; mem. SABAM (Belgian Soc. of Authors, Composers and Publrs). *Recordings include:* Soulsister: It Takes Two, Heat, Simple Rule, Live Savings, Swinging Like Big Dogs, Closer – My Velma: Exposed – Jan Leyers (solo). *Television includes:* De Weg Naar Mekka, De Weg Naar Het Avondland, Zomergasten (VPRO). *Honours:* World Music Award, Monaco 1990, Jozef Platteau 1991, BMI Country Award 1996, Golden Eye Awards 1992, 1993, Vlaamse TelevisieSter. *Address:* Mereldreef 3, 3140 Keerbergen, Belgium. *E-mail:* management@janleyers.be (office). *Website:* www.janleyers.be; www .soulsister.be.

LHASA (see de Sela, Lhasa)

LI, Yuchun, (Chris Lee); Chinese singer and actress; b. 10 March 1984, Chengdu, Sichuan. *Education:* Sichuan Music Conservatory. *Career:* winner,

Super Girl singing contest 2005; debut single 2005; several album releases 2006–; made screen debut as actress 2009; apptd Amb. for Chinese Red Cross Foundation 2006. *Films:* as actress: Bodyguards and Assassins 2009, The Flying Swords of Dragon Gate 2011. *Recordings include:* albums: The Queen and the Dreams 2006, Mine 2007, Youth of China 2008, Chris Lee 2009, The Formidable Dancing Artiste 2011, Old If Not Wild 2012. *Honours:* Metro Radio Hit Music Awards for Popularity Singer 2005, for Newcomer 2005, for King of New Singers 2005, MTV Super Festival Style Newcomer Award 2005, Chinese Music Media Award for Annual Artist 2006, Sprite Chinese Original Music Awards for Most Popular Mainland Artist 2006, for Best Performance 2006, for Most Popular Female Singer 2007, 2008, 2009, Beijing Pop Music Awards for Most Popular Female Singer 2007, 2008, 2009, for Most Popular New Singer 2007, for Golden Song (for Loving) 2007, (for Floating Subway) 2008, (for Poor Student) 2009, for Best Stage Performer 2009, MTV Asia Award for Favourite Artist for Mainland China 2008, Asia Song Festival for Best Asian Artist 2009, Mnet Asian Music Award for Best Asian Artist China 2012, MTV Europe Music Award for Best Worldwide Act 2013. *Address:* c/o EE Media, Hunan Broadcasting System, Shanghai, People's Republic of China (office). *Website:* www.eemedia.cn (office).

LIANA, BA; Canadian singer, songwriter and musician (guitar); b. (Liana C. Di Marco), 25 March 1966, Toronto, Ont. *Education:* private instruction with leading vocalists and instrumentalists. *Career:* played viola in two local orchestras prior to 1986; solo career as singer, songwriter 1988–; business ventures: LCDM Entertainments Productions, music label, and Indie Tips and The Arts, publications; mem. CCMA, SAC, Theatre Ontario, UGA. *Recordings include:* Glitters and Tumbles 1993, Amazon Trail 2000, I See No Rain 2007. *Publications:* Indie Tips and The Arts. *Honours:* Awards in Music, Journalism, French and Cinematography. *Website:* www.liana.biz.

LIBERTAD, Tania; Peruvian singer; b. Zaña. *Recordings include:* albums: Boleros Hoy 1991, México Lindo y Querido 1993, Boleros 1993, Africa en América 1994, Personalidad 1994, Libertad de Manzanero 1997, Libertad de Manzanero (with Armando Manzanero) 1997, Mujeres Apasionadas 1997, Amar Amando 1997, Tomate Esta Botella Conmigo 1998, Lo Mejor de Tania Libertad 2000, El Mismo Puerto 2000, Dos Románticos 2000, Concierto...: Libertad canta a J. A. Jiménez 2000, Tania Por Siempre 2001, Concierto Para Una Voz 2002, Costa Negra 2002, Momentos De Amor 2004, Negro Color 2004. *Honours:* UNESCO 'Singer of Peace'. *Current Management:* Mireyda Garcia, Circo 13, S.A. de C.V., México, Mexico. *Website:* www.tanialibertad.com.

LIBRA (see BT)

LIDDIARD, Brenda Christine; British writer, performer and musician (guitar, mandolin, keyboards); b. 14 Feb. 1950, Essex, England; m. Mark Clive Laurent 1990; one step-s. one d. *Education:* piano to Grade 6. *Career:* played in bands, duos, solos 1978–; major performances at UN Environmental Song Festival, Bangkok 1988, Concert for the Living Earth, Auckland 1989, QEII Arts Council six-week NZ tour 1990, Shelterbelt Festival 1993, Parachute Festival 1994, 1995, Garth Hewitt, UK support 1995, Auckland Folk Festival 1993–95, 1999; session player, recordings, concerts, tours; mem. NZ Composers' Foundation, Australasian Performing Right Asscn. *Recordings:* Land of Plenty, Spangled Drongoes 1985, Songs For Our Friends, with Mark Laurent 1989, Songs of Protest and Survival 1991, For The River, Save The Daintree, Heart Attack 1996, Millennium Hippies 1998, Trebox 2000, Background 2002, Spiritual Graffiti 2006. *Honours:* Winner, UN Asia Pacific Environmental Song Contest 1988. *Address:* 213 Tirohanga Drive, Moana Point, Whangamata 3620, New Zealand (office). *Telephone:* (7) 865-9910 (office). *E-mail:* brenda@brendaliddiard.co.nz (office). *Website:* www .brendaliddiard.co.nz.

LIDDIARD, Gareth; Australian singer and musician (guitar). *Career:* mem. and lead singer, The Drones 2001–. *Recordings include:* albums: Here Come the Lies 2002, Wait Long By the River & The Bodies of Your Enemies Will Float By (Australian Music Prize) 2005, The Miller's Daughter 2006, Gala Mill 2006, Havilah 2008. *Current Management:* One Louder, PO Box 989, Darlinghurst, NSW 1300, Australia. *Telephone:* (2) 9380-9011. *Fax:* (2) 9380-9866. *E-mail:* briese@onelouder.com.au. *Website:* www.onelouder.com .au; www.thedrones.com.au.

LIDELL, Jamie; British singer and musician; b. (Jamie Alexander Lidderdale), 18 Sept. 1973, Huntingdon, Cambs. *Education:* Univ. of Bristol. *Career:* fmr mem. Super_Collider; fmr guest vocalist with the Matthew Herbert Big Band; currently solo artist; numerous live performances. *Recordings include:* albums: with Super_Collider: Head On 1999, Raw Digits 2002; solo: Muddlin Gear 2000, Multiply 2005, Jim 2008, Compass 2010. *Current Management:* c/o Nathalie Blue, Primary Talent International, The Primary Building 10-11, Jockey's Fields, London, WC1R 4BN, England. *Website:* www.jamielidell.com.

LIEBMAN, David, BSc; American musician (saxophone), composer and teacher; *Lecturer, Manhattan School of Music Graduate Jazz Program;* b. 4 Sept. 1946, Brooklyn, NY; m. Caris Visentin 1986; one d. *Education:* New York Univ.; studied with Joseph Allard, Lennie Tristano and Charles Lloyd. *Career:* Artistic Dir and founder, International Asscn of School of Jazz; Lecturer, Manhattan School of Music Graduate Jazz Program; mem. BMI, Société de perception et de distribution des droits des artistes-interprètes de la musique et de la danse (SPEDIDAM), Gramex (copyright Soc.); mem. Bd of Advisers, Jazz Improv magazine. *Compositions:* 200 original compositions. *Recordings include:* On the Corner, Miles Davis, Live at the Lighthouse, Elvin Jones,

Lookout Farm, D Liebman, Homage To Coltrane, D Liebman, Long Distance Runner, D Liebman, West Side Story, D Liebman, New Vista, D Liebman, Water: Giver of Life, Meditation Suite, Time Immemorial 2001, Liebman Plays Puccini – A Walk In The Clouds 2001, The Unknown Jobim 2001, Conversation 2003, Colors 2003, Beyond the Line 2003, Gathering of Spirits 2004, Negative Space 2008, Lieb Plays Weill 2008, Turnaround 2009, Lieb Plays the Blues à la Trane 2010. *Publications:* Developing A Personal Saxophone Sound 1989, A Chromatic Approach to Jazz 1991, Self Portrait of a Jazz Artist 1996, Jazz Connections, Miles Davis and David Liebman 1996, On Education 2003. *Honours:* Dr hc (Sibelius Acad., Helsinki) 1997; Group Deserving of Wider Recognition Downbeat Magazine 1976, Composer Grant, Nat. Endowment of the Arts, Hall of Fame, Int. Asscn of Jazz Educators 2001, Nat. Endowment of the Arts Jazz Master Award 2011. *Current Management:* c/o Dave Love, Listen 2 Entertainment Group, PO Box 560285, Macedonia, OH 44056, USA. *Address:* Department of Jazz, Manhattan School of Music, 120 Claremont Avenue, New York, NY 10027, USA (office). *Website:* www .daveliebman.com.

LIEVEMAA, Tommi Tapani; Finnish musician (electric, acoustic guitar, mandolin); b. 10 Dec. 1966, Uusikaupunki. *Education:* Jyvaskyla School of Music, Guildhall School of Music and Drama, London. *Career:* touring with Ohilyönti 1986–93; with Dixie Fried 1987–92; tour with pop artist, Katri-Helena 1992; nat. jazz competition with Sale's Promotion 1986; int. jazz competition, Spain, Getxo, with John Crawford Group 1994; currently mem. Riverside Rascals; numerous television appearances, radio broadcasts; mem. Musicians' Union, London. *Recordings:* albums: with Dixie Fried: Dixie Fried 1988, Six Dicks of Dynamite 1990, New Deal 1991; with Ohilyonti: OHOH 1989, Himmeneuva Q 1989, Sandels On 1989, Markan Possu 1990, Soita Soita 1990, On Karhut Noussect Juhlimaan 1992, Ankkapaallikko Anna Liisa 1993; with R Keskinin and Co: Kapteeni 1993; charity album, Valaiskoon (with various Finnish stars) 1993. *Honours:* first prize Nat. Children's Song Contest, Finland 1990, 1991. *Current Management:* Jazzrytmit Agency, PO Box 141, 76101 Pieksamaki, Finland. *Telephone:* (15) 688886. *Fax:* (15) 688888.

LIFESON, Alex, OC; Canadian musician (guitar); b. 27 Aug. 1953, Fernie. *Career:* founder mem. of rock group, Rush 1969–; concerts and tours; mem. of side-project, Victor 1995–. *Recordings include:* albums: with Rush: Rush 1974, Fly By Night 1975, Caress of Steel 1975, 2112 1976, All the World's a Stage 1976, A Farewell to Kings 1977, Archives 1978, Hemispheres 1978, Permanent Waves 1980, Moving Pictures 1981, Exit... Stage Left 1981, Signals 1982, Grace Under Pressure 1984, Power Windows 1985, Hold Your Fire 1987, A Show of Hands 1988, Presto 1989, Chronicles 1990, Roll the Bones 1991, Counterparts 1993, Test for Echo 1996, Retrospective I 1997, Retrospective II 1997, Different Stages 1998, Vapor Trails 2002, The Spirit of Radio 2003, Rush in Rio 2003, Feedback 2004, R30 2005, Replay 2006, Snakes & Arrows 2007, Clockwork Angels 2012; with Victor: Victor 1996. *Honours:* Juno Awards for Most Promising Group 1975, Best Group 1978, 1979;Official Ambassadors of Music, Canadian Govt 1979. *E-mail:* info@rush.net. *Website:* www.rush.com.

LIGGINS, Len, BA; British singer, songwriter and musician (guitar, violin, bass); b. 9 Feb. 1957, London. *Education:* University of Leeds. *Career:* solo artist 1984–; lead singer, guitarist, The Sinister Cleaners 1984–87; lead singer, fiddle, balalaika and sopilka player, Ukrainian line-up of The Wedding Present 1987–89; lead singer, fiddle player, The Ukrainians 1991–. *Recordings:* albums: solo: A Remedy For Bad Nerves 1985; with The Sinister Cleaners: Lemon Meringue Bedsit 1985; with The Wedding Present: Ukrainski Vistupi V Johna Peela 1988; with The Ukrainians: The Ukrainians 1991, Pisni Iz The Smiths 1993, Vorony 1994, Kultura 1994, Drink to My Horse 2001, Respublika 2002, Istoriya 2004, Diaspora 2009. *Website:* www.the -ukrainians.com.

LIGHTBODY, Gary; Northern Irish singer, songwriter and musician (guitar); b. 15 June 1976, Bangor. *Education:* Campbell Coll., Univ. of Dundee. *Career:* Founder mem. Snow Patrol 1997–; mem. project, The Reindeer Section 2001–; Founder mem. Tired Pony 2009–; mem. Bd of Dirs Oh Yeah Music Centre. *Recordings include:* albums: with Snow Patrol: Songs For Polar Bears 1998, Little Hide 1998, One Night Is Not Enough 2001, When It's All Over We Still Have To Clear Up 2001, Final Straw (Meteor Ireland Music Award for Best Irish Album 2005, Ivor Novello Award for Best Album 2005) 2004, Eyes Open (Meteor Ireland Music Award for Best Irish Album 2007) 2006, A Hundred Million Suns 2008, Fallen Empires 2010; with The Reindeer Section: Y'all Get Scared Now, Ya Hear! 2001, Son Of Evil Reindeer 2002; with Tired Pony: The Place we Ran From 2010; with Ray Davies: See My Friends 2010. *Honours:* Meteor Ireland Music Awards for Best Irish Band (with Snow Patrol) 2005, 2007, for Most Downloaded Song and Best Live Performance 2007. *E-mail:* qprimeuk@qprime.com. *Website:* www.qprime.com. *Address:* c/o Board of Directors, Oh Yeah Music Centre, 15-21 Gordon Street, Belfast, BT1 2LG, Northern Ireland. *E-mail:* info@snowpatrol.com. *Website:* www .snowpatrol.com; www.tiredpony.com.

LIGHTFOOT, Gordon Meredith, CM; Canadian singer and songwriter; b. 17 Nov. 1938, Orilla, ON; m. Elizabeth Moon. *Education:* Westlake College of Music, Los Angeles. *Career:* singer, songwriter 1959–; mem., Swinging Singing Eight (square-dance ensemble), Canada; folk duo Two Tones 1960; solo artist 1961–; numerous concerts, television appearances. *Film appearance:* Harry Tracy 1982. *Recordings include:* albums: Lightfoot, 1965; The Way I Feel, 1967; Did She Mention My Name; Back Here On Earth; Sunday Concert; If You Could Read My Mind, 1971; Summer Side of Life; Classic

Lightfoot, 1971; Don Quixote, 1972; Old Dan's Records, 1972; Sundown, 1974; Cold On The Shoulder, 1975; Gord's Gold, 1976; Summertime Dream, 1976; Endless Wire, 1978; Dream Street Rose, 1980; Shadows, 1982; Salute, 1985; East of Midnight, 1986; The Original Lightfoot, 1992; Waiting For You, 1993; A Painter Passing Through, 1998; Singer Songwriter, 2001; Harmony 2004; All Live 2012. *Honours:* Juno Gold Leaf Awards, Canadian Male Artist of Decade 1980, Queen Elizabeth II Diamond Jubilee Medal 2012.

LIKWID BISKIT (see Ig Culture)

LIL JON; American producer and rap artist; b. (Jonathan Smith), 1971, Atlanta, GA; m.; one s. *Career:* pioneer of a style of hip hop known as Crunk; A&R Rep., So So Def Records 1993–2000; co-founder of record label, Black Market Entertainment 2002–; mem., Lil Jon and the Eastside Boyz; producer for artists, including 54th Platoon, Black Eyed Peas, Bow Wow, David Banner, E-40, Elephant Man, Juvenile, Ludacris, Master P, Mobb Deep, Petey Pablo, Snoop Dog, Too Short, Trilvilee, Little Scrappy. *Television:* presenter Pimp My Ride (MTV Europe) 2006. *Recordings include:* albums: as Lil Jon and the Eastside Boyz: Get Crunk, Who U Wit 1997, We Still Crunk 2000, Put Your Hood Up 2001, Kings of Crunk 2002, Part II 2003, Crunk Juice 2005, Crunk Rock 2010. *Film appearances:* Scary Movie 4, Date Movie. *Honours:* American Music Award 2003, two MTV Music Video Awards 2003, Grammy Award (for Yeah) 2004, BET Award (for Yeah) 2004, eight Billboard Awards, BMI Songwriter of the Year 2005. *Address:* c/o Universal Republic, Universal Motown Republic Group, 1755 Broadway, New York, NY 10019, USA (office). *Website:* www.liljononline.com.

LIL JON; American hip hop recording artist, DJ and record producer; b. (Jonathan Mortimer Smith), 17 Jan. 1971, Atlanta, Ga; m. Nicole Smith 2004; one s. *Education:* Frederick Douglass High School, Atlanta. *Career:* Founder-mem. Lil Jon and the East Side Boyz 1995–2005; f. record label BME Recordings 2000; producer of numerous recordings 2003– including tracks for Ciara, E-40, Lil Scrappy, Pitbull, Trillville, Britney Spears; featured collaborator with numerous artists including Akon, Big Boi, Bravehearts, Diddy, DJ Snake, Ice Cube, LMFAO, Ludacris, Mobb Deep, Nas, Sean Paul, Pitbull, Jay Sean, Trick Daddy, Twista. *Recordings:* with the East Side Boyz: Get Crunk, Who U Wit: Da Album 1997, We Still Crunk! 2000, Put Yo Hood Up 2001, Kings of Crunk 2002, Crunk Juice 2004; solo: Crunk Rock 2010. *Honours:* Grammy Award for Best Rap/Sung Collaboration (for Yeah!, with Usher and Ludacris) 2005, Billboard Music Award for Top Dance/Electronic Song (for Turn Down for What, with DJ Snake) 2015. *Current Management:* c/o Reservoir Media Management, 225 Varick Street, 6th Floor, New York, NY 10014, USA. *Telephone:* (212) 675-0541. *Fax:* (212) 675-0514. *Website:* www .reservoir-media.com; liljon.com.

LIL' KIM, (Queen Bee); American rap artist; b. (Kimberly Jones), 11 July 1975, Brooklyn, New York. *Career:* first appeared on Notorious B.I.G.'s Junior M.A.F.I.A. project; released debut album with production by Puff Daddy 1996; collaborations with Missy Elliott, Puff Daddy, Lil' Cease, Jay-Z, Too $hort, Sisqo. *Recordings:* albums: Conspiracy (with Junior M.A.F.I.A.) 1995, Hard Core 1996, The Notorious KIM 2000, La Bella Mafia 2003, The Naked Truth 2005. *Honours:* MTV Award for Best Female Artist 1997, Grammy Award for Best Pop Collaboration with Vocals (for Lady Marmalade, with Christina Aguilera, Mya and Pink) 2001. *Address:* c/o Atlantic Records, 1290 Avenue of the Americas, New York, NY 10104, USA. *Telephone:* (212) 707-2000. *Fax:* (212) 405-5475. *Website:* www.lilkim.com.

LIL WAYNE; American rap artist; b. (Dwayne Michael Carter, Jr), 27 Sept. 1982, New Orleans, La; one d., three s. *Career:* began career in duo, The BGs, with B.G. 1993–97; mem. The Hot Boys 1997–99; solo artist 1999–; numerous collaborations including: Destiny's Child, T.I., Kanye West, Jay-Z, Kelly Rowland, Drake, Chris Brown, Busta Rhymes; soundtrack to numerous films. *Films include:* Baller Blockin' 2000, Who's Your Caddy? 2007, The Carter 2009, Hurricane Season 2010. *Television includes:* Access Granted 2007, The Boondocks 2007, Nike Zoom VI LeBron James "Chalk" 2009, Gatorade (narrator) 1st and 10 2009, Around the Horn 2009, Behind The Music 2009, All Access With Katie Couric 2009, The Mo'Nique Show 2009, Freaknik: The Musical 2010, Saturday Night Live (performed alongside Eminem a medley of songs including No Love) 2010. *Recordings:* albums: with The Hot Boys: Get It How U Live 1997, Guerilla Warfare 1999; solo: The Block is Hot 1999, Lights Out 2000, 500 Degreez 2002, Tha Carter 2004, Tha Carter II 2005, Like Father Like Son 2006, Tha Carter III (Grammy Award for Best Rap Album 2009) 2008, Rebirth 2010, I Am Not a Human Being 2010, Tha Carter IV (Billboard Music Award for Top Rap Album 2012) 2011, I Am Not a Human Being II 2013, Free Weezy Album 2015. *Honours:* BET Award for Best Male Hip-Hop Artist 2007, World Music Award for Best Hip Hop/Rap Artist 2008, Grammy Awards for Best Rap Solo Performance (for A Milli) 2009, for Best Rap Song (for Lollipop) 2009, MOBO Award for Best Hip-Hop Act 2008, Billboard Music Awards for Top Male Artist 2012, for Top Rap Artist 2012. *Address:* c/o Cash Money Records, Universal Music Group, 1755 Broadway, New York, NY 10019, USA (office). *Website:* www.cashmoney-records.com (office); lilwayne-online.com; www.youngmoney.com.

LILES, Kevin; American music company executive and entrepreneur; b. 27 Feb. 1968, Baltimore; three c. *Education:* Morgan St Univ. *Career:* mem., Numarx 1989–91; co-founder and Co-Pres. Marx Brothers Records 1989–92; intern Def Jam Records 1991–93, Mid-Atlantic Marketing Man. 1993, Gen. Man. of Promotions 1994–96, Vice-Pres. of Promotions 1996–98, Pres. Def Jam Records 1998–2004, Exec. Vice-Pres. Island Def Jam Music Group 2002–04;

Exec. Vice-Pres. Warner Music Group 2004–09; established Kevin Liles Foundation (helping young people through sport, education and community organizations) 2004–. *Composition:* Girl You Know It's True (co-writer, performed by Milli Vanilli) 1986. *Publication:* Make It Happen: The Hip Hop Generation Guide to Success (with Samantha Marshall) 2005. *Honours:* UJA-Federation Music Visionary Award 2003. *Website:* www.kevinliles.com.

LILLYWHITE, Steve, CBE; British music producer; *Senior Vice-President of A&R, Columbia Records;* b. 1955; m. Kirsty MacColl (died 2000); two c. *Career:* tape operator, Polygram 1972; staff producer, Island Records from 1980; work as producer with artists including Joan Armatrading, Big Country, David Bowie, David Byrne, Peter Gabriel, Happy Mondays, The La's, The Dave Matthews Band, Morrissey, The Pogues, Pretenders, Psychedelic Furs, Rolling Stones, Simple Minds, Siouxsie and The Banshees, The Smiths, U2, Ultravox, XTC; Jt Man. Dir Mercury Records (UK) 2001–04; Sr Vice-Pres., A&R, Columbia Records 2005–; credited with working on more than 500 records 1977–. *Honours:* Grammy Award for Producer of the Year – Non-Classical 2006. *Address:* Columbia Records, Sony BMG, 550 Madison Avenue, New York, NY 10022, USA (office). *Website:* www.columbiarecords.com (office).

LIMERICK, Alison; British singer; b. 1959, London. *Career:* performer in stage musical, Starlight Express; backing singer, Style Council's Our Favourite Shop 1985; appeared on 4AD collective Filigree and Shadow (Acid, Bitter and Sad); worked with Peter Murphy on Holy Smoke 1992; solo artist 1991–. *Recordings include:* albums: And Still I Rise 1992, With a Twist 1994, Club Classics 1996, Spirit Rising 1998. *Honours:* Dance Record of the Year, Billboard Magazine, USA (for Where Love Lives) 1991. *Current Management:* c/o John Glover, Blueprint Management, PO Box 593, Woking, Surrey GU23 7YF, England. *Telephone:* (1483) 715336. *E-mail:* john@ blueprint-management.com. *Website:* www.blueprint-management.com.

LIMIC, Marin Kresimir; Croatian composer and musician (piano, keyboard); b. 8 Aug. 1946, Klis, Split; m. Dubravka Zauhar, 6 Feb. 1982, 2 s. *Education:* 4 semesters, Music Academy. *Career:* Over 500 television appearances including: live concerts of group Stijene, 1982–94; Television shows, 1982–83; Live concert, TV Zagreb, 1983; Tonight With You, interview, 1995; Seventh Night, HTV, 1995; Akustkoteka, unplugged concert; Fest Split, 1996, 1998–99; Voice of Asia, 1997; Cro-Turneja, 1998; Big Concert Split, 1999; International Festival, Kiev, 1999; mem, HDS (Asscn of Croatian Composers); President, Split Asscn of Musicians; Vice-President, Split Musicians' Syndicate; Artist-Composer, Republic of Croatia (ZUH Zagreb); HGU (Croatian Music Union). *Compositions:* Songs: Sve Je Neobicno Ako Te Volim; Ima Jedan Svijet; Singing That Rock 'N' Roll; Balkanska Korida; Ja Sam More Ti Si Rijeka; Zaplesimo Kao Nekada; Zbogom Prva Ljubavi; Znaj, Volim Te, 1997; Jos Te Volim Kao Nekada, 1998; Caca Moj, 1998; Dodi Nam Dodi, 1999. *Recordings:* 6 singles, 1974–84; Albums: Cementna Prasina (Silver record), 1980–81; Jedanaest I Petnaest (Gold, Silver record), 1982–83; Balkanska Korida; Stijene IV, 1994; Best of Stijene, 1995; Split, 1996, 1998–99; Stijene Promo, 1997; Voice of Asia, 1997; Obecanje, 1998. *Honours:* Gold, Silver discs; Awards from festivals: Zagreb, 1980; Split, 1981, 1982, 1990; Sarajevo, 1981, 1988; First prize, Split Fest, 1996, 1998–99; Fourth prize, Voice of Asia.

LINCE, (John) Louis James; British musician (banjo, guitar) and bandleader; b. 22 July 1941, St Helens, Lancashire; m. Gillian Everil Walker 1961; two d. *Career:* mem., Ken Colyer Allstars 1976–82, Savoy Jazzmen 1975–83, Louis Lince's New Orleans Band 1986–; Founder mem., Annie Hawkins' New Orleans Legacy 1997; occasional appearances with Jambalaya and Louisiana Joymakers 1987–; worked in New Orleans with Tuba Fats' Chosen Few 1992–95; Lionel Ferbos 1996, Reginald Koehler 1996. *Recordings include:* Just A Little While To Stay Here, Ken Colyer Allstars, 1978; You've Got the Right Key, 1979; Savoy Rag, 1981; Jubilee, 1983; Algiers Strut, 1985; Hot At The Dot, 1991; Backstairs Session, 1992; Yearning, 1993; Walking With The King, 1994; More Savoy Jazzmen, 1994; Louis Lince's Jelly Roll Kings, 1995; Good Morning to Heaven, 1996; Mardi Gras Parade, 1997. *Website:* www.louislince.co.uk.

LINDEMANN, Till; German singer and songwriter; b. 4 Jan. 1963, Leipzig; four c. *Career:* fmr mem., First Arsch; mem., Rammstein 1993–; the band has a reputation for theatrical live performances; numerous European tours. *Recordings include:* albums: Herzeleid 1995, Sehnsucht 1997, Live aus Berlin 1999, Mutter 2001, Reise, Reise 2004, Rosenrot 2005, Liebe ist für alle da 2009. *Honours:* MTV Europe Music Award for Best German Act 2005. *Current Management:* Pilgrim Management, Greifswalderstrasse 224, 10405 Berlin, Germany. *E-mail:* info@pilgrim-management.de. *Website:* www.pilgrim -management.de; www.rammstein.de.

LINDEN, Nick; British musician (bass, guitar, keyboards); b. 17 Nov. 1962, Woolwich, England. *Education:* studied music. *Career:* bass guitarist in rock band, Terraplane 1984–89; various festival appearances, tours supporting Meatloaf, Foreigner, ZZ Top; various video and television appearances; mem., Waterboys 1993–94. *Recordings include:* with Terraplane: Black and White, 1985; Moving Target, 1987; with Waterboys: Waterboys, 1983; Pagan Place, 1984; This Is The Sea, 1985; Best of the Waterboys, 1991; Secret Life of the Waterboys, 1994. *Address:* 48 Dallin Road, London, SE18 3NU, England (office).

LINDENBERG, Udo; German singer, rock musician and composer; b. 17 May 1946, Gronau. *Career:* Founder mem. and drummer, Free Orbit 1969;

collaborated with Klaus Doldinger 1970; Founder mem. and drummer, Passport 1971; mem. Niagara 1971; mem. Emergency 1971; solo career 1971–. *Recordings:* albums: solo: Lindenberg 1971, Daumen im Wind 1972, Phönix 1987, Gänsehaut 1988, Hermine 1988, Casa Nova 1988, Ich will dich haben 1991, Gustav 1992, Unter die Haut 1992, Panik-Panther 1992, Benjamin 1993, Kosmos 1995, Und ewig rauscht die Linde 1996, Zeitmaschine 1998, Der Exzessor 2000, Ich schwöre – Das volle Programm 2001, Balladen 2001, Atlantic Affairs 2002, Der Panikpräsident 2003, Absolut 2004, Stark wie zwei 2008, MTV Unplugged – Live aus dem Hotel Atlantic 2011; with Passport: Passport 1971, Doldinger 1973; with Emergency: Emergency 1971; with Niagara: Niagara 1971; with Panikorchester: Alles klar auf der Andrea Doria 1973, Ball Pompös 1974, Votan Wahnwitz 1975, Galaxo Gang 1976, Sister King Kong 1976, Panik Udo 1976, Panische Nächte 1977, Lindenbergs Rock-Revue 1978, Dröhnland-Symphonie 1978, Livehaftig 1979, Der Detektiv 1979, Panische Zeiten 1980, Meine Panik 1980, Udopia 1981, Keule 1982, Intensivstationen 1982, Odyssee 1983, Lindstärke 10 1983, Götterhämmerung 1984, Sündenknall 1985, Radio Eriwahn präsentiert 1985, Feuerland 1987; with Das Deutsche Filmorchester Babelsberg: Belcanto 1997. *Honours:* ECHO Honorary Award 1991, ECHO Awards for Best Nat. Male Artist 2009, 2012. *Address:* c/o Walentowski Galerien, Ballindamm 40, Europa-Passage 2, OG, 20095 Hamburg, Germany (office). *Telephone:* (40) 40185705 (office). *Fax:* (40) 40185709 (office). *E-mail:* info@walentowski-galerien.de (office). *Website:* www.galerie-europapassage.de (office); www.udo-lindenberg.de.

LINDENMAIER, Heinrich Lukas; musician (drums, percussion, electronics); b. 5 March 1946, Basel, Switzerland. *Education:* Acad. of Arts, Munich, Germany, private tuition at various workshops. *Career:* Eric Dolphy Memorial Band 1984; John Tchicai Workshop Orchestra 1987; Querstand, for Radio WDR and Radio RTSI; F-Orkestra 1987–; Kxutrio 1985–96; Cecil Taylor Large Ensembles 1988–92; Die Pilzfreunde 1995–2006; Words and Noises with Hartmut Geerken 2006–; Weg ins Freie, film music 1993; Jazz Swissmade, TV and film music, solo improvisations. *Compositions:* stage music for play Orestes 1992, The Break Broken, Bright Pink, Yellow and Software, Die Feenfalle, At the Hounfort for large ensemble 2003; other pieces for small ensembles or jazz orchestra. *Recordings:* Riffifi (Kxutrio), Legba Crossing (C. Taylor), Open (Stauss-Chaine-Lindenmaier), Die Pilzfreunde, En-Passent and Other Duets, Freiburg Loopholes (with F-Orkestra and John Tchicai). *Publications:* 25 Years of Fish Horn Recording 1982, The Man Who Never Sleeps 1983. *Honours:* Kulturpreis der Stadt Emmendingen 2000. *Address:* Wilhelmstr 32, 79098 Freiburg, Germany.

LINDENS, Traste; Swedish singer; b. 6 May 1960, Gävile; m. Caroline Zielfelt. *Education:* Grafic Institut, Stockholm. *Career:* mem. of band, Traste Lindens' Kvintette; tours and festival appearances. *Recordings include:* Traste Lindens' Kvintette: Sportfiskarn, 1987; Bybor, 1989; Jolly Bob Gåriland, 1991; Gud Hjåpe, 1992; Utsålt, 1993; Som På Film, 1994. *Honours:* Hälsinge Akademins Pris 1992.

LINDES, Hal; American musician (guitar) and composer; b. 30 June 1953, Monterey, CA; m. Mary Elizabeth Frampton 1979; two s. one d. *Education:* Univ. of Maryland. *Career:* fmr mem., Darling; mem., Dire Straits 1980–85; collaborations with Mark Knopfler, Tina Turner, Kiki Dee, Fish; became film and television composer; mem PRS, ASCAP, British Equity. *Television appearance:* Drowning in the Shallow End (BBC film) 1989. *Compositions:* themes for television include: Between the Lines, The Trial, Drowning in the Shallow End, Born Kicking, Joyriders, Band of Gold, The Guilty, Legacy – Great Civilisations of the World, Thieftakers, Into the Land of Oz, Bermuda Grace, The Coriolis Effect, The Infiltrator, The Great Kandinsky, Airport, Kiss and Tell, Reckless, The Vanishing Man, Forgive and Forget, Vent de Colère, The Hunt, The Whistle-Blower, Red Cap, Alibi, Nature, NY-LON, 1969, The Complete Guide to Parenting, Losing Gemma, Apparitions; film scores: Don't Do It, Gunshy, The Blind Date, Local Boys, Quicksand, Male Mail, Lucky 13, Girl 27. *Recordings:* albums: Making Movies 1980, Love Over Gold 1982, Extendeddanceplay 1983, Alchemy: Dire Straits Live 1984, Brothers In Arms 1985; singles: Tunnel of Love 1981, Private Investigations 1982, Twisting By The Pool 1983, So Far Away 1985, Money For Nothing (Grammy Awards for Best Rock Performance 1986) 1985, Brothers In Arms 1985. *Current Management:* Hot House Music Ltd, 1st Floor, 172a Arlington Road, London NW1 7HL, England. *Telephone:* (20) 7446-7446. *Fax:* (20) 7447-7448. *E-mail:* info@hot-house-music.com. *Website:* www.hot-house-music .com. *E-mail:* contactus@hallindes.com (office). *Website:* www.hallindes.com.

LINDHOLM, Dave Ralf Henrik; Finnish singer, songwriter and musician (guitar); b. 31 March 1952, Helsinki; m. Kirsi Koivunen 1993; one s. two d. *Career:* member of bands including Ferris, Orfeus, Rock 'n' Roll Band, Pen Lee and Co, Bluesounds, 12 Bar, Dave Lindholm and Ganpaza Gypsies; concerts in most of Europe and in Texas, USA; several blues festivals. *Recordings:* albums: Iso Lindholm 1972, Sirkus 1973, Musiikkia 1974, Lillam 1974, Fandjango 1975, Kenen Iaulu 1975, Vanha & uusi romanssi 1979, Aino 1982, Huoneet 6 & 14 1983, Kuutamolla 1983, Moderni hiljainen musiikki 1985, Sissi 1987, Jose Blues 1988, Sillalla 1990, Sisar 1991, Kerran 1992, Kissatanssit 1992, LLL 1993, Valmista Karnaa 1996, Just 1998, Punainen + 1998, Valkoinen & 1999, Luuttujengi tulee 2001, Lahes 50 2002, D & D 2006, Nuo Mainiot Miehet Soivine Koneineen 2007.

LINDRIDGE, Nigel Paul James; British singer and songwriter; b. 22 March 1950, Croydon, Surrey; m. Lynda Cauvain; one d. one step-d. *Education:* Medway College of Technology. *Career:* founder and lead singer,

The Menaces 1966–68; country duo with John Lynott 1970–72; solo artist 1972–76; mem. country band, The Taverners 1977–87; songwriter 1994–; mem. Musicians' Union, Performing Rights Soc. *Recordings include:* albums: Live Is Blind, You Know Me.

LINDSAY, Joe, (Ho Pepa); New Zealand musician (trombone). *Career:* mem. Fat Freddy's Drop reggae and soul band. *Recordings include:* Fat Freddy's Drop: Live at the Matterhorn 2001, Based on a True Story (first ind. release to go Gold and debut at No. 1 on NZ Music Charts, Winner, Highest Selling Album, Wandering Eye Best Video, voted Worldwide Album of the Year at Radio 1 Gilles Peterson Worldwide Music Awards 2005) 2005, Ray Ray (Best Int. Music Video, New York Ind. Film and Video Festival) 2007, Dr Boondigga and the Big BW 2009. *Honours:* Best Live Act, B-Net NZ Music Awards 2004, NZ Music Award for Best Group 2005, Outstanding Achievement in the Field of Excellence, B-Net NZ Music Awards 2006, People's Choice Award, NZ Music Awards 2006, 'Male Fox', B-Net NZ Music Awards 2006. *Address:* The Drop Ltd, PO Box 14-723, Kilbirnie, Wellington 6241, New Zealand (office). *Telephone:* (4) 934-3767 (office). *E-mail:* freddy@fatfreddysdrop.com (office). *Website:* www.fatfreddysdrop.com (office); www.fatfreddysdrop.tv (office).

LINDSTROM, Maria; Swedish singer, songwriter and musician (guitar); b. 30 Aug. 1953, Stockholm; m. Kjell Andersson 1995. *Education:* Univ. of Lund. *Career:* actress, musician, Fringe Theatre Group 1977–88; solo artist 1988–; formed trio 2003–; cabaret artist on TV; produced some 15 shows. *Compositions:* more than 100 songs including lyrics and music for stage. *Recordings include:* albums: Zingo 1998, Stockholm Boogie 2004. *Honours:* Swedish SKAP Prize 1997.

LINDUP, Mike; musician (keyboards) and singer; b. 17 March 1959. *Career:* founder mem., Level 42 1980–94; numerous live appearances, tours; solo artist 1990–. *Recordings include:* albums: with Level 42: Level 42 1981, The Pursuit of Accidents 1982, Standing In The Light 1983, True Colours 1984, A Physical Presence 1985, World Machine 1985, Running In The Family 1987, Staring At The Sun 1988, Guaranteed 1991, Forever Now 1994, Live at Wembley 1996; solo: Changes 1990, Conversations with Silence 2003. *Address:* c/o Naim Audio Ltd, Southampton Road, Salisbury, SP1 2LN, England (office). *E-mail:* info@thenaimlabel.com (office). *Website:* www.thenaimlabel.com (office); www.mikelindup.com.

LINKA, Rudolf (Rudy); Czech/Swedish/American musician (jazz guitar) and composer; *Director Bohemia JazzFest*; b. 29 May 1960, Prague, Czechoslovakia (now Czech Repub.); m. Anna Linka; one d. *Education:* Prague Conservatoire, Stockholm Musik Inst., Berklee Coll. of Music, Boston and The New School, New York, USA, private studies with Jim Hall, John Scofield and John Abercrombie. *Career:* performed with artists including Sam Rivers, Red Mitchell, Gil Goldstein, Bob Mintzer, John Abercrombie, Paul Motian; performs with own jazz group at clubs and festivlas in Europe, Canada and USA, including Birdland, Blues Alley, Blue Note, Moods, Bimhuis; Founder and Dir Bohemia JazzFest; mem. Broadcast Music, Inc. (BMI), Gesellschaft für musikalische Aufführungs- und mechanische Vervielfältigungsrechte (GEMA). *Compositions:* Room 428, Waltz for Stephanie, To Be Named Later, The Old and New Orleans, Folk Song, Simply Put, It's Just That Easy. *Recordings:* Rudy Linka 1990, News from Home 1991, Mostly Standards 1992, Live it Up 1993, Czech It Out 1995, Always Double Czech 1997, Emotions in Motion 1999, Just Between Us 2000, Every Moment 2001, Lucky Southern (voted one of 10 best new releases by Jazz Thing magazine, Germany) 2003, Trip 2005, Beyond The New York City Limits 2006, Songs 2008, Re:connect (named by DownBeat magazine as one of the best new releases of 2013) 2013. *Honours:* Jim Hall Fellowship, Berklee Coll. of Music, Jazz Composition grant, Nat. Endowment for the Arts, travel grant from Arts International, voted one of the ten best jazz guitarists by readers of Down Beat magazine (USA) 1998. *Address:* c/o Music in the Center, 2350 Broadway, Suite 203, New York, NY 10024; 55 West End Avenue, Apt 8C, New York, NY 10023, USA (home). *Telephone:* (212) 586-4899 (home). *E-mail:* linkarudy@gmail.com (office); musicinthecenter@gmail.com. *Website:* www.bohemiajazzfest.cz (office); www.facebook.com/rudy.linka.9.

LINKOLA, Jukka; Finnish composer, musician (piano) and conductor; b. 21 July 1955, Espoo; m. Marita Strömberg; one s. one d. *Education:* Sibelius Acad., Helsinki. *Career:* has conducted Danish Radio Big Band, Bohuslän Big Band, Oslo Groove Company, UMO Big Band, Prag Radio Big Band, Ljubljana Radio Big Band, Finnish Radio Big Band, Finnish Radio Symphony Orchestra, Helsinki Philharmony, Finnish Nat. Opera Orchestra; Musical Dir, Helsinki City Theatre 1979–90; currently freelance composer, opera, jazz, symphony, chamber and theatre music; mem. Soc. of Finnish Composers. *Compositions include:* Crossings for symphony orchestra 1983, Between Two Stages 1988, Ronja The Robber's Daughter (ballet) for Finnish Nat. Opera, premiered 1989, three trumpet concertos 1988, 1993, 2002, Angelika (opera) 1990, Elina (opera) 1992, Chalumeaux Suite 1993, Concerto for Tuba 1995, Concerto for Euphonium 1996, String Quartet 1996, Concerto for Flute 1997, Concerto for Trombone 1998, The Journey (opera) 1998, Concerto for Saxophone 1999, Concerto for Organ 1999, Joppe Jokamies (opera) 2004, Symphony 2004, Hallin Janne (opera) 2005, One Spooky Night (opera) 2006, Deus Protector Noster (mass) 2007, Rockland (opera) 2009, Robin Hood (opera) 2010, Piano Concerto 2011, Kaipaus (musical) 2011, Sydämeni Laulu (musical) 2012, Hölmöläiset (opera) 2012, Mere Meri Marea for SATB 2013, Piano Concerto No. 2 2013, Clarinet Concerto 2014, Väinö Metsän Jumala for SSAATTBB 2014, Euphonium Concerto No. 2 2015, Rumba Liberte 2016. *Recordings:* albums with own octet: Protofunk, Lady In Green, Scat Suite, Ben Bay; with Eija Ahvo: Kuinka Myöhään Valvoo Blues; with orchestra: Crossings and Trumpet Concerto, Euphonium Concerto, Winds, The Journey, Sisu, Astoria, The Tentet, EQ Libau (Emma Prize for Record of the Year 1998), Ronia the Robber's Daughter, Sketches from Karelia, Muisti, One Spooky Night (DVD), Robin Hood (DVD), Deus Protector Noster (DVD) 2015. *Honours:* Yrjö Award, Finnish Jazz Fed. 1979, Finnish Broadcasting Co., Record of the Year, First Prize, LUSES Competition 1993, First Prize, Paris Opera Screen 1993, First Prize, Midem Awards 1994, First Prize, Concours Int. de Composition de la Ville du Havre 1994, two Jussi Prizes for film music. *Address:* Syrene Music, Saarnitie 14, 00780 Helsinki, Finland (office). *Telephone:* 500-732423 (mobile) (office). *E-mail:* jukka.linkola@syrenemusic.fi (office). *Website:* www.fimic.fi/fimic/linkola+jukka (office).

LINNET, Anne Kristine, DipMus; Danish composer, musician, singer and songwriter; b. 30 July 1953, Århus; m. Holger Laumann (divorced); three s. three d. (including two adopted c.). *Education:* Conservatory of Music, Jutland. *Career:* mem. Tears 1970; formed own band Shit and Chanel 1974–79; formed Anne Linnet Band (with Sanne Salomonsen and Lis Soerenson) 1981, touring Scandinavia and Germany; formed band Marquis de Sade 1983; composed and recorded the musical Berlin '84 1984; formed own record co. Pladecompagniet 1988; partnership with poet and priest Johannes Moellehave composing music to his poetry; premiere of musical Krig og Kaerlighed (War and Love) 1990; worked on several major classical compositions; participated in PaPapegoje, an album of children's songs performed by major Danish rock and pop artists; composer of song for 1995 Eurovision Song Contest, performed by Ulla Henningsen; formed the band Bitch Boys 2001–02, have since released approx. one solo album annually; has written music to several musicals, films and translated ABBA's Mamma Mia for Danish Theatre. *Exhibition:* Kvindebilleder, Rundetårn, Copenhagen 2006. *Recordings include:* Kvindesind 1977, You're Crazy 1979, Anne Linnet Band 1981, Cha Cha Cha 1982, Marquis de Sade 1983, Hvid Magi 1985, En elsker 1986, Barndommens Gade 1986, Jeg er jo lige her 1988, Go' Sondag Morgen 1989, Min Sang 1989, Krig & Kaerlighed 1990, Det' saa dansk 1992, Tal til mig 1993, Pige Traed Varsomt 1995, Thorvaldsen 1996, Bitch Boys 1997, Nattog Til Venus 1999, Jeg og Du 2000, Over Mig Under Mig 2002, Relax 2003, Her hos Mig 2005, Akvarium 2007, Anne Linnet 2008, Anne Linnet Boksen 2009, Linnets Jul 2010, De Bedste 2011. *Honours:* Kt, Order of the Dannebrog 2000; Cultural Award 1996, IFPI Honor Award, Danish Music Soc. 2008. *Address:* c/o Sony BMG Music Denmark, Vognmagergade 7, 1120 Copenhagen, Denmark. *E-mail:* linnetsongs@hotmail.com. *Website:* www.annelinnet.dk.

LINS, Ivan Guimarães; Brazilian singer, songwriter and musician (piano); b. 16 June 1945, Rio de Janeiro. *Education:* Rio de Janeiro Military Coll. and Universidade Federal Rural do Rio de Janeiro. *Career:* solo artist; long-term composition collaboration with Vitor Martins; co-founder record label, Velas. *Film soundtrack compositions:* Vida e Gloria de um Canalha 1970, Dois Córregos 1999, Bens Confiscados 2004. *Film appearance:* Os Saltimbancos Trapalhões 1981. *Recordings include:* albums: Agora 1971, Deixa o trem seguir 1972, Quem sou eu 1972, Modo Livre 1974, Chama Acesa 1975, Somos todos Iguais Nesta Noite 1977, Nos dias de Hoje 1979, A Noite 1979, Novo Tempo 1980, Daquilo que eu sei 1981, Depois dos temporais 1983, Juntos 1984, Encuentro 1984, Ivan Lins 1986, Mãos 1988, Love Dance 1989, Amar assim 1989, Ivan 20 Anos Lins 1991, Awa Yiô 1993, Doce Presença 1995, Natal com Ivan Lins 1995, Anjo de Mim 1995, Ivan Lins e Irakere 1996, Viva Noel Vol. 1 1997, Viva Noel Vol. 2 1997, Millennium 1998, Live at MCG 1999, Dois Córregos 1999, Um Novo Tempo 1999, A cor Do Pôr-Do-Sol 2000, Jobiniando 2001, Love Songs: A Quem Me Faz Feliz 2002, I Love Mpb: Amor 2004, Cantando Histórias (Latin Grammy Award for Album of the Year) 2004, Acariocando 2006, Saudades de Casa 2008, Regência: Vince Mendoza (with The Metropole Orchestra) (Latin Grammy Award for Best Popular Brazilian Music Album) 2009, America, Brasil (Latin Grammy Award for Best Popular Brazilian Music Album 2015) 2014. *Current Management:* Michael Kline Artists LLC, PO Box 312, Cape May Point, NJ 08212, USA. *Telephone:* (609) 884-5986. *Fax:* (609) 884-0272. *E-mail:* info@michaelklineartists.com. *Website:* www.michaelklineartists.com. *Address:* c/o EMI Music, Praia do Flamengo 200, 15th Floor Flamengo, 22210-030 Rio de Janeiro, Brazil (office). *E-mail:* showivan@liga.br.com. *Website:* ivanlins.com.br.

LINSTEAD, Johannes; Canadian composer, musician (guitar) and author; b. Oakville, Ontario. *Career:* performer and composer of instrumental Latin and World music; also yoga and meditation instructor. *Recordings:* Sol Luna Tierra 1999, Kiss the Earth 2000, Guitarra del Fuego (NAV Music Awards Best Contemporary World Album) 2001, Zabuca 2003, Mediterranea (NAR Lifestyle Music Awards Best World Album) 2004, Cafe Tropical 2006, Encanto (NAR Lifestyle Music Awards Best Instrumental Album) 2007, Mistico 2009. *Publication:* Buddha In A Business Suit. *Honours:* Jazz Band Musician of the Year 1989, Guitarist of the Year, Candian Smooth Jazz Awards 2007. *E-mail:* info@johanneslinstead.com (home). *Website:* www.johanneslinstead.com.

LIPA, Peter; Slovak singer, songwriter and bandleader; b. 30 May 1943, Presov; m. Norina Bobrovská 1980; three s. one d. *Education:* Technical Univ., Bratislava, Slovakia. *Career:* mem. bands: Strings, Blues Five, Revival Jazz Band, Blues Band, Peter Lipa Combo, Peter Lipa and Band, Andrej Seban Band; hundreds of TV and radio performances on Slovak, Czech, German, Hungarian, Polish radio and TV; Pres. Slovak Jazz Soc., Lions Club International. *Recordings:* Moanin', That's the Way It Is, Naspat Na Stromy, Spirituals, Peter Lipa, (La, La, La) Boogie Up, Cierny Peter, V Najlepších

Rokoch 2001, Beatles in Blue(s) 2003, Lipa Spieva Lasicu 2006, Lipa 68 2012. *Publication:* Samorast – Môj život s džezom (My Life in Jazz) (autobiog.) 2003. *Honours:* Hon. Citizen of Bratislava 1995, Martonik Annual Jazz Prize 1995, Ministry of Cultural Affairs Prize 2002, Tatra Banka Prize 2002. *Current Management:* c/o East-West Promotion, Godrova 3, 81106, Bratislava, Slovakia. *E-mail:* peter@peterlipa.com (office). *Website:* www.peterlipa.com.

LIPSON, Stephen James; British record producer; b. 16 March 1954, London, England. *Career:* currently mem. The Producers. *Recordings:* Record producer for: Propaganda, A Secret Wish 1985, Grace Jones, Slave To The Rhythm 1985, Frankie Goes To Hollywood, Liverpool 1986, Pet Shop Boys, Introspective 1988, Simple Minds, Street Fighting Years 1989, Annie Lennox, Diva 1992, Prefab Sprout, If You Don't Love Me 1992, Backstreet Boys, Drowning 2001; also: Paul McCartney, Gary Barlow, Boyzone, Cher, Paul Brady, Ronan Keating, S Club 7; with The Producers: Studio 1 2007. *Honours:* Producer of the Year. *Website:* www.stevelipson.com.

LISBERG, Harvey Brian; British impresario and artist manager; b. 2 March 1940, Manchester, England; m. Carole Gottlieb 1969; two s. *Education:* Manchester Univ. *Career:* discovered Graham Gouldman, Andrew Lloyd Webber, Tim Rice, Herman's Hermits, Tony Christie, Sad Café, Godley and Creme, 10cc; represents 10cc, Graham Gouldman, Eric Stewart, George Stiles, Anthony Drewe, Cleopatra. *Current Management:* Harvey Lisberg Associates, Kennedy House, 31 Stamford Street, Altrincham, Cheshire WA14 1ES, England. *Telephone:* (161) 941-4560 (office). *Fax:* (161) 941-4199 (office). *E-mail:* harveylisberg@aol.com (office).

LISSACK, Russell; British musician (guitar); b. 11 March 1981. *Career:* founder mem., Union, later renamed Bloc Party 2003–. *Recordings include:* albums: with Bloc Party: Silent Alarm 2005, Silent Alarm Remixed 2005, A Weekend in the City 2007, Intimacy 2008, Four 2012. *Current Management:* Press Here Publicity, 138 W 25th Street, Seventh Floor, New York, NY 10001, USA. *Telephone:* (212) 246-2640. *Fax:* (212) 582-6513. *E-mail:* info@pressherepublicity.com. *Website:* www.pressherepublicity.com. *Address:* c/o V2 Music, 131 Holland Park Avenue, London, W11 4UT, England. *E-mail:* russell@blocparty.com. *Website:* www.blocparty.com.

LISTING, Georg; German musician (bass guitar); b. 31 March 1987. *Career:* mem. rock band, Tokio Hotel 2001–. *Recordings include:* albums: Schrei 2005, Schrei: So Laut Du Kannst 2006, Zimmer 483 2007, Scream 2007, Humanoid 2009. *Honours:* ECHO Award for Best National Newcomer 2006, MTV Europe Music Awards for Best Int. Act 2007, for Best Headline Act 2008, for Best Group 2009. *Address:* c/o Universal Music Deutschland, Stralauer Allee 1, 10245 Berlin, Germany (office). *Website:* www.tokiohotel.com.

LITTLE RICHARD; American rock singer and songwriter; b. (Richard Wayne Penniman), 5 Dec. 1932, Macon, Ga; adopted s. of Enotris Johnson and Ann Johnson. *Career:* R&B singer in various bands, including own band The Upsetters; gospel singer 1960–62; worldwide tours and concerts; announced retirement 2002. *Recordings include:* albums: Cast A Long Shadow 1956, Little Richard Vol. 1 1957, Little Richard Vol. 2 1957, Little Richard Vol. 3 1957, Here's Little Richard 1957, The Fabulous Little Richard 1959, Clap Your Hands 1960, Pray Along With Little Richard Vol. 1 1960, Pray Along With Little Richard Vol. 2 1960, King Of The Gospel Singers 1962, Sings Spirituals 1963, Sings the Gospel 1964, Little Richard Is Back 1965, The Wild and Frantic Little Richard 1965, The Explosive Little Richard 1967, Rock 'n' Roll Forever 1967, Good Golly Miss Molly 1969, Little Richard 1969, Right Now 1970, Rock Hard Rock Heavy 1970, Little Richard 1970, Well Alright! 1970, Mr Big 1971, The Rill Thing 1971, The Second Coming 1971, Dollars 1972, The Original 1972, You Can't Keep A Good Man Down 1972, Rip It Up 1973, Talkin' 'Bout Soul 1974, Recorded Live 1974, Keep A Knockin' 1975, Sings 1976, Little Richard Live 1976, Now 1977, Lucille 1988, Shake It All About 1992, Shag On Down By The Union Hall 1996. *Films include:* Don't Knock the Rock 1956, Mr Rock 'n' Roll 1957, The Girl Can't Help It 1957, Keep On Rockin' 1970, Down and Out in Beverly Hills 1986, Mother Goose Rock 'n' Rhyme (Disney Channel) 1989. *Honours:* Dr hc (Mercer Univ.) 2013; inducted into Rock and Roll Hall of Fame 1986, Grammy Lifetime Achievement Award 1993, American Music Award of Merit 1997, inducted into Songwriters Hall of Fame 2003. *Current Management:* Richard de la Font Agency Inc., 4845 South Sheridan Road, Suite 505, Tulsa, OK 74145-5719, USA. *Website:* www .delafont.com.

LITTLEMORE, Nicholas George (Nick); Australian musician, songwriter and producer. *Education:* Barker Coll., Coll. of Fine Arts, Univ. of New South Wales. *Career:* formed Pnau duo with Peter Mayes 1990s; founding mem. Empire of the Sun 2007–; mem. Teenager; has collaborated with Elton John, Robbie Williams, Ellie Goulding, Lost Valentinos, Groove Armada; composer and musical dir for Cirque du Soleil show, Radio City Music Hall, New York 2011–. *Recordings:* albums: with Pnau: Sambanova 1999, Again 2003, Pnau 2007; with Empire of the Sun: Walking on a Dream (ARIA Award for Album of the Year 2009) 2008. *Honours:* ARIA Music Awards for Best Dance Release 1999, for Single of the Year, Best Video, Best Group and Best Pop Release 2009, ARIA Artisan Award for Producer of the Year (with Donnie Sloan and Peter Mayes) 2009, APRA Awards for Breakthrough Songwriter of the Year and Dance Work of the Year 2010. *Address:* c/o EMI Music Australia, 98–100 Glover Street, PO Box 311, Cremorne, NSW 2090, Australia (office). *E-mail:* privacy@emimusic.com.au (office). *Website:* www.theinsoundfromwayout.com (office); www.walkingonadream.com.

LITTON, Martin, BA; British jazz musician; b. 14 May 1957, Grays, Essex, England; m. Rebekah Morley-Jones 1992 (divorced 2004). *Education:* Colchester Inst. *Career:* Pieces of Eight, with Harry Gold 1980–82; Kenny Ball and his Jazzmen 1982–84; tours of Middle East and Russia; freelance work with many American musicians, including Bob Wilbur, George Masso, Peanuts Hucko, Joe Muranyi, Al Casey, Scott Hamilton; recorded with Kenny Davern, Wild Bill Davison, Yank Lawson, Marty Grosz; work with leading British musicians includes recordings with Humphrey Lyttleton, Wally Fawkes, Digby Fairweather, Clare Teal; tours include Fabulous Fats, and Keith Smith's Hefty Jazz; Australia, New Zealand and Japan, with the Swedish Jazz Kings, latterly with Tom 'Spats' Langham; pianist with Bob Hunt's Duke Ellington Orchestra and own band, Martin Litton's Red Hot Peppers; frequent performer at London's South Bank Arts Centre; mem. Pizza Express Allstars 2002–10, A Piccadilly Dance Orchestra; mem. PRS. *Compositions:* Forever Afternoon, Striding Down 52nd Street, Litton on the Keys, Eight Bars – Eight to the Bar, For Rebekah, Elegy, Falling Castle, Laughing At Life. *Recordings include:* Martin Litton Jazz Piano, Ring Dem Bells, Falling Castle. *Radio:* Jazz Library (expert on jazz piano styles) (BBC Radio 3).

LITTRELL, Brian Thomas, (B-Rock); American singer; b. 20 Feb. 1975, Lexington, KY; m. Leighanne; one s. *Career:* mem., Backstreet Boys 1993–; numerous tours and television appearances. *Recordings include:* albums: Backstreet Boys 1996, Live in Concert 1998, Backstreet's Back 1998, Millennium 1999, Black And Blue 2000, Greatest Hits Chapter 1 2001, Never Gone 2005, Unbreakable 2007, This Is You 2009. *Honours:* Billboard Music Awards for Best Group, Best Adult Contemporary Group 1998, Album of the Year, Artist of the Year 1999, MTV Music Video Award for Best Group Video 1998, MTV European Music Awards for Best Pop Act 1997, Best Group 1999, World Music Awards for Best-Selling Pop Group 1999, 2000, Best-Selling R&B Group 1999, 2000, Best-Selling Dance Group 1999, 2000, Best American Group 2000, American Music Awards for Favorite Pop/Rock Band, Duo or Group 2000, 2001. *Current Management:* Wright Entertainment Group (WEG Music), PO Box 590009, Orlando, FL 32859, USA. *Website:* www .backstreetboys.com.

LITWIN, Ralph Henry, BFA; American singer and musician (five-string banjo, guitar, harmonica); b. 11 April 1950, Morristown, NJ; m. Stephanie Kraft 1981; one s. one d. *Education:* Rhode Island School of Design; Juris Dr, Rutgers Law School, Newark, NJ. *Career:* host and producer, Horses Sing None of It!, award-winning series, Manhattan, New York, Philadelphia, and cable stations in New Jersey; music used in soundtrack for The Black West; numerous TV and radio guest appearances, including The Today Show, The Howard Stern Show, The Uncle Floyd Show, KTV Show, Anything Goes, Jersey Beat, The Joe Franklin Show; mem. North American Folk Alliance, Folk Project. *Compositions:* The Band with a Thousand Names, Love is Like Washing a Potato, I'd Rather Say Goodbye to You than Give Up an Indoor Toilet. *Recordings include:* Makes My Heart Feel Happy 1990, Wild and Lazy 1993, Ralph Litwin and the Band with a Thousand Names 1998, Ralph Litwin and Al Podber: The Fabulous Furry Harmonica Brothers 2003. *Honours:* first place, New Jersey Old Style Banjo Championship, Cash Box Magazine Indie Album Choice, winner, Hometown Video Festival, three times; National Old Time Banjo Championship Finalist 1996; first place, Freewheelin' Style, second place, Harmonica, Uncle Dave Macon Days, Tennessee 1996. *Address:* 140 Morris Street, Morristown, NJ 07960, USA (office).

LIU, Huan; Chinese singer; b. 26 Aug. 1963, Tianjin; m. Lu Lu 1988; one d. *Education:* Beijing Int. Relations Inst. *Career:* solo artist; teacher, Univ. of Int. Relations, Beijing; currently teaching at Beijing Univ. of Int. Business and Econs; performed official theme song "You and Me" at Summer Olympic Games Opening Ceremony, Beijing, August 2008. *Stage production:* Sister Liu (opera) 2003. *Television:* The Voice of China (judge) 2012. *Compositions include:* themes to TV dramas: Plainclothes Cop 1986, The Water Margin, A Native of Beijing in New York, Snow City, Sun Rises in the East and Rain Drops in the West; songs: Asking Myself a Thousand Times for That, Helpless Love. *Address:* c/o University of International Business and Economics, No. 10 Huixin Dongjie, Chaoyang District, Beijing 100029, People's Republic of China (office). *Telephone:* (10) 64492131 (office). *Fax:* (10) 64493860 (office). *Website:* english.uibe.edu.cn/ (office).

LIVESEY, Warne; British record producer; b. 12 Feb. 1959, London, England; m. Barbara 1983. *Career:* mem. Musicians' Union. *Recordings:* albums: as producer: Diesel and Dust, Midnight Oil; Blue Sky Mining, Midnight Oil; Infected, The The; Mind Bomb, The The; When The World Knows Your Name, Deacon Blue; Perverse, Jesus Jones; Suddenly Tammy!; Prick; St Julian, Julian Cope; Babe Rainbow, House of Love; Underdogs, Matthew Good Band; Work, Lovelife, Miscellaneous, by David Devant and his Spirit Wife. *E-mail:* warne@warnelivesey.com. *Website:* www.warnelivesey .com.

LIVINGSTONE, Christian; New Zealand musician (guitar); b. Cambridge. *Career:* mem., The Datsuns 1997–; own label, Hell Squad Records. *Recordings include:* albums: The Datsuns 2002, Outta Sight Outta Mind 2004, Smoke & Mirrors 2006, Head Stunts 2008. *Current Management:* c/o Tom Dalton, Thunderbird Management, PO Box 60496, Titirangi, Waitakere 0642, New Zealand. *Telephone:* (9) 836-3232. *E-mail:* tom@thunderbirdmanagement .com. *Website:* www.thunderbirdmanagement.com. *E-mail:* enquiries@ thedatsuns.com. *Website:* www.thedatsuns.com.

LL COOL J; American rap artist; b. (James Todd Smith), 14 Jan. 1968, St Albans, Queens, NY. *Career:* began rapping aged 9; concerts include support to Run DMC, Raising Hell tour 1986; headliner, Def Jam '87 tour 1987; performed at Farm Aid IV 1990, Budweiser Superfest 1991; European tour 1993; founder, Uncle Records 1992. *Film appearances:* Krush Groove 1985, The Hard Way 1991, Toys 1992, Last Holiday 2005. *Recordings include:* albums: Radio 1985, Bigger And Deffer 1987, Walking With A Panther 1989, Mama Said Knock You Out 1990, 14 Shots To The Dome 1993, Mr Smith 1996, Phenomenon 1997, G.O.A.T. Featuring James T. Smith: The Greatest of All Time 2000, 10 2002, The DEFinition 2004, Todd Smith 2006, Exit 13 2008. *Publications:* I Make My Own Rules (autobiog.) 1997. *Honours:* Soul Train Music Awards: Best Rap Album, Best Rap Single, 1988; MTV Music Video Award, Best Rap Video, 1991; Billboard Top Rap Singles Artist, 1991; Grammy Awards, Best Rap Solo Performance, Mama Said Knock You Out, 1992, Hey Lover, 1996; MTV Video Vanguard Award, 1997. *Current Management:* Rush Artist Management, 160 Varick Street, New York, NY 10013, USA. *Address:* LL Cool J Inc, 186–39 Illian Avenue, Jamaica, NY 11412, USA (office). *Website:* www.llcoolj.com.

LLABADOR, Jean-Pierre, BA; jazz musician (guitar) and composer; b. 15 Dec. 1952, Nemours, Algeria; m. Annie Soulet-Pujol 1976, two d. *Education:* Conservatoire, France, studied in Los Angeles, USA. *Career:* mem. of various jazz, fusion and rock bands including Coincidence; Johnny Hallyday (tours, radio and television shows, recordings), 1975–85; lead guitarist, composer, with own bands 1985–; many tours, Europe and Africa; international festival appearances include: Nîmes, Montpellier-Radio-France, Nancy Jazz Pulsation, Midem, Barcelona, Laseyne sur Mer, Cardiff, Bath; numerous radio and television broadcasts; Artistic Dir, OJLR (Region Languedoc Jazz Orchestra); mem. SACEM, SPEDIDAM. *Recordings include:* albums (mostly own compostions): French Guitar Connection, quartet (USA); 5th Edition, quintet (Germany); Friendship, duo/trio (Germany); Dialogues, OJLR (France); Birds Can Fly, quintet/sextet (France); El Bobo, from duo to orchestra (France). *Address:* 700 chemin des Mendrous, 34170 Castelnau-le-Lez, France. *E-mail:* j-p.llabador@caramail.com.

LLACH, Lluís; Spanish singer, songwriter and musician (piano, guitar); b. 7 May 1948, Girona, Catalonia. *Career:* singer, songwriter, late 1960s-; pioneer, Nova Canço (Catalan protest-song movement against Gen. Franco); mem., El Setze Jutges 1967; numerous concerts; mem. Societat General d'Autors i Editors (SGAE), Associació de Cantants i Intérprets en Llengua Catalana (ACIC). *Compositions:* arranger, songwriter on albums by Teresa Rebull, Francesc Pi de la Serra, Dolors Lafitte, Marina Rossell, Josep Tero, Maria del Mar Bonet, Joan Americ, Carles Cases; music for films: Borrasca 1977, La Forja de un Rebelde 1990, El Ladrón de Niños 1992. *Recordings include:* albums: Els èxits de Lluís Llach 1968, Ara i aquí 1970, Com um arbre nu 1972, Lluís Llach a l'Olympia 1973, I si canto trist 1974, Viatge a Ítaca 1975, Barcelona Gener de 1976, Campanades a morts 1977, El meu amic el mar 1978, Somniem 1979, Verges 50 1980, I amb de somruire, la revolta 1982, T'estimo 1984, Maremar 1985, Astres 1986, Geografia 1988, La forja de un rebelde 1990, Torna aviat 1991, Ara, 25 anys en directe 1992, Un pont de mar blava 1993, A Biqi, perquê et ballis 1993, Rar 1994, Porrera-Món 1995, Nu 1997, 9 1998, Temps de Revolte 2000, Jocs 2002, Poetes 2004, i. 2006, Verges 2007 2007. *Publications:* Poemes i Cançons 1979, Lluís Llach 1979, Lluís Llach – Catalogne Vivre 1979, Un Trobador per a un Poble 1982, Història de les Seves Cançons Explicada a Josep Maria Espinàs 1986, La Dàraison d'Etat 1987, La Geografia del Cor 1992, Lluís Llach 1993. *E-mail:* contact@lluisllach.com (office). *Website:* www.lluisllach.cat.

LLOYD, Andrew Reginald, (Popman); British singer, songwriter, musician (guitar), actor and record producer; b. 2 June 1960, Halesowen, Birmingham. *Career:* mem. bands including Mickey Mouse Revival 1972–76, Andy Lloyd and the Wedge 1978–79, The Bloomsbury Set 1980–83, Popman and the Raging Bull 1986–88, Popman and the Disciple 1989–93; tours with Judie Tzuke 1981, Duran Duran 1982; various support tours 1986–92; headline tour 1993; solo acoustic US tour 1994; mem, MU, Equity, Songwriters Guild, PRS, MLPS. *Recordings:* Back To School 1978, It's Up To You 1978, Living In America 1979, Letters To Eva 1979, This Year Next Year 1981, The Other Side of You 1981, Sweet Europeans 1982, Hanging Around With The Big Boys, Getting Away From It All, Dress Parade, Serenade 1983, Just Like A Woman, Casual Acquaintance 1986, Fields In Motion, Hustling Man 1987, New Feelings, Friends and Lovers 1988, Pirate 1989, Girl of My Best Friend 1990, Little White Lies, The Same Girl 1991, Weekend 1992, Acoustic set 1994, Plugs Out 1995, Food 1996.

LLOYD, Charles; American jazz musician (alto saxophone, flute) and bandleader; b. 15 March 1938, Memphis, Tenn. *Education:* Univ. of Southern California. *Career:* began career as musician in bands of B.B. King, Howlin' Wolf, Bobby "Blue" Bland, Gerald Wilson; mem. and musical dir Chico Hamilton Band 1960–63; mem. Cannonball Adderley Sextet 1964–66; leader, Charles Lloyd Quartet 1966–68; recording and touring musician with The Beach Boys 1970s, mem. spin-off group Celebration 1979; resumed jazz career 1980s; formed group with Bobo Stenson, Palle Danielsson and Jon Christensen; also performed with Geri Allen, Jason Moran, Billy Higgins. *Recordings:* as bandleader: Discovery! 1964, Of Course, Of Course 1965, Dream Weaver 1966, Forest Flower 1966, The Flowering 1966, Charles Lloyd in Europe 1966, Love-In 1967, Journey Within 1967, Nirvana 1968, Moon Man 1970, Warm Waters 1971, Waves 1972, Geeta 1973, Morning Sunrise 1973, Weanings 1978, Koto/Painless Path 1978, Big Sur Tapestry 1979, Autumn in New York Volume One 1979, Fish Out of Water 1989, Notes from Big Sur 1992, The Call 1993, All My Relations 1994, Canto 1996, Voice in the Night 1999, The Water is Wide 2000, Lift Every Voice 2002, Which Way is East 2004, Jumping the Creek 2005, Sangam 2006, Rabo de Nube 2008, Mirror 2010; other appearances include: with Chico Hamilton: Bye Bye Birdie – Irma la Douce 1960, The Chico Hamilton Special 1960, Drumfusion 1962, Transfusion 1962, Passin' Thru 1962, A Different Journey 1963, Man from Two Worlds 1963, Chic Chic Chico 1965; with Cannonball Adderley: Cannonball Adderley's Fiddler on the Roof 1964; with The Beach Boys: Surf's Up 1971, Holland 1972, 15 Big Ones 1976, M.I.U. Album 1978; with Celebration: Celebration 1979, Disco Celebration 1979; also: Les McCann Sings, Les McCann 1961, Historical Figures and Ancient Heads, Canned Heat 1971, Full Circle, The Doors 1972, The Snake, Harvey Mandel 1972, Roger McGuinn, Roger McGuinn 1973, Breakaway, William Truckaway 1976, Old Places, Old Faces, Joe Sample 1995, Afterglow, Mark Isham 1998. *Current Management:* c/o Dorothy Darr, Forest Farm Music + Art/Dorothy Darr, PO Box 5816, Santa Barbara, CA 93150, USA. *Telephone:* (805) 969-2882. *E-mail:* info@charleslloyd.com. *Website:* www.charleslloyd.com.

LLOYD, Duncan; British musician (guitar); b. Derby, England. *Career:* founder mem., Maxïmo Park 2001–; also solo artist 2008–. *Recordings include:* albums: with Maximo Park: A Certain Trigger 2005, Our Earthly Pleasures 2007, Quicken the Heart 2009, The National Health 2012, Too Much Information 2014; solo: Seeing Double 2008. *Current Management:* Prolifica Management, Unit 1, 32 Caxton Road, London W12 8AJ, England. *Telephone:* (20) 8740-9920. *Fax:* (20) 8740-2976. *E-mail:* info@prolifica.co.uk. *Website:* www.prolificamanagement.co.uk; www.maximopark.com.

LLOYD, Gary, BA; British composer; b. 29 Jan. 1965, Ottawa, Canada. *Education:* Univ. of Liverpool, Chester Coll. *Career:* ran recording studio, 1987–89; composition and soundtrack composer since 1989; scored music for more than 400 productions including works for TV, film, theatre, contemporary dance, son et lumiere, art installations; first commission Neil Gaiman's Violent Cases, stageplay soundtrack, 1988. *Compositions include:* A Return To Love, for TV drama, 1994; Ignition, music for Fireworks, 1994; Land of Many Waters, for A/V show and CD release, 1995; Precis for String Orchestra, performed Cholmondeley Castle, Cheshire, England, 1996; The Ghost Tour (film), 1997; Curiously England (documentary), 1997; Alien Blood, filmscore, 1998. *Recordings:* Albums: The Bridge, with Iain Banks, 1996; Brought to Light, with Alan Moore, 1998.

LLOYD, Richard; American musician (drums) and producer; b. 17 Jan. 1961, Miami Beach; m. Linda Westauss 1996. *Education:* Miami Community College; studied with Cag Thaler and Charles Perry. *Career:* 20 years performing as drummer and as producer; performed across country with groups such as Stevie Ray Vaughan, The Thunderbirds, ZZ Top; mem. Department of Professional Regulation; owner, Big Beat Productions. *Recordings:* The Ones 1981, The Leap 1983, The Answer 1985, The Alternatives 1985, Lady Sabre 1987, The Sharks 1989, The Cover Doesn't Matter 2001. *Honours:* Battle of the Bands, Houston, Texas 1981. *Address:* Big Beat Productions, 1515 University Drive, Suite 108, Coral Springs, FL 33071-6085, USA (office).

LLOYD WEBBER, Baron (Life Peer), cr. 1997, of Sydmonton in the County of Hampshire; **Andrew Lloyd Webber,** FRCM; British composer; *Chairman, The Really Useful Group Ltd;* b. 22 March 1948, Kensington, London; s. of the late William Southcombe Lloyd Webber and Jean Hermione Johnstone; brother of Julian Lloyd Webber; m. 1st Sarah Jane Tudor (née Hugill) 1971 (divorced 1983); one s. one d.; m. 2nd Sarah Brightman 1984 (divorced 1990); m. 3rd Madeleine Astrid Gurdon 1991; two s. one d. *Education:* Westminster School, Magdalen Coll. Oxford, Royal Coll. of Music. *Career:* Chair. The Really Useful Group Ltd; owner of six London theatres including Theatre Royal Drury Lane and The London Palladium. *Works:* musicals: Joseph and the Amazing Technicolor Dreamcoat (lyrics by Tim Rice) 1968 (revised 1973, 1991), Jesus Christ Superstar (lyrics by Tim Rice) 1970 (revised 1996, 2012), Jeeves (lyrics by Alan Ayckbourn) 1975 (revised as By Jeeves 1996), Evita (lyrics by Tim Rice) 1976 (stage version 1978), Tell Me on a Sunday (lyrics by Don Black) 1980 (revised 2003), Cats (based on T. S. Eliot's Old Possum's Book of Practical Cats) (Tony Awards for Best Score and Best Musical 1983) 1981, Song and Dance (lyrics by Don Black) 1982, Starlight Express (lyrics by Richard Stilgoe) 1984, The Phantom of the Opera (lyrics by Richard Stilgoe and Charles Hart) (Tony Award for Best Musical 1988) 1986, Aspects of Love (lyrics by Don Black and Charles Hart) 1989, Sunset Boulevard (lyrics by Christopher Hampton and Don Black) (Tony Award for Best Score and Best Musical 1995) 1993, Whistle Down the Wind (lyrics by Jim Steinman) 1996, The Beautiful Game (lyrics by Ben Elton) (London Critics' Circle Best Musical 2000) 2000, The Woman in White (lyrics by David Zippel) 2004, Love Never Dies (lyrics by Glenn Slater) 2010, Stephen Ward (lyrics by Christopher Hampton and Don Black) 2013, School of Rock 2015; other compositions: Variations (based on A minor Caprice No. 24 by Paganini) 1977 (symphonic version 1986), Requiem Mass 1985, Amigos Para Siempre (official theme for 1992 Olympic Games), UK Eurovision entry, It's My Time (co-written with Diane Warren), Moscow 2009; film scores: Gumshoe 1971, The Odessa File 1974. *Producer:* Joseph and the Amazing Technicolor Dreamcoat 1973, 1974, 1978, 1980, 1991, Jeeves Takes Charge 1975, Cats 1981, Song & Dance 1982, Daisy Pulls it Off 1983, The Hired Man 1984, Starlight Express 1984, On Your Toes 1984, The Phantom of the Opera 1986, Café Puccini 1986, The Resistible Rise of Arturo Ui 1987, Lend Me a Tenor 1988, Aspects of Love 1989, Shirley

Valentine (Broadway) 1989, La Bête 1992, Sunset Boulevard 1993, By Jeeves 1996, Whistle Down the Wind 1996, 1998, Jesus Christ Superstar 1996, 1998, The Beautiful Game 2000, Bombay Dreams 2002, Tell Me On A Sunday, 2003, The Woman in White 2004, The Sound of Music 2006 and others. *Art collection:* Pre-Raphaelite and Other Masters: The Andrew Lloyd Webber Collection, Royal Acad., London 2003. *Film:* The Phantom of the Opera (dir Joel Schumacher) 2004. *Publications:* Evita (with Tim Rice) 1978, Cats: the book of the musical 1981, Joseph and the Amazing Technicolor Dreamcoat (with Tim Rice) 1982, The Complete Phantom of the Opera 1987, The Complete Aspects of Love 1989, Sunset Boulevard: from movie to musical 1993. *Honours:* seven Tony Awards, four Drama Desk Awards, seven Laurence Olivier Awards, 14 Ivor Novello Awards from British Acad. of Songwriters, Composers and Authors, Triple Play Award from ASCAP 1988, Star on the Hollywood Walk of Fame for live theatre 1993, Praemium Imperiale Award 1995, four Grammy Awards, Golden Globe Award, Academy Award 1996, Richard Rodgers Award for Excellence in Musical Theatre 1996, Kennedy Center Honor 2006, Woodrow Wilson Award for Public Service 2008, American Songwriters Hall of Fame, Commdr's Cross of the Order of Merit (Hungary) 2005. *Address:* c/o The Really Useful Group Ltd, 17 Slingsby Place, London, WC2E 9AB, England (office). *Telephone:* (20) 7240-0880 (office). *Fax:* (20) 7240-1204 (office). *Website:* www.reallyuseful.com (office); www.andrewlloydwebber.com.

LÔ, Cheikh N'Digel; Senegalese singer, musician (guitar) and songwriter; b. 1955, Bobo Dioulasso, Burkina Faso. *Career:* mem., Orchestra Volta Jazz 1976; moved to Dakar 1980; worked as a drummer for five years; moved to Paris 1985; continued to work as a session drummer; met Youssou N'Dour 1989, who produced Ne La Thiass album 1995; appeared in the USA with Africa Fete 1998; played at WOMAD Reading 2001; mem. and follower of the Baye Fall. *Recordings include:* albums: Ne La Thiass 1996, Bambay Gueej (featuring Juan de Marcos Gonzalez, Oumou Sangare and Bigga Morrison) 1999, Lamp Fall 2005, Jamm 2010. *Honours:* Kora Award for Best Newcomer 1997, Ordre National de Mérite de Leon (presented by the Pres. of Senegal) 2001. *Address:* c/o World Circuit Ltd, 138 Kingsland Road, London, E2 8DY, England (office). *E-mail:* post@worldcircuit.co.uk (office). *Website:* www.worldcircuit.co.uk (office).

LÔ, Ismaël; Senegalese musician; b. 30 Aug. 1956; m. *Education:* Institut des arts de Dakar. *Career:* singer and composer of African folk songs in Wolof and French. *Recordings include:* 21 albums including Iso 1995, Jammu Africa 1996, Dabah 2001, Sénégal 2006.

LOBO, Edu; singer, musician (guitar), composer and songwriter; b. (Eduardo de Goes Lobos), 1943, Rio de Janeiro, Brazil. *Career:* has written songs that combine Brazilian folk music with bossa nova harmonies; Despite being born in Rio, lyrics often object to the injustice and misery of Brazil's Northeast region; Met Carlos Lyra, mid 1960s; Greatly influenced by Lyra's new bossa style, elements of northeastern music and socially conscious lyrics; First album released, 1964; Protest songs not popular with Brazilian military dictatorship in power during late 1960s, so left for the USA, 1969; Supplied four songs and played guitar on saxophonist Paul Desmond's album From The Hot Afternoon; Since return to Brazil in 1971, has mainly written music for plays, films and ballets. *Recordings:* Albums: Musica De Edu Lobo Por Edu Lobo, 1964; Reencontro, Folklore E Bossa Nova Do Brasil, 1966; Edu, 1968; Sergio Mendes Presents Lobo, 1969; Cantiga De Longe, 1971; Nissa Breve, 1973; Limite Das Aguas, 1975; Camaleão, 1978; Tom E Edu, Jogos De Danca, 1981; O Grande Circo Mistico, 1983; Edu E Bethania, 1984; Corrupião, 1993; Meia Noite, 1995; features on: From The Hot Afternoon, Paul Desmond, 1969. *Honours:* First place TV in record festival, Borandá, 1967; Gramado Film Festival, Best Soundtrack, Barra Pesada, 1979.

LOCK, Eddie; British business executive, musician, record producer, art dealer and gallery owner and agent; *Goldie's Exclusive Worldwide Manager, Eddie Lock Management;* b. 10 Feb. 1969, Bury St Edmunds, Suffolk, England. *Education:* Maidstone Boys' Grammar School. *Career:* DJ 1987; mem. Carpe Diem, Lock & Burns; mem. Mechanical Copyright Protection Soc., British Phonographic Industry, Performing Right Soc., Music Publishers Asscn; agent and manager for the art of Goldie, Dan Baldwin, Pam Glew; Goldie's exclusive Worldwide Man., Eddie Lock Management. *Compositions:* Calling My Name, Got To Get Up 1998, La Noche Vista 1999. *Recordings:* The Buzz, Don't Wanna Be Free, Hypnotic, Music Takes You, Snakecharmer, Space is the Place, Turkish Delight, The Phuture 2000, Come Close to Me 2000, Dance to the Music 2001, Spaced 2001, Bang to the Beat of the Drum 2002, Psychology of the Dreamer 2002, Quiero Bailar la Salsa 2004. *Exhibitions:* Pepe, London 2005, Sheridans, London 2006, L.S.G Love Over Gold 2007, The Kids Are All Riot, Maverik Showroom, London 2009, Lock Up, London 2009, 2011, London Ivy 2012. *Address:* 2 The Old Parish Hall, The Square, Lenham, Kent, ME17 2PQ, England (home). *Telephone:* (1622) 858300 (office). *Fax:* (1622) 858300 (office). *E-mail:* info@eddielock.com (office). *Website:* www.eddielock.co.uk.

LOCKETT, Peter Robert; British musician (percussion); b. 8 April 1963, Portsmouth, Hampshire, England. *Education:* Madras Academy, 1991–93. *Career:* Live TV work, recording, touring with Kula Shaker; Live TV work and recording with Vanessa Mae; Duo concerts at Royal Festival Hall with Joji Hirota; Series on drum programming, The Mix, magazine; World percussion sample CDs for The Mix, magazine; Films: City of Angels; Plunkett and Maclean; The World Is Not Enough; The Bone Collector. *Recordings:* with

Bjork; Bill Bruford; David Arnold; A R Rahman; 2 albums with top Danish guitarist, Henrik Anderson; with Natacha Atlas, Transglobal Underground; Tomorrow Never Dies, Bond film; with Mel C; Pet Shop Boys; Nitin Sawhney; Junior Delgado; Arts Council CMN tour for Pete Lockett's Network of Sparks, featuring Bill Bruford, 2000; Taiko and Tabla, Joji Hirota/Pete Lockett. *Publications:* Drum technique articles for Modern Drummer and Rhythm Magazine. *E-mail:* pete@petelockett.com. *Website:* www.petelockett.com.

LOCKHEART, Mark; British musician (saxophones, clarinet, flute) and composer; b. 31 March 1961, Hampshire, England; m. Andrea Margo Tosic 1985. *Education:* Trinity Coll. of Music. *Career:* saxophone, Loose Tubes, Lysis Steve Berry Trio 1985–91; leader, Perfect Houseplants; co-leader, Matheran; mem., Django Bates' Delightful Precipice; also bands with June Tabor, Billy Jenkins; session work with Jah Wobble, Prefab Sprout, The High Llamas, Stereolab, Radiohead; solo artist. *Recordings include:* with Perfect Houseplants: Perfect Houseplants 1993, Clec 1995, Snap Clatter 1997, Extempore 1998, Extempore II New Folk Songs 2001; with Matheran: Mark Lockheart-John Paracelli 1994; with Django Bates: Summer Fruits and Unrest 1994; with June Tabor: Some Other Time 1989, Angel Tiger 1992, Against The Streams 1994, Aleyn 1997; with The Scratch Band: Through Rose-Coloured Glasses 1998; solo: Moving Air 2005, In Deep 2009, Days Like These 2010. *E-mail:* info@marklockheart.co.uk (office). *Website:* www.marklockheart.co.uk.

LOCKWOOD, Didier André Paul; French musician (violin) and jazz composer; b. 11 Feb. 1956, Calais; m. Casadesus 1993; three d. *Education:* Conservatoire de Calais, École Normale Supérieure de Musique, Paris. *Career:* first prize, at Conservatory, age 16; professional musician with French group, Magma 1973–; worked with Stéphane Grappelli 1978; formed own groups 1980–; appearances include Royal Albert Hall, Carnegie Hall, New York, Théatre des Champs Elysées; major jazz festivals; concerts worldwide incl. *Compositions:* Jazz and contemporary music; Violin concerto: Les Mouettes, (with symphony orchestra). *Recordings:* Recordings: over 20 include: New World, with Antony Williams (drums) 1981, Live In Montreux 1982, The Kid, Out of The Blue 1986, New York Rendevouz 1994, Storyboard 1996, Children's Songs 1997, Tribute To Stephane Grappelli 2000, Om Kara 2001. *Publications:* Violin Jazz Method book. *Honours:* Chevalier, Ordre des Arts et des Lettres, Grand Officier, Légion d'honneur 2002; Blue Note Award, two Victoires de la Musique Awards, Grand Prix, SACEM, Prix Charles Cross. *Current Management:* c/o Marc de Cagny, Ames Productions, 11 rue de la Forêt, 77630 Saint Martin en Bière, France. *Telephone:* 1-60-66-26-26. *Fax:* 1-60-66-26-00. *E-mail:* marcdecagny@wanadoo.fr. *Website:* www.amesproduction.com; www.didierlockwood.com.

LODDER, Stephen (Steve) John; British musician (keyboards) and composer; b. 1951. *Education:* Gonville and Caius Coll., Cambridge. *Career:* before musical freelance career worked as music teacher in a comprehensive school and ran a coffee/wholefood store; played with many artists on the London jazz scene, including Paul Nieman, Carol Grimes, Maggie Nichols, Jan Ponsford, John Etheridge, Henry Thomas, Harry Beckett late 1970s–80s; toured and recorded with George Russell's Living Time Orchestra late 1980s; mem., Brian Abrahams' District Six; tours in Germany and UK; Musical Dir for Sarah Jane Morris during a six-week tour supporting Simply Red 1989; long musical collaboration, touring and recording with Andy Sheppard, including as part of Inclassificable trio 1995; worked with John Harle on Duke Ellington tribute, Shadow of the Duke 1992; mem. ONL (with Stig Olson and Paul Nieman) 2006–; other collaborations with Mark Ramsden, Monica Vasconcelos, Carla Bley, John Harle, Paul McCartney. *Recordings include:* albums: features on: Eyes Wide Open, Carol Grimes 1987, Why Don't They Dance?, Carol Grimes 1989, Imgoma Yabantwana, Brian Abraham's District Six 1989, Introductions In The Dark, Andy Sheppard 1989, Soft On The Inside, Andy Sheppard 1989, The London Concert, George Russell's Living Time Orchestra 1990, In Co-Motion, Andy Sheppard 1991, Shadow of The Duke, John Harle 1992, Rhythm Method, Andy Sheppard 1993, Inclassificable, Andy Sheppard 1994, Delivery Suite, Andy Sheppard 1994, Terror and Magnificance, John Harle 1996, Above The Clouds, Mark Ramsden/Steve Lodder 1996, Moving Image, Andy Sheppard 1996, It's About Time, George Russell's Living Time Orchestra 1996, Nois, Monica Vasconcelos 1997, Standing Stones, Paul McCartney 1997, Learning To Wave, Andy Sheppard 1998, Nois Dos, Monica Vasconcelos 1999, Dancing Man and Woman, Andy Sheppard 2000, The Gathering, Annie Whitehead 2000, Songs of the Year, Threeway 2010; with ONL: One 2007; TV soundtracks: Ali Bongo – The Wacky Wizard; TV/radio soundtracks with Andy Sheppard: The Art Wrap, The Postman Always Rings Twice, Arena: Peter Sellers, Joseph Emidy, Syrup (short film). *E-mail:* admin@onl-music.com; steve@stevelodder.com. *Website:* www.onl-music.com; www.stevelodder.com.

LODGE, John Charles; musician (bass guitar) and singer; b. 20 July 1945, Birmingham, England; m. Kirsten 1968, one s. one d. *Education:* Birmingham Coll. of Advanced Technology. *Career:* fmr mem., El Riot and The Rebels, The Carpetbaggers, John Bullbreed; mem., Moody Blues 1966–; also solo artist; numerous tours, concerts, festival appearances. mem. PRS, BAC&S, Songwriters' Guild of America. *Recordings include:* albums: In Search of the Lost Chord, 1968; On The Threshold of a Dream, 1969; To Our Children's Children, 1969; A Question of Balance, 1970; Every Good Boy Deserves Favour, 1971; Days of Future Passed, 1972; Seventh Sojurn, 1972; This Is The Moody Blues, 1974; Blue Jays, 1975; Octave, 1978; Long Distance Voyager, 1981; Voices In The Sky/The Best of The Moody Blues, 1985; The Other Side of Life, 1986; Sur

La Mer, 1988; Greatest Hits, 1988; Keys of The Kingdom, 1991; Live At Red Rocks, 1993; Time Traveller, 1994; Anthology, 1998; Live At The Royal Albert Hall, 2000; solo: Natural Avenue, 1977. *Honours:* ASCAP Award for Best Singer in a Rock 'n' Roll Band, two Ivor Novello Awards, Ivor Novello Award for Outstanding Contribution to British Music 1985. *Address:* Threshold Record Company Limited, 90 High Street, Newmarket, Suffolk, CB8 8FE, England (office). *E-mail:* info@johnlodge.com. *Website:* www.johnlodge.com.

LOEB, Lisa; American singer, musician (guitar) and songwriter; b. Dallas, TX; m. Roey Hershkovitz 2009; one d. *Career:* solo artist, as Lisa Loeb and Nine Stories 1994–. *Recordings include:* albums: Tails 1995, Firecracker 1997, Cake and Pie 2001, Hello Lisa 2001, Catch the Moon 2003, The Way it Really Is 2004, The Purple Tape 2008, Camp Lisa 2008. *Honours:* BRIT Award for Best Int. Newcomer 1995. *Address:* 11054 Ventura Boulevard, Suite 381, Studio City, CA 91604, USA (office). *E-mail:* janet@managethismedia.com (office); webmaster@lisaloeb.com (office). *Website:* www.lisaloeb.com.

LOEFFLER, Tony; American musician (guitar) and songwriter; b. 5 April 1947, Paterson, New Jersey; m. 27 April 1968, 1 s., 2 d. *Education:* Psychology major. *Career:* Festival appearances include: Bay Shore Arts Festival, Long Island, New York, 1986; Rainbow Bash Festival, Sparta, New Jersey, 1993; Cross Rhythms Festival, Devon, UK, 1995, 1996, 1997; Sur Montreux Anniversary Jazz/Rock Festival, Switzerland, 1996, 1998; Tours throughout USA; Numerous television and radio appearances; Regular tours with Tony Loeffler and The Blue Angels; mem, Recording Industry Asscn of America (RIAA); Gospel Music Asscn; Broadcast Music Inc. *Recordings:* 12 albums including: In the Texas Heat 2001, Cuba Para Cristo 2004. *Publications:* Foundation (the Solid Rock Newsletter). *Telephone:* (561) 784-5188. *E-mail:* tloeffler@thesolidrock.org. *Website:* www.thesolidrock.org.

LOFGREN, Nils; American musician (guitar), songwriter, arranger and singer; b. 21 June 1951, Chicago, IL. *Career:* mem. Grin 1970s; solo artist 1974–; numerous live appearances. *Recordings include:* albums: Nils Lofgren 1975, Cry Tough 1976, I Came To Dance 1977, Night After Night 1977, Nils 1979, Night Fades Away 1981, Rhythm Romance 1982, Wonderland 1983, Flip 1985, Code of The Road 1986, Silver Lining 1991, Crooked Line 1992, Everybreath 1994, Damaged Goods 1995, Acoustic Live 1997, Into the Night 1998, Breakaway Angel 2001, Sacred Weapon 2006, The Loner: Nils Sings Neil 2008. *Current Management:* Anson Smith Management, LLC, 8012 Old Georgetown Road, Bethesda, MD 20814, USA. *Telephone:* (301) 654-4444. *Fax:* (301) 654-4633. *E-mail:* asmgmt@aol.com. *Website:* www.nilslofgren.com.

LOGGINS, Kenneth (Kenny) Clarke; American singer, songwriter and musician (guitar); b. 7 Jan. 1947, Everett, Washington; m. Eva Ein 1976 (divorced). *Education:* Pasadena City College. *Career:* member, Gator Creek; Second Helping; duo, Loggins and Messina (with Jim Messina) 1971–76; solo artist, songwriter 1977–. *Compositions include:* House At Pooh Corner, recorded by Nitty Gritty Dirt Band 1971, Your Mama Don't Dance, recorded by Loggins and Messina, Elvis Presley, Poison 1973, Danny's Song, recorded by Anne Murray; co-writer with Michael McDonald, What A Fool Believes, recorded by Doobie Brothers 1979; co-writer with Melissa Manchester, Whenever I Call You Friend 1979. *Recordings:* albums: with Loggins and Messina: Kenny Loggins With Jim Messina Sittin' In 1971, Loggins and Messina 1972, Full Sail 1973, On Stage 1974, Mother Lode 1974, So Fine 1975, Native Sons 1976, Finale 1977, The Best of Friends 1977; solo albums: Celebrate Me Home 1977, Nightwatch 1978, Keep The Fire 1979, Kenny Loggins: Alive 1980, High Adventure 1982, Footloose, film soundtrack 1984, Vox Humana 1985, Top Gun (film soundtrack) 1986, Back To Avalon 1987, Kenny Loggins On Broadway 1988, Leap of Faith 1991, Outside – From The Redwoods 1993, Return to Pooh Corner 1994, The Unimaginable Life 1997, December 1998, More Songs From Pooh Corner 2000, It's About Time 2003, How About Now 2007; hit singles include: This Is It 1980, I'm Alright, from film Caddyshack 1980, Don't Fight It, duet with Steve Perry 1982, Heart To Heart 1983, Footloose, from film Footloose 1984, Danger Zone, from film Top Gun 1986, Meet Me Half Way, from film Over The Top 1987, Nobody's Fool, from film Caddyshack 2 1988. *Honours:* Grammy Awards for Song of the Year (for What A Fool Believes) 1980, for Best Pop Vocal Performance (for This Is It) 1981. *Current Management:* Moir Borman Entertainment, 1250 6th Street, Santa Monica, CA 90401, USA. *Website:* www.kennyloggins.com.

LOGRÉN, Lassi; Finnish musician (fiddle, jouhikko, nyckelharpa). *Education:* Sibelius Acad. *Career:* mem., Värttinä 1985–89, 2002–; fiddle teacher, Sibelius Acad. *Music for theatre:* co-wrote score to stage musical, The Lord of the Rings (with A. R. Rahman) (Princess of Wales Theatre, Toronto) 2006. *Recordings include:* albums: Värttinä 1987, Musta Lindu 1989, iki 2003, Miero 2006. *Publication:* Harmony Parts for Finnish Fiddle (with CD) 2001. *Honours:* Kaustinen Folk Music Festival Band of the Year 1987. *Current Management:* c/o Phillip Page, Hoedown Arts Oy, Neitsytpolku 9 F 81, 00140 Helsinki, Finland. *Telephone:* (50) 5692982. *Fax:* (9) 628950. *E-mail:* pap@hoedown.com. *Website:* www.varttina.com.

LOHAN, Sinead; Irish singer and musician; b. 21 June 1971, Cork City. *Education:* piano lessons. *Career:* solo artist. *Recordings include:* albums: Who Do You Think I Am, 1995; No Mermaid, 1998. *Honours:* Irish National Entertainment Award for Best Newcomer. *Address:* c/o Pat Egan, Merchants Court 24, Merchants Quay, Dublin 8, Ireland (office). *Website:* www .sineadlohan.com.

LOHAR, Arif; Pakistani folk singer and musician (chimta); b. 1966, Lala Mussa, Gujrat District, Punjab; s. of Alam Lohar. *Career:* has released over 150 albums; has recorded over 3,000 songs; over 50 int. tours; performed at Asian Games, People's Repub. of China 2004. *Recordings include:* numerous albums including: Alif Allah Chambe Di Bootey, Ek Pal, Bol Mitti Da, Sher Punjab Da, Soniye, Aakhian, 21st Century Jugni 2006, Jugni Coke Studio 2010 and numerous other collaborative albums. *Honours:* Pride of Performance Award from Govt of Pakistan 2005.

LÖHRER, Eric; French jazz musician (guitar) and composer; b. 15 Feb. 1965, Paris; one s. *Education:* Lycée Henri IV, Univ. of Paris (Sorbonne). *Career:* bandleader for groups Eric Löhrer Trio, Open Air 1987–93, Red Whale 1991–95, Olympic Gramofón, solo programme based on music of Theolonius Monk 1995–96, Eric Löhrer Quartet, Superphenix, Julien Lourau, Kellylee Evans; tours, festivals in France, Europe, Africa; mem. Soc. des auteurs, compositeurs et éditeurs de musique (SACEM), Soc. de Perception et de Distribution des Droits des Artistes-Interprètes (SPEDIDAM). *Recordings include:* albums: with Eric Löhrer Trio: Blue Line 1989, Dans Le Bleu 1992; with Open Air: Musidisc 1991, Attitudes 1992; with Olympic Gramofon: Pee Wee 1996; with Superphenix: Superphenix 1999; with Julien Lourau: Forget 2005, Fire 2005, Julien Lourau vs Rumabierta 2007; with Eric Löhrer Quartet: Sélène Song 2008; solo: Évidence 1997; with Ibrahim Maalouf: Diachronism 2009; with Didier Malherbe: Nuit d'ombrelle 2011; with Kellylee Evans: I Remember When 2013, Come On 2015; with Hadouk: Hadoukly Yours 2014, Le Cinquieme Fruit 2016. *Publications:* Time and Improvisation In Jazz Music 1986. *Honours:* First Prize, Soloist and Band, Vienna Int. Jazz Contest 1987, two band prizes: La Défense Nat. Jazz Contest 1988, 1989. *E-mail:* info@ericlohrer.net (office). *Website:* www.ericlohrer.net.

LOKKE LARSEN, Birgit; Danish musician (percussion) and educator; b. 11 July 1967, Fr-Vaerk. *Education:* studied with Adam Nussbaum, Alex Riel. *Career:* toured with: Savage Rose; Embla; The Big Bang with Palle Danielson, Lars Jansson, Han Bennink, Alex Riel; NORDICAE with Niels Petter Molvaer, Eivin Aarset, Veslemoy Solberg, Sven Ohrvik, Rune Arnsen and Edvard Askeland; ONCE with Anders Jormin, Thomas Gustafsson; SOUK with Kim Kristensen and Thomas Agergaard; April Light Orchestra (Nordic all-women big band); mem., The Ship, tour of Denmark, Norway, Sweden and Greenland, where Marilyn Mazur composed the music; mem. of trio with Hugo Rasmussen and Arne Forchammer. *Compositions:* Dans Under Broen; Dansen; Ballovira; music for play, Mac and Beth, Copenhagen, 1997; play, Minotaurus, Copenhagen, 1999. *Recordings:* Moonchild, with Savage Rose, 1992; Strength of The Runes, with Veslemoy Solberg, 1996; Pulse of Time, with Kim Kristensen, 1999; Kjaerestebilder, with Veslemoy Solberg, 1999; Assimilation with Arne Forchhammer, 2000.

LOMAS, Roger; British record producer and sound engineer; *Managing Director, RO-LO Productions;* b. 8 Oct. 1948, Coventry, West Midlands, England; m. Linda Lomas 1966; two s. one d. *Career:* record producer for Bad Manners, The Selecter, Desmond Dekker, The Bodysnatchers, The Specials, The Modettes, Special-Beat, Roy Wood, Lee 'Scratch' Perry; also DVD audio producer for Ozzy Osbourne, ELO, Happy Mondays, Echo & The Bunnymen, The Tubes, The Bluetones, Elkie Brooks, Terrorvision, The Beat, Bad Manners, The Farm, Jeremy Spencer. *Recordings:* 18 hit singles altogether; recordings include: with Bad Manners: Can Can, Special Brew, My Girl Lollipop, Walking In The Sunshine, Lip Up Fatty; with The Selecter: On My Radio, Missing Words; with Roy Wood: I Wish it Could be Christmas Every Day (live version); with The Specials: Skinhead Girl, 2000, Conquering Ruler 2001; with Lee 'Scratch' Perry: Jamaican E.T. (Grammy Award for Best Reggae Album 2002). *Honours:* Gold and Silver awards for Bad Manners and Selecter albums and singles, Grammy Award for Best Reggae Album (by Lee 'Scratch' Perry) 2002. *Address:* 35 Dillotford Avenue, Coventry, West Midlands, CV3 5DR, England (home). *Telephone:* (24) 7641-0388 (office); 7711-817475 (mobile) (home). *E-mail:* rog@rogerlomas.com (home). *Website:* www.rogerlomas.com.

LOMAX, John, BA; American artist manager and journalist; b. 20 Aug. 1944; m. Melanie Wells; one s. one d. *Education:* University of Texas, Austin. *Career:* A & R Consultant, Demon Records; manager of three acts; freelance writer, Country Music International; founder, President, SFL Tapes and Discs, Music City Exporters; mem, CMA, IMF, NARAS (bd of govs, Nashville Chapter), NEA, CMAA. *Recordings:* Dulcimer Deluxe, Dulcimer Player, Dulcimer Sessions. *Publications:* Nashville: Music City, USA; The Country Music Book. *Honours:* Leadership Music 1998.

LOMEÑA, Paco; Spanish musician (guitar); b. 1980, Malaga. *Career:* joined Ojos de Brujo 2002, a group which fuses gypsy and flamenco music with Latin American, punk, hip hop, reggae and electronic influences; Ojos de Brujo set up own label La Fábrica de Colores 2003 and since then operate as a completely ind. org.; several tours in Europe, Latin America and USA; collaborations with Nitin Sawhney, Asian Dub Foundation. *Recordings:* albums: Barí 2002, Barí: Remezclas de la Casa 2003, Techarí 2006, Aocaná 2009; other: Girando Bari (DVD) 2005. *Honours:* World Music Award for Europe, BBC Radio 3 2004. *E-mail:* paco@ojosdebrujo.com (office). *Website:* www.ojosdebrujo.com.

THE LONE RANGER (see Q-Tip)

LONGNON, Jean-Loup; French musician (trumpet, piano), singer, arranger, composer and conductor; b. 2 Feb. 1953, Paris. *Career:* trumpet player, various bands and big bands; soloist or bandleader performing in concerts, recording studios, jazz clubs, masterclasses, festivals, tours, TV, radio, in France; throughout Europe; Turkey; Israel; Egypt; Tunisia; Morocco; Reunion Island; Mauritius; USA; Cuba (Varandero Festival); Brazil; played with artists, including Dizzy Gillespie, Stan Getz, Clark Terry, Arturo Sandoval, Martial Solal, Stéphane Grappelli, Didier Lockwood, Michel Petrucciani, Antoine Hervé, Kenny Clarke, Chet Baker, Wynton Marsalis, Michel Legrand; mem. SACEM. *Compositions:* Torride, Aquarelles, Jazz à Paris, Nathalie… Un Matin; Variations on John Coltrane themes (commissioned by National Jazz Orchestra); Suite for Orchestra on Dizzy Gillespie (commissioned by Michel Legrand for television show Grand Echiquier); Symphonic poem L'Ours (commissioned by Concert Arban brass quintet and Martin Publications); Cyclades suite for jazz soloist and symphonic orchestra (commissioned by Musique Française d'Aujourdhui). *Recordings include:* Jean-Loup Longnon and his New York Orchestra, Bop Dreamer 1998. *Honours:* winner, Festival de la Défense, Paris, 1977; Django Reinhardt Prize; Boris Vian Prize; European Audivisual Grand Prix; Django d'Or, 1995.

LONGORIA, David; American musician (keyboards). *Career:* mem., The Black 2004–, …And You Will Know Us By The Trail Of Dead 2005–. *Recordings include:* albums: with: …And You Will Know Us By The Trail of Dead: Worlds Apart 2005, So Divided 2006, The Century of Self 2009; with The Black: Tanglewood 2005. *E-mail:* merlin@trailofdead.com (office). *Website:* www.trailofdead.com; www.theblackmusic.com.

LOOP 7 (see Tomiie, Satoshi)

LOPEZ, Jennifer, (J.Lo); American actress, singer, dancer and business executive; b. (Jennifer Lynn Lopez), 24 July 1969, Bronx, New York; m. 1st Ojani Noa 1997 (divorced 1998); m. 2nd Chris Judd 2001 (divorced 2003); m. 3rd Marc Anthony 2004; one s. one d. (twins). *Education:* City Univ. of New York Baruch. *Career:* began career as a Fly Girl on TV programme In Living Color and as a back-up dancer for Janet Jackson; gained recognition in film Money Train 1995; first leading role in biographical film Selena 1997; released debut album On the 6 1999; second album J.Lo reached No. 1 on Billboard 200 the same week her film The Wedding Planner led the box office 2001; released remix album J To Tha L-O! The Remixes 2002; released first full Spanish album Como Ama una Mujer 2007; seventh album Love? gave rise to her most successful career single On the Floor; collaborations with Ja Rule, Big Pun, Fat Joe; Dance Again World Tour 2012; est. clothing and lingerie lines and various perfumes with her celebrity endorsement. *Films include:* My Little Girl 1986, My Family, Mi Familia 1995, Money Train 1995, Jack 1996, Blood and Wine 1996, Selena (ALMA Award for Outstanding Actress) 1997, Anaconda 1997, U Turn 1997, Out of Sight (ALMA Award) 1998, Antz (voice) 1998, The Cell 2000, The Wedding Planner 2001, Angel Eyes 2001, Enough 2002, Maid in Manhattan 2002, Gigli 2003, Jersey Girl 2004, Shall We Dance? 2004, Monster-in-Law 2005, An Unfinished Life 2006, El Cantante 2006, Bordertown (Artists for Amnesty Prize 2007) 2006, The Back-Up Plan 2010, Scrat's Continental Crack-Up: Part 2 (short) (voice) 2011, What to Expect When You're Expecting 2012, Ice Age: Continental Drift (voice) 2012, Parker 2013, The Boy Next Door 2015. *Television includes:* In Living Color 1990, Nurses on the Line: The Crash of Flight 7 1993, Second Chances (series) 1993–94, South Central (series) 1994, Hotel Malibu (series) 1994, How I Met Your Mother (series) 2010, judge, American Idol 2010–12. *Recordings include:* albums: On The 6 1999, J.Lo 2001, J To Tha L-O! (remixes) 2002, This Is Me… Then 2002, Rebirth 2005, Como Ama una Mujer 2007, Brave 2007, Love? 2011, Dance Again… The Hits 2012, AKA 2014. *Publication:* True Love 2014. *Honours:* Golden Globe 1998, MTV Movie Award 1999, Billboard Latin Award for Hot Latin Track of the Year 2000, MTV Video Music Award for Best Dance Video 2000, VH1/Vogue Fashion Versace Award 2000, MTV Europe Music Award for Best Female Act 2001, MTV Award for Best Female 2002, American Music Award for Favorite Pop/Rock Female Artist 2003, American Music Award for Favorite Latin Artist 2007, 2011, ranked by Forbes magazine amongst The World's 100 Most Powerful Women (38th) 2012, Vanguard Award, Glaad Media Awards 2014. *Current Management:* c/o WME Entertainment, 9601 Wilshire Boulevard, Beverly Hills, CA 90210, USA. *Telephone:* (310) 285-9000. *Fax:* (310) 285-9010. *Website:* www.wma.com; www .jenniferlopez.com.

LÓPEZ, Ramón; Spanish musician (drums, tabla); b. 6 Aug. 1961, Alicante; m. Pilar Domínguez 1992; one s. *Education:* tabla student of Krishna Govinda KC, Lucknow, India. *Career:* teacher, Indian and modal music, Paris Conservatoire (CNSMDP); plays with: Claude Tchamitchian, Philippe Deschepper, Enrico Rava, Howard Johnson, Jean-Marc Padovani, Yves Robert, François Cotinaud, Jean-Marie Machado, J. F. Jenny Clark, Glenn Ferris, Daunik Lazro, Paul Rogers, Sophia Domancich; new groups, Onj 97/ 2000, Nat. Orchestra of Jazz, conducted by Didier Levallet; many broadcasts on Radio France, television: M6 Jazz 6, Cable Paris Premiere, Capitale Jazz, F3, F3 Region, RTVE (Spain), RTSR (Switzerland), RTBF (Belgium), TRI (Indonesia), WDR (Germany), Druskininkai TV, Baltic TV (Lithuania), Armenia TV; mem. SACEM, SACD, SPEDIDAM, CNSMDP. *Recordings:* Opera (with Frantois Cotinaud) 1993, Princesse (François Cotinaud Quartet) 1990; Face Au Silence, Double Face 1991, Pyramides (featuring Enrico Rava) 1992, Lousadzak (Claude Tchamitchian Septet) 1994, Portraits (Patrice Thomas Quartet) 1995; with Marc Steckar: Elephant Tuba Horde 1987, Steckar Trinity 1988, Tubakoustic 1989, Jean-Marie Machado (Denis Colin Trio) Eleven Drums Songs 1998, Songs of The Spanish Civil War 2000, Morning Glory 2010, Freedom Now 2010, Triez 2010. *Honours:* Chevalier,

Ordre des Arts et des Lettres 2008. *E-mail:* ramon@ramonlopez.net. *Website:* www.ramonlopez.net.

LOPEZ, Trini; American singer, musician (guitar) and actor; b. (Trinidad López III), 15 May 1937, Dallas, Tex. *Career:* nightclub performer, debut appearance 1963; recorded for Frank Sinatra 1963–68; worldwide entertainer 1963–; his cover of 'Cielito Lindo' was used in film Born on the Fourth of July 1989; mem. American Fed. of Television and Radio Artists, Screen Actors Guild (merged to form SAG-AFTRA 2012). *Film roles:* Marriage on the Rocks, A Poppy is Also a Flower, The Dirty Dozen, Antonio. *Television appearances:* Adam 12, The Reluctant Heroes. *Recordings include:* albums: Trini Lopez at PJ's 1963, More Trini Lopez at PJ's 1963, On the Move 1964, Live at Basin St. East 1964, The Latin Album 1964, The Folk Album 1965, The Love Album 1965, The Rhythm and Blues Album 1965, The Sing Along World of Trini Lopez 1965, Trini Lopez Live in South Africa 1965, Trini 1966, The Second Latin Album 1966, Greatest Hits 1966, In London 1967, Now! 1967, It's a Great Life 1968, Welcome to Trini Country 1968, The Whole Enchilada 1969, The Trini Lopez Show 1969, Viva 1970, Trini Lopez Live in Tokyo 1971, Y Su Alma Latina 1977, Transformed By Time 1978, The 25th Anniversary Album 1991, Dance Party 1998, Aylole-Aylola 2000, Dance the Night Away 2001, Legacy: My Texas Roots 2002, Romantic and Sexy Guitars 2005, Ramblin' Man 2008, Into the Future 2011. *Honours:* Goodwill Amb. for USA, honoured by Congress for work in int. relations. *Current Management:* c/o OraLee Walker (PA). *Telephone:* (760) 322-5034; (760) 902-1318 (mobile). *E-mail:* oralee1oralee@aol.com. *Address:* 1139 Abrigo, Palm Springs, CA 92262, USA (home). *Telephone:* (760) 320-2634 (office). *Fax:* (760) 320-7947 (office). trini.lopez2@aol.com (office). *Website:* www.trinilopez.com.

LOPEZ-REAL, Carlos, LGSM; British musician (saxophone), composer and educator. *Education:* Oxford Univ., Guildhall School of Music and Drama; also with David Liebman in New York. *Career:* has played at most of main UK jazz venues and festivals including Ronnie Scott's, Barbican, South Bank, Cheltenham festival, Brecon jazz festival and also abroad; composes for and performs in groups; film soundtracks; teacher, Guildhall School of Music; f. e17Jazz musicians' collective 2008. *Recording:* album: Mandorla 2009; has also appeared on recordings by Justin Quinn. *Publications:* Dig It series (juvenile). *Telephone:* (7949) 408368 (home). *E-mail:* info@carloslopez-real.co .uk (office). *Website:* www.carloslopez-real.co.uk.

LORDE; New Zealand singer and songwriter; b. (Ella Maria Lani Yelich O'Connor), 7 Nov. 1996, Devonport, Auckland; d. of Vic O'Connor and Sonja Yelich. *Education:* Belmont Intermediate School, Takapuna Grammar School. *Career:* signed with Universal Records 2009; released debut EP The Love Club 2012; worldwide hit with Royals (co-written with Joel Little) 2013. *Recordings:* album: Pure Heroine 2013. *Honours:* New Zealand Music Awards for Int. Achievement 2013, for Single of the Year (for Royals), for Breakthrough Artist of the Year 2013, Award for People's Choice 2013, Silver Scroll Award for Songwriting (for Royals) 2013, MTV Europe Music Award for Best New Zealand Act 2013, mtvU Woman of the Year Award 2013, Grammy Awards for Song of the Year, for Best Pop Solo Performance (both for Royals) 2014, Billboard Music Award for Top New Artist 2014, for Top Rock Song (for Royals) 2014, iHeartRadio Music Award for Best New Artist 2014, MTV Video Music Award for Best Rock Video (for Royals) 2014, Much Music Video Award for Int. Video of the Year – Artist (for Royals) 2014. *Current Management:* c/o Scott Maclachlan, Universal Music New Zealand, PO Box 617, Shortland Street, Auckland, 1140 New Zealand. *E-mail:* scott.maclachlan@umusic.com; saikomanagement@gmail.com. *Website:* www.universalmusic.co.nz; www .lorde.co.nz.

LORENZ, Christian 'Flake'; German musician (keyboards); b. 6 Nov. 1966; m. (divorced) one d. *Career:* mem., Feeling B 1983–93; mem., Rammstein 1993–; the band has a reputation for theatrical live performances; numerous European tours. *Recordings include:* albums: Herzeleid 1995, Sehnsucht 1997, Live aus Berlin 1999, Mutter 2001, Reise, Reise 2004, Rosenrot 2005, Liebe ist für alle da 2009. *Honours:* MTV Europe Music Award for Best German Act 2005. *Current Management:* Pilgrim Management, Greifswalderstrasse 224, 10405 Berlin, Germany. *E-mail:* info@pilgrim-management .de. *Website:* www.pilgrim-management.de; www.rammstein.de.

LOTT, Pixie; British singer, songwriter and actress; b. (Victoria Louise Lott), 12 Jan. 1991, Bromley. *Career:* appeared in West End production of Chitty Chitty Bang Bang at London Palladium and Celebrate the Sound of Music BBC One 2005; performed at VE Day 70: A Party to Remember, Horse Guards Parade, London 2015. *Recordings include:* Mama Do 2009, Boys and Girls 2009, Cry Me Out 2009, Gravity 2010, Nasty 2014; albums: Turn It Up 2009, Young Foolish Happy 2011, Pixie Lott 2014. *Films include:* Fred: The Movie 2010, Sweet Baby Jesus 2011. *Honours:* MTV Europe Music Awards, Best UK & Ireland Act and Best Push Act 2009, Variety Club Awards, Breakthrough Talent Award 2009, MP3 Music Awards, Best New Act 2009, Virgin Media Music Awards, Best Newcomer 2009, Cosmopolitan Ultimate Women Awards, Ultimate Newcomer 2009, Virgin Media Music Awards, Hottest Female 2011. *Current Management:* c/o Roar Global, House 46, Charlotte Street, London, W1T 2GS, England. *Telephone:* (20) 7462-9060. *E-mail:* info@roarglobal.com. *Website:* roarglobal.com; www.pixielott.com.

LOTZ, Rainer E., MMechEng, DEcon; German discographer, music historian, engineer and economist; b. 27 Aug. 1937, Hamburg; m. Birgit Lotz; one s. three d. *Education:* Karlsruhe Tech. Univ., Univ. of Tübingen, Berlin Inst. for Devt Policy. *Career:* tech. adviser, IFCT, Bangkok, Thailand; Acting Chief of

Operations, East African Devt Bank, Kampala, Uganda; Head, Latin America Dept, Fed. German Ministry of Econ. Co-operation and Devt; contribs to 30 radio and TV documentaries; retired 2002; mem. Int. Asscn of Sound and Audiovisual Archives, Int. Asscn of Jazz Record Collectors, Asscn for Recorded Sound Collections (ARSC). *Publications:* more than 200 articles in scholarly journals; more than 60 sleeve notes for CDs and LPs; acknowledgements in more than 250 books by other authors; publr of 30 books; author of 100 monographs, including Grammophonplatten aus der Ragtime-Ära 1979, German Ragtime and Prehistory of Jazz: Vol. 1: The Sound Documents 1985, The AFRS Jubilee Show: A Discography Vols 1 and 2 1985, Mike Danzi: The Story of an American Musician in Berlin 1925–39 1986, Under the Imperial Carpet: Essays in Black History (co-ed.) 1987, The Banjo on Record: A Bio-Discography 1993, Hitler's Airwaves: The Inside Story of Nazi Radio Broadcasting and Propaganda Swing 1997, Black People: Entertainers of African Descent in Europe and Germany 1997, Vorbei—Beyond Recall: A Record of Jewish Musical Life in Nazi Berlin 1933–1938 2001, The Cotton Club 2003, 100 Jahre Jazz in Deutschland Vols 1–3 2008, Black Europe – The sounds and images of black people in Europe pre-1927 2013; Ed. German National Discography. *Honours:* ARSC Lifetime Achievement Award, for published recorded sound research 1998. *Address:* Rotdornweg 81, 53177 Bonn, Germany (home). *Website:* www.lotz-verlag.de.

LOUEKE, Lionel Gilles; Benin musician (guitar); b. 27 April 1973, Cotonou. *Education:* Institut Nat. Supérieur des Arts, Côte d'Ivoire, American School of Modern Music, Paris, France, Berklee Coll. of Music, USA, Thelonious Monk Inst. of Jazz, Univ. of S. California. *Career:* formed trio Gilferma 2005; performed with Terence Blanchard; as sideman has performed with Herbie Hancock, Kenwood Dennard, George Garzone, Bob Hurst, Alphonso Johnson, Angelique Kidjo, Dianne Reeves, Cassandra Wilson, Wayne Shorter, Jeff 'Tain' Watts, Charlie Haden, Richard Bona, Nathan East, Vinnie Colaiuta, Marcus Miller, Sting, Brian Blade, John Patitucci, Terri Lyne Carrington, Kenny Garrett, Roy Hargrove, Santana, Dennis Chambers, Magos Harrera, Gretchen Parlato. *Recordings:* albums: as leader: In a Trance 2005, Virgin Forest 2007, Karibu 2008, Mwaliku 2010, Heritage 2012; with Gilfema: ObliqSound 2005, Gilfema + 2 2008. *Honours:* United States Artists Fellow Award 2009. *Current Management:* c/o Jack Leitenberg, 12 Kent Street, New York, NY 10956, USA. *Telephone:* (845) 638-6984. *E-mail:* okaybabe@aol.com. *Address:* c/o Cem Kurosman, Blue Note Records, 150 Fifth Avenue, New York, NY 10011, USA (office). *E-mail:* cem.kurosman@bluenotelabelgroup.com (office). *Website:* www.bluenote.com (office); www.lionelloueke.com.

LOUIS, Eric; French musician (trombone) and music teacher; b. 28 Oct. 1959, Malo Les Bains; 1 d. *Education:* Conservatoires de Perpignan, 1978; St Quentin, 1979; Ville De Paris, 1980. *Career:* Played concerts with: Diana Ross; Charles Aznavour; Jerry Lewis; Lambert Wilson; Julia Migenes-Johnson; Member, jazz groups with: Michel Legrand; Patrice Caratini; Luc Lemasne; Yanko Nilovic; Laurent Cuny; 3 tours Japan with Raymond Lefèvre; Numerous revues and shows include: Cats; 42nd Street; Cabaret; Folies Bergères; Numerous appearances on French television include 4 telethons (1988–94); Several other musical and theatrical works; Performed with Orchestre Philharmonique d'Europe, Orchestre du Luxembourg and various other orchestras; Music teacher in Guéret, 1981–82; Lucé, 1988–89; Gentilly, 1989–90; Chatou, 1991–92. *Recordings:* Liza Minnelli; Charles Aznavour; Julia Migenes-Johnson; Pierre Perret; Georges Aperghis; Thomas Fersen; André Hoder.

LOUISE, (Louise Redknapp); British singer and TV presenter; b. (Louise Nurding), 1974, London; m. Jamie Redknapp; two s. *Education:* Italia Conti Stage School. *Career:* singer all-female vocal group, Eternal 1992–95; solo artist 1995–. *Recordings:* albums: with Eternal: Always and Forever 1993; solo: Louise 1996, Woman In Me 1997, Elbow Beach 2000, Best Of 2001; hit singles: with Eternal: Stay 1993, Save Your Love 1994, Just A Step From Heaven 1994, Oh Baby I 1994; solo hits: Light of My Life 1995, In Walked Love 1996, Naked 1996, Undivided Love 1996, One Kiss From Heaven 1996, Arms Around The World 1997, Let's Go Round Again 1997, All That Matters 1998, 2 Faced 2000, Beautiful Inside 2000, Stuck In The Middle With You 2001. *Honours:* Smash Hits Award. *Current Management:* Merlin Media Group, Hammersmith Studios, 55 Yeldham Road, London W6 8JF, England. *Telephone:* (20) 8834-8900. *Fax:* (20) 8834-8901. *Website:* www.merlinelite.co .uk. *E-mail:* info@louiseredknappofficial.co.uk (office). *Website:* www .louiseredknappofficial.co.uk.

LOURAU, Julien; French musician (saxophone); b. 2 March 1970, Paris; s. of René Lourau; two c. *Career:* has performed at Marciac Festival, Vienna Festival, Blue Note, New York City, Hot Brass, Paris, Auditorium des Halles, Paris, Festival Banlieues Bleues, Radio-France, Carte blanche at La Villette jazz festival 2007. *Recordings:* solo: Groove Gang 1995, Voodoo Dance 1997, City Boom Boom 1998, Gambit 1999, The Rise (Disque d'Emoi of the Year, Magazine Jazzman 2002) 2002, Forget 2005, Fire 2005, Julien Lourau vs RumbAbierta 2007, Quartet Saigon 2009; featured with Marc Ducret, Eric Legnini, David Linx, Louis Winsberg, Vincent Courtois, O. N. J. de Laurent Cugny, Minino Garay, Magic Malik. *Publications:* A Turtle's Dream, Who Used to Dance, It's Me: Abbey Lincoln, Bojan Z: Quartet, Yopla, Koreni. Olympic Gramofon 1997, Brighter Days 2009, Bozilo Live 2009. *Honours:* First Prize, soloist, Concours de la Défense 1993, Django d'Or 1996, Victoire de la Musique 1998. *Current Management:* c/o Anteprima Production, 22 rue Navarin, 75009 Paris, France. *Telephone:* 1-45-08-00-00. *E-mail:* reno .dimatteo@mac.com. *Website:* www.anteprimaproductions.com.

LOVANO, Joe; American musician (tenor saxophone, clarinet, bass clarinet) and composer; b. 29 Dec. 1952, Ohio; m. Judi Silvano 1984. *Education:* Berklee Coll. of Music, Boston. *Career:* toured with Woody Herman Big Band, Thad Jones-Mel Lewis Orchestra, John Scofield Quartet, Paul Motian Trio (with Bill Frisell); formed own bands, including Joe Lovano Ensemble, Us Five 2008–; tours worldwide; mem. AFofM. *Recordings include:* Rush Hour, Universal Language Sextet, Tenor Legacy 1993, Ten Tales 1994, Quartets: Live at the Village Vanguard 1994, Celebrating Sinatra 1996, Flying Colours 1997, Trio Fascination 1998, Friendly Fire 1999, Unknown Voyage 2000, 52nd Street Themes 2000, Flights of Fancy 2001, I'm All For You: Ballad Songbook 2004, For the Time Being (with Salvatore Bonafede) 2005, Streams of Expression 2006, Symphonica 2008, Folk Art 2009; with Us Five: Bird Songs 2011, Cross Culture 2013. *Honours:* Downbeat Magazine Critics Poll Jazz Artist of the Year 1995, Jazz Journalists' Asscn Awards for Multi-Reeds Player of the Year 2015, for Tenor Saxophonist of the Year 2015. *Telephone:* (818) 986-3985. *E-mail:* merlinco@att.net; braddlmedia@covad.net. *Address:* c/o Blue Note Records, 304 Park Avenue S, Third Floor, New York, NY 10010, USA. *Website:* www.joelovano.com.

LOVE, Courtney; American rock musician, singer and actress; b. (Love Michelle Harrison), 9 July 1964, San Francisco, Calif.; d. of Hank Harrison and Linda Carroll; m. 1st James Moreland; m. 2nd Kurt Cobain (deceased); one s. one d. *Career:* began career as occasional actress and mem. of bands Faith No More and Babes in Toyland; Founding singer and guitarist, rock band Hole 1989–2002, 2010–12; solo artist 2003–. *Films:* Sid and Nancy 1986, Straight To Hell 1987, Tapeheads 1988, Basquiat 1996, Feeling Minnesota 1996, The People vs Larry Flynt 1996, 200 Cigarettes 1999, Man on the Moon 1999, Beat 2000, Julie Johnson 2001, Trapped 2002. *Recordings include:* albums: with Hole: Retard Girl 1990, Pretty On The Inside 1991, Live Through This 1994, Celebrity Skin 1998, Nobody's Daughter 2010; solo: America's Sweetheart 2004; singles: with Hole: Beautiful Son 1993, Doll Parts 1994, Ask for It 1995, Celebrity Skin 1998, Malibu 1998, Awful 1999; solo: Mono 2004. *Publication:* Dirty Blonde (autobiog.) 2006. *Current Management:* c/o 2B Management, The Soho Building, 110 Greene Street, Suite 501, New York, NY 10012, USA. *Telephone:* (646) 370-5696. *E-mail:* info@ 2bmanagement.com. *Website:* www.2bmanagement.com.

LOVE, Mike; American singer and songwriter; b. 15 March 1941, Baldwin Hills, Calif. *Career:* mem. Beach Boys 1961–; mem. own band, Endless Summer 1981; numerous tours, concerts and festival appearances; band est. Brother Records label (also now holding co.) 1967. *Recordings include:* albums: with The Beach Boys: Surfin' Safari 1962, Surfer Girl 1963, Little Deuce Coupe 1963, Shut Down Vol. 2, All Summer Long 1964, Christmas Album 1964, The Beach Boys Today! 1965, Summer Days (and Summer Nights) 1965, Beach Boys Party 1966, Pet Sounds 1966, Smiley Smile 1967, Wild Honey 1968, Friends 1968, 20/20 1969, Sunflower 1970, Surf's Up 1971, Carl and the Passions – So Tough 1972, Holland 1973, The Beach Boys in Concert 1973, Endless Summer 1974, 15 Big Ones 1976, The Beach Boys Love You 1977, M.I.U. 1978, LA (Light Album) 1979, Keepin' The Summer Alive 1980, The Beach Boys 1985, Still Cruisin' 1989, Two Rooms 1991, Summer in Paradise 1992, The Sounds of Summer: The Very Best of The Beach Boys 2003, That's Why God Made the Radio 2012; solo: Looking Back With Love 1981. *Honours:* American Music Awards Special Award of Merit 1988, Grammy Lifetime Achievement Award 2001. *Current Management:* c/o Elliott Lott, Boulder Creek Entertainment, PO Box 91002, San Diego, CA 92169, USA. *Telephone:* (858) 793-4141. *Website:* www.thebeachboys.com.

LOVEFOXXX; Brazilian singer; b. (Luísa Hanaê Matsushita), 25 Feb. 1984, Campinas. *Career:* fmr illustrator and fashion design asst; lead singer Cansei de Ser Sexy (CSS) 2003–. *Recordings include:* Cansei de Ser Sexy 2005 (int. re-release 2006), Donkey 2008.

LOVELESS, Patty; American country singer and musician (guitar); b. 4 Jan. 1957, Pikeville, KY; m. 1st Terry Lovelace 1976; m. 2nd Emory Gordy Jr 1989. *Career:* summer job singing with the Wilburn Brothers 1971; singer, nightclubs and hotels, North Carolina; moved to Nashville 1985; worked with Vince Gill and Emmylou Harris, including CBS 70th anniversary of the Grand Ole Opry; numerous television appearances. *Recordings include:* albums: Patty Loveless 1986, If My Heart Had Windows 1988, Honky Tonk Angel 1988, On Down the Line 1990, Up Against My Heart 1991, Only What I Feel 1993, When Fallen Angels Fly 1994, The Trouble With The Truth 1996, Long Stretch of Lonesome 1998, Strong Heart 2000, Mountain Soul 2001, Bluegrass and White 2002, On Your Way Home 2003, Dreamin' My Dreams 2005, Sleepless Nights 2008, Mountain Soul II 2009. *Honours:* Country Music Awards 1993, 1995, Country Music Television Award for Female Artist of the Year 1994, Real Country Listener Award for Female Vocalist of the Year 1995, ACM Award 1997. *Current Management:* Mike Robertson Management, PO Box 120073, Nashville, TN 37212, USA. *Telephone:* (615) 329-4199. *E-mail:* mike@mrmmusic.com. *Website:* www.pattyloveless.com.

LOVERING, David; American musician (drums); b. 6 Dec. 1961, Boston, Mass. *Education:* Wentworth Inst. of Tech. *Career:* mem. Pixies 1986–93, 2004–; recorded demo, The Purple Tape 1987; formed the Martinis with Joey Santiago 1995; drummer with Cracker 1990s; est. as a 'scientific phenomenalist' (performance artist and magician) late 1990s. *Recordings:* albums with the Pixies: Come On Pilgrim (EP) 1987, Surfer Rosa 1988, Doolittle 1989, Bossanova 1990, Trompe Le Monde 1991, Death To The Pixies 1987–1991 1997, Live At The BBC 1998, Complete B-Sides 2001, Pixies (DVD) 2004,

Wave of Mutilation: The Best of the Pixies 2004, Indie Cindy 2014. *Current Management:* Richard Jones, Key Music Management Ltd, 56A Bramhall Lane South, Bramhall, Stockport, SK7 1AH, England. *Telephone:* (161) 440-0670. *E-mail:* contact@keymusicmanagement.com. *Website:* www.keymusicmanagement.com. *E-mail:* email@davidlovering.com (office). *Website:* www.pixiesmusic.com (office); www.davidlovering.com.

LOVETT, Benjamin (Ben) Walter David; British songwriter, musician (keyboards, accordion, drums) and record producer; b. 30 Sept. 1986, Cardiff, Wales. *Education:* King's Coll. School, Wimbledon. *Career:* co-founder, Communion record label and music promotions team 2006–; founder-mem. Mumford & Sons 2007–, first EP released 2008, toured as support group to Laura Marling 2009, performed with Bob Dylan at Grammy Awards 2011; musician and producer for artists including Ellie Goulding, Simon Felice. *Film:* Wuthering Heights (two songs for soundtrack) 2011. *Recordings:* albums: Sigh No More (Q Best New Act Award 2010, BRIT Award for British Album of the Year 2011, Billboard Music Awards for Top Rock Album and Top Alternative Album 2011) 2009, Babel (Grammy Award for Album of the Year 2013, Billboard Music Award for Top Rock Album 2013) 2012, Wilder Mind 2015; featured on: I Speak Because I Can, Laura Marling 2010, See My Friends, Ray Davies 2010. *Honours:* Australian Record Industry Association Music Most Popular Int. Artist Award 2010, Billboard Music Award for Top Alternative Artist 2011, Grammy Award for Best Long Form Music Video (for Big Easy Express) 2013, BRIT Award for Best British Group 2013, Ivor Novello Award for Int. Achievement (with Mumford & Sons) 2014. *Current Management:* c/o Everybody's Management, 53 Corsica Street, Highbury, London, N5 1JT, England. *Telephone:* (20) 3227-0420. *Fax:* (20) 7226-2166. *E-mail:* info@everybody-s.com. *Website:* www.everybody-s.com; www.mumfordandsons.com.

LOVETT, Lyle; American singer, songwriter and actor; b. 1 Nov. 1957, Klein, Tex.; m. Julia Roberts 1993 (divorced 1995). *Career:* backing singer for Nanci Griffith 1985; solo singer, songwriter 1986–; numerous TV appearances, regular tours. *Film appearances include:* The Player 1992, Short Cuts 1993, Prêt-à-Porter 1994, Bastard Out of Carolina 1996, Breast Men 1997, Fear and Loathing in Las Vegas 1998, The Opposite of Sex 1998, Cookie's Fortune 1999, The New Guy 2002, Three Days of Rain 2003, The Open Road 2009, Angels Sing 2013. *Recordings include:* albums: Lyle Lovett 1986, Pontiac 1988, Lyle Lovett and his Large Band 1989, Joshua Judges Ruth 1992, Leap of Faith (soundtrack) 1992, I Love Everybody 1994, Road to Ensenada 1996, Step Inside This House 1998, Live in Texas 1999, Can't Resist It 1999, Dr T and the Women 2000, My Baby Don't Tolerate 2003, It's Nor Large It's Big 2007, Natural Forces 2009, Release Me 2012. *Honours:* two Grammy Awards, four Country Music Awards. *Current Management:* c/o Michelle Findlay, Macklam Feldman Management, #200–1505 West 2nd Avenue, Vancouver, BC V6H 3Y4, Canada. *Telephone:* (604) 630-3199. *E-mail:* findlay@mfmgt.com. *Website:* www.mfmgt.com; www.lylelovett.com.

LOVLAND, Rolf U.; Norwegian songwriter, musician and producer; b. Kristiansand. *Education:* Music Conservatory, Kristiansand and Norwegian Inst. of Music, Oslo. *Career:* songwriter until mid-1990s; mem. Secret Garden 1994–. *Compositions include:* La det swinge (Let It Swing) (winner, Eurovision Song Contest) 1985, Nocturne (winner, Eurovision Song Contest) 1995. *Recordings:* albums: Songs from a Secret Garden 1994, White Stones 1995, Dawn Of A New Century 1999, Dreamcatcher 2000, Once In A Red Moon 2002, Earthsongs 2005, Inside I'm Singing 2008, Winter Poem 2011. *Honours:* Winner, Eurovision Song Contest (as composer) 1985, (composer and performer) 1995, Norwegian Grammy Award 1994, 2008. *Current Management:* c/o Trude Bø, Continental Artist Management, Kr. Augusts gate 10, 0164 Oslo, Norway. *E-mail:* trude.bo@continentalmusic.net. *Website:* www.continentalmusic.net. *E-mail:* fanmail@secretgarden.no (office). *Website:* www.secretgarden.no.

LOVSIN, Peter; Slovenian singer and songwriter; b. 27 June 1955, Ljubljana; m. Darija Lovsin 1980; one s. one d. *Education:* studied journalism. *Career:* lead singer punk bands, Pankrti 1977–87, Sokoli 1988–93; solo artist, with support band Vitezi Om'a. *Recordings:* albums: six with Pankrti, three with Sokoli, two solo. *Publications:* poetry: In The Service of Rock 'n' Roll. *Honours:* Croatian Youth Organisation Awards 1980. *Address:* Zadruzna 1, 61000 Ljubljana, Slovenia.

LOWE, Christopher (Chris) Sean; British producer and musician (keyboards); b. 4 Oct. 1959, Blackpool, Lancashire, England. *Education:* Liverpool Univ. *Career:* founder mem., West End, later renamed Pet Shop Boys 1981–; numerous television and radio appearances, worldwide tours; launched record label, Spaghetti 1991–; producer, songwriter for artists, including Dusty Springfield, Patsy Kensit, Liza Minnelli, Boy George, Electronic, Tina Turner, Kylie Minogue. *Theatre:* Closer to Heaven (musical written with Neil Tennant and Jonathan Harvey, West End, London) 2001, The Most Incredible Thing (ballet) (Beyond Theatre Award 2011) 2011. *Film:* It Couldn't Happen Here 1988. *Compositions:* new soundtrack to 1925 film Battleship Potemkin 2004. *Recordings include:* albums: Please 1986, Disco—The Remix Album 1986, Actually 1987, Introspective 1988, In Depth 1989, Behaviour 1990, Discography 1991, Very 1993, Very Relentless 1993, Disco 2 1994, Alternative 1995, Bilingual 1996, Originals (Please, Actually, Behaviour box set) 1997, Bilingual Special Edition 1997, Essential Pet Shop Boys 1998, Nightlife 1999, Please—Further Listening 1984–1986 2001, Actually—Further Listening 1987–1988 2001, Introspective—Further Listening 1988–1989 2001, Behav-

iour—Further Listening 1990–1991 2001, Very—Further Listening 1992–1994 2001, Bilingual—Further Listening 1995–1997 2001, Release 2002, Disco 3 2003, PopArt—The Hits 2003, Fundamental 2006, Concrete 2006, Disco 4 2007, Yes 2009, Format 2012, Elysium 2012, Electric 2013. *Publications:* Pet Shop Boys, Annually, Pet Shop Boys Versus America, Pet Shop Boys, Literally 1990, Catalogue 2006. *Honours:* Ivor Novello Awards 1987, 1988, BPI Award for Best Single 1987, Best Group 1988, Berolina Award (Germany) 1988, BRIT Award for Outstanding Contrib. to Music 2009, Q Magazine Outstanding Contrib. to Music 2013. *Current Management:* Becker Brown Management, 11 Knightsbridge, 3rd Floor, London, SW1X 7LY, England. *Telephone:* (20) 7838-6158. *E-mail:* info@beckerbrown.com. *Address:* Pet Shop Boys Partnership, 8th Floor, 15–19 Kingsway, London, WC2B 6UN, England (office). *Website:* www.petshopboys.co.uk.

LOWE, Jez; British singer, songwriter and musician; b. 14 July 1955, Sunderland, Tyne and Wear, England. *Education:* Sunderland Polytechnic. *Career:* professional on folk circuit 1980–; tours of Europe, USA; Musical Dir for Badapple Theatre 2002–; Amb. for the City of Sunderland; mem. Musicians' Union. *Film:* Sight Rhymes (documentary) 2004. *Radio:* contribs to BBC Radio Ballads (Sony Radio Award Winner) 2006, 2010, 2012. *Recordings include:* albums: Tou A Roue 2001, Live At The Davy Lamp 2001, Honesty Box 2002, Doolally 2005, Jack Common's Anthem 2007, Northern Echoes 2009, Wotcheor 2010, Heads Up 2012. *Publications:* Songs of Jez Lowe 1988, Songs of Jez Lowe Vol. II 1995, Songs of Jez Lowe Vol. III 2003. *Honours:* PRS Composers in Educ. Award 1993. *Address:* c/o Lowe Life Music, PO Box 57, York, YO26 8WQ, England (office). *Telephone:* (1423) 339168 (office). *E-mail:* jez@jezlowe.com (office). *Website:* www.jezlowe.com.

LOWE, Mark (see Shine, M. K.)

LOWE, Alexander (Zane) Reid; New Zealand radio disc jockey; b. 7 Aug. 1973; m.; one s. *Career:* mem., hip hop group Urban Disturbance for seven years; TV presenter, MTV 1997–; fmrly DJ, London's XFM; DJ, BBC Radio 1 2003–; mem. Breaks Co-op. *Recordings:* with Breaks Co-op: Roofers 1997, The Sound Inside 2005. *Honours:* Sony Radio Awards for Specialist Music Programme and Music Broadcaster of the Year 2006, NME Award for Best Radio Show 2006, 2007. *Current Management:* Money Management UK, 42a Berwick Street, London, W1F 8RZ, England. *Telephone:* (20) 7287-7490. *Fax:* (20) 7287-7499. *E-mail:* emma@moneymanagementuk.com. *Website:* www.moneymanagementuk.com. *Address:* BBC Radio 1, Broadcasting House, London, W1A 1AA, England (office). *Telephone:* (20) 7580-4468 (office). *E-mail:* zane@bbc.co.uk (office). *Website:* www.bbc.co.uk/radio1/zanelowe (office); www.zanelowe.com; www.breaksco-op.com.

LOYOLA FERNÁNDEZ, José, PhD; Cuban composer, teacher and musician (flute); *Professor of Composition, Orchestration and Counterpoint, Instituto Superior de Arte de La Habana;* b. 12 March 1941, Cienfuegos; s. of Efraín Loyola. *Education:* School of Music of the Nat. School of the Arts, Havana, School for Advanced Studies in Music, Warsaw, Poland and Fryderyk Chopin Acad., Warsaw. *Career:* mem., Cienfuegos Nursery Musical Band 1950, Cienfuegos Firemen's Corps Band 1952–59, Loyola Orchestra 1959–62, Central Army Band 1959–60; flautist and composer, Youth and Students Orchestra of the Eighth Festival of Youth and Students, Helsinki, Finland 1962; teacher, Nat. School of the Arts, Havana 1973–75; Dir Amadeo Roldán Conservatory, Havana 1974–75; Nat. Co-ordinator, Gen. Office of Art Schools 1975–76; teacher of composition, Faculty of Music, Higher Inst. for the Arts 1976–, currently Prof. of Composition, Orchestration and Counterpoint, teaching Vice-Rector 1976–78, Dean 1977–78; Lecturer, Second Bambuco Festival, Mexico 1990; mem. Nat. Union of Writers and Artists of Cuba (pres. music bd 1976–77, sec. 1979, deputy pres. 1983–96, pres. 1996–), Cuban Fryderyk Chopin Soc. (pres. 1983–), Union of Writers and Artists of Cuba Golden Boleros Festival (pres. 1987). *Compositions:* Los piroperos 1960–69, Mi rico chachachá 1960–69, Lo sabe Isabel 1960–69, Sinfonietta 1965, Música para flauta y cuerdas 1968, Tres imágenes poéticas 1969, Antipoemas 1970, Música viva No. 1 for percussion 1971, Monzón y el Rey de Koré (opera) 1973, Poética del guerrillero for orchestra 1976, Música viva No. 2 1976, Música viva No. 3 1978, Música viva No. 4 1979, Canto negro 1979, Variaciones folklóricas 1982, Tres piezas cubanas for piano 1985, Tropicalia I 1987, Tropicalia II 1988, Canción del Soy Todo 1990. *Publications:* Música Cabana (ed.); contrib. numerous articles. *Honours:* Eighth Festival of Youth and Students Best Soloist of Popular Music, Helsinki 1962, 26 de Julio Musical Contest Chamber Music Prize, Centenary of Karol Symanowsky medal 1982, winner Union of Writers and Artists of Cuba Nat. Composition Contest 1985, Merit of Polish Culture 1985, winner Cuban Nat. Cultural Award 1988. *Address:* c/o Ana Margarita Cabrera, Instituto Superior de Arte, Calle 120, No. 1110 entre 9na y 13, Cubanacan Playa, Havana 12100, Cuba (office).

LOZANO, Conrad; American musician (bass guitar); b. 21 March 1951, Los Angeles, CA. *Career:* mem., Los Lobos 1973–. *Recordings include:* albums: De Este De Los Angeles 1978, How Will The Wolf Survive 1984, By the Light of the Moon 1987, La Pistola y El Corazón 1988, The Neighborhood 1990, Kiko 1992, Colossal Head 1996, This Time 1999, Good Morning Aztlán 2002, The Ride 2004, The Town and the City 2006, Los Lobos Goes Disney 2009, Tin Can Trust 2010. *Current Management:* c/o Chris Tetzeli, Red Light Management, 321 East Main Street, Suite 500, Charlottesville, VA 22902, USA. *Telephone:* (434) 245-4900. *Fax:* (434) 245-4933. *E-mail:* info@redlightmanagement.com. *Website:* www.redlightmanagement.com; www.loslobos.org.

LOZANO, Ulises; Mexican musician (keyboards) and DJ. *Career:* founder mem. electro-pop band, Kinky 1998–. *Recordings include:* albums: Kinky 2002, Atlas 2003, Reina 2006. *Address:* c/o Sonic360 Records, 33 Riding House Street, London, W1 7DZ, England (office). *Website:* www.sonic360.com/kinky.

LTJ BUKEM (see WILLIAMSON, Daniel)

LU, Han; Chinese singer; b. 20 April 1990, Haidian Dist, Beijing. *Education:* Beijing Haidian Foreign Language Shi Yan School, Yonsei Univ., Seoul Inst. of the Arts. *Career:* mem. K-pop boy band Exo 2011–; mem. sub-group Exo-M 2012–; debut single 2012; numerous TV and live appearances. *Television:* EXO's Showtime 2013–. *Recordings:* albums: Mama 2012, XOXO (Mnet Asian Music Award for Album of the Year 2013) 2013. *Honours:* numerous awards including: for Exo: Mnet Asian Music Award for Best New Asian Artist/Group 2012, MTV Europe Music Award for Best Japan/Korea Act 2013, MelOn Music Award for Song of the Year (for Growl) 2013; for Exo-M: Top Chinese Music Award for Most Popular Group 2013. *Address:* c/o SM Entertainment, 521 Apgujeong 2-dong, Gangnam-gu, Seoul, South Korea (office). *Telephone:* (2) 6240-9800 (office). *Website:* www.smtown.com (office); exo.smtown.com (home).

LU WIN, Annabella, (Myant Myant Aye); singer; b. 1966, Rangoon, Burma. *Career:* singer, Bow Wow Wow 1980–83; solo artist. *Recordings:* Albums: See Jungle..., 1981; I Want Candy, 1982; When The Going Gets Tough..., 1983; The Best of Bow Wow Wow, 1989; Singles: C30, C60, C90, Go!, 1980; Chihuahua, 1981; Go Wild In The Country, 1982; I Want Candy, 1982; Louis Quatorze, 1982; Solo albums include: Fever, 1986. *Current Management:* ESP Management, 888 Seventh Ave #2904, New York, NY 10106-0001, USA.

LUBIN, Jean-Claude, DrSc; French musician (piano) and information scientist; b. 2 Oct. 1935, Paris. *Career:* mem. of various groups, New Orleans, 1953–56; Musician, Paris, with F. Jeanneau; M. Saury; A. Nicholas; A. Reweliotty; also played with B. Wilen; G. Laffite; L. Fuentes; J. L. Chautemps; S. Grapelly; J. L. Ponty; J. F. Jenny Clarke; A. Romano; H. Texier; A. Lorenzi; D. Humair; M. Roques; J. Griffin; C. Baker; D. Byrd; L. Konitz; D. Gordon; G. Coleman; J. McLean; D. Cherry; G. Barbieri. *Recordings include:* The Fabulous Pescara Jam Session (with C. Baker) 1975.

LUCENZO; Portuguese/French singer and songwriter; b. (Luis Filipe Oliveira), 27 May 1983, Bordeaux, France. *Career:* learned piano aged six and began singing aged 11; released debut single with Yanis Records Co. (Faouze Barkati) 2006; recorded int. hit single Danza Kuduro with Don Omar produced by Faouze Barkati for Yanis Records France (also co-writer and composer of worldwide hit with Fabrice Toigo) 2010; collaborations with Big Ali, Sean Paul etc. 2011. *Recordings include:* Emigrante del Mundo 2008, Dame reggaeton 2009, Baila Morena 2010, Vem Dançar Kuduro/Danza Kuduro 2011, Wine It Up 2012. *Honours:* Latin Billboard Awards for Rhythm Airplay 2011, for Latin Song of the Year (Vocal Event) 2012, for Latin Rhythm of the Year 2012, for Digital Song of the Year 2012, American Billboard Award for Top Latin Song 2012 (all for Danza Kuduro). *Address:* c/o Faouze Barkati, Yanis Records, 38 rue de la Chapelle, 95100 Argenteuil, France (office). *Telephone:* (1) 39-98-93-57 (office). *Fax:* (6) 11-62-33-89 (office). *E-mail:* faouze .yanisrecords@wanadoo.fr (office). *Website:* www.lucenzo.fr.

LUCIANO; Jamaican reggae singer; b. (Jepther Washington McClymont), 20 Oct. 1964, Davey Town. *Career:* began singing in local church, later performed with the name Stepper John; moved to Kingston 1992, began using name Luciano; has worked with producers including Herman Chin-Loy, Sky High, Freddie McGregor, Philip 'Fattis' Burrell, Joel Chin, Firehouse Crew, King Jammy; collaborations with artists including Jungle Brothers, Sizzla, Capleton. *Recordings include:* albums: One Way Ticket 1994, After All 1995, Where There Is Life 1995, Sweep Over My Soul 1999, Live 2000, Wisdom, Knowledge and Overstanding (with Mikey General) 2000, A New Day 2001, Great Controversy 2001, Serve Jah 2003, Visions 2003, Serious Times 2004, Hail the Comforter 2005, Jah Words 2005, Child of a King 2006, God Is Greater than Man 2007. *Current Management:* Sean Folkes, 6130 NW 7 Avenue, North Miami Beach, FL 33147, USA. *Telephone:* (305) 852-7275. *E-mail:* kabled@msn.com. *Current Management:* Jah Messanjah Productions, 21 Westminster Crescent, Kingston 10, Jamaica. *E-mail:* jahmessanjah@ hotmail.com. *Website:* www.lucianoreggae.com.

LUCKETT, LeToya; American singer, songwriter and actress; b. 11 March 1981, Houston, TX. *Career:* numerous print and TV commercial appearances prior to professional music career; first int. solo vocal performance in Tokyo, Japan 1990; mem., GirlsTyme (with Beyoncé Knowles, LaTavia Roberson and Kelly Rowland) 1992, renamed Something Fresh then The Dolls before settling on Destiny's Child –2000; formed group Anjel (with LaTavia Roberson) 2000–; solo artist 2006–. *Films:* Preacher's Kid 2010, Killers 2010, From the Rough 2011. *Recordings include:* albums: with Destiny's Child: Destiny's Child 1998, The Writing's On The Wall 1999; solo: LeToya 2006, Lady Love 2009. *Address:* c/o Capitol Records, 1750 North Vine Street, Hollywood, CA 90028, USA. *Website:* www.letoya.net; www.myspace.com/ letoya.

LUCKY HANDS (see U-God)

LUGER, Lex; American hip hop record producer; b. (Lexus Arnel Lewis), 6 March 1991, Suffolk, Va; two d. *Career:* collaborations with 1017 Brick Squad, Ace Hood, Jay-Z, OJ da Juiceman, Rick Ross, Slim Thug, Snoop Dogg, Styles P, Waka Flocka Flame, Kanye West. *Recordings:* albums: as producer:

Flockaveli, Waka Flocka Flame 2010, 6 Rings, OJ da Juiceman 2010; several mixtapes as producer. *Honours:* BMI Urban Producer of the Year 2011. *Address:* c/o 1017 Brick Squad, Warner Bros. Records, Warner Music Group, 75 Rockefeller Plaza, New York, NY 10019, USA (office). *Website:* www .warnerbrosrecords.com (office); www.getsmokedout.com.

LUKA BLOOM; Irish singer, musician (guitar) and songwriter; b. (Barry Moore), 23 May 1955, Newbridge, Co. Kildare; younger brother of Christy Moore. *Career:* performed in Dublin pubs and folk clubs around Europe, mid 1970s–mid 1980s; brief stint as leader of rock band Red Square; relocated to USA and changed name to Luka Bloom 1987; toured the country as opening act for the Pogues and Hothouse Flowers. *Recordings:* as Barry Moore: Treaty Stone 1978, In Groningen 1980, No Heroes 1982; as Luka Bloom: Riverside 1990, Acoustic Motorbike 1992, Turf 1994, Salty Heaven 1998, Keeper of The Flame 2000, The Barry Moore Years 2001, Between the Mountain and The Moon 2002, Before Sleep Comes 2004, Innocence 2005, Tribe 2007, The Man is Alive 2008. *E-mail:* info@lukabloom.com (office). *Website:* www.lukabloom .com.

LUKATHER, Steve; American musician (guitar); b. 21 Oct. 1957, Los Angeles, California. *Career:* Member, Toto, 1978–. *Compositions include:* Commissioned (with Toto) to write theme for Los Angeles Olympic Games 1984; Co-writer (with Randy Goodrum) I'll Be Over You 1986. *Recordings:* albums: with Toto: Toto 1979, Hydra 1979, Turn Back 1981, Toto IV 1982, Isolation 1984, Dune (film soundtrack) 1985, Fahrenheit 1986, The Seventh One 1988, Past To Present 1977–90 1990, Kingdom of Desire 1992, Tambu 1995, Toto XX 1998, Mindfields 1999, Through the Looking Glass 2002, Falling in Between 2006, Toto XIV 2015; solo: Lukather 1989, Candyman 1994, Luke 1997, Santamental 2003, Ever Changing Times 2008, All's Well That Ends Well, 2010, Transition 2013; singles: with Toto include: Hold The Line 1979, Georgy Porgy 1980, 99 1980, Rosanna 1982, Make Believe 1982, Africa (No. 1, USA) 1983, I Won't Hold You Back 1983, I'll Be Over You 1986, Without Your Love 1987, Pamela 1988; as contributor: We Are The World, USA For Africa charity single 1985. *Honours:* six Grammy Awards: Best Record, Best Album, Best Engineered Recording, Best Producer (Toto), Best Vocal Arrangement, Best Instrumental Arrangement, 1983. *Current Management:* c/o Steve Karas and Keith Hagan, SKH Music. *E-mail:* skaras@ skhmusic.com; khagan@skhmusic.com. *Website:* www.skhmusic.com. *E-mail:* luke@stevelukather.net. *Website:* www.stevelukather.net; www.totoofficial .com.

LUKKARINEN, Jaakko; Finnish musician (drums, percussion). *Education:* Sibelius Acad. with Jukkis Uotila, Marko Timonen and Mika Kallio, Espoo Pop/Jazz School, Helsinki Pop/Jazz Conservatory. *Career:* fmr mem. of numerous bands; mem., Värttinä 2000–. *Music for theatre:* co-wrote score to stage musical, The Lord of the Rings (with A. R. Rahman) (Princess of Wales Theatre, Toronto) 2006. *Recordings include:* albums: Ilmatar 2000, 6.12 2001, iki 2003, Miero 2006. *Current Management:* c/o Phillip Page, Hoedown Arts Oy, Neitsytpolku 9 F 81, 00140 Helsinki, Finland. *Telephone:* (50) 5692982. *Fax:* (9) 628950. *E-mail:* pap@hoedown.com. *Website:* www.varttina.com.

LULU; British singer and actress; b. (Marie MacDonald McLaughlin Lawrie), 3 March 1948, Glasgow. *Songs and recordings include:* Man Who Sold the World 1974, The Man with the Golden Gun (theme to Bond film) 1975, I Could Never Miss You, If I Were You 1982, Independence 1993, Absolutely 1997, The Best of Lulu 1998, Together 2002, The Greatest Hits 2003, Back on Track 2004, A Little Soul in Your Heart 2005, Shout! The Complete Decca Recordings 2009, Lulu on the Dancefloor: Remixes 2009. *Stage performances include:* Peter Pan 1975–76, 1987–88, Aladdin 1976–77, Song and Dance, Guys and Dolls, The Mystery of Edwin Drood. *Films include:* Swinging UK, Gonks Go Beat 1966, To Sir with Love, Whatever Happened to Harold Smith?. *TV appearances include:* Lulu 1966–74, 1982–83, Let's Rock 1981, Some You Win 1983–84, The Growing Pains of Adrian Mole 1987, Perfect Scoundrels 1989–90. *Website:* www.luluofficial.com.

LUMHOLDT, Sara Helena; Swedish singer; b. 25 Oct. 1984, Stockholm. *Education:* Näsbydals School, Stockholm. *Career:* mem., A*Teens 1998–2004. *Recordings include:* albums: The Abba Generation 1999, Teen Spirit 2001; solo: Back to You 2010. *Honours:* Viva Music Award for Best Int. Newcomer 2000.

LUMUMBA-KASONGO, Disashi; American guitarist; b. Congo. *Education:* Cornel Univ., Ithaca. *Career:* mem. Gym Class Heroes 2004–, numerous collaborations including Daryl Hall, Estelle, The-Dream, Busta Rhymes, Adam Levine, Neon Hitch, Ryan Tedder; Founder mem. side project Soul 2008–. *Recordings:* with Gym Class Heroes: albums: The Papercut Chronicles 2005, As Cruel as School Children 2006, The Quilt 2008, The Papercut Chronicles II 2011. *Honours:* with Gym Class Heroes: MTV Video Music Award for Best New Artist 2007. *Address:* c/o Fueled by Ramen Records, Warner Music Group, 75 Rockefeller Plaza, New York, NY 10019, USA (office). *Website:* www.fueledbyramen.com (office); www.wmg.com (office); www .gymclassheroes.com.

LUNDEN, Petri H.; Swedish promoter, booking agent and managing director; b. 29 Nov. 1963; one d. *Career:* owner, Hagenburg Law, Media Management; introduced the following acts in Scandinavia: Björk, Green Day, Nirvana, Offspring, Stereo MCs, Blue, Oasis, Prodigy, Cranberries, Soul Asylum, Weezer, The Orb; Swedish acts worked with world-wide include Clawfinger, Cardigans, Popsicle, Stanna Bo; mem. ECPA. *Honours:* Most

Interesting Promoter of the Year 1994. *Address:* Hagenburg Law, Media Management, Kyrkogatan 31, 411 08 Gothenburg, Sweden (office). *Telephone:* (31) 339-95-90 (office). *Fax:* (31) 13-95-09 (office). *E-mail:* info@hagenburg.se (office). *Website:* www.hagenburg.se (office).

LUNDSTEN, John; sound engineer. *Career:* Asst to the film editor, BBC and Yorkshire TV Productions including Horizon, Omnibus, Whicker's World 1967–69; Sound Engineer, Radio Gerinomo, live recordings, freelance film recorder for films including Pulp with Michael Caine and O Lucky Man, recorded Glastonbury festival for album and film directed by Nic Roeg, 1969–70; Assistant Recordist for film with Peter Sellers, Daily Record film contest, 1971–74; 12 concerts for Camden Jazz Festival, Raj in Orchestra, Pakistani/Western music project, started designing and building own mixing studio, 1981; Recorded live punk album for Peter and the Test Tube Babies, Pissed and Proud, 1982; Opera and masterclass recordings of Placido Domingo, Buddy Holly memorial concert with Paul McCartney, began using digital stereo recorder, 1983; Programme of music of Count Basie with Helen Shapiro on vocals, film of band Level 42 including post-production, using digital technology, also post-production for Erasure and Status Quo, 1984; Mincing Machine tour with Julian Clary, Irish Music Festival for RTE Dublin, 2 programmes on African music for S4C, Lecturer for National Film School on Digital Auto and Stereo recording techniques, 1989; Recording and post-production for Alan Price concert, recording and sound supervision for Wet Wet Wet, recordings for numerous TV programmes on world music, started work on a sound FX database, 1990–91; Recording for documentary for Rex: The Grateful and the Dead, recording for documentary on Ute Lemper, plan for building of Alchemea College of audio engineering, 1992; Lecturer, Course Co-ordinator and Curriculum Development at Alchemea, other recording projects, 1993–95; Designed 4 studios in Chipping Norton and 2 Surround-Sound mixing rooms at Alchemea, more teaching at National Film School and other projects. *Address:* Alchemea, The Windsor Centre, Islington, London N1 8QG, England.

LUNDSTEN, Ralph; Swedish composer, filmmaker, artist, author and diplomatist; *Owner, Andromeda;* b. 6 Oct. 1936, Ersnäs, northern Sweden; m. Diana Lundsten; one d. *Education:* self-taught. *Career:* Owner, Andromeda (Sweden's most famous picture and electronic music studio, including 'the Love Machine' and other invented synthesizers) since 1959, f. Andromeda Fan Soc. 1982; has worked for opera houses in Stockholm and Oslo, Modern Museum and Nat. Museum, Stockholm, the Louvre and Biennale, Paris, Triennale, Milan, Museum of Contemporary Crafts, New York, and others; more than 650 opus numbers, 122 recordings, 12 short films, as well as art exhbns, radio broadcasts; Cultural Amb. for Luleå 1999; mem. London Diplomatic Acad. 2000. *Exhibitions include:* electronic pictures, laser and sound sculptures; subject of several radio and TV portraits and special portrait exhbns at Music Museum, Stockholm 1991–92, 2000; Ralph Lundstengården, Ersnäs has hosted a perm. exhbn about him since 1998. *Compositions:* Nordic Nature Symphonies: No. 1 The Water Sprite, No. 2 Johannes and the Lady of the Woods, No. 3 A Midwinter Saga, No. 4 A Summer Saga, No. 5 Bewitched, No. 6 Landscape of Dreams, No. 7 The Seasons, No. 8 Pathways of the Soul, No. 9 In the Early Days of Summer, No. 10 Symphonia Linnæi, No. 11 In the Fairytale World; Erik XIV and Gustav III (two ballets about Swedish kings), Cosmic Love, Ourfather, Nightmare, Horrorscope, Shangri-La, Universe, Discophrenia, Alpha Ralpha Boulevard, Paradise Symphony, The New Age, Pop Age, Music for Relaxation and Meditation, Cosmic Phantazy, The Dream Master, The Gate of Time, The Ages of Man, Sea Symphony, Mindscape Music, Nordic Light, The Symphony of Joy (dedicated to the UN 50th anniversary), The Symphony of Light, The Symphony of Love, In Time and Space, Andromedian Tales, Happy Earthday, At the Fountain of Youth, A Vagabond of the Soul, Dreamlight, Suite Andromatique, Joy & Light, Prelude to the Future, Like the Wind my Longing, Out in the Wide World (Radio Sweden theme, chosen by Guinness World Records as "the most played musical composition" 2000), Lovetopia, Dance in the Endless Night, River of Time etc.; other: music for Herrskapstroll (children's opera) 1978 and for musical Glasblåsarens barn 2004. *Films include:* Främmande planet 1962–63, Komposition i tre satser 1965, EMS NR 1 1966, Hej natur 1966, Hjärtat brinner 1966–67, Reseminne 1968. *Recordings:* represented European music on EMI Classics series Inspiration 1996. *Publications:* Lustbarheter (with CD) 1992, Lustbarheter 1997, Happy Earthday (with CD) 2005, En själens vagabond 2006. *Honours:* more than 40 awards, including Grand Prix Biennale, Paris 1967, Swedish Film Inst. Prize 1964–67, Schwingungen Sonder-Preis (Oscar of electronic music) (Germany) 1997, Albert Schweitzer Medal for Science and Peace 2004, Gold Medal, Illis quorum meruere labores, given by Swedish Govt for musical and artistic works 2008. *Address:* Frankenburgs väg 1, 132 42 Saltsjö-Boo, Sweden (home). *Telephone:* (8) 715-14-37 (home). *E-mail:* ralph.lundsten@andromeda.se (office). *Website:* www.andromeda.se (office).

LUNGHINI, Elsa; French singer, actress, author and composer; b. 20 May 1973, Paris; one s. *Career:* solo artist 1986–, with tours and live appearances. *Film appearance:* Le Retour de Casanova 1991. *Recordings include:* albums: Elsa 1988, Rien Que Pour Ça 1990, Dance Violence 1992. *Honours:* Grand Prix SACEM 1993. *E-mail:* webmaster@elsalunghini.com. *Website:* www.elsalunghini.com.

LUNN, John Lawrence; British composer and musician; b. 13 May 1956, Scotland; m. Sara Lunn, one s. *Education:* Glasgow University, Royal Scottish Academy of Music, Electronic Music, Massachusetts Institute of Technology.

Career: formed pop group Earplay 1981; later joined avant garde music group The Lost Jockey; developed into Man Jumping, mid-1980s; mem. Musicians' Union, PRS. *Compositions:* films: Four Weddings and A Funeral, The Cormorant, BBC2, The Gift, BBC1, After The Dance, BBC, Life of Stuff 1998, Wisdom of Crocodiles 1998, Get Real 1998, Baby Mother 1998; other television: Finney, YTV, Hamish Macbeth, BBC, The Last Machine, BBC, Beatrix, BBC, Heart of Shelley, Anglia, The Dance House, BBC2, Focal Point, BBC Scotland, Getting Hurt (Royal Television Society Best Drama Score) 1998; ballets: Weighing The Heart, Goes Without Saying, In Dream I Loved A Dream; classical pieces: Le Voyage, Verve, Echoes, Leonce and Elena, Jazz Pointilliste, Strange Fruit, Black and Blue; operas: Mathematics of a Kiss, Misper 1998, The Maids 1998, Tangier Tattoo (premiered at Glyndebourne) 2005. *Honours:* Scottish Arts Council Scholarship. *Current Management:* Sound Track Music Associates Ltd, 22 Ives Street, Chelsea, London SW3 2ND, England.

LUNNY, Donal; Irish musician (guitar, bouzouki, bodhran) and producer; b. 1947, Newbridge, County Kildare; brother of Manus Lunny. *Career:* first musician to introduce bouzouki to Irish music; mem., Rakes of Kildare (with Christy Moore), Emmett Spiceland, Planxty, The Bothy Band, Moving Hearts, Coolfin; involved with production of first interactive CD-ROM compilation of Irish music; collaborations with Kate Bush, Mary Black, Van Morrison, Elvis Costello, Sinead O'Connor; producer for Altan, Triona and Maighread Ni Dhomhnaill, Moving Hearts, Christy Moore, Mary Black, Bill Whelan. *Television:* Bringing it All Back Home 1992, A River of Sound 1995, Sult (presenter) 1996.

LUNNY, Manus Bernard; Irish singer and musician (guitar, bouzouki, bodhran); b. 8 Feb. 1962, Dublin, Leinster; brother of Donal Lunny. *Career:* began career as mem. of The Wild Geese; toured with Andy M. Stewart and Phil Cunningham; joined Scottish folk band Capercaillie 1988–; group, along with original material, specialize in fusing traditional Gaelic songs with contemporary arrangements; act had first UK top 40 single in Gaelic, Coisich A Ruin (from A Prince Among Islands EP) 1992; in-demand session musician and composer; worked on several TV series with top folk musicians, including Tacsi, Togaidh Sinn Fonn; features as group or solo artist on film soundtracks and other artists' albums. *Film:* Rob Roy 1995. *Recordings:* albums: with Capercaillie: Sidewalk 1989, Delirium 1991, Get Out 1992, The Blood Is Strong, Secret People 1993, Capercaillie 1995, To The Moon 1996, Beautiful Wasteland 1997, Glenfinnan – Songs of The '45 (recorded 1995) 1998, Nàdurra 2000, Live in Concert 2002, Choice Language 2003, Roses and Tears 2008. *Film:* Rob Roy. *Address:* c/o Jane Skinner, Vertical Records, 19 Woodside Crescent, Glasgow, G3 7UL, Scotland (office). *Telephone:* (141) 352-6670 (office). *E-mail:* info@secretmusic.org (office). *Website:* www.verticalrecords.co.uk (office); www.capercaillie.co.uk.

LUPONE, Patti, BFA; American singer; b. 21 April 1949, Northport, Long Island, New York; d. of Orlando Joseph LuPone and Angela Louise LuPone; m. Matt Johnston; one s. *Education:* Juilliard School, New York. *Career:* has performed on Broadway in works by Stephen Sondheim, among others. *Theatre performances include:* School for Scandal, Three Sisters, The Beggar's Opera, The Robber Bridegroom, Measure for Measure, Edward II, The Water Engine, The Baker's Wife, The Woods, Working, Catchpenny Twist, As You Like It, The Cradle Will Rock, Stars of Broadway, Edmond, Evita (Tony Award 1980), Oliver!, Anything Goes, Les Misérables, Sunset Boulevard, Gypsy. *Films include:* King of the Gypsies 1978, '1941' 1979, Fighting Back 1982, Witness 1985, Wise Guys 1986, Driving Miss Daisy 1989, Family Prayers 1993, The 24 Hour Woman 1999, Summer of Sam 1999, Just Looking 1999, Bad Faith 2000, State and Main 2000, The Victim 2001, Heist 2001, City by the Sea 2002. *Television includes:* The Time of Your Life 1976, Piaf 1984, LBJ: The Early Years 1987, Life Goes On (series) 1989–93, The Water Engine 1992, The Song Spinner 1995, Her Last Chance 1996, Bonanno: A Godfather's Story 1999, Frasier (series) 2000, Falcone 2000, Sweeney Todd: The Demon Barber of Fleet Street In Concert 2001, Monday Night Mayhem 2002, Oz 2003, Strip Search 2004, Ugly Betty 2007, 30 Rock 2009–10. *Publication includes:* Patti LuPone: A Memoir 2010. *Current Management:* c/o Opus 3 Artists, 470 Park Avenue South, 9th Floor North, New York, NY 10016, USA. *Website:* www.pattilupone.net.

LURA; Portuguese singer; b. (Maria de Lurdes Pina Assunçao), 1975, Lisbon. *Career:* born into a family of Cabo Verde immigrants; became a leading exponent of Cabo Verde music; made first appearance as backing singer for Juka, later also sang for Tito Paris, Paulo Florès, Paulinho Vieira and Angolan singer Bonga. *Recordings:* albums: Nha Vida 1996, In Love 2002, Di Korpu Ku Alma 2005, M'bem di fora 2006. *Address:* c/o Lusafrica Ediçao Discográfica, 115 rue Lamarck, 75018 Paris, France. *Telephone:* 1-53-11-19-00. *Fax:* 1-53-11-19-05. *E-mail:* info@lusafrica.com. *Website:* www.lusafrica.com; www.luracriola.com.

LUSCOMBE, Stephen Alfred; British musician (keyboards), composer and producer; b. 29 Oct. 1954, Hillingdon, Middlesex. *Education:* John Steven's music workshops. *Career:* mem. Portsmouth Sinfonia, avant garde orchestra 1972–74; mem. Spontaneous Music Orchestra 1972–74; founder, performer, Music Workshop Miru 1973–77; founder, with Neil Arthur, electro-pop duo Blancmange 1979–86, 2006–; numerous tours, television and radio broadcasts, recordings; co-founder, West India Company, with Pandit Dinesh 1984–; collaborations with artists including Asha Bhosle, Boy George, Apache Indian, Saeed Jaffrey, La La La Human Steps; numerous commissions for television, radio, theatre, film productions include score for film Masala, starring Saeed Jaffrey and Zora Seghal 1991; music composition and direction for R National Theatre Production, Wicked Year 1994; mem, PRS, PPL. *Recordings:* with Portsmouth Sinfonia: Play The Popular Classics 1973, Live At The Albert Hall 1974; with Blancmange: Happy Families 1982, Mange Tout 1984, Believe You Me 1985, Greatest Hits 1990; also eight top 40 singles including Living On The Ceiling; with West India Company: Ave Maria (EP) 1984, Music From New Demons 1989, The Art of Love – Readings From The Kama Sutra, Saeed Jaffrey 1992. *E-mail:* info@blancmange.biz (office). *Website:* www.blancmange.biz.

LUTHER, Paul James; British musician (guitar); b. 1 Sept. 1974, Salisbury. *Career:* two British tours backing Toyah Willcox; concerts for British forces, Belize; Heineken festival concerts, Gateshead, Plymouth, 1994; member, Scarlet supporting Bryan Ferry, British tour, 1995; further Scarlet tour supporting Wet Wet Wet 1995; mem., Ebb 1998; numerous television appearances; mem. Musicians' Union, PAMRA. *Recordings:* with Toyah Willcox: Take The Leap 1993; with Scarlet: Naked 1995, The Friday's Duck; singles: with Scarlet: Independent Love Song, I Wanna Be Free.

LYDON, John, (Johnny Rotten); British singer; b. 31 Jan. 1956, Finsbury Park, London. *Career:* singer, punk group the Sex Pistols 1975–78; founder, Public Image Ltd 1978–; numerous live performances, tours. *Film appearances:* The Great Rock 'n' Roll Swindle 1980, The Filth and the Fury 2000. *Radio:* presenter Billion Dollar Baby: The Alice Cooper Story (BBC Radio 2) 2002. *Television:* appearance on I'm a Celebrity... Get Me Out of Here 2004. *Recordings include:* albums: Never Mind The Bollocks – Here's The Sex Pistols 1977, The Great Rock 'n' Roll Swindle 1979, Some Product – Carry On Sex Pistols 1979, Flogging A Dead Horse 1980, Kiss This 1992; with Public Image Ltd: Public Image 1978, Metal Box 1979, Paris Au Printemps 1980, Flowers of Romance 1981, This Is What You Want, This Is What You Get 1984, Album 1986, Happy? 1987, 9 1989, Greatest Hits So Far 1990, That What Is Not 1992, Plastic Box 1999, Jubilee 2002, This is PiL 2012, What the World Needs Now 2015; solo: Psycho's Path 1997, The Best of British £1 Notes 2005. *Publications:* Rotten: No Irish, No Blacks, No Dogs (autobiog.) 1994, Anger is An Energy: My Life Uncensored 2014. *E-mail:* info@pil-official.com. *Website:* www.pil-official.com; www.johnlydon.com.

LYLE, Graham; British singer, songwriter and musician (guitar); b. Largs, Ayrshire, Scotland. *Career:* songwriting partnership with Benny Gallagher 1960s; mem., McGuinness Flint 1969–71; folk duo, Gallagher & Lyle 1972–79; solo artist 1980–. *Recordings include:* albums: with Gallagher & Lyle: Gallagher & Lyle, 1972; Willie and The Lap Dog, 1973; Seeds, 1973; The Last Cowboy, 1974; Breakaway, 1976; Love On The Airwaves, 1977; Showdown, 1978; Gone Crazy, 1979; Lonesome No More, 1979; Heart On My Sleeve, 1991. *Current Management:* Hornall Brothers Music Ltd, 1 Northfields Prospect, Putney Bridge Road, London, SW18 1PE, England. *E-mail:* stuart@hobro.co.uk. *Website:* www.hobro.co.uk.

LYNCH, Colm; Irish musician; b. 29 April 1952, Dublin; 1 s., 1 d. *Education:* Social Pedegog, Denmark; Drums, piano, guitar, through school; Private tutor in School of Music, Dublin. *Career:* fmr mem. Mushroom, Irish rock band; Successful appearances on RTE (TV, Ireland): Meitheal; Saoire Samhradh; Spin Off; Jimmy Saville show, BBC; Danish radio, television; mem, KODA (Danish PRS); DJBFA (Danish Society, Jazz, Rock and Folk Composers). *Compositions:* Songwriter in Ireland, Singer/songwriter in UK, wrote hit singles. *Recordings:* Album: Early One Morning; Hit singles: Violence Has Many Faces; Devil Among The Tailors. *Honours:* Top Selling Album, 1973; Top Irish Artist, 1973; Best Group. *E-mail:* clynch@mail.tele.dk. *Website:* www.colmlynch.com.

LYNCH, Edele Claire Christina Edwina; Irish singer; b. 15 Dec. 1979, Dublin; twin sister of Keavy Lynch; one d. *Career:* mem., B*Witched 1998–2002; numerous tours and TV appearances. *Recordings include:* albums: B*Witched 1998, Awake and Breathe 1999.

LYNCH, Keavy-Jane Elizabeth Annie; Irish singer and musician (saxophone, drums, guitar); b. 15 Dec. 1979, Dublin; twin sister of Edele Lynch. *Career:* mem., B*Witched 1998–2002; numerous tours and TV appearances. *Recordings include:* albums: B*Witched 1998, Awake and Breathe 1999. *E-mail:* info@keavylynch.com (office). *Website:* www.keavylynch.com.

LYNCH, Shane Eamon Mark Stephen; Irish singer and actor; b. 3 July 1976, Donaghmede, Dublin; m. Easther Bennett. *Career:* mem., Boyzone 1993–2001, 2007–; actor 2001–. *Recordings include:* albums: Said and Done 1995, A Different Beat 1996, Where We Belong 1998, By Request 1999, Back Again... No Matter What 2008, Brother 2010. *Current Management:* ASM Damage Ltd., Unit 3, City Business Centre, St Olav's Court, Lower Road, London SE16 2XB, England. *Telephone:* (20) 7740-1600. *E-mail:* david@asmdamadge.co.uk. *Website:* www.asmanagement.co.uk; www.boyzone.net.

LYNGBO, Lasse; Danish musician (keyboards, electronics). *Career:* mem., Diefenbach 1999–; band started own label, Display Records. *Recordings include:* albums: Diefenbach 2001, Run Trip Fall 2003, Make Your Mind (EP) 2004, Re-Make Your Mind (EP) 2005, Set And Drift 2005. *E-mail:* diefenbach@diefenbach.dk (office). *Website:* www.diefenbach.dk.

LYNGSTAD, Anni-Frid (Frida); Norwegian singer; b. 15 Nov. 1945, Ballangen, Narvik, Norway; m. Benny Andersson 1978 (divorced 1981); one s. one d. (from previous relationship). *Career:* leader of own dance band Anni-

Frid Four; mem. pop group ABBA 1972–82; winner, Eurovision Song Contest 1974; world-wide tours; concerts include Royal Performance, Stockholm 1976, Royal Albert Hall, London 1977, UNICEF concert, New York 1979, Wembley Arena 1979; reunion with ABBA, Swedish TV This Is Your Life 1986; solo artist 1983–. *Film:* ABBA: The Movie 1977. *Recordings include:* albums: with ABBA: Ring Ring 1973, Waterloo 1974, ABBA 1975, Greatest Hits 1976, Arrival 1977, The Album 1978, Voulez-Vous 1979, Greatest Hits Vol. 2 1979, Super Trouper 1980, The Visitors 1981, The Singles: The First Ten Years 1982, Thank You For The Music 1983, Absolute ABBA 1988, ABBA Gold 1992, More ABBA Gold 1993, Forever Gold 1998, The Definitive Collection 2001; solo: Frida Alone 1976, Something's Going On 1982, Shine 1983, Djupa Andetag 1996, Frida 1967–72 1998, Frida: The Mixes 1998, Svenska Popfavoriter 1998; singles include: with ABBA: Ring Ring 1973, Waterloo 1974, Mamma Mia 1975, Dancing Queen 1976, Fernando 1976, Money Money Money 1976, Knowing Me Knowing You 1977, The Name Of The Game 1977, Take A Chance On Me 1978, Summer Night City 1978, Chiquitita 1979, Does Your Mother Know? 1979, Angel Eyes/Voulez-Vous 1979, Gimme Gimme Gimme (A Man After Midnight) 1979, I Have A Dream 1979, The Winner Takes It All 1980, Super Trouper 1980, On And On And On 1981, Lay All Your Love On Me 1981, One Of Us 1981, When All Is Said And Done 1982, Head Over Heels 1982, The Day Before You Came 1982, Under Attack 1982, Thank You For The Music 1983. *Honours:* World Music Award, Best Selling Swedish Artist 1993. *Website:* www.abbasite.com.

LYNN, Loretta Webb; American singer; b. 14 April 1935, Butcher Hollow, Ky; d. of Melvin (Ted) Webb and Clara Webb (née Ramey); m. Oliver V. Lynn, Jr 1948 (died 1996); two s. (one deceased) three d. *Career:* sang in local clubs with group The Trailblazers; regular appearances Grand Ole Opry; weekly TV show, with the Wilburn Brothers, Nashville; recording artist with MCA 1961–; Sec. and Treas. Loretta Lynn Enterprises; Vice-Pres. United Talent Inc.; Hon. Chair. Bd Loretta Lynn Western Stores; Hon. Rep. United Giver's Fund 1971. *Recordings include:* albums: solo: Loretta Lynn Sings 1963, Before I'm Over You 1964, Songs From The Heart 1965, Blue Kentucky Girl 1965, Hymns 1965, I Like 'Em Country 1966, You Ain't Woman Enough 1966, Don't Come Home A-Drinkin' 1967, Singin' With Feelin' 1967, Fist City 1968, Your Squaw Is On The Warpath 1969, Woman Of The World 1969, Coal Miner's Daughter 1971, I Want To Be Free 1971, Alone With You 1972, Love Is The Foundation 1973, They Don't Make 'Em Like Our Daddy 1974, Home 1975, Somebody Somewhere 1976, Out Of My Head And Back In My Bed 1976, Loretta 1980, Lookin' Good 1980, Makin' Love From Memory 1982, Just A Woman 1985, Who Was That Stranger 1989, Country's Favorite Daughter 1993, An Evening with Loretta Lynn 1995, Still Country 2000, Van Lear Rose 2004, Coal Miner's Daughter 2010; with Ernest Tubb: Mr and Mrs Used To Be 1965, Singin' Again 1967, If We Put Our Heads Together 1969; with Conway Twitty: We Only Make Believe 1971, Lead Me On 1971, Lousiana Woman, Misissipp Man 1973, Country Partners 1974, Feelin's 1975, United Talent 1976, Dynamic Duo 1977, Country Partners 1974, Honky Tonk Heroes 1978, Diamond Duets 1979, Two's A Party 1981, Making Believe 1988, Hey Good Lookin' 1993. *Publication:* Coal Miner's Daughter (autobiog.) 1976. *Honours:* Female Vocalist of the Year, Country Music Asscn 1967, 1972, 1973, Grammy Award 1971, Entertainer of the Year 1972, Top Duet 1972–75, American Music Award 1978, Entertainer of the Decade, Acad. of Country Music 1980, mem. Country Music Hall of Fame 1988. *Address:* Loretta Lynn Enterprises, Inc., PO Box 120369, Nashville, TN 37212, USA. *Website:* www.lorettalynn.com.

LYNN, Dame Vera, DBE; British singer; b. (Vera Margaret Welch), 20 March 1917, d. of Bertram Welch and Ann Welch; m. Harry Lewis 1939; one d. *Education:* Brampton Road School, East Ham. *Career:* began singing aged seven; adopted her grandmother's maiden name Lynn as her stage name; joined singing troupe 1928; ran dancing school 1932; broadcast with Joe Loss and joined Charlie Kunz band 1935; singer with Ambrose Orchestra 1937–40, then went solo; voted most popular singer in Daily Express competition 1939; own radio show Sincerely Yours 1941–47; sang to troops abroad during World War II, named 'Forces' Sweetheart'; appeared in Applesauce, London 1941; post-war radio and TV shows and numerous appearances abroad including Denmark, Canada, South Africa and Australia; most successful record Auf Wiederseh'n; became oldest living artist to reach number one in the UK album chart with We'll Meet Again – The Very Best of Vera Lynn 2009; Pres. Printers' Charitable Corpn 1980, Dame Vera Lynn Trust 2001–. *Publications:* Vocal Refrain (autobiog.) 1975, We'll Meet Again (with Robin Cross) 1989, The Woman Who Won the War (with Robin Cross and Jenny de Gex) 1990, Unsung Heroines 1990. *Honours:* Hon. Citizen, Winnipeg 1974; Freedom of City of London 1978; Commdr Order of Orange-Nassau (Holland), Burma Star Medal and War Medal 1985; Variety Club Int. Humanitarian Award, European Woman of Achievement Award 1994. *Address:* c/o The Dame Vera Lynn Trust, Ingfield Manor, Five Oaks, West Sussex RH14 9AX, England (office). *Website:* www.dvltrust.org.uk (office).

LYNNE, Jeff; British record producer, singer, songwriter, musician (guitar) and arranger; b. 30 Dec. 1947, Birmingham. *Career:* mem. Idle Race 1966–70, The Move 1970–72; founder mem., The Electric Light Orchestra (ELO) 1972–85, Jeff Lynne's ELO 2012–; regular int. tours 1973–; record producer 1983–; founder mem., Traveling Wilburys (with Bob Dylan, Roy Orbison, George Harrison, Tom Petty) 1988; solo artist; mem. American Soc. of Composers, Authors and Publishers (ASCAP), British Acad. of Composers and Songwriters (BAC&S). *Recordings:* albums include: with ELO (as singer, guitarist, writer and producer): Electric Light Orchestra 1972, ELO II 1973,

On the Third Day 1973, Eldorado 1974, The Night the Light Went On in Long Beach 1974, Face the Music 1975, Olé ELO 1976, A New World Record 1976, Out of the Blue 1977, Discovery 1979, ELO's Greatest Hits 1979, Xanadu (film soundtrack) 1980, Time (No. 1, UK) 1982, Secret Messages 1983, Perfect World of Music 1985, First Movement 1986, Balance of Power 1986, Afterglow 1990, Strange Magic 1995, Live at Wembley 1998, Flashback 2000, Zoom 2001; with Traveling Wilburys (also co-writer and co-producer): Traveling Wilburys Vol. 1 1988, Vol. 3 1991; solo: Armchair Theatre 1990, Long Wave 2012; with Jeff Lynne's ELO: Alone in the Universe 2015; as producer: Information, Dave Edmunds 1983, Cloud Nine, George Harrison 1987, Mystery Girl, Roy Orbison 1988, Full Moon Fever, Tom Petty 1989; singles include: with ELO: 10538 Overture 1972, Roll Over Beethoven 1972, Can't Get It Out of My Head 1974, Evil Woman 1976, Strange Magic 1976, Livin' Thing 1976, Telephone Line 1977, Mr Blue Sky 1978, Sweet Talkin' Woman 1978, Shine A Little Love 1979, Don't Bring Me Down 1979, Xanadu, collaboration with Olivia Newton-John (No. 1, UK) 1980, All Over the World 1980, Hold On Tight 1981, Rock 'n' Roll Is King 1983, Calling America 1986; with the Traveling Wilburys: Handle With Care 1988; solo: Doin' That Crazy Thing; as producer/co-producer: You Got It, Roy Orbison 1988; Into the Great Wide Open, Tom Petty 1991, Free as a Bird, The Beatles 1995, Real Love, The Beatles 1995, Flaming Pie, Paul McCartney 1997, Concert for George (performer/producer) 2003. *Honours:* Nationwide Music Award, Album of the Year, Out of The Blue, 1978; Ivor Novello Awards: Outstanding Contribution To British Music, 1979; Best Film Song, Xanadu, 1981; Grammy Award, Traveling Wilburys Vol. 1, 1989; Rolling Stone Award, Best Producer, 1989; BMI Songwriters Award, on broadcasts of Evil Woman, USA, 1992. *Address:* Craig Fruin, HK Management, PO Box 151470, San Rafael, CA 94901, USA. *Website:* jefflynneselo.com.

LYNNE, Shelby; American musician (guitar) and singer; b. (Shelby Lynn Moore), 22 Oct. 1968, Quantico, VA. *Career:* solo artist 1988–; numerous live appearances; f. Everso record label 2010. *Recordings include:* albums: Sunrise 1989, Tough All Over 1990, Soft Talk 1991, Temptation 1993, Restless 1995, I Am Shelby Lynne 1999, Love, Shelby 2001, Identity Crisis 2003, Suit Yourself 2005, Just a Little Lovin' 2008, Tears, Lies and Alibis 2010. *Honours:* Grammy Award for Best Newcomer 2001. *Website:* www.shelbylynne.com.

LYON, Steve; British recording engineer, producer and mixer. *Career:* trained under supervision of producer, Glyn Jones, West Sussex studio; engineer, prod., Virgin Studio Group; worked at The Townhouse, The Manor; Chief Engineer, Master Control, Los Angeles, Air Studios, London; freelance engineer and producer 1988–; owner, Panic Button Studios; has worked with Depeche Mode, The Cure, The Wedding Present, Nitzer Ebb, Suzanne Vega, Tears For Fears, Dave Stewart, Paul McCartney, Berlin, Prefab Sprout, UFO, Labi Siffre, Breathe, The Outfield, The Cure, The Creatures, The Dhamers, Recoil, Paradise Lost, Spooky Ruben, EMF, Reamonn, Thunder, Soul Asylum, Laura Pausini. *Address:* Panic Button Studios, Unit 503, Platts Eyot, Hampton, Middlesex, TW12 2HF, England (office). *E-mail:* info@steve-lyon.com (office), studio@panicbuttonstudios.com (office). *Website:* www.panicbuttonstudios.com; www.steve-lyon.com.

LYONS, Ken, (Tigger); British musician (bass guitar), songwriter and composer; b. 11 April 1951, Northallerton, Yorkshire; m. Linda Fletcher; one d. *Education:* Hammersmith Coll. of Art and Building. *Career:* with Flesh: Melody Maker Competition Finals, The Roundhouse, 1971; with Hustler: UK Queen Tour, 1974; Status Quo European Tour, 1975; Geordie Scene; Kid Jenson's 45; Radio 1 In Concert; with London club/pub band The Brain Surgeons, 1976–79; with LA band The Shots, 1980–83; KROQ Nick Stavross Show; mem. Mechanical Copyright Protection Soc., Performing Right Soc. *Compositions include:* for Hustler: Get Outta Me House (Get Out of My House); Little People; for Brain Surgeons: Me and My Guitar; for The Shots: Reject; Also appears on: Vineyard Sound Vol. 3, 1997. *Address:* Lion Music, 29 Derby Road, Uxbridge, Middx UB8 2ND, England. *E-mail:* ks.lyons@btinternet.com.

LYSDAL, Jens; Danish singer, musician (guitar), composer, producer and arranger; *Teacher, Rhythmic Music Conservatory;* b. 12 Jan. 1960, Sweden. *Education:* Royal Danish Music Conservatory. *Career:* following a year in New Orleans, USA family moved to Denmark; started his professional career by playing school-gigs with his band on the island of Thurø aged 13; invited to Beijing with Hugo Rasmussen, Dexter Gordon, Ben Webster, Coleman Hawkins, Harry Sweets Edison and Gustaf Ljunggreen, playing concerts and recording with Chinese artists, including Ai Jing and Chang Jing 2001, 2002; played at Stockholm jazz festival and Västervikfestivalen, Sweden 2003; was invited, together with Hugo Rasmussen, to play at Cornelis Vreeswijk's birthday concert in Stockholm 2003; backing musician for artists, including The Pointer Sisters, Donna Summer, Sergio Mendes, Etta Cameron, Sanne Salomonsen, Sebastian, Etta Cameron, Poul Dissing and many others. *Television appearances include:* Meyerheim After 8 (backing Lill Lindfors, TV 2), solo singer and guitarist, TV 2) 1994, Eurovision Song Contest (as mem. DR Pop-orchestra, DR) 1995, Bent Fabricius Bjerre 50-year Jubilee Show (DR) 1995, Tjek Ind Hos Mygind (TV 3) 1995, Go' Morgen TV (TV 2) 1998, Dybt vand (DR1) 1998, Årgang 0 (TV 2) 1999–2007, Til dans til vands og i luften (DR1) 2005, Krøniken (DR1) 2006, Go'morgen Danmark (TV 2) 2006. *Music for films includes:* A Day In October 1990, Treasure in the Forest 1997, Clapping with One Hand 2001, Truly Human 2001, Oh Happy Day 2004, The Scarlett Letter 2004, Veninder 2005; featured as a singer in award-winning films. *Recordings include:* solo albums: A Matter of Time (Best CD of the Year, Golden Stag Festival, Brasov, Romania 1997) 1995, It's Almost Love 2006; other albums: Danmark Dejligst (with Poul Dissing, Alberte, Kaya Brüel, Raisa Reyes Castro, Jens Lysdal and Denmark Radio Symphony Orchestra) 2001, Keep the Light in Your Eyes (with Hugo Rasmussen and Denmark Radio Concert Orchestra) 2001, Hjertekamre (with Laura Illeborg og Lysdal) 2004, It's Almost Love (with Greg Leisz, Danny Frankel and Chang Jing, among others) 2006. *Honours:* Arnold, for music to commercial, Kim's Peanuts. *Current Management:* c/o Fyns Musikkontor, Møllergade 24, 5700 Svendborg, Denmark. *Telephone:* 62-80-07-08. *Fax:* 62-80-07-27. *E-mail:* jesper@fynsmusikkontor.dk. *Website:* www.fynsmusikkontor.dk. *E-mail:* jens@lysdal.com. *Website:* www.lysdal.com.

LYTHGOE, Nigel Bruce, OBE; British choreographer, film director and television producer; b. 9 July 1949, Wirral, Merseyside, England; s. of George Percival Lythgoe and Gertrude Emily Lythgoe; m. Bonnie Shawe 1974 (divorced 2010); two s. *Education:* Hylton-Bromley School of Dance and Drama and Perry Cowell School of Dance, Wallasey, Merseyside, trained in London under Joanne Steuer and Molly Molloy. *Career:* began tap dancing aged ten; studied classical ballet, modern jazz, ballroom, character, classical Greek and nat. dance of various countries; first professional job in Corps de Ballet for nat. tour of The Merry Widow; fmr dancer with BBC's Young Generation dance troupe 1969; danced, choreographed, produced and directed a Royal Variety Performance; producer of Pop Idol and American Idol and creator and exec. producer and judge of So You Think You Can Dance; also cr. Superstars of Dance 2009; owns a vineyard in Paso Robles, Calif., USA. *Television includes:* producer of numerous series, including Popstars (series) (exec. producer) 2000, 2001, Pop Idol (series) (exec. producer) 2001, American Idol (series) (exec. producer 264 episodes 2002–14, producer two episodes 2006–09, co-exec. producer 2007, segment producer 2008) 2002–14, All American Girl (series) (exec. producer) 2003, American Juniors (series) (exec. producer) 2003, So You Think You Can Dance (series) (exec. producer) 2005–12, The Next Great American Band (series) (exec. producer) 2007, Superstars of Dance (series) (exec. producer) 2009. *Honours:* Governors Award 2007, Int. Emmy: Founders Award 2011, Ellis Island Int. Medal of Honor 2014. *Address:* Nigel Lythgoe Productions, 9000 Sunset Blvd, Suite 1560, West Hollywood, CA 90069, USA (office). *Telephone:* (310) 432-0330 (office). *Fax:* (310) 432-0331 (office). *E-mail:* info@nigellythgoeproductions.com (office). *Website:* www.nigellythgoeproductions.com (office).

M

M., Boštjan; Slovenian musician (drums, percussion). *Career:* mem., Siddharta. *Recordings include:* albums: Id 1999, Nord 2001, Silikon Delta 2002, Rh- 2003, Petrolea 2006, Maraton 2007. *Honours:* Viktor Award for Best Act 2003, 2004, 2006, for Special Achievement 2003, MTV Europe Music Award 2005. *Address:* Siddharta, PO Box 179, 1236 Trzin, Slovenia (office). *Telephone:* (4) 1382192 (office). *E-mail:* info@siddharta.net (office). *Website:* www.siddharta.net (office).

M., Tomi; Slovenian singer and musician (guitar); b. 28 Feb. 1977. *Career:* mem. Siddharta. *Recordings include:* albums: Id 1999, Nord 2001, Silikon Delta 2002, Rh- 2003, Petrolea 2006, Maraton 2007, Saga 2009, VI 2011. *Honours:* Zlati Petelin Award 2000, 2001, Bumerang Award 2000, 2002, Viktor Award for Best Act 2003, 2004, 2006, for Special Achievement 2003, MTV Europe Music Award 2005. *Address:* Siddharta, PO Box 179, 1236 Trzin, Slovenia (office). *Telephone:* (4) 1382192 (office). *E-mail:* info@siddharta.net (office). *Website:* www.siddharta.net (office).

MAAETOFT, Nils; Danish singer, songwriter and musician (guitar); b. 17 Nov. 1950, Vejle. *Career:* singer, guitarist, main songwriter for rock group, The Intellectuals; wrote, performed under pseudonym M. T. Purse, and formed group M. T. Purse 1992; mem. The Danish Soc. for Jazz Rock Folk Composers. *Recordings:* with The Intellectuals: Half A-Live 1986, Health and Happiness 1987; as M. T. Purse: Cross Talk 1992, Throwing Rocks At The Moon 1995; solo: Throwing Rocks at the Moon 1998, Five Easy Pieces 2002.

MAAL, Baaba; Senegalese singer, musician (guitar) and songwriter; b. 1953, Podor. *Education:* Dakar Conservatoire, Conservatoire des Beaux Arts, Paris, France. *Career:* fmr geography and history teacher; formed band Daande Lenol 1986–; regular collaborations with Mansour Seck; representative of UNDP speaking on the issue of HIV/AIDS in Africa; involved with HIV/AIDS awareness campaign music projects. *Recordings include:* albums: Djam Leelii 1989, Baayo 1991, Lam Toro 1993, Wango 1994, Sunugal 1995, Firin' In Fouta 1995, Gorel 1995, Taara 1997, Nomad Soul 1998, Jombaajo 2000, Missing You – Mi Yeewnii (Froots Critics' Poll Best New Album, BBC Radio 3 Critics' Award for World Music Album) 2001, Television 2009. *Address:* c/o Island Records, 364–366 Kensington High Street, London W14 8NS, England (office). *Website:* www.islandrecords.co.uk (office); www.baabamaal.tv.

MAAN, Gurdas; Indian singer, songwriter and actor; b. 4 Jan. 1957, Giddarbaha, Muktsar Dist, Punjab; m. Manjeet Mann; one s. *Education:* Nat. Inst. of Sports, Faridkot. *Career:* fmr writer and Dir of tv programmes for Doordarshan Network, Delhi; gained nat. attention with the song Dil Da Mamala Hai 1980; has recorded over 27 albums and written over 200 songs; actor in numerous Punjabi, Hindi and Tamil movies. *Recordings include:* Dil Da Mamla Hai 1981, Dil Saaf Hona Chahida 1982, Masti 1983, Peer Tere Jaan Di 1984, Kudiyan Ne Judo Sikhli 1985, Nacho Babbyo 1986, Chakkar 1988, Wah Ni Jawaniye 1988, Geeraan Di Pataari, Chugliyaan 1988, Raat Suhani 1988, Wah Ni Gental Maniye, Mohabbat Zindabad 1990, Teri Khair Hove, Aakarh Aa Hi Jaadie, , Ghar Bhulgi Morh Te Aake 1993, Than Than Gopal 1993, Ishq Da Gidda 1994, Ishq Na Dekhe Jaat 1995, Chaklo Chaklo 1996, Yaar Mera Pyar 1997, Dil Hona Chahida Jawan 1998, Jadugaarian 1999, Pya Kar Le 2001, Punjeeri, Heer (Best Song, ETC Punjabi Music Awards 2005) 2004, Vilayatan 2005, Apna Punjab (Best Song, Best Album, Asian Pop and Media Awards, Birmingham, UK 1998), Kudiye (Best Lyrics, ETC Punjabi Music Awards 2005), Boot Polishan 2008, Bekadraan Naal Pyar 2008, Dukhan Nu Bana Ke Apna 2009. *Films include:* Ucha Dar Babbe 'Nanak' Da 1982, Mamla Gadbad Hai 1984, Long Da Lashkara 1986, Ki Banu Duniyan Da 1986, Gabroo Punjab Da 1986, Chhora Haryane Da 1987, Baghavaat 1988, Qurbani Jatt Di 1990, Dushmani Di Aag 1990, Pratigya 1990, Kachehri 1994, Wanted Dead or Alive – Gurdas Maan 1994, Shaheed-e-Mohabbat (Boota Singh) 1999, Shaheed Udham Singh 2000, Zindagi Khoobsoorat Hai 2002, Des Hoyea Pardes 2004, Waris Shah-Ishq Daa Waaris (Nat. Award) 2006, Yaariyan 2008, Sukhmani – Hope for Life 2010. *Honours:* Best Int. Artist, Asian Pop and Media Awards, Birmingham, UK 1998, Best Singer of the Year, ETC Punjabi Music Awards 2005. *E-mail:* info@gurdasmaan.com (office). *Website:* www.gurdasmaan.com.

MAAS, Timo; German producer, remixer and DJ; b. 1970, Hanover. *Career:* made breakthrough as resident DJ at The Tunnel, Hamburg; produced Die Herdplatte with fellow resident Gary D, which led to recordings with Bristol's Hope Recordings; remixer; club residency at New York's Twilo; remixed: Madonna, Azzido Da Bass, Placebo, Fatboy Slim. *Recordings include:* albums: Music for the Maases 2000, Loud 2002, Music for the Maases 2 2003, Pictures 2005. *Honours:* German Dance Award for Best National DJ 2001. *E-mail:* david@itb.co.uk. *Website:* www.timomaas.com.

MABUS, Joel Dwight; American singer, songwriter and musician (guitar, banjo, fiddle, mandolin); b. 13 Sept. 1953, Belleville, Ill. *Education:* Michigan State Univ. *Career:* folk festival appearances, radio broadcasts; mem. American Fed. of Musicians, The Folk Alliance. *Recordings include:* solo albums: Fortunes 1987, Naked Truth 1988, Firelake 1990, Flatpick 1991, Short Stories 1992, Clawhammer 1993, Promised Land 1994, Rhyme Schemes 1997, Top Drawer String Band 1999, How Like the Holly, Six of One 2001, Thumb Thump 2002, Golden Willow Tree 2004, Parlor Guitar 2005, The Banjo Monologues 2007, Retold 2008, No Worries Now 2009, American Anonymous

2011. *Publication:* Big Words – the Lyrics of Joel Mabus. *Honours:* Detroit Metro Times Instrumentalist of the Year. *Address:* PO Box 306, Portage, MI 49081, USA. *E-mail:* joel.mabus@pobox.com. *Website:* www.joelmabus.com.

McALL, Barnaby (Barney) Jonathon, BMus; Australian jazz musician (piano) and composer; b. 3 Jan. 1966, Box Hill, Vic. *Education:* Melbourne Univ., Victorian Coll. of the Arts; studied in New York with Mulgrew Miller, Walter Bishop Jr, Barry Harris, Larry Goldings, Jim Beard, in Cuba with Chucho Valdez, Ramón Valle. *Career:* moved to New York 1997; toured or performed with Gary Bartz, Andy Bey, Dewey Redman, Billy Harper, Kenny Garrett, Fred Wesley, Jimmy Cobb, Vernal Fornier, Terry Clarke, Eddie Henderson, Badal Roy, Stefon Harris, Wallace Roney, Seamus Blake, Kurt Rosenwinkel; mem. The Barney McAll Sextet, Gary Bartz quartet, quintet and NTU Troop 2000, Kurt Rosenwinkel's Heart-Core Band, Fred Wesley and The JBs. *Recordings include:* solo: Release The Day, Widening Circles featuring Billy Harper, Exit, Mother of Dreams and Secrets, Flashbacks 2009. *Film and Theatre:* scores composed: Solstice (musical), Adelaide Int. Festival 1996; Homecoming (documentary), by Edwina Throsby; Necesidades (Spanish black comedy); Brother to Brother (film) 2003; performed original score, with Vince Jones, Mullaway (film), Liberia: An Uncivil War; Motherland Afghanistan; We All Fall Down: the American Mortgage Crisis. *Honours:* first prize, Wangaratta International Jazz Piano Competition 1990, Best Jazz Composition, APRA 1993, Best Jazz Composition, NSW Jazz Action Soc. 1995, 1998, Australia Council Grant to tour Europe with Bill Harper 2001, Best Newcomer CD, Los Angeles Times 2002, Jazz CD of the Year, Village Voice Pazz and Jop Awards, NYC 2002, Australia Council for the Arts Fellowship 2007. *Current Management:* Company of Heaven Management, 523–525 West 152nd Street, Apartment 42, New York, NY 10031, USA. *Telephone:* (212) 281-9785. *E-mail:* company-of-heaven@liwest.at. *E-mail:* barneymcall@gmail.com (office). *Website:* www.barneymcall.com.

McALMONT, David Irving; British singer and lyricist; b. 2 May 1967, Croydon. *Career:* mem. duo, Thieves (with Saul Freeman) 1992–93; solo artist as McAlmont 1994; mem. duo, McAlmont and Butler (with Bernard Butler) 1994–95, 2001–02; numerous live and festival appearances; solo artist 1995–; collaborations with Ultramarine, David Arnold. *Recordings include:* albums: with McAlmont and Butler: The Sound of McAlmont and Butler 1995, Bring It Back 2002; solo: A Little Communication 1998, Working 2001, Set One: You Go To My Head 2005, The Glare (with Michael Nyman) 2009. *E-mail:* home@davidmcalmont.co.uk (office). *Website:* www.davidmcalmont.co.uk.

McALOON, Patrick (Paddy) Joseph, BA; British musician, singer and songwriter; b. 7 June 1957, England. *Education:* Ushaw Coll., Co Durham, Univ. of Northumbria. *Career:* singer, songwriter, Prefab Sprout; extensive tours of the UK, Europe, Japan; numerous television appearances; mem. BAC&S. *Compositions:* songs covered by Kylie Minogue, Jimmy Nail, The Zombies, Cher; contributed songs to television series Crocodile Shoes and Where the Heart Is. *Recordings include:* albums: Swoon 1984, Steve McQueen 1985, From Langley Park To Memphis 1988, Protest Songs 1989, Jordan – The Comeback 1990, Life of Surprises: Best of Prefab Sprout 1992, Andromeda Heights 1997, The Gunman And Other Stories 2001, Let's Change the World with Music 2009, Crimson/Red 2013; solo: I Trawl the Megahertz 2003; singles: Lions In My Own Garden 1983, Don't Sing 1984, Couldn't Bear To Be Special 1984, When Love Breaks Down 1984, Faron Young 1985, Appetite 1985, Johnny Johnny 1986, Cars And Girls 1988, The King Of Rock N Roll 1988, Hey! Manhattan 1988, Nightingales 1988, The Golden Calf 1989, Looking For Atlantis 1990, We Let The Stars Go 1990, Carnival 2000 1990, The Sound of Crying 1992, If You Don't Love Me 1992, Life Of Surprises 1993, All The World Loves Lovers 1993, A Prisoner Of The Past 1997, Electric Guitars 1997. *Current Management:* Kitchenware Management, 7 The Stables, Saint Thomas Street, Newcastle Upon Tyne, NE1 4LE, England. *Telephone:* (191) 230-1970. *Fax:* (191) 232-0262. *E-mail:* info@kitchenwarerecords.com. *Website:* www.kitchenwarerecords.com.

MacALPINE, Tony; American rock musician (guitar, piano). *Education:* classical piano. *Career:* solo artist, rock guitarist 1986–90; formed short-lived supergroup, MARS 1987; founder, Squawk record label; formed band, MacAlpine 1990–; also mem. Ring of Fire, Devil's Slingshot. *Recordings include:* albums: solo: Edge of Insanity 1986, Maximum Security 1987, Freedom to Fly 1992, Madness 1992, Premonition 1994, Evolution 1995, Violent Machine 1996, Master of Paradise 1999, Chromaticity 2001, The Shrapnel Years 2006; with MARS: Project Driver 1986; with MacAlpine: Eyes of the World 1990, CAB 2000, CAB2 2000, CAB4 2003; with Ring of Fire: Dreamtower 2003, Lapse of Reality 2004. *Website:* www.tonymacalpine.com.

McANALLY, Mac; American country music singer, songwriter, record producer and musician (guitar, keyboards, mandolin, percussion); b. (Lyman Corbitt McAnally, Jr.), 15 July 1957, Red Bay, Ala. *Career:* fmr session musician, Muscle Shoals, Ala 1970s; released solo debut album 1977; writer of numerous songs for artists including Alabama, Jimmy Buffett, Ricky Van Shelton, Steve Wariner, Linda Davis; collaborated with Kenny Chesney on Down the Road single 2008; record producer for artists including Restless Heart, Sawyer Brown, John Lefebvre; mem. Jimmy Buffett's Coral Reefer Band. *Recordings:* albums: Mac McAnally 1977, No Problem Here 1978,

Cuttin' Corners 1980, Nothin' But the Truth 1983, Finish Lines 1988, Simple Life 1990, Live and Learn 1992, Knots 1994, Word of Mouth 1999, Semi-True Stories 2004, Down By the River 2009, A.K.A. Nobody 2015. *Honours:* Country Music Asscn Award for Musician of the Year 2008, 2009, 2010, 2011, 2012, 2013, 2014, 2015. *Current Management:* c/o TKO Artist Management, 2303 21st Avenue South, 3rd Floor, Nashville, TN 37212, USA. *Telephone:* (615) 383-5017. *Fax:* (615) 292-3328. *Website:* www.tkoartistmanagement.com. *E-mail:* mac@macmcanally.com (home). *Website:* www.macmcanally.com (home).

McANDREW, Ian; British artist manager; *Managing Director, Wildlife Entertainment;* b. 20 Oct. 1966, Sudbury, Suffolk. *Career:* manager of artists and producers; founder and Man. Dir, Wildlife Entertainment 1986–; manager for artists including Tasmin Archer, The Brand New Heavies, Bomb The Bass, Carleen Anderson, Tim Simenon, Travis, Conner Reeves; mem, Council Mem., International Managers Forum. *Address:* Wildlife Entertainment Ltd, Unit F, 21 Heathmans Road, London SW6 4TJ, England (office). *Telephone:* (20) 7371-7008 (office). *Fax:* (20) 7371-7708 (office). *E-mail:* info@wildlife-entertainment.com (office).

McATHEY, Brent; Canadian singer and songwriter; b. 4 Aug. 1967, Calgary, Alberta. *Career:* performs solo with pre-recorded tracks or with five-piece band in Canada; seven-piece Nashville Band in USA, Europe; opened for Joan Kennedy, Dick Damron, Michelle Wright, Prairie Oyster; mem, Country Music Asscn of Calgary, Alberta Recording Industry Asscn, Canadian Music Asscn, CMA, Nashville, Texas Country Music Asscn, Arts Touring Alliance of Alberta, Canadian Asscn of Fairs and Exhibitions, Calgary Convention and Visitors Bureau, International Fan Club Organization. *Recordings:* albums: Waiting for the Sun 1993, Believe in Me 1999, My Country Collection, I Can Go as Far as Mexico 2004, Blame it on Mexico 2004. *Honours:* Alberta's Male Recording Artist of the Year, Alberta Recording Industry Asscn 1994–95. *Address:* Box 831, Black Diamond, Alberta T0L 1H0, Canada (office). *E-mail:* brensterinmexico@hotmail.com (office). *Website:* www.brentmcathey.ca.

McAULEY, Jackie; musician (guitar) and songwriter; b. 14 Dec. 1946, Coleraine, Belfast, Northern Ireland. *Career:* member, Them (with Van Morrison), aged 17; founder member, Cult; Belfast Gypsies (with brother Pat); Trader Horn; also solo artist; mem., The Poor Mouth. *Compositions:* Dear John (recorded by Status Quo) 1982, other songs recorded by the Heptones, Jackie McAuley Plus, Bad Day At Black Rock.

McAULIFFE, Kim; British singer and musician (guitar); b. 13 April 1959, England. *Career:* co-founder, heavy metal band Painted Lady, joined by Kelly Johnson and Denise Dufort 1978–89, 1992–, band renamed Girlschool; supported Motörhead on their Overkill tour; numerous tours, television performances and hit singles; further collaborations with Motörhead; tours in Canada and the USA; tour of Russia, supporting Black Sabbath; co-founder Strangegirls, with Toyah, Denise Dufort and Enid Williams. *Recordings:* albums: Demolition 1980, Hit 'N' Run 1981, Screaming Blue Murder 1982, Play Dirty 1983, Running Wild 1995, Nightmare At Maple Cross 1986, Take A Bite 1988, Girlschool 1992, Live 1995, Race With The Devil (Live) 1998, Live On The King Biscuit Flower Hour 1998, Can't Keep A Good Girl Down 1999, Very Best Of Remastered 2002, 21st Anniversary: Not That Innocent 2002, Second Wave 2003, Believe 2004, Emergency/London 2005, Legacy 2008. *Address:* PO Box 33446, London, SW18 3XN, England (office). *E-mail:* girlschool@hotmail.com (office). *Website:* www.girlschool.co.uk.

McBEAN, Colin, (Mr G, Innersound, Mango Boy); British producer, remixer and DJ; b. London. *Career:* started as DJ with London's KCC crew; met Cisco Ferreira and started recording together 1990; formed The Advent 1994–99; continued as solo artist as Mr G; remixed: New Order, Lottie, Roger Sanchez, Hatiras; formed own Kombination Research (with Cisco Ferreira) 1990–99. *Recordings include:* albums: with The Advent: Elements of Life 1995, New Beginning 1997; solo: E.C.G.'ed', U Askin?, Makes No Sense, Still Here. *Current Management:* c/o Rekids Ltd, PO Box 42769, London, N2 0YY, England. *E-mail:* james@rekids.co.uk. *Website:* www.rekids.com. *E-mail:* colin@mr-g.org.uk. *Website:* www.mr-g.org.uk.

McBRAIN, Michael Henry (Nicko); British musician (drums); b. 5 June 1952, Hackney, London, England. *Career:* fmr mem., Streetwalkers 1975–76, McKitty, Trust; mem. heavy metal band, Iron Maiden 1983–; formed band, McBrain Damage. *Recordings include:* albums: Piece of Mind 1983, Power-slave 1984, Somewhere in Time 1986, Seventh Son of a Seventh Son 1988, No Prayer for the Dying 1990, Fear of the Dark 1992, The X-Factor 1995, Virtual XI 1998, Brave New World 2000, Dance of Death 2003, It's a Matter of Life and Death 2006, Flight 666 2009, The Final Frontier 2010, The Book of Souls 2015. *Honours:* Ivor Novello Award 2000, BRIT Award for Best British Live Act 2009. *Current Management:* c/o Phantom Music Managmnt Ltd, Bridle House 36 Bridle Lane, London, W1F 9BZ, England. *Telephone:* (845) 331-3300. *Fax:* (845) 331-3500. *Website:* www.phantom-music.com; www.ironmaiden.com.

McBRIDE, Christian; American jazz bass player; b. 31 May 1972, Philadelphia, Pa; s. of Lee Smith; m. Melissa Walker. *Education:* High School for the Creative and Performing Arts, Philadelphia, Juilliard School, New York. *Career:* began playing electric bass aged nine, followed by acoustic bass two years later; tour to Europe with Philadelphia Youth Orchestra 1989; travelling USA with classical jazz fusion group, Free Flight 1989; played with Bobby Watson, Freddie Hubbard 1990–93, Ray Brown and Jay Clayton 1991,

Benny Green, Roy Hargrove, Joshua Redman, Diana Krall, Pat Metheny 1992, Joe Henderson, D'Angelo, Kathleen Battle, Herbie Hancock, Quincy Jones, Natalie Cole and Milt Jackson; signed to Verve Records 1994; joined George Duke's band 2002; f. own groups, including Christian McBride Band; soloist; Co-Dir The Jazz Museum, Harlem 2005–; Creative Chair for Jazz, Los Angeles Philharmonic Orchestra 2005–10; mem. Heaven on Earth 2009–. *Commissions include:* Bluesin' in Alphabet City by Jazz at Lincoln Center, performed by Wynton Marsalis with Lincoln Center Jazz Orchestra, The Movement, Revisited by the Portland (ME) Arts Soc. and Nat. Endowment for the Arts, written and arranged for quartet and 30-piece gospel choir 1998. *Films include:* Café Society 1995, Kansas City 1996. *Recordings include:* albums: Ray Brown's Super Bass 1989, Roy Hargrove's Public Eye 1990, Kenny Kirkland 1991, Joshua Redman 1993, Fingerpainting: The Music of Herbie Hancock 1997, Introducing Joshua Redman 1999, Bobby Hutcherson's Skyline 1999, Don Braden's Fire Within 1999, Sting's All This Time (CD, DVD and tour) 2001, George Duke's Face the Music 2002, The Good Feeling (Grammy Award for Best Large Jazz Ensemble Album 2012) 2011, People Music 2013, Out Here 2013; with Heaven on Earth: Heaven on Earth 2009; solo albums include: Gettin' To It 1994, Number Two Express 1996, A Family Affair 1998, Sci-Fi 2000, The Philadelphia Experiment 2001, Vertical Vision (with electrical quartet) 2003, Live at Tonic 2006, Conversations with Christian 2009, Kind of Brown (with Inside Straight) 2009. *Honours:* Scholarship to Juilliard School, named by Rolling Stone magazine "Hot Jazz Artist" of 1992, Jazz Journalists' Asscn Award for Bassist of the Year 2013, 2015, Grammy Award for Best Improvised Jazz Solo 2016. *Current Management:* c/o Andre Guess, GuessWorks, Inc., 89 Elm Street, Montclair, NJ 07042, USA. *Telephone:* (212) 863-9824. *Fax:* (917) 591-5216. *E-mail:* andre@guessworks.org. *Website:* www.guessworksinc.com. *E-mail:* info@christianmcbride.com. *Website:* www.christianmcbride.com.

McBRIDE, Martina; American country singer; b. (Martina Mariea Schiff), 29 July 1966, Medicine Lodge, KS; m. John McBride; three d. *Career:* solo artist; worldwide concert tours. *Recordings include:* albums: The Time Has Come 1992, The Way That I Am 1993, Wild Angels 1995, Evolution 1997, Martina McBride Christmas 1998, Emotion 1999, White Christmas 1999, Greatest Hits 2001, Martina 2003, Timeless 2006, Wake Up Laughing 2007, Shine 2009. *Honours:* CMA Video of the Year 1994–95, Song of the Year 1995, Female Vocalist of the Year 1999, 2004, Music Row Industry Awards Breakthrough Video, Nammy Award for Video of the Year, Nashville Music Awards 1995–96, American Music Award for Best Female Country Artist 2003, Acad. of Country Music award for best female vocalist 2004. *Address:* Martina McBride Fan Club, PO Box 291627, Nashville, TN 37229-1627, USA (office). *E-mail:* fanrelations@martina-mcbride.com (office). *Website:* www.martina-mcbride.com.

McBROOM, Amanda, BA; American songwriter, singer, playwright and actress; b. 9 Aug. 1947, Los Angeles; m. George Ball 1974. *Education:* University of Texas. *Career:* several appearances on The Tonight Show, Carnegie Hall, Rainbow and Stars, The Russian Tea Room, Greek Theatre, Great American Music Hall, Kennedy Center; co-founder, Gecko Records 1985; mem, Actors Equity Asscn, Screen Actors Guild, NAS. *Plays:* Jacques Brel is Alive and Well and Living in Paris, Seesaw, Sweeney Todd, A Little Night Music, Mame, A Woman of Will. *Compositions include:* The Rose (Golden Globe Award for Best Film Song) 1980. *Recordings:* Growing Up In Hollywood Town 1980, West of Oz 1981, Dreaming 1986, Midnight Matinee 1992, A Waiting Heart 1997, Portraits: Best of Amanda McBroom 1999, A Woman of Will 2006, Chanson: Amanda McBroom Sings Jacques Brel 2009. *E-mail:* geckodisc@hotmail.com (office). *Website:* www.amcbroom.com.

McCABE, David; British musician (guitar) and singer. *Career:* Founder mem., The Zutons 2002–. *Recordings include:* albums: Who Killed... The Zutons? 2004, Tired of Hanging Around 2006, You Can Do Anything 2008.

McCABE, Nick; British musician (guitar). *Career:* founder mem., Verve 1989, renamed The Verve 1994–95, 1997–98, 2007–09; numerous festival appearances; played guitar on Prochaine Fois, Neotropic 2001. *Recordings include:* albums: A Storm in Heaven 1993, No Come Down 1994, A Northern Soul 1995, Urban Hymns (BRIT Award for Best British Album 1998, Q Award for Classic Album 2007) 1997, Forth 2008. *Honours:* BRIT Award for Best British Group 1998. *Current Management:* Big Life Management, 67–69 Chalton Street, London NW1 1HY, England. *Telephone:* (20) 7554-2100. *Fax:* (20) 7554-2154. *Website:* biglifemanagement.com.

McCABE, Zia; American musician (keyboards). *Career:* founder mem., The Dandy Warhols 1994–. *Film appearance:* Dig! 2005. *Recordings include:* albums: Dandys Rule OK 1995, Come Down 1998, Thirteen Tales From Urban Bohemia 2000, Welcome To The Monkey House 2003, The Black Album/Come On Feel The Dandy Warhols 2004, Odditorium Or Warlords Of Mars 2005, Earth to the Dandy Warhols 2008, This Machine 2012. *Address:* c/o Parlophone, EMI Group plc, 27 Wrights Lane, London, W8 5SW, England. *E-mail:* gothman@dandywarhols.com. *Website:* www.dandywarhols.com.

McCAFFERTY, Dan; Scottish singer; b. 14 Oct. 1946, Dunfermline; s. of the late Hugh McCafferty and Catherine McCafferty; m. Maryann McCafferty; two s. *Career:* Founder-mem. rock group Nazareth 1968–; regular tours, UK, USA, Europe. *Recordings:* albums: Nazareth 1971, Exercises 1972, Razamanaz 1973, Loud 'N' Proud 1974, Rampant 1974, Hair of The Dog 1975, Greatest Hits 1975, Hot Tracks 1976, Close Enough For Rock 'N' Roll 1976, Playin' The Game 1976, Expect No Mercy 1977, No Mean City 1978, Malice In Wonderland 1980, The Fool Circle 1981, 'Snaz 1981, 2XS 1982, Sound Elixir 1983, The Catch 1984, 20 Greatest Hits 1985, Play The Game 1985, Anthology – Nazareth 1988, The Early Years 1992, No Jive 1992, From The Vaults 1993, Move Me 1995, Nazareth: Greatest Hits 1996, Live at the Beeb 1998, Boogaloo 1998, Homecoming 2001, The Newz 2008. *Honours:* Nordoff Robbins Lifetime Achievement Award. *Current Management:* c/o Alan Cottam Agency, 19 Charles Street, Wigan, Lancs., WN1 2BP, England. *Telephone:* (1254) 668471. *Fax:* (1254) 697599. *E-mail:* alan@alancottamagency.co.uk. *Website:* www .alancottamagency.co.uk. *Address:* Nazareth Scotland Ltd, 5 Maree Place, Crossford, Fife, KY12 8XU, Scotland (office). *Telephone:* (1383) 738009 (office). *Fax:* (1383) 738009 (office). *E-mail:* nazarethbiz@yahoo.co.uk (office). *Website:* www.nazarethdirect.co.uk.

McCAFFERY, Craig; American musician (keyboards). *Career:* mem., The American Analog Set 2003–. *Recordings include:* albums: Promise Of Love 2003, Set Free 2005. *E-mail:* requests@amanset.com (home). *Website:* www .amanset.com.

McCANN, Eamon; British singer and musician (guitar); b. Creggan, Omagh, Northern Ireland; m. Margaret 1979; one s. three d. *Education:* FTC, IRTE. *Career:* television appearances include RTE TV: Kenny Live, Live At 3, Its Bibi, Play The Game, Live From The Olympia, Lifelines, The Big Top, Summer Cabaret, Cúrsaí, Country Cool, Winning Streak, A Stretch in the Evening, Southern Nights, The Lyric Board, Anderson On The Box, Breakfast TV, PK to Right, Anderson on the Road, BBC, Kelly, UTV, Scotch 'N' Irish, Grampian Television; radio appearances include Live on National Music Day, BBC Radio 2 1994, RTE Radio 1, 2 FM, DTR, BBC Radio Ulster; mem, PRS, IMRO. *Compositions:* Joseph's Dream, 1998. *Recordings:* albums: Touch Wood, I Will Love You ('Til This Ring Turns Green), Clear Cut Country; singles: Everything That I Am, Can't Break It To My Heart, Bunch of Bright Red Roses, Gold In The Mountains, I Give You Music, I've Gone Crazy/Happy Birthday. *Honours:* Irish Showcase Award, Best New Male Singer, 1992; Northern Sound Radio, Best Male Singer, 1993; Donegal CMC, Best Male Singer, 1993, 1994; Rehab, Person of the Year, 1992; Ready Penny Inn, Best Male Singer of New Country, 1994, 1995; Personalities Entertainment Magazine Awards: Best Singer/Songwriter, 1995–96, Best Singer of New Country, 1995–96, Favourite Male Entertainer, 1996–97; Doubla K CMC Band of the Year, Dumfries, Scotland, 1996–97; Personalities Entertainment Magazine Awards Best Album, 1997–98; Irish World Awards Best Country Singer, 1997–98. *Current Management:* Erne Promotions, 8 Forthill Road, Enniskillen, Co. Fermanagh, BT74 6AW, Northern Ireland. *Telephone:* (28) 6632-3238. *E-mail:* erneproms@btinternet.com.

McCANN, Les; American musician (piano, trumpet, keyboards); b. (Leslie Coleman), 23 Sept. 1935, Lexington, Kentucky; m. Charlotte Acentia Watkins; one s. three d. *Education:* LA City Coll., Westlake Coll. of Music, LA City Coll. *Career:* founder numerous bands including Les McCann Ltd, McCann's Magic Band, numerous concerts, TV appearances and has attended all major jazz festivals; mem. BMI, ASCAP. *Recordings include:* albums: Plays the Truth 1960, The Shout 1960, Groove 1961, In San Francisco 1961, Stormy Monday (with Lou Rawls) 1962, Somethin' Special (with Richard Holmes) 1962, In New York 1962, Jazz Waltz 1964, New From the Big City 1964, McCann/Wilson 1965, But Not Really 1965, Plays the Hits 1967, Much Les 1969, Swiss Movement 1969, Comment 1970, Second Movement 1971, Invitation to Openness 1972, Talk to the People 1972, Layers 1973, Another Beginning 1974, Hustle to Survive 1975, The Man 1978, Tall, Dark and Handsome 1979, The Longer You Wait 1983, McCann's Music Box 1984, More of Les 1989, On the Soul Side 1994, Listen Up 1996, Pacifique (with Joja Wendt) 1998, How's Your Mother? 1998, Pump It Up 2002. *Publication:* Musician as Artist (paintings). *Current Management:* Bennett Morgan and Associates, 1022 Route 276, Wappingers Falls, New York, NY 12590, USA. *Telephone:* (845) 227-6065. *Fax:* (845) 501-3013. *E-mail:* ben@bennettmorgan.com. *Website:* www.bennettmorgan.com. *E-mail:* frederic_hirsch@cyberstars.com (office). *Website:* www.lesmccann-officialwebsite.com.

McCANN, Peter; American songwriter and singer. *Education:* Fairfield University, Connecticut. *Career:* moved to Nashville 1985; songs recorded by Julio Iglesias, Anne Murray, Crystal Gayle, Kenny Rogers, Oak Ridge Boys, Isaac Hayes, K T Oslin, Lynn Anderson, Ricky Nelson, Andy Williams, Paul Anka, Karen Carpenter, Whitney Houston, Kathy Mattea; lectures on songwriting for music organizations; mem, Vice-president, Nashville Songwriters Asscn, Co-chair, Legislative committee. *Recordings:* Do You Wanna Make Love?, Peter McCann 1977, The Right Time of The Night, Jennifer Warnes 1977, One on One 1979, She's Single Again, Janie Fricke, Nobody Falls Like A Fool, Earl Thomas Conley, Treat Me Like A Stranger, Baillie and the Boys, What Christmas Really Means 1995.

McCARTHY, Nicholas (Nick); British musician (guitar, piano); b. Blackpool. *Career:* mem., Franz Ferdinand 2001–; side project, Box Codax 2006–. *Recordings include:* albums: with Franz Ferdinand: Franz Ferdinand (Mercury Music Prize 2004, NME Award for Best Album 2005, Meteor Award for Best Int. Album 2005) 2004, You Could Have It So Much Better... With Franz Ferdinand 2005, Tonight: Franz Ferdinand 2009; with Box Codax: Only an Orchard Away 2006. *Honours:* BRIT Awards for Best British Group, Best British Rock Act 2005, Meteor Award for Best Int. Band 2005, NME Award for Best Live Band 2006. *Address:* c/o Domino Recording Company, PO Box 47039, London, SW18 1WD, England. *Website:* www.franzferdinand.co.uk.

McCARTNEY, Michelle; singer and musician (bass guitar); b. 5 April 1960, Paris, France. *Career:* pop rock/folk singer; toured with Jackie Lomax (blues performer); performed at major US Theatres, int. trade shows; tours, major US college and university circuit; mem, ASCAP. *Recordings:* singles: Everybody Wants My Man, Rocomotion, Money For Honey, Michelle, Billet-Doux, Till I Get You Back. *Honours:* Best Dee-Jay Pop Pick in USA, for Till I Get You Back 1993.

McCARTNEY, Sir (James) Paul, Kt, MBE, FRCM; British singer, songwriter and musician (guitar, piano, organ); b. 18 June 1942, Liverpool; s. of James McCartney and Mary McCartney; m. 1st Linda Eastman 1969 (died 1998); one s. two d. one step-d.; m. 2nd Heather Mills 2002 (divorced 2008); one d.; m. 3rd Nancy Shevell 2011. *Education:* Stockton Wood Road Primary School, Speke, Joseph Williams Primary School, Gateacre and Liverpool Inst. *Career:* wrote first song 1956, wrote numerous songs with John Lennon; joined pop group The Quarrymen 1956; appeared under various titles until formation of The Beatles 1960; appeared with The Beatles for performances in Hamburg 1960, 1961, 1962, The Cavern, Liverpool 1961; worldwide tours 1963–66; attended Transcendental Meditation Course at Maharishi's Acad., Rishikesh, India Feb. 1968; formed Apple Ltd, parent org. of The Beatles Group of Cos 1968; left The Beatles after collapse of Apple Corpn Ltd 1970; formed MPL Group of Cos 1970; first solo album McCartney 1970; formed own pop group Wings 1971–81, tours of Britain and Europe 1972–73, UK and Australia 1975, Europe and USA 1976, UK 1979, World Tour 1989–90; also records as The Fireman, dance music duo with Youth 1994–; numerous collaborations including Elvis Costello, Dave Grohl and Krist Novoselic, Michael Jackson, Rihanna, Kanye West, Stevie Wonder; solo performances at Party at the Palace, Buckingham Palace 2002, Opening Ceremony, Summer Olympic Games, London 2012; Fellow, British Acad. of Composers and Songwriters 2000. *Recordings include:* albums: with The Beatles: Please Please Me 1963, A Hard Day's Night 1964, Beatles for Sale 1965, Help! 1965, Rubber Soul 1966, Revolver 1966, Sgt Pepper's Lonely Hearts Club Band 1967, Magical Mystery Tour 1967, The Beatles (White Album) 1968, Yellow Submarine 1969, Abbey Road 1969, Let It Be 1970, 1962–1966 (Red Album) 1973, 1967–1970 (Blue Album) 1973, Past Masters Vol. One 1988, Past Masters Vol. Two 1988, The Beatles Anthology: 1 1995, The Beatles Anthology: 2 1996, The Beatles Anthology: 3 1996, 1 2000; with Wings: Wild Life 1971, Red Rose Speedway 1973, Band On The Run (Grammy Award for Best Historical Album 2012) 1973, Venus and Mars 1975, Wings at the Speed of Sound 1976, Wings Over America 1976, London Town 1978, Wings Greatest 1978, Back To The Egg 1979, Wingspan 2001; solo: McCartney 1970, Ram 1971, McCartney II 1980, Tug of War 1982, Pipes of Peace 1983, Give My Regards to Broad Street 1984, Press To Play 1986, All the Best! 1987, CHOBA B CCCP 1988, Flowers in the Dirt 1989, Tripping the Live Fantastic 1990, Unplugged: The Official Bootleg 1991, Paul McCartney's Liverpool Oratorio (with Carl Davis) 1991, Off the Ground 1993, Paul is Live 1993, Flaming Pie 1997, Standing Stone (symphonic work) 1997, Run Devil Run 1999, Working Classical 1999, A Garland for Linda (with eight other composers for a cappella choir) 2000, Driving Rain 2001, Back in the US: Live 2002, Back in the World 2003, Chaos and Creation in the Back Yard 2005, Ecce Cor Meum (classical) (Classical BRIT Award for Best Album 2007) 2006, Memory Almost Full 2007, Kisses on the Bottom (Best Traditional Pop Vocal Album 2013) 2012, New 2013; with The Fireman: Strawberries Oceans Ships Forest 1994, Rushes 1998, Electric Arguments 2008; film soundtracks: The Family Way 1966, James Paul McCartney 1973, Live and Let Die 1973, The Zoo Gang (TV series) 1973. *Ballet:* Ocean's Kingdom (orchestral score, written for the New York City Ballet) 2011. *Films:* A Hard Day's Night 1964, Help! 1965, Magical Mystery Tour (TV film) 1967, Yellow Submarine (animated colour cartoon film) 1968, Let it Be 1970, Wings Over the World (TV) 1979, Rockshow 1981, Give My Regards to Broad Street (wrote and directed) 1984, Rupert and the Frog Song (wrote and produced) (BAFTA Award Best Animated Film) 1985, Press to Play 1986, Get Back (concert film) 1991, Live Kisses (concert film) (Grammy Award for Best Music Film 2014) 2012. *Radio:* (series) Routes of Rock (BBC) 1999. *Publications include:* Paintings 2000, The Beatles Anthology (with George Harrison and Ringo Starr) 2000, Sun Prints (with Linda McCartney) 2001, Many Years From Now (autobiography) 2001, Blackbird Singing: Poems and Lyrics 1965–1999 2001, High in the Clouds (juvenile, with Philip Ardagh and Geoff Dunbar) 2005. *Honours:* Freeman of the City of Liverpool 1984, Hon. Fellow, Liverpool John Moores Univ. 1998; Dr hc (Sussex) 1988, Hon. DMus (Yale) 2008; two Grammy Awards for Band on the Run (including Best Pop Vocal Performance) 1975, Ivor Novello Award for Best Selling British Record 1977–78 for single Mull of Kintyre, for Int. Hit of the Year 1982 for single Ebony and Ivory, for Outstanding Services to British Music 1989, Guinness Book of Records Triple Superlative Award (43 songs each selling more than 1m copies, holder of 60 gold discs, estimated sales of 100m albums and 100m singles) 1979, Lifetime Achievement Award 1990, Polar Music Prize 1992, Lifetime Achievement Award People for the Ethical Treatment of Animals (with Linda McCartney) 1996, Radio Acad. Lifetime Achievement Award 2007, Q Icon Award 2007, BRIT Award for Outstanding Contribution to Music 2008, ASCAP Award for Songwriter of the Year 2009, Gershwin Prize for Popular Song, US Library of Congress 2010, Kennedy Center Honor 2010, Grammy Award for Best Rock Song (for Cut Me Some Slack, with Dave Grohl, Krist Novoselic and Pat Smear) 2014. *Current Management:* c/o MPL Communications Ltd, 1 Soho Square, London, W1D 3BQ, England. *Website:* www.paulmccartney.com.

McCARY, Michael Shawn 'Bass'; American singer; b. 16 Dec. 1971, Philadelphia, PA. *Education:* Philadelphia High School of Creative and Performing Arts. *Career:* mem., Boyz II Men 1988–2003; established Stonecreek label. *Recordings:* albums: Cooleyhighharmony 1993, II 1995, Evolución 1997, Nathan Michael Shawn Wanya 2000, Full Circle 2002; singles: Motownphilly 1991, I'll Make Love To You, On Bended Knee, One Sweet Day (with Mariah Carey).

McCLAIN, Charlotte (Charly) Denise; American country singer, songwriter and actress; b. 26 March 1956, Jackson, Tennessee; m. Wayne Massey 1984. *Career:* sang with brother in Charlotte and the Volunteers, aged nine; worked on the mid-South Jamboree 1973–75; changed name to Charly and modelled swimsuits, early 1970s; toured with country singer O. B. McClinton; collaborations with Johnny Rodriguez, Mickey Gilley, Wayne Massey; TV appearances include Hart To Hart, CHiPS, Austin City Limits, Fantasy Island, Solid Gold, So You Want To Be A Star. *Recordings include:* albums: Here's Charly McClain 1977, Let Me Be Your Baby 1978, Alone Too Long 1979, Women Get Lonely 1980, Who's Cheatin' Who 1980, Surround Me With Love 1981, Too Good to Hurry 1982, The Woman In Me 1984, Paradise 1983, Charly 1984, It Takes Believers (with Mickey Gilley) 1984, Radio Heart 1985, When Love is Right (with Wayne Massey) 1986, Charly McClain 1988. *Honours:* Music City News, Most Promising Female Vocalist 1981. *E-mail:* charlyofficialsite@yahoo.com (office). *Website:* www.geocities.com/charlyofficialsite.

McCLARNON, Elizabeth (Liz) Margaret; British singer; b. 10 April 1981, Liverpool, England. *Career:* mem. Atomic Kitten 1999–; UK support tours 1999–2000; co-spearheaded MTV Asia Awards, 2000; Pan-European breakthrough with Whole Again single; guest at Celebrate South Africa Freedom Concert, London 2001; appearance, Party at the Palace, Buckingham Palace Jubilee celebrations 2002; recording solo album 2007. *Recordings:* albums: Right Now 2000, Feels So Good 2002, Ladies' Night 2003. *Current Management:* Integral Management, 85 Bold Street, Liverpool, L1 4HF, England. *Telephone:* (151) 709-1791. *E-mail:* kate.oshea@integralrpm.com. *Website:* www.integralrpm.com; www.lilmcclarnon.net; www.atomickitten.com.

McCLINTON, Delbert Ross; American singer, songwriter and musician (harmonica); b. 4 Nov. 1940, Lubbock, TX; m. Wendy Goldstein. *Career:* recording artist with The Straightjackets and The Rondelles; mem, BMI. *Compositions:* I Want To Love You, Two More Bottles of Wine, Giving It Up For Love, B Movie. *Recordings:* albums: Delbert and Glen 1972, Subject to Change 1973, Victim of Life's Circumstances 1975, Genuine Cowhide 1976, Love Rustler 1977, Second Wind 1978, Keeper of The Flame 1979, Plain From The Heart 1981, Honky Tonkin' 1987, Live From Austin 1989, I'm With You 1990, Never Been Rocked Enough 1992, Feelin' Alright 1993, Delbert McClinton 1993, Shot from the Saddle 1994, Let the Good Times Roll 1995, One of the Fortunate Few 1997, Nothing Personal 2001, Room to Breathe 2002, Cost of Living (Grammy Award for Best Contemporary Blues Album 2006) 2005, Rockin' Blues 2007, Acquired Taste 2009; with T Graham Brown: Wine into Water 1998; with Danny Gatton: Hot Rod Guitar 1999; with Flying Burrito Brothers: Sons of the Golden West 1999, Don't Let Go (compilation) 2000, Nothing Personal 2001. *Honours:* Top 20 Harmonica Players, Rolling Stone magazine, 1985. *Address:* PO Box 218248, Nashville, TN 37221, USA (office). *Website:* www.delbert.com.

McCLUSKEY, Andy; singer, songwriter, artist manager and producer; b. 24 June 1959, Wirral, Cheshire, England. *Career:* formed Id, 1977–78; mem., Dalek I Love You, 1978; co-founder, lead singer, Orchestral Manoeuvres In The Dark (OMD), 1978–98, 2006–; numerous tours, Europe, USA, Japan, Australia; Futurama Festival, Leeds, 1979; support to Talking Heads, Gary Numan, 1979, Festival of the 10th Summer, Manchester, 1986, Cities In The Park Festival, Prestwich, 1991, Simple Minds, Milton Keynes Bowl, 1991; created Atomic Kitten, songwriter, arranger and producer for Atomic Kitten, 1998–2002, including album Right Now. *Compositions:* Whole Again (No. 1, UK), Atomic Kitten, 2001. *Recordings:* albums: Orchestral Manoeuvres in the Dark 1980, Organisation 1980, Architecture and Morality 1981, Dazzle Ships 1983, Junk Culture 1984, Crush 1985, The Pacific Age 1986, In The Dark – The Best of OMD 1988, Sugar Tax 1991, Liberator 1993, Universal 1996, Singles 1998, Navigation (compilation) 2001, History of Modern 2010, English Electric 2013; singles: Electricity 1979, Messages 1980, Enola Gay 1980, Souvenir 1981, Joan of Arc 1981, Maid of Orleans 1982, Genetic Engineering 1983, Locomotion 1984, Talking Loud and Clear 1984, Tesla Girls 1984, So in Love 1985, If You Leave (used in film Pretty In Pink) 1986, (Forever) Live and Die 1986, Dreaming 1988, Sailing on the Seven Seas 1991, Pandora's Box 1991, Stand Above Me 1993, Dream of Me 1993, Walking on the Milky Way 1996; contributor, The Message Of Love, Arthur Baker, 1989. *Current Management:* XLTalent, Reverb House, Bennett Street, London, W4 2AH, England. *Website:* www.omd.uk.com.

McCOO, Marilyn; American singer; b. 30 Sept. 1944, Jersey City, New Jersey; m. Billy Davis Jr 1969. *Education:* Univ. of California, Los Angeles. *Career:* mem. the Hi-Fi's; vocalist, US harmony group Fifth Dimension (fmrly the Versatiles, then the Vocals) 1966–75; appearances include: San Remo Festival 1967, Bal Paree and Bambi Awards, Munich, Germany 1970, Royal Albert Hall, London 1972, Concert at the White House for President Nixon 1973, performance before Pope John Paul II, San Antonio, Texas with Billy Davis Jr; formed duo with Billy Davis Jr 1976–80; co-host, The Marilyn McCoo and Billy Davis Jr Show, CBS 1977; solo artist 1980–; television host, Solid Gold

1981–87. *Plays include:* Man of La Mancha, Anything Goes, Showboat, Broadway 1995, Showboat, Chicago 1996, Dreamgirls. *Recordings:* albums: with Fifth Dimension: Up Up and Away 1967, The Magic Garden 1968, Stoned Soul Picnic 1968, Age of Aquarius 1969, Fantastic 1970, Portrait 1970, The July 5th Album 1970, Love's Lines, Angles and Rhymes 1971, Live! 1971, Reflections 1971, Individually and Collectively 1972, Greatest Hits On Earth 1972, Living Together, Growing Together 1973, Earthbound 1975, Greatest Hits 1988, Marilyn McCoo Christmas 2000; with Billy Davis Jr: I Hope We Get To Love In Time 1977, The Two of Us 1977, Marilyn and Billy 1978; solo: Solid Gold 1983, The Me Nobody Knows 1991. *Publication:* Up, Up and Away...How We Found Love, Faith and Lasting Marriage in the Entertainment World 2004. *Honours:* Dr hc (Talladega Univ., Alabama) 1988; eight Grammy Awards, Grand Prize, Tokyo Music Festival (with Billy Davis Jr) 1977, Harvard Foundation Award. *Current Management:* c/o Guy Richard, Agency Group, 1880 Century Park East, Suite 711, Los Angeles, CA 90067, USA. *Telephone:* (310) 385-2800. *Fax:* (310) 385-1220. *E-mail:* guyrichard@theagencygroup.com. *Website:* www.theagencygroup.com; www.mccooanddavis.com.

McCOY, Travis Lazarus (Travie); American singer, rapper and songwriter; b. 6 Aug. 1981, Geneva, NY. *Education:* Geneva High School, Munson-Williams-Proctor Arts Inst. *Career:* Founder mem. Gym Class Heroes 1997–, numerous collaborations including Daryl Hall, Estelle, The-Dream, Busta Rhymes, Adam Levine, Neon Hitch, Ryan Tedder; winner of MTV Direct Effect MC competition 2002; solo career 2010, recorded with Bruno Mars and Taio Cruz, collaborated with Jessica Jarrell, Cheryl Cole. *Recordings:* albums: with Gym Class Heroes: For the Kids 2001, The Papercut Chronicles 2005, As Cruel as School Children 2006, The Quilt 2008, The Papercut Chronicles II 2011; solo: Lazarus 2010. *Honours:* with Gym Class Heroes: MTV Video Music Award for Best New Artist 2007. *Address:* c/o Fueled by Ramen Records, Warner Music Group, 75 Rockefeller Plaza, New York, NY 10019 (office); c/o Nappy Boy Entertainment, 2701 West Oakland Park Blvd, Suite 210, Oakland Park, FL 33311, USA (office). *Telephone:* (212) 275-2000 (New York) (office); (954) 733-2972 (Oakland Park) (office). *Website:* www.fueledbyramen.com (office); www.wmg.com (office); www.gymclassheroes.com; www.myspace.com/traviemccoy; www.traviemccoy.com.

McCREADY, Mike; American rock musician (guitar). *Career:* mem. rock group, Pearl Jam 1990–; numerous concert tours and festival appearances; mem., Temple of the Dog 1990. *Recordings include:* albums: with Pearl Jam: Ten 1991, Vs. 1993, Vitalogy 1994, Merkin Ball 1995, No Code 1996, Yield 1998, Live on Two Legs 1998, Binaural 2000, Riot Act 2002, Pearl Jam 2006, Backspacer 2009; with Temple of the Dog: Temple Of The Dog 1992. *Honours:* American Music Award for Favorite New Artist, Pop/Rock and Hard Rock categories 1993, Rolling Stone Readers' Award for Best New American Band, Best Video 1993. *Address:* Pearl Jam, PO Box 4570, Seattle, WA 98194-0570, USA (office). *E-mail:* contact@vandenbergcom.com (office). *Website:* www.pearljam.com.

McCULLOCH, Ian; British singer; b. 5 May 1959, Liverpool, England. *Career:* founder mem., Crucial Three 1977, group renamed Echo & The Bunnymen 1978–88, 1997–; numerous tours and festival appearances; solo artist 1988–; founder mem., The Prodigal Sons 1990, McCulloch's Mysterioso Show 1992; founder mem., Electrafixion 1994–. *Recordings include:* albums: with Echo & The Bunnymen: Crocodiles 1980, Heaven Up Here 1981, Porcupine 1983, Ocean Rain 1984, Echo & The Bunnymen 1987, Evergreen 1997, What are You Going to Do with Your Life? 1999, Flowers 2001, Siberia 2005, More Songs to Learn and Sing 2006, Me, I'm All Smiles 2006, The Fountain 2009; solo: Candleland 1989, Mysterio 1992; with Electrafixion: Burned 1995. *E-mail:* fans@bunnymen.com (office). *Website:* www.bunnymen.com.

McCULLOCH, Zoe; British musician (guitar) and guitar tutor; *Lead Guitarist, The Crickettes;* b. 25 June 1986, Newcastle upon Tyne, England. *Education:* Bridgend Coll., S Wales. *Career:* instrumental recording artist with six albums to date (two albums entered for the Grammy Awards); RGT Grade exam guitar teacher and performer; voting mem. American Recording Acad. (Grammy Awards); arena tour playing to audiences of 8–20,000; Founder and Lead Guitarist of a new all-girl rock instrumental guitar band, The Crickettes; Recipient mem. The Buddy Holly Guitar Foundation. *Television:* featured on ITV Creative Roads programme, Girls with Guitars. *Recordings include:* albums: Zoe With Love 2000, Abba Guitabba, Girls with Guitars 2001, Never Give Up Never Give In 2002, Gypsy Noodle 2004, Electrical Gas 2005. *Honours:* Best New Artiste world-wide, Instrumental Rock Guitar Hall of Fame 2000. *Current Management:* c/o Patrick Terrett, Mustang Music Ltd, Unit 21K Vale Business Park, Llandow, CF71 7PF, Wales. *Telephone:* (1446) 775050. *Fax:* (1446) 775324. *E-mail:* mail@mustang-music.com. *Website:* www.mustang-music.com. *Telephone:* (1656) 768539. *E-mail:* manager@zoemcculloch.com (office). *Website:* www.zoemcculloch.com; www.guitarteacherswales.co.uk; www.thecrickettes.com.

McCUSKER, John; British musician (fiddle, tin whistle, cittern, accordion, keyboards), composer and producer; b. 15 May 1973, Bothwell, Scotland; m. Kate Rusby 2001 (divorced). *Education:* Royal Acad., Glasgow, Scotland. *Career:* began playing whistle aged 5, and fiddle aged 7; played in youth orchestras; joined a Ceilidh band aged 12; formed folk band, Parcel O'Rogues with school friends aged 14; joined Scottish folk group, The Battlefield Band aged 17; recorded and toured internationally with The Battlefield Band; solo artist; producer for Kate Rusby, Eliza Carthy, Cathie Ryan; composed music with Kate Rusby for film Heartlands 2003. *Recordings:* albums: John McCusker 1995, Yella Hoose 2000, Goodnight Ginger 2003, Under One Sky 2008; with Parcel O' Rogues: Parcel O' Rogues 1987; with The Battlefield Band: After Hours 1987, New Spring 1991, Quiet Days 1992, Threads 1995, Across The Borders 1997, Rain Hail Or Shine 1998, Leaving Friday Harbor 1999, Happy Daze 2001; features on: Thirteen, Teenage Fanclub 1993, Kate Rusby and Kathryn Roberts 1995, Incholm, William Jackson 1996, Easter Snow, Seamus Tansey 1997, Donegal Rain, Andy Stewart 1997, Eliza Carthy and The Kings of Calicutt 1997, Hourglass, Kate Rusby 1998, Sleepless, Kate Rusby 1999, Little Lights, Kate Rusby 2001, Somewhere Along The Road, Cathie Ryan 2001. *Honours:* Glenfiddich Spirit of Scotland Award for Music 1999, Musician of the Year, BBC Radio 2 Folk Awards 2003. *E-mail:* info@johnmccusker.co.uk (office). *Website:* www.johnmccusker.demon.co.uk.

McDANIELS, Darryl, (D.M.C.); American R&B singer and rap artist; b. 31 May 1964, New York, NY; m. Zuri L. Alston 1992; one s. *Education:* Catholic schools, New York and St John's Univ., New York. *Career:* mem. duo, later trio (with Joe 'Run' Simmons and the late Jam Master Jay), Run-D.M.C. 1982–2002; solo artist 2002–. *Film appearances:* Krush Groove 1985, Tougher Than Leather 1988, Who's the Man? 1993. *Recordings include:* albums: with Run-D.M.C.: Run-D.M.C. 1984, King Of Rock 1985, Raising Hell 1986, Tougher Than Leather 1988, Back From Hell 1990, Down With The King 1993, Crown Royal 1999; solo: Checks, Thugs and Rock & Roll 2006. *Current Management:* Universal Attractions, 145 W 57th Street, 15th Floor, New York, NY 10019, USA. *Telephone:* (212) 582-7575. *Fax:* (212) 333-4508. *Website:* www.me-dmc.com.

McDILL, Robert (Bob) Lee; American songwriter; b. 5 April 1944, Beaumont, TX; m. Nancy Whitsett 1971; one s. two d. *Education:* Lamar University. *Career:* staff writer, Jack Music, Nashville 1969–75, Hall Clement Publications, Nashville 1975–84; owner, writer, Ranger Bob Music, Nashville, 1984; mem. ASCAP, NARAS. *Compositions include:* 25 US No. 1 hits include: for Don Williams: Say It Again, She Never Knew Me, Good Ole Boys Like Me; for Ronnie Milsap; Nobody Likes Sad Songs; for Dan Seals: Everything That Glitters; for Mel McDaniel: Baby's Got Her Blue Jeans On; for Waylon Jennings: Amanda. *Honours:* Distinguished Alumnus Award University, Lamar University 1989, Composer of Year, Cash Box magazine 1979, 1986, approximately 40 awards from BMI, CMA, Nashville Songwriters Asscn, 11 ASCAP Awards, two Grammy Awards; Top Songwriter, World Record magazine, 1977.

MacDONALD, Amy; British singer, songwriter and musician (guitar, keyboards); b. 25 Aug. 1987, Bishopbriggs, E Dunbartonshire. *Education:* Bishopbriggs High School. *Career:* debut album released 2007; numerous television appearances and live performances. *Recordings:* albums: This is the Life (Swiss Music Award for Best Int. Album 2009) 2007, A Curious Thing (Tartan Clef Award for Best Album 2010, Swiss Music Award for Best Int. Rock/Pop Album 2011) 2010, Life in a Beautiful Light 2012; with Ray Davies: See My Friends (duet on track Dead End Street) 2010. *Honours:* Silver Clef Award for Best Newcomer 2007, Tartan Clef Award for Best Newcomer 2008, Daily Record Award for Scottish Person of the Year 2008, ECHO Award for Best Int. Newcomer 2009, for Best Int. Rock/Pop Female 2011, Swiss Music Awards for Best Int. Song (for This is the Life) 2009. *Address:* Melodramatic Records, PO Box 623, Weybridge, Surrey, KT13 3DE, England (office). *E-mail:* info@melodramaticrecords.com (office). *Website:* www.melodramaticrecords .com (office); www.amymacdonald.co.uk.

MacDONALD, Calum; British musician (percussion, drums) and songwriter; b. 12 Nov. 1953, Lochmaddy, North Uist, Scotland. *Career:* mem. Scottish celtic rock band, Runrig 1973–; Int. concerts include Canada 1987, Berlin 1987, support to U2, Murrayfield Stadium, Edinburgh 1987, support to Genesis 1993, support to Rolling Stones 1995. *Recordings:* albums: Play Gaelic 1978, Highland Connection 1979, Recovery 1981, Heartland 1985, The Cutter and The Clan 1987, Searchlight 1989, The Big Wheel 1991, Amazing Things 1993, Mara 1995, In Search of Angels 1999, The BBC Archives 1999, The Stamping Ground 2001, Proterra 2003, Everything You See 2007. *E-mail:* mike@runrig.co.uk (office). *Website:* www.runrig.co.uk.

McDONALD, Dave; British musician (drums and drum machines) and producer; b. 1964. *Career:* engineer., Portishead 1991–; numerous live appearances. *Film:* To Kill A Dead Man (short feature, also projected on MI5 building, London) 1995. *Recordings:* albums: Dummy (Mercury Music Prize for Best Album) 1994, Herd Of Instinct 1995, Portishead 1997, PNYC (live) 1998, Glory Times 1998, Roseland, New York (DVD) 2002, Third 2008. *Current Management:* Fruit, Ground Floor, 37 Lonsdale Road, London, NW6 6RA, England. *Telephone:* (20) 7326-0848. *Fax:* (20) 7326-8070. *Website:* www .portishead.co.uk.

McDONALD, 'Country' Joe; American singer and musician (guitar); b. 1 Jan. 1942, Washington, DC. *Career:* founder, folk group, Instant Action Jug Band 1964, group became Country Joe and The Fish 1965–70; concerts with Moby Grape, Howlin' Wolf, Led Zeppelin; appeared at festivals: Monterey Festival 1967, Miami Festival 1968, Woodstock Festival 1969, New Orleans Pop Festival 1969; solo artist 1971–; sporadic line-ups as The All-Star Band, Country Joe and The Fish; also mem. Energy Crisis, Barry Melton Band, Country Joe Band. *Recordings:* albums: with Country Joe and The Fish: Electric Music For The Mind and Body 1967, I Feel Like I'm Fixin' To Die 1968, Together 1968, Here We Are Again 1969, C.J. Fish 1970; solo: Thinking

of Woody Guthrie 1969, Tonight I'm Singing Just For You 1970, Hold On It's Coming 1971, War War War 1971, Country Joe 1974, Essential Country Joe 1975, Paradise With An Ocean View 1975, Love is a Fire 1976, Goodbye Blues 1977, Rock and Roll Music from Planet Earth 1978, Leisure Suite 1979, Into the Fray 1981, On My Own 1981, Animal Tracks 1983, Child's Play 1983, Peace on Earth 1984, Vietnam Experience 1986, Classics 1989, Superstitious Blues 1991, Carry On 1995, Something Borrowed, Something New 1998, Eat Flowers and Kiss Babies 1999, I Feel Like I'm Fixing to Sing Some Songs 2000, Crossing Borders 2002, Thank the Nurse 2002, Natural Imperfections 2005, At the Borderline 2007, Vanguard Visionaries 2007. *Address:* PO Box 7064, Berkeley, CA 94707-7064, USA (office). *E-mail:* joe@countryjoe.com (office). *Website:* www.countryjoe.com.

McDONALD, Michael; American singer, musician (keyboards) and songwriter; b. 2 Dec. 1952, St Louis, Missouri; m. Amy Holland; one s. *Career:* regular session singer; Member, Steely Dan 1974; songwriter, keyboard player, Doobie Brothers 1975–82. *Compositions include:* It Keeps You Runnin', Carly Simon 1976; co-writer: You Belong To Me 1978, What A Fool Believes 1979, Minute By Minute 1979, Real Love 1980, Take It To Heart 1990; collaborations with Kenny Loggins, Michael Jackson, Brenda Russell. *Recordings:* albums: with The Doobie Brothers: Takin' It To The Streets 1976, Livin' On The Fault Line 1977, Minute By Minute 1978, One Step Closer 1980; solo: That Was Then – The Early Recordings of Michael McDonald 1982, If That's What It Takes 1982, No Lookin' Back 1985, Sweet Freedom 1986, Take It To Heart 1990, Blink of An Eye 1993, Blue Obsession 2000, In The Spirit 2001, Motown 2003, Motown 2 2004, Through the Many Winters 2005, Soul Speak 2008; other recordings (as writer and/or singer) include: Together (film soundtrack) 1979, Christopher Cross, Christopher Cross 1979, High Adventure, Kenny Loggins 1982, The Winner In You, Patti LaBelle 1986, Anywhere You Go, David Pack 1986, Decisions, The Winans 1987, Back of My Mind, Christopher Cross 1988, Love At Large (film soundtrack) 1990, The Offbeat of Avenues, Manhattan Transfer 1991. *Honours:* Grammy Awards for Record of the Year, Song of the Year, Best Pop Vocal Performance, Best Vocal Arrangement 1979, Ivor Novello Award for Best Film Theme 1987. *Current Management:* Vector Management, PO Box 120479, Nashville, TN 37212, USA. *Website:* www.michaelmcdonald.com.

McDONALD, Richie; American country singer, songwriter and musician (guitar); b. 6 Feb. 1962, Lubbock, TX. *Career:* began singing and writing music in school; moved to Dallas and sang with award-winning band, Showdown; sang on nat. commercials, later moving to Nashville to pursue music career; founder mem., Texasee 1992, became resident house band at the Wildhorse Saloon, Nashville, name changed to Lonestar 1995–2007; solo artist 2007–. *Recordings include:* albums: with Lonestar: Lonestar 1995, Crazy Nights 1997, Lonely Grill 1999, This Christmas Time 2000, I'm Already There 2001, Let's Be Us Again 2004, Coming Home 2005, Mountains 2006; solo: If Every Day Could Be Christmas 2008, I Turn to You 2008. *Current Management:* c/o Janet Bozeman, Bozeman Media. *Telephone:* (615) 376-2246. *E-mail:* janet@bozemanmedia.com. *Website:* www.richiemcdonald.com.

MacDONALD, Rory; British singer and musician (guitar, bass); b. 27 July 1949, Dornoch, Sutherland, Scotland. *Career:* founder member, Scottish folk group Runrig 1973–; Int. concerts include Canada 1987, Berlin 1987, support to U2, Murrayfield Stadium, Edinburgh 1987, support to Genesis 1993, support to Rolling Stones 1995. *Recordings:* albums: Play Gaelic 1978, Highland Connection 1979, Recovery 1981, Heartland 1985, The Cutter and The Clan 1987, Searchlight 1989, The Big Wheel 1991, Amazing Things 1993, Mara 1995, In Search of Angels 1999, The BBC Archives 1999, The Stamping Ground 2001, Proterra 2003, Everything You See 2007. *E-mail:* mike@runrig .co.uk (office). *Website:* www.runrig.co.uk.

McELHONE, Johnny; Scottish musician (bass) and producer; b. 21 April 1963, Glasgow. *Career:* mem., Altered Images 1980–84, Hipsway 1984–88; founding mem., Texas 1986–; numerous tours, festivals and TV appearances. *Recordings include:* albums: with Altered Images: Happy Birthday 1981, Pinky Blue 1982, Bite 1983; with Hipsway: Hipsway 1986; with Texas: Southside 1989, Mother's Heaven 1991, Rick's Road 1993, White on Blonde 1997, The Hush 1999, The Greatest Hits 2000, Careful What You Wish For 2003, Red Book 2005. *Current Management:* G. R. Management Ltd, 974 Pollockshaws Road, Glasgow, G41 2HA, Scotland. *Telephone:* (141) 632-1111. *Fax:* (141) 649-0042. *E-mail:* info@grmanagement.co.uk. *Website:* www.texas .uk.com.

McELHONE, Sean; British musician (guitar, keyboards); b. 4 Jan. 1970, Leeds, Yorkshire; two d. *Career:* mem. Bridewell Taxis 1987–; concerts include Reading Festival, Roundhay Park, Locomotive, Paris; supported on tour The Stone Roses, Happy Mondays, Inspiral Carpets; mem., Musicians' Union. *Recordings:* album: Invisible To You 1991; singles: Just Good Friends, Give In, Honesty, Spirit, Don't Fear The Reaper.

McENTIRE, Reba, BEd; American country music singer and actress; b. 28 March 1955, McAlester, Okla; d. of Clark McEntire and Jacqueline McEntire; m. Narvel Blackstock 1989; one s. *Education:* Southeastern Oklahoma State Univ. *Career:* Co-founder Starstruck Entertainment (with husband/manager) 1988. *Albums include:* Reba McEntire 1977, Out of a Dream 1979, Feel the Fire 1980, Heart to Heart 1981, Unlimited 1982, Behind the Scene 1983, My Kind of Country 1984, Just a Little Love 1985, Have I Got a Deal For You 1986, Whoever's in England 1986, What Am I Gonna Do About You 1986, The Last One to Know 1987, Merry Christmas to You 1987, Reba 1988, Sweet

Sixteen 1989, Reba Live! 1989, Rumor Has It 1990, For My Broken Heart 1991, It's Your Call 1992, Read My Mind 1995, Starting Over 1995, What If It's You 1996, If You See Him 1998, Secret of Giving 1999, So Good Together 1999, Room to Breathe 2003, Reba Duets 2007, Keep on Loving You 2009, All the Women I Am 2010, Love Somebody 2015. *Films:* Tremors 1990, The Gambler Returns 1991, Is There Life Out There 1994, North 1994, Little Rascals 1994, Buffalo Girls 1995, Forever Love 1998, One Night at McCool's 2001, Charlotte's Web (voice) 2006. *Television:* The Gambler Returns: The Luck of the Draw 1991, The Man from Left Field 1993, Buffalo Girls 1995, Forever Love 1998, Secret of Giving 1999, Reba (series) 2001–07. *Publications:* Reba: My Story 1994, Comfort from a Country Quilt 1999. *Honours:* Female Vocalist of the Year, Country Music Asscn Awards 1984, 1985, 1986, 1987, Grammy Award for Best Female Country Vocal Performance 1986, for Best Country Vocal Collaboration (with Linda Davis) 1993, Billboard Magazine Woman of the Year 2007, 50th Anniversary Milestone Award, Acad. of Country Music Awards 2015. *Address:* Starstruck Entertainment, 40 Music Square West, Nashville, TN 37203, USA (office). *Telephone:* (615) 259-5400 (office). *Fax:* (615) 259-5401 (office). *Website:* www.starstruckstudios.com; www.reba.com.

McERLAINE, Ally; Scottish musician (guitar); b. 31 Oct. 1968, Glasgow. *Career:* founding mem., Texas 1986–; numerous tours, festivals and TV appearances. *Recordings:* albums: Southside 1989, Mother's Heaven 1991, Rick's Road 1993, White on Blonde 1997, The Hush 1999, The Greatest Hits 2000, Careful What You Wish For 2003, Red Book 2005. *Current Management:* G. R. Management Ltd, 974 Pollockshaws Road, Glasgow, G41 2HA, Scotland. *Telephone:* (141) 632-1111. *Fax:* (141) 649-0042. *E-mail:* info@grmanagement .co.uk. *Website:* www.texas.uk.com.

McEVOY, Eleanor, BA; Irish singer, musician (guitar, violin) and songwriter; b. 22 Jan. 1967, Dublin. *Education:* Trinity College, Dublin. *Career:* played with National Symphony Orchestra of Ireland 1988; left to pursue solo career with major success on A Woman's Heart project; numerous US and European tours with band; performed for 80,000 in Dublin during US President Clinton's visit; numerous TV appearances; featured on soundtracks to TV series Clueless and films The Nephew and Some Mother's Son; board mem. IMRO, IBEC Music Industry Group. *Recordings:* albums: A Woman's Heart 1992, Eleanor McEvoy 1994, What's Following Me? 1996, Snapshots 1999, Yola 2001, Early Hours 2004, Out There 2006, Love Must be Tough 2008. *Honours:* Irish Record Industry Awards, Best Solo Artist 1992, Irish Recorded Music Asscn, Best New Artist 1992, Featured tracks on Ireland's best ever selling album, A Woman's Heart 1992, Hot Press Magazine Awards: Best Solo Performer 1992, Best Songwriter 1993, Irish National Entertainment Award, Best New Artist 1993. *Current Management:* c/o Aileen Galvin, Entertainment Architects, 117 Strand Road, Sandymount. Dublin 4, Ireland. *Telephone:* (1) 2608659. *E-mail:* aileen@ealtd.ie. *Website:* www .entertainmentarchitects.ie; www.eleanormcevoy.net.

McFADDEN, Brian; Irish singer; b. 12 April 1980, Dublin; m. 1st Kerry Katona 2002 (divorced 2006); m. 2nd Vogue Williams 2012; two d. *Career:* mem., Westlife (as Bryan McFadden) 1999–2004; solo artist 2004–. *Recordings include:* albums: with Westlife: Westlife 1999, Coast to Coast 2000, World of Our Own 2001, Unbreakable – The Greatest Hits 2002, Turnaround 2003; solo: Irish Son 2004, Set in Stone 2008, Wall of Soundz 2010, The Irish Connection 2013. *Television:* Football Superstar 2008, Australian Idol (as Guest Judge) 2009, Australia's Got Talent (as Judge) 2010–12, Stand By Your Man (as Presenter) 2014, Who's Doing the Dishes? (as Presenter) 2014–, The Chase 2014. *Honours:* BRIT Awards for Best Pop Act 2001, 2002. *Website:* www.brianmcfadden.com; www.brianmcfaddenonline.net.

MacFARLANE, Denis (Dego), (Tek 9); British producer, remixer and DJ; b. London. *Career:* mem. 4hero, Nu-Era, Jacob's Optical Stairway; co-founder, Reinforced Records 1990–, Black Records 2000; collaborations with Alex Attias, Roy Ayers, IG Culture, Jill Scott, Ursula Rucker. *Recordings include:* albums: with 4hero: In Rough Territory 1991, Parallel Universe 1995, Two Pages 1998, Creating Patterns 2001, Play With the Changes 2007; with Jacob's Optical Stairway: Jacob's Optical Stairway 1996; as Tek 9: It's Not What You Think It Is 1996, Simply 2000. *Website:* www.4hero.co.uk.

MacFARLANE, Malcolm Douglas; British musician (guitar) and composer; b. 4 April 1961, Edinburgh, Scotland. *Education:* Leeds College of Music. *Career:* member, Barbara Thompson's Paraphernalia 1988–95; several European tours; world tours with Shakatak 1992–95; formed Mulford/MacFarlane group 1992–; first British tour 1995; currently teaches music, various schools in London; mem, Performing Rights Society. *Recordings:* with Barbara Thompson's Paraphernalia: Breathless 1991, Everlasting Flame 1993; with Mulford/MacFarlane: Jamming Frequency 1995, Bright Lights, Big City 2000. *Honours:* Eric Kershaw Memorial Prize, Leeds College of Music 1984–86. *E-mail:* malc.mac@virgin.net (office). *Website:* www.jazz-in-scotland.co.uk/ malcolmmacfarlane.htm.

McFARLANE, Zara Lavinia, BMus, MMus; British jazz and soul singer and songwriter; b. 1983, Dagenham, Essex, England. *Education:* BRIT School, London Coll. of Music, Guildhall School of Music and Drama. *Career:* made TV debut aged 14 (as Lauryn Hill) on Stars in Their Eyes 1998; fmr mem. Bopstar project; featured vocalist, Jazz Jamaica; performed with numerous jazz artists including Denys Baptiste, Soweto Kinch, Orphy Robinson; currently music teacher, Southwark Music Service. *Recordings:* albums: Until Tomorrow 2011, If You Knew Her 2014. *Honours:* MOBO Award for Best Jazz Act 2014. *Address:* c/o Southwark Music Service, Children and Adults Services, 0–19

Standards Team, Hub 2, 4th Floor, PO Box 64529, London, SE1 5LX, England (office). *E-mail:* info@southwarkmusicservice.org.uk (office). *Website:* www .southwarkmusicservice.org.uk (office); www.gillespetersonworldwide.com/ brownswood-recordings (office); www.zaramcfarlane.com.

McGARRIGLE, Anna; Canadian musician (keyboards, banjo, guitar, accordion) and singer; b. 1944, Montréal, QC. *Career:* singer, performer in both French and English; fmr mem., Mountain City Four, Montréal; formed duo with sister Kate McGarrigle 1974–. *Compositions:* songs recorded by artists, including Linda Ronstadt, Maria Muldaur, Emmylou Harris. *Recordings include:* as Kate & Anna McGarrigle: Kate & Anna McGarrigle 1975, Dancer With Bruised Knees 1977, Pronto Monto 1978, French Record 1980, Love Over and Over 1983, Heartbeats Accelerating 1990, Matapedia 1996, The McGarrigle Hour 1998, La Vache Qui Pleure 2003, Entre La Jeunesse Et La Tendresse 2004, The McGarrigle Christmas Hour 2005. *Current Management:* Concerted Efforts Inc., PO Box 600099, Newtonville, MA 02460, USA. *Telephone:* (617) 969-0810. *Fax:* (617) 969-6761. *Website:* www .concertedefforts.com. *E-mail:* anna@mcgarrigles.com. *Website:* www .mcgarrigles.com.

McGARVEY, Patrick James; Irish musician (electric bass, guitar, 5 string, banjo); b. 2 Aug. 1971, Belfast, Northern Ireland. *Career:* played live/recorded with The Coal Porters (Sid Griffin's band) 1993–, The Incredibly Strange Band, Western Electric, The Arlenes, Norrin Radd, Santo El Diablo, Cool Hand, Sid Griffin, Kate St John, Greg Trooper, Amy Rigby, Bob Neuwirth, Russ Tolman, Jason Walker, Emma Tricca, Jason McNiff, The Redlands Palomino Co.; tours: All Europe, USA; also live shows with Kate St John, 1995; guitarist, bandleader, television and radio appearances; mem. Musicians' Union. *Recordings:* Land of Hope and Crosby, The Coal Porters 1994; Los London, The Coal Porters 1995. *Address:* PO Box 2539, London, NW3 6DF, England.

McGEE, Alan John; British record company executive and musician (bass guitar); b. 29 Sept. 1960, Glasgow, Scotland; m. 1st Yvonne McMurray 1980 (divorced); m. 2nd Kate Holmes 1997. *Career:* mem. H2O 1978–79, Newspeak 1979–80, The Laughing Apple 1980–83, Biff Bang Pow! 1984–88; fmr man., Jesus & Mary Chain, Primal Scream; Founder and CEO, Creation Records 1983–2000, signing artists, including Ed Ball, The Boo Radleys, Felt, House of Love, Jesus & Mary Chain, The Loft, My Bloody Valentine, Oasis, Primal Scream, Ride, Sugar, Super Furry Animals, Teenage Fanclub; Founder and CEO, Poptones Records 1999–2007, signing artists, including Arnold, BellRays, Captain Soul, Cosmic Rough Riders, The Hives, Kill City, The Others, Dirty Pretty Things; Founder and CEO 359 Music label 2013–. *Radio includes:* occasional presenter for BBC Greater London Radio, BBC Radio 1. *Honours:* New Music Seminar Weber Prize 1993. *E-mail:* infoat359music@aol .com. *Website:* 359music.co.uk.

McGINLEY, Matthew Ryan (Matt); American drummer and songwriter; b. 24 Feb. 1983, Geneva, NY. *Career:* Founder mem. Gym Class Heroes 1997–, numerous collaborations including Daryl Hall, Estelle, The-Dream, Busta Rhymes, Adam Levine, Neon Hitch, Ryan Tedder; mem. Kill the Frontman. *Recordings:* albums: with Gym Class Heroes: For the Kids 2001, The Papercut Chronicles 2005, As Cruel as School Children 2006, The Quilt 2008, The Papercut Chronicles II 2011. *Honours:* with Gym Class Heroes: MTV Video Music Award for Best New Artist 2007. *Address:* c/o Fueled by Ramen Records, Warner Music Group, 75 Rockefeller Plaza, New York, NY 10019, USA (office). *Telephone:* (212) 275-2000 (office). *Website:* www.fueledbyramen .com (office); www.wmg.com (office); www.gymclassheroes.com.

McGINLEY, Raymond; British singer and musician (guitar); b. 3 Jan. 1964, Glasgow, Scotland. *Career:* fmr mem., The Boy Hairdressers; founder mem., Teenage Fanclub 1989–. *Recordings:* albums: A Catholic Education 1990, Bandwagonesque 1991, The King 1991, Thirteen 1993, Grand Prix 1995, Songs From Northern Britain 1997, Howdy! 2000, Words Of Wisdom And Hope 2002, Man-Made 2005, Shadows 2010. *Website:* www.teenagefanclub .com.

McGOLDRICK, Michael Brendan; British musician (uilleann pipes, low whistle, wooden flute) and composer; b. 26 Nov. 1973, Manchester, England. *Career:* Founder-mem. Manchester-based Celtic rock band, Toss The Feathers; formed Flook! (with fellow flautists Brian Finnegan and Sarah Allen) 1995; joined Scottish folk band Capercaillie 1997; Co-founder Lunasa; collaborations with Jim Kerr, Youssou N'Dour, Alan Stivell, Kate Rusby, John McCusker, Afro-Celt Sound System, Idir, Karan Casey, Dezi Donnelly, Mark Knopfler. *Recordings include:* albums: with Toss The Feathers: Live At The 32 Club 1988, Columbus Eclipse 1989, Awakening 1991, TTF'94 Live 1994, The Next Round 1995; with Flook!: Flook! Live 1997; with Lunasa: Lunasa 1998, Otherworld 1999; with Capercaillie: Beautiful Wasteland 1997, Nadurra 2000; solo: Champions of the North (with Dezi Donnelly) 1995, Morning Rory 1996, Fused 2000, At First Light (with John McSherry) 2001, Wired 2005, Aurora 2010. *Honours:* All Ireland Championships, BBC Radio Two Young Tradition Award 1995, BBC Radio Two Folk Award for Best Instrumentalist 2001, BBC Radio 2 Folk Award for Musician of the Year 2006. *Address:* c/o Vertical Records, 19 Woodside Crescent, Glasgow, G3 7UL, Scotland. *Telephone:* (141) 352-6670 (office). *Fax:* (870) 762-7126 (office). *E-mail:* info@secretmusic.org (office). *Website:* www.verticalrecords.co.uk (office).

McGOVERN, Maureen; American singer, actress, producer, songwriter and teacher; b. 27 July 1949, Youngstown, OH; m. (divorced). *Career:* recording artist, concerts, stage appearances, including Broadway, television and radio; film appearances in The Towering Inferno, Airplane!, Joseph King of Dreams, The Cure For Boredom; Broadway debut in The Pirates of Penzance; played Luisa in Nine; starred with Sting in the Threepenny Opera; Mary in Brownstone; appearances in South Pacific, The Sound of Music, Guys and Dolls, I Do, I Do; The Umbrellas of Cherbourg; duet with Placido Domingo, A Love Until the End of Time, recorded with Philharmonia Virtuosi of New York; performed, Celebrating Gershwin, 50th anniversary of his death; revival of Thee I Sing/Let 'Em Eat Cake, Brooklyn Academy of Music and Kennedy Center; performed at George Gershwin Centennial Celebration, London Palladium; television special, Maureen McGovern: Live at Wolftrap; guest appearances with Boston Pops, PBS D-Day Commemorative Concert with the National Symphony; appeared with every US Symphony Orchestra; guest host, television series, Girl's Night Out; for television played Dr Berg in Pacific Blue, Mrs Hatchigan in Beyond Belief; theatre includes Letters from 'Nam, The Lion in Winter, Dear World, Marmee in Little Women; mem. Polymositis/Dermatomyositis Asscn (nat. chair.), Shamrocks Against Dystrophy (nat. chair.), Muscular Dystrophy Asscn (mem. of nat. bd), The McGovern Works of Heart Project for Music and Healing (pres.), The American Music Therapy Ass008cn. *Compositions:* The Bengal Tiger's Ball (children's musical); I Want to Learn to Fly; Born In The Heart, 2003. *Recordings:* The Morning After (Academy Award) 1973, The Continental 1976, We May Never Love Like This Again (Academy Award), Can You Read My Mind, Another Woman In Love, State of the Heart, Naughty Baby, Christmas with Maureen McGovern, Baby I'm Yours, Out of this World McGovern sings Arlen, Amen! A Gospel Celebration, The Music Never Ends: The Lyrics of Marilyn and Alan Bergman, The Pleasure of His Company; With a Song In My Heart, Works of Heart, The Music Never Ends, A Long and Winding Road. *Honours:* Hon. DMus (Youngstown State Univ.); Grand Prize, Tokyo Music Festival, 1975, Songs From The Heart Award, NARAS/The American Music Therapy Asscn, NARAS Grammy Award for participation in Songs from the Neighborhood – The Music of Mister Rogers. *Address:* 8530 Wilshire Blvd 200, Beverly Hills, CA 90211-3113, USA (office). *Telephone:* (310) 277-9137 (office). *Fax:* (310) 277-6358 (office). *E-mail:* mmprodsinc@aol .com (office). *Website:* www.maureenmcgovern.com.

MacGOWAN, Shane; British musician (guitar) and singer; b. 25 Dec. 1957, Kent. *Career:* mem., Pogues 1983–91, 2004–; numerous tours and festival appearances; solo artist with backing group, The Popes 1993–. *Film appearance:* Straight to Hell 1986. *Recordings include:* albums: with Pogues: Red Roses For Me 1984, Rum Sodomy & The Lash 1985, If I Should Fall From Grace With God 1987, Peace And Love 1989, Hell's Ditch 1990; with The Popes: The Snake 1994, Holloway Boulevard 2000, Across The Broad Atlantic 2002; singles: with Pogues: A Pair Of Brown Eyes 1985, Poguetry In Motion 1986, Sally MacLennane 1985, Dirty Old Town 1985, Haunted 1986, A Fairytale Of New York (with Kirsty MacColl) 1987, The Irish Rover (with the Dubliners) 1987, Fiesta 1988, Yeah Yeah Yeah Yeah Yeah 1988, Misty Morning, Albert Bridge 1989, Summer In Siam 1989, Jack's Heroes 1990; with The Popes: The Church of The Holy Spook, The Woman's Got Me Drinking, Haunted (duet with Sinead O'Connor) 1995, You're The One (duet with Maire Brennan) 1995. *Current Management:* Brontone Ltd, 361–373 City Road, 2nd Floor, London, EC1V 1PQ, England. *Telephone:* (20) 7278-7123. *Fax:* (20) 7837-1415. *E-mail:* enquiries@a-addis.co.uk. *Website:* www.brontone.com; www.shanemacgowan.com; www.pogues.com.

McGRATH, Robert (Bob) Emmet, BMus, MA; American singer; b. 13 June 1932, Ottawa, Illinois; m. Ann L. Sperry 1958; two s. three d. *Education:* University of Michigan, Manhattan School of Music. *Career:* original host, Bob, on Sesame Street for 30 years; tenor soloist on Sing Along With Mitch; performed with Robert Shaw Chorale, Fred Waring Pennsylvanians; host for the International Children's Festival at Wolftrap for 10 years; performed with 100 Symphony Orchestras; has performed in over 800 concerts in the USA, Canada and Japan. *Recordings:* The Baby Record, Songs and Games For Toddlers, If You're Happy and You Know It Sing Along number 1 and number 2, Bob's Favourite Street Songs, Sing Me A Story, Music for Fun, Rhythm Band Set, Christmas Sing Along. *Publications:* I'm A Good Mommy, You're A Good Daddy, Dog Lies, The Shoveller, Me Myself, Sneakers, Uh Oh! Gotta Go, Oops! Excuse Me Please!. *Honours:* Lifetime Hon. mem., Variety Club; Dr hc (Medaille College); Emmanuel Cancer Foundation Tribute, Parent's Choice, American Library Ass000cn, National Chairperson, UNICEF Day, World Children's Day Foundation, UN General Assembly, Syracuse Symphony Assocn Achievement Award for Music Education, American Eagle Award, Nat. Music Council. *Website:* www.bobmcgrath.com.

McGRATH, Mark Sayers; American singer; b. 15 March 1968; pnr Carin Kingsland; one s. one d. *Education:* University of Southern California. *Career:* became band member of The Shrinky Dinx following unscheduled leap on stage at live gig; group signed to Atlantic Records following circulation of self-made demo video; act renamed Sugar Ray owing to threat of legal action prior to record releases; built up world-wide fanbase through touring and TV appearances; cameo in Fathers Day film 1997. *Recordings:* albums: Lemonade and Brownies 1995, Floored 1997, 14–59 1999, Sugar Ray 2001, In Pursuit of Leisure 2003, Music for Cougars 2009. *Address:* PO Box 6188, Olympia, WA 98507, USA (office). *E-mail:* mark@sugarray.com (office). *Website:* www .sugarray.com.

McGRAW, Tim; American country singer, musician (guitar), songwriter and producer; b. (Tim Smith), 1 May 1967, Delhi, LA; s. of the late Tug McGraw; m. Faith Hill 1996; three d. *Education:* Northeast Louisiana Univ. *Career:* moved to Nashville and gigged around northeastern Louisiana and Jacksonville, FL; while performing in clubs around Nashville, signed deal with Curb Records; released Indian Outlaw, a song using extracts of Lament of the Cherokee Reservation Indian 1994, track attracted criticism in USA for its alleged demeaning stereotypes of Native Americans; producer for other country artists, including Jo Dee Messina. *Film appearance:* Country Strong 2010. *Recordings include:* albums: Tim McGraw 1993, Not A Moment Too Soon 1994, All I Want 1995, Everywhere 1997, A Place In The Sun 1999, Set This Circus Down (Country Albums Artist of the Year 2001, American Music Award for Favorite Country Album 2002) 2001, Tim McGraw And The Dancehall Doctors 2002, Live Like You Were Dying (American Music Award for Favorite Country Album 2005) 2004, Greatest Hits Volume 2 (American Music Award for Favorite Country Album 2006) 2006, Let It Go 2007, Southern Voice 2009, Emotional Traffic 2012, Two Lanes of Freedom 2013, Sundown Heaven Town 2014, Damn Country Music 2015. *Publications:* This is Ours 2002, My Little Girl (with Tom Douglas) 2008, Love your Heart (with Tom Douglas) 2010. *Honours:* CMA Awards for Vocal Event of the Year (for It's Your Love, with Faith Hill) 1997, for Song of the Year, Single of the Year (both for Live Like You Were Dying) 2004, for Musical Event of the Year (for Highway Don't Care, with Taylor Swift and Keith Urban) 2013, Billboard Country Artist of the Year, Male Country Artist of the Year, Country Single Artist of the Year 2001, American Music Award for Favorite Male Country Artist 2002, 2003, 2005, 2007, ACM Award for Best Single, for Best Song (both for Live Like You Were Dying) 2005, for Video of the Year (for Highway Don't Care) 2014, Grammy Award for Best Country Collaboration with Vocals (for Like We Never Loved at All, with Faith Hill) 2006, American Country Award for Single of the Year: Vocal Collaboration (for Highway Don't Care) 2013. *Current Management:* c/o EM.Co, PO Box 150366, Nashville, TN 37215, USA. *Website:* em.co; www.timmcgraw.com.

McGUINN, Roger; American singer and musician (guitar); b. (James McGuinn, III), 13 July 1942, Chicago, Illinois; m. Camilla. *Career:* touring musician with: The Limelighters, Chad Mitchell Trio, Judy Collins, Bobby Darin; founder mem. The Byrds, 1964–73; solo artist 1973–; also mem. McGuinn Clark and Hillman (with Gene Clark and Chris Hillman) 1978–79; performances include: The Beach Boys Summer Spectacular 1966, Monterey Pop Festival 1967, Grand Ole Opry 1968, Newport Festival 1969, Bath Festival 1970; tours with Bob Dylan's Rolling Thunder Revue 1975, Roy Orbison All-Star Tribute 1990. *Recordings:* albums: with the Byrds: Mr Tambourine Man 1965, Turn! Turn! Turn! 1965, Fifth Dimension 1966, Younger Than Yesterday 1967, The Notorious Byrd Brothers 1968, Sweetheart of The Rodeo 1968, The Ballad of Easy Rider 1970, Untitled 1970, Byrdmaniax 1971, Farther Along 1972, Best of The Byrds – Greatest Hits Vol. 2 1972, History of The Byrds 1973, The Byrds 1990; solo: Roger McGuinn 1973, Peace On You 1974, Cardiff Rose 1976, Thunderbyrd 1977, Back From Rio 1991, Born to Rock and Roll 1992, Nitty Gritty Dirt Band – Roger McGuinn Live 1994, Live from Mars; Folk Den, Vols 1–4 2000, McGuinn Hillman 2000, Feuding Banjos 2000, Treasures From The Folk Den 2001, The Folk Den Project 2006; with Clark and Hillman: McGuinn Clark and Hillman 1979; with Hillman: McGuinn/Hillman 1979. *Address:* Skyline Music, 28 Union Street, Whitefield, NH 03598, USA. *Telephone:* (603) 837-9600. *Fax:* (603) 837-9601. *Website:* www.skylineonline.com; www.ibiblio.org/jimmy/ mcguinn/index.html.

McHUGH, Robert (Bob), BA; American musician (piano) and composer; b. 20 July 1946, Kearney, NJ; m. Jane Belli 1970; one s. one d. *Education:* Jersey City College; private study with Bill Manzi, Morris Nanton, Don Friedman, Hester Randolfi. *Career:* performed in documentary, The Art of Worship, produced by Riverside Church, New York City, USA; appearance on Around New York, WNYC, Concert's at Count Basie Theatre, Riverfest, New York Public Library, Lincoln Center; mem, ASCAP, NJEA, MTA. *Compositions:* Steamboat Rag, Rocky Rog Tune, Bus Boy Circus, Dream Street, Three Greek Dances, Baroque Piece, Buily and The Bean, Uptown, Summer Stride, Recuperation Tango 1998. *Recordings include:* Manhattan Sunrise, Soaring on Wings of Ivory and Black, After Midnight, Interplay, American Classics, Another Sunrise, On Track. *Honours:* ASCAP Popular Award 1989, commissioned Composer for the New Jersey Music Teachers' State Piano Competition 1998–99. *Address:* Lunge Music, 902 Lincoln Avenue, Pompton Lakes, NJ 07442, USA (office). *Telephone:* (315) 287-2852 (office). *Fax:* (315) 287-2800 (office). *E-mail:* webmaster@lungemusic.com (office). *Website:* www .lungemusic.com (office).

MacINTOSH, Adrian; British jazz musician; b. 7 March 1942, Tadcaster; m. Sheila Christie 1974. *Career:* early work with John Taylor Trio and Norma Winstone; mem. Alan Elsdon Band 1970; joined Brian Leakes' Sweet and Sour 1978; joined Humphrey Lyttelton's Band 1982; work with Helen Shapiro 1984; formed Trio Time; worked with many leading jazz names including Sonny Stitt, Teddy Edwards, Jimmy Witherspoon, Harold Ashby, Nat Pierce, Scott Hamilton, Clark Terry, Warren Vache, Kenny Davern, Al Casey; mem, Musicians' Union, Chairman, Assan of British Jazz Musicians. *Recordings:* with Humphrey Lyttelton's Band: Humph and Wally Fawkes 1983, Humph and Helen Shapiro 1984, Humph, Al Casey and Kenny Davern 1984, Humph At The Bulls Head 1985, Humph and Buddy Tate 1985, Humph Gigs 1987, Humph and Lillian Boutté 1988, Humph At Breda Jazz Festival 1988, Humph

Beano Boogie 1989, Ken McCarthy Quartet (featuring Dick Pearce), Rock Me Gently, Hear Me Talkin' to Ya, Lay 'Em Straight, Between Friends, Hallelujah Howdown, Triple Exposure, Sad, Sweet Songs and Crazy Rhythms; with Trio Time: How Beautiful is Night, Sweet September, Jazz Jubilation 2004; produced album by Brian Leake's Sweet and Sour 1993.

MacISAAC, Ashley Dwayne; Canadian singer, musician (violin) and composer; b. 24 Feb. 1975, Antigonish, Nova Scotia. *Career:* fiddle player from the Cape Breton tradition, rooted in Scottish folk music; Hi, How Are You Today? album was based in Cape Breton traditional music but introduced various other musical influences. *Recordings:* albums: Close To The Floor 1992, Hi, How Are You Today? 1995, Fine, Thank You Very Much 1998, Fiddle Music 101 1999, Helter's Celtic 2000, Ashley MacIsaac 2003, Pride 2006; features on: Feelings, David Byrne 1997, Fire In The Kitchen, The Chieftains 1998, Suas E!, Mary Jane Lamond 1997, Spirit Trail, Bruce Hornsby 1998, Hanging Garden OST 1998. *Current Management:* c/o James MacLean, Talk's Cheap Management. *Telephone:* (416) 598-3330. *E-mail:* james@talks-cheap .com. *Website:* ashleymacisaac.net.

MACK, Bobby; American singer, musician (guitar) and music producer; b. 19 June 1954, Fort Worth, Texas; m. Pat Cullen 1994; one s. one d. *Education:* University of Texas, Austin. *Career:* solo artist 1974–; numerous perform-ances at Delta Blue Festival, New Orleans Jazz Festival; tours in fmr USSR, Japan, New Zealand, Australia, Scandinavia, Europe, UK. *Recordings include:* albums: Bobby Mack and Night Train: Say What 1990, Red Hot and Humid 1991, Honeytrap 1994, Sugar All Night 1996, Live at J and J Blues Bar 1997, Highway Man 1998. *Publications:* writer, Texas Blue Magazine. *Address:* PO Box 1630, Blanco, TX 78606, USA (office). *Telephone:* (830) 833-1021 (office). *Fax:* (830) 833-1282 (office). *E-mail:* bobby@bobbymack.com (office). *Website:* www.bobbymack.com.

MACK, Danny; American singer, musician (accordion, drums, trumpet, keyboards), record producer and record company executive; b. 29 March 1943, Harvey, IL; m. Caroline Panczyck 1962, one s. one d. *Career:* bandleader, 1958–; clubs circuit until 1977; songwriter 1977–; formed Syntony Publishing BMI and Briarhill Records 1984; mem. BMI, NARAS; lifetime mem. Country Music Asscns of America. *Honours:* Hon. Kentucky Col; CMAA Indie Label of the Year, Producer of the Year 1992, 1993, 1994, CMA Award for Inspirational Record of the Year 1994, World Radio Network Song of Year, Spain 1994. *Address:* c/o Briarhill Records, 3484 Nicolette Drive, Crete, IL 60417, USA.

MACK, James Joseph; British musician (percussion); b. 12 Nov. 1971, Kensington, London, England. *Education:* Guildhall School of Music and Drama; West London Institute of Higher Education. *Career:* World-wide tours and television appearances with: D:ream; Des'ree; Lonnie Liston Smith; C J Lewis; Rozalla; NYJO; Skin; mem. Musicians' Union. *Recordings:* D:ream (second album); Skin; NYJO; Various television commercials include: Ameri-can Express; Maxwell House; John Smiths Bitter. *Honours:* Performance diploma, Guildhall School of Music and Drama.

MACK, Warner; American country singer, songwriter and musician; b. (Warner McPherson), 2 April 1938, Nashville, Tenn.. *Career:* solo artist late 1950s–; regular tours, live performances. *Recordings include:* albums: The Country Touch 1966, Drifting Apart 1967, Love Hungry 1970, You Make Me Feel Like A Man 1971, Great Country 1973, Prince of Country Blues 1983, At Your Service 1984, Early Years 1998. *Current Management:* Bridgewood Music Company, PO Box 100453, Nashville, TN 37224, USA. *Website:* www .warnermack.com.

MACKAY, David; Australian record producer, composer and musician (keyboards); b. 11 May 1944, Sydney; m. Brenda Anne Challis 1973; one s. one d. *Education:* St Aloyisious Coll., Sydney, Australia, Conservatorium of Music, Sydney. *Career:* prod. of records by Blue Mink, Cliff Richard, New Seekers, Bonnie Tyler, Frankie Miller, Dusty Springfield, Johnny Hallyday, Demis Roussos, Sarah Jory, Cilla Black; mem. PRS, Repro, BAC&S, Profes-sional Composers' Guild. *Compositions:* theme and underscores for TV programmes, including Auf Wiedersehen Pet (Ivor Novello Award 1983), Bread, Blott on the Landscape. *Honours:* AKIA Award for Best Cast Album of a Musical 1990.

McKAY, Eleanora Marie (Nellie); American singer, songwriter and musician (piano); b. 13 April 1984, London, UK. *Career:* solo artist. *Film:* (original songs) Rumor Has It... 2005. *Play:* The Threepenny Opera (Theatre World Award) 2006. *Recordings:* album: Get Away From Me 2004, Pretty Little Head 2006, Obligatory Villagers 2007, Normal as Blueberry Pie: A Tribute to Doris Day 2009, Home Sweet Mobile Home 2010. *Telephone:* (973) 563-8204. *E-mail:* kidlogic@nj.rr.com. *Website:* kidlogiclovesyou.com; www .nelliemckay.com.

MACKAY, Robert Andrew, BSc, MMus, PhD; British composer, actor, singer (baritone), musician (flute, classical guitar, bass) and academic; *Lecturer in Creative Music Technology, University of Hull*; b. 12 July 1973, London. *Education:* Univs of Keele and Bangor. *Career:* session musician in Wales 1997–; Composer-in-Residence, Radio Bratislava, Slovakia 1998–99, La Muse en Circuit, Paris 2007; bass player, Gyroscope 1998; flute, guitar and bass player, Tystion 1998–2002; flute player in Drymbago 2005–; collaborator with Pwyll ap Siôn on comm. for Nat. Youth Choir of Wales and Opera Heloise 1999; comms for Twisted I Theatre Company 2003, Rotunda Mapmaker project 2005–08; works performed throughout Europe, USA and NZ; several TV appearances and radio broadcasts; mem. PRS, MCPS, PRC, Equity, Soc.

for the Promotion of New Music, BMIC, SAN. *Theatre:* Only Just 1997. *Film appearances:* Merlin, A Beautiful Mistake. *Television appearances:* I dot (S4C), Garej (S4C), 4-Track (S4C), Lois (S4C), Sesiwn Hwyr (S4C), Bandit (S4C). *Radio performances:* Late Junction (BBC Radio 3), Hear and Now (BBC Radio 3), two John Peel sessions (BBC Radio 1), various performances on BBC Radio Wales. *Compositions include:* Environs 1996, Sea Pictures 1997, Voicewind 1998, Postcards from the Summer 1999, Peiriant Gorllewinol, Meddwi Dros Gymru (BBC Radio Cymru Rap Award for Album of the Year 2000) 1999, Flute Melt 2000, Heloise 2001, Joyce's Vision 2002, Cain and Abel 2003, Phonemenon 2004, Altered Landscapes 2006, Song of Stones 2007. *Recordings:* ICMC98 1998, 1er Concurso Internacional de Miniaturas Electroacústicas 2003. *Publications:* ICMC98 1998, Shrug Off Ya Complex 1999, Mr Blaidd 2000, Hen Gelwydd Prydain Newydd 2000, Y Meistri 2001, Discontact! III 2003, Confluencias 2003, In Between 2004, Chops 2005, Costa Rita 2006, La Muse en Circuit 2007. *Honours:* Bourges Synthèse Festival Prix Résidence, France 1997, Hungarian Radio Special Prize (Ear 99) 1999, Winner, Concours Luc Ferrari 2006. *Address:* 57 Oak Road, Scarborough, North Yorkshire, YO12 4AP, England. *E-mail:* r.a.mackay@hull.ac.uk (office). *Website:* www.myspace.com/robflute.

McKEAN, Ian; British musician (guitar); b. 9 Jan. 1958, Hertford, Hertfordshire. *Education:* West Surrey College of Art and Design, City Literary Inst. *Career:* fmr mem. Twenty Flight Rockers; mem. Balaam and The Angel 1988–; played as support to Aerosmith; mem, Musicians' Union, PRS. *Recordings:* albums: Days of Madness 1989, No More Innocence 1991, Prime Time 1993. *E-mail:* bookings@balaamandtheangel.com (office). *Website:* www.balaamandtheangel.com.

McKEE, Benjamin (Ben) Arthur; American musician (bass guitar, key-boards) and songwriter; b. 7 April 1985, Forestville, Calif. *Education:* Berklee Coll. of Music. *Career:* mem. Imagine Dragons 2009–; performed at numerous festivals 2011–; signed with Interscope Records 2011; numerous TV appear-ances and tours in USA, Canada, Europe. *Recording:* albums: with Imagine Dragons: Night Visions (Billboard Music Award for Top Rock Album 2014) 2012, Smoke + Mirrors 2015. *Honours:* Teen Choice Award for Choice Rock Song (for Radioactive) 2013, American Music Awards for Favorite Alternative Rock Artist 2013, 2014, Grammy Award for Best Rock Performance (for Radioactive) 2014, Billboard Music Awards for Top Duo/Group 2014, for Top Hot 100 Artist 2014, for Top Rock Artist 2014, for Top Streaming Song (Audio) (for Radioactive) 2014, iHeartRadio Music Award for Best Alternative Rock Song of the Year (for Demons, with Imagine Dragons) 2014, Much Music Video Award for Int. Video of the Year - Group (for Demons, with Imagine Dragons) 2014. *Current Management:* c/o Mac Reynolds, Reynolds Management, 823 Las Vegas Boulevard South, Las Vegas, NV 89101, USA. *E-mail:* mac@ reynoldsmgmt.com. *Website:* www.reynoldsmgmt.com; imaginedragonsmusic .com.

McKEE, Maria; American singer and songwriter; b. 17 Aug. 1964, Los Angeles, Calif. *Career:* formed duo The Maria McKee Band (with half-brother Bryan MacLean), later renamed the Brian MacLean Band; founder mem. Lone Justice 1982–86; solo artist 1987–. *Compositions include:* A Good Heart (released by Feargal Sharkey) 1985. *Recordings include:* albums: with Lone Justice: Lone Justice 1985, Shelter 1987, This World Is Not My Home 1999, The Best of: 20th Century Masters / The Millennium Collection 2013, This Is Lone Justice: The Vaught Tapes 1983 2014; solo: Maria McKee 1990, You Gotta Sin To Be Saved 1993, Life Is Sweet 1996, Ultimate Collection 2000, Peddlin' Dreams 2005, Late December 2007, Live at the BBC 2008. *E-mail:* Management@mariamckee.com; viewfinderrecords@gmail.com. *Website:* www.mariamckee.org.

McKEE, Mike; American drummer; b. Apex, North Carolina. *Education:* Campbell Univ. *Career:* drummer and percussionist with many groups and for many artists including Triangle Jazz Quartet, Rich Emily, Santino, Jason Adamo; fmr house session drummer for K-House Recording Studios, Raleigh; private percussion teacher in Cary 2006–11; full-time mem. Delta Rae 2010–; first EP released 2010; signed to Sire Records 2011; debut album 2012; numerous live performances; support act for Edwin McCain and Hanson. *Recordings include:* album: with Delta Rae: Carry the Fire 2012. *Current Management:* c/o Jordan Burger, Fleming Artists, 543 North Main Street, Ann Arbor, MI 48104, USA. *E-mail:* Jordan@flemingartists.com; deltaraemgmt@ gmail.com. *Address:* c/o Sire Records, Warner Bros. Records, Warner Music Group, 75 Rockefeller Plaza, New York, NY 10019, USA (office). *Website:* www .deltarae.com.

McKEEGAN, Michael; Irish musician (bass guitar). *Career:* mem. rock group, Therapy? 1989–. *Recordings include:* albums: Babyteeth 1991, Pleas-ure Death 1992, Nurse 1992, Troublegum 1994, Infernal Love 1995, Semi-Detached 1998, Suicide Pack – You First 1999, So Much For The Ten Year Plan 2000, Shameless 2001, High Anxiety 2003, Never Apologise Never Explain 2004, One Cure Fits All 2006. *E-mail:* churchofnoise@ therapyquestionmark.co.uk. *Website:* www.therapyquestionmark.co.uk.

McKENNA, Mae, DipMus; British singer and songwriter; b. 23 Oct. 1955, Coatbridge, Scotland; m. James Woon 1977; one s. *Career:* recorded and toured UK and Europe as lead singer with folk rock band Contraband 1971–75; sung solo gaelic air on Ultravox tour 1983; solo singer 1985; backing singer for Scritti Politti, Blur, Madness, Jason Donovan, Cliff Richard, ABC, Wet Wet Wet, Kylie Minogue, Rick Astley, Donna Summer, David Cassidy, Steps, Westlife; mem. Musicians' Union, Equity, PRS. *Recordings:* albums: with

Contraband: Contraband 1974; solo: Mae McKenna 1975, Everything That Touches Me 1976, Walk On Water 1977, Nightfallers 1988, Mirage and Reality 1992, Shore to Shore 1999. *E-mail:* info@mae-mckenna.com (office). *Website:* www.maemckenna.com.

McKENNA, Rafe; record producer, engineer and mixer. *Career:* prod., engineer, mixer for: David Essex; UFO; Magnum; Buggles; Elkie Brooks; Steve Hackett; Steve Howe; Wishbone Ash; Danny Wilson; Roger Daltrey; Giant; Depeche Mode; Thomas Dolby; Paul McCartney; Spandau Ballet; Gary Glitter; Bad Company; Big Country; Foreigner; The Corrs; Ash; Warm Jets; Electronic; Lewis Taylor; Ronan Keating; Madness; James Taylor Quartet; Zucchero; Marco Borsato; BB Mak; Dream Kids; UB40; Brian Kennedy; Eddi Reader.

McKENNITT, Loreena; Canadian singer and songwriter; b. Manitoba. *Career:* represented Canada at UNESCO 1978, 1985; featured in festival productions as actor, singer and composer, including Shakespeare's The Tempest 1982, The Two Gentlemen of Verona 1984; solo artist 1985–. *Recordings include:* albums: Elemental 1985, To Drive the Cold Winter Away 1987, Parallel Dreams 1989, The Visit (Juno Award for Best Roots and Traditional Album 1992) 1991, The Mask & Mirror (Juno Award for Best Roots and Traditional Album 1995) 1994, A Winter Garden 1995, The Book of Secrets 1997, Live in Paris/Toronto 1999, An Ancient Muse 2006. *Honours:* won DuMaurier Search for Talent 1978, Billboard Award for Int. Achievement 1997. *Website:* www.quinlanroad.com.

McKENZIE, Derrick; British musician (drums); b. 27 March 1962, London, England. *Career:* mem., Jamiroquai 1992–; numerous tours and TV appearances. *Recordings include:* albums: Emergency On Planet Earth 1993, The Return of the Space Cowboy 1994, Travelling Without Moving (four MTV Awards, Grammy Award 1997) 1996, Synkronized 1999, A Funk Odyssey 2001, Dynamite 2005, High Times: Singles 1992–2006 2006, Rock Dust Light Star 2010. *Honours:* MTV Video Music Awards. *Current Management:* DWL, 2nd Floor, 53 Goodge Street, London, W1T 1TG, England. *Telephone:* (20) 7436-5529. *Fax:* (20) 7637-8776. *E-mail:* info@dwl.uk.net. *Website:* www.dwl .uk.net; www.jamiroquai.com.

McKENZIE, Julia Kathleen, FGSM, FRAM; British actress, director and singer; b. 17 Feb. 1941, London, England; d. of Albion McKenzie and Kathleen McKenzie (née Rowe); m. Jerry Harte 1972. *Education:* Tottenham County School and Guildhall School of Music and Drama. *Career:* actress on stage, film and TV, and in musicals; also dir. *Plays and musicals include:* Maggie May 1965, Follies, Company 1972, Side By Side By Sondheim 1977, Guys and Dolls 1982, Woman in Mind 1986, Into The Woods 1990, Sweeney Todd 1993–94, Communicating Doors 1995. *Films:* Shirley Valentine 1989, The Snow Queen (voice) 1995, Vol-au-vent 1996, Bright Young Things 2003, These Foolish Things 2006, Notes on a Scandal 2006. *TV appearances include:* Fame is the Spur, Glory Glory Days, Hotel du Lac, Absent Friends, Maggie and Her, Fresh Fields (series), French Fields (series), Julia and Co., Blott on the Landscape (series), Adam Bede 1991, The Shadowy Third 1995, The Old Curiosity Shop 1996, Jack and the Beanstalk: The Real Story 2001, The Last Detective 2003, Death in Holy Orders 2003, Philadelphia Story 2005, Celebration 2006, Midsommer Murders 2006, Where the Heart Is 2006, Celebration 2006, You Can Choose Your Friends 2007, Marple: A Pocket Full of Rye 2008, Marple: Murder Is Easy 2008, Marple: Why Didn't They Ask Evans 2009, Marple: They Do It with Mirrors 2009, Marple: The Mirror Crack'd from Side to Side 2010, Marple: The Secret of Chimneys 2010, Marple: The Blue Geranium 2010, Marple: The Pale Horse 2010, The Mystery of Edwin Drood 2012, Gangsta Granny 2013. *Plays and TV programmes directed:* Stepping Out 1984, Steel Magnolias 1989, Just So 1989, Putting it Together, The Mercury Workshop Musical Revue 1994, The Musical of the Year (for Danish TV) 1996, Honk! (Scarborough 1997, Royal Nat. Theatre, London 1999, North Shore Theatre, Beverly, USA 2000 and UK tour 2001), A Little Night Music, Tokyo 1999. *Recordings:* Album of Show Songs 1992, Anyone Can Whistle 1997, The King and I 1997, Sondheim: A Celebration 1997. *Honours:* Hon. DLitt (South Bank); two Olivier Awards, Evening Standard Best Actress Award, Critics' Award (London and New York), Variety Club Award, five consecutive TV Times Awards. *Current Management:* c/o Ken McReddie Associates Ltd, 101 Finsbury Pavement, London, EC2A 1RS, England. *Telephone:* (20) 7439-1456. *Fax:* (20) 7734-6530. *E-mail:* email@kenmcreddie.com. *Website:* www.kenmcreddie.com.

MacKENZIE, Talitha; American/British singer, musician (keyboards), composer, arranger and actress and dancer; b. 3 April 1956, Oceanside, NY, USA; m. Ian MacKenzie 1988; two s. *Education:* Connecticut College, New England Conservatory of Music, Boston, private study in classical piano, classical/jazz voice. *Career:* concerts include: Ronnie Scott's London, Chard Festival of Women in Music, WOMAD, Celts in Kent Festival, England, Edinburgh Festival Fringe, Celtic Connections Festival, Glasgow; Folk City, The Bottom Line, New York, USA, Vox Populi, Toronto, Cultures Canada, Ottawa, Winnipeg Folk Festival, Canada, Teatro Campoamor Oviedo, Juntos en Córdoba, WOMEX, Berlin, Melkweg, Amsterdam; television includes: Arts and Parts, Don't Look Down, STV, Ex-S, Ainm a'Ghàidheil, Talla a'Bhaile, Sin Agad E, Brag, BBC Scotland, Global Jukebox, BSB; mem, Musicians' Union, BMI, MCPS, PAMRA, British Equity. *Compositions:* Wall of Sound (for National Museum of Scotland event, Museum of Sound) 2001. *Recordings:* St James Gate 1985, Shantyman 1986, Mouth Music 1990, Sòlas 1993, Spiorad 1996, Indian Summer 2007; theatre includes: Réiteach, (Proiseact Naiseanta),

Russian Ritual Wedding, Harvard University. *Publications:* The Triangle Trade: African Influences in the Anglo-American Sea Shanty Tradition 1984, Song of the Scottish Highlands, Scot 1985. *Honours:* Billboard Song Contest for Owen's Boat 1994. *Current Management:* Donald MacQueen, Winning Promotions, 96/1 South Gyle Wynd, Edinburgh EH12 9HJ, Scotland. *Address:* 33 Millar Crescent, Edinburgh, EH10 5HQ, Scotland (home). *Website:* www .sonasmultimedia.com; www.talithamackenzie.com.

McKEOWN, Leslie; British singer; b. 12 Nov. 1955. *Career:* lead singer, Bay City Rollers, 1973–78; *Appearances include:* British tour, 1974; Television series featuring the group, Shang-A-Lang, 1975–77; Saturday Night Variety Show, ABC, 1975; Solo artist, 1978–; Tours as Les McKeown's 70s Bay City Rollers. *Recordings:* with The Bay City Rollers: Hit singles include: Remember (Sha La La), 1974; Shang-A-Lang, 1974; Summerlove Sensation, 1974; All of Me Loves All of You, 1974; Bye Bye Baby (No. 1, UK), 1975; Give A Little Love (No. 1, UK), 1975; Money Honey, 1975; Saturday Night (No. 1, USA), 1976; I Only Want To Be With You, 1976; It's A Game, 1977; You Make Me Believe In Magic, 1987; Albums: Rollin' (No. 1, UK), 1974; Once Upon A Star (No. 1, UK), 1975; Wouldn't You Like It, 1975; Bay City Rollers, 1976; Rock 'N' Roll Love Letter, 1976; Dedication, 1976; It's A Game, 1977; Greatest Hits, 1978; Solo albums include: All Washed Up, 1978; Rollerworld: Live At The Budokan, 2001. *Current Management:* Brian Gannon Management, PO Box 106, Rochdale OL16 4HW, England. *E-mail:* lori@lesmckeown.com (office). *Website:* www.lesmckeown.com (office).

McKERRON, Charles (Charlie) Alastair; British musician (fiddle) and composer; b. 14 June 1960, London. *Career:* mem. Capercaillie 1985–; group, along with original material, specialises in fusing traditional Gaelic songs with contemporary arrangements; had first UK top 40 single in Gaelic, Coisich A Ruin (from A Prince Among Islands EP) 1992; formed Big Sky band project with John Saich and cousin Laura McKerron; Big Sky formed from the Glasgow Celtic Grooves concerts and features many top traditional and roots musicians in its mix of traditional Celtic music and contemporary electronic instrumentation; formed Session A9. *Compositions:* contributed to the film Rob Roy; *Collaborations include:* Fish; The Pearl Fishers; Fred Morrison. *Recordings:* albums: with Capercaillie: Sidewalk 1989, Delirium 1991, Get Out 1992, The Blood Is Strong, Secret People 1993, Capercaillie 1995, To The Moon 1996, Beautiful Wasteland 1997, Glenfinnan – Songs of The '45 (recorded 1995) 1998, Nàdurra 2000, Live in Concert 2002, Choice Language 2003, Roses and Tears 2008; with Big Sky: Source 2000; with Session A9: What Road? 2003; features solo on: Music of The Fiddle 1981, Suilean Dubh, Tannas 1999, Tacsi (TV series) 2000, Pray For Rain, Andrew P White 2001. *Honours:* Daily Record Golden Fiddle Award. *Address:* c/o Jane Skinner, Vertical Records, 19 Woodside Crescent, Glasgow G3 7UL, Scotland (office). *E-mail:* info@secretmusic.org (office). *Website:* www.verticalrecords.co.uk (office); www.capercaillie.co.uk.

MACKEY, Steve; British musician (bass guitar); b. 10 Nov. 1966, Sheffield, England. *Career:* Mem., Pulp, 1987–; Numerous tours, television appearances and festival dates; Contribution to film soundtrack, Mission Impossible, 1996. *Recordings:* Albums: Freaks, 1987; Separations, 1992; His 'N' Hers, 1994; Different Class (No. 1, UK) 1995; This Is Hardcore (No. 1, UK), 1998; We Love Life, 2001; Hits, 2002. Singles: Master Of The Universe, 1987; My Legendary Girlfriend, 1990; Countdown, 1991; OU, 1992; Babies, 1992; Razzmatazz, 1993; Lipgloss, 1993; Do You Remember The First Time?, 1994; The Sisters (EP), 1994; Common People (No. 2, UK), 1995; Sorted For E's and Whizz/ Misshapes (No. 2, UK), 1995; Disco 2000, 1995; Something Changed, 1996; Help The Aged, 1997; This Is Hardcore, 1998; A Little Soul, 1998; Party Hard, 1998; The Trees/Sunrise, 2001; Bad Cover Version, 2002. *Website:* www .pulponline.com.

MACKIE, Richard James; British composer, artistic director and musician (keyboards, saxophone); b. 6 Jan. 1960, Bolton, Lancashire; m. Christine Anne Waterhouse 1985; two d. *Education:* Laban Centre for Movement and Dance. *Career:* member of bands including The Surgical Support Band, The Pharaohs, The Selecter; extensive tours in UK and Europe; replacement keyboard player for Madness; appearances at Montreux Pop Festival and Saturday Night Live in New York; many compositions for dance and dance theatre. *Recordings:* albums and single with The Selecter.

McKINNA, Iain; British producer, musician (guitar, bass, keyboards), songwriter, recording engineer and programmer; *Head Producer, Offbeat;* b. 27 Jan. 1955, Kilmarnock, Scotland; one s. *Career:* recording engineer 1977–; first production released 1993; engineer, Bay City Rollers 1984; own band, The Harmonics; Prod., Solas, Talitha MacKenzie 1994; album by Mike Heron 1996; concerts include as guitarist with Flying Colours, Level 42 tour 1982; toured with Talitha MacKenzie's band as guitarist; support Runrig 1993; WOMAD '94; Womex, Berlin 1994; Edinburgh Festival; bass player with Jimi McRae Band, concerts included Edinburgh Festival 2001, T in the Park Festival 2002–05, Beijing Spring Festival 2005; also played in Netherlands, Spain, Canada; Head Producer, Offbeat music production co.; mem. PRS, MCPS. *Recordings:* as producer, session musician, computer programmer: Solas, Talitha MacKenzie 1994; Nectarine No. 9; Spoonfed Hybrid, Hamed Kane, Jimi McRae Band, Tam White; Royal Scots Dragoon Guards, Spirit of the Glen 2007; as composer and producer: Fulgor. *Honours:* Music in Scotland Trust Award for Best Song (with The Harmonics) 1993. *Current Management:* Offbeat Scotland, 107 High Street, Royal Mile, Edinburgh, EH1 1SW,

Scotland. *Telephone:* (131) 556-4882 (office). *E-mail:* iain@offbeat.co.uk (office). *Website:* www.offbeat.co.uk (office).

MacKINTOSH, Andrew Kenneth; British musician (saxophone); b. 20 May 1953, London, England; m. Bonnie Sue 1975; one s. *Career:* played with Maynard Ferguson, Buddy Rich, Quincy Jones, James Last; involved in studio work in London; mem. PRS; Musicians' Union. *Recordings:* appeared on recordings by Paul McCartney, Elton John, Bill Wyman, Elaine Paige, Melissa Manchester, Amy Winehouse.

MACKINTOSH, Gregor; British musician (guitar); b. 20 June 1970, Halifax, West Yorkshire, England; m. 1st Mandy Taylor 1995 (divorced 2003); one d. one s.; m. 2nd Heather Thompson 2004. *Career:* festivals include Rockamring, Dynamo, Roskilde; worldwide tours, television and radio broadcasts; soundtrack for Clarion Audio advertisements; mem. PRS, Musicians' Union. *Recordings include:* albums: Icon, Draconian Times, Host 1999, Believe In Nothing 2001, Symbol of Life 2002, Paradise Lost 2005. *Honours:* Kerrang Award and MTV Best Video (both for Embers Fire) 1994. *Address:* c/o Northern Music, 43 Cheapside Chambers, Cheapside, Bradford, West Yorkshire, England (office). *Telephone:* (1274) 306361 (office). *Fax:* (1274) 730097 (office). *E-mail:* info@northernmusic.co.uk (office). *Website:* www .northernmusic.co.uk (office).

MACKLEMORE; American rapper; b. (Ben Haggerty), 19 June 1983, Seattle, Wash.; m. Tricia Davis 2015; one d. *Education:* Evergreen State Coll. *Career:* released debut EP (as Professor Macklemore) 2000; collaborations with Ryan Lewis 2008–. *Recordings include:* solo: The Language of My World 2005, The Unplanned Mixtape 2009; with Ryan Lewis: The VS. EP 2009, The Heist (American Music Award for Best Album 2013, Grammy Award for Best Rap Album 2014) 2012. *Honours:* with Ryan Lewis: BET Award for Best Group 2013, Billboard Music Awards for Rap Song of the Year (for Thrift Shop) 2013, (for Can't Hold Us) 2014, MTV Video Music Awards for Best Hip-Hop Video (for Can't Hold Us) 2013, for Best Video with a Message (for Same Love) 2013, for Best New Act 2013, mtvU Branching Out Woodie Award 2013, MuchMusic Video Award for Int. Video of the Year – Group (for Thrift Shop) 2013, Teen Choice Music Awards for Hip-Hop/Rap Artist 2013, for R&B/Hip-Hop Track (for Can't Hold Us) 2013, American Music Award for Favorite Rap/Hip-Hop Artist 2013, Grammy Awards for Best Rap Performance, for Best Rap Song (both for Thrift Shop) 2014, for Best New Artist 2014, MTV Europe Music Award for Best Video (for Downtown) 2015. *Current Management:* Zach Quillen, The Agency Group Ltd., 142 West 57th Street, 6th Floor, New York, NY 10019, USA. *Telephone:* (212) 581-3100. *Fax:* (212) 581-0015. *E-mail:* zachquillen@theagencygroup.com. *Website:* www.theagencygroup.com; www .macklemore.com.

MACKNESS, Vanessa; British painter and singer; b. Fordingbridge, Christchurch, England; one s. one d. *Education:* Camberwell School of Art, Univ. of London. *Career:* played with artists, including Derek Bailey, Barry Guy, Alexander Balanescu, Nishat Khan, Paul Lovens, Phil Minton; concert tours; duo with Barry Guy, Taktlos Festival, Switzerland 1990; Irma, (opera, USA, UK) 1992; 10th-anniversary Minton-Weston Makhno Project, Bern, Basel, Zürich, Taktlos Festival, Switzerland 1993; solo performance, Total Music Meeting, Berlin 1993; soloist, Reiner Korff's composition for 35 musicians, Peter Edel Festival, Berlin 1994; Jazz and More Festival '95, Munich, with Minton/Weston's Natural Formations 1995; formed trio with Butcher and Durrant, duo with John Butcher 1996; duo with Phil Minton 1991; mem. PRS. *Recordings include:* Company '91, with Alexander Balanescu, Derek Bailey, Paul Lovens, Paul Rogers, John Zorn, Buckethead; Respirtus, duo with John Butcher.

McLACHLAN, Sarah, OC; Canadian singer, songwriter and musician; b. 28 Jan. 1968; m. Ashwin Sood. *Education:* Nova Scotia Coll. of Art and Design. *Career:* signed recording contract with Nettwerk records 1987; collaborations with artists including Darryl 'DMC' McDaniels, Stevie Nicks, Delerium, Bryan Adams, Annie Lennox, Cyndi Lauper; f. Lilith Fair tour for female musicians to help launch the careers of female artists; raised more than $7 million for charities; f. Sarah McLachlan Foundation to promote access to music and arts for young people, launched Sarah McLachlan Music Outreach project 2003. *Recordings:* albums: Touch 1988, Solace 1991, Fumbling Towards Ecstasy 1993, The Freedom Sessions 1994, Rarities, B-Sides And Other Stuff 1996, Surfacing 1997, Mirrorball 1999, Sarah McLachlan Remixed 2001, Afterglow 2003, Afterglow Live 2004, Bloom Remix Album 2005, Wintersong 2006, Laws of Illusion 2010, Shine On (Juno Award for Adult Contemporary Album of the Year 2015) 2014. *Honours:* Order of BC 2001, Kiwanis Int. World Service Medal 2013; Hon. DIur (Univ. of Alberta) 2013 winner of Juno Awards for Best Music Video (for Into the Fire) 1992, Female Vocalist of the Year, Songwriter of the Year (with Pierre Marchand), Single of the Year (for Building A Mystery) and Album of the Year (for Surfacing) 1998, Pop Album of the Year (for Afterglow) 2000, Int. Achievement Award and Songwriter of the Year (with Pierre Marchand) 2004; Grammy Awards for Best Pop Instrumental Performance (for Last Dance) 1997, Best Female Pop Vocal Performance (for Building A Mystery) 1997, (for I Will Remember You) 1999; Elizabeth Cady Stanton Visionary Award 1998. *Website:* www.sarahmclachlan.com.

McLAUGHLIN, David Wallace; American musician (guitar, piano, mandolin, violin, bass, drums, percussion, banjo); b. 13 Feb. 1958, Washington DC; m. Marilyn Gay Harman; one d. *Education:* private music lessons. *Career:* musician 1978–; mem., The Johnson Mountain Boys; mem., Crowe and

McLaughlin; performances at venues, including Carnegie Hall, Lincoln Centre, White House, Madison Square Garden, Library of Congress, Wolf Trap, Grand Ole Opry, Ambassador Auditorium, Knoxville Worlds Fair; numerous TV appearances, tours worldwide; numerous credits on recordings by artists including Hazel Dickens, James King, The McCoury Brothers, Lynn Morris, Tony Trischka; mem. IBMA, WAMA, BMI. *Recordings include:* with The Johnson Mountain Boys: Walls of Time 1981, Working Close 1982, Live At The Birchmere 1983, We'll Still Sing On 1984, Let The Whole World Talk 1985, Play Requests 1986, At The Old School House 1988, Blue Diamond 1990; with Crowe and McLaughlin: Going Back On Rounder. *Honours:* awards from IBMA, SPBGMA, WAMA. *Current Management:* Shepherd Productions, 512 Marion Street, Winchester, VA 22601, USA.

McLAUGHLIN, Dermot, BA, MSc; Irish musician (fiddle); b. 17 Aug. 1961, Derry, County Derry. *Education:* Trinity Coll., Dublin. *Career:* Nat. Concert Hall, Dublin; frequent radio and television appearances in Ireland; concert tours and performances in Ireland, UK, Europe, Nova Scotia; record prod. for Claddagh Records, specialist Irish label; Music Officer for the Arts Council, Dublin; External Examiner in traditional music performance, Univ. of Limerick 2005–. *Publications:* Strad 1991, O Riada Lecture (Univ. Coll., Cork), Claddagh and Nimbus Records. *Honours:* Foundation Scholar of Trinity Coll., Dublin 1981–86. *Website:* dermotmclaughlinmusic.com.

McLAUGHLIN, John; British jazz musician (guitar); b. 4 Jan. 1942, Yorks., England. *Career:* played with Alexis Korner, Georgie Fame, Graham Bond, Gunter Hampel; played and recorded with John Surman, Dave Holland; mem. Tony Williams' band Lifetime 1969–70; as solo artist, recorded with Charlie Haden, Airto Moreira, Miles Davis; Founder Mahavishnu Orchestra (with Billy Cobham, Jerry Goodman, Jan Hammer, later with Jean-Luc Ponty, Michael Walden) 1971–75, 1984–86; Founder Shakti with Indian musicians L. Shankar and Zakir Hussain 1975–78; Founder One Truth Band 1979; formed trio with Larry Coryell and Paco De Lucia 1978; mem. The Translators 1991–92; Founder Free Spirits 1993–95, Heart of Things 1997–99, The 4th Dimension 2007–12, (touring) 2015–; Co-founder (with Chick Corea), Five Peace Band 2008, Remember Shatki 2010. *Compositions include:* Mediterranean Concerto, Thieves and Poets. *Recordings:* albums include: Extrapolation 1969, Devotion 1970, My Goals Beyond 1970, Inner Mounting Flame 1972, When Fortune Smiles 1972, Love Devotion Surrender 1972, Birds of Fire 1973, Between Nothingness and Eternity 1973, The Lost Trident Session 1973, Apocalypse 1974, Visions To The Emerald Beyond 1974, Inner Worlds 1975, Shakti 1976, Natural Elements 1977, A Handful of Beauty 1977, Electric Guitarist 1978, Electric Dreams 1979, Friday Night In San Francisco 1980, Passion, Grace and Fire 1982, Music Spoken Here 1982, Mahavishnu 1984, Belo Horizonte 1984, Adventures in Radioland 1986, Mediterranean 1988, Live At The Royal Festival Hall 1990, Greatest Hits 1991, Que Alegria 1992, Time Remembered 1993, Tokyo Live 1994, Mclaughlin and Santana 1994, After The Rain 1994, The Promise 1995, The Heart of Things 1997, Remember Shakti 1999, The Believer 2000, Saturday Night in Bombay 2001, Collection 2002, Thieves and Poets 2003, This is the way I do it 2004, Improvisations 2005, Industrial Zen 2006, Floating Point 2008, Five Peace Band – Live (with Chick Corea) (Grammy Award for Best Jazz Instrumental Album 2010) 2009, To the One 2010, Now Here This 2012, The Boston Live 2013, Black Light 2015. *Current Management:* c/o Musikbüro Gert Pfankuch, Alter Fischbacher Weg 8A 65817 Eppstein, Germany. *Telephone:* (6198) 5876284. *E-mail:* pfankuch@aol.com; info@musikbuero-pfankuch.de. *Website:* www.musikbuero-pfankuch.de. *E-mail:* contact@johnmclaughlin.com (home). *Website:* www.mediastarz.com (office); www.johnmclaughlin.com.

McLEAN, Alexander James; American singer and musician (bass guitar); b. 9 Jan. 1978, West Palm Beach, Fla. *Career:* puppeteer, Welcome Freshmen (Nickelodeon TV channel); mem., Backstreet Boys 1993–; numerous tours and television appearances. *Recordings include:* albums: Backstreet Boys 1996, Live in Concert 1998, Backstreet's Back 1998, Millennium 1999, Black And Blue 2000, Greatest Hits Chapter 1 2001, Never Gone 2005, Unbreakable 2007, This Is Us 2009, In A World Like This 2013. *Honours:* Billboard Music Awards for Best Group, Best Adult Contemporary Group 1998, Album of the Year, Artist of the Year 1999, MTV Music Video Award for Best Group Video 1998, MTV European Music Awards for Best Pop Act 1997, Best Group 1999, World Music Awards for Best-Selling Pop Group 1999, 2000, Best-Selling R&B Group 1999, 2000, Best-Selling Dance Group 1999, 2000, Best American Group 2000, American Music Awards for Favorite Pop/Rock Band, Duo or Group 2000, 2001. *Website:* ajmclean.com; www.backstreetboys.com.

McLEAN, Don; American singer, instrumentalist and composer; b. 2 Oct. 1945, New Rochelle, NY; s. of Donald McLean and Elizabeth Bucci; m. Patrisha Shnier 1987; one s. one d. *Education:* Iona Coll. *Career:* Pres. Benny Bird Publishing Corpn, Inc., Don McLean Music, Starry Night Music; mem. Hudson River Sloop Singers 1969; solo concert tours throughout USA, Canada, Australia, Europe, Far East etc.; numerous TV appearances; composer of film scores for Fraternity Row, Flight of Dragons; composer of over 200 songs including Prime Time, American Pie, Tapestry, Vincent (Starry, Starry Night), And I Love You So, Castles In the Air, etc.; mem. American Soc. of Composers, Authors and Publrs, BMI Broadcast Music, Inc. (BMI), Nat. Acad. of Recording Arts and Sciences, American Fed. of Television and Radio Artists, Lotos Club, Coffee House NYC, Groucho Club, London. *Recordings include:* albums: Tapestry 1970, American Pie 1971, Don McLean 1972, Playin' Favorites 1973, Homeless Brother 1974, Solo 1976, Prime Time 1977, Chain Lightning 1979, Believers 1982, Dominion 1983, Love Tracks

1988, Headroom 1991, Don McLean Christmas 1992, Favorites and Rarities (Box Set) 1993, The River of Love 1995, For the Memories Vols I and II 1996, Christmas Dreams 1997, Starry Starry Night 2000, Don McLean Sings Marty Robbins 2001, The Western Album 2003, You've Got to Share 2003, Christmastime! 2004, Rearview Mirror 2005, Addicted to Black 2009; singles include: The Mountains of Mourne 1973, Wonderful Baby 1975, Crying 1980, Since I Don't Have You 1981; hit cover versions: And I Love You So (Perry Como) 1973, American Pie (Madonna) 2000; compilation albums: The Very Best of Don McLean 1980, Don McLean's Greatest Hits – Then & Now 1987, The Best of Don McLean 1991, Favorites and Rarities 1992, Legendary Songs of Don McLean 2003, The Legendary Don McLean 2007, American Pie & Other Hits 2008. *Publications:* Songs of Don McLean 1972, The Songs of Don McLean (Vol. II) 1974. *Honours:* Dr hc (Iona Coll.) 2001; recipient of numerous gold discs in USA, Australia, UK and Ireland; Israel Cultural Award 1981, American Pie inducted into Grammy Hall of Fame 2002, inaugurated into Songwriters Hall of Fame 2004, American Pie named by New York City radio station Q104.3 FM WAXQ No. 37 in their Top 1,043 Songs Of All Time 2008, Lifetime Achievement Award for Folk Music, BBC Radio 2 2012. *Current Management:* c/o Guy Richard, 1880 Century Park East, Suite 711, Los Angeles, CA 90067, USA. *Telephone:* (310) 385-2800. *Fax:* (310) 385-1220. *E-mail:* guyrichard@theagencygroup.com. *Website:* www.theagencygroup .com; www.don-mclean.com.

MACLEAN, Dougie, OBE; British folk singer, songwriter, musician (guitar, violin, bass guitar, banjo) and record producer; b. 27 Sept. 1954, Dunblane, Scotland; m. Jennifer MacLean; one s. one d. *Career:* mem. Tannahill Weavers 1976; performed with Alan Roberts and Alex Campbell 1978–79; mem. Silly Wizard 1980; solo career 1981–; f. own record label Dunkeld Records 1983; Founder and organiser, Perthshire Amber Festival, Perthshire, Scotland 2005; numerous tours and festival appearances. *Recordings:* with Tannahill Weavers: Are Ye Sleeping Maggie 1976; with Alan Roberts: Caledonia 1978; with Alex Campbell and Alan Roberts: CRM 1979; solo: Snaigow 1980, On a Wing and a Prayer 1981, Craigie Dhu 1982, Butterstone 1983, Fiddle 1984, Singing Land 1985, Real Estate 1988, Whitewash 1990, The Search 1990, Indigenous 1991, Sunset Song 1994, Marching Mystery 1994, Tribute 1996, Riof 1997, Perthshire Amber 2000, Who Am I 2002, Inside the Thunder 2006, Muir of Gormack 2007, Resolution 2010, Till Tomorrow 2014. *Honours:* BBC Radio 2 Folk Lifetime Achievement Award for Contribution to Songwriting 2013. *Current Management:* c/o Butterstone Management and Events, The Old Schoolhouse, Butterstone, Dunkeld, Perthshire, PH8 0HA, Scotland. *Telephone:* (1350) 724281. *Fax:* (1350) 724261. *E-mail:* admin@butterstone .com. *Website:* www.dougiemaclean.com (home).

McLELLAN, Nora; Canadian actress and singer; b. 29 Oct. 1955, Vancouver, BC; d. of Godfrey and Jeanne McClelland. *Education:* Univ. of British Columbia and HB Studio, New York, USA. *Career:* stage debut aged eight, Vancouver Opera; actor with Canadian Theatre 1967–2011, with Shaw Festival Theatre, Stratford Festival of Canada, and at numerous Canadian and US theatres; co-f. AIDS Relief Fundraising (ARF) for Actors' Fund of Canada 1987; worked with Habitat for Humanity in Louisiana after Hurricane Katrina; worked in Vancouver for the Winter Olympics 2010; Founding mem. Theatre 20, Toronto. *Performances include:* La Bohème, A Respectable Wedding, Overruled, The Magistrate, Saint Joan, See How They Run, The Singular Life of Albert Nobbs, Candida, The Simpleton of the Unexpected Isles, Skin of Our Teeth, The Women, Cavalcade, Arms and the Man, Back to Methuselah, Peter Pan, Anything Goes, Julius Caesar, Scrooge, A Doll's House, Godspell, Lovers, You're a Good Man Charlie Brown, Jacques Brel is Alive and Well and Living in Paris, A Bistro Car, Starting Here Starting Now, Uncle Vanya, Harry's Back in Town, Children, Pinocchio, Time and the Conways, Road (Jessie Award), Who's Afraid of Virginia Woolf (Jessie Award) 1997, Hello Dolly! 1998, Music for Contortionist, Tarragon Theatre (Dora Mavor Moore Award) 2000, Gypsy 2005, A Little Night Music, Arms and the Man, The Heiress (all at Shaw Festival) 2006, Oklahoma and Pentacost, Stratford Festival 2007, Cabaret and Trojan Woman, Stratford Festival 2008, The Drowsy Chaperone, Vancouver Playhouse 2008, For the Pleasure of Seeing Her Again, Persephone Theatre 2009, Dirty Rotten Scoundrels, Theatre Calgary 2009. *Films:* Tart 2001, A Pair of Red Shorts, Dangerous Offender, Double Double Toil and Trouble. *Radio:* Away by Jane Urquart, numerous CBC radio plays. *Television includes:* My Own Country 1998, Dangerous Offender, The X Files. *Honours:* three Jessie Richardson Awards, Vancouver Sun Readers' Choice Award. *Current Management:* c/o Steve Young & Associates, 18 Gloucester Lane, 2nd Floor, Toronto, ON M4Y 1L5, Canada. *Telephone:* (416) 972-1046. *Fax:* (416) 972-1776. *Address:* PO Box 353, Niagara-on-the-Lake, ON L0S 1J0, Canada. *E-mail:* noramclellan@yahoo .com.

MacLEOD, James; British musician (guitar, bass guitar), singer, composer and lyricist; b. 19 Aug. 1974, Sutton Coldfield, West Midlands. *Education:* King Edward VI School, Lichfield. *Career:* bass guitarist for Birmingham four-piece band, The Cantels 1991; performances incl. Birmingham Hummingbird club; as guitarist, performed national BBC Radio sessions and residencies at Ronnie Scott's Club, Birmingham, with Lou Dalgliesh Band 1993; composer 1990s; founder, with Martin Betts, alternative power pop band, The Macleods 1998–, performing throughout UK; mem. Musicians' Union.

McLEOD, Rory; British singer, songwriter, poet, storyteller and musician (harmonica, guitar, trombone, percussion); b. 23 Jan. 1955, London, England; s. of Lewis McLeod and Shirley McLeod; two s. *Career:* ex-circus clown and fire eater; plays solo orchestra of distinctive instruments, the spoons, finger-cymbals, bandorea, Djembe-drum, harmonica, guitar, trombone and tap-dancing shoes; melodies are infused with influences from Flamenco to blues, through to Celtic, East European and Calypso rhythms; has played harmonica and guitar with Michelle Shocked, Ani Di Franco, Butch Hancock, Michael Franti, Townes van Zandt, with the West-African guitarist Ali Farka Touré, with Taj Mahal and Madagascan group Tarika; also collaborated with Hassan Eerraji (Moroccan Oud), Kathryn Tickell (Northumbrian pipes) and Paul Rodden (Irish banjo) and B. J. Cole (pedal steel guitar); has written songs and music for a BBC Radio 4 documentary (oral history project about East London's 400-year-old Spitalfields fruit and vegetable market); commissioned by Scottish dance and circus theatre-based co. Shiftwork to devise psycho-comedy theatre show based on traditional Punch and Judy puppet play; also commissioned to write music for TV animation series 'Creature Comforts' 2003, songs and music for Scottish Tabularasa Dance Co., dance-theatre piece for Children called 'Huff Puff and Away' about Wind and Breath, songs and music about Hadrian's Wall, collaborating with other poets, musicians and writers 2010–11; commissioned to compose songs for projects about convicts transported to Australia 2011; regularly plays with his band The Familiar Strangers, featuring Colombian harp, clarinet/sax, double bass, singing and playing a different repertoire of songs and tunes; various self-made scratch videos to show with his songs. *Plays:* Burston School Strike, The Powercut, The Stray Ones. *Exhibition:* Photo Competition Winner with Portrait and Montage, Camberwell 1975. *Radio:* BBC's Pick of The Week for his 'Invoking The Spirits' (recording of a personal musical journey through Zimbabwe, searching for the Mbira—African thumb piano) 1996, playing and talking with African musicians for BBC Radio 4 1996, took part in Bob Dylan birthday tribute (BBC Radio 2), rewriting and resetting an old Henry Thomas song that Dylan covered and also rewrote 2011. *Television:* has appeared on Channel 4 arts programme After Image and on Welsh TV's Television Ballads. *Recordings:* albums (self-produced): Angry Love 1985, Kicking The Sawdust 1986, Footsteps and Heartbeats 1989, Travelling Home 1992, Lullabies For Big Babies 1997, Mouth to Mouth 2000, Brave Faces 2005, Songs for Big Little People 2007, Swings and Roundabouts 2010. *Publications:* Apples and Snakes (poetry anthology), The Parrot Whisperer (tragi-comic novella), also self-published children's stories. *Honours:* Texas Harmonica Champion 1981, Edinburgh Festival Street Busker of the Year 1985, Best Live Act, BBC Radio 2 Folk Awards 2002. *Current Management:* c/o Dan Ashton (UK bookings), Ashkeys Music, 24 Camelford Road, Greenbank, Bristol, BS5 6HW, England. *Telephone:* (117) 935-5474. *E-mail:* dan@ashkeysmusic.com. *Current Management:* c/o Chris Wade (int. bookings). *E-mail:* chris.wade@adastra-music.co .uk. *Address:* Talkative Music, Whitelaw House, Earlside, Hawick, Scottish Borders, TD9 9SE, Scotland. *Telephone:* (117) 935-5474. *E-mail:* kish@ rorymcleod.com (office); info@rorymcleod.com (office); talkativemusic@dial .pipex.com. *Website:* www.rorymcleod.com.

McLIN, Lena Johnson, BMus; American composer, teacher, author and minister of religion; *Pastor, Holy Vessel Baptist Church*; b. 5 Sept. 1928, Chicago, Ill. *Education:* Booker T. Washington High School, Atlanta, Ga Spelman Coll., Atlanta, American Conservatory of Music, Chicago, Roosevelt Univ., Chicago and Chicago State Univ. *Career:* choral conductor for various community, school and church groups from 1951; accompanist Thomas Dorsey Choir, Pilgrim Baptist Church, Chicago 1952–53; founder and Dir, McLin Ensemble 1957–68; Minister of Music, Trinity Congregational Church, Chicago 1960s; Founder and Pastor, Holy Vessel Christian Center, Chicago 1980–; teacher, Julius H. Hess Upper Grade Center, Chicago 1959–60, Gurdon S. Hubbard High School, Chicago 1960–63, John Marshall Harlan Community Acad. High School, Chicago 1963–70; Head of Music Dept, Kenwood Acad., Chicago 1970–91; held choral workshops throughout USA; consultant, Westminster Choir Coll., Princeton, NJ. *Compositions include:* Impressions for piano 1957, And she Took a Ring and Placed it on his Finger 1963, A Summer Day for piano 1970, Free at Last: A Portrait of Martin Luther King Jr 1973, If I Could Give You All I Have 1986, Silence 1987, The Unlucky Apple 1987, My Love 1993, Christmas in Space 1997; choral music: All the Earth Sing Unto the Lord 1967, The Earth is the Lord's 1969, I Want Jesus to Walk With Me 1969, So Stands a College Tall of Higher Learning 1970, In This World 1970, The Colors of the Rainbow 1971, I am Somebody 1971, If They Ask You Why He Came 1971, If we Could Exchange Places 1971, I'm Moving Up 1971, We've Just Got to Have Peace All Over This World 1971, What Will You Put Under Your Christmas Tree? 1971, The Torch has been Passed 1971, For Jesus Christ is Born 1971, Psalm 100: Make a Joyful Noise 1971, Sanctus and Benedictus 1971, Psalm 117: Praise the Lord, All Ye Nations 1971, The Little Baby 1971, You and I Together 1971, Friendship 1972, Gwendolyn Brooks: A Musical Portrait 1972, New Born King 1972, Eucharist of the Soul 1972, Let the People Sing Praise Unto the Lord 1973, Winter, Spring, Summer, Autumn 1974, Memory 1976, Since He Came into my Life 1976, Challenge 1976, The Love of God 1976, Te Deum Laudamus 1976, This Land 1976, Christmas Time is Here Again 1978, Now that we are Leaving 1978, Two Introits 1978, Noel 1979, Reach Up! 1987, Introits and Responses for Worship 1990, Take Life's Challenge 1997, Makers of History 1998. *Publications:* Black Music in Church and School 1970, Pulse: A History of Music 1977; other published works include: Songs for Voice and Piano (collection of Art songs, Spirituals, and folk songs for solo voice and piano), The Christmas Cantata, The Church Cantata Songs: Don't Stop the World, When It's My Turn to Get On (light song), Follow Your First Mind, It's Usually Right Most of the Time (light song), I'm in Love, I'm Gonna Make it Anyway, I'll Be Your Friend, The Stoning of Stephen (cantata for male voices and male choirs only), Out of the Depths (anthem), Journey of Praise (instrumental march for orchestra). *Honours:* Nat. Black Music Caucus Outstanding Achievement Award 1980, Univ. of Chicago Outstanding Teacher Award 1983; scholarship American Conservatory of Music, Chicago 1951. *Address:* 6901 South Oglesby Street, Apartment 4A, Chicago, IL 60649-1827, USA (office). *Telephone:* (773) 493-3439 (office).

McLORIN SALVANT, Cécile; French/American jazz singer; b. 28 Aug. 1989, Miami, Fla, USA. *Education:* Darius Milhaud Conservatory, Aix-en-Provence. *Career:* studied voice with Edward Walker in Miami; relocated to Aix-en-Provence, France 2007–10; numerous jazz festival appearances. *Recordings:* albums: Cécile 2010, WomanChild 2013, For One to Love (Grammy Award for Best Jazz Vocal Album 2016) 2015; other appearances: Gouache, Jacky Terrasson 2012. *Honours:* winner, Thelonious Monk Competition, Washington, DC 2010, Jazz Journalists' Asscn Awards for Up and Coming Artist of the Year 2015, for Female Singer of the Year 2015. *Current Management:* c/o Edward C. Arrendell II, The Management Ark, Inc., 3 Bethesda Metro Center, Suite 700, Bethesda, MD 20814; c/o Laurel Wicks, Ted Kurland Associates, Inc., 173 Brighton Avenue, Boston, MA 02134-2003, USA. *E-mail:* ed@mngtark.com; laurel@tedkurland.com. *Website:* www .managementark.com; www.tedkurland.com. *E-mail:* cecilejazz@gmail.com (home). *Website:* cecilemclorinsalvant.com (home).

McMANUS, John Patrick, (Spudsy); Northern Irish musician (bass, low whistle) and composer; b. (John Patrick Ignatius McManus), 24 March 1961, Enniskillen, Northern Ireland; s. of John McManus and Valerie McManus; m. Lindy McManus 1996. *Career:* All-Ulster champion on tin whistle aged 7–12; formed rock band Mama's Boys with brothers Pat and Tommy; numerous TV appearances; Mama's Boys disbanded 1993 (owing to Tom McManus's leukaemia—Tom died 1994); formed new act Celtus with brother Pat 1995; manager/wife Lindy signed them to Muff Winwood, Sony S2 1996; debut performance dates for Celtus as support act to Sheryl Crow at Royal Albert Hall, Wolverhampton Civic and Manchester Apollo; tours followed with Paul Carrack; played Womad Festival; mem. Performing Right Soc., Musicians' Union. *Recordings:* with Mama's Boys: Official Bootleg, Plug It In, Turn It Up, Mama's Boys, Power and Passion, Growing Up The Hard Way, Live Tonite, Relativity; with Celtus: Moonchild (Irish World Award 1998) 1997, Portrait 1999, Live 2000 2001, What Goes Around 2001. *Current Management:* c/o Lindy McManus, Shamrock Music Ltd, 9 Thornton Place, London, W1H 1FG, England. *Telephone:* (20) 7935-9719. *Fax:* (20) 7935-0241. *E-mail:* lindy@celtus.demon.co.uk. *Website:* www.johnmcmanus.biz.

McMILLAN, Stuart; producer, remixer and DJ; b. 1966, Glasgow, Scotland. *Career:* started career as a DJ in Glasgow; met Orde Meikle and started putting on their own club nights, Atlantis and Slam; formed the Slam production duo and Soma Records label; world-wide DJ; collaborations with UNKLE; remixed Sunscreem, Mansun, Dave Angel, Phuture, Kym Sims, Underworld, Daft Punk, Dot Allison/Bryan Zentz; residencies at Pressure at the Arches, Glasgow and Fabric, London; mem. Universal Principles. *Recordings:* albums: Headstates 1996, Alien Radio, Past Lessons – Future Theories (DJ-mixed compilation) 2001, Fabric 9 (DJ mix) 2003, Human Response 2007. *Address:* c/o Soma Records, 342 Argyle Street, Glasgow, G2 8LA, Scotland. *Telephone:* (141) 229-6220. *Fax:* (141) 226-4383. *Website:* www .somarecords.com; www.slamevents.com.

McMURRAY, Rick; British musician (drums, percussion); b. 11 July 1975, Larne, Co. Antrim. *Career:* founder mem., Ash 1992–; numerous headline tours, UK festivals, television appearances and worldwide tours. *Recordings include:* albums: Trailer 1994, 1977 1996, Live At The Wireless 1997, Nu-Clear Sounds 1998, Free All Angels 2001, Cosmic Debris 2002, Intergalactic Sonic 7"s: The Best of Ash 2002, Meltdown 2004, Twilight of the Innocents 2007. *Honours:* NME BRAT Award for Best Single (for Burn Baby Burn) 2002, Q Award for Best Single (for Burn Baby Burn) 2002, Ivor Novello Award for Best Contemporary Song (for Shining Light) 2002. *Current Management:* Out There Management Ltd, Strong Room, 120–124 Curtain Road, London, EC2A 3SQ, England. *Telephone:* (20) 7739-6903. *Fax:* (20) 7613-2715. *E-mail:* outthere@outthere.co.uk. *Website:* www.ash-official.com.

McNABB, Ian; British singer and songwriter; b. 3 Nov. 1962, Liverpool; s. of Robert Gerard McNabb and Patricia Mavis Forsyth. *Career:* founder mem., Icicle Works 1980–90; founder, own record label, Fairfield; solo artist 1992–; mem., The Waterboys 2000–02. *Recordings include:* albums: with Icicle Works: Icicle Works 1984, The Small Price Of A Bicycle 1985, Understanding Jane 1986, If You Want To Defeat Your Enemy Sing His Song 1987, Blind 1987, Permanent Damage 1990; solo: Truth And Beauty 1992, Head Like A Rock 1994, My Own Way: The Words and Music of Ian McNabb 1997, Merseybeast 1996, A Party Political Broadcast On Behalf Of The Emotional Party 1998, Live At Life 2000, Ian McNabb 2001, Waifs And Strays 2001, The Gentleman Adventurer 2002, Before All Of This 2005. *E-mail:* ian@ianmcnabb.com (home). *Website:* www.ianmcnabb.com.

McNALLY, John; British entertainer and musician (guitar); b. 30 Aug. 1941, Liverpool, England; m. Mary Hollywood 1964; one s. one d. *Career:* mem., The Searchers; numerous television and live appearances. *Recordings include:* Sweets For My Sweet 1963, Sugar And Spice 1963, Needles and Pins 1964, Don't Throw Your Love Away 1964, When You Walk In The Room 1964, Goodbye My Love 1965. *Current Management:* Alan Field Associates, 3 The Spinney, Bakers Hill, Hadley Common, EN5 5BY, England. *Telephone:* (20) 8441-1137. *Fax:* (20) 8447-0657. *E-mail:* alanfielduk@aol.com.

McNALLY, Stephen Patrick; British singer, musician (guitar) and song-writer; b. 4 July 1978, Liverpool, England. *Career:* co-founder, BBMak pop group 1996–2003; signed to UK company Telstar; gained large US popularity after licence deal with Hollywood/Disney; supported Britney Spears on sell-out US tour followed by 28-date first headline US tour 2000, UK shows with The Corrs 2001. *Recordings:* albums: with BBMak: Sooner Or Later 2000, Into Your Head 2002. *E-mail:* ste@stemak.co.uk (office). *Website:* www.stemak.co .uk.

McNAMARA, Danny; British singer, songwriter and musician (guitar); b. 31 Dec. 1970, Huddersfield, England; brother of Richard McNamara. *Career:* mem., Embrace 1996–; headline tours and TV appearances. *Recordings include:* albums: The Good Will Out 1998, Drawn From Memory 2000, If You've Never Been 2001, Fireworks (Singles 1997–2002) 2002, Out Of Nothing 2004, This New Day 2006, Sleepy Sun 2009 Thick as Blood 2009. *E-mail:* tony@utdmgt.com. *Website:* www.embrace.co.uk.

McNAMARA, Richard; British musician (guitar) and singer; b. 23 Oct. 1972, Huddersfield; brother of Danny McNamara. *Career:* mem., Embrace 1996–; headline tours and TV appearances. *Recordings include:* albums: The Good Will Out 1998, Drawn From Memory 2000, If You've Never Been 2001, Fireworks (Singles 1997–2002) 2002, Out Of Nothing 2004, This New Day 2006. *Current Management:* c/o Tony Perrin, Coalition Management, Studio 2, 3A Brackenbury Road, London, W6 0BE, England. *Telephone:* (20) 8743-1000. *E-mail:* tp@coalitiongroup.co.uk. *Website:* www.coalitionmanagement.co.uk; www.embrace.co.uk.

McNEAL, Lutricia; American singer and songwriter; b. Oklahoma. *Career:* teamed up with Swedish production team Rob 'n' Raz 1991–94; solo career 1997–; numerous appearances in Europe, USA and Britain. *Recordings:* singles: Ain't That Just The Way, 1997; Someone Loves You Honey, 1998; Stranded, 1998; The Greatest Love You'll Never Know, 1998; 365, 1999; You'll Never Know, 2000; albums: My Side of Town 1997, Whatcha Been Doing? 1999, Metroplex 2002, Soulsister Ambassador 2004. *Website:* www .lutriciamcneal.net.

McNEELY, Joel; American composer; b. Madison, WI; m. Margaret Batjer; two c. *Education:* Interlochen Arts Acad., Univ. of Miami, Eastman School of Music. *Career:* mem. ASCAP. *Compositions for television:* Davy Crockett: Rainbow in the Thunder 1988, Splash, Too 1988, Parent Trap III 1989, Parent Trap Hawaiian Honeymoon 1989, Tiny Toon Adventures 1990, Appearances 1990, Frankenstein: The College Years 1991, Lady Against the Odds 1992, The Young Indiana Jones Chronicles (series) (Emmy Award) 1992, Buffalo Soldiers 1997, Buddy Faro 1998, Road Rage 1999, Sally Hemings: An American Scandal 1999, Santa Who? 2000, Dark Angel (series) 2000, All Souls (series) 2001, The Court (series) 2002, American Dad! 2009–10. *Compositions for film:* You Talkin' to Me? 1987, Polly 1989, Samantha 1991, Squanto: A Warrior's Tale 1994, Iron Will 1994, Terminal Velocity 1994, Radioland Murders 1994, Gold Diggers: The Secret of Bear Mountain 1995, Flipper 1996, Supercop 1996, Vegas Vacation 1997, Wild America 1997, Air Force One (additional music) 1997, The Avengers 1998, Soldier 1998, Virus 1999, Lover's Prayer 2000, All Forgotten 2000, Return to Neverland 2002, Ghosts of the Abyss 2003, Holes 2003, Uptown Girls 2003, Stateside 2004, America's Heart and Soul 2004, Pooh's Heffalump Movie 2005, I Know Who Killed Me 2007, Tinker Bell 2008, Tinker Bell and the Lost Treasure 2009, Tinker Bell and the Great Fairy Rescue 2010. *E-mail:* info@joelmcneely.com. *Website:* www.joelmcneely.com.

McNEW, James; American musician (bass guitar). *Career:* fmr mem. Christmas; joined Yo La Tengo 1992, have since released numerous albums and embraced many styles including indie rock, acoustic, noise, experimental, punk; frequent tours throughout USA and worldwide; collaborations with Yoko Ono, Jad Fair, Ray Davies, Robyn Hitchcock, Neil Innes, mems of the Sun Ra Arkestra; worked on soundtracks for several films; annual appearances on WFMU charity fund-raising radio show playing impromptu cover versions as requested by listeners; solo side-project, Dump. *Film soundtracks:* The Sounds of the Sounds of Science 2001, Junebug 2005, Game 6 2005, Shortbus 2006, Old Joy 2006. *Recordings:* albums: May I Sing with Me 1992, Painful 1993, Electr-O-Pura 1995, I Can Hear the Heart Beating as One 1997, Strange But True (with Jad Fair) 1998, And Then Nothing Turned Itself Inside Out 2000, The Sounds of the Sounds of Science 2002, Summer Sun 2003, Prisoners Of Love: A Smattering Of Scintillating Senescent Songs, 1985–2003 2005, I Am Not Afraid of You and I Will Beat Your Ass 2006, Yo La Tengo Is Murdering the Classics 2006, Popular Songs 2009. *Address:* PO Box 6028, Hoboken, NJ 07030, USA (office). *E-mail:* info@yolatengo.com (office). *Website:* www.yolatengo.com (office).

McPHERSON, Graham 'Suggs'; British singer; b. 13 Jan. 1961, Hastings, Sussex, England; m. Bette Bright 1982. *Career:* mem., Madness 1977–86, re-formed sporadically to perform and record albums; numerous tours and live appearances 1992–; solo artist 1988–; regular comedy host, Mean Fiddler Club, North London; Man., The Farm; musical based on Madness songs, Our House (West End, London) 2002–03. *Television:* presenter Night Fever (TV quiz, Channel 5) 1997, team captain A Question of Pop (BBC 1) 2000–01. *Film appearances:* Dance Craze 1981, Take It Or Leave It 1981, Madstock—The Movie 1992. *Recordings include:* albums: with Madness: One Step Beyond 1979, Absolutely 1980, Seven 1981, Complete Madness 1982, The Rise and Fall 1982, Madness 1983, Keep Moving 1984, Mad Not Mad 1985, Utter Madness 1986, Divine Madness 1992, Madstock! 1992, Wonderful 1999, The

Heavy Heavy Hits 1999, Our House: The Original Songs 2002, The Dangermen Sessions, Vol. 1 2005, The Liberty of Norton Folgate 2009; solo: The Lone Ranger 1995. *Publications:* That Close 2013. *Honours:* NME Singles Artists of the Year 1980, Ivor Novello Award for Best Pop Song 1983. *Current Management:* Hannah Management, Fulham Palace, London SW6 6EA, England. *Telephone:* (20) 7758-1494. *E-mail:* management@madness.co.uk. *E-mail:* info@madness.co.uk (office). *Website:* www.madness.co.uk.

McRAE, Tom; British singer, musician (guitar) and songwriter; b. 1974, Suffolk, England. *Education:* Guildhall Univ., London. *Career:* formed band while at univ.; performed at events for unsigned artists in London; solo artist. *Recordings include:* albums: Tom McRae 2000, Just Like Blood 2003, All Maps Welcome 2005, King of Cards 2007, The Alphabet of Hurricanes 2010, From the Lowlands 2012. *Address:* Tom McRae Trading, POB 380, New Malden, KT3 4XG, England (office). *E-mail:* info@tommcrae.com (office). *Website:* www.tommcrae.com.

McSHERRY, John; musician (uilleann pipes, tin whistle, low whistle) and composer; b. 1970, Belfast, Northern Ireland. *Career:* formed Tamalin with brother Paul, cousin Kevin Dorris and sisters Tina and Joanne; Played in Donal Lunny's band Coolfin with Nollaig Casey, Sharon Shannon, Ray Fean and Graham Henderson; Part of Lunasa with Michael McGoldrick; Collaborations: Niamh Parsons; Nanci Griffith; Shaun Davey; Dan Ar Braz. *Recordings:* Albums: Rhythm and Rhyme (with Tamalin), 1997; Lunasa Live, Coolfin, 1998; At First Light (with Michael McGoldrick), 2001; features on: Loosely Connected (Niamh Parsons), 1992; Each Little Thing (Sharon Shannon), 1997; Waking Ned (Soundtrack), 1998; This Is My Father (Soundtrack), 1998; Blackbirds and Thrushes (Niamh Parsons), 1999. *Honours:* All Ireland Championship, three awards by age 15; Oireachtas Piping competition, youngest ever winner at 18. *Address:* c/o Vertical Records, 19 Woodside Crescent, Glasgow, G3 7UL, Scotland (office). *Telephone:* (141) 352-6670 (office). *E-mail:* info@verticalrecords.co.uk (office). *Website:* www.johnmcsherry.com.

McTELL, Ralph; British folk singer, songwriter and musician (guitar); b. 3 Dec. 1944, Farnborough, Kent. *Recordings include:* albums: Eight Frames A Second 1968, Spiral Staircase 1969, My Side of Your Window 1970, Not Till Tomorrow 1972, Easy 1973, Streets 1975, Right Side Up 1976, Ralph, Albert and Sydney 1977, Slide Away the Screens 1979, Love Grows 1982, Sighs 1987, Stealin' Back 1990, The Boy With the Note 1992, The Silver Celebration 1992, Sand in Your Shoes 1995, Songs for Six Strings Vol. II 1996, Red Sky 2001, Alphabet Zoo 2002, National Treasure 2002, The Journey: Recordings 1965–2006 2006, Gates of Eden 2007, As Far as I Can Tell 2008. *Honours:* Ivor Novello Award, Lifetime Achievement Award, BBC Radio 2 Folk Awards. *E-mail:* queries@ralphmctell.co.uk. *Website:* www.ralphmctell.co.uk.

McVICAR, Ewan Reynolds, MSc (by research); British songwriter, singer, musician (guitar, banjo, autoharp), writer and poet; b. 17 April 1941, Inverness, Scotland; m. Linda Rosemary Gammie 1971. *Education:* Glasgow Univ., Edinburgh Univ. *Career:* f. first folk club in Scotland 1959; toured and taught music in USA 1965–67; based in Glasgow, singing and writing 1968–; wrote show for the Glasgow-Nurnberg Twinning 1985; songmaker in Schools Project 1991–99; Mungo 200 project with Amu Logotse 1992–95; Scottish Arts Council Writer-in-Residence, Craigmillar, Edinburgh 1998–2000; Chair. Sangschule, Linlithgow 1998–2000; numerous musical and educational projects organized for local and nat. orgs throughout Scotland and in Russia and several other countries; published numerous CDs on Gallus label; started Gallus Publications 2010, ten titles published by Feb. 2014. *Compositions:* Talking Army Blues 1959; 20 songs commercially covered by other singers and groups; shows written include: Salmon Spells, Church Bells, The Fyffes Banana Boat Show; wrote 16 songs for The Singing Kettle Shows 1990–98. *Recordings:* albums: Gies Peace 1987, I Was Born In Glasgow 1989, The New Songs of Fife 1999, and numerous others. *Publications:* One Singer One Song 1990, Streets, Schemes and Stages 1991, Cod Liver Oil and The Orange Juice 1993, Pictworks (booklet of Pictish poems and songs) 1999, Traditional Scottish Song & Music 2001, Doh Ray Me When Ah Wis Wee 2007. *Honours:* finalist, Songsearch 1988. *Address:* 84 High Street, Linlithgow, West Lothian, EH49 7AQ, Scotland (home). *Telephone:* (1506) 847935 (office). *E-mail:* ewanandlinda@btinternet.com (office).

McVIE, Christine; British musician (keyboards), singer and songwriter; b. (Christine Perfect), 12 July 1943, Birmingham, England; m. 1st John McVie 1971 (divorced 1976); m. 2nd Eduardo Quintela 1986. *Career:* fmr mem. Chicken Shack; mem. Fleetwood Mac 1970–94; numerous tours, concerts and television appearances. *Recordings include:* with Fleetwood Mac: Future Games 1971, Bare Trees 1971, Penguin 1973, Mystery To Me 1973, Heroes Are Hard To Find 1974, Fleetwood Mac 1975, Rumours (Billboard Award for Album of the Year 1977, American Music Award for Favorite Pop/Rock Album 1978, Grammy Award for Album of the Year 1978) 1977, Tusk 1979, Fleetwood Mac Live 1980, Mirage 1982, Tango In The Night 1987, Behind The Mask 1990; solo: Christine Perfect 1970, The Legendary Christine Perfect Album 1976, Albatross 1977, Christine McVie 1984, In The Meantime 2004. *Honours:* Melody Maker Female Vocalist of the Year 1969, American Music Award for Favorite Pop/Rock Group 1978, BRIT Award for Outstanding Contribution 1998, Ivor Novello Award for Lifetime Achievement 2014.

McVIE, John; British musician (bass); b. 26 Nov. 1945, London, England; m. Christine Perfect 1971 (divorced 1976). *Career:* mem., the Bluesbreakers 1963–67; founder mem., Fleetwood Mac, 1967–; solo artist 1992–; numerous tours, concerts and television appearances. *Recordings:* albums: with Fleetwood Mac: Peter Green's Fleetwood Mac 1968, Mr Wonderful 1968, English Rose 1969, Then Play On 1969, Kiln House 1970, Future Games 1971, Bare Trees 1971, Penguin 1973, Mystery To Me 1973, Heroes Are Hard To Find 1974, Fleetwood Mac 1975, Rumours (Billboard Award for Album of the Year 1977, American Music Award for Favorite Pop/Rock Album 1978, Grammy Award for Album of the Year 1978) 1977, Tusk 1979, Fleetwood Mac Live 1980, Mirage 1982, Tango In The Night 1987, Behind The Mask 1990, Time 1995, The Dance 1997, Say You Will 2003, Pious Bird Of Good Omen 2004; solo: John McVie's Gotta Band With Lola Thomas 1992. *Honours:* American Music Award for Favorite Band 1978, BRIT Award for Outstanding Contribution 1998. *Current Management:* Sanctuary Artist Management, 15301 Ventura Boulevard, Building B, Suite 400, Sherman Oaks, CA 91403, USA. *Telephone:* (818) 286-4800. *Fax:* (818) 286-4833. *E-mail:* blain.clausen@sanctuarygroup.com. *Website:* www.sanctuarygroup.com; www.fleetwoodmac.com.

MADDEN, Mickey; American musician (bass guitar); b. 13 May 1979, Austin, Texas. *Career:* mem., Kara's Flowers, later renamed Maroon 5 1997–. *Recordings include:* albums: with Maroon 5: Songs About Jane 2002, It Won't Be Soon Before Long (Billboard Music Award for Top Digital Album 2007) 2007, Hands All Over 2010, Overexposed 2012, V 2014. *Honours:* with Maroon 5: Grammy Awards for Best New Artist 2004, for Best Pop Performance by a Duo or Group with Vocals (for Makes me Wonder) 2008, American Music Awards for Favorite Pop/Rock Band/Duo/Group 2011, 2012, for Favorite Adult Contemporary Artist 2013, Billboard Music Award for Top Hot 100 Artist 2013, People's Choice Award for Favorite Band 2013. *Current Management:* c/o Career Artist Management, 1100 Glendon Avenue, Suite 1100, New York, NY 90024, USA. *Telephone:* (310) 776-7640. *Fax:* (310) 776-7659. *Website:* camanagement.com; www.maroon5.com.

MADFAI, Ilham al-; Iraqi guitarist and singer; b. 1942, Baghdad; m.; two s. *Education:* studied architecture. *Career:* f. The Twisters, known as Iraq's first rock band; following studies returned to Iraq, f. 13½ 1967; left Iraq 1979; performed across Arab world; returned to Iraq 1991; emigrated to Jordan 1994; based in USA in late 1990s before returning to Jordan. *Recordings include:* albums: Ilham Al-Madfai 1999, Khuttar 1999, Baghdad 2003, Dishdasha 2009. *Current Management:* PO Box 2792, Amman 11181, Jordan. *Telephone:* (6) 5828202; 777775555 (Mobile). *E-mail:* mmadfai@ilhamalmadfai.com; mmadfai@my-management.org. *Website:* www.ilhamalmadfai.com.

MADIGAN, Brian Alan; British composer and musician (drums, flute); b. 27 June 1964, Enfield, Middlesex; m. Barbara Madigan. *Education:* BA, Middlesex Polytechnic, London, 1988–91. *Career:* Composer, Performer with Hot Savoury Souffles, 1991–93; Wise Wound, 1992–96; Madigan, 1997–99; Festival appearances, 1992–99; mem, SPNM; MU. *Compositions:* Dance Notes; Coincidence; The Fisher King. *E-mail:* madmusik@brianmadigan.com. *Website:* www.brianmadigan.com.

MADLEY CROFT, Romy; British singer, songwriter and musician (guitar). *Education:* Elliott School, London. *Career:* mem. The xx 2005–. *Recordings:* albums: xx (Mercury Music Prize 2010) 2009, Coexist 2012. *Address:* c/o Young Turks, XL Recordings, 1 Codrington Mews, London, W11 2EH, England (office). *Telephone:* (20) 8870-7511 (office). *Fax:* (20) 8871-4178 (office). *E-mail:* theyoungturks@theyoungturks.co.uk (office). *Website:* thexx.info.

MADLINGOZI, Ringo; South African singer and songwriter; b. (Sindile Brian Madlingozi), 1964, Cape Town. *Career:* led school a cappella group which performed at community and youth functions; became vocalist for the group Ikwezi, and later for Peto; Peto won national Shell Road to Fame talent competition 1986; prize led to the role of support act for King's Trust concert in Swaziland headlined by Eric Clapton; moved to Johannesburg; mem., Gecko Moon 1990s; various studio session work for radio commercials, film and album recordings including: Simply Red, The Power of One soundtrack (with Teddy Pendergrass), The Lion King soundtrack, Hugh Masekela, Caiphus Semenya, Oliver Mtukudzi; performed a Xhosa version of the title song of UB40's Cover Up album 2002. *Recordings:* albums: Vukani 1996, Mamelani 1997, Sondelani (double platinum; FNB South African Music Awards, Best Adult Contemporary Performance (languages other than English and Afrikaans) 1998, Into Yam 1999, Buyisa 2000, Ntumba 2002, Baleka 2004, Ndim Lo 2006. *Honours:* Kora All-Africa Music Awards, Best Southern African Artist, Best Male Artist 1998, Best Artist/Group in Southern Africa 1999. *Address:* PO Box 815, Private Bag 9, Bonmore, Sandton 2010, South Africa (office). *Telephone:* (11) 8834667 (office). *Fax:* (11) 7849703 (office). *E-mail:* info@ring-mp.com (office). *Website:* www.ring-mp.com.

MADONNA; American singer, actress and fashion designer; b. (Madonna Louise Veronica Ciccone), 16 Aug. 1958, Bay City, Mich.; d. of Sylvio Ciccone and Madonna Ciccone; m. 1st Sean Penn 1985 (divorced 1989); one d. by Carlos Leon; m. 2nd Guy Ritchie 2000 (divorced 2008); two s. (one adopted). *Education:* Rochester Adams High School, Mich., Univ. of Michigan, Alvin Ailey Dance School. *Career:* moved to New York 1979, dancer 1979–, actress 1980–, solo singer 1983–; numerous worldwide concerts, tours, TV appearances; f. Maverick record label 1992 (sold to Warner Music Group 2004); Vice-Pres. ICA, London, UK; est. children's clothing line, Sweet Hearts 2004; launched Material Girl clothing line with daughter Lourdes 2010. *Tours:* The Virgin Tour 1985, Who's That Girl World Tour 1987, Blond Ambition World

Tour 1990, The Girlie Show World Tour 1993, Drowned World Tour 2001, Re-Invention World Tour 2004, Confessions Tour 2006, Sticky & Sweet Tour 2008–09, M.D.N.A. Tour 2012, Rebel Heart Tour 2015. *Plays:* Speed-the-Plow (Broadway) 1988, Up for Grabs (Wyndhams Theatre, London) 2002. *Films:* A Certain Sacrifice 1979, Vision Quest 1985, Desperately Seeking Susan 1985, Shanghai Surprise 1986, Who's That Girl? 1987, Bloodhounds on Broadway 1989, Dick Tracy 1990, Shadows and Fog 1991, Madonna: Truth or Dare (aka In Bed with Madonna) (documentary) 1991, A League of Their Own 1992, Body of Evidence 1993, Dangerous Game (aka Snake Eyes) 1993, Blue in the Face (aka Brooklyn Boogie) 1995, Four Rooms 1995, Girl 6 1996, Evita 1996, The Next Best Thing 2000, Swept Away 2002, I'm Going to Tell You a Secret 2005, Arthur and the Minimoys (aka Arthur and the Invisibles) (voice) 2006, Filth and Wisdom (writer and dir) 2008, I Am Because We Are (documentary, writer) 2008, W.E. (co-writer and dir) (Golden Globe Award for Best Original Song, 'Masterpiece' 2012) 2011. *Television includes:* Will & Grace (series) 2003. *Recordings include:* albums: Madonna 1983, Like A Virgin 1984, True Blue 1986, Who's That Girl? (film soundtrack) 1987, Like A Prayer 1989, I'm Breathless (soundtrack to film Dick Tracy) 1990, The Immaculate Collection 1990, Erotica 1992, Bedtime Stories 1994, Something To Remember 1995, Evita (film soundtrack) 1997, Ray Of Light (Grammy Award for Best Pop Album) 1998, Next Best Thing (film soundtrack) 2000, Music 2000, GHV2 2001, American Life 2003, Remixed and Revisited (EP) 2004, Confessions On A Dance Floor (Grammy Award for Best Electronic/Dance Album 2007) 2005, I'm Going to Tell You a Secret 2006, Hard Candy 2008, M.D.N.A. (Billboard Music Award for Top Dance Album 2013) 2012, Rebel Heart 2015. *Publications:* Sex 1992, The English Roses (juvenile) 2003, Mr Peabody's Apples (juvenile) 2003, Yakov and the Seven Thieves (juvenile) 2004, The Adventures of Abdi (juvenile) 2004, Lotsa de Casha (juvenile) 2005. *Honours:* numerous MTV Video Awards, including Vanguard Award 1986, American Music Awards for Favorite Female Video Artist 1987, Favorite Dance Single 1991, Academy Award for Best Song 1991, Juno Award for Int. Song of the Year 1991, Grammy Award for Best Longform Music Video 1992, BRIT Award for Best Int. Female 2001, 2006, numerous awards from Billboard, Vogue and Rolling Stone magazines, Echo Award for Best Int. Female Artist, Germany 2006, Ivor Novello Award for Int. Hit of the Year (for Sorry) 2007, ranked by Forbes magazine amongst The World's 100 Most Powerful Women (29th) 2010, Billboard Music Awards for Top Dance Artist 2013, for Top Touring Artist 2013. *Address:* Live Nation Inc., 9348 Civic Center Drive, Beverly Hills, CA 90210; 8491 West Sunset Boulevard, Suite 485, West Hollywood, CA 90069, USA. *Website:* www.livenationentertainment.com; www.madonna.com.

MADSEN, Bo; Danish musician (guitar). *Career:* founder mem., Mew 1996–; the band formed record label, Evil Office 2000–. *Recordings include:* albums: A Triumph For Man 1997, Half The World Is Watching Me 2000, Frengers (Danish Music Critics Award for Album of the Year) 2003, Mew And The Glass Handed Kites 2005, No More Stories 2009. *Honours:* Danish Music Critics Award for Band of the Year 2003, MTV Europe Music Award for Best Danish Act 2005. *E-mail:* hq@evil-office.net (office). *Website:* www.evil-office.net (office); www.mewsite.com.

MADSEN, Tue; Danish musician (guitar) and producer; b. 25 Jan. 1969, Hadsten. *Career:* Playing Guitar for 18 years; mem, DMF. *Recordings:* Pixie Killers: One Size Fits All; Grope: Primates, 1994; Soul Pieces, EP, 1996; The Fury, 1996; Desert Storm, 1997. *Address:* Terp Skovvej 50, 8260 Vibij, Denmark.

MAÉ, Christophe; French singer and musician; b. 16 Oct. 1975, Carpentras. *Education:* Avignon Conservatory. *Career:* began career playing violin, guitar and harmonica in jazz clubs in the South of France; moved to Paris; joined cast of Le Roi Soleil musical as Monsieur le Frère du Roi 2005–07; solo artist 2007–. *Recordings include:* albums: solo: Mon Paradis 2007, Comme à la Maison 2009, On Trace la Route 2010; also appeared on: Le Roi Soleil, Un Geste de Vous 2005, Le Roi Soleil, Tant qu'on Rêve encore 2006, Le Roi Soleil, Ca Marche 2007, Les Enfoirés, L'Amitié 2008, Les Enfoirés font leur cinéma 2009. *Honours:* NRJ Music Award for Best New Artist 2007, for Best French Male Artist 2008, 2009, Victoires de la Musique for Best New Artist 2008.

MAEL, Ronald (Ron), BA; American musician (keyboards) and songwriter; b. (Ronald Day), 12 Aug. 1950, Los Angeles; brother of Russell Mael. *Education:* Univ. of California, Los Angeles. *Career:* mem., various bands, including Moonbaker Abbey, Urban Renewal Project; mem., Halfnelson 1971, became duo, renamed Sparks 1973–; collaborations on music videos and soundtrack contributions 1970s–80s; numerous concert tours, tv appearances world-wide; mem. Sons of the Desert. *Recordings include:* albums: Halfnelson 1970, A Woofer In Tweeter's Clothing 1973, Kimono My House 1974, Propaganda 1974, Indiscreet 1975, Big Beat 1976, Introducing Sparks 1977, Number One In Heaven 1979, Terminal Jive 1980, Whomp That Sucker 1981, Angst In My Pants 1982, Sparks In Outer Space 1983, Pulling Rabbits Out Of A Hat 1984, Music That You Can Dance To 1986, Interior Design 1988, Gratuitous Sax And Senseless Violins 1994, Plagiarism 1998, Balls 2000, L'il Beethoven 2002, Hello, Young Lovers 2006, Exotic Creatures of the Deep 2008, The Seduction of Ingmar Bergman 2009. *Website:* www.allsparks.com.

MAEL, Russell; American singer and songwriter; b. (Dwight Russell Day), 5 Oct. 1953, Culver City, Los Angeles, Calif.; brother of Ron Mael. *Education:* film school. *Career:* mem., various bands, including Moonbaker Abbey, Urban Renewal Project; mem., Halfnelson 1971, became duo, renamed Sparks 1973–; collaborations on music videos and soundtrack contributions 1970s–80s; numerous concert tours, tv appearances world-wide. *Recordings include:* albums: Halfnelson 1970, A Woofer In Tweeter's Clothing 1973, Kimono My House 1974, Propaganda 1974, Indiscreet 1975, Big Beat 1976, Introducing Sparks 1977, Number One In Heaven 1979, Terminal Jive 1980, Whomp That Sucker 1981, Angst In My Pants 1982, Sparks In Outer Space 1983, Pulling Rabbits Out Of A Hat 1984, Music That You Can Dance To 1986, Interior Design 1988, Gratuitous Sax And Senseless Violins 1994, Plagiarism 1998, Balls 2000, L'il Beethoven 2002, Hello, Young Lovers 2006, Exotic Creatures of the Deep 2008, The Seduction of Ingmar Bergman 2009. *Website:* www.allsparks.com.

MAGEE, Curtis; British country singer and musician; b. 12 Aug. 1965, Strabane, Co. Tyrone, Northern Ireland; two d. *Education:* Strabane Primary and High School. *Career:* fronted own band for many years; solo; professional, 1990–; tours of UK, Ireland, Spain, Australia, Fiji, USA; mem. BCMA. *Recordings include:* 21 albums. *Honours:* numerous CMC Awards for Solo Act of the Year. *Address:* 42 Greenhall Manor, Coleraine BT51 3GN, Northern Ireland. *Website:* www.curtismagee.com.

MAGIC, Mick; British/Irish musician (guitar, keyboards), composer, writer and graphic designer; *Owner, The Magic Net/Music & Elsewhere;* b. (Russell Lancaster), 21 April 1958, Wimbledon, England; m. Samantha Taylor 2011; one d. *Education:* Weydon School, Open Univ. *Career:* fmr mem. Magic Moments At Twilight Time; now recording with Magic Moments Revival; appearance on BBC Radio 5; Owner and Ed. The Magic Net online magazine; Owner Music & Elsewhere (active again since Aug. 2012); mem. Mensa. *Recordings include:* with Magic Moments At Twilight Time: Psychotron O 1988, Zoen Nostalgia 1989, White Hawk Atomic 1992, Creavolution 1996, Flashbax Ω Ultimate: The Best Of Magic Moments At Twilight Time 2015. *Address:* Asgard, Hackensall Road, Knott End-On-Sea, Poulton-le-Fylde, FY6 0AX, England (home). *E-mail:* mickmagic_uwu@hotmail.com. *Website:* www.mickmagic.net.

MAGNET; Norwegian singer and songwriter; b. (Even Johansen), 7 June 1970, Bergen. *Recordings include:* albums: Quiet & Still 2000, On Your Side 2003, The Tourniquet 2005, The Simple Life 2007. *Honours:* Spellemannprisen for Best Male Artist 2008. *Current Management:* c/o Kathrine Synnes, Bpop Mentometer, Møllergata 4, 0179 Oslo, Norway. *Telephone:* 22-00-76-50. *Fax:* 22-00-76-59. *E-mail:* management@bpopmentometer.com. *Website:* www.bpopmentometer.com; www.homeofmagnet.com.

MAGOOGAN, Wesley; musician (saxophone); b. 11 Oct. 1951, London, England; m. Marion Willett 1973, one s. one d. (deceased). *Education:* Royal Acad. of Music. *Career:* duo with Hazel O'Connor; played with The Beat (also known as The English Beat), Joan Armatrading, Elton John, Billy Ocean; extensive world tours; mem. Royal Soc. of Musicians. *Recordings include:* albums: with O'Connor/Magoogan: Will You; with The Beat: Special Beat Service, 1982; with Hazel O'Connor: Breaking Glass, 1980; Sons and Lovers, 1980; Cover Plus, 1981: with Joan Armatrading: Secret Secrets, 1985; Sleight of Hand, 1986; Shouting Stage, 1988; two albums with Billy Ocean; with Magnum: Sleepwalking, 1992. *Address:* 5 Paddington Street, Marylebone, London W1M 3LA, England.

MAGUIRE, Martie; American musician (fiddle), singer and songwriter; b. (Martie Seidel), 12 Oct. 1969, York, PA; m. Gareth Maguire 2001. *Career:* mem. teen group, Blue Night Express 1983–89; founder mem., The Dixie Chicks 1989–, playing a mix of traditional bluegrass with mainstream country music; founder mem., Court Yard Hounds 2009–; numerous live performances. *Recordings include:* albums: with The Dixie Chicks: Little Ol' Cowgirl 1992, Thank Heavens For Dale Evans 1992, Shouldn't A Told You That 1993, Wide Open Spaces (Grammy Award for Best Country Album 1998, CMA Award for Music Video of the Year 1999) 1998, Fly (ACM Award for Album of the Year 1999, CMA Award for Album of the Year 2000) 1999, Star Profile 2000, Home (American Music Award for Best Country Album 2003) 2002, Combo 2004, Taking the Long Way (Grammy Awards for Album of the Year, Best Country Album 2007, Juno Award for Int. Album 2007) 2006; with Court Yard Hounds: Court Yard Hounds 2010. *Honours:* Grammy Award for Best Country Performance by a Duo or Group with Vocal 1998, 1999, CMA Award for Vocal Group of the Year and for Single of the Year (for Wide Open Spaces) 1999, TNN Music Award for Group/Duo of the Year 1999, ACM Award for Favorite Duo or Group 1999, American Music Award for Favorite New Country Artist 1999, Billboard Music Award for Favorite Country Artist 1999, CMA Awards for Entertainer of the Year, for Vocal Group of the Year, and for Music Video of the Year (for Goodbye Earl) 2000, American Music Award for Best Country Group 2003, Grammy Awards for Record of the Year, Song of the Year, Best Country Performance by a duo or group with Vocal (all for Not Ready To Make Nice) 2007. *Current Management:* Front Page Publicity, PO Box 90168, Nashville, TN 37209, USA. *E-mail:* info@frontpagepublicity.com. *Website:* www.frontpagepublicity.com; www.dixiechicks.com; www.courtyardhounds.com.

MAHADEVAN, Shankar; Indian singer and songwriter; b. Mumbai; m. Sangeeta Mahadevan; two c. *Education:* Ramrao Adik Inst. of Tech. *Career:* worked at Oracle Corpn and Leading Edge Systems before starting career in music; mem. Shankar-Ehsaan-Loy musical trio; f. Shankar Mahadevan Acad. 2010; mem. Indian/Swedish band Mynta; fmr judge, Fame Gurukul (TV reality show). *Recordings include:* Breathless 1998, Nine, Teri Hee Parachhayian 2011, Ganaraj Adhiraj 2011. *Songs and soundtracks include:* Humse

Hai Muqabla 1995, Auzaar 1997, Rockford 1999, Kandukondain Kandukondain (Nat. Film Award for Best Male Playback Singer 2000) 2000, Mission Kashmir 2000, Dil Chahta Hai (Star Screen Award 2001, Filmfare Award 2002) 2001, Ek Aur Ek Gyarah 2003, Kal Ho Naa Ho (Nat. Film Award for Best Male Playback Singer 2004) 2003, Rudraksh 2004, Heyy Babyy 2004, Taare Zameen Par (Nat. Film Award for Best Male Playback Singer 2008) 2007, Madampi (Kerala State Film Award for Best Male Singer 2008) 2008, Puthiya Mukham (Annual Malayalam Movie Award for Best Male Singer 2009, Asianet Film Award for Best Male Playback 2009) 2009, Karthik Calling Karthik 2010, Holidays (Kerala Film Critics Award for Best Male Playback Singer 2011) 2010, De Ghumaa Ke 2011, Zindagi Na Milegi Dobara 2011, Pilla Zamindar 2011, Don 2 2011, Chittagong (Nat. Film Award for Best Male Playback Singer 2013) 2012, Vishwaroopam 2013, Bhaag Milkha Bhaag (IIFA Award for Best Background Score 2014) 2013, D-Day 2013, One By Two 2013, 2 States 2014. *Honours:* Swaralaya-Kairali-Yesudas Award 2007; numerous other awards as part of Shankar-Ehsaan-Loy. *Address:* Shankar Mahadevan Academy, First Floor, Rathna Building, 143 Rathna Avenue, Richmond Road, Bangalore, 560025, India (office). *Website:* www.shankarmahadevanacademy .com (office).

MAHAL, Taj, BA; American composer and musician; b. (Henry St Clair Fredericks), 17 May 1942, Massachusetts; m. Inshirah Geter 1976. *Education:* Univ. Massachusetts, Amherst. *Career:* composer, musician 1964–; concert tours across USA, Europe, Africa, Australia. *Film appearances:* King of Ragtime, Sounder, Sounder II. *Theatre appearance:* Mule Bone. *Television music:* Ewoks, The Man Who Broke A Thousand Chains, Brer Rabbit, The Hot Spot. *Recordings:* albums: Taj Mahal 1967, Natch'l Blues 1968, Giant Step 1969, The Real Thing 1971, Happy Just To Be Like I Am 1971, Recycling The Blues and Other Stuff 1972, Sounder (film soundtrack) 1972, Ooh So Good 'n' Blues 1973, Mo'Roots 1974, Music Keeps Me Together 1975, Satisfied 'n Tickled Too 1976, Music Fuh Ya 1977, Brothers (film soundtrack) 1977, Evolution 1978, Taj Mahal and The International Rhythm Band 1980, Big Blues 1990, Mule Bone 1991, Like Never Before 1991, An Evening of Acoustic Music 1995, Dancing The Blues 1995, Phantom Blues 1996, Señor Blues 1997, Shakin' a Tailfeather 1997, Taj Mahal and the Hula Blues 1998, Sacred Island 1998, Kulanjan 1999, Shake it to the One you Love the Best 1999, Big Blues: Live at Ronnie Scott's, Shoutin' In Key: Live 2000, Taj Mahal Meets the Culture Musical Club of Zanzibar: Mkutano 2005, Maestro 2008. *Honours:* Best Ethnic Music Award, Brothers, 1979; Bay Area Music Awards, Brothers, 1979; Grammy Award, Contemporary Blues Album, 2001. *Current Management:* Folklore Productions, 1671 Appian Way, Santa Monica, CA 90401, USA. *Website:* www.taj-mo-roots.com.

MAHANTA, Angaraag, (Papon); Indian singer and composer; b. Assam; s. of Khagen Mahanta and Archana Mahanta. *Career:* f. band East India Co. *Recordings include:* albums: Jonaki Raati, Sinaaki Osinaaki, Gomseng, Phagunar Gaan. *Soundtracks:* Raamdhenu 2010, Dum Maaro Dum 2011. *Telephone:* 09859947596 (mobile). *Website:* www.papon.co.in.

MAHANTHAPPA, Rudresh Kalyana, BA, MFA; American (b. Italian) jazz musician (alto saxophone) and composer; b. 4 May 1971, Trieste, Italy. *Education:* Fairview High School, Berklee Coll. of Music, DePaul Univ. *Career:* grew up in Boulder, Colo; early recording credits include with The Oversize Quartet 1992, Clark Terry with DePaul Univ. Big Band 1994; moved to New York 1998; Co-founder and leader, Rudresh Mahanthappa Quartet; co-leader, Raw Materials (with Vijay Iyer); Co-founder, Indo-Pak Coalition (with Rez Abbasi and Dan Weiss); Co-founder, MSG; mem. Dakshina Ensemble septet; numerous other recording credits including: Rez Abbasi, Brooklyn Saxophone Quartet, Jack DeJohnette, Amir El Saffar, Miles From India, Anders Morgensen, Oversize Quartet, Danilo Pérez, Jason Robinson; US Artists Fellow 2015. *Recordings:* albums: as leader or co-leader: Yatra 1994, Black Water 2002, Mother Tongue 2004, Raw Materials (with Vijay Iyer) 2006, Codebook 2006, The Beautiful Enabler (as part of Mauger Trio) 2006, Kinsmen (as part of Dakshina Ensemble) 2008, Apti (with Rudresh Mahanthappa's Indo-Pak Coalition) 2008, Dual Identity (with Steve Lehman) 2010, Apex (with Bunky Green) 2010, Tasty! (with MSG) 2011, Samdhi 2011, Gamak 2013, Bird Calls 2015; with Vijay Iyer: Architextures 1998, Panoptic Modes 2001, In What Language 2003, Reimagining 2005, Blood Sutra 2006, Tragicomic 2008. *Honours:* NY Foundation for the Arts Fellow in Music 2006, three Rockefeller MAP grants, two New York State Council on the Arts grants, Guggenheim Fellow 2007, Jazz Journalists Asscn Awards for Alto Saxophonist of the Year 2009, 2010, 2011, 2013, Down Beat Critics Poll Awards for Rising Star Jazz Artist 2010, for Rising Star Alto Saxophonist 2010, for Alto Saxophonist of the Year 2011, Doris Duke Performing Artist Award 2013, No. 1 Album of the Year, No. 1 Alto Saxophonist, No. 1 Rising Star Composer in Down Beat Int. Critics Poll 2015, Best Jazz Artist, The Village Voice 2015. *Current Management:* c/o Danny Melnick, Absolutely Live Entertainment LLC, 127 Hommelville Road, Saugerties, NY 12477, USA. *Telephone:* (646) 233-2960. *E-mail:* dmelnick@absolutelylive.net. *Website:* www.absolutelylive .net. *E-mail:* info@rudreshm.com (home). *Website:* rudreshm.com (home).

MAHAR, Eric Frederick; Canadian music producer, music consultant and musician (guitar, banjo, harmonica); b. 11 Jan. 1959, Hamilton, Ontario; m. 1988. *Education:* Humber College, University of Toronto. *Career:* solo guitarist; theatre guitarist; R&B country guitarist for The Mercey Brothers, Marie Bottrell, Joan Kennedy; numerous television appearances; producer and performer for various record labels; mem, Musicians' Union.

MAHON, Kieran James, BA, MA; British musician (keyboards) and academic; *Lecturer in Interior Design History and Theory, Regent's University London;* b. 14 April 1980. *Education:* Univ. of London. *Career:* mem. The Cooper Temple Clause 1998–2007; mem. Type Two Error 2009–; Instructor in History and Theory, American InterContinental Univ. 2010–13; Lecturer in Interior Design History and Theory, Regent's Univ. London 2013–. *Recordings include:* albums: See This Through And Leave 2002, Kick Up The Fire And Let The Flames Break Loose 2003, Make This Your Own 2007. *Address:* Regent's University London, 110 Marylebone High Street, London, W1U 4RY, England. *Telephone:* (20) 7467-2484. *Website:* www.regents.ac.uk/about/who -we-are/our-staff/kieran-mahon.aspx.

MAHWASH, Ustad Farida; Afghan singer; b. 1947, Kabul; m. *Education:* studied with Ustad Nabi Gol, Khyal, Saråhang and Naynawaz. *Career:* solo artist 1970–; permanent guest artist with Radio Kabul Ensemble; awarded title of Ustad (Maestra), Ministry for Information and Culture 1977. *Recordings include:* albums: Radio Kabul 2003, Ghazals afghans 2007. *Honours:* Artist of the Year, Afghanistan 1970, Janis Joplin Award, Gold Voice Award, BBC World Music Award (Asia Category, with Radio Kabul Ensemble) 2003. *Address:* c/o Accords Croisés, 23 rue des Fontaines du Temple, Paris 75003, France (office). *E-mail:* info@accords-croises.com (office). *Website:* www.accords-croises.com (office).

MAIA, Lucio; Brazilian musician (guitar). *Career:* mem. mangue beat band, Nação Zumbi; mem., Seu Jorge and Almaz 2010–. *Recordings include:* albums: with Nação Zumbi: CSNZ 1998, Rádio SAMBA 2000, Nação Zumbi 2002, Futura 2005, Fome de Tudo 2007; with Seu Jorge and Almaz: Seu Jorge and Almaz 2010. *Honours:* São Paulo Asscn of Art Critics Award for Best Group (Nacão Zumbi) 2005. *Address:* c/o Trama, Rua Rosa Gaeta Lázara, 93 Brooklin Novo, 04570-905 São Paulo, Brazil. *Website:* www.nacaozumbi.com.br; www .seujorgealmaz.com.

MAIDMAN, Jennifer Jane; British record producer, singer, songwriter, musician (multi-instrumentalist) and actress and counsellor; b. 24 Jan. 1958, Upminster, Essex, England; d. of Brian John Maidman and Beryl Daphne Lily Maidman; m. Annie Whitehead. *Education:* studied classical guitar, piano, music theory, as adult studied counselling and psychotherapy. *Career:* producer for Paul Brady, Pili Pili, Murray Head, Mitt Gamon, Annie Whitehead, Linda McCartney; musician, toured/recorded with Loz Netto 1981, Joan Armatrading 1983–84, Murray Head 1984–, Paul Brady 1985–, Penguin Café Orchestra 1984–, Boy George 1987–89, David Sylvian 1986–88, Annie Whitehead 1990–; also worked with Steve Marriott, Van Morrison, Bonnie Raitt, Mark Knopfler, Sinead O'Connor, Rude with Harry Beckett, Soupsongs Band, Gerry Rafferty, Terry Reid, George Clinton, Stewart Levine, Alistair Anderson, Sam Brown, Northern Lights, Robert Wyatt, The Crass Collective, Penny Rimbaud, Jan Allain, Lorraine Jordan, The Proclaimers, Shakespears Sister, Sniff and the Tears, Hue and Cry; Founder-mem. The Orchestra That Fell to Earth (musicians of the Penguin Cafe Orchestra) 2009–; freelance counsellor/therapist; writes on therapy issues; Co-Ed. Self & Society 2012–13; currently playing with Murray Head Band, Tony O Malley band, Kokomo, Terry Reid, Orchestra That Fell to Earth; mem. Musicians' Union, Performing Right Soc., Mechanical-Copyright Protection Soc., PPL, Equity, British Asscn for Counselling and Psychotherapy, Asscn for Humanistic Psychology in Britain. *Plays:* appeared in Portrait in Black, The Winslow Boy, Strange Cargo. *Films:* music for All the Little Animals, Bass Desires. *Compositions:* songwriter, albums by Sam Brown and Boy George; co-writer with Annie Whitehead, Murray Head, Mitt Gamon, Ian Dury. *Radio:* Loose Ends, Jazz on 3, In Concert, Woman's Hour etc. *Television:* Old Grey Whistle Test, South Bank Show, Top of the Pops etc.. *Recordings include:* with Paul Brady, Gerry Rafferty, Joan Armatrading, Shakespears Sister, Boy George, Sam Brown, David Sylvian; including with Penguin Café Orchestra: When In Rome; with Paul Brady: Back To The Centre (Best Album, Ireland 1986–87), Primitive Dance, What A World 2000, The Paul Brady Songbook 2003, Hooba Dooba 2010; with Shakespears Sister: Hormonally Yours; with Annie Whitehead: Naked 1994, Home 1999, The Gathering 2000, Northern Lights 2002; with Robert Wyatt: Soupsongs 2002, Cuckooland 2003; with Murray Head: Restless 1985, Wave 1994, Pipe Dreams 1996, Rien est Ecrit 2009, Scrapbook 2010; played on numerous hit records, several No. 1s. *Publications:* published in Therapy Today and Self & Society; co-editor of book The Future of Humanistic Psychology 2013. *Honours:* Oustanding Contrib. Award, Thanet Coll. 2010. *E-mail:* jennifer@earthmusic.com (office). *Website:* www .earthmusic.com (office); www.facebook.com/jennifermaidmanmusic.

MAINES, Natalie Louise; American singer and songwriter; b. 14 Oct. 1974, Lubbock, Tex. *Education:* Texas Tech. Coll., Berklee Coll. of Music. *Career:* mem., The Dixie Chicks 1995–, playing a mix of traditional bluegrass with mainstream country music; numerous live performances; numerous other collaborations including Charlie Robison, Stevie Nicks, Patty Griffin, Pete Yorn, Tony Bennett, Neil Diamond. *Recordings include:* albums: Wide Open Spaces (Grammy Award for Best Country Album 1998, CMA Award for Music Video of the Year 1999) 1998, Fly (ACM Award for Album of the Year 1999, CMA Award for Album of the Year 2000) 1999, Star Profile 2000, Home (American Music Award for Best Country Album 2003) 2002, Combo 2004, Taking the Long Way (Grammy Awards for Album of the Year, Best Country Album 2007, Juno Award for Best Int. Album 2007) 2006, Mother (solo) 2013. *Honours:* Grammy Award for Best Country Performance by a Duo or Group with Vocal 1998, 1999, CMA Award for Vocal Group of the Year and for Single of the Year (for Wide Open Spaces) 1999, TNN Music Award for Group/Duo of the Year 1999, ACM Award for Favorite Duo or Group 1999, American Music Award for Favorite New Country Artist 1999, Billboard Award for Favorite Country Artist 1999, CMA Awards for Entertainer of the Year, for Vocal Group of the Year, and for Music Video of the Year (for Goodbye Earl) 2000, American Music Award for Best Country Group 2003, Grammy Awards for Record of the Year, Song of the Year, Best Country Performance by a duo or group with Vocal (all for Not Ready To Make Nice) 2007. *Current Management:* Front Page Publicity, 4505 Indiana Avenue, Nashville, TN 37209-2325, USA. *Website:* nataliemainesmusic.com; www.dixiechicks.com.

MAJID, Rashid al-; Lebanese singer. *Recordings include:* albums: Ala Meen Til'abha; Paris Concert–Live; Tidhak El Dinya; Shamaat Hayati; al-Dinya Hzooz; Khalleihom Yinfa'oonak; Ana A'ibbek; Ya Ba'd Hal Dunia Laih; Fugadnaak; Oummi; Ti'ess Tawwek; Ayallah.

MAK, Wai-Chu Clarence; composer, musician (electronics, guitar) and educator; b. 1959, Hong Kong. *Career:* Composed music for various arts groups including professional performing ensembles, dance companies and theatres; Produced concert of electronic music, computer music, contemporary music; Head of Composition and Electronic Music, Hong Kong Academy for Performing Arts; Organized projects for creative music making in Hong Kong; Radio Presenter of creative music; mem, Hong Kong Composers Guild; Composers and Authors Society of Hong Kong; International Computer Music Asscn. *Compositions:* include the works for orchestra, voice, choir, electronic means, multimedia, chamber music, Chinese music ensemble and live computer music. *Address:* School of Music, Hong Kong Academy for Performing Arts, 1 Gloucester Road, Wan Chai, Hong Kong.

MAKAREVICH, Andrei Vadimovich; Russian composer, singer and artist; b. 11 Dec. 1953, Moscow; one s. two d. *Education:* Moscow Inst. of Architecture. *Career:* Founder, Artistic Dir, soloist, Time Machine (first professional rock group in Russia) 1969–; creator, presenter Smak (TV programme); Leader, Creol Tango Orchestra; drawings have been exhibited in Moscow, St Petersburg, Riga, Caserta (Italy), London, New York. *Television:* presenter, Smak, Underwater World of Andrei Makarevich. *Recordings:* 26 albums, including music for nine films. *Publications:* nine books of poetry and prose. *Honours:* Merited Artist of RSFSR, Order of Honour, Order of Contrib. to the Motherland. *Address:* ORT (Russian Public TV), 127000 Moscow, Smak, Akademika Koroleva str. 12, Russia (office). *Telephone:* (495) 217-79-88 (office); (495) 367-63-09 (office). *Website:* www.mashina.ru (office); www.makar.info.

MAKAROFF, Edouardo; Argentine singer, musician (guitar) and composer. *Career:* solo artist; composed and performed on many film soundtracks; presenter, television shows in Buenos Aires, Argentina; moved to France 1990, as part of tango group Tango Mano; conductor, orchestra at tango club Dancing de la Coupole; founder-mem., Gotan Project 1999–; tours worldwide, mixing video, pre-recorded and live performances; collaborations with many tango musicians. *Recordings include:* albums: 12 solo albums; with Gotan Project: La Revancha del Tango 2001, Santa Maria del Buen Ayre 2002, Inspiración – Esperación 2004, Lunático 2006, Tango 3.0 2010. *Honours:* BBC Radio 3 World Music Award (Club Global) 2007. *Address:* c/o XL-Recordings, 17–19 Alma Road, London, SW18 1AA, England. *E-mail:* yabastarecords@noos.fr. *Website:* www.gotanproject.com.

MAKAROV, Jüri; Estonian promoter; b. 3 April 1959, Tallinn; m. Kirke Makarov; one s. two d. *Education:* Tallinn Tech. Univ. *Career:* staged annual Rock Summer festival 1987–; promoter for Jethro Tull, Steve Hackett, EMF, Bob Geldof, Procul Harum, Faith No More, The Pogues, Samantha Fox, Bonnie Tyler 1986–, promoter in Baltic countries for Sting, José Carreras, Bryan Adams, Depeche Mode, David Copperfield, Lord of the Dance; Chair. Makarov Music. *Address:* Makarov Muusik Management, Osmussaare 10, Tallinn 13811, Estonia (office). *Telephone:* 638-9389 (office). *Fax:* 638-9393 (office). *E-mail:* info@makarov.ee (office). *Website:* www.makarov.ee (office).

MAKHENE, Blondie Keoagile Gerald; South African singer and musician (guitar, piano); b. 16 Sept. 1955, White City Jabavu, Soweto; m. Agnes Mary 1979, three d. *Career:* numerous concerts, radio broadcasts; mem. Dorkay House. *Recordings include:* albums: Elakho Likhona, Pure Gold; Isencane, Platform 1; Amadamara, Freddy Gwala. *Honours:* Voice Education Centre Award for Most Outstanding Person, South Africa.

MALACH, Bob; American musician (saxophone, flute, clarinet); b. 23 Aug. 1954, Philadelphia, Pennsylvania; m. Janine Dreiding, 6 Jan. 1981, 1 s., 1 d. *Education:* Study with: Jow Allard; Harold Bennett; Eddie Daniels; David Weber; Keith Underwood. *Career:* Ben Sidran, 1977; Stanley Clarke, 1977–79; Stevie Wonder, 1980–85; Bob Mintzer, 1983; Horace Silver, 1986; Robben Ford, 1987; Steve Miller Band, 1987; Bill Cosby Show, 1987–92; Mike Stern, 1994; mem, AFofM; BMI. *Recordings include:* albums for: Patti Labelle, Lou Rawls, The O'Jays, Mose Allison, Regina Belle, Jean Carne, Marc Cohn, Georgie Fame, Robben Ford, The Jackson 5, Mike Stern, Stanley Clarke, Tori Amos; soundtracks to: Woman In Red (Stevie Wonder); Hoop Dreams; Miles Davis In Montreux; solo albums: Mood Swing 1990, The Searcher 1997, After Hours 1999. *Publications:* Swing Journal; Jazz Life; Ad Lib. *Address:* c/o Go Jazz Records, PO Box 763, Madison, WI 53701, USA. *E-mail:* bensidran@aol.com.

MALAKIAN, Daron V.; American musician (guitar) and producer; b. 18 July 1975, Los Angeles, CA. *Career:* fmr mem. The Soil; mem. System of a Down 1996–; founding mem. Scars on Broadway 2006–. *Recordings include:* albums:

with System of a Down: System Of A Down 1998, Toxicity 2001, Maximum 2002, Steal This Album! 2002, Mezmerize 2005, Hypnotize 2005, Vicinity of Obscenity 2006; with Scars on Broadway: Scars on Broadway 2008. *Honours:* MTV Europe Music Award for Best Alternative 2005, Grammy Award for Best Hard Rock Performance (for B.Y.O.B.) 2006. *Current Management:* Velvet Hammer, 9911 W. Pico Boulevard, 350W, Los Angeles, CA 90035, USA. *Telephone:* (310) 657-6161. *Fax:* (310) 657-0310. *Website:* www.velvethammer.net; www.systemofadown.com; www.scarsonbroadway.com.

MALCOLM, Carlos Edmond; composer and pianist; b. 24 Nov. 1945, Havana City, Cuba; one s. one d. *Education:* Vedado Inst., Havana, Amadeo Roldan Conservatory, Inst. Superior de Arte, Havana, Univ. of Music F. Chopin, Warsaw, Poland. *Career:* pianist in Havana's night clubs 1961–62; composer and pianist, Nat. Modern Dance Ensemble 1964–68, Cuban Inst. of Radio and TV, occasionally Cuban Inst. of Film 1968–70; performed at festivals 1969–85; mem. Staff of Composers, Ministry of Culture of Cuba 1970–90; toured throughout Mexico, Jamaica, Ecuador, playing own works, teaching and lecturing with choreographer Lorna Burdsal 1979–82; guest artist, New Music Concerts 1986; performed own piano compositions at Royal Conservatory of Toronto, Canada; freelance composer and pianist, living in Poland 1990–; accompanied flautist Robert Aitken during a special presentation of Quetzalcoatl for flute and piano (also recorded this piece for Cuban label EGREM with flautist Luis Bayard); recorded own music for Polish TV and Radio; works have been played in New Music Concerts, Warsaw Autumn Festival, Berlin's Biennale, Foros mexicanos de la Música Contemporanea, Japan, Argentina, Hungary, Spain; mem. Soc. of Cuban Composers and Authors. *Compositions:* Quetzalcoatl (Song of the Feathered Serpent) for flute and piano, Beny More redivivo, for string quartet, Adagio for piano (4 hands), Eclosion, Articulaciones for piano, 13 studies for piano, Sonatina (1 movement) for piano, Marionetas for orchestra (commissioned by Nat. Modern Dance Ensemble), Montaje for wind orchestra and percussion, Songs set to texts by Caribbean poets, Rumores for violin, cello and piano, Allegro en Son for wind quintet 1963–90, Autografo for piano 1998, 4 Escenas breves for piano 2005, Sonata for violin and piano 2007, Sonata Divertimento No. 1 (for piano) 2009, Sonata Divertimento No. 2 (for piano) 2012. *Honours:* several awards including UNEAC Music Awards. *Address:* ul Piękna 16 m 2, 00-539 Warsaw, Poland. *Telephone:* (22) 6290431. *E-mail:* cmalcolmw@gmail.com.

MALE, Johnny; British musician (Guitar); b. 10 Oct. 1963, Windsor, Berkshire, England. *Career:* Member, Republica; Numerous TV appearances and festival dates; Contributed track, Are Friends Electric, to Gary Numan tribute album, 1997. *Recordings:* Singles: Out of This World, 1994; Bloke, 1994; Ready To Go, 1996; Drop Dead Gorgeous, 1996; From the Rush Hour With Love, 1998; Albums: Republica, 1996; Speed Ballads, 1998. *Website:* www.republica.com.

MALIK, Anu; Indian composer; b. (Anwar Malik), 2 Nov. 1960, Mumbai; s. of Sardar Malik; m. Anju Anu Malik; two d. *Career:* composed first film song for Hunterwali 1977; became popular composer of film scores. *Compositions for films:* Aapas Ki Baat 1982, Poonam 1982, Mangal Pandey 1982, Ek Jaan Hain Hum 1983, Aasmaan 1984, Ram Tera Desh 1984, Sohni Mahiwal 1984, Love Marriage 1984, Jaan Ki Baazi 1985, Mard 1985, Phaansi Ke Baad 1985, Allah Rakha 1986, Jaal 1986, Mera Haque 1986, Ek Chadar Maili Si 1986, Pyaar Ke Do Pal 1986, Naam-O-Nishan 1987, Hawalaat 1987, Insaaniyat Ke Dushman 1987, Aakhri Adalat 1988, Ganga Jamuna Saraswathi 1988, Jeete Hain Shaan Se 1988, Maalamaal 1988, Taaqatwar 1989, Ladaai 1989, Toofan 1989, Abhimanyu 1989, Aakhri Baazi 1989, Awaargi 1990, Khatarnak 1990, Tejaa 1990, Paap Ki Kamaee 1990, Shikari 1991, Bhabhi 1991, Ramgarh Ke Sholay 1991, Radha Ka Sangam 1992, Chamatkar 1992, Police Officer 1992, Phir Teri Kahani Yaad Aayee 1993, Sir 1993, Baazigar (Filmfare Award 1994) 1993, Phool Aur Angaar 1993, Aa Gale Lag Ja 1994, The Gentleman 1994, Madam X 1994, Hum Hain Bemisaal 1994, Zaalim 1994, Yaar Gaddar 1994, Main Khiladi Tu Anari 1994, Naaraaz 1994, Vijaypath 1994, Ahankar 1995, Akele Hum Akele Tum 1995, Hulchul 1995, Imtihaan 1995, Naajayaz 1995, Ram Jaane 1995, Surakshaa 1995, Gambler 1995, Ram Shastra 1995, Yaarana 1995, Gundaraj 1995, Takkar 1995, Baazi 1995, Hathkadi 1995, Jawab 1995, Chaahat 1996, Diljale 1996, Namak 1996, Ghatak: Lethal 1996, Sapoot 1996, Zordaar 1996, Dushman Duniya Ka 1996, Krishna 1996, Daraar 1996, Khiladiyon Ka Khiladi 1996, Border 1997, Dil Deewana Maane Na 1997, Hamesha 1997, Himalay Putra 1997, Judwaa 1997, Tamanna 1997, Virasat 1997, Aankhon Mein Tum Ho 1997, Ishq 1997, Mr & Mrs Khiladi 1997, Auzaar 1997, Chhota Chetan 1998, China Gate 1998, Gharwali Baharwali 1998, Wajood 1998, Prem Aggan 1998, Hero Hindustani 1998, Soldier 1998, Iski Topi Uske Sarr 1998, Duplicate 1998, Miss 420 1998, Chehraa 1999, Baadshah 1999, Haseena Maan Jaayegi 1999, Biwi No. 1 1999, Sooryavansham 1999, Kartoos 1999, Jaanam Samjha Karo 1999, Aarzoo 1999, Hum Aapke Dil Mein Rehte Hain 1999, Champion 2000, Gang 2000, Ghaath 2000, Aaghaaz 2000, Fiza 2000, Har Dil Jo Pyar Karega 2000, Refugee (Silver Lotus Award 2001) 2000, Josh 2000, Hum To Mohabbat Karega 2000, Jung 2000, Hera Pheri 2000, Khauff 2000, Badal 2000, Mela 2000, Ajnabee 2001, Lajja 2001, Asoka 2001, Aks 2001, Yaadein... 2001, Mujhe Kucch Kehna Hai 2001, Rahul 2001, Chori Chori Chupke Chupke 2001, Kuch Khatti Kuch Meethi 2001, Shakti: The Power 2002, Chor Machaye Shor 2002, Om Jai Jagadish 2002, Kuch Tum Kaho Kuch Hum Kahein 2002, Awara Paagal Deewana 2002, Badhaai Ho Badhaai 2002, Hum Kisi Se Kum Nahin 2002, Ab Ke Baras 2002, Filhaal 2002, Munnabhai M.B.B.S. 2003, Paap 2003, LOC Kargil 2003, Inteha 2003, Ssshhh... 2003, Mumbai Se Aaya Mera Dost 2003, Saaya 2003, Main

Prem Ki Diwani Hoon 2003, Ishq Vishk 2003, Khushi 2003, Kucch To Hai 2003, Ab Tumhare Hawale Watan Saathiyon 2004, Shart: The Challenge 2004, Aan: Men at Work 2004, Murder 2004, Main Hoon Na (Filmfare Award, Screen Award, Zee Cine Award 2005) 2004, Krishna Cottage 2004, Love in Nepal 2004, Love Story 2050 2008, Mughall-E-Azam 2008, Kambakkht Ishq 2009, Teree Sang 2009. *Honours:* Filmfare Special Jury Award 2001, Screen Artist of the Decade Award 2004. *Address:* c/o Sony Music Entertainment India, Span Centre, South Avenue, Santacruz (W), Mumbai 400 054, India (office).

MALIK, Zain Javadd (Zayn); British singer; b. 12 Jan. 1993, Bradford, England; s. of Yaser Malik and Tricia Malik. *Education:* Tong High School. *Career:* mem. One Direction 2010–15; finished third in The X Factor (UK) 2010; signed to Syco Records 2010; participated in X Factor Live Tour 2011; released debut single 2011; debut album first by a British group to debut at #1 on USA Billboard 200 album chart 2011. *Recordings:* with One Direction: albums: Up All Night 2011, Take Me Home (American Music Award for Favorite Album 2013) 2012, Midnight Memories (American Music Award for Favorite Album 2014) 2013, Four 2014. *DVDs:* Up All Night: the Live Tour 2012. *Publications:* One Direction: Forever Young 2011, One Direction: The Official Annual 2012 2011, Dare to Dream: Life as One Direction 2011, Where We Are: Our Band, Our Story 2013, Who We Are: Our Official Autobiography 2014. *Honours:* numerous, including: with One Direction: Bambi Pop Int. Award 2012, BBC Radio 1 Teen Awards for Best British Music Act and Best British Single (One Thing) 2012, BRIT Awards for Best British Single (What Makes You Beautiful) 2012, for BRITs Global Success 2013, for Best British Video (for You & I) 2015, JIM Awards (Flemish TV) for Best Int. Newcomer 2012, for Best Group 2013, for Best Pop 2013, MTV Europe Music Awards for Best New Act 2012, for Best UK & Ireland Act 2012, for Biggest Fans 2012, 2014, for Best Pop Act 2013, 2014, for Best Live Act 2014, for Best Worldwide Act (Europe North) 2014, MTV Video Music Awards Brazil Award for Int. Artist 2012, MTV Video Music Awards for Best New Artist 2012, for Best Pop Video and Most Share-Worthy Video (both What Makes You Beautiful) 2012, for Song of the Summer (for Best Song Ever) 2013, 4Music Video Honours Awards for Best Breakthrough and Best Group 2012, ARIA Music Award for Best Int. Artist 2012, Billboard Music Awards for Top Duo/Group 2013, for Top New Artist 2013, for Top Pop Artist 2013, American Music Award for Favorite Band, Duo or Group 2013, 2014, for Artist of the Year 2014, Outstanding Contrib. to Music, The Asian Awards 2015. *Current Management:* c/o Modest! Management, The Matrix Complex, 91 Peterborough Road, London, SW6 3BU, England. *E-mail:* info@modestmanagement.com. *Website:* www.modestmanagement.com.

MALININ, Alexander; Russian singer and musician (guitar); b. 16 Nov. 1958, Sverdlovsk. *Education:* Sverdlov Philharmonic School of Performing Arts, Ippolitov-Ivanov Conservatory, Moscow. *Career:* soloist, military choir of Ural District, late 1977–79; played in Poyut Gitari (Singing Guitars) ensemble 1983–84; performed with Golubiye Gitari (The Blue Guitars) ensemble; soloist with Stas Namina 1984–87; toured USA 1986; recorded joint album with Dave Pomerantz 1986; world-wide tours; television appearances include: Pesnya Goda and Stariye Pesni o Glavnom. *Recordings:* over 20 solo albums. *Honours:* Honored Artist of Russia 1991, Peoples' Artist of Russia 1997; Grand Prix Prize, Yurmala Music Festival 1988, Lenin Komsomol Prize 1989. *E-mail:* info@malinin.ru (office). *Website:* www.malinin.ru.

MALKMUS, Stephen; American singer and musician (guitar); b. 30 May 1966, Santa Monica, CA. *Education:* Univ. of Virginia. *Career:* founder mem. and lead singer, Pavement 1989–2000, reunited for live performances 2010; founder mem. The Silver Jews 1989–; tours world-wide; solo artist 1998, with Stephen Malkmus and The Jicks 2000–. *Television appearance:* Space Ghost Coast to Coast (cartoon) 1997. *Recordings include:* albums: with Pavement: Slanted and Enchanted 1992, Crooked Rain, Crooked Rain 1994, Wowee Zowee 1995, Brighten the Corners 1997, Terror Twilight 1999, Crooked Rain, Crooked Rain (expanded edn) 2004; with The Silver Jews: Starlite Walker 1994, The Natural Bridge 1996, American Water 1998, Bright Flight 2001, Tanglewood Numbers 2005, Lookout Mountain, Lookout Sea 2008; with Stephen Malkmus and The Jicks: Stephen Malkmus 2001, Pig Lib 2003, Face the Truth 2005, Real Emotional Trash 2008, Mirror Traffic 2011, Wig Out at Jagbags 2014. *Address:* c/o Matador Records, 304 Hudson Street, 7th Floor, New York, NY 10013, USA (office). *Website:* www.matadorrecs.com (office); www.stephenmalkmus.com.

MALLEY, Matt; American musician (bass guitar); b. 4 July 1963. *Career:* founder mem., Counting Crows 1993–; numerous tours and live appearances. *Recordings include:* albums: August & Everything After 1993, Recovering the Satellites 1996, Across a Wire: Live in New York 1998, This Desert Life 1999, Hard Candy 2002, Saturday Nights and Sunday Mornings 2008. *Current Management:* International Talent Booking, First Floor, Ariel House, 74a Charlotte Street, London, W1T 4QJ, England. *Telephone:* (20) 7637-6979. *Fax:* (20) 7637-6978. *E-mail:* mail@itb.co.uk. *Website:* www.countingcrows.com.

MALLOZZI, Charlie; record producer, mixer and songwriter; b. Parma, Italy. *Career:* writer, producer with Marco Sabiu, known as Rapino Brothers; moved to London, 1992; mixer, producer of Pop/Dance music; mem. of groups, Tabernacle, Rapination. *Recordings:* Albums for: Take That; Kylie Minogue; Dannii Minogue; Lulu; Kym Mazelle; Rozalla; Hit singles: Could It Be Magic, Take That; Rhythm of The Night, Corona; What Is Love, Haddaway; I Know The Lord, Tabernacle; Love Me The Right Way, Rapination and Kym Mazelle;

Also produced singles for: Alicia Bridges; Heaven 17; Sparks. *Honours:* BRIT Award, Single of the Year, Take That; Triple Platinum album, Take That.

MALMI, Jani; Finnish jazz musician and record producer; b. 1959. *Education:* studied with John Abercrombie and John Scofield. *Career:* began playing with various rock bands, 1970s; bandleader, own quartet; leader, Jani Malmi trio (with Jorma Ojanperä and Markku Ounaskari). *Recordings include:* Graffiti, 1988; One Leg Duck, 1995; As producer: Kosketuksia, 1995.

MALMROS, Ted; Swedish musician (bass guitar). *Career:* founder mem., Luca Brasi, renamed Shout Out Louds 2001–. *Recordings include:* albums: 100° (EP) 2003, Oh, Sweetheart (EP) 2004, Howl Howl Gaff Gaff 2005, Very Loud (EP) 2005, Our Ill Wills 2007, Work 2010. *Current Management:* c/o Filip Wilén, Bud Fox Management, Saturnusgatan 13, 224 57 Lund, Sweden. *Telephone:* (46) 13-81-20. *E-mail:* filip@budfox.se. *Website:* www.budfox.se; www.shoutoutlouds.com.

MALMSTEEN, Yngwie; Swedish rock musician (guitar); b. 1963. *Career:* played guitar from age 8; founder, rock groups Powerhouse, Rising; lead guitarist, Steeler, Los Angeles 1983; lead guitarist, Alcatrazz 1983–84; solo artiste, with own band, Rising Force 1984–. *Recordings:* albums: with Steeler: Steeler 1983; with Alcatrazz: No Parole From Rock 'n' Roll 1984, Live Sentence 1984; solo albums: Yngwie Malmsteen's Rising Force 1984, Marching Out 1985, Trilogy 1986, Odyssey 1988, Live in Leningrad 1989, Eclipse 1990, No Mercy 1992, Concerto Suite for Electric Guitar 1998, Live in Brazil 1998, Facing the Animal 1998, Inspiration 1999, Alchemy 1999, Double Live 2000, War to End All Wars 2000, Attack! 2002, Unleash the Fury 2005, Perpetual Flame 2008, Angels of Love 2009, Relentless 2010, Spellbound 2012. *Website:* www.yngwiemalmsteen.com.

MALO, Raul F. Martinez; American musician (guitar, bass guitar, piano), singer, songwriter and producer; b. 7 Aug. 1965, Miami; m. Betty Malo. *Career:* played bass guitar in high school and joined several small bands; mem. The Basics 1987; formed the Mavericks with Robert Reynolds, late 1980s; became band's lead vocalist 1990–2001; solo artist 2001–; The Mavericks disbanded in 2004, again reformed in 2012. *Recordings include:* albums: with The Mavericks: Mavericks 1990, From Hell To Paradise 1992, What A Crying Shame 1994, Music For All Occasions 1995, Trampoline, It's Now It's Live 1998, Best of The Mavericks 2000, In Time 2013, Mono 2015; solo: Today 2001, You're Only Lonely 2006, After Hours 2007, Lucky One 2009, Sinners and Saints 2010. *Honours:* with The Mavericks: Grammy Award for I Don't Care If You Love Me Anymore 1996, CMA Awards for Top Vocal Group 1995, 1996. *Current Management:* c/o Rgk Entertainment Inc, 700 12th Avenue, S Unit 201, Nashville, TN 37203, USA. *Telephone:* (615) 921-8686. *E-mail:* info@rgkentertainment.com. *Website:* www.rgk.ca; www.themavericksband.com; www.raulmalo.com.

MALONE, Kyp; American musician (guitar) and singer. *Career:* mem., TV on the Radio 2004–; also solo artist, performing as Rain Machine. *Recordings include:* albums: with TV on the Radio: Desperate Youth, Bloodthirsty Babes 2004, Return to Cookie Mountain 2006, Dear Science 2008; solo: Rain Machine 2009. *Honours:* Shortlist Music Prize 2004. *Address:* c/o 4AD, 17–19 Alma Road, London, SW18 1AA, England (home). *E-mail:* 4ad@4ad.com (office). *Website:* www.4ad.com (office); www.tvontheradio.com.

MALONE, Russell; American jazz guitarist; b. 8 Nov. 1963, Albany, Ga. *Career:* worked with Jimmy Smith 1988–90; mem. Harry Connick Jr Big Band 1990–94; solo recording artist 1992–; mem. Diana Krall Trio 1995–99; played with Benny Green 1997–2002, then formed duo 2002–07; mem. Sonny Rollins band 2010; leader, Russell Malone Quartet, Russell Malone Trio; has toured with numerous performers including Dianne Reeves, Ron Carter, Mulgrew Miller, Romero Lubambo; special performances with Bill Frisell, Hank Jones, Dr Lonnie Smith. *Recordings:* albums: solo: Russell Malone 1992, Black Butterfly 1993, Sweet Georgia Peach 1998, Wholly Cats 1999, Look Who's Here 2000, Heartstrings 2001, Bluebird (with Benny Green) 2004, Playground 2004, Portrait (with Northwestern State Univ. Jazz Ensemble) 2009, Triple Play 2010; with Diana Krall Trio: All for You: A Dedication to the Nat King Cole Trio 1996, Love Scenes 1997, When I Look In Your Eyes (Grammy Award for Best Vocal Jazz Performance 1999) 1999; other recordings include: The Beautiful Thing, Stephen Scott 1997, Ray Brown/Monty Alexander/Russell Malone 2002, Jazz in the Key of Blue, Jimmy Cobb Quartet 2009. *Current Management:* c/o B.H. Hopper Management Ltd., 7 Netherhall Gardens, London, NW3 5RN, England. *Telephone:* (20) 7209-8609. *E-mail:* hopper@hoppermanagement.com. *Website:* www.visionsofjazz.com/web/index.php/home.html. *Address:* Verve Music Group, 1755 Broadway, 3rd Floor, New York, NY 10019, USA (office). *Telephone:* (212) 331-2000 (office). *Fax:* (212) 331-2642 (office). *E-mail:* contact@vervemusicgroup.com (office). *Website:* www.vervemusicgroup.com/russellmalone (office); www.umusic.com (office).

MALONE, Tom (Bones), BS; American musician, arranger and producer; b. 16 June 1947, Honolulu, Hawaii; two d. *Education:* North Texas State University. *Career:* as student played with Les Elgart, The Supremes, Little Stevie Wonder, Marvin Gaye, The Temptations, Gladys Knight and The Pips; joined Woody Herman's big band; tours of USA, Europe with: Frank Zappa 1972, Blood Sweat and Tears 1973, Billy Cobham 1975; joined Gil Evans Orchestra 1973; tours of Europe, Japan, Far East; tour of USA with The Band, appeared in film: The Last Waltz 1976; musician, arranger, Saturday Night Live 1975–85; Musical Dir 1981–85; played with CBS Orchestra, Late Night With David Letterman 1993–; appeared in film The Blues Brothers; tours with

The Blues Brothers Band, 1988–90; appeared in film, Blues Brothers 2000. *Compositions include:* theme song, Saturday Night Live; comedy songs for Jim Belushi, Eddie Murphy, Billy Crystal; arrangements for films: The Blues Brothers, Sister Act; television: Saturday Night Live, CBS Orchestra. *Recordings include:* albums: solo: Standards of Living, Tom 'Bones' Malone Jazz Septet 1991, Eastern Standard Time 1993; recorded with artists including Blues Brothers, Gil Evans Orchestra, Miles Davis and Quincy Jones, Blood, Sweat and Tears, Frank Zappa, Pat Metheny, Cyndi Lauper, Sister Act, Steve Winwood, David Sanborn, James Brown, Spinners, Barry Manilow, Glen Campbell, B. B. King, Billy Cobham, Lou Reed, Bonnie Tyler, Diana Ross, Carla Bley, Harry Connick Jr, Pink Floyd, Buddy Rich, Woody Herman, J Geils Band, George Benson, Paul Simon, Chaka Khan, Village People, Gloria Gaynor, Carly Simon. *Address:* c/o CBS Orchestra, Late Show, 51 West 52nd Street, New York, NY 10019-6188, USA (office). *E-mail:* cbsmailbag@aol.com (office). *Website:* lateshow.cbs.com (office).

MALONE, Walter (Wally); American musician (bass) and singer; b. 20 Sept. 1946, Pittsburgh, Pennsylvania; m. Peggy Jones 1968. *Career:* principle bassist with Bo Diddley, West Coast 1970–94; bassist, Lady Bo 1969–; backing musician for Lightning Hopkins, Richard Berry, Chuck Berry, The Olympics; concerts include HIC Arena 1971, Monterey Jazz Festival 1973, 1974, Greek Theatre 1976, Boardwalk 1988, Monterey Blues Festival 1994, 1995, 1999; tours of East Coast 1960s, West Coast; Canada, Pacific Northwest 1970s; President, AFM Local 153 1996, RMA of Northern California, Professional Musicians of California. *Play:* Tony N' Tina's Wedding, San Jose 1997–98, Cable Car Theatre, San Francisco 1998–99. *Recordings:* albums: with The Mighty Bo Diddley: Ain't It Good To Be Free 1984, The Mighty Bo Diddley 1994, Lady Bo and The BC Horns 2000. *Publications:* Listed: The Complete Bo Diddley Sessions, by George R White 1993. *Address:* PO Box 2460, Boulder Creek, CA 95006-2460, USA (office). *Telephone:* (646) 226-9070 (office). *Fax:* (831) 338-1968 (office). *E-mail:* wmalone@afm.org (office).

MAMI, Cheb; Algerian rai singer, songwriter and actor; b. (Mohamed Khélifati), 11 July 1966, Graba-el-Oved, Saïda. *Career:* signed to Disco Maghreb, after winning second prize in Ihan wa chabab contest on the radio 1982; numerous live performances at rai festivals, tours worldwide; military service, Algeria 1987–89; collaborations with Sting, K-Mel, Gordon Cyrus, Simon Law; imprisoned 2010, released 2011. *Recordings include:* albums: Douni El Bladi 1986, Prince Of Rai 1989, Let Me Rai 1990, Fatma Fatma, Saida 1994, Let Me Cry 1995, Douni El Bladi 1996, 100% Arabica (with Cheb Khaled) 1997, Meli Meli 1999, Dellali 2001, Lazrag Saani 2001, Du Sud au Nord 2004, Layali 2006. *Films include:* Automne... Octobre à Alger 1993, 100% Arabica 1997. *Honours:* World Music Award for Best Selling Arabic Artist 2001.

MAN, Aladji; Senegalese hip-hop artist; b. (Mansour Jacques Sagna). *Career:* mem., Daara J 1997–2008; currently solo artist. *Recordings include:* albums: with Daara J: Daara J 1998, Xalima 1999, Boomerang 2003. *Honours:* BBC Radio 3 World Music Award for Best African Act 2004. *Website:* www.myspace.com/lordalajiman.

MANCHESTER, Melissa; American singer, songwriter, scriptwriter and actress; b. 15 Feb. 1951, Bronx, New York; d. of the late David Manchester and of Ruth Manchester. *Career:* staff writer, Chappell Music; solo artist 1973–; actress and scriptwriter; composer of musicals I Sent a Letter to My Love, Lady and the Tramp 2. *Recordings include:* albums: Home To Myself 1973, Bright Eyes 1974, Melissa 1975, Better Days and Happy Endings 1977, Singin' 1977, Don't Cry Out Loud 1978, Melissa Manchester 1979, For The Working Girl 1980, Hey Ricky 1982, Emergency 1983, Mathematics 1985, Midnight Blue 1988, Tribute, 1989, If My Heart Had Wings 1994, Melissa Manchester performs Pocahontas, 1995, The Colours of Christmas 1997, Joy 1997, The Essence of Melissa Manchester 1997, Midnight Blue: The Encore Collection 2001, When I Look Down That Road 2004, Playlist 2012. *Television:* Blossom. *Honours:* Grammy Award for Best Female Vocalist 1982, NARAS Gov.'s Award 1997. *Address:* c/o Premier Business Management Group, LLP, 15260 Ventura Blvd, Suite 1700, Sherman Oaks, CA 91403, USA (office). *Telephone:* (818) 933-2600. *Fax:* (818) 933-2699. *E-mail:* info@premierbmg.com. *Website:* www.premierbmg.com. *E-mail:* sholder@isp.com. *Website:* www.melissa-manchester.com.

MANCINA, Mark; American composer and musician (guitar); b. 1957. *Education:* California State Fullerton and Golden West College. *Career:* mem. BMI. *Compositions:* for television: Millennium 1992, Space Rangers 1993, Lifepod 1993, Poltergeist 1996, Soldier of Fortune, Inc. 1997, Houdini 1998, From the Earth to the Moon 1998, The Strip 1999, Blood+ 2005, Criminal Minds 2006–, A House Divided 2006; for film: Rage to Kill 1987, Space Mutiny 1988, Night Wars 1988, Code Name Vengeance 1989, Hell on the Battleground 1989, Future Force 1990, Death Chase 1990, The Lost Platoon 1991, Where Sleeping Dogs Lie 1992, Taking Liberty 1993, Sniper 1993, True Romance 1993, Speed 1994, Monkey Trouble 1994, Born Wild 1995, Man of the House 1995, Bad Boys 1995, Assassins 1995, Fair Game 1995, Money Train 1995, Twister 1996, Moll Flanders 1996, Con Air 1997, Speed 2: Cruise Control 1997, Return to Paradise 1998, Tarzan 1999, Auggie Rose 2000, Bait 2001, Domestic Disturbance 2001, Training Day 2001, Early Bloomer 2003, The Reckoning 2003, Brother Bear 2003, The Haunted Mansion 2003, Asylum 2005, Tarzan II 2005, Shooter 2007, August Rush 2007, Camille 2007, Without a Badge 2009, Like Dandelion Dust 2009, First Love 2009, Stopping Power 2009, Nowherehead 2009. *Current Management:* Gorfaine/Schwartz Agency

Inc, 4111 West Alameda Avenue, Suite 509. Burbank, CA 91505, USA. *Telephone:* (818) 260-8500. *Website:* www.gsamusic.com. *E-mail:* fanmail@markmancina.com (office). *Website:* www.markmancina.com.

MANDAGI, Dougy; Australian singer and songwriter; b. Manado, Indonesia. *Career:* mem. The Temper Trap 2005–; released debut EP The Temper Trap 2006; group relocated to London 2008; released debut album 2009; int. tours. *Recordings:* albums: with The Temper Trap: Conditions 2009, The Temper Trap (ARIA Music Award for Best Rock Album 2012) 2012. *Honours:* with The Temper Trap: ARIA Music Awards for Best Group 2010, 2012, for Most Popular Australian Single (for Sweet Disposition) 2010, APRA Award for Song of the Year (for Sweet Disposition) 2010. *Current Management:* c/o Lunatic Entertainment, Level 1, 490 Crown Street, Surry Hills, NSW 2010, Australia. *E-mail:* info@lunaticentertainment.com. *Website:* www.lunaticentertainment.com. *Address:* c/o Liberation Music, 9 Dundas Lane, Albert Park, Vic. 3206, Australia (office). *Telephone:* (3) 9695-7899 (office). *Fax:* (3) 9690-8665 (office). *E-mail:* info@liberationmusic.net (office). *Website:* www.liberationmusic.net (office); www.thetempertrap.com.

MANDEL, John Alfred (Johnny); American composer and arranger; b. 23 Nov. 1925, New York; s. of Alfred Mandel and Hannah Mandel; m. Martha Blaner 1970; one d. *Education:* Manhattan School of Music, Juilliard School. *Career:* trumpeter with Joe Ventui 1943; trombonist in bands of Boyd Raeburn, Jimmy Dorsey, Buddy Rich, Georgie Auld and Chubby Jackson from 1944; accompanist to June Christy 1949; performer and arranger, Elliot Lawrence Orchestra 1951–53; performer and arranger for Count Basie 1953–54; composer for Woody Herman, Stan Getz, Count Basie, Chet Baker; session work with Frank Sinatra, Peggy Lee, Anita O'Day, Maynard Ferguson, Mel Torme, Andy Williams; arranger for Quincy Jones, Natalie Cole, Nat King Cole, Shirley Horn, Tony Bennett, Diana Krall, Barbra Streisand; composer and arranger for film and television; mem. ASCAP 1956–, mem. Bd of Dirs 1989–. *Films:* soundtrack compositions: The Americanization of Emily 1964, The Sandpiper 1965, See You in Hell, Darling 1966, Heaven with a Gun 1969, M*A*S*H 1970, Agatha 1979. *Television:* as composer: Markham 1959, Banyon 1972, M*A*S*H 1972, Too Close for Comfort 1980. *Compositions:* numerous including: Not Really the Blues 1949, Hershey Bar 1950, Pot Luck 1953, Straight Life 1953, Tommyhawk 1954, Low Life 1956, The Shadow of Your Smile 1965 (Academy Award for Best Song 1965, Grammy Award for Song of the Year 1966), Suicide is Painless 1970. *Recordings:* albums: I Want to Live! 1958, The Sandpiper 1965, The Russians Are Coming, The Russians Are Coming 1966, M*A*S*H 1970, The Last Detail 1973, Escape to Witch Mountain 1975, Freaky Friday 1976. *Honours:* Grammy Award for Best Instrumental Arrangement Accompanying Vocals 1981, 1991, 1992, Nat. Endowment for the Arts Jazz Masters Award 2011.

MANDOZA; South African singer; b. (Mduduzi Tshabalala), 17 Jan. 1978, Zola, Soweto. *Career:* as a teenager sentenced to one and a half years in prison for car theft; formed group Chiskop with three friends, launched solo career 1999; performs in kwaito style, which fuses elements of African music with Western electronic dance and urban styles. *Recordings:* albums: with Chiskop: Klaimer, Ghetto 2000; solo: 9II5 Zola South 1999, Nkalakatha (South African Music Awards for Song Of The Year and Best Kwaito Music Album 2001, Song of the Decade 2004) 2000, Godoba 2002, Tornado 2003, S'gelekeqe 2004, Same Difference with Danny K 2004, Phunyuka Bamphethe 2005, Ngalabese 2006. *Honours:* Best Artist (Southern Africa), Kora All Africa Music Awards 2001, Best Kwaito Artist, Best Male Vocalist, Best Album, Best Stylist and Song Of The Year, Metro Music Awards 2001, named in Top 100 Great South Africans 2004. *Current Management:* In Tyme Inc., POB 1347, Paulshof, Johannesburg 2056, South Africa. *Telephone:* (31) 5661650. *Fax:* (31) 5661651. *E-mail:* sue@intymeinc.com. *Website:* www.intymeinc.com. *Address:* c/o Tanith Blackbeard, CCP Records, EMI House, 1A Stan Road, Morningside, Sandton 2196, South Africa (office). *Telephone:* (11) 9111500 (office). *Fax:* (11) 9111501 (office). *E-mail:* info@esounds.co.za (office). *Website:* www.ccpworld.co.za (office); www.mandoza.co.za.

MANDRELL, Barbara Ann; American singer; b. 25 Dec. 1948, d. of Irby Matthew Mandrell and Mary Ellen Mandrell; m. Kenneth Lee Dudney 1967; three c. *Career:* country music singer and entertainer 1959–; mem. Grand Ole Opry, Nashville, Tenn. 1972–; has performed throughout USA and abroad; mem. Musicians' Union, Screen Actors' Guild, Country Music Asscn, Order of Eastern Star. *Recordings include:* Midnight Oil, Treat Him Right, This Time I Almost Made It, This is Barbara Mandrell, Midnight Angel, Barbara Mandrell's Greatest Hits, Morning Sun, Standing Room Only, The Barbara Mandrell Collection 1995, Fooled by a Feeling 1995, It Works for Me 1997, Branson City Limits 1998. *TV appearances include:* Barbara Mandrell and the Mandrell Sisters 1980–82, Barbara Mandrell: Get To the Heart 1987, The Wrong Girl 1999, Stolen from the Heart 2000. *Publications include:* Get To the Heart: My Story (co-author) 1990. *Honours:* elected Miss Oceanside (Calif.) 1965, Most Promising Female Singer, Acad. of Country and Western Music 1971, Female Vocalist of the Year 1978, 1979, 1980, Entertainer of the Year 1980, 1981, People's Choice Awards 1982–84, mem. Country Music Hall of Fame 2009. *Current Management:* c/o Creative Artists Agency, 3310 West End Avenue, 5th Floor, Nashville, TN 37203-1028, USA. *E-mail:* ressig@caa.com. *Website:* www.barbara-mandrell.com.

MANGESHKAR, Lata; Indian singer, actress and songwriter; b. (Hema Hardikar), 28 Sept. 1929, Indore; d. of actor and singer Dinanath Mangeshkar and Shudhhamati Mangeshkar; sister of Asha Bhosle. *Career:* Indian film playback singer; first sang in Kiti Hasaal 1942; has recorded thousands of songs in 20 Indian languages. *Films include:* Pahill Mangala Gaur 1942, Chimukla Sansaar 1943, Maakhe Baal 1943, Gajabhau 1944, Badi Maa 1945, Jeevan Yaatra 1946, Subhadra 1946, Mandir 1948, Chattapati Shivaji 1953, Pukar 2000. *Recordings include:* albums: soundtracks: Sargam 1979, Darr 1993, Hum Aapke Hain Koun…! 1994, Dilwale Dulhania Le Jayeng 1995, Dil To Pagal Hai 1997, Lagaan 2001; solo: Lata In Concert – An Era In An Evening 1997, Saadgi 2007. *Honours:* Hon. Citizenship of Republic of Suriname 1980, Hon. Citizenship of Houston, Texas, USA 1987; Hon. DLitt (Pune Univ.) 1990; Filmfare Awards 1958, 1962, 1965, 1969 (refused to be considered for this award after 1969 to encourage new talent), Filmfare Lifetime Achievement Award 1993, Filmfare Special Award 1994, National Awards, Best Female Playback Singer 1972, 1975, 1990, Maharashtra State Award, Best Playback Singer 1966, 1967, Bengal Film Journalist's Award, Padma Bhushan 1969, Best Female Playback Singer 1964, 1967, 1968, 1969, 1970, 1971, 1973, 1975, 1981, 1985, Key of the City of Georgetown, Guyana 1980, Dada Saheb Phalke Award 1989, Videocon Screen Lifetime Achievement Award 1996, Rajiv Gandhi Award 1997, Lux Zee Cine Lifetime Achievement Award 1998, Padma Vibhushan 1999, IIFA London, Lifetime Achievement Award 2000, Noorjehan Award 2001, Maharashtra Ratna 2001, Bharat Ratna 2001, Noorjehan Award 2001, Maharashtra Ratna 2001, Hakim Khan Sur Award 2002, Asha Bhosle Award 2002, Swar Bharati Award, One Time Award for Lifetime Achievement 2008. *Address:* Prabhu Kunj, 101 Peddar Road, Mumbai 400 026, India.

MANGIONE, Charles (Chuck) Frank, MusB; American jazz musician (trumpet) and composer; b. 29 Nov. 1940, Rochester, New York; two d. *Education:* Eastman School of Music, University of Rochester. *Career:* formed Jazz Brothers with Brother Gap 1958–64; Director, Eastman Jazz Ensemble; Teacher, Eastman School of Music 1968–72; freelance musician with Maynard Ferguson and Kai Winding 1965; trumpeter, Art Blakey's Jazz Messengers 1965–67; formed Chuck Mangione Quartet 1968–; guest conductor, Rochester Philharmonic Orchestra 1970; numerous concerts world-wide include Europe, Japan, Australia, South America Montréal Jazz Festival. *Compositions include:* Hill Where The Lord Hides, Land of Make Believe, Chase the Clouds Away, Give It All You Got (theme to Winter Olympics 1980) (Emmy Award). *Recordings:* albums include: The Jazz Brothers 1960, Hey Baby 1961, Spring Fever 1961, Recuerdo 1962, Friends and Love 1970, Together 1971, Chuck Mangione Quartet 1972, Alive 1972, Land of Make Believe 1973, Chase The Clouds Away 1975, Encore 1975, Bellavia (Grammy Award for Best Instrumental Composition) 1976, Main Squeeze 1976, Feels So Good 1977, Children of Sanchez (film soundtrack) (Grammy Award) 1978, Fun and Games 1980, Tarantella 1981, 70 Miles Young 1981, Love Notes 1982, Journey to a Rainbow 1983, Disguise 1984, Save Tonight for Me 1986, Compact Jazz 1987, Live at the Village Gate 1989, The Hat's Back 1994, Together Forever 1994, The Feeling's Back 2000, Everything For Love 2001. *Honours:* Hon. MusD 1985; Most Promising Male Jazz Artist, Record World 1975, Grammy Awards, Emmy Award for Music Composition and Direction (for Give It All You Got) 1980, Numerous Magazine Poll Wins, Georgie Award for Instrumental Act of Year 1980, Regents Medal of Excellence, New York State 1984, Jazz Music Campus Entertainment Award, NACA 1987. *Current Management:* c/o Richard A. Burkhart, DreaMakers Inc., PO Box 5359, 654 Arth Drive, Crestline, CA 92325, USA. *Telephone:* (818) 292-3090. *E-mail:* rabdreamaker@aol.com. *Website:* www.chuckmangione.com.

MANGO BOY (see McBean, Colin)

MANGRAM, Myles Edwin, BS, MBA; American artist manager and record label executive; b. 30 July 1956, Pueblo, Colorado; m. Chea Rivera 1994; two s. *Career:* founder, President and CEO, Tri-M Management (personal management company, consulting service); President, Black Lion Records Inc (independent record label); Professor, Music Business Studies; professional musician and record producer with Dizzy Gillespie, Tom Scott, Denver Symphony; mem, Conference of Personal Managers, Entertainment Law Society. *Recordings:* as producer: Alyssa Milano, Anita Whitaker. *Honours:* Outstanding Young Man of America Award, Colorado Scholars Award, Presidential Scholars Award. *Address:* Myles E. Mangram, Tri-M Management Ltd, 2060 Avenue de los Arboles, Thousand Oaks, CA 91362, USA (office). *Telephone:* (805) 493-1120 (office). *Fax:* (805) 493-1126 (office). *E-mail:* myles@tri-management.com (office). *Website:* www.tri-mmanagement.com (office).

MANGWANA, Sam; Democratic Republic of the Congo singer, musician (guitar) and songwriter; b. 1945, Kinshasa, Zaire (now Democratic Repub. of the Congo). *Education:* studied singing in the Salvation Army choir. *Career:* mem. Tabu Ley Rochereau's Africa Fiesta, c. 1962, Franco's TPOK Jazz 1972; formed Festival des Maquisards with Dizzy Mandjeku 1968; established La Belle Sonora label; founder, African All Stars 1976, based in Abidjan, toured Africa, Europe and the USA; now lives in Paris. *Recordings include:* albums: Sam and Les Maquisards 1968, Sam and African All Stars Vols 1 and 2 1982, Maria Tebbo, Rumba Music 1991, Gallo Negro (featuring Papa Noël) 1998, Sam Mangwana Plays Dino Vangu 2000, Cantos de Esperanza 2003. *Current Management:* c/o Alison Loerke, 12501 11th Avenue NW, Seattle, WA 98177, USA.

MANIAPOTO, Moana, (Ngāti Tuwharetoa, Ngāti Pikiao, Tuhourangi); New Zealand singer, songwriter and filmmaker; b. (Moana Maree Maniapoto), 1961, Invergargill; d. of Nepia Maniapoto and Bernadette Honywood; pnr

Toby Mills; one s. one d. *Career:* combines traditional Maori music and arts with Western music and modern production techniques; fmr tv and radio presenter, actor, law graduate and advocate; founding mem. Moana and the Moahunters 1990–98, performed concerts worldwide; founding mem. Moana and the Tribe 2002–, numerous tours in New Zealand and Germany and concerts in Russia, UK, Austria, Spain, Switzerland; formed film making partnership Tawera and Black Pearl Productions with Toby Mills; Trustee, Black Pearl Nat. Trust. *Recordings:* albums: with Moana and the Moahunters: Tahi 1993, Rua 1998; solo: Toru 2003; with Moana and the Tribe: Live 2004. *Honours:* Lifetime Hon. Recipient, Toi Iho-Maori Made Mark; New Zealand Order of Merit 2004; Overall Winner (first ever non-American), Int. Songwriting Competition 2003, Te Tohu Mahi Hou a Te Waka Toi in recognition of outstanding leadership and contribution to the development of Maori art 2005. *Address:* Moana Maniapoto, POB 78074, Grey Lynn, Auckland, New Zealand (office). *E-mail:* moana@moananz.com (office). *Website:* www.moananz.com; www.sol-de-sully.de.

MANILOW, Barry; American singer, musician (piano) and songwriter; b. (Barry Alan Pincus), 17 June 1946, New York; s. of Harold Manilow and Edna Manilow. *Education:* New York Coll. Music, Juilliard School of Music. *Career:* worked in mailroom at CBS; film ed. WCBS-TV; Dir Music Ed Sullivan's Pilots; Music Dir, conductor and producer for Bette Midler; Amb. for Prince's Trust 1996; solo artist 1974–; f. Manilow Health and Hope Fund (nonprofit includes Manilow Music Project). *Theatre:* Barry Manilow on Broadway (jt recipient Tony Award 1977) 1976, Barry Manilow at the Gershwin (Broadway) 1989, Copacabana (West End, London) 1994. *Television appearance:* Copacabana (film) 1985. *Recordings include:* albums: Barry Manilow I 1973, Barry Manilow II 1974, Tryin' To Get The Feelin' 1975, This One's For You 1976, Live 1977, Even Now 1978, One Voice 1979, Barry 1980, A Nice Boy Like Me 1980, If I Should Love Again 1981, Live In Britain 1982, I Wanna Do It With You 1982, Here Comes The Night 1982, Oh, Julie! 1982, 2.00 AM Paradise Café 1984, Manilow 1985, Live On Broadway 1987, Swing Street 1987, Barry Manilow 1989, Songs To Make The Whole World Sing 1989, Because It's Christmas 1990, Showstoppers 1991, Hidden Treasures 1993, Singin' With The Big Bands 1994, Another Life 1995, Summer of '78 1996, Manilow Sings Sinatra 1998, Here At The Mayflower 2001, A Christmas Gift Of Love 2002, Two Nights Live 2004, Scores: Songs From Copacabana and Harmony 2004, The Greatest Songs of the Fifties 2006, The Greatest Songs of the Sixties 2006, The Greatest Songs of the Seventies 2007, In the Swing of Christmas 2007, Beautiful Ballads and Love Songs 2008, The Greatest Songs of the Eighties 2008, Happy Holiday! 2008, In the Swing of Christmas 2009, The Greatest Love Songs of All Time 2010, 15 Minutes 2011, My Dream Duets 2014. *Publication:* Sweet Life: Adventures on the Way to Paradise 1987. *Honours:* Producer of the Year 1975, After Dark magazine Ruby Award 1976, Photoplay Gold Medal 1976, Grammy Award for Song of the Year (for I Write The Songs) 1977, Emmy Award (for The Barry Manilow Special) 1977, American Music Awards for Favorite Male Artist 1978–80, Grammy Award for Best Male Pop Vocal Performance (for At The Copa from Copacabana) 1979, Songwriters Hall of Fame Hitmaker Award 1991, Starlight Foundation Humanitarian of the Year 1991, Soc. of Singers Ella Award 2003. *Current Management:* William Morris Endeavor Entertainment, 9601 Wilshire Blvd, Suite 300, Beverly Hills, CA 90210, USA. *Website:* www.barrymanilow.com.

MANN, Aimee; American singer and songwriter; b. 8 Sept. 1960, Richmond, VA; m. Michael Penn 1998. *Career:* fmr mem., Young Snakes; lead singer, 'Til Tuesday 1982–; solo artist 1990–; formed record label, SuperEgo Records, and music publishing label, Aimee Mann Music; collaborations include Elvis Costello, Jules Shear. *Film appearance:* The Big Lebowski 1998. *Recordings include:* albums: with 'Til Tuesday: Voices Carry 1986, Welcome Home 1987, Everything's Different Now 1989, Coming Up Close: Retrospective 1999; solo: Whatever 1993, I'm With Stupid 1995, Bachelor No. 2 2000, Lost In Space 2002, The Forgotten Arm 2005, One More Drifter in the Snow 2006, #@%&*! Smilers 2008, Charmer 2012. *Current Management:* Michael Hausman Artist Management Inc., 511 Avenue of the Americas, Suite 197, New York, NY 10011, USA. *Website:* www.michaelhausman.com. *E-mail:* info@aimeemann.com (office). *Website:* www.aimeemann.com.

MANN, Jasbinder (Jas); British singer and musician (guitar); b. 24 April 1970, Dudley. *Career:* singer, The Sandkings, 1980s; tours include: Support to Happy Mondays, Stone Roses; lead singer, Babylon Zoo, 1994–; concerts include: NME Brats, Midem, 1995; The Night The Earth Stood Still, London, 1995; mem. Musicians' Union. *Recordings:* Albums: Boy With The X-Ray Eyes, 1996; King Kong Groover, 1998; Singles: Spaceman (Int. No. 1 hit), 1996; Animal Army, 1996; All The Money's Gone, 1998.

MANN, Manfred; musician (keyboards); b. (Manfred Lubowitz), 21 Oct. 1940, Johannesburg, South Africa. *Career:* founder mem., Mann-Hugg Blues Brothers 1962, became Manfred Mann 1963–69; founder, Emanon, Manfred Mann Chapter Three 1969, Manfred Mann Earth Band 1971–; nat. and int. tours; taught at Goldsmith's Coll., London late 1970s. *Recordings include:* albums with Manfred Mann: Five Faces of Manfred Mann 1964, Mann Made 1965, Mann Made Hits 1966, As Is 1966, Soul of Mann 1967, Up The Junction 1967, The Mighty Quinn 1968, This Is Manfred Mann 1971, Semi-Detached Suburban 1979, The R&B Years 1986, The Singles Plus 1987, The EP Collection 1989, The Collection 1990, Ages of Mann 1992; two albums with Manfred Mann Chapter Three; with Manfred Mann's Earth Band: Manfred Mann's Earth Band 1972, Get Your Rocks Off 1973, Solar Fire 1973, The Good Earth 1974, Nightingales and Bombers 1975, The Roaring Silence 1976, The

New Bronze Age 1977, Watch 1978, Angle Station 1979, Chance 1981, Somewhere In Africa 1983, Budapest 1983, Criminal Tango 1986, Masque 1987, Manfred Mann's Earth Band 1992; solo: Manfred Mann's Plain Music 1991, Ages of Mann 1995, Soft Vengeance 1996, Wired 2001; singles: 5–4–3–2–1 1964, Do Wah Diddy Diddy 1964, Come Tomorrow 1965, Oh No, Not My Baby 1965, If You Got To Go, Go Now 1965, Pretty Flamingo 1966, Just Like A Woman 1966, Semi-Detached Suburban Mr James 1966, Ha! Ha! Said The Clown 1967, Mighty Quinn 1968, My Name Is Jack 1968, Fox On The Run 1969, Ragamuffin Man 1969, Joybringer 1973, Blinded By The Light 1976, Davey's On The Road Again 1978, Runner 1984, Plains Music 1991–2006 2004. *Current Management:* Consolidated, PO Box 87, Tarporley, Cheshire, CW6 9FN, England. *Telephone:* (1829) 730488. *Fax:* (1829) 730499.

MANN, Steve; British musician (guitar, keyboards), sound engineer and record producer; b. 9 Aug. 1956, London. *Education:* university. *Career:* joined Liar, toured UK and Europe 1977; joined Steve Swindells, appeared on Old Grey Whistle Test 1980; formed Lionheart 1981; toured UK with Tytan 1983; joined MSG, played Monsters of Rock Festival, European and USA tours 1986; joined Sweet 1989; toured USA, Canada, Australia, Europe, Russia; producer, engineer for Shogun, Tora Tora, MSG, Rough Silk, Letter X, Sweet, Thunderhead Spice; mem, MCPS, PRS (associate mem.), Musicians' Union. *Compositions:* co-wrote Anytime. *Recordings:* with Liar: Set The World On Fire 1978; with Lionheart: Hot Tonight 1984; with Tytan: Rough Justice 1985; with MSG: Perfect Timing 1987, Save Yourself 1989; with Sweet: A 1992, Glitz, Blitz and Hits 1995.

MANNING, Barbara Lynne; American musician, songwriter and singer; b. 12 Dec. 1944, San Diego, CA. *Education:* college. *Career:* extensive tours of the USA and Europe. *Recordings include:* albums: Lately I Keep Scissors 1988, One Perfect Green Blanket 1992, Barbara Manning Sings with the Original Artists (with Stuart Moxham and Jon Langford) 1993, 1212 1997, In New Zealand 1999, You Should Know By Now 2000, Under One Roof 2000, Super Scissors 2008; other credits include: 28th Day, 28th Day 1985, The Land of Thirst, World of Pooh 1989, Nowhere, S.F. Seals 1994, Truth Walks in Sleepy Shadows, S.F. Seals 1995, Homeless Where The Heart Is, The Go-Luckys! 1999, You Should Know By Now, The Go-Luckys 2000. *Honours:* SF Goldie Award, SF Wammie Award 1992, Bay Area Music Award 1996. *Address:* PO Box 5435, Chico, CA 95927-5435, USA. *E-mail:* barbara@barbaramanning .com. *Website:* www.barbaramanning.com; www.myspace.com/ barbaramanning.

MANNING, Roger Joseph, Jr, BMus; American songwriter, arranger, record producer and musician (keyboards); b. 27 May 1966, Inglewood, CA. *Education:* Univ. of Southern California. *Career:* keyboardist, Beatnik Beatch 1987–89; keyboardist, songwriter, arranger, Jellyfish 1990–94; songwriter, arranger, producer, Imperial Drag 1995–98; keyboardist, arranger, The Moog Cookbook 1995–98, keyboardist with Beck 1998–2002; re-mixing other artists' work, including the French band, Air, Soulwax; founder mem., TV Eyes 2000–; staff mem., Expansion Team (audio and visual design co.); mem. ASCAP. *Recordings include:* albums: with Beatnik Beatch: Beatnik Beatch 1988; with Jellyfish: Bellybutton 1990, Spilt Milk 1993; with Imperial Drag: Imperial Drag 1996; with The Moog Cookbook: The Moog Cookbook 1996, The Moog Cookbook: Ye Olde Space Bande; with Beck: Mutations 1998, Midnite Vultures 1999; with Luscious Jackson: Electric Honey 1999; with TV Eyes: TV Eyes 2006; solo: Catnip Dynamite 2009. *Address:* Expansion Team, 187 Lafayette Street, New York, NY 10013, USA (office). *Telephone:* (212) 431-7508 (office). *Fax:* (212) 431-6793 (office). *Website:* www.expansionteam.org (office); www.rogerjosephmanningjr.com.

MANOV, Dragomir; Bulgarian musician (guitar). *Career:* Lead guitarist, Konkurent 1986–; numerous concerts, TV and radio appearances. *Recordings:* Konkurent 1989, Something Wet 1995, Escape from Paradise 2002, Give me Time 2007. *Honours:* First prizes: Top Rock Band, Youth Festival Vidin 1989, Rock Ring, Sofia 1990, Top Rock Composition: The Cavalry 1991, Top Rock Singer, Bulgaria 1994, Group of the Year, The Darik Radio Countdown 1994. *E-mail:* emil.anchev@abv.bg (office). *Website:* www.konkurentrockband.com.

MANSON, Marilyn; American singer and songwriter; b. (Brian Warner), 5 Jan. 1969, Canton, Ohio; m. Dita Von Teese 2005 (divorced 2007). *Career:* fmr music journalist; Founder-mem. Marilyn Manson & the Spooky Kids 1989–, later Marilyn Manson; numerous TV appearances, tours. *Recordings include:* albums: Portrait of an American Family 1994, Smells Like Children 1995, Antichrist Superstar 1996, Mechanical Animals 1998, The Last Tour on Earth 1999, Holy Wood (In the Shadow of the Valley of Death) 2000, Genesis of the Devil 2001, Live 2002, The Word According to Manson 2002, The Golden Age of Grotesque 2003, White Trash 2003, From Obscurity 2 Purgatory 2004, Eat Me, Drink Me 2007, The High End of Low 2009, Born Villain 2012, The Pale Emperor 2015. *Publication:* The Long Hard Road Out of Hell (autobiography) 1997. *Honours:* Kerrang! Icon Award 2005. *Current Management:* c/o CAA, 162 Fifth Avenue, 6th Floor, New York, NY 10010, USA. *Telephone:* (212) 277-9000. *Fax:* (212) 277-9099. *Website:* www.caa.com; www.marilynmanson.com.

MANSON, Shirley; British singer and musician (guitar); b. 3 Aug. 1966, Edinburgh, Scotland. *Career:* mem. and lead singer, August 1984, Wild Indians, Goodbye Mr McKenzie, Angel Fish; mem. and lead singer, Garbage 1994–; numerous tours, festivals, TV and radio appearances. *Recordings include:* albums: Garbage 1995, Version 2.0 1998, Beautifulgarbage 2001, Androgyny 2003, Bleed Like Me 2005, Absolute Garbage 2007, Not Your Kind of People 2012. *Film music:* The World is Not Enough (theme to James Bond:

The World is Not Enough) 1999. *Current Management:* Free Trade Agency, 20–22 Curtain Road, London, EC2A 3NF, England. *Telephone:* (20) 7655-6900. *Fax:* (20) 7655-6909. *E-mail:* info@freetradeagency.co.uk. *Website:* www .freetradeagency.co.uk; www.garbage.com.

MANTLER, Karen; American musician (glockenspiel and harmonica); b. 1966, d. of Michael Mantler and Carla Bley. *Education:* Berklee Coll. of Music, Boston. *Career:* joined the Carla Bley Band (mother) on Glockenspiel 1977, toured Europe and the USA; Carnegie Hall 1980; guest musician, Jazz Composers' Alliance; formed own band, toured; joined Carla Bley Band on harmonica for European Tour 1988; Knitting Factory with own band; played on David Sanborn's Nith Music TV show; toured alongside The Very Big Carla Bley Band; joined father as asst, Watt Works, promoted to Gen. Man.; Montréal Jazz Festival; played Synthesizer for Steve Swallow 1991; played organ with Motohiko Hino; organ player, The Very Big Carla Bley Band 1992, played Glasgow Jazz Festival, Umbria Jazz Festival, Italy; left Watt Works 1993; played again with Motohiko Hino; glockenspiel and harmonica, band with Terry Adams 1994; European tour with Carla Bley Band; worked with drummer Michael Evans as duo, gigs and recorded material; another tour with Carla Bley Big Band 1996; regular appearances at Starbuck's Coffee House 1997; rejoined Carla Bley Big Band 1997, tour of England, organ player in Fancy Chamber Music with Carla Bley. *Recordings include:* My Cat Arnold; Karen Mantler and her Cat Arnold get the Flu, Farewell, Karen Mantler's Pet Project 2000; with Robert Wyatt: Cuckooland 2002; with Carla Bley: Escalator Over the Hill, Musique Mecanique, The Very Big Carla Bley Band, Big Band Theory, The Carla Bley Big Band Goes to Church; others: The Watt Works Family Album, Carried Away, with Robbie Dupree; Swallow, with Steve Swallow; Sailing Stone, with Motohiko Hino; Folly Seeing All This, with Michael Mantler. *Address:* c/o Watt Works, PO Box 67, Willow, NY 12495, USA (office). *E-mail:* watt@ulster.net (office). *Website:* wattxtrawatt.com (office).

MANTOVANI, Gustavo Fumagalli; Brazilian rock musician (guitar) and singer. *Career:* Founder-mem. and lead guitarist, rock band Democratas 1999–2001, band name changed to Fresno 2001–; debut EP released 2001; numerous live shows and tours. *Recordings:* albums: with Fresno: Quarto dos Livros 2003, O Rio, A Cidade, A Árvore 2004, Ciano 2006, Redenção 2008, Revanche 2010, Cemitério Das Boas Intenções 2011, Infinito 2012. *Honours:* MTV VMB Awards for Best New Artist 2007, for Artist of the Year 2009, for Best Pop Artist 2009, Multishow Brazilian Music Award for Band of the Year 2009, MTV Europe Music Award for Best Brazilian Act 2013. *Current Management:* c/o Perfexx Assessoria de Comunicação, São Paulo, Brazil. *Telephone:* (11) 3064-7105. *E-mail:* contato@perfexx.com.br. *Website:* www .perfexx.com.br. *Address:* c/o Universal Music Ltd, PO Box 37133, 22.622-970, Rio de Janeiro, Brazil (office). *Telephone:* (21) 3389-7676 (office). *Fax:* (21) 2494-3035 (office). *Website:* www.universalmusic.com.br (office); www .fresnorock.com.br (home).

MANUEL, Carlos; Cuban singer; b. (Carlos Manuel Pruñeda Macias), 1972, Havana. *Career:* mem. nueva trova group, Mayohuacan 1996; collaboration and tours with Irakere 1996; formed Carlos Manuel y Su Clan 1998–; moved to USA 2003–. *Recordings:* albums: Por La Vena Del Gusto 1998, Malo Cantidad 2001, Enamora'o 2002.

MANUELLE, Victor; Puerto Rican salsa singer and songwriter; b. (Víctor Manuel Ruiz), 28 Sept. 1970, New York, NY; m. (divorced); one s. two d. *Career:* solo artist 1993–. *Recordings include:* albums: Justo a Tiempo 1993, Solo Contigo 1994, Victor Manuelle 1996, A Pesar de Todo 1997, Ironías 1998, Inconfundible 1999, Instinto y Deseo 2001, Le Preguntaba a la Luna 2002, Travesía 2004, Decisión Unánime (Billboard Latin Music Award for Male Tropical Album of the Year 2007) 2006, Una Navidad a mi Estilo 2007, Soy 2008. *Honours:* Distinguished Youngster in Music, Senate of Puerto Rico 1999, Billboard Latin Music Award for Male Tropical/Salsa Airplay Track of the Year (for Me da lo Mismo) 2002, (for Tengo Ganas) 2005, ASCAP Latin Award for Songwriter of the Year 2005, Premio Lo Nuestro for Artista del Año Tropical/Salsa 2007. *Address:* c/o Sony BMG, 550 Madison Avenue, New York, NY 10022, USA (office). *Website:* www.sonybmglatin.com (office); www .victormanuelleonline.com.

MAPFUMO, Thomas Tafirenyika Mukanya; Zimbabwean musician (mbira, guitar), singer and songwriter; b. 2 July 1945, Marondera. *Career:* important figure in local Shona music 1970s–; singer in local bands, including The Cosmic Dots, the Springfields; f. Hallelujah Chicken Run Band 1973, Black Spirits 1976; performed with The Pied Pipers 1977; f. Acid Band 1977–, later banned from the radio, renamed Blacks Unlimited 1978; Mapfumo imprisoned for subversion 1977; currently lives in exile in Eugene, Ore., USA; researcher in traditional Zimbabwean folk music. *Recordings include:* albums: Hokoya! 1977, Mbira Music of Zimba 1980, Gwindingwe 1980, Mabesa 1983, Congress 1983, The Chimurenga Singles 1983, Ndangariro 1984, Corruption 1984, Mr Music 1985, Chimurenga For Justice 1986, Zimbabwe-Mozambique 1987, Corruption 1989, Nyamaropa Nhimutimu 1989, Shumba 1990, The Spirit of the Eagle 1991, Chimurenga Masterpis 1991, Hondo 1993, Chimurenga Int'l 1993, Vanhu Vatema 1994, Chimurenga: African Spirit Music 1997, Rise Up 2006, Exile 2009. *Current Management:* c/o Linda Rowan, Midnight Productions Hawaii/International, PO Box 853, Haleiwa, HI 96712, USA. *Telephone:* (808) 637-3139. *E-mail:* lrowan39@yahoo.com. *Website:* www.thomasmapfumo.com.

MARGARIT, Bernard; French musician (guitar) and composer; b. 19 Feb. 1956, Carcassonne; one s. one d. *Education:* Academie, Toulouse. *Career:* int. tours with Johnny Hallyday; television performances with Kim Wilde, Eddy Mitchell, Johnny Hallyday; French jazz concert tours with Jean Pierre Llabador, Remy Charmasson, Philippe Petrucciani; mem. SACEM, SPEDIDAM, ADAMI. *Recordings include:* album: Friendship (with Jean Pierre Llabador), Kerala's Song, Pluma de loro, Notes de voyages. *E-mail:* b.margarit@wanadoo.fr (office). *Website:* www.bernardmargarit.com.

MARGOLIN, Bob; American blues musician (guitar) and writer; b. 9 May 1949, Boston, Massachusetts. *Education:* Graduated Boston University, 1970. *Career:* Seven years in Muddy Waters Blues Band; Leader, own blues band, 1980–. *Recordings:* sideman on 30 albums with other blues players, 1974–96; albums include: with the Band: The Last Waltz, 1978; with The Nighthawks, 1979; with Muddy Waters: Live At Mr Kellys 1971, Woodstock Album 1975, Hard Again 1977, I'm Ready 1977, Mississippi Muddy Waters Live 1977, King Bee 1980; with Johnny Winter: Nothin' But The Blues 1977, The Johnny Winter Story 1980; solo: Old School 1988, Chicago Blues 1990, Down in the Alley 1993, My Blues and My Guitar 1995, Up and In 1997, Hold Me to It 1999, In North Carolina 2006; other session work includes: Henry Gray, Roy Roberts, Daryl Davis, Toby Walker. *Publications:* senior writer, regular column for Blues Revue magazine. *E-mail:* bob@bobmargolin.com. *Website:* www.bobmargolin.com; www.myspace.com/bobmargolin.

MARGUET, Christophe; French musician (drums); b. 14 May 1965, Paris; m. Isabelle, Aug. 1992. *Career:* Played with: Barney Wilen; Vincent Herring; Bud Shank; Alain Jean Marie; Claude Barthélémy; Daunik Lazro; Noël Akchoté; Didier Levallet; Tours: People's Republic of China; Egypt; Syria; Morocco; Cameroon; Own trio with Sebastien Texier (alto sax), Olivier Sens (double bass); Played with Marc Ducret, Yves Robert, Barry Guy, Kenny Wheeler, François Jeanneau, François Corneloup, Louis Sclavis, 1997–. *Recordings:* 2 with Georges Arvanitas: Gershwin; Ellington; Altissimo, Hubert Dupont Sextet; Amazonia, Nicolas Genest; Mr Claude, Claude Barthelemy Quartet, 1997; Resistance Poetique, Christophe Marguet Trio, 1997; Strophes, Sylvain Kassap Quartet, 1998; Animal Language, 49 Nord, 1999; Ça Commence Aujourd Hui, Louis Sclavis, 1999; Les Correspondances, Christophe Marguet Quartet, 2000. *Honours:* First Prize, Orchestra, First Prize, Composition, Concours de la Défense, 1995; Django d'Or for Resistance Poetique, Best CD of Year, 1997. *Address:* 25 rue Jeanne d'Arc, 92600 Asnieres, France. *E-mail:* contact@christophemarguet.net. *Website:* www.christophemarguet.net.

MARÍA ESPINOSA SAVIÑÓN, Dulce; Mexican singer, songwriter and actress; b. 6 Dec. 1985, Mexico City. *Career:* acted in TV commercials as a child; cast mem., Plaza Sesamo 1993, group K.I.D.S. 1996–99; mem. D&D (with Daniel Habif) 1999–2000; mem. Jeans 2000–02; acted in telenovela Rebelde 2004–06; mem. group RBD 2004–08; solo artist 2009–; f. Foundation Dulce Amanecer 2009; Rep., Technology Yes 2009; numerous collaborations including with Julión Álvarez, Tiziano Ferro, Anahi, Akon, Juan Magan, J-King, Maximan, Chino & Nacho, Rio Roma, Basshunter, Henry Mendez. *Television:* as actress: Plaza Sesamo 1993–95, El Vuelo del Águila 1994, Retrato de Familia 1995, Huracán 1998, Nunca Te Olividaré 1999, Infierno en el paraíso 1999, DKDA: Sueños de Juventud 1999, Primer Amor... A Mil Por Hora 2000, Clase 2002–03, Rebelde (Premios TVyNovelas Award for Best Young Female Special Acting 2006) 2004–06, RBD: La Familia 2007, Verano de amor (People en Español Best Young Actress Award 2009) 2009, Mentir para Vivir (Premios Mas Que Telenovelas Award for Favorite Female Special Acting 2013) 2013. *Films:* as actress: Desilusiones 1997, Juguito de Ciruela 1997, Inesperado Amor 1999, Bienvenida al Clan 2000, Alguien Ha Visto A Lupita? 2011, Quiero ser Fiel 2013. *Stage:* Rock of Ages 2014. *Recordings include:* albums: with RBD: Rebelde 2004, Nuestro Amor 2005, Celestial 2006, Rebels 2006, Empezar Desde Cero 2007, Para Olvidarte de Mi 2009; solo: Extranjera (Premios Eclipse for Best Album of the Year 2010, Lo Mejor de la Música Univision Award for Best Album 2011, Premios Luminaria de Oro Award for Best Album 2011) 2010, Sin Fronteras 2014. *Publication:* Dulce Amargo 2007. *Honours:* Premios Juventud She's Got Style Awards 2006, 2011, Premios TVZ Award for Int. Artist 2010, Premios People en Español Awards for Best Pop Artist/Group 2010, for Queen of Facebook 2012, for Collaboration of the Year (with Julión Álvarez) 2013, for Favorite Female Act 2014, Premios G1 Globo Award for Best Female Singer 2010, Premios Eclipse Award for Best Pop Act 2010, Kids Choice Brazil Award for Favorite Int. Artist 2011, Kids Choice Mexico Awards for Favorite Latin Solo Artist 2011, for Prosocial Award (for Dulce Amanecer Foundation) 2011, Latin Music Italian Awards for Best Latin Female Artist 2013, for Best Latin Collaboration (with Julión Álvarez) 2013, Premios Texas Awards for Best Rock Act 2011, for Favorite Female Act 2012, for Best Pop Act 2012, MTV Millennials Awards for Best Fandom 2013, for Twitter Star 2013, for Latin Instagram Star 2013, Premios MTV Novelas for Best Musical Theme 2013, MTV Europe Music Award for Best Latin America Act 2014. *Address:* c/o Universal Music Latin Entertainment, Universal Music Group, 2220 Colorado Avenue, Santa Monica, CA 90404, USA (office). *Telephone:* (310) 865-5000 (office). *Website:* www.universalmusica.com (office); www.dulcemariamusic.com.

MARIA RITA, BA; Brazilian jazz singer; b. (Maria Rita Mariano), 9 Sept. 1977, São Paulo; d. of César Camargo Mariano and Elis Regina. *Education:* Colégio Pueri Domus, Santo Amaro, SP, New York Univ., USA. *Recordings:* album: Maria Rita (Latin Grammy Award for Most Popular Brazilian Album 2004) 2003, Segundo (Latin Grammy Award for Best Brazilian Album 2006) 2005, Samba Meu 2007. *Honours:* Latin Grammy Award for Best New Artist 2004, Latin Grammy Award for Best Brazilian Song (for Caminho das Águas) 2006. *Current Management:* Macuco Produções, rua Moviato Coelho 1266 CJ. 01, São Paulo, SP 05417-002, Brazil. *Telephone:* (11) 3034-0292. *Fax:* (11) 3813-2165. *E-mail:* macucoproducoes@uol.com.br. *Website:* www.maria-rita.com.

MARIANELLI, Dario; Italian composer; b. Pisa. *Education:* studied piano and composition in Florence and Guildhall School of Music and Drama, London, Bretton Univ. Coll., Nat. Film and Television School. *Career:* classical composer and composer of film soundtracks. *Compositions:* Canti di Uqbar 1991, Rondo for piano and orchestra 1991, Quintet for Winds No. 1 1992, Six Variations on a theme by S. Prokofief for chamber group 1993, One Movement for string quartet 1993, Fantasia for oboe and piano 1993, Four Songs for piano and tenor 1993, I Think I Do Remember Him for cello solo 1994, Pagine Di Sinfonie Perdute 1994, Variations on nought for voice, orchestra and live electronics 1994, 3 Madrigals 1994, Two Digressions for violin and piano 1995, String Quartet No. 1 1995, The Art Of Road Crossing 1996, Seeing Things (for text by Seamus Heaney) 1996, No Hot Ashes for violin solo 1996, Sohini and Mahival (cantata in Urdu, in collaboration with B.Shrivastav) 1997, Quintet for Winds No. 2 1998, Small and Neglectable Discrepancies 1998; for dance: Falling Facades 1994, Lock, Stock and Barrel 1995, Shame 1996, Amongst Shadows 1996, Sketches to Portraits 1996, Seeing Things 1996, Spool of Threads 1997, The Brutality of Fact 1998; for theatre: Molecatcher's Daughter (Production Village, London) 1992, Romeo and Juliet (Pentameters Theatre, London) 1993, Doña Rosita the Spinster (Pentameters Theatre, London) 1993, Antonio's Revenge (Chelsea Centre Theatre, London) 1994, Dr Faustus (RSC) 1997. *Compositions for film:* Models Required 1994, Ailsa 1994, The Sheep Thief 1997, Streetwise, The Long Way Home, The Key, The Man Who Held His Breath, The Stick (TV), I Don't, The Star, Meter Running, Citizen Locke (TV), I Went Down 1997, Preserve (TV) 1999, The Funeral of the Last Gypsy King 1999, Southpaw: The Francis Barrett Story 1999, Being Considered 2000, Pandaemonium 2000, The Warrior 2001, Happy Now?, The Visitor 2002, Blood Strangers (TV) 2002, In This World 2002, I Capture the Castle 2003, This Little Life (TV) 2003, September 2003, The Bypass 2003, Cheeky 2003, Burnt Out, Passer By (TV) 2004, The Brothers Grimm 2005, Shooting Dogs 2005, Opal Dream, Pride & Prejudice (Classical BRIT Award for Soundtrack/Musical Theatre Composer 2006) 2005, Pobby and Dingan 2005, V for Vendetta 2006, The Return 2006, Goodbye Bafana, Atonement 2007, We Are Together 2007, The Brave One, Far North 2007, Anna Karenina 2012; also for numerous film and TV documentaries. *Honours:* Gulbenkian Foundation scholarship; Benjamin Britten Int. Composition Prize 1997, ASCAP Award 2006. *Current Management:* Air-Edel Associates Ltd, 18 Rodmarton Street, London, W1U 8BJ, England. *Telephone:* (20) 7486-6466. *Fax:* (20) 7224-0344. *E-mail:* air-edel@air-edel.co.uk. *Website:* www.air-edel.co.uk.

MARIANO, Andrea; Italian musician (piano, synthesizer); b. 26 March 1978. *Career:* mem., Negramaro 2002–. *Recordings include:* albums: Negramaro 2003, 000577 2004, Mentre Tutto Scorre 2005, La Finestra 2007. *Honours:* MTV Europe Music Award Best Italian Act 2005. *E-mail:* management@negramaro.com. *E-mail:* band@negramaro.com (office). *Website:* www.negramaro.com.

MARIC, Dave; British musician (keyboards) and composer; b. 1970, Bedford, England. *Career:* pianist, Steve Martland Band from 1989; performances with groups, including the London Sinfonietta, London Philharmonic Orchestra, BBC Symphony Orchestra; collaborations with various jazz groups; composer 1990s–; mem., Katia Labèque Band 2001–. *Compositions include:* Trilogy for solo percussion and CD 2000, Runtime for piano, drums and electronics 2001, Breathe [Invocation] (for piano, drums and electronics 2001, Sketch for piano and electronics 2001, Shapeshifter for two percussionists 2001, Falling to the Sky for violin and piano 2001, Broken Fiction for five musicians 2002, Lifetimes for 12 strings and percussion 2002, Sense & Innocence for solo percussion and CD 2002, With No Name for piano and electronics 2002, Unspoken for piano and electronics 2002, Fields for piano, drums and electronics 2002, Hyper (from 'Falling to the Sky', version for piano, drums and electronics) 2002, Exile for two pianos, solo percussion and live electronics 2002, Predicaments for solo percussion and piano 2003, Borrowed Time for solo percussion and organ 2003, On Impulse for cello and percussion 2003, Spellbound for solo piano, digital electronics, drum kit and orchestra 2004, Music for 'You, Cuba' (dance film) for violin, piano and percussion 2004, Ghosts, ballet score for five amplified instruments and electronic score 2005, This Freedom 2005, Desert Life 2005, Designing Clouds 2005, Incantation 2005, Shore 2006, Lucid Intervals 2006, Five Movements for Arcana 2006, A Tale of Two Cities, ballet score 2008. *Recordings:* albums: Steve Martland: Crossing The Border 1992, Steve Martland: Patrol 1994, Bassistry: Bassistry 1995, Steve Martland: The Factory Masters 1996, Marc Ribot: Shoe String Symphonettes 1997, Mike Westbrook: The Orchestra of Smith's Academy 1998, John Adams: Gnarly Buttons/John's Book of Alleged Dances 1998, The Katia Labèque Band: Unspoken 2003. *E-mail:* info@davemaric.com (office). *Website:* www.davemaric.com.

MARÍN, Carlos; Spanish singer (baritone); b. 13 Oct. 1968, Rüsselsheim, Germany; m. Geraldine Larrosa 2006. *Education:* Madrid Conservatoire, studied with Montserrat Caballé and Jaime Aragall. *Career:* roles include Figaro in Il Barbiere di Siviglia, Sulpice in La Fille du Régiment, Silvio in Pagliacci, Ostasio in Francesca da Rimini, Taddeo in L'Italiana in Algeri, Ford in Falstaff, Valentin in Faust, Riccardo in I Puritani, Posa in Don Carlos,

Marcello in La Bohème, Enrico in Lucia di Lammermoor, Mercutio in Campoamor, Don Giglio in La Capricciosa Corretta, and roles in Madama Butterfly and La Traviata; performances in Spanish zarzuela include La Gran Vía, La Revoltosa, La Verbena de la Paloma; mem., Il Divo 2003–. *Films:* sang in The Nightmare Before Christmas 1993, sang the part of the Prince in Walt Disney's Cinderella (Spanish version) 2000. *Musical theatre roles:* Marius in Les Misérables 1993, The Beauty and the Beast, Vince Fontaine in Grease, Peter Pan. *Recordings include:* albums: solo: The Little Caruso, Mijn Lieve Mama; with Il Divo: Il Divo 2004, Ancora 2005, The Christmas Collection 2005, Siempre 2006, The Promise 2008, Wicked Game 2011. *Honours:* winner Jacinto Guerrero Competition, Francisco Alonso Competition, Julián Gayarre Competition 1996. *Website:* www.ildivo.com.

MARÍN ESPINOZA, Gilberto; Mexican musician (guitar); b. 26 Jan. 1983, Mexicali, Bajo California. *Education:* Universidad Autónoma de Baja California. *Career:* mem. Reik 2004–. *Recordings:* Reik 2005, Secuencia 2006, Un Día Más (Latin Grammy Award for Best Pop Album by a Duo/Group 2009) 2008. *Honours:* Premios MTV Latinoamérica for Best Group 2005, for Best Artist (Northern region) 2005, for Best New Artist (Northern region) 2005, for Best Pop Artist 2009. *Current Management:* c/o Dulce Gil, Westwood Entertainment, México, Mexico. *Telephone:* (55) 5337-2047. *E-mail:* dgil@westwoodent.com. *Website:* www.westwoodent.com; www.reik.tv.

MARINI, Giovanna Salviucci; Italian singer, composer and actress; b. 1937, Rome. *Career:* fnr mem., Il Nuovo Canzoniere Italiano; mem., vocal quartet. *Films:* Lettera aperta a un giornale della sera 1970, Il Sospetto 1975, Porci con le ali 1977, Io sono mia 1978, I giorni cantati 1979, Café Express 1980, Il Mistero del morca 1984, Storia d'amore 1986, Codice privato 1988, Il Segreto 1990, L'Alba 1990, Al centro dell'area di rigore 1996, Tarte aux pommes 2002. *Recordings include:* albums: with Il Nuovo Canzoniere Italiano: Le Canzoni Di Bella Ciao 1964, Ci Ragiono E Canto 1966; solo: Vi Parlo Dell'America 1966, Chiesa Chiesa 1967, Lunga Vita Allo Spettacolo/Viva Voltaire E Montesquieu 1970, La Nave/La Creatora 1972, L'Eroe 1974, I Treni Per Reggio Calabria 1975; with quartet: Correvano Coi Carri 1979, Cantate De Tous Les Jours 1980, Giovanna Marini Et Ses Compagnes 1982, Pour Pier Paolo 1984, Giovanna Marini 1990, Cantata Profana 1991, La Vie Au-dessus Et En-dessous Des Mille Mètres 1994, Partenze: Vent'anni Dopo La Morte di Pier Paolo Pasolini 1996, Cantate Cantata 1998, Si Bemolle 1999, Cantico Della Terra 1999, Passioni 2005. *Address:* c/o Ala Bianca Group Srl, Via Emilia est 1646/c, 41100 Modena, Italy (office). *E-mail:* giovanna@giovannamarini.it (office). *Website:* www.giovannamarini.it.

MARINO, Francesco (Frank) Antonio; Canadian rock musician (guitar) and singer; b. 22 Aug. 1954. *Career:* founder mem., Mahogany Rush 1970–80; solo artist 1981–82. *Recordings include:* albums: with Mahogany Rush: Maxoom, 1971; Child of The Novelty, 1974; Strange Universe, 1975; Mahogany Rush IV, 1976; World Anthem, 1977; Live, 1978; Tales of The Unexpected, 1979; What's Next, 1980; solo: The Power of Rock 'n' Roll, 1981; Juggernaut, 1982; Full Circle, 1986; Double Live, 1988; Eye Of The Storm, 2001. *E-mail:* frankmarino@mahoganyrush.com. *Website:* www.mahoganyrush.com.

MARIZA; Portuguese singer; b. (Mariza Nunes), Mozambique. *Career:* moved to Portugal aged three; began singing Fado aged five; solo artist, Fado singer; participated in Unity, official album of the Olympic Games, singing 'A Thousand Years' with Sting 2004; Live 8 performance under banner 'Africa Calling', Eden Project, Cornwall, UK 2005; UNICEF Nat. Amb. for Portugal 2005; Int. Ambassador for the work and spirit of Hans Christian Andersen, Denmark 2005; Portuguese Tourism Amb. *Film appearance:* Fados. *Recordings include:* albums: Fado em Mim 2001, Fado Curvo 2003, Live in London (DVD) 2004, Transparente (Golden Globe for Interpreter of the Year, Portugal) 2005, Concerto em Lisboa (live) 2006, Terra 2008. *Honours:* Voz do Fado Award 2000, Deutsche Schallplatten Kritik Award 2001, 2003, BBC Radio 3 World Music Award for Best European Artist 2003, European Border Breakers Award 2004; Ordem do Infante D. Henrique (Portugal) 2006. *Current Management:* c/o Músicas do Mundo Management Lda, Rua Castilho n° 23 4° A, 1250-067 Lisbon, Portugal. *E-mail:* info@mariza.com (office). *Website:* www.mariza.com.

MARKELIUS, Nike Maria; Swedish singer, songwriter, musician, producer and writer; b. 29 Aug. 1962; two d. *Education:* studied singing and digital audio editing. *Career:* drummer and vocals in Swedish rock groups; Usch, tours in Denmark and Sweden 1979–81, Tant Strul, Scandinavian tours 1981–85; Roskilde Festival, Slottssparken, Helsingfors 1985; singer in group, Nike, tours 1992–97; Smisk, tours in Sweden 1989–97; songwriter, solo performer, musical theatre: Puder, Teatter Tre, Stockholm 2001–02; several radio interviews; TV shows with Tant Strul 1983–85; musical theatre for children: Karameller & Karuseller 2003–05; mem. Aunt Fuzz 2008–; mem. Nike & Röda Orkestern 2009–; now working with Nike & Röda Orkestern, writing songs together with Swedish songwriters; tours 2010–; writing political articles 2013–; mem. STIM, SKAP, SAMI, SMF, Musikcentrum, DIVA. *Plays:* Fandango 1992, several theatre plays 1992–96. *Recordings include:* albums with groups: Amazon 1983, Jag Önskar Dig 1984, Samlade Singlar 1985, Hula Hula 1987; solo: Nike 1996, Karameller & Karuseller 2004, I Krumelurlandet 2005, Nike & Röda Orkestern 2012, Det står skrivet 2012. *Honours:* Kasper Priset 1983, Scholarship, SKAP 1992, Konstnärsnämnden, 1992–93, 1995–96, 1998, 1999, Stockholm City Artist Grant 1997, Hoceaniens kulturpris 2013, Svensk socialpolitisk förenings hederspris 2013, Det gyldene benet 2013. *Current Management:* c/o MNW Music AB, c/o Universal Music,

Box 55777, 114 83 Stockholm, Sweden. *Telephone:* 70-3600195 (mobile) (office). *E-mail:* nikemarkelius@glocalnet.net (home). *Website:* www.facebook .com/nikeochrodaorkestern.

MARKER, Steve; American musician (guitar, bass guitar, keyboards); b. New York, NY. *Career:* co-founder, Smart Studios; worked with Nine Inch Nails, L7; mem., Garbage 1994–; numerous tours, festivals, television and radio appearances. *Recordings include:* albums: Garbage 1995, Version 2.0 1998, Beautifulgarbage 2001, Androgyny 2003, Bleed Like Me 2005, Absolute Garbage 2007, Not Your Kind of People 2012. *Film music:* The World is Not Enough (theme to James Bond: The World is Not Enough) 1999. *Current Management:* Free Trade Agency, 20–22 Curtain Road, London, EC2A 3NF, England. *Telephone:* (20) 7655-6900. *Fax:* (20) 7655-6909. *E-mail:* info@freetradeagency.co.uk. *Website:* www.freetradeagency.co.uk; www.garbage .com.

MARKEY, Gerry, BA, PGCE; British singer, songwriter, actor and musician (guitar, piano, harmonica); b. (Gerald Murphy), 13 Nov. 1963, Liverpool. *Education:* York Univ., Univ. of London, Inst. of Linguists. *Career:* extensive tours; numerous TV appearances; project co-ordinator, The European Song Project; mem. Musicians' Union, BAC&S, Sound Sense, Equity, PRS. *Recordings:* Oh John 1984, Sweet Liberty 1987, Marvellous Marvin Gaye 1993, Ballad of Dixie Dean 1981. *Honours:* PRS John Lennon Award (for Sweet Liberty) 1987, second place Nat. Music Day Songwriter of 1993, Marvellous Marvin Gaye 1993.

MARKLEW, Leigh; British musician (bass guitar); b. 10 Aug. 1968. *Career:* founder mem. rock group, The Spoilt Bratz 1986, renamed Terrorvision 1991–2001; numerous tours, television appearances; founder mem., Malibu Stacey 2001–; currently also mem., Room Service. *Recordings include:* albums: with Terrorvision: Formaldehyde 1993, How To Make Friends And Influence People 1994, Regular Urban Survivors 1996, Shaving Peaches 1998, Good To Go 2001, Whales And Dolphins: The Very Best Of Terrorvision 2001, The First And The Last 2001, B-Sides And Rarities 2005; with Malibu Stacey: On Heat 2003. *E-mail:* leigh@malibustacey.com (office). *Website:* www .malibustacey.com.

MARKOVIC, Milivoje; Croatian musician (saxophone, clarinet), composer and conductor; b. 20 March 1939, Zagreb. *Education:* Music Acad. of Graz, Austria. *Career:* with Markovic-Gut Sextet performed at the Northsee Jazz Festival and toured Belgium, Germany, USSR, Hungary, Romania, Italy, Turkey, Bulgaria and Cuba; numerous TV and radio broadcasts; mem. Composers' Union of Yugoslavia (pres. 1987–88). *Compositions include:* Otpisani; Ballad in Escutabile; Stemi; YuN QMM; Suze. *Recordings include:* Markovic-Gut Sextet, 1980, 1981; Clark Terry Live in Belgrade with the Markovic-Gut Sextet, 1982; Message from Belgrade, 1984; Ernie Wilkins in Belgrade with Markovic-Gut Sextet; Machito and His Salsa Big Band. *Address:* Plato Jazz Club, Student TRG, Belgrade, Serbia.

MARKS, Toby Anthony; British electronic composer and musician (guitar, keyboards, electronics, percussion); b. 1 July 1964, London, England; m. Sandra Marks 1995. *Education:* Univ. of Warwick. *Career:* performed in various bands and concerts in UK and Europe 1978; formed Banco de Gaia (solo electronic project), performing world-wide 1989–; mem. Mechanical-Copyright Protection Soc., Performing Right Soc., Musicians' Union, PPL. *Recordings include:* albums: with Banco De Gaia: Maya 1994, Last Train To Lhasa 1995, Live At Glastonbury 1996, Big Men Cry 1997, The Magical Sounds of Banco De Gaia 1999, Igizeh 2000, 10 Years 2002, You Are Here 2004, Farewell Ferengistan 2006, Memories Dreams Reflections 2009. *E-mail:* info@banco.co.uk (office). *Website:* www.banco.co.uk.

MARLEY, Damian, (Jr Gong); Jamaican singer and songwriter; b. 21 July 1978, Kingston; s. of Bob Marley and Cindy Breakspeare. *Career:* released debut album Mr Marley 1996; scored a major int. hit with Welcome to Jamrock 2005; collaborations with Stephen Marley, Black Thought, Nas, Bounty Killer, Eek-A-Mouse, Cypress Hill, Snoop Dogg, Lil Kim, Gwen Stefani, Guru, Bobby Brown. *Recordings include:* albums: Mr Marley 1996, Halfway Tree (Grammy Award for Best Reggae Album) 2001, Welcome to Jamrock (Grammy Award for Best Reggae Album) 2005, Distant Relatives (with Nas) 2010. *Honours:* Best Reggae Act, MOBO Awards 2005, Best Reggae Artist, XM Nation Music Awards 2006, Bob Marley Award for Entertainer of the Year, Recording Artist of the Year, Best Song (for Welcome to Jamrock), Best Album (for Welcome to Jamrock), Best Music Video (for Welcome to Jamrock) and Songwriter of the Year (with Stephen Marley), Int. Reggae and World Music Awards 2006; Grammy Award for Best Urban/Alternative Performance (for Welcome to Jamrock) 2006. *Current Management:* c/o WME, 9601 Wilshire Boulevard, Beverly Hills, CA 90201, USA. *Website:* www.damianmarleymusic.com.

MARLEY, Rita; Jamaican singer, songwriter and philanthropist; b. (Alpharita Constantia Anderson), 25 July 1946, Santiago de Cuba, Cuba; d. of Leroy Anderson and Cynthia 'Beda' Jarrett; m. Bob Marley 1966 (died 1981); two s. one d. and three d. from various relationships. *Career:* grew up in upper level of Beachwood, Kingston, Jamaica; was singing with female ska trio named The Soulettes (later became the I-Threes), recording for Studio One, when she met her future husband mid-1960s; became involved in Rastafari Movt 1966, remains active mem. Ethiopian Orthodox Church; following her husband's death, recorded albums under her own name and looked after his estate; f. Rita Marley Foundation 2000; currently lives in Konkonuru, nr Aburi, Ghana. *Films include:* The Mighty Quinn (actress and reggae music consultant) 1989, The Reggae Movie (special thanks) 1995, How High (writer and performer, One Draw) 2001, Africa Unite (exec. producer) 2008. *Albums include:* Pied Piper (single, on Club Ska '67) 1967, Rita Marley 1980, Who Feels It Knows It 1981, Harambe (Working Together for Freedom) 1988, We Must Carry on 1988, Beauty of God's 1990, Good Girls Cult 1990, One Draw 1990, Sings Bob Marley … and Friends 2003, Play Play 2004, Sunshine After Rain 2005, Gifted Fourteen Carnation 2006. *Publication:* No Woman No Cry (book) 2004. *Honours:* honoured by Clutch magazine as one of 21 International Women of Power 2008. *Address:* c/o Rita Marley Foundation, PO Box 34, Aburi-Akwapim, Ghana www.ritamarleyfoundation.org.

MARLEY, Stephen Robert Nesta; Jamaican singer, songwriter, musician (guitar, percussion) and producer; b. 20 April 1972, Wilmington, DE, USA; s. of Bob Marley and Rita Marley. *Career:* fmr mem. The Melody Makers; solo artist; producer for artists including his brothers, Damian, Julian and Ziggy, also for Buju Banton, Spearhead, Eve, Erykah Badu, Capleton and Mr Cheeks. *Recordings include:* album: solo: Mind Control (Grammy Award for Best Reggae Album) 2007, Jah Army 2010, Revelation Pt. 1: The Root of Life (Grammy Award for Best Reggae Album 2012) 2011. *Honours:* (with The Melody Makers) Grammy Award for Best Reggae Recording (for Conscious Party) 1988, Grammy Award for Best Reggae Recording (for One Bright Day) 1989, Grammy Award for Best Reggae Album (for Fallen is Babylon) 1997, (for Mind Control-Acoustic) 2010. *Address:* c/o Tuff Gong, 220 Marcus Garvey Drive, Kingston 11, Jamaica. *E-mail:* customerservice@website .stephenmarleymusic.com. *Website:* www.tuffgong.com; www .stephenmarleymusic.com.

MARLEY, Ziggy; Jamaican singer, musician (guitar) and songwriter; b. 17 Oct. 1968, Kingston; s. of Bob Marley. *Career:* leader, Ziggy Marley and The Melody Makers, blending blues, R&B, hip-hop and roots reggae; the group mems are UN Youth Environment Ambassadors; solo artist 2003–. *Recordings include:* albums: with The Melody Makers: Play The Game Right 1985, Hey World 1986, Conscious Party (Grammy Award for Best Reggae Recording) 1988, One Bright Day (Grammy Award) 1989, Jameyka 1991, Joy and Blues 1993, Free Like We Want 2 B 1995, Fallen Is Babylon (Grammy Award) 1997, Spirit Of Music 1999, The Best of Ziggy Marley and the Melody Makers, Ziggy Marley and the Melody Makers Live Vol. 1 2000; solo: Dragonfly 2003, Love is my Religion (Grammy Award for Best Reggae Album 2007) 2006, Family Time (Grammy Award for Best Musical Album for Children 2010) 2009, Ziggy Marley in Concert (Grammy Award for Best Reggae Album 2014) 2013, Fly Rasta (Grammy Award for Best Reggae Album 2015) 2014. *Honours:* NAACP Award. *Current Management:* Tuff Gong Worldwide Inc., 269 South Beverly Drive #175, Beverly Hills, CA 90212, USA. *Address:* Ziggy Marley and the Melody Makers, 56 Hope Road, Kingston 6, Jamaica (office). *Website:* www .ziggymarley.com.

MARLIN (PEDERSEN), Lene; Norwegian singer, songwriter and musician (guitar); b. 17 Aug. 1980. *Education:* Tromsdalen Videregaende Skole, Tromsø. *Career:* recorded first album while still at school; heavy European promotion schedules throughout 1999–2000; co-wrote songs for fellow Norwegian, Sissel, 2000. *Recordings:* albums: Playing My Game 1999, Another Day 2003, Lost in a Moment 2005. *Honours:* MTV Europe Award for Best Nordic Act 1999, Spelleman Awards for Best Artist, Best New Artist, Best Pop Artist, Best Song 2000. *Address:* c/o EMI Music Norway, Karl Johans Gate 12j, PO Box 492, 0105 Oslo, Norway (office). *E-mail:* contact@lenemarlin .com (office). *Website:* www.lenemarlin.com.

MARLING, Laura; British singer, songwriter and musician (guitar); b. 1 Feb. 1990, Eversley, Hants. *Career:* mem. band Noah And The Whale –2008, currently solo artist. *Recordings include:* albums: Alas, I Cannot Swim 2008, I Speak Because I Can 2010, A Creature I Don't Know 2011, Once I Was an Eagle 2013, Short Movie 2015. *Honours:* Brit Awards, Best Female Solo Artist 2011, NME Awards, Best Solo Artist 2011. *Current Management:* Everybody's Management, 53 Corsica Street, Highbury, London, N5 1JT, England. *E-mail:* info@everybody-s.com. *Website:* www.lauramarling.com.

MARLO, Clair; American singer, producer, arranger, songwriter and composer; b. New York; m. Alex Baker 1995; one d. *Education:* Berklee Coll. of Music. *Career:* owner, Invisible Hands Productions; tours: USA, 1980; USA, 1990; Far East, 1994; mem, ASCAP, NARAS, AIMP, CC, Musicians' Union, SCL, AES. *Recordings:* Let It Go 1990, Behaviour Self 1995, Trinity; with Liquid Amber: Liquid Amber 1994, Adrift 1995; as producer: worked with Mark Winkler, Grant Geissman, The Boys, Lori Barth, David Ray, Harry Chapin, Kilauea, Michael Ruff, Pat Coil. *Honours:* 10 songwriting awards, Freedom Award for film scoring 1998. *Address:* 24307 Magic Mountain Parkway, Suite 116, Valencia 91355, USA (office). *E-mail:* info@clairmarlo .com (office). *Website:* www.clairmarlo.com.

MARLOW, Madison (Maddie) Kay; American country music singer, songwriter and guitarist; b. 7 July 1995, Sugar Land, Tex. *Career:* formed duo Sweet Aliana with Taylor Dye, renamed Maddie and Tae and moved to Nashville; debut release 2014. *Recordings:* album: with Maddie and Tae: Start Here 2015. *Honours:* ASCAP Country Music Award for Most Performed Song (for Girl in a Country Song) 2015, Country Music Assn Award for Video of the Year (for Girl in a Country Song) 2015. *Address:* c/o Dot Records, Big Machine Label Group, 1219 16th Avenue South, Nashville, TN 37212, USA (office). *E-mail:* mail@bigmachine.us (office). *Website:* www.bigmachinelabelgroup .com (office); www.maddieandtae.com.

MARQUIS, Del; American musician (guitar); b. (Derek John Gruen), 1977. *Career:* mem., Scissor Sisters 2001–. *Recordings include:* albums: Scissor Sisters (BRIT Award for Best Int. Album 2005) 2004, Ta-Dah 2006, Night Work 2010. *Honours:* BRIT Awards for Best Int. Group, Best Int. Breakthrough Act 2005, Meteor Ireland Music Award for Best Int. Group 2007. *Current Management:* c/o Dave Holmes, 3-D Management, Los Angeles, CA 90405, USA. *E-mail:* info@3dmgmt.com. *Website:* www.3dmgmt.com. *E-mail:* sisters@scissorsisters.net (office). *Website:* www.scissorsisters.com.

MARR, Johnny; British musician (guitar) and songwriter; b. (John Maher), 31 Oct. 1963, Ardwick, Manchester, England. *Career:* founder mem., The Smiths 1982–87; numerous tours and concert appearances; founder mem., Electronic 1989–; formed Johnny Marr & The Healers 2000–; mem. Modest Mouse 2006–09; The Cribs 2008–11; Visiting Prof. of Music, Univ. of Salford 2007–. *Recordings include:* albums: with The Smiths: The Smiths 1984, Hatful of Hollow 1984, Meat is Murder 1985, The Queen is Dead 1986, The World Won't Listen 1986, Louder Than Bombs 1987; with Electronic: Electronic 1991, Raise the Pressure 1996, Twisted Tenderness 1999; with Johnny Marr & The Healers: Boomslang 2003; with Modest Mouse: We were Dead Before the Ship even Sank 2007; with The Cribs: Ignore the Ignorant 2009; solo: The Messenger 2013, Playland 2014. *Honours:* Q Award for Lifetime Achievement 2007, Ivor Novello Inspiration Award 2010. *E-mail:* info@johnny-marr.com. *Website:* www.johnny-marr.com; www.modestmouse .com.

MARS, Bruno; American singer, songwriter and record producer; b. (Peter Gene Hernandez), 8 Oct. 1985, Honolulu, Hawaii; s. of Pete Hernandez and Bernadette Hernandez. *Education:* President Theodore Roosevelt High School. *Career:* moved to Los Angeles 2003; signed with Motown Records 2004; began songwriting with Philip Lawrence and Ari Levene under the name The Sneezingtons; signed with Atlantic Records 2009; songwriting credits include work for Alexandra Burke, Flo Rida, The Sugababes, Brandy, Sean Kingston, Travie McCoy, Adam Levine, Cee-Long, B.o.B.; debut EP as solo artist 2010; toured with Maroon 5, Travie McCoy 2010; collaborated with Mark Ronson on Uptown Funk single 2014. *Recordings include:* albums: solo: Doo-Wops and Hooligans 2010, Unorthodox Jukebox (Grammy Award for Best Pop Vocal Album 2014) 2012; as backing or guest vocalist: Animal, Far East Movement 2009, Uptown Funk, Mark Ronson (Grammy Awards for Record of the Year 2016, for Best Pop Duo/Group Performance 2016) 2014. *Film includes:* as child actor: Honeymoon in Vegas 1992. *Honours:* numerous awards, including: solo: Soul Train Music Award for Song of the Year 2010, ALMA! Favorite Male Music Artist Award 2011, ASCAP Top Rap Song Award 2011, BT Digital Music Best Int. Award 2011, BET Best New Artist Award 2011, BET Hip Hop Award for Best Hip Hop Video 2010, Billboard Music Award for Top Radio Song 2011, Craig Award for Best Debut 2010, Grammy Award for Best Male Pop Vocal Performance 2011, for Best Pop Vocal Album (Unorthodox Jukebox) 2014, MTV Europe Music Awards for Best New Act and Best Push 2011, for Best Song (for Locked Out of Heaven) 2013, MTV Video Music Award Japan for Best Male Video 2011, BRIT Awards for Int. Male Solo Artist 2012, for Best British Single (for Uptown Funk, with Mark Ronson) 2015, Echo Award for Best Int. Male 2012, People's Choice Award for Favorite Male Artist 2012; MTV Video Music Award for Best Male Video (for Locked Out of Heaven) 2013, for Best Choreography (for Treasure) 2013; for Cee-Lo Green: Grammy Award for Song of the Year 2011, Billboard Latin Music Award for Crossover Artist 2014. *Address:* c/o Atlantic Records, 1290 Avenue of the Americas, New York, NY 10104, USA (office). *Website:* www.brunomars .com.

MARS, Mick; American rock musician (guitar); b. (Bob Deal), 3 April 1955, Terre Haute, IN; m. Emi Canyon 1990. *Career:* mem. heavy rock group, Mötley Crüe 1981–; world-wide concert tours and festival appearances (reunion tour 2005). *Recordings include:* albums: Too Fast For Love 1981, Shout At The Devil 1983, Theatre Of Pain 1985, Girls, Girls, Girls 1987, Dr Feelgood 1989, Decade of Decadence (American Music Award for Favorite Heavy Metal Album) 1991, Mötley Crüe 1994, Generation Swine 1997, Live: Entertainment Or Death 1999, New Tattoo 2000, Red, White & Crüe 2005, Saints of Los Angeles 2008. *Publication:* The Dirt: Confessions of the World's Most Notorious Rock Band (with Mötley Crüe) 2001. *Honours:* Rolling Stone Best Heavy Metal Band 1991. *Website:* www.motley.com.

MARS, Thomas; French singer and songwriter; b. (Thomas Pablo Croquet), 21 Nov. 1976, Versailles; s. of Jean-louis Croquet and Ingrid Hedwig Karasek; m. Sofia Coppola; two d. *Education:* Lycée Hoche, Versailles. *Career:* mem. Phoenix 1997–. *Recordings:* albums: United 2000, Alphabetical 2004, It's Never Been Like That 2006, Wolfgang Amadeus Phoenix (Grammy Award for Best Alternative Album 2010) 2009; also appears on: The Virgin Suicides (original soundtrack), Air (as Gordon Tracks) 2000. *Address:* c/o Glassnote Music, 770 Lexington Avenue, New York, NY 10065, USA (office). *E-mail:* info@glassnotemusic.com (office). *Website:* www.glassnotemusic.com (office); www.wearephoenix.com.

MARSALIS, Branford; American jazz musician (saxophone), producer, composer and actor; b. 26 Aug. 1960, New Orleans, LA. *Education:* New Orleans Centre for Creative Arts, Southern Univ., Baton Rouge, Berklee Coll. of Music, Boston. *Career:* performed with Art Blakey, Lionel Hampton, Clark Terry, Bu Blakey, Wynton Marsalis, Herbie Hancock, Sting, Grateful Dead, Albert Collins, Nils Lofgren; leader of own band, with Kenny Kirkland, Jeff Watts, Bob Hurst; numerous worldwide tours, concerts, television and radio broadcasts; founder, Marsalis Music label 2002. *Radio:* host Jazzset (series) 1992, co-host Best of Disney Music 1992. *Television:* Music Dir Tonight Show 1992. *Film appearances:* School Daze, Throw Mama from the Train. *Recordings include:* albums: Scenes in the City 1984, Romances for Saxophone 1986, Royal Garden Blues 1986, Renaissance 1987, Random Abstract 1988, Trio Jeepy 1989, Do the Right Thing 1989, Mo Better Blues 1990, Crazy People Music 1990, The Beautyful Ones are Not Yet Born 1991, I Heard You Twice the First Time (Grammy Award for Best Jazz Instrumental Performance by an Individual or Group) 1992, Bloomington 1993, Buckshot LeFonque 1994, Loved Ones 1996, The Dark Keys 1996, Music Evolution 1997, Requiem 1999, Contemporary Jazz (Grammy Award for Best Jazz Instrumental Album by an Individual or Group) 2000, Creation 2001, Footsteps of Our Fathers 2002, Romare Bearden Revealed 2003, Eternal 2004, Braggtown 2006, Metamorphosen 2009. *Honours:* Nat. Endowment of the Arts Jazz Masters Award 2011. *Current Management:* c/o Ann Marie Wilkins, Wilkins Management, 323 Broadway, Cambridge, MA 02139, USA. *Telephone:* (617) 354-2736. *Fax:* (617) 354-2396. *E-mail:* info@wilkinsmanagement.com. *Website:* www .branfordmarsalis.com.

MARSALIS, Wynton; American musician (trumpet), music administrator and composer; b. 18 Oct. 1961, New Orleans, La; s. of Ellis Marsalis and Dolores Marsalis; three c. *Education:* Berkshire Music Center, Tanglewood, Juilliard School. *Career:* played with New Orleans Philharmonic age 14; joined Art Blakey and the Jazz Messengers 1980; toured with Herbie Hancock 1981; formed own group with brother Branford Marsalis 1982; leader Wynton Marsalis Septet; in addition to regular appearances in many countries with his own jazz quintet, follows a classical career and has performed with the world's top orchestras; regularly conducts master classes in schools and holds private tuition; Artistic Dir Lincoln Center Jazz Dept, New York 1990–; apptd UN Messenger of Peace 2001. *Compositions include:* Soul Gestures in Southern Blues 1988, Citi Movement 1992, Blood on the Fields (oratorio) (Pulitzer Prize for Music 1997) 1994, Jazz/Syncopated Movements 1997, Abyssinian 200: A Celebration 2008. *Recordings include:* All American Hero 1980, Wynton 1980, Wynton Marsalis 1981, Think of One 1983, Trumpet Concertos: Haydn, Hummel, Mozart 1983, English Chamber Orchestra 1984, Hot House Flowers 1984, Baroque Music: Wynton Marsalis, Edita Gruberova, Raymond Leppard and the English Chamber 1985, Black Codes (From the Underground) 1985, J Mood 1985, Live at Blues Alley 1986, Tomasi/Jolivet: Trumpet Concertos 1986, Carnaval 1987, Baroque Music for Trumpets 1988, The Majesty of the Blues 1989, Crescent City Christmas Card 1989, Tune in Tomorrow (soundtrack) 1991, Quiet City 1989, 24 1990, Trumpet Concertos 1990, Blue Interlude 1992, Citi Movement 1992, In This House, On This Morning 1992, Hot Licks: Gypsy 1993, On the Twentieth Century 1993, Joe Cool's Blues 1994, Live in Swing Town 1994, In Gabriel's Garden 1996, Jump Start and Jazz 1996, Live at Bubba's 1996, One By One 1998, The Marcial Suite 1998, At the Octoroon Ball: String Quartet No. 1 1999, Big Train 1999, Fiddler's Tale 1999, Reeltime 1999, Sweet Release and Ghost Story 1999, Listen To The Storyteller 1999, Goin' Down Home 2000, Immortal Concerts: Jody 2000, The London Concert 2000, All Rise 2002, Angel Eyes 2002, The Magic Hour 2004, Two Men with the Blues (with Willie Nelson) 2008, He and She 2009. *Television includes:* consultant on documentary series Jazz 1999. *Publications include:* Sweet Swing Blues on the Road 1994, Marsalis on Music 1995, Requiem 1999. *Honours:* Hon. RAM 1996; Chevalier, Légion d'honneur 2009; numerous hon. doctorates; Edison Award, Netherlands, Grand Prix du Disque, numerous Grammy Awards in both jazz and classical categories, Algur H. Meadows Award, Southern Methodist Univ. 1997, National Medal of Arts 2005, Ronnie Scott Award for Int. Trumpeter 2007, Gold Medal (Vitoria, Spain) 2009, Nat. Endowment of the Arts Jazz Masters Award 2011. *Current Management:* c/o James Ziefert, Kurland Agency, 173 Brighton Avenue, Boston, MA 02134-2003, USA. *Website:* www.thekurlandagency.com/artists/ wynton-marsalis. *E-mail:* info@wyntonmarsalis.org. *Website:* www .wyntonmarsalis.org.

MARSDEN, Gerald (Gerry), MBE; British singer and musician (guitar); b. 24 Sept. 1942, Liverpool, Merseyside, England; m. Pauline Ann 1965; two d. *Career:* mem., Gerry and the Pacemakers 1962–; numerous concerts and television shows worldwide; mem. Musicians' Union, Equity, PRS, Songwriters' Guild. *Plays:* Charlie Girl (West End, London), Pull Both Ends (West End, London, five years). *Recordings include:* albums: How Do You Like It 1963, Ferry Cross the Mersey 1964, Girl On A Swing 1966, 20th Anniversary Album 1983, Hit Singles Album 1986, You'll Never Walk Alone 1988, Gerry Cross the Mersey 1995, Much Missed Man 2001. *Publications:* I'll Never Walk Alone (autobiog.). *Honours:* two BMI citations, BASCA Gold Badge.

MARSH, Barbara Lynn, AA, BA; singer, songwriter and musician (guitar, piano, mandolin); b. Warwick, RI, USA; m. Peter Comley 1984 (divorced 1995). *Education:* Pensacola Jr Coll., Univ. of West Florida, Woodham High Echoes, Goldsmiths Coll., London. *Career:* mem., The Dear Janes 1992–; numerous tours, radio broadcasts; solo artist 1980–; mem. PRS, Musicians' Union, MCPS, Poetry Soc. *Television appearances:* two episodes, Broadway Stories 1994. *Recordings:* with The Dear Janes: Sometimes I 1994, No Skin 1996, Skirt 2002. *Publications:* poetry published in The Panhandler magazine 1981, The Auteur magazine 1992–93. *Address:* 10C Porchester Square, London, W2 6AN, England.

MARSH, (Ian) Henry; British composer and musician (keyboards, guitar); b. 8 Dec. 1948, Bath, Somerset, England; s. of Kenneth George Marsh and Ailsa Jean Marsh; m. 1st Susan Norddahl 1970 (divorced); two s. one d.; m. 2nd Dee Dee Wilde 2011. *Education:* studied the viola and piano. *Career:* first group, Four Pillars of Wisdom, Sherborne School; founder mem. Sailor 1970s; first musical, One Last Summer, opened in Atlanta; mem. Bd of Dirs RSC Records; writes music for theatre and television; co-composer, with Phil Pickett, Casper The Musical, West End debut 2000; Co-composer Cold Wind Blows, Eminem Recovery album; mem. PRS, MCPS, PPL. *Plays:* Dark at the Top of the Stairs, Romeo & Juliet, Grapes of Wrath, The Tempest, As You Like It, Twelfth Night, The Comedy of Errors, The Taming of the Shrew, Pericles. *Films:* Son of Nosferatu, Eye of the Storm. *Radio:* The Tics. *Television:* Bill Hicks at The Apollo Theme (BBC 1), Simpsons 'Who Killed Mr. Burns', Strike It Rich (Sky1), Backdate (Channel 4), Win Lose Or Draw (ITV). *Recordings:* hit singles with Sailor: Girls Girls Girls; A Glass of Champagne; album with Sailor: Trouble – The Third Step. *Honours:* Joseph Jefferson Award for Best Original Music in Theatre Production (for Comedy of Errors), Chicago, After Dark Award 1999, Winner, Best Original Music in a Play (Pericles), Jeff Awards, Chicago 2015. *Address:* The Red Cottage, Rood Ashton, Trowbridge, BA14 6BL, England (home). *Telephone:* (1380) 870909 (office). *E-mail:* henry_mrsh@yahoo.co.uk (home).

MARSH, Piers, (The Mountain of Love); British musician (harmonica, programming). *Career:* fmr DJ; founding mem. band Alabama 3, band's music is a unique fusion of country and gospel music with acid house and techno; band known as A3 in USA. *Recordings:* albums: with Alabama 3: Exile on Coldharbour Lane 1997, La Peste 2000, Power In The Blood 2002, The Last Train To Mashville 2003, Outlaw 2005, M.O.R. 2007, Revolver Soul 2010; solo: Ghost Flight 2006. *Honours:* ASCAP Award 2004. *Website:* www.alabama3.co .uk.

MARSHALL, Christopher William, (Matt Sinclair), BSc (Hons); British producer, musician (keyboards, bass) and composer; *Director, Rhythmshop Productions Ltd;* b. 18 Sept. 1956, Kolkata, India; s. of Hector Benjamin Marshall and Mildred Elvira Pinchbeck. *Education:* Univ. of Manchester, studied piano privately. *Career:* semi-professional until 1982; keyboard player with bands Biddie and Eve, The Next Step, Angie; started record label, Rhythm Shop Records 1994, Dir Rhythmshop Productions Ltd 2001–; Guest Lecturer, London Centre of Contemporary Music, London; mem. Asscn of Professional Recording Services, Musicians' Union, Mechanical-Copyright Protection Soc., Performing Right Soc., ANA, PPL. *Compositions:* TV soundtracks: Ad Armageddon (BBC), Zapruder Footage (BBC 2), Broken Lives (BBC 2), The No. 10 Show (Channel 4), Reputations: Hitchcock (BBC 2) 1999, The Secret History of Hackers (Channel 4); numerous albums library music; co-writer Your House Or My House, Samantha Fox 1989. *Recordings:* as producer: tracks by: Demis Roussos, Norman Wisdom; He Ain't Heavy, He's My Brother, Jonathan Paule; Blind Fool, Insane, Make Up, Dave Pop 1998–99; albums: with Tight Fit: Back To The 60s Vol. II, III; with Dream On Dream: Strangeways; with Hound Dog and The Megamixers: Junior Party Megamix 1990, This is Dave Pop! 2004, James Biddlecombe and Chris Marshall: Reflections from the Blitz (concerto, album, DVD) 2004–05. *Address:* 35 Edithna Street, London, SW9 9JR, England (office). *Telephone:* (20) 7326-1329 (office); 7956-584383 (mobile). *E-mail:* rpl@rhythmshop.com (office). *Website:* www.rhythmshop.com (office).

MARSHALL, Grant (see Daddy G)

MARSHALL, John Stanley, BA (Hons); British musician (drums, percussion); b. 28 Aug. 1941, Isleworth, Middx, England; m. Maxi Egger. *Education:* studied psychology at Univ. of Reading, studied drums privately with John Russell, Jim Marshall, Alan Ganley and Philly Joe Jones. *Career:* freelance on London jazz scene; played with Alexis Korner's Blues Incorporated 1964, Graham Collier Sextet 1965–70; played with John Surman, John McLaughlin, Dave Holland, Mike Westbrook, Graham Bond Organisation, Joe Harriot, Indo-Jazz Fusions, Keith Tippett's Sextet, Centipede, Alan Skidmore; Founder-mem. Nucleus 1969; Montreux Festival (First Prize 1970), Newport Festival, Village Gate, New York; regular mem., Mike Gibbs Orchestra, early 1970s; left Nucleus to join Jack Bruce Band 1971; joined Soft Machine 1972; played with musicians, including Larry Coryell, Gary Burton, Mary Lou Williams, Ronnie Scott, Tubby Hayes, Ben Webster, Milt Jackson, Roy Eldridge, Volker Kriegel, Gordon Beck, Charlie Mariano, Jasper van't Hof, Philip Catherine; joined Eberhard Weber's Colours 1977–81; worked with Gil Evans Orchestra, Ian Carr, Kenny Wheeler, Uli Beckerhoff, Anthony Braxton, Manfred Schoof, Joachim Kühn, Michel Portal, John Taylor, Allan Holdsworth, Norma Winstone, Gordon Beck, Jeff Clyne, Arild Andersen, John Abercrombie, John Surman Quartet, Brass Project, NDR Big Band; mem. ATM trio, recordings and concerts 2000–; concerts and recording with SoftWorks and Cercle 2003–; current projects with John Surman, Soft Machine/Soft Machine Legacy (SML), Etheridge/Andersen/Marshall Trio (EAM), Sachse/Baker/Marshall Trio; teacher, Jazz Faculty, RAM, London. *Recordings include:* more than 100 albums, including Elastic Rock, Nucleus 1970, Harmony Row, Jack Bruce 1971, Bundles, Soft Machine 1975, Stranger Than Fiction, John Surman Quartet 1994, Achirana (ATM) 2000, The Triangle (ATM) 2003, Steam (SML) 2007, In House (EAM) 2007, Live Adventures (SML) 2010, Burden of Proof (SML) 2013, Switzerland 1974 (Soft Machine) 2015. *Honours:* voted Best UK Drummer, Melody Maker 1973, 1974. *Address:* 43 Combemartin Road, London, SW18 5PP, England. *Telephone:* (20) 8788-0933. *Fax:* (20) 8788-0933. *Website:* www.drummerworld.com/ drummers/John_Marshall.html.

MARSHALL, Oren Morris, ARCM; British jazz musician (tuba, electronics) and teacher; *Head of Brass Studies, Trinity Labin Conservatoire of Music*; b. 14 June 1966, Geneva, Switzerland; m.; two c. *Education:* Shene Comprehensive School, Royal Coll. of Music. *Career:* Founder-mem. jazz and Latin sextet Oren's Panacea 1986–89; mem. Frankfurt Radio Symphony Orchestra 1986; mem. Acad. of St Martin-in-the-Fields with Sir Neville Marriner 1987–97; mem. London Brass Ensemble 1988–91; tuba teacher, Royal Coll. of Music Junior Dept 1988–93; tuba teacher and ensemble coach, Guildhall School of Music and Drama (Jr Dept) 1989–93; f. Oren Marshall Group 1992, became Charming Transport Band 1993–; Founder-mem. Oren Marshall Trio 1993–94; ensemble coach, Royal Acad. of Music 1998–; Founder, tuba ensemble Gut Rumble 2001–; tuba teacher and ensemble coach, Trinity Coll. of Music 2004–; currently Head of Brass Studies, Trinity Labin Conservatoire of Music, London; Founder-mem. Sons of Kemet 2011–; numerous masterclasses worldwide; acoustic and electric tuba player for numerous other artists and groups across many genres including Derek Bailey, Charlie Haden, Loose Tubes, Bobby McFerrin, Mark Sanders, John Dankworth Band, Julian Joseph Big Band, Creative Jazz Orchestra, Sir Peter Maxwell Davies, Bobby McFerrin, Moondog, Pan-African Orchestra, Radiohead; Fellow, Trinity Coll., London 1984. *Recordings:* albums: with Charming Transport Band: Time Spent at Traffic Lights 1993, Family Connections 2007; with Sons of Kemet: Burn 2013. *Honours:* Royal Coll. of Music Angela Bull Memorial Prize 1982; with Sons of Kemet: MOBO Award for Best Jazz Act 2013. *Address:* Trinity Labin Conservatoire of Music and Dance, Faculty of Music, King Charles Court, Old Royal Naval College, Greenwich, London, SE10 9JF (office); c/o Simon Drake, Naim Jazz Records, Southampton Road, Salisbury, Wiltshire, SP1 2LN, England (office). *Telephone:* (20) 8305-4444 (Trinity Labin) (office); (1722) 426600 (Naim Jazz) (office). *E-mail:* sonsofkemet@gmail.com; orenmarshall@hotmail.com. *Website:* trinitylabin.ac.uk (office); www.naimlabel.com (office); sonsofkemet.com; orenmarshall.com.

MARSHALL, Winston Aubrey Aladar; British songwriter and musician (banjo, dobro); b. 20 Dec. 1987, London, England. *Career:* fmr mem. Captain Kick and the Cowboy Ramblers; Founder-mem. Mumford & Sons 2007–; first EP released 2008, toured as support group to Laura Marling 2009, performed with Bob Dylan at Grammy Awards 2011. *Recordings:* albums: Sigh No More (Q Best New Act Award 2010, BRIT Award for British Album of the Year 2011, Billboard Music Awards for Top Rock Album and Top Alternative Album 2011) 2009, Babel (Grammy Award for Album of the Year 2013, Billboard Music Award for Top Rock Album 2013) 2012, Wilder Mind 2015; featured on: I Speak Because I Can, Laura Marling 2010, See My Friends, Ray Davies 2010. *Films:* Wuthering Heights (two songs for soundtrack) 2011. *Honours:* Australian Recording Industry Asscn (ARIA) Music Most Popular Int. Artist Award 2010, Billboard Music Award for Top Alternative Artist 2011, BRIT Award for Best British Group 2013, Ivor Novello Award for Int. Achievement (with Mumford & Sons) 2014. *Current Management:* c/o Everybody's Management, 53 Corsica Street, Highbury, London, N5 1JT, England. *Telephone:* (20) 3227-0420. *Fax:* (20) 7226-2166. *E-mail:* info@everybody-s.com. *Website:* www.everybody-s.com; www.mumfordandsons.com.

MARSTON, Steve; British musician (keyboards, multi-instrumentalist). *Career:* mem., jazz funk quartet, D-Influence 1990–; support to Prince, Michael Jackson; tours, television appearances; D-Influence also production team for R&B music; group owns Freakstreet label. *Recordings:* albums: Good 4 We 1992, Prayer 4 Unity 1995, London 1997, D-Influence Presents D-Vas 2002. *Address:* c/o Dome Records Ltd, PO Box 3274, East Preston, Sussex BN16 9BD, England (office). *Website:* www.domerecords.co.uk (office).

MARTELLY, Michel Joseph, (Sweet Mickey); Haitian musician, politician and fmr head of state; b. 12 Feb. 1961, Port-au-Prince; m. Sophia Martelly; four c. *Education:* Saint-Louis de Gonzague High School. *Career:* spent several years in Miami, Fla, USA employed as construction worker; successful career in Haiti as performing and recording artist, known as pioneer of 'kompas' Haitian dance music; politically active for several years but held no political positions; Pres. of Haiti 2011–16; co-f. (with wife) Rose et Blanc Foundation. *Recordings include:* singles include: Ooo La La 1988, Konpas Foret des Pins, Magouyè, 2008, Bal Bannann Nan 2016; 14 studio albums including Woule Woule 1989, Pa Manyen (Don't Touch) 1997, Dènye Okazyon 1999, SiSiSi 2001.

MARTENS, Etienne Herman Andre, (Bobby Marty); Belgian musician (bass guitar); b. 4 Oct. 1937, Bruges; m. Suffys Nicole 1963; one s. one d. *Education:* studied with Dirigent Pol Horna. *Career:* mem. Andrex, Ensemble Pol Horna, The Shamrocks, Luc Rène and the Jumps; own show with the Bobby Marty Dancers 1980–; radio broadcasts in Belgium and France, TV in France; concerts with trio Tea for Three, own songs and music of the 60s, played bass, singer. *Compositions:* Houtem Mijn Dorpje, De Bruggeling, Adieu Jacques Brel, La Maison Du Bonheur, Mon Amour, Ma Guitare et Quelques Chansons, Une Belle Nuit D'Hiver, Au Rendez-Vous des Artistes, Opa zingt zijn wiegelied voor mij (recorded with granddaughter). *Recordings:* 18 singles, one album, two compilation albums in France, with other French artists; solo albums: Bobby Marty International, Bobby Marty Sings Elvis, Country Dreams, Sixtrumentals. *Publications:* Flash (own magazine) 1989–. *Honours:* Universal Award of Accomplishment, ABI, USA 2000, Int. Peace Prize 2002. *Address:* Molenwalstraat 8A, 8630 Houtem-Veurne, Belgium (home). *Telephone:* 58 299040 (home). *E-mail:* caroline.casier@pandora.be (office); bobby.marty@telenet.be (home).

MARTENS, Everardus (Evert) Antonius Josephus Maria; Dutch musician; b. 14 July 1956, Mill and St Hubert; one s. *Career:* many TV and radio appearances; mem, NTB, VAK, SENA, BUMA, STEMRA. *Compositions:* Waltz for Rutger, La Copine, Where's My Key. *Recordings:* albums: After You're Gone, Just in Time, La Copine, Way to Go. *Honours:* First Prize, Capelino, Old Style Jazz Festival Breda 1990.

MARTENS, Hervé; Belgian keyboard player and producer; b. 11 June 1963, Louvain. *Career:* Member of Soulsister; Zap Mama World Tour, 2000; mem, Sabam; Zamu. *Recordings:* Producer for Bobby Womack, Gibson Brothers and Sophie and So Four. *Honours:* Best Belgium Band Monte Carlo Award, 1988. *E-mail:* info@hervemartens.be. *Website:* www.hervemartens.be.

MARTIN, Barrie; British musician (saxophones); b. 22 May 1944, London; m. Elizabeth Gower 1976; one s. two d. *Education:* private lessons with Leslie Evans. *Career:* member, Quotations, Walker Brothers band for 2–3 years; all concert tours except last; solo Spot, Sunday Night at London Palladium; also as guest of Walker Brothers on German TV from Berlin; played with Jet Harris' band: The Jet Blacks, One Night Stand, with Pete Murray, BBC TV 1960s; tours with Roy Orbison, Brenda Lee, Duane Eddy, Little Richard, Englebert Humperdinck, Geno Washington and The Ram Jam Band; working with Otis Grand and the Big Blues Band; mem, Musicians' Union. *Recordings:* appeared on: Walker Brothers album: Portrait; Atlantic Soul Machine album: Coast To Coast.

MARTIN, Bill; British songwriter and music publisher; b. (William Wylie MacPherson), 9 Nov. 1938, Glasgow, Scotland; m. 1972; one s., three d. *Education:* Royal Scottish Academy of Music. *Career:* tours with The Drifters; Robert Parker; Winner, Eurovision Song Contest with Puppet On A String; Congratulations; All Kinds of Everything; Co-wrote UK No. 1 hits including: Puppet On A String, Sandie Shaw, 1967; Congratulations, Cliff Richard, 1968; Back Home, England World Cup Squad, 1970; Forever And Ever, Slik, 1976; All Bay City Rollers hits including: Shang-A-Lang, 1974; Summerlove Sensation, 1974; Publisher of: Billy Connolly; Van Morrison; Sky-Songs; Writer, My Boy, for Elvis Presley; No. 1 songs world-wide; mem, BAC&S; PRS. *Honours:* 20 Gold albums; 4 Platinum albums; 3 Ivor Novello Awards; 3 ASCAP Awards. *E-mail:* bill.puppetmartin@virgin.net. *Website:* www.billmartinsongwriter.com.

MARTIN, Billie Ray; German singer. *Career:* singer, Electribe 101; solo artist. *Recordings include:* albums: Deadline For My Memories, 1995; 18 Carat Garbage, 2001; solo: Your Loving Arms, 1995; Running Around Town, 1995; You and I (Keep Holding On), 1996; Imitation of Life, 1996; Space Oasis, 1996; Pacemaker, 1998; Honey, 1999; Crimes and Punishment; 1999. *Honours:* International Dance Music Award for Best New Dance Solo Artist 1996. *Website:* www.billieraymartin.com.

MARTIN, Christopher Anthony John (Chris); British singer, musician (guitar, piano) and songwriter; b. 2 March 1977, Devon, England; m. Gwyneth Paltrow 2003 (separated 2014); one s. one d. *Education:* University Coll., London. *Career:* mem. Coldplay 1998–. *Recordings include:* albums: Parachutes (BRIT Award for Best Album 2001, Grammy Award for Best Alternative Album 2002) 2000, A Rush Of Blood To The Head (BRIT Award for Best British Album 2003, NME Award for Best Album 2003) 2002, X&Y (MasterCard British Album, BRIT Awards 2006, Juno Award for Int. Album of the Year 2006) 2005, Viva la Vida (Grammy Award for Best Rock Album 2009) 2008, Mylo Xyloto (Billboard Music Awards for Top Rock Album and Top Alternative Album 2012) 2011, Ghost Stories (Billboard Music Award for Top Rock Album 2015) 2014, A Head Full of Dreams 2015. *Honours:* BRIT Awards for Best British Group 2001, 2003, 2012, for Best British Single (for Speed of Sound) 2006, for Best Live Act 2014, MTV Europe Music Awards for Best UK and Ireland Act 2002, for Best Song (for Speed of Sound) 2005, for Best Rock Act 2015, Billboard Music Awards for Group of the Year 2002, for Top Rock Artist 2012, for Top Alternative Artist 2012, Ivor Novello Awards for Songwriters of the Year 2003, for Best Selling British Song (for Viva la Vida) 2009, Grammy Awards for Record of the Year (for Clocks) 2004, for Best Rock Vocal Performance by a Duo or Group (for In My Place) 2004, for Song of the Year 2009, for Best Pop Performance by a Duo or Group (both for Viva la Vida) 2009, Q Awards for Best Act in the World 2005, 2011, Digital Music People's Choice Award for best official site, for Best Digital Music Community (for Coldplay.com) 2005, American Music Award for Favorite Alternative Music Artist 2005, Echo Award for Best Int. Group, Germany 2006, ASCAP Award for Song of the Year (for Speed of Sound) 2006, World Music Award for Best Rock Act 2008. *Current Management:* c/o Dave Holmes, 3-D Management, 1901 Main Street, #3000, Los Angeles, CA 90405, USA. *Telephone:* (310) 314-1390. *Website:* www.coldplay.com.

MARTIN, Claire, OBE; British jazz singer; b. 6 Sept. 1967, Wimbledon, London, England. *Education:* Doris Holford Stage School, studied with Marilyn Johnson, Verona Chard. *Career:* travelled extensively in Europe, Asia; worked for The British Council in Pakistan, Cyprus, Indonesia; mem. Equity, Musicians' Union. *Recordings:* albums: The Waiting Game 1992, Devil May Care 1993, Old Boyfriends 1994, Off Beat 1995, Make This City Ours 1997, Take My Heart 1999, Perfect Alibi 2000, Every Now And Then 2001, Too Darn Hot 2002, Secret Love 2004, When Lights are Low (with Richard Rodney Bennett) 2005, He Never Mentioned Love: Remembering Shirley Horn 2007, A Modern Art 2009, Witchcraft (with Richard Rodney Bennett) 2010, Too Much in Love to Care (with Kenny Barron) 2012, Say It Isn't So (with Richard Rodney Bennett) 2013. *Honours:* British Jazz Awards for Rising Star 1994, for

Best Vocalist 1996, 1997, 2003. *E-mail:* kerstanmac@gmail.com (office). *Website:* www.clairemartinjazz.com.

MARTIN, Clive; record producer and sound engineer; b. 21 March 1963, London, England. *Career:* record prod. for Reef, Echobelly, Les Negresses Vertes, Hunters and Collectors; sound engineer for Youssou N'Dour, Echobelly, Miquel Brown, Drugstore, Llama Farmers; asst engineer for Queen, Sting, The Cure, Jesus & Mary Chain, Matt Johnson, Soft Cell. *Honours:* Academy Award (for film soundtrack, The Last Emperor), BBC Jazz Award for Best Vocalist 2003. *Address:* Paul Brown Management, 103 Devonshire Road, London, W4 2HU, England (office). *Telephone:* (20) 8994-8887 (office). *Fax:* (20) 8994-2221 (office). *E-mail:* info@pbmanagement.co.uk (office). *Website:* www.pbmanagement.co.uk/clivemartin (office).

MARTIN, Daniel-John; jazz musician (violin), composer and arranger; b. 25 Sept. 1965, Congleton, Cheshire, England. *Education:* Schola Cantorum (superieur) American School of Music. *Career:* mem., Onxtet de Violon Jazz; numerous radio and TV broadcasts, festival appearances; formed Daniel-John Martin Group; Gen. Sec. Jazz and Violin Asscn. *Recordings:* Onxtet de Violon Jazz, Djeli Moussa (African music), Public Address (rock p-4 mati). *Honours:* first prize Jazz Modern, Jazz Plus, Jazz Hot.

MARTIN, Dey, BM, MM; American songwriter, producer and musician (guitar); b. 11 Sept. 1956, Los Angeles, CA. *Education:* Univ. of Hawaii, Univ. of California at Irvine. *Career:* backing guitar, Polyphemus, Lollapalloosa tour 1995; prod. for Woodpecker, Lung Cookie, Jalopy Kinfolk, Music West, Vancouver 1995; songwriter, solo performer mid 1980s; owner, Naked Jain Records; mem. ASCAP, NAS, NARM. *Compositions:* String Quartet 1978, Three Images (text by e.e. cummings) for classical guitar, mezzo soprano vocal and piano 1979, Berlin Wall 1989. *Recording:* Mr Monotony (prod.). *Honours:* Young Composers 1978–80. *Current Management:* Naked/Jain Records Inc, PO Box 4132, Palm Springs, CA 92263, USA. *Address:* 1301 N Palm Canyon Drive, Suite 208, Palm Springs, CA 92262, USA. *E-mail:* nakedjain@aol.com. *Website:* www.deymartin.com.

MARTIN, Eric; American singer; b. Oct. 1960. *Career:* founder mem., 415 1979–82, Eric Martin Band 1982–85; solo career 1985–88, 2002–; lead singer, Mr Big 1988–2002, 2009–, Tak Matsumoto Group 2004; mem. of side project, Road Vultures. *Recordings include:* albums: with Eric Martin Band: Sucker For A Pretty Face 1983; solo: Eric Martin 1985, I'm Only Fooling Myself 1987, Somewhere in the Middle 1998, I'm Goin' Sane 2002, Destroy All Monsters 2004, Mr Vocalist 2008, Mr Vocalist 2 2009, Mr Vocalist 3 2010; with Mr Big: Mr Big 1989, Lean Into It 1991, Bump Ahead 1993; Hey Man 1996, Get Over It 1999, Actual Size 2001, What If... 2011; with Working Man: Working Man 1996, Deep House Party Vol. 4 1996; with Sammy Hagar: Marching to Mars 1997; with Gildas Arzel: Brazebeck 1999; with Supersuckers: Teachers 1999. *E-mail:* denisemartin79@aol.com. *Website:* www.ericmartin.com.

MARTIN, Sir George Henry, Kt, CBE; British music industry executive, producer and composer (retd); b. 3 Jan. 1926, s. of Henry Martin and Bertha Beatrice Martin; m. 1st Sheena Rose Chisholm 1948; one s. one d.; m. 2nd Judy Lockhart Smith 1966; one s. one d. *Education:* Bromley Co. School, Kent, Guildhall School of Music and Drama. *Career:* Sub-Lt RNVR 1944–47; worked at BBC 1950; with EMI Records Ltd 1950–65, produced all records featuring The Beatles and numerous other artists; formed AIR Group of cos 1965, Chair. 1965–; built AIR Studios 1969; built AIR Studios, Montserrat 1979; completed new AIR Studios, Lyndhurst Hall, Hampstead 1992; co. merged with Chrysalis Group 1974, Dir 1978–; Chair. Heart of London Radio 1994–; scored the music for 15 films. *Publications:* All You Need Is Ears 1979, Making Music 1983, Summer of Love 1994. *Honours:* Hon. Fellow, Guildhall School of Music, Hon. mem. Royal Acad. of Music; Hon. DMus (Berklee Coll. of Music) 1989, (Leeds Metropolitan Univ.) 2006, (Univ. of Oxford) 2011; Hon. MA (Salford) 1992; Grammy Awards 1964, 1967 (two), 1973, 1993, 1996, 2007, Ivor Novello Awards 1963, 1979, Lifetime Achievement Award (World Soundtrack Academy) 2002. *Current Management:* c/o CA Management. *Website:* www .camanagement.com. *Address:* George Martin Music, AIR Studios, Lyndhurst Hall, Lyndhurst Road, Hampstead, London, NW3 5NG, England (office). *Telephone:* (20) 7794-0660 (office). *Fax:* (20) 7916-2784 (office). *E-mail:* info@ georgemartinmusic.com (office). *Website:* www.georgemartinmusic.com.

MARTIN, Javi; Spanish musician (bass guitar); b. Barcelona. *Career:* fmr mem. De Cajón flamenco fusion band; collaborated with numerous musicians in concerts and recordings including Duquende, Montse Cortés, Peret, Parrita; joined Ojos de Brujo 2004, a group which fuses gypsy and flamenco music with Latin American, punk, hip hop, reggae and electronic influences; several tours in Europe, Latin America and USA; collaborations with Nitin Sawhney, Asian Dub Foundation. *Recordings:* albums: Barí 2002, Barí: Remezclas de la Casa 2003, Techarí 2006, Aocaná 2009; other: Girando Bari (DVD) 2005. *Honours:* World Music Award for Europe, BBC Radio 3 2004. *E-mail:* javimartin@ojosdebrujo.com (office). *Website:* www.ojosdebrujo.com.

MARTÍN, Juan; Spanish musician (guitar); b. 1 Oct. 1943, Málaga; m. Helen Foulds 1973; two s. *Career:* performed with the Royal Philharmonic and Miles Davis, worldwide solo tours; tours with own Flamenco Dance Co.; played South Bank Centre and The Barbican, London; Carnegie Hall and the Lincoln Centre, New York; numerous int. festivals, including Ludwigsburg, Montreux Jazz, The First World Guitar Congress, USA, Istanbul, Bosphorus, Bergen, Hong Kong; 18 date tours, including the Barbican, UK 1993, 1995; numerous television appearances, radio broadcasts; solo and group tours including

Australia, Far East, Iran, West Indies, Canada, Ireland, UK, Eastern Europe, N Africa, Turkey; mem. PRS, MCPS. *Recordings:* albums: Exciting Sound of Flamenco 1974, Romance 1976, Olé Don Juan, Flamenco en Andalucia 1977, Picasso Portraits 1981, Serenade (with Royal Philharmonic Orchestra) 1984, (solo album) 1985, Painter In Sounds 1986, Through The Moving Window 1988, Andalucian Suites 1990, Luna Negra 1993, Musica Alhambra 1998, El Arte Flamenco 1999, Through the Moving Window 1999, El Alquimista (Alchemist) 2000, Riqezas (with Antonio Aparecida) 2002, Camino Latino 2002, Concerto en Directo 2004. *Videos and DVDs:* video only: Live at the Barbican 1992; DVD only: The Four Martins (with Martin Taylor, Martin Carthy and Martin Simpson); teaching aids for video and DVD: La Guitarra Flamenca, Play Flamenco Guitar with Juan Martin (Grades 0–5) and (Grades 6–8, 2005). *Publications:* Guitar Method: El Arte Flamenco de la Guitarra (with CD), La Guitarra Flamenca (video/DVD series); folios: Exciting Sound of Flamenco, Guitar Solos, 12 solos, Andalucian Suites No. 1, Solos Flamenco 2002, Solos Flamencos Vol. 2 2004. *E-mail:* hvmartin@dircon.co.uk. *Current Management:* Flamencovision, PO Box 508, London, N3 3SY, England. *Telephone:* (20) 8346-4500 (office). *E-mail:* info@flamencovision.com (office). *Website:* www.flamencovision.com (office).

MARTIN, Lynne; British musician (keyboards), arranger and music director; b. 6 Nov. 1957, Bedford; one d. *Education:* college. *Career:* television appearances include Friday People, Border TV; Look Who's Talking; Laugh-In; Musical Director for numerous summer seasons and pantomimes throughout UK; Personal Musical Director for Derek Batey for 12 years; also MD for artists including Max Bygraves, Moira Anderson, Frank Carson; mem, Musicians' Union, Equity. *Compositions:* theme tune, Friday People (Border TV) 1982.

MARTIN, Marie-Ange; French jazz musician (guitar, banjo, cello); b. 18 Jan. 1948, Bois Colombes. *Education:* studied cello. *Career:* played swing and Dixieland music with Benny Waters, Bill Coleman, 1969–76; bebop and modern jazz, 1976–84; Guitar Institute of Technology, Los Angeles, 1985; guitarist with own quartet; banjo player, Hot Kings; cellist, cello quartet Cellofans, 1986–93; tours of Asia, Australia, Eastern Europe, with Christian Escoude and Marcel Azzola, 1983–95; banjo and cello player, Threepenny Opera, 1996. *Recordings:* Dixieland Parade; Cello Acoustics. *Honours:* Outstanding Award of the Year, Guitar Institute of Technology, Los Angeles, 1985. *E-mail:* marie-ange-marti@gmail.com. *Website:* marieangemartin.com.

MARTIN, Max; Swedish singer, songwriter, music engineer and producer; b. (Martin Sandberg), 26 Feb. 1971, Stockholm; m. Jenny Max; one d. *Career:* mem. (as Martin White) heavy metal band, It's Alive; songwriter, collaborating with Denniz Pop, Rami; songs recorded by 3T, Ace of Base, Bryan Adams, Christina Aguilera, Backstreet Boys, Gary Barlow, Bon Jovi, Dede, Céline Dion, Drain, E-Type, 5ive, Jessica Folker, George, Herbie, Leila K, Kahsay, Michele, *N'SYNC, Papa Dee, Rednex, Robyn, Safe, Solid Harmonie, Britney Spears, Westlife; formed music production co. (with Tom Talomaa), Maratone 2001–. *Compositions include:* ...Baby, One More Time, Britney Spears, 10,000 Promises, Backstreet Boys, As Long As You Love Me, Backstreet Boys, Don't Wanna Lose You Now, Backstreet Boys, Don't Want You Back, Backstreet Boys, Quit Playing Games, Backstreet Boys; co-writer: When You're Looking Like That (Westlife), My Life Would Suck Without You (Kelly Clarkson), I Don't Believe You (Pink), Roar (Katy Perry), Shake It Off (Taylor Swift), Blank Space (Taylor Swift), Style (Taylor Swift). *Recordings include:* album with It's Alive: Earthquake Visions 1993. *Honours:* Swedish Grammy Award (with Denniz Pop) 1998, ASCAP Songwriter of the Year Award 1999, 2000, 2001, Grammy Award for Producer of the Year, Non-Classical 2015, Polar Music Prize 2016. *E-mail:* info@maratone.se (office). *Website:* www.maratone.se.

MARTIN, Michael Anthony; British musician (piano, keyboards); b. 9 Nov. 1960, London, England; 2 d. *Education:* Post graduate diploma; O'Level Music. *Career:* keyboard player for Billy Paul; Aswad; Jean Carne; Cliff Richard; Television: Top of the Pops; Children's TV; three world tours with Aswad; Montreux Pop Festival; International AIDS Day; Nelson Mandela at Wembley; mem, PRS; Musicians' Union. *Compositions:* Music for BBC, State of Europe. *Recordings:* with Aswad: Don't Turn Around; Production on Heartbeat, Aswad, No. 1 Japan; Roots Rocking: The Island Anthology, 1997; Big Up, 1997; with Elementals: Waking on Each Other; with Dr Seuss: Dr Seuss Green Eggs and Ham; Solo Album: Odyssey, 1998. *Honours:* Platinum disc, for album: Rise and Shine, Aswad.

MARTIN, Millicent; British actress and singer; b. 8 June 1934, Romford, Essex; m. Marc Alexander 1977. *Career:* stage performances include Side By Side, London, Los Angeles, Broadway, 42nd Street, Broadway, Las Vegas, Los Angeles, The Boyfriend, London, Broadway, King of Hearts, Broadway, The Card, London, Shirley Valentine, Rise and Fall of Little Voice, Follies, The Rivals, Moon Over Buffalo, Gigi. *Television includes:* Moon and Son, Mainly Millicent, That Was The Week That Was, Downtown, LA Law, Coach, Upper Hand, Murphy Brown, Frasier. *Recordings:* Side By Side, King of Hearts, Our Man Crighton, Sondheim – A Celebration. *Honours:* TV Society Medal, Variety Club Award. *Current Management:* Amsel, Eisenstadt and Frazier, 5757 Wilshire Boulevard, Suite 510, Los Angeles, CA 90036, USA. *Telephone:* (323) 939-1188. *E-mail:* frazier@aeftalent.com.

MARTIN, Neil; British musician (drums) and teacher; b. 10 Dec. 1967. *Education:* Studied with: Paul Robinson; Ed Soph; Bob Armstrong. *Career:* Extensive sessions and television, radio appearances; Jimmy Barnes Psyclone

World Tour 95 (including support to The Rolling Stones), venues from 1,000–50,000 seaters; mem, Musicians' Union. *Compositions:* Co-writer, track Stumbling, Psyclone album, Jimmy Barnes. *Recordings:* Album: Psyclone: Jimmy Barnes. *E-mail:* enquiries@neil-martin.co.uk. *Website:* www.neil-martin.co.uk.

MARTIN, Peter Philemon Winston; musician (drums, percussion) and singer; b. 28 Jan. 1948, Tuitts Village, Montserrat; two d. *Education:* adult education courses. *Career:* first reggae performances with Owen Grey, Alton Ellis, short tours of England early 1970s; studio musician mid 1970s; tours of England, Scotland, Wales 1980s; joined Steel and Skin, art company, played Danish Festival 1983; tour of Sweden 1984; recordings, live performances, tours of Europe, West Africa, Scandinavia; tour with Dr Alban 1992; resident in Sweden 1993; taught rhythm and dance, Blå Hasten; production of Benny The Boxer, Theatre X; played djembe on dance courses; joined Afro Tiambo, West African rhythm and dance group 1994; computer course, digital music recording; sound, lighting engineer, Folkuniversitetet, theatre production, Ritten till havet; teacher, Malmö Music High School; numerous television appearances, concerts and radio broadcasts; tours and performances with Jimmy Cliff, Style Council, Papa Dee, Red Mitchell, Eek-A-Mouse, Eddie Grant; mem. Musicians' Union, Svenska Musik Forbondet.

MARTIN, Rebecca; American singer and songwriter; b. 24 April 1969, Portland, Me; m. Larry Grenadier; one c. *Career:* formed band Once Blue with musician and songwriter Jesse Harris 1990, disbanded 1997; held several man. positions at MTV Networks; f. Kingston Citizens community org. 2006, Exec. Dir Kingston Land Trust (non-profit) 2010–. *Recordings include:* albums: Once Blue 1995, Thoroughfare 1998, Middlehope 2002, People Behave Like Ballads 2004, The Growing Season (Independent Music Award 2009), When I Was Long Ago 2010. *Honours:* Community Activist of the Year 2009. *Address:* c/o Patrice Fehlen, 465 18th Street, #2, Brooklyn, NY 11215, USA. *E-mail:* patrice@septembergurl.com. *Website:* www.rebeccamartin.com.

MARTIN, Ricky; Puerto Rican singer and actor; b. (Enrique Martin Morales), 24 Dec. 1971, San José, PR; two s. *Career:* mem. Latin pop band, Menudo 1984–89; solo artist 1989–; worked as actor and singer in Mexico; f. Ricky Martin Foundation 2000. *Television:* Alcanzar una Estrella II (Mexican soap opera), played Miguel in General Hospital (US series). *Theatre:* Marius in Les Misérables (Broadway), Che in Evita (Broadway). *Film:* Hercules (voice in Spanish-language version). *Recordings include:* albums: Ricky Martin 1991, Me Amarás 1993, A Medio Vivir 1995, Vuelve (Grammy Award for Best Latin Pop Album) 1998, Ricky Martin 1999, Sound Loaded 2000, La Historia 2001, Almas de Silencio 2003, Life 2005, MTV Unplugged (Latin Grammy Awards for Best Male Pop Vocal Album and Best Long Form Music Video 2007) 2006, A Quien Quiera Escuchar (Grammy Award for Best Latin Pop Album 2016) 2015. *Publication:* Me (autobiog.) 2010. *Honours:* American Music Award for Favorite Latin Artist 2000, Int. Humanitarian Award 2005. *Address:* Columbia Records, Sony BMG Music Entertainment, 550 Madison Avenue, New York, NY 10022-3211, USA (office). *Telephone:* (212) 833-7100 (office). *Fax:* (212) 833-7416 (office). *Website:* www.sonybmg.com (office); www.rickymartin.com; www.rickymartinfoundation.org.

MARTIN, Roy; British musician (drums) and drum tutor; b. 10 July 1961, Liverpool, England; m. Margie Yates, 20 June 1985, 2 d. *Career:* Concert tours: Played for: Modern English, 1986, 1990; Shalom Hanoch, 1987, 1988; Gavin Friday, 1992; Black, 1993; Diesel, 1993. *Recordings:* Drummer on: Jimmy Barnes: Flesh and Wood; Aretha Franklin: Jimmy Lee; Cock Robin: When Your Heart Is Weak; Black: Black; Film soundtrack (The Christians): Blame It On The Bellboy; Modern English: Pillow Lips; Joe Grushecky: Pumping Iron and Sweating Steel; Jim Hunter: Fingernail Moon (bass); Tractor: Worst Enemies; Very Best of British Dance Bands (clarinet and saxophone); Patricia Kaas: Rendez-Vous and Live; Recorded with: Viv Stanshall; Regina Belle; Billy Brannigan; Shalom Hanoch. *Website:* www.roymartin.co.uk.

MARTIN, Sarah; British singer and musician (violin, recorder); b. 12 Feb. 1974. *Career:* mem., Belle & Sebastian 1996–. *Recordings include:* albums: Tigermilk 1996, If You're Feeling Sinister 1996, The Boy With The Arab Strap 1998, Fold Your Hands Child, You Walk Like A Peasant 2000, Storytelling 2002, Dear Catastrophe Waitress 2003, The Life Pursuit 2006, Write About Love 2010, Girls in Peacetime Want to Dance 2015. *Honours:* BRIT Award for Best Newcomer 1999, Q Magazine Spirit of Independence 2013. *Current Management:* Banchory Management, PO Box 25074, Glasgow, G3 8TT, Scotland. *Telephone:* (141) 204-2269. *E-mail:* banchoryman@gmail.com. *Website:* www.belleandsebastian.com.

MARTIN, Steve; American actor, comedian, writer and musician (banjo); b. 14 Aug. 1945, Waco, Tex.; s. of Glenn Martin and Mary Lee Martin; m. 1st Victoria Tennant 1986 (divorced 1994); m. 2nd Anne Stringfield 2007. *Education:* Long Beach State Coll., Univ. of California, Los Angeles. *Career:* TV writer for several shows; nightclub comedian; TV special Steve Martin: A Wild and Crazy Guy 1978. *Recordings include:* Let's Get Small 1977 (Grammy Award), A Wild and Crazy Guy 1978 (Grammy Award), Comedy is Not Pretty 1979, The Steve Martin Bros, The Crow: New Songs for the Five-String Banjo (Grammy Award for Best Bluegrass Album 2010) 2009, Rare Bird Alert (with Steep Canyon Rangers) 2011, Love Has Come for You (with Edie Brickell) 2013, So Familiar (with Edie Brickell) 2015. *Films include:* The Absent Minded Waiter 1977, Sgt Pepper's Lonely Hearts Club Band 1978, The Muppet Movie 1979, The Jerk 1979 (also screenwriter), Pennies from Heaven

1981, Dead Men Don't Wear Plaid (also writer) 1982, The Man With Two Brains (also writer) 1983, The Lonely Guy 1984, All of Me 1984 (Nat. Soc. of Film Critics Actor's Award), Three Amigos (also writer and exec. producer) 1986, Little Shop of Horrors 1986, Roxanne (also screenwriter and exec. producer) 1987, Planes, Trains and Automobiles 1987, Dirty Rotten Scoundrels 1988, Parenthood 1989, My Blue Heaven 1990, LA Story (also writer and exec. producer) 1991, Grand Canyon 1991, Father of the Bride 1991, Housesitter 1992, Leap of Faith 1992, A Simple Twist of Fate (also writer and exec. producer) 1994, Mixed Nuts 1994, Father of the Bride 2 1995, Sgt Bilko 1996, The Spanish Prisoner 1997, The Out of Towners 1999, Bowfinger (also writer) 1999, Joe Gould's Secret 2000, Novocaine 2001, Bringing Down the House 2003, Looney Tunes: Back in Action 2003, Cheaper by the Dozen 2003, Jiminy Glick in La La Wood 2004, Shopgirl (also screenplay and producer) 2005, Cheaper by the Dozen 2 2005, Pink Panther (also screenplay) 2006, It's Complicated 2009, Tangled (voice) 2010, The Big Year 2011. *Publications include:* The Pleasure of My Company 2003, Born Standing Up (autobiog.) 2007, An Object of Beauty 2010. *Honours:* Georgie Award, American Guild of Variety Artists 1977, 1978, American Cinematheque Career Achievement Honour 2004, John F. Kennedy Center for Performing Arts Mark Twain Prize for American Humor 2005, Kennedy Center Honor 2007, Academy Honorary Award 2013, Grammy Award for Best Roots Song (for Love Has Come for You, with Edie Brickell) 2014. *Website:* www.stevemartin.com.

MARTIN, Tony; British singer and songwriter; b. 19 April 1957, Birmingham, England; m. Mo Martin 1990; two s. one d. *Career:* first show aged seven; mem. of numerous local bands; mem. The Alliance 1983; mem. Black Sabbath 1987–92, 1993–, with world tours; solo artist. *Recordings include:* with Bailey Brothers: Vinyl Frontier, The Talisman, Forcefield II, Valley of the Kings, Blue Murder; with Black Sabbath: Eternal Idol 1987, Headless Cross 1989, Tyr 1990, Cross Purposes 1993, Forbidden 1995; solo: Back Where I Belong 1992. *Address:* c/o Lethal Music UK Ltd, E9 Kenilworth Court, Hagley Road, Birmingham, B16 9NU, England.

MARTÍN GARCÍA, Daniel (Dani); Spanish singer, songwriter and musician (guitar); b. 19 Feb. 1977, Madrid. *Career:* founder mem., El Canto del Loco 2000–. *Recordings include* albums: A contracorriente 2002, Sala Caracol 2003, Estados de ánimo 2003, Zapatillas 2005, Pequeños Grandes Directos 2006, Personas 2008, De Personas a Personas 2008. *Honours:* MTV Europe Music Award Best Spanish Act 2005. *Current Management:* Aire de Música, Calle Pelayo, 76 Local, 28004 Madrid, Spain. *Telephone:* (91) 7000443. *Fax:* (91) 3197946. *E-mail:* info@airedemusica.com. *Website:* www.airedemusica.com; www.elcantodelloco.com.

MARTINEZ, Cliff; American musician (drums, keyboards) and composer; b. 2 Feb. 1954, New York, NY. *Career:* worked as a session drummer; joined Captain Beefheart and The Magic Band 1982–83; mem., Red Hot Chili Peppers 1984–86; also recorded with Lydia Lunch, The Dickies and The Weirdos; began writing music for TV and films 1987–; collaborated closely with film director, Steven Soderbergh. *Compositions:* film scores written, produced or supervised include: Sex, Lies And Videotape 1989, Pump Up The Volume 1990, Kafka 1991, King Of The Hill 1993, The Underneath 1995, Schizopolis 1997, Gray's Anatomy 1997, Out Of Sight 1998, Wicked 1999, The Limey 1999, Traffic 2000, Solaris 2002, Narc 2002, Wonderland 2003, Havoc 2005, Drive 2011. *Recordings include:* albums: with Captain Beefheart and The Magic Band: Ice Cream For Crow, 1982; with The Red Hot Chili Peppers: Red Hot Chili Peppers, 1984; Freaky Styley, 1985; with Lydia Lunch: Stinkfist, 1987; with The Dickies: Second Coming, 1989; Idjit Savant, 1995; with The Weirdos: Condor, 1999; numerous soundtracks including Spring Breakers 2012. *Address:* c/o Trauma (Red) Records, 15165 Ventura Boulevard, Sherman Oaks, CA 91403, USA (office).

MARTINEZ, Lenny; Danish producer and musician; b. Honduras. *Career:* mem., Outlandish 1997–. *Recordings include:* albums: Outlands Official (Danish Music Award for Best Hip-Hop Album) 2000, Outlandish Presents... Beats, Rhymes & Life 2003, Bread & Barrels of Water 2003, Closer than Veins 2005. *Current Management:* c/o Thomas Borresen, Soulcamp Entertainment, Vester Voldgade 87, 4th., 1552 Copenhagen K, Denmark. *E-mail:* thomas.borresen@soulcamp.dk. *Website:* www.ourlandmoro.com.

MARTINEZ, Pedrito; Cuban jazz percussionist, singer and bandleader; b. (Pedro Pablo Martinez), 12 Sept. 1973, Havana. *Career:* began musical career at age 11; singer and percussionist with Cuban acts including Tata Guines and Los Munequitos de Matanzas; relocated to Canada, then New York 1998; Founder-mem. Yerba Buena, Pedrito Martinez Group; numerous collaborations live and on record including with Eric Brickell, Isaac Delgado, Paquito D'Rivera, Eliane Elias, Stefon Harris, Joe Lovano, Brian Lynch, Wynton Marsalis, Arturo O'Farrill, Eddie Palmieri, Michelle Rosewoman, Gonzalo Rubalcaba, Paul Simon, Bruce Springsteen, Sting, Bebo Valdés, Cassandra Wilson. *Films:* Calle 54 2004, Chico and Rita 2010. *Recordings:* albums: Rumba de la Isla 2013, Rumba is a Lovesome Thing (with Paul Carlton) 2013, Pedrito Martinez Group 2013. *Honours:* Thelonious Monk Award for Afro-Latin Hand Percussion 2000, Sphinx Medal of Excellence 2014, Jazz Journalists Asscn Award for Percussionist of the Year 2014, 2015. *E-mail:* paul@pedritomartinezmusic.com. *Website:* pedritomartinezmusic.com.

MARTINEZ NIEVES, José Angel; Cuban musician (double bass); b. 1977, Santiago de Cuba. *Education:* Conservatorio Esteban Salas. *Career:* several prizes at local and nat. Amadeo Roldán competitions; joined Eliades Ochoa's

Cuarteto Patria 2000–; mem. AfroCubism project 2010–; has also performed with José Mercé. *Recordings:* albums: with Eliades Ochoa: Tributo al Cuarteto Patria 2000, Estoy Como Nunca 2002; with José Mercé: Aire 2001; with AfroCubism: AfroCubism 2010. *Address:* c/o World Circuit Records, 138 Kingsland Road, London, E2 8DY, England (office). *E-mail:* post@worldcircuit.co.uk (office). *Website:* www.worldcircuit.co.uk (office).

MARTUCCI, Vincent, BA, MM; American composer, arranger, musician (piano) and educator; *Professor of Jazz Studies, State University of New York, New Paltz;* b. 21 Oct. 1954, Medford, MA; s. of the late Vincent James Martucci and Grace Alice Martucci (née Giorgio); m. Elizabeth Lawrence 1981; one s. one d. *Education:* Colby Coll., Waterville, Maine, Music State Univ. of New York, Purchase, Berklee Coll. of Music, private studies with John Mehegan, Hal Galper, Dave Holland, Baikida Carroll. *Career:* performer, synthesizer, film score My Blue Heaven (with Steve Martin); numerous tours with own group, co-lead with Dan Brubeck, The Dolphins, in USA, Europe, South America, Canada; redesign network themes, Travel Channel, Lifetime Medical Television; Showtime, children's TV series 1989; Music Dir, pianist, arranger for numerous performers incl. Eileen Fulton, Laurel Massé 1991–; producer, performer, arranger, numerous theatrical productions with Baikida Carroll and McCarter Theatre, including Tony Award-winning Having Our Say 1995; Prof. of Jazz Studies State Univ. of NY, New Paltz 2004–; mem. ASCAP, AFTRA. *Compositions:* numerous tunes for The Dolphins, scores for daytime drama As The World Turns, Guiding Light, Another World 1992–. *Recordings:* Livingston Taylor, Life is Good 1988; Dan Brubeck and the Dolphins, 3 CDs 1989–99; Rory Black, Tornado 1996. *Publications:* Introduction to Jazz Piano 1997, Introduction to Blues Piano 1997, Introduction to Rock Piano 1997. *Honours:* second place Billboard Song Contest 1988, jazz category finalist Hennessey Jazz Search 1990. *Address:* 29 Pleasant Ridge Drive, West Hurley, NY 12491, USA (home). *Telephone:* (845) 257-2710 (office). *E-mail:* martuccv@newplatz.edu (office).

MARUCCI, Mathew (Mat) Roger, III, AA; American musician (drums), producer and writer; b. 2 July 1945, Rome, NY; m. Diane Marie 1982; one s. one d. *Education:* Auburn Community College, Sacramento City Collegemat. *Career:* recording artist and jazz musician; Applied Music Instructor, American River College, Sacramento; drummer for major jazz artists, including Jimmy Smith, Kenny Burrell, James Moody, Eddie Harris, Les McCann, John Tchicai and Buddy De Franco; appeared in feature film Uncle Joe Shannon and TV series Fantasy Island; played on soundtracks for TV; leader of trio, quartet and quintet; mem. Percussive Arts Society, Broadcast Music Inc. *Compositions:* Festival, Ulterior Motif, Who Do Voo Doo Suite, Blue Suspension, Danse Desire, Lifeline, Quiescence. *Recordings:* Who Do Voo Doo 1979, Lifeline 1980, Festival 1980, Extensity 1981, Avant-Bop 1983, Body and Soul 1991, Ulterior Motif 1998, Genesis 2004, 3 The Hard Way 2006, No Lesser Evil 2007, Change-Up 2007, Partners in Crime 2008. *Publications:* contributor of articles in magazines for Modern Drummer, Percussive Notes, Percussion News, Sticks and Mallets, Upstrokes, Drum Instructors Only. *E-mail:* mat@matmarucci.com (office). *Website:* matmarucci.com.

MARVIN, Hank B.; British musician (guitar) and songwriter; b. (Brian Robson Rankin), 28 Oct. 1941, Newcastle upon Tyne, England; m. Carole; two s. *Career:* lead guitarist with Cliff Richard's backing group, The Drifters 1958, renamed The Shadows 1959–2004. *Recordings include:* albums: with The Shadows: The Shadows 1961, Out of the Shadows 1962, The Shadows Greatest Hits 1963, Dance With The Shadows 1964, The Sound of the Shadows 1965, Shadow Music 1966, Jigsaw 1967, Established 1958, 1968, Shades of Rock 1970, 20 Golden Greats 1977, Thank You Very Much, 20th Anniversary Reunion Concert, Cliff Richard and the Shadows 1978, String of Hits 1980, Change of Address 1980, Hits Right Up Your Street 1981, XXV 1983, Moonlight Shadows 1986, Simply Shadows 1987, Steppin' To the Shadows 1989, At Their Very Best 1989, Reflections 1990, Themes and Dreams 1991, Shadows in the Night 1993, Life Story 2004; solo: Hank Marvin 1969, Words and Music 1982, Into the Light 1992, Heartbeat 1993, Would You Believe It... Plus 1994, Hank Plays Cliff 1996, Marvin At The Movies 2000, Guitar Player 2002, Guitar Man 2007; singles: with The Shadows: Apache 1960, Man of Mystery 1960, FBI 1961, Kon-Tiki 1961, The Savage 1961, Wonderful Land 1962, Guitar Tango 1962, Dance On 1963, Foot Tapper 1963, Atlantis 1963, Shindig 1963, Geronimo 1963, Stingray 1965, Don't Make My Baby Blue 1965, Let Me Be The One 1975, Don't Cry For Me Argentina 1979, Cavatina (theme from film The Deerhunter) 1979, Riders in the Sky 1980, Living Doll (charity version with Cliff Richard) 1986; contributions to film soundtracks include: Serious Charge 1959, The Young Ones 1961, The Boys 1962, Summer Holiday 1963, Wonderful Life 1964, Finders Keepers 1966, The Frightened City 1961, The Deerhunter 1979, The Third Man 1981. *Honours:* winner, Split Song Festival, Yugoslavia 1967, CBS Arbiter Award for Services to British Music 1977; with the Shadows: NME Record of the Year 1960, Ivor Novello Award for Best Musical Score 1963, Special Award for 25 Years in the Music Business 1983.

MARWICK, Gavin; British musician (fiddle), composer and teacher; b. 29 Aug. 1969, Edinburgh, Scotland. *Education:* formal training with Angus Grant, Alastair Hardie, Tom Anderson, Davy Tulloch. *Career:* mem. Iron Horse 1988–2003; festivals, tours, TV and radio work across Europe, N America, Asia and Africa; formed fiddle-led trio with Jonny Hardie 1994–; Founder-mem. Burach 1994–96; mem. Cantrip 2001–08; Co-founder Bellevue Rendezvous 2006–; Journeyman Project (books, recordings and live shows featuring original tunes) 2014–; composer, recording artist; ceilidh bands include Ceilidh Minogue, The Marwicks; teaching includes Newcastle Univ., Celtic Connections Educ. Programme, Feis Rois, Falkirk Fiddle Workshop; live and/or recorded session work includes Malinky, Old Blind Dogs, Session A9, RSNO, Unusual Suspects, Wolfstone, Arz Nevez, Sogdiana; theatre work includes The Tailor of Inverness (Dogstar), Molly Whuppie (Lickityspit) and various Traverse, Dundee Rep, BBC, Sky Arts; mem. Musicians' Union, PRS, MCPS. *Commissions include:* for the Traverse: Faith Healer, The Heritage 2001, Highland Shorts, The Trestle At Pope Lick Creek, Outlying Islands; for NTS: Gobbo; for Dogstar: The Tailor of Inverness. *Recordings:* with Iron Horse: The Iron Horse 1991, Thro Water Earth And Stone (MRA for Excellence) 1993, Five Hands High 1994, Voice Of The Land 1995, Demons And Lovers 1997, The Wind Shall Blow For Evermore 2003; with Jonny Hardie: Up In The Air 1995, The Blue Lamp 1999, Moonshine 2012; with Burach: The Weird Set 1995, Unstoppable; with The Marwicks: Ceilidh Sets 1998; with Cantrip: Silver 2002, Boneshaker 2005, Piping the Fish 2008; with Bellevue Rendezvous: Tangents 2007, Salamander 2010; as Gavin Marwick: The Long Road and The Far Horizons 2014. *Publications:* contrib. to The Balnain Collection. *Honours:* Belhaven Best New Folk Band, Burach 1995. *Website:* www.gavinmarwick.co.uk.

MARX, Richard Noel; American singer, songwriter and record producer; b. 16 Sept. 1963, Chicago, IL; m. Cynthia Rhodes 1989, three s. *Career:* backing vocalist with Lionel Richie 1982; solo artist 1986–; extensive tours throughout USA, Europe and Asia; major concerts include Farm Aid V 1992, all-star benefit concert, Pediatric AIDS Foundation 1992; television and radio appearances world-wide; mem. ASCAP, SAG, AFTRA, AFofM. *Compositions:* co-writer, What About Me?, recorded by Kenny Rogers; co-writer, album tracks with Chicago, Philip Bailey; co-writer, co-producer, with Randy Meisner, David Cole, Fee Waybill, Vixen, Poco, Kevin Cronin. *Recordings:* hit singles: Don't Mean Nothing 1987, Should've Known Better 1987, Endless Summer Nights 1988, Hold On To The Nights 1988, Satisfied 1989, Right Here Waiting 1989, Angelia 1990, Too Late To Say Goodbye 1990, Children of The Night 1990, Hard To Believe 1991, Keep Coming Back 1991, Hazard 1992, Take This Heart 1992, Chains Around My Heart 1992, Now and Forever 1994, The Way She Loves Me 1994, Nothing Left Behind Us 1994, Until I Find You Again 1997, Keep Coming Back 1997; as backing singer: with Lionel Richie: All Night Long, You Are, Running With The Night; solo albums: Richard Marx 1987, Repeat Offender 1989, Rush Street 1991, Paid Vacation 1994, Flesh and Bone 1997, Greatest Hits 1997, Days Of Avalon 2000, My Own Best Enemy 2004, Duo 2008, Emotional Remains 2008. *Honours:* Billboard AC Artist of the Year 1992, first male artist with four Top 3 hits from debut album. *Website:* www.richardmarx.com.

MASAKOWSKI, Steve; American jazz musician (guitar); b. 2 Sept. 1954, New Orleans, LA; m. Ulrike Sprenger 1982; one s. one d. *Education:* Berklee Coll. of Music, Boston. *Career:* mem. Astral Project 1978–; extensive int. tours with Dianne Reeves, Rick Margitza. *Recordings:* solo: Direct AXEcess, What It Was, Friends, Mars; with Astral Project: New Orleans LA 1995, Elevado 1998, Voodoobop 2000, Big Shot, The Legend of Cowboy Bill; appears on 28 albums including Esquire Jazz Collection 1995, Philip Manuel: Time for Love 1995, Johnny Adams, Verdict 1995, Jazz: Language of New Orleans 1998. *Honours:* voted Best Jazz Guitarist in New Orleans, Offbeat Magazine, two Nat. Endowment for the Arts Fellowships. *Current Management:* c/o Tony Dagradi, 74 Egret Street, New Orleans, LA 70124, USA. *Telephone:* (504) 282-1637. *Fax:* (504) 282-1637. *E-mail:* tony@astralproject.com. *E-mail:* steve@astralproject.com (office). *Website:* www.astralproject.com.

MASEK, Jiri; Czech sound engineer; b. 15 June 1970, Prague; m. Zuzana, 22 May 1992, 1 s., 1 d. *Career:* Sound Engineer, 28 records including many well-known Czech pop, folk and jazz groups and singers. *Recordings:* Zalman and Spol, 4 CDs, Czech Republic; Ivan Hajnis, CD, Sweden; Happy to Meet, CD, Ireland; Wild West, CD, Czech Republic; Relief, CD, Czech Republic. *Honours:* Folk and Country Awards, 1997, 1998, 1999; Stereo and Video Award, 1998. *E-mail:* goodday@goodday.cz. *Website:* www.goodday.cz.

MASEKELA, Hugh; South African musician (trumpet); b. 1939, nr Johannesburg. *Education:* Guildhall School of Music, London, Manhattan School of Music, New York. *Career:* co-f. The Jazz Epistles 1959; fmrly in voluntary exile from early 1960s, in UK, USA, Ghana, Nigeria, Guinea and Botswana; f. Botswana Int. School of Music 1986; Musical Dir Graceland. *Compositions include:* wrote Sarafina (Broadway musical). *Recordings include:* Grrr 1966, The Promise of a Future 1968, Masekela 1968, Home is Where the Music Is (with Dudu Pukwana) 1972, The African Connection 1973, Techno Bush 1984, I Am Not Afraid (with Hedzoleh Soundz), Tomorrow 1987, Beatin' Aroun De Bush 1992, Stimela 1994, Reconstruction 1994, Black to the Future 1998, Boys Doin' It 1998, Sixty 2000, Time 2002, Still Grazing 2004, Revival 2005, Phola 2009, Jabulani 2010, Friends 2012, Playing @ Work 2012. *Publication:* Still Grazing: The Musical Journey of Hugh Masekela 2003. *Honours:* Order of Ikhamanga 2010; Dr hc (Univ. of York) 2014, (Rhodes Univ.) 2015; BBC Radio Jazz Int. Award of the Year 2002, Kora All African Music Award for Best Male Artist in Southern Africa 2005, Channel O Music Video Lifetime Achievement Award 2005, Ghana Music African Music Legend Award 2007. *Current Management:* c/o John Cumming, Serious Ltd, 51 Kingsway Place, Sans Walk, Clerkenwell, London, EC1R 0LU, England. *Telephone:* (82) 8818565; (20) 7324-1880. *E-mail:* josh@88.co.za; john.cumming@serious.org.uk. *Website:* www.hughmasekela.co.za; www.serious.org.uk.

MASHBURN, Robin (Rob) Arvil; American singer, songwriter and musician (guitar, bass); b. 5 April 1942, Andrews, NC; m. Catherine Stears Mashburn 1982; two s. *Career:* mem. Grand Ole Opry, Wolftrap, Bele Chere, Tennessee Homecoming – Museum of Appalachia, Georgia Mountain Fair; mem, BMI, Bluegrass Music Asscn of North Carolina, South Carolina, Georgia. *Recordings:* albums: The Picker, Another Place Another Time, Brother of Mine, It's Me Again Lord, Misty Mountain Music, The Picker's Best. *Current Management:* Catherine Mashburn, PO Box 1318, Andrews, NC 28901, USA.

MASKATIYA, Omar; British music industry executive; *Chart Director, The Official UK Charts Company. Career:* fmrly worked in Marketing Dept, Our Price Music; worked in Buying Dept, Entertainment UK; apptd Operations Man., The Official UK Charts Co., then Chart Dir 1998–. *Address:* The Official UK Charts Company, 4th Floor, 58–59 Great Marlborough Street, London, W1F 7JY, England (office). *Telephone:* (20) 7478-8500 (office). *E-mail:* info@theofficialcharts.com (office). *Website:* www.theofficialcharts.com (office).

MASON, David (Dave) Thomas; British musician (guitar); b. 10 May 1947, Worcester, England. *Career:* mem., The Hellions 1964; road man., Spencer Davis Group; founder mem. (with Steve Winwood), Traffic –1967, 1968–69; solo artist, session player and numerous collaborations; moved to USA 1973; mem., Fleetwood Mac 1993–95. *Recordings:* albums: with Traffic: Mr Fantasy 1968; solo: Alone Together 1970, Dave Mason And Cass Elliot 1971, Headkeeper 1972, Scrapbook 1972, Dave Mason Is Alive 1973, It's Like You Never Left 1973, Dave Mason 1974, Split Coconut 1975, Let It Flow 1977, Mariposa De Oro 1978, Old Crest On A New Wave 1980, Some Assembly Required 1981, Two Hearts 1987, The 40,000 Headmen Tour (live) 1999, 26 Letters - 12 Notes 2008; with Fleetwood Mac: Time 1995. *Current Management:* c/o Kristen Foster, PMKHBH, 161 Avenue of the Americas, Suite 10R, New York, NY 10013, USA. *Telephone:* (212) 373-6104. *Fax:* (212) 582-6666. *E-mail:* kristen.foster@pmkhbh.com. *Address:* c/o Barham Productions Inc., PO Box 1732, Oak View, CA 93022, USA (office). *E-mail:* dave@thedavemason.com (office). *Website:* www.dave-mason.com.

MASON, Kerry; British singer and songwriter; b. 31 March 1968, Dorking, Surrey; one d. *Education:* singing lessons with Tona de Brett. *Career:* singer in band, Hed; numerous festival appearances; session singer; mem. Musicians' Union. *Recordings:* singles: Reigndance 1994, Folklaw 1995.

MASON, Mila; American country singer; b. 22 Aug. 1963, Dawson Springs, KY. *Career:* toured with country singer mother from an early age; moved to Nashville and met songwriter Harlan Sanders, became demo singer for him and for other writers; sang jingles and appeared in several music videos, as well as developing own songwriting; solo artist 1995–. *Recordings include:* albums: That's Enough of That 1996, The Strong One 1998, Just A Peek 2001, Stained Glass Window 2003. *Address:* Mila Mason Fan Club, c/o Donna Schneidtmiller, PO Box 24392, Louisville, KY 40224, USA. *E-mail:* MilaFC@aol.com (office).

MASON, Nick; British musician (drums); b. 27 Jan. 1945, Birmingham, England. *Career:* drummer, Pink Floyd 1965–; performances include Rome International Pop Festival 1968, Hyde Park, London 1968, Bath Festival 1970, Montreux Festival 1971, Knebworth Festival 1975. *Films:* Pink Floyd Live at Pompeii 1972, The Wall 1982, Life Could be a Dream 1985. *Recordings:* albums: with Pink Floyd: Piper At The Gates Of Dawn 1967, A Saucerful Of Secrets 1968, More (film soundtrack) 1969, Ummagumma 1969, Atom Heart Mother 1970, Relics 1971, Meddle 1971, Obscured By Clouds 1972, The Dark Side Of The Moon 1972, Wish You Were Here 1975, Animals 1977, The Wall 1979, The Final Cut 1983, A Momentary Lapse Of Reason 1987, The Delicate Sound Of Thunder 1988, Shine On 1992, The Division Bell 1994, Pulse 1995, Echoes: The Very Best Of Pink Floyd 2001, The Endless River 2014; solo: Nick Mason's Fictitious Sport 1981, Profiles 1985. *Publication:* Inside Out: A Personal History of Pink Floyd 2004. *Honours:* Outstanding Contribution to British Music 1992, Polar Music Prize 2008. *Current Management:* Steve O'Rouke, EMKA Productions Ltd, 43 Portland Road, London, W11 4LJ, England. *Website:* www.pinkfloyd.com/index2.php.

MASSAQUOI, Alloysious; British rapper, singer and songwriter; b. Liberia. *Education:* Boroughmuir High School, Edinburgh, Scotland. *Career:* moved with family to Edinburgh at age four; fmr mem. 3 Style; mem. Young Fathers 2008–. *Recordings:* albums: with Young Fathers: Inconceivable Child... Conceived 2009, Dead (Mercury Music Prize 2014) 2014, White Men Are Black Men Too 2015; mixtapes: Tape One 2011, Tape Two 2013. *Address:* Big Dada Records, Big Dada HQ, PO Box 4296, London, SE11 4WW, England (office). *E-mail:* info@bigdada.com (office); youngfathers@googlemail.com (home). *Website:* www.bigdada.com (office); www.young-fathers.com.

MASSENBURG, George Y.; American producer, recording engineer and audio equipment designer; b. 1947, Baltimore, MD; one s. *Career:* ITI Studios, Huntsville, MD; Chief Engineer, Europa Sonar Studios, Paris, France 1973–74; freelance engineer and equipment designer 1973–74; designer, builder and manager of recording studios; Founder and owner, George Massenburg Labs Inc, 1982–; Adjunct Prof., Recording Arts and Sciences, McGill University, Montreal, Canada; Visiting lecturer, University of California, Los Angeles, University of Southern California, Middle Tennessee State University; worked with: Mary Chapin Carpenter, The Dixie Chicks, Earth Wind & Fire, Billy Joel, Journey, Little Feat, Kenny Loggins, Lyle Lovett, Aaron Neville, Randy Newman, Madeleine Peyroux, Linda Ronstadt,

Michael Ruff, James Taylor, Toto. *Publications:* contrib. to professional journals and trade magazines. *Honours:* Academy of Country Music Award, Record of the Year (for The Trio) 1988, Mix Magazine TEC Awards, Producer and Engineer of the Year (for Little Feat) 1989, Engineer of the Year Award, for Linda Ronstadt 1991, for Lyle Lovett 1992; Grammy Awards for Best Producer 1996, for Best Engineered Non-Classical Record 1990, for Technical Achievement 1998. *Address:* George Massenburg Labs Inc, PO Box 1366, Franklin, TN 37065, USA (office). *Telephone:* (615) 515-6656 (office). *Fax:* (615) 261-9133 (office). *Website:* www.massenburg.com (office).

MASSENBURG, Kedar, BA, JD; American record company executive; *President and CEO, Kedar Entertainment;* b. Brooklyn, NY. *Education:* Central State Univ., Univ. of North Carolina at Chapel Hill. *Career:* fmr man., Stetsasonic; fmr entertainment lawyer; signed artists D'Angelo and Erykah Badu; founder, Pres. and CEO, Kedar Entertainment 1995–; joined Motown Records 1998, signed India.Arie, Dave Hollister, Brian McKnight, Pres. and CEO 1999–2004;. *Television:* TV tribute to Stevie Wonder (prod., Black Entertainment Television) 2002, Motown Christmas Special (prod., USA Networks) 2002. *Honours:* Vibe Quincy Jones Achievement Award 2003. *Address:* Kedar Entertainment, 21 West 39th Street, New York, NY 10018, USA (office). *Telephone:* (212) 391-1111 (office). *Fax:* (212) 391-1343 (office). *E-mail:* info@kedar.com (office). *Website:* www.kedar.com (office).

MASSI, Souad; Algerian singer and musician (guitar); b. 23 Aug. 1972, Bab-el-Oued; m. *Education:* Univ. of Algiers. *Career:* began singing and playing guitar in childhood; joined flamenco group Les Trianas d'Algers 1990; joined rock group Atakor 1996; banned from TV in Algeria 1997; moved to France and began career as solo artist 1999–. *Recordings:* albums: Raoui 2001, Deb 2003, Mesk Elil 2005, Acoustic, Best of 2007, Ô Houria (Liberty) 2010. *Honours:* BBC Radio 3 Award for World Music (Mid East and North Africa) 2006. *Address:* c/o Universal Music France, 20–22 rue des Fosses Saint Jacques, 75005 Paris, France (office). *E-mail:* abdelzem@free.fr (office); souadmassiofficiel@gmail.com (office). *Website:* www.souadmassi.com.fr.

MASTA KILLA, (Noodles); American MC and rap artist; b. (Elgin Turner). *Career:* mem., Wu-Tang Clan 1993–; solo artist 2004–. *Recordings include:* albums: with Wu-Tang Clan: Enter The Wu-Tang (36 Chambers) 1993, Wu-Tang Forever 1997, The W 2000, Iron Flag 2001, Disciples Of The 36 Chambers: Chapter 1 (live) 2004, The 8 Diagrams 2007; solo: No Said Date 2004, Made in Brooklyn 2006. *Address:* c/o Sony Music Entertainment, 550 Madison Avenue, New York, NY 10022-3211, USA. *Telephone:* (212) 833-8000. *Fax:* (212) 833-4270. *Website:* www.mastakilla.net; www.myspace.com/mastakilla; www.wutangcorp.com.

MASTER GEE; American rap artist. *Career:* mem., The Sugarhill Gang 1979–85. *Recordings include:* albums: with The Sugarhill Gang: Rapper's Delight: Hip Hop Remix 1980, The Sugarhill Gang 1980, 8th Wonder 1982, Jump On It! 1999; collaborations include Bob Sinclair 2009.

MASUKA, Dorothy; Zimbabwean singer and songwriter; b. 1937, Bulawayo. *Career:* started performing with the African Jazz and Variety Show, a travelling road show with Miriam Makeba and Hugh Masekela, aged 12; started recording 1951; exiled from South Africa 1960; worked as a singer throughout Europe and Africa; returned to Zimbabwe 1980; performed several shows with The Golden Rhythm Crooners in Harare 1989; contributed to John Barry's soundtrack for Cry the Beloved Country 1995; popularly known as 'Aunty Dot' or 'Sis Do'. *Recordings include:* albums: Hamba Notsokolo 1988, Women of Africa Vol. 1 1989, Phata Phata 1990, Magumede 1998, Mzilikazi 2001, Lendaba 2003. *Honours:* award winner, Pan-African Cultural Festival in Algiers, 1969. *Address:* c/o Gallo Music South Africa. PO Box 2897, Parklands 2121, South Africa (office). *Website:* www.gallo.co.za (office).

MATHERS, Marshall Bruce, III (see Eminem)

MATHESON, Karen Elizabeth, OBE; Scottish singer; b. 11 Feb. 1963, Oban, Argyll and Bute, Scotland. *Career:* Founder-mem., Capercaillie; group, along with original material, specialize in fusing traditional Gaelic songs with contemporary arrangements; had first UK top 40 single in Gaelic, Coisich A Ruin (from A Prince Among Islands EP) 1992; also worked on solo projects and appeared on L'Heritage de Celts, a French album with Donal Lunny and Dan Ar Braz; project led to Matheson performing a Breton song, Que Naissant Les Enfants, with Dar An Braz and Elaine Morgan for France's entry in Eurovision Song Contest 1996; appeared in Rob Roy film singing an unaccompanied rendition of a Gaelic Lament; performed on TV series Transatlantic Sessions with many well-known artists including: Emmylou Harris, The MacGarrigle Sisters, Mary Black; collaborations with James Grant on solo albums and TV appearances. *Recordings include:* albums: with Capercaillie: Cascade 1984, Crosswinds 1987, Sidewalk 1989, Delirium 1991, Get Out 1992, The Blood Is Strong 1993, Secret People 1993, Capercaillie 1995, To The Moon 1996, Beautiful Wasteland 1997, Glenfinnan – Songs of The '45 (recorded 1995) 1998, Nàdurra 2000, Live in Concert 2002, Choice Language 2003, Roses and Tears 2008; solo: The Dreaming Sea 1996, Time To Fall 2002, Downriver 2005. *Address:* c/o Vertical Records, The Basement, 19 Woodside Crescent, Glasgow G3 7UL, Scotland (office). *Telephone:* (141) 352-6670 (office). *E-mail:* info@secretmusic.org (office). *Website:* www.verticalrecords.co.uk (office); www.capercaillie.co.uk; www.karenmatheson.com.

MATHEWS, Norman, BA, MA; American composer and playwright; b. (Norman Cancelose), 12 Sept. 1942, Rockford, Ill.; partner Todd Lehman. *Education:* Hunter Coll., New York and New York Univ. *Career:* composer for concert music, musical theatre, opera and jazz; mem. American Soc. of Composers, Authors and Publrs (ASCAP), American Composers' Forum. *Plays:* You Might As Well Love, Lost Empires. *Compositions:* song cycles: Songs of the Poet, Rossetti Songs; choral works: Sonnets 61, 75, 116; orchestral works: Triumph of Night, Songs of the Poet; String Quartet, Chamber Opera: Flights of the Heart; political musical work: Ye Are Many – They Are Few; musical theatre: You Might As Well Live, Lost Empires (based on the novel by J. B. Priestley); cabaret revue: Somebody Write Me A Song. *Honours:* ASCAP Standard Awards, Ludwig Vogelstein playwriting grant, VocalEssence Choral Award 2011, Puffin Foundation Grant in Composition 2012. *Address:* 667 West 161st Street, Apt 3H, New York, NY 10032, USA (office). *E-mail:* norman@normanmathews.com (office). *Website:* www .normanmathews.com.

MATHIESEN, Claus; Danish musician (clarinet, recorder); b. 13 July 1957, Copenhagen; 1 s. *Education:* Classical education, Copenhagen; Turkish Art Music, Istanbul Conservatory. *Career:* Musician with Ildfuglen, 1979–83; Kefir, 1983–86; Fuat Saka Band, 1986–; Wild East, 1989–93; Oriental Mood, 1993–; Chochek Brothers, 1994–; All these bands merging Western and Balkan/Middle Eastern music; mem. DJBFA. *Recordings:* with Fuat Saka Band: Nebengleis, 1989; Askaroz, 1991; Sen, 1994; with Anatolia: Anatolia, 1991; with Oriental Mood: Travels, 1994; Oriental Moods, 1996; Oriental Garden, 1998; with Nazê Botan: Akh Kurdistan, 1996; Kurdistan – The Forgotten World, 1998; with Chochek Brothers: Let's Chochek!, 1998. *Publications:* Contributor, Danish National Encyclopedia.

MATHIESON, Greg; American arranger, composer, producer and musician (keyboards); b. 25 Feb. 1950, Los Angeles, California; m. Barbara Price 1983; one s. *Career:* tours with Al Jarreau, Helen Reddy, Olivia Newton-John, John Travolta, Larry Carlton, Abraham Laboriel. *Recordings:* solo: Baked Potato Super Live, For My Friends, West Coast Groove; with Al Jarreau: All Fly Home, This Time, Trouble In Paradise; with Bill Champlin: Burn Down The Night, Through It All; with Laura Branigan: Gloria; with Toni Basil: Mickey; with Sheena Easton: Telefone, Strut, Almost Over You; with Donna Summer: MacArthur Park, Heaven Knows, Live and More; with Barbra Streisand: Enough Is Enough, Songbird, Wet; with Abraham Laboriel: Dear Friends, Guidem, Frontline, Koinonia, Laboriel/Mathieson; with Manhattan Transfer: Extensions: Mecca For Moderns, Bodies and Souls; with Lee Ritenour: Banded Together, Earth Run, Collection; with Deniece Williams: When Love Comes, Hot On The Trail, Special Love, From The Beginning; with Rita Coolidge: Ann; with Rickie Lee Jones: Flying Cowboys; with Jimmy Cliff: Peace; with Steven Bishop: Bowling In Paris; with Umberto Tozzi: Gloria, Notte Rosa; Umberto Tozzi – Live; Le Une Cauzui, Equivacando; with David Hasselhoff: Crazy For You; with Helen Baylor: Live; with Tina Turner: Simply the Best; keyboard player for Larry Carlton, Ringo Starr, Joe Cocker, David Foster, Tom Jones, Billy Idol, Julio Iglesias, Nils Lofgren, Simple Minds; film scores: American Flyer, Unfaithfully Yours, Midnight Express. *Address:* 2629 Manhattan Avenue, PMB 164, Hermosa Beach, CA 90254-2447, USA (office). *E-mail:* gmlmnop@aol.com (office). *Website:* www.gregmathieson.com.

MATHIESON, Ken; British musician (drums, zither), arranger and composer; b. 30 June 1942, Paisley, Scotland; m.; two s. one d. *Career:* freelance musician; 15-year residency in Black Bull Jazz Club, Milngavie, Glasgow; working and touring with leading UK and US jazz musicians including George Chisholm, Tommy Whittle, John McLevy, Jack Emblow, Sonny Stitt, Johnny Griffin, Tal Farlow, Benny Carter; played with and wrote for Fat Sam's Band (Edinburgh-based jazz group touring world-wide) 1985–96; leader, arranger and drummer for bands including Jazz Écosse All-Stars (6-piece Dixieland Band featuring top Scottish players and vocalist Fionna Duncan), Jazz Celebrities (7 piece mainstream band specialising in the music of Buck Clayton and Buddy Tate), Groovebusters (8/9 piece 'wee big-band' covering Jelly Roll Morton to Benny Golson), Brazilliance (trio plus vocalist Lynn O'Neill dedicated to Brazilian music), Ken Mathieson's Classic Jazz Orchestra (octet dedicated to interpreting jazz of all ages); latest venture a trio plus vocalist Lynn O'Neill dedicated to Brazilian music of all kinds; organized first Glasgow International Jazz Festival 1985; frequent broadcaster on Jazz and World Music. *Recordings:* with Ken Mathieson's Classic Jazz Orchestra: Jelly's New Clothes, Ken Mathieson's Classic Jazz Orchestra Salutes the Kings of Jazz. *Honours:* Scottish Jazz Award for Best Band 2009. *E-mail:* ken@kenmath.free-online.co.uk (home). *Website:* www.classicjazzorchestra .org.uk.

MATHIEU, Mireille; French singer; b. 22 July 1946, Avignon; d. of Roger and Marcelle Mathieu. *Education:* in Avignon. *Career:* singer 1962–; numerous concerts and concert tours in France and abroad, including concerts at Olympia (Paris) 1967, Palais des Congrès (Paris) 1986, 1990, New York 1986, and tours of People's Repub. of China 1986 and fmr USSR 1987. *Songs include:* Mon credo, Viens dans ma rue, Un homme et une femme, La dernière valse, Noël blanc, La première étoile, La parade des chapeaux melons, Paris un tango, Adieu je t'aime, La paloma adieu, Un jour tu reviendras, Le silence, Mille colombes, Santa Maria de la mer, A blue Bayou, Tous les enfants chantent avec moi, Toi et moi, Le village oublié, Un enfant viendra, Love story, Une femme amoureuse, L'enfant que je n'ai jamais eu, Ce soir je t'ai perdu, La Marseillaise (Nat. Anthem, with Garde Républicaine and French army choir, for the bicentenary of the French Revolution) 1989, Mireille Mathieu chante Piaf. *Publication:* Oui je crois 1988. *Honours:* Chevalier, Ordre nat. du Mérite, des Arts et des Lettres. *Current Management:* c/o Abilene Disc, 122 avenue

Wagram, 75017 Paris, France. *Fax:* 1-46-22-10-12. *E-mail:* mireillemathieu@ mireillemathieu.com (office). *Website:* www.mireillemathieu.com.

MATHIS, John (Johnny) Royce; American singer; b. 30 Sept. 1935, San Francisco. *Education:* San Francisco State College. *Career:* recording artist 1964–; tours world-wide. *Recordings include:* singles: Wonderful! Wonderful!, Chances Are 1957, Someone, The Twelfth of Never, It's Not For Me To Say, A Certain Smile, Misty, Winter Wonderland, There Goes My Heart, My Love For You, My One and Only Love, Let Me Love You, I'm Stone In Love With You, When A Child Is Born 1976, Too Much, Too Little, Too Late, duet with Deniece Williams 1978, other duets with Gladys Knight, Natalie Cole, Dionne Warwick, Stephanie Lawrence, Barbara Dickson, Nana Mouskouri; albums: Johnny Mathis 1956, Wonderful! 1957, Warm 1957, Good Night, Dear Lord 1958, Swing Softly 1958, Open Fire, Two Guitars 1959, Heavenly 1959, Faithfully 1960, Ride On A Rainbow 1960, Johnny's Mood 1960, I'll Buy You A Star 1961, Portrait of Johnny 1961, Live It Up 1962, Rapture 1962, Johnny 1963, Romantically 1963, I'll Search My Heart 1964, Olé 1965, Tender Is The Night 1965, The Wonderful World of Make Believe 1965, This Is Love 1966, The Shadow of Your Smile 1966, The Sweetheart Tree 1967, Up, Up and Away 1967, Johnny Mathis Sings 1967, Love Is Blue 1968, Those Were The Days 1968, People 1969, The Impossible Dream 1969, Raindrops Keep Fallin' On My Head 1970, The Long and Winding Road 1970, Close To You 1970, Love Story 1970, You've Got A Friend 1971, In Person 1972, The First Time Ever I Saw Your Face 1972, Make It Easy On Yourself 1972, Me and Mrs Jones 1973, Killing Me Softly With Her Song 1973, I'm Coming Home 1973, Song Sung Blue 1974, The Heart of a Woman 1974, Feelings 1975, I Only Have Eyes For You 1976, Sweet Surrender 1977, When A Child Is Born 1978, You Light Up My Life 1978, Mathis Magic 1979, Different Kinda Different 1980, Friends In Love 1982, A Special Part of Me 1984, Right From The Heart 1985, In The Still of The Night 1989, How Do You Keep The Music Playing? 1993, Celebration: Anniversary Album 1995, All About Love 1996, Because You Loved Me: Songs of Diane Warren 1998, Because you Loved Me 1998, Mathis On Broadway 2000, Isn't it Romantic 2005, Johnny Mathis Gold 2006, A Night to Remember 2008; numerous greatest hits, musical and Christmas compilations. *Address:* Rojon Production Inc, 1612 W Olive, Suite 305, Burbank, CA 91505, USA (office). *Website:* www.johnnymathis.com.

MATISYAHU; American singer and songwriter; b. (Matthew Miller), 30 June 1979, West Chester, Pa; m. Tahlia; two s. *Education:* The New School, New York. *Career:* brought up in reconstructionist Jewish family, after travels in Israel became interested in Orthodox Judaism, later moved to New York and became mem. of Hasidic movt Chabad-Lubavitch; developed performance style that combines Orthodox Jewish culture with reggae, hip hop and rock music; involved in setting up JDub Records; studio work with Bill Laswell, Sly and Robbie. *Recordings:* Shake Off the Dust . . . Arise 2004, Live At Stubb's 2005, Youth 2006, No Place to Be 2007, Light 2009. *Address:* c/o Or Music, LLC, 37 West 17th Street, #5W, New York, NY 10011, USA (office). *E-mail:* info@ormusic.com (office). *Website:* www.ormusic.com (office); www .matisyahuworld.com.

MATOLU-DODE, Papy-Tex; Democratic Republic of Congo singer; b. 28 June 1952, Kinshasa; m. Ekofo-Wando 1989, three s. eight d. *Education:* Itaga College, Kinshasa. *Career:* singer, African Choc 1968, later renamed Empire Bakuba 1979–; player, Etodle Filante football team; mem. SONECA, SACEM, SABAM, SUIZA, BURIDA. *Compositions:* Sanda; Karibu; Sanco Yamawa; Welcome in Africa; Music Clarification. *Recordings:* Bakuba Show; Full Option; Surprise; Livre D'Or; La Belle Etoire. *Honours:* Diplome of Performance for Development Initiative, 1995; Apid Certificate of Artistic Merit, 1987; Acknowledgement of Merit, Francophone Counsel of Songs, 1993. *Address:* 69 rue Luapula, Commune de Kinshasa, Democratic Republic of Congo.

MATRONIC, Ana; American singer; b. (Ana Chamberlain Lynch), 1974. *Career:* mem., Scissor Sisters 2001–. *Recordings include:* albums: Scissor Sisters (BRIT Award for Best Int. Album 2005) 2004, Ta-Dah 2006, Night Work 2010. *Honours:* BRIT Awards for Best Int. Group, Best Int. Breakthrough Act 2005, Meteor Ireland Music Award for Best Int. Group 2007. *Current Management:* c/o Dave Holmes, 3–D Management, Los Angeles, CA, USA. *E-mail:* info@3dmgmt.com. *Website:* www.3dmgmt.com. *E-mail:* sisters@scissorsisters.net (office). *Website:* www.scissorsisters.com.

MATSUDA, Seiko; Japanese singer and actress; b. (Noriko Kamachi), 10 March 1962, Fukuoka; m. 1st Masaki Kanda 1985 (divorced 1998); one c.; m. 2nd Hiroyuki Hatano 1998 (divorced 2000). *Films include:* Nogiku no haka 1981, Yume De Aetera 1982, Natsufuku no Ibu 1984, Karibu: Ai no shinfoni 1985, Final Vendetta 1996, Armageddon 1998, Drop Dead Gorgeous 1999, Partners 2000, Gedo 2000, Sennen no koi – Hikaru Genji monogatari 2002, Shanghai Baby 2007, Hotaru no Haka 2008, Yazima Beauty Salon The Movie 2010. *Television includes:* The Big Easy (series) 1996, Tattahitotsuno takaramono (film) 2004, Yo nimo kimyo na monogatari: Aki no tokubetsu hen 2005. *Recordings include:* albums: Squall 1980, North Wind 1980, Silhouette 1981, Kaze Tachi Nu 1981, Pineapple 1982, Candy 1982, Utopia 1983, Canary 1983, Tinkerbell 1984, Windy Shadow 1984, The Ninth Wave 1985, Sound of My Heart 1985, Supreme 1986, Strawberry Time 1987, Citron 1988, Precious Moment 1989, Seiko 1990, We Are Love 1990, Eternal 1991, Nouvelle Vague 1992, Sweet Memories 1992, A Time For Love 1993, Diamond Expression 1993, Glorious Revolution 1994, It's Style 1995, Was It The Future 1996, Guardian Angel 1996, Vanity Fair 1996, Sweetest Time 1997, My Story 1997, Forever 1998, Seiko Matsuda Remixes 1999, 20th Party 2000, Love &

Emotion Vol. 1 2001, Love & Emotion Vol. 2 2001, Area 62 2002, Sunshine 2004, Fairy 2006, Baby's Breath 2007, My Pure Melody 2008, My Prelude 2010, Cherish 2011, Very Very 2012, A Girl in the Wonder Land 2013, Dream and Fantasy 2014. *Publication:* Yume de Aetara 1982. *Address:* c/o Universal Music LLC, 8-5-30, Akasaka Minato-Ku, Tokyo 107-0052, Japan. *Telephone:* (3) 6406-3001. *E-mail:* office@seikomatsuda.jp (office). *Website:* www .seikomatsuda.co.jp/english/index.html.

MATSUTOYA, Yuming (Yumi); Japanese singer and songwriter; b. (Yuming Arai), 1954, Tokyo; m. Masataka Matsuyomota 1976. *Career:* achieved fame when Katsumi Kahashi recorded Ai wa totsuzen (Love, All of a Sudden), a song she had composed age 15; debut album Hikōki gumo (Airplane Clouds) released 1973; credited with coining term New Music, capturing a number of folk and popular music recording styles whose approach demanded that artistic control is placed in hands of songwriter and performer early 1970s; later work produced Orientalist motifs and landscapes; set new album and singles sales records throughout 1990s. *Recordings include:* albums: Hikōki gumo 1973, Yuming Brand 1976, Cobalt Hour. *Address:* c/o Toshiba-EMI Ltd, 2-2-17 Akasaka, Minato-ku, Tokyo 107-8510, Japan (office).

MATTACKS, David; musician (drums); b. 13 March 1948, London, England; m. Caron Woods 1993. *Career:* apprentice piano tuner; Mecca Big Band, three years; played small jazz groups; joined Fairport Convention 1969, with seven albums, tours of UK, USA, Europe, Antipodes, Japan; freelance musician 1974–; combined freelance work with re-formed Fairport Convention mid 1980s–; int. tours, festival appearances; drums and keyboards in concerts and recordings; performed with artists, including Jethro Tull, Chris Rea, Joan Armatrading, Sandy Denny, Micky Jupp, Andy Fairweather-Low, Georgie Fame, Nick Heyward, Ashley Hutchings, Ralph McTell, The McGarrigles, The Swingles; tours in UK, Europe, USA with Richard Thompson Band 1994–95; recorded, played with Liane Carroll, Everything But The Girl; week's residency, Ronnie Scott's Club, London, with Liane Carroll Trio. *Compositions:* television and film scores include: Death Wish 2; Green Ice; Give My Regards To Broad Street; Band of Gold (ITV); Love Hurts (Barbara Dickson); Time Bandits; McVicar; Lisztomania; Hussey; Hearts of Fire; Shoestring; Fox; Leo Sayer television series; Your Cheatin' Heart. *Recordings include:* with Fairport Convention: Jewel In The Crown 1995, Who Knows Where Time Goes? 1997; also with artists including: Joan Armatrading; Barbara Dickson; Elton John; Paul McCartney; Chris Rea; The Proclaimers; Jimmy Page; Alison Moyet; XTC; Beverley Craven; Richard Thompson; Gary Brooker; Elkie Brooks; John Gorka; Cat Stevens; Roger Daltrey; Mary Ann Redmond; Kimberly Rew; with Richard Thompson: Celtschmerz, 1998; with Steve Ashley: Stroll on Revisited, 1999; with Steeleye Span: Horkstow Grange, 1999; with Paul McCartney: Run Devil Run, 1999.

MATTEA, Kathy; American country singer and musician (guitar); b. 21 June 1959, South Charleston, WV; d. of John Mattea and Ruth Mattea; m. Jon Vezner 1988. *Education:* West Virginia Univ. *Career:* mem. of bluegrass group, Pennsboro; fmr tour guide, Country Music Hall of Fame, Nashville; fmr singer for demos and commercials, backing singer; currently solo artist. *Film:* Maverick. *Recordings include:* albums: Kathy Mattea 1984, From My Heart 1985, Walk The Way The Wind Blows 1986, Untasted Honey 1987, Willow in the Wind 1989, Time Passes By 1991, Lonesome Standard Time 1992, Good News Radio Special 1994, Only Everything 1995, Walking Away a Winner 1995, Ready for the Storm – Favorite Cuts 1995, Love Travels 1997, The Innocent Years 2000, Roses 2002, Joy for Christmas Day 2003, Right out of Nowhere 2005, Coal 2008. *Honours:* Dr hc (West Virginia Univ.); Best Country Song of Year (for Where've You Been), Female Vocalist of the Year, Minnie Pearl Humanitarian Award, Grammy Award (for Good News), Grammy Award (for Where've You Been?). *Current Management:* KMI, PO Box 121134, Nashville, TN 37212, USA. *Telephone:* (615) 469-7879. *Website:* www .madmanager.com; www.mattea.com.

MATTHEWS, Cerys Elizabeth Phillip, MBE; Welsh singer, songwriter, musician (guitar), author and broadcaster; b. 11 April 1969, Cardiff; m. 1st Seth Riddle 2003 (divorced 2007); one s. one d.; m. 2nd Steve Abbott; one s. *Career:* Founder-mem. Catatonia 1992–2001; solo artist 2001–; hosts a music show on BBC Radio 6 Music; has made documentaries for TV as well as BBC Radio 2 and Radio 4; has been a presenter for The Culture Show and The One Show; Artistic Dir for the opening ceremony of World Music Expo 2013; writes a column for Songlines; has written for The Guardian, The Times and Grazia; Vice-Pres. Shelter Cymru, Hay Festival of Literature and the Arts; Arts Amb. for Linden Lodge (specialist sensory and physical coll.); Patron Dylan Thomas Soc., Ballet Cymru; judge, Dylan Thomas Literary Prize, Forward Prizes for Poetry 2014; cr. cultural festival, The Good Life Experience 2014. *Recordings include:* albums: with Catatonia: Way Beyond Blue 1996, The Sublime Magic Of Catatonia 1996, International Velvet 1998, Equally Cursed and Blessed 1999, Paper Scissors Stone 2001; solo: Cockahoop 2003, Never Said Goodbye 2006, Awyren=Aeroplane 2007, Don't Look Down 2009, Tir 2010, Explorer 2011, Baby It's Cold Outside 2012, Hullabaloo 2013, Dylan Thomas - A Child's Christmas , Poems and Tiger Eggs 2014. *Television:* presented six-part series on the history of folk songs in Wales 2014. *Publications:* Hook, Line and Singer 2013; for children: Tales from the Deep 2013, Gelert, A Man's Best Friend 2013. *Honours:* Gold Medal, Sony Radio Academy Awards for BBC Radio 6 music show 2013, inaugural St David Award from First Minister of Wales 2014. *E-mail:* info@rainbowcity.co. *Website:* www.rainbowcity.co. *E-mail:*

information@cerysmatthews.co.uk (office). *Website:* www.cerysmatthews.co .uk.

MATTHEWS, David (Dave) John; South African singer, musician (guitar) and songwriter; b. 9 Jan. 1967, Johannesburg; m. Jennifer Ashley Harper 2000; two d., one s. *Career:* owner of ATO Records label; fmr mem. band, TR3; solo artist 1990–; formed the Dave Matthews Band 1991–; numerous tours and live appearances world-wide; first album released on group's own Bama Rags label; occasionally tours with Tim Reynolds as acoustic duo. *Recordings include:* albums: Remember Two Things 1993, Under The Table And Dreaming 1994, Crash 1996, Live At Red Rocks 8.15.95 1997, Before These Crowded Streets 1998, Live At Luther College (with Tim Reynolds) 1999, Listener Supported (live) 1999, Maximum Dave Matthews 2000, Everyday 2001, Live In Chicago 12.19.98 2001, Busted Stuff 2002, Live At Folsom Field, Boulder, Colorado 2002, Some Devil 2003, Central Park Concert 2003, Live Trax, Vol 1–12 2004–08, The Gorge 2004, Stand Up 2005, Big Whiskey and the GrooGrux King 2009, Away from the World 2012. *Honours:* Grammy Awards for Best Rock Performance by a Duo or Group with Vocal 1997, VH-1 Awards for Favorite Group, Must Have Album, Song of the Year 2001, Grammy Award for Best Male Rock Vocal Performance (for Gravedigger) 2004. *E-mail:* fanmail@davematthewsband.com (office). *Website:* www.davematthewsband .com.

MATTHEWS, Donna Lorraine; British musician and songwriter; b. 2 Dec. 1971, Newport, Wales. *Career:* mem., Elastica 1992–99; toured extensively world-wide; solo artist 1999–; contrib. vocals to Seven More Minutes, by The Rentals 1999. *Recordings:* albums: Elastica 1995; singles: Stutter 1993, Connection 1994, Line Up 1994, Waking Up 1995, Car Song 1996, Elastica (EP) 1999. *Honours:* NME Readers Award For Best New Band 1994.

MATTHEWS, Iain; British songwriter and singer; b. 16 June 1946, England; m. Veronique 1990, one s. one d. *Career:* mem., The Pyramid 1965; founder mem., Fairport Convention 1967; mem., Matthews Southern Comfort; solo, also Plainsong 1972; moved into A&R at Island Records; Windham Hill, early 1980s; re-formed Plainsong; founder of Hamilton Pool, singing-songwriting collective, Austin, TX; mem. NARAS. *Recordings include:* with Fairport Convention: Fairport Convention, 1968; What We Did On our Holiday, 1968; Unhalfbricking, 1968; with Matthews Southern Comfort: Matthews Southern Comfort, 1969; Second Spring, 1970; Later That Same Year, 1970; solo: If You Saw Through My Eyes, 1970; Tigers Will Survive, 1971; Journeys From Gospel Oak, 1972; Valley Hi, 1973; Some Days You Eat the Bear, 1974; Go for Broke, 1976; Hit and Run, 1977; Stealin' Home, 1978; Siamese Friends, 1979; Discreet Repeat, 1980; Spot of Interference, 1980; Shook, 1983; Walking a Changing Line (The Songs of Jules Shear), 1988; Pure and Crooked, 1990; Nights in Manhattan, 1991; Orphans and Outcasts, 1991; Live Alone, 1993; Intimate Wash, 1993; The Soul of Many Places, 1993; Skeleton Keys, 1993; Excerpts from Swine Lake, 1999; Orphans and Outcasts Vol. 3, 1999; Plainsong: In Search of Amelia Earhart, 1972; And That's That, 1992; Plainsong on the Air, 1992; Dark Side of the Room, 1992; Hi Fi: Demonstration Record, 1981; Moods for Mallards, 1982; The Dark Ride, 1994; Camouflage, 1995; God Looked Down, 1996; Nights in Manhattan, 1997; Voices Electric, 1994; Sister Flute, 1996; New Place Now, 1999. *Publication:* It's About Time (biog.). *Address:* PO Box 676, Buda, TX 78610, USA. *E-mail:* jvanmoppes@ xs4all.nl. *Website:* www.iainmatthews.com.

MATTHEWS, James (Jamie) Lindsay; British musician (harmonicas, ukulele, percussion, jaws harp, whistle, vocals); b. London, England. *Education:* church and school choirs. *Career:* extensive touring, Far East late 1960s, Europe and North America 1980s; major US tours with Daily Planet, including Telluride Festival, Colorado 1995, 1996; continuing UK tours and festivals with Daily Planet and The Fiasco Brothers, including Shetland, Sidmouth, Cambridge, Glastonbury, St Ives and other festivals; plays with Celtic-based band Arran Pilot 1977–. *Recordings:* 'Parlour Games' and 'Sunday Best', John B Spencer; 'A Month of Sundays' (double album), Johnny G; 'Clark's Secret', 'The Big Scoop' and 'Live', Daily Planet; 'Miles Apart', Leon Hunt; guest appearances and recordings with Jackie Leven, Michael Weston King, Brian Finnegan, Martin Simpson, Danny Thompson, Fast Lane Roogalator, Man, Tony Furtado, Matt Flinner, Growling Old Men etc.; numerous recordings for TV, radio, theatre, etc. *Honours:* Guinness All-Ireland Busking Champion as Gentleman Jamie 1986, BBMA Best Progressive Bluegrass Band (with Daily Planet) 1995. *Address:* 5 Cleveland Row, Bathwick, Bath, BA2 6QR, England. *Telephone:* 7721-531036 (mobile). *E-mail:* jamesmatthews5@sky.com (home). *Website:* www.dailyplanet.co.uk.

MATTHEWS, Julie; British singer, songwriter and musician (guitar, piano); b. 2 April 1963, Sheffield, South Yorkshire, England. *Career:* played in piano bars throughout Europe, Middle East for seven years; mem., Albion Band 1990–92, 1994–97; mem. Intuition project (featuring six female vocalists from South Yorkshire) 1994; formed duo with Pat Shaw, another with Chris While 1997–; co-f. Daphne's Flight 1997, Blue Tapestry; toured extensively throughout Europe, Canada; many radio appearances, sessions, festival appearances; mem. PRS, MCPS, Musicians' Union. *Compositions include:* song Thorn Upon The Rose (recorded by Mary Black). *Recordings include:* albums: with Pat Shaw: Lies and Alibis 1993; with Albion Band: Captured, Albion Heart; solo: Such Is Life 1995, Slow; with Chris While: Blue Moon On The Rise 1996, Piecework 1997, Higher Potential 1999, Quest 2001, Perfect Mistake 2003, Here and Now 2005, Together Alone 2008; with Helen Watson: Somersault

1998. *E-mail:* jil@bluemoonmusic.co.uk. *Website:* www.bluemoonmusic.co.uk; www.whileandmatthews.co.uk.

MATTHEWS, Patrick; Australian musician (bass guitar); b. 1975, Wollongong, NSW. *Career:* Founding mem. The Vines 1994–2004; joined Youth Group 2004–. *Recordings include:* albums: with The Vines: Highly Evolved 2002, Winning Days 2004; with Youth Group: Casino Twilight Dogs 2006, The Night is Ours 2008. *Honours:* ARIA Award for Breakthrough Artist Single (for Get Free) 2002, NME Award for Best Single (for Get Free) 2003, ARIA Award for Breakthrough Artist (for Forever Young, Youth Group) 2006. *Current Management:* c/o Winterman and Goldstein Management, PO Box 545, Newtown, NSW 2042, Australia. *Website:* www.thevines.com; www .youthgroup.com.au.

MATTHEWS, Roderick Newton; British composer, musician (guitar) and record producer; b. 18 May 1956, London; m. Pamela Margaret Johnson 1992; one d. *Education:* Balliol College, Oxford. *Career:* produced records for small labels, including Troggs album 1979–84; produced for majors, including Roland Rat, Musical Youth, chart entries in Germany, Norway 1984–86; remixes include Manfred Mann; session musician 1987–92; writing music for television (commercials, signatures, incidentals) 1988–; for Lenny Henry 1989–91; also appeared on soundtracks for French and Saunders, Absolutely Fabulous, Hello Mum, Alexei Sayle Shows, Lenny Henry, Rory Bremner, Harry Enfield, Girl Friday, Bad News, Blue Peter, Tracey Ullman, Newman and Baddiel, Fry and Laurie; mem, PRS, MCPS. *Compositions:* wrote for seven series of London's Burning; Newshounds (Screen Two) 1990, The Winston Pom, Funseekers (comic strip), Coffee Blues for Lenny Henry (in Lenny Live and Unleashed), Alexei Sayle: Shut Up, The Winjin Pom, Mary Whitehouse Experience; television commercials for Duracell, Burger King, Twix. *Recordings:* played or sung on recordings including: Monkey, George Michael; Don't Make Me Wait, Bomb The Bass; Cross My Heart, Patsy Kensit and Eighth Wonder; ABC; Sinitta; Charles Aznavour; Rick Astley; Pepsi and Shirlee; England Football Squad; Comic Relief; John Parr, Running the Endless Mile; George Michael, Faith; Rick Astley, Hold Me in Your Arms; London's Burning (soundtrack compilation, with Simon Brint).

MATTHEWS, Sarah; British singer; b. 22 June 1966, London. *Career:* mem. Rub Ultra; radio and television broadcasts, festival appearances and tours; mem. Musicians' Union, PRS. *Recordings include:* album: Liquid Boots and Boiled Sweets 1995.

MATTSSON, Allan; Danish singer and musician (bass guitar). *Career:* mem., Diefenbach 1999–; band started own label, Display Records. *Recordings include:* albums: Diefenbach 2001, Run Trip Fall 2003, Make Your Mind (EP) 2004, Re-Make Your Mind (EP) 2005, Set And Drift 2005. *E-mail:* diefenbach@ diefenbach.dk (office). *Website:* www.diefenbach.dk.

MATURELL ROMERO, Jorge; Cuban musician (congas, bongos, cowbell); b. 1963, Santiago de Cuba. *Education:* Escuela de Nivel Medio Superior de Superación Profesional. *Career:* f. Septeto Turquino 1984, joined Eliades Ochoa's Grupo Patria 2000 (as man. and admin. as well as percussionist); also collaborated with José Mercé and Eliades Ochoa y la Banda el Jigüe; mem. AfroCubism project 2010–. *Recordings:* albums include: with Septeto Turquino: Son para los Rumberos 2002 (EGREM Prize, Bines de Fondos Culturales); with Septeto Turquino and Alberto Tosca: Amor a Santiago 1999; with Eliades Ochoa and Cuarteto Patria: Tributo al Cuarteto Patria 2000, Estoy Como Nunca 2002; with José Mercé: Aire 2001; with AfroCubism: Afrocubism 2010. *Address:* c/o World Circuit Records, 138 Kingsland Road, London, E2 8DY, England (office). *E-mail:* post@worldcircuit.co.uk (office). *Website:* www.worldcircuit.co.uk (office).

MAULDIN, Jermaine Dupri; American rapper, producer, songwriter and record company executive; b. 23 Sept. 1972, Ashville, SC. *Career:* founder, So So Def Records; collaborations with Mariah Carey, Usher, Jay Z, Ludacris, Shade Sheist. *Recordings include:* albums: Jermaine Dupri Presents Life in 1472 1998, Instructions 2001, Young, Fly and Flashy, Vol. 1 2005. *Honours:* ASCAP Best Song of Year 1993. *Address:* c/o So So Def, Island Def Jam Records, Worldwide Plaza 825, 8th Avenue, 28th Floor, New York, NY 10019, USA (office). *Website:* www.jermainedupri.com.

MAULIS, Zbynek; Czech musician (bass guitar); b. 24 April 1975, Kladno. *Education:* Technical University, Prague, 2 years. *Career:* The Teplo, Rock and Roll group, 1992–; Brutus, Rock and Roll group, 1996–; Beatles Revival, Beatles tribute band 1996–. *Compositions:* Want You Go With Me, Brutus, 1996. *Recordings:* Best of Brutus, 1997.

MAUNICK, Jean-Paul, (Bluey); producer, musician (guitar) and songwriter; b. 1957, Mauritius. *Career:* moved to London 1967; mem. Light of the World late 1970s; formed Incognito with Paul 'Tubbs' Williams 1979; mem., Performing Right Soc.; Asscn of United Recording Artists. *Recordings include:* albums: with Incognito: Jazz Funk 1981, Inside Life 1991, Tribes Vibes and Scribes 1992, Positivity 1993, 100° and Rising 1995, Beneath The Surface, 1996, Blue Moods 1997, No Time Like The Future 1999, Life Stranger Than Fiction 2001; singles: Parisienne Girl 1980, Incognito 1981, North London Boy 1982, Inside Life, Always There (featuring Jocelyn Brown), Crazy For You (featuring Chyna) 1991, Don't You Worry About A Thing, Change 1992, Still A Friend of Mine, Givin' It Up 1993, Pieces of a Dream 1994, Everyday, I Hear Your Name 1995, Jump To My Love, Out of The Storm 1996, Nights Over Egypt 1999. *Honours:* MOBO Award, Best Jazz Act, 2001.

MAXI JAZZ; singer, rap artist and DJ. *Career:* rapper and DJ world-wide; runs record label; fmr mem., Soul Food Café Band; mem., Faithless 1995–. *Recordings include:* albums: Reverence 1996, Reverence/Irreverance, Sunday 8pm 1998, Saturday 3am 1999, Back To Mine (compilation of other artists' work) 2001, Outrospective 2001, Reperspective 2002, No Roots 2004, To All the New Arrivals 2006, The Dance 2010. *Honours:* Best Int. Act to Appear in Ireland 2001. *Address:* Faithless Live Ltd, PO Box 17336, London, NW5 4WP, England (office). *E-mail:* info@faithless.co.uk (office). *Website:* www.faithless .co.uk.

MAXI MILLION (see GZA)

MAXIM; British singer; b. (Keith Palmer), Peterborough, Cambs. *Career:* mem., The Prodigy (fmrly Maxim Reality) 1991–; numerous festival and other live appearances. *Recordings include:* albums: Music for the Jilted Generation 1994, The Fat of the Land (MTV Music Award for Best Album) 1997, The Dirtchamber Sessions 1999, Hell's Kitchen 2000, Always Outnumbered, Never Outgunned 2004, Fallen Angel 2004, Their Law: The Singles 1990–2005 2005, Invaders Must Die 2009, The Day is My Enemy 2015. *Honours:* BRIT Awards for Best British Dance Act 1997, 1998, five MTV Music Awards including for Best Live Band, Best Dance Band, Q Award for Innovation in Sound 2005, Kerrang! Spirit of Independence Award 2006, two NME awards, MOBO award 1997. *Current Management:* Supahero Media, PO Box 4205, Harlow, Essex, CM17 0LF, England. *Telephone:* (1279) 429210 (office). *E-mail:* theresa@sixfingerproductions.com. *Website:* www.theprodigy .com.

MAXWELL, Thad James, AA; American musician (guitar, bass, steel guitar, drums); b. 2 July 1945, Brooklyn, NY; m. Jeanne Cornell; one s. one d. *Education:* Glendale College. *Career:* guitarist and drummer, Tarantula 1969–70; bassist, various artists including Ricky Nelson, Arlo Guthrie, Linda Ronstadt, Flying Burrito Brothers 1970–80; steel guitarist, guitarist, Mac Davis 1973–; mem, AFofM, AFTRA. *Recordings include:* with Arlo Guthrie: Hobo's Lullabye 1972, Last of The Brooklyn Cowboys 1973; with Tarantula: Tarantula 1969. *Recordings include:* Horizon, The Carpenters 1975, A Little Warmth, Steve Gillette 1979, Sweet Country Suite, Larry Murray 1971, Sierra, Sierra 1977, Lead Free, B W Stevenson 1972, Swampwater, Swampwater 1970; with Flying Burrito Brothers: Tribute to Gram Parsons 1995.

MAXWELL, Warren, (Fulla Flesh); New Zealand musician (saxophone). *Career:* mem. reggae and soul band, Fat Freddy's Drop 2000–07. *Recordings include:* albums: Live at the Matterhorn 2001, Based on a True Story 2005. *Honours:* New Zealand Music Award for Best Group 2005. *Website:* www .fatfreddysdrop.com.

MAY, Brian, CBE, PhD; British musician (guitar), singer, composer and producer; b. 19 July 1947, Twickenham, London, England. *Education:* Imperial Coll., London. *Career:* fmr mem., The Others; mem., Smile 1967–71; founder mem. rock group, Queen 1970–; numerous tours , festival appearances; solo artist 1983–. *Theatre:* musical of Queen songs, We Will Rock You (West End, London) 2002–14; numerous productions worldwide. *Recordings include:* albums: with Queen: Queen 1973, Queen II 1974, Sheer Heart Attack 1974, A Night At The Opera 1975, A Day At The Races 1976, Good Old Fashioned 1977, News Of The World 1977, Jazz 1978, Live Killers 1979, The Game 1980, Flash Gordon (soundtrack) 1981, Hot Space 1982, The Works 1984, A Kind of Magic 1986, The Miracle 1989, Stone Cold Crazy 1991, Innuendo 1991, The Cosmos Rocks (with Paul Rodgers) 2008; solo: Star Fleet Project 1983, Back To The Light 1993, Resurrection 1994, Another World 1998, Business (EP) 1998. *Publications:* Bang! The Complete History of the Universe (with Patrick Moore and Chris Lintott) 2006, Scenes in Our Village 2009. *Honours:* Ivor Novello Award for Best Selling British Record (for Bohemian Rhapsody) 1976, Britannia Award for Best British Pop Single 1952–77 1977, Gold Ticket Madison Square Gardens 1977, American Music Award for Favorite Single 1981, Nordoff-Robbins Music Therapy Centre Silver Clef Award 1984, Ivor Novello Award for Outstanding Contribution to British Music 1987, BRIT Awards for Outstanding Contribution to British Music 1990, for Best British Single 1991, Q Classic Song Award (for Bohemian Rhapsody) 2015. *Current Management:* c/o Queen Productions Ltd, P.O. Box 141, West Horsley, Surrey KT24 9AJ, England. *Website:* www.brianmay.com; www.queenonline.com.

MAY, Derrick, (Mayday, Rhythim is Rhythim); American producer, remixer and DJ; b. 6 April 1963, Detroit, Michigan. *Career:* founder Transmat Records; credited with invention of techno genre as part of the Belleville Three (alongside Juan Atkins and Kevin Saunderson); world-wide DJ; resident DJ at the Music Institute in Detroit in the early '90s; collaborations with Juan Atkins, Kevin Saunderson, System 7, Carl Craig; Remixed: ABC, Funtopia, Yello, Inner City, DJ Rolando. *Recordings:* albums: Innovator – Soundtrack For The Tenth Planet 1992; singles: Let's Go (as X-Ray) 1986, Nude Photo (as Rhythim Is Rhythim) 1987, Strings of Life (as Rhythim Is Rhythim) 1987, It Is What It Is (as Rhythim Is Rhythim) 1988, Beyond The Dance (as Rhythim Is Rhythim) 1989, The Beginning (as Rhythim Is Rhythim) 1990, Icon (as Rhythim Is Rhythim) 1993. *E-mail:* info@derrickmay.com (office). *Website:* www.derrickmay.com.

MAY, Simon; British composer; b. 15 Aug. 1944; m. Rosie; one s. three d. *Education:* Univ. of Cambridge. *Career:* taught German, French and music, Kingston Grammar School for eight years; following commercial success of stage musical, Smike (10,000 performances world-wide, BBC TV Christmas production), became full-time composer; songwriter, record producer; songs recorded by Cliff Richard, Amii Stewart, Nick Berry, The Pointer Sisters, Al Jarreau, Marti Webb, Anita Dobson, The Shadows, Richard Clayderman, Ruby Turner, Jonathan Butler, Stephanie de Sykes, Kate Robbins; records produced for Amii Stewart include Knock On Wood, Light My Fire; Visiting Prof., Faculty of Media, Arts and Soc., Southampton Solent Univ.; Patron, Devizes juniorEisteddfod, Swindon 105.5 Community Radio Station; Vice-Pres., British Fed. of Festivals; mem. Performing Right Soc., Songwriters, British Acad. of Composers and Songwriters. *Compositions for film:* The Dawning, Caught in the Act, Return To Treasure Island. *Compositions for theatre:* musicals: Smike, Rick Van Winkel. *Compositions for television:* EastEnders theme (BBC, TRIC Award for Best TV Theme), Howard's Way (BBC, TRIC Award for Best TV Theme), Trainer (BBC, TRIC Award for Best TV Theme), Eldorado (BBC), The Holiday Programme (BBC), The Food and Drink Programme (BBC), Castaway 2000 (BBC), Don't Try This At Home (LWT), Television Weekly (TVS), Olympic Theme (Thames), The Vet (BBC), People (BBC), Paramedics (BBC), Jobs For The Girls (BBC), The Trial of James Earl Ray (Channel 4), Swiss Family Robinson 1997, Pet Rescue 1997, Lion Country 1997, Great Estates (Channel 4), A Place In The Sun (Channel 4), Animal Park, The Tribe, City Hospital, Brat Camp (Channel 4). *Honours:* Novello Award (for Every Loser Wins, Nick Berry) 1986. *E-mail:* simonmay@ musiconscreen.co.uk. *Website:* www.simonmay.co.uk.

MAY, Tina, BA; British singer; b. (Daphne Christina May), 30 March 1961, Gloucester, England; d. of Harry May and Daphne Elisabeth Walton; m. Clark Tracey 1989 (divorced 2001); one s. one d. *Education:* Univ. of Wales. *Career:* toured as singing actress, actress with own theatre co., Black Door; full-time singer; broadcasts, tours of Australia, Far East, Europe, UK with own quartet; mem. Musicians' Union, Equity, Asscn of British Jazz Music, Int. Asscn of Jazz Educators. *Recordings include:* albums: Never Let Me Go 1992, Fun 1993, It Ain't Necessarily So 1994, Time Will Tell 1995, Change Of Sky 1998, Jazz Piquant 1998, One Fine Day 1999, Live In Paris 2000, I'll Take Romance 2003, A Wing and a Prayer 2006. *Honours:* Worshipful Company of Musicians Outstanding Jazz Musician 1993. *Current Management:* c/o John Boddy, 10 Southfield Gardens, Twickenham, TW1 4SZ, England. *Telephone:* (20) 8892-0133. *Fax:* (20) 8892-4283. *E-mail:* John@johnboddyagency.co.uk. *Website:* www.tinamay.com.

MAYALL, John, OBE; British blues singer, songwriter and musician (harmonica); b. 29 Nov. 1933, Macclesfield, Cheshire, England; m. 1st Pamela; m. 2nd Maggie Parker (née Mulacek); six c. *Education:* Manchester Art Coll. *Career:* mem., The Powerhouse Four 1956–62, The Blues Syndicate 1962–63; founded John Mayall's Bluesbreakers 1963– (mems have included John McVie, Eric Clapton, Peter Green, Jack Bruce, Aynsley Dunbar, Mick Taylor, Mick Fleetwood); numerous concert tours, festival appearances; founder, Crusade record label 1969–. *Recordings include:* albums: John Mayall Plays John Mayall 1965, Blues Breakers with Eric Clapton 1966, A Hard Road 1967, Bluesbreakers with Paul Butterfield 1967, Crusade 1967, Blues Alone 1967, Diary of a Band Volume 1 1967, Diary of a Band Volume 2 1968, Bare Wires 1968, Blues From Laurel Canyon 1968, Looking Back 1969, Thru The Years 1969, Primal Solos 1969, The Turning Point 1969, Empty Rooms 1970, USA Union 1970, Back To The Roots 1971, Memories 1971, Jazz Blues Fusion 1972, Moving On 1973, Ten Years Are Gone 1973, The Latest Edition 1974, New Year New Band New Company 1975, Notice To Appear 1975, Banquet In Blues 1976, Lots of People 1977, A Hard Core Package 1977, Last Of The British Blues 1978, The Bottom Line 1979, No More Interviews 1980, Road Show Blues 1982, Return Of The Bluesbreakers 1982, Behind The Iron Curtain 1984, Chicago Line 1988, The Power Of The Blues 1988, Archives To Eighties 1988, A Sense Of Place 1990, 1982 Reunion Concert 1992, Cross Country Blues 1992, Wake Up Call 1993, Spinning Coin 1995, Blues For The Lost Days 1997, Padlock On The Blues 1999, Rock The Blues Tonight 1999, Live At The Marquee 1969 1999, Time Capsule 2000, UK Tour 2K 2001, Boogie Woogie Man 2001, Along For The Ride 2001, STORIES 2002, No Days Off 2003, Rolling With The Blues 2003, The Turning Point (soundtrack) 2004, Road Dogs 2005, In the Palace of the King 2007. *Current Management:* c/o Brodie Becker, Monterey Peninsula Inc., 200 W Superior, Suite 202, Chicago, IL 60610, USA. *Telephone:* (312) 640-7500. *Fax:* (312) 640-7515. *E-mail:* brodie@montereyinternational.net. *Address:* c/o Magnolia Blue Productions, PO Box 572188, Tarzana, CA 91357, USA (office). *E-mail:* feedback@ johnmayall.com (office). *Website:* www.johnmayall.com.

MAYDAY (see May, Derrick)

MAYER, John; American singer, songwriter and musician (guitar); b. (John Clayton Mayer), 16 Oct. 1977, Bridgeport, Conn. *Education:* Berklee Coll. of Music. *Career:* performed at South by Southwest Music Festival 2000; solo artist 2001–; formed John Mayer Trio with bassist Pino Palladino and drummer Steve Jordan 2005; collaborations with Buddy Guy, B. B. King, Eric Clapton, John Scofield, Kanye West, Common. *Television:* John Mayer Has a TV Show 2004. *Recordings:* albums: Inside Wants Out 1999, Room for Squares 2001, Heavier Things 2003, Try! (with John Mayer Trio) 2005, Continuum 2006, Battle Studies 2009, Born and Raised 2012, Paradise Valley 2013. *Honours:* Hal David Starlight Award, Songwriters Hall of Fame 2006, Grammy Awards for Best Male Pop Vocal Performance (for Daughters) 2005, (for Say) 2009, for Best Solo Rock Vocal Performance (for Gravity) 2009. *Current Management:* Michael McDonald, Mick Management, 35 Washington Street, Brooklyn, NY 11201, USA. *Telephone:* (212) 425-6425. *Fax:* (212) 422-

6814. *E-mail:* info@mickmgmt.com. *Website:* mickmanagement.com; www .johnmayer.com; www.columbiarecords.com/johnmayer.html.

MAYOR, Simon, BA; British musician (mandolin, mandola, mandocello, guitar, violin), composer and lyricist; b. Sheffield, Yorks., England. *Education:* Univ. of Reading. *Career:* regular int. concert touring includes Vancouver Festival, Rudolstadt International Festival (Germany), Varazze Int. Mandolin Festival (Italy), guest of Classical Mandolin Soc. of America Annual Conf., London's South Bank Festival, Cheltenham Literature Festival; worked as broadcaster, BBC Radios 2, 4 and 5; presented BBC Schools Radio music education programmes for six years; has written and performed many songs for children's programmes for BBC TV; currently performs in duo with Hilary James and in own quartet The Mandolinquents; has produced much educational material for the mandolin: method books, DVDs and repertoire books; continues to expand his recorded output with seven solo albums and many collaborations with others; mem. Musicians' Union, Equity, Performing Right Soc., Mechanical-Copyright Protection Soc. *Radio:* Marooned with a Mandolin (three-part documentary, BBC Radio 2); presented and played on The Song Tree (BBC Radio 4 for Schools); session musician for many other schools radio programmes. *Television:* Play School, Play Days, Greenclaws. *Recordings:* The Mandolin Album (BBC Radio 2's Album of The Week) 1990, The Second Mandolin Album 1991, Winter with Mandolins (BBC World Service Album of The Week) 1992, The English Mandolin 1995, Mandoliquents (The Simon Mayor Quintet) 1997, New Celtic Mandolin 1998, Lullabies with Mandolins 2004, Music from a Small Island 2006, The Art of Mandolin 2013, The Mandolin Albums (25th anniversary double album reissue and retrospective) 2015, Duos (with Hilary James); albums feature approximately 50% original compositions; also five albums of original songs for children in the Musical Mystery Tour series. *Publications:* The New Mandolin (original compositions in music and tablature) 1993, The Mandolin Tutor (book/CD for beginners) 1995, New Celtic Mandolin Book (Celtic tunes with detailed teaching notes) 1998, Musical Mystery Tour (children's song book) 1992, Mastering the Mandolin (book/CD for intermediate) 2003, Mandolin Essentials (DVD) 2005, New Celtic Mandolin (DVD) 2005, Great Tunes for Mandolin Vols 1 and 2 (books/mp3s) 2015, Great Traditional Tunes for Guitar (book/mp3s) 2015; regular contrib. to Acoustic Magazine. *Current Management:* c/o Acoustics Records, PO Box 350, Reading, Berks., RG6 7DQ, England. *Telephone:* (118) 926-8615. *E-mail:* mail@acousticsrecords.co.uk. *Website:* www.acousticsrecords.co.uk. *E-mail:* mail@mandolin.co.uk (office). *Website:* www.mandolin.co.uk (office).

MAYS, L. Lowry; American media executive; *Chairman, Clear Channel Communications*; b. Texas. *Career:* founder, with Red McCombs, Chair. and CEO, San Antonio Broadcasting Co 1972, acquired KEEZ-FM; renamed Clear Channel Communications 1975 (entertainment co, owning numerous radio and television stations, entertainment venues, advertising space world-wide; management and marketing cos); Created Clear Channel Sports 1989. *Address:* Clear Channel Communications, 200 East Basse Road, San Antonio, TX 78209, USA (office). *Telephone:* (210) 822-2828 (office). *E-mail:* LLowryMays@clearchannel.com (office). *Website:* www.clearchannel.com (office).

MAZETIER, Louis, MD; French jazz musician (piano) and composer; b. 17 Feb. 1960, Paris; m. Sophie Clement, 1 s., 1 d. *Career:* mem. Paris Washboard; major festivals in France: Antibes; Marciac; Bayonne; Montauban; festivals in Europe: Breda; Dresden; Plön; Tours, New Zealand; Australia; USA (including Moodus and Santa Rosa Festivals); Argentina; Uruguay; Japan; much work as a solo pianist. *Recordings:* 15 with Paris Washboard; Duet with pianist Francois Rilhac; Duet with pianist Neville Dickie; six solo piano albums; Duet with pianist Bernd Lhotzky. *Publications:* numerous articles in various French jazz reviews, mostly about stride piano. *Honours:* Prix Sidney Bechet, Prix Bill Coleman, Academie de Jazz, 1992, Prix de l'Academie du Jazz 1998, 2002, Prix du Hot Club de France 2003. *Address:* 58 rue de Vaugirard, 75006 Paris, France. *Telephone:* 1-45-49-94-27. *Website:* www.hot -club.asso.fr.

MAZUR, Marilyn; Danish composer and percussionist; b. 18 Jan. 1955, New York, USA; one s. *Education:* self taught and Royal Danish Conservatory of Music, Copenhagen. *Career:* living in Denmark 1961–; dancer with Creative Dance Theatre 1971; formed Zirenes band 1973; percussionist, drummer and singer working with various groups 1975–; mem. Miles Davis band 1985–89; has worked with groups including Six Winds, Primi Band and Mazur/ Markussen Quartet; band leader, composer and percussionist with own groups, Future Song 1989–, and Pulse Unit; mem. Jan Garbarek Group 1991–; tours with Miles Davis 1985, Gil Evans 1986, Wayne Shorter 1987; has composed numerous works for big band/orchestra, rhythmic ensembles, choirs, TV, etc.; several grants from Danish Nat. Art Foundation. *Recordings include:* Six Winds 1982, Primi Band: Primi 1984, Mazur/Markussen Quartet: MM4 1984, Ocean Fables 1986, Marilyn Mazur's Future Song 1992, Ocean Fables: Havblik 1992, Marilyn Mazur and Pulse Unit: Circular Chant 1995, Miles Davis Live (recorded 1988) 1996, Marilyn Mazur's Future Song: Small Labyrinths 1997, Jan Garbarek: RITES 1998, Future Song, Daylight Stories 2004, Elixir 2008, Tangled Temptations & The Magic Box 2010; appearances on over 50 albums 1982–2008. *Honours:* Ben Webster Prize 1983, JASA Prize 1989, Jazzpar Prize 2001, Editon Wilhelm Hansens komponistpris 2004, Django D'Or Prize 2006, Telenor Int. Culture Prize 2007, The First Int. EuroCore – JTI Jazz Award 2010. *Address:* Storegade 7, 2650 Hvidovre, Denmark (office). *Telephone:* 36-78-36-08 (office). *Fax:* 36-78-36-19 (office).

E-mail: contact@marilynmazur.com (office). *Website:* www.marilynmazur .com.

MAZWAI, Thandiswa; South African singer. *Education:* degree in int. relations and English. *Career:* mem. kwaito band, Bongo Maffin 1997–2006; numerous performances in Europe; worked with Skunk Anansie, Chaka Khan, Stevie Wonder, Boyz II Men, Hugh Masekela; solo artist 2005–. *Recordings include:* albums: with Bongo Maffin: Final Entry 1996, The Concerto 1998, IV 1999, Bongolution 2001, New Construction 2006; solo: Zabalaza 2007. *Honours:* South African Music Award for Best Kwaito Artist 1999, Kora Award for Best African Group 2001. *Address:* c/o Sony Music South Africa, 230 Jan Smuts Avenue, Dunkeld West, 2196 Gauteng, South Africa.

MAZZALAI, Christian; Italian musician (guitar) and songwriter; b. 1976, Le Chesnay, Île-de-France, France; brother of Laurent Brancowitz. *Education:* Lycée Hoche, Versailles. *Career:* mem. Phoenix 1997–. *Recordings:* albums: United 2000, Alphabetical 2004, It's Never Been Like That 2006, Wolfgang Amadeus Phoenix (Grammy Award for Best Alternative Album 2010) 2009. *Address:* c/o Glassnote Music, 770 Lexington Avenue, New York, NY 10065, USA (office). *E-mail:* info@glassnotemusic.com (office). *Website:* www .glassnotemusic.com (office); www.wearephoenix.com.

M'BANGO, Charlotte; Cameroonian singer; b. 16 April 1960, Douala; m. Mpacko Marcel 1984; one d. *Education:* in Solfège. *Career:* fmr mem., Les Têtes Brulées; tours of Ivory Coast, Cameroon, Gabon, Burkina Faso, Togo, USA, Barcelona, Madrid, Valencia, London, France; mem, ADAMI, SACEM, SPEDIDAM, SFA, ACOP, AMF. *Recordings:* albums: Nakossa Nostalgie 1987, Konkai Makossa 1988, Maloka 1995, Masoma 1996, Best of Makossa Vol. 2 1998, Cantiques 2006, Essuw'am 2006; with Paul Simon: Rhythm of the Saints 1990. *Honours:* Gold Song, Palo Rabanne 1989, Gold Lion 1994.

MBULI, Mzwakhe; South African poet and singer; b. 1959, Sophiatown. *Career:* performed with various theatre groups, performance poetry at numerous political and cultural events, despite government resistance; formed group, The Equals, for poetry, music performances 1990–; speaker at Nelson Mandela's inauguration as Pres. 1994. *Recordings include:* Change is Pain 1987, Unbroken Spirit 1989, Before Dawn 1989, Resistance is Defiance 1992, Afrika 1993, Footsteps 1994, Izigi 1995, Kwazulu Natal 1996, Umzwakhe Ubonga Ujehova 1998, Born Free but Always in Chains 2000, Mbulism 2004. *Publications include:* Before Dawn (poems) 1989.

MEADE, Bazil Leonard Duncan; musician (piano, Hammond organ); b. 4 May 1951, Montserrat; m. Andrea Encinas 1980; two s. two d. *Career:* founder and Principal, London Community Gospel Choir 1982; Man. Dir Choir Connexion Ltd, MVLS Records Ltd; Musical Dir for numerous concerts including The London Community Gospel Choir European Tours 1984–93, Freddie Mercury Tribute Concert 1991, George Michael British tour 1991, HRH Queen Elizabeth's 60th Birthday concert, Royal Opera House, Stevie Wonder Wembley concert; Luther Vandross, Royal Albert Hall 1994; Gloria Gaynor, European tour 1994; also Musical Dir for Amen Corner (theatre production) 1990, Royal Variety television shows for five years, Hallelujah Anyhow (film), Rock Gospel (television series), Desmonds (television series), Mama I Want To Sing 1995; mem. Musicians' Union, PRS, MCPS. *Recordings:* with Paul McCartney: Give My Regards To Broad Street; with The London Community Gospel Choir: Live In Sweden; The London Community Gospel Choir Sings The Gospel Greats; Christmas With The London Community Gospel Choir; Hush and Listen; with Bobby Womack: No Matter How High I Get; Circle of Life (from Walt Disney's The Lion King). *Honours:* Greenbelt Award for Services to Gospel Music 1986, Commonwealth Inst. Award for Services to Gospel Music 1986, BBC Award for Contribution to Gospel Music 1987. *Address:* Choir Connexion, Brookdale House, 75 Brookdale Road, London, E17 6QH, England (office). *Telephone:* (20) 8509-7288 (office). *Fax:* (20) 8509-7299 (office). *E-mail:* info@choirconnexion.co.uk (office). *Website:* www.lcgc.org.uk.

MEAT LOAF; American singer and actor; b. (Marvin Lee Aday), 27 Sept. 1951, Dallas, TX; m. Leslie Edmonds 1975 (divorced 2001); two d. *Education:* univ. *Film appearances:* The Rocky Horror Picture Show 1975, Americathon 1979, Scavenger Hunt 1979, Roadie 1980, Dead Ringer 1981, Out of Bounds 1986, The Squeeze 1986, Motorama 1990, Wayne's World 1992, Gun and Betty Lou's Handbag 1992, Leap of Faith 1992, Psyched for Snuppa (voice) 1993, To Catch a Yeti 1995, Spice World 1997, Gunshy 1998, Black Dog 1998, The Mighty 1998, Everything That Rises 1998, Outside Ozona 1998, A Teker-ölantos naplója 1999, Crazy in Alabama 1999, Fight Club 1999, Blacktop 2000, Trapped 2001, Polish Spaghetti 2001, The Ballad of Lucy Whipple 2001, Face to Face 2001, Rustin 2001, Focus 2001, The 51st State 2001, The Salton Sea 2002, Wishcraft 2002, The Car Kid 2003, Learning Curves 2003, Extreme Dating 2004, A Hole in One 2004, The Pleasure Drivers 2005, Chasing Ghosts 2005, Crazylove 2005, BloodRayne 2005, Tenacious D in 'The Pick of Destiny' 2006. *Plays:* Hair, Rocky Horror Show, National Lampoon Show, More Than You Deserve, Rockabye Hamlet, Billy the Kid and Jean Harlow, As You Like It, Othello. *Recordings include:* albums: Featuring Stoney and Meat Loaf 1970, Free For All (with Ted Nugent) 1976, Bat Out of Hell 1977, Dead Ringer 1981, Midnight at the Lost and Found 1983, Bad Attitude 1984, Blind Before I Stop 1986, Bat Out of Hell II: Back into Hell 1993, Welcome To the Neighbourhood 1995, Couldn't Have Said it Better 2003, Bat Out of Hell III: The Monster is Loose 2006, Hang Cool Teddy Bear 2010. *Honours:* BRIT Award 1993, Grammy Award 1993. *Website:* www.meatloaf.net.

MEDESKI, John; American musician (keyboard, organ, piano); b. 28 June 1965, Louisville, Kentucky. *Education:* New England Conservatory of Music. *Career:* co-founder Madeski Martin and Wood jazz band 1991–, festivals and concerts USA, Europe and Japan; co-founder, Indirecto Records; mem. Heaven on Earth 2009–; also solo piano recitals; has performed with The Word, Trey Anastasio Band and John Madeski and the Itch; collab. with John Scofield, John Zorn, David Fiuczynski, Marc Ribot, John Lurie, and Steve Bernstein; has recorded with artists including T-Bone Burnett, Rufus Wainwright, Ray Lamontagne, kd lang, Iggy Pop, Matthew Shipp and Maceo Parker. *Film score:* Day on Fire (also played). *Recordings include:* albums: with Medeski Martin and Wood: Notes From The Underground 1991, It's a Jungle In Here 1993, Friday Afternoon in the Universe 1994, Shack-Man 1996, Farmer's Reserve 1997, Bubblehouse 1997, Combustication 1998, Last Chance to Dance Trance (Perhaps) 1999, Tonic 2000, The Dropper 2000, Electric Tonic 2001, Uninvisible 2002, End of the World Party (Just in Case) 2004, Out Louder 2006, Mago 2007, Let's Go Everywhere (for children) 2008, Zaebos 2008, Radiolarians II 2009; with Heaven on Earth: Heaven on Earth 2009; solo: Marian McPartland's Piano Jazz: John Medeski 2006. *Address:* c/o Blue Note Group, 150 Fifth Avenue, New York, NY 10011, USA (office). *Telephone:* (212) 786-8600 (office). *Fax:* (212) 786-8613 (office). *E-mail:* info@ mmw.net (office). *Website:* www.bluenote.com (office); www.mmw.net.

MÉDIONI, Maurice el-; Algerian musician (piano); b. 1928, Oran. *Career:* self-taught musician who absorbed influences from raï, jazz and Cuban music to develop a unique and distinct playing style, sometimes described as PianOriental; built a successful career performing in Oran and surrounding areas, after end of civil war was forced to emigrate to France as Algeria became unsafe for Jewish citizens; gained further success while based in Paris and more recently has gained int. recognition; collaborated with Khaled; currently lives in Marseille. *Recordings:* albums: Café Oran 1996, Pianor-iental 1982/2000, Descarga Oriental: The New York Sessions (with Roberto Rodriguez) 2006. *Honours:* Culture Crossing Award, BBC Radio 3 World Music Awards 2007. *Address:* Piranha Musik, Bergmannstr. 102, 10961 Berlin, Germany (office). *Telephone:* (30) 31861440 (office). *Fax:* (30) 31861410 (office). *E-mail:* records@piranha.de (office). *Website:* www.piranha.de (office).

MEDLEY, Bill; American singer; b. 19 Sept. 1940, Santa Ana, CA. *Career:* mem., The Paramours; founder mem., The Righteous Brothers 1962–67, 1974–80; numerous concerts, tours, television appearances; solo artist 1967–73, 1981–; recorded collaboration with Jennifer Warnes 1987; opened Medleys Club, Los Angeles 1982. *Recordings include:* albums: with the Righteous Brothers: You've Lost That Lovin' Feelin' 1965, Right Now! 1965, Some Blue-Eyed Soul 1965, This Is New! 1965, Just Once In My Life 1965, Back To Back 1966, Go Ahead and Cry 1966, Soul and Inspiration 1966, Sayin' Something 1967, Give It To The People 1974; solo: 100% 1968, A Song For You 1971, Sweet Thunder 1981, Right Here and Now 1982, I Still Do 1984, Someone Is Standing Outside 1985, Still Hung Up On You 1985, Another Beginning 1987, The Hard Side 1987, Blue Eyed Singer 1991, Smile 1991, Christmas Memories 1996, Bridge of Words 1997, The Other Side 1997, Almost Home 1997, Damn Near Righteous 2007. *Honours:* Grammy Award for Best Pop Performance 1987. *Address:* Westlake Entertainment, 9001 Fulb-right Avenue, Chatsworth, CA 91311, USA (office). *Telephone:* (818) 716-5822 (office). *Fax:* (818) 716-5579 (office). *E-mail:* tim@billmedley.com (office). *Website:* www.westlakeent.com (office); www.billmedley.com.

MEDLEY, Sue; Canadian singer and songwriter; b. 19 Aug. 1962, Nanaimo, BC. *Career:* tours of Canada with Bob Dylan, Dwight Yoakam, Tom Cochrane (as opening act); television, radio broadcasts in Canada; mem, AFofM, CARAS, SOCAN. *Recordings:* albums: Sue Medley 1990, Inside Out 1992, Velvet Morning 2000; singles: Dangerous Times, Maybe The Next Time, That's Life, Love Thing, When The Stars Fall, Forget You, Jane's House, Inside Out. *Honours:* five West Coast Music Awards, two Juno Awards, two Songwriter Awards.

MEHLDAU, Brad; American jazz musician (piano) and composer; b. 23 Aug. 1970, Jacksonville, FL. *Education:* New School, New York. *Career:* solo artist; mem., Brad Mehldau Trio 1995–; Artistic Dir, Jazz Series, Wigmore Hall 2009–; worked with Peter Bernstein, Jimmy Cobb, Christopher Hollyday, Christian McBride, Joshua Redman, Perico Sambeat, David Sanchez, Pat Metheny, Charlie Haden, Lee Konitz, John Scofield, Charles Lloyd, Billy Higgins, Wayne Shorter, Fleurine. *Recordings include:* albums: solo: Intro-ducing Brad Mehldau 1995; with Brad Mehldau Trio: Art Of The Trio Vol. I 1996, Art Of The Trio Vol. II: Live At The Village Vanguard 1998, Art Of The Trio Vol. III: Songs 1998, Elegiac Cycle 1999, Art Of The Trio Vol. IV: Back At The Vanguard 1999, Places 2000, Art Of The Trio Vol. V: Progression, Largo 2002, Anything Goes 2004, Day Is Done 2005, House on Hill 2006, Love Sublime (with Renée Fleming) 2006, Highway Rider 2010, Love Songs (with Anne Sofie von Otter) 2010. *Current Management:* International Music Network, 278 Main Street, Gloucester, MA 01930, USA. *Telephone:* (978) 283-2883. *Fax:* (978) 283-2330. *E-mail:* scott@imnworld.com. *Website:* www .imnworld.com. *Address:* c/o Nonesuch Records, Warner Bros Jazz, 3300 Warner Blvd, Burbank, CA 91505, USA (office). *Website:* bradmehldau.com.

MEHNDI, Daler; Indian bhangra singer and musician (tabla, harmonium, tanpura); b. (Daler Singh), 18 Aug. 1967, Patna. *Career:* moved to Delhi to begin professional career 1983–; playback singer in more than 20 Hindi movies. *Recordings:* albums: Bolo Ta Ra Ra Ra 1995, Dardi Rab Rab Kardi 1996, Ho Jayegi Balle Balle 1997, Tunak Tunak Tun 1998, Ek Daana 1999,

Nabi Buba Nabi 2000, Nach Ni Shaam Kaure 2002, Mo Jaan Laen Do 2003, Shaa Ra Ra Ra 2004, Raula Pai Gaya 2007, recorded numerous devotional songs. *Honours:* Voice of Asia, Int. Ethnic and Pop Music Contest 1994, Channel V Best Male Pop Singer 1995–97, Indira Priyadarshini Award, Rajiv Gandhi Excellence Award. *Telephone:* (99) 71655555 (office). *E-mail:* mail@ dalermehndi.com (office). *Website:* www.dalermehndi.com.

MEIGHAN, Thomas Peter (Tom); British singer, songwriter and guitarist; b. 11 Jan. 1981, Leicester, England. *Education:* Countesthorpe Community Coll. *Career:* mem., Kasabian 1999–. *Recordings include:* albums: Kasabian 2004, Empire 2006, West Ryder Pauper Lunatic Asylum (Q Award for Best Album 2009, NME Award for Best Album 2010) 2009, Velociraptor! 2011, 48:13 2014. *Honours:* NME Awards for Best Live Act 2007, for Best British Band 2012, Q Awards for Best Act in the World Today 2010, 2014, for Best Live Act 2014, BRIT Award for Best British Group 2010, MOJO Award for Song of the Year 2010. *Current Management:* c/o John Coyne, The Family Entertainment. *E-mail:* coyne@thefamilyent.com. *Address:* c/o Columbia Records, 9 Derry Street, London, W8 5HY, England (office). *Website:* www .kasabian.co.uk.

MEIJS, Norbert; singer and songwriter; b. 11 July 1952; m. Marianne, two s. one d. *Career:* singer, Sophisticated Movement 1968–71; mem., Plakband 1973–74; mem., Teenager 1977–78; several appearances under pseudonym, Blackbyrd 1993–99; mem. BUMA, STEMRA, PALM. *Compositions:* Louise, Calling Richard. *Recordings include:* Baby, Hold on; Takin' My Time; Louise, recorded by the Ryes, 1999. *Address:* Keerberg 71, 6267 DB, Cadier en Keer, The Netherlands.

MEIKLE, Orde; Producer, Remixer and DJ; b. 1964, Glasgow, Scotland. *Career:* started as a DJ in Glasgow; met Stuart McMillan and started putting on their own club nights, Atlantis and Slam; formed the Slam production duo and Soma Records label; world-wide DJ; collaborations with UNKLE; remixed Sunscreem, Mansun, Dave Angel, Phuture, Kym Sims, Underworld, Daft Punk, Dot Allison/Bryan Zentz; residencies at Pressure at the Arches, Glasgow and Fabric, London. *Recordings:* albums: Headstates 1996, Alien Radio, Past Lessons – Future Theories (DJ-mixed compilation) 2001, Fabric 9 (DJ mix) 2003, Human Response 2007. *Address:* c/o Soma Records, 342 Argyle Street, Glasgow, G2 8LA, Scotland. *Telephone:* (141) 229-6220. *Fax:* (141) 226-4383. *Website:* www.somarecords.com, www.slamevents.com.

MEINE, Klaus; German singer; b. 25 May 1948, Hanover; m. Gabi Meine; one s. *Career:* lead vocalist heavy rock group, The Scorpions 1971–; regular world-wide tours, festivals and concerts. *Recordings include:* albums: Lonesome Crow 1972, Fly To The Rainbow 1974, In Trance 1975, Virgin Killer 1976, Taken By Force 1977, Tokyo Tapes 1978, Lovedrive 1979, Animal Magnetism 1980, Blackout 1982, Love At First Sting 1984, World Wide Live 1985, Savage Amusement 1988, Crazy World 1990, Face The Heat 1993, Live Bites 1995, Pure Instinct 1996, Eye II Eye 1999, Moment Of Glory 2000, Acoustica 2001, Unbreakable 2004, Humanity Hour 1 2007, Sting in the Tail 2010, Return to Forever 2015. *Honours:* ASCAP Award (for Wind of Change) 1993. *Current Management:* Peter F. Amend, Ludwigsplatz 9, 35390 Giessen, Germany. *Telephone:* (641) 32049. *Fax:* (641) 33771. *E-mail:* amend.kollegen@t-online .de. *Website:* www.amend-kollegen.de; www.the-scorpions.com (home).

MEISNER, Randy; American musician (bass) and singer; b. 8 May 1946, Scottsbluff, NV. *Career:* mem. The Dynamics early 1960s, Soul Survivors (later renamed the Poor), Poco 1968–69, 1989, Stone Canyon Band 1969; founder mem. The Eagles 1971–77; solo artist 1977–; mem. Black Tie 1990–. *Recordings include:* with The Eagles: The Eagles 1972, Desperado 1973, On The Border 1974, One Of These Nights 1975, Hotel California (American Music Award for Favorite Album 1977) 1976, The Long Run 1979, Hell Freezes Over 1994; solo: Randy Meisner 1978, One More Song 1980, Randy Meisner 1982, Meisner, Swan & Rich 2001. *Honours:* Grammy Award for Best Pop Vocal Performance (for Lyin' Eyes) 1976, Nordoff-Robbins Music Therapy Lifetime Achievement Award (with The Eagles) 2006. *Current Management:* c/o Geoffrey Blumenauer Artists, PO Box 343, Burbank, CA 91503, USA. *E-mail:* gbatalent@aol.com.

MEISSNER, Stan; Canadian songwriter; b. 28 Aug. 1956, Toronto, Ontario. *Career:* Written songs recorded by: Céline Dion; Eddie Money; Rita Coolidge; B J Thomas; Ben Orr (from the Cars); Lee Aaron; Contributing composer for several television programmes and films. *Recordings:* albums: Dangerous Games 1984, Windows To Light 1986, Undertow 1992, Metropolis 1999. *Honours:* Gemini Award. *E-mail:* stan@stanmeissner.com. *Website:* www.stanmeissner .com.

MELADZE, Valery; Georgian singer and songwriter; b. 1965, Batumi. *Education:* Nikolayev Shipbuilding Institute, Ukraine. *Career:* singer with group, Dialogue 1991–93; founder mem., Mistikana 1992; solo career, singing songs written with brother, Konstantin 1993–; numerous live appearances. *Recordings include:* albums: with Dialogue: In The Middle Of The World, 1991; Cry Of The Hawk, 1993; Solo: Saera, 1994; The Last Romantic, 1996; Live at Olympic Moscow, 1997. *Website:* www.valerymeladze.ru.

MELANDER, Anders; Swedish songwriter, composer, musician and producer; b. 7 Jan. 1948, Stockholm. *Education:* University of Lund. *Career:* bandleader, Bread 1966–68; musical leader, Nationalteatern 1970–75; score composer, SVT 1976–; songwriter, various artists; mem., CUE 1997–; mem, Swedish Composers and Authors of Popular Music, Swedish Media Composers. *Compositions:* score for SVT WW2 drama serial recorded by

Gothenburg Symphony Orchestra 1994, news themes for national network TV4 1990–, Hallå Västindien, Vikingana 1981. *Recordings include:* with Bread: singles and compilations, including Rough Lover; with Nationaltea-tern: Livet är en fest 1974, Jack the Ripper; with Speedy Gonzales; Bängen Trålar; solo: Good Luck 1981, Ebba and Didrik 1990; with CUE: Cue 2000. *Honours:* SKAP Honours 1984, Grammis Award 1997.

MELDER, Heinz; German sound engineer and music producer; b. 16 Feb. 1951, Cologne; m. Anna Maria Melder 1976; one s. *Education:* evening school. *Career:* manager, TMK Medienproduktion GmbH 1977–; mem VDT, IFPI, GVL, GEMA. *Recordings:* numerous productions in field of popular music with leading artists. *Publications:* Eimol Prinz Zo Sin en Kölle Am Rhing. *Honours:* King Eagle Award, Airplay International Record Label of the Year 1995–96. *Address:* TMK Medienproduktion GmbH, Sebastianstr. 141, 50735 Köln, Germany (office). *Telephone:* (221) 9714060 (office). *Fax:* (221) 97140617 (office). *E-mail:* info@tmk-medien.de (office). *Website:* www.tmk-medien.de (office).

MELLE MEL; American rap artist; b. (Melvin Glover). *Career:* founder member, Grandmaster Flash and The 3 MCs 1977; became Grandmaster Flash and The Furious Five 1977–83; founder, Grandmaster Flash, Melle Mel and The Furious Five 1987. *Recordings:* albums: The Message 1982, Message II 1982, Greatest Messages 1984, World War III 1984, Pump Me Up 1985, On the Strength 1988, Greatest Hits 1992, Right Now 1997, Muscles 2007; featured on: I Feel For You, Chaka Khan 1984; also collaborated with Duran Duran, Quincy Jones, The Last Poets, Bill Laswell. *Website:* www.melemel .net.

MELLENCAMP, John; American singer, musician (guitar) and songwriter; b. 7 Oct. 1951, Seymour, IN; m. 1st Priscilla, one d.; m. 2nd Victoria, two c.; m. 3rd Elaine Irwin, one s. *Education:* Vincennes Univ. *Career:* mem., Crepe Soul 1965, Snakepit Banana Barn 1966, glitter-rock group Trash 1971; solo artist 1975–; adopted name Johnny Cougar 1976; formed The Zone 1977; changed name to John Cougar Mellencamp 1983; major concerts include US Festival 1983; organizer, inaugural Farm Aid Festival 1985; also appeared in Farm Aid II–V 1986–92, Concert for the Heartland 1993; numerous North American tours; exhibition of paintings 1991. *Film appearances:* Souvenirs 1990, Falling From Grace (own project) 1992. *Recordings include:* albums: Chestnut Street Incident 1976, The Kid Inside 1977, A Biography 1978, John Cougar 1979, Nothin' Matters and What If It Did 1980, American Fool 1982, Uh-Huh 1983, Scarecrow 1985, The Lonesome Jubilee 1987, Big Daddy 1989, Souvenirs (film soundtrack) 1990, Whenever We Wanted 1991, Human Wheels 1993, Dance Naked 1994, Mr Happy Go Lucky 1996, John Mellencamp 1998, Dance Naked Bonus CD 1999, Rough Harvest 1999, Cuttin' Heads 2001, Trouble No More 2003, Freedom's Road 2007, Life, Death, Love and Freedom 2008, No Better Than This 2010. *Honours:* American Music Award for Favourite Male Artist (co-winner) 1983, Nordoff-Robbins Silver Clef 1991. *Current Management:* c/o Randy Hoffman, Hoffman Entertainment, 1 West 34th Street, Suite 306, New York, NY 10001, USA. *Telephone:* (212) 765-2525. *Website:* www .hoffmanentertainment.com. *Address:* PO Box 6777, Bloomington, IN 47407-6777, USA (office). *Website:* www.mellencamp.com.

MELLOR, David; British musician; b. 23 April 1955, Middlesborough, England. *Career:* founder mem., Evil Twin 1987–; recording and performing as The Days of the Moon 1993–. *Recordings:* The Black Spot, The Words and Music of David Mellor, The Prince.

MELUA, Katie; British singer; b. 16 Sept. 1984, Georgia. *Education:* British School of Performing Arts, Croydon, Surrey. *Career:* solo artist. *Recordings include:* albums: Call Off The Search 2003, Live And Offstage 2004, Piece By Piece 2005, Pictures 2007, The House 2010, Secret Symphony 2012. *Honours:* Echo Award for Best Int. Newcomer of the Year, Germany 2005, Variety Club Award for Recording Artist of the Year 2005, MIDEM Crossing Borders Award 2005. *Current Management:* c/o Mike Batt, Dramatico Entertainment Ltd, PO Box 214, Farnham, Surrey GU10 5XZ, England. *E-mail:* mail@dramatico.com. *Website:* www.dramatico.com. *Website:* www.katiemelua.com.

MELVOIN, Wendy Ann; American musician (guitar), producer and com-poser; b. 26 Jan. 1964, Los Angeles, California. *Career:* joined Prince's band as guitar player 1982; toured and recorded extensively; appearance in film Purple Rain; mem. recording duo, Wendy and Lisa (with Lisa Coleman); numerous TV appearances in Europe and the USA. *Compositions:* musical scores for films including Dangerous Minds, Soul Food, Hav Plenty. *Recordings:* albums: Wendy and Lisa 1987, Fruit at the Bottom 1988, Eroica 1990, Girl Bros 1998, White Flags of Winter Chimneys 2008; appearances on Prince albums: 1999 1982, Purple Rain 1984, Around The World in a Day 1985, Parade 1986, Sign O' The Times 1987; recorded with artists including Seal, Joni Mitchell, kd lang, Sheryl Crow, Neil Finn. *Website:* www.wendyandlisa .com.

MENDEL, Nathan (Nate) Gregor; American musician (bass guitar); b. 2 Dec. 1968, Richland, Wash. WA. *Career:* fmr mem. Sunny Day Real Estate; mem. Foo Fighters 1995–; side project, Fire Theft 2004–. *Recordings include:* albums: with Foo Fighters: The Colour And The Shape 1997, There Is Nothing Left To Lose (Grammy Award for Best Rock Album 2001) 1999, One By One (Grammy Award for Best Rock Album 2003) 2002, In Your Honor 2005, Skin and Bones 2006, Echoes, Silence, Patience and Grace (Grammy Award for Best Rock Album 2008, BRIT Award for Best Int. Album 2008) 2007, Wasting Light (Grammy Award for Best Rock Album 2012) 2011, Sonic Highways

2014. *Honours:* Grammy Award for Best Short Form Music Video (for Learn To Fly) 2001, Grammy Awards for Best Hard Rock Performance (for All My Life) 2003, (for The Pretender) 2008, (for White Limo) 2012, Kerrang! Award for Best Single (for Best of You) 2005, Nordoff-Robbins Silver Clef Raymond Weil Int. Award 2006, BRIT Awards for Best Int. Group 2008, 2012, 2015, Grammy Award for Best Rock Song (for Walk) 2012, Grammy Award for Best Rock Performance (for Walk) 2012. *Current Management:* Gold Mountain Entertainment, Suite 450, 3575 Cahunega Blvd West, Los Angeles, CA 90068, USA. *Address:* c/o RCA Records, 1540 Broadway, New York, NY 10036, USA. *Website:* www.foofighters.com.

MENDES, João; Cabo Verde singer; b. Palonkon, Fogo. *Career:* relocated to USA 1978; Founder-mem. Mendes Brothers (with Ramiro Mendes); co-f. MB Records 1992; co-f. Music & Life Foundation. *Recordings:* albums: with Mendes Brothers: Um Novo Método 1982, Palonkon 1992, Bandera (Boston Music Award 1995) 1995, Diplomadu 1995, Torri di Control 1997, Para Angola Com Um Xi Coração 1998, Satélite Zamby 1999, Cabo Verde 2005, Porton de Regresso 1 2010. *Honours:* Order of Volcano and Metal of Merits from Govt of Cabo Verde 2006. *Address:* c/o MB Global Media, LLC, PO Box 1641, Beverly Hills, CA 90213; c/o Music and Life Foundation, PO Box 1641, Beverly Hills, CA 90213, USA. *E-mail:* info@mbglobalmedia.com. *Website:* www .mbglobalmedia.com; www.musicandlifefoundation.org; www.mendesbros .com/home.

MENDES, Ramiro; Cabo Verde musician (guitar) and producer; b. 5 July 1961, Palonkon, Fogo. *Education:* Berklee Coll. of Music, Boston, USA. *Career:* relocated to USA 1978; record producer for numerous artists, including Bana, Tito Paris, Gil Semedo, Kafala Brothers, Tino Trimó, Talulu, Agusto Cego, Gardenia Benros, Mirri Lobo, Djosinha, Sãozinha 1980s–; Founder-mem. Mendes Brothers (with João Mendes); co-f. MB Records 1992; co-f. Music & Life Foundation. *Recordings:* albums: with Mendes Brothers: Um Novo Método 1982, Palonkon 1992, Bandera (Boston Music Award 1995) 1995, Diplomadu 1995, Torri di Control 1997, Para Angola Com Um Xi Coração 1998, Satélite Zamby 1999, Cabo Verde 2005, Porton de Regresso 1 2010; as producer: Angola Minha Namorada, Waldemar Bastos 1990, Paranoia, Mirri Lobo 1995, Sãozinha Canta Eugenio Tavares, Sãozinha 1995, Gira Sol, Bana 1998, Salipo, Moises Kafala 1999, Mar Azul, Cesaria Evora 1999, Bobosso, Augusto Cego 2001, Distinu di Belita, Cesaria Evora 2003. *Honours:* Order of Volcano and Metal of Merits from Govt of Cabo Verde 2006. *Address:* c/o MB Global Media, LLC, PO Box 1641, Beverly Hills, CA 90213 (office); c/o Music and Life Foundation, PO Box 1641, Beverly Hills, CA 90213, USA. *E-mail:* info@mbglobalmedia.com (office). *Website:* www.mbglobalmedia.com (office); www.musicandlifefoundation.org; www.mendesbros.com/home.

MENDES, Sérgio; Brazilian singer and songwriter; b. 11 Feb. 1941, Niterói; s. of Benedicto Mendes; m. Gracinha Leporace. *Education:* Music Conservatory of Niterói. *Career:* pioneered Bossa Nova movt in Brazil with Antonio Carlos Jobim, João Gilberto and Moacyr Santos; f. Bossa Rio Sextet in 1958, toured Brazil, Europe, Middle East and Japan; Bossa Nova Festival, New York 1962; moved to Calif., USA 1964; f. Brasil 64 band, toured USA, tour with Frank Sinatra 1967, tour of Japan 1968, Europe 1980; recorded albums with Black Eyed Peas 2006, 2008; continues to tour around the world. *Recordings include:* over 40 albums including Brasileiro (Grammy Award for Best World Music Album 1992) 1992, Timeless (Latin Grammy Award for Best Brazilian Pop Album 2006) 2006, Encanto 2008, Bom Tempo (Latin Grammy Award for Best Brazilian Contemporary Pop Album) 2010, Magic 2014. *Address:* c/o Concord Music Group, Inc., 23307 Commerce Park Road, Cleveland, OH 44122 USA (office). *E-mail:* press@concordmusicgroup.com (office). *Website:* www.concordmusicgroup.com (office); www.sergiomendesmusic.com.

MENDES, Shawn Peter Raul; Canadian singer, songwriter and guitarist; b. 8 Aug. 1998, Toronto, Ont.; s. of Manuel Mendes and Karen Mendes. *Education:* Pine Ridge Secondary School, Pickering. *Career:* discovered after posting videos on Vine app 2013; toured as mem. of MagCon Tour 2014; signed to Island Records 2014; first national tour as headlining act 2014; collaborated with The Vamps 2014; opening act for Taylor Swift tour 2015. *Recordings:* album: Handwritten 2015. *Honours:* Teen Choice Awards for Choice Web Star: Music 2014, 2015, MTV Europe Music Awards for Best New Artist and Best Push 2015. *E-mail:* info@agartists.com. *Website:* www .shawnmendesofficial.com.

MENEZES BASTOS, Rafael José de, AB, MA, PhD; Brazilian anthropologist, ethnomusicologist and musician (guitar); *Professor of Anthropology and Ethnomusicology, Federal University of Santa Catarina;* b. 26 Dec. 1945, Salvador, Bahia; m. 2nd Silvia de O Beraldo 1984; five s. five d. *Education:* Federal Univ. of Bahia, School of Music, Univ. of Brasilia, Univ. of São Paulo, Massachusetts Inst. of Tech., USA, Smithsonian Inst., Univ. of California at Los Angeles, École des Hautes Études en Sciences Sociales, Paris, France, New Univ. of Lisbon, Portugal. *Career:* Anthropologist, Nat. Indian Foundation 1975–80, also mem. Advisory Bd and first Vice-Pres. of Indigenous Council 1999; Asst Prof., Anthropology and Ethnomusicology, Federal Univ. of Santa Catarina 1984–90, Assoc. Prof. 1990, now Prof., Chair. Grad. Programme in Social Anthropology 1994–96, 2003–04, Chair. Research Group in Art, Culture and Society in Latin America and the Caribbean, mem. Editorial Bd Federal Univ. of Santa Catarina Press 1991–92; mem. Scientific Bd Brazilian Anthropological Asscn 1990–92, mem. Bd of Trustees 1996–98; Liason Officer in Brazil, Int. Council for Traditional Music 1993–, mem. Exec. Bd 1997–99; mem. Advisory Bd Int. Encyclopaedia of the Popular Musics of

the World 1993–, The World of Music 1997–, Critical World 2006–. *Publications include:* A Musicológica Kamayura 1978, 1999, Dioniso em Santa Catarina (ed., author of introduction and of one article) 1993, Estudos Musicais no Mercosul (co-ed. and co-author of introduction); dissertations; about 100 articles in learned journals and books. *Telephone:* (48) 3721-9714 (office). *Fax:* (48) 3721-9714 (office). *E-mail:* rafael@cfh.ufsc.br (office). *Website:* www.antropologia.ufsc.br (office); www.musa.ufsc.br (office).

MENGELBERG, Misha; Dutch musician (piano), composer, conductor and academic; b. 5 June 1935, Kiev, Ukraine. *Education:* Royal Conservatory, The Hague, The Netherlands. *Career:* emigrated to The Netherlands 1938; co-founder, Instant Composers Pool (ICP) Orchestra 1967; Artistic Dir Studio for Electro-Instrumental Music (STEIM); collaborations with artists, including Dudu Pukwana, Peter Brozmann, Steve Lacy, Joey Baron; teaches counterpoint, Sweelinck Conservatory, Amsterdam; founder, Misha Mengelberg Trio, Misha Mengelberg Quartet. *Compositions include:* three piano pieces 1961, In Memorium Hans van Zweeden 1964, Hello! Windyboys 1968, Onderweg 1973, With Well-Kind Regards from the Camel 1974, Dressoir 1977, Saxophone Concerto 1980, 3 Intermezzi 1981, Rokus de Veldmuis 1983, Zeekip Ahoy 1984, Beestebeest versus Hertie 1995, To A Deaf Man's Ears 1996. *Recordings include:* albums: with the Instant Composers Pool: Instant Composers Pool 1968, Groupcomposing 1971, Tentet in Berlin 1977, Tetterettet 1977, Live Soncino 1979, Japan Japon 1982, Two Programs: Herbie Nichols/Thelonius Monk 1984, Bospaadje konijnehol I 1986, Bospaadje konijnehol II 1990, Jubilee Varia 1995, Oh My Dog! 2001, Aan and Uit 2003; solo: Fictions 1977, Impromptus 1988, Grandpa's Spells 1992, Mix 1994, Misha Mengelberg 1996, Solo 1999, Paul Termos Sessions Vol. I 2002; with Misha Mengelberg Quartet: Driekusman Total Loss 1964, The Misha Mengelberg Quartet at the Newport Jazz Festival 1966, Four In One 2000; with Misha Mengelberg Trio: Who's Bridge 1994, No Idea 1996; collaborative albums: Last Date (with Eric Dolphy, Jacques Schols, Han Bennink) 1964, Mengelberg Bennink (with Han Bennink) 1971, Patterns (with Noah Howard) 1971, Een mirakelse tocht door het Scharrebroekse (with Han Bennink) 1972, Midwoud 77 (with Han Bennink) 1977, Yi yole (with Dudu Pukwana, Han Bennink) 1978, A European Proposal (with Han Bennink, Paul Rutherford, Mario Schiano) 1978, Three Points and a Mountain (with Han Bennink, Peter Brötzmann) 1979, Bennink Mengelberg (with Han Bennink) 1979, Willem van Manen (with Willem van Manen) 1979, Instant Replay (with Lol Coxhill) 1981, Change of Season (with Han Bennink, George Lewis, Steve Lacy, Arjen Gorter) 1984, Dutch Masters (with Han Bennink, Steve Lacy, George Lewis, Ernst Reijseger) 1987, MiHa (with Han Bennink) 1991, L'Heure bleu (with Franz Koglmann) 1991, October Meeting 1991: 3 Quartets (with Anthony Braxton, Mark Dresser, Han Bennink) 1991, October Meeting (with Sunny Murray, Ab Baars) 1991, Anatomy of a Meeting (with Sunny Murray, Ab Baars) 1991, Anthony Braxton's Charlie Parker Project (with Anthony Braxton) 1993, Live In Holland '97 (with Mats Gustafsson, Gert-Jan Prins) 1997, Lively (with Yuri Honing, Ernst Reijseger) 2000. *Current Management:* c/o Susanna von Canon, Stichting ICP, Prinseneiland 97hs, 1013 Amsterdam, Netherlands. *Telephone:* (20) 6386611. *E-mail:* canon@xs4all.nl. *Website:* www.icporchestra.com.

MENGONI, Marco; Italian singer; b. 25 Dec. 1988, Ronciglione, Viterbo. *Career:* winner, third season of Italian version of The X Factor 2009; first EP released 2009; participant, Sanremo Music Festival 2010; first national tour of Italy in 2010. *Television:* X Factor (Italian series winner) 2009. *Recordings:* albums: Solo 2.0 2010, #prontoacorrere 2013, Parole in circolo 2015, Le cose che non ho 2015. *Honours:* TRL Award, MTV Man of the Year 2010, MTV Europe Music Awards for Best Italian Act 2010, 2013, 2015, for Best European Act 2010, 2015. *Address:* Sony Music Entertainment Italy s.p.a., 20123 Milan, V. Amedei 9, Italy (office). *Telephone:* (02) 85361 (office). *Website:* www .marcomengoni.it.

MENSCH, Peter; management executive; b. 1948. *Career:* Jt Founder and head, with Cliff Burnstein, Q-Prime Management; has managed artists and groups, including AC/DC, Tal Bachman, Crazy Town, Def Leppard, Dokken, Fountains of Wayne, Garbage, Nina Gordon, Hole, Bruce Hornsby, Ivy, Madonna, Metallica, Queensryche, Red Hot Chili Peppers, Rush, Shania Twain, Smashing Pumpkins, Tesla, Veruca Salt, Warrior Soul; Q-Prime Management acquired part-ownership with Zomba Music Publishing, of Volcano Records 1998. *Address:* Q-Prime Management, 729 7th Avenue, New York, NY 10019, USA (office). *E-mail:* info@qprime.com (office). *Website:* www .qprime.com (office).

MERCÉ, José; Spanish singer; b. (José Soto Soto), 19 April 1955, Jerez de la Frontera. *Career:* singer, respected by flamenco aficionados; appeal widened with release of Aire album, which remained within flamenco tradition but updated lyrical content to reach contemporary audience. *Recordings:* Bandera de Andalucía 1977, Carmen 1983, Verde Junco 1985, Caminos Reales Del Cante 1987, Desnudando El Alma 1994, Del Amanecer 1999, Aire 2000, Lio 2004, Cuerpo y Alma 2006, La Noche y el Dia 2006, Pa' Saber de tu Querer 2006, Lo Que No Se Da 2006, Vive el Flamenco 2007, Ruido 2010. *Honours:* Cordoba Competition 1986. *Address:* c/o EMI Music Iberia, Alcalá 44, 3a, 28014 Madrid, Spain (office). *E-mail:* hablemosdemusica@emimusic.com (office). *Website:* www.josemerce.es.

MERCEL, Jeff; American musician (drums, piano). *Career:* mem. rock group Mercury Rev 1998–, fmrly drummer, switched to piano 2006; sound has gradually developed from a very experimental and psychedelic style to a more melodic approach; festival appearances in USA, Europe and Far East 2007. *Recordings include:* albums: All Is Dream 2001, The Secret Migration 2005, The Essential Mercury Rev: Stillness Breathes 1991–2006, Back to Mine compilation 2006, Hello Blackbird (soundtrack to film Bye Bye Blackbird) 2006, Snowflake Midnight 2008, Strange Attractor 2008. *Current Management:* c/o Free Trade Agency, 15 Timber Yard, Drysdale Street, London, N1 6ND, England. *Telephone:* (20) 3700-3377. *Fax:* (20) 3700-3355. *E-mail:* info@freetradeagency.co.uk. *Website:* www.freetradeagency.co.uk. *E-mail:* jm@jeffmercel.com. *Website:* www.mercuryrev.net.

MERCEY, Larry Oliver Anthony; Canadian musician; b. 12 Dec. 1939, Hanover, ON; m. June Mercey 1964; one s. one d. *Career:* mem., The Mercey Brothers 1957–90; solo artist 1990–; appeared Grand Ole Opry, Nashville, Tennessee. *Recordings include:* 17 albums with The Mercey Brothers; solo: Full Speed Ahead 1990, Let's Deal Again 1994, It's Not Over Yet 2007. *Honours:* seven Juno Awards, Top Country Vocal Group, CF Martin Lifetime Achievement Award, Canadian Country Music Award for Top Vocal Group. *Address:* Larry Mercey Productions, 590 Hunters Place, Waterloo, ON N2K 3L1, Canada (office). *Telephone:* (519) 746-8488 (office). *Fax:* (519) 746-6249 (office). *E-mail:* lmercey@rogers.com (office). *Website:* www.merceybrothers.com.

MERCHANT, Natalie; American singer, songwriter, musician (piano) and record producer; b. 26 Oct. 1963; one d. *Education:* Jamestown Community College. *Career:* founder, lead vocalist, 10,000 Maniacs 1981–93; concerts included tour with REM, USA 1987, Cambridge Folk Festival 1987, 1988, British tour 1987, US tours 1989, 1992, A Performance For The Planet, Maryland 1990, Time Capsule Tour 1990; Earth Day 1991 Concert, Massachusetts 1991, National Earth Day, Hollywood Bowl 1993; solo artist 1993–; founded own record label, Myth America Records 2003–. *Recordings:* albums: with 10,000 Maniacs: Secrets of The I Ching 1983, The Wishing Chair 1985, In My Tribe 1987, Blind Man's Zoo 1989, Hope Chest 1989, Our Time In Eden 1992; solo: Tigerlily 1995, Ophelia 1998, Motherland 2001, The House Carpenter's Daughter 2003, Campfire Songs 2004, Leave Your Sleep 2010, Natalie Merchant 2014. *Current Management:* Mick Management, 35 Washington Street, Brooklyn, NY 11201, USA. *Telephone:* (212) 425-6425. *E-mail:* info@mickmgmt.com. *Website:* www.mickmgmt.com; www.nataliemerchant.com.

MERCHANT, Ryan; American singer, songwriter, musician and record producer; b. 1981, San Francisco, Calif. *Career:* fmr writer of jingles for numerous advertising campaigns; formed Capital Cities (with Sebu Simonian) 2009–, released debut EP 2011, debut tour 2013. *Recordings:* album: with Capital Cities: In a Tidal Wave of Mystery 2013. *Honours:* MTV Video Music Award for Best Visual Effects 2013. *E-mail:* management@capitalcitiesmusic.com. *Address:* c/o Lazy Hooks Records, Capitol Records, Universal Music Group, 2220 Colorado Avenue, Santa Monica, CA 90404, USA (office). *Telephone:* (310) 865-0770 (Universal) (office); (213) 509-4083 (Lazy Hooks) (office). *E-mail:* ryan@lazyhooks.com. *Website:* www.universalmusic.com (office); www.lazyhooks.com; www.capitalcitiesmusic.com.

MERCK, Alex, DipMus; German publisher; musician (guitar) and composer; b. 8 July 1956. *Education:* Mainz Univ., Berkley Coll. of Music, USA. *Career:* tours with Raoul de Souza and as solo artist 1984–86; many TV appearances; studio recordings 1985–; composer of TV and film scores 1987–; record co. manager 1992–2000; music journalist and consultant 2000–; mem. GEMA. *Compositions:* Molthe, Adios Buenos Aires. *Recordings:* albums: Dog Days 1986, Shadowdance, Minds and Bodies. *E-mail:* info@amm-music.com (office). *Website:* www.amm-music.com.

MERCURY, Daniela; Brazilian singer, songwriter, dancer and choreographer; b. (Daniela Mercuri de Almeida Póvoas), 28 July 1965, Salvador, Bahia; d. of Antônio Fernando de Abreu Ferreira de Almeida and Liliana Mercuri; one s. one d. *Education:* Fed. Univ. of Bahia. *Career:* solo artist 1981–; performs in the energetic axé style; mem. dance group, Salta early 1990s; backing singer in Gilberto Gil band; mem., Companhia Clic; toured internationally as a solo artist; Amb. for UNICEF and Ayrton Senna Foundation. *Recordings include:* albums: Compania Clic 1990, Daniela 1992, O Canto Da Cidade 1993, Musica De Rua 1994, Feijão Com Arroz, Swing Da Cor 1997, Elétrica 1998, Sol da Liberdade 2000, Sou de Qualquer Lugar 2001, Eletrodoméstico 2002, Carnaval Electrônico 2004, Clássica 2005, Balé Mulato 2005, Balé Mulato ao Vivo (Latin Grammy Award for Best Brazilian Roots/Regional Album 2007) 2006. *Honours:* Prêmio Sharp (for Daniela) 1992. *Current Management:* Canto da Cidade, Rua São Paulo 325, Pituba, Salvador, 41830-180, Bahia, Brazil. *Telephone:* (71) 2109-5555. *Fax:* (71) 3248-9811. *E-mail:* contato@cantodacidade.com.br. *Website:* www.cantodacidade.com.br; www.danielamercury.art.br.

MERRILL, Helen; American singer; b. 21 July 1930, New York, NY. *Career:* first performed, 1944; singer with Reggie Childs' orchestra 1946–47; solo artist 1954–; collaborations with trumpeter, Clifford Brown; mem., Atco and Metrojazz 1959; tours widely. *Recordings include:* albums: Don't Explain, Helen Merrill With Clifford Brown 1954, Dream of You 1956, The Nearness of You, Merrill At Midnight 1957, You've Got A Date With The Blues 1959, The Feeling Is Mutual 1965, Shade of Difference 1969, Sposin' 1971, Chasin' The Bird 1979, Casa Forte 1980, Collaboration 1987, Alone Together 1989, Clear Out of This World 1991, Blossom of Stars 1992, Brownie – Homage To Clifford Brown 1995, Carousel 1997, You and the Night and the Music 1997, Jelena

Ana Milcactic (aka Helen Merrill), 2000, Lilac Wine 2004. *E-mail:* torriezito@aol.com; webmaster@helenmerrill.com. *Website:* www.helenmerrill.com.

MERRILL, Robbie; American musician (bass guitar); b. 13 June 1964, Lawrence, Massachusetts. *Career:* spent time in various covers bands until joining Godsmack 1995–. *Recordings include:* albums: with Godsmack: Godsmack 1998, Awake 2000, Faceless 2003, Godsmack IV 2004, The Oracle 2010. *Honours:* Boston Music Award for Act of the Year 2000, 2001, Billboard Award for Rock Artist of the Year 2001. *Current Management:* c/o Paul Geary, PGE Inc., 244 Pleasant Street, Franklin MA 02038-3600, USA. *E-mail:* pge1@prodigy.net. *Website:* www.godsmack.com.

MERRITT, Jymie; American jazz musician (bass) and composer; b. (James Raleigh), 3 May 1926, Philadelphia, PA; m. 1st Dorothy Small 1949 (divorced 1977); five s.; m. 2nd Ave Maria Davis 1981. *Career:* bass player with Art Blakey and The Jazz Messengers, Gregory and Maurice Hines, Max Roach, Dizzy Gillespie, Lee Morgan; Dir, composer, Forerunner Jazz Organization and Orchestra 1962–2005.

MERRYGOLD, Aston Iain; British singer and songwriter; b. 13 Feb. 1988, Peterborough. *Education:* Jack Hunt School, Peterborough. *Career:* competed in Stars in Their Eyes on TV (as Michael Jackson) 2002; mem. UFO 2006–08, changed group name to JLS (Jack the Lad Swing) 2008–13; competed in The X Factor (UK version) (ITV 1) 2008, placed second; signed to Epic Records 2009; toured with Lemar 2009; debut single Beat Again released 2009; debut album released 2009; first headline tour 2010; recorded single Love You More for Children in Need charity 2010; collaborations include Tinie Tempah, Dev; recorded Sport Relief charity single Proud 2012; performed at Diamond Jubilee concert, outside Buckingham Palace 2012; patron for Beatbullying charity. *Television:* JLS Revealed (special) 2009, Got to Dance (as judge) 2012–. *Film:* JLS: Eyes Wide Open 3D (concert film and documentary) 2011. *Recordings:* albums: with JLS: JLS (MOBO Award for Best Album 2010) 2009, Outta This World 2010, Jukebox 2011, Evolution 2012. *Publications:* Our Story So Far 2009, Just Between Us: Our Private Diary 2010. *Honours:* with UFO: Urban Music Award for Best Unsigned Act 2007; with JLS: MOBO Awards for Best UK Newcomer 2009, for Best Song (for Beat Again) 2009, for Best UK Act 2010, BBC Switch Live Award for Outstanding Artist 2009, BRIT Awards for British Breakthrough 2010, for Best British Single (for Beat Again) 2010, BT Digital Music Awards for Best Group 2010, 2011, for Best Video (for Everybody in Love) 2010, (for Eyes Wide Shut) 2011, (for Do You Feel What I Feel?) 2012, Urban Music Awards for Best Group 2010, for Best R&B Act 2010. *Current Management:* c/o Modest! Management, The Matrix Complex, 91 Peterborough Road, London, SW6 3BU, England. *Telephone:* (20) 7384-6410. *E-mail:* info@modestmanagement.com. *Website:* www.modestmanagement.com; www.jlsofficial.com.

MERTA, Vladimir; Czech singer, songwriter, film director, composer and musician (guitar, flute); b. 20 Jan. 1946, Prague; m. Lucie Lucka; two d. *Education:* CVUT, Faculty of Architecture, FAMU – Film Faculty, Academy of Musical Arts, Prague, LSU – People's School of Arts, Prague. *Career:* performed at: Roskilde Festival, Denmark 1988, 1990, Japan 1991, Vancouver Folk Festival 1992, Edinburgh Fringe 1993, More Than Meets The Ear, London, South Bank Centre, London 1994, Strasbourg, Mittleeuropa, Washington Folk Life Festival, Cheltenham Literary Festival 1995; mem, OSA, INTERGRAM, SAI. *Compositions include:* five television specials, Thru The Guitar Hole; one feature script, Opera In The Wineyard; music for 15 cartoons; 10 pieces of theatre music. *Recordings:* Ballade de Prague 1969, Vladimir Merta Live, Vols I and II 1989, Svatky Trpelivosti, Chtit Chytit Vitr, Biti Rublem 1993; Jewish choir Mispaha, Vols I and II 1993, 1995, Sefardic Songs (with Jana Lewitova) 1996. *Publications:* Advantage Server (novel) 1987, Born In The Bohemia (complete lyrics) 1993, Folk Blues Guitar and Harmonica (with 3 hour VHS cassette) 1993, Troubadour In The Age of Global Village 1994. *Honours:* Porta 1986. *Address:* U 5 Baterie 5, 162 00 Prague, Czech Republic (office). *Telephone:* 224313511 (office). *E-mail:* merta.vladimir@volnu.cz (office). *Website:* www.vladimirmerta.cz.

MESLIEN, Nicolas 'Kham'; French musician (bass). *Career:* mem., Lo'jo 1997–. *Recordings include:* albums: Mojo Radio 1998, Bohème de Cristal 2000, L'Une des siens/Au cabaret sauvage 2002, Ce Soir Là 2003, Bazar Savant 2006, Cosmophono 2009. *E-mail:* lojo@lojo.org (office). *Website:* www.lojo.org.

MESSINA, Jim; American musician (guitar, bass guitar), singer, record producer and engineer; b. 5 Dec. 1947, Maywood, California. *Career:* recording engineer; member, Buffalo Springfield 1966–68, Poco 1968–90, Loggins and Messina 1971–76, 2004–05; solo artist 1977–97; own studio, Gateway Studios 1983; mem, ASCAP, AFTRA. *Recordings:* albums: with The Jesters: Jim Messina and The Jesters 1967, The Dragsters 1967; with Buffalo Springfield: Again 1967, Last Time Around 1968; with Poco: Picking Up the Pieces 1968, Poco 1969, Deliverin 1971, Legacy 1989; with Loggins and Messina: Kenny Loggins With Jim Messina Sittin' In 1971, Loggins and Messina 1972, Full Sail 1973, On Stage 1974, Mother Lode 1974, So Fine 1975, Native Sons 1976, Finale 1976; solo: Oasis 1979, Messina 1981, One More Mile 1981, Watching the River Run 1996; also recordings with Hoyt Axton, Neil Young. *E-mail:* jim@jimmessina.com (office). *Website:* www.jimmessina.com.

MESSINA, Jo Dee Marie; American country singer; b. 25 Aug. 1970, Holliston, MA. *Career:* sang in country bands around New England area as a teenager; performed at local talent shows, Nashville aged 19; solo artist 1994–. *Recordings include:* albums: Jo Dee Messina 1996, I'm Alright 1998, Burn

2000, A Joyful Noise 2002, Delicious Surprise 2005. *Honours:* CMA Horizon Award 1999, ACM Top New Female Vocalist 1999. *Address:* Jo Dee Messina Fan Club, PO Box 3149, Brentwood, TN 37024, USA (office). *E-mail:* webmaster@jodeemessina.com (office). *Website:* www.jodeemessina.com.

METCALFE, Andy, BMus; British musician (bass guitar, keyboards) and producer; b. 3 March 1956, Bristol, England; m. Lilian Metcalfe 1992; one s. *Education:* Sussex Univ. *Career:* worked with Robyn Hitchcock, producing three albums and participating in nine other albums, many tours 1976–94; founder mem., Soft Boys 1976–79, 2002–; mem., Squeeze 1985–88; producer for The Reivers, Kimberley Rew, Julian Dawson, Edge Park; mem. Musicians' Union (UK), American Musicians' Union. *Recordings include:* four albums with Soft Boys, including Nextdoorland 2002; two albums with Squeeze. *Current Management:* Peter Jenner, Sincere Management, c/o 421 Harrow Road, London, W10 4RD, England.

METHENY, Patrick (Pat) Bruce; American jazz musician (guitar); b. 12 Aug. 1954, Lee's Summit, Mo. *Education:* Univ. of Miami. *Career:* taught guitar at Univ. of Miami and Berklee Coll. of Music; fmrly guitarist with Gary Burton Quintet; has performed and recorded with musicians and composers, including Ornette Coleman, Herbie Hancock and Steve Reich; formed Pat Metheny Group 1978–. *Recordings include:* albums: Bright Size Life 1976, Watercolours 1977, Pat Metheny Group 1978, New Chautauqua 1979, An Hour With Pat Metheny 1979, American Garage 1980, As Falls Wichita, So Falls Wichita Falls 1981, Offramp 1981, 80/81 1981, Travels 1983, Rejoicing 1983, Works 1984, First Circle 1984, Song X (with Ornette Coleman) 1985, Still Life (Talking) 1987, Works II 1988, Letter From Home 1989, Question And Answer (with Roy Haynes and Dave Holland) 1990, Secret Story 1992, Under Fire (film-score) 1992, Zero Tolerance For Silence 1992, I Can See Your House From Here 1993, The Road To You: Recorded Live In Europe 1993, Dream Teams 1994, Zero Tolerance for Silence 1994, We Live Here 1995, This World 1996, Quartet 1996, The Sign Of Four 1996, Imaginary Day 1997, Beyond the Missouri Sky 1997, Passaggio Per Il Paradiso (film-score) 1998, Like Minds 1998, All The Things You Are 1999, A Map Of The World (film-score) 1999, Last Train Home 1999, Jim Hall and Pat Metheny 1999, Trio 99>00 2000, Trio Live 2000, Move To The Groove 2001, Parallel Universe 2001, Sassy Samba 2001, Speaking Of Now 2002, One Quiet Night 2003, The Way Up (Grammy Award for Best Contemporary Jazz Album 2006) 2005, Metheny Mehldau 2006, Day Trip 2008, Orchestrion 2010, What's It All About (Grammy Award for Best New Age Album 2011) 2012, Unity Band (Grammy Award for Best Jazz Instrumental Album 2013) 2012, KIN 2014. *Honours:* Boston Music Awards for Outstanding Jazz Album, Outstanding Guitarist, Outstanding Jazz Fusion Group 1986, Grammy Award for Best Instrumental Composition 1990, 1993, Best Contemporary Jazz Performance 1995, Best Rock Instrumental Performance 1996, Orville H. Gibson Award for Best Jazz Guitarist 1996, Best Guitarist (Jazz Times Magazine) 2000. *Current Management:* The Kurland Agency, 173 Brighton Avenue, Boston, MA 02134-2003, USA. *Telephone:* (617) 254-0007. *Fax:* (617) 782-3524. *E-mail:* agents@thekurlandagency.com. *Website:* www.thekurlandagency.com; www.patmetheny.com.

METHOD MAN, (Iron Lung, Hott Nikkels, MZA, Ticallion Stallion, Johnny Blaze); American producer and rap artist; b. (Clifford Smith), 1 April 1971, Staten Island, New York. *Career:* mem., Wu-Tang Clan 1993–; solo artist 1994–; duo with Redman 1999–; collaborations with Texas, LL Cool J, Notorious B.I.G., Boyz II Men. *Films include:* One Eight Seven 1997, Cop Land 1997, Belly 1998, P.I.G.S. 1999, Boricua's Bond 2000, Whasango 2001, How High 2001, My Baby's Daddy 2004, Garden Slate 2004, Soul Plane 2004, Scary Movie 3 2004, Venom 2005, Meet the Spartans 2008, The Sitter 2011, The Indestructible Jimmy Brown 2011, Red Tails 2012, Mob Wives 2014. *Television includes:* Stung (series, also writer) 2002, Method & Red (series) 2004. *Recordings include:* albums: with Wu-Tang Clan: Enter The Wu-Tang Clan (36 Chambers) 1993, Wu-Tang Forever 1997, The W 2000, Iron Flag 2001, The 8 Diagrams 2007, Wu-Massacre 2010; solo: Tical 1994, Tical 2000: Judgement Day 1998, Tical 0: The Prequel 2004, 4:21 The Day After 2006, The Meth Lab 2015; with Redman: Blackout! 1999, Blackout! 2 2009. *Honours:* Grammy Award for Best Rap Performance by a Duo or Group (for I'll Be There for You, with Mary J. Blige) 1996. *Current Management:* c/o A&M Entertainment, 8605 Santa Monica Blvd, West Hollywood, CA 90069, USA. *Telephone:* (310) 295-4150. *Fax:* (310) 295-4130. *Website:* www.amentertainment.com; www.wutangcorp.com.

METSERS, Paul; New Zealand/Dutch singer, songwriter and musician (guitar, dulcimer, mandocello); b. 27 Nov. 1945, The Netherlands; partner Pauline Brocklehurst; two s. three d. *Career:* professional folk musician touring UK, Netherlands, Italy, Japan, Australia and NZ 1980–89; frequent radio coverage of songs and guest appearances; began writing and performing again 2011; mem. Performing Right Soc., Mechanical-Copyright Protection Soc. *Compositions include:* Farewell To The Gold, sung by various artists, including Bob Dylan. *Recordings:* five albums. *Publications:* song book 1986. *Honours:* voted in Top 10 of Best Male Folk Artists, Folk On 2 Poll. *Address:* Mint Cottage, Gilthwaiterigg Lane, Kendal, Cumbria, LA9 6NT, England. *Telephone:* (1539) 724707. *E-mail:* paul@mintcottage.plus.com. *Website:* www.sagemcrafts.co.uk; www.paulmetsers.com.

METZGER, Jon Frederick; American musician; b. 30 July 1959, Washington DC; m. Linda Brookshire. *Education:* BMus, 1981, MMus, 1994, North Carolina School of the Arts. *Career:* US Information Agency Arts America Program Tours of the Near East, Northern and Sub Sahara, Africa, Central America; Concert Halls, Jazz Clubs, throughout the USA, Europe, Including East Coast Jazz Festival, Lincoln Center, Kennedy Center Constitutional Hall, Smithsonian Institute, Corcoran Gallery of Art, Blues Alley, One Step Down; Artist, Clinician Musser; American Society of Composers, Authors, Publishers; International Asscn of Jazz Educators. *Compositions include:* Spiral Passages; On Verchiels Wings; Elephant Walk; The Spinner, I'll Always Be Loving You; Time Again; Credit Line; Mixed Up; Into The Light; Out of the Dark; My Lady. *Recordings:* albums: Vibes 1984, Out of the Dark 1986, Into the Light 1988, The Spinner 1997, Teach Me Tonight 1998, Times Fly 2001, Common Ground 2003; other credits include: Waltzing the Splendor, Claire Ritter 2007, Girl Trombone Player & She Sings Too, Nancy McCracken 2008, Insight at Midnight, Baron Tymas 2009. *Publications:* The Art and Language of Jazz Vibes, 1996. *Honours:* National Endowment for the Arts Grant, 1985; American Society of Composers, Authors, Publishers Popular Award, 1985–98. *E-mail:* jmetzger@elon.edu; jmetzger@triad.rr.com. *Website:* www.jonmetzger.com.

MEX, Paul; British record producer and musician; b. 25 Nov. 1962, St Albans, Hertfordshire. *Career:* recording career producing and mixing for numerous artistes; as producer, over 500,000 record sales to credit; business ventures include State Art; Mex One Recordings; mem, PRS, MCPS, Musicians' Union. *Recordings:* with Poison No. 9: Lay All Your Love On Me; with United States of Europe: Free; with Son of Space: Magic Fly; with Man 2 Man: Malestripper; with Ugly As Sin: Terminal Love. *E-mail:* info@mexonerecordings.co.uk (office). *Website:* www.mexonerecordings.co.uk.

MEYER, Edgar, BMus; American composer and double bassist; b. 24 Nov. 1960, Tulsa, Okla; s. of Edgar A. Meyer and Anna Mary Metzel; m. Cornelia (Connie) Heard 1988; one s. *Education:* Georgia Inst. of Tech., Indiana Univ. School of Music. *Career:* began playing bass aged five under tutelage of father; began composing pop songs and classical pieces as a child; studied with Stuart Stanley at univ.; formed bluegrass band Strength in Numbers, Nashville, Tenn. 1984; regular bass player, Santa Fe Chamber Music Festival 1985–93; appeared with concert artists Emanuel Ax (piano) and Yo-Yo Ma (cello); premiere of Concerto for Bass 1993; joined Chamber Music Soc., Lincoln Center, New York 1994; formed band Quintet for Bass and String Quartet, soloist debut performance 1995; premiere of Double Concerto for Bass and Cello 1995; premiere of Violin Concerto 2000; frequent collaborations with Chris Thile, Amy Dorfman, Bela Fleck, Mike Marshall; performed at Aspen, Caramoor and Marlboro Festivals; debuted with Boston Symphony Orchestra, Tanglewood, Mass 2000; Visiting Professor of Double Bass, Curtis Inst. of Music, Visiting Prof., RAM, UK. *Recordings include:* albums: Unfolding 1986, The Telluride Sessions (Strength in Numbers) 1989, Dreams of Flight 1987, Love of a Lifetime 1988, Appalachia Waltz (with Yo-Yo Ma and Mark O'Connor) 1996, Uncommon Ritual 1997, Short Trip Record 1999, Bach Unaccompanied Cello Suites Performed on a Double Bass 1999, Appalachian Journey (with Yo-Yo Ma and Mark O'Connor) (Grammy Award 2001) 2000, Perpetual Motion 2000, Edgar Meyer 2006, The Goat Rodeo Sessions (with Yo-Yo Ma, Chris Thile, and Stuart Duncan) (Grammy Award for Best Folk Album 2012) 2011, Bass and Mandolin (with Chris Thile) (Grammy Award for Best Contemporary Instrumental Album 2015) 2014; collaborated with Katty Mattea on album Where Have You Been (Grammy Award, Country Music Award, Acad. of Country Music Asscn Award) 1990. *Honours:* winner, Zimmerman-Mingus Competition, Int. Soc. of Bassists 1981, Avery Fisher Prize 2000, Grammy Award for the Best Crossover Album 2001, MacArthur Award 2002. *Current Management:* c/o Dean Shultz IMG Artists, 7 West 54th Street, New York, NY 10019, USA. *Telephone:* (212) 994-3533. *E-mail:* dshultz@imgartists.com. *Website:* edgarmeyer.com.

MEYER, Patrice; French musician (guitar); b. 18 Dec. 1957, Strasbourg. *Career:* mem., Hugh Hopper FrangloDutch Band 1989–96, Equip Out 1994–95, Richard Sinclair's Band 1994–96, Tertio 1994–96, FrangloBand 1999–, Didier Malherbe Trio 2000–, Roxongs 2000–02, Pip Pyle's Bash 2002–,. *Recordings:* albums: solo: Racines Croisées 1983, Dromadaire Vicmaois 1987; with Hugh Hopper: Mecano Pelorus 1992, Hooligan Romantics 1993, Carousel 1995; with Pip Pyle's Bash: Belle Illusion 2004. *E-mail:* p.finger@wanadoo.fr (office). *Website:* www.patrice-meyer.com.

MEYERS, Ken; French singer and musician (guitar, harmonica); b. 20 Aug. 1965, Valenciennes. *Education:* Univ. of Lille III, France. *Career:* support band for John Mayall, Calvin Russel, Bernard Allison, Peter Case, Martin Hutchinson, Patrick Verbeecke; mem. Ken Meyers Band 1991–98, now back on stage; numerous festivals and concerts, radio and TV appearances; solo artist, Unplugged 1998–, more than 350 concerts in France; Trio Unplugged 2004–; mem. SACEM. *Recordings:* albums: Ken Meyers Band Live 1994, Some Unplugged Ones, Vol. I 2001, Vol. 2 2003, 2e Saison 2005. *Television:* Report on M6. *Address:* 117 rue Lambrecht, Apt 22, 59500 Douai, France (home). *Telephone:* (6) 08-66-10-75; (3) 27-87-44-96 (home). *E-mail:* ken.meyers@free.fr. *Website:* www.ken-meyers.com.

MEZQUITA HARDY, Daniel; Spanish musician (guitar, keyboards); b. 10 June 1965. *Career:* mem. Hombres G 1983–92, 2002–; producer with Dro recording co. *Films:* Sufre mamón 1987, Suéltate el pelo 1988. *Recordings include:* Hombres G 1985, La cagaste... Burt Lancaster 1986, Estamos locos... ¿o qué? 1987, Agitar antes de usar 1988, Voy a pasármelo bien 1989, Esta es tu vida 1990, Historia del bikini 1992, Peligrosamente juntos 2004, Todo esto es muy extraño 2004, 10 2007. *Address:* c/o Dro Atlantic, Calle Juan Hurtado de Mendoza 3, 28036 Madrid, Spain (office). *Website:* www.hombres-g.com.

M'FOKO, Mansiamina; Democratic Republic of the Congo artist, composer and musician (guitar); b. (Bopol Mansiamina), 26 July 1949, Kinshasa. *Career:* mem., Orchestre Bamboula, represented Zaire in the festival of African music in Algeria 1969; founder orchestra, Rock-a-Mambo 1970; mem. orchestra, Africa Fiesta Sukisa (with Dr Nico) 1970; co-founder orchestra, Continental; began writing and composing songs 1971; mem. orchestra, Orchestre Afrisa International 1973–76; founder, Ya Toupas (with Ray Lema and Manuaku), accompanied the artist M'Pongo Love 1976; joined Africa All Stars 1978; began solo career 1979; moved to France 1982; founder, 4 Etoiles (with Nyboma-Syran Mbenza and Muta Mayi) 1983; tours to most African countries, Europe and the USA. *Recordings include:* albums: Pitié, je veux la reconciliation; Mariage forcé, Manuela.

MHOLO, Tshedi; South African singer; b. (Matshediso), Lichtenburg. *Career:* mem., Malaika. *Recordings include:* albums: Malaika 2004, Vuthelani (SAMA Award for Best African Pop Album 2006) 2005. *Honours:* Kora All Africa Music Award for Best Group from Southern Africa 2005. *Address:* West Cliff White House, 39 Jan Smuts Avenue, West Cliff, South Africa. *E-mail:* info@malaikasa.co.za. *Website:* www.malaikasa.co.za.

M.I.A.; British (b. Sri Lankan) singer and songwriter; b. (Mathangi Arulpragasam), 1977, London; one s. *Education:* Central St Martin's Coll. *Career:* moved to family's native Sri Lanka as a child, then to India, returned to England as a teenager; studied fine art and film at univ.; artwork displayed in various London galleries; solo artist 2003–; music mixes elements of dancehall, electro, hip hop and jungle. *Recordings:* albums: Arular 2005, Kala 2007, Maya 2010. *Honours:* chosen by Time magazine amongst 100 Most Influential People in the World 2009. *Address:* c/o XL Recordings, 1 Codrington Mews, London W11 2EH, England (office). *E-mail:* xl@ xlrecordings.com (office). *Website:* www.xlrecordings.com (office); www.miauk .com.

MICENMACHER, Youval; musician (percussion) and actor; b. 18 Oct. 1949, Paris, France; m. Arnelle de Frondeville 1983; one s. one d. *Career:* co-founder, jazz groups, Arcane V, L'Impossible Trio 1986, Ichthyornis (duo) 1986; played with Michel Godard, Philippe Deschepper, Gérard Marais, Vincent Courtois, Louis Sclavis, Mohamad Hamam, Fawzi Al-Aiedy, Djamchid Chémirani, Pierre Seghers, Michel Touraille, Jean-Marc Padovani, Claude Barthélemy; founder, company Solos Performances; performances include Peau à Peau, Festival d'Avignon 1983, Kaddish, Montpellier 1984, La Braraque Rouge (jazz opera) 1985, Joueurs de Jazz, Festival de Marne-La-Vallée 1987, Très Horas de Sol (jazz and flamenco), Festival Banlieues Bleues 1987, Psyché, Opera by Lully, Festival d'Aix En Provence 1987, Jubal 1988, Le Rôdeur, Festival de Marne-La-Vallée, tours of France, Austria, Hungary 1989, Opéra-Goude, with solistes de l'Ensemble Intercontemporain 1989, Jumelles, opera 1990; actor, percussionist, Black Ballad (with Archie Shepp, Dee Dee Bridgewater) 1991, Sud 1992, Echange, musical 1992, Around About Bobby, Festival de Banlieues Bleues 1993, Mister Cendron (jazz opera) 1993, Ma Nuit Chez Lucy, musical 1994, Hommage à Germaine Dulac 1994; numerous festivals with Quartet Opera de Gérard Marais 1995, The Voice in Upper Galilee Festival 1995. *Recordings:* Chants Hébreux D'Orient 1994, Fera Fera 1994, Tres Horas De Sol, Le Rodeur, L'Impossible Trio, Nimenio, Est, Lamidbar, Turkish Songs, Global Voices 1998, Chant Spirit in Sound 1999, Mediterranee. *Address:* Solos Performances, 108 rue Gambetta, 94120 Fontenay-Sous-Bois, France.

MICHAEL, George; British singer, songwriter and producer; b. (Georgios Kyriacos Panayiotou), 25 June 1963, Finchley, London; s. of Kyriacus Panayiotou and the late Lesley Panayiotou. *Education:* Bushey Meads School. *Career:* debut in group The Executive 1979; formed (with Andrew Ridgeley) Wham! 1981–86, numerous consecutive hits; toured UK, France, USA, China, etc.; launched solo career 1986–; chose to release all further music free online 2004–. *Recordings include:* albums: with Wham!: Fantastic 1983, Make It Big 1984, Music From The Edge of Heaven 1986, The Final 1986; solo: Faith (Grammy Award for Best Album 1989, American Music Awards for Favorite Album 1989) 1987, Listen Without Prejudice: Vol. 1 (BRIT Award for Best British Album 1991) 1990, Older 1996, Older and Upper 1998, Ladies and Gentlemen: The Best of George Michael 1998, Songs from the Last Century 1999, Patience 2004, Twenty Five 2006, Symphonica 2014. *Publication:* George Michael: Bare (autobiography with Tony Parsons) 1990. *Honours:* BRIT Awards for Best British Group 1985, Outstanding Contribution to British Music 1986, Best British Male Artist 1988, Best British Male Solo Artist 1997, Ivor Novello Awards for Songwriter 1985, 1989, Grammy Award (for I Knew You Were Waiting For Me, duet with Aretha Franklin) 1988, British Rock Industry Award for Best Male Artist 1988, Nordoff-Robbins Silver Clef Award 1989, American Music Awards for Favorite Pop/Rock Male Artist, Soul R&B Male Artist 1989, ASCAP Golden Note Award 1992. *Current Management:* c/o Connie Filippello Publicity, 49 Portland Road, London, W11 4LJ, England. *Telephone:* (20) 7229-5400. *Fax:* (20) 7229-4804. *E-mail:* Cfpublicity@aol.com. *Website:* www.georgemichael.com.

MICHAEL, Richard Ewen, DipMusEd; British jazz educator, musician (piano) and composer; *Honorary Professor of Jazz Piano, St Andrews University;* b. 24 July 1949, Stonehaven, Scotland; s. of John Michael and Betty Michael; m. Morag Michael 1972; one s. two d. *Education:* Mackie Acad., Royal Scottish Acad. of Music and Drama. *Career:* Founder Fife Youth Jazz Orchestra 1976, currently Man. Dir; est. jazz educ. in Fife and Scotland; gives

seminars throughout UK, Europe and in New York; one of architects of Associated Bd of Jazz Piano syllabus; teacher, then Head of Music, Beath High School, Cowdenbeath 1974–2007; mem. Mentoring Panel, Associated Bd of the Royal Schools of Music; Yamaha Educ. Expert. *Radio:* regular 'Jargon Buster' on Radio Scotland's The Jazz House. *Compositions:* Homecoming; The Shetland Suite, Young Persons Guide to the Jazz Orchestra, Jazz Suite for Vibes and Piano, Listen Up – A Young Person's Guide to the Instruments of the Orchestra, Big Band Band, Folk Group and Rock Band based on Jeremiah Clarke's well known Trumpet Tune, Beginning The Blues. *Recordings:* Homecoming, Shetland Suite, Dedication, The Deil's Awa' Wi' The Jazzman, The History of Jazz Piano, Anything but a Silent Night!, The Brothers. *Television:* appeared in episode two of Scotland's Music With Phil Cunningham (BBC) and as jazz organist in Songs of Praise. *Publications:* Creative Jazz Education 1987, Small Band Jazz for the Classroom 1996, Jazz Beginnings 1996, Jazz Suite for Vibes and Piano; various Associated Board jazz pieces and online jazz piano lessons. *Honours:* Hon. Prof. of Jazz Piano, St Andrews Univ. 2010–; BEM for services to music education 2012; Music Teacher of the Year 1984, Jr Band Winner, BBC Big Band Competition, as Director of Fife Youth Jazz Orchestra 1994, Jazz Educator of the Year, Parliamentary Jazz Awards 2009, Glasgow Herald Angel Award for Outstanding Festival Fringe Performance 2010. *Address:* 6 Dronachy Road, Kirkcaldy, Fife, KY2 5QL, Scotland. *Telephone:* (1592) 263087; 7759-98836 (mobile). *E-mail:* richardmichael@icloud.com. *Website:* www.richardmichaelsjazzschool.com.

MICHAELIS, Pasquale, (Pasquale Michaux); Belgian musician (saxophones, clarinet, keyboards, Hammond piano, electric bass), composer, arranger and singer; b. 22 Oct. 1958, Auvelais. *Career:* appearances with Deborah Brow Quartet, Art Farmer, Johnny Griffin Quartet, Kim Parker, Clark Terry Quartet, Toots, Matia Bazar, Drummin Man (P. York), Adriano Celentano, D. Geers, Bruce Adams/P. Michaux Quintet, Hammond Swing Machine, J. Halliday/T. Jones/T. Browne's Funk Machine; mem. SABAM, SIAE. *Compositions include:* My Angel's Eyes, I'll Remember You, Benny, Organology, Mild and Bourbon for Eddie Please. *Recordings include:* Atmosphere, Remember Adolf Sax, Bob Lacemant Trio. *Honours:* Best Young Saxophonist, Belgium 1979, Best Keyboards, Italy 1985.

MICHAELS, Bret; American singer; b. 15 March 1963, Pittsburgh, PA. *Career:* mem. of rock groups, The Spectres, Paris; lead singer of rock group, Poison 1984–; numerous live appearances, festivals; solo tour performing acoustic version of Poison material 1991. *Recordings include:* albums: with Poison: Look What The Cat Dragged In 1986, Open Up and Say... Aah 1988, Flesh and Blood 1990, Swallow This Live 1991, Native Tongue 1993, Letter from Death Row 1998, Crack A Smile...And More 2000, Power To The People 2000, Mamma's Fallen Angel 2000, Hollyweird 2002, The Rhapsody Interview 2006, Poison'd 2007; solo: Songs of Life 2003, Freedom of Sound 2005, Custom Built 2010. *Honours:* NARM Award for Bestselling Heavy Metal Album (for Flesh and Blood) 1991. *Address:* B*M*B/Poor Boy Records Inc., 23679 Calabasas Road, Calabasas, CA 91302-1502, USA (office). *Website:* www .bretmichaels.com; www.poisonweb.com.

MICHAELSON, Ingrid Ellen; American singer and songwriter; b. 8 Dec. 1979, Staten Island. *Education:* Staten Island Tech. High School, Binghamton Univ. *Career:* solo singer 2002–. *Recordings include:* albums: Slow the Rain 2005, Girls and Boys 2007, Be OK 2008, Everybody 2009. *Current Management:* c/o Lynn Grossman, Secret Road Artist Management, PO Box 461373, Los Angeles, CA 90046, USA. *E-mail:* lynn@secretroad.com. *Website:* www .secretroad.com. *E-mail:* info@ingridmichaelson.com (office). *Website:* www .ingridmichaelson.com.

MICHAUX, Pasquale (see Pasquale Michaelis)

MICHEL, Prazakiel (Pras); American rap artist and actor; b. 19 Oct. 1972, New Jersey. *Career:* founder mem., Tranzlator Crew, renamed The Fugees 1987–; numerous television and live appearances; solo artist 1998–. *Films:* Mystery Men (actor) 1999, Turn It Up (actor, prod.) 2000, Higher Ed (actor, exec. prod.) 2001, Go for Broke (actor, prod.) 2002, Nora's Hair Salon (actor) 2004, Careful What You Wish For (actor) 2004, First Night (prod.) 2006, Feel the Noise 2007, Skid Row (prod.) 2007, The Mutant Chronicles (actor) 2008. *Recordings include:* albums: with The Fugees: Blunted on Reality 1994, The Score 1996; solo: Ghetto Supastar 1998, Win Lose or Draw 2005. *Honours:* BRIT Award for Best Int. Group 1997.

MICHELE, Chrisette; American singer; b. (Chrisette Michele Payne), 1982, Long Island, NY. *Education:* Five Townes Coll., Long Island. *Career:* solo R&B artist. *Recordings:* albums: I Am 2007, Epiphany 2009. *Honours:* Grammy Award for Best Urban/Alternative Performance (for Be OK) 2009. *Address:* c/o Def Jam Recordings, 825 Eighth Avenue, New York, NY 10019, USA (office). *Website:* www.defjam.com (office); www.thisischrisettemichele.com.

MICHELUTTI, Andrea; Italian musician (drums); b. 20 Sept. 1962, Udine; m. Amerita Moretti 1992. *Education:* Bologna Univ., Italy, Conservatory of Music, Chatou, France. *Career:* worked with Art Farmer, Steve Grossman, Jerry Bergonzi, Ben Sidran, Harry Sweets Edison, Hal Crook, Jimmy Owens, Roger Guerin, Michelle Hendricks, Alain Jean-Marie, Paul Bollenback, Benny Golson, Jeffery Smith, Ricky Ford; appearances at numerous jazz festivals, concerts in Italy, France, Switzerland, Austria, Germany, Yugoslavia. *Recordings:* Orsa Minore, La Malaguti Quintet; Tip Of The Hat, La Malaguti Quintet, Sextet; L'Art d'Aimer, with Giovanni Licata Quintet; Les Petits Loups Du Jazz, with Michelle Hendricks and Sylvain Beuf.

MICHIELS, Paul; Belgian singer, musician (guitar, keyboards) and composer; b. 15 June 1948. *Career:* mem. Soulsister; mem. SABAM. *Recordings include:* Soulsister: It Takes Two, Heat, Simple Rule, Live Savings, Swinging Like Big Dogs, Paul Michiels: The Inner Child, Forever Young. *Honours:* Golden Eye Award 1992, 1993, World Music Award, Monaco 1990. *Address:* T.T.T. Artists, Kromstraat 60, 2520 Ranst, Belgium (home). *Telephone:* (3) 355-33-33 (office). *Fax:* (3) 353-75-20 (office). *E-mail:* info@tttartists.be (office). *Website:* www.paulmichiels.be (home).

MIDDLETON, Darren; Australian musician (guitar, keyboards); b. 4 Oct. 1972; one d. *Career:* mem. Brisbane-based rock group, Powderfinger 1992–; many Australian tours/festival appearances, also world-wide tours; vocalist/guitarist in side-project, Drag. *Recordings include:* albums: Parables For Wooden Ears 1994, Double Allergic 1996, Internationalist 1998, Odyssey Number Five 2000, Vulture Street 2003, Dream Days at the Hotel Existence 2007. *Honours:* ARIA Award for Album of the Year, Song of the Year, Best Rock Album, Best Cover Artwork 1999. *Current Management:* Secret Service Artist Management, PO Box 401, Fortitude Valley, 4006 QLD, Australia. *Telephone:* (7) 3854-1488. *Fax:* (7) 3854-0655. *E-mail:* general@secret-service .com.au. *Website:* www.secret-service.com.au; www.powderfinger.com.

MIDDLETON, Tom, (Cosmos, The Mod Wheel); British producer, remixer and DJ; b. 1971, Devon. *Education:* classically-trained cellist and pianist. *Career:* co-founder Evolution/Universal Language Records (with production partner Mark Pritchard); presenter of weekly Deep Step Breakbeat Show on London radio station Kiss 100 FM; mem. Global Communication, Link, Jedi Knights, The Bays; collaborations with Mark Pritchard, Jamie Odell, Goldfrapp, Lamb, Depeche Mode, Ian Pooley, Pulp. *Recordings:* album with Global Communication: 76–14 1994; album with Jedi Knights: New School Science 1996; solo album: Lifetracks 2007. *Website:* www.tommiddleton.com.

MIDDLETON, Tracey K., BA; British musician (accordion); b. 20 Sept. 1966, Solihull, West Midlands, England. *Education:* Christ Church Coll., Canterbury, Guildhall School of Music with John Leslie, Royal School of Music, piano, clarinet, theory with Dr Kevin Thompson. *Career:* formed accordion duo Amaryllis, with David Garwood 1986; prov. theatre work 1986–95; Cheltenham Int. Music Festival, with Amaryllis 1991; Chair. Club Accord, Midlands UK accordion club 1992–2003, 2005–09; regular performer with Amaryllis at accordion festivals such as Autumn Int. Accordion Festival 1990–93, 1996–99, 2003–05, 2007; various folk festivals in England with Amaryllis 1995–; appearances at numerous folk clubs with Amaryllis, Folk dance weekly and weekend festivals; numerous concerts at accordion clubs in England with Amaryllis; workshops and lectures on the accordion and English and American folk dance music; mem. Musicians' Union, English Folk Dance and Song Soc., Nat. Accordion Org. *Recordings:* as Amaryllis: Here, There and Everywhere, Dance and Sing 1 & 2, Mendhams Maytime, Amaryllis in Concert. *Publications:* articles on English folk music in Accordion Times and articles in Accordion World. *Address:* 16 Norgrave Road, Solihull, West Midlands, B92 9JH, England.

MIDLER, Bette; American singer, entertainer and actress; b. 1 Dec. 1945, Honolulu, Hawaii; m. Martin von Haselberg 1984; one d. *Education:* Univ. of Hawaii. *Career:* début as actress in film Hawaii 1965; mem. of cast in Fiddler on the Roof, New York 1966–69; Salvation, New York 1970, Tommy, Seattle Opera Co. 1971; night-club concert performer 1972–. *Film appearances include:* The Rose (two Golden Globe Awards) 1979, Jinxed 1982, Down and Out in Beverly Hills 1986, Ruthless People 1986, Outrageous Fortune 1987, Big Business 1988, Beaches 1989, Stella 1990, For The Boys (Golden Globe Award) 1991, Hocus Pocus 1993, Gypsy (TV), The First Wives Club 1996, That Old Feeling 1997, Get Bruce 1999, Isn't She Great? 1999, Drowning Mona 2000, What Women Want 2001, Stepford Wives 2004, Then She Found Me 2007, The Women 2008, Parental Guidance 2012. *Stage:* I'll Eat You Last: A Chat with Sue Mengers 2013. *Recordings include:* The Divine Miss M. 1973, Bette Midler 1973, Broken Blossom 1977, Live at Last 1977, Thighs and Whispers 1979, New Depression 1979, Divine Madness 1980, No Frills 1984, Some People's Lives 1991, Best Of 1993, Bette of Roses 1995, Experience the Divine 1997, Bathhouse Betty 1998, From a Distance 1998, Bette 2000, Bette Midler Sings the Rosemary Clooney Songbook 2003, Bette Midler Sings the Peggy Lee Songbook 2005, Cool Yule 2006, Memories of You 2010, It's the Girls! 2014. *Television includes:* The Tonight Show (Emmy Award) 1992, Gypsy 1993, Seinfeld 1996, Diva Las Vegas 1997, Murphy Brown 1998. *Publications include:* A View From A Broad 1980, The Saga of Baby Divine 1983. *Honours:* After Dark Ruby Award 1973, Grammy Awards for Best New Artist 1973, for Best Female Pop Vocal Performance 1981, for Record of the Year 1990, Special Tony Award 1973, Emmy Award 1978, Songwriters Hall of Fame Sammy Cahn Lifetime Achievement Award 2012. *Current Management:* c/o Creative Artists Agency, 2000 Avenue of the Stars, Los Angeles, CA 90067, USA. *Website:* www.bettemidler.com.

MIDORIN; Japanese musician (drums). *Career:* mem. jazz band, Soil & "Pimp" Sessions 2001–. *Recordings include:* albums: Pimpin' (EP) 2004, Pimp Master 2005, Summer Goddess (EP) 2005, Pimp of the Year 2006. *Address:* c/o Victor Entertainment Inc., Palacion Tower, 3-6-7 Kita-Aoyama, Minato-ku, Tokyo 107-0061, Japan (office). *E-mail:* soil@jvcmusic.co.jp. *Website:* www .soilpimp.com.

MIGLIORE, Cristiano; Italian musician (guitar); b. 20 May 1971, Milan. *Career:* mem. metal band, Lacuna Coil 1998–. *Recordings include:* albums: In a Reverie 1999, Unleashed Memories 2001, Comalies 2002, Karmacode 2006,

Shallow Life 2009. *Current Management:* Riot Rock Management, 639 Dupont Street, Unit 216, Toronto, ON M6G 1Z4, Canada. *E-mail:* info@riotrock.com. *Website:* www.riotrock.com; www.lacunacoil.it.

MIGUEL; American singer, songwriter, musician and record producer; b. (Miguel Jontel Pimentel), 23 Oct. 1985, San Pedro, Los Angeles, Calif. *Career:* signed to Jive Records 2007; supported Usher, Trey Songz on tour; numerous recording collaborations including Usher, Asher Roth, Musiq Soulchild, Mariah Carey. *Recordings:* albums: All I Want is You 2010, Kaleidoscope Dream 2012, Wildheart 2015. *Honours:* BET Awards for Best Collaboration (for Lotus Flower Bomb) 2012, for Best Male R&B Artist 2013, Soul Train Music Award for Best R&B/Soul Male Artist 2012, Grammy Award for Best R&B Song (for Adorn) 2013. *Current Management:* c/o Career Artist Management, 9350 North Civic Center Drive, Beverly Hills, CA 90210, USA. *Telephone:* (310) 776-7640 (office). *Fax:* (424) 230-7839 (office). *E-mail:* elena@camanagement.com (office). *Website:* www.camanagement.com (office); www.officialmiguel.com.

MIGUEL, Luis; Mexican singer; b. 19 April 1970, Puerto Rico. *Career:* won Grammy Award aged 15 for 'Me gustas tal como eres' (duet with Sheena Easton) 1985; duet with Frank Sinatra on recording of 'Come Fly With Me' for Sinatra's Duets Vol. 2 album 1994; tours internationally. *Recordings include:* albums: Soy Como Quiero Ser 1986, Un Hombre Busca Una Mujer 1988, 20 Años 1990, Romance 1991, Aries 1993, Segunda Romance 1994, El Concierto 1995, Amarte Es Un Placer 1999, México en la Piel (Billboard Latin Music Award for Best Regional Mexican Album by a Male Solo Artist 2005, Grammy Award for Best Mexican/Mexican-American Album 2006) 2004, Grandes Éxitos 2005, Navidades Luis Mighel 2006, Cómplices 2008, No Culpes a La Noche 2009, Luis Miguel 2010. *Honours:* various Grammy awards, European Excellence Award, Spain 1990, World Music Award for Best Selling Artist, MTV Award for Best Int. Video 1992, Recording Industry Artists of America Award 1994, Estela de Plata Award 2006. *Address:* c/o Warner Music Spain, Lopez de Hoyos 42, 28006 Madrid, Spain. *E-mail:* info.esp@warnermusic.com. *Website:* www.luismigueloficial.com.

MIKA; Lebanese/British singer, songwriter and musician (piano); b. (Michael Penniman Jr), 18 Aug. 1983, Beirut, Lebanon. *Career:* fled Beirut to Paris with family aged one, settled in London 1994; performed at Royal Opera House, and made a living from advertising jingles; solo artist 2006–; tours and festivals. *Recording:* Live in Cartoon Motion 2007, The Boy Who Knew Too Much 2009, The Origin of Love 2012, No Place in Motion 2015. *Honours:* Chevalier, ordre des Arts et des Lettres 2010; World Music Awards for Best-Selling New Artist, Best-Selling Male Entertainer, Best-Selling Pop/Rock Artist and Best-Selling British Artist 2007, BRIT Award for Best British Breakthrough Act 2008. *Current Management:* c/o Machine Management, Studio 16, London Fields Studios, 11–17 Exmouth Place, London, E8 3RW, England. *Telephone:* (20) 7923-3502. *E-mail:* info@machinemanagement.co.uk. *Website:* www .machinemanagement.co.uk; www.mikasounds.com.

MIKKELBORG, Palle; Danish musician (trumpet), composer, conductor and teacher; b. 6 March 1941, Copenhagen; m. Helen M. Davies 1989. *Career:* Leader Danish Radiojazz Group and Big Band 1964–76, Riel/Mikkelborg Quintet 1965–70, V8 1970–75, Entrance 1975–88, Heart to Heart Trio 1985–88, Palle Mikkelborg Trio 1989–; worldwide festival, radio and TV appearances as soloist and composer/conductor; Hans Christian Andersen Amb. 2005; Adjunct Prof., Det Jyske Musikkonservatorium 2012–; mem. Royal Swedish Music Acad. 2009. *Compositions:* Maya's Veil 1972, Te Faru 1979, Pictures 1983, So Many Come, So Many Go 1983, Aura, dedicated to Miles Davis 1984–85, Everything Has a Purpose 1988, Soundscape 1995, The Noone of Night 1997, A Moon of Light 1998, Ask The Wind 2000, Going To Pieces Without Falling Apart 2003, Red Dress Concert 2004, The Little Prince 2004, The Fjord Sings 2005, All Life is Your Life 2007, The Return of the Sea Stallion of Glendalough 2008, Better City – Better Life (EXPO 2010), 360 Degrees 2010, Beyond... 2010. *Recordings:* The Mysterious Corona 1967, Tempus Incertum Remanet 1970, Heart To Heart, Hommage, Aura, Anything But Grey, The Garden Is A Woman, Tread Lightly, Noone Of Night, The Voice Of Silence, To Whom It Concerns, Even Closer, Going to Pieces without Falling Apart (rev.) 2013. *Honours:* Kt, Order of Dannebrog 1996; First Prize, Montreaux 1968, Jazz Musician of the Year 1968, Lange-Müller Prize 1976, two Grammy Awards, USA 1990, Grammy Award, Denmark 1993, Wilhelm Hansen Composers Prize 1997, Carl Nielsen and Anne Marie Carl Nielsen Prize of Honour 1999, Nordic Council Music Prize 2001, D'Jango D'Or Legend of Jazz Prize 2003, Hon. Prize, IFPÍ 2006, Gentofte Council Culture Prize 2007, Poul and Sylvia Schierbeck Scholarship 2009, Velux Foundation Hon. Prize 2010, Copenhagen Jazz Festival Hon. Award 2012, Ben Webster Prize of Honour 2012. *Address:* Ellegaardsvaenge 5B, 2820 Gentofte, Copenhagen, Denmark (office). *Telephone:* 39-65-17-75 (office). *E-mail:* mikda@mail.dk (office). *Website:* www.mikkelborg.dk.

MILANÉS, Pablo; Cuban singer, musician (guitar) and songwriter; b. 1943, Bayamo. *Education:* Amadeo Roldán Conservatory, Havana. *Career:* joined vocal group, El Cuarteto del Rey aged 16; formed Los Bucaneros 1960s; embarked on solo career; prominent figure in Nueva Trova (popular song) movement late 1960s; songs recorded by many major Cuban artists, including Omara Portuonda. *Recordings include:* Versos de José Marti 1973, Canta A Nicolás Guillén 1975, Pablo Milanes 1976, No Me Pidas 1977, Aniversario 1979, Lilia Vera Y Pablo Milanes 1981, El Guerrero 1983, Querido Pablo 1985, Buenas Días América, Años Vol. 2 1986, Comienzo Y Final De Una Verde

Mañana 1987, Proposiciones 1988, Años Vol. 3 1992, Orígenes 1994, Plegaria 1995, Despertar 1997, Los Días de Gloria 2000, Pablo Querido 2002, Como Un Campo de Maíz 2005, Pueblo Unido 2006, Mas Alla de Todo 2008, Regalo 2008. *Address:* c/o Universal Music Mexico, Hegel No. 721, Col. Bosque de Chapultepec, CP 11580, México DF, Mexico (office). *E-mail:* contacto@ universal.com.mx (office). *Website:* www.universal.com.mx (office).

MILBERG, Lisa; Swedish musician (drums). *Career:* mem., The Concretes 1999–; band founded label, Licking Fingers. *Recordings include:* albums: Boyoubetterunow 2000, The Concretes 2003, Layourbattleaxedown 2005, In Colour 2006, Hey Trouble 2007. *Current Management:* EC1 Music Agency, 1 Cowcross Street, London, EC1M 6DR, England. *Telephone:* (20) 7490-8990. *Fax:* (20) 7490-8987. *E-mail:* jack@ec1music.com. *E-mail:* theconcretes@ theconcretes.com. *Website:* www.theconcretes.com.

MILENA; Bulgarian singer, musician (guitar), songwriter and lyricist; b. (Milena Slavova), 1966, Sofia; m. Robert Page-Roberts. *Career:* mem., Review 1986–90; formed own band 1991–; numerous tours and concerts in Bulgaria and Eastern Europe; writes, plays and sings own compositions with backing band. *Recordings include:* albums: with Review: Review 1989; solo: Ha-ha 1991, The Scandal 1993, Sold 1995. *Honours:* seven times voted First Lady of Bulgarian Rock, Bulgarian Nat. Award (Unison) for Best Female Voice 1994, for Best Album (for The Scandal).

MILIAN, Christina; American singer and actress; b. 26 Sept. 1981, New Jersey. *Career:* child actress; began writing songs; guest vocalist for Ja Rule; wrote songs for Jennifer Lopez, PYT. *Films include:* Love Don't Cost a Thing 2003, Be Cool 2005, Pulse 2006, Bring it On: Fight to the Finish 2009. *Recordings include:* albums: Christina Milian 2001, It's About Time 2004, So Amazin' 2006. *Address:* c/o Island Def Jam Music Group, 2220 Colorado Avenue, Santa Monica, CA 90404, USA (office). *Website:* www.christinamilian .com.

MILIČEVIĆ, Tomislav (Tomo); Bosnian-American musician (guitar, keyboards, violin, bass guitar); b. 3 Sept. 1979, Sarajevo, Bosnia; s. of Tonka Miličević and Damir Miličević; m. Vicki Bosanko 2011. *Education:* Athens High School, Troy, Mich. *Career:* mem. 30 Seconds to Mars 2003–. *Recordings:* albums: with 30 Seconds to Mars: A Beautiful Lie (MTV Asia Video Star Award 2008) 2005, This is War 2009. *Honours:* MTV2 Award at MTV Video Music Awards 2006, MTV Australia Video Music Awards for Best Rock Video and Video of the Year 2007, Kerrang! Awards for Best International Newcomer 2007, for Best Single 2007, 2008, 2011, for Best International Band 2008, 2010, 2011, TRL Award for Best New Artist 2007, Bandit Rock Award for Best International Breakthrough 2008, Los Premios MTV Award for Best International Rock Artist 2008, MTV Europe Music Rock Out Award 2008, MTV Europe Music Video Star Award 2008, MTV Video Music Award for Best Rock Video 2010, 2013, MTV Europe Music Awards for Best Rock Act 2010, for Best Alternative Act 2013. *Address:* Virgin Records America Inc., 304 Park Avenue South, 5th Floor, New York, NY 10010-4316, USA. *Website:* thirtysecondstomars.thisisthehive.net/EMAs.

MILLAR, John Jhalib; British musician (tabla, world percussion); b. 1 July 1951, Belfast, Northern Ireland; one s. one d. *Education:* Studied at Tabla Alla Rakha Institute of Music, Mumbai, 1979–. *Career:* First studied tabla, London, 1972; Played with Steve Hillage Band, 1976; Member, Nic Turner's (Hawkwind) Sphynx; Member, Monsoon, 1982–83; Interviewed on Danish radio Copenhagen, 1980; Several compositions, contemporary percussion for major UK modern dance companies; Various sessions for television, dance scores include Chakrada, 1981; Composed with Barrington Pheloung, formed Akasa, 1988; released two singles, two promo videos, one album 1990; Guest appearance with Massive Attack, Roxy Club Bologna, Italy, 1995; Joined John Mayers Inov-Jazz Fusions, 1997; mem, Musicians' Union; PRS; Mechanical Copyright Protection Society (MCPS). *Compositions:* Sitar In The Skye, BBC1 TV series Hamish Macbeth, 1996. *Recordings:* Ever So Lonely, Monsoon, (No. 12, UK charts), 1982; with Akasa: Kama Sutra, 1989; One Night In My Life, 1990; London Contemporary Dance Theatre, Under The Same Sun, 1983; Union Dance Company, Visions of Rhythm, 1985; Sangeet Sagar (Ocean of Music), CD, 1997. *Honours:* Associate mem., PRS. *Address:* 65 Bayham St, Camden Town, London NW1 0AA, England.

MILLAR, Robin, CBE, MA; British record producer; b. 18 Dec. 1951, London, England; one s. one d. *Education:* Univ. of Cambridge. *Career:* mem. Re-Pro; prod., arranger working for artists, including The Bhundu Boys, Big Country, Black, Bluebells, Sam Brown, Kate Bush, The Christians, Elvis Costello, Randy Crawford, Wazis Djop, Everything But The Girl, Fine Young Cannibals, Peter Gabriel, Herbie Hancock, Gil Scott Heron, Lavine Hudson, Patricia Kaas, The Kane Gang, Gary Kemp, Ute Lemper, Malcolm McLaren, Owen Paul, Courtney Pine, Maxi Priest, Chris Rea, Juliet Roberts, Tom Robinson, Sade, Wayne Shorter, Jimmy Somerville, The Special AKA, Sting, The Style Council, Tolu, Working Week; retd from production work 2009. *Honours:* Hon. Patron, Music Producers Guild; Hon. Prof. (Thames Valley Univ.) 2007; Brit Award, three ASCAP Awards, four American Black Music Awards, two Victoires de la Musique Awards, Windrush Award 2000. *Website:* www .robinmillar.org.uk.

MILLER, Andy; British musician (guitar); b. 18 Dec. 1968, London, England. *Career:* Joined Dodgy; Debut, Dodgy Club; Frequent live shows; Formed own record label, Bostin, 1991; Signed to A & M Records, 1992. *Recordings:* Singles: Staying Out For The Summer, 1994; So Let Me Go Far, 1995; Making

The Most Of, 1995; In A Room, 1996; If You're Thinking Of Me, 1996; Good Enough, 1996; Found You, 1997; If You're Thinking of Me, 1998; Every Single Day, 1998; Albums: The Dodgy Album, 1993; Homegrown, 1994; Free Peace Sweet, 1996; Ace A's and Killer B's, 1998; Real Estate, 2001. *Website:* www .dodgy.co.uk.

MILLER, Daniel; British record company executive and producer; *Founder and Executive Chairman, Mute Records;* b. 14 Feb. 1951, London. *Career:* solo music projects as The Normal, Silicon Teens; f. Mute Records, originally to release his own music, first release T.V.O.D./Warm Leatherette by The Normal 1978; label has reputation for signing and developing electronic and experimental pop and rock artists, acts signed include Fad Gadget, Einstürzende Neubauten, Throbbing Gristle, DAF, Cabaret Voltaire, Depeche Mode, Nitzer Ebb, Yazoo, Erasure, Moby, Goldfrapp, Nick Cave, Laibach; launched Novamute Records offshoot 1992; label sold to EMI Records 2002, currently Exec. Chair. *Honours:* Strat Award, Music Week magazine 2006. *Address:* Mute Records Ltd, 1 Albion Place , London, W6 0QT, England (office). *Telephone:* (20) 8964-2001 (office). *Fax:* (20) 8968-4977 (office). *E-mail:* info@mute.co.uk (office). *Website:* www.mute.com (office).

MILLER, David; American singer (tenor); b. 14 April 1973, San Diego, Calif. *Education:* Oberlin Conservatory, Ohio. *Career:* performed in various operas, including Baz Luhrmann's version of La Bohème; mem., Il Divo 2003–. *Recordings include:* albums: Il Divo 2004, Ancora 2005, The Christmas Collection 2005, Siempre 2006, The Promise 2008, Wicked Game 2011. *Website:* www.ildivo.com.

MILLER, Gary Alan; British singer, songwriter and musician (guitar and mandolin); b. 24 Sept. 1966, Durham; s. of Allan Miller and Mildred Cairns; m. Jane Miller 1994 (separated 2003; one s. *Education:* Durham Gilesgate Comprehensive School and Sixth Form Centre. *Career:* founded folk-rock group The Whisky Priests with twin brother Glenn, 1985–; co-founded Mad Dogs and Englishmen, 2000–; over 1,000 live club and festival performances throughout Europe; Numerous radio and TV appearances including The Tube (Channel 4), TV Española (Spain), Good Morning Croatia; 21 official releases on own label Whippet Records, formed with brother; solo work since 2002 includes recordings, tours, various theatre productions as musical dir, numerous community songwriting and music industry projects; mem, PRS; MCPS; PPL; PAMRA; Musicians' Union. *Compositions:* Alice in Wonderland; A Better Man Than You; My Ship; Song for Ewan; Side by Side; Full Circle; The Man Who Sold His Town; Success Express; When the Wind Blows, Billy Boy; Ranting Lads; The Man Who Would Be King; He's Still My Son; This Village; Forever in our Hearts; Workhorse; Halcyon Days; The Durham Light Infantry; The Hard Men; Car Boot Sale; William's Tale; Legacy of the Lionheart; Shot at Dawn; Perfect Time; The Raven; Old Man Forgotten. *Recordings:* Albums: with The Whisky Priests: Nee Gud Luck, 1989; The First Few Drops, 1991; Timeless Street, 1992; Bloody Well Live!, 1993; The Power and the Glory, 1994; Bleeding Sketches, 1995; Life's Tapestry, 1996; Think Positive!, 1998; Here Come the Ranting Lads—Live!, 1999; Story Of My Life: Pye Anthology, 2002; with Mad Dogs And Englishmen: Going Down With Alice, 2000; Video: Here Come the Ranting Lads – Live!, 1999, Gary Miller and Ralf Weihrauch: Stand Fast, Stand Steady 2005. *Theatre:* Mad Martins 2002, Radical Jack 2003. *Publications:* Our Village: Memories of the Durham Mining Communities 2000, Songs of the Durham Coalfields 2003. *Address:* 5 Springfield Close, Stockton Lane, York, YO31 1LD, England (home). *Telephone:* (1904) 425692 (home). *E-mail:* wp@whiskypriests.co.uk (office); garymillersongs@ntlworld.com (home). *Website:* www.whiskypriests.co.uk (office); www.garymillersongs.co.uk (home).

MILLER, Glenn Thomas; British musician (accordion); b. 24 Sept. 1966, Durham, England; m. Stephanie, one s. *Career:* Accordion player and songwriter with The Whisky Priests, 1985–; Over 1,000 live club and festival appearances throughout Europe; 20 official recordings released; Radio shows throughout Europe and TV appearances including Channel 4's The Tube, and shows in Spain and Germany; mem, MCPS; PRS; PPL; PAMRA; Musicians' Union. *Compositions:* Positive Steps; Death of the Shipyards; The Ghost of Geordie Jones; Jenny Grey; Goblins; Farewell Jobling!; Lament for the Setting Sons; Success Road; Durham; Epitaph for a Working Class Couple. *Recordings:* Albums: Nee Gud Luck, 1989; The First Few Drops, 1991; Timeless Street, 1992; Bloody Well Live!, 1993; The Power and the Glory, 1994; Bleeding Sketches, 1995; Life's Tapestry, 1996; Think Positive!, 1998; Here Come the Ranting Lads! – Live!, 1999; Going Down With Alice, 2000. *Address:* 14 Springfield Close, Stockton Lane, York YO31 1LD, England.

MILLER, Mac; American rapper, singer, songwriter and record producer; b. (Malcolm James McCormick), 19 Jan. 1992, Pittsburgh, Pa; s. of Mark McCormick and Karen Meyers. *Education:* Taylor Allderdice High School. *Career:* fmr mem. The Ill Spoken 2008; solo career 2009–; signed to Rostrum Records. *Recordings include:* albums: Blue Slide Park 2011, Watching Movies with the Sound Off 2013; mixtapes: with The Ill Spoken: How High 2008; solo: The Jukebox: Prelude to Class Clown 2009, The High Life 2009, K.I.D.S. 2010, I Love Life, Thank You 2011, Macadelic 2012. *Address:* c/o Rostrum Records, PO Box 4228, Pittsburgh, PA 15203, USA (office). *E-mail:* info@ rostrumrecords.com (office). *Website:* www.rostrumrecords.com (office); www .macmillerofficial.com.

MILLER, Marcus; American jazz musician, bassist, composer and record producer; b. 14 June 1959, Brooklyn, NY. *Career:* recording artist, has recorded with Joshua Redman, Lalah Hathaway, Meshell Ndegeocello, Wayne

Shorter, Herbie Hancock, Frank Sinatra, Mariah Carey and countless other recording artists; has produced Miles Davis, Luther Vandross, Chaka Khan, Wayne Shorter, David Sanborn, Herbie Hancock, George Benson, Al Jarreau, Roberta Flack and others. *Recordings include:* albums: solo: Suddenly 1983, Marcus Miller 1984, The Sun Don't Lie 1993, Tales 1994, Live And More 1998, M2: Power And Grace (Grammy Award for Best Contemporary Jazz Album) 2001, The Ozell Tapes 2002, Silver Rain 2005, Music from Siesta (with Miles Davis) 2005, Free 2007, Marcus 2008, A Night in Monte Carlo 2010; collaborations: The Jamaica Boys 1987, J Boys 1989, Music from Siesta (with Miles Davis) 2005, SMV - Stanley Clarke - Marcus Miller - Victor Wooten - Thunder 2008, Tutu Revisited 2011, Renaissance 2012, Live in Lugano - July 2008 2012. *Films:* Siesta, House Party, Boomerang, Above the Rim, Head of State, Good Hair, This Christmas, I Think I Love My Wife, King's Ransom, Deliver Us from Eva, Serving Sara, Two Can Play That Game, Trumpet of the Swan, The Brothers, The Ladies Man, The Sixth Man, The Great White Hype, Low Down Dirty Shame, "Da Butt" (School Daze). *Television:* Everybody Hates Chris, Reed Between the Lines, An American Love Story (PBS). *Notable compositions:* Jump To It (Aretha Franklin), Da Butt (E.U. from Spike Lee's School Daze), Maputo (Bob James and David Sanborn), Chicago Song (David Sanborn), Power of Love/Love Power, Any Love (Luther Vandross). *Current Management:* c/o Bibi Green, Greenhouse Management, 700 Pennsylvania Avenue, Fort Washington, PA 19034, USA. *Telephone:* (215) 283-2865. *E-mail:* bibig007@me.com. *Address:* c/o Levy and Rowe LLP, 10350 Santa Monica Blvd, #130, Los Angeles, CA 90025, USA (office). *Website:* bibig007@me.co; www.marcusmiller.com.

MILLER, Mikel; Canadian singer, songwriter and musician (guitar); b. 13 Oct. 1949, Toronto, ON; one d. *Career:* live performances in clubs and festivals throughout Canada and the USA; mem. Canadian Country Music Asscn, Folk Alliance, Music Yukon. *Recordings include:* No More Trains 1989, Another Day In Paradise 1994, The Key 1996, Rounder's Road 1999, NXNE sampler 1999, Yukon sampler RAIYA 1999, A Norm Hacking Compilation 1999, Yukon sampler 2000, Yukon sampler 2001, All Roads 2002, One Voice (tribute to Norm Hacking) 2002, Yukon Sampler 2003, 2004, Mother's Day. *Address:* PO Box 31467, Whitehorse, YT Y1A 6K8, Canada (home). *E-mail:* mallmiller@polarcom.com (home). *Website:* www.mikelmiller.ca.

MILLER, Rozalla; British singer; b. (Rozalla Sandra Miller), 18 March 1964, Ndola, Zambia. *Career:* vocalist for Band of Gypsies 1988; support act for Michael Jackson, Alexander O'Neal; joined Frontline Records 2011; numerous UK/US TV appearances; mem. Musicians' Union. *Recordings include:* albums: Everybody's Free 1992, Look No Further 1995, Coming Home 1998, Brand New Version 2009. *Website:* www.rozallaofficial.com.

MILLER, Ruth; British songwriter, singer and musician (guitar); b. 8 May 1962, Newark, Nottinghamshire, England. *Career:* founder, Rutland Records 1988; mem., PO!, Ruth's Refrigerator; mem. PRS, MCPS, PPL, Musicians' Union. *Recordings include:* with PO!: Little Stones, 1989; Ducks and Drakes, 1993; Not Marked on the Ordinance Map, 1996; Past Present Tense, 1997; Horse Blanket Weather, 1998; with Ruth's Refrigerator: Suddenly A Disfigured Head Parachuted, 1990; A Lizard Is A Submarine On Grass, 1991.

MILLER, Steve; American singer, musician (guitar) and songwriter; b. 5 Oct. 1943, Milwaukee, WI. *Education:* Wisconsin Univ., Copenhagen Univ., Denmark, studied guitar with Les Paul. *Career:* mem., Marksmen Combo 1955, The Ardells (became Fabulous Night Train); worked with Muddy Waters, James Cotton, Howling Wolf, Butterfield Blues Band; mem., World War Three Band (became Goldberg-Miller Blues Band); founding mem. Steve Miller Band 1966–; regular international appearances, festivals; founder of record label, Sailor Records 1976, Space Cowboy Records; Artist-in-Residence, Thornton School of Music, Univ. of Southern California 2010–. *Recordings include:* albums: with Steve Miller Band: Children of The Future 1968, Sailor 1968, Brave New World 1969, Your Saving Grace 1969, Number Five 1970, Rock Love 1971, Recall The Beginning... A Journey From Eden 1972, Anthology 1972, Fly Like An Eagle 1977, Book of Dreams 1977, Abracadabra 1982, The Steve Miller Band Live! 1983, Italian X-Rays 1984, Living in the 20th Century 1986, Born 2 Be Blue 1988, Wide River 1993, Bingo! 2010. *Publication:* Smart Blonde: The Life of Dolly Parton 2006. *Website:* www.stevemillerband.com.

MILLER, Steven, BA; American producer, arranger and engineer; b. 8 Nov. 1956. *Education:* San Francisco State University. *Career:* Vice-President, Windham Hill Records; Founder, Hip Pocket Records, RCA Novus Records, Windham Hill Jazz records; produced and engineered for artists including Manhattan Transfer, Juliana Hatfield, Medeski Martin and Wood, Paula Cole, Michael Hedges, Will Ackerman, Michael Brecker, Pink; mem, NARAS. *Recordings:* albums include: December, George Winston; Vapor Drawings, Mark Isham; Suzanne Vega, Suzanne Vega; Talkin' Bout You, Diane Schuur; Temporary Road, John Gorka; Mortal City, Dar Williams. *Current Management:* BK Entertainment Group, 51300 Ventura Boulevard, Suite 307A, Sherman Oaks, CA 91403, USA. *Telephone:* (818) 728-8200. *Fax:* (818) 728-8213. *E-mail:* reception@bkentertainmentgroup.com. *Website:* www.bkentertainmentgroup.com.

MILLER, William (Bill) Scott; American musician (guitar, flute) and artist; b. 23 Jan. 1955, Neenah, Wis.; m. Renee Miller 1978; two s. one d. *Career:* Tori Amos tour; TV appearances: Good Morning America, Austin City Limits. *Recordings:* Native Sons 1983, Old Dreams and New Hopes 1987, The Art of Survival 1990, Loon Mountain Moon 1991, Reservation Road 1992, The Red Road 1993, Raven in the Snow 1995, Native Suite 1996, Ghostdance 1999, Healing Waters 1999, Hear Our Prayer 2000, Spirit Rain 2002, A Sacred Gift 2003, Cedar Dream Songs (Grammy Award for Best Native American Music Album 2005) 2004, Spirit Songs 2004, Spirit Wind North (Grammy Award for Best Native American Music Album 2010) 2009, Chronicles of Hope 2010, Spirit Wind East 2010. *Current Management:* Intero Alliance LLC, PO Box 680277, Franklin, TN 37068-0277, USA. *Telephone:* (651) 221-2600. *E-mail:* artists@interoconnect.com. *Website:* www.interoconnect.com; www.billmillerarts.com (home).

MILLS, Crispian; British singer and musician (guitar); b. 18 Jan. 1973, London, England. *Career:* founder mem. Objects of Desire; founder mem. The Kays, renamed Kula Shaker; numerous TV appearances and tours, festival appearances; solo artist 1999–; founder mem., The Jeevas 2002. *Recordings include:* albums: with Kula Shaker: K 1996, Peasants, Pigs and Astronauts 1999, Strangefolk 2007; with The Jeevas: 1-2-3-4! 2002. *Honours:* BRIT Award for Best British Newcomer 1997. *Website:* www.kulashakermusic.com; www.thejeevas.com.

MILLS, Jeff, (Millsart, Purpose Maker); American producer, remixer, DJ and artist; b. 1963, Detroit, MI. *Career:* started career on Detroit radio station, WJLB, using DJ pseudonym 'The Wizard', before collaborating with Mike Banks as part of Underground Resistance 1989–91; relocated to New York as resident DJ at the Limelight club; founded Axis Records in New York; collaborations with Mike Banks, Robert Hood; remixed Maurizio, Lionrock, DJ Rolando. *Composition:* composed new soundtrack for Fritz Lang's film, Metropolis 2001. *Recordings include:* albums: Sonic Destroyer (with X101) 1991, Waveform Transmission #1 1992, Waveform Transmission #3 1994, The Other Day 1996, From the 21st 1998, Lifelike 2000, Metropolis 2000, Every Dog Has Its Day 2001, At First Sight 2002, Blue Potential 2006, One Man Spaceship 2007, Sleeper Wakes 2009, The Occurrence 2010, The Power 2011, 2087 2011, Fantastic Voyage 2011, The Messenger 2012, The Jungle Planet 2013, Woman In The Moon 2014, When Time Splits (with Mikhail Rudy) 2015, Proxima Centauri 2015. *Address:* Axis Records, 180 N. Wabash Ave. #315, Chicago, IL 60601, USA. *E-mail:* info@axisrecords.com; mills@axisrecords.com. *Website:* www.axisrecords.com.

MILLS, Martin, BA, MBE; British music executive; b. 1949; m.; two c. *Education:* Magdalen Coll. School, Oriel Coll., Oxford. *Career:* founder of music label, Beggars Banquet (later Beggars Group) 1974–; mem. BPI Council 1987–2000, IMPALA (Chair. 2006–). *Address:* Beggars Banquet, 17–19 Alma Road, London, SW18 1AA, England (office). *E-mail:* beggars@beggars.com (office). *Website:* www.beggars.com (office).

MILLS, Mike; American musician (bass); b. 17 Dec. 1958, Orange, CA. *Career:* founder mem., R.E.M. 1980–2011; numerous int. tours and festival appearances; mem. side project, Hindu Love Gods 1986–90. *Recordings:* albums: with R.E.M.: Chronic Town 1982, Murmur 1983, Reckoning 1984, Fables Of The Reconstruction 1985, Life's Rich Pageant 1986, Dead Letter Office 1987, Document 1987, Eponymous 1988, Green 1988, Out Of Time (Billboard Award for Best World Album, Q Award for Best Album) 1991, Automatic For The People (Grammy Award for Best Alternative Music Album, Atlanta Music Award for Rock Album, Q Award for Best Album, Rolling Stone Critics Award for Best Album 1993) 1992, Monster 1994, New Adventures In Hi-Fi 1996, Up 1998, Star Profiles 1999, Reveal 2001, Bad Day Pt 1 and 2 2003, Glastonbury 1999 2003, Around The Sun 2004, Accelerate 2008, Collapse into Now 2011; with Hindu Love Gods: Hindu Love Gods 1990. *Honours:* numerous MTV Music Video Awards, Earth Day Award 1990, Billboard Award for Best Modern Rock Artist 1991, BRIT Awards for Best Int. Group 1992, 1993, 1995, Grammy Awards for Best Pop Performance, Best Music Video 1992, Atlanta Music Awards for Act of the Year, Video of the Year 1992, IRMA Award for Int. Band of the Year 1993, Rolling Stone Critics Award for Best Band 1993. *Current Management:* REM/Athens Ltd, 250 W Clayton Street, Athens, GA 30601, USA. *Website:* www.remhq.com.

MILLS, Sam; musician (guitar, programmer), composer and producer; b. (Samuel Peter Landrell-Mills), 15 June 1963, London, England. *Career:* mem., 23 Skidoo; Tama (with Tom Diakite and Djanuno Dabo); collaborations: Russell Mills; Paban Das Baul; Susheela Raman. *Recordings:* Singles: with 23 Skidoo: Ethics, 1979; Last Words, 1981; Tearing Up The Plans, 1982; Albums: Seven Songs (with 23 Skidoo), 1982; Real Sugar (with Paban Das Baul), 1997; Nostalgie (with Tama), 1999; Pearl and Umbra (Russell Mills and Undark), 2000; Salt Rain (Susheela Raman), 2001.

MILLS, Vincent Delano; British musician (guitar, electric bass guitar) and composer; b. 19 April 1960, Birmingham. *Career:* performed with bands based in Birmingham and the Midlands from, late 1970s to 1990s, soul, funk, R&B, Jazz Big Bands, The Blue Pearls and numerous session gigs for Jazz combos; international tours of USA with chart topping reggae artist Pato Banton's backing band the Reggae Revolution 1992, East Coast tour, Florida and Georgia 1992, West Coast tour, with performances at The Bob Marley Day Reggae Festival, concerts in California, Washington, Arizona, Canada, Hawaii and opening for Santana in Tijuana, Mexico; performed with top Caribbean calypso/soca bands Nu-Vybes in St Kitts 1995 and Small Axe, St Kitts Music Festival 1999; performed at Birmingham, Ludlow and Keswick Jazz Festivals, Black Music Festival, London; mem, Musicians' Union. *Recordings:* Pan In Flight, Barcelona, Jamma.

MILMAN, Sophie; Russian/Canadian singer. *Education:* Univ. of Toronto, Canada. *Career:* lives in Canada; solo artist 2004–. *Recordings include:* albums: Sophie Milman 2004, Make Someone Happy (Juno Award for Best Vocal Jazz Album) 2008, Take Love Easy 2009. *Current Management:* c/o Sarah French, Linus Entertainment, 113 Lakeshore Road W, Mississauga, ON L5H 1E9, Canada. *Telephone:* (905) 278-8883. *Fax:* (905) 278-8803. *E-mail:* sarah@linusent.ca. *Website:* www.linusentertainment.com; www.sophiemilman.com.

MILSAP, Ronnie; American music artist; b. 16 Jan. 1944, Robbinsville, NC; m. Joyce. *Recordings:* Singles include: The Girl Who Waits on Tables, 1973; Please Don't Tell Me How, 1974; I'm a Stand By My Woman Man, 1976; Let My Love Be Your Pillow, 1976; Back On My Mind Again, 1978; Nobody Likes Sad Songs, 1979; Misery Loves Company, 1980; Smokey Mountain Rain, 1980; Any Day Now, 1982; Still Losing You, 1984; Only One Night of the Year, 1986; Make No Mistake, She's Mine, duet with Kenny Rogers, 1987; Button Off My Shirt, 1988; Woman in Love, 1989; Since I Don't Have You, 1991; LA to the Moon, 1992; True Believe, 1993; Albums include: Where My Heart Is, 1973; Night Things, 1975; Ronnie Milsap Live, 1976; It Was Almost Like A Song, 1977; Only One Love in My Life, 1978; Greatest Hits, Vol. 1, 1980; There's No Gettin' Over Me, 1981; Greatest Hits, Vol. 2, 1985; Lost in the Fifties Tonight, 1986; Christmas with Ronnie Milsap, 1986; Stranger Things Have Happened, 1989; Greatest Hits, Vol. 3, 1992; True Believer, 1993; Didn't We, 1996; Kentucky Woman, 1996; When It Comes To My Baby, 1996; Christmas in Dixie, 1997; Branson City Limits, 1999; Wish You Were Here, 2000, Just for a Thrill 2004, My Life 2006, Then Sings My Soul 2009, Country Again 2011. *Honours:* Grammy Awards: Best Country Male Vocal Performance, 1974, 1976, 1982, 1986, 1987, Country Song of the Year, 1984, Best Country Duet Performance, with Kenny Rogers, 1988; Billboard Awards: Best New Male Artist, 1974, Male Singles Artist of the Year, 1976, 1980, Overall Singles Artist of the Year, 1976, Bill Williams Memorial Award, Artist of the Year, 1976, Breakthrough Award, Outstanding Achievement, 1981; CMA Awards: Male Vocalist of the Year, 1974, 1976, 1977, Album of the Year, 1975, 1977, 1978, 1986, Entertainer of the Year, 1977; Numerous others. *Website:* www.ronniemilsap.com.

MINAJ, Nicki; American rapper, singer and songwriter; b. (Onika Tanya Maraj), 8 Dec. 1982, Saint James, Trinidad and Tobago; d. of Robert Maraj and Carol Maraj. *Education:* LaGuardia High School, New York. *Career:* raised in Queens, New York; rapper with quartet The Hoodstars 2004; signed contract with Young Money Entertainment record label 2009; opening act on Britney Spears US tour 2011; numerous collaborations on record including Mariah Carey, Drake, Gucci Mane, Trina, Yo Gotti, Lil Wayne, Britney Spears, Robin Thicke. *Television:* American Idol (as judge) 2012–13. *Films:* Ice Age: Continental Drift (voice) 2012, The Other Woman 2014. *Recordings include:* mixtapes: Playtime is Over 2007, Sucka Free 2008, Beam Me Up Scotty 2009; albums: Pink Friday (American Music Award for Favorite Rap/Hip-Hop Album 2011) 2010, Pink Friday: Roman Reloaded (American Music Award for Favorite Rap/Hip-Hop Album 2012, Billboard Music Award for Top Rap Album 2013) 2012, The Pinkprint (American Music Award for Favorite Rap/Hip Hop Album 2015) 2014. *Honours:* Underground Music Award for Female Artist of the Year 2008, BET Awards for Best New Artist 2010, for Best Female Hip-Hop Artist 2010, 2011, 2012, 2013, 2014, BET Hip-Hop Awards for Rookie of the Year 2010, for Made You Look 2010, 2011, 2012, 2013, for People's Champ 2010, for MVP of the Year 2011, NARM Award for Breakthrough Artist 2011, Billboard's Women in Music Rising Star Award 2011, Soul Train Music Award for Best Hip-Hop Song of the Year (for Moment 4 Life, with Drake) 2011, American Music Awards for Favorite Rap/Hip-Hop Artist 2011, 2012, 2015, MTV Video Music Awards for Best Hip-Hop Video (for Super Bass) 2011, (for Anaconda) 2015, for Best Female Video (for Starships) 2012, MTV Europe Music Awards for Best Hip-Hop Act 2012, 2014, 2015, MOBO Award for Best Int. Act 2012, Billboard Music Awards for Top Streaming Song (Video) (for Super Bass) 2012, for Top Streaming Artist 2013, for Top Rap Artist 2013, People's Choice Award for Favorite Hip-Hop Artist 2013; with Young Money label group: BET Awards for Best Group 2010, 2014, MTV Europe Music Awards (EMA) for Best Hip Hop 2015. *E-mail:* HipHopSince1987@gmail.com. *Website:* hiphopsince1987.com; mypinkfriday.com.

MINCHELLA, Damon; British musician (bass); b. 1 June 1969, Liverpool, England. *Career:* fmr mem., The Fanatics; founder mem., Ocean Colour Scene 1989–; numerous TV appearances, radio broadcasts and tours. *Recordings include:* albums: Ocean Colour Scene 1992, Moseley Shoals 1996, B-Sides, Seasides and Freerides 1997, Marchin' Already 1997, One From The Modern 1999, Mechanical Wonder 2001, Songs For The Front Row (compilation) 2001, Anthology 2003, North Atlantic Drift 2003, Marchin' Melody 2004, On The Leyline 2007, The Collection 2007. *Current Management:* Asgard Promotions Ltd, 125 Parkway, London, NW1 7PS, England. *Telephone:* (20) 7387-5090. *Fax:* (20) 7387-8740. *E-mail:* info@asgard-uk.com. *Website:* www.oceancolourscene.com.

MINDREAU, Iván; Peruvian musician (drums). *Career:* mem., Libido 2005–; numerous live performances and festival appearances. *Recordings include:* album: Lo Último Que Hablé Ayer 2005. *E-mail:* manager@libidonet.com. *E-mail:* ivan@libidonet.com (office). *Website:* www.libidonet.com.

MINGIEDI, Mawangu; Angolan musician (likembé). *Career:* founder mem. traditional Congolese band, Konono No. 1 1978–. *Recordings include:* albums

with Konono No. 1: Zaire: Musiques Urbaines a Kinshasa 1987, Lubuaku 2004, Congotronics 2005, Lubuaku - Live: Vera, Holland 2003 2005, Live at Couleur Cafe 2007, Assume Crash Position 2010; others: Raise Hope For Congo 2010, The Rough Guide to African Roots Revival 2012, Tapes 2012. *Current Management:* c/o Crammed Discs, 43 rue Général Patton, 1050 Brussels, Belgium. *E-mail:* crammed@crammed.be. *Website:* www.crammed.be; www.konono.net.

MINNELLI, Liza; American singer and actress; b. 12 March 1946, Los Angeles; d. of the late Vincente Minnelli and Judy Garland; m. 1st Peter Allen 1967 (divorced 1972); m. 2nd Jack Haley, Jr 1974 (divorced 1979); m. 3rd Mark Gero 1979 (divorced 1992); m. 4th David Gest 2002 (divorced 2007). *Films include:* Charlie Bubbles 1968, The Sterile Cuckoo 1969, Tell Me That You Love Me, Junie Moon 1971, Cabaret (played Sally Bowles) 1972 (Acad. Award for Best Actress, The Hollywood Foreign Press Golden Globe Award, the British Acad. Award and David di Donatello Award, Italy), Lucky Lady 1976, A Matter of Time 1976, New York, New York 1977, Arthur 1981, Rent-a-Cop 1988, Arthur 2: On the Rocks 1988, Sam Found Out 1988, Stepping Out 1991, Parallel Lives 1994, Sex and the City 2 2010. *Television includes:* Liza, Liza with a Z (Emmy Award) 1972, Goldie and Liza Together 1980, Baryshnikov on Broadway 1980 (Golden Globe Award), A Time to Live 1985 (Golden Globe Award), My Favourite Broadway: The Leading Ladies 1999. *Theatre:* Best Foot Forward 1963, Flora, the Red Menace 1965 (Tony Award), Chicago 1975, The Act 1977–78 (Tony Award), Liza at the Winter Garden 1973 (Special Tony Award), The Rink 1984, Victor-Victoria 1997, Liza's at the Palace 2008. *Recordings include:* Liza! Liza! 1964, It Amazes Me 1965, There is a Time 1966, Liza Minnelli 1967, Come Saturday Morning 1968, New Feelin' 1970, Liza with a Z 1972, Liza Minnelli: The Singer 1973, Tropical Nights 1977, The Act 1977, The Rink 1984, Results 1989, Maybe This Time 1996, Minnelli on Minnelli 2000, Liza's Back 2002, The Very Best of Liza Minnelli: Life is a Cabaret! 2002, Confessions 2010. *E-mail:* askliza@officiallizaminnelli.com (office). *Website:* www.officiallizaminnelli.com.

MINOGUE, Danielle (Dannii) Jane; Australian singer, actress, talent show judge, fashion designer and author; b. 20 Oct. 1971, Melbourne, Vic.; d. of Ron Minogue and Carol Minogue; one s. *Career:* actress, Australian TV drama series Skyways 1978, The Sullivans 1978, All The Way 1988, Home and Away 1989, programmes Young Talent Time 1979–88, New Generation (Australia, USA) 1988; TV presenter on Scoop, It's Not Just Saturday, Dannii on Safari (Disney), The Big Breakfast (UK) 1993, Fan T.C. (UK) 1994, Cirque du Monde (Disney) 1996, Electric Circus (UK) 1996, Disney Villains (Disney) 1997; judge, Australia's Got Talent 2007–12, The X Factor (UK) 2007–10, Britain & Ireland's Next Top Model (Sky Living) 2013–; presenter, Nickelodeon UK Kids' Choice Awards ceremony 2008; performances include Royal Children's Variety Performance 1991, Cesme Festival, Turkey 1992, Gay Pride Festival, London 1993, 1994, 1997; launched her own fashion label Project D London with her best friend Tabitha Somerset Webb 2010; mem. Media, Entertainment and Arts Alliance (Australia), APRA. *Play:* Journey to Macbeth (Edinburgh Festival) 1999. *Musical appearances:* Grease (The Arena Spectacular, Australia) 1998, Notre Dame de Paris (London West End) 2000. *Film appearance:* Secrets 1992, The Porter 2005. *Radio:* The Neon Nights Show (Capital Radio) 2003. *Recordings:* albums: Love and Kisses 1991, Get Into You 1993, Girl 1997, Neon Nights 2003, The Hits & Beyond 2006, Unleashed 2007, Club Disco 2007. *Publications:* My Story 2011, My Style 2011. *Honours:* Hon. Dr of Media and Arts (Southampton Solent Univ.) 2011; Young Variety Award (Australian Variety Club) 1989, Best New Artist, Smash Hits 1991, Best Stage Performance, Notre Dame 2001, Best Female Singer, Disney Channel 2003, TV Personality of the Year 2007, 2011, Metro No. 1 Celeb of the Year 2008, 2011, Best TV Star, Elle Style Awards 2010, Ultimate TV Personality, Cosmopolitan Awards 2009, Glamour Women of the Year 2011. *Current Management:* c/o Profile Talent Management, PO Box 650, Waltham Cross, Herts., EN8 1FF; c/o KDB Artists Pty Ltd, PO Box 46824, London SW11 3WS, England. *Telephone:* 7977-914530 (mobile). *E-mail:* nsmith@profiletalent.com.au. *Website:* www.profiletalent.com.au; www.danniiminogue.com.

MINOGUE, Kylie Ann, OBE; Australian singer, actress, producer, fashion designer and entrepreneur and philanthropist; b. 28 May 1968, Melbourne, Vic. *Career:* started acting in Skyways 1980, The Sullivans 1981, The Henderson Kids 1984–85, then Neighbours 1986–88 (all TV series); solo artist 1988–, first female vocalist to have her first (released) five singles obtain silver discs in UK; numerous tours, concerts, TV and radio performances world-wide; launched own range of lingerie 2003; labels: PWL, Mushroom, Deconstruction, Parlophone, Warner Music Australia. *Tours:* Disco in Dream 1989, Enjoy Yourself Tour 1990, Rhythm of Love Tour 1991, Let's Get to It Tour 1991, Intimate and Live 1998, On a Night Like This 2001, KylieFever2002 2002, Showgirl: The Greatest Hits Tour 2005, Showgirl: The Homecoming Tour 2006–07, KylieX2008 2008–09, For You, For Me 2009, Aphrodite World Tour 2011, Anti Tour 2012, Kiss Me Once Tour 2014. *Play:* The Tempest 1999. *Films:* The Delinquents 1989, Streetfighter 1994, Biodome 1996, Sample People 1999, Cut 1999, Sample People 2000, Moulin Rouge 2001, Holy Motors 2012. *Television:* judge and mentor, The Voice UK (BBC 1) 2014. *Recordings include:* albums: Kylie 1988, Enjoy Yourself 1989, Rhythm of Love 1990, Let's Get To It 1991, Kylie – Greatest Hits 1992, Kylie Minogue 1994, Kylie Minogue (Impossible Princess) 1997, Intimate And Live 1998, Light Years 2000, Hits + 2000, Fever (BRIT Award for Best Int. Album 2002) 2001, Confide In Me (compilation) 2002, Body Language 2003, X 2007,

Aphrodite 2010, Kiss Me Once 2014. *Publications:* Kylie 1999, Kylie La La La (with William Baker) 2003, The Showgirl Princess (juvenile) 2006. *Honours:* Ordre des Arts et des Lettres 2008; Hon. Dr of Health Sciences (Anglia Ruskin Univ.) 2011; Woman of the Decade award 1989, nine Logies (Australian TV Industry awards), six Music Week Awards (UK), three Australian Record Industry Asscn Awards, three Japanese Music Awards, Irish Record Industry Award, Canadian Record Industry Award, World Music Award, Australian Variety Club Award, MO Award (Australia), Amplex Golden Reel Award, Diamond Award (Belgium), MTV Video of the Year (for Did it Again) 1998, MTV Awards for Best Pop Act, Best Dance Act 2002, BRIT Award for Best Int. Female Solo Artist 2002, 2008, Grammy Award for Best Dance Recording (for Come into my World) 2004, Music Industry Trusts' Award 2007, Q Idol Award 2007, inducted into Australian Recording Industry Asscn (ARIA) Awards Hall of Fame 2011. *Current Management:* Terry Blamey Management Pty Ltd, 329 Montague Street, Albert Park, Vic. 3206, Australia; Terry Blamey Management, PO Box 13196, London, SW6 4WF, England. *Telephone:* (20) 7371-7627 (London). *Fax:* (20) 7731-7578 (London). *E-mail:* info@terryblamey.com (office). *Website:* www.kylie.com.

MINT SEYMALI, Noura; Mauritanian singer and musician (ardine); b. 13 Nov. 1978, Nouakchott; d. of Seymali Ould Ahmed Vall; m. Jeiche Ould Chighaly. *Career:* began performing with stepmother Dimi Mint Abba at age 13; Founder-mem. of fusion band with Jeiche Ould Chighaly 2004–10; expanded band into own quartet with Ousmane Touré and Matthew Tinari 2011–. *Recordings:* albums: Tarabe 2006, El Howl 2010, Tzenni 2014. *Current Management:* c/o Matthew C. Tinari, Luxus Live, BP 10671, Dakar–Liberté, Senegal. *Telephone:* (70) 9889462. *E-mail:* matthew.tinari@gmail.com. *Website:* www.luxuslive.com; www.nouramintseymali.com.

MINTZER, Robert (Bob); American jazz musician (saxophone, clarinet), bandleader, composer, arranger and educator; b. 27 Jan. 1953, New Rochelle, NY. *Education:* Interlochen Arts Acad., Mich., Hart Coll. of Music, Hartford, Conn., Manhattan School of Music. *Career:* toured with Eumir Deodato 1974, Tito Puente Orchestra 1974, Buddy Rich Big Band 1975–77; mem. Thad Jones and Mel Lewis Big Band 1978, Stone Alliance 1978, Jaco Pastorius' Word of Mouth Band 1981, formed own big band with Dave Sanborn, Mike and Randy Brecker, Don Grolnick and others 1983; mem. Yellowjackets 1990–; fmr Prof. of Jazz Studies, Thornton School of Music, Univ. of Southern Calif.; numerous recording sessions in jazz and pop including Randy Brecker, Mike Manieri, Eddie Palmieri, Mongo Santamaria, Aretha Franklin, James Taylor, Diana Ross, Steve Winwood; performed with New York Philharmonic, American Composers Orchestra, American Ballet Theatre. *Compositions include:* Concertino for Tenor Saxophone, Strings and Winds 1992, Rhythm of the Americas (for saxophone quartet and orchestra) 2001; several other orchestral pieces and saxophone quartets; many big band arrangements. *Recordings include:* albums: as leader of band: The Source 1981, Horn Man 1982, One Music 1991, Hymn 1991, I Remember Jaco 1991, Twin Tenors 1993, New York Ensemble – Groovetown 1996, Longing with Gil Goldstein 1997, Quality Time 1998, The Hudson Project 2000, In the Moment 2004, Bop Boy 2004, Canyon Cove 2009; as bandleader of big band: Papa Lips 1983, Incredible Journey 1985, Camouflage 1986, Spectrum 1988, Urban Contours 1989, Art of the Big Band 1991, Departure 1993, Only in New York 1994, Techno Pop 1994, The First Decade 1995, Big Band Trane 1996, Latin from Manhattan 1998, Homage to Count Basie (Grammy Award for Best Large Jazz Ensemble Recording 2001) 2000, Gently 2003, Old School: New Lessons (featuring Kurt Elling) 2006, Swing Out 2008, For the Moment 2012; with the Yellowjackets: Greenhouse 1991, Live Wires 1992, Like a River 1993, Runferyerlife 1994, Dreamland 1995, Blue Hats 1997, Club Nocturne 1998, Mint Jam 2002, Time Squared 2003, Peace Round 2003, Altered State 2005, Lifecycle (featuring Mike Stern) 2008, Timeline 2011. *Current Management:* c/o Jeff Neben, Axis Artist Management, Inc.. *Website:* www.axismanagement.com. *E-mail:* info@bobmintzer.com. *Website:* www.yellowjackets.com; www.bobmintzer.com.

MINZY; South Korean singer and rapper; b. (Gong Min-ji), 18 Jan. 1994, Seoul. *Career:* mem. 2NE1 2009–. *Television:* 2NE1 TV 2009–11; also appearances on Inkigayo (SBS) 2009–11, M! Countdown (Mnet) 2009–11, Music Bank (KBS) 2009–11. *Film:* Girlfriends 2009. *Recordings:* albums: with 2NE1: To Anyone 2010, Crush 2014. *Honours:* numerous awards for 2NE1 including: Asia Song Festival Asian Newcomer's Award 2009, Melon Music Awards for New Artist and Top 10 2009, for Top 10 2010, Mnet 20's Choice Awards for Hot New Star 2009, Hot CF Star 2009 and Hot Online Song 2009, Mnet Asian Music Awards for Best New Female Artist 2009, for Music Portal Award 2009, for Song of the Year 2009, for Best Music Video 2009, 2010, for Best Female Group 2010, for Artist of the Year 2010, Rhythmer Awards for R&B Artist of the Year and Rookie of the Year 2009 Style Icon Best Female Singer Awards 2009, 2010, MTV Daum Music Fest Award for Artist of the Year 2011, MYX Music Favorite K-pop Video Award 2011; also numerous Cyworld Digital Music Awards including Top Selling Artist Award 2009, Newcomer of the Year 2010, Bonsang Award 2010, Artist of the Year Award 2010, Song of the Year 2010. *Address:* c/o YG Entertainment, 397–5 YG Building, Hapjeong-Dong, Mapo-Gu, Seoul 109-819, South Korea (office). *Telephone:* (2) 3143-1105 (office). *Fax:* (2) 544-1546 (office). *E-mail:* web@ygmail.net (office). *Website:* eng.ygfamily.com/main/main.html (office); www.yg-2ne1.com (home).

MIOSSEC, Christophe, BA; French singer and songwriter; b. 24 Dec. 1964, Brest; one s. *Education:* Brest Univ. *Career:* fmrly music reviewer, regional newspaper Ouest France, asst to Creative Dir at TV station TF1; collabora-

tions Guillaume Jouan, Bruno Leroux, Johnny Hallyday, Jane Birkin and Axel Bauer. *Recordings include:* albums: Boire 1995, Baiser 1997, A prendre 1998, Brûle 2001, 1964 2004, L'Etreinte 2006, Chansons Ordinaires 2011, Ici-bas, Ici même 2014. *Current Management:* c/o Radical Production, 20 rue d'Anjou, 49100 Angers, France. *Telephone:* 2-41-88-19-82. *Fax:* 2-41-86-82-79. *E-mail:* info@radical-production.fr. *Website:* www.radical-production.fr. *E-mail:* postmaster@christophemiossec.com. *Website:* www.christophemiossec.com.

MIRABASSI, Gabriele; Italian musician (clarinet); b. 16 Sept. 1967, Perugia. *Education:* Morlacchi Conservatory. *Career:* mem. various jazz groups. *Recordings include:* albums: Fiabe 1995, Como una Volta 1996, Cambaluc 1997, Velho Retrato 1999, Lo Stortino 2000, Luna Park 2000, Una a Zero 2001, Fuori le Mura 2003, Latkia Blend 2004, Graffiando Vento 2007, Canto di Ebano 2008. *E-mail:* info@gabrielemirabassi.com. *Website:* www.gabrielemirabassi.com.

MIRWAIS; Italian/Afghan producer, musician (guitar) and DJ; b. (Mirwais Ahmadzai), 23 Oct. 1960, Lausanne, Switzerland. *Career:* moved to France aged six; mem. Taxi Girl 1980–87, Juliette et les Independants 1988–89; has worked as producer for several artists, including Madonna. *Recordings include:* albums: with Taxi Girl: Compilation 84–86 1990; with Juliette et les Independants: La Vie en Noir 1987, Je Suis à tes pieds 1989; solo: Mirwais 1989, Production 2000. *Website:* www.mirwais.org.

MISHALLE, Luc, Lic. Law; Belgian musician (saxophones); *Artistic Director,* Met-X vzw; b. 6 Jan. 1953, Antwerp; one s. *Education:* Univ. of Antwerp. *Career:* theatre: Musical Dir, Welfare State (UK), Dog Troop (NL), Internationale Nieuwe Scene (B), Ro-theater (NL); currently Artistic Dir, Met-X vzw; performances with Marakbar, Blindman Quartet, Galileo's Left Wing, Al Harmoniah, Marockin' Brass. *Compositions:* Mekoue, Urbanized, Akoestischo, Winterverhalen, Metropolis, Webl, Mdawa, Shark Dari. *Recordings:* Marakbar Live, Marockin' Antwerp, Blindman Poortenbos, Galileo's Left Wing Live, Marockin' Stories, El Adoua, Al Harmoniah, Marockin' Brass. *Publication:* Een stoet van kleur en klanken. *Address:* Met-X vzw, De Lenglentierstraat 20, 1000 Brussels (office); Veeartsenstraat 77, 1070 Brussels, Belgium (home). *Telephone:* (2) 218-70-52. *E-mail:* luc@met-x.be (office); veroniqueluc@skynet.be. *Website:* www.met-x.be (office).

MÍSIA; Portuguese singer; b. (Susanna Maria Alfonso), 1955, Oporto. *Career:* began singing Fado (Portuguese folk form) professionally 1991. *Recordings include:* albums: Mísia 1991, Fado 1993, Tanto Menos Tanto Mais 1994, Garros Dos Sentidos 1998, Paixões Diagonais 1999, Ritual 2001, Canto 2003, Drama Box 2005, Ruas 2009, Delikatessen Café Concerto 2013. *Honours:* Ordre des Arts et des Lettres 2004, Medal of the Order of Merit (Portugal) 2005; Grand Prix de L'Academie Charles Cross 1997. *E-mail:* misia@misia-online.com. *Website:* www.misia-online.com.

MISSEGHERS, Stéphane; Belgian musician (drums). *Career:* fmr mem., Soulwax; mem., dEUS 2004–. *Recordings include:* albums: Pocket Revolution 2005, Vantage Point 2008, Keep You Close 2011, Following Sea 2012. *Current Management:* c/o Christian Pierre, Rozenlaan 57, 2970 Schilde, Belgium. *Fax:* (3) 254-01-25. *E-mail:* info@musickness.be. *Website:* www.musickness.be; www.deus.be.

MITCHELL, Alexander; British musician (guitar, midi programming); b. 4 Nov. 1969, Minster, Kent. *Education:* Goldsmiths Coll. *Career:* guitarist with: Curve 1991–94; Choob 1993–95; Sparky Lightbourne 1997–; radio includes: John Peel Sessions for Radio 1; concerts include: Glastonbury Festival; NME Stage; major tours of USA, Europe, Japan, UK; now making techno music; mem. Musicians' Union; Performing Right Soc., Mechanical-Copyright Protection Soc. *Television includes:* The Beat. *Compositions include:* with Choob: Little Girl 1993, Choobular 1994; as Sparky Lightbourne: EP, 1997; Sparky's Secret 1998; Album 1999; Chickin Lickin', Get Your Hands Off Me. *Recordings include:* albums with Curve: Doppelganger, Cuckoo; EPs (as Choob): Little Girl, Choobular.

MITCHELL, Dryden; American singer, musician (guitar) and songwriter; b. 15 June 1976, Redondo Beach, Calif. *Career:* played with local bands Crossover, Out of Order, Dragonphlie; mem. Alien Ant Farm 1996–, released self-financed independent album 1999, signed to Papa Roach's New Noize label, second album released in conjunction with DreamWorks Records label 2001. *Recordings include:* albums: Greatest Hits (Los Angeles Music Award, Best Independent Album) 1999, ANThology 2001, Truant 2003, Up In The Attic 2006, Always and Forever 2014. *Website:* www.alienantfarm.com.

MITCHELL, Ian; American musician (guitar) and singer; b. 22 Aug. 1958, Downpatrick, Northern Ireland; m. Wendy-Ann Antanaitis 1992. *Career:* began performing aged 15; f. Albatross 1972, changed name to Young City Stars 1974–76; joined Bay City Rollers 1976, left 1976; f. Rosetta Stone 1977–79, Ian Mitchell Band 1979, Identity Crisis 1985–88, Joy Buzzers 1990–92, The Mix 1995–99; f. Flat 5 Productions 2000. *Recordings include:* albums: with Bay City Rollers: Dedication; with Rosetta Stone: Sunshine of Your Love, Try It On, Sheila; with the Ian Mitchell Band: Suddenly You Love Me, Hold On to Love, Boulevard LA, Goin Crazy 2008; solo: Edge Of The World 2000.

MITCHELL, Joni, CC; Canadian singer, songwriter, visual artist and poet; b. (Roberta Joan Anderson), 7 Nov. 1943, Fort Macleod, Alberta; d. of William A. Anderson and Myrtle Anderson (née McKee); m. 1st Chuck Mitchell 1965 (divorced); m. 2nd Larry Klein 1982; one d. by Brad McGrath. *Education:* Alberta Coll. *Recordings include:* albums: Song to a Seagull 1968, Clouds 1969, Ladies of the Canyon 1970, Blue 1971, For the Roses 1972, Court and Spark 1974, Miles of Aisles 1974, The Hissing of Summer Lawns 1975, Hejira 1976, Don Juan's Reckless Daughter 1977, Mingus 1979, Shadows and Light 1980, Wild Things Run Fast 1982, Dog Eat Dog 1985, Chalk Mark in a Rain Storm 1988, Night Ride Home 1991, Turbulent Indigo (Grammy Awards for Best Pop Album, Best Art Direction 1996) 1994, Hits 1996, Misses 1996, Taming the Tiger 1998, Both Sides Now (Grammy Award for Best Traditional Pop Vocal Album 2001) 2000, Travelog 2002, Songs of a Prairie Girl 2005, Shine 2007. *Dance:* The Fiddle and the Drum (score for ballet with the Alberta Ballet) 2007. *Exhibition:* Green Flag Song 2007. *Songs include:* Both Sides Now, Michael from Mountains, Urge for Going, Circle Game. *Television includes:* Joni Mitchell: Intimate and Interactive (Gemini Award 1996). *Publication:* Joni Mitchell: The Complete Poems and Lyrics. *Honours:* Jazz Album of Year and Rock-Blues Album of Year for Mingus, Downbeat Magazine 1979, Juno Award 1981, Century Award, Billboard Magazine 1996, Polar Music Prize (Sweden) 1996, Gov. Gen.'s Performing Arts Award 1996, Nat. Acad. of Songwriters Lifetime Achievement Award 1996; inducted into Rock & Roll Hall of Fame 1997, into Nat. Acad. of Popular Music–Songwriters Hall of Fame 1997, into Canadian Songwriters Hall of Fame 2007, Grammy Award for Best Pop Instrumental Performance (for One Week Last Summer) 2008, Jack Richardson Producer of the Year 2008. *Telephone:* (310) 288-6262. *Fax:* (310) 288-6362. *E-mail:* jtani@gtba.com. *Website:* www.jonimitchell.com.

MITCHELL, Neil; British musician (keyboards); b. 8 June 1967, Helensborough, Scotland. *Career:* mem. Wet Wet Wet 1982–. *Recordings include:* albums: Popped In Souled Out 1987, Sgt Pepper Knew My Father 1988, The Memphis Sessions 1988, Holding Back The River 1989, High On The Happy Side 1992, Wet Wet Wet Live At The Royal Albert Hall 1993, End Of Part One (Greatest Hits) 1993, Picture This 1995, 10 1997, Timeless 2007. *Honours:* BRIT Award for Best British Newcomer 1988. *Current Management:* c/o No Half Measures , 1st Floor, 5 Eagle Street, Glasgow, G4 9XA, Scotland. *Website:* nohalfmeasures.com; www.wetwetwet.co.uk; wetwetwet.ning.com.

MITCHELL, Nicole Diane, BMus, MMus; American jazz musician (flute), composer and academic; *Professor of Integrated Composition, Improvisation and Teaching, Department of Music, University of California, Irvine;* b. 17 Feb. 1967, Syracuse, NY; one d. *Education:* Univ. of California, San Diego, Oberlin Coll., Chicago State Univ., Northern Illinois Univ. *Career:* raised in New York and Calif.; moved to Chicago 1990; mem. of ensemble Samana 1990–92; collaborated with Hamid Drake, David Boykin in late 1990s; f. own group Black Earth Ensemble; co-host Avant-Garde Jazz Jam Sessions early 2000s; featured soloist with many ensembles and orchestras including Chicago Jazz Philharmonic, ICI Creative Orchestra, Germany, Vancouver NOW Orchestra, Canada, Ramsey Lewis Freedom Ensemble, New Black Repertory Ensemble, Chicago, Chicago Sinfonietta Orchestra, AACM Great Black Music Ensemble; fmr teacher at various insts including Northern Illinois Univ., Northeastern Illinois Univ., Wheaton Coll., Univ. of Illinois; Asst Prof. in Music, Univ. of Calif., Irvine 2011–, currently Prof. of Integrated Composition, Improvisation and Technology; mem. Asscn for Advancement of Creative Musicians 1995– (Co-Pres. 2006–, Pres. 2009–10); numerous collaborations with other musicians including Muhal Richard Abrams, David Boykin, Anthony Braxton, Steve Coleman, Anthony Davis, Bill Dixon, Hamid Drake, George Lewis, Rob Mazurek, Roscoe Mitchell, James Newton, Archie Shepp, Ed Wilkerson. *Recordings:* albums: Vision Quest 2001, Afrika Rising 2002, Hope, Future and Destiny 2004, Black Unstoppable 2007, Xenogenesis Suite 2008, Anaya 2009, Renegades 2009, Emerald Hills 2010, Before After 2011, Awakening 2011, The Ethiopian Princess Meets the Tantric Priest 2011, Arc of O – For Improvisers, Chamber Orchestra and Electronics 2012, Aquarius 2013, Engraved in the Wind 2013, Intergalactic Beings 2014, The Secret Escapades of Velvet Anderson 2014, Artifacts (with Tomeka Reid and Mike Reed) 2015. *Honours:* Down Beat Magazine Awards for Rising Star (Flute Category) 2004, 2005, 2006, 2007, 2008, 2009, 2010, Down Beat Int. Critics Poll Awards for Flute and Rising Star Flute categories 2010, Herb Alpert Award in the Arts 2011, Doris Duke Artist Award for Jazz 2012, Jazz Journalists Asscn Award for Best Flutist of the Year 2013, 2014, 2015. *Address:* Department of Music, Claire Trevor School of the Arts, University of California, Irvine, CA 92697, USA. *Telephone:* (949) 824-5011 (office). *E-mail:* nicole.mitchell@uci.edu (office); blackearthmusic@gmail.com (home). *Website:* music.arts.uci.edu/content/nicole-mitchell (office); www.nicolemitchell.com (home).

MITCHELL-DAVIDSON, Paul, FHEA; British composer, arranger and musician (all guitars, mandolin, banjo); b. 29 Dec. 1946, Bristol, England. *Career:* played in various bands during 1960's; played with Monad 1971–73, Maynard Ferguson Band US tour 1972, Paws For Thought 1974; freelance session musician, also musical dir, radio and TV since 1970s; played with many top UK and US jazz musicians; major concert at RNCM, 1995; mem. PRS, APC, BMWC, MCPS, Musicians' Union. *Compositions include:* Away Melancholy 1978, Steam 1980, Sonata For Solo Guitar 1981, The Lion and the Dragon 1984, A Good Time Was Had By All 1985, Oriana 1986, Plantagenet Variations 1989, Earthsongs 1990, All About Lions 1991, Gaia 1991, The Bestiary 1992, A Chorus of Inner Voices 1993, Fanfare- All Lit Up 1994, A Concert For Paul 1995, The Big Easy 1996, Towards the Rising Sun 1998, Tubafication 1998, Rhapsody For Duke 1999, Shouting on Swan Street 2000,

Kintamarni 2001, Dovestone 2002, Rainsong 2003, Saudade 2007, Dez Choros Para Tres Viloes 2008, El Libro De Parajos 2009, One Small Step 2010. *Honours:* BBC Marty Paich Award 1991–92. *Telephone:* 7902-063679 (mobile). *E-mail:* paul@paulmitchell-davidson.com. *Website:* www.paulmitchell-davidson.com.

MITON, Gilles; French musician (baritone saxophone, flute); b. 3 July 1962, Paris. *Education:* Nat. Conservatory, Versaille. *Career:* has played with: Claude Bolling, Michel Legrand, Ornical Band, Arturo Sandoval, Phil Woods, Johnny Griffin, Milky Sax, Lumiere, Laurent Cugny, Super Swing Machine, Gerard Badini, Jean-Loup Longnon, Philippe Baduoin, Antoine Hervé, Quoi de Neuf Doctor, Salena Jones, Dee Dee Bridgewater, Ray Charles, Arthur H, Charles Trenet, Michel Leeb, Le Grand Orchestre du Splendid, Manu Dibango, Sacha Distel, Eddy Mitchell. *Website:* www.cannonball-adderley.com/moi2.

MITSUI, Tôru; Japanese academic; *Professor Emeritus, Kanazawa University;* b. 31 March 1940, Saga. *Career:* Lecturer, Aichi Univ. 1964–68; Lecturer, Kanazawa Univ. 1969–71, Assoc. Prof. 1971–83, Prof. 1983–2005, Prof. Emer. 2005–; Chair. Int. Asscn for the Study of Popular Music 1993–97. *Publications:* in English: Karaoke Around The World, Global Technology, Local Singing 1998, Popular Music: Intercultural Interpretations 1998, Made in Japan: Studies in Popular Music 2014. *Address:* #25-606, 3-25 Minami-Urawa, Minami Ward, Saitama 336-0017, Japan. *E-mail:* mitsui@angel.ocn.ne.jp.

MIYAKO, Harumi; Japanese singer; b. 22 Feb. 1948, Kyoto City; d. of the late Shoji Matsuda (Yi Jong Tack) and of Matsuyo Kitamura; m. Hiroomi Asatsuki 1978 (divorced 1982); partner Ikko Nakamura. *Education:* pvt. music schools. *Career:* began traditional Japanese dancing lessons aged 6, ballet lessons aged 9, joined a theatrical co. aged 11; winner Colombia Nationwide Popular Song Contest aged 15 1963; recording debut with release of Komaru kotoyo (You Upset Me) 1964; began career singing traditional enka (ethnic) music; appeared on annual New Year's Eve Contest Kohaku uta gassen, NHK 1965–85; retd as singer 1984; worked as music producer and news commentator; special performance on music programme Kohaku uta gassen, NHK 1989; re-launched music career singing modern pop music 1990; annual concerts in Budo-Kan; regular appearances on TV music programmes. *Singles include:* Komaru kotoyo 1964, Anko tsubaki wa koi no hana (New Artist Award, Japanese Recording Industry) 1964, Namida no renraku fune 1965, Bakattcho debune 1965, Sukini natta hito 1968, Kita no shuka kara (Record of the Year, Japan Popular Music Award) 1976, I Want to Become an Everyday Woman 1984, Sennen No Koto 1990, Sakure Shigure 1993, Nana no ran 1994, Ajia Densetsu 1996, Jashu mon 1998, Ohara zessho 2000. *Honours:* Rookie of the Year Award 1964, Nihon Kayo Taisho (Japan Annual Pop Grand Prize) 1976, Nihon Record Taisho (Japan Record Annual Grand Prize) 1976.

MKANDAWIRE, Wambali; Malawi musician (guitar), singer and songwriter; b. Belgian Congo; m. Wambui Muruiki 1993, one d. *Career:* mem. of bands, Pentagon, New Song 1985–86, tours of South Africa, Namibia and Zimbabwe; solo artist 1988–; Founder and Owner, Kajimete Arts Publishing. *Recordings include:* albums: first album 1988, second album 1989, third album 1990, fourth album 1992, Zani Muwone 2000, Moto 2007. *Honours:* World Intellectual Property Org. Award for Creativity 2002, SAMA Music Award (Best African Artist) 2003. *Address:* c/o Instinct Africaine, PO Box 375, Witkoppen, Randburg, 2068, South Africa. *E-mail:* info@instinctafricaine.com. *Website:* www.instinctafricaine.com.

MOAKES, Gordon; British musician (bass guitar) and backing singer; b. 22 June 1976. *Career:* mem., Union, later renamed Bloc Party 2003–. *Recordings include:* albums: with Bloc Party: Silent Alarm 2005, Silent Alarm Remixed 2005, A Weekend in the City 2007, Intimacy 2008, Four 2012. *Current Management:* Press Here Publicity, 138 W 25th Street, Seventh Floor, New York, NY 10001, USA. *Telephone:* (212) 246-2640. *Fax:* (212) 582-6513. *E-mail:* info@pressherepublicity.com. *Website:* www.pressherepublicity.com. *Address:* c/o V2 Music, 131 Holland Park Avenue, London, W11 4UT, England. *E-mail:* gordon@blocparty.com. *Website:* www.blocparty.com.

MOBERG, Sten-Erik 'Pyret'; Swedish composer, artist and musician (piano, guitar); b. 20 Jan. 1947, Fröson; m. Karin Moberg-Hillmann; two s. one d. *Career:* tours in Ireland and England 1966–70; appearance at Olympia, Paris 1978; TV appearances and tours in Europe; mem. SKAP, STIM, SAMI, Theatre Union. *Compositions:* Kärleken Ar Vit (Love is White), various Swedish songs; Another Year of Music; An Irish Saga, symphony. *Recordings include:* Diddlers is Good For You 1969, Hai 1969, Kärleken Ar Vit 1987, Another Year of Music 1993. *Publication:* Ett Södermalm Som Gor Dig Varm (A South Part That Makes You Warm), 1987. *Honours:* STIM Award 1990; Authors Union 1991.

MOBERLEY, Gary Mark; Australian musician (keyboards), composer, writer and producer; b. Sydney. *Education:* Grade 6, Australian Music Examinations Bd. *Career:* live work and recorded with The Bee Gees, The Sweet, John Miles Band, Terence Trent D'Arby, Prefab Sprout, Wet Wet Wet, The Damned, The Alarm, Hipsway, Jody Watley, Girlschool, Drum Theatre, Sigue Sigue Sputnik, Little Richard, Haywoode, Nicole, Big Country (remix), Loose Ends, The Associates, Talk Talk, Kiki Dee, Band of Holy Joy, Tony Di Bart, Dangerous Grounds, Funkadelia, Steel Pulse, Trevor Horn, The JBs, ABC, Fine Young Cannibals, The Foundations, Jean Jacques Perrey; live work with The Bee Gees, Paul Rodgers, Bonnie Tyler, Wilson Pickett, Eddie

Floyd, Rufus Thomas, Ben E. King, Arthur Conley, The Drifters, Andrew 'Junior Boy' Jones, Cookie McGhee, Texas Blues Summit, Memphis Blues Summit, Love Affair; 34 European tours, nine American tours, three world tours, five albums of radio and TV themes used world-wide; Musical Dir of numerous British and European theatre shows.

MOBY; American musician (guitar, drums, keyboards) and producer; b. (Richard Melville Hall), 11 Sept. 1965, Harlem, New York; s. of James Hall and Elizabeth Hall. *Education:* Royle Grammar School, Darien, CT, Univ. of Connecticut. *Career:* cr. first band 1979, new wave/punk rock band Vatican Commandos 1980, new wave band AWOL 1982; DJ The Beat, Port Chester, New York 1984, Mars, Palladium, Palace de Beauté, MK, New York 1989; production and remixes for Metallica, Smashing Pumpkins, Michael Jackson, Depeche Mode, Soundgarden, Blur, David Bowie, Orbital, Prodigy, Freddie Mercury, Brian Eno, B-52s, Ozzy Osbourne, John Lydon, Butthole Surfers, Erasure, Aerosmith, OMD, Pet Shop Boys, Jon Spencer Blues Explosion; numerous tours, festival appearances, TV and radio broadcasts; owner tea shop Teany, New York; mem. BMI, PMRS, AF of M, SAG, AFTRA. *Compositions for film:* Double Tap (score) 1997, contrib. to numerous other film soundtracks. *Recordings include:* albums: Moby 1992, The Story So Far 1993, Ambient 1993, Early Underground 1993, Move (EP) 1994, Underwater 1995, Everything is Wrong (Spin Magazine Album of the Year) 1995, Voodoo Child: The End of Everything 1996, Animal Rights 1996, Rare: Collected B-Sides 1989–1993 1996, Everything is Wrong: Non-stop DJ Mix By Evil Ninja Moby 1996, I Like To Score 1997, Play 1999, Mobysongs 2000, 18 2002, Play: The B Sides 2004, Hotel 2005, Last Night 2008, Wait for Me 2009, Destroyed 2011, Innocents 2013. *Honours:* MTV Web Award 2002, Q Magazine Best Producer Award 2002, MTV Video Music Award for Best Cinematography in a Video (for We Are All Made Of Stars) 2002. *Current Management:* c/o DEF, 51 Lonsdale Road, Queen's Park, London, NW6 6RA, England. *Telephone:* (20) 7328-2922. *Fax:* (20) 7328-2322. *E-mail:* info@d-e-f.com. *Address:* c/o Mute, 429 Harrow Road, London, W10 4RE, England. *Website:* www.moby.com.

THE MOD WHEEL (see Middleton, Tom)

MODEL 500 (see Atkins, Juan)

MOFFATT, Hugh; American country singer, songwriter and musician (guitar, trumpet); b. 3 Nov. 1948, Fort Worth, Tex.; s. of Lester H. Moffatt and Sue-Jo Jarrott Moffatt; m. Mary L. Vaughan; two s. one d. *Education:* Rice Univ., Houston, Tex. *Career:* singer, songwriter, Nashville, Tenn. 1970s; recording artist 1974–; formed band Ratz early 1980s. *Compositions:* Just In Case, recorded by Ronnie Milsap 1974, Old Flames Can't Hold A Candle To You (co-writer Pebe Sebert), recorded by Joe Sun, Dolly Parton, Foster and Allen, Wild Turkey (co-writer with Pebe Sebert), recorded by Lacy J Dalton, Love Game, recorded by Jerry Lee Lewis, Praise The Lord and Send Me The Money, recorded by Bobby Bare, Why Should I Cry Over You (co-writer Ed Penney), recorded by George Hamilton IV, Words At Twenty Paces, recorded by Alabama, Rose of my Heart, recorded by Johnny Cash; operas, with Michael Ching: King of The Clouds, Out of The Rain, Corps of Discovery, new English libretto for Gluck's Orfeo e Eurydice. *Recordings:* albums: Loving You 1987, Troubadour 1989, Live and Alone 1991, The Wognum Sessions 1992, The Way Love Is 1992, Dance Me Outside (with Katy Moffatt) 1992, The Life of a Minor Poet 1996, Ghosts of The Music 1998, Songs From the Back of the Church 2006. *Address:* c/o Criterion Music, 11430 Ventura Boulevard, Studio City, CA 91604, USA (office).

MOFFATT, Katherine Louella, (Katy Moffatt); American folk musician (guitar), singer and songwriter; b. 19 Nov. 1950, Fort Worth, Tex.; d. Lester Huger Moffatt Sr and Sue-Jo Jarrott. *Education:* Sophie Newcomb Coll., St John's Coll. *Career:* folk singer 1967–68; production asst, announcer, TV stations 1970; musician, singer in blues band, Corpus Christi 1970; solo artist 1971–; recording artist 1973–; mem. American Fed. of Musicians, American Fed. of Television and Radio Artists, Screen Actors Guild, Nat. Acad. of Recording Arts and Sciences. *Film appearances:* Billy Jack, Hard Country, The Thing Called Love, Honeymoon in Vegas. *Compositions:* The Magic Ring; Kansas City Morning; Gerry's Song; Take Me Back To Texas; (Waiting For) The Real Thing; Didn't We Have Love; co-writer, Walkin' On The Moon (with Tom Russell). *Recordings include:* albums: Katy, Kissin' In The California Sun, Walkin' On The Moon, The Greatest Show on Earth, A Town South of Bakersfield, Hearts Gone Wild, Child Bride, Dance Me Outside, Sleepless Nights, Midnight Radio, Angel Town, Loose Diamond 1999, Cowboy Girl 2001, Up Close and Personal 2005, Fewer Things 2008, Trilogy 2009, Playin' Fool 2010. *Honours:* Record World Album Award 1976, Cash Box Single Award 1976, Fort Worth Weekly Award for Best Singer-Songwriter 1997. *Address:* PO Box 334, O'Fallon, IL 62269, USA (home). *Website:* www.katymoffatt.com.

MOFFETT, Johnathan Phillip; American musician (drums), music director and songwriter; b. 17 Nov. 1954, New Orleans, La; m. Rhonda Bartholomew 1976; one s. one d. *Career:* drummer for artists including Patti Austin, Cameo, Lionel Richie, Madonna, Teena Marie, Jermaine Jackson; tours and concerts with The Jacksons 1979–81, Victory Tour (also as set designer) 1984, Elton John world tours 1988–89, Madonna, Virgin and Ciao Italia tours, George Michael, Rock In Rio Festival; musical dir for concerts by Jermaine Jackson, Michael Jackson; numerous TV and video appearances with The O'Jays, Isaac Hayes, The Kane Gang, Cameo. *Recordings include:* albums include: Silk Electric (Diana Ross) 1982, Victory (The Jacksons) 1984, One More Story (Peter Cetera) 1988, Back To Avalon (Kenny Loggins) 1988, Christmas Again 2006; also recorded with Julian Lennon, Richard Marx, Jody

Watley, Chico de Barge, Brian Eno, Janet Jackson, Edgar Winter. *Address:* 2219 West Olive Avenue, Burbank, CA 91506, USA. *Website:* www.jonathan -moffett.com.

MOGENSEN, Grethe Stitz; Danish actress, author, playwright, composer and singer; b. 25 May 1937, Copenhagen; m. Axel Busch-Jensen 1964, one s. one d. *Education:* New Theatre Actors' School, Copenhagen. *Career:* mem. Danish Actors' League, Danish Popular Authors. *Stage appearances include:* Enlordag på Amàr 1957, Champagnegaloppen 1960, 1974, Farinelli 1961, Guys and Dolls 1992, No No Nanette 1973, Company 1972, Dollarprinssen 1975, Piger tilsös 1987, Sweeney Todd 1988, Nitouche 1989, Les Misérables 1991, Cirkus Mikkelikski 1991, 1997, Sommer i Tyrol 1993, Mod mig på Cassiopeia 1996, My Fair Lady 1999. *Films include:* Pigen i sogelyset 1959, Bussen 1963, Gift 1966, Flagermusen 1966, Tro, håb og Karlighed 1984, Tango for tre 1992, Klinkevals 1999. *Recordings include:* Enlordag på Amàr 1959, Farinelli 1961, En sondag på Amager 1962, Dollarprinssen 1964, Dyrene i Hakkebakkeskoven 1963, Landmandsliv 1965, Flagermusen 1966, Shehvide 1966, Bambi 1970, Askepot 1971, Pinocchio 1971, Isyngelegeland I–IV 1967–87, Jul i Syngelegeland I and II 1971–79, Lidt af hvert 1979, Cirkus Mikkeliksi 1981. *Publication:* Teaterkattens Eventyr 1993. *Honours:* Mogens Brandts Legat 1960, Kiss Gregers 1974, DPA's Haderslegat 1991, Louis Halberstadt's Haderslegat 1997.

MOGENSEN, Mogens Eddie; Danish musician (bassoon); *Principal Bassoon, Royal Danish Orchestra;* b. 31 March 1948, Odense; m. Nora Andrea Mogensen 1972; two s. one d. *Education:* Det Fynske Musikkonservatorium, Odense, with Hagbard Knudsen. *Career:* Prin. Bassoon, Royal Danish Orchestra, Copenhagen 1972–; Teacher, Royal Danish Acad. of Music, RAM, London; mem. Int. Double Reed Soc. *Honours:* Kgl. Kapelmusicus. *Address:* Mikkelborg Park 7, 2970 Hørsholm, Denmark. *Telephone:* 43-73-41-89. *E-mail:* memogensen@gmail.com.

MOGG, Phil; British rock singer; b. 1951, London, England. *Career:* founder mem. of rock group, UFO 1969–83, re-formed 1985, 1991; regular worldwide tours. *Recordings include:* albums: UFO 1971, UFO 2 – Flying 1971, Live In Japan 1972, Phenomenon 1974, Force It 1975, No Heavy Pettin' 1976, Lights Out 1977, Obsession 1978, Strangers in the Night 1979, No Place to Run 1980, The Wild, the Willing and the Innocent 1981, Mechanix 1982, Making Contact 1982, Headstone 1983, Misdemeanour 1985, Ain't Misbehavin' 1988, High Stakes and Dangerous Men 1992, Covenant 2000, Sharks 2002, You Are Here 2004, Monkey Puzzle 2006, The Visitor 2009, Seven Deadly 2012. *E-mail:* ufoweb@virginmedia.com. *Website:* www.ufo-music.info.

MOHAMED, Pops; South African musician (piano, synthesizer, keyboards, kora, mbira, didgeridu, berimbau, marimba, percussion) and programmer; b. 10 Dec. 1949, Benoni, Johannesburg; m. (divorced); two s. one d. *Education:* Fuba School of Drama and Visual Arts. *Career:* lead guitarist, Las Valiants 1969–71; band leader, The Dynamics, El Gringoes, Society's Children; solo artist 1975–; recording engineer 1981–87; record producer 1988–95; f. own record label, Kalamazoo Music 1993; mem. Royal Schools and Federated Union of Black Arts. *Recordings include:* Black Disco 1975, Night Express 1976, Black Disco 3 1978, Movement In The City 1979, BM Movement 1980, Innercity Funk 1981, Kalamazoo 1991, Sophiatown Society 1992, When In New York 1993, Ancestral Healing 1995, Music With No Name 1996, How Far We Have Come 1996, Society Vibes 1997, Timeless 1997, Africa Meltdown 2001, Yesterday, Today and Tomorrow 2002. *Honours:* Award as Original Artist (for Towntalk Show) 1979. *E-mail:* sevi@blackmajor.co.za. *Website:* www.blackmajor.co.za.

MOLDEN, Nigel Charles, BSc, MSc, PhD, FRSA, FCIM, FBIM, FIoD; British music company director; *Director, Synergie Logistics;* b. 17 Aug. 1948, Oxford, England; m. Hilary Julia Lichfield 1971; three s. *Education:* Univ. of London, Brunel Univ., Fairfax Univ. *Career:* Gen. Man. Warner Brothers Records 1977–78; Int. Gen. Man. WEA Records 1978–80; Int. Marketing Man. Thorn EMI Video 1980–84; Chair. Magnum Music Group 1984–97; Jt Chief Exec., TKO Magnum Music 1994–2002; CEO Synergie Logistics 1997–2010, Dir. *Honours:* Freeman of the City of London 1990. *Address:* Synergie Logistics Limited, Magnum House, High Street, Lane End, HP14 3JG, England (office). *Telephone:* (1494) 678177 (office). *E-mail:* synergielogistics@btconnect.com (office).

MOLINA, Carlos Anthony; American musician (bass guitar, keyboards) and record producer. *Career:* bass guitar and keyboard player with rock band Mercury Rev 2002–; festival appearances in USA, Europe and Far East 2007; has also played with Heather Nova, Longwave, Nicolai Dunger, Ras T and Asheber Posse. *Recordings include:* The Secret Migration 2005, Hello Blackbird (soundtrack to film Bye Bye Blackbird) 2006, Snowflake Midnight 2008, The Light in You 2015. *Current Management:* c/o Mag7 Management, 62 Cheever Place #1, Brooklyn, NY 11231, USA. *Telephone:* (917) 207-2023. *E-mail:* info@mag7management.com. *Website:* mag7management.com. *Current Management:* Free Trade Agency, 15 Timber Yard, Drysdale Street, London, N1 6ND, England. *Telephone:* (20) 3700-3377. *Fax:* (20) 3700-3355. *E-mail:* info@freetradeagency.co.uk. *Website:* www.freetradeagency.co.uk. *E-mail:* info@mercuryrev.com. *Website:* www.mercuryrev.com; www .anthonymolina.com.

MOLINA, Juana; Argentine singer, songwriter and actress; b. 1 Oct. 1962, Buenos Aires. *Career:* began career as actress in Argentine telenovelas; solo singer 1996–. *Television includes:* La Noticia Rebelde 1986, Gasalla 1988, El

Mundo de Gasalla 1990, Juana y sus Hermanas 1991, Nico 1995. *Recordings include:* albums: Rara 1996, Segundo 2001, Tres Cosas 2002, Son 2006, Un Día 2008, Wed 21 2013. *Current Management:* Reverse Thread Inc., Post Office Box 11, Saugerties, NY 12477, USA. *E-mail:* paul@reverse-thread.com. *E-mail:* fedemayol637@gmail.com. *Website:* www.juanamolina.com.

MOLINA BURGOS, (Francisco) Javier de; Spanish musician (drums); b. 16 June 1964. *Career:* mem. Hombres G 1983–92, 2002–. *Films include:* Sufre mamón 1987, Suéltate el pelo 1988. *Recordings include:* Hombres G 1985, La cagaste... Burt Lancaster 1986, Estamos locos... ¿o qué? 1987, Agitar antes de usar 1988, Voy a pasármelo bien 1989, Esta es tu vida 1990, Historia del bikini 1992, Peligrosamente juntos 2004, Todo esto es muy extraño 2004, 10 2007, Desayuno Continental 2010, En la playa 2011. *Website:* www.hombres-g.com.

MOLINO (COOK), Vincent; French musician (multi-instrumentalist); b. 1 Oct. 1958, Drôme. *Career:* fmr mem., Ars Antiqua Musicalis; mem., Radio Tarifa 1992–. *Recordings include:* albums: Rumba Argelina 1993, Temporal 1997, Cruzando el Rio 2001, Fiebre 2003. *Current Management:* c/o O'Donnel, Sold Out Management, 32 6°D, 28009 Madrid, Spain. *Telephone:* (91) 435-84-78. *Fax:* (91) 431-81-85. *E-mail:* recepcion@soldout.es. *Website:* www.soldout.es.

MOLKO, Brian; Scots/American singer and musician (guitar, bass); b. 10 Dec. 1972, Belgium. *Education:* Goldsmiths Coll.., London. *Career:* Founder mem., Ashtray Heart; mem., Placebo 1994–; numerous TV appearances; live tours and numerous festival dates. *Films include:* Velvet Goldmine 1998, Sue's Last Ride 2001. *Recordings include:* albums: Placebo 1996, Without You I'm Nothing 1998, Black Market Music 2000, Sleeping With Ghosts 2003, Meds 2006, Battle for the Sun 2009, Loud Like Love 2013. *Honours:* Kerrang! Classic Songwriter Award 2006, MTV Europe Music Award for Best Alternative Act 2009. *Current Management:* Riverman Management, George House, Brecon Road, London W6 8PY, England. *Telephone:* (20) 7381-4000. *Fax:* (20) 7381-9666. *E-mail:* info@riverman.co.uk. *Website:* www.riverman.co.uk; www.placeboworld.co.uk.

MOLLER, Lars Alleso, BFA; Danish musician (tenor saxophone) and composer; b. 17 Sept. 1966, Copenhagen. *Education:* New School, USA, lessons with David Liebman composer workshop with Bob Brookmeyer at Rytmekons Conservatory, Indian classical music studies, New Delhi. *Career:* own groups, with Jimmy Cobb, Niels-Henning Orsted Pedersen, Billy Hart, Mads Vinding, Alex Riel, Jukkis Outila, Thomas Clausen and John Abercrombie, 1986–91; featured soloist with Jimmy Cobb Sextet, Hermeto Pascoal Group, European Youth Big Band and European Broadcasting Union Big Band; also played with Holmes Brothers and various Danish bands such as Sound of Choice Ensemble, with Markus Stockhausen; played with leading artists including: Lee Konitz, Jimmy Cobb, Adam Nussbaum, Art Blakey, Roy Haynes and David Liebman; mem., Den 3 Vej (composer workshop group); leader, 18-piece group The Orchestra Big Band, 1997–98; Beijing Music Festival, 1998. *Recordings include:* Copenhagen Groove (with Niels-Henning Orsted Pedersen) 1989, Pyramid 1993, Cross Current 1995, Circles 1996, Colours (with John Abercrombie), 1997, Kaleidoscope Nazos/Jazz 1998, Centrifugal, 2001. *Honours:* Hon. prize from Danish Jazz Beat and Folk Authors Soc., Grammy Award (Best Danish Jazz Release) 2000, Danish Jazzmedia (JASA) Award 2000. *Telephone:* 33-22-91-89. *E-mail:* lmoller@post11.tele.dk; mail@larsmoller.com. *Website:* www.larsmoller.com.

MOLLISON, Deborah, MA; British composer and musician (piano); b. 29 May 1958, England; m. Gareth Mollison 1986. *Education:* Royal Acad. of Music, Lancaster Univ. with Craig Sheppard, Univ. of Calif., Los Angeles. *Career:* tutor of composition, Middlesex Univ.; has worked with Nik Kershaw, Marti Pellow, Brian Kennedy, Montserrat Caballe and Orchestral Manoeuvres in the Dark; has conducted London Philharmonic, BBC Concert Orchestra, Irish Film Orchestra; mem. PRS, BAC&S, Women In Film, Musicians' Union. *Film compositions include:* On the Edge 1997, Dillusc 1999, Bait 1999, East is East 1999, The Boys of Sunset Ridge 2001, Flipped 2001, The Art of the Critic 2003, The Heat of the Story 2004, Souli 2004, For Real 2006, Infinte Justice 2006, Running for River 2007, Too Much Too Young 2007, For Real 2008, On Stony Ground 2009, Tied to a Chair 2009, Godforsaken 2009, Horace K48 0.5 2013. *Television composition includes:* drama: The Gift of the Nile, Sleeping With Mickey (BBC 2), Before Your Eyes (BBC Wales), The Whistling Boy (BBC Wales), The Thing About Vince, Better by Design, Uncle Max; documentaries: Treasures At The South Pole, Thomas Cook On The Nile, Connections 2, Given Half A Chance, Amazing World of Animals, What the Romans Did For Us, Wild Weather, Better Designs, Secrets of the Ancients. *Honours:* Else Cross Prize, Royal Acad. of Music, Song '92 UK Festival. *Current Management:* c/o Air Edel, 18 Rodmarton Street, London, W1U 8BJ, England. *Telephone:* (20) 7486-6466. *Website:* www.air-edel.co.uk.

MOLLOY, Matt; Irish musician (flute, tin whistle); b. 12 Jan. 1947, Ballaghadareen Co. Roscommon. *Education:* began studying flute, aged 8. *Career:* mem. Bothy Band 1974, Planxty 1978, The Chieftains 1979–; collaborations with Paul Brady, Micheal O Suilleabhain, Donal Lunny, Irish Chamber Orchestra, Publican in Westport. *Recordings include:* with The Bothy Band: The First Album 1975, Old Hag You Have Killed Me 1976; with Planxty: After The Break 1979, The Woman I Loved So Well 1980; solo: Matt Molloy (featuring Donal Lunny) 1976, The Heathery Breeze 1981, The Gathering 1981, Contentment Is Wealth (with Sean Keane) 1985, Stony Steps 1988, The Fire Aflame (with Liam O Flynn and Sean Keane) 1992, Music At

Matt Molloy's 1992, Voyager (with Mike Oldfield), A Irmandade Das Estrellas (with Carlos Nunez) 1996, Shadows On Stone (featuring Steve Cooney, Christy Moore and Frankie Gavin) 1997, The Guiding Moon (with The West Ocean String Quartet) 2007, Pathway to the Well (with John Carty and Arty McGlynn) 2007; with The Chieftains: Chieftains 8 1978, Boil The Breakfast Early/Chieftains 9 1980, Chieftains 10 1981, The Chieftains In China 1984, Ballad Of The Irish Horse 1985, Celtic Wedding 1987, The Chieftains In Ireland (with James Galway) 1987, Year Of The French 1988, Irish Heartbeat (with Van Morrison) 1988, A Chieftains Celebration 1989, Chieftains Collection 1989, The Celtic Connection – James Galway And The Chieftains 1990, Bells Of Dublin 1991, An Irish Evening 1992, Another Country 1992, The Celtic Harp (with Belfast Harp Orchestra) 1993, The Long Black Veil 1995, Santiago 1996, Tears Of Stone 1999, Water From The Well 2000, Down The Old Plank Road: The Nashville Sessions 2002, The Wide World Over: A 40 Year Celebration 2002, San Patricio 2010, Voice of Ages 2012. *Honours:* winner, All Ireland Flute Championship, TG4 Nat. Traditional Award 1999; with The Chieftains: Grammy Awards for Best Contemporary Traditional Album (An Irish Evening – Live At The Grand Opera House 1991), for Best Traditional Album (Another Country 1992), for Best World Music Album (for Santiago) 1997. *Current Management:* c/o Macklam Feldman Management, 200–1505 West 2nd Avenue, Vancouver, BC V6H 3Y4, Canada. *Telephone:* (604) 630-3199. *E-mail:* info@mfmgt.com; management@mfmgt.com. *Website:* www.mfmgt.com. *E-mail:* info@mattmolloy.com. *Website:* www.mattmolloy.com; www.thechieftains.com.

MOLLOY, Paul; British musician (guitar). *Career:* fmr mem. The Skylarks; mem. The Zutons 2007–. *Recordings include:* album: You Can Do Anything 2008. *Current Management:* c/o Geoff Meall, The Agency Group, 361-373 City Road, London, EC1V 1PQ, England. *E-mail:* GeoffMeall@theagencygroup.com. *Website:* www.theagencygroup.com.

MOLONEY, Paddy; Irish composer and musician (uillean pipes, tin whistle); b. 1 Aug. 1938, Donnycarney, Dublin; m. Rita O'Reilly 1963; three c. *Career:* Founder Irish folk group The Chieftains 1962–; collaborations with Van Morrison and classical flute player, James Galway; Man. Dir Claddagh Records 1968–75, producing 45 albums in traditional, classical, poetry and spoken word recordings; Founding Partner, Wicklow Entertainment 1997–, producing The Long Journey Home 1998, Fire In The Kitchen 1998. *Recordings include:* albums: with The Chieftains: Chieftains 8 1978, Boil The Breakfast Early/Chieftains 9 1980, Chieftains 10 1981, The Chieftains In China 1984, Ballad Of The Irish Horse 1985, Celtic Wedding 1987, The Chieftains In Ireland (with James Galway) 1987, Year Of The French 1988, Irish Heartbeat (with Van Morrison) 1988, A Chieftains Celebration 1989, Chieftains Collection 1989, The Celtic Connection – James Galway And The Chieftains 1990, Bells Of Dublin 1991, An Irish Evening 1992, Another Country 1992, The Celtic Harp (with Belfast Harp Orchestra) 1993, The Long Black Veil 1995, Santiago 1996, Tears Of Stone 1999, Water From The Well 2000, Down The Old Plank Road: The Nashville Sessions 2002, The Wide World Over: A 40 Year Celebration 2002, San Patricio 2010, Voice of Ages 2012. *Honours:* Hon. DMus (Trinity Coll.) 1988; six Grammy Awards; Hon. Chief of the Oklahoma Choctaw Nation 1995. *Current Management:* c/o Macklam Feldman Management, 200–1505 West 2nd Avenue, Vancouver, BC V6H 3Y4, Canada. *Telephone:* (604) 630-3199. *E-mail:* info@mfmgt.com; management@mfmgt.com. *Website:* www.mfmgt.com; www.thechieftains.com.

MOMCHIL; Bulgarian musician (keyboards), singer, songwriter and arranger. *Career:* keyboard player, new wave band Class –1993; formed duo, Dony and Momchil 1993–. *Recordings include:* Albums: The Album! 1993, The Second One 1994. *Honours:* Orpheus Nat. Music Awards: Best Single: The Little Prince, Best Video For Duo Or A Group.

MOMMENS, Danny, (Danny Cool Rocket); Belgian musician (bass guitar, keyboards). *Career:* mem. dEUS 1997–2004, Vive la Fête 1997–. *Recordings include:* albums: with dEUS: In A Bar, Under The Sea 1997, The Ideal Crash 1999, Pocket Revolution 2005; with Vive la Fête: Attaque Surprise 2000, Republique 2001, Nuit Blanche 2003, Attaque Populaire 2004, Grand Prix 2005, Vive les Remixes 2006, Jour de Chance 2007, Disque d'or 2009, Produit de Belgique 2012, 2013 2013. *E-mail:* management@vivelafete.be. *Website:* www.vivelafete.be.

MOMOTA, Kanako; Japanese singer; b. 12 July 1994, Hamamatsu, Shizuoka. *Career:* Founder-mem., all-female vocal group Momoiro Clover 2008, renamed Momoiro Clover Z 2011–; first national tour 2009; debut single 2009; numerous live and TV appearances; concert appearances in Germany, Malaysia, France. *Films:* Shirome 2010. *Television:* as host: Meringue no Kimochi 2012–13. *Recordings:* albums: Battle and Romance (CD Shop Award for Best CD 2012) 2011, 5th Dimension 2013, Iriguchi no Nai Deguchi 2013. *Honours:* MTV Video Music Award Japan for Best Choreography 2013, MTV Europe Music Award for Best Japanese Act 2013. *Current Management:* c/o Stardust Promotion, 2F Takeda-Dai2 Bldg, 2-3-3 Ebisu-nishi, Shibuya, Tokyo, 150-0021, Japan. *Website:* www.stardust.co.jp; starchild.fm/special/en/momoclo.

MONAGHAN, Brendan; Irish singer, songwriter and musician (guitar); b. 3 April 1958, Newtownards, Co. Down, NI; s. of Michael Monaghan and Mary (Molly) Monaghan; m. Valerie McDonnell 1980; two s. one d. *Career:* appearances with band The Cattle Company include major country festivals, Europe; radio and TV appearances in Ireland, Europe, USA, cable TV in

Canada, USA; solo appearances at Fiddler's Green Int. Festival, Co. Down, Vlaardingen Int. Folk Festival, Netherlands 2003, Music of the Rivers Festival, Florida; writes, records and performs own songs world-wide; mem. Performing Right Soc., Int. Songwriters Asscn, BMI, USA, United Song Makers. *Compositions include:* I'm Right, You're Wrong, I Win, Love to be Loved, Sisters Lament, No More Words, Caledonian Girl, Look No Further, Love Me. *Recordings:* albums: with The Cattle Company: Hero 1996, Love to Be Loved 1998, Big Town After Dark 2000; solo: Precious Time 2004, No More Words 2006, Look No Further 2008, Flicker Of Hope 2010. *Honours:* Top Performance Award, Int. Country Music Festival, Netherlands, Publishers Award, Ray Shepherd Music, Efforts In Country Music, European Country Music Asscns, Best European Group 1995, Audio Images 2000 1997, Best Album, N America CMA Int. Awards 1999, Best Int. Songwriter, N America CMA Int. Awards 1999. *Current Management:* c/o Brambus Records, Berghalde, 8874 Muhlehorn, Switzerland. *Telephone:* (55) 6141077. *E-mail:* brambus@smile.ch. *Website:* www.brambus.com. *Address:* 5 Ballymacormick Park, Bangor, Co. Down, BT19 6BX, Northern Ireland (office). *Telephone:* (28) 9145-9350 (office). *E-mail:* info@brendanmonaghan.com (office). *Website:* www.brendanmonaghan.com.

MONAHAN, Patrick T.; American singer, songwriter and musician; b. 28 Feb. 1969, Erie, Pa; m. 2nd Amber Peterson. *Career:* Founder-mem. Train 1994–; supported bands including Barenaked Ladies, Counting Crows, Cracker, Hootie & the Blowfish; co-wrote two songs with Guy Chambers for Tina Turner; composer of song The Truth for Kris Allen (winner of American Idol); collaborations with Brandi Carlile, Martina McBride; solo career 2007–. *Recordings:* albums: with Train: Train 1998, Drops of Jupiter 2001, My Private Nation 2003, For Me, It's You 2006, Save Me, San Francisco 2009, California 37 2012, Bulletproof Picasso 2014; solo: Last of Seven 2007. *Television includes:* CSI: NY (as actor) 2009, Driver Dan's Story Train (as voice artist) 2010. *Honours:* Grammy Awards for Best Rock Song and Best Instrumental Arrangement 2002, for Best Pop Performance by a Duo or Group with Vocal 2011, Billboard Music Awards for Top Rock Artist and Top Rock Song 2011, ASCAP Pop Music Award for Song of the Year 2011. *Current Management:* c/o Crush Management, 60–62 East 11th Street, 7th Floor, New York, NY 10003, USA. *Telephone:* (646) 688-1729. *E-mail:* info@crushmm .com. *Website:* www.crushmm.com. *E-mail:* webmaster@patmonahan.net. *Website:* www.trainline.com; www.patmonahan.net.

MONDESIR, Michael Trevor Collins; British musician (bass guitar) and composer; b. 6 Feb. 1966, London, England. *Career:* in band EMJIEM (with guitarist Hawi Gondwe) 1983; performed with Courtney Pine, Iain Ballamy, Steve Williamson, Django Bates, Billy Cobham, Hermeto Pascoal, Pee Wee Ellis, Lenny White, Neneh Cherry, Jason Rebello, Annette Peacock, Bernard Purdie, Little Axe, Tackhead, Infinitum, Nikki Yeoh; Visiting Faculty, RAM, Rhythmic Conservatory, Copenhagen, British Acad. of New Music; mem. PRS, Musicians' Union. *Recordings include:* with Jason Rebello: Keeping Time 1992; with Django Bates: Summer Fruits (and Unrest) 1993, Winter Truce (and Homes Blaze) 1995, Quiet Nights 1998, Like Life 1998; with Billy Cobham: The Traveller 1994; with Oumou Sangare: Worotan 1996. *Website:* www.michaelmondesir.com.

MONDLOCK, Robert (Buddy); American singer, musician (guitar) and songwriter; b. Chicago, Ill. *Career:* performed on Chicago club scene 1980s; moved to Nashville after securing publishing contract with EMI mid-1980s; songs recorded by Garth Brooks, Joan Baez, Nanci Griffith, Janis Ian, David Wilcox, Maura O'Connell, Peter Paul and Mary. *Recordings include:* albums: solo: Buddy Mondlock 1994, Poetic Justice 1999, The Edge of the World 2007, The Memory Wall 2013. *Honours:* Kerrville Folk Festival Award 1987, Kerrville Music Award Song of the Year (The Kid) 1996. *Current Management:* c/o Terri Stewart, Stewart Management and Booking, PO Box 27581, Denver, CO 80227, USA. *Telephone:* (303) 989-1764. *Fax:* (303) 989-2783. *E-mail:* terri@stewartmgmt.com. *Website:* stewartmgmt.com; www .buddymondlock.com.

MONEYBROTHER; Swedish musician; b. (Anders Wendin). *Career:* fmr mem. punk rock band, Monster; solo artist, as Moneybrother 2003–. *Recordings include:* albums: Blood Panic (Swedish Grammy Award for Rock Album of the Year) 2003, To Die Alone 2005, Pengabrorsan 2006, Mount Pleasure 2007, Real Control 2009, This is where Life is 2012. *Honours:* MTV Europe Music Award Best Swedish Act 2005. *Current Management:* c/o Villam Artist Management, 327 W Avenue 37, Los Angeles, CA 90065, USA. *Telephone:* (323) 664-6000. *Fax:* (323) 927-1991. *E-mail:* moneybrother@villamartists .com. *Website:* www.villamartists.com; www.moneybrothermusic.com.

MONHEIT, Jane, BMus; American jazz singer and musician (clarinet); b. 3 Nov. 1977, Oakdale, LI; m. Rick Montalbano 2002. *Education:* studied with Peter Eldridge, Manhattan School of Music. *Career:* second place, Thelonious Monk Int. Jazz Competition 1998; released debut album 2000, featuring musicians including pianist Kenny Barron, bassist Ron Carter, saxophonist David 'Fathead' Newman; int. appearances include Royal Festival Hall, London 2002, Brecon Jazz Festival, Wales 2005. *Recordings:* albums: Never Never Land (Best Debut Recording, Jazz Journalists Asscn) 2000, Come Dream With Me 2001, In The Sun 2002, Live at the Rainbow Room 2003, Taking A Chance On Love 2004, The Season 2005, Surrender 2007, The Lovers, the Dreamers and Me 2009, Home 2010. *Honours:* Ronnie Scott Award for Best Female 2007. *Current Management:* c/o Cynthia B. Herbst, American International Artists, 356 Pine Valley Road, Hossick Falls, NY 12090, USA.

Telephone: (518) 686-0972. *Fax:* (518) 686-1960. *E-mail:* cynthia@aiartists .com. *Website:* www.aiartists.com. *E-mail:* info@janemonheitonline.com (office). *Website:* www.janemonheitmusic.com; www.janemonheitonline.com.

MONICA; American singer; b. (Monica Denise Arnold), 24 Oct. 1980, College Park, Atlanta, GA; m. Shannon Brown 2010. *Recordings include:* albums: Miss Thang 1995, The Boy is Mine 1998, After the Storm 2003, The Makings of Me 2007, Still Standing 2010, New Life 2012, Code Red 2015. *Honours:* Grammy Award for Best R&B Performance by a Duo or Group with Vocals (for The Girl is Mine, with Brandy) 1999. *Address:* c/o RCA Records, Sony Music Entertainment, 550 Madison Avenue, New York, NY 10022, USA (office). *Website:* www.sonymusic.com (office); www.monica.com.

MONK, Meredith Jane; American composer, singer, director and choreographer; b. 20 Nov. 1942, New York, NY; d. of Theodore G. Monk and Audrey Lois Monk (née Zellman). *Education:* Sarah Lawrence Coll. *Career:* Founder and Artistic Dir House Foundation for the Arts 1968–; formed Meredith Monk & Vocal Ensemble 1978–; Richard and Barbara Debs Composer's Chair, Carnegie Hall 2014–15; mem. American Acad. of Arts and Sciences 2006. *Films:* Book of Days, Ellis Island. *Compositions include:* Break 1964, 16 Millimeter Earrings 1966, Juice: A Theatre Cantata 1969, Key 1971, Vessel: An Opera Epic 1971, Paris 1972, Education of the Girlchild 1973, Quarry 1976, Songs from the Hill 1976, Dolmen Music 1979, Specimen Days: A Civil War Opera 1981, Ellis Island 1981, Turtle Dreams Cabaret 1983, The Games 1983, Acts from Under and Above 1986, Book of Days 1988, Facing North 1990, Three Heavens and Hells 1992, ATLAS: An Opera in Three Parts 1991, New York Requiem 1993, Volcano Songs 1994, American Archaeology 1994, The Politics of Quiet 1996, Steppe Music 1997, Magic Frequencies 1998, Micki Suite 2000, Eclipse Variations 2000, mercy 2001, Possible Sky 2003, impermanence 2004, Stringsongs 2005, Night 2005, Songs of Ascension 2008, Weave for two voices, chamber orchestra and chorus 2010, Realm Variations 2012, On Behalf of Nature 2013. *Honours:* Officer of the Order of Arts and Letters; Dr hc (Bard Coll.) 1988, (Univ. of the Arts) 1989, (Juilliard School of Music) 1998, (San Francisco Art Inst.) 1999, (Boston Conservatory) 2001; Golden Eagle Award 1981, Nat. Music Theatre Award 1986, German Critics' Award for Best Recording of the Year 1981, 1986, MacArthur Genius Award 1995, Samuel Scripps Award 1996, United States Artists Fellow 2006, Musical America Composer of the Year 2012, Doris Duke Artist 2012, NPR's 50 Great Voices 2012. *Address:* The House Foundation, 260 West Broadway, Suite 2, New York, NY 10013, USA (office). *Telephone:* (212) 904-1330 (office). *Fax:* (212) 904-1305 (office). *E-mail:* monk@meredithmonk.org (office). *Website:* www.meredithmonk.org (office).

MONTANARO, Miquieù Michel François, MA; French composer, musician (flutes, saxophone, accordion, piano) and actor; b. 13 Aug. 1955, Hyères; m. Niké Nagy 1981; two s. one d. *Career:* first concert, Edinburgh 1973; tours of Hungary, Bulgaria, Austria, Italy, Portugal, USA, Indonesia, Algeria, Morocco, Tunisia, West Africa; festivals include: Bamako, St Chartier, Nantes, Budapest, Comboscuro; has played with B Phillips, Kiss Tamàs, Konomba Traore, A Vitous, P Aledo, G Murphy, Téka, F Frith, Vujicsics, C Tyler, Sebastyén Màrta, P Neveu, Ghymes, F Richard, J Stivin, C Brazier, D Daumas, F Kop, D Regef, C Zagaria, K Ruzicka, Szabados, F Ulihr, P Vaillant, A Gabriel, J Lyonn Lieberman, L Andrst, J N Mabelly, D Phillips, Es Soundoussia, F Gaudé, S Pesce, Hayet Ayad, Christine Wodrascka, Samia Benchikh, Senem Diyici, René Sette, Mathieu Luzi, Nena Venetsanou, Sara Alexander, Michel Bianco, Carlo Rizzo, Corou de Berra, Wayal; mem. ADAMI, SPEDIDAM, SACEM, SFA. *Composition:* Cri, for symphonic orchestra and traditional instruments 1997. *Recordings include:* albums: more than 40 including: Montanaro/Collage, Bonton 1990, Mesura and Arte del Danzare 1992, Tenson – La Nef Des Musiques, Bleu Regard 1993, Vents d'Est/ Migrations 1993, Montanaro/Théâtre 1994, Galoubet-Tambourin, Musiques d'Hier Et Aujourdhui 1995; with L'Ensemble Méditerranéen P Aledo: Fusion, D'île En Ile, Tres Corpos Una Alma, Java Sapto Raharjo 1997, Vents d'Est Ballade pour une Mer qui Chante 1997, Maurin des Maures 1999, Winds of East Ungaresca 2002, Chicha 2002, Tambourinaire 2003, Bridge over the Sea 2005, Set Otramar 2006, Polonaise 2007, Duo Montanaro 2009, D'Amor de Guerra 2010, Piada Ribas 2012, Serdu 2013. *Publication:* Video K7 Noir and Blanc with Konomba Traore, CNDP, France. *Address:* MIMO, Fort Gibron, BP 4, 83570 Correns, France (office). *Telephone:* 4-94-86-15-75 (office). *Website:* www.compagnie-montanaro.com (office).

MONTANER, Ricardo; Venezuelan singer, songwriter and record producer; b. (Héctor Eduardo Reglero Montaner), 8 Sept. 1957, Buenos Aires, Argentina; m. 1st; two s.. m. 2nd Marlene Rodríguez Miranda; three c. *Career:* raised in Venezuela; debut recordings 1978; popular Latin pop artist in Mexico, Cen. America and S America late 1980s–; performed at Madison Square Garden, New York 1992; numerous albums and live tours. *Television:* as actor: Niña Bonita (telenovela) 1988; as judge/mentor: Idol Puerto Rico 2011–12, La Voz Colombia 2012. *Recordings include:* albums: Cada Día 1983, Ricardo Montaner 1987, Ricardo Montaner 1988, Un Toque de Misterio 1990, En el Último Lugar de Mundo 1991, Los Hijos del Sol 1992, Una Mañana y un Camino 1994, Viene del Alma 1995, Es Así 1997, Con la London Metropolitan Orchestra 1999, Sueño Repetido 2001, Suma 2002, Prohibido Olvidar 2003, Todo y Nada 2005, Las Mejores Canciones del Mundo 2007, Las Mejores Canciones Vol. 2 2007, Soy Feliz 2010, Viajero Frecuente 2012. *Address:* c/o Sony Music Latin, Sony Music Entertainment, 550 Madison Avenue, Room 2316, New York, NY 10022, USA (office). *E-mail:* info@montaner.com.mx (home). *Website:* www.sonymusiclatin.com (office); ricardomontaner.mx (home).

MONTE, Marisa; Brazilian singer; b. 1 July 1967, Rio de Janeiro. *Education:* studied lyrical art in Italy. *Career:* f. Tribalistas with Arnaldo Antunes and Carlinhos Brown 2002–03. *Recordings include:* Ao Vivo 1989, Rose and Charcoal, Red Hot+Rio, Aguas de Março (jtly), A Great Noise 1996, Memórias, Crônicas e Declarações de Amor 2000, Tribalistas 2003, Infinito Particular 2006, Universo ao Meu Redor (Latin Grammy Award for Best Samba/Pagode Album 2006) 2006, O Que Você Quer Saber de Verdade 2011, Verdade, Uma Ilusão 2014. *Website:* www.marisamonte.com.br.

MONTENEGRO, Oswaldo; Brazilian composer, singer, stage director and musician (guitar, piano); b. 15 March 1956, Rio de Janeiro; m. Paloma Duarte; (divorced) one s. *Education:* Univ. of Brazil, Univ. of Rio de Janeiro. *Career:* tours of Brazil 1979–; TV, radio appearances, concerts, Portugal, until 1992; collaborated with Zé Ramalho, Roberto Menescal, Milton Guedes, Eduardo Costa, Valencia Alcaeus; mem. UBC, SBAT, Warner-Chappell. *Film:* Solitudes 2013. *Compositions include:* Bandolins, Lua e Flor, Condor, Seo e Bia, Furtuiçào, Estrelas, Voz da Tela. *Recordings include:* Trilhas 1977, Poeta Maldito, Moleque Vadio 1979, Oswaldo Montenegro 1980, Asa De Lux 1981, A Dança Dos Signos 1982, Cristal 1983, Brincando em Cima Daquilo 1984, Drops De Hortelã 1985, Os Menestréis 1986, Aldeia Dos Ventos 1986, Oswaldo Montenegro ao Vivo 1989, Vida de Artista 1991, Mulungo 1992, Seu Francisco 1993, Aos Filhos Dos Hippies 1995, O Vale Encantado 1997, Noturno 1997, Letras Brasileiras 1997, Léo e Bia 1998, Aldeia dos Ventos 1998, A Lista 1999, Escondido no Tempo 1999, Entre uma Balada e um Blues 2001, Estrada Nova 2002, A Partir de Agora 2007, Intimidade 2008, Seu Francisco: Ao Vivo 2008, Quebra-cabeça Elétrico 2009, Canções De Amor 2010, De Passagem 2011, Ensaio 2013, Oswaldo Montenegro e Cia Mulungo 2013. *Honours:* winner with Agonia, TV Globo Brazilian Popular Music Festival 1980. *Address:* c/o Agência Produtora, Avenue Professor Romeu Pelegrinni, 216-Ipiranga, 04261-120 São Paulo SP, Brazil. *E-mail:* montenegro@oswaldomontenegro.com.br. *Website:* www.oswaldomontenegro.com.br.

MONTGOMERY, John Michael; American country singer, musician (guitar) and songwriter; b. 20 Jan. 1965, Danville, Ky. *Career:* began performing on parents' country music shows aged five; performed with local country bands aged 15; subsequently played with father, Harold and brother, Eddie (later of Montgomery Gentry country duo); played the Austin City Saloon in Lexington, Ky, developing local following; solo artist 1992–. *Recordings include:* Life's a Dance 1992, Kickin' It Up 1994, John Michael Montgomery 1995, What I Do the Best 1996, Leave a Mark 1998, Home to You 1999, Brand New Me 2000, Pictures 2002, Mr. Snowman 2003, Letters from Home 2004, Time Flies 2008. *Honours:* Horizon Award, Country Music Asscn 1994, Favorite Newcomer, American Music Awards (Country) 1994, New Artist of the Year, Single of the Year (for I Swear), Acad. of Country Music 1994. *Current Management:* c/o Hallmark Direction Co., 713 18th Avenue South, Nashville, TN 37203, USA. *Telephone:* (615) 320-7714.

MONTREDON, Jean-Claude Pierre; French musician (drums) and composer; b. 23 Sept. 1949, Martinique, Lesser Antilles. *Career:* mem. Frères Bernard Orchestra, Tropicana Orchestra; drums for Marius Cultier and The Surfs; formed trio with Alain Jean Marie, Winston Berkley; performances in Barbados, Trinidad 1972, Bilboquet, Paris jazz club, French Radio 1973–75; founder mem. Kominikayson (with Richard Raux, Michel Alibo) 1976, numerous live appearances; played with Didier Levellet Quintet, Chris McGregor, New Morning Jazz Club, Paris 1977–; rock concerts with Randy Weston, Claude Sommier, Michel Alibo 1978–81; tours of Finland, Sweden, West Africa with Roland Brival 1981; played with Liquid Rock Stonne, Paris; founder, The Musical Corps of Martinique 1990–94; collaborations with Luther François; mem. SACEM, SPEDIDAM, Congés Spectacle. *Recordings include:* Malavoi Tropicana Orchestre, Gisèle Baka, Al Lirvart and Didier Levallet Quintet, Brotherhood of Breath, Joby Bernabe, Doudou Guirand, 2 albums with The Caribbean Ensemble (West Indies Jazz Band) 1990, 1992, Luther François 1990, Biguine Reflections II 1996, Embarquement Créole 1996, Biguine Reflections: Délirio 2000, Wabap 2002. *Address:* 131 rue de Rome, 75017 Paris, France.

MOONEY, Gordon James, BSc; musician (bagpipes) and business executive; b. 27 May 1951, Edinburgh, Scotland; m. 1978; one s. one d. *Education:* Univ. of Dundee. *Career:* concerts include: Edinburgh Int. Festival, Sanders Tagare, Boston, Old Songs Festival USA, Tacoma Univ. USA, Québec Double Reed Convention, Vermont Bagpipe Festival; TV and radio appearances: Border TV, Canadian Nat. Radio, BBC, Radio Scotland, Radio 4, World Service; Fellow, Soc. of Antiquaries of Scotland; mem. MPRS, Pres. Lowland and Border Pipers Soc.; also manufactures Scottish small pipes, Northumbrian bagpipes, blackwood whistles. *Recordings include:* O'er The Border, Global Meditation, Song For Yarrow. *Publications include:* A Tutor for Cauld Wind Bagpipes, A Choice Collection of Tunes for the Lowland and Border Bagpipes, O'er the Border, A Scottish Wedding. *Honours:* Scottish Arts Council Award 1988, Billboard Award 1993. *Telephone:* (514) 900-1923. *E-mail:* oddscotland@ gmail.com. *Website:* www.odd-scotland.com/Gordon-Mooney-Scottish-Piper.

MOORE, Abra; American singer, songwriter and musician (guitar); b. 8 June 1969, Mission Bay, Calif. *Education:* Univ. of Hawaii. *Career:* Founder-mem. Poi Dog Pondering; solo artist, toured with Matthew Sweet, Barenaked Ladies, Medeski, Martin and Wood, Third Eye Blind, Collective Soul, Lilith Fair and Big Head Todd and the Monsters; session work with Rob Halverson;

mem. AFTRA. *Recordings include:* solo albums: Sing 1995, Strangest Places 1997, No Fear 2002, Everything Changed 2004, On the Way 2007. *Film appearances include:* Slacker 1998, Sliding Doors 1998. *Publications include:* contrib. to nat. and int. music magazines, newspapers and journals. *Current Management:* c/o Leslie Turner, PO Box 60053, Nashville, TN 37206, USA. *E-mail:* management@abramoore.com. *Website:* www.abramoore.com.

MOORE, Alecia (see Pink)

MOORE, Angelo Christopher, (Dr Madd Vibe); American singer and musician (saxophone, percussion); b. 5 Nov. 1965. *Career:* Founder-mem. Fishbone. collaborations Little Richard, Curtis Mayfield, George Clinton, Rick James, Spike Lee and others, with rap artists including the Jungle Brothers; numerous live appearances, including Lollapalooza in 1993; Co-founder (with Kris Jensen) The Brand New Step music project. *Recordings include:* albums: with Fishbone: In Your Face 1986, Truth and Soul 1988, The Reality of our Surroundings 1991, Give a Monkey a Brain and He'll… 1993, Chim Chim's Badass Revenge 1996, Fishbone and the Family Nextperience Present: The Psychotic Friends Nuttwerx 2000, Still Stuck in Your Throat 2006, Crazy Glue 2011; solo as Dr Madd Vibe: Angelo Moore Is Dr. Madd Vibe: The Ying Yang Thang 2000, Dr. Madd Vibe Comprehensive Linkology 2000, Dr. Madd Vibe's Medicine Cabinet 2005, Madd Vibe En Dub 2010, The Angelo Show - The Olegna Phenomenon 2012, Brand New Step 2012. *Website:* www.drmadvibe .com; brandnewstep.com; www.fishbone.net.

MOORE, Bob Loyce; American musician (bass guitar) and record producer; b. 30 Nov. 1932, Nashville, Tenn.; three s. one d. *Career:* mem. Nashville A-Team 1950s to 1970s; bassist for various artists including Little Jimmy Dickens 1949, Red Foley 1950, Owen Bradley 1951–66, Elvis Presley 1963–71, Crystal Gayle 1982–84; co-owner, Monument Records 1961–70; record producer for Jerry Lee Lewis, George Jones, Johnny Cash, Boxcar Willie, Roy Orbison; President, K & K Productions 1986–; Pres., Bob Moore Music 1963–; prolific studio musician, over 17,000 recording sessions for artists including Kenny Rogers, Tammy Wynette, Don McLean, Hank Williams Jr, Tom Jones, Willie Nelson, Dolly Parton, Patsy Cline, Jim Reeves, Frank Sinatra, Simon and Garfunkel, Johnny Cash, Roy Orbison, Conway Twitty, Loretta Lynn, Brenda Lee, Ernest Tubb, Andy Williams, Connie Francis, The Statler Brothers, Clyde McFatter, Marty Robbins, Eddy Arnold, Kitty Wells; mem. AFofM, NARAS. *Recordings include:* This Our Joy And This Our Feast 2000, Let Every Instrument Be Tuned For Praise 2001. *Honours:* NARAS Most Valuable Player Award 1979–82, numerous Superpicker Awards, Musicians Hall of Fame 2007. *E-mail:* rnmguard2000-nashvillesound@ yahoo.com. *Website:* www.nashvillesound.net.

MOORE, Dorothy Rudd, BMus; American composer, teacher and singer; b. 4 June 1940, Wilmington, Del.; m. Kermit Moore. *Education:* Howard High School, Wilmington School of Music, Howard Univ., American Conservatory, France, private study with Chou Wen Chung 1965, private voice lessons with Lola Hayes 1972. *Career:* teacher, Harlem School of the Arts, New York 1965–66, New York Univ. 1969, Bronx Community Coll. 1971; private piano, voice, sight singing and ear training instructor, New York 1968–; founding mem., Soc. of Black Composers 1968–75; mem., New York State Council for the Arts 1988–90; Lucy Moten Fellowship 1963; American Music Center grant 1972; New York State Council on the Arts grant 1985; mem. Nat. Endowment for the Arts, Recording and Composers (panel mem. 1986–88), New York Women Composers, New York Singing Teachers' Asscn, American Composers' Alliance, BMI. *Compositions include:* Flight for piano 1956, Symphony No. 1 1962, Songs from the Rubaiyat 1962, Reflections for concert band 1962, Baroque Suite for unaccompanied violoncello 1964, Three Pieces for Violin and piano 1966, Modes for ensemble 1968, Moods for ensemble 1969, Lament for nine instruments 1969, Trio No. 1 1969, From the Dark Tower 1970, Dirge and Deliverance for cello 1970, Weary Blues 1972, Dream and Variations for piano 1974, Sonnets on Love, Rosebuds and Death 1975, In Celebration for chorus 1977, Night Fantasy for clarinet 1978, A Little Whimsy for piano 1978, Frederick Douglass (opera) 1981, Transcension (I Have Been to the Mountaintop) for chamber orchestra 1985, Flowers of Darkness 1988, Voices From The Light for chorus 1997. *Current Management:* c/o Gina Genova, American Composers Alliance, 802 West, 190th Street, Suite 1B, New York, NY 10040, USA. *Telephone:* (212) 925-0458. *E-mail:* info@composers.com. *Website:* composers.com/dorothy-rudd-moore.

MOORE, Malcolm Charles; British musician (bass guitar, double bassist), singer and songwriter; b. 19 Jan. 1971, Chelmsford, Essex; m. Rosie Moore. *Education:* City Univ., London, Guildhall School of Music. *Career:* session bass player with Steve Martland, BBC Symphony Orchestra, London Sinfonietta, London Philharmonic Orchestra, Tommy Chase Band, Tindersticks, Swordfish, Elvis Costello, Spiritualized, Barry Adamson; toured with Westlife, A1, Girls Aloud, Sinead Quinn, James Blunt, Lulu, Fame Academy; performed in West End theatre productions Rent, Fosse, The Lion King; f. own group, themillionstars. *Recordings include:* with Steve Martland: Crossing The Border, Patrol, Horses of Instruction; with Tindersticks: This Way Up, Horses of Instruction, Trouble Everyday (soundtrack); with Swordfish: Living A Life, Frank and Walters, The Russian Ship, Lost Highway Soundtrack, Barry Adamson and David Lynch; with Lulu: I Love Xmas; with Darius: Live Twice. *Address:* 116 Skitts Hill, Braintree, Essex, CM7 1AS, England. *Telephone:* (7977) 803947. *E-mail:* mal@themillionstars.com.

MOORE, Mark; British producer, remixer and DJ; b. 1965, London, England. *Career:* began career as DJ at Phillip Sallon's Mud Club; formed S-Express with Pascal Gabriel 1988; Founder Splish Records; resident DJ at Chuff Chuff parties; collaborations: William Orbit, Billie Ray Martin, Sonique; remixed: Seal, Prince, Randy Crawford. *Recordings:* albums: Original Soundtrack 1990, Intercourse 1991; singles: Theme From S-Express, Superfly Guy 1988, Hey Music Lover, Mantra For A State of Mind 1989, Nothing To Lose 1990; Find 'Em Fool 'Em Forget 'Em 1992. *Current Management:* c/o Ultra DJ Management, 3 City Business Centre, Lower Road, London, SE16 2XB, England. *Telephone:* (20) 7740-2119. *Fax:* (20) 7252-2225. *E-mail:* cath@ultradj.co.uk. *Website:* www.ultradj.co.uk.

MOORE, Nicky; British blues singer, musician (guitar, piano, harmonica) and vocal tutor; b. 21 June 1952, Devon, England; m. Maggie Moore 1974, four s. one d. *Education:* Exeter Cathedral, RSCM. *Career:* mem. of rock bands, Hackensack, Tiger, Samson, Mammoth, Gerry Rafferty, Blues Corporation; mem. Musicians' Union. *Film appearances include:* Hearts of Fire, Just Ask for Diamond. *Recordings include:* Tiger: Up The Hard Way, Going Down Laughing, Test of Time, Before The Storm, Mammoth: Don't Get Mad Get Even, I Just Got Back, Holding On, Samson Live in London 2001, Riding With The Angels - The Anthology 2002, Hog On A Log 2006, Tomorrow & Yesterday 2006, Leftovers, Relics & Rarities 2007. *Address:* 189 Upper Fant Road, Maidstone, Kent, ME16 8BX, England. *Telephone:* (1622) 208679. *E-mail:* nickymoorevoice@hotmail.com. *Website:* www.nickymoore.com.

MOORE, Samuel (Sam) David; American singer and entertainer; b. 12 Oct. 1935, Miami, FL; m. Joyce McRae 1982. *Career:* mem. soul duo, Sam & Dave; solo artist; numerous television and live appearances; mem. NARAS. *Film appearances:* One Trick Pony, Tapeheads, Tales of the City, Soul Man. *Recordings include:* albums: as Sam & Dave: Hold On I'm Coming 1966, Double Dynamite 1967, Soul Men 1967, I Thank You 1968, Back at 'Cha 1976; solo: Plenty Good Lovin' 2002, Overnight Sensational 2006. *Honours:* Grammy Award (for Soul Man) 1967, Rhythm & Blues Foundation Pioneer Award 1991. *Website:* www.sammoore.net.

MOORE, Sean Anthony; Welsh musician (drums); b. 30 July 1968, Pontypool, Gwent. *Career:* founder mem., Betty Blue 1986, renamed Manic Street Preachers 1988–; numerous tours, festival appearances, TV and radio appearances; first Western group to play concert in Cuba since 1979, February 2001. *Recordings include:* albums: Generation Terrorists 1992, Gold Against The Soul 1993, The Holy Bible 1994, Everything Must Go (BRIT Award for Best British Album 1997) 1996, This Is My Truth, Tell Me Yours (BRIT Award for Best British Album 1999) 1998, Know Your Enemy 2001, Forever Delayed 2002, Lipstick Traces: A Secret History Of Manic Street Preachers 2003, Lifeblood 2004, Send Away the Tigers 2007, Journal for Plague Lovers 2009, Postcards from a Young Man 2010, Rewind the Film 2013, Futurology 2014. *Honours:* numerous including: with Manic Street Preachers: BRIT Awards for Best British Group 1997, 1999, Q Awards for Best Live Act 2001, for Best Track (for Your Love Alone is Not Enough) 2007, for Best Video (for Show Me the Wonder) 2013, MOJO Maverick Award 2009. *Current Management:* Gillian Porter, Hall or Nothing Independent Publicity, 2 Archer Street, Soho, London, W1D 7AW, England. *E-mail:* gillian@hallornothing.com. *Website:* www.hallornothing.com; www.manicstreetpreachers.com.

MOORE, Thurston; American singer and musician (guitar); b. 25 July 1958, Coral Gables, Fla; m. Kim Gordon, one d. *Career:* Founder mem., Sonic Youth 1981–; Founder mem., Ciccone Youth 1986–; mem. Chelsea Light Moving 2012–; Owner record label, Ecstatic Peace!; solo artist 1995–. *Recordings include:* albums: with Sonic Youth: Sonic Youth 1982, Confusion is Sex 1983, Sonic Death 1984, Bad Moon Rising 1985, E.V.O.L. 1986, Sister 1987, Daydream Nation 1988, The Whitey Album 1989, Goo 1990, Dirty 1992, Experimental Jet Set, Trash and No Star 1994, Screaming Fields of Sonic Love 1995, Made in USA 1995, Washing Machine 1995, A Thousand Leaves 1998, SYR4: Goodbye 20th Century 1999, NYC Ghosts & Flowers 2000, Murray Street 2002, Sonic Nurse 2004, Rather Ripped 2006, The Destroyed Room: B-sides and Rarities 2006, The Eternal 2009; with Ciccone Youth: The Whitey Album 1989; with Chelsea Light Moving: Chelsea Light Moving 2013; solo: Psychic Hearts 1995, Three Incredible Ideas 2001, Trees Outside the Academy 2007, Demolished Thoughts 2011, The Best Day 2014. *Publication:* No Wave: Post-Punk. Underground. New York 1976–80 (with Byron Coley) 2008. *Current Management:* c/o Michael Meisel, Silva Artist Management, 722 Seward Street, Los Angeles, CA 90038-3504, USA. *Telephone:* (323) 856-8222. *Website:* www.sonicyouth.com; www.chelsealightmoving.com.

MOORE, Vinnie; American rock musician (guitar). *Education:* jazz guitar. *Career:* member, Vicious Rumours 1985; solo artiste 1986–; guitarist, Alice Cooper, Hey Stoopid tour 1991; guitarist, UFO 2004–. *Recordings:* albums: with Vicious Rumours: Soldiers of The Night 1985; solo: Mind's Eye 1986, Time Odyssey 1988, Meltdown 1991, Out of Nowhere 1996, The Maze 1999, Live! 2000, Defying Gravity 2001, To the Core 2009; with UFO: You Are Here 2004, The Monkey Puzzle 2006, The Visitor 2009, Seven Deadly 2012. *Website:* www.ufo-music.info; www.vinniemoore.com.

MORALES, David, (The Boss, Brooklyn Friends); American producer, remixer and DJ; b. 21 Aug. 1961, Brooklyn, New York. *Career:* began DJ career at the Ozone Layer in New York and was guest at the Paradise Garage club; later resident at Better Days and Red Zone in New York; mem., Def Mix production crew (alongside Frankie Knuckles and Satoshi Tomiie); remixer from early 1990s; remixed Mariah Carey, Jody Watley, U2, Jamiroquai, Luther Vandross, Incognito, Pet Shop Boys, Basement Jaxx, Britney Spears, Janet Jackson, Spice Girls; collaborations with Albert Cabrera, Juliet Roberts,

Jocelyn Brown. *Recordings include:* singles: Congo (as The Boss), 1994; Philadelphia (as Brooklyn Friends), 1995; Needin' U, 1998; Needin' U II, 2001; albums: The Program 1993, 2 Worlds Collide 2004. *Current Management:* c/o Def Mix, 928 Broadway, Suite 400, New York, NY, USA. *Website:* www.djdavidmorales.com.

MORAN, Jason; American pianist and band leader; b. 21 Jan. 1975; m. Alicia Hall Moran; two s. *Education:* High School for the Performing and Visual Arts, Houston, Manhattan School of Music. *Career:* studied classical piano as a child; joined Greg Osby's band 1997; solo artist 1999–; collaborations with artists including Charles Lloyd, Cassandra Wilson, Joe Lovano, Don Byron, Steve Coleman, Lee Konitz, Von Freeman, Christian McBride, Ravi Coltrane; faculty mem., New England Conservatory of Music, Manhattan School of Music. *Recordings:* albums: as bandleader: Soundtrack to Human Motion 1999, Facing Left 2000, Black Stars 2001, Modernistic 2002, Same Mother 2005, Artist in Residence 2006, Ten 2010, All Rise: A Joyful Elegy for Fats Waller 2014; with Greg Osby: Further Ado 1997; other appearances: Blood from Stars, Joe Henry 2009. *Honours:* USA Prudential Fellow 2007, MacArthur Foundation Fellowship 2010, Echo Jazz Award 2011, Jazz Journalists' Asscn Award for Musician of the Year 2015. *Current Management:* c/o Louise Holland, Vision Arts Management, 16 Clintfinger Road, Saugerties, NY 12477, USA. *Telephone:* (845) 247-8969. *Fax:* (845) 247-8970. *E-mail:* louise@visionartsmgmt.com. *Website:* www.visionartsmgmt.com; www.jasonmoran.com.

MORAN, Michael John, (Triple M), BA, MA; British composer, producer, musician (electric guitar, keyboards) and programmer; *Owner/Director, Triple M Productions/The Vocal Booth;* b. 18 July 1964, Birkenhead, Merseyside, England; s. of John Moran and Pauline Moran (née Conway); m. Janette Moran; one s. one d. *Education:* Sandown Coll., Liverpool, Univ. Coll., Salford, Liverpool Hope Univ. *Career:* mem. 16 Tambourines; toured with Squeeze, Hue and Cry, Wet Wet Wet; Tour Man. 35 Summers tour with EMF; Man. N-Trust (as Decent Exposure Management); Musical Dir Jungle Book, Redgrave Theatre, Farnham, Sgt Pepper's Magical Mystery Trip, Liverpool Playhouse; Musical Dir Rockin' Robin and the Babes, Halewood Pantomime Everyman Theatre 1997–98; composer/producer for girl vocal group Dyverse; currently Dir The Vocal Booth location sound and audio post-production business; Owner Triple M Productions (music composition and production); currently producing singer-songwriter Niki Kand; mem. Performing Right Soc., Musicians' Union, Mechanical-Copyright Protection Soc. *Compositions:* co-writer: It's Better To Love, Movies, Language of Love; writer: Going Off Big Time (film music), 11 Missed Calls (winner DIY Film Festival 2009), Unseen (Fab Productions), Most Children, My Home Town (big band), Happy Animal Choir, Happy Pirate Song. *Recordings:* albums: How Green Is Your Valley, 16 Tambourines, Over You (also producer), Marc Vormawah and the L8 Connection (also producer); producer: Quiet Defiance, N-Trust; co-producer: The Happy Animal Choir, Other Favourite Nursery Rhymes for Children; singles: with 16 Tambourines: If I Should Stay, How Green Is Your Valley. *Address:* Triple M Productions, 31 Elmar Road, Aigburth, Liverpool, L17 0DA, England (office). *Telephone:* (151) 707-2833 (office). *E-mail:* triplem@thevocalbooth.com (office). *Website:* www.thevocalbooth.com (office).

MORAN, Mike, GRSM, ARCM; British composer and musician (piano, clarinet); b. 4 March 1948, Leeds, Yorkshire; m. Lynda Moran 1992; one d. *Education:* Royal Coll. of Music. *Career:* musician, arranger, record producer; as musician, arranger, worked with artists, including Paul McCartney, Stevie Wonder, Kate Bush, Paul Simon, Joe Cocker, George Harrison, Gladys Knight, Robert Plant, Cliff Richard, Carly Simon, Julio Iglesias, The Four Tops, Placido Domingo, Jose Carreras, Elvin Jones, Oliver Nelson, Leo Sayer, Lulu, Dusty Springfield, Kevin Ayers, Colin Blunstone, Chris de Burgh, Heart, Ozzy Osbourne, Chris Rea, Freddie Mercury, Elaine Paige; mem. of bands Blue Mink, Stone The Crows, Gillan; took part in Wembley tribute to Freddie Mercury 1994; Prof., Piano Jazz, Royal Coll. of Music; mem. Musicians' Union, PRS. *Compositions include:* film music: Time Bandits, The Missionary, Water, Bloodbath At The House of Death, Whoops Apocalypse, The Bitch, Top Secret, Republic of Love, The Lonely Stag, Deathwish 3, Blessed 2007, A Fox's Tale, Betrayal; co-writer, song on Innuendo album, Freddie Mercury; collaborated on album Barcelona, with Freddie Mercury and Montserrat Caballe; more than 100 songs recorded by: Freddie Mercury, Queen, George Harrison, Ian Gillan, Maggie Bell, Oliver Nelson, John Kongos, Extreme, Placido Domingo, The Hollies, Montserrat Caballe. *Honours:* Tric Best Music Award, Gold Badge (British Acad. of Songwriters & Composers). *Current Management:* c/o SMA Talent Ltd, 3rd Floor, 207 Regent Street, London, W1B 3HH, England. *Telephone:* (20) 7307-5958. *Website:* www.smatalent.com/composers/mike-moran-3.

MORAND, Roger; French musician; b. 30 Sept. 1958, Nogent sur Marne; one s. one d. *Career:* leader, Morand Cajun Band; also plays Irish and Celtic accordion and music from the centre of France (Auvergne); mem. SACEM. *Recordings include:* When I'm Up 1993, Les Blues à Bébè 1994, Nuit Cajun 1995, Hey Ariba 1997. *Publications include:* Seigneur des Mouches, contrib. to musical journals and magazines. *Honours:* European Cup, Accordion. *Address:* 3 Place du Doyen Gachon, 30610 Sauve, France (home).

MORAY, Jim; British folk singer, musician (guitar, piano, drums), composer and record producer; b. (Douglas Oates), 20 Aug. 1981, Macclesfield, England. *Education:* Birmingham Conservatoire. *Career:* solo artist 2001–; record producer or musician for many folk artists including Oysterband, James Raynard, Jackie Oates, Wheeler Street, Belshazzar's Feast, Ashley Hutchings, Cecil Sharp Project, Rose Kemp. *Recordings:* albums: solo: Sweet England (BBC Radio 2 Folk Award for Album of the Year 2004) 2003, Jim Moray 2006, Low Culture (fRoots Critics Poll Album of the Year 2008, MOJO Folk Album of the Year 2008) 2008, In Modern History 2010, Skulk 2012. *Honours:* BBC Radio 2 Folk Horizon Awards for Best Newcomer 2004, for Best Traditional Track 2013. *E-mail:* info@jimmoray.co.uk (home). *Website:* www .jimmoray.co.uk (home).

MORELLO, Tom; American musician (guitar); b. 30 May 1964, New York, NY. *Career:* fmr mem. Lock Up; mem. Rage Against the Machine 1991–2000, re-formed 2007–; supports causes such as Fairness and Accuracy in Reporting, Rock for Choice and Refuse and Resist; numerous tours and live appearances; Founder mem. Audioslave 2002–; solo artist, performing as The Nightwatchman 2003–; Founder mem. Street Sweeper Social Club 2006–. *Recordings include:* albums: with Rage Against the Machine: Rage Against The Machine 1992, Evil Empire 1996, The Battle Of Los Angeles 1998, Renegades 2000, Live And Rare 2002; with Audioslave: Audioslave 2002, Out Of Exile 2005, Revelations 2006; solo: One Man Revolution 2007, The Fabled City 2008, World Wide Rebel Songs 2011; with Street Sweeper Social Club: Street Sweeper Social Club 2009, The Ghetto Blaster 2010. *Address:* c/o Sony BMG, 550 Madison Avenue, New York, NY 10022, USA. *Website:* www.tommorello .net; www.ratm.com; www.audioslave.com; www.nightwatchmanmusic.com; streetsweepersocialclub.com.

MORENO, Chino; American singer; b. (Camillo Wong Moreno), 20 June 1973. *Career:* founder mem., Deftones 1988–; formed side project, Team Sleep 2000–, Crosses 2011–, Palms 2011–. *Recordings include:* albums: with Deftones: Adrenaline 1995, Around the Fur 1997, Live (EP) 1999, White Pony 2000, Back To School 2001, Deftones 2003, More Maximum Deftones 2003, Saturday Night Wrist 2006, Diamond Eyes 2010, Koi No Yokan 2012; with Team Sleep: Team Sleep 2005; with Crosses: Crosses 2014; with Palms: Palms 2013. *Honours:* Kerrang! Classic Songwriter Award 2007. *Current Management:* Velvet Hammer Management, 9014 Melrose Avenue, West Hollywood, CA 90069, USA. *Telephone:* (310) 657-6161. *Website:* velvethammer.net; www.deftones.com; crossesmusic.com; palmsband.com.

MORENO, Gaby; Guatemalan singer, songwriter, composer and musician (guitar); b. (Maria Gabriela Moreno Bonilla), 16 Dec. 1981, Guatemala City. *Career:* toured with Tracy Chapman 2008, Ani Difranco 2009; first headlining tours 2009; duettist with Hugh Laurie, Van Dyke Parks, Ricardo Arjado. *Television:* as co-composer: Parks and Recreation (series main theme) 2010. *Recordings:* albums: Still the Unknown 2009, Illustrated Songs 2011, Postales 2012. *Honours:* John Lennon Songwriting Contest Grand Prize (in Latin category, and overall) 2006, American Latino Award for Favorite American Latino Indie Artist 2010, Latin Grammy Award for Best New Artist 2013. *Address:* c/o Metamorfosis Records, 3449 NE 1st Street, Unit 143, Miami, FL 33137, USA (office). *Telephone:* (305) 400-0820 (office). *E-mail:* contacto@ metamorfosis.be (office); info@gaby-moreno.com (home). *Website:* www .metamorfosis.be (office); www.gaby-moreno.com (home).

MORENO, Rita; American actress, singer and entertainer; b. (Rosa Dolores Alverio), Humacao, Puerto Rico; m. Leonard Gordon; one d. *Career:* film, stage, television, concert performer; performs concerts across USA with symphony orchestras for their Pops series; mem. President's Cttee on the Arts and Humanities. *Theatre:* The Ritz (Broadway production) (Tony Award) 1975. *Films:* So Young So Bad 1950, The Toast of New Orleans 1950, Pagan Love Song 1950, The Ring 1952, Singin' in the Rain 1952, The Fabulous Señorita 1952, Cattle Town 1952, Fort Vengeance 1953, Ma and Pa Kettle on Vacation 1953, Latin Lovers 1953, El Alam"in 1953, Jivaro 1954, The Yellow Tomahawk 1954, Garden of Evil 1954, Untamed 1955, Seven Cities of Gold 1955, The Lieutenant Wore Skirts 1956, The King and I 1956, The Vagabond King 1956, The Deerslayer 1957, This Rebel Breed 1960, West Side Story (Acad. Award) 1961, Summer and Smoke 1961, Cry of Battle 1963, The Night of the Following Day 1968, Popi 1969, Marlowe 1969, Carnal Knowledge 1971, The Ritz 1976, Voodoo Passion 1977, The Boss' Son 1978, Happy Birthday, Gemini 1980, The Four Seasons 1981, Age Isn't Everything 1991, Italian Movie 1993, I Like it Like That 1994, Angus 1995, Slums of Beverly Hills 1998, Carlo's Wake 1999, Blue Moon 2001, Piñero 2001, Casa de los Babys 2003, King of the Corner 2004, Play it by Ear 2006. *Television:* sitcom version of 9 To 5, The Top of The Heap (Fox Network series) 1991–92, Cosby Mystery Series 1994. *Recordings include:* albums: Rita Moreno Sings, Warm, Wonderful and Wild, Shadow of a Bull, The Electric Company Album (Grammy Award) 1972. *Honours:* Golden Globe Award, Golden Apple, John Jefferson Award for Best Actress, Chicago's Theatrical Season 1968, Emmy Award (for The Muppet Show) 1977, Sarah Siddons Award 1985, Nat. Medal of Arts 2009, Lifetime Achievement Award, Screen Actors Guild 2014.

MORETTI, Fabrizio; Brazilian-American musician (drums); b. 2 June 1980, Rio de Janeiro, Brazil. *Education:* Dwight School, Manhattan. *Career:* mem. The Strokes 1998–; founding mem., Little Joy 2007–. *Recordings include:* albums: with The Strokes: Is This It (NME Award for Album of the Year) 2001, Room on Fire 2003, First Impressions of Earth 2006, Angles 2011, Comedown Machine 2013; with Little Joy: Little Joy 2008. *Honours:* NME Awards for Band of the Year, Best New Act 2001, for Best Int. Band 2006, BRIT Award for Best Int. Newcomer 2002. *Current Management:* c/o Ryan Michael Gentles,

Wiz Kid Management, 86 East 10th Street, Suite 1, New York, NY 10003, USA. *Telephone:* (212) 473-3600. *Website:* www.thestrokes.com.

MORGAN, Charlie; British musician (drums, electronic percussion); b. 9 Aug. 1955, Hammersmith, London, England; m. Daniela Francesca James, 6 Oct. 1992, 1 d. *Education:* College de Genève; Piano lessons; Classes with James Blades. *Career:* Mostly freelance, 1973–84; Toured, recorded with Tom Robinson Band, 1979; 2 albums, tours with Judie Tzuke, 1980–81; Numerous recordings for Nik Kershaw, Tracey Ullman, Kate Bush; 14 month world tour, as drummer with Elton John, 1992–93; Tour with Elton John, Billy Joel, USA, 1994–95; Elton John World Tour, May 1995–; mem, PRS; BAC&S; Musicians' Union. *Compositions:* Co-wrote television theme The Bill, ITV. *Recordings:* Edge of Heaven, Wham!; 2 albums with Tracey Ullman; I Am The Phoenix, Judie Tzuke; Thunderdome (Mad Max 2), Tina Turner; Iron Man, Pete Townshend; Oasis, Oasis; Out In The Fields, Gary Moore and Phil Lynott; Whose Side Are You On?, Matt Bianco; Rock and Roll Album, Johnny Logan; Human Racing, Nik Kershaw; Kane Gang album; Being There, Martyn Joseph; with Elton John: Live In Sydney (with the MSO); Made In England; Silver Bird, Justin Hayward; Go West, Go West; with Chris De Burgh: Spark To A Flame; This Way Up; Magic Ring, Clannad; Golden Days, Bucks Fizz; Theodore and Friends, The Adventures; Lionheart, Kate Bush; Cabaret (Live), Tom Robinson; Linda Thompson album, 1985; Nick Heyward album, 1985; Beverley Craven album tracks, 1991; Tasmin Archer album, 1992; The Glory of Gershwin, 1994; Plan 9, Cool Breeze, 2001. *E-mail:* cm@manicdrums .com. *Website:* www.manicdrums.com.

MORGAN, Dennis William; American songwriter and music publisher; b. 30 July 1952, Tracy, Minnesota; m. June Arnold, 27 July 1985. *Career:* songwriter, Collins Music, 1969–73; Little Shop of Morgansongs, 1974–; mem, CMA; Nashville Songwriters Asscn. *Compositions include:* Smoky Mountain Rain, Ronnie Milsap; I Wouldn't Have Missed It For The World, Ronnie Milsap; I Was Country When Country Wasn't Cool, Barbara Mandrell; I Knew You Were Waiting For Me, George Michael and Aretha Franklin; My Heart Can't Tell You Know, Rod Stewart; Jonny Lang, Lie to Me; Hank Thompson, Real Thing. *Recordings include:* albums: Salutes Don Williams 2007, A Substitute No More 2009, Songs I Wrote with Harlan, Look to God. *Honours:* Ivor Novello Award; 43 BMI Awards. *Address:* 1800 Grand Avenue, Nashville, TN 37212, USA. *Telephone:* (615) 321-9029. *Fax:* (615) 321-3640. *E-mail:* songmerch@aol.com. *Website:* www.dennismorgansongwriter.com.

MORGAN, Hugh (Huey) Angel Diaz; American singer, lyricist and musician (guitar); b. 8 Aug. 1968, New York. *Career:* Founder mem., Fun Lovin' Criminals 1993–; numerous tours, festivals and TV appearances. *Recordings include:* albums: Fun Lovin' Criminals 1995, Come Find Yourself 1996, 100% Colombian 1998, Mimosa—The Lounge Album 1999, Loco 2001, Welcome To Poppy's 2003, Livin' In The City 2005, Classic Fantastic 2010. *Film:* Clubbing to Death. *Television includes:* Liza & Huey's Pet Nation (co-host) 2010, Slips (host), Drugs Inc (narration). *Current Management:* Sidewinder Management Ltd, 10 Cambridge Mews, Hove, East Sussex, BN3 3EZ, England. *Telephone:* (1273) 774460. *E-mail:* sdw@sidewindermgmt.com. *Website:* www.sidewindermgmt.com.

MORGAN, Jeffrey, (Art Tantrum, Pokachevski); American musician and performing artist; b. 20 March 1954, Spokane, Wash. *Education:* studied under Don Cherry, Karl Berger, Dumi Maraiere, Bert Wilson, Robert Gottlieb, Greg Steinke. *Career:* concerts and festivals in Europe and USA; experimental theatre; workshops for sound and installations; mem. GEMA. *Compositions include:* Quasar-Mach 1983, Snake Eyes 1994, Near Vhana 1997, Bitin Thru 1997. *Recordings include:* albums: Quasar-Mach 1983, Pokachevski Vol. I 1990, Snake Eyes 1994, Near Vhana 1997, Bitin Thru 1997, Dial: Log-Rhythms (with Keith Rowe) 1998, Ensemble Works 81/95 1999, Electroshock 1999, Quartz And Crow Feather 2000, Sign Of The Raven 2000, Magnetic Fields (with Bert Wilson) 2002, Dubbel Duo (with Peter Kowald) 2002, Take No Prisoners (with Bert Wilson) 2003, The Chinese Smile (with Ole Lillelund) 2003, Avenue X (with Capote) 2003, Terra Incognita (with Paul Lytton) 2004, Room 2 Room (with Lawrence Casserley); solo works for piano: Ritual Space 2005. *Honours:* British Arts Council Performing Arts Grant 1992. *Address:* Gustav-Cords Street, 13 D, 50733 Cologne, Germany (home). *Telephone:* (221) 1391274 (office). *Fax:* (221) 7005952 (office). *E-mail:* morgan@jeffreymorgan .net (office). *Website:* www.jeffreymorgan.net.

MORGAN, John Marshall; American bandleader, musician (saxophone), composer and teacher; b. 3 May 1948, Clinton, Iowa; m. Nancy Eichman, 15 March 1986, 2 s. *Education:* 3 Collegiate degrees, Masters; Drake University, Des Moines, Iowa, USA. *Career:* sideman/arranger, The Russ Morgan Orchestra, The Don Hoy Orchestra; Leader, The John Morgan Band, 1984–; member Des Moines Big Band; saxophone guest artist with Drake Symphony Orchestra, Des Moines Municipal Band; educator in Drake University Community School, 1986–; Des Moines School District, 1990–; mem, Macusa (National Asscn of Composers). *Publications:* The Instrumentalist Magazine. *Honours:* Drake Soloist Artist, 1981, 1987, WO1 Radio; Phi Kappa Lamda; Omicron Delta Kappa; Phi Mu Alpha. *Address:* c/o Drake University Department of Music, 2507 University Avenue, Des Moines, IA 50311, USA (office). *Telephone:* (515) 271-4011 (office). *Website:* www.drake.edu/artsci/ Music_Dept/Ducsom%20Faculty/morgan.html (office).

MORGAN, Loretta (Lorrie) Lynn; American country singer; b. 27 June 1959, Nashville, Tenn.; one s. one d. *Career:* two years touring with George Jones; worked at Opryland, USA aged 18. *Film appearances:* Proudheart, The

Enemy Within. *Recordings include:* albums: Leave The Light On 1989, Something In Red 1991, Classics 1991, Watch Me 1992, Trainwreck of Emotion 1993, Merry Christmas From London 1993, War Paint 1994, Greater Need 1996, Shakin' Things Up 1997, Secret Love 1998, The Essential 1998, My Heart 1999, Side By Side 2000, I Finally Found Someone 2001, Show Me How 2004, A Moment in Time 2009, I Walk Alone 2010. *Honours:* CMA Award for Vocal Event of the Year (with Keith Whitley) 1990, Album of the Year (for Common Thread) 1994, TNN/Music City News Award for Video Collaboration of the Year (with Keith Whitley) 1991, Female Artist of the Year 1994, CMT Award for Female Vocalist of the Year 1992. *Current Management:* c/o Ontourage Management, 1625 Broadway, Suite 500, Nashville, TN 37203, USA. *Website:* www.lorrie.com.

MORGAN, Tudur; Welsh musician (acoustic guitar, bass, keyboards), singer, producer and songwriter; b. 18 May 1958, Bangor, Gwynedd, Wales; m. Annwen Morgan 1986; two d. *Education:* Carmarthen Trinity Coll. *Career:* radio and TV appearances; concerts throughout UK and Ireland, including Royal Albert Hall, London, Orkney Islands, Edinburgh Folk Festival; played and recorded with many top Welsh and Irish performers, including Linda Griffiths, Plethyn, 4 Yn Y Bar, Mojo, Moniars, Iona ac Andy, John ac Alun, Dylan a Neil, Bob Galvin, Tecwyn Ifan, Tudur Huws Jones, Geraint Roberts, Laura Sutton, Alistair James, Simon Gardner, Andy Moore, Keith Donald, Donal Lunny, Davy Spillane, Ronnie Drew, Dafydd Iwan, Wil Tân, Tony ac Aloma, Bryn Chamberlin, Branwen, Frank Hennessy; mem. Mechanical-Copyright Protection Soc., Performing Right Soc., Musicians' Union. *Recordings:* with numerous artists, including Branwen, Mojo, 4 Yn Y Bar, Linda Griffiths, Plethyn, Moniars, Dylan a Neil, John ac Alun, Alistair James, Laura Sutton, Heather Jones; world music albums: Narada Media's Celtic Legacy, Ellipsis Arts New York's Celtic Lullaby, World Music for Little Ears; solo: 9 Stryd Madryn 2004, Gitara 2005, Clorach 2007, Lle'r Pwll 2008, Sain y Stryt 2011. *Publications:* Anglesey in Music and Pictures 2006. *Honours:* Sain Records Special Contrib. to Welsh Pop, Folk and Rock Music Award 2006. *E-mail:* info@fflach.co.uk. *Website:* www.fflach.co.uk. *E-mail:* TUDURM@aol.com (office). *Website:* www.recordiaucraig.com; www.myspace.com/tudurmorgan.

MORGANISTIC (see Slater, Luke)

MORILLO, Erick; American DJ and producer; b. 26 March 1971, New York. *Education:* Center for Media Arts. *Career:* after a course in technical production and engineering, released first single with reggae artist The General 1992; recorded for Strictly Rhythm label Reel 2 Real featuring The Mad Stuntman (Mark Quashie); founder and dir, Subliminal Records 1997–; collaborations with Harry 'Choo Choo' Romero, Jose Nunez, Jocelyn Brown, Zig and Zag, Louie Vega; remixed Pete Heller, Madison Avenue, Whitney Houston. *Recordings include:* albums: Are You Ready For Some More (with Reel 2 Real) 1996, Live And More 1996, The Subliminal Sessions Vol. 1 2001, Subliminal Sessions, Vol. 3 2002, Subliminal Sessions, Vol. 5 2003, Subliminal Winter Sessions 2004, My World 2004, The 2 Sides of My World 2005, Subliminal Sessions, Vol. 9 2005, Subliminal Sessions, Vol. 10 2006, Subliminal Sessions 11 2007, Subliminal Sessions, Vol. 13 2009; singles: with Reel 2 Real: The New Anthem 1993, I Like To Move It, Go On Move, Can You Feel It, Raise Your Hands 1994, Conway 1995, Jazz It Up, Are You Ready For Some More 1996, Come and Take A Trip (as Smooth Touch) 1994, Reach (with Lil' Mo Yin Yang) 1995, Fun (with Da Mob) 1998, Distortion (with Pianoheadz) 1998, Believe (with Ministers De La Funk) 1999. *Honours:* Int. Producer of the Year, Canada 1994, Muzik Awards for Best Remixer (with Jose Nunez and Harry Romero) 1999, for Best Ibiza Club, Subliminal Sessions at Pacha 2001. *Telephone:* (7970) 204055 (office). *Fax:* (20) 7681-3099 (home). *E-mail:* javier@subliminalrecords.com. *Website:* www.subliminalrecords.com; www.erickmorillo.com.

MORISSETTE, Alanis Nadine; Canadian rock singer, songwriter and actor; b. 1 June 1974, Ottawa; m. Mario Treadway 2010; one s. *Career:* signed contract as songwriter with MCA Publishing aged 14, recorded two albums for MCA's recording div.; moved to Toronto, later to LA, USA. *Recordings include:* albums: Alanis 1991, Now Is The Time 1992, Jagged Little Pill (Grammy Awards for Album of the Year 1996, for Best Rock Album 1996, Juno Awards for Album of the Year 1996, for Best Rock Album 1996) 1995, Space Cakes (live) 1998, Supposed Former Infatuation Junkie (Juno Award for Album of the Year 2000) 1998, Alanis Unplugged (live) 1999, Under Rug Swept 2002, Feast On Scraps: Inside Under Rug Swept 2002, So-called Chaos 2004, Jagged Little Pill Acoustic 2005, Flavors of Entanglement (Juno Award for Pop Album of the Year 2009) 2008, Havoc and Bright Lights 2012. *Film appearances:* Anything for Love 1993, Dogma 1999, Jay and Silent Bob Strike Back 2001, De-Lovely 2004, Radio Free Albemuth 2010. *Television appearances:* as actor: You Can't Do That on Television 1986, Degrassi: the Next Generation 2005, Lovespring International 2006, Nip/Tuck 2006, Weeds 2009–10, Up All Night 2012; host of Music Works series 1994. *Honours:* BRIT Award for Best Int. Newcomer 1996, Grammy Awards for Best Female Rock Vocal Performance 1996, 1999, for Best Rock Song 1996, 1999, MTV European Music Award for Best Female Artist 1996. *Current Management:* c/o Barbara Rose Entertainment Inc., 14320 Ventura Blvd #450, Sherman Oaks, CA 91423, USA. *Telephone:* (818) 980-2899. *E-mail:* info@barbararoseent.com. *Website:* www.alanis.com.

MORLEY, Paul; British music journalist, author and music producer; b. 26 March 1957, Stockport; m. Claudia Brücken; one d. *Career:* journalist with New Musical Express 1977–83; co-founder, with Trevor Horn, ZTT Records and electronic group Art of Noise, involved in development of successful acts including Frankie Goes to Hollywood; fmr presenter The Late Show, BBC TV, contributor to numerous other tv arts and music programmes; freelance writer, Esquire, the Observer, Sunday Telegraph; formed experimental music project Infantjoy and record label ServiceAV with James Banbury. *Recordings:* with Art of Noise: albums: Into Battle With . . . 1983, Who's Afraid of The Art of Noise 1984, The Seduction of Claude Debussy 1999; singles include: Beat Box 1983, Close to the Edit 1984; with Infantjoy: albums: Where The Night Goes 2005, With 2006. *Publications:* Ask: The Chatter of Pop 1987, Nothing 2000, Words and Music: the history of pop in the shape of a city 2004, Joy Division Piece by Piece 2008, The North (And Almost Everything in It) 2013. *Current Management:* Giles Stanley, Universal Music Management, Bond House, 347–354 Chiswick High Road, London W4 4HS, England. *E-mail:* giles.stanley@umusic.com (office). *E-mail:* info@infantjoy.com (office). *Website:* www.serviceav.com (office).

MORODER, Giorgio; Italian producer, composer and artist; b. 26 April 1941, Val Gardena. *Career:* writer, producer, musician and singer on various pop projects in Germany and Italy during 1960s; formed production partnership with Pete Bellotte early 1970s, produced numerous albums for Donna Summer and Roberta Kelly; founder Musicland Studios, Munich; pioneered the use of synthesizers in 1970s popular music, also credited with laying foundations for electronic dance music and the concept of the dance remix, exemplified by Donna Summer's 'I Feel Love'; working with Bellotte, Harold Faltermeyer or solo has produced and written for numerous artists; released various solo and collaborative recordings and recordings as Munich Machine; composer of numerous film soundtracks and theme songs; composed songs for Olympic Games, Los Angeles 1984, Seoul 1988, Football World Cup, Italy 1990; has exhibited work in fields of photography and computer art; released a version of Fritz Lang's silent film Metropolis with a modern soundtrack and added colour 1984; contributed to design of Cizeta-Moroder sports car. *Recordings include:* albums: solo: Son of My Father 1972, Giorgio's Music 1974, Einzelganger 1975, Knights in White Satin 1976, From Here To Eternity 1977, E=MC2 1979, Forever Dancing 1992, Déjà Vu 2015; as Munich Machine: Introducing The Midnite Ladies 1977, A Whiter Shade of Pale 1978, Body Shine 1979; other: Giorgio and Chris, Love's in You, Love's in Me 1978, Giorgio Moroder and Joe Esposito, Solitary Men 1983, Philip Oakey and Giorgio Moroder 1985, Giorgio Moroder Project, To Be Number One 1990, Moroder and Moroder Art Show 1998. *Recordings produced include:* Donna Summer albums (with Pete Bellotte): Lady of the Night 1974, Love To Love You Baby 1975, A Love Trilogy 1976, Four Seasons of Love 1976, I Remember Yesterday 1977, Once upon a Time... 1977, Live and More 1978, Bad Girls 1979, The Wanderer 1980, I'm a Rainbow 1996; Roberta Kelly albums (with Pete Bellotte or Bob Esty): Troublemaker 1976, Zodiac Lady 1977, Gettin' the Spirit 1978; other: The Three Degrees, New Dimensions 1978, The Sylvers, Disco Fever 1979, Sparks, Terminal Jive 1980, The Three Degrees, Three D 1981, France Joli, Attitude 1983, Limahl, Colour All My Days 1986, Sigue Sigue Sputnik, S.S.S. 1986, Big Trouble, Big Trouble 1987, Koreana, Hand in Hand 1988; hit singles include: Donna Summer, Hot Stuff, Love to Love You Baby, I Feel Love, Kenny Loggins, Danger Zone, Irene Cara, Flashdance (What a Feeling!), David Bowie, Putting Out the Fire, Blondie, Call Me. *Film soundtracks include:* Midnight Express (Best Original Score, Acad. Awards 1978, Golden Globe Awards 1978), Flashdance (Best Original Score, Golden Globe Awards 1983, Grammy Awards 1983), Let It Ride, Fair Game, Over The Top, The Never Ending Story (with Klaus Doldinger), Electric Dreams, Battlestar Galactica, Scarface, Superman III, Metropolis, Another Way, American Gigolo, Cat People, Foxes. *Songs composed for films include:* Flashdance (What a Feeling!) (Flashdance) (Best Original Song, Acad. Awards 1983, Golden Globe Awards 1983), Take My Breath Away (Top Gun) (Best Original Song, Acad. Awards 1986, Golden Globe Awards 1986), The Never Ending Story (The Never Ending Story), Putting Out The Fire (Cat People), All Revved Up (Beverly Hills Cop II), Electric Dreams (Electric Dreams), Winner Takes It All (Over the Top), No See, No Cry (Superman III), Turn Out The Light (Scarface). *Honours:* Commendatore, Pres. of the Italian Repub. 2005; Dance Music Hall of Fame, New York 2004. *Address:* c/o Red Light Management, 8439 West Sunset Blvd, 2nd Floor, Los Angeles, CA 90069, USA. *Telephone:* (310) 273-2266. *Website:* redlightmanagement.com. *E-mail:* info@moroder.net. *Website:* www.moroder.net.

MORRICONE, Ennio; Italian composer; b. 10 Nov. 1928, Rome; s. of Mario Morricone and Libera Morricone; m. Maria Travia; three s. two d. *Education:* Accad. of Santa Cecilia. *Career:* began career in field of classical composition and arrangement; has composed and arranged scores for more than 500 film and TV productions; best known film scores include The Good, the Bad and the Ugly, Once Upon a Time in the West, The Mission, Le Professionnel. *Film scores include:* Il Federale 1961, La Voglia matta 1962, Diciottenni al sole 1962, La Cuccagna 1962, Il Successo 1963, Le Monachine 1963, I Basilischi 1963, Duello nel Texas (as Dan Savio) 1963, La Scoperta dell'America 1964, I Motorizzati 1964, ...e la donna creò l'uomo 1964, I Maniaci 1964, Prima della rivoluzione 1964, Per un pugno di dollari (For A Fistful of Dollars, as Leo Nichols) 1964, Le Pistole non discutono 1964, I Malamondo 1964, Thrilling 1965, Slalom 1965, Menage all'italiana 1965, Idoli controluce 1965, La Battaglia di Algeri 1965, Gli Amanti d'oltretomba 1965, Altissima pressione 1965, I Pugni in tasca 1965, Centomila dollari per Ringo 1965, Il Ritorno di Ringo 1965, Per qualche dollaro in più (For a Few Dollars More) 1965, La Ragazza del bersagliere 1966, Per Firenze 1966, Navajo Joe (as Leo Nichols)

1966, Mi vedrai tornare 1966, Matchless 1966, I Lunghi giorni della vendetta 1966, Un Fiume di dollari 1966, Uccellacci e uccellini 1966, El Greco 1966, Un Uomo a metà 1966, La Resa dei conti 1966, Il Buono, il brutto, il cattivo (The Good, the Bad and the Ugly) 1966, Sette donne per i MacGregor 1967, Pedro Páramo 1967, Il Giardino delle delizie 1967, Dalle Ardenne all'inferno 1967, L'Avventuriero 1967, Le Streghe 1967, OK Connery 1967, I Crudeli (as Leo Nichols) 1967, Per pochi dollari ancora (theme) 1967, Arabella 1967, Il Mercenario 1968, Italia vista dal cielo 1968, Grazie, zia 1968, Il Grande silenzio 1968, Ecce Homo 1968, Diabolik 1968, Da uomo a uomo 1968, La Bataille de San Sebastian 1968, Roma come Chicago 1968, C'era una volta il West (Once Upon a Time in the West) 1968, Vergogna schifosi 1969, Giotto 1969, La Donna invisibile 1969, L'Assoluto naturale 1969, Cuore di mamma 1969, L'Alibi 1969, Galileo 1969, Un Bellissimo novembre 1969, Ruba al prossimo tuo 1969, Un Tranquillo posto di campagna 1969, Una Breve stagione 1969, Le Clan des Siciliens 1969, Zenabel 1969, Uccidete il vitello grasso e arrostitelo 1970, Metello 1970, Giochi particolari 1970, La Califfa 1970, Two Mules for Sister Sara 1970, La Moglie più bella 1970, Indagine su un cittadino al di sopra di ogni sospetto 1970, Hornets' Nest 1970, Vamos a matar, compañeros 1970, Oceano 1971, Gli Occhi freddi della paura 1971, Incontro 1971, Forza 'G' 1971, Una Lucertola con la pelle di donna 1971, Veruschka 1971, Il Decameron 1971, La Tarantola dal ventre nero 1971, Giornata nera per l'ariete 1971, Il Giorno del giudizio 1971, Sacco e Vanzetti 1971, L'Istruttoria è chiusa: dimentichi 1971, Malastrana 1971, Giù la testa 1971, Maddalena 1971, ¡Viva la muerte... tua! 1971, La Violenza: Quinto potere 1972, Questa specie d'amore 1972, Quando la preda è l'uomo 1972, Perché? 1972, Il Maestro e Margherita 1972, Lui per lei 1972, Guttoso e il 'Marat morto' di David 1972, Les Deux saisons de la vie 1972, D'amore si muore 1972, Crescete e moltiplicatevi 1972, La Cosa buffa 1972, Chi l'ha vista morire? 1972, Bianchi bandinelli e la Colonna Traiana 1972, Anche se volessi lavorare, che faccio? 1972, Le Tueur 1972, Cosa avete fatto a Solange? 1972, Bluebeard 1972, J. and S. – storia criminale del far west 1972, L'Attentat 1972, Sbatti il mostro in prima pagina 1972, Un Uomo da rispettare 1972, Il Ritorno di Clint il solitario 1972, Quando le donne persero la coda 1972, La Vita, a volte, è molto dura, vero Provvidenza? 1972, Vaarwel 1973, Allonsanfan 1973, Le Serpent 1973, Le Moine 1973, La Proprietà non è più un furto 1973, Revolver 1973, Rappresaglia 1973, Il Mio nome è Nessuno 1973, Il Giro del mondo degli innamorati di Peynet 1974, Fatti di gente per bene 1974, La Cugina 1974, L'Anticristo 1974, Spasmo 1974, Mussolini: Ultimo atto 1974, Sesso in confessionale 1974, Le Trio infernal 1974, Le Secret 1974, Labbra di lurido blu 1975, Gente di rispetto 1975, Peur sur la ville 1975, Leonor 1975, Der Richter und sein Henker 1975, The Human Factor 1975, Una Vita venduta 1976, Todo modo 1976, René la canne 1976, Per amore 1976, Film 1976, Il Deserto dei Tartari 1976, L'Arriviste 1976, Ariel Limon 1976, L'Agnese va a morire 1976, Der Dritte Grad 1976, Divina creatura 1976, 1900 1976, L'Eredità Ferramonti 1976, Stato interessante 1977, Il Mostro 1977, The Dragon, the Odds 1977, Corleone 1977, Le Ricain 1977, Exorcist II: The Heretic 1977, Orca 1977, Holocaust 2000 1977, L'Immoralità 1978, Forza Italia! 1978, Il Gatto 1978, One, Two, Two: 122, rue de Provence 1978, Così come sei 1978, La Cage aux folles 1978, Ten to Survive 1979, Il Prato 1979, Il Ladrone 1979, Dedicato al mare Egeo 1979, L'Umanoide 1979, Bloodline 1979, La Luna 1979, I... comme Icare 1979, Uomini e no 1980, The Fantastic World of M.C. Escher 1980, Windows 1980, Un Sacco bello 1980, The Island 1980, L'Oeil 1980, La Banquière 1980, La Cage aux folles II 1980, La Dame aux camélias 1980, Il Pianeta azzurro 1981, Bianco, rosso e Verdone 1981, So Fine 1981, Le Professionnel 1981, La Tragedia di un uomo ridicolo 1981, Porca vacca 1982, Nana 1982, A Time to Die 1982, The Thing 1982, White Dog 1982, Blood Link 1982, Maja Plisetskaja 1982, Hundra 1983, Le Ruffian 1983, Le Marginal 1983, Sahara 1983, Pelota 1984, Once Upon a Time in America 1984, Les Voleurs de la nuit 1984, Code Name: Wild Geese 1984, Red Sonja 1985, Kommando Leopard 1985, Il Pentito 1985, La Cage aux folles 3 – 'Elles' se marient 1985, La Venexiana 1986, La Gabbia 1986, The Mission 1986, Quartiere 1987, Mosca addio 1987, Il Giorno prima 1987, The Untouchables 1987, Gli Occhiali d'oro 1987, Il Cuore di mamma 1988, Frantic 1988, A Time of Destiny 1988, Rampage 1988, Cinema Paradiso 1989, Casualties of War 1989, Fat Man and Little Boy 1989, Tre colonne in cronaca 1990, Tempo di uccidere 1990, ¡Átame! 1990, Stanno tutti bene 1990, The Big Man 1990, Tracce di vita amorosa 1990, State of Grace 1990, Hamlet 1990, Money 1991, La Domenica specialmente 1991, Bugsy 1991, A Csalás gyönyöre 1992, Beyond Justice 1992, City of Joy 1992, La Villa del venerdì 1992, Love Potion No. 9 1992, Roma imago urbis 1993, In the Line of Fire 1993, Il Lungo silenzio 1993, La Scorta 1993, Jona che visse nella balena 1994, Wolf 1994, Love Affair 1994, Disclosure 1994, The Night and the Moment 1995, Pasolini, un delitto italiano 1995, L'Uomo delle stelle 1995, I Magi randagi 1996, Vite strozzate 1996, La Lupa 1996, Cartoni animati 1997, Marianna Ucrìa 1997, U Turn 1997, Lolita 1997, Il Fantasma dell'opera 1998, Lucignolo 1999, In the Line of Fire: The Ultimate Sacrifice 2000, Canone inverso – making love 2000, Mission to Mars 2000, Malèna 2000, La Ragion pura 2001, Cowboys Don't Kiss in Public 2001, Threnody 2002, Senso '45 2002, Ripley's Game 2002, Il Diario di Matilde Manzoni 2002, L'Ultimo pistolero 2002, Arena Concerto 2003, La Luz prodigiosa 2003, The Wages of Sin 2003, 72 metra 2004, Kill Bill: Vol. 2 2004, Guardiani delle nuvole 2004, Sorstalanság 2005, Karol, un uomo diventato papa 2005, Libertas 2005, Fateless 2005, E ridendo l'uccise 2005, Adolfo Celi, un uomo per due culture 2006, A Crime 2006, La Sconosciuta 2006, The Weatherman 2007, Ultrasordine 2007, I demoni di San Pietroburgo 2008, Baaria – La porta del vento 2009, Spider Dance 2010, The Best Offer 2013, The Hateful Eight (Golden Globe Award for Best Original Score 2016, BAFTA for Best Original Music 2016) 2015, The Correspondence 2015. *Television scores include:* The Virginian (series theme) 1962, Lo Squarciagola 1966, 1943: un incontro 1969, La Sciantosa 1970, Nessuno deve sapere (series) 1971, Correva l'anno di grazia 1870 1971, L'Uomo e la magia 1972, L'Automobile 1972, Moses the Lawgiver 1975, Drammi gotichi 1976, Noi lazzaroni (series) 1978, Le Mani sporche 1978, Invito allo sport (series) 1978, Orient-Express (series) 1979, The Life and Times of David Lloyd George (series) 1981, Marco Polo (series) 1982, The Scarlet and the Black 1983, Wer war Edgar Allan? 1984, Die Försterbuben 1984, Via Mala (series) 1985, C.A.T. Squad 1986, I Promessi sposi (series) 1988, Gli Indifferenti (series) 1988, Camillo Castiglioni oder die Moral der Haifische 1988, Gli Angeli del potere 1988, C.A.T. Squad: Python Wolf 1988, Il Principe del deserto (series) 1989, The Endless Game 1990, Cacciatori di navi 1990, Una Storia italiana 1992, Piazza di Spagna (series) 1993, Missus 1993, La Piovra series 1–10 1984–99, Genesi: La creazione e il diluvio 1994, Abraham 1994, Jacob 1994, Joseph 1995, Moses (title music) 1996, Il Barone (series) 1996, Samson and Delilah 1996, In fondo al cuore 1997, Nostromo (series) 1997, David (theme) 1997, Ultimo 1998, I Guardiani del cielo 1998, Il Quarto re 1998, La Casa bruciata 1998, Ultimo 2 – La sfida 1999, Nanà 1999, Esther 1999, Padre Pio – Tra cielo e terra 2000, Un Difetto di famiglia 2002, Il Papa buono 2003, Musashi (series) 2003, Charlie Chaplin – Les années suisses 2003, Il Cuore nel pozzo 2005, Cefalonia 2005, Karol, un umono divetato Papa 2005, Lucia 2005, La Provinciale 2006, Giovanni Falcone, l'uomo che sfido Cosa Nostra 2006, L'ultimo de Corleonesi 2007, Résolution 819 2008, Pane e libertà 2009, Quatraro mysteriet 2009, Mi ricordo Anna Frank 2009. *Classical compositions:* more than 15 piano concertos, 30 symphonic pieces, choral music and one opera. *Honours:* Grand Official, Ordine al merito della Repubblica Italiana 2006, Chevalier, Légion d'honneur 2008; Dr hc (Cagliari) 2000, (Seconda Università, Rome) 2002, (New Bulgarian Univ.) 2013; numerous awards including Hon. Acad. Award 2007, Polar Music Prize 2010, Special Award for Career Achievement, Online Film Critics Soc. 2013. *Current Management:* c/o Gorfaine/Schwartz Agency Inc., 4111 West Alameda Avenue, Suite 509, Burbank, CA 91505, USA. *Telephone:* (818) 260-8500.

MORRIS, Doug; American record company executive, producer and songwriter; *Chairman and CEO, Sony Music Entertainment*; b. 23 Nov. 1938. *Education:* Columbia Univ. *Career:* fmr songwriter music publisher Robert Mellin Inc.; writer and prod. Laurie Records from 1965, later Vice-Pres. and Gen. Man.; f. Big Tree label (sold to Atlantic Records 1978); Pres. ATCO Records (part of Warner Music) 1978–80, Pres. Atlantic Records 1980–90, Co-Chair. and Co-CEO Atlantic Recording Group 1990–94, Pres. and COO, then Chair. Warner Music USA 1995; co-cr. Interscope Records; Chair. and CEO MCA Music Entertainment Group (now Universal Music Group) 1995–2011, f. Universal Records, apptd to Vivendi Universal Management Bd 2005; co-f. (with Jimmy Iovine q.v.) Jimmy and Doug's Farm Club project, comprising a record label, website and cable TV show 1999; Founder and fmr Chair. VEVO (premium music video and entertainment service) 2009; Chair. and CEO Sony Music Entertainment 2011–; Co-producer and lead financier of Broadway musical Motown: The Musical 2013; Co-owner Pressplay subscription-based music download website; mem. Bd of Dirs CBS Corpn, The Robin Hood Foundation, The Cold Spring Harbor Laboratory, Rock and Roll Hall of Fame. *Compositions include:* Sweet Talkin' Guy, The Chiffons 1966. *Honours:* Pres.'s Merit Award, Nat. Acad. of Recording Arts and Sciences (NARAS) 2003, City of Hope Spirit of Life Award 2008, NARAS Icons Award 2009, received a star on the Hollywood Walk of Fame 2009, Howie Richmond Hitmaker Award, Songwriters Hall of Fame 2014. *Address:* Sony Music Entertainment, 550 Madison Avenue, New York, NY 10022-3211, USA (office). *Telephone:* (212) 833-8000 (office). *Website:* www.sonymusic.com (office).

MORRIS, Johnny, BS; American musician (piano), singer and orchestral leader; b. 30 Oct. 1935, New York; m. 1st; two s. one d.; m. 2nd Jean Farrell; three step-s. *Education:* State Univ. of New York. *Career:* f. Johnny Morris Quartet, Johnny Morris Jazz All-Stars; numerous live performances, festivals, TV appearances. *Recordings include:* three albums with Buddy Rich, Alone Together (solo album), East Meets West (album with Johnny Morris Quartet), Romantic Jazz (album with Johnny Morris/Frank Tate Duo). *Publications:* piano arrangements for Piano Today, Keyboard, Sheet Music magazines, Steinway Library of Piano Music.

MORRIS, Lynn, BA; American musician (banjo, guitar) and singer; b. 8 Oct. 1948, San Antonio, TX; m. Marshall Wilborn 1989. *Education:* Colorado Coll., Colorado Springs. *Career:* began professionally in music 1972; performed in Europe, Asia, N America; began Lynn Morris Band 1988; numerous television appearances, radio broadcasts; mem. IBMA Bd of Dirs six years; mem. Int. Bluegrass Music Assen, Folk Alliance, Soc. for the Preservation of Bluegrass Music in America. *Recordings include:* albums: The Lynn Morris Band 1990, The Bramble and The Rose 1992, Mama's Hand 1995, You'll Never Be the Sun 1999, Shape of a Tear 2003. *Honours:* Soc. for Preservation of Bluegrass Music in America Award for Female Vocalist (traditional category) two times, Nat. Banjo Champion at Winfield, KS two times. *Address:* PO Box 2324, Winchester, VA 22604, USA. *Website:* www.lynnmorrisband.com.

MORRIS, Nathan Bartholomew 'Alex-Vanderpool'; American singer; b. 18 June 1971, USA. *Education:* Philadelphia High School of Creative and Performing Arts. *Career:* mem., Boyz II Men 1988–; established Stonecreek label. *Recordings:* albums: Cooleyhighharmony 1993, II 1995, Evolución 1997,

Nathan Michael Shawn Wanya 2000, Full Circle 2002, Motown: Hitsville USA 2007, Love 2009. *Website:* www.boyziimen.com.

MORRIS, Sarah Jane; British singer, songwriter and actress; b. 21 March 1959, Southampton, Hampshire; m. 1st David J. Coulter 1992; one s.; m. 2nd Mark Pulsford 2012. *Education:* Central School of Speech and Drama, London. *Career:* lead singer, The Republic 1980–84, The Happy End 1984–87, The Communards 1985–87; solo career; concert highlights have included a Swing Ladies concert with Chaka Khan and Monserrat Caballé, a performance in front of 10,000 fans in Athens, the Red Wedge Tour, Venice Opera House, The Verona Arena, Taormina Amphitheatre, Sicily, Royal Albert Hall, European Tour with the Royal Philharmonic Orchestra, What Women Want concert with Sinead O'Connor and Chrissie Hynde at Royal Festival Hall; lead actress in Thin Air (BBC 1), in film Expecting (Channel 4) 1995; regular residency at Ronnie Scott's, London; invited to perform at The Vatican at Christmas with orchestra and Dominic Miller, broadcast live on Italian TV; first performance of new album Where it Hurts in UK at Hay Literary Festival 2013, launched at Purcell Room, London as part of London Jazz Festival; album title is also title of her solo show which was previewed at Edinburgh Festival and co-written with Michael Crompton, with Dominic Miller accompanying on guitar, show has toured theatres and arts centres in UK; mem., PRS, MCPS, Equity, Musicians' Union. *Compositions include:* I Am A Woman; title track for television series The Men's Room (BBC) 1991–92; music for film Expecting (Channel 4) 1995. *Recordings include:* albums: Sarah Jane Morris 1989, Heaven 1992, Blue Valentine 1996, Fallen Angel 2000, August 2001, Love and Pain 2003, After All These Years 2006, Migratory Birds 2008, Where It Hurts 2009, Cello Songs 2011, Where It Hurts 2013, Bloody Rain 2015. *Honours:* Freedom of the City of Verona; Best Newcomer, Italy 1989, European Grammy, Winner, Int. Sanremo Song Festival. *Current Management:* c/o JPSM Management, 15 Culmington Road, Ealing, London, W13 9NJ, England. *Telephone:* 7967-636442 (mobile). *E-mail:* juliet@jpsm -music.co.uk. *Website:* www.sarahjanemorris.co.uk.

MORRIS, Stephen; British musician (drums); b. 28 Oct. 1957, Macclesfield, Cheshire, England; m. Gillian Gilbert 1993; two d. *Career:* mem., Joy Division 1977–80, New Order 1980–, The Other Two 1991–; tours worldwide, concerts and festival appearances. *Compositions for television:* Making Out, Common as Muck. *Recordings include:* albums: with Joy Division: Unknown Pleasures 1979, Closer 1980, Still 1981, The Peel Sessions 1988; with New Order: Movement 1981, Power, Corruption & Lies 1983, Low-Life 1985, Brotherhood 1986, Substance 1987, Technique 1989, Republic 1993, Best of New Order 1994, Rest of New Order 1995, Get Ready 2001, Back To Mine (compilation of other artists' work) 2002, In Session (live) 2004, Waiting For The Sirens' Call 2005, Lost Sirens 2013, Music Complete 2015; with The Other Two: The Other Two and You 1994, Superhighways 1999. *Honours:* NME 'Godlike Genius' Award (with New Order) 2005, Q Legend Award (with Joy Division) 2005, Ivor Novello Award for Outstanding Song Collection 2006, Q Outstanding Contribution to Music Award 2015. *Website:* www.neworder.com.

MORRIS, Wanya Jermaine 'Squirt'; American singer; b. 29 July 1973, Philadelphia, Pa. *Education:* Philadelphia High School of Creative and Performing Arts. *Career:* mem. Boyz II Men 1988–; est. Stonecreek label; signed to Arista Records. *Recordings include:* albums: Cooleyhighharmony 1993, II 1995, Evolución 1997, Nathan Michael Shawn Wanya 2000, Full Circle 2002, Motown: Hitsville USA 2007, Love 2009, Twenty 2011, Collide 2014. *Website:* www.boyziimen.com.

MORRISON, Barbara; American jazz and blues singer; b. 10 Sept. 1949, Ypsilanti, Mich. *Education:* Eastern Michigan Univ. *Career:* recorded first radio appearance aged 10; numerous musical collaborations, including Dizzy Gillespie, James Moody, Ron Carter, Etta James, Esther Phillips, David T. Walker, Jimmy Smith, Dr John, Kenny Burrell, Terence Blanchard, Joe Sample, Cedar Walton, Nancy Wilson, Mel Tormé, Joe Williams, Tony Bennett, Keb'Mo, Albert Aarons. *Recordings include:* albums: solo: Blues For Ella 1995, Doin' All Right 1995, Blues For Ella (with Thilo Berg and his Big Band) 1995, I'm Gettin' Long All Right 1997, I Know How To Do It 1998, Visit Me 1999, Live Down Under 2000, Ooh Shoobie Doo (with Johnny Otis) 2000, Live At The 9.20 Special 2002, Live at the Dakota 2005, Los Angeles, Los Angeles, The City by the Sea 2008, A Sunday Kind of Love 2013. *Address:* 4305 Degnan Blvd, Suite 101, Los Angeles, CA 90008, USA. *Telephone:* (310) 462-1439. *E-mail:* bmorrblues@aol.com. *Website:* www.barbaramorrison.com.

MORRISON, Carla; Mexican singer, songwriter and musician (guitar); b. (Carla Patricia Morrison Flores), 19 July 1986, Tecate, Baja California; d. of Porfiria Flores and Hilario Morrison. *Education:* Univ. of Arizona, Mesa Community Coll., Phoenix, USA. *Career:* fmr mem. rock bands including Revolver, Zombras; Founder mem. Babaluca 2007; solo career 2009–. *Recordings include:* albums: Mientras Tú Dormias (IMAS Best Folk Album 2011) 2010, Dejenme Llorar (Latin Grammy Award for Best Alternative Music Album 2012) 2012. *Honours:* Latin Grammy Award for Best Alternative Song (for Dejenme Llorar) 2012. *E-mail:* wakksmanejador@gmail.com. *Website:* www.carlamorrisonmusica.com.

MORRISON, James; British singer, songwriter and guitarist; b. (James Morrison Catchpole), 13 Aug. 1984, Rugby. *Career:* solo artist; tours in UK and N America. *Recordings include:* Undiscovered 2006, Songs for You, Truths for Me 2008, The Awakening 2011, Higher Than Here 2015. *Honours:* Best British Male Solo Artist, BRIT Awards 2007. *Current Management:* c/o Closer Artists, Matrix Complex, 91 Peterborough Road, London, SW6 3BU, England.

Telephone: (20) 7384-6438. *E-mail:* info@closerartists.com. *Website:* www .closerartists.com; www.jamesmorrisonmusic.com.

MORRISON, James; Australian musician (jazz trumpet); b. 11 Nov. 1962, Borrowa, NSW; m. Judi Morrison; three s. *Education:* NSW Conservatorium of Music. *Career:* Lecturer, NSW Conservatorium of Music 1981; formed Big Band 1983; numerous tours, live performances. *Recordings:* Jazz Meets The Symphony, Scream Machine 2001. *Honours:* Australian Performer of the Year, Ricky May Performer of the Year Award. *Website:* www.jamesmorrison .com.

MORRISON, Lindy, BA; Australian musician (drums); *National Coordinator Welfare, Support Act Limited;* b. (Belinda Morrison), 2 Nov. 1951, Sydney, NSW; one d. *Education:* Univs of Queensland and New South Wales. *Career:* social worker, Aboriginal and Islanders Legal Services/Dept Children's Services 1973–74; actor, Grin and Tonic Theatre and Popular Theatre Troupe 1976–79; drummer, Zero 1979, The Go-Betweens 1980–90, Cleopatra Wong 1990–92, The Rainy Season 1998–2009; community musician at regional music performances, festivals, parades, concerts 1992–; Musical Dir Junction House Band, Bondi Youth Wave, Waverley Senior Songwriters, S Sydney Youth Service; Artist Dir PPCA Bd 1993–2011; TAFE lecturer 1998–2011; Dir of Bd, Music Council of Australia 2000–03; Nat. Co-ordinator, Support Act Ltd, Australian Musicians Benevolent Soc. 2000–11. *Recordings:* albums: Send Me A Lullaby 1982, Before Hollywood 1983, Spring Hill Fair 1984, Liberty Belle and The Black Diamond Express 1986, Tallullah 1987, 16 Lovers Lane 1988, Egg 1991, Cleopatra's Lament 1992. *Honours:* Lifetime Hon. mem. Music Council of Australia 2008. *Address:* PO Box 2190, Clovelly, Sydney 2031, Australia (home). *Telephone:* (4) 0922-4720 (home). *E-mail:* lindymorrison@optushome.com.au (office).

MORRISON, Mark; British soul singer; b. 3 May 1972, Hannover, Germany. *Career:* solo artist 1994–; numerous tours and live appearances. *Recordings include:* albums: Let's Get Down 1995, Return Of The Mack 1996, Only God Can Judge Me 1997, The Judgement 2004, Just a Man 2005, Innocent Man 2006. *Current Management:* c/o Marc Connor, AirMTM, Shepherds Building West, Rockley Road, Shepherds Bush, London W14 0DA, England. *Telephone:* (20) 7386-1612. *E-mail:* connor@airmtm.com. *Website:* www.airmtm.com.

MORRISON, Patricia; British musician (bass guitar); m. Dave Vanian 2000. *Career:* mem. The Bags 1976–80, mem. Gun Club 1982–84, mem. The Sisters of Mercy, The Sisterhood 1985; mem. Punk Rock band, The Damned 1996–2004. *Recordings include:* albums: with Gun Club: The Las Vegas Story 1984, Danse Kalinda Boom 1985, Love Supreme Live Material 1985, Two Sides Of The Beast 1985, Mother Juno 1987, Pastoral Hide And Seek 1990, Divinity 1991, In Exile 1992, Live In Europe 1992, Lucky Jim 1994; solo: Reflect on This 1994; with The Damned: Fiendish Shadows 1996, Not Of This Earth 1996, Testify 1997, Eternal Damnation Live 1999, Molten Lager 2000, Grave Disorder 2001, I'm Alright Jack And The Bean Stalk 2002.

MORRISON, Sir Van, Kt, OBE; British singer, songwriter and musician; b. (George Ivan Morrison), 31 Aug. 1945, Belfast, Northern Ireland; one d. *Career:* left school aged 15; joined The Monarchs, playing in Germany; Founder and lead singer, Them 1964–67; solo artist 1967–. *Recordings include:* albums: Blowin' Your Mind 1967, Astral Weeks 1968, Moondance 1970, His Band and Street Choir 1970, Tupelo Honey 1971, Saint Dominic's Preview 1972, Hardnose the Highway 1973, It's Too Late To Stop Now 1974, Veedon Fleece 1974, This Is Where I Came In 1977, A Period of Transition 1977, Wavelength 1978, Into the Music 1979, Common One 1980, Beautiful Vision 1982, Inarticulate Speech of the Heart 1983, Live At The Royal Opera House, Belfast 1984, A Sense of Wonder 1984, No Guru, No Method, No Teacher 1986, Poetics Champion Compose 1987, Irish Heartbeat 1988, Avalon Sunset 1989, Enlightenment 1990, Bang Masters 1990, Hymns to the Silence 1991, The Best of Van Morrison 1993, Too Long in Exile 1993, A Night in San Francisco 1994, Days Like This 1995, Songs of the Mose Allison: Tell Me Something 1996, The Healing Game 1997, Brown Eyed Girl 1998, The Masters 1999, Super Hits 1999, Back On Top 1999, The Skiffle Sessions: Live in Belfast 1998 2000, You Win Again 2000, Down The Road 2002, What's Wrong With This Picture? 2003, Magic Time 2005, Pay the Devil 2006, Keep it Simple 2008, Born to Sing: No Plan B 2012, Duets: Re-working the Catalogue 2015. *Honours:* Officier, Ordre des Arts et des Lettres 1996; Dr hc (Univ. of Ulster) 1992, (Queen's Univ. Belfast) 2001; inducted into Rock and Roll Hall of Fame 1993, BRIT Award for Outstanding Contribution to British Music 1994, Ivor Novello Lifetime Achievement Award 1995, Q Award for Best Songwriter 1995, Grammy Awards for Best Pop Collaboration with Vocals 1996, 1998, BMI Icon Award 2004, Ronnie Scott Award for Int. Male Singer 2007, Freedom of Belfast 2013, GQ Legend Award 2014. *Website:* www.vanmorrison .com.

MORRISON, Will; British musician (drums, percussion) and programmer; b. 2 Feb. 1968, Tile Hill, Coventry, England. *Education:* Coventry Univ., Coventry School of Music, Drumtech, London. *Career:* tours with Don Mescall supporting: Mary Coughlan, Davey Spillane, David Thomas, Richie Havens, The Dubliners; festivals with Don Mescall, Phoenix, Larmer Bee, Berlin Music; Radio 1 Roadshows with Faun, Live Radio Sessions on Greater London Radio with Philip French, Sugartrain, Don Mescall; TV includes The Happening and Pot of Gold with Sugartrain, The Big City with Lisa Lamb Quartet; mem. Musicians' Union. *Recordings include:* She Don't Know, Faun (featuring John Entwistle, Gordon Giltrap), Here Be Dragons, Gargling With

Brains. *Publication:* Working on drum tuition book: Learning To Read and Write.

MORRISS, Mark; British singer and songwriter; b. 18 Oct. 1971, Hounslow, Middlesex, England. *Career:* founder mem., The Bluetones 1994–2011, mem. The Maypoles; numerous tours, festivals, television and radio appearances. *Recordings include:* albums: with The Bluetones: Expecting To Fly 1996, Return To The Last Chance Saloon 1998, Science And Nature 2000, The Singles 1995–2002 2002, The Bluetones 2006; solo: Memory Muscle 2008, A Flash of Darkness 2014. *E-mail:* markmorrissofficial@gmail.co.uk. *Website:* www.markmorrissmusic.co.uk.

MORRISS, Scott; British musician (bass guitar), backing singer and songwriter; b. 10 Oct. 1973, Hounslow, Middlesex, England. *Career:* Founder mem., The Bluetones 1994–2011; numerous tours, festivals, television and radio appearances; 2D Flash animator for clients including BBC, Cartoon Network, Jetix, and Lego Games. *Recordings include:* albums: Expecting To Fly 1996, Return To The Last Chance Saloon 1998, Science And Nature 2000, The Singles 1995–2002 2002, The Bluetones 2006. *Website:* scottmorriss.com.

MORRISSEY, Steven Patrick; British singer and songwriter; b. 22 May 1959, Daryhulme, Manchester. *Career:* Founder mem. The Smiths 1982–87; solo artist 1987–. *Recordings include:* albums: with The Smiths: The Smiths 1984, Hatful Of Hollow 1984, Meat Is Murder 1985, The Queen Is Dead 1986, The World Won't Listen 1987, Louder Than Bombs 1987, Strangeways Here We Come 1987, Rank 1988, Best... I 1992, Best... II 1992, Singles 1995, The Very Best Of 2001; solo: Viva Hate 1988, Bona Drag 1990, Kill Uncle 1991, Your Arsenal 1992, Beethoven Was Deaf 1993, Vauxhall And I 1994, Southpaw Grammar 1995, Maladjusted 1997, My Early Burglary Years 1998, You Are The Quarry 2004, Ringleader of the Tormentors 2006, Years of Refusal 2009, World Peace Is None of Your Business 2014. *Publications:* In Conversation: The Essential Interviews 2008, Autobiography 2013, List of the Lost 2015. *Honours:* Q Award for Best Songwriter 1994, Meteor Award for Best Int. Male Artist 2005.

MORSE, Steve; American musician (guitar); b. 28 July 1954, Hamilton, Ohio. *Education:* Miami Univ. *Career:* Founder-mem. The Dixie Dregs 1975; Founder-mem. The Steve Morse Band 1983; fmr mem. Kansas; mem. Deep Purple 1994–. *Recordings include:* albums: with The Dixie Dregs: The Great Spectacular 1975, Free Fall 1977, What If 1978, Night of the Living Dregs 1979, Dregs of the Earth 1980, Unsung Heroes 1981, Industry Standard 1982, Off the Record 1988, Full Circle 1994; with The Steve Morse Band: The Introduction 1984, Stand Up 1985, High Tension Wires 1989, Southern Steel 1991, Coast to Coast 1992, Structural Damage 1995, Stressfest 1996, Major Impacts 2000, Split Decision 2002, Major Impacts 2 2004, Prime Cuts 2005, Prime Cuts 2 2009, Out Standing in Their Field 2009; with Deep Purple: Perpendicular 1996, Abandon 1998, Butterfly Ball Wizards Convention 1998, Child In Time 1998, Under The Gun 2001, Bananas 2003, Deep Purple And Friends 2003, Total Abandon 2004, Rapture Of The Deep 2005, Now What?! 2013. *Current Management:* Frank Solomon Management, PO Box 639, Natick, MA 01760, USA. *E-mail:* info@deep-purple.com. *Website:* www.deep-purple.com; www.stevemorse.com.

MORTENSEN, Allan; Danish singer, composer and actor; b. 27 April 1946, Århus; m. Titika 1967 (divorced); one d. *Career:* singer in rock group, Midnight Sun 1971; singer in soul group, 2nd Line 1987–89; mem. Danish Artist Fed. *Stage performances include:* lead roles in Jesus Christ Superstar 1972, Hair 1972, Two Gentlemen of Verona 1973, Godspell 1979, Joseph and the Amazing Technicolour Dreamcoat 1983, Odysseus 1983, Tom Parker's Young Messiah 1986–87. *Compositions:* musicals: Thor 1989, The Concert 1991, The Three Musketeers 1995. *Recordings include:* Midnight Sun 1971, Love Ambulance (singer, composer) 1976, 2nd Line Live 1988. *Honours:* The Amber Nightingale (Poland) 1987, Helexpo (Greece) 1991. *Address:* Strandboulevarden 137, 1 sal, 2100 Copenhagen, Denmark. *E-mail:* mail@allan-mortensen.com. *Website:* www.allan-mortensen.dk.

MORTIMER, Anthony (Tony) Michael; British singer, songwriter and musician (piano); b. 21 Oct. 1970, Stepney, London; one d. *Career:* began as dancer for group Faith, Hope and Charity; mem East 17 1992–2014; joined Sub Zero 1996–. *Recordings include:* with East 17: albums: Walthamstow 1993, Steam 1994, Up All Night 1996, Around the World – The Journey So Far 1996, Resurrection 1998; singles: House of Love 1992, Deep 1993, West End Girls 1993, It's Alright 1993, Around The World 1994, Steam 1994, Stay Another Day 1994, Let It Rain 1995, Thunder 1995, Do U Still 1996, If You Ever (with Gabrielle) 1996, Hey Child 1997, Each Time 1998, Betcha Can't Wait 1999, Dark Light 2012, Songs From The Suitcase 2013. *Honours:* Ivor Novello Award. *Website:* www.asmtalent.co.uk.

MORTON, Eddie; singer and musician (mandolin, accordion, guitar). *Career:* mem. Sub Zero 1983; formed The Trick 1984; worked in production, songwriting with artists including: Phil Lynott, Slade, Ruby Turner, Rozalla, Steve Lillywhite, Roy Harper; formed own band 1988; tours of Europe, UK, USA; joined The Adventure Babies 1991; Founder-mem. The New Bushbury Mountain Daredevils, 1992–. *Recordings include:* albums: with Sub Zero: Out of The Blue; with The Trick: My World; Heart of Hearts; with Rozalla: Heartbreaker, Sunny, Spirit of Africa Perfect Kiss; as Morton: Keeper of The Light; with Adventure Babies: Adventure Babies, Laugh, Barking Mad; with Mack and The Boys: The Unknown Legends; as Eddie Morton: The Infinite

Room, Way of The World, Black and Blue; with The New Bushbury Mountain Daredevils: Bushwhacked, The Yellow Album, Bushbury Mountain.

MORTON, Nigel William; artist manager and booking agent; b. 23 Nov. 1953, Nairobi, Kenya; m. Hilary Cooper 1977 (divorced); one s. one d. *Career:* journalist for Record Mirror, Sounds, Hi-Fi Weekly; booking agent to various acts including Carmel, Marillion, Wishbone Ash, Jimmy Cliff, Billy Bragg, Angelic Upstarts, Donovan, The Exploited, Pentangle, The Twinkle Brothers 1978–84; full time manager, New Model Army 1982–91; co-manager, The Almighty 1987–90; f. Moneypenny booking agency, consultancy, clients include Bellowhead, Bruce Cockburn, Kate and Anna McGarrigle, Hot Tuna, The Ukrainians, Porcupine Tree, Test Department 1992–. *Address:* Moneypenny, The Stables, Westwood House, Main Street, North Dalton, East Yorkshire YO25 9XA, England (office). *Telephone:* (1377) 217815 (office). *E-mail:* nigel.morton@moneypennymusic.co.uk (office). *Website:* www.moneypennymusic.co.uk (office).

MORTON, Peter Michael; British singer, musician (guitar) and songwriter; b. 30 July 1964, Leicester. *Education:* Countesthorpe Community Coll. *Career:* busker –1987; concerts throughout UK, Europe, North America; British Council tours of Pakistan, Malaysia; mem. PRS. *Recordings include:* albums: Frivolous Love 1987, One Big Joke 1988, Urban Folk Vol. 1 1989, Mad World Blues 1992, Courage Love & Grace 1995, Urban Folk Vol. 2, Trespass 1999, Hunting the Heart 2000, Flying an Unknown Flag 2005, Swarthmoor 2005, Napoleon Jukebox 2007, Casa Abierta 2008, Economy 2011, The Frappin' And Ramblin' Pete Morton 2014. *Honours:* Folk Roots Magazine Award for Most Promising Newcomer 1987. *E-mail:* petermrtn1@aol.com. *Website:* www.petemorton.com.

MORYKIT, Dmytro, BEd, LRAM; British composer and musician (piano, keyboards); b. 3 Dec. 1956, Northampton, England; s. of F. Teodor Morykit and M. Carmelina Gaeta; m. Hazel Cameron. *Education:* , Univ. of Leicester; classically trained on piano from early age; studied with Graham Mayo. *Career:* mem. Nat. Student Theatre Company, 1978–80; Composer-in-Residence; session musician with various rock bands; freelance composer and musician; reinterpretations of other composers' work, including classical and pop; mem. Musicians' Union. *Compositions include:* The Wasteland by T. S. Eliot, From The Dungeons To The Skies; commissioned by Amnesty International: The Unforgiving 1997, Prisoners of Conscience 1998, Music in Manufacture 2013, Metropolis LIVE (1927) 2014, Nosferatu LIVE (1923) 2015. *Film scores include:* Portrait of Evil (Holodomor), Oasis, Buckshee Countess, Donald Trump does Bohemian Rhapsody. *Publications include:* Songs For Piano 1982, The Enchanted 1994. *Honours:* Best Original Music, Nat. Student Drama Festival. *Telephone:* (1764) 670511. *E-mail:* dmytro.morykit@yahoo.co.uk; music@dmytromorykit.co.uk. *Website:* www.dmytromorykit.co.uk.

MOS DEF, (Dante Beze); American rap artist and actor; b. (Dante Terrell Smith), 11 Dec. 1973, Brooklyn, New York. *Career:* began rapping aged nine; formed Urban Thermo Dynamics with sister; joined the Native Tongues collective, leading to guest appearance on De La Soul's Big Brother Beat; started recording solo material for independent label, Rawkus; formed rock group Black Jack Johnson; collaborations with Jill Scott, A Tribe Called Quest, DJ Krush, Common, Talib Kweli, Scritti Politti, Ghostface Killah. *Films include:* The Hard Way 1991, Bamboozled 2000, Monster's Ball 2001, Showtime 2002, Brown Sugar 2002, The Italian Job 2003, The Woodsman 2004, A Confederacy of Dunces 2004, Something the Lord Made (TV) 2004, Lackawanna Blues (TV) 2005, The Hitchhiker's Guide to the Galaxy 2005, Journey to the End of the Night 2006, Prince Among Slaves 2007, Cadillac Records 2008, Next Day Air 2009, Bouncing Cats 2010, Begin Again 2013, Life of Crime 2014. *Recordings include:* albums: Mos Def and Talib Kweli Are Black Star 1998, Black On Both Sides 1999, The New Danger 2004, True Magic 2006, The Ecstatic 2009. *Current Management:* c/o Downtown Music Publishing, 485 Broadway, 3rd Floor, New York, NY 10013, USA. *Telephone:* (212) 461-1449. *Website:* www.dmpgroup.com.

MOSER, Rudolph (Rudi); German musician (drums). *Career:* mem. experimental band, Einstürzende Neubauten 1997–. *Recordings include:* albums: Silence is Sexy 2000, Perpetuum Mobile 2004, Grundstück 2005. *Website:* www.neubauten.org.

MOSES, James Michael, (Jamie Moses); British/American musician (guitar, bass guitar, keyboards), singer, songwriter and music director; b. 30 Aug. 1955, Ipswich, Suffolk, England; s. of Harry Marcus Moses, Jr and Joan Dorothy Vera Moses; m. 1st Deborah Anne Webb 1983 (divorced); one s. one d.; m. 2nd Sarah Louise Benton 2008; one s. *Education:* Redhill Tech. Coll. *Career:* stage appearances, tours, radio and TV performances with artists including Queen, Queen Paul Rodgers, Sir Tom Jones, Mel C, Bob Geldof, Eric Burdon, Broken English, The SAS Band, The Hollies, Brian May, Deana Carter, Mike and the Mechanics, Queen, Los Pacaminos, The World Famous Red Sox, Hiding In Public, Jimmy Nail, Paul McCartney, Steve Lukather, Annie Lennox, Dave Stewart, Jamelia, Corinne Bailey Rae, Peter Gabriel, Guns 'N' Roses, Chaka Khan, Curtis Stigers, Paul Young, Roger Chapman, Roger Taylor, Extreme, Kiki Dee, U2, Beyoncé, Anastacia, Zucchero, Eurythmics, Ms Dynamite, The Corrs, Lionel Richie, Lulu, The Pretenders, Olivia Newton-John; currently freelance and singer; mem. Musicians' Union, Equity, Performing Right Soc., Mechanical-Copyright Protection Soc. *Recordings:* Live At Brixton Academy and Another World (Brian May), Return of the Champions (Queen, Paul Rodgers) 2005, The Happy Club (Bob Geldof),

Comin' On Strong and Do You Really Want Me Back? (Broken English), Various (Paul Young), Merlin (Merlin); recordings with Mike & The Mechanics, Tony Hadley, 46664 concerts (Nelson Mandela Foundation), Various (Hiding In Public), Queen's Diamond Jubilee Concert etc. (Tom Jones). *E-mail:* jamie@jamiemoses.com. *Website:* www.jamiemoses.com.

MOSLEY, Ian; British musician (drums, percussion); b. 16 June 1953, Paddington, London. *Education:* Guildhall School of Music. *Career:* fmr mem. Curved Air, Gordon Giltrap Band; duo with Steve Hackett; mem. orchestras for West End musicals, including Hair, Jesus Christ Superstar; mem. progressive rock group, Marillion 1983–; numerous tours. *Recordings include:* albums: with Gordon Giltrap: Peacock Party 1980, Live 1981; with Steve Hackett: Highly Strung 1983, Till We Have Faces 1984; with Marillion: Fugazi 1984, Real To Reel 1984, Misplaced Childhood 1985, Brief Encounter 1986, Clutching At Straws 1987, B-Sides Themselves 1988, The Thieving Magpie 1988, Season"s End 1989, Holidays In Eden 1991, Brave 1994, Marillion.com 1999, Anoraknophobia 2000, Made Again Live 2001, Anorak In The UK Live 2002, Somewhere Else 2007, Happiness is the Road 2008, Less is More 2009, Sounds That Can't Be Made 2012; solo: Postmankind (with Ben Castle) 2001. *E-mail:* info@knowmoremanagement.com. *Website:* knowmoremanagement.com. *Address:* PO Box 252, Aylesbury, Buckinghamshire, HP18 0YS, England. *Telephone:* (1296) 770839. *E-mail:* racket@marillion.com; lucy@marillion.com. *Website:* www.marillion.com.

MOSS, Jon; British musician (drums); b. 11 Sept. 1957, London, England. *Career:* session drummer, Adam and the Ants, The Damned 1977–78; mem., Sex Gang Children, renamed Culture Club 1981–87, 1998–2002; numerous TV appearances and several tours; various solo projects. *Recordings include:* albums: with Culture Club: Kissing To Be Clever 1982, Colour By Numbers 1983, Waking Up With The House On Fire 1984, From Luxury To Heartache 1986, Don't Mind If I Do 1999, 12" Mixes Plus 2003; singles: with Culture Club: Do You Really Want To Hurt Me 1982, Time (Clock of the Heart) 1982, Church Of The Poisoned Mind 1983, Victims 1983, It's A Miracle 1983, Karma Chameleon (BRIT Award for Best-Selling British Single 1984) 1983, The War Song 1984, The Medal Song 1984, Move Away 1986, I Just Wanna Be Loved 1998, Your Kisses Are Charity 1999, Cold Shoulder 1999. *Honours:* BRIT Awards for Best British Newcomer 1983, Best British Group 1984. *E-mail:* cultureclub@music3w.com (office). *Website:* www.culture-club.co.uk.

MOSS, Mick (Mix), BA; British producer; b. 25 May 1953, London. *Career:* worked with The Farm, The La's, Elvis Costello, Pete Townshend, Sonya, Racey, The Troggs; also worked with various members of The Clash, The Christians, Flock of Seagulls, Icicle Works, Tears For Fears, Suzi Quatro band, Lightning Seeds; mem. PRS, MRF, IMF. *Recordings include:* producer, engineer: singles/EPs: Bread Not Bombs 1986, What's Happening To Our Nation?, L8 Connexion, Free, Live Transmission 1986, Are U In Pain?, Gaynor Rose Madder 1987, Fading, Gaynor Rose Madder 1987, Here Comes The Floor, Benny Profane 1987, I Love You Liverpool, Steve May 1988, Worse Year of My Life, Wild Swans 1989, Soldier On, Wild Swans 1989, This Is The Age, Pupils of Parkfield School Liverpool 1989, Post Funk War, 25th of May 1989, Cynthia Payne, The Hoovers 1988, for MDM: Take What You Want 1988–94; for Awakenings: The Senses, Oh Father, Ice Factory 1990; Disease, Adams Family 1991, Cinemascope, Syndicate 1994, Greytown, Syndicate 1995. *Publications include:* contrib. articles to music magazines.

MOSUMGAARD, Niels Eliot; Danish songwriter, musician (guitar, saxophone) and singer; b. 20 Oct. 1961, Århus, mem. Eva Baadsgaard 1991, two s. *Career:* songwriter, singer, Lars Liholt Band tour 1984; toured Denmark with own band 1984–; sideman, saxophone, guitar, blues, calypso and popular bands; mem. Calypsocapellet 1984–87, Sweethearts 1989–91; lyricist for several composers on independent scene in Danish and English, and for Bamboo Brothers (Johnny Told Suzi 1993, music by Troels Skovgard); inventor, personal mix of folk, ambient, ethnic and metal called Folkadelic. *Address:* Lautrup Street No. 9 5. Sal, 2100 Copenhagen, Denmark. *Telephone:* 33-12-00-85. *E-mail:* dpa@dpa.org. *Website:* www.dpa.org.

MOTEN, Frank, Jr, (Tee Tah, Easy Mo'T); American producer and composer; b. 7 April 1967, New York. *Education:* Johnson C. Smith Univ. *Career:* live performances include Carnegie Hall and The Apollo Theater; various production projects; recorded as Tee Tah 1998; Founder OurGig.com 2000, joined Jazz Legacy Productions 2009. *Recording:* as Tee Tah: Still Boppin/Night In Tunisia 1998. *Telephone:* (305) 604-5256 (office). *E-mail:* esales@ourgig.net (office). *Website:* www.ourgig.com (office); www.frankmoten.com.

MOTION, David; British composer and wine merchant; b. (David Christopher Simon Freeman), 23 March 1959, Hamburg, Germany; s. of David Charles Freeman and Ingeborg Grete Thote; m. Vera Hegarty. *Education:* G Gaunt, G Greed, Royal Acad. of Music. *Career:* recording engineer 1982–84; record producer 1984–90; composer 1982–; wine merchant 1996–. *Compositions:* Sally Potter's film Orlando; TV: Cardiac Arrest, Trial and Retribution; commercials: HSBC, Gaviscon, BMW, Ford, Vauxhall, Audi, Sharwoods, Frontera, Tesco, Shell, Orange, Transport for London, Prada. *Recordings:* Neo-Classic, music to eat and lie down to (with Jesper Siberg), Creation, Creation 2000, Creations 3, Puro Sesso, Ultraviva. *Publication:* Groovelab (with Andy Hampton). *Honours:* D and AD Silver Award, Riesling Fellow. *Telephone:* (20) 7286-6475 (office). *E-mail:* info@davidmotion.com (office); info@thewineryuk.com (office). *Website:* www.davidmotion.com; www.thewineryuk.com.

MOTOHARU; Japanese musician (saxophone); b. 29 June 1973, Nayoro, Hokkaido. *Career:* mem. jazz band, Soil & "Pimp" Sessions 2001–. *Recordings include:* albums: Pimpin' (EP) 2004, Pimp Master 2005, Summer Goddess (EP) 2005, Pimp of the Year 2006, Pimpoint 2007, Planet Pimp 2008, 6 2009, Stoned Pirates Radio 2010, Magnetic Soil 2011, Circles 2013, Brothers & Sisters 2014. *E-mail:* soil@jvcmusic.co.jp. *Website:* www.jvcmusic.co.jp/soilpimp.

MOTTIRONI, Adriano; Italian composer, sound engineer and lecturer; b. 3 Nov. 1968, Rome, Italy. *Education:* Durham Univ., UK, Univ. of Rome 3. *Career:* music and sound designer on theatre productions; concert promoter; musical and tech. adviser; lecturer in information tech. and multimedia, secondary schools; European Computer Driving Licence examiner. *Compositions:* La Scoperta De L'America, Labyrinth, Romeo and Juliet, Sorry. *Address:* Viale Dei Gigli 75B, 00042 Lavinio, Rome, Italy (home). *Telephone:* 339-3254415 (mobile) (office). *E-mail:* adriano.mottironi@poste.it (home).

MOTTOLA, Thomas (Tommy) D.; American producer and record company executive; m. 1st Mariah Carey 1993 (divorced 1998); m. 2nd Ariadna Thalía Sodi Miranda 2000. *Career:* record prod.; joined CBS Records 1987; Pres., Columbia Records; Chair. and CEO, Sony Music Entertainment Inc 1998–2003; launched Casablanca Records 2003–. *Address:* c/o Casablanca Records, Universal Music Group, 2220 Colorado Avenue, Santa Monica, CA 90404, USA. *Website:* www.casablanca-music.com.

MOUFANG, David; German composer, producer and musician (guitar, keyboards, percussion); b. 7 Sept. 1966, Heidelberg. *Career:* runs two record labels with Jonas Grossmanns, Source Records, 1992–, KM 20 1996–; mem. Sound Works Exchange (sponsored by the Goethe Inst. and British Arts Council) 1995. *Recordings include:* Earth To Infinity 1992, Big Rooms, Deep Space Network 1993, Intergalactic Federation, Deep Space Network and Dr Atmo 1993, Intergalactic Federation 2 1994, Reagenz (with Jonah Sharp) 1994, View To View (with Rob Gordon) 1994, Kunststoff 1995, Solitaire 1995, Koolfang (with Pete Namlook) 1995, Koolgang 2 1995, Traffic (Live '95), Deep Space Network 1996, Cymbelin, Move D 1996, RO70/Move D, Roman Flügel 1996, Exploring the Psychdelic Landscape 1996, Lips, with Tobacco Rot 1997, Deep Space Network Meets Higher Intelligence Agency 1997, A Day in the Life 1997, Traffic, Deep Space Network 1999, Tomboy (with Thomas Meniecke) 1999, The Retro Rocket 1999, Conjoint 2000, Wired 2001, Home Shopping: Move D 2002, Sons of Kraut 2006, Stranger III 2010, The Silent Orbiter 2014. *Address:* c/o Source Records, Kornmarkt 9, 69117 Heidelberg, Germany.

MOULDER, Alan; British record producer and engineer; b. 11 June 1959, Boston, Lincs., England; m. Toni Halliday. *Career:* worked at Ministry of Agric. 1980–84; assistant engineer, Trident Studios, London 1984–88; Cco-founder (with Flood), Assault & Battery studio complex 2008–; production, mixing and engineering work with numerous artists including Arctic Monkeys, Atticus Ross, The Boo Radleys, The Cure, Curve, Eurythmics, Foo Fighters, Jean Michel Jarre, Jesus and Mary Chain, La Roux, Led Zeppelin, Marilyn Manson, Moby, Monster Magnet, My Bloody Valentine, Nine Inch Nails, Gary Numan, Ride, Royal Blood, Shakespear's Sister, Soulwax, The Sounds, The Sundays, Swervedriver, U2, White Lies, Wolfmother, Yeah Yeah Yeahs; numerous production collaborations with Flood including: Foals, Tom Jones, The Killers, Smashing Pumpkins. *Honours:* BRIT Award/Music Producers Guild Award for Best British Producer (with Flood) 2014. *Address:* Assault & Battery 1, Miloco Studios, 1 Maybury Gardens, London, NW10 2NB, England (office). *Telephone:* (20) 7232-0008 (office). *Website:* www.miloco.co.uk (office); www.alanmoulder.com.

MOUNFIELD, Gary 'Mani'; British musician (bass); b. 16 Nov. 1962, Manchester, England. *Education:* Xaverian Coll. *Career:* mem. Stone Roses 1987–96, 2011–; mem. Primal Scream 1999–;. *Recordings include:* albums: with Stone Roses: The Stone Roses 1989, The Second Coming 1994, The Very Best Of The Stone Roses 2002; with Primal Scream: Xtrmntr 2000, Evil Heat 2002, Dirty Hits 2003, Shoot Speed (More Dirty Hits) 2004, Riot City Blues 2006, Beautiful Future 2008, More Light 2013. *Honours:* Muso Award (Best Bass Guitar) 2005, Q Groundbreaker Award (with Primal Scream) 2006, NME Godlike Genius Award 2007. *Current Management:* G. R. Management Ltd, 974 Pollockshaws Road, Glasgow, G41 2HA, Scotland. *Telephone:* (141) 632-1111. *Website:* www.thestoneroses.org; www.primalscream.net.

MOUNSEY, Paul Fraser, GTCL, FTCL, LTCL; British composer, producer, arranger and musician (piano); b. 15 April 1959, Irvine, Scotland; m. Dorinha Carelli 1983. *Education:* Trinity Coll. of London. *Career:* part-time lecturer, Goldsmith's Coll., London Univ. 1984–85; songwriter, CBS (Sony) Brazil 1986–87; producer, arranger, Sony (Brazil), EMI (Brazil) and Independents 1987–89; Musical Director, Play It Again Studios, São Paulo, Brazil 1989–99; f. Nahoo musical collective 1994; f. production co. Junk. *Recordings include:* albums: Nahoo 1994, NahooToo 1997, Nahoo 3, Notes from the Republic 1999, City of Walls 2003, The Days Flash Past: Tha Na Laithean A'dol Seachad 2005.

MOUNT, Benjamin John David (Ben), (The Verse, MC Verse); British rapper, MC, DJ, songwriter and producer; b. 14 April 1977, London. *Education:* Univ. of Leeds. *Career:* drum and bass DJ 1996–; mem. Pendulum 2006–; drum and bass and dubstep producer; f. Crunch Recordings 2004; numerous collaborations with Ink, SP:MC, Loxy, Keaton, D-Bridge, Phobia. *Recordings:* albums: with Pendulum: In Silico 2008, Immersion 2010; solo: as contributor: Anatomy, Teebee and Calyx 2008. *Current Management:* c/o JHO Management, 1–5 Exchange Court, Maiden Lane, Covent Garden, London, WC2R 0JU, England. *Telephone:* (20) 7420-4372. *Fax:* (20) 7420-4399. *E-mail:* jho@jhooakley.com. *Website:* www.jhooakley.com. *Address:* c/o Warner Bros. Records, Warner Music UK Limited, The Warner Building, 28 Kensington Church Street, London, W8 4EP, England (office). *Website:* www .warnerbrosrecords.co.uk (office); www.pendulum.com.

MOUQUET, Eric; French musician; b. 1960, Valenciennes. *Career:* mem., Deep Forest 1991–; mem., Deo Dezi; collaborations with Abed Azrie, Peter Gabriel, Marcella Lewis, Wes Madiko, Jorge Reyes, Ana Toroja, Joe Zawinul. *Recordings include:* albums: with Deep Forest: World Mix 1994, Bohême 1996, Comparsa 1998, Made in Japan 1999, Madazulu 1997–98; with Dao Dezi: World Mix 1994, Dao Dezi 1995. *Compositions include:* Malagasy Blues Song 1993, The Greatest Hits of 1994 1994, Lullaby: A Collection 1994, Themes & Dreams 1995, Under the Monkey Puzzle Tree 1996, Solo 1997, Pure Moods 1997, Dreams/Reves 1998, Voce: Music from Women of the World 1999, Trip Around the World 2000, The Classic Chillout Album 2001, Seriously Chilled: New Arrangements of Classic Chill-Out Anthems by Anne Dudley 2003, Closer 2003, A Tribute to Josh Groban 2004, Artist's Choice: Joni Mitchell 2005, Passe Moi le Ciel 2006. *Honours:* MTV Award (Best Music Video, Sweet Lullaby) 1993, Victoires de la Musique Awards (Best World Album), 1993, 1996, World Music Award (Most Sales in the World) 1995, Grammy Award (Best World Music Album, Bohême) 1996. *Address:* c/o V.O. Music, 40 rue de la Folie Régnault, 75011 Paris, France. *Telephone:* 1-45-80-96-60. *E-mail:* info@vo-music.com. *Website:* www.vo-music.com.

MOURID, Nadia Nid al-; French singer and musician (percussion); sister of Yasmina Nid al-Mourid. *Career:* mem. Lo'jo 1995–. *Recordings include:* albums: Fils de Zamal 1993, Sin Acabar 1996, Mojo Radio 1998, Bohême de Cristal 2000, L'Une des siens/Au cabaret sauvage 2002, Ce Soir Là 2003, Bazar Savant 2006, Cosmophono 2009, Cinema El Mundo 2012, 310 Lunes 2014. *Stage productions include:* Dechpouk ze World (with Companie Jo Bithume) 1991, Triban de Lo'jo (with ZUR) 1994. *E-mail:* management@lojo .org; lojo@lojo.org. *Website:* www.lojo.org.

MOURID, Yasmina Nid al-; French singer and musician (soprano saxophone, percussion); sister of Nadia Nid al-Mourid. *Career:* mem., Lo'jo 1995–. *Recordings include:* albums: Sin Acabar 1996, Mojo Radio 1998, Bohême de Cristal 2000, L'Une des siens/Au cabaret sauvage 2002, Ce Soir Là 2003, Bazar Savant 2006, Cosmophono 2009, Cinema El Mundo 2012, 310 Lunes 2014. *E-mail:* management@lojo.org; lojo@lojo.org. *Website:* www.lojo.org.

MOUSER, Richard; American musician (guitar), record producer and engineer; *Head, The Mouse House Studio;* b. 4 June 1962, Santa Monica, Calif.; two d. *Career:* support tours with 3 Dog Night, Huey Lewis and the News, Warrant, Michael Schenker Group, Melissa Manchester, Def Leppard, Queensryche; producer, engineer, mixer for albums by Green Jelly, Corrosion of Conformity, Lucy's Fur Coat, LSD, The Coup de Grace, Black Market Flowers, The Ex-Idols, Jack Of Jill, Oleander, Blair Tefkin, Imperial Tree, Less Than Jake, Insane Clown Posse, Quickspace, The Generators, Schleprock, Clawfinger; currently Head, The Mouse House Studio; wrote and produced jingles for numerous commercials. *Telephone:* (626) 296-3224 (office). *E-mail:* themousehouse007@aol.com (office). *Website:* www .themousehousestudio.com (office).

MOUSKOURI, Ioanna (Nana); Greek singer and fmr politician; b. 13 Oct. 1934, Athens; d. of Constantin Mouskouri and Alice Mouskouri; m. 1st George Petsilas; one s. one d.; m. 2nd Andre Chapelle. *Education:* Athens Nat. Conservatory. *Career:* singer 1956–; living in Paris 1962–; has given concerts world-wide; has sold more than 300 million records world-wide; recorded more than 1,500 songs in Greek, French, English, German, Dutch, Italian and Spanish; numerous TV appearances, including Numéro 1 1979 and Nana Mouskouri à Athènes 1984; UNICEF Amb. 1993–, Special Rep. for Performing Arts and Hon. Spokesperson; mem. European Parl. 1994–99; Founder and Pres. Foundation 'Nana Mouskouri-Focus on Hope'. *Songs include:* L'enfant au tambour, Les parapluies de Cherbourg, C'est bon la vie, Plaisir d'amour, Ave Maria, L'amour en héritage, Only Love, White Rose of Athens, Je chante avec toi Liberté. *Publications:* Chanter ma vie 1989, Memoirs 2007, My Name is Nana 2007, Itinéraire intime 2013. *Honours:* Gran Cruz Placa de Plata (Dominican Repub.) 2006, Officier, Légion d'honneur 2007, Grand Commdr, Order of Benefaction (Greece) 2007, Officier, Ordre Nat. du Québec 2013; Dr hc (McGill) 2013; Greek Broadcasting Festival Award 1959, Barcelona Festival Award, No. 1 French Female Singer 1979, No. 1 Female Singer World-wide, Canada 1980, IFPI Multiplatinum Music Award 1996, UNICEF World of Children Award 1997 and numerous other awards and prizes. *Address:* c/o Nema Productions SA, 12 Robert de Traz, 1206 Geneva, Switzerland (office). *Telephone:* (22) 3460130 (home). *Fax:* (22) 7522293 (home). *E-mail:* nemaprod@bluewin.ch (home); nemaprod@mac.com (office). *Website:* www.nanamouskouri.net.

MOUTOUARI, Pierre; Republic of the Congo musician; b. 3 April 1950, Kimuimba; six d. *Career:* mem. The Super Band (later renamed Orchestre Sinza) 1968; Founder-mem. Les Sossa 1975; manager, PM Production. *Recordings include:* Le Retour de Pierre Moutouari, Tout Bouge, Dans Tremblement de Terre, Songa Nzila 2005. *Honours:* Gold Medal, Festival de Tunis 1973, Best Composer Prize 1982, Prize Zaïre 1993.

MOWER, Michael (Mike) Henry; British composer and musician (flutes, saxophones); b. 9 June 1958, Bath, England; m. Elizabeth Melia 1994. *Education:* Royal Academy of Music, London. *Career:* Mike Mower Quartet (jazz), frequent broadcasts for BBC Radio, 1980–84; wrote arrangements for BBC Radio Orchestra Big Band, 1984–86; formed Itchy Fingers, jazz saxophone quartet playing his music, won Jazz Sounds '86, 1986–95; band has toured 42 countries, playing all major European jazz festivals; commissions for soloists and ensembles specializing in jazz/classical crossover style; mem. Musicians' Union. *Compositions:* numerous for wind instruments. *Recordings:* albums: producer, writer with Itchy Fingers saxophone quartet: Quark; Teranga; Itchy Fingers Live In Europe; Full English Breakfast; with flute player Kirsten Spratt): Doodle and Flight; Triligence (titles taken from jazz sonatas for flute and piano by Mike Mower). *Honours:* Hon. ARAM. *Address:* Itchy Fingers Publications, 10 Warminster Road, Beckington, Frome, Somerset, BA11 6SY, England. *Telephone:* (1373) 831414. *Website:* www.itchyfingers.com.

MOYET, (Genevieve) Alison Jane; British singer and songwriter; b. 18 June 1961, Billericay, Essex, England; m.; three c. *Education:* Southend Technical Coll. *Career:* singer with Yazoo 1981–83; solo singer 1983–; broadcast performance with the BBC Concert Orchestra (BBC Radio 2) 2003. *Theatre:* Chicago (as Mama Morton), West End, London 2001, Smaller (Lyric Theatre, London and UK tour) 2006. *Recordings include:* albums: with Yazoo: Upstairs At Eric's 1982, You and Me Both 1983; solo: Alf 1984, Raindancing 1987, Hoodoo 1991, Essex 1994, Singles 1995, The Essential Alison Moyet 2001, Hometime 2002, Voice 2004, The Turn 2007, Best Of: 25 Years Revisited 2009, The Minutes 2013. *Honours:* BRIT Award for Best New Band (with Yazoo) 1982, for Best Female Artist 1984, 1987, Rock and Pop Award for Best Female Artist 1982. *Current Management:* c/o Georgie Gibbon, Modest Management, The Matrix Complex, 91 Peterborough Road, London, SW6 3BU; c/o Nigel Hassler, Helter Skelter, The Plaza, 535 Kings Road, London SW10 0SZ, England. *E-mail:* georgie@modestmanagement.com. *Website:* www.modestmanagement.com; www.alisonmoyet.com.

MOYSE, Nigel Arthur, BA; Irish musician (electric, semi-acoustic, acoustic guitar); b. 26 Feb. 1952, Dublin; m. Elizabeth McColl 1974; one s. one d. *Education:* Trinity Coll. Dublin, Municipal School of Music, studied guitar with Louis Stewart. *Career:* played with John Stevens Away and Dance Orchestra, Folkus, Freebop, Ed Speight, Nigel Moyse Quartet, Mike Stock Band, The Flirtations; performances include Sheffield Festivals, Round House, ICA, Hyde Park, 100 Club; visiting music teacher, Eton Coll., Windsor, Berkshire; currently also private guitar tutor; mem. Musicians' Union. *Compositions include:* co-written with Ed Speight: The Dodder Suite 1980, Complications 1981; solo: Tsk Tsk, Ballad For Mick, Martin's Dilemma 1980. *Recordings include:* with Away: Integration 1980, Mutual Benefit 1994; with Dance Orchestra: Ah 1978; with Some of: Conversation Piece 1991, A Luta Continua 1994; with Folkus: The Life of Riley 1984.

MOZEZ; British singer and producer; b. (Osmond Lloyd Wright), 1963. *Career:* mem. Spirits 1994–95; featured vocalist with Zero 7 2001–; Dir Titian Music 1999–; solo artist 2004–. *Recordings include:* albums: with Zero 7: Simple Things 2001, When It Falls 2004; solo: So Still 2005, Time Out 2011, Wings 2012, Be Like Water 2013. *Address:* c/o Numen Records, 18 Ashwin Street, Dalston, London, E8 3DL, England. *E-mail:* mozez@numenrecords.co .uk. *Website:* www.mozez.co.uk.

MOZZATI, Cristiano; Italian musician (drums); b. 13 Aug. 1973, Pesaro. *Career:* mem. metal band, Lacuna Coil 1998–. *Recordings include:* albums: In a Reverie 1999, Unleashed Memories 2001, Comalies 2002, Karmacode 2006, Shallow Life 2009, Dark Adrenaline 2012, Broken Crown Halo 2014. *Honours:* Female Metal Voices Fest Award (Lacuna Coil) 2012. *Current Management:* Riot Rock Management, 639 Dupont Street, Unit 216, Toronto, ON M6G 1Z4, Canada. *E-mail:* info@riotrock.com. *Website:* www.riotrock.com; www .lacunacoil.it.

MR G (see McBean, Colin)

MRAZ, Jason; American singer and songwriter; b. 23 June 1977, Mechanicsville, Va; m. Sheridan Edley 2001 (divorced). *Career:* solo artist 2002–, released debut 2004; performed as support act at concerts by Alanis Morrisette 2005, Rolling Stones 2005–06. *Recordings:* albums: Waiting for My Rocket to Come 2002, Mr A-Z 2005, Selections For Friends 2007, We Sing. We Dance. We Steal Things 2008, Love is a Four Letter Word 2012, Yes! 2014. *Honours:* Best Acoustic Artist, San Diego Music Awards 2002, Artist of the Year and Song of the Year, San Diego Music Awards 2003, Grammy Awards for Best Male Pop Vocal Performance (for Make it Mine) 2010, for Best Pop Collaboration with Vocals (for Lucky with Colbie Caillat) 2010. *Current Management:* Bill Silva Management, 8225 Santa Monica Blvd, West Hollywood, CA 90046, USA. *Telephone:* (310) 651-3310. *Fax:* (310) 651-3345. *Website:* www.billsilvapresents.com. *Address:* Jason Mraz, POB 69A36, Los Angeles, CA 90069, USA (office). *E-mail:* info@jasonmraz.com (office). *Website:* www.jasonmraz.com.

MTUKUDZI, Oliver 'Tuku'; Zimbabwean singer, musician (guitar) and songwriter; b. 22 Sept. 1952; one s. one d. *Career:* joined Wagon Wheels with Thomas Mapfumo 1977–79; Founder-mem. Black Spirits; sound referred to as Tuku music; tours of Africa, Australia, America and Europe; festival performances. *Theatre:* Was My Child (writer and dir, musical) 1990s. *Film appearances include:* Jit 1990, Neria (also composer). *Recordings include:*

albums: Ndipeiwo Zano 1978, Chokwadi Chichabuda 1979, Muroi Ndiani? 1979, Shanje 1980, Maungira 1981, Please Ndapota 1981, Nzara, Hwema Handirase, Mhaka, Gona, Zvauya Sei?, Wawona, Sugar Pie, Mapisarema, Strange Isn't It, Nyanga Yenzou, Grandpa Story, Live At Sakubva, Chikonzi, Kuvhaira, Mutorwa, Rombe, Rumbidzai Jehova, Ndotomuimbira, Son Of The Soil, Was My Child (Zimbabwe Writers' Union honour), Pfugama Unamate, Ivai Navo, Svovi Yangu, Chinhambwe, Africa 1980, Shoko 1990, Ziwere 1992, Tuku Music 1999, Paivepo 2000, Ndega Zvangu 2001, Neria (M-Net Award for Best Soundtrack) 2001, Bvuma 2001, Vhunze Moto 2002, Shanda 2003, Bira Rekunze 2003, Tsivo 2004, Nhava 2005, Tsimba Itsoka 2007, Dairai 2008, Rudaviro 2010, Sarawoga 2013. *Honours:* Celebration of African Artists Ceremony (CAMA) Award 2001, Kora Award for Best African Arrangement 2002, for Best Male Artist, Southern Africa 2004, Kora Lifetime Achievement Award 2004. *Address:* Tukumusic Ltd, Bassline Building, 10 Henry Nxumalo Street, Newtown, Johannesburg 2001, South Africa (office). *Telephone:* (11) 8389145 (office). *Fax:* (11) 8389149 (office). *E-mail:* smataure@gmail.com. *Website:* www.tukumusic.com.

MUBARAK, Abdel Aziz al-; Sudanese singer and musician (oud); b. 1951, Wad Madani. *Education:* Inst. of Music and Drama, Khartoum. *Career:* solo artist; tours extensively in Africa and Arab States, including Ethiopia, Somalia, Nigeria, Chad, Cameroon, Egypt, Kuwait, UAE; mem. trio with Abdel Gadir Salim and Mohammed Gubara. *Recordings include:* Straight from the Heart 1985, The Sounds of Sudan (with Mohammed Gubara and Abdel Gadir Salim) 1986, Abdel Aziz El Mubarak 1987, Rough Guide to the Music of North Africa (compilation album) 2013. *Address:* c/o World Circuit Records, 138 Kingsland Road, London, E2 8DY, England.

MUES, Jan; Belgian musician (flugelhorn, trumpet), composer and arranger; b. 8 Feb. 1955, Zichem; m. Marie Paule Branders 1976; one d. *Education:* Acad. des Beaux Arts. *Career:* soloist, Belgian Jazz Orchestra; mem. SABAM, Int. Jazz Festival. *Compositions include:* Mystic Smile, Whippy Lippy, Why Do You Skip So Tippy, Hayday, Who's Watching Who, Lullaby For the Sun, I Hope the Guys Like It, Foolish Enter, Peter's Egg. *Recordings include:* Mystic Smile (album), Jan Mües Cool Cargo 2004. *Publication:* De Koning the Rijk. *Honours:* Laureate, 11th European Jazz Contest 1989, SABAM Award 1997. *Address:* Jan Mües, Mannenberg 70, 3270 Scherpenheuvel, Belgium (office). *Telephone:* (1) 377-53-38 (office). *Fax:* (1) 377-53-38 (office). *E-mail:* jan.mues@scarlet.be. *Website:* www.janmues.be.

MUGGERUD, Lawrence (see DJ Muggs)

MUGGLETON, Paul Frank; British record producer; b. 27 Feb. 1947, London; partner Judie Tzuke; two s. three d. *Education:* Univ. of Madrid, Spain. *Career:* tours with Judie Tzuke including tour of America with Elton John; played Central Park, New York (with Judie Tzuke); f. Big Moon Records 1996; mem. PRS, Musicians' Union. *Recordings include:* co-producer (with Mike Paxman) all Judie Tzuke albums. *Honours:* Song Award, Festival De Malaga 1970. *Address:* Big Moon Records, PO Box 347, Weybridge, KT13 9WZ, England (office). *Telephone:* (1932) 590169 (office). *E-mail:* paul@tzuke.com. *Website:* www.tzuke.com.

DJ MUGGS; American DJ and producer; b. (Lawrence Muggerud), 28 Jan. 1968, New York. *Career:* Founder-mem. DVX 1986, renamed Cypress Hill 1988–; solo artist 1996–. *Recordings include:* albums: with Cypress Hill: Cypress Hill 1991, Black Sunday 1993, Cypress Hill III: Temples of Boom 1995, IV 1998, Skull & Bones 2000, Live at the Fillmore 2000, Stoned Raiders 2001, Till Death Do Us Part 2004, Rise Up 2010; solo: Muggs Presents... The Soul Assassins Chapter I 1997, Muggs Presents... The Soul Assassins Chapter II 2000, Dust 2003, Grandmasters (with GZA) 2005, Pain Language (with Planet Asia) 2008, Soul Assassins: Intermission 2009, Kill Devil Hills 2010. *Current Management:* Goliath Artists, 151 Lafayette Street, 6th Floor, New York, NY 10013, USA. *Telephone:* (212) 324-2410. *E-mail:* howard@goliath-management.com. *Website:* goliath-management.com; www.cypresshill.com; www.djmuggs.com.

MUHANDIS, Majid al-; Iraqi singer and composer; b. (Majid al-Utaybi), 25 Oct. 1971, Baghdad. *Career:* fmr engineer (Muhandis means engineer in Arabic); solo artist 2005–. *Recordings include:* albums: Waheshni Moot 2005, Enjanet 2006, Ensa 2008, Sarharni Halaha 2012. *Current Management:* c/o Kingdom Tower, 58th Floor, King Fahd Road, Olaya District, Riyadh, Saudi Arabia. *Telephone:* (1) 211-0000. *Fax:* (1) 211-0011. *E-mail:* info@rotana.net. *Website:* www.rotana.net.

MUHL, Lars; Danish singer, songwriter, musician and writer; b. 14 Nov. 1950, Århus; m. Githa Ben-David. *Education:* Jutland Conservatory of Music. *Career:* mem. Daisy 1968; formed Warm Guns 1978–; solo artist 1986–; songwriter for European Artists; Founder Hearts & Hands 2003, Gilalai -Inst. for Energy & Consciousness; mem. DJBFA, Danish Artists Asscn. *Compositions include:* One More Minute, Open Up My Heart. *Recordings include:* albums: with Warm Guns: First Shot Live 1979, Instant Schlager 1980, Italiano Moderno 1981, Follow Your Heart or Fall 1983; solo: The Glorious Art of Breakin Little Girls' Hearts and Blowin' Big Boys' Brains 1986, King of Croon 1988, When Angels Fall 1991, From All of Us 1993, Kingdom Come 1994, Regnfang 1996, Mandolina 1997, Till the End of Time 1998, To Heal the Space Between Us 2011. *Publications include:* Soul at Fire (autobiography), Zoé (novel), The O Manuscript (trilogy). *Honours:* DJBFA Prize of Honour 1990, WCM Songwriters Million Certificate 1996. *E-mail:* dharma@larsmuhl.com. *Website:* www.larsmuhl.com.

MÜHLEIS, Daniela; Swiss singer and musician (guitar, piano); b. 27 April 1955, St Gallen; m. Hans Georg Huber 1986; one adopted d. *Education:* commercial school, commercial association, St Gallen, took guitar, piano lessons. *Career:* joined Cargo 1979; Nat. Country and Western Festival in Zürich, Open-Air Festival, St Gallen 1981; Swiss finals, European Song Contest; debut album 1983; band renamed, Daniela Mühleis and Band 1984; successful concerts in Switzerland, Italy; country festivals; Swiss television includes Sonntagsmagazin 1989, Country Roads; Holansky kapr Country Music Festival, Prague 1989; Int. Country Festival, Geiselwind 1990; German cable TV includes Offener Kanal Dortmund 1991; PORTA Country Festival, Czech Republic 1992; Int. Visagino Country Festival, Lithuania 1993; TV appearances in Lithuania and Malta; video clip produced in Malta 1994; own radio show in St Gallen, Country Music 1984–97; mem. CMA (USA), CMFS (Switzerland), ECMA, NACMAI (USA), ECMA (Europe). *Recordings include:* albums: Stage-fright 1983, Die Sieger des 1 Country und Western Festivals Zürich 1986, Far Away 1987, Animals 1990, Far Away 1991, Better Life 1993, Open Minds 1997. *Honours:* winner of Modern Country Music section, Swiss Country Open Air 1985, SRI Selection 1997, North America Country Music Asscn Int. Rising Star Award 1999. *Current Management:* DMB, Lehnackerstrasse 9a, 9033 Untereggen, Switzerland.

MUIR, Mike; American singer. *Career:* mem., Suicidal Tendencies; numerous live gigs in USA; also mem. of side project, Infectious Grooves. *Recordings include:* albums: with Suicidal Tendencies: Suicidal Tendencies 1983, Join the Army 1987, How Will I Laugh Tomorrow When I Can't Even Smile Today 1988, Controlled by Hatred 1989, Lights, Camera, Revolution! 1990, F.N.G. (compilation) 1992, The Art of Rebellion 1992, Still Cyco After All These Years 1993, Suicidal for Life, 1994, Prime Cuts 1997, Friends and Family (compilation) 1998, FreeDumb 1999, Free Your Soul And Save Your Mind 2000, Friends and Family Vol. 2 (compilation) 2001, Year of the Cycos 2008, No Mercy Fool!/The Suicidal Family 2010; with Infectious Grooves: The Plague that Makes Your Booty Move 1991, Sarsippius' Ark, 1993, Groove Family Cyco 1994, Mas Borracho, 2000; solo (as Cyco Miko): Lost My Brain! (Once Again) 1996, Schizophrenic Born Again Problem Child 2001, The Mad Mad Muir Musical Tour 2011. *E-mail:* stigfamilia@aol.com. *Website:* www.suicidaltendencies.com.

MUIRHEAD, Dennis Richard; Australian lawyer, music agent and mediator; *Founder and CEO, Muirhead Management;* b. 7 Oct. 1941, Dubbo, NSW; m. 1st Elizabeth 1966; three s.; m. 2nd Angel 1988; one s. one d. *Education:* Univ. of Adelaide, S Australian. *Career:* consultant lawyer, Simons, Muirhead and Burton; Founder and CEO Dennis Muirhead Co. Ltd, Muirhead Man. 1982–; man., business, legal services to record producers, engineers, studios, artists, songwriters; clients included producers Clive Langer and Alan Winstanley, Hugh Padgham, Denis Woods, Richard Bennett, R.S. Field, Sun Studio Entertainment (Memphis), Australian jazz pianist and composer Paul Grabowsky, Missouri rockabilly singer and songwriter Billy Swan; mem. Counsel Assisting the S Australian Royal Comm. into the non-medical use of Drugs; Chair. City Roads (Crisis Intervention), Inst. for the Study of Drug Dependence; Founding Chair. and Council mem. The Music Managers' Forum; CEO Muirhead Music and Hugely Music Publishing; consultant New Media; mem. Country Music Asscn, NARAS, Nashville; Mediator with ADR Chambers, Asscn of Cambridge Mediators and Clerksroom 2002–; Trustee, Australian Music Foundation UK 2010–. *Honours:* British Music Roll of Honour 2008. *Address:* Association of Cambridge Mediators, Sheraton House, Castle Park, Cambridge, CB3 0AX, England (office). *Telephone:* (1223) 370063 (office). *E-mail:* enquiries@cambridgemediators.co.uk (office). *Website:* www.cambridgemediators.co.uk (office).

MUKHTAR, Ahmed, BA, MA; Iraqi/British musician (oud) and teacher; b. 1969, Baghdad. *Education:* Inst. of Fine Arts, High Inst. of Music, Syria, London Coll. of Music, School of Oriental and African Studies, UK. *Career:* oud and other Arabic percussion artist 1979–; music teacher, Al Arabi Inst., Syria 1993, SOAS; Chair. Oriental Culture Forum, London 2009–. *Television:* Speech of the Oud (presenter, Almustaklah TV, London) 2001–. *Recordings include:* album: Words from Eden 1996, Tajwal 1999, Rhythms Of Baghdad 2003, The Road to Baghdad 2005. *Honours:* British Musicians' Union Award 1999. *Address:* Flat 17, 23 Stukeley Street, London WC2B 5LT, England (home). *Telephone:* (20) 7404-1627 (home). *E-mail:* info@amukhtar.com; oud15@hotmail.com. *Website:* www.amukhtar.com.

MULDAUR, Maria; American singer; b. (Maria Grazia Rosa Domenica d'Avato), 12 Sept. 1943, Greenwich Village, New York; m. Jeff Muldaur (divorced 1972). *Career:* mem. Even Dozen Jug Band (with John Sebastian, Stefan Grossman, Joshua Rifkin, Steve Katz), Jim Kweskin Jug Band; solo artist 1973–. *Recordings include:* albums: Maria Muldaur 1973, Waitress In A Donut Shop 1974, Sweet Harmony 1976, Southern Winds 1978, Open Your Eyes 1979, Gospel Nights 1981, There Is A Love 1982, Sweet and Slow 1984, Transblucency 1986, On The Sunnyside 1990, Louisiana Love Call 1992, Meet Me at Midnite 1994, Jazzabelle 1994, Fanning the Flames 1996, Southland of the Heart 1998, Meet Me Where They Play the Blues 1999, Richland Woman Blues 2000, Animal Crackers in my Soup 2002, A Woman Alone with the Blues, Sisters and Brothers 2004, Love Wants to Dance 2004, Sweet Lovin' Ol' Soul 2005, Heart of Mine 2006, Naughty, Bawdy and Blue 2007, Yes We Can! 2008, Maria Muldaur and Her Garden of Joy 2009, Maria Muldaur's Barnyard Dance 2010, Steady Love 2011. *Current Management:* c/o Mindy Giles, Swell Productions, 1526 Caramay Way, Sacramento, CA 95818, USA. *Telephone:*

(916) 447-6508. *E-mail:* mindy@swell-productions.com. *Website:* www.swell-productions.com; www.mariamuldaur.com.

MULDOON, Paul Gerrard 'Mule'; British musician (bass, guitar) and singer; b. 29 Oct. 1958, Huddersfield, Yorkshire; m. C. A. Nester 1995. *Career:* f. own band Muldoon Brothers; appeared at many major country festivals throughout Europe; appearances on British, Irish and Scandinavian TV and radio; mem. Musicians' Union. *Compositions include:* Back O' The Barn, Following The Trail, Brandin' Time, Ya'll Know It's Christmas. *Honours:* Most Promising Country Act 1992.

MULET, Sergio Roberto; Uruguayan musician (drums, congas, timbales, Brazillian percussion), arranger and music teacher; b. 2 Nov. 1958, Montevideo; m. Eloisa Valeria; one s. two d. *Career:* supported Gipsy Kings in Sydney 1989; numerous Australian TV appearances; formed Sandunga (Australia's first Afro-Cuban band); Artistic Dir and Event Co-ordinator, Manly World Music Concert Series; Man. and Co-ordinator, Manly Int. Jazz Festival 1998–; mem. Australian Jazz Soc. *E-mail:* sergiomulet@yahoo.com.

MULLEN, Larry, Jr; Irish musician (drums) and actor; b. 31 Oct. 1961, Dublin. *Education:* Mount Temple School, Dublin. *Career:* Founder-mem. and drummer with the Feedback 1976, renamed the Hype, finally renamed U2 1978–; major concerts include Live Aid Wembley 1985, Self Aid Dublin, A Conspiracy of Hope (Amnesty Int. Tour) 1986, Smile Jamaica (hurricane relief fundraiser) 1988, Very Special Arts Festival, White House, Washington, DC 1988; numerous tours world-wide. *Films include:* Rattle and Hum 1988, Man on the Train 2011, A Thousand Times Good Night 2013. *Recordings include:* albums: Boy 1980, October 1981, War 1983, Under a Blood Red Sky 1983, The Unforgettable Fire 1984, Wide Awake In America 1985, The Joshua Tree (Grammy Award for Album of the Year, Best Rock Performance by a Duo or Group with Vocal) 1987, Rattle and Hum 1988, Achtung Baby (Grammy Award for Best Rock Performance by a Duo or Group with Vocal 1992) 1991, Zooropa (Grammy Award for Best Alternative Music Album) 1993, Passengers (film soundtrack with Brian Eno) 1995, Pop 1997, The Best Of 1980–90 1998, All That You Can't Leave Behind (Grammy Award for Best Rock Album 2001) 2000, The Best Of 1990–2000 2002, How To Dismantle An Atomic Bomb (Meteor Ireland Music Award for Best Irish Album 2006, Grammy Awards for Album of the Year, for Best Rock Album 2006) 2004, No Line on the Horizon 2009, Songs of Innocence 2014. *Honours:* U2 have won 22 Grammy Awards, including Best Rock Performance by a Duo or Group with Vocal (for Desire) 1988, BRIT Awards for Best Int. Act 1988–90, 1992, 1998, 2001, Best Live Act 1993, Outstanding Contribution to the British Music Industry 2001, JUNO Award 1993, World Music Award 1993, Grammy Award for Song of the Year, Record of the Year, Best Rock Performance by a Duo or Group with Vocal (all for Beautiful Day) 2000, Grammy Awards for Best Pop Performance by a Duo or Group with Vocal (for Stuck In A Moment You Can't Get Out Of), for Record of the Year (for Walk On), for Best Rock Performance by a Duo or Group with Vocal (for Elevation) 2001, American Music Award for Favorite Internet Artist of the Year 2002, Ivor Novello Award for Best Song Musically and Lyrically (for Walk On) 2002, Golden Globe for Best Original Song (for The Hands That Built America, from film Gangs of New York) 2003, Grammy Awards for Best Rock Performance by a Duo or Group with Vocal, Best Rock Song, Best Short Form Music Video (all for Vertigo) 2004, Nordoff-Robbins Silver Clef Award for lifetime achievement 2005, Q Award for Best Live Act 2005, Digital Music Award for Favourite Download Single (for Vertigo) 2005, Meteor Ireland Music Award for Best Irish Band, Best Live Performance 2006, Grammy Awards for Song of the Year, for Best Rock Performance by a Duo or Group with Vocal (both for Sometimes You Can't Make it on Your Own), for Best Rock Song (for City of Blinding Lights) 2006, Amnesty International Ambassadors of Conscience Award 2006, Golden Globe Award for Best Original Score, Motion Picture (Ordinary Love in Mandela: Long Walk to Freedom) 2014, Palm Springs Film Festival Sonny Bono Visionary Award 2014; Portuguese Order of Liberty 2005. *Current Management:* c/o Principle Management, 30–32 Sir John Rogersons Quay, Dublin 2, Ireland. *E-mail:* nadine@numb.ie. *Website:* www.u2.com.

MÜLLER, Anders; Danish musician (piano, keyboards), composer, arranger and academic; *Associate Professor, Rhythmic Music Conservatory;* b. 2 Feb. 1955, Copenhagen; m. Anne Macholm, 6 June 1987, two s. one d. *Education:* Univ. of Copenhagen, studied with Ole Kock Hansen. *Career:* leader, own jazz trio and quartets 1975–; mem. orchestras led by Erling Kroner, Leif Johansson, Per Goldschmidt 1979–92; co-leader, jazz-rock group, Ariel 1979–83; appeared with New Music Orchestra as pianist 1985, 1992, as conductor 1990, composer 1985, 1988; also worked with Thad Jones, Eddie Bert, Red Rodney, Etta Cameron; currently Assoc. Prof., Rhythmic Music Conservatory, Copenhagen; mem. Danske Jazz, Beat og Folkemusik Autorer. *Compositions:* Tashmia, Woody's Blues, recorded by Lee Konitz. *Recordings:* with Erling Kroner, Leif Johansson, Ariel. *Honours:* First Prize, Dunkerque Jazz Festival, with Soren Bogelund Quartet. *Address:* Mazurka Music, Gammel Kongevej 78, 2 tv, 1850 Frederiksberg C, Denmark (office). *Telephone:* 33-23-21-31 (office). *E-mail:* am@mzm.dk (office). *Website:* www.mzm.dk (office).

MÜLLER, Christoph H., (Roy Dubb); Swiss producer, musician and composer. *Career:* fmr mem. band Touch el Arab; mem. Boyz From Brazil (with Philippe Cohen Solal); founder mem., band Gotan Project 1999–; tours worldwide, mixing video, pre-recorded and live performances; collaborations with many tango musicians, including with musicians from coastal Peru

(Radiokijada project). *Film music:* Je ne suis pas là pour être aimé 2005. *Recordings include:* albums: with Gotan Project: La Revancha del Tango 2001, Inspiración – Esperación 2004, Nuevos sonidos Afro Peruanos Part 1 (EP, with RadioKijada) 2005, Lunático 2006, Tango 3.0 2010; with Radiokijada: Nuevos Sonidos Afro Peruanos 2009. *Honours:* BBC Radio 3 World Music Award (Club Global) 2007. *Address:* c/o XL-Recordings, 17–19 Alma Road, London, SW18 1AA, England. *E-mail:* yabastarecords@noos.fr; info@radiokijada.com. *Website:* www.gotanproject.com; www.radiokijada.com (office).

MÜLLER, Ina; German singer and musician (guitar); b. 25 July 1965, Köhlen. *Career:* trained as a pharmaceutical-technical asst; Founder mem. cabaret duo Queen Bee (with Edda Schnittgard) 1994–2005; solo artist 2002–; collaborates with singer-songwriter Johannes Oerding. *Television:* as host: Inas Nacht 2007–. *Recordings:* albums: with Queen Bee: Die eine singt, die andere auch 1996, Wenn Du aufhörst, fang ich an 1998, Freundinnen 2000, Volle Kanne Kerzenschein 2002; solo: Das grosse Du 2004, Weiblich Ledig 40 2006, Liebe macht taub 2008, Die Schallplatte – nied opleggt 2009, Das wär dein Lied gewesen 2011. *Honours:* with Queen Bee: Mindener Stichling Gruppenpreis 2000, Deutscher Kleinkunstpreis in der Sparte 2001, Garchinger Kleinkunstmaske 2002; solo: ECHO Award for Best Nat. Female Artist 2012. *Current Management:* c/o Presse Peter, Peter Goebel, St Georgs Kirchhof 23, 20099 Hamburg, Germany. *Telephone:* (40) 3170-7526. *E-mail:* hallo@presse-peter.de. *Website:* www.presse-peter.de. *Address:* c/o 105 Music GmbH, Hopfensack 20, 20457 Hamburg, Germany (office). *Telephone:* (8) 222151-0 (office). *Fax:* (8) 222151-25 (office). *E-mail:* info@105music.com (office). *Website:* www.105music.com (office); www.inamueller.de.

MULLIGAN, Néillidh (Neil); Irish musician (Uilleann pipes) and public servant; b. 13 May 1955, Dublin; s. of Tom Mulligan; m. Sandra Ní Gharbháin 1993; one s. one d. *Education:* Municipal School of Music, studied with Tom Mulligan (father) and Leo Rowsome. *Career:* played and toured many parts of the world including: Europe, America, New Zealand; concerts in major cities; represented Ireland at various Int. Bagpipe Festivals; Founder-mem. Na Píobairí Uilleann, mem. Folk Music Soc. of Ireland, Irish Traditional Music Archive. *Compositions include:* Tom Mulligan's Hornpipe, Wings of My Soul, When Harry Became a Tree (film). *Recordings include:* albums: Barr Na Cúille 1991, The Leitrim Thrush 1997, An Tobar Glé 2005. *Publications include:* contrib. to piping publs. *Honours:* All-Ireland Champion at various age levels. *E-mail:* neillidh@hotmail.com. *Website:* www.neilmulligan.com.

MUMBA, Samantha Tamania Anne Cecilia; Irish singer and actress; b. 18 Jan. 1983, Dublin; m. Torray Scales. *Education:* Billie Barry Stage School. *Career:* lead role in Dublin stage musical, The Hot Mikado 1998; various Irish TV appearances; solo artist 2000–. *Film appearances include:* The Time Machine 2001, Spin The Bottle 2003, Boy Eats Girl 2005, Nailed 2006, Johnny Was 2006, 3 Crosses 2007, Shifter 2007, Loftus Hall 2011. *Television includes:* Get Your Act Together with Harvey Goldsmith 2008, Dancing on Ice 2008. *Recordings include:* Gotta Tell You 2000, The Collection (compilation album) 2006. *Honours:* Smash Hits Award for Best New Female Artist 2000, Meteor Music Award (Best Female Singer) 2002,. *Telephone:* (323)-461-5900. *E-mail:* dino@dinomaymgmt.com. *Website:* www.dinomaymgmt.com.

MUMFORD, Marcus Oliver Johnston; British singer, songwriter and musician (guitar, drums, mandolin); b. 31 Jan. 1987, Anaheim, Calif., USA; s. of John Mumford and Eleanor Mumford; m. Carey Mulligan 2012. *Education:* King's Coll. School, Wimbledon. *Career:* Founder-mem. Mumford & Sons 2007–, debut release in 2008, toured as support group to Laura Marling 2009, performed with Bob Dylan at Grammy Awards 2011; drummer for Laura Marling on Australian tour 2008. *Film:* Wuthering Heights (two songs for soundtrack) 2011. *Recordings include:* albums: Sigh No More (Q Best New Act Award 2010, BRIT Award for British Album of the Year 2011, Billboard Music Awards for Top Rock Album and Top Alternative Album 2011) 2009, Babel (Grammy Award for Album of the Year 2013, Billboard Music Award for Top Rock Album 2013) 2012, Wilder Mind 2015; featured on: I Speak Because I Can, Laura Marling 2010, See My Friends, Ray Davies 2010. *Honours:* Australian Recording Industry Asscn (ARIA) Music Most Popular Int. Artist Award 2010, Billboard Music Award for Top Alternative Artist 2011, Grammy Award for Best Long Form Music Video (for Big Easy Express) 2013, BRIT Award for Best British Group 2013, Ivor Novello Award for Int. Achievement (with Mumford & Sons) 2014. *Current Management:* c/o Everybody's Management, 53 Corsica Street, Highbury, London, N5 1JT, England. *Telephone:* (20) 3227-0420. *Fax:* (20) 7226-2166. *E-mail:* info@everybody-s.com. *Website:* www.everybody-s.com; www.mumfordandsons.com.

MUNCEY, Cameron (Cam); Australian rock musician (guitar) and singer; b. 4 Feb. 1980, Melbourne; m. Sarah Rumbelow. *Education:* St Bedes High School. *Career:* Founder-mem. (with brothers Nic and Chris Cester) rock band Jet 2001–12, lead guitarist and songwriter, sang lead vocals on some songs; toured as support act with the Rolling Stones, Australia 2003; toured USA with other Australian bands The Vines and The Living End 2004; tours of USA, UK, Europe, Japan, Australia 2006–07. *Recordings include:* albums: with Jet: Get Born 2003, Shine On 2006, Shaka Rock 2009; others: 90210 2009, Les Petits Mouchoirs 2010, 100 Hits: Rock Anthems 2011, Dad: The Collection 2013, Latest & Greatest Festival Anthems 2014. *Honours:* APRA Award for Most Performed Australian Work Overseas 2006, 2007.

MUNDEN, David Charles; British musician (drums) and singer; b. 2 Dec. 1943, Dagenham, Essex, England; m. Andrée Munden 1969; one s. one d. *Career:* mem. The Tremeloes; mem. Musicians' Union, Equity, PRS. *Record-*

ings include: albums: Shiner 1974, As It Happened 1983, Best of the Tremeloes 1992. Television includes: Big Beat '64 (TV movie) 1964, UK Swings Again 1964, Go-Go Bigbeat (documentary) 1965, Ready, Steady, Go! (TV series) 1963–65, Thank Your Lucky Stars (TV series) 1962–65, All Systems Freeman (TV series) 1968. Honours: Carl Alan Awards. Current Management: Wayne Denton Associates, Premier House, 283 Causeway Green Road, Oldbury, B68 8LU, England. Address: 21 Oleander Close, Crowthorne, RG45 6TU, England (home). E-mail: d.munden@btinternet.com. Website: www.thetremeloes.co.uk.

MUNIS, Krummi; Icelandic singer. Career: mem. and lead singer of rock band, Mínus 1998–2012. Recordings include: albums: Hey Johnny! 1999, Jesus Christ Bobby 2001, Halldor Laxness 2004, The Great Northern Whalekill 2008.

MUNKGAARD, Peer; Danish music teacher and musician (viola, violin); b. 29 March 1965, Vejle. Education: Esbjerg Kommunale Gymnasium, Music Acad. in Esbjerg with Gert Inge Andersson. Career: danced folkdances since 1969; played folk music (fiddle) 1973–; danced on TV show Les Lanciers 1983; danced and played for numerous folkdance groups including Udöbt on their first tours in England; Danish representative on the Comhaltas Ceoltoiri Eireann European Tour 1985; Instructor, folk dance and music at seminars, music schools and evening schools; teacher, viola, violin, cello, chamber music, orchestras and choirs; mem. West Jutland Symphony Orchestra, Jutland Sinfonietta; assisted in various symphony orchestras and Esbjerg Ensemble; also played in musicals including: The King and I, Showboat and the Phantom of the Opera; mem. Danish Musicians' Union. Address: Peder Skrams Gade 5, II tv, 6700 Esbjerg, Denmark.

MUNRO, Donnie, DA, DipEd; Scottish musician (singer/guitarist), songwriter, art teacher, columnist and broadcaster; b. 2 Aug. 1953, Uig, Isle of Skye, Scotland; s. of James Munro and Christina Robertson; m. 1980; two s. one d. Education: Gray's School of Art, Robert Gordon Univ., Univ. of Edinburgh. Career: mem. and lead singer, Scottish rock group Runrig 1973–97; Rector, Edinburgh Univ. 1991–94; First Rector, Univ. of the Highlands and Islands Project; solo artist 1997–; Chair. Tobar an Dualchais Digitisation Programme; Dir of Devt, Fundraising and the Arts, Sabhal Mor Ostaig Int. Centre for Gaelic Language, Culture and the Arts; Chief Trust Officer SMO Development Trust; mem. Musicians' Union; mem. Bd PNE Nat. Gaelic Arts Agency; mem. Management Group Scottish Drama Training Network; Patron Scottish Child Psychotherapy Trust, Highland Soc. for the Blind, MYPAS. Recordings include: albums: with Runrig: Play Gaelic 1978, The Highland Connection 1979, Recovery 1981, Heartland 1985, The Cutter And The Clan 1987, Once In A Lifetime 1988, Searchlight 1989, The Big Wheel 1991, Amazing Things 1993, Townsmitting Live 1995, Mara 1996, Beat The Drum 1999, Gaelic Collection; solo: On The West Side 1999, Donnie Munro Live, Across The City And The World 2002, Gaelic Heart 2003, Friends of the Young 2004, Heart of America: Across the Great Divide 2006, An Turas Live; contrib. to Troubadours of British Folk Vol. 3 1995, Best of British Folk Rock 1996, Sweet Surrender. Films include: City of Lights, The Wheel in Motion, Aig an Oir, Fields of the Young, Donnie Munro and Friends Special. Television includes: Wilderness Walks (BBC TV), Hogmanay Live (BBC TV), Boxed Set (STV), Hogmanay Live BBC Alba. Honours: Dr hc (Edin. Univ.) 1994; Scottish Band of the Year 1990, Scottish Male Vocalist of the Year1990, Scottish Music Hall of Fame 2004, Album of the Year Award 2008. Telephone: (1478) 612177 (office). E-mail: info@donniemunro.co.uk (office). Website: www .donniemunro.co.uk (office).

MUPEMHI, Adrian Stoan; South African singer. Career: backing vocalist for Thebe; mem. kwaito band, Bongo Maffin 1996–, World Wild Grooves tour, France 2000; performances in UK, Denmark 2000; worked with Skunk Anansie, Chaka Khan, Stevie Wonder, Boyz II Men, Hugh Masekela. Recordings include: albums: Final Entry 1996, The Concerto 1998, IV 1999, Bongolution 2001, New Construction 2006. Honours: South African Music Award, (Best Kwaito Artist) 1999, (Best Duo/Group) 2002, 2006, Best African Group 2001, Metro FM Award 2002, Kora Africa Music Award 2006. Current Management: c/o Exclusive Management Services, 12 Leogem Commercial Park, 16/48 Richards Drive, Halfway-House, Midrand 1685, South Africa. Telephone: (11) 8052245. Fax: (11) 8052604. E-mail: info@exclusivems.co.za. Website: www.exclusivems.co.za; www.bongomaffin.co.za.

MURCIA, Joey; American musician (guitar); b. 21 March 1948, Brooklyn, New York; one s. Education: Grove School of Music. Career: session guitarist; tours with: Benny Lattimore, support to James Brown 1975, Bee Gees, Here At Last Tour 1976, Spirits Having Flown Tour 1979, Jay Ferguson, support to Foreigner 1977, Andy Gibb, Shadow Dancing Tour 1978; performances with Ann Jillian include: Tahoe, Las Vegas 1984, Trump Plaza Atlantic City 1989, 1990; mem. AFofM. Compositions include: Cozumel (Jay Ferguson) 1978, Jennifer Slept Here (Joey Scarborough), theme for NBC 1985, 1990. Recordings include: albums: with Betty Wright: Clean Up Women; with Gwen McCrae: Rockin Chair; with Benny Lattimore: Lattimore III, Latimore, Straighten It Out: The Best of Latimore; with Bill Wyman: Monkey Grip Glue; with Bee Gees: Here At Last-Bee Gees Live, Saturday Night Fever; with Jay Ferguson: Thunder Island; with Joe Walsh: But Seriously Folks; with Joe Cocker: A Luxury You Can Afford; with Frankie Valli: Grease; with Bellamy Brothers: Restless; with Andy Gibb: Flowing Rivers, Shadow Dancing, After Dark, Andy Gibb's Greatest Hits; singles with Andy Gibb: I Just Want To Be Your Everything, Thicker Than Water, Shadow Dancing, Everlasting Love.

MURDOCH, Stuart; British singer, musician (guitar) and songwriter; b. 25 Aug. 1968, Scotland. Career: mem., Belle & Sebastian 1996–; collaborations with Future Pilot AKA, Arab Strap, Hefner. Recordings include: albums: Tigermilk 1996, If You're Feeling Sinister 1996, The Boy With The Arab Strap 1998, Fold Your Hands Child, You Walk Like A Peasant 2000, Storytelling 2002, Dear Catastrophe Waitress 2003, The Life Pursuit 2006, Write About Love 2010, Girls in Peacetime Want to Dance 2015. Publications: The Celestial Cafe (memoir) 2010. Honours: BRIT Award for Best Newcomer 1999, Q Magazine Spirit of Independence Award 2013. Current Management: Banchory Management, PO Box 25074, Glasgow, G3 8TT, Scotland. Telephone: (141) 204-2269. E-mail: banchoryman@gmail.com. Website: www .belleandsebastian.com.

MURISON, Krissi; Briitsh journalist. Career: joined NME (New Musical Express) as staff writer 2003, then New Music Ed., Features Ed., Deputy Ed. 2003–09, Ed. 2009–12; Music Dir, Nylon magazine Feb.–Sept. 2009; Features Ed., Sunday Times Magazine 2012–, currently Assoc. Ed. Honours: Breaking Music Writer 2005. Address: c/o The Sunday Times, News UK and Ireland, 1 London Bridge Street, London, SE1 9GF, England (office). Telephone: (20) 7782-5000 (office). Website: www.thesundaytimes.co.uk (office).

MURPHY, James, (LCD Soundsystem); American producer, engineer and record label owner; b. 4 Feb. 1970, New York. Career: formed The DFA (Death From Above) production duo and record label (with Tim Goldsworthy) 2002–, worked with Turing Machine, BS 2000, Zero Zero, The Rapture, David Holmes, Primal Scream, Radio 4, The Juan Maclean, Echoes, Gotham'; solo artist as LCD Soundsystem 2002–2011; Owner, Plantain Studios, New York. Recordings include: albums: as The DFA: Dance To The Underground 2003; as LCD Soundsystem: LCD Soundsystem 2005, Sound of Silver 2007, This is Happening 2010; other: Reflektor (Arcade Fire), Mosquito (producer) 2013. E-mail: jamesmurphy@monotoneinc.com; dfaweb@dfarecords.com. Website: www.dfarecords.com; lcdsoundsystem.com.

MURPHY, Jamie; British musician (guitar), singer and songwriter; b. 23 Dec. 1976. Career: Founder-mem. Space 1993–2002, 2011–12; Founder-mem. Firehead. Recordings include: albums: Spiders 1996, Remixes and B-Sides 1996, Tin Planet 1998, Love You More than Football 2000.

MURPHY, John; British composer and musician (guitar); b. 4 March 1965, Liverpool, England. Career: session guitarist, worked with The Lotus Eaters, Thomas Lang, Gary Wall and Claudia Brücken, Thomas Langcollaborations with Vadim Jean, Danny Boyle, Guy Ritchie; mem. PRS, Musicians' Union. Compositions include: with David Hughes: Films: Leon The Pig Farmer, Solitaire For 2, Clockwork Mice, Welcome To The Terrordome, Beyond Bedlam, A Feast At Midnight, Body Memories, Dinner In Purgatory, Destroying Angels, Proteus, Flame, Giving Tongue, Lock, Stock and Two Smoking Barrels, Stiff Upper Lips, The Real Howard Spitz; Miami Vice (with Klaus Badelt) 2006; other: Sunshine, 28 Weeks Later, TV: White Men Are Cracking Up, BBC2; All The President's Women; Eunice The Gladiator (Channel 4); Where The Bad Girls Go, Granada; Black Velvet Band, Yorkshire.

MURPHY, Robert Joseph, BA, LLB; American musician (saxophone, piano, percussion); b. 3 June 1936, Summit, NJ; m. Judith Ann Miller 1962; two d. Education: Brown Univ., Stanford Univ., Deanza Coll., Cupertino, Calif. Career: solo artist; numerous tours, festival appearances; plays with Natural Gas Jazz Band 1970–; Faculty mem. Stanford Jazz Workshop; mem. Broadcast Music, Inc. Compositions: Red Neck Blues, To the Emerald Isle. Recordings: 16 albums with Natural Gas Jazz Band. Address: 8 Portola Green Circle, Portola Valley, CA 94028-7833, USA (office). Telephone: (650) 493-3636 (office). E-mail: murphjazz@yahoo.com (office). Website: www.murphjazz.com.

MURPHY, Róisín Marie; Irish singer, composer and producer; b. 5 July 1973, Dublin; d. of James Michael Murphy; two c. Career: fmr mem. And Turquoise Car Crash, The; mem. Moloko 1995–2004; solo artist 2005–. Recordings include: albums: with Moloko: Do You Like My Tight Sweater? 1995, I Am Not A Doctor 1998, Things To Make And Do 2000, Statues 2003; solo: Ruby Blue 2005, Overpowered 2007, Live At Ancienne Belgique 2007, Hairless Toys 2015. E-mail: hopeless.optimist@yahoo.com. Website: www .roisinmurphyofficial.com.

MURRAY, Anne, CC, ONS; Canadian singer; b. 20 June 1945, Springhill, NS; d. of Carson Murray and Marion Murray. Education: Univ. of New Brunswick. Career: teacher 1966–67; musician 1967–. Recordings include: What About Me 1968, This is My Way 1969, Honey, Wheat and Laughter 1970, Snowbird 1970, Straight, Clean and Simple 1971, Talk It Over in the Morning 1971, Anne Murray/Glen Campbell 1971, Annie 1972, Danny's Song 1973, Love Song 1974, Country 1974, Highly Prized Possession 1974, Together 1975, Keeping in Touch 1976, There's a Hippo in My Tub 1977, Let's Keep it that Way 1978, New Kind of Feeling 1979, I'll Always Love You 1979, A Country Collection 1980, Somebody's Waiting 1980, Where do you go to Dream 1981, Christmas Wishes 1981, The Hottest Night of the Year 1982, A Little Good News 1983, Heart over Mind 1984, Something to Talk About 1986, Harmony 1987, Country Hits 1987, Songs of the Heart 1987, As I Am 1988, Anne Murray Christmas 1988, Love Songs 1989, From Springhill to the World 1990, You Will 1990, Yes I Do 1991, Croonin' 1993, The Season Will Never Grow Old 1993, Anne Murray 1996, The Signature Series 1998–2002, What a Wonderful Christmas 2001, Country Croonin' 2002, I'll Be Seeing You 2004, Duets: Friends and Legends 2007, Christmas Album 2008. TV Specials include: Anne

Murray's Christmas Special 1981, Anne Murray's Caribbean Cruise 1983, Anne Murray's Winter Carnival from Quebec 1984, Sounds of London 1985, Anne Murray's Family Christmas 1988, Anne Murray in DisneyWorld 1991, Anne Murray in Nova Scotia 1999, Croonin' 1993. *Publication:* All Of Me 2009. *Honours:* Top Canadian Female Vocalist 1970, Top Canadian Female Entertainer of the Year 1970, Best Female Newcomer of the Year (Record World Magazine, USA) 1970–71, Top Newcomer Female Vocalist of the Year (Cashbox Magazine, USA), Juno Award, Top Female Vocalist 1970–86, Best Female Vocalist Grammy Award 1974, Nashville's Country Music Hall of Fame, Walkway of Stars 1974, Vanier Award, Outstanding Young Canadian, Canadian Female Recording Artist of Decade, star placed in Walkway of Stars 1980, Best Female Vocal Performance 1978–80. *Address:* PO Box 69030, 12 St Clair Avenue East, Toronto, ON M4T 1K0, Canada (office). *E-mail:* anne@annemurray.com (office). *Website:* www.annemurray.com.

MURRAY, David (Dave) Michael; British musician (guitar) and songwriter; b. 23 Dec. 1958; m. Tamar Murray; one d. *Career:* Founder-mem. heavy metal band, Iron Maiden 1975–. *Recordings include:* albums: Iron Maiden 1980, Killers 1981, The Number of the Beast 1982, Piece of Mind 1983, Powerslave 1984, Somewhere in Time 1986, Seventh Son of a Seventh Son 1988, No Prayer for the Dying 1990, Fear of the Dark 1992, The X-Factor 1995, Virtual XI 1998, Brave New World 2000, Dance of Death 2003, It's a Matter of Life and Death 2006, Flight 666 2009, The Final Frontier 2010, The Book of Souls 2015. *Honours:* Ivor Novello Award 2000, BRIT Award for Best British Live Act 2009, Grammy Award for Best Metal Performance 2011, Metal Hammer Award (Best UK Band) 2011, 2014. *Current Management:* c/o Phantom Music Managment Ltd, Bridle House 36 Bridle Lane, London, W1F 9BZ, England. *Telephone:* (845) 331-3300. *Fax:* (845) 331-3500. *Website:* www.phantom-music.com; www.ironmaiden.com.

MURRAY, Neil; British musician (bass guitar); b. 27 Aug. 1950, Edinburgh, Scotland. *Education:* London Coll. of Printing. *Career:* mem. Gilgamesh 1973, Hanson 1974, Colosseum II 1975–76, National Health 1976–77, Whitesnake 1978–82, 1984–86, Gary Moore Band 1982–83, Vow Wow 1987–89, Black Sabbath 1989–90, 1994–, Brian May Band 1992–93. *Recordings include:* albums: with Whitesnake: Trouble 1978, Lovehunter 1979, Ready An' Willing 1980, Live In The Heart of The City 1980, Come An' Get It 1981, Saints An' Sinners 1982, Slide It In 1984, Whitesnake 1987, Whitesnake's Greatest Hits 1994, The Early Years 2004; with Black Sabbath: Tyr 1990, Forbidden 1995; with Empire: Hypnotica 2001, Trading Souls 2003, The Raven Ride 2006, Chasing Shadows 2007; contrib. to Gary Moore Corridors of Power (The Early Years) 1982, Rockin' Every Night 1983, Victims of the Future 1983, Back to the Light (Brian May) 1993, Another World 1998, Twang!: A Tribute to Hank Marvin 1996, Company Of Snakes, Here They Go Again (Live) 2001, Burst the Bubble 2002, Space Elevator Album 2014. *Website:* www.neilbass.com.

MURRAY, Phil; British writer and performer; b. 18 Nov. 1953, North Shields; m. Allison Longstaff 1980; two s. one d. *Career:* singer, songwriter with U Boat; mem. of Blackie; actor, TV programmes, including Dempsey and Makepeace, Cats' Eyes, Les Dawson Show; many theatre tours; personal development author and presenter; mem. Equity, Musicians' Union, PRS, MCPS, PPS. *Recordings include:* album with U Boat: End of My Time; other: Talk Talk, Separate Holiday, Forever Again (love songs), Plus, Inspirational Stories, Superman, 2001: A Success Odyssey 2001. *Publications include:* You Can Always Get What You Want, Before the Beginning is a Thought, Empowerment 1995, The 49 Steps to a Bright Life 1996, Phil Murray Bites on Personal Development 1997, You and Me Make Three 1997, Staying Awake Forever 1997, The Flow of Life 1998.

MURRELL, David (Dave) Evan; British musician, arranger and academic; b. 22 Jan. 1952, London; m. Debora Anne Diamond 1980; two d. *Education:* Humber Coll., Canada. *Career:* tours in Canada, USA with Ken Tobias, Tommy Hunter, Ronnie Prophet; British artists: Psychic TV, Long John Baldry, Zoot Money; mem. Musicians' Union. *Recordings include:* MD, Yamaha Jazz Connection; film music: Words of Love (BBC) 1990, Long Way Home (ITV) 1991. *Telephone:* (1243) 602956. *E-mail:* dave@davemurrellmusic.com. *Website:* www.davemurrellmusic.com.

MURTO, Janne; Finnish musician (saxophone, flutes) and music teacher; b. 26 Oct. 1964. *Education:* Oulunkylä Pop/Jazz Conservatoire, Sibelius Acad., and studied musical culture in Cuba. *Career:* mem. various big bands, including Espoo Big Band, Big Bad Family (with Upi Sorvali), UMO Big Band; 10 years with Fiestacita (Afro-Cuban ensemble); freelance musician for recording studios, radio and theatre; Rector, Helsinki Pop and Jazz Conservatory 1999; mem. Paroni Paakunainen's Saxperiment Quartet, Kari Tenkanen Quintet. *Recordings include:* albums with John Adams: I Was Looking at the Ceiling and Then I Saw the Sky 1998, The Earbox: 10-CD Retrospective 1999, John Adams: Hallelujah Junction: A Nonesuch Retrospective 2008.

MUSGRAVES, Kacey Lee; American country music singer, songwriter and musician (guitar, mandolin, harmonica); b. 21 Aug. 1988, Mineola, Tex. *Career:* raised in Golden, Tex.; self-released three albums 2002–07; moved to Austin, Tex. 2006; competed in TV talent show Nashville Star (USA Network) (placed fifth) 2007; signed to Mercury Nashville Records 2012; released major label debut album 2012; toured USA with Alison Krauss and Willie Nelson, UK and Europe with Lady Antebellum, Little Big Town, Kenny Chesney; songwriter for Martina McBride, Miranda Lambert, Gretchen Wilson, Aubrey Peeples, Clare Bowen, Deana Carter, Hayden Panettiere and Charles Esten.

Television: Nashville Star (contestant) 2007. *Recordings:* albums: Movin' On 2002, Wanted: One Good Cowboy 2003, Kacey Musgraves 2007, Same Trailer Different Park (Grammy Award for Best Country Album 2014, Acad. of Country Music Award for Album of the Year 2014) 2013, Pageant Material 2015. *Honours:* CMA Award for New Artist of the Year 2013, for Song of the Year (for Follow Your Arrow) 2014, Grammy Award for Best Country Song (for Merry Go 'Round) 2014,. *Current Management:* c/o Sandbox Management, 54 Music Square East, Nashville, TN 37203, USA. *E-mail:* info@sandboxmgmt.com. *Website:* sandboxmgmt.com. *Address:* c/o Mercury Nashville Records, Universal Music Group Nashville, 54 Music Square East, Suite 300, Nashville, TN 37203, USA (office). *Telephone:* (615) 524-7500 (office). *Fax:* (615) 524-7600 (office). *Website:* www.umgnashville.com (office); www.kaceymusgraves.com.

MUSHOK, Mike; American musician (guitar); b. 10 April 1970, Manhasset, New York. *Career:* fmrly worked with HVAC Applications; Founder-mem. Staind 1995–; joined Jason Newsted 2013. *Recordings include:* albums: Tormented 1996, Dysfunction 1999, Break The Cycle 2001, 14 Shades of Grey 2003, Chapter V 2005, The Illusion of Progress 2008, Staind 2011, Live from Mohegan Sun 2012. *Honours:* VH-1 Award (for Your Song Kicked Ass But Was Played Too Damn Much) 2001, Guitar World Readers' Poll Award for Best New Talent 2000. *Website:* www.staind.com.

MUSHROOM; British musician (keyboards) and producer; b. (Andrew Vowles), 10 Nov. 1967, Bristol. *Career:* mem. collective The Wild Bunch; Founder-mem. Massive Attack 1987–; collaborations with Shara Nelson, Tricky, Horace Andy, Madonna, Tracey Thorn (Everything But The Girl), Liz Fraser (Cocteau Twins). *Recordings include:* albums: Blue Lines 1991, Protection 1994, No Protection: Massive Attack vs Mad Professor 1995, Mezzanine 1998, 100th Window 2003, Danny the Dog 2004, Collected 2006, Heligoland 2010. *Honours:* BRIT Award for Best British Dance Act 1996, Q Award for Innovation in Sound (Massive Attack) 2008. *Website:* www.massiveattack.co.uk.

MUSSELWHITE, Charlie, (Memphis Charlie, Charlie Kelly, Mussels); American blues-harp player; b. (Charles Douglas Musselwhite III), 31 Jan. 1944, Kosciusko, Miss.; s. of the late Charles Douglas Musselwhite, Jr and Ruth Maxine Musselwhite; m. Henrietta Musselwhite; one s. one d. *Education:* Memphis Tech. High School. *Career:* concerts tours in USA; performed on albums with Bonnie Raitt, The Blind Boys of Alabama, Tom Waits, Mickey Hart and INXS; Presenter, weekly radio show Charlie's Back Room (KRSH). *Recordings include:* Stand Back! 1967, Louisiana Fog 1968, Stone Blues 1968, Tennessee Woman 1968, Memphis, Tennessee 1970, The Harmonica According to Charlie Musselwhite 1979, Curtain Call Cocktails 1982, Mellow-Dee 1986, Ace of Harps 1990, Signature 1991, Where Have All the Good Times Gone? 1992, In My Time 1993, Memphis Charlie 1993, The Blues Never Die 1994, Takin' Care of Business 1995, Rough News 1997, Continental Drifter 1999, Best of the Vanguard Years 2000, One Night in America 2002, Sanctuary 2004, Delta Hardware 2006, Rough Dried 2007, Get Up! (with Ben Harper) (Grammy Award for Best Blues Album 2014) 2013. *Honours:* 24 W.C. Handy Awards, Lifetime Achievement Awards (Monterey Blues Festival, San Javier Jazz Festival, Spain), Mississippi Gov.'s Award for Excellence in the Arts, Pete Pedersen Lifetime Achievement Award, Howlin' Wolf Award, Trophées France Blues 2000, 2002, Blues Music Hall of Fame 2010. *Current Management:* c/o Morrow Management, 5003 Westpark Drive, Suite 102, Valley Village, CA 91601, USA. *Telephone:* (818) 642-9217. *E-mail:* JParker@morrowmanagement.com; henri@sonic.net. *Website:* www.morrowmanagement.com. *Current Management:* c/o The Rosebud Music Booking Agency, PO Box 170429, San Francisco, CA 94117, USA. *Telephone:* (415) 386-3456. *Fax:* (415) 386-0599. *E-mail:* info@rosebudus.com. *Website:* www.rosebudus.com. *Address:* c/o Real World Studios, Box Mill, Mill Lane, Box, Wilts., SN13 8PL, England. *Fax:* (1225) 743787. *Website:* www.realworldrecords.com; www.charliemusselwhite.com.

MUSTAINE, Dave; American singer, musician (guitar) and songwriter; b. 13 Sept. 1961, La Mesa, Calif.; s. of John Mustaine and Emily Mustaine (née David); m. Pamela Anne Casselberry; one s. one d. *Career:* Founder-mem. Metallica 1981–83; Founder-mem. Megadeth 1983–; worldwide tours and concerts. *Recordings include:* albums: with Metallica: Kill 'Em All 1983; with Megadeth: Killing Is My Business... And Business Is Good! 1985, Peace Sells... But Who's Buying? 1986, So Far So Good... So What! 1988, Rust In Peace 1990, Countdown To Extinction 1992, Youthanasia 1994, Cryptic Writings 1997, Risk 1999, The World Needs A Hero 2001, Rude Awakening 2002, The System Has Failed 2004, United Abominations 2007, Endgame 2009, Thirteen 2011, Super Collider 2013. *Honours:* Genesis Doris Day Music Award. *Current Management:* c/o Ron Laffitte, Laffitte Management Group, 9350 Civic Center Drive, Suite 100, Beverly Hills, CA 90210, USA. *Telephone:* (310) 209-6460. *Website:* www.megadeth.com.

MVULA, Laura; British singer, songwriter and musician (piano); b. (Laura Douglas), 23 April 1986, Kings Heath, Birmingham, England; m. Themba Mvula 2010. *Education:* Birmingham Conservatoire. *Career:* as teenager, violinist with Birmingham Schools Concert Orchestra; fmr teacher; singer with Black Voices acappella group 2005; Founder-mem. jazz/soul group Judyshouse 2008; Dir, Lichfield Community Gospel Choir 2009–. *Recordings:* album: Sing to the Moon 2013. *Honours:* MOBO Awards for Best Female Act 2013, for Best R&B/Soul Artist 2013. *Address:* c/o RCA Records, Sony Music

UK, 9 Derry Street, London, W8 5HY, England (office). *Telephone:* (20) 7361-8000 (office). *Website:* www.sonymusic.com (office); www.lauramvula.com.

MYATT, Charlie; British booking agent; b. 24 June, Bristol, England. *Education:* Royal Holloway and Bedford New Coll., Clifton Coll. *Career:* many years as agent for Arctic Monkeys, Radiohead, Suede, Skunk Anansie, The Stone Roses, Tame Impala, Royal Blood among many others. *Address:* 13 Artists, 11–14 Kensington Street, Brighton BN1 4AJ, England (office). *Telephone:* (1273) 601355 (office). *Fax:* (1273) 626854 (office). *E-mail:* admin@13artists.com (office). *Website:* www.13artists.co.uk (office).

MYCKA, Katarzyna, MMus; Polish/German marimba player; b. 27 Oct. 1972, Leningrad, Russia. *Education:* Music School and Acad. of Music, Gdansk, Poland, Mozarteum, Salzburg, Austria, Stuttgart Music Acad., Germany, Music Acad., Wrocław, Poland. *Career:* master classes in Germany, USA, Poland, Switzerland, Luxembourg; concerts in USA, Asia and Europe; mem. Percussive Arts Soc. (PAS), USA; Percussion Creative, Germany; Amb. of Polish Percussive Arts, Polish Percussive Arts Soc. 1999; teacher, Acad. of Music, Poznań 2006–09; Founder and Artistic Dir Int. Katarzyna Mycka Marimba Acad.; Pres. PAS chapter, Germany; mem. of jury, various int. and nat. percussion and marimba competitions; commissioned and premiered many works for marimba; performed with numerous orchestras, choirs and chamber music groups, including Mandelring String Quartet. *Recordings:* solo: Katarzyna Mycka: Marimba Spiritual 1997, Katarzyna Mycka: Marimba Dance 1999, Katarzyna Mycka: Marimba Concerto 2001, Katarzyna Mycka: Marimba Sculpture 2003, Mycka/Bacanu, Bach/Marimba Concertos 2005, Katarzyna Mycka: Marimba Classica 2008. *Honours:* First Prize Opole Percussion Competition, Poland 1991, First Prize and Audience Prize Solo Marimba Competition, Luxembourg 1995, First Prize, First World Marimba Competition, Stuttgart 1996, Scholarship for Young Artists, Rotary Club, Stuttgart 1997, Promotional Scholarship, Foundation of the Arts, Baden Wurttemberg 1998, Festival Artist, First World Marimba Festival, Osaka, Japan 1998, Soloist of the Year, Neubrandenburg 2005–06, Soloist at the Marimba Festival, Minneapolis 2010. *Current Management:* c/o SKS-Russ GmbH, PO Box 104262, 70180 Stuttgart, Germany. *Telephone:* (71) 11635311. *Fax:* (71) 11635330. *E-mail:* info@sks-russ.de. *Website:* www.sks-russ.de. *E-mail:* info@marimbasolo.com (office). *Website:* www.marimbasolo.com.

MYHRE, Wenche Synnöve; Norwegian entertainer and singer; b. 15 Feb. 1947, Kjelsås, Oslo; m. Arthur Bucharot (divorced); three s. one d.; m. Michael Pfleghar 1980. *Career:* appeared on German TV and personality shows 1974–87; solo shows 1978–98. *Stage performances include:* The Wizard of Oz (musical) 1965, Cabaret (in Sweden) 1968, 1969–70, 1974, 1993, lead in Sweet Charity (Norway) 1989–90. *Recordings include:* albums: Wenche Myhre 1963, Sanger Fra Dengang 1967, Powshow 1970, Wenche 1976, Vi Lever 1983, Wenches Jul 1991, Co-Wenches Beste 1997, Du og jeg og vi to! 2001, 50 beste gjennom 50 år 2004, Tulla vår 2004, Lykkeliten 2004, Wenche Myhre in Concert 2008, 66 2013. *Honours:* Knight of St Olav 2004; five Otto Awards, Germany 1966–70, Midem Award 1966–67, Silver Microphone 1967, Norwegian Grammy Award 1976, Gammleng Award 2003, Hon. Award Spellemannprisen 2003, Rockheim Hall of Fame 2011.

MYLES, Heather, BA; American singer, songwriter and musician (bass); b. 31 July 1964, Riverside, CA. *Career:* solo artist. *Recordings:* albums: Just Like Old Times 1992, Untamed 1995, Sweet Little Dangerous (Live In London) 1996, Highways and Honky Tonks 1998, Sweet Talk and Good Lies 2002, In the Wind 2011. *Address:* PO Box 2133, Riverside, CA 92516, USA. *Website:* www.heathermyles.com.

MYLLÄRI, Mika; Finnish musician (trumpet) and composer; b. 17 June 1966, Kokkola. *Education:* Jazz Dept Sibelius Acad. 1986, jazz composition with Jukka Linkola 1991. *Career:* mem., Espoo Big Band; freelance musician with UMO Big Band; formed own quintet, playing own material, 1990; Founder MMQ 1990; mem. 10-man ensemble Zone, 1991–. *Recordings include:* An Ordinary Day in an Unusual Place 2001, Helsinki-Shangri-La 2010, Stones Grow Her Name 2012. *Honours:* Finnish Jazz Federation Award, Band of the Year, Mika Mylläri Quintet.

MYLO, BA, PhD; British electronic musician, producer and DJ; b. (Myles MacInnes), 10 May 1978, Isle of Skye, Scotland. *Education:* George Watson's Coll., Univ. of Edinburgh, Brasenose Coll., Univ. of Oxford, Univ. of California, Los Angeles, USA. *Career:* Co-founder Breastfed Records; played headline tours and festivals worldwide with live band, including Fuji Rock Festival, Japan 2005, M8 Ibiza Dance Awards 2006, Oxegen Festival, Ireland 2006, Rhythm & Vines Festival, New Zealand 2006; collaborations with Kylie Minogue. *Recordings include:* albums: Destroy Rock & Roll 2004, Mylo's Rough Guide to Rave 2005, Live: Glasgow Barrowlands 10-27-05 2006, Live: London Brixton Academy 11-05-05 2006, The Return of Mylo 2009. *Current*

Management: DEF Management, 51 Lonsdale Road, Queens Park, London, NW6 6RA, England. *Telephone:* (20) 7328-2922. *E-mail:* info@d-e-f.com. *Website:* www.d-e-f.com.

MYROL, Keith; Canadian musician (guitar); b. 19 July 1950, Maple Creek, Sask.; m. Trish Myrol 1972; one s. one d. *Career:* mem. The Myrol Brothers; appearances: Capital Country CFAC TV Calgary, SCMA Awards Show 1990–94, seven Sunday In the Park concerts, Right Tracks, Gold Rush Cafe, Saskatchewan Showcase of The Arts, CBC Arts Reel, Project Discovery; mem. CCMA,. *Recordings include:* albums: The Singles Collection, Raisin' The Roof, :Best of the West, Vols I and II, CFAC Country Showdown. *Honours:* Non-Touring Band of the Year, Saskatchewan Country Music Asscn, inducted into Saskatchewan Country Music Asscn Hall of Famer.

MYROL, Myles; Canadian musician (bass guitar); b. 6 March 1957, Maple Creek, Saskatchewan; m. Diane, 31 July 1976, 1 s., 1 d. *Career:* The Myrol Brothers; Appearances: Capital Country CFAC TV Calgary; SCMA Awards Show, 1990–94; 7 Sunday In The Park concerts; Right Tracks; Gold Rush Cafe; Sask Showcase of the Arts; CBC Arts Reel; Project Discovery; mem, CCMA; SCMA Hall of Fame. *Recordings:* albums: The Singles Collection; Raisin' The Roof; Also on: Best of the West, Vols I and II, CFAC Country Showdown. *Honours:* SCMA Non Touring Band of the Year. *Address:* The Myrol Brothers, Box 969 Outlook, Saskatchewan S0L 2N0, Canada.

MYROL, Rick; Canadian musician (guitar); b. 30 May 1948, Maple Creek, Sask.; m. Violet Myrol 1968; two s. *Career:* mem. The Myrol Brothers; appearances: Capital Country CFAC TV Calgary SCMA Awards Show 1990–94, 7 Sunday In The Park, Right Tracks, Gold Rush Cafe, Saskatchewan Showcase of the Arts, CBC Arts Reel, Project Discovery; mem. CCMA. *Recordings include:* albums: The Singles Collection, Raisin' The Roof, Best of West Vols I and II, CFAC Country Showdown. *Honours:* Non-Touring Band of the Year, Saskatchewan Country Music Asscn, inducted into Saskatchewan Country Music Asscn Hall of Fame.

MYSLIKOVJAN, Ivan M.; Czech/French musician (alto saxophone, electric wind instrument), music arranger, composer and teacher; b. 24 Sept. 1960, Ostrava, Czech Republic; m.; one s. *Education:* Conservatory of Ostrava, Jazz Studio, with Karel Velebny. *Career:* studio musician and soloist; appearances at jazz and pop festivals, clubs and concerts in Czech Republic and abroad; numerous TV and radio broadcasts; teacher, bass clarinet and saxophone, improvisation lessons, Conservatory of Ostrava 1982–86; regular tours to Brazil, Middle East and Arabia; collaborations with Karel Ruzicka, Milan Svoboda, Jiri Stivin, Emil Viklicky, Tony Trishka, Breakfast Special, Second Grass, Patrick Bergman, Charlie 1, DJs Diome, Maxx, Hector Lopez, Vandoren, Selmer, B. G. France, Josef Mazan, Prague Philharmonic Orchestra, Prague Chamber Orchestra, Atlantis; producer of all his solo albums; Sax Horoscope live in Prague Planetarium 2002; week-long festival of Czech Culture in Paris 1995; mem. jazz fusion group Blue Birds, DJ project Sax'o'phono, jazz duo Two, classic duo Duo Concertinissimo. *Recordings include:* solo: Nice To Meet You 1995, Information Of My Soul 1995, Christmas Inspiration 1996, Sax And Love 1998, Sax Art 1998, Sax Horoscope 1999, Harmonie, Look Better Naked, Sax 'N Dance, Two, Music Vars 2002, Look Better Naked 2003, Duo Concertinissimo 2004, Wingra 2004; soloist on more than 60 albums, including film music of Bernard Herrmann, Floodland. *Compositions include:* many jazz pieces, contemporary pieces. *Publication:* Modern Lessons for Saxophone 1998. *E-mail:* info@ivan-sax.com (office). *Website:* www.ivan-sax.com.

MYSZOR, Przemysław; Polish rock musician (keyboards, guitar); b. 1969. *Career:* joined band Myslovitz 1996, first int. concerts, Sweden, Germany, USA 1998; numerous European festival appearances and support act for Iggy Pop and Simple Minds 2002; began releasing English-language versions of their music 2002; European tour and support act for Iggy Pop and The Corrs 2004; contributed to soundtracks for films Młode wilki ½ (Young Wolves ½), Duże zwierzę (The Big Animal), To my (That's us). *Recordings:* albums: Z rozmyślań przy śniadaniu 1997, Miłość w czasach popkultury 1999, Korova Milky Bar 2002, The Best Of 2003, Korova Milky Bar (English version) 2003, Skalary, mieczyki, neonki 2004, Happiness Is Easy 2006. *Honours:* Music Video of The Year 1998, Band of The Year and Rock Album of The Year 1999, Song of the Year and Video of The Year 2000, Album of The Year 2003, all Fryderyk awards; Polityka's Paszport award 1999, Best Polish Act, MTV Europe Music Awards 2002, 2003, Border Breakers European Breakthrough award (for Korova Milky Bar) 2005. *Current Management:* Maciej Pilarczyk, Chaos Management Group, ul. Karowa 31, 00-324 Warsaw, Poland. *E-mail:* m.pil@myslovitz.pl (office). *Website:* www.chaos.com.pl (office); www.myslovitz.pl.

MZA (see Method Man)

N

NABORS, James (Jim) Thurston; American entertainer, actor and musician (piano); b. 12 June 1930, Sylacauga, Ala. *Education:* Univ. of Alabama. *Films include:* A Different Approach 1978, The Best Little Whorehouse in Texas 1982, Stroker Ace 1983, Cannonball Run II 1984. *Television includes* The Andy Griffith Show (series) 1962–64, Gomer Pyle, U.S.M.C. (series) 1964–69, The Jim Nabors Hour (series) 1969, Return to Mayberry 1986; numerous guest appearances. *Recordings include:* albums: Jim Nabors by Request 1967, 16 Most Requested Songs 1989, Jim Nabors' Christmas Album 1990, 22 Great Hymn and Country Favorites 2000, When He Spoke 2000. *Address:* Naborly Productions, PO Box 60159, Nashville, TN 37206, USA. *E-mail:* webmaster@jimnabors.com. *Website:* www.jimnabors.com.

NAFAR, Tamer; Israeli (Arabic) rapper; b. 6 June 1979, Lod. *Career:* mem. Arabic rap act DAM with his brother Suhell and Mahmoud Jrere 1999–, group performs in Arabic, Hebrew and English, songs are inspired by the Israeli–Palestinian conflict and the problems facing Arab-Israelis; performances in USA, UK, Germany, Italy; documentary film Channels of Rage deals with his rivalry with Jewish rapper Kobi Shimoni (Subliminal). *Recordings include:* albums: Stop Selling Drugs 1998, Mir Irhabi (Who's the Terrorist?) 2001, Dedication 2006, Dabke on the Moon 2012, The Rough Guide to the Music of Palestine 2014. *Films include:* Innocent Criminals 2003, Forgiveness 2006, Slingshot Hip Shop. *Website:* www.damrap.com.

NAGA, Alobo; Indian singer, songwriter and musician (piano, guitar). *Career:* songwriter and performer from age of 12; fmr mem. groups Nice and Ugly, Spark; fmr Christian worship leader, Sumi Baptist Church, Delhi 2004, Freedom Church, Delhi 2005, Church of the Nation and Kingdom Int., Delhi 2006; Founder mem. lead singer and keyboard player, Alobo Naga and the Band 2010–; currently music teacher, Furtados School of Music. *Recordings:* albums: Yesterday Today Forever 2001, Road of Thousand Dreams 2010. *Honours:* Nagaland State Music Awards for Best Rock Song of the Year, Best Rock Band of the Year, Best Producer of the Year 2011, Best Folk Fusion Song 2011, MTV Europe Music Award for Best Indian Act 2012. *Address:* c/o Betoka Swu, Hiyo Cafe, Aiko Building, Bank Colony, Dimapur, Nagaland, 797 112, India. *Telephone:* 9615102545. *E-mail:* booking@alobonaga.com. *Website:* www.alobonaga.com/en.

NAGAI, Yohei, DEA; Japanese musical instrument researcher; b. 5 Nov. 1938, Tokyo. *Education:* Tokyo Univ., Univ. of Marseilles, France. *Career:* 38 years in Musical Instrument Research and Design Dept, Yamaha Co. Ltd, three years as Gen. Man. of Research Labs; mem. Acoustical Soc. of Japan, Acoustical Soc. of America, Acoustical Soc. of Europe. *Publications:* numerous research papers and patents on piano, wind instruments and electronic instruments. *Address:* 1-31-8, Ohiradai Nishi-ku, Hamamatsu-shi 432-8068, Japan (home). *Telephone:* (53) 415-8610 (office). *Fax:* (53) 415-8610 (office). *E-mail:* y-nagai68@rmail.plala.or.jp (office).

NAIDENOV, Vassil; Bulgarian singer; b. 3 Sept. 1950, Sofia. *Education:* Music Acad., Bulgaria. *Career:* mem. Diana Express 1973–79; solo artist 1979–, with numerous TV and radio broadcasts, tours across Western and Eastern Europe; mem. Union of Bulgarian Musicians. *Recordings include:* fifteen albums. *Honours:* Second Place, Eurovision Belgium, First Prize, The Golden Orpheus Festival 1981, int. prizes in Cuba 1982, USSR, Belgium, Canada, Silver Orpheus 1983. *E-mail:* vasil_naidenov@bulgaria.com. *Website:* vassil-n.hit.bg.

NAIDOO, Xavier Kurt, (Kobra); German singer, songwriter and record producer; b. 2 Oct. 1971, Mannheim. *Career:* released debut album as Kobra 1993; changed performing name; solo albums as Xavier Naidoo 1998–; numerous collaborations including RZA, Deborah Cox, Sabrina Setlur, Illmat!c, Moses Pelham, Söhne Mannheims, Reamonn, Ben Becker, Sommersault, Erkan Aki, Stress, Bintia, Majestic 12, Schiller. *Recordings include:* albums: as Kobra: Seeing is Believing 1993; as Xavier Naidoo: Nicht von dieser Welt (ECHO Award and MTV Europe Music Award) 1998, Zwischenspiel – Alles für den Herrn 2002, Telegramm für X 2005, Alles kann besser werden 2009. *Stage:* Human Pacific 1995, People 1998. *Film:* Auf Herz und Nieren 2001. *Honours:* MTV Europe Music Awards for Best German Act 1999, 2002, ECHO Awards for Best National Male Artist – Rock/Pop 2000, 2006, Goldene Stimmgabel Award 2002, Comet Award for Best National Act 2002, Amadeus Award for Record of the Year 2004, Goldene Kamera Pop National Award 2006. *Address:* Naidoo Records GmbH, Kamenzerstrasse 10, 68309 Mannheim, Germany (office). *Telephone:* (621) 18144000 (office). *Fax:* (621) 18144144 (office). *Website:* www.xaviernaidoo.de.

NAIFF, Richard; British musician (keyboards, flute). *Education:* Guildhall School of Music. *Career:* joined The Waterboys 2000; currently also mem. Soulsec. *Recordings include:* albums: Rock in the Weary Land 2000, Universal Hall 2003, Book of Lightning 2007. *Address:* Soulsec, 40 Broadhope Avenue, Stanford Le-Hope, Essex, SS17 0SJ, England. *E-mail:* info@soulsec.com. *Website:* www.soulsec.com; www.mikescottwaterboys.com.

NAIL, Jimmy; British singer and actor; b. (James Michael Aloyisius Bradford), 16 March 1954, Newcastle upon Tyne, England. *Career:* solo recording artist 1992–; Owner, Big Boy Productions. *Film appearances*

include: Morons from Outer Space 1985, Howling II: Stirba - Werewolf Bitch 1985, Dream Demon 1987, Just Ask for Diamond 1988, Crusoe 1989, Danny, the Champion of the World 1990, Still Crazy 1998, The 10th Kingdom 2000. *Television includes:* Minder 1984, Blott on the Landscape 1985, Master of the Game 1985, Raoul Wallenberg 1986, Spender (BBC, also co-writer) 1991–93, Crocodile Shoes (BBC), Auf Wiedersehen Pet (ITV) 1983–2004, Parents of the Band 2008. *Recordings include:* albums: Growing Up In Public 1992, Crocodile Shoes 1994, Big River 1995, Crocodile Shoes II 1996, The Nail File: The Best of Jimmy Nail 1997, Tadpoles In A Jar 2000, 10 Great Songs And An OK Voice 2001; singles: Love Don't Live Here Anymore 1985, Ain't No Doubt 1992, Crocodile Shoes 1994, Big River 1995; appeared on: Gary Moore, We Want Moore 1984, Evita (film soundtrack) 1996, Carnival: Rainforest Foundation 1997. *Publication:* Northern Soul 2004. *Honours:* Best Album and Best Song, Great British Country Music Awards 1996.

NAISSOO, Tõnu; Estonian jazz musician (piano, organ, synthesizers) and composer; *Associate Professor of Jazz Piano, Estonian Academy of Music and Theatre;* b. 18 March 1951, Tallinn; m. Kersti Johanson 1977; one s. one d. *Education:* Tallinn Music School 1970, Tallinn State Conservatory 1982, Berklee Coll. of Music, Boston, USA (scholarship) 1989–90. *Career:* jazz pianist, bandleader (trio, quartet), solo pianist 1967–; keyboardist, pop/showgroup Laine 1972–76; as solo artist or with Tõnu Naissoo Trio/Quartet, played at jazz festivals, solo concerts in the fmr USSR 1978–89; jazz pianist, sideman, int. projects including EBU Big Band, Pori Jazz, Finland 1985, Trio Eckert-Gaivoronski-Naissoo, Turku Jazz, Finland 1992, Baltic Trio, Schleswig-Holstein Musik Festival, Germany 1992, Vladimir Tarasov's Baltic Art Orchestra, Jazz Baltica 1994, Munster Jazz Festival, Germany 1994; pianist, soloist, Alfred Schnittke's First Symphony, Symphony Orchestra of the USSR Ministry of Culture 1987; Boston Symphony Orchestra, US premiere 1988; Rotterdam Philharmonic Orchestra, Netherlands premiere 1991; pianist, entertainer 1991–; Assoc. Prof. of Jazz Piano, Estonian Acad. of Music and Theatre 2001–; Tõnu Naissoo Trio concert tours in Japan 2007, 2008, 2011, 2012, solo piano tour 2009; mem. Estonian Composers' Union, Estonian Arnold Schoenberg Soc. 2006. *Compositions:* for films, TV, theatre 1967–; Jazz: First Flight 1981, A Time There Was 1983, There Is Nothing New For You 2011, Red Wind 2011; chamber: Johnny, You Had A Nice Car 1994, Concerto for jazz group and orchestra 2006, Moog Concerto 2011, Moogtrane 2011. *Recordings:* Tõnu Naissoo Trio 1968, Turning Point 1980, Dedication 1993, Relaxin' at Viru 1998, With A Song In My Heart 2005, You Stepped Out Of A Dream 2006, Estonian Wind 2007, For Now And Forever 2008, Alone 2009, If You Want To Be Good 2009, Blue Pearl 2010, A Time There Was 2011, My Back Pages 2011, Memories Of Tomorrow (with Laura Põldvere) 2012, Live In Osaka (double CD) 2012, Fire 2012. *Honours:* Estonian Radio Musician of the Year 1991, Estonian Music Council's Interpretation Prize 2011. *Current Management:* c/o Estonian Composers' Union, Lauteri 7, 10145 Tallinn, Estonia. *E-mail:* naissoo@hot.ee; tnaissoo@gmail.com. *Website:* www.tonunaissoojazz.com.

NAKAJIMA, Miyuki; Japanese singer, songwriter and DJ; b. 23 Feb. 1952, Sapporo, Hokkaido. *Career:* folk and rock solo artist 1975–; performer in experimental theater, Yakai 1989–98; numerous compositions for other singers; participant, Nat. Language Council of Japan. *Films include:* Yousei Florence (voice) 1985, Tokyo Biyori 1997, Sayonara Color 2005, Glass no Tsukai 2005, The Mamiya Brothers 2006. *Recordings include:* albums: Aishiteiru to Ittekure 1978, Sinainaru Monoe 1979, Okaerinasai 1979, Kansuigyo 1982, The Change 1985, Goodbye Girl 1988, Love or Nothing 1994, Lullaby for the Soul 2001, Lullaby Singer 2006, I Love You, Do You Hear Me? 2007, Drama! 2009, Midnight Zoo 2010, From the Icy Reaches 2011, Night-light 2012, Hard Problems 2014. *Address:* c/o Yamaha Music Communications, 3-24-22, Shimo-Meguro, Meguro-ku, Tokyo 153-8666, Japan. *Website:* www.miyuki.jp.

NAMBA, Akihiro; Japanese musician (bass guitar) and singer. *Career:* Founder-mem. Hi-Standard 1991–. *Recordings include:* albums: Growing Up 1995, Angry Fist 1997, Making the Road 1999, Last of Sunny Day 2000, Kids Are Alright 2003. *Address:* c/o Fat Wreck Chords, PO Box 193690, San Francisco, CA 94119-3690, USA.

NAMYSŁOWSKI, Zbigniew; Polish jazz musician (trombone) and composer; b. 9 Sept. 1939, Warsaw; m. Maria Małgorzata Ostaszewska; one s. two d. *Education:* in Warsaw. *Career:* trombone player, leader of Modern Dixielanders 1957–60, sideman with Zygmunt Wichary Group 1960, New Orleans Stompers 1960–61, alto sax player and leader of Jazz Rockers 1961–62, Air Condition 1980–82, Zbigniew Namysłowski Quartet and Quintet 1973–; Air Condition 1980–83; Kalatówki Big Band 2001–03, sideman in the Wreckers 1962–63, Krzysztof Komeda Quintet 1965; mem. Polish Composer Asscn 1972–; participant in festivals including Students' Group Festival, Wrocław (Award for the Best Soloist – trombone) 1957, Int. Jazz Festival, Prague (Award for the Best Soloist) 1964, Lugano 1961, Tauranga (NZ) 1969, 1978, Bombay (now Mumbai) 1969, 1978, Paris 1974, Ivrea (Italy) 1979, Montreal 1984, Copenhagen 1989, Århus 1989, several times Jazz Jamboree, Warsaw and Molde, Kongsberg, Bergen (Norway), Zurich, Christianstadt, Stockholm, North Sea-Haag, Pori Jazz Festival (Finland), Red Sea (Israel) 1991, Int. Festival Wien, Kuwait 2002 and others; has toured in countries including

Denmark, USA, Italy, New Zealand, Australia, India, Netherlands, Greece, Canada, Mexico, Sweden, Norway, Switzerland. *Compositions include:* Der Schmalz Tango 1976, Convenient Circumstances 1980, Speed Limit 1981, Kuyawiak Goes Funky 1984, After Perturbation 1985, Quiet Afternoon 1985, Double-Trouble Blues 1985, Cuban Tango Mojito 1986, Seven-Eleven 1987, Western Ballade 1992, Oriental Food 1994, Mazurka Uborka 1996. *Recordings include:* Polish Jazz – Zbigniew Namysłowski Quartet, Kuyawiak Goes Funky, Zbigniew Namysłowski with Symphony Orchestra, Song of the Pterodactil, Jasmine Lady, Song of Innocence, Double Trouble, Open, Without Talk; adaptations of compositions by Mozart, Gershwin and Chopin for string quartet, clarinet and jazz band. *Honours:* State Prize (First Class) 1984, Fryderyk (Polish music award for Best Polish Jazz Record of the Year – Zbigniew Namysłowski Quartet and Zakopane Highlanders Band) 1995, Jazz Forum Award 1997, 1998, Gold Cross of Merit 1974, Meritorious Activist of Culture Award 1982. *E-mail:* quartet@poczta.onet.pl (office).

NAOKI; Japanese musician (drums); b. Tokyo. *Career:* Founder-mem. punk band, Nicotine 1994–; band formed its own record label, Sky Records 1997. *Recordings include:* albums: Royal Mellow Day 1996, ¡Hola Amigo! 1997, Will Kill You... (EP) 1998, Pleeeeeeeez! Who Are You? 2000, Fitness Dayz 2001, Samurai Shot 2002, School Of Liberty 2003, Hey Dude! We Love the Beatles 2005, Desperado 2006, Carnival 2006, Sound from the Schizoid Core 2006, Probably the Best 2007, Liberation 2007, Achromatic Ambitious 2007, Soundquake 2008. *E-mail:* nicotine@skyrecords.net. *Website:* skyrecords.net/nicotine.

NAPOLITANO, Johnette Lin; American singer, songwriter and musician (bass guitar, keyboards); b. 22 Sept. 1957, Hollywood, Calif.; d. of John Louis Napolitano II. *Career:* fmr mem. Dream 6; mem. Concrete Blonde 1982–95, 2002–06. *Recordings include:* albums: with Dream 6: Dream 6 1982; with Concrete Blonde: Concrete Blonde 1988, Free 1989, Bloodletting 1990, Walking In London 1992, Mexican Moon 1993, Concrete Blonde y los Illegals 1997, Group Therapy 2002, Live In Brazil 2003, Mojave 2004; solo: Sketchbook 2002, Various Works 1 2006, Sketchbook Vol. 2 2006, Scarred 2007. *Publication:* Rough Mix 2013. *Current Management:* c/o APA, 405 South Beverly Drive, Beverly Hills, CA 90212, USA. *E-mail:* jnroughmix@gmail.com. *Website:* www.concreteblondeofficialwebsite.com.

NARANJO, Mónica; Spanish singer, songwriter and producer; b. (Mónica Naranjo Carrasco), 23 May 1974, Figueras, Catalonia. *Recordings:* albums: Monica Naranjo 1994, Palabra de Mujer 1997, Minage (Shangay Award for Best Pop Album 2001) 2000, Chicas Malas 2001 (released in English as Bad Girls 2002), Tarantula 2008. *Honours:* Acapulco Festival Gold Medals for Best Solo Female (Audience Award) 1995, 1997, World Music Awards for Best Selling Spanish Artist 1996, 1998, 2010, Cadena Dial Awards for Best Nat. Soloist 1998 and Special Public Prize 2002, Amigo Best Solo Spanish Artist Award 1998, Shangay Award for Best Female Artist 2001. *Current Management:* c/o Alaia Productions SL, Calle Diputacio 79 – pta 1, Barcelona, 08015, Spain. *E-mail:* contacto@alaiaproductions.com. *Website:* www.alaiaproductions.com. *Address:* c/o Sony Music Entertainment Spain S.A., Avda de los Madronos 27, Madrid 28043, Spain (office). *Website:* www.monicanaranjo.com.

NAS, (Nas Escobar, Nasty Nas); American rap artist; b. (Nasir Jones), 1973, Queensbridge, NY; m. Kelis 2005. *Career:* first appearance aged 18 with Main Source on Live at the Barbecue 1991; first solo single, Halftime, appeared on Zebrahead soundtrack; solo recording artist 1994–; collaborations with Will Smith, Puff Daddy, Missy Elliott, Notorious BIG, Mary J. Blige, Allure, R. Kelly. *Recordings include:* albums: Illmatic 1994, It Was Written 1996, I Am 1999, Nastradamus 2001, Hip Hop is Dead 2006, Untitled 2008, Distant Relatives (with Damian Marley) 2010, Life is Good 2012. *Address:* c/o Def Jam Recordings, Worldwide Plaza, 825 Eighth Avenue, 28th Floor, New York, NY 10019, USA (office). *Website:* nas.defjam.com (office).

NASCIMENTO, Milton; Brazilian singer, songwriter, composer and musician (piano, accordion, guitar, bass guitar); b. 26 Oct. 1942, Rio de Janeiro; one s. *Career:* DJ, announcer, dir, Rádio Três Pontas, early 1960s; composer 1963–; played Carnegie Hall 1994; collaborations with Art Blakey, Laudir De Oliviera, Deodato, João Gilberto, Herbie Hancock, Airto Moreira, Flora Purim, Charlie Rouse, Wayne Shorter, Roberto Silva. *Recordings include:* albums: Milton Nascimento (aka Travessia) 1967, Courage 1968, Milton Nascimento 1969, Milton 1970, Clube Da Esquina – Milton Nascimento E Lo Borges 1972, Milagre Dos Peixes 1973, Milagre Dos Peixes – Gravado Ao Vivo – Milton Nascimento E Som Imaginário 1974, Native Dancer 1974, Minas 1975, Geraes 1976, Clube Da Esquina Dois 1978, Journey To Dawn 1979, Sentinela 1980, Caçador De Mim 1981, Missa Dos Quilombos 1982, Anima 1982, Milton Nascimento Ao Vivo 1983, Encontros E Despedidas 1985, A Barca Dos Amantes 1986, Yauarete 1987, Miltons 1988, Taxi 1990, O Planeta Blue Na Estrada Do Sol 1991, Ângelus 1993, Amigo 1995, Nascimento (Grammy Award for Best World Music Record of the Year 1998) 1997, Tambores De Minas – Ao Vivo 1998, Crooner (Latin Grammy Award for Best Brazilian Contemporary Pop Album 2000) 1999, Gil E Milton (with Gilberto Gil) 2001, Pietá 2002, Bossas Novas (with Jobim Trio) 2008, ...E a Gente Sonhando 2010. *Honours:* Chevalier des Arts et des Lettres 1984, Ordem do Rio Branco 1985; Dr hc (Universidade Federal de Ouro Preto) 2000; Festival of Brazilian Popular Music Best Performer 1965, Villa-Lobos Prize 1977, Santos Dumont Medal 1998, Sisac Gold Medal, Chile 2000, Latin Grammy Awards for Best Brazilian song (for Tristesse) 2004, (for A Festa) 2005, Gold Medal, Acad. des Arts, Sciences et Belles-Lettres (France) 2006. *Current Management:* c/o Tribo Produções Artísticas, Avenida Armando Lombardi 800, gr 225, Barra da Tijuca, 22640-000 Rio de Janeiro, RJ, Brazil. *Telephone:* (21) 3154-8200; (21) 2294-7294. *Fax:* (21) 3154-8220. *E-mail:* miltonnascimento@triboproducoes.com.br; amaurylinhares@mpbproducoes.com.br. *Website:* www.triboproducoes.com.br; www.miltonnascimento.com.br.

NASH, Gary Powell, BM, MM, PhD; American composer, musician (clarinet, saxophone) and academic; *Associate Professor of Music, Fisk University*; b. 2 Aug. 1964, Flint, Mich. *Education:* Mich. State Univ., Western Mich. Univ. *Career:* began composing arrangements and transcriptions for bands; first compositions 1981; Choir Dir, Central Christian Church, Flint 1991–94; Conductor, Clarinet Ensemble, Miss. Valley State Univ., Itta Bena 1996–2003, Asst Prof. of Theory and Composition 1996, later Assoc. Prof. of Music –2003; Artist-in-Residence, Western Mich. Univ. 1997; Visiting Prof. of Music Composition, Univ. of the Philippines-Diliman 2000–01; Assoc. Prof. of Music, Fisk Univ. 2003–; mem. American Composers Forum. *Compositions include:* Fanfare for woodwinds 1985, Necrology 1985, Two Relatively Short Pieces for piano 1986, Aura 1986, Deformation and Tranquillity for clarinet 1987, Easter Music for woodwind 1987, Five Etudes plus One More 1987, Deformation II for trombone 1988, Life, War and Death (choral music) 1988, Elemental Surprise 1988, Saturday Drive (electronic music) 1988, Variants on the Holiday Season for orchestra 1989, Deformation III for percussion 1991, In Memoriam: Sojourner Truth for orchestra 1992, Deformation IV for tuba 1992, Heroes for orchestra 1992, Mountain Rhapsody 1992, Enigmatic Fanfare for brass 1993, Improvisation for solo marimba 1993, For Two for violin 1993, Deformation V for bassoon 1993, Scherzando for thirteen clarinets 1994, Two Psalms of the Sons of Korah (choral music) 1994, Blues Impromptu for solo cello 1995, Two Songs (of Paul Laurence Dunbar) 1995, Zuilhou de Lianqu (The Last Love Song) 1995, A Romantic Prelude for brass 1996, Sphinx 1996, Valley Music for percussion 1997, Rhapsody for Three 1997, A Fraternal Prelude 1997, Lux Nova (electronic music) 1998, Threnody for solo marimba 1998, Why Fades A Dream? 1998, Brass Magnolia Suite 1999, Fire of Love 1999, Valse and Intermezzo 1999, Mu Gua (The Quince) 1999, Nie Ni Ren (You And I) 1999, Psalm 149 (choral music) 2000, Galaw Ng Sayaw Sa Apat At Tatio for flute and piano 2001, Delta Flourish for woodwind 2002, Three Ivory Magnolia Fantasies for piano 2003, A Romantic Prelude and March for brass 2003, Tradition and Innovation 2004, Psalms of Ascents for mixed choir, piano and clarinet 2004, So Cal Dream 2010, Giovanna's Song and Dance 2011, African Diaspora Suite 2012. *Honours:* winner, Baltimore Symphony Orchestra African-American Composer Composition Contest 1991, winner, Chicago Civic Orchestra Black Composer Composition Contest 1992, Mich. State Univ. School of Music Honors Concert Best Student Composition 1994, ASCAP Foundation Grants to Young Composers Award 1994, NEA Minority Outreach Fellowship 1995, Miss. Humanities Council Teachers Award 2001–02. *Address:* Music Department, Fisk University, 1000 17th Avenue, Nashville, TN 37208-3051, USA (office). *Telephone:* (615) 329-8528 (office). *E-mail:* gnash@fisk.edu (office). *Website:* www.fisk.edu (office).

NASH, Graham; British singer and musician (guitar); b. 2 Feb. 1942, Blackpool, Lancashire, England; m. Susan. *Career:* touring musician with the Hollies; mem., Crosby Stills and Nash 1968–, later Crosby, Stills, Nash and Young; also solo artist; also f. Nash Editions (photographic printmaking house) 1990; numerous live performances, festival appearances. *Television:* presenter, The Inside Track interview show (cable) 1990. *Recordings include:* albums: with The Hollies: Stay With The Hollies 1964, In The Hollies Style 1964, The Hollies 1965, Would You Believe? 1966, For Certain Because 1966, Evolution 1967, Butterfly 1967, The Hollies At Abbey Road 2000; with Crosby Stills and Nash: Crosby Stills and Nash 1969, Déjà Vu 1970, CSN 1977, Daylight Again 1982, American Dream 1988, Live It Up 1990, After the Storm 1994, Looking Forward 1999; solo: Songs For Beginners 1971, Wild Tales 1974, Earth and Sky 1980, Innocent Eyes 1986, Songs for Survivors 2002; with David Crosby: Graham Nash/David Crosby 1972, Wind On The Water 1975, Whistling Down The Wire 1976, Crosby/Nash Live 1977, The Best Of 1978. *Honours:* Grammy Award for Best New Artist (with Crosby, Stills and Nash) 1970. *Current Management:* c/o Michael Jensen, Jensen Communications, 709 East Colorado Boulevard, Suite 220, Pasadena, CA 91101, USA. *Telephone:* (626) 585-9575. *Fax:* (626) 564-8920. *E-mail:* info@jensencom.com. *Website:* www.jensencom.com; www.grahamnash.com; www.csny.com.

NASH, John (Johnny) Lester; American singer and actor; b. 9 Aug. 1940, Houston, TX. *Career:* lead soprano, gospel choir; singer on television variety show; mem., Teen Commandments (with Paul Anka and George Hamilton IV); solo artist 1960s–70s; involved in recording and production. *Films:* Take a Giant Step 1958, Key Witness 1960. *Recordings include:* Hold Me Tight 1968, Let's Go Dancing 1969, I Can See Clearly Now 1972, My Merry-Go-Round 1973, What A Wonderful World 1977, Stir It Up 1981, Johnny Nash 1985, Here Again 1986, Tears On My Pillow 1987, The Very Best of Johnny Nash 1995, The Best of Johnny Nash 1996.

NASH, Rob; singing coach and musician (keyboards, guitar); b. 30 May 1956, Boston, Lincolnshire, England; m. Nic Bagguley 1989, three s. one d. *Education:* Loughborough Univ., Ely Cathedral Chorister, Cambridge Coll. of Arts and Technology. *Career:* vocal coach to Michael Barrymore (for television series Barrymore), Jeremy Irons (for films The Lion King, Chorus of Disapproval); work with Marc Almond, Simon Climie, Dion Estes, Stephanie Lawrence, Colin Blunstone, Nick Cave; mem. Equity, Musicians' Union. *Recordings:* albums: solo: With Love, A Touch of Music in the Night. *Honours:*

Vivien Ellis Awards 1990. *Address:* 31 Tyne Street, St Werburgh, Bristol BS2 9UA, England.

NASH, Su-Elise; British singer; b. London. *Education:* Middlesex Univ. *Career:* Founder mem. Mis-Teeq 2001–05; live appearances include 'Party at the Palace' for Golden Jubilee celebrations 2002; solo artist 2005–; founder and Principal, Su-Elise Nash Stage School. *Recordings include:* albums: Lickin' On Both Sides 2001, Eyecandy 2003; singles: Why? 2001, All I Want 2001, One Night Stand 2001, B With Me 2002, Roll On 2002, Scandalous 2003, Can't Get It Back 2003, Style 2003, Shoo Shoo Baby 2005. *Honours:* UK Garage Award for Best Artist 2001, MOBO Award for Best Garage Act 2002. *E-mail:* talent@mobmanagement.co.uk. *Website:* www.mobmanagement.co.uk.

NASHID, Ahmed; Maldivian singer and songwriter. *Career:* mem., Zero Degree Atoll; solo blues artist. *Recordings include:* Bird in Flight (New York Int. Music Festival Best Blues Album 2003). *Honours:* Nat. Award of Recognition for Outstanding Public Service in Music, Maldives 1990.

NASRI, Assala; Syrian singer; b. 15 May 1969, Damascus; m. 1st Ayman al-Zahabi (divorced 2005); two c.; m. 2nd Tarek al-Eryan 2006. *Recordings include:* albums: Ya Sabra Yana 1993, Tawam al-Rooh 1994, Egdab 1994, Wala Tesaddeq 1995, Rahal 1996, Qalbi Beyirtahlak 1998, Ya Majnoon 1999, Moushtaaqah 2001, Yakhy Esaal 2002, Yameen Allah – Haqeeqat Waqi'ei 2001, Qad al-Herouf 2003, Awqaat 2004, Aadi 2005, Hayati 2006, Sawaha Galbi 2007. *Address:* c/o Rotana Music, Kingdom Tower, 58th Floor, King Fahd Road, Olaya District, Riyadh, Saudi Arabia. *Website:* www.assalanasry.com.

NASRI, Maya; Lebanese singer and actress; b. (Maya Hussam Asmar), 14 Aug. 1976, Tripoli. *Education:* Univ. of Fine Arts, Beirut. *Career:* solo artist 1999–. *Film and television appearances:* Code 36 (film) 2007, Sultan el-Gharam (TV series, Egypt) 2007, Kharej an el-Qanoun (film) 2007, Wekalet atiyya (TV series, Egypt) 2008. *Recordings include:* albums: Akhbarak eih? 2002, Law kan lak alb 2003, Izzay taa'rafni 2005, Jayi lwa't 2008. *Address:* c/o Rotana, Burj al-Ghazal, 11th Floor, al-Tabaris, Achrafieh, Beirut, Lebanon (office). *E-mail:* nasri.maya@gmail.com (office). *Website:* www.rotana.net (office); www.maya-nasri.net.

NASTANOVICH, Bob; American musician (drums); b. 1968, Rochester, NY. *Education:* Univ. of Virginia. *Career:* mem., Pavement 1991–2000, reunited for live performances 2010; tours world-wide; contrib. to Starlite Walker by the Silver Jews 1994. *Television appearance:* Space Ghost Coast to Coast (cartoon) 1997. *Recordings include:* albums: Slanted and Enchanted 1992, Crooked Rain, Crooked Rain 1994, Wowee Zowee 1995, Brighten the Corners 1997, Terror Twilight 1999, Crooked Rain, Crooked Rain (expanded edn) 2004.

NASTASIA, Nina Maria; American singer and songwriter; b. Hollywood, CA. *Recordings include:* albums: The Blackened Air 2002, Run To Ruin 2003, Dogs 2004, On Leaving 2006, You Follow Me (with Jim White) 2007, Outlaster 2010. *Address:* c/o FatCat Records, PO Box 3400, Brighton, BN1 4WG, UK (office). *E-mail:* info@fat-cat.co.uk (office). *Website:* fat-cat.co.uk (office); www.ninanastasia.com.

NATTHEW; Thai singer and actor; b. (Nat Thewphaigam), 5 June 1989, Bangkok. *Education:* Kasetsart Univ. *Career:* participated in reality TV talent show Academy Fantasia (Season 5 winner) 2008; debut single 2008; debut album 2011; actor in several TV drama series. *Television:* as participant: Academy Fantasia (series winner) 2008; as actor: drama series including: Wai Puan Kuan La Fun 2010, Nuea Ma Nut 2011, Sane Bangkok 2011, Thida-Wanon 3 2011, Sue-Saming 2012. *Recordings include:* album: Natthew the Passion 2011. *Honours:* Mnet Asian Music Award for Best New Asian Artist (Thailand) 2012. *Address:* c/o CJ Entertainment, CJ Group, Seoul, South Korea (office). *E-mail:* red414@cj.net (office). *Website:* english.cj.net (office); www.cjent.co.kr (office).

NAUGHTY BOY; British R&B musician, singer, songwriter and record producer; b. (Shahid Khan), 1 Jan. 1985, Watford, Herts., England. *Education:* London Guildhall Univ. *Career:* signed publishing deal with Sony ATV Music 2012; Founder, Naughty Boy Recordings; songwriter for Wiley, Chipmunk; collaborator with Emeli Sandé on her debut album Our Version of Events 2012; also collaborator as writer or producer on songs for Alexandra Burke, Cheryl Cole, Devlin, Alesha Dixon, Jennifer Hudson, JLS, Leona Lewis, Professor Green, Rihanna, Emeli Sande, Tinie Tempah, wil.i.am; debut solo album released 2013 featuring contribs from Gabrielle, Ed Sheeran, Sam Smith, Tinie Tempah. *Recordings:* album: Hotel Cabana 2013. *Honours:* Prince's Trust Grant Award 2005, MOBO Awards for Best Song and Best Video (for La La La) 2013. *Address:* c/o Virgin EMI Records, Universal Music UK, 364–366 Kensington High Street, London, W14 8NS, England (office). *Telephone:* (20) 7471-5000 (office). *E-mail:* contact@virginemirecords.com (office). *Website:* www.virginemirecords.com (office); www.hotel-cabana.com.

NAUMOV, Julian; Bulgarian musician (drums). *Career:* mem., Konkurent 1986–95; numerous concerts, television and radio appearances. *Recordings:* Rock For Peace 1988, Rock Festival In Mitchurin 1989, The Black Sheep (rock collection) 1992, Something Wet 1994. *Honours:* First Prizes; Top Rock Band, Youth Festival, Vidin 1989, Rock Ring, Sofia 1990, Top Rock Composition: The Cavalry 1991, Group of the Year, The Darik Radio Countdown 1994.

NAVARRO, Dave; American musician (guitar); b. 7 June 1967, Santa Monica, Calif.; m. Carmen Electra 2003 (divorced 2007). *Career:* mem. Jane's Addiction 1984–91, 1997–; mem. Deconstruction 1994, Red Hot Chili Peppers 1993–97; numerous sessions for artists including Christina Aguilera, Marilyn Manson, Alanis Morrisette, Nine Inch Nails, P. Diddy, Janet Jackson. *Recordings include:* albums: with Jane's Addiction: Jane's Addiction 1987, Nothing's Shocking 1988, Ritual do lo Habitual 1990, Kettle Whistle 1997, Strays 2003, The Great Escape Artist 2011; with Deconstruction: Deconstruction 1994; with Red Hot Chili Peppers: One Hot Minute 1995; solo: Rhimorse 1995, Trust No One 2001. *Website:* www.janesaddiction.com.

NAVARRO ROSAS, Jesús Alberto; Mexican singer; b. 9 July 1986, Mexicali, Bajo California. *Career:* founding mem. and lead singer, Reik 2003–. *Recordings:* Reik 2005, Secuencia 2006, Un Día Más (Latin Grammy Award for Best Pop Album by a Duo/Group 2009) 2008. *Honours:* Premios MTV Latinoamérica for Best Group 2005, for Best Artist (Northern region) 2005, for Best New Artist (Northern region) 2005, for Best Pop Artist 2009. *Current Management:* c/o Dulce Gil, Westwood Entertainment, México, Mexico. *Telephone:* (55) 5337-2047. *E-mail:* dgil@westwoodent.com. *Website:* www.westwoodent.com; www.reik.tv.

NAWASADIO, Sylvie Kihanga; Belgian musician; b. 8 Jan. 1965, Ixelles. *Career:* mem. Zap Mama –1995, Barut Trio. *Composition:* Sab Syl Ma. *Recordings include:* albums: with Zap Mama: Zap Mama 1993, Sab Syl Ma; with Barut Trio: Ndugu Yangu; with Toni Child: The Woman's Boat; with Sally Nyolo: Tribu, Multiculti, Beti; with Kadja Nin: Free; with Uinckx: I Love My Job; with Jaques Higelin: Au Rex, Paradis Païen; with Arthur H.: Bachibouzouk; with H. Felix Thiéfaine: Le Bonheur De La Tentation; other: Y-a-t'il Une Femme Noire Dans Cette Ville? 1998, La Voix Dans Tous Ses États 2000. *Honours:* SABAM Prize 1997.

NAWAZ, Aki, (Propa-Ghandi); British hip-hop artist, musician (drums, guitar), producer and filmmaker; *Director, Nation Records Limited;* b. (Haq Qureshi), Pakistan. *Career:* musician in Southern Death Cult, Getting The Fear, Fun Da Mental; record label producer, currently Dir, Nation Records; film and documentary producer. *Films:* To Gaza With Love, Bosnia – A Painful Peace. *Recordings include:* albums: Seize the Time 1994, With Intent to Pervert the Cause of Injustice 1995, Erotic Terrorism 1998, Why America Will Go to Hell 1999, There Shall Be Love! 2001, Voice of Mass Destruction 2003, All is War (The Benefits of G-Had) 2006. *Address:* Nation Records Ltd, 19 All Saints Road, London, W11 1HE, England (office). *Telephone:* (20) 7792-8167 (office). *E-mail:* akination@btopenworld.com (office). *Website:* www.fun-da-mental.co (office).

NAZARKHAN, Sevara; Uzbekistani singer, songwriter and musician (doutar); b. 1976. *Education:* Tashkent State Conservatoire. *Career:* first recordings released, Uzbekistan 1999. *Recordings:* albums: Yol Bolsin 2003. *Address:* c/o Real World Records, Box Mill, Mill Lane, Box, Wiltshire SN13 8PL, England (office). *Website:* www.sevara.uz.

NAZERI, Hafez; Iranian composer and musician; s. of Shahram Nazeri. *Education:* Mannes Coll., New York. *Career:* performances with his father, Shahram Nazeri in Europe and Middle East; has performed as musician at Sfinks Festival, Belgium, Festa Del Popolo, Italy, Théâtre de la Ville, Paris, Beiteddine Festival, Lebanon, Walt Disney Concert Hall, Los Angeles, Carnegie Hall, New York; compositions performed by Armenian Philharmonic Orchestra at Royal Albert Hall, Sodra Theare, Stockholm, De Bijlike, Ghent, Fez Festival, Morocco; founder, the Rumi Ensemble 2000–, the Rumi Symphony Project (ensemble playing a mix of Eastern and Western classical string music); created a new musical instrument based on traditional four-string sitar, The Hafez. *Compositions include:* The Passion of Rumi, The Rumi Symphony 2007, Iranian Sounds of Peace 2009, Night Angel 2010. *Honours:* UCLA Creativity Award for Most Distinguished Young Composer, Irvine City Hall Award of Distinction in Kurdish Music. *Current Management:* International Music Network, 278 Main Street, Gloucester, MA 01930, USA. *Telephone:* (978) 283-2883. *Fax:* (978) 283-2330. *Website:* www.imnworld.com.

NAZERI, Shahram; Iranian singer and musician; b. 1950, Kermanshah; father of Hafez Nazeri. *Education:* studied with Persian masters including Abdullah Davami, Abdol Ali Vaziri, Jalal Zolfonoun, Mohammad Reza Shajarian, Nourali Boroumand, Mahmood Karimi. *Career:* singer of Persian classical and Sufi music; started singing in public aged eight years, performed on tv aged eleven years; first vocalist to set Sufi poetry of Mawlana Jalal ad-Din Rumi to music; concerts worldwide; numerous performances with s. Hafez Nazeri including biggest-ever concert in Middle East, Iran 2000, US Tour 2005–06, Walt Disney Concert Hall, Los Angeles, USA 2007, Barbican Centre, London, UK 2007; performances and lectures at Stanford, Columbia, Calif. – Berkeley, UCLA, Emory and Harvard univs 2006. *Recordings include:* albums: Gol e Sad Barg (The one-hundred-leaf-flower), Yadegar e doust (In remembrance of a friend), She'r va Erfan (Poetry and Mysticism), Motreb Mahtabroo, Shour Angiz (Joy giver) 1989, Zemesstan, Heyrani (Mystified) 1997, Seda ye Sokhan e Eshgh (The veiled voice of love) 2001, Leili o Majnoon 2002, Gham e ziba 2003, Shahram Nazeri and The Dastan Group 2003, The Passion of Rumi 2007. *Honours:* Chevalier des Arts et Lettres 2007; First Prize, Concours de Musique Traditionelle 1975, Best Singer of Classical Persian and Sufi Music, Ministry of Culture, Iran, Living Legend Award, UCLA, Irvine City Hall Award of Distinction in Persian music. *Address:* c/o Kereshmeh Records, 12021 Wilshire Boulevard, #420, Los Angeles, CA 90025,

USA (office). *Telephone:* (310) 400-4161 (office). *Website:* www.kereshmeh.com (office).

NCHANGA, Bongani; South African singer; b. Klerksdrop. *Career:* mem., Malaika. *Recordings include:* albums: Malaika 2004, Vuthelani (SAMA Award for Best African Pop Album 2006) 2005. *Honours:* Kora All Africa Music Award for Best Group from Southern Africa 2005. *Current Management:* Dara House, 46B Wierda Road West, Wierda Valley, Sandton, South Africa. *Telephone:* (11) 7317000. *Fax:* (11) 8835022. *E-mail:* bookings@ beyonddestiny.co.za. *Website:* www.beyonddestiny.co.za. *E-mail:* info@ malaikasa.co.za. *Website:* www.malaikasa.co.za.

NDABA, Jabulani; South African singer; b. Klerksdrop. *Career:* mem., Malaika. *Recordings include:* albums: Malaika 2004, Vuthelani (SAMA Award for Best African Pop Album 2006) 2005. *Honours:* Kora All Africa Music Award for Best Group from Southern Africa 2005. *Address:* Dara House, 46B Wierda Road West, Wierda Valley, Sandton, South Africa. *Telephone:* (11) 7317000. *Fax:* (11) 8835022. *E-mail:* bookings@beyonddestiny .co.za. *Website:* www.beyonddestiny.co.za. *E-mail:* info@malaikasa.co.za. *Website:* www.malaikasa.co.za.

N'DJOCK, Yves; Cameroonian musician (guitar), producer and composer. *Career:* fmr mem., Kékélé collective; collaborations with Salif Keita, Khaled, Talking Heads, Mario Caonge, Touré Kunda, Ismael Lô and Sekouba Bambino. *Address:* c/o Mad Minute Music, 5–7 rue Paul Bert, 93400 St Ouen, France. *E-mail:* corinne@madminutemusic.com. *Website:* www .madminutemusic.com.

N'DOUR, Youssou; Senegalese singer, songwriter and government official; *Minister-Counsellor to the Presidency;* b. Oct. 1959, Dakar; s. of Elimane N'Dour and Ndeye Sokhna Mboup; m. 1st Mami Camara (divorced), four c.; m. 2nd Aida Coulibaly, two. d. *Career:* mem. Sine Dramatic 1972, Orchestre Diamono 1975, The Star Band (house band of Dakar nightclub, the Miami Club) 1976–79; formed band Etoile de Dakar (changed name to Super Etoile 1982) 1979–; has performed with Peter Gabriel, Paul Simon, Bob Dylan, Branford Marsalis; sings in English, French, Fulani, Serer and native Wolof; Goodwill Amb. to UN, UNICEF, Int. Bureau of Work; Owner Jololi Records recording studio, radio station, Thoissane nightclub, Dakar; f. political group Fekke ma ci bolle (I am involved) Nov. 2011, announced candidacy for presidential election 2012 (subsequently barred from standing by Constitutional Council ruling); Minister of Tourism and Culture 2012–13, Minister-Counsellor to the Presidency 2013–. *Recordings include:* albums: A Abijan 1980, Xalis 1980, Tabaski 1981, Thiapathioly 1983, Absa Gueye 1983, Immigrès 1984, Nelson Mandela 1985, Inedits (1984–1985) 1988, The Lion 1989, African Editions Vols 5–14 1990, Africa Deebeub 1990, Jamm La Prix 1990, Kocc Barma 1990, Set 1990, Hey You: The Essential Collection 1988–90, Eyes Open 1992, The Best of Youssou N'Dour 1994, The Guide 1994, Gainde– Voices From The Heart Of Africa (with Yande Codou Sene) 1996, Lii 1996, Immigrès/Bitim Rew 1997, St Louis 1997, Best of the 80s 1998, Special Fin D'annee Plus Djamil 1999, Rewmi 1999, Joko: From Village to Town 2000, Le Grand Bal, Bercy 2000, Le Grand Bal 1 & 2 2001, Batay 2001, Birth of a Star 2001, Nothing's In Vain (Coono Du Réér) 2002, Et Ses Amis 2002, Sant Allah (Homage to God) 2003, Egypt (BBC Radio 3 World Music Award for Album of the Year 2005) 2004, Hey You! The Essential Collection 2005, Rokku Mi Rokka 2007, I Bring What I Love 2010, Etoile de Dakar/Once Upon a Time in Senegal 2010, Dakar-Kingston 2010. *Film roles include:* Picc Mi 1992, Amazing Grace 2006. *Honours:* Hon. DMus (Yale) 2011; Best African Artist 1996, African Artist of the Century 1999, MOBO Award for Best African Act 2005. *Address:* c/o Office of the President, ave Léopold Sédar Senghor, BP 168, Dakar, Dakar (office); Youssou N'Dour Head Office, 8 Route des Almadies Parcelle, BP 1310, Dakar, Senegal. *Telephone:* 33-822-4303 (office); 33-865-1039. *Fax:* 33-822-1638 (office); 33-865-1068. *E-mail:* yncontact@yahoo.fr. *Website:* www.youssou.com.

NE-YO; American songwriter and singer; b. (Shaffer Chimere Smith), 18 Oct. 1979, Arkansas; one d. *Career:* songwriter for R & B, rap and pop artists 1999–; has written songs for artists including Youngstown, Christina Milian, Dawn Angelique, Rhianna, Mary J. Blige, B2K, Faith Evans, Paula DeAnda, Beyoncé, Snoop Dogg, Jay Z, Mario, Musiq Soulchild, Britney Spears, Corbin Bleu, Celine Dion; solo recording artist 2005–, guest appearances on songs by Remy Ma, Ghostface Killah, Busta Rhymes, Jay-Z, Mic Little, Rihanna, City Boy, Fabolous, Foxy Brown. *Compositions include:* Unfaithful (Rhianna), Let Me Love You (Mario), Gallery (Mario Vazquez), Walk Away (Remember Me) (Paula DeAnda), Irreplaceable (Beyoncé), Minority Report (Jay Z), Impossible (Britney Spears). *Recordings:* albums: In My Own Words 2006, Because of You (Grammy Award for Best Contemporary R&B Album 2008) 2007, Year of the Gentleman 2008, Libra Scale 2010, R.E.D. 2012, Non-Fiction 2015. *Honours:* Best R & B Male Artist, BET Awards 2007, Best Song (for Because of You), MOBO Awards 2007, Best R & B/Soul New Artist, Soul Train Music Awards 2007, Grammy Award for Best Male R&B Vocal Performance (for Miss Independent) 2009. *Address:* c/o Def Jam Recordings, 825 Eighth Avenue, New York, NY 10019, USA (office). *Website:* www.neyothegentleman.com (office).

THE NEANDERTHAL (see Sanchez, Roger)

NED B; musician (guitar, keyboards); b. (Ed Baden Powell). *Career:* mem., jazz funk quartet, D-Influence, 1990–; Support to Prince, Michael Jackson; Tours, television appearances; D-Influence also production team for R&B

music; Group owns Freakstreet label. *Recordings:* albums: Good 4 We 1992, Prayer 4 Unity 1995, London 1997, D-Influence Presents D-Vas 2002. *Address:* c/o Dome Records Ltd, PO Box 3274, East Preston, Sussex BN16 9BD, England (office). *Website:* www.domerecords.co.uk (office).

NEDELCHEV, Boyko; Bulgarian singer, songwriter and composer; b. 24 April 1965, Rousse. *Career:* singer, songwriter and composer with brother Deyan 1987–; numerous live appearances, festivals, concerts, television and radio broadcasts, and tours; mem. FIDOF. *Recordings:* A Plea To The World, 1990; A Game of Love, 1991; Madly In Love, 1992; The Best of Deyan and Boyko Nedelchev, 1993; Love and Dream, 1993; La Mia Musica, 1994; Love For Love, 1994; The Hits of Deyan and Boyko Nedelchev, 1995; Atlanta, 1996; Brothers, 1996; Gently News, 1997; Grande Amore, 1998. *Honours:* Contest for Youth Pop Singers, Bulgaria, 1988–89; Union of Bulgarian Writers, 1989–90, 1992, 1996; Grand Prix, Nashville, USA, 1989; Golden Orpheus International Festival, Bulgaria, 1990, 1993–96; International Festival of Melody of the Friends, Ulan-Bator, Mongolia, 1990; Step To Parnasus International Festival, Moscow, Russia, 1994; Voice of Asia International Festival, Kazakhstan, 1995; International Song Festival, Cairo, Egypt, 1995–97; Silver Eros Festival, Bulgaria, 1996; Golden Stang International Festival, Romania, 1996; Love Duets Festival, Bulgaria, 1996; Annual National Music Awards, Bulgaria, 1996–98; South Pacific International Song Contest, Australia, 1998.

NEDELCHEV, Deyan, (Deyan Angeloff); Bulgarian singer, songwriter, composer and musician; b. (Deyan Angelov), 16 Jan. 1964, Ruse. *Career:* singer, songwriter, composer with brother, Boyko 1987–; appearances at many festivals, concerts, TV and radio broadcasts in Bulgaria, Russia, Kazakhstan, Mongolia, Egypt, Italy, Canary Islands, France, UK, S Africa, Romania, N Korea, Belarus. *Recordings include:* albums: Greetings from Struma 1987, A Plea To The World 1990, Deyan Nedelchev 1990, A Game of Love 1991, Madly in Love 1992, The Best of Deyan and Boyko Nedeltchev 1992, Love-dream: Dedication 1993, La Mia Musica 1993, Love For Love 1993, La Palestride 1993, The Hits of Deyan and Boyko Nedelchev 1995, Brothers 1996, Atlanta 1996, Gently News 1997, Grande Amore 1998, The Big Ones 2001, Oh God, How Lovely You Are 2002, To You 2005, Nessun Dorma 2008, The Old Man 2012, To Be 2015. *Honours:* contest for Youth Pop Singers, Bulgaria 1988–89, Union of Bulgarian Writers 1989–90, 1996, Hon. Prize, Nashville, USA 1989, First Prize, Bulgarian Nat. Radio Contest 1990, Golden Orpheus Int. Festival, Bulgaria 1990, 1993–96, Int. Festival of Melody of The Friends, Ulan-Bator, Mongolia 1990, Step to Parnasus Int. Festival, Moscow, Russia 1994, Voice of Asia Int. Festival, Kazakhstan 1995, Int. Song Festival, Cairo, Egypt 1995–97, Silver Eros Festival, Bulgaria 1996, Golden Stang Int. Festival, Romania 1996, Love Duets Festival, Bulgaria 1996, Annual Nat. Music Awards, Bulgaria 1996, 1998, South Pacific Int. Song Contest, Australia 1998, Gold Cup, Int. Spring Festival, Democratic People's Repub. of Korea 2000, First Award, XIVth European Youth Pop-Rock Concert, Bulgaria 2002, First Prize, Pres.'s Choice Award, Bilboard USA 2006, amongst others. *Address:* 7005 Ruse, Lipnik Blvd 62, Entr G, Apt 16, Bulgaria (home). *E-mail:* deyanangel@gmail.com (home); deyanangeloff@abv.bg (home); deyanangelov@mail.bg (home).

NEECE, Timothy G.; American artist manager; *General Manager, Austin City Limits Live;* b. 2 Oct. 1946, Abilene, Texas; m. 1st Lynda Hunnicutt, one d.; m. 2nd Deborah Chaffey 1988. *Education:* BA, Business, McMurry University. *Career:* manager, prior to release and through 3 albums for Christopher Cross; Bruce Hornsby and the Range; Charlie Sexton; Manager, Rickie Lee Jones during Flying Cowboys release; General Manager, Austin City Limits Live 2010–. *Honours:* launched careers of 2 Best New Artist Grammy Award Winners; many Gold, Platinum awards world-wide for artistes managed. *Address:* ACL Live, 310 Willie Nelson Boulevard, Austin, TX 78701, USA (office). *Telephone:* (512) 225-7999 (office). *E-mail:* info@acl -live.com (office). *Website:* www.acl-live.com (office).

NEFF, John; American recording engineer, producer and musician; b. 13 March 1951, Birmingham, Michigan; m. Nancy L. B. Neff; two s. one d. *Career:* chief engineer, David Lynch's Asymmetrical Studio; re-recording mixer, The Straight Story, Mulholland Drive; engineer, Walter Becker, Donald Fagen; Morning Radio Host; mem. Japancakes 1996–; mem, ASCAP, Audio Engineering Society. *Compositions:* The Straight Story, Mulholland Drive, Lux Vivens. *Recordings:* albums: with Japancakes: If I Could See Dallas 1999, Down the Elements 2000, Sleepy Strange 2001, Belmondo 2002, Waking Hours 2004, Giving Machines 2007, Loveless 2007. *E-mail:* japancakesmusic@ gmail.com (office). *Website:* www.japancakesmusic.com.

NEGRAO, Mario Borganovi; Brazilian musician (drums, percussion, flute); b. 18 Nov. 1945; m. Sonia Dias; two s. *Education:* studied with Guirra Peixe. *Career:* drummer in shows with Brazilian artists, including Chico Buarque Vinicius de Moraes, Quartet em CY, Leila Pinheiro, Baden Powell, Carlinhos Lyra, Paulinho Nogueira, Topm Jobim; worked with ensembles, including the Brazilian Symphony Orchestra, Rio Jazz Orchestra, Bebeto (Tamba Trio), Edson Lobo and Osmar Milito; participated in shows in Brazil with Toquinho, Vinicius and Clara Nunes, in the Sistine Theatre with Chico Buarque, Italy, in Mexico with local orchestras, in Argentina with Chico Buarque, Marilia Barbosa, Maria Creuza, Toquinho, Vicinius and MPB4; Prof. of Drumming, Conservatório Brasileiro de Música 2007–. *Compositions:* Canela de Velho, Fruta Doce, Mata Mato, Joao Mole, Orelma de Onca, Farinma Seca, Respira Fundo, Zaratudo, Samba Antigo,. *Recordings:* solo album of his own compositions; recordings with other artists, including Chico Buarque, Aresar de Voce, Calicz and Homenagem ao Malandao, Vinicius, Toquinho, Regna Très, Samba de Orly. *Honours:* Panama State Critics Best Original Instrumental Recording, Brazil. *Address:* Conservatório Brasileiro de Música, Centro Universitário, Avenida Graça Aranha, 57, 12° andar, Castelo, 20030-002 Rio de Janeiro, RJ, Brazil (office). *Telephone:* (21) 3478-7600. *E-mail:* marionegraob@hotmail.com (office). *Website:* www.cbm-musica.org.br (office).

NEGRIJN, Thomas; Danish singer and musician (guitar); b. 19 Oct. 1959, Copenhagen. *Education:* H. F. Music School, Copenhagen. *Career:* own big band, Simcess 1985–92; played Roskilde Festival, Midfyn Festival; many Danish television and radio broadcasts, tours; founder mem., Blink 1995–; mem. Danish Soc. for Jazz Rock Folk Composers. *Recordings:* with Simcess: Play With Your Life 1988, The House 1990; with Tam Tam Top: Secrets 1993; with Blink: Blink 1994. *Honours:* John (Lennon) Award for Best Band, Copenhagen 1987. *Address:* Hjort Lorenzensgade 6 4tv, 2200 Copenhagen N, Denmark.

NEIL, Simon Alexander; British singer, songwriter and musician (guitar); b. 31 Aug. 1979, Irvine, Scotland; m. Francesca Neil 2008. *Education:* Univ. of Glasgow. *Career:* Founder-mem. Biffy Clyro (initially called Screwfish) 1995–; signed to Beggars Banquet Records 2001, numerous tours; mem. Marmaduke Duke 2005–. *Recordings:* albums: with Biffy Clyro: Blackened Sky 2002, The Vertigo of Bliss 2003, Infinity Land 2004, Puzzle 2007, Only Revolutions 2009, Opposites (Kerrang! Award for Best Album 2013, Q Magazine Award for Best Album 2013) 2013; with Marmaduke Duke: The Magnificent Duke 2005, Duke Pandemonium 2009. *Honours:* with Biffy Clyro: Kerrang! Awards for Best Music Video (for The Captain) 2010, for Classic Songwriter 2011, NME Awards for Best Music Video (for The Captain) 2010, for Best Live Band 2011, for Best British Band 2013, Q Magazine Award for Best Live Band 2011. *Address:* c/o 14th Floor Records, Warner Music UK Limited, The Warner Building, 28a Kensington Church Street, London, W8 4EP, England (office). *Telephone:* (20) 7368-2500 (office). *Fax:* (20) 7368-2770 (office). *Website:* www .14thfloorrecords.com (office); www.wmg.com (office); biffyclyro.com.

NEIL, Vince; American singer; b. (Vincent Neil Wharton), 8 Feb. 1961, Hollywood, CA; m. 4th Lia Gerardini 2005. *Career:* fmr mem. and lead singer, Rock Candy; mem. heavy rock group, Mötley Crüe 1981–92, reformed 2005–; solo artist 1992–. *Film appearance:* The Adventures of Ford Fairlane 1990. *Recordings include:* albums: with Mötley Crüe: Too Fast For Love 1981, Shout At The Devil 1983, Theatre Of Pain 1985, Girls, Girls, Girls 1987, Dr Feelgood 1989, Decade of Decadence (American Music Award for Favorite Heavy Metal Album) 1991, Mötley Crüe 1994, Generation Swine 1997, Live: Entertainment Or Death 1999, New Tattoo 2000, Red, White & Crüe 2005, Saints of Los Angeles 2008; solo: Exposed 1993, Carved In Stone 1995, Live At The Whisky: One Night Only 2003, Tattoos & Tequila 2010. *Publication:* The Dirt: Confessions of the World's Most Notorious Rock Band (with Mötley Crüe) 2001, Tattoos & Tequila (with Mike Sager) 2010. *Honours:* Rolling Stone Best Heavy Metal Band 1991. *Website:* www.motley.com; www.vinceneil.net.

NELLY; American singer and musician; b. (Cornell Haynes Jr), Austin, TX. *Career:* founder mem., St Lunatics 1993–; solo artist 1999–; signed to Universal Records; official clothing line, Vokal; film appearance, Snipes 2002. *Film appearance:* The Longest Yard 2005. *Recordings:* albums: with St Lunatics: Free City 2001; solo: Country Grammar 2000, Nellyville 2002, Sweat 2004, Suit 2004, Brass Knuckles 2008, 5.0 2010, M.O. 2013. *Honours:* two Source Awards, MTV Video Music Award, Soul Train Award, American Music Awards for Favorite Rap/Hip Hop Artist 2002, Fans' Choice Artist 2003, Billboard Music Award for Top Country Song (for Cruise) (with Florida Georgia Line) 2014. *Address:* c/o Universal Music Group, Universal Studios, 100 Universal City Plaza, Universal City, CA 91608, USA. *Website:* www.nelly .net.

NELSON, Bonita (Bonnie) Rae; American singer (country and Christian music); *President, Firestorm Ministries International;* b. 11 April 1949, Denver, Colo. *Education:* Douglas Co. High School, Castle Rock. *Career:* ordained minister; spokeswoman for International Harvester for 12 years; Ralph Emery Radio Show, Tenn Network Show, Nashville Now, German ZDE TV Special; Centecor Drug Programme; Donna Fargo Special; Girl in My Life, TV; NBC 's Real People; teacher and praise and worship leader, Christian Prophetic Worship; Pres. FireStorm Ministries Int. *Recordings:* 13 albums, 16 singles, seven videos, one movie. *Publications:* It's Not Luck, It's God 1998, Women In The Church, The Cremation Issue Revealed, I'm Not Wild About Harry, The 10 Plagues of Egypt. *Honours:* Entertainer and Female Vocalist, Colorado and New York, State Country Music Asscn . *Address:* PO Box 25050, Nashville, TN 37202, USA (office). *Telephone:* (615) 562-2790 (office). *E-mail:* bonnienelp@aol.com (office). *Website:* www.FirestormMinistry.com.

NELSON, Matthew Edward; British singer and songwriter; b. 20 March 1968, Colne, England. *Education:* Manchester Polytechnic. *Career:* lead singer with Milltown Brothers, with television appearances, tours of Britain, USA, Europe and Japan, and appearing at various British festivals; mem. PRS. *Compositions:* wrote songs for the BBC TV series, All Quiet on the Preston Front. *Recordings include:* albums: Slinky, 1991; Valve, 1993; The Best Of, 1997.

NELSON, Shara; British singer and songwriter; b. London. *Career:* singer, Massive Attack; solo artist. *Recordings include:* albums: with Massive Attack: Blue Lines 1991; solo: What Silence Knows 1993, Down That Road 1994,

Friendly Fire 1995. *Current Management:* Def Mix Productions, 938 Broadway, Suite 400, New York, NY 10010, USA. *E-mail:* info@sharanelson.com (home). *Website:* www.sharanelson.com (home).

NELSON, Tracy; American singer and musician; b. 27 Dec. 1944, Madison, WI. *Education:* college. *Career:* lead singer, Mother Earth 1968–73; solo artist 1965–. *Recordings include:* albums: with Mother Earth: Living With The Animals, 1968; Make A Joyful Noise, 1969; Mother Earth Presents – Tracy Nelson Country, 1970; Satisfied, 1970; Bring Me Home, 1971; Tracy Nelson / Mother Earth, 1972; Poor Man's Paradise, 1973; solo: Deep Are The Roots, 1965; Tracy Nelson, 1974; Sweet Soul Music, 1975; Time Is On My Side, 1976; Doin' It My Way, 1978; Homemade Songs, 1978; Come See About Me, 1980; In The Here and Now, 1993; I Feel So Good, 1995; Move On, 1996; Tracy Nelson Country, 1996; The Best of Tracy Nelson/Mother Earth, 1996; Ebony And Irony, 2001, Victim of the Blues 2011. *Honours:* Nashville Music Award for Best Blues Album 1996. *Current Management:* Julie Devereux, Lucks Management, 817 18th Avenue S, Nashville, TN 37203; Ronnie Narmour, RNA, PO Box 19289, Austin, TX 78760, USA. *Website:* www.tracynelson.com.

NELSON, Trevor, MBE; British DJ; b. 7 Jan. 1964, London; two c. *Career:* founder, Madhatter sound system; DJ, Kiss FM Radio, London, later dir; DJ, Soul II Soul session, Africa Centre, later co-established Soul II Soul shop, London; Head of A&R, EMI's Cooltempo label 1993–98; joined BBC Radio 1 1996, presenting Rhythm Nation 1996, R&B Chart 1997, 1Xtra Breakfast Show 2007, Soul Show, BBC Radio 2 2008–; Club DJ, sessions all over Europe; presenter, The Lick, MTV 1998–; presenter, nfluk, Channel 5 2009–. *Honours:* MOBO Awards for Best DJ 1999, for Best Radio DJ 2008, 2009. *Address:* BBC 1Xtra, Broadcasting House, London, W1A 1AA, England (office). *E-mail:* trevor.nelson@bbc.co.uk (office). *Website:* www.bbc.co.uk/radio1/trevornelson (office); www.trevornelson.com (home).

NELSON, Willie Hugh; American country and western singer, musician and songwriter; b. 30 April 1933, Abbott, Tex.; m. Annie Marie Nelson; three s. four d. *Education:* Baylor Univ. *Career:* fmr salesman, announcer, host and DJ, country music shows in Tex.; bass player, Ray Price's band; formed own band; appearances at Grand Ole Opry, Nashville and throughout USA 1964–; tours to NZ, Australia, USA, Canada, Europe, Japan; annual Fourth of July picnics throughout USA 1972–; performed with Frank Sinatra, Neil Young, Dolly Parton, Linda Ronstadt, ZZ Top, Waylon Jennings, Ray Charles, Santana, Joni Mitchell, Kris Kristofferson, Bob Dylan, Patsy Cline. *Film appearances:* Electric Horseman 1980, Honeysuckle Rose 1980. *Compositions include:* Crazy (performed by Patsy Cline), Hello Walls (performed by Faron Young). *Recordings include:* albums: The Sound In Your Mind 1976, The Troublemaker 1976, Willie Nelson And His Friends 1976, To Lefty From Willie 1977, Willie Before His Time 1978, Wanted/The Outlaw 1978, The Willie Way 1978, Stardust 1978, One For The Road 1979, Willie And Family Live 1979, Pretty Paper 1979, Willie Sings Kristofferson 1979, San Antonio Rose 1980, Honeysuckle Rose 1980, Family Bible 1980, Tougher Than Leather 1983, City Of New Orleans 1984, Me And Paul 1985, Highwayman 1985, The Promised Land 1986, Partners 1986, Island In The Sea 1987, Seashores Of Old Mexico 1987, What A Wonderful World 1988, A Horse Called Music 1989, Highwayman II 1990, Born For Trouble 1990, Clean Shirt Waylon And Willie 1991, Across The Borderline 1993, Six Hours At Pedernales 1994, Healing Hands Of Time 1994, Just One Love 1995, Spirit 1996, How Great Thou Art 1996, Christmas With Willie Nelson 1997, Hill Country Christmas 1997, Teatro 1998, Nashville Was The Roughest 1998, Night And Day 1999, Forever Gold 2000, Me And The Drummer 2000, Milk Cow Blues 2000, Rainbow Connection 2001, Joy 2001, The Great Divide 2002, All The Songs I've Loved Before 2002, Crazy: The Demo Sessions 2003, Picture In A Frame (with Kimmie Rhodes) 2003, It Always Will Be 2004, Countryman 2005, Songbird 2006, Last Of The Breed (with Merle Haggard and Ray Price) 2007, Moment Of Forever 2008, Two Men With The Blues (with Wynton Marsalis) 2008, Willie And The Wheel (with Asleep at the Wheel) 2009, American Classic 2009, Country Music 2010, Remember Me Volume 1 2011, Heroes 2012, Let's Face the Music and Dance 2013, To All the Girls... 2013, Band of Brothers 2014, December Day 2014. *Honours:* six Grammy (NARAS) Awards, eight CMA Awards, Nashville Songwriters' Asscn Hall of Fame 1973, Nat. Acad. of Popular Music Lifetime Achievement Award 1983, three ACM Awards, Tex Ritter Songwriting Award (with Kris Kristofferson) 1984. *Current Management:* c/o Mark Rothbaum and Associates Inc., PO Box 2689, Danbury, CT 06813-2689, USA. *Telephone:* (203) 792-2400. *Address:* 12400 St Hwy 71 West, Suite 350, Austin, TX 78738, USA. *E-mail:* info@willienelson.com. *Website:* www.willienelson.com.

NERGAARD, Silje; Norwegian jazz singer and songwriter. *Career:* performances world-wide, including the North Sea and Montreal Jazz Festivals, the Edinburgh Festival 2004. *Recordings:* albums: Tell Me Where You're Going 1990, Silje 1991, Cow on the Highway 1995, Brevet 1995, Huemmefra, Port of Call 2000, At First Light 2001, Nightwatch 2003, Darkness Out of Blue 2007. *Honours:* Spellemannspris Artist of the Year 2004. *Current Management:* c/o Pernille Torp-Hoite, Unit AS, Eilert Sundsgate 14, 0259 Oslo, Norway. *Telephone:* 22-12-90-50. *Fax:* 22-12-90-51. *E-mail:* pernille@unit.nu. *Website:* www.unit.nu; www.siljenergaard.com.

NESMITH, (Robert) Michael (Mike); American singer, songwriter, musician (guitar) and actor; b. 30 Dec. 1942, Houston, TX. *Career:* mem. of folk duo, Mike and John (with John London) 1965; mem., The Monkees 1966–69; founder mem., First National Band 1970, re-formed as Second National Band

1972; founder and Pres. of own Countryside and Pacific Arts Corporation record label 1974; financed and produced films Repo Man, Elephant Parts, Time Rider. *Television as actor:* The Monkees (series) 1966–68, 33 1/3 Revolutions per Monkee (NBC special). *Recordings include:* albums: with the Monkees: The Monkees 1966; More of The Monkees 1967; Headquarters 1967; Pisces, Aquarius, Capricorn and Jones Ltd 1967; The Birds, The Bees and The Monkees, 1968; Head (soundtrack), 1969; The Monkees Present, 1969; solo: The Wichita Train Whistle Sings, 1968; Magnetic South, 1970; Treason, 1972; And The Hits Just Keep On Comin', 1972; Pretty Much Your Standard Ranch Hash, 1973; The Prison, 1974; From A Radio Engine To The Photon Wing, 1977; Live At The Palais, 1978; Infinite Rider On The Big Dogma, 1979; Tropical Campfires, 1992; The Garden, 1994; Listen To The Band, 1997; Timerider–The Adventures Of Lyle Swann, 2000, Rays 2005. *Publication:* The Prison 1974. *Honours:* NARM Award for Best Selling Group, for Best Album 1967, Emmy Award for Outstanding Comedy Series 1967, three BMI Awards 1968, Grammy Award (for video Elephant Parts) 1982. *Website:* www .videoranch.com.

NESTOROVIC, Sascha; Croatian musician (saxophone), composer and arranger; b. 27 Aug. 1964, Zagreb; m. Vlasta Gyrura 1993. *Education:* Zagreb Academy of Music. *Career:* first alto in big band, Croatian State Television; live concerts with Zagreb Saxophone Quartet, Muscora, Paris; World Saxophone Congress, Pesaro, Italy; tours with Zagreb Jazz Portrait to Germany, Austria, Italy, France; mem. Croatian Musicians' Union, Jazz Club Zagreb. *Recordings:* with Zagreb Saxophone Quartet: Croatian Contemporary Music for Saxophones; Zagreb 900; with Slovenian RTV Big Band: Peter Herbolzheimer; Moments Notice, Zagreb Jazz Portrait. *Honours:* classical awards: Darko Lukic; Milka Trnina. *Address:* Sascha Nestorovic, Kustossijanska 316, 10000 Zagreb, Croatia.

NETO, José Pires de Almeida; Brazilian musician (electric guitar); b. 1954, São Paulo; m. Flora Purim. *Career:* musical dir for Harry Belafonte 1972–92; mem., Fourth World; founder mem., Netoband; collaborations with Tony Bird, Suzanne Ciani, Paquito D'Rivera, Jorge Dalto, Madala Kunene, Tania Maria, Airto Moreira, Flora Purim, Filó Machado. *Recordings include:* albums: with Fourth World: Fourth World 1992, Encounters of the Fourth World 1995, Last Journey 1999; solo: Mountains And The Sea 1986, Neto 1993, In Memory Of Thunder 1996, Live At Guiting Power 1998, 7th Wave: The Lucky One 2000, About Time (with Steve Winwood) 2003, Lua's Dance 2004. *Address:* c/o Robert Trunz, Melt 2000 Records (office). *E-mail:* robert@melt.co.za (office). *Website:* www.melt2000.com (office).

NETTLES, Jennifer Odessa; American country music singer, songwriter and musician (guitar, percussion, keyboards, harmonica); b. 12 Sept. 1974, Douglas, GA; m. 1st Todd Van Sickle 1998 (divorced); m. 2nd Justin Miller 2011. *Education:* Agnes Scott College. *Career:* fmr mem. Soul Miner's Daughter 1995–98; fmr mem. Jennifer Nettles Band 1998–2002; mem. and singer Sugarland 2002–, toured with Brad Paisley 2005, Kenny Chesney 2006–07, Keith Urban 2009; guest appearance on Bon Jovi single Who Says You Can't Go Home 2006; launched Common Thread charity music events 2008; guest appearance on USA for Haiti charity single We Are the World 25 for Haiti 2010. *Television:* Country Music Awards Country Christmas (host and performer) 2010, Duets (regular mentor) 2012–. *Recordings include:* albums: with Soul Miner's Daughter: The Sacred and Profane 1996, Hallelujah 1998; with Jennifer Nettles Band: Story of Your Bones 2000, Gravity: Drag Me Down 2002, Rewind 2002; with Sugarland: Twice the Speed of Life 2004, Enjoy the Ride 2006, Love on the Inside 2008, Gold and Green 2009, The Incredible Machine 2010. *Honours:* with Soul Miner's Daughter: Lilith Fair Acoustic Talent Search Winner 1999; with Sugarland: American Music Award for Favorite Breakthrough Artist 2005, Country Music Television Awards for Collaborative Video of the Year 2006, for Duo Video of the Year 2011, Country Music Association Awards for Vocal Duo of the Year 2007, 2008, 2011, Grammy Awards for Best Collaboration (with Bon Jovi) 2007, for Best Country Song 2009, for Best Country Performance by a Duo or Group 2009, Academy of Country Music Awards for Song of the Year 2008, Milestone Award 2009, for Vocal Duo of the Year 2009, 2011. *Current Management:* c/o Gail Gellman Management, 22917 Pacific Coast Highway, Suite 920, Malibu, CA 90265-4879, USA. *E-mail:* gail@gellmanmgmt.com. *Website:* www .gellmanmgmt.com. *Address:* c/o Mercury Nashville, Universal Music Group, 2220 Colorado Avenue, Santa Monica, CA 90265-4879, USA (office). *Website:* www.sugarlandmusic.com; www.jennifernettles.com.

NETTLETON, Christopher; singer, songwriter, composer and musician (guitar, keyboards); b. 25 Sept. 1968, Cardiff, Wales. *Education:* studied piano. *Career:* played with Hollyweird 1989–92, The Nubiles 1993–98; toured UK 1994–97; mem. Musicians' Union, PRS. *Recordings:* Mindblower, album; Layabout/Mother and Father; Without Waking; Tatjana; Kunta Kinté; Layabout vs Mindblower. *Address:* c/o 5 Clare Court, Lime Street, Bedford MK40 1NH, England.

NEUFELD, Sarah; Canadian musician (violin); b. 27 Aug. 1979. *Career:* mem. Arcade Fire 2003–, The Luyas 2009–. *Recordings include:* with Arcade Fire: Funeral 2004, Neon Bible (Juno Award for Alternative Album of the Year 2008) 2007, The Suburbs (Grammy Award for Album of the Year 2011) 2010, Reflektor 2013; with The Luyas: Too Beautiful to Work 2011, Animator 2012; solo album: Hero Brother 2013. *E-mail:* contact@estuaryartists.com. *Website:* www.sarahneufeldmusic.com; www.arcadefire.com.

NEUMANN, Bob, BSc; American producer, engineer, musician (keyboards), electronic music composer and synthesist; b. Chicago, Illinois; m. Carolyn 1992; one s. one d. *Career:* 25 years' performance experience, Chicago area pop bands; 18 years recording, composition; Owner, Project Studio, Lemont, Illinois; mem, EARS Society, Chicago BMI. *Recordings:* three albums, one dance single released on independent labels. *Honours:* Discoveries Column Alumni, State Fair, Illinois Awards.

NEUWIRTH, Olga, MA; Austrian composer; b. 4 Aug. 1968, Graz. *Education:* Conservatory of Music, San Francisco, USA, Vienna Acad. of Music and Performing Arts, Electroacoustic Inst., studied composition under Erich Urbanner, Elinor Armer, Adriana Hölszky, Tristan Murail and Luigi Nono; studied music technology at IRCAM, Paris. *Career:* jury mem. Munich Biennale 1994; mem. Composers' Forum, Darmstadt Summer School; Composer-in-Residence, Royal Philharmonic Orchestra of Flanders, Antwerp, Belgium 2000, Lucerne Festival 2002; mem. Acad. of the Arts, Berlin 2006. *Radio music:* Punch & Judy 1994. *Theatre music:* Ein Sportstück 1997, Abenteuer in Sachen Haut 2000, Virus 2000, Ein Sommernachtstraum 2000, Totenauberg 2001, Philoktet 2002, Lost Highway 2003, Der jüngste Tag 2004. *Film score:* The Long Rain 1999, Das Vaterspiel 2009. *Compositions include:* Locus... doublure... solos 2001, Ecstaloop 2001, Torsion: transparent variation 2001, Verfremdung/Entfremdung 2002, Lost Highway 2003, ...ce qui arrive... 2004, ...miramondo multiplo... (trumpet concerto) 2006, Remnants of Songs... an Amphigory (viola concerto) 2009. *Recordings include:* Vexierbilder 1993, Loncera Caprifolium 1993, Sans Soleil 1994, Five Daily Miniatures 1994, Spleen 1994, Vampyrotheone 1995, Akroate Hadal 1995, Risonanze! 1996, Pallas/Construction 1996, Hooloomooloo 1996, Bählamms Fest 1997, Photophorus 1997, Todesraten 1997, Nova/Minraud 1998, Hommage à Klaus Nomi 1998, Ad auras... in memoriam H 1999, Settori 1999, Morphologische Fragmente 1999, Clinamen/Nodus 1999, The Long Rain 2000, Construction in Space 2000, Inciendo/fluido 2000, Settori, Quasare/ Pulsare, Neuwirth Music for Films 2009. *Honours:* Publicity Prize, austro mechana 1994, Ernst von Siemens Foundation Composers Prize, Munich, Hindemith Prize, Schleswig-Holstein Music Festival 1999, Ernst Krenek Prize 1999, Heidelberg Artist Prize 2008, Louis Spohr Music Prize, Braunschweig 2010, Österreichischer Staatspreis 2010. *Current Management:* c/o Frank Harders, Boosey & Hawkes, Bote & Bock GmbH, Lützowufer 26, 10787 Berlin, Germany. *Telephone:* (30) 25001300. *Fax:* (30) 25001399. *E-mail:* frank.harders@boosey.com. *Website:* www.boosey.com; www .olganeuwirth.com.

NEVILL, Brian Roy; British musician (drums, piano); *Music Consultant, Ace Records (London) Ltd;* b. 4 Jan. 1948, Wuppertal, Germany; divorced; remarried 2006. *Education:* Royal Soc. of Arts School Certificate. *Career:* numerous recording sessions and broadcasts with various artists, including Graham Parker, Flying Lizards, Kirsty MacColl, Shriekback, Virginia Astley; mem. Pigbag; worked in Brussels 1984–85; formed record label 1989; recorded and played with numerous American blues and rock 'n' roll artists 1992–98; lived and worked in USA as musician with Deke Dickerson, Big Sandy, the Collins Kids, Ray Campi, Sammy Masters and others; Music Consultant, Ace Records (London) Ltd 2001–; has compiled and annotated two dozen albums for BMG and Ace 1999–; still active as session player, including Holly Golightly, Duffy Power, Pete Molinari, Carlos Bandido, Joe Clay, Jamie Rowan; mem. PRS, Mechanical Copyright Protection Soc. *Television:* Top of the Pops, TOTP 2. *Recordings:* albums: Lend An Ear, Pigbag; The Best Of Pigbag; The BBC Sessions, Pigbag 1998; The Infinite, Shriekback; Blues and Stomps, Carl Sonny Leyland; The Panasonics; Eddie Angel's Guitar Party; Big Sixteen, Big Joe Louis and the Blues Kings; Laugh It Up, Holly Golightly, Number One Hit Record, Deke Dickerson; The Legend Is Now, Joe Clay. *Publications:* articles in Goldmine; sleeve notes to album Soul Classics, The Best of Bell; compiled and annotated 12 CDs by Elvis Presley for BMG 1999–2000, many CDs for Ace/Kent Records, London 2001–. *Address:* 6 Lancaster Lodge, 83–85 Lancaster Road, London, W11 1QH, England. *E-mail:* brianrnevill@googlemail.com (home); brian.nevill@acerecords.com (office). *Website:* acerecords.com (office).

NEVILLE, Aaron; American singer; b. 24 Jan. 1941, New Orleans, LA. *Career:* solo artist early 1960s–; mem., The Neville Brothers 1977–; numerous live appearances. *Recordings include:* with The Neville Brothers: Wild Tchoupitoulas 1976, The Neville Brothers 1977, Fiyo On The Bayou 1981, Nevillization 1984, Uptown 1987, Yellow Moon 1989, Brother's Keeper 1990, Family Groove 1992, Live on Planet Earth 1994, Mitakuye Oyasin Oyasin/All My Relations 1996, Valence Street 1999, Uptown Rulin' 1999, Valence Street 1999, Walkin' in the Shadow of Life 2004; solo: Orchid in the Storm 1986, Warm Your Heart 1991, Tell It Like It Is 1991, Aaron Neville's Soulful Christmas 1993, The Grand Tour 1993, The Tattooed Heart 1995, Doing It Their Way 1996, To Make Me Who I Am 1997, Devotion 2000, Gospel Roots 2003, Love Songs 2003, Nature Boy 2003, Christmas Prayer 2005, Bring It On Home 2006. *Honours:* Grammy Awards for Best Pop Vocal Group 1989, 1990, for Best Country and Western Vocal Collaboration (for I Fall to Pieces with Trisha Yearwood) 1994, Rolling Stone Critics Award for Best Band 1990, Downbeat Award for Best Blues/Soul/R&B Group 1990. *Current Management:* Elevation Group Inc, 1408 Encinal Avenue, Suite A, Alameda, CA 94501, USA. *Telephone:* (510) 864-2600. *Fax:* (510) 864-2615. *E-mail:* info@ elevationgroup.net. *Website:* www.elevationgroup.net; www.nevilles.com; www.aaronneville.com.

NEVILLE, Alaric James, BA; British sound engineer, record producer and musician (guitar); b. 28 July 1961, Derby. *Education:* Univ. of Leeds. *Career:* sound engineer to Oysterband, The Ukrainians; producer for artists, including Cud, Bridewell Taxis, The Ukrainians, Ringo's High, Lazer Boy, Oyster Band; mem, Musicians' Union.

NEVILLE, Art; American musician (piano) and singer; b. 17 Dec. 1937, New Orleans. *Career:* mem., The Neville Sound 1962–68, Art Neville and the Sounds 1967, renamed The Meters 1968–77; mem., The Neville Brothers 1977–; with the Meters worked with Dr John, Robert Palmer, Labelle; with the Neville Brothers numerous tours and live appearances. *Recordings:* albums: with the Meters: The Meters 1969, Look-Ka Py Py 1970, Struttin' 1970, Cabbage Alley 1972, Rejuvenation 1974, Fire On The Bayou 1975, Trick Bag 1976, New Directions 1977; with The Neville Brothers: Wild Tchoupitoulas 1976, The Neville Brothers 1977, Fiyo On The Bayou 1981, Nevillization 1984, Uptown 1987, Yellow Moon 1989, Brother's Keeper 1990, Family Groove 1992, Live on Planet Earth 1994, Mitakuye Oyasin Oyasin/All My Relations 1996, Valence Street 1999, Uptown Rulin' 1999, Valence Street 1999, Walkin' in the Shadow of Life 2004; solo: Mardi Gras Rock 'n' Roll 1987, That Old Time Rock 'n' Roll 1992, Art Neville – His Speciality Recordings 1956–58 1993. *Honours:* Grammy Awards for Best Pop Vocal Group 1989, 1990, Rolling Stone Critics Award for Best Band 1990, Downbeat Award for Best Blues/Soul/R&B Group 1990. *Current Management:* Elevation Group Inc, 1408 Encinal Avenue, Suite A, Alameda, CA 94501, USA. *Telephone:* (510) 864-2600. *Fax:* (510) 864-2615. *E-mail:* info@elevationgroup.net. *Website:* www.elevationgroup.net; www.nevilles.com.

NEVILLE, Charles; American musician (saxophone); b. 28 Dec. 1938, New Orleans. *Career:* toured USA with various blues players, including Jimmy Reed, Little Walter; played with Joey Dee and The Starliters 1962; mem., The Wild Tchoupitoulas 1976–77, The Neville Brothers 1977–; numerous live appearances. *Recordings:* with The Neville Brothers: Wild Tchoupitoulas 1976, The Neville Brothers 1977, Fiyo On The Bayou 1981, Nevillization 1984, Uptown 1987, Yellow Moon 1989, Brother's Keeper 1990, Family Groove 1992, Live on Planet Earth 1994, Mitakuye Oyasin Oyasin/All My Relations 1996, Valence Street 1999, Uptown Rulin' 1999, Valence Street 1999, Walkin' in the Shadow of Life 2004; solo: Charles Neville & Diversity 1991. *Honours:* Grammy Awards for Best Pop Vocal Group 1989, 1990, Rolling Stone Critics Award for Best Band 1990, Downbeat Award for Best Blues/Soul/R&B Group 1990. *Current Management:* Elevation Group Inc, 1408 Encinal Avenue, Suite A, Alameda, CA 94501, USA. *Telephone:* (510) 864-2600. *Fax:* (510) 864-2615. *E-mail:* info@elevationgroup.net. *Website:* www.elevationgroup.net; www.nevilles.com.

NEVILLE, Cyril; American singer and musician (percussion); b. 10 Jan. 1948, New Orleans; m. Gaynielle Neville. *Career:* mem., The Neville Sound 1962–68, Soul Machine 1968–75, The Meters 1975, The Wild Tchoupitoulas 1976, The Neville Brothers 1977–; numerous live appearances. *Recordings:* with The Neville Brothers: Wild Tchoupitoulas 1976, The Neville Brothers 1977, Fiyo On The Bayou 1981, Nevillization 1984, Uptown 1987, Yellow Moon 1989, Brother's Keeper 1990, Family Groove 1992, Live on Planet Earth 1994, Mitakuye Oyasin Oyasin/All My Relations 1996, Valence Street 1999, Uptown Rulin' 1999, Valence Street 1999, Walkin' in the Shadow of Life 2004; solo: The Fire This Time 1995, New Orleans Cookin' 2000, Soulo 2000, Brand New Blues 2009. *Honours:* Grammy Awards for Best Pop Vocal Group 1989, 1990, Rolling Stone Critics Award for Best Band 1990, Downbeat Award for Best Blues/Soul/R&B Group 1990. *Current Management:* Elevation Group Inc, 1408 Encinal Avenue, Suite A, Alameda, CA 94501, USA. *Telephone:* (510) 864-2600. *Fax:* (510) 864-2615. *E-mail:* info@elevationgroup.net. *Website:* www.elevationgroup.net; www.nevilles.com.

NEW ELECTRO SOUND OF LONDON (see Pilgrem, Rennie)

NEWCOMER, Carrie Ann; American singer, musician (guitar, dulcimer) and songwriter; b. 25 May 1958, Dawajack, MI. *Education:* studied the flute as a child. *Career:* singer-songwriter who uses folk country, jazz and blues influences; began playing guitar at around aged 14; played dulcimer and was lead vocalist and songwriter in folk trio, Stone Soup 1981–87; solo artist 1991–; toured regularly and made appearances at events such as Newport folk festival. *Recordings include:* with Stone Soup: Long Fields 1984, October Nights 1987; solo: Visions and Dreams 1991, An Angel at my Shoulder 1994, The Bird on the Wing 1995, My Father's Only Son 1996, My True Name 1998, The Age of Possibility 2000, The Gathering of Spirits 2002, Betty's Diner 2004, Regulars and Refugees 2005, Wilderness Plots 2007, The Geography of Light 2008. *Current Management:* Meltus Gelbert Rose, 47 South Meridian Street, Suite 400, Indianapolis, IN 46204, USA. *Telephone:* (317) 464-5366. *Fax:* (317) 464-5111. *E-mail:* ealexander@mgrfirm.com. *Website:* www.mgrfirm.com. *E-mail:* info@carrienewcomer.com (office). *Website:* www.carrienewcomer.com.

NEWMAN, David; American composer, musician (violin) and conductor; b. 11 March 1954, Los Angeles, CA. *Education:* classically trained. *Career:* mem. BMI. *Compositions:* For film: Frankenweenie, 1984; Vendetta, 1986; The Kindred, 1986; Critters, 1986; Throw Momma from the Train, 1987; My Demon Lover, 1987; Malone, 1987; The Brave Little Toaster, 1987; The War of the Roses, 1989; R.O.T.O.R., 1989; Little Monsters, 1989; Heathers, 1989; Gross Anatomy, 1989; Disorganized Crime, 1989; Bill & Ted's Excellent Adventure, 1989; The Runestone, 1990; Mr Destiny, 1990; Madhouse, 1990; Fire Birds, 1990; DuckTales: The Movie–Treasure of the Lost Lamp, 1990; The

Freshman, 1990; Talent for the Game, 1991; Rover Dangerfield, 1991; Paradise, 1991; Don't Tell Mom the Babysitter's Dead, 1991; Bill & Ted's Bogus Journey, 1991; The Marrying Man, 1991; Other People's Money, 1991; That Night, 1992; The Itsy Bitsy Spider, 1992; The Mighty Ducks, 1992; Honeymoon in Vegas, 1992; Hoffa, 1992; Undercover Blues, 1993; The Sandlot, 1993; Coneheads, 1993; The Flintstones, 1994; The Air Up There, 1994; My Father the Hero, 1994; The Cowboy Way, 1994; I Love Trouble, 1994; Boys on the Side, 1995; Tommy Boy, 1995; Operation Dumbo Drop, 1995; Jingle All the Way, 1996; Big Bully, 1996; The Phantom, 1996; The Nutty Professor, 1996; Matilda, 1996; Out to Sea, 1997; Anastasia, 1997; Never Been Kissed, 1999; Bowfinger, 1999; Brokedown Palace, 1999; Galaxy Quest, 1999; The Flintstones in Viva Rock Vegas, 2000; Duets, 2000; The Nutty Professor II: The Klumps, 2000; Bedazzled, 2000; 102 Dalmatians, 2000; Dr Dolittle 2, 2001; The Affair of the Necklace, 2001; Death to Smoochy, 2002, Welcome Home Roscoe Jenkins 2007. *Honours:* Emmy Award, for The Young Indiana Jones Chronicles: The Scandal of 1920. *Current Management:* Blue Focus Management, 15233 Ventura Blvd, Suite 200, Sherman Oaks, CA 91403, USA.

NEWMAN, Randy; American singer, songwriter, musician (piano) and arranger; b. 28 Nov. 1943, Los Angeles, Calif.; m. Gretchen Newman; one d. *Education:* Univ. of California, Los Angeles. *Career:* staff songwriter, Metric Music 1962; numerous concerts and festival appearances; mem. The American Soc. of Composers, Authors and Publrs (ASCAP). *Compositions include:* They Tell Me It's Summer, The Fleetwoods; I Don't Want To Hear It Anymore, Jerry Butler; I've Been Wrong Before, Cilla Black; Simon Smith and His Amazing Dancing Bear, Alan Price; Nobody Needs Your Love and Just One Smile, Gene Pitney; Mama Told Me (Not To Come), Three Dog Night; I Think It's Going To Rain Today (also recorded by UB40); I Love L.A. (used to promote 1984 Olympic Games); songs also recorded by artistes including Judy Collins; Harry Nilsson; Manfred Mann; Frankie Laine; Jackie DeShannon; Walker Brothers; as arranger: Is That All There Is?, Peggy Lee; for film: Cold Turkey 1971, Ragtime 1981, The Natural (Grammy Award for Best Instrumental Composition 1985) 1984, Three Amigos! (also script writer) 1986, Parenthood 1989, Awakenings 1990, Avalon 1990, The Paper 1994, Maverick 1994, Toy Story (Annie Award 1996) 1995, James and the Giant Peach 1996, Michael 1996, Cats Don't Dance (Annie Award 1997) 1997, Pleasantville 1998, A Bug's Life (Grammy Award for Best Instrumental Composition 2000) 1998, Toy Story 2 (Grammy Award for Best Song for Motion Picture (for When She Loved Me) 2001, Annie Award 2000) 1999, Meet the Parents 2000, Monsters, Inc. (Academy Award for Best Original Song (for I Didn't Have You) 2002) 2001, Seabiscuit 2003, Meet the Fockers 2004, Cars (Grammy Award for Best Song for Motion Picture (for Cars) 2007, Annie Award 2007) 2006, Leatherheads 2008, The Princess and the Frog 2009, Toy Story 3 (Academy Award for Best Original Song (for We Belong Together) 2011, Grammy Award for Best Score Soundtrack Album 2011) 2010, Monsters University 2013; for television: The Marshall Chronicles 1990, Cop Rock (ABC TV) (Emmy Award for Achievement in Music and Lyrics 1991) 1991, Monk (series) (Emmy Awards (for It's a Jungle Out There (theme song) 2004, When I'm Gone 2010) 2003–09. *Recordings include:* albums: Randy Newman 1968, Twelve Songs 1970, Randy Newman Live 1971, Good Old Boys 1974, Little Criminals 1978, Born Again 1979, Trouble in Paradise 1983, Lonely at the Top 1987, Land of Dreams 1988, Music from the Motion Picture The Paper 1994, Faust 1995, Bad Love 1999, The Randy Newman Songbook Vol. I 2003, Harps and Angels 2008. *Honours:* Frederick Loewe Award 2001, Ivor Novello Award 2013. *Current Management:* Gorfaine/Schwartz Agency Inc., 4111 West Alameda Avenue, Suite 509, Burbank, CA 91505, USA. *Telephone:* (818) 260-8500. *Website:* www.gsamusic.com; www.randynewman.com.

NEWMAN, Thomas Montgomery, MMus; American composer; b. 29 Oct. 1955, Los Angeles, Calif.; s. of Alfred Newman; m. Ann Marie Zirbes; three c. *Education:* Univ. of Southern California, Yale Univ. *Career:* mem. Broadcast Music, Inc. *Compositions for film:* Summer's End 1984, Reckless 1984, Revenge of the Nerds 1984, Grandview, USA 1984, Desperately Seeking Susan 1985, Girls Just Want to Have Fun 1985, The Man with One Red Shoe 1985, Real Genius 1985, Gung Ho 1986, Jumpin' Jack Flash 1986, Light of Day 1987, The Lost Boys 1987, Less Than Zero 1987, The Great Outdoors 1988, The Prince of Pennsylvania 1988, Cookie 1989, Men Don't Leave 1990, Welcome Home, Roxy Carmichael 1990, Career Opportunities 1991, Naked Tango 1991, The Rapture 1991, Deceived 1991, The Linguini Incident 1991, Fried Green Tomatoes 1991, The Player 1992, Whispers in the Dark 1992, Scent of a Woman 1992, Flesh and Bone 1993, Josh and S.A.M. 1993, Threesome 1994, The Favor 1994, Corrina, Corrina 1994, The Shawshank Redemption 1994, The War 1994, Little Women 1994, Unstrung Heroes 1995, How to Make an American Quilt 1995, Up Close & Personal 1996, Phenomenon 1996, American Buffalo 1996, The People vs Larry Flynt 1996, Mad City 1997, Red Corner 1997, Oscar and Lucinda 1997, The Horse Whisperer 1998, Meet Joe Black 1998, American Beauty (Grammy Award, BAFTA 2000) 1999, The Green Mile 1999, Erin Brockovich 2000, My Khmer Heart 2000, Pay It Forward 2000, In the Bedroom 2001, The Execution of Wanda Jean 2002, The Salton Sea 2002, Road to Perdition 2002, White Oleander 2002, Finding Nemo 2003, Lemony Snicket's A Series of Unfortunate Events 2004, Cinderella Man 2005, Jarhead 2005, Little Children 2006, The Good German 2006, Nothing is Private 2007, Wall-E 2008, Revolutionary Road 2009, Brothers 2009, The Debt 2010, Skyfall (BAFTA 2013, Grammy Award for Best Score Soundtrack for Visual Media 2014) 2012, Side Effects 2013, Saving Mr. Banks 2013. *Compositions for television:* The Paper Chase (series) 1978, The Seduction of

Gina (film) 1984, Amazing Stories (episode 'Santa 85') 1985, Heat Wave (film) 1990, Against the Law (series) 1990, Those Secrets (film) 1992, Citizen Cohn (film) 1992, Arli$$ (series) 1996, Boston Public (series theme) 2000, Six Feet Under (series theme) 2001, Angels in America (mini-series) 2003, Katedralen 1.z 2004, The Newsroom (series) 2012, Lauren (series) 2013. *Current Management:* c/o Gorfaine/Schwartz Agency Inc., 4111 West Alameda Avenue, Suite 509, Burbank, CA 91505, USA. *Telephone:* (818) 260-8500. *Website:* www.gsamusic.com.

NEWSOM, Joanna Caroline; American singer, songwriter and musician (harp, piano); b. 18 Jan. 1982, Nevada City, Calif.; m. Andy Samberg 2013. *Education:* Mills Coll., Calif. *Career:* toured with Will Oldham, Devendra Banhart; concerts worldwide, US tour performing with various orchestras, with London Symphony Orchestra, London 2007; collaborations and guest appearances include Golden Shoulders, The Pleased, Nervous Cop, Vetiver, Smog, Vashti Bunyan, RF & Lili De La Mora. *Recordings:* albums: The Milk-Eyed Mender 2004, Ys 2006, Have One on Me 2010, Divers 2015. *Current Management:* c/o David T. Viecelli, The Billions Corporation, 3522 West Armitage Avenue, Chicago, IL 60647, USA. *Telephone:* (312) 997-9999. *Fax:* (773) 278-3721. *E-mail:* boche@billions.com. *Website:* billions.com. *Address:* Drag City, POB 476867, Chicago, IL 60647, USA (office). *Telephone:* (312) 455-1015 (office). *E-mail:* press@dragcity.com (office). *Website:* www.dragcity.com (office); www.joanna-newsom.com.

NEWSTED, Jason; American musician (bass guitar); b. 4 March 1963, Battle Creek, MI. *Career:* fmr mem. heavy rock group, Flotsam and Jetsam; mem. heavy rock group, Metallica 1986–2001; numerous world-wide tours, television and radio appearances; mem. Echobrain 2002–04, band's exec. prod. 2004–; mem. Voivod 2003–09, Rock Star Supernova 2006–08; mem. AFofM San Francisco, ASCAP. *Recordings:* albums: with Flotsam and Jetsam: Flotsam and Jetsam 1986; with Metallica: …And Justice For All 1988, The Good, The Bad And The Live 1990, Metallica 1991, Load 1996, Reload 1997, Early Days 1997, S&M (live) 1999; with Echobrain: Echobrain 2002; with Voivod: Voivod 2003, Katorz 2006, Infini 2009. *Honours:* American Music Award for Favorite Heavy Metal Artist (with Metallica) 1993. *Current Management:* Echobrain, 454 Las Gallinas Avenue, Suite 353, San Rafael, CA 94903-3618, USA. *E-mail:* info@echobrain.com. *Website:* www.echobrain.com.

NEWTON, Colin; British musician (drums); b. 18 April 1977. *Career:* founder mem., Idlewild 1995–. *Recordings include:* albums: Captain 1998, Hope Is Important 1998, 100 Broken Windows 2001, The Remote Part 2002, Warnings/Promises 2005, Make Another World 2007, Scottish Fiction: Best of Idlewild 2007, Post Electric Blues 2009. *Current Management:* c/o Steve Nice, Nice Management, 2109 Cooley Place, Pasadena, CA 91104-4111, England. *Telephone:* (626) 345-9794. *E-mail:* steve@nicemgmt.com. *Website:* www .nicemgmt.com; www.idlewild.co.uk.

NEWTON, Robert Arthur William (Tad), BA; British jazz musician (trombone) and singer; b. 25 June 1946, Marlborough, Wiltshire, England; m. Anne Marie Newton 1969; two s. two d. *Education:* Univ. of Southampton. *Career:* bandleader, trombonist and singer, Tad Newton's Jazzfriends (seven-piece dixieland and mainstream jazz band); numerous concert appearances, festivals; mem. Musicians' Union. *Recordings include:* albums: Basin St To Harlem 1988, Drivin' 1989, Jumpin' For Joy 1991, Journey Thru' Jazz 1994, Jazz Portraits 1999. *Address:* 23 Windmill Avenue, Blisworth, Northamptonshire NN7 3EQ, England. *E-mail:* tadnewton@fsmail.net. *Website:* www .jazzbandsuk.com.

NEWTON, (Carson) Wayne; American entertainer, singer, musician (trumpet, piano, guitars, violin, drums, valve trombone), actor and writer; b. 3 April 1942, Norfolk, Va; m. Kathleen McCrone 1994; one d. *Career:* performances include over 30,000 solo shows in Las Vegas and USA tours; over 2,000 TV shows and films including The Lucy Show, Jackie Gleason, Roseanne, Full House; Chair. USO Celebrity Circle 2005; mem. American Federation of TV and Radio Artists, Screen Actors Guild, American Federation of Musicians. *Films include:* 80 Steps to Jonah 1969, North and South 1986, Licence to Kill 1989, The Adventures of Ford Fairlane 1990, The Dark Backward 1991, Best of the Best 2 1993, Night of the Running Man 1995, Vegas Vacation 1997, Ocean's Eleven 2001, Who's Your Daddy? 2003, Elvis Has Left the Building 2004, Smokin' Aces 2006, Ellen's Really Big Show 2007, The Hour 2008, Here's to Lucy 2009, Getting Back to Zero 2010, Hoodwinked Too! Hood vs. Evil (voice) 2011. *Recordings include:* Danke Schoen 1963, Red Roses For A Blue Lady 1965, The Letter, Daddy Don't You Walk So Fast 1972; 142 albums released, 300 singles. *Publication:* Once Before I Go (autobiography). *Honours:* Medal for Distinguished Public Service; Jimmie E. Howard Award, Gaming Hall of Fame 2000, Woodrow Wilson Award for Public Service 2008. . *Website:* www.waynenewton.com.

NEWTON-JOHN, Olivia, AO, OBE; British singer and actress; b. 26 Sept. 1948, Cambridge, England; d. of Brin Newton-John and Irene Born; m. Matt Lattanzi 1984; one d. *Career:* Co-owner Koala Blue 1982–; UNEP Goodwill Amb. 1989–. *Albums include:* If Not For You 1971, Let Me Be There (American Music Award for Favorite Country Album 1974) 1974, Music Makes My Day 1974, Long Live Love 1974, If You Love Me Let Me Know (No. 1, USA) 1974, Have You Never Been Mellow (American Music Award for Favorite Pop/Rock Album 1975) 1975, Clearly Love 1975, Come On Over 1976, Don't Stop Believin' 1976, Making A Good Thing Better 1977, Greatest Hits 1978, Grease (film soundtrack) (American Music Award for Favorite Pop/Rock Album 1978) 1978, Totally Hot 1979, Xanadu (film soundtrack) 1980, Physical 1981, 20

Greatest Hits 1982, Olivia's Greatest Hits Vol. 2 1983, Two Of A Kind 1984, Soul Kiss 1986, The Rumour 1988, Warm And Tender 1990, Back To Basics: The Essential Collection 1971–92 1992, Gaia – One Woman's Journey 1995, More Than Physical 1995, Greatest Hits 1996, Olivia 1998, Back With A Heart 1998, Highlights From The Main Event 1999, Greatest Hits: First Impressions 1999, Country Girl 1999, Best Of Olivia Newton John 1999, Love Songs: A Collection: One Woman's Live Journey 2000, Grace and Gratitude 2007, Christmas Collection 2010, Magic 2011, This Christmas 2012. *Films include:* Grease 1978, Xanadu 1980, Two of a Kind 1983, It's My Party 1995, Sordid Wives 1999, 1 a Minute (documentary) 2009, A Few Best Men 2012. *Television includes:* It's Cliff Richard (BBC series). *Publication:* LivWise: Easy Recipes for a Healthy, Happy Life 2011. *Honours:* Grammy Awards for Best Female Country Vocal Performance 1973, for Record of the Year 1974, for Best Female Pop Vocal Performance 1974, American Music Awards for Favorite Female Country Artist 1974, 1975, for Favorite Female Pop/Rock Artist 1974, 1975, 1976, 1982, Humanitarian Award, US Red Cross 1999, People's Choice Awards, Medal of the Order of Australia 2010 and numerous other awards. *Current Management:* c/o Fitzgerald Hartley Co., 34 North Palm Avenue, Suite 100, Ventura, CA 93001, USA. *Website:* www.olivianewton-john.com.

NGUYA-TRASA, Papy; musician (guitar) and singer; b. 6 March 1973, Bas-Congo. *Education:* College of Arts. *Career:* appearances at Musical Festival of Africa 1996; musical research performance, 1997; Festival of Jazz, 1999; mem. Asscn of Research Music. *Recordings:* Owala, 1994; Gaby Kwambamba, 1995; Let Them Say, 1996. *Honours:* Medal of Flying Musician of China 1997.

NGWENYA, Moses; South African musician (keyboards, guitar, drums); b. Soweto. *Career:* mem., The Crocodiles; worked with Intombi Zesi Manje Manje; mem., The Young Brothers 1976, renamed Soul Brothers; producer with own Black Moses Productions. *Recordings include:* albums: Umshoza Wami, 1974; Isiphiwo, 1982; Xola, 1987; Jive Explosion, 1988; Impimpi, 1989; Isighebhezana, 1999; Induk' Enhle, 2001. *Honours:* FNB South African Music Award for Best Mbaqanga Performance. *Website:* www.gallo.co.za.

NÍ MHAONAIGH, Mairéad; Irish singer and musician (fiddle); b. 26 July 1959, Gaoth Dobhair, Co Donegal; m. 1st Frankie Kennedy (died 1994); m. 2nd Dermot Byrne. *Career:* founding mem., Ragairne; recorded for RTE and performed at numerous festivals; played in USA with Kennedy 1984–85; founding mem., Altan 1983–. *Television:* presenter, traditional music radio show The Long Note, series The Pure Drop, The Full Set 2008. *Recordings include:* albums: solo: Ceol Aduaidh (with Frankie Kennedy) 1983, Imeall; with Altan: Altan 1987, Horse With A Heart 1988, The Red Crow 1990, Harvest Storm 1992, Island Angel 1993, Blackwater 1996, Runaway Sunday 1997, Another Sky 2000, The Blue Idol 2002, Local Ground 2005. *Website:* www.altan.ie; www.mairead.ie.

NÍ RIAIN, Nóirín, DipPhil, BMus, MA, PhD; Irish singer, musician (various Indian drones), theologian and teacher; b. (Nora Mary Antoinette Ryan), 12 June 1951, Limerick; two s. *Education:* Univ. Coll., Cork, MIC, Univ. of Limerick. *Career:* performed at UN conferences in Costa Rica, Brazil, Denmark, Poland, India, People's Repub. of China; worked with John Cage; numerous worldwide TV and radio broadcasts; worked extensively in Cathedral of St John the Divine, New York; Artist-in-Residence, Co. Laois, Ireland 1999–2000, Co. Wexford 2004; currently a Dir of a Glenstal/MIC theology course entitled 'Liturgy and Life'; offers chant workshops in Glenstal Abbey both privately and sanctioned by Dept of Educ. for primary school teachers. *Recordings include:* Caoineadh Na Maighdine, Good People All, Vox De Nube, Soundings, Gregorian Chant Experience, Stór Amhrán, Darkest Midnight, Virgin's Lament, Biscantorat, A.M.E.N, Celtic Soul, Hearth Songs 2013. *Publications include:* Gregorian Chant Experience 1999, Stór Amhrán 2008, Listen With the Ear of the Heart: An Autobiography 2009, Theosony: A Theology of Listening 2011. *Honours:* Millenium Scholarship, Univ. of Limerick 2000. *Address:* Glenstal Abbey, Murroe, Co. Limerick, Ireland. *Telephone:* (61) 621079; 86-8137040 (mobile). *E-mail:* nniriain@gmail.com. *Website:* ww.theosony.com.

NICALLS, Murdoc; musician (bass guitar). *Career:* animated mem. of virtual band, Gorillaz 1998– (see creator and Musical Dir, Damon Albarn and creator and Visual Dir, Jamie Hewlett). *Website:* www.gorillaz.com.

NICHOLAS, Grant; British singer, songwriter and musician (guitar). *Career:* fmr mem., Temper Temper; founder mem., Reel, later renamed Feeder 1985–. *Recordings include:* albums: Polythene 1997, Yesterday Went Too Soon 1999, Echo Park 2001, Comfort In Sound 2002, Pushing The Senses 2005, Silent Cry 2008. *Address:* Feeder Central, PO Box 2539, London, W1A 3HZ, England. *E-mail:* info@feederweb.com. *Website:* www.feederweb.com.

NICHOLAS, Julian Conan, BA; British musician (saxophone) and composer; b. 13 Jan. 1965, London; m.; one d. *Education:* Univ. of York. *Career:* saxophonist with Loose Tubes 1989–91; own group, Mountain People 1989–98; toured Europe extensively 1989–98; lecturer and educationist, Bishop Otter Coll., West Sussex 1993–96; Access to Music 1992–98; launched first South Coast Jazz Festival Jan. 2015 with Claire Martin; mem. Mr Vertigo 1991–2005, Curious Paradise 2003–, eJazz, Carmina 1997–; mem. Musicians' Union, PRS. *Compositions:* Fools Gold (film score), Brinksmat Robbery (TV score, LWT) 1992. *Recordings include:* Mountain People, RS001, Square Groove, Food of Love, Transformations, Everything You Do To Me; with Carmina: Love Like Angels 2000, Curious Paradise 2004, Now! 2007, My Crescent City 2007. *Honours:* Brighton Festival Zap Award for Jazz 1989,

1991. *Address:* Hawthbush Farm, Gun Hill, Heathfield, TN21 0JY, England. *E-mail:* jnicholas126@gmail.com. *Website:* www.carmina.co.uk.

NICHOLLS, Alan (Al) Charles; British musician (saxophone) and arranger; b. 27 Feb. 1957, Wrexham, Wales. *Education:* City of Leeds Coll. of Music. *Career:* mem., Big Town Playboys 1987–91, 1999–; numerous tours, television appearances; mem., King Pleasure and The Biscuit Boys 1991–94; leader of own band, Blue Harlem 1996–; freelance musician, solo jazz performer in clubs and at festivals; mem. Musicians' Union, British Music Writers' Council. *Stage:* Elvis: The Musical (Prince of Wales Theatre, West End) 1996. *Recordings:* albums: Now Appearing, Big Town Playboys; Don't Mess With The Boogieman, Big Joe Duskin; Live At The Burnley Blues Festival, Champion Jack Dupree; The Full Flavour, Ray Gelato and The Giants; with King Pleasure and The Biscuit Boys: Live At Ronnie Scott's; with Blue Harlem: Hot News! 2001, Oooh! That Kiss! 2003, Uptown Swing 2006, Talk to Me 2007, I Dare You! 2008; solo: I'm Old Fashioned 2004. *Honours:* Hot News International Best Dep of the Year Award 1999. *E-mail:* al@alnicholls.co.uk (office). *Website:* www.blueharlem.co.uk.

NICHOLLS, William (Billy) Morris; British singer, songwriter and producer; b. 15 Feb. 1949, London; m. Anne Dupée; two s. one d. *Career:* songs recorded by Del Shannon, Pete Townshend, Leo Sayer, Long John Baldry, The Babies, The Outlaws, Roger Daltrey, Justin Hayward, Kiki Dee, Marilyn Martin, Jon Astley, Little Angels, Phil Manzanera, Ruby Turner, The Chieftains and Phil Collins; Musical Dir, The Who tour 1989, Pete Townshend's Psychoderelict tour 1993, Roger Daltrey's tour 1996–97; f. Southwest Records 1998. *Compositions include:* Can't Stop Loving You, Leo Sayer; Without Your Love, Roger Daltrey; Fake It, Pete Townshend; music for the McVicar film. *Recordings:* albums: solo: Would You Believe 1968, Love Songs 1974, White Horse 1977, Under One Banner 1990, Snapshot 2000, Penumbra Moon 2001, Still Entwined 2001, Forever's No Time At All 2005, Rosslyn Road 2008. *Website:* www.billynicholls.com.

NICHOLLS, Craig; Australian singer and musician (guitar); b. 1978. *Career:* founding mem., The Vines 1994–; numerous tours and festival appearances. *Recordings include:* albums: Highly Evolved 2002, Winning Days 2004, Vision Valley 2006, Melodia 2008. *Honours:* ARIA Award for Breakthrough Artist Single (for Get Free) 2002, NME Award for Best Single (for Get Free) 2003. *Current Management:* Winterman and Goldstein Management, PO Box 545, Newtown, NSW 2042, Australia. *Website:* www.thevines.com.

NICHOLS, Keith Charles, GGSM; British musician (piano, trombone) and arranger; b. 13 Feb. 1945, London, England; m. Eve Nichols 1976. *Education:* Guildhall School of Music. *Career:* mem. jazz-comedy band, Levity Lancers, seven years; regular ragtime concerts, South Bank, London as soloist and with small ensembles; mem., Richard Sudhalter's New Paul Whiteman Orchestra; formed Midnite Follies Orchestra 1977; freelance musician, performing throughout UK, Europe and USA; Lecturer in Jazz History, Royal Acad, of Music, Trinity Coll. of Music. *Recordings:* numerous solo albums; many albums as bandleader and sideman; album recreated music of Fletcher Henderson; album of rare Duke Ellington and Fats Waller pieces. *Honours:* Hon. ARAM 1998; Great British Jr Champion, Accordion 1960, BBC Jazz Heritage Award 2004. *E-mail:* jazz@keithnicholsjazz.co.uk (office). *Website:* www.keithnicholsjazz.co.uk.

NICKS, Stephanie (Stevie); American singer and songwriter; b. 26 May 1948, Phoenix, Ariz.; m. Kim Anderson 1983 (divorced 1984). *Career:* fmr mem. Fritz (with Lindsey Buckingham); mem. duo, Buckingham Nicks (with Lindsey Buckingham) 1971–74; mem. Fleetwood Mac 1975–93, 1997–; solo artist 1978–; numerous world-wide tours and concert appearances. *Recordings include:* albums: with Lindsey Buckingham: Buckingham Nicks 1973; with Fleetwood Mac: Fleetwood Mac 1975, Rumours (Billboard Award for Album of the Year 1977, American Music Award for Favorite Pop/Rock Album 1978, Grammy Award for Album of the Year 1978) 1977, Tusk 1979, Fleetwood Mac Live 1980, Mirage 1982, Tango In The Night 1987, Behind The Mask 1990, The Dance 1997, Say You Will 2003, Pious Bird Of Good Omen 2004; solo: Bella Donna 1981, The Wild Heart 1983, Rock A Little 1985, The Other Side Of The Mirror 1989, Street Angel 1994, Maybe Love Will Change Your Mind 1994, Trouble In Shangri-La 2001, The Divine 2001, The Soundstage Sessions 2009, In Your Dreams 2011, 24 Karat Gold 2014. *Honours:* American Music Award for Favorite Pop/Rock Group 1978, Billboard Award for Group of the Year 1977, BRIT Award for Outstanding Contribution 1998, Grammy Hall of Fame Award 2003. *Address:* PO Box 112083, Carrolton, TX 75011-2083, USA (office). *E-mail:* jk@nicksfix.com. *Website:* www.nicksfix.com.

NICOL, Ken, BA (Hons); British musician (guitar), writer and performer; b. 27 May 1951, Preston, Lancs., England. *Education:* Univ. of Central Lancashire. *Career:* performed as Nicol & Marsh and as Nicol & Marsh's Easy Street 1974–78; played lead guitar and recorded with Al Stewart; mem. Albion Band 1996–2001; lead guitarist, singer and writer with Steeleye Span 2002–10; performs as solo artist; mem. Musicians' Union, Performing Right Soc., Mechanical-Copyright Protection Soc., Performing Artists Media Rights Assen, Phonographic Performance Ltd (PPL). *Recordings:* with Nicol and Marsh: Nicol & Marsh's Easy Street 1974, Easy Street 1976, Under The Glass 1977, Nicol and Marsh 1978; with The Albion Band: Happy Accident 1998, Road Movies 2001; with Steeleye Span: They Called Her Babylon 2004, Bloody Men 2006, Cogs Wheels & Lovers 2009; solo albums: Living In A Spanish Town 1991, 2 Frets from the Blues 1994, Clean Feet – No Shoes 1997, The

Bridge 2001, 13 Reasons 2005, Tidings 2006, Initial Variations 2008, The Glass Chronicles 2012, Historic Events and Other Subjects 2012. *Publications:* blogs: On The Road 2009, The Glass Chronicles 2012. *E-mail:* jim@fofpromotions.org.uk. *Website:* www.friendsoffolk.org.uk. *Address:* MVS Sound, 298 Tag Lane, Preston, Lancs., PR2 3UY, England (office). *Telephone:* (1772) 510144 (office). *E-mail:* kennicol298@gmail.com (office). *Website:* kennicolmusic.com (office).

NICOL, Simon; British folk musician (guitar, keyboards); b. 13 Oct. 1950, Muswell Hill, London, England. *Career:* founder mem., Fairport Convention 1967–71, 1977–; founder mem., Albion Country Band 1971; numerous live appearances, tours and festivals; annual Fairport Convention reunion concerts from 1980. *Recordings include:* albums: with Fairport Convention: Fairport Convention, 1968; What We Did On Our Holidays, 1969; Unhalfbricking, 1969; Liege and Lief, 1970; Full House, 1970; Angel Delight, 1971; Babbacombe Lee, 1971; A Bonny Band Of Roses, 1977; Moat On The Ledge, 1982; The Best Of. . ., 1988; Red And Gold, 1989; Fairport Convention, 1990; Them Five Seasons, 1991; Jewel In The Crown, 1995; Old-New-Borrowed-Blue, 1996; Who Knows Where The Time Goes?, 1997; Encore, Encore, 1997; Fiddlestix 1970–84: The Best of Fairport Convention, 1998; Fairport Convention, Woodworm Years, 1998; Wood And The Wire, 2000; XXXV, 2002; Heyday: BBC Radio Sessions 1968–69, 2002; with Albion Country Band: Battle of The Field, 1976; Prospect Before Us, 1977; Rise Up Like The Sun, 1978; Albion River Hymn March, 1979; Light Shining Albino, 1984; Shuffle Off, 1984. *E-mail:* faircrop@aol.com. *Website:* www.fairportconvention.co.uk.

NICOLI, Eric Luciano, CBE, BSc; British business executive; b. 5 Aug. 1950, Pulham Market, Norfolk, England; s. of Virgilio Nicoli and Ida Nicoli; m. Rosalind West 1977; one s. one d. *Education:* Diss Grammar School, Norfolk, King's Coll. London. *Career:* worked briefly in market research, then various positions with Rowntree Marketing Dept 1972–80; Sr Marketing Controller Biscuit Div., United Biscuits 1980–81, Marketing Dir Biscuits 1981–84, and Confectionery 1982–84; UK Business Planning Dir 1984, Man. Dir UB Frozen Foods 1985, UB Brands 1986–89, apptd. to Bd of UB (Holdings) PLC 1989, CEO European Operations 1989–90, Group CEO United Biscuits (Holdings) PLC 1991–99, Acting Chair. 2001; Non-Exec. Dir EMI Group PLC 1993–99, Exec. Dir and Chair. 1999–2007, CEO Jan.–Aug. 2007; Deputy Chair. Business in the Community 1991–2003; Chair. (non-exec.) HMV Media Group PLC 2001–04, Tussauds Group Ltd 2001–, Vue Entertainment 2006–10, R&R Music 2008–, Wentworth Media and Arts 2013–; Chair. Per Cent Club 1993–, EMI Music Sound Foundation 2003–07; adviser, Nick Stewart and Assocs 2008–. *Honours:* Hon. degree (Brunel) 2011. *Address:* R&R Music Ltd, 2 Melville Street, Falkirk, FK1 1HZ, Scotland.

NICOLS, Maggie; British musician (piano, keyboards), singer, teacher and composer; b. 24 Feb. 1948, Edinburgh, Scotland; one d. *Education:* studied with Dennis Rose and John Stevens. *Career:* dancer, Windmill Theatre; sang with Great Bebop Pianist, Dennis Rose; joined innovator John Stevens' Spontaneous Music Ensemble; pioneer of vocal and instrumental music workshops, Oval House Theatre 1970–; joined Keith Tippett's Centipede, formed duo with Julie Tippett, co-founder, feminist improvising group; performed internationally at festivals, Moers Music Festival, Berlin Jazz Festival, Bath and Bracknell Jazz Festivals; radio broadcasts include Jazz in Britain; television appearances in Germany, Italy, France and Switzerland; mem. Musicians' Union, Equity, PRS, BAC&S, PAMRA. *Recordings include:* Sweet and S'ours; Les Diaboliques; Nevergreens; Cats Cradle.

NIEBLA, Salvador; Spanish musician (drums), producer and composer; b. 28 Dec. 1960, Ceuta, Spain. *Education:* Isaac Albeniz Conservatory (Girona), Drummer Collective (New York), Taller de Musics (Barcelona). *Career:* Spanish TV shows with Big Bands (TV 1, TV 2, TV 3); session master with more of 150 recordings; producer of first online school for drummers, Virtual Drummer School 2001; composer for film and for Spanish Olympic Swimming Team 2001–; masterclasses in schools and conservatories; mem. SGAE, AIE (counsellor), AMSC, APE, Drummer Collective (delegate). *Recordings:* over 150 albums of jazz, rock, flamenco, fusion, etc. with J. Manel Serrat, Max Sunyer Trio, Deborah Carter, Paquito De Ribera, Didier Lockwood, Sabandeños, Alameda, Enrique Morente, Benavent-Amargos Band, Orquestra Mondragon, Miguel Rios; Amalgamas y Poliritmias (DVD) 2005. *Compositions:* music for films, jingles, ballet, theatre and for Spanish Olympic Swimming Team (Sydney 2000, Athens 2004, Beijing 2008). *Publications:* Drum Guide for Pop and Rock 1998, The Virtual Drummer (CD-ROM) 1999. *Honours:* hon. mem. PERCUBA, Bateria Total magazine Best Drummer and Best Educator 2003, 2004, prizes from El País Popular1 magazine. *Telephone:* (934) 539 099. *E-mail:* salvadorniebla@virtualdrummerschool.com. *Website:* www.virtualdrummerschool.com.

NIEDECKEN, Wolfgang; German rock musician and singer; b. 30 March 1951, Cologne. *Education:* Cologne Univ. of Applied Sciences. *Career:* Founder mem. Wolfgang Niedecken's BAP (later BAP) 1976–; also solo artist; many albums and tours. *Recordings include:* albums: with BAP: Wolfgang Niedecken's BAP rockt andere kölsche Leeder 1979, Affjetaut 1980, Für usszeschnigge! 1981, Vun drinne noh drusse 1982, Zwesche Salzjebäck un Bier 1984, Ahl Männer, aalglatt 1986, Da Capo 1988, X für 'e U 1990, Pik Sibbe 1993, Amerika 1996, Comics & Pin-Ups 1999, Tonfilm 1999, Aff un zo 2001, Sonx 2004, Dreimal zehn Jahre 2005, Halv su wild 2011; solo: Schlagzeiten 1987, Leopardefell 1995, NiedeckenKöln 2004. *Honours:* Frankfurter Musikpreis 1996, ECHO Honorary Award 2012. *Current Management:*

c/o Travelling Tunes Productions GmbH, Sternengasse 3, 50676 Cologne, Germany. *E-mail:* kontakt@bap.de. *Website:* www.bap.de. *Address:* c/o EMI Music Germany GmbH & Co. KG, Vogelsanger Strasse 321, 50827 Cologne, Germany (office). *E-mail:* info@emimusic.de (office). *Website:* www.emimusic .de (office).

NIELSEN, Ib Lund; Danish musician (bass) and music teacher (retd); b. 9 Oct. 1941, Vamdrup, Jylland; m. Inge Holten Nielsen 1964; two s. *Education:* studied bass with John Nielsen. *Career:* school teacher 1966–2004; mem. Niels Husum Septet, Body 'n' Soul jazz choir with rhythm-section; mem. Leonardo Pedersens Jazz (LPJ) Kapel (12-piece swing band) 1968–, also playing with Nielsenswingtime Quartet; mem. DMF, NDJ. *Recordings:* Lockjaw, Sweets 1976, Bass Relief 1980, I Want A Roof 1994, LPJ 1976–77 2000, LPJ Portalen Live 2000, LPJ featuring Bobo Moreno and Etta Cameron 2002, Shiny Stockins (Body 'n' Soul) 2006, LPJ Evil Gal Blues 2006, Undecided (Body 'n' Soul) 2009. *Honours:* winner, jazz competition (with Stormy's Quartet), Denmark 1960. *Address:* Hvidager 42, 2620 Albertslund, Denmark (home). *Telephone:* 43-64-81-36 (home). *E-mail:* iblundnielsen@webspeed.dk (home).

NIELSEN, Jens G.; Danish musician (drums), record producer and record company executive; b. 1 Aug. 1951. *Career:* founder mem., Gnags (with brother Peter Nielsen and others) 1974–2000; world-wide tours; co-founder, Genlyd record label (later bought by BMG); A&R Dir, BMG, Denmark, producer of albums for various artists. *Recordings:* albums: På vej... 1973, Del af en ring 1975, Det er det 1976, La det gro 1977, Er du hjemme i aften 1978, Burhøns 1979, Intercity 1980, Live vol. 1 1981, Safari 1982, X 1983, Den blå hund 1984, En underlig fisk 1985, Plads til begejstring 1986, Har de puttet noget i kaffen 1987, Under bøgen 1988, Mr Swing King (Danish Grammy 1990) 1989, Lygtemandens sang 1991, Live vol. 2 1992, Øjne på stilke 1994, Gösta Hammerfedt 1996, Gnags Greatest 1999, Ridser, Revner og Buler 2000.

NIELSEN, Peter A. G.; Danish singer, composer and musician (keyboards, guitar, harmonica); b. 17 Dec. 1952, Skjern; m. Katrine Nyholm 1923; one s. one d. *Education:* Århus Univ. *Career:* founder mem., singer, Gnags (with brother, Jens Nielsen and others) 1966–. *Recordings:* albums: På vej... 1973, Del af en ring 1975, Det er det 1976, La det gro 1977, Er du hjemme i aften 1978, Burhøns 1979, Intercity 1980, Live vol. 1 1981, Safari 1982, X 1983, Den blå hund 1984, En underlig fisk 1985, Plads til begejstring 1986, Har de puttet noget i kaffen 1987, Under bøgen 1988, Mr Swing King (Danish Grammy 1990) 1989, Lygtemandens sang 1991, Live vol. 2 1992, Øjne på stilke 1994, Gösta Hammerfedt 1996, Gnags Greatest 1999, Ridser, Revner og Buler 2000, Skønhedspletter 2002, Skitsernes Drøm 2003, Legepladsen 2008. *E-mail:* gnags@gnags.dk (office). *Website:* www.gnags.dk.

NIELSEN, Rick; American musician (guitar) and singer; b. Rockford, IL. *Career:* mem. various bands, including Fuse, Sick Man of Europe; founder mem. rock group, Cheap Trick 1974–; numerous live appearances, festivals, tours; solo performance, Concerto for electric guitar and orchestra, by Michael Kamen (with Rockford Symphony Orchestra) 1993. *Recordings include:* albums: Cheap Trick 1977, Heaven Tonight 1978, Cheap Trick At Budokan 1979, Dream Police 1979, Found All The Parts 1980, All Shook Up 1980, One On One 1982, Next Position Please 1983, The Doctor 1986, Lap of Luxury 1988, Busted 1990, Silver 2001, Rockford 2006, The Latest 2009. *Address:* Trick International, 8225 Fifth Avenue, Suite 803, Brooklyn, NY 11209, USA (office). *Website:* www.cheaptrick.com.

NIEMELÄINEN, Ilkka; Finnish musician (guitar) and composer; b. 9 March 1956. *Education:* Helsinki Conservatory. *Career:* writer, performer of electronic music with Otto Romanowski, Esa Kotilainen 1970s; founder, composer, musical dir, Wasama Quartet 1976–85; numerous concerts, festival appearances; founder, composer, musical dir, Instinct 1985; founder mem. of trio, IN2á3 1990–; founder SynChronos, musical project 1997–; founder UNI trio 2008–. *E-mail:* ilkka.niemelainen@intelligentinstruments.fi (office). *Website:* www.intelligentinstruments.fi/koti.html.

NIGAM, Sonu; Indian singer and actor; b. 30 July 1973, Faridabad, Haryana; s. of Agam Kumar Nigam and Shobha Nigam; m. Madhurima 2002; one s. *Education:* J.D.Tyler School, Delhi, Univ. of Delhi. *Career:* successful as both film playback singer and pop star; spent childhood in Delhi, often singing at functions with father; went to Mumbai to try and break into films, aged 18; began by taking acting roles whilst attempting to become a playback singer; first found fame with song Achha Sila Diya Tune Mere Pyaar Ka from the film Bewafa Sanam; other film offers followed along with the chance to record pop albums. *Television:* host of music show TVS Sa Re Ga Ma, Kisme Kitna Hai Dum. *Recordings:* albums: Sapnon Ki Baat 1997, Kismat 1998, Mausam 1999, Pariyon se 1999, Deewana 1999, Jaan 2000, Yaad 2001, Chanda ki Doli (Anadolok Award) 2005, Classically Mild 2008, Kal Aaj Aur Kal 2008, Punjabi Please 2008, Rafi Resurrected 2008, Maha Ganesha 2008, Neene Bari Neene 2009. *Films include:* Jaani Dushman: Ek Anokhi Kahani, Kaash..Aap Hamare Hote, Love in Nepal. *Film soundtrack recordings:* Jeet, Papa Kehte Hain 1996, Border, Tamanna 1997, China-Gate, Dil Se..., Dulhe Raja, Jab Pyaar Kisise Hota Hai, Jeans, Keemat 1998, Dillagi, Hum Saath-Saath Hain, Jaanwar, Mast, Shool, Taal, Vaastav 1999, Chori Chori Chupke Chupke, Dhadkan, Fiza, Hadh Kar Di Aapne, Har Dil Jo Pyar Karega, Jungle, Kahin Pyar Na Ho Jaaye, Kurukshetra, Kya Kehna, Mela, Phir Bhi Dil Hai Hindustani, Pukar, Refugee, Tera Jadoo Chal Gayaa 2000, Dil Chahta Hai, One 2 Ka 4, Pyaar Ishq Aur Mohabbat, Pyaar Tune Kya Kiya.., Yaadein 2001, Saathiya 2002, Kabhi Khushi Kabhi Gham, Kal Ho Na Ho, Tumko Na Bhool Payenge, Rehna Hai Tere Dil Mein, Pardes, Kaante and several others.

Honours: Immie Award for Best Male Singer 2003, Teachers' Achievement Award 2005, Swaralaya Yesudas Award 2005; numerous other awards. *Website:* www.sonuniigaam.in.

NIGHTINGALE, Annie, MBE; British radio DJ; b. London, England; m. (divorced); one s. *Career:* fmr journalist, columnist, music reviewer for numerous nat. newspapers and magazines, including The Daily Express and Cosmopolitan magazine; TV presenter Old Grey Whistle Test (BBC) 1978–82; BBC Radio One's first female DJ 1970–, presenting programmes, including Sunday Night Request Show 1982–94, Chill Out Zone 1993–2004, Annie Nightingale 2004–; also worked for the BBC World Service, BBC Radio 4 and Radio 5, British Forces Broadcasting; has made numerous documentaries for BBC TV and radio, and for ITV; numerous live broadcasts from festivals and events worldwide; regularly works as a DJ, having played across the UK and in Baghdad, Barcelona, Los Angeles, New York, Paris and Warsaw; Ambassador, The Prince's Trust. *Recording:* Annie On One. *Publications:* Chase the Fade: Music Memoirs and Memorabilia (autobiog.) 1981, Wicked Speed (autobiog.) 1999. *Honours:* Music Industry and Related Media Organisation Woman of the Year Award 1998, Muzik Magazine Caner of the Year Award 2002, PRS John Peel Award for Outstanding Contribution to Music Radio 2008. *Address:* c/o BBC Radio 1, London, W1N 4DJ, England (office). *E-mail:* annie.nightingale@bbc.co.uk (office). *Website:* www.bbc.co.uk/radio1/dance/ nightingale.

NIGO; Japanese fashion designer, music producer and DJ; b. (Tomoaki Nagao), 23 Dec. 1970. *Education:* Bunka Fashion Coll., Tokyo. *Career:* fashion student, magazine stylist, DJ early 1990s; DJ of Japanese hip hop group Teriyaki Boyz; began making T-shirts and selling them at parties and DJ shows; opened store Nowhere with Jun Takahashi 1993; set up A Bathing Ape fashion label 1993, label now has stores across Japan and in Hong Kong, Taiwan, London, New York; built Ape Sounds the studio and f. The Bapesounds music label; f. A Bathing Ape fashion label 1993 with stores across Japan and in Hong Kong and London, opened New York store 2005, Los Angeles (closed 2010); with Pharrell Williams, responsible for helping produce the Billionaire Boys Club and Ice Cream Footwear brands; Creative Dir for Uniqlo's UT brand; also has interests in music, art, cafés, hairstyling; f. Bapesta!!Wrestling (professional wrestling), Bape Gallery. *Exhibition:* participated in Coloriage Exhbn Fondation Cartier pour l'art contemporain, Paris, France. *Television:* Nigoldeneye (MTV Japan). *Broadcasts:* (B)ape TV, live show Bape Heads Show. *Recordings include:* Ape Sounds 2000, Return of the Ape Sounds 2005. *Honours:* Best Producer Award, Tokyo Art Dirs Club (ACD) 2002, one of 30 Best Asian Heroes, Time Asia 2004, Style Award, MTV Asia Awards 2005.

NILES, Richard, BMus; American composer, producer, arranger, journalist and broadcaster; b. 28 May 1951, Hollywood, California. *Education:* Berklee Coll. of Music, Boston. *Career:* arranger for: Pet Shop Boys; Kate Dimbleby; Heather Small; Westlife; Samantha Mumba; Joe Cocker; Paul McCartney; Cher; Take That; Boyzone; Tears For Fears; Kiri Te Kanawa; producer for: Pet Shop Boys; Hue and Cry; Dusty Springfield; Pat Metheny; The Troggs; musical director for TV series: David Essex; Leo Sayer; Michael Ball; Ruby Wax; composer of numerous TV commercials; broadcaster: writer and presenter of New Jazz Standards, BBC Radio 2; Recording Artiste: Santa Rita, Black Box Records; mem, Musicians' Union; PRS; BMI; MPG. *Compositions:* Recorded by: Ray Charles; Tina Turner; Hue and Cry; Bobby Womack; Deniece Williams; Spike Milligan. *Honours:* Golden Rose of Montreux, Score for The Strike (Comic Strip). *Address:* Niles Productions, 34 Beaumont Road, London W4 5AP, England. *Website:* www.richardniles.com (office).

NIMMERSJÖ, Conny; Swedish musician (guitar); b. 20 March 1967, Angelholm; one d. *Career:* mem., bob hund 1991–; numerous concerts in Scandinavia, including Roskilde, Lollipop, Ruisrock, Quartfestivalen and Hultsfred festivals; mem. STIM, SAMI. *Recordings:* bob hund 1993, Edvin Medvind, 7 1994, I släktet för Musik: förvirring 1996, Omslag: Martin Kann 1996, Düsseldorf 3:53 1996, Ett fall och en lösning 1997, Nu är det väl revolution på gång? 1998, Jag rear ut min själ! Allt skal bort!!! 1998, Helgen V.48 1999, Sover aldrig 1999, Stenåldem kan börja 2001, Ingenting 2002. *Honours:* Swedish Grammy Awards for Best Live Act 1994, Best Lyrics 1996. *Website:* www.bobhund.nu.

NINO, Harold Michael; American musician (guitar) and blues singer; b. 29 Nov. 1950, New York, NY; m. Julie Hebner; one s. *Education:* Manhattan Community Coll., New School for Social Research, studied with Robert Yelin and Ted Meckler. *Career:* studio musician, New York 1977–82; travelling road musician 1978–; appeared regularly on The Music Art Show, Huntsville, AL 1978–79; mem. blues band, Oysters Rockefeller; mem. American Federation of Musicians, Blues Music Assen, BMI. *Film appearance:* They Want To Know Too!. *Compositions:* You're Never Going to Understand (recorded by Oysters Rockefeller) 1996. *Recordings include:* Past and Present (with Oysters Rockefeller). *Honours:* Addy Award (for Villa Esperanza commercial) 1979.

NISBETT, Steve 'Grizzly'; British musician (drums). *Career:* mem., Steel Pulse 1977–2001; f. Grazzily Records, Birmingham 2004–; numerous television appearances, world-wide tours. *Recordings:* albums: Handsworth Revolution 1978, Tribute To The Martyrs 1979, Caught You (aka Reggae Fever) 1980, True Democracy 1982, Earth Crisis 1984, Reggae Refreshers 1985, Babylon The Bandit (Grammy Award) 1985, State of Emergency 1988, Victims 1991, Rastafari Centennial 1992, Smash Hits 1993, Vex 1994,

Rastanthology 1996, Rage & Fury 1997, Sound System: The Island Anthology 1996, Living Legacy 1999.

NKETIA, Joseph Hanson Kwabena; Ghanaian composer, academic and writer; *Director, International Centre for African Music and Dance, University of Ghana*; b. 22 June 1921, Mampong, Ashanti Region. *Education:* Presbyterian Training Coll. and Theological Seminary, Akropong, School of Oriental and African Studies, London, Trinity Coll. of Music, London, Birkbeck Coll., London, Columbia Univ. and Juilliard School of Music, New York, Northwestern Univ., Evnaston, IL. *Career:* composer from 1940; teacher, Presbyterian Training Coll. 1941–44, 1949–52, acting Principal 1954; Asst, SOAS, Univ. of London 1946–49; Research Fellow, Univ. Coll. of Ghana 1952–59, Sr Research Fellow 1959–61; Assoc. Prof., Univ. of Ghana, Legon 1962, Prof. 1963–65, Dir Inst. of African Studies 1965–79, Prof. Emeritus 1990–, Dir Int. Centre for African Music and Dance 1993–; Dir musical ensemble for Ghana Dance Troupe 1963–70; Prof., Univ. of Calif. at Los Angeles 1969–82, Prof. Emeritus 1982–; Horatio Appleton Lamb Visiting Prof. of Music, Harvard Univ. 1971; Visiting Prof. of Music, Univ. of Queensland, Brisbane, Australia 1979; Andrew Mellon Prof. of Music, Univ. of Pittsburgh, PA 1982–91, Chair. Dept of Music 1986–89, Andrew Mellon Prof. Emeritus 1992; Visiting Prof., China Conservatory of Music, Beijing; Langston Hughes Visiting Prof., Univ. of Kansas-Lawrence 1992; Cornell Visiting Prof. Dept of Music and Dance, Swarthmore Coll., PA 1995; Distinguished Hannah Prof. of Integrative Studies, Mich. State Univ., East Lansing 1997; Fellow, Ghana Acad. of Arts and Sciences 1959; mem. Exec Bd, Int. Folk Music Council 1959–70; mem. Int. Music Council 1962–66, 1978, exec. mem. 1971–77, mem. of honour 1980; mem. Scientific Bd, Int. Inst. for Comparative Music Studies and Documentation (Berlin) 1964; mem. Soc. for Ethnomusicology Council (dir at large 1968, vice-pres. 1972–73); mem. Int. Soc. for Music Educ. (bd dirs 1967–74, vice-pres. 1968–74); Chair. African Regional Secretariat, Int. Music Council (UNESCO) 1972; Regional Co-ordinator for Africa, Bd Dirs Universe of Music: A World History (UNESCO) 1980; mem. Int. Comm. for a Scientific and Cultural History of Mankind, UNESCO 1980–; mem. Scientific Cttee, Institut des Peuples Noir, Burkina Faso 1986; mem. Bd Dirs, African Studies Asscn 1986–90; mem. Int. Semiotic Inst. 1987; mem. African Music Soc., Historical Soc. of Ghana, Int. Council for Traditional Music, Nat. Music Assocn of Ghana (pres.). *Compositions include:* Adanse Kronkron (Divine Testimony) 1940, African Pianism: Twelve Pedagogical Pieces 1946–75, Suite for flute and piano 1959, Four Akan Solo Songs 1962, Canzona 1963, Antubam (Dirge for cello and piano) 1965, For Violin 1967, Four Flute Pieces 1969, Quartet No. 1 for Atenteben 1969, Quartet No. 2 for Ateneben 1969, Chamber Music in the African Idiom 1976. *Publications:* Akanfoo Anansesem 1949, Akanfoo Nnwom Bi 1949, Ananwoma 1951, Anwonsem 1952, Kwabena Amoa 1952, Akwansosem Bi 1952, Adae 1953, Semode 1954, Funeral Dirges of the Akan People 1955, The Writing of Twi: Asante Spelling 1955, Possession Dances in African Societies 1956, Kookoo ho Mpanisem 1959, African Music in Ghana: A Survey of Traditional Forms 1962, Drumming in Akan Communities of Ghana 1963, Folk Songs of Ghana 1963, Ghana: Music, Dance and Drama: A Review of the Performing Arts of Ghana 1965, Music in African Cultures: A Review of the Meaning and Significance of Traditional African Music 1966, Adowa Songs 1966, The Place of Authentic Folk Music in Music Education 1966, Our Drums and Drummers 1968, Creating a Wider Interest in Traditional Music: The Place of Traditional Music in the Musical Life of Ghana 1969, Ethnomusicology in Ghana 1970, Kokofu Ayan: Drum Language of Kokofu (Ashanti) 1973, The Music of Africa 1974, Ayan 1975, Collating and Disseminating Oral Sources of Musical Information 1977, Amoma 1978, Selected Reports in Ethnomusicology: Studies in African Music (ed., with Jacqueline C. DjeDje) 1984. *Honours:* elected to Ghana Acad. of Arts and Sciences 1959, hon. mem. Royal Anthropological Inst. of Great Britain and Ireland 1972; African Music Soc. Cowell Award 1958, Rockefeller Foundation Fellowship 1958–59; Ford Foundation Fellowship 1961, Grand Medal of Ghana 1968, Ghana Arts Award 1972, ASCAP Deems Taylor Award 1975, Int. Music Council-UNESCO Music Prize for Distinguished Service to Music 1981, Nat. Entertainment Critics and Reviewers Asscn of Ghana Flagstar Award 1993. *Address:* International Centre for African Music and Dance, University of Ghana, PO Box 25, Legon, Accra, Ghana (office). *Telephone:* (233) 21-500381 (office). *Website:* www.ug .edu.gh (office).

NNEKA; Nigerian/German singer; b. (Nneka Egbuna), Warri, Nigeria. *Education:* Univ. of Hamburg. *Career:* moved to Hamburg, Germany, aged 19; began working with producer, DJ Farhot; professional solo artist 2005–. *Recordings:* albums: Victim of Truth 2005, No Longer at Ease 2008, Concrete Jungle 2010. *Honours:* MOBO Award for Best Africa Act 2009. *Address:* c/o Yo Mama Recordings, Four Music Productions, Schlegelstrasse 26B, Gartenhaus 2, 10115 Berlin, Germany (office). *E-mail:* mgmt@neverlandmusic.net (office). *Website:* www.fourmusic.com; www.nnekaworld.com.

NOBES, Roger Michael; British musician (vibraphone, piano, drums) and arranger; b. 26 Dec. 1939, Abbots Langley, Hertfordshire; m. Maureen Payne 1987; one d. *Education:* Guildhall School of Music and Drama. *Career:* fmrly worked in holiday camps and function bands; played for West End, London musicals, including West Side Story, A Chorus Line, Fiddler on the Roof; mem., The Alex Welsh Band eight years, touring with numerous American artists; fmr mem., The Dave Shepherd Quintet; formed The Roger Nobes Quartet; mem. Musicians' Union.

NOBLE; British musician (guitar); b. (Martin Noble), Leeds. *Career:* founder mem., British Sea Power 2000–; the band runs Club Sea Power, a monthly variety show in Brighton, England; numerous live performances and festival appearances. *Recordings include:* albums: The Decline of British Sea Power 2003, Open Season 2005, Do You Like Rock Music? 2008, Man of Aran (film soundtrack) 2009. *Honours:* Time Out Award for Live Band of the Year 2004. *Address:* British Sea Power, PO Box 5123, Hove, East Sussex BN52 9ET, England. *Website:* www.britishseapower.co.uk.

NOBLE, Douglas, BSc, LLCM (TD); British guitar teacher and music journalist; b. 9 July 1964, Edinburgh, Scotland. *Education:* Edinburgh University, London College of Music. *Career:* freelance music journalist, regular contributor to the Guitar Magazine (UK); occasional contributor to Guitar Player (USA), Bass Player (USA); contributions to several books on the electric guitar; sleeve notes for several albums; Music Director for Univibes, international Jimi Hendrix magazine; Examiner, Rock School, Trinity College of Music. *Publications:* Instant Hendrix 1988, Instant Peter Green 1990.

NOBLE, Stephen Francis Paterson; British musician (drums, percussion, musical saw, bugle); b. 26 March 1960, Wallingford, Oxfordshire. *Career:* contemporary Music Network Tour, with Alex Maguire 1994; performed at festivals including Glasgow Jazz 1989–94, New Music America, New York 1989, Sitges International Dance 1991, Taklos (Swizz) 1990–92, London Jazz 1993–94; mem, Musicians' Union, PRS. *Compositions:* commissioned by South Bank Centre, London to compose music for collaboration with Spanish Dance Company Mal Pelo 1993. *Recordings:* Duo with Alex Maguire: Live At Oscar's; (voted one of top jazz albums of 1980s) Once, recordings from Derek Bailey's Company Week, featuring Bailey and Lee Konitz 1987; The Shakedown Club.

NOGA, Mike; Australian musician (drums). *Career:* mem., The Drones 2005–. *Recordings include:* album: Gala Mill 2006, Havilah 2008. *Current Management:* One Louder, PO Box 989, Darlinghurst, NSW 1300, Australia. *Telephone:* (2) 9380-9011. *Fax:* (2) 9380-9866. *E-mail:* briese@onelouder .au. *Website:* www.onelouder.com.au; www.thedrones.com.au.

NOMIYA, Maki; Japanese singer; b. Hokkaido. *Career:* fmr mem., Portable Rock (releasing singles) late 1980s; mem., Pizzicato Five 1991–2001; solo artist 2000–; founder mem., Oui Oui 2001–02, 2004–; launched fashion label, Mini She by Maki Nomiya 2004–. *Recordings include:* albums: with Pizzicato Five: Hi Guys! Let Me Teach You 1991, This Year's Model 1991, London Paris Tokyo 1991, Readymade Recordings 1991, Instant Replay 1993, Made in USA 1994, A Television's Workshop 1994, Five by Five 1994, Romantique 96 1995, The Sound of Music by Pizzicato Five 1995, Antique 96 1995, A Quiet Couple 1995, Great White Wonder 1996, Sister Freedom Tapes 1996, Combinaison Spaciale 1997, Happy End of the World 1997, Happy End of You 1998, Pizzicatomania! 1998, Playboy & Playgirl 1998, Darlin' of Discotheque 1999, Nonstop to Tokyo 1999, Overdose 1999, Perfect World 1999, Pizzicato Five TM 1999, Sweet Pizzicato Five 2000, Voyage a Tokyo 2000, Bossa Nova 2001, 24 December 2001, Ca Et La Du Japon 2001; solo: Pink no Kokoro 1981, Miss Maki Nomiya Sings 2000, Lady Miss Warp 2002, Dress Code 2004, Party People 2005,. *Publication:* Dress Code 2004. *Current Management:* The Billions Corporation, 833 W Chicago Avenue, Suite 101, Chicago, IL 60622-5497, USA. *Address:* c/o Matador Records, PO Box 20125, London, W10 5BN, England. *Website:* www.matadorrecords.com/pizzicato_five; www .missmakinomiya.com.

NOODLE; musician (guitar) and backing singer. *Career:* animated mem. of virtual band, Gorillaz 1998– (see creator and Musical Dir, Damon Albarn and creator and Visual Dir, Jamie Hewlett). *Website:* www.gorillaz.com.

NOODLES (see Masta Killa)

NOODLES; American musician (guitar); b. (Kevin Wasserman), 4 Feb. 1963, Los Angeles, Calif.; m. Jackie Wasserman 1998; one d. *Career:* fmr mem., Clowns of Death, Dirty Dot; mem. Manic Subsidal 1985, renamed The Offspring 1986–; numerous live shows, festival appearances and tours. *Recordings include:* albums: The Offspring 1989, Ignition 1992, Smash! 1994, Ixnay On The Hombre 1997, Americana 1998, Conspiracy Of One 2000, Splinter 2003, Greatest Hits 2005, Rise and Fall, Rage and Grace 2008, Days Go By 2012. *Honours:* Kerrang! Award for Classic Songwriter (with The Offspring) 2002. *Address:* The Offspring, PO Box 3479, Huntington Beach, CA 92605-3479, USA. *Website:* www.offspring.com.

NOONE, Peter; British singer; b. 5 Nov. 1947, Davyhulme, Manchester, England; m. Mireille Strasser. *Education:* Manchester School of Music and Drama. *Career:* lead singer, Herman's Hermits 1963–71; solo artist 1971–; numerous tours; mem., The Tremblers 1980; business partnership with Graham Gouldman, studio production work, New York boutique, Zoo 1968; video jockey, US cable TV 1990s. *Film appearance:* Mrs Brown You've Got A Lovely Daughter 1968. *Television:* The Canterville Ghost 1966. *Plays:* Pinocchio 1968, Pirates of Penzance (Broadway and London) 1982–83. *Recordings include:* Introducing Herman's Hermits, 1965; Herman's Hermits on Tour, 1965; Hold On!, 1966; Both Sides of Herman's Hermits, 1966; Vol. III, 1968; I'm Into Something Good, 1964; Silhouettes, 1965; Wonderful World, 1965; I'm Henry VIII, I Am, 1965; Just a Little Better, 1965; A Must To Avoid, 1965; Dandy, 1966; No Milk Today, 1966; There's A Kind Of Hush (All Over The World), 1967; Sleepy Joe, 1968; Sunshine Girl, 1968; Something's Happening, 1969; Years May Come Years May Go, 1970; Bet Yer Life I Do, 1970; Lady Barbara, 1970; solo: Oh You Pretty Thing, 1971; One of the Glory Boys, 1982; Pirates of Penzance, 1986; I'm into Something Good, 1989. *Address:* c/o NoOne Records Inc., 1187 Coast Village Road, #525, Santa

Barbara, CA 93108, USA. *Telephone:* (805) 969-5792. *Website:* www
.peternoone.com.

NORBY, Caecilie; Danish singer, composer, lyricist and arranger; b. 9 Sept.
1964, Frederiksberg; d. of Erik Norby and Solveig Lumholt; partner Lars
Danielsson; one d. *Education:* Sct Annae Gymnasium Music School, Music
Theatre School, also self taught. *Career:* mem. various performing groups
1980–81; lead singer funk rock band, Street Beat 1982–84; lead singer,
Frontline 1983–92; lead singer, One Two (with Nina Forsberg) 1985–93; tours
and performances as a soloist world-wide 1983–; mem. Danish Artists' Soc.,
Danske Jazz, Beat og Folkemusik Autorer (DJBFA). *Recordings include:*
albums: with Frontline: Frontline 1985, Frontlife 1986; with One Two: One
Two 1986, Hyide Løgne 1989, Getting Better 1993; solo: Caecilie Norby 1995,
My Corner of the Sky 1996, Queen of Bad Excuses 1999, First Conversation
2002, London/Paris 2003, Slow Fruit 2005, I Had a Ball 2007, Arabesque 2010,
Silent Ways 2013, Just the Two of Us 2015. *Honours:* Ben Webster Prize 1986,
Japan Music Award for Best Sound 1996, Simon Spies Soloist Prize 1997,
Wilhelm Hansen Music Prize 2000, Danish Music Award IFPI's Prize of
Honour 2010. *Current Management:* c/o Denise Thigpen (Personal Manager).
Telephone: 27-29-40-94. *E-mail:* denise@thigpen.dk. *Current Management:* c/o
Micky Pramming, PDH Dansk Musikformidling, Ny Vesterdage 7, 1471
Copenhagen, Denmark. *Telephone:* 33-11-22-00. *E-mail:* mp@pdh.dk. *Website:*
www.pdh.dk. *Current Management:* c/o Eva Maria Thiessen, XJAZZ Booking
& Production, c/o Contemplate 360° music network GBR, Alte Schönhauser
Str. 39, 10245 Berlin, Germany. *Telephone:* 17-24525192 (mobile). *E-mail:*
eva@xjazz.net. *Website:* prod.xjazz.net. *Telephone:* 40-75-70-19 (office).
E-mail: info@caecilienorby.com (office). *Website:* www.caecilienorby.com.

NORCROSS, Richard (Rick) Charles, BA; American singer, songwriter,
musician (guitar) and band leader; *President, Airflyte Productions;* b. 23
March 1945, Waltham, Mass. *Education:* Univ. of South Florida. *Career:* solo
artist 1963–80; three tours of England 1965–75; Entertainment Ed., The
Tampa Times 1969–74; lead singer and band leader, Rick and The Ramblers
Western Swing Band 1980–; tours include central Florida, New England Fair
& Festival Circuit, Murcia, Spain 2010; producer, more than 75 festivals and
special events 1974–; celebrated his 50-year anniversary as a performing
artist with Riding My Guitar Tour in New England 2013; currently Pres.
Airflyte Productions; Sec./Treas., Vermont Musicians Asscn Local 351,
American Fed. of Musicians 1999–2011; Vice-Pres. New England Conf. of
Musicians. *Recordings:* albums: Nashfull 1980, Fairly Live 1983, Tour du Jour
1989, You Can't Get There From Here 1991, You Can't Catch A Rambler 1994,
The Legend of Scratch Leroux 1995, I Heard the Highway 2001, I Rode The Ti
2009, Riding My Guitar 2013, Welcome to OUR Vermont 2014. *Art exhibitions:*
Rick's Pix: The Faces of Rock & Roll 1969 to 1974, The South End Art Hop,
Burlington, Vt 2008 and Whitewater Gallery, East Hardwick, Vt 2009, Village
Wine & Coffee Gallery, Shelburne, Vt 2013, Island Arts Gallery, Merchants
Bank, South Hero, Vt 2013), Rick Norcross: The Faces of Rock & Roll,
Burlington City Arts BCA Center 2015. *Publication:* Riding My Guitar: The
Rick Norcross Story (biog. by Stephen Russell Payne) 2013. *Address:* Airflyte
Productions, 216 Battery Street, Burlington, VT 05401, USA (office).
Telephone: (802) 864-6674 (office). *E-mail:* rick.norcross@gmail.com.
Website: www.rickandtheramblers.com (home).

NORDWIND, Timothy (Tim) Jay; American bass guitarist and singer; b. 28
June 1976, Kalamazoo, Mich. *Career:* Founder-mem. Stanley's Joyful Noise
1997–98; mem. OK Go 1998–; signed to Capitol Records 2001; f. own label for
OK Go recordings, Paracadute Recordings 2010. *Recordings:* albums: with OK
Go: OK Go 2002, Oh No 2004, Of the Blue Colour of the Sky 2010, Hungry
Ghosts 2014. *Honours:* Grammy Award for Best Music Video 2007, UK Music
Video Awards for Video of the Year and Best Rock Video 2010, CLIO Gold
Award in Branded Entertainment 2013, MTV Video Music Award for Best
Visual Effects 2014. *Address:* c/o Mike Rosenthal, Paracadute, 236 Hoyt
Street, Suite 2, Brooklyn, New York, NY 11217, USA (office). *E-mail:*
Rosenthal@paracadute.net (office); paracadute@okgo.net (office); info@okgo
.net. *Website:* www.paracadute.net (office); www.okgo.net.

NORÉN, Gustaf; Swedish singer, songwriter and musician (guitar, harmonica); b. 1 Feb. 1981. *Career:* founder mem., Mando Diao 1999–. *Recordings
include:* albums: Bring 'Em In 2002, Hurricane Bar 2005, Ode to Ochrasy
2006, Never Seen the Light of Day 2007, Give Me Fire 2009. *Current
Management:* Flagstone Management, Götabergsgatan 2, 411 34 Gothenburg,
Sweden. *Telephone:* (3) 170-175-20. *Fax:* (3) 170-175-30. *E-mail:* info@
flagstone.se. *Website:* www.flagstone.se; www.mandodiao.com.

NORMAN, Chris; British singer, songwriter, musician (guitar) and record
producer; b. 25 Oct. 1950, Redcar, Yorks.; m. Linda Heddle 1970; four s. two d.
Career: lead singer, Kindness, backing group to Peter Noone (ex Herman's
Hermits) 1960s, group later became Smokie 1970s; solo artist 1980s–; mem.
Performing Right Soc., Mechanical-Copyright Protection Soc., British Acad. of
Composers and Songwriters. *Recordings:* albums: with Smokie: Changing All
the Time 1975, Pass It Around 1975, Midnight Cafe 1976, Smokie 1976, Bright
Lights and Back Allies 1977, The Montreux Album 1978, The Other Side of the
Road 1979, Solid Ground 1981, Midnight Delight 1982, Stangers in Paradise
1982; solo: Rock Away Your Teardrops 1982, Some Hearts are Diamonds 1986,
Different Shades 1987, Break the Ice 1989, The Interchange 1991, The
Growing Years 1992, Jealous Heart 1993, The Album 1994, Scrreaming Love
Album 1994, Every Little Thing 1995, Reflections 1995, Into the Night 1997,
Christmas Together 1997, Full Circle 1999, Breathe Me In 2001, Handmade

2003, Break Away 2004, Million Miles 2006, Coming Home 2006, Close Up
2007, The Hits! 2009, Time Traveller 2011, There & Back 2013, Crossover
2015. *Honours:* three Bravo Awards 1976–86, Golden Europa 1986, CMT
Europe 1994. *Current Management:* c/o Ina D. Keilitz, K-Musix, A.S.S.
Concert & Promotion GmbH, Rahlstedter Str. 92, 22149 Hamburg, Germany.
Telephone: (474) 403070. *Fax:* (474) 403071. *E-mail:* ina.keilitz@k-musix.com.
Website: www.k-musix.com; www.chris-norman.co.uk.

NORMAN, David; British tour and production manager and sound engineer;
b. 19 May 1962, London, England; m. Suzanne Feit 1992. *Career:* television
and live appearances, tours and festivals; engineer on albums for Peabo
Bryson, Arrested Development, Bare E'ssentials. *Address:* 639 Gardenwalk
Blvd, Suite 1632, College Park, GA 30349, USA.

NORMAN, Michael, DipMus; Canadian musician (keyboards, saxophones,
guitar), singer, producer and songwriter; b. 16 June 1970. *Education:*
Malaspina College. *Career:* Canadian Country Music Award shows with
Lisa Brokop, 1993; Patricia Conroy, 1995, 1999; Patricia Conroy: Wild As The
Wind, 1999; mem. AFM, CCMA. *Compositions:* Too Late; Bring It On; Put A
Little Distance. *Recordings:* Girls Will Be Girls; Living Beyond Our Dreams;
The Message, Alpha Yaya Diallo, 1999. *Honours:* BCCMA Keyboard Player of
the Year 1999.

NORREEN, Claus; Danish musician (keyboards, drum machines); b. 5 June
1970, Charlottenlund. *Career:* Worked with Soeren Rasted on film, Fraekke
Frida; Formed Joyspeed; Changed name to Aqua; Obtained major record deal
in Denmark; Numerous TV and live appearances. *Recordings:* Singles: Itsy
Blitzy, as Joyspeed; Roses Are Red; Barbie Girl (No. 1, UK), 1997; Doctor
Jones (No. 1, UK), 1998; Turn Back Time (theme from film Sliding Doors) (No.
1, UK), 1998; My Oh My, 1998; Good Morning Sunshine, 1998; Cartoon
Heroes, 2000; Around The World, 2000; Lollipop; Albums: Aquarium, 1997;
Bubble Mix, 1998; We Belong To The Sea, 2001.

NORREMOLLE, Jens; Danish composer, producer and musician (key-
boards); b. 12 Aug. 1956, Vejle; one s. *Career:* mem. various bands –1987;
composer, singer, keyboard player, Singing Zoo; record prod. for Anne Dorte
Michelsen and Venter På Far 1987–95; mem. DMF, DJBFA. *Recordings:* with
Anne Dorte Michelsen: Elskerindens Have; Den Ordlose Time; Min Karriere
Som Kvinde (producer, arranger, musician); also albums with Singing Zoo and
Venter På Far. *Honours:* Best Band 1988, Musikcafé Prize with Singing Zoo.

NORRIS, Richard; British musician (keyboards, saxophone, drums), pro-
ducer and remixer; b. 23 June 1965, London. *Education:* Univ. of Liverpool.
Career: mem. musical duo, The Grid; met pnr Dave Ball, recording Jack The
Tab compilation 1988; tours, UK, Japan, Thailand, Singapore, New Zealand,
Australia; producer, remixer, artists including: Pet Shop Boys, Boy George,
Marc Almond, Brian Eno, Billie Ray Martin, Black Grape, Happy Mondays
1990–95; Director of Areeba Records; A&R Manager for Creation Records;
mem. PRS, PPL, Musicians' Union. *Recordings:* albums: Electric Head 1990,
456 1992, Evolver 1994, Music For Dancing 1995, Doppelgänger 2008.

NORRIS, Richard T.; British music programmer, writer and recording
engineer; b. 9 Feb. 1966, Epping, Essex. *Career:* programmer, engineer for
Bryan Ferry, including albums Taxi, Mamouna 1990–95; co-writer with Little
Annie 1989–94; co-writer with Guy Pratt (Pink Floyd) under joint name Deep
Cover. *Recordings:* albums: Taxi, Bryan Ferry 1993; Deboravation, Deborah
Harry 1993; Mix-ism, Mad Capsule Markets 1994; Mamouna, Bryan Ferry
1994; Grand Central, Deep Cover, from Hackers film soundtrack 1995;
Goodbye, Dubstar 1997; Neapolis, Simple Minds 1998; Invincible, Five 2000;
Interview With The Angel, Ghostland 2001.

NORTON, Gil; British producer. *Career:* producer for artists, including The
Pixies, Foo Fighters, Counting Crows, Feeder, James and Del Amitri. *Current
Management:* c/o JPR Management Ltd, Suite 25, 9–12 Middle Street,
Brighton, BN1 1AL, England. *Telephone:* (1273) 236969. *Fax:* (1273)
386291. *E-mail:* info@jprmanagement.co.uk. *Website:* www.jprmanagement
.co.uk; kadazan.net/gilweb.

NOVA, Aldo; Canadian rock musician (guitar) and singer; b. (Aldo
Caporuscio). *Career:* solo recording artist 1980–. *Recordings include:* albums:
Aldo Nova, 1982; Subject, 1984; Twitch, 1985; Blood On The Bricks, 1991;
Nova's Dream, 1997.

NOVAKOVIČ, Mojmir; Croatian traditional musician. *Career:* founder
mem. and lead singer, Legen 1992–2002, band performed live for play, Quai
Ouest 1998–99, numerous other live performances and int. tours; co-founder
Ethnoambient festival, Salona 1995–; founder mem., Kries 2002–; mem.
Croatian Musicians' Union (pres. of ethno-music section). *Recordings include:*
albums: with Legen: Kolo – Tribal Music from Forsaken Place 1995, Peacock's
Dance 1997, Transatlantic (film soundtrack) 1998, Sky – Satellites (film
soundtrack) 2000, Seljaèka Buna 2000; with Kries: Konjanik (film soundtrack)
(Croatian Music Award for Best Original Music for Film 2005) 2002, Ivo i
Mara 2004, Kocijani. *Current Management:* c/o Goran Cvok, 44320 Kutina,
Eugena Kvaternika 3, Croatia. *Telephone:* (44) 631521. *E-mail:* kopito@ak.t
-com.hr. *Website:* www.kries.info.

NOVOSELIC, Krist; American musician (bass); b. 16 May 1965, Croatia.
Career: member, Nirvana, 1987–94; worldwide tours; Concerts include:
Reading Festival, 1991, 1992; Transmusicales Festival, Rennes, France,
1991; Benefit concert, Washington State Music Coalition, 1992; Benefit
concert, Tresnjevka Women's Group, Cow Palace, San Francisco, 1993;

Founder, Sweet 75, 1995; mem. Flipper 2006–. *Recordings:* Albums: Bleach, 1989; Nevermind 1991; Incesticide, 1993; In Utero 1993; Unplugged In New York, 1994; Singles, 1996; Box, 1998; Singles include: Smells Like Teen Spirit, 1991; Come As You Are, 1992; Lithium, 1992; In Bloom, 1992; Oh, The Guilt, 1993; Heart-Shaped Box, 1993; All Apologies, 1993; Track, I Hate Myself and Wanna Die, featured on Beavis and Butthead Experience, 1993; Appears on: Live From The Battle In Seattle, The No WTO Combo, 2000. *Honours:* with Nirvana: Platinum disc, Nevermind; Best Alternative Music Video, Best New Artist Video, Smells Like Teen Spirit, MTV Music Video Awards, 1992; Best International Newcomer, BRIT Awards, 1993; other: Grammy Award for Best Rock Song (for Cut Me Some Slack, with Dave Grohl, Paul McCartney and Pat Smear) 2014. *E-mail:* flipperfriends@ISPwest.com. *Website:* www.200pockets .com/projects/flipper/.

NOWELS, Rick; American songwriter, record producer and musician. *Education:* Univ. of California at Berkeley. *Career:* prod. and songwriter; worked with Kelli Ali, All Saints, Belinda Carlisle, Boy George, Cher, The Corrs, Des'ree, Dido, Céline Dion, Nelly Furtado, Geri Halliwell, Enrique Iglesias, Jewel, Ronan Keating, Madonna, Melanie C., Stevie Nicks, Nerina Pallot, Sinead O'Connor, New Radicals, Stevie Nicks, *NSYNC, Eros Ramazotti, Leann Rimes, Santana, Sonique, Cat Stevens, Texas, Ed Tracy, Keith Urban; mem. ASCAP. *Compositions:* for Madonna: The Power of Good-bye, To Have and Not to Hold, Little Star; for Céline Dion: Falling Into You (Grammy Award); for Robert Miles: One and One; for Des'ree: Time, Get a Life; for Anita Baker: Body and Soul; for Belinda Carlisle: Heaven is a Place on Earth, Circle in the Sand, Leave a Light On, Live Your Life Be Free, In Too Deep, We Want the Same Thing, La Lune, Runaway Horses, Vision of You, Do You Feel Like I Feel?; for Stevie Nicks: I Can't Wait, Rooms on Fire, Maybe Love Will Change Your Mind; for Roachford: Naked Without You; for The Corrs: Intimacy; for Maria Nayler: Naked and Sacred; for New Radicals: You Get What You Give; for k. d. lang: Anywhere But Here; for Mel C.: Northern Star, I Turn To You 2000; for Enrique Iglesias: I Have Always Loved You; for Ronan Keating: Life Is A Rollercoaster 2000; for Geri Halliwell: Scream If You Wanna Go Faster 2001; for John Legend: Green Light 2008. *Honours:* Ivor Novello Award 2004, nine ASCAP Awards. *Current Management:* Stephen Budd Management, 59–65 Worship Street, London, EC2A 2DU, England. *Website:* www.record-producers.com. *E-mail:* rnowels@mindspring.com (office). *Website:* www.ricknowels.com.

NOYCE, Jonathan; British musician (bass guitar) and composer; b. 15 July 1971, Sutton Coldfield, West Midlands; m. Sara Joanna King 1995. *Education:* North Herts College, Royal Acad. of Music. *Career:* with Ian Anderson (Jethro Tull) 1995–2005: tours, USA, Canada, Europe; VH-1 radio broadcast, Secret Life; TV: Pebble Mill; What's Up Doc?; videos; with C J Lewis: The White Room; with David Palmer: concerts in Venezuela; Belgium; Estonia; Romania; Germany; various concerts and recordings; Summer of Rock shows with Gary Moore throughout Europe 2010; mem. Archive 2007–; mem. Three Friends 2015–; mem. Musicians' Union. *Recordings include:* with Take That: Relight My Fire 1993; with Al Green: Keep On Pushing Love 1994; with Sister Sledge: Thinking of You (remix) 1993; with Diana Ross: Love Hangover (remix) 1994; with Joey Negro: Universe of Love 1993; with David Palmer: Sgt Pepper; with Jethro Tull: J-Tull.Com 1999; with Mylène Farmer: Bleu Noir 2010; with Martin Barre: Away With Words 2013; with Archive: Restriction 2015. *Honours:* LRAM, Professional Certificate of Royal Acad. of Music. *E-mail:* tullmanagement@aol.com. *E-mail:* jo.cosbert@emimusic.com. *Website:* www.j -tull.com.

NOZEDAR, Adele; British record company executive and musician (piano, harp); b. 7 Aug. 1966, Yorkshire, England; m. Adam Fuest 1993. *Career:* formed the band Indians in Moscow (with Pete Riches and Stuart Walton) 1981, later formed band The Fever Tree (with Tom Hosie and Nik Corfield); Man. Dir, Rhythm King Records, independent label f. in 1986 with Martin Heath; owner of recording studio Twin Peaks (with Adam Fuest); co-founder of Renegade Software; mem. Musicians' Union, PRS. *Recordings include:* with Indians in Moscow: Your Secret's Safe With Us 1982, Indians in Moscow 1985. *Honours:* Leslie Perrin Award for Public Relations 1992.

N-TRANCE; British musician (keyboards); b. (Dale Longworth), 19 June 1966, Middleton, Manchester. *Career:* f. N-Trance 1990; sound engineer, leading PA company, most aspects of live sound (rock and roll, musicals, classical, television); signed to PWL while working on the Hitman and Her; mem, Musicians' Union. *Recordings:* albums: Electronic Pleasure 1995, Happy Hour 1999; singles: Back To The Bass (unreleased), Set You Free, Turn Up The Power, Tears in the rain 1999, Do Ya Think I'm Sexy? 1999, Paradise City 1999, Shake Ya Body 2000; as producer: 200% Energy 1995, N Trance, Stayin' Alive 1995, Now Dance '95 1995, Dance '96 Supermix 1996, goodtime disco Dance Hits 1997, Euromix Vol. 3 1997, Night at the Roxbury 1998, House of Boogie 1998. *Honours:* Best UK Dance Record 1994. *Current Management:* All Around The World, 9–13 Penny Street, Blackburn, BB1 6HJ, England. *Telephone:* (1254) 264120. *Fax:* (1254) 692768. *E-mail:* info@ aatw.com. *Website:* www.aatw.com; www.n-trance.co.uk.

DJ NU-MARK; American producer and DJ. *Career:* mem., Jurassic 5 1993–2006; numerous live performances. *Recordings include:* albums: with Jurassic 5: Jurassic 5 (EP) 1997, Quality Control 2000, Power in Numbers 2002, Feedback 2006; solo: Hands On 2004, Take Me With You 2011. *E-mail:* rick@aproposmanagement.com. *Website:* www.aproposmm.com; www .unclenu.com.

NUGENT, Ted; American rock musician (guitar) and singer; b. 13 Dec. 1948, Detroit. *Career:* Founder mem., The Amboy Dukes 1966–75; solo artist 1975–89; Founder mem., Damn Yankees 1989–; numerous live appearances. *Recordings include:* albums: with The Amboy Dukes: Call Of The Wild 1973, Tooth Fang And Claw 1974; solo: Ted Nugent 1975, Free For All 1976, Cat Scratch Fever 1977, Double Live Gonzo 1978, Weekend Warriors 1978, State of Shock 1979, Scream Dream 1980, Great Gonzos – The Best of Ted Nugent 1981, Intensities In Ten Cities 1981, Nugent 1982, Penetrator 1984, Little Miss Dangerous 1986, Anthology 1986, If You Can't Lick 'Em, Lick 'Em! 1988, Spirit Of The Wild 1995, Full Bluntal Nugity 2001, Craveman 2002, Love Grenade 2007; with Damn Yankees: Damn Yankees 1990. *Address:* 4008 West Michigan Avenue, Jackson, MI 49202, USA (office). *Telephone:* (517) 750-9060 (office). *Fax:* (517) 750-3640 (office). *E-mail:* linda@tednugent.com (office). *Website:* www.tednugent.com.

NUMAN, Gary; British singer and songwriter; b. (Gary Webb), 8 March 1958, Hammersmith, London, England. *Career:* singer, Tubeway Army 1978–79; solo artist 1979–; own record labels, Numa Records 1984–87, Mortal Records 2006–; extensive tours, regular television appearances. *Recordings include:* albums: Replicas 1979, The Pleasure Principle 1979, Telekon 1980, Living Ornaments 1979–80 1981, Dance 1981, I Assassin 1982, The Plan 1984, White Noise Live 1985, Strange Charm 1986, Exhibition 1987, Metal Rhythm 1988, Skin Mechanic 1989, Outland 1991, Machine + Soul 1992, Dream Corrosion 1994, Exile 1997, Dramatis Project 2000, Pure 2000, Hybrid 2003, Jagged 2006, Dead Son Rising 2011, Splinter (Songs from a Broken Mind) 2013. *Honours:* Q Innovation in Sound Award 2015. *Current Management:* Flick Productions, PO Box 888, Penzance, Cornwall TR20 8ZP, England. *E-mail:* flickprouk@aol.com. *Website:* www.numan.co.uk.

NÚÑEZ (MUÑOZ), Carlos; Spanish musician (gaita, recorder, tin whistle) and composer; b. Spain. *Education:* Royal Conservatory, Madrid. *Career:* began playing the gaita (Galician bagpipes), aged 8; invited to play as soloist with Lorient Symphony Orchestra, Britanny, aged 13; studied at the Royal Conservatory of Music in Madrid, received highest ever marks achieved for Baroque recorder; brought new life to neglected Galician folk tradition by studying the style of Irish and Scottish pipers and bringing ornamentation into the playing of the pipes; reached wider audience by collaborating with other Celtic musicians including Chieftains, Dan Ar Braz. *Recordings:* albums: A Irmandade Das Estrelas (Brotherhood of Stars) 1996, Os Amores Libres 1999, Mayo Longo 2000, Todos os Mundos 2002, Almas de Fisterra 2003, Carlos Nuñez y Amigos 2004; features on: Treasure Island OST 1989, The Long Black Veil, The Chieftains 1995, Santiago, The Chieftains 1996, Finisterres, Dan Ar Braz 1997, Zenith, Dan Ar Braz 1998, Silent Night – A Christmas In Rome, Paddy Moloney 1998, Caminhos, Dulce Pontes 1998, Bilbao Oh, Kepa Junkera 1999. *Honours:* Folkest 2001, Special Award, Rome. *Website:* www.carlos-nunez.com.

NUTINI, Paolo; British singer, songwriter and musician (guitar); b. 9 Jan. 1987, Paisley, Scotland. *Education:* St Andrews Acad. *Career:* fmr studio engineer; professional solo artist 2004–. *Recordings:* albums: These Streets 2006, Sunny Side Up (Ivor Novello Award for Best Album 2010, Meteor Ireland Award for Best Int. Album 2010) 2009, Caustic Love 2014. *Honours:* Q Award for Best Male 2010. *Current Management:* c/o Brendan Moon, Morsecode Management, 41-42 Berners Street, London, W1T 3NB, England. *E-mail:* info@morsecodemanagement.com. *Website:* www .morsecodemanagement.com; www.paolonutini.com.

NYE, Cheryl, BFA (Music); Canadian/American singer, songwriter, musician (keyboards), publisher and producer and model; b. Montreal, QC, Canada; d. of Wilfred Donald Nye and Esther Kalan Nye; single. *Education:* Concordia Univ., Montreal. *Career:* sang anthems at Toronto Skydome, Montreal Forum, Montreal Bell Centre, Olympic Stadium, Lansdowne Park; appearances in Las Vegas, Nashville, as well as throughout Canada and USA; judge, Songwriters of Wisconsin International 2001–; image used as 3D Bond Girl in an Internet video 2008; numerous TV appearances and radio interviews; mem. BMI. *Radio:* guest on numerous radio stations throughout Canada, USA and UK. *Television:* CBC, CFCF, Videotron, Télé-Métropole, RDS, CHRO, Radio-Québec, CFCL-CITO, CHNB-CKNY and numerous others. *Recordings include:* albums: Loving You 1993, With Goodbyes 2001, Eyes Of A Stranger (in English, Spanish and French) (No. 1 on the ReverbNation Charts for Montreal 2011–15, Featured Album on SplashRadio.org (UK) for two weeks 2012) 2011, I Surrender To My Heart, Hommage To The James Bond Films 2016. *Honours:* B100 Pepsi Entertainer Award (USA), Winner Country Music News Singing Competition, Knights of Pythias Certificates, Canada Day statuette for performances at Canada Day celebrations. *E-mail:* violetowl11@ yahoo.com. *Website:* www.cherylnye.com; www.reverbnation.com/cherylnye; www.facebook.com/cheryl.nye.7.

NYMAN, Michael, CBE; British composer; b. 23 March 1944, London. *Education:* Royal Acad. of Music, King's Coll. London. *Career:* composer, writer and music critic 1968–78; lecturer 1976–80; f. MN Records label 2005–. *Film and television soundtracks:* Peter Greenaway films: Postcards from Capital Cities 1967, Vertical Features Remake 1976, Goole by Numbers 1976, A Walk Through H: The Reincarnation of an Ornithologist 1978, 1–100 1978, The Falls 1980, Act of God 1980, Terence Conran 1981, The Draughtsman's Contract 1982, The Coastline 1983, Making a Splash 1984, A Zed and Two Noughts 1985, Inside Rooms: 26 Bathrooms, London & Oxfordshire 1985, Drowning by Numbers 1988, Fear of Drowning 1988, Death in the Seine 1988,

The Cook, The Thief, His Wife and Her Lover 1989, Hubert Bals Handshake 1989, Prospero's Books 1991; other films: Keep It Downstairs 1976, Tom Phillips 1977, Brimstone and Treacle 1982, Nelly's Version 1983, Frozen Music 1983, The Cold Room 1984, Fairly Secret Army 1984, The Kiss 1985, L'ange frénétique 1985, I'll Stake My Cremona to a Jew's Trump 1985, The Disputation 1986, Ballet méchanique 1986, Le miraculé 1987, The Man Who Mistook His Wife for a Hat 1987, Monsieur Hire 1989, Out of the Ruins 1989, Le mari de la coiffeuse 1990, Men of Steel 1990, Les enfants volants 1990, Not Mozart: Letters, Riddles and Writs 1991, The Final Score 1992, The Fall of Icarus 1992, The Piano 1993, Ryori no tetsujin 1993, Mesmer 1994, A la folie (Six Days, Six Nights) 1994, Carrington 1995, Anne no nikki (The Diary of Anne Frank) 1995, Der Unhold (The Ogre) 1996, Enemy Zero 1996, Gattaca 1997, Titch 1998, Ravenous 1999, How to Make Dhyrak: A Dramatic Work for Three Players and Camera, Truncated with Only Two Players 1999, Wonderland 1999, Nabbie no koi (Nabbie's Love) 1999, The End of the Affair 1999, The Claim 2000, Act Without Words I 2000, That Sinking Feeling 2000, La Stanza del figlio 2001, Subterrain 2001, 24 heures de la vie d'une femme 2002, The Man with a Movie Camera 2002, The Actors 2003, Nathalie... 2003, Charged 2003, Ident (Channel 5) 2004, Man on Wire 2007, The Eleventh Year 2009, The Trip 2010, 2 Graves 2010, Everyday 2012. *Other compositions:* orchestral: A Handsome, Smooth, Sweet, Smart, Clear Stroke: Or Else Play Not At All 1983, Taking a Line for a Second Walk 1986, L'Orgie Parisienne 1989, Six Celan Songs 1990, Where the Bee Dances 1991, Self Laudatory Hymn of Inanna and Her Omnipotence 1992, The Upside-Down Violin 1992, MGV (Musique à Grande Vitesse) 1993, On the Fiddle 1993, Concerto for Harpsichord and Strings 1995, Concerto for Trombone 1995, Double Concerto 1996, Strong on Oaks, Strong on the Causes of Oaks 1997, Cycle of Disquietude 1998, a dance he little thinks of 2001, The Draughtsman's Contract for Orchestra 2001, Dance of the Engines 2002, Gattaca for Orchestra 2003, The Claim for Orchestra 2003, The Piano: Concert Suite 2003, Violin Concerto 2003; chamber music: First Waltz in D, Bell Set No. 1 1974, 1–100 1976, Waltz in F 1976, Think Slow, Act Fast 1981, 2 Violins 1981, Four Saxes (Real Slow Drag) 1982, I'll Stake My Cremona to a Jew's Crump 1983, Time's Up 1983, Child's Play 1985, String Quartet No. 1 1985, Taking a Line for a Second Walk 1986, String Quartet No. 2 1988, String Quartet No. 3 1990, In Re Don Giovanni 1991, Masque Arias 1991, Time Will Pronounce 1992, Songs for Tony 1993, Three Quartets 1994, H.R.T. 1995, String Quartet No. 4 1995, Free for All 2001, Five Who Figured Four Years Ago 2002, Mapping 2002, Yellow Beach 2002, 24 Hour Sax Quartet 2004, For John Peel 2004; instrumental: Shaping the Curve 1990, Six Celan Songs 1990, Flugel-horn and Piano 1991, For John Cage 1992, The Convertibility of Lute Strings 1992, Here to There 1993, Yamamoto Perpetuo 1993, On the Fiddle 1993, To Morrow 1994, Tango for Tim 1994, Elisabeth Gets Her Way 1995, Viola and Piano 1995, Titch 1997, Fourths, Mostly (for organ) 2001; dramatic works: Strange Attractors, The Princess of Milan, A Broken Set of Rules 1984, Basic Black 1984, Portraits in Reflection 1985, And Do They Do 1986, The Man Who Mistook His Wife for a Hat 1986, Miniatures/Configurations 1988, Letters, Riddles and Writs 1991, Noises, Sounds and Sweet Airs 1994, Facing Goya 2000, Man and Boy: Dada (opera) 2003, Love Counts 2004; vocal: A Neat Slice of Time 1980, The Abbess of Andouillets 1984, Out of the Ruins 1989, Polish Love Song 1990, Shaping the Curve 1991, Anne de Lucy Songs 1992, Mozart on Mortality 1992, Grounded 1995, The Waltz Song 1995, The Ballad of Kastriot Rexhepi 2001, Mosè 2001, A Child's View of Colour 2003, Acts of Beauty 2004; with Michael Nyman Band: In Re Don Giovanni 1977, The Masterwork/Award-Winning Fishknife 1979, Bird List Song 1979, Five Orchestral Pieces Opus Tree 1981, Bird Anthem 1981, M-Work 1981, Love is Certainly, at Least Alphabetically Speaking 1983, Bird Work 1984, The Fall of Icarus 1989, La Traversée de Paris 1989, The Final Score 1992, AET (After Extra Time) 1996, De Granada a la Luna 1998, Orfeu 1998, The Commissar Vanishes 1999, Man with a Movie Camera 2001, Compiling the Colours (Samhitha) 2003, Three Ways of Describing Rain (Sawan; Rang; Dhyan) 2003, Zeit und Ziel 1814–2002, Manhatta 2003; dance: Flicker 2005. *Films:* Cine Opera 2009, Nyman with a Movie Camera 2010. *Recordings include:* film soundtracks, The Piano Sings 2005. *Publications:* Libretto for Birtwistle's Dramatic Pastoral, Down by the Greenwood Side 1968–69, Experimental Music: Cage and Beyond 1974; contribs: critical articles to journals, including The Spectator. *Honours:* Hon. DLitt. *E-mail:* myriam@michaelnyman.com. *E-mail:* office@michaelnyman.com. *Website:* www.michaelnyman.com.

NYS, (Magthea) Sandy; Belgian graphic designer; b. 30 July 1959, Mechelen. *Education:* Art School, School for Electronic Music, Conservatorium Antwerpen. *Career:* tours Europe, with bands including: Klinik, Hybryds 1983–; world-wide radio broadcast, in ind. charts; SABAM, Belgian copyright org.; soundtrack for Aquaria of Antwerp Zoo. *Recordings include:* Music For Rituals – An Ongoing Musical Spiritual Quest; More than 10 album releases, more than 100 hours music registered at SABAM. *Publications include:* contrib. to official and underground press.

NYSTROM, Lene Grawford; Norwegian singer; b. 2 Oct. 1973, Tonsberg. *Career:* mem., Joyspeed, renamed Aqua; numerous TV and live appearances in Scandinavia and UK. *Recordings include:* albums: Aquarium, 1997; Bubble Mix, 1998; We Belong to the Sea, 2001. *Website:* www.lene.net.ms.

NYSTRÖM, Per; Swedish musician (organ). *Career:* mem., The Concretes 1999–; band founded label, Licking Fingers. *Recordings include:* albums: Boyoubetterunow 2000, The Concretes 2003, Layourbattleaxedown 2005, In Colour 2006, Hey Trouble 2007. *Current Management:* EC1 Music Agency, 1 Cowcross Street, London, EC1M 6DR, England. *Telephone:* (20) 7490-8990. *Fax:* (20) 7490-8987. *E-mail:* jack@ec1music.com. *E-mail:* theconcretes@theconcretes.com. *Website:* www.theconcretes.com.

O

O, Karen; American singer; b. (Karen Lee Orzolek), 1978. *Education:* Oberlin Coll., New York Univ. *Career:* mem. (lead singer) Yeah Yeah Yeahs 2000–. *Recordings include:* albums: Fever To Tell 2002, Show Your Bones 2006, It's Blitz! 2009. *Theatre includes:* Stop the Virgens 2011. *Films:* wrote songs for Where the Wild Things Are 2009. *E-mail:* mail@ciullamgmt.com. *E-mail:* yeahyeahyeahsctc@hotmail.com. *Website:* www.yeahyeahyeahs.com.

Ó LIONÁIRD, Iarla, BEd, MA; Irish singer and record producer; b. 18 June 1964, Cúil Aodha, Co. Cork; m.; three c. *Education:* Carysfort Coll., Univ. of Limerick. *Career:* began performing at age of five; made first recording (Aisling Gheal) for Gael Linn record label 1976; singer with Afro Celt Sound System 1995–; Founder-mem., The Gloaming 2011–. *Recordings:* albums: with Tony MacMahon and Noel Hill: Aisling Gheal/Music of Dreams 1993; with Afro Celt Sound System: Volume 1: Sound Magic 1996, Volume 2: Release 1999, Volume 3: Further in Time 2001, Seed 2003, Pod 2004, Volume 5: Anatomic 2005; solo: The Seven Steps to Mercy 1997, I Could Read the Sky 2000, Invisible Fields 2005, Foxlight 2011; with Crash Ensemble: Donnacha Dennehy: Grá Agus Bás 2011; with The Gloaming: The Gloaming 2014. *E-mail:* m@barquemgmt.com. *Website:* thegloaming.net; iarla-o-lionaird.com.

O. R., Tomaž, (Tomaž Okroglič Rous); Slovenian musician (keyboards), songwriter and programmer. *Career:* mem. Siddharta; also mem. Revolute. *Recordings include:* albums: Id 1999, Nord 2001, Silikon Delta 2002, Rh- 2003, Petrolea 2006, Maraton 2007. *Honours:* Viktor Award for Best Act 2003, 2004, 2006, for Special Achievement 2003, MTV Europe Music Award 2005. *Address:* Siddharta, PO Box 179, 1236 Trzin, Slovenia (office). *Telephone:* (4) 1382192 (office). *E-mail:* info@siddharta.net (office). *Website:* www .siddharta.net (office).

Ó RAGHALLAIGH, Caoimhín; Irish folk musician (violin, hardanger fiddle); b. 1979, Dublin. *Career:* released debut solo album 1999; Founder-mem., The Gloaming 2011–; This Is How We Fly 2013–; numerous collaborations including with Brendan Begley, Martin Hayes, Catherine McEvoy, Peadar Ó Riada, Mick O'Brien, Dan Trueman. *Television:* as musician: Ainmhithe na Héireann 2008. *Films:* as musician: Dambé 2008, i 2008. *Recordings:* albums: solo: Turas Go Tir Na Nóg 1999, Where the One Eyed Man is King 2007, Music for an Elliptical Orbit 2014; with Peadar Ó Riada and Martin Hayes: Triúr Sa Draighean 2010, Triúr Aris 2012, Triúr Omós 2013; with This Is How We Fly: This Is How We Fly 2013; with The Gloaming: The Gloaming 2014; other: Kitty Lie Over (with Mick O'Brien) 2003, FYH (with Brendan Begley) 2007, Comb Your Hair and Curl (with Catherine McEvoy and Micheál Ó Raghallagh) 2010, A Moment of Madness (with Brendan Begley) 2010, Deadly Buzz (with Mick O'Brien) 2011, Laghdú (with Dan Trueman) 2014; spoken word (as accompanist): Sanas 2007, Súil Seilge 2008. *E-mail:* m@barquemgmt.com. *Website:* thegloaming.net; caoimhinoraghallaigh.com.

Ó SÚILLEABHÁIN, Mícheál, BMus, MA, PhD; Irish musician (piano), composer, educator and musicologist; *Professor of Music and Founding Director, Irish World Academy of Music and Dance, University of Limerick;* b. 10 Dec. 1950, Co. Tipperary. *Education:* Univ. Coll. Cork, Queen's Univ. Belfast, Trinity Coll., London. *Career:* Lecturer at Univ. Coll. Cork 1975–93; Inaugural Chair. of Music, Univ. of Limerick 1994–, Founder-Dir Irish World Acad. of Music and Dance 1994–, Founder Irish World Music Centre; leading figure in the integration of traditional music into Irish higher education; Visiting Prof., Boston Coll., USA 1990; Inaugural Chair. Culture Ireland 2006–14; Visiting O'Donnell Chair in Irish Studies, Keogh Naughton Inst., Univ. of Notre Dame, USA. *Films:* Irish Destiny 1994. *Radio:* broadcasts on RTÉ 1, RTÉ Lyric FM, BBC World Service. *Television:* contributed to RTÉ/ BBC TV series Bringing It All Back Home 1992; wrote and presented TV series A River of Sound 1995. *Recordings include:* albums: Mícheál Ó Súilleabháin 1975, Óró Damhnaigh 1977, Cry of the Mountain 1982, The Dolphin's Way 1987, Oilean/Island 1989, Casadh/Turning 1990, Gaiseadh/ Flowing (with the Irish Chamber Orchestra) 1992, A River of Sound 1995, Becoming 1998, Templum (featuring Nat. Chamber Choir) 2001, Irish Destiny 2005, Elver Gleams 2010. *Publication:* Fleischmann's Source of Irish Traditional Music Vols 1 and 2 (asst ed.) 1998. *Honours:* Hon. DMus (Nat. Univ. of Ireland) 2005; Hon. Alumnus Award, Boston Coll., Ard-Ollamh na hÉigse, Comhaltas Ceóltoirí Éireann 2004. *Address:* Irish World Academy of Music and Dance, University of Limerick, Limerick, Ireland (office). *Telephone:* (61) 202590 (office). *Fax:* (61) 202589 (office). *E-mail:* paula.dundion@ul.ie (office). *Website:* www.irishworldacademy.ie (office); www.mosmusic.ie (office).

OAKENFOLD, Paul; British DJ, remixer and producer; b. 30 Aug. 1963, London, England. *Career:* fmr chef; DJ in Covent Garden, London from 1982; resident, Heaven Club; mem. Steve Hillage's collective, System 7 1990s; numerous concerts, radio and TV broadcasts; produced and remixed for artists, including Boy George, U2, Happy Mondays, Olive, Cure, Insider; founder and owner Perfecto Records; wrote and produced (along with Andy Gray) theme tune to Big Brother (Channel 4) 2000. *Music for film:* Vexille 2007. *Recordings include:* albums: Journeys by Stadium DJ 1994, Journeys by DJ, Vol. 15: Paul Oakenfold in... 1995, Journeys by DJ Marathon 1996, Global Underground: Oslo 1997, Fantazia Presents the House Collection 1997, Cream Anthems '97 1997, Global Underground: New York 1998, Tranceport

1998, Resident: Two Years of Oakenfold at Cream 1999, A Sample from Essential Selection, Vol. 1 2000, Another World 2000, Travelling 2000, Sampladelica: The Roots of Paul Oakenfold 2000, Voyage into Trance 2001, Swordfish (film soundtrack) 2001, Ibiza 2001, Bust A Groove 2002, Bunkka 2002, Perfecto Presents... Paul Oakenfold Travelling 2000, Perfecto Presents... Paul Oakenfold in Ibiza 2001, A Lively Mind 2006, Paul Oakenfold, Greatest Hits and Remixes 2007, Perfecto in Las Vegas 2009, Pop Killer 2010. *Honours:* Q Award for Best Producer 1990. *E-mail:* info@pauloakenfold.com. *Website:* www.pauloakenfold.com; www.perfectorecords.com.

OAKES, Richard; British musician (guitar) and songwriter; b. 1 Oct. 1976, Perivale, Middlesex, England. *Career:* mem., Suede 1995–2004, 2010–; numerous tours, festival dates and TV appearances. *Recordings include:* albums: with Suede: Coming Up 1996, Sci-Fi Lullabies 1997, Head Music 1999, A New Morning 2002, Bloodsports 2013, Night Thoughts 2016. *Honours:* with Suede: Q Icon Award 2013. *Current Management:* Quietus Management Limited, 13 Bramley Road, 2nd Floor Phoenix Brewery, London, W10 6SP, England. *Telephone:* (20) 3220-0310. *Website:* www.quietusmanagement.com; www.suede.co.uk.

OAKEY, Philip; British singer and musician (synthesizer); b. 2 Oct. 1955, Sheffield, South Yorkshire, England. *Career:* fmr hospital porter; lead singer, Human League 1978–; numerous concerts, tours worldwide. *Recordings include:* albums: with Human League: Reproduction 1979, Travelogue 1980, Dare! 1981, Hysteria 1984, Crash 1986, Romantic? 1990, Octopus 1995, Secrets, 2001, Credo 2011. *Honours:* BRIT Award for Best Newcomer 1982. *Website:* www.thehumanleague.co.uk.

OANA, Augustin; Romanian folk singer; b. 26 July 1942, Cabesti-Hunedoara; m. 1972, two s. *Education:* Hunedoara Musical Assembly. *Career:* several television and radio broadcasts, including Bucharest radio; concerts throughout Romania, tours of Turkey and Austria; adapted poems for folk music of region; participated in many shows and television appearances with Bucharest Radio Orchestra.

OATES, John; American singer, songwriter and musician (guitar); b. 7 April 1949, New York. *Education:* Temple Univ. *Career:* fmr mem., The Masters, Gulliver; mem. duo, Hall and Oates 1969–; concerts worldwide. *Compositions include:* numerous hit songs co-written with Daryl Hall; film soundtrack, Outlaw Blues 1979; co-writer, Electric Blue, Icehouse 1988. *Recordings include:* albums: albums: with Hall and Oates: Whole Oats 1972, Abandoned Luncheonette 1974, War Babies 1974, Daryl Hall and John Oates 1975, Bigger Than Both of Us 1976, No Goodbyes 1977, Beauty On A Back Street 1977, Livetime 1978, Along The Red Edge 1978, X-Static 1979, Voices 1980, Private Eyes 1981, H2O 1982, Rock n' Roll Soul, Part 1 1983, Big Bam Boom 1984, Live At The Apollo With David Ruffin and Eddie Kendricks 1985, Ooh Yeah! 1988, Change of Season 1990, Marigold Sky 1997, Behind the Music 2002, Do It for Love 2003, Our Kind of Soul 2004, Home for Christmas 2006, Do What You Want, Be What You Are 2009; solo: Phunk Shiu 2002, 1000 Miles of Life 2008. *Honours:* American Music Awards for Favorite Duo or Band 1983–85. *Current Management:* Wolfson Entertainment Inc., 22201 Ventura Boulevard, Suite 207, Woodland Hills, CA 913649, USA. *Telephone:* (818) 615-0499. *Fax:* (818) 615-0498. *E-mail:* info@wolfsonent.com. *Website:* www.wolfsonent .com. *E-mail:* admin@hallandoates.com (office). *Website:* www.hallandoates .com.

OBA FUNKE (see King Britt)

OBERG, Rolf Thomas; Swedish singer and musician (melodica, synthesizer); b. 15 March 1967, Helsingborg. *Career:* mem., bob hund 1991–; numerous concerts in Scandinavia, including Roskilde, Lollipop, Ruisrock, Quartfestivalen and Hultsfred festivals; mem. STIM, SAMI. *Recordings:* bob hund 1993, Edvin Medvind, 7 1994, I Stället för Musik: förvirring 1996, Omslag: Martin Kann 1996, Düsseldorf 3:53 1996, Ett fall och en lösning 1997, Nu är det väl revolution på gång? 1998, Jag rear ut min själ! Allt skal bort!!! 1998, Helgen V.48 1999, Sover aldrig 1999, Stenáldem kan börja 2001, Ingenting 2002. *Honours:* Swedish Grammy Awards for Best Live Act 1994, Best Lyrics 1996. *Website:* www.bobhund.nu.

OBERST, Conor, (Bright Eyes); American singer, songwriter and musician; b. 15 Feb. 1980, Omaha, Neb. *Career:* released debut album aged 14 1993; mem. band Commander Venus 1995–98; played in various bands including Desaparecidos, Park Ave.; prin. mem. Bright Eyes 1995–; co-founder (with Robb Nansel) Saddle Creek Records; f. Team Love record label; toured with Bruce Springsteen and R.E.M. on Vote for Change tour during US presidential election campaign 2004; mem. Monsters of Folk 2004–. *Films:* Spend an Evening with Saddle Creek 2005, Coachella: The Movie 2005. *Recordings:* albums: as Conor Oberst: Water 1993, Here's to Special Treatment 1994, The Soundtrack to My Movie 1996, Conor Oberst 2008, Outer South 2009; with Commander Venus: Do You Feel at Home? 1995, The Uneventful Vacation 1997; with Bright Eyes: A Collection of Songs Written and Recorded 1995–1997 1998, Letting Off the Happiness 1998, Fevers and Mirrors 2000, Lifted or The Story Is in the Soil 2002, Keep Your Ear to the Ground 2002, A Christmas Album 2002, I'm Wide Awake, It's Morning 2005, Digital Ash in a Digital Urn 2005, Motion Sickness: Live Recordings 2005, Noise Floor

(Rarities: 1998–2005) 2006, Cassadaga 2007, One Jug of Wine, Two Vessels (with Neva Dinova) 2010; with Monsters of Folk: Monsters of Folk 2009. *Honours:* Artist of the Year and Song of the Year (for When the President Talks to God), PLUG Independent Music Awards 2006. *Address:* Saddle Creek, POB 8554, Omaha, NE 68108-0554, USA (office). *E-mail:* info@saddle-creek.com (office); info@monstersoffolk.com (office). *Website:* www.saddle-creek.com (office); www.thisisbrighteyes.com; monstersoffolk.com.

OBI, Ben; British producer; *Producer, Savannah Street Music;* b. London, England. *Education:* coll. and Univ. of Minnesota. *Career:* producer, Alexander O'Neal 1996; producer for The Sunset Music Band and other Minneapolis groups; f. Savannah Street Music, artist agency, music production and recording co.; mem. ASCAP. *Recordings include:* Alexander O'Neal: Lovers Again, Timotha Lanae: Red, Rewind. *Address:* Savannah Street Music (office). *Telephone:* (651) 501-3958 (office). *E-mail:* benobi@savannahstreet.com (office). *Website:* www.savannahstreet.com (office).

O'BRIEN, Edward (Ed) John; British musician (rhythm guitar, percussion) and songwriter; b. 15 April 1968, Oxford, England. *Education:* Manchester Univ. *Career:* mem. On A Friday 1987, renamed Radiohead 1991–; numerous tours, festivals and television appearances. *Recordings include:* albums: Pablo Honey 1993, The Bends 1995, OK Computer (Grammy Award for Best Alternative Music Performance) 1997, Kid A (Grammy Award for Best Alternative Music Album) 2000, Amnesiac 2001, I Might Be Wrong (live recordings) 2001, Hail To The Thief 2003, In Rainbows (Grammy Award for Best Alternative Music Album 2009) 2007, The King of Limbs 2011. *Honours:* Q Award for Best Act in the World Today 2001, 2002, 2003. *Current Management:* Courtyard Management, 21 The Nursery, Sutton Courtenay, Abingdon, Oxfordshire OX14 4UA, England. *Website:* www.radiohead.com.

O'BRIEN, Steve, (Steve-O); American musician. *Career:* founder mem., Fun Lovin' Criminals 1993–99; numerous tours, festivals and television appearances. *Recordings include:* albums: Fun Lovin' Criminals 1995, Come Find Yourself 1996, 100% Colombian 1998, Mimosa—The Lounge Album 1999.

OBROVAC, Tamara; Croatian singer, musician (flute) and composer; b. 1962, Pula. *Education:* High School of Music, Ljubljana and Pula. *Career:* f. and leader, The Tamara Obrovac Quartet, Tamara Obrovac Quintet, Tamara Obrovac Transhistria Electric, Tamara Obrovac Transhistria Ensemble, Tamara Obrovac Istria/Ireland Ensemble, Transhistria Juniors; collaborations with Balkan Winds, Transbaikanika ensemble, Matija Dediá; also composes music for film and theatre. *Recordings include:* albums: solo: Triade 1996, Črni Kos (with Georg Kuszrich) 2006; with Tamara Obrovac Quartet: Ulika 1998; with Transhistria Ensemble: Transhistria 2001, Sve Passiva (All Fades Away) 2003, Daleko Je (Is Faraway) 2005; with Transhistria Electric: Neću više jazz kantati 2009. *Address:* 52342 Svetvinčenat, Krančići 21, Croatia (office). *E-mail:* tamara.obrovac@gmail.com (office). *Website:* www.tamaraobrovac.com (home).

O'CARROLL, Sinéad Maria; Irish singer; b. 14 May 1978, Dublin; one d. *Career:* mem., B*Witched 1998–2002; numerous tours and television appearances. *Recordings:* albums: B*Witched 1998, Awake and Breathe 1999. *Website:* www.bwitched.com.

OCASEK, Richard (Ric); American singer, songwriter, musician (guitar) and record producer; b. 23 March 1949, Baltimore, MD; m. Paulina Porizkova 1989. *Career:* founder mem., The Cars 1976–88; numerous live appearances with The Cars; founded Synchro Sound recording studio, Boston 1981; solo artist 1990–; record prod. for artists, including Bad Brains, Black 47, Guided By Voices, No Doubt, Hole, Jonathan Richman, The Wannadies, Weezer. *Recordings include:* albums: with The Cars: The Cars 1979, Candy-O 1979, Panorama 1980, Shake It Up 1982, Heartbeat City 1984, Door To Door 1987; solo: Beatitude 1983, This Side of Paradise 1986, Fireball Zone 1991, Negative Theater 1993, Quick Change World 1993, Getchertikitz 1996, Troublizing 1997, Learner's Permit 1999, Nexterday 2005. *Honours:* Rolling Stone Best New Band of the Year 1979, MTV Award (for You Might Think) 1984. *Website:* www.ricocasek.com.

OCEAN, Billy; singer and songwriter; b. (Leslie Sebastian Charles), 21 Jan. 1950, Trinidad. *Career:* solo artist 1975–; numerous concerts internationally. *Compositions include:* co-writer of own hits Loverboy, There'll Be Sad Songs, Get Outta My Dreams. *Recordings include:* albums: Billy Ocean 1976, City Limit 1980, Nights (I Feel Like Getting Down) 1981, Inner Feeling 1982, Suddenly 1984, Love Zone 1986, Tear Down These Walls 1988, Time To Move On 1993, L.I.F.E. 1997, Emotions In Motion 2002, On the Run 2003, Let's Get Back Together 2003, Showdown 2004, YBC! 2007. *Honours:* Grammy Award for Best R&B Performance 1985, American Music Awards for Favorite Male Video Artist, Favorite Single 1988, ASCAP Award for Caribbean Queen, Most Played Song in USA 1996. *Current Management:* LJE, 32 Willesden Lane, London NW6 7ST, England. *Website:* www.billyocean.co.uk.

OCEAN, (Christopher Francis) Frank; American singer, songwriter and musician (keyboards); b. (Christopher Breaux), 28 Oct. 1987, Long Beach, Calif. *Education:* Univ. of New Orleans. *Career:* raised in New Orleans, La; moved to Los Angeles; became songwriter for artists including Brandy, Justin Bieber, John Legend, Beyoncé; joined hip hop collective OFWGKTA (aka Odd Future) 2009; signed to Def Jam Recordings; released debut album 2012; has collaborated with Nas, Pharrell Williams, Kanye West and Jay-Z. *Recordings include:* mixtape: Nostalgia, Ultra 2011; album: Channel Orange (Soul Train Music Award for Album of the Year 2012, Grammy Award for Best Urban Contemporary Album 2013) 2012. *Honours:* GQ Award for Rookie of the Year 2011, Vibe Award for Man of the Year 2012, mtvU Award for Man of the Year 2012, Grammy Award for Best Rap/Sung Collaboration (for No Church In The Wild) 2013, BRIT Award for Int. Male Artist 2013. *Address:* c/o Def Jam Records, Island Def Jam Group, Universal Music Group, Worldwide Plaza, 825 Eighth Avenue, 28th Floor, New York, NY 10019, USA (office). *Website:* www.defjam.com (office); www.frankocean.com.

OCHOA, Eliades; Cuban singer and musician (guitar); b. 22 June 1946, Songo La Maya, Santiago de Cuba. *Career:* worked in radio 1960s; fmr mem., Trova Cubano, Quinteto Oriente, Septeto Típico; leader, Cuarteto Patria 1978–; session work; solo artist; mem. Buena Vista Social Club; mem. AfroCubism project 2010–. *Film:* Buena Vista Social Club 1997. *Recordings include:* albums: A Una Coqueta 1993, Lion Is Loose 1996, Buena Vista Social Club (with others) (Grammy Award) 1997, Cubafrica 1998, Sublime Illusió 1999, Son de Santiago 1999, Llego el Cuarteto Patria 1999, Tributo al Cuarteto Patria 2000, Cuidadito Compay Gallo 2001, Grandes Exitos 2001, Son de Oriente 2001, Estoy como nunca 2002, Ochoa y Segundo 2003; with AfroCubism: AfroCubism 2010. *Address:* c/o World Circuit Records, First Floor, Shoreditch Stables, 138 Kingsland Road, London, E2 8DY, England (office). *E-mail:* post@worldcircuit.co.uk (office). *Website:* www.worldcircuit.co.uk; www.buenavistasocialclub.com.

OCHOA HIDALGO, Eglis; Cuban singer and musician (congas, bongos, cowbell); b. 1972, Santiago de Cuba. *Education:* Esteban Salas Conservatory. *Career:* early career as a violinist; as a student performed with Quinteto Oriente; mem. Grupo Patria 1994–; mem. AfroCubism 2010–; has performed with Eliades Ochoa's Cuarteto Patria, Buena Vista Social Club. *Recordings:* albums include: with Eliades Ochoa: Sublime Illusion 1999, Tributo al Cuarteto Patria 2000, Estoy Como Nunca 2002; with AfroCubism: AfroCubism 2010. *Address:* c/o World Circuit Records, 138 Kingsland Road, London, E2 8DY, England (office). *E-mail:* post@worldcircuit.co.uk (office). *Website:* www.worldcircuit.co.uk (office).

O CONGHAILE, Micheál, BA, MA, DipEd; Irish writer, managing director and record company executive; b. 14 March 1962, Galway. *Career:* fmr coll. lecturer; Founder Cló Iar-Chonnacht (Irish traditional music label) 1985–; mem. Performing Right Soc., IMRO. *Publications:* song collections: Croch Suas é, Up Seanamhach!; ten books in the Irish language. *Honours:* elected mem. of Aosdána for outstanding contrib. to the arts in Ireland; numerous nat. literary awards. *Address:* Cló Iar-Chonnacht, Indreabhán, Conamara, Co. Galway, Ireland. *E-mail:* moccic@eircom.net.

O'CONNELL, Brian; American musician (bass guitar); b. Queens, NY; m. Ayesha Alam; one d. *Education:* State Univ. of New York. *Career:* mem., Junoon (with Ali Azmat and Salman Ahmad) 1992–2005, banned by Pakistani authorities for criticism of govt corruption early 1990s; upon invitation of UN Sec.-Gen., Kofi Annan, performed at UN Gen. Ass. (first band to play at Gen. Ass.); tours throughout Asia, N America, Middle East and Europe; Jazbe-e-Junoon selected as official song of cricket world cup, hosted by Pakistan 1996. *Recordings include:* albums: Junoon 1990, Talaash 1993, Inquilaab 1995, Khashmakash 1996, Azaadi 1997, Parvaaz 1999, Andaz 2001, The Millennium Edition (compilation) 2000, Daur-e-Junoon 2002, Dewaar 2003. *Honours:* Channel V Music Award for Int. Group 1998, UNESCO Award for Outstanding Achievement in Music and Peace 1999, BBC Asia Award 1999.

O'CONNOR, Gerry; Irish composer and musician (banjo, guitar, violin); b. 20 July 1960, Tipperary; m. Marie, 13 May 1980, 1 s., 1 d. *Education:* Third level, UCD, Dublin. *Career:* Solo albums; Member, 4 Men and A Dog; Performances, television, radio: Britain; Europe; Scandinavia; Canada; USA; Australia; Workshop; Festivals; Tutor publications, book, cassette, video; mem, IMRO; PRS; MCPS. *Recordings:* Time To Time; Trad At Heart; Funk The Cajun Blues; 4 Men and A Dog: Shifting Gravel; Dr A's Secret Remedies; Niamh Parsons: Loosen Up; Gordon Duncan: Circular Breath; Gaelic roots; Mighty Session; Mists of Morning; Moving Cloud: Foxglove; Other collaborations include: Maire Brennan; Luka Bloom. *Publications:* 50 Solos For Tenor Banjo; Tenor Banjo Techniques. *Honours:* International Radio Festival: Bratislava, 1989; Folk Album of the Year, 1991, (4 Men and A Dog). *E-mail:* christinekeenan@eircom.net. *Website:* www.gerryoconnor.com.

O'CONNOR, Mark; American musician (violin, guitar, bass, mandolin); b. 5 Aug. 1961, Seattle, Washington. *Career:* leader, own group, Nashville Strings; musician with artists including Paul Simon, James Taylor, Dolly Parton, Willie Nelson, Chet Atkins, Randy Travis, Michael Brecker; concerts include Barbican Hall (with Yo-Yo Ma), Montreux Jazz Festival, Carnegie Hall, New York; founder and Pres., Mark O'Connor Fiddle Camp and Strings Conference; Artist-in-Residence, UCLA 2008–09; mem, CMA. *Compositions include:* Fiddle Concerto 1995, The American Seasons: Seasons of an American Life 2000, Double Violin Concerto 2000, Double Concerto for Violin and Cello 2003, Violin Concerto No. 6: Old Brass 2003, Poets and Prophets. *Recordings include:* Pickin' in the Wind 1975, Markology 1978, On the Rampage 1979, Soppin' the Gravy 1979, False Dawn 1982, Meanings Of 1985, Stone from Which the Arch Was Made 1986, Elysian Forest 1988, Championship Years 1989, On the Mark 1989, Retrospective 1990, New Nashville Cats 1991, Johnny Appleseed (children's album with Garrison Keillor) 1992, Heroes 1993, The Night Before Christmas 1993, Fiddle Concerto for violin and orchestra 1994, Appalachia Waltz 1996, Liberty! 1997, Midnight on the Water 1998, Fanfare for the Volunteer 1999, Appalachian Journey (Grammy Award 2001) 2000, Hot Swing 2001, The American Seasons 2001, In Full Swing 2003,

Crossing Bridges 2004, Double Violin Concerto 2005, Fiddle Camp, Vol. 1 2006, Folk Mass 2007. *Honours:* winner, classical guitar competition, aged 11, Country Music Asscn 's Musician of the Year, four times, Grammy Award, New Nashville Cats. *Current Management:* c/o Mark Alpert, Columbia Artists Management, 1790 Broadway, New York, NY 10019-1412, USA. *Telephone:* (212) 841-9500. *Fax:* (212) 841-9744. *E-mail:* info@cami.com. *Website:* www.cami.com. *E-mail:* mark@markoconnor.com (office). *Website:* www.markoconnor.com.

O'CONNOR, Martin (Mairtin); Irish musician (accordion); b. 28 March 1955, Galway, Ireland; m. Sietske Van Minnen 1983; one s. three d. *Career:* tours of America, Europe, Middle East, Hong Kong; soloist, Bill Whelan's Seville Suite, with RTE Concert Orchestra, World Expo, Seville 1993; soloist in Riverdance; featured in television documentaries Bringing It All Back Home, River of Sound; mem, IMRO, Musicians' Union. *Compositions:* music for 2 short films, many local theatre productions. *Recordings:* albums: solo: The Connachtman's Rambles 1979, Perpetual Motion 1990, Chatterbox (featuring own compositions) 1993, The Road West 2005; featured as accordion player on: Riverdance, Bill Whelan 1996, Golden Heart, Mark Knopfler 1996, Eileen Ivers, So Far: The collection 1979–95, Legends of Ireland 1998, Ellen Cranitch, Karst 1998, Maire Brennan, Whisper to the Wild Water 1999, Retrospective, Mark O'Connor 1999, Keeper Of The Flame, Luka Bloom 2000, Os Amores Libres, Carlos Nunez 2000, Little Lights, Kate Rusby 2001, Dreamcatcher, Secret Garden 2001. *Honours:* AIB (Allied Irish Bank) Traditional Musician of the Year 1995. *Address:* c/o Tara Music, Basement, 18 Upper Mount Street, Dublin 2, Ireland (office). *E-mail:* info@taramusic.com (office). *Website:* www.taramusic.com (office).

O'CONNOR, Sinéad; Irish singer, songwriter and musician (guitar, piano, keyboards, percussion, low whistle); b. (Sinéad Marie Bernadette O'Connor), 8 Dec. 1966, Glenageary, Co. Dublin; d. of John O'Connor and the late Marie O'Connor; m. 1st John Reynolds (divorced); one d. (by John Waters); m. 2nd Nicholas Sommerland 2002; one c. with Frank Bonadio 2007; m. 3rd Steve Cooney 2010 (divorced 2011); m. 4th Barry Herridge 9 Dec. 2011 (divorced 26 Dec. 2011). *Education:* Dublin Coll. of Music. *Career:* mem. Ton Ton Macoute 1985–87; refused to accept Grammy Award for Best Alternative Album 1991; now Tridentine priest Mother Bernadette Mary. *Recordings include:* albums: The Lion and the Cobra 1987, I Do Not Want What I Have Not Got (Grammy Award for Best Alternative Album 1991) 1990, Am I Not Your Girl? 1992, Universal Mother 1994, Gospeloak 1997, Sean-Nós Nua 2002, Throw Down Your Arms 2005, Theology 2007, How About I Be Me (And You Be You)? 2012, I'm Not Bossy, I'm the Boss 2014. *Video films:* Value of Ignorance 1989, The Year of the Horse 1991. *Television:* Hush-a-Bye-Baby. *Honours:* MTV Award for Best Video, MTV Award for Best Single (both for Nothing Compares 2 U) 1990, MTV Award for Best Female Singer 1990, Rolling Stone Artist of the Year Award 1991, BRIT Award for Best Int. Solo Artist 1991. *Website:* www.sineadoconnor.com.

DR OCTAGON (see Kool Keith)

ODADJIAN, Shavo; Armenian/American musician (bass guitar); b. 22 April 1974, Armenia. *Career:* moved to USA as a child; mem., System of a Down 1996–. *Recordings include:* albums: System Of A Down 1998, Toxicity 2001, Maximum 2002, Steal This Album! 2002, Mezmerize 2005, Hypnotize 2005, Vicinity of Obscenity 2006. *Honours:* MTV Europe Music Award for Best Alternative 2005, Grammy Award for Best Hard Rock Performance (for B.Y.O.B.) 2006. *Current Management:* Velvet Hammer, 9911 W. Pico Boulevard, 350W, Los Angeles, CA 90035, USA. *Telephone:* (310) 657-6161. *Fax:* (310) 657-0310. *Website:* www.velvethammer.net; www.systemofadown.com.

ODDE, Knud; Danish composer and painter; b. 25 Jan. 1955, Fröslev. *Education:* Gen. Certificate of Educ., Research Librarian. *Career:* mem. The Sods 1977, name changed to Sort Sol 1980–2001; toured USA, 1982, Russia 1988; Music for Danish Royal Ballet production of Hamlet 1996. *Solo exhibitions:* Esbjerg Art Museum 1994, Heartart Museum 1995, 2000, DCA Gallery, New York 1999, 2005, Randers Art Museum 2002, Ystat Konstmuseum 2003. *Group exhibitions:* about Mark E. Smith/The Fall in Hamburg, Berlin, London 2007–09. *Recordings:* Minutes To Go 1979, Under En Sort Sol 1980, Dagger and Guitar 1983, Everything That Rises Must Converge 1987, Flow My Firetear 1990, Glamourpuss 1993, Unspoiled Monsters 1996, Blackbox 1997, Snakecharmer 2001, Circle Hits The Flame 2002, Lonely Nudist 2008. *Publications:* biography: Knud Odde by Henrik Wivel 1994, Erich Von Stroheim, by Knud Odde 1994, Knud Oddes kabinet 2004, North Star Serenade 2005. *Honours:* three (local) Grammy Awards 1991; five Grammy Awards in 1994, with Sort Sol; Nat. Art Council grant 1999–2001. *Address:* Esromgade 15, OPG.2, 3rd Floor, Room 2301, 2200 Copenhagen N, Denmark (office). *Website:* www.knudodde.dk.

ODELL, Ann Mary, LRAM; British musician (keyboards), singer and arranger; b. 18 April 1947, London, England; m. Stephen R. Spurling 1980 (divorced 1994); two s. *Education:* Royal Acad. of Music. *Career:* fmr mem., Ivy Benson Orchestra; mem., Anna Dell Trio (for QE2 maiden voyage) 1969; session musician and arranger 1972–81; various tours, TV broadcasts; formed own band, Blue Mink 1992–94; runs Watermill Jazz Club, Dorking, Surrey; owner of agency and MIDI recording studio, Take Note Ltd; mem. PRS, Musicians' Union, Asscn of British Jazz Musicians. *Recordings include:* with Blue Mink: Fruity, Blue Mink; solo: Ann Odell; A Little Taste. *E-mail:* ann.odell@lineone.net (office). *Website:* www.annodell.com.

ODELL, Roger Keith; musician (drums, percussion) and songwriter; b. 7 Dec. 1941, Epping, Essex, England; m. Larraine 1968, one s. one d. *Education:* Guildhall School of Music. *Career:* toured throughout the world in concert, with numerous broadcasts on television and radio; mem. PRS, International Percussion Soc., BAC&S. *Compositions include:* contributed to over 20 recordings by Shakatak, as drummer and songwriter; co-writer: Night Birds; Down On The Street. *Recordings include:* with Shakatak: Live at Ronnie Scott's, 1998; Shinin On, 1998; Magic, 1999; Invitations, 1999; Christmas Dreams, 1999; Collection Volume 2, 2000; with Martini Grooves: Martini Grooves, 1999; Welcome to the Jazz Cafe, 1999. *Honours:* silver prize Tokyo International Song Festival. *Address:* 81, Crabtree Lane, London SW6 6LW, England.

ODGERS, Brian Norman; British musician (bass, bass guitar); b. 9 Feb. 1942, Forest Gate, London; m. Jahnet McIlwain 1976; four d. (three by previous marriage). *Career:* Played with: Herbie Hancock; Chick Corea; Freddie Hubbard; Larry Carlton; Van Morrison; Georgie Fame on Herbie's 50th birthday; TV special in Los Angeles; Tours: two years Van Morrison; six months Andy Williams; 26 years Georgie Fame; three years Winifred Atwell; TV, radio appearances over 30 years with most UK and World stars, include: Tom Jones; Englebert Humperdinck; Elton John; Eric Clapton; Cliff Richard; Sarah Vaughan; Shirley Bassey; Neil Diamond; Tony Bennett; Abba; Andre Previn; mem., Musicians' Union. *Recordings:* John McLaughlin: Extrapolation; Van Morrison: Enlightenment; Orginal Evita recording with Andrew Lloyd Webber; Roger Daltrey: White Horse; Jimmy Webb: Land's End; Georgie Fame: That's What Friends Are For; Marc Bolan: Cat Black; Roger Daltrey, Martyrs and Madmen; Sweet Thursday; Session musician for 20 years; Recorded with artistes from rock through jazz to light classical, including: Pete Atkin; Jane Birkin; Chris De Burgh; Serge Gainsbourg; Lou Reed; Al Stewart. *Address:* c/o Ronnie Scott's Club, Frith Street, London W1, England.

ODIT BAVASTRO, Osnel; Cuban singer, musician (guitar) and composer; b. 1965, Granma. *Career:* fmr mem. Grupo los Olivos, Grupo AKAN; mem. Septeto Turquino 1984–2000; mem. Grupo Patria 2005–; mem. AfroCubism project 2010–; has performed with variety of Cuban artists. *Compositions:* numerous compositions performed by artists including Sexteto Moneda Nacional, Morena Son, Adalberto Álvarez, Roberto Torres, Tamara, Eduardo Sosa, Oscar de León. *Recordings:* albums: with AfroCubism: AfroCubism 2010. *Honours:* OTI Performance Competition First Prize 1998. *Address:* c/o World Circuit Records, 138 Kingsland Road, London, E2 8DY, England (office). *E-mail:* post@worldcircuit.co.uk (office). *Website:* www.worldcircuit.co.uk (office).

Ó DOCHARTAIGH, Seoirse, BA, MA; Northern Irish painter, musician, researcher and writer; b. 17 June 1946, Belfast, Northern Ireland. *Education:* Univ. Coll., Cork. *Career:* born into musical Co. Armagh/Donegal family; began with singing, later, guitar and tin whistle; public performances increased 1970s, including TV appearances and radio broadcasts, tours of Europe and USA; Musical and Artistic Dir of own band, Dúlamán 1995–; mem. Performing Right Soc., Irish Music Rights Org., Mechanical-Copyright Protection Soc., PPI. *Recordings include:* Slán Agus Beannacht 1988, Seoirse O Dochartaigh: Live 1989, Bláth Buí 1992, Amhráin Agus Bodhráin 1994, Oíche Go Maidin 1994, Tabhair ar Ais an Oíche Aréir 2000, Dúlamán A' tSléibhe 2002, Seoirse 2006, Another Side of Seoirse (box set of five CDs) 2012, Windmills of the Mind 2013. *Honours:* music prizes in the Oireachtas. *Address:* 1 John's, Mossyglen, Leckemy, Carndonagh PO, Inishowen, Co. Donegal, Ireland (home). *Telephone:* (87) 2475371 (home). *E-mail:* seoirseod@eircom.net (home). *Website:* www.seoirse.com; www.seoirseodochartaigh.ie.

O'DONNELL, Daniel, MBE; Irish singer; b. 12 Dec. 1961, Kincasslagh, Co. Donegal; m. Majella McLennan 2002. *Career:* backing vocalist for sister Margo O'Donnell early 1980s; tours of UK and Ireland 1985–, Australia and NZ 1993–, USA 2003–; numerous live appearances. *Radio:* numerous interviews in Ireland, UK, USA and Australia. *Television:* series, Ireland, Pledges (PBS TV, USA). *Recordings include:* albums: Two Sides Of Daniel O'Donnell 1985, I Need You 1986, Don't Forget To Remember 1987, The Boy From Donegal 1987, Love Songs 1988, From The Heart 1988, Thoughts Of Home 1989, Favourites 1990, The Last Waltz 1990, The Very Best Of… 1991, Follow Your Dream 1992, Christmas With Daniel 1994, Especially For You 1994, The Classic Collection 1995, Irish Collection 1996, Timeless (with Mary Duff) 1996, Songs Of Inspiration 1996, Country Collection 1997, This Is Daniel O'Donnell 1997, I Believe 1997, Love Hope & Faith 1998, Greatest Hits 1999, Faith And Inspiration 2000, Live Laugh Love 2001, Heartbreakers 2002, Songs Of Love 2002, Irish Album 2002, Yesterday's Memories 2002, Dreaming 2002, The Daniel O'Donnell Show 2003, Welcome To North America 2003, Date With (live) 2003, Daniel In Blue Jeans 2003, Daniel O'Donnell And Friends (live) 2003, At The End Of The Day 2003, The Jukebox Years 2004, Welcome To My World 2004, Until The Next Time 2006, Together Again (with Mary Duff) 2008, Country Boy 2008, Peace In The Valley 2009, O Holy Night 2010. *Videos include:* Daniel O'Donnell Live In Concert 1988, Thoughts Of Home 1989, TV Show Favourites 1990, An Evening With Daniel O'Donnell 1990, Follow Your Dream 1992, Daniel And Friends Live 1993, Just For You 1994, The Classic Concert 1995, Christmas With Daniel 1996, The Gospel Show, Live At The Point 1997, Give A Little Love 1998, Peaceful Waters 1999, Faith And Inspiration 2000, Live Laugh Love 2001, The Daniel O'Donnell Show 2001, Shades Of Green 2002, Songs Of Faith 2003, Daniel in Blue Jeans 2003, At the End of the Day 2003, The Jukebox Years 2004, Welcome to My

World 2004, Teenage Dreams 2005, From Daniel with Love 2006, Until the Next Time 2006, Together Again (with Mary Duff) 2007, Country Boy 2008, Peace in the Valley 2009, O Holy Night 2010, Moon Over Ireland 2011, Songs from the Movies and More 2012, A Picture of You 2013, Stand Beside Me 2014. *Publications:* My Story (autobiog.) 2000, Daniel O'Donnell: My Pictures and Places 2004. *Current Management:* c/o Brockwell Ltd, Unit 6, 90B Lagan Road, Dublin Industrial Estate, Glasnevin, Dublin 11, Ireland. *Telephone:* (1) 830-1707. *Fax:* (1) 830-1981. *E-mail:* srmanagement@eircom.net. *Website:* www.danielodonnell.org.

O'DONOGHUE, Daniel (Danny) John Mark Luke; Irish singer, songwriter and musician (keyboards); b. 3 Oct. 1980, Dublin. *Career:* fmr R&B producer in USA; mem. MyTown 1996–2001; mem. The Script 2001–. *Television:* The Voice UK (mentor and judge) 2012–13. *Recordings:* albums: The Script 2008, Science and Faith 2010, #3 2012, No Sound Without Silence 2014. *Honours:* World Music Award for Best Selling Irish Act 2008, Meteor Ireland Music Awards for Best Band 2009, for Best Irish Album 2009. *Address:* c/o RCA Group, 9 Derry Street, London W8 5HY, England (office). *Website:* www.rcalabelgroup.co.uk (office); www.thescriptmusic.com.

Ó FARACHÁIN, Antaine, BEd; Irish singer and musician; b. 6 Feb. 1959, Dublin. *Career:* organizer, Sean-Nós Cois Life Festival; guest at various music and vocal festivals including Sidmouth Folk Festival, Inishowen Singers Festival, Ennistymon Singers Festival, Willie Clancy Summer School, Milwaukee Irish Fest; numerous radio and television broadcasts. *Compositions:* songs in traditional style, in both English and Irish language. *Recordings include:* Seachrán Sí. *Honours:* prizes at Oireachtas na Gaeilge (Irish Cultural Festival).

O'FARRILL, Arturo; Mexican Latin jazz musician (piano) and bandleader; *Assistant Professor and Director of Jazz Ensembles, Brooklyn College;* b. (Arturo O'Farrill Valero), 22 June 1960, Mexico City; s. of Chico O'Farrill and Lupe Valero; m. Alison Deane; two s. *Education:* LaGuardia High School for Music and Art, New York, Manhattan School of Music, Brooklyn Coll. Conservatory of Music, Aaron Copland School of Music at Queens Coll. *Career:* raised in Mexico and New York; recruited by Carla Bley to join her band 1979–83; solo work with Lester Bowie, Dizzy Gillespie, Howard Johnson, Steve Turre 1982–87; apptd musical dir for Harry Belafonte 1987; pianist for Andy Gonzalez during early 1990s; joined with father as pianist and musical dir, Chico O'Farrill Afro-Cuban Jazz Orchestra 1995–2001, bandleader (on father's death) 2001–11; Founder Afro-Latin Jazz Orchestra 2002–; Asst Prof. of Jazz, Univ. of Mass, Amherst 2007–08; est. Afro Latin Jazz Alliance 2007–; Asst Prof., State Univ. of New York at Purchase 2008–10; currently Asst Prof. and Dir of Jazz Ensembles, Jazz Studies, Brooklyn Coll. *Recordings include:* with Chico O'Farrill: Pure Emotion 1995, Heart of a Legend 1999, Carambola 2000; as bandleader: Blood Lines 1999, A Night in Tunisia 2000, Cumana 2004, Una Noche Inolvidable 2005, Song for Chico (Grammy Award for Best Latin Jazz Album 2008) 2008, Risa Negra 2009, 40 Acres and a Burro 2011, The Noguchi Sessions 2012, Final Night at Birdland 2013, The Offense of the Drum (Latin Grammy Award for Best Instrumental Album 2014, Grammy Award for Best Latin Jazz Album 2015) 2014, Cuba: the Conversation Continues 2015; with Jim Seeley: The Jim Seeley/Arturo O'Farrill Quintet 2005; with Claudia Acuna: In These Shoes 2008; with Bebo Valdés: Chico & Rita 2011. *Honours:* Jazz Journalists' Asscn Award for Large Ensemble of the Year 2015, Grammy Award for Best Instrumental Composition (for The Afro Latin Jazz Suite) 2016. *Address:* Conservatory of Music, School of Visual, Media and Performing Arts, Brooklyn College, 2900 Bedford Avenue, Brooklyn, NY 11210, USA (office). *Telephone:* (718) 951-5000 (office). *E-mail:* Arturo@arturoofarrill.com. *Website:* www.brooklyn.cuny.edu (office); arturoofarrill.com.

OFFSET (see Slater, Luke)

O'FLYNN, Liam; Irish musician (uillean pipes); b. 1945, County Kildare. *Career:* Born into family of traditional musicians; Founding member: Planxty; One of the first musicians to bring classical and traditional music together as soloist in Shaun Davey's The Brendan Voyage; Appeared on film soundtracks: Cal, 1992; The Field, 1990; A River Runs Through It, 1992; Collaborations: Mark Knopfler; Kate Bush; Enya; Sinead O'Connor; International tours; Performed at the first BBC Proms night of Irish music, 1999; Recorded over 50 albums. *Recordings:* Albums include: The Brendan Voyage, 1980; The Fine Art of Piping, 1989; Out To An Other Side, 1993; The Given Note, 1995; The Piper's Call, 1998. *Honours:* Golden Insignia of the University of La Coruna, Spain, 2000. *E-mail:* amaia@syntorama.com. *Website:* www.syntorama.com. *Address:* c/o Tara Music, Basement, 18 Upper Mount Street, Dublin 2, Ireland. *Website:* www.taramusic.com.

OGAN, Toca; Brazilian musician (percussion). *Career:* mem. mangue beat band, Nação Zumbi. *Recordings include:* albums: CSNZ 1998, Rádio SAMBA 2000, Nação Zumbi 2002, Futura 2005, Fome de Tudo 2007. *Honours:* Award for Best Group, São Paulo Asscn of Art Critics (Naçao Zumbi) 2005. *Address:* c/o Trama, Rua Rosa Gaeta Lázara, 93 Brooklin Novo, 04570-905 São Paulo, Brazil. *Website:* www.nacaozumbi.com/br.

O'GRUAMA, Aindrías; musician (guitar); b. 9 May 1957, Dun Laoighaire, Ireland. *Career:* guitarist, The Fatima Mansions; many radio and television broadcasts, tours; mem. Musicians' Union. *Recordings:* albums: Zerra, My Baby's Arm, Viva Dead Ponies, Valhalla Avenue, Lost in the Former West.

Honours: Hot Press Critics Poll for Album of the Year 1990. *Address:* 49 Chartham Court, Brixton, London SW9 7PT, England.

O'HIGGINS, David (Dave) Charles; British musician (saxophones) and composer; b. 1 Sept. 1964, Birmingham, England. *Education:* City Univ., London. *Career:* mem., Nat. Youth Jazz Orchestra 1983–86; leader, Dave O'Higgins Quartet/Quintet 1983–, Mezzoforte 1986–89; co-leader, Roadside Picnic 1986–90; leader, The Gang of Three 1987–89; leader, Dave O'Higgins and The Oblivion Brothers 1989–91; also played with Cleo Laine and The John Dankworth Quintet, Sax Appeal, Pizza Express Modern Jazz Sextet, Jason Rebello, Jim Mullen Quartet, Itchy Fingers, Clark Tracey Sextet, Martin Taylor's Spirit of Django, Stepping Stones; tours of Europe, Japan, Cuba, South Africa and Namibia, Tunisia, Sri Lanka, Bangladesh; played at venues, including Montreux Jazz Festival 1989, Havana Jazz Festival 1993; several residencies, including Ronnie Scott's, New York's Visionez; television appearances, radio broadcasts. *Recordings include:* with NYJO: Full Score, Concrete Cows, With An Open Mind; with Mezzoforte: No Limits; with Roadside Picnic: Roadside Picnic, For Madmen Only; with Jim Mullen: Soundbites, Rule of Thumb; with Jason Rebello: A Clearer View; with Sax Appeal: Flat Out; Let's Go; with Dave Higgins bands: All Good Things, Beats Working For A Living, Under the Stone, The Secret Ingredient, The Grinder's Monkey, Big Shake Up, Fast Foot Shuffle; with Clark Tracey: Full Speed Sideways; with Itchy Fingers: Full English Breakfast; with Martin Taylor: Spirit of Django; with John Dankworth: Live At Ronnie Scott's; with Matt Bianco: Another Time Another Place; with Simon Hale: East Fifteen; with Ray Charles: Strong Love Affair; with Stephane Grappelli: Celebrating Grappelli; with Colosseum: Breads and Circuses; with James Galway: Un-Break My Heart; with US3: Ordinary Day In An Unusual World; with Eric Alexander: Sketchbook. *Honours:* British Jazz Award for Best New Band 1988, 1989, Cleo Laine Personal Award 1990, BT British Jazz Award for Best Tenor Sax, for Rising Star 1995. *Website:* www.daveohiggins.com.

OITO, Gilmar Bola; Brazilian musician (percussion). *Career:* mem. mangue beat band, Nação Zumbi. *Recordings include:* albums: CSNZ 1998, Rádio SAMBA 2000, Nação Zumbi 2002, Futura 2005, Fome de Tudo 2007. *Honours:* Award for Best Group, São Paulo Asscn of Art Critics (Naçao Zumbi) 2005. *Address:* c/o Trama, Rua Rosa Gaeta Lázara, 93 Brooklin Novo, 04570-905 São Paulo, Brazil. *Website:* www.nacaozumbi.com.br.

OJANEN, Eero; Finnish musician (piano) and composer; b. 3 Jan. 1943. *Career:* played with Juhani Vilkki's sextet 1960s; mem. Otto Donner Treatment 1960s; pianist for Pekka Pöyry, Montreux Festival 1968; theatre and film work 1970s; played improvised music with Jouni Kesti projects; accompanist to numerous singers; mem. duo with bass player Teppo Hauta-Aho. *Compositions:* Väinämöinen's Music (cantata based on epic Kalevala), Pori Jazz Festival 1974, ballet, based on Aleksis Kivi's Seitsemän Veljestä (The Seven Brothers) 1980. *Honours:* Yrjö Award, Finnish Jazz Fed. 1968, Jussi Award for Best Film Music 2002. *E-mail:* eero.ojanen@pp.inet.fi (office).

OJANPERÄ, Jorma; Finnish musician (bass); b. 24 March 1961, Alahärmä. *Education:* Oulunkylä Inst., Helsinki Univ., Sibelius Acad., Helsinki. *Career:* performances with The Nat. Theatre and symphony orchestras; mem., Pori Big Band 1983; regular bassist at Helsinki clubs Groovy, Jumo, Orfeus; played Bengt Hallberg's music, directed by Hannu Hoivula 1989; regular appearances at Pori Jazz Festival; fmr mem., The Seppo Kantonene Trio, Markku Johansson Quintet; also plays with saxophonist Ion Muniz. *Address:* Rike 24 B, 07700 Koskenkylän Saha, Finland.

OKABAYASHI, Nobuyasu; Japanese singer, songwriter and folk musician; b. 1946, Shiga Pref. *Career:* leading figure of Osaka underground folk scene 1968–71; collaborated with rock band Happy Endo; retired from public performance 1971, re-emerged 1985. *Recordings:* albums: Danzai seyo (Condemn Me) 1969, Miru Mae ni Tobe 1970, Kuruizaki 1971, Graffiti, Machi wa Suteki na Carnival, Storm, Kiniro No Lion, 1973 PM 9:00 – 1974 AM 3:00, Tarezo Konoko ni Ainote wo, Good Evening 1980. *Films:* Nihon no Akuryo (Evil Spirits of Japan) 1970, Kitsune (The Fox) 1983. *Address:* c/o Victor Entertainment, Inc., Shibuya First Tower, 1-2-20 Higashi, Shibuya-ku, Tokyo 150-0011, Japan (office).

OKEREKE, Kele; British singer and musician (guitar); b. 13 Oct. 1981, Liverpool. *Career:* founder mem., Union, later renamed Bloc Party 2003–; solo artist 2010–. *Recordings include:* albums: with Bloc Party: Silent Alarm 2005, Silent Alarm Remixed 2005, A Weekend in the City 2007, Intimacy 2008, Four 2012; solo: The Boxer 2010. *Current Management:* Press Here Publicity, 138 W 25th Street, Seventh Floor, New York, NY 10001, USA. *Telephone:* (212) 246-2640. *Fax:* (212) 582-6513. *E-mail:* info@pressherepublicity.com. *Website:* www.pressherepublicity.com. *Address:* c/o V2 Music, 131 Holland Park Avenue, London, W11 4UT, England. *E-mail:* kele@blocparty.com. *Website:* www.blocparty.com; www.iamkele.com.

OKIN, Earl, BA; British singer, songwriter, musician (guitar, piano, vocal trumpet) and comedian; b. 31 Jan. 1947, Carshalton, Surrey; s. of the late Woolf Okin and Helma Okin. *Education:* Univ. of Kent, Canterbury. *Career:* various TV appearances world-wide, including Belgium, Germany, USA, Australia, UK; first UK TV appearance 1959; Edinburgh Festival 1983–2000; opening act with Paul McCartney and Wings, Van Morrison, Stéphane Grappelli; tours of Brazil as Bossa Nova singer/songwriter; presenter, MTV2 2002–03; performed cabarets for King & Queen of Sweden, Duke & Duchess of Northumberland, shows at Ronnie Scott's, London, etc. 2005–09; Jazz/Bossa

Nova Concert, São Paulo and Adelaide Cabaret Gala with Natalie Cole 2010; mem. Performing Right Soc., Musicians' Union, British Equity. *Compositions:* more than 100 songs; classical pieces include a string quartet. *Television:* O Programo do Jo (Brazil) 2004, De Laatsche Show (Belgium) 2004, Raymann is Laat (Netherlands) 2004, Adelaide Cabaret Festival TV Gala (Australia) 2010. *Recordings:* albums include: Bossa Britanica, Earl Okin: Musical Genius and Sex Symbol 2004, Songs From A Garden Shed; singles include: Yellow Petals 1967, Stop!, You Will Become Aware 1969. *Publications:* various articles, liner notes on opera and jazz. *Current Management:* c/o Spats Music Ltd, 248 Portobello Road (Upper Floors), London, W11 1LL, England. *Telephone:* (20) 7727-6375. *E-mail:* spats47@ntlworld.com. *Website:* www.earlokin.com; earlokin.blogspot.com; www.myspace.com/earlokin.

OKOYE, Paul; Nigerian rapper, singer, songwriter and record producer; b. 18 Nov. 1981, Lagos; brother of Peter Okoye; m. Anita Isama 2014; one s. *Education:* St Murumba Coll., Jos, Univ. of Abuja. *Career:* founding mem., several groups also featuring twin brother Peter including acapella group, MMMPP (later MMPP), Smooth Criminals 1997, P-Square (duo) 2001–. *Recordings include:* albums: with P-Square: Last Nite 2003, Get Squared (Headies Awards for Best R&B/Pop Album 2006, for Album of the Year 2006, Nigerian Music Award for Album of the Year 2006) 2005, Game Over 2007, Danger 2009, The Invasion 2011, Double Trouble 2014. *Honours:* with P-Square: Grab Da Mic competition winners 2001, Amen Best R&B Group Award 2003, Headies Awards for Artiste of the Year 2006, for Song of the Year (for Bizzy Body) 2006, for Best Music Video (for Get Squared) 2006, Nigerian Music Award for Music Video of the Year (for Get Squared) 2006, Channel O Music Video Awards for Best Duo or Group 2007, 2008, for Most Gifted Group 2012, MTV Africa Music Awards for Best Group 2008, 2009, 2015, for Artist of the Decade 2015, Kora Award for Artist of the Year 2010. *E-mail:* jude@northsidegroup.net (office); northsidemusicinc@yahoo.com (office). *Website:* www.mypsquare.com.

OKOYE, Peter; Nigerian rapper, singer, songwriter and record producer; b. 18 Nov. 1981, Lagos; brother of Paul Okoye; m. Loretta Omotayo 2013; one s., one d. *Education:* St Murumba Coll., Jos, Univ. of Abuja. *Career:* founding mem., several groups also featuring twin brother Paul including acapella group, MMMPP (later MMPP), Smooth Criminals 1997, P-Square (duo) 2001–. *Recordings include:* albums: with P-Square: Last Nite 2003, Get Squared (Headies Awards for Best R&B/Pop Album 2006, for Album of the Year 2006, Nigerian Music Award for Album of the Year 2006) 2005, Game Over 2007, Danger 2009, The Invasion 2011, Double Trouble 2014. *Honours:* with P-Square: Grab Da Mic competition winners 2001, Amen Best R&B Group Award 2003, Headies Awards for Artiste of the Year 2006, for Song of the Year (for Bizzy Body) 2006, for Best Music Video (for Get Squared) 2006, Nigerian Music Award for Music Video of the Year (for Get Squared) 2006, Channel O Music Video Awards for Best Duo or Group 2007, 2008, for Most Gifted Group 2012, MTV Africa Music Awards for Best Group 2008, 2009, 2015, for Artist of the Decade 2015, Kora Award for Artist of the Year 2010. *E-mail:* jude@northsidegroup.net (office); northsidemusicinc@yahoo.com (office). *Website:* www.mypsquare.com.

OLAFSSON, Arnar; Icelandic musician (guitar). *Career:* founder mem., Leaves 2001–. *Recordings include:* albums: Breathe 2002, The Angela Test 2005. *Website:* www.leaves.tv.

OLDFIELD, Michael (Mike) Gordon; British musician (multi-instrumentalist) and composer; b. 15 May 1953, Reading, Berks., England; three s. two d. *Career:* solo artist; numerous tours, worldwide TV and radio broadcasts. *Recordings include:* albums: Tubular Bells (Grammy Award) 1973, Hergest Ridge 1974, Ommadawn 1975, Incantations 1978, Platinum 1979, QE2 1980, Five Miles Out 1982, Crises 1983, Discovery 1984, Islands 1987, Earthmoving 1989, Amarok 1990, Heaven's Open 1991, Tubular Bells II 1992, Elements 1994, The Songs of Distant Earth 1996, Voyager 1996, XXV The Essential 1997, Tubular Bells III 1998, Guitars 1999, Millennium Bell 1999, Tres Lunas 2002, Tubular Bells 2003 2003, Light + Shade 2005, Music of the Spheres 2008, Man on the Rocks 2014. *Website:* www.mikeoldfieldofficial.com.

OLDHAM, Spooner; American musician (keyboards) and songwriter; b. (Dewey Lyndon Oldham), Center Star, Ala. *Education:* Univ. of N Ala. *Career:* worked as backing musician, FAME Studios, Muscle Shoals, Ala, played on recordings by Percy Sledge, Wilson Pickett, Aretha Franklin, James and Bobby Purify, Clarence Carter; formed songwriting partnership with Dan Penn; moved to Memphis 1966, worked with Penn and Chips Moman at American Studios, co-wrote numerous hits for The Box Tops; later moved to Los Angeles and worked as backing musician, recording and performing with artists including Neil Young, Bob Dylan, Joe Cocker, Linda Ronstadt, Jackson Browne, The Flying Burrito Brothers, The Everly Brothers, Dickey Betts, J. J. Cale, Frank Black; tours with Neil Young, Bob Dylan, Crosby, Stills, Nash & Young 2006, Drive-By Truckers 2007, also performs regularly with Dan Penn; other songwriting collaborators include John Prine, Hal Newman. *Compositions:* songs as writer or co-writer include: Cry Like A Baby (The Box Tops), I'm Your Puppet (James and Bobby Purify), Sweet Inspiration (Sweet Inspirations), It Tears Me Up (Percy Sledge), Take Me Just As I Am (Solomon Burke), Let's Do It Over (Joe Simon), Out Of Left Field (Percy Sledge), Wish You Didn't Have To Go (James and Bobby Purify), Let It Happen (James Carr), Lonely Women Make Good Lovers (Bob Luman), Another Night Of Love (Freddy Weller), Love Got In The Way (Freddy Weller), In The Same Old Way (Bobby Bare). *Recordings:* albums: Potluck (solo), Moments From This

Theatre (live recording, with Dan Penn) 1999; guest musician on albums including: Aretha Franklin's Aretha Arrives, I Never Loved a Man the Way I Love You, Aretha Now, Aretha's Jazz, Neil Young's Silver and Gold, Comes a Time, Luck Thirteen, Prairie Wind, Bob Dylan's Saved, Frank Black's Honeycomb, John Hammond's Can't Beat the Kid, Kate Campbell's Moonpie Dreams, J. J. Cale's Closer to You, Janis Joplin's Pearl, Jewel's Pieces of You. *E-mail:* booking@spooneroldham.com (office). *Website:* www.spooneroldham .com.

OLDHAM, Will, (Bonnie 'Prince' Billy); American alternative singer, songwriter and actor; b. 24 Dec. 1970. *Career:* has performed and recorded as Will Oldham, Bonnie 'Prince' Billy, Palace Brothers, Palace Songs; collaborations with David Pajo, Box of Chocolates, Amalgamated Sons of Rest, The Anomoanon, The Boxhead Ensemble, Matt Sweeney, Continental OP, Current 93, The Silver Jews, Johnny Cash. *Recordings include:* albums: as Palace Music/Palace Brothers: There Is No One That Will Take Care of You 1993, Days in the Wake 1994, Viva Last Blues 1995, Lost Blues and Other Songs 1997; as Will Oldham: Arise Therefore 1996, Joya 1997, Guarapero/Lost Blues 2 2000, Ode Music (film soundtrack) 2000, Seafarers Music (film soundtrack) 2004; as Bonnie 'Prince' Billy: I See A Darkness 1999, Ease Down the Road 2001, Master and Everyone 2003, Sings Greatest Palace Music 2004, Superwolf (with Matt Sweeney) 2005, Summer in the Southeast 2005, The Letting Go 2006, Ask Forgiveness 2007, Lie Down in the Light 2008, Is It the Sea? 2008, Beware 2009, The Wonder Show of the World 2010. *Films:* actor: Matewan 1987, Thousand Pieces of Gold 1991, Elysian Fields 1993, Radiation 1998, Julien Donkey-Boy 1999, Slitch 2003, Tripping with Caveh 2004, Junebug 2005, Old Joy 2005, The Guatemalan Handshake 2006, The Edge of Town 2006, The Land 2006. *Current Management:* The Billions Corporation, 833 West Chicago Avenue, Suite 101, Chicago, IL 60622-5497, USA. *Telephone:* (312) 997-9999. *Fax:* (312) 977-2287. *E-mail:* boche@billions.com. *Website:* www.billions.com.

OLENIUS, Adam; Swedish singer and musician (guitar). *Career:* founder mem., Luca Brasi, renamed Shout Out Louds 2001–. *Recordings include:* albums: 100° (EP) 2003, Oh, Sweetheart (EP) 2004, Howl Howl Gaff Gaff 2005, Very Loud (EP) 2005, Our Ill Wills 2007, Work 2010. *Current Management:* c/o Filip Wilén, Bud Fox Management, Saturnusgatan 13, 224 57 Lund, Sweden. *Telephone:* (46) 13-81-20. *E-mail:* filip@budfox.se. *Website:* www.budfox.se; www.shoutoutlouds.com.

OLIVA, Stéphan; French jazz musician (piano) and composer; b. 7 Jan. 1959, Montmorency; m. Cathy Frantz, 14 Oct. 1982, one s. *Education:* Classical training, Ecole Normale De Musique De Paris. *Career:* Teacher, performer, Jah, Grim, Ajmi, Roy Hart Theatre (France); Concerts in jazz festivals with trios (with drums, bass, violin, saxophone); Selected to Biennale Des Jeunes Createurs D'Europe De La Mediterranée, 1990; Selected to Jeunes Affiches '94, SACEM, 1994; Conferences: History of Jazz Piano, 1995; Trio Jade Visions, tribute to Bill Evans, 1995; mem, Archipel Mozaïque (Montpellier). *Music for film:* Les Liens du Sang (Rivals) 2008. *Recordings:* with trio: Novembre, 1991; Jade Visions, 1996; Tristano, 1999; Piano solo: Clair Obscur, 1994. *Honours:* Django D'Or, 1992. *Address:* 2 rue du Levant, 93100 Montreuil, France.

OLIVER, Jamie; Welsh musician (piano). *Career:* mem. rock bands, Lostprophets 2000–13, No Devotion 2014–. *Recordings include:* albums: Start Something 2004, Liberation Transmission 2006, The Betrayed 2010, Permanence 2015. *Honours:* Kerrang! Award for Best British Band 2007. *Website:* nodevotion.com.

OLIVER, Tim, BSc; British producer and engineer; b. 6 Sept. 1959, England. *Career:* freelance engineer 1981–; sound engineer 1985–; Prod. 1990–; worked with artists, including Temper Temper, M People, Happy Mondays, Definition of Sound, The Other Two, Sinead O'Connor, Cara Dillon, New Order, Gene, Indigo Girls, Carlos Nunez; mem. Musicians' Union. *Address:* Positive Management, 4th Floor Studio, 16 Abbey Churchyard, Bath BA1 1LY, England (office). *Telephone:* (1225) 311661 (office). *Fax:* (1225) 482013 (office). *E-mail:* info@positiveproducermanagement.com (office). *Website:* www .positiveproducermanagement.com (office).

OLIVER, Vaughan, BA; British graphic designer. *Education:* Newcastle-upon-Tyne Polytechnic. *Career:* Visiting Lecturer in Graphic Design, Newcastle-upon-Tyne Polytechnic, Liverpool Univ., Kingston Univ., Central St Martin's Coll., Epsom Coll. 1981–2007; f. (with photographer, Nigel Grierson) design co., 23 Envelope 1980, renamed v23 1988–, following Grierson's departure; designed record sleeves, principally for record label 4AD, for artists, including Frank Black, Clan of Xymox, Cocteau Twins, Robert Fripp, His Name is Alive, Lush, Modern English, The Pixies, This Mortal Coil, Ultra Vivid Scene; collaborations with David Sylvian. *Exhibitions:* solo: 23 Envelope, CSV Corpn, Tokyo 1986, Sleeves By, Rotterdam ABK 1988, Espace Graslin (CRDC), Nantes, France 1990, Festival Art Rock '90, Centre d'Action Cuturelle, St Brieuc, France 1990, Pavillon Tusquets, Parc de Villette, Paris 1990, Expo 23, Parco, Tokyo 1991, Glove, GGG Gallery, Tokyo, DDD Gallery, Osaka 1992–93, This Rimy River, Pacific Design Center, Los Angeles 1994, Is Minty a Man?, Univ. of Northumbria, Norwich School of Art and Design, Cornerhouse, Manchester 1996, To Have and To Hold, Athens, Greece, 2001, Slightly off the Ground, Stanley Picker Gallery, Surrey 2007; group: Swinging London: Graphisme and Musique Aujourd'hui, France 2004, Designing Modern Life, Design Museum, London 2004, Communicate: Independent British Graphic Design Since the Sixties, Barbican Art Gallery, London 2004,

The Contemporary Poster: A Global Perspective, GGG Gallery, Tokyo, Basel School of Design, Basel 2005, Urban Forest Project, Times Square, New York 2006, Exhibitions: Graphic Messages from GGG Gallery amd DDD Gallery 1986–2006, GGG Gallery, Tokyo, DDD Gallery, Osaka 2006, Our Friends in the North, Robert Stephenson Buliding, Newcastle-upon-Tyne 2007, Helvetica 50, Design Museum, London 2007. *Publications include:* This Rimy River: Vaughan Oliver and V23, Graphic Works 1988–94 1994, Vaughan Oliver: Visceral Pleasures 2000, Vaughan Oliver and v23 Poster Designs 2005. *Honours:* Hon. MA (Univ. for the Creative Arts) 2011. *E-mail:* info@v23.biz. *Website:* www.v23.biz.

OLIVOR, Jane; American singer; b. 1947, Brooklyn, NY. *Career:* began in night clubs in New York early 1970s; solo artist 1976–; played major venues across USA; career break; returned to live performing early 1990s; tours extensively. *Recordings include:* albums: First Night 1976, Chasing Rainbows 1977, Stay the Night 1978, The Best Side of Goodbye 1980, In Concert 1982, Love Decides 2000, Songs of the Season 2001, Safe Return 2004. *E-mail:* missjaneo@aol.com. *Website:* www.janeolivor.com; www.members.com/missjaneo.

OLOMIDE, Koffi, MA; Democratic Republic of the Congo singer, songwriter and musician (guitar); b. (Antoine Agpeba), 13 Aug. 1956, Kisangani. *Education:* studied in Bordeaux and at Univ. of Paris. *Career:* began composing while a student; composed for Papa Wemba, Viva La Música, Zaiko Langa Langa, Defao; joined Viva La Música as backing singer late 1970s; formed Quartier Latin 1986; devised Tcha Tcho style. *Recordings include:* albums: Kiki Ewing 1987, Henriquet 1988, Elle Et Moi 1989, Tcha Tcho 1990, Pas De Faux Pas, Diva 1992, Noblesse Oblige 1993, Magie 1994, V12 1995, Wake Up 1996, Loi 1997, Ngounda, Ba La Joie 1998, Droit De Veto 1999, Live A Bercy, Force De Frappe 2000, Effrakata 2001, Affaire d'Etat 2003, Monde Arabe 2004, Danger de Mort 2006, African Classics 2007, Bord Ezanga Kombo 2008, Mandra Manda Skol 2010. *Honours:* Best Singer award (Abidjan) 1998, Kora Awards for Best Male African Artist 1998, 2002, Best Artist – Central Africa 2002, Best Video – Africa 2002.

OLSDAL, Stefan; musician (guitar, bass, keyboards); b. 31 March 1974, Sweden. *Career:* played drums in school orchestra 1987; founder mem., Ashtray Heart; mem., Placebo 1994–; numerous television appearances; live tours and numerous major festival dates. *Recordings include:* albums: Placebo 1996, Without You I'm Nothing 1998, Black Market Music 2000, Sleeping With Ghosts 2003, Meds 2006, Battle for the Sun 2009. *Honours:* Kerrang! Classic Songwriter Award 2006, MTV Europe Music Award for Best Alternative Act 2009. *Current Management:* Riverman Management, George House, Brecon Road, London W6 8PY, England. *Telephone:* (20) 7381-4000. *Fax:* (20) 7381-9666. *E-mail:* info@riverman.co.uk. *Website:* www.riverman.co.uk; www.placeboworld.co.uk.

OLSEN, Allan; Danish singer and songwriter; b. 18 March 1956, Frederikshavn. *Career:* intensive touring from mid-1970s, solo, then with own band 1988–; festival and television appearances; mem. Danish Musicians' Union, DJFBA. *Recordings include:* Norlan 1989, Gaio 1991, Pindsvin I Pigsko 1992, Dalton (with Johnny Madsen and Lars Liholt) 1994, Dubble Live-Rygter Fra Randområderne. *Honours:* Grammy Award 1994, Denmark Labour Union Great Award of Culture. *Address:* Mollevej 35, 9520 Skorping, Denmark (home). *E-mail:* misja@allanolsen.dk (home). *Website:* www.allanolsen.dk.

OLSEN, Jørgen; Danish singer, musician (guitar) and songwriter; b. 15 March 1950, Odense. *Career:* moved to Copenhagen aged 12; formed beat group The Kids with brother Noller, aged 15; released three singles; supported The Kinks; group renamed the Olsen Brothers 1970; starred in Danish production of musical Hair 1970; Scandinavian pop star in the 1970s; worked in education 1990–94; winner (with his brother), Eurovision Song Contest, Stockholm with the song Fly on the Wings of Love 2000. *Recordings:* albums: with Olsen Brothers: Olsen 1972, For What We Are 1973, For The Children of The World (in conjunction with UNICEF) 1973, Back On The Tracks 1976, You're The One 1977, San Francisco 1978, Dans – Dans – Dans 1979, Rockstalgi 1987, Det Stille Ocean 1990, Angelina 1999, Fly on the Wings of Love 2000, The Story of The Olsen Brothers 2000, Neon Madonna 2001, Walk Right Back 2001, Songs 2002, More Songs 2003, Our New Songs 2005, Celebration 2005, Respect 2008; numerous Olsen Brothers singles, Brothers to Brothers (CD) 2013. *Current Management:* c/o Steen Wittrock, International Personal Management, Solkaer 7, 3100 Hornbaek, Denmark. *Telephone:* 33-11-52-25. *E-mail:* ipmsw@mail.tele.dk. *Website:* www.olsen-brothers.dk.

OLSEN, Keith; American producer, musician, recording engineer and arranger; *Owner, Pogologo Corporation;* b. Sioux Falls, SDak. *Career:* Founding mem. Ragamuffins 1965, later Music Machine; engineer, Sound City Studios, Los Angeles; Founder Pogologo Productions 1973–; Owner Goodnight LA Studios, Los Angeles 1980–99; Founder Bursen Music Group 1996–99; Dir Professional Recording Products Div., Mackie Designs Inc., Seattle, Wash. 1999–2003; produced project by The Babys, Bad Company, Russ Ballard, Pat Benatar, Kim Carnes, Sheena Easton, Emerson Lake & Palmer, Fleetwood Mac, Foreigner, Lou Gramm, Grateful Dead, Sammy Hagar, Heart, Journey, Loverboy, Eddie Money, Stevie Nicks, Ozzy Osbourne, Steve Perry, REO Speedwagon, Santana, Scorpions, Rick Springfield, Starship, 38 Special, Jethro Tull, Joe Walsh, Bob Weir, Whitesnake and many others; contributed to movie soundtracks: Flashdance, Footloose, Top Gun, Tron, Vision Quest, amongst many others. *Recordings:* production appears on more than 550 albums and in numerous films. *Publication:* A Music Producer's Thoughts to Create By. *Honours:* six Grammy Awards, Hollywood Walk of Fame Lifetime Achievement. *Address:* Pogologo Productions Group, 17837 First Avenue South, Suite 3, Seattle, WA 98148-1728, USA (office). *Telephone:* (206) 444-0300 (office). *Fax:* (206) 244-0066 (office). *E-mail:* keith@pogologoproductions.com (office). *Website:* www.keitholsenproductions.com (office).

OLSEN, Noller Niels; Danish singer, musician (guitar) and songwriter; b. 13 April 1954, Odense. *Career:* moved to Copenhagen aged 8; formed beat group The Kids with brother Jørgen, aged 11; released three singles; supported The Kinks; group renamed the Olsen Brothers 1970; appeared in Danish production of musical Hair 1970; Scandinavian pop star in the 1970s; worked in education 1990–94; winner with his brother, Eurovision Song Contest, Stockholm with the song, Fly on the Wings of Love 2000. *Recordings:* albums: with Olsen Brothers: Olsen 1972, For What We Are 1973, For The Children of The World (in conjunction with UNICEF) 1973, Back On The Tracks 1976, You're The One 1977, San Francisco 1978, Dans – Dans – Dans 1979, Rockstalgi 1987, Det Stille Ocean 1990, Angelina 1999, Fly on the Wings of Love 2000, The Story of The Olsen Brothers 2000, Neon Madonna 2001, Walk Right Back 2001, Songs 2002, More Songs 2003, Our New Songs 2005, Celebration 2005, Respect 2008; numerous Olsen Brothers singles, Brothers to Brothers (CD) 2013. *Honours:* Kt, Order of the Kts Hospitaller of St John of Jerusalem. *Current Management:* c/o Steen Wittrock, International Personal Management, Solkaer 7, 3100 Hornbaek, Denmark. *Telephone:* 33-11-52-25. *E-mail:* ipmsw@mail.tele.dk. *Website:* www.olsen-brothers.dk.

OLSON, Carla; American musician (guitar), singer, songwriter and producer; b. 3 July 1952, Austin, Tex.; d. of Carl and Robbie Olson; m. Saul Davis 1987. *Career:* worked in various capacities with Paul Jones, Joe Louis Walker, Ana Gazzola, Chubby Tavares, Mick Taylor, Ry Cooder, Don Henley, Barry Goldberg, Gene Clark, Phil Seymour; appearances include Radio City Music Hall, New York; tours to Europe, Japan; contrib. to film soundtracks, including Real Genius, Blue City, Sylvester, Saturday Night Special, A Tiger's Tale, and TV including Eastbound & Down; mem. American Fed. of Television and Radio Artists (AFTRA), Nat. Acad. of Recording Arts and Sciences (NARAS), Broadcast Music, Inc. (BMI). *Compositions:* Why Did You Stop (recorded by Percy Sledge), Number One Is To Survive (recorded with Gene Clark), Trail of Tears (co-writer with Eric Johnson), Midnight Mission (recorded with The Textones), Misty Morning (with Percy Sledge) 2004, Road of no Return (with Percy Sledge) 2004, Rubies & Diamonds (with Percy Sledge) 2004. *Recordings:* as producer: albums by Paul Jones 2009, 2014, Chubby Tavares 2012, Ana Gazzola 2012 as well as Joe Louis Walker, Mare Winningham, Barry Goldberg, Jake Andrews, Davis Gaines, Phil Upchurch; individual tracks by Son Seals, Roy Gaines, Sugar Blue, Ernie Watts, Taj Mahal, Peter Noone, The Ventures, Otis Rush, Brenton Wood, Sugar Blue, Charlie Musselwhite, Kim Wilson, Billy Joe Royal. *Recordings include:* albums: So Rebellious A Lover 1986, Too Hot For Snakes 1991, Live 1991, Within An Ace 1993, Reap The Whirlwind 1994, The Ring Of Truth 2001, Honest As Daylight 2001, Have Harmony, Will Travel 2013; contrib. guitar and vocals to Percy Sledge album, Shining Through the Rain 2004. *Current Management:* c/o Saul Davis Management, 11684 Ventura Blvd, #583, Studio City, CA 91604, USA. *Website:* www.carlaolson.com.

OLVERA, (José Fernando Emilio) Fher; Mexican singer, songwriter and musician (guitar); b. 8 Dec. 1959, Puebla; m. Ana Ivette Verduzco; one c. *Education:* Universidad Iberoamericana. *Career:* performed with Gustavo Orozco during teenage years; mem. Sombrero Verde 1978–85; Founder mem. Maná 1986–; group f. Salva Negra Foundation (financing and supporting projects to protect environment) 1995–; over 25 million records sold worldwide; numerous int. tours; numerous collaborations including Rubén Blades, Miguel Bosé, Juan Luis Guerra, Carlos Santana, Zucchero. *Recordings include:* albums: with Sombrero Verde: Sombrero Verde 1981, A Tiempo de Rock 1983; with Maná: Falta Amor 1990, ¿Dónde Jugarán Los Niños? 1992, Cuando los Ángeles Lloran 1995, Sueños Liquidos (Grammy Award for Best Latin Rock/Alternative Performance 1999, Premio Lo Nuestro for Pop Album of the Year 1999) 1997, Maná MTV Unplugged (Ritmo Latino Music Award for Album of the Year 2000) 1999, Revolución de Amor (Billboard Latin Music Awards for Latin Rock Album of the Year 2003, for Latin Pop Album of the Year – Duo or Group 2003, Grammy Award for Best Latin Rock/Alternative Album 2003, Latin Grammy Award for Best Rock Album by a Duo or Group 2003, Premio Lo Nuestro for Rock Album of the Year 2003, Ritmo Latino Music Award for Album of the Year 2003) 2002, Amar es Combatir (Billboard Latin Music Award for Latin Rock/Alternative Album of the Year 2007, Grammy Award for Best Latin Rock/Alternative Album 2007, Premio Lo Nuestro for Rock Album of the Year 2007) 2007, Arde el Cielo (Billboard Latin Music Awards for Latin Pop Album of the Year – Duo or Group 2009, for Latin Rock/Alternative Album of the Year 2009) 2008, Drama y Luz (Latin Grammy Award for Best Rock Album 2011, Premio People en Español Award for Best Album 2011, Grammy Award for Best Latin Pop, Rock or Urban Album 2012, Premio Lo Nuestro Award for Rock/Alternative Award of the Year 2012) 2011, Cama Incendiada (Latin Grammy Award for Best Pop/Rock Album 2015) 2015; other contribs include: Supernatural, Santana 1999. *Honours:* FAO Goodwill Amb. 2003; with Maná: Premios Lo Nuestro for Best Pop Group 1997, 1999, 2000, for Pop Song of the Year (for Mariposa Traicionera) 2004, for Rock Song of the Year (for Labios Compartidos) 2007, (for Bendita Tu Luz) 2008, for Rock Artist of the Year 2007, 2008, for Lifetime Achievement 2011, for Rock/Alternative Artist of the Year 2012, Ritmo Latino Music Award for Best Solo or Rock Group Artist 1999, Premios Oye! Special Social Prize to Music 2002, Award for Best Solo or Group Artist 2003, Mexican Public Commercial Award 2004, MasterTone Award (for Labios Compartidos) 2007, Latin Grammy Awards for Record of the Year 2000, for Best Rock Performance by a Duo or Group (both with Santana, for Corazón Espinado) 2000, for Best Pop Performance by a Duo or Group with Vocal (for Se Me Olvidó Otra Vez) 2000, Latin Grammy Special Award for Musical Accomplishments 2006, Billboard Latin Awards for Pop Airplay Song of the Year – Duo or Group (for Labios Compartidos) 2007, for Latin Tour of the Year 2008, for Hot Latin Song of the Year – Duo or Group (for Si No Te Hubieras Ido) 2009, for Latin Pop Airplay Song of the Year – Duo or Group (for Si No Te Hubieras Ido) 2009, for Latin Duet or Group Songs 2012, for Latin Duet or Group Album 2012, for Latin Pop Duet or Group of the Year Songs 2012, for Latin Pop Duet or Group of the Year Album 2012, Premio Juventud Supernova Award 2006, Premios Juventud for Favorite Rock Artist 2007, 2008, 2009, 2011, 2012, World Music Awards for World's Best Selling Latin Group 2007, for Best Selling Latin American Artist 2007, Los Premios 40 Principales for Best Concert/Tour 2007, 2011, Pan American Health Org. Champions of Health (for Salva Negra Foundation), World Health Day 2008, Premios Telehit for Best Int. Mexican Band 2011, Premio People en Español Award for Best Rock Artist or Group 2011, Premio Cadena Dial 2011, Premio Casandra Internacional 2012. *Address:* c/o Warner Music Mexico, SA de C.V. Leibnitz 32 Col., Nueva Anzures, México, DF 11590, Mexico (office). *Telephone:* (55) 5279-3800 (office). *Website:* www.warnermusic.com.mx (office); www.mana.com.mx.

O'MALLEY, Nick; British musician (bass guitar); b. 5 July 1985, Sheffield. *Career:* fmr mem., The Dodgems –2006; mem., Arctic Monkeys 2006–. *Recordings include:* albums: with Arctic Monkeys: Favourite Worst Nightmare (BRIT Award for Best British Album 2008) 2007, Humbug 2009, Suck It and See (MOJO Award for Best Album 2011) 2011, AM 2013. *Honours:* with Arctic Monkeys: BRIT Awards for Best British Group 2007, 2008, NME Awards for Best British Band 2008, for Best Track (for Flourescent Adolescent) 2008, for Best Music DVD (for Scummy Man) 2007, (for Arctic Monkeys at the Apollo) 2009, for Best Live Band 2010, 2013, Q Magazine Awards for People's Choice 2006, for Best Act in the World Today 2007, for Best Live Act 2009, for Best Track (for Do I Wanna Know?) 2013. *Current Management:* Press Here Publicity, 138 West 25th Street, Seventh Floor, New York, NY 10001, USA. *E-mail:* info@pressherepublicity.com. *Website:* www .pressherepublicity.com. *E-mail:* arctic.monkeys@gmail.com. *Website:* www .arcticmonkeys.com.

Ó MAONLAÍ, Liam; Irish singer and musician (piano); b. Dublin. *Career:* mem. punk group, Congress (later became My Bloody Valentine), Dublin; busker in duo, Incomparable Benzini Brothers (with Fiachna O'Brainain) 1985; Founder mem., Hothouse Flowers 1986–. *Recordings include:* albums: with Hothouse Flowers: People (No. 2, UK), 1988; Home, 1990; Songs From The Rain, 1993; Best Of, 2000; with Def Leppard, Retro Active, 1993; with Sharon Shannon, Sharon Shannon, 1993; with Liam O'Flynn, Out to the Other Side, 1993; with the Rankin Family, North country, 1994; with ALT, Altitude, 1995; with Altan, Best of Altan, 1997; with Sharon Shannon, Spellbound: The Best of Sharon Shannon, 1999; with Maire Breatnach, Angels Candles, 1999; Singles: Don't Go, 1988; I Can See Clearly Now, 1990; Give It Up, 1990; Movies, 1990; Emotional Time, 1993; One Tongue, 1993; You Can Love Me Now, 1998. *Honours:* Street Entertainers of the Year Award 1985. *Address:* c/o Rian Records, 33 Charlemont Street, Dublin 2, Ireland. *Website:* www.liamomaonlai.ie.

OMAR, Don, (El Rey); Puerto Rican singer and record company executive; b. (William Omar Landrón Rivera), 10 Feb. 1978, San Juan; s. of William Landrón and Luz Antonia Rivera; m. Jackie Guerrido 2008 (divorced); four c. *Career:* fmr backing singer for duo Hector & Tito; released debut album 2003; f. Orfanato Music Group record label 2007; recorded int. hit single Danza Kuduro with Lucenzo 2010. *Recordings include:* albums: The Last Don (Billboard Latin Music Awards for Latin Pop Album of the Year 2003, for New Artist and Latin Rap/Hip-Hop Album of the Year) 2003, King of Kings (Billboard Latin Award for Reggaeton Album of the Year 2006) 2006, iDon 2009, Don Omar Presents: Meet the Orphans 2010, Don Omar Presents MTO2: The New Generation (Latin Grammy Award for Best Urban Music Album 2012) 2012. *Honours:* Latin Billboard Awards for Rhythm Airplay 2011, for Latin Song of the Year (Vocal Event) 2012, for Latin Rhythm of the Year 2012, for Digital Song of the Year 2012, American Billboard Award for Top Latin Song 2012 (all for Danza Kuduro). *Current Management:* c/o Adam Torres, Arrow Management, 365 River Drive, 2nd Floor, Garfield, NJ 07026, USA. *Website:* www.arrowmgt.com. *Address:* c/o Orfanato Music Group, Machete Music, Universal Music Group, 2220 Colorado Avenue, Santa Monica, CA 90404, USA (office). *Website:* www.orfanatomusicgroup.com (office).

O'NEAL, Alexander; American singer; b. 14 Nov. 1954, Natchez, Miss. *Career:* singer 1972–; mem. Flyte Time; solo artist 1984–. *Recordings include:* albums: Alexander O'Neal 1985, Hearsay 1986, All Mixed Up 1988, My Gift To You 1988, Hearsay All Mixed Up 1988, All True Man 1991, Loves Makes No Sense 1993, Lovers Again 1997, Saga of a Married Man 2002, Live at the Hammersmith Apollo London 2005, Alex Loves 2008, Five Questions: The New Journey 2010. *Current Management:* Tony Denton Promotions Ltd, 19 South Molton Lane, Mayfair, London, W1K 5LE, England. *Telephone:* (20)

7629-4666. *Fax:* (20) 7629-4777. *E-mail:* info@tdpromo.com. *Website:* www .tdpromo.com; www.alexanderoneal.net.

O'NEIL, Liam; Canadian musician (keyboards, percussion). *Career:* mem., The Stills 2005–. *Recordings:* albums: Without Feathers 2005, Oceans Will Rise (Juno Award for Best Alternative Album of the Year 2009) 2008. *Honours:* Juno Award for Best New Group of the Year 2009. *Address:* c/o Arts&Crafts, 460 Richmond Street W, Suite 402, Toronto, ON M5V 1Y1, Canada (office). *Website:* www.arts-crafts.ca/thestills (office).

O'NEILL, Bernard Anthony, ARCM; Irish musician (double bass, cello, bass guitar, keyboards); b. 4 Sept. 1961, Dublin. *Education:* Royal Irish Acad. of Music, Royal Coll. of Music. *Career:* teacher, composer, performer; Musical Director for numerous acts including: Rolf Harris, Viv Stanshall, Jon Spencer, Flower Sermon, Aqua Rhythms, Ether, Zumzeaux, Kimbara Brothers, Silly Sisters, June Tabor; founding mem., Syriana. *Recordings include:* with Zumzeaux: Wolf At Your Door, Live In Edinburgh; with Silly Sisters: No More To The Dance; with Andrew Cronshaw: The Language of Snakes; with Jon Spencer Band: Parlour Games; Echoes And Whispers 2001; with Syriana: Al Bidayeh 2010. *Honours:* Associate of Royal Irish Acad. of Music. *Address:* c/o Real World Records, Mill Lane, Wiltshire SN13 8PL, England (office). *Website:* realworldrecords.com (office).

O'NEILL, Keith; British musician (drums); b. 18 Feb. 1969, Liverpool, England. *Career:* mem., Cast 1993–2002; numerous tours, festival, TV appearances and radio sessions; mem., Kealer 2002–. *Recordings include:* albums with Cast: All Change 1995, Mother Nature Calls 1997, Magic Hour 1999.

ONEIRO (see Carter, Derrick)

ÖNEY, Özgür Can; Turkish musician (drums); b. 21 July 1980, Ankara; m. Pelin Öney. *Education:* Anadolu Univ. *Career:* mem., alternative rock band, maNga 2002–; concerts, festivals include Sziget Festival, Mannheim Turkish Rock Festival, Rock'n Coke Turkey, also London; composes music for theatre. *Recordings:* albums: maNga 2004, Şehr-i Hüzün 2009, We Could Be the Same, Fly to Stay Alive 2010. *Honours:* MTV Europe Music Award for Best European Act 2009. *Current Management:* Hadi Elazzi, GRGDN, Mübayacı sok. 5, Rumelihisarı, 34470 İstanbul, Turkey. *Telephone:* (212) 2876287. *Fax:* (212) 2876216. *E-mail:* manga@grgdn.com. *Website:* www.grgdn.com. *Address:* c/o Sony Music Entertainment, Sony Music Türkiye, Ticaret A.Ş. Oteller Sokak 1/ 5, Tepebaşı, 34430 İstanbul, Turkey. *Website:* manga.web.tr.

ONGG, Judy, BA; Japanese actress, singer and woodcut artist; b. 24 Jan. 1950, Taipei, Taiwan; d. of Pin Y. and Yun Ngo Ongg; m. H. Suzuki 1991. *Education:* American School, Tokyo and Sophia Univ. Int. Div., Tokyo. *Career:* joined Himawari Theatre 1960; film and TV debuts 1961; has starred in Chinese and Japanese films, TV shows and plays, nat. and int. variety shows, and made 50 records; host World Popular Song Festival 1975–89; Amb. of Friendship UNICEF Japan Aqua Aid Project 1987; Producer Judy Collection (fashion) and Pres. Heemory Co. and Judy Ongg Tennis Classic Tournament; Organizer Great Wall Peace Project for 1995. *Plays include:* Hobson's Choice 1983, The World of Suzie Wong 1984, Fiddler on the Roof 1985, Roots 1987. *TV appearances include:* Story of a Boy Called Santa 1961, Judy Ongg Talk Show 1967–70, Young 720 (talk show) 1967–71; That's Music 1983, Liegui Aisha 1986, Tian xia 1988, Kaseifu ha mita! 19 2001, Mahô shôjo Alys (Tweeny Witches) 2003. *Films include:* The Big Wave 1961, Goodbye Mr Tears 1968, Forgive, Forgot, Forgotten 1974, Suk san: Sun Suk san geen hap 1983, Tanba Tetsuro no daireikai shindara odoroita!! 1990, The Pillow Book 1996, Vampire Hunter D: Bloodlust 2000, American Pastime 2007. *Recordings include:* Tasogare no Akai Tsuki (Red Moon at Dusk) 1967, Miserarete (Enchanted) 1979, Oshin (theme music, Golden Record Grand Prix, Hong Kong) 1988. *Woodcut prints include:* Fuyunohi (First Prize Japan Fine Art Acad.) 1983, Abura-ya II (Second Prize Japan Fine Art Acad.) 1984, Ageya (Third Prize Japan Fine Art Acad.) 1985, Iris 1987. *Publications:* Enchanted (essays) 1981, Judy's Healthy Food 1988, My Grandfather (fiction) 1991. *Honours:* Order of Brightness Medal, People's Repub. of China; other awards include Best Actress in a Leading Role Award (Golden Horse, Asian Film Festival) 1972, Special Performance Award (19th Annual Asia Film Festival) 1973, Best Actress in a TV Drama Series (Kyoto Film Festival) 1974, Golden Canary Award (Tokyo Music Festival) 1979, Best Vocalist of the Year (Japanese Recording Acad.) 1979; 3 Feb. designated Judy Ongg Day, NV, USA 1990. *Telephone:* (3) 3265-7895. *Fax:* (3) 3265-7896.

ORANGE, Jason Thomas; British singer, musician, guitar), songwriter and actor; b. 10 July 1970, Crumpsall, North Manchester, England. *Education:* South Trafford Coll. *Career:* mem. all-male vocal group Take That 1990–96, 2005–14; pursued a career in acting and appeared in TV thriller Killer Net 1998; lead actor with Tom Hayes in London stage production of Gob by Jim Kenworth 1999; numerous TV appearances, tours and concerts. *Recordings include:* albums: Take That And Party 1992, Everything Changes 1993, Nobody Else 1995, Beautiful World 2006, The Circus 2008, Progress 2010. *Television appearances:* Killer Net (drama) 1998, cameo role in Shameless (Channel 4) 2013. *Honours:* Nordoff Robbins Silver Clef Award for Best Band 1995, 2009, Golden Camera Award (Berlin), Golden Otto Award for best band, MTV Award for Best Group in Europe, seven Smash Hits Awards, BRIT Award for Best British Single 1994, (for Patience) 2007, (for Shine) 2008, for Best British Live Act 2008, for Best British Group 2011, Q Idol Award (with Take That) 2006. *Current Management:* c/o Jonathan Wild, 10 Management,

36 Phillimore Walk, London, W8 7SA, England. *Telephone:* (20) 8747-4534. *E-mail:* jonathan@10management.com. *Address:* c/o Polydor Records, 364–366 Kensington High Street, London, W14 8NS, England (office). *Website:* www.takethat.com.

ORBIT, William; British producer and remixer; b. (William Wainwright), 1 Oct. 1956, England. *Career:* mem., Torch Song 1980s; remixer for artists, including Human League, Erasure, Belinda Carlisle, S'Express, Prince, Jimmy Somerville, The Cure, Oleta Adams, Kraftwerk, Seal, The Shamen, Madonna, Peter Gabriel, Beth Orton, Depeche Mode, 18 Wheeler, Dreadzone, Blur, Melanie C., Sasha, All Saints; recorded own material under names, Strange Cargo, Bass-o-Matic, Spill, N-Gram Recordings; founder, O Records. *Recordings include:* albums: with Torch Song: Wish Thing 1984, Ecstasy 1986, Toward the Unknown Region 1995; solo: Strange Cargo 1987, Orbit 1987, Strange Cargo II 1990, Set The Controls For The Heart Of The Bass 1990, Science And Melody 1991, Strange Cargo III 1993, Trance Europe Express 3 1994, The Electric Chamber 1995, Pieces In A Modern Style 1995, Hinterland 1995, Invisible 1997, Harald (OST) 1997, Audio Visual (compilation) 1998, Pieces In A Modern Style 2000, Hello Waveforms 2006, My Oracle Lives Uptown 2009. *E-mail:* andy@aaminc.com. *Website:* www.williamorbit.com.

ORCHIN, Mark Alan; British musician (guitar); *Head of Music, Lewes Old Grammar School;* b. 3 Oct. 1957, London, England; m. Valerie Orchin 1979; one s. one d. *Career:* lead guitar with band, Possum and various pub, club bands late 1970s; mem. Touchstone; played for festivals, theatres, TV broadcasts; formed duo with singer, Bonnie Burden; freelance music tutor; working with Herbie Flowers at Rockshops summer schools including Dartington Int. Summer School 2005–09 (five years as main guitar tutor); Head of Music, Lewes Old Grammar School; mem. Musicians' Union; currently studying Humanities with Music degree at Open Univ. *Recordings include:* albums: with Touchstone: The Night The Snow Came Down 1991, One The Rum 1995, Silently Calling 1998, Wine Barrel Jigtarrel 2001, Sea of Providence 2006. *Address:* Lewes Old Grammar School, 140 High Street, Lewes, East Sussex, BN7 1XS, England (office). *Telephone:* (1273) 472634 (office). *E-mail:* mark@allwoodmusic.co.uk (office). *Website:* www .allwoodmusic.co.uk (office).

ORFORD, Tim; British sound engineer and programmer; b. 10 March 1964, Cambridge, England. *Education:* BSc Electronic Engineering. *Recordings:* Dina Carroll; EYC; Young Disciples; Carleen Anderson; Billie Curry; West End; Outlaw Posse; Watergates; Brand New Heavies; S'Express; PJ and Duncan; Sandals; Mary Kiani; Kym Mazelle; Marshall Jefferson; Alex Party; Mike; Rebecca Ryan; Grace; Kicks Like A Mule; Greatest 90s Dance Hits, 1996; Massive Dance Mix '96, 1996; Glen Scott, Without Vertigo, 1999; Kylie Minogue, Fever, 2001.

ORIDJANSKI, Zlatko; Macedonian musician (guitar, mandolin, flute) and backing singer; b. 13 Nov. 1963, Skopje; m. Magda Origjanska; one d. *Career:* mem. band Anastasia 1991–; numerous concerts and tours world-wide; contributed music to film 'Before the Rain' and other film, television and theatre projects. *Recordings:* albums: Mansarda (with Lola V. Stain) 1992, Pred Do'dot (Before The Rain) (soundtrack) 1994, Melurgia 1997, Nocurnal 1998. *Current Management:* c/o Ivo Jankoski, Third Ear Music, 1000 Skopje, Leninova 29/3/6, Macedonia. *Telephone:* (2) 3236990. *Fax:* (2) 3136906. *E-mail:* info@thirdear.com.mk. *Website:* www.thirdear.com.mk. *E-mail:* neubauten@plugin.com.mk (office). *Website:* www.unet.com.mk/anastasia/ Main.htm.

O'RIORDAN BURTON, Dolores Mary; Irish singer, songwriter and musician (guitar, keyboards); b. 6 Sept. 1971, Limerick; m. Don Burton 1994; three c. *Career:* mem. and lead singer, The Cranberries 1990–2003, 2009–; numerous headlining tours, festivals, radio and television appearances; collaborations with Jah Wobble, Devil's Own and Amazing Grace, Zucchero, Jam & Spoon, Angelo Badalamenti; solo artist 2003–. *Films:* Click 2006. *Recordings include:* albums: with The Cranberries: Everybody Else is Doing it, So Why Can't We? 1993, No Need to Argue 1994, To the Faithful Departed 1996, Bury the Hatchet 1999, Bury the Hatchet: The Complete Sessions 2000, Wake Up and Smell the Coffee 2001, Treasure Box 2002, Roses 2012; solo: Are You Listening? 2007, No Baggage 2009. *Honours:* European Border Breakers Award 2008. *Current Management:* c/o Danny Goldberg, Gold Village Entertainment, 72 Madison Avenue, 8th Floor, New York, NY 10016, USA. *Telephone:* (212) 741-2400. *Fax:* (212) 741-4871. *E-mail:* info@ goldve.com. *Website:* www.goldve.com; www.cranberries.com; www .doloresoriordan.ie.

ORLANDO, Tony; American singer; b. (Michael Anthony Orlando Cassivitis), 3 April 1944, Manhattan. *Career:* demo singer 1960; worked for music publishers 1963–70; lead singer trio, Dawn (later billed as Tony Orlando and Dawn) 1970–77, reunion 1990; own TV series (CBS) 1974–75; solo artist 1977–; performed over 2000 shows. *Television appearance:* Three Hundred Miles for Stephanie (film) 1979. *Play:* Barnum (lead role, musical) 1981. *Recordings include:* albums: Bless You 1961, Candida 1970, Dawn Featuring Tony Orlando 1971, Tuneweaving 1973, Dawn's New Ragtime Follies 1973, Golden Ribbons 1974, Prime Time 1974, Tony Orlando and Dawn II 1975, He Don't Love You (Like I Love You) 1975, Skybird 1975, To Be With You 1976, Tony Orlando 1978; hit singles: Tie a Yellow Ribbon Round the Ole Oak Tree, Sweet Gypsy Rose, He Don't Love You, Who's In The Strawberry Patch With Sally, Cupid, Steppin' Out (Gonna Boogie Tonight), Mornin' Beautiful. *Honours:* American Music Award for Favorite Single 1974, for Favorite Pop/

Rock Group 1976. *Current Management:* c/o David Brokaw, The Brokaw Company, 9255 Sunset Boulevard, Suite 804, Los Angeles, CA 90069, USA. *Telephone:* (310) 273-2060. *Fax:* (310) 276-4037. *E-mail:* db@brokawco.com. *Website:* www.brokawco.com; www.tonyorlando.com.

O'ROURKE, Aidan Joseph; British folk musician (fiddle) and composer; b. 1975, Oban, Scotland. *Career:* professional musician from age of 15; toured Scotland, Europe and N America with Caledonia Ramblers; Founder-mem. Tabache (with Claire Mann) 1998–2000; mem. Blazin' Fiddles big band 1998–; Founder-mem. folk trio Lau 2005–, collaborations with Karine Polwart, Adem; solo artist 2006–; mem. Kan 2010–; mem. Unusual Suspects; session musician on numerous albums for artists including Karen Matheson, Michael McGoldrick, Runrig. *Recordings:* with Tabache: Are You Willing 1999, Waves of Rush 2000; with Lau: Lightweights and Gentlemen 2007, Arc Light 2009, Race the Loser 2012; solo: Sirius 2006, An Tobar 2008, Hotline 2013; with Kan: Sleeper 2012. *Honours:* Scottish Traditional Music Awards for Instrumentalist of the Year 2006, for Composer of the Year 2011; with Lau: BBC Radio 2 Folk Awards for Best Band 2008, 2009, 2010, for Best Group 2013, Scottish Traditional Music Award for Best Live Act 2009. *E-mail:* tomreveal@mac.com. *Website:* www.revealrecords.co.uk; www.lau-music.co .uk; www.aidanorourke.net.

O'ROURKE, Jim; American musician. *Career:* collaborated with Sonic Youth 1997, joined band 2001–05; founder mem., Loose Fur 2002–, Fenn O'Berg. *Recordings include:* albums: with Sonic Youth: Murray Street 2002, Sonic Nurse 2004, Rather Ripped 2006, The Destroyed Room: B-sides and Rarities 2006; with Loose Fur: Loose Fur 2002, Sleeps With Fishes 2003, Born Again in the USA 2006; with Fenn O'Berg: The Magic Sound of Fenn O'Berg 1999, The Return of Fenn O'Berg 2002, In Stereo 2010. *Address:* c/o Drag City, PO Box 476867, Chicago, IL 60647, USA (office). *E-mail:* press@dragcity.com (office). *Website:* www.dragcity.com (office).

ORRALL, Robert Ellis; American songwriter, producer, singer and musician; b. 4 May 1955, Winthrop. *Career:* solo artist and songwriter 1980–; producer, Flying Colors 1991, Orrall and Wright 1993, Michael Peterson 1997; mem. ASCAP, AFTRA, CMA. *Recordings include:* Sweet Nothing 1979, Fixation 1981, Special Pain 1983, Contain Yourself 1984, Flying Colors 1991, Orrall and Wright 1993, Mistakes 1998, The Book of Lies 2008; with Michael Peterson: Michael Peterson 1997, Drink, Swear, Steal and Lie 1997, Being Human 1999; with Wedding Day Music: Wedding Day Music 1998; with Yankee Grey: All Things Considered 1999, Untamed, 1999; as Monkey Bowl: Plastic 350 2004, Lowe Profile 2005. *Honours:* ASCAP Country Awards 1990, 1993, 1994, CMA Number One Awards 1990, 1993, 1997, World Festival Charleston Grand Award for Best Music Video 1994, ASCAP Pop Award 1995. *Address:* 35 Music Square E, Nashville, TN 37203, USA. *E-mail:* hello@ infinitycat.com. *Website:* www.robertellisorrall.com.

ORTI, Guillaume; French musician (saxophones) and composer; b. 8 Dec. 1969, Nyons. *Career:* fmr mem., Pepa Päivinen Trio + Orti, 7 Wheels, Urban Mood, Thôt Agrandi, François Merville Quintet, Aghia Triada, Le Sacre du Tympan, Christophe Marguet Quartet, Los Incontrolados, Triple Gee, Paintings, Altissimo; mem., Reverse, Octurn, Kartet, Opus Incertum on C, Osmosis, Thôt Twin; mem. collective, Hask 1993–2005; mem., Mercoledi & Co. 1997–2000; mem. Oxymore Quintet 2006–; frequent work with theatre and dance cos; played with Steve Argüelles, Marc Ducret, Aldo Romano, Steve Lacy, Dominique Pifarely, Thierry Madiot, Noël Akchoté, Benoît Delbecq. *Compositions:* Dix + Orti 1996, À Mesure 1998, CCC suite for eight musicians 1998. *Recordings include:* albums: Triple Gee (with Mercoledi), Sous les Pattes du Lion (with Mercoledi), Paintings (with Benoît Delkbecq) 1993, Altissimo (with Hubert Dupont) 1995, A l'envers – Quoi de neuf Dr big band 1995, Pression (with Kartet) 1995, Compli X cités (with Malo Vallois) 1997, Si loin, si proche (with Pascale Labbé) 1997, New Songs (with Manu Pekar) 1998, Oxymore Quintet 2008. *Current Management:* c/o Mark Haanstra, Hudsonstraat 91-2, 1057 Amsterdam, Netherlands. *Telephone:* (20) 6119109. *E-mail:* info@oxymoremusic.org (office). *Website:* www.oxymorequintet.org.

ORTMANN, Carsten, MA; Danish television producer, musician (drums) and singer; b. 4 Aug. 1965, Copenhagen. *Education:* Inst. of Music, Univ. of Århus. *Career:* drummer, Picnic 1986–96, Hunk Ai 1986–89; founder mem., drummer and lead singer, Fullface Storband 1987–89; drums, percussion and backing vocals, Shirtsville 1989–91; percussion and backing vocals, Tintin og HårtGírrerne 1993–95; singer, Guttermændenen 1989–. *Recordings:* with Hunk Ai: Hunk Ai 1986, Alene Hjemme 1989; with Picnic: Barking Up the Wrong Tree 1987, Meat King 1990, Reverse Ahead 1992, Lemming Nation 1995; with Shirtsville: Secrets 3 1990, Girls Deserve the Best 1991; with Tintin og Hårtgírrerne: Dance Crazy 1994, Mad Guppies Fighting the Food Chain 1995.

ORTON, Beth; British singer, songwriter and musician (guitar); b. Dec. 1970, Norwich, England. *Career:* mem. of duo, Spill; formed backing band; numerous live appearances and appearances at festivals; guest or backing vocalist with Red Snapper, William Orbit, Chemical Brothers, Strange Cargo, Beck, Terry Callier; solo artist 1996–. *Recordings include:* albums: Trailer Park 1996, Central Reservation 1999, Daybreaker 2002, Comfort of Strangers 2006. *Honours:* BRIT Award for Best British Female Solo Artist 2000. *Current Management:* azoffmusic Management, 22 Gordon Avenue, St Margarets, Twickenham TW1 1NQ, England. *Telephone:* (20) 8744-2404. *Fax:* (20) 8744-2406. *Website:* www.bethorton.mu.

ORTON, Kenneth, LLCM, TD, DipLAC (Hons); British musician (saxophones, woodwind), teacher, arranger and writer; b. 26 March 1934, Bedworth, Warwicks., England; m. 1st Jean Finlay 1960 (died 1996); one d.; m. 2nd Marie-Claire Davidson 2004. *Education:* Tech. Coll., City & Guilds, London Art Coll., London Coll. of Music. *Career:* qualified electrical engineer 1955; Army Band 1955–58; performed with Big Bands including Syd Dean, Ken Turner; Geraldo; Soul Bands including Ray King; tours with numerous artistes 1960s; formed Don Ellis Connection Big Band, only band dedicated to the late jazz star; retired from teaching 1998; re-formed Don Ellis Connection Orchestra 1999–2001; est. Don Ellis library in UK, relocated to France 2004; directed four-day seminar, with final radio broadcast concert, of the music of Don Ellis at Conservatoire Nat. Supérieur de Musique et de Danse de Paris 2007; major project of more than 20 years of research-related work and author of biog. of Don Ellis. *Compositions:* two songs, recorded by Ray King; major work reconstructing Don Ellis scores; rearranged and set to lyrics (SATB choir) certain Ellis material; reconstructed all Ellis 1960s vocal arrangements for Karin Krog, and presented concert for Karin Krog 1994. *Publications:* Forgotten Genius (biog.) 2006, In Search of Don Ellis – Forgotten Genius (three-vol. biog.) 2010, Don Ellis' Jazz Journal, Encyclopaedia of Pop Music, Who's Who In Jazz; new booklet and album liner notes for CD re-release of Don Ellis's Haiku 2010, exec. producer and liner notes (booklet) for CD Don Ellis Live in India 2010. *Honours:* Freeman of Coventry 1955; GSM Cyprus Clasp 1955–58. *Address:* L'Ellisée, 94 avenue Frédéric Garnier, 17640 Vaux-sur-Mer, France (home). *Telephone:* (5) 46-08-35-18 (home). *E-mail:* ken.orton@orange.fr.

ORZABAL, Roland; British singer, songwriter, musician (guitar, keyboards) and record producer; b. 22 Aug. 1961, Portsmouth, Hampshire, England. *Career:* founder mem., The Graduate 1979–81; founder mem., Tears for Fears 1981–; co-producer for artists, including Oleta Adams, Emiliana Torrini. *Compositions include:* Everybody Wants To Run The World (amended from hit single, theme for Sport Aid famine relief) 1986. *Recordings include:* albums: with Graduate: Acting Your Age 1979; with Tears for Fears: The Hurting 1983, Songs From The Big Chair 1985, The Seeds Of Love 1989, Elemental 1993, Raoul And The Kings Of Spain 1995, Everybody Loves A Happy Ending 2004; solo: Tomcats Screaming Outside 2001. *Honours:* Smash Hits Award for Most Promising New Act 1982, BRIT Award for Best British Single 1985, Ivor Novello Award for Songwriter of the Year 1986, BMI Performance Award (for single Head Over Heels 1985) 1991. *Website:* www.tearsforfears.net.

OSBORN, Kassidy; American country singer; b. Magna, UT. *Career:* mem. country group, SheDaisy (with sisters Kristyn and Kelsi). *Recordings include:* albums: The Whole Shebang 1999, Brand New Year 2001, Knock On The Sky 2002, Sweet Right Here 2004, Fortuneteller's Melody 2006, A Story to Tell 2010. *Address:* c/o PO Box 150638, Nashville, TN 37215-0638, USA (office). *E-mail:* chrisbrunton@mac.com (office). *Website:* www.shedaisy.com.

OSBORN, Kelsi; American country singer; b. Magna, UT. *Career:* mem. country group, SheDaisy (with sisters Kassidy and Kristyn). *Recordings include:* albums: The Whole Shebang 1999, Brand New Year 2001, Knock On The Sky 2002, Sweet Right Here 2004, Fortuneteller's Melody 2006, A Story to Tell 2010. *Address:* c/o PO Box 150638, Nashville, TN 37215-0638, USA (office). *E-mail:* chrisbrunton@mac.com (office). *Website:* www.shedaisy.com.

OSBORN, Kristyn; American country singer and songwriter; b. Magna, Utah. *Career:* mem. and lead singer of country group, SheDaisy (with sisters Kassidy and Kelsi). *Recordings include:* albums: The Whole Shebang 1999, Brand New Year 2001, Knock On The Sky 2002, Sweet Right Here 2004, Fortuneteller's Melody 2006, A Story to Tell 2010. *Address:* c/o PO Box 150638, Nashville, TN 37215-0638, USA (office). *Website:* www.shedaisy.com.

OSBORNE, Jeffrey; American singer, songwriter and producer; b. 9 March 1948, Providence, Rhode Island. *Career:* singer, Love Men Ltd. 1969, changed name to LTD (Love Togetherness and Devotion) 1970–82; solo artist 1982–. *Recordings:* albums: Jeffrey Osborne 1982, Stay With Me Tonight 1983, Don't Stop 1984, Emotional 1986, One Love One Dream 1988, Only Human 1991, Something Warm for Christmas 1997, Ultimate Collection 1999, That's for Sure 2000, Music is Life 2004, From the Soul 2005. *Website:* www.jeffreyosborne.com.

OSBORNE, Joan; American singer and songwriter; b. 1962, Anchorage, Kentucky. *Career:* performer on New York blues circuit 1988; solo artist; numerous concerts and live appearances; own record label, Womanly Hips Music. *Recordings include:* albums: Relish 1995, Righteous Love 2000, How Sweet It Is 2002, Christmas Means Love 2005, Pretty Little Stranger 2006, Breakfast in Bed 2008, Little Wild One 2008. *Current Management:* c/o Jason Richardson, DAS Communications Ltd. *E-mail:* jason@dasgroup.com. *Website:* www.joanosborne.com.

OSBORNE, John Michael; British artist agent and record company owner; b. 28 Sept. 1960, London. *Education:* Royal College of Art. *Career:* owner, Slate Records; own management co., John Osborne Management, looking after many top radio DJs. *Honours:* BEDA DJ of the Year 1992, Disco International 1992.

OSBORNE, Pete; British musician (saxophones, clarinet) and composer; b. 15 Sept. 1957, London; m. Sally Bowring 1983. *Education:* studied classical, jazz, clarinet, saxophone with Prof. Malcolm Ellingworth. *Career:* worked in England, USA, Denmark, Belgium, Germany, Sweden, Italy, France; concerts with Herb Jeffries, Andy Sheppard, John Taylor 1980, Georgie Fame, Andy Sheppard, Spirit Level 1985, Bobby Shew; Mark Murphy, 1986; radio broadcasts with Rhythm Machine, Nightride, BBC Radio 2 1987, with Lars Sjosten Trio, Radio Stockholm 1989; moved to Paris, concerts with Liz McComb 1991, 1995; mem, Musicians' Union, London, SACEM, France, SPEDIDAM. *Compositions:* Jazz suite for Paris, and 50 original compositions (to be released) for jazz sextet. *Recordings:* with Billy Joel: Just The Way You Are 1979; with James Brown: album and video 1991; with Vanessa Paradis 1992; with MC Solaar (Caroline Re-mix) 1993; with Cat Stevens: album 1994; with Abbey Lincoln Trio: title film track, Tom Est Tout Seul 1994. *Honours:* Best Saxophone Player, SW England, Bath Evening Chronicle 1985, 1986, 1987.

OSBOURNE, Kelly Lee; American singer and actor; b. 27 Oct. 1984, London, England; d. of Ozzy Osbourne and Sharon Osbourne. *Career:* solo artist; presenter Sunday Surgery (BBC Radio 1) 2007–. *Television includes:* The Osbournes 2002–05, Life As We Know It 2004–05, Dancing with the Stars (Season 9) 2009, Fashion Police 2010–. *Films include:* Austin Powers in Goldmember 2002, Live Freaky Die Freaky (voice) 2006. *Recordings include:* albums: Shut Up 2003, Changes 2003, Sleeping in the Nothing 2005. *Publications include:* Ordinary People (autobiography with Ozzy, Sharon, Aimee and Jack Osbourne) 2004, Fierce 2009. *Honours:* Teen Choice Award 2002, 2003, LK Today High Street Fashion Award 2008, Glamour Award 2008, Young Hollywood Award 2013. *Current Management:* c/o Marcel Pariseau, True Public Relations, 6725 Sunset Blvd, Suite 470, Los Angeles, CA 90028, USA. *Telephone:* (323) 957-0710. *Website:* www.truepublicrelations.com; www.kellyosbourne.com.

OSBOURNE, John (Ozzy); British musician and singer; b. 3 Dec. 1948, Aston, Warwicks., England; m. 1st Thelma; two d.; m. 2nd Sharon Arden 1982; two d. one s. *Career:* mem. and lead singer, Black Sabbath (fmrly Polka Tulk, then Earth) 1967–77 (reunion tour 1998–99); solo artist with backing group Blizzard of Ozz 1979–; cr. annual touring festival Ozzfest 1996–; numerous live performances and festival appearances. *Television series:* The Osbournes (MTV) 2001–05. *Recordings include:* albums: with Black Sabbath: Black Sabbath 1969, Paranoid 1970, Master Of Reality 1971, Black Sabbath Vol. 4 1972, Sabbath Bloody Sabbath 1973, Sabotage 1975, Technical Ecstasy 1976, Never Say Die! 1978, Reunion 1998, 13 2013; solo: Blizzard Of Ozz 1980, Diary Of A Madman 1981, Speak Of The Devil 1982, Bark At The Moon 1983, The Ultimate Sin 1986, Tribute 1987, No Rest For The Wicked 1988, Just Say Ozzy 1990, No More Tears 1991, Live & Loud 1993, Ozzmosis 1995, The Ozzman Cometh 1997, OzzFest Vol. 1 1997, Down To Earth 2001, Live At Budokan 2002, X-Posed 2002, Under Cover 2005, Black Rain 2007, Scream 2010. *Publication:* I Am Ozzy (autobiog.) 2009. *Honours:* Grammy Awards for Best Metal Performance (for I Don't Want to Change the World) 1994, (for Iron Man) 2000, (for God is Dead?) 2014, Nordoff-Robbins O2 Silver Clef Award (with Sharon Osbourne) 2006, MTV Europe Music Award for Global Icon 2014. *Current Management:* c/o Sharon Osbourne Management, 9292 Civic Centre Drive, Beverly Hills, CA 90210, USA. *Website:* www.ozzy.com.

OSCAR; South African DJ and musician. *Career:* founding mem., kwaito band, Bongo Maffin 1996–; performances in UK, Denmark 2000; worked with Skunk Anansie, Chaka Khan, Stevie Wonder, Boyz II Men, Hugh Masekela. *Recordings:* albums: Final Entry 1996, The Concerto 1998, IV 1999, Bongolution 2001, New Construction 2006. *Honours:* South African Music Award, Best Kwaito Artist 1999, Kora Award, Best African Group 2001. *E-mail:* info@exclusivems.co.za (office). *Website:* www.bongomaffin.co.za.

OSEI, Teddy; Ghanaian highlife musician (saxophone, drums) and composer. *Career:* fmr mem. highlife band, Star Gazers, and Comets; moved to London to study music 1962; formed Cat's Paw 1964; founder mem. Osibisa 1969–. *Recordings include:* albums: Osibisa 1971, Woyaya 1971, Heads 1972, Superfly TNT 1973, Happy Children 1973, Osibirock 1974, Welcome Home 1975, Ojah Awake 1976, Black Magic Night 1977, Mystic Energy 1980, African Flight 1981, Unleashed 1983, Live At The Marquee 1983, Movements 1989, Monsore 1995, Aka Kakra 2000, African Dawn African Flight 2003, Wango Wango 2004, Blue Black Night (Live) 2005, Osee Yee 2009. *E-mail:* contact@osibisa.co.uk. *Website:* www.osibisa.co.uk.

OSLIN, Kay Toinette; American country music singer, songwriter and actress; b. Crossett, Arkansas. *Education:* Lon Morris College, Texas. *Career:* folk singer in Houston; touring and Broadway productions of: Hello Dolly; Promises, Promises; West Side Story; began songwriting 1978; backing singer for Guy Clark; numerous television appearances. *Television appearances:* Paradise, Evening Shade, Poisoned By Love. *Film:* The Thing Called Love. *Compositions:* songs: Do Ya?, Round The Clock Lovin', Where Is A Woman To Go, 80s Ladies, Hold Me, Come Next Monday, Younger Men. *Recordings include:* albums: 80's Ladies 1988, This Woman 1989, Love In A Small Town 1990, My Roots are Showing 1996, Super Hits 1997, At Her Best 1998, Live Close By, Visit Often 2001. *Honours:* three Grammy Awards, CMA Award for Best Female Vocalist 1988, CMA Award for Song of the Year 1988, ACM Award for Best Female Country Vocalist 1989. *Website:* www.ktoslin.net.

OSMAN, Mat; British musician (bass); b. 9 Oct. 1967, Welwyn Garden City, England. *Career:* mem., Geoff 1985, Suave and Elegant 1989, Suede 1990–2004, 2010–; numerous concerts, festivals, tours and television appearances. *Recordings include:* albums: with Suede: Suede, 1993, Dog Man Star 1994, Coming Up 1996, Sci-Fi Lullabies 1997, Head Music 1999, A New Morning 2002, Bloodsports 2013, Night Thoughts 2016. *Honours:* with Suede: Mercury Music Prize 1993, Q Icon Award 2013. *Current Management:* Quietus Management Limited, 13 Bramley Road, 2nd Floor Phoenix Brewery,

London, W10 6SP England. *Telephone:* (20) 3220-0310. *Website:* www .quietusmanagement.com; www.suede.co.uk.

OSMENT, Matt; New Zealand musician (drums); b. Cambridge. *Career:* founder mem., Trinket 1996, renamed The Datsuns 1997–; own label, Hell Squad Records. *Recordings include:* albums: The Datsuns 2002, Outta Sight Outta Mind 2004, Smoke & Mirrors 2006, Head Stunts 2008. *Current Management:* c/o Tom Dalton, Thunderbird Management, PO Box 60496, Titirangi, Waitakere 0642, New Zealand. *Telephone:* (9) 836-3232. *E-mail:* tom@thunderbirdmanagement.com. *Website:* www.thunderbirdmanagement .com. *E-mail:* enquiries@thedatsuns.com. *Website:* www.thedatsuns.com.

OSMOND, Donald (Donny) Clark; American singer; b. 9 Dec. 1957, Ogden, Utah; m. Debra Glenn 1978; five c. *Education:* Brigham Young Univ. *Career:* singer with The Osmonds 1963–80; solo artist 1971–78, 1988–; also duo with sister Marie; head of own TV production co., Night Star 1980s; f. Donny Osmond Home. *Television includes:* Donny and Marie (show) 1976–79, Osmond Family (show) 1980, Dancing With The Stars (winner) 2009. *Films include:* Goin' Coconuts 1978, College Road Trip 2008. *Theatre includes:* Joseph and his Amazing Technicolour Dreamcoat, Toronto, Canada 1992–93, Beauty and the Beast, New York 2006. *Recordings include:* albums: with The Osmonds: Homemade 1971, Osmonds 1971, Crazy Horses 1972, Phase-III 1972, The Osmonds Live 1972, The Plan 1973, Love Me For A Reason 1974, Around The World: Live In Concert 1975, The Proud One 1975, Brainstorm 1976, The Osmond Christmas Album 1976, Osmond Family Christmas 1991; solo: The Donny Osmond Album 1971, To You With Love, Donny 1971, Portrait of Donny 1972, Too Young 1972, My Best To You 1972, A Time For Us 1973, Alone Together 1973, Donny Osmond Superstar 1973, Donny 1974, I'm Leaving It All Up To You (with Marie Osmond) 1974, Love Me For A Reason 1974, Make The World Go Away (with Marie Osmond) 1975, Donny and Marie – Featuring Songs From Their Television Show (with Marie Osmond) 1976, Donny and Marie: New Season (with Marie Osmond) 1976, Deep Purple (with Marie Osmond) 1976, Disco Train 1976, Donald Clark Osmond 1977, Goin' Coconuts (with Marie Osmond) 1978, Winning Combination 1978, Donny Osmond 1989, Eyes Don't Lie 1990, Christmas At Home 1998, This Is The Moment 2001, Somewhere In Time 2002, What I Meant To Say 2004, Love Songs of the '70s 2007, From Donny with Love 2008, Duets (with Marie Osmond) 2009, Donny & Marie (with Marie Osmond) 2011, The Soundtrack of My Life 2014. *Publication:* Life is Just What You Make of It (autobiography) 2005. *Honours:* Georgie Award for Best Vocal Team (with Marie Osmond) 1978. *E-mail:* info@donnyosmond.com. *Website:* www.donnyosmond.com; donny.com.

OSMOND, Jimmy; American singer and business executive; b. 16 April 1963, Canoga Park, Calif.. *Career:* solo artist from 1972; rock impressario and restaurateur; owner, Oz-Art advertising and design co.; owner, Osmond's family film and video centre, Utah 1988–. *Recordings include:* albums: Killer Joe 1973, Little Arrows 1975.

OSMOND, Marie; American singer; b. 13 Oct. 1959, Ogden, UT; m. 1st Stephen Craig 1982 (divorced, remarried 2011); m. 2nd Brian Blosil 1986 (divorced 2007); eight c. *Career:* mem. of family singing group, The Osmonds 1966–73; solo artist 1973–; mem. of duo (with brother Donny Osmond); numerous television appearances, including Donny and Marie Show 1976–81, Osmond Family Show 1980, Marie (NBC) 1980, Maybe This Time 1995, Donny & Marie 1998–2000, several Osmonds Christmas specials; co-founder, Children's Miracle Network. *Films:* Goin' Coconuts 1978, The Gift of Love 1979, Side by Side 1982, I Married Wyatt Earp 1983. *Plays:* The Sound of Music, The King and I. *Recordings include:* albums: with Donny Osmond: I'm Leaving It Up To You 1974, Make The World Go Away 1975, Donny and Marie – Songs from Their Television Show 1976, Deep Purple 1976, Donny and Marie – A New Season 1977, Winning Combination 1978, Duets 2009; solo: Paper Roses 1974, In My Little Corner of The World 1974, Who's Sorry Now 1975, This Is The Way That I Feel 1977, There's No Stopping Your Heart 1985, I Only Wanted You 1987, All in Love 1988, Steppin' Stone 1989. *Publications:* Behind the Smile 2001, Might as Well Laugh About It Now 2009. *Honours:* American Music Award for Best Country Band, Duo or Group (with Donny Osmond) 1976, Georgie Award for Best Vocal Team (with Donny Osmond) 1978, for Best Country Duo of Year (with Dan Seals) 1986, Roy Acuff Community Service Award 1988. *Website:* www.marieosmond.com.

OSTERMANN, Flemming; Danish musician (guitar), singer and producer; b. 2 June 1947, Århus; m. Annette Stenbjoern 1988; two s. one d. *Career:* tours with: Savage Rose 1969–70; Cox Orange 1972–76; Anne Linnet Band 1977–80; Billy Cross and All Stars 1980–95; Assoc. Prof., Rhythmic Music Conservatory, Copenhagen; mem. Danish Music Soc., DJBFA. *Recordings:* with Savage Rose, Cox Orange, Anne Linnet, Pia Raug, Billy Cross, Jens Rugsted; as producer: Keep The Light In Your Eyes, Lysdal & Rasmussen 2001. *Publications:* Rhythmic Guitar for Beginners 1995. *Address:* Brumleby 25, 2100 Copenhagen O, Denmark (home).

OSTEŠ, Tin; Croatian musician (drums). *Career:* mem., Pipschips&videoclips 2002–. *Recordings include:* album: Drveće i rijeke 2003. *Address:* c/o Menart Records, Bencekovićeva 19, 10 000 Zagreb, Croatia. *Website:* www .pipschipsvideoclips.com.

O'SULLIVAN, Gilbert Raymond; Irish singer and musician (piano); b. (Raymond Edward O'Sullivan), 1 Dec. 1946, Waterford. *Education:* St Joseph's Comprehensive School, Swindon, UK, Swindon Art Coll. *Career:*

solo artist 1970–. *Recordings include:* albums: Himself 1971, Back To Front 1972, I'm A Writer Not A Fighter 1973, Stranger In My Own Backyard 1974, Southpaw 1977, Odd Centre 1980, Life and Rhymes 1982, Frobisher Drive 1988, Sounds of the Loop 1993, Every Song Has Its Play 1995, Live In Japan 1993, By Larry 1994, Singer Sowing Machine 1998, Little Album 2001, Irlish 2002, Piano Foreplay 2004, The Berry Vest Of Gilbert O'Sullivan 2004, A Scruff At Heart 2007. *Address:* c/o Park Promotions, PO Box 651k, Oxford, OX2 9RB, England. *Website:* www.gilbertosullivan.net.

OTERO MARTÍN, David; Spanish musician (guitar) and songwriter; b. 17 April 1980, Madrid. *Career:* mem., El Canto del Loco 2000–. *Recordings include* albums: A contracorriente 2002, Sala Caracol 2003, Estados de ánimo 2003, Zapatillas 2005, Pequeños Grandes Directos 2006, Personas 2008, De Personas a Personas 2008. *Honours:* MTV Europe Music Award Best Spanish Act 2005. *Current Management:* Aire de Música, Calle Pelayo, 76 Local, 28004 Madrid, Spain. *Telephone:* (91) 7000443. *Fax:* (91) 3197946. *E-mail:* info@airedemusica .com. *Website:* www.airedemusica.com; www.elcantodelloco.com.

O'TOOLE, Steve; musician (guitar); b. 4 April 1969, Chesterfield, England. *Career:* mem., Slaughterhouse 5; mem., Enormous; mem. Musicians' Union. *Compositions:* Pathetic; Things She Did; Wide Open; Cigarette Machine From God; My Type. *Address:* 31A Bishop Street, Mansfield, Nottingham NG18 1HJ, England.

OTTEWELL, Ben; British musician (guitar, bass) and singer; b. 1975, Chesterfield, England. *Career:* mem., Gomez 1996–; numerous concerts, festival, radio and television appearances. *Recordings include:* albums: Bring It On 1998, Liquid Skin 1999, Abandoned Shopping Trolley Hotline 2000, In Our Gun 2002, Out West: Live at the Fillmore 2005, How We Operate 2006, A New Tide 2009. *Honours:* Mercury Music Prize 1998. *Current Management:* c/o Jason Colton, Red Light Management, 321 East Main Street, Charlottesville, VA 22902, USA. *Telephone:* (434) 245-4900. *Fax:* (434) 245-4933. *E-mail:* gomez@redlightmanagement.com. *Website:* www.redlightmanagement.com. *E-mail:* gomez@gomeztheband.com (office). *Website:* www.gomeztheband.com.

OTTO, John; American musician (drums); b. Jacksonville, FL. *Education:* private lessons in jazz drumming. *Career:* fmrly played in jazz band; mem., Limp Bizkit 1994–. *Recordings:* albums: Three Dollar Bill Y'All 1997, Significant Other 1999, Chocolate Starfish And The Hotdog Flavored Water 2000, New Old Songs 2001, Bipolar 2003, Results May Vary 2003, The Unquestionable Truth (Part 1) 2005, Gold Cobra 2010. *Honours:* American Music Award for Favorite Alternative Artist 2002. *Current Management:* c/o Peter Katsis, The Firm, 9100 Wilshire Boulevard, Beverly Hills, CA 90212, USA. *Website:* www.limpbizkit.com.

DJ ÖTZI; Austrian singer and DJ; b. (Gernot Friedle), 7 Jan. 1971, St Johann, Tyrol; m. Sonja Kein 2001. *Education:* Imst Agricultural Coll. *Recordings include:* albums: Anton – Das Album 2000, Never Stop The Alpenpop 2001, Love Peace and Vollgas 2001, Today is the Day 2002, Flying to the Sky 2003, Ich war immer der Clown 2004, Stemstunden 2007. *Honours:* German Echo Music Award for Best Int. Rock/Pop Single (for Anton Aus Tirol) 2001. *Current Management:* c/o Kunstlermanagement Wolfgang Kaminski, Unterer Ahlenbergweg 47a. 58313 Herdecke, Germany. *Telephone:* (2330) 13344. *Fax:* (2330) 13343. *E-mail:* w-kaminski@t-online.de. *Website:* www.kaminski -kuenstlermanagement.de; www.maxkaminski.com; www.dj-oetzi.com.

OUZOUNOFF, Alexandre; French musician (bassoon) and composer; b. 15 Nov. 1955, Suresnes; m. 28 Aug. 1993, 1 d. *Education:* Student of Maurice Allard. *Career:* Trio Ozi (with C Villevielle, L Aubert), Festivals: France, Europe, Africa, Republic of Korea; Brazil; Middle East; Russia, 1976–96; Contemporary repertory Constitution; Solo bassoon recitals: Radio France; Centre Pompidou; IRCAM; Festival d'Automne à Paris; INA-GRM; MANCA (Strasbourg; GMEB (Bourges); GRAMW (Lyon); Germany; USA; Italy; Poland, 1979–87; Member, Blue Ensemble, contemporary jazz group (with T. Gubitsch, J. F. Jenny-Clarck, J. Schwartz), 1991–94; Appearances, festivals include: De La Butte Montmarte; Festival de Paris; Hyères; Presences 93/Radio France; La Rochelle; Aix En Musique; Heures Musicales de Chatres; Futurs Musiques; D'Automne; Prague; Presence 95/Radio France; Uzès; Breme; Théatre du Châtelet; Moscow-Idaho; Contemporary bassoon masterclasses, France and abroad, 1985–95; mem, IDRS (International Double Reed Society). *Recordings include:* Jazz: Palissander's Night, 1988; Sokoa Tanz, 1991; with KOQ Trio: Made In Nigeria, 1993; Contemporary: with Jean Schwartz: Assolutamente, 1990; Canto, 1993; Destroy, 1990; with François Bousch: Espace-Temps, 1992; Classical: Heitor Villa Lobos, Trio d'Anches, 1989; Francis Poulenc, Trio d'Anches, 1991; Etienne Ozi, Trio d'Anches Ozi, 1991; André Caplet/Alberic Magnard, Trio d'Anches Ozi, 1994. *Publications:* Actually The Bassoon. *Honours:* First Prize, Music History, CNSM, Paris; Certificate, International Chamber Music Competition, Martigny (Switzerland).

OVADIA, Salomone (Moni); Italian playwright, singer, actor, musician and writer; b. 1946, Plovdiv, Bulgaria. *Education:* Univ. of Milan. *Career:* fmr mem. of band Almanacco Popolare; Founder-mem. Gruppo Folk Internazionale 1972; Founder-mem. Theather Orchestra 1990–; apptd Artistic Dir, Mittelfest, Cividale del Friuli 2004. *Stage productions include:* Oylem Goylem 1990, Dybbuk 1995, Taibele e il suo demone 1995, Diario ironico dall'esilio 1995, Ballata di fine millennio 1996, Pallida madre, tenera sorella 1996, Il Caso Kafka 1997, Trieste, ebrei e dintorni 1998, Mame, mamele, mamma, mamà... 1998, Joss Rakover si rivolge a Dio 1999, Il Banchiere errante 2001, L'Armata a cavallo 2003. *Film:* Memories of Anne Frank 2009. *Publications* *include:* Perché no? 1996, Oylem Goylem 1998, L'ebreo che ride 1998, La porta di sion 1999, Ballata di fine millennio 1999, Speriamo che tenga 2001, Le Baladin du monde yiddish 2002, Vai a te stesso 2002, Contro l'idolatria 2005, Lavoratori di tutto il mondo ridete 2007, Il conto dell'Ultima cena 2010. *Address:* Promo Music Sas, Via dalla Volta, 21, 40131 Bologna, Italy. *Telephone:* (51) 313530. *Fax:* (51) 383001. *E-mail:* info@promomusic.it. *Website:* www.moniovadia.it.

OVERETT, Kelly; British singer and dancer; b. Ipswich. *Career:* dancer, SL2; singer in dance-music group, Cappella 1993–95. *Recordings include:* albums: U Got To Know 1994, Remixes 1994.

OVERON, Geoffrey (Geoff) John, (Jet Overcoat); British musician (electric and acoustic guitar, electric sitar, guitar-banjo, bass guitar), singer, song-writer, teacher and promoter and record producer; b. 26 Nov. 1953, Leicester, England. *Education:* De Montfort Univ. *Career:* professional musician 1978–; played with artists, including Ric Grech, Jimmy Witherspoon, Van Morrison Band, The Foundations; shared tour dates with Thin Lizzy, The Animals, Taj Mahal, at Montreux Jazz Festival; Founder-mem Geoff Overon Band; session player, producer, teacher and impresario; mem. British Music Writers' Council, Musicians' Union, Registry of Electric Guitar Tutors, Leicester Rhythm and Blues Soc. (Life Pres.). *Compositions:* Loving With A Loaded Dice, If It Don't Come Easy, My Feet, She Didn't Say Diddley, etc. *Recording:* Switchmaster compilation CD 2007. *Address:* Go Promotions, 12 Somerville Road, Leicester, LE3 2ET, England. *Telephone:* (116) 289-1919.

OVERWATER, Tony; Dutch musician (acoustic bass, contrabass, bass guitar); b. 24 March 1965, Rotterdam, Netherlands; one c. *Education:* Royal Conservatory, The Hague. *Career:* played at Ronnie Scott's, London, with David Murray; North Sea Jazz Festival with Yuri Honing Trio; Montréal Jazz Festival; solo TV appearance in Reiziger in Muziek; wrote music for documentary. *Compositions:* Le Petit Prince for double bass and mezzo soprano, Eter/Ether (for dancer/choreographer Anouk van Dijk). *Recordings:* Tony Overwater OP, Faces of China, Upclose, Motion Music, Treya Quartet Plays, Gabriel Fauré, Yuri Honing Trio: Sequel, Star Tracks; Tony Overwater Group Calefax: Ellington Suites; Yuri Honing Wired Paradise: Temptation. *Honours:* podium prize Most Promising Musician of the Year 1989, Boy Edgar Prize 2003, Edison Award. *E-mail:* sophie@jazzinmotion.com. *Website:* www.jazzinmotion.com. *Address:* kol Verveerstraat 19, 1411 VB, Naarden, The Netherlands (home). *E-mail:* info@tonyoverwater.com (home). *Website:* www.tonyoverwater.com.

OWEN, Huw Dylan; British musician and singer; b. 20 May 1971, Nantwich, Cheshire. *Education:* Polytechnic of Wales, Univ. of Glamorgan, All Wales Occupational Therapy Programme. *Career:* lead singer with Y Celtiaid Anhysbus 1987–89; singer and mandolin player with folk rock group Gwerinos 1988–95; regular appearances on Welsh TV and radio 1988–; lead singer and guitarist with folk punk group Defaid, 1989–92. *Compositions include:* composed 7 songs on the album Tocio Mogia, Defaid 1992, Dolgellau 1992, Hydref 1992, 100,000,000 1992, Llanfair Bryn Meurig 1992, Gobaith 1992, Fy Allwedd I Afallon 1994. *Recordings include:* Tocio Mogia, Defaid 1992, Di-Didlan, Gwerinos 1994, Lleuad Llawn 1999. *Publications include:* Editor of Welsh language magazine Sothach! 1991–94.

OWEN, Jake; American country music singer, songwriter and musician (guitar); b. (Joshua Ryan Owen), 28 Aug. 1981, Vero Beach, Fla; m. Lacey Buchanan 2012; one d. *Education:* Vero Beach High School, Florida State Univ. *Career:* songwriting collaborator with Chuck Jones and Jimmy Ritchey 2005; signed to RCA Records Nashville 2005; released debut single Yee Haw 2006; opening act on tour for numerous acts including Jason Aldean, Brooks & Dunn, Kenny Chesney, Alan Jackson, Little Big Town, Brad Paisley, Sugarland, Keith Urban. *Recordings:* albums: Startin' With Me 2006, Easy Does It 2009, Barefoot Blue Jean Night 2011, Days of Gold 2013. *Honours:* Acad. of Country Music Award for Top New Male Vocalist 2009, American Country Award for Breakthrough Artist of the Year 2012. *Current Management:* c/o Morris Artists Management LLC, 818 19th Avenue South, Nashville, TN 37203, USA. *Telephone:* (615) 327-3400. *E-mail:* info@morrisartistsmanagement.com. *Website:* www.morrisartistsmanagement.com. *Address:* c/o RCA Records Nashville, Sony Music Nashville, 1400 18th Avenue South, Nashville, TN 37212, USA (office). *Telephone:* (615) 301-4300 (office). *Fax:* (615) 301-4392 (office). *Website:* www.jakeowen.net.

OWEN, Mark; British singer and composer; b. 27 Jan. 1972; m. Emma Ferguson 2009; one s. one d. *Career:* mem. all-male vocal group, Take That 1990–96, 2006–; solo artist 1996–; numerous TV appearances; owner Sedna Records 2004–; mem. PRS, Equity, MCPS. *Television:* winner Celebrity Big Brother (Channel 4) 2002. *Recordings include:* albums: with Take That: Take That and Party 1992, Everything Changes 1993, Nobody Else 1995, Beautiful World 2006, The Circus 2008, Progress 2010, III 2014; solo: Green Man 1996, In Your Own Time 2004, How the Mighty Fall 2005, The Art of Doing Nothing 2013. *Honours:* Nordoff Robbins Silver Clef Award for Best Band 1995, 2009, Golden Camera Award (Berlin), Golden Otto Award for best band, MTV Award for Best Group in Europe, seven Smash Hits Awards, BRIT Award for Best British Single 1994, (for Patience) 2007, (for Shine) 2008, for Best British Live Act 2008, Q Idol Award (with Take That) 2006. *Current Management:* c/o Jonathan Wild, 10 Management, 36 Phillimore Walk, London, W8 7SA, England. *Telephone:* (20) 8747-4534. *E-mail:* jonathan@10management.com. *Address:* c/o Polydor Records, 364–366 Kensington High Street, London, W14

8NS, England (office). *Website:* www.markowenofficial.com; www.takethat.com.

OWEN, Randy Yeuell; American musician (rhythm guitar) and singer; b. 13 Dec. 1949, Fort Payne, AL; m.; three c. *Education:* Jacksonville State Univ. *Career:* founder mem. of country music group, Young Country 1969, renamed Wild Country 1972, renamed Alabama 1977–. *Recordings include:* albums: My Home's In Alabama 1980, Feels So Right 1981, Mountain Music 1982, The Closer You Get 1983, Roll On 1984, 40 Hour Week 1985, Alabama Christmas 1985, The Touch 1986, Just Us 1987, Live 1988, Southern Star 1989, Pass It On Down 1990, American Pride 1992, Gonna Have A Party… Live 1993, Cheap Seats 1993, In Pictures 1995, Dancin' on the Boulevard 1997, For the Record 1998, 20th Century 1999, When It All Goes South 2001, In the Mood: The Love Songs 2003, The American Farewell Tour 2003, Livin', Lovin', Rockin', Rollin' 2006, Songs of Inspiration 2006, Songs of Inspiration, Vol. 2 2007; solo: One on One 2008. *Publications:* Born Country (auto-biog.) 2008. *Honours:* numerous Country Music Assen Awards 1981–84, Acad. of Country Music Award for Artist of the Decade 1989, American Music Award of Merit 2003, Grammy Award (for Mountain Music) 1983, (for The Closer You Get) 1984, BMI President's Award 2000, numerous Billboard Awards. *E-mail:* info@brokenbowrecords.com (office). *Website:* www.thealabamaband.com; www.randyowen.com.

OWENS, Virginia (Ginny) Lee, BMusEd; American singer and musician (piano); b. 22 April 1975, Jackson, MS. *Education:* Belmont Univ. *Career:* numerous live performances, TV and radio broadcasts. *Recordings include:* Without Condition 1999, Something More 2002, Blueprint 2002, Beautiful 2004, Long Way Home 2005, Bring Us Peace 2008. *Honours:* winner Lilith Fair Talent Search, Nashville 1999, Dove Award for New Artist of the Year 2000, for Best Enhanced CD (for Without Condition) 2000, for Inspirational Recorded Song of the Year (for Blessed) 2001. *Website:* www.ginnyowens.com.

OWENS, James (Jimmy) Robert, Jr, MEd; American jazz musician (trumpet), composer and arranger; b. 9 Dec. 1943, New York; m. Lola Mae Brown 1965. *Education:* University of Massachusetts. *Career:* musician with Lionel Hampton 1963–64, Slide Hampton 1963, Hank Crawford 1964–65, Charlie Mingus 1964–65, Thad Jones/Mel Lewis Jazz Orchestra 1965–66, Duke Ellington 1968, Count Basie 1968, Billy Taylor Quintet, David Frost 1969–72; world-wide appearances as Jimmy Owens Plus; panelist, New York State Council of Arts 1978–81; Director, Jazzmobile Inc, jazz workshops 1974–90, Blackarts, National Diaspora (board member) 1986–; faculty member, SUNY 1981–86; panelist, National Endowment for Arts 1972–76; 1990–; panelist, Ohio Arts Council 1981–82; Fellow, National Endowment Arts 1980–; mem, AFofM, BMI, National Jazz Service Organization, Jazz Foundation of America. *Recordings include:* appearance on: Impressions of The Middle East, Herbie Mann 1967, Coming At You, Junior Wells 1968, Zawinul, Joe Zawinul 1971, Spectrum, Billy Cobham 1973, Cosmic Vortex, Weldon Irvine 1974, Sound of a Drum, Ralph MacDonald 1976, Inner Conflicts, Billy Cobham 1978, Anthology, Yusef Lateef 1994, Things to Come, Dizzy Gillespie 1996, New York, New Sound, Gerald Wilson 2003, In My Time, Gerald Wilson 2005, Monterey Moods, Gerald Wilson 2007, The Masters Return!, Gerald Wilson 2007; solo: Pure Be-Bop 1998, Autumn Jazz 1999, The Best of Duke Ellington 1999; other collaborations include: Herbie Mann, George Benson, Eddie Harris. *Honours:* Drumbeat Award, Talent deserving wider recognition 1967, Award for Excellence in Arts, Manhattan Borough 1986, Benny Golson Jazz Master Award, Howard Univ. 2008. *E-mail:* esemnyc@aol.com (office). *Website:* www.jimmyowensjazz.com.

OXAAL, Adrian; musician (guitar). *Career:* mem., James 1996–2001; numerous tours, festival dates and television appearances. *Recordings include:* albums: Whiplash 1997, The Best Of James 1998, Millionaires 1999, B-Sides Ultra 2001, Pleased To Meet You 2001, Getting Away With It 2002.

OXFORD, Tim; Canadian drummer. *Career:* Founder mem. Charlemagne, formed in Hamilton, Ont. 2006, renamed Arkells 2008–; signed to Dine Alone Records 2006; released debut EP Deadlines 2007; opening act for Matt Mayes & El Torpedo on Canadian tour 2008; toured with Waking Eyes on Canadian tour 2009; toured USA with The Maine and Lydia 2012; toured Europe with Billy Talent and Anti-Flag 2012; support act for Tragically Hip on Canadian tour 2013. *Recordings include:* albums: with Arkells: Jackson Square 2008, Michigan Left 2011, High Noon (Juno Award for Rock Album of the Year 2015) 2014. *Honours:* 102.1 The Edge CASBY Award 2009, Juno Awards for New Group of the Year 2010, for Group of the Year 2012, 2015. *Current Management:* c/o Tom Sarig, Kari Dexter and Christine Carson, ECG Management; Adam Countryman and Jack Ross, The Agency Group Ltd, 2 Berkeley Street, Suite 202, Toronto, ON M5A 4J5, Canada. *E-mail:* tom@ecgnyc.com; kari@ecgnyc.com; christine@ecgnyc.com. *Website:* www.theagencygroup.com; www.arkells.ca.

ØYE, Erlend; Norwegian singer, songwriter, musician (guitar) and DJ; b. Bergen. *Career:* founder mem. (with Erik Glambek Bøe) Kings of Convenience 2000–; solo artist 2003–, and solo project The Whitest Boy Alive; collaborations with Röyksopp, Jolly Music, Schneider TM, Morgan Geist. *Recordings include:* albums: with Kings of Convenience: The Kings of Convenience 2000, Quiet Is The New Loud 2001, Versus 2001, Riot On An Empty Street 2004, Declaration of Dependence 2009; solo: Unrest 2003. *E-mail:* management@kingsofconvenience.com. *E-mail:* erlend@kingsofconvenience.com (office). *Website:* www.kingsofconvenience.com; www.erlendoye.com.

P

PAAKKUNAINEN, Seppo Toivo Juhani 'Baron', (Baron von Klumpenfrau); Finnish jazz and folk composer, arranger and musician (flute, saxophone); b. 24 Oct. 1943, Tuusula; m. Ritva Marjatta Ikävalko; one s. one d. *Education:* Sibelius Acad., Helsinki, Berklee Coll. of Music, USA. *Career:* mem. of jazz groups including Soulset, Tuohi Quartet, George Gruntz Concert Jazz Band, Braxtonia (with Anthony Braxton), Saxperiment, Trio Nueva Finlandia; Karelia tours in USA and Europe; worldwide tours, including Norway Winter Olympics, Lillehammer 1993–94 with artists Nils-Aslak Valkeapää, Juhan Anders Bær and Esa Kotilainen; played with most top Finnish jazz musicians, including Jan Garbarek, Jon Christensen, Palle Danielsson, Terje Rypdal, Heikki Sarmanto, Charlie Mariano, Mal Waldron, Palle Mikkelborg and all top jazz artists of GG-CJB 1980–84; first Finnish jazz musician to play at Carnegie Hall, New York; mem. TEOSTO (Finnish Composers' Copyright Soc.), Suomen Säveltäjät, ELVIS, Musicians' Union, Jazzmuusikot ry, Suomen Saksofoniseura, Kalevalaseura, Tonkonstnärsmedlem Sällskapet MM. *Compositions include:* more than 1,000 compositions/arrangements registered in TEOSTO, including Nunnu 1971, Whale Conphony 1974, Nahant Suite 1976–77, Sami Luondu, Gollerisku 1980–81, 1989 (yoik symphony), Kalevala Drama 1984–85, Immanuel 1989–2003, Kaikkeuden ytimessä (Christian opera) 1993–94, Dalvi Duoddar Luohti 1994, Amazon 1994, Christmas Oratorium 2006, Fin – Got Suite 2008, Sami Eatnan Jahkiaigii (Sameland's seasons) 2009–11; numerous works for orchestra, choir, theatre, radio feature, various ensembles and big bands. *Recordings include:* albums include: Plastic Maailma 1971; with Edward Vesala: Nan Madol 1974, Unisono 1975, No Comments 1975, Kissapa Uu 1977, Baron Disco-Go 1978, Kanteletar 1980, Sami Luondu Gollerisku, with Nils-Aslak Valkeapää 1980; with Karelia: Nunnu 1971, Tuohihuilu 1981, Hyvää Joulua 1981, Maanitus 1983; with George Gruntz: Theatre 1983, Karelia 1986, Best of Karelia 1990, Sápmi Lottázan with Nils-Aslak Valkeapää and Ingor Ante Ailu Gaup 1992; with George Gruntz: George Gruntz Concert Jazz Band 1981, Theatre 1984, Dálveleaikkat Wintergames with Nils-Aslak Valkeapää 1994, Saxperiment 1997, Two Compositions (Järvenpää), with Anthony Braxton and Ensemble Braxtonia 1996, Ha! – What's Going On?, with Trio Nueva Finlandia 1998, Baritone, Paroni Paakkunainen 2002, Silmäni ovat nähneet, Chorus Cantorum Finlandie (including Baron's male choir suite Minun silmäni ovat nähneet Jumalan) 2005, Vuoi, Biret – Maret, vuoi! with Nils-Aslak Valkeapää 1974, 2009, Alit idja lahkona (Blue Night Moving Closer) with Nils-Aslak Valkeapää 1992, 2009, RAUK, Gunnel Mauritzson voc and UMO Jazz Orchestra 2011. *Honours:* Gold Medal, Student Youth Festival 1968, Best Ensemble, Montreux Jazz Competition (with Tuohi Quartet) 1971, Yrjö Award, Finnish Jazz Fed. 1973, Jazz Composer of Year, Helsinki Festival 1981, Arrangers Prize, Nordring Competition 1982, Prix Future, West Berlin Festival 1989, GullinPriset, Lars Gullin sällskapet 2001. *Address:* Papintie 2 B 3, 59730 Uukuniemi, Finland (home). *E-mail:* paroni.paakkunainen@gmail.com (office).

PACKHAM, Blair James Marc, BA; Canadian singer, songwriter, composer and musician (guitar); *President, Blare! Music Inc.*; b. 23 April 1959, North Bay, Ont.; s. of James McLeod Packham and Madeleine Matte; m. Arlene Marie Bishop 1998 (separated 2007); one s. *Education:* Univ. of Toronto. *Career:* rock 'n' roll group leader, The Jitters 1980s; engineer, live recordings of Bryan Adams, Stevie Ray Vaughan; film and TV music composer; Program Dir Humber Coll. Summer Songwriting Workshop 2005–08, SongStudio Summer Songwriting Workshop 2009–; Vice-Pres. Songwriters Assen of Canada 2000–05; mem. American Fed. of Musicians, Guild of Canadian Film Composers, Soc. of Canadian Composers Authors and Publishers. *Compositions:* TV themes: Spliced!, Isla des Mutantes, Beyblade, Pecola, Destiny Ridge, NHL Tonight, World Cup Soccer '94, The Jane Show; film scores: Hollywood North, Move Your World, Triggermen, Fall: The Price of Silence. *Plays:* Joan of Montreal, Toronto Fringe Festival 1998. *Radio:* presenter, In the Studio (Newstalk 1010 Toronto). *Television:* Joan of Montreal 2000. *Recordings include:* with The Jitters: The Jitters 1987, Louder Than Words 1990; solo albums: Everything That's Good 2000, Could've Been King 2004; as producer: Andy Kim (with Ron Sexsmith), Arlene Bishop, Stacey Kaniuk, Bob Reid. *Honours:* Toronto Music Award 1990. *Address:* Blare! Music Inc., 260 Adelaide Street East, Suite 131, Toronto, ON M5A 1N1, Canada (office). *E-mail:* blair@blairpackham.com (office). *Website:* www.blairpackham.com.

PACZYNSKI, Georges; French musician (drums); b. 30 March 1943, Grenoble; m. Sophie Tret 1995; one d. *Career:* represented France, Festival of Montreux, Festival of Zurich 1968; broadcasts, France Culture, with Black and Blue, Radio France 1981, 1998–; founded trio with Jean-Christophe Levinson and Jean-François Jenny-Clark 1984; Une Histoire De La Batterie De Jazz, broadcast, France Culture 1993; Prof., Conservatoire National de Cergy-Pontoise; founded trio with Philippe Macé and Ricardo del Fra 1996; founded trio with Edouard Ferlet and Yves Torchinsky; Concert historique à l'Ambassade de Pologne en France 2002. *Compositions:* more than 22 pieces for percussion and piano, Paris, Zurfluh 1985–2003. *Recordings:* Eight Years Old 1992, Levin's Song 1994, Générations 2006. *Publications:* Thesis: Baudelaire Et La Musique 1973, La Genèse Du Rythme Et L'Anthropologie Gestuelle 1984, Book: Rythme Et Geste, Les Racines Du Rythme Musical 1988, Une Histoire de La Batterie, Vol. 1 1997, Une Histoire de La Batterie de Jazz, Vol. 2 2000, Vol. 3 2004, Dictionnaire du Jazz (co-author) 2000, The Art

of Melodic Drumming (L'Art de Travailler un Thème de Jazz à la Batterie) 2002, L'Art de Travailler les Accords de Jazz au Piano 2003, Six Blues pour Piano et Percussion 2004. *Honours:* Medal of the Society of Encouragement For Progress 1989, Charge de Cours sur le jazz et le rythme au Conservatoire National Superieur de Lyon. *Address:* Georges Paczynski, 89 rue Nationale, 95000 Cergy-Village, France. *Telephone:* (1) 30-32-13-52. *Fax:* (1) 30-32-13-52.

PADEN, Jurica; Croatian composer, musician (guitar) and singer; b. 3 Feb. 1955, Zagreb. *Education:* univ. *Career:* mem. of groups including Aerodrom, Paden Band; numerous concerts in Croatia, television appearances, tour of former CCCP, concerts in Netherlands, Germany; mem. HGY (Croatian Music Union), DHS (Composers' Union of Croatia). *Recordings include:* some 30 albums. *Honours:* first prize Arena-Fest, Pula. *Address:* Vidriceva 31, 91000 Zagreb, Croatia.

PADEN, Thomas (Tom) C., BS; American songwriter, publisher and musician (piano); *Owner, Paden Place Music;* b. 13 Oct. 1956, Chattanooga, Tenn.; s. of Carter Paden and Janet Paden; m. Grace Michele Paden 1993. *Education:* Univ. of Tennessee. *Career:* staff writer, Starstruck Writer's Group, Reba McEntire's publishing co.; Owner Paden Place Music; mem. Nat. Acad. of Recording Arts and Sciences, Inc., Country Music Assen, Nashville Songwriters Assen Int. *Compositions:* numerous songs include Same Time Each Year, nat. theme song for Ducko Unlimited. *Recordings:* songs recorded by numerous artists, including Aaron Neville, Tammy Wynette, Restless Heart, Kenny Rogers, Lee Greenwood. *Address:* 437 Essex Park Circle, Franklin, TN 37069, USA (office). *Telephone:* (615) 794-6757 (office). *E-mail:* thomaspaden@comcast.net (office). *Website:* www.padenplacemusic.

PADGHAM, Hugh Charles; British, record producer and engineer; b. 15 Feb. 1955, London; partner Cath Kidston; one d. *Education:* St Edward's School, Oxford. *Career:* mem. Re-Pro, Aura. *Recordings include:* as producer, engineer, mixer include: with Split Enz: Conflicting Emotions, Time and Tide; with The Police: Synchronicity, Ghost In The Machine; with Phil Collins: Face Value, Hello I Must Be Going, No Jacket Required, But Seriously; with Genesis: Genesis, Invisible Touch; with Sting: Ten Summoner's Tales, The Soul Cages, Fields of Gold–The Best of Sting; with Julia Fordham: Porcelain, Swept; with Melissa Etheridge: Yes I Am, Your Little Secret, No One Is To Blame, Howard Jones, Hysteria, Human League, English Settlement, XTC, Between Two Fires, Paul Young: Press To Play, Paul McCartney, Tonight, David Bowie, Two Rooms, Elton John and Bernie Taupin, Walkaway Joe (single), Trisha Yearwood, Clannad 1996, Beth Hart Band 1996, Bee Gees: Still Waters 1997, Phil Collins: Hits 1998, Julia Fordham: Collection 1999, Mansun, Little Kix 2000; engineering/mixing credits include: tracks from World Outside, Psychedelic Furs, Where's The Light, Toni Childs, Just Like Us, Robbie Nevil, Nothing Like The Sun, Sting, Love and Affection, Joan Armatrading, Days of Open Hand, Suzanne Vega, Shakin' The Tree, Youssou N'Dour, The Scattering, Cutting Crew, My Nation Underground, Julian Cope, In The Air Tonight (88 Remix), Phil Collins, Abacab, Genesis, The Third, Peter Gabriel, Black Sea, Drums and Wires, XTC; with Hall and Oates: Starting All Over Again, H2O, Dead Man on Campus, Happy Texas, Yes. *Honours:* four Grammy Awards, BRIT Awards, Music Week Award, TEC Award For Outstanding Creative Achievement. *E-mail:* hughpadgham@mac.com. *Website:* www.hughpadgham.com.

PADILLA, José; Spanish producer, remixer and DJ; b. 1955. *Career:* began DJ career in Ibiza 1975; resident DJ at the island's Café Del Mar; compiled first Vol. of Café Del Mar CD series and several further editions; collaborations with A Man Called Adam, Phil Mison, Seal, N'Dea Davenport. *Recordings:* albums: Souvenir 1998, Navigator 2001, Cafe Solo 2006, Bella Musica 2 2007.

PADOVANI, Jean-Marc; French musician (saxophone) and composer; b. 2 Feb. 1956, Villeneuve les Avignon; m. Françoise Piotelat 1987; two s. *Education:* High School of Music, Avignon and Marseille. *Career:* played with Miles Davis; performs with his quartet, Tres Horas de Sol, Mingus, Cuernavaca, Quartet with Paul Motian, Sketches septet and others. *Recordings include:* Tres Horas de Sol 1986, One For Pablo 1989, Nîmeño 1990, Sud 1992, Mingus, Cuernavaca 1992, Nocturne 1994, Takiya! Tokaya! 1997, Jazz Angkor 1998, Minotaure Jazz Orchestra 2000. *Current Management:* c/o Soleart Productions, 3 rue des Quatre Cheminées, 92514 Boulogne Cedex, France. *Telephone:* 1-47-61-56-82. *E-mail:* soleart@wanadoo.fr. *Address:* 6 rue Pédro Gailhard, 31100 Toulouse, France (home). *Telephone:* 5-62-87-97-39 (home). *E-mail:* jean.marc.padovani@orange.fr (home). *Website:* www.jeanmarcpadovani.fr.

PAEFFGEN, Gilbert; German musician (drums, hammered dulcimer) and composer; b. 21 Jan. 1958, Würzburg; m. Bettina Paeffgen Hehl, 16 Feb. 1990, 1 s., 1 d. *Career:* Member, Aventure Dupont, 1983–93, over 500 performances; Expo Sevilla, Pabellón de la Suiza; Member, The Treya Quartet, 1997–2003; leads own trio; numerous TV appearances. *Recordings:* Offshore (with Joe McHugh) 1996, Dices (with Del Ferro, Paeffgen, Overwater) 1997, The Treya Quartet Plays Gabriel Fauré 1998; Pedestrian Tales 2001, Sketches from Europe 2004, Joran 2005, The Story of Major Tom (with Hasler, Paeffgen, Audetat). *Honours:* Mentor, Swiss New Jazz Festival, 1997. *E-mail:* makedam@bluewin.ch (home). *Website:* www.gilbertpaeffgen.com.

PÁEZ ÁVALOS, Rodolfo (Fito); Argentine musician (piano), singer, songwriter, film director and scriptwriter; b. 13 March 1963, Rosario; one adopted s. *Career:* fmr mem. El Banquete; solo artist 1978–; owns recording studio, Circo Beat Studio. *Films:* as writer, director and producer: La Balada de Donna Helena 1994, Vidas Privadas 2001, ¿De Quién es el Portaligas? 2007. *Recordings include:* albums: Del '63 1984, Giros 1985, Corazón Clandestino 1986, Ciudad de Pobres Corazones 1987, Ey! 1988, Tercer Mundo 1990, El Amor Después del Amor 1992, Circo Beat 1994, Euforia 1996, Enemigos Íntimos (with Joaquín Sabina) 1998, Abre 1999, Rey Sol 2000, Naturaleza Sangre 2003, Moda y Pueblo 2005, El Mundo Cabe en una Canción (Latin Grammy Award for Best Rock Solo Vocal Album 2007) 2006, Rodolfo (Latin Grammy Award for Best Singer-Songwriter Album 2008) 2007, No se si es Baires o Madrid (Latin Grammy Award for Best Male Pop Vocal Album 2009) 2008. *Honours:* two Latin Grammy Awards 2000. *Telephone:* (11) 4776-6111 (Argentina) (office). *E-mail:* norakoblinc@circobeat.com.ar (office). *Website:* www.mpaez.com.ar.

PAGE, James (Jimmy) Patrick, OBE; British musician (guitar) and songwriter; b. 9 Jan. 1944, Heston, Middlesex, England; m. Jimena Page; one d. from previous relationship. *Career:* mem., Neil Christian and the Crusaders 1959, The Yardbirds 1966–68; numerous concerts and tours; founder mem., The New Yardbirds 1968, renamed Led Zeppelin 1968–80, re-formed for one-off performance 2007; tours and concerts; formed band's own record label, Swan Song 1974; mem., Honeydrippers (with Robert Plant, Nile Rodgers, Jeff Beck) 1984–85, Coverdale/Page (with David Coverdale) 1993, Page/Plant (with Robert Plant) 1994–. *Recordings include:* albums: with the Yardbirds: Over Under Sideways Down 1966, Little Games 1967; with Led Zeppelin: Led Zeppelin 1969, Led Zeppelin II 1969, Led Zeppelin III 1970, Led Zeppelin IV 1971, Houses Of The Holy 1973, Physical Graffiti 1975, Presence 1976, The Song Remains The Same (live) 1976, In Through The Out Door 1979, How The West Was Won 2003, Mothership 2007, Celebration Day (Grammy Award for Best Rock Album 2014) 2012; solo: Death Wish II (OST) 1982, Outrider 1988, Coverdale/Page (with David Coverdale) 1993, Live At The Greek 2000, Rock And Roll Highway 2000; with The Honeydrippers: The Honeydrippers Vol. 1 1984; with Page & Plant: No Quarter 1994, Walking Into Clarksdale 1998, Masters 1998, Before the Balloon Went Up 1998, More Oar 1999. *Honours:* Ivor Novello Award for Outstanding Contribution to British Music 1977, Q magazine Merit Award 1992, Grammy lifetime achievement award 2005, Q Icon Award 2005, Royal Swedish Acad. of Music Polar Music Prize 2006, Kennedy Center Honor 2012. *Current Management:* International Talent Booking, First Floor, Ariel House, 74a Charlotte Street, London, W1T 4QJ, England. *Telephone:* (20) 7637-6979. *Fax:* (20) 7637-6978. *E-mail:* mail@itb.co.uk. *Website:* www.ledzeppelin.com.

PAGNY, Florent Maurice; French singer and actor; b. 6 Nov. 1961, Chalon-sur-Saône; one s. *Education:* Conservatoire de Levallois-Perret, Paris. *Films:* La Balance 1982, L'As des as 1982, Effraction 1983, Les Fauves 1984, Fort Saganne 1984, Blessure 1985, La Femme de ma vie 1986, Les Keufs 1987, Francois Villon, Poetul vagabond 1987, La Fille des collines 1990, Tom est tout seul 1995, Quand je vois le soleil 2003, Les Visages d'Alice 2005. *Television:* La Mariage blues 1985, La Chaine 1988, Jo et Milou 1992, Milady 2005. *Recordings include:* Merci 1990, Réaliste 1992, Rester vrai 1994, Savoir aimer 1997, Ré-création 1999, Châtelet les Halles 2000, 2 2001, Ailleurs Land 2003, Live Olympia 2003, Baryton 2004, Abracadabra 2006, Pagny Chant Brel 2007. *Honours:* Victoires de la Musique Award for Best Male Artist of the Year 1998. *Address:* c/o Universal Music France, 20 rue des Fossés-Saint-Jacques, 75235 Paris, Cédex 05, France (office). *Website:* www.universalmusic.fr (office); www.florentpagny.org.

PAHLAVAN, Ali, BSc; Iranian singer, songwriter and musician (guitar); b. 1975, Tehran; m. *Education:* Azad Univ., Tehran (industrial engineering). *Career:* founder mem., The Arian Band (the first officially sanctioned mixed-gender pop band in Iran); Planning and Project Control Man., Iranian oil and gas projects (engineering office www.eied.com). *Recordings:* albums: Sunflower, And But Love!, Till Eternity, Without You With You 2008. *Current Management:* c/o Mr Mohsen Rajabpour, Taraneh Sharghee Cultural & Artistic Co., Apt No. 26, Seventh Floor, Suite 22, Second Alley, Shahnazri Street, Mohseni Square, Mirdamad Avenue, Tehran 1547914415, Iran. *Telephone:* (21) 22223513 (office). *Fax:* (21) 22223670 (office). *E-mail:* president@taranehsh.com (office). *Website:* www.taranehsh.com (office). *E-mail:* ali@arianmusic.com (home). *Website:* www.arianmusic.com.

PAICE, Ian Anderson; British musician (drums) and writer; b. 29 June 1948, Nottingham, England; m. Jacky 1976; one s. one d. *Education:* technical coll. *Career:* founder mem., Deep Purple 1968–76, 1984–; numerous live appearances, tours worldwide; founder mem., Paice Ashton Lord 1976–77. *Recordings include:* albums: with Deep Purple: Shades Of Deep Purple 1968, The Book Of Taliesyn 1969, Deep Purple 1969, Concerto For Group And Orchestra 1969, Deep Purple In Rock 1970, Fireball 1971, Machine Head 1972, Who Do We Think We Are? 1973, Burn 1974, Stormbringer 1974, Come Taste The Band 1975, Deep Purple 1977, Power House 1977, Perfect Strangers 1985, Fireworks 1985, The House Of Blue Light 1987, Slaves And Masters 1990, The Battle Rages On 1992, Perpendicular 1996, Abandon 1998, Butterfly Ball Wizards Convention 1998, Child In Time 1998, Under The Gun 2001, Bananas 2003, Deep Purple And Friends 2003, Total Abandon 2004, Rapture Of The Deep 2005, numerous live albums; with Paice Ashton Lord: Malice In Wonderland 1977; with Paul McCartney: Run Devil Run 1999. *Current Management:* The Agency Group Ltd, 361–373 City Road, London,

EC1V 1PQ, England. *Telephone:* (20) 7278-3331. *Fax:* (20) 7837-4672. *E-mail:* agencylondon@theagencygroup.com. *E-mail:* info@deep-purple.com. *Website:* www.deep-purple.com.

PAICH, David; American singer and musician (keyboards); b. 25 June 1954, Los Angeles, CA. *Career:* mem., Rural Still Life, Toto 1978–. *Recordings include:* albums: Toto 1979, Hydra 1979, Turn Back 1981, Toto IV 1982, Isolation 1984, Dune (film soundtrack) 1985, Fahrenheit 1986, The Seventh One 1988, Past to Present 1977–90 1990, Kingdom of Desire 1992, Tambu 1995, Sax for Lovers 1996, Toto XX, 1977–97 1998, Mindfields 1999, Through the Looking Glass 2002, Falling in Between 2006, Toto XIV 2015. *Honours:* Grammy Award for Best Record, Best Album, Best Vocal Arrangement, Best Instrumental Arrangement, Best Engineered Recording, Best Producer (with Toto) 1983. *Current Management:* c/o Steve Karas and Keith Hagan, SKH Music. *E-mail:* skaras@skhmusic.com; khagan@skhmusic.com. *Website:* www.skhmusic.com; www.totoofficial.com.

PAIGE, Elaine, OBE; British singer and actress; b. (Elaine Bickerstaff), 5 March 1948, Barnet, England; d. of Eric Bickerstaff and Irene Bickerstaff. *Education:* Aida Foster Stage school. *Theatre:* West End, London appearances in Hair 1968, Jesus Christ Superstar 1973, Grease (played Sandy) 1973, Billy (played Rita) 1974, Evita (created role of Eva Perón) (Soc. of West End Theatre Award for Best Actress in a Musical 1978) 1978, Cats (created role of Grizabella) 1981, Abbacadabra (played Carabosse) 1983, Chess (played Florence) 1986, Anything Goes (played Reno Sweeney) 1989, Piaf 1993–94, Sunset Boulevard (played Norma Desmond) 1995–96, The Misanthrope (played Célimène) 1998, The King and I (played Anna) 2000, The Drowsy Chaperone (Novello Theatre, London) 2007. *Recordings include:* albums: Sitting Pretty 1978, Elaine Paige 1981, Stages 1983, Cinema 1984, Love Hurts 1985, Christmas 1986, Memories: The Best Of Elaine Paige 1987, The Queen Album 1988, Elaine Paige: The Collection 1990, Love Can Do That 1991, An Evening With Elaine Paige 1991, Elaine Paige And Barbara Dickson 'Together' 1992, Romance And The Stage 1993, Piaf 1994, Encore 1995, Performance 1996, From A Distance 1997, On Reflection 1998, Centre Stage: The Best of Elaine Paige 2004, Essential Musicals 2006, Elaine Paige and Friends 2010; contributions to soundtrack recordings, including Nine, Anything Goes, Chess, Cats, Evita, Billy, The King And I; appears on: Tim Rice Collection: Stage and Screen Classics 1996, Christmas with the Stars Vol. 2 1999. *Honours:* Variety Club Award for Showbusiness Personality of the Year and Recording Artist of the Year 1986, BASCA Award 1993, Lifetime Achievement Award, Nat. Operatic and Dramatic Asscn 1999. *Current Management:* c/o Nick Fiveash, The Works PR, 11 Marshalsea Road, London, SE1 1EN, England. *Telephone:* (20) 7940-4686. *E-mail:* nick@theworkspr.com. *Website:* www.theworkspr.com; www.elainepaige.com.

PAINE, Brace, (DJ Nightschool, The Chain); American musician (guitarist); b. (Nathan Howdeshell), Ark. *Career:* fmr mem. bands including Die Monitr Batss, A.S.T., Deep Jail, Xeaxx Xeaxx; lead guitarist with band Gossip 1999–. *Recordings:* albums: That's Not What I Heard 2001, Movement 2003, Undead in NYC 2003, Standing in the Way of Control 2006, Music for Men 2009. *Address:* Music With A Twist, POB 1998, Radio City Station, New York, NY 10101, USA (office). *E-mail:* info@musicwithatwist.com (office). *Website:* www.musicwithatwist.com (office); www.gossipyouth.com (office).

PAINTAL, Priti, BSc, MSc, MMus, PGCE; British composer; *Artistic Director, ShivaNova/Equator;* b. Delhi, India; partner Robert Maycock (deceased); one s. one d. *Education:* studied piano and composition in India and moved on to Univ. of York, Royal Northern Coll. of Music, Manchester and Inst. of Educ., London. *Career:* joined a family that included musicians trained in both Indian and Western traditions alongside eminent scientists and doctors; established herself writing for leading British performers; now based in UK and well known as a composer, performer, music producer and promoter; f. ensemble ShivaNova, brings together traditional, classical and jazz performers; has written group pieces and a mini-opera, Survival Song, for the Royal Opera's Garden Venture contemporary opera programme, led to full-length Biko, Royal Opera's first commission from an Asian and a woman composer, staged in London and Birmingham; other performers have included the Philharmonia Orchestra in premiere of Secret Chants, City of London Sinfonia, Bournemouth Sinfonietta, East of England Orchestra, Balanescu and Bingham string quartets, Park Lane Sextet, and numerous singers and instrumentalists; contrib. to radio and TV; has written for The Guardian; featured in The Independent and The Daily Telegraph, on Songlines, and BBC Radio 3 and on Womans' Hour (BBC Radio 4); mem. Bd Kent Music; fmr mem. Arts Council Music panel, Bd of South-East Arts, Bd of Overtones; Artistic Dir Women of the World, Equator World music and dance (promotions of ShivaNova). *Works include:* Survival Song 1988, Biko 1992, Gulliver 1995, Polygamy, Improvisations and other chamber works. *Recordings include:* Polygamy, Urban Mantras, Flying to the Sun, Moonlighting, Seventh Heaven, Secret Chants 2009. *Address:* Peregrine, Grange Road, St Michaels, Tenterden, Kent, TN30 6TJ, England (office). *E-mail:* PPaintal@aol.com (office); shivanova@aol.com (office); admin@shivanova.co.uk (office). *Website:* www.shivanova.com (office); www.myspace.com/shivanovacom; www.equatorfestival.com.

PAISLEY, Brad; American country singer, songwriter and musician (guitar); b. 28 Oct. 1972, Glen Dale, W Va; m. Kimberly Williams; two s. *Education:* Belmont Univ., Tenn. *Recordings include:* albums: Who Needs Pictures 1999, Part II 2001, Mud on the Tires 2003, Time Well Wasted (Acad. of Country

Music Award for Album of the Year 2006, CMA Award for Album of the Year 2006) 2005, Brad Paisley Christmas 2006, 5th Gear 2007, Play 2008, American Saturday Night 2009, This Is Country Music 2011, Wheelhouse 2013. *Honours:* Acad. of Country Music Award for Vocal Event of the Year, for Best Video 2005, for Best Male Vocalist 2007, 2008, 2009, 2010, 2011, CMA Awards for Musical Event of the Year (for When I Get Where I'm Going) 2006, for Male Vocalist of the Year 2007, 2008, 2009, for Music Video of the Year (for Online) 2007, for Entertainer of the Year 2010, Grammy Awards for Best Country Instrumental Performance (for Throttleneck) 2008, (for Cluster Pluck) 2009, for Best Male Country Vocal Performance (for Letter to Me) 2009, American Country Award for Artist of the Year 2011, for Video Visionary Artist 2013. *Address:* c/o Arista Records, 1540 Broadway, New York, NY 10036, USA. *Website:* www.bradpaisley.com.

PÄIVINEN, Pertti (Pepa); Finnish musician (saxophones, flutes, clarinets); *Baritone Saxophonist, UMO Big Band;* b. 2 June 1955, Vantaa; m. Marit Päivinen 1978; two s. one d. *Education:* Vantaa Music Inst., Oulunkyla Pop-Jazz Conservatory. *Career:* toured in Europe with Jukka Tolonen Band 1979–80; freelance work, TV, theatre and teaching 1980–85; touring with Edward Vesala Sound and Fury 1985–, UMO Big Band 1985–; mem. saxophone quartet Saxperiment 1989–2007; tour with Anthony Braxton 1988; touring with own trio 1998–2003; mem. Pepa Päivinen Quartet 2004–, Pepa Päivinen Quintet 2008–13; performances with Lenny Pickett 2008, 2012, 2015; Pepa Päivinen and Good Romans 2012–, Duo Pepa Päivinen and Hannu Risku 2015–; mem. Finnish Saxophone Soc. *Recordings include:* with Jukka Tolonen: Just Those Boys 1980; with Edward Vesala: Death of Jazz 1990, Invisible Storm 1992, Nordic Gallery 1995; with UMO: UMO Plays the Music of Muhal Abrams 1986, Selected Standards 1993, Green and Yellow 1994; Umo Jazz Orchestra 1998, Electrifying Miles 1998, Sauna palaa 2005, Traveller (also with Mikko Hassinen) 2008, UMO on UMO 2009; with Anthony Braxton: two compositions 1988; with Saxperiment: Saxperiment 1997; with Pepa Päivinen Trio: Saxigon 1998, Umpsukkelis 1999, Fun Faraway 2002; with Jro Haarla Duo: Yarra, Yarra 2001; with Jarmo Saari Filmtet: A Tribute to Finnish Cinema; Samuli Mikkonen & 7 henkeä 2003; with Pepa Päivinen Quartet: Tiram num 2005, North Pipe 2009, Otto Donner: And It Happened 2013, Sound and Fury: Pulsacion 2013, Pepa Päivinen and Good Romans: Ghost of a Dog 2014. *Honours:* Pekka Poyry Reward 1984, Award from Finnish Govt for artistic working 1998–2000, Georgie Award 2000, Finnish Culture Foundation Award 2001–03, Finnish Musicians Union Award 2003. *Address:* Rajakulmantie 108, 04170 Paippinen, Finland. *E-mail:* pepapaivinen@hotmail.com. *Website:* www.vapaataanet.fi/pepapaivinen; www.sound-and-fury.weebly.com.

PALLADINO, Pino; British musician (electric bass guitar); b. 17 Oct. 1957, Cardiff, Wales; m. Marilyn Roberts, 13 Oct. 1992, 1 s., 2 d. *Education:* 1 year classical guitar lessons, age 14. *Career:* Bass guitar for Paul Young, 1982–87; Recording sessions for artists including: Don Henley; Eric Clapton; Phil Collins; Elton John; Chaka Khan; Jeff Beck; Pete Townshend; Michael McDonald; John McLaughlin; Joan Armatrading. *Recordings:* No Parlez, Paul Young; Journeyman, Eric Clapton; But Seriously, Phil Collins; Building The Perfect Beast, Don Henley; Sowing The Seeds Of Love, Tears For Fears; Who Else, Jeff Beck; Pilgrim, Eric Clapton; Breakdown, Melissa Etheridge; Emotional Blends, Robbie McIntosh; Oltre, Claudio Baglioni; Naked Flame, Tony O'Malley; Human, Rod Stewart, 2000; Alone With Everybody, Richard Ashcroft, 2000; Reptile, Eric Clapton, 2001. *Publications:* Standing In The Shadows of Motown. *Address:* 250 W 57th St, Suite 1502, New York, NY 10019, USA. *E-mail:* info@pinopalladino.com. *Website:* www.pinopalladino.com.

PALLETT, Owen, BMus; Canadian singer, musician (violin), producer and arranger; b. (Michael James Owen Pallett-Plowright), 7 Sept. 1979, Toronto. *Education:* Univ. of Toronto. *Career:* fmr mem. bands Les Mouches, Picastro; prin. mem. band Final Fantasy; strings arranger for Funeral and Neon Bible by Arcade Fire, The Flying Club Cup by Beirut; collaborations with Jim Guthrie, The Hidden Cameras, The Vinyl Cafe; remixes for Stars, Bloc Party; composed music for computer game Traffic Department 2192. *Recordings:* albums: Has a Good Home 2005, He Poos Clouds 2006, Heartland 2010. *Honours:* Polaris Music Prize, Canada 2006. *E-mail:* patrick@ boyfriendmanagement.com (office); info@finalfantasyeternal.com (office). *Website:* www.owenpalletteternal.com.

PALMER, Carl; British musician (drums, percussion); b. 20 March 1950, Handsworth Wood, Birmingham; m. Maureen Fraser 1985; one d. *Education:* Royal Acad. with James Blades, Guildhall with Gilbert Webster. *Career:* Founder mem., Emerson Lake and Palmer 1970–81; Founder mem., Asia 1982–86; numerous world-wide concerts, television, radio broadcasts. *Recordings include:* albums: with Emerson Lake and Palmer: Emerson Lake and Palmer 1970, Tarkus 1971, Pictures At An Exhibition 1971, Trilogy 1972, Brain Salad Surgery 1973, Welcome My Friends 1974, Works 1974, Works Vol. II 1977, Love Beach 1978, In Concert 1979; with Asia: Asia 1982, Alpha 1983, Astra 1985; solo: Percussion Concerto 1995, One More Time – The Anthology 2001. *Publications include:* Applied Rhythms. *Honours:* Playboy Magazine Award 1977. *Current Management:* c/o Bruce Pilato, Pilato Entertainment, 482 Bay Meadows Drive, Webster, NY 14580, USA. *Website:* www.carlpalmer.com.

PALMER, Dave, (Yorkie); musician (bass), backing singer and songwriter. *Career:* mem., Space 1997–; numerous world-wide tours and television

appearances. *Recordings include:* albums: Tin Planet 1998, Greatest Hits 2001.

PALMER, Florrie; British songwriter, singer and musician (keyboards); b. 14 Nov. 1947, Broxted, Essex; one s. one d. *Career:* mem. PRS. *Compositions:* singles: I Get Lonely; Nine to Five, retitled Morning Train (USA), Sheena Easton; The Heat is On, Agnetha Faltskog; When He Shines, Sheena Easton 1980; various album tracks including Halfway There, The Last One to Leave, I Want to Marry You. *Recordings:* I Get Lonely, The Mellen Bird, as Susie Mellen 1973; Hi-fi Love. *Publications:* Never Final Till It's Vinyl 1994. *Honours:* Ivor Novello Award for Best Lyric of the Year (for When He Shines).

PALMER, Tim; British music producer and mixer; b. 4 Oct. 1962, North Shields; m. Veronica Palmer; four d. *Career:* Assistant Engineer, Utopia Studios early 1980s; Engineer, Producer in England and USA for Mark Knopfler, Dead or Alive, Texas, David Bowie, Robert Plant, Pearl Jam, Tears For Fears and numerous others; Director, Re-Pro (British Record Producers Guild). *Recordings:* Now and Zen, Shaken and Stirred, Robert Plant; Tin Machine, Tin Machine 2, David Bowie; Elemental, Tears For Fears; Southside, Texas; Carved In Sand, The Mission; Ten, Pearl Jam; Reel Big Fish, Why Do They Rock so Hard; Michael Hutchence; American Pie; Gene Loves Jezebel, Voodoo Dollies: The Best of Gene Loves Jezebel; Legal Reins, Please, the Pleasure; tracks on All That You Can't Leave Behind, U2 2000. *Website:* www.timpalmer.com.

PALMIERI, Edward (Eddie); American musician (piano, percussion) and composer; b. 15 Dec. 1936, Spanish Harlem, New York; m. 1955; one s. four d. *Career:* started playing timbales in Chino y Sus Almas Tropicales band aged 13; switched to piano 1951, and formed group with singer Joe Quijano; became pianist in Johnny Segui's band 1955; joined Tito Rodriguez's Mambo Orchestra 1958; formed La Perfecta 1961–68; collaborations 1966–73 include Tico All Stars, Fania All Stars, Harlem Drive, Cheo Feliciano, Brian Lynch; went to Puerto Rico 1980s; formed Eddie Palmieri Orchestra; returned to New York late 1980s; played in numerous festivals, including North Sea Jazz Festival, Montréal Jazz Festival, Nice Jazz Festival, New Orleans, JVC Festival (New York); mem. bd of govs (New York) Nat. Asscn of Recording Arts and Sciences. *Recordings include:* albums: La Perfecta, El Molestoso, Lo Que Traigo Es Sabroso, Enchando Pa'lante, Azucar Pa'Ti, Mambo Con Conga Es Mozambique, Palmiere and Tjader: El Sonido Nuevo, Molasses, Palmiere and Tjader: Bamboleate, Champagne, Justicia, Superimposition, Vamonos Pa'l Monte, Harlem River Drive, Live At Sing Sing (Vols 1 and 2), Sentido, Live At the University of Puerto Rico, The Sun of Latin Music, Unfinished Masterpiece, Lucumi Macumba Voodoo, Eddie Palmieri, Palo Pa'Rumba, Solito, La Verdad, Sueño, Llego La India Via Eddie Palmieri, Palmas, Arete, Vortex, Jazz Latino Vol. I, El Rumbero del Piano, Live, Verdad: The Truth, Eddie's Concerto, Music Man, Salsa-Jazz-Descarga: Exploration, Live 1999, The Best Of… 1999, Listen Here! (Grammy Award for Best Latin Jazz Album 2006) 2005, Simpático (with Brian Lynch) (Grammy Award for Best Latin Jazz Album 2007) 2006, Eddie Palmieri 2010, Salsa Brothers (with Charlie Palmieri) 2011. *Honours:* Grammy Awards for Best Latin Album 1975, 1976, Best Tropical Latin Performance 1984, 1985, 1987, Best Salsa Album (for Masterpiece, with Tito Puente) 2001. *Current Management:* Edward Palmieri II Music Management, 1908 Parker Street, Berkeley, CA 94704, USA. *Website:* www.eddiepalmierimusic.com.

PALUMBO OF SOUTHWARK, Baron (Life Peer), cr. 2013, of Southwark, in the London Borough of Southwark; **James (Jamie) Palumbo;** British entrepreneur and author; b. 6 June 1963, London, England; s. of Baron Peter Palumbo; one s. with Atoosa Hariri. *Education:* Eton Coll., Worcester Coll., Oxford. *Career:* worked for Merrill Lynch and Morgan Grenfell, City of London 1984–92; Co-founder Ministry of Sound nightclub, South London 1991, Owner, Ministry of Sound Group, incorporating book and magazine publishing, fashion, a record label, sold 16% of the business to 3i 2001; mem. (Liberal Democrat), House of Lords 2013–. *Publication:* Tomas (novel) 2009. *Address:* Ministry of Sound, 103 Gaunt Street, London, SE1 6DP, England (office); House of Lords, Westminster, London, SW1A 0PW, England. *Telephone:* (870) 060-0010 (office). *E-mail:* info@ministryofsound.com (office); contactholmember@parliament.uk. *Website:* www.ministryofsound .com (office); www.parliament.uk/biographies/lords/lord-palumbo-of -southwark/4310.

PAMPARIUS, Pål Pot; Norwegian musician (keyboards, guitar); b. (Pål Bøttger Kjærnes), 18 June 1969. *Career:* founder mem. glam-punk band, Turbonegro 1988–98, 2002–. *Recordings include:* albums: Turboloid 1990, Hot Cars and Spent Contraceptives 1992, Helta Skelta 1993, Never is Forever 1994, Ass Cobra 1996, Apocalypse Dudes 1998, Scandinavian Leather 2003, Party Animals 2005, Retox 2007. *Honours:* MTV Europe Music Award for Best Norwegian Act 2005. *Address:* c/o Burning Heart Records, PO Box 441, 70148 Örebro, Sweden (office). *Website:* www.burningheart.com (office); www .turbonegro.nu.

PANDIT G; British producer, DJ and composer; b. (John Ashok Pandit), 1962. *Career:* Founder mem., Asian Dub Foundation 1993–. *Recordings include:* albums: Concious (EP) 1994, Facts and Fictions 1995, R.A.F.I. 1997, Rafi's Revenge 1998, Conscious Party 1998, Community Music 2000, Enemy of the Enemy 2003, Bangin' On The Walls 2003, Tank 2005, Punkara 2008, A History of Now 2011. *Honours:* BBC Asian Award for Music 1998. *Website:* www.asiandubfoundation.com.

PANJABI MC, (PMC); British hip-hop and bhangra musician; b. (Rajinder Rai), Coventry, England. *Career:* solo artist 1993–. *Recordings:* albums: The CD 1993, Another Sellout 1994, 100% Proof 1995, Grass Roots 1996, Panjabi MC 1998, Beware 2003, Desi 2003, Dhol Jageero 2003, Mundian To Bach Ke 2004. *Current Management:* c/o Compagnia Nuove Indye Management and Booking, Via Vivaldi 9, 00199 Rome, Italy. *Website:* www.panjabi-mc.com.

DJ PANKO; Spanish musician, DJ and producer; b. Barcelona. *Career:* fmr guitarist in punk rock group Soplamocos; fmr actor, singer and bass player, The World project, Amsterdam; fmr guitarist with La Esencia rumba fusion band; performed with electronic group ON; began working as DJ and producer; joined Ojos de Brujo, a group which fuses gypsy and flamenco music with Latin American, punk, hip hop, reggae and electronic influences, set up own label La Fábrica de Colores 2001 and since then operates as a completely ind. org.; remixed group's music for Remezclas de la Casa album 2003; several tours in Europe, Latin America and USA; collaborations with Nitin Sawhney, Asian Dub Foundation. *Recordings:* albums: Vengue 1999, Barí 2002, Barí: Remezclas de la Casa 2003, Techarí 2006, Aocaná 2009; other: Girando Bari (DVD) 2005. *Honours:* World Music Award for Europe, BBC Radio 3 2004. *E-mail:* panko@ojosdebrujo.com (office). *Website:* www.ojosdebrujo.com.

PANTAZIS, Lefteris; Greek singer and actor; b. Ascend, Russia. *Career:* moved to Greece 1969; performed with numerous artists, including Giannis Karabenissis, Panos Gavalas, Maria Linda, Genie Vanou, Vicky Mosholiou, Giannis Efstratiou, Catherine Gray, Johana Lydia, Pitsa Papadopoulou. *Films:* Mages kai mortisses 1982, Glentiste mazi mas 1988, Sapounopetra: To hrima sto laimo sas 1995. *Recordings include:* albums: Agapiomaste 1980, Pali Monoi 1981, Dio Lekseis 1982, Mia zoi Erotefmenos 1983, Deste me alisides tin Karadia mou 1984, Tha Figo monos mou 1985, Se Nostalgo 1986, Kai me Xathoume 1987, Ekeini 1988, Taraxi 1989, Yparxei Kaneis 1990, Tilepatheia 1991, Lefteris & Mimis Plessa 1991, Thimise mou to Onoma sou 1992, Theleis 1992, Salonikiotiko Feggari 1993, Ego den eimai ego 1993, O Paiktis 1994, O Pantazis erminevei Tsitsani 1994, Xrisa Soukse 1994, Dikaioma Mou 1995, Empeiries 1996, Eleftheros 1996, O Lepa Tragoudaei Zampeta 1996, Erxetai 1997, An me Agapas 1998, Den tha me Deis na Klaio 1999, Filakia 2000, Oti Kalitero 2000, Evdomos Ouranos 2000, Ena asteri sta asteria 2001, Kati Trexei 2002, Gia proti Fora 2002, Le Cabaret 2003, 1000 Vanilla 2004, Allos Anthropos 2005, Alli mia Nixta 2006, Exo Trelanei Ton Yheo 2008. *Website:* www.lefteris-pantazis.gr.

PANZU-NIOSI, Papy; Democratic Republic of the Congo musician (guitar, piano); b. 21 Jan. 1975, Kinshasa. *Education:* Studied composition and musical writing. *Career:* TV and radio appearances, 1999; mem, Arts National Institute. *Compositions:* Heritage; Testimony; Marriage; The Richness; Alleluia; Charity; Alienation; Lamb's Glory. *Honours:* Academic competition, 1997.

PAPA DEE; Swedish singer and reggae MC; b. (Daniel David Christopher Wahlgren), 13 July 1966, Gothenburg. *Education:* Church Sweden. *Career:* tours of Scandinavia with The Stonefunkers 1987–89; mem. Brooklyn Funk Essentials; mem, Swedish Musicians' Union. *Recordings:* albums: Lettin' Off Steam 1990, One Step Ahead 1993, Original Master 1994, The Journey 1996, Island Rock 1998, The Man Who Couldn't Say No 2001, Live It Up! 2004, A Little Way Different 2008. *Honours:* Swedish Dance Music Awards for Hip Hop Album of the Year, for Best Male Vocalist 1991, for Best Male Vocalist 1995, for Best Pop Album, 1995. *Current Management:* c/o Magnus Nygren, Stockhouse, Box 63, 182 05 Djursholm, Sweden. *Telephone:* (8) 856-80-0. *Fax:* (8) 624-00-51. *E-mail:* info@stockhouse.se. *Website:* www.stockhouse.se; www.papadee.se.

PAPA GEORGE; British singer, songwriter and blues musician (guitar); b. (George Papanicola), 9 May 1953, London. *Career:* leader, The Papa George Band 1986–; tours of Europe, Texas, Columbia; also performed in duos with Micky Moody, Zoot Money, Alan Glen, Steve Simpson, Ian Hunt, Ken Emerson, the late Gary Moore; mem. Musicians' Union; PRS and MCPS, Barnes Bowling Club, London. *Compositions include:* Heading South, title track (co-writer with Ian Hunt), Guilty (for Paul Williams) 1995. *Recordings:* Papa George 1986, Nite With You 1996, Being Free... Ain't no Crime 2002, Down at the Station 2004. *Radio:* Blues n Soul, UK Jazz Radio 2010, Theme for Pienaar's Politics 2010–11 (author-composer), BBC Radio 5 live. *Honours:* Hawaii Music Award 2004. *Address:* Barnes Station House, Station Road, London SW13 0HT, England (office). *Telephone:* (7957) 543010 (office). *Fax:* (20) 8876-2748 (office). *E-mail:* papageorgeblues@btinternet.com (office). *Website:* www.papageorge.co.uk.

PAPA NOEL; Democratic Republic of the Congo singer, musician (guitar) and songwriter; b. (Antoine Nedule Monswet), 25 Dec. 1940, Kinshasa. *Career:* first recording 1957; mem. Rock-a-Mambo 1957–60, Orchestre Bantou 1960–63, Orchestre African Jazz 1963–68; f. own band, Orchestre Bamboula 1968; mem. OK Jazz 1978–89, Kékélé project 2001–; collaborations with Sam Mangwana, Mose Fan Fan, Adan Pedroso; int. tours as part of Kekele and with Adan Pedroso including WOMAD Reading 2000. *Recordings:* Bon Samaritain 1984, Allegria 1986, Bakitani (reunion with ex-members of OK Jazz) 1992, Haute Tension 1994, Bel Ami 2000, Rumba Congo 2001; as part of Kekele: Mosala Makasi (with Adan Pedroso) 2001.

PAPASOV, Ivo; Bulgarian clarinettist; b. (Ibrahim Hapasov), 16 Feb. 1952, Kurdzali; s. of Mehmed Sali and Zeliha Mümün Sali; m. Maria Karafizieva;

two s. *Career:* founder Trakija Band 1974; leader Ivo Papasov and His Wedding Band; performed at venues including Palais des Beaux Arts, Paris, Ronnie Scott's, London, Szena, Vienna, Treibhaus, Innsbruck, Moods, Zurich, Bimhuis, Amsterdam; collab. with Johnny Griffin, Hector Zazou, Okay Temiz, Glen Velez, Kepa Junkera, Arild Andersen, Kalman Balogh, Iva Bitova, Sergei Starostin. *Film:* The World Is Big and Salvation Lurks Around the Corner 2008. *Recordings:* Orpheus Ascending 1989, Balkanology 1991, Fairground 2004, Dance of the Falcon 2008. *Honours:* Hon. Citizen Stara Zagora; Dr hc (State Univ. of Library Studies and Information Technologies, Sofia); Audience Award, BBC Radio 3 World Music Awards 2005, Special BG Radio Prize, World Amb. of Bulgarian Music 2005, Great Inspiration Prize on 10th anniversary of the House of the Arts 2005, Famous Alley Star, Arena Mladost (Sofia), The Golden Award of the Atlantic Club. *Current Management:* c/o Victor Lilov, Messechina Music, POB 49, 1700 Sofia, Bulgaria. *Telephone:* (2) 9463070. *Fax:* (2) 9463070. *E-mail:* office@messechina-music.com. *Website:* www.messechina-music.com. *E-mail:* papasov@messechina-music.com. *Website:* ivo-papasov.com.

PAPER MACHE (see Chandler, Kerri)

PAPERCLIP PEOPLE (see Craig, Carl)

PARADA, Pete; American musician (drums). *Career:* mem. Steel Prophet 1996–98, Face to Face 1998–2002, Saves the Day 2002–07, The Offspring 2007–. *Recordings include:* albums: with The Offspring: Rise and Fall, Rage and Grace 2008, Days Go By 2012. *Address:* The Offspring, PO Box 3479, Huntington Beach, CA 92605–3479, USA (office). *E-mail:* info@offspring.com (office). *Website:* www.offspring.com (office); web.mac.com/peteparada.

PARADIS, Vanessa; French singer and model; b. 22 Dec. 1972, Saint-Maur-des-Fossés, Val-de-Marne, Île-de-France; pnr Johnny Depp; one s. one d.. *Films:* Noce blanche (César Award for Most Promising Actress) 1989, Elisa 1995, Un Amour de sorcière 1997, Une Chance sur deux 1998, Le Plaisir (et ses petits tracas) 1998, La Fille sur le pont 1999, Tony N' Tina's Wedding 2004, Le Retour de James Bataille 2004, Mon ange 2004, The Magic Roundabout (voice) 2005, La Clef 2007. *Recordings:* albums: M & J, 1987, Variations sur le meme t'aime 1990, Vanessa Paradis 1992, Live 1994, Bliss 2000, Vanessa Paradis au Zenith 2001, Divinidylle 2007. *Address:* c/o Universal Music Deutschland, Stralauer Allee 1, 10245 Berlin, Germany.

PARDESI, Silinder, BSc; British singer; b. 1 Sept. 1957, Kenya; m. R. K. Bhooal; one s. two d. *Education:* MISTC. *Career:* formed 'Pardesi' 1982; TV broadcasts; mem. MISTC, Musicians' Union. *Recordings include:* albums: Shabad Gurbani and Geet Guran De, Pump Up The Bhangra, Full Badmashi, Planet Earth, No To Nasha, Bollywood Seduction, On A Dance Trip, Pump n' Up Again, Seduction 2, Firing on All Silinders, Destiny, Hey Soniye, Akhiyeen. *Honours:* Winner Asian Song Contest 1986, Best Album of 1990, Best Track of 1990, Top Selling Album of 1990, Best Live Band of 1990, Outstanding Singing Achievement 1995, Award for Achievement for Enhanced CD-ROM by Indian High Commr HE Lalit Mann Singh, Punjabi Cultural Award 2009. *Address:* Pardesi World HQ, PO Box 525, Coventry, CV3 2YW, England (office). *Telephone:* (845) 226-5518 (office). *Fax:* (845) 226-5518 (office). *E-mail:* silinder@pardesi.co.uk (office); management@pardesi.co.uk (office). *Website:* www.pardesi.co.uk.

PARDY, Richard Alan, PGCE; British musician (saxophones, clarinet, flute, piano), composer and arranger; b. 17 April 1966, Grimsby, Lincolnshire; m. 1993; two s. *Education:* studied clarinet with Jack Brymer and saxophone with Al Wood, GCLCM. *Career:* tours include Ben E. King, Marty Wilde, Cao Quin, Martha Reeves and the Vandellas, Drifters, Westlife; tributes to Carpenters, Steely Dan/Donald Fagen, Burt Bacharach, Big Bands/Jazz Combos; mem., Pardy Quintet (appeared at South Bank International Jazz Festival), Impulse; West End shows and touring shows in UK, Europe and world-wide; mem. CASS, MU. *Recordings:* Under the Orange Tree; session player on advertisement and film music; featured soloist: Song for the United Nations, Just Can't Give It Up, Nirvana Remix-Hustler's Convention, Blue Lagoon, Living Planet, Lennon. *Publications:* Development/Evolution of the Big Bands 1987. *Address:* c/o Impulse Music, 83 Church Avenue, Humberton, Lincolnshire DN36 4HR, England (office). *Telephone:* (1472) 598784 (office). *E-mail:* sales@impulselive.co.uk (office). *Website:* www.impulselive.co.uk.

PARFITT, Andy; British broadcasting executive; *Chair, Youth Music*; b. 24 Sept. 1958. *Education:* Old Vic Theatre, Bristol. *Career:* joined BBC as Studio Man. 1980; seconded to BFBS, posted to Falkland Islands 1984; Producer, BBC Educ. 1984–87, BBC Radio Four 1987–89 (programmes including Pick of the Week, Bookshelf); joined BBC Radio Five 1989 (for launch in 1990), Asst Ed. 1990; Ed., Danny Baker's Morning Edition 1992–93, Six-O-Six 1991–93; Chief Asst to Controller, BBC Radio One 1993–94; Ed. Commissioning and Planning, then Man. Ed., BBC Radio One 1994–97; Deputy Controller BBC Radio One 1997–98, Controller 1998–2011, also fmr controller for BBC 1Xtra, BBC Switch, BBC Asian Network, BBC popular music; currently Chair., Youth Music. *Address:* Youth Music, Suites 3–5, Swan Court, 9 Tanner Street, London, SE1 9LE, England (office). *Telephone:* (20) 7902-1060 (office). *Website:* www.youthmusic.org.uk (office).

PARFITT, Rick, OBE; British musician (guitar) and singer; b. (Rick Harrison), 12 Oct. 1948, Woking, Surrey, England. *Career:* fmr mem., the Highlights; mem. rock group Status Quo (originally the Spectres) 1967–; extensive tours worldwide, concerts and festivals; played four venues in 12 hours, entered in Guinness Book of Records 1991. *Recordings include:* albums:

Picturesque Matchstickable Messages 1968, Spare Parts 1969, Ma Kelly's Greasy Spoon 1970, Dog of Two Heads 1971, Piledriver 1973, Hello! 1973, Quo 1974, Encore 1974, On The Level 1975, Pop Chronik 5 1975, Blue For You 1976, Live 1977, Rockin' All Over The World 1977, If You Can't Stand The Heat 1978, Whatever You Want 1979, Just Supposin' 1980, Never Too Late 1981, Now Hear This 1981, 1+9+8+2 1982, Live At The N.E.C. 1984, Status Quo 1984, To Be Or Not To Be 1983, Back To Back 1983, In The Army Now 1986, Ain't Complaining 1988, Rock 'Til You Drop 1991, Live Alive Quo 1992, The Other Side Of Status Quo 1995, Thirsty Work 1995, Don't Stop 1996, Whatever You Want 1997, Under The Influence 1999, Famous In The Last Century 2000, Rockin' And Rollin' 2001, Heavy Traffic 2002, Riffs 2003, XS All Areas 2004, The Party Ain't Over Yet 2005, In Search of the Fourth Chord 2007. *Publication:* XS All Areas: The Status Quo Autobiography (with Francis Rossi) 2004. *Honours:* Nordoff-Robbins Music Therapy Centre Silver Clef Award 1981, Ivor Novello Award 1983, BRIT Award for Outstanding Contribution to the British Music Industry 1991, World Music Award for Outstanding Contribution to Music 1991. *Current Management:* Duroc Media Ltd, Riverside House, 10–12 Victoria Road, Uxbridge, Middlesex UB8 2TW, England. *Telephone:* (1895) 810831. *Fax:* (1895) 231499. *E-mail:* info@durocmedia.com. *Website:* www.statusquo.co.uk.

PARIDJANIAN, Gale; British singer and musician (guitar). *Career:* founder mem. Turin Brakes 1999–. *Recordings include:* albums: The Door (EP) 1999, The State of Things (EP) 2000, The Optimist 2001, Ether Song 2003, JackInABox 2005, Dark on Fire 2007, Outbursts 2010. *Current Management:* CMO Management International Ltd, Studio 2.6, Shepherds East, Richmond Way, London, W14 0DQ, England. *Telephone:* (20) 7316-6969. *Fax:* (20) 7316-6970. *E-mail:* reception@cmomanagement.co.uk. *Website:* www .cmomanagement.co.uk; www.turinbrakes.com.

PARIS, Mica; British singer; b. (Michelle Warren), 27 April 1969, London, England. *Career:* singer in church choir early 1980s; session singer, notably with Shakatak; mem. gospel group, Spirit of Watts; Hollywood Beyond; solo artist 1988–. *Radio:* presenter, BBC Radio 2 2001. *Television:* presenter, What Not to Wear 2007–. *Recordings:* albums: So Good 1988, Contribution 1990, Whisper A Prayer 1993, Black Angel 1998, If You Could Love Me 2005, Born Again 2009; appears on: Stereo MCs, Connected 1992; Courtney Pine, To the Eyes of Creation 1992; Brenda Russell, Soul Talkin' 1993; Omar, For Pleasure 1995; Guru Jazzmatazz, Vol. 2: The New Reality 1995. *Publication:* Beautiful Within 2007. *E-mail:* info@micaparis.com (office). *Website:* www.micaparis .com.

PARISH, Alan Victor; British musician (drums); b. 22 Oct. 1951, Edmonton, London; Divorced, two s. *Career:* television and radio jingles; played with Top 40 bands; urrently member of The Hamsters, 8 years; numerous concerts, television and radio appearances; toured UK and Europe. *Recordings:* On all Hamsters albums and video. *Website:* www.thehamsters.co.uk.

PARISH, John, (Scott Tracey); British record producer, composer, musician (guitar, drums, percussion) and singer; b. 11 April 1959, Yeovil, Somerset. *Career:* mem. new wave group, Thieves Like Us 1979–81; founder, singer and guitarist, The Headless Horsemen (as Scott Tracey); mem. experimental West Country band, Automatic Dlamini (with Polly Harvey and Robert Ellis) 1983–92; began production career, specialising in independent guitar groups; Prod. for artists, including The Chesterfields, Becketts, PJ Harvey, The Harvest Ministers, 16 Horsepower, Elliot Green; Assoc. Lecturer in rock music and recording techniques, Yeovil Coll. 1991–94; recorded with Bettie Seevert, eels, Goldfrapp; mem. PRS, Musicians' Union. *Compositions include:* Dance Hall at Louse Point (music, with lyrics by PJ Harvey) 1996, Rosie (OST) (Bonn Int. Film Music Biennale Special Appreciation Prize) 1998. *Recordings include:* with Automatic Dlamini: The D is for Drum 1988, From a Diva to a Diver 1992; solo: How Animals Move 2003, Once Upon a Time 2005, A Woman A Man Walked By (with PJ Harvey) 2009. *Current Management:* Dnotice Ltd, PO Box 33808, London N8 9GY, England. *E-mail:* info@dnotice.net. *Website:* www.dnotice.net; www.johnparish.com.

PARK, Graeme; British dj, remixer and musician; b. 4 Aug. 1963, Aberdeen, Scotland; m. Anne-Marie Curtis. *Career:* DJ, Garage, Nottingham, 1982; Started Hacienda, Manchester, 1988; Saturday Night resident, Hacienda, 1988–; DJ world-wide including: Australia; South America; USA; Yugoslavia; Iceland; mem, Musicians' Union. *Recordings:* Remixed acts including: Brand New Heavies; Inner City; New Order; ABC; Jan Hammer; Eric B; Dubstar; M People; K Klass; Ace Remix Vol. 16; Recent remixes include: Take Me Home and Murder On The Dancefloor, both by Sophie Ellis-Bextor, 2001. *Honours:* Dance-Aid DJ of Year, 1991, 1992, 1993. *Website:* www.trustthedj.com/graemepark/.

PARK, Jin-young, (J.Y. Park, JYP); South Korean singer, musician, songwriter, record producer and music executive; *Founder and CEO, JYP Entertainment;* b. 13 Dec. 1971, Seoul; m. 1st Seo Yoon-jeong 1999 (divorced); m. 2nd 2013. *Education:* Baemyung High School, Yonsei Univ. *Career:* frontman, Park Jin-Young and the New Generation 1992; solo performer 1994–; producer for numerous acts in S Korea and USA including Cassie, Mase, Rain, Will Smith, Wonder Girls; Founder, JYP Entertainment 2001–, currently CEO. *Television:* Dream High 2011–12, K-pop Star (as judge) 2011–. *Film:* as actor: Five Million Dollar Man 2012. *Recordings include:* albums: solo: Blue City 1994, Tantara 1995, Summer Jingle Bell 1997, Even After 10 Years 1998, Kiss Me 1998, Game 2001, Back to Stage 2007, White in Snow 2013. *Honours:* Mnet Asian Music Awards for Best Asian Composer (for

Nobody) 2009, for Best Male Artist 2015. *Address:* JYP Entertainment, JYP Center, 41, 79-gil, Apgujeong-ro, Gangnam-gu, Seoul, South Korea (office). *Telephone:* (2) 3438-2300. *Website:* english.jype.com.

PARKER, Alan; British composer and musician (guitar); b. 26 Aug. 1944, England; m. Stephanie; one s. one d. *Education:* Royal Acad. of Music, London. *Career:* session guitarist 1960s–70s; worked with artists, including Stevie Wonder, Frank Sinatra, Elton John, Dusty Springfield, Andy Williams, Tony Bennett, Mick Jagger, David Bowie, Paul McCartney, John Lennon, Jimi Hendrix, John Denver, Johnny Cash, Dame Kiri Te Kanawa, Placido Domingo; founder mem. and songwriter, Blue Mink; mem., The Congregation; session musician on soundtracks by John Barry, John Williams, Jerry Goldsmith, Lalo Schifrin; mem. PRS, Musicians' Union. *Compositions:* songs recorded by: Blue Mink; The Congregation; The Walker Brothers; Dusty Springfield; CCS; Arrangements for: Neil Diamond; John Denver; Dusty Springfield; The Walker Brothers; 21 films, 75 television productions include: What's Eating Gilbert Grape; Rhodes, BBC; Up on the Roof, Granada Films; Red Fox, LWT; Jaws 3; To Be The Best; Voice of The Heart; American Gothic; The Glory Boys; Dempsey and Makepeace; Firm Friends; Van Der Valk, Thames TV; Minder, Thames TV; Wild Justice; The Danedyke Mystery, Granada; Mirage; Philby Burgess and McClean; Moody and Pegg; Mixed Doubles; Pop Quest, YTV; Children's ITV; Thames News; River Journeys, BBC TV; Oktober, ITV; Unknown Soldier, Carlton; Round Tower, ITV; Colour Blind, ITV; Nancherrow, BBC; Victoria And Albert; Movie scores include: Come See The Paradise; Angela's Ashes; Commercial jingles include: Kellogg's; Wrangler Jeans; Levi's Jeans; Volkswagen; Heinz; Citröen; Tuborg Lager; Mass performed at the Vatican, 1993; work for music libraries. *Honours:* Ivor Novello Award. *Address:* Soundtrack Music Associates Ltd, 25 Ives Street, Chelsea, London SW3 2ND, England.

PARKER, Ed, BS, MD; American country singer and musician (guitar); b. 16 July 1929, Goose Creek (now Baytown), TX; m. Carey Ruth Parker 1962. *Education:* FBI National Academy. *Career:* solo artist, with live appearances, festivals and guitar conventions; mem. CMA, ACM, ROPE, CMOA. *Film appearance:* Tomboy and the Champ. *Recordings include:* albums: Ed Parker Sings Just For You, From My Heart, I'd Like to Live It Again, One Ole Texan, Vol. 1, Still a Lot of Good Miles Left in Me. *Honours:* Airplay International Trailblazer Leadership Award, International Star Music Award for Special Achievement.

PARKER, Graham; British singer and songwriter; b. 18 Nov. 1950, London, England. *Career:* mem. R&B groups, The Black Rockers, Deep Cut; mem., Graham Parker and The Rumour 1975–80; solo artist 1980–; numerous concert tours, festival appearances. *Recordings include:* albums: with Graham Parker and The Rumour: Howlin' Wind 1976, Heat Treatment 1976, Stick To Me 1977, The Parkerilla 1978, Squeezing Out Sparks 1979, The Up Escalator 1980, The Best of Graham Parker and The Rumour 1980; solo: Another Grey Area 1982, The Real McCaw 1983, Steady Nerves 1985, Mona Lisa's Sister 1988, Human Soul 1989, Live! Alone In America 1989, Struck By Lightning 1991, Burning Questions 1992, Passion Word—The Graham Parker Anthology 1976–91 1993, Live on the Test 1995, Squeezing Out Sparks/Live Sparks 1996, The Last Rock and Roll Tour 1997, Loose Monkeys, Spare Tracks and Lost Demos 1999, Parkerilla 1999, Master Hits: Graham Parker; Deepcut To Nowhere 2001. *Telephone:* (805) 646-8433. *Fax:* (805) 646-3367. *E-mail:* trip@paradiseartists.com. *Website:* www.grahamparker.net.

PARKER, Kevin Richard; Australian musician (guitar, keyboards, drums), singer, songwriter and record producer; b. 17 Dec. 1986, Sydney, NSW; s. of Jerry Parker and Rosalind Parker. *Career:* raised in Perth; Founder-mem. The Dee Dee Dums 2005–07; Founder-mem. Tame Impala 2007–, signed to Modular Recordings label 2008, numerous live appearances; drummer with group Pond 2009; other collaborations include Canyons, Relation Longue Distance, Discodeine. *Recordings:* albums: Innerspeaker (Triple J's J Award for Album of the Year 2010) 2010, Lonerism (Triple J's J Award for Album of the Year 2012, ARIA Awards for Album of the Year 2013, for Best Rock Album 2013) 2012. *Honours:* EG Music Award for Best Song (for Elephant) 2012, ARIA Award for Best Group 2013, APRA Award for Song of the Year (for Feels Like We Only Go Backwards) 2013. *Current Management:* c/o Spinning Top Music, PO Box 769, Fremantle, WA 6959, Australia. *E-mail:* tameimpala@spinningtopmusic.com. *Website:* www.spinningtopmusic.com; www .tameimpala.com (home).

PARKER, Mick; British musician (piano, keyboards, accordion) and composer; b. 12 June 1952, London, England; m. Angelika Helm 1992; one s. *Education:* To degree level; All piano academy grades 1–8. *Career:* Toured with: Joan Armatrading, 1976–79; Billy Ocean, 1979–80; Linda Lewis, 1980–82; Television with all the above; Touring and recording for Gilbert O'Sullivan as MD, 1991–; Toured Japan with Linda Lewis, 1997; mem, PRS; MCPS; Musicians' Union. *Compositions:* Many jingles and film music, includes Merchant Ivory film Heat and Dust, 1985; Soundtrack for Thief-takers, ITV, 1996. *Recordings:* As producer: Single: So Macho, Sinitta, 1986; As arranger: Album: Aqaba Beach, Mory Kante, 1986; As musician: Album: Este Mundo, Gipsy Kings, 1992; with Gilbert O'Sullivan: Sounds of The Loop, 1992; Live In Japan, 1993; Singer Sewing Machine, Gilbert O'Sullivan, 1996; Bare Bones, Wishbone Ash, 2000. *Honours:* Ampex Golden Reel Awards, Sinitta; Azucar Moreno.

PARKER, Peter Paul; British musician (bass) and songwriter; b. 31 Aug. 1964, Kingston, Surrey. *Education:* Basstech Coll., Acton. *Career:* bassist,

Heaven Can Wait 1982–86; mem. Musicians' Union, Guild of Master Songwriters. *Recordings:* album: Out of the Blue, by Emily's Sister 1996.

PARKER, Ray, Jr; American musician (guitar); b. 1 May 1954, Detroit, Mich.; m. Elaine Parker. *Career:* mem. houseband 20 Grand Club late 1960s; toured with Detroit Spinners; studio musician for Invicta Wax; formed Raydio 1977–; solo artist 1982–. *Recordings:* albums: as Raydio: Raydio 1977, Rock On 1979, Two Places At The Same Time 1980, A Woman Needs Love 1981; solo: The Other Woman 1982, Greatest Hits 1982, Woman Out of Control 1983, Chartbusters 1984, Sex and The Single Man 1985, After Dark 1987, I Love You Like You Are 1991, The Heritage Collection 2000, I'm Free 2006; as musician, albums by Stevie Wonder: Talking Book 1972, Innervisions 1973; by Marvin Gaye: Master 1961–84; by Diana Ross: Greatest Hits The RCA Years; by Boz Scaggs: My Time the Anthology 1969–97, Dig 2001; by Nona Hendryx: Transformation; by Herbie Hancock: VSOP. *Honours:* Grammy Award for Best Pop Instrumental Performance 1984, BAFTRA Award, Star on Hollywood Walk of Fame 2014. *Address:* Raydio Music Corpn, 23679 Calabasas Road, Suite 501, Calabasas, CA 91302, USA (office). *Telephone:* (818) 225-2412 (office). *E-mail:* info@rayparkerjr.com (office). *Website:* www.rayparkerjr.com.

PARKINSON, Bill; British musician (guitar), songwriter and producer; b. 28 Nov. 1941, Lancaster, England; m. Jennifer 1965; two d. *Career:* has worked with The Fourmost, P J Proby, Screaming Lord Sutch, The Savages, Tom Jones backing group, The Squires, Chuck Berry, The Beatles, Sammy Davis Jr, Shirley Bassey, Bobby Vee, Petula Clark, Vic Damone, Englebert Humperdinck, Ted Heath Orchestra, Freddie Starr; mem, PRS, MCPS, Musicians' Union. *Compositions:* Neil Reid: Mother of Mine, Jimmy Osmond, Deep Purple: Theme to Mandrake Root. *E-mail:* info@bill-parkinson.co.uk (office). *Website:* www.bill-parkinson.co.uk.

PARKS, Van Dyke; American singer, songwriter, producer and musician (piano, clarinet); b. 3 Jan. 1943, Hattiesburg, MS. *Education:* American Boychoir School, Princeton, NJ, Carnegie Institute. *Career:* child actor; mem., Greenwood County Singers; signed to MGM as songwriter for Walt Disney Studios 1964, Warner Bros 1966; Dir, Warner Bros Audio/Visual Services 1970–71; worked with Fiona Apple, Tango Argentino, Tim Buckley, The Buena Vista Social Club, T Bone Burnett, The Byrds, Eliza Carthy, Peter Case, Cher, Natalie Cole, Judy Collins, Ry Cooder, Sheryl Crow, Kathy Dalton, The Everly Brothers, Kinky Friedman, Lowell George, Eliza Gilkyson, Arlo Guthrie, Harpers Bizarre, Peter Ivers, Leo Kottke, Little Feat, Mojo Men, Keith Moon, Aaron Neville, Randy Newman, Harry Nilsson, Phil Ochs, Sam Phillips, Bonnie Raitt, The Rembrandts, Stan Ridgway, Linda Ronstadt, Carly Simon, Mighty Sparrow, Bruce Springsteen, Ringo Starr, Syd Straw, Meryl Streep, Three Dog Night, U2, Jennifer Warnes, Victoria Williams, Brian Wilson, Steve Young. *Compositions include:* High Coin; Come To The Sunshine; for television: Chesapeake Borne, Polar Bears/Season of Fear, The Billy Crystal Comedy Hour, Alfred Hitchcock Mystery Theatre, Fairy Tale Theatre, The Marshal, Hallmark Hall of Fame, Movies of the Week; for film: Goin' South 1978, Two Jakes, One Christmas, Wild Bill, Club Paradise, Bastard Out of Carolina, The Brave Little Toaster (three songs), Shadrach, Harland County; for theatre: Mother Courage by Brecht (Boston Shakespeare Theatre), Henry IV Part II (Kennedy Center); music for The Triumph of Love (Broadway). *Recordings:* albums: Song Cycle 1967, Discover America 1971, Clang Of The Yankee Reaper 1975, Jump! 1982, Tokyo Rose 1990, Orange Crate Art 1995, Moonlighting: Live At The Ash Grove 1997. *Publications:* children's book: Jump, Jump Again, Jump on Over. *E-mail:* therealvandykeparks@gmail.com (office). *Website:* www.vandykeparks.com.

PARLATO, Gretchen, BA; American jazz singer; b. Los Angeles; d. of David Parlato and Judy Frisk. *Education:* Los Angeles County High School for the Arts, Univ. of California, Los Angeles, Thelonious Monk Inst. of Jazz Performance. *Career:* has performed with Lionel Loueke, Wayne Shorter and Kenny Barron. *Recordings:* Gretchen Parlato 2005, In a Dream 2009. *Honours:* first prize, Thelonious Monk Int. Jazz Vocals Competition 2009. *Current Management:* c/o Karen Kennedy, 24 Seven Artist Development, 6 Richmond Street, Newark, NJ 07103, USA. *Telephone:* (973) 230-3160. *Fax:* (973) 353-9477. *E-mail:* karen@karenkennedy.net. *Address:* c/o Stephanie Jo Klein, Obliq Sound, 373 Broadway, Suite F11, New York, NY 10013, USA (office). *Telephone:* (212) 274-8640 (office). *Fax:* (212) 274-8641 (office). *Website:* www.gretchenparlato.com.

PARLETT, Michael John, BMus, PGCE; British musician (saxophones, flute, percussion, windsynth) and producer; *CEO, Talented Productions Inc.*; b. 19 July 1963, Bexleyheath, Kent, England. *Education:* Goldsmiths Coll., Middlesex Univ. *Career:* currently solo performer and producer throughout Southern California; CEO, Talented Productions Inc. *Radio:* host, Mike Parlett radio show, Solar Radio. *Recordings:* solo: Waiting on You; sessions with: Lulu, Take That, Mica Paris, Eternal, Gabrielle, Yazz, The Jones Girls, 911, M People, Geno Washington, Simply Red, Norman Brown, Jeff Lorber, Ricky Lawson, Randy Crawford, Brian Culbertson, Deborah Laws. *Current Management:* Talented Productions, 2010 South Crescent Heights, Los Angeles, CA 90034, USA. *Telephone:* (818) 284-3943. *Fax:* (818) 424-6782. *E-mail:* mike@talentedstudios.com. *Address:* 11271 Ventura Boulevard, Studio City, CA 91604, USA (office). *Website:* www.parlett.net; www.talentinternational.com (home).

PARNELL, Lee Roy; American country musician (slide guitar); b. 21 Dec. 1956, Abilene, Texas; 1 s., 1 d. *Career:* Ten Feet Tall and Bulletproof tour, with Travis Tritt and Joe Diffie, 1994; Late Show With David Letterman; The Tonight Show; Live With Regis and Kathie Lee; Music City Tonight; Happy New Year America from the House of Blues; Miller Genuine Draft radio commercial; CocaCola Radio commercial; Theme song for 'The Road' radio and television programme; mem, BMI; ACM; CMA. *Recordings:* albums: Lee Roy Parnell 1990, Love Without Mercy 1992, On the Road 1993, We All Get Lucky Sometimes 1995, Every Night's a Saturday Night 1997, Hits and Highways Ahead 1999, Tell The Truth 2001, Back to the Well 2006. *Address:* Universal South Records, Nashville, TN, USA. *E-mail:* info@leeroyparnell.com. *Website:* www.leeroyparnell.com.

PARR, John; British singer, songwriter and producer; b. 19 Nov. 1957, Nr. Sherwood Forest, Nottinghamshire; m. Sharon 1980; two s. *Education:* guitar lessons. *Career:* tours 1985–, including tours with: Tina Turner, Bryan Adams, Toto, Heart, Beach Boys; mem, PRS, MCPS, ASCAP, AFTRA, Equity, Musicians' Union. *Recordings:* hit singles: Naughty Naughty 1985, St Elmo's Fire 1985, Rock 'N' Roll Mercenaries (with Meatloaf) 1986, Paris (with LSO and Philarmonic Choir), Miami Vice; as producer: Web Of Love, Sarah Jory 1994, If I Love You, Sarah Jory 1999; movie soundtracks: 3 Men and A Baby, Quicksilver, American Anthem, The Running Man, St Elmo's Fire 1985, Near Dark 1987, Spruce Goose 1986; covers with Tom Jones, The Monkees, Meatloaf, Roger Daltrey. *Honours:* ASCAP Award, Most Performed Song; MIDEM Award. *Website:* www.johnparr.net.

PARRA, Samuel, (Samo); Mexican singer; b. Veracruz. *Career:* trained as a classical singer; participated in Festival Valores Juveniles 1995; founding mem. Camila 2006–; collaborations with Yuri, Alan, Maria del Sol, Cristian Castor, Eugenia Leon, Reyli. *Recordings:* albums: with Camila: Todo Cambió 2006, Dejarte de Amar (Latin Grammy Award for Best Pop Album by a Duo or Group) 2010. *Honours:* Premio Lo Nuesto for Song of the Year (for Todo Cambió) 2008, Premio Lo Nuesto for Group of the Year 2008, two Latin Billbaord Awards 2008, Latin Grammy Awards for Record of the Year (for Mientes) 2010, for Song of the Year (for Mientes) 2010. *Address:* c/o Sony Music Entertainment Mexico, Horacio 1855, piso 2, Col. Los Morales Polanco, México 11510, Mexico (office). *Telephone:* (55) 5249-3200 (office). *Website:* www.sonymusic.com.mx (office); www.camila.tv.

PARRISH, Man; American producer, musician (keyboards) and artist manager; b. 6 May 1958, Brooklyn, New York. *Education:* American Academy of Dramatic Arts, High School of Performing Arts, New School for Social Research, New York. *Career:* owner, production company, Man Made Productions 1983–; partner, Artist Management Company; manager, Village People 1988–93; mem., group Man 2 Man; mem, ASCAP, National Music Publishers, Harry Fox Agency. *Recordings:* albums: solo: Man Parrish 1983, 2 1996, Hip Hop Bee Bop (Don't Stop) 1996, The Best of Man Parrish: Heartstroke 1996, Dream Man 1998, Dreamtime 1998; producer/writer on approximately 50 recordings, including Village People, Michael Jackson, Boy George, Gloria Gaynor, Omar Santana, Klaus Nomi. *Honours:* Billboard Award for Best Dance Artist, Bessie Smith Award. *Current Management:* c/o Vito Bruno, Am/Pm Entertainment, 415 63rd Street, Brooklyn, NY 11213, USA. *Telephone:* (718) 492-0100. *E-mail:* info@manparrish.com (office). *Website:* www.manparrish.com.

PARRY, J. Chris; record company executive and record producer; b. 7 Jan. 1949, Wellington, New Zealand; m. (divorced); one s. two d. *Education:* HND business studies. *Career:* professional drummer 1968–71; A&R Manager, Polydor Records 1974–78; Owner, Fiction Records 1978–; Managing Director, Fiction Records, Fiction Songs; Managing Director, XFM Radio; mem, BPI, Institute of Marketing. *Recordings:* appearances on: albums: by The Jam: In The City 1977, Modern World 1977, All Mod Cons 1978; various recordings by The Cure (as co-producer) including Japanese Whispers 1983, The Top 1984, Disintegration 1989, Wish 1992, Greatest Hits 2001, Three Imaginary Boys.

PARRY, Richard Reed; Canadian musician (tambourine, keyboards, guitar, accordion, bass) and singer; s. of David Parry and Caroline Parry. *Education:* Canterbury High School, Ottawa, ON. *Career:* fmr mem., New International Standards; mem. own band, Bell Orchestre; founder mem., Arcade Fire 2003–. *Recordings include:* albums: Funeral 2004, Neon Bible (Juno Award for Alternative Album of the Year 2008) 2007, The Suburbs (Grammy Award for Album of the Year 2011) 2010, Reflektor (Juno Awards for Album of the Year and Alternative Album of the Year 2014) 2013. *Address:* Quest Management, 1D–36 Warple Way, London, W3 0DY, England. *Telephone:* (20) 8749-0088. *Fax:* (20) 8749-0080. *E-mail:* info@quest-management.com. *Website:* www.quest-management.com; www.arcadefire.com.

PARRY, Tim; British music industry executive. *Career:* fmr mem. The Crooks, later Blue Zoo (managed by Jazz Summers); began career in man. with The March Violets; f. Big Life Management with Jazz Summers 1986, also launched Big Life Records and Big Life Music (publishing co.), initial success with acts including Lisa Stansfield, Coldcut, Yazz, Soup Dragons, Soul II Soul, De La Soul, The Orb; Big Life Records closed down 1998; current acts managed include Badly Drawn Boy, Snow Patrol, Embrace, The Verve, The Futureheads, Klaxons, The Wyos and producers Youth, Jacknife Lee, Jagz Kooner, Andy Gill, Clive Godard; Music Man., Power Amp Music (investment co.) 2008–09. *Address:* Big Life Management, 67–69 Chalton Street, London NW1 1HY, England (office). *Telephone:* (20) 7554-2100 (office). *Fax:* (20) 7554-2154 (office). *E-mail:* tim@biglifemanagement.com (office). *Website:* www.biglifemanagement.com (office).

PARSLEY, Ambrosia; American singer; b. 1971, Los Angeles, CA. *Career:* sang and played banjo as child; left home and toured country playing music aged 13 years; unsuccessful career as solo artist; f. Junebug with Danny McGough 1993, name changed to Shivaree 1995–. *Recordings:* albums: I Oughtta Give You A Shot In The Head For Making Me Live In This Dump 1999, Rough Dreams 2002, Who's Got Trouble? 2005, Tainted Love: Mating Calls and Fight Songs 2007. *Address:* c/o Capitol Records, 1750 N Vine Street, Hollywood, CA 90028-5209, USA (office). *Website:* www.shivaree.com.

PARSONS, Alan; British musician, record producer and engineer; b. 20 Dec. 1948. *Career:* former recording engineer, EMI Records; founder, Alan Parsons Project 1975–; The Alan Parsons Live Project have toured 19 different countries around the world 1994–. *Recordings:* albums: with Alan Parsons Project: Tales of Mystery and Imagination 1976, I Robot 1977, Pyramid 1978, Eve 1979, The Turn of a Friendly Card 1980, Eye In The Sky 1981, Ammonia Avenue 1983, Vulture Culture 1984, Stereotomy 1985, Gaudi 1987, Instrumental Works – Best of Alan Parsons Project 1983, Limelight – Best of (Vol. II) 1988, Try Anything Once 1992, On Air 1996, Definitive Collection 1997, The Time Machine 1999; recording engineer for artists including The Beatles, Wings, Pilot, Cockney Rebel, Al Stewart, Pink Floyd. *E-mail:* contact@alanparsonsmusic.com (office). *Website:* www.alanparsonsmusic.com.

PARSONS, David John, BA; British record company executive and artist manager; b. 30 Aug. 1962, Colchester, Essex; m. Stephanie Bowyer 1992; one s. *Career:* lead vocalist, Splat! 1981–83; Owner, Ron Johnson Records 1983–90; Director, Submission Records Ltd 1987–90; Owner, Zung Records 1994; Director, Too Pye Ahh Records 1995; lead vocalist, Chod 1995; mem, PRS, MCPS, PPL. *Recordings:* 1936, The Ex; Mud On A Colon, Stump; Two Kan Guru, Big Flame; I Am John's Pancreas, A Witness; Dudley Dorite Wristwatch, Chod; Debut album, Wholesome Fish. *Honours:* Ron Johnson Records, Independent Label of the Year 1986.

PARSONS, David Richard; British musician (guitar, violin) and songwriter; b. 12 April 1959, Woking, England; one s. *Education:* studied violin. *Career:* Founder-mem. Sham 69 1976–; mem. The Wanderers; also solo artist; various TV appearances, concerts; mem. PRS, MCPS, Musicians' Union. *Recordings include:* albums: with Sham 69: Tell Us the Truth 1978, That's Life 1978, The Adventures of the Hersham Boys 1979, The Game 1980, Volunteer 1988, Information Libre 1991, Kings and Queens 1993, Soapy Water & Mr Marmalade 1995, The A Files 1997, Direct Action: Day 21 2001, Western Culture 2008; solo: Reconcile 1995, Unstable 2014. *E-mail:* daveparsons69@aol.com. *Website:* www.daveparsons69.co.uk.

PARSONS, Niamh; Irish singer; b. 1958, Dublin. *Education:* learned singing from father. *Career:* first sang with band Killera; formed The Loose Connections with Dee Moore; joined Arcady 1992; Lecturer, Ballyfermot School of Music. *Recordings include:* albums: Loosely Connected 1992, Many Happy Returns 1995, A Celtic Tapestry 1996, A Celtic Tapestry II 1997, Loosen Up 1997, Holding Up Half The Sky 1997, Celtic Love Songs 1998, Blackbirds and Thrushes 1999, In My Prime 2000, The Old Simplicity 2006. *Current Management:* c/o Ken and Sue Bradburn, Emerging Music, Sarah's Cottage, Horns Cross, Bideford, Devon EX39 5DW, England. *Telephone:* (1237) 451933. *Fax:* (1237) 451931. *E-mail:* ken@emerging.demon.co.uk. *Website:* www.emergingmusic.co.uk; www.niamhparsons.com.

PARTON, Dolly Rebecca; American singer, songwriter and actress; b. 19 Jan. 1946, Sevier County, Tenn.; d. of Robert Lee Parton and Avie Lee Parton (née Owens); m. Carl Dean 1966. *Career:* Owner, Dollywood Entertainment Complex, including Dollywood Theme Park. *Films include:* Nine to Five 1980, The Best Little Whorehouse in Texas 1982, Rhinestone 1984, Steel Magnolias 1989, Straight Talk 1991, The Beverly Hillbillies 1993, Frank McKlusky, C.I. 2002, Miss Congeniality 2: Armed and Fabulous 2005, Joyful Noise 2012. *Stage:* as score writer: Nine to Five: The Musical, Broadway 2009. *Recordings include:* albums: Here You Come Again (Grammy Award 1978), Real Love 1985, Just the Way I Am 1986, Heartbreaker, Great Balls of Fire, Rainbow 1988, White Limozeen 1989, Home for Christmas 1990, Eagle When She Flies 1991, Slow Dancing with the Moon 1993, Honky Tonk Angels 1994, The Essential Dolly Parton 1995, Just the Way I Am 1996, Super Hits 1996, I Will Always Love You and Other Greatest Hits (with others) 1996, Hungary Again 1998, Grass is Blue 1999, Best of the Best-Porter 2 Doll 1999, Halos and Horns 2002, Those Were The Days 2006, Backwoods Barbie 2008, Better Day 2011, Blue Smoke 2014. *Composed numerous songs including:* Nine to Five (Grammy Award 1981). *Radio includes:* Grand Ole Opry, WSM Radio, Cass Walker Program. *Publication:* Dolly: My Life and Other Unfinished Business 1994, Dream More: Celebrate the Dreamer in You 2012. *Honours:* CMA Vocal Group of the Year (with Porter Wagoner) 1968, Vocal Duo of the Year 1970, 1971, Female Vocalist of the Year 1975, 1976, Country Star of the Year 1978, Nashville Metronome Award 1979, People's Choice 1980, ACM Female Vocalist of the Year 1980, ACM Vocal Event of the Year and Video of the Year (both for When I Get Where I'm Going, with Brad Paisley) 2006, Kennedy Center Honor 2006, US Songwriters' Hall of Fame Johnny Mercer Award 2007, Grammy Lifetime Achievement Award 2011. *Address:* PO Box 150307, Nashville, TN 37215, USA. *Website:* www.dollypartonmusic.net.

PARTON, Stella; American singer, songwriter, actress, speaker and author; b. 4 May 1949, Sevierville, Tenn.; sister of Dolly Parton. *Career:* solo artist 1955–. *Stage appearances:* The Best Little Whorehouse in Texas, Seven Brides for Seven Brothers, Pump Boys & Dinettes, Gentlemen Prefer Blondes. *Films:* The Color of Love, Ghost Town, Phoenix Falling, Seven to Midnight;

Television includes: The Dukes Of Hazzard, Live with Regis & Kathie Lee, Oprah!, Good Morning America, The Today Show, Crook & Chase, American Music Awards, Music City Tonight, Hee Haw, Entertainment Tonight, Grand Ole Opry. *Recordings include:* albums: In The Garden (Gospel), Stella And The Gospel Carrolls, I Want To Hold You In My Dreams Tonight (ASCAP Award (Songwriter)) 1975, Country Sweet, Stella Parton, Love Ya, The Best Of Stella Parton, So Far So Good, True To Me, Always Tomorrow, Stella Parton Favorites, Vol. 1, Picture In A Frame, A Woman's Touch, Anthology, Appalachian Blues, Blue Heart, Appalachian Gospel, Stella Parton Favorites, Vol. 2, Stella Parton Favorites, Vol. 3, Songwriter Sessions, Holiday Magic, Testimony, Hits Collection, Mountain Rose, American Coal, Tell It Sister Tell It. *Honours:* ASCAP Award (Recording Artist) for Stormy Weather, GBCM Award for Most Promising Int. Act, ASCAP Award (Recording Artist) for It's Not Funny Anymore, Tennessee Democratic Chair.'s Award 2001, Summerfest Country Female Vocalist and Entertainer 2001, Canadian Country Music Asscn (CCMA) Mainstream Country Artist 2002, CCMA Female Vocalist 2004, American Old-Time Country Music Hall of Fame Inductee 2006, Alabama Country and Gospel Music Hall of Fame Album of the Year 2006, Alabama Country and Gospel Music Hall of Fame Entertainer of the Year 2006. *Address:* PO Box 120871, Nashville, TN 37212-0871, USA. *Telephone:* (615) 924-6284. *E-mail:* stella@stellaparton.com. *Website:* www.stellaparton.com.

PARTRIDGE, Andy; musician (guitar), singer, songwriter and record producer; b. 11 Nov. 1953, Malta. *Career:* mem., XTC 1977–82, work as studio band only 1982–; numerous tours and live appearances; mem. send-up 60s group, The Dukes of Stratosphear 1985–87; producer 1983–, working with artists including The Mission, The Lilac Time, Peter Blegvad, Wallflowers, Woodentops. *Recordings include:* albums: as XTC: White Music 1978, Go 2 1978, Drums And Wires 1979, Black Sea 1980, English Settlement 1982, Waxworks: Some Singles 1977–82 1982, Mummer 1983, The Big Express 1984, The Compact XTC 1986, Skylarking 1986, Chips From The Chocolate Fireball 1987, Oranges And Lemons 1989, Nonsuch 1992, Fossil Fuel 1996, Transistor Blast 1998, Apple Venus Vol. I 1999, Homespun 1999, Wasp Star (Apple Venus Vol. 2) 2000, Homegrown 2001, Waspstrumental 2002, Fuzzy Warbles Vols 1–4 2002–03, The Fuzzy Warbles Collectors' Album 2006; solo: The Lure of Salvage 1980, Takeaway 1980, The Greatest Living Englishman (with Martin Newell) 1993, Through The Hill (with Harold Budd) 1994, Orpheus The Lowdown (with Peter Blegvad) 2004; as The Dukes of Stratosphear: 25 O'Clock 1985, Psonic Psunspot 1987. *Honours:* Edison Award 1982. *E-mail:* info@xtcidearecords.co.uk (office). *Website:* www.xtcidearecords.co.uk.

PARVEEN, Abida; Pakistani singer; b. 1954, Larkana, Sindh; d. of Ghulam Haider; m. Ghulam Hussain Sheikh (deceased); one s. two d. *Education:* attended father's music school; studied classical music with Salamat Ali Khan. *Career:* debut on Hyderabad Radio Station; repertoire includes classical music, ghazals, traditional Sufiana kalaam and Punjabi folk music; worldwide tours and performances before heads of state; made recordings of original works of Sufi poets. *Recordings include:* Pakistani Sufi Songs 1995, The Best of Abida Parveen 1997, Ho Jamalo 2000, Songs of the Mystics 2000, Tere Ishq Nachaya 2001, Raqs-e-Bismil 2001, Faiz by Abida 2001, Jahan E. Khusrau 2001, Visal – The Meeting Mystic Poets from the Hind & Mind 2002, Baba Bulleh Shah 2003, Mere Dil Se 2005, Ishq: l'Amour Absolu (Supreme Love) 2005, Svar Utsav 2006, Abida Parveen-The Sufi Queen 2011, Treasures Vol 1 2012, Lal De Rang Vich Rangi Aan 2012, Sufiana Safar 2012, Tera Lal Sakhi Mera Lai Sakhi 2012, Shaane-e-Ali 2012, Ghazal Ka Safar Vol 2 2013, Ru-e-Ali 2013, Treasures Vol 2 2014, Tasawwuf 2014. *Honours:* President's Award for Pride of Performance 1982, Sitara-i-Imtiaz Award 2005, Lifetime Achievement Award, Kaladharmi Begum Akhtar Academy of Ghaza, India 2012.

PASCAL, Michel; French electro-acoustic composer and academic; *Professor of Electro-acoustic Composition, Conservatoire de Nice;* b. 12 Oct. 1958, Avignon; m. Maxime Pascal; two d. *Education:* CNSM Paris, CNR Marseille, INA-GRM and IRCAM, Paris with I. Xenakis, H. Dutilleux, W. Lutosławski and L. Berio. *Career:* debut as asst of Jean Etienne Marie, CIRM, Nice 1985–87, for studio and Festival of Contemporary Music; composer in many fields, including acoustic, choir, instrumental, dance music, music for theatre, film, video and television production; as synthesist, performer and creator of the Studio Instrumental, works played on hyperinstruments with live electronics; Prof. of Electro-acoustic Composition, Conservatoire de Nice 1986–; Artistic Dir acousmatic festival Microfolies, Aix en Provence – Acousmonium Rime Monaco 2005–10; mem., SACEM, SACD, Rainbow Across Europe. *Compositions include:* Falaises et Emergences, for tape 1981, Voiles, for choir and synthesizers 1987, Protos, for symphonic orchestra 1989, Sonic Waters No. 2 1989, Nausicaä 1991, Berceuses 1992, Puzzle 1995–99, Puissance 3, for string trio 1997, V° Concours Noroit 1997, Répertoires Polychromes 2 1998, Répliques 2007, Beyond 2009. *Recordings:* albums: Contribution to Nausicaa, Centre de la Mer, Boulogne 1990, Sonic Waters, with Michel Redolfi-Berceuse/Albin Michel 1990, Répertoires Polychromes 1999, Puzzle 1999; videos: Mille Mètres sous la Jungle 1995, Les Grottes ornées de Borneo 1996; other: music for Luc Henri Fage's film, French national television. *Publications:* Les Nouveaux Gestes de la Musique 1999, La composition est-elle transmissible? 2010. *Address:* Conservatoire à Rayonnement Régional, 127 Avenue de Brancolar, 06364 Nice, France (office). *Telephone:* 4-97-13-50-00 (office). *Fax:* 4-97-13-50-25 (office). *E-mail:* info@crr

-nice.org (office); michel.pascal@freesbcc.fr (home). *Website:* www.crr-nice.org (office); studio-instrumental.org (home).

PASCOAL, Hermeto; Brazilian musician (multi-instrumentalist), arranger and composer; b. 22 June 1936, Lagoa da Canoa; brother of José Neto; m. Ilza da Silva Pascoal 1955; three s. three d. *Career:* accordion, flute, with Quarteto Novo –1969; solo artist 1970–; formed Hermeto Pascoal Group, playing at festivals, tours, on television and radio; mem. SACEM (France). *Recordings:* Quarteto Novo, 1967; Hermeto, 1979; A Musica Livre De Hermeto Pascoal, 1973; Slaves Mass, 1976; Zabumbe-bum-a, 1978; Montreux ao Vivo, 1978; Cerebro Magnetico, 1980; Hermeto Pascoal and Grupo, 1982; Lagoa da Canoa Municipalo de Arapiraca, 1984; Brasil Universo, 1986; So Nao Toca Quem Nao Quer, 1987; Por Diferentes Caminhos/Piano solo, 1988; Festa Dos Deuses, 1992; Hermeta Pascoal E Grupo, 1992; Eu E Eles, 1999; Calendário do Som, 2000; Mundo Verde Esperança, 2002; Chimarrão com Rapadura (with Aline Morena) 2006. *Honours:* Best Soloist, Associação Paulista de Criticos de Arte, Brazil, 1972; Best Group, Brazil, 1988; Best Cover and Best Tune: Pixitotina, Brazil, 1989; Concert of Year and Decade, Guardian, Q Magazine, 1994. *Address:* Rua Inácio Slompo 55, Santa Felicidade, 82320-070 Curitiba, Paraná, Brazil.

PASCU, Ioan Gyuri; Romanian teacher, songwriter, entertainer and actor, musician (guitar, drums), writer and radio, television producer; b. 31 Aug. 1961, Agnita; m. Daniela Marin, 15 Aug. 1993. *Education:* University of Cluj, Faculty of Philology; Private piano lessons. *Career:* Member, Divertis Group (humour, political satire shows) since 1990; Many radio and television shows, 1989–92; Soloist, 1991–; Established the Ioan Gyuri Pascu and The Blues Workers Band; International Jazz and Blues Festivals: Brasov, 1992; Bucharest, 1992; Russe, 1992; Brasov, 1993, 1994; International Rock Festivals: Bucharest, 1993; Dracula, Brasov, 1993; Skip Rock, Bucharest, 1994; International Pop Festival, Golden Stag, Brasov (record debut contest), 1993; Opened the Romanian tours of Beats International, 1993, Asia, 1994; Acted in Unforgettable Summer, by Lucian Pintilie (offically selected for Cannes film festival); TV specials: Stars Duel, 1993; VIP, 1993; Many Divertis Group shows, soloist in musical shows; mem, Divertis Cultural Asscn. *Compositions:* Over 30 songs; Original music for television film: Teapa, 1993; Stars School, 1995. *Recordings:* It Could Be, 1992; Mixed Grill, 1993; The Machine With Jazzoline, 1994; Video: Divertis Group, 1995. *Publications:* Short stories in Apostrof (literature magazine), 1990; Cuvantul magazine (serial). Showman of the Year: Pop Rock and Show magazine; Major Personality of the Year, 1993; The Song of the Year, The Songwriter of the Year, Radio Contact, 1994; Record of the Year, Vox, Pop, Rock magazine. *Website:* www.ioangyuripascu.ro.

PASILLAS, José Antonio, II; musician (drums); b. 26 April 1976. *Career:* started drumming 1990; founder mem., Incubus 1991–; tours and live appearances. *Recordings include:* albums: Fungus Amongus 1995, S.C.I.E.N.C.E. 1997, Make Yourself 1999, Morning View 2001, A Crow Left Of The Murder 2004, Light Grenades 2006, Monuments and Melodies 2009. *Honours:* Billboard Award for Modern Rock Single of the Year 2001. *Address:* c/o Epic Records, 550 Madison Avenue, New York, NY 10022, USA (office). *Website:* www.enjoyincubus.com.

PASKIN, Layo; producer, remixer and DJ; b. London, England. *Career:* opened London's The End nightclub with pnr, Mr C 1995; co-founder, End Recordings; mem., Killer Loop (with Mr C); mem., Layo and Bushwacka!. *Recordings include:* albums: Lowlife (with Bushwacka!) 1999, Night Works (with Bushwacka!) 2002, Feels Closer (with Bushwacka!) 2006. *E-mail:* mail@itb.co.uk. *E-mail:* info@olmetorecords.com. *Website:* www.layoandbushwacka.com.

PATTERSON, Jack Robert; British musician (bass guitar, keyboards), songwriter and singer; b. 1986, Birkenhead, England. *Education:* Jesus Coll., Cambridge. *Career:* Founder-mem. Clean Bandit (with brother Luke Patterson) 2009–; released debut single A+E 2012; toured UK with Disclosure 2013; released single Rather Be (with Jess Glynne) 2014; numerous collaborations with other artists including Noonie Bao, Sharna Bass, Gorgon City, Love Ssega, Kandaka Moore and Nikki Cislyn, Stylo G. *Recordings:* albums: with Clean Bandit: New Eyes 2014. *Honours:* Grammy Award for Best Dance Recording (for Rather Be) 2015. *Current Management:* c/o Machine Management, Studio 16, London Fields Studios, 11–17 Exmouth Place, London, E8 3RW, England. *Telephone:* (20) 7923-3502. *E-mail:* info@machinemanagement.co.uk. *Website:* machinemanagement.co.uk; cleanbandit.co.uk.

PATTERSON, Luke; British musician (drums) and songwriter; b. 1993, Birkenhead, England. *Career:* Founder-mem. Clean Bandit (with brother Jack Patterson) 2009–; released debut single A+E 2012; toured UK with Disclosure 2013; released single Rather Be (with Jess Glynne) 2014; numerous collaborations with other artists including Noonie Bao, Sharna Bass, Gorgon City, Love Ssega, Kandaka Moore and Nikki Cislyn, Stylo G. *Recordings:* albums: with Clean Bandit: New Eyes 2014. *Honours:* Grammy Award for Best Dance Recording (for Rather Be) 2015. *Current Management:* c/o Machine Management, Studio 16, London Fields Studios, 11–17 Exmouth Place, London, E8 3RW, England. *Telephone:* (20) 7923-3502. *E-mail:* info@machinemanagement.co.uk. *Website:* machinemanagement.co.uk; cleanbandit.co.uk.

PATTON, Mike; American singer, songwriter and dancer; b. 27 Jan. 1968, Eureka, Calif.; several c. *Career:* fmr mem. Mr Bungle 1985–2000; lead singer rock group, Faith No More 1988–98, 2009–; numerous int. concerts and festival appearances; mem. Fantômas 1998–; mem. Tomahawk, Mondo Cane; numerous collaborations; Co-founder of label, Ipecac Recordings. *Film scores:* A Perfect Place 2008, Crank: High Voltage 2009, The Solitude of Prime Numbers 2011, The Place Beyond the Pines 2013. *Recordings include:* albums: with Faith No More: The Real Thing 1989, Live At Brixton Academy 1991, Angel Dust 1992, King For A Day... Fool For A Lifetime 1995, Adult Themes for Voice 1996, Pranzo Oltranzis 1997, Album of the Year 1997, Faith No More, Greatest Hits 1998, Sol Invictus 2015; with Mr Bungle: Mr Bungle 1991, Disco Volante 1995, California 1999; with Fantômas: Fantômas 1999, Director's Cut 2001, Delìrium Còrdia 2004, Suspended Animation 2005; with Tomahawk: Tomahawk 2001, Mit Gas 2003, Anonymous 2007, Oddfellows 2013; solo: Adult Themes for Voice 1996, Pranzo Oltranzista 1997, Peeping Tom 2006, Mondo Cane 2010. *E-mail:* info@ipecac.com. *Website:* www.ipecac.com; www.fnm.com.

PATTULLO, Gordon James; British musician (accordion); b. 8 Sept. 1961, Dundee, Scotland; m. June Elspeth McLaren 1984, two s. one d. *Education:* Dundee Accordion School of Music. *Career:* concert tours world-wide with Andy Stewart Show 1977–; TV appearances; mem. Musicians' Union. *Compositions include:* The Furrows End. *Recordings include:* Hand Made in Scotland, Sure as the Sunrise, Gordon Pattullo, his Accordion and his Friends (DVD) Vols 1 and 2, 7 Star Ceilidh. *Publication:* The Furrows End. *Honours:* Jr Accordion Champion of Scotland 1974, Guest Artist of the Year, Nat. Asscn of Accordion and Fiddle Clubs 2007. *Address:* Tullybaccart Farmhouse, Coupar Angus, Blairgowrie, Perthshire, PH13 9LA, Scotland. *Telephone:* (1382) 581265. *E-mail:* gordonpattullo@hotmail.com. *Website:* www.gordonpattullo.co.uk.

PAUL, Amit Sebastian; Swedish singer; b. 29 Oct. 1983, Boden. *Education:* Kungsholmens School, Stockholm. *Career:* mem., A*Teens 1998–2004. *Recordings include:* albums: The Abba Generation 1999, Teen Spirit 2001. *Honours:* Viva Music Award for Best Int. Newcomer 2000. *Website:* amitpaul.se.

PAUL, Oskar; songwriter, producer and programmer. *Career:* worked with as prod. and songwriter: Isabelle A, Marc Almond, David Chavet, Hear'say, Emma Holland, Ladies First, Jamie Pearce, S Club 7, Steps; worked with as programmer: Curve, Depeche Mode, Seal, SJ.

PAUL, Sean; Jamaican reggae artist and DJ; b. (Sean Paul Henriques), 8 Jan. 1973. *Career:* began music career performing in Jamaican dancehalls; solo artist 1996–. *Recordings:* albums: Stage One 2000, Dutty Rock (Grammy Award for Best Reggae Album 2004) 2002, The Trinity 2005, Imperial Blaze 2009, Tomahawk Technique 2012. *Honours:* American Music Award for Best Pop/Rock Male Artist 2006, MOBO Award for Best Reggae Act 2006, 2009, 2013. *Current Management:* William Morris Agency, 1325 Avenue of the Americas, New York, NY 10019, USA. *Telephone:* (212) 586-5100. *Fax:* (212) 246-3583. *Current Management:* c/o Jerome Hamilton, Headline Entertainment, 8 Haughton Avenue, Kingston 10; c/o Jeremy Harding, 2 Hard Records, 8 Jacks Hill Road, Kingston 6, Jamaica. *Telephone:* (876) 754-1526 (Headline); (876) 960-0382 (2 Hard Records). *Fax:* (876) 906-3634 (Headline). *E-mail:* headline@headlinejamaica.com. *Website:* www.headlinejamaica.com; www.allseanpaul.com.

PAULIK, Dalibor; Croatian composer, musician (piano) and theatre critic; b. 22 Dec. 1953, Zagreb; m. Vesna Paulik, 7 June 1980, one s. *Education:* MSc, Theatrology; Professor, Music theatre; Secondary music school, private music seminars. *Career:* Croatian and international festivals of popular music; 500 concerts with popular Croatian singers; Music for theatre and television; Festivals in: Ireland; Latin America; Finland; Los Angeles; Croatia (Zagreb, Krapina, Split); Sarjevo; Songs for organizations: Stars of Hope (Sweden); World For Two (UK); mem, Croatian Composers' Society (FIDOF). *Compositions:* Over 200 include: Your Face In My Mirror; Goodbye Is Not For You; Love Is A Game; Never In My Life; Memories; The Violin Song; Stars of Hope; Today I'm Sad My Love; Together Forever; Dancing With The Moonlight. *Publications:* Scientific publications of HAZU; Who Is Who In Croatia; Directory of Croatian Composers Society. *Honours:* 20 at Croatian festivals; 1 in Ireland. *E-mail:* dpaulik@net.hr. *Website:* www.adu.hr.

PAUPEQUENO, Pupilo; Brazilian musician (drums). *Career:* mem. mangue beat band, Nação Zumbi; mem., Seu Jorge and Almaz 2010–. *Recordings include:* albums: with Nação Zumbi: CSNZ 1998, Rádio SAMBA 2000, Nação Zumbi 2002, Futura 2005, Fome de Tudo 2007; with Seu Jorge and Almaz: Seu Jorge and Almaz 2010. *Honours:* Award for Best Group, São Paulo Asscn of Art Critics (Nação Zumbi) 2005. *Address:* c/o Trama, Rua Rosa Gaeta Lázara, 93 Brooklin Novo, 04570-905 São Paulo, Brazil. *Website:* www.nacaozumbi.com.br; www.seujorgealmaz.com.

PAUSINI, Laura; Italian singer and songwriter. *Career:* solo artist, sings in Italian, Spanish and English; numerous concert appearances. *Recordings include:* albums: Laura Pausini 1993, Laura 1994, Le Cose Che Vivi 1996, La Mia Risposta 1998, Tra Te E Il Mare 2000, Lo Mejor de Laura Pausini 2002, From the Inside (in English) 2002, Escucha (Grammy Award for Best Latin Pop Album 2006, Latin Grammy Award for Best Female Pop Vocal Album 2006) 2005, Io Canto (also recorded as Yo Canto in Spanish; Latin Grammy Award for Best Female Pop Vocal Album 2007) 2006, Primavera in Anticipio

(Latin Grammy Award for Best Female Pop Vocal Album 2009) 2008. *Honours:* Festival de la Cancion Italiana 1993, World Music Award for Best Selling Italian Artist 1994, 2003, 2007, Premio Lo Nuestro for Most Promising Latin Artist, Latin Grammy Award for Best Female Pop Vocalist 2005. *Address:* Atlantic Records, 1290 Avenue of the Americas, New York, NY 10104, USA (office). *Telephone:* (212) 707-2000 (office). *Fax:* (212) 405-5475 (office). *E-mail:* info@laurapausini.com (office). *Website:* www.atlanticrecords.com (office); www.laurapausini.com.

PAWLOWSKI, Mauro; Belgian musician (guitar). *Career:* fmr lead singer, Evil Superstars, Mitsoobishi Jacson; mem., dEUS 2004–. *Recordings include:* albums: Pocket Revolution 2005, Vantage Point 2008, Keep You Close 2011, Following Sea 2012. *Current Management:* c/o Christian Pierre, Musickness Bvba, Rozenlaan 57, 2970 Schilde, Belgium. *Telephone:* (3) 254-01-25. *E-mail:* info@musickness.be. *Website:* musickness.be. *E-mail:* mauroworld@outlook.com. *Website:* www.mauroworld.net; www.deus.be.

PAXTON, Tom, BFA; American folk singer, songwriter and writer; b. 31 Oct. 1937, Chicago, IL; m. Margaret Ann Cummings 1963; three d. *Education:* Univ. of Oklahoma. *Career:* folk recording artist 1962–; early concerts on Greenwich Village circuit; world-wide tours and concerts 1960–; mem. bd of dirs, Kerrville Folk Festival 1990; mem. ASCAP, AFTRA, AFofM, Screen Actors' Guild, World Folk Music Asscn (hon. chair. of bd). *Compositions include:* Lyndon Johnson Told The Nation; Talkin' Vietnam Pot Luck Blues, Leaving London, The Hostage (also recorded by Judy Collins). *Recordings include:* albums: Ramblin' Boy 1964, Ain't That News 1965, Outward Bound 1968, Morning Again 1968, The Things I Notice Now 1969, Tom Paxton 6 1970, The Compleat Tom Paxton 1971, How Come The Sun 1971, Peace Will Come 1972, New Songs Old Friends 1973, Something In My Life 1975, Saturday Night 1976, Heroes 1978, Up and Up 1980, The Paxton Report 1981, In The Orchard 1985, One Million Lawyers and Other Disasters 1985, Even A Gray Day 1986, And Loving You 1988, Politics – Live 1989, Storyteller 1989, Suzy is a Rocker 1992, Goin' to the Zoo 1997, I Can't Help Wonder Where I'm Bound 1999, Live From Mountain Stage 2001, Under American Skies 2001, Looking for the Moon 2002, Comedians and Angels 2008; for children: A Child's Christmas 1997, I've Got a Yo-Yo 1997, Goin' to the Zoo 1997, Fun Food Songs 1999, Your Shoes, My Shoes 2001. *Publications:* Ramblin' Boy and Other Songs 1965, Tom Paxton Anthology 1971, Politics 1989, The Authentic Guitar of Tom Paxton 1989, The Tom Paxton Children's Song Book 1990; children's books: Jennifer's Rabbit 1988, Belling The Cat 1990, Englebert The Elephant 1990, Aesop's Fables Retold In Verse 1988, Androcles and The Lion 1991. *Honours:* BBC Radio 2 Folk Lifetime Achievement Award 2005. *Current Management:* Fleming Artists, 543 North Main Street, Ann Arbor, MI 48104, USA. *Telephone:* (734) 995-9066. *Fax:* (734) 662-6502. *E-mail:* contact@flemingartists.com. *Website:* www.flemingartists.com; www.tompaxton.com.

PAYNE, Douglas (Dougie); British musician (bass); b. 14 Nov. 1972, Scotland. *Career:* mem., Travis, 1997–; numerous tours, festivals and television appearances. *Recordings include:* albums: Good Feeling 1997, The Man Who 1999, The Invisible Band 2001, 12 Memories 2003, The Boy With No Name 2007, Ode to J. Smith 2008. *Honours:* Q Magazine Award for Best Single 1999, Select Magazine Award for Album of the Year 1999, BRIT Awards for Best British Group 2000, 2002, Best British Album 2000. *Current Management:* Wildlife Entertainment, Unit F, 21 Heathmans Road, London SW6 4TJ, England. *Telephone:* (20) 7371-7008. *Fax:* (20) 7371-7708. *E-mail:* info@wildlife-entertainment.com. *Website:* www.travisonline.com.

PAYNE, Freda; American singer and actress; b. 19 Sept. 1945, Detroit, MI; m. Gregory Abbott 1976, one s. *Education:* Detroit Institute of Musical Arts, studied acting with Al Mancini. *Career:* began singing career aged 17; toured with Quincy Jones; numerous tours. *Stage appearances include:* Hallelujah Baby (musical), Linda in Lost in the Stars, The Book of Numbers, Daddy Goodness, Ain't Misbehavin', Sophisticated Ladies, Blues in the Night (musical) 1990–91, Jelly's Last Jam (musical drama). *Television appearances:* Freda Payne and The Stylistics, The Legendary Ladies of Rock (HBO), host of talk show Today's Black Woman. *Recordings include:* albums: After the Lights Go Down Low and Much More!! 1964, How Do You Say I Don't Love You Anymore 1966, Band of Gold 1970, Contact 1971, Reaching Out 1973, Payne and Pleasure 1974, Out of Payne Comes Love 1975, Stares and Whispers 1977, Supernatural High 1978, Hot 1979, I Hate Barney; An Evening with Freda Payne: Live 1995, Live in Concert 1999, Lost In Love, 2000, Come See About Me 2001, On the Inside 2007. *Honours:* Dame of Malta – The Sovereign Military and Hospital Order of St John of Jerusalem 1994; Drama-Logue Award for Best Ensemble Performance (for Blues in the Night) 1990. *E-mail:* utopiaartists@aol.com. *Website:* www.fredapayne.com.

PAYNE, John Devereux; American musician and music teacher; b. 16 Dec. 1945, Virginia, USA; m. Francine Rota, four s. *Education:* BA, Harvard University, 1972. *Career:* played and recorded with Van Morrison 1968, Bonnie Raitt 1972–78; led own jazz band 1973–77; toured with Dave Bromberg 1973–74, Phoebe Snow 1977, Michael Franks 1978, 1979; directs his own music school; plays local Boston area jazz clubs. *Compositions:* Scenes From A Journey; Rush; Reaching. *Recordings:* albums: John Payne's First Album 1975, Bedtime Stories 1976, The Razor's Edge 1978, Hurt 1992, Gotta Live Together; with Van Morrison: Astral Weeks 1968; with Bonnie Raitt: Give It Up 1972; with Krisanthi Pappas: My Backyard, 2000. *Honours:* Best of Boston Jazz Bands, 1970s. *Current Management:* John Payne Music Center, 9A Station Street, Brookline, MA 02445, USA. *E-mail:* jpayne5355@aol.com. *Website:* www.artsforall.com/jp.html; www.johnpayneband.com.

PAYNE, Les Alexander; singer, songwriter and musician (guitar, keyboards); b. 22 Aug. 1943, Newport, Isle of Wight; m. 1st Brigitte Jean Wilson 1965 (divorced 1971); one s.; m. 2nd Rosalind Jean Butler 1974 (divorced 1993); two s.; m. 3rd Pennie Hawkes 1994; one step-s. one step-d. *Career:* solo artist; numerous concerts, radio and television broadcasts; mem. PRS, Musicians' Union. *Recordings include:* Who Am I?, 1971; I Can't Help To Feel The Love, 1974; Don't Say Goodbye, 1975; Who Do You Love, 1978; By Yourside, 1979; No Money, 1979; Exposure album, 1979; Who Will Be The Winner, (single in Japan), 1982; album: 47 Summers.

PAYNE, Liam James; British singer; b. 29 Aug. 1993, Wolverhampton; s. of Geoff Payne and Karen Payne. *Education:* City of Wolverhampton Coll. *Career:* mem. One Direction 2010–; finished third in The X Factor (UK), ITV 1 2010; signed to Syco Records 2010; participated in X Factor Live Tour 2011; released debut single 2011; debut album first by a British group to debut at number one on USA Billboard 200 album chart 2011; numerous TV appearances and tours; group hiatus 2016–. *Recordings include:* with One Direction: albums: Up All Night 2011, Take Me Home (American Music Award for Favorite Album 2013) 2012, Midnight Memories (American Music Award for Favorite Album 2014) 2013, Four 2014, Made in the A.M. 2015. *DVDs:* Up All Night: the Live Tour 2012. *Publications:* One Direction: Forever Young 2011, One Direction: The Official Annual 2012 2011, Dare to Dream: Life as One Direction 2011, Where We Are: Our Band, Our Story 2013, Who We Are: Our Official Autobiography 2014. *Honours:* numerous including: with One Direction: Bambi Pop Int. Award 2012, BBC Radio 1 Teen Awards for Best British Music Act 2012, for Best British Single 2012, 2013, 2014, 2015, for Best British Group 2013, 2015, BRIT Awards for Best British Single (What Makes You Beautiful) 2012, for BRITs Global Success 2013, for Best British Video (for You & I) 2015, JIM Awards (Flemish TV) for Best International Newcomer 2012, for Best Group 2013, for Best Pop 2013, MTV Europe Music Awards for Best New Act 2012, for Best UK & Ireland Act 2012, 2013, 2014, for Biggest Fans 2012, 2014, for Best Pop Act 2013, 2014, 2015, for Best Live Act 2014, for Best Worldwide Act (Europe North) 2014, MTV Video Music Awards Brazil Award for International Artist 2012, MTV Video Music Awards for Best New Artist 2012, for Best Pop Video and Most Share-Worthy Video (both What Makes You Beautiful) 2012, for Song of the Summer (for Best Song Ever) 2013, 4Music Video Honours Awards for Best Breakthrough and Best Group 2012, ARIA Music Awards for Best Int. Artist 2012, 2013, 2014, Billboard Music Awards for Top Duo/Group 2013, 2015, for Top New Artist 2013, for Top Pop Artist 2013, for Top Touring Artist 2015, American Music Awards for Favorite Band, Duo or Group 2013, 2014, 2015, for Artist of the Year 2014, 2015. *Current Management:* c/o Modest! Management, The Matrix Complex, 91 Peterborough Road, London, SW6 3BU, England. *E-mail:* info@modestmanagement.com. *Website:* www.modestmanagement.com; www.onedirectionmusic.com.

PAYNE, Sean; British musician (drums). *Career:* Founder mem., The Zutons 2002–. *Recordings include:* albums: Who Killed... The Zutons? 2004, Tired of Hanging Around 2006, You Can Do Anything 2008.

PAYTON, Nicholas; American musician (trumpet); b. 26 Sept. 1973, New Orleans; s. of Walter Payton; m. Cecilia Payton 2003. *Education:* New Orleans Center for Creative Arts, Univ. of New Orleans. *Career:* regular performer at Jazz at Lincoln Center, New York 1990s; has worked with Doc Cheatham, Hank Jones, Elvin Jones, Ray Brown; tours of USA and in Europe; mem., The Blue Note 7 2009–. *Recordings include:* From This Moment 1994, Gumbo Nouveau 1996, Doc Cheatham & Nicholas Payton (Grammy Award for Best Instrumental Solo) 1997, Payton's Place 1998, Nick@Night 2000, Dear Louis 2001, Sonic Trance 2003, Mysterious Shorter 2006, Into the Blue 2008, Mosaic (with The Blue Note 7) 2009, Bitches 2011. *Current Management:* c/o Anna M. Sala, AMS Artists. *Telephone:* (201) 928-0513. *Fax:* (201) 215-9589. *E-mail:* amsala@aol.com. *Website:* amsartists.com; www.nicholaspayton.com.

PAYTON, Nicholas (Nik) Edward, GCLCM; British jazz musician (saxophone, clarinet) and composer; *Artistic Director, Jazz Festival Brasil;* b. 14 Feb. 1972, Birmingham; m.; one c. *Education:* City of Leeds Coll. of Music, studied with Bob Wilber. *Career:* toured with The Duke Ellington Orchestra; lead alto saxophone with The Pasadena Roof Orchestra, The Charleston Chasers; major jazz festivals in UK, Europe and S America, including North Sea Jazz Festival, Nairn Jazz Festival, Umbria Jazz, Pori Jazz Festival, Edinburgh, Cork, Breda, Jazz Gerais, Ouro Preto; extensive touring in USA, Europe and S America; major concerts at the Southbank Centre, London (International Jazz Orchestra), Kuala Lumpur, Hong Kong; numerous appearances on TV and radio; performed with The Duke Ellington Orchestra, Maria Schneider, Wynton Marsalis, Bob Wilber, Kenny Davern, Judy Carmichael, Spike Robinson, Marty Grosz, Mark Shane; Artistic Dir Jazz Festival Brasil 2009–; Artistic Dir Estação New Orleans. *Films:* performs on soundtracks of Olga, Filhos do Vento, The Comedian Harmonists. *Recordings:* Henderson Stomp 1993, Pleasure Mad 1995, Steaming South 1996, Rompin' With Buck 1998, Swing That Music 1998, What A Life 1999, The Pasadena Roof Orchestra Live At Regents Park 1999, Turn On The Heat 2000, Misty Morning 2001, If Dreams Come True 2001, Smilin' Skies 2002, Here And Now 2002, Mists of Avalon 2004, Jimmy/Nik Project 2005, In The Spirit of Swing 2006, Swingin' the Changes (with Bob Wilber) 2008, Come and

Get It (with Judy Carmichael) 2009. *E-mail:* info@nikpayton.com (office). *Website:* www.nikpayton.com; www.cdbaby.com/nikpayton.

PAZ, Ania; Peruvian musician (piano) and composer; b. 18 June 1966, Lima. *Education:* Bachelor of Music, University of Detmold, Germany; Master of Music, University of the Arts, Philadelphia, USA. *Career:* Performances at festivals including International Jazz Festival, Lima, 1996, Jazz Astwood Festivals, 1995, 1997, 1998, San Jose Jazz Festival, 1998; Numerous television appearances; mem, ASCAP. *Compositions:* San Pedro de Macorrs; Classic Night; San Francisco. *Recordings:* Meta Arará. *Honours:* ASCAP Special award; Hon. Mention, USA Songwriting Contest, 1998; Plaque of Recognition, University of Missouri ALARA Conference. *Address:* c/o Jazzymas, Manzana D-29 A, Residencial Villa Claudia, Altos de Arroyo Hondo I, Santo Domingo, Dominican Republic. *E-mail:* jazzymas@hispavista.com.

PEACOCK, Dave; British musician (bass guitar, banjo, guitar) and singer; b. 24 May 1945; m. Sue Peacock (died 2009). *Career:* fmr mem., The Tumbleweeds, Black Claw; mem. cockney duo, Chas & Dave (with Chas Hodges) 1960s–2009, 2011–; world-wide tours, numerous radio, television and live appearances. *Recordings include:* albums: with Chas & Dave: Oily Rags 1974, One Fing 'n' Anuvver 1975, Rockney 1978, Don't Give a Monkeys 1979, Mustn't Grumble 1981, Joblot 1982, Well Pleased 1984, Flying 1987, The EMI Years 2005, That's What Happens 2013. *Current Management:* Barry Collings Entertainments, 21a Clifftown Road, Southend-on-Sea, Essex SS1 1AB, England. *Telephone:* (1702) 201880. *Fax:* (1702) 333309. *E-mail:* barry-collings@btconnect.com. *E-mail:* mail@chasndave.com (office). *Website:* www.chasndave.com.

PEACOCK, Olly; British musician (guitar, drums, percussion, piano); b. 1974, England. *Career:* founding mem., Gomez 1996–; numerous concerts, festival, radio and television appearances. *Recordings include:* albums: Bring It On 1998, Liquid Skin 1999, Abandoned Shopping Trolley Hotline 2000, In Our Gun 2002, Out West: Live at the Fillmore 2005, How We Operate 2006, A New Tide 2009. *Honours:* Mercury Music Prize 1998. *Current Management:* c/o Jason Colton, Red Light Management, 321 East Main Street, Charlottesville, VA 22902, USA. *Telephone:* (434) 245-4900. *Fax:* (434) 245-4933. *E-mail:* gomez@redlightmanagement.com. *Website:* www.redlightmanagement.com. *E-mail:* gomez@gomeztheband.com (office). *Website:* www.gomeztheband.com.

PEAKE, Ryan; Canadian musician (guitar) and singer; b. 1 March 1973. *Career:* mem. rock band, Nickelback 1996–; extensive tours. *Recordings include:* albums: Curb 1996, The State 1999, Silver Side Up (Juno Award for Best Rock Album 2002) 2001, The Long Road 2003, All The Right Reasons (Juno Award for Best Rock Album 2006, American Music Award for Favorite Pop/Rock Album 2006, Billboard Award for Rock Album of the Year 2006) 2005, Dark Horse (Juno Award for Album of the Year 2009) 2008, Here and Now 2011, No Fixed Address 2014. *Honours:* Juno Award for Best New Group 2001, Best Group, Best Single (for How You Remind Me) 2002, MuchMusic Video Award for Best Video (for Too Bad), Best Rock Video (for How You Remind Me) 2002, Juno Award for Best Group 2006, 2009, Billboard Award for Artist Duo/Group of the Year, for Hot 100 Artist Duo/Group of the Year 2006, American Music Award for Favorite Pop/Rock Band, Duo or Group 2007, Juno Fan Choice Award 2009. *Address:* c/o Roadrunner Records Inc., 902 Broadway, Eighth Floor, New York, NY 10010, USA. *Website:* www.nickelback.com.

PÉAN, Denis; French singer, poet, lyricist and musician (keyboard). *Career:* Founding mem., Lo'jo Triban, later renamed Lo'jo 1982–; helped organize inaugural Festival in the Desert, Sahara Desert 2001. *Recordings include:* albums: Depuis Très Longtemps 1989, International Courabou 1990, Fils de Zamal 1993, Sin Acabar 1996, Mojo Radio 1998, Bohême de Cristal 2000, L'Une des siens/Au cabaret sauvage 2002, Ce Soir Là 2003, Bazar Savant 2006, Cosmophono 2009. *Stage productions:* Décrocher La Lune (with Companie Jo Bithume) 1988, Dechpouk ze World (with Companie Jo Bithume) 1991, Triban de Lo'jo (with ZUR) 1994. *Publications:* Les Passagers ordinaires des temps 1996, Sommeil Sommeil 2000. *E-mail:* lojo@lojo.org (office). *Website:* www.lojo.org.

PEARCE, Dave; British DJ, broadcaster and company director; b. 14 June 1963. *Career:* began career as DJ on pirate radio, Radio Jackie, South London and in clubs; presented Funk Fantasy, BBC Radio London; created and presented BBC's first hip hop show, A Fresh Start to the Week; helped create BBC's first dance show, Behind the Beat; presenter, BBC GLR nightly dance show; first presenter signed to launch Kiss 100; joined BBC Radio 1 1995, hosting Early Breakfast Show; Weekend Breakfast Presenter 1997–99; Dance Anthems 1998–; also int. club DJ; est. Reachin' Records; A&R Dir, Nulife Records; Founder and A&R Dir, Nulife Records. *Radio:* Kiss FM, BBC Radio 1, BBC Radio 2, BBC 6 Music. *Television:* presenter, Dance Years (ITV), Behind the Beat (BBC 2). *Recordings:* Dave Pearce Dance Anthems compilations; mixed Transcendental Euphoria, Mixed Delirium, Vols 1 and 2; soundtrack to film South West 9 (Best Movie Soundtrack, British Independent Film Awards 2001); Dave Pearce Trance Anthems, Ministry Of Sound. *Honours:* Sony Silver Award for Best Drivetime Presenter. *Address:* PO Box 5181, Brighton, BN2 1AL, England (office). *Website:* www.davepearce.co.uk.

PEARSON, Dan; American musician (bass guitar). *Career:* founder mem., American Music Club 1983–96, 2003–04. *Recordings:* albums: The Restless Stranger 1986, Engine 1987, California 1988, United Kingdom 1990, Ever-

clear 1991, Mercury 1993, San Francisco 1994, Love Songs for Patriots 2004. *Current Management:* Bob Andrews, Undertow Music Management, 4217 W Grace Street, Chicago, IL 60641, USA. *Telephone:* (773) 205-9823. *Website:* www.undertowmusic.com.

PEARSON, John; British musician (6- and 12-string guitar) and singer; b. 5 Oct. 1948, Liverpool. *Career:* leader, John Pearson' Blues and Beyond; collaborations with Alexis Korner, Davey Graham, Jo Ann Kelly, Bert Jansch, Sonny Terry and Brownie McGhee, Louisiana Red, Rory Gallagher, Big Moose Walker, Woody Mann, Wizz Jones, Cephas and Wiggins, Roy Rogers and his Delta Rhythm Kings. *Recordings:* albums: solo: Drive My Blues Away 1989, Streamline Train 1990, Busy Bootin' 1992 (with Roger Hubbard), Grasshoppers In My Pillow 1995; with: John Pearson's Blues and Beyond: Rhythm Oil 2000, Just Blowed In Your Town 2002, Rhythm Oil, Eucalypso Furioso. *E-mail:* john@johnpearsonblues.com (office). *Website:* www.johnpearsonblues.com.

PEART, Neil; Canadian musician (drums); b. 12 Sept. 1952, Hamilton, ON. *Career:* mem. of rock group, Rush 1974–; tours and live appearances. *Recordings include:* albums: Rush 1974, Fly By Night 1975, Caress of Steel 1975, 2112 1976, All the World's a Stage 1976, A Farewell to Kings 1977, Archives 1978, Hemispheres 1978, Permanent Waves 1980, Moving Pictures 1981, Exit... Stage Left 1981, Signals 1982, Grace Under Pressure 1984, Power Windows 1985, Hold Your Fire 1987, A Show of Hands 1988, Presto 1989, Chronicles 1990, Roll the Bones 1991, Counterparts 1993, Test for Echo 1996, Retrospective I 1997, Retrospective II 1997, Different Stages 1998, Vapor Trails 2002, The Spirit of Radio 2003, Rush in Rio 2003, Feedback 2004, R30 2005, Replay 2006, Snakes & Arrows 2007, Clockwork Angels 2012. *Honours:* Juno Awards for Most Promising Group 1975, Best Group 1978, 1979;Official Ambassadors of Music, Canadian Govt 1979. *E-mail:* tag@neilpeart.net; info@rush.net. *Website:* www.neilpeart.net; www.rush.com.

PEDERSEN, Karl-Erik; Danish singer, songwriter, musician (guitar, bass) and music teacher; b. 17 Nov. 1960, Hobro, Jutland; m. Anne Iben Hansen. *Education:* university. *Career:* mem. of band, Yellow Moon; played concerts in Denmark, Sweden, Finland, Iceland; live concerts on national radio; touring festivals, with Tears for Jeanie 1998; touring as a solo artist 1998; mem. KODA, Danish Jazz Beat and Folk Authors, Danish Musicians' Union. *Compositions:* songwriter for: Nikolaj and Piloterne, 1989; Björn Afzelius (Sweden), 1994; Kim C. (Denmark), 1994; music for films, documentaries with director Ole Henning Hansen. *Recordings include:* Albums: Tears For Jeanie, 1997; Fishjoint, 1997; Album with Yellow Moon; Det Kinesiske Hav, 1989; Nitton Ar, 1994; Out There, 1997; You Gotta Believe It, 1997; Days, 1997; Crawling To You, 1998; with Naked Fish: Takin' It To The Bone, 2001. *Address:* Terp Skovvej 46, 8260 Viby J, Denmark.

PEDERSEN, Leonardo; Danish musician (saxophone, clarinet, flute) and songwriter; *Leader, Leonardo Pedersen's Jazzkapel;* b. (Hans Leonardo Pedersen), 2 July 1942, Copenhagen; s. of Peter Leonardo Pedersen and Lilli Pedersen; m. Annelise Pedersen 1972; one s. one d. *Career:* formed first jazz band in 1958, becoming Leonardo Pedersen's Jazzkapel 1962; tours of Germany, Scandinavia, Eastern Europe, Italy, France, Belgium, Spain, Greenland, UK, USA; performed with numerous leading jazz artists, including Albert Nicolas, Ben Webster, Benny Waters, Al Grey, Bennie Bailey, Harry 'Sweets' Edison and Eddie 'Lockjaw' Davis, Abdul Ibrahim, Johnny Griffin, Cootie Williams, Svend Asmussen, Etta Cameron; appearances on nat. and int. TV and radio; also played with Barbarossa, 1978–88, Van Dango 1986–89, The Original Danish Polcalypso Orchestra 1989–, Hans Knudsen Jumpband 1992–, Zebrass 2001–; studio musician with various bands; currently songwriter musician with bands St Croix, USA. *Recordings:* with Leonardo Pedersen's Jazzkapel: Danish Traditional Jazz 1963, Leonardo Pedersens Jazzkapel 1975, Leonardo Pedersen's Jazzkapel with Harry 'Sweets' Eddison, Eddie 'Lockjaw' Davis and Richard Boone 1977, I Want A Roof 1994, Portalen Live 2000, Swinging the Blues 2002, Evil Gal Blues 2007, The Danish Connection 2007, The First Fifty Years 2012; with Polcalypso: Karlekammeret 1989, Polcalypso II 1991, The Original Danish Polcalypso Orchestra featuring James 'Jamesie' Brewster 1996, SE ACABO Polcalypso & Jamesie Live 2000; with Hans Knudsen Jumpband: So Long John 1994, Jump In Focus 1997, Caldonia 2002, Every Day Hans Knudsen Jumpband og Troels Jensen 2011; with Zebrass: En Rose Så Jeg Skyde 2001, Zebrass på Afveje 2002, Safari 2004, N'city Blues feat. Hans Leonardo Pedersen 2010, En æften med Flemming Fuglsang i Galleri Stalden 2012, Vejen til Loussa/Peter Abrahamsen 2012. *Honours:* winner, annual jazz competition 1962. *Address:* Bisserup Havnevej 62, 4243 Rude, Denmark (home). *Telephone:* 55-45-92-14 (home); 39-69-05-25 (home); 21-95-39-69 (office). *E-mail:* mail@leonardo-music.dk (home). *Website:* www.leonardo-pedersen.dk.

PEGG, David; British musician (bass guitar, guitar, mandolin) and producer; b. 2 Nov. 1947, Birmingham; m. Christine 1966, one s. one d. *Career:* mem. of various Birmingham bands playing R&B; double bass, Ian Campbell Folk Group; mem., Fairport Convention, 1969–79, 1985–, Jethro Tull, 1979–96; sessions 1970s, with many folk artists, including Nick Drake, John Martyn, Sandy Denny, Ralph McTell; co-organizer, Cropredy Festival with Christine Pegg; founder and owner, Woodworm Studios, 1978–; mem. Musicians' Union, Mechanical-Copyright Protection Soc., Performing Artists Media Rights Asscn. *Recordings include:* with Fairport Convention: What We Did On Our Holidays, 1969; Unhalfbricking, 1969; Liege and Lief, 1970; Full House, 1970; Angel Delight, 1971; Babbacombe Lee, 1971; A Bonny Band Of Roses, 1977;

Red and Gold, 1989; Fairport Convention, 1990; Them Five Seasons, 1991; Jewel In The Crown, 1995; Old-New-Borrowed-Blue, 1996; Who Knows Where The Time Goes?, 1997; Encore, Encore, 1997; Fairport Convention, Woodworm Years, 1998; Wood and the Wire, 2000; XXXV, 2002; Heyday: BBC Radio Sessions 1968–69, 2002, Over the Next Hill 2004; with Jethro Tull: albums 1979–96. *Honours:* Midland Beat Bassist of the Year, 1967; Grammy Award for Crest of a Knave, with Jethro Tull, 1988. *Address:* Fairport Convention Ltd, PO Box 263, Chipping Norton OX7 9DF, England; 22 Britannia Wharf, Britannia Road, Banbury, OX16 5PS, England (home). *Telephone:* (1295) 251447 (home). *E-mail:* mattygroovesrecs@aol.com (office); peggyonthebass@aol.com (home). *Website:* www.fairportconvention.com (office).

PEKAREK, Neyla Michel Collins; American folk rock musician (cello, piano) and singer; b. 1986. *Education:* Univ. of Northern Colorado. *Career:* fmr teacher; mem. The Lumineers 2010–, released debut EP 2011; numerous tours. *Recordings:* album: The Lumineers 2012. *Current Management:* c/o Christen Greene and David Meinert, Onto Entertainment, 2611 5th Avenue, Seattle, WA 98121-1517, USA. *Address:* c/o Dualtone Records, Dualtone Music Group, 203 North 11th Street, Suite B, Nashville, TN 37206, USA (office). *Telephone:* (615) 320-0620 (office). *Fax:* (615) 320-0692 (office). *E-mail:* info@dualtone.com (office); info@thelumineers.com. *Website:* www.dualtone.com (office); www.thelumineers.com.

PELLEN, Jacques; French musician (guitar); b. April 1957, Brest. *Education:* University. *Career:* European tours, 1980–95; Celtic Procession (guest Kenny Wheeler), 1991; Europe Jazz Festival, Le Mans, 1994; Festival Quimper (guest Didier Lockwood); Zénith Paris, with Dan Ar Bras, 1995. *Recordings:* Celtic Progression, 1996; La Tombees De La Nuit, 2000; Sorserez (with Riccardo Del Fra); Condaghès, trio with Jacques Pellen, Paolo Fresu and Erik Marchand, 1998.

PELLOW, Marti; British singer; b. (Mark McLoughlin), 23 March 1966, Clydebank, Scotland. *Career:* lead singer, Wet Wet Wet 1982–97, 2004–; solo artist 2001–. *Theatre:* appeared as Billy Flynn in musical, Chicago, West End, London 2002, Dublin, Tokyo and Broadway, New York 2003. *Recordings* include: albums: with Wet Wet Wet: Popped In Souled Out 1987, Sgt Pepper Knew My Father 1988, The Memphis Sessions 1988, Holding Back The River 1989, High On The Happy Side 1992, Wet Wet Wet Live At The Royal Albert Hall 1993, End of Part One (Their Greatest Hits) 1993, Picture This 1995, 10 1997, Timeless 2007; solo: Smile 2001, Between The Covers 2003, Moonlight Over Memphis 2006, Sentimental Me 2008, Devil and the Monkey 2010, Love to Love 2011, Hope 2013. *Honours:* BRIT Award for Best British Newcomer 1988. *Website:* www.martipellowofficial.co.uk; www.wetwetwet.co.uk.

PEMELTON, Bret; American gospel singer; m. Diana Pemelton, two s. *Career:* fmr mem., Christian pop group, Dream of Eden; mem. Uthanda 1988–94; two major tours of USA; numerous TV and radio appearances; mem. Gospel Music Asscn. *Recordings:* album: Into Here and Now; singles: Wonderful Thing 1993, Into The Here and Now 1995.

PEÑA, Paco; Spanish flamenco guitarist, musical director and professor of flamenco guitar; *Director, Paco Peña Flamenco Company;* b. (Francisco Peña Perez), 1 June 1942, Córdoba; s. of Antonio Peña and Rosario Pérez; m. Karin Vaessen 1982; two d. *Career:* int. concert artist since 1968; f. Paco Peña Flamenco Co. 1970, Centro Flamenco Paco Peña, Córdoba 1981; Prof. of Flamenco, Rotterdam Conservatory, Netherlands 1985; composed Misa Flamenca 1991; produced Musa Gitana 1999, Voces y Ecos 2002; composed Flamenco Requiem 2004; produced flamenco dance show A Compas! 2006; devised dance productions Flamenco sin Fronteras 2009, Quimeras 2010, Flamenco Vivo 2011, Quimeras 2012. *Publication:* Toques Flamencos. *Honours:* Oficial de la Cruz de la Orden del Mérito Civil; Ramón Montoya Prize 1983, Arts Gold Medal in the Arts, John F. Kennedy Centre for the Performing Arts, Washington, DC 2012. *Current Management:* c/o MPM London, Suite 20, 1 Prince of Wales Road, London, NW5 3LW, England. *Telephone:* (20) 7681-7475. *Fax:* (20) 7681-7476. *E-mail:* MPM@pacopena.com. *Website:* www.pacopena.com.

PENAVA, Pista (Pishta) Gordan; Croatian singer, musician (guitar), songwriter, broadcaster and journalist; b. 29 Oct. 1967, Zagreb. *Career:* mem. Hard Time; tours and live appearances, festivals; mem. HGU (Croatian Musicians' Union), HDS ZAMP (Croatian Composers' Soc., Collecting Soc.). *Recordings* include: albums: Kiss My Ass and Go To Hell 1992, Kad Poludim... 1996, Through the Hard Times 2002, No. 3 2006, Live in Jabuka 2008. *Film:* Kad Muzičari Šokiraju 2005. *Publication:* Suuca. *Honours:* Best Hard Rock Band of Croatia 1992, Best Video Clip (for Hit and Run) 1993, Fender Mega Muzika Award for Best Hard Rock Album 2006. *Address:* Siget 7, 1000 Zagreb, Croatia (office). *Telephone:* (1) 6524166 (home); (91) 5457056 (office). *E-mail:* gpenava@hgu.hr (home); hardtime@hgu.hr (office). *Website:* www.hardtime-band.com.

PENDER, Mike; British musician (guitar) and singer; b. (Michael John Prendergast), 3 March 1942, Liverpool, England; s. of John Pender and Elizabeth Pender. *Career:* founder mem. and lead vocalist, The Searchers early 1960s–85; numerous tours and concerts; left The Searchers to form Mike Pender's Searchers 1985–; regular live performances UK, Japan, South Africa and Australia; appeared in Reelinandarockin touring show through UK, Australia, Far East, Europe 2002–05. *Recordings* include: albums: Meet The Searchers 1963, Sugar and Spice 1963, It's The Searchers 1964, Sounds Like Searchers 1965, Take Me For What I'm Worth 1965, Needles and Pins 1974,

The Searchers 1979, Play For Today 1981, 100 Minutes of The Searchers 1982, The EP Collection, Vol. 1 1989, 30th Anniversary Collection 1992, The EP Collection, Vol. 2 1992, Searchers 2001. *Current Management:* Tony Sherwood Entertainment, 5 Castleton Avenue, Carlton, Nottingham, NG4 3NZ, England. *Telephone:* (115) 940-0130. *Fax:* (115) 940-0130. *E-mail:* tony@sherwoodent.freeserve.co.uk.

PENDLEBURY, Andrew Scott; Australian musician (guitar); b. 30 Nov. 1951, Melbourne. *Career:* Member, Australian band, The Sports; Recorded 8 albums; Toured England twice; First major tour, Graham Parker and The Rumour; Finished 3 nights at Hammersmith Odeon, London, England. *Compositions:* Who Listens to the Radio, 1979. *Recordings:* 8 sports albums including: Don't Throw Stones, 1979; 4 solo albums; with Peter Lawler, King Rooster, 1998. *Address:* 34 Wellington St, Richmond 3121, Melbourne, Victoria, Australia.

PENG, Liyuan; Chinese singer and actress; *First Lady;* b. 20 Nov. 1962, Yuncheng, Shandong Prov.; d. of Peng Longkun; m. Xi Jinping (Pres. of People's Repub. of China 2013–) 1987; one d. *Education:* Shandong Acad. of Arts, China Acad. of Music. *Career:* solo singer, Qianwei Song and Dance Troupe of Ji'nan Mil. Command 1980–84; appeared on China Central TV (CCTV) New Year Gala 1983; solo singer and civilian mem., Song and Dance Troupe, PLA Gen. Political Dept 1984–; nicknamed 'The Peony Fairy'; specializes in traditional Chinese folk music and patriotic songs; frequent appearances on stage and on state TV; has performed overseas in USA, Canada, Japan and Austria; part-time Prof., Central Beijing Conservatory; Ministry of Health Amb. for HIV/AIDS Prevention 2006–; Amb. Chinese Asscn on Tobacco Control 2009–; WHO Goodwill Amb. for Tuberculosis and HIV 2011–; UNESCO Amb. for Women's Education 2014–; mem. CCP 1985–, mem. 11th CPPCC Nat. Cttee. *Works include:* People from Our Village, Mount Everest, On the Plains of Hope, Mountain Song, I Love You Saibei Snow, High Heaven Clouds, We are the Yellow Tarzan, Folks, Exalted, Sunnyway. *Operas include:* White Haired Girl, The Daughter of the Party, Melancholy Dawn, Poems of Mulan. *Television:* regular appearances on China Central TV (CCTV) New Year Gala. *Honours:* several awards including Plum Blossom Award 1985, Nat. Cultural Projects Award, China Golden Records Award, Lincoln Center for the Arts Distinguished Artist Award, ranked by Forbes magazine amongst The World's 100 Most Powerful Women (54th) 2013, (57th) 2014, (68th) 2015. *Address:* Song and Dance Troupe, People's Liberation Army General Political Department, A-16, East Huayuan Road, Haidian District, Beijing 100083, People's Republic of China (office). *Telephone:* (10) 62010693 (office). *Fax:* (10) 62369748 (office).

PENGILLY, Kirk; Australian musician (guitar, saxophone), songwriter and producer; b. 4 July 1958, Kew, Vic.; one d. *Career:* fmr mem., Guiness; founder mem., The Farriss Brothers 1977, renamed INXS 1979–; production work and collaborations with other artists. *Recordings* include: albums: INXS 1980, Underneath The Colours 1981, Shabooh Shoobah 1982, The Swing 1984, Listen Like Thieves 1985, Kick 1987, X 1990, Live Baby Live 1991, Welcome To Wherever You Are 1992, Full Moon Dirty Hearts 1993, Elegantly Wasted 1997, Switch 2006. *Honours:* Brit Award for Best Int. Group 1991, World Music Award for Outstanding Contribution To The Music Industry 1992. *E-mail:* info@inxs.com. *Website:* www.inxs.com.

PENISTON, CeCe; American singer and songwriter; b. 6 Sept. 1969, Dayton, OH. *Education:* Phoenix Coll., studied with Seth Riggs. *Career:* solo artist 1991–; numerous concerts and tours. *Recordings* include: albums: Finally 1992, Thought 'Ya Knew 1994, I'm Movin' On 1996, Winning Combination 2000. *E-mail:* cece@cecepeniston.com. *Website:* www.cecepeniston.com.

PENN, Dan; American songwriter, singer and producer; b. (Wallace Daniel Pennington), 16 Dec. 1941, Vernon, Ala. *Career:* began career in music business as lead singer, The Mark V Combo; wrote his first successful song, Conway Twitty's Is A Bluebird Blue 1960; worked with Rick Hall at FAME Studios, Muscle Shoals, Ala, firstly as performer using the name Lonnie Wray, later as songwriter and producer; wrote or co-wrote numerous hits for soul artists including Joe Simon, Aretha Franklin, James and Bobby Purify, Jimmy Hughes, Percy Sledge, Wilson Pickett; moved to Memphis, worked for Press Publishing Company and with Chips Moman at American Studios 1966, wrote and produced numerous hit songs for The Box Tops; f. Dan Penn Music 1970; has written many songs in partnership with Spooner Oldham and Chips Moman; released debut solo album Nobody's Fool 1972; continues to write and produce often in collaboration with Spooner Oldham, Carson Whitsett, Hoy Lindsey, Donnie Fritts, Gary Nicholson, Norbert Putnam; co-producer Solomon Burke, Don't Give Up On Me (album) 2002, producer and co-writer Bobby Purify, Better to Have It (album) 2005; currently owner Dandy Records; concerts and tours performing with Spooner Oldham. *Compositions:* songs as writer or co-writer include: The Letter (The Box Tops), Cry Like A Baby (The Box Tops), I'm Your Puppet (James and Bobby Purify), Sweet Inspiration (Sweet Inspirations), It Tears Me Up (Percy Sledge), Dark End Of The Street (James Carr), Take Me Just As I Am (Solomon Burke), Let's Do It Over (Joe Simon), Where There's A Will There's A Way (Bobby Womack), I'll Be Your Everything (Percy Sledge), Out Of Left Field (Percy Sledge), Wish You Didn't Have To Go (James and Bobby Purify), Let It Happen (James Carr), Do Right Woman, Do Right Man (Aretha Franklin), Woman Left Lonely (Charlie Rich), You Left The Water Running (Otis Redding). *Recordings:* albums: Nobody's Fool 1973, Do Right Man 1994, Moments From This Theatre (live recording, with Spooner Oldham) 1999, Blue Nite Lounge 1999. *Address:* Dandy Records,

POB 40891, Nashville, TN 37204-0891, USA (office). *E-mail:* webmaster@ danpenn.com (office). *Website:* www.danpenn.com.

PENNEY, John; British singer and lyricist; b. 17 Sept. 1968, Birmingham, England. *Career:* mem., Ned's Atomic Dustbin 1987–; numerous festival appearances worldwide; mem. Musicians' Union. *Recordings include:* albums: Bite 1990, God Fodder 1991, And Besides. . . 1992, Are You Normal? 1993, 0.522 1994, Brainbloodvolume 1995, Intact 1998, One More, No More 2001, Terminally Groovy 2003, Session 2004. *Website:* www.nedsatomicdustbin .com.

PEÓN (MOSTEIRO), Mercedes; singer, musician (gaita, percussion) and composer; b. 1967, La Coruña, Spain. *Career:* collects tunes, researches, teaches, lectures around the world to help preserve Galician folk tradition; Runs Discotrompo record label promoting Galician folk and traditional music; Organized several festivals including Federation of European Cultural Associations traditional music festival and Galicia Terra Unica; Previously member of Arjú before releasing solo material; Collaborations: Carlos Nunes; Xosé Manuel Budino; Manu Chao; Composed theme for Galician TV soap opera Mareas Vivas. *Recordings:* Single: Mareas Vivas; Albums: Isué, 2000; features on: Naciones Celtas II (Celtic Nations). *Honours:* Cídade Vella festival in Santiago de Compostela, special Jury Award; Santiago de Compostela Folk Days, Best Performer of Voice and Bagpipes; Lorient's Festival Interceltique, Macallan Award for Galician Pipers. *Website:* www .mercedespeon.com.

PEPA; Jamaican rap artist, songwriter and producer; b. (Sandra Denton), 9 Nov. 1969, Kingston; one c. *Career:* formed US female rap duo Super Nature with Cheryl James 1985, signed to Next Plateau Records and group re-named Salt-N-Pepa 1986, group joined by DJ 'Spinderella', in form of Pamela Green, then Latoya Hanson, then Dee Dee Roper; created Jireh Records company with Cheryl James 1997; opened clothing store Hollyhood, Atlanta, USA. *Recordings:* albums: Hot Cool & Vicious 1986, A Salt With A Deadly Pepa 1988, Blacks' Magic 1990, A Blitz of Hits: The Hits Remixed 1990, Very Necessary 1993, Brand New 1997, Salt-N-Pepa. . . The Best Of 2000; singles include: as Super Nature: Showstopper 1985, as Salt-N-Pepa: My Mike Sounds Nice 1987, Push It 1988, Shake Your Thang (It's Your Thing) 1988, Twist and Shout 1988, Expression 1990, Do You Want Me 1991, Let's Talk About Sex 1991, You Showed Me 1991, Let's Talk About AIDS (re-write of Let's Talk About Sex) 1992, Start Me Up 1992, Shoop 1993, Whatta Man (with En Vogue) 1994, Ain't Nothin But A She Thing 1995, Champagne 1996, R U Ready 1997, Gitty Up 1998, Brick Track Vs Gitty Up, Pt I and II 2000. *Honours:* Grammy Award for Best Rap Performance by a Duo or Group (for None Of Your Business) 1994, three MTV Awards 1994.

PERCIVAL, John Graham; British musician (clarinet, saxophone, musical saw); b. 7 March 1938, Northampton; m. Jane Allsop 1960; three d. *Career:* ran own jazzband, Horace M. Smith 1971–87; member, Bob Kerr's Whoopee Band; television appearances in Germany, Netherlands, France, Switzerland, Belgium, Sweden, Denmark, Russia; mem, Musicians' Union. *Recordings:* as Horace M Smith: Hold That Tiger; with Bob Kerr Whoopee Band: Molotov Cocktails; Happy Daze; Videos: Live At The Half Moon; From Russia With Laughs; Films with Bob Godfrey: French Revolution; Happy Birthday Switzerland. *Address:* c/o Bob Kerr's Whoopee Band, PO Box 59, Diss, Suffolk IP21 5HF, England (office). *Telephone:* (1379) 384775 (office). *E-mail:* bobwhoopee@aol.com (office). *Website:* www.whoopeeband.de.

PERCIVAL, Lynne, MScS; British teacher, singer and musician (guitar, mandolin); b. 24 Nov. 1954, Altrincham, Cheshire, England. *Career:* semi-professional singer, guitarist and mandolin player; mem., The Fluence Band 1988–, specialising in Irish traditional dance music and song, performing regularly in Northern England, local residencies and ceilidhs; co-ordinator of Irish music promotions, Club Cheoil, Manchester; mem. PRS, Musicians' Union. *Recordings include:* Goodwill (with Wild Bill Flatpick and The Bindle Stiffs).

PEREIRA, Francis Martin Purcell; Singaporean producer, arranger and musician (guitar); b. 1 May 1950; m. Ann Toh Swee Hua 1985. *Education:* Royal School of Music, Singapore Armed Forces Band, Gateway School of Audio Engineering. *Career:* arranger, EMI, Singapore 1975–83; television Brunei; played for Sultan of Brunei 1985–87; First Asean Festival of Songs 1986; Director, Shekinah Music Trading 1992–. *Composition for film:* Eye of the Tiger. *Recordings:* Guitar Indigo Series, Guitar Latino Series, Guitar Memories, Different Class Harmonica Series, Sax with Love, Dijazz Series, Contemporary Saxophone, Vols I and II, Todos Latino, Guitarra Series, Hymns, Asia. *Honours:* Affiliated Mem., Ferrum University, Virginia, USA.

PEREIRA, Rui; Australian musician (guitar); b. (Rui Telmo Prata Dias Gonçalves Pereira), Mozambique. *Career:* mem., The Gutterville Splendour Six 1996–2000, The Drones 2001–06, The Selfish Gene 2006–. *Recordings include:* albums: with The Drones: Here Come the Lies 2002, Wait Long By the River & the Bodies of Your Enemies Will Float By (Australian Music Prize 2005) 2005, The Miller's Daughter 2006, Gala Mill 2006. *E-mail:* ruismonsters@hotmail.com (home).

PERES, Vivian; French musician (drums). *Career:* Participated in first Francofolies de la Rochelle; Leader, own group Traction Ailleurs; Worked at Béziers Conservatoire with René Nan; Founder member, La Campagnie du Jazz; Member, quartet Golem; Salsa group with Juan Quintana; Accompanist with numerous singers; Member, Slax; Mezcal Jazz Unit, European tour,

1994; Jazz Festival, Lithuania, 1994; Also performs with groups: Swing; Planete Jazz. *Honours:* Agfa Song Contest Winner, with group Traction Ailleurs, 1986.

PÉREZ, Danilo; Panamanian jazz musician (piano), composer and philanthropist; *Director, Global Jazz Institute, Berklee College of Music;* b. (Danilo Enrico Pérez Samudio), 29 Dec. 1965, Panama City. *Education:* Nat. Conservatory, Panama, Berklee Coll. of Music, USA. *Career:* while studying jazz composition performed with Jon Hendricks, Terence Blanchard, Claudio Roditi, Paquito D'Rivera 1985–88; youngest mem., Dizzy Gillespie's United Nations Orchestra 1989–92, toured worldwide; has performed and recorded with musicians including Steve Lacy, Jack DeJohnette, Charlie Haden, Michael Brecker, Joe Lovano, Tito Puente, John Patitucci, Tom Harrell, Gary Burton, Roy Haynes; first Latin member of Wynton Marsalis' band 1995; regular mem. Wayne Shorter Quartet; concerts worldwide as leader of own band 1993–; performed with Panamanian Symphony Orchestra; Prof. of Improvisation and Jazz Studies, New England Conservatory of Music 1995–2009; artist-in-residence: Irving Gilmore Int. Keyboard Festival 1998–99; Prof., Berklee Coll. of Music 2002–, Dir, Global Jazz Inst. 2009–; clinician/performer, Ravinia Music Festival 2001, 2002; judge, American Jazz Piano Competition, incl. 1998, Thelonious Monk Int. Jazz Competitions; Cultural Amb. for Panama 1999–2004; UNICEF Goodwill Amb. 2005–; Cultural Amb. of Panama to Chicago 2008; Founder and Pres., Panama Jazz Festival; Pres., Danilo Pérez Foundation; Artistic Advisor to Mellon Jazz Up Close series, Kimmel Center, Phila. *Recordings:* solo: Danilo Perez 1993, The Journey 1994, Panamonk (Outstanding Jazz Album, Boston Music Awards) 1996, Central Avenue (Outstanding Jazz Album, Boston Music Awards) 1998, Motherland (Outstanding Jazz Album, Boston Music Awards) 2000, Till Then 2003, Danilo Perez Trio Live at the Jazz Showcase 2005, Providencia 2010; with Wayne Shorter: Alegria 2002, Footprints Live! 2001, Beyond The Sound Barrier 2005; other: Paquito D'Rivera & Arturo Sandoval, Reunion 1990, Dizzy Gillespie, Live At The Royal Festival Hall 1991, Arturo Sandoval, Danzon 1994, Roy Haynes Trio 2000. *Honours:* Boston Music Awards 1996, 1999, 2000, Best Artist in Performance, Jazz Journalists Asscn Awards 1998, Distinguished Alumnus Award, Berklee Coll. of Music 2000, Talent Deserving Wider Recognition, DownBeat Awards 2002, Best Small Ensemble of the Year (for Wayne Shorter Quartet), Jazz Journalists Asscn Awards 2002, Grammy Award 2005. *Address:* c/o Cholo Music Inc. (office). *Telephone:* (857) 891-9018 (office). *E-mail:* patricia@cholomusicinc.com (office). *Website:* www.daniloperez.com.

PEREZ, Ivan; French musician (guitar) and composer; b. 11 Nov. 1964, Orange. *Education:* BPA Floriculture; Conservatoire de Music; Studied improvised music with bassist B Santacruz and saxophonist Andre Jaume. *Career:* Jazz Festivals: Avignon; Sorgues; Carpentras; Music for Florence Saul contemporary dance company; Member, duo with Frederic Duvivier; Trio with Colin McKellar and Tox Drohead; Trio with Simon Fayolle and Lionel Villard.

PÉREZ, Louie; American musician (guitar, percussion); b. 29 Jan. 1953, Los Angeles, CA. *Career:* mem., Los Lobos 1973–. *Recordings include:* albums: De Este De Los Angeles 1978, How Will The Wolf Survive 1984, By the Light of the Moon 1987, La Pistola y El Corazón 1988, The Neighborhood 1990, Kiko 1992, Colossal Head 1996, This Time 1999, Good Morning Aztlán 2002, The Ride 2004, The Town and the City 2006, Los Lobos Goes Disney 2009, Tin Can Trust 2010. *Current Management:* c/o Chris Tetzeli, Red Light Management, 321 East Main Street, Suite 500, Charlottesville, VA 22902, USA. *Telephone:* (434) 245-4900. *Fax:* (434) 245-4933. *E-mail:* info@redlightmanagement.com. *Website:* www.redlightmanagement.com; www.loslobos.org.

PEREZ, Michel; French musician (guitar); b. 2 Jan. 1946, St Priest, France; m. Patricia Van Ginneken, 31 Dec. 1977, 1 s., 2 d. *Career:* Concert first part of Miles Davis, Vienne Festival, 1984; Nice Jazz Festival, 1984; Casino de Paris, 1989; Film in concert, Lyon, 1986; Around Midnight (Bertrand Taverner) with Herbie Hancock, Tony Williams, Wayne Shorter; Concert, first part of Zawinul Syndicate, 1992. *Recordings:* 2 with Spheroe: Spheroe, 1976; Primadonna, 1979; Kaleidoscope, 1982; Virgile, 1986; Orange, 1991; Toujours, Ron Carter, 1992; Film: Around Midnight, 1986. *Publications:* 3 compositions to be published in: Le Livre Du Jazz En France. *E-mail:* michelperez@ michelperez-jazz.com. *Website:* michelperez.jazz.free.fr.

PÉREZ JOGLAR, René, (Residente), MFA; Puerto Rican rapper; b. 23 Feb. 1978, Hato Rey; s. of Flor Joglar de Gracia; half-brother of Eduardo José Cabra Martínez (aka Visitante). *Education:* Escuela de Artes Plásticas, Puerto Rico and Savannah Coll. of Art and Design, USA. *Career:* fmr mem. rock group Bayanga; formed Calle 13 with half-brother Eduardo José Cabra Martínez, music combines influences from hip hop, reggaeton, cumbia, tango, electronica; collaborations with Voltio, Three 6 Mafia, Nelly Furtado, Alejandro Sanz. *Recordings include:* albums: Calle 13 (Latin Grammy Award for Best Urban Music Album 2006) 2005, Residente O Visitante (Latin Grammy Award for Best Urban Music Album 2007, Grammy Award for Best Latin Urban Album 2008) 2007, Los de Atrás Vienen Conmigo (Latin Grammy Awards for Best Album, for Best Urban Album 2009, Grammy Award for Best Latin Urban Album 2010) 2008, Entren Los Que Quieran (Latin Grammy Award for Album of the Year 2011) 2010, Latinoamerica (Latin Grammy Award for Song of the Year 2011) 2011, Multi Viral (Grammy Award fpr Best Latin Pop, Rock or Urban Album 2015) 2014. *Honours:* Best New Artist, MTV Latin Awards 2006, Latin Grammy Awards for Best New Artist and Best Short Form Music Video 2006, for Best Urban Song (for Pal Norte with Panasuyo and Orishas)

2007, for Best Recording (for No Hay Nadie Como Tú) 2009, for Best Alternative Song (for No Hay Nadie Como Tú) 2009. *Address:* c/o Sony Music Latin, 555 Madison Avenue, New York, NY 10022-3211, USA. *Website:* lacalle13.com.

PERKINS, Stephen; American musician (drums). *Career:* mem. Jane's Addiction 1984–91, 1997–; mem. Porno for Pyros 1993–98; mem. Infectious Grooves 1991, Banyan 1997–99, Hellflower; session drummer for Sheryl Crow, Jewel, Rage Against the Machine, Nine Inch Nails, No Doubt, Red Hot Chili Peppers; own company, Perkana Percussion. *Recordings include:* albums: with Jane's Addiction: Jane's Addiction 1987, Nothing's Shocking 1988, Ritual do lo Habitual 1990, Kettle Whistle 1997, Strays 2003, The Great Escape Artist 2011; with Infectious Grooves: The Plague That Makes Your Booty Move... It's the Infectious Grooves 1991; with Porno for Pyros: Porno for Pyros 1993, Good God's Urge 1996; with Banyan: Banyan 1997, Anytime at All 1999; with Hellflower: Us You 2010. *Website:* www.janesaddiction.com; www.stephenperkins.com.

PERKIÖMÄKI, Jari, DMus; Finnish musician (alto saxophone, reeds, flutes); *Vice-Rector, Sibelius Academy, University of the Arts Helsinki;* b. 13 April 1961, Pori. *Education:* Sibelius Acad. *Career:* joined Pori Big Band aged 15; represented Finland, EBU Big Band 1981; Conductor Pori Big Band; own quartet, appearances in Europe, Venezuela, Mexico, China and Australia; Lecturer and Head, Jazz Dept, Sibelius Acad., currently Vice-Rector, Lecturer in Jazz Music, Univ. of the Arts Helsinki (formed from merger of Finnish Acad. of Fine Arts, Sibelius Acad. and Theatre Acad. Helsinki 2013); Chair. Int. Asscn of Schools of Jazz; mem. Finnish Higher Educ. Evaluation Council 2010–. *Compositions include:* Music for 2 plays by Ilpo Tuomarila. *Recordings:* Jari Perkiömäki Quartet 1985, Shades 1997. *Publication:* Music Theory! (co-author) (in Finnish) 2008. *Honours:* Pekka Pöyry Award 1985, Musician of the Year, RYTMI magazine 1985, Thalia Award, for music to play Exit 1988, Yrjö Award 2005. *Address:* Kielonkuja 5, 04260 Kerava, Finland (home). *Telephone:* (50) 3843454 (office). *E-mail:* jari.perkiomaki@siba.fi (office). *Website:* www.jariperkiomaki.com.

PERKO, Jukka; musician (alto and soprano saxophone); b. 18 Feb. 1968, Huittinen, Finland. *Education:* Saxophone from 1982; Sibelius Academy, 1988. *Career:* Played Pori Jazz Festival, 1985; Played in Dizzy Gillespie 70th Anniversary Big Band, 1987; Tour with Dizzy Gillespie, 1988; Regular member, UMO (New Music Orchestra), 1989; Formed Jukka Perko Quartet; Finnish Jazz Federation Tour, 1990; Played with Horace Tapscott, Ultra Music Meeting workshop, Pori, 1990; Member, Perko-Pyysalo Poppoo, with Severi Pyysalo. *Recordings:* Albums: Portrait By Heart, Jukka Perko Quartet, 1990; Uuno Kailas, Perko-Pyysalo Poppoo, 1995. *Honours:* Yrjö Award, Finnish Jazz Federation, 1989. *E-mail:* jukka.perko@hidas.fi. *Website:* www.jukkaperko.com.

PERRET, Pierre; French singer, actor, musician and writer; b. 9 July 1934, Castelsarrasin, France; m. Rebecca Perret 1964; one s. two d. *Education:* Conservatoires de Musique, Toulouse and Paris. *Career:* played saxophone; formed group while a student; began writing songs while performing military service; associated with Georges Brassens; f. Adèle music and book publisher 1967–; wrote numerous books on subject of language; mem. Conseil Supérieur de la Langue Français. *Recordings include:* albums: Le Bonheur Conjugal 1960, Le Zizi 1974, Mon P'tit Loup 1979, Comment C'est La Chine 1983, Bercy Madeleine 1992, Chansons Eroticocoquines 1996, Casino De Paris 1997, La Bête Est Revenue 1998, Çui-là 2002, Du rire aux larmes 2003, Mélangez-vous 2006, Le plaisir des Dieux 2007, numerous compilation albums; singles: Le Tord-Boyaux, Trop Contente, La Corrida, Les Jolies Colonies De Vacances, Tonton Cristobal, La Cage Aux Oiseaux, Lily. *Publications include:* Adieu M. Léautaud, Au Petit Perret Gourmand, Le Petit Perret Illustré 1985, Le Parler Des Métiers 2003, Le café du Pont 2005. *Address:* c/o Warner Music France, 29 Avenue MacMahon, 75890 Paris Cédex 17, France (office).

PERRIN, Roland; musician (piano), composer, arranger and teacher; b. 18 Jan. 1959, New York, NY, USA. *Education:* BA Hons, Music, University of York, England. *Career:* Played in professional jazz/blues bands from age 15; Plays wide variety of music, specialising often in Afro-Cuban, Brazilian and South African Music; Played Mandela 70th birthday concert with Jonas Gwangwa, Wembley Stadium; Tours, sessions; Own band, Evidence, 1987–94; new band, The Blue Planet Orchestra, 1999. *Compositions:* With Evidence: Later; Kinacho; Golden Road; Salsa Diferente; Sleeping City; With South African Friends: DP; With Beaujolais Band: The New World; El Monte; Sister Grace; Songs from the Cage (Big Band setting for Charles Bukowski poems), 2002. *Recordings:* Evidence, See You Later; It's A Triple Earth, Westway; Mark Ramsden, Above the Clouds; The Beaujolais Band, Mind How You Go; Talk, Talk and More Talk; Aster Aweke, Kabu; Dudu Pukwana, Cosmics '90; Brotherhood of Breath, In Memorium; Tumbaito, Otros Tiempos; Introducing The Blue Planet Orchestra, 1999; Mose, Congo Acoustic, 1999. *Publications:* 3 piano pieces for First Associated Board Jazz Piano Exams. *E-mail:* roland.perrin@btconnect.com. *Website:* www.rolandperrin.com.

PERRONE, Marc; French musician (diatonic accordion); b. 8 Oct. 1951, Villejuif (Paris); m. Marie Odile Chantran, 27 June 1995. *Career:* Montparnasse, 1994; Olympia, Paris, 1995; Carnaval de Venise; Numerous foreign tours include: Africa; USA; Canada; South America; Asia; Japan, 1995; Films: La Trace, 1984; Un Dimanche à La Campagne, 1985; Maine Océan, 1986; La Vie Et Rien d'Autre, 1989; L-627, 1992; mem, Administration Council of ADAMI. *Recordings:* Gabriel Valse, 1974; Perlinpinpin, 1974; Rondeaux Et

Autres Danses Gasconnes à Samatan, 1976; Accordéons Diatoniques, 1979; Country Dances (Les Lendemains Qui Dansent), 1980; La Forcelle, 1983; La Trace (film score), 1984; Un Dimanche à La Campagne (film score), 1985; Velverde, 1988; Paris Musette, 1990; Cinéma Mémoire, 1993; Paris Musette Living It (Vol. 2), 1993; Jacaranda, 1995; Voyages, 2001. *Honours:* Prix de l'Academie Charles Cros for: La Forcelle. *E-mail:* marcperrone@noos.fr. *Website:* www.marcperrone.net.

PERRONI BEORLEGUI, Maite; Mexican singer and actress; b. 9 March 1983, Mexico City. *Education:* CEA. *Career:* actress; mem. RDB 2004–. *Theatre:* Usted tiene ojos de mujer fatal, Las cosas simples, Los enamorados, Cyrano de Bergerac, Cats. *Television:* Rebelde (series) 2004, RBD: La Familia (series) 2007. *Recordings include:* albums: Rebelde 2004, Nuestro Amor 2005, Celestial (Billboard Latin Music Award for Latin Pop Album of the Year by a Duo or Group 2007) 2006, Rebels (in English) 2006, Empezar Desde Cero 2007. *Honours:* Billboard Latin Music Award for Top Latin Albums Artist of the Year, for Latin Tour of the Year 2007, some 24 Premios Juventud, Billboard Latin Music 'Tu Mundo' Award 2008. *Address:* c/o EMI Latin, 404 Washington Avenue, Suite 700, Miami Beach, FL 33139, USA (office). *Website:* www.emimusic.com.mx (office); www.grupo-rbd.com.

PERRY, André; Canadian record company executive and record producer; b. (André Perrotte), 12 Feb. 1937, Montréal; m. (divorced); two c. *Career:* founder, Studio André Perry 1962; founder, André Perry Productions 1968–70, Son Québec 1970–73; Founder, President, Groupe André Perry Inc. 1974–88, André Perry Video 1980–88; Founder, on board of directors, Québec Assoc Record and Entertainment Industry, Independent Record Producers Association of Canada; Founder, Le Studio (recording studios); Music co-ordinator, Montréal Olympic Games 1976; record producer for John Lennon, Charles Aznavour, Wilson Pickett, numerous Canadian artists; mem, Audio Engineering Society, Pro-Can, Composers, Authors and Publishers Asscn of Canada, Canadian Recording Industry Asscn, Société d'Auteurs, Compositeurs et Editeurs de Musique. *E-mail:* info@andreperrystudio.com (office). *Website:* andreperrystudio.com.

PERRY, Barney Blair; American composer, musician (guitar), singer and teacher; b. 2 Nov. 1953, Buffalo, New York; m. Ethlene Perry 1982; two s. two d. *Education:* Buffalo State College, Howard University, Canada Christian College, University of Buffalo, Catholic University; jazz guitar with George Benson, classical guitar with Bill Harris and Oswald Rentucci, symphonic music with Russell Wollen and William Penn. *Career:* activist for intellectual property rights, state courts and federal courts, New York and California; TV, Blair, Invitation to Dance Show; numerous radio shows; Concerts and performances as soloist, quartet; band and show with Herbie Hancock, Lenny Williams; co-founder, Blackbyrds 1973–78; backing guitarist for Donald Byrd, Phyllis Hyman, Bobbi Humphrey, Vivian Reed, Jack McDuff; mem, BTF, UTLA, Musicians Local, NRA, Blessed Trinity Holy Name Society. *Compositions:* Walking in Rhythm, Nightlife, A Hot Day Today, Virgo Princess, Who is Blair. *Recordings:* albums: with the Blackbyrds: The Blackbyrds 1973, Flying Start 1974, Cornbread, Earl and Me 1975, City Life 1975, Unfinished Business 1976, Action 1977, Night Grooves 1978; solo: Blair 1978. *Honours:* Outstanding Citation of Achievement, BMI, Million Plus Performance Composer; Pop Music Award, BMI.

PERRY, Joe; American musician (guitar); b. 10 Sept. 1950, Boston. *Career:* lead guitarist rock band, Aerosmith 1970–79, 1984–; solo work as leader, Joe Perry Project 1980–83; numerous concerts and festival appearances. *Film appearances include:* as the Future Villain Band in Sgt Pepper's Lonely Hearts Club Band 1978. *Television appearance:* guest voice on The Simpsons (Fox TV) 1990. *Recordings include:* albums: with Aerosmith: Aerosmith 1973, Toys In The Attic 1975, Get Your Wings 1975, Rocks 1976, Draw The Line 1977, Greatest Hits 1981, Done With Mirrors 1985, Classic Live! 1986, Permanent Vacation 1987, Retrospective Gems 1988, Pump 1989, Pandora's Box 1992, Get A Grip 1993, Big Ones 1994, Nine Lives 1997, Little South of Sanity 1998, Young Lust – The Aerosmith Anthology 2001, O'Yeah! Ultimate Aerosmith Hits 2002, Honkin' On Bobo 2004; with Joe Perry Project/solo: Let The Music Do The Talking 1980, I've Got The Rock 'n' Roll Again 1981, Once A Rocker, Always A Rocker 1983, Joe Perry 2005, Have Guitar, Will Travel 2009, Music from Another Dimension! 2012. *Honours:* Grammy Award for Best Rock Performance 1991, American Music Award 1991. *Current Management:* c/o Richard De La Font Agency, 4845 South Sheridan Road, Tulsa, OK 74145, USA. *Telephone:* (918) 665-6200. *Website:* www.delafont.com. *Address:* c/o Aero Force One, 40 Washington Street, Suite 3000, Westborough, MA 01581, USA. *Telephone:* (508) 791-3807. *E-mail:* customerservice@joeperry.com. *Website:* www.aerosmith.com; www.joeperry.com.

PERRY, Katy; American singer; b. (Katheryn Elizabeth Hudson), 25 Oct. 1984, Santa Barbara, Calif.; m. Russell Brand 2010 (divorced). *Career:* as a child sang in local church, at family functions; moved to Nashville to work with professional songwriters and producers, aged 15; solo artist 2007–; UNICEF Goodwill Amb. 2013–. *Recordings include:* albums: Katy Hudson 2001, One of the Boys 2008, Teenage Dream 2010, Prism 2013. *Honours:* MTV Europe Music Awards for Best New Act 2008, for Best Female 2013, for Best Video (featuring Juicy J, for Dark Horse) 2014, for Best Look 2014, People's Choice Award for Favorite Pop Song (for I Kissed a Girl) 2009, BRIT Award for Best Int. Female Artist 2009, People's Choice Award 2012, Billboard Music Awards for Top Female Artist 2014, for Top Digital Songs Artist 2014, MTV Video Music Award for Best Female Video (featuring Juicy J, for Dark Horse)

2014, American Music Awards for Favorite Pop/Rock Female Artist 2014, for Favorite Adult Contemporary Artist 2014, for Single of the Year (featuring Juicy J, for Dark Horse) 2014. *Current Management:* c/o Bradford Cobb, Direct Management Group Inc., 8332 Melrose Avenue, Top Floor, Los Angeles, CA 90069, USA. *Telephone:* (310) 854-3535. *E-mail:* bradford@directmanagement .com. *Website:* www.directmanagement.com; www.katyperry.com.

PERRY, Kimberly Marie; American country music singer, songwriter and musician (guitar, piano); b. 12 July 1983, Greeneville, Tenn.; d. of Steve Perry and Marie Perry. *Career:* raised in Ala; mem. The Band Perry (with siblings Reid and Neil); fmrly toured with Tim McGraw, Keith Urban; signed to Republic Nashville record label 2009. *Recordings include:* albums: The Band Perry 2010, Pioneer 2013. *Honours:* Academy of Country Music Awards for Top New Vocal Duo or Group 2011, for Top Vocal Group 2011, for Vocal Group of the Year 2014, CMT Awards for USA Weekend Breakthrough Video of the Year 2011, for Nationwide Insurance On Your Side Award 2011, Country Music Asscn Awards for New Artist of the Year 2011, for Single of the Year and Song of the Year (for If I Die Young) 2011, Grammy Award for Best Country Duo/Group Performance (for Gentle on My Mind) 2015. *Current Management:* c/o Rob Beckham, William Morris Endeavor Entertainment, 1600 Division Street, #300, Nashville, TN 37203, USA. *E-mail:* BEC@ wmeentertainment.com. *Website:* www.wmeentertainment.com. *Address:* c/o Republic Nashville, Records, Big Machine Label Group, 1219 16th Avenue South, Nashville, TN 37212, USA (office). *Website:* www .bigmachinelabelgroup.com (office); www.republicnashville.com (office); www .thebandperry.com.

PERRY, Lee 'Scratch'; musician and producer; b. (Rainford Hugh Perry), 1936, Hanover, Jamaica. *Career:* also known as 'Scratch and the Upsetter'; record scout 1950s–60s; prod. and songwriter for Delroy Wilson 1963; solo artist 1963–; formed own label, Upsetter 1968–; prod. for artists, including Susan Cadogan, Junior Marvin, Bob Marley and The Wailers. *Recordings include:* albums: The Upsetter 1969, Many Moods of the Upsetter 1970, Scratch the Upsetter Again 1970, Prisoner of Love – Dave Barker Meets the Upsetters 1970, Africa's Blood 1972, Battle Axe 1972, Cloak and Dagger 1972, Double Seven 1973, Rhythm Shower 1973, Blackboard Jungle 1974, Kung Fu Meets the Dragon 1974, DIP Presents the Upsetter 1974, Revolution Dub 1975, Scratch the Upper Ape 1976, Jah Lion – Columbia Colly 1976, Return of the Super Ape 1977, Roast Fish, Collie Weed and Corn Bread 1978, Scratch on the Wire 1979, Scratch and Company – Chapter 1 1980, Return of Pipecock Jackson 1981, Heart of the Ark, Vol. 1 1982, Vol. 2 1983, Megaton Dub 1983, Megaton Dub 2 1983, History, Mystery and Prophecy 1984, Black Ark in Dub 1985, Battle of Armagideon – Millionaire Liquidator 1986, Time Boom X De Devil Dead 1987, Satan Kicked the Bucket 1988, Scratch Attack 1988, Chicken Scratch 1989, Build the Ark 1990, Meets Bullwackie – Satan's Dub 1990, Meets the Mad Professor 1990, The Upsetter and the Beat 1992, Soundz from the Hot Line 1993, Black Art in Dub 1993, Larks from the Ark 1995, Experryments at the Grassroots of Dub 1995, Voodooism 1996, Technomajikal 1997, Dub Fire 1998, Lick Shot 1999, Lost Treasures of the Ark 2000, Techno Party 2000, Station Underground 2001, Divine Madness – Definitely! 2001, Jamaican E.T. 2002, Sensimilla Showdown 2002, Scratch 2002, The Compiler, Vol. 1: Rude Walking 2002, Alien Starman 2003, Dub Around the World 2005, Panic in Babylon 2006, The Upsetter Selection: a Lee Perry Jukebox 2007, Repentance 2008, Revelation 2010. *Current Management:* c/o Michel Jovanovic, Mediacom Agency, BP 231, 51058 Reims, France. *Telephone:* 3-26-40-96-71. *Fax:* 3-26-40-23-13. *E-mail:* michel@mediacom-agency.com. *Website:* www.mediacom-agency.com. *Address:* c/o Trojan Records, Sanctuary House, 45–53 Sinclair Road, London, W14 0NS, England (office). *Website:* www .trojanrecords.com (office); www.lee-perry.com.

PERRY, Linda; American singer, songwriter and producer; b. 15 April 1965. *Career:* fmr mem. and lead singer, 4 Non-Blondes; solo artist and songwriter for Pink, Christina Aguilera, Courtney Love, Alicia Keys, Vanessa Carlton, Gwen Stefani; founder member, Deep Dark Robot 2010–. *Recordings include:* albums: with 4 Non-Blondes: Bigger, Better, Faster, More! 1992; solo: In Flight 1996, After Hours 1999; with Deep Dark Robot: 8 Songs About a Girl 2011. *Address:* c/o Rebel Management, 8939 1/2 Santa Monica Blvd, West Hollywood, CA 90069, USA (office). *Telephone:* (310) 275-5900 (office). *Fax:* (310) 275-5905 (office). *Website:* www.deepdarkrobot.com.

PERRY, Neil Clark; American country music musician (drums, mandolin, accordion); b. 23 July 1990, Jackson, Miss.; s. of Steve Perry and Marie Perry. *Career:* raised in Ala; mem. The Band Perry (with siblings Kimberly and Reid); fmrly toured with Tim McGraw, Keith Urban; signed to Republic Nashville record label 2009. *Recordings include:* albums: The Band Perry 2010, Pioneer 2013. *Honours:* Academy of Country Music Awards for Top New Vocal Duo or Group 2011, for Top Vocal Group 2011, for Vocal Group of the Year 2014, CMT Awards for USA Weekend Breakthrough Video of the Year 2011, for Nationwide Insurance On Your Side Award 2011, Country Music Asscn Awards for New Artist of the Year 2011, for Single of the Year and Song of the Year (for If I Die Young) 2011, Grammy Award for Best Country Duo/ Group Performance (for Gentle on My Mind) 2015. *Current Management:* c/o Rob Beckham, William Morris Endeavor Entertainment, 1600 Division Street #300, Nashville, TN 37203, USA. *Address:* c/o Republic Nashville, Records, Big Machine Label Group, 1219 16th Avenue South, Nashville, TN 37212, USA (office). *Website:* www.bigmachinelabelgroup.com (office); www .republicnashville.com (office); www.thebandperry.com (home).

PERRY, Reid Hogan; American country music musician (bass guitar); b. 17 Nov. 1988, Jackson, Miss.; s. of Steve Perry and Marie Perry. *Career:* raised in Ala; mem. The Band Perry (with siblings Kimberly and Neil); fmrly toured with Tim McGraw, Keith Urban; signed to Republic Nashville record label 2009. *Recordings include:* albums: The Band Perry 2010, Pioneer 2013. *Honours:* Academy of Country Music Awards for Top New Vocal Duo or Group 2011, for Top Vocal Group 2011, for Vocal Group of the Year 2014, CMT Awards for USA Weekend Breakthrough Video of the Year 2011, for Nationwide Insurance On Your Side Award 2011, Country Music Asscn Awards for New Artist of the Year 2011, for Single of the Year and Song of the Year (for If I Die Young) 2011, Grammy Award for Best Country Duo/Group Performance (for Gentle on My Mind) 2015. *Current Management:* c/o Rob Beckham, William Morris Endeavor Entertainment, 1600 Division Street #300, Nashville, TN 37203, USA. *Address:* c/o Republic Nashville, Records, Big Machine Label Group, 1219 16th Avenue South, Nashville, TN 37212, USA (office). *Website:* www.bigmachinelabelgroup.com (office); www .republicnashville.com (office); www.thebandperry.com (home).

PERRY, Steve; American singer; b. 22 Jan. 1949, Hanford, CA. *Career:* mem., Alien Project; lead singer, Journey 1978–97; solo artist 1987–; numerous concerts, tours and festival appearances. *Recordings include:* albums: with Journey: Journey 1975, Look Into The Future 1976, Next 1977, Infinity 1978, Evolution 1979, In The Beginning 1979, Departure 1980, Dream After Dream 1980, Captured 1981, Escape 1981, Frontiers 1983, Raised On Radio 1986, Time 3 1992, Trial By Fire 1996; solo: Street Talk 1984, For the Love of Strange Medicine 1994. *Honours:* Bay Area Music Award for Best Vocalist, for Best Performance 1987.

PERSSON, Nina Elisabet; Swedish singer, songwriter and musician (harmonica); b. 6 Sept. 1974, Örebro; m. *Career:* fmr mem., Green Camels; lead singer, The Cardigans 1992–; numerous concert tours, festivals, television and radio appearances; founder mem., A Camp 2001–. *Music for TV and film:* contributed tracks to films Romeo and Juliet and A Life Less Ordinary, theme to 'Randall & Hopkirk Deceased' (BBC1, with David Arnold) 2000. *Recordings include:* albums: with The Cardigans: Emmerdale 1994, Life 1995, First Band On The Moon 1996, Other Side Of The Moon 1998, Gran Turismo 1998, Long Gone Before Daylight 2003, Super Extra Gravity 2005; with A Camp: A Camp 2000, Colonia 2009. *Honours:* Slitz Magazine Award for Best Band 1994, Swedish Government Export Prize 1997, BMI Award for Best Song 1997, Best Album 1998, Best Group 1996, 1998. *Current Management:* Hagenburg Management, Kyrkogaten 31, 411 08 Gothenburg, Sweden. *Telephone:* (31) 339-95-90. *Fax:* (31) 13-95-09. *E-mail:* info@hagenburg.se. *Website:* www.hagenburg.se; www.cardigans.com.

PESCE, Serge; French musician (guitar) and composer; b. 7 Sept. 1959, Nice. *Career:* Performed with: Alan Vitous, Barre Phillips, Miquel Montanaro, Yves Rousguisto, Patrick Vaillant, Alex Grillo, Jean-Louis Ruf; Festival appearances at: Nantes, Toulon, Confolens, Uzeste, Avignon, Parthenay, St Chartier Miskols, Szeged, Hungary; mem, SACEM; SPEDIDAM; SACD; SFA. *Compositions:* L'odore del caffe, guitar solo. *Recordings:* Guitare Attitude; Couples; Le Gaboulet, Tambourin – Ocora Radio France; Ballade Pour Une Mer Qui Chante, Vols 2 and 3; L'odore Del Caffè; Jazzd'aià; Tenson, with Alan Vitous and Miqueu Montanaro; Silence de faune, with Yves Rousguisto; Amb la doçor, Aguillera, Zagaria. *Publications:* Yes Bomb'ai. *Website:* www .sergepesce.org.

PETEJ, Peco Petar; Croatian musician (drums, piano); b. 18 March 1949, Split; m. Nada Vicic 1973; two s. *Education:* College degree; Academy for Jazz Music and Theatre Arts, Graz, Austria. *Career:* Delfini, Split, 1972; Played with leading jazz musicians with Hans Koller Free Sound; Member, rock band Time, 1973–79; Moved to Britain, 1974; Played with Jackie McAuley Throat, 1975; The Foundations vocalist Collin Young; Zagreb Jazz scene, TV Big Band, 1979; Returned to London blues scene, 1990; Back to Croatia, war humanitarian work, 1991; Indexi Sarajevo, 1994; mem, Musicians' Union (UK); Croatian Music Union; Croatian Asscn of Orchestral Musicians. *Recordings:* 2100 recorded minutes for TV Big Band; Recorded over 150 albums with various artists; Original music, theatre play, Hamlet and Tarzan. *Honours:* Numerous Pop and Rock Festival Awards, jazz fairs, Zagreb, Slovenia, Germany; Original Music Theatre Award, 1994.

PETERS, Mike; Welsh musician (guitar) and singer; b. 25 Feb. 1963, St Asaph. *Education:* School Bands, Stripey. *Career:* founder and lead singer, The Alarm 1981–92, with David Sharp, Eddie MacDonald and Nigel Twist; concerts include Spirit of '86 (audience of 26,000), Univ. of California, Los Angeles, worldwide broadcast on MTV; percussionist with Colin Vearncombe 2000–; drummer with Lucky Luciano 2001–; solo artist; mem. Musicians' Union, PRS. *Recordings:* albums: with The Alarm: Declaration 1984, Strength 1985, Eye Of The Hurricane 1987, Change 1989, Standards 1990, Raw 1991, Greatest Hits Live 2001; solo: Breathe 1994, Second Generation Vol. 1 1996, Feel Free 1996, Rise 1998, Flatiron, History; singles: with The Alarm: 68 Guns 1983, Where Were You Hiding When The Storm Broke? 1984, Absolute Reality 1985, Spirit Of '76 1986, Rain In The Summertime 1987, A New South Wales 1989, Raw 1991, 45RPM 2004. *Publications:* The Words and Music of The Alarm. *E-mail:* mpo@alarmpo.demon.co.uk (office). *Website:* www .thealarm.com.

PETERS, Robert (Rob) Philip; British musician (guitar, drums, percussion), songwriter, performer and producer; *Sole Proprietor, Wafer Thin Music Production Services;* b. 4 Oct. 1954, Birmingham, England; one d. *Education:*

Univ. of Exeter. *Career:* songwriter 1973–; formed Dangerous Girls 1978; drummer with Everything But The Girl 1985–87; tour manager 1988–; percussionist with Boo Hewerdine 1991–, Colin Vearncombe/Black 2000–; guitarist 1996–; studio engineer, Highbury Studio, Birmingham; mem. Performing Right Soc., Mechanical-Copyright Protection Soc., PPL. *Compositions:* Step Out, Dangerous Girls, Long Ride Home, Georgie's Back in Town, Sister Smile. *Recordings:* Fantasy Shift, Baby The Stars Shine Bright, Ignorance, Zinc, Flatiron, Copper Heart,Twelve golden Greats, Decree Neicey, Dangerous Girls, Taaga, Men In The Glass, Step Out. *E-mail:* waferthin@ hotmail.com (home). *Website:* www.facebook.com/waferthin.

PETERSEN, Erik; Swedish musician, composer and actor; b. 25 Jan. 1953, Uppsala; two s. one d. *Education:* Sämus Malmö, Musikhögskolan, Stockholm. *Career:* Skottes Musikteater, Gävle 1983–86; Den goda människan i Sezvan, Gävle, Drottningens Juvelsmycke, Dramaten, Den Perfekta Kyssen, Angered, Det Susar i Säven, Stockholm, Oliver Twist, Turteatern, Kärlekens himmelska helvete (film), Variété Velociped; mem. Föreningen Svenska Kompositörer Av Populärmusik (SKAP). *Compositions:* Skrotsymfoni 1999, Glas mellan vänner 2004. *Recordings:* Den passionerade hästen 1986, Propeller 1997. *Address:* Oxelvägen 38, 141 41 Huddinge, Sweden (home). *Telephone:* (8) 711-11-85 (home). *E-mail:* petersenmusik@yahoo.se (office). *Website:* www.erikpetersen.se.

PETERSON, Deborah (Debbi) Mary; American musician (drums) and singer; b. 22 Aug. 1961, Northridge, San Fernando Valley, CA; sister of Vicki Peterson; m. Steve Botting; one s. *Career:* mem., The Bangles 1981–90, 2002–; other collaborations include Gina Schock, Siobhan Maher (as Kindred Spirit). *Recordings include:* albums: with The Bangles: The Bangles 1982, All Over The Place 1984, Different Light 1985, Everything 1988, Doll Revolution 2003, Sweetheart of the Sun 2011; with Kindred Spirit: Kindred Spirit 1995. *Current Management:* c/o Brett Steinberg, Creative Artists Agency, 9830 Wilshire Blvd, Beverly Hills, CA 90212-1825, USA. *Telephone:* (310) 288-4545. *Fax:* (310) 288-4800. *E-mail:* management@thebangles.com. *Website:* www .thebangles.com.

PETERSON, Gilles; DJ; b. 28 Sept. 1964, Switzerland. *Career:* began DJ career aged 18, Jazz Rooms, Electric Ballroom, Camden, London; regularly ran Sunday afternoon session at Dingwalls, Camden; worked on Acid Jazz label, Talkin Loud label; DJ's at Bar Rumba and Atmapuri, Eve Club; Presenter, Jazz FM 1990–91, Kiss FM 1991–98, BBC Radio 1 1998–2012, BBC Radio 6 Music 2012–. *Recordings include:* The INCredible Sound Of. . . 1999, Worldwide 2000, Fania DJ Series 2007, Gilles Peterson presents Brazilika 2009. *Website:* gillespetersonworldwide.com.

PETERSON, Victoria (Vicki) Anne; American musician (guitar) and singer; b. 11 Jan. 1958, Burbank, Los Angeles, CA; sister of Debbi Peterson. *Career:* mem. The Bangles 1981–90, 2002–; mem. groups, including Psycho Sisters, Double Date, Continental Drifters; other collaborations include John Doe, Belinda Carlisle, Jules Shear, Kevin Salem. *Recordings include:* albums: with The Bangles: The Bangles 1982, All Over The Place 1984, Different Light 1985, Everything 1988, Doll Revolution 2003, Sweetheart of the Sun 2011; with Continental Drifters: Vermillion 2001. *Current Management:* c/o Brett Steinberg, Creative Artists Agency, 9830 Wilshire Blvd, Beverly Hills, CA 90212-1825, USA. *Telephone:* (310) 288-4545. *Fax:* (310) 288-4800. *E-mail:* management@thebangles.com. *Website:* www.thebangles.com.

PETIT, Philippe; French jazz musician (guitar) and composer; b. 23 Nov. 1954, Marmande. *Education:* Bordeaux Conservatory of Music. *Career:* Tours with Philip Catherine; Tal Farlow; Barney Wilen; Miroslav Vitous; Eliot Zigmund; With own group including: Michel Graillier; Alain Jean Marie; Riccardo Del Fra; Al Levitt; Aldo Romano; J F Jenny-Clark; mem, SACEM. *Compositions:* Sigmanialogie 21, for jazz quartet and symphony orchestra, 1985. *Recordings:* Parfums, 1977; For All The Life, 1979; La Note Bleue, with Barney Wilen, 1986; Impressions of Paris, with Miroslav Vitous, 1989; Solo: Guitar Reflections, 1991; Standards Recital, with Tal Farlow, 1993; Guitar Attitude, 1996.

PETRI, Michala; Danish musician (recorder player); b. 7 July 1958, Copenhagen; d. of Kanny Sambleben and Hanne Petri; m. Lars Hannibal 1992 (divorced 2010); two d. *Education:* Staatliche Hochschule für Musik und Theater, Hannover. *Career:* debut aged five, Danish Radio 1964; soloist with Orchestra Tivoli, Copenhagen 1969; over 4,000 concerts in Europe, USA, Japan, China, Korea, Mexico, Canada and Australia; numerous appearances at festivals, performances on TV and radio; performs frequently with orchestras worldwide, also as duo with lutenist and guitarist, Lars Hannibal; has inspired and initiated various contemporary compositions by Malcolm Arnold, Vagn Holmboe, Per Nørgård, Thomas Koppel, Daniel Boertz, Gary Kulesha, Stephen Stucky, Joan Albert Amargos, Chen Yi and others; mem. Presidium, UNICEF Denmark; Vice-Pres. Cancer Asscn (Denmark). *Recordings include:* more than 60 albums, including 12 with Academy of St Martin-in-the-Fields, Bach Sonatas and Handel Sonatas with Keith Jarrett, Vivaldi Concertos with Heinz Holliger, Henryk Szeryng, contemporary concerts with English Chamber Orchestra and Danish Nat. Symphony Orchestra, six albums with Lars Hannibal, albums with Chen Yue, Kremerata Baltica, Chinese Recorder Concertos, English Recorder Concertos, Uģis Prauliņš: The Nightingale (ECHO Klassik Award for World Premiere Recording of the Year 2012) 2011, two albums with Danish Nat. Vocal Ensemble. *Publications:* ed. of several works for Wilhelm Hansen and Moeck; Sheet Music Now. *Honours:* Hon. Prof., Royal Danish Acad. of Music; Kt of the Dannebrog 1995, Order Kt

of First Grade 2010; Jacob Gade Prize 1969, 1975, Critics' Prize of Honour 1976, Nording Radio Prize 1977, Niels Prize 1980, Tagea Brandts Prize 1980, Maarum Prize 1981, Schroder Prize 1982, Deutscher Schallplattenpreis 1997, 2002, Sonning Music Prize 2000, H. C. Lumbye Prize 2000, European Soloist Prize 'Pro Europa' 2005, Danish Music Award 2006, three ECHO Klassik Awards. *Current Management:* c/o Lars Hannibal, Borgergade 142, 3rd, 1300 Copenhagen K, Denmark. *Telephone:* 40-15-05-77. *E-mail:* hannibal@ michalapetri.com. *Website:* www.ourrecordings.com. *Address:* Nordskraenten 3, 2980 Kokkedal, Denmark (office). *Telephone:* 26-13-58-77 (office). *E-mail:* mail@michalapetri.com (office). *Website:* www.michalapetri.com.

PETROV, Petar; Bulgarian musician (bass). *Career:* member, Konkurent 1986–; numerous concerts, TV, radio appearances, Bulgaria. *Recordings:* Konkurent 1989, Something Wet 1995, Escape from Paradise 2002, Give me Time 2007. *Honours:* First prizes: Top Rock Band, Youth Festival Vidin 1989, Rock Ring, Sofia 1990, Top Rock Composition: The Cavalry 1991, Top Rock Singer, Bulgaria 1994, Group of the Year, The Darik Radio Countdown 1994. *E-mail:* emil.anchev@abv.bg (office). *Website:* www.konkurentrockband.com.

PETROV, Vadim; Czech composer and academic; *President, The Dilia;* b. 24 May 1932, Prague; m. Marta Votápková 1954; one s. two d. *Education:* Acad. of Fine Arts, Prague. *Career:* Head Music Dept Soc. of Music, Prague 1957–66; Dir Conservatory of Dance Music and Jazz 1966–70; Prof. of Composition Prague Conservatory 1970–92; Pres. The Dilia 1998–; specialist in music for film and stage. *Compositions include:* for animation films: The Little Mole, The Brave Soldier Svejk, Lucas (Gottwaldov Festival Award 1982, West Berlin Festival Award 1983), The Little Mole in the City (Gottwaldov Festival Award 1983), The Little Mole in a Dream (Moscow Festival Award 1985, Gottwaldov Festival Award 1985, Gijon Festival Award 1985), The Giant Mountains Fairly Tales; for children's films: Jonas and the Lizinka the Whale (Best Film for Children, Tokyo 1980), Lucas Brave Vladislav (Gottwaldov Festival Award 1985); for TV films: The Swan (Plovdiv Festival Award, Bulgaria 1983), There Are Some Limits (Japanese Festival of TV Film Award 1989), Hope's Bottom is Deep (Prague Festival Gold Award 1989),Evangelium (Banff Festival Award, Canada 1993), The Romance of the Water Spirit, Forgotten Faces, The Devil in Prague; for film documentaries: The Prague Castle (Madrid Film Festival Award 1982); for TV plays: Adriena (Award of A. Zapotocky 1979); for stage: Opera Buffo: Taming of the Shrewd, Courtship and Marriage, The Good Old Band; for radio plays: Sonnets Chiseled in Stone, Pax Rerum Optima, The Swan's Lament, The Nightingale and the Rose, The Twelve (Radio Harvest CSR Award 1958), The Season in the Lower Class Settlement (Radio Harvest CSR Award 1960), Johan Doctor Faust, The Avenue of Cherry Trees (Prix Bohemia 1982), The Hare's Tale (Prix Bohemia 1982), How to Bake the Luck (Prix Bohemia 1983), Pax rerum optima (Prix Bohemia 1984); symphonic work: The Beskydfy Episodes, The Ballet Miniature, Tarantela, The Overture of 89, Violin concerto in D, The Salt of the Earth – poem for symphonic orchestra and concert piano; popular music: Nocturno in G, Burlesque, The Valessian Intermezzo, Song of the Night, The Ditty, Scherzo poetico, Danse pastorale; for voice: Ballad cycles based on folk texts with piano accompaniment, Maple Violin choir cycle, One Day and Yet, Another One. *Recordings include:* The Maple Violin, Lucy and Miracles, Anna Snegina, Don Quixote, Don Jean and others. *Publications include:* Czech and Slovak Composer 1980, Film and Time 1983, The Little Czechoslovak Encyclopedia 1986. *Honours:* numerous nat. and int. awards including Czechoslovak Television Award for Best Scenic Music 1987, Czechoslovak Composer Asscn Award for Life Work 1987, Award of Asscn of Czechoslovak Composers, Czech Television 1997, Svobodné Slovo, Prague 1997. *Address:* Krátkého 1, 15000 Prague (office); Hlubočinka 844, 25168 Kamenice, Czech Republic (home). *Telephone:* (283) 893603 (office); (323) 671490 (home). *Fax:* (283) 893599 (office). *E-mail:* petrov@dilia.cz (office); prof.petrov@quick.cz. *Website:* www.dilia.cz (office); www.prof-vadim-petrov.cz (home).

PETROV, Vassil; Bulgarian pop and jazz musician and singer; b. 1964, Sofia. *Education:* Acad. of Popular Music, Sofia. *Career:* numerous appearances at jazz, popular music festivals; performances in Helsinki, Oslo, Stockholm, Belgrade, at the Winter Olympics, Lillehammer, Norway; worked with Villi Kazassyan's Big Band; mem. jazz group, Acoustic Version; concerts with Pleven's Philharmonic Orchestra; worked on albums with composer Vassil Parmakov, lyricist Terry Kaliski; plays and sings own compositions. *Recordings include:* albums: The Other One (Best Hit of the Year, Best Album of the Year), Castrol Presents: Vassil Petrov, Duets (with pianist Rumen Toskov), Petrov Sings Parmakoff 1994. *Honours:* Nat. Music Award for Number One Male Voice, Orpheus Award for Best Male Vocalist.

PETRUCCIANI, Louis; French musician (contrabass). *Education:* Studies with Chuck Israël, USA, 1980. *Career:* Played with Barre Phillips, 1975–80; European tour with brother Michel Petrucciani; Also played with Lenny White; Trio with brother Michel; Quartet with brother Philippe. *Recordings:* Solo albums: Loï's Blues; The Librarian; MisterLight; with Tony Petrucianni: Nuages; with Orchestre de Jazz du Languedoc-Rousillon: Dialogues; Recordings with numerous artists including: Bernard Lubat; Lee Konitz; Alain Jean-Marie; Philippe Petit. *E-mail:* louis.petrucciani@wanadoo.fr. *Website:* www .petrucciani.com.

PETTAN, Svanibor Hubert, BA, MA, PhD; Slovenian ethnomusicologist and academic; *Professor and Chairman of Ethnomusicology Programme, Faculty of Arts, University of Ljubljana;* b. 11 Feb. 1960, Zagreb. *Education:* Univ. of Zagreb, Univ. of Ljubljana, Univ. of Maryland, USA. *Career:* Music Ed., Radio

Zagreb 1984–88; Research Scholar, Inst. of Ethnology and Folklore Research, Zagreb 1988–98; adjunct staff, Univs of Zagreb 1993–2010, Maribor 1995–2010, Pula 2003–, Split 2011–; Asst Prof., Univ. of Ljubljana 1995–, Assoc. Prof. 2001–, Full Prof. 2006–, Chair. Ethnomusicology Programme, Faculty of Arts; Visiting Scholar/Prof., Norway 1994, 1996, USA 1998, 2001, 2004, 2006, 2010, 2012, Taiwan 2013, Australia 2013; frequent guest lectures and conf. participations; mem. Int. Council for Traditional Music (Sec. Gen.), Soc. for Ethnomusicology, European Seminar in Ethnomusicology, Cultural and Ethnomusicological Soc. Folk Slovenia (Pres.). *Recordings:* Folk Songs and Dances of Banija, selection and sleeve notes, Croatia, Vols 2 and 3, 1988, Croatia: Traditional Music of Today selection and sleeve notes, 1998, Folk Revival in Slovenia, sleeve notes, 1998, Kosovo Roma, selection and sleeve notes, 2001. *Film:* Kosovo through the Eyes of Local Rom (Gypsy) Musicians 2012. *Recordings:* Folk Songs and Dances of Banija, Croatia, Vols 2 and 3 (selection and sleeve notes) 1988, Croatia: Traditional Music of Today (selection and sleeve notes) 1998, Folk Revival in Slovenia (sleeve notes) 1998, Ethnophonia (sleeve notes) 1999, Kosovo Roma (selection and sleeve notes) 2001, Suita Romani (sleeve notes) 2005, Etno (selection and sleeve notes) 2011, Hubert Pettan (selection and sleeve notes) 2012. *Publications:* Gypsies, Music and Politics, Balkans: A Case Study from Kosovo 1996, Music, Politics and War: Views from Croatia (ed.) 1998, Rom Musicians in Kosovo: Interaction and Creativity 2002, Music and Music Research in Croatia (ed.) 1998, Music and Minorities (ed.) 2001, Glasba in Manjšine/Music and Minorities (ed.) 2001, Rom (co-ed.) 2001, Kosovo Roma 2001, Encounter with 'The Others from Within': The Case of Gypsy Musicians in Former Yugoslavia 2001, Creativity 2002, Male, Female, and Beyond in Culture and Music of the Roma in Kosovo 2003, Balkan Boundaries and How to Cross Them: A Postlude 2007, Applied Ethnomusicology (ed.) 2008, Musical Perceptions of the Turks in the Territories of Former Yugoslavia: An Ethnomusicological Plea for Inclusiveness 2009, War, Music, and Ethnomusicology at the Break-up of Yugoslavia 2009, Dance House: European Models of Folk Music and Dance Revival in Urban Settings 2009, Music in War, Music for Peace: Experiences in Applied Ethnomusicology 2010, Lambada na Kosovu: etnomuzikološki ogledi 2010, Applied Ethnomusicology: Historical and Contemporary Approaches (co-ed.) 2010, Etnomuzikologija na razpotju: iz glasbene zakladnice kosovskih Romov 2011. *Honours:* Golden Lent, Univ. of Ljubljana. *Address:* University of Ljubljana, Department of Musicology, Aškerčeva 2, 1000 Ljubljana, Slovenia (office). *Telephone:* (1) 2411326 (office). *E-mail:* svanibor.pettan@guest.arnes.si.

PETTERS, John David; British traditional and swing jazz musician (drums) and bandleader; b. 13 April 1953, Stratford, London, England; m. Teresa Mellerick 1980; two s. *Career:* formed New Dixie Syncopators 1976; worked with John Gill and Ronn Weatherburn 1977; joined Ken Sims Dixie Kings 1979; formed John Petters Swing Band 1982; opened Jazz Club, The Square, Harlow, Essex; American soloists include Wild Bill Davison, Art Hodes, Kenny Davern, George Masso, Yank Lawson, Slim Gaillard, Al Casey, Billy Butterfield; British artists include Georgie Fame, Ken Colyer, Monty Sunshine, Humphrey Lyttelton, Cy Laurie, Maxine Daniels, George Chisholm; stage shows and concerts include Queens of The Blues 1986, Roarin' 20s Show 1987, concerts with Lonnie Donegan, George Chisholm, Yank Lawson, Legends of American Dixieland 1988, Swinging Down Memory Lane 1989, Legends of British Trad 1991, This Joint Is Jumpin' 1993, Special Magic of Benny Goodman 1994, Boogie Woogie and All That Jazz 1994; ran Honky Tonk Train, Severn Valley Railway 1995; formed National Traditional Mailing List; Dir, Mundesley Jazz Weekend Festival 1995, Drum Crazy show and workshops 1996, This Joint Is Jumping, Blackpool 1996, first Prestatyn Jazz 'n' Swing Forum 1997; This Is Jazz festival, Torquay 1997; Now You Has Jazz Jazz Jazz, Pontins; toured UK theatres with 'S Wonderful, Gershwin centenary show 1998; toured with Hoagy – Old Music Master, Hoagy Carmichael centenary show 1999; toured Bing – The Road to Rhythm and Romance 2003, Swinging Down Memory Lane 2 2004; dir and promoter William Shakespeare Jazz Festival, Stratford upon Avon 2001–04, Simply Sinatra 2006; toured Germany with Herbert Christ International Band 2007; Upton Jazz Festival with Swing Band 2008; regular gigs with Alan Gresty/ Brian White Ragtimers 2008–09, 2010; appeared on BBC Radio Gold For Grown-ups and BBC Ulster Jazz Club as part of the Krupa Centenary; A Centenary Celebration of Gene Krupa & Benny Goodman, tour with Swing Band 2009; directed Now You Has Jazz Jazz Jazz Festival at Pontins Pakefield 2010, Louis Armstrong Celebration Jazz Festival, Bracklesham Bay, Sussex 2010, 2011, William Shakespeare Jazz 'n' Swing Festival, Stratford upon Avon 2010; worked with Pete Allen Traditional Jazz Band 2011; solo guest with Herbert Christ band in Frankfurt 2011, Caveau de la Huchette, Paris 2011, promoted First Louis Armstrong Celebration Jazz Festival at Mundesley, Norfolk 2012; 13th Louis Armstrong Festival at Bracklesham Bay, Sussex 2012; 10th William Shakespeare Jazz 'n' Swing Festival at Stratford upon Avon 2012; continues to run successful jazz concerts at St John's Arts Centre, Old Harlow, Essex; appeared on BBC 4 documentary Trad Jazz Britannia 2013; played Goodnight Sweethearts Dance Camp and Barrellhouse Stomp Swing Dances with John Petters Swing Band 2013. *Recordings include:* Live and Swinging, with Kenny Davern 1985, Mixed Salad, with Wally Fawkes 1986, Together Again, with Art Hodes and Wild Bill Davison 1988, Swinging Down Memory Lane, with George Chisholm and Maxine Daniels 1989, Rags Boogie and Swing, with Simon Holliday 1989, Mixed Salad 1989, The Legends of British Trad 1991, Blowin' A Storm 1991, This Joint Is Jumping 1992, John Petters' Red Hot Seven 1994, Walking With

The King 1994, Boogie Woogie and All That Jazz, with Duncan Swift 1995, Makin' Whoopee, with John Petters Dixielanders, Swing Band with Yank Lawson and Kenny Davern, 1996, Bechet Centenary Band, Blame It On The Blues, with Trevor Whiting, John Wurr, Martin Litton, Dave Green 1997, It's Me, O Lord 1998, Shades of Jazz, with John Cherry, It's Alright With Me, with Nick Dawson, 'S Wonderful, John Petters Broadway Melodists 1998, Hoagy – The Old Music Master, John Petters and His Music Masters 1999, Goin' Bananas, John Petters Jazz 'n' Swing Band, Very Live at Pakefield, Down in Honky Tonk Town, with Sammy Rimington 2000, Eye to Eye, with Dave Bailey and Annie Hawkins 2000, Flamingo, with Trevor Whiting 2000, Coalition, with Wild Bill Davison and Art Hodes 2000, Stompin' at the Savoy – A Tribute to Benny Goodman, with Trevor Whiting and Nick Dawson 2001, Havin' Fun, with Pete Allen 2001, Keepin' Out of Mischief, with Cuff Billett 2002, Bing The Road to Rhythm & Romance, with Martin Litton 2003, Tailgate Ramble – A Salute to Kid Ory, with Mike Pointon and Cuff Billett 2003, Swinging Down Memory Lane 2, with Val Wiseman and Nick Dawson 2003, An Evening with George Webb and John Petters Hot Five 2004, Heah me Talkin': A Tribute to Johnny Dodds 2004, 'S Wonderful Vol. 2 2005, Simply Sinatra 2006, Sing Sing Sing, with John Petters Swing Band 2007, A Centenary Tribute to Gene Krupa & Benny Goodman, with James Evans & Paolo Alderighi 2008, Ragtime Revisited, with Martin Litton & James Evans 2009, Sing Sing Sing (digital download) 2013. *Publications:* contrib. to Jazz Journal (History of Jazz Drumming) 1985, Just Jazz magazine 2003. *Address:* John Petters Productions, New House Farm, Hospital Drove, Long Sutton, Lincs., PE12 9EN, England (office). *Telephone:* (1406) 365731 (office). *E-mail:* tjpost@traditional-jazz.com (office). *Website:* www.traditional-jazz.com (office).

PETTY, Tom; American singer, songwriter and musician (guitar); b. 20 Oct. 1953, Gainesville, Fla. *Career:* guitarist with local groups, Sundowners, Epics, Mudcrutch; founder mem., Tom Petty and The Heartbreakers 1975–; mem., The Traveling Wilburys 1988–; regular US and int. tours, concert and festival appearances. *Film appearances:* FM 1978, Made in Heaven 1987, The Postman 1997. *Recordings include:* albums: with the Heartbreakers: Tom Petty and The Heartbreakers 1976, You Gonna Get It! 1978, Damn The Torpedoes 1979, Hard Promises 1981, Long After Dark 1982, Southern Accents 1985, Pack Up The Plantation 1986, Let Me Up (I've Had Enough) 1987, Full Moon Fever 1989, Into The Great Wide Open 1991, Greatest Hits 1993, Take The Highway 1994, She's The One (OST) 1996, Echo 1999, Anthology: Through The Years 2000, The Last DJ 2002, Mojo 2010, Hypnotic Eye 2014; with The Traveling Wilburys: Traveling Wilburys 1988, Vol. 2 1989, Vol. 3 1990; solo: Wildflowers 1994, Highway Companion 2006; with Mudcrutch: Mudcrutch 2008. *Honours:* MTV Music Video Award (for Don't Come Around Here No More) 1985, Billboard Century Award 2005. *Current Management:* East End Management, 12441 Ventura Court, Studio City, CA 91604, USA. *Telephone:* (818) 985-5060. *Fax:* (818) 985-5069. *Website:* www.tompetty.com; www.mudcrutchmusic.com.

PEWNY, Michael; Austrian boogie woogie and blues musician (piano); b. 11 Nov. 1963, Vienna. *Education:* MBA; Private classical education on piano, started playing age 7. *Career:* First concert, Vienna, 1981; Several radio and television appearances, ORF, Austria; US tours; Festivals include: Blues Spring Festival, Belgium, 1992; Le Nuits Jazz and Boogie Festival, Paris, 1993, 1994. *Recordings:* Left Hand Roller, featuring Dana Gillespie, 1990; Boogie On My Mind, featuring Sabine Ruzicka, 1992; Vienna Boogie Woogie, featuring Torsten Zwingenberger, 1994; Crazy Bout Boogie, 1996; Movin' To Chicago; 20th Anniversary, 2000. *E-mail:* pewny@gmx.at. *Website:* www.pewnyboogie.at.

PEYROUX, Madeleine E.; American jazz singer; b. 1974, Athens, GA. *Career:* fmr street musician in Paris, France. *Recordings include:* albums: Dreamland 1996, Careless Love 2004, Half the Perfect World 2006, Bare Bones 2009, Standing on the Rooftop 2011, The Blue Room 2013. *Current Management:* c/o Cynthia B. Herbst, American International Artists, 356 Pine Valley Road, Hoosick Falls, NY 12090, USA. *E-mail:* Cynthia@aiartists.com (office). *Website:* www.aiartists.com (office); www.madeleinepeyroux.com.

PHILIPPAKIS, Yannis Barnabas Emanuel; British singer, songwriter and musician (guitar); b. 23 April 1986, Karpathos, Greece. *Education:* Magdalen Coll. School, St John's Coll., Oxford. *Career:* fmr mem. The Edmund Fitzgerald; Founder-mem. Foals 2005–. *Recordings:* albums: with Foals: Antidotes 2008, Total Life Forever 2010, Holy Fire 2013, What Went Down 2015. *Honours:* with Foals: NME Awards for Best Track (for Spanish Sahara) 2011, (for Inhaler) 2013, Q Magazine Awards for Best Live Act 2013, for Best Act in the World Today 2015. *Current Management:* c/o Steve Matthews, Q Prime Management, 729 Seventh Avenue, #1600, New York, NY 10019, USA. *Telephone:* (212) 302-9790. *E-mail:* info@qprime.com. *Website:* www.qprime.com; www.foals.co.uk.

PHILIPS, Ross; British musician (guitar); b. Chertsey, Surrey. *Career:* previously worked in a hi-fi shop; guitar player with band Hard-Fi 2003–. *Recordings:* albums: Stars of CCTV 2005, Once Upon a Time in the West 2007; other: In Operation (DVD) 2006. *Current Management:* Necessary Records, PO Box 28362, London SE20 7WH, England. *Telephone:* (7832) 141503. *E-mail:* info@necessaryrecords.com. *Website:* www.necessaryrecords.com; www.hard-fi.com (office).

PHILLIPPS, Martin John James; New Zealand songwriter, singer and musician (guitar); b. 2 July 1963, Wellington. *Career:* band mem., The Same

1978–80, The Chills 1980–92 (relaunched as Martin Phillipps and The Chills 1995–); tours: Australasia, Europe, USA late 1980s–early 1990s; also played with The Clean (re-formed), Snapper, Pop Art Toasters, April Fools. *Recordings include:* albums: Kaleidoscope World (compilation) 1986, Brave Words 1987, Submarine Bells 1989, Soft Bomb 1992, Pop Art Toasters (EP) 1994, Heavenly Pop Hits (Best of. . .) 1994, Sunburnt 1996, Sketch Book Vol. One 1999, Secret Box 2001. *Honours:* New Zealand Music Awards: Top Group 1987 and Top Group, Album, Single, Songwriter 1990. *Address:* PO Box 705, Dunedin Central, New Zealand.

PHILLIPS, Dudley; British musician (electric bass, bass) and composer; b. 9 June 1960, Maidenhead, Berkshire. *Career:* fmr mem. soul bands; world tour with Womack and Womack, Bill Withers, Mica Paris; jazz touring with Annie Whitehead, Andy Sheppard, Orphy Robinson, Perfect Houseplants; appearances at numerous jazz festivals, television and radio appearances; projects include Balanescu Quartet, London Sinfonietta, Orlando Consort, Ernestine Anderson, Ronny Jordan, Dave Valentin, Najma. *Compositions include:* Sextet for Vanessa Smith, for string quartet, electric bass and drums; Arrangement of early vocal music for Orlando Consort plus Perfect Houseplants; Writing for own jazz sextet. *Recordings:* albums: six with Perfect Houseplants (first album voted Best Jazz Album of the Year), Life Without Trousers 2005; Andy Sheppard's Moving Image; two with Orphy Robinson; three with Colin Town's Mask; four with June Tabor; albums with Annie Whitehead, John Etheridge, Tim Whitehead, Permission, Huw Warren, Mark Lockheart band. *Address:* c/o Oliver Weindling, Babel Label, 9 Gillett Square, London N16 8AZ, England (office). *Website:* www.babellabel.co.uk (office).

PHILLIPS, John Keith Andrew; Australian composer, producer and musician (guitar, bass); b. 9 June 1961, Darlinghurst, Sydney; m. Emily Humphries; one s. one d. *Education:* Latrobe Univ., Melbourne. *Career:* founder mem., Easter 1983–85; mem., Not Drowning, Waving 1984–95. *Compositions for films:* Body Work 1988, Proof 1991, Say A Little Prayer 1993, Greenkeeping 1993, That Eye The Sky 1994, What I Have Written 1995, River Street 1996, Idiot Box 1996, The Myth of Fingerprints 1997; contrib. to Malcolm 1985. *Recordings:* Another Pond, Little Desert, Cold and the Crackle, Claim, Tabaran, Circus, Stylin Up, by Christine Anu, Telek, by Telek, World Turning, by Yothu Yindi. *Honours:* Aria Award, Proof, film soundtrack CD; Aria Award, Telek, album, 1997. *Current Management:* Loud and Clear Management, PO Box 276, Albert Park, 2306, Australia.

PHILLIPS, Josh; British musician (keyboards) and producer; b. 12 Dec. 1962, Rochester, Kent. *Education:* Guildhall School of Music. *Career:* professional musician 1982–; tours with Diamond Head 1983–85, Heatwave (world tour) 1986–88, Big Country (Russia, Estonia, Europe, UK) 1988–90, Midge Ure (Europe, UK) 1991, 1992, Procul Harum (Europe) 1993–94, 2004–, Steve Roux Band (UK and Europe) 1993–94, Moody Marsden Band (Europe) 1994–95, Gary Brooker All-Star Band Annual Charity Christmas Show 1990–; contrib. to music videos by numerous artists; many television appearances; recorded with Mark Brzezicki, Tony Butler, Steve Roux. *Compositions:* incidental television music; Meltdown ITV Rock Music Show; Comment; music for various commercials.

PHILLIPS, Martyn John Courtenay, BA; British record producer, recording engineer and musician (guitar, keyboards, viola); b. 24 Nov. 1960. *Education:* Univ. of Oxford. *Career:* recording engineer, London 1982; synthesizer programmer 1983–; record producer 1989–. *Compositions:* Dolphin Stories/Out of the Blue, music for TV series; Living with the Enemy, Title music; Songs for Lindy Layton, Akasa, Signs of Life, Deep. *Recordings:* producer of albums by Amina Anabi, The Beloved, Cause and Effect, Erasure, Jesus Jones, London Beat, Roachford, Soul II Soul, Swing Out Sister. *Website:* www.martynphillips.com.

PHILLIPS, (Holly) Michelle; American singer and actress; b. 4 June 1944, Long Beach, CA; m. 1st John Phillips 1962 (died 2001); two s. one d.; m. 2nd Dennis Hopper 1970 (divorced); m. 3rd Robert Burch 1978 (divorced); m. 4th Steven Zax 2000. *Career:* mem., The Mamas and the Papas; mem, NARAS; ACOMPAS. *Films:* The Last Movie 1971, Dillinger 1973, Miracle 1975, Valentino 1977, Bloodline 1979, The Man with Bogart's Face 1980, Savage Harvest 1981, American Anthem 1986, Let It Ride 1989, Keep on Running 1990, Scissors 1991, Joshua Tree 1993, Lost in the Parshing Point Hotel 2000, The Price of Air 2000, March 2001, Harry and Max 2004, Kids in America 2005, Unbeatable Harold 2006. *Television includes:* Fantasy Island 1979–84, The Love Boat 1981–84, Hotel 1983–86, Knots Landing 1987–93, Second Chances 1993–94, Malibu Shores 1996, Spicy City 1997, Beverly Hills 90210 1997–98, The Magnificent Seven 1998–2000, 7th Heaven 2001–04. *Compositions:* Co-wrote California Dreamin'; Creque Alley. *Recordings:* albums: If You Can Believe Your Eyes and Ears 1966, Cass John Michelle Denny 1966, Deliver 1967, Presenting The Papas And The Mamas 1968, Singles+ 1999. *Publications:* California Dreamin'. *Honours:* Grammy Award.

PHILLIPS, Phillip; American singer, songwriter and musician (guitar); b. (Phillip LaDon Phillips Jr), 20 Sept. 1990, Albany, Ga; s. of Phillip LaDon Phillips Sr and Sheryl Phillips. *Education:* Lee County High School, Albany Technical Coll. *Career:* winner of American Idol series 11 2012; toured North America supporting Matchbox Twenty 2013, John Mayer 2013; solo tour 2013. *Television:* American Idol (series winner) 2012. *Recordings:* album: The World from the Side of the Moon 2012. *Current Management:* c/o 19 Entertainment, CORE Media Group, 8560 West Sunset Boulevard, 9th Floor, West Hollywood, CA 90069, USA. *Telephone:* (310) 777-1940. *E-mail:* inquiries@

19entertainment.com. *Website:* coremediagroup.com/19.html; www .phillipphillips.com.

PHILLIPS, Roy; British musician (keyboards) and singer; b. 5 May 1941, Parkstone, Poole, England. *Career:* own trio, The Peddlers 15 years; worked in Las Vegas for 15 seasons; world tours, regular radio and TV world-wide; mem. Performing Right Soc., British Acad. of Songwriters, Composers and Authors. *Recordings include:* 17 albums, one DVD. *Current Management:* c/o Robyn Promotions, 27A King Street, Christchurch 8023, New Zealand. *E-mail:* info@ royphillips.org. *Website:* www.royphillips.org.

PHILLIPS, Shawn; American musician (guitar, keyboards, sitar), composer and firefighter; *Senior Officer, National Sea Rescue Institute, Port Elizabeth, South Africa;* b. 3 Feb. 1943, Fort Worth, Tex.; s. of James Atlee Phillips and Joyce Clayton Phillips; m. Juliette Phillips; one s. *Education:* achieved Gen. Educational Devt while in USN. *Career:* Lead singer, Broadway musical, Jesus Christ Superstar; tours include South Africa, S Korea, England, Canada, USA, Japan, France, Holland; First Officer, Navigator, Extrication Specialist, Nat. Sea Rescue Inst., Port Elizabeth (S Africa); EMT-B, Scuba Rescue Diver; mem. Soc. of Composers, Authors and Music Publrs of Canada (SOCAN), Broadcast Music, Inc. (BMI). *Film appearance:* Run With The Wind, Futurekick. *Television appearances:* Midnight Special (four times), CBS; In Concert, NBC. *Compositions include:* Sunshine Superman album (co-writer, with Donovan), Disturbing Horizons, Events In The Life Of A Prince (performed by the Nashville Symphony Orchestra) 2006. *Recordings:* albums: Contribution 1970, Second Contribution (three platinum discs) 1971, Collaboration 1972, Faces 1973, Furthermore 1974, Bright White 1975, Do You Wonder 1976, Rumplestiltskin's Resolve 1977, Spaced 1978, Transcendence 1980, Best of Shawn Phillips 1986, Beyond Here Be Dragons 1988, The Truth If It Kills 1994, Another Contribution 1995, No Category 2002, Living Contribution, Live At The Kirstenbosch Botanical Gardens 2008, Living Collaboration, Live at the Minneapolist Zoo Amphitheaer 2009, Reflections 2012, Perspective 2013. *Honours:* Paramedic Honoraire, Urgences-Santé Emergency Medical Services, Montreal 2003; First Prize, Yamaha World Popular Song Festival 1973, First Responder Of The Year 2000, Commendation For Bravery Above And Beyond, Pedernales Emergency Services, Austin, Tex. 2001. *Current Management:* c/o Juliette Phillips. *Telephone:* (72) 478-1896. *Address:* 20 Goedehoop Way, Seaview, Port Elizabeth, South Africa (home). *Telephone:* (631) 459-1547 (office). *E-mail:* sflips2003@yahoo.com (home). *Website:* www.shawnphillipsmusic.com.

PHILLIPS, (Nicholas) Stephen (Steve); British singer and musician (guitar); b. 18 Feb. 1948, London, England; two d. *Career:* semi-professional musician 1961–86; professional solo artist 1986–; also duo with Brendan Croker; collaborations with Paul Judge; mem., Notting Hillbillies 1990; own band, Steve Phillips and The Rough Diamonds; mem. PRS, PAMRA. *Recordings include:* albums: The Best of Steve Phillips 1987, Steel Rail Blues 1989; with Notting Hillbillies: Missing Presumed Having A Good Time 1990, Been A Long Time Gone 1995, Just Pickin' 1996. *Current Management:* GTA, Wisteria House, 14 Glamorgan Road, Hampton Wick, Surrey KT1 4HB, England.

PHIMISTER, Glen; British recording engineer; b. 15 Sept. 1953, London; m. Hortensze. *Education:* Ealing Mead Academy, London. *Career:* Engineer, Unity Gain Studio and freelance; Previously with: Studios 301, Sydney; Air Studios, London; Trident Studios, London; Worked on various pop, rock, jazz and orchestral recordings, mid 1970s–; Worked on Sydney Olympics, 2000; TV work includes: Home and Away; The Farm. *Recordings:* Olivia Newton-John; INXS; Pseudo Echo; Prague Symphony Orchestra; Split Enz; Slim Dusty; David Campbell; Iota; Jazz Police.

PHOENIX; American musician (bass guitar); b. (David Michael Farrell), 8 Feb. 1977, Plymouth, MA. *Education:* private guitar lessons. *Career:* mem., high school group The Snax; mem., Xero 1996, left band after completion of coll.; rejoined group, now named Linkin Park 2000–; numerous int. concerts. *Recordings include:* albums: Hybrid Theory (Rock Bear Awards for Best Int. Album 2001) 2000, Reanimation 2002, In The End: Live & Rare 2002, Meteora 2003, Live In Texas 2003, Collision Course (Jay-Z) 2004, Minutes to Midnight 2007, A Thousand Suns 2010. *Honours:* Billboard Award for Best Modern Rock Artist 2001, Rock Bear Award for Best Int. Band 2001, Kerrang! Award for Best Int. Newcomer 2001, Rolling Stone Award for Best Hard Rock/Metal Band 2001, MTV Awards for Best Group, Best Hard Rock 2002, MTV Europe Awards for Best Rock Band 2004, for Best World Stage Performance 2009, Grammy Award for Best Rap/Sung Collaboration (for Numb/Encore, with Jay-Z) 2006, MTV Europe Music Award for Best Band 2007, American Music Award for Favorite Alternative Rock Music Artist 2007. *Current Management:* Andy Gould Management, 8484 Wilshire Boulevard, Suite 425, Beverly Hills, CA 90211, USA. *Website:* www.linkinpark.com.

PIANO OVERLORD (see Herren, Scott)

PIATKOWSKI, Dioniszy, MA; Polish critic, jazz historian, journalist, DJ and producer; *President, Era Jazzu;* b. 1954, Poznań; m. Irena; one s. two d. *Education:* Poznań Univ. *Career:* music journalist, Jazz Forum, Express Poznanski, Glos Wielkopolski, Wprost, Jazz a Go Go, Jazz Magazine; freelance journalist for several jazz magazines in Europe and the USA; jazz and music publicist, producer and organizer in Poland; Lecturer on Jazz, Black Music and Folklore, Univ. of Graz, Austria, Poznań Univ., Pittsburgh Univ., USA; DJ and Producer, Polish radio stations, shows include Jazz Acad. and Let's

Play Folklore; Producer, Dir and A&R, jazz festivals and concerts including Dave Brubeck, Stephane Grappelli, B. B. King, Jan Garbarek and Kronos Quartet; Man. Dir, Poznań Jazz Festival; founder, Programme and Music Dir, first Polish music radio station, Radio 88.4 Jazz/FM; Pres. Era Jazzu 1998–; mem. Int. Asscn for Jazz Research, Austria; Friends of Polish Music, USA; Int. Jazz Hall of Fame, Pittsburgh Univ., USA. *Publications:* Not Only Music, Fan Club Special, Komeda's Time, Jazz Giants, Blues Punk Disco, Encyclopaedia of Popular Music – Jazz; contrib. numerous articles in Polish and int. journals. *Address:* Strzelecka 37, 62-050 Mosina, Poland (home). *Fax:* (61) 8132566 (office). *E-mail:* erajazzu@jazz.pl (office). *Website:* www.jazz.pl (office).

PICCHIOTTI, Mark; producer, remixer and DJ. *Career:* worked with: Adeva, Basstoy & The Absolute, Mariah Carey, Eternal, Enrique Iglesias, Michael Jackson, Jamiroquai, Kylie Minogue, Madonna.

PICKERING, Michael (Mike) Duncan; British musician (saxophone), singer, composer and DJ; b. 24 Feb. 1958, Manchester, England. *Career:* DJ, Manchester clubs, including the Haçienda; fmr mem., Quando Quango; worked in A&R, Factory Records mid-1980s, then DeConstruction Records; founder mem., T-Coy; founder mem. dance group, M People 1990–; Sr Vice-Pres. of A&R, Columbia Records; numerous concerts and festival appearances. *Recordings include:* albums: Northern Soul 1992, Northern Soul Extended 1992, Elegant Slumming (Mercury Music Prize 1994) 1993, Bizarre Fruit 1994, Bizarre Fruit Vol. 2 1995, Fresco 1997, Testify 1999, 3 Originals 2003. *Honours:* BRIT Award for Best Dance Act 1994, 1995, Freedom of Manchester 1999. *Website:* www.m-people.com.

PICKERING, Phil; British musician (bass guitar, didgeridoo, synthesizer); b. 27 June 1960, Pembury, Kent, England; three s. one d. *Education:* guitar tuition. *Career:* mem. Webcore, Goat, Tribal Drift, Fun-Da-Mental, Lights In A Fat City, Zuvuya; mem. PRS, Musicians' Union. *Recordings include:* albums: with Vane: Glamorous Boys 1981; with Webcore: Webcore 1987, Webcore Webcore 1988; with Goat: Goat; with Tribal Drift: Like This! 1992, Medicine Hat 1992; with Zuvuya: DMT, 1994, Shamania 1994, Zuvuya: The Goat Faced Girl 1994, Driving The Monkey Insane 1994, Moose Jaw 1994, Away The Crow Road 1994, The Trance End of Dreaming 1994, Turn Around 1994, Quadruped, Quadruped 1995, with Fun-Da-Mental: Seize The Time 1994, With Intent To Pervert The Cause Of Injustice 1995, Erotic Terrorism 1998, There Shall Be Love 2001, All is War 2006. *Address:* c/o Nation Records, 19 All Saints Road, London, W11 1HE, England (office). *E-mail:* akination@btopenworld.com (office). *Website:* www.dicklaurentisdead.com/nation-records; www.fun-da-mental.co.uk.

PICKFORD, Andrew Cliffe; British musician (electronic keyboards); b. 22 Oct. 1965, Kegworth, Nottinghamshire, England. *Career:* Solo artist, Electronic music; Concerts include: Derby Cathedral, Derby Assembly Rooms and Guildhall (several times); Radio and television: Interviews and broadcasts on BBC local radio; BBC Radio 1 including John Peel show; Formed Electronic Music and Musicians Association; mem, PRS; Past Secretary, EMMA. *Recordings:* Albums: Replicant, 1993; Terraformer, 1994; Maelstrom, 1995 (all No. 1, Electronic music charts); 2 EPs; Dystopia, 1996; Xenomorph, 1996; Works Vol. 1, Works Vol. 2 (both live at Derby), 1997. *Address:* The Bryans, 89 Dundee Rd, West Ferry, Dundee DD5 3LZ, Scotland.

PIERCE, Jason, (J. Spaceman); British singer and musician (guitar, organ); b. 19 Nov. 1965, Rugby. *Career:* mem. Spacemen 3 1982–91; Founder-mem. Spiritualized 1989–; worked with Dr John and Spring Heeled Jack. *Recordings:* albums: with Spacemen 3: Sound Of Confusion 1986, Perfect Prescription 1987, Performance 1988, Playing With Fire 1989, Dreamweapon: An Evening Of Contemporary Sitar Music 1990, Taking Drugs To Make Music To Take Drugs To 1990, Recurring 1991; with Spiritualized: Lazer Guided Melodies 1992, Fucked Up Inside (live) 1993, Pure Phase 1995, Ladies and Gentlemen We Are Floating In Space 1997, Royal Albert Hall October 10 1997 (live) 1998, Let It Come Down 2001, Amazing Grace 2003, Complete Works Vol. 1 2003, Complete Works Vol. 2 2004, Songs in A&E 2008, Sweet Heart, Sweet Light 2012. . *Website:* www.spiritualized.com.

PIERSON, Kate; American singer and musician (organ); b. 27 April 1948, Weehawken, NJ. *Career:* founder mem., The B-52s 1976–, numerous live performances, particularly as successful touring band 1989–. *Recordings include:* albums: The B-52s 1979, Wild Planet 1980, Rock Lobster 1980, Party Mix! 1981, Whammy! 1983, Bouncing Off The Satellites 1986, Cosmic Thing 1989, Good Stuff 1992, Associate, Associate 1996, Nude on the Moon: the B-52s Anthology 2002; singles: Mesopotamia 1982, Channel Z 1989, Deadbeat Club 1989, Love Shack 1989, Roam 1990, Megamix 1991, Good Stuff 1992, Is That You Mo-Dean? 1992, Revolution Earth 1992, Tell It Like It T-I-Is 1992, Hot Pants Explosion 1993, Meet The Flintstones 1994, Time Capsule 1998, Funplex 2008. *Current Management:* Vector Management, PO Box 120479, Nashville, TN 37203, USA. *E-mail:* info@vectormgmt.com. *Website:* www.theb52s.com.

PIG CITY (see Clarke, Dave)

PILAROVÁ, Eva; Czech singer and actress; b. 9 Aug. 1939, Brno; d. of Ladislav Bojanovský and Fransiška Horčičková Bojanovská; m. Van Koloma-tuík 1952; one s. *Education:* Brno School of Econs and Acad. of Music. *Career:* actress and singer, Semafor Theatre 1960–62, 1964–65, 1992–, Pokoko Theatre 1962–64; singer with her own group 1965–. *Films include:* Good Walking Trip 1966, Crime in Cabinet 1968. *Publication:* I Remember 1991. *Honours:* Grand Prix du Disque 1967. *Address:* Pod Královkov 5, 169 00

Prague 6, Czech Republic. *Telephone:* (2) 357854. *Website:* www.evapilarova.cz.

PILC, Jean-Michel; American (b. French) pianist, composer and academic; *Associate Professor of Jazz Music and Improvisation, Schulich School of Music, McGill University;* b. 19 Oct. 1960, Paris, France; m; two c. *Education:* Ecole Polytechnique, Paris, France. *Career:* played in numerous concerts, festivals, tours to over 40 countries including Africa, Asia, Europe; has played with Roy Haynes, Michael Brecker, Dave Liebman, Marcus Miller, Kenny Garrett, Lenny White, Chris Potter, John Abercrombie, Mingus Dynasty & Big Band, Lew Soloff, Richard Bona and many others; composer, leader, arranger playing solo, in duo, trio and big band; European tour, Germany, Switzerland, France; moved to New York City 1995; Musical Dir to Harry Belafonte 1995–; plays in Sweet Basil, New York City, with his trio 1999–; int. touring including most major European and American festivals (North Sea, Montreal, Monterey, Juan) 2000–05; Co-Dir New York Univ. Summer Jazz Improvisation Workshop 2010; Prof. of Jazz Studies, New York Univ. 2006–15; currently Assoc. Prof. of Jazz and Improvisation, Schulich School of Music, McGill Univ., Canada. *Compositions:* music played throughout Europe, covered by many other artists; Many film scores. *Recordings include:* albums as leader: Electrochoc 1987, Funambule 1989, Big One 1993, Welcome Home 2002, Cardinal Points 2003, Follow Me 2004, Jean-Michel Pilc Trio: Together Live at Iridium, NYC 2005, New Dreams 2007, True Story 2010, Essential 2011, Threedom 2011, What is This Thing Called 2015; other recordings with Richard Bona, Mads Vinding, Hein Van De Geyn, Elizabeth Kontomanou, Eric Le Lann, J-Loup Longnon, Andre Ceccarelli, Aldo Romano etc. *Honours:* Django Reinhardt Prize, Acad. du Jazz, France 2000. *Current Management:* c/o The Janet Williamson Music Agency, PO Box 27114, Los Angeles, CA 90027, USA. *Telephone:* (323) 661-0800. *Fax:* (323) 906-8797. *E-mail:* jwilliamsonmusagency@earthlink.net. *Website:* www.janetwilliamsonmusicagency.com. *E-mail:* jmpilcinfo@aol.com (office). *Website:* www.jeanmichelpilc.com (home).

PILGREM, Rennie, (Thursday Club, New Electro Sound of London, Tribal Underground); British producer, remixer and DJ; b. 15 Jan. 1961, London. *Career:* formed Rhythm Section (with Ellis Dee), early 1990s; Founder, Thursday Club Recordings 1993; major figure in Nu Skool Breakz scene during late 1990s; co-promoter, Friction night in London (with Adam Freeland) 1996; formed Rennie Pilgrem and The TCR Allstars 2005; collaborations with Ellis Dee, Arthur Baker, Will South, B.L.I.M., Uberzone, BT, Quivver, Kosheen. *Recordings include:* albums: Philadelphia Bluntz (with Philadelphia Bluntz) 1998, Selected Werks (compilation) 2000, Perfecto Breaks 2004, Skin 2008; singles: Feel The Rhythm (with Rhythm Section), Check Out The Bass (with Rhythm Section) 1991, A Place Called Acid (as Thursday Club) 1995, Sister Sister (with Philadelphia Bluntz), Like No Other (with Arthur Baker) 1998, Eskimo (with B.L.I.M.) 2001, Tribalizm 2002, Perfecto Breaks 2003, Y4K 2004, TCR100 2006, Live in the Cavern Club 2007. *Address:* Thursday Club Recordings, Unit 2, 11 Colville Road, London W3 8BL, England (office). *Telephone:* (7764) 938907 (office). *E-mail:* info@pocketgallery.co.uk (office). *Website:* www.pocketgallery.co.uk (office).

PILKINGTON, Stephen Roy, GRSM, ARMCM, LRAM, ARCO; British music director and musician (piano, organ); *Musical Director, Opera Teifi;* b. 5 Oct. 1946, Bakewell, Derbyshire; m. Patricia Anne Wall 1970; one s. one d. *Education:* Royal Manchester Coll. of Music. *Career:* Music Dir of numerous shows, including Royal Shows for The Princess Royal, Princess Margaret 1975–; music dir for TV series; keyboard backing for TV signature tunes and plays; pianist for Welsh musical programmes; Musical Dir Artswave 1985–2010; Vocal Tutor, Music Theatre Dept, Trinity Coll., Camarthen 1997–2007; Musical Dir Opera Teifi 2000–07, 2009–; musical arranger, Fflach recording studio; accompanist and arranger, Ysgol Gerdd Ceredigion. *Recordings include:* Romance (solo piano ballads and orchestra accompaniment), Stephen Pilkington Organ Collection. *Address:* 5 New Close, Hampton Magna, Warwick, Warwicks., CV35 8TL, England (office). *Telephone:* 7887-866693 (mobile) (office). *(1926) 493691 (home). *E-mail:* stephenpilkington@sky.com.

PINE, Courtney Fitzgerald, CBE; British jazz musician (saxophone) and composer; b. 18 March 1964, London; m. June Guishard 1997; one s. three d. *Career:* Founder-mem. Jazz Warriors 1985–, The Abiba Jazz Arts 1985–; tours internationally with reggae and acoustic jazz bands; Musical Dir Windrush Gala Concert, BBC TV 1998; organizes free workshops for young people in many countries; regular presenter of radio shows (BBC); bandleader at concerts worldwide. *Recordings include:* albums: Journey to the Urge Within 1986, Destiny's Song and The Image of Pursuance 1988, The Vision's Tale 1989, Closer to Home 1990, Within the Realm of Our Dreams 1991, To the Eyes of Creation 1993, Modern Day Jazz Stories (Mercury Music Prize for Best Album of the Year 1996) 1996, Underground 1997, Another Story 1998, History is Made at Night (soundtrack) 1999, Back in the Day 2000, Devotion 2003, Resistance 2005, Transition in Tradition 2009, Europa 2011, House of Legends 2012, Song (The Ballad Book) 2015. *Television:* soundtrack to BBC documentary Mandela: Living Legend 2002. *Radio:* presented BBC Radio 2 series Millennium Jazz 1999, five series of BBC Radio 2 Jazz Crusade 1999–2004, UK Black 2003, Jazz Makers, weekly show on digital station The Jazz 2007–. *Honours:* Dr hc (Univ. of Westminster) 2004, (Univ. of Southampton) 2010; Fellow Leeds Coll. of Music, MOBO for Best Jazz Act 1996, BBC Jazz Award for Best Jazz Act 2001, Acad. of Composers and Songwriters Gold Badge 2002, Urban Music Award for Best Jazz Act 2005,

Ronnie Scott Award for Int. Saxophonist 2007, Lifetime Achievement Award, Brecon Jazz Festival 2009. *Address:* Collaboration, 33 Montpelier Street, Brighton, BN1 3DL, England (office). *Telephone:* (1273) 730744 (office). *Fax:* (1273) 775135 (office). *E-mail:* nikki@collaborationuk.com (office). *Website:* www.courtney-pine.com (office).

PINHEIRO, Chico; Brazilian composer, arranger and musician (guitar, violin); b. São Paulo. *Education:* Berklee Coll. of Music, Boston, USA. *Career:* solo artist 1991–; worked with artists, including Chico César, Rosa Passos, Luciana Souza, Jair Rodrigues, Danilo Caymmi, Zé Miguel Wisnik, Luciana Mello, Daniela Mercury, Pedro Mariano, Vicente Barreto, César Camargo Mariano, Victor Mendoza, Greg Hopkins Big Band, Giovanni Hidalgo, Vincent Borgeaux, Franck Oberson, Batiste Trotignon, Tom Jobim Orchestra. *Recordings:* album: Meia-noite Meio-dia 2003; Chico Pinheiro 2005. *Honours:* Prêmio Projeto Nascente 1994. *Current Management:* Buriti Produções, Rua Oscar Caravelas, 63, São Paulo, SP 05441–000, Brazil. *Telephone:* (11) 3812-7333. *E-mail:* buritiproducoes@uol.com.br. *Website:* www.chicopinheiro.com .br.

PINK; American singer and songwriter; b. (Alecia Moore), 8 Sept. 1979; m. Carey Hart 2006. *Career:* started singing and dancing in local bands aged 13; fmr mem. of groups, Basic Instinct and Choice; teamed up with producers LA Reid and Babyface. *Recordings include:* albums: Can't Take Me Home 2000, Missundaztood 2001, Try This 2003, I'm Not Dead 2006, Funhouse 2008, The Truth About Love 2012. *Honours:* numerous awards including: seven MTV Video Awards including for Best New Artist, for Best Song (for Get the Party Started) 2002, for Best Collaboration (for Just Give Me a Reason, with Nate Ruess) 2013, Grammy Awards for Best Pop Collaboration with Vocals (for Lady Marmalade with Christina Aguilera, Lil' Kim and Mya), (for Imagine) 2011, for Best Female Rock Vocal Performance (for Trouble) 2004, BRIT Award for Best Int. Female Solo Artist 2003, Billboard Music Award for Woman of the Year 2013. *Address:* c/o RCA Records, Sony Music Entertainment, 550 Madison Avenue, New York, NY 10022, USA (office). *Telephone:* (212) 930-4000 (office). *Fax:* (212) 930-4512 (office). *Website:* www.rcarecords .com (office); www.pinkspage.com.

PINKSTON, Steven Ray; record producer, engineer and songwriter; b. 12 Dec. 1960, Columbus, Ohio, USA; m. Angie Akin 1993. *Education:* Belmont University, Nashville, TN. *Career:* concert tours: Linda Ronstadt; Steven Curtis Chapman; Shelley West; The Commodores; Geoff Moore and The Distance; ABC; Amy Grant; mem. GMA; NARAS. *Compositions:* Cleansing Rain, Kelli Reisen (No. 3, CCM hit); 50 albums include: 4Him; Commissioned; Angelo and Veronica; Brian White; J J Cale; Dallas Brass; Midnight Clear; Graham Maw; Videos: 4Him; Commissioned; Harvest; Brian White; Wellington Boone; Grace Lazenby; Becky Tirabassi. *Recordings include:* Natural Encounters, 1998; Mark Baldwin, In the pocket, 1999; Contemporary Christian Hits, 1999; Four Him, Basics of Life, 1999. *Address:* PO Box 40784, Nashville, TN 37204, USA.

PİŞMİŞOĞLU, Raci, BA; Turkish musician (bass guitar); b. 1954, Antalya. *Education:* İzmir Univ. *Career:* teacher of music; fmr mem., Acid Tripping; mem., Yeni Türkü 1994–; concerts world-wide. *Recordings by band:* albums (does not play on all): "Yeni", Her Dem Yeni, Telli Telli Remixes, Süper Baba (film music), Ask Yeniden, Rumeli Konseri, Külhani Şarkilar, Vira Vira, Yeşilmişik?, Günebakan: Dünyanin Kapilari, Akdeniz Akdeniz. *Publications:* five books on music teaching techniques. *E-mail:* raci@yeniturku.com (office). *Website:* www.yeniturku.com.

PITCHFORD, Dean; American songwriter, screenwriter, director and author; b. 29 July 1951, Honolulu, Hawaii. *Education:* Yale Univ. *Career:* actor, singer, New York City in Godspell 1971–72, Pippin 1972–75, The Umbrellas of Cherbourg 1978; songwriter: Fame 1980, 2009, Footloose 1984, 2011, Chances Are 1989, more than 80 motion pictures; screenwriter: Footloose 1984, 2011, Sing 1989, Broadway: Carrie 1988, 2012, Footloose 1998; mem. Broadcast Music, Inc. (BMI), NAS, Nat. Acad. of Recording Arts and Sciences, Acad. of Motion Picture Arts and Sciences, Acad. of TV Arts & Sciences, Screen Actors Guild, American Fed. of TV and Radio Artists. *Compositions include:* songs: Fame (Acad. Award 1980, Golden Globe Award 1981), recorded by Irene Cara 1980, Footloose, recorded by Kenny Loggins 1984, Let's Hear It For The Boy, recorded by Deniece Williams 1984, You Should Hear How She Talks About You, recorded by Melissa Manchester 1982, After All, Almost Paradise, Holding Out For A Hero, recorded by Bonnie Tyler 1984, All The Man That I Need, recorded by Whitney Houston 1990, Love Moves In Mysterious Ways, recorded by Julia Fordham 1992, Footloose, on Broadway 1998. *Publications include:* The Big One-Oh 2008, Captain Nobody 2009, Nickel Bay Nick 2013. *Address:* PO Box 111, 8491 Sunset Blvd, Hollywood, CA 90069, USA (office). *Website:* www.deanpitchford.com.

PITICCO, Steve; Canadian musician (guitar, bass, steel, dobro); b. 6 July 1961, Toronto, Ont.; m. Laurie Laporte 1983; one s. one d.; partner, Spike McNaughton 2002. *Career:* performs professionally with Fender Telecaster guitars; regular performer with Tommy Hunter, John Landry, John Cody Carter, Kevin Collins; formed own band, South Mountain 1989; toured with Sweethearts of the Rodeo, Marty Stuart, Conway Twitty, Charley Pride; played shows supporting Vince Gill, George Jones, Johnny Cash, Ricky Skaggs; Mid-Canada TV network with South Mountain 17 years; picker, various bands, including South Mountain, on Canadian Country Music Awards' Annual Telecast 1984–94; tours in Canada and Europe 2008. *Recordings:* 17 albums with South Mountain; session player on recordings

by Patricia Conroy, Tracy Prescott, Don Neilson, John Cody Carter; released own self-titled CD 2005. *Honours:* seven CCMA Instrumentalist of Year Awards 1985–94, CCMA Rising Star Award 1991, CCMA Guitar Player of the Year 1990–93, DCMA Awards for Int. Instrumentalist 1993, 1994, 2000, 2001, 2002, 2003. *Telephone:* (613) 967-8969 (home). *E-mail:* SPiticco@sympatico.ca (home). *Website:* www3.sympatico.ca/spiticco; www.myspace.com/ StevePiticco.

PIZZARELLI, John 'Bucky'; American jazz musician (guitar); b. 9 Jan. 1926; m. Ruth Litchult Pizzarelli 1954; two s. two d. *Education:* studied with Peter and Robert Domenick. *Career:* fmr mem., Vaughn Monroe Orchestra; fmr staff musician with NBC, ABC, Skitch Henderson, Doc Severinson, Mitch Miller; concerts and tours with artists, including George Barnes and Les Paul, Stéphane Grappelli, Skitch Henderson, Bobby Short, Benny Goodman, Zoot Sims, Peter Appleyard, Barney Kessel and Charlie Byrd, Howard Alden; recorded with George Barnes, Zoot Sims, Eddie Daniels, Benny Goodman, Joe Venuti; festival appearances; Faculty Member Emeritus, William Paterson College, Wayne, New Jersey. *Recordings include:* albums: Midnite Mood 1960, Music Minus Many Men 1961, Green Guitar Blues 1972, Nightwings 1975, Buck and Bud 1977, Bucky's Bunch 1977, 2x7= Pizzarelli 1979, Cafe Pierre Trio 1982, Swinging Stevens 1984, Solo Flight 1986, Guitar Quintet 1988, Nirvana 1995, Solos and Duets 1996, Contrasts 1999, Passion Guitars 1999, April Kisses 1999, Italian Intermezzo 2000, One Morning in May 2001, Passionate Guitars 2001, Twogether 2001, Hot Club of 52nd Street 2004, Moonglow 2005, Around the World in 80 Years 2006, Doug and Bucky 2006, Five for Freddie 2007, Generations 2007. *Current Management:* c/o Andrew Tenenbaum, MBST Entertainment, 345 N Maple Drive, Beverly Hills, CA 90210, USA. *Telephone:* (310) 385-1760. *E-mail:* andy@mbst.com.

PIZZORNO, Sergio Lorenzo; British musician (guitar), songwriter and backing singer; b. 15 Dec. 1980, Newton Abbot, Devon, England. *Education:* Countesthorpe Community Coll. *Career:* mem., Kasabian 1999–. *Recordings include:* albums: Kasabian 2004, Empire 2006, West Ryder Pauper Lunatic Asylum (Q Award for Best Album 2009, NME Award for Best Album 2010) 2009, Velociraptor! 2011, 48:13 2014. *Honours:* NME Awards for Best Live Act 2007, for Best British Band 2012, Q Awards for Best Act in the World Today 2010, 2014, for Best Live Act 2014, BRIT Award for Best British Group 2010, MOJO Award for Song of the Year 2010. *Current Management:* c/o John Coyne, The Family Entertainment. *E-mail:* coyne@thefamilyent.com. *Address:* c/o Columbia Records, 9 Derry Street, London, W8 5HY, England (office). *Website:* www.kasabian.co.uk.

PLA, Roberto Enrique; Colombian musician (timbales, bongos, congas, drums) and bandleader; b. Barranquilla; m. Dominique Roome 1992. *Education:* Nat. Univ. of Bogotá, studied percussion with Pompelio Rodríguez. *Career:* session musician with artists, including Los Ocho de Colombia; drummer, Orquesta Lucho Bermudez 1968–78, with tours of Latin America and USA; regular TV appearances; moved to New York, USA 1979; salsa session percussionist with bands, including Orquesta La Tradicion; moved to London, England 1979; mem. jazz-fusion band, Cayenne; founder mem. bands, including Valdez, Sonido de Londres (co-founder), Roberto Pla Latin Ensemble (12-piece all-star band) 1988; has toured with Boney M, Joe Strummer, Arrow, Radio Futura, The Frank Chickens, Motorhead, Slim Gaillard, Alfredo Rodriguez, Carlos Valdez, Trevor Watts. *Recordings include:* Cumbia Dominique 1990, Danzas Delrenacimento 2001. *Telephone:* (20) 8472-8712 (office). *E-mail:* domroome@hotmail.com (office). *Website:* www.roberto -pla.150m.com.

PLAN B; British rapper, singer, songwriter and actor; b. (Benjamin Paul Balance-Drew), 22 Oct. 1983, Forest Gate, London; s. of Paul Balance. *Education:* Anglo European School, Ingatestone, Essex, Tom Hood School, Leytonstone. *Career:* made recording debut in 2005; first tour in 2006; collaborations with Chase & Status, Epic Man, Professor Green, Killa Kela, Skrein, Shameless, The Mitchell Brothers, Jacob Anderson, Adam Deacon, Elton John; screen actor 2008–, film dir 2011–; supported Noel Gallagher at Royal Albert Hall concert 2010. *Recordings:* albums: Who Needs Actions When You Got Words 2006, The Defamation of Strickland Banks (BBC Radio 1 Teen Award for Best Album 2010, Ivor Novello Album Award 2011, South Bank Sky Arts Pop Music Award 2011) 2010. *Films:* as actor: Adulthood 2008, Harry Brown 2009, 4.3.2.1 2010, Turnout 2011; as dir: Ill Manors 2012. *Honours:* MOBO Award for Best UK R&B/Soul Act 2010, Q Awards for Breakthrough Artist and Best Video 2010, ASCAP Vanguard Award 2011, BRIT Award for Best British Male Solo Artist 2011, Ivor Novello Awards for Songwriter of the Year and Most Performed Work 2011, Music Producers Guild Award for UK Single of the Year 2010 2011, Virgin Media Music Best Solo Male 2011. *Address:* c/o 679 Artists, 3rd Floor, 140 Wardour Street, London, W1F 8ZT, England (office). *Telephone:* (20) 3367-6613 (office). *E-mail:* hello@679artists.com (office). *Website:* www.679artists.com (office); www .time4planb.co.uk.

PLANETARY ASSAULT SYSTEMS (see Slater, Luke)

PLANKA, Pavel; Czech musician; b. 29 May 1962, Pilsn. *Education:* Public School of Arts; Prague Conservatoire. *Career:* Performances with several top Czech ensembles, jazz, rock, pop, classical, orchestral, folk; Support to Rolling Stones, Voodoo Lounge. *Recordings:* Nerez, Ke Zdi, 1990; Tutu, Mr Jazz Man, 1991; Zuzana Navarová, Caribe, 1992; Vitacit, Mate Se Hnout; Hot line, Still Callin', 1993; Merinsky-Lewitova, Sefardske Pisne; Dan Barta Alice, Usta Hromu, 1994; Lucie, Cerny Kocky Mokry Zaby; Janek Ledecky, Jenom Tak;

Michal Pavlicek, Na Kloboucku II, 1995; Tresnak-Korman-Koller, Kolaz; Roman Dragoun, Stin My Krve; Veleband All Stars Big-Band, 1996; Jarek Nohavica, Divne Stoleti; Musical, Hair, 1997; Daniel Hulka, Mise, 1998; Karel Gott, Souhvezdi Gott; Lucie Bila, Uplne Naha, 1999; Jaromir Nohavica, Moje Smutne Srdce, 2000; Marie Rottrova Podivej; Nerez, Ještě Jednou, 2001; Support Lesbians, Tune Da Radio, 2002. *Honours:* Prize, Authors Competition, Porta, 1986. *E-mail:* pavel.planka@volny.cz.

PLANT, Robert Anthony, CBE; British singer and songwriter; b. 20 Aug. 1948, West Bromwich, Warwickshire, England; m. Maureen; three s. one d. *Career:* mem. various R&B groups, including Listen, Band of Joy; Founder-mem. The New Yardbirds 1968, renamed Led Zeppelin 1968–80, re-formed for one-off performance 2007; numerous tours and concert appearances worldwide; formed band's own label, Swan Song 1974; solo artist 1980–; mem. The Honeydrippers (with Jimmy Page, Nile Rodgers, Jeff Beck) 1984–85; mem. Page & Plant (with Jimmy Page) 1994–; Founder-mem. The Strange Sensation, The Sensational Space Shifters. *Recordings include:* albums: with Led Zeppelin: Led Zeppelin 1969, Led Zeppelin II 1969, Led Zeppelin III 1970, Led Zeppelin IV 1971, Houses Of The Holy 1973, Physical Graffiti 1975, Presence 1976, The Song Remains The Same (live) 1976, In Through The Out Door 1979, How The West Was Won 2003, Mothership 2007, Celebration Day (Grammy Award for Best Rock Album 2014) 2012; solo: Pictures At Eleven 1982, The Principle Of Moments 1983, Shaken 'N' Stirred 1985, Now & Zen 1988, Manic Nirvana 1990, Fate Of Nations 1993, If I Was A Carpenter 1993, Divinity 2000, Dreamland 2002, Raising Sand (with Alison Krauss) (Grammy Awards for Album of the Year 2009, for Best Contemporary Folk/Americana Album 2009) 2007, Band of Joy 2010, Lullaby and...The Ceaseless Roar 2014; with The Honeydrippers: The Honeydrippers Vol. 1 1984; with Page & Plant: No Quarter 1994, Walking Into Clarksdale 1998, Masters 1998, Before the Balloon Went Up 1998, More Oar 1999; with The Strange Sensation: Mighty Rearranger 2005, Raising Sand (with Alison Krauss) 2007, Band of Joy 2010, Lullaby and the Ceaseless Roar 2014. *Honours:* Ivor Novello Award for Outstanding Contribution to British Music 1977, Nordoff-Robbins Music Therapy Foundation Silver Clef Award 1990, Q magazine Merit Award 1992, Grammy Lifetime Achievement Award 2005, Royal Swedish Acad. of Music Polar Music Prize 2006, Grammy Awards for Best Pop Collaboration with Vocals (for Gone Gone Gone with Alison Krauss) 2008, (for Rich Woman with Alison Krauss) 2009, for Record of the Year (for Please Read the Letter with Alison Krauss) 2009, for Best Country Collaboration with Vocals (for Killing the Blues with Alison Krauss) 2009, CMA Award for Musical Event of the Year (for Gone Gone Gone with Alison Krauss) 2008, Kennedy Center Honor 2012. *Current Management:* Yam Yam 345, 110 Gloucester Avenue, London, NW1 8HX, England. *Telephone:* (20) 7586-1815. *E-mail:* nicola@yamyam345.com. *Website:* www.ledzeppelin.com; www.robertplant.com.

PLASKETT, Joel; Canadian singer, songwriter, musician (guitar) and producer; b. 18 April 1975, Lunenberg, NS; m. Rebecca Krantz. *Career:* founder mem. Thrush Hermit 1992–99; solo artist 1999–; founder mem. Joel Plaskett and the Emergency 2001–; record producer for Two Hours Traffic, Little Miss Moffet. *Films:* One Week 2008; DVD releases: Make a Little Noise (East Coast Music Award for DVD of the Year 2007) 2006. *Television:* Rock Camp (CBC documentary series) 2004, The Berkeley Sessions (performance), (Bravo!) 2008. *Recordings:* albums: with Thrush Hermit: Sweet Homewrecker 1997, Clayton Park 1999; solo: In Need of Medical Attention 1999, La De Da 2005, Three 2009 (Juno Award for Adult Alternative Album of the Year, East Coast Music Awards for Pop Recording of the Year, Recording of the Year and Male Solo Recording of the Year 2010); with Joel Plaskett and the Emergency: Down at the Khyber 2001, Truthfully Truthfully (East Coast Music Award for Rock Recording of the Year 2005) 2003, Ashtray Rock 2007. *Honours:* East Coast Music Awards for Male Artist of the Year 2005, 2006, for Songwriter of the Year 2005, 2006, 2008, 2010, for Single of the Year 2006, 2008, 2009, 2010, Video of the Year 2006, 2008, for Group of the Year 2008, FACTOR Recording of the Year 2008, for Entertainer of the Year 2009, 2010, for Pop Recording of the Year 2010, Billboard World Song Contest Pop Category Winner 2008, Great American Song Contest Pop Category Winner 2006, 2008, 2009. *Current Management:* c/o Sheri Jones, Jones and Co. Artist Management, PO Box 25072, Halifax, NS B3M 4H4, Canada. *Telephone:* (902) 429-9005. *Fax:* (902) 457-1187. *E-mail:* sheri@jonesandcompany.ca. *Website:* www.jonesandcoartistmanagement.com. *Address:* c/o MapleMusic Recordings, 230 Richmond Street West, 11th Floor, Toronto, ON M5V 3E5, Canada (office). *E-mail:* mary.mill@maplemusicrecordings.com (office). *Website:* www.maplemusicrecordings.com (office); www.joelplaskett.com.

PLASTIKMAN (see Hawtin, Richie)

PLATE, Peter; German musician and songwriter; b. 1 July 1967, New Delhi, India; m. Ulf Sommer 2002. *Career:* moved to Goslar, Braunschweig, Germany, then to Berlin 1990; Founder mem. Rosenstolz 1991–2012, released debut album 1992. *Recordings include:* albums: with Rosenstolz: Soubrette werd' ich nie 1992, Nur einmal noch 1994, Sanfte Verführer 1994, Mittwoch is' er fällig 1995, Objekt der Begierde 1996, Die Schlampen sind müde 1997, Zucker 1999, Kassengift 2000, Macht Liebe 2002, Herz 2004, Das grosse Leben 2006, Die Suche geht weiter 2008, Wir sind am Leben 2011. *Honours:* ECHO Award for Best Nat. Rock/Pop Group 2012. *Current Management:* c/o Pop-out Management, Forster Strasse 5, 10999 Berlin, Germany. *Address:* c/o Universal Music GmbH, Stralauer Allee 1, 10245 Berlin, Germany (office). *Website:* www.rosenstolz.de.

PLATT, Tony; British record producer and engineer; b. 21 Jan. 1952, Yorkshire, England; m. Jacqueline 1974; one s. one d. *Career:* Trident Studios, London, England; Asst Engineer, Island Studios, Basing Street 1969–70; Recording Engineer for Bob Marley, Toots, Free, etc; freelance 1975–; Mutt Lange's Engineer on Highway to Hell, Back in Black, AC/DC and Foreigner 4; mem. Re-Pro, PAMRA. *Recordings include:* Producer, Engineer, Marche ou Creve, Trust, 1981; Producer, Engineer, Shock Tactics, Samson, 1981; Producer, Engineer, One Vice at a Time, Krokus, 1982; Producer, Engineer, Another Perfect Day, Motörhead, 1983; Engineer, Co-Producer, Flick of the Switch, AC/DC, 1983; Remix, Producer, All Men Play on Ten, Manowar, 1984; Producer, Engineer, We Want Moore, Gary Moore, 1984; Producer, Engineer, Equator, Uriah Heep, 1984–85; Producer, Engineer, Brave the Storm, Shy, 1985; Producer, Engineer, Nightless City, VowWow, 1985; Producer, Engineer, Live and Dangerous, Krokus, 1986; Producer, Engineer, The Doctor, Cheap Trick, 1986; Producer, Engineer, Wired, Jeff Paris, 1986–87; Producer, BBC–Late Night in Concert, The Cult, 1987; Producer, Engineer, Cold Lake, Celtic Frost, 1988; Producer, Engineer, Love and War, Lillian Axe, 1988–89; Co-Producer, Engineer, Never Turn Your Back on the Blues, Moody Marsden Band, 1991; Producer, Engineer, The Ritual, Testament, 1992; Co-Producer, Engineer, Live in Hell, Moody Marsden Band, 1994; Co-Producer, Green and Blues, Bernie Marsden, 1995; Producer, Engineer, Eternity, Anathema, 1996; Producer, Engineer, Ten, 1997; Producer, Engineer, Mau Mau, 1997; Producer, Mixer, Huge Baby, 1997–98; other productions include: Aswad; Dio. *Publication:* Music Industry Management and Promotion, by Chris Kemp (contrib.). *Current Management:* CMI (USA), 201 E 87th Street, New York, 10128, USA.

PLATZMAN, Daniel; American musician (drums, viola, trumpet) and composer; b. 28 Sept. 1986, Atlanta, Ga. *Education:* Berklee Coll. of Music. *Career:* studied film scoring; fmr mem. Berklee Concert Jazz Orchestra, Urban Outreach Jazz Orchestra, Berklee Rainbow Big Band; Founder-mem. Daniel Platzman Quintet; mem. Imagine Dragons 2011–, has performed at numerous festivals 2011–; signed with Interscope Records 2011; numerous TV appearances and tours in USA, Canada, Europe. *Films include:* composed scores for: Golden Minutes 2009, Eagles Are Turning People into Horses 2009, Cherrylocks and the Three Mexicans 2011, Pierre the Pickpocket 2012. *Recordings include:* albums: with Imagine Dragons: Night Visions (Billboard Music Award for Top Rock Album 2014) 2012, Smoke + Mirrors 2015; with Daniel Platzman Quintet: Pun and Games Vol. 1 2012. *Honours:* Vic Firth Award for Outstanding Musicianship, Michael Rendish Award in Film Scoring; with Imagine Dragons: Teen Choice Award for Choice Rock Song (for Radioactive) 2013, American Music Awards for Favorite Alternative Rock Artist 2013, 2014, Grammy Award for Best Rock Performance (for Radioactive) 2014, Billboard Music Awards for Top Duo/Group 2014, for Top Hot 100 Artist 2014, for Top Rock Artist 2014, for Top Streaming Song (Audio) (for Radioactive) 2014, iHeartRadio Music Award for Best Alternative Rock Song of the Year (for Demons, with Imagine Dragons) 2014, Much Music Video Award for Int. Video of the Year - Group (for Demons, with Imagine Dragons) 2014. *Current Management:* c/o Mac Reynolds, Reynolds Management, 823 Las Vegas Boulevard South, Las Vegas, NV 89101, USA. *Telephone:* (702) 445-7000. *Fax:* (702) 385-7743. *E-mail:* mac@reynoldsmgmt.com. *Website:* www.reynoldsmgmt.com. *E-mail:* danielplatzman@mindspring.com. *Website:* www.danielplatzman.com; imaginedragonsmusic.com.

PLAYFORD, Robert; British record producer, engineer, remixer, programmer and record company executive; b. 25 March 1968, Ware, Hertfordshire, England. *Career:* formed Moving Shadow Music 1990, pioneering and establishing Jungle music; concerts, festivals, television and radio broadcasts; worked with 2 Bad Mice, Audioweb, Babylon Zoo, Black Grape, David Bowie, Melanie C., Corduroy, Dom & Rob, Fugees, Garbage, Goldie, Lionrock, Marlo, Metalheads, Monday Michuru, Sly & Robbie, Ingrid Schroeder, Snowpony, Tin Star; mem. Musicians' Union. *Address:* 55 Conifer Walk, Stevenage, Herts SG2 7QS, England.

PLIEGO, César; Mexican musician (bass guitar). *Career:* mem. electro-pop band, Kinky 2000–. *Recordings include:* albums: Kinky 2002, Atlas 2003, Reina 2006. *Address:* c/o Sonic360 Records, 33 Riding House Street, London, W1 7DZ, England. *Website:* www.sonic360.com/kinky.

PLIERS; Jamaican DJ; b. (Everton Banner), 1965, Kingston. *Career:* recording with Black Scorpio; recorded for numerous labels, including: Pickout, Pioneer Musik, Jammys, Harry J. and Studio One; pnr in duo, Chaka Demus and Pliers 1991–. *Recordings:* albums: with Chaka Demus and Pliers: Gal Wine 1992, Ruff This Year 1992, Chaka Demus and Pliers 1992, Tease Me 1993, Help Them Lord 2001, So Proud 2008. *E-mail:* annidc@orange.fr. *Address:* c/o Yes Music, 20 rue Saint Joseph, 42000 Saint Etienne, France (office). *E-mail:* contact@yesmusic.fr (office). *Website:* www.yesmusic.fr.

PLOTNIKOFF, Mike; Canadian audio engineer. *Career:* started at Vancouver's Little Mountain Sound; worked with producers, including Bruce Faibairn, Bob Rock, Chris Thomas, Howard Benson; has worked on albums for Aerosmith, All American Rejects, Buck Cherry, The Cranberries, Daughtry, Delerium, Kelly Clarkson, Kiss, Motley Crue, My Chemical Romance, Papa Roach, The Scorpions, Van Halen, Yes, Bon Jovi. *Current Management:* c/o Alia Fahlborg, Nettwerk Producer Management, 6525 Sunset Blvd, 8th Floor, Hollywood, CA 90028, USA. *Telephone:* (323) 310-4200. *Fax:* (323) 301-4195. *E-mail:* alia@producermgmt.com. *Website:* www.nettwerk.com/producer.

POE, David, BS; American singer, songwriter and musician (guitar); b. 20 July 1969, Ann Arbor, Michigan; m. *Education:* Miami Univ., Oxford. *Career:* solo artist 1990–; produced debut recording for Melissa Sheehan, Jenifer Jackson. *Compositions include:* for films: Pocket Pair 2007, Capers 2008, Dare 2009, Harvest 2009. *Recordings:* Glass Suit 1996, David Poe 1999, The Late Album 2002, Love is Red 2004. *Website:* www.davidpoe.com.

POHJOLA, Mika, BM, MM; Finnish musician (jazz piano) and composer (classical, jazz); b. 1 Dec. 1971, Helsinki; s. of Heikki Pohjola and Saga Pohjola. *Education:* Vantaa Conservatory, Royal Coll. of Stockholm, Sweden, Berklee Coll. of Music, Mass, USA. *Career:* performances in Europe, USA, Canada, S America and Japan 1993–; Blue Note debut 1996; Composer, music to Tove Jansson's Moomin fairy-tales; Visiting Artist, Berklee Coll. of Music 2006–; Steinway Distinguished Artist 1997–; recorded over 40 albums; featured on recordings with Fernando Huergo, Miguel Zenón, Ben Monder, Steve Wilson, Rigmor Gustafsson and others. *Recordings include:* Reflections in Real Time 1994, Myths and Beliefs 1996, Jazz Capital of the World 1996, On the Move 1997, The Secret of the Castle 1997, Announcement 1998, English Breakfast 1999, Live at the Blue Note 2000, Hur man räddar kärleken and annat 2000, Still Alive 2001, Sound of Village 2001, Landmark 2002, Moomin in Swedish 2003, Ball Play 2003, Scandinavian Yuletide Voices 2005, Muumilauluja 2005, A Lark in the Snowstorm 2006, Ballads 2006, Swedish Traditional Songs 2006, Nu blir sommar 2007, Two For the Road 2008, Live Jazz on Broadway 2009, Northern Sunrise 2009, Christmas Carols 2009, Das Wörterbuch 2009, Great Tunes by My Friends 2009, The Red Bicycle 2010, Trio Hour 2013, Chick Corea: Children's Songs 2014. *Radio:* airplay on BBC Radio (UK), NRK (Norway), DR (Denmark), SR (Sweden), YLE (Finland), several NPR stations (USA). *Honours:* The Downbeat Magazine Award 1994, American-Scandinavian Soc. Award 1996, Swedish Cultural Endowments 1998, 2002, 2007, Performance and Recording Endowments 1996, 1997, 2000, 2003, 2004, 2005, 2008. *E-mail:* info@bluemusicgroup.com. *Website:* bluemusicgroup.com. *Telephone:* (347) 688-6452 (New York) (office). *E-mail:* newyork@mikapohjola .com (office). *Website:* mikapohjola.com.

POINTER, Anita; American singer; b. 23 Jan. 1948, East Oakland, CA. *Career:* mem. (with sisters), Pointers 1969–71, recording as session singers for Elvin Bishop, Ray Charles, Cold Blood, Céline Dion, Robert Foreman, Iron Eagle 2, Kenny Loggins, Taj Mahal, Dave Mason, Oliver and Company, Rockets, Boz Scaggs, Bruce Willis, Bill Wyman; mem. female vocal quartet, The Pointer Sisters 1972–78, later trio 1978–; numerous concerts, festival appearances, television and radio broadcasts. *Recordings include:* albums: with The Pointer Sisters: The Pointer Sisters 1973, Live At The Opera House 1974, Steppin' 1975, Having A Party 1978, Energy 1979, Priority 1979, Special Things 1980, Black and White 1981, So Excited 1982, Break Out 1984, Contact 1985, Hot Together 1986, Serious Slammin' 1988, Right Rhythm 1990, Only Sisters Can Do That 1993; solo: Love For What It Is 1987. *Honours:* Grammy Awards for Best Country Vocal Performance 1974, Best Performance by a Group and Best Vocal Arrangement 1985, Billboard Awards for Top Dance Single and Album 1984, American Music Awards for Favorite Soul/R&B Band 1985, for Favorite Soul/R&B Video 1985, 1986. *Current Management:* Konrad Leh, Creative Talent Group, 1900 Avenue of the Stars, Suite 2475, Los Angeles, CA 90067, USA. *Telephone:* (424) 239-1050. *Fax:* (424) 239-1051. *E-mail:* konrad@creativetalentgroup.com. *Website:* www.thepointersisters .com.

POINTER, Ruth; American singer; b. 19 March 1946, Oakland, CA; m. Michael Sayles 1990. *Career:* mem. (with sisters), Pointers 1969–71, recording as session singers for Elvin Bishop, Ray Charles, Cold Blood, Céline Dion, Robert Foreman, Iron Eagle 2, Kenny Loggins, Taj Mahal, Dave Mason, Oliver and Company, Rockets, Boz Scaggs, Bruce Willis, Bill Wyman; mem. female vocal quartet, The Pointer Sisters 1972–78, later trio 1978–; numerous concerts, festival appearances, television and radio broadcasts. *Recordings include:* albums: The Pointer Sisters 1973, Live At The Opera House 1974, Steppin' 1975, Having A Party 1978, Energy 1979, Priority 1979, Special Things 1980, Black and White 1981, So Excited 1982, Break Out 1984, Contact 1985, Hot Together 1986, Serious Slammin' 1988, Right Rhythm 1990, Only Sisters Can Do That 1993. *Honours:* Grammy Awards for Best Country Vocal Performance 1974, Best Performance by a Group and Best Vocal Arrangement 1985, Billboard Awards for Top Dance Single and Album 1984, American Music Awards for Favorite Soul/R&B Band 1985, for Favorite Soul/R&B Video 1985, 1986. *Current Management:* Konrad Leh, Creative Talent Group, 1900 Avenue of the Stars, Los Angeles, CA 90067, USA. *Telephone:* (424) 239-1050. *Fax:* (424) 239-1051. *E-mail:* konrad@creativetalentgroup.com. *Website:* www .thepointersisters.com.

POINTON, Michael John (Mike); British musician (trombonist), singer, writer and broadcaster; b. 25 April 1941, London, England; s. of Frederick Pointon and Josephine Day. *Education:* Elmwood School and Rose Bruford Coll. of Speech and Drama. *Career:* f. own band 1950s; worked with many European New Orleans style groups and American jazzmen and toured many countries; documentaries for BBC Radio include Swingtime for Hitler 1987, Bunk and Bill 1992, Preservation Hall 1998, Up A Lazy River (with George Melly) 1998, Echoes of Harlem (with George Melly) 1999, Ride, Red, Ride 2000, The Unknown Satchmo 2001, Benny Carter at 95 2002, The Count (with John Dankworth) 2003, Memories of the Blues (with George Melly) 2004, Chicken Inspector No. 23 (with Woody Allen) 2005, Empress of the Blues (with George Melly) 2005, Cooke's Jazz Tour, Jazz Indaba 2005, Pee Wee's Blues and Black British Swing 2006, Dust Bowl Balladeer (with Billy Bragg) 2006.

Recordings: recorded with: Barry Martyn's Band 1961, Mezz Mezzrow/Cotton City Jazz Band 1964, Young Olympia Brass Band 1965, Eagle Brass Band 1966, European Classic Jazz Band 1983, British All-Stars 1993, Apex Jazzband of Northern Ireland 1997, Kid Martyn Alumni 1998, Sammy Rimington and John Petters' All Stars 1999, Pat Hawes' All-Stars 2000, John Petters' Creole Jazzband 2003. *Publications:* Goin' Home – The Uncompromising Life and Music of Ken Colyer (with Ray Smith) (House of Commons All Party Jazz Book of the Year Award) 2010; contrib. to New Orleans Music, Just Jazz, I.A.J.R.C. journal, Jazz Journal. *Address:* 11 Kings Court, Kings Road, Wimbledon, London, SW19 8QP, England (home). *Telephone:* (20) 8542-7193 (office). *E-mail:* michael.pointon@btopenworld.com (home).

POLAND, Chris; American musician (guitar, bass guitar); b. Dunkirk, NY. *Career:* mem., New Yorkers 1977–82; mem., Megadeth 1984–87; solo artist 1987–; mem., Damn The Machine 1991–93, renamed Mumbo's Brain; world tours with all bands; founder mem., OHM 2003–. *Recordings include:* albums: with Megadeath: Killing Is My Business. . . And Business Is Good! 1985, Peace Sells. . . But Who's Buying? 1986, The System Has Failed 2004; solo: Return To Metalopolis 1990, Chasing The Sun 2000, Rare Trax 2000; with Damn The Machine: Damn The Machine 1993; with Mumbo's Brain: Excerpts From The Book Of Mumbo 1995; with Lamb of God: As the Palaces Burn 2003, Ashes of the Wake 2004; with OHM: OHM 2003, Amino Acid Flashback 2005, Circus of Sound 2008; with OHMPHREY: OHMPHREY 2009. *Address:* c/o Grooveyard Records, PO Box 26871, Rochester, NY 14626, USA. *Website:* www .chrispoland.com.

POLCER, Edward (Ed) Joseph, BSE; American jazz musician (cornet) and bandleader; b. 10 Feb. 1937, Paterson, NJ; m. Judy Kurtz 1976; three s. one d. *Education:* Princeton Univ., music lessons with Prof. James V. Dittamo, Prospect Park, NJ. *Career:* cornettist, Stan Rubin's Tigertown Five; concerts include: Carnegie Hall, Europe, Prince Rainier and Grace Kelly wedding 1956, Congressional Ball, White House, by Presidential invitation 1994, official opening of the Louis Armstrong House museum 2004; played with Benny Goodman Sextet 1973; solo artist, band leader, international Jazz Festival circuit 1975–; owner, manager, bandleader, Eddie Condon's NY 1975–85; bandleader, eight major US tours for Columbia Artists, several European tours 1992–97; Pres., International Art of Jazz 1982–89. *Recordings:* albums include: Ed Polcer–Live In Concert 1988; with Ed Polcer's All Stars: Coast To Coast–Swinging Jazz 1990, Some Sunny Day 1991, Barbara Lea 1992, A Night At Eddie Condon's 1992, The Magic of Swing Street 1993, A Salute To Eddie Condon 1993, Jammin' A La Condon 1994, At The Ball (with Jim Galloway) 1998, The Magic Of Swing 2000, Let's Hit It 2003, Everything We've Got (with Judy Kurtz) 2004, Lionel, Red and Bunny 2007, When Broadway Meets Swing Street 2007. *Publications:* Carmina Princetonia – The Song Book of Princeton University Centennial Edition (co-ed.) 1968. *E-mail:* edpolcer@edpolcer.com (office). *Website:* www.edpolcer.com.

POLCHENKO, Yuri, (Tobto); Ukrainian singer, songwriter, producer and musician (guitar); b. 10 Oct. 1959, Kyiv; m.; two s. *Education:* Kyiv Polytechical Inst., Kyiv Jazz School. *Career:* composer, singer for Night Saxophone Film; leader of Nebesna Kopalyna and Celestial Mine groups. *Compositions:* Night Saxophone (UNICEF, music for film) 1997, Out of the Time 1997, Chas Ide 1998, Chekai 1998. *Recordings:* Mist Of Dance (sponsored by British Embassy in Ukraine) 1998, Splyat Yangoly 2002, Music for Love FM. *Address:* V. Pika 10, kv 46, 04111 Kiev, Ukraine (office). *E-mail:* tobto@ukr.net (home); seo@tobto.org (office). *Website:* tobto.org (office).

POLNAREFF, Michel; French singer, musician (piano, guitar) and songwriter; b. 3 July 1944, Nérac (Lot-et-Garonne); s. of Leib Polnareff (Léo Polland) and Simone Lane. *Career:* learned piano by age five and then the guitar, followed by music studies, military service and a brief time in insurance; began to play his guitar on the steps of the Sacré Cœur; popular in France from mid-1960s until early 1990s; still critically acclaimed and occasionally tours in France. *Compositions:* for theatre: Rebelais 1968, La Folie des Grandeurs 1971; for film: Erotissimo 1969, L'Indiscret 1969, La pomme de son œil (TV) 1970, Ça n'arrive qu'aux autres 1971, La folie des grandeurs 1971, D'Artagnan l'Intrépide 1974, Lipstick 1976, La Vengeance du serpent à plumes 1984. *Recordings include:* albums: Love Me Please Love Me 1966, Le Bal Des Laze 1967, Polnareff's 1971, Polnarévolution (live) 1972, Michel Polnareff 1974, Tibilli 1974, USA 1975, Fame à la mode 1975, Coucou Me Revoilou 1978, Bulles 1981, Show Télé 82/Public (live) 1982, Incognito 1985, Kâmâ Sutrâ 1990, Live At The Roxy (live) 1996, Nos Mots D'Amour (compilation) 1999, Ze Re Tour 2007 (live) 2007. *Publications:* Polnaréflexions (with Jean-Michel Desjeunes) 1974, Polnareff par Polnareff (with Philippe Manœuvre) 2004, Le Polnabook 2013. *Honours:* Disco Revue Prize, Paris 1965. *E-mail:* michel@polnaweb.com. *Website:* www.polnaweb.com.

POLYGON WINDOW (see James, Richard David)

PONOMAREVA, Valentina; Russian singer; *Solo Vocalist and Art Director, Valentina Ponomareva Musical Theatre;* b. 10 July 1939, Moscow; m. Konstantin Gogunskiy 1954; one s. *Education:* Khabarovsk Inst. of Arts. *Career:* solo vocalist, Tula Jazz big band 1967–70; actress, singer, dancer, Moscow Gypsy Theatre Romen 1971–78; solo vocalist of The Trio Romen 1973–83, int. concerts 1974–84, Metropolitan Opera, New York 1976, Midem-76 Festival, Cannes 1976, Edinburgh Int. Festival 1977; numerous nat. TV and radio appearances 1973–; solo artist, Russian and int. concerts and tours 1978–, including Soviet Avantgarde Jazz Festival, Zurich 1989; int. workshop on free improvised music, Tokyo, Osaka 1989; festivals world-wide, including

Tateyama Int. Folk Music Festival, Japan 1989, Huddersfield Contemporary Music Festival, UK 1990, Voice Over Festival, London 1990, Novosibirsk Int. Festival 1990, Int. Music Festival, Davos 1991, Imola and Europa Festival Jazz, Italy 1991, Jazz Summer, Bolzano, Italy 1991, seven-month USA tour, including Los Angeles, San Francisco, Chicago, Boston, New York 1992, Music Unlimited Festival, Wels, Austria 1993, Musique Action Nancy, France 1993, Fringe Int. Festival, Edinburgh 1999, Festival des Arts et du Cinema Russes, Cannes 1999, Bohème Jazz Festival Int., Moscow 2001, 2002, Int. Odessa Jazz-Carnival, Odessa 2001, 2002; Solo Vocalist and Art Dir Valentina Ponomareva Musical Theatre; mem. Performing Right Soc., Mechanical-Copyright Protection Soc., PPL. *Film:* Karnavalnaya noch II 2007. *Recordings:* solo albums: Fortune-teller 1985, Intrusion 1988, At Parting I Say 1989, Temptation 1989, Don't Rise My Recollection 1990, Terra Incognita 1990, Live In Japan 1991, The Romances Of The Friends Or Mine 1992, Dve Gitary 1994, At Parting I Say 1996, We Strangely Happen To Meet 1997, Forte 1999, The Russian Gypsy Queen: Ochi Chiornye 2001, Avangarde roman s Yuri Kuznetsov 2003, Kak khoroshi te ochi 2003, Gypsy Romances 2004, Grand Collection 2008, Trio Romen: The Russian Gypsy Queen 2008, Nochnye Tsvety 2009, Luchshie romansy i pesni 2010. *Address:* Valentina Ponomareva Musical Theatre, 16 Samotechny 3 pereulok, Apt 89, 127473 Moscow, Russia (office). *Telephone:* (495) 600-64-40 (office); (495) 600-63-30 (home). *Fax:* (495) 600-69-19 (office). *E-mail:* kosta@aha.ru (office). *Website:* ValentinaPonomareva.ru (home).

PONOMARYOV, Olexander; Ukrainian singer, musician (piano) and arranger; *Director*, *The Producer's Center*; b. 9 Aug. 1973, Khmelnitsky; two d. *Education:* Kyev Conservatory. *Career:* jt concert with Patricia Kaas; festival appearances include All-Ukrainian Chervona Ruta (first grant) 1993, Int. Festival Slavonic Bazaar (second grant) 1994, All-Ukranian Festival in memory of Volodymyra Ivasiuka 1995, All-Ukranian Festival Yalta 1996; rep. Ukraine, Eurovision Song Contest 2003; currently Dir The Producer's Center. *Film:* Private Life 2003. *Television:* Tasty Country (presenter, 1+1 channel) 2006. *Recordings:* albums: Z ranku do nochi (From Morning till Night) 1996, Perhsa i ostannia liubov (The First and the Last Love) 1997, Vona (She) 2000, Vin (He) 2001, Krashche (The Best) 2004. *Publications:* contrib. articles on music items to Republican press. *Honours:* Best Newcomer 1993, Best Ukrainian Singer in Popular Music 1996–99, 2001–04, Zirka Estrady Roku (Star of Stage), Liudyna Roku (Person of the Year) 1997, Honoured Artist of Ukraine 1998, Kumir natsii (Idol of the Nation 2003) 2004. *Address:* 9A Tarasivs'ka Str, Kiev, 01033, Ukraine (office). *Telephone:* (44) 2352565 (office). *Fax:* (44) 4566863 (office). *E-mail:* zrdn@ukr.net (office); zrdn@bigmir.net (office). *Website:* www.ponomarev.kiev.ua.

PONTIEUX, Loic; French musician (drums); b. 10 June 1967, Harfleur; m. 1994. *Education:* conservatoire. *Career:* drummer with many artists including: Michel Jonasz, Claude Nougaro, Didier Lockwood, Birelli Lagrene, Al Jarreau, Pascal Obispo, Veronique Sanson, Francis Cabrel, Mauranne, Maxime Le Forestier and Bernard Cavilliers. *Recordings:* with various artists including: Didier Lockwood, Bernard Cavilliers, Claude Nougaro, Birelli Lagrene, Solensi, Jean Michel Kajdan, Pascal Obispo, Idrissa Diop, Jean Jacques Milteau, Babik Reihardt, Grappelli Trio, Patrick Bruel.

PONTY, Jean-Luc; musician (jazz violin, synthesizers), composer and bandleader; b. 29 Sept. 1942, Avranches, France; m. Claudia Bosco 1966; two d. *Education:* Conservatoire National de Musique, Paris. *Career:* classical violinist to 1964; jazz violinist, Europe, 1964–69; night clubs, music festivals, in collaboration with the George Duke Trio, USA, 1969; toured with own group, Europe, 1970–72; moved to USA, 1973; pioneer electric violin, jazz innovator; headlined international concerts with own group, 1975–; music festivals in USA include: Meadowbrook; Artpark; Wolf Trap; in Europe: Montreux; North Sea Festival; Paris Jazz Festival; Guest soloist, Montréal Symphony Orchestra, 1984; Toronto Symphony Orchestra, 1986; New Japan Philharmonic, 1987; New York Radio City Orchestra; 1990; Oklahoma Symphony Orchestra, 1995; numerous television appearances. *Recordings:* (own productions) Albums include: Upon The Wings of Music; Aurora; Imaginary Voyage; Enigmatic Ocean; Cosmic Messenger; Jean-Luc Ponty – Live; Civilised Evil; A Taste For Passion; Mystical Adventures; Individual Choice; Open Mind; Fables; The Gift of Time; Storytelling; Tchokola (with African musicians); No Absolute Time; Life Enigman, 2001; The Rite of Strings (with Stanley Clarke, Al DiMeola); Jean-Luc Ponty with the George Duke Trio; With Kurt Edelhagen and His Orchestra; Live at Chene Park; Sonata Erotica; As; Far from the Beaten Paths; Also recorded with: Elton John; Honky Chateau, 1972; Frank Zappa and the Mothers of Invention, 1973; Mahavishnu Orchestra, 1974–75; Stephane Grappelli, 1996. *Current Management:* c/o Mario Tirado, APA, 888 Seventh Avenue, Suite 602, New York, NY 10106, USA; c/o Pascal Bernardin, Encore Productions, 6 rue du Mont Thabor, 75001 Paris, France.

POOK, Jocelyn; British composer and violist; b. 14 Feb. 1960, Birmingham, England; d. of Wilfred Pook and Mary Cecil Williams. *Education:* King Edward VI School, Bury St Edmunds and Guildhall School of Music and Drama. *Career:* composes music for film, TV, theatre, dance and the concert platform; has toured and recorded with many leading names in pop, rock and classical music including The Communards (three-year tour), Laurie Anderson, Massive Attack, Ryuichi Sakamoto and Peter Gabriel; Assoc. Guildhall School of Music and Drama; mem. Jocelyn Pook Ensemble. *Musical scores include:* films: Strange Fish (Prix Italia 1994) 1994, Mothers and Daughters (Mention Speciale at Grand Prix Int. Video-Danse 1994) 1994, Blight (Golden Plaque Award, Chicago Int. Film Festival 1997) 1996, Eyes Wide Shut (Chicago Film Critics' Award 2000, ASCAP Award 2000) 1999, Comment j'ai tué mon père 2000, Time Out/L'emploi du Temps (Golden Lion Award) 2001, La Repentie 2002, Gangs of New York (featuring her track Dionysus from Untold Things album) 2003, Wild Side 2004, The Merchant of Venice 2004, Heidi 2005, Brick Lane (ASCAP Award) 2007, Caótica Ana 2007, The People v. Leo Frank 2009, Habitación en Roma 2010, Room 304 2011; TV: People's Century/Half the People (BBC) 1996, Saints and Sinners (S4C documentary series) 1997, The Lost Supper (Channel 4) 1998, Just Enough Distance (BBC 2) 1998, Trouble at the House (BBC 2) 1998, The Establishment (Channel 4 documentary series) 1999, Dancing Inside (BBC 2) 1999, Butterfly Collectors (Granada) (Best Title Music, Royal TV Soc.) 1999, In a Land of Plenty (BBC 2, co-written with Harvey Brough) 2001, Death on the Staircase 2004, The Government Inspector 2005, Storm Over Everest 2008, Going South 2009, DESH (British Composer Award 2012); opera: Ingerland 2010. *Dance includes:* Phantasmaton (Shobana Jeyasingh Dance Co.), Requiem (Darshan Singh Bhuller, performed by the Phoenix Dance Co. *Television commercials include:* Blow the Wind/Pie Jesu (Orange Mobile Phone TV advert) (Designers and Art Dirs Asscn Silver Award 1997) 1997, Ode to Why (Enron advertising campaign) 2000–01. *Recordings include:* Deluge 1997, Flood 1999, Untold Things 2001, Wild Side 2004, The Merchant of Venice 2004, Saint Joan 2008 (Olivier Award). *Honours:* American Soc. of Authors Composers and Publrs' Prize 1999, Multi-Media Award, British Composer Awards 2003. *Address:* c/o Laurence Aston, First Name, Suite 302, 43 Lancaster Gate, London, W2 3NA, England (office). *Telephone:* (20) 7706-8484 (office). *Fax:* (20) 7706-3434 (office). *E-mail:* info@firstname.org.uk (office). *Website:* www.jocelynpook.com (office).

POOLE, Brian; British singer; b. 2 Nov. 1941, Barking, Essex. *Career:* lead singer, Brian Poole and The Tremeloes 1961–66; numerous live appearances; formed backing group, The Seychelles 1969; left music scene 1969–88; briefly re-formed the Tremeloes 1988; mem., The Corporation 1989; lead singer, Electrix. *Recordings:* albums: Twist and Shout 1963, Brian Poole and the Tremeloes 1964, It's About Time 1965, Brian Poole is Here 1966, Silence is Golden 1995, Time is on My Side 1995, Twenty Miles 1995, The World Of Brian Poole & The Tremeloes; hit singles include: Twist and Shout 1963, Do You Love Me? 1963, I Can Dance 1963, Candy Man 1964, Someone Someone 1964, Twelve Steps To Love 1964, The Three Bells 1965, I Want Candy 1965, Good Lovin' 1965.

POOLE, Chris, BA; Danish musician (flutes, tenor saxophone) and composer; b. 23 June 1952, New York, USA. *Education:* Berklee Coll. of Music, Boston (first woman to complete Berklee applied music programme); studied with Gary Burton, Andy McGee, Joe Viola, James Newton. *Career:* moved to Denmark from USA 1975; performed in jazz and latin bands; numerous television and radio appearances; solo performances 1988–; mem. Danish Musicians' Union, Danish Asscn of Jazz and Rock Composers, Women in Music. *Compositions:* writer for theatre, film and modern dance, including score for Troll, Norwegian film, The Lady From the Sea (Bay Area Critics Award, Best Musical Score For A Drama, USA) 1993; plays: Joan of Arc: Vision through Fire, Ibsen Women, Maria. *Recordings:* Chris Poole-Solo Flute 1990, To The Powers That Be (with Pia Rasmussen) 1993, In Search of Solace 1998, Breaking The Malestream, Waterlights (with Kaspre Søeborg). *Telephone:* 33799301 (home). *E-mail:* chrispoole0@gmail.com (home). *Website:* www.chrispoole.dk.

POOLEY, Ian, (Ansicht); German producer, remixer and DJ; b. (Ian Pinnekamp), Mainz. *Career:* started producing tracks while still a student in Mainz; first releases were collaborations with DJ Tonka; remixed: DJ Sneak, Daft Punk, Yello, Sven Vath, Modjo. *Recordings:* albums: Relations 1995, Meridian 1998, The Allnighter/Calypso1999, Since Then 2000, The IP Series 2002, Souvenirs 2004, A Subterranean Soundtrack 2005, In Other Words 2008. *Website:* www.ianpooley.com.

POP, Iggy; American singer, musician (guitar) and actor; b. (James Jewel Osterberg), 21 April 1947, Ann Arbor, Mich. *Education:* Univ. of Michigan. *Career:* formed high-school band Iguanas 1962, Prime Movers 1966; concerts in Michigan, Detroit and Chicago; formed The Stooges (originally the Psychedelic Stooges) 1967, re-formed 2007–; solo artist 1976–; collaborations with David Bowie 1972–; numerous tours and TV appearances. *Film appearances:* Rock & Rule (voice) 1983, Sid and Nancy 1986, The Color of Money 1986, Hardware 1990, Cry-Baby 1990, Atolladero 1995, Tank Girl 1995, Dead Man 1995, The Crow – City of Angels (also known as The Crow II) 1996, The Brave 1997, The Rugrats Movie (voice) 1998, Snow Day 2000, Coffee and Cigarettes 2003, Persepolis (voice) 2007. *Television appearances:* Miami Vice (series), The Adventures of Pete & Pete (series). *Radio:* as regular presenter: BBC 6 Music programme 2014–. *Other appearances include:* Driv3r (video game, voice) 2004. *Compositions include:* China Girl (with David Bowie). *Film songs include:* Repo Man (theme song 'Repo Man') 1984, Sid and Nancy (song 'I Wanna Be Your Dog') 1986, Dogs in Space (songs 'Dog Food' and 'Endless Sea') 1987, Slaves of New York (song 'Fall in Love with Me') 1989, Tales from the Crypt (TV series, songs 'Kill City' and 'Five Foot One' for episode 'For Cryin' Out Loud') 1989, Va mourire (1995), Trainspotting (song 'Nightclubbing') 1996, Space Goofs (series theme song) 1997, Full Blast (song 'Loose') 1997, The Brave 1997, Home to Rent (TV series theme song) 1997, Great Expectations (song) 1998, The Wedding Singer (song 'China Girl') 1998, Velvet Goldmine (song 'T.V. Eye') 1998, Whatever (song 'Gimme Danger') 1998, Lock, Stock and Two Smoking Barrels (song 'I Wanna Be Your Dog', as

James Oaterberg, Jr) 1998, Radiofreccia (song 'The Passenger') 1998, Born to Lose (song 'Tight Pants') 1999, The Filth and the Fury (song 'No Fun') 2000, Almost Famous (song 'Search and Destroy') 2000, Dogtown and Z-Boys (song 'I Wanna Be Your Dog') 2001, Intimacy (songs 'Consolation Prizes' and 'Penetration', as J. Osterberg alias I. Pop) 2001, Gran Turismo 3: A-Spec (video game) 2001, Killer Barbys vs. Dracula (song 'Candy') 2002, Pro BMX 2 (video game) (song 'The Passenger') 2002, Rugrats Go Wild! (song 'Lust for Life') 2003, Wonderland (song 'Search and Destroy') 2003, The School of Rock (song 'T.V. Eye', as James Osterberg) 2003, The Life Aquatic with Steve Zissou (song 'Search and Destroy') 2004. *Recordings:* albums: with The Stooges: The Stooges 1969, Fun House 1970, Jesus Loves The Stooges 1977, I'm Sick of You 1977, Raw Stooges 1988, Raw Stooges 2 1988, The Weirdness 2007; solo: Raw Power 1973, Metallic KO 1976, The Idiot 1977, Lust For Life 1977, TV Eye Live 1978, Kill City 1978, New Values 1979, Soldier 1980, Party 1981, I'm Sick of You 1981, Zombie Birdhouse 1982, I Got The Right 1983, Blah Blah Blah 1986, Rubber Legs 1987, Live At The Whiskey A Go Go 1988, Death Trip 1988, Instinct 1988, Brick By Brick 1990, American Caesar 1994, Naughty Little Doggie 1996, Heroin Hates You 1997, King Biscuit Flower Hour 1997, Your Pretty Face is Going to Hell 1998, Sister Midnight 1999, Avenue B 1999, Iggy Pop 1999, Hippodrome Paris '77 (live) 1999, Beat 'Em Up 2001, Skull Ring 2003, Preliminaires 2009, Après 2012. *Publications:* I Need More (autobiog.), Iggy Pop's A–Z (autobiog.) 2005. *Honours:* inducted into Rock and Roll Hall of Fame 2010. *Website:* www.iggypop.com.

POPMAN (see Lloyd, Andrew Reginald)

PORCARO, Steve; American singer and musician (keyboards); b. 2 Sept. 1957, Hartford, Conn. *Career:* support musician to artists, including Jackson Browne, Aretha Franklin, Barbra Streisand, Jennifer Warnes, Jim Wilson, Yes, Jefferson Airplane; mem., Toto 1978–87, 2010–, Chris Squire Experiment 1992. *Television:* as composer: Justified 2010–15. *Recordings include:* albums: with Toto: Toto 1979, Hydra 1979, Turn Back 1981, Toto IV 1982, Isolation 1985, Dune (film soundtrack) 1985, Fahrenheit 1986, Toto XIV 2015. *Honours:* Grammy Award for Record of the Year, Album of the Year, Best Vocal Arrangement, Best Instrumental Arrangement, Best Producer (Toto), Best Engineered Recording 1983. *Current Management:* c/o Steve Karas and Keith Hagan, SKH Music. *E-mail:* skaras@skhmusic.com; khagan@skhmusic.com. *Website:* www.skhmusic.com; www.totoofficial.com.

PORTEJOIE, Philippe René Paul; French musician (saxophone); b. 28 Dec. 1956, Niort; m. Frederique Lagarde, 15 Sept. 1990, 1 s. *Education:* First Prize, CNSM, Paris. *Career:* Member duo Portejoie-Lagarde; 2 albums; 100 concerts, France; Italy; Belgium; Norway; Radio: Radio France (France Inter; France Musique); Premier alto saxophone, Big Band with Claude de Bolling; mem, Yehudi Menuhin Foundation; Professor, Conservatoire Superieur de Paris (CNR). *Recordings:* 20 recordings include Musique Francaise Du XXe Siècle; Stéphane Grappelli; Strictly Classical; Saxomania Et Clark Terry; with Tsf: Ca Va Ca Va, 1996; with Claude Bolling: First Class 1991; Black Brown and Beige, 1993; Victory Concert, 1994; Cinema Dreams, 1996; Drum is a Woman, 1996; Tone Parallel to Harlem, 1999. *Honours:* Premier Prix d'Honneur à l'Unanité (Concours de Musique d'Ensemble de l'UFAM); Meilleur Formation Française (Musique de Chambre de Paris). *Website:* www.hexagone.net/music/cvprofs/philippe%20portejoie.htm.

PORTELLI, Rose-Marie; French singer and composer; b. Toulon. *Career:* appeared at Festival of Traditional Music, Birmingham, England, 1991, Olympia in 1994, Congrés Mondial Acadien, Canada, 1994, Fête de la Musique at American Center in Paris, 1995, Francofolies de la Rochelle, 1995, Disneyland in Paris, 1995; Tour of USA and Canada, 1995; mem. SACEM. *Recordings include:* Marine Marine 1993. *Publication:* Fabienne Thibeau (biog.). *Honours:* First Prize for Interpretation, SACEM, 1992. *Current Management:* Dolphin Dreams Productions, 98 Blvd Poniatowski, 75012 Paris, France.

PORTEOUS, Michael Lindsay; British ethnomusicologist and musician (Jew's harp, folk insruments); b. 2 Feb. 1948, The Mytertoun Menstrie, Clackmannanshire, Scotland. *Career:* several TV appearances for various cos, and radio including several of own on folk instruments; mem. Musicians' Union, The Traditional Music and Song Asscn of Scotland. *Compositions:* Dunblane (lament cassette), Farewell to Lizziewells. *Recordings:* Recordings with Heritage 1978–93, Tell Tae Me 1993, Greentrax, 1988, Tracks on various CD samplers 1987–97; cassettes. *Publication:* How to Play and Have Fun with the Jew's-Harp 1990. *Honours:* Competition Certificates, Traditional Music Song Asscn of Scotland 1976–2007, One Man Band Champion, Edinburgh Folk Festival 1982, 1983, 1984. *Address:* Lindsay Porteous, Tron House, Culross, Fife, KY12 8JG, Scotland (home). *Telephone:* (1383) 880271 (home).

PORTER, Christopher; British record producer; b. 4 May 1954, Southampton, Hampshire; m. Virginia Guarlez 1977; two d. *Education:* art coll. *Career:* began as engineer at Good Earth Studios under Tony Visconti 1980; early engineering success with Lynx and Junior Giscombe; long-standing collaboration with George Michael; co-producer with Tim Simenon for Whycliffe and Zan Jam. *Recordings:* producer, engineer: albums: George Michael: Faith, Listen Without Prejudice, Part 1; Wham!: The Final, Make It Big; Breaking Glass film soundtrack; recordings for: Living In A Box, Robbie Nevil, Hall and Oates, Debbie Gibson, Diana Ross, Omar, Breathe, Gary Moore, The Christians, The Alarm, Simple Minds, David Bowie, Dexy's Midnight Runners, Junior Giscombe, Boomtown Rats, Thin Lizzy, A Flock of Seagulls, Steps; singles/tracks include: Take That: Back For Good 1995, Babe;

George Michael: tracks for Red Hot and Dance; Elton John: Don't Let The Sun Go Down On Me, Some Other World; Aswad: On and On, Don't Turn Around, Beauty's Only Skin Deep; Wham!: Wham! Rap; Pet Shop Boys: Se A Vida É; Diana Princess of Wales: Tribute; Robbie Nevil: Wot's It to Ya, Music of the Heart.

PORTER, Gregory; American jazz singer; b. 4 Nov. 1971, Sacramento, Calif. *Education:* Highland High School, San Diego State Univ. *Career:* guest performer, Jazz at Lincoln Center Jazz Orchestra; residency at Smoke Jazz, NY; appearances at many festivals including ELB Jazz Festival, Germany, London Jazz Festival, North Sea Jazz Festival, The Netherlands, Nat. Black Arts Festival, Atlanta; sang with Cyrus Chestnut Trio, Wynton Marsalis's Lincoln Center Jazz Orchestra; numerous collaborators including Jools Holland, Disclosure, Renée Fleming, Jamie Cullum. *Recordings:* albums: Water 2010, Be Good 2012, Liquid Spirit (Grammy Award for Best Jazz Vocal Album 2014) 2013; as Broadway cast mem.: It Ain't Nothin' But the Blues 2000; also featured on Love & Revolution, Nicola Conte 2011. *Stage appearances include:* It Ain't Nothin' But the Blues, Denver, Colorado 1998, and Broadway 1999, Nat King Cole and Me, Denver 2004. *Honours:* Village Voice Jazz Critics' Best Debut 2010, Jazz Journalists' Asscn Award for Male Vocalist of the Year 2013, 2014, 2015. *Current Management:* Paul Ewing, Wingsmusic Entertainment Inc., 530 East 76th Street, # 24C, New York, NY 10021; Maria Matias Music, 316 Mid Valley Center, Suite 203, Carmel, CA 93923, USA. *Telephone:* (212) 879-3747 (New York); (831) 625-0344 (Carmel). *Fax:* (831) 536-1040 (Carmel). *E-mail:* wingsmusicinc@gmail.com; office@mariamatiasmusic.com; maria@mariamatiasmusic.com. *Website:* www.wingsmusic.com; www.mariamatiasmusic.com; www.gregoryporter.com.

PORTER, Bishop Henry L.; singer, author, musician (piano, organ) and songwriter, lecturer, poet and cleric; *Bishop and Pastor, HLPEA, Inc., Westcoast Centers For Human Development;* b. 2 Jan. 1948, Sarasota, Fla; m. Cynthia E. Porter (deceased); three s. one d. *Education:* Florida A&M Univ., Tallahassee, Yale Univ., New Haven, CT. *Career:* music featured in adapted version of Black Nativity (Christmas musical) and on nationwide radio; performed at the White House, Pentagon, throughout continental USA and abroad; Founder and Pres. Prelate, Westcoast Centers for Human Devt; mem. American Asscn of Univ. Profs, Yale Club, League Club, Sarasota Chamber of Commerce; mem. Senate Advisory Bd on Educ. (Nigeria). *Television:* The HLP Love Campaign – BET, The Guardian Network, The Word Network, CTN Reflections, Bobby Jones Gospel. *Compositions:* over 2,000 compositions. *Recordings:* 17 albums, including Keep Making Tracks, He's Real, The Love Campaign (TLC), The Encyclopedia of Praise, Shout. *Publications:* Grief, A Sure Thing, Higher Thoughts and Peaceful Ways, Children of the Thought, Leaders a Rare Breed, Duties of an Assistant, Seasons of the Rain. *Honours:* Hon. DLitt (United Bible Coll. and Seminary); Hon. DD (Trinity Coll. of Ministerial Arts); Gospel Award for Music that Does More than Sound, State of Florida Gospel Hall of Fame, Sarasota Hall of Fame, Broadcasters' Hall of Fame, Freedom Award in Educ. to his school (Westcoast School for Human Devt). *Current Management:* c/o Dr Mariea E. Watkins, Watkins Music LLC, Jewelstone Records, PO Box 49052, Sarasota, FL 34230-6052, USA. *Telephone:* (866) 271-2071. *E-mail:* dw@watkinsmusic.biz; watkinsmusic@yahoo.com. *Website:* www.watkinsmusic.biz; www.thegospelawards.com. *Address:* HLPEA Inc., PO Box 49168, Sarasota, FL 34230-6168, USA (office). *Telephone:* (941) 365-7543 (office). *Fax:* (941) 954-1057 (office). *E-mail:* WCHDhdqrs@aol.com (office). *Website:* www.henryporter.com (office); www.lovecampaign.tv (office); www.westcoastcenter.org (office).

PORTER, K. C.; American record producer and musician (keyboards); b. 27 June 1962, Encino, CA; m. Aimée Porter; one d. *Education:* CSUN University. *Career:* producer for Santana, Ricky Martin, Selena, Patti LaBelle, Ednita Nazario, Los Fabulosos Cadillacs; Alan Azul; Laura Pausini; mem, SAG, AFTRA, ASCAP, BMI, SESAC, NARAS, LARAS. *Recordings:* produced albums for: Boyz II Men, Toni Braxton, Sting, Bon Jovi, Brian McKnight, Geri Halliwell, Montell Jordan, Lara Fabian, La India; Az Yet (Producer of Spanish Crossover Versions), Ozomatli, Carlos Santana, Laura Pausini. *Honours:* ASCAP/SESAC Writer Awards 1994, Grammy Awards 1998–99, BMI, Song of the Year 1997–98, Latin Grammy Award for Producer of the Year 2001. *Address:* c/o Worldbeat Productions, 24522 Dry Canyon Cold Creek Road, Calabasas, CA 91302, USA (office). *Telephone:* (818) 225-0082 (office). *Fax:* (818) 225-0084 (office). *Website:* www.kcporter.com.

PORTER, Steve; British music industry executive. *Career:* worked in sr man. positions in the music industry and with Price Waterhouse, London; joined MCPS-PRS Alliance as Finance Dir 1998, later Man. Dir, CEO 2007–09; Chair. Central European Licensing and Admin Service. *Address:* c/o MCPS-PRS Alliance, Copyright House, 29-33 Berners Street, London W1T 3AB, England (office).

PORTMAN, Emily Gwyneth, BA, MA; British folk singer, musician (concertina) and songwriter; b. 1982; one d. *Education:* Univ. of Newcastle. *Career:* fmr mem. The Devil's Interval a cappella folk vocal group 2002–07; f. Emily Portman Trio (with Lucy Farrell and Rachel Newton); other collaborations include Lauren McCormick, Rubus, the Furrow Collective; currently singing teacher, Univ. of Newcastle; Co-founder, Furrow Records 2010. *Recordings:* albums: with the Devil's Interval: Blood and Honey 2006; with Rubus: Nine Witch Knots 2008; solo: The Glamoury 2010, Hatchling 2012; with the Furrow Collective: At Our Next Meeting 2014. *Honours:* BBC Radio 2 Folk Award for

Best Original Song 2013. *Address:* Furrow Records, 22 St Michael's Road, Aigburth, Liverpool, L17 7AR, England (office). *Website:* furrowrecords .bandcamp.com (office); www.emilyportman.co.uk (home).

PORTMAN, Rachel Mary Berkeley, OBE; British composer; b. 11 Dec. 1960, Haslemere, Surrey, England; m. Uberto Pasolini; three d. *Education:* Worcester Coll., Oxford. *Career:* composer of film and TV scores, for US productions 1992–. *Compositions for film and television:* Experience Preferred… But Not Essential 1982, The Storyteller (TV series) 1986–88, 1990, Life is Sweet 1990, Oranges Are Not the Only Fruit (TV drama) 1990, Antonia and Jane 1991, Where Angels Fear to Tread 1991, Used People 1992, The Joy Luck Club 1993, Benny and Joon 1993, Friends 1993, Sirens 1994, Only You 1994, War of the Buttons 1994, To Wong Foo – Thanks for Everything! 1995, A Pyromaniac's Love Story 1995, Smoke 1995, The Adventures of Pinocchio 1996, Marvin's Room 1996, Emma (Academy Award for Best Music, Original Music or Comedy Score 1997) 1996, Addicted to Love 1997, The Cider House Rules 1999, Ratcatcher (Georges Delerue Prize, Ghent Int. Film Festival) 1999, Chocolat 2000, The Legend of Bagger Vance (Phoenix Film Critics Soc. Award for Best Original Score) 2000, The Emperor's New Clothes 2001, Hart's War 2002, The Truth About Charlie 2002, Nicholas Nickleby 2002, The Human Stain 2003, Mona Lisa Smile 2003, The Little Prince 2003, Lard 2004, The Manchurian Candidate 2004, Because of Winn-Dixie 2005, Oliver Twist 2006, The Lake House 2006, Miss Potter 2006, Infamous 2006, H2hOpe: The Water Diviner's Tale (BBC Proms) 2007, Little House on the Prairie Musical (theatre) 2008, The Duchess 2008, Grey Gardens (TV) 2009, London Assurance (Royal Nat. Theatre) 2010, Never Let Me Go (San Diego Film Critics Soc. Award for Best Score) 2010, Snowflower and the Secret Fan 2011, One Day 2011, The Vow 2012, Bel Ami 2012, Private Peaceful 2012, The Right Kind of Wrong 2013, Paradise 2013, Still Life 2013, Belle 2013, Dolphin Tale 2 2014, Bessie (Primetime Emmy Award for Outstanding Music Composition for a Limited Series, Movie or a Special (Original Dramatic Score) 2015) 2015. *Recordings include:* Rachel Portman Soundtracks (compilation album), numerous soundtrack recordings. *Honours:* British Film Inst. Young Composer of the Year Award 1988, Carlton TV/Rank Films Laboratories Award for Creative Originality 1996, Muse Award from New York Women in Film and Television 2000, BMI Richard Kirk Award 2010. *Current Management:* c/o Robert Messinger, First Artists Management, 4764 Park Granada, Suite 210, Calabasa, CA 91302, USA; Simon Platz, Bucks Music, Onward House, 11 Uxbridge Street, London, W8 7TQ, England. *Website:* www.rachelportman.co .uk.

PORTNOW, Neil; American music company executive and musician; *President, NARAS;* b. New York, NY. *Career:* played with various bands; studio sideman, playing bass and guitar; Pres., Portnow-Miller Company Inc 1971; Man., Talent Acquisition and Development, Screen Gems Publishing Group 1972; Staff Producer, RCA Records, promoted to Exec. Producer 1977; Senior Vice-Pres., 20th Century Fox Records 1979; Vice-Pres., Artists and Repertoire, EMI America Records 1985; Senior Vice-Pres., West Coast Operations for Zomba Group of Companies, including Jive Records, Silvertone Records, Zomba Music Publishing, Zomba Management, Segue Music, Zomba Music Clearance; music supervision, Wired (motion picture) 1988–2002; music supervisor for Frank Mancuso Jr's production of Permanent Record (Paramount Pictures) 1987; Pres. NARAS (Nat. Acad. of Recording Arts and Sciences) 2002–; mem. Recording Academy (nat. trustee, former nat. vice-pres., bd of trustees), Los Angeles Chapter (fmr mem. and treasurer, bd of govs, Songwriters Resources and Services (advisory bd), Los Angeles City of Hope Music Chapter (team captain). *Address:* NARAS, 3030 Olympic Boulevard, Santa Monica, CA 90404, USA (office). *Telephone:* (310) 392-3777 (office). *Fax:* (310) 399-3090 (office). *Website:* www.grammy.com (office).

PORTUONDO, Omara; Cuban singer; b. 30 Oct. 1930, Havana; d. of Bartolomes Portunondo and Esperanza Pelaez; one s. *Education:* Univ. of Havana. *Career:* professional debut at Caberet Tropicana 1945; sang in Loquibambla Swing; became known as 'La novia del filin' (The Fiancée of Filin) after the Cuban music form combining bossa nova with American jazz influences; founder mem. Cuarteto Las D'Aida 1952–67; mem. Orquesta Aragón 1970s; recorded a track for film Buena Vista Social Club; participated in Buena Vista performances Amsterdam and New York; collaborations with Ry Cooder, Ibrahim Ferrer, Afro-Cuban All-Stars. *Recordings:* albums: Buena Vista Social Club 1997, Distinto Diferente (with Afro Cuban All-Stars) 1999; solo: Magia Negra 1958, Esta es Omara Portuondo 1967, Omara Portuondo 1967, Omara 1974, Y Tal Vez Omara Portuondo 1981, Palabras 1995, Pensamientos 1995, La Novia del Feeling 1997, Buena Vista Social Club Presents Omara Portuondo 2000, Flor de Amor (Billboard Music Award for Best Female Tropical Album 2005) 2004, Gracias (Latin Grammy Award for Best Contemporary Tropical Album 2009) 2008, Omara Portuondo e Maria Bethânia 2008. *Honours:* Guardia Nacional de Cuba (five times), Federación de Mujeres Cubanas Hon. Prize. *Current Management:* Montuno Producciones, Provenza, 112 bis, Escalera A, Entlo. 3a, 08029 Barcelona, Spain. *Telephone:* (93) 3633600. *Fax:* (93) 3633450. *E-mail:* info@montuno.com. *Website:* www.montuno,com.

POST, Mike; composer, musician (guitar), producer and arranger; b. 29 Sept. 1944, San Fernando Valley, CA, USA. *Career:* founder, Wellingbrook Singers, First Edition; guitarist with Dick and Dee, Sammy Davis Jr, Dean Martin, Sonny and Cher; Musical Dir, Andy Williams Show; Prod., Mac Davis Show. *Compositions:* music scores and theme music for numerous television shows, including Rockford Files, LA Law, Hill Street Blues, The A-Team, Magnum

PI, Doogie Howser MD, Quantum Leap, Hardcastle and McCormick, Riptide, NYPD Blue, Law and Order, Silk Stalkings, Wiseguy, Hunter, News Radio, The Commish, Blossom, Hooperman, White Shadow, Renegade. *Recordings include:* as producer and/or arranger: Photograph, Mason Williams; various albums by Ray Charles; Nine To Five, Dolly Parton; I Could've Been A Sailor, Peter Allen; Greatest American Hero, Joey Scarbury (also as musician and writer), 1981; as musician: All I Really Want To Do, Cher, 1965; Sandman, Herb Pedersen, 1977; compilations: Television Theme Songs, 1982; Music From LA Law and Otherwise; NYPD Blue–The Best Of 1999. *Honours:* Grammy Awards for Rockford Files, LA Law, Hill Street Blues, Greatest American Hero, Murder 1 1995–96.

POTGER, Keith, AO; British singer, musician (guitar, banjo, mandolin) and songwriter; b. 21 March 1941, Colombo, Sri Lanka; m. Nicki Paull. *Career:* Founding mem. folk/pop group The Seekers, with Judith Durham, Athol Guy and Bruce Woodley; formed The New Seekers 1969; reunited with original Seekers members 1993; musical activities in Australia and UK including solo touring, songwriting, music publishing and recording. *Recordings include:* with The Seekers: The Four & Only Seekers 1964, The New Seekers 1965, Come the Day 1966, Seen in Green 1967, Georgy Girl 1967, Live at the Talk of the Town 1968, Future Road 1997; solo: Secrets of the Heart 2005, Sunday 2007, Smile Now 2010. *Honours:* with The Seekers: Australians of the Year 1967, ARIA Hall of Fame 1995. *E-mail:* circle@vianet.net.au. *Website:* www .artistsbusiness.info.

POTT, Joel; British singer and musician (guitar); b. Lincolnshire; m. Zoë; one d. *Career:* founder mem., Athlete 1997–; tours throughout Europe. *Recordings include:* albums: Vehicles & Animals 2003, Tourist 2005, Beyond the Neighbourhood 2007, Black Swan 2009. *Honours:* Ivor Novello Award for Best Contemporary Song (for Wires) 2006. *Website:* www.athlete.mu.

POTTER, Chris; American jazz musician (tenor saxophonist) and composer; b. 1 Jan. 1971, Chicago, Ill. *Education:* Dreher High School, New School, New York, Manhattan School of Music. *Career:* grew up in Columbia; made professional jazz debut 1984; performer on over 150 albums; numerous collaborators including Patricia Barber, Joanne Brackeen, Dave Holland, Joe Lovano, Marian McPartland, Pat Metheny, Steely Dan, Kenny Werner; regular collaborator with Adam Rogers, Wayne Krantz, Nate Smith. *Recordings:* as leader: Presenting Chris Potter 1994, Concentric Circles 1994, Sundiata 1995, Pure 1995, Moving In 1996, Unspoken 1997, Vertigo 1998, Gratitude 2001, Traveling Mercies 2002, Underground 2006, 10: Song for Anyone 2007, Ultrahang 2009, Transatlantic 2011, The Sirens 2013, Imaginary Cities 2015; as sideman: with Paul Motian: Reincarnation of a Love Bird 1994, Flight of the Blue Jay 1996, 2000 + One 1997, Play Monk and Powell 1998, On Broadway Vol. 4 or the Paradox of Continuity 2005, Lost in a Dream 2010; with Dave Holland: Prime Detective 2000, Not for Nothin' 2001, Overtime 2005, Critical Mass 2006, Pathways 2010; other credits include: Sea Jam Blues (with Urbie Green) 1997, Damaged in Transit (with Steve Swallow) 2003, Unity Band (with Pat Metheny) 2012, All Over the Place (with Mike Stern) 2012, Circle of Life (with Burak Bedikyan) 2013, KIN (with Pat Metheny) 2014. *Honours:* Jazz Journalists Asscn Awards for Best Tenor Saxophonist Rising Star 2004, 2005, 2006, 2007, for Tenor Saxophonist of the Year 2013, 2015. *Address:* c/o ECM Records, Postfach 600 331, 81203 Munich, Germany (office). *E-mail:* ecm@ecmrecords.com (office). *Website:* www .ecmrecords.com (office); www.chrispottermusic.com.

POTTER, Craig Lee; British musician (keyboards) and songwriter. *Career:* joined band Mr Soft with his brother Mark, Guy Garvey, Richard Jupp and Pete Turner, renamed Soft and eventually renamed Elbow 1997–; numerous tours throughout UK, Europe and USA; played concerts in Cuba 2004, becoming first British band to perform outside Havana; headlined UKULA Bright Lights Festival, Toronto, Canada 2006. *Recordings:* albums: Asleep in the Back 2001, Cast of Thousands 2003, Leaders of the Free World 2005, The Seldom Seen Kid (Mercury Music Prize) 2008, Build a Rocket Boys! 2011, The Take Off and Landing of Everything 2014. *Honours:* BRIT Award for Best British Group 2009, Ivor Novello Awards for Best Song Musically and Lyrically (for One Day Like This) 2009, for Best Contemporary Song (for Grounds for Divorce) 2009. *Current Management:* TRC Management, 10c Whitworth Court, Manor Park, Manor Farm Road, Runcorn, Cheshire, WA7 1TE, England. *Telephone:* (1928) 571111. *E-mail:* mail@trcmanagement.com. *Website:* www.trcmanagement.com; www.elbow.co.uk.

POTTER, Mark Ellis; British musician (guitar) and songwriter. *Career:* formed band Mr Soft with his brother Craig, Guy Garvey, Richard Jupp and Pete Turner 1990, renamed Soft and eventually renamed Elbow 1997–; numerous concerts and tours throughout UK, Europe and USA; played concerts in Cuba 2004, becoming first British band to perform outside Havana; headlined UKULA Bright Lights Festival, Toronto, Canada 2006. *Recordings:* albums: Asleep in the Back 2001, Cast of Thousands 2003, Leaders of the Free World 2005, The Seldom Seen Kid (Mercury Music Prize) 2008, Build a Rocket Boys! 2011, The Take Off and Landing of Everything 2014. *Honours:* BRIT Award for Best British Group 2009, Ivor Novello Awards for Best Song Musically and Lyrically (for One Day Like This) 2009, for Best Contemporary Song (for Grounds for Divorce) 2009. *Current Management:* TRC Management, 10c Whitworth Court, Manor Park, Manor Farm Road, Runcorn, Cheshire, WA7 1TE, England. *Telephone:* (1928) 571111. *E-mail:* mail@ trcmanagement.com. *Website:* www.trcmanagement.com; www.elbow.co.uk.

POUGET, Nelly; French musician (saxophone) and composer; b. 19 May 1955, Dijon, Côte d'Or. *Education:* Classique Conservatoire, School of Art, Beaune, Côte d'Or with Jean-Marie Londeix. *Career:* began her jazz music career in 1982; Founder Nelly Pouget Quartet; Jazz Festival Dudelange Luxembourg 1992, Foyer Boris Vian Ulis 1992, Theatre Maubel Galabru, Paris 1992, Espace 1789, St Ouen 1992; duo with Belgium drummer Micheline Pelzer at Tourcoing Jazz Festival, A.M.R. Geneva and Bern, Switzerland, Tours, Mont de Marsan, Bruges and Thorout Belgium 1993–95; played with Horace Tapscott and led a septet 1993; played at Word Stage, Los Angeles, USA 1994; led int. quartet with James Lewis, Noah Rosen and Makoto Sato 1995; led duo with Sunny Murray at Frankfurt Festival 1998; performed solo at Contemporary Art Centre, Vassivière 1998, Culture Centre, Limoges 1999, Europa Jazz Festival, Le Mans 1999, Culture Centre, Bron 2000, Grenoble Jazz Festival 2001, 2002; first solo CD Fraîcheur Cuivrée 1999; recorded for Radio France an original composition in five parts for Allabreves, France Musique, France Culture; mem. SACEM France. *Recordings:* albums: Le Dire 1991, Le Vivre 1993, Nelly Pouget Quartet Live at Procreart Paris 1996, Le Voir 1997, Fraîcheur Cuivrée 1999, Le Waw (Nelly Pouget Duo with organ) 2002. *Address:* c/o Minuit Regards, 56 rue de la Sablière, 75014 Paris, France. *Telephone:* 1-40-44-98-28; (6) 82-24-36-68 (mobile). *Fax:* 1-40-44-98-28. *E-mail:* nellypouget@minuitregards.com; nellypouget@wanadoo.fr. *Website:* www.minuitregards.com/fr/nellypouget/.

POULIOT, George Stephen; American record producer, sound engineer and composer; b. 12 June 1954, North Hollywood, CA; m. Erica Gardner 1989. *Education:* Sherwood Oaks Coll. *Career:* recording engineer, Steve Pouliot Music 1979–; sound engineer for Rita Coolidge and Dwight Yoakam; also collaborated with: Bonnie Bramlett, Peaches & Herb, Robin Pearl; mem. BMI. *Compositions:* songwriter for Micky Martin, Billy Burnett. *Recordings:* as engineer: Behind The Mask, Fleetwood Mac 1990; as producer: Rick Vito 1991, The Honest 1991; In Trouble Again. *Honours:* Grammy Award 1978.

POULLAIN, Francis (Frankie); British musician (bass); b. (Francis Gilles Poullain-Patterson), 15 April 1967, Scotland. *Career:* f. band Empire (with Justin and Dan Hawkins), band split 1999, reconstituted as The Darkness 2000–05, 2011–. *Recordings include:* albums: with The Darkness: Permission To Land (Best Album, Kerrang! Awards, BRIT Award for Best British Album 2004) 2003, Hot Cakes 2012, Last of Our Time 2015. *Publications:* Dancing in the Darkness 2008. *Honours:* Kerrang! Award for Best Live Act 2003, The Observer Band of the Year 2003, BRIT Award for Best British Group, Best British Rock Act 2004. *Website:* www.thedarkness.com.

POUSSY, Moussa; Niger singer, songwriter and dancer; b. 5 May 1962, Niamey; m. Adama Tahirou 1988; two s. three d. *Education:* Centre de Formation et de Promotion Musicales, Hadj Taya. *Career:* comic actor and musician; began as entertainment singer in night clubs; leader of many orchestras in Niamey; concerts in Nigeria, Côte d'Ivoire, Burkina Faso and Mali; Leader, Le Degara-Band, Niamey; mem. Nigerian Asscn of Musicians. *Compositions include:* Adama; Tchirey; Nafissa; Kokaina; Waimo; Sibo; Toro. *Recordings include:* compilation albums Vols I, II and III 1988, Toro 1991, Niamey Twice 1994. *Honours:* first prize Concours de Musique Nigerienne Moderne 1987. *E-mail:* MoussaPoussy@PlaneteAfrique.com.

POWAGA, Wojciech; Polish rock musician (guitar); b. 1972, Mysłowice. *Career:* formed band The Freshmen with Artur Rojek 1992, changed band's name to Myslovitz 1994; first int. concerts, Sweden, Germany, USA 1998; numerous European festival appearances and support act for Iggy Pop and Simple Minds 2002; began releasing English-language versions of their music 2002; European tour and support act for Iggy Pop and The Corrs 2004; contributed to soundtracks for films Młode wilki ½ (Young Wolves ½), Duże zwierzę (The Big Animal), To my (That's us). *Recordings:* albums: Myslovitz 1995, Sun Machine 1996, Z rozmyślań przy śniadaniu 1997, Miłość w czasach popkultury 1999, Korova Milky Bar 2002, The Best Of 2003, Korova Milky Bar (English version) 2003, Skalary, mieczyki, neonki 2004, Happiness Is Easy 2006. *Honours:* Music Video of The Year 1998, Band of The Year and Rock Album of The Year 1999, Song of The Year and Video of The Year 2000, Album of The Year 2003, all Fryderyk awards; Polityka's Paszport award 1999, Best Polish Act, MTV Europe Music Awards 2002, 2003, Border Breakers European Breakthrough award (for Korova Milky Bar) 2005. *Current Management:* Maciej Pilarczyk, Chaos Management Group, ul. Karowa 31, 00-324 Warsaw, Poland. *E-mail:* m.pil@myslovitz.pl (office). *Website:* www.chaos.com.pl (office); www.myslovitz.pl.

POWELL, Claire-Louise; singer, actress and producer; b. Norfolk, England. *Career:* lead singer, Pentangle; lead singer, Sugar Mice; Cabaret at La Parisien; Ma Kindley's Musical Extravaganza; extensive musicals, film, television, radio and opera Don Giovanni; Director, Osiris Productions; Director, Chucklefactory; Production Executive, Sound Pound; Casting Consultant, Good Vibrations. *Recordings:* Cabaret Cage; Poison Dwarf; Sacred Songs of Scotland; Rock Opera 1; Soul Sounds, Mellow Yellow. *Honours:* Le Sarlation, Most Outstanding Female Vocalist, three times.

POWELL, Don; British musician (drums) and producer; b. 10 Sept. 1950, Bilston, Warwickshire, England. *Career:* mem. rock group, Slade (formerly N'Betweens, Ambrose Slade) 1966–; numerous concert tours and festival appearances. *Film appearance:* Flame 1974. *Recordings include:* albums: Beginnings (as Ambrose Slade) 1969, Play It Loud 1970, Slade Alive 1972, Slayed 1973, Sladest 1973, Old New Borrowed Blue 1974, Slade In Flame (soundtrack) 1974, Nobody's Fool 1976, Slade Alive Vol. 2 1978, Return To

Base 1979, Slade Smashes 1980, Till Deaf Do Us Part 1981, We'll Bring The House Down 1981, Slade On Stage 1982, The Amazing Kamikaze Syndrome 1983, Slade's Greats 1984, Rogue's Gallery 1985, Crackers 1985, You Boyz Make Big Noize 1987, Wall of Hits 1991, Keep On Rockin' 1996, Fantastic World of Spaghetti Westerns 1999, Slade II 2001, Slayed? 2006. *Honours:* Hon. Fellow (Univ. of Wolverhampton) 2002.

POWELL, Gary Armstrong; American drummer; b. 11 Nov. 1969, New York. *Career:* mem. The Libertines 2001–04, 2014–; mem. Dirty Pretty Things 2005–08; drummer for Eddy Grant. *Recordings:* albums: with The Libertines: Up the Bracket 2002, The Libertines 2004, Anthems for Doomed Youth 2015; with Dirty Pretty Things: Waterloo to Anywhere 2006, Romance at Short Notice 2008. *Honours:* Q Best Track Award (for Gunga Din) 2015. *Current Management:* c/o Various Artists Management, 17 Lonsdale Road, London, NW6 6RA, England. *Telephone:* (20) 7372-6075. *E-mail:* info@variousartistsmanagement.com. *Website:* www.variousartistsmanagement.com; www.thelibertines.com.

POWELL, James Michael; British musician (drums); b. 25 March 1973, London; s. of Georgie Fame. *Education:* Tuition from John Parish. *Career:* Numerous Tours with Georgie Fame; Stephen Duffy; Alan Price; Van Morrison; Lloyd Cole; Orchestra for Whistle Down The Wind and Mamma Mia; mem. Musicians' Union. *Recordings:* Relationships, Georgie Fame, 2001.

POWELL, John James; British composer, conductor, pianist and producer; b. 18 Sept. 1963, London; m. Melinda Lerner. *Education:* Trinity Coll. of Music, London. *Career:* composer for commercials and TV, Air-Edel Music 1988–95; co-f. Independently Thinking Music (commercial music house) 1995; moved to USA 1997. *Films:* scores: Stay Lucky 1990, The Wild Heels 1994, High Incident 1996, Human Bomb 1996, Face/Off (ASCAP Award for Top Box Office Film 1998) 1997, Antz (with Harry Gregson-Williams) (ASCAP Award for Top Box Office Film 1999) 1998, With Friends Like These 1998, Endurance 1998, Chill Factor 1999, Forces of Nature 1999, Chicken Run (with Harry Gregson-Williams) (ASCAP Award for Top Box Office Film 2001) 2000, The Road to El Dorado (with Hans Zimmer) 2000, Shrek (with Harry Gregson-Williams) (Annie Award for Outstanding Individual Achievement for Music Score in an Animated Feature Production) 2001, Evolution 2001, I Am Sam 2001, Just Visiting 2001, Rat Race 2001, The Bourne Identity (ASCAP Award for Top Box Office Film 2003) 2002, D-Tox 2002, Drumline 2002, The Adventures of Pluto Nash 2002, Two Weeks Notice 2002, Agent Cody Banks 2003, Gigli 2003, Paycheck 2003, Stealing Sinatra 2003, The Italian Job (ASCAP Award for Top Box Office Films 2004) 2003, Alfie 2004, Mr 3000 2004, The Bourne Supremacy (ASCAP Award for Top Box Office Films 2005) 2004, Be Cool 2005, Mr and Mrs Smith (ASCAP Award for Top Box Office Films 2006) 2005, Robots (ASCAP Award for Top Box Office Films 2006) 2005, Ice Age: The Meltdown 2006, United 93 2006, X-Men: The Last Stand 2006, Happy Feet (Film and TV Music Award for Best Score for an Animated Feature Film 2007) 2006, The Bourne Ultimatum 2007, Stop-Loss 2007, PS, I Love You 2007, Horton Hears a Who! 2008, Jumper 2008, Kung Fu Panda (with Hans Zimmer) (Annie Award for Best Music in an Animated Feature Production 2009) 2008, Hancock 2008, Bolt 2008, Ice Age 3: Dawn of the Dinosaurs (Ivor Novello Award for Best Original Film Score 2010) 2009, How to Train Your Dragon 2010, Green Zone 2010, Knight and Day 2010, Mars Needs Moms! 2011, Rio 2011, Kung Fu Panda 2 2011, Happy Feet 2 2011, Continental Drift 2012. *Television:* theme music: High Incident 1997, Kung Fu Panda: Secrets of the Furious Five (with Henry Jackman and Hans Zimmer) (Annie Award for Best Music in an Animated Television Production or Short Form 2009) 2008. *Current Management:* c/o Kraft-Engel Management, 15233 Ventura Boulevard, Suite 200, Sherman Oaks, CA 91403, USA. *Telephone:* (818) 380-1918. *E-mail:* info@kraft-engel.com. *Website:* www.kraft-engel.com.

POWELL, Owen; British musician (guitar); b. 9 July 1967, Cambridge, England. *Career:* fmr mem. various bands, including Y Crumblowers, Colour 45, The Family; mem. Catatonia 1995–2001; judge, Wawffactor talent show 2003–06. *Recordings include:* albums: Way Beyond Blue 1996, The Sublime Magic of Catatonia 1996, International Velvet 1998, Equally Cursed and Blessed 1999, Paper Scissors Stone 2001.

POWELLS, Jimmy; British musician (mandolin, guitar) and singer; b. 18 March 1947, Arbroath, Scotland; two s. *Education:* Leith Acad. *Career:* Company Accountant, The Travel Bureau, Gosforth; mem. folk groups, Town Choice, Carterbar. *Recordings:* albums: Romantic Mandolin/Mandolin Moments, Mandolin Magic 2000, Mandolin Memoirs. *Address:* 32 Minting Place, Cramlington, Northumberland, NE23 6AX, England. *Telephone:* (191) 285-9321 (office); (1670) 734547 (home). *Fax:* (1670) 715564 (office); (1670) 715564 (office). *E-mail:* jpowells@trowelbureaugosforth.co.uk (office); jim.powells@btopenworld.com (home). *Website:* www.btinternet.com/~jim.powells.

POWER, Brendan, BA, MA; New Zealand musician (chromatic and diatonic harmonica); b. 20 Feb. 1956, Mombasa, Kenya; m. Lorraine Power 1991. *Career:* session harmonica player; moved to Britain 1992; in band for Riverdance; Irish TV series: A River of Sound; mem. Musicians' Union (UK). *Recordings:* State of The Harp, Harmonica Nights, Digging In, Harmonica After Hours, Jig Jazz, Blow In, Music from Riverdance, Dawn to Dusk, Two Trains Running, Tradish, Farrago, Iron Lung, BP and the Swingfellas, Black to Back, Lament for the 21st Century, Power and White. *Honours:* All-Ireland

Champion 1993. *E-mail:* bren@brendan-power.com (office). *Website:* www .brendan-power.com.

POWER, Cat; American singer and songwriter; b. (Charlyn Marie Marshall), 21 Jan. 1972, Atlanta, GA. *Films:* Speaking For Trees: A Film By Mark Borthwick 2004, Sleepwalkers 2007, My Blueberry Nights 2007, American Widow 2008. *Recordings include:* albums: Dear Sir 1995, Myra Lee 1996, What Would The Community Think 1996, Moon Pix 1998, The Covers Record 2000, You Are Free 2003, Willie Deadwilder 2004, The Greatest (Shortlist Music Prize 2007) 2006, Jukebox 2008, Dark End of the Street 2008. *Address:* c/o Matador Records, 304 Hudson Street, 7th Floor, New York, NY 10013, USA (office). *Telephone:* (212) 995-5882 (office). *Fax:* (212) 995-5883 (office). *E-mail:* info@matadorrecords.com (office). *Website:* www.matadorrecords.com (office); www.catpowermusic.com.

POWER, Glen Joseph; Irish musician (drums) and singer; b. 5 July 1980, Dublin. *Career:* fmr session musician; mem. The Script 2003–. *Recordings:* albums: The Script 2008, Science and Faith 2010, #3 2012, No Sound Without Silence 2014. *Honours:* World Music Award for Best Selling Irish Act 2008, Meteor Ireland Music Awards for Best Band 2009, for Best Irish Album 2009. *Address:* c/o RCA Group, 9 Derry Street, London W8 5HY, England (office). *Website:* www.rcalabelgroup.co.uk (office); www.thescriptmusic.com.

POWER, John Timothy; British singer, songwriter and musician (guitar); b. 14 Sept. 1967, Liverpool, England; m. Belinda Stone 1996; two c. *Career:* bassist with The La's –1993, 2005–; founder mem., Cast 1993–2002; solo artist 2002–; mem. PPL, PRS, Musicians' Union. *Recordings include:* albums: with The La's: The La's 1990, Breakloose–Lost La's 1984–87 2001; with Cast: All Change 1997, Magic Hour 1999; solo: Happening for Love 2003, Willow She Weeps 2006, Stormbreaker 2008. *E-mail:* z@tanukitanuki.com. *Website:* www .johnpower.uk.com.

POWER, Nick; British musician (organ); b. Hoylake, Wirral, England. *Education:* Hilbre High School, Hoylake. *Career:* Founder mem., The Coral 1996–. *Recordings include:* albums: The Coral 2002, Magic and Medicine 2003, Secret Kiss 2003, Nightfreak and the Sons of Becker 2004, The Invisible Invasion 2005, Roots and Echoes 2007, The Singles Collection 2008, Butterfly House 2010.

POWER, Vince; Irish music promoter; b. 29 April 1947, Co. Waterford; m. 1st; m. 2nd; m. 3rd; eight c. *Education:* Kilmacthomas Primary School, Co. Waterford. *Career:* fmr second-hand furniture retailer; opened The Mean Fiddler club in Harlesden High Street, London 1982, with a broad range of musicians performing; expanded co. with ownership of numerous venues (including clubs like London Astoria, restaurants like The Jazz Café, and bars), and to promote festivals (including Reading, Carling Weekend, Phoenix, Tribal Gathering, Homelands and Glastonbury Festivals), individual artists' concerts and tours, sports events, etc.; Chief Exec., The Mean Fiddler Music Group –2004, Exec. Chair. 2004–05 (sold co.); owner of numerous bars and restaurants in London, including Pigalle supper club (opened 2006); owner Benicàssim Festival, Spain 2006–. *Honours:* Hon. CBE 2007. *Address:* c/o Festival Internacional de Benicàssim, PO Box 18240, 28080 Madrid, Spain. *E-mail:* infoenglish@fiberfib.com. *Website:* www.fiberfib.com.

POWERHOUSE (see Gonzalez, Kenny)

POWERPILL (see James, Richard David)

POWERS, Stephen H.; American record producer and entrepreneur; b. 22 Aug. 1951, Rockford, IL. *Education:* MIT. *Career:* founder, Manager, Charlotte's Web Performing Arts Center, Rockford, Illinois 1992; Founder, President, Mountain Railroad Records Inc 1974; Producer, over 50 folk, blues, rock, reggae albums; Director of Entertainment, Los Angeles Olympics 1984; Director, A & R, Capitol Records, Hollywood 1984–87; worked with artists including: The Beach Boys, Duran Duran, Duane Eddy, The Eurythmics, Bryan Ferry, Tina Turner; Founder, President, Chameleon Music Group 1987–92; co-founder, CEO, Drive Entertainment Inc, 1992–2001; Pres. Miller & Kreisel Sound Inc. 2001–06; Man. Dir Agape Media International 2006–; also CEO Powers Commnications and Media; mem, NARAS, National Academy of Songwriters (Board of Directors), Country Music Asscn, NAIRD, NARM. *Honours:* Producer of the Year, Wisconsin Music Awards 1982, Independent Executive of the Year, Los Angles Music Council 1991. *Address:* Agape Media International, 5601 West Slauson Avenue, Suite 180A, Culver City, CA 90230, USA (office). *Telephone:* (310) 348-1260 (office). *E-mail:* info@agapemedia-film.com (office). *Website:* www.agapemedia-film.com (office).

POWLES, Tim; New Zealand musician (drums) and producer; b. 21 Dec. 1959, Wellington. *Career:* fmr mem. The Venetians; Founder Spacejunk Production House; mem. The Church 1996–; solo artist 1999–. *Recordings include:* albums: with The Church: Magician Among the Spirits 1996, Hologram of Baal 1998, After Everything Now This 2002, Parallel Universe 2002, Forget Yourself 2003, El Momento Descuidado 2004, Uninvited, Like the Clouds 2006, El Momento Siguiente 2007; solo: Tygs in Space 1999. *Address:* Spacejunk Production House, PO Box 3041, Putney, NSW 2112, Australia (office). *E-mail:* info@spacejunk.biz (office). *Website:* spacejunk.biz (office); www.thechurchband.com (office).

POWTER, Daniel; Canadian singer and songwriter; b. 25 Feb. 1971, Vernon, BC. *Career:* solo artist 2000–. *Recordings:* albums: I'm Your Betty 2000, Daniel Powter 2005, Under the Radar 2008. *Honours:* Best New Artist, Canadian Juno Awards 2006, Album Of The Year, MTV Japan Video Music

Awards 2007. *Address:* c/o Warner Bros. Records Inc., 3300 Warner Boulevard, Burbank, CA 91505, USA (office). *Telephone:* (818) 846-9090 (office). *Website:* www.warnerbrosrecords.com (office); www.danielpowter.com.

POYNTER, Dougie; British musician (bass guitar) and singer; b. 30 Nov. 1987. *Career:* Founder mem., McFly 2004–. *Recordings include:* albums: Room on the Third Floor (Smash Hits Award for Best Album 2005) 2004, Wonderland 2005, Motion in the Ocean 2006, Radio:Active 2008, Above the Noise 2010. *Honours:* BRIT Award for Best Pop Act 2005, Smash Hits Awards for Smash Hits Star of the Year, for Best UK Band, for Best Video (for That Girl) 2005. *Website:* www.mcflyofficial.com.

POZGAJEC, Branko; Croatian singer and musician (flute); b. 23 July 1950, Zagreb; m. Margita Pozgajec 1983; one s. one d. *Education:* High School of Music, univ. *Career:* leader rock group, Drugi način; numerous nat. and int. concerts, TV and radio broadcasts; mem. Croatian Composers' Union, Croatian Artists' Union, Croatian Musicians' Union (vice-pres. 1998–). *Compositions include:* The Right Words (Prave Rijeci); Dilemmas (Dileme); Again (Opet); Promise Me Springtime (Obecaj Mi Proljece); I'd Like To Get Back (Htio Bih Vratiti). *Recordings include:* four albums with Drugi način.

PRATT, Guy Adam; British musician (bass guitar), record producer and songwriter; b. 3 Jan. 1962, London. *Career:* tours and television appearances with: Icehouse, Bryan Ferry, Scritti Politti, Pink Floyd, Coverdale/Page, Womack and Womack, Bobby Womack and Jeff Beck; mem. PRS; Musicians' Union. *Recordings:* with Madonna: Like A Virgin, Hanky Panky; with Robert Palmer: Riptide, Don't Explain; with Bryan Ferry: Bête Noire, Mamounia; with Pink Floyd: The Division Bell, Delicate Sound of Thunder, Pulse; Jimmy Nail: Ain't No Doubt; Robbie Robertson: Storyville; Power Station: Power Station; Michael Jackson: History; The Orb: The Orb; Debbie Harry: Communion; Third Matinee: Toy Matinee; Dream Academy; Junior Reid: Long Road; Last Action Hero; Ted Hawkins: Ted Hawkins Story; In Dreams: In Dreams; Natalie Imbruglia: White Lillies Island; Ronan Keating: Ronan; Naimee Coleman: Bring Down The Moon. *Honours:* Grammy Award. *Current Management:* RBM, 3rd Floor, 168 Victoria Street, London SW1E 5LB, England. *Telephone:* (20) 7630-7733. *Fax:* (20) 7630-6549. *E-mail:* info@rbmcomedy.com. *Website:* www.rbmcomedy.com.

PREFUSE 73 (see Herren, Scott)

DJ PREMIER, (Primo); American producer and DJ; b. (Chris Edward Martin), 21 March 1966, Houston, TX. *Career:* formed Gang Starr with rapping partner Guru 1989; producer for acts, including Common, Black Eyed Peas; collaborations with Rakim, Jay-Z, Mos Def, Jeru the Damaja. *Recordings include:* albums: No More Mr Nice Guy 1989, Step In The Arena 1990, Daily Operation 1992, Hard To Earn 1994, Moment of Truth 1998, The Ownerz 2003, Kings of Hip-Hop (compilation, with Mr Thing) 2005, Checc Ya Mail 2005, Holiday Hell 2005, Inside Lookin' Out 2007, Inside Lookin' In 2007, Beats That Collected Dust, Vol. 1 2008, On Tha Road Again 2009. *Website:* www.djpremierblog.com.

PRESCOTT, Peter James; British singer; b. 20 Oct. 1956, Erith, Kent, England; m. Wendy Patricia Lewsley 1978, two d. *Career:* singer for 23 years; television appearances, festival performances; mem. Musicians' Union, PRS, MCPS. *Recordings include:* albums with Forcefield; two albums with Paul Sinden: Turn It Up, 1993; Mean Business, 1995; three albums with Swiss band Sergeant; Time Stands Still (with band Passion Play). *Publications:* over 70 songs published.

PRESENCER, Gerard; British musician (trumpet, piano) and composer; b. 12 Sept. 1972, London. *Career:* jazz musician and session player; played trumpet from age 10, first performing with National Youth Jazz Orchestra, aged 11; performed and recorded with many jazz artists and ensembles including Roadside Picnic, Clark Tracey, Pizza Express Modern Jazz Sextet, Charlie Watts Quintet, Dankworth Generation Band, Pete King, Gail Thompson's Gail Force, Stan Tracey, Tina May, Martin Taylor, Tim Garland, Ian Barnes, Don Weller; made a number of solo albums; leads own band, Platypus; regular session work, both as an individual and as a member of the Horny Horns (with Denis Rollins and Michael Smith); appearances on a wide range of artists' recordings including The Brand New Heavies, Tina Turner, Tindersticks, Gabrielle, Beverley Knight, Incognito, Joni Mitchell. *Recordings:* albums: Platypus 1998, The Optimist 2000, Dreams (with Tony Coe) 2001; features on: Brand New Heavies albums: The Brand New Heavies 1990, Brother Sister 1994, Shelter 1997; Alec and John Dankworth Generation Band albums: Nebuchadnezzar 1994, Rhythm Changes 1995; Martin Taylor albums: Years Apart (Martin Taylor's Spirit of Django) 1996, Gold 1997, Celebrating Grappelli 1998; Tim Garland albums: Enter The Fire 1997, Made By Walking 2000; Pete King Quartet albums: Speed Trap 1996, Lush Life 1999; others include From One Charlie, Charlie Watts 1991, Hand On The Torch, US3 1993, Fun, Tina May 1993, Live At The QEH, Stan Tracey 1994, 100 Degrees and Rising, Incognito 1995, For Heaven's Sake, New Stan Tracey Quartet 1996, Wildest Dreams, Tina Turner 1996, Young Mind – Old Hands, Alan Barnes and Brian Lemon 1997, 10, Wet Wet Wet 1997, Curtains, Tindersticks 1997, A Dotty Blues, Alan Barnes 1998, Prodigal Sista, Beverley Knight 1998, Peasants Pigs and Astronauts, Kula Shaker 1999, Rise, Gabrielle 2000, Still, Field of Blue 2000, Both Sides Now, Joni Mitchell 2000. *Honours:* Best Trumpeter, BT Jazz Awards 1995, 1997. *Address:* c/o Linn Records, Glasgow Road, Waterfoot, Eaglesham, Glasgow G76 0EQ,

Scotland (office). *E-mail:* info@linnrecords.co.uk (office). *Website:* www
.linnrecords.com (office).

PRESLAND, Frank; British music executive; *Chairman, Rocket Music
Management. Career:* solicitor specialising in music and copyright for 25
years, advising artists and companies in the industry; Sr partner, Frere
Cholmeley, then (following acquisition by Eversheds) Jt Chair.; est. music
man. co., Twenty-First Artists Management Ltd 1999, CEO –2006; apptd
Group CEO, Sanctuary Group 2006; currently Chair., Rocket Music Management. *Address:* Rocket Music Management, 1 Blythe Road, London, W14 0HG,
England (office). *Telephone:* (20) 7348-4800 (office). *E-mail:* contact@
rocketmusic.com (office). *Website:* www.rocketmusic.com (office).

PRESLEY, Lisa Marie; American singer; b. 1 Feb. 1968, Memphis, TN; d. of
Elvis Presley and Priscilla Presley; m. 1st Danny Keough 1988 (divorced
1994); one s. one d.; m. 2nd Michael Jackson 1994 (divorced 1997); m. 3rd
Nicolas Cage 2002 (divorced); m. 4th Michael Lockwood 2006; two d.
Recordings include: album: To Whom It May Concern 2003, Now What
2005. *Address:* LMP Fan Mail, PO Box 4084, Santa Monica, CA 90411-4084,
USA (office). *Website:* www.lisapresley.com.

PRESTON, Frances W.; American music industry executive; *President
Emerita, Broadcast Music Inc.*; three s. *Education:* Lincoln Coll., Ill. *Career:*
mem. staff, Broadcast Music Inc., Nashville 1958, Vice-Pres. 1964–85, Sr Vice-
Pres. of Performing Rights New York 1985, Exec. Vice-Pres. and CEO 1986,
Pres. and CEO 1986–2004, now Pres. Emer. and consultant; Pres. T. J.
Martell Foundation for Leukemia, Cancer and AIDS Research; mem. Film,
Entertainment and Music Comm. Advisory Council, TN, John Work Memorial
Foundation, Leadership Nashville, Admin. Council Confed. of Int. Socs of
Authors and Composers; Trustee Country Music Foundation Inc.; fmr mem.
Comm. on White House Record Library; mem. Bd of Dirs Rock and Roll Hall of
Fame, Peabody Awards; Vice-Pres. Nat. Music Council; Founder-mem. Black
Music Assen; mem. Country Music Assen, Nat. Acad. of Recording Arts and
Sciences, Gospel Music Assen, American Women in Radio and TV, Nashville
Songwriters' Assen. *Honours:* Hon. Trustee, Nat. Acad. of Popular Music; Dr
hc (Illinois); awards include Women's Equity Action League Achievement
Award, Nat. Acad. of TV Arts and Sciences Citation Award, Young Musicians'
Foundation Golden Baton Award, Country Music Assen Irving Waugh Award
of Excellence, named One of America's 50 Most Powerful Women by Ladies'
Home Journal, Indie Award from Association of Independent Music Publish-
ers 2004. *Address:* Broadcast Music Inc. (BMI), 320 West 57th Street, New
York, NY 10019, USA (office). *Telephone:* (212) 586-2000 (office). *Website:*
www.bmi.com (office).

PRICE, Alan; British musician, singer and composer; b. 14 April 1941,
Fatfield, Co. Durham. *Career:* formed Alan Price Combo 1958, The Animals
1963–65, 1983, Alan Price Set 1965, Alan Price and Friends 1968–69; teamed
up with Georgie Fame, many TV appearances 1971–74; acted in Alfie Darling
1975; two British tours 1976; Dir Fulham Football Club 1978; British tour
1979; series of shows, BBC 2 1980; formed own record label Key Records 1981;
appeared in Andy Capp, Manchester, London 1982; tours of Canada, USA,
Hawaii, Japan, France, UK; two concerts, Royal Albert Hall; Wembley, with
The Police, New Year's Eve 1983; 21st Anniversary tour 1986; Travelling Man
Tour 1987; Liberty Tour 1990–91; Greatest Hits Tour 1992–93; formed Alan
Price and the Electric Blues Company. *Compositions include:* The House That
Jack Built, Jarrow Song, Just For You; film scores include: O Lucky Man 1973,
The Plague Dogs 1982, Britannia Hospital 1982, Whales of August 1988;
theatre music: Home 1970, Early Days 1980; musical: Andy Capp 1982.
Recordings: hit singles include (with The Animals): House of The Rising Sun
(No. 1, UK and USA) 1964, Don't Let Me Be Misunderstood 1965, We've Gotta
Get Out of This Place 1965; with Alan Price Set: I Put A Spell On You 1966, Hi-
Lili Hi-Lo 1966, Simon Smith And His Amazing Dancing Bear 1967, The
House That Jack Built 1967, Don't Stop The Carnival 1968, Rosetta, with
Georgie Fame 1971, Jarrow Song 1974, Just For You 1978, Baby Of Mine
1979, Goodnight Irene, Changes 1988; albums: Metropolitan Man, Performing
Price, Shouts Across The Street, Travelling Man, Liberty, Covers, A Gigster's
Life For Me, A Rock 'N' Roll Night At The Royal Court Theatre 2000, Geordie
Boy – The Anthology 2002, Based On A True Story 2002. *Television
appearances:* Turtles' Progress, World's End, Fame is the Spur, A Night on
the Tyne, The Chalk Face. *Honours:* BAFTA Gold Badge of Merit 1973,
inducted into American Rock 'N' Roll Hall of Fame 1994. *Current Management:* c/o V. Gibbons, Cromwell Management, 20 Drayhorse Road, Ramsey,
Cambs, PE26 1SD, England. *Telephone:* (1487) 815063. *Fax:* (1487) 711896.
E-mail: cromwellmanagement@hotmail.co.uk; alanpriceonline@
absoluteelsewhere.net.

PRICE, James; Danish composer, orchestrator and conductor; b. 20 Nov.
1959, Copenhagen; m. Kirsten 1992; one s. *Education:* Composition, Royal
Danish Academy of Music. *Career:* Debut, 1979; Musical Director, Arranger
and Pianist; Revues, Vaudevilles, Musicals including Nitouche, Sound of
Music, HMS Pinafore, Annie Get Your Gun, Cabaret, Annie; Host in television
show; Around a Piano; Compositions for theatre, radio, television, film; mem,
Danish Songwriters' Guild; Danish Conductors' Society. *Compositions:* Ved
Frokosten (Opera-Monologue, Royal Theatre, 1983); Underscore for TV
Serials: Two People in Love; Karrusel; Musicals: Tordenskiold; Livsens
Ondskab. *Recordings:* Tordenskiold, 1994. *Honours:* Wilhelm Hansens Grant,
1992; Revue Composer of the Year, 1983, 1996.

PRICE, Kelly; American singer; b. Queens, New York. *Career:* received
musical foundation in church; began as backing vocalist and moved into vocal
arranging and writing; solo artist 1997–; collaborations with Puff Daddy,
Faith Evans, Whitney Houston, Brian McKnight. *Recordings include:* albums:
Soul of a Woman 1997, Mirror Mirror 2000, One Family 2001, Priceless 2003,
This is Who I Am 2006, Kelly 2011. *Honours:* Kora Award for Best Female
African Diaspora Artist 2002. *E-mail:* TheBookingStaff@kellyprice.com.
Website: www.kellyprice.com.

PRICE, P. J.; American singer, songwriter and musician (guitar, keyboards);
b. 8 July 1964, Houston, TX; two s. *Career:* various radio releases, television
appearances; solo artist on Entertainment Unlimited; Owner, Priceless
Records; Owner, Taste of Texas Music; mem, GSCMA; NCMO. *Recordings:*
albums: P. J. Price 1994, Movin' On 2008; Singles: Runnin' On Love; What's A
Heart Like Yours. *Honours:* Star of Tomorrow, Airplay International,
1993–94; Best Female Indie and Album of the Year, World Country Music
Network, 1994; No. 1, GSCMA European Chart, 1995. *Address:* 111 Pine
Valley, Huntsville, TX 77340, USA. *Website:* www.myspace.com/pjprice.

PRICE, Rick; Australian singer and songwriter. *Career:* solo artist. *Record-
ings include:* albums: Heaven Knows (Australian Music Award for Album of
the Year 1993) 1992, Tambourine Mountain 1995, Another Place 1999.
Honours: Apra Award for Song of the Year (for Heaven Knows) 1992,
Australian Music Award for Song of the Year (for Walk Away Renée) 1993,
Advance Australia Foundation 1993, Australia Export Award 1993, Singapore
Music Award for Song of Year (for Heaven Knows) 1993. *Current Manage-
ment:* c/o Dion Durante, Ralph Carr Management, Lennox House, 229 Lennox
Street, Richmond, Vic. 3121, Australia. *Telephone:* (3) 9428-4862. *Fax:* (3)
9429-9137. *Website:* www.ralphcarr.com.

PRICE, Stuart, (Jacques Lu Cont); British producer, songwriter, musician
and DJ; b. 1977, Reading. *Career:* debut release as Zoot Woman (with Adam
and John Blake) Sweet to the Wind EP 1995; released first record as Les
Rythmes Digitales 1996, worked under pseudonym Jacques Lu Cont; began
performing live as Les Rythmes Digitales, toured Europe with other Wall of
Sound artists Wiseguys, Dirty Beatniks, Propellerheads etc. 1997, also
performances worldwide as club DJ; keyboard player on Madonna's Drowned
World Tour 2001, Music Dir for subsequent Madonna tours, Re-Invention
Tour 2004, Confessions Tour 2006; keyboards and programming, Madonna,
American Life album 2003, co-producer and co-writer, Confessions on a Dance
Floor 2005; producer Seal, System 2007; remixes for numerous artists using
names Thin White Duke, Paper Faces, Jacques Lu Cont, Man With Guitar.
Compositions: co-writer with Madonna: X-Static Process, Hung Up, Get
Together, Sorry, I Love New York, Forbidden Love, Push. *Production work
includes:* Madonna, Confessions on a Dance Floor 2005, Seal, System 2007;
remixes for artists including Aloud, Armand Van Helden, Beck, Bis, Britney
Spears, Cassius, Chromeo, Coldplay, Cornershop, Depeche Mode, Electric Six,
Felix da Housecat, Fischerspooner, Goldfrapp, Gwen Stefani, Juliet, Justice,
Kasabian, The Killers, Madonna, Mirwais, Missy Elliott, The Music, New
Order, No Doubt, Placebo, Röyksopp, Scissor Sisters, Seal, Starsailor, Texas.
Recordings: as Les Rythmes Digitales: albums: Libération 1996, Darkdancer
1999; with Zoot Woman: albums: Living In A Magazine 2001, Zoot Woman
2003; other: Fabric Live 09 (DJ mix album) 2003. *Honours:* Grammy Award
for Best Remixed Recording (for It's My Life) 2005. *Current Management:* Alex
Hardee, Coda Agency, 229 Shoreditch High Street, London E1 6PJ, England.
Telephone: (20) 7456-8802 (office). *E-mail:* alex@codaagency.com (office).
Address: Wall of Sound Recordings, 338A Ladbroke Grove, London W10
5AH, England (office). *E-mail:* info@zootwoman.com (office). *Website:* www
.zootwoman.com.

PRIDE, Charley Frank; American musician (guitar) and singer; b. 18
March 1938, Sledge, MS. *Career:* fmr baseball player; solo artist 1965–; first
appeared at Grand Ole Opry 1967. *Recordings include:* albums: Country
Charley Pride 1966, Songs of Pride... Charley That Is 1968, I'm Just Me 1971,
Pride of America 1974, Charley 1975, The Happiness of Having You 1975,
Sunday Morning With Charley Pride 1976, She's Just An Old Love Turned
Memory 1977, Someone Loves You Honey 1978, Burgers and Fries 1978,
You're My Jamaica 1979, There's A Little Bit of Hank In Me 1980, Roll On
Mississippi 1981, Charley Sings Everybody's Choice 1982, Live 1982, Night
Games 1983, The Power of Love 1984, After All This Time 1987, I'm Gonna
Love Her on the Radio 1988, In Person (Special Music) 1989, Moody Woman
1989, Amy's Eyes 1990, Classics With Pride 1991, My Six Latest and Six
Greatest 1994, Branson City Limits (live) 1998, A Tribute to Jim Reeves 2000,
Comfort of Her Wings 2003, Choices 2010. *Honours:* Grammy Award for Best
Male Country Record (for Just Between You and Me). *E-mail:* johndaines@
charleypride.com. *Website:* www.charleypride.com.

PRIEST; American singer, musician and producer. *Career:* released cassette-
only recordings on Anti-Pop Recordings label; mem., The Anti-Pop Consortium 1997–2002, 2007–; supported DJ Shadow's US tour 2002; solo artist
2002–; collaboration with Matthew Shipp; prod., remixer; joint founder, Anti-
Pop Records. *Recordings:* albums: with Anti-Pop Consortium: Tragic Epilogue
2000, Shopping Carts Crashing 2000, Arrhythmia 2002, Fluorescent Black
2009. *Current Management:* c/o Joseph Noon, Spectrum Music, 235 Nassau
Avenue, Suite 2L, Brooklyn, NY 11222, USA. *Telephone:* (718) 383-2313. *Fax:*
(718) 383-2373. *E-mail:* joseph@spectrummusic.net. *Website:* www
.spectrummusic.net.

PRIEST, Mathew; British musician (drums); b. 3 April 1970, Birmingham, England. *Career:* Formed Dodgy with Nigel Clarke (left band, 1998); Joined by Andy Miller; Frequent live shows and festival appearances; Formed own record label, Bostin, 1991; Signed to A & M records, 1992; Presenter, BBC Greater London Radio (GLR), 1997–99. *Recordings:* Singles: Staying Out For The Summer, 1994; In A Room, 1996; Good Enough, 1996; Found You, 1997; If You're Thinking of Me, 1998; Every Single Day, 1998; Feather Cuts And Monkey Boots, 2000; Albums: The Dodgy Album, 1993; Homegrown, 1994; Free Peace Sweet, 1996; Ace A's and Killer B's, 1998; Real Estate, 2001.

PRIEST, Maxi; British reggae singer; b. (Max Elliot), 1962, London, England. *Career:* fmr carpenter, builder of sound systems; DJ and solo artist; numerous live appearances. *Recordings include:* albums: You're Safe 1985, Intentions 1986, Maxi Priest 1988, Bonafide 1990, Best Of Me 1991, Fe Real 1992, Man With The Fun 1996, CombiNation 1999, Collection 2000, 2 The Max 2005, Refused 2007. *Honours:* Urban Music Award for Best Reggae Act 2005. *Current Management:* 21st Century Artists Inc., 853 Broadway, Suite 1711, New York, NY 10003, USA. *Telephone:* (212) 254-5500. *Fax:* (212) 254-4800. *E-mail:* tobyinnyc@aol.com. *Website:* www.maxipriest.com.

PRIESTLEY, Brian, BA, DipEd; British writer and musician; b. 10 July 1946, Manchester, England. *Education:* Univ. of Leeds. *Recordings:* You Taught My Heart To Sing, 1996; Love You Madly, with Louise Gibbs, 1999. *Publications:* Mingus, A Critical Biography, 1982; Jazz Piano, 6 Vols, 1983–90; Charlie Parker, 1984; John Coltrane, 1987; Jazz – The Essential Companion (with Ian Carr and Digby Fairweather), 1987; Jazz on Record, A History, 1988; Jazz – The Rough Guide (with Ian Carr and Digby Fairweather), 1995; contrib. reviews and articles; The Gramophone; New Grove Encyclopedia of Jazz; The Cambridge Companion to the Piano; The International Directory of Black Composers; liner notes for recordings by artists, including Charlie Parker, Charles Mingus, Thelonius Monk, Ben Webster, Duke Ellington, Ella Fitzgerald, Lionel Hampton. Literary Agent: Barbara Levy.

PRIESTMAN, Henry; British singer and songwriter; b. 21 July 1955, Hull, England. *Career:* founder mem. The Yachts 1976–81, It's Immaterial 1981–84; mem., The Christians 1984–95; also mem., Echo and the Bunnymen; songwriter; 1991–; solo artist 2008–; numerous live appearances and tours. *Recordings include:* albums: with the Yachts: Yachts 1979, Yachts without Radar 1989; with The Christians: The Christians 1987, Colour 1990, Happy In Hell 1992, The Best of The Christians 1993; with Echo and the Bunnymen, Echo and the Bunnymen 1987, Summer Olympic Album 1998; with Lightning Seeds: Cloudcuckooland 1989; with Mike Peters: Feel Free 1996; with Ian McNabb: Waifs And Strays 2000; with Enemy Within: Death Blues 2000; solo: The Chronicles of Modern Life 2009. *Current Management:* c/o Jessica Brandon, Bright Artist Management, 1st Floor, 50 Great Portland Street, London W1W 7ND, England. *Telephone:* (20) 7631-4638. *E-mail:* jessica@brightartistmanagement.com. *Website:* brightartistmanagement.com; www.henrypriestman.com.

PRIMO (see DJ Premier)

PRIMORAC, Vanja; Croatian promoter, manager, booking agent and producer; b. 1 Jan. 1966, Zagreb; one s. *Education:* Univ. of Theatre and Film Art. *Career:* columnist, musical critic, promotional work, 1985–; manager of several Croatian, Slovenian, American/English artists; producer, manager, first Yugoslavian alternative music festival: Offestum; work with Siouxsie and The Banshees, Laurie Anderson, Tuxedomoon, The Young Gods; first private promoter in ex-Yugoslavia; mem., Croatian (HGU, HGS). *Honours:* Japan Award for Festival Design. *Address:* Podvrsje 2, Zagreb 41000, Croatia.

PRIMROSE, Neil; British musician (drums); b. 20 Feb. 1972, Scotland. *Career:* mem., Travis 1997–; numerous tours, festivals and television appearances. *Recordings include:* albums: Good Feeling 1997, The Man Who 1999, The Invisible Band 2001, 12 Memories 2003, The Boy With No Name 2007, Ode to J. Smith 2008. *Honours:* Q Magazine Award for Best Single 1999, Select Magazine Award for Album of the Year 1999, BRIT Awards for Best British Group 2000, 2002, Best British Album 2000. *Current Management:* Wildlife Entertainment, Unit F, 21 Heathmans Road, London SW6 4TJ, England. *Telephone:* (20) 7371-7008. *Fax:* (20) 7371-7708. *E-mail:* info@wildlife-entertainment.com. *Website:* www.travisonline.com.

PRINCE; American musician, singer, producer and actor; b. (Prince Rogers Nelson), 7 June 1958, Minneapolis, Minn.; s. of John L. Nelson and Mattie Nelson (née Shaw); m. 1st Mayté Garcia 1996 (divorced 1998); one s. (deceased); m. 2nd Manuela Testolini Nelson. *Career:* alternatively known as The Artist Formerly Known as Prince (AFKAP) and Symbol; fmr lead singer, Prince and The Revolution; singer with own backing group the New Power Generation 1991–; numerous tours, concerts; own recording studio and record label, Paisley Park. *Recordings include:* albums: For You 1978, Prince 1979, Dirty Mind 1980, Controversy 1981, 1999 1982, Purple Rain (Acad. Award for Best Original Score, BRIT Award for Best Soundtrack 1985) 1984, Around the World in a Day (Best Soul/Rhythm and Blues Album of the Year, Down Beat Readers' Poll) 1985, Parade 1986, Sign O' The Times 1987, Lovesexy 1988, Batman (film soundtrack) (BRIT Award for Best Soundtrack 1990) 1989, Graffiti Bridge (film soundtrack) 1990, Diamonds and Pearls 1991, (symbol as title) 1992, Come 1994, The Black Album (recorded 1987) 1994, The Gold Experience 1995, Emancipation 1996, Chaos and Disorder 1996, New Power Soul 1998, Rave Un2 The Joy Fantastic 1999, The Rainbow Children 2002, One Nite Alone – Live! 2002, Musicology 2004, 3121 2006,

Planet Earth 2007, LotusFlow3r 2009, 20Ten 2010, Art Official Age 2014, Plectrumelectrum 2014, HITnRUN Phase One 2015, HITnRUN Phase Two 2015. *Films include:* Purple Rain 1984, Under the Cherry Moon 1986, Sign O' The Times 1987, Graffiti Bridge 1990. *Honours:* three Grammy awards 1985, Nat. Asscn for the Advancement of Colored People Special Achievement Award 1997, Q Award for Best Songwriter 1990, BRIT Awards for Best International Male Artist 1992, 1993, 1995, 1996, BET Award for Best Male R&B Artist 2006, Grammy Award for Best Male R&B Vocal Performance (for Future Baby Mama) 2008. *Current Management:* Paisley Park Enterprises, 7801 Audoban Road, Chanhassen, MN 55317, USA. *Website:* www.npgmusicclub.com.

PRINCE, Anna Lou, MusD; American composer, publisher, construction executive and author; b. 28 May 1935, Isabella; d. of Bishop Ulysses G. Prince and Della Hawkins Prince; m. Eddie Joe McCurry; three c. *Education:* Carolina School of Broadcasting, Israel Bible School, Jerusalem, South West Tech. Coll., London Inst. of Applied Research, Academia Argentina de Diplomacia. *Career:* songwriter, Hank Locklin Music Co., Nashville, Tennessee 1963–70; entertainer, World's Fair, Knoxville, Tennessee 1982; Partner and Owner, Prince Wholesale Bait Co., Canton, North Carolina 1976–82; Prince TV Co. 1986–2003; Music Publr, Anna Prince Publishing Co., Broadcast Music Inc., Nashville 1982–; mem. production staff, Talent Co-ordinator TV series, Down Home, Down Under 1989–90; appeared on Grand Ole Opry; Exec. Producer and Host of music show and TV talk show, Real Heroes of Country Music 1996–2003; Man., WJIZ-FM radio station, Albany, Georgia; apptd Dir of Community Access Television Station, Nashville; Mayoral appointment as Dir of Community Access Television, Channel 19, Nashville, Tennessee; mem. BMI, Nashville Songwriters' Asscn, Country Music Asscn, Songwriters' Guild of America. *Recordings:* I Feel A Cry Coming On 1965, Best Part of Loving You 1969, Anna 1969, I'm In Love with You 1995, We're Making Memories 2000, Anna Prince Writes Hit Songs (with Eddie Joe McCurry) 2009. *Television:* producer/host: Real Heroes of Country Music, Celebrity Cooking; 200 shows produced and hosted. *Publications include:* The Strange Life of Anna Prince (autobiog.) 2006, Anna from Prince Mountain. *Honours:* Order of Kt of Templars (Dame), Lofsensic Order (Dame), Maison Internationale des Intellectuals; several hon. doctorates; Talk Show Host of the Year 2000, Airplay Int. King Eagle Award 2000. *Address:* Anna Prince Publishing Co., PO Box 622, Marble, NC 28905, USA (office). *Telephone:* (828) 837-0510 (office). *E-mail:* DocAPrince@aol.com (office).

PRINCE BUSTER; Jamaican singer and record producer; b. (Cecil Bustamante Campbell), 28 May 1938, Kingston. *Career:* boxer; worked for Clement 'Coxsone' Dodd's Down Beat sound system; founded Voice Of The People sound system, Wild Bells, Islam, Buster's Record Shack labels, and numerous record stores; worked with artists, including Big Youth, Dennis Brown, Alton Ellis, John Holt. *Recordings:* albums: I Feel the Spirit 1963, Fly Flying Ska 1964, It's Burke's Law 1965, Pain in My Belly 1965, Ten Commandments 1967, Judge Dread Rock Steady 1967, What a Hard Man Fe Dead 1967, The Outlaw 1969, Big Five 1972, Dance Cleopatra Dance 1972, Message Dubwise 1972, Sisters Big Stuff 1976, Wreck a Pum Pum 1976, She Was a Rough Rider 1978, Prophet 1994.

PRINCE PICHO; singer, actor and musician (guitar, keyboards); b. (Emmanuel Volel), 24 April 1942, Port-au-Prince, Haiti; one s. two d. *Education:* College, Hotel Management; Music studies, New-Sewell Music Conservatory, Washington, DC. *Career:* Appearances include: Cable TV channel 45; Cable TV channel 33; Annual guest at Marvin Gaye Festival, African festival, Washington DC; Performed at benefit for homeless; mem, New Sewell Music Conservatory. *Recordings:* Numerous albums for Henri Debs record company, Guadaloupe, FWI; Also for Marc Recors, New York, USA. *Publications:* numerous articles, Montgomery Journal, La Nación. *Honours:* Masons of Washington DC Award.

PRINCE RAKEEM (see RZA)

PRINCE ROYCE; American singer, songwriter and record producer; b. (Geoffrey Royce Rojas), 11 May 1989, New York. *Career:* fmr mem. of Jino and Royce, El Duo Real; collaborations with producer Donzell Rodriguez and Vincent Outerbridge 2005–08; solo career 2008–; numerous recording collaborators including Daddy Yankee, Maná. *Recordings:* albums: Prince Royce (Billboard Latin Music Award for Tropical Album of the Year 2011, for Album of the Year 2012) 2010, Phase II (Lo Nuestro Award for Tropical Album of the Year 2013) 2012, Soy el Mismo 2013. *Honours:* numerous awards including: Casandra Awards for Revelación del Año 2011, for Artista Popular en el Extranjero 2012, Billboard Latin Music Awards for New Latin Artist of the Year 2011, Solo Tropical Airplay and Albums Artist of the Year 2011, for Hot Latin Songs Artist of the Year 2012, for Tropical Song of the Year (for Corazon sin Cara 2012) 2012, for Tropical Album Artist of the Year 2012, Premios Juventud for Favorite Tropical Artist 2011, 2012, for Best Artist 2011, Lo Nuestro Awards for Tropical Song of the Year (for Stand By Me) 2011, (for El Amor Que Perdimos) 2012, (for Incondicional) 2013, for Tropical Male Artist of the Year 2011, 2012, 2013, for Collaboration of the Year (for Ven Commigo) 2012, (for El Verdadero Amor Perdona) 2013, for Tropical Traditional Artist of the Year 2012, 2013. *Current Management:* David Sonenberg, DAS Communications, 83 Riverside Drive, New York, NY 10024, USA. *Telephone:* (212) 877-0400. *Website:* www.princeroyce.com.

PRINE, John; American singer and songwriter; b. 10 Oct. 1946, Maywood, Illinois. *Career:* began writing folk songs as teenager; regular on Chicago club circuit 1970; recording artist 1972–; Founder-Pres. Oh Boy Records 1980–; numerous tours and festival appearances. *Film appearance:* Falling From Grace 1992. *Compositions include:* Love is on a Roll, sung by Don Williams 1980. *Recordings include:* albums: John Prine 1971, Diamonds In The Rough 1972, Sweet Revenge 1973, Common Sense 1975, We're Children Of Coincidence 1976, Bruised Orange 1978, Pink Cadillac 1979, Storm Windows 1980, Aimless Love 1984, German Afternoons 1986, Live 1988, The Missing Years (Grammy Award for Best Contemporary Folk Album) 1991, A John Prine Christmas 1994, Lost Dogs And Mixed Blessings 1995, Live On Tour 1997, In Spite Of Ourselves 1999, Souvenirs 2000, Fair & Square (Grammy Award for Best Contemporary Folk Album 2006) 2005, Standard Songs for Average People (with Mac Wiseman) 2009. *Current Management:* c/o Al Bunetta Management, 33 Music Square West, Suite 102B, Nashville, TN 37203, USA. *Telephone:* (615) 742-1250. *Fax:* (615) 742-1360. *E-mail:* jon@ohboy.com. *Address:* Oh Boy Records, 33 Music Square West, Suite 102B, Nashville, TN 37203, USA (office). *Website:* www.ohboy.com (office); www.johnprine.net.

PRIOR, Maddy, MBE; British folk singer and songwriter; b. Blackpool, England; m. Rick Kemp, two c. *Career:* founder mem. and lead singer of folk group, Steeleye Span 1969–; solo artist 1978–; mem., The Carnival Band 1982–; collaborations with guitarist, Tim Hart and keyboard player, Nick Holland. *Recordings include:* albums: solo: Woman In The Wings 1978, Changing Winds 1978, Hooked On Winning 1982, Going For Glory 1983, Happy Families 1991, Sing Lustily and with Good Cheer 1994, Year 1994, Hang Up Sorrow and Care 1996, Flesh and Blood 1998, Ravenchild 2000, Ballads And Candles 2001, Arthur the King 2001, Bib and Tuck 2002, Lionhearts 2003, Under the Covers 2005, Paradise Found 2007, The Quest 2007, Seven for Old England 2008; with Steeleye Span: Hark the Village Wait 1970, Please to see the King 1971, Ten Man Mop, or Mr. Resevoir Butler Rides Again 1971, Below the Salt 1972, Parcel of Rogues 1973, Now We Are Six 1974, Commoners Crown 1975, All Around My Hat 1975, Rocket Cottage 1976, Storm Force Ten 1977, Live at Last 1978, Sails of Silver 1980, Back in Line 1986, Tempted and Tried 1989, Tonight's the Night 1992, Time 1996, Horkstow Grange 1998, The Journey 1999, Bedlam Born 2000, They Called Her Babylon 2004, Winter 2004, Bloody Men 2006, Cogs Wheels and Lovers 2009; with The Carnival Band: A Tapestry of Carols 1987, Sing Lustily and with Good Courage 1990, Carols and Capers 1991, Hang Up Sorrow and Care 1993, Carols at Christmas 1998, Hoi Polloi 1999, Gold, Frankincense and Myrrh 2001, An Evening of Carols and Capers 2005, Paradise Found 2007, Ringing the Changes 2007. *Current Management:* Park Promotions, PO Box 651, Oxford, OX2 9RB, England. *Telephone:* (1865) 241717. *E-mail:* info@parkrecords.com. *Website:* www.parkrecords.com. *Address:* c/o Stones Barn, Roweltown, Cumbria CA6 6LA, England (office). *Telephone:* (1697) 748424 (office). *E-mail:* sbadmin@maddyprior.co.uk (office). *Website:* www.maddyprior.co.uk.

PRITCHARD, Peter Andrew; British musician (bass guitar, double bass); b. 13 Aug. 1955, London, England; m. Chrystella Maria Nicholas 1978; one s. one d. *Education:* Trinity College of Music. *Career:* Member of Flying Saucers with numerous appearances on German, Dutch and British television and radio; Tours with Chuck Berry, Bill Haley, Scotty Moore, D J Fontana, and The Jordonaires; Film, Blue Suede Shoes; mem, Musicians' Union. *Compositions:* 10 compositions. *Recordings:* Several singles and albums with Flying Saucers including: The Rawking Sandy Ford, 1994; Albums and singles with Avengers include: She Walks Right In, 2001; CD with the Jordonaires.

PRITCHARD, Russell; British musician (bass guitar). *Career:* Founder mem., The Zutons 2002–. *Recordings include:* albums: Who Killed... The Zutons? 2004, Tired of Hanging Around 2006, You Can Do Anything 2008.

PROBY, P. J.; American singer and songwriter; b. (James Marcus Smith), 6 Nov. 1938, Houston, TX. *Career:* founder, The Moondogs 1958; worked as demo singer, recording under names Jett Powers, Orville Wood; appeared on Beatles TV Special, London 1964; stage performances include: Catch My Soul (rock version of Othello), West End 1970, Elvis (musical) 1977; cabaret circuit and recording career continued to 1991. *Recordings include:* albums include: I Am PJ Proby 1964, Go Go P.J. Proby 1965, P.J. Proby's In Town 1965, P.J. Proby 1965, Enigma 1966, Phenomenon 1967, Believe It or Not 1968, What's Wrong with my World? 1968, California License 1969, Three Week Hero 1969, I'm Yours 1973, Somewhere 1975, Elvis 1978, The Hero 1981, Heroes 1998, Sentimental Journeys, Memories, Wanted, His Hand in Mine, Songwriter 2006; hit singles include: Hold Me 1964, Together 1964, Somewhere 1965, I Apologise 1965, Let The Water Run Down 1965, That Means A Lot 1965, Maria 1965, You've Come Back 1966, Niki Hoeky 1967, Yesterday Has Gone, with Marc Almond 1996. *Honours:* Best Musical of the Year for Elvis 1977. *Current Management:* c/o Robert Pratt, Chimes International, PO Box 26312, Glasgow G76 7WX, Scotland. *Telephone:* (141) 577-7798. *E-mail:* mary@chimesinternational.co.uk. *Website:* www.chimesinternational.com; www.pjproby.net.

PRODIGY; American rap artist and producer; b. (Albert J. Johnson), 11 Feb. 1974, New York, NY. *Education:* Graphic Arts High School, Manhattan, NY. *Career:* mem., Mobb Deep 1992–. *Recordings include:* albums: with Mobb Deep: Juvenile Hell 1993, The Infamous Mobb Deep 1995, Hell on Earth 1996, Murda Muzik 1999, Infamy 2001, Free Agents 2003, Amerikaz Nightmare 2004, Blood Money 2006; solo: HNIC 2000, Return of the Mack 2007, Product of the 80s 2008. *Address:* c/o Universal Music Group, 2220 Colorado Avenue,

Santa Monica, CA 90404, USA (office). *Website:* www.mobbdeep.net; www.hnic2.com.

PROFESSOR GRIFF; American rap artist; b. (Richard Griffin). *Career:* mem. rap group, Public Enemy 1984–89, 1997–; solo artist with own band the Asiatic Disciples 1989–. *Recordings include:* albums: with Public Enemy: Yo! Bum Rush The Show 1987, It Takes A Nation of Millions To Hold Us Back 1988, He Got Game (film soundtrack) 1998, There's a Poison Goin' On... 1999, Revolverlution 2002, Rebirth of a Nation 2005, New Whirl Odor 2005, How you Sell Soul to a Soulless People who Sold their Soul ??? 2007, The Evil Empire of Everything 2012, Man Plans God Laughs 2015; solo: Pawns In The Game 1990, Kao's II Wiz-7-Dome 1991, Disturb N Tha Peace 1992, Blood of the Profit 1998, And The Word Became Flesh 2001. *Publication:* Atlanta Musick Bizness Resource Information Publication (R.I.P.) 2004. *Honours:* MOBO Award for Outstanding Contribution to Black Music 2005. *E-mail:* Mistachuck@rapstation.com (office). *Website:* www.publicenemy.com; professorgriff.wordpress.com/professor-griffs-online-network.

PROKOFIEV, Gabriel; British composer, musician and producer; s. of Oleg Prokoviev, grandson of Sergei Prokoviev. *Career:* with father recorded spoken parts for a recording of Peter and the Wolf 1991; formed band Spektrum with singer Lola Olafisoye 1999; produces electronic dance music as Caspa Codina and Medasyn; producer for Lady Sovereign, MC Envy; founder, Nonclassical record label 2004; collaborations with Heritage Orchestra, Elysian Quartet. *Compositions:* String Quartet No. 1, No. 2, Concerto for Turntables and Orchestra. *Recordings:* albums with Spektrum: Enter The Spektrum, Fun at the Gymkhana Club. *E-mail:* lulu@lululevay.com. *Website:* www.lululevay.com. *Address:* Nonclassical, Cambridge Heath Road, Bethnal Green, London E2 9DA, England (office). *E-mail:* info@spektrum.co.uk (office). info@nonclassical.co.uk (office). *Website:* www.spektrum.co.uk; www.nonclassical.co.uk.

PROKOP, Michal; Czech singer, composer, musician (guitar, harmonica) and broadcaster; b. 13 Aug. 1946, Prague; m. Nina 1972; one s. one d. *Education:* Univ. of Economics, Charles Univ., Prague. *Career:* rock singer 1967–90; mem. Parl. 1990–92, 1996–98; Deputy Minister of Culture 1992–95; Dir European City of Culture (Prague) initiative 2000; Pres. Council Czech Radio. *Television:* TV talk show host, I Mean It Well 1998–99, Fine Losses 2000–13. *Recordings include:* albums: Blues in Soul, Mesto Er, Holubi Dante, Kolej Yesterday, Nic Ve Zlým, nic v Dobrým, Snad Nam Naše Deti Prominou, Az Si Pro Mne Prijdou, Cerný Ovce, Odněkud někam, Poprvé naposledy, Live 60, Prokop, Andršt, Hrubý Unplugged, Sto roků na cestě. *Honours:* Officier des Arts et des Lettres 1995; Melodia Award (Czechoslovakia) 1988, Hall of Fame of Radio Beat (Czech Repub.) 2007. *Website:* www.michalprokop.cz.

PROPHET, Ronnie; Canadian entertainer, musician (guitar, singer); b. 26 Dec. 1937, Hawksbury, ON; m. Glory-Anne 1986, two s. *Career:* duo with wife, Glory-Anne; numerous tours, festival appearances, television and radio broadcasts; mem. AFofM, ACTRA, ROPE. *Television includes:* host Grand Ole Country six years, host Ronnie Prophet Show, host Music Hall America, host Ronnie Prophet Entertains. *Recordings include:* 32 albums: The Phantom, No Holiday In LA., Ronnie Prophet 1977, I'm Gonna Love Him out of You 1983, Sure Thing 1987. *Honours:* CCM Award 1976, 1980, 1984, Juno Awards 1977, 1978, TV Country Show of the Year, Canada 1977–80, St Jude Children's Research Hospital Angel Award. *E-mail:* ronnieprophet@hotmail.com. *Website:* www.ronnieprophet.com.

PROWSE, Ian; British musician and songwriter; b. 10 Jan. 1967, Ellesmere Port. *Career:* lead singer, Pele 1990–96; founder mem. Amsterdam 1999–; various tours, television and live appearances; mem. PRS, Musicians' Union. *Recordings include:* albums with Pele: Fireworks, The Sport of Kings, Alive, Alive-O; with Amsterdam: Attitunes 2001, Live, Left and Covered 2001, The Curse 2002, The Journey 2005, Arm in Arm 2008. *E-mail:* amsterdamhq@hotmail.co.uk (office). *Website:* www.amsterdam-music.com.

PRYCE, Guto; Welsh musician (bass guitar); b. 4 Sept. 1972, Cardiff. *Career:* mem., Catatonia 1992–93; mem., Super Furry Animals 1996–; early releases on small indie label before obtaining major indie label deal; numerous tours in the UK and internationally, many festival appearances. *Recordings:* albums: Fuzzy Logic 1996, Radiator 1997, Guerrilla 1999, Mwng 2000, Rings Around The World 2001, Phantom Power 2003, Love Kraft 2005, Hey Venus 2007, Dark Days/Light Years 2009. *E-mail:* info@superfurry.com (office). *Website:* www.superfurry.com.

PRZYGODDA, Johannes Pit; German musician and composer; b. 2 June 1968, Luthe. *Career:* some pieces for film and music in Germany 1980s; worked in Hamburg with band, Go Plus 1990–; experimental music, together with Burkhard Beins, Rudi Mahall, Michal Griener; film music composer. *Compositions:* Schwerelos, Definitiv, Song For Brian, Superfreunde. *Recordings:* Go Plus, La Montanara, Largo. *Current Management:* Kitty Yo, Torstrasse 172, 10115 Berlin, Germany. *Address:* Oelmuehle 2, 20357 Hamburg, Germany.

PSY; South Korean rapper, dancer, songwriter and record producer; b. (Park Jae-sang), 31 Dec. 1977, Gangnam Dist, Seoul; s. of Park Won-ho; m. Yoo Hye-yeon 2006; two d. *Education:* Berklee Coll. of Music, Boston, USA. *Career:* released debut album 2001; served in military 2003–05, 2007–09; signed to YG Entertainment label 2010; released Gangnam Style 2012, first single by South Korean artist to chart at number one on the iTunes Music Video Charts. *Films:* Mong Jung Gi 2002, Mong Jung Gi 2 2005. *Television includes:*

Superstar K4 (as regular judge) 2012–; numerous guest appearances. *Recordings include:* albums: PSY from the PSYcho World! 2001, Sa 2 2002, 3 PSY 2003, Sa Jib 2006, PSY Five (Seoul Music Award for Record of the Year 2011) 2010, PSY 6 (Six Rules) 2012; single: Gentleman 2013. *Honours:* Goodwill Amb., UNICEF 2012; Military Grand Award 2009, Dept of Defense Plaque of Appreciation 2011, Okgwan Order 2012; Mnet Asian Music Awards for Best Video Performer 2005, for Best Music Video 2006, for Best Producer 2010, Seoul Music Award for Best Performance 2010, Melon Music Award for Best Performance 2010, 1st Korea Music Copyright Target Singer Awards for Songwriting and Composition 2011, Cyworld Digital Music Award for Song of the Month 2012, MTV Europe Music Award for Best Video 2012, American Music Award New Media Award 2012, Billboard Music Award for Top Streaming Song (Video) 2013. *Address:* c/o YG Entertainment, 397-5 YG Building, Hapjeong-Dong, Mapo-Gu, Seoul, 121-886, South Korea (office). *Website:* www.psypark.com.

PSYCHE (see Craig, Carl)

P'TAAH (see Brann, Chris)

PUENTE PORTILLO, Anahí Giovanna; Mexican singer and actress; b. 14 May 1983, Mexico City. *Career:* actress from childhood; mem. RDB 2004–. *Television:* Chiquilladazas 1985, Te Doy un Besito, Mujer casos de la vida real, Hora Marcada, La Telaraña, Clase 406 – 2da Temporada, Rebelde (series) 2004, RBD: La Familia (series) 2007. *Films:* Nacidos para Morir, Había una vez una Estrella. *Recordings include:* albums: Rebelde 2004, Nuestro Amor 2005, Celestial (Billboard Latin Music Award for Latin Pop Album of the Year by a Duo or Group 2007) 2006, Rebels (in English) 2006, Empezar Desde Cero 2007. *Honours:* Ariel Award 1991, Palma de Oro 1991, Billboard Latin Music Award for Top Latin Albums Artist of the Year, for Latin Tour of the Year 2007, some 24 Premios Juventud, Billboard Latin Music 'Tu Mundo' Award 2008. *Address:* c/o EMI Latin, 404 Washington Avenue, Suite 700, Miami Beach, FL 33139, USA (office). *Website:* www.emimusic.com.mx (office); www.grupo-rbd.com.

PUEYRREDON, César 'Banana'; Argentine singer, composer and musician (keyboards); b. 7 July 1952, Buenos Aires; m. Cecilia Garcia Laborde 1979, one s. one d. *Education:* Universidad Católica Argentina. *Career:* mem. of group, Banana, with tours of Argentina, Uruguay, Chile, Paraguay 1969–84, Central America 1977; solo artist 1984–; numerous concerts; mem. SADAIC (composers' society). *Recordings include:* albums: with Banana: Negra no te vayas de mi lado 1971, Conociéndote 1973, Aún es tiempo de soñar 1979; solo: Asi de simple 1984, Solo un poco mas 1985, Está en vivo 1986, Mas cerca de la vida 1987, Ser uno mismo 1988, Tarde o temprano 1990, 20 años 1991, Armonia 1992, De la ternura a la pasión 1993. *Honours:* Premio Santa Clara de Asis. *E-mail:* info@cesarpueyrredon.com.ar. *Website:* www.cesarpueyrredon.com.ar.

PUGACHEVA, Alla Borisovna; Russian singer; b. 15 April 1949, Moscow; m. 1st Mykolas Orbakas 1969 (divorced 1973); m. 2nd Alexander Stefanovich 1976 (divorced 1980); m. 3rd Yevgeniy Boldin 1985 (divorced 1993); m. 4th Filipp Kirkorov 1994 (divorced 2005); one d. *Education:* M. Ippolitov-Ivanov Music High School, A. Lunacharsky State Inst. of Theatre Art. *Career:* debut as soloist of Lipetsk vocal-instrumental group 1970; with O Lundstrem Jazz orchestra 1971; soloist, Veselye Rebyata Ensemble 1973–78; f. Song Theatre 1988; numerous prizes and awards including 3rd prize All-Union Contest Moscow, 1974; Grand Prix Int. Competition Golden Orpheus Bulgaria 1975, Int. Festival Sopot 1978; acted in films; tours in USA, Germany, Switzerland, India, France, Italy and other countries; f. Theatre of Songs 1988, Alla Co. 1993, Alla Magazine 1993; toured Russia and other countries in honour of her 60th birthday 2009. *Repertoire includes:* numerous songs by popular Soviet composers such as R. Pauls, A. Muromtsev, A. Zatsepin and others, also songs of her own; albums: Alla 1990, Yes! 1998, River Tram 2001, Was There a Boy? 2002, Live Peacefully, My Country! 2003, Invitation to a Sunset 2008. *Honours:* Order of Merit for the Fatherland, 2nd degree 1999, 3rd degree 2009, Order of Dostlugn (Friendship) (Azerbaijan) 2009, Order of St Mesrop Mashtots (Armenia) 2009; USSR People's Artist 1991, Ovation Prize 1994, State Prize of Russia 1995. *Address:* Tverskaya-Yamskaya str., Apt 57, Moscow, Russia (home). *Telephone:* (495) 250-95-78 (home).

PULLEN, Doug, BA; American writer on music; b. 9 April 1957, Loring, MN; m. Teresa Pullen; one s. *Education:* Texas Technical Univ. *Career:* journalist, El Paso Times, El Paso Herald and Post, Kalamazoo Gazette, Metro Times (Detroit), Flint Journal, MusicHound; writer on rock, country, blues, R & B music; mem. Nat. Music Critics' Asscn. *Address:* El Paso Times, Times Plaze, El Paso, TX 79901-1470, USA (office). *E-mail:* dpullen@elpasotimes.com (office). *Website:* elpasotimes.typepad.com/pullen (office).

PULSFORD, (Howard) Nigel; British musician (guitar); b. 11 April 1963, Newport, Gwent, Wales. *Career:* mem., Future Primitive, changed name to Bush 1992–2001; numerous headlining tours, festival appearances. *Recordings:* albums: with Bush: Sixteen Stone 1994, Razorblade Suitcase 1996, Deconstructed 1997, Science Of Things 2000, Golden State 2001; solo: Heavenly Toast on Paradise Road.

PUOLIS, Rolandas; Lithuanian artist manager and broadcaster; b. 20 Nov. 1969. *Education:* Vilnius Technical University. *Career:* radio and television DJ 1987–92; Manager, rock group BIX, 1991–. *Recordings:* Blind Soldiers (Best Record in Lithuania) 1991, Labomba 1992, Doozgle (Best CD, Lithuania) 1994. *Honours:* Band of the Year, 1991, 1992, 1994, Science of Things 2001, Golden State, 2000. *Address:* PO Box 552, 2024 Vilnius, Lithuania.

PURI, Premlata, BSc, MMus; Indian musician; b. 30 May 1939, Dehradun; d. of Bihari Lal Puri and Maya Devi Puri. *Education:* Univs of Lucknow and Delhi. *Career:* lecturer on Indian culture in Europe, USA and Japan, Indian Del. to UNESCO confs on educ., art, culture 1968–95; mem. Exec. Cttee India Int. Centre, Kendriya Vidyalaya Sangatan, Steering Cttee of Working Group on Art and Culture (Dept of Educ.), Cen. Bd of Secondary Educ., Nat. Council of Science Museums; Dir-Gen. Centre for Cultural Resources and Training, New Delhi 1992–97. *Publications:* has contributed articles and papers on Indian culture to numerous books and journals. *Honours:* Govt of India Scholarship in Music 1964, Italian Scholarship for the Study of Italian Language and Western Music 1967, Padma Shri 2004. *Address:* c/o Centre for Cultural Resources and Training, 15-A, Sector 7, Pappankalan, Dwarka, New Delhi 110 075; Triveni Kala Sangam, Flat 4, 205 Tansen Marg, New Delhi, India (home). *Telephone:* (11) 3714506 (home).

PURIM, Flora; Brazilian jazz singer; b. 6 March 1942, Rio De Janeiro; m. 1st; one d.; m. 2nd Airto Moreira 1972; one d. *Education:* Univ. of California, Long Beach, California State Univ. *Career:* moved to New York, USA 1967. *Compositions include:* with Airto Moreira: Seeds On The Ground 1970, Natural Feelings 1969, Free 1971, Fingers 1972, Identity 1975, Promises of The Sun 1976. *Recordings:* solo albums: Butterfly Dreams 1973, 500 Miles High 1974, Stories To Tell 1974, Open Your Eyes You Can Fly 1976, Encounter 1976, Nothing Will Be As It Was Tomorrow 1977, Everyday Everynight 1978, That's What She Said 1978, Carry On 1979, The Midnight Sun 1988, Queen of the Night 1992, Speed of Light 1995, Perpetual Emotion 2001, Wings Of Imagination 2001, Sings Nascimento 2002, Speak No Evil 2003, Flora's Song 2005; with Chick Corea: Return To Forever 1972, Light As A Feather 1973; with Carlos Santana: Welcome 1973; Borboletta 1974; with Airto Moreira, Neville Potter: San Francisco River 1972; with McCoy Tyner: Search for Peace 1974; with George Duke: Love Reborn 1973; Feel 1974; with Airto Moreira: Three Way Mirror 1985, Humble People 1985, The Magicians 1986, The Colours of Life 1988, The Sun Is Out 1989; with Hermeto Pascoal: We Love 1970, A Brazilian Love Affair; with Ernie Hood: Mountain Train 1974; with Duke Pearson: How Insensitive 1969, It Could Only Happen With You 1970; with Airto and Deodato: Deodato/Airto In Concert 1973, That's What She Said, Everyday Every Night, Humble People 1985; with The Magicians; The Sun Is Out 1987. *Honours:* Ordem do Rio Branco, Brazil 2002; Downbeat Critics Poll, Established Singer 1974–76, 1978; Record World, Top Female Jazz Artist 1974, 1976; Cash Box Award, Top New Female Jazz Artist 1974. *Current Management:* A Train Management, PO Box 29242, Oakland, CA 94604, USA. *Telephone:* (510) 893-4705. *Fax:* (510) 893-4807. *E-mail:* alevers@a-train.com. *Website:* www.a-train.com; www.florapurim.com.

PURPOSE MAKER (see Mills, Jeff)

Q

QADRI, Waqas; Danish producer and MC; b. Pakistan. *Career:* mem., Outlandish 1997–. *Recordings include:* albums with Outlandish: Outlands Official (Danish Music Award for Best Hip-Hop Album) 2000, Outlandish Presents... Beats, Rhymes & Life 2003, Bread & Barrels of Water 2003, Closer than Veins 2005, Sound of a Rebel 2009, Warrior // Worrier 2012: solo: Ajooba 1999, Øko Logik 2008, Basement Biriyani Vol. 1 2013. *Current Management:* c/o Tajmer Booking & Management, Søndre Allé 17, 4600 Køge, Denmark. *Telephone:* 46-15-37-00. *E-mail:* tajmer@tajmer.dk. *Website:* www.tajmer.dk.

QASIMOV, Alim; Azerbaijani singer and musician (mugham); b. 14 Aug. 1957, Shamakha. *Education:* Mugham School, Baku. *Career:* leader, Alim Qasimov Ensemble; collaborations with Malik Mansurov and Eshan Mansurov 1989–, with Jeff Buckley, Yo-Yo Ma and The Silk Road Ensemble. *Recordings include:* albums: Classical Mugham 1996, Azerbaijan: Art of the Mugham 1998, Love's Deep Ocean 2000, Art of the Mugham 2001, Spiritual Music of Azerbaijan (with daughter, Fergana Qasimova) 2007, Music of Central Asia, Vol. 8: Rainbow 2010; with Alim Qasimov Ensemble: The Legendary Art of Mugham 2004. *Honours:* Int. IMC/UNESCO Music Prize 1999.

QIZILBASH, Asad; Pakistani musician (sarod); b. 1963, Islamabad; s. of K. H. Qizilbash. *Education:* Tagore Inst., Germany. *Career:* first public performance at UNICEF Universal Children Day, Islamabad 1973; mem. Children's Art Workshop, Pakistan Council of Arts 1975–82; contract musician at Pakistan TV for programmes, including Kasbey Qamal 1983, Pangnat 1984, Raselay Log 1993, Satnby Studio 1994; worked for oil drilling co. in the Middle East; moved to Germany 1989; returned to Pakistan 1992; numerous live and festival performances. *Honours:* Festival of Pakistan Musician of the Year 1999. *Address:* c/o Laurent Barbiot, Asad Team Connection, rue des Hayettes 14/2, 5000 Namur, Belgium (office). *E-mail:* aqizilbash_63@yahoo.com (office); aqizilbash@mail.com (office); Lbarbiot@voila.fr. *Website:* asadsarod.webs.com.

Q-TIP, (The Lone Ranger); American rap artist; b. (John William Davis), 20 Nov. 1970, Brooklyn, New York. *Career:* Co-founder A Tribe Called Quest 1988; part of the Native Tongues collective with De La Soul and Queen Latifah; collaborations with Lucy Pearl, Slick Rick, Mos Def, Jay-Z, Janet Jackson, Deee-Lite. *Recordings include:* albums: with A Tribe Called Quest: People's Instinctive Travels and The Paths of Rhythm 1990, The Low End Theory 1991, Midnight Marauders 1993, Beats Rhymes and Life 1996, The Love Movement 1998; solo: Amplified 1999, The Renaissance 2008, Kamaal The Abstract 2009. *Honours:* Grammy Award for Best Dance Recording (Galvanize) 2006. *Address:* c/o Universal Motown, 1755 Broadway, New York, NY 10019, USA.

QUATRO, Susan Kay (Suzi); American rock singer, songwriter, musician (bass guitar, drums, piano), radio presenter and actor; b. 3 June 1950, Detroit, Mich.; d. of Arthur Quatro and Ilona Sanisly; m. 1st Len Tuckey; m. 2nd Rainer Haas 1993; one s. one d. *Education:* Brownell Junior High School, Grosse Pointe South. *Career:* professional artist 1964–, solo artist 1971–; own chat show (ITV) for one year, own radio show (BBC Radio 2) 1998–; worldwide concert tours, stage and TV appearances; Unzipped (one-woman show) performed, London Hippodrome Oct. 2013; several events to celebrate 50th year in music business 2014. *Stage roles include:* Annie Get Your Gun (West End, London), Tallulah Who? (actor and writer). *Radio:* as presenter: Rockin' with Suzi Q (BBC Radio 2) 1998– (show now called Wake Up Little Suzi), documentaries for BBC Radio 2 including those on Elvis Presley, Otis Redding, Janis Joplin, Jim Morrison, Patsy Cline, Suzi Quatro's Detroit 2012. *Television includes:* as actor: Happy Days (series) 1977–79; appearances in Minder 1982, Dempsey and Makepeace 1985, Absolutely Fabulous 1994, Gene Simmons' Rock School 2006, Trust Me – I'm a Beauty Therapist 2006, Countdown 2007, The Weakest Link, Eggheads, Midsomer Murders 2007, Australian Idol (as guest judge) 2009, RocKwiz (as performer and quiz contestant) 2011. *Recordings include:* albums: Suzi Quatro 1973, Quatro 1974, Your Mama Won't Like Me 1975, Aggro Phobia 1977, If You Knew Suzi 1978, Suzi and Other 4-Letter Words 1979, Rock Hard 1980, Main Attraction 1982, Baby You're a Star 1989, The Wild One 1990, Oh Suzi Q 1990, The Latest and Greatest 1992, Unreleased Emotion 1998, The Best of Suzi Quatro 1998, Leather Forever (live DVD) 2004, Naked Under Leather 2006, Back to the Drive 2006, In The Spotlight 2011; appearance on Bob the Builder – Built to Be Wild (voice of Rio Rogers) 2006. *Publication:* Unzipped (memoir) 2007. *Honours:* six Brit Awards Awards, six Brave Otto Awards (Germany) 1973, 1974, 1975, 1978, 1979, 1980, numerous Artist of the Year Awards (Japan), selected by BBC TV as one of the Queens of British Pop 2009, Distinguished Achievement Award, Detroit Music Awards 2013, Woman of Valor, Meow, Austin, Texas 2013. *Telephone:* (1245) 362670 (home). *Fax:* (1245) 361510 (home). *E-mail:* sqrocks1@aol.com (home). *Website:* www.suziquatro.com.

QUAYE, Finley, BTEC in Music Production; British singer; b. 1974, Edinburgh, Scotland. *Career:* worked with A Guy Called Gerald, Graham Massey, Rainbow Tribe; solo artist 1996–. *Recordings include:* albums: Maverick A Strike 1997, Vanguard 2000, Much More Than Much Love 2003. *Honours:* BRIT Award for Best Male Solo Artist 1998. *Address:* c/o Epic Records, 10 Great Marlborough Street, London, W1V 2LP, England.

QUEEN BEE (see Lil' Kim)

QUEEN LATIFAH; American rap artist and actress; b. (Dana Owens), 18 March 1970, East Orange, NJ; d. of Lance Owens and Rita Bray. *Career:* worked with female rap act, Ladies Fresh; recorded with producers Dady-O, KRS-1, DJ Mark the 45 King and mems of De La Soul; moved to Motown Records; began acting career with sitcom Living Single; established management company, Flavor Unit Entertainment and label, Flavor Unit Records 1993–; guest appearance on Shabba Ranks' single, Watcha Gonna Do; other recording collaborations with De La Soul and Monie Love. *Films include:* Living Single, Jungle Fever 1991, House Party 2 1991, Juice 1992, My Life 1993, Set It Off 1996, Hoodlum 1997, Sphere 1998, Living Out Loud 1998, The Bone Collector 1999, Bringing Out the Dead 1999, The Country Bears 2002, Brown Sugar 2002, Chicago 2002, Bringing Down the House (also exec. producer) 2003, Scary Movie 3 2003, Barbershop 2: Back in Business 2004, The Cookout (also writer and producer) 2004, Beauty Shop (also producer) 2005, Last Holiday 2006, Ice Age: The Meltdown (voice) 2006, Stranger Than Fiction 2006, Hairspray 2007, The Perfect Holiday 2007, Mad Money 2008, What Happens in Vegas 2008, The Secret Life of Bees 2008, Joyful Noise 2012, House of Bodies 2013, 22 Jump Street 2014. *Television includes:* Living Single (series) 1993, Mama Flora's Family 1998, Queen Latifah Show 1999–2001, 2013–15, Living with the Dead (mini series) 2002, The Muppets' Wizard of Oz 2005, Life Support (Golden Globe Award for Outstanding Performance by a Female Actor in a Television Movie or Miniseries 2008) 2007, Steel Magnolias 2012, Bessie (exec. producer), The Wiz 2015. *Recordings include:* albums: All Hail The Queen 1989, Latifah's Had It Up 2 Here 1989, Nature Of A Sista 1991, Black Reign 1993, Queen Latifah and Original Flava Unit 1996, Order In The Court 1998, The Dana Owens Album 2004, Trav'lin' Light 2008, Persona 2009. *Publications include:* Ladies First 2000, Queen of the Scene 2006, Put On Your Crown 2010. *Honours:* Grammy Award for Best Rap Solo Performance 1994.

QUERALT, Stephen Paul; British musician (bass guitar); b. 4 Feb. 1968, Oxford; one s. *Career:* bass guitarist in rock band Ride; numerous concerts, festival and TV appearances. *Recordings include:* albums: with Ride: Nowhere 1991, Going Blank Again 1992, Carnival of Light 1994, Live Light 1995, Tarantula, 1996, Poptopia! 90s Power Pop Classics 1997, OX4 2001; with Sharks Patrol These Waters: Sharks Patrol These Waters 1995; with The Postmarks: By-the-Numbers 2008. *Website:* www.ridemusic.net.

QUILLIVIC, Jean, BA, MA, DE; French composer and musician (saxophone); b. 10 Jan. 1960, Rabat, Morocco; m. Josiane Robakowski; two s. two d. *Education:* studied science in Brest, studied musicology in Paris (Diplôme d'Etat de Professeur de Jazz). *Career:* CIM School of Jazz, Paris, 1985; first alto saxophone in Pierre Sellin Big Band, 1985–; formed group Oxyde de Cuivre, 1987; formed own group Jean Quillivic Quartet, 1988; concerts in festivals, summer tours, 1989–; mem. Soc. des auteurs, compositeurs et éditeurs de musique (SACEM). *Recordings:* Prise de Bec, Zap 1989, La Femme à La Valise, Jean Quillivic Quartet 1990, En Public Au Fourneau 1995, Oxyde de Cuivre 1995, Au Studio Toot 1999, 6 rue Traverse de la Rive 2004. *Current Management:* c/o Promoart, L'Asterie, 29470 Plougastel-Daoulas, France. *Telephone:* 2-98-07-06-23 (home). *E-mail:* jean@quillivic.com. *Website:* www.quillivic.com/jean.

QUIN, Andrew James, BA; British composer, musician (keyboards, percussion) and music lecturer; b. 12 Aug. 1960, London; m. Anne Perrett 1983; one s. one d. *Education:* Keele Univ. *Career:* mem., Dewolfe 1984–; freelance lecturer in music technology, univs. and conservatories throughout UK; regular jazz performer, with broadcasts in 36 countries; mem. Musicians' Union, PRS, APC. *Recordings include:* Albums: Mirage 1985, The Cutting Edge 1987, Four Minus One 1988, The Corporate Net, 1995; Colours Of Classical Piano, 1997; Television themes: Something To Treasure, 1988; Central Weekend, 1985; Scandal, 1988; Commercials: Fairy Snow 1989, Canderel 1990, Webster's Bitter 1991, Lynx Deoderant 1992, Season's Greetings 2006. *Address:* De Wolfe Ltd., Shropshire House, 11-20 Capper Street, London WC1E 6JA, England. *Telephone:* (20) 7631-3600. *Fax:* (20) 7631-3700. *E-mail:* info@dewolfemusic.co.uk. *Website:* www.dewolfe.co.uk; www.andyquin.com.

QUINN, Aidy; Irish singer; b. Co. Tyrone; s. of Tom Quinn and Philomena Quinn. *Education:* St Patrick's Coll., Dungannon. *Career:* country music singer. *Recordings include:* albums: Born and Bred on Country Music (Irish Country Music Award for Best New Album) 2006. *Honours:* Irish World Award for Most Promising New Act 2006, Irish Entertainment Award for Best New Artist 2007. *Current Management:* c/o Purple Heather Promotions, 8 Forthill Road, Enniskillen, BT74 6AW, Northern Ireland. *Telephone:* (28) 6632-3238. *Fax:* (28) 6632-3225. *E-mail:* erneproms@btinternet.com. *Address:* Millbrook House, Galbally, BT70 2NR, Northern Ireland (home). *Telephone:* (28) 8775-8526 (home). *Website:* www.aidyquinn.com.

QUINN, John; British musician (drums); b. Northern Ireland. *Education:* Univ. of Dundee. *Career:* Founder-mem., Snow Patrol 1997–; mem. project, The Reindeer Section 2001–. *Recordings include:* albums: with Snow Patrol: Songs For Polar Bears 1998, Little Hide 1998, One Night Is Not Enough 2001, When It's All Over We Still Have To Clear Up 2001, Final Straw (Meteor Ireland Music Award for Best Irish Album 2005, Ivor Novello Award for Best

Album 2005) 2004, Eyes Open (Meteor Ireland Music Award for Best Irish Album 2007) 2006, A Hundred Million Suns 2008, Fallen Empires 2011; with The Reindeer Section: Y'all Get Scared Now, Ya Hear! 2001, Son Of Evil Reindeer 2002. *Honours:* Meteor Ireland Music Awards for Best Irish Band (with Snow Patrol) 2005, 2007, for Most Downloaded Song and Best Live Performance 2007. *E-mail:* qprimeuk@qprime.com. *Website:* www.qprime .com. *E-mail:* info@snowpatrol.com. *Website:* www.snowpatrol.com.

QUINN, Mick; British musician (bass guitar); b. 17 Dec. 1969; m. *Career:* mem., Supergrass 1993–2010; numerous concerts and festival appearances. *Recordings include:* albums: I Should Coco 1995, Bag O Grass (compilation) 1996, In It For The Money 1997, Supergrass 1999, B-Side Trax (compilation) 2000, Life On Other Planets 2002, Road To Rouen 2005, Diamond Hoo Ha 2008. *Honours:* Q Award for Best New Act 1995, BRIT Award for Best British Newcomer 1996, UK Music Video Award for Best Rock Video (Bad Blood) 2008. *Current Management:* Courtyard Management, 22 The Nursery, Sutton Courtenay, Abingdon, Oxfordshire, OX14 4UA, England. *Telephone:* (1235) 845800. *E-mail:* kate@cyard.com. *Website:* www.supergrass.com.

QUINTERO, Gabriela; Mexican musician (guitar); b. México. *Career:* mem. bands Las Brujas, Subterraneo and Las Formigas in México; met Rodrigo Sánchez at Casa de Cultura, México, formed heavy metal band Tierra Acida; moved to Dublin, Ireland with Sánchez 1999, busked on streets and collaborated with local musicians; travelled and busked in Copenhagen and Barcelona; support act at various Damien Rice concerts, performing as Rodrigo y Gabriela 2003–. *Recordings include:* albums: Re-Foc 2003, Live in Manchester and Dublin 2004, Rodrigo y Gabriela 2006, 11:11 2009, Live in France 2011, Area 52 2012. *Current Management:* Niall Muckian, Rubyworks, 6 Park Road, Dun Laoghaire, County Dublin, Ireland. *Telephone:* (1) 2841747. *Fax:* (1) 2841767. *E-mail:* nmuckian@rubyworks.com. *Website:* www .rubyworks.com; www.rodgab.com.

QURESHI, Fazal; Indian musician (tabla, dholak, kanjira); b. 1961, s. of Ustad Allarakha Qureshi. *Career:* Founder-mem. Surya, Mynta 1979–;

participant, Zakir Hussain's Masters of Percussion 2002; collaborations with numerous artists. *Recordings include:* albums: with Mynta: Havanna Club 1983, Short Conversation 1985, Indian Time 1988, Hot Madras 1991, Is It Possible 1994, Nandu's Dance 1994, First Summer 1998, Mynta Live 1999, Cool Nights 2001, Teabreak 2003, Hot Days 2006, Meetings in India 2009. *Address:* c/o Christian Paulin, Odengatan 91, 11322 Stockholm, Sweden. *E-mail:* info@mynta.net; fazalbirwa@yahoo.co.in. *Website:* www.mynta.net.

QURESHI, Haq Nawaz (Aki), (PropaGhandi); British producer. *Career:* fmr mem., Southern Death Cult; Co-founder Nation Records 1988–; Founder-mem., Fun'Da'Mental 1991–. *Recordings include:* albums: with Fun'Da'Mental: Seize The Time 1994, With Intent To Pervert The Cause Of Injustice 1995, Erotic Terrorism 1998, There Shall Be Love 2001, All is War 2006. *Address:* c/o Nation Records, 19 All Saints Road, London, W11 1HE, England. *Telephone:* (20) 7792-8167. *E-mail:* akination@btopenworld.com. *Website:* www.fun-da -mental.co.

QURESHI, Taufiq; Indian musician (percussion); b. 9 Aug. 1963, Mumbai; s. of Ustad Allarakha Qureshi; m. Geetika Varde 1993; one s. *Education:* Hill Grange High School, St Xavier's Coll. *Career:* fmr mem. Surya, Indus Creed; later solo artist; participant, Zakir Hussain's Masters of Percussion 2002; Founder, Mumbai Stamp percussion group; assisted Ustad Zakir Hussain on thematic, feature film albums; featured on several int. albums. *Recordings include:* albums: solo: Colours of Rajasthan 1995, Rhydhun 2000, Taalisma 2002, Taufiq – The Other Rhythm, Perc Jam 2002, Maestros in Concert – Taufiq Live at Swarutsav 2003, Amazing Fusion Concerts 2004, Bombay Fever 2006, Forest: Mystic Soundscapes 2007; appeared on Global Drum Project recording 2008; composed music for various Hindi movies. *Address:* 12/ A Purushottam Towers, 884, off Gokhale Road, Prabhadevi, Mumbai 400 028, India (office). *Telephone:* (98) 20500553 (office). *Website:* www.taufiqqureshi .com.

R

R., Cene; Slovenian musician (saxophone, ewi, keyboard). *Career:* mem., Siddharta. *Recordings include:* albums: Id 1999, Nord 2001, Silikon Delta 2002, Rh- 2003, Petrolea 2006, Maraton 2007. *Honours:* Viktor Award for Best Act 2003, 2004, 2006, for Special Achievement 2003, MTV Europe Music Award 2005. *Address:* Siddharta, PO Box 179, 1236 Trzin, Slovenia (office). *Telephone:* (4) 1382192 (office). *E-mail:* info@siddharta.net (office). *Website:* www.siddharta.net (office).

RABIN, Trevor; South African musician (guitar, keyboards), songwriter and record producer; b. 13 Jan. 1954, Johannesburg, South Africa; m. Shelley May 1979; one s. *Education:* private studies with Walter Mony. *Career:* formed band, Rabbitt age 14; moved to England 1977; solo artist 1977–; mem. progressive rock group, Yes 1983–89, 1991; numerous concerts, festivals and tours; composer for film; mem. AFTRA, Musicians' Union. *Composition for film:* Death of a Snowman 1982, Eraser 1996, The Glimmer Man 1996, Con Air 1997, Homegrown (song) 1998, Armageddon 1998, Enemy of the State 1998, Jack Frost 1998, Deep Blue Sea 1999, Whispers: An Elephant's Tale 2000, Gone in Sixty Seconds 2000, Remember the Titans 2000, The 6th Day 2000, Texas Rangers 2001, American Outlaws 2001, Rock Star 2001, The One 2001, Bad Company 2002, The Banger Sisters 2002, Kangaroo Jack 2003, Bad Boys II 2003, Torque 2004, Exorcist: The Beginning 2004, National Treasure 2004, Ripley's Return 2004, The Great Raid 2005, Snakes on a Plane 2006, The Guardian 2006, Gridiron Gang 2006, Hot Rod 2007, National Treasure Book of Secrets 2007, Get Smart 2008. *Other compositions:* music for computer games, including Grand Theft Auto: Vice City; theme tune to Soldier of Fortune Inc. (TV series). *Recordings:* albums: two albums with Rabbitt; solo: Trevor Rabin 1978, Face To Face 1979, Wolf 1981, Can't Look Away 1989, Live in LA 2003, Jacaranda 2012; with Yes: 90125 1983, 9012 Live: The Solos 1985, Big Generator 1987, Union 1991, Talk 1994, Active 1994. *Publications:* instructional guitar video. *Honours:* Grammy Award for Best Instrumental Performance (for Cinema) 1985. *Website:* trevorrabin.net.

RABINOWITZ, Harry, (Henry Oliver, Andy Thurlow), MBE; British composer and conductor; b. 26 March 1916, Johannesburg, S Africa; s. of Israel Rabinowitz and Eva Rabinowitz (née Kirkel); m. 1st Lorna T. Anderson 1944 (divorced); one s. two d.; m. 2nd Mitzi Scott 2001. *Education:* Athlone High School, Johannesburg, Univ. of the Witwatersrand and Guildhall School of Music, London. *Career:* Conductor, BBC Radio 1953–60; Musical Dir BBC TV Light Entertainment 1960–68; Head of Music, London Weekend TV 1968–77; freelance composer and conductor 1977–; appeared with London Symphony and Royal Philharmonic Orchestras in UK and with the Los Angeles Philharmonic and Boston Pops Orchestras and Orchestra of St Luke's in USA; Musical Dir for world premieres of Cats and Song & Dance; composed and conducted several TV scores including The Charlie Drake Show (series) 1960, BBC Top of the Pops Theme, The Marquise 1980, The Sign of Four 1983, Reilly: The Ace of Spies (mini-series) 1983, The Ewok Adventure 1984, The Insurance Man 1986, Agatha Christie Hour 1987, In a Glass Darkly (aka Agatha Christie's In a Glass Darkly) 1987, L'Amérique en otage 1991, Memento Mori 1992, Alien Empire (BBC); mem. British Acad. of Songwriters, Composers and Authors, Composers' Guild (BASCA). *Television:* Musical Dir: Julia and Friends 1986, Paul Nicholas and Friends 1987, New Faces 1987. *Films:* Musical Dir: Funeral in Berlin 1966, Puppet on a Chain 1970, Inside Out 1975, All This and World War II 1976, The Greek Tycoon 1978, Roberte 1979, Hanover Street 1979, Goldengirl 1979, La mort en direct 1980, Mon oncle d'Amérique 1980, Chariots of Fire 1981, Time Bandits 1981, Heat and Dust 1983, The Bostonians 1984, Electric Dreams (also actor) 1984, Nemo 1984, Revolution 1985, Return to Oz 1985, Lady Jane 1986, F/X 1986, The Manhattan Project 1986, RoboCop 1987, Masters of the Universe 1987, Maurice 1987, Mangoecus 1988, Camille Claudel 1988, Queen of Hearts 1989, Shirley Valentine 1989, L'Argent, Lord of the Flies 1990, La Voix, Les Carnassiers, Le Petit Garçon, La Baule-les Pins, La Fille des Collines, Eve of Destruction, Jesuit Joe, Jeanne, Putain du Roi, The Ballad of the Sad Café 1991, J'embrasse pas 1991, Howards End 1992, The Remains of the Day 1993, A Business Affair 1994, Gross Fatigue 1994, La Fille de d'Artagnan, Death and the Maiden 1994, Jefferson in Paris 1995, Secret Agent 1996, The Proprietor 1996, The Stupids, The English Patient 1996, Tonka, Surviving Picasso 1996, Wings of the Dove, Amour Sorcier, My Story So Far, City of Angels 1998, A Soldier's Daughter Never Cries 1998, Message in a Bottle 1999, My Life So Far 1999, Cotton Mary 1999, The Talented Mr. Ripley 1999, Place Vendome, The Golden Bowl 2000, Possession 2002, Bon Voyage 2003, Le Divorce 2003, Cold Mountain 2003. *Honours:* Freeman of the City of London 1995; BASCA Gold Badge for Services to British Music 1985, Radio and TV Industries Award for Best TV Theme 1984, All-Music Gold Award 1991. *Address:* Yellow Cottage, Walking Bottom, Peaslake, Surrey, GU5 9RR, England (home). *Telephone:* (1306) 730674 (home); (503) 224-2541 (USA) (home); (4) 90-75-89-47 (France) (home). *E-mail:* mitziscott@aol.com (office).

RADCLIFFE, Mark, BA; British DJ and broadcaster; b. 29 June 1958, Bolton, Lancs., England; m.; three d. *Education:* Univ. of Manchester. *Career:* Jr Asst Producer, Piccadilly Radio, Manchester 1979; Producer, Radio 1, Saturday Live and John Peel session 1983; Head of Music, Piccadilly Radio 1985; began DJ work; Popular Music Producer, BBC North, including Martin Kelner on Radio 2 and In Concert series for Radio 1; presenter, Hit the North

evening programme (Radio 5) 1990, Out on Blue Six (indie show) 1991; returned to Radio 1, four evenings weekly show 1993; stand-in, Radio 1 Breakfast Show with Lard 1996, Breakfast Show presenter 1997; afternoon show, Radio 1 1998–2004; other radio work includes How Tickled Am I (BBC Radio 4) 1999, Hope I Die Before I Get Old (BBC Radio 2) 1999–2000, Heroes or Zeroes (BBC Radio 2) 2001, Count Arthur Strong's Radio Show (producer; BBC Radio 4); TV work includes Pop Upstairs Downstairs (UK Play) 1998, Next (BSkyB) 2001, Match of the Nineties (BBC) 2001; drums/vocals for The Shirehorses 1996–; presenter, BBC Radio 2 folk show 2004–, BBC 6Music 2011–. *Recordings:* with The Shirehorses: The Worst Album In The World Ever. . . Ever! 1997, Our Kid Eh 2001; with The Family Mahone: Songs Of The Back Bar 1999, On The Razzle 2003, Mahone Brew 2006, The Four Counts: Out for the Counts 2007; solo: What Remains of the Day 2011. *Publications:* Showbusiness – Diary of a Rock 'n' Roll Nobody (memoirs) 2001, Northern Sky (novel) 2005, Thank You for the Days (memoirs) 2008, Reelin' in the Years (memoirs) 2011. *Honours:* Sony Best Specialist Music Programme Award 1992, Sony Gold for Daytime Award – Music 1998, 1999, Sony Gold for Music Programming – Daily Sequence 2001, 2007. *Address:* BBC Radio, Dock House, Mediacity, Salford, M50 2LH, England. *Website:* www.bbc.co.uk.

RADIO BOY (see Herbert, Matthew)

RADMAN, Nikola; Croatian musician (guitar). *Career:* mem., Pipschips&videoclips 2000–. *Recordings include:* album: Drveće i rijeke 2003. *Address:* c/o Menart Records, Bencekovićeva 19, 10 000 Zagreb, Croatia. *Website:* www .pipschipsvideoclips.com.

RAE, Corinne Bailey; British jazz singer; b. 1979, Leeds. *Education:* Univ. of Leeds. *Recordings include:* albums: Corinne Bailey Rae 2005, Live in London and New York 2007, The Sea 2010; EP: The Love EP 2011. *Honours:* Mobo Award for Best UK Newcomer, Best UK Female 2006, Q Award for Best New Act 2006, Grammy Award for Best R&B Performance (for Is This Love) 2012. *Current Management:* c/o Running Media, 14 Victoria Road, Douglas, IM2 4ER, Isle of Man. *Telephone:* (1624) 677214. *E-mail:* management@ runningmedia.com. *Website:* www.runningmedia.com; www.corinnebaileyrae .net.

RAE, Dashiell; American composer, musician (flute, piano) and singer; b. 10 Jan. 1956, New Jersey. *Education:* Eastman School of Music, New York. *Career:* orchestral musician, principal flautist, soloist, New York; worked with Julia Fordham (keyboards, flute, backing vocals) 1989–, Level 42, The Style Council, Womack and Womack, Midge Ure, Aztec Camera, Paul Young, Colin Towns; composer of film and television music 1992–; music editor for films and television 1997–; mem. Musicians' Union, PRS, Equity (UK), AFTRA, ASCAP, Women in Film and TV (UK). *Compositions include:* film: Keys, The Queen's House; The Docket Box; Tea and Bullets; television: Hidden Hands; Art and The CIA, CH4; The Dream, BBC Wales; Children's Ward, Granada; Last Days At Forchwen, BBC Wales; Touch, BBC Wales; commercials: Onken Yogurt, 1994; various: Sky Sports, 1993; Anglia, Survival, 1994; Channel Islands TV News Theme, 1994–; promos for BBC, ITV. *Classical compositions:* La Chasse (piano duet), Misere (string orchestra). *Recordings include:* solo album: Songs Without Words 1985.

RAEKWON, (Lex Diamonds, Shallah Raekwon); American MC and rap artist; b. (Corey Woods), 12 Jan. 1968. *Career:* mem., Wu-Tang Clan 1993–; solo artist 1995–. *Recordings include:* with Wu-Tang Clan: Enter The Wu-Tang (36 Chambers) 1993, Wu-Tang Forever 1997, The W 2000, Iron Flag 2001, Disciples Of The 36 Chambers: Chapter 1 (live) 2004, The 8 Diagrams 2007; solo: Only Built 4 Cuban Linx 1995, Immobilarity 1999, The Lex Diamond Story 2003, Only Built 4 Cuban Linx...Pt II 2009, Wu-Massacre 2010, Shaolin vs Wu-Tang 2011, Fly International Luxurious Art 2015. *Website:* www.raekwonchronicles.com; www.wutangcorp.com.

RAESIDE, Diane Lesley Cameron; Canadian country and blues singer; b. Scarborough, ON. *Education:* Canadian Academy for the Performing Arts with Ian Garrett. *Career:* professional singer from age 18; concert and television appearances; mem. Songwriters' Asscn, Canadian Country Music Asscn. *Recordings include:* album: Crazy Infatuation, 1992; Since You Went Away, 1995. *Honours:* Labatts-Guinness Travel Bursary; Numerous Song Contests; RPM Big Country Award, Outstanding New Artist, 1992. *Address:* 23 Timgren Drive, Scarborough, ON M1R 3R4, Canada.

RAFFIT, Jean-Paul; French musician (guitar); b. 2 Aug. 1964, Patiers. *Career:* jazz festivals include Montréal with B. Sandoval, Kalamata (Greece) with B. Sandoval, Dortmund, Bonn, Frankfurt, Petit Journal, Passage Nordouest, Cartou Cherie; television appearances; mem. SACEM, SPEDIDAM. *Recordings include:* albums: with B. Sandoval: Camino del Alba, 1992; Caracola, 1993; Vida, 1994; with S. Lopez, 1993; All the Generics, 1994–95; Graffiti 1995. *Publications:* Jean-Paul Raffit, Un Amour de Guitare 1995, Flash 1995. *Address:* Plaisance, 09100 Madiere, France.

RAFIATOU, Fifi; Togolese singer and composer; b. (Rafiatou Bellow-Adjani), 2 Oct. 1963, Atakpame; one s. one d. *Career:* backing singer in Togo; mem., National Presbyterian Choir; int. concerts with Papa Wemba; Alpha Blondy; Ossibissa; Miriam Makeba; Masa; performed at St Martin Black Festival; mem. SACEM; ADAMI. *Compositions:* Ibama; Ahe; Ile; Wawa; Ikoule.

Publications: Priere Pour La Paix, 1980; Nwassa, 1985; Djofe, 1990; Motus, 1997. *Honours:* Pan-African Fair of Art and Music Award, 1990; First Prize, Afrovision, 1991; Spring Festival of Dion-Yang. *Current Management:* c/o Georges Konila Figah, Discorama Production, PO Box 12629 Lomé, Togo.

RAFLI; Indonesian singer, songwriter and musician (percussion, flute); b. Aceh. *Career:* mem. and lead singer, Kande. *Address:* c/o Ministry of Culture and Tourism, Sapta Pesona Bldg, Jalan Medan Merdeka Barat 17, Jakarta Pusat 10110, Indonesia.

RAGUNATHAN, Sudha, MA; Indian classical Karnatic musician; *Founder and Managing Trustee, Samudhaaya Foundation*; b. (Geeta Sudha), 30 April 1968, Chennai; d. of Smt. Choodamani and Sri Venkatraman; m. M. C. Ragunathan; two c. *Education:* Ethiraj Coll. *Career:* vocalist specializing in Karnatic music; studied under Padmavibushan Sangeetha Kalanidhi, Dr M. L. Vasanthakumari; has travelled world-wide and participated in global music festivals; host of lecture demonstrations and conductor of workshops incorporating her diverse repertoire; participated in celebration of 50th Anniversary of Repub. of India with Vande Mataram by A. R. Rahman; has performed at Alice Tully Hall, Lincoln Centre and Broadway, New York to commemorate 50 years of the Bharatiya Vidya Bhavan; performed with Théâtre de la Ville, Paris; only Indian vocalist to have participated in Global Vocal Meeting organized by the Burghof Acad. of Music and Arts, Lorrach, Germany and produced by Stimmen Voices Int. Vocal Festival; performances in Norway, Switzerland, Tunisia and Israel 2011; teamed up with Amit Heri to present concerts in Karnatic fusion at The Hindu and The Times of India music festivals; forays into film music has had her singing for Ivan, Morning Raagas, Vaaranam Aayiram, Aadhavan, Mandhirappunnagai and Narthaki; has also composed pieces; Founder and Man. Trustee, Samudhaaya Foundation (charity) 1999–; took Karnatic music to the Corporation Schools 2010, 2011; lecture demonstrations and performances at select schools in Chennai. *Films:* has sung many film songs across all genres in Tamil, Telugu and Malayalam. *Radio:* 'A' Grade Artist, All India Radio. *Television:* numerous music programmes during key festivals; chief guest and judge for several reality shows. *Recordings include:* more than 200 albums, including San Marga 1994, Kaleeya Krishna 1994, Classical Vocal 1994, Padmashri 2004, Om Meditation 2004, Shakti 2005, Raagamala, 7th Sense. *Honours:* Amutha Isai Vani by Ikankai Thamil Sangam, USA 1988, Kalaimamani Award, Tamil Nadu Govt 1993, Sangeetha Choodamani, Sri Krishna Gana Sabha, Chennai 1997, Sangeetha Kala Sarathy, Sri Parthasarathy Swami Sabha, Chennai, Sangeetha Ratna 2003, Sangeetha Kalasagaram 2003, Padma Shri 2004, Award of Excellence, Rotary Club of Madras 2004, Virtuoso Award 2005, Gowri Manohari Award 2007, Gaana Padmam Award 2007, Rajiv Gandhi-Moopanar Award 2007, Best Performing Artist of the Season, Music Acad., Chennai 2008, Acharya Award 2008, Sangeetha Kala Sasagara, Visakha Music Acad. of Visakhapatnam 2009, Pannisai Arasi, Thamizh Isai Manram, Thiruvaiyaru 2009, Sangeetha Rathnakara, Bhairavi Fine Arts Soc. 2010, Sangeetha Sampoorna, Poornathrayeesa Sangeetha Sabha, Tripunithura 2010, Sangeetha Kala Vishaaradh, Dombivili Fine Arts Soc., Mumbai 2010, Padmabhushan 2015; numerous other awards and titles. *Address:* 'Vasantham', 18/3 Cenotaph First Street, Alwarpet, Chennai 600 018, India (office). *Telephone:* (44) 24345001 (office). *E-mail:* sudha.sudharagunathan@gmail .com (office). *Website:* www.sudharagunathan.com.

RAHBANI, Ziad; Lebanese composer, singer and playwright; b. 1956, Antelias; s. of Assi Rahbani and Nuhad Haddad (née Fairuz); m. Dalal Karam (divorced). *Career:* composer of numerous songs for mother Fairuz (successful Lebanese singer); contributor to several political radio shows including Bazdna Taybeen Oulou Allah and El Akl Zeeneh; columnist, Al-Akhbar (daily newspaper) 2006–; well known as satirist of Lebanese politics. *Recordings:* solo albums: Belly Dance 1972, Bil Afrah 1972, Sahrieh - Songs 1973, Abou Ali 1979, Ana Mosh Kafer 1985, Hodou' Nisbi 1985, Bema Enno 1996, Amrak Seedna 2000, Bnisba la boukra shou Monodose 2001, Live at Damascus Citadel 2009; with Music for Fairuz: Wahdon 1979, Maarefti Fik 1987, Kifak Inta 1991, Ila Assi 1995, Mich Kayen Hayk Tkoun 1999, Wala Kif 2002, Eh, Fi Amal 2010. *Plays:* Sahriyyeh 1973, Nazl el Sourour 1974, Bennesbe La Boukra Shou? 1978, Film Ameriki Taweel 1980, Shi fashel 1983, Bikhsous el Karameh wel Shaab el aaneed 1993, Lawla Fos'hat el Amali 1994. *Address:* c/o Al-Akhbar, POB 5963-113, 6th Floor, Concorde Centre, rue Verdun, Beirut, Lebanon (office).

RAHMAN, Allah Rakha (A. R.); Indian musician (keyboards), singer and composer; b. (A. S. Dileep Kumar), 6 Jan. 1967, Chennai; s. of the late R. K. Sekhar and of Kareema Begum; m. Saira Banu; three c. *Education:* Padma Seshadri Bal Bhavan, Madras Christian Coll. and Trinity Coll. of Music, London. *Career:* studied piano aged four; began musical career aged 11 as keyboard player, performing with Illaiyaraja's troupe, later with orchestras of M. S. Vishwanathan and Ramesh Naidu; mem. local rock bands, including Roots, Magic and Nemesis Avenue; began composing 1987–; f. Panchathan Record Inn studio 1989; performances and recordings with many artists, including Nusrat Fateh Ali Khan, Apache Indian, Zakir Hussain, Dr L. Shankar, Talvin Singh, Dominic Miller, David Byrne and Michael Jackson (Friends of the World, Munich 2002); has created music for many TV and radio advertisements as well as scores for corp. videos and documentaries; fuses music of different traditions (Western classical, reggae, rock and Karnatic music); apptd Global Amb. of WHO Stop TB Partnership project 2004; UN Amb. for 2015 Millennium Devt Goals; f. A R Rahman Foundation, KM Music Conservatory, Chennai. *Selected film soundtracks include:* Roja (Nat. Film Award 1993, Cinema Express Award 1993) 1992, Gentleman (Cinema Express Award 1994) 1993, Kadhalan (Cinema Express Award 1995) 1994, Kadhal Desam (Screen-Videocon Awards 1997, Cinema Express Award 1997) 1996, Minsaara Kanavu (Nat. Film Award for Best Music Direction 1998, Screen-Videocon Award 1998) 1997, Dil Se. . . (Zee Sangeet Award, MTV-VMA Award 1999) 1998 Jeans (Cinema Express Award 1999) 1998, Taal (Screen-Videocon Award 2000, Zee Cine Award 2000, Zee Gold Bollywood Award 2000, Int. India Film Award 2000) 1999, Lagaan (Nat. Film Award) 2001, Elizabeth – The Golden Age 2007, Slumdog Millionaire (Golden Globe Award for Best Musical Score 2009, BAFTA Award for Best Film Music 2009, Academy Award for Best Original Score 2009, Academy Award for Best Original Song (music) 2009, Grammy Awards for Best Compilation Soundtrack Album for Motion Picture 2010, Best Song Written for Motion Picture 2010) 2008, Vinnaithaandi Varuvaayaa (Filmfare Best Music Dir Award (Tamil), Vijay Best Music Dir Award) 2010, Ye Maaya Chesave (CineMAA Award for Best Music Dir, Filmfare Best Music Dir Award (Telugu) 2010, 127 Hours (Denver Film Critics Soc. Award) 2010, Rockstar (Filmfare Best Music Dir Award, Zee Cine Best Music Dir Award, Screen Best Music Dir Award) 2011, Ekk Deewana Tha 2012. *TV soundtracks include:* Vande Mataram (Screen-Videocon Award 1998) 1997. *Musicals include:* Bombay Dreams (with Don Black) 2001, The Lord of the Rings (with Varttina) (Princess of Wales Theatre, Toronto) 2006. *Recordings include:* Deen Isai Malai (Muslim devotional songs) 1988, Set Me Free (launch album of Malgudi Subha) 1992, Vande Mataram 1997, Jana Gana Mana 2000, Pray For Me Brother 2007, Thenvandhu Paayedhu, Connections, Andhi Maalai, Gurus of Peace, Harem, Indian Mantra. *Honours:* Dr hc (Aligarh Muslim Univ.), (Middlesex Univ.); SuMu Music Award 1993, R. D. Burman Awards 1993, 1995, Telega Purashkar Award 1992, 1993, 1994, Filmfare Awards 1992–2002, Padma Shree 2000, Awadh Sammaan UP govt 2001, Al-Ameen Educ. Soc. Community Award 2001, Amir Khusro Sangeet Nawaz Award 2002, Lata Mangeshkar Samman, MP govt 2005, Mahavir Mahatma Award, Oneness Foundation 2005, Stanford Univ. Award for contrib. to Global Music 2006, Bommai Nagi Reddy Award, Rajiv Gandhi Award, Padma Bhushan 2010; several other nat. and int. awards. *Address:* c/o The Really Useful Group, 22 Tower Street, London, WC2H 9TW, England. *E-mail:* info@arrahman.com. *Website:* www.arrahman.com.

RAIMON; Spanish singer and songwriter; b. (Raimon Pelegero Sanchis), 2 Dec. 1940, Xàtiva; m. Annalisa Corti 1966. *Education:* university. *Career:* tours of France, Mexico, USA, Argentina, Japan; concerts include Olympia Theatre, Paris 1966, 1969, 1974, Teatro Español, Madrid 1988; many appearances, Barcelona, Valencia; previously banned during Franco Dictatorship –1977. *Compositions include:* Al Vent, Diguem No, Jo Vinc d'un Silenci, Com Un Puny. *Recordings include:* Raimon 1963, A L'Olympia 1966, Diguem No 1971, Catalonian Protest Songs 1971, T'Adones Amic 1974, Raimon 1977, Quan L'Aigua Es Queixa 1980, Entre La Nota I El So 1984, Canta Ausiàs March 1989, Cançons 1993, Integral 1993, Spain 1994, Cancons 1996, Integral 1999, Dotze Cancons 2002, Per Destruir Aquell Qui l'Ha 2002, Recitals al Palau 2002, Poesia Cantada 2004, Campos de Bellaterra 2004, Les Cancons d'Amor 2004. *Publications:* Canzoni Contro 1971, Poemes I Cançons 1973, Poemas y Canciones 1976, Les Hores Guanyades 1983, D'Aquest Viure Insistent 1986, Les Paraules Del Meu Cant 1993. *Honours:* Grand Prix Francis Carco, Académie Du Disque, Paris 1967, City of Barcelona Prize 1982, Fundació Jaume Primer, Barcelona 1987, Aportació Musical, Valencia 1993, The Best Show of the Year, Barcelona 1994, Premi Nacional de Música 1993, Grand Prix, Nouvelle Academie Du Disque, Integral Raimon, France 1994. *Address:* c/o PICAP, PO Box 253, 08200 Sabadell, Spain (office). *E-mail:* picap@picap.cat (office). *Website:* www.picap.com.

RAIN; South Korean singer and actor; b. (Jeong Ji-hoon), 25 June 1982. *Career:* reported for mil. service 2011. *Television:* leading roles in series, Dang Doo! Let's Go To School 2003, Full House 2004, A Love to Kill 2005, The Fugitive: Plan B 2010. *Recordings include:* albums: Rain 2002, Ways to Avoid the Sun 2003, It's Raining 2005, Rain's World 2006, Rainism 2008. *Honours:* MTV Asia Award for Favourite Artist 2005, Time Magazine's 100 Most Influential People Who Shape the World Award 2006, 2011, Bonsang Golden Disk Award 2008, Green Planet Movie Award 2010. *Address:* c/o JYP Entertainment, JYP Centre, 123-50 Kangnam-Gu Sheongdam-Dong, Seoul, Korea. *Website:* www.jype.com.

RAINEY, Ronald Paul; American artist manager; *President and CEO, Ron Rainey Management Inc.*; b. 3 Feb. 1946, East Stroudsburg, PA; s. of Donald Rainey and Genevieve Rainey; m. Vivienne Rainey. *Career:* concert agent, Int. Famous Agency (now Int. Creative Management), New York 1969–71; Vice-Pres., concert dept Agency for the Performing Arts, New York and Los Angeles 1971–73; Chair., CEO, Magna Artists Corporation, Los Angeles 1974–81; Pres. and CEO, Ron Rainey Management Inc., Beverly Hills, CA 1981–; owner, Raineyville Music Publishing 1990; Pres. and CEO, American Artists Corpn 1996–; Pres. and CEO Ramblin' Records 1998–; Pres. and CEO Rainman Records 1999–; Pres. and CEO, MT Industries 2000–. *Address:* 315 S Beverly Drive, Suite 407, Beverly Hills, CA 90212, USA (office). *Telephone:* (310) 557-0661 (office). *Fax:* (310) 557-8421 (office). *E-mail:* rrmgmt@aol.com (office). *Website:* www.ronrainey.com.

RAINWATER, Keech; American country musician (drums, banjo, percussion); b. 24 Jan. 1963, Plano, TX. *Career:* mem., Canyon 1988–90; founder mem., Texasee 1992, became resident house band at the Wildhorse Saloon, Nashville, name changed to Lonestar 1995–. *Recordings include:* albums: Lonestar 1995, Crazy Nights 1997, Lonely Grill 1999, This Christmas Time

2000, I'm Already There 2001, Let's Be Us Again 2004, Coming Home 2005, Mountains 2006, My Christmas List 2007. *Address:* c/o BNA Records, Sony BMG, 1400 18th Avenue, South Nashville, TN 37212, USA (office). *Website:* www.lonestarnow.com.

RAITT, Bonnie Lynn; American blues singer and musician (guitar, piano); b. 8 Nov. 1949, Burbank, Calif.; d. of the late John Raitt; m. Michael O'Keefe 1991 (divorced 1999). *Education:* Radcliffe Coll. *Career:* performer in blues clubs on American E Coast; numerous concert tours and live appearances. *Recordings include:* albums: Bonnie Raitt 1971, Give It Up 1972, Takin' My Time 1973, Streetlights 1974, Home Plate 1975, Sweet Forgiveness 1977, The Glow 1979, Green Light 1982, Nine Lives 1986, Nick of Time (Grammy Awards for Best Female Rock Vocal Performance, Best Female Pop Vocal Performance, Album of the Year 1990) 1989, I'm in the Mood (with John Lee Hooker) (Grammy Award for Best Blues Traditional Record 1990), The Bonnie Raitt Collection 1990, Luck of the Draw (Grammy Award for Best Female Rock Vocal Performance, Best Duet 1992) 1991, Longing in Their Hearts (Grammy Award for Best Pop Album) 1994, Road Tested (Grammy Award for Best Rock Instrumental Performance 1997) 1995, Fundamental 1998, Silver Lining 2002, Souls Alike 2005, Bonnie Raitt and Friends 2006, SlipStream (Grammy Award for Best Americana Album 2013) 2012. *Address:* PO Box 626, Los Angeles, CA 90078, USA. *Website:* www.bonnieraitt.com.

RAJERY; Malagasy composer, singer, musician (percussion, valiha) and writer; b. (Randrianarisoa Germain), 1965, Analamihantona. *Career:* mem., Tsilavena 1982; solo artist 1983–; founder mem. valiha group, Akombaliha (later orchestra). *Recordings include:* albums: Dorotanety 1999, Fanamby 2002, Volantany 2004, Sofera 2007. *Publication:* The Secret of the Valiha. *Honours:* RFI Musiques du Monde Award 2002. *Address:* c/o Marabi Productions, 9 rue de Point du Jour, 16000 Angouleme, France (office). *E-mail:* marabi@wanadoo.fr (office). *Website:* www.marabi.net (office).

RAKIM; American MC; b. (William Griffin Jr), 28 Jan. 1968, Wyandanch, NY. *Career:* converted to Islam aged 16, adopting the name Rakim Allah; part of duo Eric B. & Rakim 1985–92. *Recordings:* albums: as Eric B. & Rakim: Paid In Full 1987, Follow The Leader 1988, Let The Rhythm Hit 'Em 1990, Don't Sweat The Technique 1992; solo: The 18th Letter 1997, The Master 1999, The Seventh Seal 2009; singles: as Eric B. & Rakim: Eric B Is President 1986, Just A Beat 1988, Let The Rhythm Hit 'Em 1990, Move The Crowd 1990, Mahogany 1990, In The Ghetto 1990, What's On Your Mind 1991, Juice 1992, Don't Sweat The Technique 1992, Casualties Of War 1992, Microphone Fiend 1992, Eric B. Is President 1997, I Ain't No Joke 1997, I Know You Got Soul 1997. *Website:* www.myspace.com/rakim.

RALPHES, Paul Stuart, BA; British record producer, songwriter and musician (guitar, bass guitar); b. 23 Feb. 1962, Shrewsbury, England; m. Rosana Ferrao 1991. *Education:* Univ. of Warwick. *Career:* producer, songwriter, musician, Bliss 1987–92; tours with Van Morrison, Paul Simon, Gipsy Kings, Chris Isaak; worked with: Rupert Hine, Jon Kelly, John Shaw, Hugh Jones, Duke Baysee; mem. PRS, Musicians' Union. *Recordings:* as producer, writer, musician: Loveprayer Bliss, 1989, Change In The Weather, Bliss 1991, Sugar Sugar, Duke Baysee 1994, Do You Love Me?, Duke Baysee 1995, Siderado, Skank 1999, Cidade Negra, Cinquante 2000. *Honours:* Best International Act, Bliss, Italy, Brazil 1989.

RALPHS, Mick; British musician (guitar) and songwriter; b. 31 March 1944, Hereford; two s. one d. *Career:* founder mem., Mott the Hoople 1969–73, reformed for live performances 2009; founder mem., Bad Company 1973–83, re-formed 1986, 2009; toured worldwide; fmr mem., Amazing Blondell; solo recording artist 1983; mem. Musicians' Union, PRS. *Recordings include:* albums: with Mott the Hoople: Mott the Hoople 1969, Mad Shadows 1970, Wild Life 1971, Brain Capers 1971, All the Young Dudes 1972, Mott 1973, All the Way From Stockholm (live in 1971) 1999, Live Dudes 2000; with Amazing Blondell: Blondell 1973, Mulgrave Street 1974; with Bad Company: Bad Company 1974, Straight Shooter 1975, Run With The Pack 1976, Burnin' Sky 1977, Desolation Angels 1979, Rough Diamonds 1982, 10 from 6 1985, Fame and Fortune 1986, Dangerous Age 1988, Holy Water 1990, Here Comes Trouble 1992, Company of Strangers 1995, Stories Told + Untold 1996, The Original Bad Co Anthology 1999; solo: Take This 1984, It's All Good 2002, That's Life 2003. *Honours:* Grammy Award 1975; Hon. Col of Louisiana (with Bad Company). *Website:* www.mottthehoople.com; www.mickralphs.co.uk.

RAMAGE, Andrew; British musician (guitar, bass, contra); b. 24 Sept. 1949, Edinburgh, Scotland; m. Anita 1975. *Education:* Telford College. *Career:* numerous TV and radio broadcasts; mem. Musicians' Union. *Recordings:* Golden Bird Vols 1 and 2, 1968; Bitter Withy Sampler, 1973; Bridging The Gap, 1983; Two For The Road, 1986; Silver Darlings, 1988; Dancing On A Wave, 1989; Naturally, 1991; Family Ties, 1993; Scotland The Brave, 1995; Songs You Heard Tonight, 1999. *Honours:* RBI, 1970; Glenfarg Quaich, 1980.

RAMAN, Susheela; singer; b. 20 July 1973, London, England. *Education:* studied with Shruti Sadolikar in India. *Career:* moved to Australia 1977; learned and gave recitals of South Indian classical music; moved into blues-based music as a teenager; moved to England 1997. *Recordings:* Salt Rain 2001, Love Trap 2003, Music for Crocodiles 2005, 33 1/3 2007. *Honours:* BBC Radio 3 World Music Award for Best Newcomer 2002. *E-mail:* cbitton@wanadoo.fr (office). *Website:* www.susheelaraman.com.

RAMAZZOTTI, Eros; Italian singer, musician (guitar) and songwriter; b. 28 Oct. 1963, Rome. *Career:* participated in Castrocaro Music Festival 1981; solo artist 1982–; numerous tours and live appearances; created own management co., Radiorama 1993–. *Recordings include:* albums: Cuori Agitati 1985, Nuovi Eroi 1986, In Certi Momenti 1987, Musica e 1988, In Ogni Senso 1990, Eros in Concert 1991, Tutte Storie 1993, Dove C'e Musica 1996, Eros 1997, Eros Live 1998, Stile Libero 2000, 9 (Best Italian Album Award) 2003, Calma apparente 2005, Ali e radici 2009, Eros Best Love Songs 2012. *Honours:* Commendatore dell'Ordine al Merito della Repubblica Italiana 2006; San Remo Festival Best Young Artist Award 1984, MTV Music Award for Best Italian Singer 1996, Echo Award for Best Int. Singer, Germany 1997, Best Italian Male Artist 2003. *Telephone:* (02) 89546454 (office). *Fax:* (02) 89546197 (office). *E-mail:* info@radioramaasrl.it (office). *Website:* www.ramazzotti.com.

RAMIREZ, Humberto, BMus; Puerto Rican musician (trumpet), composer, producer and arranger; b. 31 Jan. 1963, San Juan; m. Ivette Maritza Negron 1988; one s. one d. *Education:* Escuela Libre de Musica, San Juan, Puerto Rico and Berklee Coll. of Music, Boston. *Career:* leader, Jazz Project band, Humberto Ramirez Jazz Orchestra; concerts played at Madison Square Garden, Hollywood Bowl, Miami Arena, Blue Note Jazz Club, Blues Alley; mem, NARAS; ASCAP. *Recordings:* with Jazz Project: Jazz Project 1992; solo: Aspects 1993, Portrait of a Stranger 1996, Canciones de Amor 1996, Treasures 1998, Best Friends 1999, Paradise 2002, Passions of Latin Jazz 2002, Dos Almas 2003. *Honours:* Diplo Award Best Jazz Recording 1992, TU Musica Award for Best Jazz Recording 1994, 1995, 1996.

RAMIREZ, Juan; British flamenco musician (guitar), songwriter and producer; *Artistic Director, Viva Flamenco Dance Company;* b. 17 Oct. 1947, London, England; m. Marsha 1972. *Education:* studied flamenco guitar and dance accompaniment in Spain and London. *Career:* full time 1974–; formed Viva Flamenco Dance Co. 1976; performed at Royal Albert Hall, Barbican, Royal Festival Hall, London; world's then-largest production of Carmen 1992; numerous TV appearances; mem. Musicians' Union 1972–. *Films:* The Curse of The Pink Panther 1983, The Dark Border 1989, Kevin and Perry Go Large 2000. *Compositions include:* Viva Flamenco – Juan Ramirez. *Recordings include:* with Marc Almond: The Desperate Hours; with Gary Barlow: Stronger; with Vanessa Mae: Pasha; recorded and produced three albums with Sir Christopher Lee: Revelation 2009, Charlemagne, by the Sword and the Cross 2010, The Omens of Death 2013. *Address:* Orchard Cottage, Little Green, Burgate, Diss, Norfolk, IP22 1QQ, England (home). *Telephone:* (1379) 788840 (home); 7850-843880 (mobile) (office). *E-mail:* info@vivaflamenco.com. *Website:* www.vivaflamenco.com; www.vivaflamenco.co.uk; www.juanmoretime.co.uk.

RAMIREZ, Karen; British singer; b. 1972, Islington, London, England. *Career:* vocalist for producers, Souled Out; solo artist. *Recordings include:* album: Distant Dreams 1998. *E-mail:* info@karenramirez.net. *Website:* www.karenramirez.net.

RAMIREZ EGUÍA, Julio; Mexican musician (guitar) and singer; b. 21 Dec. 1987, Mexicali, Bajo California. *Career:* founding mem., Reik 2003–. *Recordings:* Reik 2005, Secuencia 2006, Un Día Más (Latin Grammy Award for Best Pop Album by a Duo/Group 2009) 2008. *Honours:* Premios MTV Latinoamérica for Best Group 2005, for Best Artist (Northern region) 2005, for Best New Artist (Northern region) 2005, for Best Pop Artist 2009. *Current Management:* c/o Dulce Gil, Westwood Entertainment, México, Mexico. *Telephone:* (55) 5337-2047. *E-mail:* dgil@westwoodent.com. *Website:* www.westwoodent.com; www.reik.tv.

RAMOS, Ruben, (El Gato Negro); American singer and bandleader; b. Sugarland, Tex.; s. of Alfonso Ramos and Elvira Perez. *Career:* mem., Alfonso Ramos Orchestra 1960s; founder and bandleader, The Mexican Revolution 1969–; co-f. Los Super Seven 1998. *Recordings:* Los Super Seven (Grammy Award for Best Mexican American Music Performance 1999); with The Mexican Revolution: Viva La Revolución (Grammy Award for Best Tejano Album 2009), Christmas Cool, On the Prawl, By Popular Demand, A Class Act, Smooth, El Chupa Chavas, Amor y Paz, Tejanisimo, Yo No Se, Revolutionized. *Honours:* Best Male Vocalist, Tejano Music Awards 1999. *Website:* www.rubenramos.com.

RAMOS, Sergio; Spanish musician (percussion). *Career:* fmr mem. Calixto Bieto Nat. Theatre; worked with groups including Los Negativos, Goma 2, Primera Línea, Acción-Reacción Percusión trio; joined Ojos de Brujo, a group which fuses gypsy and flamenco music with Latin American, punk, hip hop, reggae and electronic influences; originally a temporary replacement for Xavier Turull but became perm. mem.; Ojos de Brujo set up own label La Fábrica de Colores 2001 and since then operate as a completely ind. org., Ramos is responsible for org.'s accounts; several tours in Europe, Latin America and USA; collaborations with Nitin Sawhney, Asian Dub Foundation. *Recordings:* albums: with Ojos de Brujo: Barí 2002, Barí: Remezclas de la Casa 2003, Techarí 2006, Aocaná 2009; other: Girando Bari (DVD) 2005. *Honours:* World Music Award for Europe, BBC Radio 3 2004. *E-mail:* sergio@ojosdebrujo.com (office). *Website:* www.ojosdebrujo.com.

RANALDO, Lee, BFA; American artist, poet, musician and composer; b. 3 Feb. 1956, Glen Cove, NY. *Education:* State Univ. of NY, Binghampton. *Career:* soloist, performer with Glenn Branca and Rhys Chatham; Founder-mem. Sonic Youth 1981–; duo performances: spoken word/film/music with filmmaker Leah Singer; numerous exhbns world-wide since early 1990s; mem. American Fed. of Musicians. *Recordings include:* albums: with Sonic Youth: Sonic Youth 1982, Confusion is Sex 1983, Sonic Death 1984, Bad Moon Rising

1985, E.V.O.L. 1986, Sister 1987, Daydream Nation 1988, The Whitey Album 1989, Goo 1990, Dirty 1992, Experimental Jet Set, Trash and No Star 1994, Screaming Fields of Sonic Love 1995, Made in USA 1995, Washing Machine 1995, A Thousand Leaves 1998, SYR4: Goodbye 20th Century 1999, NYC Ghosts & Flowers 2000, Murray Street 2002, Sonic Nurse 2004, Rather Ripped 2006, The Destroyed Room: B-sides and Rarities 2006, The Eternal 2009; with Ciccone Youth: The Whitey Album 1989; solo: Scriptures of the Golden Eternity 1993, East Jesus 1995, Dirty Windows 1998, Amarillo Ramp (for Robert Smithson) 1998, Text of Light 2004, The Celestial Answer (with William Hooker) 2006, Between The Times And The Tides 2012. *Publications:* Road Movies: Poems 1998, Bookstore, Jrnls 80s (poems) 1999, Moroccan Journal (with Leah Singer) 2001, Lengths and Breaths 2005, DRIFT (with Leah Singer) 2005. *Current Management:* c/o Michele Fleischli, Silva Artist Management, 722 Seward Street, Los Angeles, CA 90038-3504, USA. *Telephone:* (323) 856-8222. *E-mail:* mfleischli@sammusicbiz.com. *Website:* www.sammusicbiz.com. *Address:* PO Box 6179, Hoboken, NJ 07030, USA (home). *Website:* www.leeranaldo.com; www.sonicyouth.com.

RANEY, Sue; American singer; b. (Raelene Claire Claussen), 18 June 1939, McPhearson, Kan.; m. Carmen Fanzone 1985. *Career:* recording debut aged 16; performed worldwide, with artists, including Don Rickles, Dean Martin, Bob Hope, Henry Mancini, Michel Legrand, Bob Newhart, Flip Wilson, Rosemary Clooney; mem. Faculty, Dick Grove School of Music; mem. Soc. of Singers. *Film:* The Road Hustler 1968. *Recordings include:* albums: When Your Lover Has Gone 1959, Songs for a Raney Day 1960, All By Myself 1964, Happiness is a Warm Sue Raney 1965, Alive and In Love 1966, New and Now 1967, With a Little Help from My Friends 1969, The People Tree 1972, Ridin' High 1984, Flight of Fancy 1986, In Good Company 1990, Dreamsville (The Music of Henry Mancini) 1992, Autumn in the Air 1997, Breathless 1997, Heart's Desire: A Tribute to Doris Day 2006, Listen Here: Alone with Alan Broadbent 2011, Late In Life 2014. *Honours:* Most Valuable Player, Los Angeles Naras Chapter 1981, Los Angeles Jazz Soc. Female Vocalist 1996, New York Bistro Award 2013. *E-mail:* info@sueraneysro.com. *Website:* www.sueraneysro.com.

RANGE, Heidi; British singer; b. 23 May 1982, Liverpool, England. *Career:* fmr mem., Atomic Kitten; solo artist; mem., Sugababes 2001–. *Recordings include:* albums: Angels With Dirty Faces 2002, Three 2003, Taller In More Ways 2005, Change 2007, Catfights and Spotlights 2008, Sweet 7 2010. *Honours:* Q Award (for Freak Like Me) 2002, BRIT Award for Best Dance Act 2003. *Current Management:* Crown Music Management, 91 Peterborough Road, London SW6 3BU, England. *Telephone:* (20) 7371-5444. *Fax:* (20) 7371-5454. *E-mail:* info@crownmusic.co.uk. *Website:* www.crownmusic.co.uk. *Address:* c/o Island Records Group, 22 St Peters Square, Hammersmith, London, W6 9NW, England (office). *Website:* www.sugababes.com.

RANGEL, Enrique; Mexican musician (bass guitar) and singer. *Career:* founding mem., Café Tacvba 1989–; contrib. to film soundtracks, including Y tu mamá también, Vivir Mata, Amores Perros; collaborations with artists, including Celso Piña, El Gran Silencio, Inspector, Kronos Quartet, Ofelia Medina, David Byrne. *Recordings:* albums: Café Tacuba 1992, Re 1994, Avalancha de Éxitos (EP) 1996, Reves/YoSoy (Latin Grammy Award for best rock album) 1999, Tiempo Transcurrido 2001, Vale Callampa (EP) 2002, Cuatro Caminos (Latin Grammy Award for best alternative music album 2004) 2003, SiNo 2007. *Honours:* Latin Grammy Awards for Best Rock Song (for Esta Vez) 2008, for Best Alternative Song (for Volver a Comenzar) 2008. *Address:* Universal Music Latino, 1425 Collins Avenue, Miami Beach, FL 33139, USA (office). *Telephone:* (305) 604-1380 (office). *Fax:* (305) 604-1343 (office). *Website:* www.universalmusica.com (office); www.cafetacuba.com.mx.

RANGEL, Joselo; Mexican musician (guitar) and singer. *Career:* founding mem., Café Tacvba 1989–; contrib. to film soundtracks, including Y tu mamá también, Vivir Mata, Amores Perros; collaborations with artists, including Celso Piña, El Gran Silencio, Inspector, Kronos Quartet, Ofelia Medina, David Byrne. *Recordings:* albums: Café Tacuba 1992, Re 1994, Avalancha de Éxitos (EP) 1996, Reves/YoSoy (Latin Grammy Award for best rock album) 1999, Tiempo Transcurrido 2001, Vale Callampa (EP) 2002, Cuatro Caminos (Latin Grammy Award for best alternative music album 2004) 2003, SiNo 2007. *Honours:* Latin Grammy Awards for Best Rock Song (for Esta Vez) 2008, for Best Alternative Song (for Volver a Comenzar) 2008. *Address:* Universal Music Latino, 1425 Collins Avenue, Miami Beach, FL 33139, USA (office). *Telephone:* (305) 604-1380 (office). *Fax:* (305) 604-1343 (office). *Website:* www.universalmusica.com (office); www.cafetacuba.com.mx.

RANKIN, Mark; Scottish singer; b. Glasgow, Scotland. *Career:* singer in rock group, Gun 1989–; numerous international tours and live performances. *Recordings include:* albums: Taking On The World, 1989; Gallus, 1992; Swagger, 1994; 0141 632 6326, 1997. *Current Management:* G R Management, 974 Pollockshaw Rd, Glasgow G41 2HA, Scotland.

RANKINE, Graham, (Graham Fenton); British singer; b. 28 May 1947, London, England; m. Caroline Rankine 1991. *Career:* mem. various bands 1970s; mem. Matchbox 1979–86, 1996–; radio and TV, tours of Germany, the Netherlands, Switzerland, Spain, Austria, Belgium, Yugoslavia; mem. Musicians' Union. *Recordings:* albums: with Matchbox: Matchbox 1979, Midnight Dynamos 1980, Flying Colours 1981, Crossed Line 1982, Coming Home 1998. *E-mail:* matchbox@freenetname.co.uk. *Website:* www.rockabillyrebel.co.uk.

RANKS, Shabba, (Rexton Gordon); Jamaican reggae, ragga singer; b. 17 Jan. 1966, Sturgetown. *Career:* club artist as DJ Don, early 1980s; solo artist, mid-1980s; prolific local recording artist, Caribbean; support to Bobby Brown, USA 1992. *Recordings:* As Raw As Ever, 1991; Rough and Ready Vol. 1, 1992; Xtra Naked, 1992; Mr Maximum, 1992; Love Punanny Bad, 1993; No Competition, 1993; A Mi Shabba, 1995; Shine Eye Gal, 1995; Holding On, 1998; King of Dancehall, 1998; Get Up Stand Up, 1998; Loverman, 1999; Shabba Ranks and Friends, 1999; Greatest Hits, 2001; Hit singles: She's A Woman (with Scritti Politti), 1991; Housecall (with Maxi Priest), 1991; Mr Loverman, used in film soundtrack Deep Cover, 1993; Slow and Sexy, 1992; What'cha Gonna Do? (with Queen Latifah), 1993; Family Affair, used in film soundtrack Addams Family, 1993. *Honours:* Grammy Awards: Best Reggae Album, As Raw As Ever, 1992; Xtra Naked, 1993; 2 Caribbean Music Awards, 1992; 6 International Reggae Awards, 1992. *Current Management:* Shang Artist Management, 850 Seventh Ave, Suite 500, New York, NY 10019, USA.

RANSOME, Steve; British musician (keyboards), composer and record producer; b. 24 Aug. 1961, London; m. Shirley Peterson 1994. *Education:* Grangewood School in London. *Career:* ATV Production Assistant 1977–78; played keyboards in various bands at Wembley, Peterborough and Glasgow Festivals; toured UK, Ireland, Europe and America; appeared on BBC TV, ITV, MTV, Channel 4 TV and Cable TV; Yamaha demonstration concerts given; played at Bahai Festivals, the University circuits in Scotland and on most radio stations; owns recording studio; mem, PRS; MCPS; Musicians' Union. *Compositions include:* about 12 television themes and soundtracks; arranger for 1988 special Olympics theme. *Recordings:* Single: Peace Moves, world-wide release; Many major artists as production assistant. *Publications:* Peace Moves; Storming The Gates; Bahai Song Book Vol. 1. *Address:* Donfield House, Backmill by Turriff, Aberdeenshire AB53 8ET, Scotland.

RANTANEN, Hannu; Finnish musician (bass guitar, double bass). *Education:* Helsinki Pop Jazz Conservatory. *Career:* fmr mem. UMO Big Band, Pepa Päivinen Trio, Raoul Björkenheim Triad, Unto Tango Orchestra, Rajaton, Avanti, Helsinki Symphony, Lahti Symphony; mem. Värttinä 2001–; teacher, Helsinki Pop Jazz Conservatory. *Music for theatre:* co-wrote score to stage musical, The Lord of the Rings (with A. R. Rahman) (Princess of Wales Theatre, Toronto) 2006. *Recordings include:* albums: 6.12 2001, iki 2003, Miero 2006. *Current Management:* c/o Phillip Page, Hoedown Arts Oy, Neitsytpolku 9 F 81, 00140 Helsinki, Finland. *Telephone:* (50) 5692982. *Fax:* (9) 628950. *E-mail:* pap@hoedown.com. *E-mail:* hannu.rantanen@pp5.inet.fi (office). *Website:* www.varttina.com.

RANTASALMI, Pauli Antero; Finnish musician (guitar) and producer; b. 1 May 1979, Helsinki. *Career:* mem., The Rasmus 1994–. *Recordings include:* albums: Peep 1996, Playboys (Emma Award) 1997, Hell Of A Tester 1998, Into 2001, Dead Letters 2003, Hide From The Sun 2005, Black Roses 2008. *Honours:* Emma Award for Best New Artist 1996, MTV Europe Music Award Best Finnish Act 2005. *Address:* c/o Playground Music, Box 3171, 200 22 Malmö, Sweden (office). *E-mail:* info@playgroundmusic.com (office). *Website:* www.playgroundmusic.com (office); www.therasmus.com.

RAPHAEL; Spanish singer; b. (Rafael Martos), 5 May 1942, Linares, Jaén; m. Natalia Figueroa 1972; two s. one d. *Career:* first prize winner at Salzburg Festival children's singing competition aged nine; subsequently won numerous other competitions; began professional career in Madrid nightclub 1960; rep. of Spain, Eurovision Song Contest 1966, 1967; US debut 1967; toured USSR 1968, Japan 1970, Australia 1971; Broadway debut 1974; celebrated 25th anniversary as professional singer with open-air concert at Bernabé Stadium, Madrid 1985. *Films include:* Las gemelas 1963, Cuando tú no estás 1966, Al ponerse el sol 1967, Digan lo que digan 1968, El Ángel 1969, El golfo 1969, Sin un adiós 1970, Volveré a nacer 1973, Ritmo, amor y primavera 1981. *Television include:* Donde termina el camino (series) 1978, Horas doradas (series) 1980. *Recordings include:* Los hombres lloran también 1964, Sigo siendo aquel 1985, Toda una vida 1985, Las apariencias engañan 1988, Maravilloso corazón 1989, El monstruo de la canción 1990, Andaluz 1990, Fantasia 1994, Brillantes 1994, Monstruo 1995, Desde el fondo de mi alma 1995, Raphael 1998, Dama Dama 1999, Sentado a la vera del camino 1999, Hotel de l'universe 2001, Yo soy aquel 2001, Maldito Raphael 2001, Realite 2003, De vuelta 2003, Vuelve Por Navidad 2004, A Que No Te Vas 2006, Cerca de ti 2006, 50 Años Despues 2008, Viva Raphael! 2009, Te Llevo En El Corazón 2010, El Reencuentro 2012, Mi gran noche 2013. *Current Management:* Arie Kaduri Agency, Inc., 16125 NE 18th Avenue, North Miami Beach, FL 33162, USA. *Website:* www.raphaelnet.com.

RASHAD, Essam; Egyptian musician (oud) and composer; b. 1935, Cairo. *Career:* fmrly composer, Egyptian nat. radio; joined Egyptian Nat. Orchestra as oud player; played oud on records by Natacha Atlas, Hossam Ramzy, Transglobal Underground. *Recordings:* albums: Big Heart 1989, Ro-He 1994, Arabic Oud, Classical Egyptian Dance, Vol 1 2004.

RASMUSSEN, Pia, CandPhil, MA; Danish musician (piano), composer and music teacher; *Associate Teaching Professor and Head, Department of Musicology, Århus University;* b. 10 Nov. 1954, Århus. *Education:* Copenhagen Univ. *Career:* pianist and composer, all-woman groups Sosterrock and Lilith 1976–83; composer for documentaries, films and theatre; solo concerts, piano, synthesizers 1991–; duo with flautist Chris Poole 1992–; Assoc. Teaching Prof. and Head, Dept of Musicology, Århus Univ.; teaching and research in jazz, entrepreneurship, music production and film music; mem. Danske Jazz, Beat og Folkemusik Autorer (DJBFA), Danish Musicians'

Union, Women In Music, Women in Film and Television. *Recordings:* album: To The Powers That Be; theme song, Nordic Women's Conference, Oslo 1988. *Publications:* Entreprenørskabsundervisning – proces, refleksion og handling (co-author) 2010, Blues For Klaver, Vols 1 and 2 (educational books on blues piano) (co-author) 2013. *Address:* Afdeling for Musikvidenskab, Bygning 1580, Langelandsgade 139, 8000 Århus C, Denmark (office). *Telephone:* 87-16-31-01 (office). *E-mail:* muspr@hum.au.dk (office). *Website:* person.au.dk/da/muspr@hum.

RASOANAIVO ANDERSON, Hanitrarivo, BA; British/Malagasy singer, dancer, musician (percussion) and songwriter; *Director, Antshow Malagasy Arts & Centre;* b. 1 Oct. 1964, Antananarivo; m. Ian Anderson. *Career:* lead singer and founding mem., Tarika 1994; band toured USA and Europe; performed with Weave, Gogmagogs; Women of Africa collaboration (with Oumou Sangare, Sally Nyolo and Sibongile Khumalo), performing on tour 1998; worked on project to build an arts centre in Antananarivo, now Dir, Antshow, Malagasy Arts & Centre; theatre projects in Norway and France. *Recordings include:* albums: Fanafody 1990, Balance 1992, Bibiango 1994, Avelo 1997, Son Egal (Asscn for Independent Music Indie Award for Best Contemporary World Music Album 1998) 1997, D 1998, Soul Makassar 2001, Beasts, Ghosts & Dancing With History 2004, Tapan Routes 2007. *Address:* c/o Rogue Productions, PO Box 337, London, N4 1TW, England. *E-mail:* info@tarika.nu (home).

RASTED, Peter; Danish musician (trumpet, flugelhorn), arranger and conductor; b. 28 July 1958, Copenhagen; m. Annette Frandsen; one s. *Education:* Royal Acad. of Music, Copenhagen. *Career:* mem. several big bands, including Kluvers Big Band (also production man.), Blast, The Franks, Cordero et Los Gran Daneses, Orquestra Llego la Hora, Sexteto; theatre appearances in Copenhagen, Ålborg, Århus and Fredericia; Danish television show, Showbizzerne; studio sessions; teacher, Det Jyske Musikkonservatorium. *Recordings:* with Blast: all recordings except Blast, SKO/Torp: I Ain't Got Too Many Problems, Cordero et Los Gran Daneses: Del Norte Y Tropical, Hej Frede; and others. *Address:* Sandogade 4, 8200 Århus N, Denmark (office); Arnagervej 3, 1208 Århus V, Denmark (home). *Telephone:* 26-15-84-93 (office); 86-10-12-08 (home). *E-mail:* lper@nordkons.dk (home).

RASTED, Soeren; Danish musician (keyboards, drum machines); b. 13 June 1969, Blovstrod. *Career:* Worked with Claus Norreen on film Fraekke Frida; Formed Joyspeed; Changed name to Aqua; Obtained major label deal in Denmark; Numerous TV and live appearances. *Recordings:* Singles: Itsy Blitzy, as Joyspeed; Roses Are Red; My Oh My; Barbie Girl (No. 1, UK), 1997; Doctor Jones (No. 1, UK), 1998; Lollipop; Turn Back Time (theme from film Sliding Doors) (No. 1, UK), 1998; Good Morning Sunshine; Albums: Aquarium, 1997; Bubble Mix, 1998; We Belong To The Sea, 2001. *Website:* www.aqua.dk.tp.

RAT SCABIES; British musician (drums); b. (Chris Miller), 30 July 1957, Kingston upon Thames, Surrey, England. *Career:* fmr mem., Rat, London SS; founder mem. punk rock band, The Damned 1976–77, 1979–89, 1991–95; mem., the White Cats 1978; world-wide concerts; mem. side project, Naz and the Nomads 1984–88. *Recordings:* albums: with The Damned: Damned, Damned, Damned 1977, Music For Pleasure 1977, Machine Gun Etiquette 1979, The Black Album 1980, Live At Shepperton 1980 1982, Strawberries 1982, Live At Newcastle 1983, Damned But Not Forgotten 1985, Phantasmagoria 1985, Anything 1986, Not The Captain's Birthday Party? 1986, The Captain's Birthday Party 1986, Light At The End Of The Tunnel 1987, Mindless, Directionless, Energy: Live At The Lyceum 1987, Final Damnation 1989, Live 1991, Ballroom Blitz 1992, Music For Pleasure 1995, Eternally Damned 1995; with Naz and the Nomads: Give Daddy The Knife, Cindy 1988.

RATCLIFFE, Simon; British DJ, producer and songwriter; b. 1969. *Career:* founder mem., Basement Jaxx 1994–; co-founder and owner, Atlantic Jaxx records 1994–; remixes for acts, including Pet Shop Boys, Roger Sanchez, Lil' Mo Yin Yang; worked with vocalist Corrina Josephs; numerous gigs and television appearances. *Recordings include:* albums: Atlantic Jaxx (compilation) 1997, Remedy 1999, Rooty 2001, Kish Kash (Grammy Award for Best Electronic/Dance Album 2005) 2003, The Singles 2005, Crazy Itch Radio 2006, Scars 2009, Junto 2014. *Honours:* BRIT Awards for Best British Dance Act 2002, 2004. *Address:* c/o XL Recordings, One Codrington Mews, London, W11 2EH, England (office). *Telephone:* (20) 8870-7511. *Website:* www.xlrecordings.com; www.basementjaxx.co.uk.

RATHBOURNE, Andie; British musician (drums); b. 8 Sept. 1971, Blacon, Chester, England. *Career:* mem., Mansun 1996–2003; numerous TV and live appearances. *Recordings include:* albums: Attack Of The Grey Lantern 1996, Desperate Icons 1997, Legacy 1998, Six 1998, Little Kix 2000, Electric Man 2000, Kleptomania 2004. *Website:* www.mansun.net.

RATZER, Karl; Austrian musician (guitar), composer and singer; b. 4 July 1950, Vienna. *Career:* mem., C Department 1969, Gipsy Love 1970, High Voltage (later known as Rufus and Chaka Khan); worked with Chet Baker, Eddie Gomez, Joe Chambers, Steve Gadd, Joe Farrell, Sal Nistico, Bob Mintzer, Johnny Griffin, Clark Terry, Art Farmer, Fritz Baver, Lee Konitz, James Moody, Chaka Khan, Jenny Evans; formed band project, Beat the Heat 1991; tours, festival appearances. *Recordings include:* solo albums: In Search of the Ghost; Street-Talk; Fingerprints; Serenade; Happy Floating; Electric Finger; Dancing on a String; Fool for Your Sake; That's Jazz; Gitarre;

Gitarrenfever; Gumbo Dive; Waltz for Ann; Bayou; Coasting; Saturn Returning. *E-mail:* office@karlratzer.com. *Website:* www.karlratzer.com.

RAULIN, Francois; French musician (piano) and composer; b. 17 March 1956, Annecy; 3 s. *Education:* Mathematics; Piano lessons from age 9. *Career:* Founder, Association Grenoble Espace Musical (AGEM), 1981; Duo, with pianist Pascal Lloret, tour, France, 1981; Studied African music, 1980–83; Pianist, La Marmite Infernale, 1982; Tours, France; Festivals include: Paris; Le Mans; Nancy; Milan, 1982; Zürich, 1984; Moers, 1984; Hofheim, 1985; Nickelsdorf, 1986; Tours: Algeria; Germany; Switzerland; Italy; Austria; Member, Louis Sclavis Group, 1985; Festivals world-wide include: All over Europe; Canada; Japan; India; Turkey; Algeria; Mexico; Festival appearances with Claude Barthelemy, Jean-Marc Padovani, 1986; Antoine Herve, 1988; Philippe Deschepper, 1992; Solo performances at festivals including: Grenoble; Lausanne; Geneva; Cologne, 1992–; Tours with trio and quartet. *Compositions include:* Quelque Chose Du Sud, with Maurice Merle; Battleship Potemkin (film music); with Louis Sclavis: Chamber Music, 1988; Clarinettes: Indigène, 1989; Duke On The Air, 1990; Face Nord, with Mathilde Monnier's Dance Company, 1991; Vue Sur Tower Bridge (Travelling) (co-writer), 1992; Work for 5 Pianos, 1993; Hit Parada, Jean Mereu, 1993; Les Violences de Rameau, with Louis Sclavis, 1993, reissued 2001; Music for theatre, film and dance, with Louis Sclavis, J Mereux, A Gibert. *Recordings include:* Chine; Rouge; First Flush; Duke on The Air. *Honours:* Winner, Biennale, Barcelona (with Louis Scalvis Quartet), 1988. *Address:* 686 Ave Saint Jean, 38360 Noyarey, France. *Website:* www.laforgecir.com/pages/F-Raulin.html.

RAUX, Richard; French musician (saxophone, flute), composer and bandleader; b. 17 July 1945, Perigaux; m. Helena, 25 May 1970, one s., one d. *Education:* Bac Philo; 2 years university; Saxophone, Phil Woods; Flute, Caratgt; Composition, G Russell. *Career:* Played, recorded with Eddy Louis; Magma; Luther Allison; Kenny Clarke; Mal Waldron; Charlie Haden; Memphis Slim; Dizzy Gillespie; Roy Burrowes Sextet; John Greaves; Festivals, concerts, clubs, Telé France; Nice, 1991, 93; London; Berlin; Jazz teacher, saxophone, flute. *Recordings:* Feel Good At Last, Richard Raux Quartet; S Murray; Eddy Louis; Under The Magnolias, Richard Raux Quartet, 1989; Live At The Dreyer, Roy Burrowes, Mal Waldron; Won't Rain in California, Sonny Rhodes, 1996; House Rent Party, 1998. *E-mail:* dir.tech@cinethea.com. *Website:* www.cinethea.com.

RAVEN, Eddy; American musician, singer and songwriter; b. (Edward Garvin Futch), 19 Aug. 1944, Lafayette, LA; two s. *Career:* has worked with Hank Williams Jr, Alabama, Tracy Lawrence, George Strait, Reba McEntire, Alan Jackson, Charlie Daniels, Stevie Ray Vaughan, The Judds, George Jones, Conway Twitty, Merle Haggard, Dolly Parton, Roy Acuff, Barbara Mandrell, Marty Robbins; numerous television appearances; founder, own publishing company; staff writer on La Louisianne 1963–69, Acriff Rose 1970–83; mem. ASCAP, BMI, AFTRA, AFofM, Tennessee Film and Entertainment Commission; lifetime mem. Songwriters' Asscn. *Television:* co-host Yesteryear (TNN). *Compositions:* Country Green, Don Gibson; Touch The Morning, Don Gibson; Good Morning Country Rain, Jeannie C Riley; Thank God For Kids, Mel Tillis. *Recordings:* albums: That Cajun Country Sound 1969, This Is Eddy Raven 1976, Eyes 1979, Desperate Dreams 1981, Thank God For Kids 1984, I Could Use Another You 1984, Love and Other Hard Times 1985, Right Hand Man 1986, Temporary Sanity 1989, Greatest Country Hits 1990, Right For Flight 1991, Wild Eyed and Crazy 1994, Cookin' Cajun 1996, Eddy Raven I Got Mexico 1997, Living In Black And White 2001, House of the Rising Sun 2006. *Address:* PO Box 2476, Hendersonville, TN 37077, USA (office). *E-mail:* info@eddyraven.com (office). *Website:* www.eddyraven.com.

RAVEN MAIZE (see Lee, Dave)

RAWLINGS, David Todd; American singer and musician (guitar); m. Gillian Welch. *Education:* Berklee School of Music, Boston, MA. *Career:* duo with Gillian Welch; later solo artist, performing as Dave Rawlings Machine; numerous appearances, collaborations. *Recordings include:* albums: with Gillian Welch: Revival 1996, Hell Among The Yearlings 1998, Time (The Revelator) 2001, Soul Journey 2003; solo: A Friend of a Friend 2009. *Website:* www.gillianwelch.com; www.myspace.com/daverawlingsmachine.

RAYE, Collin; American singer; b. (Floyd E. Wray), 22 Aug. 1960, De Queen, Arkansas. *Career:* numerous television appearances; mem. SAG, AFTRA. *Recordings:* albums: All I Can Be 1990, In This Life 1992, Extremes 1994, I Think About You 1995, Christmas The Gift 1996, The Walls Came Down 1998, Tracks 2000, Can't Back Down 2001, Twenty Years and Change 2005, Fearless 2006, Never Going Back 2009. *Honours:* Dove Award for Country Recorded Song of the Year (for The Gift) 1998. *Current Management:* c/o Matthew Stevens, Stevens Management Group, 5016 Spedale Court, Suite 179, Spring Hill, TN 37174, USA. *E-mail:* stevensmgmtgroup@gmail.com. *Website:* www.collinraye.com.

RAYMONDE, Simon; British musician (bass, keyboards); b. 3 April 1962, London, England; m.; one c. *Career:* mem., Cocteau Twins 1984–98; collaboration with 4AD collective, This Mortal Coil; collaboration with pianist Harold Budd and on Spooky's Found Sound 1996; own band 1997–. *Recordings include:* albums: Treasure 1984, The Pink Opaque 1985, The Moon and the Melodies 1986, Blue Bell Knoll 1988, Heaven or Las Vegas 1990, Four Calendar Café 1993, Milk and Kisses 1996, Stars and Topsoil 2000; solo:

Blame Someone Else 1997. *E-mail:* michael@etherweave.com. *Website:* www.cocteautwins.com.

REA, Chris; British singer, songwriter and musician (guitar); b. 4 March 1951, Middlesbrough, Cleveland, England; m. Joan 1980. *Career:* mem., Magdelene 1973–75, name changed to The Beautiful Losers 1975–76; solo artist 1977–; regular UK and European tours and appearances. *Compositions for film and television:* Black Joy 1977, Cross Country 1983, Auf immer und ewig 1986, The Krays 1990, Joking Apart (TV series, theme tune) 1991, Soft Top Hard Shoulder 1992, Cold Sweat (theme tune) 1993, La Passione 1996, Schimanski – Blutsbrüder (TV) 1997, Parting Shots (songs) 1999, Steel River Blues (TV series, theme tune) 2004. *Recordings include:* albums: Whatever Happened To Benny Santini? 1978, Deltics 1979, Tennis 1980, Chris Rea 1982, Water Sign 1983, Wired To The Moon 1984, Shamrock Diaries 1985, On The Beach 1986, Dancing With Strangers 1987, The Road To Hell 1989, Auberge 1991, God's Great Banana Skin 1992, Espresso Logic 1993, The Blue Café 1998, The Road To Hell Pt 2 1999, King Of The Beach 2000, Dancing Down The Stony Road 2002, Blue Street (Five Guitars) 2003, The Blue Jukebox 2004, Blue Guitars 2005, The Return of the Fabulous Hofner Bluenotes 2008. *Honours:* Melody Maker Award for Best Newcomers (with The Beautiful Losers) 1975. *Current Management:* GAA (Gold Artist Agency), 16 Princedale Road, London, W11 4NJ, England. *Telephone:* (20) 7221-1864. *Fax:* (20) 7221-1606. *Website:* www.chrisrea.com.

READER, Eddi, MBE; British singer; b. (Sadenia Reader), 29 Aug. 1959, Glasgow, Scotland; two s. *Career:* fmr lead singer, Fairground Attraction; solo artist 1992–; tours of the UK, Europe, America, Japan; mem. Equity, Musicians' Union. *Recordings include:* albums: with Fairground Attraction: First of a Million Kisses 1988, Ay Fond Kiss 1990; solo: Mirmama 1992, Eddi Reader 1994, Candyfloss and Medicine 1996, Angels and Electricity 1999, Simple Soul 2001, Driftwood 2002, Eddi Reader Sings the Songs of Robert Burns 2003, Peacetime 2006, Love is the Way 2009, Vagabond 2014. *Honours:* BRIT Awards for Best Single, Best Band, Best British Female Artist. *Current Management:* c/o Jane Skinner, Secret Music, 752 Argyle Street, Glasgow, G3 8UJ, Scotland. *Telephone:* (141) 847 0002. *Fax:* (870) 762 7126. *E-mail:* jane@eddireader.com. *E-mail:* info@eddireader.com. *Website:* www.eddireader.co.uk.

REBEL INS (see Inspectah Deck)

REBELLION, Rune; Norwegian musician (guitar); b. (Rune Grønn). *Career:* mem. glam-punk band, Turbonegro 1989–98, 2002–07. *Recordings include:* albums: Turboloid 1990, Hot Cars and Spent Contraceptives 1992, Helta Skelta 1993, Never is Forever 1994, Ass Cobra 1996, Apocalypse Dudes 1998, Scandinavian Leather 2003, Party Animals 2005, Retox 2007. *Honours:* MTV Europe Music Award for Best Norwegian Act 2005.

REBELLO, Jason Matthew; British jazz musician (piano); b. 29 March 1969, Carshalton, Surrey. *Education:* Guildhall School of Music and Drama. *Career:* concerts with Halle Orchestra; played with Wayne Shorter, Freddie Jackson, Claire Martin, Gerard Presencer, Tony Remy and Mica Paris; television presenter, Artrageous. *Recordings include:* albums: A Clearer View 1990, Keeping Time 1993, Make it Real 1995, Last Dance. *Honours:* The Wire Jazz Album of the Year, Perrier British Jazz Pianist of the Year. *E-mail:* info@jasonrebello.co.uk. *Website:* www.jasonrebello.co.uk.

RED, Axelle; Belgian singer; b. (Fabienne Demal), 15 Feb. 1968, Hasselt; m. Filip Vanes 1998; two d. *Career:* released single Little Girl aged 15 years; studied law at univ. before signing recording contract; Sans Plus Attendre became biggest-selling album in Belgian history; records in Dutch, English and French. *Recordings include:* albums: Sans Plus Attendre 1993, A Tâtons 1996, Con Solo Pensarlo 1996, Toujours Moi 1999, Alive 2000, Face A/Face B 2003; singles: Little Girl 1983, Kennedy Boulevard 1988, Arétha Et Moi 1989, Sensualité 1998, Elle Danse Seul 1993, Je T'Attends 1998, La Cour Des Grands (with Youssou N'Dour) 1998, Ce Matin 1999, Manhattan-Kaboul (with Renaud, Best Single Victoires de la Musique) 2002, Je Me Fâche 2003, Toujours 2003, French Soul 2004, J'ai fait un rêve 2005. *Honours:* Victoires de la Musique Award for Best Female Artist 1999. *Address:* c/o Music and Roses, avenue Winston Churchill 157, 1180 Brussels, Belgium (office). *E-mail:* info@music-and-roses.be (office). *Website:* www.axelle-red.com.

REDBONE, Leon; American singer and musician (guitar); two d. *Career:* solo artist 1975–; numerous television, film and radio performances; mem. AFofM, SAG, AFTRA, Equity. *Recordings include:* albums: On The Track 1975, Double Time 1977, Champagne Charlie 1978, From Branch To Branch 1981, Red To Blue 1985, No Regrets 1988, Christmas Island 1988, Sugar 1990, Up A Lazy River 1992, Whistling In The Wind 1994, Any Time 2001. *Honours:* Silver Lion 1989, London International Advertising Award 1989. *Website:* www.leonredbone.com.

REDDOG, Jeff Higgins; American singer and musician (guitar); b. 28 Feb. 1954, Alexandria VA. *Career:* blues player, Southeast USA; founder mem. Reddog. *Recordings include:* albums: with Reddog: Reincarnation 1988, Standing in the Shadow 1989, After the Rain 1993, Early Years 1994.

REDDY, Helen; Australian singer and actress; b. 25 Oct. 1942, Melbourne, Vic.; m. 1st Jeff Wald; m. 2nd Milton Robert Ruth; one s. one d. *Education:* UCLA. *Career:* singer 1966–; numerous concerts worldwide; campaign work for women's political movement and women in prison. *Film appearances:* Airport 1975, Pete's Dragon 1977. *Recordings include:* albums: I Don't Know How To Love Him, 1971; Helen Reddy, 1971; I Am Woman, 1972; Long Hard Climb, 1973; Love Song For Jeffrey, 1974; Free and Easy, 1974; No Way To Treat A Lady, 1975; Music Music, 1976; Ear Candy, 1977; We'll Sing In The Sunshine, 1978; Live In London, 1979; Reddy, 1979; Take What You Find, 1980; Play Me Out, 1981; Imagination, 1983; Take It Home, 1984; When I Dream, 1996; Center Stage, 1998; Christmas, 2001. *Honours:* LA Times Woman of the Year 1975, NAACP Image Award 1974, Maggie Award 1976, Humanitarian Award, B'nai B'rith 1975. *E-mail:* info@helenreddy.com. *Website:* www.helenreddy.com.

REDMAN, (Dr Trevis, Funk Docta Spock); American rap artist; b. (Reggie Noble), Newark, NJ. *Career:* first appeared on friend Erick Sermon's group EPMD's Hardcore and Headbanger; signed to Def Jam on the strength of those performances; starred in How High film with Method Man 2002; collaborations: LL Cool J, Adam F, Lil' Cease, Dave Hollister, D'Angelo, De La Soul. *Recordings:* albums: Whut? Thee Album 1992, Dare Iz A Darkside 1994, Muddy Waters 1997, Doc's Da Name 1998, Blackout! (with Method Man) 2000, Malpractice 2001, Red Gone Wild 2007, Blackout! 2 (with Method Man) 2009. *Address:* c/o Def Jam, 825 Eighth Avenue, New York, NY 10019, USA (office). *Website:* www.funkdoc.com.

REECE, Alex; British DJ and producer; b. 18 Feb. 1970, London. *Career:* early releases on Goldie's Metalheadz label; additional recordings as Jazz Juice, Lunar Funk and Original Playboy; mem. PRS; Musicians' Union. *Recordings:* Basic Principles 1995, I Want You 1995, So Far 1996; singles: Feel the Sunshine, Candles, I Want You/B-Boy Flavour 1995, Acid Lab 1996, Candles 1996; as producer: Platinum Breakz 1996, Rawworks, for Laurent Garnier 1996, Jungle Jazz 1996, In Flux (remixing) 1997, Incredible Sound of Drum 'n' Bass, with Goldie 1999, Remixer of: Mandalay, Solace 2001. *Honours:* Best Jungle Single, Pulp Fiction, Dance Awards, Kiss FM 1995.

REECE, Jason; American singer and musician (drums). *Career:* mem., ...And You Will Know Us By The Trail Of Dead 1993–. *Recordings include:* albums: ...And You Will Know Us By The Trail of Dead 1998, Madonna 1999, Source Tags and Codes 2002, The Secret of Elena's Tomb 2003, Worlds Apart 2005, So Divided 2006, The Century of Self 2009. *E-mail:* merlin@trailofdead.com (office). *Website:* www.trailofdead.com.

REED, Brett; American musician (drums); b. 1972. *Career:* mem. Rancid 1993–2006; numerous live shows. *Recordings:* albums: Rancid 1993, Let's Go 1994, And Out Come The Wolves 1995, Life Won't Wait 1998, Rancid 2000, Indestructible 2003; other collaborations include: Peter Garland, Wayne Kramer.

REED, Leslie (Les) David, OBE; British composer, songwriter, arranger, conductor and musician (multi-instrumentalist); *Chairman, Chapter One Records Ltd;* b. 24 July 1935, Westfield, Woking, Surrey, England; s. of Ralph Henry Reed and Beatrice Caroline Budgen; m. June Williams 1960; one d. *Education:* Kingfield Secondary School, Woking. *Career:* joined John Barry Seven 1958; hit records, numerous concerts, TV appearances; with Roger Cook, launched Beautiful and Damned (musical based on lives of Zelda and Scott Fitzgerald) in the West End, London 2004, with Edward Seago, launched That Woman (musical); mem. Performing Right Soc., British Acad. of Songwriters, Composers and Authors; currently Chair. Chapter One Records Ltd, Rebecca Music Ltd, The Windsors Ltd; Amb., Fed. Int. des Orgs de Festivals (FIDOF); Patron, The Epworth Choir; Dir The Heritage Foundation (GB) 2013. *Compositions include:* for Tom Jones: It's Not Unusual 1965, I'm Coming Home 1967, Delilah 1968, Daughter of Darkness 1970; for Engelbert Humperdinck: The Last Waltz 1967, Les Bicyclettes de Belsize, Winter World of Love; for Des O'Connor: I Pretend 1968, Elvis Presley: Sylvia 1972, Bing Crosby: That's What Life is All About; other: There's A Kind of a Hush, Love is All, Tell Me When, Here it Comes Again, I'm Coming Home, 24 Sycamore, Everybody Knows, Hello Happiness, Gina, Leave a Little Love, I've Got my Eyes on You; numerous other; classical: The Niagara Suite, The Jubilation Suite, The Erin Symphony, The Grand National Anthem, The Olympus Suite. *Television:* Musical Dir: Ready Steady Go, International Pop Proms, The Paul Daniels Show, The Music of Les Reed (BBC), Gadzooks, The Rolf Harris Show (A Swinging Time); guest: Drumbeat; 6-5 Special, Thank Your lucky Stars, Juke Box Jury, New Faces. *Recordings include:* as arranger, conductor: Green Green Grass of Home, Tom Jones 1966; You've Got Your Troubles, The Fortunes; hits recorded by Dave Clark Five, P. J. Proby, Sammy Davis Jr, Connie Francis, Tony Henry with Royal Philharmonic Orchestra (classical tenor version of Delilah); film soundtrack albums: The Girl on a Motorcycle 1968, The Bushbaby 1969, One More Time 1970, George and Mildred 1980, Creepshow 2 1987, Parting Shots 1999; songs have appeared in more than 280 major films; The Les Reed Orchestra orchestral albums: Man of Action; signature tune of Radio Northsea International maintains great interest from pirate radio audiences since early 1970s. *Honours:* Freeman of the City of London 1994; Jimmy Kennedy Award for Outstanding Contrib. to the Art and Heritage of the British Songwriting Industry 1993, 10 Ivor Novello Awards, BMI 'Millionaire' Award for over four million broadcasts in the USA of 'It's Not Unusual', British Heritage Foundation Tribute Award, Grammy Award amongst various European awards, placed by Guinness Book of Hit Records as eighth most successful songwriter of the 1960s 2009. *Address:* Terwick Place, Rogate, nr Petersfield, Hants., GU31 5BY, England (office). *Telephone:* (1730) 821644 (office). *Fax:* (1730) 821597 (office). *E-mail:* les@lesreed.com (office). *Website:* www.chapteronerecords.com (office); www.lesreed.com.

REES, Paul, BA; British journalist; b. West Bromwich; m. Denise Jeffrey; one s. *Education:* Alsager Coll. *Career:* contrib. to Brum Beat; News Ed. Raw – 1995; News Ed. freelance writer, Ed. Kerrang! 1995–2002; Ed. Q magazine 2002–08, Ed.-in-Chief 2008–12. *Publications:* Robert Plant: A Life 2013. *Address:* c/o HarperCollins, 77–85 Fulham Palace Road, Hammersmith, London, W6 8JB, England (office). *Telephone:* (20) 8741-7070 (office). *E-mail:* enquiries@harpercollins.co.uk (office). *Website:* www.harpercollins.co.uk (office).

REES-JONES, John, GLCM, LLCM (TD), CertEd (London); British musician (double bass, electric upright bass); b. 9 Nov. 1948, Cardiff, Wales. *Education:* London Coll. of Music, Univ. of London. *Career:* toured and recorded with Keith Tippett's Centipede in early 70s, and has subsequently worked in theatre, concert, cabaret, studio and jazz fields; deputised in many West End shows, including Me and My Girl, Crazy for You, Miss Saigon, Kiss Me Kate and Guys and Dolls (Nat. Theatre); worked in concert with Vera Lynn, Roy Castle, Helen Shapiro, Anita Harris, Richard Stilgoe, Peter Skellern and Salena Jones; TV appearances include South Bank Show with Petula Clark, the Noel Edmonds Show, Soldier Soldier, numerous other TV and radio appearances in the UK and abroad; toured with the Inkspots 1988–89; worked with many top jazz musicians, including Harry 'Sweets' Edison, Herb Ellis, Barney Kessell, Charlie Byrd and 'Peanuts' Hucko; toured, recorded and appeared on TV as part of Giants of Jazz tour 1993; mem. Humphrey Lyttelton Band from 2004; Campbell Burnap's All Stars; deputiser for the bands of George Melly, Kenny Ball, Acker Bilk, and the Great British Jazz Band; worked in most European countries and in Hong Kong, Pakistan, South America and Lapland; visiting teacher of jazz double bass, Eton Coll. *Recordings include:* Septober Energy (Centipede) 1971, The Giants of Jazz (with Kenny Baker, Don Lusher and Eric Delaney) 1993, The Memory of Tonight (Maxine Daniels) 1996, Sad, Sweet Songs and Crazy Rhythms (with Humphrey Lyttelton and his Band) 2005, and subsequent Humphrey Lyttelton albums. *Address:* May Cottage, 39 Slough Road, Datchet, Berks., SL3 9AL, England (home). *Telephone:* (1753) 581413 (office). *E-mail:* john@rees-jones.co.uk (home).

REESE (see Saunderson, Kevin)

REESE, Della; American gospel singer; b. (Deloreese Patricia Early), 6 July 1931, Detroit, MI; m. 1st Vermont Adolphus Bon Taliaferro (divorced); m. 2nd Leroy Basil Gray (divorced); m. 3rd Franklin Thomas Lett Jr. *Education:* Wayne Univ. *Career:* choir singer 1938–; singer with Mahalia Jackson 1945–49, with Clara Ward; lead singer, Meditation Singers; Erskine Hawkins Orchestra 1956; solo artist 1957–; organized gospel group at Wayne Univ.; numerous television appearances; ordained as minister 2010. *Recordings include:* albums: Special Delivery 1961, The Classic Della 1962, Waltz With Me Della 1964, Let Me Into Your Life 1975, The Classical Della 1980, Della By Starlight 1982, I Like It Like That 1984, Sure Like Lovin' You 1985, And Brilliance 1990, Voice of an Angel 1996, My Soul Feels Better Right Now 1998, All Of Me 2000, Della Reese Sings 2001, Della Young 2002, Touch Me Again 2003, Give It to God 2006, Some of My Best Friends are the Blues 2007. *Honours:* voted Most Promising Singer of the Year 1957. *Current Management:* William Morris Agency, 151 El Camino Drive, Beverly Hills, CA 90212, USA. *Website:* www.dellareese.com.

REEVES, Dianne E.; American jazz singer; b. 23 Oct. 1956, Detroit, MI. *Education:* Univ. of Colorado. *Career:* performed with trumpeter, Clark Terry while at coll.; session work in Los Angeles from 1976; toured with Sergio Mendes 1978, Harry Belafonte 1984; solo artist 1982–; performer, Salt Lake City Winter Olympic Games closing ceremony 2002; collaborations include Affirmation, Charles Aznavour, Daniel Barenboim, Bob Belden, David Benoit, Tom Browne, Wynton Marsalis, Lincoln Center Jazz Orchestra; Creative Chair. in Jazz, LA Philharmonic 2002–. *Recordings include:* albums: Welcome To My Love 1977, For Every Heart 1985, Dianne Reeves 1987, Better Days 1987, I Remember 1988, Come In 1989, Never Too Far 1989, Dianne Reeves 1991, Art And Survival 1993, Quiet After The Storm 1994, The Grand Encounter 1996, That Day 1997, Bridges 1999, In The Moment: Live in Concert (Grammy Award for Best Jazz Vocal Album 2001) 2000, The Calling: Celebrating Sarah Vaughan (Grammy Award for Best Jazz Vocal Album 2002) 2001, A Little Moonlight (Grammy Award for Best Jazz Vocal Album 2004) 2003, Christmas Time Is Here 2004, Good Night, and Good Luck (Grammy Award for Best Jazz Vocal Album 2006) 2005, When You Know 2009, Beautiful Life (Grammy Award for Best Jazz Vocal Album 2015) 2013. *Honours:* Dr hc (Berklee Coll. of Music, Boston) 2003; Montreal Int. Jazz Festival Ella Fitzgerald Award 2002. *Current Management:* Depth of Field Management, 1501 Broadway, Suite 1304, New York, NY 10036, USA. *Telephone:* (212) 302-9200. *Fax:* (212) 382-1639. *Address:* c/o Blue Note Records, 150 Fifth Avenue, New York, NY 10011, USA (office). *Website:* www.diannereeves.com.

REEVES, Martha; American singer, musician (piano, tambourine) and politician; b. 18 July 1941, Eufaula, Ala; d. of Elijah Reeves and Ruby Reeves; m. (divorced); one s. *Education:* Motown Univ., Lee Strassberg's Theatre Inst. *Career:* began as Martha LaVaille, blues singer; lead singer, Martha Reeves and The Vandellas; numerous live appearances and TV and radio broadcasts; music featured in films, including Thelma and Louise, Good Morning Vietnam, Carrie; tours of USA and other countries; performances for charitable organizations; mem. AFTRA, Screen Actors' Guild; spokesperson for Rite-Aid, Breast Cancer Foundation; mem. Detroit City Council 2005–. *Film appearance:* Fairy Tales 1979. *Compositions:* Love is Like a Heatwave, Nowhere to Run, Dancing in the Street. *Recordings include:* albums: with the Vandellas: Come and Get These Memories 1963, Love Is Like A Heat Wave 1963, A Love Like Yours 1963, Quicksand 1963, Live Wire 1964, In My Lonely Room 1964, Dancing In The Street 1964, Wild One 1964, Nowhere To Run 1965, Love (Makes Me Do Foolish Things) 1965, You've Been In Love Too Long 1965, My Baby Loves Me 1966, I'm Ready For Love 1966, Jimmy Mack 1967, Third Finger, Left Hand 1967, Honey Chile 1967, Live Wire!: The Singles 1962–72 1993, Dancing in the Street: Their Greatest Hits 1995, Motown Milestones 1995, Best Of 1999; solo: Martha Reeves 1974, Rainbow 1975, For the Rest of My Life 1977, We Meet Again 1978, Gotta Keep Moving 1980, Home to You 2004. *Publications:* Dancing in the Street (Confessions of a Motown Diva) (autobiog.), Martha Reeves Exclusive Newsletter. *Honours:* Dick Clark Soul of America Award 1992, Rhythm and Blues Foundation Pioneer Award 1993, Black Women in Publishing Award 1994. *Current Management:* c/o The Booking Entertainment Agency Ltd, 275 Madison Avenue, Sixth Floor, New York, NY 10016, USA. *Address:* c/o Detroit City Council, 1340 Coleman A. Young Municipal Center, 2 Woodward Avenue, Detroit MI 48226, USA. *Website:* www.missmarthareeves.com.

REEVES, Thomas (Tom) W., Jr; Welsh sound engineer, DJ and musician (electric bass); *Owner and Engineer, Cat's Voice Productions;* b. 14 Feb. 1953, Boston, MA, USA; m. Carol Reeves 1998; one s. one d. *Education:* ATI Technical Inst., School of Contemporary Music, Brookline, MA, Cabrillo Coll., CA, Graduate School of Contemporary Music. *Career:* owner, Cat's Voice Productions; Asst Man., Vibrations 1988; DJ, Encore Entertainment, Newbury, MA 1989–; Prod., Sound Block Studios, Salem, NH 1990–; owner and engineer, Cat's Voice Productions, MA 1990–; owner, Reel Adventures II Recording Studio; representative, Market America Inc.; Man. and mem., Protex Blues Band 1991; Marketing Agent, Tennie Komar, Fine and Devine; mem. American Federation of Musicians, ASCAP, DJs of America, Brotherhood of Electrical Workers, Nat. Asscn of Independent Record Distributors, Nat. Asscn of Music Merchants. *Recordings as producer:* MC Chill 1990, Clean Shot 1988–, One Groove At A Time 1991, The Mangled Ducklings 1993, Hot, Moist, Pink and Stinky 1993, Paul Wilcox: Signature 1996. *Recordings:* Dust of Adam 2004, Falling Upward 2005. *Address:* 114 Kennebunk Pond Road, Lyman, ME 04002-7719, USA. *Telephone:* (207) 499-2646. *E-mail:* catsvoice21@hotmail.com (office); catreeves@adelphia.net (home).

REGAN, Julianne; British singer and musician (bass); b. England. *Career:* fmr music journalist; backing singer, The Mission; mem., Gene Loves Jezebel; founder mem. and lead singer, All About Eve 1986–. *Recordings:* albums: with All About Eve: All About Eve 1988, Scarlet And Other Stories 1989, Touched By Jesus 1991, Ultraviolet 1992, Fairy Light Nights Vol. 1 2000, Fairy Light Nights Vol. 2 2001, Live and Electric At The Union Chapel 2002, Live At Brixton 2003, Iceland 2003, Cinemasonic 2003, Acoustic Nights 2003, Keepsakes 2006.

RÉGINE, (Régina Zylberberg); Belgian singer and cabaret artist; b. 26 Dec. 1929, Etterbeck; d. of Joseph Zylberberg and Tauba Zylberberg (née Rodstein); m. 2nd Roger Choukroun 1969; one s. (from previous m.). *Education:* privately in Aix-en-Provence, Lyon and Paris. *Career:* cabaret compère at Chez Régine, Paris (first discotheque) 1958–61, in Paris 1961–81, Deauville, France 1965, Régine's Club, Paris 1971–, Monte-Carlo 1971–, Régine's, Rio de Janeiro and Bahia,Brazil, Régine's New York, USA, Le Palace, Paris 1992–; has performed in numerous nat. and int. concerts and tours, including concerts at L'Olympia 1968, 1990 and Bobino, Paris 1973, Bouffes-du-Nord 1993, tours of Belgium 1970, Canada and USA; Creator 'Régine's' perfumes 1989; Co-founder Presse et Public public relations co. 1990–; Pres. SOS Drogue International 1985–. *Songs include:* J'ai la boule au plafond, La Grande Zoa, Rue des rosiers, Patchouli-Chinchilla, Mille fois par jour, Les balayeurs, La fille que je suis, Fais-moi danser, La bonne adresse pour chiens perdus, La guimauve. *Films include:* Le Couteau dans la plaie 1962, Jeu de massacre 1967, Mazel Tov ou le mariage 1969, Sortie de secours 1970, Le train 1973, The Seven-Per-Cent Solution 1976, Les Ripoux 1984, Grosse fatigue 1996. *Publications include:* Appelle-moi par mon prénom (Prix Bruno Coquatrix) 1985, La drogue, parlons-en 1987. *Honours:* Chevalier des Arts et des Lettres; Grand Prix Acad. du Disque Français 1969, Ruban Rouge, Chanson Française. *Address:* Patrick Goavec, 10 avenue Georges V, 75008 Paris, France. *Website:* www.regine-lesite.com.

REHMAN, Wajid; singer. *Career:* mem. Anglo-Asian duo, Sweetblood 2005–. *Recordings include:* album: Friendly Infidel 2005.

REICHMANN DE SALAS, Silke, DipJug; German musician (hurdy-gurdy, flute); b. 1 March 1966, Frankfurt. *Education:* Kassel Univ., Frankfurt Conservatory, masterclass with Valentin Clastrier, studied with Helmut Eisel. *Career:* musician, folk dance coach with Die Hummel 1982–86; teacher at workshops in Germany, The Netherlands, France 1983–; musician in folk and world music band, Trio Grande 1984–; with Paul Engel, world premiere in Philharmonic Hall, Munich 1987; solo radio broadcasts, Berlin 1994; special concert for the visit of Germany's Pres., Dr Roman Herzog 1996; mem. EU World Music Project, Kaleidoscope, touring in Sweden, Norway and Finland 1998; concert at reception of Minister of Women's Affairs, Int. Women's Day 1999; teacher of hurdy-gurdy, Music School, Berlin 1999–; mem. ProFolk, GEMA, GVL. *Compositions:* Mazurka des amis, Laisser tomber!, Symbati, Zwei Lieben, Ghostdance, Vielfaches Fuer Aspe. *Recordings:* with Trio Grande: Nabucodonosor 1990, Bagage 1994, PiloPao 1998; with Madre:

Ghostdance on Mesmerismo 1997. *Honours:* first prize Hurdy Gurdy Duo Competition, St Chartier, France 1991. *Address:* Hasenheide 51, 10967 Berlin, Germany (home). *Telephone:* (30) 42851734 (home).

REID, Antonio 'LA'; American record company executive, producer and musician; *Chairman, Island Def Jam Music Group. Career:* producer, Boyz II Men, Whitney Houston; co-founder, Co-Pres., LaFace Records 1989–2000; Pres. and CEO, Arista Records 2000–04; Chair., Island Def Jam Music Group 2004–. *Honours:* Grammy Award for Producer. *Address:* Island Def Jam Group, Worldwide Plaza, 825 Eighth Avenue, 28th Floor, New York, NY 10019, USA (office). *Website:* www.islanddefjam.com (office).

REID, Charlie; British singer and songwriter; twin brother of Craig Reid. *Career:* co-founder, The Proclaimers 1983–; numerous tours, live appearances and TV and radio broadcasts; song, I'm Gonna Be (500 Miles) played on the Mars space probe. *Recordings include:* albums: Sunshine On Leith 1988, This Is The Story 1994, Hit The Highway 1994, Persevere 2001, Born Innocent 2003, Restless Soul 2005, Life With You 2007, Notes and Rhymes 2009, Like Comedy 2012. *Current Management:* Braw Music Management, 31 Hartington Place, Edinburgh, EH10 4LF, Scotland. *Telephone:* (131) 221-0011. *Fax:* (131) 221-1313. *E-mail:* kenny@brawmusic.com. *Website:* www.proclaimers.co.uk.

REID, Craig; British singer and songwriter; twin brother of Charlie Reid. *Career:* co-founder, The Proclaimers 1983–; numerous tours, live appearances and TV and radio broadcasts; song, I'm Gonna Be (500 Miles) played on the Mars space probe. *Recordings:* albums: Sunshine On Leith 1988, This Is The Story 1994, Hit The Highway 1994, Persevere 2001, Born Innocent 2003, Restless Soul 2005, Life With You 2007, Notes and Rhymes 2009, Like Comedy 2012. *Current Management:* Braw Music Management, 31 Hartington Place, Edinburgh, EH10 4LF, Scotland. *Telephone:* (131) 221-0011. *Fax:* (131) 221-1313. *E-mail:* kenny@brawmusic.com. *Website:* www.proclaimers.co.uk.

REID, Jim; British singer and musician (guitar); b. 1961, East Kilbride, Scotland; brother of William Reid. *Career:* founder mem., The Jesus & Mary Chain 1984–99, 2007–. *Recordings include:* albums: Psychocandy 1985, Darklands 1987, Automatic 1989, Honey's Dead 1992, Stoned & Dethroned 1994, Munki 1998. *Website:* www.thejesusandmarychain.org.

REID, Johnny; Canadian (b. British) country music singer; b. 21 Aug. 1974, Lanark, Scotland; m. Jennifer Reid 2000. *Education:* Bishop's Univ., Lennoxville, PQ. *Career:* moved to Canada 1988; signed to JCD Records for first album 1997; later signed to Open Road Records 2005–09, with EMI 2009–. *Recordings:* albums: Another Day, Another Dime 1997, Johnny Reid 2000, Born to Roll 2005, Kicking Stones (Canadian Country Music Asscn Award for Album of the Year 2008) 2007, Dance with Me (Canadian Country Music Asscn Awards for Album of the Year 2009, for Top Selling Canadian Album 2010) 2009, Christmas 2009, A Place Called Love (Juno Award for Country Album of the Year 2011, Canadian Country Music Asscn Award for Top Selling Canadian Album 2011) 2010, Fire It Up (Canadian Country Music Asscn Award for Top Selling Canadian Album 2012, Juno Awards for Country Album of the Year 2013, for Top Selling Canadian Album 2013) 2012, A Christmas Gift to You (Juno Awards for Adult Contemporary Album of the Year 2014, for Top Selling Canadian Album 2014) 2014; also appears on: The Long Way Home, Terri Clark 2010. *Honours:* Canadian Country Music Asscn Awards for Ind. Male Artist of the Year 2007, for Male Artist of the Year 2008, 2009, 2011, for Video of the Year 2009, 2011, Fan's Choice Awards 2009, 2010, 2011, 2012, 2014, 2015, for Single of the Year 2010. *Current Management:* c/o Tracey Wilder, Johnny Mac Entertainment. *E-mail:* souledout@johnnyreid.com. *Website:* www.johnnymacentertainment.com; www.johnnyreid.com.

REID, Delroy (Junior); Jamaican reggae singer and record producer; b. 1965, Kingston. *Career:* first recording aged 13; mem. Voice of Progress group; solo artist early 1980s, 1989–; singer, Black Uhuru 1985–88; Founder JR Productions record label and recording studio; record producer for artists including Junior Demus, Ninjaman, Dennis Brown and Gregory Isaacs. *Recordings include:* albums: with Voice of Progress: Mini-Bus Driver; with Black Uhuru: Brutal 1986, Positive; solo: Boom Shack A Lack, Back To Back, Original Foreign Mind, Visa 1994, Junior Reid and the Bloods 1995, Listen to the Voices 1996, Big Timer 2000. *Address:* JR Productions, 39b Eastwood Park Road, Kingston, Jamaica.

REID, Terrance (Terry) James; British singer and musician (guitar, piano); b. 13 Nov. 1949, Huntingdon, Cambridgeshire; two d. *Career:* toured with P.J. and the Jaywalkers, The Rolling Stones, Ike and Tina Turner, The Hollies, Scott Walker, The Small Faces, Paul Jones, Cream, The Beach Boys, Jethro Tull, Del Shannon; television includes: Whistle Test; Lulu, David Frost; mem, PRS. *Compositions:* albums: Bang Bang You're Terry Reid 1968, Terry Reid 1969, River 1973, Seed Of Memory 1976, Rogue Wave 1979, The Driver 1991, Terry Reid (compilation) 1992, Alive 2004, Silver White Light 2004, Superlungs 2004. *Website:* www.terryreid.com.

REID, Vernon; American musician (guitar) and songwriter; b. London, England; m. Mia McLeod 1991. *Education:* Manhattan Community Coll., studied with Ted Dunbar and Rodney Jones. *Career:* musician with Defunkt, Decoding Society; founder mem. of funk rock group, Living Colour 1985–95, 2000–; numerous tours and concerts, festival appearances; mem. Black Rock Coalition. *Photography exhibition:* Once Upon A Time, Called Now (Chicago) 1991. *Compositions include:* writer and producer of tracks for B. B. King 1990.

Recordings include: albums: Vivid 1988, Time's Up 1991, Biscuits 1991, Stain 1993, Collideøscope 2003, The Chair in the Doorway 2009. *Honours:* International Rock Awards Elvis Award for Best New Band 1989, MTV Award for Best New Artist, for Best Group Video, for Best Stage Performance 1989, Grammy Awards for Best Hard Rock Performance (for Cult of Personality) 1990, (for Time's Up) 1991, Rolling Stone Critics' Poll Winner of Best Band 1991. *E-mail:* livingcolourinfo@yahoo.com (office). *Website:* www .livingcolourmusic.com.

REID, William; British singer and musician (guitar); b. 1958, East Kilbride, Scotland; brother of Jim Reid. *Career:* founder mem., The Jesus & Mary Chain 1984–99, 2007–. *Recordings include:* albums: Psychocandy 1985, Darklands 1987, Automatic 1989, Stoned & Dethroned 1994, Munki 1998. *Website:* www.thejesusandmarychain.org.

REID, Wilson; singer and musician (guitar); b. 28 Feb. 1961, Accra, Ghana. *Education:* qualified teacher. *Career:* lead singer, songwriter, Death Bang Party 1986–94; various tours and live appearances; singer and guitarist, The Tarantinos; mem. Musicians' Union, Equity. *Publication:* Thrills, Pills and Backache: The Hank Williams Story 1995. *Address:* 842 Garratt Lane, London SW17 0NA, England.

REID DICK, William F.; audio producer and engineer; b. 19 July 1952, London, England; m. Lorna Hewitt 1982. *Career:* CBS Studios, Whitfield Street, West Indies, 1972–73; Ramport Studios, London, 1973–83; Freelance, 1983–95; mem, Re-Pro; PRS. *Recordings:* with Thin Lizzy: Jailbreak; Johnny The Fox; Live and Dangerous; also Saxon: Wheels of Steel; Strong Arm of The Law; Motörhead: Iron Fist; also Carlene Carter; Curved Air; Roger Daltrey. *Honours:* 2 Platinum, 5 Gold, 6 Silver albums; Ampex Gold Reel Award. *Address:* No. 1, 35 Wemyss Road, Blackheath, London SE3 0TG, England.

REIFF, Soren; Danish musician (guitar, keyboard, bass), producer, composer and writer; b. 22 Oct. 1962, Butterup. *Education:* music coll., Holstebro. *Career:* toured Europe and USA with different artists and as a solo artist 1989–98; guitarist in TV house band appearing on some 200 chatshows, Meyerheim and Co. 1991–94; played with Robert Palmer, Randy Crawford, Paul Young, Toots Thielemanns, Jamie Walters, Curtis Stigers, Bonnie Tyler, Robin Beck and Suzi Q 1991–98; played in house band on TV show, Don't Forget Your Toothbrush, Denmark 1995, on Safari TV show 1996; founder and owner, DaRoof production company 1996–; Musical Dir of house band on It's Saturday Night, Denmark 1997; appeared on 199 shows with Danish trio, Linie 3 1997–98; bd mem. Music Highschool of Jyderup, Denmark 1998. *Recordings:* numerous recordings as session musician with Tower of Power, Michael Brecker and Madness 4 Real and artists from the UK, Scandinavia, Japan, India and Mexico; solo albums: Funky Flavas 2003, Miss You 2010, Gratitude 2015. *Publications:* Reiffs riffs 2004, Reiffs rytmer 2005, Reiffs riffs vol 2 2007, Reiffs rytmer vol 2 2008, Gode Råd 2010. *Telephone:* 32-84-68-46 (office). *E-mail:* info@reiff.dk (office). *Website:* www.sorenreiff.com.

REIHSE, Andreas, (April); German musician (keyboards, electronics, vocals); b. 21 Jan. 1968, Bad Säckingen, Waldshut, Baden-Württemberg; s. of Uwe Reihse and Brigitte Reihse; one s. *Education:* studied media science, German language and literature, philosophy and audio-visual communications in Düsseldorf. *Career:* mem. electro-pop group, Kreidler 1994–; mem. Klaus Dinger's la!NEU?; mem. techno project, Binford; performs solo as Andreas Reihse, also as April; music for artists, films, theatre plays; curator for artists' music and events at Image Movement, Berlin. *Plays:* Alexij Koshkarov's Tortenschlacht, Malkasten Düsseldorf 2001, I Will, Düsseldorf 2005, Südstadtvirus (with Thea Djordjadze), Studio Voltaire, London 2005, Untitled (with Thea Djordjadze), Serpentine Gallery, London 2010, A&R (with Annika Henderson), PSM Gallery, Berlin, Musée d'Art Moderne, Strasbourg, Salon des Amateurs, Düsseldorf, Inkonst, Malmö 2015, The General Line (with Redmond Entwistle), Pompidou Centre, Paris, South London Gallery, Synagogue Delme 2015, Awst & Walther, Berlin 2015, Der Tag… (Kreidler with Sibylle Berg), Berlin, Hamburg, Munich, Cologne 2015, A&W: Prometheus Nu, Betty Nansen Teatret, Copenhagen 2015. *Dance:* Untitled (with Sigal Zouk), Wales 2014, Untitled (with Sigal Zouk), Berlin 2015. *Recordings include:* albums with Kreidler: Riva 1994, Weekend 1996, Resport 1997, Appearance and The Park 1998, Kreidler 2000, Chicks on Speed/ Kreidler Sessions 2001, Eve Future 2002, Eve Future Recall 2004, OST Durchfahrtsland 2006, Mosaik 2014 2010, Tank 2011, Untitled 2011, Mars Chronicles 2011, DEN 2012, OST The Last Hijack 2013, ABC 2014; albums with la!NEU?: Düsseldorf 1996, Zeeland 1997, Live in Tokyo 1998, Live in Tokyo #2 1999, Cha Cha 2000; Andreas Reihse: Romantic Comedy 2011; with Conrad Schnitzler: Con-Struct 2012; with Isaac B. Trogdon. Entropie OST 2015; with Annika H.enderson: A&R Weeping Willow 2015. *Honours:* Type Directors Club, New York 1997, scholarship Atelierprogramm Imhoff-Stiftung/Kölnischer Kunstverein, Cologne 2008, Interactive Emmy, Last Hijack Website 2015. *Current Management:* c/o Jonas Förster, Howdy Partner Booking, Stahltwiete 10, 22761 Hamburg, Germany. *Telephone:* (1573) 3872409. *Fax:* (40) 88166622. *E-mail:* jonas@howdypartnerbooking.com. *Website:* www.howdypartnerbooking.com. *Address:* c/o Spreepark Studios, Gutenbergstrasse 6, 10587 Berlin, Germany (office). *E-mail:* a@reihse.de (office); a@i-april.de. *Website:* www.ikreidler.de; www.reihse.de.

REIMERS-WESSBERG, Marianne, BA; Swedish music publisher; b. 6 Aug. 1957, Stockholm; m. H G Wessberg; one s., two d. *Career:* Editor, Music Teachers' Magazine, Musik Kultur, 1983–88; Managing Director, Reimers AB, 1990–; mem, Music Publishers Asscn; STIM; Swedish Music Information

Center. *Publications:* Lyssna ar Silver, Spela ar Guld, (To Listen Is Silver – To Play Is Gold), 1991.

REIS, Sérgio; Brazilian singer and actor; b. (Sérgio Bavini), 23 June 1940, São Paulo; s. of Erico Bavini and Clara Reis Bavini; m. Ruth Bavini; two s. *Career:* solo recording artist, specialising in sertanejo style 1958–. *Television:* as actor: O Menino da Porteira 1976, Mágoa de Boiadeiro 1977, Paraíso 1982, O Filho Adotivo 1984, Pantanal 1990, O Rei do Gado 1996, Bicho do Mato 2006. *Recordings include:* over 40 albums including: Compacto 1966, Coração de Papel 1967, Anjo Triste 1969, Sérgo Reis 1973, João de Barro 1974, Saudades da Minha Terra 1975, Retrato do Meu Sertão 1976, Disco de Ouro 1977, O Menino da Porteira 1977, Relaciones Internacionales 1977, Mágoa de Boiadeiro 1978, Natureza 1978, Boiadeiro Errante 1981, O Melhor de Sérgo Reis 1982, A Sanfona do Menino 1982, Acervo Especial 1993, Ventos Uivantes 1994, Marcando Estrada 1996, O Rei do Gado 1996, Vida Violeira 1997, Boiadeiro 1997, Sérgio Reis do Tamanho do Brazil 1998, Essencial 1998, Popularidade 1999, Jovem Guarda 2000, Dose Dupla 2000, Sérgio Reis e Convidados 2000, 100 Anos de Música 2001, Nossas Canções 2002, O Divino Espírito do Sertão 2003, Sérgio Reis e Filhos: Violas e Violeiros 2003, Tributo a Goiá 2006, Em Foco 2007, Coração Estradeiro (Latin Grammy Award for Best Sertanejo Album 2009) 2008. *Current Management:* Consumídia Publicidade, Rua Maestro João Gomes de Araújo, 106, 3° andar, 02332-020 São Paulo, Brazil. *Telephone:* (11) 2959-0322. *Fax:* (11) 2959-0856. *E-mail:* souza@consumidia.com.br. *Website:* www.consumidia.com.br; sergioreis.uol.com.br.

REISIG, Bernd; German media manager; b. 10 March 1963, Frankfurt. *Career:* founded concert agency, working with artists including Purple Schulz, Bruce Cockburn, Extrabeit 1984; founded music publishing agency 1985; founded management agency 1987, representing artists including Nena, Badesalz, Thomas Koschwitz, Matthias Beltz, Christian Kahrman; founded RMG Merchandising and RMG Music Entertainment 1993, representing artists including Nena, The Stroke, Mellow D, McDowell-Tarr, Dan, Badesalz, Bodo Bach; several dance projects; share in radio station, Radio 01 1994; share in advertising agency Koschwitz-Kommunikation; share in television production company Feedback; mem, IFPI, GEMA. *Honours:* Grimme-Preis.

REMI, Salaam; American hip-hop and R&B record producer and musician (guitar, bass guitar, keyboards, percussion); *Executive Vice-President of A&R, Sony Music Entertainment*; s. of Van Gibbs. *Career:* made recording debut on Kurtis Blow album Kingdom Blow 1986; record producer 1992–; has produced numerous artists including Corinne Bailey Rae, Big Boi, B.o.B., Jamie Cullum, Craig David, Faith Evans, Fugees, Nelly Furtado, Cee Lo Green, Whitney Houston, Ini Kamoze, Jurassic 5, Alicia Keys, Leona Lewis, Biz Markie, Mis-Teeq, Monica, Ms Dynamite, Nas, Ne-Yo, Pras, Usher, Amy Winehouse, Zhigge; Exec. Vice-Pres. of A&R, Sony Music Entertainment 2012–. *Recordings include:* albums: as musician: Kingdom Blow, Kurtis Blow 1986; as producer: Zhigge, Zhigge 1992, Rough & Ready Vol. 2, Shabba Ranks 1993, Non-Fiction, Black Sheep 1994, Blunted on Reality, Fugees 1994, The Score, Fugees 1996, Can-I-Bus, Canibus 1998, Art and Life, Beenie Man 2000, Stillmatic, Nas 2001, A Little Deeper, Ms Dynamite 2002, Frank, Amy Winehouse 2003, Mis-Teeq, Mis-Teeq 2004, Mind, Body & Soul, Joss Stone 2004, Feedback, Jurassic 5 2006, Back to Black, Amy Winehouse 2006, Spirit, Leona Lewis 2007, The Reason, Lemar 2008, Fearless, Jazmine Sullivan 2008, Mi Plan, Nelly Furtado 2009, Hidden Treasures, Amy Winehouse 2011, I Remember Me, Jennifer Hudson 2011, R.E.D., Ne-Yo 2012. *Address:* c/o Sony Music Entertainment, 550 Madison Avenue, New York, NY 10022, USA (office). *Telephone:* (212) 833-8000 (office). *Fax:* (212) 833-5828 (office). *Website:* www.sonymusic.com (office); www.salaamremi.com.

RENAUD, Line, (Jacqueline Gasté); French singer and actress; b. 2 July 1928, Nieppe; d. of Edmond Enté and Simone Enté (née Renard); m. Louis Gasté 1950 (died 1995). *Career:* singing debut, Paris 1945; singer in cabaret shows including the Moulin Rouge, Paris 1950, 1954, 1957, Casino de Paris 1959–63, 1966–67, 1976–79, Las Vegas, USA 1964–65, 1968–70, 1970–71; nat. and int. tours; numerous TV appearances, also co-producer of shows broadcast by Office de Radiodiffusion-Télévision Française (ORTF) 1972–73; f. Asscn des Artistes Contre le Sida (Artists Against AIDS). *Plays and cabaret shows include:* Désirs 1966–67, Flesh (producer) 1970–71, Parisline 1978–79, Folle Amanda (Archange for Best Actress of the Year) 1982, Pleins feux 1991, La Visite de la Vieille Dame 1995, Poste restante 2002. *Films include:* La route du bonheur, La Madelon (Prix du Prestige français) 1955, Mademoiselle et son gang 1956, Sur la piste du rock and roll 1959, Le mariage de Figaro 1989, Ripoux contre Ripoux 1990, The Sands of Time 1992, I Can't Sleep 1994, Ma Femme Me Quitte 1996, Belle-maman 1999, Chaos 2001, 18 Ans Apres 2003, Men and Women 2005, La Maison du Bonheur 2006, Bienvenue chez les Ch'tis 2007. *Publications include:* Bonsoir mes souvenirs 1963, Les brumes d'où je viens 1989, Loulou, envoie-moi un arc-en-ciel 2002. *Honours:* Chevalier, Légion d'honneur, Officier des Arts et des Lettres; Médaille de Vermeil, Ville de Paris, Silver Mask for Career (Italy) 1988. *Address:* 5 rue du Bois-de-Boulogne, 75116 Paris (home); Les Cèdres bleus, La Jonchère, 92500 Rueil-Malmaison, France (home).

RENAULT, Nathalie; French musician (banjo, trumpet and guitar); b. 26 Nov. 1966, Paris. *Education:* Ecole Nat. Supérieure des Beaux-Arts, Paris, Conservatoire de Musique, Clamart, Hauts-de-Seine. *Career:* concerts include Int. Music Festival, Riga, Latvia, Centre Culturel Français, Skopje, Macedonia, Jazz Festival, Corinth, Greece, Malmö Festival, Sweden, Cromwell Festival, Upton Upon Severn, UK, Oude Stijl Jazz Festival, Breda,

Netherlands, 12 tage Jazz, Frankfurt, Germany, Dixie Jazz Festival, Sargans, Switzerland, Jazz Festival, Vannes, Jazz Band Ball, Paris, Nice Jazz Festival, Jazz à Vienne, Bix Festival, Chicago USA, Jazz in Toronto, Canada, Dubai. *Recordings:* with female jazz (old style) band Certains L'Aiment Chaud (Some Like It Hot), (album) 1985, (album) 1991, J'ai Deux Amours 1995, April In Paris 2002, En concert 2010; with quartet Jazz at Four: Come Back Sweet Papa 2005; with quartet Le Fil à Monique de Pantin: 1,000 tours minute 2006; with Be Bop Stompers: Giant Stomps 2010. *Honours:* Jazz Acad. Sidney Bechet Prize, Paris 1992. *Address:* 4 rue des Pommiers, 93500 Pantin, France (office). *Telephone:* 1-48-40-99-89 (office). *Fax:* 1-48-40-99-89 (office). *E-mail:* nathaliebanjo@orange.fr (office). *Website:* www.supermoniqueclub.com.

RENE, Tawamba; Central African Republic author, composer and singer; b. 27 July 1962, Bangassou; m. Fozen Brigitte; one s. one d. *Career:* dancer, Johny Tezano 1987–91; many TV and radio broadcasts, festival appearances. *Compositions include:* Bibi Kitoko, Palauce Sonkouss, Bjamena, Sambara Reko, Kibindo Lauce, Tika Kolela. *Recordings include:* Bibi Kotoko, Confiance Perdue, Palauce Sonkouss, Bjamena, Sambara Perko, Kibindo Lauce, Tika Kolela.

RENLIDEN, Ivan; Swedish musician (piano) and arranger; b. 27 Sept. 1936, Mönsterås; m. Sonja 1956; one s. one d. *Education:* Academy of Music, Stockholm. *Career:* musical leader, arranger and pianist, major stages in Stockholm; numerous radio and TV appearances, recordings with popular Swedish artists; mem. STIM, SAMI. *Recordings:* Svenska Melodier, Ivan Renliden Spelar Ivan Renliden, Ain't Misbehavin, Spectrum, Ivan Renliden Spelar Chopin. *Honours:* Cultural Prize of Stockholm 1975. *Address:* Ullerudsb 79, 12373 Farsta, Sweden.

RENO, Mike; Canadian singer and songwriter. *Career:* fmr mem., Moxy; founder mem. rock group, Loverboy 1980–89; extensive tours. *Compositions include:* co-writer, with Bryan Adams, Jon Bon Jovi, Richie Sambora, for Loverboy tracks. *Recordings include:* Albums: Loverboy 1980, Get Lucky 1981, Keep It Up 1983, Lovin' Every Minute of It 1985, Wildside 1987, Big Ones (compilation) 1989, Six 1997, Live, Loud And Loose 1982–86, 2001, Singles: Turn Me Loose; The Kid Is Hot Tonite, Working For The Weekend, Hot Girls In Love, Lovin' Every Minute of It. *Honours:* JUNO Awards: Album of the Year, Loverboy 1981, Get Lucky 1982, Single of the Year, Turn Me Loose 1981, Group of Year 1981, 1982, Composer of the Year (with Paul Dean) 1981, Tribute To West Coast Music Awards: Best Group 1981, 1982, Best Album 1981, 1982, Song of the Year, The Kid Is Hot Tonite 1981, Most Promising Act 1981; International Achievement Award 1984, Rock Band of Year 1981. *Website:* www.loverboyband.com.

RENZER, David, BA; American music industry executive; *Chairman and CEO, Universal Music Publishing Group*. *Education:* New York Univ. *Career:* began career at Zomba Music Publishing, served as Sr Vice-Pres. and Gen. Man.; joined MCA Music Publishing (later Universal Music Publishing Group) 1996, currently Chair. and CEO; mem. Bd of Dirs ASCAP, Nat. Music Publishers' Asscn, Foundation for Ethnic Understanding; mem. Exec. Bd City of Hope, founder Songs of Hope Celebrity Sheet Music Auction. *Address:* UMPG, 2440 Sepulveda Boulevard, Suite 100, Los Angeles, CA 90064-1712, USA (office). *Telephone:* (310) 235-4700 (office). *Fax:* (310) 235-4900 (office). *Website:* www.universalmusicpublishing.com (office).

RESCALA, Tim; Brazilian composer, arranger and musician (piano); b. (Luiz Augusto), 21 Nov. 1961, Rio de Janeiro; m. Claudia Mele 1995; one d. *Education:* Universidade Federal do Rio de Janeiro, studies piano with Maria Yêda Cadah, composition with Hans-Joachim Koellreutter. *Career:* works with both classical and popular music; founding mem. Estúdio da Glória (composers' cooperative) 1981; Musical Producer, TV Globo 1988–; Dir, Sala Baden Powell, Rio de Janeiro 2005–. *Compositions:* opera: O Homem que Sabia Português 1998, A Redenção pelo Sonho 1998, 22 Antes Depois 2002, À Sombra do Sucesso 2002; children's musical: Pianíssimo 1993, A Orquestra das Sonhos 1996, Papagueno 1997, O Cavalinho Azul 2001, A Turma do Pererê 2004; over 50 instrumental pieces. *Recordings:* Cliché Music, Estudio da Glória, Romance Policial, Desritmificações, Dolores, Giramundo. *Honours:* first prize, Villa-Lobos competition, Mambembe Prize 1993, Prize of Rio de Janeiro Municipality to write an opera, Shell Prize for Music 2001. *Website:* www.timrescala.com.br.

RESHAMMIYA, Himesh; Indian composer for film; b. 23 July 1973, Bhavnagar, Gujarat; s. of Vipin Reshammiya and Madhu Reshammiya. *Education:* Hill Grange School, Mumbai. *Career:* fmr producer of Gujarati TV serials, later Nat. Network and Hindi serials; composed for TV serials, later films; acted in Hindi films. *Compositions for film:* Pyar Kiya To Darna Kya (title song) 1998, Hello Brother 1999, Dulhan Hum Le Jayenge 2000, Kurukshetra 2000, Kahin Pyaar Na Ho Jaaye 2000, Aamdani Atthanni Kharcha Rupaiya 2001, Kyaa Dil Ne Kahaa 2002, Humraaz 2002, Yeh Hai Jalwa 2002, Chalo Ishq Ladaaye 2002, Chura Liyaa Hai Tumne 2003, Tere Naam 2003, Zameen 2003, Ishq Hai Tumse 2004, Bardaasht 2004, Julie 2004, Taarzan 2004, Dil ne Jise Apna Kaha 2004, Aitraaz 2004, Dil Maange More!! 2004, Vaada 2005, Insan 2005, Blackmail 2005, Nigehbeen 2005, Kuchh Meetha Ho Jaye 2005, Main Aisa Hi Hoon 2005, Silsilay 2005, Yakeen 2005, Maine Pyar Kyun Kiya? 2005, Aashiq Banaya Aapne 2005, Koi Aap Sa 2005, Kyon Ki 2005, Vaah! 2005, Anjaane 2005, Tom, Dick and Harry 2006, Aksar 2006, Shaadi se Pehle 2006, Banaras 2007, 36 China Town 2006, Phir Hera Pheri 2006, Chuo Chuo Ke 2006, Anthony Kaun Hai? 2006, Aap Ki Khatir 2006, Rocky: The Rebel 2006, Anjaam 2007, Red: The Dark Side 2007,

Namastey London 2007, Shakalaka Boom Boom 2007, Good Boy, Bad Boy 2007, Fool N Final 2007, Apne 2007, Aap kaa Surroor 2007, Darling 2007, Nanhe Jaisalmer 2007, Welcome 2007, My Name is Anthony Gonsalves 2008, Dasavatharam 2008, Karzzz 2008, Radio 2009. *Honours:* Filmfare Best Male Playback Award 2005. *Address:* A/403 Sea Shell Apartments, 7 Bungalows, Versova, Andheri (w), Mumbai 400 061, India.

REVELL, Graeme; composer; b. 23 Oct. 1955, Auckland, New Zealand. *Education:* University of Auckland. *Career:* mem. BMI. *Compositions:* For TV: Bangkok Hilton, 1989; Psycho IV: The Beginning, 1991; Dune, 2000; For film: Dead Calm, 1989; Spontaneous Combustion, 1989; Till There was You, 1990; Child's Play 2, 1990; Love Crimes, 1991; Until the End of the World, 1991; Traces of Red, 1992; Deadly, 1992; The People Under the Stairs (additional music), 1992; The Hand That Rocks the Cradle, 1992; Hear No Evil, 1993; Ghost in the Machine, 1993; The Crush, 1993; Body of Evidence, 1993; Boxing Helena, 1993; Hard Target, 1993; Street Fighter, 1994; S.F.W., 1994; No Escape, 1994; The Crow, 1994; Killer: A Journal of Murder, 1995; Tank Girl, 1995; The Basketball Diaries, 1995; Mighty Morphin Power Rangers: The Movie, 1995; The Tie That Binds, 1995; Strange Days, 1995; From Dusk Till Dawn, 1996; Race the Sun, 1996; The Craft, 1996; Fled, 1996; The Crow: City of Angels, 1996; Suicide Kings, 1997; Chinese Box, 1997; The Saint, 1997; Spawn, 1997; Phoenix, 1998; Bride of Chucky, 1998; The Big Hit, 1998; The Negotiator, 1998; Lulu on the Bridge, 1998; Strike, 1998; The Siege, 1998; Idle Hands, 1999; Buddy Boy, 1999; Three to Tango, 1999; Bats, 1999; The Insider (additional music), 1999; Pitch Black, 2000; Gossip, 2000; Attraction, 2000; Titan A.E., 2000; Red Planet, 2000; Double Take, 2001; Blow, 2001; Tomb Raider, 2001; Collateral Damage, 2001; High Crimes, 2002; Out of Time, 2003; Freddy vs Jason, 2003; Daredevil, 2003; Open Water, 2003; Walking Tall, 2004; Assault on Precinct 13, 2005; Sin City, 2005; Aeon Flux, 2005; Magnolia 2006; Goal! The Dream Begins 2006; Harsh Times 2006, Man of the Year 2006, Street Kings 2008, The Ruins 2008, Pineapple Express 2008. *Current Management:* Kraft Engel Management, 15233 Ventura Boulevard, Suite 200, Sherman Oaks, CA 91403, USA. *Telephone:* (818) 380-1918. *Fax:* (818) 380-2609. *E-mail:* dawna@kraftengel.com.

REYES, Andre; French musician (guitar). *Career:* guitarist and backing singer with The Gipsy Kings; group was formed in Arles (originally named Los Reyes) 1976; collaborations with Ruben Blades, Joan Baez, Bananarama; group performs a style of music known as Rumba Flamenca or Rumba Catalana; pioneered the introduction of drum kits, electronic bass, electronic keyboards, pop and reggae rhythms and modern recording techniques into flamenco music. *Film:* Tierra Gitana (Gipsy Ground) 1996. *Recordings:* albums: Gitan Poete (as Los Reyes) 1977, Allegria 1982, Luna de Fuegos 1983, Gipsy Kings 1988, Mosaique 1989, Allegria US Version 1990, Este Mundo 1991, Live 1992, Love and Liberté (Best Pop Album of the Year, Latin Grammy Awards) 1993, Greatest Hits 1994, The Best of the Gipsy Kings 1995, Estrellas 1995, Tierra Gitana 1996, Compas 1997, Cantos de Amor 1998, Volare: The Very Best of the Gipsy Kings 1999, Somos Gitanos 2001, Tonino Baliardo 2003, Roots 2004, Pasajero 2006, Savor Flamenco (Grammy Award for Best World Music Album 2014) 2013. *Current Management:* Impact Artist Management, 356 West 123rd Street, New York, NY 10027, USA. *Telephone:* (212) 280-0800. *Fax:* (212) 280-0808. *E-mail:* info@impactartist.com. *Website:* www.impactartist.com; www.gipsykings.com.

REYES, Canut; French musician (guitar); s. of Jose Reyes. *Career:* guitarist and backing singer with The Gipsy Kings; as a teenager performed with his father, a renowned flamenco singer; joined Gipsy Kings 1989, has performed throughout Europe, USA and N Africa; collaborations with Ruben Blades, Joan Baez, Bananarama; group performs a style of music known as Rumba Flamenca or Rumba Catalana; pioneered the introduction of drum kits, electronic bass, electronic keyboards, pop and reggae rhythms and modern recording techniques into flamenco music. *Film:* Tierra Gitana (Gipsy Ground) 1996. *Recordings:* albums: solo: Bolero 1989; with Jose Reyes: Flamenco Passion 1995; with Gipsy Kings: Mosaique 1989, Allegria US Version 1990, Este Mundo 1991, Live 1992, Love and Liberté (Best Pop Album of the Year, Latin Grammy Awards) 1993, Greatest Hits 1994, The Best of the Gipsy Kings 1995, Estrellas 1995, Tierra Gitana 1996, Compas 1997, Cantos de Amor 1998, Volare: The Very Best of the Gipsy Kings 1999, Somos Gitanos 2001, Tonino Baliardo 2003, Roots 2004, Pasajero 2006, Savor Flamenco (Grammy Award for Best World Music Album 2014) 2013. *Current Management:* Impact Artist Management, 356 West 123rd Street, New York, NY 10027, USA. *Telephone:* (212) 280-0800. *Fax:* (212) 280-0808. *E-mail:* info@impactartist.com. *Website:* www.impactartist.com; www.gipsykings.com.

REYES, Fernando; Spanish flamenco singer and flamenco musician (guitar); b. 4 Feb. 1939, Conil de la Frontera, Cádiz; m. Gillian Carol Hamling 1975, one s. one d. *Education:* private musical tuition. *Career:* performed throughout Spain and across Europe, Canada, USA, Asia; played for Antonio and Paco Romero and the King and Queen of Belgium; toured with Los Paraguayos; performances include Madison Square Gardens, Palais de Beaux Arts, Royal Albert Hall, Royal Festival Hall, Sadler's Wells, Covent Garden, QEH, Fairfield Hall, Purcell Room, numerous provincial theatres; sang in opera Carmen in UK and Germany; television appearances; live musical soundtrack for film, Pain Is... 1998; also various film scores; mem. Musicians' Union. *Recordings:* albums: Spanish, South American music, Flamenco Songs, Spanish Popular Songs, Encuentros, Flamenco, Flamenco Gypsy, Canciones de Pasión, Flamenco En Vivo, Fernando Reyes Live in London. *Honours:* various medals, trophies, awards from flamenco competitions in

Spain. *Address:* 19 Fairmount Road, London, SW2 2BJ, England (home). *Telephone:* (20) 8671-1317 (home). *E-mail:* reyes131@btinternet.com (home).

REYES, Nicolas; French singer; s. of Jose Reyes. *Career:* lead singer with The Gipsy Kings; as a teenager performed with his father, a renowned flamenco singer; group was formed in Arles (originally named Los Reyes) 1976; performed throughout Europe and N Africa, collaborations with Ruben Blades, Joan Baez, Bananarama; group performs a style of music known as Rumba Flamenca or Rumba Catalana; pioneered the introduction of drum kits, electronic bass, electronic keyboards, pop and reggae rhythms and modern recording techniques into flamenco music. *Film:* Tierra Gitana (Gipsy Ground) 1996. *Recordings:* albums: Gitan Poete (as Los Reyes) 1977, Allegria 1982, Luna de Fuegos 1983, Gipsy Kings 1988, Mosaique 1989, Allegria US Version 1990, Este Mundo 1991, Live 1992, Love and Liberté (Best Pop Album of the Year, Latin Grammy Awards) 1993, Greatest Hits 1994, The Best of the Gipsy Kings 1995, Estrellas 1995, Tierra Gitana 1996, Compas 1997, Cantos de Amor 1998, Volare: The Very Best of the Gipsy Kings 1999, Somos Gitanos 2001, Tonino Baliardo 2003, Roots 2004, Pasajero 2006, Savor Flamenco (Grammy Award for Best World Music Album 2014) 2013. *Current Management:* Impact Artist Management, 356 West 123rd Street, New York, NY 10027, USA. *Telephone:* (212) 280-0800. *Fax:* (212) 280-0808. *E-mail:* info@impactartist.com. *Website:* www.impactartist.com; www.gipsykings.com.

REYES, Pablo; French musician (guitar); s. of Jose Reyes. *Career:* guitarist and backing singer with The Gipsy Kings; as a teenager performed with his father, a renowned flamenco singer; group was formed in Arles (originally named Los Reyes) 1976; performed throughout Europe and N Africa; collaborations with Ruben Blades, Joan Baez, Bananarama; group performs a style of music known as Rumba Flamenca or Rumba Catalana; pioneered the introduction of drum kits, electronic bass, electronic keyboards, pop and reggae rhythms and modern recording techniques into flamenco music. *Film:* Tierra Gitana (Gipsy Ground) 1996. *Recordings:* albums: Gitan Poete (as Los Reyes) 1977, Allegria 1982, Luna de Fuegos 1983, Gipsy Kings 1988, Mosaique 1989, Allegria US Version 1990, Este Mundo 1991, Live 1992, Love and Liberté (Best Pop Album of the Year, Latin Grammy Awards) 1993, Greatest Hits 1994, The Best of the Gipsy Kings 1995, Estrellas 1995, Tierra Gitana 1996, Compas 1997, Cantos de Amor 1998, Volare: The Very Best of the Gipsy Kings 1999, Somos Gitanos 2001, Tonino Baliardo 2003, Roots 2004, Pasajero 2006, Savor Flamenco (Grammy Award for Best World Music Album 2014) 2013. *Current Management:* Impact Artist Management, 356 West 123rd Street, New York, NY 10027, USA. *Telephone:* (212) 280-0800. *Fax:* (212) 280-0808. *E-mail:* info@impactartist.com. *Website:* www.impactartist.com; www.gipsykings.com.

REYES, Patchai; French musician (guitar). *Career:* guitarist and backing singer with The Gipsy Kings; group was formed in Arles (originally named Los Reyes) 1976; performed throughout Europe and N Africa; collaborations with Ruben Blades, Joan Baez, Bananarama; group performs a style of music known as Rumba Flamenca or Rumba Catalana; pioneered the introduction of drum kits, electronic bass, electronic keyboards, pop and reggae rhythms and modern recording techniques into flamenco music. *Film:* Tierra Gitana (Gipsy Ground) 1996. *Recordings:* albums: Gitan Poete (as Los Reyes) 1977, Allegria 1982, Luna de Fuegos 1983, Gipsy Kings 1988, Mosaique 1989, Allegria US Version 1990, Este Mundo 1991, Live 1992, Love and Liberté (Best Pop Album of the Year, Latin Grammy Awards) 1993, Greatest Hits 1994, The Best of the Gipsy Kings 1995, Estrellas 1995, Tierra Gitana 1996, Compas 1997, Cantos de Amor 1998, Volare: The Very Best of the Gipsy Kings 1999, Somos Gitanos 2001, Tonino Baliardo 2003, Roots 2004, Pasajero 2006, Savor Flamenco (Grammy Award for Best World Music Album 2014) 2013. *Current Management:* Impact Artist Management, 356 West 123rd Street, New York, NY 10027, USA. *Telephone:* (212) 280-0800. *Fax:* (212) 280-0808. *E-mail:* info@impactartist.com. *Website:* www.impactartist.com; www.gipsykings.com.

REYNOLDS, (Lee) Allen; American country music record producer, songwriter and music publisher; b. North Little Rock, Arkansas. *Education:* Rhodes College, Memphis. *Career:* began songwriting partnership with long-term collaborator and friend, Dickey Lee at college; moved to Texas; joint composition I Saw Linda Yesterday became US hit for Lee 1962; composition about day job in a bank, Five O'Clock World, subsequently a Top 5 US pop hit for the Vogues; moved to Nashville and began production work, including Don Williams' recording of I Recall A Gypsy Woman; purchased Jack's Tracks Recording Studio in Nashville 1976; set up self-contained recording and publishing operation; own recording career 1978; productions include: Crystal Gayle, Kathy Mattea, O'Kanes, Bobby Bare, George Hamilton IV, Daniel O'Donnell, Randy Vanwarmer, Hal Ketchum, Emmylou Harris, all of Garth Brooks' country albums; songs recorded by artists including: Waylon Jennings, Johnny Russell, Marianne Faithfull. *Compositions include:* Catfish John, Everybody's Reaching Out For Someone, Five O'Clock World, I Saw Linda Yesterday, Ready For The Times To Get Better, Somebody Loves You, We Should Be Together, Dreaming My Dreams With You. *Honours:* sales of albums produced for Garth Brooks surpass the 100 m. mark; inducted into Nashville Songwriters Asscn Inc (NSAI) Hall of Fame 2000. *Address:* c/o Jack's Tracks Recording Studio, 1308 16th Avenue S, Nashville 37212, USA (office).

REYNOLDS, Daniel Coulter; American singer, songwriter and musician (guitar, percussion); b. 14 July 1987, Las Vegas, Nev.; s. of Ronald Reynolds and Christine Reynolds; m. Aja Volkman Reynolds 2011; one d. *Education:*

Brigham Young Univ. *Career:* Founder-mem., Imagine Dragons 2008–, performed at numerous festivals 2011–; signed with Interscope Records 2011; numerous TV appearances and tours in USA, Canada, Europe; also collaborated with Aja Volkman in duo Egyptian 2010. *Recording:* album: with Imagine Dragons: Night Visions (Billboard Music Award for Top Rock Album 2014) 2012, Smoke + Mirrors 2015. *Honours:* Teen Choice Award for Choice Rock Song (for Radioactive) 2013, American Music Awards for Favorite Alternative Rock Artist 2013, 2014, Grammy Award for Best Rock Performance (for Radioactive) 2014, Billboard Music Awards for Top Duo/Group 2014, for Top Hot 100 Artist 2014, for Top Rock Artist 2014, for Top Streaming Song (Audio) (for Radioactive) 2014, iHeartRadio Music Award for Best Alternative Rock Song of the Year (for Demons, with Imagine Dragons) 2014. *Current Management:* c/o Mac Reynolds, Reynolds Management, 823 Las Vegas Boulevard South, Las Vegas, NV 89101, USA. *Telephone:* (702) 445-7000. *Fax:* (702) 385-7743. *E-mail:* mac@reynoldsmgmt.com. *Website:* www .reynoldsmgmt.com; imaginedragonsmusic.com.

REYNOLDS, Debbie Mary Frances; American actress and singer; b. 1 April 1932, El Paso, Tex.; m. 1st Eddie Fisher 1955 (divorced 1959); one d. (Carrie Fisher) one s.; m. 2nd Harry Karl 1960 (divorced 1973); m. 3rd Richard Hamlett 1985 (divorced 1994). *Career:* film debut in June Bride 1948; stage debut at Blis-Hayden Theater 1952; nightclub act mid-1960s–; founder Debbie Reynolds Professional Rehearsal Studios, North Hollywood late 1970s; Prin. Debbie Reynolds Hotel/Casino and Hollywood Motion Picture Museum, Las Vegas 1993–. *Theatre includes:* Irene 1973, Annie Get Your Gun, Woman of the Year 1983, The Unsinkable Molly Brown (nat. tour) 1989. *Films:* June Bride 1948, The Daughter of Rosie O'Grady 1950, Three Little Words 1950, Two Weeks with Love 1950, Mr Imperium 1951, Singin' in the Rain 1952, I Love Melvin 1953, The Affairs of Dobie Gillis 1953, Give a Girl a Break 1953, Susan Slept Here 1954, Athena 1954, Hit the Deck 1955, The Tender Trap 1955, The Catered Affair 1956, Bundle of Joy 1956, Tammy and the Bachelor 1957, This Happy Feeling 1958, The Mating Game 1959, Say One for Me 1959, It Started with a Kiss 1959, The Gazebo 1959, The Rat Race 1960, The Pleasure of his Company 1961, The Second Time Around 1961, How the West Was Won 1962, Mary, Mary 1963, My Six Loves 1963, The Unsinkable Molly Brown 1964, Goodbye Charlie 1964, The Singing Nun 1966, Divorce American Style 1967, How Sweet It Is! 1968, What's the Matter with Helen? 1971, Charlotte's Web (voice) 1973, Kiki's Delivery Service (voice) 1989, Heaven & Earth 1993, Mother 1996, In & Out 1997, Zack and Reba 1998, Rudolph the Red-Nosed Reindeer: The Movie (voice) 1998, Rugrats in Paris: The Movie – Rugrats II (voice) 2000. *Television:* The Debbie Reynolds Show 1969, Aloha Paradise (series) 1981, Sadie and Son 1987, Perry Mason: The Case of the Musical Murder 1989, Battling for Baby 1992, Halloweentown 1998, The Christmas Wish 1998, A Gift of Love: The Daniel Huffman Story 1999, Virtual Mom 2000, Rugrats (series, voice) 2000–04, These Old Broads 2001, Halloweentown II: Kalabar's Revenge 2001, Halloweentown III: Halloweentown High 2004, Lolo's Cafe (voice) 2006, Will & Grace (series) 1999–2006, Return to Halloweentown 2006. *Publications:* Debbie: My Life (with David Patrick Colombia) 1987, Unsinkable: A Memoir 2013. *Honours:* Dr hc (Univ. of Nevada, Reno) 2007; Nat. Hon. presented by Girl Scouts USA 1966–69, Lifetime Achievement Award, American Comedy Awards 1996, Lifetime Achievement Award, Palm Springs Int. Film Festival 1999, Lifetime Achievement Award, Savannah Film and Video Festival 2002, Pres.'s Award, Costume Designers Guild 2005, Lifetime Achievement Award, Chapman Univ. 2006, Nat. Film Soc. Humanitarian Award, Life Achievement Award, Screen Actors Guild 2014, Jean Hersholt Humanitarian Award, Acad. of Motion Picture Arts and Sciences 2015. *Address:* William Morris Endeavor, 1 William Morris Place, Beverly Hills, CA 90212 (office); Debbie Reynolds Studios, 6514 Lankershim Blvd, North Hollywood, CA 91606-2409, USA (office). *Telephone:* (818) 985-3193 (office). *Fax:* (818) 985-6927 (office). *E-mail:* DRStudios@sbcglobal.net (office).

REZNOR, (Michael) Trent; American rock musician, singer and songwriter; b. 17 May 1965, Mercer, Pa. *Career:* previously associated with bands Option 30, Exotic Birds, Tapeworm; Founder-mem. and lead vocalist of rock group, Nine Inch Nails 1989–; currently mem. of How to Destroy Angels; left Interscope Records 2007, now an ind. musician. *Compositions include:* soundtracks: Natural Born Killers (film) 1994, Quake (video game) 1996, Closure (film) 1997, CSI: Crime Scene Investigation (TV series) 2000, Wanted (film) 2008, The Social Network (with Atticus Ross) (film) (Golden Globe for Best Original Score 2010, Academy Award for Best Original Score 2011) 2010, The Girl with the Dragon Tattoo (with Atticus Ross) (film) (Grammy Award for Best Score Soundtrack 2013) 2011; songs for films, including The Young Americans 1993, Se7en 1995, The Fan 1996, Lost Highway 1997, Final Destination 2000, Freeman 2004, Man on Fire 2004. *Recordings include:* albums: with Nine Inch Nails: Pretty Hate Machine 1989, Broken (mini album) 1992, The Downward Spiral 1994, The Fragile 1999, Things Falling Apart 2000, And All That Could Have Been (live) 2002, With Teeth 2005, Year Zero 2007, Ghosts I–IV 2008, The Slip 2008, Hesitation Marks 2013. *Website:* www.nin.com.

RHODES, Louise (Lou); British singer and songwriter. *Career:* founder mem., Lamb 1994–2004; solo artist 2004–; established Infinite Bloom Recordings 2005–07. *Recordings include:* albums: with Lamb: Lamb 1996, Fear of Fours 1999, What Sound 2001, Between Darkness and Wonder 2003, Best Kept Secrets: The Best of Lamb 1996–2004 2004; solo: Beloved One 2005, Bloom 2007, One Good Thing 2010; vocalist on The Cinematic Orchestra's

album Ma Fleur 2007. *E-mail:* gordon@stratamusicgroup.com (office). *Website:* www.lourhodes.com.

RHODES, Nick; British musician (keyboards); b. (Nicholas James Bates), 8 June 1962, Moseley, West Midlands, England. *Career:* founder mem., Duran Duran 1978–; founder mem., Arcadia 1985–86. *Recordings include:* albums: with Duran Duran: Duran Duran 1981, Rio 1982, Seven And The Ragged Tiger 1983, Arena 1984, Notorious 1986, Big Thing 1988, Liberty 1990, Duran Duran (The Wedding Album) 1993, Thank You 1995, Medazzaland 1997, Pop Trash 2000, online-only releases of Duran Duran recordings of live shows in Japan 2003, Astronaut 2004, Red Carpet Massacre 2007, All You Need is Now 2010, Paper Gods 2015; with Arcadia: So Red The Rose 1985. *Honours:* MTV Music Video Lifetime Achievement Award 2003, Q Magazine Lifetime Achievement Award 2003, BRIT Outstanding Contribution to Music Award 2004, Q Icon Award 2015, MTV Europe Music Video Visionary Award 2015. *Current Management:* c/o Ms Wendy Laister, Magus Entertainment Inc., 33 Greene Street, #3W, New York, NY 10013, USA. *Telephone:* (212) 343-1577. *Fax:* (212) 925-4007. *E-mail:* info@magusentertainment.com. *Website:* www .magusentertainment.com; www.duranduran.com.

RHYS, Gruff; Welsh singer, musician, songwriter and record producer; b. 18 July 1970, Haverfordwest. *Career:* mem. Super Furry Animals 1993–; recorded two EPs on indie label, then obtained independent label deal; numerous tours in the UK and abroad; appearances at numerous festivals; solo artist 2004–; mem. Neon Neon (with Boom Bip) 2008; collaborated with Tony da Gatorra on album 2010; collaborations as soloist with several other artists including De La Soul, Gorillaz, Mogwai, Sparklehouse. *Recordings include:* albums: with Super Furry Animals: Fuzzy Logic 1996, Radiator 1997, Guerrilla 1999, Mwng 2000, Rings Around The World 2001, Phantom Power 2003, Love Kraft 2005, Hey Venus 2007, Dark Days/Light Years 2009; solo: Yr Atal Genhedlaeth 2005, Candylion 2006, Hotel Shampoo (Welsh Music Prize 2011) 2011; with Neon Neon: Stainless Style 2008; with Tony da Gatorra: The Terror of Cosmic Loneliness 2010. *Films:* Separado (documentary) 2010. *E-mail:* turnstilemusic@gmail.com (office); info@superfurry.com (office). *Website:* www.gruffrhys.com; www.superfurry.com; www.turnstilemusic.net.

RHYS-JONES, Merlin; British musician (guitar), songwriter and arranger; b. 15 June 1958, Brighton, Sussex, England. *Career:* recorded with Lipservice; toured with Ian Dury and The Music Students 1983, Ian Dury and The Blockheads 1992, 1994–95, Ellis, Beggs and Howard 1989; currently teaching at Musicians' Inst., Wapping; mem. Publishing agreement with Mute Song, Musicians' Union, PRS. *Radio:* Capital Radio. *Television includes:* The Tube with Ian Dury, Sight and Sound, Martin Dobson's Main Course; several sessions for TV shows. *Recordings:* albums with Ian Dury: 4000 Weeks Holiday, Apples, Bus-Drivers Prayer and Other Stories (includes some co-writes), Warts and Audience (Live Blockheads at Brixton Academy), Guitar on Strange Liquid, Recoil 2000. *Address:* Flat 21, 318 Hornsey Road, London, N7 7HE, England (home).

RHYTHIM IS RHYTHIM (see May, Derrick)

RHYTHM X (see Kool Keith)

RIBOT, Marc; American musician (guitar); b. 21 May 1954, Newark, New Jersey. *Education:* studied with Frantz Casseus. *Career:* moved to New York 1978; mem. Realtones/Uptown Horns Band 1979–83, John Lurie's Lounge Lizards 1984–89; freelance musician 1989–; played with Jack MacDuff, Wilson Pickett, Chuck Berry, Solomon Burke, Tom Waits, Elvis Costello, John Zorn, Henry Grimes; founder mem. trio, Ceramic Dog 2006–. *Films:* The Lost String 2007. *Recordings include:* albums: with Lounge Lizards: No Pain For Cakes 1987, Voice Of Chunk 1988; solo: Hatian Suite, Marc Ribot Plays Solo Guitar Works Of Frantz Casseus, The Book Of Heads (with John Zorn), Subsonic 1 (with Fred Frith), Rootless Cosmopolitans 1990, Requiem For What's his Name 1992, Shrek 1994, Don't Blame Me 1995, Shoe String Symphonettes 1997, The Prosthetic Cubans 1998, A Yo I Killed Your God 1999, Muy Divertido 2000, Saints 2001, Scelsi Morning 2003, Spiritual Unity 2005, Exercises in Futility 2008, Party Intellectuals 2008, Silent Movies 2010, Your Turn 2013, Live at the Village Vanguard 2014. *E-mail:* info@marcribot .com. *Website:* www.marcribot.com.

RICE, Damien; Irish singer, songwriter and musician (guitar); b. Dublin. *Career:* mem. Juniper 1997–99; solo artist 1999–; six-week tour of Ireland, the UK, Germany, France and Spain 2002, festival appearances at Glastonbury, V2002, Edinburgh Fringe, London Fleadh, support to McAlmont and Butler, Counting Crows and Kathryn Williams; owner drm record label. *Recordings include:* albums: O 2002, 9 2006. *Honours:* XPN Award for an Emerging Artist 2003, Shortlist Music Prize 2003. *Current Management:* Mondo Management, Unit 2D, Clapham North Arts Centre, 26–32 Voltaire Road, London, SW4 6DH, England. *Telephone:* (20) 7720-7411. *Fax:* (20) 7720-8095. *E-mail:* info@ damienrice.com. *Website:* www.damienrice.com.

RICE, Melanie Ailene, BA; American singer and music contractor; b. 4 Nov. 1957, Philadelphia, Pennsylvania. *Education:* Rowan Coll., Univ. of Delaware. *Career:* tours: opening act for: Joan Rivers, Smokey Robinson, Shecky Greene, David Brenner, Susan Anton, George Kirby, Bobby Vinton; backing vocalist for: Grover Washington, James Darren, Joe Piscopo, Bobby Rydell; founder and Pres., Melanie Rice Entertainment, music and event production co. 1995; mem, NACE. *Recordings:* solo: He Loves She Loves 2000. *Honours:* John Phillip Sousa Award. *Address:* Melanie Rice Entertainment, 1 North New York Road, Smithville Commons, Suite 34, Smithville, NJ 08205, USA (office). *Telephone:* (609) 748-3900 (office). *Fax:* (609) 748-8814 (office). *E-mail:* contactus@melanierice.com (office). *Website:* www.melanierice.com.

RICE, Sir Timothy (Tim) Miles Bindon, Kt; British songwriter; b. 10 Nov. 1944, Amersham; s. of Hugh Gordon Rice and Joan Odette Rice; m. Jane Artereta McIntosh 1974, one s. one d.; pnr Nell Sully, one d. *Education:* Lancing Coll. *Career:* with EMI Records 1966–68, Norrie Paramor Org. 1968–69; founder and fmr Dir GRRR Books Ltd 1978, Pavilion Books Ltd 1981; Chair. Foundation for Sport and the Arts 1991–; mem. Main Cttee MCC 1992–94, 1995– (Pres. 2002–03). *Lyrics for musicals:* (music by Andrew Lloyd Webber q.v. unless otherwise specified): The Likes of Us 1965, Joseph and the Amazing Technicolor Dreamcoat 1968, Jesus Christ Superstar 1970, Evita 1976, Blondel (music by Stephen Oliver) 1983, Chess (music by Benny Andersson and Bjorn Ulvaeus) 1984, Cricket 1986, Starmania/Tycoon (with music by Michael Berger) 1989–90, Aladdin (film musical, music by Alan Menken) 1992, The Lion King (film musical, music by Elton John) 1993 (theatre version 1997), Beauty and the Beast (music by Alan Menken) 1994 (some lyrics for stage version), Heathcliff (music by John Farrar) 1995, King David (music by Alan Menken) 1997, Aida (music by Elton John) 1998, The Road to El Dorado (music by Elton John) 1999, The Wizard of Oz (music by Andrew Lloyd Webber, and Harold Arlen and E.Y. Harburg) 2011, From Here to Eternity (music by Stuart Bryson) 2013; songs include: Don't Cry For Me Argentina, I Know Him So Well, Can You Feel The Love Tonight? (Acad. Award, Golden Globe, with Elton John 1994), I Don't Know How To Love Him, A Winter's Tale, Circle Of Life, Any Dream Will Do, A Whole New World (Acad. Award, Golden Globe, with Alan Menken 1992), All Time High (from film Octopussy), You Must Love Me (Acad. Award, Golden Globe, with Andrew Lloyd Webber 1996), One Night In Bangkok; lyrics for songs with composers, including Paul McCartney, Mike Batt, Freddie Mercury, Graham Gouldman, Marvin Hamlisch, Rick Wakeman, John Barry. *Publications:* Evita (with Andrew Lloyd Webber) 1978, Joseph and the Amazing Technicolor Dreamcoat 1982, Treasures of Lords 1989, Oh, What a Circus (autobiog.) 1995, The Complete Eurovision Song Contest Companion (jtly) 1998, founder and original author, with Paul Gambaccini, Jonathan Rice and Mike Read, of the Guinness Book of Hit Singles and related titles. *Honours:* Dr hc (Univ. of Sunderland) 2006; 12 Ivor Novello Awards, three Tony Awards, six Grammy Awards, British Acad. of Songwriters, Composers and Authors Fellowship 2010. *Current Management:* Lewis & Golden, 40 Queen Anne Street, London, W1G 9EL, England. *Telephone:* (20) 7580-7313. *Website:* www.timrice.co.uk.

RICE-OXLEY, Tim; British musician (piano, keyboards) and songwriter; b. 2 June 1976, Battle, East Sussex, England; m. *Education:* Univ. Coll. London. *Career:* founder mem. Keane 1997–; founder mem. Mt Desolation 2010–. *Recordings include:* album: with Keane: Hopes and Fears (Best Album, Q Awards 2004, BRIT Award for Best British Album 2005) 2004, Under the Iron Sea 2006, Perfect Symmetry 2008, Night Train (mini-album) 2010; with Mt Desolation: Mt Desolation 2010. *Honours:* Best Int. Band, Premios Onda, Spain 2004, BRIT Award for Best British Breakthrough Act 2005, Songwriter of the Year (with Tom Chaplin), Ivor Novello Awards 2005, Band of the Year, GQ Awards 2006. *Current Management:* c/o Adam Tudhope, Everybody's, 21–22 Great Castle Street, London, W1G 0HY, England. *Telephone:* (20) 7907-2667. *Fax:* (20) 7493-8416. *E-mail:* info@everybody-s.com. *Website:* www.everybody-s.com; www.keanemusic.com; www.mtdesolation.com.

RICH, John; American country singer and musician (pedal steel guitar, bass guitar); b. 7 Jan. 1974, Amarillo, TX. *Career:* began career as singer and performer in the bluegrass field; founder mem., Texasee 1992, became resident house band at the Wildhorse Saloon, Nashville, name changed to Lonestar 1995–98; solo artist 1998–; mem. Big and Rich (with Big Kenny); co-f. MuzikMafia (country music collective) 2001. *Recordings include:* albums: with Lonestar: Lonestar 1995, Crazy Nights 1997; solo: Underneath The Same Moon 2006; with Big and Rich: Horse of a Different Colour 2004, Big and Rich's Super Galactic Fanpark 2004, Comin' to Your City 2005, Between Raising Hell and Amazing Grace 2007. *Address:* c/o BNA Records, Sony BMG, 1400 18th Avenue, South Nashville, TN 37212, USA (office). *Website:* www.johnrich.com; www.bigandrich.com.

RICH, Rishi; British musician, songwriter and producer; b. 1978, London. *Career:* worked in recording studio from age 11; formed 2Kool 1993; began producing traditional Asian music; toured India with leading Asian artists, including Kumar Sanu, Udit Narayan, Kavita Krishnamurti; produced and wrote songs for Mary J. Blige, Craig David, Liberty X, Ricky Martin, Mis-Teeq, Britney Spears, Westlife; formed The Rishi Rich Project to work with new artists 2002–. *Recordings include:* albums: Love2Love 1994, Play Back 2001, Simply Rich 2002, The Project 2006. *Honours:* UK Asian Music Award for Best Producer 2003, for Best Single (for Dance With You) 2003. *Address:* Rishi Rich Productions, 9 Lydden Road, London, SW18 4LT, England (office). *Telephone:* (20) 3004-0771 (office). *Fax:* (75) 1528-4377 (office). *E-mail:* info@rishirichproductions.com (office). *Website:* www.rishirichproductions.com (office).

RICHARD, Sir Cliff, Kt, OBE; British singer, musician (guitar) and actor; b. (Harry Rodger Webb), 14 Oct. 1940, India; s. of Rodger Webb and the late Dorothy Webb. *Education:* Riversmead School, Cheshunt, Herts. *Career:* Leader, Cliff Richard and The Shadows; later, solo artist; regular int. concert tours, various repertory and variety seasons; own TV series on BBC and ITV; numerous radio and TV interviews and performances since 1958; mem. Equity. *Films include:* Serious Charge 1959, Expresso Bongo 1960, The Young Ones 1961, Summer Holiday 1962, Wonderful Life 1964, Finders Keepers 1966, Two a Penny 1968, His Land, Take Me High 1973. *Stage appearances include:* musicals Time, Dominion Theatre, London 1986–87, Heathcliff, UK tour and Hammersmith Apollo, London 1996–97. *Recordings include:* albums: Cliff 1959, Cliff Sings 1959, Me And My Shadows 1960, Listen To Cliff 1961, 21 Today 1961, The Young Ones 1961, 32 Minutes And 17 Seconds With Cliff Richard 1962, Summer Holiday 1963, Cliff's Hit Album 1963, When In Spain 1963, Wonderful Life 1964, Aladdin And His Wonderful Lamp 1964, Cliff Richard 1965, More Hits By Cliff 1965, When In Rome 1965, Love Is Forever 1965, Kinda Latin 1966, Finders Keepers 1966, Cinderella 1967, Don't Stop Me Now 1967, Good News 1967, Cliff In Japan 1968, Two A Penny 1968, Established 1968, The Best Of Cliff 1969, Sincerely 1969, It'll Be Me 1969, Cliff Live At The Talk of The Town 1970, About That Man 1970, His Land 1970, Tracks 'n' Grooves 1970, The Best Of Cliff Vol. Two 1972, Take Me High 1973, Help It Along 1974, The 31st February Street 1974, I'm Nearly Famous 1976, Every Face Tells A Story 1977, 40 Golden Greats 1977, Small Corners 1978, Green Light 1978, Thank You Very Much (Cliff & The Shadows) 1979, Rock 'n' Roll Juvenile 1979, I'm No Hero 1980, Love Songs 1981, Wired For Sound 1981, Now You See Me... Now You Don't 1982, Dressed For The Occasion 1983, Silver 1983, Rock 'n' Roll Silver 1983, Cliff & The Shadows 1984, Always Guaranteed 1987, Private Collection 1988, Stronger 1989, From A Distance – The Event 1990, Together 1991, Cliff Richard: The Album 1993, The Hit List 1994, Songs From Heathcliff 1995, Heathcliff Live 1996, Cliff Richard At The Movies 1996, The Rock 'n' Roll Years 1997, Real As I Wanna Be 1998, The Whole Story 2001, Wanted 2001, The Singles Collection 2002, Cliff At Christmas 2003, Something's Goin' On 2004, Two's Company: The Duets 2006, Love: The Album 2007, 50th Anniversary Album 2008, Reunited (with The Shadows) 2009, Bold As Brass 2010, Soulicious 2011, The Fabulous Rock 'N' Roll Songbook 2013, Cliff Richard 75 at 75 2015. *Publications include:* Questions 1970, The Way I See It 1972, The Way I See It Now 1975, Which One's Cliff? 1977, Happy Christmas from Cliff 1980, You, Me and Jesus 1983, Mine to Share 1984, Jesus, Me and You 1985, Single-Minded 1988, Mine Forever 1989, My Story: A Celebration of 40 Years in Showbusiness 1998, My Life, My Way (with Penny Junor) 2008. *Honours:* Hon. DUniv (Middlesex) 2003; numerous awards. *Address:* Cliff Richard Organisation, PO Box 423, Leatherhead, Surrey, KT22 2HJ, England (office). *Telephone:* (1372) 467752 (office). *E-mail:* general@cliffrichard.org (office). *Website:* www.cliffrichard.org (home).

RICHARD, Marc; French jazz musician (saxophone, clarinet), composer and arranger; b. 22 Nov. 1946, Neuilly-Sur-Seine. *Education:* 3 years of courses for arrangement. *Career:* Played cornet with Haricots Rouges, 1963; Played saxophone and clarinet with many different bands including: Irakli; François Biensan; Founder, Anachronic Jazz Band, 1976; Played as sideman in Paris for many years with prominent jazzmen, including: Cab Calloway; Dee Dee Bridgewater; Harry Edison; Teacher, Jazz History, various schools. *Recordings:* Anachronic Jazz Band, Vol. 1, 1977; Vol. 2, 1980; Also appears on: Duke Ellington Complete Edition Vol. 1; Accident, John Greaves, 1982; Bix Beiderbecke, Vols 2, 4, 5, 7, 8, 1994–96; Solo: After You've Gone.

RICHARD, Zachary, CM, BA; American singer, songwriter, musician (guitar, piano, cajun accordion, harmonica) and poet; b. 8 Sept. 1950; m. Claude Thomas 1992. *Education:* Tulane Univ. *Career:* innovator, Cajun and Zydeco musical styles; composer and producer, TV documentaries, Against the Tide 2000, Contre vents, contre mareés 2002. *Recordings:* albums: Bayou des Mystères 1976, Mardi Gras 1977, Migration 1978, Allons Danser 1979, Live in Montréal 1980, Vent d'Été 1981, Zack Attack 1984, Zack's Bon Ton 1987, Mardi Gras Mambo 1989, Women in the Room 1990, Snake Bite Love 1992, Looking Back (compilation) 1995, Cap Enragé 1996, Travailler C'est Trop Dur (anthology) 1999, Coeur Fidèle 2000, Lumière dans le noir 2007, Last Kiss 2009, Le Fou 2012. *Television:* producer, narrator and musical supervisor, Against the Tide: The Story of the Cajun People of Louisiana (NET Authority Award for Best Historical Documentary, USA 2000); narrator and composer, Contre Vents, Contre Marées (Prix Historia de l'Institut d'histoire d'Amérique Française) 2002; narrator, Coeurs Batalliaiers; narrator and composer, Migration 2003; narrator and host, Vu du large 2005. *Publications:* poetry: Voyage de Nuit 1980, Faire Récolte 1997, Feu 2001 Fables: Conte Cajun, L'Histoire de Télésphore et 'Tit Edvard 1999, L'Histoire de Télésphore et 'Tit Edvard dans le grand nord 2007, Télésphore et Petit Edvard au Vieux Pays 2010, L'Histoire des Acadiennes et Acadiens de la Louisiane 2012. *Honours:* Officier des Arts et des Lettres 1996; Membre, Ordre de Francophones d'Amérique, Québec 1998; Chevalier, Ordre de la Pléiade 2000; Order of Canada 2009; Dr hc (Université de Moncton) 2005, Univ. of Louisiana at Lafayette) 2008, (Université de Sainte-Anne, NS) 2008, (Univ. of Ottawa) 2011; Prix de la Jeune Chanson Française 1980, Prix Miroir de Québec 1996, Felix de l'ADISQ 1997, 1998, 1999, 2000, Prix Littéraire Champlain 1998, Int. Achievement Award, Centre Int. de Louisiane 1999, Prix du Publique, Salon du Livre de la Côte Nord 2000, Acadiana Arts Council Distinguished Artist 2000, Meritas Acadien, Fédération Acadienne du Québec 2000, Prix Roland Gasparic 2001, Chanson de l'année, Cajun French Music Asscn 2002, Chanson populaire de l'année, Soc. of Composers, Authors and Music Publrs of Canada 2002, Louisiana Legend, Louisiana Public Broadcasting 2002, Prix Historia, Institut d'Histoire de l'Amérique Française 2003. *Current Management:* c/o Claude Thomas, 802 Cayret Street, Scott, LA 70583, USA. *Telephone:* (318) 269-9926. *Website:* www.zacharyrichard.com.

RICHARDEAU, Xavier Jacques; French musician (baritone and soprano saxophones); b. 1965, St Jean d'Angely. *Education:* Versailles Conservatoire, studied with Jean-Claude Forenbach and Jacques Charles. *Career:* formed Xavier Richardeau Quartet 1990. *Recordings include:* Aube Brune 1998, Live In Paris 1999, Hit and Run. *Address:* c/o Taxi Records, 60 rue Victor Bash, 76140 Petit-Quevilly, France (office). *E-mail:* taxirecords@wanadoo.fr (office). *Website:* www.taxirecords.net (office).

RICHARDS, Aled; British musician (drums); b. 5 July 1969, Camarthen, Wales. *Career:* mem., The Hepburns; mem. Catatonia 1996–2001; mem. Killing for Company 2010–; numerous festival appearances and live gigs; many appearances on music shows on TV and radio. *Recordings:* albums: with Catatonia: Way Beyond Blue 1996, The Sublime Magic of Catatonia 1996, International Velvet 1998, Equally Cursed and Blessed 1999, Paper Scissors Stone 2001, Greatest Catatonia Hits 2002. *E-mail:* info@killingforcompany.com (office). *Website:* www.killingforcompany.com.

RICHARDS, Andy; producer, programmer and musician (keyboards). *Career:* as programmer and keyboard player has worked with Trevor Horn and Stephen Lipson on many projects including: Frankie Goes to Hollywood, Propaganda, Grace Jones; other artists include: George Michael, The Pet Shop Boys, Chris De Burgh, Def Leppard, Wet Wet Wet, Cher, Ronan Keating, Annie Lennox and Tina Turner; as producer and programmer clients include: Alphaville; Prefab Sprout; The Pet Shop Boys; Fuzzbox; OMD; T'Pau; Dusty Springfield; Boyzone; Seal; Orchestral Manoeuvres in the Dark; Art of Noise; Genesis. *Current Management:* SARM Management, The Blue Building, 42/46 St Luke's Mews, London W11 1DG, England.

RICHARDS, Dick; American musician (drums) and singer; b. Philadelphia, PA. *Career:* mem., Bill Haley's Comets 1953–55; theatre and film actor (as Richard Boccelli). *Recordings:* Rock Around The Clock, See You Later Alligator, Crazy Man Crazy, Shake Rattle and Roll, Rock The Joint, Mambo Rock, Rudy's Rock, Florida Twist, Shimmie Minnie; with Bill Haley: From the Original Master Tapes 1985, Decca Years and More 1991, We're Gonna Rock Around The Clock 2001. *Publications:* Rock Around The Clock, Stage Clear, We're Gonna Party, Never Too Old To Rock, Let's All Rock Together, Now Dig This. *Honours:* Best Vocal group of 1953.

RICHARDS, Eddie, (Jolly Roger); British producer, remixer and DJ; b. Amersham, Buckinghamshire. *Career:* started as a DJ at the Camden Palace in London; instrumental in introducing house music to the UK as resident DJ at the Clink Street parties, 1988; founder: Dy-na-mix DJ agency; Lunar Records; collaborations with Mr C, Richie Hawtin, Kid Bachelor, The Shamen, Orbital. *Recordings:* Zig Zag, Love Is/House, Yeyo/iMove/Oyea, D-Comm/Someday/Xtrk, Dark 1.1/Dark1.2/Dark1.3, Open the Pod Door, Tileefuoynac/Soul is Life, Rewind, Crying/Werks, Mnbaby/Aali, Be Still, Chicken or Beef. *Telephone:* (1908) 270811 (office). *E-mail:* eviled@mac.com (office). *Website:* www.eddierichards.net.

RICHARDS, Eric Thomas, BA; British musician (bass guitar, piano); b. 21 July 1953, Alnwick, England; two d. *Education:* City of Leeds Coll. of Music, Univ. of Durham, Newcastle Coll. of Arts and Tech. *Career:* with Gloria Gaynor British tour, live TV; with Dudu Pukwana's Zila tours, television and radio in UK, Europe, Africa; UK radio with Lloyd Ryan; Rhythm on Two with Tony Evans Orchestra, John West Orchestra. *Recordings:* with Dudu Pukwana: Sounds Zila 1981, Tom Christie: Beautiful Noise 1982, Zila: Life in Bracknell and Willisau 1983, Tony Evans: The Beat Goes On 1983, Dudu Pukwana: Zila 86 1986, Lloyd Ryan: Circular Storm 1989, Dudu Pukwana: Cosmics Chapter 90 1990, Stick Jam: Stick Jam 1991, Die Big-Band der Stadt Hamm: Die 'Hammer' Big-Band 1995, For Everyman: Four Songs From Under Mount Nephin 1997, Selma Garcia: Smilin' Samba 1998, rocksiechor!: She's got it 1999, Crazy Chris Kramer: Guarantee for the Blues 2000, Crazy Chris Kramer and Friends Vol. 1 – Guarantee for the Blues 2001, Crazy Chris Kramer and Friends Vol. 3 – Guarantee for the Blues – second set 2003, rocksiechor!: splash! 2003, Igel-Records: Der Bär auf dem Seil 2004, Soulful Swinging Singers: Praise The Lord! 2004, Igel-Records: Kindergarten Geschichten 2005, Inez Timmer: nichts haut mich um… 2005, Inez Timmer singt Cole Porter 2005, jan bierther trio & gäste: jazz in der fabrik 2005. *Publications:* The Music Factory (bass guitar instrumental workbooks). *Address:* Behringstr. 45, 44225 Dortmund, Germany (office). *E-mail:* pianoman@ericrichards.de (office); eric@pianoandbass.de (home). *Website:* www.the-pianoman.de; www.pianoandbass.de.

RICHARDS, Keith; British musician (guitar), singer and songwriter; b. (Keith Richard), 18 Dec. 1943, Dartford, Kent; s. of Bert Richards and Doris Richards; m. 1st Anita Pallenberg; two s. (one deceased) one d.; m. 2nd Patti Hansen 1983; two d. *Education:* Sidcup Art School. *Career:* Founder mem., The Rolling Stones 1962–; composer (with Mick Jagger) of numerous songs 1964–. *Films:* Sympathy for the Devil 1970, Gimme Shelter 1970, Ladies and Gentlemen, the Rolling Stones 1974, Let's Spend the Night Together 1983, Hail Hail Rock 'n' Roll 1987 (with Chuck Berry, Eric Clapton and Friends), Flashpoint 1991, Voodoo Lounge 1994, Pirates of the Caribbean: At World's End (actor) 2007, Shine a Light 2007. *Recordings include:* albums: with The Rolling Stones: The Rolling Stones 1964, The Rolling Stones No. 2 1965, Out Of Our Heads 1965, Aftermath 1966, Between The Buttons 1967, Their Satanic Majesties Request 1967, Beggar's Banquet 1968, Let It Bleed 1969, Get Yer Ya-Ya's Out 1969, Sticky Fingers 1971, Exile On Main Street 1972, Goat's Head Soup 1973, It's Only Rock And Roll 1974, Black And Blue 1976, Some Girls 1978, Emotional Rescue 1980, Tattoo You 1981, Still Life 1982,

Undercover 1983, Dirty Work 1986, Steel Wheels 1989, Flashpoint 1991, Voodoo Lounge 1994, Stripped 1995, Bridges to Babylon 1997, Forty Licks 2002, Live Licks 2004, A Bigger Bang 2005; solo: Hail Hail Rock 'n' Roll (with Chuck Berry) 1987, Talk Is Cheap 1988, Live At The Hollywood Palladium 1991, Main Offender 1992, Crosseyed Heart 2015. *Publications:* According to the Rolling Stones (jt autobiography) 2003, Life (autobiography) 2010. *Honours:* Nordoff-Robbins Silver Clef 1982, Grammy Lifetime Achievement Award 1986, Ivor Novello Award for Outstanding Contribution to British Music 1991. *Current Management:* Munro Sounds, 5 Wandsworth Plain, London, SW18 1ES, England. *Telephone:* (20) 8877-3111. *Fax:* (20) 8877-3033. *Website:* www.rollingstones.com; www.keithrichards.com.

RICHARDS, Ryan; British musician (drums). *Career:* mem. rock band, Funeral for a Friend 2001–12. *Recordings include:* albums: Casually Dressed & Deep in Conversation 2003, Hours 2005, Tales Don't Tell Themselves 2007, Memory and Humanity 2008, Welcome Home Armageddon 2011. *Honours:* Kerrang! Award for Best British Band 2006.

RICHARDSON, Garth John; Canadian record producer; b. 23 July 1958, Toronto, ON; s. of Jack Richardson; m. Jennifer Quinn 1989; two d. *Education:* Fanshawe Music Coll. *Career:* producer for Rage Against The Machine, L7, The Melvins, Ugly Kid Joe, POL, Houdini, Chase the Sun, State; engineer for Red Hot Chili Peppers, Ozzy Osbourne, Kiss, Mötley Crüe, Alice Cooper, American Man, Bulletboys; co-founder, Nimbus School of Recording Arts. *Address:* Nimbus School of Recording Arts, 242 East 2nd Avenue, Vancouver, V5T 1B7, Canada (office). *Telephone:* (604) 875-8998 (office). *Fax:* (604) 875-8959 (office). *Website:* www.nimbusrecording.com (office).

RICHARDSON, Kevin Scott; American singer and actor; b. 3 Oct. 1971, Lexington, KY. *Career:* qualified ballroom dancing instructor; mem., Backstreet Boys 1993–2006; numerous tours and television appearances. *Recordings include:* albums: with Backstreet Boys: Backstreet Boys 1996, Live in Concert 1998, Backstreet's Back 1998, Millennium 1999, Black And Blue 2000, Greatest Hits Chapter 1 2001, Never Gone 2005. *Honours:* Billboard Music Awards for Best Group, Best Adult Contemporary Group 1998, Album of the Year, Artist of the Year 1999, MTV Music Video Award for Best Group Video 1998, MTV European Music Awards for Best Pop Act 1997, Best Group 1999, World Music Awards for Best-Selling Pop Group 1999, 2000, Best-Selling R&B Group 1999, 2000, Best-Selling Dance Group 1999, 2000, Best American Group 2000, American Music Awards for Favorite Pop/Rock Band, Duo or Group 2000, 2001.

RICHARDSON, Mark; British musician (drums); b. 28 May 1970, Leeds, England. *Career:* founder mem., Skunk Anansie 1994–2001, 2009–; numerous headlining tours, festival appearances, television and radio shows; mem., Feeder 2002–09. *Recordings include:* albums: with Skunk Anansie: Paranoid and Sunburnt 1995, Stoosh 1996, Post Orgasmic Chill 1999, Smashes and Trashes 2009, Wonderlustre 2010; with Feeder: Comfort In Sound 2002, Pushing The Senses 2005, Silent Cry 2008. *Website:* www.skunkanansie.net.

RICHARDSON, Stuart; Welsh musician (bass guitar); b. Ferndale. *Career:* mem. rock band, Lostprophets 1999–2013, No Devotion 2014–. *Recordings include:* albums: thefakesoundofprogress 2000, Start Something 2004, Liberation Transmission 2006, The Betrayed 2010, Permanence 2015. *Honours:* Kerrang! Award for Best British Band 2007. *Website:* www.nodevotion.com.

RICHEY, David Andrew; musician (guitar), composer, actor and playwright; b. 21 Sept. 1965, Edgbaston, Birmingham, England; m. Gillian MacKenzie 1988; one d. *Career:* lead guitarist, vocalist with many bands, including YZI; founder mem., Aquila, Wayzgoose, Lyra and The Fianna; created Dave Richey Music, Media Music Production co. 1993; appeared in numerous stage plays, pantomimes; writer, composer, numerous songs and instrumentals; mem. Musicians' Union, SPAM. *Plays:* The Thorn in the Rose (writer), The Parkie (dir, writer).

RICHIE, Lionel, BS (Econs); American singer, songwriter and musician; b. 20 June 1949, Tuskegee, Ala; m. Diane Alexander 1996. *Education:* Tuskegee Univ. *Career:* mem. The Commodores 1968–82; various tours, concerts; solo artist 1982–. *Compositions include:* with The Commodores: Sweet Love 1975, Just To Be Close To You 1976, Easy 1977, Three Times A Lady 1979, Sail On 1980, Still 1980, Oh No 1981; for Kenny Rogers: Lady 1981; for Diana Ross: Missing You 1984; solo hits: Endless Love, film theme duet with Diana Ross 1981, Truly 1982, All Night Long 1983, Running With The Night 1984, Hello 1984, Stuck On You 1984, Penny Lover (with Brenda Harvey) 1984, Say You Say Me 1986, Dancing On The Ceiling 1987, Love Will Conquer All 1987, Ballerina Girl 1987, My Destiny 1992, Don't Wanna Lose You 1996; contrib. We are the World (with Michael Jackson), USA for Africa 1985. *Recordings include:* albums: with The Commodores: Machine Gun 1974, Caught In The Act 1975, Movin' On 1975, Hot On The Tracks 1976, Commodores 1977, Commodores Live! 1977, Natural High 1978, Greatest Hits 1978, Midnight Magic 1979, Heroes 1980, In The Pocket 1981; solo: Lionel Richie 1982, Can't Slow Down 1983, Dancing On The Ceiling 1986, Back To Front 1992, Louder Than Words 1996, Time 1998, Encore 2002, Coming Home 2006, Just Go 2009, Tuskegee 2012. *Honours:* ASCAP Songwriter Awards 1979, 1984–96, numerous American Music Awards 1979–, Grammy Awards include: Best Pop Vocal Performance 1982, Album of the Year 1985, Producer of the Year (shared) 1986; Lionel Richie Day, Los Angeles 1983, two Nat. Asscn. for the Advancement of Colored People (NAACP) Image Awards 1983, NAACP Entertainer of the Year 1987, Acad. Award for Best Song 1986, Golden Globe

Award for Best Song 1986. *Current Management:* c/o Bruce Eskowitz, Red Light Management, 8439 West Sunset Boulevard, 2nd Floor, Los Angeles, CA 90069, USA. *Telephone:* (310) 273-2266. *Website:* redlightmanagement.com. *E-mail:* web@lionelrichie.com. *Website:* www.lionelrichie.com.

RICHMAN, Guy Charles; British musician (drums); b. 3 June 1965, Rush Green, England; m. Alison Murray, 20 June 1994. *Education:* Taught by Maz Abrams and Bobby Armstrong. *Career:* Concert dates with Kylie Minogue, 1995; World tours and television appearances with: Black; Patricia Kaas; British tours with: Joe Longthorne (including television); Sister Sledge; Odyssey; Harold Melvin; mem, Musicians' Union. *Recordings:* Black; Boy George; Bucks Fizz; Patricia Kaas; Joe Longthorne; Two People; Sister Sledge; Odyssey; Howard Jones.

RICHMOND, Kim, BA, BM; American musician, composer and arranger; b. 24 July 1940, Champaign, Ill.; d. of Don Richmond and Edna Richmond; m. Chris Zambon 1989. *Education:* Univ. of Illinois. *Career:* has written and conducted original musical scores for several TV series, including Kojak, Harry O, Lazarus Syndrome, ABC Movie of the Week, and assorted cues for other shows; composed new works for concert stage (mostly jazz); arranger and music dir for singers, including Ann Jillian, Buddy Greco, Helen Reddy and Johnnie Ray; arranged for many acts, including Pat Boone, Diahann Carroll, Thelma Houston, Jaye P. Morgan, Kaye Ballard; has written for jazz groups of Stan Kenton, Buddy Rich, Louis Bellson, Stan Getz; toured with Percy Faith Orchestra in Japan and Australia for several years; freelance studio work, TV shows, theatre orchestras, concerts and other musical activities in Los Angeles; mem. Composers Ensemble of LA Chamber Orchestra; Artist-in-Residence, Univ. of Sydney Music Conservatorium Jazz Studies programme, Australia; fmr Adjunct Prof. in Jazz Studies, Thornton School of Music, Univ. of Southern California; occasional jazz radio host; mem. American Fed. of Musicians, American Soc. of Composers, Authors and Publrs, American Soc. of Music Arrangers and Composers, Los Angeles Jazz Soc., Nat. Acad. of Recording Arts and Sciences, Royal Musical Asscn, Pacific Composers Forum, Chamber Music Soc.; maintains the Kim Richmond Concert Jazz Orchestra (23 players) and the Kim Richmond Ensemble (six players). *Compositions include:* for large concert jazz ensemble: Augustana, Trump Card I, Trump Card II, Viridian, Range, Variations, All Together, Back A Tad, Bhakti, Big Mama Louise, The Big Sur, Brain Trouble, Chester's Way, Chic-a-brac, City of LA, Clear Command, Continued Obscurity, Fantasia for alto sax and jazz orchestra (three movements), Firebush (three movements), Flapjacks and Maple Syrup, Franz, Gems, Image, Blues and Likeness, Mayo, Melon Bells, Nicé, Old Acquaintances, Osage Autumn, Passages, Planos, Realization for guitar and jazz orchestra (three movements), Soft Feelings, Sojourn, Three Refractions, Tributaries, White Tornado, Wind Chimes, Wind-up, Trains; for small jazz ensemble: Range, Tracks, Cal 20, Common Denominator, Data Bank, Trains, Corrective Measures, Precious Promises, Anchor of Hope, Horizon; classical: Centuria for symphony orchestra, Movements for brass quintet, strings and percussion, Mixtures for brass quintet, Travels, Romanza Italian, Dreams, Waltz and Variations. *Recordings:* as leader: Look At The Time, Range, Passage, Looking In Looking Out, Ballads 2001, Refractions, Cross Weave, Live at Cafe Metropol; three CDs for the Kim Richmond Ensemble with Clay Jenkins (trumpet); many others for other leaders. *Publications:* writes articles and reviews for jazz magazines. *Address:* 6248 Rogerton Drive, Hollywood, CA 90068, USA. *Telephone:* (323) 466-3934. *Fax:* (323) 466-1970. *E-mail:* jazzkim@kimrichmond.com. *Website:* www.kimrichmond.com.

RICKFORS, Mikael; Swedish singer, musician (guitar, piano) and song-writer; b. 4 Dec. 1948; m. Mia (divorced); two s. one d. *Career:* founder mem. Bamboo 1967-70; mem., The Hollies 1971-73; solo artist 1973-; founder mem. Grymlings 1990-2005; concert tours and television appearances in Europe and the USA. *Compositions:* Yeah Yeah (recorded by Cyndi Lauper), Blue Night (Percy Sledge), Road Of No Return (co-written with and recorded by Percy Sledge), Misty Morning (co-written with and recorded by Percy Sledge), Shining Through The Rain (co-written with and recorded by Percy Sledge), Daughter of The Night (Carlos Santana), The Last Wind (Carla Olson), Touch (Carla Olson); recorded by The Hollies: Don't Leave The Child Alone, They Don't Realise I'm Down. *Recordings include:* albums: with the Hollies: Romany 1972, Out On The Road 1972, solo: Mikael Rickfors 1975, The Wheel 1976, Kickin' A Dream 1979, Tender Turns Tuff 1979, Blue Fun 1980, Rickfors 1983, Hearthunters 1985, Vingar 1988, Judas River 1991, Happy Man Don't Kill 1997, Greatest Hits 1999, The Mikael Rickfors Years 2000, Lush Life 2004, Away Again 2009; with Grymlings: Grymlings 1990, Grymlings Vol. 2 1992, Grymlings Vol. 3 2005. *E-mail:* info@mikaelrickfors.com (office). *Website:* www.rickfors.se.

RIDGELEY, Andrew; British singer and musician (guitar); b. 26 Jan. 1963, Windlesham, Surrey, England; m. Keren Woodward; one s. *Career:* mem., The Executive 1979-80; mem. duo, Wham! 1982-86, with world-wide tours and concerts; solo artist, actor and racing driver 1986-. *Recordings include:* albums: with Wham!: Fantastic 1983, Make It Big 1984, The Final 1986, If You Were There 1997; solo: Son Of Albert 1990. *Honours:* BRIT Award for Best British Group 1985, Outstanding Contribution to British Music 1986.

RIDGWAY, Stanard (Stan); American singer, songwriter and composer; b. 5 April 1956, Los Angeles, CA; m. Pietra Wexstun 1981; one s. *Career:* singer, Wall of Voodoo; solo recordings; numerous television appearances; mem. BMI. *Recordings include:* albums: with Wall of Voodoo: Wall of Voodoo 1979, Dark

Continent 1980, Call of The West 1981; solo: The Big Heat 1985, Mosquitos 1990, Party Ball 1991, Songs That Made This Country Great 1992, Anatomy 1999, Snakebite 2004, Neon Mirage 2010, Mr Trouble 2012. *E-mail:* stanmanager@stanridgway.com (office). *Website:* www.stanridgway.com.

RIDING, Jules; British Christian musician and singer; b. 22 May 1949, Cheltenham, Gloucestershire, England; m. Lynn Gousmett 1980, two s. two d. *Education:* Univ. of Auckland, New Zealand. *Career:* full-time professional 1988-; founder, Elkanah School of Music Ministry 1995; mem. APRA, New Zealand. *Recordings include:* albums: On This Night, 1984; Heartstrings, 1987; Revelation, 1991; Homecoming, 1992; The Fisherman, 1994; Kids Time, 1997; Amazing Sacrifice, 1998. *Publications:* Don't Let Poor Nellie Starve (poems) 1975, New Zealand Lamb (poems) 1981. *Honours:* New Zealand Music Award for Gospel Album of the Year 1984, 1987.

RIDLEY, Laurence (Larry) Howard, II, BS, MA, DPA; American jazz musician and music educator; *Professor Emeritus, Rutgers University;* b. 3 Sept. 1937, Indianapolis, Ind.; s. of Laurence H. Ridley and Nevoleane Morris Ridley; m. Magdalena Benitez-Ridley; one d. *Education:* Indiana Univ., New York Univ., Empire State Coll., State Univ. of New York, Univ. of Maryland-Eastern Shore. *Career:* Assoc. Prof. of Music, Livingston Coll./Rutgers Univ., New Jersey 1971-99, Chair. Dept of Music 1972-80, Prof. Emer. 1999-; Artist-in-Residence at numerous univs in USA and South Africa; bandleader, Jazz Legacy Ensemble; recordings and int. performances with numerous leading musicians, including Dizzy Gillespie, Duke Ellington, Wes Montgomery, Art Farmer, Thelonious Monk, Dinah Washington, Coleman Hawkins, Benny Goodman, Dexter Gordon, Benny Carter, Herbie Hancock, Freddie Hubbard, Mercer Ellington, Sonny Rollins, Philly Joe Jones, Chet Baker, Kenny Burrell, Stephane Grappelli, Joe Venuti, Roy Haynes, Lee Morgan; Jazz Artist-in-Residence, Schomburg Centre/New York Public Library 1993-; Exec. Dir African American Jazz Caucus Inc. 2000-; Chair. Jazz Panel, Nat. Endow-ment for the Arts (NEA) 1976-78, Nat. Co-ordinator, NEA Jazz Artists in Schools pilot programme 1978-82; Lecturer, Jazz at Lincoln Center/Swing Univ. 2011-; mem. Nat. Asscn of Jazz Educators (Advisory Bd 1981-), Jazz Educ. Network (JEN). *Honours:* Mid-Atlantic Arts Foundation Living Legacy Jazz Award 1997, inducted into Int. Assicn for Jazz Educ and Downbeat Magazine Halls of Fame, inducted into Indianapolis Jazz Hall of Fame 2013, honouree at 43rd Annual USA Congressional Black Caucus Foundation, Inc. 2013, Donald Meade Legacy Griot Award, JEN/African American Jazz Caucus 2014. *Address:* 3 Stuyvesant Oval, Apartment 9B, New York, NY 10009, USA (home). *Telephone:* (212) 979-0304 (office). *Fax:* (212) 260-5937 (office). *E-mail:* LHRidley@aol.com. *Website:* www.aajc.us (office); www.larryridley.com.

RIDLEY, Tim, GRSM, LRAM, PhD, FRSA; British teacher, musician (keyboards, drums, percussion) and conductor; *Director of Music, Glenalmond College;* b. 5 Aug. 1967, Portsmouth, Hants., England; s. of Captain Peter Ridley (RN Retrd) and Mrs Jenifer Ridley (nee Teale); Married Mrs Judith Ridley (nee Cutter), children Christopher (b.1989), Molly (b.1999) and Eleanor (b.2001). *Education:* Marlborough Coll., Wilts., Royal Acad. of Music, London, Brunel Univ., Uxbridge, West London. *Career:* freelance session keyboard player, composer, choral conductor and organist 1988-; keyboard player/composer, Mentaur 1988-94; keyboard player, Brotherhood of Man 1988-99; peripatetic teacher of drums, percussion and jazz piano 1988-96; keyboard player, The Sounds of The Supremes Show 1993-96; Head of Music Tech. and Dir of Chapel Music, Marlborough Coll. 1996-2009; Dir of Music, Glenalmond Coll., Perthshire 2009-; examiner for both Main and Jazz Panels, Associated Bd of the Royal Schools of Music 2009-; mem. Royal Coll. of Organists. *Compos-itions:* Magnificat and Nunc Dimittis (Collegium Marlburiense) 1996, Trom-bone Sonata 2003, Trumpet Sonata 2003, Oboe Sonata 2004, Rhapsodic Variations for clarinet and piano 2004, An Eiger Fantasia for horn and piano 2005, Modal Partita for bassoon and piano 2006, Sonatina upon Old English Heavy Guitar Riffs for tuba and piano 2006, Fugal Nonet for wind octet and piano 2006, Six Graded Miniatures for alto, tenor and baritone saxophones 2007, Suite of Graded Variations for euphonium and piano 2007, Sonatina for horn and piano 2007, Four Mood Movements for flute and piano 2007, A Spotless Rose (carol) 2008. *Recordings:* Darkness Before Dawn, Mentaur 1995, Live In Germany, The Sounds of The Supremes 1995. *Address:* Glenalmond College, Perth, SN8 1PA, Scotland (office). *Website:* www .myspace.com/mentaurmusic.

RIEDEL, Oliver (Ollie); German musician (bass guitar); b. 11 April 1971, Schwerin; m. (divorced); two c. *Career:* mem., The Inchtabokatables 1990-93; mem., Rammstein 1993-; the band has a reputation for theatrical live performances; numerous European tours. *Recordings include:* albums: Herzeleid 1995, Sehnsucht 1997, Live aus Berlin 1999, Mutter 2001, Reise, Reise 2004, Rosenrot 2005, Liebe ist für alle da 2009. *Honours:* MTV Europe Music Award for Best German Act 2005. *Current Management:* Pilgrim Management, Greifswalderstrasse 224, 10405 Berlin, Germany. *E-mail:* info@ pilgrim-management.de. *Website:* www.pilgrim-management.de; www .rammstein.de.

RIEL, Alex; Danish musician (drums); b. 13 Sept. 1940, Copenhagen. *Education:* Berklee Coll. of Music, Boston, USA. *Career:* career began as house drummer, Montmartre jazz club, Copenhagen; founder, Alex Riel Trio; member, Niels Lan Doky Trio; freelance solo musician; founding mem. The Savage Rose; television appearances with: Nancy Wilson, Manhattan Trans-fer, Stan Getz, Bill Evans, Eddie Gomez, Toots Thielemans, Gerry Mulligan, Roland Kirk, Niels Henning, Orsted Petersen; played concerts with: John

Scofield, Michel Petrucianni, Dizzy Gillespie, Wayne Shorter, Dollar Brand, Archie Shepp, Don Cherry; mem, Dansk Musiker Forbund. *Recordings include:* Alex Riel Trio 1967, Emerge 1993, Emergence 1994, The Riel Deal 1996, Unriel 1997, DSB Kino 1998, Rielatin' 1999, Celebration 2000, What Happened? 2004, The High and the Mighty 2007, Riel Time 2008; recorded as guest musician with numerous artists including Dexter Gordon, Ben Webster, Gary Burton, Thomas Clausen, Palle Mikkelborg, Karin Krog, Archie Shepp, Toots Thielmans, Jean Luc Ponty, Eddie Lockjaw Davis, Marilyn Mazur, Stéphane Grappelli. *Honours:* Danish Jazz Musician of Year 1965, Palace Jazz Award 1991, Ben Webster Award 1999, Django d'Or Award 2001. *E-mail:* drummer@alexriel.dk (office). *Website:* www.alexriel.dk.

RIENIETS, Andrea, BA; Australian singer, songwriter and composer; b. Feb. 1963, Shepparton, Vic.. *Career:* 17 scores for stage; founder/Dir of Before You Were Blonde choir 1991–96; Guest Dir, Sing It Up BIG, Indigenous Australian Choir 1997–98; WOMAD 1997. *Compositions:* Wooden Child, 1995; Love of a Lifetime, 1995; Something So Simple, 1998. *Recordings:* Fluently Helvetica 1995, Something So Simple 1998. *Address:* PO Box 10059, Adelaide, BC 5000, Australia.

RIHANNA; Barbadian singer; b. (Robyn Rihanna Fenty), 20 Feb. 1988, Saint Michael. *Education:* Combermere School, Barbados. *Career:* moved to USA aged 16 to pursue recording career under guidance of producer Evan Rogers, subsequently signed contract with Def Jam Recordings after auditioning for then-label head Jay-Z; solo artist 2005–; released debut studio album, Music of the Sun 2005; numerous collaborations with other artists including: Sean Paul, Maroon 5, T.I., Jay-Z, Kanye West, Eminem, Drake, Nicki Minaj, Mikky Ekko, Coldplay, Paul McCartney, David Guetta, Shakira. *Recordings include:* albums: Music of the Sun 2005, A Girl Like Me 2006, Good Girl Gone Bad (Juno Award for Int. Album of the Year 2008) 2007, Rated R 2009, Loud 2010, Talk That Talk (American Music Award for Favorite Soul/R&B Album 2012) 2011, Unapologetic (Billboard Music Award for Top R&B Album 2013, Grammy Award for Best Urban Contemporary Album 2014) 2012. *Film appearances:* Bring It On: All or Nothing 2006, Battleship 2012, Katy Perry: Part of Me 2012, This Is The End 2013, Annie 2014, Home 2015. *Honours:* numerous awards including: MOBO Awards for Best R&B Artist 2006, for Best Int. Act 2007, BMI Urban Award (for Pon de Replay) 2006, MTV European Music Award for Best R&B Artist 2006, Billboard Awards for Female Artist of the Year, for Female Hot 100 Artist of the Year, for Pop 100 Artist of the Year 2006, MTV Video Music Awards for Best Single (for Umbrella), for Best Video (for Umbrella) 2007, MTV Europe Music Awards for Best Urban Act 2007, for Best Female Artist 2015, American Music Awards for Favorite Female Soul/R&B Artist 2007, 2013, 2015, for Icon 2013, for Favorite American Music Award Icon Award 2013, Grammy Awards for Best Rap/Sung Collaboration (for Umbrella with Jay-Z) 2008, (for Run This Town with Jay-Z and Kanye West) 2010, for Best Dance Recording (for Only Girl (in the World)) 2011, for Best Rap/Sung Collaboration (for All of the Lights, with Kanye West) 2012, BRIT Awards for Best Int. Female Solo Artist 2011, 2012, Grammy Awards for Best Rap/Sung Collaboration (for All Of The Lights with Kanye West, Kid Cudi and Fergie) 2012, for Best Short Form Music Video (for We Found Love) 2013, for Best Rap/Sung Collaboration (for The Monster with Eminem) 2015, Billboard Music Awards for Top Radio Songs Artist 2013, for Top R&B Artist 2013, for Top R&B Song (for Diamonds) 2013, Icon Award, American Music Awards 2013, Fashion Icon Lifetime Achievement Award, Council of Fashion Designers of America 2014, iHeartRadio Music Award for Artist of the Year 2014, for Hip Hop and R&B Song of the Year (for Pour It Up) 2014, for Song of the Year (for Stay) 2014, MTV Europe Music Award (EMA) for Best Female Singer 2015. *Current Management:* c/o Roc Nation, 19348 Civic Center Drive, Beverly Hills, CA 90210, USA. *Telephone:* (310) 975-6854. *Website:* rocnation.com. *E-mail:* sos@rihannanow.com. *Website:* www .rihannanow.com.

RIIS-OLSEN, Jacob; Danish musician (guitar); b. 23 Aug. 1951. *Career:* founder mem., Gnags 1974–. *Recordings:* albums: På vej... 1973, Del af en ring 1975, Det er det 1976, La det gro 1977, Er du hjemme i aften 1978, Burhøns 1979, Intercity 1980, Live vol. 1 1981, Safari 1982, X 1983, Den blå hund 1984, En underlig fisk 1985, Plads til begejstring 1986, Har de puttet noget i kaffen 1987, Under bøgen 1988, Mr Swing King (Danish Grammy 1990) 1989, Lygtemandens sang 1991, Live vol. 2 1992, Øjne på stilke 1994, Gösta Hammerfedt 1996, Gnags Greatest 1999, Ridser, Revner og Buler 2000, Skønhedspletter 2002, Skitsernes Drøm 2003, Legepladen 2008. *E-mail:* gnags@gnags.dk (office). *Website:* www.gnags.dk.

RILEY, Howard, BA, MA, MMus, MPh; British musician (piano) and composer; b. 16 Feb. 1943, Huddersfield, Yorks., England. *Education:* Univ. of Wales, Indiana Univ., USA, York Univ. *Career:* festival, club, TV and radio appearances as solo and group pianist, throughout Europe and N America 1967–; Creative Assoc., Centre of the Creative and Performing Arts, Buffalo, NY, USA 1976–77. *Recordings include:* albums: Facets 1983, For Four On Two Two 1984, In Focus 1985, Live At The Royal Festival Hall 1985, Feathers 1988, Procession 1990, The Heat Of Moments 1991, Beyond Category 1993, The Bern Concert 1993, Inner Mirror 1996, Making Moves 1997, Short Stories 1998, One to One 1999, Synopsis 2000, Overground 2001, Airplay 2001, Consequences 2005, Two Is One 2006, Short Stories (Volume Two) 2007, Three is One 2008, The Monk and Ellington Sessions 2009, Solo in Vilnius 2010, The Complete Short Stories 1998–2010 2010, Live with Repertoire 2011, To Be Continued 2013. *Publications:* The Contemporary Piano Folio 1982. *Honours:* Bicentennial Arts Fellowship 1976. *Address:* Flat 2, 53 Tweedy

Road, Bromley, Kent, BR1 3NH, England (home). *Telephone:* (20) 8290-5917 (home).

RILEY, Jeannie Carolyn; American singer; b. (Jeannie Carolyn Stephenson), 19 Oct. 1944, Stamford, TX; d. of Oscar Stephenson and Nora Stephenson; m. Mickey Riley; one d. *Recordings:* albums: Harper Valley PTA 1968, Yearbooks and Yesterdays 1968, Things Go Better With Love 1969, Country Girl 1970, Generation Gap 1970, Jeannie 1971, Give Myself a Party 1972, Down to Earth 1973, When the Love Has Gone Away 1973, Just Jeannie 1973, Jeannie C Riley and Fancy Friends 1977, Wings to Fly 1979, From Harper Valley to the Mountain Top 1981, Total Woman 1984, Jeannie C. Riley 1986, Here's Jeannie C 1991, Praise Him 1995, Good Old Country 2000. *Honours:* Grammy Award 1968, CMA Record of Year 1969, Music Operators of America Award 1969. *E-mail:* jeanniecriley@mac.com (office). *Website:* www .jeanniec.com.

RILEY, Marc; British musician (guitar, bass, keyboards), producer and broadcaster; b. 10 July 1961, Manchester, England; m.; two d. *Education:* Saint Gregory's Grammar School. *Career:* mem., The Fall 1978–82; founder mem., The Creepers 1982–89; public relations for labels such as 4AD and Factory Records 1989; mem., The Shirehorses 1997; researcher and prod. for radio, later presenter. *Radio:* Hit the North (fortnightly music news show), joined Mark Radcliffe on BBC Radio 1 evening slot (as 'The Hapless Boy Lard') 1993, stand-in on the breakfast show 1996, permanent presenter on Breakfast Show 1997, afternoon show 1998–2005, Rocket Science show (BBC 6 Music) 2005–. *Recordings include:* albums: with The Fall: Live At The Witch Trials 1979, Dragnet 1979, Totale's Turns (It's Now Or Never) 1980, Grotesque (After The Gramme) 1980, Slates 1981, Hex Enduction Hour 1982, Room To Love 1982; with The Shirehorses: The Worst Album In The World Ever... Ever! 1997. *Address:* c/o BBC 6 Music, Broadcasting House, 1 Portland Place, London, W1A 1AA, England. *Website:* www.bbc.co.uk/6music.

RILEY, Teddy; American musician (multi-instrumentalist) and record producer; b. 8 Oct. 1967, Harlem, New York. *Career:* considered pioneer of 'New Jack Swing'; produced underground hit, Raps New Generation aged 15; member, groups Guy, Blackstreet; collaborated with various artists including Kool Moe Dee, Heavy D, Michael Jackson, Roy Brown, Aretha Franklin, Whitney Houston, Billy Ocean, Blondie, Boy George, Hi-Five, Stephanie Mills, The Jacksons; own recording studio, Future Records. *Recordings:* albums: with Guy: Guy 1987; as producer: with Michael Jackson, Dangerous 1991, Blood on the Dance Floor 1997, Invincible 2001; with Bobby Brown: Don't Be Cruel; with Wreckx 'N' Effects: Hard or Smooth, Rap's New Generation; with Keith Sweat: Make It Last Forever; with Men of Vision: Personal; with Blackstreet, Another Level; with Foxy Brown: Get on the Bus, Ill Na Na; with Nate Dogg: G-Funk Classics; other recordings for: Heavy D, James Ingram, Jazzy Jeff and The Fresh Prince, Profyle, K-Ci and Jo-Jo. *E-mail:* tr@ trmusicgroup.com (office). *Website:* www.trmusicgroup.com.

RILEY, Terry Mitchell, MA; American composer, pianist and raga singer; b. 24 June 1935, Colfax, Calif.; s. of Charles Riley and Wilma Ridlofi; m. Ann Yvonne Smith 1958; three c. *Education:* San Francisco State Univ., Univ. of California, studied with Duane Hampton, Adolf Baller and Pandit Pran Nath. *Career:* joined La Monte Young's Theater of Eternal Music 1965; Creative Assoc., Center for Creative and Performing Arts, Buffalo 1967; taught music composition and N Indian raga at Mills Coll. 1971–83; freelance composer and performer 1961–; launched Minimal Music Movt with composition and first performance of In C 1964; Founder-mem., Khaval ensemble 1989–93; f. The Travelling-Avantt-Gaard (theatre co.) 1992. *Compositions include:* The Harp of New Albion for solo piano in just intonation, Sunrise of the Planetary Dream Collector, Sri Camel, The Ten Voices of the Two Prophets, Chorale of the Blessed Day, Eastern Man, Embroidery, Song from the Old Country, G-Song, Remember This Oh Mind, The Ethereal Time Shadow, Offering to Chief Crazy Horse, Rites of the Imitators, The Medicine Wheel, Song of the Emerald Runner, Cycle of five string quartets, Trio for violin, clarinet and cello 1957, Concert for two pianos and tape 1960, String Trio 1961, Keyboard Studies 1963, Dorian Reeds for ensemble 1964, In C 1964, A Rainbow in the Curved Air 1968, Persian Surgery Dervishes for electronic keyboard 1971, Descending Moonshine Dervishes 1975, Do You Know How it Sounds? for low voice, piano and tabla 1983, Cadenza on the Night Plain for string quartet 1984, Salome Dances for Peace string quartet 1988, Jade Palace for orchestra and synthesiser 1989, Cactus Rosary for synthesiser and ensemble 1990, June Buddhas for chorus and orchestra 1991, The Sands for string quartet and orchestra 1991, Four Woelfi Portraits for ensemble 1992, The Saint Adolf Ring chamber opera 1993, Ritmos and Melos 1993, El Hombre string quartet 1993, Ascension for solo guitar 1993, The Heaven Ladder for piano four hands 1996, Three Requiem Quartets 1997, Autodreamographical Tales for narrator and instruments 1997, Uncle Jard for saxophone quartet and piano 1998, MissiGono 1998, DeepChandi for string orchestra, dancer and tape 1998, Banana Humberto 2000, Assassin Reverie for saxophone quartet 2001, Sun Rings for string quartet, choir and backing track 2002, ArchAngels for eight cellos 2003, Quando Cosas Malas Caen del Cielo 2003, Crazy World 2003, Worksong 2003, Baghdad Highway 2003, The Cusp of Magic 2004, Melodious Junkyard for piano 2004, Bruce's Travelling Machine for solo cello 2005, The Heaven Ladder, Book 6 2006, Giant-Hairy Nude-Warriors Racing down the Slopes of Battle 2006, SolTierraLuna 2007, The Universal Bridge 2008, The Transylvanian Horn Courtship 2009. *Honours:* Guggenheim Fellowship 1980. *Current Management:* c/o Tom Walsh, Associate Director of Music, The Cleveland Museum of Art, 11150 East Boulevard, Cleveland, OH 44106, USA. *Telephone:*

(216) 707-2281. *E-mail:* tom@elisionfields.com. *Address:* Sri Moonshine Music, 13699 Moonshine Road, Camptonville, CA 95922, USA (office). *E-mail:* srimoonshinemusic@gmail.com (office). *Website:* www.terryriley.com.

RIMES, (Margaret) LeAnn; American country singer; b. 28 Aug. 1982, Jackson, MS; d. of Wilbur Rimes; m. Dean Sheremet 2002 (divorced 2009). *Career:* was winning talent shows aged five; her parents recorded an album to sell aged seven; released first commercial album aged 11. *Film appearances:* Holiday in Your Heart 1997, Dill Scallion 1999. *Recordings include:* albums: Blue (Grammy Award for Best Female Country Vocal Performance 1997) 1996, You Light Up My Life – Inspirational Songs 1997, Sittin' On Top Of The World 1998, LeAnn Rimes 1999, I Need You, God Bless America 2001, Twisted Angel 2002, This Woman 2005, Whatever We Wanna 2006, Family 2007, Spitfire 2013. *Publications:* Jag 2003, Jag's New Friend 2004. *Honours:* American Music Award, three Acad. of Country Music Awards, twelve Billboard Awards, Grammy Award for Best New Artist 1997. *Address:* LeAnn Rimes All Access, PO Box 150667, Nashville, TN 37215, USA (office). *Website:* www.leannrimesworld.com.

RINGO, Sheena; Japanese singer, musician (piano, bass guitar) and songwriter; b. 15 Nov. 1978, Fukuoka, Japan; m. Junji Yayoshi 2001. *Education:* trained as classical pianist and ballerina. *Career:* fmr mem. various semi-professional groups, including The Marvelous Marbles; solo artist 1999–. *Music for film:* Sakuran 2007. *Recordings include:* albums: Muzai Moratorium 1999, Shoso Strip 2000, Utaite Myōri 2002, Kalk Samen Kuri no Hana 2003, Heisei Fūzoku 2007, Sanmon Gossip 2009, Gyakuyunyū 2014, Hi Izuru Tokoro 2014. *Honours:* Annual Music Quest Award of Excellence 1996, Newcomer Prize, Ministry of Educ., Culture, Sports, Science and Tech's Fine Arts Award in the Popular Culture 2009, Best Artist, Space Shower Music Video Awards 2010.

RIPPER, Dubravko Ivaniš; Croatian singer. *Career:* mem. and lead singer, Pipschips&videoclips 1992–. *Recordings include:* albums: Shimpoo Pimpoo 1993, Dernjava 1995, Fred Astaire (Porin Award for Best Rock Album 1997) 1997, Bog (Porin Award for Best Rock Album 2000) 1999, Drveće i rijeke 2003. *Address:* c/o Menart Records, Bencekovićeva 19, 10 000 Zagreb, Croatia. *Website:* www.pipschipsvideoclips.com.

RIPPLE, Sean; American musician (guitar, vibraphone). *Career:* mem., The American Analog Set 2000–. *Recordings include:* albums: Know By Heart 2001, Updates 2002, Through The 1990s: Singles & Unreleased 2001, Promise Of Love 2003, Set Free 2005. *E-mail:* requests@amanset.com (home). *Website:* www.amanset.com.

RISDON, Ronald Valentine; artist manager and television and film producer; b. 14 Feb. 1950, Dorking, Surrey, England; m. Jane Risdon 1972; one s. *Career:* bassist, then guitarist, with Marjorine, including UK, Europe tours, 1968–; re-named Jungle Jim, 1972; Tours, North Africa, UK and Europe; television and radio: Europe, UK, Channel Islands; manager of various acts including: Tag, Ignorance, Heat featuring T J Felton, Treana, Craig Thomson, actor, Lucy, Gita, Blackout; Co-owner, production company Everyday Productions; mem, PRS; BAC&S. *Recordings:* Singles: I Live, 1968; Big Fat Orangoman, (Top 20, UK, No. 1, France, Germany); Manager, recording artists 1980–; Released: Tag, USA; Ignorance, USA; Treana, USA; Rain; Manages record producers: G Young and K Holland; Manages Songwriters: Young/Morris, A Hayman, Holland/Palmer/Wilcocks. *Address:* Showcase Management International, 3217 Overland Ave, Suite 7115, Los Angeles, CA 90034, USA. *E-mail:* selectevents@mediaone.net.

RITCHIE, Billy Darrell, Jr, BA; American singer and songwriter; b. High Point, North Carolina; m. Michelle Ritchie 1990; one d. *Education:* Gardner-Webb College. *Career:* full-time concert artist, songwriter; over 500 concerts 1991–; mem. Gospel Music Asscn, BMI. *Recordings:* albums: Stand and Believe 1992, No Turning Back 1993, Big Time 1995. *Website:* darrellritchie.org.

RITENOUR, Lee; American jazz musician (guitar); b. 11 Jan. 1952, Los Angeles, Calif. *Career:* session player, as Captain Fingers, mid 1970s; also jazz fusion solo artist; has played with artists including Herbie Hancock, Steely Dan, Eddie Henderson, Stanley Clarke; mem. Friendship (with Don Grusin). *Recordings include:* albums: First Course 1976, Lee Ritenour and His Gentle Thoughts 1977, Captain Fingers 1977, Sugar Loaf Express 1977, Friendship 1978, The Captain's Journey 1978, Rio 1979, Feel The Night 1979, Rit 1981, Rit 2 1982, On The Line 1983, Banded Together 1984, Harlequin (with Dave Grusin) 1985, Earth Run 1986, Portrait 1987, Festival 1988, Color Rit 1990, Stolen Moments 1990, Collection 1991, Fourplay 1991, Wes Bound 1993, Between the Sheets 1993, Larry and Lee (with Larry Carlton) 1995, Elixir 1995, Alive in LA 1997, A Twist of Jobim 1997, Best of Fourplay 1997, This is Love 1998, Two Worlds 1999, A Twist of Marley 2001, Rit's House 2002, A Twist of Motown 2003, Overtime 2005, World of Brazil 2005, Smoke N Mirrors 2006, Amparo 2008, 6 String Theory 2010, Rhythm Sessions 2012. *Honours:* Echo Award for Best Int. Instrumentalist 2011. *E-mail:* ritsguitar@aol.com. *Website:* www.leeritenour.com; www.sixstringtheory.com.

RITTER, Josh; American singer and songwriter; b. 21 Oct. 1976, Moscow, ID. *Education:* Oberlin Coll. *Career:* solo artist 1999–. *Recordings include:* albums: Josh Ritter 1999, Golden Age of Radio 2002, Hello Starling 2003, The Animal Years 2006, The Historical Conquests of Josh Ritter 2007, So Runs the World Away 2010, The Beast in Its Tracks 2013. *Publication:* Bright's Passage (novel) 2011. *Current Management:* Darius Zelkha, Tough Love Artist Management, 660 York Street, Suite 212, San Francisco, CA 94110, USA.

Telephone: (415) 651-4509. *E-mail:* darius@thisistoughlove.com. *Website:* www.thisistoughlove.com; www.joshritter.com.

RIVERA, Chita; American actress, singer and dancer; b. (Dolores Conchita Figueroa del Rivero), 23 Jan. 1933, Washington, DC; d. of Pedro Julio Figuerva del Rivero and Katherine Anderson del Rivero; m. Anthony Mordente (divorced); one d. *Education:* American School of Ballet, New York. *Career:* performs in nightclubs and cabarets around the world. *Stage appearances include:* Father's Day, Threepenny Opera, Born Yesterday, Jacques is Alive and Well and Living in Paris, Ivanhoe, Call Me Madam 1951, Guys and Dolls 1951, Can-Can 1953, Seventh Heaven 1955, Mister Wonderful 1956, West Side Story 1957, Bye Bye Birdie 1960, Flower Drum Song 1966, Sweet Charity 1967, Zorba 1969, Sondheim–A Musical Tribute 1973, Kiss Me Kate 1974, Chicago 1975, Bring Back Birdie 1981, Merlin 1983, The Rink (Tony Award 1984) 1984, Jerry's Girls 1985, Kiss of the Spider Woman (Tony Award for Best Actress in a Musical 1993) 1992, Chita Rivera: The Dancer's Life 2005, Chita Rivera: My Broadway 2010, The Mystery of Edwin Drood 2012, The Visit 2015. *Films:* Chicago 2002, Kalamazoo? 2006. *Television includes:* Kojak and the Marcus Nelson Murders 1973, The New Dick Van Dyke Show 1973–74, Kennedy Center Tonight–Broadway to Washington!, Pippin 1982, The Mayflower Madam 1987. *Recordings include:* And Now I Swing 2009. *Honours:* Kennedy Center Honor 2002, Presidential Medal of Freedom 2009, League of Professional Theatre Women's Lifetime Achievement Award 2010. *Current Management:* c/o Ken DiCamillo, William Morris Agency, 1325 Avenue of the Americas, New York, NY 10019, USA. *Telephone:* (212) 586-5100. *Fax:* (212) 246-3583. *E-mail:* kdicamillo@wmeentertainment.com. *Website:* www.wma.com; www.chitarivera.com.

RIVERA, Sandy; American producer, remixer and DJ; b. San Diego, California. *Career:* founder: Blackwiz Records, 1992; Deep Vision Records; Remixed: Moloko Eddie Amador; Ladysmith Black Mambazo; member: Kings of Tomorrow; Soul Vision; numerous collaborations including Everything But The Girl, Jose Burgos, Julie McKnight, DADA, Robert Owens, HAZE, Andy Daniell, Rae. *Recordings:* albums: with Jose Burgos: The Calling 1999; with Kings of Tomorrow: It's In The Lifestyle 2000, Trouble 2005; singles: with Kings of Tomorrow: Fade II Black, 1997; Tear It Up, 2000; Finally, 2001; Tracey In My Room (as Soul Vision with EBTG), 2001. *Address:* c/o KOT, Suite 244, 22 Notting Hill Gate, London, W11 3JE, England. *E-mail:* hello@sandyrivera.dj. *Website:* www.sandyrivera.dj.

RIVERS, Johnny; American musician, singer and songwriter; b. (Johnny Henry Ramistella), 7 Nov. 1942, New York, NY. *Career:* formed band, The Spades 1956; solo artist 1958–; Pres., record and publishing co., singer and songwriter by age 25; started American discotheque craze at Whiskey A Go Go, Los Angeles 1963; appeared La Riviera, with Nancy Wilson 1966; first rock and roll act to play Copacabana, New York; formed record co., Soul City Records; owner, manager, Rivers Music; mem. BMI, ASCAP, AFTRA, AFofM. *Recordings:* albums: At the Whiskey A Go-Go 1964, Here We Go-Go Again 1964, In Action 1964, Meanwhile 1965, ...and I Know You Want to Dance 1966, Changes 1966, Rewind 1967, Realization 1968, Touch of Gold 1969, Home-grown 1971, L.A. Reggae 1972, Blue Suede Shoes 1973, Last Boogie in Paris 1974, Road 1974, New Lovers and Old Friends 1975, Wild Night 1976, Outside Help 1979, Borrowed Time 1980, Not a Through Street 1983, Memphis Sun 1991, Last Train to Memphis 1998, Shadows on the Moon 2009; hits include: Memphis, Maybelline, Mountain of Love, Seventh Son, Midnight Special, Secret Agent Man, Poor Side of Town, Baby, I Need Your Lovin', Tracks of My Tears, Summer Rain, Look To Your Soul, Rockin' Pneumonia and The Boogie Woogie Flu, Sea Cruise, Blue Suede Shoes, Help Me Rhonda, Swayin' To The Music (Slow Dancin'), Curious Mind (Um Um Um Um Um), Last Train to Memphis. *Honours:* two Grammy Awards, BMI Awards. *Website:* www.johnnyrivers.com.

RIVERS, Sam; American musician (bass guitar); b. 21 Sept. 1977, Jacksonville, FL; m. Kinter 2001. *Education:* Arlington Middle School, Jacksonville, Douglas Anderson School of the Arts. *Career:* mem., Limp Bizkit 1994–. *Recordings:* albums: Three Dollar Bill Y'All 1997, Significant Other 1999, Chocolate Starfish And The Hotdog Flavored Water 2000, New Old Songs 2001, Bipolar 2003, Results May Vary 2003, The Unquestionable Truth (Part 1) 2005, Gold Cobra 2010. *Honours:* Orville H. Gibson Guitar Award for Best Rock Bass Player 2000, American Music Award for Favorite Alternative Artist 2002. *Current Management:* c/o Peter Katsis, The Firm, 9100 Wilshire Boulevard, Beverly Hills, CA 90212, USA. *Website:* www.limpbizkit.com.

RIX, (Leon) Luther, MusB; American musician (percussion, drums) and composer; b. 11 Feb. 1942, Lansing, Michigan; m. Ellen Garrett 1973; one s. *Education:* Indiana Univ., Jordan Conservatory of Music, Indianapolis. *Career:* percussionist with Indianapolis Symphony Orchestra 1965–67, Winter Consort 1968, Doc Severinsen 1970; drummer with Bette Midler 1971–72, Manhattan Transfer 1974–75, Mary Travers 1975–76, Bob Dylan 1975–76, Leonard Cohen, Laura Branigan 1976, Peter, Paul and Mary 1978; freelance musician 1979–; drummer with Rosenhontz 1986–, Richard Reiter Swing band 1987–, Crossing Point 1990–; musician, shows including The Wiz, Grease, Barnum, Little Shop of Horrors; mem, ASCAP, AFTRA, BMI, AFofM. *Compositions:* Boogaloother 1972, Like A Beautiful Song 1980, Tightrope (also arranger) 1969; compositions recorded by Genya Raven, Buzzy Lindhart, Kaleidoscope. *Recordings include:* with Loudon Wainwright III: Fame and Wealth 1983; Tommy (original Broadway cast) 1993; with Bob Dylan:

Greatest Hits Vol. 3 1994; with Labelle: Something Silver 1997; also with Topaz, Bette Midler.

RIX, Simon; British musician (bass guitar). *Career:* founder mem. Runston Parva 1997, renamed Parva, renamed Kaiser Chiefs 2003–. *Recordings include:* albums: Employment (Meteor Ireland Music Award for Best Int. Album 2006, NME Award for Best Album 2006, Ivor Novello Award for Best Album 2006) 2005, Yours Truly, Angry Mob 2007, Off With Their Heads 2008, The Future Is Medieval 2011, Education, Education, Education & War 2014. *Honours:* BRIT Awards for Best British Rock Act, Best British Live Act, Best British Group 2006, Nordoff-Robbins Silver Clef Award for Best Group 2006, Q Award for Best Video (for 'Ruby') 2007. *E-mail:* james.sandom@ redlightmanagement.com; jessica.lord@redlightmanagement.com. *Website:* www.redlightmanagement.com; www.kaiserchiefs.com.

RIZZO, Carmen; American record producer, engineer, mixer and musician; b. 8 April 1964, Akron, Ohio; m. 1993. *Career:* writer, engineer and programmer on Seal's classic album Seal 2; producer and writer for Paul Oakenfold's Bunka album; collaborated with Tuvan throat singers Huun Huur Tu; Co-founder world music/electronic act Niyaz (three albums all debuted at No. 1 on iTunes world music chart); has worked with artists including Coldplay, Seal, Perry Farrell, Alanis Morissette, Dido, Jem, A. R. Rahman, Ryuichi Sakamoto, Khaled, Michael Nyman and Pete Townshend as well as record producers Trevor Horn, Rob Cavallo, David Foster and Marius De Vries; has recorded world-wide, including at Abbey Road Studios, UK, Studio Plus XXX, Paris, Record Plant, Los Angeles, Studio 301, Australia, amongst others; debut solo album selected by USA Today as No. 1 in their autumn music guide; music for numerous films and TV shows, including CSI Miami, True Blood (HBO), and numerous Buddha Bar compilations and on KCRW radio station; also contributed original music to the David Lynch Foundation album alongside Moby and Peter Gabriel; wrote score for several films directed by Michael Apted, score for Perfect Sisters, end title for Uncharted 2 video game; co-wrote and introduced the new category Best Electronic Album as well as writing technical Grammys for Apple and Roger Linn 2005; has lectured at insts including TED convention, Berklee School of Music, Univ. of Southern California, UCLA, Los Angeles Film School, Univ. of Audiovisual Arts – European Film Acad. ESRA, Skopje, Macedonia; Owner Electrofone Music label; mem. Nat. Acad. of Recording Arts and Sciences (mem. Bd Govs and Trustees, Producer and Eng Advisory Bd). *Recordings include:* Niyaz 2005, Nine Heavens 2008, Sumud 2012; solo: The Lost Art of the Idle Moment 2005, Ornament of an Imposter 2008, Looking Through Leaves 2010, The Space Left Behind 2010, Romancia 2013. *Current Management:* c/o WME Entertainment, 9601 Wilshire Boulevard, Beverly Hills, CA 90210-5213, USA. *Telephone:* (310) 285-9000. *Fax:* (310) 285-9010. *Website:* www.wma.com. *E-mail:* info@ carmenrizzo.com. *Website:* www.carmenrizzo.com.

RJD2; American hip-hop producer and DJ; b. 27 May 1976, Eugene, OR. *Career:* DJ and prod. for group, Megahertz 1998–99; prod. for artists, including Copywrite; solo artist 2001–; formed Icebird (duo with Aaron Livingston) 2011. *Recordings include:* albums: Your Face Or Your Kneecaps 2001, Dead Ringer 2002, The Horror 2003, Since We Last Spoke 2004, The Third Hand 2007, The Colossus 2010; as The Insane Warrior: We Are the Doorways 2011; with Icebird: The Abandoned Lullaby 2011. *Current Management:* c/o Cris Hearn, Primary Talent International, 2–12 Pentonville Road, London, N1 9PL, England. *Telephone:* (20) 7833-8998. *Fax:* (20) 7833-5992. *E-mail:* cris@primary.uk.com. *Website:* www.primary.uk.com. *E-mail:* rjd2management@hotmail.com. *Website:* www.rjd2.net.

ROACH, Archie; Australian singer and songwriter; b. 1956, Framlingham, Vic.; pnr Ruby Hunter; five c. *Career:* singer, songwriter; numerous tours, festival appearances. *Recordings include:* albums: Charcoal Lane, 1990; Jamu Dreaming, 1994; Looking for Butter Boy, 1997. *Publication:* You Have the Power (anthology of lyrics) 1994. *Address:* 25 Overend Street, Brunswick, Vic. 3056, Australia. *Website:* www.loreoftheland.com.au/indigenous/archie.

ROACHFORD, Andrew; singer and musician (keyboards, percussion). *Career:* performer in Soho jazz clubs, London aged 14; founder own band, Roachford 1987–. *Recordings include:* albums: Roachford 1988, Get Ready! 1991, Feel 1997, The Roachford Files 2000, Word of Mouth 2006. *Address:* c/o M3 Records, PO Box 52803, London, SW11 5RS, England. *Telephone:* (20) 7228-1011. *Website:* www.roachford.co.uk.

ROBBINS, Dennis Anthony; American country musician (guitar); b. Hazelwood, NC; m. Helen Hughs; two c. *Career:* US Marines, toured Viet Nam 1968; joined the Rockets 1976; moved to Nashville, solo artist and songwriter 1985–; mem. of band, Billy Hill 1988–90. *Compositions include:* Do You Love Me, Just Say Yes, Highway 101 1987; Church On Cumberland Road, Shenandoah; Two of a Kind, Working On A Full House, Garth Brooks; Finally Friday, by both Earl Thomas Connelly, George Jones; Paris Tennessee, Tracy Lawrence; I'm Just A Rebel, by both Confederate Railroad, Joy Lynn White; Home Sweet Home, Dennis Robbins. *Recordings include:* albums: The First of Me 1986, I Am Just a Rebel 1989, Man with a Plan 1992, Born Ready 1994. *Website:* www.myspace.com/iplayslide.

ROBERSON, LaTavia; American singer and songwriter; b. 1 Nov. 1981, Houston, TX. *Career:* first TV appearance on Ed McMann's Star Search, aged nine; package model for Pro-Line Hair Corpn 1989–98; various other nat. TV and print advertising work; mem., GirlsTyme (with Beyoncé Knowles, Kelly Rowland and LaToya Luckett) 1992, renamed Something Fresh then The

Dolls before settling on Destiny's Child; acrimonious split from group 2000; formed group Anjel (with LaToya Luckett) 2000. *Recordings:* albums: with Destiny's Child: Destiny's Child 1998, The Writing's On The Wall 1999.

DR ROBERT; British singer; b. (Bruce Robert Howard), 2 May 1961, Norfolk. *Career:* fmr footballer, Norwich City Football Club; fmr pop music journalist; mem. The Blow Monkeys 1984–90, reformed 2007–; est. Artbus record label 1992. *Recordings:* albums with The Blow Monkeys: Limping For A Generation 1984, Animal Magic 1986, She Was Only A Grocer's Daughter 1987, Whoops There Goes The Neighbourhood 1989, Choices 1989, Springtime for the World 1990, Atomic Lullabies (compilation) 2001, Devil's Tavern 2008; solo albums: Realms of Gold 1994, Bethesda 1995, Flatlands 1999, Birds Gotta Fly 2001, Keep on Digging for Gold 2002, Five in the Afternoon (with P.P. Arnold) 2007; also recorded with: Paul Weller, Beth Orton; contrib. to soundtracks for film Dirty Dancing and TV documentaries Dave's World, Gangsters. *Current Management:* East Central One, Creeting House, All Saints Road, Creeting St Mary, Suffolk, IP6 8PR, England. *Telephone:* (1449) 723244. *Fax:* (1449) 726067. *E-mail:* enquiries@eastcentralone.com. *Website:* www.eastcentralone .com. *E-mail:* fencatonline@mac.com (home). *Website:* www.theblowmonkeys .com; www.drrobert.net.

ROBERT, George Paul, BA, MMus; Swiss/American musician (saxophones, clarinet, piano); b. 15 Sept. 1960, Geneva, Switzerland; s. of Marcel Robert and Joan Robert; m. Joan Yap 1991. *Education:* Conservatoire de Musique de Genève, Berklee Coll. of Music, Manhattan School of Music, USA. *Career:* toured Europe with own quartet 1983, lead alto saxophone, MSM Big Band; formed George Robert/Tom Harrell Quintet 1987, toured throughout USA, Canada and Europe; freelance musician with many groups, including Lionel Hampton and Toshiko Akiyoshi Jazz Orchestras, Buster Williams, Ray Drummond, Ron McClure; first Swiss jazz musician to lead successful career in USA; formed George Robert Quartet, worked with Clark Terry, numerous tours including 16-week world tour in top jazz clubs with Clark Terry; Teacher and Jazz Clinician, USA, Canada and Europe; performed in numerous top clubs as leader; Dir Swiss Jazz School, Berne 1995; organized USA tours for SJS Big Band; teacher, Interlaken Jazz Workshop teaching and performing with leading names including Billy Hart, Phil Woods, Lionel Hampton, Tony Bennett, Benny Green; mem. American Soc. of Composers, Authors and Publrs (ASCAP), SUISse Auteurs (SUISA), American Fed. of Musicians. *Recordings include:* First Encounter 1985, Shades of Time 1987, Sun Dance 1988, Lonely Eyes 1989, Looking Ahead 1989, Visions 1991, Swiss Kiss 1992, Jazz on the Mountain 1992, Cape Verde 1993, Youngbloods 1993, The Good Things in Life 1994, Tribute 1994, Remember the Time 1994, Voyage 1995, George Robert with the Metropole Orchestra 1995, The Big Summit 1999, Italian Jazz Machine 2001, Paradise Found 2001, Shades of Time 2003, I Wish I Knew 2003, Soul Eyes 2003, Peace 2003, Reflections Vol. III 2004, First Encounter 2005, Soul Searching 2005, Wingspan 2006. *Honours:* Down Beat Awards, Outstanding Performance 1983, Best Coll. Band 1987. *Address:* GPR Productions, PO Box 357, 1009 Pully, Switzerland (office). *E-mail:* george .robert@bluewin.ch (office). *Website:* ww.georgerobert.com.

ROBERTS, Austin; American songwriter, artist, producer and publisher; b. 19 Sept. 1945, Newport News, Virginia. *Career:* songs featured, films and television series; wrote and sang many of the Scooby-Doo songs, Josie and the Pussycats; wrote musicals: Damon's Song, Rachinoff; formed Hot House Music 1992. *Compositions:* hits include: Something's Wrong With Me, Keep on Singing, Rocky, When You Put Your Heart In It, Honor Bound, Strong Heart, IOV, My Night To Howl, Desesperados, You Lie; songs recorded by: Reba McEntire, Kenny Rogers, Crystal Gayle, Michelle Wright, Lee Greenwood, Oak Ridge Boys, Charley Pride, Lulu, Julio Iglesias, Glen Campbell, Tanya Tucker, Sonny and Cher, Dan Seals, Englebert Humperdinck, Vikki Carr, Loverboy, Billy Crash Craddock, The Osmonds, Rosa Reeves, Marta Sanchez. *Honours:* Grammy Award, Music City News Award, NSAI Award, numerous ASCAP Airplay Awards, one German Grammy Award, four JUNO Awards, SESAC Airplay Award.

ROBERTS, Eric; American bass guitarist. *Career:* fmr bassist, Kill the Frontman; mem. Gym Class Heroes 2005–, numerous collaborations including Daryl Hall, Estelle, The-Dream, Busta Rhymes, Adam Levine, Neon Hitch, Ryan Tedder. *Recordings include:* with Gym Class Heroes: albums: The Papercut Chronicles 2005, As Cruel as School Children 2006, The Quilt 2008, The Papercut Chronicles II 2011. *Honours:* with Gym Class Heroes: MTV Video Music Award for Best New Artist 2007. *Address:* c/o Fueled by Ramen Records, Warner Music Group, 75 Rockefeller Plaza, New York, NY 10019, USA (office). *Website:* www.fueledbyramen.com (office); www.gymclassheroes.com.

ROBERTS, Graham Andrew; musician (guitar); b. 3 Feb. 1964, North-ampton, England. *Education:* Royal Academy of Music. *Career:* numerous concerts, television, radio, for BBC, ITV, various European stations; Tours, USA, Europe, Far East. *Recordings:* with Grahamphones: Let's Do It Again, 1990; with Pasadena Roof Orchestra: Breakaway, 1991; Swing That Music, 2000; with Swing Sisters: Swing, 1992; Take Me Back, 1994; with Tetra Guitar Quartet: By Arrangement, 1993; Pasadena, 1994. *Honours:* Julian Bream Guitar Competition 1988. *Current Management:* Hothouse Entertainments, 7 Wychwood Close, New Duston, Northampton, NN5 6QL, England.

ROBERTS, J. Patricia, BSc, DipEd; British scottish traditional singer and musician (celtic harp (clarsach), guitar); b. 17 Feb. 1954, Aberdeen, Scotland. *Education:* Hamilton Academy, Stirling University, studied clarsach with Sanchia Pielou. *Career:* science teacher and guidance counsellor in high school

1977–93; numerous live appearances, festivals, television and radio broadcasts; mem. Musicians' Union, Scotland. *Recordings include:* Just As I Am, 1993; Glamis, A Trysting Place; Patricia Roberts and Lorna Swan. *Telephone:* (1786) 465065. *E-mail:* patriciaroberts@totalise.co.uk. *Website:* www .patriciaroberts.com.

ROBERTS, Kathryn; British folk singer, songwriter and musician (piano, woodwind); b. 1975, Barnsley, S Yorks., England; pnr Sean Lakeman; two d. *Career:* formed duo with Kate Rusby 1995; mem. and lead singer, Equation, with Kate Rusby, and Sean, Sam and Seth Lakeman 1995–; formed duo with Sean Lakeman 2003–; session work with Seth Lakeman. *Recordings:* albums: as contrib.: Intuition (compilation) 1993; with Kate Rusby: Kate Rusby & Kathryn Roberts 1995; with Equation: Hazy Daze 1998, The Lucky Few 1999, First Name Terms 2002, Return to Me 2003; with Sean Lakeman: 1 2003, 2 2004, Hidden People 2012. *Honours:* BBC Radio 2 Folk Music Award for Best Duo 2013. *Current Management:* c/o Matt Bartlett, Midnight Mango Limited, The Old Stables, Moorlinch, Bridgwater, Somerset, TA7 9DD, England. *Telephone:* (1458) 211117. *E-mail:* matt@midnightmango.co.uk. *Website:* www .midnightmango.co.uk; www.kathrynrobertsandseanlakeman.com.

ROBERTS, Mark; British musician (guitar); b. 3 Nov. 1969, Colwyn Bay, Wales. *Career:* Member, Welsh-language band, Y Cyrff, –1991; Founder member, Catatonia, 1992–2001; First release on Welsh Indie label Crai; Signed to Blanco Y Negro, 1996; Numerous tours and festival appearances; Many TV appearances. *Recordings:* Albums: Way Beyond Blue, 1996; The Sublime Magic of Catatonia, 1996; International Velvet (No. 1, UK), 1998; Equally Cursed and Blessed (No. 1, UK), 1999; Paper Scissors Stone, 2001; Greatest Catatonia Hits, 2002. Singles: For Tinkerbell (EP), 1993; Hooked (EP), 1994; Bleed/Do You Believe In Me, 1996; You've Got A Lot To Answer For, 1996; Mulder and Scully, 1998; Road Rage, 1998; Strange Glue, 1998; Dead From The Waist Down, 1999; Londinium, 1999; Karaoke Queen, 1999; Stone By Stone, 2001.

ROBERTS, Nicola Maria; British singer; b. 5 Oct. 1985, Runcorn. *Career:* mem. Girls Aloud, pop group created from winning contestants on reality tv show Popstars: The Rivals 2002–03; solo career 2011–. *Compositions:* co-writer of songs including It's Magic, I Say A Prayer For You, I Don't Really Hate You. *Recordings:* albums: with Girls Aloud: Sound of the Underground 2003, What Will the Neighbours Say? 2004, Chemistry 2005, Tangled Up 2007, Out of Control 2008; solo: Cinderella's Eyes 2011. *Television:* Girls Aloud: Off the Record 2006, Nicola Roberts: The Truth About Tanning 2010. *Films:* St Trinian's 2007. *Honours:* Best Single, Disney Channel Awards 2003, Popjustice Music Prize 2003, 2005, 2006, BRIT Award for Best British Single (for The Promise) 2009. *Current Management:* Shaw Thing Management, Unit 12A, Utopia Village, 7 Chalcot Road, London, NW1 8LH, England. *Telephone:* (20) 7722-6161. *Fax:* (20) 7722-9661. *E-mail:* info@ shawthingmanagement.com. *Website:* www.shawthingmanagement.com. *Address:* c/o A&M Records, Universal Music UK, 364–366 Kensington High Street, London, W14 8NS, England (office). *Telephone:* (20) 7471-5000 (office). *E-mail:* info@umusic.com (office). *Website:* www.umusic.com (office); www .girlsaloud.co.uk; www.nicolarobertsmusic.com.

ROBERTS, Rudy; French rock musician (guitar); b. 9 April 1966, Nantes. *Education:* American School of Modern Music, Paris. *Career:* mem. Squealer 1991; mem. Starmania/Tycoon 1993–95; solo artist 1991–; numerous concerts, France, Belgium, Switzerland, Canada, played to over 1 m. people; has played with Stuart Hamm, Jonathon Mover; Electric guitar teacher, Vitré Conservatory of Music 1991–93; demonstrator for Jackson guitars; Hughes and Kettner amplifiers; mem. SACEM, SPEDIDAM. *Recordings:* albums: with Squealer: This Is What The World Is About 1991; with Starmania: Starmania 1994; solo: Passion Colors 1994, Rudy Roberts Live 1994, Acoustique Influence 1996, Arabesque 1997, Esperanza 2008. *Publications:* Instruction video, Plans and Techniques Hard Rock. *Honours:* Victoire de la Musique Award (for Best Live Show with Starmania) 1994. *E-mail:* ricardo.guinee@rudy-roberts.com (office); rudyroberts44@yahoo.fr (office). *Website:* www.rudy-roberts.com.

ROBERTS, Sam; Canadian singer, songwriter and bandleader; b. 2 Oct. 1974, Pointe-Claire, Quebec; m. Jen Roberts; two d. *Education:* Loyola High School, McGill Univ. *Career:* f. William 1993 (renamed Northstar 1996, disbanded 1999), Sam Roberts Band 2001–. *Recordings include:* The Inhuman Condition 2002, We Were Born In A Flame 2003, Chemical City 2006, Love At The End Of The World 2008. *Honours:* four Juno Awards. *Current Management:* c/o Dave Spencer, Secret Weapon Management, Toronto, Ontario, Canada. *E-mail:* management@samrobertsband.com. *Website:* www .samrobertsband.com. *E-mail:* contact@samrobertsband.com (office). *Website:* samrobertsband.com.

ROBERTS, Stephen; British musician (drums) and singer. *Career:* founder mem., Athlete 1997–; tours throughout Europe. *Recordings include:* albums: Vehicles & Animals 2003, Tourist 2005, Beyond the Neighbourhood 2007, Black Swan 2009. *Honours:* Ivor Novello Award for Best Contemporary Song (for Wires) 2006. *Website:* www.athlete.mu.

ROBERTS, Stephen; British musician (drums); b. 27 March 1958, London, England; m. Philippa Jane 1991. *Career:* founder mem. heavy metal group, Silverwing (with brother Dave) 1980–83; formed Pet Hate, toured USA and Canada; formed Wild Ones 1989; session musician with Belinda Carlisle and Rick Astley; mem., No Fit State; mem. Musicians' Union. *Recordings:* with Silverwing: Rock and Roll Are Four Letter Words 1980, Sittin' Pretty 1981,

Alive and Kicking 1982; with Pet Hate: The Bride Wore Red 1984, Bad Publicity 1985; with Wild Ones: Writing On The Wall 1991; with No Fit State: Welcome To... 1995.

ROBERTSON, Brian; British rock musician (guitar); b. 12 Sept. 1956, Glasgow, Scotland. *Career:* mem. rock group, Thin Lizzy 1974–78; briefly with Graham Parker and The Rumour 1977; founder mem., Wild Horses 1978–81; mem. heavy metal group, Motörhead 1982–83. *Recordings include:* albums: with Thin Lizzy: Nightlife 1974, Fighting 1975, Jailbreak 1976, Johnny The Fox 1976, Bad Reputation 1977, Live and Dangerous 1978, Japanese Compilation 1980, Adventures of Thin Lizzy 1981, Life 1983, Dedication 1991; with Motörhead: Another Perfect Day 1983.

ROBERTSON, Robbie Jaime; Canadian musician (guitar) and singer; b. 5 July 1944, Toronto, ON. *Career:* guitarist, singer with The Band (formerly the Hawks) 1964–78; long association with Bob Dylan; as backing band for Bob Dylan, appearances include: Don't Look Back British tour 1965, Royal Albert Hall 1966, Isle of Wight Festival 1969, US tour 1974; solo artist 1978–. *Compositions:* Much of Band's material including: 4% Pantomime (co-written with Van Morrison). *Films:* working on soundtracks: The Last Waltz 1978, Carny 1980, Raging Bull 1980, The King of Comedy 1983, The Color of Money 1986, Until the End of the World 1991, Jimmy Hollywood 1994, Casino 1995, Phenomenon 1996, Forces of Nature 1999, Any Given Sunday 1999, Gangs of New York 2002, Jenifa 2004, The Departed 2006. *Recordings:* albums: with The Band: The Basement Tapes (with Bob Dylan) 1967, Music From Big Pink 1968, The Band 1969, Stage Fright 1970, Cahoots 1971, Rock of Ages 1972, Moondog Matinee 1973, Before The Flood (with Bob Dylan) 1974, Northern Lights Southern Cross 1976, Best Of... 1976, Islands 1977, The Last Waltz 1978; solo: Robbie Robertson 1987, Storyville 1991, Music For The Native Americans 1994, Contact from the Underworld of Red Boy 1998; producer: Beautiful Noise, Neil Diamond 1976; contributor, Planet Waves, Bob Dylan 1974, Beauty, Ryuichi Sakamoto 1989, Rainbow Warriors, Greenpeace charity album 1979; also appeared on recordings by Eric Clapton, John Hammond, Emmylou Harris, B. B. King, Joni Mitchell, Tom Petty, Carly Simon, Ringo Starr. *Honours:* The Band, inducted into Canadian Hall of Fame 1989.

ROBIN, Thierry (Titi); French composer and musician (guitar, oriental lute, bouzouq); b. 26 Aug. 1957. *Career:* performances at venues, including Théatre de la Ville de Paris, Arabic World Inst., UNESCO, most European festivals (including Transmusicales, WOMAD, Angoulême, WOMEX); tours of Japan, Africa, Indian Ocean, Europe, USA, Canada, North Africa, Middle East; mem. SACEM. *Recordings:* Luth et Tablá 1985, An Henchoû Treûz 1989, An Tri Breur 1991, Gitans 1993, Le Regard Nu 1996, Payo Michto 1997, Kali Gadji 1998, Un Ciel de Cuivre 2000, Rakhî 2002, Alezane 2004, Ces Vagues que L'Amour Soulève 2005, Anita! 2006, L'Ombre du Ghazal 2008. *Honours:* Grand Prix de l'Academie Charles Cros 1990. *Current Management:* Zamora Productions, 84 avenue de la République, 75011 Paris, France. *Telephone:* 1-43-72-42-42. *Fax:* 1-43-72-42-00. *E-mail:* bookingfrance@zamoraprod.com. *Website:* www.zamoraprod.com. *E-mail:* thierry.titi.robin@club-internet.fr (office). *Website:* www.thierrytitirobin.com.

ROBINSON, Barry; British music director, composer, conductor, arranger and musician (piano, keyboards); b. 10 Sept. 1963, Bushey, Watford. *Education:* Grove School of Music, Los Angeles. *Career:* fmr Music Dir, Sporting Club, Monte Carlo; collaborations with Whitney Houston, Natalie Cole, Kool and the Gang, Sammy Davis Jr, The Temptations, The Three Degrees, The Supremes, Odyssey, Rose Royce, Cliff Richard, Kiki Dee, Madeline Bell, Salena Jones, Joe Longthorne, Lily Savage, Des O'Connor, Jane McDonald, Michael Barrymore; music for television includes Big Stage Indie Awards, Come Dancing, Variety Club Awards, Children In Need, The Accountant; West End Shows include Saturday Night Fever, Smokey Joe's Cafe, Fame, Jesus Christ Superstar, Kat and The Kings; founder and owner, BazzaMusic production co.; mem. PRS. *Compositions:* composer, arranger, Midas Touch, game show, Central Television. *Current Management:* Tony Clayman Promotions, Suite 25, Vicarage House, 58/60 Kensington Church Street, London W8 4DB, England. *Telephone:* (20) 7368-3336. *Fax:* (20) 7368-3338. *E-mail:* tony@tonyclayman.com. *Website:* www.tonyclayman.com. *E-mail:* barry@barryrobinson.net (office). *Website:* www.barryrobinson.net.

ROBINSON, Christopher (Chris) Mark; American rock singer and songwriter; b. 20 Dec. 1966, Atlanta, GA; m. 1st Kate Hudson 2000 (divorced 2007); one s.; m. 2nd Allison Bridges; one d. *Career:* founding mem., rock group, Mr Crowe's Garden, later renamed The Black Crowes 1984–2002, 2005–; major concerts include support tours to Heart 1990, Robert Plant 1990, ZZ Top 1991, Memphis in May Festival 1991, Monsters of Rock Festival, Castle Donington 1991, Glastonbury Festival 1993, Phoenix Festival 1993; solo artist 2002–; founding mem. Chris Robinson Brotherhood 2011–. *Recordings:* albums: with The Black Crowes: Shake Your Money Maker 1990, The Southern Harmony and Musical Companion 1992, Amorica, 1994, Three Snakes and One Charm 1996, Sho Nuff: The Complete Black Crowes 1998, By Your Side 1999, Live At The Greek 2000, Tribute To A Work In Progress: Greatest Hits 1990–1999 2001, Lions 2001, Warpaint 2008, Before the Frost... Until the Freeze 2009, Croweology 2010; solo: New Earth Mud 2002; with Chris Robinson Brotherhood: Big Moon Ritual 2011, The Magic Door 2012. *Honours:* Rolling Stone magazine, Best New American Band, Best Male New Singer, 1991. *Current Management:* Angelus Entertainment, 269 S. Beverley Drive, Beverly Hills, CA 90212, USA. *E-mail:* info@blackcrowes.com (office). *Website:* www .blackcrowes.com; www.chrisrobinsonbrotherhood.com/Big-Moon-Ritual/.

ROBINSON, Crispin, (Bro Spry); British musician (congas, shakers, djembs, drums, percussion); b. 3 Nov. 1966, London; m.; two d. *Education:* City and East London Coll., Kent Univ.; studied with Bobby Sanabria, John Amira, Bob Armstrong, Robin Jones. *Career:* first recordings with Manassah, Soul II Soul, Yazz, Youth, Young Disciples; mem., Galliano 1991–97; wrote and performed with artists such as Brian Eno, Courtney Pine, Paul Weller, others; currently Lecturer, School of Oriental and African Studies, Univ. of London. *Recordings:* albums: first and second albums: Soul II Soul; with Galliano: In Pursuit of the 13th Note 1991, A Joyful Noise unto the Creator 1992, What Colour Our Flag 1994, The Plot Thickens 1994, 4 1996. *Address:* c/o Trade Secrets, The Jam Factory, Block B604, 27 Green Walk, London SE1 4TX, England. *Website:* www.tradesecrets-uk.com.

ROBINSON, Orphy; British jazz musician (vibraphone, drums, percussion, keyboards) and composer; b. 13 Oct. 1960, London, England; one s. *Education:* Hackney Coll. *Career:* played with Savanna, Courtney Pine, Andy Sheppard, Balanescu String Quartet, Mica Paris, David Murray, Jazz Warriors; lead soloist, Shivanova 1990–; solo artist 1990–; mem. PRS, Musicians' Union. *Recordings include:* I Can't Turn Away, Savanna; In and Out of Love, Imagination; Journey To The Urge Within, Courtney Pine; Out of Many One People, Jazz Warriors; When Tomorrow Comes, The Vibes Describes, Orphy Robinson; Introductions In The Dark, Andy Sheppard; Suite de Lorenzo, Ensemble Bash; Singles include: Life; Makes A Change; film soundtracks: Men of The Month; Bloodrights. *Honours:* British Jazz Award for Most Promising Newcomer 1989, Best Miscellaneous Instrumentalist 1993. *E-mail:* orphy@orphyrobinson.com. *Website:* www.orphyrobinson.com.

ROBINSON, Pat; American songwriter, singer and musician (guitar, piano); b. 7 April 1948; two d. *Career:* mem. BMI. *Compositions:* You Got Away With Love, recorded by Percy Sledge; Civilised Man, Joe Cocker; No Promise No Guarantee, Laura Branigan; Jokers Are Wild, Gene Clark; also compositions for Glen Campbell, Jill Michaels, Moon Martin. *Recordings:* contrib. to: Wave of the Hand: The Best of Carla Olson, Carla Olson 1995, Honest As Daylight, Carla Olson 2001; with The Textones: Cedar Creek 1987, Through The Canyon 1989, Back In Time 1990; other: Revenge of the Nerds (soundtrack) 1998. *Current Management:* Saul Davis, 11864 Ventura Blvd, #583, Studio City, CA 91604, USA. *E-mail:* patagoura@earthlink.net. *Website:* www .patrobinson.net.

ROBINSON, Richard (Rich) S.; American musician (guitar); b. 24 May 1969, Atlanta, GA. *Career:* founding mem., US rock group, Mr Crowe's Garden, later renamed The Black Crowes 1984–2002, 2005–; major concerts include Support tours to Heart 1990, Robert Plant 1990, ZZ Top 1991, Memphis In May Festival 1991, Monsters of Rock Festival, Castle Donington 1991, Glastonbury Festival 1993, Phoenix Festival 1993. *Recordings:* albums: Shake Your Money Maker 1990, The Southern Harmony and Musical Companion 1992, Amorica 1994, Three Snakes and One Charm 1996, Sho Nuff: The Complete Black Crowes 1998, By Your Side 1999, Live At The Greek 2000, Tribute To A Work In Progress: Greatest Hits 1990–1999 2001, Lions 2001, Warpaint 2008, Before the Frost... Until the Freeze 2009, Croweology 2010. *Honours:* Rolling Stone magazine, Best New American Band, Best Male New Singer 1991. *Current Management:* Angelus Entertainment, 269 S. Beverley Drive, Beverly Hills, CA 90212, USA. *E-mail:* info@blackcrowes.com (office). *Website:* www.blackcrowes.com.

ROBINSON, Ross; American record producer and musician (guitar); b. 1969. *Career:* mem. and prod., thrash metal group Detente; debut as Prod., Korn's first album, Korn, 1995; producer of albums by: Amen, At The Drive In, Deftones, Glassjaw, Korn, Limp Bizkit, Sepultura, Slipknot, Soulfly, Vanilla Ice, Vex Red; Owner and Pres., record label, I Am Recordings. *Recordings:* with Detente: Recognize No Authority, 1983. *E-mail:* ross@iamrecordings .com. *Website:* www.iamrecordings.com.

ROBINSON, William (Smokey), Jr; American R&B and soul singer, songwriter and producer; b. 19 Feb. 1940, Detroit, Mich.; m. 1st Claudette Robinson 1959; two c.; m. 2nd Frances Robinson. *Career:* fmr singer with The Matadors; singer with The Miracles 1954–72, also billed as Smokey Robinson and The Miracles 1967–72; solo artist 1973–; Vice Pres. Motown 1961–88; Exec. Producer and composer on film, Big Time 1977; numerous TV appearances; f. SFGL Foods, Inc. *Compositions include:* most recordings with The Miracles – 1968; also The Way You Do The Things You Do (recorded by The Temptations) 1964, My Guy (co-writer, recorded by Mary Wells) 1964, My Girl (recorded by The Temptations) 1965. *Recordings include:* albums: with The Miracles: The Fabulous Miracles 1963, The Miracles On Stage 1963, Doin' Mickey's Monkey 1964, Going To A Go-Go 1966, Make It Happen 1967, Special Occasion 1968, Time Out For... 1969, What Love Has Joined Together 1970, A Pocketful Of Miracles 1970, One Dozen Roses 1971, Flying High Together 1972; solo: Smokey 1973, Pure Smokey 1974, A Quiet Storm 1975, Smokey's Family Robinson 1976, Deep In My Soul 1977, Big Time (OST) 1977, Love Breeze 1978, Smokin' Motown 1979, Where There's Smoke 1979, Warm Thoughts 1980, Being With You 1981, Yes It's You Lady 1982, Touch The Sky 1983, Essar 1984, Smoke Signals 1986, One Heartbeat 1987, Love Songs 1988, Love, Smokey 1990, Double Good Everything 1991, Ballads 1995, Our Very Best Christmas 1999, Intimate 1999, Food For The Spirit 2004, Timeless Love 2006, Time Flies When You're Having Fun 2009, Smokey & Friends 2014. *Honours:* Dr hc (Howard Univ.) 2006, (Berklee Coll. of Music) 2009; Grammy Award for Best R&B Vocal Performance 1988, Grammy Living Legend Award 1989, Soul Train Heritage Award 1991, Motor City Music Award for Lifetime Achievement 1992,

Grammy Lifetime Achievement Award 1999, Kennedy Center Honor 2006, Q Award for Outstanding Contribution to Music 2006, Ivor Novello Special Int. Award 2009. *Current Management:* c/o WME, 9601 Wilshire Blvd, Beverly Hills, CA 90201, USA. *Website:* www.smokeyrobinson.com.

ROBINSON, Tom; British songwriter and broadcaster; b. 1 June 1950, Cambridge, England. *Career:* joined first band Café Soc., London 1973; Album produced by Ray Davies 1975; formed Tom Robinson Band (TRB) 1976; Chart success; founder mem. of Rock Against Racism; Formed Sector 27 1979; USA tour with Police 1981; lived and worked in East Germany 1982; further chart success 1983–84; tours of Japan, Italy, UK 1987; hit show Private View, Edinburgh Fringe 1987; presenter BBC World Service, Radio 1 1988; briefly re-formed Tom Robinson Band 1989; solo tours throughout UK, Europe, Canada, USA, Australia 1991–95; presenter BBC Radio 4 series, The Locker Room 1992–95; presenter The Evening Sequence, BBC Introducing: Fresh on the Net, BBC 6 Music. *Compositions include:* Co-writer with Peter Gabriel: Bully For You; Merrily Up On High, 1979; Atmospherics: Listen To The Radio, 1983; Co-writer with Elton John: Sartorial Eloquence; Elton's Song; Never Gonna Fall In Love Again, 1979–80; Composed music for: More Lives Than One, BBC2 TV, 1985; with Jakko Jakszyk: Hard Cases, Central TV, 1988; Lyrics for It's About Time, Manu Katché, 1991. *Recordings:* Singles include: 2–4–6–8 Motorway, 1977; Glad To Be Gay, 1978; War Baby, 1983; Atmospherics: Listen To The Radio, 1983; Hard, 1994; Albums include: Café Society, 1975; Power In The Darkness, 1978; TRB Two, 1979; Sector 27, 1981; North By Northwest, 1982; Cabaret 79, 1982; Hope and Glory, 1984; Still Loving You, 1986; We Never Had It So Good (with Jakko Jakszyk) 1990; Living In A Boom Time, 1992; Love Over Rage, 1994; Having It Both Ways, 1996; Holidays in the Sun, 1997; Smelling Dogs, 2001. *Honours:* Gold Winner with You've Got to Hide Your Love Away, UK Sony Awards, 1997. *Current Management:* Leporine Ltd, PO Box 3185, London SW18 3JG, England. *E-mail:* tom.6music@bbc.co.uk. *Website:* www.tomrobinson.com.

ROBISON, Emily Burns; American musician (guitar, banjo, resophonic guitar, fiddle, mandolin, keyboards), singer and songwriter; b. (Emily Erwin), 16 Aug. 1972, Pittsfield, MA; m. Charlie Robison 1999. *Career:* mem. teen group, Blue Night Express 1983–89; founder mem., The Dixie Chicks 1989–, playing a mix of traditional bluegrass with mainstream country music; founder mem., Court Yard Hounds 2009–; numerous live performances. *Recordings include:* albums: with The Dixie Chicks: Little Ol' Cowgirl 1992, Thank Heavens For Dale Evans 1992, Shouldn't A Told You That 1993, Wide Open Spaces (Grammy Award for Best Country Album 1998, CMA Award for Music Video of the Year 1999) 1998, Fly (ACM Award for Album of the Year 1999, CMA Award for Album of the Year 2000) 1999, Star Profile 2000, Home (American Music Award for Best Country Album 2003) 2002, Combo 2004, Taking the Long Way (Grammy Awards for Album of the Year, Best Country Album 2007, Juno Award for Best Int. Album of the Year 2007) 2006; with Court Yard Hounds: Court Yard Hounds 2010. *Honours:* Grammy Award for Best Country Performance by a Duo or Group with Vocal 1998, 1999, CMA Award for Vocal Group of the Year and for Single of the Year (for Wide Open Spaces) 1999, TNN Music Award for Group/Duo of the Year 1999, ACM Award for Favorite Duo or Group 1999, American Music Award for Favorite New Country Artist 1999, Billboard Award for Favorite Country Artist 1999, CMA Awards for Entertainer of the Year, for Vocal Group of the Year, and for Music Video of the Year (for Goodbye Earl) 2000, American Music Award for Best Country Group 2003, Grammy Awards for Record of the Year, Song of the Year, Best Country Performance by a duo or group with Vocal (all for Not Ready To Make Nice) 2007. *Current Management:* Front Page Publicity, PO Box 90168, Nashville, TN 37209, USA. *E-mail:* info@frontpagepublicity.com. *Website:* www.frontpagepublicity.com; www.dixiechicks.com; www .courtyardhounds.com.

ROBYN; Swedish singer and songwriter; b. (Robin Miriam Carlsson), 12 June 1979, Stockholm. *Career:* released first album aged 16; Founder and CEO Konichiwa Records 2005–. *Recordings:* albums: Robyn is Here 1995, My Truth (Swedish Grammy Award for Best Female Pop/Rock Artist 1999) 1999, Don't Stop the Music (Swedish Grammy Award for Best Female Pop/Rock Artist 2002) 2002, Robyn (Swedish Grammy Award for Best Album 2005) 2005, Body Talk (Swedish Grammy Award for Best Album 2011) 2010, Do It Again (with Röyksopp) 2014, Love is Free (with La Bagatelle Magique) 2015. *Honours:* Swedish Grammy Awards for Best Composer 2005, 2011, for Best Live Act 2005, for Best Female Artist 2011, for Best Artist 2011, for Best Song (for Dancing on My Own) 2011, KTH Royal Inst. of Tech. in Stockholm Great Prize 2013. *Current Management:* DEF Management, 51 Lonsdale Road, Queen's Park, London, NW6 6RA, England. *E-mail:* info@d-e-f.com. *Website:* www.d-e -f.com; www.robyn.com.

ROCCOFORTE, Vito; American musician (drums); m. *Career:* founder mem., The Rapture 1998–. *Recordings include:* albums: Mirror 1999, Out Of The Races And Onto The Tracks 2001, Echoes 2003, Pieces of People We Love 2006. *Current Management:* Principle Management, 30–32 Sir John Rogerson's Quay, Dublin 2, Ireland. *Telephone:* (1) 6777330. *Fax:* (1) 6777276. *Website:* www.therapturemusic.co.uk.

ROCHEMAN, Manuel David; French musician (piano) and composer; b. 23 July 1964, Paris. *Education:* CNR de Paris with Alberto Neuman, studied jazz with Martial Solal. *Career:* appearances with own trio on radio and at festivals; tours worldwide; also played with Jean-Luc Ponty, Anthony Ortega, Johnny Griffin, Kyle Eastwood, Al Foster, George Mraz, Scott Colley, Antonio

Sanchez, Didier Lockwood, Dusko Goykovich, Eddie Gomez, Bill Mobley, Patrice Caratini, Charles Aznavour, Chuck Israels, Olivier Ker Ourio, Rick Margitza, Brasil Project with Toninho Horta; mem. Soc. des auteurs, compositeurs et éditeurs de musique (SACEM), SPEDIDAM, Admin des droits des artistes et musiciens interprètes (ADAMI). *Compositions include:* Concerto for piano and orchestra 1988, San Felipe for jazz band and philharmonic orchestra 1995, Concerto for piano and orchestra 1999. *Recordings include:* albums: Trio Urbain 1989, White Keys 1992, Tropic City 1995, Come Shine (with George Mraz and Al Foster) 1998, I'm Old Fashioned 2000, Alone at Last 2003, Cactus Dance (with Scott Colley and Antonio Sanchez) 2007, The Touch of Your Lips-Tribute to Bill Evans 2010, Café & Alegria (meets Toninho Horta) 2012, Paris-Maurice 2014, misTeRIO 2016. *Honours:* Prix Boris Vian 1991, Django D'Or 1992, Prix Django Reinhardt 1998. *Address:* 14 rue Camille Pelletan, 93600 Aulnay-sous-bois, France (home). *E-mail:* contact@manuelrocheman.com. *Website:* manuelrocheman.com.

ROCHFORD, Sebastian (Seb); British jazz musician (percussion, drums), songwriter and bandleader; b. 1973, Aberdeen, Scotland; s. of Gerald Rochford. *Education:* Newcastle Coll. of Music. *Career:* fmr mem. hardcore band Cabbage 1988; percussionist for numerous jazz artists in London including Julian Joseph, Andy Sheppard, Stan Tracey, Tim Richards, Joanna MacGregor; Founder-mem. Fulborn Teversham; mem. rock band Menlo Park 1999–2003; regular mem. Pete Wareham's Acoustic Ladyland group 2001–10; Founder-mem. quartet Polar Bear 2003–; mem. Oriole 2005–11; Founder-mem. Sons of Kemet 2011–; numerous session credits including Adele, Babyshambles, Carl Barat, Brian Eno, Rick Holland, David Byrne, Corinne Bailey Rae, Herbie Hancock. *Recordings:* albums: with Menlo Park: Menlo Park 2000; with Acoustic Ladyland: Camouflage 2004, Last Chance Disco (Jazzwise Album of the Year 2005) 2005, Skinny Grin 2006, Living with a Tiger 2009; with Polar Bear: Dim Lit 2004, Held on the Tips of Fingers 2005, Polar Bear 2008, Peepers 2010; with Oriole: Song for the Sleeping 2005, Migration 2006, Every New Day 2011; with Basquiat Strings: Basquiat Strings with Seb Rochford 2007; with Sons of Kemet: Burn 2013. *Honours:* solo: BBC Jazz Award for Best Newcomer 2004; with Acoustic Ladyland: BBC Jazz Award for Best Band 2005; with Sons of Kemet: MOBO Award for Best Jazz Act 2013. *Address:* c/o Simon Drake, Naim Jazz Records, Southampton Road, Salisbury, Wiltshire, SP1 5LN, England (office). *Telephone:* (1722) 426600 (office). *Fax:* (871) 230-1012 (office). *E-mail:* info@naimlabel.com (office), sonsofkemet@gmail.com (office). *Website:* www.naimlabel.com (office), sonsofkemet.com.

ROCK, Bob; Canadian producer. *Career:* mem. punk band, The Payolas, changed name to Rock and Hyde 1987; worked alongside producer Bruce Fairbairn; producer, secured gigs with Blue Murder, Loverboy, The Cult, Motley Crue, David Lee Roth, Cher; teamed up with Metallica 1991; has also worked with Aerosmith, Michael Bublé, Bon Jovi, David Lee Roth, Skid Row, The Offspring, 311. *Recordings include:* Sonic Temple; A Little Ain't Enough; Bitter, Sweet and Twisted; Keep The Faith; The Cult; Subhuman Race; Load; Eight Arms To Hold You; Tal Bachman; On A Day Like Today; Load; Reload; Garage Inc; American Hi-Fi. *Honours:* Juno/Jack Richardson Award for Producer of the Year 2010. *Address:* c/o Michael McCarty, EMI Music Publishing, 119 Spadina Avenue, Suite 604, Toronto, ON M5V 2L1, Canada (office). *E-mail:* mmccarty@emimusicpub.com (office). *Website:* www.emimusicpub.com (office).

ROCKY; British producer, remixer and DJ; b. (Darren Rock), 25 Sept. 1967, Hayes, London, England. *Career:* started DJ career with pnr, Diesel; mem., Ballistic Brothers, Problem Kids; founder mem., X-Press 2 1993–; co-founder, Low Pressings Records; mem. MCPS/PRS. *Recordings include:* albums: Ballistic Brothers vs The Eccentric Afro's 1995, London Hooligan Soul (with Ballistic Brothers) 1995, My First Acid House (with Problem Kids) 2001, X-Press-2 2002, Muzikizum 2002, Makeshift Feelgood (with X-Press 2) 2006. *Honours:* Muzik Award for Best Producer (with X-Press 2) 2001. *Address:* c/o Skint Records, 73A Middle Street, Brighton, Sussex BN1 4BA, England. *Website:* www.xpress2.com.

RODE, Birgitte; Danish singer, composer, producer and musician (keyboards); *CEO, Soundbranding;* b. 26 Feb. 1956, Copenhagen; m. Claus Hvass 1992; two c. *Education:* Acad. of Music, Ålborg. *Career:* sound branding and sound identity for brands including Bang & Olufsen, Martin Lindstrom; producer of records, radio and TV programmes; various festival appearances, tours, radio and TV broadcasts; CEO Soundbranding; mem. Nat. Musicians' Soc., Danish Songwriters and Authors Org. (DJBFA). *Plays:* Winnie the Pooh, Medea. *Exhibitions:* North Jutland Museum of Art, Herning Kunstmuseum, Esbjerg Museum, The Experimentarium, Copenhagen, Arken, The Arch, Koege. *Radio:* Rock News, The Rolling Roc. *Television:* The Wise Women, Live Aid. *Recordings:* with Johnny Og de Kolde Dæmoner: Paraneuropa; with Walk the Walk: Walk the Walk, Feet on the Ground, Frog Dance; The Untold Scandinavian story of Martin Hannett and Johnny and the Cold Demons (book and CD). *Honours:* four Nat. Music Council Awards 1991–94. *Address:* Marienhaab, Kirkegaardsgade 3, 9000 Ålborg, Denmark (home). *Telephone:* 39-40-64-60 (office), 98-16-64-62 (office). *E-mail:* br@marienhaab.dk (office), br@soundbranding.com (office). *Website:* www.soundbranding.com (office), www.marienhaab.dk (office).

RODGERS, Nile; American guitarist and record producer; b. 19 Sept. 1952, New York. *Career:* mem. New World Rising 1960s; Founder-mem. Big Apple Band 1972–76; became Chic 1977–; also solo artiste and record producer;

mem. The Honeydrippers with Robert Plant, Jimmy Page, Jeff Beck; leader own trio, Outloud; numerous collaborations including Daft Punk, Pharrell Williams, Avicii, Disclosure; co-founder Ear Candy record label 1989; owner Sumthing Distribution (music distribution co.). *Recordings include:* albums: with Chic: C'Est Chic 1978, Risqué 1979, The Best of Chic 1980, Real People 1982, Take It Off 1982, Tongue In Chic 1982, Believer 1983, Freak Out 1987, Chic-Ism 1992; solo albums: Adventures In The Land of The Good Groove 1983, B-Movie Matinee 1985, Singles include: Dance Dance Dance 1977, Everybody Dance 1978, Le Freak (No. 1, USA) 1978, I Want Your Love 1979, Good Times (No. 1, USA) 1979, My Forbidden Lover 1979, My Feet Keep Dancing 1980, Soup For One 1982, Jack Le Freak 1987, Chic Mystique 1992; as writer, producer with Bernard Edwards: Norma Jean, Norma Jean Wright 1977, He's The Greatest Dancer, Sister Sledge 1979, We Are Family, Sister Sledge 1979, Love Somebody Today, Sister Sledge 1979, Upside Down, Diana Ross 1980, Diana, Diana Ross 1980, Why, Carly Simon 1982; record producer for artists including David Bowie, Madonna, Duran Duran, Aretha Franklin, Jeff Beck, Mick Jagger, Al Jarreau, Grace Jones, Johnny Mathis, Marta Sanchez. *Honours:* Grammy Awards for Record of the Year, for Best Pop Duo/Group Performance (both for Get Lucky, with Daft Punk) 2014, Ivor Novello Special Int. Award 2014. *Address:* Sumthing Distribution, 9 East 45th Street, 3rd Floor, New York, NY 10017, USA (office). *Telephone:* (212) 818-0047 (office). *Website:* www.nilerodgers.com; www.sumthing.com (office).

RODGERS, Paul; British singer, songwriter and musician (guitar, piano); b. 17 Dec. 1949, Middlesborough, Cleveland, England; m. Cynthia Rodgers; one s. two d. *Career:* singer with Roadrunners, Brown Sugar; founder mem., Free 1968–73; numerous tours and festival appearances; founder mem., Peace 1971; founder mem. and lead singer, Bad Company 1973–83; founder mem. and lead singer, The Firm 1984–86; founder mem. and lead singer, The Law 1991; solo artist with backing band, Paul Rodgers 1993–; toured with Queen as lead singer 2005–09; mem. Musicians' Union, PRS, MCPS. *Recordings include:* albums: with Free: Tons Of Sobs 1968, Free 1969, Fire And Water 1970, Highway 1971, Free Live 1971, Free At Last 1972, Heartbreaker 1973, The Free Story 1973, Best Of Free 1991, Walk In My Shadow – An Introduction To Free 1998; with Bad Company: Bad Company 1974, Straight Shooter 1975, Run With The Pack 1976, Burnin' Sky 1977, Desolation Angels 1979, Rough Diamonds 1982, 10 From 6 1985, The Original Bad Company Anthology 1999; with The Firm: The Firm 1985, Mean Business 1986; with The Law: The Law 1991; solo: Cut Loose 1983, Muddy Waters Blues 1993, The Hendrix Set 1993, Live (The Loreley Tapes) 1995, Now 1997, Electric 1999, The Royal Sessions 2014; with Queen: The Cosmos Rocks 2008. *Honours:* Dr hc (Teesside) 2009; Grammy Award (with Bad Company) 1975, Hon. Col of Louisiana 1977. *Current Management:* c/o Chris Crawford, Millennium Management, PO Box 6052, Bellingham, WA 98227, USA. *Telephone:* (360) 383-0583. *Fax:* (360) 383-0583. *E-mail:* crawford76@aol.com. *Website:* www.paulrodgers.com.

RODNEY, (Godfrey) Winston, (Burning Spear); singer and songwriter; b. 1 March 1945, St Ann's Bay, Jamaica; m. Sonia Marlene Thompson 1981; one s. three d. *Career:* reggae singer, songwriter also known as Burning Spear; numerous tours, TV appearances, radio broadcasts; mem. PRS, ASCAP. *Recordings include:* albums: Burning Spear, Rocking Time, Marcus Garvey, Man In The Hills, Garvey's Ghost, Hail H I M 1981, Farover 1982, Resistance 1984, Mek We Dweet 1990, Jah Kingdom 1992, The World Should Know 1993, Rasta Business 1995, Best Of The Fittest 2001, Our Music 2006, Jab is Real (Grammy Award for Best Reggae Album 2009) 2008. *Honours:* Musicians Merit Award, Album of the Year 1990, Martin's Int. Reggae Award for Most Educational Entertainer of the 1980s 1991, Album of the Year, Best Arranger (reggae), Caribbean Music Awards, Best Reggae Album, NAIRD Indie Awards 1992; four IRMA Awards, including Best Music Video, 1995, Bob Marley Award for Entertainer of the Year, Int. Reggae Hall of Fame, Marcus Garvey Humanitarian Award, Grammy Award. *Address:* Burning Music Productions, 130–34 231st Street, Laurelton, NY 11413, USA (office). *E-mail:* burningspear.net@gmail.com (home). *Website:* www.burningspear.net.

RODRIGUES, Virginia; Brazilian singer; b. 31 March 1964. *Career:* singer in the Afro-Bahia style. *Recordings include:* albums: Sol Negro 1998, Nós 2000, Mares Profundos 2004. *Address:* c/o Deutsche Grammophon GmbH, Alte Rabenstrasse 2, 20148 Hamburg, Germany.

RODRIGUEZ, Arabella Sabina; recording and mixing engineer; b. Norfolk, England; one s. one d. *Education:* Piano, Harmony, Violin, Flute. *Career:* sound engineer 1986–; mem, Repro; PRS; MCPS. *Recordings:* Credits as Engineer include: Motörhead; Scritti Politti; Soul II Soul; Black Rain; Caron Wheeler; Manu Dibango; Angelique Kidjo; D-Influence; East 17; Sinead O'Connor; Natacha Atlas; Tama; Jack Roberts; Busi Mholongo; Ghostland. *Address:* 106 Albion Road, London, N16 9AD, England.

RODRIGUEZ, Juan (Johnny) Raoul Davis; American country singer, songwriter and musician (guitar); b. 10 Dec. 1951, Sabinal, TX. *Career:* performed with high school rock band The Spocks, late 1960s; discovered by Tom T Hall and Bobby Bare while performing at Alamo Village Amusement Park, Brackettville, Texas 1971; moved to Nashville; worked as guitarist with Tom T Hall's band; signed to Mercury Records; first chart appearance 1972; most successful Chicano country singer of all time, recording in both English and Spanish; peak period early to mid-1970s but continued to chart until 1989; appeared in TV show Adam-12, 1974; movies include: Rio Diablo, Nashville Girl (aka Country Music Daughter/New Girl In Town) 1976, La Bamba Party,

The Runaway Barge (aka River Bandits 1975; charity work includes helping underprivileged Mexican-American children through the Life Enrichment Center. *Compositions include:* Dance With Me (Just One More Time), Down On The Rio Grande, Ridin' My Thumb To Mexico. *Recordings include:* albums: Introducing Johnny Rodriguez 1973, All I Ever Meant To Do Was Sing 1973, My Third Album 1974, Songs About Ladies and Love 1974, Just Get Up and Close the Door 1975, Love Put a Song in My Heart 1975, Reflecting 1975, Practice Makes Perfect 1977, Just for You 1977, Love Me with All Your Heart 1978, Rodriguez was Here 1978, Sketches 1979, Through My Eyes 1980, Gypsy 1980, After the Rain 1981, For Every Rose 1983, Foolin' with Fire 1984, Full Circle 1986, Gracias 1988, Run for the Border 1993, You Can Say That Again 1996, Funny Things Happen to Fun Lovin' People 1996, Back to Back 2001, Desperado 2002. *Honours:* various including: ACM, Most Promising Male Vocalist 1972, Cash Box, New Male Vocalist, Singles and Albums 1973, Music City News, Most Promising Male Vocalist 1973, 1974, Billboard Trendsetter Award 1973, Cash Box Upcoming Male Award 1973, Record Review, Most Promising Male Vocalist, Album Charts and Singles Chart 1973.

RODRIGUEZ, Mala; Spanish rapper, singer and songwriter; b. (Maria Rodriguez Garrido), 13 Feb. 1979, Jerez de la Frontera, Cádiz. *Career:* raised in Seville; began music career under name of La Mala 1996; early guest appearances on recordings by hip-hop acts including La Gota Que Colma, SFDK, La Alta Escuela late 1990s; debut solo single released 1999; collaborations with numerous artists including Nelly Furtado, R de Rumba, Full Nelson, Vico C, Kultama, Calle 13, Antonio Carmona, Tego Calderón, Julieta Venegas, Romeo Santos, Kinky, Diego Torres. *Recordings:* albums: Lujo Ibérico 2000, Alevosia 2003, Malamarismo 2007, Dirty Bailarina 2010, Bruja (Latin Grammy Award for Best Urban Album 2013) 2013. *Honours:* Latin Grammy Award for Best Urban Song (for No Pidas Perdón) 2010. *Current Management:* c/o Norkin Talent Agency, 888 Biscayne Boulevard, Suite 1112, Miami, FL 33132, USA. *Telephone:* (305) 433-5953. *E-mail:* jnorkin@norkintalent.com; info@norkintalent.com. *Website:* www .norkintalent.com. *E-mail:* anaarias@malarodriguez.com (home). *Website:* malarodriguez.com (home).

RODRIGUEZ, Roberto Juan; Cuban/American musician (drums, percussion) and composer; b. El Vedado, Havana; s. of Roberto Luis Rodriguez. *Education:* Caturla Conservatory of Music, Havana, Univ. of Miami. *Career:* left Cuba with his family at age nine, moved to Miami USA; while still a teenager performed with his father and with Israel 'Cachao' Lopez; developed an interest in the music of the Jewish diaspora, worked on numerous projects with Jewish and klezmer musicians; moved to New York City; numerous concerts with his own band Septeto Rodriguez; performed and recorded with musicians including Rufus Wainwright, Joe Jackson, John Zorn, Marc Ribot, Celia Cruz, Paquito D'Rivera, Julio Iglesias, Miami Sound Machine, Paul Simon, T-Bone Burnett, Lloyd Cole, Reuben Blades, Susie Ibarra, Larry Coryell, Dr L Subramaniam, Kavita Krishnamurti, Randy Brecker, Dave Liebman, Kim Carnes, Phoebe Snow, Dianne Shure, Lester Bowie, Wadada Leo Smith; involved in several projects with Susie Ibarra; performs with Anthony Coleman Trio. *Recordings:* El Danzon de Moises 2001, Baila! Gitano Baila! 2004, Descarga Oriental: The New York Sessions (with Maurice El Medioni) 2006, Oy Vey! Vey! 2006; other: guest musician on recordings including Joe Jackson's Two Rainy Days, Marc Ribot's !Muy Divertido!, John Zorn's Taboo and Exile, Miami Sound Machine's Into the Light. *Honours:* American Music Award, Culture Crossing Award, BBC Radio 3 World Music Awards 2007. *E-mail:* roberto1rodriguez@earthlink.net (office). *Website:* www .robertojuanrodriguez.com.

RODRÍGUEZ, Silvio; Cuban singer, songwriter and musician (guitar); b. 29 Nov. 1946, San Antonio de los Baños; s. of Víctor Dagoberto Rodríguez Ortega and Argelia Domínguez León. *Career:* a leading figure in the Cuban 'nueva trova' movt of 1960s, combining progressive and political lyrics with traditional folk music; many of his songs considered classics in Spanish-speaking world, lyrics have been studied on univ. courses; mil. service 1964; made first tv appearance 1967; served as Cuban cultural emissary, Argentina 1984, Chile 1991; performed at Barbican Centre, London 2006; tour of Spain 2007. *Recordings:* albums: Ineditas 1967, Días y flores 1975, Mujeres 1978, Al final de este viaje...? 1978, Mujeres 1979, Rabo de Nube 1980, Unicornio 1982, Tríptico 1984, Causas y azares 1986, Oh melancolía 1988, Silvio Rodríguez in Chile, Vols I and II 1991, Silvio 1992, Mano a Mano (with Luis Eduardo Aute) 1992, Rodríguez 1994, El Hombre Extraño 1995, Domínguez 1996, Descartes 1998, Mariposas 1999, Expedición 2002, Cita con ángeles 2003, Érase que se Era 2006, Seguna Cita 2010. *Publications:* Canciones del Mar 1999. *Honours:* Dr hc, Universidad Nacional Mayor de San Marcos, Lima, Peru 2007. *Website:* www.silvio-rodriguez.org.

RODRÍGUEZ-LÓPEZ, Marcel; American musician (percussion, keyboards, drums); brother of Omar Rodríguez-Lopez. *Career:* mem. The Mars Volta 2003–; mem. Zechs Marquise 2003–; has also played with Omar Rodríguez-Lopez Quintet, Thieves of Always. *Recordings:* albums: with The Mars Volta: De-Loused in the Comatorium 2003, Frances the Mute 2005, Amputechture 2006, The Bedlam in Goliath 2008, Octahedron 2009; with Zechs Marquise: Our Delicate Stranded Nightmare 2008. *Honours:* Grammy Award for Best Hard Rock Performance (for Wax Simulacra) 2009. *Address:* c/o Warner Bros. Records Inc., 3300 Warner Boulevard, Burbank, CA 91505, USA (office). *Website:* www.themarsvolta.com.

RODRÍGUEZ-LÓPEZ, Omar; American singer, musician (guitar) and songwriter; b. 1 Sept. 1975, Bayamón, Puerto Rico. *Career:* fmr mem. At the Drive-In; founding mem. and lead, The Mars Volta 2001–; moved to Amsterdam, Netherlands 2005; f. the Omar Rodríguez-López Quintet 2005, later renamed the Omar Rodríguez-López Quintet; also solo artist. *Recordings:* albums: with At the Drive-In: Acrobatic Tenement 1996, In Casino Out 1998, Relationship of Command 2000; with The Mars Volta: De-Loused in the Comatorium 2003, Frances the Mute 2005, Amputechture 2006, The Bedlam in Goliath 2008, Octahedron 2009; with the Omar Rodríguez-López Quintet/Group: Omar Rodriguez 2005, The Apocalypse Inside of an Orange 2007, Los Sueños de un Higado 2009; solo: A Manual Dexterity 2004, Se Dice Bisonte, No Búfalo 2007, Calibration 2007, Absence Makes the Heart Grow Fungus 2008, Minor Cuts and Scrapes in the Bushes Ahead 2008, Old Money 2009, Megaritual 2009, Despair 2009. *Honours:* Grammy Award for Best Hard Rock Performance (for Wax Simulacra) 2009. *Address:* c/o Warner Bros. Records Inc., 3300 Warner Boulevard, Burbank, CA 91505, USA (office). *Website:* www .themarsvolta.com.

ROE, Tommy; American entertainer, musician (guitar), songwriter and music publisher; b. 9 May 1942, Atlanta, Georgia. *Career:* Performances and concerts world-wide; Appearances, all major television and radio shows in 1960s; Sold 40 m. records; mem. Society of Singers; Academy of Country Music. *Recordings:* albums include: Sheila 1963, Something for Everybody 1963, Everybody Likes Tommy Roe 1964, Ballads and Beat 1965, Sweet Pea 1966, Phantasy 1967, It's Now Winter's Day 1967, Dizzy 1969, 12 in a Roe 1970, We Can Make Music 1970, Beginnings 1971, Energy 1976, Full Bloom 1977, Golden Legends 2000, High Profile 2000, Salute 2006. *Honours:* 4 Gold Singles; Georgy Award; BMI Awards. *Address:* PO Box 26037, Minneapolis, MN 55426, USA. *Website:* www.tommyroe.com.

ROEL, (Anne) Charlotte; singer; b. 3 Dec. 1964, Copenhagen, Denmark; m. Floyd Adams III 1990. *Education:* Manhattan School of Music, New York, Greve Coll. *Career:* solo performer 1992–; concerts: Copenhagen Gospel Rock Festival, Opstand Festival, Glumsö Gospel Festival, Västervik Gospel Festival Sweden; performed at Montmartre, Copenhagen Jazz House, Huset, KB Hallen; radio: Strax, Denmark Nat. Radio, More Than Music, Tjek Listen, Danish local radio, NIK Kolding, Radio Roskilde, Naestved Radio, Copenhagen FM, Radio Ballerup, Swedish radio, KFUM Sweden; TV: KKR/TV Charlotte Roel – A Musical Portrait, Norwegian TV, Hello Norden; hostess, producer, The Five Blind Boys of Alabama; mem. DAF (Danish Artist Soc.). *Recordings include:* single: Perfect Love (No. 1, Denmark) 1994, debut album 1995.

ROESER, Donald, (Buck Dharma); American musician (guitar) and singer; b. 12 Nov. 1947. *Career:* lead guitarist and singer of rock group, Blue Öyster Cult 1971–; numerous concerts, tours and festival appearances; solo artist as Buck Dharma. *Recordings include:* albums: Blue Öyster Cult, 1972; Tyranny and Mutation, 1973; Live On Your Feet Or On Your Knees, 1975; Agents of Fortune, 1976; Spectres, 1978; Some Enchanted Evening, 1978; Mirrors, 1979; Cultosaurus Erectus, 1980; Fire of Unknown Origin, 1981; ETL (Extra-Terrestrial Live), 1982; Club Ninja, 1986; Imaginos, 1988; Career of Evil: The Metal Years, 1990; Live 1976, 1994; Cult Classic, 1994; The Curse Of The Hidden Mirror, 2001; solo (as Buck Dharma): Flat Out; with Blotto: Collected Words, 1994; with Summerdaze: Summerdaze, 1997; other credits include: ZKG, Tommy Zvoncheck 2000, Music Machine, Erik Norlander 2003, River to the Sea, Simon Apple 2004. *Address:* PO Box 99, Port Richey, FL 34668, USA. *Website:* www.buckdharma.com.

ROGERS, Adam; American musician (jazz guitar); b. New York City. *Education:* Mannes Coll. of Music. *Career:* fmrly co-leader, Lost Tribe; leader, various ensembles, also sideman; has toured USA, Canada, Europe, Japan, Southeast Asia, Middle East, S America, Russia; collab. with Michael Brecker, Mingus Orchestra, Cassandra Wilson, Norah Jones, Chris Potter, John Zorn, Randy Brecker and others; played music for Great Lakes Theater Co., Joseph Papp's Public Theater, Metropolitan Opera; featured soloist in John McLaughlin's Apocalypse with Dresden Symphony Orchestra 1999. *Film soundtracks:* as performer: Hamlet, Jim Brown: All American, What Just Happened. *Recordings include:* as leader: Art of the Invisible 2002, Allegory 2003, Apparitions 2005, Time and the Infinite 2007, Sight 2009; as co-leader, with Lost Tribe: Lost Tribe 1993, Soulfish 1994, Many Lifetimes 1998. *Current Management:* c/o Gille Amaral, Dog and Pony Industries. *Telephone:* (603) 379-6602. *E-mail:* gille@dogandponyindustries.com. *Website:* www .adamrogersmusic.com.

ROGERS, David; British composer (keyboards), programmer and producer; b. 3 Jan. 1963, Dartford, Kent; m. Sue Ward 1992; two s. *Education:* Univ. of London. *Career:* founder member, Daybreak Productions 1987; numerous television, radio broadcasts; mem. Musicians' Union, PRS. *Compositions:* 346 works published by 1995; works include: Mr Blobby, Light of Summer, Peanuts, Steady, Blobby – The Album, The Dream, Boing, Probe. *Honours:* Ivor Novello Award for Best Selling Song (for Mr Blobby) 1993.

ROGERS, Kenneth (Kenny) David; American country singer and songwriter; b. 21 Aug. 1938, Houston, TX; m. Wanda Miller. *Career:* mem., The Scholars 1955; founder, Ken-Lee record label (with brother Lelan), Jolly Rogers record label; bass player, Bobby Doyle Three 1962; mem., New Christy Minstrels 1967; founder mem., First Edition 1967–74; solo artist 1974–; established Dreamcatcher Entertainment 1998. *Television films:* The Dream Makers 1975, Easter By the Sea 1978, The Gambler 1980, Coward of the

County 1981, I Love Liberty 1982, Six Pack 1982, The Gambler: The Adventure Continues 1983, Wild Horses 1985, The Gambler Part III: The Legend Continues 1987, Christmas in America 1990, The Gambler Returns: The Luck of the Draw 1991, Rio Diablo 1993, MacShayne: Winner Takes All 1994, MacShayne: The Final Roll of the Dice 1994, Gambler V: Playing for Keeps 1994, Get to the Heart: The Barbara Mandrell Story 1997, Snowden on Ice 1997, Longshot 2000. *Recordings:* albums: with First Edition: The First Edition 1967, The First Editions Second 1968, Ruby Don't Take Your Love To Town 1969, Something's Burning 1970, Fools 1970, Tell It All Brother 1971, Transition 1971, Backroads 1972, Planet Texas 1972, The Ballad of Calico 1972, Monumental 1973, Rollin' 1974; solo: Kenny Rogers 1976, Love Lifted Me 1976, Daytime Friends 1977, Every Time Two Fools Collide (with Dottie West) 1978, Love Or Something Like It 1978, The Gambler 1978, Kenny 1978, Gideon 1980, Shine Out 1980, Christmas 1981, Lady 1981, Ruby 1981, Share Your Love 1981, Love Will Turn You Around 1982, Eyes That See In The Dark 1983, We've Got Tonight 1983, Once Upon A Christmas 1984, What About Me? 1984, The Heart Of The Matter 1985, Love Is What We Make It 1985, Short Stories 1986, They Don't Make Them Like They Used To 1986, I Prefer The Moonlight 1987, Christmas In America 1989, Something Inside So Strong 1989, Love Is Strange 1990, Back Home Again 1992, Some Prisons Don't Have Walls 1991, Heart To Heart 1992, Lucille 1992, If Only My Heart Had A Voice 1993, Timepiece 1994, The Gift 1996, Across My Heart 1997, Branson City Limits 1998, Christmas From The Heart 1998, She Rides Wild Horses 1999, After Dark 1999, Christmas Greetings 2000, There You Go Again 2000, The Way It Used To Be 2001, Sing You A Sad Song 2001, Calico Silver 2002, Back To The Well 2003, Kenny Rogers: 50 Years 2008. *Publication:* Making It in Music (with Len England). *Honours:* numerous Grammy Awards, People's Choice Awards, Acad. of Country Music Awards, Sammy Cahn Lifetime Achievement Award 1999, RIAA Diamond Award 1999, LeRoy Neiman Award for Artistic Excellence 1999. *Current Management:* Dreamcatcher Entertainment, 2910 Poston Avenue, Nashville, TN 37203, USA. *Telephone:* (615) 329-2303. *E-mail:* ccook@dreamcatcherenter.com. *Website:* www .dreamcatcherenter.com; www.kennyrogers.com.

ROGERS, Robert; British bandleader, musician (guitar) and singer; b. 27 Jan. 1926, London, England; m. Olive 1950; one s. *Television and radio:* more than 200 TV Tonight shows with Ted Taylor Four, Don Lang's Frantic Five, 6.5 Special, Saturday Club and Country Club on radio; hundreds of radio shows as Sounds Bob Rogers; own series, The Towncriers; Things Are Swinging; Skinnerette in the Frank Skinner TV Shows, BBC 1995–99, ITV 2000–05. *Recordings:* 11 albums; session guitarist with artists, including John Barry Seven, Adam Faith, Freddie and The Dreamers, Les Reed; banjo player with artists, including Mike Daniels Delta Jazzmen, Sid Phillips, Joe Henderson. *Address:* 11 Darwin Close, Orpington, Kent, BR6 7EP, England (home). *Telephone:* (1689) 858164 (home).

ROGERS, Roy, BA; American producer and musician (slide guitar); b. 28 July 1950, Redding, California; m. Gaynell Toler Rogers 1984; one s. one d. *Education:* Hayward State Univ., California. *Career:* mem., Delta Rhythm Kings; producer/musician, John Lee Hooker 1989–; world-wide tours, major jazz festivals; numerous television and radio shows; performed with Carlos Santana, Miles Davis, Albert Collins, B. B. King, Bonnie Raitt, Robert Cray; mem, AFofM, NARAS, BMI. *Compositions:* The Healer, with John Lee Hooker. *Recordings:* albums: solo: Chops Not Chaps 1985, Slidewinder 1987, Blues On The Range 1989, Slide of Hand 1993, Slide Zone 1994, Rhythm and groove 1996, Pleasure and Pain 1998, Everybody's Angel (with Shana Morrison) 1999, Sideways 2002, The Crossing in Norway (with Reidar Larsen) 2006, Ballads Before the Rain (with Ray Manzarek) 2008, Split Decision 2009; with Norton Buffalo: R&B 1991, Travelin' Tracks 1992, Rhythm and Groove 1996, Everybody's Angel 1999; soundtracks: The Hot Spot; One Flew Over The Cuckoo's Nest. *Honours:* Best Emerging Blues Artist, Jazz Times Critics Poll 1990, NARAS Award of Recognition, two Grammy Awards. *Current Management:* c/o Stephen Gordon, Savoy Music, 1844 SW Troy Street, Portland, OR 97219, USA. *Telephone:* (503) 245-2321. *E-mail:* gordoom@aol.com. *Website:* www.savoymusicinternational.com; www .roy-rogers.com.

ROGERS, Timothy (Tim) Adrian; Australian singer, musician (guitar), songwriter and producer; b. 20 Sept. 1969, Kalgoorlie, WA; m. Rocío García Rodríquez 1999. *Education:* Australian Nat. Univ. *Career:* Founding mem. and lead singer rock band, You Am I 1989–; numerous world-wide tours; Founder mem. The Brides, later renamed The Twin Set, to back his solo career 1999–. *Film appearance:* Holy Smoke. *Recordings include:* albums: with You Am I: Sound As Ever 1993, Hi Fi Way 1995, Hourly, Daily 1996, # 4 Record 1998, What Rhymes With Cars And Girls 1999, …Saturday Night, 'Round Ten 1999, Dress Me Slowly 2001, Deliverance 2002, Spit Polish 2005, Convicts 2007; with The Twin Set: What Rhymes With Cars and Girls? 1998. *Honours:* ARIA Award for Best Alternative Release 1995, six Industry Awards 1996. *Current Management:* c/o Scott McKenzie, Premier Artists, Dundas La, Albert Park, Vic. 3206, Australia. *Telephone:* (3) 9699-9555. *E-mail:* scotty@ premierartists.com.au. *Website:* www.premierartists.com.au; www.timrogers .com.au; www.youami.com.au.

ROGERS, Tony; British musician (mellotron, organ, piano) and singer. *Career:* mem., The Charlatans 1999–; numerous tours, festivals, television and radio appearances. *Recordings include:* albums: Us And Us Only 1999, Songs From The Other Side 2000, Wonderland 2001, Live It Like You Love It 2002, Up At The Lake 2004, Simpatico 2006, You Cross My Path 2008, Who

We Touch 2010, Modern Nature 2015. *Current Management:* Big Life Management, 67–69 Chalton Street, London, NW1 1HY, England. *Telephone:* (20) 7554-2100. *Fax:* (20) 7554-2101. *E-mail:* tim@biglifemanagement.com. *Website:* www.biglifemanagement.com. *Address:* The Charlatans, PO Box 134, Sandbach, Cheshire CW11 1AE, England (office). *E-mail:* info@ thecharlatans.net (office). *Website:* www.thecharlatans.net.

ROJEK, Artur; Polish rock musician (guitar), singer and songwriter; b. 6 May 1972, Mysłowice. *Career:* formed band The Freshmen with Wojciech Powaga 1992, changed band's name to Myslovitz 1994; first int. concerts, Sweden, Germany, USA 1998; numerous European festival appearances and support act for Iggy Pop and Simple Minds 2002; began releasing English-language versions of their music 2002; contributed to soundtracks for films Młode wilki ½ (Young Wolves ½), Duże zwierzę (The Big Animal), To my (That's us). *Recordings:* albums: Myslovitz 1995, Sun Machine 1996, Z rozmyślań przy śniadaniu 1997, Miłość w czasach popkultury 1999, Korova Milky Bar 2002, The Best Of 2003, Korova Milky Bar (English version) 2003, Skalary, mieczyki, neonki 2004, Happiness Is Easy 2006. *Honours:* Music Video of The Year 1998, Band of The Year and Rock Album of The Year 1999, Song of The Year and Video of The Year 2000, Album of The Year 2003, all Fryderyk awards; Polityka's Paszport award 1999, Best Polish Act, MTV Europe Music Awards 2002, 2003, Border Breakers European Breakthrough award (for Korova Milky Bar) 2005. *Current Management:* Maciej Pilarczyk, Chaos Management Group, ul. Karowa 31, 00-324 Warsaw, Poland. *E-mail:* m.pil@myslovitz.pl (office). *Website:* www.chaos.com.pl (office); www .myslovitz.pl.

ROKER, Ron; British composer, songwriter, record producer and publisher; b. 23 Jan. 1941, Lincoln; m. Karol Roker 1977; one s. one d. *Career:* Founder and lead vocalist of own group with guitarist Albert Lee 1960s; toured, worked with various headliners; turned to writing and producing; co-writers include Gerry Shury, Barry Blue, Lynsey De Paul, Roger Greenaway, Howard Greenfield; formed own publishing and producing company, Karon Productions; mem. IPA, Term, BAC&S Council. *Recordings include:* UK top 10 hits include: Rupert (Jackie Lee), Storm In A Teacup (The Fortunes), Do You Wanna Dance (Barry Blue), Dance Little Lady Dance (Tina Charles), Guilty (The Pearls); US top 20 hits include: Guilty, First Choice; Up In A Puff of Smoke, Polly Brown; Devils Gun, CJ and Co; Funk Theory, Rokotto and BT Express; Do You Believe In Love At First Sight, Dionne Warwick; Honey Honey, Sweet Dreams. *Honours:* Never Giving Up (composer), performed by Sweet Dreams in 1983 Eurovision Song Contest (placed sixth). *E-mail:* enquiries@ronroker.com. *Website:* ronroker.com.

ROLLE, Leon, (DJ Locksmith); British DJ, songwriter and record producer. *Career:* Founder-mem. Rudimental 2010–; released debut single Deep in the Valley 2011; collaborations with MC Shantie, Adiyam, MNEK and Syron, John Newman, Alex Clare, Angel Haze, Ella Eyre, Emeli Sandé, Nas, Foxes. *Recordings:* album: with Rudimental: Home (MOBO Award for Best Album 2013) 2013. *Current Management:* c/o Coda Music Agency LLP, CODA House, 56 Compton Street, Clerkenwell, London, EC1V 0ET, England. *Telephone:* (20) 7017-2500. *Fax:* (20) 7017-2555. *Website:* www.codaagency.com; www .rudimental.co.uk; www.majortoms.co.uk.

ROLLINS, Henry; American singer, author and actor; b. 13 Feb. 1961, Washington, DC. *Career:* mem. punk rock group, Black Flag 1981–86; numerous concert and spoken word tours; leader, Henry Rollins Band 1986–; publisher with 2.13.61 Publications 1984–. *Film appearances:* The Right Side of My Brain 1985, The Chase 1994, Johnny Mnemonic 1995, Heat 1995, Lost Highway 1997, Jack Frost 1998, Morgan's Ferry 1999, Desperate But Not Serious 1999, Batman Beyond: Return of the Joker (voice) 2000, Scenes of the Crime 2001, Time Lapse 2001, Psychic Murders 2002, The New Guy 2002, Bad Boys II 2003, A House on a Hill 2003, Live Freaky Die Freaky (voice) 2003, Deathdealer: A Documentary 2004, Feast 2005, Lies & Alibis 2006, Wrong Turn 2: Dead End 2007. *Television:* Words in Your Face (film) 1991, Shadow Realm (film) 2002, Henry's Film Corner (series host) 2004, The Henry Rollins Show (series host) 2006. *Recordings include:* albums: with Black Flag: Everything Went Black 1982, Damaged 1982, Slip It In 1984, Loose Nut 1985, The Process of Weeding Out 1985, In My Head 1985, Who's Got The Ten 1986; with Henry Rollins Band: Hot Animal Machine, Drive By Shooting 1987, Life Time 1988, Do It 1989, Hard Volume 1989, Turned On 1990, The End of Silence 1992, Electro Convulsive Therapy 1993, The Weight 1994, Everything 1996, Black Coffee Blues 1997, Think Tank 1998, Live in Australia 1999, Get Some Go Again 2000, A Rollins In The Wry 2001, Nice 2001, Rise Above 2002, The End of Silence Demos 2002, The Only Way To Know For Sure 2002, Weighting 2003; spoken works include: Short Walk On A Long Pier 1987, Live At McCabe's 1992, Deep Throat 1992, The Boxed Life 1993. *Publications:* contrib. to Details, Face, Interview, Melody Maker, Sounds, Village Voice. *Current Management:* 3 Artist Management, 14260 Ventura Boulevard, Suite 201, Sherman Oaks, CA 91423, USA. *Address:* c/o 2.13.61 Publications, 7510 Sunset Blvd, #602, Los Angeles, CA 90046, USA. *Telephone:* (818) 380-0303 (office). *E-mail:* info@threeam.net (office). *Website:* www.henryrollins.com.

ROLLINS, Theodore Walter (Sonny); American jazz musician (tenor saxophone); b. 7 Sept. 1930, New York, NY; s. of Walter Rollins and Valborg Solomon; m. 1st Dawn Finney 1956 (divorced); m. 2nd Lucille Pearson 1959 (died 2004). *Education:* High School, New York. *Career:* began rehearsing while in high school, with Thelonious Monk; recorded with Bud Powell 1949;

wrote standards 'Airegin' and 'Oleo' recorded with Miles Davis 1953; played and recorded with Clifford Brown/Max Roach 1955; took sabbatical playing on Williamsburg Bridge, New York 1959–61; scored and played music for film Alfie 1966; has appeared in Jazz Heritage series, Smithsonian Inst. and at Newport Jazz Festival; numerous concert tours in Europe and Far East; annual concert tours of Europe, Japan, USA with Concert Orchestra 1973–; mem. American Acad. of Arts and Sciences 2010–. *Recordings include:* albums: Sonny Rollins with the Modern Jazz Quartet 1953, Moving Out 1954, Work Time 1955, Sonny Rollins Plus 4 1956, Tenor Madness 1956, Saxophone Colossus 1956, Rollins Plays for Bird 1956, Tour de Force 1956, Sonny Boy 1956, Sonny Rollins, Vol. 1 1957, Way Out West 1957, Sonny Rollins, Vol. 2 1957, The Sound of Sonny 1957, Newk's Time 1957, A Night at the Village 1957, Sonny Rollins Plays/Thad Jones Plays 1957, Freedom Suite 1958, Brass/Trio 1958, Sonny Rollins and the Big Brass 1958, Sonny Rollins and the Contemporary Leaders 1958, Sonny Rollins 'At Music Inn' (split LP with Teddy Edwards At Falcon Lair with Joe Castro) 1959, The Bridge 1962, What's New? 1962, Our Man in Jazz 1962, Sonny Meets Hawk! 1963, Now's the Time 1964, The Standard Sonny Rollins 1964, There Will Never Be Another You 1965, Sonny Rollins on Impulse! 1965, Alfie 1966, East Broadway Run Down 1966, Next Album 1972, Horn Culture 1973, Sonny Rollins in Japan 1973, The Cutting Edge 1974, Nucleus 1975, The Way I Feel 1976, Easy Living 1977, Don't Stop the Carnival 1978, Don't Ask 1979, Love at First Sight 1980, No Problem 1981, Reel Life 1982, Sunny Days, Starry Nights 1984, The Solo Album 1985, G-Man 1986, Dancing in the Dark 1987, Falling in Love with Jazz 1989, Here's to the People 1991, Old Flames 1993, Sonny Rollins + 3 1996, Global Warming 1998, This Is What I Do 2000, Without a Song: The 9/11 Concert 2001, Sonny, Please 2006, Road Shows 2008, Road Shows Vol. 2 2011, Road Shows Vol. 3 2014. *Honours:* Dr hc (Bard Coll.) 1993, Hon. DMus (Long Island Univ.) 1998, (New England Conservatory of Music) 2002, (Juilliard School) 2013, Hon. DArts (Wesleyan Univ.) 1998, Hon. DFA (Duke Univ.) 1999; Guggenheim Fellow 1972, Lifetime Achievement Award, Tufts Univ. 1996, Lifetime Achievement Award, Nat. Asscn of Recording Arts and Science 2005, Grammy Award for Best Jazz Instrumental Solo (for Why Was I Born?) 2006, Edward MacDowell Medal 2010, Honoree, 34th Annual Kennedy Center Honors 2011, Jazz Journalists Asscn Award 2011. *Current Management:* c/o Ted Kurland, The Kurland Agency, 173 Brighton Avenue, Boston, MA 02134-2003, USA. *Telephone:* (617) 254-0007. *E-mail:* ted@thekurlandagency.com. *Website:* www.thekurlandagency.com. *Address:* Route 9G, Germantown, NY 12526, USA. *Telephone:* (518) 537-6112 (office). *Fax:* (518) 537-4342 (office). *Website:* www.sonnyrollins.com.

ROMAN-SMITH, Lu Lu; American singer and songwriter; b. 6 May 1946, Pilot Point, TX; m. (divorced); two s. *Career:* gospel and country music and contemporary Christian singer; numerous live appearances and concerts; mem. CCMA, GMA. *Television includes:* Hee-Haw (series) 1968–93. *Recordings include:* albums: Now Let Me Sing 1974, One Day At A Time 1975, Love Coming Down 1976, Lulu's Testimony 1978, Sing For My Friends 1979, You Were Loving Me 1984, Take Me There 1985, Hymns That Light The Way 1987, Joy 1988, Key To The Kingdom 1990, Best Friend 1991, Hymns, Promises and Praises 1997, Inspired 2001. *Honours:* Dove Award for Best Album by a Secular Artist (for You Were Loving Me) 1985. *Address:* Rainey Steele, 1300 Division Street, Suite 206, Nashville, TN 37203, USA. *E-mail:* info@luluroman.net. *Website:* www.luluroman.net.

ROMANO, Aldo; musician (drums); b. 16 Jan. 1941, Belluno, Italy. *Career:* family relocated to France, played guitar and drums in Paris jazz clubs; concentrated on drums 1961–; accompanied numerous visiting musicians at Paris clubs; collaborated with artists including Chet Baker, Keith Jarrett, Michel Petrucciani, Henri Texier; mem., various groups including Total Issue, Pork Pie; released first album as band leader 1978; f. Italian Quartet 1988, Palatino 1995–; founding pres., Union des Musiciens de Jazz. *Recordings:* albums: as band leader: Divieto di Santoficazione 1977, Il Piacere 1978, Night Diary 1980, Alma Latina 1983, Ritual 1988, To Be Ornette To Be 1989, Latin Memories 1991, Prosodie 1995, Canzoni 1997, Tempo 1999, Non Dimenticar 1999, Corners 2000, Because of Bechet 2002, Palatino 2002, Threesome 2005, Chante 2006, Flower Power 2006, Intervista 2007, Night Diary 2007, Etat de Fait 2008, Just Jazz 2008. *Honours:* Jazzpar Prize 2004.

ROMBOLA, Tony; American musician (guitar); b. 24 Nov. 1964, Norwood, Mass.; m. Sue Rombola; three c. *Career:* fmrly mem. The Crushed Tomatoes; mem. Godsmack 1995–. *Recordings include:* albums: with Godsmack: Godsmack 1998, Awake 2000, Faceless 2003, Godsmack IV 2004, The Oracle 2010. *Honours:* Boston Music Award for Act of the Year 2000, 2001, Billboard Award for Rock Artist of the Year 2001. *Website:* www.godsmack.com.

ROMCESCU, Mircea; Romanian musician (violin, piano, guitar), songwriter and singer; b. 5 Feb. 1957, Bucharest; m. Olimpia Panciu Romcescu 1986. *Education:* George Enesco School of Music, Ciprian Porumbesco Acad. of Music. *Career:* concerts, tours, TV, radio, with own group Academica; big band arranging, directing; film music; studio musician, producer; owner of 16-track digital studio; violin soloist, Acad. Symphony Orchestra 1980; mem. Danish Composers' Union, Romanian Composers' Union. *Recordings include:* albums: Academica 1980, Music Is My Life 1981, Olimpia, 1983, Words Against Words 1989, Free 1993, Together Forever 2003. *Honours:* Composer of the Year 1982, Billboard Song Contest winner three times.

RØMER, Hanne; Danish composer, conductor and musician (saxophone, vocals, guitar, piano); b. 29 July 1949, Copenhagen; two d. *Education:* Dick Grove School of Music, Los Angeles, Univ. of Copenhagen, Danish Royal Conservatory. *Career:* Founder, singer, guitarist, all-woman rock group, Hos Anna 1975–81; Hexethyl Big Band 1978–81; duo with pianist Marietta Wandell 1980–; Conductor, several choirs and big bands; Leader, Nordic All-Women Big Band: April Light Orchestra 1994–2000; tours throughout Denmark and Finland, the Baltic countries, China, Iceland, Sweden; Founder, Amanda Music Edition 1994, which has released several CDs and some books on ear-training; currently performs as saxophone player and singer in various quartets and with saxophone quintet Sax in the City. *Compositions:* Piano feature, for Danish Radio Light Music Orchestra 1985, Saxophone Concert 1987, several symphonic poems, music for string orchestras, choirs, big bands and jazz ensembles. *Recordings:* four albums with Hos Anna; with Marietta Wandall: Akijava 1990, Ametyst 1994, Between Pain and Joy 2000, Walking with the Slow Turtle 2005; with the Nordic All-Women Big Band: Somewhere In Time 1994; with the Hanne Romer Quartet: Come Rain Or Come Shine 1994; with Mads Granum Quartet: Early Spring 1999, Everything You Wanna Know about Spring 2004, Fantasia with the saxophone quintet 'Sax in the City' 2005. *Address:* Amanda Music, 6200 Aabenraa, Denmark (office). *Telephone:* 22-17-99-15 (office). *Fax:* 74-62-99-15 (office). *E-mail:* hr@amanda-music.dk (office). *Website:* www.amanda-music.dk (office).

ROMMEL, Bernd; German musician (drums); b. 10 June 1967, Waiblingen; m. Monika, 1 d. *Education:* Music High School (MHS, Graz, Austria) with jazz diploma. *Career:* Several R&B projects throughout Germany including: White Bread; Paddy Corn Band; Member, Lizl, 1990; Member, The Solutions, 1991; Member, Blues Pumpm, 1992; mem, AKM; Austromecha; LSG. *Recordings:* with Lizl: Talk About Jobsharing; All Blues Pumpm productions, (1993–) including; Single: Men From Milwaukee, 1993; Album: Living Loving Riding, 1994. *Honours:* Winner, Bigband Contest Festival with High School Big Band, Graz, Austria. *E-mail:* office@bluespumpm.at. *Website:* www.bluespumpm.at.

ROMO, Olle; Swedish programmer, engineer and musician (drums); b. 3 July 1958, Stockholm; m. Mary Beth Romo 1991; one d. *Education:* Stockholm Music Conservatory. *Career:* Two Eurythmics world tours as drummer; Recording career as drummer, programmer, engineer; mem, Musicians' Union. *Recordings:* Contributions (as drummer/programmer): Feargal Sharkey, 1985; Eurythmics, Savage, 1987; Shakespears Sister, Sacred Heart, 1989; Eurythmics, We Too Are One, 1989; Neville Brothers, Brother's Keeper, 1990; Pulp, Different Class, 1996; Alisha's Attic, Alisha Rules the World, 1996; Shania Twain, Come On Over, 1997; Bryan Adams, MTV Unplugged, 1997; Pulp, This is Hardcore, 1998; Céline Dion, These Are Special Times, 1998; Also programmer for Backstreet Boys.

RONCHETTI, Francesco, MA, DMus,; Italian singer, composer and performer; b. 18 Feb. 1962, Florence; m. Lyall Forsyth Harris 1998. *Education:* University of Bologna. *Career:* mem. of vocal trio, Trinovox; numerous TV and radio broadcasts, concerts; wrote soundtrack for radio play, Bavarian State Radio 1995; voice specialist, teacher; collaborations with American and Italian singers, composers, musical producers; founder acoustic improvisational duo, The Dedications 1999; founder artistic co., Ars Una; mem. SIAE, GEMA, SIEM, Contemporary a cappella Soc. of America. *Recordings include:* albums: with Trinovox: Incanto, 1994; Voices, (Trinovox, Sarband, The Bulgarian Voices), 1994; Earborn, Trinovox and Various Artists, 1994; Mediterranea, 1997. *Publications:* contrib. articles, including 'Pop-Rock Singing', in Suonare uno Strumento 1989, 'Tell Me How He Sings...', in Imparerock 1994; The Sound of Colors (poems, paintings and music, with album). *Honours:* Premio Quartetto Cetra, Italy (with Trinovox) 1994.

RÖNNBLOM, Anders F.; Swedish singer, songwriter, musician (guitar) and designer; b. 9 May 1946, Stockholm. *Education:* coll., art and design school. *Career:* first recording 1959; played with numerous bands in the 1960s with recordings 1963–66; solo artist 1971–; f. EFX Art & Design magazine 1991, Digital Hall of Fame art exhbn 1995. *Recordings include:* Jag Kysste Henne Våldsamt, Europa Brinner, Det Är Inte Snön Som Faller, The F-BOX (18 CDs and 40 Years of Music). *Publications:* publishes own magazine, Mac Art and Design; graphic books include Metalheart, Metalheart is Movement. *Current Management:* Studio Matchbox, Roslagsgatan 11, 11355 Stockholm, Sweden. *E-mail:* andersf@andersf.com (office). *Website:* www.andersf.com (office).

RONSON, Mark; British/American music producer; b. 4 Sept. 1975, London; s. of Laurence Ronson and Ann Dexter-Jones. *Education:* Vassar Coll., New York Univ. *Career:* fmr mem. Whole Earth Mamas; made his name as DJ on New York club scene in mid-1990s; after producing a song for Nikka Costa signed a recording contract with Elektra Records; solo recording artist and producer of songs by Christina Aguilera, Amy Winehouse, Lily Allen, Robbie Williams, Paul McCartney, Estelle, Bruno Mars, Duran Duran; formed own record label Allido Records 2004. *Recordings include:* albums: Here Comes the Fuzz 2003, Version 2007, Record Collection 2010, Uptown Special 2015; as producer: Powerule, Heatin' Up/P.R.I.S.M., Rhymes To Bust/It's Your Right, Nikka Costa, Everybody Got Their Something, Like A Feather, Lily Allen, Littlest Things, Robbie Williams, Rudebox (four songs), Sean Paul, International Affair, J-Live, School's In, Teriyaki Boyz, The Takeover, Rhymefest, These Days, Ol' Dirty Bastard, Dirty Dirty, Christina Aguilera, Slow Down Baby, Amy Winehouse, Back To Black (six songs), Rhymefest, Blue Collar (three songs). *Film includes:* Amy 2015. *Honours:* Grammy Awards for Best Non-Classical Producer 2008, for Record of the Year and Best Pop Duo/Group Performance (both for Uptown Funk; featuring Bruno Mars) 2016, BRIT Awards for Best British Male Solo Artist 2008, for Best British Single (for

Uptown Funk) 2015, MTV Video Music Award for Best Male Video (for Uptown Funk) 2015, Q Hero Award 2015. *Current Management:* c/o Paradigm Talent Agency, 360 North Crescent Drive North Building, Beverly Hills, CA 90210, USA. *Telephone:* (310) 288-8000. *Fax:* (310) 288-2000. *Website:* www .paradigmagency.com; www.markronson.co.uk.

RONSTADT, Linda Marie; American singer; b. 15 July 1946, Tucson, Ariz.; d. of Gilbert Ronstadt and Ruthmary Ronstadt (née Copeman). *Career:* debut album with Stone Poneys 1967; appeared in stage version of Pirates of Penzance 1981, film version 1983; featured in La Bohème 1984; American Music Award 1978; Grammy Awards 1975, 1976, 1987, 1988 (with Emmylou Harris q.v. and Dolly Parton q.v.), 1989, 1990 (jtly); Emmy Award 1988, 1989, Acad. of Country Music Award 1987, 1988. *Recordings include:* albums: Evergreen 1967, Home Sown, Home Grown 1969, Silk Purse 1970, Don't Cry Now 1973, Heart Like a Wheel 1974, Different Drum 1974, Prisoner in Disguise 1975, Hasten Down the Wind 1976, Simple Dreams, Blue Bayou 1977, Living in the USA 1978, Get Closer 1982, What's New 1983, Lush Life 1984, For Sentimental Reasons 1986, Trio (with Emmylou Harris and Dolly Parton, Country Music Album of the Year 1987) 1986, Canciones de Mi Padre 1987, Cry Like a Rainstorm—Howl Like the Wind 1989, All My Life 1990, Mas Canciones 1991, Frenesi 1992, Winter Light 1993, Feels Like Home 1995, Dedicated to the One I Love 1996, We Ran 1998, Trio 2 (with Emmylou Harris and Dolly Parton) 1999, Western Wall: The Tucson Sessions (wih Emmylou Harris), A Merry Little Christmas 2000, Hummin' to Myself 2004, Adieu False Heart (with Ann Savoy) 2006. *E-mail:* info@vanguardrecords.com (office). *Website:* www.vanguardrecords.com.

ROONEY, Joe Don; American musician (guitar) and songwriter; b. 13 Sept. 1975, Picher, OK; m. Tiffany Fallon; one s. one d. *Career:* mem., Rascal Flatts 2000–. *Recordings include:* albums: Rascal Flatts 2000, Melt 2002, Feels Like Today 2004, Me and My Gang 2006, Still Feels Good 2007, Unstoppable 2009. *Honours:* CMA Horizon Award 2002, CMA Awards for Best Vocal Group 2003, 2004, 2005, 2006, 2007, 2008, ACM Awards for Best New Vocal Group 2001, for Best Vocal Group 2002, 2003, 2004, 2005, 2006, 2007, 2008, 2009, and for Song of the Year (for I'm Movin' On), ASCAP Vocal Group of the Year 2004, American Music Award for Favorite Country Band, Duo or Group 2006, 2007, 2008, 2009, CMT Group Music Video of the Year Award 2003, 2004, 2005, 2006, 2007, 2008, Radio Music Award Country Song of the Year for "God Bless Broken Road" 2005, People's Choice Award for Favourite Remake for "Life is a Highway" 2007, People's Choice Award for Favourite Song from a Movie for "Life is a Highway" 2007. *Current Management:* William Morris Agency, 1660 Division Street, Suite 300, Nashville, TN 37203, USA. *Website:* www.wma .com; www.rascalflatts.com.

ROOTS MANUVA; British rap artist and producer; b. (Rodney Hylton Smith), 1972, Stockwell, London. *Career:* fmr poet. *Recordings include:* albums: Brand New Second Hand 1999, Run Come Save Me 2001, Dub Come Save Me 2002, Awfully Deep 2004, Alternately Deep 2006, Slime and Reason 2008, Duppy Writer 2010, 4everevolution 2011, Bleeds 2015. *Honours:* MOBO Award for Best Hip Hop Act 1999. *Current Management:* c/o Lisa Horan Management, 189 Ellesmere Road, London, NW10 1LG, UK. *Telephone:* (20) 8450 3084. *E-mail:* lisahoran@btinternet.com (office). *Website:* www .rootsmanuva.co.uk.

ROSA, Draco; Puerto Rican singer, songwriter, musician, record producer and entrepreneur; b. (Robert Edward Rosa Suarez), 27 June 1969, Long Island, New York, USA; m. Angela Alvarado; two s. *Career:* raised in Peñuelas, Puerto Rico; mem. (as Robi Rosa) boy band Menudo (featuring Ricky Martin) 1984–87; solo artist based in Brazil (as Robby Rosa) 1988–89; relocated to New York and f. group Maggie's Dream 1990; solo artist 1993–; f. own production co. Phantom Vox Corporation 1998–; songwriter and producer, several Ricky Martin hits including Maria, Livin' La Vida Loca, She Bangs 1998–2000; songwriter for other artists including Julio Iglesias, Ednita Nazario; toured with Lenny Kravitz 2004; numerous tours and live appearances. *Films:* Salsa 1988. *Recordings:* albums: with Menudo: Reaching Out 1984, Mania 1984, Evolución 1984, Menudo 1985, Ayer Y Hoy/A Festa Vai Começar 1985, Viva! Bravo! 1986, Refrescante 1986, Can't Get Enough 1986; solo, as Robby Rosa: Robby Rosa 1988, Robby 1989; with Maggie's Dream: Maggie's Dream 1990; solo, as Draco Rosa: Frio 1994, Vagabundo 1996, Songbirds & Roosters 1998, Libertad del Alma 2001, Mad Love 2004, Como Me Acuerdo 2004, Draco y El Teatro del Absurdo 2007, Vino 2008, Teatro (Latin Grammy Award for Best Rock Solo Vocal Album 2009) 2008, Amor Vincit Omnia (Lo Nuestro Award for Album of the Year: Rock 2011) 2009, Vida (Latin Grammy Award for Album of the Year 2013, Grammy Award for Best Latin Pop Album 2014) 2013. *Honours:* Latin Grammy Award for Best Music Video (for Más y Más) 2004, Latin Songwriters Hall of Fame Premio Conquistador 2013. *E-mail:* info@dracorosa.com (home). *Website:* www .dracorosa.com (home); www.phvx.com.

ROSAS, César; American musician (guitar, mandolin), singer and songwriter; b. 26 Sept. 1954, Hermosillo, Mexico. *Career:* mem., Los Lobos 1973–; solo artist 1999–. *Recordings include:* albums: with Los Lobos: De Este De Los Angeles 1978, How Will The Wolf Survive 1984, By the Light of the Moon 1987, La Pistola y El Corazón 1988, The Neighborhood 1990, Kiko 1992, Colossal Head 1996, This Time 1999, Good Morning Aztlán 2002, The Ride 2004, The Town and the City 2006, Los Lobos Goes Disney 2009, Tin Can Trust 2010; solo: Soul Disguise 1999. *Current Management:* c/o Chris Tetzeli, Red Light Management, 321 East Main Street, Suite 500, Charlottesville, VA

22902, USA. *Telephone:* (434) 245-4900. *Fax:* (434) 245-4933. *E-mail:* info@ redlightmanagement.com. *Website:* www.redlightmanagement.com; www .loslobos.org.

ROSCHMANN, Lisa; American musician (keyboards). *Career:* mem. Electric Company –1994; Founder-mem. The American Analog Set 1995–99. *Recordings include:* albums: The Fun Of Watching Fireworks 1996, From Our Living Room To Yours 1997, The Golden Band 1999. *Website:* www.amanset.com.

ROSE, Axl; American rock singer; b. (William Bailey), 6 Feb. 1962, Lafayette, Ind.; m. Erin Everly 1990 (annulled 1991). *Career:* mem. heavy rock group Guns N' Roses 1985–; regular int. tours, concerts. *Recordings include:* albums: Appetite For Destruction (American Music Award for Favorite Heavy Metal/ Hard Rock Album 1990) 1987, G 'N' R Lies 1988, Use Your Illusion I and II 1991, The Spaghetti Incident 1993, Live Era '87–'93 1999, Chinese Democracy 2008. *Honours:* American Music Award for Favourite Heavy Metal Artist 1990, 1992, two MTV Music Video Awards, World Music Award for Best Selling Hard Rock Artists of the Year 1993, Rolling Stone and Billboard magazine awards. *Website:* www.gunsnroses.com.

ROSE, David Richard; Canadian promoter and musician (drums); b. Chatham, Ontario; three d. *Career:* agent for 3 years; promoter for 4 years; owner of promotion company, Rose Concert Productions Inc., producing many concerts including Blue Rodeo, Jefferson Starship, Procol Harum, 54–40, Rusty, King Cobb Steelie, Change of Heart, Big Sugar, Nazareth; mem CCMA, CARAS, CAE, SOCAN. *Address:* PO Box 23053, London, ON N6A 5N9, Canada. *E-mail:* rcpinc@home.com.

ROSENTHAL, David Michael; American musician (keyboards), producer, orchestrator, composer and synthesizer programmer; b. 1 Jan. 1961, New York; m. Michelle Christo, 11 Sept. 1999. *Education:* BA in Professional Music, Berklee College of Music, Boston, 1981. *Career:* World Tours: Rainbow: Straight Between The Eyes, 1982–83; Bent Out of Shape, 1983–84; Little Steven, Voice of America; Robert Palmer, Heavy Nova; Cyndi Lauper: True Colors, 1986–87; Japan Tour, 1991; Enrique Iglesias, Vivir, 1997; Billy Joel and Elton John, Face To Face, 1994–95, 1998; Billy Joel: River of Dreams, 1993–95; Greatest Hits World Tour, 1998–99; Two Thousand Years Tour, 1999–2000; Numerous TV and video appearances; mem, BMI; American Federation of Musicians. *Compositions:* Producer and songwriter for Red Dawn, Never Say Surrender; Orchestrator for Yngwie Malmsteen's Millennium Concerto Suite. *Recordings:* Albums: Billy Joel: The Complete Hits Collection, 1997; Greatest Hits Vol. III, 1997; A Voyage On The River of Dreams, 1994; Yngwie Malmsteen: Millennium Concerto Suite, 1998; Inspiration, 1997; Archives, 2001; Vinnie Moore: Defying Gravity, 2001; Niji-Densetsu, Legends of Rainbow, 1998; Departure: Open Your Mind, 1999; Departure, 1998; Good Rats, Tasty Seconds, 1996; Dream Theater, A Change of Seasons, 1995; Red Dawn, Never Say Surrender, 1993; Deborah Blando, A Different Story, 1991; Steve Vai, Passion and Warfare, 1990; Whitesnake, Slip of The Tongue, 1989; Nicole McCloud: Jam Packed, 1989; Love Town, 1998; Donna Allen, Heaven Goodwin, 1988; Stacy Lattisaw: Very Best of Stacy Lattisaw, 1998; Personal Attention, 1987; Rainbow: The Very Best of Rainbow, 1997; Finyl Vinyl, 1986; Bent Out of Shape, 1983; Straight Between The Eyes, 1982; Roger Glover, Mask, 1984; Hit Singles: Billy Joel, Hey Girl; Will To Power, Baby I Love Your Way/Freebird Medley; Stacy Lattisaw, Let Me Take You Down; Donna Allen, Joy and Pain; Rainbow: Stone Cold; Street of Dreams; Can't Let You Go. *Publications:* Multi-Keyboard Master Class with David Rosenthal; Macintosh, MIDI and Music: The Open Door; Columnist for Keyboard Magazine and Electronic Musician. *Honours:* Keyboard Magazine Reader's Poll Winner, 1993; Berklee College of Music, Distinguished Alumnus Award, 1994. *E-mail:* david@davidrosenthal.com. *Website:* www .davidrosenthal.com.

ROSENTHAL, Phil, BA; American singer, musician (guitar), producer and songwriter; b. 30 Sept. 1948, New Haven, Conn.; m. Elizabeth Sommers 1977; one s. one d. *Education:* Univ. of Chicago. *Career:* lead singer and guitarist, bluegrass band The Seldom Scene, singer, guitarist, banjo player, The Sommers Rosenthal Family Band 1993–; Founder and Pres. American Melody Records 1986–; has performed with Jerry Douglas, Bill Monroe, Emmylou Harris, Jonathan Edwards and many others; Co-founder (with s. and d.) The Rosenthals; mem. Int. Bluegrass Music Asscn. *Recordings include:* seven albums with The Seldom Scene 1977–86; solo albums: Indian Summer 1978, A Matter of Time 1981, Turkey In The Straw 1985, The Paw Paw Patch 1987, Chickens In The Garden 1991, Comin' Round The Mountain 1994, The Green Grass All Around 1995, Animal Songs 1996, This Land Is Your Land 1999, Folk Song Lullabies 2001, Grandma's Patchwork Quilt: A Children's Sampler 2003; with The Rosenthals: Fly Away 2013. *Honours:* Connecticut State Troubadour 1994; four Parents' Choice Awards; three American Library Asscn Awards for solo children's music recordings. *Address:* American Melody, PO Box 270, Guilford, CT 06437, USA (office). *Telephone:* (203) 457-0881 (office). *E-mail:* phil@americanmelody.com. *Website:* www .americanmelody.com; www.therosenthals.org.

ROSKO, Emperor; American DJ and broadcaster; b. (Mike Pasternak), 26 Dec. 1942, Los Angeles, Calif. *Career:* shows on Radio Monte Carlo, Europe No 1, Radio Caroline, Radio Luxembourg, France and 208 UK, BBC Radio 1, Virgin Radio, Nostalgie FM and many others; ran his own soul music station Rosko Radio for Live 365. *Publication:* Emperor Rosko's DJ Book 1976. *Honours:* Best DJ (UK), Billboard, Top DJ, R&R, inducted into Radio Acad.

Hall of Fame 2008, Lifetime Achievement Award, Int. Radio Festival, Zurich 2011. *Website:* www.emperorrosko.net.

ROSNAY, Xavier de; French musician and producer; b. 22 July 1982. *Career:* mem. Justice 2003–. *Recordings include:* albums: Waters of Nazareth 2005, Phantom 2007, DANCE 2007, † 2007, DVNO 2008, Audio, Video, Disco 2011, Access All Arenas 2013. *Honours:* MTV Europe Music Award for Best Video (for We Are Your Friends) 2006, (for DANCE) 2007, for Best French Act 2007, Victoires de la Musique for Best Electronic/Dance Act 2008, Grammy Award for Best Remixed Recording (for Electric Feel, MGMT) 2009. *Address:* c/o Ed Banger Records, Headbangers Entertainment, 10 rue Ramey, 75018 Paris, France. *Website:* myspace.com/etjusticepourtous.

ROSS, Andrew (Andy); American musician (guitar, bass guitar, keyboards), songwriter and singer; b. 8 March 1979, Worcester, Mass. *Education:* Columbia Univ. *Career:* fmr bass guitarist, Unsacred Hearts; fmr guitarist, DraculaZombieUSA; fmr bass guitarist, Cold Memory; solo project, as Secret Dakota Ring 2004–; Co-founder, Serious Business Records 2004–; mem. OK Go 2005–; f. own label for OK Go recordings, Paracadute Recordings 2010. *Recordings:* albums: solo (as Secret Dakota Ring): Do Not Leave the Baggage All the Way 2004, Cantarell 2008; with OK Go: Of the Blue Colour of the Sky 2010, Hungry Ghosts 2014. *Honours:* Grammy Award for Best Music Video 2007, UK Music Video Awards for Video of the Year and Best Rock Video 2010, CLIO Gold Award in Branded Entertainment 2013, MTV Video Music Award for Best Visual Effects 2014. *Address:* c/o Mike Rosenthal, Paracadute, 236 Hoyt Street, Suite 2, Brooklyn, NY 11217, USA (office). *E-mail:* Rosenthal@paracadute.net (office); paracadute@okgo.net (office); info@okgo.net. *Website:* www.paracadute.net (office); www.okgo.net.

ROSS, Andrew David; British producer, songwriter and musician (guitar); b. 24 Feb. 1960, Bromley, Kent; s. of jazz saxophonist Ronnie Ross; m. Dina Burnstock 1994. *Career:* mem. band Immaculate Fools 1984–97; worked with Howard Jones, Miguel Bosé, Tori Amos; co-f. (with Robbie Bronnimann) band Tek^tonik; mem. Musicians' Union, PRS, MCPS. *Recordings include:* with Immaculate Fools: Immaculate Fools, Hearts of Fortune 1985, Dumb Poet 1987, Another Man's World 1990, The Toy Shop 1992, Woodhouse 1995, Kiss and Punch 1996; with Propaganda: 1234 1990; with Miguel Bosé: Bajo el signo de cain 1993; with Howard Jones: Working In The Back Room 1994; with Tori Amos: Crucify (song) 1992; with Nan Vernon: Manta Ray 1995.

ROSS, Annie; British jazz singer, actress and lyricist; b. (Annabelle Short Lynch), 25 July 1930, Mitcham, Surrey; one s. *Career:* emigrated to USA 1934; entered radio talent show with Paul Whiteman Orchestra, won six-month contract with MGM; returned to London 1947, then to Paris in singing trio with Hugh Martin and Timothy Gray; recording debut in Le Vent Vert (with James Moody) 1950; returned to New York 1952, recording with Modern Jazz Quartet, King Pleasure and for HMV and Pye labels; toured with Lionel Hampton 1953; mem. Lambert, Hendricks and Ross (with Dave Lambert and Jon Hendricks) 1957–62; successful solo career in theatre, film and music; reformed Hendricks and Ross 1999; other collaborations include Harry 'Sweets' Edison, Frank Wess, Sonny Payne, Joe Williams, Al Grey, Eddie Jones, Snooky Young, Benny Powel, Charlie Fowlkes, Frank Foster, Henry Coker, Kenny Clarke, Marshall Royal, Joe Newman, Thad Jones, Wendell Culley, George Duvivier, Chet Baker, John Barry, Count Basie, Dave Brubeck, Georgie Fame. *Films include:* The Little Rascals: Our Gang Follies 1938, Presenting Lily Mars 1943, Straight on Till Morning 1972, Yanks 1979, Funny Money 1982, Superman III 1983, Throw Momma from the Train 1987, Witchery 1988, Pump Up the Volume 1990, The Player 1992, Short Cuts 1993, Blue Sky 1994. *Theatre:* Cranks, The Threepenny Opera, The Seven Deadly Sins, Kennedy's Children, The Pirates of Penzance, Side by Side by Sondheim. *Recordings include:* albums: with Lambert, Hendricks and Ross: Sing A Song Of Basie 1957, Sing Along With Basie 1958, The Swingers! 1959, Everybody's Boppin' 1959, The Real Ambassadors (with Louis Armstrong and The All-Stars, Dave Brubeck) 1961, High Flying 1962; solo: Skylark 1956, Cranks 1956, Annie By Candlelight 1956, Sings A Song With Mulligan (with Gerry Mulligan) 1958, A Gasser! (with Zoot Sims) 1959, Gypsy 1959, Loguerhythms 1962, Sings A Handful Of Songs 1963, Annie Ross And Pony Poindexter 1967, Fill My Heart With Song 1967, Music Is Forever 1995, Cool For Kids 2001, A Handful Of Songs And More 2002, Let me Sing 2005, To Lady With Love 2013. *Honours:* inducted into ASCAP Jazz Wall of Fame 2009, Nat. Endowment for the Arts Jazz Master Award 2010. *E-mail:* info@annieross.net. *Website:* www .annieross.net.

ROSS, Brian; American record producer, music publisher, personal manager and musician (keyboards); *Chairman and CEO, Brian Ross Productions*; b. 13 Feb. 1953, Chicago, Ill.; two s. *Education:* Univ. of California, Los Angeles. *Career:* Chair. and CEO Brian Ross Productions, Starborn Records, Int. Music Comm.; creates Global Cultural Exchange Programs in China, Japan, Middle East (MENA), India and Southeast Asia; licenses masters and music publishing rights to labels and music firms within USA and globally; produced records for Universal Records, CBS/Sony, Phonogram, Warner Bros, RCA, A&M and MCA Record labels; Life mem. Nat. Acad. of Recording Arts and Sciences (Grammys), American Fed. of Musicians, AFL-CEO, Hollywood Musicians Union Local 47, Japan America Soc., Asian Business League, California Copyright Conf.; Producer and Signatory, SAG-AFTRA. *Recordings:* producer, publisher, Music Machine, Talk Talk 1966; released children's version of We Are The World on Starborn Records, written by Michael Jackson, Lionel Richie; publisher, I'm On Fire, Barry White; licensed La

Bamba, Ritchie Valens. *Publication:* Business Aspects of the Music Industry. *Address:* 3884 Franklin Avenue, Los Angeles, CA 90027-4661, USA (office). *Telephone:* (213) 662-3121 (office). *E-mail:* brianrossmusic@gmail.com (office). *Website:* www.starbornrecords.com.

ROSS, Diana; American singer and actress; b. 26 March 1944, Detroit, Mich.; d. of Fred Ross and Ernestine Ross; m. 1st Robert Ellis Silberstein 1971 (divorced 1976); three d.; m. 2nd Arne Naess 1985 (divorced, died 2004); one s. *Career:* fmr lead singer, The Supremes (later Diana Ross and the Supremes), solo singer 1970–. *Films include:* Lady Sings the Blues 1972, Mahogany 1975, The Wiz 1978. *Television includes:* Out of Darkness (film) 1993, Double Platinum, (film) 1999. *Recordings include:* albums: I'm Still Waiting 1971, Touch Me In The Morning 1973, Diana 1980, Why Do Fools Fall in Love? 1981, Eaten Alive 1984, Chain Reaction 1986, Workin' Overtime 1989, Surrender 1989, Ain't No Mountain High Enough 1989, The Forces Behind the Power 1991, The Remixes 1994, Take me Higher 1995, Gift of Love 1996, The Real Thing 1998, Every Day is a New Day 1999, Voice of Love 2000, Gift of Love 2000, Blue 2006, I Love You 2006. *Publications include:* Secrets of a Sparrow (autobiog.) 1993. *Honours:* citation from US Vice-Pres. Hubert Humphrey for efforts on behalf of Pres. Lyndon Johnson's Youth Opportunity Programme, from Mrs. Martin Luther King and Rev. Abernathy for contrib. to Southern Christian Leadership Conf., Billboard, Cash Box and Record World magazine awards as world's outstanding female singer, Grammy Award 1970, Female Entertainer of the Year, Nat. Asscn for the Advancement of Colored People 1970, Cue Award as Entertainer of the Year 1972, Golden Apple Award 1972, Gold Medal Award, Photoplay 1972, Antoinette Perry Award 1977, Golden Globe Award 1972, Kennedy Center Honor 2007, BET Lifetime Achievement Award 2007, Grammy Lifetime Achievement Award 2012, Ella Fitzgerald Award, Festival International de Jazz de Montréal 2014. *Website:* www .dianaross.com.

ROSS, Rick; American rapper and record company executive; b. (William Leonard Roberts II), 28 Jan. 1976, Coahoma Co., Miss. *Education:* Carol City Sr High School, Florida, Albany State Univ. *Career:* signed recording deal with Suave House Records, then Slip-n-Slide Records; f. record label Maybach Music Group; numerous collaborators including Nelly, Trey Songz, Avery Storm, R Kelly, DJ Khaled, Ne-Yo, Kanye West, Diddy. *Recordings include:* albums: Port of Miami 2006, Trilla 2008, Deeper Than Rap 2009, Teflon Don 2010, God Forgives, I Don't 2012, Mastermind 2014, Hood Billionaire 2014, Black Market 2015; with Triple C's: Custom Cars & Cycles 2009. *Address:* c/o Maybach Music Group, Warner Bros. Records, Warner Music Group, 75 Rockefeller Plaza, New York, NY 10019, USA (office). *Telephone:* (212) 275-2000 (office). *Website:* www.wmg.com (office); www.maybachmusic.net (office); www.godforgivesidont.com.

ROSS, Ricky; British singer and songwriter; b. 22 Dec. 1957, Dundee, Tayside, Scotland; m. Lorraine McIntosh 1990. *Career:* Founder-mem., Deacon Blue 1985–94, 2000–; also solo artist; numerous live and festival appearances. *Recordings include:* albums: with Deacon Blue: Raintown 1987, When the World Knows Your Name 1989, Ooh Las Vegas 1990, Fellow Hoodlums 1991, Whatever You Say, Say Nothing 1993, Our Town: The Greatest Hits 1994, A New House 2014; solo: What You Are 1996, New Recording 1997, This Is The Life 2002, Pale Rider 2005, The Great Lakes 2009, Trouble Came Looking 2013. *Current Management:* c/o One Fifteen Management, 1 Globe House, Middle Lane Mews, London, N8 8PN, England. *Website:* www.rickyross.com; www.deaconblue.com.

ROSSDALE, Gavin McGregor; British singer, songwriter and musician (guitar); b. 30 Oct. 1967, London, England; m. Gwen Stefani 2002; two s. *Career:* mem. Future Primitive (changed name to Bush) 1992–2002, 2010–; mem. Institute 2004–06; also solo artist. *Recordings include:* albums: with Bush: Sixteen Stone 1994, Razorblade Suitcase 1996, Deconstructed 1997, Science Of Things 2000, Golden State 2001, Man on the Run 2014; with Institute: Distort Yourself 2005; solo: Wanderlust 2008. *Films include:* Constantine 2005, How to Rob a Bank 2008, The Bling Ring 2013. *E-mail:* themgmtcompany@gmail.com. *Website:* www.gavinrossdale.com.

ROSSELL, Marina; Spanish singer; b. 17 Jan. 1954, Barcelona. *Education:* studied in Solfege. *Career:* professional singer 1970–; collaborations with composers, including Georges Moustaki, Tomatito, Antoni Ros Marbà, Manzanita, Maria del Mar Bonet, Joan Bibloni, Pau Riba. *Film appearance:* El Vicari d'Olot 1981. *Recordings include:* Llegendes de Catalunya 1975, Si Volieu Escolatar 1977, Penyora, Premio Fotogramas Vol. 1 1978, Festival Internacional Vol. 1 1979, Cos Meu Recorda 1982, Victoria (Banda Sonora Pelicula) 1983, Maremar – Lluis Llach 1985, Barca del Temps, Disco de Oro 1986, Les Millors Cançons de Marina Rossell 1990, Cinema Blau 1990, Marina 1993, Gracies (Recopilacions) 1994, Cinema Blau + La Gavina 1994, Y Rodara el Mundo 2000, Cap al cell 2002, Maritim 2003, Nadal 2005, Vistas al mar 2006, Clàssics catalans 2007, Inicis 1977-1990 2011, Marina Rossell canta Moustaki 2011. *Honours:* Silver Shot Award 1979, Award for Best Catalan Record of the Year 1981, Best Catalan Record of the Year (for Rosa de Foc) 1989. *E-mail:* marina@marinarossell.com. *Website:* www.marinarossell.com.

ROSSELSON, Leon, BA; British singer, songwriter, musician (guitar) and children's author; b. 22 June 1934, London, England; m. Rina Picciotto 1959; two d. *Career:* mem. Galliards Folk Group 1959–61; BBC radio Easy Beat and Saturday Club, solo performer 1961–; folk clubs, arts centres, univs and concert halls, including Royal Festival Hall, Royal Albert Hall; tours worldwide; mem. Mechanical-Copyright Protection Soc., Performing Right Soc.,

Musicians' Union. *Radio:* The Last of the Studleys, BBC Afternoon Theatre 1971. *Recordings include:* albums: Songs For Sceptical Circles 1967, A Laugh a Song and a Handgrenade 1968, Hugga Mugga 1971, That's Not the Way It's Got to Be 1974, Palaces of Gold 1975, Love Loneliness and Laundry 1976, If I Knew Who the Enemy Was 1979, For the Good of the Nation 1981, Temporary Loss of Vision 1984, Bringing the News from Nowhere 1986, I Didn't Mean It 1988, Rosselsongs 1989, Wo Sind Die Elefanten? 1991, The Happiness Counter 1992, Intruders 1995, Perspectives 1997, Harry's Gone Fishing 1999, The Last Chance (EP) 2002, Turning Silence into Song 2004, And They All Sang Rosselsongs 2005, A Proper State 2008, The World Turned Upside Down (four-CD box set) 2011. *Publications include:* Bringing The News From Nowhere: 125 selected songs 1993, Turning Silence into Song: 39 Songs 2003; 20 children's books, including Rosa's Singing Grandfather. *Address:* 28 Park Chase, Wembley Park, Middx, HA9 8EH, England (home). *E-mail:* leonrosselson@mac.com. *Website:* www.leonrosselson.co.uk.

ROSSER, Hamish; Australian musician (drums); b. 1978; m. Kristy Rosser. *Education:* Univ. of Sydney. *Career:* mem. bands Sixties Mania, The Vines 2001–11, Wolfmother 2012–13; numerous tours and festival appearances. *Recordings include:* albums: with The Wines: Highly Evolved 2002, Winning Days 2004, Vision Valley 2006, Melodia 2008, Future Primitive 2011; with Wolfmother: Keep Moving 2013. *Honours:* ARIA Award Breakthrough Artist Single (for Get Free) 2002, NME Award for Best Single (for Get Free) 2003.

ROSSI, Francis, OBE; British musician (guitar) and singer; b. 29 May 1949, Peckham, London. *Career:* founder mem. rock group, Status Quo 1967–; extensive tours worldwide, concerts and festivals; played four venues in 12 hours, entered in Guinness Book of Records 1991. *Recordings include:* albums with Status Quo: Picturesque Matchstickable Messages 1968, Spare Parts 1969, Ma Kelly's Greasy Spoon 1970, Dog of Two Heads 1971, Piledriver 1973, Hello! 1973, Quo 1974, Encore 1974, On The Level 1975, Pop Chronik 5 1975, Blue For You 1976, Live 1977, Rockin' All Over The World 1977, If You Can't Stand The Heat 1978, Whatever You Want 1979, Just Supposin' 1980, Never Too Late 1981, Now Hear This 1981, 1+9+8+2 1982, Live At The N.E.C. 1984, Status Quo 1984, To Be Or Not To Be 1983, Back To Back 1983, In The Army Now 1986, Ain't Complaining 1988, Rock 'Til You Drop 1991, Live Alive Quo 1992, The Other Side Of Status Quo 1995, Thirsty Work 1995, Don't Stop 1996, Whatever You Want 1997, Under The Influence 1999, Famous In The Last Century 2000, Rockin' And Rollin' 2001, Heavy Traffic 2002, Riffs 2003, XS All Areas 2004, The Party Ain't Over Yet 2005, In Search of the Fourth Chord 2007; solo album: One Step at a Time 2010. *Publication:* XS All Areas: The Status Quo Autobiography (with Rick Parfitt) 2004. *Honours:* Nordoff-Robbins Music Therapy Centre Silver Clef Award 1981, Ivor Novello Award 1983, BRIT Award for Outstanding Contribution to the British Music Industry 1991, World Music Award for Outstanding Contribution to Music 1991. *Current Management:* Duroc Media Ltd, Riverside House, 10–12 Victoria Road, Uxbridge, Middlesex UB8 2TW, England. *Telephone:* (1895) 810831. *Fax:* (1895) 231499. *E-mail:* info@durocmedia.com. *Website:* www.statusquo.co.uk.

ROSSINGTON, Gary; American musician (guitar) and songwriter; b. 4 Dec. 1951, Jacksonville, Fla; m. Dale Krantz; two d. *Career:* mem. rock group, Lynyrd Skynyrd 1970–77, 1987–2014; formed Rossington-Collins Band (with Allen Collins), later The Rossington Band 1979–88; numerous tours, festival appearances; suffered serious injury in plane crash 1977. *Recordings include:* albums: with Lynyrd Skynyrd: Pronounced Leh-nerd Skin-Nerd 1973, Second Helping 1974, Nuthin' Fancy 1975, Gimme Back My Bullets 1976, One More For The Road 1976, Street Survivors 1977, Skynyrd's First and Last 1978, Gold and Platinum 1980, Best of The Rest 1985, Legend 1987, Southern By The Grace of God/Lynyrd Skynyrd Tribute Tour 1988, Lynyrd Skynyrd 1991, The Last Rebel 1993, Endangered Species 1994, Freebird 1996, Lyve 1998, Edge of Forever 1999, Then And Now 2000, Christmas Time Again 2000, Vicious Cycle 2003, Gods and Guns 2009, Live from Freedom Hall 2010; with the Rossington-Collins Band: Anytime Anyplace Anywhere 1980, This Is The Way 1981, Love Your Man 1988. *Current Management:* c/o Ken Levitan, Vector Management, PO Box 120479, Nashville, TN 37212, USA. *E-mail:* info@vectormgmt.com. *Website:* www.lynyrdskynyrd.com.

ROTH, David Lee; American rock singer; b. 10 Oct. 1955, Bloomington, IN. *Career:* fmr singer, Red Ball Jets; founder mem. rock group, Van Halen 1974–85, 1996–97, 2007–; numerous tours worldwide, festival appearances; solo artist 1985–. *Recordings include:* albums: with Van Halen: Van Halen 1978, Women and Children First 1980, Fair Warning 1981, Diver Down 1982, 1984 1983, Live Anthology, 1975–81 2000, A Different Kind of Truth 2012; solo: Eat 'Em and Smile 1986, Skyscraper 1988, A Little Ain't Enough 1991, Your Filthy Little Mouth 1994, DLR Band 1998, Diamond Dave 2003, Strummin' with the Devil 2006. *Honours:* MTV Music Video Award 1984. *Website:* www.van-halen.com; www.davidleeroth.com.

ROTHERAY, David; British musician (guitar); b. 9 Feb. 1963, Hull, England. *Education:* Univ. of Hull. *Career:* mem. The Beautiful South 1989–2007; Founder-mem. Homespun 2003–08; solo artist 2009–. *Recordings include:* albums: with The Beautiful South: Welcome To The Beautiful South 1989, Choke 1990, 0898 1992, Miaow 1994, Blue Is The Colour 1996, Quench 1998, Painting It Red 2000, Gaze 2002, Golddiggas, Headnodders & Pholk Songs 2004, Superbi 2006; with Homespun: Homespun 2003, Effortless Cool 2005, Short Stories from East Yorkshire 2008; solo: The Life of Birds 2010, Answer Ballads 2013. *Website:* davidrotheray.com.

ROTHERY, Steve; British musician (guitar); b. 25 Nov. 1959, Brampton, South Yorkshire, England. *Career:* mem. progressive rock band, Marillion 1980–; numerous tours; collaborations with artists, including Enchant, Arena, John Wesley, Jadis, Arrakeen, Mr So and So, Stranger by the Minute; solo project as The Wishing Tree 1996–. *Recordings include:* albums: Script For A Jester's Tear 1983, Fugazi 1984, Real To Reel 1984, Misplaced Childhood 1985, Brief Encounter 1986, Clutching At Straws 1987, B-Sides Themselves 1988, The Thieving Magpie 1988, Season's End 1989, Holidays In Eden 1991, Brave 1994, Afraid of Sunlight 1995, Blueprint of the World 1995, Made Again 1996, This Strange Engine 1997, Radiation 1998, Clutching At Straws 1999, Marillion.com 1999, Made Again Live 2001, Anorak In The UK Live 2002, Somewhere Else 2007; with The Wishing Tree: Carnival of Souls 1996, Ostara 2009; solo: Live in Rome 2014, The Ghosts of Pripyat 2014. *E-mail:* info@knowmoremanagement.com. *Website:* www.knowmoremanagement.com. *E-mail:* lucy@marillion.com; band@marillion.com. *Website:* www.marillion.com; www.steverothery.com.

ROTTEN, Johnny (see Lydon, John)

ROUCAN, Jean-Yves; French musician (drums); b. 2 June 1962, Neuilly Sur Seine; one s. one d. *Education:* CIM, Berklee Coll. of Music, USA. *Career:* jazz drummer, Triode 1986–87; formed trio (with M. Bismut and B. Paillard), Trio Paillard-Bismut-Roucan 1987–; numerous concerts and festival appearances, radio and TV broadcasts; worked with R. Beirach, D. Liebman's Quest, P. Motian, D. Holland, B. Frisell, J. Lovano, D. Humair; freelance jazz drummer; played with Passage (big band), Interplay Collectif, Switzerland. *Recordings include:* Trio de Jazz Quartet, Socco, Trio Paillard-Bismut-Roucan 1992; With Interplay Collectif: S. Duner Project. *Honours:* First Prize, Concours International de Vienne.

ROUGVIE, Jeff James; American music producer; b. 4 March 1963, Quincy, Mass. *Education:* Hartford Art School. *Career:* signings include Sugar, Golden Smog, Alejandro Escovedo, Martin Zellar, Morphine; responsible for catalogue development for Badfinger, Big Star, David Bowie, Elvis Costello, Bill Hicks; fmr Project Manager, Rykodisc; Vice-Pres. of Repertoire, Caroline Records 2006–. *Recordings include:* as producer: Ned Kelly, 1970; Jimmy Buffett, Rancho Deluxe, 1975; Born to Choose, 1993; Chitty Chitty Bang Bang, 1997; Across 10th Street, 1997. *E-mail:* caroline.distribution@gmail.com. *Website:* www.carolinedist.com.

ROUISSI, Walid; Tunisian singer and songwriter. *Career:* creates dance music from hybrid of European and Afro-Arabic traditional music. *Recordings include:* album: The Desert Shadow. *Website:* en.hibamusic.com/Tunisie/walid-rouissi/walid-rouissi-2194.htm.

ROUMI, Magida El-; Lebanese singer; b. 13 Dec. 1956, Kfarchima; d. of Halim El Roumi and Marie Loutfi; m. Antoine Dfouni 1977; two d. *Education:* Lebanese Univ. *Career:* appearances include Carthage Festival, Tunisia 1980, 1987, 1990, 1997, 1999, Sound and Light International Song Festival, Egypt 1985, Jerash Festival, Jordan 1986, 1988, 1991, 1996, 1999, UAE 1987, 1991, Rashana Festival, Japan 1988, Beirut, Syria and Bahrain 1988, USA Convention Center (Los Angeles, Calif.) 1989, 1990, Palais des Congrès, Paris 1991, 1996, Beit El Din Festival and Sour Festival, Lebanon 1991, Busra Festival, Syria 1991, Qatar and Bahrain 1991, The Oriental Music Festival, Egypt 1997, Akhbar El Negoum Festival, Marina Village, Alexandria, Egypt 1998. *Recordings include:* Widaa 1982, Men Zaman (live recording) 1982, El Asfoura (for children) 1983, Dawy Ya Kamar 1986, Ya Saken Afkary 1988, Kalimat 1991, Ebhath Anny 1994, Rasael 1996, Oheboka Wa Baad 1998. *Film:* Return of the Prodigal (Egyptian Critics' Prize) 1975. *Honours:* has won several int. awards, including two Platinum Record Awards (first Arabic singer). *Address:* PO Box 352, Jounieh, Lebanon (home). *Telephone:* (9) 916543 (office); (9) 637777 (office). *E-mail:* management@magidaelroumy.com (office). *Website:* www.magidaelroumy.com (office).

ROUND, Carina Dianne; British singer and songwriter; b. 1979, Low Hill, Wolverhampton, W Midlands. *Recordings include:* albums: The First Blood Mystery 2001, The Disconnection 2003, Slow Motion Addict 2006, Tigermending 2012. *Website:* www.carinaround.com.

ROUNDS, James, BA; American musician (guitar) and songwriter; b. 16 Oct. 1951, Tokyo, Japan. *Education:* Dickinson Coll., Carlisle, Pa. *Career:* played on stage with John Lee Hooker, Charlie Gracie and others; mem. ASCAP Writer and Publr; NARAS voting mem. (Grammys). *Compositions:* Go Man Go, Charlie Gracie (with the Jordanaires) 1988, Where Everybody Stays, Liars Club, 1991. *Recordings:* The Metropolitans 1996. *Honours:* Help Heal LA Award 1992, Music City (Nashville) Award for R&B Category 1988, ASCAP PLUS Award for composing Dayton Peace Accords theme song 1996–2001. *Address:* 514 Fairline Drive, Nashville, TN 37211-2167, USA. *Website:* www.jamierounds.net.

ROUNDS, Michelle; Australian singer, songwriter and composer; b. Australia; d. of John Victor Derek Rounds and Barbara May Bennett; m. Ali El-Mahdy; one s. *Career:* first performed live in Sydney 1989; int. solo jazz/R&B/reggae artist; created soul band Michelle Rounds and Get Funked, jazz band Michelle Rounds and The Souljazz; performed live in Australia, New Zealand, Indonesia, Japan, Egypt. *Recordings include:* Never Been In Love Before 1992, Draw Blood 1994, Contrasts 1996, Culture Cross 1998, Era Bini Tu 1998, Coffee Time Jazz 2005, A Matcha Chocolate Love Adventure 2005, Coffee Time Jazz 2005, Autumn Leaves 2010, Michelle Rounds and Her Amazing Friends 2013, Hold On 2014. *Honours:* Vakalutuivoce Award for Best

Female Artist and Best Album, Mai Time Award. *E-mail:* mr@michellerounds .com; ali@michellerounds.com. *Website:* www.michellerounds.com.

ROUSÉ, Guillaume; French musician (drums); b. 25 Dec. 1970. *Career:* mem. Superbus 1998–2006, La Phaze 2006. *Recordings include:* albums: Aéromusical 2002, Pop'N'Gum 2004, Wow 2006, Lova Lova 2009, Sunset 2012; with La Phaze: Miracle 2007. *Honours:* MTV Europe Music Award Best French Act 2005.

ROWBOTTOM, Simon (Sice), (Eggman); British singer; b. Wallasey, England. *Career:* singer, The Boo Radleys 1989–99; mem. Paperlung 2005–. *Recordings include:* albums: with The Boo Radleys: Ichabod and I 1989, Everything's Alright Forever 1992, Giant Steps 1993, Learning To Walk 1994, Wake Up 1995, C'mon Kids 1996; solo (as Eggman): First Fruits, Kingsize 1998, Find the Way Out 2005; with Paperlung: Balance. *Honours:* NME magazine Album of the Year 1993.

ROWLAND, Henry Cottrell (Broz), BA; American producer, songwriter and musician (guitar, bass, keyboards, drums); b. 30 July 1949, Dallas, TX. *Education:* Univ. of Colorado. *Career:* mem., Blue Pearl band, 1978; formed Alpha Wave, 1980; mem., Modern Kids, 1982; producer, co-songwriter, Bodyhouse album with Allen Ginsberg, 1986; formed The Pilots, 1990; joined Flying Perfect, 1994; mem. ASCAP. *Recordings include:* albums: You Know It's Coming, Alpha Wave 1980; album with Modern Kids, 1982; solo: It's All Right Here 1997, The Edge of Nothing 1997; with Rowland Brothers, No Sleep for the Dreamers 1998; as producer: Ruff N Wicked, Max-E 1994, The Bees, The Bees 1997, Angels Whisper, The Dreamers 2000, Cowboy Buddhist, Les Pillitteri 2001, Come Back to the Heart, Allen Ginsberg and Bodyhouse 2007. *Honours:* KBCO Eighth Boulder Music Invitational, 1984; Houston International Film Festival, 1986. *Address:* High Kite Productions, 1245 Elizabeth Street, Denver, CO 80206, USA. *E-mail:* info@highkite.com. *Website:* www .highkite.com.

ROWLAND, Kelendria (Kelly); American singer; b. 11 Feb. 1981, Atlanta, GA. *Career:* founding mem., GirlsTyme (with Beyoncé Knowles, later joined by LaTavia Roberson and LeToya Luckett), group renamed Something Fresh, then The Dolls before settling on Destiny's Child 1989–2005; numerous live performances, tours; solo artist 2001–. *Films:* Beverly Hood 1999, Freddy vs Jason 2003, The Seat Filler 2004. *Recordings include:* albums: with Destiny's Child: Destiny's Child 1998, The Writing's On The Wall 1999, Survivor (American Music Award for Favorite Pop/Rock Album 2002) 2001, Eight Days Of Christmas 2001, Destiny Fulfilled (Lady of Soul Award for Best Group Album 2005, American Music Award for Favorite Soul/R & B Album 2005) 2004; solo: Simply Deep 2003, Ms Kelly 2007, Kelly Rowland 2010, Here I Am 2011, Talk a Good Game 2013. *Honours:* (with Destiny's Child) Billboard Award for Artist of the Year, Group of the Year, Hot 100 Singles Artist of the Year, Hot 100 Group of the Year 2000, Grammy Award for Best R&B Song, Best R&B Performance by a Duo or Group with Vocal (for Say My Name) 2001, NAACP Image Award for Outstanding Duo or Group (for Say My Name) 2001, MTV Video Award for Best R&B Video (for Say My Name) 2001, American Music Award for Favorite Soul/R&B Group 2001, Soul Train Sammy Davis Jr Award for Entertainer of the Year 2001, American Music Award for Favorite Pop/Rock Band, Duo or Group 2002, BRIT Award for Best Int. Group 2002, MOBO Award for Best Gospel Act 2002, World Music Award for World's Best Pop Group 2005, Lady of Soul Award for Best Group Single (for Soldier) 2005, American Music Award for Favorite Soul/R&B Band, Duo or Group 2005, Billboard Music Award for R&B/Hip-Hop Group of the Year 2005. *Current Management:* Music World Entertainment, 9898 Bissonnet, Suite 625, Houston, TX 77036, USA. *Website:* www.destinyschild.com; www .kellyrowlandonline.com.

ROWLAND, Kevin; British singer and musician (guitar); b. 17 Aug. 1953, Wolverhampton, West Midlands, England. *Career:* mem., Lacy and The Lovers, The Killjoys; lead singer, Dexy's Midnight Runners 1978–; solo artist 1988–. *Recordings include:* albums: with Dexy's Midnight Runners: Searching for the Young Soul Rebels 1980, Too-Rye-Ay 1982, Geno 1983, Don't Stand Me Down 1985, It Was Like This 1996, One Day I'm Going to Soar 2012; solo: The Wanderer 1988, My Beauty 1999. *Honours:* BRIT Award for Best British Single (Come on Eileen) 1983. *Address:* c/o BMG Records, Sony Music Entertainment, 9 Derry Street, London, W8 5HY, England (office). *Telephone:* (20) 7361-8000 (office). *Website:* www.sonymusic.com (office); www.myspace .com/dexysmidnightrunners; www.dexys.org.

ROWLANDS, Tom; British musician; b. 11 Jan. 1971, England. *Education:* Univ. of Manchester. *Career:* formed first band, Ariel; formed The Dust Brothers (with Ed Simons); Founder-mem. The Chemical Brothers (with Ed Simons) 1989–. *Recordings include:* albums: Exit Planet Dust 1995, Live At The Social, Vol. 1 1996, Dig Your Own Hole 1997, Brothers Gonna Work It Out (DJ mix album) 1998, Surrender 1999, Come With Us 2002, Singles 93–03 2003, Push the Button (Grammy Award for Best Electronic/Dance Album 2006) 2005, We Are The Night (Grammy Award for Best Electronic/Dance Album 2008) 2007, Brotherhood 2008, Further 2010, Hanna 2011, Don't Think (live album) 2012, Born in the Echoes 2015. *Honours:* Grammy Award 1997, BRIT Award for Best British Dance Act 2000, MTV Europe Music Award for Best Video (for Believe) 2005, Grammy Award for Best Dance Recording (for Galvanize) 2006, Belgian TMF Award for Best Int. Dance 2007, Q Hero 2010, Ivor Novello Award for Outstanding Song Collection 2014. *Current Management:* c/o Fleet River, 1 Cowcross Street, London, EC1M 6DR,

England. *Telephone:* (20) 7253-7755. *E-mail:* kathryn@fleetrivermusic.com. *Website:* fleetrivermusic.com; www.thechemicalbrothers.com.

ROWLES, Greg; American musician (guitar, bass guitar, pedal-steel guitar); b. 6 Sept. 1965, Fredericksburg, Va; m. Brandee Ann Courtney 1992; one d. *Career:* professional songwriter signed with Music For The Future 1995–. *Address:* Music For The Future, Inc., PO Box 291802, Nashville, TN 37229, USA. *Website:* www.musicforthefuture.com.

ROWNTREE, Dave; British musician (drums), animator, solicitor and political activist; b. (David Alexander De Horne Rowntree), 8 May 1964, Colchester, Essex, England; s. of John Rowntree and Susan Rowntree; m. 1994. *Education:* Gilberd School, Colchester, Landermere Music School, Thorpe-le-Soken, Thames Polytechnic. *Career:* began career as computer programmer for Colchester Borough Council; Founder-mem. Idle Vice; played in clubs for two years, France; mem. Blur 1989–; mem. The Ailerons; extensive TV, radio and festival appearances; owns animation co. Nanomation; training to become solicitor 2006–, currently working at Kingsley Napley, East London; mem. Labour Party 2002–, unsuccessful cand. in local and general elections. *Television includes:* directed two series of animated show Empire Square (Channel 4) 2005. *Recordings include:* albums: Leisure 1991, Modern Life Is Rubbish 1993, Parklife (Best Album, Q Awards 1994, Best Album, Best Single, Best British Video, BRIT Awards 1995, Best Album, NME Awards 1995) 1994, The Great Escape (Best Album, Q Awards 1995) 1995, Blur 1997, 13 1999, The Best Of Blur 2000, Think Tank (Best Album, Q Awards 2003, Best Album, South Bank Show Awards 2003) 2003, Midlife 2009, The Magic Whip 2015. *Honours:* with Blur: BRIT Awards for Best Single, Best Video, Best Album, Best Band 1995, for Outstanding Contrib. to Music 2012, Best Alternative Band, Smash Hits Awards 1994, Best Band and Best Live Act, NME Awards 1995, Best Act in the World Today, Q Awards 1999, Best Band, Best Single (Tender), NME Awards 2000, NME Award for Best Live Event (Blur at Hyde Park) 2010. *E-mail:* david@davidrowntree.org. *Website:* www.blur.co.uk.

ROY, Pola; German musician (drums); b. 1975, Karlsruhe; m. Judith Holofernes. *Career:* mem. Wir sind Helden 2001–. *Recordings include:* albums: Die Reklamation 2003, Von hier an blind 2005, Soundso 2007, Bring mich nach Hause 2010. *Honours:* ECHO Award for Best Nat. Group 2006. *Address:* Wir sind Helden GbR, Weidenallee 27, 20357 Hamburg, Germany. *E-mail:* gutentag@wirsindhelden.com. *Website:* www.wirsindhelden.com.

ROY, Stephane, BA, MA, PhD; Canadian electronic music composer; b. 2 July 1959, Québec; m. Claudine Jomphe; one s. one d. *Education:* Univ. of Montréal. *Career:* Prof., Queens Univ., Kingston, 1993–94; Guest Composer, son Mu 95 Concert, Paris 1995; Guest Composer, Los Andes Univ., Colombia 1995; Guest Lecturer, Conservatoire Superieur de Mons, Belgium 1996; Prof., Univ. of Montréal 1993–97; spent five years in St Louis, Mo. and then returned to Montreal; currently mem. Faculty, Conservatoire de musique du Québec à Montréal; Vice-Pres. Canadian Electroacoustic Community 2002–04; mem. Canadian Music Centre, Int. Computer Music Asscn. *Compositions:* Paysages Interieurs 1988, Mimetismo 1992, Crystal Music 1994, Inaccessible Azur 1997, Trois Petites Histoires Concretes 1998, Une âme nue glisse à l'eau vive 2005. *Recordings include:* Crystal Music, Mimetismo, Paysages Intérieurs, Ondes Arborescences, Resonances D'Arabesques, Kaleidos 1996, Migrations 2003. *Publications include:* Functional and Implicative Analysis of Ombres Blaches of Francois Bayle, La Serie Schonberg, Form and Referential Citation in a Work By Francis Dhomont. *Honours:* Hon. Mention, Int. Computer Music Competition Ars Electronica; First Prize, 14th Luigi Russolo Int. Competition, Noroit Prize. *E-mail:* stephanearoy@videotron.ca.

ROYAL HOUSE (see Terry, Todd)

RUBEL, Mark, BA; American academic, musician (bass guitar), record producer and engineer; *Professor of Music Business, Millkin University;* b. 1 May 1958, s. of Lee and Nina Rubel; m. *Education:* Univ. of Illinois. *Career:* professional musician 1973–; freelance and studio musician 1978–; recording engineer and producer 1980–; Prof. of Audio, Parkuano Coll. 1985–; Prof. of Music Business, Millkin Univ., Decatur 2003–; bassist, Captain Rat and the Blind Rivets 1980; bassist, J. B. Hutto and the Hawks 1980; produced over 1,000 records and recorded for numerous artists, including Hum, Poster Children, Menthol, Alison Krauss, Adrian Belew, Mojo Nixon, Shiner; mem. Production Cttee NARAS; mem. AES, ASCAP, MEIEA, EARS (Vice-Pres.). *Publications:* contrib. to Tape Op and Mix Magazines, including interviews with Les Paul 2005, Terry Manning 2007. *Address:* Pogo Studio, 35 Taylor Street, Champaign, IL 61820, USA. *Telephone:* (217) 351-8155 (office). *E-mail:* mark@pogostudio.net (office); info@pogostudio.net (office). *Website:* www .pogostudio.net.

RUBIE, Stephen Mark; British musician (flute, saxophone), jazz club proprietor and actor; b. 14 Oct. 1952, Marlow, Buckinghamshire, England. *Education:* University College Hospital, Dental School, London; Flutes with William Bartlett, Principal with BBC Concert Orchestra, Trinity College, London; Jazz theory, harmony, with Peter Ind. *Career:* professional freelance musiican 1974–; toured Italy 1975; peripatetic teacher 1978–85; proprietor, 606 Jazz Club 1976–; leader, 606 Club Big Band 1985–; bandleader, Jazz/ Latin sextet, Samara 1991–; featured flute player, Julian Joseph Big Band, BBC Prom, live broadcast 1995; African band, Amabutho, live television in Germany 1995; appeared on BBC 2 TV series, Jazz 606 1998; mem, Musicians' Union, Equity. *Honours:* Hon. ARAM . *Current Management:* 90 Lots Road,

London SW10 0QD, England. *Telephone:* (20) 7352-5953. *E-mail:* jazz@
606club.co.uk (office). *Website:* www.606club.co.uk.

RUBIN, Joel; American musician (clarinet) and ethnomusicologist; b. 17 Oct.
1955, Los Angeles. *Education:* California Institute of the Arts, 1973–75; BA,
State University of New York, 1978; PhD, City University, London, 2001.
Career: Including film, television and radio appearances; Gewandhaus
Leipzig, 1993; Berlin Philharmonic, 1994; Tonhalle Zurich, 1994; Cité de la
Musique, Paris, 1996; Co-Author, Musical and Research Consultant, A Tickle
in the Heart, 1996; mem, Society for Ethnomusicology; International Council
for Traditional Music; American Folklore Society; College Music Society;
International Clarinet Society. *Recordings include:* albums: Bessarabian
Symphony 1994, Zeydes un Eyniklekh 1995, Beregovskis Khasene 1997,
Hungry Hearts 1998; with Uri Caine Duo: Azoy Tsu Tsveyt 2011; with Joel
Rubin Ensemble: Midnight Prayer 2007, The Nign of Reb Mendel (with Rabbi
Eli Silberstein) 2010. *Publications:* Kol Rino, The Voice of Jubilation; Mazltov:
Jewish American Wedding Music for Clarinet; Klezmer-Musik; Jewish
Musical Traditions, 2001. *Honours:* State University of NY, Most Outstanding
Student, 1978; German Record Critics Prize, 1992, 1995; Artur Brauner Prize,
1996; Prix Europa, 1996; 18th Bavarian Film Prize, 1996. *Telephone:* (434)
326-4864. *E-mail:* info@rubin-ottens.com; rubin@joelrubinklezmer.com.
Website: www.rubin-ottens.com; www.joelrubinklezmer.com.

RUBIN, Rick, BFA; American record producer and record company executive;
b. 10 March 1963, Long Beach, New York. *Education:* New York Univ. *Career:*
Owner and Founding Pres., Def Jam Recordings 1984–88, Def American
Recordings 1988– (renamed American Recordings 1993); Co-Chair. Columbia
Records 2007–12; revived American Recordings imprint 2012; producer for
numerous artists, including American Head Charge, Beastie Boys, Black
Crowes, Melanie C., Johnny Cash, Eagle-Eye Cherry, Sheryl Crow, Macy
Gray, Krishna Das, Kula Shaker, LL Cool J, Neil Diamond, Paloalto, Tom
Petty, Public Enemy, Red Hot Chili Peppers, Run D.M.C., Justin Timberlake,
U2. *Film:* Tougher Than Leather (dir, co-producer) 1987; numerous cameo
appearances. *Honours:* Rolling Stone Award for Hot Producer of Year 1988,
New Music Seminar Joel Weber Award 1990, Grammy Awards for Producer of
the Year (Non-Classical) 2007, 2009.

RUBIN, Vanessa Kay, BA; American jazz singer, composer and producer; b.
14 March 1957, Cleveland, Ohio. *Education:* Ohio State Univ. *Career:* fmr
teacher; sang with and managed The Blackshaw Brothers; recorded with The
Cleveland Jazz All-Stars; moved to New York 1982; studied with Barry
Harris; teacher, New York public school system; collaborations include
Pharoah Sanders, Frank Foster's Loud Minority, Mercer Ellington and Lionel
Hampton's Big Bands; toured with Herbie Hancock, Woody Herman Orches-
tra, The Jazz Crusaders. *Recordings include:* albums: Soul Eyes 1991,
Pastiche 1993, I'm Glad There Is You: A Tribute To Carmen McRae 1994,
Vanessa Rubin Sings 1995, New Horizons 1997, Language Of Love 1999, Girl
Talk 2001. *Honours:* numerous decorations from the cities of New Orleans, St
Louis and Memphis; Lionel Hampton Jazz Festival Awards 1993, 1995, Int.
Asscn of Jazz Educators Outstanding Service to Jazz Educ. Award 1997.
E-mail: vanessa@vanessarubin.com. *Website:* www.vanessarubin.com.

RUBINI, Michel; American music director, composer, musician and record
producer; b. 3 Dec. 1942, Los Angeles, Calif. *Career:* music dir for Johnny
Mathis 1968, Nancy Wilson 1969–70; producer, arranger for Sonny and Cher
1971–73; artist, producer, Motown Records 1975–78; worked with numerous
artists including Elvis Presley, John Lennon, Diana Ross, Quincy Jones,
Frank Zappa, Linda Ronstadt; toured with numerous bands including Seals
and Crofts, Loggins and Messina; f. Rubini Gallery of Fine Art, Palm Springs,
Calif.; mem. BMI, Composers and Lyricists Guild. *Compositions:* numerous
TV and film soundtracks, including The Hunger, Manhunter, Band of The
Hand, The Hitchhiker (TV series). *Recordings include:* albums: solo: Secret
Dreams 1988, Secret Dreams: Improvisations I–VII 1995, The Hunger,
original soundtrack 1995, Theme from Joe's Death 1995; as record producer:
Stoney End, Barbra Streisand; California Dreamin', Johnny Mathis; All I
Ever Need Is You, Sonny and Cher; Country Class, Jerry Lee Lewis; So Fine,
Loggins and Messina. *Honours:* BMI Writers Award 1985. *Address:* Rubini
Gallery, 1833 Araby Drive, #31, Suite 1015, Palm Springs, CA 92264, USA.
E-mail: michelrubini@yahoo.com. *Website:* www.rubinigallery.com.

RUBIO, Paulina; Mexican singer and actress; b. 17 June 1971, Mexico City;
d. of Susana Dosamantes; m. Nicolas Vallejo-Nagera 2007. *Career:* began
singing career in children's dancing and singing group Timbiriche, formed by
producers for the Mexican TV network Televisa 1981; began acting in soap
operas and TV series 1998; left Timbiriche and recorded first solo album
1992–. *Film and television:* El Día del compadre 1983, Pasión y poder (TV
series) 1988, Vaselina, Baila conmigo (TV series) 1992, Bésame en la boca
1995, Pobre niña rica (TV series) 1995. *Recordings include:* albums: La Chica
Dorada 1992, 24 Kilates 1993, Tiempo Es Oro 1995, Planeta Paulina 1996,
Paulina 2000, Border Girl (in English) 2002, Pau-Latina (Billboard Latin
Music Award for Best Female Latin Pop Album 2005) 2004, Viva La Diva (live)
2004, Ananda 2006, Gran City Pop 2009, Brava! 2011, TBA 2014. *Honours:*
Billboard Latin Music Award for Best Hot Latin Tracks Artist 2005, for Best
Female Pop Airplay Track (for Te Quise Tanto) 2005. *Website:* www
.paulinarubio.com.

RUCKER, Darius; American singer, songwriter and musician (guitar); b. S
Carolina; two d. *Education:* Univ. of S Carolina. *Career:* lead singer, Hootie
and the Blowfish 1986–; also solo artist 2001–, singing country music 2008–.

Recordings: albums: with Hootie and the Blowfish: Cracked Rear View 1994,
Fairweather Johnson 1996, Musical Chairs 1998, Scattered, Smothered and
Covered 2000, Hootie and the Blowfish 2003, Looking for Lucky 2005; solo:
Back to Then 2002, Learn to Live 2008, Charleston SC 1966 2010, True
Believers 2013. *Honours:* MTV Video Music Award for Best New Artist 1994,
Grammy Awards for Best New Artist 1994, for Song of the Year (for Let Her
Cry) 1994, for Best Solo Country Performance (for Wagon Wheel) 2014, CMA
Award for Best New Artist of the Year 2009. *Address:* 2238 Dundas Street
West, PO Box 59039, Toronto, ON M6R 3B5, Canada (office). *Telephone:* (416)
469-9808 (office). *E-mail:* help@dariusrucker.com (office). *Website:* www
.hootie.com; www.dariusrucker.com.

RUDD, Phil; Australian musician (drums); b. 19 May 1954, Melbourne.
Career: mem. Australian heavy rock group, AC/DC 1975–83, 1994–; numerous
tours worldwide, festival appearances. *Recordings include:* albums: High
Voltage 1975, TNT 1975, High Voltage 1975, Dirty Deeds Done Dirt Cheap
1976, Let There Be Rock 1977, Powerage 1978, Highway to Hell 1979, Back in
Black 1980, For Those About to Rock 1981, Flick of the Switch 1983,
Ballbreaker 1995, Volts 1997, Private Parts 1997, Bonfire 1997, Stiff Upper
Lip 2000, Satellite Blues 2001, Black Ice 2008, Rock or Bust 2014; solo: Head
Job 2014. *Honours:* Grammy Award for Best Hard Rock Performance (for War
Machine) 2010. *Website:* www.acdc.com.

RUDD, Roswell; American jazz trombonist, composer and teacher; b.
(Roswell Hopkins Rudd, Jr), 17 Nov. 1935, Sharon, Conn.; m. 1st Marilyn
Schwartz (divorced); one s.; m. 2nd Moselle Galbraith (died 2004); one s.
Education: Hotchkiss School, Yale Univ. *Career:* fmr mem. Eli's Chosen Six;
moved to New York 1960; debut recording (with New York City R&B) 1961;
mem. Bill Dixon's free jazz group 1962–68; mem. Steve Lacy's School Days
Quartet 1963; Founder-mem. New York Art Quartet 1963–65; staff musicol-
ogist, Alan Lomax projects including Cantometrics and Cantometrics Teach-
ing Tapes and Global Jukebox 1964–94; regular collaborator with Archie
Shepp 1964–68; Founder-mem. Primordial Group 1968; Visiting Lecturer,
Bard Coll., Annandale-on-Hudson 1972–76; teacher of ethnomusicology, Univ.
of Maine 1976–82; regular collaborator with Verna Gillis 1998–; Jazz Artist
Residency, Harvard Univ. 2002–03; currently leader of own quartet; numer-
ous collaborations as sideman including with Albert Ayler, Gato Barbieri,
Carla Bley, Kent Carter, Dennis Charles, Don Cherry, Toumani Diabate,
Milford Graves, Henry Grimes, Charlie Haden, Paul Haines, Beaver Harris,
Robin Kenyatta, Steve Lacy, Michael Mantler, Buell Neidlinger, David
Oquendo, Gary Peacock, Archie Shepp, Cecil Taylor, John Tchicai. *Recordings
include:* albums: as bandleader: Roswell Rudd 1965, Everywhere 1966,
Numatik Swing Band 1973, Flexible Fryer 1974, Blown Bone 1976, Inside
Job 1976, Regeneration 1982, New York Art Quartet 1999, Monk's Dream
(with Steve Lacy) 1999, MALIcool 2002, Blue Mongol (with Mongolian Buryat
Band) 2005, El Espiritu Jibaro (as Trombone Tribe) 2006, Keep Your Heart
Right 2007, El Encuentro 2008, Trombone for Lovers 2013. *Honours:*
Guggenheim Fellowship for Composition 2000, Jazz Journalists Asscn Award
for Trombonist of the Year 2003, 2004, 2005, 2014. *E-mail:* soundscape@
soundscapepresents.com. *Website:* www.roswellrudd.com.

RUESS, (Nathaniel Joseph) Nate; American singer, songwriter and
musician; b. 26 Feb. 1982, Iowa City, Ia. *Education:* Deer Valley High School.
Career: raised in Glendale, Ariz.; Founder mem. The Format 2001–08; other
appearances include recordings by Anthony Green, P!nk; songwriter for
Ke$ha; Founder mem. fun. 2008–; toured with Jack's Mannequin 2008, 2010;
support act for Vedera, Paramore, Panic at the Disco; first single release 2009;
collaborations include Janelle Monáe (We Are Young); solo artist 2015–.
Recordings include: albums: with The Format: Interventions + Lullabies 2003,
Dog Problems 2006; with fun.: Aim and Ignite 2009, Some Nights 2012; solo:
Grand Romantic 2015. *Honours:* with fun.: Teen Choice Awards for Choice
Rock Group 2012, for Choice Single by a Group (for We Are Young) 2012,
Billboard Music Award for Top Rock Artist 2013; other: MTV Video Music
Award for Best Collaboration (for Just Give Me a Reason; with Pink) 2013.
Address: c/o Fueled by Ramen Records, Warner Music Group, 75 Rockefeller
Plaza, New York, NY 10019, USA (office). *Website:* www.fueledbyramen.com
(office); www.ournameisfun.com; www.nateruess.com.

RUFFIN, Bruce, LLB; Jamaican musician (guitar, piano); b. (Bernardo
Constantine Balderamus), 17 Feb. 1952, St Catherine; three d. *Career:*
discovered in Vere John's Talent Contest, Jamaica; joined The Techniques
1967; formed The Shades 1969; joined Inner Circle Band; also solo artist;
formed Chain Reaction 1977; formed Slick Records and Smash Music 1980;
Man. Dir, Jeunesse Cosmetics Ltd, Yak Yak Babywear Co.; CEO BRM Music
Co.; mem. PRS, BAC&S, ASCAP, MCPS. *Recordings:* albums: Rain - the Best
of Bruce Ruffin and Friends 2001, Mad About You - The Anthology 2004; hit
singles include, as solo artist: Rain, Candida, Mad About You; with The
Techniques: Queen Majesty, You Don't Care. *E-mail:* bruce@brmmusic.com.
Website: www.bruceruffin.com.

RUFFNER, Mason; American musician (guitar) and singer; b. 29 Nov. 1952,
Fort Worth, TX. *Career:* solo artist; has also recorded with Bob Dylan, Daniel
Lanois. *Recordings include:* albums: Mason Ruffner 1985, Gypsy Blood 1987,
Evolution 1994, You Can't Win 1999; other credits: Acadie, Daniel Lanois
1989, Oh Mercy, Bob Dylan 1989. *Address:* Rt 2 Box 592, Wimberley, TX
78676, USA. *Website:* www.masonruffner.com.

RUHLMANN, Jean-Jacques; French musician (saxophone, clarinet) and
composer; b. 18 May 1952, Nogent-le-Rotrou. *Education:* Univ. of Paris

(Sorbonne). *Career:* f. J. J. Ruhlmann Big Band; also leader, Le Big Band de Chartres; played with numerous musicians, including J. Thollot, F. Jeanneau, J. Gilson, E. Watson, A. Mangelsdorf, A. Hervé, Michael O'Neil, B. Renaudin, F. Moerman, J. F. Jenny-Clark; performed at many festivals in France, Belgium, Netherlands, Germany, Colombia, Tunisia, Spain. *Recordings include:* albums: Evensong, Michael O'Neil; Valses Manouches, with F. A. Moerman; Windows, J. J. Ruhlmann Big Band.

RUIZ CASARES, Chema; Spanish musician (bass guitar); b. 9 March 1978, Madrid. *Career:* mem. El Canto del Loco 2000–. *Recordings include* albums: with El Canto del Loco: A contracorriente 2002, Sala Caracol 2003, Estados de ánimo 2003, Zapatillas 2005, Pequeños Grandes Directos 2006, Personas 2008, De Personas a Personas 2008, Por todos por mí y mis compañeros 2009. *Honours:* MTV Europe Music Award Best Spanish Act 2005.

RUN (see Joseph Simmons)

RUNDGREN, Todd; American singer, songwriter, musician (guitar) and record producer; b. 22 June 1948, Philadelphia, Pa; m. Michele Gray 1998. *Career:* mem. Woody's Truck Stop; Founder-mem. The Nazz 1967–70; solo recording artist 1970–; formed progressive rock group Utopia 1974–. *Recordings include:* albums: with The Nazz: Nazz 1968, Nazz Nazz 1969, Nazz III 1970; with Utopia: Todd Rundgren's Utopia 1974, Another Live 1975, Ra 1977, Oops! Wrong Planet 1977, Adventures In Utopia 1980, Deface The Music 1980, Swing To The Right 1982, Utopia 1982, Oblivion 1984; solo: Runt 1970, The Ballad of Todd Rundgren 1971, Something / Anything? 1972, A Wizard, A True Star 1973, Todd 1974, Initiation 1975, Faithful 1976, Hermit of Mink Hollow 1978, Back To The Bars 1978, Healing 1981, The Ever Popular Tortured Artist Effect 1983, A Cappella 1985, POV 1985, Anthology – Todd Rundgren 1988, Nearly Human 1989, Second Wind 1991, No World Order 1993, No World Order Lite 1994, The Individualist 1995, With a Twist 1997, Up Against It 1998, Live in Chicago 1991 1999, One Long Year 2000, Liars 2004, Arena 2008, (re)Production 2011, State 2013; record producer, Bat Out of Hell, Meat Loaf 1977; also producer/engineer, recordings by New York Dolls, Grand Funk Railroad, Hall and Oates, XTC, The Band. *Website:* www.tr-i.com.

RUNGA, Bic, MNZM; New Zealand singer and composer; b. (Briolette Kah Bic Runga), 13 Jan. 1976, Christchurch. *Recordings include:* albums: Drive 1997, Together In Concert (with Tim Finn and Dave Dobbyn) 2000, Beautiful Collision 2002, Live In Concert (with The Christchurch Symphony Orchestra) 2003, Birds 2005, Belle 2011, Anthology 2012. *Honours:* Tui Awards for Album of the Year, Record of the Year, Best Vocal Performance, Best Songwriter 1997, Silver Scroll for Songwriting 1997. *Website:* www.bicrunga.com.

RUNGE, Jens Christian; Danish musician (guitar) and singer; b. 28 Nov. 1961, Malaysia. *Career:* toured Scandinavia with Hanne Boel 1989, 1993, 1994, 1996, 1997, 1998; Sanne Salomonsen 1990, 1991, 1992, 1995; Kasper Winding 1987, 1988, 1989, 1990; Anne Linnet 1988, 1989, 1991, 1992; toured Europe with Hanne Boel 1995; played at Roskilde Festival with Hanne Boel 1989, 1993, 1998, Sanne Salomonsen 1992, 1995, Anne Linnet 1989; mem. The Danish Artist Union. *Recordings include:* Hanne Boel: Dark Passion 1990, Misty Paradise 1994, Silent Violence 1996, Need 1998, Strangely Disturbed 2001, Abaco 2004, Private Eye 2007, Kasper Winding: No 5 1989, Blue Isis: Kalder Pa Tiden 1989, Paris Paris: Paris Paris 1986, Love Construction: Caught in the Act 1988, Simon Mathew: All for Fame 2008, Ulrik Elholm: It All Comes Back to You 2009, Rasmus Nøhr: Samlesaet, Vol. 1 2011.

RUOCCO, Joanne, BA; musician (drums, percussion); b. 26 May 1961, New Jersey, USA; m. Douglas Newbery 1989. *Education:* Farleigh Dickenson University, New Jersey. *Career:* mem. Musicians' Union; AFofM. *Recordings:* Duke Ellington Orchestra (Mercer Ellington); Chuck Berry; Bobby Womack; J Geils Band; Ron Wood; Hollywood Beyond; Jellybean; Mick Hucknall (Simply Red); The Style Council (Paul Weller). *Address:* 7 Linwood Road, Harpenden, Hertfordshire AL5 1RR, England.

RUPČIĆ, Hrvoje; Croatian musician (percussion); b. 2 March 1970, Zagreb. *Education:* Latin Percussion, Drum Teaching Studios, London. *Career:* Founder and leader of latin-jazz group, Cubismo; collaboration, concerts and recordings with Toots Thielemans, Philippe Catherine, Bob Mover, Gianni Basso, Yolanda Duke, Mind Games; workshops for hand-drumming and Afro-Cuban rhythms; teacher of hand-drumming at Classical Academy, Zagreb; mem. HGU, Croatian Musicians' Union, HUOKU, Croation Asscn of Orchestral and Chamber Musicians, HZSU, Croation Asscn of Freelance Artists. *Recordings include:* Cubismo: Cubismo, Viva La Habana, Csaba Deseo, The Swinging Violin, Mind Games, Pretty Fonky, Bob Mover, Yesterdays, Soul Fingers, Live In BP Club. *Honours:* STATUS (Croatian Musicians' Union Award) 1996–97, Porin (Croatian Discography Award), seven awards with Cubismo for numerous recordings.

RUSBY, Kate Anna; British folk singer, musician (guitar, piano, fiddle) and songwriter; b. 4 Dec. 1973; m. 1st John McCusker 2001 (divorced); m. 2nd Damien O'Kane 2010. *Career:* performed with all-female folk group The Poozies; as solo artist performs traditional songs and own folk-influenced material. *Recordings include:* albums: with The Poozies: Come Raise Your Head 1997, Infinite Blue 1998; solo: Kate Rusby and Kathryn Roberts 1995, Hourglass 1997, Sleepless (BBC Folk Album of the Year) 1999, Little Lights 2001, 10 2002, Heartlands (film soundtrack) 2003, Underneath the Stars 2003, The Girl Who Couldn't Fly 2005, Awkward Annie 2007, Sweet Bells 2008, Make the Light 2010, 20 2012, Ghost 2014. *Honours:* BBC Radio 2 Folk Award for Best Live Act 2006. *Address:* c/o Steve Rusby, Pure Records, PO Box

174, Sheffield, South Yorkshire, S36 8XB, England. *Telephone:* (1226) 767872. *E-mail:* info@purerecords.net. *Website:* www.purerecords.net; www .katerusby.com.

RUSCHKOWSKI, André, PhD; German composer; *Professor of Electronic and Computer Music, Music University Mozarteum, Salzburg;* b. 25 March 1959, Berlin. *Education:* Humboldt Univ., Berlin. *Career:* composer-in-residence at several studios for electronic music, including Berlin, Budapest, Paris, Vienna; Lecturer in Electronic Music and Music of the 20th Century, Music Univ. Mozarteum, Salzburg, Austria 1992–, Technische Universität Berlin, Univ. of Cologne, Prof. of Electronic Music and Dir Electronic Music Studio, Composition Dept 1995–; Vice-Pres., Austrian Soc. for Electroacoustic Music; mem. Int. Computer Music Asscn. *Compositions:* Zeichen for tape 1989, Nasca for tape 1993, Succubus Quartet for tape 1994, Salzburgtrum for flute, violin and percussion and tape 1995–98, Four Short Studies for tape 1995, Sonama for flute, violin and percussion 1996, Karabontara for piano and tape 1996, Arara and Araku for percussion and tape 1997, Trakl Cycle (In blauem Kristall, Weisser Scheaf, Dunkle Stunde, Unter steinernen Bogen) for soprano, flute, clarinet, violin, cello, piano and tape 1997, Les pas intérieurs for female dancer, percussion and tape 1997, Arion, Dione, Cento, Boreas for tape 1998, Doxa for female dancer, video, percussion and tape 1999, Ondit for tape 2002, Farbklang Raum multimedia performance 2003, Xenon Loops for tape and video 2004, Shadow of a Hare for guitar, interactive computer control and video 2005, Shadow of a Dog for string trio, interactive computer control and video 2005, Twigs and Grains for tape and video 2005. *Publications:* Soundscapes 1990, Electronic Sound Synthesis and Musical Discoverings 1998, Space and Time in Electroacoustic Music 2000, 'Scientifically Exact Music' with the means of electronic techniques 2004. *Honours:* Prize of the City of Varese, Italy 1990, Bourges, France 1985, 1989, 2000, Int. Competition for Audio Art, Paris 1997, prize Composition Competition for Computer Music, Braunschweig 1998, American Composers Forum Sonic Circuits Prize 1998. *Address:* Strauss Str 3, 83457 Bayerisch Gmain, Germany (home). *E-mail:* andre.ruschkowski@moz.ac.at (office); ruschkowski@web.de (home). *Website:* www.moz.ac.at/sem (office); www.ryscgjiwsju,de (home).

RUSSELL, Brenda; American singer, songwriter, musician and producer; b. (Brenda Gordon), 8 April 1949, Brooklyn, New York; m. Brian Russell 1974 (divorced); one d. *Career:* toured with David Sanborn, Billy Ocean, Jeffrey Osborne; numerous television appearances; toured as singer (pre-solo career) with Mac Davis, Elton John; solo artist. *Plays:* co-writer, The Color Purple 2005. *Compositions:* songs recorded by: Herb Alpert, Ray Charles, Joe Cocker, Rita Coolidge, Earth Wind and Fire, Roberta Flack, Chaka Khan, Johnny Mathis, Diana Ross, Donna Summer, Dionne Warwick, Oleta Adams, Regina Belle, Peabo Bryson, Alex Bugnon, Don Grusin, Layla Hathaway, George Howard, Bunny Hull, Jermaine Jackson, Walter Jackson, Al Jarreau, Koinonea, Ivan Lins, Byron Miller, Ann Murray, Phil Perry, Anita Pointer, Rufus, Patrice Rushen, Tom Scott, Marilyn Scott, Tavares, Luther Vandross, Tata Vega, Sudao Watanabe, Kirk Whalum, David Williams, Pauline Wilson, Phillip Wynne. *Recordings include:* albums: Brenda Russell 1979, Love Life 1980, Two Eyes 1983, Get Here 1988, Kiss Me With The Wind 1990, Soul Talkin' 1993, Paris Rain 2000, Between the Sun 2004. *E-mail:* brenda@ brendarussell.com. *Website:* www.brendarussell.com.

RUSSELL, Graham Cyril; British singer, musician (piano, guitar) and composer; b. 11 June 1950, Nottingham; m. Jodi Varble 1986; one s. one d. *Career:* Founder-mem. and singer, Air Supply 1975–; mem. BMI, 2 Million Plays Club. *Recordings include:* Air Supply 1976, Love and Other Bruises 1977, The Whole Thing Started 1977, Life Support 1979, Lost in Love 1980, The One That You Love 1981, Now and Forever 1982, Air Supply 1985, Hearts in Motion 1986, The Christmas Album 1987, The Earth Is ... 1991, The Vanishing Race 1993, News from Nowhere 1995, The Book of Love 1997, Yours Truly 2001, The Singer and the Song 2005, Mumbo Jumbo 2009, The Ultimate Collection 2012. *Honours:* Artist of the Year, American Music Awards 1980, Song of the Year 1980. *Current Management:* c/o Jim Gosnell, APA Agency, 405 South Beverly Drive, Beverly Hills, CA 90212, USA. *Telephone:* (310) 888-4201. *Fax:* (310) 888-4242. *Website:* www.apa-agency .com; www.airsupplymusic.com.

RUSSELL, Jack Patrick; American singer; b. 5 Dec. 1960, Montebello, CA; m. Jana Whisenant 1991, one s. *Career:* singer with rock group, Great White 1981–2010; various tours and live appearances. *Recordings include:* albums: Great White 1984, Shot In The Dark 1986, Once Bitten 1987, Recovery Live 1987, Twice Shy 1989, Hooked 1991, Psycho City 1992, Best of Great White 1994, Sail Away 1994, Let It Rock 1996, Can't Get There From Here 1999, Latest and Greatest 2000, Back to the Rhythm 2007, Rising 2009; solo: Shelter Me 1996, For You 2002. *Address:* c/o Siegl, Feldstein, Duffin and Vuylstehe Inc., 10345 W Olympic Blvd, Los Angeles, CA 90064-2524, USA. *Website:* www .callitrocknroll.com.

RUSSELL, John William Edward; British musician (guitar); b. 19 Dec. 1954, London, England. *Education:* private lessons. *Career:* Co-founder Acta Records 1987; Co-founder MOPOMOSO concert series 1988; mem. London Musicians' Collective. *Compositions:* QuaQua. *Recordings include:* albums: Teatime 1974, Home Cooking 1978, Artless Sky 1979, Forward of Short Leg 1980, Vario II 1980, The Fairly Young Bean 1981, Conceits 1987, Wild Pathway Favourites 1988, News from the Shed 1989, Cultural Baggage 1990, The Place 1991, Ohrkiste 1992, Strakt 1994, Birthdays 1996, London Air Lift 1996, Navigations 1997, Interplay 1997, String with Evan Parker 1997, The

Scenic Route 1998, Refrain 1998, Excerpts and Offerings 2000, The Second Sky 2001, Freedom of the City 2001, Horizontals White 2001, Grain 2001, From Next to Last 2001, Frequency of Use 2002, Mopomoso Solos 2002, Three Planets 2003, Analekta 2004, Crossing the River 2005, More Together than Alone 2005, 2006 Duos 2006, Vario-44 2006, House Full of Floors 2008, No Room for Doubt 2009, Duet 2009, The Cigar That Talks 2010, Birds 2012, Home 2012, No Step 2014. *Publications:* essays, interviews in: Musics, Rubberneck, The Wire. *Honours:* Arts Council development bursary. *E-mail:* jrussell@mopomoso.com. *Website:* john-russell.co.uk.

RUSSELL, Leon; American musician (guitar, piano, trumpet) and singer; b. (Hank Wilson), 1942, Lawton, OK; m. Mary McCreary 1976; one s. one d. *Career:* multi-instrumental session musician; regular mem., Phil Spector's Wall of Sound session crew 1962; pianist, television series Shindig! (NBC); built own recording studio 1967; played with Bob Dylan, The Rolling Stones, Eric Clapton, Jerry Lee Lewis, George Harrison, Ringo Starr, B.B. King, Elton John, Frank Sinatra; owner, video production co. *Film appearance:* Mad Dogs and Englishmen 1970. *Compositions include:* co-writer, singer, theme to Flesh and Blood, NBC TV; Delta Lady, recorded by Joe Cocker; A Song For You, recorded by The Carpenters, Donny Hathaway; This Masquerade, recorded by George Benson; Co-writer, Superstar, recorded by The Carpenters. *Recordings include:* albums: Asylum Choir 1968, Leon Russell 1970, Leon Russell and The Shelter People 1971, Asylum Choir II 1972, Carney 1972, Leon Live 1973, Hank Wilson's Back 1973, Stop All That Jazz 1974, Will O'The Wisp 1975, The Wedding Album 1976, Make Love To The Music 1977, Americana 1978, Willie and Leon (with Willie Nelson) 1979, Life and Love 1979, The Live Album 1981, Hank Wilson Vol. II 1984, Anything Can Happen 1992, Hank Wilson Vol. 3 1998, Face in a Crowd 1999, Blues: Same Old Song 1999, Face in the Crowd 1999, Guitar Blues 2001, Signature Songs 2001, Hank Wilson, Vol. 4 2001, Moonlight & Love Songs 2002, In Your Dreams 2003, Bad Country 2003, Almost Piano 2003, A Mighty Flood 2006, Angel in Disguise 2006, The Union (with Elton John) 2010. *Honours:* Grammy Award for Record of the Year (for This Masquerade) 1976. *E-mail:* LRRecords@LeonRussellRecords.com (office). *Website:* www.leonrussellrecords.com.

RUSSELL, Mark J., BA; British composer; m. Joanne Whitworth 1997. *Career:* joined BBC Television's music department for three years, then left to start own recording studio; as musician and arranger has worked with Tanita Tikaram, Julia Fordham and acclaimed Chinese flautist Guo Yue, with whom he appeared in concerts throughout Europe and Australia; Writer and presenter of BBC Radio 3's music programme Mixing It which covers jazz through to world music and experimental techno, drum and bass. *Compositions include:* for film: Saving Grace 2000, Embrassez qui vous voudrex 2002; for television: Barnados Children 1995, The Peter Principle 1995, Going to Chelsea 1996, Officers and Gentlemen 1997, The Aviators 1998, In Love with Elizabeth 1998, Cold Feet 1998–2003, Passion Killers 1999, The Elevator 2000, Fat Friends 2000, Bubbles 2001, The Eustace Brothers 2003, The Return 2003, Donovan 2004, Rose and Maloney 2004, Cherished 2005, All About George 2005, Murder City 2004–06, Angel Cake 2006, The Bad Mother's Handbook 2007, Kingdom 2007–09, What's Virgin Mean? 2008, Sons of Cuba 2009. *Publication:* Film Music. *Current Management:* Cool Music Ltd, 1A Fishers Lane, Chiswick, London W4 1RX, England. *Telephone:* (20) 8995-7766. *Fax:* (20) 8987-8996. *E-mail:* enquiries@coolmusicltd.com. *Website:* www.coolmusicltd.com.

RUSSELL, Paul Stuart Rupert, CertArch; British musician (drums, New Orleans style); b. 13 Feb. 1934, Nuthall, Nottingham, England; m. June Vivian Hill 1958; three s. one d. *Education:* Leicester School of Architecture, studied drumming in New Orleans. *Career:* mem. Mercia Jazz Band (Nottingham) 1954–58; then musician with various bands: Mike Casimir; Chris Blount; Chris Burke; Spirits of Rhythm (own band); Oriole Brass Band (own band); Dave Donohoe; Louisiana Joymakers; worked with Sammy Rimington, accompanied many visiting Americans, including Alton Purnell, Kid Thomas, Louis Nelson, Benny Waters, Herb Hall, Sam Lee, Captain John Handy; played at Jazz Festivals in New Orleans, Nice, Ascona, Lugano, Milan, Breda, Cork, Gent; mem. The Teddy Fullick Quintet and Frank Brooker New Orleans Swingtet; mem. Musicians' Union. *Recordings include:* with Dave Donohoe, Jimmy Noone Jr. *E-mail:* paul@paulrussellmusic.com. *Website:* www.paulrussellmusic.com.

RUSSELL, Richard; British musician and record executive; *Label Manager and Owner, XL Recordings;* b. 18 March 1971, Dollis Hill, London, England. *Career:* pirate radio DJ during late 1980s; worked for City Beat record label 1990–91; mem. rave and electronic duo Kicks Like a Mule (with Nick Halkes) 1991–; A&R scout, XL Recordings 1991–94, Label Man. and Owner 1994–; numerous albums released on XL by acts including The Prodigy, Radiohead, Adele, The White Stripes, Dizzee Rascal, M.I.A., Vampire Weekend, Gil Scott-Heron, Damon Albarn and Bobby Womack. *Honours:* Music Week Strat Award 2012, Music Week Label of the Year Award 2012, Q Award for Outstanding Contribution to Music 2014. *Address:* XL Recordings, One Codrington Mews, London, W11 2EH, England (office). *Telephone:* (20) 8870-7511 (office). *Fax:* (20) 8871-1766 (office). *Website:* www.xlrecordings.com (office).

RUSSELL, Thomas (Tom); American country musician (guitar) and singer; b. 1953, Los Angeles, CA. *Education:* Univ. of Calif. at Santa Barbara. *Career:* worked as a schoolteacher in Nigeria during the Biafran War; wrote songs for leading country and country-rock artists, including Johnny Cash and Guy Clark. *Recordings:* albums: with Patricia Hardin: Ring Of Bone 1976, Wax

Museum 1978; solo or as band leader: Heart On A Sleeve 1984, Road To Bayamon 1987, Poor Man's Dream 1989, Hurricane Season 1991, Cowboy Real 1991, Beyond St Olav's Gate 1992, Hillbilly Voodoo 1993, Box Of Visions 1993, Cowboy Mambo 1994, Rose Of The San Joaquin 1995, The Long Way Around 1997, Song Of The West 1997, The Man From God Knows Where 1998, All Around These Northern Towns 2001, Borderland 2001, Museum Of Memories 1972–2002 2002, Modern Art 2003, Indians Cowboys Horses Dogs 2004, Hotwalker 2005, Love and Fear 2006, The Wounded Heart of America 2007, Blood and Candle Smoke 2009. *E-mail:* jy@tomrussell.com (office). *Website:* www.tomrussell.com.

RUTHERFORD, Mike; British musician (guitar, bass) and record producer; b. 2 Oct. 1950, Guildford, Surrey, England. *Career:* mem. Genesis 1970–99, 2006–; solo artist 1980–; Founder and producer Mike and the Mechanics 1986–; numerous worldwide tours and concerts. *Recordings include:* albums: with Genesis: Foxtrot 1972, Selling England by the Pound 1973, Genesis Live 1973, The Lamb Lies Down on Broadway 1974, Trick of the Tail 1976, Wind and Wuthering 1977, Seconds Out 1977, And Then There Were Three 1978, Duke 1980, Abacab 1981, Three Sides Live 1982, Genesis 1983, Invisible Touch 1986, We Can't Dance 1991, Calling All Stations 1997, Not About Us 1997; with Mike and the Mechanics: Mike and the Mechanics 1986, The Living Years 1988, Word of Mouth 1991, Beggar on a Beach of Gold 1995, Mike & The Mechanics 1999, Rewired 2004, The Road 2011; solo: Small Creep's Day 1980, Acting Very Strange 1982. *Publication:* Genesis: Chapter and Verse (with other band mems) 2007. *E-mail:* info@genesis-music.com. *Website:* www .genesis-music.com; mikeandthemechanics.com.

RUTTEN, Leo; Belgian engineer and musician (melodeon, bagpipes, hurdy-gurdy, flute, saxophone, taragot); *Lecturer, Katholieke Universiteit Leuven;* b. 25 Dec. 1957, Tongeren; m. Lieve Veulemans 1988; two s. two d. *Education:* KHLim Diepenbeek. *Career:* hurdy-gurdy and melodeon player with Limburgs Dansorkest 1984–93; TV programme De Milieu-Karavaan 1987; Concert, Zoo Leipzig, DDR 1988; Concert, BRT Radio 3 1993; Concert, Festival St Chartier, France 1993; fmr mem. SLEMP, Papaver; playing with Katskoo, Concert Poescafe Ancienne Belgique, Brussels 1998; currently Lecturer, KHLim Diepenbeek, Katholieke Universiteit Leuven. *Compositions:* Biesenwals, Wals Voor Mathilde, De Groene Wants, Alvers in De Lucht, Vals i Fem, Vrijdag 13, Boer ree naar Huis, De Blinde Ekster. *Recordings:* Volksmuziek 1985, Limburgsdans Orkest 1990, Folk Music from Belgium 1997, Poescafe 1997, Klankkleuren 2009. *E-mail:* leo.rutten@skynet.be (office). *Website:* www.katskoo.be.

RUUSUKALLIO, Sami-Kalle; Finnish musician (bass guitar) and singer; b. 25 Dec. 1963. *Career:* mem. Eppu Normaali 1989–. *Recordings include:* albums: Historian suurmiehiä 1990, Studio etana 1993, Sadan vuoden päästäkin 2004, Syvään päähän 2007, Mutala 2011. *Website:* www .eppunormaali.fi.

RYABTSEV, Sergey; Russian musician (violin, bass) and singer; b. 11 Sept. 1958. *Career:* mem. gypsy punk band Gogol Bordello 1999–. *Film:* Kill Your Idols (as Sergey Rjabtzev) 2004, Everything Is Illuminated (as Sergej Rjabcev) 2005, The Pied Piper of Hützovina 2006, Filth and Wisdom 2008. *Recordings include:* with Gogol Bordello: Voi-La Intruder 1999, Multi Kontra Culti vs Irony 2002, East Infection 2005, Gypsy Punks 2005, Super Taranta! 2007, Trans-Continental Hustle 2010, My Tsyganiada 2011, Pura Vida Conspiracy 2013. *Current Management:* c/o Red Light Management, 8439 Sunset Blvd, 2nd Floor, Los Angeles, CA 90069, USA. *E-mail:* gogolbordello@ redlightmanagement.com. *Website:* redlightmanagement.com. *E-mail:* gogolbordello@mac.com (office). *Website:* www.gogolbordello.com.

RYAN, Barbara Tresidder, BA; American singer, Celtic musician (guitar, bouzouki, bodhrán) and teacher (voice and bodhrán); *President, Barnaby Productions, Inc.;* b. (Barbara Ellen Tresidder), 29 May 1950, Colombo, Sri Lanka; d. of Argus J. Tresidder and Nancy Tresidder (née Palmer); m. 1st David B. Ryan (divorced 1986), two s.; m. 2nd Bernard W. Argent 2010. *Education:* George Washington Univ., studied voice with Lida Brodenova, Jane White and Rilla Mervine. *Career:* f. traditional Celtic music group, Iona 1986–; performed at major Celtic festivals and venues throughout USA and UK; voice and bodhrán teacher 1986–; solo work includes broadcasts on Voice of America, singing for the National Geographic Explorer special series; Pres., Barnaby Productions Inc. 1993–; f. Potomac Celtic Festival 1994–2001; Exec. Dir Inst. of Musical Traditions 2003–10, Publicist 2011–; mem. Washington Area Music Asscn, Folk Alliance, Virginia Comm. for the Arts, Maryland State Arts Council Touring Programs. *Recordings include:* albums: IONA 1986, Off the Beaten Track 1987, Back to Our Roots 1992, Holding Our Own 1994, Nutmeg and Ginger 1996, The Sound of Iona 1998, Birken Tree 2001, Branching Out 2003, A Celebration of 20 (Washington Area Music Asscn Award for Best Folk/Traditional Album) 2006, Mid-Winter Light 2009, Silver 2011; DVD: Live! At the 333 2012. *Honours:* Award for Best Event 2002, Loudoun Convention and Visitor Assen . *Address:* Barnaby Productions Inc., 7116 Swift Run Trails Drive, Fairfax Station, VA 22039, USA (office). *Telephone:* (703) 426-1450 (office). *E-mail:* ionavoice@pobox.com (office). *Website:* www.ionamusic.com (home); www.voiceandbodhranteacher.com (office); www.imtfolk.org (office).

RYAN, Kate; Belgian singer; b. (Katrien Verbeeck), 22 July 1980. *Career:* fmr mem. Melt; solo recording artist 2001–; rep. Belgium in Eurovision Song Contest 2006. *Recordings:* Different 2002, Stronger 2004, Alive 2006, Free 2008, French Connection 2009, Electroshock 2012. *Address:* c/o Nextar,

Kerkstraat 28, 2850 Boom, Belgium (office). *Telephone:* (3) 292-88-22 (office). *Fax:* (3) 646-84-67 (office). *E-mail:* management@kateryan.be (office). *Website:* www.kateryan.be.

RYAN, Lee; British singer; b. 17 June 1983, Chatham, Kent, England. *Career:* mem. band, Blue 2001–05, 2009–; solo artist 2005–. *Recordings include:* albums: with Blue: All Rise 2001, One Love 2002, Guilty 2004, Roulette 2013; solo: Lee Ryan 2005. *Honours:* Smash Hits Awards for Best Newcomer 2001, Best Live Act, Best UK Band 2002, Interactive Music Award for Artist of the Year 2002, BRIT Award for Best British Newcomer 2002, NRJ Music Award for Best Int. Group (France) 2005. *Address:* Blue, 52-54 High Holborn, London, WC1V 6RB, England. *Website:* wp.officialblue.com.

RYAN, Nicky; Irish music producer and sound engineer; b. Dublin. *Career:* formed Aigle Music/Enya partnership (with Enya and Roma Ryan) as sound engineer and producer 1982–. *Recordings include* Enya albums: Enya 1987, Watermark (IFPI Platinum European Award) 1988, Shepherd Moons (IFPI Platinum European Award, Grammy Award, Billboard Music Award, NARM Best-Selling Album Award) 1991, The Celts 1992, The Memory of Trees (Grammy Award) 1995, Paint the Sky with Stars (Japanese Grand Prix Album of the Year) 1997, A Day Without Rain (Grammy Award, Japanese Grand Prix Album of the Year) 2000, Amarantine (Grammy Award for Best New Age Album 2006) 2005, And Winter Came... 2008, Dark Sky Island 2015. *Honours:* Grammy Awards for producing and engineering on soundtracks for The Lord of the Rings: The Fellowship of the Rings, Ivor Novello International Achievement Award 1998, Echo Award (for Only Time), BMI Special Citation of Achievement (for Only Time, for Orinoco Flow, I Don't Wanna Know), Las Vegas Film Critics Soc. Award for Best Original Song (for May It Be), Phoenix Film Critics Award for Best Original Song (for May It Be), Broadcast Film Critics Award for Best Song (for May It Be), Hot Press Music Critics Award for Best Producer. *Website:* www.nickyryan.net; www.enya.com.

RYAN, Roma; British lyricist and music manager; b. Belfast, Northern Ireland; m. Nicky Ryan; two d. *Career:* formed Aigle Music/Enya partnership (with Enya and Nicky Ryan) as lyricist and manager 1982–. *Recordings include* albums with Enya: Enya 1987, Watermark (IFPI Platinum European Award) 1988, Shepherd Moons (IFPI Platinum European Award, Grammy Award, Billboard Music Award, NARM Best-Selling Album Award) 1991, The Celts 1992, The Memory of Trees (Grammy Award) 1995, Paint the Sky with Stars (Japanese Grand Prix Album of the Year) 1997, A Day Without Rain (Grammy Award, Japanese Grand Prix Album of the Year) 2000, Amarantine (Grammy Award for Best New Age Album 2007) 2005, And Winter Came... 2008, Dark Sky Island 2015. *Art exhibitions:* exhibitions of art in Ireland and in Switzerland. *Publication:* Water Shows the Hidden Heart 2005. *Honours:* Ivor Novello Int. Achievement Award 1998, Echo Award (for Only Time), BMI Special Citation of Achievement (for Only Time, for Orinoco Flow, I Don't Wanna Know), Las Vegas Film Critics Soc. Award for Best Original Song (for May It Be), Phoenix Film Critics Award for Best Original Song (for May It Be), Broadcast Film Critics Award for Best Song (for May It Be). *Address:* Treesdale, Church Road, Killiney, Co. Dublin, Ireland (office). *Website:* www.romaryan.com; www.enya.com.

RYDELL, Bobby; American singer and musician (drums); b. (Robert Ridarelli), 26 April 1942, Philadelphia, PA. *Career:* drummer, Teen Club television show for three years; duo with Frankie Avalon 1954; mem., Rocco and the Saints; solo artist 1959–63; cabaret and club singer. *Film appearance:* Bye Bye Birdie. *Recordings include:* albums: We Got Love 1959, Bobby Sings, Bobby Swings 1960, Bobby Salutes the Great Ones 1961, Rydell At The Copa 1961, Bobby Rydell/Chubby Checker 1961, Bobby's Biggest Hits 1961, All The Hits 1962, An Era Reborn 1962, Bye Bye Birdie 1963, Wildwood Days 1963, Top Hits of 1963 1964, Forget Him 1964, Somebody Loves You 1965, Born with a Smile 1976, The Best of Bobby Rydell 2000, Bobby's Biggest Hits 1999, Now And Then 2000. *Current Management:* Fox Entertainment, 1650 Broadway, Suite 503, New York, NY 10019, USA. *E-mail:* bobbyrydell@gmail.com. *Website:* www.bobbyrydell.com.

RYDER, Paul; British musician (bass guitar); b. 24 April 1964, Salford, Greater Manchester; s. of Derek Ryder and Linda Ryder; m. Angela Smith; three s. one d. *Education:* St Ambrose Barlow School, Salford. *Career:* Founder-mem., bass player, songwriter, Happy Mondays 1985–93, 1999–2000, 2012–, Big Arm 2007–; numerous tours and festival appearances; also appeared in feature film 24 Hour Party People 2002 and TV series Burn It (BBC 3) 2003–04. *Recordings include:* albums: with Happy Mondays: Squirrel and G-Man Twenty-Four Hour Party People Plastic Face Carnt Smile (White Out) 1986, Bummed (Q Magazine Classic Album Award 2013) 1988, Pills 'n' Thrills and Bellyaches 1990, ...Yes Please! 1992; with Big Arm: Radiator 2008. *Honours:* DMC World DJ Award for Best Indie Act 1991. *Current Management:* c/o Angela Smith, Turn on Talent, Suite 2B, 22 Lever Street, Manchester, M1 1EA, England. *Telephone:* (161) 247-7700. *E-mail:* angela .smith@turnontv.co.uk. *Website:* www.turnontv.co.uk/turnontalent.html. *Telephone:* (161) 408-9616 (UK) (office); (310) 729-7043 (USA) (office). *Website:* www.happymondaysonline.com; www.paulryder.info.

RYDER, Shaun; British singer; b. 23 Aug. 1962, Little Hulton, Lancashire, England; two d. one s. *Career:* founder mem. and lead singer, Happy Mondays 1985–92, 1999–2000, 2004–; numerous tours and festival appearances; founder mem., Black Grape 1995–98. *Film appearance:* The Ghost of Oxford Street (Channel 4) 1990. *Recordings include:* albums: with Happy Mondays: Squirrel and G-Man Twenty-Four Hour Party People Plastic Face Carnt

Smile (White Out) 1986, Bummed (Q Magazine Classic Album Award 2013) 1988, Pills 'n' Thrills and Bellyaches 1990, ...Yes Please! 1992; with Black Grape: It's Great When You're Straight... Yeah! 1995, Stupid, Stupid, Stupid 1997; solo: Planet Groove – The Shaun Ryder Session (selected tracks) 2000, Clowns and Pet Sounds 2002, Amateur Night in the Big Top 2003, Uncle Dysfunktional 2007. *Honours:* DMC World DJ Award for Best Indie Act 1991. *Current Management:* c/o Warren Askew Management, Woodhead House, 44/ 46 Market Street, Hyde, Cheshire, SK14 1AH, England. *Telephone:* (7818) 888368. *E-mail:* weaentertainment@gmail.com. *Website:* www .happymondaysonline.com; www.shaunryderofficial.com.

RYDER-JONES, Bill; British singer and musician (guitar, trumpet); b. Hoylake, Wirral, England. *Education:* Hilbre High School, Hoylake. *Career:* Founder-mem. The Coral 1996–2008. *Recordings include:* albums: The Coral 2002, Magic and Medicine 2003, Secret Kiss 2003, Nightfreak and the Sons of Becker 2004, The Invisible Invasion 2005, Roots and Echoes 2007; solo: If 2011, A Bad Wind Blows in My Heart 2013. *E-mail:* ellie@jigsawmusicmgmt .com. *Website:* www.jigsawmusicmgmt.com.

RYGERT, Göran T., MArch; Swedish composer and musician; b. 1 May 1935, Tranås; s. of Torsten Rygert; m. 1st; two s.; m. 2nd Janet A. Rybka 1997. *Education:* Chalmers Univ. of Technology, Göteborg. *Career:* arranger and composer, ballad and folk music; string bass musician, Swedish song – ballad artists, in many folk music orchestras, Sweden and USA; appearances in Swedish, American and Russian radio and TV; song festivals; produced 40 song books; freelance ed., Warner/Chappell Music Scandinavia AB, Sweden; Founder and leader of men's choir Vasa Drangar, Atlanta, GA; mem. Swedish Composers of Popular Music, Balalaika and Domra Asscn of America. *Compositions:* numerous songs with words by Swedish poets and writers, pieces for Russian folk instrument orchestras, orchestral arrangements. *Recordings:* Visituder 2004, Ta Dej En Jamare 2010, Jul Jul 2011. *Publications:* 60 Folkvisor Från Hela Världen 1977, Visor För Törstiga 1980, Ölands Folkliga Visor och Melodier Genom Tiderna 1987, Låtar Vid Strandkanten 1988, Poeten Pihl 1992, Visor Kring Bordet 1993, Festvisor 1994, Disney Sångboken 1996, 2000, 2001, 2003, 2007, Evert Taubes Bästa 1998, Musical Hits 1998, 2002, Bellmans Bästa 1999, FilmHits 2002, Sångboken (Chalmers 1870–2007) 2007, The Very Best of Swedish Schnapps Songs 2008, numerous other song books. *Honours:* Hon. mem. Visans Vänner, Stockholm; Lion's Club Cultural Award 1984, Royal Gustav Adolf's Acad. Prize 1991, Kalmar County Council Cultural Award 1997, Swedish Council of America Award of Merit 2007, Nordic Lodge of the Vasa Order Award 2013. *Address:* 4390 Ivywood NE, Marietta, GA 30062, USA. *Telephone:* (770) 977-8537. *E-mail:* goran@ rygert.se; rygert@bellsouth.net. *Website:* www.rygert.se.

RYLANDER, Ludvig; Swedish musician (horns); b. Uppsala. *Career:* mem. The Concretes 2001–; band founded label, Licking Fingers. *Recordings include:* albums: The Concretes 2003, Layourbattleaxedown 2005, In Colour 2006, Hey Trouble 2007, WYWH 2010. *E-mail:* theconcretessweden@gmail .com. *Website:* www.theconcretes.com.

RYPDAL, Terje; Norwegian musician (guitar, piano) and composer; b. 23 Aug. 1947, Oslo; m. Elin Kristin Rypdal 1988; three s. one d. *Education:* Univ. of Oslo. *Career:* musician with The Vanguards 1962–67, The Dream 1967–69, Jan Garbarek Group 1969–71; leader of own groups 1971–; mem. Norwegian Composers Guild. *Compositions include:* six symphonies, two operas. *Recordings include:* albums: Bleak House 1968, Ved Sorevatn (on album of Baden Baden Free Jazz Meeting) 1969, Terje Rypdal 1971, What Comes After 1974, Whenever I Seem To Be Far Away 1974, Odyssey 1975, After The Rain 1976, Waves 1978, Descendre 1980, To Be Continued 1981, Eos 1984, Chaser 1986, Works 1989, Undisonus 1990, QED 1993, If Mountains Could Sing 1995, Nordic Quartet (with John Surman, Karin Krog, Vigleik Storaas) 1995, Skywards 1997, Double Concerto/Fifth Symphony 2000, Selected Recordings 2002, Melodic Warrior 2006, Vossabrygg 2006, Crime Scene 2010; also collaborated with Robert Wyatt, Ketil Bjornstad. *Honours:* Deutscher Schallplattenpreis. *Current Management:* c/o Kjell Kalleklev Management AS Georgernes Verft 12, N-5011 Bergen, Norway. *Telephone:* 55-55-76-30. *Fax:* 55-55-76-31. *E-mail:* kjell@kalleklev.no. *Website:* www.kalleklev.no.

RZA, (The Abbott, Prince Rakeem, RZArector, Bobby Steels, Bobby Digital); American rap artist, producer and actor; b. (Robert Diggs), 5 July 1969, Brooklyn, New York. *Career:* fmr mem. rap group All in Together Now; solo artist as Prince Rakeem 1991; mem. Wu-Tang Clan 1993–; mem., Gravediggaz 1995, as RZArector; solo artist 1998–; producer for artists, including Raekwon, Ol' Dirty Bastard, Method Man, GZA, Ghostface Killah, Gravediggaz, Bjork, Notorious B.I.G., Big Pun. *Films include:* Ghost Dog: The Way of the Samurai 1999, Coffee and Cigarettes 2003, Derailed 2005, American Gangster 2007, Gospel Hill 2008, Life Is Hot in Cracktown, Funny People 2009, Due Date, Repo Men 2010, The Man with the Iron Fists (directorial debut) 2012, G.I. Joe: Retaliation 2013. *Television include:* Californication (TV series). *Recordings include:* albums: with Wu-Tang Clan: Enter the Wu-Tang (36 Chambers) 1993, Wu-Tang Forever 1997, The W 2000, Iron Flag 2001, Disciples of the 36 Chambers 2004, The 8 Diagrams 2007; Only Built 4 Cuban Linx II (with Raekwon) 2009; solo: RZA as Bobby Digital in Stereo 1998, Ghost Dog: The Way of the Samurai (film soundtrack) 2000, Digital Bullet 2001, The World According to RZA 2003, Birth of a Prince 2003, The RZA-Instrumental Experience 2007, RZA as Bobby Digital, Digi Snacks 2008. *Publications:* The Wu-Tang Manual 2005, The Tao of Wu (memoir) 2009. *Website:* www .wutangcorp.com.

S

SA DINGDING; Chinese singer, songwriter and musician (zheng, Chinese drum, gong, horse-head fiddle); b. 23 Dec. 1983, Inner Mongolia. *Education:* Beijing Central Conservatory of Music. *Career:* merges modern and traditional music, sings in Sanskrit, Tibetan and other languages; solo artist 2001–. *Recordings include:* albums: Dong Ba La 2001, Alive (BBC Award for World Music, Asia/Pacific Region 2008) 2007, Harmony 2010, The Coming Ones 2012, Wonderland 2014. *Honours:* China's Best Dance Music Singer 2001.

SAADIQ, Raphael; American R&B singer, songwriter and producer; b. (Raphael Wiggins), 14 May 1966, Oakland, Calif. *Career:* formed vocal trio Tony! Toni! Toné! (with brother, Dwayne and cousin Timothy Christian) 1988; founder, Pookie Records; formed Lucy Pearl (with Dawn Robinson and Ali Shaheed Muhammad) 2000–01; collaborations with Q-Tip, Snoop Doggy Dogg, Willie Max, Vanessa Williams, D'Angelo, Bilal, Whitney Houston, Angie Stone; producer for Flo-Ology, Anthony Hamilton, Teedra Moses, Mary J. Blige, Kelis, Lionel Richie, John Legend, Musiq Soulchild, Joss Stone. *Recordings include:* albums: with Tony! Toni! Toné!: Who? 1988, The Revival 1990, Sons of Soul 1993, House of Music 1996; with Lucy Pearl: Lucy Pearl 2000; solo: Instant Vintage 2002, All Hits at the House of Blues 2003, Ray Ray 2004, The Way I See It 2008, Stone Rollin' 2011. *Website:* www.raphaelsaadiq.com.

SAARI, Sami; Finnish singer; b. 21 Jan. 1962, Kokkola. *Career:* fmr mem. Veeti & the Velvets, Aki Sirkesalo ja Lemmen jättiläiset and Sami Saari & Cosmo Sonic; Founder Wicked Recordings (with Timo Juuti) 2008–. *Recordings include:* albums: Do Re Mi 1997, Samtheman 1999, Turisti 2002, Hits 2003, Neljas 2005, Vapaa 2009, Soulklassikot 2012. *Website:* www.wicked-recordings.com.

SABINA, Leslie Michael, BMus, BEd, MM, PhD; American jazz composer and academic; *Professor of Music, St Bonaventure University;* b. 21 Sept. 1958, Neb.; m. Evelyn May Rennie; one s. one d. *Education:* Univ. of Toronto, Univ. of Windsor, Univ. of Miami, Michigan State Univ. *Career:* Prof. of Music, Univ. of Windsor 1988–90, St Bonaventure Univ. 1991–; jazz performances with Dizzy Gillespie, J.C. Heard Jazz Orchestra, Joe Coughlin, Joe Williams, Billy Eckstine, Della Reese, The Temptations; mem. The American Soc. of Composers, Authors and Publrs (ASCAP), JEN, College Music Soc., North American Saxophone Alliance. *Compositions:* 100 jazz compositions. *Honours:* Hon. Visiting Fellow, Univ. of York 1998; PROCAN Jazz Composers Award 1986, 1988, PROCAN Jazz Composer of the Year 1988, ASCAP Composition Award 1995–2011. *Address:* Department of Music, St Bonaventure University, 3261 West State Road, St Bonaventure, NY 14778, USA (office). *Telephone:* (716) 375-2320 (office). *Fax:* (716) 375-7667 (office). *E-mail:* lsabina@sbu.edu (office). *Website:* www.sbu.edu/music (office).

SABIU, Marco; record producer, mixer and songwriter; b. Forli, Italy. *Career:* writer, producer with Charlie Mallozzi, known as Rapino Brothers; moved to London 1992; classically trained pianist; programmer, mixer, producer of pop/dance music; mem. of groups, Tabernacle, Rapination. *Recordings include:* Albums for: Take That, Kylie Minogue, Dannii Minogue, Lulu, Kym Mazelle, Filippa Giordano, Rozalla; Hit singles: Could It Be Magic, Take That; Rhythm of The Night, Corona; What Is Love, Haddaway; I Know The Lord, Tabernacle; Love Me The Right Way, Rapination and Kym Mazelle; I Love My Radio, Taffy; T'pau, Red; Also singles for: Alicia Bridges, Heaven 17, Sparks. *Website:* www.worldconcertartists.org.

SADASHIGE, Yuzuru; American (b. Japan) composer and musician; b. 12 May 1966, Chiba, Japan; m. Wendy Griffiths, 4 Sept. 1998. *Education:* Univ. of Tokyo , Japan, Berklee Coll. of Music, Manhattan School of Music,. *Career:* Co-Founder, Co-Artistic Dir, NeWorks, contemporary music group; Composer In Residence, American Chamber Music Festival at Edsvik, Sweden, 1999; Assistant Conductor, Pianist, Golden Fleece Chamber Opera, 1995; US Premiere of Maurice Ohana's Three Stories of Honorable Flower, 1996; Pianist for ballet classes, Rehearsal Pianist for Musical Theatre; Pianist, Scott Wolson's Folk-Rock CD, Anything Left to Say; Jazz/Pop Pianist/Keyboardist, Arranger for bands, sessions and parties; bass player Changing Modes alternative rock group; Adjunct Mem. The Actors Company Theatre; mem, ASCAP; American Music Center; Actors' Company Theatre. *Compositions:* Third Tribe, for flute, djembe drums and piano, 1992; Electric Ice Dream, for clarinet quartet, 1996; Fractured Skies, 1998; eX-s-Tet, for clarinet, 2 violins, viola, cello, piano, 1999; Concert music performed throughout USA and Mexico by Civic Orchestra of Chicago; ONIX New Music Ensemble; The New York Clarinet Quintet; NewEar Ensemble of Kansas City; Synchronia of St Louis; numerous commissions, theatre scores, dance scores; film score for ANA: Portrait in Days 1995. *Honours:* Brian M Israel Award, Society for New Music 1996. *E-mail:* info@changingmodes.com. *Website:* www.changingmodes.com.

SADE, OBE; British singer and songwriter; b. (Helen Folasade Adu), 16 Jan. 1959, Ibadan, Nigeria. *Education:* St Martin's School of Art. *Career:* mem. Arriva, Pride; Founder own band Sade 1983–; appearances include Montreux Jazz Festival 1984, Live Aid, Wembley Stadium 1985; film appearance in Absolute Beginners 1987. *Recordings include:* albums: Diamond Life (BRIT Award for Best British Album 1985) 1984, Promise 1985, Stronger Than Pride 1988, Love Deluxe 1992, Best Of 1994, Lovers Rock (Grammy Award for Pop Vocal Album 2002) 2000, Soldier of Love 2010; singles: Your Love Is King 1984, When Am I Going To Make A Living 1984, Smooth Operator (co-writer) 1984, The Sweetest Taboo 1985, Is It A Crime? 1986, Never As Good As The First Time 1986, Love Is Stronger Than Pride 1988, Paradise 1988, No Ordinary Love (used in film Indecent Proposal) 1993, Feel No Pain 1993, By Your Side 2000, King Of Sorrow 2001; contrib. film soundtrack Absolute Beginners 1987. *Honours:* BRIT Award for Best New Artist 1986, Black Music Award 1992, American Music Award for Favourite Adult Contemporary Artist 2002. *Website:* www.sade.com.

SADIER, Laetitia; French singer, musician (keyboards, guitar, trombone) and songwriter; b. 6 May 1968, Paris; partner Tim Gane; one s. *Career:* Founder-mem. Stereolab 1991–; also mem. Monade; Stereolab formed record label, Duophonic 1994. *Recordings include:* albums: with Stereolab: Switched On 1992, Peng! 1992, Lo-Fi (EP) 1992, The Groop Played 'Space Age Batchelor Pad Music' 1993, Transient Random Noise Bursts With Announcements 1993, Mars Audiac Quintet 1994, Music For The Amorphous Body Study Center (EP) 1995, Emperor Tomato Ketchup 1996, Fluorescences (EP) 1996, Dots And Loops 1997, Cobra And Phases Group Play Voltage In The Milky Night 1999, The First Of The Microbe Hunters 2000, Sound-Dust 2001, ABC Music: The Radio 1 Sessions 2002, Margerine Eclipse 2004, Fab Four Suture 2006, Chemical Chords 2008, Not Music 2010; with Monade: Socialisme ou Barbarie 2003, A Few Steps More 2005, Monstre cosmic 2008; solo: The Trip 2010, Silencio 2012, Something Shines 2014. *Address:* Stereolab, PO Box 3787, London, SE22 9DZ, England (office). *E-mail:* duophonic@btopenworld.com (office). *Website:* www.stereolab.co.uk.

SAFARI, Jean Bosco; Belgian singer and songwriter; b. (Jean Vijdt), 10 May 1954, Rubago, Rwanda; one s. one d. *Career:* solo artist, originally as Kid Safari, billed as Jean Bosco Safari 1995–; mem. SABAM, ZAMU. *Recordings include:* Wow 1991, The Romantic Heroes 1993, Little Boy Blue 1995, Visions Of Home 1997, Nomad 2003, Private Revolution 2008. *Website:* www.jeanboscosafari.be.

SAFER, Mattie; American musician (bass guitar, keyboards), backing singer and songwriter; b. 11 Dec. 1980. *Career:* mem. The Rapture 1999–2009; currently solo artist. *Recordings include:* albums: Mirror 1999, Out Of The Races And Onto The Tracks 2001, Echoes 2003, Pieces of People We Love 2006. *Website:* www.mattiesafer.com.

SAFFRON; Nigerian singer; b. (Samantha Sprackling), 3 June 1968. *Career:* former ballet dancer; lead singer, N-Joi 1995–; lead singer, Republica 1994–98, 2008–. *Recordings include:* albums: with N-Joi: Anthem 1990; with Republica: Republica 1997, Speed Ballads 1998; guest vocals on: Fat Of The Land by Prodigy 1997, Drums Are Dangerous by The Drum Club, Smile by Deepsky, Crusher, Spirits by Junkie XL; solo singles: One Love 1992, Circles 1993, World of You 1993.

SAGER, Carole Bayer; American songwriter and singer; b. 1946, New York, NY; m. Burt Bacharach. *Education:* High School of Music and Art, New York. *Career:* songwriter 1960s; solo artist 1970s–. *Compositions:* Groovy Kind of Love (recorded by Patti Labelle, The Mindbenders, Phil Collins); That's What Friends Are For (recorded by Dionne Warwick and Friends); co-writer, Midnight Blue (recorded by Melissa Manchester); When I Need You (recorded by Leo Sayer); They're Playing Our Song, with Marvin Hamlisch; Arthur's Theme, with Burt Bacharach (recorded by Christopher Cross); Nobody Does It Better, Carly Simon (James Bond theme); On My Own, Patti Labelle, Michael McDonald; also composed songs for: Roberta Flack; Taja Sevelle; Neil Diamond; Aretha Franklin; The Monkees; Andrea Bocelli; Céline Dion, Bette Midler, Doobie Brothers, Daian Ross, Liza Minnelli, Michael Jackson. *Recordings include:* albums: Carole Bayer Sager 1977, Too 1978, Sometimes Late at Night 1981. *Honours:* Academy Award (for Arthur's Theme). *Current Management:* Maureen O'Connor, 8687 Melrose Avenue, Seventh Floor, Los Angeles, CA 90069, USA. *Telephone:* (310) 854-8116. *E-mail:* moconnor@rogersandcowan.com. *Website:* www.carolebayersager.com.

SAGOV, Margo Leona, MA; British musician (guitar), singer, songwriter, producer and studio designer and architect; *Architect, Margo Sagov Architect and Murray John Architects;* b. 22 Dec. 1952, Cape Town, South Africa; m. (divorced); partner Gary Curson. *Education:* Univ. of Cape Town School of Architecture, Architectural Asscn School of Architecture, London, Univ. of East London. *Career:* registered architect; Founder-mem. group, Amazulu, guitarist, backing vocalist 1982–86; toured extensively, UK, Europe; numerous TV appearances, radio and recording sessions; mem. JackOut 1995–, Hip Replacement' 2009–, The Antoinettes' 2011–; currently architect, Margo Sagov Architect, Murray John Architects; mem. Musicians' Union, Equity, ACTT as sound recordist (membership on hold), ARB. *Recordings include:* with Amazulu: Cairo 1984, Smiley Stylee 1984, Excitable 1985, Moonlight Romance, Don't You Just Know It 1985, Too Good To Be Forgotten 1986; with Clicking The Mouse: I Must Be Dreaming; with JackOut: Saturnalia 2009; sessions include: Happiness, The Beloved 1990, Zeke Manyika. *Address:* 10 Brookfield Mansions, Highgate West Hill, London, N6 6AS, England (home). *Fax:* (20) 7720-0377 (office); (20) 8348-2148 (office). *E-mail:* bilikins@mac.com (home). *Website:* www.murrayjohn.com (office).

ŞAHIN, Timuçin; Turkish musician (jazz guitar) and composer; b. 3 Feb. 1973. *Education:* Hilversum and Amsterdam Conservatories, Manhattan School of Music. *Career:* moved to Netherlands 1992, then New York 2003; leader, jazz ensembles including Greg Osby-Timucin Sahin Quartet, Rare Falcons, Timucin Sahin Trio and contemporary chamber music ensemble, Occult Ensemble; played/recorded with Randy Brecker, Greg Osby, Robin Eubanks, Hein vd Geyn, Kai Eckhardt, Mike Mainieri, Tony Moreno, Aydin Esenal and others; solo performances at int. festivals; has composed for and been commissioned by Amsterdam Percussion Group, Occult Ensemble, Enric Monfort Ensemble, Ere Lievonen, Verso, Amsterdam Conservatory Symphonic Orchestra, Brisk Quartet, TobeSung, and others; teaches in conservatories and schools worldwide. *Recordings include:* as leader: with On the Line: The Unexpected (First Prize, Dutch Jazz Competition) 2001; with others: Slick Road 2003, Window for My Breath 2005. *E-mail:* tsahinmusic@yahoo.com (office). *Website:* myspace.com/timucinsahin.

SAHIR, Kazem Jabbar Ibrahim as-; Iraqi singer, songwriter and musician (guitar, oud); b. 9 Dec. 1961, Nainawa; m. (divorced); two s. *Education:* Baghdad Music Acad. *Career:* worked as songwriter; first song, Ladghat El Hayya banned, owing to lyrical content; collaborations with Syrian poet Nizar Qabbani, with music artists Sarah Brightman, Lenny Kravitz. *Recordings include:* albums: Ghazal 1989, Abart Al-Shat 1989, Al-Aziz 1990, Haza Allon 1992, Banat Alaebak 1993, La Ya Sadiqi 1993, Salamtek Min Al-Ah 1994, Baad Al-Hob 1995, Ighlesi Belbarad 1996, Fi Medreset Al-Hob 1996, Ana Wa Laila 1998, Habibeti Wa Al-Matar 1999, Al-Hob Al-Mustahil 2000, Abbathu Anki 2001, Quasat Habebain 2002, Haibibati Wal Matar 2003, Hafiat Al Kadamain 2003, Ila Tilmitha 2004, Entaha al Mushwar 2005, Yawmiyat Rajul Mahzoum 2007, Souwar– Pictures 2008, Al Rasm Bel Kalimat 2009, La Tazeedeeh Lowa'a 2011. *Honours:* UNICEF Award, BBC Radio 3 World Music Award for Middle East Artist of the Year 2004. *Current Management:* c/o Dawn Elder Management, 303 Lorna Alta Drive, Suite #31, Santa Barbara, CA 93109, USA. *Telephone:* (805) 963-2415. *Fax:* (805) 965-4075. *E-mail:* demgmt@aol.com. *Website:* www.demgmt.com.

SAID, Samira; Morrocan singer; b. (Samira Bensaid), 10 Jan. 1957, Rabat; m. Moustapha Naboulssi; one s. *Recordings include:* albums: El hob elli ana a'aycheh 1980, Bitaqat hob 1980, Ben lif 1981, Hikaya 1982, Allemnah el-hob 1983, Ketr al-kalam 1983, Methaya'li 1984, Lilet el-ouns 1984, Ya damaiti haddi 1984, Ehki ya Shehrazade 1985, Youm akablak fih 1985, Ech gab li gab 1985, Amrak ajib en 1986, Ana walla anta 1989, Moch hatnazel a'anak 1986, Sibak 1986, Ya ebn el-halel 1987, Ghariba 1988, Sibni louahdi 1988, Ensani 1989, Ba'adin neta'ateb 1990, Choft el-amar 1991, Hannitlak 1992, Khayfa 1992, a'ach'a 1993, Enta habibi 1995, Kolli de echa'at 1996, a'al bal 1998, Rouhi 1999, Laila habibi 2001, Youm wara youm (BBC Award for World Music, Middle East Region 2003) 2002, Awweeni beek 2004, Ayam hayati 2008, Khallouh 2010, Mazal 2013. *Website:* www.diva.vze.com.

SAIJO, Hideki; Japanese singer; b. (Kimoto Tatsuo), 13 May 1955, Hiroshima; m.; two s. one d. *Career:* popular recording artist 1972–; has released over 80 singles, appeared in six feature films, four plays, seven musicals and 23 TV dramas; producer and performer annual Stop AIDS benefit concert. *Singles include:* Ai Suru Kisetsu, Jyonetsu no Arashi, Chigereta Ai, Young Man, Itsumo no Hoshi ga Nagare. *Publications:* Bali Sutairu no Ie. *Website:* www.earth-corp.co.jp/HIDEKI.

SAINSBURY, Roy; British musician (guitar); b. 12 April 1942, Birmingham; m. Wendy Sainsbury; two s. one d. *Education:* studied guitar with Reg Bishop and Jack Toogood. *Career:* numerous TV and radio broadcasts; played with BBC Midland Radio Orchestra and New Millionaires' Band; solo appearances. *Compositions include:* Love and Sunshine, Crieff Melody, Wendy's Blues. *Recordings include:* album: Gentle Guitar, I've Got It Bad (with Jane Christie). *E-mail:* info@roysainsbury.com. *Website:* www.roysainsbury.com.

ST JAMES, Rebecca; Australian Christian musician; b. 26 July 1977, Sydney. *Education:* high school music group, studied with Norris Brannstrom. *Career:* solo artist 1994–; numerous tours, TV appearances; mem. BMI, GMA. *Recordings include:* albums: Refresh My Heart 1991, Rebecca St James 1994, One Way 1995, God 1996, Pray 1998, Transform 2000, Worship God 2002, Wait for Me: The Best from Rebecca St James 2003, If I Had One Chance To Tell You Something 2005, I Will Praise You 2011. *Publications include:* You're the Voice 1997, Wait for Me 2002, SHE: Safe, Healthy, Empowered 2004, Sister Freaks 2005, Pure 2008, Loved: Stories of Forgiveness 2009. *E-mail:* rebeccastjames@rsjames.com. *Website:* www.rsjames.com.

ST JOHN, Kate Elinor Margaret, BSc; British musician (oboe, saxophone), singer, composer and arranger; b. 2 Oct. 1957, London; d. of John St. John and Diana St. John; m. Neill MacColl 2014. *Education:* City Univ., Guildhall School of Music and Drama. *Career:* mem., Ravishing Beauties 1981–82; mem., Dream Academy 1983–91; oboe/saxophone session player in many bands; mem., Channel Light Vessel 1994; mem., Van Morrison's live and recording band 1991–95; toured with Nigel Kennedy 1998; also worked with Hal Wilner, Tom Waits, Philip Glass, Damon Albarn, Vashti Bunyan, Kathryn Williams, Marianne Faithfull; mem. Musicians' Union, PRS, MCPS. *Compositions for television:* Harry Enfield's Television Show, Harry Enfield and Chums. *Recordings:* albums: with Dream Academy: The Dream Academy, Remembrance Days, A Different Kind of Weather, Somewhere In The Sun (compilation); with Channel Light Vessel: Automatic 1994, Excellent Spirits 1996; solo albums: Indescribable Night 1995, Second Sight 1997. *E-mail:* info@katestjohn.co.uk (office). *Website:* www.katestjohn.co.uk.

ST VINCENT; American singer, songwriter and musician (guitar, bass guitar, keyboards, theremin); b. (Anne Erin Clark), 28 Sept. 1982, Tulsa, Okla. *Education:* Lake Highlands High School, Berklee Coll. of Music. *Career:* mem. The Polyphonic Spree 2004–06; touring musician with Sufjan Stevens 2006; solo career with own band 2006–; numerous collaborations including with David Byrne, Andrew Bird, Swans. *Recordings:* albums: Marry Me 2007, Actor 2009, Strange Mercy 2011, Love This Giant (with David Byrne) 2012, St Vincent (Grammy Award for Best Alternative Rock Album 2015) 2014. *Honours:* PLUG Independent Music Award for Female Artist of the Year 2008, Q Maverick Award 2014. *Current Management:* c/o Austen Holman, Lever and Beam LLC, 325 West 38th Street, Suite 1101, New York, 10018, USA. *Telephone:* (212) 217-9448 (ext 7231). *E-mail:* austen@leverandbeam.com. *Website:* www.leverandbeam.com; ilovestvincent.com.

SAINTE-MARIE, Buffy, PhD; Canadian singer, songwriter and musician (keyboards, guitar, mouthbow, computer); b. 20 Feb. 1941, Sask.; one s. *Education:* Univ. of Massachusetts, USA. *Career:* solo concerts worldwide 1963–; symphony concerts with Calgary Symphony, National Arts Centre Orchestra, Vancouver Opera Symphony; toured with various bands major cities, Indian reservations, indigenous area worldwide; Founder The Cradleboard Teaching Project 1996–; mem. American Soc. of Composers, Authors and Publrs, American Fed. of Musicians. *Recordings include:* albums: It's My Way 1964, Many a Mile 1965, Little Wheel Spin and Spin 1966, Fire and Fleet and Candlelight 1967, I'm Gonna Be a Country Girl Again 1968, Illuminations 1969, She Used to Wanna be a Ballerina 1971, Moonshot 1972, Quiet Places 1973, Native North American Child 1974, Buffy 1974, Changing Woman 1975, Sweet America 1976, Coincidence and Likely Stories 1992, Up Where We Belong 1996, Running for the Drum (Juno Award for Aboriginal Album of the Year) 2009. *Honours:* Academy Award for Best Original Song (for Up Where We Belong from An Officer and a Gentleman), Billboard Best New Artist Award 1964, Premico Award, Italy 1972, Queen Elizabeth Jubilee Medal, Charles de Gaulle Grand Prix for Best Int. Artist 1994, Saskatchewan Lifetime Achievement Award 1994, Gov.-Gen's Performing Arts Award for Lifetime Artistic Achievement 2010. *Current Management:* c/o Gilles Paquin, Paquin Entertainment, 2628 5th Street, Suite C, Santa Monica, CA 90405, USA. *Telephone:* (310) 905-9289. *E-mail:* management@paquinentertainment.com. *Website:* www.creative-native.com; buffysainte-marie.com.

SAKAMOTO, Ryûichi, MA; Japanese composer, musician and actor; b. 17 Jan. 1952, Tokyo; m. Akiko Yano 1979. *Education:* Shinjuku High School, Composition Dept, Tokyo Fine Arts Univ. *Career:* began composing at age of ten; mem. group Yellow Magic Orchestra 1978–83; worked with David Sylvian 1982–83; solo recording artist, composer 1982–; conductor, arranger, music for Olympic Games opening ceremony, Barcelona, Spain 1992. *Film appearances:* Merry Christmas Mr Lawrence 1982, The Last Emperor 1987, New Rose Hotel 1998. *Film soundtracks:* Merry Christmas Mr Lawrence (BAFTA Award 1983) 1982, Daijôbu, mai furendo 1983, Koneko monogatari 1986, The Last Emperor (with David Byrne and Cong Su, Academy Award, Golden Globe Award, Grammy Award) 1987, Ôritsu uchûgun Oneamisu no tsubasa 1987, The Laser Man (title song) 1988, The Handmaid's Tale 1990, The Sheltering Sky (Golden Globe Award) 1990, Tacones lejanos 1991, Topâzu 1992, Wuthering Heights 1992, Wild Palms (TV series) 1993, Little Buddha 1993, Rabbit Ears: Peachboy 1993, Wild Side 1995, Snake Eyes 1998, Love is the Devil 1998, Gohatto 1999, Poppoya (theme) 1999, Femme Fatale 2002, Alexei to izumi 2003, Derrida 2003, Los Rubios 2003, Life Is Journey 2003, Appurushîdo 2004, Original Child Bomb 2004, Hoshi ni natta shonen 2005, Zarin 2005, Tony Takitani 2007, Silk 2007. *Recordings include:* albums: Thousand Knives 1978, B-2 Unit 1980, Hidariudeno (A Dream Of The Left Arm) 1981, Coda 1983, Ongaku Zukan (A Picture Book Of Music) 1984, Illustrated Musical Encyclopedia 1984, Esperanto 1985, Miraiha Yarô (A Futurist Chap) 1986, Media Bahn Live 1986, Oneamisno Tsubasa (The Wings Of Oneamis) 1986, Neo Geo 1987, Playing The Orchestra 1988, Tokyo Joe 1988, Sakamoto Plays Sakamoto 1989, Grupo Musicale 1989, Beauty 1989, Heartbeat 1991, Neo Geo (with Iggy Pop) 1992, Sweet Revenge 1994, Soundbites 1994, Hard To Get 1995, 1996 1996, Music For Yohji Yamamoto 1997, Smoochy 1997, Discord 1998, Love Is The Devil 1998, Raw Life 1999, Intimate 1999, Space 1999, BTTB 1999, Gohatto 1999, Complete Index of Gut 1999, Cinemage 2000, Casa 2002; singles: Bamboo Houses (with David Sylvian) 1982, Forbidden Colours (with David Sylvian) 1983, Field Work (with Thomas Dolby) 1986, Risky 1988, We Love You 1991, Moving On 1994, Prayer/Salvation 1998, Anger 1998, O Grande Amor 2001, World Citizen 2003, Sala Santa Cecillia 2005, Revep 2006, Koko 2008, Nord 2009, Three 2013. *Honours:* Order of the Cavaleiro Admissão (Brazil), Ordre des Arts et des Lettres 2009; UN Environment Programme's Echo Award, Golden Pine Award for Lifetime Achievement, Int. Samobor Film Music Festival 2013. *Current Management:* David Rubinson Management, PO Box 411197, San Francisco, CA 94141, USA. *Website:* www.sitesakamoto.com.

SALAH, Baba; Malian musician (guitar); b. 23 March 1974, Gao; s. of Salah Baba and Niamoyé Touré; m. Alimatou Cissé. *Education:* Institut National des Arts. *Career:* plays with Oumou Sangare; numerous live performances, including Festival in the Desert 2003. *Recordings include:* albums: Gao, Borey; contrib. to album Le Festival au désert 2003. *Website:* studiomali.com.

SALEHI, Payam; Iranian singer, songwriter and musician (guitar, santour); b. 1975, Tehran; divorced; one d. *Education:* Azad Univ., Shahriar (veterinary surgery). *Career:* veterinary surgeon; Founder-mem. The Arian Band (the first officially sanctioned mixed-gender pop band in Iran); Man.-Dir of Co. 'Seven'. *Recordings include:* albums: Sunflower, And But Love!, Till Eternity,

Without You With You 2008. *Current Management:* c/o Mr Mohsen Rajabpour, Taraneh Shargheh Cultural & Artistic Co., Apt No. 26, Seventh Floor, Suite 22, Second Alley, Shahnazari Street, Mohseni Square, Mirdamad Avenue, Tehran 1547914415, Iran. *Telephone:* (21) 22223513. *Fax:* (21) 22223670. *E-mail:* president@taranehsh.com. *Website:* www.taranehsh.com; www .payam-salehi.com.

SALIM, Abdel Gadir; Sudanese singer, musician (oud) and teacher; b. Kordofan Province. *Education:* Inst. for Music and Drama. *Career:* Headmaster in Chad; regular nat. TV and radio appearances popularizing traditional folk music. *Recordings include:* The Sounds of Sudan (with Abdel Aziz el Mubarak and Mohammed Gubara) 1991, Blues in Khartoum 1999, Ceasefire (with Emmanuel Jal) 2005, The Nile: Song of the Rivers 2012.

SALINAS, Luis; Argentine jazz guitarist. *Career:* guitarist for Egle Martin 1985–91; performed on tour with Anders Person 1993; solo recording career 1995–; also performed with Adolfo Abalos, Horacio Salgan, Jaime Torres, Maria Graña. *Recordings:* albums: with Egle Martin: El Atre del Encuentro 1991; solo: Aire de Tango 1995, Salinas 1997, Solo Guitarra 2001, Ahi Va 2003, Musica Argentina 2003, Luis Salinas y Amigos en Espana 2005, Muchas Cosas 2006, En Vivo 2009, Sin Tiempo 2010; other appearances: Corazon Libre, Mercedes Sosa 2005, Rio de Los Canasteros, Diego Amador 2008. *E-mail:* info@salinasluis.com.ar. *Website:* www.salinasluis.com.ar.

SALISBURY, Peter; British musician (drums); b. 24 Sept. 1971, Bath, Avon, England. *Career:* Founder-mem. Verve, later renamed The Verve 1989–99, 2007–09; numerous festival appearances; played drums on Alone With Everybody, Richard Ashcroft 2000, The Charlatans UK tour 2010. *Recordings include:* albums: A Storm in Heaven 1993, No Come Down 1994, A Northern Soul 1995, Urban Hymns (BRIT Award for Best British Album 1998, Q Award for Classic Album 2007) 1997, Forth 2008. *Honours:* BRIT Award for Best British Group 1998. *Current Management:* c/o Big Life Management, 67–69 Chalton Street, London, NW1 1HY, England. *Telephone:* (20) 7554-2100. *Fax:* (20) 7554-2154. *Website:* www.biglifemanagement.com.

SALLEY, Jerry; American singer, songwriter and producer; b. Chillicothe, Ohio; m.; three d. *Career:* regular performer, Nashville Showcase Circuit 1982–; appearances, Grand Ole Opry; regular TV appearances; staff writer, Warner Chappell; instructor, music business, Belmont Univ.; backing vocals on Love Letters (Leslie Satcher) 2000; mem. Gospel Music Asscn, Country Music Asscn, Nashville Songwriters Asscn, SESAC. *Compositions include:* I Fell In The Water, John Anderson; Breakin' New Ground, Wild Rose; His Strength is Perfect, Real Life Conversations, Stephen Curtis Chapman; Tracy Byrd; Roger Brown and Swing City; Songs for: Patty Loveless; The Hutchins; Woody Lee; Rhonda Vincent. *Recordings include:* albums: Tell Everyone You Know, Country, Take this Road, Lonesome Cafe, Against the Grain, Livin', Lovin', Losin', New Songs, Old Friends, Showing My Age. *Honours:* Dove Award (for His Strength is Perfect) 1990, four SESAC Nat. Performance Activity Awards. *Current Management:* 1110 17th Avenue South, Suite 2, Nashville, TN 37212, USA. *Telephone:* (615) 345-9461. *Fax:* (615) 751-9978. *E-mail:* tom@rutledgeentertainment.com. *Website:* www .rutledgeentertainment.com. *E-mail:* jerrysalley@comcast.net (office). *Website:* www.jerrysalley.com.

SALMINEN, Teemu Tapio; Finnish musician (saxophones, clarinet, flutes); *Principal Tenor Saxophone, UMO Jazz Orchestra;* b. 5 June 1953, Helsinki; m. Eija Salminen. *Education:* Sibelius Acad. *Career:* has played in UMO Jazz Orchestra 1976–; played in several small groups, including Teemu Salminen Quartet, Septet, Jukka Linkolas Octet, Quintet, Quartet, Jarmo Savolainen Nonet, Edward Vesala Group, Jukkis Uotila Quartet; teacher of music educ. in Jazz Dept, Sibelius Acad.; mem. Musicians' Union, Flute Players Asscn, Jazz Players Asscn. *Compositions:* Mystery, Yes, Please, Gaudi, Minguish, Fryyginen. *Recordings include:* 32 albums with The UMO Jazz Orchestra, including Selected Standards, Day Dreamin, Lady in Green, Green and Yellow, Electrifying Miles, Linkola's Orchestral Works 1997. *Address:* Tollinpolku 1B 20, 00410 Helsinki, Finland.

SALT; American rap artist, songwriter and producer; b. (Cheryl James), 8 March 1964, Brooklyn, New York; one d. *Career:* formed US female rap duo Super Nature with Cheryl James 1985, signed to Next Plateau Records and group re-named Salt-N-Pepa 1986, group joined by DJ 'Spinderella' (Pamela Green, then Latoya Hanson, then Dee Dee Roper); f. Jireh Records 1997. *Recordings include:* albums: Hot Cool & Vicious 1986, A Salt With A Deadly Pepa 1988, Blacks' Magic 1990, A Blitz of Hits: The Hits Remixed 1990, Very Necessary 1993, Brand New 1997, Salt-N-Pepa... The Best Of 2000; singles include: as Super Nature: Showstopper 1985, as Salt-N-Pepa: My Mike Sounds Nice 1987, Push It 1988, Shake Your Thang (It's Your Thing) 1988, Twist and Shout 1988, Expression 1990, Do You Want Me 1991, Let's Talk About Sex 1991, You Showed Me 1991, Let's Talk About AIDS (re-write of Let's Talk About Sex) 1992, Start Me Up 1992, Shoop 1993, Whatta Man (with En Vogue) 1994, Ain't Nothin But A She Thing 1995, Champagne 1996, R U Ready 1997, Gitty Up 1998, Brick Track Vs Gitty Up, Pt I and II 2000. *Honours:* Grammy Award for Best Rap Performance by a Duo or Group (for None Of Your Business) 1994, three MTV Awards 1994.

SALUT, Christian, (Ton Ton Salut), MA; French musician (jazz drummer), composer and instructor; b. 2 Feb. 1953, Montauban; two d. *Education:* Univ. of Toulouse, Drummers' Collective, New York, USA. *Career:* founder, Ton-Ton Quartet 1980–84; Co-founder, Drumpact 1985–95, The Hip Jazz Trio 1993–;

accompanist for soloists including: Sonny Stitt, Georges Coleman, Ted Curson, Philip Harper, Lou Bennett, Glenn Ferris, Frank Lacy, Georges Cables, Jorge Pardo, Steve Turre, Dee Dee Bridgewater, Lucky Peterson and numerous others; currently teacher of jazz history and rhythm, Nat. Conservatory of Toulouse (France). *Play:* 'Peter Pan, Karl Valentin, Boris Vian' by The Théâtre Réel – Théâtre Jules Julien, Toulouse, directed by Luc Montech and Monique Demay. *Compositions include:* Creation for a Double Trio, in festival Jazz sur Son 31 1997, Le Bruissement de la langue (after Roland Barthes with Richard Calleja) 2003–05. *Films:* Expérience africaine de Laurent Chevallier 2009. *Radio:* France Musique, France Culture (French nat. radio), Deutsche Welle. *Television:* Arte, Mezzo, FR3. *Recordings include:* solo: Ali-Aba 1995, Be Hip Be Bop 2001; with Drumpact: Journey into the World 1985, Percussion Unlimited 1988, New Music 1991; with The Hip Jazz Trio: Don't Stop the Carnival 1997, Out of Africa 2010: as musician for other artists: Big Band, Big Band 31 1987, Billie, Big Band 31 1989, Mauresaca, Jazz Time Big Band 1993, In the Path of the Light, Abdu Salim 1994, Samantha's Dance, Steve Mabry 1996, Street Music, Sonny Simmons 1997, Mélodies, Chris Brun 1999, Memoire, Joshua Breakstone 2004, Passages, Judy Blair 2005, B'luz, Juan Martin 2006, In Exile, Abdu Salim 2008, La Paz Congo, Quartier Sud 2008. *Publication:* Methode de rythme pour tous instrumentistes. *Address:* 55 rue Saint-Savournin, 13005 Marseille, France (home). *Telephone:* (4) 91-58-59-76 (office); 6-11-48-55-31 (mobile) (office). *E-mail:* jazzunit@orange.fr (office); salut-tonton@orange.fr. *Website:* www .thejazznetworkworldwide.com/profile/ChristianTonTonSalut.

SALUZZI, Dino; Argentine musician (bandoneon, flute) and composer; b. 20 May 1935, Campo Santo; s. of José María Saluzzi. *Career:* began career in Radio El Mundo Stable Orchestra; later solo artist; several European, US and South American tours with George Gruntz, Mark Egan, Charlie Haden, Palle Mikkelbourg, Bob Moses and Enrico Rava. *Recordings include:* Kultrum 1982, Once Upon a Time–Far Away in the South 1985, Volver 1986, Andina 1988, Argentina 1990, Mojotoro 1991, Rios 1995, Cite de la Musique 1997, Responsorium 2003, Senderos 2005, Juan Condori 2006, Ojos Negros 2007, El Encuentro 2010, Navidad de Los Andes 2011, El Valle De La Infancia 2014. *Address:* San Luis 2421 4A- CP 1056 Buenos Aires Cap. Fed., Argentina. *Telephone:* (11) 4963-3317. *E-mail:* dino@saluzzimusic.com. *Website:* www .saluzzimusic.com.

SALUZZI, José María; Argentine guitarist; b. 1975, s. of Dino Saluzzi. *Education:* studied with Liliana Manzitti, Walter Malsetti, Aníbal Arias. *Career:* mem. Dino Saluzzi Group 1990, also Shades of Light trio; solo collaborations with César Franov, Sebastián Zambrana, Enrique Sinesi, Javier Malosetti, Beto Satragni, Alejandro Franov, Matias Cifuentes, Carlos Rivero, Mariana Baraj, Jaime Torres, Lito Epumer, Walter Rios, Rodolfo Mederos. *Recordings:* albums: with Dino Saluzzi Group: Mojotoro 1991, Juan Condori 2006; with Shades of Light Trio: Shades of Light 2004; other: Cité de la Musique 1996, Responsorium 2003. *E-mail:* jose@saluzzimusic.com (office); josesaluzzi@hotmail.com (office). *Website:* www.saluzzimusic.com.

SAMAHA, Carole, MA; Lebanese singer and actress; b. 1973, Beirut. *Career:* actress, particularly in musical theatre 1995–; solo artist 2003–. *Theatre:* The House of Bernarda Alba (Beirut Theatre) 1995, Al-Mohajer (Al-Medina Theatre, Beirut) 1996, Toukous isharat wal tahawoulat (Lebanon, France, Syria and Jordan) 1997, The Last Days of Socrates (Casino du Liban, Abu Dhabi, Syria and Egypt) 1998, Hiya fi ghiyab al-hob wal maout (Theatre Monot) 1998, Imara min Hal Zaman (Baalbek Festival) 1999, Gardenia (Jordan) 2000, He Rose on the Third Day (Casino du Liban) 2001, Abu Tayyeb al-Mutanabbi (Baalbek Festival, Jordan and Lebanon) 2002, Moulouk al-tawa'ef (Casino du Liban) 2003, Zenobia 2007. *Television appearances:* Talbin el-orb (series) 1999, Noura (drama) 1999, Ismouha La (series) 2000. *Recordings include:* albums: Helm 2003, Ana hura 2004, Adhwaa el-shohra (Arab Music Award for Album of the Year 2006, Cairo Cinema Festival of Art Award for Best Album 2007) 2006, Hdoudi Sama (Best album of the year, Murex d'Or 2010) 2009, Ehssas 2013. *Honours:* Lions Club Murex d'Or for Arab Artist of the Year 2003, Arab Music Award for Female Artist of the Year 2004, Best Lebanese Female Singer, Murex d'Or 2007. *E-mail:* info@carolesamaha.com. *Website:* www.carolesamaha.com.

SAMARASINGHE, Dhanushka; Sri Lankan musician (guitar); s. of Chula Samarasinghe and Suri Samarasinghe. *Education:* Trinity Coll., Kandy. *Career:* Founder mem., rock group Paranoid Earthling 2000–, debut live performance 2001; released several EPs and singles 2005–, including Rock'n'Roll is My Anarchy, Playtime Music 2007, Bringing Down the Sun 2008; live performances in India 2009, Afghanistan 2012. *Recordings include:* several EPs and singles. *E-mail:* manager@paranoidearthling.com (office); manager.paranoidearthling@gmail.com (office). *Website:* www .paranoidearthling.com.

SAMARASINGHE, Shanka; Sri Lankan musician (drums); b. 18 June 1984, s. of Chula Samarasinghe and Suri Samarasinghe. *Education:* Trinity Coll., Kandy. *Career:* Founder mem., rock group Paranoid Earthling 2000–, debut live performance 2001; released several EPs and singles 2005–, including Rock'n'Roll is My Anarchy, Playtime Music 2007, Bringing Down the Sun 2008; live performances in India 2009, Afghanistan 2012. *Recordings include:* several EPs and singles. *E-mail:* manager@paranoidearthling.com (office); manager.paranoidearthling@gmail.com (office). *Website:* www .paranoidearthling.com.

SAMBORA, Richie; American musician (guitar), singer and songwriter; b. 1 July 1959, New Jersey. *Career:* mem. rock band Bon Jovi 1983–88, 1992–2013; simultaneous solo career 1991–; numerous tours, television, radio and live appearances worldwide. *Recordings include:* albums: with Bon Jovi: Bon Jovi 1984, 7800° Fahrenheit 1985, Slippery When Wet 1986, Bon Jovi Live 1987, New Jersey 1988, Keep The Faith 1991, Cross Road 1994, These Days 1995, Crush 2000, One Wild Night 1985–2001 2001, Bounce 2002, Distance 2003, This Left Feels Right 2003, Have A Nice Day 2005, Lost Highway 2007, The Circle 2009, What About Now 2013; solo: Stranger In This Town 1991, Undiscovered Soul 1999, Aftermath of the Lowdown 2012. *Honours:* American Music Awards for Favorite Pop/Rock Band 1988, for Favorite Pop/Rock Single 1991, Nordoff-Robbins Music Therapy Silver Clef 1990, BRIT Award for Best Int. Group (with band) 1995, Billboard Music Award for Top Touring Artist 2014. *Current Management:* Bon Jovi Management, PO Box 237040, New York, NY 10023, USA. *Telephone:* (212) 336-9413. *Fax:* (212) 336-5385. *Website:* www.bonjovi.com.

SAMI KHAN, Adnan; Pakistani singer, composer, musician (piano) and actor; b. 15 Sept. 1973, London, England; s. of Arshad Sami Khan and Naureen Khan; m. 1st Zeba Bakhtiar 1996 (divorced); one c.; m. 2nd Sabah Galadari 2001 (divorced); m. 3rd Roya Faryabi 2010. *Education:* Rugby School, King's Coll., Univ. of London. *Career:* raised in UK; learnt piano and sitar; debut album 1991; debuted as film composer 1994, playback singer for numerous films; collaborations with many artists including Namrata Shirodkar, Raveena Tandon, Rani Mukerji, Govinda, Amitabh Bachchan. *Films:* as composer or playback singer: Sargam (also lead actor and composer) 1995, Ajnabee 2001, Yeh Teraa Ghar Yeh Meraa Ghar 2001, Deewaanapan 2001, Junoon 2002, Ab Ke Baras 2002, Awara Paagal Deewana 2002, Chor Machaaye Shor 2002, Shakti: The Power 2002, Pyaasa 2002, Annarth 2002, Kehtaa Hai Dil Baar Baar 2002, Karz: The Burden of Truth 2002, Saathiya 2002, Love at Times Square (also composer) 2003, Calcutta Mail 2003, Chori Chori 2003, Koi... Mil Gaya 2003, Boys 2003, Joggers' Park 2003, Janasheen 2003, Sssshhh...? 2003, Plan 2004, Tum – A Dangerous Obsession 2004, Muskaan 2004, Yuva 2004, Aayatha Ezhuthu 2004, Chot (Aaj Isko, Kal Tere Ko) 2004, Shankar Dada MBBS 2004, Naach 2004, Aitraaz 2004, Sullan 2004, Sehar 2005, Page 3 2005, Jurm 2005, Lucky: No Time for Love (also composer) 2005, Waqt: The Race Against Time 2005, Koi Mere Dil Mein Hai 2005, Garam Masala 2005, Mahanandi 2005, Makalkku 2005, Rehguzar 2006, Khosla Ka Ghosla 2006, Jaan-E-Mann 2006, Salaam-e-Ishq: A Tribute to Love 2007, Soundarya 2007, Yogi 2007, Aadavari Matalaku Ardhalu Verule 2007, Mumbai Salsa (also composer) 2007, Life in a... Metro 2007, Shankar Dada Zindabad 2007, Darling 2007, Dhamaal (also composer) 2007, Satham Podathey 2007, No Smoking 2007, Taare Zameen Par 2007, Return of Hanuman 2007, Shaurya (also composer) 2008, Dheemaku 2008, Superstar 2008, U Me Aur Hum 2008, Tahaan 2008, Khushboo (also composer) 2008, 1920 (also composer) 2008, Money Hai Toh Honey Hai 2008, Kidnap 2008, Gumnaam – The Mystery 2008, Jayeebhava 2009, Siva Manasula Sakthi 2009, Sulha Mil Gaya 2010, My Name is Khan 2010, Click 2010, Sadiyaan (also composer) 2010, Ek Second... Jo Zindagi Badal De? 2010, Chikku Bukku 2010, 100% Love 2011, Oosaravelli 2011, Ishq 2012, Julayi 2012, Devudu Chesina Manushulu 2012. *Recordings include:* albums: Ecstasy 1990, Raag Time 1991, Sargam 1995, Badaltey Mausam 1997, Always Yours 2000, Kabhi to Nazar Milao (with Asha Bhosle) 2000, Tera Chehra 2002, Kahbi To Nazar Milao 2003, Teri Kasam 2004, Kisi Din 2007, Ek Ladki Deewani Si 2009. *Honours:* Nigar Award, Bolan Academy Award, Graduate Award, UNICEF Award, UN Peace Medal, MTV Breakthrough Artist of the Year 2001, Andhra Pradesh Dept of Culture Naushad Music Award, Hyderabad 2008, UK Asian Music Award for Best Int. Act 2008. *Website:* www.adnansamikhan.com.

SAMINI, Batman; Ghanaian singer; b. (Emmanuel Andrews Samini), 22 Dec. 1981, Wa; s. of G. A Samini and Theresa Nusala. *Career:* musical style is a fusion of African highlife, dancehall reggae and hip hop often called 'raglife' or 'hiplife'; developed talents singing for a local church; appeared as guest vocalist on recordings by numerous artists including Mary Agyapong, Kokoveli; has collaborated with artists including Akon, Beenie Man, Wayne Wonder, Kevin Little; performances in Africa, UK, Italy, Germany, Holland. *Recordings include:* albums: Dankwansere 2002, Samini 2006, Dagaati 2008. *Honours:* Hiplife Artist of the Year and New Hiplife Artist of the Year, Ghana Music Awards, Best African Act, MOBO Awards 2006, Artiste of the Year, Ghana Music Awards 2007, Reggae Artiste of the Year, Golden Jubilee Ghana Music Awards Festival 2007, Best Performer, MTV Africa Music Awards 2009. *Current Management:* c/o List Entertainment, 137 Ogunlana Drive, off Masha Road, Surulere, Lagos, Nigeria. *Telephone:* (1) 8103797. *E-mail:* contact@listentertainmentng.com. *Website:* www.listentertainmentng.com.

SAMKOPF, Kjell, DipMus, BMus; Norwegian composer and musician (percussion); b. 6 April 1952, Baerum; m. 1st Mona Walderhaug 1994 (divorced 2006); two s.; m. 2nd Caroline Ho-Bich-Tuyen Dang 2007. *Education:* Norwegian State Acad. of Music, Berklee Coll. of Music, USA, Inst. for Sonology, Utrecht, Netherlands. *Career:* timpanist, Trondheim Symphony Orchestra 1974–75; freelance percussionist, Norwegian Opera Orchestra and Oslo Philharmonic Orchestra 1975–82; teacher of percussion, East Norway Conservatory 1979–85; Prof. and Head of Percussion Dept, Norwegian State Acad. of Music 1988–2008; mem. Soc. of Norwegian Composers (Vice-Pres. 1988–90), Norwegian Music Information Centre (Pres. Bd 1994–95). *Compositions include:* Associations for large orchestra with live electronics and four-channel tape 1984, Invention No. 5 for solo percussion and electronics 1981, Aqua for tape and two percussionists 1986, Tide for five tapes 1990, Harstad for symphonic band and percussion soloist 1991, Did You Sing This For Grieg? (electroacoustic) 1993, Mårådalen Walk (electroacoustic) 1994, Bergen for woodwind quintet and two percussion players 1996, Concerto for vibraphone and strings 2008, Music for two marimbas, one playing softer than the other 2012, A Book of Études 2014. *Recordings include:* Invention No. 5, On The Way, Because of GH, Intention, solo percussion with electronics, Asphyxy, Positive Frustrations, Waltz Around The Circle, Intention, Blues Extract (with Sandvika Storband), Aqua (with Rob Waring Duo), Did You Sing This For Grieg?, electroacoustic, Self-Portrait, Invention No. 3, solo piece for snare drum, Tokke Kraftverk, Mårådalen Walk, electroacoustic, Mountain Listening 1998, Burragorangian Stones 2011, Study in Playing for the Crows 2014, The Sounds of 60 Things Given to Me 2015. *Publications:* Practical Drum Method vols 1A, 1B, 2 1981, A Workbook for Vibraphone and Marimba Players vols 1 and 2 2013. *Honours:* Concours Int. de Composition de la Ville du Havre, Special Mention of the Jury (for Harstad). *Address:* Sørhågåvegen 37, 2864 Fall, Norway (home). *Telephone:* 97-73-05-32 (home). *E-mail:* kjell@samkopf .no. *Website:* www.samkopf.no.

SAMS, Dean; American country singer, songwriter and musician (keyboards, harmonica); b. 3 Aug. 1966, Garland, TX. *Education:* Southwest Texas State Univ. *Career:* moved to Nashville to pursue a career in country music late 1980s; secured a job at Opryland Theme Park singing in Country Music USA show; owner 16-track recording studio, engineering and producing demos for himself and others; founder mem., Texasee 1992, became resident house band at the Wildhorse Saloon, Nashville, name changed to Lonestar 1995–; simultaneous solo career, as songwriter and with collaborations with other Nashville writers. *Film appearance:* New Horizons 2001. *Recordings include:* albums: Lonestar 1995, Crazy Nights 1997, Lonely Grill 1999, This Christmas Time 2000, I'm Already There 2001, Let's Be Us Again 2004, Coming Home 2005, Mountains 2006, My Christmas List 2007. *Address:* c/o BNA Records, Sony BMG, 1400 18th Avenue, South Nashville, TN 37212, USA (office). *Website:* www.lonestarnow.com.

SAMS, Mark, (Rock Freebase); British musician (guitar). *Career:* mem. Alabama 3, band's music is a fusion of country and gospel music with acid house and techno; band known as A3 in USA. *Recordings include:* with Alabama 3: albums: Exile on Coldharbour Lane 1997, La Peste 2000, Power In The Blood 2002, The Last Train To Mashville 2003, Outlaw 2005, M.O.R. 2007, Revolver Soul 2010, There Will Be Peace in the Valley When We Get the Keys to the Mansion on the Hill 2011, Shoplifting 4 Jesus 2011, The Men From W.O.M.B.L.E 2013. *Website:* www.alabama3.co.uk.

SAMUEL, Julie; British artist manager; b. 15 May 1949, London, England; m. (deceased); one d. *Education:* Italia Conti Stage School. *Career:* began as actress, singer 1962; appeared in numerous TV shows, films and stage plays; started music man. 1980; artist man. for rock group Mexico 70, Sarah Cracknell (vocalist with Saint Etienne), Janey Lee Grace (recording artist, TV presenter, DJ for Virgin Radio), Donna Air, Janey Hoy, Vicky Taylor (vocal act from Byker Grove); Co-founder Loose Cannonz music promotion co. 2006–. *E-mail:* julie@loosecannonz.biz (office). *Website:* www.loosecannonz.biz (office).

SAMUELS, Elaine Mary, BSc (Eng); British singer, songwriter, folk, blues, bluegrass musician (guitar, banjo, cittern, bodhran) and electronic engineer, tutor, band manager, artist and graphic designer and publicist and academic; b. 17 Sept. 1962, Hampton, Middx; d. of Desmond Jones and Doris Jones (née Markham); m. 1st Michael Paul Samuels 1982 (divorced 2000); one s.; m. 2nd Clive Robert Turner 2000. *Education:* St David's School, Ashford, Middx, University Coll., London. *Career:* featured on HTV singing own songs; numerous nat. and int. radio broadcasts and TV appearances; performances at Barbican, Marquee, Weavers, Half Moon, Mean Fiddler; UK tour, including Glastonbury 1995; f. band Kindred Spirit, band leader, front person (singer/ guitar player) and solo performer; f. Songwriter Festivals (first, Windsor Songwriter Festival 2003); mem. Girls With Guitars UK 2003–; mem. Musicians' Union; Scout Leader, canoe instructor, web designer. *Achievements include:* Second Place, Devizes to Westminster canoe race (women's section); first female electronic engineer to go on Challenger and Chieftain tank firing trials, Scotland 1980. *Recordings include:* albums: solo: Obsession, Reach Out For Me, Blue Skies, Dragonfire; with Now and Then: New Country, Best of British Bluegrass, Vol. 1; with Kindred Spirit: Dance Of Life, Origins, Free Spirit, Spirit Rising, The Watchers, Mystic Journey, Metamorphosis, Phoenix Rising. *Publications include:* articles on performing and songwriting in Music Maker magazine, Tradition magazine 2002–. *Honours:* awarded second place in Leicester Live at Y Song Competition, Duke of Edinburgh Gold Award. *Address:* 9 Church Stretton Road, Hounslow, Middx, TW3 2QP, England (home). *Telephone:* (20) 8898-6040 (office). *E-mail:* elaine@ elainesamuels.co.uk. *Website:* www.elainesamuels.co.uk (office).

SANABRIA, Robert (Bobby) Dennis, BM; American Latin jazz percussionist, drummer, composer and record producer; b. 2 June 1957, New York, NY; s. of José Sanabria and Juanita Sanabria. *Education:* Berklee Coll. of Music. *Career:* fmr drummer, Mario Bauza's Afro-Cuban Jazz Orchestra; f. own nonet Ascensión; f. Bobby Sanabria Big Band; numerous collaborations including Francisco Aguabella, Ray Barretto, Paquito D'Rivera, Dizzy Gillespie, Charles McPherson, Chico O'Farrill, Tito Puente, Marco Rizo, Roswell Rudd, Arturo Sandoval, Mongo Santamaria, Henry Threadgill, Yomo Toro; currently teacher of Afro-Cuban Big Band ensemble, Manhattan School of Music and

New School for Jazz and Contemporary Music. *Recordings:* albums: as leader: New York City Ache! 1993, Live and In Clave!!! 2000, Bobby Sanabria & Quarteto Aché! 2002, Big Band Urban Folktales (Jazz Journalists Award for Best Latin Jazz Recording 2008) 2007, Kenya Revisited Live!!! 2009, Tito Puente Master Works Live!!! 2011, Multiverse 2012. *Honours:* Nat. Endowment for the Arts grant 1983, Berklee Coll. of Music Faculty Asscn Award, Latin Jazz USA Outstanding Lifetime Achievement Award 2003, JJA Jazz Award for Percussionist of the Year 2013. *Telephone:* (917) 539-4647. *E-mail:* nujackrican@yahoo.com. *Website:* www.bobbysanabria.com.

SANBORN, David; American musician (alto saxophone); b. 30 July 1945, Tampa, Fla. *Career:* fmr mem. Paul Butterfield group; leading session player with artists including David Bowie, James Taylor, Stevie Wonder, Albert King, Dean Brown, Linda Ronstadt; solo artist 1975–. *Recordings include:* albums: Taking Off 1975, David Sanborn 1976, Promise Me The Moon 1977, Heart To Heart 1978, Hideaway 1980, Voyeur (Grammy Award 1982) 1981, As We Speak 1982, Backstreet 1983, Straight To The Heart 1984, Double Vision (with Bob James) 1986, A Change of Heart 1987, Close Up 1988, Another Hand 1991, Upfront 1992, Hearsay 1994, Pearls 1995, Songs From The Night Before 1996, Inside 1999, Love and Happiness 1999, Camel Island 1999, I Told U So 1999, Inside 1999, Closer 2005, Here and Gone 2008, Only Everything 2010, Original Album Series 2010, Quartette Humaine 2013. *Current Management:* c/o Patrick Rains and Associates, 1543 Seventh Street, Third Floor, Santa Monica, CA 90401, USA. *Telephone:* (212) 860-3233. *Fax:* (212) 860-5556. *E-mail:* pra@prarecords.com. *Website:* www.prarecords.com; www .davidsanborn.com.

SANCHEZ (DeLEON), (José) David; Puerto Rican jazz musician (tenor, soprano saxophones); b. 3 Sept. 1968, Guaynabo. *Education:* La Escuela Libre de Música, San Juan, Rutgers Univ. *Career:* member, Slide Hampton and The Jazzmasters 1993–95; leader, David Sanchez Quintet 1994–99; leader, David Sanchez Sextet 1999–; has played with Dizzy Gillespie and The United Nation Orchestra, Phillip Morris Superband, Eddie Palmieri, Hitton Ruiz, Claudio Roditti, Miriam Makeba, Kenny Barron, Roy Haynes, Charlie Haden, Lalo Schifrin, Tom Harrell, Elvin Jones; mem, AFofM, BMI. *Recordings:* albums: The Departure 1994, Sketches of Dreams 1995, Street Scenes 1996, Obsession 1998, Melaza 2000, Y Sus Corridos Bravos 2001, Travesia 2001, Coral (Latin Grammy Award for Best Instrumental Album 2005) 2004, Cultural Survival 2008. *Current Management:* The AMI Agency, New York, NY 20009, USA. *Telephone:* (212) 260-2921. *Fax:* (212) 260-8920. *E-mail:* info@theamiagency .com. *Website:* www.theamiagency.com. *E-mail:* mkdeleon@gmail.com (office). *Website:* www.davidsanchezmusic.com.

SANCHEZ, Michel; French musician; b. 1 July 1957. *Career:* Founder-mem. Deep Forest (with Éric Mouquet) 1991–; solo artist; collaborations with Abed Azrie, Peter Gabriel, Marcella Lewis, Wes Madiko, Jorge Reyes, Ana Toroja, Joe Zawinul. *Recordings include:* albums: with Deep Forest: World Mix 1994, Bohème (Grammy Award for Best World Music Album, World Music Award for Most Sales in the World) 1996, Comparsa 1998, Madazulu 1997–98, Made in Japan 1999, Pacifique 2000, Music Detected 2002, Essence of Deep Forest 2004; solo: Windows 1995, Welenga 1997, Hieroglyphes 2000, The Touch 2008, The Day of a Paper Bird 2008, Eliott 2012. *Honours:* MTV Award for Best Music Video (for Sweet Lullaby) 1993, Victoires de la Musique Award for Best World Album 1993, 1996, 1995. *E-mail:* contact@deep-forest.fr. *Website:* www .michelsanchez.com.

SANCHEZ, Paco; Spanish musician (drums); b. 7 June 1956, Murcia. *Education:* Univ. of Human Sciences, Paris VII Conservatory. *Career:* played with the International Orchestra of Tchicai John in Denmark and Morocco; played in West Africa, Benin, Festival of Brazzville, Bangui, Trio Soledad, France; mem. SACEM. *Recordings include:* Soledad, with Carlos Acciari and Michel Fernandez 1996, Itinerances 1996, Narvalo, Gypsy Flamenco Music 1998, Danza Fuego, Flamenco Poetry 1998, Adam Del Monte, Heart and Soul: Romantic Dedications 1999. *Honours:* First Excellency Prize.

SANCHEZ, Ildefonso 'Poncho'; American singer; b. 30 Oct. 1951, Laredo, TX; m. Stella Martinez 1973; two s. *Career:* performances with Poncho Sanchez Latin Jazz Band at Klon, Monterey Jazz Festival, Long Beach Jazz Festival, Playboy Jazz Festival, Jazz Central B E T (58); Japanese tour; European tour. *Recordings:* Sonando 1982, Bien Sabroso 1983, El Conguero 1985, Papa Gato 1986, Fuerte 1987, La Familia 1988, Chile con Soul 1989, Cambios 1990, Bailar 1990, El Mejor 1992, Para Todos 1993, Soul Sauce 1995, Conga Blue 1995, Freedom Sound 1997, Afro-Cuban Fantasy 1998, Latin Soul (Grammy Award 2000) 1999, Soul of the Conga 2000, Latin Spirits 2001, Instant Party 2004, Out of Sight! 2004, Do It! 2005, Raise Your Hand 2007, Psychedelic Blues 2009. *Publications:* Concord Jazz Picante. *Current Management:* c/o Jim Cassell, The Berkeley Agency, 2608 Ninth Street, Berkeley, CA 94710, USA. *Telephone:* (510) 843-4902. *Fax:* (510) 843-7271. *E-mail:* mail@berkeleyagency.com. *Website:* www.berkeleyagency.com. *E-mail:* poncho@ponchosanchez.com (office). *Website:* www.ponchosanchez.com.

SÁNCHEZ, Rodrigo; Mexican musician (guitar); b. México. *Career:* played drums in heavy metal band Castlow, met guitarist Gabriela Quintero at Casa de Cultura, México, she joined band, changed band name to Tierra Acida; moved to Dublin, Ireland with Quintero 1999, busked on streets and collaborated with local musicians; travelled and busked in Copenhagen and Barcelona; support act at various Damien Rice concerts, performing as Rodrigo y Gabriela 2003–; musical style fuses elements of Latin American music and rock. *Recordings:* albums: Re-Foc 2003, Live in Manchester and

Dublin 2004, Rodrigo y Gabriela 2006, 11:11 2009. *Current Management:* Niall Muckian, Rubyworks, 6 Park Road, Dun Laoghaire, County Dublin, Ireland. *Telephone:* (1) 2841747. *Fax:* (1) 2841767. *E-mail:* nmuckian@rubyworks.com. *Website:* www.rubyworks.com; www.rodgab.com.

SANCHEZ, Roger, (The S-Man, Roger S, Funk Junkeez, The Neanderthal); American producer, remixer and DJ; b. 1 June 1967, New York, NY. *Career:* began as a New York club DJ; progressed to producing, recording for Strictly Rhythm in New York; founder R-Senal Records, Stealth Records 2002; presents weekly radio show on London radio station Kiss 100 FM; summer DJ residency, Ibiza 2000–; collaborations with Armand Van Helden, Todd Terry, Judy Cheeks, Kathy Sledge, Juliet Roberts, Incognito, Brand New Heavies, Michael Jackson. *Honours:* Grammy Award 2004. *Current Management:* Unmanageable Artists, Krijn Taconiskade 348, 1087 Amsterdam, Netherlands. *Telephone:* (20) 6944097. *Fax:* (20) 4630331. *E-mail:* info@ unmanageableartists.com. *Website:* www.unmanageableartists.com; www .rogersanchez.com.

SANCHEZ DUEÑAS, (Rafael) Fain; Spanish musician (percussion); b. 12 Nov. 1951. *Career:* fmr architect; fmr mem., Ars Antiqua Musicalis; mem., Radio Tarifa 1992–. *Recordings include:* albums: Rumba Argelina 1993, Temporal 1997, Cruzando el Rio 2001, Fiebre 2003. *Current Management:* Sold Out Management, Alcalá 114, 6°B, 28009 Madrid, Spain. *Telephone:* (91) 435-84-78. *Fax:* (91) 431-81-85. *E-mail:* mkt@soldout.es. *Website:* www.soldout .es. *Address:* c/o World Circuit Records, 138 Kingsland Road, London, E2 8DY, England. *Website:* www.radiotarifa.com.

SANDERS, (James) Edward, BA; American poet, writer, singer and lecturer; b. 17 Aug. 1939, Kansas City, Mo.; m. Miriam Kittell 1961; one c. *Education:* New York Univ. *Career:* Ed. and Publisher, Fuck You/A Magazine of the Arts 1962–65; Founder and lead singer, The Fugs, satiric folk-rock-theatre group 1964–69, 1985–; Owner, Peace Eye Bookstore, New York City 1964–70; Visiting Prof. of Language and Literature, Bard Coll., New York 1979, 1983; Founder and Ed., Woodstock Journal; lectures, readings, performances throughout the US and Europe; mem. New York Foundation for the Arts, PEN. *Compositions:* musical drama: The Municipal Power Cantata 1977, The Karen Silkwood Cantata 1979, Star Peace 1986, Cassandra 1992. *Recordings:* albums: with The Fugs: The Village Fugs 1965, The Fugs 1966, Virgin Fugs 1967, Tenderness Junction 1968, It Crawled into my Hand, Honest 1968, Belle of Avenue A 1969, Golden Filth 1970, Refuse to be Burnt Out 1984, No More Slavery 1985, Star Peace 1986, The Fugs Final CD 2003, Be Free 2010; solo: Sanders' Truckstop 1969, Beer Cans on the Moon 1972, Songs in Ancient Greek 1990, American Bard 1996. *Publications include:* poetry: Poem from Jail 1963, Peace Eye 1966, Egyptian Hieroglyphics 1973, 20,000 A.D. 1976, Hymn to Maple Syrup and Other Poems 1985, Poems for Robin 1987, The Ocean Étude and Other Poems 1990, Thirsting for Peace in a Raging Century: Selected Poems 1961–1985 1987, Hymn to the Rebel Cafe: Poems 1987–1991 1993, Cracks of Grace 1994, Chekhov: A Biography in Verse 1995, 1968: A History in Verse 1997, America: A History in Verse, nine vols 2000–, The Poetry and Life of Allen Ginsberg 2000, Stanzas for Social Change 2004, Poems for New Orleans 2007, This Morning's Joy 2008, Revs of the Morrow 2008; fiction: Shards of God: A Novel of the Yippies 1970, Tales of Beatnik Glory, four vols 1975–2003, Fame and Love in New York 1980; non-fiction: The Family: The Story of Charles Manson's Dune Buggy Attack Battalion 1971, Vote! (with Abbie Hoffman and Jerry Rubin) 1972, Investigative Poetry 1976, The Z-D Generation 1980, The Family: The Manson Group and Aftermath 1990. *Honours:* Frank O'Hara Prize, Modern Poetry Asscn 1967, National Endowment for the Arts Awards 1966, 1970, Fellowship 1987–88, Guggenheim Fellowship 1983–84, American Book Award 1988. *Address:* PO Box 729, Woodstock, NY 12498, USA (office). *Telephone:* (845) 679-6556 (office). *Fax:* (845) 679-3290 (office). *E-mail:* info@woodstockjournal .com (office); info@thefugs.com (office). *Website:* www.woodstockjournal.com (office); www.thefugs.com.

SANDERS, Kevin Bruce; British freelance musician (double bass, bass guitar) and arranger; b. 22 May 1962, Torquay; m. 6 June 1987, 1 d. *Education:* college; private classical double bass tuition. *Career:* started with Dennis Rowland Trio; later joined Lawrie Dixon Trio; since worked with: Mornington Lockett; Kathy Stobart; Don Weller; Michael Hashim; Tony Lee; Stan Grieg; worked with Dave Thompson Quartet, 1992–94; lectured in bass studies at Dartington College of Music and contemporary jazz ensemble; mem, Musicians' Union. *Recordings:* Rayas Pictures, 1992. *Honours:* Musicians' Union Award, Most Promising Bass Player, 1984. *Current Management:* Music à la Carte Ent. Services; Bette Holman (For Rhythm Machine). *Address:* 30 Elm Park, Paignton, Devon TQ3 3QH, England.

SANDERS, Tim Bryan; British singer and songwriter; b. 16 April 1962, Stoke-on-Trent, Staffordshire, England; m. Jynine James 1993; three s. *Education:* Cauldon Coll. *Career:* founder mem., City Zones 1979, re-formed 1992; radio and TV appearances; supported many early 1980s artists; mem. PAMRA, PRS, MCPS. *Television:* actor Joy Swift's original Murder Weekends (German satellite TV and BBC) 1990–91. *Compositions:* Don't Stop Me Now (with Muchin/Ainsworth/O'Dowd) 1996. *Recordings:* La Maison De L'Amour, The City Zones 1992, Live At The BBC, The City Zones 1992, Born To Win, Knock Me Down Pick Me Up, Pain of Love, When I Dream, Spoils of Humanity, Past Shadows, Knock Me Down Pick Me Up, Legendary Lonnie 1994, Sexual Affection, Stacy Grant 2001.

SANDISON, Michael; British composer and producer; b. 1 June 1970, Scotland; three c. *Career:* Founder-mem. Boards of Canada 1989–; Remix and production for various artists including Beck, Meat Beat Manifesto, Clouddead, Why?, The Sexual Objects, Boom Bip, Mira Calix, Nevermen and Odd Nosdam; collaboration with dir Chris Cunningham on TV commercials. *Art exhibition:* No More Stars, in collaboration with Polarcap Contemporary Arts Projects, Edinburgh 2007. *Recordings include:* albums: Twoism 1995, Hi Scores 1996, Music Has The Right To Children 1998, BBC Peel Session 1999, In A Beautiful Place Out In The Country 2000, Geogaddi 2002, The Campfire Headphase 2005, Trans Canada Highway 2006, Tomorrow's Harvest 2013. *Current Management:* c/o Hexagon Sun, PO Box 28607, Edinburgh, EH14 7YA, Scotland. *E-mail:* mark@hexagonsun.com. *Address:* Warp Records, Spectrum House, 32–34 Gordon House Road, London, NW5 1LP, England (office). *Website:* www.warp.net (office); www.boardsofcanada .com.

SANDKE, Randy; American composer, arranger and musician (trumpet); b. 23 May 1949, Chicago, Illinois; m. Karen Kelly, 15 Sept. 1990. *Education:* University of Chicago Lab School; Indiana University; Studied TPT with Renold Shilke, Vince Penzerella; Arranging with Oliver Nelson; Composing with Henry Brant and Easley Blackwood. *Career:* TPT with Benny Goodman, 1985–86, with Buck Clayton, 1986–90; Concord Recording Artist, 1993–; Written several suites for Carnegie Hall Jazz Band; Performed on soundtracks of three Woody Allen films; mem, NARAS; IAJRC; Musicians' Union Local 802. *Compositions:* Orphic Mystery, 1997; Overture For the Year 2000, 1997. *Recordings:* NY Stories, 1986; I Hear Music, 1993; Get Happy, 1994; The Chase, 1995; Calling All Cats, 1996; Awakening, 1997; Count Basie Remembered, 1998; Rediscovered Louis And Bix, 2000. *Publications:* Introduction to Metatonal Music, 1997; Bix Beiderbecke From a Musician's Perspective, 1998; Annual Review of Jazz Studies. *E-mail:* randysandke@earthlink.net. *Website:* www.randysandke.com.

SANDOVAL, Arturo; American (b. Cuban) musician (trumpet); b. 6 Nov. 1949, Artemisa, Cuba; m. Marianela Sandoval; one s. *Education:* Nat. School of Art. *Career:* began trumpet playing aged 12 and made first public appearances in Cuba aged 13; played in group with Chucho Váldez until 1981; formed own group, Irakere, in 1981 and now undertakes annual maj. world tour; granted political asylum in USA 1990; currently Prof. of Music, Florida Int. Univ.; opened Arturo Sandoval Jazz Club, Miami Beach 2006; festival appearances at Tokyo, Newport, Montreux, Antibes, Chicago, The Hague and the Hollywood Bowl; several record albums. *Recordings include:* albums: Havana (with David Amram) 1976, New York (with David Amram) 1977, Irakere 1979, To a Finland Station (with Dizzy Gillespie) 1982, Breaking the Sound Barrier 1983, No Problem 1986, Tumbaito 1987, Straight Ahead 1988, Classics 1989, Arturo Sandoval 1989, Flight to Freedom 1991, I Remember Clifford 1992, Danzón 1993, Dream Come True 1993, Passion 1993, Cubano 1994, Arturo Sandoval y el Tren Latino 1995, Double Talk (with Ed Calle) 1996, Swingin' 1996, Just Music 1997, Hot House 1998, Americana 1999, Sunset Harbour (with Ed Calle) 1999, Los Elefantes (with Wynton Marsalis) 1999, For Love or Country 2000, Piedras y Flores (with Amaury Gutiérrez) 2001, L.A. Meetings 2001, My Passion for the Piano 2002, From Havana With Love 2003, Trumpet Evolution 2003, Rumba Palace (Latin Grammy Award for Best Latin Jazz Album 2007) 2007, Arturo Sandoval & the Latin Jazz Orchestra 2007, A Time for Love (Latin Grammy Award for Best Instrumental Album) 2010, Dear Diz (Grammy Award for Best Large Jazz Ensemble Album 2013) 2012. *Honours:* numerous Grammy and Billboard Awards. *Current Management:* Turi's Music Enterprises Inc., 6701 Collins Avenue, Regency No. 1, Miami Beach, FL 33141, USA. *Telephone:* (305) 866-6511. *Fax:* (305) 866-6516. *E-mail:* fanmail@arturosandoval.com. *Website:* www.arturosandoval.com.

SANDREN, Heikki; Finnish musician (drums); b. 1 June 1960. *Education:* clarinet and drums; Sibelius Academy, Helsinki. *Career:* began in music shop, early 1980s; became professional musician; member, Pekka Toivanen quartet; played for Severi Pyysalo's No Hope Band; stayed with Pyysalo's re-formed band The Front; played on tour with leading Finnish trumpeter Markku Johansson. *Website:* www.ebeli.info.

SANDRESKY, Eleonor; American composer, pianist, performance artist and producer; b. 5 Oct. 1957, NC; d. of Clemens Sandresky and Margaret Sandresky. *Education:* North Carolina School of Arts, Wisconsin Conservatory of Music, Eastman School of Music, Yale Univ. School of Music. *Career:* music featured in both narrative and art film, at film festivals world-wide, including Cannes Film Festival; recent collaboration was part of Venice Biennale 2013; grants and commissions from Lower Manhattan Cultural Council, New York State Council on the Arts, Jerome Foundation, ASCAP, American Music Center, Meet the Composer; Composer-in-Residence, Yaddo, STEIM, The MacDowell Colony, among others; recent works include Meditation 2, for choreographed orchestra, The Mary Oliver Songs Book 1: The Return, for choreographed pianist and Wonder Suit, a remote sensor system, with live electronics, and an ongoing series of piano etudes, Strange Energies; latest composition, commissioned by Parthenia, for baroque triple harp and consort of viols, premiered in New York 2015; performs and premieres new works by composers including Don Byron, Philip Glass, Egberto Gismonti; concerts world-wide; initiated a series of collaboration projects that she presented at Spectrum called Rétes: collaboration series 2013; collaborators include Du Yun, Andrew Sterman, Martha Mooke, Pat Irwin, Kevin Norton, Kamala Sankaram, Jim Pugliese, Randy Gibson and Mary Rowell; f. Ensemble 50, a group of composer/performers including Mary Rowell, Kevin Norton, Jim Pugliese and Eleonor Sandresky; has led ensembles in various theatrical settings, from dance performances with Susan Marshall, to conducting live ensemble, to film with Philip Glass Ensemble (mem. 1991–2004); Co-founder MATA Festival with Lisa Bielawa and Philip Glass. *Compositions:* works for large ensemble: before and after for chamber orchestra 1994–2002, Meditation for string orchestra 2003, Meditation 2 for orchestra 2012; choral works: The Fall of America for women's SSAA chorus and violin, with texts by William Blake, additional text by Allen Ginsberg 2003, The Fall of America for mixed SATB chorus, with violin and violoncello, with texts by William Blake, additional text by Allen Ginsberg 2004; vocal works: Someone Comes By, for soprano & piano, text by William Bronk 2003, Manifest; and Furthermore, 12 songs for mezzo soprano and string quartet, text by William Bronk 2004–06, Someone Comes By, arranged for baritone and harp, text by William Bronk 2012; cabaret works: My Goddess, for soprano and chamber ensemble 1998, How Would You Know, for soprano and piano 2000; chamber works: Duo for marimba and piano 1991, Carry Me Down to the River of Grace, for brass quintet 1995, Mathematically Inclined, for percussion quartet 1997, Homage to Egberto, for soprano, soprano saxophone, keyboards and bass 1999, It's Come Undone, for trumpet, percussion and digital effects 1999, Suburban Suite, aka Scenes from Suburbia, for clarinet and piano 2000, Homage to Egberto, arranged for piano four-hands 2001, Suite for string quartet 2000–06, In the Cracks Between, arranged for vibraphone and piano 2013, Numbers for piano and drum set 2013, A Summer Evening, for electric guitar 2013, Conversation 3, for electric guitar and piano 2013, The Donne Songs without Words for 4 viols and triple harp 2014; works for solo piano: Chrysalis, variations for piano solo 1988–92, Regarding Women, for piano solo 1991–92, Homage to Egberto, arranged for solo piano 2001, A Sleeper's Notebook, for solo piano 2000–03, The Mary Oliver Songs Book 1: The Return, for solo piano and Wonder Suit 2012, Strange Energies, a set of etudes for solo piano 2012–14; other solo works: Etude, for solo violin 2003, On the Lip of Insanity, for solo contrabass 2004, Contemplation 1, for electric guitar and pre-recorded track 2007; works for flexible instrumentation: Everybody Keep Calm, for 3 players 2013, Spice Mixes 1–3, for between 2 and 6 players 2013–14, In Short, Db for a minimum of 10 players 2014; works with electronics and Wonder Suit: The Mary Oliver Songs Book 1: The Return, for solo piano and Wonder Suit 2012, Improvisations 1, for solo piano and Wonder Suit, a set of 6 pieces improvised on lines of poetry 2014; film scores: Wunderkammern: The Private Life of Objects, for chamber ensemble 2014. *Recordings:* Les Enfants Terrible, La Belle et le Bête, Complete Works of William Russell, A Sleeper's Notebook, Tell the Birds, Innocence Lost: The Berg-Debussy Project, To Have and to Hold 2007. *Honours:* ASACP Special Awards 1998–2014, grants from Meet the Composer, Jerome Foundation and NYSCA, Most Promising Composer Award, Yale School of Music. *Current Management:* c/o Varsa Publishing. *Telephone:* (718) 284-0648. *E-mail:* varsa@sandresky.com. *E-mail:* eleonor@sandresky.com; info@sandresky.com. *Website:* www.esandresky.com; www.facebook.com/ChoreographicPianist; soundcloud.com/eleonor-sandresky/sets.

SANDS, Colum; Irish singer, songwriter and musician; b. 26 May 1951, Newry; m. Barbara Wendel 1978; three s. one d. *Career:* tours with Sands Family 1972–; also solo artist 1981–; mem. Performing Right Soc., Mechanical-Copyright Protection Soc. *Recordings:* solo albums: Unapproved Road 1981, March Ditch 1989, All My Winding Journeys 1996, The note that Lingers On 2001, Live! In Concert 2007, Look where I've Ended Up Now 2009, The Seedboat (with Maggie MacInnes) 2010, Turn the Corner 2012. *Publication:* Between the Earth and the Sky (song book) 2001. *Honours:* Living Tradition Award, Glasgow 1996. *Address:* Spring Records, 50 Shore Road, Rostrevor, Co. Down, BT34 3AA, Northern Ireland (office). *E-mail:* columsands@live.com (office). *Website:* www.columsands.com.

SANDS, Tommy; Northern Irish singer, songwriter and musician (guitar, whistle, banjo, bodhran); b. (Michael Thomas), 19 Dec. 1945, Mayobridge, Co. Down. *Education:* Newry St Colman's Coll., St Patrick's, Carlow. *Career:* began playing with Sands Family 1968; solo artist; numerous concerts, world tours; mem. Performing Right Soc., Mechanical-Copyright Protection Soc., MIMA. *Recordings include:* solo albums: Singing of the Times 1985, Beyond the Shadows 1992, Down By Bendys Lane 1993, Hedges of County Down 1994, The Hearts A Wonder 1995, To Shorten The Winter 2001, Let the Circle be Wide 2009; 20 albums with the Sands Family. *Publications:* Tommy Sands Song Book 1986, The Songman (autobiog.). *Honours:* Hon. DHumLitt (Nevada) 2005; Best Irish Single of the Year (for There Were Roses) 1986, Living Tradition Award 1995, BBC Folk Song of the Year 2005. *Current Management:* c/o Spring Records, 50 Shore Road, Rostrevor, Co. Down, BT34 3AA, Northern Ireland. *E-mail:* tsands@dnet.co.uk (home); info@tommysands .com (office). *Website:* www.tommysands.com.

SANGALO, Ivete; Brazilian singer and songwriter; b. 27 May 1972, Juazeiro, Bahia. *Career:* associated with both Axé and MPB (Música Popular Brasileira) styles; lead singer with group Banda Eva 1993–98; solo artist 1999–, has had numerous No. 1 singles and sold millions of records in Brazil and worldwide. *Recordings:* albums: with Banda Eva: Autêntico 1993, Pra Abalar 1994, Hora H 1995, Beleza Rara 1996, Banda Eva ao Vivo 1997, Eva, Você e Eu 1998; solo: Ivete Sangalo 1999, Beat Beleza 2000, Festa 2001, Se Eu Não Te Amasse Tanto Assim 2002, Clube Carnavalesco 2003, MTV Ao Vivo 2004, As Super Novas 2005, Novo Millennium 2005, As Melhores 2006, Multishow 2007, A Casa Amarela (for children) 2008, Pode Entrar 2008. *Honours:* Prêmio Dorival

Caimmy 1992, Latin Grammy Award for Best Brazilian Song 2014. *Current Management:* Caco de Telha Produções, Avenida Otávio Magabeira 6000, Aeroclube Plaza Show, 41706–690 Salvador, Brazil. *Telephone:* (71) 3462-9999. *E-mail:* artistas@cacodetelha.com.br. *Website:* www.cacodetelha.com.br; www.ivetesangalo.com.br.

SANGARE, Oumou; Malian singer and songwriter; b. 25 Feb. 1968, Bamako; m. Ousmane Haidara; one c. *Career:* began singing aged five; first performance at Stade des Omnisports aged six; mem. Nat. Ensemble of Mali; mem. Djoliba percussion 1986–89; solo artiste with own backing group 1989–; regular concert tours in W Africa and Europe; first US concert 1994; campaigner for women's rights; apptd Amb. to FAO 2003. *Recordings include:* Moussolou (Women) (Best Selling Album of the Year 1990) 1990, Ko Sira (Marriage Today) (European World Music Album of the Year 1993) 1993, Worotan 1996, Moussolou 1999, Ko Sira 2000, Oumou (compilation) 2003, Seya 2009, Kounadia 2012; appears on African Blues 1998, Beloved 1998; also recordings with Ali Farka Touré, Trilok Gurtu, Herbie Hancock. *Honours:* Performance of the Year 1993, IMO-UNESCO Int. Music Prize 2001, Grammy Award for Best Pop Collaboration with Vocals (with Herbie Hancock) 2011; numerous African Music Awards. *Current Management:* c/o World Circuit Records, First Floor, Shoreditch Stables, 138 Kingsland Road, London, E2 8DY, England. *E-mail:* post@worldcircuit.co.uk. *Website:* www.worldcircuit.co.uk.

SANGIORGI, Giuliano; Italian singer, songwriter and musician (guitar); b. 12 Dec. 1977. *Career:* mem., Negramaro 2002–. *Recordings include:* albums: Negramaro 2003, 000577 2004, Mentre Tutto Scorre 2005, La Finestra 2007. *Honours:* MTV Europe Music Award Best Italian Act 2005. *E-mail:* management@negramaro.com. *E-mail:* band@negramaro.com (office). *Website:* www.negramaro.com.

SANLUCAR, Manolo; Spanish composer and musician (flamenco guitar); b. 24 Nov. 1943, Sanlucar De Barrameda, Cádiz. *Education:* learnt to play guitar with father Isidro Sanlúcar (famous Flamenco guitarist). *Career:* Musical Dir, Sevillanas a Carlos Saura, film; La Gallarda, Rafael Alberti. *Compositions include:* Medea, composed for Ballet Nacional de España 1987, Tauromagia 1988, Solea 1989, Aljibe 1992, Locura De Brisa y Trino 2000, La Voz del Color 2008. *Honours:* Prize Spanish Guitarist, Record World, USA 1978; First Prize, Concurso Mundial de Guitarra, Italy 1972; Premio Nacional de Música for interpretation 2000; Nat.Music Prize, Caja Madrid Flamenco Festival 2001. *Address:* Huerta Iraola, c/ Bahía s/n, 11540 Sanlúcar de Barrameda, Cádiz, Spain (home). *E-mail:* informacion@manolosanlucar.com. *Website:* www.manolosanlucar.com.

SANSOM, Frank Roger Charles; British record company executive; *Managing Director, Amazon Music;* b. 3 Dec. 1946, London; m. Frances Sansom 1976; two s. one d. *Education:* Christopher Wren, Gloucestershire and Wimbledon Coll. of Art; Postgraduate, London Film School; Diploma in Fine Art. *Career:* Art Dir BandC Records 1971; Marketing Dir Charisma Records 1973–78; Man. 1979–81; set up First Bill Ltd (First Independent Tele-Sales Team) 1981, First Strike 1985; sold companies to Stylus Music 1987; TV Marketing Consultant 1987–98; Man. Dir, shareholder, Pulse Records launched 1990–95; Man. Dir Cowboy Records 1993–, Avenue Pictures 1993–, Amazon Records Ltd 2000–05, Amazon Music 2000–, prizeproperty.co.uk Ltd 2004–; mem. BPI. *Address:* Amazon Records, PO Box 5109, Hove, East Sussex, BN52 9EA, England. *Telephone:* (1273) 726414 (office). *Fax:* (1273) 726414 (office). *E-mail:* frank@amazonrecords.co.uk (office). *Website:* www.amazonrecords.co.uk (office).

SANSON, Véronique; French singer and songwriter; b. 24 April 1949, Boulogne, Paris; d. of René Sanson and Colette Sanson; m. 1st Stephen Stills 1973 (divorced 1976); one s.; m. 2nd Pierre Palmade 1995 (divorced 2004). *Career:* began career in group Roche Martin with sister Violaine and François Bernheim; recorded debut solo single Le printemps est là/Le feu du ciel with Michel Berger 1969; Berger became a lifetime collaborator; based in USA 1973–83; toured with Johnny Hallyday, Michel Sardou, Eddy Mitchell, Jean-Jacques Goldman for charity Restos du Coeur 1989; performed series of concerts with Prague Symphony Orchestra, Théâtre du Châtelet, Paris 1989. *Recordings include:* albums: Amoureuse 1972, De l'autre côté de mon rêve 1972, Le maudit 1974, Vancouver 1976, Live at the Olympia 1976, Hollywood 1977, 7ème 1979, Laisse-la vivre 1981, Au Palais des Sports 1981, Véronique Sanson 1985, Olympia 85 1986, Moi le venin 1988, A l'Olympia 89 (Académie Charles Cros award) 1989, Symphonique Sanson 1990, Sans regrets 1992, Zénith 93 1993, Comme ils l'imaginent 1995, Indestructible 1998, D'un papillon à une étoile 1999, Avec vous 2000, Longue distance 2004, Olympia 2005 2005, Petits Moments Choisis 2007, Plusieurs Lunes 2010, Coffret 2013. *Honours:* Ordre national du Mérite 1992, Ordre des Arts et des Lettres 2005; Grand Prix de la SACEM 1991, Best Female Artist, Victoires de la Musique 1992, 1996. *Website:* www.veronique-sanson.net.

SANTA ROSA, Gilberto; Puerto Rican singer and bandleader; b. 21 Aug. 1962, San Juan; m. Alexandra Malagón. *Career:* known as El Caballero de la Salsa; made formal singing debut on TV, aged 13 1975; began professional career as backing singer with Orquesta Mario Ortiz 1976; later performed and recorded with Orquesta La Grande 1976–78, Puerto Rico All Stars 1980, Orquesta Willie Rosario 1981–86; made debut with own salsa orchestra 1986–; solo artist 1990–. *Recordings:* albums: Good Vibrations 1986, Keeping Cool! 1987, De Amor Y Salsa 1988, Salsa....en Movimiento 1988, Punto de Vista 1990, Perspectiva 1991, A Dos Tiempos de Un Tiempo 1992, Nace Aquí 1993,

De Cara Al Viento 1994, Esencia 1996, De Corazón 1997, Salsa Sinfonica en Venezuela 1998, Expresión 1999, Perdóname... Exitos! 2000, Romántico 2001, Intenso 2001, Viceversa 2002, Sólo Bolero 2003, Auténtico 2004, Dos Soneros, Una Historia 2005, Directo Al Corazón 2006, Contraste 2007, Contraste en Salsa 2008, Una Navidad con Gilberto 2008, El Caballero de la Salsa Historia Tropical 2009, Irrepetible (Latin Grammy Award for Best Salsa Album) 2010, Gilberto Santa Rosa 2012, Necesito Un Bolero (Latin Grammy Award for Best Traditional Pop Vocal Album 2015) 2014. *Honours:* Billboard Lo Nuesto Award for Best Male Singer 1990. *Current Management:* Miredys Santa Rosa, Producciones PMC, Inc., Avenue Ashford 1450, Apartado 2A, San Juan, Puerto Rico. *Telephone:* (787) 723-5183. *Fax:* (787) 723-7344. *E-mail:* miredys@gilbertosantarosa.com. *Website:* www.gilbertosantarosa.com.

SANTANA, Carlos; Mexican musician; b. 20 July 1947, Autlán de Navarro; s. of José Santana; m. Cindy Blackman 2010. *Career:* played Tijuana night clubs; debut with the Santana Blues Band 1966, played at Woodstock Festival Aug. 1969; guitarist, Santana Man. 1987–; Prin. Guts and Grace Records 1993; performed with Mike Bloomfield, Al Kooper, Buddy Miles, McCoy Turner, Jose Feliciano, Herbie Hancock, Wayne Shorter, Alice Coltrane, Aretha Franklin, Mahavishnu, John McLaughlin; co-founder Milagro Foundation supporting young people in the arts, health and education 1998. *Films:* Viva Santana 1988, Sacred Fire 1993, A History of Santana: The River Of Color And Sound 1997, A Supernatural Evening With Santana 2000. *Recordings include:* albums: Santana 1969, Abraxas 1970, Santana III 1971, Greatest Hits 1974, Moonflower 1977, Inner Secrets 1978, Zebop! 1981, Shango 1982, Freedom 1987, Freedom 1987, Viva Santana 1988, Milagro 1992, Sacred Fire 1993, Dance Of The Rainbow Serpent 1995, Live At The Fillmore 1997, Best of Santana 1998, Supernatural 1999, All That I Am 2005, Guitar Heaven: The Greatest Guitar Classics of All Time 2010, Shape Shifter 2012, Corazón 2014. *Honours:* Santana Band first to earn CBS Records' Crystal Globe Award, multiple Best Pop-Rock Guitarist in Playboy Magazine's Readers' Poll, Grammy for Best Rock Instrumental Performance 1988, Nosotros Golden Eagle Legend Award 1992, Recording Acad. (NARAS) tribute concert and induction into Hollywood Rock Walk, Billboard Magazine Century Award 1996, ten Bay Area Music Awards, BAMMY Hall of Fame, Chicano Music Awards Latino Music Legend of the Year 1997, Rock 'n' Roll Hall of Fame, Hollywood Walk of Fame 1998, also won nine Grammys Feb. 2000, Latin Recording Acad. Person of the Year 2004; numerous civic and humanitarian commendations. *Address:* Santana Management, PO Box 10348, San Rafael, CA 94912, USA (office). *E-mail:* info@jensencom.com. *Website:* www.santana.com (office).

SANTAOLALLA, Gustavo; Argentine musician, producer and composer; b. 19 Aug. 1951, El Palomar, Buenos Aires. *Career:* mem. Arco Iris 1967–75; Founder-mem. Soluna 1976; moved to Calif., USA 1978, formed group Wet Picnic; producer for Argentine and Latin American rock artists, including Leon Gieco, Fobia, Molotov, Café Tacvba, Julieta Venegas, Juanes, Maldita Vecindad y Los Hijos del Quinto Patio; formed label, Surco, signed and produced artists, including Bersuit, Erica García, Arbol, La Vela Puerca; also recorded as a solo artist; also worked with Gaby Kerpel, the Kronos Quartet, Bajofondo Tango Club; film music composer 1999–. *Film soundtracks:* She Dances Alone 1981, The Insider 1999, Amores Perros 2000, 11'09"01: September 11 (Mexico segment) 2002, 21 Grams 2003, Rendezvous 2004, The Motorcycle Diaries (BAFTA Award) 2004, Brokeback Mountain (Acad. Award for Original Score 2006, Golden Globe Award for Best Original Song 2006) 2005, North Country 2005, Babel (BAFTA Award for Achievement in Film Music 2007, Acad. Award for Best Original Score 2007) 2006, Linha de passe 2008, Into the Wild 2007, I Come With The Rain 2009, Nanga Parbat 2010, Dhobi Ghaat 2010, On the Road 2012, August: Osage County 2013, The Book of Life 2014, Wild Tales 2014. *Recordings include:* albums: Energia Natural (with Soluna) 1977, Santaolalla (solo) 1982, Gas (solo) 1995, Ronroco (solo) 1998. *Current Management:* c/o First Artists Management, 4764 Park Granda, Suite 210, Calabasas, CA 91302, USA. *Telephone:* (818) 377-7750. *Fax:* (818) 377-7760. *E-mail:* fam-info@firstartistsmgmt.com. *Website:* www.firstartistsmgmt.com.

SANTIAGO, Joey; American musician (guitar); b. 10 June 1965, Manila, Philippines; m. Linda Mallari. *Career:* formed the Pixies with Frank Black 1986–93, 2004–; recorded demo, The Purple Tape 1987; worked with Frank Black on his solo material; formed the Martinis with David Lovering 1995–; composer of film soundtracks and incidental music. *Compositions:* Crime and Punishment in Suburbia (film) 2000, Undeclared (TV series) 2001, The Low Budget Time Machine (film) 2003. *Recordings:* albums with the Pixies: Come On Pilgrim (EP) 1987, Surfer Rosa 1988, Doolittle 1989, Bossanova 1990, Trompe Le Monde 1991, Death To The Pixies 1987–1991 1997, Live At The BBC 1998, Complete B-Sides 2001, Pixies (DVD) 2004, Wave of Mutilation: The Best of the Pixies 2004, Indie Cindy 2014; with The Martinis: Smitten 2004. *Current Management:* Richard Jones, Key Music Management Limited, 56A Bramhall Lane South, Bramhall, Stockport, SK7 1AH, England. *Telephone:* (161) 440-0670. *E-mail:* contact@keymusicmanagement.com. *Website:* www.keymusicmanagement.com; www.pixiesmusic.com.

SANTORO DE SOUSA LIMA, Paula; Brazilian singer; b. Belo Horizonte. *Education:* Universidade Federal de Minas Gerais, studied singing, violin at Fundação de Educação Artística. *Career:* mem. Nós e Voz 1988–90, later with Sagrado Coração da Terra –1993; solo artist 1995–. *Recordings:* albums: with Nós e Voz: Hum 1991; with Sagrado Coração da Terra: Farol da Liberdade 1991; solo: Santo 1996, Sabiá 2004, Paula Santoro 2005, Casa de Vila (with

Guinga) 2007. *Telephone:* (21) 2225-5197 (office). *E-mail:* paulasantoro@paulosantoro.com.br (office); paulasantoro@terra.com.br (office). *Website:* www.paulasantoro.com.br.

SANTOS, Lenny; American musician (guitar) and producer; b. 24 Oct. 1979, Bronx, New York. *Education:* South Bronx High School. *Career:* mem. Aventura, a Dominican Bachata music group 1996–2010; co-f. (with brother Max Santos) bachata group D'Element 2011; co-f. (with Max Santos and Steve Styles) bachata group Vena 2013; as a producer, worked with Optima, Huellas de Tiempo. *Recordings include:* albums: Generation Next 1999, We Broke the Rules 2002, Love and Hate 2003, God's Project 2005, The Last 2009. *Honours:* Billboard Award for Song of the Year (for Mi Corazoncito) 2008, American Music Award for Best Latin Music Artist 2009. *Website:* www.itsvena.com.

SANTOS, Max; American musician (bass) and rapper; b. 30 Jan. 1982, Bronx, New York. *Education:* South Bronx High School. *Career:* began playing bass, aged 12; mem. (with brother Lenny Santos) Dominican bachata music group Aventura 1996–2010; co-f. (with Lenny Santos) bachata music group D'Element 2011; co-f. (with Lenny Santos and Steve Styles) bachata music group Vena 2013; also solo rapper. *Recordings include:* albums: Generation Next 1999, We Broke the Rules 2002, Love and Hate 2003, God's Project 2005, The Last 2009. *Honours:* Billboard Award for Song of the Year (for Mi Corazoncito) 2008, American Music Award for Best Latin Music Artist 2009. *Website:* www.itsvena.com.

SANTOS, Romeo; American singer, songwriter and actor; b. (Anthony Santos), 21 June 1981, Bronx, New York. *Education:* South Bronx High School. *Career:* as a child, sang in church choir; founding mem. and lead singer, Aventura 1994–2011 (Dominican Bachata music group); solo career 2011–; has written music for Wisin y Yandel, Thalia and El Torito; many solo collaborators including Enrique Iglesias, Drake, Nicki Minaj. *Recordings:* albums: with Aventura: Generation Next 1999, We Broke the Rules 2002, Love and Hate 2003, God's Project 2005, The Last 2009; solo: Formula Vol. 1 (Premios Juventud Lo Toco Todo Award 2012, Billboard Music Award for Top Latin Album 2012, Billboard Latin Music Awards for Album of the Year 2013, for Digital Album of the Year 2013) 2011, The King Stays King: Sold Out at Madison Square Garden (Billboard Latin Music Award for Tropical Album of the Year 2013) 2012, Formula Vol. 2 2015. *Honours:* numerous including: with Aventura: ASCAP Award for Tropical Music (for Obsesion) 2006, Billboard Music Awards for Composer of the Year 2007, for Song of the Year (for Mi Corazoncito) 2008, American Music Award for Best Latin Music Artist 2009; solo: Premios Juventud Perfect Combination Award (for Promise) 2012, MTV Video Music Award for Best Latino Artist 2012, Billboard Music Award for Top Latin Artist 2015. *Website:* www.romeosantosofficial.com/us/home.

SANTOS JETER, Henry; American singer, songwriter and producer; b. 15 Sept. 1979, Moca, Dominican Repub. *Education:* South Bronx High School. *Career:* moved to New York, aged 14; mem. Aventura 1996–, a Dominican Bachata music group; as producer, worked with Los Robacorazones. *Films include:* Sanky Panky, La Soga. *Recordings include:* albums: Generation Next 1999, We Broke the Rules 2002, Love and Hate 2003, God's Project 2005, The Last 2009; solo: Henry Santos' My Way 2013. *Honours:* Billboard Award for Song of the Year (for Mi Corazoncito) 2008, American Music Award for Best Latin Music Artist 2009. *E-mail:* johnnymarines@gmail.com. *Website:* www.henrysantos.com.

SANZ, Alejandro; Spanish singer and songwriter; b. 18 Dec. 1968, Madrid; m. Raquel Perera 2012. *Career:* solo artist. *Recordings include:* albums: Viviendo Deprisa 1991, Si Tú Me Miras 1992, 3 1995, Más 1997, Básico 1998, El Alma Al Aire 2000, MTV Unplugged (Latin Grammy Award for Album of the Year 2002) 2001, El Concierto Tour Mas 98 2002, Canta Como 2002, No Es Lo Mismo (Latin Grammy Awards for Album of the Year, for Best Pop Male Album 2004) 2003, El Tren de los Momentos (Grammy Award for Best Latin Pop Album 2008) 2006, Paraíso Express (Latin Grammy Award for Best Male Pop Vocal Album 2010, Grammy Award for Best Latin Pop Album 2011) 2009, La Música No Se Toca (Latin Grammy Award for Best Contemporary Pop Vocal Album 2013) 2012, Sirope. *Honours:* Dr hc (Berklee Coll. of Music) 2013; Amigo Award for Best Nat. Male Artist 1997, Special Tribute 1998, Ondas Awards for Best Nat. Artist 1997, for Best Song (for Corazón Partío) 1998, World Music Award for Best Selling Spanish Artist 1999, Premio Gardel de la Música for Best Male Artist, for Album of the Year 2002, Latin Grammy Awards for Record of the Year (for Y Solo Se Me Ocurre Amarte), for Song of the Year (for Y Solo Se Me Ocurre Amarte) 2002, for Best Song, for Best Record 2004, Latin Grammy Awards for Song of the Year, for Record of the Year 2005. *Address:* Warner Music Spain, Calle Lopez de Hoyos 42, Madrid, Spain (office). *Telephone:* (91) 7454200 (office). *E-mail:* info.esp@warnermusic.com (office). *Website:* www.warnermusic.es (office); www.alejandrosanz.com.

SAPUNDZIJEV, Mary, BA, PhD; Australian musicologist, composer, songwriter and librettist; b. 1965, Melbourne, Vic. *Education:* Monash Univ. *Career:* Artistic Dir, folk dance co. 1984–92; film appearance, The John Sullivan Story 1979; Production Asst, ethnic radio, Victoria; dancer and co-organizer, cultural festivals throughout Australia. *Publications:* Politics in Music – Music of Politics: The Choral Miniature Repertoire of First Generation Macedonian Composers (PhD dissertation); Motivation, Function and Value (article in IRASM) 2002. *Honours:* shared Ernst Morawetz Prize for Music, Monash Univ. 1987, Australian Postgraduate Research Award 1988–91. *Fax:* (3) 9877-3810 (home).

SARDUY, Carlos; Cuban musician (trumpet, congas); b. Havana. *Education:* Amadeo Roldán Music School. *Career:* fmr trumpet player with groups Rumbatere and Interactivo; released solo album 2005; joined Ojos de Brujo as conga player 2005, a group which fuses gypsy and flamenco music with Latin American, punk, hip hop, reggae and electronic influences; concerts worldwide; collaborations with Nitin Sawhney, Asian Dub Foundation. *Recordings include:* albums: solo: Charly En La Habana 2005; with Ojos de Brujo: Techarí 2006, Aocaná 2009. *Honours:* winner, several Jojazz contests, Havana.

SARGAM, Sadhana; Indian playback singer; b. (Sadhana Ghanekar), d. of Purshotam Ghanekar and Neelatai Ghanekar. *Career:* trained in Indian classical music by mother Neelatai Ghanekar, then by Pandit Jasraj; released debut single 1982 (for film Vidhaata); sings in 27 languages (including Hindi, Tamil, Kannada, Telugu, Malayalam); playback singer for numerous films in Hindi and Tamil film industry. *Films:* singing contributor to numerous titles including: Hindi: Janbaaz 1986, Khoon Bhari Maang 1988, Tridev 1989, Dil 1990, Jurm 1990, Kishen Kanhaiya 1990, Jo Jeeta Wohi Sikandar 1992, Deewana 1992, Dil Ka Kya Kasoor 1992, Phir Teri Kahani Yaad Aayee 1993, Mohra 1994, Vijaypath 1994, Barsaat 1995, Karan Arjun 1995, Tere Mere Sapne 1996, Hero No. 1 1997, Hameshaa 1997, Gupt 1997, Sapnay 1997, Dahek 1998, Jeans 1998, Doli Saja Ke Rakhna 1998, 1947 Earth 1998, Saathiya 2002, Kehtaa Hai Dil Baar Baar 2002, 16 December 2002, Warriors of Heaven and Earth 2003, Tujhe Meri Kasam 2003, Kuch Naa Kaho 2003, Kal Ho Naa Ho 2004, Maqbool 2004, Kyun! Ho Gaya Na... 2004, Hum Tum 2004, Swades 2004, Water 2005, Jaan-E-Mann 2006, Salaam-e-Ishq 2007, Black & White 2008, Mukhbiir 2008, Damadamm! 2011; South: Coimbatore Mappillai 1996, Minsara Kanavu 1997, Ratchagan 1997, Naam Iruvar Namakku Iruvar 1998, Poovellam Kettuppar 1999, Alaipayuthey 2000, Kandukondain Kandukondain 2000, Kushi 2000, Rhythm 2000, Thenali 2000, Hoo Antheeya Uhoo Antheeya 2000, Alli Arjuna 2001, Azhagi 2001, Citizen 2001, Dumm Dumm Dumm 2001, Manadhai Thirudivittai 2001, Paarthale Paravasam 2001, Poovellam Un Vasam 2001, Samudhiram 2001, Star 2001, Thavasi 2001, Virumbugiren 2001, Anbe Sivam 2002, Holi 2002, Yuvarathna 2002, April Maadhathil 2002, Album 2002, Baba 2002, Bagavathi 2002, En Mana Vaanil 2002, Gemini 2002, Ramanaa 2002, Roja Kootam 2002, Run 2002, Villain 2002, Anbe Anbe 2003, Anbu 2003, Boys 2003, Dum 2003, Ninuchoodaka Nenundalenu 2003, Manasellam 2003, Parasuram 2003, Priyamana Thozhi 2003, Thithikudhe 2003, Madhurey 2004, Manmadhan 2004, New 2004, News 2004, Vasool Raja MBBS 2004, Anbe Aaruyire 2005, Ayya 2005, Ponniyin Selvan 2005, Bambara Kannaley 2005, Muddula Koduku 2005, Daas 2005, Sankranthi 2005, February 14 2005, Kalvannin Kaadhali 2005, Kanda Naal Mudhal 2005, Majaa 2005, Oru Naal Oru Kanavu 2005, Aadhi 2006, Manathodu Mazhaikalam 2006, Thiruttu Payale 2006, Varalaru 2006, Stalin 2006, Aalwar 2007, Koodal Nagar 2007, Ninaithu Ninaithu Paarthen 2007, Munna 2007, Kireedam 2007, Anumanaspadam 2007, Ee Bandhana 2007, Nenjaithodu 2007, Pirivom Santhippom 2008, Dasavathaaram 2008, Kuselan 2008, Maska 2008, Sathyam 2008, Jayamkondaan 2008, Abhiyum Naanum 2008, Naan Kadavul 2009, Konchem Ishtam Konchem Kashtam 2009, Savari 2009, Baana Kaathadi 2010, Enthiran 2010, Mynaa 2010, Shambo Shiva Shambo 2010, Neneyuve Ninna 2010, Ayyan 2011, Bombay March 12 2011, Oru Nuna Kadha 2011, Prema Kaidhi 2011, Rowthiram 2011, Naaku O Loverundi 2011, Parie 2011, Udumban 2012. *Recordings:* numerous albums including: Vaada, Oh My Love, Kabhi Aasoon Kabhi Khushboo Kabhi Nagma. *Honours:* National Film Award for Best Female Playback Singer (for Paattu Cholli from film Azhagi) 2002, Star Screen Award for Best Female Playback (for Chupke Se from film Saathiya) 2003, Zee Cine Award for Best Playback Singer – Female (for Kuch Naa Kaho from film Kuch Naa Kaho) 2004, Filmfare Awards South for Best Female Playback Singer (Tamil) (for Akkam Pakkam from film Kireedom) 2007, for Best Female Playback Singer (Telugu) (for Manasa from film Munna) 2007. *Current Management:* c/o Lakshman Sruthi, 72 2nd Avenue, Off 100 Feet Road, Ashok Nagar, Chennai, 600 083, India. *Telephone:* 7299110101. *E-mail:* info@lakshmansruthi.com. *Website:* www.lakshmansruthi.com.

SARIC, Stanko; Croatian musician (tambura); b. 26 June 1960, Stitar; m. Verca Saric (Salopek) 1984; one s. one d. *Career:* appearances with group Zlatni Dukati (Golden Coins) in biggest concert halls in Croatia; tours to USA, Canada, Australia, Western Europe; mem., Croatian Musicians' Union. *Recordings include:* albums: Nek zvone tambure 1988, Hrvatska pjesmarica 1989, Pjevaj kad dusa boli 1989, Dao bih zlatne dukate 1990, Hrvatska domovina 1990, Klasika 1991, U meni Hrvatska 1991, 16 zlatnih hitova 1992, Da su meni krila laka 1993, Sretan Bozic 1993, Od dvora do dvora 1994, Satrogradska pjesmarica 1994, Vranac 1996, Nek me pamte gradovi 1998, Sedam dana 2001, Divne godine 2003, Tamburica od javora suva 2004, Sretan Bozic 2005, Nostalgija 2007, Zlatna kolekcija 2007, Slavonijo, biseru Hrvatske 2010. *Honours:* 10 Golden discs, many other awards. *E-mail:* stanko.saric@zg.t-com.hr. *Website:* www.najboljihrvatskitamburasi.com.

SARİGÜL, Yağmur; Turkish musician (electric guitar), songwriter and producer; b. 26 Aug. 1979, Antalya. *Education:* Hacettepe Univ. State Conservatory, Bilkent Univ. Stage Arts Faculty, Ankara Anadolu Fine Arts High School, Gazi Univ. *Career:* played with bands including Laterna and 6/8; f. and mem., alternative rock band maNga 2002–; concerts, festivals include Sziget Festival, Mannheim Turkish Rock Festival, also London. *Recordings:* albums: maNga 2004, Şehr-i Hüzün 2009. *Honours:* MTV Europe Music Award for Best European Act 2009. *Current Management:* c/o Hadi Elazzi, GRGDN, Mübayacı sok. 5, Rumelihisarı, 34470 İstanbul, Turkey. *Telephone:*

(212) 2876287. *Fax:* (212) 2876216. *E-mail:* manga@grgdn.com. *Website:* www .grgdn.com. *Address:* c/o Sony Music Entertainment, Sony Music Türkiye, Ticaret A.Ş. Oteller Sokak 1/5, Tepebaşı, 34430 İstanbul, Turkey (office). *Website:* manga.web.tr.

SARJEANT, Derek; folk singer and musician (concertina, guitar, trumpet); b. 7 June 1930, Chatham, Kent, England; m. 1st Diane Doherty 1966; two s.; m. 2nd Hazel King 1977 (died 2003); one s. one d. *Education:* Kingston Coll. *Career:* mem. of jazz bands; leader, Golden Gate Jazzmen 1950s; part of British Folk revival 1960s; organizer of one of Britain's largest Folk clubs, Surbiton and Kingston for 14 years; assisted with organization of English Folk Dance and Songs Soc. first Folk Festival 1965; radio and television broadcasts; tours solo, also with wife, Hazel of folk clubs, concerts, festivals in UK, Europe, America; work as session musician; teaches folk guitar at adult education centre; mem. Musicians' Union. *Recordings:* 24 albums, including Derek Sarjeant Sings English Folk Songs (Melody Maker Folk Medal of Year for Best First Record 1962). *Publication:* How Do You Do stages 1–5 (English Folk Songs for German Schools). *Address:* 4 Coneygar House, Coneygar Park, Bridport, Dorset DT6 3BA, England. *E-mail:* dereksarjeant@hotmail.com. *Website:* www.dereksarjeant.co.uk.

SARMANTO, Heikki; Finnish composer and musician (piano); b. 22 June 1939. *Education:* Music and language, Helsinki University and Sibelius Academy, 1962–64; Lessons with Margaret Chaloff, Berklee College of Music, Boston, USA, 1968–71. *Career:* Regular visits to East Coast of USA; Own ensemble became UMO (New Music Orchestra); Played Jazz Mass, Newport Festival, 1979. *Compositions include:* New Hope Jazz Mass (premiered in New York); Jazz Mass; Jazz opera; Songs to words by Finnish poets including: Edith Södergran; Laura Vita; Eino Leino; 3 suites for soloists: Maija Hapuoja; Juhani Aaltonen; Pekka Sarmanto; Suomi, suite for jazz ensemble and strings; Passions of Man, ballet suite; Music for radio stories by Robert Shure: Man With A Sax; Felix The Great; Hearts (commissioned by WHO), 1995. *Recordings include:* Distant Dreams; The Traveller; Tales of Max; Orchestral Works. *Honours:* First prize, Jazz composition contest, Minneapolis, 1961; Yrjö Award, Finnish Jazz Federation, 1970. *Website:* www.sarmanto.com.

SARMANTO, Pekka; Finnish musician (double bass); b. (Pekka Eerik Juhani Sarmanto), 15 Feb. 1945, Helsinki; s. Hillel Sarmanto and Laura Pajumäki; m. Raija Hurme; one d. *Education:* Sibelius Acad. *Career:* one of Finland's most recorded artists 1965–; long term partnership playing with brother Heikki Sarmanto; played with artists including Benny Carter, Toots Thielemans, Dizzy Gillespie, Gil Evans, Michael Brecker, Dexter Gordon, Ben Webster, Billy Eckstine, Clifford Jordan, Joe Williams, Roy Hanes, Joe Morello, Mel, Thad Jones, McCoy Tyner, Bengt Hallberg, Sonny Rollins and others; mem. UMO Jazz Orchestra 1975–2006; festival appearances include Warsaw, London, Paris, Newport, Montreal, Stockholm, Copenhagen, Havana, Tokyo and elsewhere; soloist, performance of Heikki Sarmanto's suite, Song For My Brother 1982. *Recordings:* with Dizzy Gillespie, Clark Terry, Ted Curson, Charlie Mariano and most of the UMO recordings 1975–2006. *Honours:* Yrjö Award, Finnish Jazz Fed. 1978. *Address:* Kuurinniityntie 11 Ab, 02750 Espoo, Finland. *Telephone:* 40-823720 (mobile). *E-mail:* pekka.sarmanto@saunalahti.fi.

SÁROSI, Bálint, PhD, DrSc; Hungarian ethnomusicologist; b. 1 Jan. 1925, Csíkrákos, Harghita, Romania; m. Benkö Jolán 1952; two d. *Education:* Composition and Musicology, Liszt Ferenc High School of Music, Budapest. *Career:* Research Fellow, Inst. for Musicology, Budapest 1956–, Dir Ethnomusicological Section 1974–88 (retd); lectures on folk music, Hungarian Radio, weekly programme 1969–87; Guest Prof., Univ. of Innsbruck 1985–86, Univ. of Göttingen 1989, 1994; Invited Lecturer, most countries of Europe and USA, Japan, Armenia and Samarkand, Jerusalem; mem. Exec. Bd Int. Council for Traditional Music 1978–91. *Recordings:* Hungarian Instrumental Folk Music, two discs 1980, Anthology of Hungarian Folk Music V and VI 1993, 1995, The Hungarian Musical Mother Tongue 2003. *Publications include:* Die Volksmusikinstrumente Ungarus 1967, Gypsy Music 1978, Folk Music 1986, Sackpfeifer Zigeunermusikanten… 1999, A cigányzenekar múltja (The History of the Gypsy Band) Vol. 1 1776–1903 2004, Vol. 2 1904–1944 2012, Nótáskönyv (song book) 2010. *Honours:* Order of Labour, Golden Degree 1988, Middle Cross, Order of Hungarian Repub. 1995; Erkel Prize 1976, Presidential Gold Medal 2000, Széchenyi Prize 2005, Hazám Prize 2007, Eötvös József Wreath 2012, Prima primissima-prize. *Address:* Áldás u 11, 1025 Budapest, Hungary (home). *E-mail:* sarosib@ella.hu.

SARPILA, Antti Juhani; Finnish musician (clarinet, saxophones), composer and arranger; b. 11 June 1964, Helsinki; m. Minna Niemela 1994; three s. *Education:* pvt. studies with Bob Wilber, USA 1981–83. *Career:* freelance jazz musician; performances as soloist with different jazz orchestras world-wide including Tribute to Benny Goodman Concert at the Carnegie Hall, New York and Royal Ellington Concert at Royal Festival Hall, London; mem. Finnish Composers and Authors' Soc. *Compositions:* more than 300 published compositions and arrangements, mostly recorded. *Recordings:* numerous recordings under own name and around 100 recordings as guest musician, including: Peter Meyer, Ralph Sutton, Allan Vache, Bob Wilber. *Honours:* George Award, Finnish Jazz Fed. 1997, Louis Armstrong Award, Classic Jazz Soc. *Address:* Museokatu 26 A 14, 00100 Helsinki, Finland. *Telephone:* 400501702 (home). *Fax:* 401501702 (home). *E-mail:* antti.sarpila@co.inet.fi (home). *Website:* www.anttisarpila.com.

SARSTEDT, Peter; British folk singer and songwriter; b. Delhi, India; m. Joanna. *Recordings include:* albums: Peter Sarstedt 1969; PS…, 1979; Up Date, 1981; Asia Minor, 1987; Never Say Goodbye, 1987; Where Do You Go To, 2000; The Legends Collection, 2001; with Eden Kane and Robin Sarstedt: Worlds Apart Together, 1973. *E-mail:* petersarstedt@blueyonder.co.uk. *Website:* www.petersarstedt.com.

SARTORIUS, Paula, BA; American artist manager; b. New York. *Education:* Fordham Univ. *Career:* Artist Manager, Side One Management, for Los Lobos, Luscious Jackson.

SARUP, Kenneth; Danish singer and musician (guitar). *Career:* founder mem., Diefenbach 1999–; band started own label, Display Records. *Recordings include:* albums: Diefenbach 2001, Run Trip Fall 2003, Make Your Mind (EP) 2004, Re-Make Your Mind (EP) 2005, Set And Drift 2005. *E-mail:* diefenbach@ diefenbach.dk (office). *Website:* www.diefenbach.dk.

SARYGLAR, Alexei; Russian (Tuvan) singer and musician (percussion, strings). *Career:* mem. folk singing quartet, Huun-Huur-Tu 1995–. *Recordings include:* albums: If I'd Been Born an Eagle 1997, Where Young Grass Grows 1999, Malerija 2003. *Address:* c/o JARO Record Company, Bismarckstr. 43, 28203 Bremen, Germany. *E-mail:* mail@jaro.de. *Website:* www.huunhuurtu .com.

SASAKI, Ayaka; Japanese singer; b. 11 June 1996, Kanagawa. *Career:* Founder-mem., all-female vocal group Momoiro Clover 2008, renamed Momoiro Clover Z 2011–; first national tour 2009; debut single 2009; numerous live and TV appearances; concert appearances in Germany, Malaysia, France. *Films:* Shirome 2010. *Recordings:* albums: Battle and Romance (CD Shop Award for Best CD 2012) 2011, 5th Dimension 2013, Iriguchi no Nai Deguchi 2013. *Honours:* MTV Video Music Award Japan for Best Choreography 2013, MTV Europe Music Award for Best Japanese Act 2013. *Current Management:* c/o Stardust Promotion, 2F Takeda-Dai2 Bldg, 2-3-3 Ebisu-nishi, Shibuya, Tokyo, 150-0021, Japan. *Website:* www.stardust.co .jp; starchild.fm/special/en/momoclo.

SASH!; German DJ and producer; b. (Sascha Lappessen), 1970, Nettetal. *Career:* electrical engineer; started as DJ; began producing as Sash!, with Thomas Lüdke and Ralf Kappmeier; numerous gigs, television appearances and hit singles throughout Europe; remixer for Jean-Michel Jarre and Dr Alban. *Recordings:* albums: It's My Life 1997, Life Goes On 1998, Trillennium 2000, S4! Sash! 2003, 10th Anniversary 2007; hit singles include: It's My Life 1996, Ecuador 1997, Stay 1997, Encore Une Fois 1997, La Primavera 1998, Mysterious Times 1998, Ma Baker 1998, Colour the World 1998, Adelante 1999, Just Around The Hill 2000, With My Own Eyes 2000. *E-mail:* office@ mibd-agency.com (office). *Website:* www.sashworld.com.

SASHA; Nigerian singer; b. (Antonia Yetunde Alabi), 21 May 1983. *Education:* Univ. of Lagos. *Career:* began professional singing career 2002–. *Recordings:* albums: First Lady 2007. *Honours:* Kora Award for Most Promising Artist, West Africa 2004, Amen Award for Most Promising Female Artist 2005, Channel O Award for Best Female Video 2009. *Address:* c/o Storm Records, Plot 77, 22b Admiralty Way, Lekki Phase 1, Lagos, Nigeria (office). *E-mail:* info@storm360degrees.com (office). *Website:* storm360degrees.com/ music_sasha.php.

SASHA; British producer, remixer and DJ; b. (Alexander Coe), 4 Sept. 1969, Bangor, Wales. *Career:* began DJ career at the Hacienda in Manchester, then Shelly's in Stoke; worldwide DJ; various mix compilations for Renaissance and Global Underground labels; collaborations with Brian Transeau, Maria Nayler, Charlie May. *Recordings include:* album: Airdrawndagger 2002. *Honours:* Muzik Award for Best DJ 2001. *Current Management:* c/o Three Six Zero Group Ltd, 11 Jack's Place, 6 Corbet Place, London, E1 6NN, England. *Telephone:* (20) 3051-7930. *Fax:* (20) 3004-1589. *E-mail:* office@tszgrp.com. *Website:* www.threesixzerogroup.com; www.djsasha.com.

SATRIANI, Joe; American musician (guitar, banjo, harmonica) and educator; b. 1956, Long Island, NY. *Career:* founder mem., The Squares; mem., Greg Kihn Band; solo artist 1984–; played with Deep Purple 1992; numerous tours; guitar tutor to musicians Steve Vai, Kirk Hammett. *Recordings include:* with Greg Kihn Band: Love and Rock 'N' Roll 1986; solo: Not Of This Earth 1986, Surfing With The Alien 1987, Dreaming #11 1988, Flying In A Blue Dream 1989, The Extremist 1992, The Beautiful Guitar 1993, Time Machine 1993, Joe Satriani 1995, Crystal Planet 1998, Engines Of Creation 2000, Additional Creations 2000, Strange Beautiful Music 2002, The Satch Tapes 2003, Is There Love in Space? 2004, Super Colossal 2006, Professor Satchafunkilus and the Musterion of Rock 2008, Black Swans and Wormhole Wizards 2010, Unstoppable Momentum 2013, Shockwave Supernova 2015. *Honours:* several Grammy Awards. *E-mail:* webmaster@satriani.com (office). *Website:* www .satriani.com.

SAUNDERS, Edward (Eddie) John; British singer, composer, lyricist and musician (percussion); b. 6 July 1965, London. *Career:* founder member, lead vocalist, Push 1987–96; lead and backing vocals, Groove Nation; has worked with Reuben Wilson (Push was his UK pick-up band), Omar, Leon Ware, Jo Cang, Boogie Back All Stars; support to Curtis Mayfield, Airto Moreira and Flora Purim, Maceo Parker, Average White Band; mem, PRS, Musicians' Union, MCPS. *Recordings:* Traffic, track on Acid Jazz and Other Illicit Grooves compilation (first ever Acid Jazz record) 1988; further recordings with

Push, Talbot/White, Jo Cang, Galliano, Groove Nation, Steve Beresford, Cue Sheets.

SAUNDERS, Gerald (Gerry) Ivor Ewart, (Radio Call Sign 2B3GS); British musician (percussion), radio presenter, writer and lecturer; b. 3 Nov. 1929, Plymouth, Devon. *Career:* ENSA 1943–45; Theatre Pit 1945–47; RAF 1947–49; Big band/Orchestra tours 1949–55; magazine proprietor, broadcasting, writing 1955–65; jazz club propr (six clubs), music/stage producer, jazz tours 1965–80; musical/stage tours, writing, band man., broadcasting 1980–93; Nat. Exec., South East Dist Council; Chair. Bournemouth Br. Musicians' Union, British Citizens Band Conf.; jazz tours 1980–; mem. Nat. Exec. Musicians' Union; Chief Exec. Nat. Citizens Band Conf.; Dir Coastal Radio (community radio station); retd from all official orgs 2001; continues jazz tours of UK and Europe; lectures on mil. history; broadcasts and records for SAGA music holidays and others; after-dinner speaker for many orgs. *Publications:* 'Playtime' Entertainment Newspaper; Editor and Publisher, Secretary, 'Video Record'; numerous feature articles on music, jazz history, broadcasting history, radio communication and public relations for various magazines. *Address:* 12 Lincoln Avenue, Springbourne, Bournemouth, Dorset, BH1 4QS, England (home). *Telephone:* (1202) 302414 (office). *Fax:* (1202) 302414 (office). *E-mail:* gerrysaundersjazz@ntlworld.com (home). *Website:* Skype name: picturepost.

SAUNDERS, Mark; British mixing engineer and record producer; b. 20 March 1959, Basingstoke, Hampshire. *Career:* began career as asst, West Side Studios, London. *Recordings include:* albums as producer: Raw Like Sushi, Neneh Cherry; Wild!, Erasure; Maxinquaye, Tricky; singles: with The Cure: Lullaby; Lovesong; with The Farm: Groovy Train; with Lisa Stansfield: This Is The Right Time; Erasure: Little Respect; Drama (remix); Blue Savannah; Star; Buffalo Stance, Neneh Cherry; Rapture, Siouxsie and the Banshees; Madder Rose, Tragic Magic; David Byrne, Feelings; John Lydon, Psycho's Path; Depeche Mode, Strangelove (remix); Cathy Dennis; The Chameleons; Coldcut; Laptop; Madness; The Mission. *Address:* Beat 360 Studios, 630 Ninth Avenue, Suite 710, New York, NY 10036, USA (office). *Telephone:* (212) 262-4932 (office). *Fax:* (212) 262-4969 (office). *E-mail:* info@marksaunders.com (office). *Website:* www.marksaunders.com.

SAUNDERSON, Kevin, (Reese, E-Dancer); American producer, remixer and DJ; b. 5 Sept. 1964, Brooklyn, New York. *Career:* formed the Belleville Three with Juan Atkins and Derrick May; founder: KMS Records; member: Inner City, The Reese Project; collaborations with Santonio Echols, Juan Atkins, Paris Grey, Pet Shop Boys, Paula Abdul, New Order. *Recordings include:* albums: with Inner City: Paradise 1989, Fire 1990, Praise 1992; with The Reese Project: Faith, Hope and Clarity 1993; as E-Dancer: Heavenly 1998; as Kevin Saunderson: Prelude to Rave 1988, The Groove That Won't Stop 1988, Faces and Phrases 1996, Elevator 2001, KS01 2002, Say Something 2005, History Elevate 1 2007, History Elevate 2 2007, History Elevate 3 2008, History Elevate 4 2008. *Website:* www.kevinsaunderson.com.

SAVAGE, Matt; British musician (keyboards) and backing singer; b. (Matthew James Savage), 23 Aug. 1972, Reading, England; s. of David Savage and Catherine Savage. *Career:* mem. The Levellers 1990–; numerous concerts, festival appearances. *Recordings include:* albums: Weapon Called The Word 1990, Levelling The Land 1991, See Nothing, Hear Nothing, Do Something 1993, Levellers 1993, Zeitgeist 1995, Mouth To Mouth 1997, Special Brew 2000, Hello Pig 2000, Green Blade Rising 2002, Truth & Lies 2005, Letters from the Underground 2008, Static on the Airwaves 2012, Greatest Hits 2014. *Address:* The Levellers, PO Box 29, Winkleigh, Devon, EX19 8WE, England (office). *Telephone:* (1273) 608887 (office). *E-mail:* otf@levellers.co.uk (office). *Website:* www.levellers.co.uk.

SAVAGE, Richard (Rick); British rock musician (bass guitar) and singer; b. 2 Dec. 1960, Sheffield, England; m. Paige; two c. *Career:* founder mem., Atomic Mass, band later became Def Leppard 1977–; numerous concerts and tours worldwide, festival appearances. *Recordings include:* albums: The Def Leppard EP 1978, On Through the Night 1980, High 'n' Dry 1981, Pyromania 1983, Hysteria 1987, Adrenalize 1992, Retro Active 1993, Vault 1980–95 1995, Slang 1996, Euphoria 1999, X 2002, Yeah 2006, Songs from the Sparkle Lounge 2008, Def Leppard 2015. *Television:* Behind the Music (documentary series, VH1) 1998, Storytellers (documentary, VH1), Hysteria: The Def Leppard Story (documentary, VH1), Ultimate Albums (documentary, VH1). *Honours:* American Music Awards for Favorite Heavy Metal Album, for Favorite Heavy Metal Artist 1989. *Current Management:* c/o Primary Wave Music, 116 East 16th Street, 9th Floor, New York, NY 10003, USA. *E-mail:* info@primarywave.com. *Website:* www.defleppard.com.

SAVALE, Steve Chandra, (Chandrasonic); British musician (guitar) and producer; b. 26 May 1963, London; s. of Sharad Savale and Jean Savale; one s. *Education:* Univ. of Essex. *Career:* fmr mem., Higher Intelligence Agency; mem., Asian Dub Foundation 1994–. *Compositions include:* Gaddafi: The Opera, ENO 2006. *Radio:* guest ed., Today programme (BBC Radio 4) 2005. *Recordings include:* albums: Concious (EP) 1994, Facts and Fictions 1995, R.A.F.I. 1997, Rafi's Revenge 1998, Conscious Party 1998, Community Music 2000, Enemy of the Enemy 2003, Bangin' On The Walls 2003, Tank 2005, Punkara 2008. *Honours:* BBC Asian Award for Music 1998, NME Bratz Award 1998, Asian Music Award for Best Underground Act 2005.

SAVALL, Jordi; Spanish musician (viola da gamba) and conductor; b. 1 Aug. 1941, Igualada, Barcelona; m. Montserrat Figueras (died 2011). *Education:*

Barcelona Conservatory of Music and Schola Cantorum Basiliensis, Switzerland. *Career:* early collaborations with Ars Musica mid-1960s; teacher at Schola Cantorum Basiliensis from 1973; formed Hespèrion XX 1974; returned to Barcelona 1988; formed La Capela Reial de Catalunya 1988; created Le Concert des Nations 1989; many collaborations, including John Williams, Rafael Puyana, Michel Piguet, Stephen Preston, Trevor Pinnock, Ton Koopman, Christophe Coin, Christopher Hogwood; f. own label Alia Vox 1998, more than 70 titles published; EU Amb. for Cultural Dialogue 2008; UNESCO Amb. – Artists of Peace 2009. *Recordings include:* solo: Del Romànic Al Renaixement 1968, Recercadas Del Tratado De Glosas 1970, Canti amorosi 1975, François Couperin: Pièces De Viole 1976, Marin Marais: Pièces De Viole 1976, Sainte-Colombe: Concerts A Deux Violes Esgales 1976, Marin Marais: Pièces De Viole Du Quatrième Livre 1977, De Mr Demachy: Pièces De Viole 1977, The Punckes Delight And Other 17th Century English Music For Viol and Keyboard 1978, Antoine Forqueray: Pièces De Viole 1978, J. S. Bach: 3 Sonaten Für Viola Da Gamba Und Cembalo 1978, Lessons For The Lyra Viol 1980, Tobias Hume: Musical Humors 1983; with Hespèrion XX: Weltiche Musik Im Christlichen Und Jüdischen Spanien 1976, Canciones Y Danzas De España: Songs And Dances From The Time Of Cervantes 1977, Musicque De Loye 1978, Cansós De Trobairitz 1978, El Barroco Español 1978, Scheidt: Ludi Musici 1978, Music From The Armada Years 1978, Libre Vermell De Montserrat 1979, Battaglie E Lamenti Schlacht Und Klage 1982, Couperin: Les Nations 1983, Brade: Consort Music 1983, Viva Rey Ferrando 1984, Hume: Poeticall Musicke 1985, Couperin: Les Apothéoses 1985, J. S. Bach: Die Kunst Der Fuge 1985, A. de Cabezón 1985, Johann Hermann Schein: Banchetto Musicale 1985, Harmmerschmidt: Vier Suiten Aus Erster Fleiss 1987, Ensaladas 1987, Eustache Du Caurroy: XXIII Fantasies 1988, Dowland: Lachrimae Or Seven Teares 1988, Juan del Enzina: Romances And Villancicos 1988, Tye: Lawdes Deo, Complete Consort Musicke 1989, Rosenmüller: Sonata Da Camera And Sinfonie 1989, Jenkins: Consort Music In Six Parts 1991, J. S. Bach: The Four Overtures 1991, Lope de Vega: Intermedios Del Barroco Hispánico 1991, J. S. Bach: The Brandenburg Concertos 1991, El Cancionero De Palacio 1992, El Cancionero De La Colombina 1992, Guerrero: Sacrae Cantiones 1993, Victoria: Cantica Beatae Virginis 1992, Folias And Canarios 1994, Locke: Consort Of Four Parts 1994, Jeanne La Pucelle 1994, Purcell: Fantasias For The Viol 1995, Scheidt: Ludi Musici 1997, Cabanilles 1644–1712 1998, William Lawes 1602–1645: Consort Sets in Five And Six Parts 2002, Istanbul: Dimitrie Cantemir 2009; with Le Concert des Nations: Marc-Antoine Charpentier: Canticum Ad Beatam Virginem Mariam 1989, Haydn: Seven Last Words Of Our Savior On The Cross 1991, Mozart: Requiem 1992, Vicent Martin I Soler: Una Cosa Rara 1992, Handel: Water Music/Music For The Royal Fireworks 1993, Marais: Alcione: Suites Des Airs À Jouer 1994, Arriaga: Symphony In D 1995, Beethoven: Symphony No. 3 1997, Purcell: The Fairy Queen/Prophetess 1997, Dinastia Borja with Hespèrion XXI (Grammy Award for Best Small Ensemble Performance) 2011, Rameau: L'Orchestre de Louis XV (Int. Classical Music Award for Best Baroque Instrumental Recording 2012) 2011. *Honours:* Officer, Ordre des Arts et des Lettres 1988; Grand Prix de l' Acad. du Disque Lyrique 1990, Generalitat de Catalunya Creu de Sant Jordi Award 1990, Medalla d'Or Parlament de Catalunya 2003, Prix Nat. de la Culture 2009, Léonie Sonning Music Prize 2012, York Early Music Festival Lifetime Achievement Award 2012. *Current Management:* c/o Fundació CIMA, Camí de la Font, 08193 Bellaterra, Spain. *Telephone:* (93) 594-47-60. *Fax:* (93) 594-47-70. *E-mail:* info@fundaciocima.org. *Website:* www .fundaciocima.org. *Address:* Alia Vox, Avinguda Bartomeu 11, 08193 Bellaterra, Spain (office). *E-mail:* aliavox@alia-vox.com (office). *Website:* www.alia-vox.com (office).

SAVANNAH, Jonn; British musician; b. 13 Jan. 1957, Nairobi, Kenya; m. Marie Savannah. *Education:* one year at coll.; Grade 4 piano. *Career:* toured with Tina Turner, Squeeze, Van Morrison; session work; backing vocals, Kylie Minogue, Light Years 2000; signed publishing deal with EMI UK 1994; mem. PAMRA, Musicians' Union, MCPS. *Recordings:* The Catch: 25 Years (No. 3, Germany) 1984. *Address:* Little Barn, Plaistow Road, Loxwood, W Sussex, RH14 0SX, England.

SAVATH Y SAVALAS (see Herren, Scott)

SAVILLE, Peter, RDI; British artist; b. 1955, Manchester, England. *Education:* Manchester Polytechnic. *Career:* designed poster for Factory club, Manchester 1978; Co-founder and Art Dir Factory Records 1979–81, collaborating on design for Haçienda nightclub, consultant 1981–91; Art Dir, Dindisc, part of Virgin Records 1981; f. design firm (with Brett Wickens), Peter Saville Associates 1983–90; partner, Pentagram design studio, London 1990–93; worked for Frankfurt Balkind advertising agency, Los Angeles, USA 1993–94; freelance art dir, London 1994–, opening The Apartment, Mayfair 1995; co-f. Nick Knight's SHOWstudio website 2000; Royal Designer to Industry, Royal Soc. of Arts 2011; comms include Channel One (Los Angeles), Design Museum (London), Christian Dior, EMI, Givenchy, Stella McCartney, Ministry of Culture (France), Natural History Museum (London), Pompidou Centre (Paris), Pringle, Jil Sander, Selfridges (London), Martin Sitbon, Whitechapel Art Gallery (London), Yohji Yamamoto; work for music industry includes David Byrne, Brian Eno, Peter Gabriel, Joy Division, George Michael, Monaco, New Order, OMD, Orchestral Manoeuvres in the Dark, Beth Orton, The Other Two, Pulp, Roxy Music, Suede, Ultravox, Wham!. *Exhibition:* The Peter Saville Show, Design Museum, London 2003. *Publications:* Designed by Peter Saville (ed. Emily King) 2003, Peter Saville Estate (ed. Heike Munder) 2007. *Honours:* Prince Philip Designers Prize,

Design Council 2009, London Design Medal 2013. *Website:* www.petersavillestudio.com (office).

SAWHNEY, Nitin; British musician (keyboards, guitar), remixer, producer and composer; b. 1964, Kent. *Education:* Liverpool Univ. *Career:* solo recordings feature influences of many cultures, including Indian, Flamenco, Jazz, Dance; also composed for commercials, TV and film soundtracks; produced and remixed other artists' work; toured with the James Taylor Quartet; formed The Jazztones; worked with Talvin Singh in the Tihai Trio; Musical Dir, Theatre Royal (Stratford East), London; provided music for Nat. Theatre; written and produced for Amar and Aya; songs recorded by Sinéad O'Connor, Shara Nelson; remixed Mandalay, Khaled, Mondo Gross; worked on Sir Paul McCartney's project The Fireman; performed Royal Albert Hall, London Sept. 2014. *Television appearances:* Secret Asians double act, Goodness Gracious Me (BBC). *Radio includes:* Nitin Sawhney Spins the Globe (BBC Radio 2). *Compositions include:* The Sikhs (documentary series soundtrack); for film: The Dance of Shiva, Split Wide Open, Blindsight 2006; Urban Prophecies (premiered at the Proms, Albert Hall, conducted by Cameron Sinclair, featuring Joanna MacGregor on piano and Aref Durvesh on tabla) 2000, score for BBC series Wonders of the Monsoon (Royal TV Society award for best composer 2015) 2014. *Recordings:* albums: Spirit Dance 1993, Migration 1995, Displacing The Priest 1996, Introduction To Nitin Sawhney, Beyond Skin 1999, Prophesy 2001, Human 2003, Philtre 2005, London Undersound 2008, Last Days of Meaning 2011, OneZero 2013, Dystopian Dream 2015. *Honours:* South Bank Show Award for Popular Music 2000, BBC Radio 3 Award for World Music (Boundary Crossing) 2002, 2006. *E-mail:* tina@positiv-id.co.uk. *Website:* www.nitinsawhney.com.

SAWKA, Kevin Joseph; American musician (drums) and producer; b. 10 Oct. 1977, Seattle, Wash. *Education:* Skyview Middle School. *Career:* solo artist (performing as KJ Sawka) 2005–; mem. Pendulum 2009–. *Recordings:* albums: as KJ Sawka: Synchronized Compression 2005, Cyclonic Steel 2007; with Pendulum: Immersion 2010. *Current Management:* c/o JHO Management, 1–5 Exchange Court, Maiden Lane, Covent Garden, London, WC2R 0JU, England. *Telephone:* (20) 7420-4372. *Fax:* (20) 7420-4399. *E-mail:* jho@jhooakley.com. *Website:* www.jhooakley.com. *Address:* c/o Warner Bros. Records, Warner Music UK Limited, The Warner Building, 28 Kensington Church Street, London, W8 4EP, England (office). *Website:* www.warnerbrosrecords.co.uk (office); www.pendulum.com.

SAWTELL, Paul, LLB; British arranger, composer and musician (piano, vibraphone); b. 1 May 1959, Stourbridge, West Midlands, England. *Education:* classical training. *Career:* numerous BBC radio sessions, television broadcasts, with Tom Jones, Shirley Bassey, Neil Sedaka, BBC Radio Big Band; worked with Peter King, Dick Morrisey, Jim Mullen, Norma Whinstone; f. The Test Card Circle music archive 1989. *Compositions:* over 200 pieces. *Recordings:* 10 albums. *Publication:* The Paul Sawtell Collection of BBC Television Test Card Music. *Address:* Esgair Geiliod, Old Hall, Mochdre, Powys SY16 4JW, Wales (home).

SAYYID, M.; American singer. *Career:* released recordings on Anti-Pop Recordings label; mem. The Anti-Pop Consortium 1997–2002, 2007–; solo artist 2002–; technical advisor, film Hurricane Streets. *Recordings include:* albums: Tragic Epilogue 2000, Arrhythmia 2002, Fluorescent Black 2009. *Current Management:* c/o Joseph Noon, Spectrum Music, 235 Nassau Avenue, Suite 2L, Brooklyn, NY 11222, USA. *Telephone:* (718) 383-2313. *Fax:* (718) 383-2373. *E-mail:* joseph@spectrummusic.net. *Website:* www.spectrummusic.net. *E-mail:* sayyidairborn@gmail.com.

SCABBIA, Cristina; Italian singer; b. 6 June 1972, Milan. *Career:* mem. metal band, Lacuna Coil 1994–. *Recordings include:* albums: In a Reverie 1999, Unleashed Memories 2001, Comalies 2002, Karmacode 2006, Shallow Life 2009, Dark Adrenaline 2012, Broken Crown Halo 2012. *Current Management:* c/o Riot Rock Management, 639 Dupont Street, Unit 216, Toronto, ON M6G 1Z4, Canada. *E-mail:* info@riotrock.com. *Website:* www.lacunacoil.it.

SCAGGS, Boz; American musician (guitar) and singer; b. 8 June 1944, Ohio. *Career:* mem. of groups, The Marksmen, The Ardells; formed R&B group, The Wigs; mem., Steve Miller Band 1967; solo artist 1968–. *Recordings include:* albums: Boz Scaggs 1969, Moments 1971, Boz Scaggs and Band 1971, My Time 1972, Slow Dancer 1974, Silk Degrees 1976, Down Two Then Left 1977, Middle Man 1980, Other Roads 1988, Some Change 1994, Come on Home 1997, Dig 2001, But Beautiful 2003, Fade into Light 2005, Speak Low 2008. *Address:* c/o Decca Records, 1755 Broadway, New York, NY 10019, USA (office). *Website:* www.deccarecords-us.com (office); www.bozscaggs.com.

SCARTH, Andrew; record producer. *Career:* as prod., worked with Levellers; Heather Nova; Blameless; Skunk Anansie; Killing Joke; Mundy; Credit to the Nation; Addict; Underworld; Mainstream; Diamond Head; Bad Company; as engineer: Howard Jones: Dream Into Action; Cross That Line; Prefab Sprout, Two Wheels Good; Tina Turner, Foreign Affair; Tesla, Time's Makin' Changes: The Best of Tesla; Drain STH, Freaks of Nature; Backyard Babies; Bob Geldof; Honeymoon Suite.

SCHACK, Michael; Belgian musician (drums), producer and remixer; b. 11 May 1966, Sint-Niklaas. *Education:* Sint-Michielscollege, Brasschaat, UFSIA, Antwerp, Sint-Eligius/KDGH, Antwerp. *Career:* drummer with Blue Blot 1987–93, Clouseau 1995–97, Roland Demoband/Roland Rocks 1992–, Ozark Henry 2006–10, Milk Inc 2006–, Kate Ryan 2006–10, Soulsister 2008–, Netsky

2011–, also with own project SquarElectric 2008–; drums demonstrator; columnist, Slagwerkkrant (Netherlands) 2005–, Poppunt (Belgium) 2007–12; mem. Soc. Belge des Auteurs, Compositeurs et Editeurs (SABAM), Uradex/PlayRight Belgium. *Compositions:* for Blue Blot: Pretty Good, New Blunk; for Groovemania: Posativity; for Mich van Hautem: Jacky; also for Franste, SquarElectric; jingles/work for Belgian TV; miscellaneous preset instrument music contribs for Roland Corpn. *Recordings:* Blue Blot albums 1990–94, Orphan; September Rain; True Blue, Calvin Owens 1993; De 7 Drumzonden; Live for Life 1993; MichaelSchack.Drums 2005, SquarElectric (solo) 2009. *Honours:* Drum Video of the Year 1996, TMF Best Live (Milk Inc), MIA Best Live (Netsky). *Current Management:* c/o Boem Labo, Antwerp, Belgium. *E-mail:* boemlabo@telenet.be (office). *Website:* www.michaelschack.com.

SCHÄFER, Gustav; German musician (drums); b. 8 Sept. 1988. *Career:* mem. rock band, Tokio Hotel 2001–. *Recordings include:* albums: Schrei 2005, Schrei: So Laut Du Kannst 2006, Zimmer 483 2007, Scream 2007, Humanoid 2009. *Honours:* ECHO Award for Best National Newcomer 2006, MTV Europe Music Awards for Best Int. Act 2007, for Best Headline Act 2008, for Best Group 2009. *Address:* c/o Universal Music Deutschland, Stralauer Allee 1, 10245 Berlin, Germany (office). *Website:* www.tokiohotel.com.

SCHEINER, Elliot; American music director, producer, engineer and musician (percussion). *Career:* percussionist, bands including Jimmy Buffett's Coral Reefers; asst to Phil Ramone, A&R Recording 1967, becoming engineer; ind. engineer and producer 1973–; Co-founder Bop City Records 2002–; Co-Music Dir, DH 1 2002–; currently Strategic Partner, Hollywood Studios Int.; authority on 5.1 surround sound mixing and DVD audio; has worked with Aerosmith, George Benson, The Eagles, Fleetwood Mac, John Fogerty, Bruce Hornsby, Billy Joel, B. B. King, Ricky Martin, Steely Dan, Sting, Van Morrison. *Honours:* Hon. DMus (Berklee Coll. of Music) 2006; Surround Pioneer Award, seven Grammy Awards including Grammy Award for Best Surround Sound Album (for Eric Clapton's Layla And Other Assorted Love Songs) 2012. *Address:* c/o Hollywood Studios International, 257 West 52nd Street, New York, NY 10019, USA.

SCHENKER, Michael; German musician (guitar); b. 10 Jan. 1955, Savstedt. *Career:* founder mem. heavy rock group The Scorpions 1971–73, 1979; mem. UFO 1973–78; founder mem. The Michael Schenker Group (MSG) 1979–; contrib. to Contraband recording project (with mems of Shark Island, Vixen, Ratt, LA Guns) 1991. *Recordings include:* albums: with The Scorpions: Lonesome Crow 1972, Lovedrive 1979; with UFO: Phenomenon 1974, Force It 1975, No Heavy Pettin' 1976, Lights Out 1977, Strangers In The Night 1977, Obsession 1978, Deadly Sting: The Mercury Years 1997; with MSG: The Michael Schenker Group 1980, MSG 1981, One Night At Budokan 1982, Assault Attack 1982, Built To Destroy 1983, Rock Will Never Die 1984, Perfect Timing 1987, Save Yourself 1989, Never Ending Nightmare 1992, The Michael Schenker Life Story 1997, Unforgiven 1999, Written in Sand 1999, The Unforgiven World Tour: Live 1999, Unplugged (live) 1999, Adventures of the Imagination 2000, Be Aware Of Scorpions 2001, Heavy Hitters 2005; with Contraband: Contraband 1991; with Michael Schenker's Temple of Rock: Temple of Rock 2011, Temple of Rock - Live in Europe 2012, Bridge the Gap 2013, Spirit On A Mission 2015. *E-mail:* mwschenker@earthlink.net (office). *Website:* www.michaelschenkerhimself.com.

SCHENKER, Rudolf; German musician (guitar), songwriter and writer; b. 31 Aug. 1948, Hildesheim; partner Tatyana Sazonova; one s. *Career:* Founder-mem. German heavy rock group The Scorpions 1965–2014; numerous worldwide tours, festivals and concerts. *Recordings include:* albums: Lonesome Crow 1972, Fly to the Rainbow 1974, In Trance 1975, Virgin Killer 1976, Taken by Force 1977, Tokyo Tapes 1978, Lovedrive 1979, Animal Magnetism 1980, Blackout 1982, Love at First Sting 1984, World Wide Live 1985, Savage Amusement 1988, Crazy World 1990, Face the Heat 1993, Live Bites 1995, Pure Instinct 1996, Deadly Sting: The Mercury Years 1997, Eye II Eye 1999, Moment of Glory 2000, Acoustica 2001, Unbreakable 2004, Humanity Hour 1 2007, Sting in the Tail 2010, Get Your Sting and Blackout 2011, Comeblack 2011, MTV Unplugged 2013, Return to Forever 2015. *Publication:* Rock Your Life 2009. *Honours:* Goldene Europa 1985, 1992, Bravo-Otto in Silver 1986, Bravo-Otto in Gold 1991, Bravo-Otto in Bronze 1992, World Music Award 1992, 1994, 2010, Radio Regenbogen Award Rock Int. 1998, RSH-Gold 1999, Echo für das Lebenswerk 2009, Goldene Henne 2009, Rock Legend Award 2010, GQ Männer des Jahres Award 2010, World Music Award, Monte Carlo 2010, Lifetime Achievement Awards der Hard Rock Cafe-Kette 2010, Radio Regenbogen Award in der Kategorie Lifetime Rock 2011, Metal Guru Award des Classic-Rock Magazins 2011. *Current Management:* c/o Peter F. Amend, Ludwigsplatz 9, 35390 Giessen, Germany. *Telephone:* (641) 32049. *Fax:* (641) 33771. *E-mail:* amend.kollegen@t-online.de. *Website:* www.amend-kollegen.de; www.the-scorpions.com; www.rockyourlife-yeah.com.

SCHEUERELL, Douglas Andrew, BMus with distinction; American musician (tabla, guitar, voice) and academic; *Tabla Specialist, School of Music and Dance, University of Oregon*; b. 31 May 1948, Madison, Wis.; m. Victoria Ann Scheuerell 1992; one s. *Education:* Univ. of Wisconsin, Madison, Ali Akbar Coll. of Music, San Rafael, Calif., studied with Ali Akbar Khan, Swapan Chaudhuri, Jnan Prakash Ghosh, Samir Chatterjee. *Career:* musician, Madison 1966–74; Intern Choral Dir Sun Prairie High School, Wis. 1970; recording artist, Stas WHA and WHA-TV, Madison 1973–74; musician, composer, Missing Link Theatre Co., Berkeley, Calif. 1977–78; Faculty mem. East Bay Center for the Performing Arts, Berkeley 1977–78; Family Light

Music School, Sausalito, Calif. 1978; Elizabeth Waters Dance Ensemble, Albuquerque, New Mexico 1979–80; accompanist, Univ. of New Mexico School of Dance, Albuquerque 1979–80; tabla soloist and accompanist, North Indian classical music 1988–; tabla tutor, Eugene, Ore. 1988–93; Faculty mem. and tabla specialist, Univ. of Oregon School of Music and Dance, Eugene 1993–; residencies in California schools, Nat. Endowment for the Arts 1977–78; performance grantee, Lane Regional Arts Council, Eugene 1989, 2010; faculty devt grantee, Univ. of Oregon, Eugene 1996; performances for Percussive Arts Soc., Asia Soc. *Film:* Musical Dir Wisconsin We Care. *Radio:* composed music for educational programming, WHA. *Recordings:* Badger A Go-Go, Vanish Into Blue, Communion, Loss, Structures. *Address:* School of Music and Dance, 1225 University of Oregon, Eugene, OR 97403-1225 (office); 1557 D Street, Springfield, OR 97477, USA (home). *Telephone:* (541) 346-5642 (office); (541) 484-9305 (home). *Fax:* (541) 346-0723 (office). *E-mail:* dougsch@uoregon.edu (office). *Website:* music.uoregon.edu/people/faculty/scheuerell.htm (office); dougmusic.info.

SCHICK, Ignaz; German musician (saxophone, electronics); b. 9 Sept. 1972, Tostberg. *Education:* Academy of Fine Arts, studied with Josef Anton Riedl. *Career:* toured, played concerts and festivals of experimental music 1989–; f. Edition Zangi (production co.) 1998, Zarek (record label) 2000; Sales Man., Staalplat Amsterdam 2004–07; festivals include Bonner Herbst, Donaueschingen, Autumn Concerts, Graz, Austria, FEAM, Berlin; collaborations with Mathias Bauer, Tony Buck, Jason Kahn, Tarwater, Kalle Laar; mem. GEMA, GVL, JIM. *Compositions:* Che, Die Wueste Bleibt Leer, Liebe Macht Blind, Koerper Im Abseits, Tools And Tales Against Radio Agents, Puppy Love, Perm, Vononoch. *Recordings include:* albums: Kratzen 1990, Kaeseplatte 1991, Donaueschingen 1995, Lonely Woman 1997, Tales And Tools Against Radio Agents 1997, Nuts 1998, Petit Pale 2001. *Honours:* Foerderstipendium fur Musik 1994, Künstlerhaus Worpswede 2008.

SCHIFRIN, Lalo; Argentine pianist, composer, conductor and educator; b. 21 June 1932, Buenos Aires; m. Donna; three c. *Education:* Paris Conservatoire with Olivier Messiaen. *Career:* professional jazz pianist, composer and arranger 1950s–; represented Argentina, Paris Int. Jazz Festival 1955; founder of big band late 1950s; moved to USA 1958; played with Dizzy Gillespie, including European tour with Jazz at the Philharmonic Ensemble 1960–62; also played with Quincy Jones, Jimmy Smith, Sarah Vaughan, Ella Fitzgerald, Stan Getz and Count Basie; Tutor of Composition, Univ. of California at Los Angeles 1968–71; Musical Dir, Paris Philharmonic Orchestra 1987–92; Music Dir, Glendale Symphony Orchestra 1989–95; guest conductor of orchestras, including Atlanta Symphony Orchestra, Georgian State Symphony Orchestra, Houston Symphony Orchestra, Israel Philharmonic, London Philharmonic Orchestra, London Symphony Orchestra, Los Angeles Chamber Orchestra, Los Angeles Philharmonic, Mexico City Philharmonic, Mexico Philharmonic, Moscow Symphony Orchestra, National Symphony Orchestra of Argentina, Orchestra of Saint Luke (New York), Orchestre de la Suisse Romande (Geneva, Switzerland), Vienna Symphony Orchestra; Adviser to the Pres. in Cultural Affairs (Sec. of the Cabinet), Argentina 1998. *Compositions include:* Concerto for double bass, Concerto for guitar and orchestra, Down Here on the Ground, Gone with the Wave, Harp Aujourd'hui, La Clave, Music for harp, Invocations, La Nouvelle Orleans, New Continent Suite, Pulsations, Rain Dance, Resonances, Spectrum, Tristeza on Piano, Tropicos, Piano Concerto No. 1, Piano Concerto No. 2 1992, Cantares Argentinos 1992, Christmas in Vienna 1992, Lili'Uokalani Symphony 1995, Rhapsody for Bix 1996, Concerto Caribeño for flute and orchestra 1997, Gillespiana Suite 1998, Latin Jazz Suite 1999, Esperanto 2000, Fantasy for screenplay and orchestra 2002, Symphonic Impressions of Oman 2003, Letters from Argentina 2005, Double Concerto for Piano, Trumpet and Orchestra 2007, Tangos Concertantes 2008, Elegy and Meditation 2009, Pampas (Latin Grammy Award for Best Classical Contemporary Composition 2010) 2009. *Compositions for film include:* Venga a bailar el rock 1957, El Jefe 1958, Rhino! 1964, Les Félins 1964, See How They Run 1964, The Way Out Men 1965, Once a Thief 1965, Dark Intruder 1965, The Cincinnati Kid 1965, The Liquidator 1965, Blindfold 1965, Wall Street: Where the Money Is 1966, Way... Way Out 1966, The Making of a President: 1966, The Doomsday Flight 1966, Murderers' Row 1966, I Deal in Danger 1966, How I Spent My Summer Vacation 1967, The Venetian Affair 1967, Sullivan's Empire 1967, Cool Hand Luke 1967, The Fox 1967, The President's Analyst 1967, Mission Impossible Versus the Mob 1968, Coogan's Bluff 1968, Bullitt 1968, Hell in the Pacific 1968, The Rise and Fall of the Third Reich 1968, The Brotherhood 1968, U.M.C. 1969, Che! 1969, Eye of the Cat 1969, The Young Lawyers 1969, Pussycat, Pussycat, I Love You 1970, Kelly's Heroes 1970, The Aquarians 1970, I Love My Wife 1970, The Beguiled 1971, Pretty Maids All in a Row 1971, The Hellstrom Chronicle 1971, Earth II 1971, The Christian Licorice Store 1971, Dirty Harry 1971, Prime Cut 1972, The Wrath of God 1972, The Neptune Factor 1973, Enter the Dragon 1973, Hit! 1973, Egan 1973, Magnum Force 1973, Up from the Ape 1974, Night Games 1974, The Four Musketeers 1974, The Master Gunfighter 1975, Sky Riders 1976, Special Delivery 1976, Voyage of the Damned 1976, The Eagle has Landed 1976, Day of the Animals 1977, Good Against Evil 1977, Rollercoaster 1977, Telefon 1977, The President's Mistress 1978, Return from Witch Mountain 1978, Nunzio 1978, Escape to Athena 1979, Boulevard Nights 1979, Love and Bullets 1979, The Amityville Horror 1979, The Concorde... Airport '79 1979, The Nude Bomb 1980, The Big Brawl 1980, The Competition 1980, Chicago Story 1981, Caveman 1981, Los Viernes de la eternidad 1981, La Pelle 1981, Wait Until Dark 1982, The Seduction 1982, A Stranger is Watching 1982, Class of 1984

1982, Amityville II: The Possession 1982, The Sting II 1983, The Osterman Weekend 1983, The New Kids 1985, Private Sessions 1985, Command 5 1985, Bad Medicine 1985, Bridge Across Time 1985, Black Moon Rising 1986, Kung Fu: The Movie 1986, Triplecross 1986, Beverly Hills Madam 1986, The Ladies' Club 1986, Out on a Limb 1987, The Fourth Protocol 1987, Earth Star Voyager 1988, The Dead Pool 1988, Berlin Blues 1988, The Neon Empire 1989, Original Sin 1989, Return from the River Kwai 1989, Face to Face 1990, F/X2 1991, The Beverly Hillbillies 1993, Scorpion Spring 1996, Money Talks 1997, Something to Believe In 1998, Tango, no me dejes nunca 1998, Rush Hour 1998, Longshot 2000, Rush Hour 2 2001, Tom the Cat 2002, Bringing Down the House 2003, Biyik 2004, After the Sunset 2004, The Bridge of San Luis Rey 2004, Abominable 2006, Rush Hour 3 2007, Love and Virtue 2008, Love Story 2011, Sweetwater 2013, Tales of Halloween 2015. *Compositions for television:* music for episodes of The Man from U.N.C.L.E. 1965, Shipwrecked 1966, T.H.E. Cat 1966, Jericho 1966, National Geographic documentaries 1966, Mannix 1967, The Big Valley 1968–69, Medical Center 1969, The Young Lawyers 1970, The Partners 1971, Night Gallery 1972, The Sixth Sense 1972, Mission Impossible (BMI Composer's Award 2001) 1966–73, Petrocelli 1974, Planet of the Apes 1974, Bronk 1975, Starsky and Hutch 1975, Hollywood Wives 1985, A.D. 1985, El Quijote de Miguel de Cervantes 1991, A Woman Named Jackie 1991, Danger Theatre 1993. *Honours:* four Grammy Awards, Cable ACE Award, BMI Lifetime Achievement Award 1988, MIDEM Classique Festival Award 1990, Los Angeles Music Center Distinguished Artist Award 1998, SACEM Award for contribution to music, film and culture 2004, American Soc. of Music Arrangers & Composers Golden Score Award 2004; Chevalier, Ordre des Arts et des Lettres; Dr hc (Rhode Island School of Design), (Univ. of La Plata, Argentina). *Current Management:* c/o Rich Jacobellis, First Artists Management, 4764 Park Granada, Suite 210, Calabasas, CA 91302, USA. *Telephone:* (818) 377-7750. *E-mail:* rjacobellis@firstartistsmgmt.com. *Website:* www.firstartistsmgmt.com. *E-mail:* l2schifrin@aol.com (office). *Website:* www.schifrin.com.

SCHLAPMAN, Kimberly; American country music singer and songwriter; b. (Kimberly A. Bramlett), 15 Oct. 1969, Toccoa, Ga; m. 1st Steven Roads (died 2005); m. 2nd Stephen Schlapman 2006; one d. *Education:* Samford Univ. *Career:* raised in Cornelia, Ga; met and sang with Karen Fairchild at univ. in late 1980s; Founder-mem. Little Big Town (with Karen Fairchild and Jimi Westbrook) 1998, appeared at Grand Old Opry 1999, released debut album 2002; toured with Keith Urban 2006, Sugarland and Jake Owen 2007, Martina McBride 2007–08, George Strait 2008, Carrie Underwood 2009, Sugarland 2010, Rascal Flatts 2012; numerous collaborations including Ashley Monroe, John Mellencamp, Collin Raye. *Recordings:* albums: with Little Big Town: Little Big Town 2002, The Road to Here 2005, A Place to Land 2007, The Reason Why 2010, Tornado 2012, Pain Killer 2014. *Honours:* Acad. of Country Music Awards for Top New Vocal Duo/Group 2007, for Top Vocal Group 2013, for Music Video of the Year (for Tornado) 2013, for Vocal Group of the Year 2014, 2015, Country Music Asscn Awards for Vocal Group of the Year 2012, 2013, 2014, 2015, for Single of the Year (for Pontoon) 2012, for Single and Song of the Year (both for Girl Crush) 2015, American Country Award for Music Video of the Year: Group or Collaboration (for Pontoon) 2012, Daytime Emmy Award for Outstanding Original Song (for Good Afternoon) 2013, Grammy Awards for Best Country Duo/Group Performance (for Pontoon) 2013, (for Girl Crush) 2016, for Best Country Song (for Girl Crush) 2016. *Current Management:* c/o Sandbox Entertainment, 54 Music Square East, Nashville, TN 37203, USA. *E-mail:* info@sandboxmgmt.com. *Website:* sandboxmgmt.com; littlebigtown.com.

SCHMIDT, Bjarne Gregers; musician (tenor banjo, Irish bouzouki, guitar); b. 3 Nov. 1957, Copenhagen, Denmark. *Education:* piano lessons, sound engineering course, musical studies in Ireland. *Career:* mem. band, Foxhunters, Trad Lads; Scandinavian Tour with Irish top acts, Mary Bergin and Mick Conneely Gin Whistle and Fiddle 1991. *Compositions:* The Moth in the Lampshade; Happy Days 1997. *Recordings:* Same Old Story, contributor 1990, Folk music in Denmark 1 1992, Folk music in Denmark 2 1993, Trad Lads, Happy Days 1997, Eck D'Ville, contributor 1997, Folk music of Denmark 1997. *Publications:* Trad Lads, Happy Days 1997, Eck D'Ville 1997.

SCHMIDT-DECKER, Petra, (Felix Spengler); German songwriter, record producer and writer; b. Berlin; d. of Felix-Peter Schmidt-Decker and Ingeborg Schmidt-Decker (née Lohse). *Education:* acting classes. *Career:* actress on stage, TV and in films for 13 years; songwriter, then producer of children's records, produced 150 records, including 30 records for Disney and 25 recorded biographies of composers from Vivaldi to Ravel (with Karlheinz Böhm) 1976–92; writer of TV and theatre scripts; leading companion of START Wort-Ton-Bild Verlags GmbH Hamburg, Germany; has worked on Jungle Book and Sesame Street productions. *Achievements include:* one Double Platinum CD, six Platinum CDs, one Triple Gold CD, eighteen Gold CDs. *Publications include:* novels: Die jungen Bosse, Unternehmer Portraits 1984, Das große Buch des guten Benehmens 1985, Die Seherin 1996, Der Schildkröteninstinkt, Motivationsbuch 2003; plays: In Between (TV), Casanova bevorzugt (theatre) 1998; short stories: Der Verlorene Blitz 2005, 52 Verträge mit mir selbst 2010, L'Istinto della Tartaruga (also published as Scelte di Vita) 2010. *Address:* Papenhuder Str. 42, 22087 Hamburg-Uhlenhorst, Germany (home). *Telephone:* (40) 2202203 (home).

SCHMIT, Timothy B.; American musician; b. 30 Oct. 1947, Sacramento, CA. *Career:* mem. folk trio, Tim, Tom and Ron 1962; mem. groups, The Contenders, New Breed, Glad; mem., Poco 1970–77, The Eagles 1977–.

Recordings include: with Poco: Poco 1970, Deliverin' 1971, From The Inside 1971, A Good Feelin' To Know 1973, Crazy Eyes 1973, Seven 1974, Cantamos 1974, Head Over Heels 1975, The Very Best of Poco 1975, Poco Live 1976, Rose Of Cimarron 1976, Indian Summer 1977; with The Eagles: The Long Run 1979, Long Road out of Eden 2007; solo: Playin' It Cool 1981, Timothy B 1987, Tell Me The Truth 1990, Feed The Fire 2001, Expando 2009. *Honours:* Grammy Awards for Best Rock Vocal Performance (for Heartache Tonight) 1980, for Best Country Performance by a Duo or Group with Vocals (for How Long) 2008, for Best Pop Instrumental Performance (for I Dreamed There Was No War) 2009, American Music Award for Favorite Album, Favorite Band 1981, Nordoff-Robbins Music Therapy Lifetime Achievement Award (with The Eagles) 2006. *Current Management:* William Morris Agency, 1350 Avenue of the Americas, New York, NY 10019, USA. *E-mail:* info@timothybschmit.com (office). *Website:* www.timothybschmit.com.

SCHMITT, Al; American music company director, producer and music engineer. *Career:* worked at Apex Studios, New York; independent engineer, Atlantic Records, Prestige Records, Radio Records; Staff Prod. for label, RCA Records; staff engineer, RCA studio; Music Dir, DH1 Studios 2001–; co-founder, Bop City Records 2002–; currently Strategic Partner, Hollywood Studios Int.; has worked with Jefferson Airplane, David Benoit, George Benson, Tony Braxton, Dee Dee Bridgewater, Les Brown, Ray Charles, Natalie Cole, David Grusin, Al Jarreau, Doctor John, Quincy Jones, Diana Krall, Madonna, Luis Miguel, John Raitt, Kenny Rankin, Joe Sample, Diane Schuur, Frank Sinatra, Steely Dan, Barbra Streisand, Luther Vandross, Vanessa Williams, Yasuka Agawa. *Honours:* nine Grammy Awards for Best Engineering 1962, 1976, 1977, 1978, 1982, 1991, 1996, 2002, two Latin Grammy Awards for Best Engineering 2000; inducted, Technical Excellence and Creativity Awards Hall of Fame 1997, Grammy Trustees Lifetime Achievement Award 2006. *Address:* c/o Hollywood Studios International, 257 W 52nd Street, New York, NY 10019, USA (office).

SCHNEIDER, Christoph 'Doom'; German musician (drums); b. 11 May 1966. *Career:* fmr mem., Die Firma; mem., Rammstein 1993–; the band has a reputation for theatrical live performances; numerous European tours. *Recordings include:* albums: Herzeleid 1995, Sehnsucht 1997, Live aus Berlin 1999, Mutter 2001, Reise, Reise 2004, Rosenrot 2005, Liebe ist für alle da 2009. *Honours:* MTV Europe Music Award for Best German Act 2005. *Current Management:* Pilgrim Management, Greifswalderstrasse 224, 10405 Berlin, Germany. *E-mail:* info@pilgrim-management.de. *Website:* www.pilgrim -management.de; www.rammstein.de.

SCHNEIDER, Florian; German musician (flute, electronics); b. 7 April 1947, Düsseldorf. *Education:* Düsseldorf Conservatory. *Career:* met Ralf Hütter while both were students, the two began collaborating on musical projects soon afterwards, forming Organisation 1970; group re-formed as Kraftwerk 1971–2009. *Recordings include:* albums: with Organisation: Tone Float 1970; with Kraftwerk: Kraftwerk 1 1971, Kraftwerk 2 1972, Ralf and Florian 1973, Autobahn 1974, Radio-Activity 1975, Trans-Europe Express 1977, The Man-Machine 1978, Computer World 1981, Electric Café 1986, Tour De France Soundtracks 2003, Minimum-Maximum 2005. *Address:* c/o Astralwerks Records, 150 Fifth Avenue, New York, NY 10001, USA (office). *Website:* www.astralwerks.com (office).

SCHNEIDER, Fred; American singer; b. 1 July 1951, Newark, GA. *Career:* founder mem., The B-52s 1976–, numerous live performances, particularly as successful touring band 1989–; solo artist 1991–; founded The Superions 2010. *Film appearances:* A Matter of Degrees 1990, Hangfire 1991, The Flintstones 1994, Desert Blue (voice) 1998, The Rugrats Movie (voice) 1998, Godass 2000, Each Time I Kill 2002. *Recordings include:* albums: with The B-52s: The B-52s 1979, Wild Planet 1980, Whammy! 1983, Bouncing Off The Satellites 1986, Cosmic Thing 1989, Good Stuff 1992, Associate, Associate 1996, Nude on the Moon: the B-52's Anthology 2002, Funplex 2008; solo: Fred Schneider And The Shake Society 1991, Just Fred 1996; with The Superions: Destination... Christmas 2010. *Current Management:* Vector Management, PO Box 120479, Nashville, TN 37203, USA. *E-mail:* info@vectormgmt.com. *Website:* www .theb52s.com.

SCHNEIDER, John; American country singer and actor; b. 8 April 1954, Mount Kisco, NY. *Career:* performed in musicals from age 14; television and film actor; solo artist 1981–. *Television includes:* The Dukes of Hazzard 1979–85, Grand Slam 1990–, Smallville 2000–. *Films include:* Snow Day 2000. *Recordings include:* albums: Now Or Never, 1981, Dukes of Hazzard (cast album) 1982, Quiet Man 1982, If You Believe, with Jill Michaels 1983, Too Good To Stop Now 1984, Trying to Outrun the Wind 1985, A Memory Like You 1986, Take The Long Way Home 1986, You Ain't Seen The Last of Me 1987, Worth the Wait 1996, John's Acoustic Christmas 2009, The Promise 2010. *Website:* www.johnschneideronline.com.

SCHNEIDER, Maria; BM, MM; American jazz composer, arranger and conductor; b. 27 Nov. 1960, Windom, MN. *Education:* Univ. of Minnesota, Univ. of Miami and Eastman School of Music. *Career:* fmr asst to Gil Evans; formed Maria Schneider Jazz Orchestra, New York 1993–, with weekly appearances at Visiones, Greenwich Village for five years, numerous tours, jazz festival appearances; she has also conducted jazz orchestras in Australia, Austria, Belgium, Canada, Denmark, Finland, France, Germany, Greenland, Holland, Iceland, Italy, Norway, Portugal, Scotland, Slovenia, Sweden, and across the USA; owner record label, ArtistShare. *Compositions:* Aires de Lando, Allegresse, Anthem, Baytrail Shuffle, Bird Count, Bombshelter Beast,

Buleria, Soleá y Rumba, Cerulean Skies, Choro Dançado, City Sunrise, Coming About, Cool Stew, Dança Ilusória, Dance You Monster to My Soft Song, Days of Wine and Roses, Dissolution, El Viento, Evanescence, Green Piece, Gumba Blue, Gush, Hang Gliding, In a Pinch, Journey Home, Ladybird, Last Season, Lately, My Lament, Night Watchmen, Nocturne, Pas de Deux, Recapitulation, Rich's Piece, Salina, Samba Solstice, Scenes from a Childhood, Sea of Tranquility, Sky Blue, Smooth Talk, Some Circles, The Pretty Road, The Willow, Three Romances, Tork's Cafe, Waltz for Toots, Waxwing, Wyrgly. *Recordings include:* albums: Evanescence 1994, Coming About 1996, Allegresse 2000, Days of Wine and Roses – live at the Jazz Standard 2000, Concert in the Garden (Grammy Award 2005) 2004, Sky Blue 2007, Winter Morning Walks (with Dawn Upshaw) 2010, The Thompson Fields (Grammy Award for Best Large Jazz Ensemble Album 2016) 2015. *Honours:* Doris Duke Award (composed dance work, Dissolution, in collaboration with the Pilobolus dance group), two Jazz Journalists' Asscn Jazz Awards for Best Composer, for Best Big Band, for Best Recording (for Concert in the Garden), for Best Arranger, for Composer/Arranger of the Year 2013, Grammy Awards for Best Instrumental Composition (for Cerulean Skies) 2008, for Composer/Arranger of the Year (for Concert in the Garden) 2013, for Arranger of the Year 2015, for Best Arrangement (for Sue (Or In A Season of Crime), for David Bowie) 2016, numerous Down Beat Magazine Critics' and Readers' Polls wins as composer, arranger. *Current Management:* Ted Kurland Associates. *Telephone:* (617) 254-0007. *E-mail:* ted@tedkurland .com. *E-mail:* marlene@mariaschneider.com (office). *Website:* www .mariaschneider.com (office).

SCHOCK, Gina; American musician (drums); b. 31 Aug. 1957, Baltimore, MD. *Career:* joined the Go-Go's (formerly The Misfits) 1980–85; formed House of Schock; The Go-Go's re-formed briefly for PETA benefit concert 1990; mem., re-formed Go-Go's 1994, shows in Las Vegas; The Go-Go's re-formed 2000–, for an album and tours, including US tour with B-52s. *Recordings:* albums: with the Go-Go's: Beauty And The Beat 1981, Vacation 1982, Talk Show 1984, Return To The Valley Of The Go-Go's 1994, God Bless The Go-Go's 2001; with House of Schock: House of Schock 1988. *E-mail:* gogos@beyondmusic.com (office). *Website:* www.gogos.com.

SCHOELINCK, Roland; Belgian musician and composer; b. 3 Jan. 1951, Anderlues, Hainaut; m. Chantal Lefevre; two s. one d. *Career:* dir, private music school; composer, arranger and performer, jazz, classical, opera, popular music and studio work; music for ballet and film; mem. Belgian Composers Union, SABAM. *Compositions:* Toots Concerto, for harmonica and symphony orchestra, Safety First, official safety hymn, Complicity, for flute and piano, Symphony, symphony poem, String Quartet, Wind Quintet, Pieces for Solo Piano, Dr Theodore, for symphony orchestra 1998, Lions Ceremony, Bouglione Parade, Infinitude, horn concerto, Jazz Quartet Concerto, Vent Dominant, concerto for horn quartet and harmony orchestra, Le vrai secret, opera, Namasté, cello concerto. *Music for film:* as arranger/composer: Gérard Corbiau's L'année de l'éveil, 12 short films and 30 advertisements. *Recordings:* Safety First, Dolphin Tears (performed by Toots Thielemans), Complicity. *Publications:* Sur La Voie de l'improvisation 1996, Easy to Write 1997, Petit Livre de Jazz 1 and 2 1997, Complicity 1997, 26 Airs de Gilles, for piano, Bb and Eb tuba, tambours et grosse-caisse. *Address:* 6 Chemin Brulotte, 7063 Neufvilles, Belgium (home). *Telephone:* (65) 723279 (office). *Fax:* (65) 728473 (office). *E-mail:* roland.schoelinck@skynet.be (home). *Website:* www.myspace .com/schoelinck (office).

SCHOLZ, Drazen; Croatian musician (drums); b. 25 June 1961, Zagreb; m. 1986, one d. *Career:* drummer with Parni Valjak (Steam Roller); Promise of Spring; Parliament; Film: Some Like It Hot; Le Cinema; mem, HGU (Croatian Music Union). *Recordings:* with Parni Valjak: Live In ZKM (Unplugged), Parni Valjak – All 15 Years (3 LPs live) 1990, Dream Hunters 1990, Awakenings 1994, Samo snovi teku uzvodno 1998, Zastave 2000. *Honours:* seven Porin Awards (Croatian equivalent of Grammy) with Parni Valjak. *Current Management:* Nenad Drobnjak, Miramarska 15b, Zagreb, Croatia. *Website:* scena.hgu.hr/parni%2Dvaljak/.

SCHOLZ, Tom, MEng; American singer and musician; b. 10 March 1947, Toledo, OH. *Education:* Massachusetts Inst. of Technology. *Career:* founder of rock group, Boston 1976–; various tours and live appearances. *Recordings include:* albums: Boston 1976, Don't Look Back 1978, Third Stage 1986, Walk On 1994, Corporate America 2002. *Website:* www.bandboston.com.

SCHON, Neal; American musician (guitar) and singer; b. 27 Feb. 1954, Tinker Air Force Base, Okla. *Career:* guitarist with Carlos Santana; Founder, Azteca; Founder-mem. rock group Journey 1973–; mem. HSAS 1984, Bad English 1988–91, Hardline 1992–; partnership with Jan Hammer 1981–82; also solo artist. *Recordings include:* with Santana: Santana 1972, Santana/Abraxas/Santana 1997, Santana/Abraxas/Santana 1998; with Journey: Journey 1975, Look into the Future 1976, Next 1977, Infinity 1978, Evolution 1979, Departure 1980, Dream After Dream 1980, Escape 1981, Frontiers 1983, Raised on Radio 1986, Trial by Fire 1996, Arrival 2001, Generations 2005, Revelation 2008, Eclipse 2011; with HSAS: Through The Fire 1984; with Jan Hammer: Untold Passion 1981, Here To Stay 1982; with Bad English: Bad English 1989, Backlash 1991; solo: Late Nite 1989, Beyond The Thunder 1995, Electric World 1997, Piranha Blues 1999, Voice 2001, I on U 2005, The Calling 2012, So U 2014. *Website:* www.schonmusic.com; www.journeymusic.com.

SCHÖNBERG, Claude-Michel; French composer; b. 6 July 1944, s. of Adolphe Schönberg and Julie Nadás; one s. two d.; m. Charlotte Talbot 2003.

Career: started as producer for EMI France and as pop song writer 1967–72; recording his own songs in France 1974–77. *Ballet:* Wuthering Heights with the Northern Ballet Theatre 2002, cr. Cleopatra 2011. *Films:* Les Misérables (screenplay) 2012. *Compositions:* musicals: La Révolution Française 1973, Les Misérables 1980–85, Miss Saigon 1989, Martin Guerre 1996–, Pirate Queen 2006–, Marguerite 2008; for cinema: Les Misérables 2012. *Honours:* recipient of Tony, Grammy, Evening Standard and Laurence Olivier Awards, French 'Molière' and 'Victoires de la musique' for musicals; Grammy Award for Outstanding Contrib. to the Creative Community. *Current Management:* c/o Cameron Mackintosh Limited, 1 Bedford Square, London, WC1B 3RA, England. *Telephone:* (20) 7637-8866.

SCHREURS, Dirk, MA; Belgian musician (piano) and academic; *Professor of Jazz Piano, Brussels Royal Conservatory of Music;* b. 23 May 1966, Neerpelt; m. Sabine Tielens 2007. *Education:* Music Acad., Neerpelt, Univ. of Louvain; master-classes with John Abercrombie, Dave Kikoski, Trilok Gurtu, Reggie Washington, Martial Solal, David Gilmour. *Career:* pianist and composer with Real Deal, DSWB 4, Jan Mues Quartet, Jive Talk, Scora, Chromatic Banana, Enrique Tarde; appearances on Belgian Radio and TV; Prof. of Jazz Piano, Brussels Royal Conservatory 1994–; mem. SABAM. *Exhibitions include:* Minds of Glass (video art with Marta Bressi), Los Angeles Int. Film Festival 2009, New York 2010. *Compositions:* more than 250 compositions and arrangements. *Recordings include:* Passage in Beauty 1991, Flexibility 1992, Beyond Ballads 1993, Echoing Delight 1994, Parallel Flaming 1994, Still Fragments 1994, From Blues to Funk 1995, River of Appearance 1996, Crossing the Trail 1998, The Shape of Solitude 1999, Echo Passage 2000, Tremor 2001, Spore 2002, Legacy 2004, Minds of Glass 2009, I Found You Found Me 2014, Bragasinga 2015. *Publications:* Jazzics 1984. *Honours:* Int. Jazz Composition Award, Hoeilaart 2001, 2013. *E-mail:* blizz@skynet.be (office). *Website:* www.dirkschreurs.com.

SCHROADER, Doni; American musician (percussion). *Career:* mem., ...And You Will Know Us By The Trail Of Dead 1995–. *Recordings include:* albums: ...And You Will Know Us By The Trail Of Dead 1998, Madonna 1999, Source Tags and Codes 2002, The Secret of Elena's Tomb 2003, Worlds Apart 2005, So Divided 2006, The Century of Self 2009. *E-mail:* merlin@trailofdead.com (office). *Website:* www.trailofdead.com.

SCHULTZ, Debra Kay; American gospel singer; b. 30 Oct. 1955, Holden, W Va; m. Robert A. Schultz 1974; two s. *Education:* studied with Robert Turner. *Career:* numerous appearances at gospel concerts, on Gospel TV stations, throughout USA; radio stations internationally; mem. Gospel Music Asscn. *Recordings include:* singles: Lord You're My Strength 1991, Don't Lift The Anchor 1992, I Just Found Jesus 1993. *Honours:* Airplay Int. King Eagle Award for Christian Female Artist of the Year 1994–95. *Address:* PO Box 88, Route 17, Sharples, WV 25183, USA.

SCHULTZ, Eric, BA; American musician (guitar, electric bass), composer, arranger and teacher; b. 11 Sept. 1960, Los Angeles, Calif. *Education:* California State Univ., Northridge, guitar studies with Ralph Towner, Joe Diorio, John Abercrombie and Ron Escheté. *Career:* professional jazz player 1982; resident in Paris 1986–; worked regularly with jazz drummers including Oliver Johnson, Barry Altschul, Sunny Murray, Frank Butler, Alan Jones, Peter Perfido; especially with Paul Carman 1984–85, Onzy Matthews Quartet, Peter Perfido/Andy Laster Group; Eric Schultz Trio (with Oliver Johnson, Jack Gregg) 1991–; Eric Schultz Nonet; Jean Michel Couchet/Eric Schultz Quartet 1993–; Eric Schultz Space and Time Ensemble 1995; Viviane Ginapé/Eric Schultz duo; mem. Soc. des auteurs, compositeurs et éditeurs de musique (SACEM). *Recordings:* Eric Schultz Space And Time Ensemble 1995. *Address:* Space and Time Productions, 8 rue de la Pompe, 94410 St Maurice, France.

SCHULTZ, Irma; Swedish singer, songwriter and actress; b. 1 Oct. 1965, Stockholm. *Career:* tours of Sweden and numerous television performances; backing singer for many artists; solo artist. *Recordings include:* Da Staden Vaknat, 1989; Irma, 1991; Tröst för Stygga Barn, 1993; Andas Fritt, 1995; A Bird That Whistles, Songs of Joni Mitchell, 1996. *Honours:* scholarships from STIM, SKAP, Grammy Award for Best Female Artist in Sweden 1989. *E-mail:* isk@tele2.se. *Website:* www.irmaschultzkeller.se.

SCHULTZ, Wesley Keith; American folk rock singer, songwriter and guitarist; b. 30 Dec. 1982, Ramsey, NJ. *Education:* Univ. of Richmond. *Career:* fmr mem. Free Beer, 6Cheek; Founder-mem. (with Jeremiah Fraites) Wesley Jeremiah, changed name to The Lumineers 2009–; released debut EP 2011, numerous tours. *Recordings:* album: The Lumineers 2012. *Current Management:* c/o Christen Greene and David Meinert, Onto Entertainment, 2611 5th Avenue, Seattle, WA 98121-1517, USA. *Address:* c/o Dualtone Records, Dualtone Music Group, 203 North 11th Street, Suite B, Nashville, TN 37206, USA (office). *Telephone:* (615) 320-0620 (office). *Fax:* (615) 320-0692 (office). *E-mail:* info@dualtone.com; info@thelumineers.com. *Website:* www.dualtone.com (office); www.thelumineers.com.

SCHUMAN, Tom; American musician (piano, keyboards) and songwriter; b. 31 Jan. 1958, Buffalo, NY; s. of Wally Schuman and Marion Schuman; m. Yvonne Schuman. *Career:* played with pop and jazz bands including The Existing Reality and Birthright; mem. jazz band, Spyro Gyra 1977–; also guest appearances and collab. with other artists, and solo projects. *Recordings:* with Spyro Gyra: Spyro Gyra 1978, Morning Dance 1979, Catching the Sun 1980, Carnaval 1980, Freetime 1981, Incognito 1982, City Kids 1983, Access All

Areas 1984, Alternating Currents 1985, Breakout 1986, Stories Without Words 1987, Rites of Summer 1988, Point of View 1989, Fast Forward 1990, Three Wishes 1992, Dreams Beyond Control 1993, Love & Other Obsessions 1995, Heart of the Night 1996, 20/20 1997, Road Scholars 1998, Got the Magic 1999, In Modern Times 2001, Original Cinema 2003, The Deep End 2004, Wrapped in a Dream 2006, Good to Go-Go 2007, Down the Wire 2009; solo: Extremities 1990, Into Your Heart 2002, Schuman Nature 2003, Deep Chill 2006. *Current Management:* c/o Phil Brennan, Crosseyed Bear Productions, 270 Olympic Avenue, Buffalo, NY 14215-3258, USA. *Telephone:* (845) 827-6426. *E-mail:* phil@philbrennan.com. *Address:* JazzBridge Music, POB 750186, Las Vegas, NV 89136-0186, USA (office). *Telephone:* (702) 553-1757 (office). *Fax:* (702) 515-0783 (office). *E-mail:* info@jazzbridge.com (office); info@spyrogyra.com (office). *Website:* www.jazzbridgellc.com (office); www.spyrogyra.com (office).

SCHUUR, Diane; American singer; b. 1953, Tacoma, Washington. *Recordings include:* albums: Pilot of My Destiny 1982, Deedles 1984, Schuur Thing 1985, Timeless 1986, Diane Schuur and the Count Basie Orchestra 1987, Talkin" About You 1988, Collection 1989, Pure Schuur 1991, In Tribute 1992, Love Songs 1993, 1994, Heart To Heart (With B. B. King), Love Walked In 1996, Blues For Schuur 1997, The Best of Diane Schuur 1997, Music Is My Life 1999, Friends For Schuur 2000, Swingin' For Schuur (with Maynard Ferguson) 2001, Midnight 2003, Schuur Fire 2005, Live In London 2006, Some Other Time 2008, The Gathering 2011, Diane Schuur Live 2012. *Honours:* two Grammy Awards 1987–88, Manhattan Asscn of Cabarets and Clubs Award 1997, Bagley Wright Award 1997, First Annual Ella Fitzgerald Award from the Montréal Int. Jazz Festival 1999, Helen Keller Achievement Award 2000, AFTRA Disability Awareness Award 2003, Disability Rights Legal Center DREAM Award 2006. *Current Management:* c/o Donald Marsh, Deedles Music Inc., PO Box 1530, Sumner, WA 98390, USA. *Telephone:* (253) 862-3179. *Website:* www.dianeschuur.com.

SCHWARTZ, Stephen, BFA; American songwriter and composer; b. 6 March 1948, New York, NY. *Education:* Juilliard School of Music, Carnegie Mellon Univ. *Career:* Producer, RCA Records; Producer, Original Cast album of Godspell; runs ASCAP Foundation musical theatre workshops; mem. Bd ASCAP Foundation, Council of Dramatists' Guild. *Recordings:* Reluctant Pilgrim 1997, Uncharted Territory 2001. *Compositions:* title song, play Butterflies Are Free, Broadway 1969; for musicals: Music and lyrics, Godspell (two Grammy Awards) 1971, Pippin 1972, The Magic Show 1974, The Baker's Wife 1976, Children Of Eden 1991, Wicked 2003, Snapshots 2011; lyrics, Rags 1986; music, Working (Drama Desk Award for Best Dir) 1978, Personals; for film: Score, Pocahontas (with Alan Menken) (Acad. Awards for Original Musical or Comedy Score and Original Song) 1995, The Hunchback of Notre Dame (with Alan Menken) 1996; songs, The Prince of Egypt (Acad. Award for Original Song, for When You Believe 1999), Enchanted 2007; for TV: Geppetto 2000. *Publication:* The Perfect Peach. *Honours:* ASCAP Award for Most Performed Motion Picture Song, inducted into American Theatre Hall of Fame 2010. *Current Management:* c/o Harry Fox Agency, 711 Third Avenue, New York, NY 10017, USA. *E-mail:* schwartz@stephenschwartz.com. *Website:* www.stephenschwartz.com.

SCHWARZ, Alexander (Ali); German DJ and producer; b. 7 June 1967, Stuttgart. *Career:* ran club nights in Stuttgart, ON-U 1990–93, Red Dog 1993–97; set up Tiefschwarz DJ/production team with brother Sebastian (Basti) and Peter Hoff 1996; debut single 24 Seven released on Continuemusics label 1997, more than 50 remixes released 1996–; regular DJ appearances throughout Europe, USA, Australia, Brazil, Russia, as well as residencies in London, Berlin, Frankfurt; relocated to Berlin, set up recording studio 2003; set up own label Souvenir 2006. *Recordings:* albums: RAL9005 2000, Eat Books 2005, 10 Years Of Blackmusik 2007; singles include: 24 Seven 1997, Music 1999, Holy Music 2000, I'll Be Around 2000, Never 2001, Thru A Little Window 2001, You 2001, Hello Again 2002, Nix 2002, Ghostrack 2003, Blow 2004, Issst 2005, Wait & See 2005, Warning Siren 2005, Damage 2005, Fly 2006, Original 2007, Hey! (as Ichundu) 2007; other: remixes for artists including Masters at Work, Ultra Naté, Boogie Solitaire, Freaks, Isolee, Groove Armada, The Rapture, Cassius, Spektrum, Micatone, Lost & Alive, Lopazz, Osunlade, Minimal Compact, Trüby Trio, DJ Hell, Kelis, Missy Elliott, Depeche Mode, Madonna, Roxy Music, Booka Shade, Soft Cell, Goldfrapp. *Address:* Souvenir, Kremmenerstr. 9-11, 10435 Berlin, Germany (office). *E-mail:* arthur@souvenir-music.com (office). *Website:* www.tiefschwarz.net (office).

SCHWARZ, Jean; French composer; b. 20 May 1939, Lille. *Career:* worked in Dept of Ethnomusicology, Musée de l'Homme 1965–99; Prof., Gennevilliers Conservatoire 1979–97; mem. GRM de l'INA 1969–99. *Compositions include:* Hoiku 1971, Erda 1972, Anticycle 1972, Tracés sonores 1973, Sonances pour bande 1973, Le Pays au quarante horloges 1974, Il Était une fois pour bande 1974, Comodulation 1974, Histoires d'A 1974, Symphonie pour bande 1975, Eclats 1975, Les Cahiers de Malte 1976, Un Enfant dans la foule 1976, Variations pour bande 1976, Nuit d'or 1976, Providence 1976, Don Quichotte pour bande 1976, Comment ça va 1976, Ici et ailleurs 1976, Fotoband pour bande 1977, Roundtrip 1977, Pour Clémence 1977, Louis Rossel et la commune de Paris 1977, La Justice 1977, Guillevic 1977, L'Enfance d'hier 1977, Klavierband pour bande et piano 1978, Le Voyage au pays de l'abandon 1978, Le Brave soldat Sveik 1978, Le Dossier 51 1978, Danses en liberté 1978, Year of the Horse 1978, Henri Michaux 1978, Pianoband 1978, Writings on the Wall 1979, L'Enfance de Vladimir Kobalt 1979, Roundaboutnow 1979, Le

Prince de Hombourg 1979, Appelez moi Ferdinand 1979, Wheels 1979, Thomson 1979, Blue Chicken 1979, Gamma plus 1979, Surroundings 1980, Windmills 1980, Maison rouge 1980, Dune 1980, Jackson Pollock 1980, De profundis 1980, Just for Fun 1980, Undici onde 1981, La Glace à trois faces 1981, And Around 1981, One to Two 1981, La Guele du loup 1981, Eaux profondes 1981, Les Gens d'ici 1981, Mon enfant ma mère 1981, Eveil 1981, Suite N pour bande 1982, Bran pour bande 1982, Les Terroristes à la retraite 1982, Interurbain 1982, Le Grand braquet 1982, Tous ensemble 1983, Les Frères de Soledad 1983, Souvenir de la maison des morts 1983, Quatre saisons (Vierjahreszeiten) 1983, L'Automne 1983, Nocturne pour flûte et bande 1983, Les Nouvelles de l'histoire 1983, La Célestine 1983, La Femme au Japon 1983, Sonal France culture 1984, Saturday Matinée 1984, En Désespoir de causes 1984, L'Ivrogne dans la brousse 1984, Perpetuum mobile I: cycles 1984, Perpetuum mobile II: Mécaniques 1984, Thrillers 1984, Perpetuum mobile III: Tensions 1985, Issue de secours 1985, Détective (éléments) 1985, Les Battants 1985, Little Suite 1985, Cendrillon 1985, Still Waters 1986, Chantakoa 1986, A toute Villette 1986, Tokyo 1987, Quatre vingts 1987, Le Concert était-il réussi? 1987, Medley Body Music 1987, Suite symphonique 1989, Vent d'est 1990, The Seamaid's Music 1990, Pyramides 1990, L'Ours et le rat 1990, Assolutamente 1990, Voicescape 1990, Up 1990, Sculptures 1990, Mi 1990, So Long 1990, Encore 1990, Nouvelle vague 1990, La Barque sacrée 1991, Mano a mano 1991, Acaousmatique 1991, Sokoa Tanz 1991, Concertino 1992, Olé 1992, Milesan 1992, Silky 1992, Elles 1992, Bluesie 1992, Canto 1993, Capriccio 1993, Le Chevalier de Goñi 1993, Transe 1993, Makinak 1995, Chasin' 1996, Courrier du pacifique 1996, Octosax 1997, Mixed Up 1997, Dall'Interno 1998, Etudes 1998, Dilin dalan 1999, Calypso 2000. *Recordings include:* albums: Quatre Saisons 1988, Suite Symphonique: Anticycle 1988, Chantakoa: And Around 1989, Assolutamente 1990, Destroy 1990, Sokoa Tanz 1992, The Sea Maid's Music 1992, Mano A Mano 1993, Canto 1994, Quatre Vingts 1995, Makinak/Capriccio 1995, Transe 1995, Gamma Plus 1997, Mosaique: Il Était Une Fois (Variations) 1998, Oeuvres 1998, Erda Symphonie Surroundings 2000, Dilin Dalan 2001.

SCHWARZ, Sebastian (Basti); German DJ and producer; b. 28 Dec. 1969, Stuttgart. *Career:* set up Tiefschwarz DJ/production team with brother Sebastian (Basti) and Peter Hoff 1996; debut single 24 Seven released on Continuemusics label 1997, more than 50 remixes released 1996–; regular DJ appearances throughout Europe, USA, Australia, Brazil, Russia, as well as residencies in London, Berlin, Frankfurt; relocated to Berlin, set up recording studio 2003; set up own label Souvenir 2006. *Recordings:* albums: RAL9005 2000, Eat Books 2005, 10 Years Of Blackmusik 2007; singles include: 24 Seven 1997, Music 1999, Holy Music 2000, I'll Be Around 2000, Never 2001, Thru A Little Window 2001, You 2001, Hello Again 2002, Nix 2002, Ghostrack 2003, Blow 2004, Issst 2005, Wait & See 2005, Warning Siren 2005, Damage 2005, Fly 2006, Original 2007, Hey! (as Ichundu) 2007; other: remixes for artists including Masters at Work, Ultra Naté, Boogie Solitaire, Freaks, Isolee, Groove Armada, The Rapture, Cassius, Spektrum, Micatone, Lost & Alive, Lopazz, Osunlade, Minimal Compact, Trüby Trio, DJ Hell, Kelis, Missy Elliott, Depeche Mode, Madonna, Roxy Music, Booka Shade, Soft Cell, Goldfrapp. *Address:* Souvenir, Kremmenerstr. 9-11, 10435 Berlin, Germany (office). *E-mail:* arthur@souvenir-music.com (office). *Website:* www .tiefschwarz.net (office).

SCHWISBERG, Arnold, BA, BSc, LLB; Canadian music company executive; b. 17 Nov. 1961, Montréal, QC; m. Kathrine Brodie; two s. *Education:* Queens Faculty of Law, Kingston, ON. *Career:* founder and co-owner, Pres., independent label Jazz Inspiration Records. *Address:* Jazz Inspiration Records, 5510 Robinson Avenue, Suite 206, Cote St Luc, QC H4V 2P5, Canada (office). *E-mail:* abslegal@total.net (office). *Website:* www .jazzinspiration.com.

SCHWISBERG, David; Canadian music company executive; b. 20 July 1966, Montréal, QC. *Career:* co-owner, Vice-Pres., independent label Jazz Inspiration Records. *Address:* Jazz Inspiration Records, 5510 Robinson Avenue, Suite 206, Cote St Luc, QC H4V 2P5, Canada (office). *E-mail:* abslegal@total .net (office). *Website:* www.jazzinspiration.com.

SCOCCO, Mauro; Swedish artist and composer; b. 11 Sept. 1962, Stockholm. *Career:* singer Ratata 1980–83; part of duo with Johan Ekelund 1983–89; currently solo artist. *Recordings include:* with Ratata: Ratata 1982; with duo: Äventyr 1983, Paradis 1984, Sent i September 1985, Mellan Dröm och Verklighet 1989; Människor under molnen 1989; solo: Mauro Scocco 1988, Dr. Space Dagbok 1991, Ciao! 1992, 28 Grader i Skuggan 1994, Godmorgon Sverige 1996, Tillbaks Till Världen 1999, Beat Hotel 2003, Herr Jimsons Äventyr 2005, Ljudet Av Tiden Som Går 2007, Musik för nyskilda 2011, Årets Julklapp! 2013; with Plura Jonsson: Mauro & Plura 2014. *Honours:* four Swedish Grammy Awards; numerous other awards. *Current Management:* c/o Diesel Music, Saltmätargatan 7, 113 59 Stockholm, Sweden. *Telephone:* (8) 615-67-80. *Fax:* (8) 615-67-88. *E-mail:* info@dieselmusic.se. *Website:* www .dieselmusic.se; www.mauroscocco.se.

SCOFIELD, John; American jazz musician (guitar) and composer; b. 26 Dec. 1951, Ohio. *Education:* Berklee College of Music, Boston. *Career:* began playing in local R&B groups; solo artiste, 1970s–; Played with Billy Cobham; Gary Burton; Dave Liebman; Charlie Haden; Jack DeJohnette; McCoy Tyner; Marc Johnson; French National Orchestra; Mike Gibbs Orchestra; member, Miles Davis' group, 1983–85. *Recordings:* albums include: John Scofield Live 1977, Rough House 1978, Who's Who 1979, Bar Talk 1980, Shinola 1981, Out

Like A Light 1981, Electric Outlet 1984, Still Warm 1987, Blue Matter 1987, Loud Jazz 1987, Flat Out 1989, Pick Hits Live 1989, Time On My Hands 1990, Slo Sco 1990, Meant To Be 1991, Blue Matter 1991, Grace Under Pressure 1992, What We Do 1993, Bump 2000, Steady Groovin' 2000, Works For Me 2001, Uberjam 2002, Up All Night 2003, That's What I Say: John Scofield Plays the Music of Ray Charles 2005, This Meets That 2007, Piety Street 2009, A Moment's Peace 2011, Past Present (Grammy Award for Best Jazz Instrumental Album 2016) 2015; with Miles Davis: Decoy, 1984, You're Under Arrest 1985, Star People 1989, Groove Elation 1996; with Herbie Hancock: The New Standard 1996; with Medeski Scofield Martin & Wood: Out Louder 2006; Also recorded with Gerry Mulligan, Chet Baker, John Abercrombie. *E-mail:* sco@johnscofield.com. *Website:* www.johnscofield.com.

SCOTT, David Andrew; British songwriter, musician (guitar, keyboards), singer, lecturer and broadcaster; *Lecturer in Music, University of the West of Scotland;* b. 20 Aug. 1964, Falkirk, Scotland; m. 1st Julie Parker 1989; m. 2nd Margaret Daly 2007. *Education:* Falkirk College, Glasgow School of Art. *Career:* recordings as Chewy Raccoon, Hearts and Minds; film and television commissions; founder, My Dark Star record label to release records by The Pearlfishers 1991–; numerous concert appearances; producer for BMX Bandits, Ricky Ross and others, BBC Radio presenter 1998–; Lecturer in Music, Univ. of the West of Scotland; mem. PRS, Musicians' Union. *Recordings include:* with The Pearlfishers: Sacred 1991, Hurt 1991, Za Za's Garden 1993, The Strange World of the Tall Poppies 1997, The Young Picnickers 1999, Across the Milky Way 2001, Sky Meadows 2003, A Sunflower At Christmas 2004, Up with the Larks 2007; with BMX Bandits: My Chain 2005, Bee Stings 2007. *Radio:* Silverscreen Beats, series 1 and 2, Classic Scottish Albums, series 1–3, Waxing Lyrical series 1. *Address:* Marina Records, Kassel/Lähnemann GbR, Margaretenstrasse 39, 20357 Hamburg, Germany (office). *E-mail:* info@marinarecords.com (office). *Website:* www .marinarecords.com (office); www.pearlfishers.co.uk (home).

SCOTT, Don E.; Canadian singer, songwriter and musician (guitar, steel guitar, mandolin, harmonica, resophonic guitar, drums); b. 12 Feb. 1937; m. Marie; one s. two d. *Education:* diplomas in Real Property Management, Public Relations, Interpersonal Skills, Economics and Social Philosophy. *Career:* TV, radio, video and stage performances; fmr businessman and consultant; currently active volunteer with community agencies and charities. *Compositions:* over 600 songs. *Recordings:* The Real Deal, Beginnings, Room In My Heart. *Honours:* numerous awards and prizes in songwriting and singing; also numerous honours for community service. *Current Management:* The Management Centre, 13808, 110A Avenue, Edmonton, Alberta, T5M 2M9, Canada. *Telephone:* (780) 934-0571. *E-mail:* tmc.cci@telus.net (office).

SCOTT, Hammond; American record producer and attorney; b. 15 May 1950, Alexandria, Louisiana. *Education:* Dr of Law. *Career:* co-owner, Black Top Records Inc (internationally distributed and recognized blues, R&B and roots label); produced over 100 albums; served as personal manager of blues artist Clarence 'Gatemouth' Brown 1970s; former writer, Living Blues Magazine; hosted radio show on WWOZ FM, New Orleans, for 5 years; produced recordings by R&B artists including: Buckwheat Zydeco, WC Clark, Albert Collins, Robert Ward, Solomon Burke, Maria Muldaur, Earl King, Snooks Eaglin, Bobby Parker, Neville Brothers, Anson Funderburgh and the Rockets, Former Prosecutor, District Attorney's Office of Harry Connick Sr; Neville Brothers; Bobby Radcliff; Bobby Parker; Robert Ward; Ronnie Earl; Earl Gaines. *Honours:* Numerous W. C. Handy Awards.

SCOTT, Hillary; American singer and songwriter; b. 1 April 1984, d. of Lang Scott and Linda Davis; m. Chris Tyrrell 2012; one d. *Career:* mem. country music group Lady Antebellum 2006–; performed at Grand Old Opry; songwriter for Sara Evans, Blake Shelton. *Recordings include:* albums: Lady Antebellum 2008, Need You Now (Grammy Award for Best Country Album 2011, Acad. of Country Music Award for Album of the Year 2011) 2010, Own the Night (Grammy Award for Best Country Album 2012) 2011, On This Winter's Night 2012, Golden 2013, 747 2014. *Honours:* numerous including: Acad. of Country Music Awards for Best New Group 2008, for Best Vocal Group 2010, for Best Single Record of the Year (for Need You Now) 2010, for Best Song of the Year (for Need You Now) 2010, for Top Vocal Group 2011, for Vocal Group of the Year 2012, Jim Reeves Int. Award 2013, Country Music Asscn Awards for New Artist of the Year 2008, for Single of the Year (for I Run to You) 2009, (for Need You Now) 2010, for Vocal Group of the Year 2009, 2010, for Int. Artist Achievement 2012, Grammy Award for Best Country Performance by a Duo or Group with Vocals (for I Run to You) 2010, Grammy Award for Record of the Year, Song of the Year, Best Performance by a Duo or Group (all for Need You Now) 2011, Billboard Music Award for Top Country Artist 2012, American Music Awards for Favorite Band, Duo or Group – Country 2012, 2013, American Country Awards for Duo/Group Artist of the Year 2012, 2013, for Single by a Duo/Group (for We Owned the Night) 2012, (for Downtown) 2013. *Address:* c/o Capitol Nashville Records, 3322 West End Avenue, 11th Floor, Nashville, TN 37203-1100, USA. *Telephone:* (615) 269-2000. *Fax:* (615) 269-2059. *E-mail:* support@ladyantebellum.com. *Website:* www.ladyantebellum.com.

SCOTT, Jill; American singer and poet; b. 4 April 1972, Philadelphia. *Career:* started career reading poetry until spotted by local hip hop outfit The Roots; wrote lyrics for their Grammy Award-winning first single You Got Me; performed with Canadian cast of stage musical Rent; collaborations: Eric Benet, Will Smith, Common, 4 Hero. *Films include:* Hounddog 2007, Why Did

I Get Married? 2007, The No. 1 Ladies Detective Agency 2008. *Recordings include:* albums: Who Is Jill Scott?: Words and Sounds Vol. 1 2000, Experience 2001, Beautifully Human: Words and Sounds Vol. 2 2004, Collaborations 2007, The Real Thing: Words and Sounds Vol. 3 2007, Light of the Sun 2011, Woman 2015. *Website:* www.missjillscott.com.

SCOTT, Lydia; Canadian country singer and musician (guitar); b. 9 Aug. 1953, Montréal, QC. *Education:* Montréal University. *Compositions:* The Moon She Knows, True Love, I Could Love You, As Good As You Look. *Recordings:* Isn't It Always Love, You Can Crash Here. *Honours:* Talent Contest Winner 1989, BC Award for Female Vocalist of the Year 1999. *Address:* Suite 704, 2121 W 44th Avenue, Vancouver, BC V6M 2G5, Canada.

SCOTT, Matthew James; musician (piano) and composer; b. 11 Oct. 1967, London, England. *Career:* resident pianist, The Vortex 1994–95; regular appearances on London jazz/pop circuit, London jazz festivals 1994–95; clubs include: The 606; The Orange; The King's Head, Upper Street; Chat's Palace. *Compositions:* L'Esquisse, film soundtrack, 1995; Trio for strings, 1995; The Land Girls, film soundtrack, 1998; The Mrs. Bradley Mysteries, BBC drama serial, 2000. *Recordings include:* albums: Improvisations for Solo Piano 1995, Standards 1995. *Address:* 249 Goswell Road, London EC1V 7JD, England.

SCOTT, Mike; singer, songwriter and musician (guitar); b. 14 Dec. 1958, Edinburgh, Scotland. *Career:* lead singer, Another Pretty Face 1978–81, Funhouse 1981–82, The Red and The Black 1982; Founder mem. The Waterboys 1983–93, 1999–; solo artist 1994–; numerous tours and festival appearances. *Recordings include:* albums: with The Waterboys: A Pagan Place 1984, This Is The Sea 1985, Fisherman's Blues 1988, Room To Roam 1990, Dream Harder 1993, Secret Life of the Waterboys 1994, Rock in the Weary Land 2000, Universal Hall 2003, Book of Lightning 2007, An Appointment with Mr Yeats 2011, In A Special Place 2011; solo: Bring 'Em All In 1995, Still Burning 1997, Whole of the Moon 1998; with Characters: Characters 1997; with Angel Grant: Album 1998. *Publications:* Jungleland 1977–80, Adventures of a Waterboy 2012. *Honours:* Ivor Novello Award (for The Whole of the Moon) 1992. *Website:* www.mikescottwaterboys.com.

SCOTT, Rick; singer, songwriter, actor and musician (dulcimer, whimmy-diddle, guitar, trombone, tuba, Japanese flute); b. 14 July 1948, New Jersey, USA. *Career:* Pied Pumpkin String Ensemble 1975–76; Pied Pear 1976–83; Rick Scott Band 1985–86; concert tours throughout Canada, USA, Australia, Asia as solo family performer; starred in numerous stage plays, musicals including Barnum (title role), The Late Blumer, Angry Housewives; mem. AFofM, SOCAN, ACTRA, Canadian Actors Equity. *Recordings include:* albums for children: The Electric Snowshoe, 1989; Rick Around the Rock, 1992; Philharmonic Fool, 1995. *Honours:* Pacific Music Industry Award for Best Children's Album 1997. *Address:* 2736 W 13 Ave, Vancouver, BC V6K 2T4, Canada.

SCOTT, Tommy; British singer and songwriter; b. 18 Feb. 1966. *Career:* founder mem., Space –1997; numerous television appearances and live performances. *Recordings include:* albums: Spiders, 1996; Remixes and B-Sides, 1996; Tin Planet, 1998.

SCOTT, Toni Lee; American singer; b. 15 Jan. 1933, San Francisco, CA; m. Angelo Ligi 1989. *Career:* professional singer from age 14; mem., Bob Scobey's Band, Bob Crosby's Band; numerous television appearances, radio broadcasts and club appearances; mem. Soc. of Singers, Women in Music Business. *Recordings include:* albums: San Francisco, Goody Goody, Something's Always Happening On The River 1959, Volume Lonely 1963, Songs of My Friends 1996. *Publication:* A Kind of Loving (autobiog.) 2002. *Honours:* Cerebral Palsy Fade To Gold Award for Entertainer of the Year, Heart Assen Woman of the Year Award. *Address:* 6 Haverhill Court, Novato, CA 94947, USA. *E-mail:* tonileescott@webtv.net. *Website:* www.tonileescott.com.

SCOTT, Tony; Suriname rap artist, dancer, singer and composer; b. 3 Oct. 1973, Paramaribo. *Career:* solo artist 1987–; mem. FNV Kunstenbond. *Recordings include:* The Piece 1990, Expressions Of The Soul 1991, Chameleon 1993. *Honours:* Dance Artist Award 1989, 1990. *E-mail:* info@eurotrophic.nl. *Website:* www.tonyscott.nl.

SCOTT-FRANCIS, Chris, (Chris Francis); British bandleader, jazz musician (alto/soprano saxophone, G flute) and photographer; b. 11 Aug. 1948, London, England; m. Penny 1976; one s. *Education:* Manchester and Chelsea Art Schools, studied music privately. *Career:* f. Naima, band ranging from trio to fifteen piece, toured Europe; Founder-mem. Joy quintet; recorded with many pop stars, toured with rock bands and folk groups; active teacher of saxophone and jazz studies; widely exhibited artist, both paintings and constructions; inventor of the Novacal(TM) calendar system; mem. Musicians' Union, Performing Right Soc., Mechanical-Copyright Protection Soc. *Recordings:* Herm Island Suite (BBC Radio), Joy, Ming Hat, Baltic Suite, (session man) Adam Ant: Goody Two Shoes; numerous broadcasts of own compositions. *Honours:* GLAA Young Jazz Musicans Award (jtly) 1976. *Address:* 10A Putney High Street, London, SW15 1SL, England (office). *Telephone:* (20) 8788-2551 (office). *E-mail:* chris@scott-francis.co.uk (office).

SCOTT-KEY, Joules; American musician (drums); b. Flint, Mich. *Education:* Univ. of North Texas. *Career:* mem. Metric 1998–; founding mem. Bang Lime. *Films:* soundtrack contributions: Scott Pilgrim vs the World 2010, The Twilight Saga: Eclipse 2010. *Recordings:* albums: with Metric: Old World Underground Where Are You Now 2003, Live it Out 2005, Grow Up and Blow Away 2007, Fantasies (Juno Award for Alternative Album of the Year 2010) 2009; with Bang Lime: Best Friends in Love 2007; other credits include: Spirit If, Kevin Drew 2007. *Honours:* Juno Award for Group of the Year 2010. *Address:* c/o Last Gang Records, 171 East Liberty Street, Suite 330, Toronto, ON M6K 3P6, Canada (office). *Telephone:* (416) 534-3000 (office). *Fax:* (416) 534-3005 (office). *E-mail:* management@ilovemetric.com (office); contact@banglime.com (office). *Website:* www.ilovemetric.com; www.banglime.com.

SCURLOCK, Clifton Thomas (Kliph); American musician (drums, percussion) and songwriter; b. 16 June 1973, Topeka, Kan.; s. of Roger W. Scurlock and Linda Louise Rokey. *Career:* fmr mem. Slackjaw 1990–93; played in several other bands including Kill Creek, Sleeztax, Panel Donor, The Rohypnol Rangers, Contortion Horse during 1990s; mem. The Flaming Lips 2002–, full-time mem. 2009–; also performs in Paris Gun. *Recordings:* albums: with The Flaming Lips: At War with the Mystics 2006 (Grammy Award for Best Engineered Album, Non-Classical 2007), Embryonic 2009; with Stardeath and White Dwarfs: The Flaming Lips and Stardeath and White Dwarfs with Henry Rollins and Peaches Doing Dark Side of the Moon 2010; other credits: Cinemagic, Cinemagic 2000, Age of the Sun, The Sunshine Fix 2001. *Honours:* Grammy Award for Best Rock Instrumental Performance 2006. *Current Management:* c/o Scott Booker, Hellfire Enterprises Limited, 1208 Chowning Avenue, Edmond, OK 73034, USA. *Telephone:* (405) 715-0600. *Fax:* (405) 715-0632. *E-mail:* SDBMKTG@hellfireltdcom. *Website:* www.hellfireltd .com. *Address:* c/o Warner Bros. Records Inc., 3300 Warner Boulevard, Burbank, CA 91505, USA (office). *Website:* www.theflaminglips.com.

SEAL; British singer and songwriter; b. (Henry Olusegun Adeola Samuel), 19 Feb. 1963, London, England; m. Heidi Klum 2005 (divorced 2012); two s. two d. *Career:* singer, Adamski 1990; solo artist 1991–; numerous concerts and tours. *Recordings include:* albums: Seal 1991, Seal 1994, Human Being 1998, Seal IV 2003, System 2007, Soul 2008, Commitment 2010, Soul 2 2011, 7 2015. *Honours:* Ivor Novello Award for Best Contemporary Song (for Killer) 1991, Q Award for Best New Act 1991, Variety Club of Great Britain Recording Artist of 1991, BRIT Awards for Best Male Artist, for Best British Album, for Best British Video 1992, Grammy Awards for Best Record, for Best Song 1996, Ivor Novello Awards for Best Contemporary Song, for Int. Hit of the Year (for Crazy) 1992. *Current Management:* c/o Ric Salmon, Harvest Entertainment, Unit 217, Buspace Studios, Conlan Street, London, W10 5AP, England. *E-mail:* ric@harvestentertainment.com. *Website:* www.harvestentertainment .com; www.seal.com.

SEALS, Troy; American songwriter and musician (guitar); b. 16 Nov. 1938, Big Hill, KY; m. Jo Ann Campbell. *Career:* guitarist, club bands, Ohio 1960s; formed duo with Jo Ann Campbell; moved to Nashville as songwriter; session guitarist and solo artist. *Compositions:* There's A Honky Tonk Angel (Who'll Take Me Back In), recorded by Elvis Presley, Conway Twitty; Pieces of My Life, recorded by Elvis Presley; We Had It All (co-written with Donnie Fritts), recorded by Rita Coolidge, Brenda Lee, Scott Walker, Waylon Jennings; Feeling (co-written with Will Jennings and Don Goodman), recorded by Loretta Lynn and Conway Twitty; Storms (co-written with Max Barnes), recorded by Randy Travis; Seven Spanish Angels (co-written with Eddie Setser), recorded by Willie Nelson and Ray Charles; other compositions recorded by Eric Clapton, George Jones, Reba McEntire, Roy Orbison and others. *Recordings include:* solo albums: Now Presenting Troy Seals 1973, Troy Seals 1976. *Honours:* Nashville Songwriters Hall of Fame 1988.

SEALY, Denice; British backing singer; b. 25 Nov. 1964, London. *Education:* University of East London. *Career:* Greenbelt Christian Festival, with Bryan Powell 1989–91; Hammersmith Odeon, with Jennifer Holliday 1993; EMI Music Conference, with Kenny Thomas 1993; Wembley Arena, with Dina Carroll 1994; with Carleen Anderson, British tour 1993; Motor Traders Awards 1995; with D. C. Lee, UK promo tour 1995; backing vocals, World (Pentecostal Conference), Jerusalem, Israel 1995; mem. Musicians' Union. *Recordings include:* Albums: I Think of You, Bryan Powell 1992; Michelle Gayle 1993; Nu Inspirational Album, Soul Stirrings; Backing vocals on: Mama, The Spice Girls 1997.

SEAMONE, Joyce Evelyn; Canadian singer and songwriter; b. 21 May 1946, Maplewood; m. Gerald Ivan Seamone 1964; three d. *Education:* high school graduate. *Career:* solo artist; numerous tours, TV appearances and other live performances; performs with own band Total Country; mem. Soc. of Composers, Authors and Music Publrs of Canada (SOCAN), Nova Scotia Country Music Hall of Fame (NSCMHF). *Recordings include:* Testing 1–2–3 1972, Merry Christmas from Joyce Seamone 1972, Stand By for a Special Announcement 1973, I Can See It in His Eyes 1976, The Other Side of Me 1994. *Honours:* inducted into NSCMHF 2004, Stompin' Tom Award, East Coast Music Assen 2009. *Address:* RR2, New Germany, NS B0R 1E0, Canada (home). *Telephone:* (902) 543-5053 (office). *E-mail:* joyceseamone@bwr .eastlink.ca (office). *Website:* www.joyceseamone.com.

SEASICK STEVE; American blues singer and musician (guitar); b. (Steven Gene Wold), 1941, Oakland, CA; m. 2nd Elisabeth Wold; three s. *Career:* worked at intervals as studio engineer, session musician, producer; began touring as solo blues performer 1960s–; appeared on BBC TV on Jools Holland's Hootenanny 2006, Later with Jools Holland 2009; extensive tours in UK. *Recordings include:* Cheap 2001, Dog House Music 2006, I Started Out with Nothin' and I Still Got Most of It Left 2008, Man From Another Time 2009, Songs for Elisabeth 2010. *Honours:* MOJO Award for Best Breakthrough Act 2007. *Website:* www.bronzerat.com (office); www.seasicksteve .com.

SEATE, Tshepo, (Appleseed); Zimbabwean musician. *Career:* mem. kwaito band, Bongo Maffin 1996–; World Wild Grooves tour, France 2000; performances in UK, Denmark 2000; worked with Skunk Anansie, Chaka Khan, Stevie Wonder, Boyz II Men, Hugh Masekela. *Recordings include:* albums: Final Entry 1996, The Concerto 1998, IV 1999, Bongolution 2001, New Construction 2006. *Honours:* South African Music Award, Best Kwaito Artist 1999, Kora Award, Best African Group 2001. *Current Management:* c/o Exclusive Management Services, 12 Leogem Commercial Park, 16/48 Richards Drive, Halfway-house, Midrand, South Africa. *E-mail:* info@ exclusivems.co.za. *Website:* www.bongomaffin.co.za.

SEBÁSTIAN, Joan; Mexican/American singer and songwriter; b. (José Manuel Figueroa), 8 April 1951, Juliantla, Guerrero; m. 1st Maribel Guardia (divorced); four s. four d. *Recordings include:* El Camino de Amor 1977, Rumores 1985, Mascarada 1988, Al Rojo Vivo 1995, Bandido de Amores 1995, Gracias Por Tanto Amor 1998, Secreto de Amor 2000, Lo Dijo El Corazón (Grammy Award for Best Mexican/American Album) 2002, Afortunado (Grammy Award for Best Mexican/American Album 2003) 2002, Que Amarren A Cupido 2004, Inventario 2005, Más Allá Del Sol (Grammy Award for Best Banda Album) 2006, No Es De Madera (Grammy Award for Best Banda Album 2008) 2007, Corridos y Algo Mas 2007, Pegadito al Corazon 2009. *Honours:* ASCAP Silver Pen Award 2000, ASCAP Award for Songwriter of the Year 2003, Golden Note Award 2007, Latin Music Awards Premio Lo Nuestro 2001, 2004, 2007. *Address:* POB 1974, Tustin, CA 92780, USA (office). *Telephone:* (714) 349-7208 (office). *Fax:* (714) 242-6651 (office). *E-mail:* info@ suaveconcerts.com (office). *Website:* www.joansebastian.com.

SEBASTIAN, John; American singer, songwriter and musician (guitar, harmonica, autoharp); b. 17 March 1944, New York; two s. *Career:* founder mem., The Lovin' Spoonful 1965–68; solo artist 1969–; numerous live appearances, tours and festivals; session musician for artists, including Stephen Stills, Rita Coolidge, Everly Brothers. *Television:* host The Golden Age of Rock 'N' Roll (A&E cable channel) 1991, appeared in one episode of Married with Children (Fox) 1992. *Compositions include:* music for television and films, including Welcome Back, Kotter (ABC TV) 1976, The Care Bears, Strawberry Shortcake, The Jerk II (NBC TV). *Recordings include:* albums: with The Lovin' Spoonful: Do You Believe in Magic 1965, Daydream 1966, What's Shakin' 1966, Hums of The Lovin' Spoonful 1966, Everything Playing 1968; solo: John B. Sebastian 1970, John Sebastian Live 1970, Cheapo Cheapo Productions Present 1971, The Four of Us 1971, The Tarzana Kid 1974, Welcome Back 1976, Tar Beach 1993, John Sebastian 1995, I Want My Roots 1996, King Biscuit Flower Hour Live 1996, Chasin' Gus' Ghost 1999, Satisfied (with David Grisman) 2007. *Honours:* Songwriters' Hall of Fame 2008. *Address:* c/o David Bendett, 2431 Briar Crest Road, Beverly Hills, CA 90210, USA (office). *Website:* www.johnbsebastian.com.

SEBASTIAN, Mark Douglas; American musician (guitar, bass, keyboards), songwriter, screenwriter and film producer; b. 20 Feb. 1951, New York. *Education:* Kim Stanley Drama Study. *Career:* performances in New York clubs including Gaslight, Wetlands, Lone Star; theatre Music: La Mama; TV; Solid Gold, Cheers, Wizards and Warriors; Los Angeles clubs: The Strand, Wadsworth Theatre; also performing member, Second City Emperor (Santa Monica group); mem. BMI, American Soc. of Composers, Authors and Publrs, Screen Actors Guild, American Fed. of TV and Radio Artists. *Compositions include:* Summer In The City (Lovin' Spoonful 1966, co-written with brother John Sebastian and Steve Boone).

SEBESTYÉN, Márta; Hungarian singer, musician (recorder) and songwriter; b. 1957, Budapest. *Career:* sings, researches and promotes roots music of Hungary and Transylvania; grew up surrounded by folk music, mother had studied with composer Zoltan Kodaly and collected folk songs; started singing at Budapest 'dance houses' while still at school; joined Sebö Halmos group 1975; became part of Hungary's leading folk group Muszikás 1980–; also sang with renowned group Vujicsics; appeared in musical based on the life of King Stephen 1984; apptd Amb. of Hungarian Culture 2007, UNESCO Artist for Peace 2010. *Recordings:* albums: Transylvanian Portraits 1993, Kismet 1996, I Can See the Gates of Heaven 2009; with Karoly Csereps: Hungarian Christmas Songs 1984, Loverecord 1985, Emigration 1986; with Muzsikás: The Prisoner's Song 1986, Muzsikás 1987, Blues For Transylvania 1991, Maramaros – The Lost Jewish Music of Transylvania 1993, The Bartok Album 1999; with Vujicsics: Serbian Music From Southern Hungary 1988; features on: East Wind, Andy Irvine and Davy Spillane 1992, Bohème, Deep Forest (Grammy Award for Best World Music Recording 1996) 1995, The English Patient (film soundtrack) (Acad. Award for Best Film Music 1998) 1996, Flirt (film soundtrack) 1996, Coolfin, Donal Lunny 1998, American Rhapsody 2001, Big Blue Ball 2008. *Honours:* Hon. mem., Hungarian Acad. of Arts 2007–; Officer, Cross of the Hungarian Republic 1994, Middle Cross with the Star of the Hungarian Republic 2005, Knight's Cross of the Italian Republic 2005; Hungarian Female Singer of the Year 1984, Niveau Prize for Hungarian Culture 1988, Liszt Ferenc Prize 1991, Emerton Prize 1995, 1997, Int. Interlira Prize 1998, Déri János Prize 1998, Kossuth Prize 1999, Hungarian Arts Award 2000, Prima Primissima Award 2003, Chianciano Fellini Award 2004, Kolcsey Prize 2012, Lanchid Award 2012. *Website:* www .martasebestyen.com.

SECADA, Jon, MA; Cuban/American singer, songwriter and producer; b. 10 April 1961, Havana. *Education:* Univ. of Miami. *Career:* appearances include National Anthem World Series 1992, Central and South America Tour 1994, Lifebeat concert 1994, World Cup 1994, X-Mas in Washington 1994, Grease, Broadway 1995, US Tour 1995; mem. Nat. Acad. of Recording Arts and Sciences. *Recordings include:* albums: Jon Secada 1992, Otro Dia Mas Sin Verte (Grammy Award for Best Latin Pop Album) 1992, Heart Soul and A Voice 1994, Si Te Vas 1994, Frank Sinatra Duets II: The Best Is Yet To Come 1994, Heart Soul and Voice 1994, Amor (Grammy Award for Best Latin Pop Performance) 1995, Secada 1997, Better Part Of Me 2000, The Gift 2001, Amanecer 2002, Same Dream 2005, A Christmas Fiesta 2006, Expressions: The Jazz Album 2009, Expressions 2009, Classics 2010, Otra Vez 2011, Stage Rio 2011. *Honours:* Alumnus of Distinction Award, Univ. of Miami. *Website:* www.jonsecada.com.

SECK, Cheick Amadou Tidiane; Malian musician (keyboards, African percussion) and singer; b. 11 Dec. 1953, Segou; one s. *Education:* Diplome Institut National des Arts; learned lear organ and solfege in church. *Career:* concert with Jimmy Cliff 1977; African and European tours with The Ambassadors of Mali and Salif Keita; world tour with Amina 1992–93, Printemps de Bourges Festival; mem. SACEM, SPEDIDAM. *Recordings include:* albums: solo: Laada 1995, Sarala 1995, MandinGroove 2005, Sabaly 2008, Guerrier 2013; with Salif Keita: Soro, Folon; Amen; with Graham Haynes: The Griots Footsteps, Transition; with Joe Zawinul: Next; Hank Jones, Cheick Tidiane Seck: My People. *E-mail:* catsmanagement@yahoo.fr. *E-mail:* chafia.pencreach@wanadoo.fr. *Website:* www.cheick-tidiane-seck .com.

SEDAKA, Neil; American singer, pianist, songwriter and record producer; b. 13 March 1939, Brooklyn, New York; s. of Mac Sedaka and Eleanor Appel; m. Leba M. Strassberg 1962; one s. one d. *Education:* Juilliard School of Music, New York. Composed numerous popular songs including: Breaking Up Is Hard to Do, Stupid Cupid, Calendar Girl, Oh! Carol, Stairway to Heaven, Happy Birthday Sweet Sixteen, Laughter in the Rain, Bad Blood, Love Will Keep Us Together, Lonely Night (Angel Face). *Recordings include:* Rock with Sedaka 1959, Circulate 1961, Neil Sedaka Sings His Greatest Hits 1963, Smile 1965, Sounds of Sedaka 1969, Workin' on a Groovy Thing 1969, Emergence 1971, Solitaire 1972, The Tra-La Days Are Over (UK) 1973, Sedaka's Back 1974, The Hungry Years 1975, Steppin' Out 1976, A Song 1977, All You Need Is The Music 1978, In the Pocket 1980, Neil Sedaka Canta en Espanol 1983, Come See About Me 1984, All Time Greatest Hits 1988, Oh! Carol and Other Hits 1990, Timeless – The Very Best of Neil Sedaka 1991, Tales of Love (and Other Passions) 1998, The Show Goes On 2003, Neil Sedaka in Italiano 1999, The Singer and His Songs 2000, RCA 100th Anniversary Series: The Very Best of Neil Sedaka 2001, Brighton Beach Memories – Neil Sedaka Sings Yiddish 2003, Oh! Carol: The Complete Recordings, 1955–66 2003, Stairway to Heaven: The Best of Neil Sedaka 2004, Love Songs 2005, The Very Best of Neil Sedaka: The Show Goes On 2006, Neil Sedaka: Live at the Royal Albert Hall – The Show Goes On (2 DVD set filmed in London) 2006, The Definitive Collection 2007, Oh! Carol (LT Series album, compilation of 1970s hits recorded live in concert) 2007, The Miracle of Christmas 2008, Waking Up Is Hard to Do 2009, Flashback (compilation of Italian recordings) 2009, The Music of My Life (UK) 2009, The Miracle of Christmas: The Deluxe Edition 2009, The Music of My Life 2010, Neil Sedaka Sings Little Devil and His Other Hits/The Many Sides of Neil Sedaka 2010, I Must Be Dreaming 2011, The Things I Love 2013. *Honours:* recipient of numerous gold records and recording industry awards, Ivor Novello Special Int. Award 2010. *Current Management:* c/o Leba Sedaka, Neil Sedaka Music, 641 Lexington Avenue, 14th Floor, New York, NY 10022, USA. *Fax:* (212) 593-0526 (office). *E-mail:* leba@neilsedaka.com (home). *Website:* www.neilsedaka.com.

SEDGWICK, Amanda; Swedish musician (saxophone), songwriter and composer; b. 7 Oct. 1970, Stockholm. *Education:* Royal Swedish Univ. Coll. of Music, Stockholm. *Career:* toured Sweden; appeared on Swedish TV and radio, including live broadcasts; mem., Swedish Soc. of Popular Music Composers, Swedish Performing Rights Soc. *Compositions include:* Volt, 3 movement suite for jazz group, string quartet and woodwinds. *Recordings include:* Volt, 1996; contrib. to So Many Stars, 1996, Kalabra, 1997. *Honours:* Debut of the Year, Swedish National Radio. *Current Management:* c/o Touché Music, Karlbergsvägen 14 , 113 27 Stockholm, Sweden. *Telephone:* (8) 30-13-50. *Fax:* (8) 30-13-80. *E-mail:* info@touchemusic.se. *Website:* www .touchemusic.se; www.amandasedgwick.com.

SEEGER, Peggy; American singer, songwriter and musician (guitar, piano, five-string banjo, autoharp, Appalachian dulcimer, English concertina); b. 17 June 1935, New York; d. of Charles Louis Seeger and Ruth Crawford Seeger; partner Ewan MacColl 1978, two s. one d. *Education:* Radcliffe Coll. *Career:* fmr mem. London Critics Group; solo artist 1955–, with numerous live concerts, TV and radio broadcasts; mem. Musicians' Union (USA and UK). *Recordings include:* solo albums: Folksongs of Courting and Complaint 1955, Animal Folksongs for Children 1957, Folksongs and Ballads 1958, American Folksongs for Banjo 1960, Popular Ballads 1960, A Song for You and Me 1960, Long Harvest (ten Vols) 1966–67, Peggy Alone 1967, Peggy 'n' Mike 1967, The Amorous Muse 1968, The Angry Muse 1968, Paper Stage (two Vols) 1968, From Where I Stand 1982, The Folkways Years 1992, Period Pieces: Women's Songs for Men and Women 1998, Love Will Linger On 2000, Almost Commercially Viable 2000, Peaceful Woman Fighting Hard 2002, Heading for Home 2003, Songs for October 2004, Ballad of Jimmy Massey 2005, Three

Score and Ten 2005, Enough is Enough 2006, Bring Me Home 2007, Peggy Seeger Live 2012, Everything Changes 2014. *Publications include:* Travellers' Songs of England and Ireland (with Ewan MacColl), Doomsday in The Afternoon (with Ewan MacColl), Peggy Seeger Song Book: Forty Years of Songmaking, The Essential Ewan MacColl Song Book. *Honours:* Italia Prize, Inspirational Artist Award, Women in Music. *E-mail:* info@peggyseeger.com. *Website:* www.pegseeger.com.

SÉGAL, Vincent; French cellist and bassist; b. 1967, Reims. *Education:* Nat. Music Acad. of Lyon, Banff Centre for the Arts, Canada. *Career:* Founder-mem. (with Cyril Atef), Bumcello 1996–; numerous recordings and performances as soloist and as guest musician including with Dick Annegarn, Alain Bashung, Blackalicious, Carlinhos Brown, Jeanne Cherhal, Elvis Costello, Piers Faccini, Brigitte Fontaine, Keziah Jones, Vanessa Paradis, Susheela Raman, Sting. *Recordings include:* with Bumcello: Bumcello 1999, Booty Time 2001, Bude for Love 2002, Animal sophistiqué 2005, Lychee Queen 2008, Al 2012; solo: T-Bone Guarnerius 2002, Cello 2007; with -M-: Le Baptême 1997, Je dis aime 1999, Qui de nous deux 2003; with Piers Faccini: Songs of Time Lost 2014. *Address:* c/o Tôt ou tard, 68 rue de la folie-méricourt, 75011 Paris, France (office). *Telephone:* (1) 55-28-85-85 (office). *Fax:* (1) 55-28-34-35 (office). *E-mail:* info@totoutard.net (office); Vincent@bumcello.com. *Website:* www .totoutard.com (office); www.bumcello.com.

SEGER, Robert (Bob) Clark; American singer, songwriter and musician (keyboards); b. 6 May 1945, Detroit, Mich. *Education:* Pioneer High School, Ann Arbor, Mich. *Career:* mem., The Town Criers, Doug Brown and The Omens 1965–66, Bob Seger and the Last Heard 1966–67, The Bob Seger System 1967–70, The Silver Bullet Band 1974–. *Recordings include:* albums: with The Bob Seger System: Ramblin' Gamblin' Man 1969, Noah 1970, Mongrel 1970; solo: Brand New Morning 1971, Smokin' OPs 1972, Back In '72 1973, Seven/Contrasts 1974, Beautiful Loser 1975, Live Bullet 1976; with the Silver Bullet Band: Night Moves 1976, Stranger In Town 1978, Against The Wind 1980, Nine Tonight 1981, The Distance 1983, Like A Rock 1986, The Fire Inside 1991, It's A Mystery 1995, Face the Promise 2006, Ride Out 2014. *Honours:* Grammy Award for Best Rock Performance 1981, NARAS Governor's Award 1992, Motor City Music Award for Musician of the Year, Outstanding National Rock 'n' Pop Album 1992, inducted into Rock and Roll Hall of Fame 2004, Songwriters Hall of Fame 2012. *Current Management:* Punch Enterprises, 567 Purdy, Birmingham, MI 48009, USA. *Website:* www .bobseger.com.

SEGLEM, Karl; Norwegian musician (tenor saxophone, goat horn), composer and arranger; *Managing Director, NORCD AS;* b. 8 July 1961, Ardalstangen; s. of Kirsten Lægreid Seglam and Ingvald Emil Seglem. *Education:* private music lessons. *Career:* toured Norway and abroad with jazz and folk bands since 1980s; producer and record label manager for NORCD AS 1991–, currently Man. Dir; worked with own music mixing jazz and Norwegian folk music; numerous TV and radio broadcasts, concert tours; mem. TONO, NOPA, GRAMO, Norwegian Musician Asscn. *Recordings include:* albums: solo: Poems for Trio 1988, Sogn-a-Song 1991, Rit 1994, Spir 1998, Nye Nord 2002, New North 2004, Femstein 2004, Urbs 2006, Norskjazz.no 2009, Ossicles 2010, NyeSongar.no 2013, Som spor 2014; with Isglem: Rom 1991, To Steg 1992, Null G 1996, Fire 2003; with Utla: Juv 1993, Brodd 1995, Dans 1999, Song 2003, Som Spor 2014, Laerad 2015, Live in Germany 2015, Worldjazz 2015. *Publications include:* Stilla er ein åker (poetry) 2006, Kvit frekvens (poetry) 2013. *Honours:* Edvard Prize 1998, Folkelarmprisen 2010, The Buddy Award 2010, Luttprisen 2013. *Current Management:* Artist Vision, Dicks Vei 12, 1362 Lysaker, Norway. *E-mail:* eivind@artist.vision. *Website:* www.artist.vision. *Address:* NORCD AS, Kongens gt. 16, 0153 Oslo, Norway (office). *E-mail:* karl@karlseglem.no; norcd@norcd.no (office). *Website:* www .norcd.no (office); www.karlseglem.no.

SEHUN; South Korean singer and rapper; b. (Oh Sehun), 12 April 1994, Seoul. *Education:* School of Performing Arts, Seoul. *Career:* trainee at SM Entertainment 2008–12; mem. K-pop boy band Exo 2012–; mem. sub-group Exo-K 2012–; debut single 2012; numerous TV and live appearances. *Television:* EXO's Showtime 2013–, Royal Villa (as guest star) 2013. *Recordings:* albums: Mama 2012, XOXO (Mnet Asian Music Award for Album of the Year 2013) 2013. *Honours:* numerous awards including: for Exo: Mnet Asian Music Award for Best New Asian Artist/Group 2012, MTV Europe Music Award for Best Japan/Korea Act 2013, MelOn Music Award for Song of the Year (for Growl) 2013; for Exo-K: Golden Disk Newcomer Award 2012. *Address:* c/o SM Entertainment, 521 Apgujeong 2-dong, Gangnam-gu, Seoul, South Korea (office). *Telephone:* (2) 6240-9800 (office). *Website:* www.smtown .com (office); exo.smtown.com (home).

SEINE, Johannes (John) Hendricus; Dutch artist manager and agent; *Managing Director, Europop International;* b. 30 March 1946, Amsterdam; m. Coline Flentrop; two s. *Education:* Univ. of Amsterdam. *Career:* Man., Amsterdam bands 1964; Producer, Dutch radio 3 Vara Drive-in show 1969; Producer, Radio Northsea Mobile Show 1972; Man. Dir Europop International; Man., agent for American Gipsy, Lois Lane, Boney M, Doop; tours organized with Divine, Inner Circle, LaToya Jackson, Tower of Power, Capella, Prodigy, Boney M. *Address:* Europop International, Valkenburgerlaan 2, 2103 AN Heemstede, The Netherlands (office). *Telephone:* 62-1578281 (mobile) (home). *E-mail:* john.seine@planet.nl (office). *Website:* www.euro-pop .nl.

SELIGMAN, Matthew; British musician (bass guitar); b. 14 July 1955, Cyprus. *Career:* mem. The Soft Boys 1979–80, 2002–, The Thompson Twins 1981–82, Thomas Dolby 1982–84; toured USA, Europe, with Thomas Dolby 1984; session bassist, London 1986–94; mem. Radio Science Orchestra 1994–98; performed at Live Aid concert with David Bowie, Wembley Stadium, London 1985; recorded songs with David Bowie, Transvision Vamp, Morrissey, Sinead O'Connor, Stereo MCs; mem. Musicians' Union. *Compositions as co-writer:* The Brightest Star, Now and Forever, Motorcycle, Neon Sisters, Slipping You The Midnight Fish, Daddy, Stabbed In The Heart Again. *Recordings include:* albums: with The Soft Boys: Underwater Moonlight 1980, Lope At The Hive 1981, Invisible Hits 1983, The Soft Boys 1979–81 1994, Nextdoorland 2002; with The Thompson Twins: In The Name Of Love 1982; with Thomas Dolby: Blinded By Science 1982, The Flat Earth 1983, Retrospectacle 1994, A Map of the Floating City 2011; with The Radio Science Orchestra: Theme From The Electronic City, The Architect, Beachcombing Man, The Brightest Star 1995, Strange Weather (with Grace Jones). *E-mail:* reverbe@aol.com; reverbe@netscape.net.

SELLAM, Philippe; French musician (saxophone); b. 24 Oct. 1960, Algeria. *Career:* concerts with John Scofield, Gil Evans, European Union Radio Big Band, Michel Portal, Michel Petruciani, Mino Cinelu, NOJAZZ; numerous tours in Africa. *Recordings include:* Abidjan, Live at Saint-Louis du Sénégal, Traditional Odyssey, Serenade, Afrique; with Gil Evans, Laurent Cugny, French National Jazz Orchestra, Michel Legrand; six records with own band African Project, Nojazz. *Honours:* Best Soloist, Concours Nat. de Jazz de Paris La Défense 1987. *Address:* c/o Cristal Records, BP 138, 17005 La Rochelle Cedex 1, France (office). *Website:* www.cristalrecords.com (office); www .myspace.com/philippesellam (home).

SELLAR, Gordon Maxwell; British musican (bass guitar, guitar); b. 13 June 1947, Glasgow, Scotland; m. Julie Sellar 1975; one s. one d. *Career:* mem. Beggar's Opera, The Alex Harvey Band, The Denny Laine Band, Jackie Lynton Band, The Freddie Starr Band; mem. Musicians' Union. *Compositions include:* featured on two Gordon Neville albums. *Recordings include:* Joseph and His Amazing Technicolour Dreamcoat, Evita, Robson and Jerome1995, including Unchained Melody and Up On The Roof.

SELLERS, Joey Elton; American musician (trombone) and composer; b. 5 May 1962, Phoenix, Arizona. *Education:* BS, Music Education, State University, Arizona; Studied improvisation with Warne Marsh; Chuck Mahronic; Bobby Shew; Gary Foster. *Career:* Merv Griffin with Side Street Strutters, 1984; US Presidents dinner, 1986; Numerous radio broadcasts; Brass quintets, I and II, St Louis Brass; Trombone with California Arts Trombone Quartet; mem. BMI; AFofM. *Recordings:* Joey Sellers Jazz Aggregation: Something For Nothing 1989, Pastels, Ashes 1991, Payaso 2005, with Malby/Sellers Quartet: Cosas 1993; with Kim Richmond/Clay Jenkins Ensemble: Range 1994; with Satoko Fujii: South Wind 1997, Jo 2000, Double Take 2000, Future of the Past 2003, Blueprint 2005, Undulation 2006; Commission for Gil Evans Fellowship: Seeds; Trumpet Summit for Summit Records featuring: Bobby Shew; Alan Vizzetti; Vince D'Marino; Satoko Fujii Orchestra. *Honours:* Gil Evans Fellowship in Jazz Composition. *Address:* 4243 E Fifth St, 1, Long Beach, CA 90814, USA. *Website:* joeysellers.com.

SELTMANN, Darren; Australian musician; m. Sally Russell 2003; one d. *Career:* founder mem. punk band, later electronic music collective, The Avalanches 1997–2014. *Recordings include:* album: Since I Left You 2000; with New Buffalo: Last Beautiful Day 2005, Somewhere, Anywhere 2007; with Sally Seltmann: Hey Daydreamer 2014.

SELWAY, Phillip James; British musician (drums); b. 23 May 1967, Hemingford Grey, Cambridgeshire, England; m. Kate Selway; three c. *Education:* Liverpool Polytechnic. *Career:* mem. On A Friday 1987, renamed Radiohead 1991–; also solo artist 2010–; numerous tours, festivals and television appearances. *Recordings include:* albums: with Radiohead: Pablo Honey 1993, The Bends 1995, OK Computer (Grammy Award for Best Alternative Music Performance) 1997, Kid A (Grammy Award for Best Alternative Music Album) 2000, Amnesiac 2001, I Might Be Wrong (live recordings) 2001, Hail To The Thief 2003, In Rainbows (Grammy Award for Best Alternative Music Album 2009) 2007, The King of Limbs 2011; solo: Familial 2010, Weatherhouse 2014. *Honours:* Q Award for Best Act in the World Today 2001, 2002, 2003. *Current Management:* Courtyard Management, 21 The Nursery, Sutton Courtenay, Abingdon, Oxfordshire OX14 4UA, England. *Website:* www.radiohead.com; www.philipselway.com.

SELWYN, Esmond Wayne, BA; British musician (guitar); b. 18 Feb. 1948, London, England. *Education:* Kings Coll. London; studied with Ivor Mairants, Tal Farlow, Ike Isaacs, Chuck Wayne. *Career:* professional musician from age 12; varied career especially in jazz including opposite Chick Corea and Elvin Jones 1993; tour with Salena Jones, Thailand 1994; mem. Musicians' Union. *Recordings include:* Matt Bianco: Tequila, Melanie Marshall: Cocktail, Robin Jones Quartet: Eye of The Hurricane, Don Rendell, Follow That 2003. *Publications include:* Jake Lee Arrives, The Jakes Progress, included in Guildhall Guitar Syllabus. *E-mail:* esmondselwyn@btinternet.com. *Website:* www.esmondselwyn.com.

SEN, Palash, MBBS; Indian singer, songwriter, musician (guitar), actor and physician; b. 23 Sept. 1965, New Delhi; s. of Dr Rupendra Kumar Sen and Dr Pushpa Sen; m. Shalini Sen; two s. *Education:* Univ. Coll. of Medical Sciences. *Career:* worked as physician then formed band Euphoria in New Delhi in

1988; fmr judge, Indian Popstars TV show. *Recordings include:* albums: Dhoom 1998, Phir Dhoom 2000, Gully 2003, Mehfuz 2006, Redhoom 2008, Item 2011. *Films include:* as actor: Filhaal 2002, Mumbai Cutting 2010; as singer: Filhaal 2002, Hanuman, Dhoondte Reh Jaoge, Lamhaa. *E-mail:* polly@dhoom.com. *Website:* www.dhoom.com.

SEN, Susmit; Indian singer and musician (guitar). *Career:* Founder-mem. and lead guitarist of band Indian Ocean. *Recordings include:* Indian Ocean 1993, Desert Rain 1997, Kandisa 2000, Jhini (AVMax Award) 2003, 16/330 Khajoor Road 2010. *Soundtracks include:* Swaraj–The Little Republic 2002, Black Friday 2004, Hulla 2008, Beware Dogs 2008, Bhoomi 2009, Yeh Mera India 2009, Mumbai Cutting 2009, Leaving Home–The Life and Music Of Indian Ocean 2010. *Address:* Indian Ocean, 1224, Sector 37, Faridabad, 121 003, India (office). *Telephone:* 09810138921 (mobile); 09811130451 (mobile). *E-mail:* indianoceanmusic@gmail.com (office). *Website:* www.indianoceanmusic.com (office); www.susmitsen.com (office).

SEN DOG; American (b. Cuban) singer; b. (Senen Reyes), 20 Nov. 1965, Cuba. *Career:* founder mem., DVX 1986, renamed Cypress Hill 1988–96, 1998–; co-f. The Reyes Brothers 2006–. *Recordings:* albums: with Cypress Hill: Cypress Hill 1991, Black Sunday 1993, Cypress Hill III: Temples of Boom 1995, IV 1998, Skull & Bones 2000, Live at the Fillmore 2000, Stoned Raiders 2001, Till Death Do Us Part 2004, Rise Up 2010; with The Reyes Brothers: Ghetto Therapy 2006. *Website:* www.cypresshill.com.

SENFLUK, Jaromir (Jerry); jazz musician (clarinet); b. 17 March 1946, Prague, Czechoslovakia; m. Jirina 1973; one s. *Education:* clarinet with Karel Dlouhy, Conservatoire in Prague. *Career:* frequent bookings in West Germany, worked with a band accompanying Freddie Kohlman, and with Savoy Gang, swing quartet 1975–77; founded Hallmark Swingtet, Berlin 1979–84; West End venues and composing, London, England 1985–90; with pianist Mick Pyne, guitarist Nils Solberg, double bassist John Rees-Jones and drummer Rex Bennett, formed Capital Swing, 1991; Yves 'Little Fats' Guyot and Eric Luter, residencies at Hotel Ermitage Golf near Gstaad, Switzerland 1991–94; mem, Musicians' Union, Asscn of British Jazz Musicians. *Compositions:* Pas De Chat; Air Condition Breakdown. *Recordings:* From East to West 1974, We Swing – Take It From Me 1995, Swing Express 1997.

SENIOR, Russell; British musician (guitar, violin); b. 18 May 1961, Sheffield, England. *Career:* Mem., Pulp, –1996; Numerous tours, television appearances and festival dates; Contribution to film soundtrack, Mission Impossible, 1996; Founding mem., Venini, 1999–2000. *Recordings:* albums: with Pulp: It 1983, Freaks 1987, Separations 1992, His 'N' Hers 1994, Different Class 1995. *Publications:* Freak Out the Squares (memoir) 2015. *Website:* www.pulponline.com.

SENNETT, Blake; American singer, songwriter, guitarist and actor; b. (Blake Sennett Swendson), 22 Sept. 1976, San Diego, Calif. *Career:* fmr child actor (performing as Blake Soper and Blake Swendson); founder mem. Rilo Kiley 1998–; mem. The Elected 2004–06. *Television:* as actor: TV series: His & Hers 1990, Salute Your Shorts 1991–92, Boy Meets World 1993–98; other appearances include Highway to Heaven 1987, Family Ties 1987, My Two Dads 1989, It's Garry Shandling's Show 1990, The Wonder Years 1990–91, Melrose Place 1996, 3rd Rock from the Sun 1997–99, Buffy the Vampire Slayer 1999, Once and Again 2000. *Recordings:* albums: with Rilo Kiley: Take Offs and Landings 2001, The Execution of All Things 2002, More Adventurous 2004, Under the Blacklight 2007, with The Elected: Me First 2004, Sun, Sun, Sun 2006. *Current Management:* c/o Jessica Massa, Press Here Publicity, 138 West 25th Street, 9th Floor, New York, NY 10001, USA. *Telephone:* (212) 246-2640. *Fax:* (212) 582-6513. *E-mail:* jessica@pressherepublicity.com. *Website:* www.pressherepublicity.com. *Address:* c/o Brant Weil, Warner Bros. Records Inc., 3300 Warner Boulevard, Burbank, CA 91505-4694, USA (office). *E-mail:* brant.weil@wbr.com (office). *Website:* www.warnerbrosrecords.com (office); www.rilokiley.com.

ŞENOL, Erdinç; Turkish musician (drums); b. 1975, Manisa. *Education:* studied music. *Career:* mem., Yeni Türkü 1996–; concerts world-wide. *Recordings by band:* albums (does not play on all): "Yeni", Her Dem Yeni, Telli Telli Remixes, Süper Baba (film music), Ask Yeniden, Rumeli Konseri, Külhani Şarkilar, Vira Vira, Yeşilmişik?, Günebakan: Dünyanin Kapilari, Akdeniz Akdeniz. *E-mail:* erdinc@yeniturku.com (office). *Website:* www.yeniturku.com.

SEPE, Daniele; Italian musician (wind instruments); b. 17 April 1960, Naples. *Education:* Graduated, flute, Conservatorio Sanpietro A Masella, Naples. *Career:* Formed group, Gruppo Operaio 'E Zezi Di Pomigliano; Appeared festivals: Rennes; Martigues; Bonn, 1976; Played at festivals including: Les Allumnes, Nanates; Vignola; Atina; Ravenna; Horizontal Radio Linz; Rai Stereonette; Audio Box; DOC; Radiotresuite. *Compositions include:* Arrangements for groups including: Little Italy; Bisca; Walhalla; Degrado; Music for theatre, ballet, cinema. *Recordings:* Malamusica, 1983; L'Uscita dei Gladiatori, 1991; Plays Standards and More, 1991; Vite Perdite, 1993; Spiritus Mundi, 1995; Contribututions to: Roberto Murolo, Tu Si Na Cosa Grande, 1995. *Publications:* L'Italia Del Rock; Encyclopedia Del Rock. *Honours:* Academia International Del Tango. *Address:* Via Manzoni 191, 80123 Naples, Italy. *E-mail:* danielesepe@libero.it. *Website:* www.danielesepe.com.

SERGEANT, Will; British musician (guitar); b. 12 April 1958, Liverpool, England. *Career:* mem., Echo & The Bunnymen 1978–94, 1997–; founder

mem., Electrafixion 1994–; numerous tours and festival appearances; solo artist, under the name Glide. *Recordings include:* albums: with Echo & The Bunnymen: Crocodiles 1980, Heaven Up Here 1981, Porcupine 1983, Ocean Rain 1984, Echo & The Bunnymen 1987, Reverberation 1990, Evergreen 1997, What Are You Going To Do With Your Life? 1999, Flowers 2001, Siberia 2005, More Songs to Learn and Sing 2006, Me, I'm All Smiles 2006, The Fountain 2009; solo: as Glide: Weird As Fish 1978, Themes For Grind 1982, Space Age Freak Out 1997, Performance 2000, Blue Sunshine (film soundtrack) 2001, Curvature of the Earth 2004; with Electrafixion: Burned 1995. *E-mail:* fans@bunnymen.com (office). *Website:* www.bunnymen.com.

SERGENT, Carole; French singer, entertainer, author, composer and actress; b. 22 Jan. 1962, Montargis, Loiret; one d. *Education:* CIM, ARIAM. *Career:* festivals include Jacques Brel, Jazz Amiens, Jazz Montlouis, Printemps Bourges, Choralies, Jazz Paris, Tourtour Paris, Jazz Sous les Pommiers, Estival, France Television 2, MCM Telsat 1988–, 673rd concert 1997; mem. Soc. des auteurs, compositeurs et éditeurs de musique (SACEM). *Recordings include:* albums: Chant du corps 1994, Cherche Passion 1997, Sur ta Peau 2005; DVD: Live at Royale Factory 2012. *Honours:* Ellipse d'Or Canal 1992. *Current Management:* 45 rue Jussieu, 78150 Le Chesnay, France. *Telephone:* 6-80-61-79-76 (mobile); one d. *E-mail:* carolesergent@orange.fr (home). *Website:* myspace.com/carolesergent.

SERMILÄ, Jarmo Kalevi, MA; Finnish composer and musician (trumpet, flugelhorn); b. 16 Aug. 1939, Hämeenlinna; m. Ritva Vuorinen 1962. *Education:* Helsinki Univ., Sibelius Acad. *Career:* worked for Finnish broadcasting co. (YLE), Artistic Dir YLE Experimental Studio 1973–79; Pres. Finnish Section, Int. Soc. for Contemporary Music 1975–79; Composer-in-Residence, Hämeenlinna 1977–82; freelance composer 1982–; Artistic Dir Time of Music Contemporary Music Festival, Viitasaari 1987–99; state grant for composition 1990; mem. Soc. of Finnish Composers, Vice-Pres. 1981–2005. *Compositions include:* A Circle of the Moon, Allegria, At Bizarre Exits, La Place Revisitée, Labor, Manifesto, Merlin's Mascarade (ballet), Mimesis 2, Movimenti, On the Road, Pentagram, Quattro Rilievi, Random Infinities, Technogourmet, Train of Thoughts, Wolf Bride (ballet). *Recordings:* Quattro Rilievi, At Bizarre Exits, Random Infinities, Movimenti, Technogourmet, Citymusic. *Honours:* Hon. Prof. 2005; hon. mem. Finnish Composers' Soc. 2005; Hon. Reward, Sibelius Fund of the Finnish Composers' Soc. 2006; Janáček Medal 1978, Hämeenlinna City Music Prize 1981, Smetana Medal 1984, Häme Prov. Art Soc. Award 1988, State Grant for Composition 1990–2003. *Address:* Niittykatu 7 A 7, 13100 Hämeenlinna, Finland (home). *E-mail:* jarmo@sermila.net (home). *Website:* www.sermila.net.

SERMON, (Daniel) Wayne; American guitarist and songwriter; b. 15 June 1984, American Fork, Utah; s. of Jeff Sermon and Debbie Sermon. *Education:* Berklee Coll. of Music. *Career:* mem. Imagine Dragons 2009–, performed at numerous festivals 2011–; signed with Interscope Records 2011; numerous TV appearances and tours in USA, Canada, Europe. *Recording:* album: with Imagine Dragons: Night Visions (Billboard Music Award for Top Rock Album 2014) 2012, Smoke + Mirrors 2015. *Honours:* Teen Choice Award for Choice Rock Song (for Radioactive) 2013, American Music Awards for Favorite Alternative Rock Artist 2013, 2014, Grammy Award for Best Rock Performance (for Radioactive) 2014, Billboard Music Awards for Top Duo/Group 2014, for Top Hot 100 Artist 2014, for Top Rock Artist 2014, for Top Streaming Song (Audio) (for Radioactive) 2014, iHeartRadio Music Award for Best Alternative Rock Song of the Year (for Demons, with Imagine Dragons) 2014, Much Music Video Award for Int. Video of the Year - Group (for Demons, with Imagine Dragons) 2014. *Current Management:* c/o Mac Reynolds, Reynolds Management, 823 Las Vegas Boulevard South, Las Vegas, NV 89101, USA. *Telephone:* (702) 445-7000. *Fax:* (702) 385-7743. *E-mail:* mac@reynoldsmgmt.com. *Website:* www.reynoldsmgmt.com; imaginedragonsmusic.com.

SERNEHOLT, Marie Eleonor; Swedish singer and TV presenter; b. 11 July 1983, Stockholm. *Education:* Rytmus School, Stockholm. *Career:* mem., A*Teens 1998–2004; solo career 2006–. *Television:* The X Factor (Swedish version) 2012, Bingoletto 2013. *Recordings include:* albums: The Abba Generation 1999, Teen Spirit 2001. *Honours:* Viva Music Award for Best Int. Newcomer 2000. *Website:* www.marieserneholt.se.

SERVI, Jo; British singer and actor; b. 17 May 1970, Aylesbury, Bucks.. *Career:* session singer 1988–; steel pan player, singer, Radcliffe Rollers Steel Band; TV appearances; backing vocalist, duo, Sister-Brother; lead singer, keyboards, The Bizz 1993; Wind Parade 1994; joined Southlanders vocal quartet 1995; vocals for The Foundations, Mark Williamson, Vince Cross, Nashleigh Hill, Marcus Collins, Leanne Mitchell, Janet Devlin, Boyzone, My Name; Disney's Dinosaur, Skins, Maurice: A Life With Bells On (Soundtracks), Original Cast Recordings: Peter Pan - A Musical Adventure, Sweet Charity (English Theatre Frankfurt), Bush Tales; Before The Dawn with the KT Fellowship (Kate Bush) 2014; recent acting perfs. with Birmingham Rep., Regent's Park's Open Air Theatre and in West End, London; mem. Musicians' Union, Equity. *Address:* 2 Bateman Drive, Brookhurst, Aylesbury, Buckinghamshire, WP21 8AF, England (home).

SERYABKINA, Olga; Russian singer, songwriter and producer; b. 12 April 1985, Moscow. *Career:* mem. Serebro 2006–, formed for Eurovision Song Contest 2007 with song Song #1, finished in third place; signed to Monolit Records; many hits in Russia; international hits with Song #1 2007, Mama Lover 2011. *Recordings include:* with Serebro: albums: OpiumRoz 2009, Mama Lover 2011. *Honours:* MTV Russian Music Awards for Best Debut

2007, for Best Group 2008, Golden Gramophone Award 2007, World Music Award for Best Selling Russian Artist 2007. *Address:* c/o Monolit Records, Studio Monolit office, Moscow, 117105, 4a Novodanilovskaya naberezhnaya, Russia (office). *Telephone:* (495) 5102255 (office). *E-mail:* pkmonolit@mail.ru (office). *Website:* www.pkmonolit.ru/english.php (office); www.serebro.su.

SESSOMATO (see Lee, Dave)

SEULONG; South Korean singer; b. (Im Seulong), 11 May 1987. *Education:* Daejin Univ. *Career:* mem. 2AM 2008–, live debut in 2010; has also recorded with IU. *Television:* as actor: Personal Preference 2010. *Recordings:* albums: with 2AM: Saint o'Clock 2010; other 2AM appearances include: Personal Preference (soundtrack) 2010, Listen Up!: The Official 2010 FIFA World Cup Album 2010, Acoustic (soundtrack) 2010. *Honours:* Mnet Asian Music Award for Best Vocal Performance by a Group 2011. *Address:* c/o JYP Entertainment, JYP Center, 41, 79-gil Apgujeong-ro, Gangnam-gu, Seoul, South Korea (office). *Telephone:* (2) 3438-2300 (office). *Fax:* (2) 3438-2330 (office). *E-mail:* publicity@jype.com (office). *Website:* www.jype.com (office); 2am.ibighit.com (home).

SEUNGRI; South Korean singer, songwriter, producer and actor; b. (Lee Seung-hyun), 12 Dec. 1990, Gwangju. *Education:* Chung-Ang Univ. *Career:* fmr mem. Il Hwa; mem. Big Bang 2006–; solo career 2009–. *Stage:* Sonagi 2008, Shouting 2009. *Films:* Why Did You Come to My House? 2009, My 19 2009. *Recordings:* albums: with Big Bang: Bigbang Vol 1 2007, Remember 2008, Number 1 2008, Big Bang 2009, Big Bang 2 2011, Alive 2012; solo: VVIP 2011. *Honours:* Mnet KM Music Festival Awards for Best Male Group 2007, 2008, 2012, for Song of the Year 2007, for Digital Music 2008, for Artist of the Year 2008, 2012, for Guardian Angel Worldwide Performer 2012, Golden Disk Bonsang Award 2007, Mnet Music Portal Award 2008, Seoul Music Awards for Digital Music 2008, for Bonsang 2008, 2009, for Best Album 2009, for Popular Mobile 2009, Nickelodeon Korea Kids' Choice Best Male Artists Award 2008, 2009, Hiwon Award 2009, Korea PD Best Singer Award 2009, Best Hits Song Festival Gold Artist Award 2009, Japan Cable Broadcasting Best Newcomer Award 2009, Ministry of Culture, Sports and Tourism Artist of the Year 2009, Japan Record Awards for New Artist and Best New Artist 2009, Gold Award 2010, Japanese Grand Prix du Disque for Best Newcomer 2010, Japan Gold Disc Awards for Best Five New Artists and Best New Artist 2010, MTV Video Music Awards Japan for Best New Artist Video and Best Pop Video 2010. *Address:* c/o YG Entertainment, 397–5 YG Building, Hapjeong-Dong, Mapo-Gu, Seoul 109-819, South Korea (office). *Telephone:* (2) 3143-1105 (office). *Fax:* (2) 544-1546 (office). *E-mail:* web@ygmail.net (office). *Website:* eng.ygfamily.com/main/main.html (office); www.ybigbang.com (home); www.ybigbang.jp (home).

7EVEN, Marc; American rap artist. *Career:* mem., Jurassic 5 1993–2006; numerous live performances. *Recordings include:* albums: Jurassic 5 (EP) 1997, Quality Control 2000, Power in Numbers 2002, Feedback 2006.

THE 7TH PLAIN (see Slater, Luke)

SEVERINSEN, Carl H. (Doc); American musician (trumpet) and music director; b. 7 July 1927, Arlington, OR; m. Emily Marshall 1980; two s. three d. *Career:* musician with Ted Fio Rito 1945, Charlie Barnet 1947–49; also with Tommy Dorsey, Benny Goodman; mem. house band, Steve Allen Show, NBC 1954–55, NBC Orchestra for Tonight Show 1962–92; owner, Severinsen Custom Trumpets. *Recordings:* over 30 albums including: Brass Roots 1971, Facets 1988, Night Journey, Doc Severinsen and Friends, Ja-Da, Two Sides of Doc Severinsen, Brass on Ivory, Skyliner, Doc Severinsen and Xebron, Doc Severinsen with Strings, The Very Best of Doc Severinsen. *E-mail:* severinsendocinfo@gmail.com (office). *Website:* www.docseverinsen.com.

SEVINK, Jon; British musician (violin); b. 15 May 1965, Harlow, Essex. *Career:* founder-mem. The Levellers 1988–; numerous concerts, festival appearances. *Recordings include:* albums: Weapon Called The Word 1990, Levelling The Land 1991, See Nothing, Hear Nothing, Do Something 1993, Levellers 1993, Zeitgeist 1995, Mouth To Mouth 1997, Special Brew 2000, Hello Pig 2000, Green Blade Rising 2002, Truth & Lies 2005, Letters from the Underground 2008. *Film:* Chaos Theory 2006. *Publication:* Dance Before The Storm (official biog.) 1998. *Address:* The Levellers, PO Box 2600, Brighton, BN2 0DX, England (office). *Telephone:* (1273) 608887 (office). *E-mail:* otf@levellers.co.uk (office). *Website:* www.levellers.co.uk.

SEXSMITH, Ronald (Ron) Eldon; Canadian singer, musician (guitar) and songwriter; b. 8 Jan. 1964, St Catharine's, ON. *Career:* formed first band at age of 14; founder mem., The Uncool. *Films:* as himself: Love Shines 2010. *Recordings include:* albums: solo: Out Of The Duff 1985, There's A Way 1986, Grand Opera Lane 1991, Ron Sexsmith 1995, Other Songs 1997, Whereabouts 1999, Blue Boy 2001, Cobblestone Runway 2002, Retriever 2004, Time Being 2006, Exit Strategy of the Soul 2008, Long Player Late Bloomer 2011, Forever Endeavour (Juno Award for Adult Alternative Album of the Year 2014) 2013, Carousel One 2015. *Honours:* Canadian Ind. Music Awards Critics' Choice Major Independent Album of the Year 2002, 2003. *Current Management:* Michael Dixon Management, 119 Pebble Creek Road, Franklin, TN 37064, USA. *Telephone:* (615) 791-7731. *Fax:* (615) 791-7732. *E-mail:* sodarock@mac.com. *E-mail:* info@ronsexsmith.com (office). *Website:* www.ronsexsmith.com.

SEXTON, Charlie; American singer, songwriter, musician (guitar) and producer; b. 11 Aug. 1968, San Antonio, Tex.; brother of Will Sexton. *Career:* solo artist; formed The Nauts 2013 (with Jakob Dylan, Brady Blade and Dave Matthews); numerous collaborations. *Recordings include:* solo albums: Pictures for Pleasure 1985, Charlie Sexton 1989, Arc Angels 1992, Under the Wishing Tree 1995, Cruel and Gentle Things 2005; as producer: Marc Cohn's Giving up the Ghost, Edie Brickell's Volcano, Shannon McNally's Geronimo. *Current Management:* c/o Jim Phelan or Jerimaya Grabher, GPS/Global Positioning Services, 3435 Ocean Park Boulevard, Suite 107, #191, Santa Monica, CA 90405, USA. *E-mail:* info@globalpositioningservices.net. *Website:* www.globalpositioningservices.net.

SEXTON, Will; American musician (guitar); b. 10 Aug. 1970, San Antonio, TX; brother of Charlie Sexton. *Career:* bassist for W.C. Clark Bires Band, performed and recorded with Stevie Ray Vaughan, Speedy Spaks, Joe Ely, Stephen Stills, Waylon Jennings, Steve Earle, Alejandro Escovedo; mem., The Kill; mem., The Sexton Sextet. *Website:* www.willsexton.com.

SEYMOUR, Nick; Australian musician (bass); b. 9 Dec. 1958, Benalla, Vic.; m. Brenda Bentleigh 1989 (divorced 1993). *Career:* mem., Glory Boys 1979–80, Romantics 1980, Scratch Record Scratch 1981, plays with Marionettes 1981–84; mem., the Mullanes 1985, later renamed Crowded House –1996, re-formed 2007–; numerous early acoustic gigs in restaurants and clubs, later headlining tours, festival dates and TV and radio appearances; founder mem., Akimbo 1998–. *Recordings include:* albums: with Crowded House: Crowded House 1986, Temple of Low Men 1988, Woodface 1991, Together Alone 1993, Recurring Dream: The Best of Crowded House 1996, Farewell to the World 2006, Time on Earth 2007, Intriguer 2010; with Akimbo: Invasion of the Happy People 1998, On Top 2000. *Current Management:* c/o Mike Bradshaw, Meniscus Media, PO Box 136-150, Parnell, Auckland, New Zealand. *Website:* www.crowdedhouse.com.

SEYMOUR, Patrick, BA; British composer, musician (keyboard) and producer; b. 11 Dec. 1958, Reading, Berkshire. *Education:* Univ. of Oxford. *Career:* film composer, songwriter; world tours with The Eurythmics 1986, 1989. *Compositions for film:* The Feast of All Saints, Tricks, The End of Summer, Northern Lights. *Compositions:* co-writer: Revival, When Tomorrow Comes, Eurythmics; You're History, Shakespears Sister. *Recordings:* keyboard player on albums with Eurythmics: Revenge 1986, We Too Are One 1989; with The Pretenders: Get Close; with The Jayhawks: Smile 2000; other albums by: Mick Jagger, Bob Dylan.

SHABALALA, Joseph Bhekizizwe; South African singer, dancer and songwriter; *Associate Professor of Ethnomusicology, University of Natal;* b. 28 Aug. 1940, Ladysmith. *Career:* founding mem. and lead singer, Ladysmith Black Mambazo 1970–; Assoc. Prof. of Ethnomusicology, Univ. of Natal; part-time lecturer, UCLA, USA, Univ. of Zululand. *Recordings include:* albums: Induku Zethu 1984, Ulwandle Oluncgwele 1985, Inala 1986, Shaka Zulu 1987, Journey of Dreams 1988, Umthombo Wamanzi 1988, How the Leopard got his Spots 1989, Two Worlds One Heart 1990, Zibuyinhlazane 1992, Gift of the Tortoise 1993, Liph' Iquiniso 1994, Thuthukani Ngoxolo 1996, Heavenly 1997, The Star and the Wise Man 1998, African Lullaby 1999, In Harmony 1999, Gospel Songs 2000, Lihl'lxhiba Likagogo (SAMA Award for Best Zulu Album) 2001, Wenyukela (SAMA Award for Best Zulu Album) 2003, Chillout Sessions 2004, Long Walk to Freedom 2006, Ilembe: Honoring Shaka Zulu (Grammy Award for Best Traditional World Music Album 2009) 2008. *Honours:* Grammy Award for Best Traditional Folk Recording (for Shaka Zulu) 1987, JEFF Award for Best Original Musical Score (for Nomathemba stage production), Kora Special Judges' Award for Contribution to African Music 2000, Kora All African Music Award for Best Traditional Group 2005. *Address:* c/o Gallo, PO Box 2897, Parklands 2121; 38 St Mary's Road, Kloof 3610, South Africa (home). *Telephone:* (31) 764-0147 (home). *Fax:* (31) 764-0665 (home). *Website:* www.ladysmithblackmambazo.com.

SHACHO; Japanese singer. *Career:* mem. and lead singer of jazz band, Soil & "Pimp" Sessions 2001–. *Recordings include:* albums: Pimpin' (EP) 2004, Pimp Master 2005, Summer Goddess (EP) 2005, Pimp of the Year 2006. *Address:* c/o Victor Entertainment Inc., Palacion Tower, 3-6-7 Kita-Aoyama, Minato-ku, Tokyo 107-0061, Japan (office). *E-mail:* soil@jvcmusic.co.jp. *Website:* www.soilpimp.com.

SHACKLETON, Danny J.; engineer, producer, programmer, writer and musician (keyboards); b. 7 April 1966, Wegberg, Germany. *Education:* art college. *Career:* freelance engineer, producer, studios throughout UK, for several years; Programmed for various projects including specialist jazz ventures, library music; Taught Music Technology to A Level; Various chart entries for albums, singles; Major jazz pieces July 1995; various dance projects 1995; mem, Musicians' Union. *Address:* c/o Fairview Music, Fairview Studio, Willerby, Hull HU10 6DP, England.

DJ SHADOW; American producer and hip-hop DJ; b. (Josh Davis), 1 Jan. 1973, Hayward, CA. *Career:* joined artists' collective, Sole Sides; worked with Paris, DJ Krush, Depeche Mode and Massive Attack; work on collective, U.N.K.L.E. (with James Lavelle and Thom Yorke of Radiohead); f. record label, Cali-Tex 2000–. *Film soundtrack contributions:* The End of Violence 1997, One Eight Seven 1997, Dark Days 2000, Keepintime: Talking Drums and Whispering Vinyl 2000, Brothers 2000, Jam (TV series) 2000, Phone Booth 2002, Better Luck Tomorrow 2002. *Recordings include:* albums: Endtroducing 1996, Preemptive Strike 1998, The Private Press 2002, In Tune and On Time 2004, The Outsider 2006, The Less You Know, the Better 2011. *E-mail:* jamal@djshadow.com (office). *Website:* www.djshadow.com.

SHADY, Slim (see Eminem)

SHAFER, Sanger D. (Whitey); American songwriter; b. 24 Oct. 1934, Whitney, TX; m. Lyndia Shafer. *Education:* Whitney High School. *Career:* signed publishing contract with Blue Crest Music Publishing, Nashville 1967; signed contract with Acuff-Rose Music; inducted, Songwriters Hall of Fame 1989; songs recorded by Moe Bandy, Lefty Frizzell, Jack Greene, Merle Haggard, George Jones, The Oak Ridge Boys, Johnny Rodriguez, Johnny Russell, Connie Smith, George Strait, Keith Whitley. *Compositions include:* solo: Between My House And Town, I'm A New Man In Town, Soft Lights And Hard Country Music, I Can't Get Over You To Save My Life, I Wonder Do You Think Of Me, Overnight Success, Lefty's Gone, I Never Knew, Dream Painter, Lord Is That Me?, Honky Tonk Amnesia, Soft Lights & Hard Country Music, You Babe, Overnight Success, Birmingham Turnaround; with Lefty Frizzell: That's The Way Love Goes, Bandy The Rodeo Clown, I Never Go Around Mirrors, I Can't Get Over You to Save My Life (with Lefty Frizzell), Lucky Arms (with Lefty Frizzell); with Darlene Shafer: Does Fort Worth Ever Cross Your Mind; with Lyndia Shafer: All My Ex's Live In Texas; with Dallas Frazier: The Baptism Of Jesse Taylor; Tell Me My Lying Eyes Are Wrong; with A. L. Owens: I Just Started Hatin' Cheatin' Songs Today. *Recordings:* albums: I Never Go Around Mirrors; So Good For So Long. *Address:* c/o Nashville Songwriters Foundation, PO Box 121775, Nashville, TN 37212-1775, USA (office).

SHAFFER, James 'Munky'; American musician (guitar). *Career:* founder mem., L.A.P.D. (Love and Peace, Dude) 1989, renamed KoRn 1992–; numerous tours and live appearances. *Recordings include:* albums: with L.A.P.D.: Love And Peace, Dude (EP) 1989, Who's Laughing Now 1991, L.A.P.D. 1997; with KoRn: Korn 1994, Life Is Peachy 1996, Follow The Leader 1998, Issues 1999, Untouchables 2002, Take A Look In The Mirror 2003, See You On The Other Side 2005, Untitled 2007, Korn III: Remember Who You Are 2010. *Current Management:* International Talent Booking, First Floor, Ariel House, 74a Charlotte Street, London, W1T 4QJ, England. *Telephone:* (20) 7637-6979. *Fax:* (20) 7637-6978. *E-mail:* mail@itb.co.uk. *Website:* www.korn.com.

SHAFRANOV, Vladimir 'Vova'; Finnish musician (piano); b. 1946, Leningrad, Russia. *Education:* Rimsky-Korsakov Conservatory. *Career:* played with various bands throughout USSR; worked in Finnish jazz trios with Eero Koivistoinen; represented Finland at Middleheim Festivals, Belgium 1978, Ljubljana 1979; lived and worked in New York 1983–; performed duos, trios in local clubs with American jazz artists including Ron Carter, Eddie Gomez, Mark Johnson, Al Foster, Mel Lewis. *Recordings:* album: with Al Foster and George Moraz: White Nights 1992.

SHAGGY; Jamaican/American singer and songwriter; b. (Orville Richard Burrell), 22 Oct. 1968, Kingston. *Career:* left Jamaica to live with mother in Brooklyn, New York, USA, aged 18; former Gulf War veteran with US Marines; reggae/dancehall hits with independent label releases; co-owner Big Yard record label (with man., Robert Livingston and others); collaborations with Rayvon, Ricardo 'RikRok' Ducent, Grand Puba, Wayne Wonder. *Recordings include:* albums: Pure Pleasure 1993, Original Doberman 1994, Boombastic (Grammy Award for Best Reggae Album 1996) 1995, Midnite Lover 1997, Ultimate Shaggy Collection 1999, Hotshot (Billboard Music Award for Album of the Year 2001, Best-Selling Album 2001) 2000, Lucky Day 2002, Clothes Drop 2005, Intoxication 2007. *Honours:* Billboard Music Award for Male Artist of the Year 2001, BRIT Award for Int. Male Solo Artist 2002. *Address:* c/o Big Yard Music Group, PO Box 1060, Valley Stream, NY 11580, USA (office). *E-mail:* info@bigyardmusic.com (office). *Website:* www.bigyardmusic.com (office); www.shaggyonline.com.

SHAHIDA, Shahin; Iranian/American musician (guitar). *Education:* American Univ., Washington, DC, USA. *Career:* met Sepehr Haddad while at school; joined band Amsterdam while studying in USA; mem., Feast or Famine; formed duo with Haddad, early 1990s. *Recordings include:* albums: One Thousand And One Nights 1994, Shahin And Sepehr 1995, Aria 1996, World Café 1998, East/West Highway (compilation) 2000, Nostalgia 2002. *E-mail:* Shahin@shahinmusic.com. *Website:* www.shahinmusic.com.

SHAIMAN, Marc; American composer; b. 22 Oct. 1959, Newark, NJ. *Career:* mem. ASCAP. *Compositions for television:* What's Alan Watching Now? 1989, From the Earth to the Moon 1998, Jackie's Back! 1999, Bette 2000. *Compositions for film:* When Harry Met Sally... 1989, Misery 1990, Scenes from a Mall 1991, City Slickers 1991, The Addams Family 1991, Mr Saturday Night 1992, Sister Act 1992, A Few Good Men 1992, Heart and Souls 1993, Sleepless in Seattle 1993, Addams Family Values 1993, Speechless 1994, City Slickers II: The Legend of Curly's Gold 1994, North 1994, Stuart Saves his Family 1995, Forget Paris 1995, The American President 1995, Mother 1996, Ghosts from the Past 1996, The First Wives Club 1996, Bogus 1996, In & Out 1997, George of the Jungle 1997, Patch Adams 1998, My Giant 1998, Simon Birch 1998, The Out-of-Towners 1999, South Park: Bigger, Longer and Uncut 1999, The Story of Us 1999, The Kid 2000, One Night at McCool's 2000, What's the Worst That Could Happen? 2001, Down with Love 2003, Alex & Emma 2003, Rumor Has It... 2005, Hairspray 2007, The Bucket List 2007, Parental Guidance 2012. *Current Management:* Kraft-Engel Management, 15233 Ventura Blvd, Suite 200, Sherman Oaks, CA 91403, USA. *Telephone:* (818) 380-1918 (office). *Fax:* (818) 380-2609 (office). *E-mail:* dawna@kraft-engel.com (office). *Website:* shaiman.filmmusic.com.

SHAJARIAN, Mohammed-Reza; Iranian singer; b. 23 Sept. 1940, Mashhad; m.; one s. three d. *Career:* began singing career at Radio Khorasan 1959; became master (ostad) of traditional Persian music; collaborations with Parviz Meshkatian, Mohammad Reza Lotfi, Hossein Alizadeh, Keyhan Kalhor and Faramarz Payvar; has taught at Dept of Fine Arts, Tehran Univ.; mem., Masters of Persian Music –2007; performances with other ensembles; tours in USA and Europe. *Recordings include:* with Masters of Persian Music: Zemestan ast 2000, Bi To Be Sar Nemishavad 2002, Faryad 2005, Soroude Mehr 2007; with others: Bidad 2005, Shajarian Golden Songs 2008, Bote Chin 2008, Khazan 2008, Beyade Aref 2008. *Honours:* Picasso Award, UNESCO 1999, Mozart Medal, UNESCO 2006, Nushin Medal 2008. *E-mail:* info@delawaz.ir (office). *Website:* www.delawaz.ir/default.htm.

SHAKER, Fadl; Lebanese singer; b. (Fadl Abd al-Rahman Shamander), 1 April 1969, Sidon; m., three c. *Career:* solo artist 1998–. *Recordings include:* albums: Wallah zaman 1998, Baya'a el-qolob 1999, Al-hob al-kadim 2000, Hobak khayal 2001, Sidi rohi 2003, Haflah 2004, Saharni ash-shok 2005, Allah weallam 2006, Yamusaherni al-lail 2007. *Address:* c/o Rotana, Burj al-Ghazal, 11th Floor, al-Tabaris, Achrafieh, Beirut, Lebanon (office). *E-mail:* info@rotana.net (office). *Website:* www.rotana.net (office); www.fadl-shaker.com.

SHAKER, Hani; Egyptian singer, songwriter and actor; b. 21 Dec. 1952, Cairo. *Education:* Cairo Conservatoire. *Career:* solo artist 1972–. *Recordings include:* albums: Wasalna lefain, Sadaany, Ya retak ma'aia, Teslamly oyouno, Howa eli ekhtar, Hekayet kol 'asheq, Baasha dehketak, Maak, Elhob malosh kabeer, Ally el-dehkaiya, Shawer, Kolo yehoun, Albi malo, Wala kan baamry, Leh manehlamsh, Tekhsary, El-helm el-gamel, Yaretny, Garhy ana, Men ghair leh 2001, Na'am ya habibi na'am 2001, Bahebak ana 2002, Bahebak ya ghaly 2004, Arabny leek 2005, A'la il layali 2007. *Address:* c/o EMI Music Arabia, PO Box 61003, Dubai, United Arab Emirates (office). *E-mail:* info@emimusicarabia.com (office). *Website:* www.emimusicarabia.com (office); www.hanishakeronline.com.

SHAKESPEARE, Robbie; Jamaican reggae musician (bass) and producer; b. 27 Sept. 1953, Kingston. *Career:* mem. rhythm partnership, Sly and Robbie (with Sly Dunbar) 1975–; prolific session musician with artists including Peter Tosh, Bunny Wailer, Black Uhuru, Grace Jones, Bob Dylan, Ian Dury, Joan Armatrading, Horace Andy, Mikey Dread, Gregory Isaacs, Augustus Pablo; formed own label, Taxi; tours with Black Uhuru. *Recordings:* with Sly and Robbie: Sly and Robbie Present Taxi 1981, A Dub Extravaganza 1984, Language Barrier 1985, Sly and Robbie Meet King Tubby 1985, The Sound of Taxi Vol. 1, Vol. 2 1986, Rhythm Killers 1987, Taxi Fare 1987, Uhuru In Dub 1987, The Summit 1988, Hardcore Dub 1989, Silent Assassin 1990, Remember Precious Times 1993, Mambo Taxi 1997, Hail Up Taxi 2 1998, Taxi Christmas 1998, Fatigue Chic 1999, Massive 1999, Dub Fire 2000, In Good Company 2001, Version Born 2004, Inspiration Information Vol. 1 2008. *E-mail:* gbougard@gmail.com (office). *Website:* www.officialslyandrobbie.com.

SHAKIRA; Colombian singer, songwriter, dancer, record producer and choreographer and model; b. (Shakira Isabel Mebarak Ripoll), 2 Feb. 1977, Barranquilla; d. of William Mebarak Chadid and Nidia Ripoll. *Career:* wrote first song aged eight, signed recording contract with Sony Music Colombia aged 13; f. Fundación Pies Descalzos (Barefoot Foundation) 1997; Founding mem. Fundación América Latina en Acción Solidaria; apptd UNICEF Goodwill Amb. 2003; helped organize Live Aid Latino series of concerts 2008–; Hon. Chair. for Educ. Action Week, Global Campaign for Educ. April 2008; mem. White House Initiative on Educational Excellence for Hispanics 2011. *Recordings include:* albums: Magia 1991, Peligro 1993, Pies Descalzos 1996, ¿Dónde Están Los Ladrones? 1998, Laundry Service 2002, Washed And Dried: Laundry Service Limited Edition 2002, Fijación Oral Vol. 1 (Billboard Music Award for Latin Pop Album of the Year 2005, Grammy Award for Best Latin Rock/Alternative Album 2006, Latin Grammy Awards for Best Album and Best Female Pop Vocal Album 2006) 2005, Fijación Oral Vol. 2 2005, She Wolf 2009, Sale el Sol (Premios Lo Nuestro Award for Album of the Year 2012) 2010, Shakira 2014. *Television includes:* El oasis (Colombian TV drama series) 1996, Taina (series) 2002, coach and judge on The Voice (NBC) 2013, 2014. *Honours:* Latin Grammy Awards for Best Female Vocal Performance 2000, for Best Music Video (for Suerte) 2002, five MTV Video Awards 2002, MTV Europe Music Award for Best Female 2005, American Music Award for Favorite Latin Music Artist 2005, 2006, Billboard Music Awards for Latin Song of the Year (for La Tortura), for Latin Pop Album Artist of the Year 2005, MTV Video Award for Best Choreography 2006, MTV Latin America Music Award for Song of the Year (for Hips Don't Lie) 2006, Latin Grammy Award for Best Song (for La Totura), for Record of the Year (for La Totura) 2006, MTV Video Music Award for Best Collaboration (for Beautiful Liar with Beyoncé) 2007, Latin Recording Academy Person of the Year 2011, Premios Lo Nuestro Award for Artist of the Year 2012, Premios Lo Nuestro Award for Female Artist of the Year 2012, Premios Lo Nuestro Award for Song of the Year (for Rabiosa) 2012, ranked by Forbes magazine amongst The World's 100 Most Powerful Women (40th) 2012, (52nd) 2013, (58th) 2014, (81st) 2015. *Current Management:* c/o ROC Nation, 1411 Broadway, New York, NY 10018, USA. *Telephone:* (212) 292-8500. *Website:* www.rocnation.com. *Address:* c/o Sony BMG Entertainment, 550 Madison Avenue, New York, NY 10022-3211, USA (office). *Website:* www.shakira.com.

SHALIT, Jonathan Sigmund, OBE; British music manager; *Managing Director, ROAR Global;* b. 17 April 1962, London, England; s. of David Shalit and Sophie Shalit (née Gestetner). *Education:* City of London School. *Career:* worked at Saatchi & Saatchi; est. Shalit Global Entertainment and Management (now ROAR Global); recorded or managed Big Brovaz, Carly Simon, Charlotte Church, Cher, Chris de Burgh, Claire Sweeney, Courtney Pine, Elton John, Elvis Costello, Esther McVey, Jamelia, Javine, Jon Bon Jovi, Kate Bush, Larry Adler, Leo Sayer, Lisa Stansfield, Meat Loaf, Oleta Adams, Peter Gabriel, Robert Palmer, Ruthie Henshall, Sinead O'Connor, Sting, Willard White; Trustee, Variety Club of GB, The Chicken Shed Theatre Co., Regain; mem. Annabel's, Queens, Tramp. *Honours:* Freeman of the City of London, Liveryman of the Worshipful Co. of Coach Makers and Coach Harness Makers. *Address:* ROAR Global, ROAR House, 46 Charlotte Street, London, W1T 2GS, England (office). *Telephone:* (20) 7462-9060 (office). *E-mail:* jessica@roarglobal.com (office). *Website:* roarglobal.com (office).

SHANKAR, Anoushka; Indian sitar player, conductor and composer; b. 9 June 1981, London; d. of Ravi Shankar and Sukanya Shankar. *Education:* San Dieguito Acad., San Diego, Calif., USA. *Career:* professional debut in New Delhi 1995, aged 13; regular performances since 1997 at major concert halls in India, Europe, USA and Asia, including tours with Ravi Shankar ensemble; first solo tour 2000; fundraising concerts for the Tibet Foundation Peace Garden 2000, Ramakrishna Centre, Kolkata 2000, Siri Fort Auditorium, New Delhi (conducting debut) 2001, World Economic Forum, New York 2002, Rainforest Foundation Benefit Concert, Carnegie Hall 2002, Elizabeth Glazer Pediatric AIDS Foundation Concert 2002, A Concert for Peace and Reconciliation, Lincoln Center's Avery Fisher Hall, New York 2003, Adopt a Minefield, Germany 2005. *Film appearance:* Dance Like a Man 2003. *Recordings include:* solo: Anoushka 1998, Anourag 2000, Live at Carnegie Hall 2002, Rise 2006, Breathing Under Water (with Karsh Kale) 2007, Traveller (Best Artist, Songlines Music Awards) 2012, Traces of You 2013, Home 2015. *Publication:* Bapi, the Love of My Life (pictorial biog. of Ravi Shankar) 2002. *Honours:* House of Commons Shield 1998, Nat. Council on Youth Leadership Award 1998, San Dieguito Acad. Award 1999, Woman of the Year (India) Award 2003. *Current Management:* Sulivan Sweetland, 1 Hillgate Place, Balham Hill, London, SW12 9ER, England. *Telephone:* (20) 8772-3470 (home). *Fax:* (20) 8673-8959 (home). *E-mail:* info@sulivansweetland.co.uk. *Website:* www .sulivansweetland.co.uk; www.anoushkashankar.com.

SHANKAR (KATHAK), (Pandit) Bhavani; Indian composer and musician (pakhawaj, tabla); b. 1950. *Career:* mem. Zakir Hussain and The Rhythm Experience; collaborations with Hariprasad Chaurasia, Shivkumar Sharma. *Recordings include:* album: Pakhawaj Beat 2002. *Honours:* Taal Shri 1986, Taal Vilas 1996, Sangeet Natak Acad. Award, Pandit Jasraj Gaurav Puraskar, Maharashtra Kala Niketan Award.

SHANNON, Sharon; Irish folk musician; b. 1968, Corofin, County Clare. *Education:* Cork Univ. *Career:* mem., The Waterboys 1989–90; played with Adam Clayton, Van Morrison, Sinead O'Connor, Dennis Bovell; solo artist 1991–; regular festival appearances and tours. *Recordings include:* albums: Sharon Shannon 1991, Out The Gap 1994, Each Little Thing 1997, The Diamond Mountain Sessions 2000, Live In Galway 2001, Tunes 2005. *Honours:* Meteor Ireland Music Award for Best Folk/Traditional Music 2007. *Current Management:* Asgard Promotions Ltd, 125 Parkway, London, NW1 7PS, England. *Telephone:* (20) 7387-5090. *Fax:* (20) 7387-8740. *E-mail:* info@asgard-uk.com.

SHAPIRO, Helen; British singer; b. 28 Sept. 1946, Bethnal Green, London; d. of Barney Shapiro and Rachel Shapiro; m. John Williams. *Education:* Maurice Berman Singing Acad. *Career:* solo artist aged 14; numerous radio and TV appearances by age 15; tours worldwide; concerts with own band 1963–2003; Humph 'n' Helen Show (with Humphrey Lyttelton) 1984–2001; singer and speaker at Messianic Gospel events. *Film appearances:* It's Trad Dad 1962, Play It Cool 1962. *Theatre includes:* I'll Get My Man 1967, Never Too Late 1968, The French Have A Song For It 1979, Oliver 1979–80, Cabaret 1982, Goose Pimples 1982, Ello Ello Ello 1982, One For The Road 1985, Seesaw 1987, numerous pantomimes. *Recordings include:* albums: Tops With Me 1962, It's Trad, Dad (film soundtrack) 1962, Helen's Sixteen 1963, Helen Hits Out 1964, All for the Love of Music 1978, Straighten Up and Fly Right 1983, Echoes of the Duke 1985, Humph 'n' Helen 1990, The Pearl 1990, Helen Shapiro 25th Anniversary Album 1991, Kadosh 1992, Nothing But The Best 1995, The Essential Helen Shapiro 1997, Enter Into His Gates 1997, The Best of the 80s 1997, Helen Shapiro 1997, Helen 'n' Humph Mark II 1998, Helen Shapiro at Abbey Road 1998, By Request 1998, Simply Shapiro 2000, Gospel Collection 2002, What Wondrous Love is This 2010, The Ultimate Helen Shapiro 2011, For Such a Time As This (with Hebron) 2015; numerous singles, including several hit records in early 1960s. *Publications include:* Walking Back to Happiness (autobiography) 1993. *Honours:* NME Readers' Poll winner of Best British Female Singer 1961, Variety Club Silver Heart Award for Most Promising Newcomer 1962, BASCA Gold Badge of Merit 1991. *Address:* PO Box 35619, London, SE9 4ZQ, England (office). *Telephone:* (20) 8851-9049 (office). *Fax:* (20) 8851-9049 (office). *E-mail:* mannamusic@freeuk.com (office). *Website:* www.mannamusic.co.uk (office).

SHARAM; Iranian producer and remixer; b. (Sharam Tayebi), 12 Aug. 1970. *Career:* formed Deep Dish and founded Deep Dish/Yoshitoshi Records with partner, Dubfire 1992; also solo artist; collaborations with Danny Tenaglia, John Selway, Everything But The Girl; remixed Madonna, De'Lacy, Billie Ray Martin, Joi Cardwell, Dusted, Sven Vath, The Shamen, Eddie Amador. *Recordings include:* albums: Junk Science 1998, George Is On 2005; solo Get Wild 2009. *Honours:* Grammy Award for Remixer of the Year 2001. *Current Management:* c/o Bullitt Agency, 320/a M Street, NW, Washington, DC 20007,

USA. *Website:* www.thebullittagency.com. *E-mail:* mail@kurosh.net. *Website:* www.deepdish.com.

SHARDA, Anju, BA; British singer and songwriter; b. 17 March 1969, Perivale, Middlesex. *Career:* mem. of Cardiff-based trio, Banana Cat (later Glorious) 1991–93; various television appearances; co-writer with Simon and Diamond Dougal 1994, with Jon Moss (ex-Culture Club) 1995; mem. Musicians' Union, PRS. *Recordings:* album, with 3rd Core: Pandemic 2000. *Address:* 13 Elvendon Road, London N13 4SJ, England.

SHARKEY, Feargal; Northern Irish singer and music industry representative; *CEO, British Music Rights;* b. 13 Aug. 1958, Londonderry. *Career:* fmr mem., The Undertones –1983; numerous hit singles and live appearances, television and radio appearances; worked with Vince Clarke (of Erasure) on project The Assembly 1983; solo artist; A & R man; with Radio Authority 1998–2003; Chair. Live Music Forum, Dept for Culture, Media and Sport 2004–07; CEO British Music Rights (industry organization) 2008–. *Recordings include:* albums: with The Undertones: Teenage Kicks 1978, Undertones 1979, Hypnotised 1980, Positive Touch 1981, The Sin of Pride 1983, Peel Sessions 1986, The Very Best of The Undertones 1994; solo: Feargal Sharkey 1985, Wish 1988, Song from the Mardi Gras 1991. *Honours:* Dr hc (Univ. of Hertfordshire) 2008, Hon. DLitt (Ulster) 2010. *Address:* British Music Rights, British Music House, 26 Berners Street, London, W1T 3LR, England (office). *Telephone:* (20) 7306-4446 (office). *Fax:* (20) 7306-4449 (office). *E-mail:* britishmusic@bmr.org (office). *Website:* www.bmr.org (office).

SHARKIMAXX (see Felix Da Housecat)

SHARROCK, Chris; British musician (drums); b. 1964, Bebington, Wirral. *Career:* mem. The Icicle Works 1980–88, The La's 1989; fmr mem. World Party, The Lightning Seeds; mem. backing band for Robbie Williams 2000–08; mem. Oasis 2008–10, Beady Eye 2010–14.

SHAVERZASHVILI, George; Georgian composer and classical and jazz pianist; *Head of Jazz Department, Georgian-Anglo International Association for Culture and the Arts;* b. 4 Aug. 1950, Tbilisi; s. of Alexander Shaverzashvili and Aza Kavtaradze; m. Nino Meskhi; one d. *Education:* State Conservatory, Tbilisi. *Career:* debut, piano 1970, composer 1980, Tbilisi; concerts in Tbilisi, Moscow, St Petersburg, Tallinn, Budapest, Bratislava; Prof. of Composition, Tbilisi State Conservatory; Head of Jazz Dept, Georgian-Anglo Int. Assn for Culture and the Arts 2005–; mem. Georgian Composers' Union. *Compositions:* Quintet for piano and string quartet, three Sonatas for piano, two Concertos for piano and orchestra 1984, 1991, two Concertos for violin 1990, 1995, Sonata for violin, Trio for piano, flute and clarinet 1997, Alegg for string orchestra 1998, two Piano Fantasies 1998, 1999, Mass for chorus and orchestra 1999, Maestoso for piano 2000, Clouds for symphony orchestra 2003, Trio for piano, violin and cello 2004, Piano Suite from five pieces 2005, String Quartet No. 1 2006, No. 2 2010. *Honours:* Laureate of Transcaucasus Int. Piano Competition, Baku 1972, second prize Moscow Int. Competition of Composers 1985. *Address:* D. Agmashenebeli str. 123, 0164 Tbilisi (office); Mosashvili Street 8, Ap 6, 380062 Tbilisi, Georgia (home). *Telephone:* (32) 968678 (office); (32) 954861 (office); (32) 224157 (home). *Fax:* (32) 968678 (office). *E-mail:* geomic@mail.ru (office). *Website:* www.geomic.org.ge (office).

SHAW, Donald Patrick; British musician (keyboards, accordion) and composer; b. 6 May 1967, Ketton, Leicestershire, England. *Career:* founder mem., Capercaillie; group, along with original material, specialise in fusing traditional Gaelic songs with contemporary arrangements; had first UK top 40 single in Gaelic, Coisich A Ruin (from A Prince Among Islands EP), 1992; Produced and performed on fellow Capercaillie members' solo albums: Karen Matheson, The Dreaming Sea, 1996; Michael McGoldrick, Fused, 2000; written music for television documentaries, dramas and the feature film Rob Roy. *Recordings:* albums: with Capercaillie: Sidewalk 1989, Delirium 1991, Get Out 1992, The Blood Is Strong, Secret People 1993, Capercaillie 1995, To The Moon 1996, Beautiful Wasteland 1997, Glenfinnan – Songs of The '45 (recorded 1995) 1998, Nàdurra 2000, Live in Concert 2002, Choice Language 2003, Roses and Tears 2008; features solo on: L'Heritage De Celts 1994, The Dreaming Sea, Karen Matheson 1996, Finisterres, Dan Ar Braz 1997, Zenith, Dan Ar Braz 1998, Identities, Idir 1999, Suilean Dubh, Tannas 1999, Ru-Ra, Tannas 2000, Sawdust In My Veins, James Grant 2000, My Thrawn Glory, James Grant 2000, Fused, Michael McGoldrick 2000, Source, Big Sky 2000, Magaid A Phipir, Rory Campbell 2000, Tacsi (TV series) 2000. *Honours:* All-Britain Accordion Champion 1984. *Address:* c/o Jane Skinner, Vertical Records, 19 Woodside Crescent, Glasgow G3 7UL, Scotland (office). *Telephone:* (141) 352-6670 (office). *E-mail:* info@secretmusic.org.uk (office). *Website:* www .verticalrecords.co.uk (office); www.capercaillie.co.uk.

SHAW, Ian, BMus; British jazz singer, musician (piano), actor, broadcaster and presenter and producer; b. 2 June 1962, North Wales. *Education:* King's Coll., London. *Career:* plays regularly at Ronnie Scott's, London; tours in UK, Europe, USA and world-wide; has worked with Mark Murphy, Cedar Walton, Kenny Wheeler, John Taylor, Carol Grimes, Ruby Turner, Madeline Bell, Michael McDonald, Quincy Jones, Abdullah Ibrahim, Mari Wilson, Claire Martin, Guy Barker, Nigel Kennedy, amongst others. *Films:* Pierrepoint 2005, Titus 2013. *Radio:* Kaleidoscope, Nicky Campbell (BBC Radio 1), Big Band Special (BBC Radio 2), In Tune (BBC Radio 3), Jazz Library (BBC Radio 4), Dinner Jazz (Jazz FM), Ronnie Scott's Radio Show. *Television includes:* Top of the Pops, Pebble Mill, Jools Holland's The Happening, The Jack Dee Show, The Late Show. *Recordings include:* Lazy Blue Eyes (album of jazz love songs with Carol Grimes) 1990, Ghostsongs, Live At Ronnie Scott's 1992, Zebra (guest singer with Yello) 1994, Taking It To Hart, A Tribute To Rodgers And Hart 1995, Famous Rainy Day 1996, The Echo Of A Song 1996, In A New York Minute 1999, Soho Stories 2001, A World Still Turning 2003, Drawn To All Things: The Songs Of Joni Mitchell 2006, Lifejacket 2008, Somewhere Towards Love 2009, The Abbey Road Sessions 2011, A Ghost In Every Bar: The Lyrics Of Fran Landesman 2013, The Theory Of Joy 2016. *Publications:* Making it in the Music Business 1993. *Honours:* Perrier Award, Edinburgh 1991, BBC Jazz Award for Best Vocalist 2004, 2007. *Current Management:* c/o Charlotte Keech, Viva Voce, 17 Macroom Road, London, W9 3HY, England. *Telephone:* (20) 8960-0315 (home). *E-mail:* charlottekeech@yahoo.co.uk. *Website:* www.ianshaw.biz.

SHAW, James (Jimmy); Canadian musician (guitar, theremin, trumpet) and producer; b. London, England. *Career:* mem. Metric 1998–. *Films:* soundtrack contributions: Scott Pilgrim vs the World 2010, The Twilight Saga: Eclipse 2010. *Recordings:* albums: with Metric: Old World Underground Where Are You Now 2003, Live it Out 2005, Grow Up and Blow Away 2007, Fantasies (Juno Awards for Alternative Album of the Year 2010) 2009; as producer: Hind Hind Legs, The Lovely Feathers 2006. *Honours:* Juno Award for Group of the Year 2010. *Address:* c/o Last Gang Records, 171 East Liberty Street, Suite 330, Toronto, ON M6K 3P6, Canada (office). *Telephone:* (416) 534-3000 (office). *Fax:* (416) 534-3005 (office). *E-mail:* management@ilovemetric.com (office). *Website:* www.ilovemetric.com.

SHAW, Mark; British singer and songwriter; b. (Mark Robert Tiplady), 10 June 1961, Chesterfield, Derbyshire. *Career:* mem., Then Jerico 1985–90, 1994–; solo artist 1990–91; mem., Shaw Etc. 1991. *Television appearances:* Dream Team (Hewland Int./Sky One), Reborn in the USA (ITV 1). *Recordings include:* albums: with Then Jerico: First (The Sound Of Music) 1987, Big Area 1989, Electric 1994, Radio Jerico 1997, Orgasmaphobia 1998, Alive And Exposed 2000; solo: Almost 1991; singles: with Then Jerico: The Big Sweep 1985, Let Her Fall 1987, Prairie Rose 1987, Muscle Deep 1987, The Motive 1987, Big Area 1989, What Does It Take? 1989, Sugar Box 1989, Let Her Fall 1989; solo: Love So Bright 1990, Under Your Spell 1991. *Address:* c/o TJNC, The Old Bake House, 16a Barnes High Street, London, SW13 9LW, England (office). *Website:* www.thenjerico.com.

SHAW, Marlena; American jazz singer; b. (Marlena Burgess), 22 Sept. 1942, Valhalla, New York. *Education:* State Teachers' Coll., Potsdam. *Career:* performer Harlem's Apollo Theater 1952; singer with Count Basie Orchestra 1968–72; toured with Sammy Davis Jr early 1970s; first female singer signed to Blue Note Records 1972; collaborations include Benny Carter, Bruno Coulais and Akhenaton. *Recordings include:* albums: Out Of Different Bags 1967, Spice Of Life 1969, Marlena 1972, From The Depths Of My Soul 1973, Live At Montreux 1973, Who Is This Bitch, Anyway? 1974, Just A Matter Of Time 1976, Sweet Beginnings 1977, Acting Up 1978, Take A Bite 1980, Let Me In Your Life 1982, It Is Love 1986, Love Is In Flight 1988, Dangerous 1996, Elemental Soul 1997, Memories 2001, Live In Tokyo 2002, Lookin' For Love 2004. *Current Management:* c/o The Berkeley Agency, 2608 Ninth Street, Suite 301, Berkeley, CA 94710, USA. *Telephone:* (510) 843-4902. *Fax:* (510) 843-7271. *E-mail:* jim@berkeleyagency.com; connie@berkeleyagency.com. *Website:* www.berkeleyagency.com.

SHAW, Ryan Christopher; American R&B and soul and singer; b. 25 Dec. 1980, Decatur, Ga. *Education:* Georgia State Univ. *Career:* mem. Fabulous Soul Shakers group 2004; signed to Columbia record label 2006; opening act for Van Halen tour 2007–08; also supported Joss Stone and John Legend; numerous TV and live appearances. *Recordings:* albums: This is Ryan Shaw 2007, Real Love 2012. *E-mail:* jimmy@dynotonerecords.com (office). *Website:* www.dynotonerecords.com (office); www.thisisryanshaw.com.

SHAW, Sandie; British singer, songwriter and record producer; b. (Sandra Ann Goodrich), 26 Feb. 1947, Dagenham, Essex; m. 1st Jeff Banks 1968 (divorced 1978); one d.; m. 2nd Nik Powell 1982; two c.; m. 3rd Tony Bedford. *Education:* univ. *Career:* int. recording artist, singer, composer and producer; numerous hit singles, over 30 years; Winner, Eurovision Song Contest with the song Puppet On A String 1967; semi-retirement 1970s; relaunched music career with Morrissey 1984; numerous concerts, TV and radio broadcasts world-wide; sang the theme song to the film Made in Dagenham 2010; special guest on Jools Holland's Tour 2011; joined an Amnesty International campaign to end human rights abuses in Azerbaijan, host country of the 2012 Eurovision Song Contest April 2012; announced retirement from music April 2013; Founder Arts Clinic, psychological counsellor, writer and lecturer; Int. Amb. for Women Aid, UN 1985; mem. Royal Soc. of Musicians. *Compositions:* numerous collaborations with Chris Andrews. *Recordings include:* albums: Sandie 1965, Me 1965, The Golden Hits of Sandie Shaw 1966, Love Me, Please Love Me 1967, Puppet on a String 1967, The Sandie Shaw Supplement 1968, Reviewing the Situation 1969 (re-released 2013), Choose Life 1983, Hello Angel 1988, Nothing Less Than Brilliant 1994, The Pye Anthology 2000, Pourvu Que Ça Dure – Chante En Français 2003, La Cantante Scalza – Canta In Italiano 2003, Wiedehopf Im Mai – Sandie Shaw Singt Auf Deutsch 2004, Marionetas En La Cuerda – Sandie Shaw Canta En Español 2004, Nothing Comes Easy (four-CD box set) 2004, The Very Best of Sandie Shaw 2005, The Collection 2007. *Radio includes:* Sounds of the 60s (BBC Radio 2) 2006, Desert Island Discs (BBC Radio 4) 2010. *Television includes:* Making Your Mind Up (BBC), Loose Women (ITV) 2010, Hootenanny (BBC 2) 2011. *Publications:* The World At My Feet, Stress in Rock

Musicians: The Phenomena of Fame and Its Psychological Effect on the Developmental Processes of Artists. *Honours:* Hon. Prof. of Music, Royal Soc. of Musicians 1998. *Address:* Shavian Enterprises Ltd, 14 Devonshire Place, London, W1G 6HX, England. *E-mail:* info@sandieshaw.com. *Website:* www.sandieshaw.com.

SHAW, Tommy; American musician (guitar), singer and songwriter; b. 11 Sept. 1953, Montgomery, AL. *Career:* guitarist, Styx 1975–89, Damn Yankees 1989–; also mem. of side project, Shaw Blades 1995; worldwide tours and concerts. *Recordings include:* albums: with Styx: Crystal Ball 1976, The Grand Illusion 1977, Pieces of Eight 1978, Cornerstone 1979, Paradise Theater 1980, Kilroy Was Here 1983, Caught in the Act 1984, Brave New World 1999, Styx World (live) 2001; solo: Girls with Guns 1984, What If 1986, Ambition 1987, 7 Deadly Zens 1998, The Great Divide 2011; with Damn Yankees: Damn Yankees 1990, Don't Tread 1992; with Shaw Blades: Hallucination, 1995, Influence 2008. *Honours:* Motor City Music Award for Outstanding National Rock/Pop Single 1992. *E-mail:* tommy@tommyshaw.net. *Website:* www.tommyshaw.net.

SHBEIR, Ghada, BMus, MMus; Lebanese singer and teacher; b. 1969. *Education:* Université Saint-Esprit de Kaslik. *Career:* exponent of traditional Middle Eastern folk, Arabo-Andalusian singing and Assyrian religious chants; first gained acclaim as soloist with Université Saint-Esprit de Kaslik choir; has performed concerts in Lebanon, Egypt, Jordan, Cyprus, Greece, UK, France, Italy, Canada; festivals have included Festival of Oriental, Sacred and Andalusian Songs, Greece, Festival of Sacred Syriac and Byzantine Music, Venice, Italy 2001, Lebanon 2002, Festival of the Sacred Musical Traditions in the Middle East, Beirut 2002, Chants Liturgiques Syriaques, France, Belgium, Germany 2007; currently Prof., Université Saint-Esprit de Kaslik, Lebanese Univ., Nat. Conservatory of Lebanon. *Recordings include:* Chants Maronites de la Nativiteln, Kiddissa Min Ardina, Al Muwashahat 2006, Passion: Chants Syriaques 2008; guest vocalist on Carrefour de la Méditerranée by Constantinople 2003. *Publications include:* The Muwashah After the Cairo Caucus of 1932, Sayyed Darwish, Mouwashah et Dawr 2006; several articles on Arabic music in journals. *Honours:* Third World Festival of Arabic Music Award, Cairo 1997, Philippe Akiki Award from Ghosta Community 1997, Winner, Audience Award and Middle East and N Africa Award, BBC World Music Awards 2007. *E-mail:* info@ghadashbeir.com; chelayel@zamanme.com. *Website:* www.ghadashbeir.com.

SHCHEDRIN, Rodion Konstantinovich; Russian composer and pianist; b. 16 Dec. 1932, Moscow; s. of Konstantin Mikhailovich Shchedrin and Konkordia Ivanovna Shchedrin; m. Maya Plisetskaya 1958. *Education:* Moscow Conservatoire. *Career:* Chair. RSFSR (now Russian) Union of Composers 1973–90; USSR People's Deputy 1989–91; f. International Maya Plisetskaya and Rodion Shchedrin Foundation 2000; mem. Acad. of Fine Arts, Berlin 1989–, Bavarian Acad. of Fine Arts. *Compositions include:* operas: Not Only Love 1961, Lenin Oratory 1972, Dead Souls 1976, Lolita 1994, The Enchanted Wanderer 2002, Boyarinya Morozova 2006; ballets: Little Humpbacked Horse 1960, Carmen Suite 1967, Anna Karenina 1972, The Seagull 1980, Lady with a Lapdog 1985; for orchestra: three symphonies 1958, 1965, 2000, 5 concertos for orchestra 1963, 1968, 1988, 1989, 1998; Self-Portrait 1984, Stykhira 1988, Old Russian Circus Music 1989; 6 concertos for piano and orchestra 1954, 1966, 1973, 1992, 1999, 2003, Concerto for cello and orchestra 1994, Concerto for trumpet and orchestra 1995, Two Tangos by Albéniz for orchestra 1996, Concerto dolce for viola and string orchestra 1997; other: Poetoria 1974, Musical Offering for organ and nine soloists 1983, The Sealed Angel (Russian Liturgy) 1988, Nina and the Twelve Months (musical) 1988, Piano Terzetto 1996, Concerto Cantabile (for violin and strings) 1997, Preludium for 9th Symphony by Beethoven 1999, Lolita-serenade 2001, Parabola concertante (for cello and strings) 2001, Dialogue with Shostakovich 2001, The Enchanted Wanderer (concert opera) 2002, Tanja-Katya 2002, My Age, My Wild Beast 2003; works for chamber orchestra, piano, violin, organ and cello and song cycles, music for theatre and cinema. *Honours:* Hon. mem. American Liszt Soc., Rachmaninov Soc., Int. Music Council, Hon. Prof., Moscow Conservatoire, St Petersburg Conservatoire; Lenin Prize, USSR and Russian State Prizes, Russian Union of Composers Prize, Shostakovich Prize, Beethoven Soc. Prize. *Address:* International Maya Plisetskaya and Rodion Shchedrin Foundation, Weihergarten 9, 55116 Mainz (office); Theresienstrasse 23, 80333 Munich, Germany (home); 25/9, Tverskaya St, apt. 31, 103050 Moscow, Russia (home). *Telephone:* (89) 285834 (home); (495) 299-72-39 (home). *Fax:* (89) 282057 (home). *E-mail:* infoplisetskaya.de (office); infoshchedrin.de (home); rshchedrin@yahoo.com. *Website:* www.shchedrin.de (office).

SHEA, Pat; American singer, songwriter and musician (guitar, piano); b. 7 Dec. 1957, Buffalo, NY. *Career:* grand prize winner, TNN's Be A Star Talent Show 1991; numerous live appearances; solo artist; mem. ASCAP. *Recordings include:* albums: The Road Less Traveled 1996, The Rocky Road to Dublin 2008, Christmas, Christmas II, Christmas III, Pearls. *Address:* PBS Records, PO Box 991, Orchard Park, NY 14127, USA. *Telephone:* (716) 870-4709. *E-mail:* pat@patshea.com. *Website:* www.patshea.com.

SHEARS, Jake; American singer; b. (Jason Sellards), 1978. *Career:* mem., Scissor Sisters 2001–. *Recordings include:* albums: Scissor Sisters (BRIT Award for Best Int. Album 2005) 2004, Ta-Dah 2006, Night Work 2010. *Honours:* BRIT Awards for Best Int. Group, Best Int. Breakthrough Act 2005, Meteor Ireland Music Award for Best Int. Group 2007. *Current Management:*

c/o Dave Holmes, 3-D Management, Los Angeles, CA 90405, USA. *E-mail:* info@3dmgmt.com. *Website:* www.3dmgmt.com. *E-mail:* sisters@scissorsisters .net (office). *Website:* www.scissorsisters.com.

SHEEHAN, Billy; American musician (bass guitar). *Career:* founder member, rock group Talas 1980–83; bass player, David Lee Roth 1985–88; founder member, Mr Big 1989–. *Recordings:* albums: with Talas: Talas 1980, Sink Your Teeth Into That 1982, High Speed On Ice 1983, The Talas Years 1990; with David Lee Roth: Eat 'Em and Smile 1986, Skyscraper 1988; with Mr Big: Mr Big 1989, Raw Like Sushi 1 1990, Lean Into It 1991, Raw Like Sushi 2 1992, Bump Ahead 1993, Japandemonium 1994, Hey Man 1996, Get Over It 2000, Deep Cuts 2000, Actual Size 2001; solo: Compression 2001. *E-mail:* billy@billysheehan.com (office). *Website:* www.billysheehan.com.

SHEEHAN, Mark; Irish musician (guitar) and singer; b. 29 Oct. 1981, Dublin. *Career:* fmr R&B producer in USA; mem. MyTown 1996–2001; mem. The Script 2001–. *Recordings:* albums: The Script 2008, Science and Faith 2010, #3 2012, No Sound Without Silence 2014. *Honours:* World Music Award for Best Selling Irish Act 2008, Meteor Ireland Music Awards for Best Band 2009, for Best Irish Album 2009. *Address:* c/o RCA Group, 9 Derry Street, London W8 5HY, England (office). *Website:* www.rcalabelgroup.co.uk (office); www.thescriptmusic.com.

SHEERAN, (Edward Christopher) Ed; British singer, songwriter, musician (guitar) and record producer; b. 17 Feb. 1991, Halifax; s. of John Sheeran and Imogen Sheeran. *Education:* Thomas Mills High School, Framlingham. *Career:* first EP The Orange Room released 2005; toured with Just Jack 2009; signed to Asylum/Atlantic record label 2011; released debut single, The A Team 2011; songwriting credits include material for Olly Murs, One Direction, Taylor Swift; special guest on Taylor Swift's Red tour, N America 2013. *Recordings include:* albums: Ed Sheeran 2006, Want Some? 2007, + 2011, x (BRIT Award for Best British Album 2015) 2014; as contrib.: Red, Taylor Swift 2012. *Publications:* Ed Sheeran: A Visual Journey 2014. *Honours:* Q Awards for Breakthrough Artist 2011, for Best Solo Artist 2014, 2015, Ivor Novello Award for Best Song Musically and Lyrically 2012, BRIT Awards for Best British Male Solo Artist 2012, 2015, for British Breakthrough of the Year 2012, MTV Video Music Award for Best Male Video (for Sing) 2014, MTV Europe Music Awards for Best Live Act 2015, for Best World Stage Performance 2015, American Music Award for Favorite Male Artist 2015, Grammy Awards for Song of the Year, for Best Pop Solo Performance (both for Thinking Out Loud) 2016. *Current Management:* c/o Stuart Camp, Rocket Music Management, 1 Blythe Road, London, W14 0HG, England. *Telephone:* (20) 7348-4800. *E-mail:* contact@rocketmusic.com. *Website:* www.rocketmusic .com. *E-mail:* info@edsheeran.com. *Website:* www.edsheeran.com.

SHEHAN, Steve; American/French composer and musician (percussion, bass, keyboards); b. 18 Jan. 1957, Fort Eustis, Va, USA. *Education:* classical piano and guitar, Balinese gamelan; qualified aeroplane pilot. *Career:* concerts and recordings with Didier Lockwood 1978–2002, John McLaughlin 1981, Yves Montand 1982, Alan Stivell 1982, Jacques Higelin 1983, Magma 1984, Michael Jonasz 1984, Veronique Samson 1984, Kim Wilde 1984, Richard Horowitz 1985–98, Liane Foly 1986–96, Gipsy Kings 1987–89, Amina 1987–2002, Leonard Bernstein at Carnegie Hall 1989, Peter Gabriel's band and Akiro Inoué 1989, Les Polyphonies Corses 1989–90, Le Mystere des voix Bulgares 1991, Paco de Lucia's band 1991, David Sylvian and Riyuchi Sakamoto 1991, Jon Hassell, John Cage, Manu Dibango 1991–92, Wasis Diop 1992–2002, Paul Winter 1995, Zazie 1997–98, Nitin Sawhney 1998–2002, Paul Simon 1998–2002, Michael Brecker 1999, Jerry Douglas 1999, Alan Simon 2000–02, Simon Shaheen 2000, Bob Dylan 2000, Paul McCartney 2001, Cheb Mami 2001, Angun 2002, Supertramp 2002, Natacha Atlas 2002, Cirque du Soleil 2002, Rokia Traore 2002, Billy Preston 2002, Fleetwood Mac 2002, Carla Bruni 2002; recorded film music with Elliot Goldenthal 1991, Gabriel Yared (L'AMANT), Costa Gravas, Jonathan Dem; played and composed for several fashion shows by Antonio Miro 1989–92, Yves Saint Laurent 1989; owner publishing, production and record label, Safar Production Inc; mem. trio, Hadouk; producer and arranger, Omar Farouk Tekbilek with Natacha Atlas 2000; mem. SACEM, SDRM, BMI, SPEDIDAM. *Compositions:* ballet music with Ismaël Ivo, Bibliotheca of Babel, Weimar Opera 2000, Beijo Asfalto 1998, Ballet Jazz Art 1999, 2000, Metropolis, Dresden 2004, Shakespeare's The Tempest, Bangkok 2004, Haus der Kultur der Welt Berlin 2004, music for Israel Ivo 2004. *Recordings:* Impressions de Voyages 1984, Arrows 1989, Assouf (with Baly Otmani) 1994, 1997, Figaro Si! 1995, Indigo Dreams 1995, Safar – A Journey 1997, Ikewan 1997, Assarouf 1997, Versecrêt 1997, Shamanimal (with Hadouk) 1997, Awham (with Youssef el Idrissi) 1998, Amok 1998, Plenitude 1998, Alif (with Omar Farouk Tekbilek) 2001, Roads 2002, Now (with Hadouk) 2002, Elevations (with Reza Derakshani) 2004, Trio Hadouk Live 2004, Indigo Dreams 2006, Elevations 2006, Assikel (with Baly Othmani) 2008, Awalin with Nabil Othmani 2010, Hang with You 2013. *Address:* Safar, 11 rue Jean Jaurés, 94000 Créteil, France (office). *Telephone:* 1-48-99-59-58 (office). *E-mail:* contact@steveshehan.com (office). *Website:* www.steveshehan.com.

SHEILA, (Annie Chancel); French singer; b. 16 Aug. 1946, Créteil; d. of André Chancel and Micheline Chancel (née Gaultier); m. Guy (Ringo) Bayle (divorced); one s. *Education:* Rue de Patay School, Paris. *Career:* singer 1962–; numerous concerts including performances at Zénith 1985 and Olympia, Paris 1989; performer Bang Bang (film) 1967; scaled back in music business 1989 to concentrate on writing and sculpture, returned 1998 and

continues to perform. *Recordings include:* Sheila, L'école est finie, Première surprise partie, Papa t'es dans le coup, Ne raccroche pas, Pendant les vacances, Chaque instant de chaque jour, Ecoute ce disque, C'est toi que j'aime, Le folklore américain, Le cinéma, Bang Bang, L'heure de la sortie, La famille, Adios amor, Dans une heure, Dalila, Petite fille de français moyen, Arlequin, La colline de Santa Maria, Oncle Jo, Julietta, Reviens je t'aime, Les rois mages, Blancs, jaunes, rouges, noirs, Mélancolie, Le couple, Tu es le soleil, On dit, Tangue Au, Vis vas, Je suis comme toi, Emmenez-moi, Vivre mieux, On s'dit plus rien, Seulement pour toi, Dense 1999, Sheila Live 1999. *Publications:* Chemin de lumière 1993, Et si c'etait vrai 1995, La Captive (novel) 1997. *Address:* c/o EMI Music, 43 rue Camille Desmoulin, 92130 Issy-les-Moulineaux; c/o Editions Ramsay, 103 blvd Murat, 75016 Paris, France.

SHELLEY, Steve; American musician (drums), producer and record label executive; b. 23 June 1962, Midland, MI. *Career:* mem., Sonic Youth 1985–; founder Smells Like Records 1992–; collaborations with The Raincoats, Two Dollar Guitar, Cat Power, Chris Lee, Christina Rosenvinge. *Recordings include:* albums: with Sonic Youth: E.V.O.L. 1986, Sister 1987, Daydream Nation 1988, The Whitey Album 1989, Goo 1990, Dirty 1992, Experimental Jet Set, Trash and No Star 1994, Screaming Fields of Sonic Love 1995, Made in USA 1995, Washing Machine 1995, A Thousand Leaves 1998, SYR4: Goodbye 20th Century 1999, NYC Ghosts & Flowers 2000, Murray Street 2002, Sonic Nurse 2004, Rather Ripped 2006, The Destroyed Room: B-sides and Rarities 2006, The Eternal 2009. *Current Management:* c/o Michele Fleischli, Silva Artist Management, 722 Seward Street, Los Angeles, CA 90038-3504, USA. *Telephone:* (323) 856-8222. *E-mail:* mfleischli@ sammusicbiz.com. *Website:* www.sammusicbiz.com. *Address:* Smells Like Records, POB 6179, Hoboken, NJ 07030, USA (office). *E-mail:* steve@ smellslikerecords.com (office). *Website:* www.smellslikerecords.com (office); www.sonicyouth.com.

SHELTON, Blake Tollison; American country music singer and songwriter; b. 18 June 1976, Ada, Okla; s. of Richard Shelton and Dorothy Shelton; m. 1st Kaynette Gern 2003 (divorced 2006); m. 2nd Miranda Lambert 2011 (divorced 2015). *Career:* moved to Nashville, Tenn. 1993; signed to Giant Records 1998; debut single Austin released in 2001; guest vocalist on Tracy Byrd's single The Truth About Men 2003; duet with Trace Adkins on Hillbilly Bone in 2010. *Recordings include:* albums: Blake Shelton 2000, The Dreamer 2003, Blake Shelton's Barn & Grill 2004, Pure BS 2007, Startin' Fires 2009, Red River Blue 2011, Based on a True Story… (American Country Award for Album of the Year 2013, Country Music Asscn Award for Album of the Year 2013) 2013, Bringing Back the Sunshine 2014. *Television:* judge on Nashville Star 2007, Clash of the Choirs 2007; vocal coach on The Voice (NBC) 2011–. *Film:* The Christmas Blessing (TV film) 2005. *Honours:* with Trace Adkins: Acad. of Country Music Award for Vocal Event of the Year 2010, Country Music Asscn Award for Vocal Event of the Year 2010, Country Music Television Music Award for Collaborative Video of the Year 2010; solo: Country Music Asscn Awards for Male Vocalist of the Year 2010, 2011, 2013, 2014, Country Music Television Music Awards for Male Video and Best Web Video of the Year 2011, American Music Award for Favorite Country Male Artist 2011, Acad. of Country Music Award for Male Vocalist of the Year 2012, for Song of the Year (with Miranda Lambert for Over You) 2013, American Country Awards for Single of the Year: Male (for Sure Be Cool if You Did) 2013, iHeartRadio Music Award for Best Country Song of the Year (for Boys 'Round Here) 2014. *Current Management:* c/o Starstruck Management, 4445 Corporation Lane, Suite 268, Virginia Beach, VA 23462, USA. *Telephone:* (757) 213-6833. *Fax:* (757) 213-6801. *E-mail:* info@starstruckmanagement.com. *Website:* www .starstruckmanagement.com; www.blakeshelton.com.

SHELTON, Ricky Van; American country singer and songwriter; b. 12 Jan. 1952, Danville, Virginia; s. of Jenks Shelton and Eloise Shelton; m. Bettye Witt 1986. *Career:* fmr pipefitter, plumber, car salesman; country singer 1985–; mem. Country Music Asscn, Acad. of Country Music. *Recordings:* albums: Wild-Eyed Dream 1987, Loving Proof 1988, Ricky Van Shelton Sings Christmas 1989, Ricky Van Shelton III 1990, Backroads 1991, Don't Overlook Salvation 1992, A Bridge I Didn't Burn 1992, Greatest Hits Plus 1992, Love and Honor 1994, Ultimately Fine 1994, Making Plans 1998. *Honours:* CMA Awards: Horizon Award 1988, Male Vocalist of Year 1989; Nashville Network Viewer's Choice: Male Vocalist of Year, Album of Year 1989. *E-mail:* rvshelton2@yahoo.com (office). *Website:* www.rickyvanshelton.com.

SHEPHERD, Ben; American musician (bass); b. 20 Sept. 1968, Okinawa, Japan. *Career:* former mem. March of Crimes; mem. US heavy rock group, Soundgarden, 1990–97, 2010–; mem. Hater 1993–97; mem. Wellwater Conspiracy 1993–98; numerous tours and festival appearances. *Recordings:* albums: with Soundgarden: Badmotorfinger 1991, Superunknown 1994, Down on the Upside 1996, A-Sides 1997; with Hater: Hater 1993, The 2nd 2005; with Wellwater Conspiracy: Declaration of Conformity 1997; singles: Rusty Cage; Spoonman; The Day I Tried To Live; Black Hole Sun; Fell on Black Days; Pretty Noose; Burden in My Hand; Blow Up The Outside World; Ty Cobb; Bleed Together. *Website:* www.soundgardenworld.com.

SHEPHERD, Ollie Imogene (Jean); American country singer, songwriter and musician (bass); b. 21 Nov. 1933, Paul's Valley, OK; m. Hawkshaw Hawkins (died 1963). *Career:* formed all-girl band, Melody Ranch Girls 1948; worked with Red Foley's Ozark Jubilee 1955–57; debut country hit, A Dear John Letter (with Ferlin Huskey) 1953; solo artist until 1978; mem. Grand Ole Opry 1955. *Recordings include:* albums: Songs of a Love Affair 1956,

Lonesome Love 1959, This is Jean Shepherd 1959, Got You on My Mind 1961, Heartaches and Tears 1962, Lighthearted and Blue 1964, It's a Man Every Time 1965, Many Happy Hangovers 1966, I'll Take The Dog (with Ray Pillow) 1966, Heart We Did all That We Could 1967, Your Forevers Don't Last Very Long 1967, Hello Old Broken Heart 1967, Heart to Heart 1968, A Real Good Woman 1968, I'll Fly Away 1969, Seven Lonely Days 1969, Under Your Spell Again 1969, Best by Request 1970, A Woman's Hand 1970, Here and Now 1971, Just as Soon As I Get Over Loving You 1971, Just Like Walkin' in the Sunshine 1972, Slippin' Away 1973, I'll Do Anything It Takes 1974, Poor Sweet Baby 1975, I'm a Believer 1975, Jean Shepherd and the Second Fiddles 1975, For the Good Times 1975, Mercy 1976, Dear John 1981, Star of the Grand Ole Opry 1981, Honky Tonk Heroine 1995, The Melody Ranch Girl 1995, Satisfied Mind 1995. *Honours:* Cash Box Award for Top Female Singer 1959. *E-mail:* oprylady@comcast.net (office). *Website:* www .jeanshepardcountry.com.

SHEPHERDSON, Paul; British musician (drums), drama teacher and theatre director; b. 23 June 1941, Hull; m. Sandra Nicholl 1963; one s. one d. *Education:* studied piano. *Career:* member, Mike Peters Florida Jazz Band; supporting Kenny Ball Band, Roy Williams, Terry Lightfoot Band; backing residental musician to most cabaret acts including Marti Caine, The Nolans, Norman Collier, Faith Brown; own band with Martin Jones; mem. Musicians' Union. *Compositions:* co-writer, various musicals for local performance. *Address:* 73 The Wolds, Castle Park, Cottingham, Nr Hull HU16 5LQ, England.

SHEPPARD, Andy; British jazz musician (saxophones); b. 20 Jan. 1957, Bristol. *Education:* studied clarinet, saxophone, flute and guitar. *Career:* fmr mem., Sphere; played with Klaunstance, Big Band Lumière, Urban Sax; joined George Russell's Living Time Orchestra 1987; fmr mem., Carla Bley Big Band; leader of own band 1987–90; founder, Soft on the Inside Big Band 1990, Co-Motion 1991–98 (later Big Co-Motion); formed trio with Steve Lodder and Nana Vasconcelos, Inclassifiable 1995; formed sextet 1998–. *Compositions include:* music for the Gateshead Millennium Bridge project (with Kathryn Tickell) 2001, Arthur Miller's The Man Who Had All the Luck (Bristol Theatre Royal), Modern Living (dance piece), Syrup (Channel 4 TV), and music for various TV documentaries. *Recordings include:* albums: with Sphere: Sphere 1988, Present Tense 1988; with own bands: Andy Sheppard 1988, Introductions in the Dark 1989, Soft on the Inside 1990, In Co-Motion 1991, Rhythm Method 1993, Delivery Suite 1994, Inclassifiable 1995, Moving Image 1996, Learning to Wave 1998, Dancing Man & Woman 2000, Music for a New Crossing 2001, Nocturnal Tourist 2002, PS 2003, Deep River (with Joanna MacGregor) 2006, The Birds 2006, Movements in Colour 2009. *Honours:* British Jazz Awards for Best Newcomer 1987, for Best Instrumentalist 1988, for Best Album and Best Instrumentalist 1989, Big Band Award 1990. *Current Management:* c/o John Cumming, Serious, 51 Kingsway Place, Sans Walk, Clerkenwell, London, EC1R 0LU, England. *Telephone:* (20) 7324-1880. *Fax:* (20) 7324-1881. *E-mail:* info@serious.org.uk. *Website:* www.serious.org.uk; www.andysheppard.co.uk.

SHEPPARD, Rodney Charles; American musician (guitar); b. 25 Nov. 1967; m. Gretchen, one s. *Career:* played colleges and parties with local group The Tories; group became The Shrinky Dinx; signed to Atlantic Records following circulation of self-made demo video; act renamed Sugar Ray owing to threat of legal action prior to record releases; built up world-wide fanbase through touring and TV appearances; cameo in Fathers Day film, 1997. *Recordings:* albums: Lemonade and Brownies 1995, Floored 1997, 14–59 1999, Sugar Ray 2001, In Pursuit of Leisure 2003, Music for Cougars 2009. *Honours:* second/third albums certified double/triple platinum by RIAA respectively. *Address:* PO Box 6188, Olympia, WA 98507, USA (office). *E-mail:* rodney@sugarray.com (office). *Website:* www.sugarray.com.

SHEPPARD, T. G.; American country singer, songwriter and musician (guitar, saxophone, piano); b. (William Neal Browder), 20 July 1944, Humboldt, Tennessee; m. Kelly Lang 2007. *Career:* moved to Memphis 1960; worked as backup singer with Travis Wammack's band; recorded High School Days as Brian Stacey for Atlantic 1966; brief stint as record promoter for Stax label; first charted on pop and country chart with Devil In The Bottle for Motown's country subsidiary, Melodyland 1974; collaborations with Karen Brooks, Clint Eastwood, Judy Collins. *Recordings include:* albums: T.G. Sheppard 1975, Motels and Memories 1976, Solitary Man 1976, T.G. 1978, Daylight 1979, 3/4 Lonely 1979, Smooth Sailin' 1980, I Love 'Em All 1981, Finally! 1982, Perfect Stranger 1982, Greatest Hits 1983, Slow Burn 1983, One Owner Heart 1984, Livin' on the Edge 1984, It Still Rains in Memphis 1986, One for the Money 1987, Crossroads 1988, Nothin' on but the Radio 1997, Timeless 2004. *Current Management:* R. J. Kaltenbach Personal Management, PO Box 550, Harvard, IL 60033, USA. *E-mail:* rjkmgmt@aol .com. *Website:* tgsheppard.com.

SHERGILL, Rabbi; Indian singer, songwriter and musician (guitar); b. (Gurpreet Singh Shergill), 1975. *Education:* Sri Guru Tegh Bahadur Khalsa Coll., Univ. of Delhi. *Career:* f. band Kaffir (later disbanded); performs for Coke Studio (TV series). *Recordings include:* Rabbi 2004, Avengi Ja Nahin 2008. *Films include:* as music dir: Delhii Heights; soundtracks include: Dharti 2011. *Website:* www.rabbishergill.com (home).

SHERINE, BMus; Egyptian singer and actress; b. (Sherine Abd al-Wahab), 10 Oct. 1980, Cairo; m. Mohammad Mustafa 2007. *Career:* solo artist 2000–. *Film:* Mido mashakel 2003. *Recordings include:* albums: Garh tany 2002,

Lazim aish 2005, Bataminak 2008, Habeat 2009, Esaal Alaya 2012, Ana Keteer 2014.

SHERMAN, Cary; American lawyer; *Chairman and CEO, Recording Industry Association of America*; b. 10 April 1948, New York. *Education:* Cornell Univ., Harvard Law School. *Career:* worked for Arnold & Porter law firm, Washington, DC, later Sr Partner 1971–97, served as Head, Intellectual Property and Technology Practice Group; joined Recording Industry Asscn of America 1997, Pres. 2001–11, Chair. and CEO 2011–; Chair. of Bd, Levine School of Music, Washington, DC; bd mem. BNA's Patent, Trademark and Copyright Journal; fmr bd mem. Washington Area Lawyers for the Arts, Computer Law Asscn, The Computer Lawyer, Copyright Soc. *Publications include:* Computer Software Protection Law (co-author, two vols). *Address:* Recording Industry Association of America, 1025 F Street, NW, Tenth Floor, Washington, DC 20004, USA (office). *Telephone:* (202) 775-0101 (office). *Fax:* (202) 775-7253 (office). *E-mail:* csherman@riaa.com (office). *Website:* www .riaa.com (office).

SHERMAN, Richard M.; American songwriter; b. 12 June 1928, New York. *Career:* wrote as duo with late brother, Robert; staff songwriter, Walt Disney 1960–70. *Compositions:* film scores: Bambi 1942, Alice in Wonderland 1951, Peter Pan 1953, Lady and the Tramp 1955, Sleeping Beauty 1959, Rocky and Bullwinkle 1959, One Hundred and One Dalmatians 1961, The Parent Trap 1961, In Search of the Castaways 1962, Summer Magic 1963, The Sword in the Stone 1963, Big Red 1963, Mary Poppins 1964, The Happiest Millionaire 1967, The Jungle Book 1967, The One and Only, Genuine, Original Family Band 1968, Chitty Chitty Bang Bang 1968, The Aristocats 1970, Bedknobs and Broomsticks 1971, Snoopy, Come Home 1972, Charlotte's Web 1973, Tom Sawyer 1973, Huckleberry Finn 1974, The Slipper and the Rose 1976, The Many Adventures of Winnie the Pooh 1977, The Rescuers 1977, The Magic of Lassie 1978, The Fox and the Hound 1981, Magic Journeys 1982, Winnie the Pooh and a Day for Eeyore 1983, An American Tail 1986, All Dogs go to Heaven 1989, Little Nemo 1992, The Mighty Kong 1998, The Tigger Movie 2000; musicals: Victory Canteen 1971, Over Here! 1974, Dawgs 1983, Busker Alley 1995, Chitty Chitty Bang Bang 2002, Mary Poppins 2004. *Honours:* Acad. Awards for Best Original Song (for Chim Chim Cher-ee from Mary Poppins) 1965, for Best Music Score (for Mary Poppins) 1965, Grammy Award for Best Original Score for a Motion Picture (for Mary Poppins) 1965, Nat. Medal of Arts 2008. *E-mail:* rjsherman@shermanmusic.com (office). *Website:* www.shermanmusic.com.

SHERRY, Fionnuala; Irish violinist; *Concert Violinist, Secret Garden*; b. 20 Sept. 1962, Dublin; d. of Bernard Sherry and Breeda Sherry; m. Bernard Doyle. *Education:* Trinity Coll. of Music, Dublin. *Career:* mem. Radio Telefís Éireann (RTÉ) Concert Orchestra for ten years; contrib. to RTÉ children's programming; session work with The Chieftains, Sinead O'Connor, Van Morrison, Chris de Burgh, Bono, Wet Wet Wet; mem. Secret Garden 1994–, won Eurovision Song Contest with 'Nocturne' 1995. *Films:* recorded several Hollywood film scores with Irish Film Orchestra, including A Room with a View, The Mask. *Television:* A Little Bit of Eurovision (RTÉ) 2011, own TV double series, Tune In (RTÉ), numerous guest appearances on TV shows in Ireland, Norway, UK, USA, China, Taiwan, South Korea and Australia. *Recordings:* albums: Songs from a Secret Garden 1994, White Stones 1995, Dawn Of A New Century 1999, Dreamcatcher 2000, Once In A Red Moon 2002, Earthsongs 2005, Inside I'm Singing 2008; solo album: Songs From Before 2010. *Honours:* quadruple platinum (Norway), 25 Gold Albums worldwide, also platinum and double platinum, voted Best Int. Production, Shanghai. *Current Management:* c/o Trude Bø, Continental Artist Management, Kr. Augusts gate 10, 0164 Oslo, Norway. *Telephone:* 22-06-27-70. *E-mail:* trude.bo@continentalmusic.net. *E-mail:* fanmail@secretgarden.no (office). *Website:* www.secretgarden.no; www.fionnualasherry.com.

SHERRY, Rachel Patricia; musician (harp) and singer; b. 16 March 1960, Nottingham, England; m. John Byron 1993. *Education:* Birmingham Univ. and Royal Acad. of Music. *Career:* appearances at Purcell Room and QEH; concert tours to France, Italy, Spain and throughout UK; numerous television appearances as actress, singer and harpist; four programmes of music for harp and voice for BBC radio and numerous broadcasts with BBC Singers; mem. Musicians' Union, Equity. *Recordings include:* Rachel Sherry – Voice and Harp. *Address:* 16 Roughdown Avenue, Hemel Hempstead, Hertfordshire HP3 9BN, England.

SHERWOOD, John Torrance; South African composer, producer, musician (guitar) and engineer. *Education:* Architectural Association of Architecture; classical guitar with Patrick Bashford and Hector Quine. *Career:* mem. Musicians' Union; Performing Right Soc. *Compositions include:* soundtracks: Rumours of Rain, Channel 4 1992, Spoilt For Choice, BBC 2 1993, Trouble, Channel 4 1993. *Recordings include:* albums: as guitarist with Haysi Fantayzee: Battle Hymns For Children Singing; as engineer with PM Dawn: of The Heart of The Soul and of The Cross; Single: Set Adrift On Memory Bliss; as engineer: Project One and Irresistible Force: Outlaw Posse: My Afro's On Fire. *Honours:* Gold records for PM Dawn: Set Adrift On Memory Bliss; Of The Heart of The Soul and of The Cross.

SHIBAYAMA, Shinji; Japanese songwriter, musician (multi-instrumentalist) and producer. *Career:* previously recorded under the name Team Spirit; fmr mem., Idiot O'Clock, the Hallelujahs –1988; founder and owner, Org Records; founder mem., Nagisa Ni te 1990–. *Recordings:* albums: True Sun 1998, The True World 1999, Feel 2001, On the Love Beach 2001, The Same as a Flower 2004, Dream Sounds 2005, III 2005, Yosuga 2008. *Website:* www.p -vine.com.

SHIFLETT, Christopher (Chris) Aubrey; American musician (guitar); b. 6 May 1971, Santa Barbara, Calif.; m. Cara Shiflett; three s. *Career:* mem. Foo Fighters 1999–; side project, Jackson United 2004–. *Recordings include:* albums: with Foo Fighters: There Is Nothing Left To Lose (Grammy Award for Best Rock Album 2001) 1999, One By One (Grammy Award for Best Rock Album 2003) 2002, In Your Honor 2005, Skin and Bones 2006, Echoes, Silence, Patience and Grace (Grammy Award for Best Rock Album 2008, BRIT Award for Best Int. Album 2008) 2007, Wasting Light (Grammy Award for Best Rock Album 2012) 2011, Sonic Highways 2014. *Honours:* Grammy Award for Best Short Form Music Video (for Learn To Fly) 2001, Grammy Award for Best Hard Rock Performance (for All My Life) 2003, (for The Pretender) 2008, (for White Limo) 2010, Kerrang! Award for Best Single (for Best of You) 2005, Nordoff-Robbins Silver Clef Raymond Weil Int. Award 2006, BRIT Award for Best Int. Group 2008, 2012, 2015, Grammy Award for Best Rock Performance (for Walk) 2012, Grammy Award for Best Rock Song (for Walk) 2012. *Current Management:* c/o Gold Mountain Entertainment, Suite 450, 3575 Cahunega Blvd West, Los Angeles, CA 90068, USA. *Address:* c/o RCA Records, 1540 Broadway, New York, NY 10036, USA. *Website:* www.foofighters.com.

SHILKLOPER, Arkady; Russian musician (horn); b. 17 Oct. 1956, Moscow; m. Olga Goloborodko 1981, one s., one d. *Education:* Moscow Gnesin Institut, 1976–81. *Career:* Bolshoi Theatre Orchestra, 1978–85; Moscow Philharmonic Orchestra, 1985–89; Freelance musician (jazz, classical, folk), since 1990; Hornplayer (also alphorn, corno du caccio); Jazz podium; Jazz time; Jazz kwadrat; mem, International Horn Society. *Recordings:* with Pago Libre: Titles, 1996; Wake Up Call, 1998; Sheffield Jazz Experience, 1996; with Karl Berger: No Man Is An Island, 1996; with Misha Alperin: North Story, 1998. *Address:* Schwarzbach 21, 42277 Wuppertal, Germany (home). *Telephone:* (20) 24298749 (home). *E-mail:* arkady.shilkloper@gmx.de (home). *Website:* www.arkadyshilkloper.com (home).

SHIMONI, Ya'akov (Kobi), (Subliminal); Israeli rapper and producer; b. 13 Nov. 1979, Tel-Aviv. *Career:* formed rap duo with Yoav Eliasi (The Shadow) mid-1990s, gained popularity performing in clubs in Tel-Aviv; co-founder TACT Records; since 2000 associated with political and patriotic songs, labelled 'Zionist hip hop'; collaborations with Wyclef Jean, Joe Budden, Killah Priest, Remedy. *Recordings:* albums: Ha'Or m'Zion (The Light From Zion) 2000, Ha'Or Ve'HaTzel (The Light and the Shadow) 2002, TACT All-Stars 2004, Bediuk Kshe'Hashavtem she'Hakol Nigmar (Just When You Thought It Was Over) 2006. *Address:* TACT, Hanahalatact Ltd, 84 Derech Ben-Zvi, Tel-Aviv 68104, Israel (office). *Telephone:* (3) 6091826 (office). *E-mail:* office@wmwm.co.il (office). *Website:* www.tact-records.com (office).

SHIN, Lee Jung; South Korean musician (bass guitar), rapper and singer; b. 15 Sept. 1991. *Career:* mem. CN Blue 2009–. *Recordings:* albums: with CN Blue: Thank U 2010, First Step 2011, 392 2011. *Honours:* Male Rookie Award, Mnet Asian Music Awards 2010, Golden Disk Bonsang Award 2010, Melon Music Awards for Best New Artist and 2010 TOP 2010, Seoul Music Award for Best Newcomer 2011. *Address:* c/o FNC Music, Mnet Media Building, Apgujeong-dong, Gangnam-gu, Seoul, South Korea (office). *Telephone:* (2) 2517-5426 (office). *Fax:* (2) 2518-5428 (office). *E-mail:* fncmusic1@naver.com (office). *Website:* www.fncmusic.com (office); cnblue.co.kr/cnblue/kor (home).

SHINE, M. K.; British singer, songwriter and reggae club owner; b. (Mark Lowe), *Education:* School of Music, London. *Career:* Founder and lead singer of group Destiny, with brother 1986; solo artist as M. K. Shine 1991–; represented Jamaica in the Caribbean Broadcasting Union 1990. *Recordings include:* Wild Gilbert 1988, My Dream 1994, Simply Magic.

SHINODA, Mike Kenji; American singer; b. 11 Feb. 1977, Agoura, CA. *Education:* Pasadena Art Coll. of Design. *Career:* founding mem., Xero 1996, renamed Hybrid Theory, later renamed Linkin Park 1999–; also performed as Fort Minor 2004–; numerous int. concerts. *Recordings include:* albums: with Linkin Park: Hybrid Theory (Rock Bear Awards for Best Int. Album 2001) 2000, Reanimation 2002, In The End: Live & Rare 2002, Meteora 2003, Live In Texas 2003, Collision Course (with Jay-Z) 2004, Minutes to Midnight 2007, A Thousand Suns 2010, Living Things 2012, The Hunting Party 2014; as Fort Minor: The Rising Tied 2005. *Honours:* Billboard Award for Best Modern Rock Artist 2001, Rock Bear Award for Best Int. Band 2001, Kerrang! Award for Best Int. Newcomer 2001, Rolling Stone Award for Best Hard Rock/Metal Band 2001, World Music Awards for Best Selling Rock Group 2002, 2003, 2007, MTV Awards for Best Group, Best Hard Rock 2002, MTV Europe Awards for Best Rock Act 2004, 2011, 2012, 2014, for Best World Stage Performance 2009, 2013, for Best Live Act 2010, Grammy Award for Best Rap/ Sung Collaboration (for Numb/Encore, with Jay-Z) 2006, MTV Europe Music Award for Best Band 2007, American Music Awards for Favorite Alternative Rock Music Artist 2007, 2008, 2012. *Current Management:* Andy Gould Management, 8484 Wilshire Boulevard, Suite 425, Beverly Hills, CA 90211, USA. *Website:* www.linkinpark.com; mikeshinoda.com.

SHIPP, Matthew; American musician (piano); b. 7 Dec. 1960, Wilmington, DE; m. Delia Scaife 1990. *Education:* New England Conservatory of Music. *Career:* formed asscn with bassist William Parker, both joining the David S. Ware Quartet; played as session pianist on numerous jazz recordings; curated Thirsty Ear Records' Blue Series. *Recordings:* albums: solo or as band leader: Sonic Explorations 1987, Points 1990, Prism 1993, Critical Mass 1994, Zo

1994, Circular Temple 1995, Symbol Systems 1995, Before The World 1995, By The Law Of Music 1996, 2-Z 1996, Thesis 1997, Flow Of X 1997, Gravitational Systems 1998, Strata 1998, Multiplication Table 1998, Magnetism 1999, DNA 1999, Pastoral Composure 2000, Matthew Shipp's New Orbit 2001, Expansion, Power, Release 2001, Nu Bop 2002, Songs 2002, Equilibrium 2002, Antipop Consortium Vs. Matthew Shipp 2003, The Good and Evil Sessions 2003, The Sorceror Sessions 2003, The Trio Plays Ware 2004, Harmony and Abyss 2004, One 2006, Phenomena of Interference 2007, Piano Vortex 2007, Un Piano 2009, Right Hemisphere 2009, Telephone Popcorn 2009, Cosmic Suite 2009, Culture Catch 2009, Harmonic Disorder 2009, 4D 2010; with The David S. Ware Quartet: Great Bliss 1991, Flight Of I 1992, Third Ear Recitation 1993, Cryptology 1995, Earthquation 1995, Godspelized 1996, DAO 1996, Oblations And Blessing 1996, Wisdom Of Uncertainty 1997, Go See The World 1998, Surrendered 2000, Corridors & Parellels 2001, The Freedom Suite 2002. *E-mail:* booking-usa@matthewshipp .com (office). *Website:* www.matthewshipp.com.

SHIPSTON, Roy; British musician (keyboards, vocals), composer, songwriter, arranger and producer; *Chairman and CEO, Rococo Productions Limited;* b. 25 Aug. 1951, London, England; s. of Reginald Jarrett Shipston and Mabel Shipston; m. Julia Diane Twigg 1968 (divorced 1994); one s. one d. *Career:* music journalist, Disc and Music Echo 1969–71; musician since 1971; mem., Formerly Fat Harry 1972; leader, own bands Rococo, The Legendary Brats, Future; performed on more than 45 albums; sessions for Peter Green, Carl Palmer (ELP), Mike Harrison (Spooky Tooth), Chris Thompson, Peter Cox (Go West), Jake Sollo (Osibisa), Biddu, Jim Diamond; Chair. and Dir HSH Music Ltd; Co-owner The Mill Recording Studios, Cookham, Berks. 1989–94; clients included George Harrison, Elton John, Chris Rea, Clannad; mem. Rococo, First Light, WireHead, Mick Underwood's Glory Road; reformed Rococo 2004; Chair. and CEO Rococo Productions Ltd; mem. Performing Right Soc. *Recordings:* albums with Rococo: Run From The Wildfire 2010, The Firestorm and Other Love Songs 2011; with First Light: How The Land Lies, Field Day; singles with Rococo: Ultrastar/Wildfire 1973, Follow That Car/ Lucinda 1976, Home Town Girls/Quicksilver Mail 1981. *Honours:* two BASF/ Studio Master Awards for The Mill Recording Studios, Music Week Top European Engineer Award, 3M Award. *Address:* c/o 2 Selwyn Court, Church Road, Richmond, Surrey, TW10 6LR, England (office). *Telephone:* (20) 8940-4508 (office). *E-mail:* rococoprod@yahoo.co.uk (office); royshipston@yahoo.com (home). *Website:* www.rococo.ws (office).

SHIPWAY, Nigel Howard, FRSA; British musician (percussion, timpani, mallets); *Managing Director, Drumroll Productions;* b. 29 March 1953, Reading, Berks. *Education:* studied with James Blades, Royal Academy of Music, with Reg Barker, Bobby Christian, Paul Patterson, Nadia Boulanger. *Career:* Principal timpanist, Nat. Symphony Orchestra 1968–93, New London Orchestra 1980–, principal percussionist, Cats, New London Theatre for 20 years; principal percussionist, Academy of St Martin in the Fields, English Chamber Orchestra, Orchestre Revolutionnaire et Romantique (with conductor Sir John Eliot Gardiner) 2002–; played on film scores The Far Pavilions, Knight's Move, The Tall Guy, Morons from Outer Space, The Honorary Consul, The Killing Fields, Gangster No. 1; appearances with The Moody Blues, Pink Floyd, Bob Geldof, Gene Pitney, Dionne Warwick, Bob Hoskins, José Carreras, Kiri Te Kanawa, Placido Domingo, Frankie Laine, The Pointer Sisters, Billy Daniels, Katherine Jenkins, Russell Watson; Man. Dir, Drumroll Productions 2005–; mem. Percussive Arts Soc. (founding pres., UK chapter), Royal Soc. of Musicians. *Film appearances:* Hunchback, The Wall, Return To Oz. *Compositions:* 44 studies for timpani; Style Studies For Xylophone; Concert Marimba Etude. *Recordings:* over 1,000 with National Symphony Orchestra, English Chamber Orchestra, Royal Opera House Orchestra, Alyn Ainsworth Orchestra, Ron Goodwin Orchestra. *Publications:* book: The Percussionist's Essential Survival Guide; contrib. articles to Talking Drums, Percussive Notes. *Honours:* ARAM 2013. *Address:* Masters Yard, 180A South Street, Dorking, Surrey RH4 2ES, England. *Telephone:* (1306) 500022. *E-mail:* nigel@drumrollproductions.co.uk. *Website:* drumrollproductions.co.uk.

SHIRE, David Lee, BA; American composer; b. 3 July 1937, Buffalo, NY; s. of Irving Shire and Esther Sheinberg Shire; m. 1st Talia Rose Coppola 1970 (divorced); one s.; m. 2nd Didi Conn 1984; one s. *Education:* Yale Univ. *Career:* mem. Composers' and Lyricists' Guild of America, Acad. of Motion Picture Arts and Sciences, Nat. Acad. of Television Arts and Sciences, Dramatists' Guild of America (Council mem.). *Film scores include:* The Conversation 1973, The Taking of Pelham 1-2-3 1974, Farewell, My Lovely 1975, All the President's Men 1977, Saturday Night Fever 1977, Norma Rae 1979, Return To Oz 1985, Short Circuit 1986, Night, Mother 1986, Vice Versa 1988, Monkey Shines 1988, Paris Trout 1991, Bed and Breakfast 1992, The Journey Inside 1993, One Night Stand 1994, Zodiac 2008. *Television scores include:* Raid on Entebbe 1977, The Defection of Simas Kudirka 1978, Do You Remember Love? 1985, Promise 1986, Echoes in the Darkness 1987, The Women of Brewster Place 1989, The Kennedys of Massachusetts 1990, Common Ground 1990, Sarah Plain and Tall 1991, Last Wish 1992, Broadway Bound 1992, Skylark 1993, Remember 1993, The Companion 1994, My Brother's Keeper 1995, Serving in Silence 1995, The Heidi Chronicles 1995, My Antonia 1995, The Streets of Laredo 1995, Big 1996, Last Stand at Saber River 1997, Double Platinum 1999, Small Vices 1999, Rear Window 1999, These Old Broads 2001, Two Against Time 2001. *Theatre scores:* Starting Here, Starting Now 1975, Baby 1983, Closer Than Ever 1989, Big 1997, Take Flight 2005–10.

Recordings include: album: David Shire at the Movies 1991; songs: What About Today? 1965, The Promise 1978, It Goes Like It Goes 1979, With You I'm Born Again 1979. *Honours:* Grammy Award (two) 1977, Academy Award 1979. *Current Management:* c/o Geibelson Young Inc., 21700 Oxnard Street, Suite 2030, Woodland Hills, CA 91367, USA. *Telephone:* (818) 971-7300. *Fax:* (818) 971-7334. *E-mail:* rhonda@gyco.com (office). *Fax:* (845) 365-4786 (office). *E-mail:* dshire2@gmail.com (office). *Website:* www.davidshiremusic.com.

SHIRLEY, Andrew (Drew); American musician (guitar); b. 3 April 1976. *Education:* California Baptist Coll., CA. *Career:* mem., Switchfoot 2003–. *Recordings include:* albums: Nothing is Sound 2005, Oh! Gravity 2006, Hello Hurricane 2009. *Address:* c/o Bruce Flohr, Red Light Management, 9200 Sunset Boulevard, Los Angeles, CA 90069, USA. *E-mail:* switchfoot@redlightmanagement.com. *Website:* www.redlightmanagement.com; www .switchfoot.com.

SHIVY, Sylvia Massey; American record producer; *Head, RadioStar Studios;* m. Greg Shivy. *Career:* producer Zoo Records; worked with Johnny Cash, Cowboy Mouth, Cyclefly, The Deadlights, Deftones, Dig, Econoline Crush, Firewater, Glueleg, Green Jelly, Greta, Horsehead, Insolence, Luscious Jackson, Lollipop Lust Kill, Loudermilk, Love & Rockets, Lustra, Machines of Loving Grace, Oingo Boingo, Powerman 5000, Artist formerly known as Prince, Red Hot Chili Peppers, R.E.M., Seigmen, Sevendust, Skunk Anansie, System Of A Down, Tallman, Tom Petty and the Heartbreakers, Tool, Toyshop, Virgos; f. RadioStar Studios 2001. *Address:* RadioStar Studios, Weed Palace Theater, 180 Main Street, Weed, CA 96094, USA (office). *Telephone:* (530) 938-1108 (office). *Fax:* (530) 938-9904 (office). *E-mail:* sylvia@radiostarstudios.com (office). *Website:* www.radiostarstudios.com (office).

SHOCKED, Michelle, BSc; American artist, singer, songwriter, musician (guitar) and music publisher; b. (Karen Michelle Johnston), 24 Feb. 1962, Dallas, Tex.; d. of Bill Johnston and Karen Tutor; m. 1992 (divorced 2004). *Education:* Univ. of Texas. *Career:* world-wide tours, numerous concerts and festival appearances; Owner, Mighty Sound label; Publr, Campfire Girl Publishing; mem. American Society of Composers, Authors and Publrs, American Fed. of TV and Radio Artists, NARAS, Folk Alliance, Rhythm and Blues Foundation. *Recordings include:* The Texas Campfire Tapes 1986, Short Sharp Shocked 1988, Captain Swing 1989, Arkansas Traveller 1992, Kind Hearted Woman 1994, Mercury Poise 1996, Artists Make Lousy Slaves (with Fiachnia O'Braonain) 1996, Good News 1998, Dub Natural 2001, Deep Natural 2002, Texas Campfire Takes 2003, Don't Ask Don't Tell 2005, Got No Strings 2005, Mexican Standoff 2005, Soul of My Soul 2009. *Address:* 1850 Industrial Street, Suite 709, Los Angeles, CA 90021, USA (office). *E-mail:* mshocked@yahoo.com. *Website:* www.michelleshocked.com.

SHORE, Howard; Canadian film score composer; b. 18 Oct. 1946, Toronto, Ont. *Education:* Berklee Coll. of Music, Boston. *Career:* f. rock band Lighthouse; Musical Dir Saturday Night Live TV comedy show 1970s; began composing film music 1978; has collaborated on films by David Cronenberg, Peter Jackson; mem. ASCAP. *Film scores include:* I Miss You, Hugs and Kisses 1978, The Brood 1979, Scanners 1980, Videodrome 1983, Nothing Lasts Forever 1984, After Hours 1985, Fire with Fire 1986, The Fly 1986, Heaven 1987, Nadine 1987, Dead Ringers 1988, Big 1988, Signs of Life 1989, She-Devil 1989, The Local Stigmatic 1989, An Innocent Man 1989, Made in Milan 1990, The Lemon Sisters 1990, Naked Lunch 1991, The Silence of the Lambs 1991, A Kiss Before Dying 1991, Prelude to a Kiss 1992, Single White Female 1992, Philadelphia 1993, Mrs Doubtfire 1993, Guilty As Sin 1993, Sliver 1993, M. Butterfly 1993, Nobody's Fool 1994, The Client 1994, Ed Wood (Los Angeles Film Critics' Asscn Award) 1994, Se7en 1995, Moonlight and Valentino 1995, White Man's Burden 1995, Before and After 1996, The Truth About Cats and Dogs 1996, Striptease 1996, Looking For Richard 1996, Crash 1996, That Thing You Do! 1996, The Game 1997, Cop Land 1997, Gloria 1999, Existenz 1999, Dogma 1999, Analyze This 1999, The Yards 2000, High Fidelity 2000, Esther Kahn 2000, The Cell 2000, Camera 2000, The Score 2001, The Lord of the Rings: The Fellowship of the Ring (Acad. Award for Best Original Score 2002, Grammy Award for Best Soundtrack) 2001, Spider 2002, Panic Room 2002, The Lord of the Rings: The Two Towers 2002, Gangs of New York 2002, The Lord of the Rings: The Return of the King (Golden Globe Award for Best Original Score 2004, Acad. Award for Best Song, for 'Into the West' 2004) 2003, The Aviator (Golden Globe Award for Best Original Score 2005) 2004, The Departed 2006, The Last Mimzy 2007, Eastern Promises 2007, Doubt 2008, The Betrayal 2008, The Twilight Saga: Eclipse 2010, Edge of Darkness 2010, A Dangerous Method 2011, Hugo (Frederick Loewe Award) 2011, The Spider 2011, The Rise of Theodore Roosevelt 2011, The Hobbit: An Unexpected Journey 2012, Cosmopolis 2012. *Opera:* The Fly. *Honours:* Officier, Ordre des Arts et des Lettres; Dr hc (Berklee Coll. of Music), Hon. DLitt (York Univ., Toronto) 2007; Career Achievement for Music Composition Award, Nat. Bd of Review of Motion Pictures, ASCAP Lifetime Achievement Award 2004, Max Steiner Film Music Achievement Award, City of Vienna 2005. *Current Management:* Gorfaine/Schwartz Agency Inc, 4111 West Alameda Avenue, Suite 509, Burbank, CA 91505-4161, USA. *Telephone:* (818) 260-8500 (office). *Website:* www.gsamusic.com (office); www.howardshore.com.

SHORROCK, Glenn; Australian singer; b. 30 July 1944, Rochester, Kent, England. *Career:* mem., The Twilights, Axiom, then Esperanto; mem., Little River Band (formerly Mississippi) 1975–83, 1988–; also solo career; mem. APRA (bd mem. 1980–98). *Recordings include:* albums: Little River Band, 1975; After Hours, 1976; Diamantina Cocktail, 1977; Sleeper Catcher, 1978;

First Under The Wire, 1979; Backstage Pass, 1980; Time Exposure, 1981; Monsoon, 1988; Too Late To Load, 1989; Get Lucky, 1990; Reminiscing – The 20th Anniversary Concert, 1995; Little River Band Greatest Hits, 2000; solo: Villain of The Peace, 1983; The First 20 Years, 1985; with The Twilights: '64– '69; with Axiom: '69–'71. *Website:* www.littleriverband.com.

SHORTER, Wayne, BA; American jazz musician (saxophone); b. 25 Aug. 1933, Newark, New Jersey. *Education:* New York Univ. *Career:* served in US Army 1956–58; played saxophone with Art Blakey 1959–63, Miles Davis 1964–70, Weather Report 1970–86, Miles Davis Tribute Band 1992; solo artist 1962–, and with Wayne Shorter Quartet. *Recordings include:* albums: solo: Blues á la Carte 1959, Introducing Wayne Shorter 1959, Second Genesis 1960, Free Form 1961, Wayning Moments 1962, Search for a New Land 1964, Night Dreamer 1964, Some Other Stuff 1964, JuJu 1964, Speak No Evil 1964, The Soothsayer 1965, Et Cetera 1965, The Collector 1965, The All Seeing Eye 1965, Adam's Apple 1966, Schizophrenia 1967, Super Nova 1969, Moto Grosso Felo 1970, Odyssey of Iska 1970, Shorter Moments 1972, Wayne Shorter 1974, Native Dancer 1974, Atlantis 1985, Phantom Navigator 1986, Joy Ryder 1988, High Life (Grammy Award for Best Contemporary Jazz Album 1996) 1994, Portrait 2000, All or Nothing at All 2002, Footprints Live! 2002, Alegría (Grammy Award for Best Jazz Instrumental Album by an Individual or Group) 2003, Footprints 2005, Beyond the Sound Barrier (Grammy Award for Best Jazz Instrumental Album by an Individual or Group 2006) 2005, Without a Net (Jazz Journalists' Asscn Award for Record of the Year 2014) 2013; with Weather Report: Weather Report 1971, I Sing the Body Electric 1972, Sweetnighter 1973, Mysterious Traveler 1974, Tail Spinnin' 1975, Black Market 1976, Black Market/Heavy Weather 1978, Mr Gone 1978, 8.30 (Grammy Awards for Best Jazz Fusion Performance) 1979, Night Passage 1980, Procession 1983, Domino Theory 1984, Sportin' Life 1985, This is This! 1986. *Honours:* Hon. DMus (Berklee Coll. of Music) 1999; winner of numerous Down Beat Magazine Awards, Best Soprano Sax 1984, 1985, Grammy Awards for Best Jazz Instrumental Performance (for A Tribute to Miles) 1994, for Best Jazz Instrumental Solo (for In Walked Wayne) 1999, for Best Instrumental Composition (for Sacajawea) 2003, for Best Improvised Jazz Solo (for Orbits) 2014, Jazz Journalists' Asscn Awards for Lifetime Achievement in Jazz 2013, for Musician of the Year 2014, for Soprano Saxophonist of the Year 2013, for Small Ensemble 2013, for Midsize Ensemble 2014, 2015. *Current Management:* c/o International Music Network, 278 Main Street, Gloucester, MA 01930, USA. *Telephone:* (978) 283-2883. *Fax:* (978) 283-2330. *E-mail:* info@imnworld.com. *Website:* www.imnworld.com; www.wayneshorter.com.

SHOVELL; musician (percussion); b. (Andrew Lovell), 11 Feb. 1969, Jamaica. *Career:* fmr mem. Natural Life; member, M People 1993–; numerous live dates and television appearances; Song, Search for the Hero used in TV advertisement. *Recordings include:* albums: with M People: Elegant Slumming (Mercury Music Prize 1994) 1993, Bizarre Fruit 1994, Bizarre Fruit Vol. 2 1995, Fresco 1997, Testify 1999, 3 Originals 2003. *Honours:* BRIT Award for Best Dance Act 1994, 1995, Freedom of Manchester 1999. *Current Management:* Take 3 Management, 110 Gloucester Avenue, Primrose Hill, London NW1 8HX, England. *Telephone:* (20) 7209-3777. *Fax:* (20) 7209-3770. *E-mail:* info@take3management.co.uk. *Website:* www.take3management.co.uk; www .m-people.com.

SHOW LUO, (Xiao Zhu); Taiwanese singer, actor and television presenter; b. (Lo Chih Hsiang), 30 July 1979, Keelung. *Career:* fmr mem., Romeo 1996; host of TV variety shows 2000–02; TV and film actor 2000–; solo recording artist 2003–; several int. tours including Show Luo Show on Stage 2007, Dance Without Limits 2010, 10001st Night 2011, Over the Limit 2013. *Films:* as actor: Journey to the West: Conquering the Demons 2013. *Television:* as actor: Shao nin liang zhu 2000, Hi! Working Girl 2003, Outsiders II 2004, Corner with Love 2007, Hot Shot 2008, Hi My Sweetheart 2009, Three Women and a Man 2014. *Recordings:* albums: ShowTime 2003, Expert Show 2004, Hypnosis Show 2005, SPESHOW 2006, Show Your Dance 2007, Trendy Man 2008, The Show (released in Japan) 2009, Rashomon 2010, Only You 2011, Good Show 2012, Lion Roar 2013. *Publications:* Zhu Shi Hui She (autobiography) 2002, Show on Stage 2007, Logic (co-author) 2010. *Honours:* numerous awards including: Hong Kong TVB8 Award for Most Popular Male Artist (China) 2005, Golden Melody Award for Most Popular Male Artist 2007, HITO Radio Music Awards for Most Popular Male Singer 2007, 2008, 2012, MTV Mandarin Music Awards for Male Artist of the Year 2011, for Asia Artist of the Year 2011. *E-mail:* dkdssh@universes.com.tw. *Website:* universes-star.com; www .sonymusic.com (office).

SHREEVE, Mark; composer and musician (keyboards, synthesizers, guitar); b. 2 June 1957, Great Yarmouth, Norfolk, England. *Education:* studied architecture. *Career:* numerous festival appearances; mem. PRS. *Compositions include:* Touch Me 1986, I Surrender 1987, True Devotion 1988 (all recorded by Samantha Fox). *Recordings include:* albums: Phantom, 1980; Embryo, 1980; Thoughts Of War, 1981; Assassin, 1983; Legion, 1985; Crash Head, 1988; Nocturne, 1988; soundtracks: Turnaround, 1986; Buy and Cell, 1988; Honor Bound, 1989. *Honours:* ASCAP Awards for various songs. *Address:* 155 Prince George Avenue, Southgate, London N14 4TD, England.

SHRIEVE, Michael; American musician (drums); b. 6 July 1949, San Francisco, California; m. Cindy Weintraub, 1 May 1982, 1 s. *Education:* BA, San Mateo Jr College; BA studies with Anthony Cirome. *Career:* long involvement as drummer/percussionist with Santana; recorded with artists such as: The Rolling Stones; Steve Winwood; David Crosby; also with experimental jazz musicians: Stomu Yamashta; Klaus Schulze; John McLaughlin; Bill Frisell; one of first to experiment with electronic drums, 1973–; mem, BMI; NARAS; Percussive Arts Society. *Compositions include:* (for film and television) The Tempest 1982, The Bedroom Window 1987. *Recordings:* with Santana: Santana 1969, Abraxas 1970, Santana III 1971, Caravansérail 1972, Welcome 1973, Barboletta 1974; with David Crosby: If Only I Could Remember My Name 1971; with Steve Winwood: Automatic Man 1976; with Stomu Yamashta: Go 1976; with John McLaughlin: Love Devotion and Surrender; with The Rolling Stones: Emotional Rescue 1980, Tattoo You 1981; solo: Transfer Station Blue 1984, Stiletto 1989, Big Picture 1989, The Leaving Time 1989, Two Doors 1996, Fascination (with Bill Frisell) 2001, Drums of Compassion 2006; as producer: Bittersweet Lullabies, Sam Shrieve 2009. *Honours:* Melody Maker; Modern Drummer. *E-mail:* contact@ michaelshrieve.com. *Website:* www.michaelshrieve.com.

SHUMAN, Earl Stanley; American songwriter (lyrics) and music publisher; b. 2 Aug. 1923, Boston, Massachusetts; m. Margaret Stein 1956; two s. one d. *Education:* BA, Yale College, 1945. *Career:* owner, Earl/Peg Music Co. 1965–; appeared with Georgia Gibbs on The Perry Como Show, 1953, Jackie Gleason Show, 1953, Red Buttons Show, 1953; mem, ASCAP; NARAS; SGA. *Compositions:* Seven Lonely Days; Banjo's Back in Town; I Am; Left, Right, Out of Your Heart; Theme For a Dream; Starry-Eyed; Most People Get Married; Caterina; Hotel Happiness; Hey There Lonely Boy (Girl); The River; My Shy Violet; Young New Mexican Puppeteer; Clinging Vine; Close to Cathy; I've Been Here; Time, Time; Leaves are the Tears of Autumn, Nothing to Lose, Love is a Christmas Rose, Marriage is for Old Folks, Friendship's a Holly Tree; Off-Broadway Production, Secret Life of Walter Mitty, 1964; Movie Title Songs: Disorderly Orderly; Carpetbaggers; Judith; Dondi; Situation Hopeless But Not Serious, Robin Crusoe on Mars. *Honours:* Gold Record, Hey There Lonely Girl 1970; Country Music Award, Leaves Are The Tears of Autumn 1970; Platinum Record, Bat Out of Hell 1978. *Address:* Earl/Peg Music Company, 111 East 88th St, Apt 3 B, New York, NY 10128, USA (office). *Telephone:* (212) 289-9036 (office).

SHUTTLEWORTH, David (Shutty); British musician (drums); b. 20 March 1967, Keighley, Yorkshire, England. *Career:* founder mem. rock group, The Spoilt Bratz 1986, renamed Terrorvision 1991–2001; numerous tours, television appearances. *Recordings include:* albums: Formaldehyde 1993, How To Make Friends And Influence People 1994, Regular Urban Survivors 1996, Shaving Peaches 1998, Good To Go 2001, Whales And Dolphins: The Very Best Of Terrorvision 2001, The First And The Last 2001, B-Sides And Rarities 2005.

SHVEDOVA, Irina; singer; b. 28 April 1959, Kishivev, Moldova; m. (divorced); one d. *Education:* Kiev State Institute of Theatre Art, Music School, Kiev. *Career:* lead role, children's radio play, 1968; Ukrainian pop concert, 1986; mem. Theatre Artists' Union, Ukraine. *Recordings include:* The Witch 1993, We'll Meet Again 1996. *Honours:* Diploma for Song of the Year 1990, 1991. *Address:* Frumenskaya na 6, 27/1, ap 50, 119196 Moscow, Russia.

SHY'M; French singer and dancer; b. (Tamara Marthe), 28 Nov. 1985, Trappes, Paris. *Career:* featured on K-Maro song Histoire de Luv 2005; debut as solo artist 2006–. *Television includes:* Danse avec les stars (contestant; series winner) 2011; many guest appearances. *Recordings include:* albums: Mes fantaisies 2006, Reflets 2008, Prendre l'air 2010, Caméléon 2012. *Honours:* NRJ Music Award for Francophone Female Artist of the Year 2012. *Address:* c/o Warner Music France, 29 avenue Mac-Mahon, 75017 Paris, France (office). *Telephone:* 1-56-60-40-00 (office). *Website:* www.warnermusic .fr (office); www.wmg.com (office); www.shymofficiel.com.

SHYNKARUK, Iryna Volodymyrivna; Ukrainian singer; b. 31 July 1979, Fastiv, Kiev; d. of Volodymyr Shynkaruk and Liudmyla Shynkaruk; m. Vitaliy Selivanov; two s. *Education:* Musical Coll., Zhitomyr-city, Ukraine, Zhitomyr State Pedagogical Institute, Kiev Nat. Univ. of Culture and Arts. *Career:* tours of Ukraine, France, Germany, Hungary, USA, Cuba, other countries 1994–2000; concerts include World Youth Festival, Cuba 1998, Int. Music Festival, Sharc Taronalari (Melodies of Asia), Uzbekistan 2003; currently soloist, Nat. Radio Co. of Ukraine; faculty mem. giving voice training, Kiev Nat. Univ. of Culture and Arts 2002; mem. FIDOF. *Compositions:* Mermaid's Week 1993, The Moon Talisman (Misiachny Oberih), Ty Mynaesh 2003, Akacia (Locust) 2004, Bjut' Porogy 2006, Nemichna 2006, Glybokyj Kolodiaz (Deep Well) 2006, Plyve choven 2007, Tuman Yarom 2007. *Plays:* Mykhola Hvyliovy 1994, Sad Bozhestvennyh Pisen (Garden of God Songs) 1997, Tenderness 2008. *Films:* Cheremkhova Vikhola 1993, Ty Mynaesh 2003, Liudy i Doli 2004, De Ty, De Ja 2004, Zyma 2005. *Television:* appeared in TV show Ukraine, Spring, Slavutych (commemorating Chernobyl) 1995; currently TV announcer, Culture Channel, Ukrainian Nat. TV. *Recordings:* I'm Like A Bird (14 Songs of the Period) 1993, The Fifth Season Of The Year (The Season of Love) 1995, Step Towards The Summer 1996, I'm Coming 2000, Vidchuvaju (I'm feeling) 2004, This is mine and yours Ukraine 2006, Mira 2006. *Publications:* The Stars of Chervona Ruta 1993, Ukrainian Show Business 2003. *Honours:* Honoured Artist of Ukraine; First Prize Chervona Ruta 1993, Grand Prize, Int. Festival Bilostotsky Malvy, Poland 1993, Diploma FIDOF V Int. Festival, The Voice of Asia 1994, Grand Prix Yalta Int. Festival, The Sea of Friends 1998, Grand Prix TV Festival, Melodia 1998, Second Prize, Volodymyr Ivasiuk Int. Festival 1999. *Address:* c/o Spromo Agency, 76 Velyka Vasylkivska str., Office 17, Kiev 03150, Ukraine.

Telephone: (44) 451-40-24. *Fax:* (44) 451-40-23. *E-mail:* office@spromo.com .ua. *E-mail:* iryna_shynkaruk@ukr.net (home). *Website:* www.iryna.com.ua.

SIA; Australian singer and songwriter; b. (Sia Kate Isobelle Furler), 18 Dec. 1975, Adelaide; d. of Phil B. Colson and Loene Furler. *Education:* Adelaide High School, Univ. of Adelaide. *Career:* vocalist with jazz funk band Crisp 1993–97; solo career 1997–; backing vocalist for Jamiroquai 2000; guest vocalist with Zero 7 2001–06; numerous other collaborations as vocalist or songwriter including Christina Aguilera, Beck, David Guetta, The Birds and the Bee, Lior, David Byrne/Fatboy Slim, Flight of the Conchords, Shakira, Flo Rida, Afrojack, Rihanna. *Recordings include:* albums: with Crisp: Word and the Deal 1996, Delerium 1997; solo: OnlySee 1997, Healing is Difficult 2001, Colour the Small One 2004, Some People Have Real Problems 2008, We Are Born (ARIA Award for Album of the Year 2010, for Best Independent Release 2010, for Best Pop Release 2010) 2010, 1000 Forms of Fear 2014, This is Acting 2016; as contrib.: with Zero 7: Simple Things 2001, When It Falls 2004, The Garden 2006. *Honours:* APRA Award for Breakthrough Songwriter of the Year 2002, ARIA Award for Best Music DVD 2009. *Current Management:* c/o Crush Management, 60–62 East 11th Street, 7th Floor, New York, NY 10003, USA. *Telephone:* (212) 334-4446. *E-mail:* info@crushmm.com. *Website:* www .crushmm.com; www.siamusic.net (home).

SIBERIL, Soïg; French musician (Celtic guitar); b. 1 Feb. 1955; one s. *Career:* guitarist for 20 years; mem. Sked 1975, Kornog 1980, Gwerz 1980, Pennou Skoulm 1989, Kemia 1989, Orion 1992, La Rouchta 1992; numerous concerts and festivals all over Europe and USA. *Recordings include:* solo albums: Digor 1993, Entre Ardoise et Granit 1996, Du côté de chez Soïg! 2003, Lammat 2006, Botcanou 2009, La guitare celtique de Soïg Sibéril 2011, Dek 2014; 15 albums with other bands, including five with Kornog, three with Gwerz; with Den Quintet: Just Around The Window 2001. *Honours:* Prix Acad. du Disque Charles Cros, Gwertz 1987, Le Sours du Scorff 1995. *Address:* Le Presbytère, 1 rue de Carhaix, 22340 Trébrivan, France (home). *E-mail:* contact@soigsiberil .com (home). *Website:* www.soigsiberil.com.

SIBERRY, Jane, BSc; Canadian singer; b. 12 Oct. 1955, Toronto. *Education:* Univ. of Guelph. *Career:* recorded with Windham Hill/A&M 1984–87, with Reprise/Warner 1987–96; Founder and Pres. Sheeba Records 1996–; has contributed to several soundtracks including Until The End Of The World, Faraway So Close, The Crow, Songs From The Cold Seas; Casby Awards for Producer and Album of the Year. *Albums include:* Jane Siberry 1981, No Borders Here 1984, The Speckless Here 1985, The Walking 1987, Bound By The Beauty 1989, When I Was A Boy 1993, Maria 1995, Teenager 1996, Child 1997, Lips 1999, Tree 1999, Hush 2000, City 2001, Love Is Everything 2002, Shushan the Palace 2003, Dragon Dreams 2008, With What Shall I Keep Warm? 2009. *Honours:* Victor Martyn Lynch-Staunton Award, Canada Council 2005. *Address:* SHEEBA Music Inc., 4438 West 10th Avenue, Suite 523, Vancouver, BC V6R 4R8, Canada (office). *Website:* www.janesiberry.com; www.issalight.com.

SIDDIQUI, Khalid, BA; British singer, musician, songwriter and producer; b. 14 Feb. 1970, Oxford, England. *Education:* Univ. of East London. *Career:* f. Doleboy Cowboy record label 1994 (later defunct); stand-up acts such as The Loving Bucket and The Thief O'Badgags 1997–98; f. Knockback Music 2002–; started DJ set as Evil Elvis 2002–; involved in running comedy club and novelty band The Admirals; formed K.S. & The Mystery Jet Set 1999–; joined The Action Men dance troupe 2011–; returned to comedy writing with the Juke Box Stories writing group alongside DJing 2013. *Recordings:* with K.S. & The Mystery Jet Set: Savage Kitsch, Without Rock & Roll, Exotic Emotions (split 7" with The Sayme,) Thirtysomething & A Third RPM; Doleboy Cowboy Records: Gew Gaw Mule 7" EP; Knockback Music: Knockback in Anger, Front Row Sleeze (Luxury Condo). *E-mail:* knockbackmusic@yahoo.co.uk (office). *Website:* www.myspace.com/ksandthemysteryjetset (office).

SIDIBE, Balla; Senegalese singer and musician (percussion); b. Casamance. *Career:* fmr mem. Star Band, Club Miami, Dakar –1970; founder mem. Orchestra Baobab 1970–85, originally at Club Baobab to 1977, then Jandeer Club, Balafon Club to 1978, time in Paris, then at Ngalam Club to 1985; Orchestra Baobab re-formed 2001–, resident at Just 4U Club, Dakar. *Recordings include:* albums: M'Beugene 1972, Hommage a Lay M'Boop 1974, Orchestre Baobab '75 1975, Guy Gu Rey Gi 1975, Senegaal Sunugaal 1975, Visage du Senegal 1975, Aduna Jarul Naawoo 1975, N'Deleng N'Deleng 1977, Une Nuit Aun Jandeer 1978, Baobab à Paris Vols 1 and 2 1978, Gouygui Dou Daanou 1979, Mohamadou Bamba 1980, Sibou Odia 1980, Ken Dou Werente (re-released as Pirate's Choice 2001) 1982, On Verra Ça: The 1978 Paris Sessions 1992, Bamba 1993, Specialist in All Styles (BBC Radio 3 Awards for World Music Critic's Award for Album of the Year 2003) 2002, A Night at Club Baobab 2006, Made in Dakar 2007. *Honours:* BBC Radio 3 Awards for World Music, Africa Region 2003. *Address:* World Circuit Records, First Floor, Shoreditch Stables, 138 Kingsland Road, London, E2 8DY, England (office). *E-mail:* post@worldcircuit.co.uk (office). *Website:* www .worldcircuit.co.uk (office); www.orchestrabaobab.com (office).

SIEGEL, Janis; American singer, arranger and producer; b. 23 July 1952, Brooklyn, NY; d. of Edward Siegel and Joan Siegel; one s. *Education:* James Madison High School, State Univ. of NY at Buffalo (nursing programme). *Career:* fmr mem. The Young Generation, Laurel Canyon; mem. The Manhattan Transfer 1972–; solo artist 1982–; collaborations include Richie Cole, Steve Hass, Jon Hendricks, Jeff Lorber, Ilhan Mimaroglu and the Beaux Arts String Quartet, Jay McShann, Lew Soloff, Robert Kraft, Leon Ware,

Natalie Cole, Bobby McFerrin's Voicestra, Fred Hersch, Frank Vignola, JaLaLa (Janis Siegel, Laurel Massé and Lauren Kinhan). *Recordings include:* albums: with The Manhattan Transfer: The Manhattan Transfer 1975, Coming Out 1976, Pastiche 1978, The Manhattan Transfer Live 1978, Extensions 1979, Mecca For Moderns 1981, Bodies And Souls 1983, Bop Doo Wopp 1985, Vocalese 1985, Live 1987, Brasil 1987, The Offbeat Of Avenues 1992, The Christmas Album 1992, The Manhattan Transfer Meets Tubby The Tuba 1994, Tonin' 1995, Man Tora!: Live In Tokyo 1996, Swing 1997, Spirit of St Louis 2000, Couldn't Be Hotter 2003, Vibrate 2004, An Acapella Christmas 2004, The Chick Corea Songbook 2009; solo: Experiment In White 1982, At Home 1987, Short Stories (with Fred Hersch) 1989, Slow Hot Wind (with Fred Hersch) 1995, Tender Trap 1999, I Wish You Love 2002, Friday Night Special 2003, Sketches Of Broadway 2004, A Thousand Beautiful Things 2006, That Old Mercer Magic (with JaLala) 2009; featured soloist: The Gene Krupa Songbook, The Lionel Hampton Songbook, Americana Songbook, A Jazz Tribute to The Carpenters, Circlesongs (Bobby McFerrin), Mr X (with Jason Miles), Blo (with Jane Rutter), Traveler (with Steve Hass). *Honours:* incomplete hon. doctorate (Berklee School of Music, Boston) 1993; Grammy Awards for Best Jazz Fusion Performance 1980, Best Arrangement for Voices 1980, Best Pop Performance by a Duo or Group 1981, Best Jazz Fusion Performance 1981, Best Jazz Vocal Performance 1982, 1983, 1985, Best Pop Performance by a Duo or Group 1987, Best Contemporary Jazz Performance 1992, New York Music Award for Best Female Jazz Singer 1989. *Current Management:* c/o Paul Goldman, Monterey International, PO Box 297, Carmel-by-the-Sea, CA 93921, USA. *Telephone:* (831) 625-6300. *Fax:* (831) 625-6335. *E-mail:* paul@montereyinternational.net. *Website:* www .montereyinternational.net. *E-mail:* info@janissiegel.com (office). *Website:* www.manhattantransfer.net; www.janissiegel.com.

SIFFRE, Labi; British singer, musician (guitar) and poet; b. Bayswater, London, England. *Education:* studied music harmonics. *Career:* mem. of various soul bands in Cannes, France; solo artist late 1960s–. *Recordings include:* albums: Labi Siffre, 1970; Singer and the Song, 1971; Crying, Laughing, Loving, Lying, 1972; So Strong, 1988; Make My Day, 1989, Man of Reason 1991, The Last Songs 1998. *Website:* www.so-strong.com; www .intothelight.info.

SIIKASAARI, Eerik; Finnish musician (bass); b. 8 Oct. 1957, Kotka. *Education:* Piano, electric and acoustic bass; Oulunkylä; Diploma, Sibelius Academy. *Career:* Appeared with Jukkis Uotila Quartet, Middelheim Festival, Belgium, 1978; Association with Seppo Paakkunainen's Karelia, 1980–; Plays regularly with bands: Jukka Perko Quartet; Trio Töykeät; Espoo Big Band; Jukka Linkola Quintet; Perko-Pyysalo Poppoo; Concerts with Karelia and big bands in France, Switzerland, Germany, UK, USA. *Recordings include:* Kudos. *Honours:* First prize, with Trio Töykeät, Belgian jazz contest, 1988; Yrjö Award, Finnish Jazz Federation, 1995. *E-mail:* anssi.koivusalo@ emimusic.com. *Website:* www.emi.fi; www.triotoykeat.fi.

SILAG, Marc; American tour production manager and artist manager; b. 22 May 1953, New York; m. Susan Brown. *Education:* coll. *Career:* Gen. Man., Bitter End, New York 1974; Stage Man., Bottom Line Theatre, New York 1975–77; tour and artist man. 1977–; currently Pres., Right Side Management; tour, Production Man. for Michael Urbaniak, John McLaughlin, David Sanborn, Herb Alpert, Patti Labelle, Pat Metheny Group, Paul Simon, Simon and Garfunkel; Personal Man. for Ladysmith Black Mambazo, Chris Botti; musical contractor, The Capeman, Broadway; mem. AFM, AFTRA. *Address:* Right Side Management, PO Box 250806, New York, NY 10025-1509, USA (office). *Telephone:* (212) 586-1223 (office).

SILLITTO, Lorenzo; Australian guitarist and songwriter. *Education:* Wesley Coll., Melbourne. *Career:* mem. The Temper Trap 2005–; released debut EP The Temper Trap 2006; group relocated to London 2008; released debut album 2009; int. tours. *Recordings include:* albums: with The Temper Trap: Conditions 2009, The Temper Trap (ARIA Music Award for Best Rock Album 2012) 2012. *Honours:* with The Temper Trap: ARIA Music Awards for Best Group 2010, 2012, for Most Popular Australian Single (for Sweet Disposition) 2010, APRA Award for Song of the Year (for Sweet Disposition) 2010. *Current Management:* c/o Lunatic Entertainment, 53 Corsica Street, London, N5 1JT, England. *E-mail:* info@lunaticentertainment.com. *Website:* www.lunaticentertainment.com. *Address:* c/o Liberation Music, 9 Dundas Lane, Albert Park, Vic. 3206, Australia (office). *E-mail:* info@liberationmusic .net (office). *Website:* www.liberationmusic.net; www.thetempertrap .com.

SILSON, Alan; British musician (guitar) and singer; b. 21 June 1951, Bradford, West Yorkshire; m. Angela 1986; one d. *Career:* founder mem., Smokie 1975–81, 1986–95; founder mem., Silson; numerous television and radio broadcasts; mem, Musicians' Union; PRS; MCPS; PPL; BAC&S. *Compositions include:* Boulevard of Broken Dreams. *Recordings include:* albums: Pass It Round 1975, Changing All the Time 1975, Midnight Cafe 1976, Bright Lights and Back Alleys 1977, The Other Side of The Road 1979, Solid Ground 1981, Strangers In Paradise 1982, Midnight Delight 1982, All Fired Up 1987, Boulevard of Broken Dreams 1989, Whose Are These Boots? 1990, Chasing Shadows 1992, Burnin' Ambition 1993, Celebration 1994; solo: Solitary Bird 2008. *E-mail:* info@alansilson.com (office). *Website:* www .alansilson.com.

SILVANO, Judi; American songwriter, singer, composer and teacher; b. (Judith Silverman), 8 May 1951, Philadelphia, Pa; d. of Arthur Silverman and Miriam 'Mimi' Schwartz; m. Joe Lovano 1984. *Education:* Pennsylvania Ballet School, Murray Louis/Alwin Nikolais Dance Theatre School, Temple Univ. Coll. of Music, BMI Composers' Workshop, private studies with Anne Marie Moss, Mark Murphy, Kirk Nurock, Yolanda Picucci Radlowski, Sheila Jordan, Jay Clayton, Jeanne Lee. *Career:* mem. Group Motion Dance Troupe, Residency, Berlin Arts Festival 1975; European Tour and live recording at Amiens, France, Joe Lovano, Worlds 1989; Montreal Jazz Festival, European Tours, Montreux, Switzerland, Scandinavia, Italy, Paris, Israel, Festivals 1991–; BET Jazz Showcase, Judi Silvano Vocalise Band 1997; concerts at Carnegie Hall, Lincoln Center, Chicago Symphony Hall, Canadian Jazz Festivals; Faculty, Lake Placid Inst. and BANFF Jazz Workshop; Voice Instructor, Rutgers Univ. 1994–2004, Newburgh Performing Arts Acad. 2004–08; mem. AFTRA, New York Local 802 Musicians Union, Int. Asscn of Women Composers, New York Women Composers; recorded 10 CDs as leader including Indigo Moods 2012; toured and played with Joe Lovano, Kenny Werner, Mal Waldron, Michael Abene, George Garzone, Gerry Hemingway, Michael Formanek, Dick Oatts, Rufus Reid, Ingrid Jensen, The Bad Plus, George Cables, amongst others; Clinician, Stanford Jazz Workshop, Danish Jazz Workshop, Banff Int. Summer Jazz, Janice Borla Jazz Camp. *Exhibition:* Emerging Artist Exhbn, Walkill River Valley Art School 2013. *Compositions:* jazz: Bass Space and Left Behind recorded by Joe Lovano; Ecstasy, Isadora, 23rd St, Calypso, on Dancing Voices album; Heuchera Americana, It's So Amazing, At Home, Bass Space on Vocalise (Blue Note); chamber music: Nature of Life, American Festival of American Composers, Three Songs for Bryant and Early Evening, Symphony Space Thalia theatre by the Aviva Players 2012. *Recordings:* as leader: Dancing Voices 1992, Vocalise (Blue Note) 1997, Songs I Wrote or Wish I Did 2000, Riding A Zephyr (duo with Mal Waldron) 2002, Let Yourself Go 2004, Sound Garden – Spirit Music 2005, Sound Garden – Celestial Voices 2006, Woman's Work (songs by American Women Composers) 2007, Cleome: Live Takes (original songs) 2008, Indigo Moods 2012; featured with Joe Lovano on Worlds: Universal Language, Celebrating Sinatra, Rush Hour, Viva Caruso; with Kenny Werner on Paintings and No Beginning, No End; Jim Pepper on Comin' and Goin'; with Adam Kolker on Reflections. *Radio:* guest DJ host, WKCR Columbia Univ. Musicians Show 2004, 2009, 2012, KCSM Santa Monica Desert Island Jazz show 2012. *Publications:* contrib. to All About Jazz, Jazz Improv Magazine, D & H Canvas. *Honours:* Down Beat magazine Top 10 Vocalist 1995, 1998, 2000, 2005, BS inEd Grant from Meet The Composer, two grants from NY State Council on the Arts, Hudson Valley Best Jazz Singer. *Address:* 66 Beaver Brook Road, New Windsor, NY 12577, USA (home). *Telephone:* (914) 213-2292 (office). *E-mail:* silvano@hvc.rr.com (home); booking@ judisilvano.com (office). *Website:* www.judisilvano.com.

SILVEIRA, Lucas Cesar Lima; Brazilian rock singer, musician (rhythm guitar, keyboards) and songwriter; b. 1 Dec. 1983, Rio Grande do Sul. *Career:* Founder-mem. and rhythm guitarist, rock band Democratas 1999–2001, changed band name to Fresno and became lead singer 2001–; debut EP released 2001; numerous live shows and tours. *Recordings:* albums: with Fresno: Quarto dos Livros 2003, O Rio, A Cidade, A Árvore 2004, Ciano 2006, Redenção 2008, Revanche 2010, Cemitério Das Boas Intenções 2011, Infinito 2012. *Honours:* MTV VMB Awards for Best New Artist 2007, for Artist of the Year 2009, for Best Pop Artist 2009, Multishow Brazilian Music Award for Band of the Year 2009, MTV Europe Music Award for Best Brazilian Act 2013. *Current Management:* c/o Perfexx Assessoria de Comunicação, São Paulo, Brazil. *Telephone:* (11) 3064-7105. *E-mail:* contato@perfexx.com.br. *Website:* www.perfexx.com.br. *Address:* c/o Universal Music Ltd, PO Box 37133, 22.622-970, Rio de Janeiro, Brazil (office). *Telephone:* (21) 3389-7676 (office). *Fax:* (21) 2494-3035 (office). *Website:* www.universalmusic.com.br (office); www.fresnorock.com.br (home).

SILVERIA, David; American musician (drums). *Career:* founder mem., L.A.P.D. (Love and Peace, Dude) 1989, renamed KoRn 1992–2007; numerous tours and live appearances. *Recordings include:* albums: with L.A.P.D.: Love And Peace, Dude (EP) 1989, Who's Laughing Now 1991, L.A.P.D. 1997; with KoRn: Korn 1994, Life Is Peachy 1996, Follow The Leader 1998, Issues 1999, Untouchables 2002, Take A Look In The Mirror 2003, See You On The Other Side 2005. *Current Management:* International Talent Booking, First Floor, Ariel House, 74a Charlotte Street, London, W1T 4QJ, England. *Telephone:* (20) 7637-6979. *Fax:* (20) 7637-6978. *E-mail:* mail@itb.co.uk. *Website:* www .korn.com.

SILVERLIGHT, Terry; American composer, producer, musician (drums) and arranger; b. 8 Sept. 1972, Tulsa, Okla. *Education:* Princeton Univ.; studied piano with Olga Von Til, percussion with Morris Lang. *Career:* mem. ASCAP. *Films:* Head Over Heels, Invincible, Mad About Mambo, Sunshine Cleaning. *Television includes:* songs aired on TV shows Melrose Place, Pacific Palisades, Beverly Hills 90210, Guiding Light, CNN Lifestyles, Jag, Clueless, Seventh Heaven, The Sopranos; TV appearances as drummer with Roberta Flack and Marvin Hamlisch at White House, appearances with Peabo Bryson, Natalie Merchant on Rosie O'Donnell Show, Sheena Easton, Barry Miles, Al DiMeola, Stephen Stills. *Compositions include:* All That Matters, Louise; Chasin' a Dream, Nancy Wilson; All I Wanna Do, Carl Anderson; Love's The Key, Maria Amada; Take My Love For Real, Yasuko Agawa and Philip Ingram. *Recordings include:* albums: solo: Terry Silverlight, Wild!!, Diamond in the Riff; played drums on records for Billy Ocean, Mel Tormé, Laura Nyro, Anne Murray, Tom Jones, Barry Miles, Phil Woods, Stephanie Mills, George Benson, David Matthews, Don Johnson, Freddie Jackson, Eric Kloss,

Jonathan Butler, Melba Moore, David Sancious, Odyssey, Jeffrey Osborne. *Publication:* The Featured Drummer (instruction book) 1981. *Honours:* 12 gold and platinum record awards. *E-mail:* tsilverlight@att.net (office). *Website:* www.terrysilverlight.com.

SILVESTRI, Alan; American composer; b. 26 March 1950, New York, NY. *Education:* Berklee Coll. of Music. *Career:* collaborations with Howard Deutch, Stephen Hopkins, Mick Jackson, Nancy Meyers, Donald Petrie, Robert Zemeckis; mem. BMI. *Compositions include:* The Doberman Gang 1972, The Mack 1973, Starsky and Hutch (TV) 1975, The Amazing Dobermans 1976, Chips (TV) 1977, The Fifth Floor 1980, Romancing the Stone 1984, Summer Rental 1985, Fandango 1985, Back to the Future 1985, Cat's Eye 1985, No Mercy 1986, Flight of the Navigator 1986, Amazing Stories (TV) 1986, American Anthem 1986, The Clan of the Cave Bear 1986, The Delta Force 1986, Overboard 1987, Critical Condition 1987, Predator (Saturn Award for Best Music 1988) 1987, Outrageous Fortune 1987, My Stepmother is an Alien 1988, Mac and Me 1988, Who Framed Roger Rabbit 1988, She's Out of Control 1989, Tales from the Crypt (TV series) (Cable Ace Award for Best Original Score 1990) 1989, The Abyss 1989, Back to the Future Part II (Saturn Award for Best Music 1991) 1989, Downtown 1990, Back to the Future Part III 1990, Young Guns II 1990, Predator 2 1990, Father of the Bride 1991, Dutch 1991, Soapdish 1991, Shattered 1991, Ricochet 1991, Stop! Or My Mom Will Shoot 1992, Death Becomes Her 1992, Ferngully: The Last Rainforest 1992, The Bodyguard 1992, Sidekicks 1992, Judgment Night 1993, In Search of the Obelisk 1993, Grumpy Old Men 1993, Cop and a Half 1993, Super Mario Bros 1993, Richie Rich 1994, Clean Slate 1994, Blown Away 1994, Forrest Gump 1994, The Quick and the Dead 1995, The Perez Family 1995, Judge Dredd 1995, Father of the Bride Part II 1995, Grumpier Old Men 1995, Sgt Bilko 1996, Eraser 1996, The Long Kiss Goodnight 1996, Fools Rush In 1997, Volcano 1997, Contact 1997, Mouse Hunt 1997, The Odd Couple II 1998, The Parent Trap 1998, Holy Man 1998, Practical Magic 1998, Stuart Little 1999, Reindeer Games 2000, What Lies Beneath 2000, Cast Away (Grammy Award for Best Instrumental Composition 2002) 2000, What Women Want 2001, The Mexican 2001, The Mummy Returns 2001, Serendipity 2001, Show Time 2002, Lilo And Stitch 2002, Stuart Little 2 2002, Maid in Manhattan 2002, Pirates of the Caribbean 2003, Polar Express (Grammy Award for Best Song Written for Motion Picture, Television or Other Visual Media, with Glen Ballard 2006) 2004, The Wild 2006, Night at the Museum 2006, Beowulf 2007, Night at the Museum 2 2009, G.I. Joe: The Rise of the Cobra 2009, A Christmas Carol 2009, The A-Team 2010, Avengers Assemble 2012, Flight 2012, The Croods 2013. *Honours:* BMI Richard Kirk Award for Outstanding Career Achievement 1995, ASCAP Henry Mancini Award for Lifetime Achievement 2002. *Current Management:* Gorfaine/Schwartz Agency Inc., 4111 West Alameda Avenue, Suite 509, Burbank, CA 91505, USA. *Telephone:* (818) 260-8500. *Website:* www.gsamusic.com.

SIM, Oliver; British singer, songwriter and musician (bass guitar). *Education:* Elliott School, London. *Career:* mem. The xx 2005–. *Recordings:* albums: xx (Mercury Music Prize 2010) 2009, Coexist 2012. *Address:* c/o Young Turks, XL Recordings, 1 Codrington Mews, London, W11 2EH, England (office). *Telephone:* (20) 8870-7511 (office). *Fax:* (20) 8871-4178 (office). *E-mail:* theyoungturks@theyoungturks.co.uk (office). *Website:* thexx.info.

SIMARD, Bernard; Canadian musician (guitar) and singer; b. 27 Aug. 1959, Valleyfield, QC; m. 1994; one s. one d. *Career:* mem., La Bottine Souriante 1983–87; mem., Manigance 1987–90, tours of France, Canada; lived in France 1992–2001; mem., Gwazigan 1994–2001, tours to USA, Canada, Europe 1984–87; mem., Cabestan 1996–2001; mem. Le Vent du Nord 2002–04; numerous collaborations with groups including Les Clochards Célestes, Migration, Matante Alys, Matawin, Nuked, Tabarnak, Ben Embelle, Les P'tits Bûcheux, La Tuque Bleue; mem. SOCAN. *Recordings include:* with La Bottine Souriante: La Traversée de l'Atlantique 1986; with Manigance: Album Souvenir Vol. 1 1988, Nouvelles Manigances 1991; with Cabestan: Tempête pour sortir... 1995, Femmes de Marin 1997, Le mer est trop vieille pour qu'on se moque d'elle 2000; with Gwazigan: Dessus La Fougère 1997, Y'Avait Du Monde 2000; with Christian Maes: Coup de Vent 1998; with Le Vent du Nord: Maudite Moisson 2003; solo: Spectacle Solo 2001. *Address:* 150 rue Rosaire, Saint-Alphonse-Rodriguez, Québec J0K 1W0, Canada (office). *Telephone:* (450) 883-1015 (office). *E-mail:* simardbernard@hotmail.com (office). *Website:* www.bernardsimard.com.

SIMINS, Russell; American musician (drums); b. 1964, Long Island, NY. *Career:* mem., Jon Spencer Blues Explosion, 1990–. *Recordings:* Albums: with Jon Spencer Blues Explosion: Jon Spencer Blues Explosion, 1992; Crypt Style, 1992; Extra Width, 1993; Mo' Width, 1994; Orange, 1994; Experimental Remixes, 1995; Now I Got Worry, 1996; Controversial Negro, 1997; Rocketship, 1997; ACME, 1998; Magical Colours, 2000; Plastic Fang, 2002; Solo: Public Places, 2000. Singles: The Sound Of The Future Is Here Today, 1992; Shirt-jac, 1992; Son Of Sam, 1992; Big Yule Log Boogie, 1992; Train 3, 1993; Bellbottoms, 1995; Get With It, 1996; 2 Kindsa Love, 1996; Wail, 1997; Rocketship, 1997; Talk About The Blues, 1998. *Website:* www .thejonspencerbluesexplosion.com.

SIMMONS, Gene, ABA, BA; American musician (bass guitar), singer, songwriter and actor; b. (Chaim Witz), 25 Aug. 1949, Haifa, Israel; m. Shannon Tweed 2011; two c. *Education:* Sullivan Coll., State Univ. of New York, Richmond Coll., City Univ. of New York. *Career:* Founder mem., Wicked Lester 1972; founder mem. Kiss 1973–; tours worldwide; also solo artist;

inventor, Axe bass guitar 1980; established Simmons record label 1988–. *Films:* The Runaway 1984, Never Too Young To Die 1986, Trick Or Treat, Dead Or Alive 1986, Kiss Attack of the Phantom. *Television:* Rock School (documentary series, Channel 4) 2005, Gene Simmons Family Jewels 2011. *Recordings include:* albums: with Kiss: Kiss 1974, Hotter Than Hell 1974, Dressed To Kill 1975, Alive! 1975, Destroyer 1976, The Originals 1976, Rock and Roll Over 1976, Kiss Alive II 1977, Love Gun 1977, Double Platinum 1978, Dynasty 1979, Kiss Unmasked 1980, Music From The Elder 1981, Creatures of the Night 1982, Lick It Up 1983, Animalize 1984, Asylum 1985, Crazy Nights 1987, Smashes, Thrashes and Hits 1988, Hot In The Shade 1989, Revenge 1992, Kiss Alive III 1993, Unplugged 1996, Greatest Kiss 1997, Carnival of Souls: The Final Sessions 1997, Kiss, The Second Coming I and II 1998, Psycho Circus 1999, Sonic Boom 2009; solo: Gene Simmons 1978. *Honours:* footprints at Grauman's Chinese Theater, Hollywood 1976, Gold Ticket, Madison Square Garden 1979, inducted into Hollywood's Rock Walk, Kiss Day proclaimed, Los Angeles 1993. *Current Management:* c/o Doc McGhee, McGhee Entertainment, 8730 Sunset Boulevard, Suite 2000, Los Angeles, CA 90069, USA. *E-mail:* info@mcgheela.com. *Website:* www .mcgheela.com; www.kissonline.com.

SIMMONS, Rev. Joseph 'Run'; American hip-hop, R&B and rap artist; b. 14 Nov. 1964, New York; brother of Russell Simmons; m. Justine Jones 1994; five c. *Career:* mem. duo, later trio (with Darryl 'D.M.C.' McDaniels and the late Jam Master Jay), Run-D.M.C. 1982–2002; ordained minister 1995; solo artist 2005–. *Film appearances:* Krush Groove 1985, Tougher Than Leather 1988, Who's the Man? 1993, Red Dragon 2002. *Television:* Run''s House 2005–09. *Recordings include:* albums: with Run-D.M.C.: Run-D.M.C. 1984, King Of Rock 1985, Raising Hell 1986, Tougher Than Leather 1988, Back From Hell 1990, Down With The King 1993, Crown Royal 1999; solo: Distortion 2005. *Publication:* It's Like That: A Spiritual Memoir 2000.

SIMMONS, Kyle Jonathan; British musician (keyboards); b. 5 Feb. 1988, London, England. *Education:* Univ. of Leeds. *Career:* Founder-mem., Bastille 2010–; released debut single 2011; signed to Virgin Records 2011. *Recordings:* album: with Bastille: Bad Blood 2013. *Honours:* BRIT Award for British Breakthrough Act 2014. *Address:* c/o Virgin EMI Records, Universal Music Group, 364–366 Kensington High Street, London, W14 8NS, England (office). *Telephone:* (20) 7471-5000 (office). *E-mail:* contact@virginemirecords.com (office). *Website:* www.virginemirecords.com (office); bastillebastille.com.

SIMMONS, Russell W.; American producer and record company executive; *Chairman, President and CEO, Rush Communications Inc.*; b. 4 Oct. 1957, New York, NY; brother of Joseph Simmons; m. Kimora Lee; two d. *Education:* City Coll. of New York, Harlem. *Career:* man., Run-D.M.C., Oran 'Juice' Jones, LL Cool J, The Beastie Boys, Public Enemy; co-founder, Def Jam Records 1984–99 (sold co.); founder, Rush Artist Management 1985–; currently Chair., Pres. and CEO Rush Communications Inc.; co-founder, Phat Farm clothing; founder, Russell Simmons Music Group 1999–2005 (merged with Def Jam); apptd UN Goodwill Amb. 2009. *Television as producer:* Russell Simmons' Def Comedy Jam (HBO), Russell Simmons Presents Def Poetry (HBO) 2001. *Films:* Krush Groove (prod.) 1985, Tougher Than Leather (prod.) 1988, The Nutty Professor (prod.) 1995, The Addiction (exec. prod.) 1995, Gridlock'd (exec. prod.) 1997, The Industry (prod.) 2004, The History Makers (prod.) 2005, Russell Simmons Presents Yoga Live (fitness video) 2005, Waist Deep (prod.) 2006, The Hip Hop Project 2006. *Plays:* Russell Simmons Def Poetry Jam (creator), Broadway 2002. *Publication:* A Super Rich: A Guide to Having It All (with Chris Morrow) 2011. *Address:* Rush Communications Inc., 512 Seventh Avenue, Suite 43–45, New York, NY 10018, USA (office). *Telephone:* (212) 840-9399 (office). *Fax:* (212) 840-9390 (office).

SIMON, Carly; American singer, songwriter and musician (piano, guitar); b. 25 June 1945, New York; d. of Richard Simon; m. 1st James Taylor 1972 (divorced 1983); one d. one s.; m. 2nd James Hart 1987 (divorced 2007). *Education:* Sarah Lawrence Coll. *Film appearance:* No Nukes 1980. *Compositions include:* Romulus Hunt (opera) 1993; film scores for Heartburn 1986, Working Girl 1988, Postcards From the Edge 1990, This Is My Life 1992; theme tunes for Torchlight 1985, Phenom (TV) 1993; contrib. songs to other films. *Recordings include:* albums: Carly Simon 1971, Anticipation 1972, No Secrets 1973, Hotcakes 1974, Playing Possum 1975, Another Passenger 1976, Boys In The Trees 1978, Spy 1979, Come Upstairs 1980, Torch 1981, Hello Big Man 1983, Spoiled Girl 1985, Coming Around Again 1987, My Romance 1990, Have You Seen Me Lately? 1991, This Is My Life 1992, Letters Never Sent 1994, Clouds In My Coffee 1965–95 1996, Film Noir 1997, The Bedroom Tapes 2000, This Kind of Love 2008, Never Been Gone 2009. *Publications include:* Boys in the Trees: A Memoir 2015; juvenile: Amy the Dancing Bear 1989, The Boy of the Bells 1990, The Fisherman's Song 1990, The Nighttime Chauffeur 1993, Midnight Farm 1997, Basket Full of Rhymes 2000, Take Me Out to the Ball Game 2011; several songbooks. *Honours:* Grammy Award for Best New Artist 1971, Acad. Award (for Let The River Run) 1989, Golden Globe Award for Best Original Song (for Let the River Run) 1990. *Current Management:* c/o Larry Ciancia, Ciancia Management, 5419 Evergreen Heights Drive, Evergreen, CO 80439, USA. *Telephone:* (213) 925-7117. *Fax:* (310) 388-5353. *E-mail:* larry@cianciamanagement.com. *Website:* www.cianciamanagement .com; www.carlysimon.com.

SIMON, Edward; jazz musician (piano); b. 27 July 1969, Comunidad Cardom, Falcon State, Venezuela; m. Maria A. Simon 1994. *Education:*

Univ. of the Arts, Manhattan School of Music. *Career:* mem., Bobby Watson's Horizon 1988–92; played with Greg Osby, Kevin Eubanks, Paquito D'Rivera, Herbie Mann, Charlie Sepulveda, Jerry Gonzalez; mem., The Terence Blanchard Quartet; mem. NARAS, BMI. *Recordings:* albums: solo: Beauty Within 1994, Edward Simon 1994, La Bikina 1998, Afinidad, The Process, Fiestas de Agosto, Simplicitas, Unicity, Océanos; with Edward Simon: The Searcher 1989, Promise of Tomorrow 1990; with Greg Osby: Mind Games 1988, Season of Renewal 1989, Man-Talk 1990; with Bobby Watson: The Inventor 1990, Post Motown Bop 1991, Present Tense 1992, Midwest and Shuffle 1993; with Herbie Mann: Caminho de Casa 1990; with Dave Binney: Point Game 1990; with Victor Lewis: Family Portrait 1992, Know It Today, Know It Tomorrow 1993; with Claudio Roditi: Two of Swords 1991; with Craig Handy: Split Second Timing, 1992; with Charlie Sepulveda: Algo Nuestro, 1993; with Terence Blanchard: Romantic Defiance 1995, The Heart Speaks 1996, Wandering Moon 2000; with Carl Allen: The Pursuer 1994; with Terell Stafford: Time To Let Go 1995; with Mark Shim: Turbulent Flow 2000; with Marlon Simon: Rumaba A La Potato 2000; with John Patitucci: Communion 2001. *Current Management:* Hans Wendl Production. *Telephone:* (510) 848-3864. *Fax:* (510) 848-3972. *E-mail:* artists@hanswendl.com. *Website:* www .hanswendl.com. *E-mail:* info@edwardsimon.com (office). *Website:* www .edwardsimon.com.

SIMON, Paul F., BA; American singer and composer; b. 13 Oct. 1941, Newark, NJ; s. of Louis Simon and Belle Simon; m. 1st Peggy Harper (divorced); one s.; m. 2nd Carrie Fisher 1983 (divorced 1984); m. 3rd Edie Brickell 1992; two s. one d. *Education:* Queens Coll., Brooklyn Law School. *Career:* mem. singing duo Simon & Garfunkel (with Art Garfunkel) 1964–71; solo artist 1972–. *Compositions:* The Capeman (musical) (Antoinette Perry Award for Best Original Score Written for the Theatre 1998) 1997. *Film appearances:* Annie Hall 1977, The Rutles (TV) 1978, All You Need Is Cash 1978, One-Trick Pony 1980. *Recordings include:* albums: as Simon & Garfunkel: Wednesday Morning 3AM 1964, Sounds Of Silence 1966, Parsley, Sage, Rosemary And Thyme 1966, The Graduate (film soundtrack) (two Grammy Awards) 1968, Bookends 1968, Bridge Over Troubled Water (six Grammy Awards 1971) 1970, Concert In Central Park (live) 1982, Early Simon & Garfunkel 1993, Old Friends 1997; solo: The Paul Simon Songbook 1965, Paul Simon 1972, There Goes Rhymin' Simon 1973, Live Rhymin': Paul Simon In Concert 1974, Still Crazy After All These Years (two Grammy Awards) 1975, One-Trick Pony 1980, Hearts And Bones 1983, Graceland (Grammy Award 1987) 1986, Negotiations And Love Songs 1988, Rhythm Of The Saints 1990, Paul Simon's Concert In The Park 1991, Songs From The Capeman 1997, You're The One 2000, Surprise 2006. *Publications:* The Songs of Paul Simon 1972, New Songs 1975, One-Trick Pony (screenplay) 1980, At The Zoo (juvenile) 1991. *Honours:* Hon. DMus (Berklee Coll.) 1986, (Yale) 1996, (Queens Coll.) 1997; Emmy Award (for Paul Simon Special, NBC) 1977, inducted into Songwriters Hall of Fame 1982, Simon & Garfunkel inducted into Rock and Roll Hall of Fame 1990, inducted as solo artist 2001, Kennedy Center Honor 2002, Grammy Lifetime Achievement Award 2003, Gershwin Prize for Popular Song, US Library of Congress 2007, Polar Music Prize (Sweden) 2012. *Address:* c/o C. Vaughn Hazell, Paul Simon Music, Suite 500, 1619 Broadway, New York, NY 10019, USA (office). *Website:* www.paulsimon .com.

SIMONIAN, Sebu; American/Armenian singer, songwriter, musician and record producer; b. 1979, Syria. *Education:* California State Univ., Northridge. *Career:* raised in Lebanon and Calif.; learnt piano and voice as a child; record producer from age of 16; Editorial Asst, Asbarez English Section during late 1990s; formed Capital Cities (with Ryan Merchant) 2009–, released debut EP 2011, debut tour 2013. *Recordings:* album: with Capital Cities: In a Tidal Wave of Mystery 2013. *Honours:* MTV Video Music Award for Best Visual Effects 2013. *Address:* c/o Lazy Hooks Records, Capitol Records, Universal Music Group, 2220 Colorado Avenue, Santa Monica, CA 90404, USA (office). *Telephone:* (213) 509-4083 (office). *E-mail:* ryan@lazyhooks.com. *Website:* www.lazyhooks.com; www.capitalcitiesmusic.com.

SIMONON, Paul; British musician (bass guitar) and artist; b. 15 Dec. 1955, London. *Education:* Byam Shaw School of Art. *Career:* bass guitar player with The Clash 1976–; founder mem. Havana 3am 1986; retired from music business to become full-time artist; mem. The Good, The Bad and The Queen 2006–. *Film:* Ladies and Gentleman the Fabulous Stains. *Exhibitions:* From Hammersmith to Greenwich, Hazlitt, Gooden & Fox, London 2002, collaboration with Damien Hirst, Scottish Nat. Gallery. *Compositions:* with The Clash: The Guns of Brixton, The Crooked Beat, Long Time Jerk. *Recordings:* albums: with The Clash: The Clash 1977, Give 'Em Enough Rope 1978, London Calling 1979, Sandinista! 1980, Combat Rock 1982, Cut the Crap 1985; other: Havana 3am 1991, The Good, the Bad and the Queen 2007. *Address:* c/o Honest Jon's, 278 Portobello Road, London W10 5TE, England (office). *Telephone:* (20) 8969-9822 (office). *E-mail:* mail@honestjons.com (office). *Website:* www.thegoodthebadandthequeen.com.

SIMONS, Edward (Ed); British musician; b. 9 June 1970, England. *Education:* Univ. of Manchester. *Career:* formed The Dust Brothers (with Tom Rowlands); Founder-mem. The Chemical Brothers (with Tom Rowlands) 1989–. *Recordings include:* albums: Exit Planet Dust 1995, Live At The Social, Vol. 1 1996, Dig Your Own Hole 1997, Brothers Gonna Work It Out (DJ mix album) 1998, Surrender 1999, Come With Us 2002, Singles 93–03 2003, Push the Button (Grammy Award for Best Electronic/Dance Album 2006) 2005, We Are The Night (Grammy Award for Best Electronic/Dance Album 2008) 2007,

Brotherhood 2008, Further 2010, Hanna (soundtrack) 2011, Don't Think 2012, Born in the Echoes 2015. *Honours:* Grammy Award 1997, BRIT Award for Best British Dance Act 2000, MTV Europe Music Award for Best Video (for Believe) 2005, Grammy Award for Best Dance Recording (for Galvanize) 2006, Belgian TMF Award for Best Int. Dance 2007, Q Hero 2010, Ivor Novello Award for Outstanding Song Collection 2014. *Current Management:* c/o Fleet River, 1 Cowcross Street, London, EC1M 6DR, England. *Telephone:* (20) 7253-7755. *E-mail:* kathryn@fleetrivermusic.com. *Website:* fleetrivermusic.com; www.thechemicalbrothers.com.

SIMPER, Dominic; Australian musician (bass guitar). *Career:* raised in Perth; Founder-mem. The Dee Dee Dums 2005–07; mem. Tame Impala 2007–, signed to Modular Recordings label 2008, numerous live appearances. *Recordings:* albums: with Pond: Psychedelic Mango 2009, Corridors of Blissterday 2009, Frond 2010, Beard, Wives, Denim 2012, Hobo Rocket 2013; with Tame Impala: Innerspeaker (Triple J's J Award for Album of the Year 2010) 2010, Lonerism (Triple J's J Award for Album of the Year 2012, ARIA Awards for Album of the Year 2013, for Best Rock Album 2013) 2012. *Honours:* with Tame Impala: ARIA Award for Best Group 2013. *Current Management:* c/o Spinning Top Music, PO Box 769, Fremantle, WA 6959, Australia. *E-mail:* tameimpala@spinningtopmusic.com. *Website:* www .spinningtopmusic.com; www.tameimpala.com (home).

SIMPSON, James (Jim); British music company executive, record producer, journalist and musician (trumpet); *Managing Director, Big Bear Music Group*; b. 27 Jan. 1938, Westminster, London, England; s. of William Simpson and Dorothy Simpson; one s. *Education:* trumpet tuition with Dougie Roberts, Dennis Darlowe. *Career:* played with Locomotive 1964–69; managed Black Sabbath 1969–71; recorded and toured with American Bluesmen Lightnin' Slim, Homesick James, Doctor Ross, Snooky Pryor, through 1970s; established Birmingham Int. Jazz Festival 1985, BT British Jazz Awards 1987; Ed. The Jazz Rag 1990–; formed Bruce Adams/Alan Barnes Quintet 1995; reformed Kenny Baker's Dozen 1997; Man. Dir, Big Bear Music Group 1968–; Dir Birmingham Int. Jazz Festival 1985–; Man. King Pleasure & The Biscuit Boys 1986–; Artistic Dir Marbella Int. Jazz Festival 2003–06. *Recordings:* with Locomotive: Rudi's In Love; 11 albums with King Pleasure & The Biscuit Boys; with Black Sabbath: Black Sabbath, Paranoid; with The Quads: There Must Be Thousands. *Photography:* Just Another Whistle Stop, photographic exhbn sponsored by Kodak and shown in Birmingham, Solihull and Marbella. *Publications:* launched nat. jazz magazine, The Jazz Rag 1990. *Honours:* British Jazz Award for Jazz CD of the Year 1994. *Address:* Big Bear Music, PO Box 944, Edgbaston, Birmingham, B16 8UT, England (office). *Telephone:* (121) 454-7020 (office). *E-mail:* jim@bigbearmusic.com (office). *Website:* www.bigbearmusic.com (office); www.birminghamjazzfestival.com.

SIMPSON, Kerri; Australian musician; b. 15 Nov. 1960, Melbourne. *Career:* performed, toured, nationally and internationally in New Orleans, Chicago, London, Barcelona, Blues, Gospel, Alternative Dance; Regular House Artist, ABC TV 's Big Gig 1989–91; Int. supports for Kylie Minogue 1991, Charlie Musselwhite 1991, The Church 1995; mem. MU; Australian Performing Rights Asscn. *Recordings:* albums: Veve 1992, The Arousing 1995, Speak 1996, Higher; Turkey Necklasso 1996, Psy Harmonica, Vol. 1, Confessin' The Blues 1998, Vodou – Songs of The Spirits 2001. *Honours:* Australian Nat. Female Blues Performer of the Year Award 2005. *Current Management:* Carolyn Logan Management, PO Box 406, Fairfield 3078, Victoria, Australia. *E-mail:* carolynlogan38@hotmail.com. *E-mail:* music@kerrisimpson.com (home). *Website:* www.kerrisimpson.com.

SIMPSON, Martin Stewart; British singer, musician (guitar, banjo), composer and songwriter; b. 5 May 1953, Scunthorpe, Lincs., England; m. 1st Jessica Ruby Radcliffe 1985; m. 2nd Kit Bailey 2005. *Career:* folk musician; began playing guitar aged 12 and banjo soon after; performed professionally from age 15; recorded first album, Golden Vanity, at 22 and toured supporting Steeleye Span; worked with June Tabor for more than a decade and recorded three albums together; relocated to USA 1988, returned to UK 2002; worked with many folk greats, including Martin Carthy, Dave Mattacks, Ashley Hutchings, Simon Nicol, Richard Thompson; also performed more recently with musicians from diverse backgrounds, including Wu Man (Chinese pipa player), Bob Brozman, Debashish Bhattacharya; Cool and Unusual album draws on Celtic, American and Afro-American music, featuring David Lindley, Joe Phelps and mems of Tarika; album Bramble Briar concentrates on English folk material; further collaborations with Danu, Nancy Kerr and James Fagan, Danny Thompson, Andy Cutting, Alistair Anderson, Barry Phillips, Kate Rusby, Jackson Browne. *Recordings:* Golden Vanity 1976, Special Agent, A Cut Above (with June Tabor) 1981, Grinning In Your Face 1983, Nobody's Fault But Mine 1985, True Dare Or Promise (with Jessica Simpson) 1987, Leaves of Life 1989, When I Was On Horseback 1991, A Closer Walk With Thee 1994, Smoke and Mirrors, Red Roses 1995, Band of Angels, Music For The Motherless Child 1996, Live, Cool and Unusual (AFIM Award for Acoustic Instrumental Album of the Year) 1997, The Bramble Briar (BBC Radio 2 Folk Award for Best Album 2002) 2001, Righteousness & Humidity 2003, Kind Letters 2005, Prodigal Son (BBC Radio 2 Folk Award for Best Album 2008) 2007, True Stories 2009; features on: Albion Band, Larkrise To Candleford 1980; June Tabor, Aqaba 1988, Abyssinians 1989; Sit Down & Sing, Roy Bailey 2005. *Television:* Cambridge Folk Festival (BBC 4) 2004, 2007, Dick Gaughan documentary (BBC 4) 2004, Later With Jools Holland (BBC 2) 2007. *Honours:* BBC Radio 2 Folk Awards for Best Instrumentalist 2002, for Musician of the Year 2004, Ards Guitar Festival Lifetime Achievement Award 2006. *Current Management:* c/o Alan Bearman Music, Unit 604, Oxford House, 49A Oxford Road, London, N4 3EY, England. *Telephone:* (20) 8347-4200. *E-mail:* bearman@btinternet.com. *Website:* www .alanbearmanmusic.co.uk. *Address:* Simpsonian Music Ltd, PO Box 4450, Sheffield, S11 9DU, England (office). *Telephone:* (114) 266-5642 (office). *E-mail:* info@martinsimpson.com (office). *Website:* www.martinsimpson.com.

SIMPSON, Tom; Scottish musician (keyboards) and programmer. *Career:* mem., Snow Patrol 2005–. *Recordings include:* album: Eyes Open (Meteor Ireland Music Award for Best Irish Album 2007) 2006, A Hundred Million Suns 2008. *Honours:* Meteor Ireland Music Awards for Best Irish Band 2007, for Most Downloaded Song and Best Live Performance 2007. *E-mail:* qprimeuk@qprime.com. *Website:* www.qprime.com. *E-mail:* info@snowpatrol .com. *Website:* www.snowpatrol.com.

SIMPSON, Valerie; American singer and songwriter; b. 26 Aug. 1946, Bronx, NY; m. Nickolas Ashford 1974 (died 2011). *Career:* performing and songwriting duo with husband; collaborations with Marvin Gaye; solo artist 1971–73. *Compositions:* co-writer with Nickolas Ashford: Never Had It So Good, Ronnie Milsap; One Step At a Time, Maxine Brown, The Shirelles; Let's Go Get Stoned, Ray Charles; songs include: Ain't No Mountain High Enough; You're All I Need To Get By; Reach Out and Touch Somebody's Hand; Remember Me; Solid. *Recordings include:* albums: solo: Exposed! 1971, Valerie Simpson 1972; with Nickolas Ashford: Keep It Comin' 1973, Gimme Something Real 1973, I Wanna Be Selfish 1974, Come As You Are 1976, So So Satisfied 1977, Send It 1977, Is It Still Good To Ya? 1978, Stay Free 1979, A Musical Affair 1980, Performance 1981, Street Opera 1982, High-Rise 1983, Solid 1984, Real Love 1986, Love Or Physical 1989, Been Found 1996, The Real Thing 2000. *Honours:* more than 50 ASCAP Awards. *E-mail:* info@ valeriesimpson.net. *Website:* valeriesimpson.net.

SINATRA, Nancy; American singer and writer; b. 8 June 1940, Jersey City, NJ; d. of the late Frank Sinatra and Nancy Sinatra (née Barbato). *Career:* appearances include Sinatra/Elvis Presley TV special 1959; recording debut 1961; numerous TV appearances, including Movin' With Nancy (also prod.) 1967. *Film appearances:* For Those Who Think Young 1964, Get Yourself a College Girl 1964, Marriage on the Rocks 1965, The Ghost in the Invisible Bikini 1966, The Last of the Secret Agents? 1966, The Wild Angels 1966, Speedway 1968. *Film music:* You Only Live Twice (singer of title song) 1967, Now and Then (singer of These Boots Are Made for Walking) 1995, Kill Bill: Vol. 1 (singer of Bang Bang – My Baby Shot Me Down) 2003. *Recordings include:* albums: Boots 1966, How Does That Grab You? 1966, Nancy In London 1966, Sugar 1967, Country, My Way 1967, Movin' With Nancy 1968, Nancy & Lee (with Lee Hazlewood) 1968, Nancy 1969, Woman 1970, This Is Nancy Sinatra 1971, Did You Ever (with Lee Hazlewood) 1972, California Girl 2002, Nancy Sinatra 2004, Nancy and Lee 3 (with Lee Hazlewood) 2004. *Publications:* Frank Sinatra My Father 1985, Frank Sinatra – An American Legend 1995. *Current Management:* John Dubuque, TECS Worldwide Inc., 330 Merwin Avenue, Unit # F1, Milford, CT 06460, USA. *Address:* c/o Delsener/Saleter, 27 E 67th Street, New York, NY 10021, USA. *Website:* www .nancysinatra.com; www.sinatrafamily.com.

SINCLAIR, Gord; Canadian musician (bass guitar); b. Ontario. *Career:* mem., The Tragically Hip 1983–. *Recordings include:* albums: Up to Here 1989, Road Apples 1991, Fully Completely 1992, Day for Night 1994, Trouble at the Henhouse 1996, Live Between Us 1997, Phantom Power 1998, Music @ Work 2000, In Violet Light 2002, In Between Revolution 2004, World Container 2006. *Honours:* inducted into the Canadian Music Hall of Fame 2005. *Address:* c/o Universal Music, 2450 Victoria Park Avenue, Suite 1, Toronto, ON M2J 5H3, Canada (office). *Website:* www.thehip.com.

SINCLAR, Bob; French DJ and producer; b. (Christophe Le Friant), 1970, Paris. *Career:* DJ 1986–; co-f. Yellow Productions label; releases DJ albums under pseudonyms including The Mighty Bop, Reminiscence Quartet, and through the Africanism project. *Recordings include:* albums: Paradise 1998, Champs-Élysées 2000, III 2003, Western Dream 2006, Soundz of Freedom (compilation of remixes) 2007. *Current Management:* Mona Rennalls Agency, Paseo San Gervasio 28 (1-1), 08022 Barcelona, Spain. *Telephone:* (93) 4-18-96-37. *Fax:* (93) 4-18-50-21. *E-mail:* mona@mona-rennalls.de. *Website:* www.mona-rennalls.com. *E-mail:* info@yellowprod.fr (office). *Website:* www.bobsinclar.com.

SINFIELD, Peter John; British producer; b. 27 Dec. 1943, Fulham, London; (divorced). *Career:* King Crimson, writer, producer, 1969–72; Roxy Music, Producer, 1973; Solo album, 1974; Greg Lake, Co-writer, co-producer, 1974–80; Songwriting with Andy Hill, Albert Hammond, Bill Livsey and others, 1981–; mem, PRS; BAC&S Council, Chair of IT Committee. *Compositions:* King Crimson: In the Court of the Crimson King; 21st Century Schizoid Man; I Talk to the Wind; Emerson Lake and Palmer: Karnevil 9; Pirates; Greg Lake: C'est La Vie; I Believe in Father Xmas; The Land of Make Believe, for Bucks Fizz (No. 1, UK), 1982; Allstars, 2001; Rain or Shine, for Five Star; Don't Walk Away; Have You Ever Been in Love, for Leo Sayer; Keep Each Other Warm, for Barry Manilow; Peace in Our Time, for Cliff Richard; Waiting in the Wings, for Diana Ross; As Dreams Go By, for Bette Midler; Think Twice; Call the Man, for Céline Dion. *Honours:* Ivor Novello Awards for Best Song, Have You Ever Been in Love, 1981, Think Twice, 1992; Call The Man, 30 m. album sales; Solo album: Still, 1973. *Current Management:* David Ravden, MGR Ltd, 55 Loudoun Road, St Johns Wood, London NW8 0DL,

England. *Telephone:* (20) 7625-4545. *Fax:* (20) 7625-5365. *E-mail:* davidr@mgr .co.uk. *Website:* www.songsouponsea.com (home).

SINGER, Ray; British record producer, film music supervisor and musician (percussion); b. 4 July 1946, Tonbridge, Kent; m. Janine Turkie 1987; one s. two d. *Education:* London Film School. *Career:* singer, with numerous television appearances; percussionist; collaborations with David Knopfler, Cinema, Japan, Peter Sarstedt, Joan Armatrading, Average White Band; founder, Singer Records 2005; mem, PRS, Musicians' Union, Equity. *Recordings:* as producer: Peter Sarstedt: Where Do You Go To My Lovely, Frozen Orange Juice; Child: It's Only Make Believe; Japan: Assemblage; Robin Sarstedt: My Resistance Is Low; David Knopfler: Giver; Small Mercies; produced music to over 100 TV commercials. *Honours:* Ivor Novello Award, Best TV Series Music (for Civvies). *E-mail:* sales@singerrecords.com (office). *Website:* www.singerrecords.com (office).

SINGH, Arijit; Indian playback singer and musician (guitar, piano); b. 25 April 1987, Jiaganj Azimganj, Murshidabad, W Bengal; m. Koel Roy 2014. *Education:* Raja Bijay Singh High School, Sripat Singh Coll. *Career:* participant, reality TV shows Fame Gurukul (as finalist) 2005, 10 Ke 10 Le Gaye Dil (winner); fmr asst music programmer to Pritam Chakraborty, Shankar-Ehsaan-Loy, Vishal-Shekhar, Mithoon; made Bollywood music debut with song Phir Mohabbat (from film Murder 2) 2011; playback singer for numerous films. *Films include:* as playback singer: Murder 2 2011, Agent Vinod 2012, Players 2012, Cocktail 2012, Barfi! 2012, Shanghai (Mirchi Music Award for Upcoming Male Playback Singer 2013) 2012, 1920: Evil Returns 2012, 3G 2013, Aashiqui 2 (Apsara Film and Television Producers Guild Award 2014, Filmfare Award for Best Male Playback Singer 2014, Global Indian Music Award for Best Male Playback Singer 2014, Int. Indian Film Acad. Award 2014, Mirchi Music Award for Best Male Playback Singer 2014, Screen Award 2014, Zee Cine Award 2014, Gaana Award for Most Popular Male Singer 2014, all for song Tum Hi Ho) 2013, Yeh Jawaani Hai Deewani 2013, Chennai Express 2013, Phata Poster Nikhia Hero 2013, Boss 2013, Shahid 2013, Mickey Virus 2013, Ishk Actually 2013, Goliyon Ki Raasleela: Ram-Leela 2013, Club 60 2013, R... Rajkumar 2013, Jackpot 2013. Yaariyan 2014, Karle Pyaar Karle 2014, One by Two 2014, Heartless 2014, Gunday 2014, Shaadi Ke Side Effects 2014, Queen 2014, Dishkiyaoon 2014, Young-istaan 2014, Main Tera Hero 2014, 2 States 2014, Samrat & Co 2014, Heropanti 2014, Kochadaiiyaan 2014, CityLights (Global Indian Music Award for Best Male Playback Singer (for Muskurane) 2015, Screen Award 2015) 2014, Holiday: A Soldier is Never Off Duty 2014, Fugly 2014, Ek Villain 2014, Humpty Sharma Ki Dulhania (Global Indian Music Award for Best Duet (for Samjhawan, with Shreya Ghoshal) 2015, Mirchi Music Award for Best Male Playback Singer 2015) 2014, Hate Story 2 2014, Singham Returns 2014, Raja Natwarlal 2014, Mary Kom 2014, Creature 3D 2014, Haider 2014, Happy New Year 2014, Kill Dil 2014, Happy Ending 2014, Titoo MBA 2014, Hum Hai Teen Khurafaati 2014, Zid 2014, I 2015, Khamoshiyan 2015, Roy 2015, Badlapur 2015, NH10 2015, Hunterrr 2015, Dilliiwali Zaalim Girlfriend 2015, Ek Paheli Leela 2015, Mr X 2015, Gabbar is Back 2015, Ishqedarriyaan 2015, Hamari Adhuri Kahani 2015, ABCD 2 2015, Guddu Rangeela 2015, Drishyam 2015, All is Well 2015, Phantom 2015, Calendar Girls 2015, Talvar 2015, Singh is Bliing 2015, Wedding Pullav 2015, Shaandaar 2015, Tamasha 2015; as director: Bhalobasar Rojnamcha 2015. *Honours:* Nat. Indian Students Union UK Youth Icon Music Award 2014. *Current Management:* c/o Tarsame Mittal Talent Management, Bungalow no. 181, 1st floor, Aram Nagar part 2, Versova, Andheri (W), Mumbai, 400 061, India. *Telephone:* (22) 26358498. *E-mail:* info@tmtalentmanagement.com. *Website:* www.tmtalentmanagement .com.

SINGH, Malkit, MBE, BA; Indian bhangra singer and songwriter; b. 1962, Hussainpur, Punjab. *Education:* Khalsa Coll., Jalandhar. *Career:* solo artist with Golden Star backing band 1986–. *Film and TV appearances:* Mehndi Shagna Di 1992, En kort en lang 2001, Hvor svaert kan det vaere (one episode, TV series) 2002. *Recordings include:* albums: Nach Gidhe Wich 1986, I Love Golden Star 1987, Put Sardaren De 1988, Chott Nigary Lawo 1988, Up Front 1988, Fast Forward 1989, Hai Shava 1989, Jind Mahi Dee 1989, Dhotakada Bai Dhotakada 1990, Ragga Muffin Mix 1991, Gal Sun Ja 1991, Tere Ishq Nachiyanv 1992, Singho Ho Jo Kathe 1992, Chak De Dholia 1993, Midas Touch 1994, Akh Larr Gayee 1997, Malkit Millennium Mixes 'Kini Sohni' 1999, Nach Nach 2000, Kudi Patole Wargi 2000, Murh Watna Nu Jana, Paaro 2001, Mighty Boliyan 2001, Midas Touch II 2003, 21st Chapter Nachna Aaj Nachna 2005, Billo Rani 2009. *Honours:* Guru Nanak Dev Univ. Convocation Gold Medal 2001. *Telephone:* (121) 580-8080 (UK) (office). *Fax:* (121) 580-8080 (UK) (office). *E-mail:* malkit@malkitsingh.com (office). *Website:* www .malkitsingh.com.

SINGH, Talvin, OBE; British musician (tabla), composer and arranger; b. (Talvinder Singh Matharoo), 1970, London, England. *Career:* began playing tablas as a child; went to India to study tabla under Pandit Lashman Singh 1986–87; head of Omni Records; worked with artists including Björk, Sun Ra and Future Sound of London; f. Anokha club night with promoter Sweety Kapoor at East London's Blue Note 1995; solo artist 1997–; producer, One World One Drum percussion album; worked on projects with numerous other Asian artists, including Osmani Soundz, Amar, Milky Bar Kid, Niladri Kumar, also with Madonna, Siouxsie and the Banshees, Sun Ra, Massive Attack, Jay Z, Blondie. *Recordings:* albums: Drum + Space (as Calcutta Cyber Cafe) 1996, Anokha: Soundz of the Asian Underground 1997, Ok (Mercury Music Prize 1999) 1998, Ha 2001, Back To Mine (compilation of other artists' work) 2001, Vira (with Rakesh Chaurasia) 2002, Sweet Box 2008, Skin 2009. *Honours:* Award at UK Asian Music Awards 2010. *Address:* c/o Chilly Media, 3 Avenue de Beaulieu, 1004 Lausanne, Switzerland (office). *E-mail:* info@unitedsound.ch (office). *Website:* www.talvinsingh.com.

SINGH, Tjinder; British singer, songwriter and musician (guitar, dholki); one s. *Career:* mem., General Havoc –1991; founder mem., Cornershop 1992–; mem., Clinton; founder and owner, Meccico label 1998–. *Recordings include:* albums: with Cornershop: Hold On It Hurts, 1994; Woman's Gotta Have It, 1995; When I Was Born For The 7th Time, 1997; Handcream for a Generation, 2002; with Clinton: Disco and the Halfway to Discontent, 1998. *E-mail:* info@cornershop.com. *Website:* www.cornershop.com.

SINGLETON, Alvin; American composer; b. 28 Dec. 1940, Brooklyn, NY; m. Lisa D. Cooper. *Education:* New York Univ., Columbia Univ., Juilliard School, Berkshire Music Center, Tanglewood, Mass, Yale Univ., Accad. Naz. di Santa Cecilia, Rome, Italy, Ferienkurse für Neue Musik, Darmstadt, Germany and Instituto Musicale, Vicenza, Italy. *Career:* mem. Woodwind Quintet, Berkshire Music Festvial 1969; freelance composer, Graz, Austria 1973; Composer-in-Rresidence, Atlanta Symphony Orchestra 1985–88, Spelman Coll. 1988–91; Master Artist, Atlantic Center for the Arts 1992; Composer-in-Residence, Calif. State Univ., Los Angeles 1996; UNISYS Composer-in-Residence, Detroit Symphony Orchestra 1996–97, Ritz Chamber Players, Jacksonville, Fla 2002–03, Visiting Composer-in-Residence, Tirana, Albania 2008. *Compositions include:* Epitaph (choral) 1966, String Quartet No. 1 1967, Woodwind Quintet 1968–69, Cinque for piano 1969, Argoru I for piano 1970, Argoru II for cello 1970, A Seasoning 1971, Argoru III for flute 1971, Be Natural for strings 1974, Kwitana for chamber orchestra 1974, Messa (soprano, chorus and chamber ensemble) 1975, Dream Sequence (opera) 1976, Extension of a Dream (percussion) 1977, Le Tombeau du Petit Prince for harpsichord 1978, Argoru IV for viola 1978, Again for chamber orchestra 1979, Et nunc (alto flute, bass clarinet and double bass) 1980, Necessity is a Mother (drama) 1981, A Yellow Rose Petal for orchestra 1982, Inside-Out for piano four hands 1983–84, La flora (chamber ensemble) 1983, Argoru Va for bass clarinet 1984, Argoru Vb for alto flute 1984, Apple for clarinet quartet 1984, Akwaaba (chamber orchestra) 1985, Changing Faces for piano 1986, Shadows for orchestra 1987, After Fallen Crumbs for orchestra 1987, Fallen Crumbs (choral) 1987, Alleluia (choral) 1987, Gospel (choral) 1988, Argoru VI for marimba 1988, Bernsteinlied (soprano, flute and piano)1988, Eine Idee ist ein Stück Stoff (An Idea is a Piece of Cloth, for string orchestra) 1988, Secret Desire to be Black for string quartet 1988, Between Sisters (soprano, flute, vibraphone and piano)1990, Sinfonia Diaspora (orchestra) 1991, Even Tomorrow for orchestra 1991, Durch Alles for orchestra 1992, 56 Blows for orchestra 1993, Intezar for string trio 1993, Cara Mia Gwen for orchestra 1993, Fifty Times Around the Sun (for clarinet and piano) 1994, Argoru VII for vibraphone 1994, Somehow We Can for string quartet 1994, Sing to the Sun (for narrator, children's chorus, chamber ensemble) 1995, Blues Konzert (piano concerto) 1995, Umoja: Each One of us Counts for narrator and orchestra 1996, Ein kleines Volkslied (chamber ensemble) 1997, In Our Own House (for chamber ensemble) 1998, Praisemaker (for chorus and orchestra) 1998, Mookestueck for electric viola 1999, Jasper Drag (for clarinet, violin and piano) 2000, When Given a Choice (for orchestra) 2004, Truth (for chamber orchestra) 2006, Through It All (for wind quintet) 2008, Brooklyn Bones (for tenor, chorus and orchestra) 2008, After Choice (for string orchestra) 2009. *Recordings including:* albums: Shadows 1992, Extension of a Dream 2002, Somehow We Can 2002, Sing to the Sun 2007, Sweet Chariot 2014. *Honours:* New York Univ. Marion Bauer Memorial Award 1967, Yale Univ. Rena Greenwald Memorial Prize 1969–70, Yale Univ. Woods Chandler Memorial Prize 1970–71, Kranischsteiner Musikpreis, Darmstadt 1974, Austrian Radio Musik-protokoll Kompositionpreis, Graz 1979, 1981, NEA grants 1980, 1990, MacDowell Colony fellowships 1987, 1989, 1991, 1994, 1995, 1997, City of Atlanta Mayor's Fellowship in the Arts 1989, ASCAP Standard Award 1997–98, Guggenheim Fellowship 2003. *Current Management:* c/o Norman D. Ryan, Schott Music Corporation, 254 West 31st Street, 15th Floor, New York, NY 10001, USA. *Telephone:* (212) 461-6940. *E-mail:* norman.ryan@schott-music.com. *Website:* www.schott-music.com; www.alvinsingleton.com.

SIOUX, Siouxsie; British singer and songwriter; b. (Susan Janet Dallion), 27 May 1957, Chislehurst, Kent; m. Peter Clark (aka Budgie). *Education:* Mottingham Secondary Modern School for Girls, Kent. *Career:* punk rock singer 1970s; singer and songwriter with Siouxsie & the Banshees 1976–96; singer with The Creatures 1981–; lives in France. *Film appearances:* Jubilee 1977, Punk Rock Movie 1978, The Court of Miracles 1982, Out of Bounds 1986. *Recordings:* albums: with Siouxsie and the Banshees: The Scream 1978, Join Hands 1979, Kaleidoscope 1980, Ju Ju 1981, Kiss in the Dream House 1982, Nocturne 1983, Hyaena 1984, Tinderbox 1986, Through The Looking Glass 1987, Peepshow 1988, Superstition 1991, Twice Upon a Time 1992, Rapture 1995, Seven Year Itch (live) 2003; with The Creatures: Feast 1983, Boomerang 1989, Anima Animus 1999, Hybrids 1999, Sequins In The Sun 2001, Hai! 2003; solo: Mantaray 2007. *Honours:* Mojo Icon Award 2005. *Current Management:* Mission Impossible Management, 102A Western Road, Hove, East Sussex, BN3 1FA, England. *Website:* siouxsie.trinitystreetdirect.com; www.thecreatures.com.

SIRACUSA, Gérard; French musician (drums, percussion) and composer; b. 6 Oct. 1957, Tunis, Tunisia; m. Sophie Schneider 1984; one s. one d. *Education:* National Conservatory, Rueil-Malmaison, France. *Career:* mem., Goah 1974; formed G. S. Duo with André Jaume 1975; trios with Raymond Boni and Michel Redolfi 1976; Blaguebolle (musical theatre) 1974–78; Groupe de Recherche et d'Improvisation Musicales de Marseille (GRIM) 1978–84; Molto Mobile 1980; Touchers (percussion quartet) 1981–83; solo percussionist 1981–86; formed G. S. Quartet 1985; G. S. Alma Ata Quintet formed for Banlieues Bleues Festival 1986–87; Ensemble Musique Vivante 1982–87; Un Drame Musical Instantané 1982–84, 1991–94; Solibrius, solo percussion 1986–; Claude Barthélémy – G. S. Quintet/Nonet formed for Vandoeuvre-les-Nancy Festival 1988–91; Collectif Incidences 1990–94; G. S. Trio 1991; Pied de Poule 1991–93; Bûcher des Silences formed for Moers Festival 1991–95; Trio Bal(l)ade 1993–95; duo with Valentin Clastrier 1995–97; duo with Michael Riessler 1996–99; duo with Daniel Petitjean 1997–2000; trio with Valentin Clastrier and Youval Micenmacher 1997–; quintet with Jouk Minor, Bernard Vitet and others 2001–; duo with Garth Knox 2002–; solo drums 2002–; numerous radio and TV broadcasts; mem. SACEM, SPEDIDAM, ADAMI, SACD. *Compositions include:* Jardins de Paille 1982, Titchak 1985, Music for Radio France Culture: Les Chiennes 1987, Nationalité Française 1988, Executeur 14 1989, M'Arco Polo 1989, Kaling 1990, Pas Oui C'Est Non 1993, Diptères (with Daniel Petitjean) 1993, Les Matins De Blanche 1993, Le Dîner Percutant 1993, Ballade Sur Une Autoroute Et Ses Sept Bretelles (with Jean-Marie Maddeddu) 1994, Les Petits Endroits Du Corps 1994, 3 Minutes De Gloire 1994, L'Argent 1994, Special Percussion 1997, Discontinuo 1997, Le long voyage vers le jour 1997, Les demeurés 1997, Ah, Vous Dirai-je… 1998, Les histoires du Prince Oreille au Salon du livre Jeunesse de Montreuil 1998, Jeanne en fragments 2000, Belleville sans laisser d'adresse 2001, Orphee Studio 2002–03. *Recordings:* Musique Pour 8 – L'Oc (with André Jaume) 1982, Anna S. Et Autres Histoires (with Trio MRS) 1983, Jardins De Paille 1982, Terra, Michel Doneda 1985, Slumberland 1986, Kind Lieder 1991, What a Time, Michael Riessler 1991, Hérésie, Valentin Clastrier 1992, Crasse Tignasse 1993, Héloïse 1993, Jamais Tranquille 1993, Le Bûcher Des Silences 1994, Les Tentations d'Abelard 1995, Stations Avant L'oubli 1998, La Jardinière De Légumes 1999. *Honours:* First Prize, Academie Charles Cros, for Le Bûcher Des Silences, 1995. *Address:* c/o En L'Air Association, 27 rue des Papillons, 93100 Montreuil, France (office). *E-mail:* g.siracusa@free.fr (office).

SIRUSHO; Armenian singer and songwriter; b. (Siranush Harutyunyan), 7 Jan. 1987, Yerevan; d. of Hrachya Harutyunyan and Syuzan Margaryan; m. Levon Kocharyan 2009. *Education:* Khachik Dashtents School, Sayat-Nova Music School, Yerevan State Univ. *Career:* recording debut as a child; released debut album 2000; represented Armenia in Eurovision Song Contest 2008. *Recordings:* albums: Sirusho 2000, Sheram (Armenian Nat. Music Award for Best Album 2005) 2005, Hima 2007, Havatum Em (Armenian Nat. Music Award for Best-Selling Album 2010) 2010. *Honours:* numerous awards, including Armenian Music Award (for Lusabats) 1996, Armenian Nat. Music Awards for Future of Armenian Music 2003, for Best Female Artist 2005, 2008, for Best Song (for Havatum Em) 2010, for Best Performance 2013, for Queen of Armenian Pop Music 2013, Krunk Award for Best Female Artist 2004, Voske Qnar Awards for Best Song 2005, 2007, Diaspora Music Awards for Best Female Artist 2005, 2006, for Best Int. Armenian Singer 2009, Special Award 2010, Top 10 Awards for Best Video 2007, 2008, Luxury Awards for Best Singer 2010, for Best Media Star 2010, Armenian Pulse Award for Best Female Artist 2012, World Music Awards for Best Armenian Song 2014, for Best Armenian Video (both for PreGomesh) 2014. *Website:* www.sirusho.am.

SISQÓ, (Sisqó The Golden Child, Dru Nasty); American singer; b. (Mark Andrews), 1977, Baltimore, MD. *Career:* originally worked as a dancer; Formed group Dru Hill with college friends, named after Druid Hill Park in Baltimore; first release Tell Me from the soundtrack of film Eddie; after two hit albums, group decided to pursue solo projects; solo career 1999–; collaborations with Foxy Brown, Mya, Kelly Price. *Recordings:* albums: with Dru Hill: Dru Hill 1997, Enter The Dru 1999; solo: Unleash The Dragon 1999, Return of Dragon 2001. *Honours:* Billboard Award, Male Artist of the Year 2000.

SISSEL (see Kyrkjebo, Sissel)

SISSOKO, Baba; Malian singer and musician (tanami, ngoni, kamelngoni, bala, calabash); b. 8 March 1963, Bamako. *Career:* tamani accompanist at local festivals and ceremonies, as part of group Le Griottes 1970–78; first concert 1978; mem. Mali Instrumental Assembly 1985–90; toured Europe with Griot Ami Koita 1985– 87; mem. Griot Ami Koita 1988–91; formed own group, Baba Sissoko Taman-Kan 1991; accompanist, Souleymane Koli Koteba 1993–94; toured and recorded with singer Habib Koite 1994–98; accompanist to Rokia Traore 1997; mem. AfroCubism project 2010–; has performed with artists including Marie-Veronique Brasseur, Myriam Mollet, Cachaito Lopez, Gregorio Hernandez Rios, Dom Um Romeo, formed trio with Roger Sabal Lecco and Reynaldo Hernandez; other collaborations with Youssou N'Dour, Salif Keita, Habib Koite, Rokia Traore, Ibrahim Ferrer, Buena Vista Social Club, Dee Dee Bridgewater, Don Moye & the Art Ensemble of Chicago, Mamady Keita. *Recordings:* albums: solo: Djana 1999, Live in Studio 2000, Djeliya 2004, Bolokan 2005, Djekafo 2006, Bamako Jazz 2007, Mali mali 2007; with AfroCubism: AfroCubism 2010; other collaborations: Songs of Praises, Ami Kota 1993, Muso Ko, Habib Koite & Bamada 1995, 3, Lokua Kanza 1998, Macire, Boubacar Traore 1998, Maya, Habib Koite & Bamada 1998, Mouneissa, Rokia Traore 1998, Chicago Express, Famoudou Don Moye Bamako 2002, Bowmboi, Rokia Traore 2003, Reunion, Art Ensemble of Chicago 2003, Al Majmaa, Maak's Spirit and Gnawa Ensemble 2004, Tarantella Bruna, Enzo Avitabile & Bottari 2004, Echu Mingua, Miguel Anga Diaz 2005, Rainbow Country, Chris Joris and Bob Stewart 2006, Red

Earth, Dee Dee Bridgewater 2006. *Current Management:* c/o Poney Gross, Zig Zag World Management, 9 rue P.E. Janson, 1050 Brussels, Belgium. *Telephone:* (2) 537-25-25. *Fax:* (2) 538-11-17. *E-mail:* info@zigzagworld.be. *Website:* www.zigzagworld.be. *Address:* c/o World Circuit Records, 138 Kingsland Road, London, E2 8DY, England (office). *E-mail:* sissoko@tiscali .it (office). *Website:* www.worldcircuit.co.uk (office); www.babasissoko.com.

SISSOKO, Ballaké; Malian musician (kora) and composer; b. 1967, s. of Jelimady Sissoko; m. Mama Draba. *Career:* mem. Ensemble Instrumental National from age of 14; worked with artists, including Toumani Diabaté, Taj Mahal. *Recordings include:* albums: New Ancient Strings (with Toumani Diabaté) 1999, Deli 2001, Ballake: Kora Music from Mali 2002, Tomora 2005, 3MA 2008, Chamber Music (with Vincent Segal) 2010, Humbling Tides 2011, At Peace 2013.

SISTER BLISS; British musician (keyboards, violin, piano), remixer, DJ and producer; b. (Ayalah Bentovim), 1970, London, England. *Career:* DJ at London's Bar Industria club; Founder-mem. Faithless 1995–2011; f. Nate's Tunes record label; f. Junkdog Records 2013; collaborations with numerous artists including Dido, Boy George, Cat Power; mem. MCPS, PRS. *Compositions include:* incidental music for TV serial Life Begins (ITV) 2003. *Recordings include:* albums: with Faithless: Reverence 1996, Reverence/ Irreverance, Sunday 8pm 1998, Saturday 3am 1999, Back To Mine (compilation of other artists' work) 2001, Outrospective 2001, Reperspective 2002, No Roots 2004, To All the New Arrivals 2006, The Dance 2010; solo: Headliners: 02 2001, Nightmoves 2008. *Honours:* Best Int. Act to Appear in Ireland 2001. *Current Management:* c/o Craig Newman, ATC Management, The Hat Factory, 166-168 Camden Street, NW1 9PT, London, England. *E-mail:* craig@atcmanagement.com. *Website:* www.atcmanagement.com. *E-mail:* info@junkdogrecords.com. *Website:* thesisterbliss.com.

SITBON, Franck; French musician (keyboards) and singer; b. 15 May 1957, Paris; m. Brigitte Silverio 1982, two s. *Education:* rivate piano lessons. *Career:* tours and performances with artists, including Nicole Croiselle, Bernard Lavilliers, Jacques Higelin, Pino Danielle, Patrick Bruel; mem. SACEM, SPEDIDAM. *Recordings include:* Serge Guirao: Enchanteur, 1988; Nicole Croiselle: Black and Blanche, 1990; Joelle Ursule: Comme dans un film, 1993; with Richard Galliano: Gallianissimo, 2001. *Publication:* Method Up Clavies 1991. *E-mail:* contact@francksitbon.com. *Website:* www.francksitbon.com.

SITEK, David Andrew; American musician (multi-instrumentalist) and producer. *Career:* founder mem., TV on the Radio 2001–; producer, working with bands, including the Yeah Yeah Yeahs; also solo artist, performing as Maximum Balloon 2010–. *Recordings include:* albums: with TV on the Radio: Desperate Youth, Bloodthirsty Babes 2004, Return to Cookie Mountain 2006, Dear Science 2008; as Maximum Balloon: Maximum Balloon 2010. *Honours:* Shortlist Music Prize 2004. *Address:* c/o 4AD, 17–19 Alma Road, London, SW18 1AA, England (office). *E-mail:* 4ad@4ad.com (office). *Website:* www4ad .com (office); www.tvontheradio.com; www.maximumballoon.com.

SIXX, Nikki; American musician (bass guitar) and songwriter; b. (Frank Carlton Serafino Ferrano), 11 Dec. 1958, San Jose, CA. *Career:* fmr mem. groups, London, Christmas; founder mem. heavy rock group, Mötley Crüe 1981–; founder mem., 58 2000–. *Recordings include:* albums: with Mötley Crüe: Too Fast For Love 1981, Shout At The Devil 1983, Theatre Of Pain 1985, Girls, Girls, Girls 1987, Dr Feelgood 1989, Decade of Decadence (American Music Award for Favorite Heavy Metal Album) 1991, Mötley Crüe 1994, Generation Swine 1997, Live: Entertainment Or Death 1999, New Tattoo 2000, Red, White & Crüe 2005, Saints of Los Angeles 2008; with 58: Diet for a New America 2000; solo: The Heroin Diaries: The Soundtrack 2007. *Publication:* The Dirt: Confessions of the World's Most Notorious Rock Band (with Mötley Crüe) 2001, The Heroin Diaries: A Year in the Life of a Shattered Rock Star (with Ian Gittins) 2008. *Honours:* Rolling Stone Best Heavy Metal Band 1991. *Website:* www.motley.com.

SIXX-SCHMULEWITZ, Aaron, BA; American record company executive; b. 4 Aug. 1947, Feldafing, Germany; m. Lynda M. Jones 1977; one s. one d. *Education:* Univ. of California at Los Angeles. *Career:* European A & R Dir, United Artists Records 1973–74; Dir of Int. Operations, Arista Records 1975–77; Music and Entertainment Man. Dir, Aura Records 1978–.

SIZE, Roni; British musician (keyboards, drums, programming) and produccer; b. (Ryan Williams), 29 Oct. 1969, Bristol; one s. *Career:* began as DJ in clubs; co-founder, Full Cycle Records 1993; creative leader of Bristol-based collective, Reprazent; with Reprazent, numerous performances at concert venues and festivals worldwide. *Recordings include:* with DJ Die, Music Box; Agility; solo: Jazz Thing, Return To V 2004; with Reprazent: Reasons For Sharing (EP) 1996, New Forms (Mercury Music Prize) 1997, In The Mode 2000, Touching Down 2002, Return to V 2005, Touching Down Vol. 2 2005, Friends 2006, New Forms 2 2008. *Honours:* Urban Music Award for Best Drum and Bass Act 2005. *Current Management:* HDM Group, The Paintworks, Unit 4.16, Bath Road, Bristol, BS4 3EH, England. *Telephone:* (117) 971-2397. *Fax:* (117) 972-8981. *E-mail:* info@hdmgroup.co.uk. *Website:* www .hdmgroup.co.uk.

SJÖBLOM, Titti, (Sigrid); Swedish singer, songwriter and entertainer; *Producer, Seaflower Music;* b. (Titti Sigrid Renée Sjöblom), 29 Aug. 1949, Stockholm; d. of Nils Ivar Sjöblom and Alice Babs Sjöblom; m. Ehrling Eliasson; two s. *Education:* pvt. singing lessons, Acad. of Ballet, Musicology Univ. of Uppsala. *Career:* played Maria Magdalena in Jesus Christ Superstar 1972; children's shows on TV 1980s; tours annually to entertainment parks, restaurants, churches; entertained UN troops; f. own record label Seaflower Music; Chair. Bd of Entertainers of the Swedish Armed Forces. *Compositions include:* Trumman, Det Tanker jag ofta pa. *Recordings include:* Sjung Med Oss Mamma, For Sjal Och Hjarta, Världsarvets Serenad, Titti & Ehrling sjunger Kai Gullmar, ALICE BABS - Mamma & Idol. *Honours:* Expressens Best Television Entertainment for Children 1964, Perne Paddock Award 1994, HKH Kronprinsessan Margaretas Medal, Entertainer for the UN – The Nobel Peace Prize 1988, Goldmedal of the CFB. *Address:* Seaflower Music, Hall 205, 87032 Ullanger (office); Seaflower Music, Hälsingegatan 37 5 tr, 11331 Stockholm, Sweden (office). *Telephone:* (70) 372-94-04 (office). *E-mail:* info@seaflowermusic.se (office). *Website:* www.seaflowermusic.se (office).

SKAGGS, Ricky Lee; American musician (guitar, banjo, mandolin, fiddle); b. 18 July 1954, Cordell, KY; m. Sharon White 1981; two s. two d. *Career:* mem., Ralph Stanley and the Clinch Mountain Boys 1970, Country Gentlemen 1974; formed own band, Boone Creek 1975; mem., Emmylou Harris' Hot Band 1977–, Whites 1980–; solo artist 1981–, with own backing band, Kentucky Thunder; host of own radio series, Simple Life with Ricky Skaggs; numerous television appearances; mem. AFTRA, AFofM. *Recordings include:* albums: Waitin' for the Sun to Shine 1981, Highways and Heartaches 1982, Don't Cheat in Our Hometown 1983, Country Boy 1984, Favorite Country Songs 1985, Live in London 1985, Love's Gonna Get Ya! 1986, Comin' Home to Stay 1988, Kentucky Thunder 1989, My Father's Son 1991, Ricky Skaggs Portrait 1992, Solid Ground 1995, Bluegrass Rules 1997, Ancient Tones 1999, Soldier of the Cross 2000, History of the Future 2001, Instrumentals (Grammy Award for Best Bluegrass Album 2007) 2006, Salt of the Earth (Grammy Award for Best Southern, Country or Bluegrass Gospel Album 2008) 2007, Honoring the Fathers of Bluegrass: Tribute to 1946 and 1947 (Grammy Award for Best Bluegrass Album 2009) 2008, Songs My Dad Loved 2009. *Honours:* Ralph Stanley Dove Award 1982, eight Grammy Awards 1984–2001, eight ACM Awards, including Best Touring Band 1983–87, Edison Award, The Netherlands 1987, eight CMA Awards, six Music City News Awards, BBC Radio 2 Artist of the Decade, Guitar Player Readers' Poll Best Country Guitarist 1987–89, Gospel Voice Diamond Award 1993, Bluegrass Instrumentalist Group of the Year (with Kentucky Thunder) 1998–99. *Address:* c/o Skaggs Family Records, PO Box 2478, Hendersonville, TN 37077, USA (office). *Telephone:* (615) 264-8877 (office). *Fax:* (615) 264-8899 (office). *E-mail:* charlotte@skaggsfamilyrecords.com (office). *Website:* www .skaggsfamilyrecords.com; www.rickyskaggs.com.

SKELLERN, Peter; British musician (piano), singer and songwriter; b. 14 March 1947, Bury, Lancashire, England; m.; two c. *Education:* Guildhall School of Music. *Career:* mem. March Hare (recorded as Harlan County) 1971; series of musical plays, Happy Endings; host of chat show Private Lives 1983; formed Oasis group (with Julian Lloyd Webber, Mary Hopkin, Bill Lovelady) 1984, 1996. *Recordings include:* Peter Skellern with Harlan County 1971, Peter Skellern 1972, Not Without a Friend 1973, Holding My Own 1974, Hold On To Love 1975, Hard Times 1976, Skellern 1978, Astaire 1979, Still Magic 1980, Happy Endings 1981, Introducing Right from the Start 1981, A String of Pearls 1982, Oasis 1984, Love Light 1987, Sentimentally Yours 1996, The Masters 1997, A Quiet Night Out 2000. *Honours:* Music Trades Asscn Best MOR Album 1979.

SKELLY, Ian; British musician (drums); b. Hoylake, Wirral. *Education:* Hilbre High School, Hoylake. *Career:* Founder mem., The Coral 1996–. *Recordings:* albums: The Coral 2002, Magic and Medicine 2003, Secret Kiss 2003, Nightfreak and the Sons of Becker 2004, The Invisible Invasion 2005, Roots and Echoes 2007, The Singles Collection 2008, Butterfly House 2010. *Website:* www.thecoral.co.uk.

SKELLY, James; British musician (guitar); b. Hoylake, Wirral, England. *Education:* Hilbre High School, Hoylake. *Career:* Founder mem., The Coral 1996–. *Recordings include:* albums: The Coral 2002, Magic and Medicine 2003, Secret Kiss 2003, Nightfreak and the Sons of Becker 2004, The Invisible Invasion 2005, Roots and Echoes 2007, The Singles Collection 2008, Butterfly House 2010. *Website:* www.thecoral.co.uk.

SKEPTA; British hip hop and grime rapper, songwriter and record producer; b. (Joseph Junior Adenuga), 19 Sept. 1982, Tottenham, London, England. *Career:* DJ for Meridian Crew –2005; mem. Roll Deep 2005–06; Founder-mem. Boy Better Know 2006; solo career 2007–. *Recordings include:* albums: Greatest Hits 2007, Microphone Champion 2009, Doin' It Again 2011; mixtapes: Been There Done That 2010, Community Payback 2011, Blacklisted 2012. *Honours:* MOBO Award for Best Video 2014. *Address:* c/o All Around the World, Universal Island, Universal Music Group, 364–366 Kensington High Street, London, W14 8NS, England (office). *Telephone:* (20) 7471-5000 (office). *Website:* www.aatw.com (office).

SKI; British musician (keyboards, zither), producer and writer; b. (Dominic Oakenfull), 28 Jan. 1971, Sevenoaks, Kent. *Education:* City Univ., London; music lessons with Keith Rusling, Kent; K. B. Wizard, London. *Career:* keyboard player, writer, producer for the K-Creative 1991–93, Raw Stylus 1993, Palm Skin Productions 1993, Thats How It Is 1994, Galliano 1994, 1995; solo artist performing as Ski 1993–; founder, Primaudial Records 2007; writer, jingles for various radio commercials. *Recordings:* albums: QED, K-Creative 1992, The Plot Thickens, Galliano 1994, Marla Glen, Marla Glen 1995, Pushing, Raw Stylus 1995, Galliano (fourth album) 1996; solo: Life Changes

2001, Rising Sun 2005. *Publications:* Fender Rhodes, A Brief History 1994. *Website:* www.primaudialrecords.com; www.skioakenfull.com.

SKIFS, Björn Nils Olof; Swedish singer, composer and actor; b. 20 April 1947, Vansbro; m. Pernilla Skifs 1988; two s. *Career:* major concert tours and TV shows 1970–; Eurovision Song Festival 1978 and 1981; musicals. *Plays:* leading role: Spök 1981, 1991, Some Like It Hot 1992, Guys & Dolls 1996. *Films:* screenplay, leading role: Strul 1986, Joker 1989, Drömåken 1993. *Recordings include:* Hooked On A Feeling 1974, Never My Love 1974, Michaelangelo 1975–76, Håll Mitt Hjärta (Hold My Heart) 2002, Skifs Hits! 2004, When You Tell the World You're Mine (with Agnes Carlsson) 2010, Break the Spell 2011, Step Right Up 2012. *Current Management:* Desert AB, PO Box 103, 70142 Orebro, Sweden. *Website:* www.skifs.se.

SKILLINGS, Manuel (Muzz); American musician (bass); b. 6 Jan. 1960, New York. *Career:* mem., Living Colour –1993; session work with Mick Jagger, support slots live to Rolling Stones. *Recordings:* albums: with Living Colour: Vivid 1988, Time's Up 1990, Biscuits 1991; other appearances include: This What I Do, Sir Mack Rice 2000, Brand New Man, Freddie Scott 2001.

SKIN; British singer and songwriter; b. (Deborah Ann Dyer), 3 Aug. 1967, Brixton, London. *Education:* Teesside Polytechnic. *Career:* founder mem. and lead singer, Skunk Anansie 1994–2001, 2009–; numerous headlining tours, festival appearances, TV and radio shows; contributed songs to films Timecode 2000, Princess and the Warrior; solo artist 2001–. *Recordings include:* albums: with Skunk Anansie: Paranoid and Sunburnt 1995, Stoosh 1996, Post Orgasmic Chill 1999, Smashes and Trashes 2009, Wonderlustre 2010; solo: Fleshwounds 2003, Fake Chemical State 2006. *Film:* Strange Days (cameo appearance by Skunk Anansie). *Honours:* Kerrang!! Best Rock Band Award 1995, Best British Live Act Award 1996. *Website:* www.skunkanansie.net; www.skinmusic.net.

SKINNER, Harry; British musician (guitar), singer, composer and songwriter; b. 30 April 1958, Barking, Essex; m. Elizabeth Vango 1991; one s. one d. *Education:* Southampton Univ., RMSM, Kneller Hall, Twickenham, Bournemouth and Poole Coll., Poole. *Career:* oboist, Rhine Staff Band RTR 1976–81; formed band, Manitou, touring UK, Gemany and Japan; founder mem., The Producers 1990–2002, 2009–; festival appearances throughout Europe; tours of UK, Germany, France, Belgium and Ireland; mem. Musicians' Union; assoc. mem. PRS, MCPS. *Recordings include:* albums: with Manitou: Manitou At The Electric Drum I and II 1987, Looking For The Lost 1991; with The Producers: Escape From Muswell Hell 1991, Ain't No Love In The World 1993, For This Night Only 1994, Nearly Wired 1996, Really Wired 1996, Somewhere Down the Line, Harry Skinner and Dave Saunders, Into the Blues, Arizona. *E-mail:* davesau@ntlworld.com (office). *Website:* www .producersbluesband.co.uk.

SKINNER, Tom; British jazz musician (percussion, drums, keyboards). *Education:* Goldsmiths Coll., Univ. of London. *Career:* fmr mem. Zero 7; mem. Zed-U 2007–; Founder-mem. Hello Skinny 2010–; Founder-mem. Sons of Kemet 2011–; collaborator, Owiny Sigoma Band, Mulatu Astatke, Matthew Herbert, Eska, Finn Peters. *Recordings:* albums: with Zed-U: Night Time on the Middle Passage 2009; as Hello Skinny: Smash + Grab 2012; with Sons of Kemet: Burn 2013. *Honours:* MOBO Award for Best Jazz Act 2013. *Current Management:* c/o Sinan Ors, Elastic Artists Agency Limited, Targetspace: Room 104, 1st Floor, 70 St Mary Avenue, London, EC3A 8BE, England. *Telephone:* (20) 7336-8340. *Fax:* (20) 7608-1471. *E-mail:* sinan@elasticartists .net. *Website:* www.elasticartists.net. *Address:* c/o Simon Drake, Naim Jazz Records, Southampton Road, Salisbury, Wiltshire, SP1 SLN, England (office). *Telephone:* (1722) 426600 (office). *Fax:* (871) 230-1012 (office). *E-mail:* info@ naimlabel.com (office); sonsofkemet@gmail.com. *Website:* www.naimlabel.com (office); sonsofkemet.com.

SKIPPER, Svend; Danish musician (piano), conductor, composer and arranger; b. 22 April 1947, Naestved; m. Ghita Noerby, 15 July 1984. *Education:* Studied piano, solfeggio, conducting, Royal Danish Conservatory, 1970–77. *Career:* Musical Director, all Danish theatres, Directed musicals: The Peanuts; No No Nanette; Promises Promises; Showboat; Pal Joey; Oliver; They're Playing Our Song; Chicago; My Fair Lady; Orpheus In The Underworld; Parisian Life; Beggar's Opera (Weill); Jesus Christ Superstar; Teenage Love (Finn Savery); Starting Here Starting Now; Sunday In The Park With George; Sweeney Todd; Side By Side By Sondheim; A Little Night Music; En Spurv I Tranedans (Danish vaudeville, 1880); I'm Getting My Act Together; Les Miserables, Odense and Copenhagen; Conducted all Danish symphony orchestras; Also Danish Light Music Orchestra playing jazz, rock, musicals, Indian, classical repertoire; Concerts, television and radio appearances in Denmark and Sweden; Performed with instrumentalists and singers including: Birgit Nilsson; Elizabeth Soderstroem; Anne Sofie von Otter; Indian violinist, Supramaniam; Hubert Laws; Ben Webster; Harry 'Sweets' Edison; Bob Rockwell; Doug Rayney; Touring Europe with pioneer jazz/ classical Skipper-Lund-Simonsen Trio (piano, flute, bass); Own recording studio, The Holtewood Studio; Song coach for Danish version of Prince of Egypt; Conductor, Evita, recorded with Bournemouth Sinphonietta (conducting), The Little Mermaid, drama theatre, 1998; mem, Danish Conductors Society; DJBFA. *Compositions:* Composer for Danish films, television series, songs, signatures, 8 minute comic opera, Bread; Arranger: orchestra, theatre, live and recorded music. *Recordings:* More than 100, including musicals: The Peanuts; Starting Here Starting Now; Oliver; Les Miserables, Danish cast, Spanish cast; Miss Saigon, Danish cast.

SKIRVING, Mark Antony; British singer, musician (saxophone) and painter; b. 13 March 1966, Wednesbury, West Midlands, England; one s. *Career:* numerous TV appearances world-wide; played with B. B. King, Cab Calloway, Slim Gaillard, Matt (Guitar) Murphy, Steve Cropper, Donald Dunn, Eddie Floyd, Bruce Adams, Alan Barnes, Val Wiseman; several small film appearances; mem., Birmingham Jazz Festival Bd, British Jazz Awards Cttee. *Art exhibition:* paintings exhibited at Walsall Art Gallery. *Recordings:* albums: King Pleasure and the Biscuit Boys, This Is It, Better Beware, King Pleasure and the Biscuit Boys Live at Ronnie Scott's, Blues and Rhythm Revue, Vol. 1, Smack Dab in the Middle, Let 'Em Roll, Hey Puerto Rico!, Live at Last. *Current Management:* c/o Big Bear Music, PO Box 944, Edgbaston, Birmingham, B16 8UT, England. *Telephone:* (121) 454-7020. *E-mail:* kp@ bigbearmusic.com. *Website:* www.bigbearmusic.com.

SKOLNICK, Alex; American rock musician (guitar); b. 29 Sept. 1968, Berkeley, California. *Education:* studied with Joe Satriani. *Career:* toured and recorded with US heavy rock group Testament; toured with Stu Hamm; recorded with Michael Manring; founded Alex Skolnick Trio; mem, ASCAP. *Recordings:* albums with Testament: The Legacy 1987, The New Order 1988, Practice What You Preach 1989, Souls of Black 1990, The Ritual 1992, The Formation of Damnation 2008; with Savatage: Handful of Rain, 1994; with Attention Deficit: Attention Deficit 1998, The Idiot King 2001; with Alex Skolnick Trio: Goodbye to Romance: Standards for a New Generation 2002, Transformation 2004, Last Day in Paradise 2007, Veritas 2011; with Michael Manring: The Skol-Patrol 1997; compilations: Guitars That Rule The World; Guitars Practicing Musicians. *Publications:* Columnist for magazines: Guitar; Guitar Player; Guitar World. *Address:* Skol Productions, PO Box 2271, Radio City Station, New York, NY 10101-2271, USA. *Website:* www.alexskolnick .com.

SKOVBYE, Kim Lind; Danish musician (harp, guitar, violin, bouzouki, mandolin, recorder), composer, songwriter and poet; b. 10 Jan. 1955, Copenhagen; partner Anne Ostrup; two s. two d. *Education:* private lessons from age 9; 3 years study at Danish Music Acad. *Career:* 10 years teaching children; 7 years, teaching music and drama, adult training coll.; 10 years as street musician with the juggler and singer Herman; Several TV and radio shows; two big concerts at the Tivoli; Several shows and tours with keyboard player, Klaus Schonning, Denmark, Germany and Netherlands. *Compositions:* Skygge Boxer (songs) 1986, Barsebeck (songs) 1987, Scandinavia (instrumental) 1990, Heartland (instrumental) 1992, Aftermath (instrumental) 1993, Ask and Riana (children) 1994, Mountains of Fire (song) 1995, Coming Albums: Wayfarer 1995, Lord of The Rings Part 1 1996, There and Back Again 1997, Eventide 2000, The Fullmoon Concert 2000, Hvidt Sa Vidt 2001, The Ring, Vol. 1 2002, The Ring, Vol. 2 2003, The Tolkien Collection 2004; film music: Holografi 1988, The Glassheart 1989, Song of a Tiger 1989, Landscapes of Childhood 1992. *Honours:* awards from Danish Jazz Beat Folk Soc. *Address:* Strandvejen 324, 3060 Espergaerde, Denmark. *E-mail:* mail@ kimskovbye.dk. *Website:* www.kimskovbye.dk.

SKRILLEX; American musician, DJ, music producer and singer-songwriter; b. (Sonny John Moore), 15 Jan. 1988, Los Angeles, Calif. *Career:* joined post-hardcore band From First to Last as lead singer 2004, recorded two studio albums Dear Diary, My Teen Angst Has a Body Count 2004, Heroine 2006; left to follow solo career 2007; first tour as a solo artist 2007; joined Alternative Press Tour to support bands including All Time Low and The Rocket Summer; appeared on cover of Alternative Press' annual 100 Bands You Need to Know issue; releasing Gypsyhook EP 2009; began performing as Skrillex later that year; formed Jack Ü with Diplo 2013–. *Recordings include:* albums: Gypsyhook EP (as Sonny) 2009, My Name Is Skrillex 2010, Scary Monsters and Nice Sprites 2010, More Monsters and Sprites 2011, Bangarang (Grammy Award for Best Dance/Electronica Album 2013) 2011, Make It Bun Dem After Hours 2012, Leaving 2013, Recess 2014; with Diplo: Skrillex and Diplo Present Jack Ü (Grammy Award for Best Dance/Electronic Album 2016) 2015; singles as lead artist: WEEKENDS!!! (featuring Sirah) 2010, Kill Everybody 2010, Scary Monsters and Nice Sprites (Grammy Award for Best Dance Recording) 2010, Reptile's Theme 2011, First of the Year (Equinox) 2011, Bangarang (featuring Sirah) (Grammy Award for Best Dance Recording 2013, Billboard Music Award for Top Electronic Dance Music Album 2013) 2012, Make It Bun Dem (with Damian Jr Gong Marley) 2012; singles as featured performer: Get Up! (Korn featuring Skrillex) 2011, Still Gettin' It (Foreign Beggars featuring Skrillex) 2011, Burst (12th Planet featuring Skrillex and Kill the Noise) 2011, Narcissistic Cannibal (Korn featuring Skrillex and Kill the Noise) 2011, Bring Out the Devil (SOFI featuring Skrillex and Kill the Noise) 2011, Chaos Lives in Everything (Korn featuring Skrillex) 2012; promotional single: Lick It (with Kaskade from album Fire & Ice) 2012. *Honours:* Grammy Awards for Best Remixed Recording Non-Classical (for Cinema) 2012, (for Promises) 2013, for Best Dance Recording (for Where Are Ü Now? with Justin Bieber and Diplo) 2016, MTV's Electronic Dance Music Artist of the Year 2011, MTV Europe Music Award (EMA) for Best Collaboration (for Where Are Ü Now?) 2015, American Music Award for Collaboration of the Year (for Where Are Ü Now?) 2015. *Website:* www.skrillex.com; bloodcompany.net/skrillex.

SKYE (see Edwards, Skye)

SLABAK, Jan; Czech musician (trumpet), composer, conductor and band master; b. 24 March 1941, Kelcany, Kyjova; m. 1st Jitka Janowskova, 18 Nov. 1960, m. 2nd Ivana Soutalova, 22 July 1976, one s., one d. *Education:* State Conservatoire (Academy of Music), Brno; Janacek's Academy of Music Arts,

Brno. *Career:* State Philharmonic Orchestra, Brno; Moravanta of Jan Slabak; Many film, TV, radio appearances; mem, OSA; Chair, Competition juries. *Compositions:* 210 compositions for brass band, published and recorded on LPs, MCs, and CDs. *Publications:* Hundreds of reviews and contributions, Kaoje Kdo, 1991–92; Mijosua ic Moravanka, 1997. *Honours:* TV Prize, 1973; Ministry of Culture, 1975; Golden Key, Cleveland, USA, 1978; 3 times Golden Disc, 1980, 1985, 1991; 1 Platinum Disc, 1995; 1 Diamond Disc, 1996. *Current Management:* Jan Hlaváček, Merhautova 66, 613 00 Brno, Czech Republic. *E-mail:* moravanka@moravanka.net. *Website:* www.moravanka.de.

SLADE, Isaac; American singer and musician (piano); b. 1981. *Career:* founder mem. and lead singer, The Fray 2002–. *Recordings include:* album: How to Save a Life (Billboard Award for Digital Album of the Year 2006) 2005, The Fray 2009. *Honours:* Billboard Award for Digital Album Artist of the Year, for Digital Songs Artist of the Year 2006. *Address:* c/o Sony BMG, 550 Madison Avenue, New York, NY 10022, USA. *E-mail:* fraymanagement@gmail.com. *Website:* www.thefray.net.

SLASH; rock musician (guitar); b. (Saul Hudson), 23 July 1965, Stoke-on-Trent, Staffordshire, England; m. Renee Suran 1992. *Career:* mem. heavy rock group, Guns N' Roses 1985–97; int. tours, festival appearances; lead singer, Slash's Snakepit 1994–2001; mem., Velvet Revolver (VR) 2002–; also solo artist. *Recordings include:* albums: with Guns N' Roses: Appetite For Destruction 1987, G 'N' R Lies 1988, Use Your Illusion I and II 1991, The Spaghetti Incident 1993, Live Era '87–'93 1999; with Velvet Revolver: Contraband 2004, Libertad 2007; with Slash's Snakepit: It's Five O'Clock Somewhere 1995, Ain't Life Grand 2000; solo: Slash 2010; with Myles Kennedy and the Conspirators: Apocalyptic Love 2012, World on Fire 2014. *Publication:* Slash (auto-biog.) 2007. *Honours:* American Music Award for Favorite Heavy Metal Single, for Favorite Heavy Metal Artist and Album 1989, for Favorite Heavy Metal Artist 1992; several MTV Awards; World Music Award for Best Selling Artist of the Year 1993; Rolling Stone and Billboard Magazine Awards. *Address:* c/o Columbia Records, 550 Madison Avenue, New York, NY 10022, USA (office). *Website:* www.velvetrevolver.com; www.gnronline.com; slashonline.com.

SLATER, John; British artist manager and tour manager; b. 12 Jan. 1957, London, England. *Education:* Essex Univ. *Career:* Stage Manager, Edinburgh Playhouse 1976–77; sound engineer 1977–80, radio presenter, BRMB Radio Birmingham, hosting and producing indie and rock evening show 1980–91, with interviews, sessions and concert recordings; partnership with Danny Kenny managing various bands.

SLATER, Luke, (Offset, Clementine, Morganistic, Planetary Assault Systems, The 7th Plain); British producer, remixer and DJ; b. 12 June 1968, Reading, Berkshire, England. *Career:* DJ at Troll club, London 1988; worked in Jelly Jam Records shop in Brighton, East Sussex; first recordings appeared on shop's own label; f. Mote-Evolver record label 2006; remixed Madonna, Depeche Mode, Ballistic Brothers, Slam; composed music for Shut Up and Dance, Staatsballet, Munich 2007. *Recordings include:* albums: Fluids Amniotic 1994, The Four Cornered Room 1994, My Yellow Wise Rug 1995, X-Tront, Vol. 2 1996, Electric Funk Machine 1997, Freek Funk 1997, The Drone Sector 1998, Wireless 1999, Atomic Funkster 2001, Fear and Loathing 2001, Alright On Top 2002, Fear and Loathing Vol. 2 2004, Fabric 23 2007. *Address:* c/o Fabric, 77a Charterhouse Street, London, EC1M 3HN, England. *Website:* www.lukeslater.com.

SLEDGE, Robert; American musician (bass guitar, synthesizer) and songwriter; b. 9 March 1968. *Career:* fmr mem. of several groups including The Beam, Toxic Popsicle, Lexx Luthor; mem. Ben Folds Five 1993–2000, 2011–; mem. International Orange 2003–05; Founder mem. The Bob Sledge Band. *Recordings include:* with Ben Folds Five: Ben Folds Five 1995, Whatever and Ever Amen 1997, Naked Baby Photos 1998, The Unauthorised Biography of Reinhold Messner 1999, The Sound of the Life of the Mind 2012. *Address:* c/o Epic Records, Sony Music Entertainment, 550 Madison Avenue, New York, NY 10022, USA (office). *Website:* www.benfoldsfive.com.

SLICK, Grace; American singer, songwriter and entertainer; b. (Grace Barnett Wing), 30 Oct. 1939, Evanstown, IL; m. 1st Gerald Robert Slick 1961 (divorced); one d.; m. 2nd Skip Johnson 1976. *Education:* Finch Coll. *Career:* singer, Great Society 1965–66, Jefferson Airplane 1966–72, Jefferson Starship (later known as Starship) 1972–88; numerous concerts, including Woodstock and Altamont, television appearances; mem. AFofM. *Recordings include:* albums: solo: Manhole 1973, Dreams 1980, Welcome To The Wrecking Ball 1981, Software 1984; with Jefferson Airplane/Starship: Surrealistic Pillow 1967, Dragon Fly 1974, Red Octopus 1975, Earth 1978, Modern Times 1981, Winds of Change 1982, Nuclear Furniture 1984; with Starship: Knee-Deep in the Hoopla 1985, No Protection 1987. *Honours:* four Bay Area Music Awards for Best Singer. *Address:* 8900 Wilshire Blvd #300, Beverly Hills, CA 90211-1906, USA. *Website:* www.jeffersonairplane.com.

SLIGER, Robert Earl; American singer, songwriter, composer, producer and educator and musician (guitar, piano/keyboards, drums); b. 31 Oct. 1962, Detroit, MI. *Education:* Community Coll. of the Air Force, USA, USAF Chorale with Martha Daige (Dir), Denver, CO, voice instruction with Bill White and Sid Wright, Austin, TX, Tom Prebble, Torejon, Spain, Gene Nice, Pensacola Civic Opera, FL, Vaccai, Italian Opera (English); Chris Beatty, TN, Thomas Appell, CA. *Career:* Tenor/MC, USAF Air Force Chorale 1980–81; Co-leader/lead singer, background, with Star Fire 1982; tenor, Gospel Quartet,

Germany 1983; lead singer, background, with Angel Band 1990–92; producer, lead and background singer, with Liberty-N-Justice 1991–93; Lost In Eden tour, with Liberty-N-Justice 1993; filmed two music videos with Liberty-N-Justice: All Your Love 1992, We Are Family 1993; solo career 1993–; radio interview, WQFL, WGSL, Rockford, IL 1995; tenor, Mendelssohn's Elijah, Bradley Community Chorus and Chamber Orchestra, Bradley Univ., IL,1996; lead vocalist, with Marvin Lee Zilch 1997–98; Tenor/First Tenor, Celebrate America – a Patriotic Celebration, Great Hills Worship Choir and Orchestra in conjunction with USAF, US Army, USN, US Marines and Special Cavalry, The Austin Police Dept/SWAT Teams, Austin, TX 2003, 2004; mem, ASCAP. *Compositions:* Christ You Share 1991, Through The Night 1992, You're Not Alone 1993, LORD Jesus Christ 1993, In Your Arms 1993, Dr Werking's Office 1993, Your Open Door (with Marvin Zilch) 1994, When You're Needing a Friend (with Marvin Zilch) 1994, Show The Way 1995, Majestic (instrumental) 1995, When I Walk With You (Road to Emmaus) 1997. *Recordings:* with Liberty-N-Justice: Armed With The Cross 1992, Big Guns 1994; with Angel Band: Down To Earth 1992, Down To Earth (remastered) 1993; solo: The Practices (EP) 1998, The Aunt Gloria Project 1999; with Marvin Zilch: LOVE 1999, You Are So Beautiful 2001, Anytime 2002, Sliger – Family Christmas 2003, I'm A Believer 2004. *Publications:* How To Read The Holy Bible – The Basics 1988. *Honours:* Most Valuable Player Trophy, South Summer High Track-n-Field Team, Fla 1980, USAF Colour Guard Selectee, Spain 1982, USAF Good Conduct Medal 1983, Honor Grad USAF School of Aerospace Applied Sciences (Phase I), Texas 1985, Weigel Music Award Scholarship, Tennessee Temple Univ. 1986. *Address:* C & R Productions, PO Box 10763, Austin, TX 78766, USA (office). *E-mail:* robmusic001@yahoo.com (office).

SLIJNGAARD, Ray; Belgian rap artist and songwriter. *Career:* mem. of dance music group, 2 Unlimited 1991–. *Recordings include:* albums: No Limits, 1993; Real Things, 1994; Hits Unlimited, 1995. *Current Management:* CBA Artists, PO Box 1495, 1200 BL Hilversum, The Netherlands.

SLOANE, Carol; American jazz singer; b. 5 March 1937, Providence, RI; d. of Frank Morvan and Claudia Morvan; m. Edward 'Buck' Spurr 1986. *Education:* business coll. *Career:* professional singer from age 14, with Ed Drew's Dance Band; tours with Larry Elgart Orchestra, 1958–60; singer with Hendricks (Dave) Lambert and Ross Trio, 1960; shared bills with Bill Cosby, Woody Allen, Lenny Bruce, Richard Pryor, 1960s; singer with Tonight Show Band, Johnny Carson's Tonight Show; supper club work, regular public radio show, North Carolina, 1981–85; moved to Boston, 1986; DJ, WGBH, 1986–95; played Starlight Roof, Boston, 1985; signed with Concord Jazz, 1991; featured artist, Pre-Fujitsu/Concord Jazz Festival party, honouring Carl Jefferson (pres., Concord Jazz), 1993; 10 consecutive appearances festival season, Japan; DJ, national public radio station, WICN, in Worcester, MA, 2000–. *Recordings include:* albums: A Night of Ballads (duets with Don Abney) 1984, But Not For Me (with Tommy Flanagan, George Mraz, Al Foster, Frank Wess) 1986, Love You Madly (with Richard Rodney Bennett, Kenny Barron, Kenny Burrell) 1988, The Real Thing (with Phil Woods, Grady Tate, Mike Renzi, Rufus Reid) 1989, Heart's Desire (Stef Scaggiari, John Lockwood, Colin Bailey) 1990, Concord All Stars On Cape Cod (with Scott Hamilton and Dave McKenna) 1991, Sweet and Slow (with Frank Wess, Tenor Sax) 1992, Concord Christmas (Mel Torme, Rosemary Clooney, various artists) 1993, When I Look In Your Eyes (with Bill Charlap, Steve Gilmore, Ron Vincent) 1994, The Songs Carmen Sang (with Phil Woods, Bill Charlap, Michael Moore, Ron Vincent) 1995, The Songs Ella and Louis Sang with Clark Terry 1996, Romantic Ellington with Benny Golson 1999, I Never Went Away (with Norman Simmons, Paul West, Paul Bollenback, Kenny Washington and Grady Tate) 2001, Whisper Sweet (with Norman Simmons, Paul West, Paul Bollenback, Kenny Washington, Grady Tate, Houston Person) 2003, Dearest Duke 2007. *Current Management:* Buck Spurr, Spurr Marketing Group, 215 Salem Street, Woburn, MA 01801, USA. *Telephone:* (781) 438-3814. *E-mail:* rumhilda@aol.com. *Website:* www.carolsloane.com.

SLUIJS, Ben, MMus; Belgian jazz musician (saxophone); *Teacher, Conservatory and Academy of Antwerp;* b. 6 March 1967, Antwerp; two d. *Education:* Antwerp Jazz Studio with John Ruocco, Brussels Conservatory with Steve Houben, classes with David Liebman in USA. *Career:* has played with Philippe Catherine, Toots Thielemans, Bert Van den Brink, Michel Herr, Bert Joris, Dre Pallemaerts, Hein Van De Geijn, Nathalie Loriers, Chris Joris, Joe Fonda, John Betsch; Serge Lazarevitch, represented Belgium, EBU Big Band in Slovenia; Tutor, Brussels Conservatory. *Recordings include:* Till Next Time, with Ben Sluijs Quintet 1991, Reminiscense, with Miriam Alter Quintet 1994, Chromatic History, with Octurn 1994, Silent Walk, with Miriam Alter Quintet 1996, Ocean, with Octurn 1996, Hamp Digs Ham, with François Descamps octet 1997, Food for Free, with Ben Sluijs Quartet 1997, Coast to Coast, with Paolo Radoni Quartet 1999, Candy Century with Ben Sluijs Quartet 1999, Round, with Octurn 2000, Stones, with Eric Vermeulen 2001, Seasounds, with Ben Sluijs Quartet 2001, Flying Circles, with Ben Sluijs Quartet 2002, Ancesthree, with Hendrik Braekman & Piet Verbist 2002, True Nature, with Ben Sluijs Quartet 2005, Somewhere in Between, with Ben Sluijs Quartet 2006, The Unplayables, with Ben Sluijs Quartet 2007, Let Me Hear A Simple Song, with Radonis Tribe 2009, Brick Quartet, with the Brick Quartet 2010, Parity, in duo with Erik Vermeulen 2010, 3/4 Peace, Christian Mendoza and Brice Soniano 2012, Decades, in duo with Erik Vermeulen 2014, A Turkey Is Better Eaten, with Augusto Pirodda Quartet 2014, Rainy Days on the Common Land, with 3/4 Peace 2015. *Honours:* Jack Van Poll Award 1991, Antoon Van Dijck Award 1999. *Telephone:* (8) 710-77-79. *E-mail:* bensluijs@

hotmail.com. *Address:* Jean de la Hoeselaan 48, 1080 Brussels, Belgium (home). *Telephone:* (8) 710-77-79 (home). *E-mail:* bensluijs@hotmail.com. *Website:* bensluijs.be.

SLUSHER, Michael Dennis, BS; American musician (trombone), arranger and producer; b. 13 Nov. 1949, Oliver Springs, Tennessee, USA. *Education:* Brevard Community College, North Texas State University. *Career:* musician, Elvis Presley 1977–79; resident musician, venues in Las Vegas 1977–82; producer, arranger, Take Cover Enterprises, Beverly Hills 1983–86; Associate Producer, television and radio commercials 1984–86; independent producer, arranger, Seattle 1986–; musician with artists including: Frank Sinatra, Sammy Davis Jr, Tony Bennett, Righteous Brothers, Tom Jones, Glen Campbell, Paul Anka, Pearl Bailey; also played for orchestras with Tommy Dorsey, Si Zentner, Tex Beneke, Thad Jones, Mel Lewis.

SMALE, Joanne R. Muroff, BA; American/Canadian public relations executive and consultant; *CEO, Planet3 Communications Ltd;* b. 20 June 1949, Brooklyn, New York, USA. *Education:* Univ. of Miami. *Career:* Pres. Joanne Smale Productions Ltd 1980–; currently CEO Planet3 Communications Ltd; fmr mem. Nat. Bd of Dirs, Acad. of Canadian Cinema and Television, Bd of Canadian Ind. Recording Producers Asscn (fmr Vice-Pres.), Metronome and the World of Comedy Int. Film Festival; has also been involved with Canadian Women in Radio and Television (CWRT/CWC, Founding Bd mem.), Toronto Women in Film and Television (TWIFT/WIFT), Canadian Showcasing Internationally, Toronto Entertainment Dist Asscn, Canadian Ind. Film Caucus, Int. Fed. of Festival Orgs (FIDOF), VideoFact; projects in entertainment industry have varied from performers, cultural events, charities and benefits to industry conferences and awards; works as producer and publicist for numerous theatre productions, nightclub openings, sports, arts and cultural events as well as entertainment industry events; has represented The Juno Awards, du Maurier Downtown Jazz Festival, WOMAD, Molson Million Thoroughbred Race/Woodbine Race Course, The Moscow Circus (nat. tour), Caribana, Mariposa Folk Festival, Toronto Int. Film Festival Symposium, Toronto Jewish Film Festival, Hot Docs, imagineNATIVE, ReelWorld Film Festival, Toronto Corso Fiesta, Taste of Little Italy, Gov.-Gen. Awards in Visual Arts, amongst others; involved in numerous charities and benefits, including Freeing The Human Spirit: Jeremy Irons and Kate McGarrigle 07, Sistering: 5th Annual Funny Girls and Dynamic Divas 07, Rekindle The Light Festival (held in conjunction with Commonwealth Foreign Ministers Conf.) 1988; part of successful Arts Against Apartheid week-long festival held in Toronto under auspices of Toronto Arts Against Apartheid Foundation; acted as Toronto base on behalf of Nelson Mandela Reception Cttee during visit of Nelson Mandela to Canada 1990; has worked with United Way of Greater Toronto, Seva Service Soc., Tears Are Not Enough, EcoFest, Lake Ontario Keepers, Family Farm Tributes, Canadian Give the Gift of Literacy Foundation and Canadian Landmine Foundation – Peacekeepers Initiative; clients include the Toronto Star – launch of entertainment section 'What's ON', NOW, eye Weekly, CFNY, True North Records, Putumayo Records, Eagle Rock Entertainment Canada, Sam the Record Man, as well as Molson Ontario Breweries Ltd, Harbourfront Centre, icebergMedia.com and Chart Communications Inc.; served as Canadian Rep. for events including New Music Seminar in New York, Int. Music and Media Conf., Montreux, Switzerland, American Video Conf. and Awards, Los Angeles; has prepared publicity campaigns for premiers of Allan King's most recent films and other film and TV campaigns. *Films:* two documentaries: Mondo Moscow, The Un-Canadians. *Honours:* six gold and two platinum albums for her work with Rough Trade, Murray McLauchlan and Bruce Cockburn, platinum album for contrib. with 'Oh What A Feeling – A Vital Collection of Canadian Music' by CARAS, platinum album for work on The World Wrestling Fed.'s album 'WWF – The Music Vol. 4', Canadian Music Week Award for Best Ind. Publicist 2000. *Address:* Planet3 Communications Ltd, 612-103 Avenue Road, Toronto, ON M5R 2G9, Canada (office). *Telephone:* (647) 346-4101 (office). *Fax:* (647) 346-4104 (office). *E-mail:* info@planet3com.net (office). *Website:* www.planet3com.net (office).

SMALL, Heather; British singer; b. 20 Jan. 1965, London. *Career:* fmr singer in soul group, Hothouse; lead singer dance group, M People 1990–; numerous concerts and festival appearances; solo artist 2000–. *Play:* The Vagina Monologues (West End, London) 2005. *Recordings include:* albums: with M People: Northern Soul 1992, Northern Soul Extended 1992, Elegant Slumming (Mercury Music Prize 1994) 1993, Bizarre Fruit 1994, Bizarre Fruit Vol. 2 1995, Fresco 1997, Testify 1999, 3 Originals 2003; solo: Proud 2000, Close to a Miracle 2006. *Honours:* BRIT Award for Best Dance Act 1994, 1995, Freedom of Manchester 1999, Urban Music Award for lifetime's work 2005. *Current Management:* c/o Joe McGairl, Bandana Management Ltd, Apartment 1, 100 Kings Road, London, SW6 4LZ, England. *Telephone:* (20) 7736-4810. *E-mail:* joe@banman.co.uk. *Website:* www.banman.co.uk.

SMÁRASON, Örvar Þóreyjarson; Icelandic musician (electronics). *Career:* mem. experimental group, Múm 1997–. *Recordings include:* albums: Yesterday Was Dramatic – Today Was OK 2000, Please Smile My Noise Bleed 2001, Finally We Are No One 2002, Summer Make Good 2004. *Address:* c/o Fat Cat Records, PO Box 3400, Brighton, BN1 4WD, England. *Website:* www.randomsummer.com.

SMBATYAN, Armen B.; Armenian diplomatist, musician and composer; *Executive Director, Humanitarian Co-operation Council, Commonwealth of Independent States;* b. 17 Nov. 1954, Yerevan. *Education:* Yerevan State

Conservatoire. *Career:* pianist and composer; Rector, Yerevan State Conservatoire 1995, 1998–2002; Minister of Culture, Youth Affairs and Sport 1996–98; Amb. to Russian Fed. 2002–09; Exec. Dir, Humanitarian Co-operation Council, CIS 2010–. *Address:* The Commonwealth of Independent States, 220000 Minsk, Kirava 17, Belarus (office). *Telephone:* (17) 222-35-17 (office). *Website:* www.cis.minsk.by (office).

SMEAR, Pat; American rock musician (guitar, bass guitar, piano), songwriter and singer; b. (Georg Albert Ruthenberg), 5 Aug. 1959, Los Angeles, Calif. *Career:* mem., numerous punk and rock bands including Germs 1977–80, The Adolescents 1980, Twisted Roots 1981, 45 Grave 1981; solo artist 1982–; mem. Deathfolk 1989–92; touring guitarist, Nirvana 1993–94; mem. Foo Fighters (with ex-Nirvana mem. Dave Grohl) 1995–97, touring mem. 2006–10, rejoined as full-time mem. 2010–, collaborators include Paul McCartney, Mike Watt, Nina Hagen. *Films:* Back and Forth (Grammy Award for Best Long Form Music Video) 2012. *Recordings:* albums: with Germs: GI 1979; solo: Ruthensmear 1987, So You Fell in Love with a Musician 1992; with Deathfolk: Deathfolk 1989, Deathfolk II 1992; with Nirvana: MTV Unplugged in New York 1994; with Foo Fighters: The Colour and the Shape 1997, Skin and Bones (certain tracks only) 2006, Echoes, Silence, Patience & Grace (certain tracks only) 2007, Wasting Light (Grammy Award for Best Rock Album 2012) 2011, Sonic Highways 2014. *Honours:* with Foo Fighters: American Music Award for Favorite Alternative Artist 2011, BRIT Awards for Int. Group 2012, 2015, Grammy Awards for Best Rock Performance (for Walk) 2012, for Best Rock Song (for Walk) 2012, (for Cut Me Some Slack) 2014, for Best Hard Rock/Metal Performance (for White Limo) 2012, NME Award for Best Int. Band 2012. *Current Management:* c/o Gold Mountain Entertainment, 12400 Ventura Boulevard, #444, Studio City, CA 91604, USA. *Telephone:* (818) 508-2210. *Website:* www.gmemusic.com.

SMIETANA, Jarek Zdzislaw; Polish musician (guitar); b. 29 March 1951, Krakow; m. Anna Smietana 1978; one d. *Education:* Studied Class Composition and Arranging, Academy of Music, Katowice, Poland. *Career:* One of the major jazz musicians in Poland; First Band, Extra Ball, formed 1974; One of the most successful European jazz groups; mem, Polish Jazz Society. *Compositions:* A Few Warm Words; Follow the Fellow; Flowers in Mind; Children of Time; Sounds and Colours. *Recordings:* Ballads and Other Songs, 1996; Jarek Smietana Quintet Live, 1996; Phone Consultations, 1997; Songs and Other Ballads, 1998; Art Farmer Plays Standards, 1998; Speak Easy, 1999. *Publications:* Jazz Songs by Smietana. *Honours:* No 1 Jazz Guitarist in Poland, prizes every year since 1983; Fryderyk, Polish Music Award, 1998. *E-mail:* smietana@onet.pl. *Website:* www.jareksmietana.pl.

SMITH, Adrian Frederick; British musician (guitar) and songwriter; b. 27 Feb. 1957, Hackney, London, England. *Career:* fmr mem. Urchin; mem. heavy metal band Iron Maiden 1980–90, 1999–; formed ASAP (Adrian Smith And Project) 1989–; Founder-mem. Psycho Motel 1996–97. *Recordings include:* albums: with Iron Maiden: Killers 1981, The Number of the Beast 1982, Piece of Mind 1983, Powerslave 1984, Somewhere in Time 1986, Seventh Son of a Seventh Son 1988, Brave New World 2000, Dance of Death 2003, It's a Matter of Life and Death 2006, Flight 666 2009, The Final Frontier 2010, The Book of Souls 2015; with ASAP: Silver and Gold 1989; with Psycho Motel: State of Mind 1996, Welcome to the World 1997. *Honours:* Ivor Novello Award 2000, BRIT Award for Best British Live Act 2009. *Current Management:* c/o Phantom Music Managment Ltd, Bridle House 36 Bridle Lane, London, W1F 9BZ, England. *Telephone:* (845) 331-3300. *Fax:* (845) 331-3500. *Website:* www.phantom-music.com; www.ironmaiden.com.

SMITH, Bryan Christopher; British recording engineer, producer, programmer and musician (guitar, keyboards); b. 21 Dec. 1954, St Albans, Hertfordshire; m. Denise 1974; one s. one d. *Career:* Red Bus Records 1980–82; member, French Impression 1984–86; member, The Big Push 1992–; founded Farm Factory Studios 1990; support tours: Jools Holland, Cool Notes; member, Hello 1993; mem. PRS. *Recordings:* musician, engineer, programmer for Move Your Skin, And Why Not, Amazing Colossal Men: Buddy's Song, Chesney Hawkes; also recorded Jon Anderson/Francis Dunnery 1991, Steve Harley demos 1994.

SMITH, Chad; American musician (drums); b. 25 Oct. 1962, St Paul, MN. *Career:* mem., Red Hot Chili Peppers 1988–; numerous tours, festivals and television appearances; simultaneous mem., Honeymoon Stitch, Chickenfoot, Chad Smith's Bombastic Meatballs. *Recordings include:* albums: with Red Hot Chili Peppers: Mother's Milk 1989, Blood Sugar Sex Magik 1991, One Hot Minute 1995, Californication 1999, By The Way 2002, Live In Hyde Park 2004, Stadium Arcadium (MTV Europe Music Award for Best Album) 2006, I'm With You 2011; solo: Cyberfunk 1993, Rhythm Train 2010; with John Fogerty: Blue Moon Swamp 1997; with Private Parts: Private Parts 1997; with Leah Andreone: Alchemy 1998; with Chickenfoot: Chickenfoot 2009, Chickenfoot III 2011; with Chad Smith's Bombastic Meatbats: Meet the Meatbats 2009, More Meat 2010; other credits include: George Clinton, Dixie Chicks, John Fogerty, Glenn Hughes, Kid Rock. *Honours:* MTV Music Video Award 1992, American Music Award for Favorite Alternative Artist 2000, MTV Awards for Best Live Act, Best Rock 2002, American Music Award for Favorite Pop/Rock Band 2006, for Favorite Alternative Music Artist 2006, Grammy Award for Best Rock Performance by a Duo or Group with Vocal (for Dani California) 2007. *Current Management:* Lindy Goetz Management, 11116 Aqua Vista, Suite 39, Studio City, CA 91602, USA. *Address:* c/o Rockinfreakapotamus, The Red Hot

Chili Peppers Official Fan Club, PO Box 801, Rockford, MI 49341, USA. *Website:* www.redhotchilipeppers.com; www.therhythmtrain.com.

SMITH, Connie; American country singer, songwriter and musician (guitar, piano); b. (Constance June Meador), 14 Aug. 1941, Elkhart, Indiana, USA; m. 1st Jerry Smith; m. 2nd Marty Stuart 1997. *Career:* as a teenager, appearances with Floyd Miller's Square Dance Band; weekly appearances on West Virginia local TV; solo artist 1963–; became a Christian and recorded gospel material as well as country music, early 1970s–; mem. Grand Ole Opry 1971. *Film appearances:* Second Fiddle to a Steel Guitar 1965, The Las Vegas Hillbillys 1966, The Road to Nashville 1967, Hell on Wheels 1967, The Hi-Lo Country 1998. *Compositions include:* I'll Come Running. *Recordings include:* albums: Connie Smith 1965, Cute 'n' Country 1965, Miss Smith Goes To Nashville 1966, Sings Great Sacred Songs 1966, Born to Sing 1966, Downtown Country 1967, Connie in the Country 1967, Sings Bill Anderson 1967, Soul of Country Music 1967, I Love Charley Brown 1968, Sunshine and Rain 1968, Connie's Country 1969, Back in Baby's Arms 1969, I Never Once Stopped Loving You 1970, Where Is My Castle 1971, Just One Time 1971, Come Along and Walk With Me 1972, Ain't We Havin' Us a Good Time 1972, If It Ain't Love and Other Great Dallas Frazier Songs 1972, A Lady Named Smith 1973, God is Abundant 1973, That's the Way Love Goes 1974, Sings Hank Williams Gospel 1975, The Song We Fell in Love To 1976, I Don't Wanna Talk it Over Anymore 1976, Pure Connie Smith 1977, New Horizons 1978, Connie Smith 1998, Long Line of Heartaches 2011; with Barbara Fairchild and Sharon White: Love Never Fails 2003. *Honours:* CMA Award for Song of the Year (for Once A Day) 1971. *Address:* c/o Fat City Artists, 1226 17th Avenue S, Suite 2, Nashville, TN 37212, USA. *Website:* www.conniesmithmusic.com.

SMITH, Curt; American musician (bass guitar) and singer; b. 24 June 1961, Bath, Avon, England; m.; two d. *Education:* attended coll. *Career:* professional musician from age 18; founder mem., Graduate 1979–81; founder mem., Tears For Fears 1981–92, 2003–; solo artist 1991–; mem. concert band Mayfield; mem. Musicians' Union, PRS, AFTRA, BMI. *Recordings include:* albums: with Graduate: Acting Your Age 1979; with Tears for Fears: The Hurting 1983, Songs From The Big Chair 1985, The Seeds Of Love 1989, Everybody Loves A Happy Ending 2004; solo: Soul On Board 1993, Aeroplane 2000, Halfway, pleased 2008; with Mayfield: Mayfield 1998. *Honours:* Smash Hits Award for Most Promising New Act 1982, BRIT Award for Best British Single 1985, BMI Performance Award (for single Head Over Heels 1985) 1991. *Current Management:* c/o Arlene Wszalek, SW14 Group, 2934 Beverly Glen Circle, Suite 428, Los Angeles, CA 90077, USA. *Telephone:* (818) 232-5620. *Fax:* (818) 232-5620. *E-mail:* aw@sw14group.com. *Website:* sw14group.com; new .curtsmithofficial.com.

SMITH, Daniel Campbell; British singer, songwriter, musician (keyboards, percussion) and record producer; b. 14 July 1986, London, England. *Education:* King's Coll. School, Wimbledon, Univ. of Leeds. *Career:* Founder-mem., Bastille 2010–; released debut single 2011; signed to Virgin Records 2011. *Recordings:* album: with Bastille: Bad Blood 2013. *Honours:* BRIT Award for British Breakthrough Act 2014. *Address:* c/o Virgin EMI Records, Universal Music Group, 364–366 Kensington High Street, London, W14 8NS, England (office). *Telephone:* (20) 7471-5000 (office). *E-mail:* contact@virginemirecords .com (office). *Website:* www.virginemirecords.com (office); bastillebastille.com.

SMITH, Darran; British musician (guitar). *Career:* mem. rock band, Funeral for a Friend 2001–10. *Recordings include:* albums: Casually Dressed & Deep in Conversation 2003, Hours 2005, Tales Don't Tell Themselves 2007, Memory and Humanity 2008; with Tim McGraw: Let It Go/Set This Circus Down 2008, Greatest Hits Vols 1-3 2008, Southern Voice 2009, Number One Hits 2010, Emotional Traffic 2012. *Honours:* Kerrang! Award for Best British Band 2006.

SMITH, Geoff, BA, MBA, PhD; British songwriter and musician (piano); *Deputy Vice-Chancellor, Falmouth University;* b. 11 May 1966, Tynemouth, England; m. Nicola Walker Smith 1989; two s. *Education:* Nottingham Univ., Oxford Univ., Huddersfield Univ. *Career:* Head of Music, Bath Spa Univ.; f. School of Music and Performing Arts at Bath 2002; Deputy Vice-Chancellor, Falmouth Univ. 2008–; exec. mem., Music subject asscn; mem. exec. cttee, Universities South West. *Recordings include:* Albums: Gas Food Lodging 1993, Fifteen Wild Decembers 1994, Black Flowers 1997; with Mono: Formica Blues 1997; with Gap Mangione: Planet Gap: Big Band 1998; with Burning Bush: Klezmer and Hassidic Music 1998; others: The Garden 1991, Spaces and Places 2009. *Publications include:* American Originals (co-author) 1994; interviews with Harold Budd, Philip Glass, Steve Reich. *Honours:* debut album selected as Top 40 Album of the Year, BBC Music Magazine. *Address:* Falmouth University, Falmouth Campus, Woodlane, Falmouth, Cornwall, TR11 4RH, England (office). *Telephone:* (1326) 370423 (office). *E-mail:* geoff .smith@falmouth.ac.uk (office). *Website:* www.falmouth.ac.uk/content/ professor-geoff-smith (office).

SMITH, James (Jimmy); British musician (guitar, synthesizer) and songwriter; b. 2 Aug. 1984, Reading, Berks. *Education:* Abingdon School, Univ. of Hull. *Career:* fmr mem. Face Meets Grill; Founder-mem. Foals 2005–. *Recordings:* albums: with Foals: Antidotes 2008, Total Life Forever 2010, Holy Fire 2013, What Went Down 2015. *Honours:* with Foals: NME Awards for Best Track (for Spanish Sahara) 2011, (for Inhaler) 2013, Q Magazine Awards for Best Live Act 2013, for Best Act in the World Today 2015. *Current Management:* c/o Steve Matthews, Q Prime Management, 729 Seventh Avenue, #1600, New York, NY 10019, USA. *Telephone:* (212) 302-9790. *E-mail:* info@qprime.com. *Website:* www.qprime.com; www.foals.co.uk.

SMITH, James Edward, BA, MM; American jazz musician (guitar); *Professor of Jazz Studies, Central St University and University of Cincinnati College-Conservatory of Music;* b. 2 Aug. 1952, San Diego, Calif.; divorced; two s. two d. *Education:* Univ. of New Mexico, Wisconsin Conservatory of Music. *Career:* Prof. of Jazz Studies, Central St Univ. 1980–, Chair. Fine and Performing Arts 1999–2007; Adjunct, Assoc. Prof. of Jazz Guitar, Univ. of Cincinnati Coll., Conservatory of Music 1984–; four Nat. Public Radio Broadcasts 1992; performance at Nancy Jazz Festival, Nancy, France 1992, Newport Jazz Festival, Saratoga Springs, NY 2004, three pieces for Dayton Philharmonic Orchestra 2006; scholarly paper presented at Leeds Int. Jazz Conf., Leeds, UK 2002, 2010; mem. American Asscn of Univ. Profs. *Compositions:* Song For Om 1992, Second Sight 2004. *Recording:* Cincinnati Seven. *Publications:* Jazz Guitar: Theory and Technique 1982, Bebop Riffs 1990, Guitarists Guide To Technique 1992, Chord Thesaurus For Jazz Guitar 1994. *Honours:* Outstanding Service To Jazz Educ. 1988, 1997. *Current Management:* c/o Smith Management, 4189 Sugar Leaf, Dayton, OH 45440, USA. *Telephone:* (937) 369-7595. *Fax:* (937) 376-6415. *E-mail:* jazzgt01@gmail.com. *Address:* PO Box 1004, 1400 Brush Row Road, CSU, Wilberforce, OH 45384, USA (office). *Telephone:* (937) 369-7595 (office). *Fax:* (937) 376-6415 (office). *E-mail:* jim@ jazzgt.com (office). *Website:* jazzgt.com (office).

SMITH, Jamie; British musician (keyboards, drums) and producer. *Education:* Elliott School, London. *Career:* mem. The xx 2005–; collaborator with Gil Scott-Heron; producer and remixer for Drake, Radiohead. *Recordings:* albums: with The xx: xx (Mercury Music Prize 2010) 2009, Coexist 2012; with Gil Scott-Heron: We're New Here 2011. *Address:* c/o Young Turks, XL Recordings, 1 Codrington Mews, London, W11 2EH, England (office). *Telephone:* (20) 8870-7511 (office). *Fax:* (20) 8871-4178 (office). *E-mail:* theyoungturks@theyoungturks.co.uk (office). *Website:* thexx.info.

SMITH, Josh; American blues musician (guitar); b. 10 July 1979, Middletown, Connecticut. *Education:* Private study, 9 years. *Career:* member, band, the Rhino Cats, 1993–96; mem. Josh Smith and the Frost; opened for bands including Buddy Guy; The Fabulous T-Birds; Allman Brothers Band; mem, ASCAD. *Recordings:* albums: with the Rhino Cats: Born Under a Blue Sign 1995, Woodsheddin 1996; with the Frost: Too Damn Cold 1997, Woman 2000; with High Karate: High Karate, 1998; with One Eighty: Crackerjack, 1998; solo: Deep Roots 2006, Inception 2009. *Honours:* Best Blues Band, State of Florida, Florida Jam Magazine, Jammy Awards, 1994. *Address:* 8920 N W 14th St, Pembroke Pines, FL 33024, USA. *E-mail:* joshandniki@aol.com. *Website:* www.joshsmithguitar.com.

SMITH, Karen M.; American artist development and record company executive; b. 23 July 1958, Chicago, Illinois, USA; m. A. J. Smith 1994. *Education:* college. *Career:* owner, Glow In The Dark Rehearsals, (rehearsal space in Chicago); owner, record company Conscience Music/TOW Records, Chicago 1989–98; Consultant for Ex-Idols; PO! Exec. Producer for: Wait For Light; S Is For Space; Artist Developer and Property Man., Feather Building 1995–2006; Consultant and Program Dir, Hubbard Street Mural Project 2000–; Property Man., Two Ponyz Ranceh 2006–; Grant Writer and Volunteer Manzano Mountain Art Council 2008–; mem, NAMM; NARAS. *Honours:* Gottlieb Award, Best Rehearsal Studio, 1994. *Address:* PO Box 740, Oak Park, IL 60303, USA.

SMITH, Keely; American singer and actor; b. 9 March 1932, Norfolk, VA; m. Louis Prima 1953 (divorced 1961). *Career:* joined Louis Prima's band aged 16 1948; settled in Las Vegas, establishing a 'lounge act'; solo artist 1956–; occasional live performances in Las Vegas. *Film appearances:* Thunder Road 1958, Senior Prom 1958, Hey Boy Hey Girl 1959. *Recordings include:* I Wish You Love 1957, Politely 1958, Swingin' Pretty 1959, Because You're Mine 1959, Be My Love 1960, Swing You Lovers 1960, Dearly Beloved 1961, What Kind of Fool Am I 1961, Cherokeely Swings 1962, Keely Smith Wishes You A Merry Christmas 1963, Little Girl Blue Little Girl New 1964, Keely Smith Sings The Lennon and McCartney Song Book 1965, That Old Black Magic 1965, I'm In Love Again 1985, Swing Swing Swing 2000, Keely Sings Sinatra 2001, Keely Sings Count Basie Style with Strings 2002. *Honours:* Cherokee Medal of Honor 2000.

SMITH, Laura; Canadian singer, songwriter and musician (guitar); b. 18 March 1952, Ontario. *Career:* solo artist; numerous collaborations; mem. SOCAN, CARAS, ECMA, AVLA. *Recordings include:* Between the Earth and My Soul; It's a Personal Thing; Agnes Browne (soundtrack, with Ed Shearmur). *Honours:* ECMA Female Artist 1996, ECMA Album 1996, Gemini Award for Best Performance 1997. *E-mail:* laura.smith@laurasmith.ca. *Website:* www.laurasmith.ca.

SMITH, Lonnie, (Dr Lonnie Smith); American jazz musician (organ); b. 3 July 1942, Lackawanna, NY. *Career:* formed quartet with George Benson 1966; solo recordings 1966–; numerous collaborations and credits including Eric Allison, Ray Brown, Jr., Lou Donaldson, Marvin Gaye, Monty Guy, Dave Hubbard, Javon Jackson, Jimmy McGriff, Cyrus Pace; f. own record label, Pilgrimage Productions 2012. *Recordings:* albums: Finger-Lickin' Good 1966, Think! 1968, Turning Point 1969, Move Your Hand 1970, Drives 1970, Mama Wailer 1971, When the Night is Right! 1975, Afrodesia 1975, Keep on Lovin' 1976, Funk Reaction 1977, Gotcha 1978, Afro Blue 1993, Foxy Lady: A Tribute to Hendrix 1994, Purple Haze 1995, The Turbanator 2000, Boogaloo to Beck 2003, Too Damn Hot 2004, Jungle Soul 2006, Rise Up! 2009, Spiral 2010, The Healer 2012. *Honours:* Jazz Journalists Asscn Award for Keyboards Player of the Year 2003, 2005, 2008, 2009, 2012, 2013, 2014. *Current Management:* c/o

Myles Weinstein, Unlimited Myles, 6 Imaginary Place, Matawan, NJ 07747, USA. *Telephone:* (732) 566-2881. *Fax:* (732) 566-8157. *E-mail:* myles@unlimitedmyles.com. *Website:* www.unlimitedmyles.com. *E-mail:* info@drlonniesmith.com (home). *Website:* www.drlonniesmith.com (home).

SMITH, Mark; American musician (drums). *Career:* mem., Electric Company –1994; founder mem., The American Analog Set 1995–. *Recordings include:* albums: The Fun Of Watching Fireworks 1996, From Our Living Room To Yours 1997, The Golden Band 1999, Know By Heart 2001, Through The 1990s: Singles & Unreleased 2001, Updates 2002, Promise Of Love 2003, Set Free 2005. *E-mail:* requests@amanset.com (home). *Website:* www.amanset.com.

SMITH, Mark 'Hitman'; British producer, remixer, programmer and musician (keyboards); b. 20 Oct. 1972, Doncaster, Yorkshire. *Education:* High Melton Coll., Doncaster, Royal School of Music. *Career:* producer, remixer, for Music Factory Records; commercial DJ; mem. Musicians' Union. *Recordings:* Mixes include: Rock 'N' Roll Dance Party, Jive Bunny; Nolans Hitmix; Hot Chocolate Hitmix; Glamma; Paradox; Remixes include: Kylie Minogue; 2 Unlimited; Kelly Marie. *Publications:* contrib. to Mixology Magazine.

SMITH, Mark Edward; British singer, songwriter and musician (guitar, bass guitar); b. 5 March 1957, Salford, Manchester, England; m. Laura Elise (Brix) Smith (divorced 1990). *Career:* founder mem., The Fall 1977–. *Recordings include:* albums: Live At The Witch Trials 1979, Dragnet 1979, Totale's Turns (It's Now Or Never) 1980, Grotesque (After The Gramme) 1980, Slates 1981, Hex Enduction Hour 1982, Room To Love 1982, Perverted By Language 1983, The Wonderful And Frightening World Of... 1984, This Nation's Saving Grace 1985, Bend Sinister 1986, The Frenz Experiment 1988, I Am Kurious Oranji 1988, Seminal Live 1989, Extricate 1990, 458489 1990, 458489: B Sides 1990, Shiftwork 1991, Code Selfish 1992, The Infotainment Scan 1993, Sinister Waltz 1996, The Marshall Suite 1999, The Unutterable 2000, Are You Are Missing Winner 2001, 2G + 2 2002, Fall Heads Roll 2005, Reformation! Post-TLC 2007, Imperial Wax Solvent 2008, Your Future Our Clutter 2010, Ersatz GB 2011, Re-Mit 2013. *Publication:* Hey! Luciani (play), Renegade: The Lives and Tales of Mark E Smith (auto-biog.) 2008. *Address:* c/o Domino Records, PO Box 47029, London, SW18 1WD, England (office). *Website:* www.dominorecordco.com (office).

SMITH, Michael (Mike) John; British artist manager, music publisher and media consultant; b. 16 Nov. 1946, Edgware, Middx; m. Sally James 1978; four s. *Career:* producer, Asst Head, Light Entertainment, London Weekend Television 1968–76; Head of A&R, Decca Records 1976–78; Gen. Man., Vice-Pres. GTO Records 1978–80; Owner, Yellow Balloon Productions Ltd, Mike Music Ltd, Yellow Balloon Music, Yellow Balloon Records, Universal Media Management Ltd, Unitapes UK Ltd, Unismart Ltd, Locationsurrey.com Ltd; man. or producer of: Rick Wakeman, Bruce Foxton, Adam and The Ants, Billy Ocean, The Moody Blues, The Smurfs, The Dooleys, Rolf Harris, Hazel O'Connor; mem. Musicians' Union, ACCA, Performing Rights Soc. *Honours:* Tokyo Music Festival Award, award-winning producer of London Bridge TV programme, 30 Gold and Silver discs as producer or man. of established acts. *Address:* Freshwater House, Outdowns, Effingham, Surrey, KT24 5QR, England (home). *Telephone:* (1483) 281500 (home). *Fax:* (1483) 281501 (home). *E-mail:* yellowbal@aol.com (office); unimediaman@aol.com (office). *Website:* www.locationsurrey.com (office).

SMITH, Patti; American singer, songwriter, musician (guitar), poet and artist; b. 30 Dec. 1946, Chicago, Ill.; d. of Grant Smith and Beverly Smith; m. Fred 'Sonic' Smith 1980 (died 1994); two s. *Education:* Glassboro State Teachers Coll., NJ. *Career:* avant-garde poet, singer and artist; fmr rock critic for Creem, Rock, Crawdaddy and Rolling Stone magazines 1970s; solo artist 1972–, forming Patti Smith Group 1974; Artistic Dir Meltdown Festival, South Bank Centre, London 2005. *Recordings include:* albums: Horses 1975, Radio Ethiopia 1976, Easter 1978, Wave 1979, Dream Of Life 1988, Gone Again 1996, Peace And Noise 1997, Gung Ho 2000, Land 1975–2002 2002, Twelve 2007, The Coral Sea (with Kevin Shields) 2008, Banga 2012. *Publications:* Seventh Heaven (poems) 1971, Kodak (poems) 1972, Cowboy Mouth (play, with Sam Shepard) 1972, Witt (poems) 1973, Babel 1978, Early Work 1970–1979 (poems) 1980, Woolgathering (short stories) 1993, The Coral Sea (prose poems in memory of Robert Mapplethorpe) 1996, Auguries of Innocence (poems) 2006, Just Kids (Nat. Book Award for Non-Fiction 2010) 2010, M Train 2015. *Honours:* Commdr, Ordre des Arts et des Lettres 2005; inducted into Rock and Roll Hall of Fame 2007, ASCAP Founders Award 2010, Polar Music Prize, Royal Swedish Acad. of Music 2011, Katharine Hepburn Medal, Bryn Mawr Coll. 2013. *Address:* c/o Ecco Press, HarperCollins, 195 Broadway, New York, NY 10007, USA (office). *Fax:* (212) 207-7145 (office). *Website:* www.pattismith.net (home).

SMITH, Paul, BA, MA; British singer; b. 13 March 1979, Billingham, Stockton-on-Tees, England. *Education:* Univ. of Newcastle. *Career:* mem., Maxïmo Park 2001–; also solo artist 2010–. *Recordings include:* albums: with Maxïmo Park: A Certain Trigger 2005, Our Earthly Pleasures 2007, Quicken the Heart 2009, The National Health 2012, Too Much Information 2014; solo: Margins 2010. *Current Management:* Prolifica Management, Unit 1, 32 Caxton Road, London W12 8AJ, England. *Telephone:* (20) 8740-9920. *Fax:* (20) 8740-2976. *E-mail:* info@prolifica.co.uk. *Website:* www.prolificamanagement.co.uk; www.maximopark.com.

SMITH, Richard (Rick) David; British programmer, musician (keyboard), composer and producer; b. 1960, South Wales. *Education:* Univ. of Wales, Cardiff. *Career:* mem. The Screen Gemz 1981–83, Freur 1983–86, Underworld 1986–, Lemon Interrupt 1992; remixer for artists, including Bjork, The Chemical Brothers, Depeche Mode, Dreadzone, Fire Island, Front 242, Gat Decor, Leftfield, Massive Attack, One Dove, Orbital, Shakespears Sister, Saint Etienne, U2, William Orbit. *Recordings include:* albums: with Freur: Doot Doot 1983, Get Us Out Of Here 1985; with Underworld: Underneath The Radar 1988, Change The Weather 1989, Dubnobasswithmyheadman 1993, Second Toughest In The Infants 1996, Beaucoup Fish 1999, Everything Everything 2000, A Hundred Days Off 2002, Anthology 1992–2002 (compilation) 2002, Back To Mine (selection of other artists' work) 2003, Oblivion with Bells 2007, Barking 2010. *Current Management:* Jukes Productions Ltd, PO Box 13995, London, W9 2FL, England. *Telephone:* (20) 7286-9532. *Fax:* (20) 7286-4739. *E-mail:* jukes@easynet.co.uk. *Website:* www.jukesproductions.co.uk; www.underworldlive.com.

SMITH, Robert; British singer and musician (guitar); b. 21 April 1959, Blackpool, England; m. Mary Poole 1988. *Career:* founder mem., Easy Cure (with Laurence Tolhurst and Michael Dempsey) while at school 1976, band changed name to The Cure; temporary mem., Siouxsie & The Banshees 1979, 1983–84; mem., Glove 1983; numerous world tours with The Cure. *Recordings:* albums: with The Cure: Three Imaginary Boys 1979, Seventeen Seconds 1980, Faith 1981, Pornography 1982, The Top 1984, Concert 1984, The Head On The Door 1985, Staring At The Sea 1986, Kiss Me, Kiss Me, Kiss Me 1987, Disintegration 1989, Mixed Up 1990, Wish 1992, Show 1993, Paris 1993, Wild Mood Swings 1996, Galore 1997, Bloodflowers 2000, Greatest Hits 2001, Join the Dots: B-Sides and Rarities 1978–2001 2004, The Cure 2004, 4:13 Dream 2008; with Siouxsie & The Banshees: Hyaena 1983; with Glove: Blue Sunshine 1983. *Honours:* BRIT Award for Best British Group 1992. *Address:* c/o Geffen Records, Polydor, 364–366 Kensington High Street, London W14 8NS, England (office). *Website:* www.polydor.co.uk (office); www.thecure.com.

SMITH, Robert (Rob) Kevin, BA, MMus; British musician (saxophones, clarinets, keyboards, percussion, electronics); b. 17 Dec. 1960, West Yorks., England; s. of Harold Smith and Marian Smith; m. Sarah Stone 1990; two d. *Education:* Univ. of Nottingham, King's Coll., London, Royal Welsh Coll. of Music and Drama, Cardiff. *Career:* with Four Quartets, appeared on HTV 1987, at 'Outside In' jazz festivals 1988, 1993; Brecon Jazz Festival 1984–; two Arctic Songs with London Sinfonietta Voices 1994; Lecturer in Composition, Bath Spa Univ. Coll. 1996–2006; Musical Dir, Wonderbrass Community Jazz Orchestra, Moving Being Theatre (for Tesla and Brecht's Galileo projects) 2004–06; Sr Lecturer in Popular Music, Cardiff School of Creative and Cultural Industries, Univ. of Glamorgan, S Wales 2006–; composer, writer, presenter, Radio Tesla (STAR Radio) 2006; mem. Performing Right Soc., Soc. for Promotion of New Music. *Compositions:* Anonymous Twentieth Century 1998, Toccata Lachrymae and Tenebrae 2001, Gwen John Suite 2002, I Thought I Heard Buddy Bolden Shout 2006, The Idea of North (for Bath Int. Music Festival) 2006, Sacred Sites (for Improvisation Continuums Festival, Cardiff) 2007. *Film scores:* The Knowledge 1996, The Confectioner 1997, Minim 1999, Overland 2001, Strange Beauty 2002, Cardiff/River 2011. *Radio:* music for I Thought I Heard Buddy Bolden Shout (BBC Radio 3) 2006. *Recordings:* with Heavy Quartet: Poum 1988, A Screaming Tradition 1989, Short Stories 1991, Carnivore 1995, Delete Memory 2001, Machine 2004, Hardware 2009; with The Diggers: Imbolc 1993; with Wonderbrass: Daisy Roots 2001, Jive at a Five 2007, Bone Drops 2009, Blown Away 2011; musicals: Race 1989, Starcross'd 1991, Dangerous Acquaintances 1997. *Honours:* Fellow, Higher Educ. Acad.. *Address:* Edge of Europe Productions, 93 Pencisely Road, Llandaf, Cardiff, CF5 1DJ, Wales (office). *E-mail:* rksmith@glam.ac.uk (office).

SMITH, Ruthie Elaine Foster, BA, PG Dip Social Work; British jazz/classical musician (saxophones), singer, composer and psychotherapist; *Psychotherapist, The Flame Centre*; b. 24 Nov. 1950, Manchester, England; d. of Malcolm Pascoe Smith and Elaine Smith. *Education:* York Univ., UK Council for Psychotherapy registered psychotherapist. *Career:* musical career spanning jazz and classical music; recorded contemporary songs for BBC while at York Univ.; mem. feminist rock band, Stepney Sisters 1974–76; Founder-mem. all-female jazz band, The Guest Stars, British Council tour 1985; UK and world tours, int. jazz festival, radio, TV and club appearances, including Ronnie Scott's, London and The Blue Note Club, New York; played and recorded with Stepney Sisters, The Guest Stars, Toot Sweet (with Jim Dvorak, Bass Julia Doyle and Frances Knight) and in South African band, District Six; currently sings in classical ensembles (Thomas Tallis Chamber Choir and Illuminations), voice recitals (St James's, Piccadilly), plays in soul band Xpensive, Stepney Sisters, Toot Sweet and The Guest Stars (London Jazz Festival 2013); served on Greater London Arts Council panel for two years; also has a separate career as a psychotherapist; mem. Musicians' Union. *Recordings include:* three albums with The Guest Stars, two albums with District Six, albums with Toot Sweet, Stepney Sisters; live recordings for BBC. *Honours:* Arts Council of GB Jazz Bursary to compose and perform a jazz suite on Radio 3 Jazz in Britain with Toot Sweet. *Address:* The Flame Centre, Unit 3, The Chandlery, 50 Westminster Bridge Road, London, SE1 7QY, England (office). *Telephone:* 7971-964438 (mobile) (office). *Fax:* (20) 7928-2752 (office). *E-mail:* ruthie.efsmith@gmail.com (office); ruthie@theflamecentre.co.uk (office). *Website:* www.theflamecentre.co.uk (office).

SMITH, Samuel (Sam) Frederick; British singer and songwriter; b. 19 May 1992, London, England; s. of Frederick Smith and Kate Cassidy. *Education:* St Mary's Catholic School, Bishop's Stortford. *Career:* fmr mem. Youth Music Theatre UK; backing singer for Joanna Eden 2007; featured singer on Disclosure's single Latch 2012, on Naughty Boy's single La La La 2013; released debut solo single Lay Me Down 2014; sang Writing on the Wall, theme song for James Bond film Spectre 2015. *Recordings include:* album: In the Lonely Hour (MOBO Award for Best Album 2014, Grammy Award for Best Pop Vocal Album 2015, Juno Award for Best Int. Album 2015) 2014. *Honours:* MOBO Awards for Best Video 2013, for Best Song 2013, 2014, for Best R&B/Soul Act 2014, for Best Male Act 2014, BBC's Sound of 2014 Award Winner 2014, Q Award for Best New Act 2014, American Music Award for Favorite Male Artist, Pop/Rock 2014, BRIT Awards for Critics' Choice 2014, for British Breakthrough Artist 2015, for Global Success 2015, Grammy Awards for Record of the Year, Song of the Year (both for Stay With Me, Darkchild Version) 2015, for Best New Artist 2015, Billboard Music Awards for Top New Artist 2015, for Top Male Artist 2015, for Top Radio Songs Artist 2015, Golden Globe Award for Best Original Song (for Writing's on the Wall) 2016. *Current Management:* c/o Elvin Smith, Mansion Artists. *E-mail:* elv@mansionartists.co.uk. *Website:* www.mansionartists.co.uk (office). *Address:* c/o PMR Records, Capitol Records, Universal Music Group, 364–366 Kensington High Street, London, W14 8NS, England (office). *Telephone:* (20) 7471-5000 (office). *Website:* www.capitolrecords.co.uk (office); samsmithworld.com.

SMITH, Spencer John; British musician (drums); b. 8 Feb. 1967, London, England. *Career:* mem., North of Cornwallis; concert appearances; mem., Saint Etienne 1992, with tours worldwide, television and festival appearances; mem. Musicians' Union, PRS. *Recordings include:* albums: with East Village: Dropout, Hotrod Hotel; with Saint Etienne: Tiger Bay. *Current Management:* Heavenly Management, 47 Frith Street, London W1V 5TE, England.

SMITH, Tom; British musician (keyboards, guitar), singer and songwriter; b. 1981, Stroud; one s. *Education:* Staffordshire Univ. *Career:* Founder mem., Snowfield 2003, renamed Editors 2004–. *Recordings include:* albums: The Back Room 2005, An End Has a Start 2007, In This Light And On This Evening 2009. *Website:* www.editorsofficial.com.

SMITH, Tommy; Scottish musician (tenor saxophone), bandleader, composer, arranger and educator and producer; *Founder and Director, Scottish National Jazz Orchestra;* b. (Thomas William Ellis), 27 April 1967, Edinburgh, Scotland; s. of William Ellis and Brenda Urquhart. *Education:* Berklee Coll. of Music, USA. *Career:* career began when he recorded first album Giant Strides aged 16; gained scholarship to Berklee Coll. of Music; Founder/Dir Scottish Nat. Jazz Orchestra (SNJO) 1995–, Tommy Smith Youth Jazz Orchestra, performances and recordings of programmed and commissioned works, including popular treatments of Ellington, Gershwin, Weather Report and Miles Davis; numerous solo albums as a leader for Blue Note, Linn and own label Spartacus Records; has collaborated with Gary Burton, Chick Corea, Jack DeJohnette, Kenny Barron, Arild Andersen, John Scofield and Trilok Gurtu amongst others; Prof., Royal Conservatoire of Scotland, Head of Jazz. *Compositions include:* Unirsi in Matrimono 1988, Hall of Mirrors 1993, Dreaming with Eyes Open 1995, Planet Wave 1997, Hiroshima and Monte Cristo 1998, ALBA 2000, Torah 2000, Beauty and the Beast 2002, Edinburgh, Evolution 2003, Karma 2010. *Films:* Talented Mr Ripley, Complicity. *Recordings:* 26 albums under his own name, including Giant Strides 1983, Taking Off 1984, Forward Motion: The Berklee Tapes 1984, Progressions 1985, Whiz Kids 1986, Step By Step 1988, Peeping Tom 1990, Standards 1991, Paris 1992, Reminiscence 1993, Misty Morning and No Time 1994, Azure 1995, Beasts of Scotland 1996, Sound of Love 1997, Gymnopedie 1998, Blue Smith 1999, Spartacus 2000, Into Silence 2001, Alone at Last 2002, The Christmas Concert 2002, Bezique 2002, Miles Ahead 2002, Evolution 2003, Symbiosis (with Brian Kellock) 2004, Forbidden Fruit 2005, Live at Belleville (with Arild Andersen) (Acad. du Jazz European CD of the Year 2009) 2008, Torah 2010, Karma (Best Album, Scottish Jazz Awards 2012) 2011, Emergence 2011, Celebration (SNJO) 2012, In the Spirit of Duke (SNJO) 2013, Mira (with Arild Andersen), Whispering of the Star 2013, American Adventure (SNJO) 2013, Jeunehomme (SNJO) 2014. *Honours:* Dr hc (Heriot-Watt Univ.) 1999, (Glasgow Caledonian Univ.) 2008, (Edinburgh) 2013; Hon. Fellow, Royal Incorporation of Architects of Scotland 2000; Best Young Musician, Edinburgh Jazz Festival, 1981, Best Band, Edinburgh Jazz Festival 1981, Outstanding Musician Award, Nat. Big Band Competition 1986, British Jazz Award 1989, Wavendon All Music Award for Services to Music 1992, BT British Jazz Award 1996, Fellowship Prize, Arts Foundation/Barclays Bank Jazz Composition 1996, ScotRail Award for Best Performance, Glasgow Jazz Festival 1996, Creative Scotland Award, Scottish Arts Council 2000, Best Tenor Saxophonist, British Jazz Awards 2002, Heart of Jazz Award, BBC Jazz Awards 2008, Best Woodwind, Scottish Jazz Awards 2009, Best Big Band for SNJO, Scottish Jazz Awards 2009, Best Educator, Best Big Band, Scottish Jazz Awards 2011, Best Educator, Scottish Jazz Awards 2012, Best Big Band, British Jazz Award 2012, Best Live Performance, SNJO, Scottish Jazz Awards 2012. *Address:* c/o Spartacus Records Ltd, PO Box 3743, Lanark, ML11 9WD, Scotland (office). *E-mail:* ts@snjo.co.uk (office). *Website:* www.spartacusrecords.com (office); www.snjo.co.uk (office); www.tsyjo.com (office); www.tommysmith.co.uk.

SMITH, (Ishmael) Wadada Leo; American jazz musician (trumpet) and composer; *Director, African-American Improvisational Music Program,* *California Institute of the Arts;* b. 18 Dec. 1941, Leland, Miss. *Education:* Sherwood School of Music, Wesleyan Univ. *Career:* fmr mem., R&B groups 1960s; Co-founder and mem. of trio, Creative Construction Company (with Leroy Jenkins and Anthony Braxton); f. own record label, Kabell 1971; debut album as leader 1972; Founder-mem. of several ensembles, New Dalta Ahkri, Golden Quartet, Silver Orchestra, Organic; teacher, Univ. of New Haven 1975–76, Creative Music Studio, Woodstock 1975–78, Bard Coll. 1987–93; mem. Faculty, Herb Alpert School of Music, California Inst. of the Arts 1993–, currently Dir, African-American Improvisational Music Program; numerous collaborations including Muhal Richard Abrams, Derek Bailey, Carla Bley, Anthony Braxton, Jack DeJohnette, Henry Kaiser, Frank Lowe, Matthew Shipp, Cecil Taylor, John Zorn; mem. ASCAP, Chamber Music America, Asscn for the Advancement of Creative Musicians; Fellow, Atlantic Center for the Arts 2001, Civitela Foundation 203, Jurassic Foundation 2008, John Simon Guggenheim Memorial Foundation 2009–10. *Compositions include:* Odwira (for 12 multi-ensembles) 1995, Heart Reflections 1996, Tabligh 2006. *Recordings:* albums: as leader: Creative Music – 1 1972, Reflectativity 1974, Song of Humanity 1976, Divine Love 1978, Mass on the World 1978, Budding of a Rose 1979, Go in Numbers 1980, Spirit Catcher 1980, Akhreanvention 1981, Human Rights 1982, Procession of the Great Ancestry 1983, Rastafari 1983, If You Want the Kernels, You Have to Break the Shells 1985, Kulture Jazz 1995, Tao-Nija 1996, Golden Hearts Remembrance 1997, Prataksis 1997, Condor, Autumn Wind 1998, Light Upon Light 1999, Reflectativity 2000, Golden Quartet 2000, Red Sulphur Sky 2001, The Year of the Elephant 2002, Luminous Axis 2002, Organic Resonance 2003, Lake Biwa 2004, Saturn, Conjunct the Grand Canyon in a Sweet Embrace 2004, Snakish 2005, Compassion 2006, Wisdom in Time 2007, Tabligh 2008, America 2009, Spiritual Dimensions 2009, The Blue Mountain's Sun Drummer (with Ed Blackwell) 2010, Heart's Reflections 2011, Ten Freedom Summers (MAP Fund Award 2011) 2012, Ancestors 2012, Occupy the World 2013, The Great Lakes Suites 2014, Celestial Weather (with John Lindberg) 2015; as sideman: 3 Compositions of New Jazz (with Anthony Braxton) 1968, Anthony Braxton (with Anthony Braxton) 1969, This Time (with Anthony Braxton) 1970, Geechee Recollections (with Marion Brown) 1973, Young at Heart/Wise in Time (with Muhal Richard Abrams) 1974, The Flam (with Frank Lowe) 1975, Creative Orchestra Music (with Anthony Braxton) 1976, Yo, Miles! (with Henry Kaiser) 1998, New Orbit (with Matthew Shipp) 2001, Sky Garden (with Henry Kaiser) 2004, Upriver (with Henry Kaiser) 2004, 50th Birthday Celebration Vol. 8 (with John Zorn) 2003, The Unknown Masada (with John Zorn) 2003, The Sweetness of the Water (with Spring Heel Jack) 2004. *Publications:* Notes (8 Pieces), Source of a New World Music: Creative Music 1973. *Honours:* Nat. Endowment for the Arts Music Grants 1972, 1974, 1981, New York Foundation on the Arts Fellowship in Music 1990, Jazz Journalists Asscn Jazz Awards 2004, for Trumpeter of the Year 2013, for Musician of the Year 2013, for Composer of the Year 2015, Festival of New Trumpet Award of Recognition 2008. *Address:* Room B204, California Institute of the Arts, 24700 McBean Parkway, Valencia, CA 91355, USA (office). *Telephone:* (661) 255-1050, ext 2049 (office). *Fax:* (661) 255-0938 (office). *E-mail:* wlsmith@calarts.edu (office). *Website:* directory.calarts.edu/node/767 (office); www.wadawaleosmith.com (home).

SMITH, Wendy; British singer, musician and voice movement therapist; b. 31 May 1963, Middlesbrough, Cleveland, England. *Career:* mem., Prefab Sprout 1982–99; extensive tours to Europe, UK, Japan; numerous TV appearances; practitioner of Voice Movement Therapy, trained with Paul Newham, founder of Voice Movement Therapy; mem., Int. Network of Voice Movement Therapy Assocs. *Recordings include:* albums: Swoon 1984, Steve McQueen 1985, From Langley Park To Memphis 1988, Protest Songs 1989, Jordan: The Comeback 1990, Life of Surprises: The Best of Prefab Sprout 1992, Andromeda Heights 1997; with Bryan Savage: Cat Food 1996; with James Bignon: What a Mighty God We Serve 1996; with Special Delivery: This is Special Delivery 1996; singles include: When Love Breaks Down 1985, Cars And Girls 1988, The King Of Rock'n'Roll 1988, Carnival 2000 1990, The Sound Of Crying 1992, If You Don't Love Me 1992, Life Of Surprises 1993, Prisoner Of The Past 1997. *Honours:* six Gold discs.

SMITH, Will; American actor and singer; b. (Willard Christopher Smith II), 25 Sept. 1968, Philadelphia, Pa; s. of Willard Smith, Sr and Caroline Smith; m. 1st Sheree Zampino 1992 (divorced); one s.; m. 2nd Jada Pinkett 1997; one s. one d. *Education:* Overbrook High School, Winfield, Pa. *Career:* formed duo DJ Jazzy Jeff and the Fresh Prince; f. Overbrook Entertainment (production co.); developer and owner The Boom Boom Room (recording studio). *Films include:* Where the Day Takes You 1992, Made in America 1993, Six Degrees of Separation 1993, Bad Boys 1995, Independence Day 1996, Men in Black 1997, Enemy of the State 1998, Wild Wild West 1999, Legend of Bagger Vance 2000, Ali 2002, Men in Black II: Alien Attack 2002, Bad Boys II 2003, Shark Tale (voice) 2004, I, Robot 2004, Hitch 2005, The Pursuit of Happyness 2006, I Am Legend 2007, Hancock 2008, Seven Pounds 2009, The Karate Kid (producer) 2010, Men in Black 3 2012, After Earth 2013, Winter's Tale 2014, Focus 2015. *Television includes:* The Fresh Prince of Bel Air (series) 1990–96, Happily Ever After: Fairy Tales for Every Child (episode 'Pinocchio'; voice) 1997, All of Us Johnny (three episodes) 2003–04, Nur die Liebe zählt (episode) 2008. *Recordings include:* albums: as The Fresh Prince with DJ Jazzy Jeff: He's the DJ, I'm the Rapper 1988, And in This Corner... 1989, Homebase 1991, Rock the House 1991, Code Red 1993; solo: Big Willie Style 1997, Willennium 1999, Born to Reign 2002, Lost and Found 2005. *Publication:* Just the Two of Us (juvenile) 2005. *Honours:* with DJ Jazzy Jeff: Grammy Awards Best Rap

Performance 1988, 1991; as solo artist: Grammy Awards Best Rap Solo Performance 1998, MTV Music Video Awards Best Male Video, Best Rap Video 1998, American Music Awards Favorite Pop/Rock Male Artist, Favorite Album, Favorite Male Soul/R&B Artist 1998, Favorite Pop/Rock Male Artist 2000; César d'honneur 2005, American Music Award for Favorite Male Pop/Rock Artist 2005, Kora All African Music Award for Best African American Diaspora Artist (for song, Switch) 2005. *Current Management:* c/o Overbrook Entertainment, 450 North Roxbury Drive, 4th Floor, Beverly Hills, CA 90210; c/o Ken Stovicz, Creative Artists Agency, 9830 Wilshire Boulevard, Beverly Hills, CA 90212, USA. *Telephone:* (310) 432-2400 (Overbrook). *Fax:* (310) 432-2410 (Overbrook). *Website:* www.overbrookent.com.

SMULYAN, Gary; American jazz musician (baritone saxophone); b. 4 April 1956, Bethpage, NY; m. Joan Cornachio. *Education:* State Univ. of New York - Potsdam, Hofstra Univ. *Career:* mem., Woody Herman's Young Thundering Herd 1978–80; mem. Mel Lewis Jazz Orchestra 1980; played in other ensembles including Mingus Big Band, Smithsonian Jazz Masterworks Orchestra; formed trio with Ray Drummond and Kenny Washington; currently baritone saxophonist, Vanguard Jazz Orchestra, Dave Holland Big Band and Octet, Dizzy Gillespie All Star Big Band; Artistic Dir, Berkshire Hills Music Acad., South Hadley, Mass 2006–; collaborators include Woody Herman, Carla Bley Big Band, Michel Camilo, Chick Corea, Stan Getz, Dizzy Gillespie, Gene Harris, Freddie Hubbard, B.B. King, Joe Lovano, Tito Puente, Diana Ross, John Scofield. *Recordings:* albums: The Lure of Beauty 1990, Homage 1991, Saxophone Mosaic 1993, With Strings 1997, Blues Suite 2000, The Real Deal 2003, Hidden Treasures 2006, More Treasures 2007, High Noon: The Jazz Soul of Frankie Laine 2007, Smul's Paradise 2012, Bella Napoli 2013. *Honours:* Jazz Journalists Asscn Awards for Baritone Saxophonist of the Year 2009, 2010, 2012, 2013, 2014, 2015. *Address:* c/o Capri Records Limited, PO Box 892, Bailey, CO 80421, USA (office). *Telephone:* (303) 816-1367 (office); (914) 924-8640 (home). *Fax:* (303) 816-1362 (office). *E-mail:* gary@garysmulyan.com (home). *Website:* caprirecords.com (office); www.garysmulyan.com (home).

SMYTH, James (Jimmy) Patrick; Irish musician (guitar, keyboards), singer and producer; b. 22 April 1958, Navan; m. Jenny Newman 1994. *Education:* RIAM, Dublin. *Career:* toured with The Kinks, Thin Lizzy, Bob Dylan, Rory Gallagher, Bon Jovi; played guitar with Bogey Boys, Toni Childs (all world tours), Van Morrison, Paul Brady, Don Baker; numerous television appearances world-wide, including performance at Grammy Awards Ceremony 1989; mem, Musicians' Union, ASCAP, IMRO, MCPS. *Compositions:* co-wrote six songs on Toni Childs' album The Woman's Boat; many songs covered. *Recordings:* two albums as singer, guitarist with The Bogey Boys; played on over 150 major release albums including Daniel O'Donnell's Love Hope and Faith 1998, Winter's Tale's Winter's Tale 1998, Lisa Stansfield's Face Up 2001. *Honours:* twice voted in Top 5 guitarists in Ireland, Hot Press magazine.

SNIDER, Dee; American rock singer and lyricist; b. 15 March 1955, New York. *Career:* founder mem. of rock group, Twisted Sister 1972–87, 1997–; worldwide tours, festival appearances; founder mem., Desperado, Widowmaker 1991–. *Recordings include:* albums: with Twisted Sister: Under The Blade 1982, You Can't Stop Rock and Roll 1983, Stay Hungry 1984, Come Out and Play 1985, Love is for Suckers 1987, Live at Hammersmith 1994, Early Works 1999, Still Hungry; with Widowmaker: Blood and Bullets 1992, Stand By For Pain 1994, Thunderbolt: A Tribute to AC/DC 1998; with Strangeland (executive producer): Strangeland 1998; with Bernie Torme: White Trash Guitar 1999; Never Let The Bastards Wear You Down 2000. *Website:* www.deesnider.com.

SNOOP LION, (Snoop Dogg, Snoop Doggy Dogg); American rap artist and actor; b. (Calvin Broadus), 20 Oct. 1971, Long Beach, Calif. *Career:* mem. 213 (with Warren G. and Nate Dogg) early 1990s, re-formed 2005; collaborations with Dr Dre, Rage Against the Machine, K-Ci, JoJo; numerous live appearances; Exec. Producer, satellite radio network, XM 2005–. *Songs for film:* In Prison My Whole Life 2008. *Film appearances:* Half Baked 1998, Caught Up 1998, Ride 1998, Da Game of Life 1998, Urban Menace 1999, The Wrecking Crew 1999, Hot Boyz 1999, 3 the Hard Way 1999, Tha Eastsidaz 2000, Baby Boy 2001, Training Day 2001, Bones 2001, The Wash 2001, Crime Partners 2000 2001, Snoop Dogg's Hustlaz: Diary of a Pimp 2002, Malibu's Most Wanted (voice) 2003, Starsky & Hutch 2004, Soul Plane 2004, Racing Stripes (voice) 2005, Boss'n Up 2005, The Tenants 2005, Arthur and the Invisibles (voice) 2007, Falling Up 2009, Arthur and the Revenge of Maltazard 2009, The Big Bang 2011, We the Party 2012, Mac and Devin Go to High School 2012, Turbo (voice) 2013, Scary Movie 5 2013. *Recordings include:* albums: solo: Doggystyle 1993, Tha Doggfather 1996, Da Game Is To Be Sold, Not To Be Told 1998, Top Dogg 1999, The Last Meal 2000, Death Row's Greatest Hits 2001, Paid Tha Cost To Be Da Boss 2002, Rhythm & Gangsta: The Masterpiece 2004, The Blue Carpet Treatment 2006, Ego Trippin' 2008, Malice n' Wonderland 2009, Doggumentary 2011, Reincarnated (as Snoop Lion) 2013, Bush 2015; with 213: The Hard Way 2005. *Honours:* MTV Europe Music Award for Best Hip-hop 2005. *Current Management:* c/o William Morris Endeavor Entertainment, 1325 Avenue of the Americas, New York, NY 10019, USA. *Telephone:* (212) 586-5100. *Fax:* (212) 246-3583. *Website:* www.wmeentertainment.com; snooplion.com; snoopdogg.com.

SNYMAN, Jean Corneille (Neil), Higher Nat. Dipl., Electrical Eng LC; South African producer, engineer and musician (multi-instrumentalist); *Owner, Big Ears Productions;* b. 3 Nov. 1956, Bellville; m. 1977; one s. one d. *Education:* Wits Univ. of Tech. *Career:* specialist in Zulu ethnic recordings; engineer and producer, South African Broadcasting Corpn (SABC) 1976–89; Owner Durban Beach Studios 1989–99; Owner and Producer, Eagle Records 1992–2000; Head of Sound Dept, The Playhouse Co. 1999–2009; Owner, Big Ears Productions 2009–; mem. Asscn of South African Music Industry, Southern African Music Rights Org. *Recordings:* recorded Ladysmith Black Mambazo for Rugby World Cup 1995; for album Anthems: Swing Low; Sosholoza; World In Union. *Honours:* SABC Artes Awards, for traditional music, two years in succession, Asst Engineer for Grammy Award, Best World Album 2004, Engineering. *Address:* 30 Kinmont Crescent, Glenmore, Durban (office); 210 Grosvenor Road, Carrington Heights, Durban, South Africa (office). *Telephone:* 71-6459520 (mobile). *Fax:* 86-2408565 (mobile). *E-mail:* jeancsnyman@gmail.com (office); neil@bigears.co.za (office). *Website:* www.bigears.co.za (office).

SOARES, Elza; Brazilian singer and songwriter; b. 23 June 1937, Rio de Janeiro; m. Garrincha (died 1983). *Career:* singer in the jazz and samba styles. *Recordings include:* albums: A Bossa Negra 1961, Baterista: Wilson das Neves 1968, Pede Passagem 1972, Trajeitoria 1997, Do Coccix ate o pescoco 2003, Vivo Feliz 2003, Elza, Carnaval e Samba 2004. *E-mail:* danielsetti@recohead.com.br. *Website:* www.recohead.com.br.

SÖDERBERG, Johanna Kajsa; Swedish singer, songwriter and musician (keyboards); b. 31 Oct. 1990, Enskede, Stockholm; d. of Benkt Söderberg. *Career:* Founder-mem. First Aid Kit (with sister Klara) 2007–; released debut EP Drunken Trees 2008; toured Europe with Conor Oberst 2013; numerous live and TV appearances. *Recordings include:* albums: with First Aid Kit: The Big Black & the Blue 2010, The Lion's Roar (Swedish Grammis Award for Album of the Year 2013, Nordic Music Prize for Best Album 2013) 2012, Stay Gold 2014; as contrib.: Upside Down Mountain, Conor Oberst 2014, The Voyager, Jenny Lewis 2014. *Honours:* Swedish Music Publishers Asscn Awards for Composer of the Year 2012, for Breakthrough of the Year 2012, Swedish Grammis Awards for Artist of the Year 2013, for Songwriter of the Year 2013, for Best Pop Act of the Year 2013. *Current Management:* c/o Laura Haber, Ciulla Management, 8515 Santa Monica Blvd, West Hollywood, CA 90069, USA. *Telephone:* (310) 659-9200. *Fax:* (323) 654-3111. *E-mail:* Laura@ciullamgmt.com. *Website:* www.ciullamgmt.com; thisisfirstaidkit.com.

SÖDERBERG, Klara Maria; Swedish singer, songwriter and musician (guitar); b. 8 Jan. 1993, Enskede, Stockholm; d. of Benkt Söderberg. *Career:* Founder-mem. First Aid Kit (with sister Johanna) 2007–; released debut EP Drunken Trees 2008; toured Europe with Conor Oberst 2013; numerous live and TV appearances. *Recordings include:* albums: with First Aid Kit: The Big Black & the Blue 2010, The Lion's Roar (Swedish Grammis Award for Album of the Year 2013, Nordic Music Prize for Best Album 2013) 2012, Stay Gold 2014; as contrib.: Upside Down Mountain, Conor Oberst 2014, The Voyager, Jenny Lewis 2014. *Honours:* Swedish Music Publishers Asscn Awards for Composer of the Year 2012, for Breakthrough of the Year 2012, Swedish Grammis Awards for Artist of the Year 2013, for Songwriter of the Year 2013, for Best Pop Act of the Year 2013. *Current Management:* c/o Laura Haber, Ciulla Management, 8515 Santa Monica Blvd, West Hollywood, CA 90069, USA. *Telephone:* (310) 659-9200. *Fax:* (323) 654-3111. *E-mail:* Laura@ciullamgmt.com. *Website:* www.ciullamgmt.com; thisisfirstaidkit.com.

SOENEN, Geert; Belgian teacher and conductor; b. (Geert Herbé Simon), 25 April 1963, Wervik; m. Elly Deflo 1988. *Education:* Royal Conservatory of Ghent, Conservatory of The Hague, Netherlands. *Career:* soloist, played on trumpet and piano, classical, popular and chamber music; Conductor, Accad. Amanti Dell'Arte, Symphony Orchestra of Flanders, Prague Philharmonic Chamber Orchestra, Euregion Symphony Orchestra; Conductor, Young Ghent and Ensemble 1828; teacher of Solfège, Ear Training and Music Theory, Royal Conservatory of Ghent School of Arts. *Compositions:* arrangements for Pitti Polak, Raymond Van Het Groenewoud, for proms with symphony orchestra. *Address:* Mispelbilk 14, 9030 Mariakerke-Gent, Belgium (home). *Telephone:* (9) 329-61-49 (home). *E-mail:* geert.soenen@pandora.be (home); info@jemoo.be (office). *Website:* www.jemoo.be (office).

SOERENSEN, Kim Hougaard; Danish composer, lyricist, journalist and music theatre critic; b. 21 May 1956, Haldum. *Education:* Journalism, Danish University, 1981; Private lessons by Danish composers. *Career:* Keyboard player, numerous Danish pop and rockbands, 1980–90; Composer, lyricist, Danish National Concert musical, The Egtved Chronicle, tour, 1993; mem, Danish Jazz, Folk and Rock Composers; Danish Board of Journalists. *Recordings:* The Egtved Chronicle, 1993. *Publications:* Songs From The Egtved Chronicle, 1993. *Honours:* The Cultural Award, 1993; The VAF Foundation Award, 1993.

SOHEE; South Korean singer, rapper and actress; b. (Ahn So-hee), 27 June 1992, Seoul. *Education:* Changmun's All Girls High School. *Career:* mem. Wonder Girls 2006–; first int. tour (including Thailand and USA) 2009; first S Korean group to enter the Billboard Hot 100 chart (with Nobody) 2009; world tour with Jonas Brothers 2009; supported Justin Bieber at Valentine's Day Concert 2010; toured USA and Canada with Wonder World Tour 2010; collaborated with Akon on single Like Money 2012; numerous festival appearances and tours. *Films:* Hellcats (I Like It Hot) 2008, The Last Godfather 2010, The Wonder Girls 2012. *Television includes:* MTV Wonder Girls 2006–10, Welcome to Wonderland 2009, Made in Wonder Girls 2010; numerous guest appearances. *Recordings include:* albums: The Wonder Years

(Golden Disk Main Award Winners (Bonsang) 2007) 2007, The Wonder Years: Trilogy (Seoul Music Awards for Record of the Year in Digital Release 2009, Bonsang Award 2009, Daesang Award 2009) 2009, Wonder World 2011. *Honours:* Golden Disk Awards for Popularity 2007, Seoul Music Award for Best New Artist 2008, Korean Music Awards for Best Dance and Electronic Song (for Tell Me) 2008, for Group Musician of the Year Netizen Vote (for Wonder Girls) 2009, Golden Disk Awards Main Award Winners 2008, MNet KM Music Festival Awards for Best New Female Group 2007, for Song of the Year 2008, for Best Music Video (for Nobody) 2008, for Best Female Group 2008. *Current Management:* c/o Creative Artists Agency, 162 Fifth Avenue, 6th Floor, New York, NY 10010, USA. *Address:* c/o JYP Entertainment, JYP Center, 123-50 Cheongdam-dong, Gangnam-gu, Seoul, South Korea (office). *Telephone:* (2) 3438-2300 (office). *Website:* www.jype.com (office); www .wondergirlsworld.com.

SOIRAT, Philippe; French jazz musician (drums); b. 11 March 1961, Menton. *Education:* Jazz Acad., Monaco, Centre Musical Contemporain. *Career:* Concerts with: J R Monterose, Warren Bernhardt, Barney Wilen, John Stubblefield, Duke Jordan, Ray Brown, Walter Bishop Jr, Bob Mover, Alain Jean-Marie, Jacky Terrasson, Georges Cables, LaVelle, James Moddy, Lou Donaldson, Horace Parlan, Emmanuel Bex, Jimmy Gourley, Dee Dee Bridgwater, Larry Schneider, Andy Laverne, Enrico Rava, Eric Lelann; Tours: Turkey (Armen Donelian Trio) 1990, France (Lee Konitz Quartet) 1992, Viet Nam, Thailand, Malaysia, Singapore (Laurent de Wilde, Ira Coleman, Eric Barret) 1993, Australia, New Zealand (Laurent de Wilde Quartet) 1995, Portugal (Carlos Barretto Quintet), Canada (Yannick Rieu Quartet), Singapore, Brunei, Poland (Laurent de Wilde Trio) 1995, Africa (Belmondo Quintet) 1996. *Recordings include:* What Is The Color of Love?, Yannick Rieu Quartet; Passione, Barney Wilen Quintet; Alone Together, Georges Cables Trio; Going Up, Carlos Barretto Quintet.

MC SOLAAR; French rap artist; b. (Claude M'Barali), Dakar, Senegal; m.; one c. *Recordings:* albums: Qui Sème Le Vent Récolte Le Tempo 1993, Prose Combat 1994, Paradisiaque 1997, Le Tour De La Question 1999, Cinquieme As 2002, Mach 6 2004, Chapitre 7 2007. *Address:* c/o Eastwest Records: A&R Abteilung HipHop/Black Music, Postfach 106524, 20044 Hamburg, Germany. *Website:* www.solaarsystem.net.

SOLAL, Martial; French musician (piano) and composer; b. 23 Aug. 1927, Algiers, Algeria. *Career:* mem. of various trios, quartets, and arranger for big bands; also solo jazz artist; composer of film music. *Film soundtracks:* Deux hommes dans Manhattan 1959, Match contre la mort 1959, Le Testament d'Orphée, ou ne me demandez pas pourquoi! 1960, À bout de souffle 1960, Si le vent le fait peur 1960, L'Affaire d'une nuit 1960, Léon Morin, prêtre 1961, Les Ennemis 1962, Svenska flickor i Paris 1962, Le Bougnat 1963, Le Temps d'une nuit 1964, Échappement libre 1964, Trois chambres à Manhattan 1965, Timber – ØK i Canada 1967, Ballade à blanc 1983, Les Acteurs 2000. *Recordings include:* albums: Martial Solal Trio 1953, French Modern Sounds 1954, Martial Solal 1961, Martial Solal Trio 1965, Son 66 1965, 7 + 4 = X 1975, Nothing but Piano 1975, Movability 1976, Duplicity 1977, Suite for Trio 1978, Four Keys 1979, Big Band 1981, Bluesine 1983, Big Band 1984, Plays Hodeir 1984, Duo in Paris 1991, Triptyque 1991, Martial Solal & Toots Thielemans 1992, Martial Solal/Didier Lockwood 1993, Difficult Blues 1996, Triangle 1996, Silent Cinema – Cinema Muet 1998, Just Friends 1998, Martial Solal (Vol. 2) 1998, Balade du 10 Mars 1999, En Solo 1999, Plays Ellington 2000, A Piacere: Triptyque 2000, Gaveau et Autres Pieces 2000, Sans Tambour Ni Trompette 2000, Solos-Trios-Big Band 2000, In & Out 2000, Les Acteurs 2000, Locomotion 2002, Jazz 'N (E)motion 2003, Newdecaband 2007, Exposition Sans Tableau 2007, Solitude 2007, Longitude 2008. *Address:* c/o Sunnyside Records, 348 W 38th Street, Suite 12B, New York, NY 10018, USA (office). *E-mail:* francois@sunnysiderecords.com (office). *Website:* www .sunnysiderecords.com.

SOLEM, Phil; American singer, songwriter and musician. *Career:* mem., Great Buildings late 1970s; mem., The Rembrandts 1989–96, 2000–; mem. Thrush 1995–; mem. ASCAP, SAG. *Recordings include:* albums: with Great Buildings: Apart from the Crowd 1981; with the Rembrandts: The Rembrandts 1990, Untitled 1991, LP 1995, Lost Together 2001; Poptopia! 80s Power Pop Clasics, 1997; Poptopia! 90s Power Pop Classics, 1997; with Mango Jam: Preserves, 1998; with Thrush: Thrush 2000; solo: Hodgepodge 2011. *Honours:* ASCAP and BMI Awards 1995–97, LA Music Award. *Address:* 9744 Wilshire Blvd, Suite 305, Beverly Hills, CA 90212, USA. *Website:* philsolem.therembrandts.net.

SOLIS, Marco Antonio; Mexican singer and songwriter; b. 29 Dec. 1959, Michoacan; m. Beatriz (divorced); one d. *Career:* fmr mem. Los Hermanitos Solis aged 12; formed Los Bukis 1970s; songwriter for singers, including Beatriz and Marisela; wrote for Mexican soap operas, Amor en Silencio and El Alma no Tiene Color; compositions recorded by singers, including Lucero, Enrique Iglesias; solo career 1995–. *Recordings include:* albums: Por Amor A Mi Pueblo 1995, En Pleno Vuelo 1996, Marco 1997, 20 Aniversario 1999, Trozos De Mi Alma 1999, Marco Antonio Solís En Vivo 2000, Más De Mi Alma 2001, Tu Amor O Tu Desprecio (Billboard Latin Music Award for Album of the Year 2004) 2003, La Historia Continúa 2003, Dos Grandes (Billboard Latin Music Award for Best Latin Greatest Hits Album 2005) 2004, Razón de sobra 2004, Trozos De Mi Alma, Vol. 2 2006, No Molestar 2008, En Total Plenitud 2010. *Honours:* Pride of SESAC Award 2000, Latin Grammy Awards for Best Regional Mexican Song (for Tu Amor O Tu Desprecio) 2003, (for No Molestar)

2009, (for A Donde Vamos a Parar) 2011, Billboard Latin Music Award for Best Male Regional Mexican Solo Artist 2004, Billboard Latin Music Award for Lifetime Achievement 2005. *Address:* c/o Fonovisa Records, 5820 Canoga Avenue, Suite #300, Woodland Hills, CA 91367, USA. *Website:* www.fonovisa .com; www.marcoantoniosolis.com.mx.

SOLO, Sal; British singer, songwriter and broadcaster; b. Hatfield, England. *Career:* lead singer, Classix Nouveaux 1979–85; numerous tours; lead singer, Rockets 1984–92; solo artist 1984–; host, radio shows 1988–; mem. Christian Music Asscn. *Recordings include:* Guilty, Night People, 1981; Is It a Dream, La Verité, 1982; Secret, Imperception, Under The Sun, 1983; San Damiano, Heart and Soul, 1985; Look At Christ, 1991; Another Future, 1992; Through Ancient Eyes, 1994; Anno Domini, 1999. *Publication:* For God's Sake 1993. *Honours:* CACLB Radio Award 1990. *Address:* Acts E & W Inc., PO Box 1128, Bolingbrook, IL 60440, USA. *E-mail:* salsoloacts@aol.com. *Website:* www .salsolo.com.

SOLOMON, Sophie, MSc, BA; British violinist and composer; b. 6 June 1978, Manchester; d. of Michael Brodie Solomon and Juniper Mary Makin; m. Ivan Jankovic 2011; one d. *Education:* Cheltenham Ladies Coll., Univ. of Oxford, LSE. *Career:* studied violin with Suzuki method from age of two; worked with Nat. Children's Orchestra and ProCorda; DJ in techno clubs in London as teenager; travelled in Russia, Poland and Eastern Europe, DJ residency at Propaganda nightclub, Moscow, also developed interest in Eastern European music including gypsy and klezmer styles; founder mem. Oi Va Voi klezmer fusion band 1999–2005, guest musician with artists including Paul Weller, Rufus Wainwright, Heather Nova, Theodor Bikel; collaborated with hip hop producer Socalled, also with Gary Lucas, Bacon and Quarmby, Luke Toms, The Real Tuesday Weld, Nayekhovichi, Alan Bern and Brave Old World, Maurice el Medioni, th'Legendary Shackshakers, Hazmat Modine, Avishai Cohen, Yasmin Levy, Ludovico Einaudi, Marius de Vries, Temposhark, Jon Thorne, Smadj, Ben Parker, Beshodrom; numerous appearances with London Symphony Orchestra including Genius of the Violin concert, with Roby Lakatos, Nikolaj Znaider and Mark O'Connor, Barbican Hall, London 2006, also BBC Concert Orchestra; musical arranger, Fiddler on the Roof, London 2006; performed in world premiere of Wiesenberg's Suite Concertante for Klezmer and Classical Violins with Dora Schwarzberg and the Yehudi Menuhin School Orchestra 2007; teaches klezmer music at School of Oriental and African Studies (SOAS), London, RAM, London, Weimar Conservatoire; Artistic Dir Jewish Music Inst, SOAS 2012–. *Film:* Easy Virtue (tango violin solo) 2008. *Recordings:* albums: with Oi Va Voi: Digital Folklore 2003, Laughter Through Tears (Edison World Music Album of the Year) 2004; solo: Poison Sweet Madeira 2006; other: Solomon & Socalled, Hiphopkhasene (German Record Critics' Album of the Year 2004) 2003. *E-mail:* manager@ sophiesolomon.com (office). *Website:* www.sophiesolomon.com.

SOMACH, Denny, BA; American producer and record company executive; b. 30 Sept. 1952, Allentown, Pennsylvania; m. Kathy Levinsky Somach 1995; two s. one d. *Education:* Moravian College. *Career:* radio announcer, Station WSAN, Allentown 1971–75; programme director 1975; announcer, music director, Station WYSP-FM, Philadelphia 1975–81; record producer; television producer for Hot Spots, USA Network 1982–84, Rock 'n' Roll Show, CBS 1982, John Debella Show 1990; radio producer, Psychedelic Snack 1985–, Ticket To Ride 1985–, Legends of Rock 1985–, Don Kirshner's History of Rock 'n' Roll 1990; producer, President, Denny Somach Productions 1979–; President, Cinema Records 1986–; President, founder, Musicom International 1992; mem. NARAS. *Recordings:* albums produced for: Dave Mason 1987, Patrick Moraz 1987, Johnny Winter 1988, Eric Johnson 1990, Barbara Mandrell 1997, Alan Parsons 1997. *Publications:* Ticket To Ride 1989. *Honours:* Grammy Award for Best Rock Instrumentalist, Eric Johnson, Cliffs of Dover. *Address:* Denny Somach Productions, 812 Darby Road, Havertown, PA 19083-4684, USA (office). *Telephone:* (610) 446-7100 (office). *Fax:* (610) 446-7721 (office).

SOMERVILLE, Jimmy; British singer and songwriter; b. 22 June 1961, Glasgow, Scotland. *Career:* founder mem., Bronski Beat 1984–85; formed The Communards (with Richard Coles) 1985–89; solo artist 1989–; numerous tours and live appearances. *Recordings:* albums: with Bronski Beat: The Age of Consent 1984, Hundreds and Thousands 1985; with the Communards: Communards 1986, Red 1987; solo: Read My Lips 1990, The Singles Collection 1984–90 1991, Dare To Love 1995, Manage the Damage 1999, Rootbeer 2000, Very Best Of 2001, Home Again 2005. *Current Management:* Solar Management Ltd, 13 Rosemont Road, London, NW3 6NG, England. *Telephone:* (20) 7794-3388. *Fax:* (20) 7794-5588. *E-mail:* info@solarmanagement.co.uk. *Website:* www.solarmanagement.co.uk; www.jimmysomerville.co.uk.

SON OF SCIENTIST (see Ig Culture)

SONDHEIM, Stephen Joshua, BA; American composer and lyricist; b. 22 March 1930, New York, NY; s. of Herbert Sondheim and Janet Fox. *Education:* George School, Newtown, Pa, Williams Coll., private instruction. *Career:* Pres. Dramatists' Guild 1973–81, Council mem. 1981–; Visiting Prof. of Drama and Musical Theatre, Univ. of Oxford, UK Jan.–June 1990; mem. American Acad. and Inst. of Arts and Letters 1983–, American Theater Hall of Fame 2014–. *Compositions include:* television: Topper (co-author) 1953, Evening Primrose (music and lyrics) 1967; lyrics: West Side Story 1957, Gypsy 1959, Do I Hear a Waltz? 1965, Candide 1973; music and lyrics: A Funny Thing Happened on the Way to the Forum 1962, Anyone Can Whistle 1964, Evening Primrose 1966, Company 1970, Follies 1971, A Little Night

Music 1973, The Frogs 1974, Pacific Overtures 1976, Sweeney Todd 1978, Merrily We Roll Along 1981, Sunday in the Park with George 1984, Into the Woods (Drama Critics' Circle Award 1988) 1986, Follies 1987, Assassins 1990, Passion 1994, Bounce 2003 (renamed Road Show 2008); anthologies: Side by Side by Sondheim 1976, Marry Me a Little 1980, You're Gonna Love Tomorrow 1983, Putting It Together 1993; screenplays: (with Anthony Perkins) The Last of Sheila 1973, Birdcage 1996, Getting Away with Murder 1996; film scores: Stavisky 1974, Reds 1981, Dick Tracy 1989; incidental music: The Girls of Summer 1956, Invitation to a March 1961, Twigs 1971, Company: A Musical 2007, Sweeney Todd 2007, Into the Woods 2014. *Publications:* Finishing the Hat 2010, Look, I Made a Hat: Collected Lyrics (1981–2011) 2011. *Honours:* Antoinette Perry Awards for Company 1971, Follies 1972, A Little Night Music 1973, Sweeney Todd 1979; Drama Critics' Awards 1971, 1972, 1973, 1976, 1979; Evening Standard Drama Award 1996; Grammy Awards 1984, 1986; Nat. Medal of Arts 1997, Praemium Imperial 2000, Special Tony Award for Lifetime Achievement in the Theatre 2008, Presidential Medal of Freedom 2015. *Current Management:* c/o John Breglio, 1285 Avenue of the Americas, New York, NY 10019, USA.

SONIQUE; British singer, producer and DJ; b. (Sonia Clarke), 21 June 1968, London. *Career:* vocalist with S-Express; started as a DJ in the 1990s, singing over the records; Resident DJ for Manumission in Ibiza 1997–99; solo recording career 1998–; mem. MCPS/PRS. *Recordings include:* albums: Hear My Cry 2000, Serious Sounds of Sonique (mixed multi-artist compilation) 2000, Born to Be Free 2003, On Kosmo 2006, Sweet Vibrations 2011. *Honours:* BRIT Award, Best British Female Artist 2001. *E-mail:* info@sonique.co.uk. *Website:* www.sonique.co.uk.

SONNEBORN, Daniel Atesh, BA (Hons), MA, PhD; American ethnomusicologist, producer, educator, composer and music director; *Associate Director, Smithsonian Folkways Recordings*; b. 31 Oct. 1949, Illinois; m. Patrizia Pallaro; two s. *Education:* Univ. of California, Santa Cruz, Univ. of California, San Diego, Univ. of California, Los Angeles. *Career:* musician 1967–; theatre, opera, film composer, USA and Europe 1970–; consultant, educator 1975–; Project Dir, Drumming at the Edge of Magic 1988–92; Co-Producer, Remembrance 1991; Exec. Co-Producer, Available Sound 1995; currently Assoc. Dir Smithsonian Folkways Recordings; mem. Soc. for Ethnomusicology, Int. Council for Traditional Music; mem. Advisory Bd Al Ain Centre for Music in the World of Islam 2007–. *Radio:* Latitudes: Music and Migration; Sound Sessions. *Music:* incidental music for two dozen original theatre works. *Recordings:* Jumping Over the Fence: XA: A Vietnam Primer; Delta Prime; Production Supervisor and Exec. Co-Producer of more than 200 Smithsonian Folkways albums. *Publications:* Planet Drum (co-author), Sufi Music, Smithsonian Folkways Recordings: A Museum of Sound. *Honours:* Int. Herald Tribune Best Show of the Year 1973, LA Drama Critics Circle 1971, 1972, Dept of Music Fellowship 1984, 1985, Pres.'s Fellowship 1981, Honors in the Major (Music Composition), Univ. of California, Santa Cruz. *Address:* Smithsonian Folkways, 600 Maryland Avenue SW, Suite 2001, Washington, DC 20024-2520, USA (office). *Telephone:* (202) 633-6450 (office). *Fax:* (202) 633-6477 (office). *E-mail:* sonneborna@si.edu (office). *Website:* www.folkways.si.edu (office).

SONNIER, Jo-El; American country and Cajun music singer, songwriter and musician (accordion); b. (Joel Sonnier), 2 Oct. 1946, Rayne, La. *Career:* made radio debut aged six; recording debut aged 11; numerous albums and live appearances; numerous session credits as accordionist including albums for Johnny Cash, Elvis Costello, Robert Cray, Neil Diamond, Merle Haggard, Alan Jackson, Mark Knopfler, Dolly Parton, Hank Williams, Jr. *Recordings:* albums: Hurricane Audrey 1967, The Scene Today in Cajun Music 1968, Yesterdays 1969, The Cajun Valentino 1969, The Cajun Troubadour 1969, Cajun Life 1980, Come On Joe 1987, Right Next Door to Texas 1989, Have a Little Faith 1990, Tears of Joy 1991, Hello Happiness Again 1992, Cajun Roots 1994, Cajun Kids 1995, Cookin' Cajun (with Eddy Raven) 1996, Cajun Young Blood 1997, Cajun Pride 1997, Here to Stay 1998, Cajun Memories 1998, Cajun Blood 1999, Cajun Tradition 2000, Back by Request 2005, Where's That Music Comin' From 2011, The Legacy (Grammy Award for Best Regional Roots Album 2015) 2013. *Honours:* inducted into Louisiana Music Hall of Fame 2009. *Address:* Bobbye Sonnier, PO Box 13253, Lake Charles, LA 70612, USA. *Telephone:* (337) 429-2820; (337) 842-4212. *E-mail:* bobbye1959@gmail.com. *Website:* www.jo-elsonnier.com.

SOSA, Omar; Cuban composer, musician (piano, percussion) and producer; b. 10 April 1965, Camagüey; s. of Sindulfo Jacinto Sosa Adan and Maria Gricelia Palacios Cadena; one s. two d. *Education:* Escuela Nacional de Música, Havana. *Career:* independent artist, working with various artists and groups. *Recordings include:* albums: Omar Omar 1996, Free Roots 1997, Spirit Of The Roots 1998, Inside 1998, Bembon 2000, Prietos 2001, Sentir (Jazz Journalists' Assen Afro-Caribbean Jazz Album of the Year) 2002, Ayaguna 2003, A New Life 2003, Pictures of Soul 2004, Mulatos 2004 (Remix 2005), Promise 2006, Afreecanos 2008, Across the Divide: A Tale of Rhythm and Ancestry 2009, Tales From The Earth 2009, Ceremony 2010, Calma 2011, Alma 2012, Eggun: The Afri-Lectric Experience 2013. *Honours:* San Francisco Bay Guardian Goldie Award 1997, San Francisco Weekly Wammie Award 1998, Smithsonian Institution Lifetime Achievement Award 2003, Jazz Journalists Assen Best Latin Jazz CD. *Address:* Otá Records, 484 Lake Park Avenue, Suite 32, Oakland, CA 94610, USA (office). *Telephone:* (510) 339-3389 (office). *Fax:* (510) 339-0389 (office). *E-mail:* otarecords@melodia.com (office). *Website:* www.melodia.com (office); www.omarsosa.com.

SOSSIN, Stephen Mark; American music producer, engineer and musician (guitar, bass guitar, keyboards, violin); *Founder, Vizion Productions, New Vizion Studio and TMM-Music;* b. 28 Sept. 1956, Hartford, Conn.; s. of Roy H. Sossin and Connie M. Sossin. *Education:* Manchester Coll., Conn., studied Heil Sound Engineering and with Capitol Records promoter Merv Amols. *Career:* early performing career with many artists, including Mike Ruff (keyboards, songwriter) 1973–75, Tom Chapin (saxophone, horns) 1973–76; est. songwriter/arranger in original music scene, New England 1975–; Founder Vizion Productions Studio digital recording facility, photo, video services; began artist devt programme 1983–; works mainly with emerging artist, custom writing for individual's voice; producer/engineer in major recording/music industry 1990–2001; Founder-Producer New Vizion Studios working with Merv Amols, Capitol Records 1995–2000; mem. Ind. Producer's Guild, US Naval Inst.; Second Lt, USSF Reserves 1993. *Compositions:* professional 'ghoster' for many artists and groups 1971–2001. *Recordings:* with Bonnie Lynn: Embrace of My Heart 1993; with Dianne Glynn: I Can't Find The Words 1995, That's Why I Ran 1996, Take My Hand 1996. *Publications:* Recording Industry Sourcebook 1991–2001; contrib. to Mix, Onstage etc. *Honours:* Nat. Defense Service Medal, Cold War Certificate; Kt Chevalier Medal, Pres.'s Nat. Patriotism Medal, AFP, Guardian Certificate of Recognition 2010. *Address:* Box 53, Manchester, CT 06045-0053, USA (office). *Telephone:* (860) 221-9813 (office); (860) 647-9883 (home). *E-mail:* Vizionmusic@aol.com (office).

SOUL BOY (see Tenaglia, Danny)

SOULTAN, Ahmed; Moroccan singer, musician, songwriter and producer; *Owner, Somum Records & Publishing;* b. 1978, Taroudant. *Career:* supported Tiken Jah Fakoly Kora Awards, S Africa 2005; collaborated with Ne-Yo on Amazing You 2010; featured on song People Power for Radiowaves Project (campaign to oppose climate change) 2011, with Talib Kweli, Zap Mama, Angelique Kidjo; collaborating with George Clinton, Femi Kuti, RZA, Fred Wesley, Pee Wee Ellis, Bootsy Collins, Questlove; appearances at numerous festivals and concerts world-wide. *Television:* Rhimou (soundtrack). *Recordings include:* albums: solo: Tolerance 2005, Coda 2009, Best Of 2013, MHNB (music has no boundaries) 2014; singles: Jokko feat. Fafadi & Amajang 2010, Amazing You feat. Ne-Yo 2010, My Jailer 2012, It's Alright (Denia Hania) 2013. *Honours:* MTV Europe Music Award for Best Africa/Middle East/India Act 2012, 2013, Moroccan Music Award (Best Pop) 2013, named to Forbes List of 13 African celebrities to watch in 2013. *E-mail:* mgmt@ahmedsoultan.com. *Address:* c/o SOMUM (Soul of Moroccan Urban Music) Records and Publishing, Taroudant, Morocco (office). *E-mail:* somumrecords@ahmedsoultan.com (office). *Website:* www.ahmedsoultan.com; www.facebook.com/ahmedsoultan2009; www.twitter.com/SoultanAhmed.

SOUMANO, Adja; Malian singer. *Recordings include:* albums: N'teri Diaba 1989, Aigles du Mali, Kokabéré 2004. *Honours:* Kora All African Music Award for Best Female Artist (West Africa) 2006. *Address:* c/o All Africa Music Awards, PO Box 785643, Sandton 2146, South Africa.

SOUND PATROL (see Carter, Derrick)

SOUQUES, Laurent; French musician (double bass), composer and arranger; b. 27 Oct. 1963, Paris. *Education:* Conservatoire Nat. Supérieur de Musique et de Danse, Paris. *Career:* Jazz Festival, Franche Comté 1986, 1987, 1989; Jazz Festival Suedine Bleue (Dijon) 1986; Jazz Festival Aiguillon 1990; jazz clubs in Paris 1991–95; Jazz Festival Banlieue Bleue, with G. Russell, Living Time Orchestra 1993; Banlieue Bleue, G. Russell, Cité de la Musique 1995; JVC Halle That Jazz, Paris 1995; Duc des Lombards, Baiser salé, Marciac 2006; Langourla Jazz Festival 2007; Jersey Jazz Festival 2009; Jersey Jazz Festival 2011; Altitude Jazz Festival Briançon 2012; Tonnerres de Brest 2012. *Compositions include:* film music; Syndrome de l'Espion – Zooleil, N. Joyeux; Paris des Frères Ténèbres; Muriel Mazières; Double Face 2014, Ravages 2015. *Radio:* G. Russell for Radio France 1993, 1995, Déborah Seffer New Group, France musique 2003. *Recordings include:* Just Back From New Orleans, Fidgety Feet 1989; Fire Beat, Ralph Thomas Sextet 1996; Un Charivari Entre Chien Et Loup, Skymnningsslandet 1998; Caravansérail, Olivier Savariaux 2000; Quintescence, Déborah Seffer 2001; New Group, Déborah Seffer 2003; Puig et les Voisins 'déménagent', Décib'ailes Productions 2004; At the Jimmy's Bar, Quintet Marie-Ange Martin et Gérard Siffert 2005; Live at the Café du Parc, Laurent Souques Trio 2005; GMS trio Live in Lorient 2008; Proud to Call It Home, Fidgety Feet 2009; Trio Denis Castelli 2010; The Seasons, Gilles Blandin Trio Live 2012, Emosongs, Madalenn Trio 2015. *Address:* 42 Allée des Soudanes, 78430 Louveciennes, France (home). *Telephone:* 6-15-45-14-48 (mobile) (office). *E-mail:* laurent@souques.com (office). *Website:* www.souques.com.

SOUSA, Duane 'Beans'; American musician (bass) and singer; b. 22 July 1951; m. Barbara Runnion 1989; one s. *Career:* bassist for major country and rock artists including Lacy J. Dalton, Phoebe Snow, Larry Hosford; studio work for major recording companies including CBS, MCA, Capitol and Shelter Records; mem. AFofM. *Recordings include:* albums: solo: You Don't Know, Into the Blue; appeared on Dream Baby, Lacy J. Dalton. *E-mail:* beans44@aol.com (office). *Website:* www.shoprecords.com/duane.htm.

SOUTHALL, Lee; British singer and musician (guitar); b. Hoylake, Wirral, England. *Education:* Hilbre High School, Hoylake. *Career:* Founder mem., The Coral 1996–. *Recordings:* albums: The Coral 2002, Magic and Medicine 2003, Secret Kiss 2003, Nightfreak and the Sons of Becker 2004, The Invisible

Invasion 2005, Roots and Echoes 2007, The Singles Collection 2008, Butterfly House 2010. *Website:* www.thecoral.co.uk.

SOUZA, Luciana, BA, MA; Brazilian jazz singer and composer; b. 14 June 1966, São Paulo; d. of Walter Santos and Tereza Souza; m. Larry Klein 2006. *Education:* Berklee Coll. of Music, New England Conservatory of Music, USA. *Career:* recorded 200 advertising jingles and soundtracks in childhood; teacher, Berklee Coll. of Music, Manhattan School of Music, New York; Jazz Artist-in-Residence, San Francisco Performances 2004–10; numerous collaborators including Herbie Hancock, Bobby McFerrin, Danilo Perez, Maria Schneider, Paul Simon, James Taylor; singer with many ensembles and orchestras including Bach Akademie Stuttgart, Boston Symphony Orchestra, Brooklyn Philharmonic Orchestra, Los Angeles Guitar Quintet, New York Philharmonic Orchestra, Atlanta Symphony Orchestra, Los Angeles Philharmonic Orchestra, Los Angeles Chamber Orchestra. *Recordings:* albums: An Answer to Your Silence 1999, The Poems of Elizabeth Bishop and Other Songs 2000, Brazilian Duos 2001, North and South 2003, Neruda 2004, Duos II 2005, The New Bossa Nova 2007, Tide 2009, Duos 2012, Book of Chet 2012; as featured artist: River: The Joni Letters, Herbie Hancock (Grammy Award for Album of the Year 2008) 2008. *Honours:* Jazz Journalists Asscn Award for Best Female Vocalist 2005, 2013. *Address:* c/o John Newcott, Universal Jazz France S.A.S., 20/22 Rue des Fossés Saint Jacques, 75235 Paris, France (office); c/o Sunnyside Records, Sunnyside Communications, 348 West 38th Street, Suite 12B, New York, NY 10018, USA (office). *Telephone:* (1) 44-41-91-40 (Paris) (office); (212) 564-4606 (New York) (office). *Fax:* (1) 44-41-91-40 (Paris) (office). *E-mail:* john.newcott@umusic.com (office); francois@ sunnysiderecords.com (office). *Website:* www.sunnysiderecords.com (office); www.lucianasouza.com.

SPAGNA, Ivana; Italian singer and songwriter. *Career:* fmrly sang in rock group with her brother; now solo singer; numerous concerts in Italy and France. *Recordings include:* albums: No Way Out, Diario di bordo 2005. *Telephone:* (0338) 4652047. *E-mail:* info@ivanaspagna.it (office). *Website:* www.ivanaspagna.it.

SPALDING, Esperanza; American singer and jazz musician (bass); b. 18 Oct. 1984, Portland, Ore. *Education:* Northwest Acad., Portland State Univ., Berklee Coll. of Music. *Career:* as teenager played bass for different groups throughout Portland area, including two jazz septets, a trio, and fusion group Noise for Pretend; instructor, Berklee Coll. of Music 2009. *Recordings include:* Junjo 2005, Esperanza 2008, Chamber Music Society 2010, Radio Music Society 2012; numerous collaborations. *Honours:* Up and Coming Artist of the Year, Jazz Journalists Association 2009, Rising Star Acoustic Bass Award 2010, Grammy Award for Best New Artist 2011, for Best Instrumental Arrangement Accompanying Vocalist(s) (for City of Roses) 2013, Boston Music Award 2011, Soul Train Music Award for Best Contemporary Jazz Artist 2012. *Website:* www.esperanzaspalding.com (home).

SPANG-HANSSEN, Simon Cato; Danish musician (saxophone) and composer; b. 13 April 1955, Hellerup; m. Mariane Bitran, 23 Jan. 1987, 1 s. *Career:* Tours with: John Tchicai and Strange Brothers, Scandinavia, Germany, Italy; Andy Emler's Mega-Octet, Europe; French National Jazz Orchestra, 1991–94, Europe; Leader of Quartet, Muluankh; Duo with Denis Badault, France, Denmark, Central Africa; mem, Union de Musicians de Jazz (Paris). *Recordings:* Darktown Highlights; Ten By Two; Because Forever; Mardi Gras, Chez Toi; Instant Blue, 1998; Wondering, 1999; Identified, 1999, Noctiflore 2005. *Honours:* Ben Webster Prize, 1978. *E-mail:* simonspang@ get2net.dk. *Website:* hjem.get2net.dk/simon_spang-hanssen/.

SPARKES, Neil Charles Lawrence; British programmer, musician, DJ and producer. *Career:* mem., TransGlobal Underground collective 1992–99; founder mem., Neil Sparkes & The Last Tribe 1996–; mem., Temple of Sound 1999–. *Recordings:* albums: with TransGlobal Underground: Dream Of 100 Nations 1993, International Times 1994, Interplanetary Meltdown 1995, Psychic Karaoke 1996, Innernation Vol. 2 1998, Rejoice Rejoice 1998; with The Last Tribe: Confessions of a Mask 1997, Burning Mask 2001; with Temple of Sound: Black Orchid 1998, People's Colony No. 1 (with Rizwan-Muazzam Qawwali) 2001, First Edition 2002, Shout At The Devil (with Jah Wobble) 2002, Gold Of The Sun Live 2004, Globalhead 2007. *Current Management:* c/o Steven Machat, Namaste, 59 Maiden Lane, 27th Floor, New York, NY 10038, USA. *E-mail:* management@templeofsound.org.uk; smachat@gmail.com. *E-mail:* neil@templeofsound.org.uk (office). *Website:* www.templeofsound.org .uk.

SPARKS, Jordin; American singer; b. 22 Dec. 1989, Phoenix, Ariz. *Career:* winner, American Idol singing contest 2007; solo recording artist 2007–. *Film:* Sparkle 2012. *Recordings:* Jordin Sparks 2007, Battlefield 2009. *Honours:* American Music Award for Favorite Adult Contemporary Artist 2008. *Address:* c/o Jive Records, Zomba Music Group, 550 Madison Avenue, New York, NY 10022-3211, USA (office). *Website:* www.jordinsparks.com.

SPARROW, Edwin Harold James, ARCM, LTCL, LLCM; musician (drums, timpani, percussion); b. 28 Jan. 1943, Harrogate, Yorkshire, England. *Education:* piano with Evelyn Gunnar, Trinity College with Lewis Pocock. *Career:* many years in France, worked with top light entertainment artistes including: Johnny Hallyday; Sylvie Vartan; Charles Aznavour; Appeared in film Les Jeunes Loups, directed by Marcel Carné; Appeared with Kevin Ayers; Mike Oldfield; Nico and others connected with The Velvet Underground; Gerry Rafferty, 1970s; Closely connected with Ballet Rambert; London

Contemporary Dance Theatre; Contemporary Dance and Therapy in UK; Featured on: June The 1st, 1974; Bannamour, Kevin Ayers; Banana Follies, Kevin Ayers, 2000.

SPASIUK, Horacio (Chango); Argentine musician (accordion); b. 23 Sept. 1968, Misiones. *Career:* chamame musician. *Recordings include:* albums: Chango Spasiuk 1989, Contrastes 1990, Bailemos y... 1992, La ponzoña 1996, Polcas de mi tierra 1999, Chamamé crudo 2001, Tarefero de mis Pagos (Piranha) 2004, Pynandi 2009. *Honours:* BBC World Music Award for Best Newcomer 2005. *Address:* c/o Piranha Musik, Bergmannstr. 102, 10961 Berlin, Germany (office). *Website:* www.changospasiuk.com.ar.

SPASOVSKI, Zoran; Macedonian musician (drums, percussions, keyboards) and backing singer. *Career:* mem. band Anastasia 1991–; numerous concerts and tours world-wide; contributed music to film 'Before the Rain' and other film, television and theatre projects. *Recordings:* albums: Mansarda (with Lola V. Stain) 1992, Pred Do'dot (Before The Rain) (soundtrack) 1994, Melurgia 1997, Nocturnal 1998, Mizar Harmosini 2010. *Current Management:* c/o Ivo Jankoski, Third Ear Music, 1000 Skopje, Leninova 29/3/6, Macedonia. *Telephone:* (2) 3236990. *Fax:* (2) 3136906. *E-mail:* info@thirdear .com.mk. *Website:* www.thirdear.com.mk. *E-mail:* neubauten@plugin.com.mk (office). *Website:* www.unet.com.mk/anastasia/Main.htm.

SPEAKE, Martin John, LTCL, FTCL; British musician (alto saxophone), jazz educator and composer; *Saxophone Professor, Royal Academy of Music;* b. 3 April 1958, Barnet, Hertfordshire, England; s. of the late John Speake and of Betty McCall; m. Rachel Cutler 1990 (divorced); one d. *Education:* Trinity Coll. of Music, Banff Centre for the Arts. *Career:* teacher, Royal Acad. of Music 1989–, Middlesex Univ. 1989–, Guildhall School of Music and Drama 1997–, Trinity Coll. of Music 2001–; external examiner, Birmingham Conservatoire; tours of West Africa, Latin America, Europe, with saxophone quartet Itchy Fingers; tours of Indonesia, Philippines, Croatia, UK, with seven-piece Fever Pitch; own quartet, and duo with guitarist Phil Lee; tours with pianist Ethan Iverson, Int. Quartet with Bobo Stenson, Mick Hutton and Paul Motian, trio with Indian musicians Dharambir Singh and Sarvar Sabri, Constellation celebrating Charlie Parker's music; various radio and television appearances; BBC live recording, Royal Opera House of Martin Speake Group; Contemporary Music Network tour with Sam Rivers Big Band; founded own record label 2006; mem. Musicians' Union. *Recordings include:* with John Parricelli, Steve Watts and Steve Arguelles: In Our Time 1994, Trust 1998; with Nikki Iles: The Tan T'ien 1997; with Phil Lee, Pete Saberton, Mick Hutton and Bryan Spring: Amazing Grace 1997; with Paul Clarvis, Dave Hassell, Dawson Miller, Oren Marshall, Chris Batchelor, Stuart Hall: Fever Pitch; with Nikki Iles, Duncan Hopkins, Anthony Michelli: Secret 2002, Bloor Street 2010; with John Parricelli, Mick Hutton, Tom Skinner: Hullabaloo 2002; with Mick Hutton, Tom Skinner: Exploring Standards; with Ethan Iverson: My Ideal 2004; with Dharambir Singh and Sarvar Sabri: The Journey 2004; with Mike Outram, Simon Thorpe, Dave Wickins: Charlie Parker 2005; with Bobo Stenson, Mick Hutton and Paul Motian: Change of Heart 2006; with Mark Sanders: Spark 2007; with Barry Green, Dave Green and Jeff Williams: Generations 2008. *Honours:* Hon. ARAM, FHEA; Dame Ruth Railton Prize for woodwind playing, Schlitz Young Jazz Musicians Winner (with Itchy Fingers) 1986, Peter Whittingham Award 1999. *E-mail:* martin.speake@virgin.net (home). *Website:* www.martinspeake.co.uk (home).

SPEARE, Paul, GLCM, LLCM, CertEd; British musician (saxophone, flute), arranger, producer and composer; b. 1955, Romford, Essex, England. *Education:* London Coll. of Music, Birmingham Polytechnic. *Career:* mem. Dexy's Midnight Runners 1980–82; Q-Tips British tour 1982; Elvis Costello, USA, UK and European tours 1983; Man., Expresso Bongo Studios, Tamworth 1985–94; Leader, Expresso Bongo Orchestra 1988–94; Lecturer and Moderator in Popular Music, Music Tech. and Media Production, Lewisham Coll., London 1995–2005; now semi-retd/freelance, currently baritone sax and arranger with The Lisa Davies Big Band, baritone sax and composer for Burrito Cat (jazz fusion). *Recordings include:* singles: Show Me 1981, Liars A–E 1981, Celtic Soul Brothers 1982, Come On Eileen, Too-Rye-Ay (Dexy's Midnight Runners) 1982, Punch The Clock (Elvis Costello) 1983, Free Nelson Mandela (Special AKA) 1984, Keep Moving (Madness) 1984, Nick Lowe and his Cowboy Outfit 1984, Hold Back The Night (KWS/The Tramps) 1992. *E-mail:* pspeare@hotmail.com (home). *Website:* www.paulspeare.com; www .burritocatband.com.

SPEARS, Britney Jean; American singer and entertainer; b. 2 Dec. 1981, McComb, Miss.; m. Kevin Federline 2004 (divorced 2007); two s. *Career:* raised in Kentwood, La; began performing as a child, landing acting roles in stage productions and TV shows; signed with Jive Records 1997, released debut album Baby One More Time 1999 (best-selling album by a teenage solo artist); presenter, Mickey Mouse Club; numerous tours, radio and TV appearances; judge, The X Factor (USA) 2012; owner of southern grill restaurant, Nyla; f. The Britney Spears Foundation. *Films:* Longshot (cameo) 2000, Austin Powers in Goldmember (cameo) 2002, Crossroads 2002, Fahrenheit 9/11 (cameo) 2004. *Recordings include:* albums: Baby One More Time 1999, Oops! I Did It Again 2000, Britney 2001, In The Zone 2003, My Prerogative 2004, Blackout 2007, Circus 2008, Femme Fatale 2011, Britney Jean 2013. *Honours:* MTV Europe Music Awards for Best Female Artist 1999, 2004, for Best Song (for Baby One More Time) 1999, Best Breakthrough Act 1999, Best Pop Act 1999, several MTV Video Music Awards 1999, and Best Female Pop Vocal Performance 2000, Billboard Music Award 2000, American Music Award for

Favourite New Artist 2000, Grammy Award for Best Dance Recording (for Toxic) 2005, MTV Video Music Award for Best Female Video (for Piece of Me) 2008, Best Celebrity Fragrance For Women, Cosmopolitan Fragrance Awards 2010, Best Celebrity Fragrance For Women – Readers' Award, Cosmopolitan Fragrance Awards 2011. *Website:* www.britneyspears.com (office); www .britney.com.

SPECTOR, (Harvey) Phillip (Phil); American record producer, composer and musician; b. 26 Dec. 1940, Bronx, NY; m. Ronnie Spector (divorced). *Career:* mem., The Teddy Bears, The Spectors Three; formed Philles Records 1961–66; produced albums for Beatles' Apple label; formed Phil Spector International; producer for artists, including LaVern Baker, Ruth Brown, Billy Storm, The Top Notes, Ray Petersen, Curtis Lee, Paris Sisters, the Crystals, the Ronettes, Sonny Charles and The Checkmates, John Lennon, George Harrison, Leonard Cohen, Ramones. *Recordings include:* Phil Spector Wall of Sound volumes, The Phil Spector Story 1976, Echoes of The Sixties 1977, Phil Spector 1974–79 1979, The Early Productions 1958–61, Twist and Shout: Twelve Atlantic Tracks Produced By Phil Spector 1989. *Honours:* Q Award 1999.

SPECTOR, Ronnie; American singer; b. (Veronica Bennett), 10 Aug. 1943, New York; m. 1st Phil Spector; m. 2nd Jonathan Greenfield 1982; five c. *Career:* dancer in New York 1962–63; lead singer, choreographer, dancer, Ronnie and The Relatives (later renamed The Ronettes) 1962–67; numerous live appearances; solo artist 1969–; writer 1988–90. *Publications:* Be My Baby (autobiog., with Vince Waldron) 1990. *Current Management:* GreenSpec Properties, Suite 233, 39B Mill Plain Road, Danbury, CT 06811, USA. *E-mail:* info@ronniespector.com. *Website:* www.ronniespector.com.

SPEDDING, Paul Brian; British musician (drums); b. 28 Sept. 1945, Birmingham, England. *Career:* Various Jazz Festivals Throught UK and Europe; Stage, Royal Festival Hall with Fats Domino Band; Capital Radio Jazz Festival; Worked with Olympia Brass Band, Tuxedo BB; mem, Musicians' Union. *Recordings:* The John Handy Memorial; Dan Pawson's Buddies. *Honours:* Musical Prize Breda, Holland.

SPEDICATO, Emanuele; Italian musician (guitar); b. 24 Jan. 1979. *Career:* mem., Negramaro 2002–. *Recordings include:* albums: Negramaro 2003, 000577 2004, Mentre Tutto Scorre 2005, La Finestra 2007. *Honours:* MTV Europe Music Award Best Italian Act 2005. *E-mail:* management@negramaro .com. *E-mail:* band@negramaro.com (office). *Website:* www.negramaro.com.

SPEECH; American singer and lyricist; b. (Todd Thomas), 1968, Milwaukee, WI. *Education:* Art Inst. of Atlanta. *Career:* originally known as DJ Peech; formed gangsta rap act, DLR (Disciples of a Lyrical Rebellion), renamed Secret Society, later evolved into hip-hop act, Arrested Development 1988–96, 2003–; numerous live performances, tours; also solo artist 1996–. *Recordings include:* albums: with Arrested Development: 3 Years, 5 Months & 2 Days in the Life Of... 1992, Unplugged 1993, Zingalamaduni 1994, Extended Revolution 2003, Among the Trees 2004, Since the Last Time 2006, Strong 2010; solo: Speech 1996, Hoopla 1999, Down South Produckshuns 2002, Spiritual People 2002, Peechy 2003, The Vagabond 2005, Love Life Music 2006, The Grown Folks Table 2009. *Honours:* Grammy Award for Best New Artist, Best Rap Group 1993, Soul Train Award for Best Rap Album 1993, seven Atlanta Music Awards 1993. *Current Management:* Elevation Group Inc., 401 Devon Drive, Birmingham, AL 35209, USA. *Telephone:* (510) 213-2013. *E-mail:* jay@ elevationgroup.net. *Address:* Vagabond Music Enterprises, PO Box 1539, Fayetteville, GA 30214, USA. *E-mail:* mike@speechmusic.com. *Website:* www .speechmusic.com; www.arresteddevelopmentmusic.com.

SPEECH DEBELLE; British singer and songwriter; b. (Corynne Elliott), 1983, London. *Education:* Harris City Acad. *Career:* solo rapper 2006–. *Recordings:* album: Speech Therapy (Mercury Music Prize) 2009. *E-mail:* 2diceproductionz@googlemail.com (office). *Website:* www.speechdebelle.com.

SPEIDEL, Paul, BA, MMus; American jazz and blues musician (guitar) and educator; b. 15 Feb. 1965, Kenmare, ND; m. Adlin Quiles 1991. *Education:* Augustana Coll., Univ. of Northern Colorado. *Career:* freelance guitarist, bassist in Chicago, Denver, Boston; vocal performances with Univ. of Northern Colorado Vocal Jazz I; performances with Patti Page, Gerry Beaudoin, Jeff Benedict, Terry Cooke, Ted Pilzecker; numerous musical shows; three tours of Latin and Central America with the Latin Continental Singers, as Instrumental Dir; guitarist with the Monique Weiss Quartet; guitarist, vocalist with the Paul Speidel Band; CD reviewer in bi-monthly 'No Name Jazz News'; mem. International Asscn of Jazz Educators, Boston Jazz Soc., Boston Blues Soc., Gospel Music Asscn, Music Educators Nat. Conference. *Recordings:* with The Paul Speidel Band: The Paul Speidel Band 2004, Guitar Bass Drums 2005, Taped Together 2006, Hey Everybody 2007, Previous Engagements 2008. *Honours:* Illinois State Scholar, Colorado National Scholar. *Address:* PO Box 600770, Newton, MA 02460, USA (office). *Telephone:* (617) 965-9848 (office). *E-mail:* feedback@paulspeidelband.com (office). *Website:* www.paulspeidelband.com.

SPEKTOR, Regina; American singer, songwriter, musician (keyboards), arranger and producer; b. 18 Feb. 1980, Moscow, Russia; m. Jack Dishel 2011. *Education:* Purchase Coll., SUNY. *Recordings include:* albums: 11-11 2001, Songs 2002, Soviet Kitsch 2004, Mary Ann Meets the Grave Diggers and Other Short Stories 2006, Begin to Hope 2006, Far 2009, What We Saw from the Cheap Seats 2012. *Current Management:* Ron Shapiro Management, 56 West 22nd Street, 6th Floor, New York, NY 10010, USA. *Telephone:* (212) 337-

2034. *E-mail:* info@ronshapiro.com. *Website:* www.ronshapiro.com; www .reginaspektor.com.

SPENCER, Jon; American musician (guitar); b. 1966, Hanover, NH; m. Cristina Martinez. *Career:* fmr mem., Pussy Galore 1985–89, Boss Hog 1989–2000; founder mem., Jon Spencer Blues Explosion 1990–2005; founder, Heavy Trash (with Matt Verta-Ray) 2004–. *Recordings include:* albums: with Boss Hog: Drinkin', Lechin' and Lyin' 1989, Cold Hands 1990, Boss Hog 1995; with Jon Spencer Blues Explosion: Jon Spencer Blues Explosion 1992, Crypt Style 1992, Extra Width 1993, Mo' Width 1994, Orange 1994, Experimental Remixes 1995, Now I Got Worry 1996, Controversial Negro 1997, Rocketship 1997, Acme 1998, Magical Colours 2000, Plastic Fang 2002, Jukebox Explosion 2007; with Heavy Trash: Heavy Trash 2005, Going Way Out with Heavy Trash 2007, Mightnight Soul Serenade 2009; solo: The Man Who Lives for Love (with Luther Dickinson) 2006. *Address:* In the Red Records, P.O. Box 50777, Los Angeles, CA 90050, USA (office). *E-mail:* info@intheredrecords .com (office). *Website:* www.intheredrecords.com (office); www.heavytrash .net.

SPILLANE, Davy; Irish musician (uillean pipes, whistle); b. 1959, Dublin. *Career:* began playing pipes aged 13; Founder-mem. Moving Hearts; solo artist; formed the Davy Spillane Band; launched label, Burrenstone Records 2000–; soloist in Riverdance; instrument maker; collaborations with Elvis Costello, Bryan Adams, Kate Bush, Van Morrison, Tim Finn, Baba Maal, Afro Celt Sound System. *Film appearance:* Traveller. *Recordings include:* Out of The Air (featuring Rory Gallagher), Atlantic Bridge 1988, The Storm (with Moving Hearts) 1989, Shadow Hunter 1990, Pipedreams, A Place Among The Stones 1994, Sea of Dreams 1998. *Honours:* Grammy Award for Best New Age Album (for Celtic Solstice, Paul Winter and Friends) 2000. *E-mail:* davy@ davyspillane.com (office). *Website:* www.davyspillane.com.

SPILLANE, John; Irish musician, singer, songwriter, storyteller and poet; b. (John Mary Spillane), 3 Jan. 1961, Cork. *Education:* Univ. Coll. Cork. *Career:* performer and recording artist; fmr mem. of traditional band, Nomos; solo artist; songs recorded by artists including Christy Moore, Karan Casey, Pauline Scanlon, Cathy Ryan, Sharon Shannon, Sean Keane, George Murphy; has toured Europe, Japan, Ireland and USA; visited Senegal to film a 'musical visit' for an Irish TV series, met and played music with, among others, the legendary Baaba Maal; tour to Australia 2008, sang Irish Nat. Anthem before 45,000 people attending the Australia vs Ireland Ozzie Rules Football and also sang for Pres. of Ireland, Mary McAleese (by invitation). *Recordings include:* with Nomos: I Won't Be Afraid Anymore 1995, Set You Free 1997; solo: The Wells of The World 1997, Will We Be Brilliant Or What? 2002, The Boy who had no Story (film soundtrack) 2003, Hey Dreamer 2005, The Gaelic Hit Factory 2006, Dark Rosaleen and the Island of Dreams 2008. *Radio:* hosts weekly radio show, Rogha John Spillane. *Television:* presenter of Chúrsaí Ceoil series for RTÉ. *Honours:* Winner Realta Irish Song Contest (with Louis de Paor) 2001, Meteor Ireland Music Award for Best Folk/Traditional Artist 2003, 2006. *Current Management:* c/o Verge Management Ltd, 4 Mountain Villa, Killiney, Co. Dublin, Ireland. *Telephone:* (1) 2722799. *Fax:* (1) 2721212. *E-mail:* verge@johnspillane.ie. *Website:* www.johnspillane.ie.

SPINDERELLA; American DJ and producer; b. (Deidre (Dee Dee) Roper), 3 Aug. 1971, New York; one c. *Career:* joined female rap duo Salt-N-Pepa 1987, as DJ 'Spinderella'. *Recordings include:* albums: A Salt With A Deadly Pepa 1988, Blacks' Magic 1990, Very Necessary 1993, Brand New 1997, Salt-N-Pepa... The Best Of 2000; singles include: Push It 1988, Shake Your Thang (It's Your Thing) 1988, Twist and Shout 1988, Expression 1990, Do You Want Me 1991, Let's Talk About Sex 1991, Let's Talk About AIDS (re-write of Let's Talk About Sex) 1992, You Showed Me 1991, Start Me Up 1992, Shoop 1993, Whatta Man (with En Vogue) 1994, Ain't Nothin But A She Thing 1995, Champagne 1996, Gitty Up 1998, Brick Track Vs Gitty Up, Pt I and II 2000;. *Films:* Stay Tuned 1992, Kazaam 1996. *Honours:* Grammy for Best Rap Performance by a Duo or Group (for None Of Your Business) 1994, three MTV Awards 1994. *Telephone:* (469) 426-1148. *E-mail:* dlquinn@achievepr.net.

SPINELLI, Philip Antony; British musician (drums, keyboards) and singer; b. 30 March 1950, Newcastle upon Tyne, England; m. Biliana Mancheva 1994; one s. *Education:* Berklee Coll., Boston, USA, masterclass with Bob Armstrong, PIT, London. *Career:* founder mem., Brand X; tours with Atomic Rooster, Edwin Starr, Rick Kenton; session work with Chris Wood, Pino Palladino; several UK television appearances; mem. PRS. *Recordings include:* albums: Brand X: First album (with Phil Collins); Locust: Alpha Waves. *Address:* 19 Wharfdale, Hemel Hempstead, Herts HP2 5TQ, England.

SPINETTA SALAZAR, Dante; Argentine singer, composer and musician (guitar); b. 9 Dec. 1976, Buenos Aires; s. of Luis Alberto Spinetta; m. Majo Carnero 2001; one s., one d. *Career:* mem., group Pechugo (with Emmanuel Horvilleur) 1987–88; Founder-mem., duo Illya Kuryaki and the Valderramas (IKV) (with Emmanuel Horvilleur) 1990–2001, 2011–; solo artist 2001–. *Recordings:* albums: with Illya Kuryaki and the Valderramas: Fabrico cuero 1991, Horno para calendar los mares 1993, Chaco 1995, Versus 1997, Leche 1999, Kuryakistan 2001, Chances 2012; solo: Elevado 2002, El Apagón 2007, Pyramide 2010. *Honours:* Latin MTV Award for Best Latin Video of the Year (for Abarájame) 1996, Latin Grammy Award for Best Urban Song (for Ula Ula) 2013. *Website:* www.dantespinetta.com; ikvoficial.com.

SPINETTI, Henry Anthony George; British musician (drums); b. 31 March 1951, Cwm, Wales; m. (divorced); two s. *Career:* tours, concerts with artists, including Eric Clapton, Tina Turner, Joan Armatrading, Neil Sedaka, Andy Fairweather-Low, Procol Harum, Bill Wyman; various television and radio broadcasts; mem. Musicians' Union.

SPITERI, Sharleen Eugenie; Scottish singer, songwriter and musician (guitar, piano, organ, harmonica); b. 7 Nov. 1967, Glasgow; one d. *Career:* founding mem., Texas 1986–; guest vocals on Bad Time, The Jayhawks 1995. *Recordings include:* albums: with Texas: Southside 1989, Mother's Heaven 1991, Rick's Road 1993, White on Blonde 1997, The Hush 1999, The Greatest Hits 2000, Careful What You Wish For 2003, Red Book 2005; solo: Melody 2008. *Honours:* Capital Radio Best Female Vocal, Malta Music Prize for Best Int., Ivor Novello Award for Best Collection of Songs 1998. *Current Management:* G. R. Management Ltd, 974 Pollockshaws Road, Glasgow, G41 2HA, Scotland. *Telephone:* (141) 632-1111. *E-mail:* info@grmanagement.co.uk. *Website:* www.texas.uk.com; www.sharleenspiteri.co.uk.

SPIZZ, Julian, (Spizzman); singer and composer; b. 17 Sept. 1968, Florence, Italy. *Education:* studies in field of experimental singing. *Career:* mem. Trinovox; appearances in major German TV and radio programmes 1994; concerts in major German, Swiss, Austrian towns (Berlin, Bremen, Lübeck, Stuttgart, Basel, Vienna, Innsbruck) 1994–95; soundtrack, radio play, Bavarian State radio 1995; mem. SIAE, GEMA. *Recordings include:* albums: Incanto, Trinovox 1994, Voices, Trinovox; Sarband, The Bulgarian Voices 1994; Earborn, Trinovox and Various Artists 1995; other: Incipit 2004. *Honours:* Italian Nat. Award, vocal artists: Quartetto Cetra (with Trinovox) 1994.

SPRAGG, Rob, (Larry Love, Robert Love); British singer and songwriter; b. Nelson, Caerphilly, Wales. *Career:* singer and founder mem. (with Jake Black (aka The Very Reverend Dr D. Wayne Love)) Alabama 3 1988–, band's music is a unique fusion of country and gospel music with acid house and techno; band known as A3 in USA; solo recordings as Robert Love. *Recordings:* albums: with Alabama 3: Exile on Coldharbour Lane 1997, La Peste 2000, Power In The Blood 2002, The Last Train To Mashville 2003, Outlaw 2005, M.O.R. 2007, Revolver Soul 2010; solo: Ghost Flight 2006. *Honours:* ASCAP Award 2004. *Website:* www.alabama3.co.uk.

SPRINGFIELD, Rick; Australian/American singer, musician (guitar, piano) and actor; b. (Richard Lewis Springthorpe), 23 Aug. 1949, Merrylands, Sydney; s. of Norman Springthorpe and Eileen Springthorpe; two s. *Career:* fmr mem., Jordy Boys, Rock House, MPD Band, Zoot; solo artist 1972–. *Television:* General Hospital, High Tide; guest appearances on The Rockford Files, Wonder Woman, The Six Million Dollar Man. *Film:* Hard To Hold 1984. *Recordings include:* albums: Beginnings 1972, Comic Book Heroes 1973, Mission Magic 1974, Wait For Night 1976, Working Class Dog 1981, Success Hasn't Spoiled Me Yet 1982, Living In Oz 1983, Hard to Hold 1984, Tao 1985, Rock of Life 1988, Sahara Snow 1997, Karma 1999, Legendary 2003, Shock/Denial/Anger/Acceptance 2004, The Day After Yesterday 2005, Christmas With You 2007, Venus in Overdrive 2008, My Precious Little One 2009. *Honours:* Grammy Award for Best Male Vocal Performance (for Jessie's Girl) 1982, American Music Award for Best Rock Male Artist 1983. *Current Management:* Doyle-Kos Entertainment, 1 Penn Plaza, Suite 2107, New York, NY 10119, USA. *Telephone:* (646) 674-1500. *Fax:* (646) 674-1513. *E-mail:* info@doylekos.com. *Website:* www.doylekos.com; www.rickspringfield.com.

SPRINGSTEEN, Bruce; American singer, songwriter and musician (guitar); b. 23 Sept. 1949, Freehold, NJ; s. of Douglas Springsteen and Adele Springsteen; m. 1st Julianne Phillips 1985 (divorced 1990); m. 2nd Patti Scialfa 1991; two s. one d. *Education:* community coll. *Career:* performed in New York and NJ nightclubs; solo artist 1972–; numerous tours of USA and Europe; formed backing group the E-Street Band 1974. *Recordings include:* albums: Greetings from Asbury Park, New Jersey 1973, The Wild, The Innocent And The E-Street Shuffle 1973, Born To Run 1975, Darkness On The Edge Of Town 1978, The River 1980, Nebraska 1982, Born In The USA 1984, Bruce Springsteen And The E Street Band Live 1975–85 1986, Tunnel Of Love 1987, Chimes of Freedom 1988, Human Touch 1992, Lucky Town 1992, The Ghost Of Tom Joad 1995, The Rising (Grammy Award for Best Rock Album 2003) 2002, Roll Of The Dice 2003, Devils & Dust 2005, We Shall Overcome: The Seeger Sessions (Grammy Award for Best Traditional Folk Album 2007) 2006, Magic 2007, Working on a Dream 2009, Wrecking Ball 2012, High Hopes 2014. *Honours:* Grammy Award for Best Male Vocalist 1984, 1987, for Best Rock Performance by a Duo (jtly) 2004, BRIT Award for Best Int. Solo Artist 1986, Acad. Award for Best Original Song in a Film (for Streets of Philadelphia) 1994, MTV Best Video from a Film Award (for Streets of Philadelphia) 1994, Grammy Awards for Best Solo Rock Vocal Performance (for Devils & Dust) 2006, (for Radio Nowhere) 2008, (for Working on a Dream) 2010, for Best Rock Instrumental Performance (for Once Upon a Time in the West) 2008, for Best Rock Song (for Radio Nowhere) 2008, (for Girls in Their Summer Clothes) 2009, Golden Globe Award for Best Original Song (for The Wrestler) 2009, Kennedy Center Honor 2009. *Current Management:* Premier Talent Agency, 3 East 54th Street, New York, NY 10022, USA. *Website:* www.brucespringsteen.net.

SPRUNG, Roger; American folk singer, musician (five-string banjo), teacher and entertainer; b. 29 Aug. 1930, New York; m. Nancy 1990, two d. *Career:* tours with numerous artists, TV appearances and concerts. *Recordings include:* Bluegrass Gold, Vols 1–2 1976, The Philadelphia Folk Festival 1977, 44th Annual Galax Fiddler's Convention 1980, Pound Ridge Fiddler's Celebration 1981, Irish Grass 1983, The Irish Bluegrass Connection 1983,

Southwest Winds 1983, Let's Pick 1988, Thyme and Beyond 1989, Stompin' Stuff 1990. *Address:* 7 Papoose Hill Road, Newtown, CT 06470, USA. *E-mail:* rogersprung@gmail.com. *Website:* www.stockbridgeandberry.com/magento/Roger_Sprung/RS_Home.htm.

SQUAREPUSHER (see Jenkinson, Tom)

SQUIRE, John; British musician (guitar), singer, songwriter and artist; b. 24 Nov. 1962, Broadheath, Greater Manchester, England. *Career:* mem., the Stone Roses 1984–96; formed The Seahorses 1997–99; solo artist 2001–. *Recordings:* albums: with the Stone Roses: The Stone Roses 1989, Turn Into Stone 1992, Second Coming 1994, The Very Best Of The Stone Roses 2002; with The Seahorses: Do It Yourself 1997; solo: Time Changes Everything 2002, Marshall's House 2004. *Exhibitions:* The Smithfield Gallery, London 2007, Dazed and Confused Gallery, London 2007, Signal Gallery, London 2007, Graffle, London 2008, SW1 Gallery, London 2008, The Front Room, London 2009, Tokyo Hipsters Club, Tokyo 2009, Gallery Thiele, Austria 2009, Gallery Oldham, London 2009. *Current Management:* c/o Emma Petit, Margaret PR, 10 Victoria Park Road, London E9 7ND, England. *Telephone:* (7852) 196539. *E-mail:* emma@margaretlondon.com. *Website:* www.margaretlondon.com; www.johnsquire.com.

STAFF, Bryan Alastair, BA; New Zealand DJ, rock music journalist and photographer; b. 16 May 1950, Christchurch. *Education:* Auckland Univ. *Career:* became an announcer on commercial radio aged 19; specialized in local music; formed punk label, Ripper Records 1979–83 (producing five albums, 20 singles); continued as rock writer, reviewer, photographer; mem. Recording Industry Asscn of New Zealand. *Publication:* The Record Years (with Sheran Ashley).

STAFFORD, Jimmy W.; American musician (guitar) and songwriter; b. 26 April 1964, Morris, Ill. *Career:* fmr mem. The Apostles; Founder-mem. Train 1994–, supported bands including Barenaked Ladies, Counting Crows, Cracker, Hootie & the Blowfish. *Recordings:* albums: with The Apostles: The Apostles 1992; with Train: Train 1998, Drops of Jupiter 2001, My Private Nation 2003, For Me, It's You 2006, Save Me, San Francisco 2009, California 37 2012, Bulletproof Picasso 2014. *Honours:* Grammy Awards for Best Rock Song and Best Instrumental Arrangement 2002, for Best Pop Performance by a Duo or Group with Vocal 2011, Billboard Music Awards for Top Rock Artist and Top Rock Song 2011, ASCAP Pop Music Award for Song of the Year 2011. *Current Management:* c/o Crush Management, 60-62 East 11th Street, 7th Floor, New York, NY 10003, USA. *Telephone:* (646) 688-1729. *E-mail:* info@crushmm.com. *Website:* www.crushmm.com; www.trainline.com.

STAFFORD, Simon; British musician (bass); b. Sheffield, England. *Career:* fmr mem., The Longpigs; worked with Richard Hawley, Joe Strummer. *Recordings:* Singles: Happy Again, 1995; She Said, 1995; Jesus Christ, 1995; Far, 1996; On and On, 1996; Lost Myself, 1996; Blue Skies, 1999; The Frank Sonata, 1999; Albums: The Sun Is Often Out, 1996; Mobile Home, 1999; Also features on: Late Night Final, Richard Hawley, 2001.

STAGG, Mark Jeffrey; British producer, engineer, programmer and remixer; b. 26 May 1961, Sheffield, Yorkshire. *Education:* Manchester School of Sound Recording. *Career:* mem. of bands, Lionrock, Pro-Gress; studio work includes production for: Eskimos and Egypt, Sparks, Pro-Gress, MC Tunes; engineering for: K-Klass, Lionrock, The Grip, Björk, TC 1992, Rednex, Erasure; remixing for: Nitzer Ebb, The Shamen, Supreme Love Gods, Sweet Mercy; mem., Musicians' Union, PRS. *Recordings:* co-writer and engineer, Rhythm is a Mystery, K-Klass. *E-mail:* info@markjstagg.com. *Website:* www.markjstagg.com.

STAKENAS, Virgis; Lithuanian country singer, songwriter, musician and producer; b. 10 Aug. 1953; m. Ramute Stakeniene; one d. *Education:* Siauliai Univ., Siauliai Music School. *Career:* produced country music festivals in Lithuania; played in more than 40 big country, bluegrass, pop music festivals in USA, Canada, Holland, Germany, Denmark, Sweden, Czechoslovakia, Poland, Russia, Latvia, Estonia, Lithuania; mem. Int. Bluegrass Music Asscn. *Compositions:* more than 250 songs 1973–98. *Recordings:* Gyvenimas 1979, Vakaras 1986, Čia Tavo Namai 1989, Šiauliai 1991, Dainynas 1995, Jumbo 1997, 615 1998, SV 2000, Country Mama 2001, Tavo Zona 2002, Actros 2003, Country'Be 2003. *E-mail:* virgis@stakenas.ot.lt (office). *Website:* www.stakenas.com.

STALLINGS, Mary; American jazz singer; b. San Francisco, CA; one d. *Career:* performed with Louis Jordan's Tympani Five, Ben Webster, Wes Montgomery, Dizzy Gillespie, Billy Eckstine 1960s, Count Basie Orchestra 1969–72; solo artist. *Recordings include:* albums: solo: Cal Tjader Plays, Mary Stallings Sings 1961, Fine And Mellow 1990, I Waited For You 1994, Fine And Well 1995, Spectrum 1995, Yesterday Today And Forever 1996, Manhattan Moods 1996, Trust Your Heart 2000, Live At The Village Vanguard 2001, Remember Love 2005. *Address:* c/o Maxjazz, 115 W Lockwood Avenue, St Louis, MO 63119, USA (office). *Website:* www.maxjazz.com/stallings (office).

STAMPLEY, Joe Ronald; American country singer, musician (guitar, piano, ukulele) and songwriter; b. 6 June 1943, Springhill, LA. *Career:* solo artist 1957–; lead singer and mem. pop/rock group, The Cutups 1960, renamed The Uniques 1963–; staff writer for Gallico Music; collaborations with Moe Bandy (as Moe and Joe) 1971–89, including controversial parody of Boy George, Where's The Dress 1984; mem., The Tennessee Fat Cats. *Compositions include:* Bring It On Home To Your Woman, How Lucky Can One Man Be.

Recordings include: albums: If You Touch Me 1972, Soul Song 1973, Take Me Home To Somewhere, I'm Still Loving You 1974, Joe Stampley 1975, Billy, Get Me a Woman 1975, The Sheik of Chicago 1976, All These Things 1976, Ten Songs About Her 1976, Saturday Nite Dance 1977, Red Wine and Blue Memories 1978, I Don't Lie 1979, After Hours 1980, I'm Gonna Love You Back to Loving Me Again 1981, Backslidin' 1982, Memory Lane 1983, I'll Still Be Loving You 1985, Somewhere Under the Rainbow 2001. *Honours:* CMA Award, Vocal Duo of the Year (with Moe Bandy) 1980, Acad. of Country Music Awards, Vocal Duo of the Year (with Moe Bandy) 1979, 1980. *Address:* PO Box 150006, Nashville, TN 37215, USA (office). *Website:* www.joestampley.com.

STAN, Mircea; Romanian musician (trombone); b. 2 Oct. 1943. *Education:* 11 years study at Music High School and Conservatory in Bucharest, 1958–69. *Career:* Moved to Finland, 1970s; Formed own quartet, 1972; Ran several groups including: Sextet formed for Pori Festival, 1978; Trombone quartet, toured Finland, 1980s; Played in UMO (New Music Orchestra); Also in bands run by: Heikki Sarmanto; Edward Vesala; Seppo Paakunainen; Taught trombone at Sibelius Academy; Coaches amateur jazz bands. *Recordings:* Album: Para Los Trombones, with own sextet, late 1980s; Also appears on: Mau-mau, Edward Vesala, 1982; Thad Jones, Mel Lewis and UMO; Anthony Braxton. *E-mail:* info@mirceastan.com. *Website:* www.mirceastan.com.

STAN, Ollie; German composer, arranger, musician (keyboards) and producer; b. 28 May 1969, Kronstadt. *Career:* tour with group: Bang!, Germany, with Dr Alban; 2 Unlimited; DJ Bobo, Mega Dance Festival 1994. *Recordings include:* Papa Winnie: You Are My Sunshine 1994, Go: Your Body My Body 1994, Bang! You Know I Know 1994, Slavik/Kemmler: Indian Spirits (Dance Mixes) 1994, Powersound and Lori Glori: Freedom Forever 1995.

STANCHEV, Georgi; Bulgarian composer, arranger, lyricist and producer; b. 1 June 1951, Sofia; m. Tsvetanca Georgieva 1976; one s. two d. *Career:* solo singer, guitarist, Diana Express 1979–81; worked with Hungarian group The Times 1986; President, Georgia-Venice Music House; Executive Musical Director, Peak Music Record Company. *Recordings:* albums Lovers 1983, A Handful of Sands 1985, Be a Star Up To The End 1991, Venice 1995. *Honours:* prizes, Bulgarian Television, Knoque Festival, Belgium 1982, Dresden Festival 1983, Best Singer, Caven, Ireland 1984, Performer's Prize, Valletta, Malta 1984, Grand Prize, Composer, Siofok, Hungary 1986. *E-mail:* georgistan4ev01@abx.bg (office). *Website:* georgistanchev.com.

STANDAERT, Luc; Belgian music publisher and artist manager; b. 17 Jan. 1958, Ghent; m. Tine Lecompte 1981. *Education:* studied architecture, scenography. *Career:* scenographer 1979–82; show dir, tour manager 1982–88; music publr, artist manager 1988–; business ventures include Tempo BVBA, Tempo Media Nv, Yellow House BVBA, Taste My Music; publr of songs performed by Arno, Dinky Toys, Francis Goya, Viktor Lazlo, Jack Radics, Jean Bosco Safari; music for films includes Koko Flanel, Daens, Marie; mem. SABAM, URBEM, BVBI. *Publications:* Vrije Radio In Vlaanderen 1986. *E-mail:* info@lucstandaert.be (office). *Website:* www.lucstandaert.be.

STANGER, William John Nigel, BA, BArch, MA; British musician (saxophone, keyboards); b. 16 Jan. 1943, Newcastle upon Tyne, England; two d. *Education:* Univ. of Oxford, Univ. of Newcastle. *Career:* performed with various bands in London, including Alexis Korner, John Mayall Bluesbreakers, Alan Price Set, Herbie Goins, Night Timers 1963–66; performed with Newcastle Big Band, East Side Torpedoes, Little Mo 1996–; mem., Crosbys; various television and radio broadcasts; mem. ARCUK, Musicians' Union, Equity. *Recordings:* with John Mayall: Live At Klooks Kleek; with Alan Price: Any Day Now; Album with Newcastle Big Band; with Alexis Korner: Bootleg Him, 1993. *Address:* 51 Brandling Place South, Jesmond, Newcastle upon Tyne NE2 4RU, England.

STAŃKO, Tomasz; Polish musician (trumpet) and composer; b. 11 July 1942, Rzeszów. *Career:* mem., Kryzsztof Komeda Group 1963–67; performed with Andrzej Trzaskowski mid-1960s; leader, Tomasz Stańko Quintet 1968–73; performed with Edward Vesala in quartet 1974–78; mem., Cecil Taylor Big Band 1984; founder mem., Freelectronic mid-1980s; numerous collaborations include The Globe Unity Orchestra, Michael Urbaniak, Cecil Taylor, Gary Peacock, Bobo Stenson, Chico Freeman in Heavy Life, James Spaulding, Jack DeJohnette, Rufus Reid. *Recordings include:* albums: with Freelectronic: The Montreux Performance 1987; solo: Leosia 1996, Litania 1997, From the Green Hill 2000, Soul of Things 2002, Suspended Night 2004, Levitation (with Mark O'Leary and Billy Hart) 2005, Lontano 2006. *Honours:* European Prize in Jazz 2002. *E-mail:* book@tomaszstanko.com (office). *Website:* www.tomaszstanko.com.

STANLEY, Bob; British musician (keyboards, programming) and producer; b. 25 Dec. 1964, Horsham, Sussex, England. *Career:* journalist and writer, NME, Melody Maker, MOJO; Founder-mem. Saint Etienne 1988–; launched own label, Emidisc; Artist-in-Residence, Southbank Centre 2006–07. *Films:* writer: Finisterre 2002, Curator: Gonna Make You A Star, Pop Fiction, Britain Learns To Rock, programmes of British TV documentaries/films about popular music (Barbican, London) 2005–09; Producer: Monty the Lamb 2006. *Recordings include:* albums: Foxbase Alpha 1991, So Tough 1993, Tiger Bay 1994, Continental 1997, Good Humor 1998, The Misadventures Of Saint Etienne (soundtrack) 1999, Sound Of Water 2000, Finisterre 2002, Tales From Turnpike House 2005, Words and Music by Saint Etienne 2012. *Publications:* Match Day 2005, Yeah Yeah Yeah: The Story of Modern Pop 2013. *E-mail:*

martin@heavenlymanagement.com. *Website:* www.heavenly100.com; www.saintetienne.com; croydonmunicipal.blogspot.com.

STANLEY, Damian Mark; British producer, writer, engineer and musician (keyboards); b. 18 Aug. 1967, Nottingham, England. *Career:* recording artist as Mad, Overview, The Deadbeats, DIY, DEA, Love Brothers; owner, Spacehopper Records and DIY Communications; remixes of Moodswings, Whycliffe, Turntable Orchestra, Ashley Beedle, Jimi Polo, Alabama 3 (DIY Dub), Humdrum (soundtrack to film Hackers), Chrissie Hynde, Sly and Love Child, Chumbawamba, Mind the Gap, Leena Conquest, Secret Knowledge, Century Falls; mem. PRS, MCPS.

STANLEY, Ian Christopher; British record producer and musician (keyboards); b. 28 Feb. 1957; m. Louise; one s. *Career:* mem., Tears for Fears early 1980s; producer for artists, including Lloyd Cole & The Commotions, A-ha, Pretenders, Human League, Saturnine, Tori Amos, Mozaic, Jimmy Nail, Propaganda, Rialto, The Aloof and Ultra; produced Republica, Natalie Imbruglia, Hal, The Beautiful South, Bryan Adams, Peter Gabriel, Paul Oakenfold. *Recordings include:* albums with Tears for Fears: The Hurting 1983, Songs from the Big Chair 1985. *Current Management:* Sanctuary Producer Management, Sanctuary Townhouse, 150 Goldhawk Road, London, W12 8HH, England.

STANLEY, Paul; American singer and musician (guitar); b. (Paul Eisen), 20 Jan. 1950, Queens, NY. *Career:* mem. rock group, Kiss 1973–; numerous live appearances, tours. *Compositions:* Many for Kiss. *Recordings include:* albums: Kiss 1974, Hotter Than Hell 1974, Dressed To Kill 1975, Destroyer 1976, The Originals 1976, Rock and Roll Over 1976, Kiss Alive II 1977, Double Platinum 1978, Dynasty 1979, Kiss Unmasked 1980, Music From The Elder 1981, Creatures of The Night 1982, Lick It Up 1983, Animalize 1984, Asylum 1985, Crazy Nights 1987, Smashes Thrashes and Hits 1988, Hot In The Shade 1989, Revenge 1992, Kiss Alive III 1993, Unplugged 1996, Psycho Circus 1998, Sonic Boom 2009; solo: Paul Stanley 1978. *Current Management:* c/o Doc McGhee, McGhee Entertainment, 8730 Sunset Boulevard, Suite 2000, Los Angeles, CA 90069, USA. *E-mail:* info@mcgheela.com. *Website:* www.mcgheela.com; www.kissonline.com.

STANLEY, Ralph; American bluegrass singer and musician (banjo); b. 25 Feb. 1927, Stratton, USA; brother of Carter Stanley (deceased); m. Jimmi Stanley; one s. two d. *Career:* Founder-mem. The Lazy Ramblers 1941, touring and recording from 1946; Founder-mem. Clinch Mountain Boys 1946–51, 1967–; Founder-mem. The Stanley Brothers 1947–66; also recorded with Bob Dylan, Joan Baez, Jim Lauderdale, Iris DeMent. *Film:* Down from the Mountain 2000. *Recordings include:* with The Stanley Brothers: The Stanley Brothers: Hymns And Sacred Songs 1959, The Stanley Brothers And The Clinch Mountain Boys 1959, Sacred Songs From The Hills 1960, Long Journey Home 1961, Old Country Church 1961, Hymns Of The Cross 1964, Over The Sunset Hill 1968, Precious Memories 2002, Traditional Bluegrass Gospel 2004, An Evening Long Ago: Live 1956 2004, Choo Choo Coming 2004; with The Clinch Mountain Boys: Sing Michigan Bluegrass 1971, Sing Gospel Echoes Of The Stanley Brothers 1973; solo: Cry From The Cross 1971, Something Old Something New 1971, Old Country Church 1972, Plays Requests 1972, I Want To Preach The Gospel 1973, A Man And His Music 1973, Let Me Rest On A Peaceful Mountain 1975, Old Home Place 1976, Clinch Mountain Gospel 1977, Down Where The River Bends 1978, I'll Wear A White Robe 1980, The Stanley Sound Today 1981, The Memory Of Your Smile 1982, Snow Covered Mound 1983, Child Of The King 1983, Live! At The Old Home Place 1984, I Can Tell You The Time 1985, Live In Japan 1985, Lonesome And Blue 1986, I'll Answer The Call 1988, Like Father Like Son (with Ralph Stanley II) 1989, Pray For The Boys 1991, Christmas Time With Ralph Stanley 1993, Back To The Cross 1994, Gospel Gathering (with Joe Isaacs) 1995, Saturday Night And Sunday Morning 1996, Short Life Of Trouble: Songs Of Grayson And Whitter 1996, Clinch Mountain Country 1997, My All And All 1997, I Feel Like Singing Today (with Jim Lauderdale) 1999, While The Ages Roll On 2000, Lost In The Lonesome Pines (with Jim Lauderdale) 2002, Ralph Stanley 2002, Poor Rambler 2003, Great High Mountain 2004, Shine On 2005, A Distant Land to Roam 2006, Mountain Preacher's Son 2011, A Mother's Prayer 2011, Old Songs & Ballads 2012, Side by Side 2014, My Life & Legacy: The Very Best of Ralph Stanley 2014. *Publication:* Man of Constant Sorrow: My Life and Times 2009. *Honours:* Dr hc (Lincoln Memorial Univ.) 1976; CMA Living Legend Award, ACM Living Legend Award, IBMA Living Legend Award, three Grammy Awards, including for Best Male Country Vocalist 2001. *Current Management:* c/o Ken Levitan, Vector Management, PO Box 120479, Nashville, TN 37212, USA. *Telephone:* (615) 269-6600. *Website:* vectormgmt.com; drralphstanley.com.

STANNERS, Malcolm James, DipMus; British sound engineer, programmer and producer; b. 27 Dec. 1965, Derby, England. *Career:* sound engineer, programmer, Paradise Studios, London 1988–89, clients include: Boy George, Bill Wyman, Errol Brown; films: Madame Suzatska; Incredibly Strange Picture Show; studio owner, 4 Real Studios, 1989–; dance music producer and artist; co-founder, Salt Tank, London Records; mem, MCPS; PRS. *Recordings include:* albums: Science and Nature 1996, Wavebreaks 1998, The Energy 2001; compilation albums: Cafe Del Mar 2, Ministry of Sound, Cream, In the Mix 96, Horizons, Chill Out 2, Trance Europe Express, Essential Mix 2; remixes: Sueño Latino, Chakra, Paul Van Dyk, Orbital, Chicane, Man With No Name, Hawkwind. *E-mail:* salttank@talk21.com (office). *Website:* www.salttank.co.uk.

STANSFIELD, Lisa; British singer and actress; b. 11 April 1966, Rochdale, Lancs. *Career:* fmr presenter, Razzmatazz children's TV programme. *Recordings include:* Affection 1989, All Around the World (single) 1989, Live Together 1990, What Did I Do To You 1990, Change 1991, Real Love 1991, All Woman (single) 1991, Set Your Loving Free 1992, Time To Make You Mine (single) 1992, So Natural 1993, Lisa Stansfield 1997, Swing 1999, Never, Never Gonna Give You Up 1999, Face Up 2001, Biography 2003, The Moment 2004, Seven 2013, The Collection 1989–2003 2014. *Films include:* Swing 1999, Monkey Trousers 2005, Goldplated 2006, Agatha Christie's Marple 2007, Quest for a Heart 2007, The Edge of Love 2008, Dean Street Shuffle 2009, Northern Soul 2014. *Honours:* three Brit Awards for Best Female Vocalist. *Current Management:* c/o Neil Warnock, The Agency Group Ltd, 361-373 City Road, London, EC1V 1PQ, England. *E-mail:* london@theagencygroup.com. *Website:* www.theagencygroup.com; www.lisa-stansfield.com.

STAPLE, Neville; British singer and musician (percussion); b. 1955, Jamaica. *Career:* founder mem., Coventry Automatics, later renamed Special A.K.A., then The Specials 1977–84, 1996, 2008–; founder mem., Fun Boy Three 1981–83; solo artist 1998–; tours and live appearances world-wide. *Recordings:* albums: with The Specials: The Specials 1979, More Specials 1980, Today's Specials 1996, Guilty 'Til Proved Innocent! 1998, Conquering Ruler 2001; with Fun Boy Three: The Fun Boy Three 1982, Waiting 1983; solo: Skantastic 1998, Neville Staple From The Specials 2001, The Rude Boy Returns 2004. *E-mail:* info@nevillestaple.com (office). *Website:* www .thespecials.com; www.nevillestaple.com.

STAPLETON, Christopher (Chris) Alvin; American country music singer, songwriter and guitarist; b. 15 April 1978, Lexington, Ky; m. Morgane Stapleton; two c. *Education:* Johnson Central High School, Vanderbilt Univ. *Career:* songwriter for numerous other artists 2003–, including Adele, Trace Adkins, Luke Bryan, Kenny Chesney, Alan Jackson, Alison Krauss and Union Station, Patty Loveless, Tim McGraw, George Strait, Lee Ann Womack; lead singer and guitarist, The SteelDrivers bluegrass band 2008–10; Founder, Jompson Brothers rock band 2010; solo artist 2013–. *Recordings:* albums: with The SteelDrivers: The SteelDrivers 2008, Reckless 2010; with The Jompson Brothers: The Jompson Brothers 2010; solo: Traveller (CMA Award for Album of the Year 2015, Grammy Award for Best Country Album 2016) 2015. *Honours:* as songwriter: ASCAP Awards 2006, 2007, 2008, 2009, 2010, 2011, 2012; with The SteelDrivers: Int. Bluegrass Music Asscn Award for Emerging Artist of the Year 2010; as solo artist: Country Music Asscn (CMA) Awards for Male Vocalist of the Year and New Artist of the Year 2015, Grammy Award for Best Country Solo Performance (for Traveller) 2016. *Current Management:* c/o Red Light Management, 1101 McGavock Street, Suite 300, Nashville, TN 37203, USA. *Telephone:* (615) 279-3784. *Website:* www.redlightmanagement .com; chrisstapleton.com.

STAPLEY, Jay; British musician (guitar), producer and writer; b. 13 April 1957; m. 1990; two d. *Career:* session and live work, London 1979–; world tours and albums with Roger Waters, Tubular Bells II tours with Mike Oldfield; tours and albums with Westernhagen; mem. Songwriting Faculty, Institute of Contemporary Music Performance; mem. PRS, MCPS. *Recordings:* four solo albums; also appears on When the Wind Blows, with Roger Waters 1987, Kiss My Soul, with Roger Chapman 1996, Phoenix, with Toyah 1997, Schwarz Oder Weiss, with Klaus Schulze 1998, Just Good Stuff, Just Good Stuff 1998, All Stars And All Sorts, with Nigel Dick 2000. *Publications include:* articles on technical subjects in trade press. *Address:* Institute of Contemporary Music Performance, Foundation House, 1A Dyne Road, London, NW6 7XG, England (office). *Telephone:* (207) 328-0222 (office). *Fax:* (207) 372-4603 (office). *Website:* icmp.co.uk/teachers/jay-stapley (office). *E-mail:* jay@jaystapley.co .uk. *Website:* www.jaystapley.co.uk.

STARKEY, Zak; British musician (drums, guitar); b. 13 Sept. 1965, London, England; s. of Ringo Starr and Maureen Starkey; m. Sarah Menikides 1985; one d. *Career:* mem., The Next 1978–80, Dead Meat 1980, Monopacific 1981–83, ICE 1988–90, Animal Soup 1995; session drummer for Spencer Davis Group, The Icicle Works, The Waterboys, The Lightning Seeds, The Face, Oasis 2004–08; mem. Johnny Marr & The Healers 2000–. *Recordings include:* album: with Johnny Marr & The Healers: Boomslang 2003. *Website:* www.jmarr.com.

STARKS, Tony (see Ghostface)

STARR, Lucille; Canadian entertainer, singer and musician (guitar, bass); b. St Boniface, MB; m. 1st Bob Reagan 1955 (divorced); one s.; m. 2nd Bryan Cunningham 1978; one step-s. one step-d. *Career:* first Grand Ole Opry tour with Hank Snow 1961; television shows in Los Angeles; yodelling for Cousin Pearl on Beverly Hillbillies; mem. AFTRA, Television Screen Actors' Guild, Musicians' Union, Canadian Country Music Asscn. *Recordings include:* hits include: The French Song; Jolie Jacqueline; Colinda; Yours; Crazy Arms; Pepères Mill; First Time I've Ever Been In Love; Freight Train; Leaving It Up To You; Send Me No Roses; Collaborations include: Sylvia Tyson, 1994.

STARR, Ringo, MBE; British musician (drums); b. (Richard Starkey), 7 July 1940, Dingle, Liverpool; m. 1st Maureen Cox 1965 (divorced 1975); two s. one d.; m. 2nd Barbara Bach 1981. *Education:* Dingle Vale Secondary Modern School. *Career:* fmrly an apprentice engineer; played with Rory Storme and The Hurricanes 1959–62; mem. The Beatles 1962–70; numerous performances and tours world-wide; attended Transcendental Meditation Course at Maharishi's Acad., Rishikesh, India Feb. 1968; formed Apple Corps Ltd,

parent org. of The Beatles Group of Companies 1968; solo artist 1969–. *Film appearances include:* with The Beatles: A Hard Day's Night 1964, Help! 1965, Magical Mystery Tour (TV film) 1967, Yellow Submarine (animated film) 1968, Let it Be 1970; solo: Candy 1968, The Magic Christian 1969, 200 Motels 1971, Blindman 1971, That'll be the Day 1973, Born to Boogie (also dir and producer) 1974, Son of Dracula (also producer) 1975, Lisztomania 1975, Ringo Stars 1976, Caveman 1981, The Cooler 1982, Give My Regards to Broad Street 1984. *Television:* narrator of Thomas the Tank Engine (children's programme) 1980s. *Recordings include:* albums: with The Beatles: Please, Please Me 1963, Introducing... The Beatles 1963, With The Beatles 1963, Meet The Beatles! 1964, A Hard Day's Night 1964, Something New 1964, Beatles For Sale 1965, Help! 1965, Rubber Soul 1966, Yesterday... And Today 1966, Revolver 1966, Sgt. Pepper's Lonely Hearts Club Band (BPI Award for Best British Album) 1967, Magical Mystery Tour 1967, The Beatles (White Album) 1968, Yellow Submarine 1969, Abbey Road 1969, Let It Be 1970, At The Beeb 1994, 1 2000; solo: Sentimental Journey 1969, Beaucoups Of Blues 1970, Ringo 1973, Goodnight Vienna 1974, Blasts From Your Past 1975, Ringo's Rotogravure 1976, Ringo The 4th 1977, Bad Boy 1977, Stop And Smell The Roses 1981, Old Wave 1983, All-Starr Band 1990, Time Takes Time 1992, Live From Montreaux 1994, Vertical Man 1998, I Wanna Be Santa Claus 1999, Ringo Starr & His All-Star Band: The Anthology 2001, King Biscuit Flower Hour 2002, Ringorama 2003, Anthology... So Far 2004, Choose Love 2005, Liverpool 8 2008, Y Not 2010, Ringo 2012 2012, Postcards from Paradise 2015. *Honours:* BPI Award for Best British Group 1977, Lifetime of Peace and Love Award, David Lynch Foundation 2014. *Current Management:* c/o Elizabeth Freund, Beautiful Day Media & Management LLC, 128 Coffey Street, 1R, Brooklyn, NY 11231, USA. *E-mail:* elizabeth@beautifuldaymedia .com. *Website:* www.beautifuldaymedia.com; www.ringostarr.com.

STATHAM, Robert; Brtish musician (fretless bass guitar); b. 4 April 1959, Bournemouth, Dorset, England. *Education:* Certificate of Advanced Studies, Jazz/Rock, Guildhall School of Music. *Career:* Played with John Etheridge; Dick Heckstall-Smith; Ed Jones; Paz – Keith Emerson; Theo Travis; Radio broadcasts with Paz; Ed Jones; Theo Travis; Tours with Ed Jones; Theo Travis; mem, Musicians' Union; PRS. *Compositions:* Featured on Ed Jones album; also Ed Jones radio broadcasts, Jazz Today, 1989. *Recordings:* Ed Jones; Paz; Kelvin Christiane; Theo Travis; Totally Wired compilation (acid jazz); Bop Brothers compilation: ...And Sisters, 2000.

STATON, Canzetta (Candi); American singer; b. 13 March 1940, Alabama. *Career:* solo artist in the gospel, disco and R&B styles. *Recordings include:* albums: I'm Just a Prisoner 1969, Stand By Your Man 1971, Candi 1974, Young Hearts Run Free 1976, Music Speaks Louder Than Words 1977, House of Love 1978, Chance 1979, Nitelites 1982, Make Me an Instrument 1983, The Anointing 1985, Tell It Like it Is 1986, Sing a Song 1986, Love Lifted Me 1988, Nightlites 1989, Stand Up and Be a Witness 1990, Standing on the Promises 1991, I Give You Praise 1993, It's Time 1995, Cover Me 1997, Outside In 1999, Here's a Blessing 2000, Christmas in my Heart 2001, Proverbs 31 Woman 2002, His Hands 2006, Who's Hurting Now? 2009. *Current Management:* Beracah Ministries, PO Box 870567, Stone Mountain, GA 30087, USA. *Telephone:* (770) 266-0718. *Fax:* (770) 266-6479. *E-mail:* candistaton1@altel .net. *Website:* www.candi-staton.com.

STAVNSTRUP, Jens Peter Fjeder, (Noddy Mud); Danish singer and songwriter; b. 18 Oct. 1954, Naestved; two d. *Career:* fmr mem. of rock group Harlot, The Savage Affair; Founder-mem. Shiner (later renamed Shiner 22), Glam Gang, Queen Of Denmark, Stiff Upper Lip. *Compositions include:* Power Flower, Rain, Love Junkie, How Many?, Whole New World, Pollution Gnome, Daddy's Girl. *Recordings include:* albums: Velvet Revolution, The Savage Affair, Shiner, Mint 2001. *Telephone:* 22-14-10-84. *E-mail:* mail@fast -entertainment.dk. *Website:* www.fast-entertainment.dk. *Address:* Moldaugade 6 st th, 2300 Copenhagen, Denmark (home). *E-mail:* jenspeter .stavnstrup@kadk.dk (office); jensfjeder@gmail.com. *Website:* www.glamgang .com; www.queenofdenmark.net.

STEAD, Dave; British musician (drums); b. 15 Oct. 1966, Huddersfield, Yorkshire, England. *Career:* mem. The Beautiful South 1989–2007, 2009–; formed The New Beautiful South (with Dave Hemingway and Alison Wheeler) 2008. *Recordings include:* albums: Welcome To The Beautiful South 1989, Choke 1990, 0898 1992, Miaow 1994, Blue Is The Colour 1996, Quench 1998, Painting It Red 2000, Gaze 2002, Golddiggas, Headnodders & Pholk Songs 2004, Superbi 2006.

STEELE, Kevin; American singer, songwriter and musician (harmonica); b. Cleveland, OH. *Career:* lead singer of rock groups, Roxx Gang, Mojo Gurus; numerous live performances, tours, television and radio broadcasts. *Recordings include:* with Roxx Gang: Things You've Never Done Before 1988, The Voodoo You Love 1995, Love 'Em and Leave 'Em 1997, Mojo Gurus 1998, Roxx Gang: Old, New, Borrowed and Blue 1998, Bodacious Ta Tas 2001; with Mojo Gurus: Drinking TNT and Smokin' Dynamite 2000, Hot Damn 2003, Shakin' in the Barn 2005, Let's Get Lit with the Mojo Gurus 2009. *Address:* 7002 124th Terrace N, Largo, FL 33773, USA. *Website:* www.mojogurus.com.

STEELE, Luke James; Australian singer, musician (guitar) and songwriter; b. 13 Dec. 1979, Perth; s. of Rick Steele; one d. *Career:* singer and songwriter, The Sleepy Jackson 1998–2007; founder mem. Empire of the Sun 2006–; other appearances with Nations by the River, Pnau, Yoko Ono. *Recordings:* albums with The Sleepy Jackson: Lovers (ARIA Awards for Album of the Year, Best New Artist and Best Rock Album) 2003, Personality–One Was a Spider, One

Was a Bird (ARIA Award for Album of the Year 2006, J Award 2006) 2006; with Rick Steele: Through My Eyes 2008; with Empire of the Sun: Walking on a Dream (ARIA Award for Album of the Year 2009) 2008. *Honours:* ARIA Award for Best New Artist 2003, WAMI Award for Most Popular Local Original Single or EP 2003. *Address:* c/o EMI Music Australia, 98–100 Glover Street, PO Box 311, Cremorne, NSW 2090, Australia (office). *E-mail:* privacy@emimusic.com.au (office). *Website:* www.theinsoundfromwayout.com (office); www.walkingonadream.com.

STEELE, Michael Susan; American musician (bass guitar) and singer; b. 2 June 1959, Los Angeles, CA. *Career:* fmr mem., The Runaways 1975, Toni and the Movers 1981; mem., The Bangles 1981–90, 2002–04. *Recordings include:* albums: with The Runaways: Born to Be Bad 1975; with The Bangles: The Bangles 1982, All Over The Place 1984, Different Light 1985, Everything 1988, Doll Revolution 2003; with Lisa Dewey: Weather Changer Girl 2000, Busk 2004.

STEELE, Tommy, OBE; British actor and singer; b. (Thomas Hicks), 17 Dec. 1936, Bermondsey, London; s. of Thomas Walter Hicks and Elizabeth Ellen Bennett; m. Ann Donoughue 1960; one d. *Education:* Bacon's School for Boys, Bermondsey. *Career:* entered Merchant Navy 1952; first stage appearance Empire Theatre, Sunderland 1956, London debut 1957; roles include Buttons (Cinderella), London 1958/59, Tony Lumpkin (She Stoops to Conquer) 1960, Arthur Kipps (Half A Sixpence) 1963/64, New York 1965/66, Truffaldino (The Servant of Two Masters) 1968, title role in Hans Andersen, London 1974/75, 1977/78, 1981, Don Lockwood (Singin' in the Rain), London (also dir) 1983–85, 1989 Some Like it Hot (also dir) 1991, What a Show! 1995; film debut in Kill Me Tomorrow 1956; sculpted tribute to the Beatles' Eleanor Rigby 1982. *Films include:* The Tommy Steele Story, The Duke Wore Jeans 1957, Tommy the Toreador 1959, Light Up the Sky 1963, Its All Happening 1966, The Happiest Millionaire 1967, Half A Sixpence, Finian's Rainbow 1968, Where's Jack 1971; TV debut in Off the Record 1956, cabaret debut, Caesar's Palace, Las Vegas 1974; composed and recorded musical autobiog. My Life, My Song 1974. *Live performances include:* An Evening with Tommy Steele 1979, Tommy Steele in Concert 1998, lead role in Bill Kenwright's stage production of Scrooge (UK tour) 2003–04; Quincy's Quest (TV) 1979. *Publications include:* Hans Andersen (co-author, stage version), Quincy 1981, The Final Run 1983, Bermondsey Boy (autobiog.) 2006. *Honours:* Hon. DLitt (South Bank) 1998. *Current Management:* c/o Laurie Mansfield, International Artistes, Suite 17, Adam House, 7-10 Adam Street, London, WC2N 6AA, England. *Telephone:* (20) 7520-9411. *E-mail:* info@lauriemansfield.co.uk. *Website:* www.lauriemansfield.co.uk.

STEELS, Bobby (see RZA)

STEFANI, Gwendolyn (Gwen) Renee; American singer; b. 3 Oct. 1969, Fullerton, Calif.; m. Gavin Rossdale 2002; two s. *Career:* founder mem. and lead singer, No Doubt 1986–; simultaneous solo career 2004–; established L.A.M.B. (Love, Angel, Music, Baby) fashion label 2003–; owner publishing co., Harajuku Lover Music. *Recordings include:* albums: with No Doubt: No Doubt 1992, Beacon Street Collection 1994, Tragic Kingdom 1995, Return Of Saturn 2000, Rock Steady 2001, Everything In Time 2004, Push and Shove 2012; solo: Love Angel Music Baby 2004, The Sweet Escape 2006. *Film:* The Aviator 2004. *Honours:* Grammy Award for Best Rap/Sung Collaboration 2002, Grammy Award for Best Performance by a Duo or Group with Vocal (for Underneath It All) 2004, BRIT Award for Best Int. Female Solo Artist 2005, MTV Award for Best Art Direction (for What Are You Waiting For?) 2005, World Music Award for Bestselling Female Artist 2005, American Music Award for Favorite Female Pop/Rock Artist 2005, Billboard Music Awards for New Artist of the Year, for Digital Song of the Year (for Hollaback Girl) 2005. *Website:* www.nodoubt.com; www.gwenstefani.com.

STEINBERG, Billy; songwriter. *Career:* songs recorded by Ace Of Base, Amber, Atomic Kitten, The Bangles, Meredith Brooks, Melanie C, The Corrs, Celine Dion, Whitney Houston, Ronan Keating, Cyndi Lauper, Madonna, Robert Miles, The Pretenders, Tina Turner.

STEINCKE, Viggo; Danish musician (guitar, bass) and composer; b. 15 Nov. 1951, Viborg. *Career:* several live performances on Danish radio; mem, KODA; Danish Music Foundation. *Recordings:* with Coma: Financial Tycoon, 1977; Amoc, 1980; Love and Madness, 1986; with Colours of Blue: Colours of Blue, 1989; Workshop, 1994. *Honours:* North Jutland Country Music Award, 1991. *Address:* Schleppegrellsgade 11, 9000 Ålborg, Denmark. *E-mail:* info@steincke.dk. *Website:* www.steincke.dk.

STEINMETZ, Hugh, MA; Danish composer, conductor and musician (trumpet); *Board Member, ToneArt;* b. (Carl-Jørgen Gradt Steinmetz), 15 Feb. 1943, Copenhagen; s. of Hendrik Steinmetz and Elna Steinmetz; m. Anna Lise Malmros; one d. *Education:* Univ. of Copenhagen. *Career:* trumpet player, composer, conductor, soloist, The Danish Radio Jazz Group, The Contemporary Jazz Quintet, Cadentia Nova Danica, Hugh Steinmetz Octet, Communio Musica, VogelSteinmetz Quartet, Hugh Steinmetz Quartet, Hugh Steinmetz Sextet, ToneArt Ensemble; mem. Danish Musicians' Union, KODA, Danske Jazz, Beat og Folkemusik Autorer (DJBFA), ToneArt. *Compositions include:* Fujiama, Gizzy, Sound Like Arnoldi, Nisshinbo, Afrodisiaca, Stars and Mirrors, Mandra, Magic Waters, Relief, Traffic War Victims, Memory of a Face, Opus Statium, Electric Dancer, Flower Power, Global Community, Many Faces, Ah-Wah-Pah, Janus Head (with Hugh Steinmetz Quartet and featuring Luther Thomas), Sweet and Aggressive (with VogelSteinmetz

Quartet). *Recordings include:* Action, Nu, Afrodisiaca, City Music, Gate of Changes, Special Alloy, Flower Suite (15 pieces), Autumn Colours (for symphony orchestra), Human Ghettos (symphony), O Nightingale (choir), The Cherry Blossom (suite), Conductors Day Off (chamber orchestra), Screwball (big-band). *Honours:* Danish Jazz Musician of the Year 1966, grants from Danish State Art Foundation 1967, 1997, 1998, 1999, 2000, 2001, 2002, 2003, 2004, 2006. *Address:* Hyldegårdsvej 7, 1 tv, 2920 Charlottenlund, Copenhagen, Denmark (home). *Telephone:* 39-63-11-76 (office); 26-36-11-76 (office). *E-mail:* hugh@steinmetz.dk (home). *Website:* www.hughsteinmetz.dk.

STEINVIG, Peter, BA, MA; Danish musician (organ) and music director; b. 20 July 1955, Ronne; m. Anette; two s. three d. *Education:* Univ. of Copenhagen, Royal Danish Music Conservatory, Duke Univ. *Career:* Music Director, organist, Karlslunde Strandkirke; gospel choir leader and clinician; founder, KEFAS 1975–; originator, Copenhagen Gospel Festival 1992–; performances with Edwin Hawkins, Andrae Crouch, Richard Smallwood; mem. Danish Guild of Organists, DOKS. *Recordings:* Blessed Be The Rock, Copenhagen Gospel Festival Live 1997–99. *Publications:* 88 Salmer and Sange (hymn book), Dig Til Aere (song book). *E-mail:* kontakt@kefas.dk (office). *Website:* www.kefas.dk.

STELFOX, James Paul; British musician (bass guitar); b. 23 March 1976. *Career:* mem., Starsailor 2000–. *Recordings include:* albums: Love Is Here 2001, Silence Is Easy 2003, On the Outside 2005, All the Plans 2009. *Current Management:* Heavenly Management, 47 Frith Street, London, W1D 4SE, England. *Telephone:* (20) 7494-2998. *Fax:* (20) 7437-3317. *E-mail:* info@heavenlymanagement.com. *Website:* www.starsailor.mu.

STEN, Helge, (Deathprod); Norwegian producer and musician (electronic); b. 26 Jan. 1971, Røros. *Career:* mem. rock group Motorpsycho 1993–94; mem. experimental group, Supersilent 1997–; collaborated with Biosphere, Motorpsycho and Food. *Recordings include:* albums: solo as Deathprod: Treetop Drive 1–3 1994, Towboat 1996, Imaginary Songs from Tristan Da Cunha 1996, Nordheim Transformed 1998, Morals and Dogma 2004, 6-Track 2006; with Supersilent: 1–3 1997, 4 1998, 5 2001, 6 (Alarmprisen Award for Jazz 2004) 2003, 7 2005, 8 2007. *Address:* c/o Rune Grammofon, Akersgaten 7, 0158 Oslo, Norway (office). *E-mail:* rune@grappa.no (office). *Website:* www.runegrammofon.com (office).

STENBORG, Bebban; Swedish musician (keyboards) and singer. *Career:* mem., Shout Out Louds 2001–. *Recordings include:* albums: 100° (EP) 2003, Oh, Sweetheart (EP) 2004, Howl Howl Gaff Gaff 2005, Very Loud (EP) 2005, Our Ill Wills 2007, Work 2010. *Current Management:* c/o Filip Wilén, Bud Fox Management, Saturnusgatan 13, 224 57 Lund, Sweden. *Telephone:* (46) 13-81-20. *E-mail:* filip@budfox.se. *Website:* www.budfox.se; www.shoutoutlouds.com.

STEPHENS, Kai; British musician (bass guitar). *Career:* previously worked in pest control; bass guitar player with band Hard-Fi 2003–. *Recordings:* albums: Stars of CCTV 2005, Once Upon a Time in the West 2007; other: In Operation (DVD) 2006. *Current Management:* Necessary Records, PO Box 28362, London SE20 7WH, England. *Telephone:* (7832) 141503. *E-mail:* info@necessaryrecords.com. *Website:* www.necessaryrecords.com; www.hard-fi.com (office).

STEPHENS, Tanya; Jamaican reggae artist; b. (Vivienne Stephenson), 2 July 1973; one d. *Recordings:* albums: Too Hype 1997, Ruff Rider 1998, Sintoxicated 2001, Gangsta Blues 2004, Rebelution 2006, Infallible 2009. *Address:* c/o VP Records, 89-05 138th Street, Jamaica, New York, NY 11435, USA (office). *E-mail:* press@vprecords.com (office). *Website:* www.vprecords.com (office).

STEPHENSON, Larry Lee; American musician (mandolin, guitar); b. 24 Oct. 1956, Harrisonburg, Virginia. *Career:* Four years with Bill Harrell and The Virginians; Five years with The Bluegrass Cardinals; Six years with The Larry Stephenson Band; Tours: The Middle East; Europe; Japan; Travelled USA, Canada; Appearances: Nashville Network; Grand Ole Opry; Many Bluegrass Festivals world-wide; mem. International Bluegrass Music Asscn; BMI, Writer and Publisher; Musicians' Union. *Recordings:* albums: five with Bill Harrell; with The Bluegrass Cardinals: Home is Where the Heart Is 1984; with The Larry Stephenson Band: Everytime I Sing a Love Song 1988, Can't Stop Myself 1991, Wash My Blues Away 1993, Born to Sing 1994, Far Away in Tennessee 1995, On Fire 1998, Two Hearts On The Borderline 2001, Heavenward Bound 2001, Clinch Mountain Mystery 2004, Life Stories 2006, Thankful 2007, 20th Anniversary 2010; featured musician on about 25 other Bluegrass albums. *E-mail:* info@LarryStephensonBand.com. *Website:* www.larrystephensonband.com; www.myspace.com/larrystephensonband.

STEPHENSON, Robert; music promoter, artist manager and agent; b. 30 June 1953, Dublin, Ireland. *Education:* Belvedere Coll., Roscrea Coll., Blackrock Coll. and Trinity Coll., Dublin. *Career:* Sense of Ireland Festival, London, 1980; organizer of Irish rock festivals in London, 1986–90; Paris, 1992; manager of bands, tour organizer, agent and promoter; Managing Director of Treasure Island Promotions, Media, Music, Discs; acts on record label: Dr Millar; Ruby Horse. *Address:* Bartra Lodge, Harbour Rd, Dalkey, Co Dublin, Ireland.

STEPHENSON, Wilfredo, BA; Peruvian musician (percussion); b. 27 Feb. 1948, Lima; m. Maria Stephenson 1988; three s. two d. *Education:* Howard Univ., USA, Stockholm Univ., NM School, Stockholm, Lima Musical Conservatory. *Career:* mem. Swedish salsa group, Hot Salsa (toured Scandinavia, Europe and USA) 1979–95; percussionist, Aston Reymers Riivaler 1981–86; co-owner, Rub a Dub Records and Studio 1988–97; Co-Prod., Rub a Dub Catalogue (19 productions with salsa, Afro, flamenco and world music) 1997; mem. STIM, SAMI, SKAP, Swedish Socs. for Musicians. *Compositions include:* Lana Turkaleza 1997. *Recordings include:* albums: Hot Salsa 1979, Ensemble of Salsa Percussion (solo) 1981, Maldito Primitivo 1985, Hot Salsa Meets Swedish Jazz 1988, Lamowosbacuba 1989, Ilusiones 1992, With Friends for Friends 1995, First Summer 1998. *Honours:* Swedish Grammy (for Per Mernberg).

STERIAN, Valeriu; Romanian singer and musician (guitar, drums); b. 21 Sept. 1952, Rîmnicu Sárat; m. Lucia Sterian 1976, one s. *Education:* music school. *Career:* mem. of folk-rock group, Vali and Carmen 1973; lead singer and guitarist of rock group, Valeriu Sterian and Compania de Sunet 1975–; tours across Eastern and Western Europe. *Recordings include:* albums: Folk, 1977; Antirazbolnica, 1979; Veac XX, 1982; Nimic Fara Oameni, 1989; Noati in Norway, 1990; Vino Doamne, 1991; S-A Votat Codul Penal, 1993; Evenimentul Zilei, 1994. *Address:* Str Ion Cîmpineanu-27, Ap 75, Sect L, Bucharest, Romania.

STES, Walter; Belgian musician (bass); b. 24 Jan. 1950, Heist-Aan-Zee; m.; 3 c. *Career:* Musical Dir, Theatre Arena, Ghent 1975–85; Musical Dir, Royal Ballet of Flanders 1985–90; Leader, Blues band, Red Rooster; Sales Man., EAITC (producer of stringed instruments). *Recordings include:* Albums: Straight From the Heart, Bluesin' Up, On the Move, Never Alone.

STETSON, Colin; American musician (saxophone, clarinet); b. Ann Arbor, Mich. *Education:* Univ. of Michigan. *Career:* currently mem. of band Bon Iver; also solo performer; regular mem. of bands Sway Machinery and Bell Orchestre; numerous credits performing and recording with other artists including: Arcade Fire, LCD Soundsystem, Feist, Tom Waits. *Recordings include:* albums: New History Warfare, Volume 1 2008, New History Warfare, Volume 2: Judges 2011; Those Who Didn't Run (EP) 2011. *Address:* Billions Corporation, 3522 West Armitage Avenue, Chicago, IL 60647, USA (office); Ian Ilavsky, Constellation Records, PO Box 55012, CSP Fairmount, Montreal, Quebec, H2T 3E2, Canada (office). *Telephone:* (514) 279-9705 (office). *Fax:* (253) 736-1966 (office). *E-mail:* ian@cstrecords.com (office); colin@colinstetson.com. *Website:* www.cstrecords.com (office); colinstetson.com.

STEVENS, Cat (see ISLAM, Yusuf)

STEVENS, Craig Ronald, MS, BA, AAS; American singer; b. 30 Sept. 1959, Syracuse, NY; m. Mary L. Sinclair 1986. *Career:* touring artist, session musician, RCA Canada and Wurlitzer; contract artist, keyboardist for Thrill of a Lifetime, Canada, 1982; mem. GMA, ASCAP, CAPAC (SOCAN). *Recordings include:* Just Another Night 1980, 1981, Live At The Grand 1983, Terminal Barber Shop 1984, Risin' Child 1994. *Publication:* Poems on the Road 1983. *Honours:* Excellence in Music Education 1992. *Address:* Division Street, #1300, Suite 200, Nashville, TN 37203, USA.

STEVENS, Dane; British country singer, songwriter and musician (guitar); b. 31 July 1942, Colchester, Essex; m. Kathleen Marian 1985, three s. one d. (by a previous m.). *Career:* solo artist, working in country music clubs, major country festivals; radio plays; tours nationwide; mem. Performing Rights Soc. *Compositions include:* songs recorded by The Haleys, Jolene and Barry. *Recordings include:* albums: TBL: New Country, Across the Miles, We Danced 1998, Love is my Life 2000. *Honours:* Country Music Club Best Act.

STEVENS, Michael Jefry, MMus; musician (piano), composer and educator; b. 13 March 1951, New York, USA. *Education:* Queens Coll., New York. *Career:* extensive tours of Europe with Stevens Siegel and Ferguson Trio and the Lily White Band; various other tours including David Clayton Thomas Band; worked with Cecil Bridgewater, Dakota Staton, Charnott Moffett, Mark Whitfield, Ira Sullivan, Harold Vick, Ralph Lalama, Billy Drewes, Mark Feldman, Pheeroan Aklaff, Leo Smith, Gerry Hemingway, Phil Haynes, Perry Robinson, Ed Schuller, Thomas Chapin, Herb Robertson, Mark Whitecage, Billy Martin, Dave Douglas, Blood Sweat and Tears, The Platters, Carlos Patato Valdez, Jeff Andrews, Frank Gambale, Jaco Pastorius, Suzanne Vega; Head of Keyboard Dept, National Guitar Summer Workshop; Musical Dir, Music Theatre Ensemble, Barnard Coll. 1980–84; mem. BMI, Minnesota Composers Forum. *Compositions:* music for vocal and instrumental ensembles, dance, music-theatre, film. *Recordings:* with Mark Whitecage and Liquid Time: Liquid Time; Live At Brandeis; with Jim Finn: Jim Finn; Talking With Angels; with Tim Ferguson Trio: Habitat; Dedication; Vagabond Blues; with The Lily White Band: Somewhere Between Truth and Fiction; with Phil Haynes/Michael Stevens: Music For Percussion and Piano; with The Mosaic Sextet: Today This Moment; Live At Brandeis; with Stevens/Siegel/Ferguson: One of a Kind; with Mark Whitecage/Michael Jefry Stevens: Duo Improvisations; Live At Greenwich House; Haiku, 1995; Elements, 1996; Points of View, 1996; Short Stories, 1998. *Honours:* BMI Composers' Workshop, Eurie Blake Scholar. *Website:* michaeljefrystevens.com.

STEVENS, Michael William, ARCM, ABSM; British musician (saxophone, keyboards), producer and songwriter; b. 26 Jan. 1957, Wisbech, Cambridgeshire; m. Susan Borthwick. *Education:* Birmingham School of Music. *Career:* Musical Dir, Bill Withers 1988, Take That 1993–2011, Deni Hines 1997, Geri Halliwell 1998, B*Witched 1999, Gary Barlow 1999, Billie Piper 1999, Atomic Kitten 2001, Annie Lennox 2003, Mark Owen 2003, Gareth Gates 2004, Donny Osmond 2004, Sugababes 2005, Eurythmics 2005, Patrizio Buanne 2006, Mika 2007, Will Young 2008, James Morrison 2008; Musical Supervisor, Clandestine Marriage (film) 1997, Oh What a Night (musical theatre) 1999, Britain's Got the Pop Factor (TV) 2008; mem. LA mix. *Recordings:* solo albums: Light Up The Night 1988, Set the Spirit Free 1990, Joy 1995; as writer and producer: Songs of Mass Destruction, Annie Lennox 2007, The Annie Lennox Collection 2009, A Christmas Cornucopia 2010; as writer: Can I Go Now, Jennifer Love Hewitt, Forever Begins Tonight, Patrizio Buanne, Take That (incidental). *E-mail:* saxes1@aol.com (office).

STEVENS, Mike; Canadian musician (harmonica); b. 9 Oct. 1957, Sarnia, Ontario; m. Jane Gosselin, 8 Nov. 1986, one s. *Education:* Electrical Instrumentation at college. *Career:* First played The Grand Ole Opry, guest of Jim and Jesse, 1989; Guested over 100 times since; Tours: Canada; USA; Japan; Bahamas; Mexico; mem. SOCAN; CMRAA; HFA; AFofM; NARAS; CARAS. *Recordings:* Harmonica, 1990; Blowing Up a Storm, 1992; Life's Railway To Heaven, 1994; Joy, 1998; With Mike Stevens Project: Normally Anomaly, 1998; The World Is Only Air, 2000. *Publications:* Mike Stevens Harmonica Techniques For Bluegrass and Beyond. *Honours:* Recording of the Year, Central Canada, Bluegrass, 1990; 5 times Entertainer of the Year, Central Canada, Bluegrass; Best Selling Album, PRC, 1992; Made a Kentucky Col, 1994. *Address:* 1595 Blackwell Rd, Sarnia, ON N7X 1A4, Canada. *E-mail:* mikestevensmusic@sympatico.ca. *Website:* www.mikestevensmusic.com.

STEVENS, Paul; British musician (electric, acoustic, classical guitars) and electronics and sound engineer; b. 30 June 1969, Hammersmith, London. *Education:* Chelmsford College of Further Education, Anglia Polytechnic, Colchester Music College, Martin Smith LLCM. *Career:* parallel careers as musician and electronics/sound engineer; sessions in London, Essex and Suffolk; numeous live performances with bands including: Real Lives (early version of Blur), Hot Wired, Customs Men, Colours, Dream Age, Empathy; Product Design and Engineering Manager for Trace Elliot, designed several ranges of guitar and bass amplifiers for Trace Elliot, 1994–, Orange and Gibson, 1998–; mem. Musicians' Union; Institute of Incorporated Engineers. *Recordings:* produced solo work of guitar instrumentals 1991; session for U2: I Can't Help Falling In Love (remix at SARM West) 1992; producer for: Empathy, Universal (EP) 1995. *Honours:* HNC Electronic Engineering, 1990.

STEVENS, Roj; British musician (keyboards). *Career:* mem., Broadcast 1995–2011; signed recording contract with Duophonic label 1996, moved to Warp Records 1997. *Recordings:* albums: Work and Non Work 1997, The Noise Made By People 2000, HAHA Sound 2003, Tender Buttons 2005, The Future Crayon 2006. *Current Management:* Stereophonic Management, PO Box 3787, London, SE22 9DZ, England. *Telephone:* (20) 8299-1650. *Fax:* (20) 8693-5514. *E-mail:* duophonic@btopenworld.com. *Website:* www.broadcast.uk.net.

STEVENS, Shakin'; British singer and songwriter; b. (Michael Barratt), 4 March 1948, Ely, Cardiff, South Wales. *Career:* enjoyed much success touring for many years with his band, the Sunsets; signed as solo artist with Epic Records worldwide 1978; first UK Top 30 single, Hot Dog, charted 1980; first European chart entry, Marie Marie 1980; first UK No. 1, later an int. hit, This Ole House 1981; 39 hit singles, 37 of which were consecutive, throughout the 1980s and 1990s; UK hits: four No. 1 hits, three No. 2 hits, 12 Top 5 hits, 15 Top 10 hits, 26 Top 20 hits, 31 Top 30 hits and 33 Top 40 hits (success was mirrored across Europe and worldwide); musical collaborations incl. Bonnie Tyler, Roger Taylor, Hank Marvin, Albert Lee, Tony Joe White; tours, personal appearances and television performances worldwide, including headlining to an audience of 200,000 in Vienna 2003; most successful hit-maker of the 1980s in the UK, with more weeks in the charts (254 in the 1980s alone) than any other int. recording artist; his work has been covered by many artists, incl. Eddy Raven (A Letter To You), Sylvia (Cry Just A Little Bit) No. 1 and No. 9 in the Nashville charts, Barry Manilow (Oh Julie) US hit 1982. *Theatre:* starred in the multi-award-winning West End musical, Elvis, which ran for 19 months from 1977 (awarded Best Musical of 1977). *Recordings include:* albums: Shakin' Stevens Take One!, This Ole House, Shaky, Give Me Your Heart Tonight, The Bop Won't Stop, Greatest Hits, Lipstick, Powder And Paint, Let's Boogie, A Whole Lotta Shaky, There's Two Kinds Of Music—Rock 'N' Roll, The Epic Years, Now Listen 2007; UK hit singles include: Hot Dog 1980, Marie Marie 1980, This Ole House (No. 1, UK) 1981, You Drive Me Crazy 1981, Green Door (No. 1, UK) 1981, It's Raining 1981, Oh Julie (No. 1, UK) 1982, Shirley 1982, I'll Be Satisfied 1982, The Shakin' Stevens EP 1982, It's Late 1983, Cry Just A Little Bit 1983, A Rockin' Good Way (To Mess Around And Fall In Love) (duet with Bonnie Tyler) 1984, A Love Worth Waiting For 1984, A Letter To You 1984, Teardrops 1984, Breakin' Up My Heart 1985, Lipstick Powder And Paint 1985, Merry Christmas Everyone (No. 1, UK) 1985, Turning Away 1986, Because I Love You 1986, A Little Boogie Woogie (In The Back Of My Mind) 1987, What Do You Want To Make Those Eyes At Me For? 1987, Feel The Need In Me 1988, Love Attack 1988, I Might 1990, The Best Christmas Of Them All 1990, Radio 1992, Trouble 2005. *Honours:* 30 Top 30 hits in a decade, unsurpassed by any other artist; Best Singer/Performer, MIDEM; Chartmaker Award for four simultaneous singles in the German chart; numerous Gold and Platinum discs worldwide; first double platinum single ever to an international artist, Sweden; shares with the Beatles and Elton John the distinction of being the most successful British chart performer of a decade; Gold Badge Award, British Acad. of Composers and Songwriters, for contribution to the music industry 2000; Guinness Book of British Hit Singles, Number One Gold Award 2002; ranked 16th highest selling artist ever (UK) 2004. *Current Management:* Sue Davies, The HEC

Organisation, PO Box 3586, Bucks. SL8 5GW, England. *E-mail:* contactus@shakinstevens.com. *Website:* www.shakinstevens.com.

STEVENS, Steve; American musician (guitar); b. New York. *Career:* lead guitarist, Billy Idol 1981–88; solo artist and leader of own group, Atomic Playboys 1996–; mem. Bozzio Levin Stevens; also worked with Michael Jackson, Ric Ocasek, Steve Lukather, Thompson Twins; mem. ASCAP. *Recordings include:* albums: with Billy Idol: Don't Stop 1981, Billy Idol 1982, Rebel Yell 1983, Whiplash Smile 1986, Vital Idol 1987, Devil's Playground 2005; solo: Steve Stevens' Atomic Playboys 1989, Flamenco A Go-Go 1999, Steve Stevens 2000, Memory Crash 2008; with Bozzio Levin Stevens: Black Light Syndrome 1997, Situation Dangerous 2000. *Film:* DogTown (music score) 2000. *Honours:* Grammy Award for Best Pop Instrumental Performance (for Top Gun Anthem) 1986. *Address:* c/o J.H. Cohn, 720 Palisade Avenue, Englewood Cliffs, NJ 07632, USA. *Telephone:* (201) 567-2600. *E-mail:* stevensagogo@hotmail.com. *Website:* www.myspace.com/stevestevensmemorycrash.

STEVENS, Sufjan; American singer, songwriter and musician; b. 1 July 1975, Detroit, Mich. *Education:* Interlochen Arts Acad., Hope College, Mich., New School for Social Research, New York. *Career:* multi-instrumentalist who plays banjo, guitar, piano, drums, oboe and English horn; began musical career as mem. folk-rock band Marzuki; set up Asthmatic Kitty Records with step-father 1999; moved to New York; announced plan to record an album based on each of 50 US states entitled The Fifty States Project; commissioned by Brooklyn Acad. of Music to create music and film work exploring the Brooklyn-Queens Expressway in New York City 2007; collaborated with Rosie Thomas, Denison Witmer, Soul Junk, Half-handed Cloud, Brother Danielson, Danielson Famile, Serena Maneesh, Castanets, Shannon Stephens, Liz Janes, The National, David Garland, Ben & Vesper. *Recordings:* albums: A Sun Came 2000, Enjoy Your Rabbit (later released as Run Rabbit Run 2009) 2001, Michigan 2003, Seven Swans 2004, Illinois 2005, The Avalanche 2006, Songs for Christmas 2006, The BQE 2009, Run Rabbit Run 2009, The Age of Adz 2010, All Delighted People 2010, Carrie and Lowell 2015. *Publications:* contribs to Topic Magazine, McSweeney's The Best American Nonrequired Reading. *Honours:* New Pantheon Prize 2005, Album Of The Year, Best Album Art/Packaging and Male Artist Of The Year, PLUG Independent Music Awards 2006, Municipal Art Soc. of New York Brendan Gill Prize 2008. *Address:* Asthmatic Kitty Records, POB 1282, Lander, WY 82520, USA (office). *E-mail:* info@asthmatickitty.com (office). *Website:* asthmatickitty.com (office); sufjan.com.

STEVENSON, Jeffrey; British musician (guitar, piano), singer and songwriter; b. 14 Jan. 1947, Leeds, Yorkshire, England; m. Cecile Louise McDonald 1969, two d. *Career:* singer, guitarist, co-writer, television series Spider, BBC; support to Labi Siffre in concert; staff writer for programme Watch, BBC TV; mem. Musicians' Union, Songwriters' Guild, PRS, MCPS. *Stage appearance:* played Woof in production of musical, Hair 1970. *Compositions:* over 80 titles published and/or recorded. *Recordings include:* Spider, One Day 2000.

STEWART, Al; British singer, songwriter and musician (guitar); b. 5 Sept. 1945, Glasgow, Scotland; two d. *Career:* solo artist 1967–; numerous festival appearances and tours. *Recordings:* albums: Bedsitter Images 1967, Love Chronicles 1969, Zero She Flies 1970, Orange 1972, Past Present And Future 1974, Modern Times 1975, Year Of The Cat 1976, Time Passages 1978, Carrots 1980, Live/Indian Summer 1981, Russians And Americans 1984, Last Days Of The Century 1988, Rock The World 1990, Rhymes In Rooms (live) 1993, Between The Wars (with Laurence Juber) 1995, Seemed Like A Good Idea 1996, Live At The Roxy 1997, Acoustic Evening 1998, Down In The Cellar 2000, A Beach Full Of Shells 2005, Just Yesterday (box set) 2005. *Current Management:* Chapman and Associates Management, PO Box 55246, Sherman Oaks, CA 91413, USA. *Website:* www.alstewart.com.

STEWART, Allan, (Saigon Vietnam), BA (Hons); British musician (guitar); b. (Allan William Stewart), 21 Jan. 1977, s. of William Robert Stewart and Norma Stewart; m. Sandra Anderson. *Education:* Univ. of Glasgow. *Career:* mem. Idlewild 2002–. *Recordings include:* albums: The Remote Part 2002, Warnings/Promises 2005, Make Another World 2007, Scottish Fiction: Best of Idlewild 2007, Post Electric Blues 2009. *Current Management:* c/o Steve Nice, Nice Management, 2109 Cooley Place, Pasadena, CA 91104-4111, USA. *Telephone:* (626) 345-9794. *E-mail:* steve@nicemgmt.com. *Website:* www.nicemgmt.com; www.idlewild.co.uk.

STEWART, David (Dave) A.; British musician (guitar, keyboards) and songwriter; b. 9 Sept. 1952, Sunderland; m. 1st Pam Stewart (divorced); m. 2nd Siobhan Fahey 1987 (divorced); two s.; m. 3rd Anoushka Fisz 2001; two d. *Career:* fmr mem., Harrison and Stewart (with Brian Harrison); Founder mem. Longdancer 1973; Founder mem. The Catch 1977, later renamed The Tourists 1979–80; Founder mem. Eurythmics (with Annie Lennox) 1980–89, 1999–, live appearances worldwide; solo artist 1990–; Founder mem. The Spiritual Cowboys 1990–92; mem. Vegas 1992–93; f. record label Anxious Records 1988; founder, Dave Stewart Entertainment; Weapons of Mass Entertainment; produces and directs films, including computer-enhanced films; writes film soundtracks; owner of recording studio, The Church 1992; producer and session musician for artists, including Mick Jagger, Bob Dylan, Tom Petty, Daryl Hall, Bob Geldof, Boris Grebenshikov, Sinead O'Connor, Feargal Sharkey. *Compositions for film and television:* Rooftops 1989, De Kassière (with Candy Dulfer) 1989, Jute City (BBC1) 1991, GFI (TV series, with Gerry Anderson) 1992, No Worries 1993, The Ref 1994, Showgirls 1995, Beautiful Girls 1996, Crimetime 1996, Cookie's Fortune 1999, Honest 2000, Le Pont du trieur 2000, Chaos 2002, Around the World in 80 Days 2004, Alfie 2004; contrib. songs to numerous other films. *Film directed:* Honest 2000. *Television:* Malibu Country (co-creator) 2012. *Stage musicals:* as composer: Barbarella 2004, Ghost: the Musical 2011. *Recordings include:* albums: with The Tourists: The Tourists 1979, Reality Affect 1979, Luminous Basement 1980; with Eurythmics: In The Garden 1981, Sweet Dreams 1982, Touch 1983, Be Yourself Tonight 1985, Revenge 1986, Savage 1987, We Too Are One 1989, Eurythmics Live 1983–89 1992, Peace 1999; with The Spiritual Cowboys: Dave Stewart And The Spiritual Cowboys 1990; with Vegas: Vegas 1992; solo: Greetings From The Gutter 1994, The Blackbird Diaries 2011, The Ringmaster General 2012, Lucky Numbers 2013; with SuperHeavy: SuperHeavy 2009. *Honours:* Hon. DMus (Westminster) 1998; Ivor Novello Award for Songwriter of the Year (for Sweet Dreams, with Annie Lennox) 1984, MTV Music Award for Best New Artist Video (for Sweet Dreams (Are Made Of This)) 1984, Ivor Novello Award for Best Song (for It's Alright (Baby's Coming Back, with Annie Lennox) 1987, Grammy Award for Best Rock Performance (for Missionary Man) 1987, BRIT Awards for Best Producer 1986, 1987, 1990, for Oustanding Contribution 1999, Golden Globe Award for Best Original Song (with Mick Jagger, for Old Habits Die Hard, from the film Alfie) 2005. *Current Management:* 19 Management Ltd, Unit 33, Ransomes Dock, 35–37 Park Gate Road, London, SW11 4NP, England. *Telephone:* (20) 7801-1919. *Fax:* (20) 7801-1920. *Address:* Dave Stewart Entertainment, 6253 Hollywood Blvd, Suite 1104, Hollywood, CA 90028, USA (office). *Telephone:* (323) 871-8112 (office). *Fax:* (323) 871-8132 (office). *E-mail:* info@davestewartent.com (office). *Website:* www.davestewartent.com (office); www.davestewart.com; www.eurythmics.com.

STEWART, Donald George, MusB; American musician (clarinet), composer and music industry executive; *President, Trillenium Music Company*; b. 8 Jan. 1935, Sterling, Ill.; s. of Donald Balmer Stewart and Elinore Maud Denison; m. Susan Ann Trainer 1963 (divorced 1979); one d. *Education:* Indiana Univ., Manhattan School of Music, School of Jazz; studied with Ray Harris, Bernhard Heiden, Gunther Schuller, clarinet with Russianoff, Cioffi and Moyse. *Career:* second clarinet, Birmingham Symphony Orchestra, Ala 1954–56, Florida Symphony, Orlando 1963; played with numerous jazz ensembles, including Ornette Coleman, David Baker, Sammy Davis 1957–65; freelance copyist 1958–88; woodwind in Orchestra USA 1963–65, various orchestras, New York 1967–72; arranger and orchestrator, Harkness Ballet 1968–71; Founder Boehm Quintette, New York 1968–88, debut at Carnegie Recital Hall 1972; more than 1,000 chamber music concerts, festival appearances, with Boehm Quintette and other groups; Co-Prin. Clarinet, Sarasota Pops 2005–08; Lead Alto, Sarasota Jazz Ensemble and Good Time Groove 2005–10; Music Asst, New York State Council on Arts 1970–74; panellist, Vermont Council on the Arts 1976–78; Founder Chamber Music America 1978, Bd mem., Treas. 1982; Founder and Pres. Trillenium Music Co. 1986–; Pres. Opera North, Norwich, Vt 1987–89, Bd mem. 1985–95; mem. Bd Vermont Symphony Orchestra 1989–93; mem. ASCAP, American Fed. of Musicians, American Soc. of Music Copyists (mem. Bd Dirs 1970–87, Treas. 1984–87), American Music Centre, Music Publrs' Asscn, Retail Print Music Dealers' Asscn. *Compositions include:* Seven Little Etudes for orchestral woodwind section, Gesualdo Stanzas for large ensemble, 200-bar Passacaglia, two string quartets, Sonata No. 1 for horn and piano, No. 2 for wind quintet, String Quartet Nos 1 and 2, Saxophone Quartet, Brass Quintet, Duet for flute and bass clarinet, Violin Sonatina, Never Leave Me Blue for SSAATTBB, piano and string bass, Piccolo Concerto 1973, August Lions for youth orchestra 1978, Song of Arion 1985, First Blue Symphony for large orchestra 1988, A Book of Sliding Things for eight trombones, tuba and bass 1989, Green Mountain Christmas Card (opera) 1993, Never Seek to Tell Thy Love for voice and ensemble 1998, Duo for violin and cello 1999, Sinfonia for strings and percussion 2000, A Quartet of Flutes 2003, Third Symphony (Op. 43) Continuo Canti, Period Pieces with NooGlu (Op. 47), Third Wind Quintet, Metric Measures (Op. 48) 2008, Fourth Symphony (Music for Clarinet and Orchestra Op. 49), The Good Time Groove Op. 50 2010; transcriber, composer, arranger. *Recordings include:* three records with Boehm Quintette, Marlboro Recordings, Music of Arthur Berger. *Publications:* more than 100 titles in print 1970–. *Address:* Trillenium Music Co., PO Box 51059, Sarasota, FL 34232-0329 (office); 1515 Firethorne Lakes Drive, Sarasota, FL 34240, USA (home). *Telephone:* (941) 377-7375 (office). *Fax:* (941) 377-9043 (office). *E-mail:* don@trillmusic.com (office). *Website:* www.trillmusic.com (office).

STEWART, James (Jimmy) Otto, AA, BA; American musician (guitar), producer, composer and writer; b. 8 Sept. 1935, San Francisco, California; m. Terri Tilton 1988. *Education:* Coll. of San Mateo, Chicago School of Music, Berklee Coll. of Music, Boston. *Career:* featured soloist with: Los Angeles Philharmonic, Dallas Symphony Orchestra, St Louis Symphony Orchestra, San Francisco Light Opera; guitarist with artists including Ray Charles, Stan Getz, David Grisman, Dave Grusin, Michael Jackson, Quincy Jones, Herbie Mann, Shelly Manne, Gary McFarland, Carlos Santana, Sonny Stitt, Gabor Szabo; Musical Dir for Lainie Kazan, Chita Rivera, Andy Williams; vocal coach for Linda Ronstadt, Juice Newton, Lee Ritenour; master class tutor at Dick Grove School of Music, Musicians Inst. of Technology, Audio/Video Inst. of Technology, Hollywood, Univ. of Southern California; mem, ASCAP, NARAS, IAJE, AFM. *Compositions include:* classical pieces, music for commercials, television, films. *Recordings:* solo albums include: Once Around the Block 1964, Fire Flower 1977, Street Jazz 1981, The Touch 1987,

Evolution of Jazz Guitar 1987, Rock Tracks 1989, Power Trax 1991, Blues Trax 1992, Heavy Metal Guitar 1992, The Art, History and Style of Jazz Guitar 1993, The Complete Jazz Guitarist 1994, Tribute To Classical Guitar 1995, Memorabillia 1998; also recorded with artists including: Gabor Szabo (seven albums, including The Sorcerer 1967), Burt Bacharach, James Brown, Sammy Davis Jr, Neil Diamond, Barbra Streisand, Everly Brothers, Maurice Jarre, Dusty Springfield; featured on 1200 recordings. *Publications:* 21 guitar books include: Mode Mania 1992, Heavy Metal Guitar 1992, The Art History and Style of Jazz Guitar 1993, The Complete Jazz Guitarist 1994, Tribute To Classical Guitar 1995; numerous song books; contributor to Guitar Player, Recording Engineer and Producer magazine; Wes Montgomery Jazz Guitar Method 1968. *Honours:* Alabama Jazz Hall of Fame, Decade of Service, Guitar Player Magazine, Communicator Award, Crystal Award of Excellence 1998. *E-mail:* jimmy@thecompletemusician.com (office). *Website:* www .thecompletemusician.com.

STEWART, Jon Randall; American singer and musician (guitar, mandolin); b. 14 Feb. 1949. *Career:* lead guitar, harmony, vocals for Emmylou Harris with The Nash Ramblers 1990–95; solo artist 1998–. *Recordings include:* albums: What You Don't Know, 1995; Emmylou Harris and The Nash Ramblers of The Ryman; Cold Coffee Morning, 1999; Willin', 2000. *Address:* PO Box 159007, Nashville, TN 37215, USA.

STEWART, Natalie, (The Floacist); British singer and songwriter. *Education:* London Metropolitan Univ. *Career:* mem., Floetry 2002–; co-songwriter for Michael Jackson, Jill Scott and Jazz (Dru Hill). *Recordings include:* albums: Floetry Floetic (Soul Train Lady of Soul Award for Best Album 2003) 2002, Floetry Floacism 2003, Flo'Ology 2005. *Address:* c/o Geffen Records, 2220 Colorado Avenue, Santa Monica, CA 90404, USA (office). *Website:* www .floetry.net.

STEWART, Roderick (Rod) David, CBE; British singer; b. 10 Jan. 1945, London; m. 1st Alana Collins 1979 (divorced 1984), one s. one d.; one d. with Kelly Emberg; m. 2nd Rachel Hunter 1990 (divorced), one d. one s.; m. 3rd Penny Lancaster 2007, two s. *Career:* singer with Steampacket, Shotgun Express, Jeff Beck Group 1968–69, Faces 1969–75; solo artist 1971–. *Recordings include:* albums: two with Jeff Beck, four with Faces; solo: Every Picture Tells a Story 1971, Never a Dull Moment 1972, Atlantic Crossing 1975, A Night On The Town 1976, Foot Loose and Fancy Free 1977, Blondes Have More Fun 1978, Foolish Behaviour 1980, Tonight I'm Yours 1981, Camouflage 1984, Love Touch 1986, Out of Order 1988, The Best Of 1989, Downtown Train 1990, Vagabond Heart 1991, Lead Vocalist 1992, Unplugged… and Seated 1993, A Spanner In The Works 1995, When We Were the New Boys 1998, Human 2000, It Had To Be You… The Great American Songbook 2002, The Story So Far: The Best of Rod Stewart 2003, Thanks for the Memory 2005, Still the Same 2006, Some Guys Have All the Luck 2008, Songbook 2009, Merry Christmas, Baby 2012, Time 2013, Another Country 2015. *Publication:* Rod: The Autobiography 2012. *Honours:* Rolling Stone Magazine Rock Star of the Year 1971, British Rock and Pop Award for Lifetime Achievement 1992, BRIT Lifetime Achievement Award 1993. *Website:* www.rodstewart.com.

STEWART, Tommy; American musician (drums); b. 26 May 1966, Flint, Michigan, USA. *Career:* fmr mem. Lillian Axe and various covers groups; joined Boston-based band Godsmack for short period 1995, 1997–2002. *Recordings include:* albums: with Godsmack: Godsmack 1998, Awake 20000. *Honours:* Boston Music Award for Act of the Year 2000, 2001, Billboard Award for Rock Artist of the Year 2001.

STIEF, Bo; Danish musician (bass guitar, double bass), composer, bandleader and teacher; b. 15 Oct. 1946, Copenhagen; one s. two d. *Career:* started in Jazzhus Montmartre, accompanying Ben Webster, Stuff Smith, Roland Kirk, Yousef Lateef, New York Contemporary Five, Dexter Gordon, Roy Eldridge, Kenny Dorham, Kenny Drew and others; bass player for touring soloists, including Dexter Gordon, Chet Baker, John Scofield, Don Cherry, Stan Getz, Dizzy Gillespie; mem. Don Cherry's quintet 1966, touring Europe; mem. Pork Pie 1970s, Peter Herboltzheimer's Rhythm and Brass Combination, Entrance, Midnight Sun; composer and bandleader of own bands, Bo Stief 5, Chasing Dreams, Dream Machine 1980–; major tours, festivals throughout Europe; also played with Miles Davis, Toots Thielmans, Joe Henderson, Larry Coryell, Alex Riel, Clark Terry, Archie Shepp, Yusef Lateef, Gato Barbieri, Art Farmer, Terje Rypdal, Jan Garbarek, George Russell, Astrid Gilberto, Zoot Sims, Carla Bley, AMO, Just Friends, Palle Mikkelborg, Barbara Thompson, Ernie Watts, Jasper van't Hof Quartet, Lena Ericsson, Vince Nilsson Quartet; creator of a series of concerts under the heading The Nordic Tone. *Compositions:* Simple Song, Miss Julie (used for UN educational film), jingles for Danish programmes, Hvornår var det nu det var (DR TV) and Fredags Kanalen (Denmarks Radio). *Recordings:* albums: with Hidden Frontiers 1987, Chasing Dreams 1994, One Song III, Duo (with Arild Andersen). *Honours:* Jazz Musician of the Year 1988, Composers' Award of Honour, DJBFA 1990, Ben Webster Prize 2011. *Address:* www.thecompletemusician.comKaermindevej 11, 2820 Gentofte, Denmark (office). *E-mail:* stief@mail.tele.dk (office). *Website:* www.bostief.com.

STIGERS, Curtis; American jazz singer, songwriter and musician (clarinet, saxophone); b. 1965, Boise, ID. *Education:* classical training in clarinet. *Career:* fmr mem. of local punk and blues bands, later played in blues groups, New York; solo artist 1991–. *Recordings include:* albums: Curtis Stigers 1992, Time Was 1995, Brighter Days 1999, Baby Plays Around 2001, Secret Heart

2002, Real Emotional 2007, Lost in Dreams 2009, Let's Go Out Tonight 2012, Hooray for Love 2014. *E-mail:* comments@curtisstigers.com. *Website:* www .curtisstigers.com.

STILLS, Stephen; American singer and musician (guitar); b. 3 Jan. 1945, Dallas, TX; m. Veronique Sanson 1971. *Career:* mem., Au Go Go Singers, Buffalo Springfield 1966–68, Crosby Stills and Nash 1968–, also Crosby Stills Nash and Young, Manassas 1971–74; solo artist 1969–; numerous live performances, festivals and tours. *Recordings include:* albums: with Buffalo Springfield: Buffalo Springfield 1967, Stampede 1967, Buffalo Springfield Again 1967; with Crosby Still and Nash: Crosby Stills and Nash 1969, Déjà Vu 1970, 4-Way Street 1971, So Far 1974, Daylight Again 1982, What Goes Around 1983, Allies 1983, American Dream 1989, Live It Up 1990, Looking Forward 1999; solo: The Stooges 1969, Stephen Stills 1970, Fun House 1970, Stephen Stills 2 1971, Manassas 1972, Down the Road 1973, Stills 1975, Stephen Stills – Live On Atlantic 1976, Illegal Stills 1976, Long May You Run 1976, Still Stills – The Best of Stephen Stills 1977, Thoroughfare Gap 1978, Right By You 1984, Stills Alone 1991, Turnin' Back the Pages 2003, Man Alive! 2006, Just Roll Tape 2007; with Manassas: Manassas 1972, Down The Road 1973; with Stills/Young: Long May You Run 1976, Manassas: Pieces 2009. *Honours:* Grammy Award for Best New Artist (with Crosby Stills and Nash) 1970. *Address:* Rhino Records, 3400 W. Olive Avenue, 5th Floor, Burbank, CA 91505, USA (office). *Telephone:* (818) 238-6200 (office). *Fax:* (818) 562-9242 (office). *Website:* www.rhino.com (office); www.stephenstills.com; www.crosbystillsnash.com.

STING, CBE; British singer, musician (bass guitar), songwriter and actor; b. (Gordon Matthew Thomas Sumner), 2 Oct. 1951, Wallsend, Newcastle upon Tyne; s. of the late Ernest Sumner and Audrey Sumner (née Cowell); m. 1st Frances Tomelty 1976 (divorced 1984); one s. one d.; m. 2nd Trudie Styler 1992; two s. two d. *Education:* St Cuthbert's High School, Newcastle upon Tyne, Univ. of Warwick, Coventry, Northern Counties Coll. of Educ. *Career:* worked as bus conductor, construction labourer and tax officer –1971; primary school teacher, St Paul's First School, Cramlington, Newcastle 1975–77; played with local jazz bands, including Phoenix Jazzmen, the Newcastle Big Band, and Last Exit; mem., with Stewart Copeland and Henry Padovani (replaced by Andy Summers), and lead singer of rock group, The Police 1977–84, re-formed to tour 2007–08; solo artist 1985–; numerous tours, TV and radio broadcasts in Europe and USA. *Stage appearance:* The Threepenny Opera (Broadway) 1989, Twin Spirits 2009. *Play:* The Last Ship, writer and producer 2013, actor 2014. *Film appearances include:* Quadrophenia 1979, Radio On 1980, Artemis 81 (BBC TV) 1981, Brimstone and Treacle 1982, Dune 1984, The Bride 1985, Plenty 1985, Bring on the Night 1985, Giulia and Giulia 1987, The Adventures of Baron Munchausen 1988, Stormy Monday 1988, The Grotesque 1995, Lock, Stock and Two Smoking Barrels 1998, The Tulse Luper Suitcases: The Moab Story 2003, Bee Movie 2007. *Recordings include:* albums: with the Police: Outlandos D'Amour 1977, Regatta De Blanc 1979, Zenyatta Mondatta 1980, Ghost In The Machine 1981, Synchronicity 1983, Every Breath You Take: The Classics 1995, Sting & The Police—The Very Best Of 1997, 2002, The Police 2007; solo: The Dream of The Blue Turtles 1985, Bring On The Night 1986, Nothing Like The Sun 1987, The Soul Cages 1991, Ten Summoner's Tales 1994, Mercury Falling 1996, Brand New Day 1999, All This Time 2001, Sacred Love 2003, Songs of Love 2003, My Funny Valentine 2005, Songs From The Labyrinth 2007, Songs for Tibet – The Art of Peace 2008, If On a Winter's Night 2009, Symphonicities 2010, The Last Ship 2013. *Publications:* Jungle Stories: The Fight for the Amazon 1989, Escape Artist (memoir) 2003. *Honours:* Chevalier, Ordre des Arts et Lettres 2007; Hon. DMus (Northumbria) 1992; Ivor Novello Awards for Best Song (for They Dance Alone) 1989, four BMI songwriting awards 1998, BMI Award for Int. Achievement 2002, BRIT Award for Best Male Artist 1994, for Outstanding Contribution to Music 2002, Emmy Award for Best Performance (Sting in Tuscany… All This Time) 2002, 14 Grammy Awards (with The Police and solo), Grammy Award for Best Pop Collaboration with Vocals (for Whenever I Say Your Name, with Mary J. Blige) 2004, MusiCares Foundation Person of the Year 2003, Billboard Music Century Award for Creative Achievement 2003, Kennedy Center Honor 2014. *Current Management:* Kathryn Shenker Associates, 12th Floor, 1776 Broadway, New York, NY 10019, USA; c/o Publicity Department, Polydor Records, 72 Black Lane, London, W6, England. *Website:* www.sting.com.

STIPE, (John) Michael; American musician and songwriter; b. 1 April 1960, Decatur, Ga. *Education:* Univ. of Georgia. *Career:* Founder mem. and lead singer, R.E.M. 1980–2011; Owner, C-00 (film co.) and Single Cell Pictures 1987–; Owner, Grit vegetarian restaurant, Athens, Ga. *Films:* as composer: The Cold Lands 2014. *Recordings:* albums: Chronic Town 1982, Murmur 1983, Reckoning 1984, Fables Of The Reconstruction 1985, Life's Rich Pageant 1986, Dead Letter Office 1987, Document 1987, Eponymous 1988, Green 1988, Out Of Time (Billboard Award for Best World Album, Q Award for Best Album) 1991, Automatic For The People (Grammy Award for Best Alternative Music Album, Atlanta Music Award for Rock Album, Q Award for Best Album, Rolling Stone Critics Award for Best Album 1993) 1992, Monster 1994, New Adventures In Hi-Fi 1996, Up 1998, Star Profiles 1999, Reveal 2001, Bad Day Pt 1 and 2 2003, Glastonbury 1999 2003, Around The Sun 2004, Accelerate 2008, Collapse into Now 2011. *Honours:* numerous MTV Music Video Awards, Earth Day Award 1990, Billboard Award for Best Modern Rock Artist 1991, BRIT Awards for Best Int. Group 1992, 1993, 1995, Grammy Awards for Best Pop Performance, Best Music Video 1992, Atlanta Music Awards for Act of the

Year, Video of the Year 1992, IRMA Award for Int. Band of the Year 1993, Rolling Stone Critics Award for Best Band 1993. *Website:* www.michaelstipe .com; www.remhq.com.

STIRLING, Lindsey, BS; American violinist, singer and composer; b. 21 Sept. 1986, Santa Ana, Calif. *Education:* Mesquite High School, Brigham Young Univ. *Career:* quarter-finalist on America's Got Talent competition 2010; released debut solo album 2012; debut national tour 2012; toured UK and Ireland with Andrea Bocelli 2014; numerous collaborators including John Legend, Pentatonix, LMFAO, Decemberists, Tyler Ward. *Television:* America's Got Talent 2010. *Recordings:* albums: Lindsey Stirling 2012, Shatter Me (Billboard Music Award for Top Dance/Electronic Album 2015) 2014. *Publication:* The Only Pirate at the Party (autobiography) 2015. *Honours:* Echo Music Crossover Nat./Int. Awards 2014, 2015. *Address:* c/o Jennifer Fletcher, PO Box 87146, Phoenix, AZ 85080, USA (office). *Website:* www.lindseystirling .com.

STIRRATT, John Chadwick; American musician (bass guitar) and singer; b. 1967. *Education:* Univ. of Mississippi, Oxford. *Career:* mem., The Hilltops 1987–90; solo artist (as The Gimmecaps) 1991–93; mem., Uncle Tupelo 1993–94; mem., Wilco 1994–; mem., The Autumn Defense 1999–; mem., Laurie & John 2003–. *Recordings include:* albums: with The Hilltops: Holler 1989, Big Bad River 1990; with Uncle Tupelo: Anodyne 1993, Songs From Uncle Tupelo 89/93: An Anthology 1994, Live And Otherwise 1994; with Wilco: A.M. 1995, Being There 1996, Summerteeth 1998, Yankee Hotel Foxtrot 2002, A Ghost Is Born 2004, Sky Blue Sky 2007, Wilco (The Album) 2009, The Whole Love 2011, Star Wars 2015; with The Autumn Defense: The Green Hour 2001, Circles 2003, The Autumn Defense 2008; with Laurie & John: Arabella 2004. *Film:* I Am Trying To Break Your Heart 2002. *Current Management:* Tony Margherita Management, 116 Pleasant Street, Suite 245, Easthampton, MA 01027, USA. *E-mail:* info@tmmchi.com. *Website:* tmmchi.com; www .wilcoworld.net; www.theautumndefense.com; www.thestirratts.com.

STOCK, Michael; British songwriter, record producer and musician; b. 3 Dec. 1951, Margate, Kent; m. Frances Roberta 1975; two s. one d. *Education:* Univ. of Hull. *Career:* signed first publishing deal 1970; mem. Mirage 1976–84, Nightwork 1981–84; Founding Partner, Stock Aitken Waterman writing/production team 1984–93; Founder production co. Love This International, including Love This Records 1994–99; Co-founder Better the Devil Records 2003; writer/producer for numerous artists, including Princess, Hazell Dean, Dead or Alive, Bananarama, Mel and Kim, Rick Astley, Kylie Minogue, Jason Donovan, Donna Summer, Cliff Richard, Sybil, Kym Mazelle, Sonia, Big Fun, Sinitta, Jocelyn Brown, Nicki French, Power Rangers, Robson and Jerome, Scooch; mem. PRS, BAC&S. *Publication:* The Hit Factory 2004. *Honours:* BPI Best Producer 1988, three-time winner, Ivor Novello Songwriter of Year Award, four BMI Awards. *Website:* www.mikestockmusic.com.

STOCKMAN, Shawn Patrick 'Slim'; American singer; b. 26 Sept. 1972. *Education:* Philadelphia High School of Creative and Performing Arts. *Career:* mem., Boyz II Men 1988–; est. Stonecreek label. *Recordings:* albums: Cooleyhighharmony 1993, II 1995, Evolución 1997, Nathan Michael Shawn Wanya 2000, Full Circle 2002, Motown: Hitsville USA 2007, Love 2009. *Website:* www.boyziimen.com.

STODART, Michele; British musician (bass guitar) and singer; b. Trinidad; sister of Romeo Stodart. *Career:* mem., The Magic Numbers 2002–. *Recordings include:* albums: The Magic Numbers 2005, Those The Brokes 2006, The Runaway 2010. *Current Management:* c/o Stephen Budd, SuperVision Management Group, 59–65 Worship Street, London, EC2A 2DU, England. *Telephone:* (20) 7688-9000. *Fax:* (20) 7688-8999. *E-mail:* info@ supervisionmgt.com. *Website:* www.themagicnumbers.net.

STODART, Romeo; British musician (guitar) and singer; b. Trinidad; brother of Michele Stodart. *Career:* mem., The Magic Numbers 2002–. *Recordings include:* albums: The Magic Numbers 2005, Those The Brokes 2006, The Runaway 2010. *Current Management:* c/o Stephen Budd, SuperVision Management Group, 59–65 Worship Street, London, EC2A 2DU, England. *Telephone:* (20) 7688-9000. *Fax:* (20) 7688-8999. *E-mail:* info@ supervisionmgt.com. *Website:* www.themagicnumbers.net.

STOERMER, Mark; American musician (bass guitar); b. Las Vegas, NV. *Career:* founder mem., The Killers 2002–. *Recordings include:* albums: Hot Fuss 2004, Sam's Town (BRIT Award for Best Int. Album 2007) 2006, Sawdust 2007, Day and Age 2008, Battle Born 2012. *Honours:* NME Award for Best Int. Band 2005, for Best Video 2007, MTV Video Award for Best New Artist 2005, MTV Europe Music Award for Best Rock Act 2006, BRIT Award for Best Int. Group 2007, ASCAP Vanguard Award 2010. *E-mail:* lauren.schneider@ umusic.com. *Website:* www.thekillersmusic.com.

STOIKOV, Youri; Bulgarian composer and musician (keyboards); b. 1 March 1962, Varna; m. Savina Stoikova 1994. *Education:* St Kliment Ochridski State Univ., Varna College of Musical Harmony and Composition, with Petke Mechkev. *Career:* First and Second Festivals of Electronic Music, Getse Delchev, Bulgaria; mem. Jury, Diskovery 1994–96 Festival, Varna. *Recordings include:* Window to the Soul, cassette 1988, Things, cassette 1990, Transfiguration 1992, The Legends 1996. *Honours:* First Prize for Song dedicated to the Sea, Maritime Navigation Competition, Bulgaria 1992, Jury's Prize, Badalona, Spain. *Website:* yri.tripod.com.

STOKER, Richard, FRAM, ARAM, ARCM; British composer, actor, conductor, writer and poet and painter; b. 8 Nov. 1938, Castleford, Yorks.; s. of Bower Morrell Stoker and Winifred Stoker; m. Gillian Patricia Watson 1986. *Education:* Breadalbane House School, Castleford, Univ. of Huddersfield with Harold Truscott, Coll. of Art, Royal Acad. of Music and Drama, composition with Sir Lennox Berkeley, conducting with Maurice Miles, pvt. study with Nadia Boulanger in Paris (Mendelssohn Scholarship), Arthur Benjamin, Eric Fenby, Benjamin Britten. *Career:* performance debut with BBC Home Service 1953, Nat. and Int. Eisteddfods, Wales 1955–58; conducting debut 1956; Asst Librarian, London Symphony Orchestra 1962–63; Prof. of Composition, RAM 1963–87 (tutor 1970–80); composition teacher, St Paul's School 1972–74, Magdalene Coll., Cambridge 1974–76; Ed. The Composer magazine 1969–80; Magistrate, Inner London Comm. 1995–2003, Crown Court 1998–2003; Adjudicator, Royal Philharmonic Soc. Composer's Award, Cyprus Orchestral Composer's Award from Ministry of Culture 2001–, BBC Composer's Awards; mem. Composers' Guild 1962– (mem. Exec. Cttee 1969–80); Founder-mem. RAM Guild Cttee 1994– (Hon. Treas. 1995–); Founder-mem. European-Atlantic Group 1993–; mem. Byron Soc. 1993–2000, Magistrates' Asscn 1995–2003, English and Int. PEN 1996–2005; mem. and Treas. Steering Cttee Lewisham Arts Festival 1990, 1992; Founder-mem. Atlantic Council 1993, RSL, Creative Rights Alliance 2001–; concert appearances as pianist including Queen Elizabeth Hall, Purcell Room, Leighton House, RAM, Pizza on the Park, Barnet Festival; mem. RAM Guild. *Art exhibitions:* various works in pvt. collections including Trinity Coll. of Music. *Compositions include:* four symphonies 1961, 1976, 1981, 1991; 12 nocturnes; two jazz preludes; overtures: Antic Hay, Feast of Fools, Heroic Overture; three string quartets, three violin sonatas, Partita for Violin and Harp or Piano, Sonatina for Guitar, two piano sonatas, three piano trios, A York Suite for piano, Piano Variations, Piano Concerto, Partita for Clarinet and Piano, Wind Quintet; organ works: Partita, Little Organ Book, Three Improvisations, Symphony; Monologue, Passacaglia, Serenade, Petite Suite, Nocturnal, Festival Suite; choral works and song cycles: Benedictus, Ecce Homo, Proverb, Psalms, Make Me a Willow Cabin, Canticle of the Rose, O Be Joyful, A Landscape of Truth; piano works: Zodiac Variations, Regency Suite, A Poet's Notebook; vocal works: Music That Brings Sweet Sleep, Aspects of Flight, Four Yeats Songs, Four Shakespeare Songs, Johnson Preserv'd (three-act opera), Thérèse Raquin, Chinese Canticle, Birthday of the Infanta; music for film and stage includes Troilus and Cressida, Portrait of a Town, Garden Party, My Friend – My Enemy. *Recordings:* appearances on numerous CDs and records. *Films:* appearances include Red Mercury Rising, Woken, Daddy's Girl, Portrait of a Town, Lear and Goneril, The Shrink, Bedtime Story, The Usual, The End of the Line, The Queen, The Da Vinci Code, Ancient Cataclysms, Vagabond Shoes, Encounter, Bouquet, Interval, Home Guard Ron, Pirates of the Caribbean IV. *Television:* Mary Tudor (four-part series), Comment (Channel 4), Europe, Dirty Weekend in Hospital, Happiness (BBC), Troilus and Cressida. *Radio:* interviews and discussions on BBC Radio 3, 4, World Service, Radio Leeds, New York Times Radio, Radio New York, Wall Street Radio, Radio Algonquin. *Publications include:* Portrait of a Town 1970, Words Without Music 1974, Strolling Players 1978, Open Window – Open Door (autobiog.) 1985, Tanglewood (novel) 1990, Between the Lines 1991, Diva (novel) 1992, Collected Short Stories 1993, Sir Thomas Armstrong: A Celebration 1998, Turn Back the Clock 1998, A Passage of Time 1999; contrib. to anthologies, including Triumph, Forward, Outposts, Spotlight, Strolling Players, American Poetry Soc. publs, reviews and articles for periodicals, including Records and Recording, Books and Bookmen, Guardian, Performance, The Magistrate, poems in numerous anthologies and internet publs; contrib. to Oxford Dictionary of Nat. Biography (nine entries) 2004, 2006 (adviser 2003–). *Honours:* BBC Music Award 1952, Eric Coates Award 1962, Dove Prize 1962, Nat. Library of Poetry (USA) Editors' Choice Award 1995, 1996, 1997. *Telephone:* 7906-843812 (mobile). *E-mail:* r_stoker@ btinternet.com. *Website:* www.richardstoker.co.uk.

STOKES, Mary Teresa, BA, MA; Irish singer; b. 25 Aug. 1962, Dublin; m. Brian Palm 1994. *Career:* formed blues band, The Mary Stokes Band 1988 (later became five-piece); concerts, radio and television broadcasts; composer 1993–. *Recordings include:* three albums. *Honours:* Smithwicks Hot Press Best Newcomer Award 1989.

STOLTING, Arnold Hugo; singer, songwriter, producer and business executive; *Owner, Stolting Media Group;* b. 12 Aug. 1969, Georgetown, Guyana. *Education:* National Inst. of Broadcasting, Toronto. *Career:* productions aired on radio world-wide; producer for songwriter demo tapes; fmr producer for professional recording artists, also involved with devt of new talent; Owner, Stolting Media Group; numerous compositions in styles of dance, R&B, pop, reggae, hiphop, rap; mem. SOCAN, CMRRA. *Recordings:* Think I'm In Love, Hugo; Hey Pretty Boy, Crystal; Give It To Me Baby, Azz; In the Distance, Sona; Summatime, Blakborough. *E-mail:* info@ stoltingmediagroup.com (office). *Website:* www.stoltingmediagroup.com.

STONE, Angie; American singer and songwriter; b. Columbia, SC. *Career:* daughter of a gospel singer, started singing in church choir with father; member of rap trio The Sequence on Sugarhill records; reached the attention of Prince protégé Jill Jones and was recruited to work on her album; formed vocal trio Vertical Hold; solo artist 1999–; collaborations with Mantronix, Lenny Kravitz, D'Angelo, Omar, Mary J Blige, Guru, Alicia Keys, Prince, Gerry DeVeaux. *Recordings:* albums: A Matter of Time (with Vertical Hold) 1993, Head First (with Vertical Hold) 1995, Black Diamond 1999, Mahogany

Soul 2001, Stone Love 2004, The Art of Love and War 2007, Unexpected 2010. *Honours:* Soul Train Award for Best R&B/Soul New Artist 2000, Kora Award for Best Video of the African-American Diaspora 2002, Kora Award for Best Female Artist of the African-American Diaspora 2004. *Current Management:* c/o Ari Bernstein, ICM Talent, 825 Eighth Avenue, New York, NY 10019, USA. *Telephone:* (212) 556-5690. *E-mail:* azbernstein@icmtalent.com. *Website:* www.icmtalent.com. *E-mail:* tay24_2000@yahoo.com (office). *Website:* www.angiestoneonline.net.

STONE, Angus; Australian singer, songwriter and musician (guitar); b. 27 April 1986, Newport, NSW. *Career:* studied trombone as a child; Founder of duo Angus & Julia Stone (with sister Julia) 2006–; played as support act to The Magic Numbers, Newton Faulkner, David Gray, Martha Wainwright; solo act (as Lady of the Sunshine) 2009. *Recordings:* albums: with Angus and Julia Stone: A Book Like This 2007, Down the Way (ARIA Awards for Album of the Year and Best Adult Alternative Album 2010) 2010, Angus and Julia Stone 2014; as Lady of the Sunshine: Smoking Gun 2009. *Honours:* Australian Recording Industry Assen (ARIA) Single of the Year 2010, Australasian Performing Right Assen Awards for Songwriter of the Year Award and Song of the Year 2011. *Telephone:* (77) 17893201; 466981987 (mobile). *E-mail:* info@ originalmatters.com. *Website:* www.angusandjuliastone.com.

STONE, Doug; American musician (piano, electric and acoustic guitars, bass, mandolin, drums) and mechanic; b. 19 June 1956, Nashville, TN. *Career:* eight-year tenure with Sony Nashville; signed with Atlantic Records. *Recordings:* albums: Doug Stone 1990, I Thought It Was You 1991, From the Heart 1992, More Love 1993, Faith in Me, Faith in You 1995, Make Up in Love 1999, The Long Way 2002, In a Different Light 2005, My Turn 2007. *Honours:* Grammy Award for Best Male Vocal Performance, Horizon Award, Acad. of Country Music Awards, TNN Music City News Awards. *Current Management:* c/o Ben Ewing, Progression Music Group LLC, 530 Third Avenue South, Nashville, TN 37210, USA. *Telephone:* (615) 847-3702. *E-mail:* ben@progressionmusicgroup.com. *Website:* progressionmusicgroup.com; www .dougstone.com.

STONE, Joss; British soul singer; b. (Joscelyn Eve Stoker), 11 April 1987, Dover, Kent, England. *Recordings include:* albums: The Soul Sessions 2003, Mind Body And Soul 2004, Introducing Joss Stone 2007, Colour Me Free 2009, LP1 2011, The Soul Sessions Volume 2 2012, Water for Your Soul 2015. *Television:* The Tudors 2009–10. *Films:* Eragon 2006, Tomorrow 2015. *Honours:* BRIT Awards for Best British Female Solo Artist, Best British Urban Act 2005, Grammy Award for Best R&B Performance by a Duo or Group with Vocals (for Family Affair, with John Legend and Van Hunt) 2007. *Current Management:* c/o David Levy, William Morris Agency, Centrepoint Tower, 103 New Oxford Street, London, WC1A 1DD, England. *Telephone:* (20) 7534-6800. *Fax:* (20) 7534-6900. *E-mail:* dlevy@wma.com. *Website:* www.wma .com; www.jossstone.com.

STONE, Julia; Australian singer, songwriter and musician (guitar); b. 13 April 1984, Newport, NSW. *Career:* studied trumpet as a child; formed duo Angus & Julia Stone (with brother Angus) 2006–; played as support act to The Magic Numbers, Newton Faulkner, David Gray, Martha Wainwright; solo act 2010. *Recordings:* albums: with Angus and Julia Stone: A Book Like This 2007, Down the Way (ARIA Awards for Album of the Year and Best Adult Alternative Album 2010) 2010, Angus and Julia Stone 2014; solo: The Memory Machine 2010. *Honours:* Australian Recording Industry Assen (ARIA) Single of the Year 2010, Australasian Performing Right Assen Awards for Songwriter of the Year Award and Song of the Year 2011. *Telephone:* (77) 17893201; 466981987 (mobile). *E-mail:* info@originalmatters.com. *Website:* www .angusandjuliastone.com.

STONE, Ronald William, (Ronnie Stone); British record producer, engineer, programmer, musician (guitar) and songwriter; *Media Designer (Music and Visual), Area 5.1 Management;* b. 27 March 1959, Merseyside, England. *Education:* Union of Lancashire and Cheshire Insts. *Career:* mem. Afraid of Mice 1978; backing musician for China Crisis 1982; formed Freeze Frame 1984; producer/engineer for Easterhouse, Throwing Muses, The Pixies, Oceanic, River City People, Audioweb, Pete Wylie, Shack, Sarah Cracknell, Mansun, Christians, Connie Lush, Sian James, Lotus Eaters, TNT, Marli (singer, Fame Acad. BBC TV); live sound for Easterhouse, Jason Donovan, WOMAD 1996, 1997; consultant A&R for major record labels; has helped raise money for various charities over past ten years through Lukemia research cycling events, open garden events for Oxton Soc. *Compositions:* composer and producer for TV and cinema advertisements, including Commonwealth Games 2002, Morrisons Supermarkets 2003–06, Co-Op Banking, Yorkshire Tourist Board, Philips CD/DVD players, Yves St Laurent, BMG/Zomba TV/ film soundtrack albums, Liverpool, City of Culture (writer and exec. producer) 2008, Tesco Supermarkets 2008, Delta Airlines 2006–09, IBuyeco, Diamond Car insurance, Circulon Vodaphone Sagem, Oprah Winfrey show, Miami Ink, Nokia phones 2010, Hills and the City 2010, Olympic Games London 2012, Music for MTV show, I Just Want My Pants Back 2012. *Films:* music for soundtrack of Max-N 2004, Liverpool, Gateway to the North (3D film for EXPO China) 2010, Gobby (film about Liverpool and its sayings for Museum of Life, Liverpool 2012), Standing in the Wings 2016, ten other short films about the life and times of Liverpool, also for the museum. *Recordings as producer and engineer:* albums: Say Something Good (River City People), all works by Oceanic 1991–93, Attack of the Grey Lantern (Mansun) 1997, Connie Lush (Blues Album of the Year, TNT Best New Band) 2003, Hope (music for film

soundtrack) 2003; dance album: Insanity (producer) 1991, Loving Cup 2012, James J Turner 'Walk the Bridge' 2012, Speed of Life 2012, Nothing Lasts Forever (single) 2013, Standing in the Wings for Joe Flannery (book of same name about his work with The Beatles written with singer/writer Sue Hedges) 2014;. *Television:* music production and composition for BBC TV series, Birdman 1999, 2013, Blue Inc (Officers Club, Petroleum, Twisted Soul) music and video production. *Honours:* gold and silver discs for work with Mansun, Oceanic, River City People, Pixies, Commendation from Pres. Obama for music. *Current Management:* c/o Area 5.1 Management, TMW House, 5A Shrewsbury Road, Prenton, CH43 1UU, England. *Telephone:* 7743-385529 (mobile) (home). *E-mail:* studio@rsopro51.plus.com.

STONE, Sly; American songwriter, musician (drums, guitar) and producer; b. (Sylvester Stewart), 15 March 1944, Dallas, TX. *Career:* mem., The Stewart Four, several other bands; songwriter (as Sylvester Stewart) and Prod., Autumn Records; founder mem., The Stoners 1966, Sly and the Family Stone 1967–; numerous live appearances, festivals; worked with The Beau Brummels, Bobby Freeman, Mojo Men, The Tikis. *Recordings include:* albums: A Whole New Thing 1967, Dance To The Music 1968, Life 1968, Stand! 1969, There's A Riot Going On 1971, Fresh 1973, Small Talk 1974, High On You 1975, Heard Ya Missed Me, Well I'm Back 1976, Back On The Right Track 1979, Ain't But The One Way 1982. *Website:* www.slystonemusic .com.

STONEBRIDGE; Swedish record producer, DJ and songwriter; *Chief Executive Officer, StoneBridge Productions;* b. 2 July 1961, Stockholm. *Career:* formed Swemix, DJ service and promotion group, late 1980s; formed BTB record label 1992; formed Stoney Boy Music record label 1997; solo artist 2002; producer and songwriter; mem. STIM. *Compositions include:* Jazzy John's Freestyle Dub 1990, Back It Up 1994, Satisfy My Love 1994, Earthbeat 1996, Boy You Knock Me Out 1997, The Beach 1999, Calling 2000, Something About You 2001. *Recordings include:* All Nite Long 1999, Sometimes 2002, Can't Get Enough (artist album) 2004, The Flavour The Vibe (mix album) 2006, Music Takes Me (artist album) 2007, The Flavour The Vibe Vol II (mix album) 2008, Let It Go (with Wawa) 2008; as producer: Show Me Love, Robin S.; Make My Love, Shawn Christopher; Satisfy My Love, Sabrina Johnston; Boy You Knock Me Out, Tatyana Ali and Will Smith; The Beach, Coco and StoneBridge; remixes include: Escape, Enrique Iglesias; I Turn To You, Melanie C. (No. 1, UK), 2000; Inner Smile, Texas; Wish I Could Fly, Roxette, Feel's Good, David Morales; Lose Control, Missy Elliott; The Girl You Lost, Sia; Gimme More, Britney Spears; Love In This Club, Usher; Closer, Ne-Yo; If She Knew, Lemar; Pocketful of Sunshine, Natasha Bedingfield; Whatcha Think About That, Pussycat Dolls ft Missy Elliott; The Fear, Lily Allen; If This Isn't Love, Jennifer Hudson; Dream Big, Jazmin Sullivan. *Honours:* Best DJ, Sweden 2001, Best Remixer, Swedish Dance Awards 1991, 1993, 1994, 1996, Best 12", Winter Music Conference 1994. *Current Management:* Stonebridge Productions, Eremitvagen 6, 112 64 Stockholm, Sweden. *Website:* www .stoneyboy.com.

STONER, Joel; American recording engineer and producer; b. 13 Jan. 1964, Sewickley, PA; m. Clare B. McDonald 1991; one s. *Education:* Berklee Coll. of Music, Boston. *Career:* recording and mixing albums including Fishbone, Susanna Hoffs, Kazo Matsui, Keiko Matsui, Roxx Gang, Steve Stevens; music for film, television and commercials in all styles for major record labels and film companies. *Publications:* contrib. to professional magazines including Billboard and Mix. *Telephone:* (818) 802-3926 (office). *E-mail:* joel@studiosuite .com (office). *Website:* www.studioexpresso.com (office).

STOOKEY, Noel Paul; American singer, songwriter and producer; b. 30 Dec. 1937; m. Betty; three d. *Education:* Michigan State Univ. *Career:* mem., Peter, Paul & Mary 1960–70, 1978–; also solo artist 1971–. *Recordings include:* albums: with Peter, Paul & Mary: Peter, Paul & Mary 1962, (Moving) 1963, In the Wind 1963, In Concert 1964, A Song Will Rise 1965, See What Tomorrow Brings 1965, (untitled) 1966, 1700 1967, In Japan 1967, Late Again 1968, Peter, Paul & Mommy 1969, Ten Years Together 1970, Reunion 1978, Such is Love 1983, No Easy Walk to Freedom 1986, A Holiday Celebration 1988, Flowers and Stones 1990, Peter, Paul & Mommy Too 1993, PP M& (LifeLines) 1995, Lifelines Live 1996, Around the Campfire 1998, Songs of Conscience and Concern 1999, In These Times 2004, Carry it On 2004, The Solo Recordings 1971–1972 2008; solo: Paul and 1971, One Night Stand 1973, Real to Reel 1977, Something New and Fresh 1978, Band and Bodyworks 1979, Wait'll You Hear This! 1982, There is Love 1984, State of the Heart 1985, In Love Beyond Our Lives 1990, Circuit Rider 2002, Virtual Party 2004, Facets 2007. *Honours:* Grammy Awards 1962, 1963, 1969, Songwriters Hall of Fame Lifetime Achievement Award 2006. *Current Management:* c/o Martha Hertzberg, Walk Street Management, 22 Wavecrest Avenue, Venice, CA 90291, USA. *Telephone:* (310) 399-5001. *Fax:* (310) 399-6350. *E-mail:* information@ peterpaulandmary.com (office). *Website:* www.peterpaulandmary.com; www .noelpaulstookey.com.

STORAAS, Vigleik; Norwegian musician (piano, synthesizer); b. 9 Feb. 1963, Bergen; m. Astrid Vasseljen 1994; one s. one d. *Education:* Jazz Dept, Conservatory of Trondheim (now part of Univ. of Trondheim-NTNU). *Career:* festival appearances with Karin Krog, John Surman and Terje Rypdal and with others world-wide; also performances with NHØP, Bobby McFerrin, John Scofield and Jack DeJohnette and with most Norwegian musicians; seven albums as a leader; approx. 20 as a sideman; mem. Norsk Musikerfor- bund, NJF, Norway. *Compositions:* co-wrote many compositions, including

Nordic Quartet. *Recordings include:* Nordic Quartet (with John Surman, Karin Krog, Terje Rypdal), 1995; other albums with artists including Bjorn Alterhaug; Soyr; Norma Winstone, Karin Krog, Excess Luggage Trio. *Honours:* Spellemannprisen ('Norwegian Grammy') 1995, 1997. *Address:* Bromstadekra 21C, 7046 Trondheim, Norway (home). *Telephone:* 98-48-03-34 (office). *E-mail:* vigleikv@broadpark.no. *Website:* www.vigleikstoraas.no.

STORB, Ilse, MusD; German academic; b. 18 June 1929, Essen; d. of Friedrich Storb and Maria Storb. *Education:* girls' school, Essen, Musikhochschule, Cologne, Univ. of Cologne, Univ. of Paris (Sorbonne), France. *Career:* secondary school teacher 1957–68; Sr Teacher, Pädagogische Hochschule Ruhr, Duisburg 1968; Co-Founder Jazz Lab. for music teacher training, Munich 1971; took part in Jazz Summer Workshops for Music Educators, Berklee Coll. of Music, USA 1980, 1981; Prof. of Musicology and Jazz Research, Head of Jazz Lab., Univ. Duisburg Gesamthochschule 1982–; organizer of int. congresses on Jazz Teaching and Improvized Music 1985, 1987, 1990, 1995; Founder Ilse and her Satchmos, Jazz History Live group 1991; has given concert-lectures in Brazil, Nigeria and Tunisia; TV and radio performances. *Recordings:* Interaction 1989, Ilse and her Satchmos 1995. *Publications:* Claude Debussy 1966, Jazz: Musik in der Schule 1983, 1987, 1990, Louis Armstrong 1989, Dave Brubeck: Improvisationen und Kompositionen, die Idee der kulturellen Wechselbeziehungen 1990 (English trans. 1994), Jazz und Neue Musik im Unterricht (with CD) 2001. *Honours:* awards for Outstanding Service to Jazz Educ., Detroit, USA 1988 and Miami, USA 1992. *Address:* Bredeneyer Straße 44, 4300 Essen 1, Germany (home). *Telephone:* (201) 411079 (home).

STORCH, Scott; Canadian producer and musician (keyboards); b. 16 Dec. 1973, Halifax, Nova Scotia. *Career:* fmr keyboard player with hip-hop group The Roots; working primarily as producer, on hip-hop, R 'n' B and pop music 2000–; set up own production co. Tuff Jew Productions LLC and own record co. Storch Music Company (SMC); has produced successful tracks for artists including The Roots, Jazzyfatnastees, Busta Rhymes, Snoop Dogg, Xzibit, Eve, Mobb Deep, Mystikal, Mos Def, Justin Timberlake, Pink, Slum Village, Christina Aguilera, Onyx, Lil Kim, Britney Spears, Ginuwine, Beyoncé, Nelly, Ja Rule, Memphis Bleek, G Unit, Janet Jackson, Jadakiss, Fabolous, Mario, 50 Cent, Corey Clark, Vivian Green, Fat Joe, R. Kelly, Missy Elliot, Jason Mraz, Ricky Martin, Twista, Chris Brown, Ice Cube, MC Hammer, DMX, Paris Hilton, Kelis, Beenie Man, Brooke Hogan, The Game, Nas, Daddy Yankee, Kelly Rowland; keyboard player on tracks by Spearhead, Dr Dre, D12, Bubba Sparxxx; has incorporated influences from Middle Eastern and Indian music in many of his productions.

STORRY, Richard, DipRAM, GRSM, LRAM; British composer and musician (guitar, keyboards); b. 8 Sept. 1965, Ontario, Canada. *Education:* Royal Acad. of Music. *Career:* television appearances, radio broadcasts and live performances; tours throughout UK with the Tetra Guitar Quartet; accompanist for West End singers and Recreation Theatre Co. The Rivals; music consultant and tutor for Uncle Vanya; public speaker; examiner, Associated Bd of the Royal Schools of Music; mem. PRS, BAC&S, MCPS, PAMRA. *Compositions:* musicals: A Musical Term, Arthur, Spellbyte, Kennedy, The Fiery Phoenix, Three Sisters by Chekhov, The Brothers Lionheart. *Recordings:* Tetra by Arrangement, Tetra play Vivaldi's Four Seasons, Carmen 1999. *Publication:* The Cryptic Lines. *Honours:* Julian Bream Prize, Lady Holland Award. *Address:* 43 Orchard Gardens, London SE20 8DN, England (home). *Telephone:* (20) 8659-0069 (home).

STOTZEM, Jacques; Belgian musician (acoustic guitar); b. 17 July 1959, Verviers; one s. *Career:* major concerts include Guitar Festival of Liege 1983, 1985, Inner Circle Concert, Los Angeles, USA 1994, Int. Guitar Tour, Germany 1994, Belga Jazz Festival 1994; clinics for Fishman Transducers and Lowden Guitars, Direction, Fingerstyle Workshops, in Europe; concerts during the Namm Show, Los Angeles 1996, 1997, Int. Jazz Festival of Montreal, QC 1997, Int. Guitar Festival of Birkenhead, UK 1997, Int. Acoustic Guitar Night, Germany 1997, Japan tour 1998, concert tour of Taiwan 2002, regular concert tours in China 2005–; mem. Asscn of Stringed Instrument Artisans; Jacques Stotzem Custom Signature Edn guitar produced by Martin Guitar Co. 2007. *Recordings:* Last Thought Before Sleeping 1982, Training 1985, Words From The Heart 1988, Clear Night 1991, Straight On 1993, Two Bridges 1995, Different Ways 1996, Fingerprint 1997, Connections 2000, Sur Vesdre 2002, Jacques Stotzem in Concert 2004, Colours of Turner 2006, Simple Pleasure 2007, Catch the Spirit (lasted 43 weeks in Belgian Pop Charts 2009) 2009, Lonely Road 2011. *Publications:* Selections from Two Bridges, Straight On and Clear Night 1996. *Address:* 24 rue Francval, 4800 Lambermont, Belgium (home). *Telephone:* (87) 339050 (office). *E-mail:* jacques@stotzem.com (office). *Website:* www.stotzem.com.

STOVEY, Martin Trevor; British musician (keyboards), songwriter and arranger; b. 27 Feb. 1971, Bushey, Hertfordshire, England. *Education:* HNC Civil Engineering. *Career:* Kings College, Cambridge, 1990–92; Flavour of the Month at Borderline, 1993; Lindsay Wesker Show (Kiss FM); mem. Elixir 1995–; mem, Musicians' Union. *Recordings:* Driftings; Oh La La; Love Season; Chosen Child; Populus; I Witness, as Sykes, 2000. *E-mail:* elixir@ elixirphobos3sykes.co.uk. *Website:* www.elixirphobos3sykes.co.uk.

STOYA; German singer; b. Düsseldorf. *Career:* Founder-mem. Bombay1 2001–. *Recordings include:* albums: The Identity Thing 2001, Me Like You 2003, Strobl 2005.

STRADLIN, Izzy; American rock musician (guitar); b. (Jeffrey Isabelle), 8 April 1961, Lafayette, IN. *Career:* mem. heavy rock group, Guns N' Roses 1985–91; regular nat. and int. tours; founder mem., Izzy Stradlin and the Ju Ju Hounds 1992–. *Recordings include:* albums: with Guns N' Roses: Appetite For Destruction 1987, G 'N' R Lies 1988, Use Your Illusion I and II 1991; with the Ju Ju Hounds: Izzy Stradlin and the Ju Ju Hounds 1992, 117° 1998; solo: Ride On 1999, River 2001, On Down the Road 2002, Like a Dog 2005, Miami 2007, Fire: the Acoustic Album 2007, Concrete 2008. *Honours:* American Music Award for Favorite Heavy Metal Single, for Favorite Heavy Metal Artist and Album 1989, Rolling Stone and Billboard magazine awards. *Website:* www.chopaway.com.

STRAHAN, Derek William, BA; Australian composer, actor, singer and writer; *Director, Revolve Pty Ltd*; b. 28 May 1935, Penang, Malaysia; m. (divorced); one s. one d. *Education:* Campbell Coll., Belfast, Univ. of Cambridge. *Career:* Dir, Revolve Pty Ltd; script assessor and mem., Australian Writers' Guild; mem. Australian Music Centre, APRA, Music Arrangers' Guild of Australia, Media Entertainment and Arts Alliance; represented artist with Australia Cultural Fund of Australian Business Arts Foundation. *Radio:* presenter Words and Music, Sweet and Hot (Eastside Radio FM) 1984–2010. *Television:* Number 96 (212 episodes), Chopper Squad, Glenview High, Carrots!, Flying Start. *Film and TV appearances:* Fantasy 1991, Inspector Shanahan Mysteries (episode, Cult of Diana) 1992. *Film and TV writing:* The Unisexers (TV series) 1975, Chopper Squad (TV series) 1978, Leonora (screenplay, also dir) 1984, Fantasy (screenplay, also dir) 1991. *Compositions for film:* 30 documentaries, including Shell's Australia 1969–73, Aliens Among Us 1974, Garden Jungle 1974, Artisans of Australia 1985; films, including Leonora 1984, Fantasy 1991. *Compositions include:* String Quartet No. 1: The Key 1980, Clarinet Quintet No. 1 in D: The Princess 1980, The Quay for orchestra 1986, Rose of the Bay song cycle for mezzo-soprano, clarinet and piano 1987, String Trio No. 1 in F 1987, Piano Trio in F 1987, Sydney 200 for orchestra 1988, China Spring for cello and piano 1989, Escorts Trio 1989, Atlantis for flute and piano 1990, Solo Cello Suite No. 1 1991, Solo Cello Suite No. 2 1992, Atlantis Variations for piano 1992, Voodoo Fire for clarinet, percussion and keyboards 1994, Eden in Atlantis for soprano, flute and piano 1994, Clarinet Concerto No. 1 2001, Eden in Atlantis (opera libretto) 2002, Calypso in Exile for soprano and wind quintet 2003, Space Trilogy for trumpet and piano 2009. *Publications:* contrib. numerous articles to music publs and websites. *Address:* POB 422, Cronulla, NSW 2230, Australia (office). *Telephone:* (2) 8544-0184 (office). *Fax:* (2) 8544-0184 (office). *E-mail:* dstrahan@ revolve.com.au (home). *Website:* www.revolve.com.au (home).

STRAIT, George; American country singer; b. 18 May 1952, Poteet, Tex.; m. Norma Voss 1971; one d. (deceased) one s. *Education:* South West Texas State Univ. *Career:* solo artist, with own band, Ace in the Hole 1981–; mem. ACM, CMA. *Film appearances:* The Soldier 1982, Pure Country 1992. *Recordings include:* albums: Strait Country 1981, Strait From The Heart 1982, Right Or Wrong 1983, Does Fort Worth Ever Cross Your Mind 1984, Something Special 1985, Number 7 1986, Merry Christmas Strait To You 1986, Ocean Front Property 1987, If You Ain't Lovin', You Ain't Livin' 1988, Beyond The Blue Neon 1989, Livin' It Up 1990, Chill Of An Early Fall 1991, Holding My Own 1992, Pure Country 1992, Easy Come, Easy Go 1993, Lead On 1995, Strait Out Of The Box 1996, Blue Clear Sky 1996, Carrying Your Love With Me 1997, One Step At A Time 1998, Always Never The Same 1999, Merry Christmas Wherever You Are 1999, George Strait 2000, The Road Less Traveled 2001, Honkytonkville 2003, Somewhere Down In Texas 2005, Strait Hits 2006, It Just Comes Natural (CMA Award for Album of the Year 2007) 2006, Fresh Cut Christmas 2006, 22 More Hits 2007, Troubadour (CMA Award for Album of the Year, Grammy Award for Best Country Album 2009) 2008, Twang 2009, Here for a Good Time 2011, Love is Everything 2013. *Honours:* ACM Award for Male Vocalist of the Year 1984, 1985, 1989, CMA Award for Male Vocalist of the Year 1985, 1986, 1996, 2000, CMA Award for Album of the Year 1985, 1996, 2000, CMA Award for Entertainer of the Year 1989, 1990, 2013, ACM Awards for Entertainer of the Year 1990, 2014, SRO Touring Artist of the Year 1990, American Music Award for Top Country Vocalist 1991, CMA Award for Single of the Year 1996, CMA Award for Vocal Event of the Year 2000, CMA Award for Musical Event of the Year (for Good News Bad News, with Lee Ann Womack) 2005, ACM Awards for Single of the Year (for Give it Away) 2007, (for I Saw God Today) 2008, ACM Artist of the Decade Award 2008, 50th Anniversary Milestone Award, Acad. of Country Music 2015. *Website:* www .georgestrait.com.

STRAND, Arthur John Philip; British musician (fretboards, lute, flamenco), composer and songwriter; *Proprietor, Escutcheon Records, Music & Media;* b. 8 Oct. 1948, Finchampstead, Berks.; s. of John Strand and Ruby Strand. *Education:* South East Berks Coll., Bracknell, pvt. cornet tuition. *Career:* Six Minus Two; Sketch; Misty; BBC radio and TV (sound only); US Forces Europe, tours and residencies; own record label; folk session singarounds, acoustic; Ed. Escutcheon Magazine 1997– (now on website); mem. Asscn of British Jazz Musicians, British Acad. of Songwriters, Composers and Authors, Musicians' Union, Guild of International Songwriters and Composers, FSB, PPL, Lute Soc., Peña Flamenca, Performing Right Soc. for Music, American Soc. of Composers, Authors and Publrs (ASCAP), Asscn of Cricket Statisticians and Historians, Finchampstead Football Club (Vice-Pres. and press reporter); currently running 30 websites, including Escutcheon Media, sports websites and traders websites. *Compositions include:* 214 songs 1964–94; 150 instrumental melodies; five fusion longer works, one orchestral work 1985; supplied sequence for Figure of Eight on Flowers in the Dirt album, Paul McCartney. *Radio include:* BBC Radio 2 as bassist for Misty on Wogan show 1970. *Television include:* Space Cathedrals section of instrumentals used for US Army documentary 1980s or 1990s; song, 'Crazy Adventures' on UK TV. *Recordings as bassist:* If Not For You, Olivia Newton-John. *Publications include:* Time Itself Imploded (poem, in Poetry Now) 1996, The Last Straw and Metaphorically Communicating (poetry) 2010. *Address:* Escutcheon Media, 7 Grove Close, Nine Mile Ride, Wokingham, Berks., RG40 3NB, England (office). *Telephone:* (1344) 775566 (office); (1344) 752255 (home). *Fax:* (1344) 775566 (office); (1344) 752255 (home). *E-mail:* strand_arthur@yahoo.co.uk (office); arthur@escutcheonmedia.com (office). *Website:* www.escutcheonmedia.com (office); www.arthur -escutcheonsongs.moonfruit.com.

STRAND-HOLM, Klaus; Danish musician, singer and producer; b. 6 May 1951, Praestoe; m. Karin Maud Mortensen 1985. *Career:* recording artist 1969–; appearances on television; mem. Dansk Musiker Forbund, KODA, NCB, DPA. *Recordings include:* Den Bedste Pige, Lad mig Vaere den, Der' Rock, Der' Pop, 60'er musik, Herstedvester, Bank 3 gange, Oresund, Herlig Herlig, Ring Ring, Ska'det vaere os to, 25 Rode Roser, Vi Maa Passe Bedre Paa Vor Jord (with Klaus and Servants) 1999, Naar Et Hjerte Slaar, Jeg Vil leve, Do You Still Remember?, Pop Juhiliaren, Beach Party. *Address:* Key Sound ApS, Stadionvej 15, 4720 Praestoe, Denmark (office). *Telephone:* 55-99-21-95 (office). *E-mail:* ks-h@post8.tele.dk (office).

STRANDBERG, Orjan; Swedish composer, lyricist and musician (guitar); b. 22 Aug. 1956, Stockholm; m. Carina Strandberg 1981; one d. *Career:* musician, TV, 1970; mem. Dice (progressive rock group) 1971–80; toured in Sweden and Denmark until 1980; Signed by Peer Music as Songwriter; fmr mem JetSet group; fulltime composer, commercials and industry 1980–; Owner, Vision & Sound AB 1980–; responsible for Swedish script and lyrics for Walt Disney's World On Ice 1989–; Production Man., Producer, MicroSound AB 2000–08; mem, Bd mem., Swedish Soc. of Popular Music Composers; Bd Mem., Swedish Performing Rights Soc. 1997–2005; fmr Chair, Swedish Soc. of Media Composers, Swedish Artists' and Musicians Org. *Compositions:* commercials and industrial assignments. *Recordings:* albums: with Dice: Dice 1978, The Four Riders of the Apocalypse 1992, Live Dice 1993; Singles: with JetSet: Rock 'n' Roller Skates 1980, Diamonds for My Hands 1980; as producer, arranger: All Up to You, by World Youth Choir 1989. *Publications:* Grönsakernas Hemliga Liv (The Secret Life of Vegetables) 1986; several papers on music and copyright. *Honours:* several awards, including Silver Screen Award 1985, STIM Atterberg Prize 2014. *E-mail:* orjan@visionandsound.se. *Website:* www .visionandsound.se.

STRANDBERG, Paul Bocciolone; Swedish musician; b. 21 July 1949, Malmö. *Career:* Guitar and Cornet player; Formed Scaniazz ensemble, regular performances in Malmö and throughout Sweden; Festival appearances throughout Europe, 1975–77; Tours of Holland, Belgium, Germany, England; Played in pop and folk group playing guitar and banjo, many appearances on radio and TV; Started Absalon Orchestra, '20s style dance music band, played Breda festival, 1987; Played New Orleans Jazz and Heritage festival with Scaniazz, 1982; Band disbanded, 1987; Played cornet, Peruna Jazzmen, tours of Holland and Germany, 1983; Teacher, Jazz Institute of Malmö; Participated in events organized by Malmö College of Music; Board Member of new jazz club; Founded Paul and his Gang, 1990; Tours of Hungary and Czech Republic and at European jazz festivals including International Dixieland Festival in Dresden, Germany, 1997; Chicago, USA and Toronto, Canada, 2000; Regular tours in Europe with Hot House Jazzmen and also Original Jazzmakers; Sousaphone with Swing Kings quartet. *Recordings include:* With Scaniajazz: Some Like it Hot, 1977; Messin' Around, 1980; Sunset Café Stomp, 1982; In New Orleans, 1982; Jazzfestival Dresden, 1985–86; With Absalon Orchestra: Reaching for Someone, 1985; Stardust, 1986; Paul and His Gang: Jazzfestival Breda, 1982; Futuristic Rhythm, 1994; Hot House Jazzmen: Storyville's Sensation, 1994; Anthology; Hot House Jubilee, 1999. *Publications:* Essays and reviews of classical jazz in periodicals. *Honours:* Certificate of Merit, City of New Orleans, 1982; Cultural Award, Malmö, 1989; Grant, Arts Council of Sweden, 1991, 1994; Winner, Competition for Jazz Bands in Breda, Holland, 1992. *E-mail:* digitpaul@bredband.net. *Website:* www.paulandhisgang.com.

STRAYBLOVA, Blanka; Czech musician, composer and singer; b. 1952, Prague. *Career:* played in several alternative rock groups; mem. The Rock and Joces Extempore Band 1978–; innumerable concerts, tours; Founder-mem. MCH Band. *Recordings include:* with The Extempere Band: nine albums; with MCH Band: seven albums. *E-mail:* blankas@volny.cz.

STREET, Stephen; British record producer and musician (guitar, bass, keyboards); b. 29 March 1960, London, England; m. Sarah Street 1987; two s. one d. *Career:* recording engineer, Island Records 1980s; freelance producer, after working with The Smiths on three albums 1980s; co-wrote and produced Morrissey's first solo LP, Viva Hate 1988; pursued production career, working with artists including Blur, Lloyd Cole & The Negatives, The Cranberries, Kaiser Chiefs, The Ordinary Boys, The Pretenders, The Promise Ring, Psychedelic Furs, Shed Seven, Sleeper, Suede, Triffids, The Webb Brothers; mem. Re-Pro. *Honours:* Q Magazine Award for Best Producer 1995, Music Week Award for Producer of the Year 2006. *Website:* www.stephenstreet.net.

THE STREETS; British producer, MC and musician (keyboards); b. (Mike Skinner), 1979, Birmingham, England. *Career:* garage prod., MC and musician as 'The Streets'; numerous live appearances, including Prince's

Trust Urban Music Festival, London 2004. *Recordings include:* albums: Original Pirate Material 2002, A Grand Don't Come For Free 2004, The Hardest Way To Make An Easy Living 2006, Everything is Borrowed 2008. *Honours:* BRIT Award for Best British Male Solo Artist 2005. *Current Management:* Coalition Management, Devonshire House, 12 Barley Mow Passage, London, W4 4PH, England. *Telephone:* (20) 8987-0123. *Fax:* (20) 8987-0345. *E-mail:* management@coalitiongroup.co.uk. *Website:* www.the -streets.co.uk.

STREISAND, Barbra Joan; American singer and actress; b. 24 April 1942, Brooklyn, New York; d. of Emanuel Streisand and Diana Streisand (née Rosen); m. 1st Elliot Gould 1963 (divorced 1971); one s.; m. 2nd James Brolin 1998. *Education:* Erasmus Hall High School. *Career:* nightclub debut at Bon Soir 1961; appeared in off-Broadway revue Another Evening with Harry Stoones 1961; appeared at Caucus Club, Detroit and Blue Angel, New York 1961; played in musical comedy I Can Get It for You Wholesale 1962; began recording career with Columbia records 1963; appeared in musical play Funny Girl, New York 1964, London 1966; TV programme My Name is Barbra shown in England, Holland, Australia, Sweden, Bermuda and the Philippines, winning five Emmy awards; second programme Color Me Barbra also shown abroad; numerous concert and nightclub appearances; f. Barwood Films (film production co.) 1972; f. Streisand Foundation. *Recordings include:* albums: The Barbra Streisand Album 1963, The Second Barbra Streisand Album 1963, The Third Album 1964, My Name Is Barbra 1965, People 1965, Color Me Barbra 1966, Je m'appelle Barbra 1967, Barbra Streisand: A Happening In Central Park 1968, What About Me? 1969, Stoney End 1970, Barbra Joan Streisand 1972, Classical Barbra 1974, The Way We Were 1974, Lazy Afternoon 1975, A Star Is Born 1976, Superman 1977, Songbird, 1978, Wet 1979, Guilty (with Barry Gibb) 1980, Memories 1981, Emotion 1984, The Broadway Album 1986, One Voice 1986, Til I Loved You 1989, Just For The Record 1991, Butterfly 1992, Back To Broadway 1993, Barbra Streisand – The Concert 1994, The Concert – Highlights 1995, Mirror Has Two Faces 1996, Higher Ground 1997, A Love Like Ours 1999, Timeless 2000, Christmas Memories 2001, The Essential Barbra Streisand 2002, Duets 2002, The Movie Album 2003, Guilty Pleasures 2005, Love is the Answer 2009, One Night Only 2010, What Matters Most 2011, Release Me 2012, Partners 2014; soundtracks include: Funny Girl 1968, Yentl 1983, Nuts 1987, The Prince of Tides 1991. *Films include:* Funny Girl (Acad. Award (Oscar)) 1968, Hello Dolly 1969, On a Clear Day You Can See Forever 1969, The Owl and the Pussycat 1971, What's up Doc? 1972, Up the Sandbox 1973, The Way We Were 1973, For Pete's Sake 1974, Funny Lady 1975, A Star is Born 1977, Yentl 1983 (also dir and producer), Nuts 1987, Sing 1989, Prince of Tides 1990 (also dir, co-producer), The Mirror Has Two Faces (also dir) 1996, Meet the Fockers 2004. *Honours:* Commdr des Arts et Lettres 1984; Dr hc (Hebrew Univ. of Jerusalem) 2013; New York, Critics Best Supporting Actress Award 1962, Grammy Awards for Best Female Pop Vocalist 1963, 1964, 1965, 1977, 1986, London Critics' Musical Award 1966, American Guild of Variety Artists' Entertainer of the Year Award 1970, Nat. Medal of Arts, Emmy Award for Best Individual Performance in a Music or Variety Programme (for Barbra Streisand: Timeless) 2001, American Film Inst. Lifetime Achievement Award 2001, Kennedy Center Honor 2008, Chaplin Award, Film Soc. of Lincoln Center 2013, Presidential Medal of Freedom 2015, Sherry Lansing Leadership Award 2015. *Current Management:* Martin Erlichman Associates, 5670 Wilshire Boulevard, Suite 2400, Los Angeles, CA 90036, USA. *Address:* Barwood Films, 40 West 57th Street, #18, New York, NY 10019, USA (office). *Telephone:* (212) 762-7191 (office). *Website:* www.barbrastreisand.com.

STRICKLAND, Keith; American musician (drums); b. 26 Oct. 1953, Athens, GA. *Career:* founder mem., The B-52s 1976–, numerous live performances, particularly as touring band 1989–. *Recordings include:* albums: The B-52s 1979, Wild Planet 1980, Whammy! 1983, Bouncing Off The Satellites 1986, Cosmic Thing 1989, Good Stuff 1992, Associate, Associate 1996, Nude on the Moon: the B-52s Anthology 2002; singles: Rock Lobster 1980, Party Mix! 1981, Mesopotamia 1982, Channel Z 1989, Deadbeat Club 1989, Love Shack 1989, Roam 1990, Megamix 1991, Good Stuff 1992, Is That You Mo-Dean? 1992, Revolution Earth 1992, Tell It Like It T-I-Is 1992, Hot Pants Explosion 1993, Meet The Flintstones 1994, Time Capsule 1998, Funplex 2008. *Current Management:* Vector Management, PO Box 120479, Nashville, TN 37203, USA. *E-mail:* info@vectormgmt.com. *Website:* www.theb52s.com.

STRINGER, Sir Howard, Kt, MA; American/British electronics industry executive and broadcasting executive; b. 19 Feb. 1942, Cardiff, Wales; s. of Harry Stringer and Marjorie Mary Pook; m. Jennifer A. Kinmond Patterson 1978; two c. *Education:* Oundle School, Northants., Merton Coll., Oxford. *Career:* emigrated to USA 1965; served with US Army in Viet Nam 1965–67; researcher and producer, CBS News 1967–76; Exec. Producer, CBS Reports 1976–81, CBS Evening News 1981–84; naturalized US citizen 1985; Exec. Vice-Pres. CBS News 1984–86, Pres. 1986–88; Pres. CBS Broadcast Group 1988–95; Chair. and CEO Tele-TV 1995–97; Pres. Sony Corpn of America 1997, Chair. and CEO 1998–2012, Pres. and CEO Sony Corpn 2005–12, Chair. 2005–12, Chair. of the Bd of Sony Corpn 2012–13; Vice-Chair. American Film Inst. –1999, Chair. Bd of Trustees 1999–; non-exec. mem. Exec. Bd, BBC 2014–; mem. Bd of Dirs Six Continents PLC, BBC 2013–; Gov. Motion Picture and TV Fund Foundation; Trustee, Presbyterian Hosp., Museum of TV and Radio. *Television includes:* CBS Reports (exec. producer) 1976–81, CBS Evening News with Dan Rather (exec. producer) 1981–84. *Honours:* Hon. Fellow, Merton Coll., Oxford 2000, Royal Welsh Coll. of Music and Drama

2001; US Army Commendation Medal; Dr hc (Univ. of Glamorgan, Univ. of the Arts, London); nine Emmy Awards for: The Rockefellers, The Palestinians, A Tale of Two Irelands, The Defense of the United States, The Boat People, The Boston Goes to China, The Fire Next Door, and The CIA's Secret Army 1974–76; First Amendment Leadership Award, Radio and Television News Dirs Foundation 1996, inducted into Broadcasting and Cable Hall of Fame 1996, Steven J. Ross Humanitarian Award, UJA-Fed. of New York 1999, inducted into Royal Television Soc.'s Welsh Hall of Fame 1999, Visionary Award for Innovative Leadership in Media and Entertainment, Museum of Television and Radio 2007, honoured by Lincoln Center, Big Brothers Big Sisters and New York Hall of Science.

STRINGER, Rob; British music executive; *Chairman and CEO, Columbia Records. Career:* graduate trainee, Columbia Records 1985, worked his way up to A&R Dir 1991–93; Man. Dir Epic Records 1993–2000; Chair. and CEO, Sony Music Entertainment UK 2000–04, Sony BMG Music Entertainment UK & Ireland (following merger in 2004), Chair. Sony Music Labels Group, USA 2006–; mem. Bd of Dirs Official Chart Co.; mem. BPI Council, BRITS Cttee, Chart Supervisory Cttee. *Address:* Sony Music Entertainment, 550 Madison Avenue, New York, NY 10022-3211, USA (office). *Telephone:* (212) 833-8000 (office). *Website:* www.sonymusic.com/executives/rob-stringer (office).

STROMAE; Belgian singer and songwriter; b. (Paul Van Haver), 12 March 1985, Brussels. *Education:* Institut national de radioélectricité et cinématographie, Brussels. *Career:* launched rap career under the name Opsmaestro 2000–03; Co-founder of rap group Suspicion 2003; released debut solo EP 2007; worked at NRJ radio, Brussels 2009; released single Alors on danse 2009; support act to Black Eyed Peas 2011; numerous collaborations including with Kanye West, Major Lazer. *Recordings include:* albums: Cheese (Victoires de la musique Award for Best Dance Album 2011) 2010, Racine Carrée (Square Root) (Victoires de la Musique Award for Song/Variety Album of the Year 2014, Octaves de la musique Award for Best Album of French Songs 2014) 2013. *Honours:* NRJ Music Awards for Belgian Francophone Musical Breakthrough 2009, for Best French-Language Song (for Formidable) 2013, for Best French-Speaking Male Artist 2013, Ultratop Download Award 2011, Octaves de la musique Awards for Artist of the Year 2011, 2014, for Show of the Year 2011, Bel RTL Public Prize 2014, SACEM Rolf Marbot Prize for Song of the Year (for Formidable) 2013, MTV Europe Music Award for Best Belgian Act 2013, Victoires de la musique Awards for Male Artist of the Year 2014, for Music Video of the Year 2014, Globes de Cristal Award for Best Male Singer 2014, World Music Award for Best-Selling Benelux Artist 2014. *E-mail:* events@stromae.net. *Website:* www.stromae.net.

STUART, Gareth Ian; British recording engineer, lecturer and musician (clarinet, saxophone, guitar); b. 26 March 1963, Bracknell, Berkshire; m. Amanda Jane 1989; one s. *Education:* Guildhall School of Music, CCAT, Surrey Univ. *Career:* recording studio owner, engineer 1986–; partner, Zigzag Music Productions 1992–; sound projectionist for Tim Souster (equalisation and trumpet concerto), Equale Brass, Chelmsford Festival, Philharmonia, Queen Elizabeth Hall; Sinetone generator operator for Stockhausen 'Mixtur' with BBC Symphony Orchestra, Barbican; mem. APRS (assoc.), Musicians' Union, MCPS. *Recordings include:* Sin Ti Por El Alma Adentro, for album Culture Electroniques, Julio D'Escrivan; Lady of The Grave, Faith; Hard 2 Get, Interlude; My Guitar, Bongo Blister; Hold On Tight, Bob and The Bearcats; Rollin' To The Jukebox Rock, Bob And The Bearcats. *Publications include:* articles on recording equipment, Sound On Sound 1987–89. *Address:* Zigzag Music Productions, Croeso, Church Lane, Hilton, Huntingdon, Cambridgeshire, PE28 9NH, England (office). *Telephone:* (1480) 830073 (office). *E-mail:* info@zigzagmusic.com (office). *Website:* www.zigzagmusic.com (office).

STUART, George K.; British musician (drums, percussion); b. 25 Jan. 1951, Edinburgh, Scotland; one s. *Career:* tour with Scottie 1975; support to Showaddywaddy, Shakin' Stevens, and Hello; German tour of American air bases 1974, 1976; mem. Distraction 1983–93, Blues Inc. 1996–98; freelance 2000–; mem. Musicians' Union. *Radio:* broadcasts with Scottie. *Television:* appearance, Arrows (Granada TV, with Scottie) 1976. *Recordings:* with Scottie: Happy Together 1975, Sweet Rock 'N' Roll 1976, The Time Has Come 1976; with West Side Strut: Nothing I Can Do 1978, Living 1979, Song for Chris 1980; with Distraction: Let Me Know 1983. *Address:* 9 Victoria Road, Victoria Park, Newton Grange, Edinburgh, EH22 4NN, Scotland (home). *Telephone:* (131) 663-1753 (home). *E-mail:* blint73@talktalk.net.

STUART, Glenn Douglas, BS, MA; American musician (trumpet); b. 8 May 1932, Elmira, NY; m. Laverne 1981; one s. two d. *Education:* Ithaca Coll., New York Univ. *Career:* played trumpet with orchestras lead by Tony Pastor, Richard Hayman, Noro Morales, Ralph Marterie, Vaughn Monroe, Les and Larry Elgart, Tommy Tucker, Hank Levy, Jimmy Dorsey, Stan Kenton, Don Ellis 1965–; tours in Canada, Bermuda, Japan, Hawaii, Europe with Don Ellis 1969, 1977; festivals include Monterey, New Port, North Sea, Montreux, Pacific, Antibes; television, films include: Emmy Awards Banquet, Ed Sullivan Show, Shirley MacLaine Special, Mission Impossible, French Connection I and II, Soupy Sales Special, California; played with artists including The Supremes, Frankie Avalon, Joe Williams, Jack Jones, Frankie Valli, Chubby Checker, Cleo Laine, Johnny Mathis, Jose Feliciano, Steve Lawrence, Phyllis Diller, Pat Boone, Louis Armstrong, Paul Anka; teaches trumpet, schools, colleges in California; lecturer, clinics, universities, colleges;

mem, NA of Jazz Educators. *Publications:* The Art of Playing Lead Trumpet. *Honours:* featured soloist at International Trumpet Guild 1977.

STUART, (James) Hamish; British singer, musician (guitar, bass) and writer; b. 8 Oct. 1949, Glasgow, Scotland; m. Lyn; one s. two d. *Career:* mem., Dream Police 1969, Average White Band 1972–82; numerous tours, television shows; numerous writing, production credits 1982–87; mem. ASCAP, AFTRA, PRS. *Recordings include:* solo album: Sooner Or Later 1999. *E-mail:* info@sulphuricrecords.co.uk. *Website:* www.sulphuricrecords.co.uk.

STUART, Marty; American singer and musician (guitar, mandolin); b. 30 Sept. 1958, Philadelphia, PA; m. 1st Cindy Cash (divorced); m. 2nd Connie Smith. *Career:* fmr mem., the Sullivan Family, Lester Flatt and the Nashville Grass; solo artist; also leader, The Fabulous Superlatives; concerts, tours and television appearances. *Recordings include:* albums: solo: The Slim Richey Sessions 1978, Busy Bee Cafe 1982, Marty Stuart 1986, Hillbilly Rock 1989, Tempted 1991, Let There Be Country 1992, This One's Gonna Hurt You 1992, Once Upon a Time 1992, Love and Luck 1994, The Marty Party Hit Pack 1995, Honky Tonkin's What I Do Best 1996, The Pilgrim 1999, Livin' Lovin' Losin': Songs of the Louvin Brothers 2003, Compadres 2007, Ghost Train 2010; with The Fabulous Superlatives: Country Music 2003, Souls' Chapel 2005, Badlands 2005, Live at the Ryman 2006. *Publication:* Country Music: The Masters 2008. *Honours:* CMA Award for Best Vocal Event (with Travis Tritt) 1992, Grammy Award for Best Vocal Collaboration (with Travis Tritt) 1993, Best Country Instrumental (with Bob Wills) 1994. *E-mail:* madmanager@mac .com. *Website:* www.madmanager.com. *E-mail:* martystuartfc@aol.com (office). *Website:* www.martystuart.net.

STUBER, William Charles; American producer, engineer, musician (percussion) and arranger, writer, lecturer and lighting designer; *Owner, Shabda Publishing;* b. 25 Sept. 1951, Rochester, New York; s. of W. James Stuber; m. Irene Stuber; three s. *Education:* Recording Inst. of America, Stonybrook Univ., Cleveland Inst. of Electronics. *Career:* more than 30 years as recording engineer, producer for artists including Hall and Oates, Rachael Sweet, Nitty Gritty, Supersonics, Ted Nugent, Scorpions, The Hooters, Hart, Jesse Colin Young, Tommy Bolin, Sammy Hagar, Judas Priest, Judy Collins, Arlo Guthrie, The Beach Boys, Devo, Emmylou Harris, Bonnie Raitt, London Ballet, Moscow Ballet; KONP, KCTS, KZOK, KZAM, KISW, KZFM, KBPI, King TV, KIRO TV, EMI, RCA, Warner Brothers, Sands Hotel, MGM Grand; scores for several films; music for radio plays, multiple interviews and programmes; lighting designer and stage manager for Juan de Fuca Festival of the Arts and various theatre, ballet and variety shows; various art shows; writer, producer, lighting designer, arranger, stage designer, set designer, Visioneering/Shabda Publishing; mem. RIAA. *Exhibitions include:* Juan De Fuca Festival of the Arts, Sequim Arts. *Compositions include:* Devotion, Love's Heavenly Dream, Seattle Super Sonics Theme, Winter Olympics, Various Commercials. *Radio includes:* numerous interviews. *Television includes:* several interviews, including on Good Morning Phoenix, Seattle Cable Today, soundtracks for TV films. *Recordings include:* recordings in various Seattle Best Of Compilations, albums with various artists. *Publications include:* Love's Heavenly Dream 1995, Devotion 1996, Ultimate Love 1997, Gems of The Seven Color Rays 2000, What is My Color Ray 2002, Fingers of Fire 2003. *Honours:* Seattle's Best Recordings 1979. *Address:* 2076 Taylor Cutoff Road, Sequim, WA 98382 (office); 5610 Woodville Road, Northwood, OH 43619 (office); PO Box 21, Carlsborg, WA 98324, USA (home). *Telephone:* (360) 683-2385 (office); (567) 694-7933 (home). *Fax:* (360) 683-2385 (office).

STUMP, Patrick; American singer, songwriter, musician (guitar) and producer; b. (Patrick Martin Stumph), 27 April 1984, Glenview, Ill. *Career:* Founder-mem., lead singer, rhythm guitarist band Fall Out Boy 2001–09, 2013–; headline act Nintendo Fusion Tour 2005, Black Clouds and Underdogs Tour 2005, Honda Civic Tour 2007, Young Wild Things Tour 2007; collaborations with Gym Class Heroes, Motion City Soundtrack, Misery Signals, Kanye West, Timbaland, Lupe Fiasco; has produced tracks for The Hush Sound and Gym Class Heroes. *Recordings include:* albums: Fall Out Boy's Evening Out with Your Girlfriend (mini-LP) 2002, Take This to Your Grave 2003, From Under the Cork Tree 2005, Infinity on High 2007, Folie à Deux 2008, Save Rock and Roll 2013, American Beauty/American Psycho 2015; solo: Soul Punk 2011. *Honours:* People's Choice Awards for Favorite Int. Group 2006, for Favorite Alternative Band 2014, Kerrang! Awards for Best Video (for Sugar, We're Going Down) 2006, (for This Ain't a Scene, It's an Arms Race) 2007, for Best Single (for The Phoenix) 2013, for Best Int. Band 2014, Teen Choice Awards for Best Rock Track and Best Single (for Dance, Dance) 2006, for Best Single (for Thnks Fr Th Mmrs) 2007, MTV Video Music Awards for Viewers Choice 2007, for Best Group 2007, for Best Rock Video (for Uma Thurman) 2015, World Music Award for Best Alternative Act 2014, American Music Award for Favorite Alternative Rock Artist 2015. *Website:* www .falloutboy.com; www.patrickstump.com.

STÜRMER, Christina; Austrian singer; b. 9 June 1982. *Career:* won second place in tv talent show Starmania 2003; numerous tours and concerts in Austria, Germany, Switzerland, Italy. *Recordings include:* albums: Freier Fall 2003, Soll das wirklich alles sein? 2004, Schwarz Weiss 2005, Lebe Lauter 2006, In dieser Stadt 2009, Nahaufnahme 2010. *Honours:* Best Nat. Pop/Rock Act 2004, 2005, 2006, Nat. Newcomer of the Year 2004, Best Single 2005, 2006, Amadeus Austrian Music Awards, Best Nat. Female Artist, ECHO Awards 2006, Best German Rock/Pop Artist, Goldene Stimmgabel 2006. *Address:* Büro

Christina Stürmer, PO Box 113, 1218 Vienna, Austria (office). *E-mail:* office@christinastuermer.at (office). *Website:* www.christinaonline.at.

STURR, Jimmy; American bandleader, musician (trumpeter, clarinet, saxophone) and business executive; b. 1941, Florida, NY. *Education:* Valley Forge Military Acad. *Career:* leader of polka band, Jimmy Sturr And His Orchestra 1960s–; presenter, The Jimmy Sturr Show (Red TV); f. own record label, travel firm, artists' management and music publishing companies, local radio station. *Recordings:* over 100 albums including Polka Your Troubles Away 1994, When It's Polka Time At Your House 1994, Polka! All Night Long (with Willie Nelson) 1997, Living on Polka Time (with Bill Anderson and Flaco Jiménez) 1998, Life's A Polka 1998, Polkapalooza 1999, Dance with Me (with Oak Ridge Boys and Flaco Jiménez) 1999, Touched By a Polka (with Mel Tillis) 2001, Gone Polka (with Willie Nelson and Brenda Lee) 2002, Top of the World 2003, Let's Polka 'Round 2004, Shake, Rattle and Polka! 2006, Polka in Paradise (with Bobby Vinton) 2007, Come Share the Wine 2007, Let the Whole World Sing 2009. *Honours:* 18 Grammy Awards for Best Polka Album or Best Polka Recording. *Address:* United Polka Artists, Box One, Florida, NY 10921, USA (office). *Telephone:* (800) 724-0727 (office). *E-mail:* jspolka@warwick.net (office). *Website:* jimmysturrbio.blogspot.com.

STYLES, Harry Edward; British singer; b. 1 Feb. 1994, Holmes Chapel, Cheshire; s. of Des Styles and Anne Cox. *Education:* Holmes Chapel Comprehensive School. *Career:* fmr mem. White Eskimo; mem. One Direction 2010–; finished third in The X Factor (UK) 2010; signed to Syco Records 2010; participated in X Factor Live Tour 2011; released debut single 2011; debut album first by a British group to debut at number one on USA Billboard 200 album chart 2011; numerous TV appearances and tours; group hiatus 2016–. *Recordings include:* with One Direction: albums: Up All Night 2011, Take Me Home (American Music Award for Favorite Album 2013) 2012, Midnight Memories (American Music Award for Favorite Album 2014) 2013, Four 2014, Made in the A.M. 2015. *DVDs:* Up All Night: The Live Tour 2012. *Publications include:* One Direction: Forever Young 2011, One Direction: The Official Annual 2012 2011, Dare to Dream: Life as One Direction 2011, Where We Are: Our Band, Our Story 2013, Who We Are: Our Official Autobiography 2014. *Honours:* numerous including: with One Direction: Bambi Pop Int. Award 2012, BBC Radio 1 Teen Awards for Best British Music Act 2012, for Best British Single 2012, 2013, 2014, 2015, for Best British Group 2013, 2015, BRIT Awards for Best British Single (What Makes You Beautiful) 2012, for BRITs Global Success 2013, for Best British Video (for You & I) 2015, JIM Awards (Flemish TV) for Best International Newcomer 2012, for Best Group 2013, for Best Pop 2013, MTV Europe Music Awards for Best New Act 2012, for Best UK & Ireland Act 2012, 2013, 2014, for Biggest Fans 2012, 2014, for Best Pop Act 2013, 2014, 2015, for Best Live Act 2014, for Best Worldwide Act (Europe North) 2014, MTV Video Music Awards Brazil Award for International Artist 2012, MTV Video Music Awards for Best New Artist 2012, for Best Pop Video and Most Share-Worthy Video (both What Makes You Beautiful) 2012, for Song of the Summer (for Best Song Ever) 2013, 4Music Video Honours Awards for Best Breakthrough and Best Group 2012, ARIA Music Awards for Best Int. Artist 2012, 2013, 2014, Billboard Music Awards for Top Duo/Group 2013, 2015, for Top New Artist 2013, for Top Pop Artist 2013, for Top Touring Artist 2015, American Music Awards for Favorite Band, Duo or Group 2013, 2014, 2015, for Artist of the Year 2014, 2015. *Current Management:* c/o Modest! Management, The Matrix Complex, 91 Peterborough Road, London, SW6 3BU, England. *Telephone:* (20) 7384-6410. *E-mail:* info@modestmanagement.com. *Website:* www.modestmanagement.com; www.onedirectionmusic.com.

STYLUS TROUBLE (see Heller, Pete)

SUCH, Alec John; American musician (bass guitar); b. 14 Nov. 1956. *Career:* Founder-mem. rock group Bon Jovi 1983–88, 1992–94, 2001; numerous tours, TV, radio and live appearances worldwide. *Recordings include:* albums: Bon Jovi 1984, 7800° Fahrenheit 1985, Slippery When Wet 1986, Bon Jovi Live 1987, New Jersey 1988, Keep The Faith 1991, Cross Road 1994. *Honours:* American Music Awards for Favorite Pop/Rock Band 1988, for Favorite Pop/Rock Single 1991, Nordoff-Robbins Music Therapy Silver Clef 1990, BRIT Award for Best Int. Group (with band) 1995, VH-1 Award for Favorite Video (for It's My Life) 2000.

SUGAR, BTec; British musician (bouzouki, Cypriot flute) and producer; b. (Zacharia Hajishacalli), 8 July 1954, London; m. Androulla 1977; two d. *Education:* masterclasses in bouzouki, Greece. *Career:* toured with Boy George's Jesus Loves You Band; concerts include Town and Country, Ronnie Scott's, Royal Festival Hall; TV and radio appearances; runs ethnic music recording studio; mem. Musicians' Union, PRS, MCPS. *Recordings include:* produced and recorded four Greek albums for ARC Music; Bouzouki player on Mathilda May album; Yamaha instruments for sampling bouzouki for new synth; Bouzouki player on four tracks for Boy George; composer, producer, Cypriot Flute of Sugar; composer, music for film, The Odyssey. *Publications include:* Cypriot Flute of Sugar; Turning Point, Angela 2001; Haji-Mike album.

SUGIYAMA, Kazunori, BS, MA; Japanese record producer; b. 18 Aug. 1950, Tokyo; s. of Hiroshi Sugiyama and Michiko Sugiyama; m. Emi Fukui 1981. *Education:* Waseda Univ., Tokyo, Boston Univ., USA. *Career:* New York Rep., Jazz Division, Toshiba EMI 1990–93; US Rep. and Exec. Producer, DIW/Avant Records 1991–; Exec. Producer, Tzadik Records 1995–; Advisory Bd, New Grove Dictionary of Jazz 1997; mem. NARAS. *Recordings:* Bud and Bird/Gil Evans (engineer) 1988, V/Ralph Peterson Jr (producer) 1990, Big Band

and Quartet, David Murray (producer) 1992, producer for many other artists, including George Adams, Derek Bailey, Steven Bernstein, Greg Cohen, Joe Henderson, John Patton. *Publications:* autobiography of Miles Davis (trans.) 1989. *Honours:* Grammy Award 1988, Jazz Album of the Year (producer) 1990, Album of the Year in Japan, Best Production 1992. *Address:* 93 Mercer Street 3W, New York, NY 10012, USA (office). *Telephone:* (212) 334-8427 (office). *E-mail:* tzadik@nyc.rr.com (office). *Website:* www.tzadik.com (office).

SUHO; South Korean singer; b. (Kim Joon Myun), 22 May 1991, Seoul. *Education:* Korea Nat. Univ. of Arts. *Career:* mem., K-pop boy band Exo 2012–; mem. sub-group Exo-K 2012–; debut single 2012; numerous TV and live appearances. *Television:* EXO's Showtime 2013–. *Recordings:* albums: Mama 2012, XOXO (Mnet Asian Music Award for Album of the Year 2013) 2013. *Honours:* numerous awards including: for Exo: Mnet Asian Music Award for Best New Asian Artist/Group 2012, MTV Europe Music Award for Best Japan/Korea Act 2013, MelOn Music Award for Song of the Year (for Growl) 2013; for Exo-K: Golden Disk Newcomer Award 2012. *Address:* c/o SM Entertainment, 521 Apgujeong 2-dong, Gangnam-gu, Seoul, South Korea (office). *Telephone:* (2) 6240-9800 (office). *Website:* www.smtown.com (office); exo.smtown.com (home).

SULTON, Kasim Anthony; American musician (bass guitar, guitar, keyboards) and singer; b. 8 Dec. 1955, New York; m. Laurie Rampulla, one s., two d. *Career:* joined band, Utopia as bassist and vocalist, 1976–86; bassist with Joan Jett 1986; bassist with Hall and Oates 1990; guitarist with Meat Loaf 1993; bassist, musical director, Meat Loaf 1998; mem, American Federation of Musicians; American Federation Radio and Television Artists. *Compositions:* Set Me Free; Love Is The Answer; Mated. *Recordings:* albums: with Utopia: Ra 1977, Oops! Wrong Planet 1977, Adventures in Utopia 1980, Deface the Music 1980, Swing to the Right 1982, Utopia 1982, Oblivion 1984, P.O.V. 1985 1976–86; other credits include: Bat Out of Hell, Meat Loaf 1977, I Hate Myself for Loving You, Joan Jett 1988, Bat Out of Hell II, Meat Loaf 1993, Falling into You, Céline Dion 1996, One Long Year, Todd Rundgren 2000; solo: Kasim 1982, The Bassment Tapes 1993, Quid Pro Quo 2002, All Sides 2007. *Honours:* Best Video and Grammy Award, 1995, 1996. *Address:* PO Box 060 106, Staten Island, New York 10306, USA. *Website:* www.kasimsulton.com.

SUMMER; Estonian singer. *Career:* mem., Tuberkuloited 1988–. *Recordings include:* albums: Klassiõhtu 1992, Lilleke rohus 1993, Religioon 1995, Õhtupimedas 1997, Seitseteist lillekest rohus 1999, D-Tuur, Vol. 6 1999, Kiirteel 2000, Wiimane 2001, Tuberkuloited unplugged 2001, Estraadialbum 2003, Põlevad väljad 2004. *Current Management:* MMM Agentuur OÜ, Risti 2-21, 11624 Tallinn, Estonia. *E-mail:* mm@mmagentuur.ee. *Website:* www.mmagentuur.ee. *E-mail:* Summer@tuberkuloited.ee. *Website:* www.tuberkuloited.ee.

SUMMER, Henry Lee; American singer, songwriter, record producer and musician (multi-instrumentalist); b. 7 May 1960, Evansville, Indiana. *Education:* Western Wyoming Univ. *Career:* nat. support tours with Stevie Ray Vaughan, Don Henley, Eddie Money, Richard Marx, .38 Special, Chicago, Cheap Trick, The Doobie Brothers, The Allman Brothers, REO Speedwagon; also played with John Mellencamp, Willie Nelson, Guns N' Roses, Neil Young, Bonnie Raitt, Indiana; mem. BMI, American Fed. of TV and Radio Artists, American Fed. of Musicians. *Recordings include:* albums: Stay With Me 1984, Time For Big Fun 1986, Henry Lee Summer 1988, I've Got Everything 1989, Way Past Midnight 1991, Slam Drunk 1993, Smoke And Mirrors 1999, Big Drum 2001. *Honours:* BMI Award for Hey Baby 1991. *E-mail:* info@henryleesummer.com. *Website:* www.henryleesummer.com.

SUMMERS, Andy; British musician (guitar) and singer; b. (Andrew Somers), 31 Dec. 1942, Poulton-Le-Fylde, Lancashire, England. *Career:* mem. of rock group, The Police 1977–86, re-formed to tour 2007–; numerous worldwide tours, television, radio broadcasts; solo artist 1987–; live music dir, The Dennis Miller Show (US TV) 1992; composer of film scores; session work with Joan Armatrading, Kevin Ayers, David Bedford, Toni Childs. *Recordings include:* albums: with The Police: Outlandos D'Amour 1977, Regatta De Blanc 1979, Zenyatta Mondatta 1980, Ghost in the Machine 1981, Synchronicity 1983; solo: I Advance Masked (with Robert Fripp) 1982, XYZ 1987, Mysterious Barricades 1988, Golden Wire 1989, Charming Snakes 1990, World Gone Strange 1991, Synaesthesia 1995, The Last Dance of Mr X 1998, Strings of Desire 1998, Green Chimneys 1999, Peggy's Blue Skylight 2000, Earth + Sky 2003. *Publication:* One Train Later: A Memoir 2006. *Honours:* Chevalier, Ordre des Arts et des Lettres 2007; Grammy Awards (with The Police). *Current Management:* Firstars/Talent Bank Management, Bugle House, 21A Noel Street, London, W1V 3PD, England. *E-mail:* info@andysummers.com. *Website:* www.andysummers.com.

SUMMERS, Chris; Norwegian musician (drums); b. (Christer Engen). *Career:* mem. punk band, Turbonegro 1988–98, 2002–08; also played for band Bigbang. *Recordings include:* albums: Turboloid 1990, Hot Cars and Spent Contraceptives 1992, Helta Skelta 1993, Never is Forever 1994, Ass Cobra 1996, Apocalypse Dudes 1998, Scandinavian Leather 2003, Party Animals 2005. *Honours:* MTV Europe Music Award for Best Norwegian Act 2005.

SUMMERS RODRÍGUEZ, David; Spanish singer and musician (bass guitar); b. 26 Feb. 1964. *Career:* mem. Hombres G 1983–92, 2002–; solo artist 1992–2002. *Films:* Sufre mamón 1987, Suéltate el pelo 1988. *Recordings* *include:* Hombres G 1985, La cagaste... Burt Lancaster 1986, Estamos locos... ¿o qué? 1987, Agitar antes de usar 1988, Voy a pasármelo bien 1989, Esta es tu vida 1990, Historia del bikini 1992, Peligrosamente juntos 2004, Todo esto es muy extraño 2004, 10 2007. *Address:* c/o Dro Atlantic, Calle Juan Hurtado de Mendoza 3, 28036 Madrid, Spain (office). *Website:* www.hombres-g.com.

SUMNER, Bernard; British singer and musician (guitar, keyboards); b. (Bernard Dicken), 4 Jan. 1956, Salford, Lancashire, England. *Career:* mem., Joy Division (under name, Bernard Albrecht) 1977–80, New Order 1980–, Electronic 1989–, Bad Lieutenant 2007–; worldwide tours, concerts and festival appearances. *Recordings include:* albums: with Joy Division: Unknown Pleasures 1979, Closer 1980, Still 1981, The Peel Sessions 1988; with New Order: Movement 1981, Power, Corruption & Lies 1983, Low-Life 1985, Brotherhood 1986, Substance 1987, Technique 1989, Republic 1993, Best of New Order 1994, Rest of New Order 1995, Get Ready 2001, Back To Mine (compilation of other artists' work) 2002, In Session (live) 2004, Waiting For The Sirens' Call 2005, Lost Sirens 2013, Music Complete 2015; with Electronic: Electronic 1991, Raise the Pressure 1996, Twisted Tenderness 1999; with Bad Lieutenant: Never Cry Another Tear 2009. *Publications:* Chapter and Verse – New Order, Joy Division and Me 2014. *Honours:* NME 'Godlike Genius' Award (with New Order) 2005, Q Legend Award (with Joy Division) 2005, Ivor Novello Award for Outstanding Song Collection 2006, Q Outstanding Contribution to Music Award (with New Order) 2015. *Current Management:* c/o Jayne Houghton, Excess Press, The Metway, 55 Canning Street, Brighton BN2 0EF, England. *Telephone:* (1273) 667991. *E-mail:* jayne@excesspress.co.uk. *Website:* www.excesspress.co.uk; www.neworder .com.

SUMNER, Gordon Matthew (see STING)

SUN, Hongjun; Chinese musician (accordion); b. 6 Dec. 1934, Liaoyang District, Liaoning Province; m. Cui Min 1957; two s. two d. *Education:* ShenYang Musical College. *Career:* Attended PLA China, Liaoning Military Org. 1956; attended Fu Shun song and dance ensemble, assigned as accordion player 1959; Chief, Main Ed., Fushun Office, Chinese National Music 1979; programmed Russian Red Army song and dance ensemble, many others; mem. Cui Min; Sun Like; S Dongke; Sun Qiuke; Xiake. *Compositions:* North East Drum and Wind Music 1986, Chao Xian Folk Songs 1991. *Recordings include:* 100 Man Folk Songs of China, Xi Bo Music, Chaoxian Folk Songs, North East Drum and Wind Music. *Publications:* National Folk Musician essay 1995. *Honours:* Man Musical Essay, First Festival of Asian Pacific Soc. for Ethnomusicology.

SUN, Joe; American musician and songwriter; b. 25 Sept. 1943, Rochester, Minnesota; m. Inka Sun Paulsen, 10 Oct. 1965. *Education:* Brown School of Broadcasting, Minneapolis, 1967. *Career:* National promotions director, Ovation Records, Nashville, 1976–78; Recording artist, 1978–82; Touring musician, songwriter, 1987–; Actor, film Marie – A True Story, 1986. *Recordings include:* albums: Old Flames 1978, Out of Your Mind 1979, Livin' on Honky Tonk Time 1980, I Ain't Honky Tonkin' No More 1981, The Best 1982, Sun Never Sets 1984, Twilight Zone 1988, Hank Bogart Still Lives 1989, Heartbreak Saloon 1996, Dixie and Me 2006. *Honours:* Most Promising New Country Artist, Billboard, 1979. *Website:* www.myspace.com/ joesunandtheallstars.

SUN, Stefanie, (Sun Yanzi); Singaporean singer and songwriter; b. (Sng Ee Tze), 23 July 1978; m. Nadim Van Der Ros 2011. *Education:* St Andrew's Jr Coll., Nanyang Technological Univ. *Career:* f. Make Music (artist man. and music publishing co.) 2003; served as Singapore's Mercy Relief Goodwill Amb. for survivors of Sichuan earthquake 2008. *Recordings include:* albums: Yan Zi 2000, My Desired Happiness 2000, Kite 2001, Leave 2002, Start 2002, Yanzi Start World Tour Live 2002, To Be Continued 2003, Stefanie 2004, A Perfect Day 2005, Against The Light 2007, It's Time 2011. *Films include:* as actor: 12 Lotus; soundtrack: Mu Lan 2009. *Honours:* numerous awards, including Channel V Music Awards, Best Newcomer 2000, China Music Awards, Best Newcomer 2000, Singapore Hit Awards, Best New Act (Gold) 2001, Singapore Hit Awards, Most Popular Female Artiste 2002, MTV Asia Awards, Favourite Artist Singapore 2003, 2004, 2005, 2006, 2008, Global Chinese Music Awards, Most Popular Female Singer 2002, 2003, 2004, 2006, 2007, Golden Melody Awards (Taiwan), Best Female Mandarin Singer 2005, Singapore Hit Awards, Best Female Vocalist 2005, Singapore Hit Awards, Asian Media Recognition Award 2007, Business China Young Achiever Award 2011. *Address:* Make Music, 391B Orchard Road, #13-09, Ngee Ann Tower B, 238874 Singapore (office). *Website:* www.makemusic-asia.com (office).

SUN GOD (see Ghostface)

SUN-J; British DJ, musician and producer; b. (Sunjay Tailor), 15 Dec. 1969, Hampstead, London, England; m. Sophie Tailor; one d. *Career:* writer, programmer, prod. and DJ, Asian Dub Foundation 1995–. *Recordings include:* albums: Facts and Fictions 1995, R.A.F.I. 1997, Rafi's Revenge 1998, Conscious Party 1998, Community Music 2000, Enemy of the Enemy 2003, Bangin' On The Walls 2003, Tank 2005, Punkara 2008. *Honours:* BBC Asian Award for Music 1998. *Current Management:* c/o Cris Hearn, Primary Talent International, Fifth Floor, 2–12 Pentonville Road, London, N1 9PL, England. *Telephone:* (20) 7833-8998. *Fax:* (20) 7833-5992. *E-mail:* emailcris@primary .uk.com. *Website:* www.ilmc.com/primary; www.asiandubfoundation.com.

SUND, John; Danish musician (guitar) and composer; b. 6 Jan. 1957, Copenhagen. *Career:* debut at age 18 as soloist with the Danish Radio Big Band 1976; mem. Creme Fraiche Big Band, broadcasting in radio and TV 1978; permanent mem., Danish Radio Jazzgroup, including appearances at Montmartre 1976–80; mem. and contrib. to Danish Radio Workshop/Palle Mikkelborg 1978–80; formed own band, John Sund Group 1977–79; own trio, Trigon, broadcast on DR TV 1982; played with Bo Stief, Thomas Clausen, Alex Reel, Mads Vinding, Debbie Cameron, South Indian musicians Ganesh and Kumaresh, Mariam Mursal, among others; leader of jazz/ethnic-fusion ensemble, Special Venture, and world/fusion group Acoustic Sense; co-leader jazz/world quartet, World on a String, with violinist Bjarke Falgren; mem. Soc. of Danish Jazz, Rock and Folk Composers (DJBFA), KODA, Danish Musicians' Union. *Compositions:* Fusion Symphony, extended suite of eight compositions 1993. *Recordings include:* with the Neumann Brothers, 3 x Neumann: Song Hits From 1920–70 1977; with Creme Fraiche Big Band: Creme Fraiche 1978; with Richard Boone and Debbie Cameron: Brief Encounter 1978; Yadam: Cosas De La Vida 2001; Ayi Solomon: Back Home 2002; solo: John Sund And The Danish Radio Big Band—Fusion Symphony 1993, The Open Road 2011, Here and Now 2012; with Special Venture: Special Venture 1999, Twice 2007; John Sund and Acoustic Sense—New Gems 2003, Absorption 2014; John Sund and Ayi Solomon: Duometric Events 2009. *E-mail:* johnsund@johnsund.dk. *Website:* www.johnsund.dk.

SUNDING, Per Gunnar; Swedish singer, musician (bass guitar), songwriter and producer; b. 23 Nov. 1967, Lomma, nr Malmö. *Career:* founder mem., Eggstone 1986–; the band established Tambourine Studios (with Tore Johansson and Anders Nordgren) 1991–, Vibrafon Records 1995–; studios used by artists, including Saint Etienne and The Cardigans; prod. for artists, including Wannadies, Bob Hund, Ray Wonder; mem. SKAP. *Recordings include:* albums: In San Diego 1992, Somersault 1994, Vive La Différence 1997, Spanish Slalom 1998, Ça chauffe en Suede! 1999. *Address:* Tambourine Studios, Sofielundsvägen 57, 214 34 Malmö, Sweden (office). *Telephone:* (40) 87-08-8 (office). *Fax:* (40) 87-08-0 (office). *E-mail:* info@tambourinestudios.com (office). *Website:* www.tambourinestudios.com (office).

SUNYE; South Korean singer and actress; b. (Min Seon-ye), 12 Aug. 1989, Seoul. *Education:* Korea Arts High School, Dongguk Univ. *Career:* numerous collaborations including Mighty Mouth, Park Jin Young, Davichi, Taeyeon, 8eight; mem. Wonder Girls 2006–; first int. tour (including Thailand and USA) 2009; first S Korean group to enter the Billboard Hot 100 chart (with Nobody) 2009; world tour with Jonas Brothers 2009; supported Justin Bieber at Valentine's Day Concert 2010; toured USA and Canada with Wonder World Tour 2010; collaborated with Akon on single Like Money 2012; numerous festival appearances and tours. *Films:* The Last Godfather 2010, The Wonder Girls 2012. *Television includes:* MTV Wonder Girls 2006–10, Welcome to Wonderland 2009, Made in Wonder Girls 2010; numerous guest appearances. *Recordings include:* albums: The Wonder Years (Golden Disk Main Award Winners (Bonsang) 2007) 2007, The Wonder Years: Trilogy (Seoul Music Awards for Record of the Year in Digital Release 2009, Bonsang Award 2009, Daesang Award 2009) 2009, Wonder World 2011. *Honours:* Golden Disk Awards for Popularity 2007, Seoul Music Award for Best New Artist 2008, Korean Music Awards for Best Dance and Electronic Song (for Tell Me) 2008, for Group Musician of the Year Netizen Vote (for Wonder Girls) 2009, Golden Disk Awards Main Award Winners 2008, MNet KM Music Festival Awards for Best New Female Group 2007, for Song of the Year 2008, for Best Music Video (for Nobody) 2008, for Best Female Group 2008. *Current Management:* c/o Creative Artists Agency, 162 Fifth Avenue, 6th Floor, New York, NY 10010, USA. *Address:* c/o JYP Entertainment, JYP Center, 123-50 Cheongdam-dong, Gangnam-gu, Seoul, South Korea (office). *Telephone:* (2) 3438-2300 (office). *Website:* www.jype.com (office); www.wondergirlsworld.com.

SUONSAARI, Klaus; Finnish musician (drums) and composer; b. 7 Nov. 1959. *Education:* Lahti Conservatory, Eastman School of Music, USA, Berklee College of Music, USA, private studies with Billy Higgins, Jeff Hamilton, Alan Dawson, Kauko Saari, Jorma Alanne. *Career:* played with musicians including Bob Berg, Niels-Henning Orsted-Pedersen, Ray Drummond, Tom Harrell, Mike Mainieri, Niels Lan Doky, Muhal Richard Abrams; int. appearances in USA, Canada, UK, Scandinavia, Central Europe; performances with Jerry Bergonzi, Randy Brecker, Geri Allen, Joe Henderson, Toots Thielemans, David Sanborn; mem. American Fed. of Musicians, Associated Musicians of Greater New York. *Recordings include:* Inside Out 1995, Something In Common 1998, With Every Breath I Take 1999, Portrait In Sound 2003, Offering 2003. *Honours:* Buddy Rich Jazz Masters Award 1983, Quincy Jones Jazz Masters Award 1984, Artist of the Year Award, Finland 1992. *Current Management:* c/o Charlie Ellicott, Ellicott Talent Group, 2503 Marylyn Circle, Petaluma, CA 94954, USA. *Telephone:* (707) 773-3170. *Fax:* (707) 773-3173. *E-mail:* etgjazz@attbi.com. *E-mail:* klaus@klaussuonsaari.com. *Website:* www .klaussuonsaari.com.

SUTCLIFFE, Jeremy (Jess); British recording engineer and producer; b. 25 Nov. 1958, London, England; m. Shari Lee Inoue 1987; one s. one d. *Career:* tape operator and assistant engineer, London Recording Studios 1977; independent first engineer 1979; engineer for Vangelis 1982–86; recording engineer for films, records, and TV commercials; freelance engineer and producer 1987; moved to Los Angeles 1988; has worked with artists including Prince, Vangelis, Toto, Manu Dibango, Warren Hill, Aretha Franklin, Jon and Vangelis, Carlene Carter, Sheila E, Quincy Jones, Patti LaBelle, Willie Nelson, Patti Austin, Gary Numan, Elvis Costello, Sheena Easton, Wall of Voodoo, The Fall, Handel's Messiah, Meat Loaf, LeAnn Rimes; mem, NARAS. *E-mail:* jesssutcliffe@earthlink.net (office). *Website:* www.jesssutcliffe.com.

SUTTON, Chris; British singer, songwriter, musician (piano, keyboards) and producer; b. 25 Dec. 1960, Essex, England; m. Elaine Sutton, one d. *Career:* solo artist; mem. PRS. *Recordings include:* album: Songs into the Light. *Website:* www.myspace.com/chrissuttonproductions.

SUTTON, Graham Paul; British songwriter, singer, producer and musician (multi-instrumentalist); b. 1 April 1972, Stratford, London. *Career:* formed Bark Psychosis 1987; pursued music from age 16; recorded several independently released EPs; has worked with: Lee Harris, Paul Webb of Talk Talk under name Orang; also records under name Boymerang; worked as producer with Jarvis Cocker, British Sea Power, The Delays; mem Musicians' Union, PRS, MCPS. *Recordings:* albums: with Bark Psychosis: Hex 1994, Independency 1994, Game Over 1997, '///Codename: Dustsucker' 2006; as Boymerang: Balance of the Force 1996; also appears on: Orang's Herd of Instinct, Fields and Waves; as producer worked on: The Delays' Faded Seaside Glamour 2004, You See Colours 2006, Pellumair's Summer Storm 2005, Jarvis Cocker's Jarvis 2006, British Sea Power's Open Season 2006, Do You Like Rock Music? 2008. *Address:* 40 Abbotsford Gardens, Woodford Green, Essex IG8 9HW, England (home).

SUTTON, Tierney; American jazz singer and educator; *Vocal Department Chair, Los Angeles Music Academy;* b. 28 June 1963, Omaha, Neb. *Education:* Nicolet High School, Milwaukee, Wis., Wesleyan Univ., Berklee Coll. of Music. *Career:* singer with Tierney Sutton Band; headliner at Carnegie Hall, Jazz at Lincoln Center, Hollywood Bowl; numerous int. tours; teacher, Jazz Studies Dept, Univ. of Southern Calif. 1997–2008; Vocal Dept Chair, Los Angeles Music Acad., Pasadena 2008–. *Recordings:* albums: Introducing Tierney Sutton 1998, Unsung Heroes 2000, Blue in Green 2001, Something Cool 2002, Dancing in the Dark 2004, I'm with the Band 2005, On the Other Side 2007, Desire 2009, American Road 2011, After Blue 2013. *Honours:* Jazzweek Vocalist of the Year 2005. *Current Management:* c/o Lorraine Kelley Weinstein, Unlimited Myles, 6 Imaginary Place, Matawan, NJ 07747, USA. *Telephone:* (732) 566-2880. *Fax:* (732) 566-8157. *E-mail:* lorraine@unlimitedmyles.com. *Website:* www.unlimitedmyles.com. *Address:* Los Angeles Music Academy College of Music, 370 South Fair Oaks Avenue, Pasadena, CA 91105, USA (office). *Telephone:* (626) 568-8850 (office). *Fax:* (626) 568-8854 (office). *E-mail:* info@lama.edu (office). *Website:* www.lama.edu (office). *Website:* www.tierneysutton.com (home).

SVARE, Jørgen Christian; Danish musician (clarinet); b. 28 Dec. 1935, Copenhagen; m. Susanne Svare 2004; two s. one d. *Career:* clarinet player in local bands 1950s; Founder-mem. Papa Bue's Viking Jazz Band 1956; played and toured world-wide for 30 years; own quartet 1986–95; jazz club owner, Slukefter Jazzhus, Tivoli Gardens, Copenhagen 1994–97; Co-leader of Stolle and Svare Jazz Quintet 1995–2004; currently freelance and playing in own trio; mem. Danish Soc. of Band Leaders. *Compositions include:* Slukefter Blues, Blues for Omer, Falling Down, Jazz Air. *Recordings include:* more than 60 albums with Papa Bue, six albums with quartet, three albums with Stolle and Svare Jazz Quintet 1998, 2003, two albums with Svare/Thoroddsen 2003, 2006, Jørgen Svare Jazz Vibes 2015. *Honours:* Sorens Penge, Denmark 1996. *Address:* Mitchellsgade 18, 1568 Copenhagen V (home); Weidekampsgade 59, 2300 Copenhagen S, Denmark. *Telephone:* 52-64-11-21 (home). *E-mail:* jcsvare@gmail.com. *Website:* www.jazzvibes.dk.

SVEINSSON, Kjartan (Kjarri); Icelandic musician (keyboards). *Career:* mem., Sigur Rós 1995–; numerous tours. *Recordings include:* albums: Von, Agœtis Byrjun 2000, ( ) 2002, Takk... 2005, Hvarf-Heim 2007, Með Suð Í Eyrum Við Spilum Endalaust 2008, Valtari 2012; DVD: Heima 2007. *Honours:* Shortlist Music Prize 2001. *Address:* c/o Smekkleysa Records, PO Box 1263, 121 Reykjavík, Iceland (office). *Website:* www.sigur-ros.com.

SVENINGSSON, (Johan) Magnus; Swedish musician (bass guitar) and songwriter; b. 4 April 1972, Falköping. *Career:* founder mem., The Cardigans 1992–; numerous concert tours, festivals, television and radio appearances; simultaneous solo career as Righteous Boy 2000–. *Music for TV and film:* contributed tracks to films Romeo and Juliet and A Life Less Ordinary, theme to 'Randall & Hopkirk Deceased' (BBC1, with David Arnold) 2000. *Recordings include:* albums: with The Cardigans: Emmerdale 1994, Life 1995, First Band On The Moon 1996, Other Side Of The Moon 1998, Gran Turismo 1998, Long Gone Before Daylight 2003, Super Extra Gravity 2005; solo: I Sing Because of You 2000. *Honours:* Slitz Magazine Award for Best Band 1994, Swedish Government Export Prize 1997, BMI Award for Best Song 1997, Best Album 1998, Best Group 1996, 1998. *Current Management:* Hagenburg Management, Kyrkogaten 31, 411 08 Gothenburg, Sweden. *Telephone:* (31) 339-95-90. *Fax:* (31) 13-95-09. *E-mail:* info@hagenburg.se. *Website:* www.hagenburg.se; www.cardigans.com.

SVENNINGSSON, Uno; Swedish singer and songwriter; b. 1 July 1959, Jönköping, Småland; m. Carina Bihli 1993; one s. *Career:* singer and songwriter of rock group, Freda 1983–93; solo artist 1994–; numerous tours, TV and radio broadcasts. *Recordings include:* albums: with Freda: En Människa 1984, Välkommen Hero 1986, Tusen Eldar 1988, Undan För Undan 1990, Alla Behöver 1993, Freda Samling 1993; solo: Uno 1994, ...due! 1996, Möss & människor 1998, Möss & människor 2001, Ett andetag från dig 2004, ag sjunger för dig 2008, December -En svensk jul (with Irma Schultz Keller) 2011, 7 2013. *Honours:* Swedish Grammy Award for Best Rock Group 1991, Rock Björnen Award for Best Male Artist 1994, The Mozart Prize for Best Male Artist 1994.

SVENSSON, (Anders) Peter; Swedish musician (guitar) and composer; b. 18 Oct. 1974, Jönköping. *Education:* music coll., Jönköping. *Career:* founder mem., The Cardigans 1992–; numerous concert tours, festivals, television and radio appearances; writer and prod. for Titiyo Cherry 2000; mem. Soc. for Swedish Composers of Pop Music. *Music for TV and film:* contributed tracks to films Romeo and Juliet and A Life Less Ordinary, theme to 'Randall & Hopkirk Deceased' (BBC1, with David Arnold) 2000. *Recordings include:* albums: Emmerdale 1994, Life 1995, First Band On The Moon 1996, Other Side Of The Moon 1998, Gran Turismo 1998, Long Gone Before Daylight 2003, Super Extra Gravity 2005. *Honours:* Slitz Magazine Award for Best Band 1994, Swedish Government Export Prize 1997, BMI Award for Best Song 1997, Best Album 1998, Best Group 1996, 1998. *Current Management:* Hagenburg Management, Kyrkogaten 31, 411 08 Gothenburg, Sweden. *Telephone:* (31) 339-95-90. *Fax:* (31) 13-95-09. *E-mail:* info@hagenburg.se. *Website:* www.hagenburg.se; www.cardigans.com.

SVIRIDOVA, Alena; Russian singer and actor; b. 14 Aug. 1962. *Career:* solo artist; numerous acting roles, including Buro Shchastya (TV series); mem. Russian Union of Writers. *Recordings include:* albums: Pink Flamingoes 1994, At Night, It's Different 1997, Life Line 2000, Hopscotch 2002, Just Ran Out Winter 2003, Siren or 12 Stories Told at Dawn 2008. *Current Management:* Empire of Music Management, 125222 Moscow, 1-ya Tverskaya-Yamskaya 6/ 38, Russia. *E-mail:* pr@tabriz.ru; pr@empireofmusic.ru. *Website:* www .empireofmusic.ru; www.sviridova.ru.

SWALLOW, Steve; American musician; b. 1940, New York, NY. *Education:* Yale Univ., studied piano with Howard Kasschau. *Career:* tours and recordings with Paul Bley, Jimmy Giuffre Trio and George Russell Sextet 1960; performances with other noted jazz musicians; joined Art Farmer Quartet 1964; toured with Stan Getz Quartet 1965–67; joined Gary Burton Quartet 1968; took up electric bass; teacher, Berklee Coll. of Music 1974–76; performed with Dizzy Gillespie, George Benson, Herbie Hancock and played on numerous recordings with other musicians; joined Carla Bley Band 1978, numerous recordings and tours; toured and recorded with John Scofield 1980–84, and produced many recordings; production for numerous artists, including Andy Sheppard, Karen Mantler, Lew Soloff; numerous tours with Paul Bley, Ernie Watts, Allen Ginsberg; reunited with Jimmy Giuffre and Paul Bley 1989, numerous tours; contributions to numerous recordings 1993; many concert appearances with Carla Bley, Jimmy Giuffre, Andy Sheppard 1994; numerous tours with many artists 1994–98; played with Harvard Univ. Jazz Band. *Recordings include:* Deconstructed, Real Book, Go Together, Swallow, Duets, Carla, Home, Hotel Hello (with Gary Burton), Always Pack Your Uniform On Top 2000, Are We There Yet?, Damaged in Transit 2003, So There (with Robert Creeley) 2006, Playing in Traffic (with Adam Nussbaum and Ohad Talmor) 2010; with Carla Bley: Night-Glo, Sextet; with John Scofield: Shinola, Out Like a Light. *Honours:* Nat. Endowment for the Arts grant 1976, first place Downbeat Int. Critics' Poll, Electric Bass 1983–, Readers' Poll 1985–, winner Jazz Times Poll, Electric Bass several times. *Current Management:* c/o Laurel Wicks, Ted Kurland Associates, 173 Brighton Avenue, Boston, MA 02134-2003, USA. *Telephone:* (617) 254-0007. *Fax:* (617) 782-3524. *E-mail:* agents@tedkurland.com. *Website:* www .tedkurland.com. *Address:* c/o Watt Works, PO Box 67, Willow, NY 12495, USA (office). *Website:* www.wattxtrawatt.com/stevecell.html.

SWAN, Billy; American singer, songwriter, musician (guitar, bass, keyboards) and producer; b. 12 May 1942, Cape Giardeau, Mo.; m. Marlu Swan (deceased); two d. *Career:* Musical Dir, A Thing Called Love, Wild At Heart (actor and singer); songwriter for Willie Nelson and Kris Kristofferson; Asst Music Dir, Great Balls of Fire, As You Like It (scored and played singing minstrel); toured with T Bone Burnett, Kinky Friedman and The Texas Jewboys, Billy Joe Shaver, Black Tie, Harry Dean Stanton and Kris Kristofferson. *Recordings include:* albums: I Can Help 1974, Rock 'n' Roll Moon 1975, Billy Swan 1976, Four, You're OK, I'm OK, I'm Into Lovin' You, Billy Swan's Best 1993, Vinyl Junkie Country, Undying Love 1995, The Sun Studio Story: Rockabilly B, Lonely Weekends 1995, Bop To Be 1995, Billy Swan Live 1996, Billy Swan, Choice Cuts 1997, The Best of Billy Swan 1997, Billy Swan: Collectibles 1997, I Can Help/Rock 'n' Roll Moon and Billy Swan/ Four: See For Miles 1997, Like Elvis Used To Do 2000, Greatest Hits 2005, Sunatra 2005, Do With Me What You Will 2009; with Black Tie: When the Night Falls 1990. *Honours:* Memphis Producer Award 2005. *E-mail:* info@ billyswanmusic.com. *Website:* www.billyswanmusic.com.

SWAN, Ren; British sound engineer. *Career:* Engineering work includes albums for KT Tunstall (Eye to the Telescope), Ronan Keating, Lionel Richie, Il Divo, Seth Lakeman, The Waterboys, Rex Radio, Westlife, The Faders, Gary Barlow, Dee Ellington, Conner Reeves, All Saints; worked on singles for Craig David, Salt 'N' Pepa, Michelle Gayle, Sensational; Remix of Clementine for Mark Owen with Grant Mitchell (3 UK charts); Remixed, Above the Law, The Evil That Men Do; Engineering and mixing credits include: George Michael, Older; Eternal, including: Stay, Oh Baby I, Good Thing; Michael Jackson, Wanna Be Starting Something mix; De La Soul, Ring Ring; Aswad, Close to You, 7 and 12 remix; Pet Shop Boys, Where The Streets Have No Name 7; Other engineering work for: Rick Astley, The Beloved, Betty Boo, Boyzone, Dina Carroll, Tom Jones, Kylie Minogue, 911, Tina Turner. *Address:* c/o SARM Studios, 8–10 Basing Street, London W11 1ET, USA. *Website:* www .myspace.com/renswan.

SWAN LAKE (see Terry, Todd)

SWANK, Ben; American musician (drums). *Career:* mem., Henry & June 1994–96, Soledad Brothers 1998–2006; co-founder Third Man Records. *Recordings include:* albums: with Soledad Brothers: Soledad Brothers 2000, Steal Your Soul (And Dare Your Spirit To Move) 2002, Live 2003, Voice Of Treason 2003, The Hardest Walk 2006. *Address:* 1203 Ferdinand, Detroit, MI 48209, USA. *E-mail:* soledadbrothers@hotmail.com. *Website:* www .soledadbrothers.com; www.thirdmanrecords.com.

SWANSON, David James; British musician (percussion); b. 15 Aug. 1951, Edinburgh, Scotland; one d. *Education:* studied with James Catherwood, coll. music course. *Career:* played with many jazz stars including: Joe Temperley; Roy Williams; Kenny Davern; Buddy DeFranco; Tal Farlow; Louis Stewart; tour of Middle East with Demis Roussos; television appearances with Tam White; Benny Waters; Healing Force; Craig McMurdo; radio with George Chisholm; tour with Herb Geller; featured in Edinburgh Jazzfest with Alex Shaw Trio, 1997; tutor with Fyjo and Nyjos; mem., Jack Duff Quintet, Freddy King Quintet, Edinburgh Light Orchestra; Chair., Edinburgh Branch, Musicians' Union.

SWEET, Phillip S.; American country music singer, songwriter and musician (guitar); b. 18 March 1974, Pocahontas, Ark.; m. Rebecca Arthur; one d. *Education:* Arkansas State Univ. *Career:* songwriter for The Martins 1998; mem. Little Big Town 1999–, appeared at Grand Old Opry 1999; toured with Keith Urban 2006, Sugarland and Jake Owen 2007, Martina McBride 2007–08, George Strait 2008, Carrie Underwood 2009, Sugarland 2010, Rascal Flatts 2012; numerous collaborations including Ashley Monroe, John Mellencamp, Collin Raye. *Recordings:* albums: with Little Big Town: Little Big Town 2002, The Road to Here 2005, A Place to Land 2007, The Reason Why 2010, Tornado 2012, Pain Killer 2014. *Honours:* Acad. of Country Music Awards for Top New Vocal Duo/Group 2007, for Top Vocal Group 2013, for Music Video of the Year (for Tornado) 2013, for Vocal Group of the Year 2014, 2015, Country Music Asscn Awards for Vocal Group of the Year 2012, 2013, 2014, 2015, for Single of the Year (for Pontoon) 2012, for Single and Song of the Year (both for Girl Crush) 2015, American Country Award for Music Video of the Year: Group or Collaboration (for Pontoon) 2012, Daytime Emmy Award for Outstanding Original Song (for Good Afternoon) 2013, Grammy Awards for Best Country Duo/Group Performance (for Pontoon) 2013, (for Girl Crush) 2016, for Best Country Song (for Girl Crush) 2016. *Current Management:* c/o Sandbox Entertainment, 54 Music Square East, Nashville, TN 37203, USA. *E-mail:* info@sandboxmgmt.com. *Website:* sandboxmgmt.com; littlebigtown .com.

SWIFT, Taylor Alison; American singer and songwriter; b. 13 Dec. 1989, Wyomissing, Pa; d. of Scott Swift and Andrea Swift. *Career:* began songwriting 2001; solo artist 2006–. *Recordings include:* albums: Taylor Swift 2006, Sound of the Season 2007, Fearless (Acad. of Country Music Award for Best Album 2009, CMA Award for Album of the Year 2009, American Music Award for Favorite Country Album 2009, Grammy Award for Album of the Year 2010) 2008, Speak Now 2010, Red (Billboard Music Awards for Top Billboard 200 Album 2013, for Top Country Album 2013, American Music Award for Favorite Country Album 2013) 2012, 1989 (American Music Award for Favorite Pop/Rock Album 2015, Grammy Awards for Album of the Year 2016, for Best Pop Album 2016) 2014. *Film appearances:* Valentine's Day 2010, Dr Seuss' The Lorax (voice) 2012, The Giver 2014. *Honours:* CMA Horizon Award 2007, CMT Award for Female Video of the Year 2008, Acad. of Country Music Awards for Best New Female Vocalist 2008, for Entertainer of the Year 2011, 2012, for Video of the Year (for Highway Don't Care) 2014, CMA Awards for Female Vocalist of the Year 2009, for Entertainer of the Year 2009, 2011, for Music Video of the Year 2009, for Int. Artist Achievement 2009, American Music Award for Artist of the Year 2009, 2013, for Favorite Female Artist 2009, for Favorite Pop/Rock Female Artist 2009, 2013, for Favorite Adult Contemporary Artist 2009, 2015, for Favorite Country Female Artist 2013, for Musical Event of the Year (for Highway Don't Care) 2013, for Song of the Year (for Blank Space) 2015, American Music Dick Clark Award for Excellence 2014, CMA Pinnacle Award 2013, Grammy Awards for Best Female Country Vocal Performance (for White Horse) 2010, for Best Country Song (for White Horse) 2010, for Country Solo Performance (for Mean) 2012, for Country Song (for Mean) 2012, for Best Song Written for Visual Media (for Safe & Sound) 2013, Woman of the Year, Billboard magazine 2011, 2014, MTV Europe Music Awards for Best Female 2012, for Best Live Act 2012, for Best Look 2012, for Best US Act 2015, for Best Song (Bad Blood) (with Kendrick Lamar) 2015, Billboard Music Awards for Top Artist 2013, 2015, for Top Female Artist 2013, 2015, for Top Country Artist 2013, for Top Billboard 200 Artist 2013, 2015, for Top Digital Songs Artist 2013, 2015, for Top Country Song (for We Are Never Ever Getting Back Together) 2013, for Top Streaming Song (Video) 2015, for Chart Achievement 2015, American Country Award for Single of the Year: Vocal Collaboration (for Highway Don't Care) 2013, for Worldwide Artist of the Year 2013, MTV Video Music Awards for Best Female Video (for I Knew You Were Trouble) 2013, for Video of the Year and Best Collaboration (for Bad Blood) 2015, for Best Female Video and Best Pop Video (both for Blank Space) 2015, BRIT Award for Best Int. Female Solo Artist 2015, 50th Anniversary Milestone Award, Acad. of Country Music Awards 2015, Primetime Emmy Award for Outstanding Creative Achievement In Interactive Media (for AMEX Unstaged: Taylor Swift Experience) 2015; ranked by Forbes magazine amongst The World's 100 Most Powerful Women (64th) 2015. *Address:* c/o Big Machine Records, 1219 16th Avenue South, Nashville, TN 37212, USA. *Website:* www .bigmachinerecords.com; www.taylorswift.com.

SWINFIELD, Raymond; musician (saxophone, clarinet, flutes); b. 14 Dec. 1939, Sydney, Australia; m. Rosemarie, Sept. 1970, divorced 1991. *Career:* Played on recordings by: Quincy Jones; Robert Farnon; Henry Mancini; Pat Williams; Ella Fitzgerald; The Beatles; Phil Woods; Michel Legrand; Kiri Te Kanawa; Stéphane Grappelli; Johnny Mercer; J J Johnson; Bjork; Everything But The Girl; Mel Torme; Chicago film soundtrack; mem, PRS; British Jazz Musicians. *Compositions:* Sydney Suite; Rain Curtain; Caroline; Thinking On It. *Recordings:* Albums: Rain Curtain; The Winged Cliff; Angel Eyes. *Honours:* Own albums listed amongst jazz records of the Year in Gramophone Jazz Journal magazines.

SWING KIDS (see Gonzalez, Kenny)

SWIRE, Rob; Australian singer, songwriter, musician (keyboards) and producer; b. (Robert Swire-Thompson), 5 Nov. 1982, Perth, WA. *Education:* Scotch Coll., Swanbourne. *Career:* musician and producer for Hardline Rekordingz –2002; fmr mem. Breakbeat; founder mem. Pendulum 2002–. *Compositions:* as co-writer: Rude Boy (for Rihanna) 2010. *Recordings:* albums: with Pendulum: Hold Your Colour 2005, In Silico 2008, Immersion 2010. *Honours:* Knowledge Magazine Awards for Best Single and Best Breakthrough Producers 2003. *Current Management:* c/o JHO Management, 1–5 Exchange Court, Maiden Lane, Covent Garden, London, WC2R 0JU, England. *Telephone:* (20) 7420-4372. *Fax:* (20) 7420-4399. *E-mail:* jho@jhooakley.com. *Website:* www.jhooakley.com. *Address:* c/o Warner Bros. Records, Warner Music UK Limited, The Warner Building, 28 Kensington Church Street, London, W8 4EP, England (office). *Website:* www.warnerbrosrecords.co.uk (office); www.pendulum.com.

SWIZZ BEATZ; American record producer, DJ and rapper; b. (Kasseem Dean), 13 Sept. 1978, Bronx, New York; m. 1st Mashonda Tifere 2004 (divorced 2008); m. 2nd Alicia Keys 2011; one s.; also one s. and one d. from other relationships. *Career:* produced first tracks 1994; producer and collaborator for numerous artists including: Beyoncé, Mary J. Blige, Bone Thugs-n-Harmony, Bow Wow, Chris Brown, Foxy Brown, Cam'ron, Mariah Carey, Cassidy, DJ Clue, DMX, Drag-On, Estelle, Eve, Fantasia, Flipmode Squad, Whitney Houston, Jennifer Hudson, Jadakiss, Jay-Z, Alicia Keys, Lil' Kim, The LOX, Ludacris, Mashonda, Mya, Nas, Nicki Minaj, Busta Rhymes, Ruff Ryders, Angie Stone, Strings, Kanye West, Yung Wun; founder Full Surface Records 2001; released first compilation album of tracks 2002; pnr in clothing co. Kidrobot 2006. *Recordings:* albums: solo: One Man Band Man 2007, Haute Living 2011. *Honours:* Producer-in-Residence, New York Univ. 2010–11; solo: Urban Music Award for Best Producer 2009; with Jay-Z: Grammy Award for Best Rap Performance by a Duo or Group 2011. *Address:* c/o Full Surface Records, 36 West 37th Street, New York, NY 10018, USA (office). *Telephone:* (646) 837-3297 (office). *Website:* www.fullsurfacerecords.com (office); www .swizzbeatzonline.com; www.swizzworld.com.

SYKES, John; British rock musician (guitar) and songwriter; b. 29 July 1959, Reading, Berkshire. *Career:* with UK rock groups Streetfighters, Tygers of Pan Tang 1980–81, Thin Lizzy 1982–83, Whitesnake 1984–86; formed Blue Murder; concerts include: British tour 1982, tours of Europe, Japan 1983, Reading Festival 1983, Monsters of Rock European tour 1983; US tours with Dio and Quiet Riot 1984, Rock In Rio 1985. *Compositions:* Co-writer with David Coverdale: Still of The Night; Is This Love?. *Recordings include:* Albums: with Tygers of Pan Tang: Spellbound 1981, Crazy Nights 1981, the Cage 1983; with Thin Lizzy: Thunder and Lightning 1983, Life 1983, One Night Only 2000; with Whitesnake: Slide It In 1984, Whitesnake (No. 2, USA) 1987; with Blue Murder: Demo 1988, Blue Murder 1989, Nothin' but Trouble 1993, Screaming Blue Murder: Dedicated to Phil Lynott 1994; Solo: Loveland 1997, Best of John Sykes 1998, Please Don't Leave Me 1999, Chapter One 2000, Out Of My Tree 2000, Nuclear Boy 2000; Singles: with Thin Lizzy: Hollywood, Cold Sweat, Thunder and Lightning, The Sun Goes Down; with Whitesnake: Give Me More Time, Standing In The Shadow, Love Ain't No Stranger. *Honours:* Platinum and Gold discs. *Website:* www .johnsykes.com.

SYLVAIN, Dominique, DEA; Haitian singer, writer and composer; b. 17 Nov. 1959, New York, USA; one d. *Education:* studied piano, guitar, percussion, voice. *Career:* solo artist; numerous concerts, festival appearances, broadcasts; mem. SACEM, ADAMI, SACED. *Recording:* Reconnais 1994, Merci la Vie, Respire, Joyshanti. *Honours:* first prize for choreography and interpretation, FFD 1990. *Address:* c/o Sanandaya Productions, 23 rue de la Gare, 78940 La Queue lez Yvelines, France (office). *Telephone:* 1-34-86-86-97 (office). *E-mail:* info@dominique-sylvain.com (office). *Website:* www.chant-dominique-sylvain .com.

SYLVAIN SYLVAIN; American musician (piano, guitar) and singer; b. (Sylvain Mizrahi), 1953, Cairo, Egypt. *Career:* founder mem., New York Dolls 1971–75, re-formed 2003–; solo artist. *Recordings include:* albums: with New York Dolls: New York Dolls 1973, Too Much Too Soon 1974, One Day it Will Please Us to Remember Even This 2006, Cause I Sez So 2009; solo: Bowery Butterflies 1978, (Sleep) Baby Doll 1998, New York's a Go Go 2004. *Address:* c/o Roadrunner Records, 902 Broadway, Eighth Floor, New York, NY 10010, USA (office). *E-mail:* roadrunner@roadrunnerrecords.com. *Website:* www .nydolls.org.

SYLVIAN, David; British rock singer, songwriter and musician (guitar); b. (David Alan Batt), 23 Feb. 1958, Beckenham, Kent; brother of Steve Jansen. *Career:* Founding mem. and lead singer, Japan 1974–82; solo artist 1982–; mem. Rain Tree Crow (with the mems of Japan) 1991; collaborations with artists including Ryuichi Sakamoto, dancer Gaby Abis, Holger Czukay, Christian Fennesz, Joan Wasser. *Recordings:* albums: with Japan: Adolescent Sex 1978, Obscure Alternatives 1978, Quiet Life 1979, Gentlemen Take Polaroids 1980, Tin Drum 1981, Oil On Canvas 1983; solo: Brilliant Trees 1984, Words With The Shaman (EP) 1985, Alchemy, An Index Of Possibilities 1985, Gone To Earth 1986, Secrets Of The Beehive 1987, Plight & Premonition (with Holger Czukay) 1988, Flux & Mutability (with Holger Czukay) 1989, Weather Box 1989, The First Day (with Robert Fripp) 1993, Damage: Live (with Robert Fripp) 1994, Dead Bees On A Cake 1999, Approaching Silence 1999, Everything & Nothing 2000, Blemish 2003, The Good Son Vs The Only Daughter 2005, Nine Horses: Snow Borne Sorrow (with Steve Jansen and Burnt Friedman) 2005, When Loud Weather Buffeted Naoshima 2007, Manafon 2009, Sleepwalkers 2010; with Rain Tree Crow: Rain Tree Crow 1991; with Stephan Mathieu: Wandermüde 2013. *Films:* Preparations for the Journey (documentary) 1985, Amplified Gesture (documentary) 2009. *Art Exhibitions:* Ember Glance: the permanence of memory (art installation, with Russell Mills), Tokyo Bay, Shinagawa 1990, Redemption (art installation, with Robert Fripp), Japan 1994, Naoshima Island (art installation), Japan 2007, When We Return You Won't Recognise Us (art installation), Gran Canaria 2009. *Publications:* Perspectives: Polaroids 82/84 (photographs) 1984, Trophies: The Lyrics of David Sylvian 1987. *Current Management:* c/o Opium (Arts) Ltd, 49 Portland Road, London, W11 4LJ, England. *Telephone:* (20) 7229-5080. *Fax:* (20) 7229-4841. *E-mail:* opiumartsinfo@aol.com. *Website:* www.davidsylvian.net.

SYNTEK, Aleks; Mexican singer, songwriter and producer; b. (Raúl Alejandro Escajadillo Peña), 29 Sept. 1969, Mérida, Yucatán; m. Karen Coronado. *Education:* Univ. of Granada. *Career:* began composing songs at age 11; professional solo singer at age 15; fmr lead singer, Aleks Syntek y La Gente Normal 1990–99; solo artist 1999–; has composed, arranged or produced songs for Sasha Sokol, Pandora, Timbiriche, Alejandro Fernandez, Enrique Iglesias, Paulina Rubio. *Films:* Robots (voice) 2005, Despicable Me (voice) 2010. *Recordings:* albums: with La Gente Normal: Hey Tú 1990, Más fuerte de lo que pensaba 1993, Bienvenido a la vida 1995, Lugar secreto 1997; solo: Sexo, pudor y lágrimas (soundtrack) (Mexican Academy Movie Award for Best Score) 1999, De noche en la ciudad 2001, Multiple 2003, Mundo lite 2004, Lección de vuelo 2007, Juntos 2008, Plug & Play 2008, Métodos de Placer Instantáneo 2009. *Current Management:* c/o Verónica Ramirez (PR/Marketing), Crack Producciones, México, Mexico. *Telephone:* 56584592. *E-mail:* veronica@crack.com.mx; management@crack.com.mx. *Website:* www.crack .com.mx. *Address:* c/o Jorge Chiwo, EMI-México, 36 Tultitlán, Estado de México, México CP 54900, Mexico (office). *Telephone:* 55881686 (office). *Fax:* 55881296 (office). *E-mail:* jorge.chiwo@emimusic.com (office); ventas@emi -mexico.com (office). *Website:* www.emi-mexico.com (office); www.alekssyntek .com.mx.

SYRJÄ, Aku; Finnish musician (drums); b. 4 April 1959. *Career:* Founder-mem. Eppu Normaali 1976–. *Recordings include:* albums: Aknepop 1978, Maximum Jee&Jee 1979, Akun tehdas 1980, Cocktail Bar – Musiikkia Rantalasta 1981, Tie vie 1982, Aku ja köyhät pojat 1983, Rupisia riimejä karmeita tarinoita 1984, Kahdeksas ihme 1985, Valkoinen kupla 1986, Imperiumin vastaisku 1988, Historian suurmiehiä 1990, Studio etana 1993, Sadan vuoden päästäkin 2004, Syvään päähän 2007, Mutala 2011. *Website:* www.eppunormaali.fi.

SYRJÄ, Martti Ilmari; Finnish singer; b. 17 May 1959. *Career:* founder mem., Eppu Normaali 1976–. *Recordings include:* albums: Aknepop 1978, Maximum Jee&Jee 1979, Akun tehdas 1980, Cocktail Bar – Musiikkia Rantalasta 1981, Tie vie 1982, Aku ja köyhät pojat 1983, Rupisia riimejä karmeita tarinoita 1984, Kahdeksas ihme 1985, Valkoinen kupla 1986, Imperiumin vastaisku 1988, Historian suurmiehiä 1990, Studio etana 1993, Sadan vuoden päästäkin 2004, Syvään päähän 2007. *Address:* c/o Poko Records, PO Box 483, 33101 Tampere, Finland (office). *E-mail:* poko@poko.fi (office). *Website:* www.eppunormaali.fi.

SYRJÄ, Mikko Juhana; Finnish musician (guitar), singer, artist manager and producer; b. 15 Nov. 1957. *Career:* founder mem., Eppu Normaali 1976–. *Recordings include:* albums: Aknepop 1978, Maximum Jee&Jee 1979, Akun tehdas 1980, Cocktail Bar – Musiikkia Rantalasta 1981, Tie vie 1982, Aku ja köyhät pojat 1983, Rupisia riimejä karmeita tarinoita 1984, Kahdeksas ihme 1985, Valkoinen kupla 1986, Imperiumin vastaisku 1988, Historian suurmiehiä 1990, Studio etana 1993, Sadan vuoden päästäkin 2004, Syvään päähän 2007. *Address:* c/o Poko Records, PO Box 483, 33101 Tampere, Finland (office). *E-mail:* poko@poko.fi (office). *Website:* www .eppunormaali.fi.

SZABO, Richard Wayne, BA; American musician (trumpet) and bandleader; b. 16 March 1956, Newark, NJ. *Education:* Fairleigh Dickinson Univ., Madison. *Career:* played in bands of Maynard Ferguson, Buddy Rich, Ray Anthony, Sammy Kaye, Guy Lombardo, Tito Puente, Billy May, Xavier Cugat, Frank Sinatra Jr; appeared or recorded with Melissa Manchester, The Grass Roots, Mel Torme, Johnny Desmond, Margaret Whiting, Helen Forrest, Regis Philbin, The Four Tops, The Four Lads, The Four Aces, The Chordettes; Music Dir, Station WPCN-AM Radio, Pennsylvania 1988; mem,

Songwriters Hall of Fame, NARAS, AFofM, AFTRA, IJAE. *Recording:* Manhattan At Dusk 1994. *Current Management:* Fame Management, PO Box 262, Livingston, NJ 07039, USA. *Telephone:* (973) 994-1902. *Fax:* (973) 994-2301. *E-mail:* famemgt@aol.com. *E-mail:* info@richszabo.com (office). *Website:* www.richszabo.com.

SZAWLOWSKI, William Stephen; Canadian record producer, engineer, arranger and writer; *Active Recording Engineer and Producer, William Szawlowski Productions & Ventura Digital Audio*; b. 24 March 1955, Montréal, Québec. *Career:* asst recording engineer 1974–75; recording engineer 1976–83; Pres. SCI Productions, Record Producer 1984–90; ind. record producer, engineer, arranger, 1991–2007; producer for: Marjo, Marie-Carmen, Ray Lyell; engineer for: April Wine, Aldo Nova, Frank Marino, Robbie Robertson, Helix, Luba, Teaze, Murray Head, Walter Rossi, Cirque du Soleil, Diane DuFresne, Kashtin, Pagliaro, Nanette Workman Discography-C (partial listing 1999–2005), Eye Of The Storm, Frank Marino, WSQ 25th World Saxaphone Quartet, The Calling Bluiett/Jackson/El Zabar Like A Kiss..., David Murray, This Is Carmen, Lundy Nuage, Jeff Johnson, All 'Alba, Francois Carriere, Rendez Vous, Jean Seb, Accapella Plus One, Montreal Jubilation Choir, Pennies From Heaven, Suzie Arioli Crossroad Diaries, Adam Karch, Blue Until June, Ballets Jazz de Montreal, Waiting For The Dawn, Emerald City, Goin Up Yonder, Firm Roots, Jeri Brown, Gagner Sa, Vie Bourbon, Gautier Suite For New York, dd Jackson, Performance Quartango, Something To Believe In, Carmen Lundy, Nasty Reputation, Mathew Enright, Travelling Lights, Francois Carrier, Gwo Ka Masters, David Murray, The English House, J.P. Mortier, That's For Me, Susie Arioli, Rhapsody of Blues, Mathew Enright, Best Of Cirque du Soleil, Cirque du Soleil Just You, Just Me Ranee, Lee & Oliver Jones, Learn To Smile..., Susie Arioli/Jordan Officer, Le Passant, Michel Lambert, Echos From The Blue Angel, Craig Morrison, I'll Take You There, Montreal Jubilation Choir, Sand Underfoot, Jeannette Lambert, Turquoise Marjo, Live At The Oscar, Craig Morrison, Introduction To Wood, Lew Dite; mem. Soc. of Composers, Authors and Music Publrs of Canada. *Films:* Time At The Top, T'Choupi (children's series), SOF (Special Ops Force) EFX (action series), Jules Verne FilmLine (TV series), Heavy Metal 2000, Cine Groupe/ Das Werk Production (feature). *Recordings:* Producer for: Marjo; Marie-Carmen; Ray Lyell; Engineer for: April Wine; Aldo Nova; Frank Marino; Robbie Robertson; Helix; Luba; Teaze; Murray Head; Walter Rossi; Cirque du Soleil; Diane DuFresne; Kashtin; Pagliaro; Nanette Workman. *Honours:* ADISQ Award, Best Engineer 1987, Gemini Award for Best Sound (Cirque du Soleil) 1996, Double Platinum albums (CRIA certified): Standback, April Wine Greatest Hits, April Wine Celle Qui Va Marjo; Platinum albums (CRIA certified): Standback, April Wine Whole World iGoin' Crazy, April Wine Forever For Now, April Wine First Glance, April Wine Greatest Hits, April Wine; Gold albums (CRIA certified): Standback, April Wine, Whole World's Goin' Crazy, April Wine Forever For Now, April Wine Boogie, Home Billy Workman Live, Frank Marino & Mahogany Rush, First Glance, April Wine Tour Of Japan, Teaze Greatest Hits, April Wine Aldo Nova Aldo Nova, RPM #1 Award (April Wine), ADISQ Best Engineered Recording (Marjo), ADISQ Best Rock Album (Nanette Workman), Startrack Songwriter's Award (Denise Murray), Juno Best New Jazz (D.D. Jackson), Best Jazz CD (Ranee Lee/Oliver Jones), Canadian Nat. Jazz Awards. *E-mail:* info@ venturadigitalaudio.com (office). *Website:* www.venturadigitalaudio.com (office).

SZCZESNIAK, Mieczyslaw Wojciech; Polish singer; b. 9 July 1964, Kalisz. *Education:* Acad. of Music. *Career:* many TV and radio broadcasts, concerts and recitals, festivals; mem. STOMUR (Polish Soc. of Pop Musicians), PSJ (Polish Soc. of Jazz). *Recordings include:* Niby Nowy 1990, Czarno na białym 1998, Spoza nas 2000, Kiedyś 2002, Zwykły cud 2006, Signs 2011. *Honours:* Sopot Festival 1989, Bresenz Interlatent 1989, Golden Orpheus 1990, Cesmè Festival 1990, Golden Record of Nashville (FIDOF) 1990. *Telephone:* 607401207. *E-mail:* koncerty@mieczu.pl; mietek@mieczu.pl. *Website:* www .mietekszczesniak.pl.

SZE, Jean Yi-Ching, BA, BS, MA, MS; American (b. Chinese) composer, zheng player and music teacher; b. 14 May 1956, Shanghai, China. *Education:* Shanghai Conservatory of Music, Coll. of St Elizabeth and Virginia Tech Univ., USA. *Career:* mem. American Music Center, American Soc. of Composers, Authors and Publrs (ASCAP), New Jersey Music Teachers Asscn. *Compositions include:* Shi for string quartet, Mountain for electric violin, zheng, bamboo flute, Autumn for string orchestra with bamboo flute, Flute Solo, Eastern View and Tradition Suite for violin and zheng, A Spring Morning at Miao Mountain for bamboo flute and zheng, Three Poems of Tang Dynasty for soprano, bamboo flute, yang qing, zheng, ban hu and pipa, The Sword and the Silk for lute and zheng and pipa 2000, The Pearl and the Thread for viola and pipa 2001, Nature for violin and piano 2003, White, Peace, Snow Mountains V for flute, piano and narrator 2006, Jasmin Flower Capriccio for zheng 2008, The Only Time Left for chorus 2010, A Letter from Mountain Village for er hu and flute 2010, A Brook at My Backyard for piano. *Publication:* Twentieth Century Music for Flute and Piano or Flute Solo. *Honours:* Second Prize, Shanghai Nat. Music Competition 1983, Asia Artist Award, USA 2001. *Address:* 13 Joann Court, Monmouth Junction, NJ 08852, USA (home). *Telephone:* (732) 329-3245 (home). *E-mail:* jeansze@comcast.net (office).

SZE, Kwan Leung; Chinese musician; b. 11 Dec. 1938; m. Chi Wan Sze Siu; one s. *Education:* Tianjin Conservatory of Music, People's Republic of China.

Career: The Choir of Hong Kong, Professional Teacher, Conductor; Radio Television Hong Kong; Hong Kong Chinese Folk Song Group; Recital, 1982, 1983; Professor, Tsing Hua College Music Department; mem, Hong Kong Ethnomusicology Society. *Publications:* Chorus and Chorus Conductor; The Great Singers In Record.

SZÖRÉNYI, Levente; Hungarian musician, composer and songwriter; b. 26 April 1945, Gmunden, Austria; m. (divorced). *Education:* Coll. of Music. *Career:* guitar player; worked with János Bródy 1965–; pop musician with Mediterrán and Balassa 1963–64, with Illés 1965–73; dance participant, Még fáj minden csók (song festival) 1966; Founding mem. Fonográf (band) 1974–81; retd from theatre 1984. *Soundtracks include:* Ezek a fiatalok 1967, Extázis 5-7-ig 1969, Eltávozott a nap, Locsolókocsi, Pókfoci, A Koncert 1982, István a Király 1983, Attila Isten kardja (opera) 1993, Veled Uram! (opera) 2000, Ének a csodaszarvasról 2001. *Compositions include:* Human Rights (Oratory) 1968, Kömíves Kelemen (rock ballad) 1982, István a Király (rock opera) 1983, Fehér Anna (rock ballad) 1988, Fénylő Ölednek édes Örömében (Innin and Dumuzi—oratory) 1989. *Honours:* First Prize Hungarian Radio Amateur Competition 1965, SZOT (Trade Union) Award 1981, Composer of the Year 1983, Erkel Ferenc Award 1983, KISZ (Youth Org.) Award. *Address:* Mátru u. 9, 1029 Budapest, Hungary (office). *E-mail:* szorenyi@c2.hu (office). *Website:* ummagumma.hu/szorenyi.

T, Jamie; British singer and songwriter; b. (Jamie Alexander Treays), 8 Jan. 1986, Wimbledon, London, England. *Career:* solo artist 2006–; signed to Virgin Records; released debut EP Betty and the Selfish Sons on own label Pacemaker Records 2006. *Recordings:* albums: Panic Prevention 2007, Kings & Queens 2009. *Honours:* Best Solo Artist, Shockwave NME Awards 2007. *Website:* www.jamie-t.com; www.myspace.com/jamietwimbledon.

TABATABAEE, Alireza; Iranian musician (drums); b. 1971, Mashhad; m.; one d. *Career:* qualified interpreter of German; mem. The Arian Band (first officially sanctioned mixed-gender pop band in Iran). *Recordings include:* albums: Sunflower, And But Love!, Ta Binahayat (Till Eternity), Without You With You 2008, Farewell 2015. *Current Management:* c/o Mr Mohsen Rajabpour, Taraneh Sharghee Cultural & Artistic Co., Apt No. 26, Seventh Floor, Suite 22, Second Alley, Shahnazari Street, Mohseni Square, Mirdamad Avenue, Tehran 1547914415, Iran. *Telephone:* (21) 22223670. *Fax:* (21) 22906211. *E-mail:* president@taranehsh.com. *Website:* www.taranehsh.com; www.arianmusic.com.

TABLO, (Supreme T), BA, MA; South Korean rapper, songwriter, musician, actor and record producer; b. (Lee Seon-woong), 22 July 1980, Seoul; m. Kang Hye-jung 2009; one d. *Education:* Seoul Int. School, Stanford Univ., USA. *Career:* raised in Switzerland, Hong Kong, Canada; several side-project groups including Eternal Morning, Anyband; Founder mem. hip hop group Epik High 2003–; co-f. Map the Soul record label 2009. *Television:* as actor: Nonstop 2005, Fantastic Parasuicides 2007. *Recordings include:* albums: with Epik High: Map of the Human Soul 2003, High Society 2004, Swan Songs 2005, Remapping the Human Soul (Mnet KM Music Festival Award for Album of the Year 2007) 2007, Pieces Part One 2008, (e) 2009, Epilogue 2010, 99 2012; solo: Fever's End Part I 2011, Fever's End Part II 2011. *Publication:* Pieces of You 2008. *Honours:* Golden Disk Awards for Best Hip-Hop Artist 2005, 2009, for Bonsang (Fan) 2007, KBS Music Award for Best Hip-Hop Artist 2005, SBS Music Award for Best Hip Hop Artist 2006, M.net KM Music Festival Awards for Best Hip-Hop Artist 2005, 2008, for Bonsang (Fan) 2007, Seoul Music Award for Bonsang (Fan) 2008, Mnet Asian Music Award for Best Rap Performance (for UP) 2012. *Address:* c/o YG Entertainment, 397-5 YG Building, 5th Floor, Hapjeong-Dong, Mapo-Gu, Seoul, 121886, South Korea (office). *Website:* www.mapthesoul.com; www.vgtablo.com; www.vg-epikhigh .com.

TABOO; American MC and dancer. *Career:* mem., Black Eyed Peas 1995–. *Recordings include:* albums: Behind The Front 1998, Bridging The Gap 2000, Elephunk (NRJ Music Award for Best Int. Album, France 2005) 2003, Monkey Business (Juno Award for Int. Album of the Year 2006, American Music Award for Favorite Rap/Hip-Hop Album 2006) 2005, The E.N.D. (Grammy Award for Best Pop Vocal Album 2010) 2009, The Beginning 2010. *Honours:* MTV Europe Award for Best Pop Act 2004, 2005, Australian MTV Awards for Best R&B Video, for Sexiest Video (both for Hey Mama) 2005, American Music Award for Favorite Pop/Rock Band, Duo or Group 2005, 2009, for Favorite Rap/Hip-Hop Band, Duo or Group 2005, 2006, 2009, Grammy Award for Best Rap Performance by a Duo or Group (for Don't Phunk with my Heart) 2006, MOBO Award for Best Group 2006, American Music Award for Favorite Soul/R&B Band, Duo or Group 2006, Grammy Awards for Best Pop Performance by a Duo or Group with Vocal (for My Humps) 2007, (for I Gotta Feeling) 2010. *Website:* www.blackeyedpeas.com; taboo.blackeyedpeas.com.

TABOR, June, MA; British singer and fmr librarian and fmr restaurateur; b. 31 Dec. 1947, Warwick, Warwicks. *Education:* St Hugh's Coll., Univ. of Oxford. *Career:* singer and interpreter of both traditional and contemporary song; solo artist; collaborations including with pianist/composer Huw Warren, guitarist Martin Simpson, harpist/composer Savourna Stevenson, Oysterband, Maddy Prior (as Silly Sisters), The Creative Jazz Orchestra, saxophonist Iain Ballamy (in Quercus), Renga Ensemble of the London Philharmonic Orchestra. *Television:* BBC 4 Sessions (filmed concert 2005), Later With Jools Holland (twice), BBC Proms (Grainger) 2011, Later With Jools Holland with Oysterband 2013. *Recordings include:* albums: Silly Sisters (with Maddy Prior) 1976, Airs And Graces 1976, Ashes And Diamonds 1977, A Cut Above 1980, Abyssinians 1983, Aqaba 1988, No More To The Dance (with Maddy Prior) 1988, Some Other Time 1989, Freedom And Rain (with Oysterband) 1990, Angel Tiger 1992, Anthology (compilation) 1993, Against The Streams 1994, Singing The Storm (with Savourna Stevenson) 1996, Aleyn (live) 1997, A Quiet Eye 1999, Rosa Mundi 2001, An Echo of Hooves 2003, Always (four-CD boxed set) 2005, At The Wood's Heart 2005, Apples 2007, Ashore 2011, Ragged Kingdom (with Oysterband) 2011, Quercus (with Huw Warren and Iain Ballamy) 2013. *Honours:* BBC Radio 2 Folk Award for Folk Singer of the Year 2004, 2012. *Current Management:* c/o Mark Emerson. *Telephone:* (1547) 528112. *E-mail:* taborinfo@yahoo.co.uk (office). *Website:* www.junetabor.co .uk.

TABORN, Craig Marvin, BA; American jazz pianist, keyboardist, bandleader and composer; b. 20 Feb. 1970, Minneapolis, Minn.; s. of John Taborn and Marjorie Taborn. *Education:* Breck School, Univ. of Michigan. *Career:* Founder-mem. (with Gerald Cleaver), Tracey Science Quartet during early 1990s; mem. James Carter's band during early 1990s; formed Craig Taborn Trio 1994; debut recording as bandleader 1994; collaboration with techno

producer Carl Craig during late 1990s; toured internationally with Dave Holland's Prism quartet 2012–; collaborations as sideman on more than 70 albums including recordings by Lotte Anker, Diego Barber, Tim Berne, David Binney, Jakob Bro, Rob Brown, Francisco Mora Catlett, Gerald Cleaver, Scott Colley, Dave Douglas, Marty Ehrlich, Shane Endsley, Gang Font, Michael Formanek, Ya Ya Fornier, Drew Gress, Susie Ibarra, Innerzone Orchestra (with techno producer Carl Craig), Bill Laswell, Okkyung Lee, Chris Lightcap, Mat Maneri, Nicole Mitchell, Roscoe Mitchell, Eivind Opsvik, Evan Parker, Mario Pavone, Chris Potter, Hugh Ragin, Mike Reed, Pete Robbins, Roberto Rodriguez, David Rogers, Leo Sclavis, Alex Sipiagin, Wadada Leo Smith, Assif Tsahar, David Torn. *Recordings:* as leader: Craig Taborn Trio 1994, Light Made Lighter 2001, Junk Magic 2004, Avenging Angel 2011, Chants 2013. *Honours:* Down Beat Critics' Awards for Electric Keyboard 2011, for Rising Star in Piano and Organ 2011, North Sea Jazz Festival Paul Acket Award 2012, Jazz Journalists Asscn Award for Pianist of the Year 2014. *Address:* c/o ECM Records/Verlag, Edition Zeitgenössische Musik GmbH, Postfach 600 331, 81203 Munich, Germany (office). *Telephone:* (89) 851048 (office). *Fax:* (89) 8545652 (office). *E-mail:* ecmrecords@ecmrecords.com (office). *Website:* www .ecmrecords.com (office); www.craigtaborn.com (office).

TABU ZOMBIE; Japanese musician (trumpet). *Career:* mem. jazz band, Soil & 'Pimp' Sessions 2001–. *Recordings include:* albums: Pimpin' (EP) 2004, Pimp Master 2005, Summer Goddess (EP) 2005, Pimp of the Year 2006. *Current Management:* c/o Victor Entertainment Inc., Palacion Tower, 3-6-7 Kita-Aoyama, Minato-ku, Tokyo 107-0061, Japan. *E-mail:* soil@jvcmusic.co .jp. *Website:* www.soilpimp.com.

TACUMA, Jamaaladeen; American musician (double bass) and composer; b. (Rudy MacDaniel), 11 June 1956, Hempstead, New York. *Career:* session musician 1977–; played with Charles Earland, Ornette Coleman's Prime Time, Jeff Beck, Jayne Cortez (poet); solo recording artist 1983–; f. own dance band, Cosmetic 1983–; Founder-mem., Golden Palominos; Founder-mem., Free Form Funky Freqs 2007–; numerous concerts. *Recordings include:* albums: solo: Showstopper 1983, Renaissance Man 1984, So Tranquilizin' 1984, Music World 1986, Jukebox 1989, Boss of The Bass 1993, Sound Symphony 1994, Night of Chamber Music 1994, Intense 1995, Gemini-Gemini 1995, Journey into Gemini Territory 1996, Dreamscape 1998, Live in Cologne 1998, Meet The Podium Three 2000, Brotherzone 2001, All Basses Covered 2005, Flavors of Thelonius Monk Reloaded 2007, Coltrane Configurations 2009, For the Love of Ornette 2010; with Free Form Funky Freqs: Urban Mythology, Volume 1 2008. *Current Management:* c/o Maurice Montoya, 11 Island Avenue, Suite 1711, Miami, FL 33139, USA. *Telephone:* (305) 763-8961. *Fax:* (305) 831-4472. *E-mail:* maurice@mmmusicagency.com; info@ mmmusicagency.com. *Website:* www.mmmusicagency.com.

TAEYANG; South Korean singer; b. (Doug Youngbae), 18 May 1988, Pocheon, Gyeonggi-do. *Career:* signed to YG Entertainment 2000; mem. Big Bang 2006–; collaborations with Weesung, Teddy Park, Big Tone. *Recordings:* albums: with Big Bang: Bigbang Vol 1 2007, Remember 2008, Number 1 2008, Big Bang 2009, Big Bang 2 2011, Alive 2012; solo: Hot 2008, Solar 2010, RISE 2014. *Honours:* Mnet KM Music Festival Awards for Best Male Group 2007, 2008, 2012, for Song of the Year 2007, for Digital Music 2008, for Artist of the Year 2008, 2012, for Guardian Angel Worldwide Performer 2012, Golden Disk Bonsang Award 2007, Mnet Music Portal Award 2008, Korean Music Awards for Best R&B/Soul Music 2008, for Male Musician of the Year 2011, Naver Music Song of the Year Award 2008, Seoul Music Awards for Digital Music 2008, for Bonsang 2008, 2009, for Best Album 2009, for Popular Mobile 2009, Nickelodeon Korea Kids' Choice Best Male Artists Award 2008, 2009, Hiwon Award 2009, Korea PD Best Singer Award 2009, Best Hits Song Festival Gold Artist Award 2009, Japan Cable Broadcasting Best Newcomer Award 2009, Ministry of Culture, Sports and Tourism Artist of the Year 2009, Japan Record Awards for New Artist and Best New Artist 2009, Gold Award 2010, Japanese Grand Prix du Disque for Best Newcomer 2010, Japan Gold Disc Awards for Best Five New Artists and Best New Artist 2010, MTV Video Music Awards Japan for Best New Artist Video and Best Pop Video 2010, Mnet Asian Music Awards for Best Male Singer 2011, for Song of the Year 2014, for Best Vocal Performance 2014, for Best Male Artist 2014. *Address:* c/o YG Entertainment, 397–5 YG Building, Hapjeong-Dong, Mapo-Gu, Seoul 109-819, South Korea (office). *Telephone:* (2) 3143-1105 (office). *Fax:* (2) 544-1546 (office). *E-mail:* web@ygmail.net (office). *Website:* eng.ygfamily.com/main/main.html (office); www.ybigbang.com (home); www.ybigbang.jp (home).

TAEYEON; South Korean singer; b. (Kim Tae-yeon), 9 March 1989, Jeonju, N Jeolla. *Education:* Jeonju Art High School. *Career:* lead singer, Girls' Generation 2007–; solo singer 2008–; mem. Girls' Generation-TTS (or TTS) 2012–; mem., SM the Ballad 2014–; collaborations include Kangta, Sunny, Kim Bum-soo, Amber, Yim Jae-beom, Verbal Jint. *Stage:* Midnight Sun (musical) 2010. *Radio:* host, Taeyeon's Chin Chin Radio (MBC Radio) 2008–10. *Television:* host, Win Win 2010, Music Core 2012–13. *Recordings include:* with Girls' Generation: Girls' Generation 2007, Oh! 2010, The Boys 2011, I Got a Boy 2013, Lion Heart 2015; with SM the Ballad: Breath 2014. *Honours:* numerous awards including: solo: Golden Disk Popularity Award (for Can You Hear Me) 2008, Mnet Asian Music Awards for Best OST 2008, for Best Female Artist 2015; with Girls' Generation: Golden Disk Popularity

Awards 2007, 2010, 2014, 2015, Digital Daesang Awards 2009, 2012, Disk Bonsang Awards 2009, 2010, 2014, 2015, Seoul Music Best Newcomer Award 2007, Seoul Music Popularity Awards 2009, 2010, 2011, Mnet Asian Music Awards for Best Female Group 2011, 2013, 2015, for Artist of the Year 2011. *Current Management:* c/o SM Entertainment, 114 Seolleung-ro 190-gil, Gangnam-gu, Seoul, South Korea. *Telephone:* (2) 6240-9800. *Website:* www .smtown.com.

TAFJORD, Stein Erik; Norwegian musician (tuba), conductor and composer; b. 2 Nov. 1953, Aalesund, Norway; m.; four c. *Education:* Norwegian State Acad. of Music. *Career:* played with Norwegian Radio Symphony Orchestra, Carla Bley Scandinavian Orchestra, Lester Bowie, David Murrey's Jazz Baltica Ensemble, The Brazz Brothers; soloist, with several TV and radio productions in Europe, USA, Asia, Africa, South America; mem. Norwegian Musicians' Union. *Recordings include:* contrib. to some 120 recordings, 35 with own band. *Honours:* Jazz Musician of the Year 1991. *Address:* Stein Erik Tafjord ENK, Løvenskioldsgt 10 B, 0263 Oslo, Norway (home). *Telephone:* 95-00-48-86 (mobile). *E-mail:* steinerik@tafjord.com. *Website:* www .brazzbrothers.com.

TAGAQ, Tanya; Canadian (Inuit) singer. *Education:* Nova Scotia Coll. of Art and Design. *Career:* throat singer; collaborated with Björk 2004. *Recordings include:* album: Sinaa 2005, Auk/Blood 2008, Anuraaqtuq 2011, Animism (Polaris Music Prize 2014, Juno Award for Best Aboriginal Recording 2015) 2014. *Honours:* Canada Aboriginal Music Award for Best Female Artist 2005. *Current Management:* c/o Helen Britton and Shauna de Cartier, Six Shooter Inc., PO 98038, 970 Queen Street East, Toronto, ON M4M 1J0, Canada. *Telephone:* (416) 465-2459. *E-mail:* helen@sixshooterrecords.com; shauna@ sixshooterrecords.com. *Website:* www.tanyatagaq.com.

TAHA, Rachid; Algerian rai singer and songwriter; b. 18 Sept. 1958, Oran; one s. *Career:* family emigrated to Alsace, France 1968; Founding mem. Carte de Séjour 1981–89; solo artist 1991–; numerous tours, live performances and festival appearances world-wide. *Recordings:* albums: with Carte de Séjour: Rhoromanie 1984, Deux Et Demi 1986; solo: Barbès 1990, Rachid Taha 1993, Olé Olé 1995, Carte Blanche 1997, Diwân 1998, 1 2 3 Soleil (with Khaled and Faudel), Ach Adani, Made In Medina 2000, Live 2001, Takitoi 2004, Rock El Casbah 2005, Diwan 2 (BBC Radio 3 World Music Award, Middle East and North Africa Region 2008) 2006, Bonjour 2009, Zoum 2013. *Honours:* World Music Album of the Year (France) 2000. *Current Management:* c/o La Cile, 41 rue de La Duée, 75020 Paris, France. *Telephone:* 6-13-42-36-84 (mobile). *E-mail:* amblanc@labelleaffaire.eu. *Website:* www.rachidtaha.fr.

TAKAGI, Reni; Japanese singer; b. 21 June 1993, Kanagawa. *Career:* mem., all-female vocal group Momoiro Clover 2010, renamed Momoiro Clover Z 2011–; numerous live and TV appearances; concert appearances in Germany, Malaysia, France. *Radio:* as host: Takagi Reni no King of Rock 2012. *Films:* Shirome 2010. *Recordings:* albums: Battle and Romance (CD Shop Award for Best CD 2012) 2011, 5th Dimension 2013, Iriguchi no Nai Deguchi 2013. *Honours:* MTV Video Music Award Japan for Best Choreography 2013, MTV Europe Music Award for Best Japanese Act 2013. *Current Management:* c/o Stardust Promotion, 2F Takeda-Dai2 Bldg, 2-3-3 Ebisu-nishi, Shibuya, Tokyo, 150-0021, Japan. *Website:* www.stardust.co.jp; starchild.fm/special/en/ momoclo.

TAKEDA, Masako; Japanese singer. *Career:* Founder-mem. Nagisa Ni te 1990–. *Recordings include:* albums: True Sun 1998, The True World 1999, Feel 2001, On the Love Beach 2001, The Same as a Flower 2004, Dream Sounds 2005, III 2005, Yosuga 2008, Destination Tokyo 2009.

TAKURO; Japanese musician (guitar) and songwriter; b. (Kubo Takuro), 26 May 1971, Hakodate. *Career:* Founder-mem. pop/rock band, Glay 1988, moved band to Tokyo 1990–; numerous live performances and tours, numerous radio broadcasts. *Recordings include:* albums: Hai to Daiyamondo 1994, Speed Pop 1995, BEAT out! 1996, Beloved (Nihon Record Grand Prize 1997) 1996, Review: Best of Glay 1997, Pure Soul (Nihon Record Best Album) 1998, Heavy Gauge 1999, Mirai Diary (film soundtrack) 2000, One Love 2001, Unity Roots & Family, Away 2002, The Frustrated 2004, Love is Beautiful 2007; singles: Rain 1994, Manatsuno Tobira 1994, Kanojo no Modern 1994, Freeze My Love 1995, Zutto Futari de 1995, Yes, Summerdays 1995, Ikiteju Tsuyosa 1995, Glorious 1996, Beloved (Japan Usen Broadcast Networks Gold Request Prize) 1996, Zutto Wasurenai (A Boy) 1996, Kuchibiru 1997, However (Nihon Record Excellent Work Award) 1997, Yuuwaku 1998, Soul Love 1998, Be With You 1998, Winter Again (Nihon Record Grand Prize) 1999, Kokodewanai, Dokokae 1999, Happiness 2000, Mermaid 2000, Tomadoi/Special Thanks 2000, Missing You 2000, Global Communication 2001, Stay Tuned 2001, Hitohira no Jiyuu 2001, Way Of Difference 2002, Mata Kokode Aimashou 2002, Aitai Kimochi 2002, Beautiful Dreamer/Street Life 2003, Blue Jean 2004, Verb 2007. *Honours:* Japan Usen Broadcast Networks Grand Prize 1997, 1999, Golden Arrow Music Prize 1998, Gold Disc Awards for Best Rock Artist of the Year, Best Music Video of the Year, Artist of the Year 1998. *Website:* www.glay.co.jp.

TALBOT, Joby, BMus, MMus; British composer, arranger, musician (piano, oboe) and conductor; b. 25 Aug. 1971, Wimbledon, London; m. Claire Burbridge. *Education:* Guildhall School of Music and Drama, Univ. of London. *Career:* composer of concert music for groups, including London Sinfonietta, RRC Philharmonic, Britten Sinfonia Crouch End Festival Chorus; keyboard player and arranger, The Divine Comedy 1993–; composer 1996–; Composer-in-Residence, Classic FM in asscn with the PRS Foundation for New Music

2004; formed the Joby Talbot Quartet; mem. Musicians' Union, PRS. *Compositions include:* Incandescence, Luminescence, Young Musician of the Year theme, Tomorrow's World theme, League of Gentlemen theme (BBC TV) (RTS Award for Best Title Music 2000) 1999–2000, BFI commission for a new score to Alfred Hitchcock's The Lodger 2000, Sneaker Wave (for Proms) 2004, The Hitchhiker's Guide to the Galaxy (film score) 2005, The League of Gentlemen's Apocalypse (film score) 2005, Sixty Six (film score) 2006, Penelope (film score) 2007, Son of Rambow (film score) 2007, Arctic Tale (film score) 2007, Angus, Thongs and Perfect Snogging (film score) 2008. *Recordings include:* albums: with The Divine Comedy: Promenade 1994, Casanova 1996, A Short Album About Love 1997, Fin de Siecle 1998, A Secret History (compilation) 1999, Regeneration 2001, Absent Friends 2004, Victory for the Comic Muse (Choice Music Prize for Irish Album of the Year) 2006; solo: Once Around the Sun 2005. *Honours:* BBC Young Composer of the Year 1996, ASCAP Award 2006. *Address:* c/o Catherine Manners, Manners McDade Artist Management, 4th Floor, 40 Mortimer Street, London, W1W 7RQ, England (office). *Telephone:* (20) 7928-9939 (office). *Fax:* (20) 7277 7630. *E-mail:* info@mannersmcdade.co.uk (office). *Website:* www.mannersmcdade .co.uk; www.jobytalbot.com.

TALBOT, Martin; British journalist; *Managing Director, Official UK Charts Company. Career:* fmr Ed., Fono magazine –2002; Exec. Ed., Music Week 2002–07; Man. Dir, Official UK Charts Co. 2007–. *Address:* The Official UK Charts Company, 2nd Floor, Riverside Building, County Hall, Westminster Bridge Road, London, SE1 7JA, England (office). *Telephone:* (20) 7620-7450 (office). *Fax:* (20) 7620-7469 (office). *Website:* www.theofficialcharts.com (office).

TALLARICO, Thomas (Tommy) V.; American composer and broadcaster; *President, Tommy Tallarico Studios.* b. 18 Feb. 1968, Orange County, Calif. *Career:* fmr games tester, product man., producer, writer and designer; Head of Music and Video Div., Virgin Interactive 1991–94; Founder and Pres., Tommy Tallarico Studios 1994–, producing music for the multimedia industry, including computer games, TV, film and radio; Co-founder and Pres., Game Audio Network Guild (GANG) 2002–, co-creator of Video Games Live 2002–; mem. advisory bd, Game Developers Conf.; Nominating Cttee mem. Acad. of Interactive Arts and Sciences. *Television:* host, Judgment Day (G4), host, writer and co-producer, The Electric Playground (Telly Award for Best Entertainment Cable Program 2001) 1995–. *Television writing:* Mohr Sports (series writer) 2002, Judgment Day (series writer) 2002. *Compositions for television:* Electric Playground (series) 1997, Judgment Day (series) 2002. *Compositions for computer games include:* Batman: Revenge of the Joker 1992, Aladdin 1993, RoboCop vs the Terminator (music dir) 1994, Earthworm Jim 1994, Demolition Man 1994, Earthworm Jim 2 1995, MDK 1997, Wargames 1998, Wild 9 1998, Apocalypse 1998, Pac-Man World 1999, Spider-Man 2000, Evil Dead: Hail to the King 2000, Scooby-Doo: Night of 100 Frights 2002, Maximo Vs Army of Zin 2004, The Bard's Tale 2004, James Bond Tomorrow Never Dies,. *Honours:* winner of numerous industry awards for best video game audio. *Address:* Tommy Tallarico Studios, PO Box 507, 31868 Del Obispo, Suite 118, San Juan Capistrano, CA 92675-3224, USA (office). *E-mail:* mike@tallarico.com (office). *Website:* www.tallarico.com.

TAMAI, Shiori; Japanese singer; b. 4 June 1995, Kanagawa. *Career:* mem., all-female vocal group Momoiro Clover 2010, renamed Momoiro Clover Z 2011–; numerous live and TV appearances; concert appearances in Germany, Malaysia, France. *Films:* Shirome 2010. *Television:* as voice artist: Akumu-chan 2012–. *Recordings:* albums: Battle and Romance (CD Shop Award for Best CD 2012) 2011, 5th Dimension 2013, Iriguchi no Nai Deguchi 2013. *Honours:* MTV Video Music Award Japan for Best Choreography 2013, MTV Europe Music Award for Best Japanese Act 2013. *Current Management:* c/o Stardust Promotion, 2F Takeda-Dai2 Bldg, 2-3-3 Ebisu-nishi, Shibuya, Tokyo, 150-0021, Japan. *Website:* www.stardust.co.jp; starchild.fm/special/en/ momoclo.

TAMAIRA, Dallas, (Joe Dukie); New Zealand singer. *Career:* mem. reggae and soul band, Fat Freddy's Drop. *Recordings include:* albums: Live at the Matterhorn 2001, Based on a True Story 2005, Dr Boondigga and the Big BW 2009, Live at Roundhouse 2010. *Honours:* Fat Freddy's Drop: Best Live Act, b-Net NZ Music Awards 2004, New Zealand Music Award for Best Group 2005, Best Vocalist, b-Net NZ Music Awards 2005, DJ Fitchie, Best Producer and Most Outstanding Musician, b-Net NZ Music Awards 2005. *Address:* The Drop Ltd, PO Box 14-723, Kilbirnie, Wellington 6241, New Zealand (office). *Telephone:* (4) 934-3767 (office). *E-mail:* freddy@fatfreddysdrop.com (office). *Website:* www.fatfreddysdrop.com.

TAMIA; Canadian R&B singer, songwriter and musician (piano); b. (Tamia Marilyn Hill), 9 May 1975, Windsor, Ont.; m. Grant Hill 1999; two d. *Education:* Walkerville Collegiate Institute, Windsor. *Career:* studied with Eugene Davis; sang gospel in church; appeared with Gladys Knight, Chaka Khan and Brandy for single Missing You 1996; other collaborations including Fabolous, Deborah Cox and Kelly Price; toured with R. Kelly 2012. *Films:* Speed 2: Cruise Control 1997. *Recordings include:* albums: Tamia 1998, A Nu Day 2000, More 2004, Between Friends 2006, Beautiful Surprise 2012, Love Life 2015. *Honours:* YTV Vocal Achievement Award 1993, NAACP Image Award Winner for Outstanding Song (for Spend My Life With You) 2000. *Current Management:* c/o Chris Smith, Chris Smith Management Inc., 110 Cumberland Street, Suite 322, Toronto, ON M5R 3V5, Canada. *E-mail:* chris@

chrissmithmanagement.com. *Website:* www.chrissmithmanagement.com. *E-mail:* gramos@tamiaworld.com. *Website:* www.tamiaworld.com.

TAMPIER, Karel; Czech composer and songwriter; b. 24 June 1946, Ceské Budejovice; m.; three d. *Education:* studied piano. *Career:* leader, guitar and mandolin player in bluegrass group, Bobri 1970–84; leader, piano player, Zridlo 1979–85; mem. Countryfuga (family group with wife and three d.) 1989–93; numerous concerts in clubs and at nat. festivals, performances on Czech and Slovak TV; Founder-mem. and Man. Vera Klaskova. *Compositions:* Proc Jsem Mrtev?, Postel (song and music). *Recordings include:* Bobri 1977–80 1994, De Tampier 1999. *Honours:* Czech Country and Folk Festival prizes for interpretation, Porta 1978, 1979, 1980, Songwriting Prize 1984. *Telephone:* 72 8369392 (mobile). *E-mail:* manazer@klaskova.cz. *Website:* www .klaskova.cz. *Address:* Staromestská 9, 37004 Ceské Budejovice, Czech Republic. *E-mail:* ktampier@gmail.com. *Website:* www.tampier.cz.

TAMS, John Murray; British singer, musician (guitar, melodeon, fiddle, banjo, harmonica), actor, songwriter and producer; b. 16 Feb. 1949. *Career:* regular on British folk scene for many years before recording first solo album 2000; played trumpet in brass band as a child but is known in folk circles as vocalist/guitarist; mem., Ashley Hutchings' Albion Band 1976–87; leader, Home Service (folk rock band); Musical Dir, production of the Mysteries (Nat. Theatre); launched record label, No Masters Co-operative (with Jim Boyes); Assoc. Dir, Crucible Theatre, Sheffield; producer of radio dramas; appeared in and composed music for TV series Sharpe. *Recordings include:* albums: with Albion Band: The Prospect Before Us 1977, Rise Up Like The Sun 1978, Larkrise To Candleford 1980; with Home Service: The Mysteries 1985, Alright Jack 1986, Live 1986 2011; solo: Unity (Radio 2 Folk Award for Album of the Year 2001) 2000, Home 2002, The Reckoning (BBC Radio 2 Folk Award for Album of the Year 2006) 2005. *Honours:* BBC Radio 2 Folk Award for Folk Singer of the Year 2006. *Current Management:* c/o Topic Records Ltd, 7 Fernie Court, Station Road, Uppingham, Rutland, LE15 9TX, England. *E-mail:* info@ johntams.co.uk. *Website:* www.johntams.co.uk.

TAN, Dun, MA; Chinese composer; b. 18 Aug. 1957, Si Mao, Hunan Province; s. of Tan Xiang Qiu and Fang Qun Ying; m. Jane Huang 1994. *Education:* Cen. Conservatory of Music, Beijing and Columbia Univ., USA. *Career:* violist, Beijing Opera Orchestra 1976–77; Vice-Pres. Cen. Conservatory of Music 1978–; works performed by major orchestras in China and at festivals world-wide; has conducted orchestras including Royal Concertgebouw, London Symphony, New York Philharmonic, Berlin Philharmonic, BBC Symphony and Filarmonica della Scala; four recordings of his major orchestral works, oriental instrumental music, chamber music and electronic music issued by China Nat. Recording Co.; orchestral piece commissioned by Inst. for Devt of Intercultural Relations Through the Arts, USA for Beijing Int. Music Festival 1988; Artistic Dir Fire Crossing Water Festival, Barbican Centre, London 2000; composed music for Olympic Games medal ceremonies, Beijing 2008; commissioned by Google/YouTube to compose internet Symphony Eroica; named UNESCO Goodwill Amb. 2013. *Film scores:* Aktion K 1994, Nanjing 1937 1995, Fallen 1997, In the Name of the Emperor 1998, Wo hu cang long (Crouching Tiger Hidden Dragon) (Grammy Award 2001, Acad. Award 2001, British Acad. Film Award 2001, Classical BRIT Contemporary Music Award 2001) 2000, Ying xiong (Hero) 2002. *Compositions:* orchestral works: Li Sao (symphony) 1979, Five Pieces in Human Accent for piano 1980, Feng Ya Song for string quartet 1982, Fu for two sopranos, bass and ensemble 1982, Piano Concerto 1983, Symphony in two movements 1985, On Taoism for orchestra 1985, Traces for piano 1989, Eight Colours for string quartet 1989, Silk Road for soprano and percussion 1989, Orchestral Theatre I: Xun 1990, Soundshape 1990, Silent Earth 1991, Elegy: Snow in June 1991, Jo-Ha-Kyu 1992, Death and Fire: Dialogue with Paul Klee 1992, Orchestral Theatre II: Re 1992, CAGE for piano 1993, Circle for four trios, conductor and audience 1993, The Pink 1993, Autumn Winds for instruments and conductor ad lib 1993, Memorial Nineteen for voice, piano and double paper 1993, Orchestral Theatre III: Red 1993, Yi concerto for cello 1994, Ghost Opera 1994, Marco Polo 1995, A Sinking Love 1995, Heaven, Earth, Mankind symphony for the 'Bian Zhong' bronze bells (composed in celebration of the Hong Kong handover) 1997, Concerto for Six 1997, Heaven Earth Mankind 1997, Peony Pavilion 1998, 2000 Today: A World Symphony for the Millennium: A Musical Odyssey for the Ages 1999, Water Passion after St Matthew 2000, Crouching Tiger Concerto 2000, The Map concerto for cello, video and orchestra 2003, Eight Memories in Watercolor 2003, Secret Land: for Orchestra and 12 Violoncelli 2004; opera: Out of Beijing 1987, Nine Songs 1989, Marco Polo 1994, Peony Pavilion 1998, Tea 2002, Eight Memories in Watercolor 2003, The First Emperor (opera score, libretto co-writer) 2006. *Honours:* second place, Weber Int. Chamber Music Composition Competition, Dresden 1983, Suntory Prize 1992, Grawemeyer Award 1998, Musical America Composer of the Year 2003. *Address:* 367 West 19th Street, Suite A, New York, NY 10011, USA (office). *Telephone:* (212) 627-0410 (office). *Fax:* (917) 606-0247 (office). *E-mail:* tan_dun@hotmail.com (office). *Website:* tandun.com (office).

TANK; American R&B singer, songwriter and record producer; b. (Durrell Babbs), 1 Jan. 1976, Milwaukee, Wis.; four c. *Education:* Crossland High School. *Career:* raised in Clinton, Md; fmr backing singer for Ginuwine –2001; Founder-mem., supergroup TGT (with Tyrese and Ginuwine) 2007–; numerous collaborators including Aaliyah, Chris Brown, Drake, Ja Rule, Kelly Rowland, Lil Wayne, Willie Taylor. *Films:* It Ain't Easy 2006, Preacher's Kid 2010. *Recordings:* albums: Force of Nature 2001, One Man 2002, Sex, Love & Pain 2007, Now or Never 2010, This Is How I Feel 2012; with TGT: Three

Kings 2013. *Address:* c/o Atlantic Records, Warner Music Group, 75 Rockefeller Plaza, New York, NY 10019, USA (office). *E-mail:* contact@ atlanticrecords.com (office); WebCrew@TheRealTank.com (home). *Website:* atlanticrecords.com (office); www.wmg.com (office); www.TheRealTank.com (home).

TANKIAN, Serj; American singer and musician (keyboard); b. 21 Aug. 1967, Beirut, Lebanon. *Career:* moved to USA as a child; fmr mem. The Soil; mem., System of a Down 1996–; Co-founder, Axis of Justice Org., Serjical Strike label. *Recordings include:* albums with System of a Down: System Of A Down 1998, Toxicity 2001, Maximum 2002, Steal This Album! 2002, Mezmerize 2005, Hypnotize 2005, Vicinity of Obscenity 2006; solo: Elect the Dead 2007, Imperfect Harmonies 2010, Harakiri 2012. *Publication:* Cool Gardens 2002. *Honours:* MTV Europe Music Award for Best Alternative 2005, Grammy Award for Best Hard Rock Performance (for B.Y.O.B.) 2006. *Current Management:* Velvet Hammer, 9911 West Pico Blvd, 350W, Los Angeles, CA 90035, USA. *Telephone:* (310) 657-6161. *Fax:* (310) 657-0310. *Website:* www .velvethammer.net; www.systemofadown.com; www.axisofjustice.com; www .serjtankian.com.

TANNEN, Amanda; American musician (bass guitar). *Education:* Pratt Inst. of the Arts, NY. *Career:* mem., Stellastarr 2000–. *Recordings include:* albums: with Stellastarr: Stellastarr 2003, Harmonies for the Haunted 2005, Civilized 2009. *Current Management:* c/o Plus One Music, Studio 6, Brooklyn, New York, NY 11211, USA. *Telephone:* (718) 599-3740. *Fax:* (718) 599-0998. *E-mail:* jonnykaps@plusonemusic.net. *Address:* c/o Sony BMG, 550 Madison Avenue, New York, NY 10022, USA. *E-mail:* band@stellastarr.com. *Website:* www.stellastarr.com.

TAÑÓN, Olga; Puerto Rican singer; b. 13 April 1967, Santurce. *Career:* first sang with Orchestra las Nenas de Ringo y Jossie; joined Chantelle; solo artist 1992–; tours internationally. *Recordings include:* Sola 1992, Mujer de Fuego 1993, Siente el Amor 1994, Exitos y Más 1995, Nuevos Senderos 1996, Llévame Contigo 1997, Te Acordarás de Mi 1998, Olga Viva – Viva Olga (Grammy Award for Best Merengue Album 2000) 1999, Yo Por Ti (Grammy Award and Latin Grammy Award for Best Merengue Album 2002) 2001, Nueva Mujer 2005, Soy Como Tú 2006, Exitos en 2 Tiempos 2007, Ni Una Lagrima Más 2011, Una Mujer 2013. *Honours:* Asscn of Entertainment Critics of New York Award 1994, ASCAP Award 1993, Billboard Int. Latin Music Award for Best Female Album of the Year 1998. *Current Management:* c/o Olga Tañón Music, Inc., PO Box 50599, Levittown Station, Toa Baja 00950-0599, Puerto Rico. *Telephone:* (787) 620-9001. *Fax:* (787) 620-9004. *E-mail:* management@olgatanon.com. *E-mail:* olga@olgatanon.com (office). *Website:* www.olgatanon.com.

TANT, Jean-Christophe; French singer, composer and musician (guitar); b. 12 Feb. 1962, Lille. *Education:* Acad. of Music, Lille. *Career:* performed at festivals, including Montréal, Munchen-Gladbach, Edinburgh, Lille, Jelena Gora, Jazz Valley, Paris, Singapore; tv appearances and radio broadcasts; mem. SACEM. *Honours:* Golden Nono (Wazemmes), France.

TAO; Chinese singer and rapper; b. (Huang Zitao), 2 May 1993, Qingdao, Shandong. *Career:* trainee, SM Entertainment 2010–11; mem. K-pop boy band Exo 2011–; mem. sub-group Exo-M 2012–; debut single 2012; numerous TV and live appearances. *Television:* EXO's Showtime 2013–. *Recordings:* albums: Mama 2012, XOXO (Mnet Asian Music Award for Album of the Year 2013) 2013. *Honours:* numerous awards including: for Exo: Mnet Asian Music Award for Best New Asian Artist/Group 2012, MTV Europe Music Award for Best Japan/Korea Act 2013, MelOn Music Award for Song of the Year (for Growl) 2013; for Exo-M: Top Chinese Music Award for Most Popular Group 2013. *Address:* c/o SM Entertainment, 521 Apgujeong 2-dong, Gang-nam-gu, Seoul, South Korea (office). *Telephone:* (2) 6240-9800 (office). *Website:* www.smtown.com (office); exo.smtown.com (home).

TAPIO, Jorma Ilmari; Finnish musician (alto saxophone, bass clarinet, flute, percussion); b. 6 Aug. 1957, Mikkeli. *Education:* private piano lessons at music school, studied with Pekka Pöyry, Juhani Aaltonen and Edward Vesala. *Career:* mem. trio, Lavantairyhmä 1980–82; mem. traditional tango band, rock groups and big bands; own tapes for radio, TV documentaries, theatre, film pieces and dance performances; tours with Krakatau; int. tours, recordings, TV appearances and two documentary films with Edward Vesala's Sound & Fury; tours and recordings with Norwegian drummer, Terje Isungset; performances with Terje Isungset, Shoji Hano, Kenji Haino, Tesu Saitoh and butodancers in Japan; f. own group, Rolling Thunder 1995–97, 2001–02; leader, Tse-tse Club (music club), Helsinki 1998–2001; toured hospitals with dancer Kirsi Heimonen 2002–04; Founder-mem., KASKI 2004–; also solo appearances. *Recordings include:* with Krakatau: Ritual 1988; with Edward Vesala's Sound & Fury: Lumi 1985, Ode To The Death of Jazz 1989, Invisible Storm 1991, Nordic Gallery 1994; with Rolling Thunder: Live in Japan (Aketa) 2003; also appears on Terje Isungset: Floating Rhythms 2000; solo: Aihki 2007. *Address:* Agricolankuja 2 C 96, 00530 Helsinki, Finland. *Telephone:* (9) 7741612. *E-mail:* jorma.tapio@pp.inet.fi.

TARDLEY, Ken, BSc, MSc; British musician (resophonic guitar), bandleader and lecturer; b. 5 Oct. 1949, Rotherham, Yorkshire, England; m. Lorretta Tardley 1982; one d. *Education:* Davis and Elkins Coll., USA. *Career:* mem. bands, Muleskinner, 1990–92, Sound In Mind, 1985–93, Generation Gap, 1992–94; toured USA 1994; DJ, WTHO radio, Thompson, Ga, USA; curator, Dalebilly Museum, Airdale Drive, Howarth; Founder-mem., British Bluegrass

Music Asscn, staff writer, British Bluegrass News. *Recordings include:* Riding Down The Canyon, Sound In Mind 1989, Muleskinner 1990. *Honours:* King of The Dalebilly Dobro Players 1995. *Address:* 65 Gledholt Bank, Huddersfield, West Yorkshire, HD1 4HE, England.

TARKAN; Turkish singer; b. (Tarkan Tevetoglu), 17 Oct. 1972, Alzey, nr Frankfurt, Germany; s. of Ali and Neşe Tevetçioğlu. *Education:* Karamürsel Music High School, studied music in Istanbul, Turkey, Baruch Coll., New York, USA. *Career:* solo artist 1993–; numerous concerts worldwide. *Recordings include:* albums: Yine Sensiz 1993, A-Acayipsin 1995, Ölürüm Sana 1997, Tarkan 1999, Karma 2001, Dudu 2003 (, Come Closer 2006, Metamorfoz 2007, Adımı Kalbine Yaz 2010. *Honours:* numerous awards including World Music Award for Best Selling Turkish Act 1999, Asscn of Turkish Journalists Award for Most Successful Turkish Artist, Song of the Year (Russia) for Dudu, 17th Kral TV Music Awards for Best Turkish Album, Best Song, Best Composition and Best Lyrics (for Adımı Kalbine Yaz). *Current Management:* Hitt Productions, 5 Gazeteciler Sitesi Söltaş Evleri Hare Sok., G.12 No. 5, 34355 Levent-Beşiktaş, Istanbul, Turkey. *Website:* www.tarkan.com.

TASCO, Danilo, (Data); Italian musician (drums); b. 26 March 1979. *Career:* mem., Negramaro 2002–. *Recordings include:* albums: Negramaro 2003, 000577 2004, Mentre Tutto Scorre 2005, La Finestra 2007, Via le Mani Dagli Occhi 2008, Casa 69 2010, La Rivoluzione Sta Arrivando 2015. *Honours:* MTV Europe Music Award Best Italian Act 2005. *E-mail:* management@negramaro .com. *E-mail:* management@negramaro.com (office). *Website:* www .negramaro.com.

TASHIAN, Barry M.; American singer, musician (guitar), songwriter and music publisher; b. 5 Aug. 1945, Oak Park, Ill.; m. Holly Paige Tashian (née Kimball), two s. *Education:* Boston Univ., private lessons in guitar, piano and voice. *Career:* Founder rock band, Barry & The Remains 1964–66; toured with The Beatles, USA 1966; plays as duo with Holly Tashian; mem. Emmylou Harris and The Hot Band 1980–90; compositions recorded by Kenny Rogers, Solomon Burke, Daniel O'Donnell, The Nashville Bluegrass Band, Ty England, Roland White, Lynn Morris Band; owner, Barry Boy Songs (music publisher), Nashville. *Compositions include:* Why Do I Cry, Two Ways To Fall, Ooh Las Vegas, Spinning Straw into Gold, Heaven With You, Ring of Gold, Long Train of Fools, Honey, Where's the Money Gone. *Recordings include:* albums: as Barry & The Remains: The Remains 1966, Movin' On 2005; as Barry & Holly Tashian: Trust In Me 1989, Live In Holland 1991, Ready For Love 1993, Straw Into Gold (Nat. Asscn of Independent Record Distributors Country Album of the Year 1995) 1994, Harmony 1997, At Home 2002, Summervilla: We Got Work To Do 2005. *Publication:* Ticket To Ride: The Extraordinary Diary of the Beatles Last Tour. *Honours:* Boston Music Award 1990, Indie Album of the Year 1996. *Address:* Tashian Music, PO Box 150921, Nashville, TN 37215-0921, USA (office). *Telephone:* (615) 383-8948 (office). *E-mail:* harmony@tashian.com (office). *Website:* www.tashianmusic.com; www.theremains.com.

TASHIAN, Holly Paige, BA (Cum laude); American singer, songwriter and musician (guitar, upright bass); b. (Holly Paige Kimball), 8 Jan. 1946, New York; m. Barry M. Tashian 1972; two s. *Education:* Univ. of Hartford, Mills Coll. *Career:* duo as Barry & Holly Tashian 1972–; numerous TV and radio broadcasts; mem. American Soc. of Composers, Authors and Publrs (ASCAP), Int. Bluegrass Music Asscn, Folk Alliance. *Compositions include:* songs recorded by Nashville Bluegrass Band, Ty England, Daniel O'Donnell, Roland White, Jody Stecher, Kate Brislin, Mick Flavin. *Recordings include:* albums as Barry & Holly Tashian: Trust in Me 1989, Live in Holland 1991, Ready For Love 1993, Straw into Gold (Nat. Asscn of Ind. Record Distributors Country Album of the Year) 1994, Harmony 1997, At Home 2002, Summervilla: We Got Work to Do 2005, Long Story Short 2008. *Address:* Tashian Music, PO Box 150921, Nashville, TN 37215, USA. *Telephone:* (615) 383-8948. *E-mail:* harmony@tashian.com. *Website:* www.tashianmusic.com.

TASHIRO, Hidehiko; Japanese music company executive. *Career:* fmr Programme Dir, Franklin Mint, USA, Exec. Vice-Pres. of Marketing, Franklin Mint Japan; Founder and Pres., The Imperial Enterprises Inc.; Pres. and CEO, BMG Funhouse Inc., Japan 1998–2006; mem. Exec. Bd Recording Industry Asscn of Japan. *Address:* c/o 11F Kita-Aoyama Yoshikawa Building, 2-12-16 Kita-Aoyama, Minato-ku, Tokyo 107-0061, Japan.

TATE, Geoff; American singer. *Career:* lead singer rock group, Queensrÿche 1981–. *Stage productions:* Operation: Mindcrime 1988, Operation: Mindcrime II 2006. *Recordings include:* albums: with Queensrÿche: The Warning 1984, Rage For Order 1985, Operation: Mindcrime 1988, Empire 1990, Operation: LiveCrime 1991, Promised Land 1994, Hear in the Now Frontier 1997, Q2K 1999, Live Evolution 2001, Classic Masters 2003, Tribe 2003, The Art of Live 2004, Operation: Mindcrime II 2006, Take Cover 2007, American Soldier 2009, Dedicated to Chaos 2011; solo: Geoff Tate 2002. *Address:* The Queensrÿche Campaign, PO Box 5000, PMB 168, Duvall, WA 98019, USA. *Telephone:* (866) 843-4719. *Website:* www.queensryche.com; www.geofftate .com.

TAUPIN, Bernie; British songwriter; b. 22 May 1950, Lincolnshire, England. *Career:* long-term songwriting partnership with Elton John 1967–. *Compositions include:* with Elton John: albums with Elton John: all albums 1969–77, Too Low for Zero 1983, Sleeping with the Past 1989, Two Rooms – Celebrating the Songs of Elton John and Bernie Taupin 1992; solo: albums: Bernie Taupin 1970, Taupin 1971, He Who Rides the Tiger 1980, Tribe 1987; individual songs: Don't Let the Sun Go Down on Me, Crocodile Rock, Rocket Man, Sacrifice, Goodbye Yellow Brick Road, Bennie & The Jets, Your Song, Candle in the Wind, Don't Go Breaking My Heart, Sorry Seems to Be the Hardest Word, Daniel, Saturday Night's Alright for Fighting, I'm Still Standing; other co-compositions: Skyline Pigeon, Roger Cook 1968; I Can't Go on Living Without You 1969; Snookeroo 1975; These Dreams, Heart 1985; A Love that Will Never Grow Old (with Gustavo Santaolalla, for film Brokeback Mountain) (Golden Globe for Best Original Song in a Motion Picture 2006) 2005. *Honours:* Ivor Novello Awards for Best Song (Daniel) 1974, (Sacrifice) 1991, MTV Special Recognition Trophy 1987. *Current Management:* c/o Lippman Entertainment, 8900 Wilshire Blvd, Suite 340, Beverly Hills, CA 90211, USA. *Telephone:* (818) 225-7480. *Fax:* (818) 900-0749. *E-mail:* music@lippmanent .com. *Website:* www.berniejtaupin.com.

TAVASSOL, Mark; German musician (bass guitar); b. 1974, Bremen. *Career:* mem. Wir sind Helden 2001–. *Recordings include:* albums: Die Reklamation 2003, Von hier an blind (Eins Live Krone for Best Album) 2005, Soundso 2007, Bring mich nach Hause 2010. *Honours:* ECHO Award for Best Nat. Group 2006. *Current Management:* c/o Labels Germany, Leuschnerdamm 13, 10999 Berlin, Germany. *E-mail:* info@labelsmusic.de. *Website:* www.wirsindhelden .com.

TAVERNER, Tony; British producer and engineer; b. 20 Sept. 1951, London, England; m. Ruth Taverner; four c. *Career:* engineered Duran Duran's single, Ordinary World and The Wedding Album, and Thank You, albums; co-produced and engineered, Warren Cuccurullo's solo album project; engineered and produced two albums in Spain with Duncan Dhu; worked with Mikel Erentxum and Diego Vasallo; Sr Engineer, Maison Rouge Studios, London 1977–88; engineer for various albums with Jeff Beck 1973–99; partnered with songwriter and producer, Simon Ellis (Spice Girls, S Club 7), sound mixing on two Spice Girl videos, and on TV series Sex Chips and Rock 'N' Roll, Taggart, The Turnaround; worked with artists, including Jeff Beck, Bill Wyman & The Rhythm Kings, Mick Taylor, The Damned, Cutting Crew.

TAWFIK, Ehab, MA, PhD; Egyptian singer; b. 7 Jan. 1966, Cairo; m. *Career:* solo artist 1990–. *Recordings include:* albums: Ekmeny 1990, Marasil 1992, Rasamtek 1993, Hat'ade 1994, Adda el-leil 1995, El-donya 1996, Ye'sha' el-amar 1997, Sahrany 1999, Habeb el-alb 2000, Homa kelmeten 2002, Leh el-khesam 2003, Esmak eih 2004, Hobak alemni 2005, Ahla menhom 2007, Ella rasol Allah 2007, Sahrany 2008, El Doniya 2008, Lezem Tesmaa 2009, Ahla Samrah 2010. *Honours:* Commdr, Order of Nat. Merit for Culture, Tunisia 2003. *Current Management:* c/o Alam el-Phan, 4 Soliman El Halaby Street, downtown, Cairo, Egypt. *Telephone:* (2) 25742418. *Website:* www.alamelphan .com.

TAWIL, Adel; German singer; b. 15 Aug. 1978, Berlin; s. of Salah Tawil and Fatima Tawil; m. Jasmin Weber 2011. *Career:* mem. The Boyz 1996–99; Founder-mem. Ich + Ich 2004–; other collaborations with Azad, Tobias Schenke. *Recordings:* albums: with The Boyz: Boyz in Da House 1997, Next Level 1998; with Ich + Ich: Ich + Ich 2005, Vom selben Stern 2007, Gute Reise 2009. *Honours:* Best National Rock/Pop Group, ECHO Awards 2009, 2011. *Current Management:* Artist Legend Management GmbH, Kurfürstendamm 186, 10707 Berlin, Germany. *E-mail:* ich-und-ich@artist-legend.de. *Website:* www.ich-und-ich.de.

TAYLER, Stephen William; British recording and mixing engineer, producer, programmer and musician; b. 20 Sept. 1953, High Wycombe, Buckinghamshire. *Education:* New College School, Shrewsbury School, Royal Coll. of Music. *Career:* House Engineer, Trident Studios 1974–80; freelance engineer, musician, producer, programmer 1980–; worked on over 120 album projects; mem., Re-pro; Musicians' Union. *Recordings include:* engineer/mixer for Tina Turner, Stevie Nicks, Peter Gabriel, Bob Geldof, Rush, Howard Jones, The Fixx, Suzanne Vega, others. *Honours:* numerous awards, including Ampex Golden Reel, two BASF/Studio Awards for Excellence. *Current Management:* c/o Chimera Records, 41 Rosebank, Holyport Road, London, SW6 6LQ, England. *E-mail:* stephen@chimera-arts.com (office). *Website:* www .chimera-arts.com (office).

TAYLOR, Andy; British musician (guitar); b. 16 Feb. 1961, Tynemouth, England; m. Tracey Wilson 1982. *Career:* mem., Duran Duran 1980–85, 2001–06; mem., Power Station 1985–96; solo artist 1986; numerous concert tours world-wide. *Recordings include:* albums: with Duran Duran: Duran Duran 1981, Rio 1982, Seven and the Ragged Tiger 1983, Arena 1984, online-only releases of Duran Duran recordings of live shows in Japan 2003, Astronaut 2004; with Power Station: The Power Station 1985, Living in Fear 1996; solo: Thunder 1987, Dangerous 1990, The Spanish Sessions (with Luke Morley). *Publication:* Wild Boy (auto-biog.) 2008. *Honours:* MTV Video Music Lifetime Achievement Award 2003, Q Magazine Lifetime Achievement Award 2003, BRIT Outstanding Contrib. to Music Award 2004.

TAYLOR, Cecil Percival; American musician (piano); b. 15 March 1929, Long Island City, New York. *Education:* New England Conservatory of Music. *Career:* began performing in early 1950s; played in numerous groups; f. quartet 1955; f. Cecil Taylor Unit; mem., Jazz Composers Guild group; led numerous formations throughout 1970s and 1980s; continued to teach various music courses at academic insts, including Antioch Coll., Glassboro State Coll., Univ. of Wisconsin, numerous others. *Recordings include:* albums: Jazz Advance 1955, Looking Ahead! 1958, Coltrane Time 1958, Love For Sale 1959, The World Of Cecil Taylor 1960, Cell Walk For Celeste 1961, Nefertiti, The

Beautiful One Has Come 1962, Unit Structures 1966, Conquistador 1966, Praxis 1968, The Great Concert Of Cecil Taylor 1969, Indent 1973, Spring Of 2 Blue Js 1973, Silent Tongues 1974, Air Above Mountains (Buildings Within) 1974, Dark Unto Themselves 1976, Cecil Taylor Unit 1978, 3 Phasis 1978, It Is In The Brewing Luminous 1980, Fly! Fly! Fly! Fly! Fly! 1980, Garden 1981, For Olim 1986, Olu Iwa 1986, Chinampas 1987, Cecil Taylor In Berlin 88 1988, In Fluorescence 1989, Burning Poles 1990, Always A Pleasure 1993, Mixed 1998, Port Of Call 2002, Piano Cecil 2003, The Owner of the Riverbank 2004, Algonquin 2004, All the Notes 2004, The Dance Project 2008, The Last Dance 2009. *Honours:* Guggenheim Fellowship.

TAYLOR, Christopher Gordon; British musician (keyboards, drums), composer and arranger; b. 24 Nov. 1966, Birmingham. *Career:* Musical Dir, Central TV, Central Weekend; keyboard player and Music Dir, Ruby Turner 1988–95; Music Dir and accompanist for many UK cabaret artists; Musical Dir, Sheila Ferguson 1996; Musical Dir, Three Degrees and The Supremes 1997; Oh What a Night, The Musical, Opera House 1997; worked with Rose Royce, Heatwave, Jools Holland, Gloria Gaynor, Leo Sayer, Boyzone, Peter Andre; mem. Musicians' Union, British Music Writers' Council, PRS, MCPS, PAMRA. *Compositions for television:* Gardener's World (BBC) 1990, Central Weekend (Central TV) 1993, Home Run (Central TV) 1993, Sunday Supplement (Central TV) 1993, Millionaires 1995, Wednesday Night Live 1998.

TAYLOR, Courtney A.; American singer and musician (guitar, keyboards). *Career:* founder mem., The Dandy Warhols 1994–. *Film appearance:* Dig! 2005. *Recordings include:* albums: Dandys Rule OK 1995, Come Down 1998, Thirteen Tales From Urban Bohemia 2000, Welcome To The Monkey House 2003, The Black Album/Come On Feel The Dandy Warhols 2004, Odditorium Or Warlords Of Mars 2005, Earth to the Dandy Warhols 2008, This Machine 2012. *Address:* c/o Parlophone, EMI Group plc, 27 Wrights Lane, London, W8 5SW, England. *E-mail:* gothman@dandywarhols.com. *Website:* www .dandywarhols.com.

TAYLOR, Crispin Luke; British musician (drums, percussion); b. 1 July 1961, London, England; m. Rosamond Howe 1994; two d. *Career:* fmr mem. Galliano; currently mem. Push; concerts include Montreux Jazz Festival, Nice Jazz Festival, Glastonbury Festival; numerous TV appearances; mem. PRS. *Recordings include:* with Galliano: The Plot Thickens; Joyful Noise Unto the Creator; A Thicker Plot; with Urban Species: Spiritual Love; Listen; with Oui 3: Oui Love You; Tracks/singles: Long Time Gone, Twyford Down, both with Galliano, 1994; Wear your Love Like Heaven, Definition of Sound; Let It Last, Carleen Anderson; Mathar, Indian Vibes; as co-writer, producer: Scratchmo 1988, Same Feeling, Mica Paris 1988. *E-mail:* theband@pushband.com (office). *Website:* www.pushband.com.

TAYLOR, Gary; American singer, songwriter and musician (keyboards); b. 18 Jan. 1951, Los Angeles, Calif.; two s. one d. *Education:* studied psychology. *Career:* worked in studios; began songwriting early 80s; has written, produced records for numerous artists; radio and television commercials; solo artist 1988–. *Compositions include:* Good Love (Anita Baker); I'm Coming Back (Lalah Hathaway), Square One (Ray Parker Jr), One Day At A Time (Vanessa Williams), songs also recorded by Grover Washington Jr, Vesta Williams, Chico Debarge, Joyce Kennedy, The Whispers, Mac Band, Jennifer Holliday, Stephanie Mills, Will Downing, Najee. *Recordings include:* albums: Compassion 1988, Take Control 1990, Square One 1993, The Mood of Midnight 1995, Love Dance 1998, Under the Nightlight 2001, Eclectic Bohemian 2003, Retro Blackness 2006. *Telephone:* (818) 419-4887. *E-mail:* info@morningcrew.com. *Website:* www.morningcrew.com.

TAYLOR, Geoff, LLB; British music industry executive; CEO, *British Phonographic Industry (BPI)*; b. 26 May 1986. *Education:* Univ. of Sussex, Coll. of Europe, Belgium. *Career:* trainee solicitor, Cameron McKenna 1993–94; Assoc., WilmerHale law firm, Brussels 1995–97; held various legal positions, Int. Fed. of the Phonographic Industry (IFPI) 1997–2004, Gen. Counsel and Exec. Vice-Pres. 2005–07; Gen. Counsel, British Phonographic Industry 2004–05, CEO 2007–. *Address:* BPI, Riverside Building, County Hall, Westminster Bridge Road, London, SE1 7JA, England (office). *Telephone:* (20) 7803-1300 (office). *Fax:* (20) 7803-1310 (office). *E-mail:* general@ bpi.co.uk (office). *Website:* www.bpi.co.uk (office).

TAYLOR, Graeme David; British musician (guitar, mandolin, banjo, piano); b. 2 Feb. 1954, Stockwell, London; m. Sue Meldon 1974; one d. *Career:* tours with Gryphon, Europe, USA, supporting Yes, 1971; many TV and radio appearances; mem. Albion Band 1977–; mem. Home Service; guitarist to Rolf Harris; theatre includes Cats, Joseph and The Technicolour Dreamcoat, The Mysteries; mem. Musicians' Union, PRS. *Recordings include:* albums include: with Gryphon: Gryphon 1973, Red Queen to Gryphon Three 1974, Midnight Mushrumps 1974, Raindance 1975; with Albion Band: Prospect Before Us 1977, Rise Up Like the Sun 1978, Larkrise to Candleford 1980; with Home Service: Mysteries 1998, Alright Jack 1998. *Telephone:* (20) 8544-9609 (office). *Fax:* (20) 8287-6552 (office). *E-mail:* gt@graemetaylor.com (office). *Website:* www.graemetaylor.com.

TAYLOR, James; American singer and songwriter; b. 12 March 1948, Boston, Mass; s. of Dr. Isaac Taylor and Gertrude Taylor; m. 1st Carly Simon 1972; m. 2nd Kathryn Walker 1985; m. 3rd Carolyn Smedvig 2001. *Career:* solo artist 1968–; numerous tours world-wide, concerts and festival appearances. *Film appearances:* Two Lane Blacktop 1971, No-Nukes 1980. *Recordings include:* albums: James Taylor 1968, Sweet Baby James 1970, Mud Slide

Slim and the Blue Horizon 1971, One Man Dog 1972, Walking Man 1974, Gorilla 1975, In The Pocket 1976, Greatest Hits 1976, JT 1977, Flag 1979, Dad Loves His Work 1981, That's Why I'm Here 1985, Never Die Young 1988, New Moon Shine 1991, James Taylor (Live) 1993, In The Hands of The Inevitable 1995, Original Flying Machine 1996, Hourglass (Grammy Award for Best Pop Vocal Album 1997) 1997, Live at the Beacon Theatre 1998, October Road 2002, Rhino Hi-Five 2005, James Taylor at Christmas 2006, One Man Band 2007, Covers 2008, Other Covers 2009, Live At The Troubadour 2010, The Essential 2013, Before This World 2015. *Honours:* Grammy Awards for Best Male Pop Vocal Performance 1971, 1977, 2001, for Best Country Collaboration with Vocals 2003, Musicares Person of the Year, Nat. Acad. of Recording Arts and Sciences 2006, BBC Radio 2 Folk Awards Lifetime Achievement Award 2009, Presidential Medal of Freedom 2015. *Current Management:* c/o Jane Muckle, Macklam Feldman Management, #200–1505 West 2nd Avenue, Vancouver, BC V6H 3Y4, Canada. *Telephone:* (604) 630-3199. *E-mail:* muckle@slfa.com. *Website:* www.mfmgt.com; www.jamestaylor.com.

TAYLOR, Jeremy; British singer and composer; b. 24 Nov. 1937, Newbury, Berkshire, England. *Education:* Univ. of Oxford. *Career:* taught at Eton Coll.; taught in S Africa; wrote hit show, Wait a Minim, W End and Broadway; worked with Sydney Carter, Spike Milligan; one-man shows throughout S Africa. *Recordings include:* Ag Please Daddy 1961, Piece of Ground 1972, Jobsworth 1973, The Very Best of Jeremy Taylor 1996, Live in Chicago 2005. *E-mail:* TaylorsJandS@yahoo.co.uk; JeremyTaylorUSA@gmail.com. *Website:* www.jeremytaylormusic.com.

TAYLOR, (Nigel) John; British musician (bass guitar) and songwriter; b. 20 June 1960, Birmingham; one d. *Career:* Founder-mem., Duran Duran 1978–97, 2001–; mem., Power Station 1985–96; mem. Neurotic Outsiders; solo artist 1996–; rejoined Duran Duran for a reunion of the original five members 2001; numerous concert tours world-wide. *Recordings include:* albums: with Duran Duran: Duran Duran 1981, Rio 1982, Seven And The Ragged Tiger 1983, Arena 1984, Notorious 1986, Big Thing 1988, Liberty 1990, Duran Duran (The Wedding Album) 1993, Thank You 1995, online-only releases of Duran Duran recordings of live shows in Japan 2003, Astronaut 2004, Red Carpet Massacre 2007, All You Need is Now 2010, Paper Gods 2015; with Power Station: The Power Station 1985, Living In Fear 1996; solo: Feelings Are Good and Other Lies 1997. *Publication:* In the Pleasure Groove: Love, Death and Duran Duran 2012. *Honours:* MTV Video Music Lifetime Achievement Award 2003, Q Magazine Lifetime Achievement Award 2003, BRIT Outstanding Contribution to Music Award 2004, Q Icon Award 2015, MTV Europe Music Video Visionary Award 2015. *Current Management:* c/o Ms Wendy Laister, Magus Entertainment Inc., 33 Greene Street, #3W, New York, NY 10013, USA. *Telephone:* (212) 343-1577. *Fax:* (212) 925-4007. *E-mail:* info@magusentertainment.com. *Website:* www.magusentertainment .com; www.duranduran.com.

TAYLOR, John Michael (Mike); British musician (trumpet, piano, keyboards, organ); b. 24 March 1934, Retford, Nottinghamshire, England;18-Feb.2016 s. of Thomas Taylor and Daisy Taylor. *Career:* with Mike Taylor Jazzmen 1956–59, Micky Askman Ragtime Jazzband 1959–63, Midland Allstars 1964–66, City Jazzmen 1969–75; numerous live and TV appearances; accompanied various American artists, including Billy Butterfield, Wild Bill Davidson, Eddie Miller, Bud Freeman, Art Hodes, Earl Warren, Kenny Daverne, John Handy; Derby Big Band 1976–79; Burton MU Big Band 1977–80; All That Jazz Parade band 1984–89; festival appearances include Tilburg, Giethoorn, Breda, Kassel, Ascona, Upton, Bude, Cork, Keswick, Edinburgh, Keswick; Duke Ellington Conf., Harlem 1985–94; several London Night at the Cotton Club shows with Doc Cheetham, Benny Waters, Adelaide Hall, Bertice Reading, Herb Jeffries, Juanita Brooks; freelance musician on piano, trumpet, with numerous groups; mem. Musicians' Union.

TAYLOR, Jon 'T-Bone'; British blues and jazz musician (guitar); b. 29 Aug. 1963, London; m. Andrie Reid. *Education:* Guildhall School of Music. *Career:* Leader, Bop Brothers 1986–2000; guitarist with Tim Richards' bands Roogalator and Grooveyard; Daniel Smith Blues Band and Duo 2000–10; Shakey Vick Blues Band 2010–; toured with Charlie Sayles, Champion Jack Dupree, Mojo Buford, Lefty Dizz, Deitra Farr, Dick Heckstall-Smith; mem. Musicians' Union. *Recordings include:* Strange News, Bop Brothers 1995, Bop Brothers… and Sisters, with Earl Green, Dana Gillespie and Ruby Turner 1998, Bop Brothers… and Sisters, with Deitra Farr, Taka Boom and Connie Lush 2000, Dreamtime, with Daniel Smith Blues Band 2002, You're Not Far Away, with John Stapelton and The Big Easy 2002. *Address:* 24B Walterton Road, London, W9 3PN (home). *E-mail:* jontbonetaylor@gmail.com. *Current Management:* c/o Abacabe Ltd, 10 Messaline Avenue, London, W3 6JX, England.

TAYLOR, Linda Christina; singer and songwriter; b. 27 July 1950, Cleveland, England; m. Jeff Taylor 1968; one s. *Education:* studied piano with Prof. Larman in Bedford, voice with Jean Knight in London. *Career:* backing vocals, worked on albums for Chris Rea, Tom Jones, Céline Dion, Gary Moore, Kylie Minogue, Doctor John, Mike and The Mechanics, Julien Clerc, ABC, Paul Young, Jimmy Nail, Sting, Johnny Hallyday, Zucchero, Fish Tree Water Blues, Then Jerico, Sam Brown, Bananarama; tours with: Go West, Art of Noise, Jocelyn Brown, Marvin Gaye, EPO (Japan), Chris Rea; Impressions: Spitting Image, Prime Suspect III, Crazy Horse, Paris; TV commercials; mem. Equity, Musicians' Union, PAMRA, PRS. *Compositions include:* Angel, Everybody Knows, Taylor Made (solo album, 1981), Morrisey/

Mullen 1981, Cayenne Gary Numan, Bill Sharpe, Every Waking Hour, You and Me Just Started 1981.

TAYLOR, Martin, MBE; British jazz musician (guitar) and composer; b. 20 Oct. 1956, Harlow, Essex; s. of William 'Buck' Taylor. *Education:* Passmore Comprehensive School, Harlow. *Career:* began playing aged four, playing in local bands aged 12, professional musician 1972–; support act for Count Basie and his Orchestra, QE2; performed and recorded regularly with violinist Stéphane Grappelli; formed Martin Taylor's Spirit of Django 1994–; played and recorded with Bill Wyman's Rhythm Kings 1998, 1999; featured on Prefab Sprout album Andromeda Heights; recordings (with Steve Howe) of guitars from Chinery Collection. *Recordings include:* albums: Taylor Made 1978, Skye Boat 1981, Sarabanda (with John Patitucci and Paulinho Da Costa) 1987, Don't Fret 1990, Change Of Heart 1991, Artistry 1993, Reunion (with Stéphane Grappelli) 1993, Spirit of Django (British Jazz Awards for Best Album 1995) 1994, Portraits 1995, Years Apart 1996, Gypsy 1998, Two's Company 1999, I'm Beginning To See The Light 1999, Kiss & Tell 1999, In Concert (live) 2000, Stepping Stones 2000, Nitelife 2001, Solo (Int. Guitar Foundation Award for Best Album) 2002, Valley 2005, Gypsy Journey 2005, Freternity 2007, Double Standards 2008, Last Train to Hauteville 2010. *Film soundtracks include:* (with Stéphane Grappelli) Milou en Mai, Dirty Rotten Scoundrels. *Publication includes:* Martin Taylor: Autobiography of a Travelling Musician, The Martin Taylor Guitar Method. *Honours:* Freeman of the City of London 1998; Dr hc (Paisley) 1999, (Royal Scottish Acad. of Music and Drama) 2010; Music Retailers Asscn Award for Excellence 1985, British Jazz Award for Best Guitarist 1987, 1988, 1989, 1990, 1991, 1993, 1995, 1997, 1999, 2001, British Acad. of Composers & Songwriters Gold Badge of Merit 1999, Pioneer to the Life of the Nation 2003, BBC Radio 2 Jazz Award 2007, British Jazz Award 2007, Scottish Jazz Award 2012, Lifetime Achievement Award, Ards Int. Guitar Festival 2012. *Current Management:* P3 Music Ltd, Incheoch, Alyth, Perthshire, PH11 8HJ, Scotland. *E-mail:* management@p3music.com. *Website:* www.p3music.com. *E-mail:* martin@martintaylor.com. *Website:* www .martintaylor.com.

TAYLOR, Mick; British musician (guitar); b. 17 Jan. 1948, Hemstead, England. *Career:* mem. John Mayall's Bluesbreakers 1960s; mem. The Rolling Stones 1969–75; recorded and toured with Bob Dylan; session player and solo artist 1975–. *Recordings include:* albums: with John Mayall's Bluesbreakers: Bare Wires 1968; with The Rolling Stones: Let It Bleed 1969, Get Yer Ya Ya's Out 1970, Sticky Fingers 1971, Exile on Main Street 1972, Goat's Head Soup 1973, It's Only Rock and Roll 1974, Made in the Shade 1975, Metamorphosis 1975, Forty Licks 2002, Brussels Affair 2011, GRRR! 2012; solo: Mick Taylor 1979, Stranger in this Town 1990, Too Hot for Snakes 1991, Coastin' Home 1995, Live at 14 Below 1995, A Stone's Throw 1998, Shadow Man 2003, Little Red Rooster 2007. *Website:* www.rollingstones.com/artist/mick-taylor.

TAYLOR, Otis; American blues singer and musician (guitar, banjo, mandolin, harmonica); b. 30 July 1948, Chicago, Ill.; m. Carol Taylor; two d. *Career:* formed bands Butterscotch Fire Dept Blues Band, Otis Taylor Blues Band; played in bands T&O Short Line (with Tommy Bolin), 4-Nikators, Zephyr; retired from music 1977, worked as antiques dealer; returned to professional music 1995; collaborations with Gary Moore, Charlie Musselwhite, Hiromi Uehara, Cassie Taylor (d.); designed and delivers Writing the Blues educational workshops in schools and colls. *Recordings include:* albums: Blue-Eyed Monster (Best New Artist Debut, W. C. Handy Awards) 1997, When Negroes Walked the Earth 1998, White African 2001, Respect the Dead 2002, Truth Is Not Fiction (Blues Album of the Year, DownBeat) 2003, Double V (Blues Album of the Year, DownBeat) 2004, Below the Fold 2005, Definition of a Circle 2007, Recapturing the Banjo 2008, Clovis People 2010, Contraband 2012, My World Is Gone 2013. *Honours:* Best Blues Entertainer, Living Blues Readers' Poll 2004. *Current Management:* c/o Shoelace Music, PO Box 3564, Boulder, CO 80307, USA. *Telephone:* (303) 579-4917. *E-mail:* shoelacemusic@ indra.com. *Website:* www.otistaylor.com.

TAYLOR, Robin Christian; British composer, musician (guitar, bass, keyboards, percussion) and producer; b. 17 May 1956, Copenhagen, Denmark. *Education:* Acad. for Free and Commercial Art, Copenhagen. *Career:* mem. several local rock groups 1970s; first radio appearance 1978; record debut 1991; composer of film music; Founder-mem. progressive jazz/rock fusion group Taylor's Universe 1993–98, 2003–, free jazz ensemble Taylor's Free Universe 2000–05, Art Cinema 2007; mem. avant-garde big band Communio Musica, led by Hugh Steinmetz 1996–97; mem. Danish Musicians' Union, Danish Jazz Beat and Folk Authors. *Recordings:* albums: solo: Essay 1991, Cloze Test Terror 1992, Heart Disc 1999, The Bândbix Tapes 2000, Edge of Darkness 2000, Samplicity 2001, November 2003, X Position Vol. 1 2004, X Position Vol. 2: Project '85 2005, Deutsche Schule 2006, Isle of Black 2008, Two-Pack 2010; with Taylor's Universe: Taylor's Universe 1994, Pork 1996, Experimental Health 1998, Once Again 2004, Oyster Apprentice 2005, Certain Undiscoveries 2006, Terra Nova 2007, Soundwall 2007, Return to Whatever 2009, Artificial Joy 2009, Kind of Red 2012, Worn Out 2013, Evidence 2013, From Scratch 2015, Across the Universe 2015; with Communio Musica: Special Alloy 2000; with Taylor's Free Universe: File Under Extreme 2002, Unplugged in Elsinore 2003, 9 Eleven: Live at Copenhagen JazzHouse 2004, Once Again 2004, Family Shot 2005, Manipulated by Taylor 2006; with Art Cinema: Art Cinema 2008. *Honours:* Danish Arts Foundation work grants. *Address:* c/o Marvel of Beauty Records, Listedvej 40, 3. mf., 2770 Kastrup, Denmark (home). *E-mail:* marvelofbeauty@hotmail.com. *Website:* www.progressor.net/robin-taylor.

TAYLOR, Roger; British musician (drums); b. 26 April 1960. *Career:* mem. Duran Duran 1979–85, 2001–; Founder-mem. Arcadia 1985–86. *Recordings include:* albums: with Duran Duran: Duran Duran 1981, Rio 1982, Seven and the Ragged Tiger 1983, Arena 1984, online-only releases of Duran Duran recordings of live shows in Japan 2003, Astronaut 2004, Red Carpet Massacre 2007, All You Need is Now 2010, Paper Gods 2015; with Arcadia: So Red the Rose 1985. *Honours:* MTV Video Music Lifetime Achievement Award 2003, Q Magazine Lifetime Achievement Award 2003, BRIT Outstanding Contrib. to Music Award 2004, Q Icon Award 2015, MTV Europe Music Video Visionary Award 2015. *Current Management:* c/o Ms Wendy Laister, Magus Entertainment Inc., 33 Greene Street, #3W, New York, NY 10013, USA. *Telephone:* (212) 343-1577. *Fax:* (212) 925-4007. *E-mail:* info@magusentertainment.com. *Website:* www.magusentertainment.com; www.duranduran.com.

TAYLOR, Roger; British musician (drums), singer and producer; b. (Roger Meddows-Taylor), 26 July 1949, Kings Lynn, Norfolk, England. *Education:* studied biology. *Career:* mem. Smile 1967–71; Founder-mem. rock group Queen 1970–; Founder-mem. The Cross 1987–; numerous tours, festival appearances. *Theatre:* musical of Queen songs, We Will Rock You (West End, London) 2002–14; numerous productions worldwide. *Recordings include:* albums: with Queen: Queen 1973, Queen II 1974, Sheer Heart Attack 1974, A Night At The Opera 1975, A Day At The Races 1976, Good Old Fashioned 1977, News Of The World 1977, Jazz 1978, Live Killers 1979, The Game 1980, Flash Gordon (soundtrack) 1981, Hot Space 1982, The Works 1984, A Kind of Magic 1986, The Miracle 1989, Stone Cold Crazy 1991, Innuendo 1991, The Cosmos Rocks (with Paul Rodgers) 2008; with The Cross: Shove It! 1988, Mad, Bad and Dangerous to Know 1990, Blue Rock 1991; solo: Fun In Space 1981, Strange Frontier 1984, Happiness? 1994, Electric Fire 1998, Fun on Earth 2013. *Honours:* Ivor Novello Award for Best Selling British Record (for Bohemian Rhapsody) 1976, Britannia Award for Best British Pop Single 1952–77 1977, Gold Ticket Madison Square Gardens 1977, American Music Award for Favorite Single 1981, Nordoff-Robbins Music Therapy Centre Silver Clef Award 1984, Ivor Novello Award for Outstanding Contribution to British Music 1987, BRIT Awards for Outstanding Contribution to British Music 1990, for Best British Single 1991, Q Classic Song Award (for Bohemian Rhapsody) 2015. *Website:* www.queenonline.com; www.rogertaylorofficial .com.

TAYLOR, Steve, BA; American songwriter, producer and filmmaker; b. 9 Dec. 1957, Brawley, Calif., USA; m. Debbie L. Taylor 1985. *Education:* Univ. of Colorado, Boulder. *Career:* producer, co-writer for Newsboys. *Recordings include:* I Want To Be A Clone 1983, Meltdown 1984, On The Fritz 1985, I Predict 1990 1987, Chagall Guevara 1991, Squint 1993, Liver 1995; Video: Squint: Movies From The Soundtrack, 1994; Producer, Co-writer, The Newsboys: Not Ashamed, 1992; Going Public, 1994; Take Me To Your Leader, 1996; Producer, Guardian: Buzz, 1995, Sixpence None the Richer, 1997. *Honours:* Three Dove Awards; 2 Billboard Music Video Awards (as artist and director); Contemporary Christian Music Magazine, Producer of the Year, 1994, 1995.

TAYLOR, Steven Vernard, BMus; American producer and director of A&R; b. 24 Dec. 1950, Norton, Va. *Education:* Univ. of Tennessee, Los Angeles Valley Coll. *Career:* 16 years touring as vocalist, musician; engineered for Jimmy Buffett, Michael McDonald, Jeff Berlin; Asst to dir on Boys of Summer (Don Henley); musical consultant for TV shows Gimme A Break, Facts of Life, Diff'rent Strokes, One Day At A Time; Dir of A&R, RCM Recordings. *Recordings include:* Unknown Soul (producer), Sugar Jones, Argument Clinic (producer), Choral Collection, Women Of Faith, Truth, First Call, Alleluia Worship Band, Gary Sadler. *Address:* PO Box 4735, Austin, TX 78765-4735, USA.

TAYLOR-GOOD, Karen; American singer and songwriter; b. El Paso, Tex. *Career:* began as folk singer in Austin, Tex.; radio, TV commercials; backing singer for Willie Nelson, Merle Haggard, Randy Travis, Roy Rogers, George Jones; solo artist and songwriter for Warner Chappell; represented USA on musical peace mission to USSR 1988; Founder-mem. Planet Earth Project. *Compositions for:* Laura Branigan, Patty Loveless, Melanie, Nana Mouskouri, Diamond Rio. *Recordings include:* solo album: Karen 1984, One Mile Apart 1994, On Angels' Wings 2001, Song Guru 2006. *Honours:* ACM Award for Best New Female, Kerrville Festival Award for New Folk Winner 1992, SESAC Songwriter of the Year 1994, two CMA Awards (for How I Can I Help You Say Goodbye), SESAC Music Video Awards. *Current Management:* c/o Dennis Good, PO Box 122194, Nashville, TN 37212, USA. *Telephone:* (615) 479-7535. *E-mail:* dennis@karentaylorgood.com. *Website:* www.karentaylorgood.com.

T-BOZ (see Watkins, Tionne Tenese)

TCHANDO; Danish composer, musician (guitar) and singer; b. (Salvador Embalo), 22 March 1957, Bafata, Guinea-Bissau. *Education:* Superior Economic Inst. of Lisbon. *Career:* guitarist and backing singer for N'kassa Kobra, Issabari, Hanne Boel, Kaba Mane; lead singer for Zebra, Continental Heat, Kilimandjaro; solo artist 1991–; TV appearances, radio broadcasts; mem. Danish Musicians' and Composers' Union, Koda. *Recordings include:* albums: Naton (solo) 1994, Chefo Mae Mae (with Kabe Mane), Kungha (with Kabe Mane), Dark Passion (with Hanne Boel).

TE, Carlos; Portuguese composer, lyricist and musician (guitar); m. Olga Fortes; one s. one d. *Education:* Univ. of Porto. *Career:* worked with Rui VeLoso, writing and producing records 1979–; collaborations with Trovante

1983, Gabriela Schaff 1983, Jáfumega 1982, 1983, CLÃ, writing and producing 1995, Mãozinha 1997, Santos and Pecadores 1999; mem. SPA. *Compositions include:* Chico Fininho, Porto Covo, Porto Sentido, Nao Há Estrelas No Céu, A Paixão, Lado Lunar, GTI, Novas Babilónias. *Recordings include:* Mingos and Os Samurais, Auto da Pimenta, Kazoo, Lado Lunar, Avenidas. *Publications include:* Ar de Rock 1980, Rui VeLoso 1987, Mingos and Os Samurais 1990, Auto da Pimenta 1991, Avenidas 1998. *Honours:* Caras magazine award for Album of the Year 1980, Nove Gente magazine award for Song of the Year 1998. *Address:* Praceta Joao Moreira Bastos 468, 4400 Vila Nova de Gaia, Portugal.

TEDDER, Ryan; American singer, songwriter, musician (guitar, piano) and producer; b. 26 June 1979, Tulsa, Okla; m. Genevieve Tedder; one s. *Career:* began career as solo artist and producer, working with Timbaland; Founding mem. OneRepublic 2002–; f. own record label, Patriot Records 2009; as producer, worked with Adele, Stan Walker, Leona Lewis, Jordin Sparks, Beyoncé. *Recordings include:* albums: Dreaming Out Loud 2007, Waking Up 2009, Native 2013. *Honours:* Grammy Award for Album of the Year (as producer with Taylor Swift for 1989) 2016. *Address:* Patriot Records, c/o Interscope, 1755 Broadway, New York, NY 10019, USA (office). *Website:* www .patriotrecords.com (office); www.onerepublic.net.

TEE-BIRDD, Jamaka; Jamaican musician (keyboards, guitar, percussion) and publisher; b. (Richard Anthony Johnson), 15 Sept. 1952, Kingston; m. Celia Caiz. *Education:* Kingston Coll., Coll. of Art, Science and Tech. *Career:* mem. bands, Bare Essentials, Zap-Pow, In-Crowd, Soul Syndicate, Burning Spear, Judy Mowatt, Bunny Wailer, Boris Gardiner, Top Notch, Roots Radics, Home T; performed in Reggae Sunsplash I–V, X, XI, reggae Sunsplash Pay Per View 1991; tours world-wide; mem. PRS, JFM, Musicians' Union (UK). *Recordings include:* albums: with Zap-Pow: Now, LoveHits, ZapPow; with Soul Syndicate: Harvest Uptown-Famine Downtown, Was Is and Always, Friends of Soul Syndicate, FM, Freddie McGregor; with In-Crowd: His Majesty is Coming, Man From New Guinea, Best of In-Crowd; with Burning Spear: Far Over, Fittest of The Fittest, Resistance, People of the World, Live in Paris, Jah Kingdom; with Israel Vibration: Forever, Vibes Alive, IV, Free to Love, On the Rock, Dub-the-Rock, Live Again, IV Dub, Cry Blood, Charlie Chaplin, Party, Yellowman, World Peace Three, Radically Radics, Roots Radics; with Bare Essentials: Back-a-Yard, No Loafin', Soca With You; with various artists; Reggae for Kids; RORXX (Reggae on the Rocks X), Tee-Bird Showcase; Heart Monitor. *Publications include:* Jamaka comic magazines, Jamaka serial cartoon in The Star daily newspaper.

TEE TAH (see Moten, Frank, Jr)

TEIMOSO (see Da Silva, Rui)

TEK 9 (see MacFarlane, Denis)

TELLIER, Sébastien; French singer, songwriter and musician; b. 1975, Paris. *Career:* solo artist 2001–; rep. France in Eurovision Song Contest 2008. *Recordings include:* albums: L'incroyable Vérité 2001, Politics 2004, Sessions (re-released as Universe) 2006, Sexuality 2008, My God is Blue 2012, Cochon Ville 2012, Narco 2013, Confection 2013. *Current Management:* c/o Record Makers, 6 rue André Messager, 75018 Paris, France. *E-mail:* recordmakers@ recordmakers.com. *Website:* www.recordmakers.com; www.sebastientellier .com.

TEMIME, Olivier; French musician (saxophone); b. 30 Jan. 1974, Aix-en-Provence. *Career:* performed in public six months after beginning saxophone aged 14 years; f. club nights in Paris; performed regularly at jazz festivals in France, accompanying artists including Johnny Griffin, Wynton Marsalis; f. numerous projects, including Electric Volunteered Slaves 2002. *Recordings include:* albums: Le Douze 1998, Saï Saï Saï 2003, Streetwise 2005, Breakfast in Babylon, Massaliaz, The Intruder. *Honours:* First Prize, JazzFutur90, best soloist La Défense Jazz contest 1997. *Current Management:* c/o Elabeth, Studio du Petit Pont, 12 rue du Petit Pont, 78310 Maurepas, France. *E-mail:* elabeth@elabeth.com (office). *Website:* www.elabeth.com (office). *Telephone:* 06-22-84-03-91. *E-mail:* olivier.temime@laposte.net. *Website:* www .oliviertemime.com.

TEMIZ, Okay; Turkish/Swedish musician (percussion); b. 11 Feb. 1939, Ankara; one s. *Education:* music conservatory. *Career:* world tours with Don Cherry, Karnata Ka Coll. of Percussion, Oriental Wind, Okay Temiz Magnetic Band; mem. Swedish and Finnish Jazz Org. *Recordings include:* Music For Axaba 1974, Oriental Wind, 12 records 1947–86, Fis Fis Tziganes 1992, Fish Market 1993, Don Cherry/Bobo Stainson/Okay Temiz 1993, Ranarop, Gjallarhorn 1998, Peregrina World 1999, Hammage An Istanbul 2000. *Current Management:* c/o Denis Leblond, 99 avenue de Clichy, 75017 Paris; c/o Orane Senly, Artalene, 15 passage de la Main d'Or, 75001, Paris, France; c/o Werner Oberender, PO Box 1926, 5450 Neuvied 1, Germany. *E-mail:* okaytm@ okaytemiz.com. *Address:* Lüleci Trench Cad. Tatarbey Sk. No. 15, Kuledibi, Istanbul, Turkey. *Telephone:* (533) 7709967 (office); (533) 3749062. *E-mail:* okaytm@superonline.com (office). *Website:* www.okaytemiz.com.

TEMNIKOVA, Elena; Russian singer; b. 18 April 1985, Kurgan. *Career:* contestant on TV talent show Star Factory 2003; released two solo singles; mem. Serebro 2006–, formed for Eurovision Song Contest 2007 with song Song #1, finished in third place; signed to Monolit Records; many hits in Russia; international hits with Song #1 2007, Mama Lover 2011. *Recordings include:* with Serebro: albums: OpiumRoz 2009, Mama Lover 2011. *Honours:* MTV

Russian Music Awards for Best Debut 2007, for Best Group 2008, Golden Gramophone Award 2007, World Music Award for Best Selling Russian Artist 2007. *Address:* c/o Monolit Records, Studio Monolit office, Moscow, 117105, 4a Novodanilovskaya naberezhnaya, Russia (office). *Telephone:* (495) 5102255 (office). *E-mail:* pkmonolit@mail.ru (office). *Website:* www.pkmonolit.ru/ english.php (office); www.serebro.su.

TEMPEST, Joey; Swedish singer and songwriter; b. 19 Aug. 1963, Stockholm. *Career:* Co-founder of rock group, Force 1982, later renamed Europe 1985–92, re-formed 2003; won nat. rock talent contest, Sweden; solo artist 1993–; int. tours. *Recordings include:* albums: with Europe: Wings of Tomorrow 1985, The Final Countdown 1986, Out of this World 1988, Prisoners in Paradise 1991, Super Hits 2000; solo: A Place to Call Home 1995, Azalea Place 1999, Joey Tempest 2002. *Current Management:* c/o Siren Artist Management Inc., 4446 West 169th Street, Lawndale, CA 90260, USA. *Telephone:* (310) 371-0476. *Website:* www.europetheband.com.

TEMPLETON, David Joseph; American composer, performer and musician (piano, guitar, violin, cello, percussion, voice); *Owner, Mason Ridge Records;* b. 18 June 1960, Chicago, Ill.; s. of David Edward Templeton and Patricia Ann Templeton. *Education:* Univ. of Washington, studied jazz improvisation with Bill Smith, film scoring with Hummie Mann. *Career:* numerous live performances, including Carnegie Hall, New York, Benaroya Hall, Seattle; mem. American Soc. of Composers, Authors and Publrs (ASCAP). *Compositions:* Time Alone, Promise, Elisha, Only With You, The Crossing, Under the Willow Tree, Radiance, Once on Blueberry Lake. *Recordings:* albums: Time Alone, Promise, The Deepest Water, Change, The Crossing, Under the Willow Tree. *Publication:* Under the Willow Tree, Songbook 2012. *Honours:* Innovation Lab Award, Washington Filmworks at Seattle Int. Film Festival (for The Maury Island Incident) 2013, People's Choice Award, Gig Harbor Int. Film Festival 2014. *Address:* Mason Ridge Records, PO Box 942, Seahurst, WA 98062-0942, USA (office). *Telephone:* (206) 242-4129 (office). *E-mail:* mason.ridge@juno .com; david@davidtempleton.com. *Website:* www.davidtempleton.com; www .davidtempleton.com.

TEMS, Michael (Mick) James Anthony; British singer and musician; *Editor, Folkwales Online Magazine;* b. 3 Jan. 1950, London, England. *Career:* mem. Welsh traditional groups Swansea Jack 1973–78, Calennig and the Calennig Big Band 1978–2001; suffered major stroke 2001; mem. twmpath/ceilidh group Dr Price's Fire Band 2007–, Welsh dance group Gwerinwyr Gwent; researcher and collector of The South Wales Archive; Ed. Folkwales Online Magazine; mem. Equity, Musicians' Union, Mechanical-Copyright Protection Soc., Nat. Union of Journalists, CDdWC, COTC, PPL TSF, CAMRA, RATS, Pontyclun Inst. Athletic Club. *Recordings include:* solo: Gowerton Fair 1977; with Swansea Jack: The Seven Wonders 1978; with Calennig: Songs and Tunes From Wales 1980, You Can Take a White Horse Anywhere 1983, Dyddiau Gwynion Ionawr 1985, Dwr Glan 1990, Trade Winds 1994, A Gower Garland 2000; numerous compilations. *Address:* 88 Manor Chase, Beddau, Pontypridd, CF38 2JE, Wales (office). *Telephone:* (1443) 206689 (office). *E-mail:* micktems@folkwales.org.uk (office). *Website:* www.folkwales.org.uk (office).

TENAGLIA, Danny, (Soul Boy); American producer, remixer and DJ; b. 7 March 1961, New York. *Career:* began as a DJ in New York; relocation to Miami during 1980s, led to production work; returned to New York 1990; resident DJ at Vinyl, Roxy , Twilo, Tunnel, New York; collaborations with Peter Daou, Liz Torres, Celeda; remixed Deep Dish, East 17, D*Note, Pet Shop Boys, Faithless, Kings of Tomorrow, Depeche Mode, Jamiroquai. *Recordings include:* albums: Bottom Heavy 1994, Hard and Soul 1995, ohno 1996, Elements 1997, Tourism 1998, Back to Mine 1999, Athens 2000, Back to Basics 2002, Choice 2003, DIBIZA 2006, The Space Dance 2008, Futurism 2008. *Honours:* Dancestar Lifetime Achievement Award. *Website:* www .dannytenaglia.com.

TENNANT, Neil Francis; British singer, songwriter and producer; b. 10 July 1954, North Shields, Northumberland, England. *Education:* North London Polytechnic. *Career:* mem, Dust 1970–71; worked in publishing 1975–; Founder-mem., West End, later renamed Pet Shop Boys 1981–; numerous television and radio appearances, worldwide tours; launched record label, Spaghetti 1991; producer, songwriter for numerous artists, including Dusty Springfield, Patsy Kensit, Liza Minnelli, Boy George, Electronic, Tina Turner, Kylie Minogue; songwriter and singer on electronic tracks, including Getting Away With It 1989, Patience Of A Saint 1991, Disappointed 1992; Visiting Fellow, Lady Margaret Hall, Oxford 2016–. *Theatre:* Closer to Heaven (musical written with Chris Lowe and Jonathan Harvey, West End, London) 2001, The Most Incredible Thing (ballet) (Beyond Theatre Award 2011) 2011. *Film:* It Couldn't Happen Here 1988. *Compositions:* new soundtrack to 1925 film Battleship Potemkin 2004. *Recordings include:* albums: Please 1986, Disco—The Remix Album 1986, Actually 1987, Introspective 1988, In Depth 1989, Behaviour 1990, Discography 1991, Very 1993, Very Relentless 1993, Disco 2 1994, Alternative 1995, Bilingual 1996, Originals (Please, Actually, Behaviour box set) 1997, Bilingual Special Edition 1997, Essential Pet Shop Boys 1998, Nightlife 1999, Please—Further Listening 1984–1986 2001, Actually—Further Listening 1987–1988 2001, Introspective—Further Listening 1988–1989 2001, Behaviour—Further Listening 1990–1991 2001, Very—Further Listening 1992–1994 2001, Bilingual—Further Listening 1995–1997 2001, Release 2002, Disco 3 2003, PopArt—The Hits 2003, Fundamental 2006, Concrete 2006, Disco 4 2007, Yes 2009, Format 2012,

Elysium 2012, Electric 2013. *Publications:* Pet Shop Boys, Annually, Pet Shop Boys Versus America, Pet Shop Boys, Literally 1990, Catalogue 2012. *Honours:* Ivor Novello Awards 1987, 1988, BPI Award for Best Single 1987, Best Group 1988, Berolina Award (Germany) 1988, BRIT Award for Outstanding Contrib. to Music 2009, Q Magazine Outstanding Contrib. to Music Award 2013. *Current Management:* Becker Brown Management, 11 Knightsbridge, 3rd Floor, London, SW1X 7LY, England. *Telephone:* (20) 7838-6158. *E-mail:* info@beckerbrown.com. *Address:* Pet Shop Boys Partnership, 8th Floor, 15–19 Kingsway, London, WC2B 6UN, England (office). *Website:* www.petshopboys.co.uk.

TENNILLE, Toni; American singer; b. 8 May 1943, Montgomery, AL; m. Daryl Dragon 1974. *Career:* co-writer and performer, musical Mother Earth, San Francisco 1972; mem. of duo, Captain & Tennille 1972–; numerous tours and live appearances; musical variety show, Captain & Tennille (ABC TV) 1976; solo artist 1980–; Nevada Ambassador for the Arts 1998. *Stage appearances:* Stardust (Broadway) 1991, The Rainmaker. *Recordings include:* albums: with Captain & Tennille: The Secret of Christmas 1974, Love Will Keep Us Together 1975, Song of Joy 1976, Come in from the Rain 1977, Dream 1978, Make Your Move 1980, Keeping Our Love Warm, Twenty Years of Romance 1995, Size 14 1997, Tennille Sings Big Band 1998, Incurably Romantic 2001, More Than Dancing... Much More 2002; other credits include: Elton John, Pink Floyd, Art Garfunkel. *Honours:* Grammy Award for Record of the Year (for Love Will Keep Us Together) 1976, Juno Award for Best Int. Single (for Love Will Keep Us Together) 1976. *E-mail:* NAAProd@aol.com (office); tonifans@aol.com (office). *Website:* www.captainandtennille.net.

TERMINATOR X; American DJ and rap artist; b. (Norman Lee Rogers), 25 Aug. 1966. *Career:* mem. rap group, Public Enemy 1984–90; solo artist 1990–; man., The Entourage (hip hop club), Long Island, New York 1986. *Recordings include:* albums: with Public Enemy: Yo! Bum Rush The Show 1987, It Takes A Nation of Millions To Hold Us Back 1988, Fear of a Black Planet 1990, Apocalypse 91... The Enemy Strikes Black (Soul Train Music Award for Best Rap Album 1992) 1991, Greatest Misses 1992, Muse Sick-n-Hour Mess Age 1994, He Got Game (film soundtrack) 1998, There's a Poison Goin' On... 1999, Revolverlution 2002, Rebirth of a Nation 2005, New Whirl Odor 2005, How you Sell Soul to a Soulless People who Sold their Soul ??? 2007; solo: Terminator X and The Valley of The Jeep Beets 1991, Superbad 1994, Judgment Day 2011. *Honours:* MOBO Award for Outstanding Contribution to Black Music 2005. *E-mail:* Mistachuck@rapstation.com (office). *Website:* www.publicenemy.com.

TERRASSON, Jacques (Jacky) Laurent; French/American jazz musician (piano); b. 27 Nov. 1966, Berlin, Germany. *Education:* Berklee Coll. of Music, Boston, USA. *Career:* collaborations include Ray Brown, Art Taylor's Wailers; accompanist for Dee Dee Bridgewater, Betty Carter, Cassandra Wilson, Dianne Reeves. *Recordings include:* albums: Lover Man 1993, What's News 1994, Terrasson 1994, Reach 1995, Rendezvous (with Cassandra Wilson) 1997, Alive 1998, What Is It 1999, Kindred (with Stefon Harris) 2001, A Paris 2001, Smile 2003, Mirror 2007, Push 2010. *Honours:* Thelonious Monk Int. Jazz Competition 1993. *Current Management:* Christophe Deghelt Productions, Résidence Castel Régina, 41 avenue du Mont-Alban, 06300 Nice, France. *Telephone:* 4-93-89-71-24. *Fax:* 4-93-89-71-24. *E-mail:* info@deghelt-productions.com. *Website:* www.deghelt-productions.com; www.jackyterrasson.com.

TERRY, Todd, (Swan Lake, Royal House, Gypsymen); American producer, remixer and DJ; b. 18 April 1967, Brooklyn, New York. *Career:* mem. Masters At Work (with Kenny Dope); house music producer under various pseudonyms; Founder, Freeze Records, Sound Design Records; collaborations with Kenny Dope, Roland Clark, T La Rock; has remixed Martha Wash, Janet Jackson, Jamiroquai, Everything But The Girl, Michael Jackson, Kylie Minogue, The Corrs. *Recordings include:* albums: To The Batmobile – Let's Go 1988, Todd Terry Project 1992, Sound Design 1992, Todd, Louie and Kenny 1994, Sound Design, Vol. 2 1995, Todd Terry Presents Ready for a New Day 1997, Sessions, Vol. 8 1997, House Music Movement 1999, Resolutions 1999, Penthouse: La Nuit Luxure 2007, Strictly 2007. *Address:* 769 Sunset Terrace, Franklin Lakes, NJ 07417, USA. *Website:* www.toddterry.com.

TERU; Japanese singer; b. (Kobashi Teruhiko), 8 June 1971, Hakodate; m. 1st (divorced); m. 2nd. *Career:* Founder-mem. and lead singer pop/rock band, Glay 1988, moved band to Tokyo 1990–; numerous live performances and tours, numerous radio broadcasts. *Recordings include:* albums: Hai to Daiyamondo 1994, Speed Pop 1995, BEAT out! 1996, Beloved (Nihon Record Grand Prize 1997) 1996, Review: Best of Glay 1997, Pure Soul (Nihon Record Best Album) 1998, Heavy Gauge 1999, Mirai Diary (film soundtrack) 2000, One Love 2001, Unity Roots & Family, Away 2002, The Frustrated 2004, Love is Beautiful 2007; singles: Rain 1994, Manatsuno Tobira 1994, Kanojo no Modern 1994, Freeze My Love 1995, Zutto Futari de 1995, Yes, Summerdays 1995, Ikiteju Tsuyosa 1995, Glorious 1996, Beloved (Japan Usen Broadcast Networks Gold Request Prize) 1996, Zutto Wasurenai (A Boy) 1996, Kuchibiru 1997, However (Nihon Record Excellent Work Award) 1997, Yuuwaku 1998, Soul Love 1998, Be With You 1998, Winter Again (Nihon Record Grand Prize) 1999, Kokodewanai, Dokokae 1999, Happiness 2000, Mermaid 2000, Tomadoi/Special Thanks 2000, Missing You 2000, Global Communication 2001, Stay Tuned 2001, Hitohira no Jiyuu 2001, Way Of Difference 2002, Mata Kokode Aimashou 2002, Aitai Kimochi 2002, Beautiful Dreamer/Street Life 2003, Blue Jean 2004. *Honours:* Japan Usen Broadcast Networks Grand Prize 1997,

1999, Golden Arrow Music Prize 1998, Gold Disc Awards for Best Rock Artist of the Year, Best Music Video of the Year, Artist of the Year 1998. *Website:* www.glay.co.jp.

TESORI, Jeanine, (Jeanine Levenson); American composer, conductor and music arranger; b. 1961; m. Michael Rafter; one d. *Education:* Barnard Coll. *Career:* Broadway debut with arrangement of dance music for revival of How to Succeed in Business Without Really Trying 1995; arranger and conductor for numerous Broadway productions; Artistic Dir 'Encores! Off-Center' (concert series of Off-Broadway musicals); mem. Dramatists Guild of America. *Theatre scores include:* Violet (with Brian Crawley) (Obie Award, New York Drama Critics Circle Award for Best Musical 1997, Lucille Lortel Award for Outstanding Musical, Richard Rodgers Production Award) 1997, Thoroughly Modern Millie (with Dick Scanlan) (Tony Award winner for Best Musical 2003) 2000, Caroline, or Change (with Tony Kushner) 2004, Shrek the Musical 2008, Mother Courage and Her Children (with Tony Kushner) 2006, A Blizzard on Marblehead Neck (with Tony Kushner) 2011, Fun Home (with Lisa Kron) 2011, The Lion, The Unicorn, and Me (opera) 2013. *Film scores include:* Mulan II (with Alexa Junge) 2004, The Emperor's New Groove 2: Kronk's New Groove 2005, Shrek the Third 2007, Nights in Rodanthe 2008, The Loss of a Teardrop Diamond 2008, The Little Mermaid: Ariel's Beginning 2008. *Current Management:* Josef Weinberger Ltd, 12–14 Mortimer Street, London, W1T 3JJ, England. *Telephone:* (20) 7580-2827. *Fax:* (20) 7436-9616. *Website:* www.josef-weinberger.com/musicals/author/jeanine-tesori.html.

TESTA, Gianmaria; Italian singer, songwriter and musician (guitar); b. (Giovanni Maria), 17 Oct. 1958, Cuneo, Piedmont. *Recordings include:* albums: Montgolfières 1995, Extra-muros 1996, Lampo 1999, Il Valzer Di Un Giorno 2000, Altre Latitudini 2003, Da questa parte del mare (Premio Tenco 2007) 2006, F-à Lèo 2007, Solo dal vivo 2008, Vitamia 2011, Men at Work 2013. *Plays include:* Guarda che luna 2001, Attraverso 2003, RossinTesta 2004, Chisciotte e gli invincibili 2004–08, even in France, Che storia è questa 2010, 18mila giorni - Il Pitone 2010–11, Italy 2011, Chisciottimisti 2013–14. *Publications include:* Ninna nanna dei sogni 2012, 20mila Leghe (in fondo al mare) 2013, Biancaluna 2014, Il sentiero e altre filastrocche 2015. *Honours:* Chevalier des Arts et des Lettres; First Prize, Recanati Festival 1993–94, Premio Tenco 2007. *Current Management:* c/o Produzioni Fuorivia Sas di Paola Farinetti, Via Paruzza 18, 12051 Alba (CN), Italy. *Telephone:* (0173) 366549. *Fax:* (0173) 223183. *E-mail:* info@produzionifuorivia.it. *Website:* www.produzionifuorivia.it. *Telephone:* (0173) 366549. *Fax:* (0173) 223183. *E-mail:* info@gianmariatesta.com (office). *Website:* www.gianmariatesta.com.

TÉTÉ; French singer and songwriter; b. (Mahmoud Tété Niang), 25 July 1975, Dakar, Senegal. *Career:* moved with family to Saint-Dizier, France 1978. *Recordings include:* albums: Le Préambule 2000, L'air de rien 2001, A la faveur de l'automne 2003, Le Sacre des Lemmings 2006, On Dirait Nino 2007, Le Premier Clair De L'Aube 2010, Nu là-bas 2013. *Current Management:* c/o Sony Music France, 20–26 rue Morel, 92110 Clichy, France. *E-mail:* ffw75@mac.com. *Website:* www.tete.tv.

TETTEH-LARTEY, Benedict Julien (Benny); British singer, songwriter, musician, arranger and carpenter; *Partner, Creative Records;* b. 29 Sept. 1965, Mayfield, Dalkieth, Scotland; s. of Andrew J. V. Tetteh-Lartey and Barbara Liaudinski; m. Ms Lesley Moss 1999; one s. two d. *Education:* Rudolf Steiner School, Edin. *Career:* bassist and vocalist in Edinburgh band, Makossa 1987–91; bass player and backing vocalist on Dave Robb's album, Capture an Image 1992; plays eight-string acoustic guitar; solo career; numerous live sessions, performances and TV and radio interviews; played alongside Nick Harper at 12 Bar Club in London 1999; cr. original 18-string instrument called a combuitar 2007; mem. Mechanical-Copyright Protection Soc., Performing Right Soc., Musicians' Union. *Exhibition:* Driven Creativity, Brick Lane Gallery, London. *Compositions include:* In the Same Boat 1987, Song to Papa 1996, Injustice (BBC Scotland Tympanali Award (songwriter showcase) 1998) 1997, Head in the Sand 1998, Don't be Sad 1998. *Plays:* Roses are Red, All the Night, Song to Papa, Same Boat, Afro Scot. *Film:* music for Salome. *Television:* UK Nat. Star for a Night and Edinburgh Live TV, Sony TV 2009, BIC TV (Bahrain). *Recordings include:* albums: Don't Be Sad 1998, See The Wonder 2010. *Honours:* BBC Tympanali Singer Songwriter 1998, SME Small Business of the Year 2009, Professional Music Award Winner for Hitachi Europe sponsored Driven Creativity Competition. *Address:* Creative Records, 50 Paradykes Avenue, Loanhead, Midlothian, EH20 9LD, Scotland (office). *Telephone:* (131) 440-0076 (office). *E-mail:* music@bennytetteh-lartey.co.uk (office); bennytet@talktalk.net (home). *Website:* www.bennytetteh-lartey.co.uk; www.aardvarkrecords.co.uk/benny_tettehlartey.htm.

TEXIER, Henri; French jazz musician (double bass) and composer; b. 27 Jan. 1945, Paris; one s. *Career:* collaborations with artists, including Bud Powell, Dexter Gordon, Johnny Griffin, Louis Sclavis, John Abercrombie, Paul Motian, Bob Brookmeyer, Joe Lovano; founder mem., Phil Woods' European Rhythm Machine; fmr mem., The Azur Quintet late 1990s, Mad Nomads. *Recordings include:* albums: Amir 1975, Varech 1977, La Companera 1983, Paris: Batignolles 1986, Colonel Skopje/Izlaz 1988, The Scene Is Clean 1991, An Indian's Week (with Louis Sclavis, Aldo Romano) 1993, Carnet De Routes 1995, Respect 1997, Mosaic Man 1998, Suite Africaine 1999, Remparts d'Argile 2000, (V)ivre 2005, Holy Lola 2005, Love Songs Reflexions 2009, Canto Negro 2011, 3 + 3 (Romano Sclavis Texier) 2012, Improviste 2013, Sky Dancers 2016. *Address:* Label Bleu, Maison de la Culture d'Amiens, CS 60631,

80006 Amiens, Cedex 1, France (office). *Telephone:* (3) 22-97-79-79 (office). *Fax:* (3) 22-97-79-90 (office). *E-mail:* contact@label-bleu.com (office). *Website:* www.label-bleu.com (office); www.maisondelaculture-amiens.com.

THAIN, Laurie Anne, BPE, MSc, TEYL; Canadian singer, songwriter, English teacher and musician (guitar); *President, Pure Pacific Music;* b. 18 Feb. 1955, New Westminster, BC; d. of William Ransom Thain and Evelyn Anne Thain. *Career:* concert artist specializing in the intimate singer/songwriter approach; writer and producer of numerous custom entertainment shows and corporate events, concerts, opening shows for Lee Greenwood, Gary Morris, Rita MacNeil, Pam Tillis; Pres. Pure Pacific Music; worldwide tours; lived in Japan for ten years, now back in Canada teaching English and writing and recording music for children to learn English by; concerts. *Recordings include:* Hopeless Romantic 1984, Matters of the Heart 1987, Stages 1992, Preview 1996. *Publications:* Rhythm, Music, and Young Learners: A Winning Combination. In, A. M. Stoke (Ed.), JALT 2009 Conf. Proceedings, Tokyo: JALT 2010. *Honours:* Winner, Canadian Nat. Du Maurier Search for Stars. *Address:* #205, 6359 198th Street, Langley, BC V2Y 2E3, Canada (home). *Telephone:* (604) 530-6530 (office). *E-mail:* lauriethain@hotmail.com. *Website:* purepacificmusic .com.

THALÍA; Mexican actress and singer; b. (Ariadna Thalía Sodi Miranda), 27 Aug. 1971, Mexico City; m. Tommy Mottola 2000. *Career:* mem. children's group Din-Din; mem. Timbiriche 1984; solo artist 1990–. *Films include:* Vamos al baile 1996, Mambo Café 2000. *Television:* La pobre señorita Limantour 1983, Quinceañera 1987, Luz y sombra 1989, Maria Mercedes 1992, Marimar 1994, Maria la del barrio 1995, Rosalinda 1999. *Recordings include:* albums: with Din-Din: four albums; with Timbiriche: three albums; solo: Thalia I 1990, Mundo De Cristal 1991, Love 1992, Marimar 1994, En Éxtasis 1995, Nandito Ako 1997, Amor A La Mexicana 1997, Arrasando (Latin Grammy Award for Best Engineered Album) 2000, Thalia con Banda 2001, Thalia II 2002, Thalia (I Want You) 2003, El Sexto Sentido 2005, Lunada 2008, Habítame siempre 2012, Viva Tour (Live) 2013. *Website:* www.thalia.com.

THANDISWA (see Mazwai, Thandiswa)

THANGER, Hakan; Swedish musician (electric bass, guitar), singer and composer; b. 23 Oct. 1943, Boo, Stockholm; m. (divorced). *Career:* formed band The Thundermen; joined Weine Renlidens Orchestra; mem. vocal group Country Four; played and wrote songs and arrangements for many artists including Lill Babs, Jerry Williams, Family Four; mem. STIM, SAMI, SKAP, TSO; currently owns a digital studio. *Compositions include:* Dagar Jag Ner I Min Källare; Slices with Wild Cactus: The Time Machine 1970, Our Bikes 1971, Night 1972, Ibis 1974.

THATCHER, Benjamin (Ben) Peter; British rock music drummer and songwriter; b. 12 Feb. 1988, Rustington, E Sussex, England; m. *Career:* fmr mem. Flavour Country; Founder-mem. Royal Blood 2013–; released debut single Out of the Black 2013, supported Arctic Monkeys 2014, Foo Fighters 2015; performed at numerous music festivals including South by Southwest, Liverpool Sound City, Glastonbury Festival, T in the Park, Reading Festival. *Recordings:* album: Royal Blood 2014. *Honours:* Kerrang! Best British Newcomer 2015, BRIT Award for Best British Group 2015, Q Best Live Band Award 2015. *Current Management:* c/o Wildlife Entertainment, 21 Heathman's Road, London, SW6 4TJ, England. *Telephone:* (20) 7371-7008. *E-mail:* info@wildlife-entertainment.com. *Website:* www.wildlife -entertainment.com; www.royalbloodband.com.

THAYIL, Kim; American musician (guitar); b. 4 Sept. 1960, Seattle, WA. *Education:* Philosophy Degree, University of Washington. *Career:* mem., US heavy rock group, Soundgarden, 1984–97, 2010–; mem. the No WTO Combo 1999, Probot 2004; numerous live tours and festival appearances. *Recordings:* albums: with Soundgarden: Screaming Life 1987, Fopp 1988, Ultramega OK 1988, Louder than Love 1989, Badmotorfinger 1991, Superunknown 1994, Down on the Upside 1996, A-Sides 1997, Telephantism 2010; with The No WTO Combo: Live From The Battle In Seattle 2000; with Probot: Probot 2004; guitarist on: Wellwater Conspiracy, Scroll And Its Combinations, 2001. *Address:* c/o A&M Records, Interscope Records, 2220 Colorado Ave, Santa Monica, CA 90404, USA. *Website:* www.soundgardenworld.com.

THE WEEKND; Canadian R&B recording artist and record producer; b. (Abel Tesfaye), 16 Feb. 1990, Scarborough, Ont. *Career:* released debut mixtape 2011; first headlining tour 2011; numerous live appearances. *Recordings:* mixtapes: House of Balloons 2011, Thursday 2011, Echoes of Silence 2011, Trilogy (Juno Award for R&B/Soul Recording of the Year 2013) 2012; albums: Kiss Land (Juno Award for R&B/Soul Recording of the Year 2015) 2013, Beauty Behind the Madness (American Music Award for Favorite R&B/Soul Album 2015, Grammy Award for Best Urban Contemporary Album 2016) 2015. *Honours:* Sirius XM Indie Award for Solo Artist of the Year 2012, MTV O Music Award for Best Web-born Artist 2012, Juno Awards for Breakthrough Artist of the Year 2013, for Artist of the Year 2015, American Music Award for Favorite R&B/Soul Male Artist 2015, Grammy Award for Best R&B Performance (for Earned It) 2016. *Address:* c/o XO Recordings, Republic Records, Universal Music Group, 2220 Colorado Avenue, Santa Monica, CA 90404, USA (office). *Telephone:* (310) 865-5000 (office). *E-mail:* contact@theweeknd.com (home). *Website:* www.republicrecords.com (office); www.TheWeeknd.com (home).

THEMIS, John, BSc; British producer, musician (guitar), writer and music director; b. 13 Oct. 1954; m. Anne Lawrence 1981; one s. two d. *Career:* as producer, writer and arranger has worked with leading artists including Kylie Minogue, Elton John, Cat Stevens (Yusuf Islam), Craig David, Lemar, George Michael, Rod Stewart, Gabrielle, Will Young, The Spice Girls, Dido, Boyzone, Tori Amos, Cher, Bryan Ferry, Dolly Parton, Malcolm McLaren, Chris De Burgh, Sugababes; session musician with Blue featuring Stevie Wonder, Dido; conductor and string arranger for Victoria's Secrets' fashion productions with Mary J. Blige; co-wrote songs with Boy George for musical Taboo. *Compositions include:* What Took You So Long (Emma Bunton), Please Stay (Kylie Minogue), Even God Can't Change the Past; BBC TV Olympic Theme Tune 2004, music for Christian Dior TV commercial. *Recordings include:* Atmospheric Conditions 1985, The Other Side of John Themis 2007. *Films include:* soloist on Don Juan de Marco, The Saint, Othello, Sleeping with the Fishes. *Address:* 46 The Limes Avenue, London, N11 1RH, England (home). *Website:* www.freshmanguitars.net/artists/john-themis.

THERRIEN, Lucille (Lucie), MA; American singer and musician (piano, guitar, ethnic instruments); b. 1945. *Education:* UNH, Ecole des Beaux Arts. *Career:* numerous TV and radio broadcasts, performances and tours; mem. Le Conseil Francophone de la Chanson, NH Council of the Arts, NH Humanities Council, NH American Canadian French Cultural Exchange Comm. (govt bd mem.); owns teaching studio, Do-Re-Mi, Portsmouth, NH. *Compositions include:* Cousins, Memere. *Recordings inlcude:* Noel c'est l'amour, Cousins, Pot Pourri Folklorique, Un Tresor. *Honours:* four NH Council on the Arts Traditional Arts Program Awards, one NH Council on the Arts film award. *Current Management:* French American Music Enterprises, 5 Junkins Avenue, Suite 106, Portsmouth, NH 03801, USA. *E-mail:* lth@star.net. *Website:* www.luciet.com.

THICKE, Robin Alan; Canadian/American singer, songwriter, musician and actor; b. 10 March 1977, Los Angeles, Calif.; s. of Alan Thicke and Gloria Loring; m. Paula Patton 2005 (divorced 2014); one s. *Career:* songwriter for Color Me Badd, Christina Aguilera, Brandy, 3T, Jordan Knight, Mya in late 1990s; solo artist, as Thicke 2000–; released debut single When I Get You Alone 2002; recorded and toured as Robin Thicke 2005–; toured as support to India Arie 2006, John Legend 2006, Beyoncé 2007, Jennifer Hudson 2009, Alicia Keys 2010; numerous recording collaborations including: Jay-Z, Snoop Dogg, Nicki Minaj, Leighton Meester, Lil Wayne, Usher, Jennifer Hudson, R. Kelly, Ashanti, 50 Cent. *Films:* as actor: Abby in the Summer 2012. *Television:* as mentor and judge: Duets (ABC Television) 2012. *Recordings:* albums: as Thicke: A Beautiful World 2003; as Robin Thicke: The Evolution of Robin Thicke 2006, Something Else 2008, Sex Therapy 2009, Love After War 2011, Blurred Lines 2013, Paula 2014. *Honours:* ASCAP Rhythm & Soul Music Award for Top R&B/Hip-Hop Song (for Lost Without U) 2008, Billboard Music Awards for Top Hot 100 Song, for Top Digital Song, for Top Radio Song, for Top R&B Song (all for Blurred Lines) 2014. *Address:* c/o Interscope Records, Universal Music Group, 2220 Colorado Avenue, Santa Monica, CA 90404, USA (office). *Telephone:* (310) 865-5000 (office). *Website:* www.interscope.com (office); www.robinthicke.com.

THIELEMANS, Baron; **Jean Baptiste (Toots);** Belgian/American jazz musician (harmonica); b. 29 April 1922, Brussels; m. Huguette Thielemans. *Career:* began playing accordion, aged three; started playing with Bobby Jaspar, René Thomas; joined Benny Goodman on European tour 1950; moved to USA 1952; mem., Charlie Parker's All-Stars, George Shearing Quintet; collaborations include Ella Fitzgerald, Quincy Jones, Bill Evans, Jaco Pastorius, Paul Simon, Billy Joel, Elis Regina. *Television:* played harmonica on theme to Sesame Street 1969. *Recordings include:* albums: The Sound 1955, Man Bites Harmonica 1957, Time Out For Toots 1958, The Soul Of Toots Thielemans 1959, Toots Thielemans 1961, The Whistler And His Guitar 1962, Toots And Svend (with Svend Asmussen) 1972, Captured Alive 1974, Live 1974, Images 1974, Two Generations 1974, Live Vol. 2 1975, Apple Dimple 1979, Live In The Netherlands 1980, All Night Long 1981, Autumn Leaves 1984, Your Precious Love 1984, Just Friends 1986, Ne Me Quitte Pas 1986, Aquarela Do Brasil 1987, Only Trust Your Heart 1988, Footprints 1989, In Tokyo 1989, For My Lady 1991, The Brasil Project 1992, The Brasil Project Vol. 2 1993, East Coast West Coast 1994, Concerto For Harmonica 1995, Toots 75: The Birthday Album 1998, Chez Toots 1998, The Live Takes Vol. 1 1999, Toots Thielemans And Kenny Werner 2001, Wilsamba 2001, Witse (OST) 2004, One More for the Road 2006, Toots Thielemans, European Quartet – Live 2010. *Honours:* Chevalier des Arts et des Lettres, Commdr, Order of Leopold II (Belgium), Comendador, Ordem de Rio Branco (Brazil); Dr hc (Univ. Libre de Bruxelles), (Vrije Universiteit Brussel); Nat. Endowment for the Arts Jazz Master Award 2009, Concertgebouw Jazz Award 2009. *Address:* Toots BVBA, Veerle Van de Poel, Zagerijstraat 41, 2530 Boechout, Belgium. *Telephone:* (3) 337-31-73 (office). *E-mail:* info@tootsthielemans.com (office). *Website:* www.tootsthielemans.com.

THILE, Christopher (Chris) Scott; American musician (mandolin, banjo, guitar, violin, piano), singer and songwriter; b. 20 Feb. 1981, Oceanside, Calif.; m. 1st Jesse Meighan 2003 (divorced); m. 2nd Claire Coffee 2013; one s. *Education:* Murray State Univ. *Career:* began learning mandolin aged five; mem. bluegrass trio Nickel Creek 1989–2007, 2014–; won Nat. Mandolin Championship, Walnut Valley Festival, Winfield, Kan. 1993; Founder-mem. How to Grow a Band 2006, renamed Punch Brothers 2007–; collaborations with numerous musicians including Michael Daves, Stuart Duncan, Yo-Yo Ma, Mike Marshall, Edgar Meyer, Mark O'Connor; MacArthur Fellowship 2012. *Radio:* numerous guest appearances on A Prairie Home Companion 1996–, guest host 2015, regular host 2016–. *Compositions include:* Ad astra per alas porci (Concerto for Mandolin and Orchestra) 2009. *Recordings include:* solo albums: Leading Off 1994, True Life Blues: The Songs of Bill Monroe (Grammy Award for Best Bluegrass Album 1997) 1997, Stealing Second 1997, Not All Who Wander Are Lost 2001, Into the Cauldron (with Mike Marshall) 2003, Deceiver 2004, The Goat Rodeo Sessions (with Yo-Yo Ma, Stuart Duncan and Edgar Meyer) (Grammy Award for Best Folk Album 2013) 2011, Bach: Sonatas and Partitas Volume 1 2013; with Nickel Creek: Little Cowpoke 1993, Here to There 1997, This Side 2002, Why Should the Fire Die? 2005, A Dotted Line 2014; with Punch Brothers: How to Grow a Woman from the Ground (as How to Grow a Band) 2006, Punch 2008, Antifogmatic 2010, Who's Feeling Young Now? 2012, The Phosphorescent Blues 2015; with Edgar Meyer: Edgar Meyer and Chris Thile 2008, Bass & Mandolin (Grammy Award for Best Contemporary Instrumental Album 2015) 2014; with Michael Daves: Sleep with One Eye Open 2011. *Honours:* Emerging Artist of the Year (with Nickel Creek), Int. Bluegrass Music Asscn Awards 2000, Instrumental Group of the Year (with Nickel Creek), Int. Bluegrass Music Asscn Awards 2001, Mandolinist of the Year, Int. Bluegrass Music Asscn Awards 2001, Musician of the Year, BBC Folk Awards 2007. *Current Management:* c/o Ladd Circle Productions; c/o Jason Colton and Eric Mayers, Red Light Management. *Telephone:* (425) 491-5076 (Ladd Circle). *E-mail:* info@laddcircleproductions.com; punchbrothers@ redlightmanagement.com. *Website:* www.laddcircleproductions.com; www .redlightmanagement.com; www.nickelcreek.com; www.punchbrothers.com.

THOMAS, Billie Joe (B. J.); American singer, songwriter and entertainer; b. 7 Aug. 1942, Hugo, Okla; m. Gloria Richardson 1968; three d. *Career:* lead singer, The Triumphs; opened for acts including Roy Orbison, The Dave Clark Five, the Four Tops; solo artist; toured with Dick Clark Caravan of Stars; became 60th mem., Grand Ole Opry; mem. American Fed. of TV and Radio Artists, SAG, American Fed. of Musicians, CMA, Nat. Acad. of Recording Arts and Sciences, Nat. Songwriters' Asscn. *Recordings include:* albums include: I'm So Lonesome I Could Cry 1966, Tomorrow Never Comes 1966, Sings for Lovers and Losers 1967, On My Way 1968, Young and In Love 1969, Raindrops Keep Fallin' On My Head 1970, Everybody's Out of Town 1970, Most Of All 1971, The Scepter Citation Series 1972, Country 1972, Longhorns and Londonbridges 1974, Help Me Make It 1975, Home Where I Belong 1976, Everybody Loves a Rain Song 1978, Happy Man 1978, You Gave Me Love 1979, For the Best 1980, Amazing Grace 1981, As We Know Him 1981, Miracle 1982, Peace In The Valley 1982, Love Shines 1983, New Looks 1983, Great American Dream 1983, Shining 1984, All Is Calm, All Is Bright 1985, Throwin' Rocks At The Moon 1985, Nightlife 1986, Midnite Minute 1989, Back Against the Wall 1992, Still Standing Here 1993, Back Forward 1994, I Believe 1995, Precious Memories 1995, Scenes of Christmas 1995, Christmas is Coming Home 1997, You Call That A Mountain 2000, Love to Burn 2009, The Complete Scepter Singles 2012, The Living Room Sessions 2013. *Publications include:* Home Where I Belong; In Tune. *Honours:* six Grammy Awards, two Dove Awards, Lifetime Achievement Award, Univ. Coll. of Berkeley, Acad. Award 1970, Country Song of the Year 1975. *Address:* Honeyman Music, PO Box 12003, Arlington, TX 76012, USA (office). *Telephone:* (817) 261-4022 (office). *E-mail:* bjthomasoffice@tx.rr.com (office). *Website:* www.bjthomas .com.

THOMAS, Irma Lee; American R&B singer; b. 18 Feb. 1941, Pontchatoula, La. *Career:* known as 'The Soul Queen of New Orleans'. *Recordings include:* albums: Wish Somone Would Care 1964, Take A Look 1968, In Between Tears 1973, Live 1977, Soul Queen of New Orleans 1978, Safe With Me 1979, Hip Shakin' Mama 1981, The New Rules 1986, The Way I Feel 1988, Simply The Best 1991, True Believer 1992, Turn My World Around 1993, Walk Around Heaven 1993, The Story of My Life 1997, My Heart's In Memphis 2000, After the Rain (Grammy Award for Best Contemporary Blues Album 2007) 2006, Simply Grand 2008, The Soul Queen of New Orleans: 50th Anniversary Celebration 2009. *Current Management:* c/o Emile Jackson, PO Box 26126, New Orleans, LA 70185-6126, USA. *Telephone:* (504) 245-1719. *Fax:* (504) 246-2542. *Website:* www.irmathomas.com.

THOMAS, Patrick, BA; British musician (keyboards), composer and producer; b. 27 July 1960, Oxford, England. *Education:* Open Univ. St Edmund Campion School, Oxford with Mary Howell-Pryce. *Career:* Paris with Chuck Berry, Continental Drift 1989; London with Derek Bailey, Eugene Chadbourne, Keith Rowe 1990; London with John Zorn, Bucket Head, Paul Lovens 1991; Germany with Tony Oxley, Sirone, Larry Stabbins, Manfred Schoof 1992; Glasgow with Lol Coxhill 1993; Berlin Jazz Festival with Bill Dixon 1994; London Jazz Cafe with Thurston Moore, Lee Renaldo 1996; solo: Copenhagen 1997; Austria Graz Music Protocol with And 1997; CMN Tour with Butch Morris; London Sky Scraper; Vancouver Jazz Festival with Eugene Chadborne and Alex Ward 1998; Cologne, Germany with Celebration Orchestra 1998; Uncool Festival, Switzerland with Scatter 1999; Freedom of the City Festival solo 2001; pianoforte tour with Keith Tippett, Howard Riley, Stephen Grew 2003; Newcastle Jazz Festival with Roy Campbell 2004; mem. Performing Rights Soc., London Musicians' Collective. *Compositions include:* Ensemble WX7e Turntables Dialogue (with interruptions), Pulse for drum machine and two percussionists, Reflex for ensemble and computers. *Recordings include:* with Tony Oxley Quartet: Incus 1992, Lol Coxhill: Halim Nato 1993, One Night in Glasgow: Scatter 1994, Company 91 (three vols) 1994, Mike Cooper Island Songs 1995, Celebration Orchestra: The Enchanted Messenger 1996, Tones of Life: Guidance 1997, solo: Remembering 1998, Total Tuesday: Hellington Country 1998, And: Intakt 1998, with Rhys Chatham:

Hard Edge 1999, Powerfield: EEE 1999, Nur: Solo Piano 1999, with Tony Oxley Quartet: Phantom Navigator 1999, Strong Language Lunge 2002, Pianoforte 2004. *Publications include:* Islam's Contribution to Jazz and Improvised Music 1993, Upside Down (The Myth of Jazz History) 1998, The Trouble with Jazz History 2004. *Honours:* Arts Council of Great Britain Jazz Bursary for three electro- acoustic compositions, Paul Hamlyn Foundation Award for Composers 2014. *Address:* 5 Saint Omer Road, Cowley, Oxford, OX4 3HB, England (home).

THOMAS, Rhozanda, (Chilli); American singer and choreographer; b. 27 Feb. 1971, Atlanta, Ga; one s. *Career:* professional dancer, Damian Dame; mem. TLC 1991–; appeared in film Have Plenty; started own publishing co., T-Ron Music. *Recordings include:* Albums: Ooooooohhh… On The TLC Tip 1992, Crazysexycool (Grammy Award for Best R&B Album) 1994, Fanmail 1999, 3D 2002, Now and Forever 2003, Crazy Sexy Hits 2007. *Television:* What Chilli Wants 2010–11. *Honours:* Grammy Award, for Best R&B Performance by Duo/Group, two Lady of Soul Awards, two Billboard Music Awards, three Soul Train Awards, Blockbuster Entertainment Award, four MTV Music Video Awards (for Waterfalls). *Address:* LaFace Records, 1 Capital City Plaza, 3350 Peachtree Road, Suite 1500, Atlanta, GA 30326, USA.

THOMAS, Richard; British composer and writer; b. 1965. *Education:* Univ. of Cambridge. *Career:* mem. of musical and comic duo Miles & Milner 1987–93; Co-founder and mem. Club Zarathustra 1993–98; Co-founder Kombat Opera 1996. *Compositions include:* Jerry Springer: The Opera (music and lyrics, with Stewart Lee) (Evening Standard Theatre Award for Best New Musical 2004) 2001, Shoes (dance piece) 2010, Anna Nicole 2011. *Radio:* performer: The Miles & Milner Show (BBC Radio 4) 1991, Rainer Hersch's All Classical Music Explained (BBC Radio 4) 1998. *Television include:* performer: Beethoven's Not Dead (Spitting Image/BBC 2) 1992, This Morning With Richard Not Judy (BBC 2) 1998–99, Either/Or (PlayUK) 1999, Attention Scum (BBC Choice/BBC 2) 2001; Musical Dir The Frank Skinner Show (Avalon TV/ BBC 1, later ITV) 1995–2001, This Morning With Richard Not Judy (BBC 2) 1998–99, Baddiel & Skinner Unplanned (Avalon TV/ITV) 2000–03, Jerry Springer: The Opera (BBC 2) 2004, Kombat Opera 2007. *Address:* c/o Avalon, 4A Exmoor Street, London, W10 6BD, England. *Telephone:* (20) 7598-8000.

THOMAS, Rob (Robert Kelly); American singer, songwriter and musician (piano); b. 14 Feb. 1972, Landstuhl, Germany. *Career:* lead singer, Tabitha's Secret 1993–96; lead singer and songwriter Matchbox Twenty 1996–, numerous tours worldwide with Matchbox Twenty; wrote and recorded song Smooth with Santana 1999; collaborations with Willie Nelson, Marc Anthony, Mick Jagger, Bernie Taupin; solo artist 2005–; Founder Sidewalk Angels Foundation homeless charity. *Recordings include:* albums: with Matchbox Twenty: Yourself or Someone Like You 1996, Mad Season 2000, More Than You Think You Are 2002, Exile on Mainstream 2007; solo: Something to Be 2005, Cradlesong 2009. *Honours:* South Carolina Music and Entertainment Hall of Fame 2001, Billboard's Songwriter of the Year (twice), Starlight Award, Songwriters Hall of Fame 2004, 13 BMI Awards. *Website:* www .matchboxtwenty.com; www.robthomasmusic.com.

THOMPSON, (Richard E.) Butch, BA; American musician (piano, clarinet); b. 28 Nov. 1943, Stillwater, Minn.; m. Mary Ellen Niedenfuer 1991. *Education:* Univ. of Minnesota. *Career:* clarinettist, Hall Brothers Jazz Band, 1962–94; pianist, leader, Butch Thompson Trio in residency, National Public Radio, 1974–86; world tours as pianist include Cairo, Egypt, 1994, 1997, 1998; European festivals, appearances with orchestras include: Hartford Symphony; Minnesota Orchestra; St Louis Symphony and many more; national tour of off-Broadway show, Jelly Roll, 1994–97; pianist on Grammy winning Verve album, Doc Cheatham and Nicholas Payton, 1997; major US jazz festivals, 1968–; mem. American Federation of Musicians, local 30–73. *Compositions include:* Ecuadorean Memories; Yancey On My Mind; Eduadorean Suite, for piano and orchestra, premiered with Minnesota Orchestra in 1998. *Recordings include:* albums: Butch Thompson 1979, 'A' Solas 1982, If You Don't Shake 1984, Milenberg Joys 1984, Butch Thompson and His Boys in Chicago 1985, Chicago Breakdown 1989, Good Old New York 1989, Minnesota Wonder 1992, Yulestride 1994, Butch & Doc 1994, Lincoln Avenue Blues 1995, Lincoln Avenue Express 1997, Thompson Plays Joplin 1998, Bethlehem After Dark 2000, Tain't Nobody's Business 2005, Plays Jelly Roll Morton Solos 2008; over 100 other recordings, 25 as leader or soloist. *Address:* PO Box 7023, Ann Arbor, MI 48107, USA. *Website:* www.butchthompson.com.

THOMPSON, Chris; American country music drummer; m. Candace Thompson 2011. *Education:* Univ. of North Texas. *Career:* mem. Eli Young Band 2002–. *Recordings:* albums: with Eli Young Band: Eli Young Band 2002, Level 2005, Jet Black & Jealous 2008, Life at Best 2011, 10,000 Towns 2014. *Honours:* Acad. of Country Music Award for Song of the Year 2012, MusicRow Breakthrough Artist Award 2012. *Current Management:* c/o George Couri, Triple 8 Management, 5524 West Highway 290, Austin, TX 78735, USA. *Telephone:* (512) 444-7600. *Fax:* (512) 444-7601. *Website:* www.eliyoungband .com.

THOMPSON, Christopher Hamlet; British musician; b. 9 March 1947, Hertford, Herefords.; m. Maggie, 4 Jan. 1995, one s. *Career:* mem. Manfred Mann's Earth Band 1975–86; formed own band Night 1979; tours throughout USA, Europe: with Manfred Mann's Earth Band 1975–86, with Night 1979–83; working in Europe under own name 1986–; with The Alan Parsons

Project; mem. PRS, SAG, Equity. *Recordings include:* with Manfred Mann's Earth Band: The Roaring Silence 1976, Watch 1978, Angel Station 1979, Chance 1980, Somewhere In Africa 1982, Live In Budapest 1983, Criminal Tango 1986, The Best Of, Remastered 1998, Blindin' 2000; singles: Blinded By The Light, Davys On The Road Again; solo albums: Radio Voices 1983, High Cost of Living 1986, Beat of Love 1989, Rediscovery 2004, Do Nothing Till You Hear from Me 2012; Hits in Germany with: The Challenge 1989, The Joker 1991, Florida Lady 1994; songs and vocals to albums by: The Doobie Brothers, Tina Turner, Elton John, Roger Daltrey, Jefferson Starship, Brian May, Barbara Dickson, Ozzy Osbourne. *E-mail:* chris.thompson@christhompson-central.com. *Website:* www.christhompson-central.com.

THOMPSON, Danny; British musician (double bass, trombone); b. 4 April 1939, Teignmouth, S Devon, England; s. of Edward Hutchison Thompson and Florence Selina Thompson; m. Sylvia E. Thompson; one s. two step-s. *Education:* Salesian Coll. Grammar. *Career:* worked with Alexis Korner 1964–67, Roy Orbison tour 1964; recording sessions 1960s including Marianne Faithfull, Incredible String Band, Nick Drake, Donovan; co-founded Pentangle 1968; own trio with John McLaughlin 1966; Tubby Hayes Quartet, Phil Seamen Quartet, Harold McNair Quartet; numerous concert and club dates with artists including Brook Benton, Josh White Sr, Red Rodney, Joe Williams, Freddy Hubbard, Mark Murphy, John Hendricks, Blind Boys of Alabama, Roger Daltrey and Pete Townsend, Mark Knopfler; studio work including Bert Jansch, Rod Stewart, Kate Bush, Talk Talk 1970s, 1980s; formed own band Whatever 1989, toured 1992–97; studio work 1990s to present includes Tasmin Archer, Billy Bragg, David Sylvian, Norma Waterson, Loreena McKennitt, Peter Gabriel, Paul Brady, Paul Weller, Barbara Dickson, Yusuf Islam, Darrell Scott, Richard Thompson, Eric Bibb, Baaba Maal, Martin Simpson, Graham Coxon; numerous TV appearances on Jools Holland Show, Transatlantic Sessions, John Martyn (BBC). *Television:* Faces of Islam (BBC films), The Furthest Mosque (documentary). *Compositions include:* Take 3 Girls Theme (Ivor Novello Award, BBC 1969), Light Flight, Musing Mingus Til Minne Av Jan, Children of the Dark, Pitfalls, New Rhythms, No Love is Sorrow, Passion to Protect (film), Swedish Dance, Fair Isle Friends. *Recordings include:* albums with: Pentangle: The Pentangles 1968, Sweet Child 1968, Basket of Light 1969, Cruel Sister 1970, Reflection 1971, Solomon's Seal 1972, Open the Door 1985; as Danny Thompson: Whatever 1987, Whatever Next 1989, Elemental 1990, Whatever's Best 1995; others: Dizrhythmia, Songhai, Solid Air, Live at Leeds (with John Martyn), Industry, Spirit of the Century (with Peter Gabriel) 2002, Martin Simpson 2009. *Honours:* Hugo, Chicago Int. Film Festival, two Grammy Awards for Five Blind Boys of Alabama 2003, Lifetime Achievement Award, BBC 2 Ivor Novello Awards 2007, Lifetime Achievement Award with group Pentangle 2007, Lifetime Achievement Award, BBC 2 Folk Awards 2007. *Current Management:* c/o Paul Crockford, PCM, Latimer House, Latimer Road, London, W10 6QY, England. *Telephone:* (20) 8962-8272 (home). *Fax:* (20) 8962-8243 (office). *E-mail:* dannythompson@paulcrockfordmanagement.com. *Website:* www.therealdannythompson.co.uk.

THOMPSON, Darrion Keith (Keifer); American country music singer, songwriter and musician (guitar); b. 17 March 1976, Miami, Okla; s. of Darien Thompson; m. Shawna Thompson 1999. *Career:* mem. Thompson Square (with wife Shawna Thompson) 2002–, signed to Stoney Creek Records 2010, released debut single Let's Fight 2010, opening act on Lady Antellebum tour 2012. *Recordings:* albums: Thompson Square 2011, Just Feels Good 2013. *Honours:* American Country Awards for Best Single by a Duo/Group, for Single by a Breakthrough Artist, for Music Video by a Duo/Group/Collaboration (all for Are You Gonna Kiss Me or Not) 2011, Acad. of Country Music Awards for Top Vocal Duo 2012, 2013, CMT Music Award for Duo Video of the Year (for I Got You) 2012, Country Music Assen Award for Vocal Duo of the Year 2012. *Address:* c/o Stoney Creek Records, 704 18th Avenue South, Nashville, TN 37203, USA (office). *Telephone:* (615) 244-8600 (office). *E-mail:* contactus@thompsonsquare.com. *Website:* www.thompsonsquare.com.

THOMPSON, Gail; British musician (saxophone, clarinet), composer and conductor; b. 15 June 1958, London, England; m. Tim May, 10 May 1994. *Career:* West End hit show Bubbling Brown Sugar 1977; music teacher, South East London Tech. Coll. 1977; Manageress, Macari's Music Shop, Charing Cross Road 1980; formed jazz funk band The Gail Thompson Approach, featured Camden Jazz Week 1980; f. Women In Music 1986; est. Sax Council tuition school; cr. Gail Force 1986; f. Jazz Warriors with Courtney Pine 1986; played regularly with Charlie Watts Big Band, Art Blakey's Jazz Messengers; f. Music Work Resource Centre, music school; joined Greater London Arts, Arts Council of Great Britain advisory panels 1987; travelled Africa, studying African music 1988; set up Frontline Productions to promote jazz music; MC, various major jazz festivals; Reggae Philharmonic Orchestra, on Highway, ITV 1990–91; vocalist, panelist, The Music Game Show, Channel 4 1992; Admin., National Music Day (with Harvey Goldsmith) 1992; freelance consultant, music schools, projects 1992; Chair. Arts Council Jazz Cttee; Founder and Chief Exec. Turnaround Project for music media and film for the disabled; Jazz Africa appearances at Berlin Jazz Festival; Chair. Arts Council Jazz Review; started Jazz in Women Festival 1997. *Television:* presented jazz programmes with Russell Davies, BBC 2 1978; Sang solo with Reggae Philharmonic Orchestra, Highway, ITV 1990–91. *Compositions include:* commissioned by BBC 2, composition for Midland Big Band featuring Courtney Pine, performed, televised, Royal Albert Hall; various compositions commissioned include: Royal Opera House Covent Garden, featuring Stan Tracey, Andy Sheppard 1989; Jazz Africa (suite) by Apples and Snakes 1991; TV themes for Carlton TV. *Recordings include:* albums: Gail Force Big Band, Jazz Africa Big Band 1996, Jadu 2001.

THOMPSON, Rev. John Alexander; American gospel singer, choir leader and songwriter; b. 15 Aug. 1942, Philadelphia, Pa. *Career:* Founder-mem. Sunlight Jubilee Juniors 1955, Johnny Thompson Singers 1965, Pennsylavania District F B H Choir 1970, Sanctification 1983; mem. Philadelphia Mass Choir and Gospel Music Preservation Alliance Choir; Johnny Thompson Singers, numerous tours, Europe and Africa, including first gospel act to play Montreux Festival, with Bessie Griffin 1972, first black gospel act to produce own video 1980, first gospel act behind the iron curtain, Poland 1981, first black American gospel act to play Russia, Bulgaria and Egypt; countless radio and TV broadcasts in Europe; performed with numerous gospel acts, including Marion Wlliams, Bessie Griffin, Dorothy Love-Coates, Rev. James Cleveland, Evangelist Shirley Caesar, Dorothy Norwood; gospel minister, Gospel Music Workshop of America; Choral Dir, Wynnefield Acad., Philadelphia; mem. Nat. Convention of Gospel Choirs and Choruses. *Plays:* Master I Want to Live 1965, The Judgement Bar 1973, The Capricorn King 1973, The Gospelers 1974, These are the Books of the Bible 1974, Little Dark Baby 1978, Virgil Jones 1979, Holiness by Choice 1992, Anointed to Sing the Gospel 1995. *Compositions include:* The Creation, Stranger On The Road, Get Up My Brother, If I Perish, Hold Out, Happy On My Way, There Must Be A Reason, If You Gonna Pray. *Recordings include:* albums: I'm His 1971, I'm On My Way 1972, I'm On My Way To Zion 1972, Little Willie Jr's Resurrection 1973, Look Over Your Shoulders 1974, A Gospel Gathering 1 1976, A Gospel Gathering 2 1976, God Be With Me 1976, Hour of Prayer 1976, I've Found a Refuge 1976, Precious Memories 1976, Gospelsongs Vol. 1 1977, It's Here Again Christmas Time 1977, Negro Spirituals 1977, Lord I Belong to You 1982, On the Battlefield 1982, Gospel At The Opera 1985, Who Shall Abide 1985, Glorious Feeling 1986, Gospel Christmas 1986, Silent Night 1986, Spirit of Gospel 1987, Swing Low, Sweet Chariot 1988, Gospel Christmas 1991, Gospel Feeling 1991, Wake Up Now 1994, Master I Want to Live 1995, Wake Up Now 1995, Gospel Stars 1997, Master I Want to Live 1998, The Soul of Gospel 1998, Rev. Johnny Thompson Presents 1999, Gospels Éternels 2002. *Honours:* Prix Mahalia Jackson, Philadelphia 1975. *Address:* c/o bAld & bOld Ltd, Obergass 3, 8260 Stein am Rhein, Switzerland (office). *Telephone:* (52) 7416688 (office). *Fax:* (52) 7416689 (office). *E-mail:* bald-bold@bald-bold.com (office). *Website:* www.johnnythompsonsingers.com.

THOMPSON, Keith; British blues and rock musician (electric and acoustic guitar, harmonica, piano, bass); b. 29 Jan. 1956, Worcester, Worcs., England; m. Janette Kathleen Thompson 1982; one s. two d. *Career:* solo artist; also Leader Keith Thompson Band; mem. Musicians' Union, Performing Right Soc., Mechanical-Copyright Protection Soc. *Television:* Road Dreams (Tortworth Television). *Recordings:* albums: Are You Ready 1981, Consuming Fire 1987, The Six Faces of Third Day 1987, The Ship 1989, Against the Odds 1989, From the Battle Place 1987, Young Hearts 1991, Voice From Heaven 1994, Reputation 1995, Strange Brew 1998, Face Up 1999, Out of the Smoke 2000, Independence 2006, Steel Strings and Bruised Reed 2009, Snapshot of Reality 2012, Catch the Fire 2015. *Honours:* Songwriter of the Year, Six Counties Festival 1990. *Address:* Libertus Road, Cheltenham, Glos., GL51 7EP, England (home). *E-mail:* info@densitymusic.com (office). *Website:* www.densitymusic.com (office).

THOMPSON, Linda; British singer and songwriter; b. (Linda Peters), London, England; m. 1st Richard Thompson (divorced); three c.; m. 2nd Steve Kenis. *Education:* Queen's Park Grammar School, Glasgow. *Career:* British tour as mem. of folk group Albion Band 1972; duo with Richard Thompson 1972–82; appearances include Reading Festival 1975, regular British tours; co-writer, appeared in The Mysteries 1975; solo artist 2000–. *Compositions include:* Telling Me Lies (with Betsy Cook, recorded by Emmylou Harris, Linda Ronstadt, Reba McEntire). *Recordings include:* albums: with Richard Thompson: Henry The Human Fly 1972, I Want To See The Bright Lights Tonight 1974, Hokey Pokey 1975, Pour Like Silver 1975, First Light 1978, Sunnyvista 1979, Shoot Out The Lights 1982; solo: One Clear Moment 1985, Give Me A Sad Song 2000, Fashionably Late 2002, Versatile Heart 2007, Won't Be Long Now 2013; contrib. to Guv'nor Vol. 3 (Ashley Hutchings) 1999, Mirror Man (David Thomas) 1999, Long Expectant Comes Last (Cathal McConnell) 1999. *E-mail:* info@2jakesmanagement.com. *Website:* www.2jakesmanagement.com. *Address:* 95 Barkston Gardens, London, SW5 0EU, England (home). *Telephone:* (20) 7370-6641 (home). *E-mail:* lkenis@attglobal.net. *Website:* www.lindathompsonmusic.com.

THOMPSON, Richard, OBE; British singer, songwriter and musician (guitar); b. 3 April 1949, London, England; m. Linda Peters (divorced). *Career:* Founder-mem. folk group, Fairport Convention 1968–71, reunion concert 1980; numerous concert performances; partnership with wife, Linda 1972–82; appeared in groups Albion Country Band, Hokey Pokey, Sour Grapes; solo artist 1982–; regular worldwide appearances. *Recordings include:* albums: with Fairport Convention: Fairport Convention 1968, What We Did On Our Holidays 1969, Unhalfbricking 1969, Liege and Lief 1970, Full House 1970; with Linda Thompson: I Want To See The Bright Lights Tonight 1974, Hokey Pokey 1975, Pour Like Silver 1975, First Light 1978, Sunnyvista 1979, Shoot Out The Lights 1982, Small Town Romance 1982; solo: Henry The Human Fly 1972, Guitar Vocal 1976, Strict Tempo 1981, Hand Of Kindness 1983, Across a Crowded Room 1985, Daring Adventures 1986, The Marksman (soundtrack to BBC drama series) 1987, Live, Love, Larf and Loaf 1987,

Amnesia 1988, Rumour and Sigh 1991, Sweet Talker 1992, Watching the Dark – The History of Richard Thompson 1993, You? Me? Us? 1996, Industry 1997, Mock Tudor 1999, Action Packed 2001, The Old Kit Bag 2003, Front Parlour Ballads 2005, Grizzly Man (OST) 2005, Sweet Warrior 2007, Walking on a Wire: 1968–2009 2009, Dream Attic 2010. *Honours:* New Music Award for Solo Artist, Songwriter of the Year, Life Achievement Trophy 1991, Q Award for Best Songwriter 1991, BBC Radio 2 Folk Awards lifetime achievement award 2006. *Current Management:* c/o Gary Stamler, Suite 2400, 1801 Century Park East, Los Angeles, CA 90067, USA. *Website:* www.richardthompson-music .com.

THOMPSON, Robert Scott; American engineer, producer, singer and musician (keyboards, guitar); b. 17 Feb. 1959, California; m. Debra Mobley. *Education:* Campbell College; University of Oregon; University of California; Compostion and Computer Music With Bernard Rands, Roger Reynolds, Joji Yuasa and F Richard Moore. *Recordings:* albums: Deeper In The Dreamtime 1991, The Strong Eye 1992, Ginnungagap 1993, Shadow Gazing 1994, Air Friction 1995, Elemental Folklore 1996, The Silent Shore 1996, Music for a Summer Evening 1998, Frontier 1998, Blue Day 2000, Forgotten Places (with James Johnson) 2001, At the Still Point of the Turning World 2005, Poesis Athesis 2008, Gold Flowers Bloom Mercury Petals 2009, as Fountainheat: Voice of Reason 1998, Drain 1997, Cloud Cover 1998. *Honours:* Bourges Electro Acoustic, 1984; Fulbright Scholar, 1991; Luiy Russolo, 1994; Irino Prize, 1996. *Address:* PO Box 2231, Roswell, GA 30075, USA. *Website:* www .robertscottthompson.com.

THOMPSON, Shawna; American country music singer and songwriter; b. (Shawna McIlwain), 25 Feb. 1978, Chatom, Ala; d. of the late George Michael McIlwain; m. Keifer Thompson 1999. *Education:* Fruitdale High School. *Career:* mem. Thompson Square (with husband Keifer Thompson) 2002–, signed to Stoney Creek Records 2010, released debut single Let's Fight 2010, opening act on Lady Antellebum tour 2012. *Recordings:* albums: Thompson Square 2011, Just Feels Good 2013. *Honours:* American Country Awards for Best Single by a Duo/Group, for Single by a Breakthrough Artist, for Music Video by a Duo/Group/Collaboration (all for Are You Gonna Kiss Me or Not) 2011, Acad. of Country Music Awards for Top Vocal Duo 2012, 2013, CMT Music Award for Duo Video of the Year (for I Got You) 2012, Country Music Asscn Award for Vocal Duo of the Year 2012. *Address:* c/o Stoney Creek Records, 704 18th Avenue South, Nashville, TN 37203, USA (office). *Telephone:* (615) 244-8600 (office). *E-mail:* contactus@thompsonsquare.com. *Website:* www.thompsonsquare.com.

THOMPSON, Teddy; British singer, musician (guitar) and songwriter; b. 1976, s. of Richard Thompson and Linda Thompson. *Career:* first recording singing backing vocals on his father's You? Me? Us? album 1996; support slot on subsequent promotional tour; solo artist 2000–. *Recordings include:* albums: Teddy Thompson 2000, Separate Ways 2005, Up Front and Down Low 2007, A Piece of What You Need 2008. *Current Management:* Morebarn Music, 628 Broadway, Suite 502, New York, NY 10012, USA. *E-mail:* gary@ morebarn.com. *Website:* www.morebarn.com; www.teddythompson.com.

THOMSON, Paul; British musician (percussion); b. Glasgow, Scotland; m. Esther Thomson. *Career:* fmr mem. Yummy Fur; mem. Franz Ferdinand 2001–. *Recordings include:* albums: Franz Ferdinand (Mercury Music Prize 2004, NME Award for Best Album 2005, Meteor Award for Best Int. Album 2005) 2004, You Could Have It So Much Better... With Franz Ferdinand 2005, Tonight: Franz Ferdinand 2009. *Honours:* BRIT Awards for Best British Group, Best British Rock Act 2005, Meteor Award for Best Int. Band 2005, NME Award for Best Live Band 2006. *Address:* c/o Domino Recording Company, PO Box 47039, London, SW18 1WD, England. *Website:* www .franzferdinand.co.uk.

THORDARSON, Gunnar; Icelandic composer, producer and arranger; *CEO, Arco;* b. 4 Jan. 1945, Holmavík; s. of Þórður Björnsson and Guðrún Guðbjörnsdóttir; m. Sigrun Toby Herman; two s. three d. *Education:* studied counterpoint. *Career:* record producer and writer 1966–; mem. Hljomar 1963–69, Trubrot 1969–73; record producer, more than 100 records; CEO Arco; has written hundreds of TV commercials, music for three Icelandic films and scores for three musicals; has composed two masses, one in Icelandic, the other in Latin; first opera, Ragnheidur, libretto by Fridrik Erlingsson, concert performance 2013; mem. Samband tónskálda og eigenda flutningsréttar, FIH, Iceland. *Compositions:* 670 songs as songwriter; songs recorded by various artists; work performed by Icelandic Symphony Orchestra; film music. *Recordings:* in own name: Gunnar Thordarson 1 1975, Himimm og jörð 1981, Islensk alpýðulög 1980, Reykjavikurflugur 1986, Í loftinu 1987, Borgarbragur 1986, Þitt Fyrsta 1994, bros 1994, Agnes 1996, Heilög messa (Mass) 2000, Brynjolfsmessa (Mass) 2002, Bæn (in French) 2006, Vetrarsól 2008. *Honours:* Order of the Falcon; Hon. Prize for Service in Icelandic Music 1997. *Address:* Aegisgata 10, Reykjavík 101, Iceland. *Telephone:* 5513032 (office); 8999932 (office). *E-mail:* arpa@centrum.is (office).

THORN, Tracey; British singer and songwriter; b. 26 Sept. 1962; m. Ben Watt 2009; three c. *Education:* Univ. of Hull. *Career:* mem. of trio Marine Girls 1980–83; Founder-mem. of duo Everything But The Girl 1983–2000; numerous live appearances, tours; also solo artist; worked with Massive Attack; numerous collaborations. *Recordings include:* albums: solo: A Distant Shore 1982, Out of the Woods 2007, Love and Its Opposite 2010, Tinsel and Lights 2012; with Marine Girls: Beach Party 1980, Lazy Ways 1983; with Everything But The Girl: Eden 1984, Love Not Money 1985, Baby, The Stars Shine Bright

1986, Idlewild 1988, The Language of Life 1990, Worldwide 1991, Amplified Heart 1994, Walking Wounded 1996, Temperamental 1999, Back To Mine (mix album) 2001. *Publication:* Bedsit Disco Queen: How I Grew Up and Tried to Be a Pop Star (autobiography) 2013. *Address:* c/o Strange Feeling Records, 31 Camden Lock Place, London, NW1 8AL, England (office). *E-mail:* lizzi@ buzzinfly.com (office). *Website:* www.traceythorn.com.

THORNTON, Julia; British musician (harp, percussion). *Education:* Royal Acad. of Music. *Career:* began playing harp at aged 11; mem. Nat. Youth Orchestra; solo artist; collaborated with Roxy Music 1999–; numerous tours and concerts; participated in tour As Time Goes By with Bryan Ferry; mem. band The Metaphors. *Recordings include:* albums: Harpistry 2003, Eye of the Storm 2004, The Bench Connection 2007, Breathe with Me 2008. *E-mail:* julia@juliathornton.net; heidi@zestproductions.com. *Website:* www .juliathornton.net; www.themetaphors.com.

THOROGOOD, George; American blues musician (guitar); b. 31 Dec. 1952, Wilmington, Delaware. *Career:* former baseball player; Formed own group the Destroyers, 1973–; opened for the Rolling Stones, 1981; appeared at Live Aid with Albert Collins, 1985. *Recordings:* albums: George Thorogood and The Destroyers 1978, Move It On Over 1978, Better Than The Rest 1979, More George Thorogood and The Destroyers 1980, Bad To The Bone 1982, Maverick 1985, Live 1986, Born To Be Bad 1988, Let's Work Together 1995, Rockin' My Life Away 1997, Half a Boy Half a Man 1999, Live In 1999, Anthology 2000, The Hard Stuff 2006, The Dirty Dozen 2009, 2120 South Michigan Avenue 2011. *E-mail:* gtandd@gthorogood.com. *Website:* www.georgethorogood.com.

THORUP, Jesper; Danish composer, singer and musician (drums); b. 9 June 1952, Copenhagen. *Education:* studied with Alex Riel, Hans Fülling, Ed Thigpen. *Career:* played with artists including Dana Gillespie, The Rustics, Mal Waldren Trio, Benny Waters, Peter Thorup and Jesper Band, Paul Millins, Sam Mitchel Blue Vikings, Dexter Gordon, Jackie McLean, Danish Radio Jazzgroup; mem. DMF, DJFBA. *Recordings include:* Annegrete: Hvem Sir, Duggen Falder: Drops Koernes Sang, Aorta: Havnerfunk. *Honours:* Dunquerque Int. Jazz Festival Prize for Best Soloist, France 1975.

THRALE, Carlos Heinrich, BA (Hons), MA (Ed); British/Swiss musician (guitar/bass), music teacher and examiner; b. 3 Aug. 1962, London, England. *Education:* Nottingham Trent Univ., Open Univ. *Career:* session guitarist for artists including Queen, Pet Shop Boys, Kate Bush, Dr Egg, Iron Maiden; teacher and guitar examiner in further/higher educ.; External Examiner, London Coll. of Music, Univ. of West London, Registry of Guitar Teachers (also consultant); freelance musician and recording artist. *Films:* Guitar Theory and Technique (video) 1985, Working As A Session Musician 1998; DVDs: Funk Guitar 2003, Session Musician Training 2008, Carlos & Edd's Guitar Workout 2013. *Publication:* How To Teach Guitar 2010; contrib. to Guitar Coach Magazine 2013–. *Telephone:* (1636) 830282 (office). *E-mail:* info@carlosthrale.com (home). *Website:* www.carlosthrale.com (office).

THREADGILL, Henry Luther, BM; American composer, musician (saxophone, clarinet, percussion) and teacher; b. 15 Feb. 1944, Chicago, Ill. *Education:* Wilson Jr Coll., American Conservatory of Music. *Career:* served in US Army c. 1968–69; mem. Muhal Richard Abrams' Experimental Band; Founder-mem. Air 1971–82; Founder-mem. Henry Threadgill Sextet 1982–91; Founder-mem. Very Very Circus 1992–; music instructor and choral dir Brooklyn Acad. of Music from mid-1960s; mem. Asscn for the Advancement of Creative Musicians. *Compositions include:* Be Ever Out 1976, Keep Right on Playing thru the Mirror over the Water 1977, No. 2 1977, Subtraction 1977, Abra 1978, Let's All Go Down to the Footwash 1978, Open Air Suite 1978, Suisse Air 1978, Air Song 1979, Celebrations 1979, Paille Street 1979, Sir Simpleton 1979, C.T., J.L. 1980, Dance of the Beast 1982, Do Tell 1982, 80 Below '82 1982, Great Body of the Riddle (Where Were the Dodge Boys When My Clay Started to Slide) 1982, The Traveller 1982, Unrealistic Love 1982, Untitled Tango 1982, Cover 1983, Cremation 1983, Difda Dance 1983, Gateway 1983, Just the Facts and Pass the Bucket 1983, No. 1 1983, Tragedy on a Thursday Afternoon 1983, Air Raid 1984, Midnight Sun 1984, Release 1984, Roll On 1984, Through a Keyhole Darkly 1984, Homeostasis 1985, Just Trinity the Man 1985, A Piece of Software 1985, This 1985, Achtud El Buod (Children's Song) 1986, Air Show 1986, Apricots On Their Wings 1986, Bermuda Blues 1986, Don't Drink That Corner My Life is in the Bush 1986, Good Times 1986, Salute to the Enema Bandit 1986, Side Step 1986, Silver and Gold Baby, Silver and Gold 1986, Theme from Thomas Cole 1986, Those Who Eat Cookies 1986, To Be Announced 1986, Award the Squadrett 1987, Black Hands Bejeweled 1987, Dancin' with a Monkey 1987, The Devil Is on the Loose and Dancin' with a Monkey 1987, Gift 1987, Hall 1987, Let Me Look Down Your Throat and Say Ah 1987, My Rock 1987, Off The Rag 1987, Spotted Dick Is Pudding 1987, Sweet Holy Rag 1987, Background 1989, Background quartet for saxophones 1989, Bee Dee Aff 1990, Drivin' You Slow and Crazy 1990, Exacto 1990, First Church of This 1990, Hope a Hope a 1990, In the Ring 1990, Breach of Protocol 1991, Dangerously Slippy 1991, I Love You with an Asterisk 1991, King Kong 1991, Next 1991, Snakes Don't Do Suicide 1991, Better Wrapped/Better Unrapped 1992, In Touch 1992, Little Pocket Size Demons 1992, Paper Toilet 1992, Too Much Sugar 1992, Try Some Ammonia 1992, Mix for Orchestra 1992, Crea 1993, Grief 1993, Over the River Club 1993, Song Out of My Trees 1993, Come Carry the Day 1994, Growing a Big Banana 1994, Hyla Crucifer... Silence Of 1994, Jenkins Boys Again, Wish Somebody Die, It's Hot 1994, Vivjanrondirkskij 1994, Between Orchid Lilies Blind Eyes and Cricket 1994, Dirty in the Right Places 1995, Like It Feels

1995, Make Hot and Give 1995, The Mockingbird Sin 1995, Noisy Flowers 1995, Official Silence 1995, Refined Poverty 1995, And This 1997, Feels Like It 1997, The Flew 1997, Go to Far 1997, Laughing Club 1997, One Hundred Year Old Game 1997, Where's Your Cup? 1997. *Recording includes:* albums: solo: X-75 Volume 1 1979, Makin' a Move 1995, Where's Your Cup 1996, Up Popped The Two Lips 2001, Everybody's A Book 2001, Up Popped the Two Lips 2001, Pop Start the Tape, Stop 2005, This Brings Us To 2009; with Air: Air Song 1975, Live Air 1976, Air Raid 1976, Air Time 1977, Open Air Suite 1978, Live At Montreux 1978 1978, Air Lore 1979, Air Mail 1980, 80 Degrees Below '82 1982, New Air: Live at the Montreux International Jazz Festival 1983, Air Show No. 1 1987; with The Henry Threadgill Sextet: When Was That? 1982, Facts 1983, Just The Facts And Pass The Bucket 1983, Subject To Change 1984, You Know The Number 1986, Easily Slip Into Another World 1987, Rag, Bush And All 1988; with Very Very Circus: Spirit of Nuff... Nuff 1990, Live at Koncepts 1991, Too Much Sugar For A Dime 1993, Carry The Day 1995; with Billy Bang and Craig Harris: Hip Hop Be Bop 1993; with Make A Move: Where's Your Cup 1996; with David Murray: Ming 1980, Home 1981, Murray's Steps 1982; Vietnam Reflections (with Billy Bang) 1996; Absolute Quintet (with Dafnis Prieto) 2006. *Honours:* Down Beat Magazine Readers Poll Award for Best Composer 1988, 1989, Int. Jazz Critics Poll Award for Best Composer 1988–91, Critics Poll Award for Best Composer 1995. *E-mail:* info@pirecordings.com (office). *Website:* pirecordings.com (office).

3-D; British singer; b. (Robert del Naja), 21 Jan. 1965, Brighton, England. *Career:* Founder mem., Massive Attack 1987–; collaborations with Shara Nelson, Tricky, Horace Andy, Madonna, Tracey Thorn (Everything But The Girl), Liz Fraser (Cocteau Twins), Damon Albarn (Blur). *Recordings include:* albums: with Massive Attack: Blue Lines 1991, Protection 1994, No Protection: Massive Attack vs Mad Professor 1995, Mezzanine 1998, 100th Window 2003, Danny the Dog 2004, Collected 2006, Heligoland 2010; solo: Bullet Boy (EP, soundtrack) 2005. *Honours:* BRIT Award for Best British Dance Act 1996, Ivor Novello Award for Outstanding Contrib. to British Music 2009. *Website:* www.massiveattack.com.

THROCKMORTON, James Fron (Sonny); American songwriter and musician (bass guitar); b. 2 April 1941, Carlsbad, Calif. *Career:* country music songwriter; worked for small record co. 1961–62; played bass for Carl and Pearl Butler 1964–66; signed to Capitol, Mercury, MCA, Warner Bros; songs recorded by George Burns, Johnny Duncan, Emmylou Harris, Alan Jackson, Millie Jackson, the Judds, Jerry Lee Lewis, George Strait; mem. Nashville Songwriters Assen. *Compositions include:* I Feel Like Loving You Again, I Had a Lovely Time, Thinking Of A Rendezvous, I'm Knee Deep In Loving You, If We're Not Back In Love By Monday, Middle Age Crazy, When Can We Do This Again, Smooth Sailing, Fadin' In Fadin' Out, Lovin' You Lovin' Me, I Wish You Could Have Turned My Head (and Left My Heart Alone), I Wish I Was Eighteen Again, Last Cheater's Waltz, It's A Cheatin' Situation, The Way I Am, Trying To Love Two Women, Friday Night Blues, Why Not Me, Where The Cowboy Rides Away, She Can't Say That Anymore, Stand Up, Made for Loving You. *Recordings include:* albums: The Last Cheater's Waltz 1978, Southern Train 1986, Ten Number Ones 1986. *Honours:* Nashville Songwriters Assen Songwriter of the Year 1978, 1979, 1980, BMI Songwriter of the Year (jtly) 1980.

THUNDERBITCH (see Kelis)

THURSDAY CLUB (see Pilgrem, Rennie)

T.I. (see Harris, Clifford Joseph)

TICALLION STALLION (see Method Man)

TICKELL, Kathryn Derran, OBE; British musician (northumbrian pipes, fiddle) and composer; b. 8 June 1967, England. *Career:* plays traditional folk material from the North-East of England and composes own tunes; began playing Northumbrian smallpipes aged nine; recorded The Long Tradition TV documentary 1987; performed on the Sting hit Fields of Gold; performed and recorded with Jimmy Nail; composed, performed and recorded Music For A New Crossing with saxophonist Andy Sheppard (commissioned for the opening of the Gateshead Millennium Bridge); broadcast live on the Last Night of the Proms 2001; Founder The Young Musicians Fund; Lecturer on Folk and Traditional Music degree course, Newcastle Univ. *Recordings:* albums: On Kielderside 1984, Borderlands 1986, Common Ground 1988, The Kathryn Tickell Band 1991, Signs 1993, The Gathering 1997, The Northumberland Collection 1998, Debateable Lands 1999, Kathryn Tickell and Ensemble Mystical 2000, Music For A New Crossing 2001, Back To The Hills 2002, Air Dancing 2004, Kathryn Tickell & Corrina Hewat, The Sky Don't Fall 2006, Strange But True 2006, Instrumental 2007, Durham Concerto (with Jon Lord) 2008, What We Do (with Peter Tickell) 2008, Northumbrian Voices 2012. *Honours:* Musician of the Year, BBC Radio 2 Folk Awards 2005, 2013, Queen's Medal for Music 2009. *Current Management:* c/o Karen McWilliams, PO Box 130, Morpeth, Northumberland, NE65 7WD, England. *E-mail:* info@kathryntickell.com. *Website:* www.kathryntickell.com.

TIELENS, Louis, (Country Lewis); Belgian broadcaster and DJ; b. 2 Aug. 1942, Beringen; m. Germa Baelen 1984; one s. one d. *Education:* coll. *Career:* DJ as 'Country Lewis'; fmr man., Radio Animo, Station Man., Radio Loksbergen; Prod., syndicated country music programmes, De Bazuin non-profit organisation; with wife, producer, gospel programme Good News. *Address:* Botermijnstraat 6, Bus 1, 3580 Beringen, Belgium (home).

TIERS, Wharton, BA; American producer, musician (drums, keyboards, guitar), songwriter and engineer; b. 11 Feb. 1953, Philadelphia, PA. *Education:* Villanova Univ., Pennsylvania. *Career:* producer, engineer, indie records 1980s–90s; over 120 records produced; mem., Laurie Anderson's Band, Glenn Branca's Band; played with Theatrical Girls, Glorious Strangers; producer for artists, including Sonic Youth, Dinosaur, Jr, Gumball, Biohazard, Helmet, Teenage Fanclub, Prong, Cop Shoot Cop, Pussy Galore; founded The Kennel Studio, Brooklyn, NY 2008–. *Recordings include:* albums: Brighter Than Life 1996, Twilight of the Computer Age 1999, I, Rasputin 2000, Freedom Incorporated 2005. *E-mail:* wharton@thekennelstudio. *Website:* www.whartontiers.com.

TIERSEN, Yann; French composer and musician (multi-instrumentalist); b. 23 June 1970, Brest. *Education:* Rennes Conservatoire. *Career:* composed incidental music for plays and films before recording first album; collaborated with Françoiz Breut, Lisa Germano, Neil Hannon, The Married Monk, Noir Désir, Claire Pichet. *Compositions for film:* scores to Le Dernier bip 1998, Les Grandes batailles de monsieur le Maire (TV) 1998, La Vie rêvée des anges 1998, Alice et Martin (songs) 1998, Qui plume la lune..? (songs) 1999, Le Cyclope de la mer 1999, Notre besoin de consolation... 2001, Trois huit 2001, Le Fabuleux destin d'Amélie Poulain 2000, Primitifs 2002, Le Poteau rose 2002, Good Bye Lenin! 2003, Tabarly 2008. *Recordings include:* albums: La Valse Des Monstres 1995, Rue Des Cascades 1997, Le Phare 1998, Tout Est Calme 1999, Black Session 1999, L'Absente 2001, C'Etait Ici 2003, Les Retrouvailles 2005, Dust Lane 2010, Skyline 2011. *Address:* c/o Mute, 1 Albion Place, London, W6 0QT, England (office). *E-mail:* info@yanntiersen.com (office). *Website:* www.yanntiersen.com.

TIËSTO; Dutch musician, DJ and producer; b. (Tijs Michiel Verwest), 17 Jan. 1969, Breda, North Brabant. *Career:* performing since 1985; worldwide tours, including opening ceremony of Athens Olympics 2004 and festivals such as Coachella; remixed artists including The Killers, Yeah Yeah Yeahs, Bloc Party; co-f. Black Hole Recordings with Arny Bink. *Tours:* Area2 Tour 2002, Just Be: Train Tour 2004, Tiësto In Concert: North America Tour 2005, Central Eastern European Tour 2005, In Search of Sunrise 5 Asia Tour 2006, Elements of Life World Tour 2007–08, In Search of Sunrise: Summer Tour 2008, Kaleidoscope World Tour 2009–10, College Invasion Tour 2011. *Recordings include:* albums: In My Memory 2001, Just Be 2004, Elements of Life 2007, In Search of Sunrise 7 2008, Kaleidoscope 2009, Kiss From The Past (as Allure) 2011. *Honours:* numerous nat. and int. dance music awards. *E-mail:* mgmt@controlny.com. *E-mail:* tiesto@controlny.com. *Website:* www.tiesto.com.

TIFFANY; American singer; b. (Tiffany Renee Darwish), 2 Oct. 1971; m. Bulmaro Garcia 1992; one s. *Career:* solo artist 1986–; numerous tours, TV and radio broadcasts. *Films include:* voice of Judy Jetson, The Jetsons Movie 1990. *Recordings include:* albums: Tiffany 1987, Hold An Old Friend's Hand 1988, New Inside 1990, Dreams Never Die 1993, All The Best 1995, The Color Of Silence 2000, Dust Off And Dance 2005, Just Me 2007, Rose Tattoo 2011. *Current Management:* c/o Charlie Davis, Paradise Artists Inc., PO Box 1821, Ojai, CA 93024-1821, USA. *Telephone:* (805) 646-8433. *Fax:* (805) 646-3367. *E-mail:* charlie@paradiseartists.com. *Website:* www.tiffanymusicsite.com.

TIGA; Canadian DJ and producer; b. (Tiga James Sontag), 1974, Montreal. *Education:* Selwyn House School. *Career:* involved in promoting rave parties and clubs in Montreal during early 1990s; opened DNA Records store 1994; set up own record label Turbo Recordings 1998; works with Mateo Murphy as TGV; other collaborations with Jesper Dahlbäck, Jori Hulkkonen, Richard X, Jake Shears, Soulwax; has remixed tracks for many leading artists. *Recordings include:* albums: DJ-Kicks (DJ mix) 2002, INTHEMIX.05 (DJ mix) 2005, Sexor 2006, Ciao! 2009; singles include: Sunglasses at Night (as Tiga & Zyntherius, with Jori Hulkkonen) 2001, TGV EP (as TGV) 2002, Running out of Time EP (as TGV) 2003, Hot in Herre (with Mateo Murphy and Jake Shears) 2003, Burning Down (with Richard X) 2003, Pleasure from the Bass (with Jesper Dahlbäck) 2004, Louder than a Bomb (with Jesper Dahlbäck) 2005, You Gonna Want Me (with Soulwax and Jake Shears) 2005, Good as Gold (with Soulwax) 2005, Far From Home 2006, 3 Weeks 2006, Move My Body 2006, Lower State of Consciousness (with Zombie Nation) 2007, The Worm (with Zombie Nation) 2008, Beep Beep Beep 2009, Hands Up 2010, Partys Over Los Angeles (with Zombie Nation) 2011, Plush 2013; other: remixes for artists including Bran Van 3000, Depeche Mode, Dannii Minogue, Scissor Sisters, Peaches, Felix Da Housecat, Cabaret Voltaire, Soulwax, LCD Soundsystem, FC Kahuna, Télépopmusik, Märtini Brös, The Killers, Pet Shop Boys, Moby, Mylo; DJ mix compilations: Montreal Mix Sessions Vol. 1 1998, American Gogolo 2001, Inthemix.05 2005, Tiga: Non Stop 2012. *Radio:* My Name is Tiga (BBC Radio 6). *Current Management:* c/o Nerve Artist Management, 1st Floor, 24 Denmark Street, London, WC2H 8NJ, England. *E-mail:* info@nervemanagement.com. *Website:* www.tiga.ca.

TIGER, Flower; Chinese composer; b. 29 Sept. 1934, Baojing County, Hunan Province; m. Zhang Xiangming, 20 Oct. 1968, 2 s. *Education:* Minzu Normal School, Jishou City, studied under Professor of Music Liu Tianlin, Shanghai Conservatory, studied with He Luding, Sha Hankun, Liu Zhuang, Deng Erjing. *Career:* mem. Chinese Musicians' Assen; Vice-President, China Minorities Music Soc. *Compositions include:* Beautiful Peacock, Please Fly Back Soon, The Charming Moonlight of Tujia Home Villages; many other ethnic minority folk songs. *Recordings include:* Hunting in Wuling Mountains, Grand Chorus in Praise of National Unity, Wind and Percussion

Concerto, Miao Music Dance, Polyphonic Piano Suite for Chinese Folk Songs, The Drum of Blood. *Publications include:* Beacon Fire in Miao Borders 1988, A New Song Anthology of National Art 1990. *Honours:* Nat. Music Prize 1983, 1988.

TIGGER (see LYONS, Ken)

TIJOUX, Ana; French/Chilean musician and rapper; b. (Anamaría Merino Tijoux), 12 June 1977, Lille, France. *Career:* raised in Paris and Chile; f. own group Los Gemelos 1995; mem. group Los Tetas 1997; MC for hip hop group Makiza 1997–2006; solo career 2006–; collaborated with Barrio Santo, Julieta Venegas, Jorge Drexler. *Recordings:* albums: with Makiza: Vida Salvaje 1997, Aerolineas Makiza 1999, Casino Royale 2005; solo: Kaos 2007, 1977 2009, La Bala 2011, Vengo 2014. *Honours:* Latin Grammy Award for Record of the Year (for Universos Paralelos, with Jorge Drexler) 2014. *Address:* c/o Nacional Records, 10627 Burbank Boulevard, North Hollywood, CA 91601, USA (office). *Telephone:* (818) 763-1397 (office). *Fax:* (818) 763-1398 (office). *Website:* www .nacionalrecords.com (office).

TIJSSENS, Michael Warren, (Mike Sens), MA; Dutch lyricist, screenwriter, playwright and literary translator; b. 27 March 1961, Amersfoort, The Netherlands; m. Dyna Justin 1987; two s. *Education:* Royal Acad. of Dramatic Art, UK, Univ. of Paris (Sorbonne), France. *Career:* numerous roles as actor, singer, writer, director, dramatist and producer; writing for artists in music business; has worked with Bob Geldof, Rick Smith, Karl Hyde, Lou Reed, Tom Waits; mem. Soc. des auteurs, compositeurs et éditeurs de musique, Soc. des Auteurs et Compositeurs Dramatiques. *Plays:* La Trilogie Manticore, Le Pont Tournant de la Rue Dieu, Rushes Instables. *Film:* Dialogues 'Flowers of Evil' by David Dusa. *Recordings:* Tropical Corridor, Blanc Nègre, Destination Tomorrow. *Publications include:* L'Arche, Les Solitaires Intempestifs, Théâtrales, Lansman, Actes Sud, Alna Editeur. *Honours:* Prix d'Honneur, Institut Radiodiffusion Suisse. *Address:* 13 boulevard de la Marne, 77420 Champs-Sur-Marne, France (office). *Telephone:* 1-64-68-43-29 (office). *E-mail:* miketijssens@yahoo.com (home).

TIKARAM, Tanita; German singer, songwriter and musician (guitar); b. 12 Aug. 1969, Münster, Germany. *Career:* moved to UK 1982; numerous collaborations; numerous stage performances. *Recordings include:* albums: Ancient Heart 1988, The Sweet Keeper 1990, Everybody's Angel 1991, Eleven Kinds of Loneliness 1992, Lovers In The City 1995, The Cappuccino Songs 1998, Sentimental 2005, Best Good Tradition 2008, Can't Go Back 2012. *Current Management:* c/o Sarah Pearson, Wasted Youth PR, 53 Corsica Street, London, N5 IJT, England. *E-mail:* sarah@wastedyouthpr.com. *Website:* www.wastedyouthpr.com; www.tanita-tikaram.com.

TIKHONOV, Dimitri; Russian/French musician (keyboards), singer and composer; b. 6 Aug. 1964, Vladivostok, Russia; m. Juliette Alix 1994; one s. *Education:* Jazz School, St Petersburg. *Career:* composer, lead singer and keyboard player Nom 1987–94; tours of Europe; solo career as composer and bass player Geneva Opera Choir 1995–. *Recordings include:* albums: Brutto 1989, To Hell With It 1990, Senka – Mosgaz 1992, Live is Game 1995, In the Name of Mind 1995, Les Sons De Carton (solo) 1997, Some Original Melodies 1998, Jban D (film soundtrack) 2000, What a Wonderful Liver 2000. *Honours:* Skotinorap, Best Alternative Video of Russia 1993, Nina-2, Grand Prix Exotica 1994, Ukr Blues, Best Low Budget Video 1996. *Address:* 9 rue Mont-Blanc, 74100 Ville-La-Grand, France (home). *Telephone:* 4-50-38-23-31 (home).

TIKU, Archis; British musician (bass guitar); b. 6 May 1977, Bombay (now Mumbai), India. *Education:* Bolton School, Univ. of Newcastle. *Career:* raised in Wigan, England; founder-mem. Maxïmo Park 2001–. *Recordings include:* albums: A Certain Trigger 2005, Our Earthly Pleasures 2007, Quicken the Heart 2009, The National Health 2012, Too Much Information 2014. *Current Management:* Prolifica Management, Unit 1, 32 Caxton Road, London, W12 8AJ, England. *Telephone:* (20) 8740-9920. *Fax:* (20) 8740-2976. *E-mail:* info@ prolifica.co.uk. *Website:* www.prolificamanagement.co.uk; www.maximopark .com.

TILBROOK, Glenn; British singer, musician (guitar) and songwriter; b. 31 Aug. 1957, London, England. *Career:* writing partnership with Chris Difford 1973–; Founder-mem. Squeeze 1974–98, 2007–; numerous tours, festival appearances; solo artist 2000–; Founder-mem. The Fluffers 2008–; owns recording studio 35 RPM. *Compositions include:* From a Whisper to a Scream (with Elvis Costello) 1981, Labelled with Love (songs for musical) 1983. *Recordings include:* albums: with Squeeze: Squeeze 1978, Cool For Cats 1979, Argy Bargy 1980, East Side Story 1981, Sweets From A Stranger 1982, Cosi Fan Tutti Frutti 1985, Babylon And On 1987, Frank 1989, A Round And A Bout 1990, Play 1991, Some Fantastic Place 1993, Ridiculous 1995, Domino 1998, Live At Royal Albert Hall 1999, Essential Squeeze 2007, Spot the Difference 2010; with Chris Difford: Difford and Tilbrook 1984; solo: The Incomplete Glenn Tilbrook 2001, The Completely Acoustic Glenn Tilbrook 2001, Transatlantic Ping Pong 2004; with The Fluffers: Pandemonium Ensues 2009. *Current Management:* c/o Suzanne Hunt, Stress Management, PO Box 27947, London, SE7 8WN, England. *Telephone:* (20) 8269-0352. *Fax:* (20) 8269-0353. *E-mail:* suzanne@quixoticrecords.com. *Website:* www .squeezeofficial.com; www.glenntilbrook.com.

TILBURY, John; British musician (piano); b. 1 Feb. 1936, London, England; one s. two d. *Education:* Royal College of Music, and privately with James Gibb; Warsaw Conservatory with Zbigniew Drzewecki. *Recordings:* Cage:

Sonatas And Interludes; Feldman: Complete Solo Piano Music; Skempton: Solo Piano Music; Christian Wolff: Early Piano Music; Cornelius Cardew: Early Piano Music; Many recordings as member of AMM Free Improvisation group including: Tunes Without Measure Or End, 2001.

TILLIS, Frederick C., PhD; American composer, musician (trumpet, saxophone) and teacher; b. 5 Jan. 1930, Galveston, Tex. *Education:* Wiley Coll., Univ. of Iowa, Univ. of North Texas. *Career:* military service, Webb Air Force Base, Big Springs, Tex. 1952–56; began composing 1948; saxophonist, Tradewinds Jazz Ensemble, touring from 1982; made appearances with Billy Taylor Trio 1985–; formed Tillis-Holmes Jazz Duo 1985; recorded with Billy Taylor Trio 1992; instructor and dir, Wiley Coll. 1949–51, Asst Prof. and Dir of Instrumental Music 1956–61, Assoc. Prof. and Chair Music Dept 1963–64; Prof. of Music, Head of Music Theory Dept, Grambling Coll. 1964–67; Prof. and Head of Music Dept, Kentucky State Univ. 1967–70; Assoc. Prof. Music Dept, Univ. of Mass at Amherst 1970–73, Prof. of Music Theory and Composition, Dir Afro-American Music and Jazz Programme 1973–97, Dir, UMass Jazz Workshop 1974–80, Assoc. Provost, Faculty Relations, Special Asst to Provost for the Arts, Assoc. Vice-Chancellor for Faculty 1974–90, Dir, Univ. Fine Arts Center 1978–97, Dir Emeritus 1998–, Assoc. Chancellor for Equal Opportunity and Diversity 1990–97; mem. Bd of Trustees, Springfield Symphony 1997–; mem.-elect Mass Cultural Council 1997–; Chair., Nat. Music Foundation Educ. Advisory Cttee 1998–; mem., Center for Black Music Research Assocs., TransAfrica Forum, American Music Center, American Composers Alliance, BMI, Music Educators Nat. Conference, Int. Asscn of Jazz Educators, Mass Music Educators Asscn, American Fed. of Musicians, United Negro Coll. Fund. *Compositions include:* Passacaglia for brass quintet 1950, Quartet for flute, clarinet, bassoon and cello 1952, Concert Piece for clarinet and piano 1955, Capriccio for viola and piano 1960, Militant Mood for brass sextet 1961, String Trio 1961, Quintet for four woodwinds and percussion 1962, Quintet for brass 1962, Phantasy for viola and piano 1962, Passacaglia for organ in baroque style 1962, Three Chorale Settings for organ in baroque style 1962, Motions for trombone and piano 1964, Three Movements for piano 1964, Music for alto flute, cello and piano 1966, Three Showpieces for viola 1966, Music for an Experimental Lab: Ensemble No. 1 1967, Music for tape recorder No. 1 1968, Freedom 1968, Poems for piano 1970, Music for an Experimental Lab: Ensemble No. 3 1970, Music for violin, cello and piano 1972, Blue Stone Differencia for jazz ensemble 1972, Music for Recorders 1972, Reflections 1973, The Blue Express for jazz ensemble 1973, Niger Symphony 1975, Autumn Concerto for trumpet 1979, Spiritual Fantasy No. 2 for double bass 1980, Spiritual Fantasy No. 3 for piano four hands 1981, Spiritual Fantasy No. 4 for piano 1981, Spiritual Fantasy No. 5 for French horn 1982, Elegy for jazz orchestra 1983, Spiritual Fantasy No. 7 for cello 1984, In Memory Of 1984, In the Spirit and the Flesh 1985, Fantasy on a Scheme by J. S. Bach for saxophone 1987, Spiritual Fantasy No. 12: Suite for string quartet 1988, Inauguration Overture 1988, Spiritual Fantasy No. 13 for harp 1989, The Time Has Come 1989, Voices and Colors for jazz ensemble 1989, Fantasy on a Chopin Prelude for saxophone 1990, Fantasy on a Volga Boat Song for saxophone 1990, Images of the Blue Earth 1990, Kabuki Scenes 1991, Holiday Waltz for saxophone 1991, Spiritual Fantasy No. 16: Death's Cold Icy Hands On Me for saxophone 1991, Trilogy for saxophone 1991, Ai-Midori for jazz ensemble 1991, A Festival Journey 1992, The Best Times 1993, The Rain Forest 1993, In Celebration 1993, Walking Wind 1993, A Latin Fringe 1994, A Wintering for jazz ensemble 1994, Spiritual Fantasy No. 17: Were You There?/Mary Don't You Weep 1994, Little David 1995, Bolero 1995, Play On Your Flute Little Mary 1995, Poem for Orchestra Nos. 1–4 1996, Celebration: Grand March 1996. *Publications:* Jazz Theory and Improvisation: A Manual of Keyboard, Instrumental (or vocal), and Aural Practice 1977. *Honours:* United Negro Coll. Fund Fellowship 1961–62, 1962–63, Danforth Associateship 1969, Rockefeller Foundation grant for composition 1978, NEA composer's grant 1979, DeWitt Wallace-Reader's Digest Fellow 1993, Int. Asscn of Jazz Educators Outstanding Service Award 1994, Mass Cultural Council Commonwealth Award in Organizational Leadership 1997, Black Musicians' Conference Distinguished Achievement Award, Amherst 1998. *Website:* www.fredericktillis.com.

TILLIS, (Lonnie) Melvin (Mel); American country singer, songwriter and musician (guitar, fiddle); b. 8 Aug. 1932, Tampa, Fla. *Education:* Univ. of Florida. *Career:* began performing, recording 1956–57; has toured extensively with The Statesiders 1960s–; numerous tours and TV appearances; recorded duets with Glen Campbell and Nancy Sinatra; owned several publishing companies; also cattle breeder. *Films include:* WW and The Dixie Dance Kings, Smokey and The Bandit 2, Murder in Music City, Uphill All the Way. *Compositions include:* I'm Tired, Tupelo County Jail, I Ain't Never (all hits for Webb Pierce), Lonely Island Pearl, Johnny and Jack; Heart Over Mind, Ray Price; Ten Thousand Drums, Carl Smith; Detroit City (co-written with Danny Dill) Bobby Bare 1963; The Snakes Crawl At Night, Charley Pride 1966; Ruby Don't Take Your Love To Town, Johnny Darrell 1967 (Also hit for Kenny Rogers and The First Edition 1969). *Recordings include:* albums include: Heart Over Mind 1961, Stateside 1966, Mr Mel 1967, One More Time 1970, Mel Tillis 1972, Sawmill 1973, M-M-Mel and The Statesiders 1975, Are You Sincere 1979, The Great Mel Tillis 1979, Southern Rain 1980, M-M-Mel Live 1980, It's A Long Way To Daytona 1982, After All This Time 1983, New Patches 1984, California Road 1985, Four Legends (with Jerry Lee Lewis, Webb Pierce, Faron Young) 1985, Branson City Limits (live) 1999, You Ain't Gonna Believe This 2010, Brand New Mister Me, I Believe in You, M-M-Mel Live, Wings of My Victory, The Father's Son, Snowflake; also recorded with:

Glen Campbell, Nancy Sinatra, Sherry Bryce. *Publications include:* Stutterin' Boy, The Autobiography of Mel Tillis (with Walter Wager). *Honours:* inducted into Nashville Songwriters Int. Hall of Fame 1976, CMA Entertainer of the Year 1976. *Address:* Mel Tillis Enterprises, POB 305, Silver Springs, FL 34489, USA (office). *E-mail:* mmel@meltillis.com (office). *Website:* www .meltillis.com.

TILLIS, Pamela (Pam) Yvonne; American country singer, musician (guitar, piano), songwriter and actress; b. 24 July 1957, Plant City, Fla; m. Bob DiPiero. *Education:* Univ. of Tennessee; studied classical piano. *Career:* member of group Billy Hill; debut appearance with father, country vocalist Mel Tillis and family on stage of the Grand Ole Opry singing Tom Dooley, aged 8; performed solo at Nashville's Exit/In during teens; at 16, car crash shattered face in 30 places requiring five years of surgery; formed first band High Country Swing Band at univ., also appearing in duo with Ashley Cleveland; worked for father's publishing company, Sawgrass Music; left for San Francisco, formed the Pam Tillis Band; returned to Nashville singing backing vocals in father's band 1978; solo artist 1979–. *Television:* LA Law 1986, Hot Country Nights 1991, Diagnosis Murder 1993, The Thing Called Love 1993, XXXs and OOOs 1994, The Best of Country 1995, Promised Land 1996. *Compositions include:* Cleopatra – Queen of Denial, Spilled Perfume, Mi Vida Loca, Put Yourself In My Place, Someone Else's Trouble Now. *Recordings include:* albums include: Put Yourself In My Place 1991, Sweetheart's Dance 1994, Greatest Hits 1997, Thunder and Roses 2001, It's All Relative 2002, Rhinestoned 2007, Just in Time for Christmas 2007, Recollection 2012, Dos Divas 2013. *Honours:* CMA Female Vocalist of the Year 1994. *E-mail:* info@ pamtillis.com (office). *Website:* www.pamtillis.com.

TILLOTSON, Paul, AAS, BMus; American musician (piano) and composer; b. 18 Dec. 1964, Boise, Ida. *Education:* Edmonds Community Coll., Univ. of Miami, William Patterson Univ. of New Jersey. *Career:* perfomed at North Sea Jazz Festival, Montreux Jazz Festival, Gene Harris Jazz Festival; mem. Local 802, Sun Valley Lodge, Sun Valley, Ida. *Radio:* FM Radio KSKI, Pandora. *Compositions:* Simple Pleasures, Tulips, Big Valley, Tidbits, Tebadadeda, Loungin' @ The Evelyn, Chartreuse, Seltzer, Centipede, Morphine, Charlotte's Blues, Janie's Song. *Recordings:* The Paul Tillotson Trio: Tulips, Live At The Lock, Tidbits, Sweet Mystery, Tasty Morsels, Drinkin' Wine With Pauli, Duck Callin' Man, Funky Good Time, The New York City Connection, Tequila Time, Lindy Hop Blues. *Address:* PO Box 3201, Ketchum, ID 83340, USA (home). *Telephone:* (208) 928-6554 (office). *E-mail:* paul@paultillotson.com (office). *Website:* www.paultillotson.com (home).

TILSTON, Stephen (Steve) Thomas Gregory; British musician (guitar), singer and songwriter; b. 26 March 1950, Liverpool; s. of Thomas James Tilston and Bettine Spence; m. 1st Maggie Boyle 1984; one s. three d.; m. 2nd Margaret Robson 2004. *Education:* trained as graphic artist. *Career:* solo artist; also duo with Maggie Boyle; mem. Ship of Fools (with John Renbourn); guitarist, Ballet Rambert; mem. British Longbow Soc. *Recordings include:* albums: Acoustic Confusion 1971, Collection 1973, Songs From The Dress Rehearsal 1977, In For A Penny 1983, Life By Misadventure 1987, Swans At Goole 1990, Of Moor and Mesa 1992, And So It Goes 1995, All Under The Sun 1996, Solorubato 1998, The Greening Wind 1999, Of Many Hands 2005, Reaching Back 2007, Ziggurat 2009, Ghosts from the Basement (with Wizz Jones and Dave Evans) 2010, The Oxenhope (with the Durbervilles) 2012. *Honours:* Songwriter of the Year Award, BBC Radio 2 2012. *Current Management:* c/o Lorraine Carpenter, Different Strings. *Telephone:* (117) 904-1870; 7929 135744 (mobile). *E-mail:* lorraine@differentstrings.co.uk. *Website:* www.differentstrings.co.uk. *Address:* c/o Hubris Records, PO Box 100, Hebden Bridge, W Yorks., HX7 9AB, England. *E-mail:* mail@steve-tilston .co.uk (office). *Website:* www.steve-tilston.com.

TIMATI; Russian rapper, singer, songwriter, record producer and entrepreneur and actor; b. (Timur Ildarovich Yunusov), 15 Aug. 1983, Moscow; s. of Ildar Yunusov and Simona Yunusova (née Chervomorskaya). *Education:* State Univ. – Higher School of Econs. *Career:* came to prominence on TV show Star Factory 4; fmr mem. Banda; CEO of own record label Black Star Inc.; numerous collaborations including with Snoop Dogg, Blue Marine, Wolffman, DJ Antoine, Kalenna, P. Diddy, Dirty Money, La La Land Timbaland, Grooya, Craig David; featured performer on tracks by Sergey Lazarev, DJ Smash, Evii, DJ M.E.G., Jean-Roch, Nick Mccord, Mario Winans, Detsi, Fat Joe, Busta Rhymes. *Films:* as actor: Countdown 2004, Heat 2006, Albania! 2008, Monday Twist 2008. *Recordings include:* albums: Black Star 2006, The Boss (MUZ-TV Award for Best Album 2010) 2009, SWAGG 2012. *Honours:* MUZ-TV Award for Best Hip-Hop Artist 2010. *E-mail:* info@levelamanagement .com. *Website:* www.levelamanagement.com; www.black-star.ru; www .timatimusic.com.

TIMBALAND; American hip-hop and R&B producer, remixer and songwriter; b. (Timothy Z. Mosley), 10 March 1971, Norfolk, Va. *Career:* f. Beat Club record label; mem. of hip-hop group Timbaland & Magoo; production credits include Destiny's Child, Jay-Z, Usher, The Lox; collaborations with Missy Elliott, Aaliyah, Ginuwine, Magoo, Bubba Sparxx, Justin Timberlake, Nelly Furtado. *Recordings include:* albums: as Timbaland & Magoo: Welcome to Our World 1997, Indecent Proposal 2001, Under Construction Part II 2003, Timbaland & Magoo Present: Greatest Hits 2004; solo: Tim's Bio: Life from da Bassment 1998, Shock Value 2007, Shock Value II 2009, Textbook Timbo 2014. *Website:* www.timbalandmusic.com.

TIMBERLAKE, Justin Randall; American singer, songwriter and actor; b. 31 Jan. 1981, Memphis, Tenn.; m. Jessica Biel 2012; one s. *Career:* started vocal training aged eight; guest appearance at Grand Ole Opry 1991; early TV appearances include Star Search 1992, The Mickey Mouse Club 1993–94; mem. *NSYNC vocal quintet 1995–, first headline US tour 1998; also solo artist 2002–; f. Justin Timberlake Foundation, a charity to fund music and art programmes in schools; founder, Chair. and CEO Tennman Records 2007–. *Film appearances:* Longshot 2000, On the Line 2001, Edison 2005, Alpha Dog 2006, Southland Tales 2006, Black Snake Moan 2006, Shrek the Third (voice) 2007, The Open Road 2009, The Social Network 2010, Bad Teacher 2011, Friends with Benefits 2011, In Time 2011, Trouble with the Curve 2012, Runner, Runner 2013, Inside Llewyn Davis 2013. *Recordings include:* albums: with *NSYNC: *NSYNC 1998, Home For The Holidays 1998, The Winter Album 1998, No Strings Attached 2000, Celebrity 2001; solo: Justified (Grammy Award for Best Pop Vocal Album, BRIT Award for Best Int. Album 2004) 2002, FutureSex/LoveSounds (American Music Award for Favorite Soul/R&B Album 2007) 2006, The 20/20 Experience (American Music Award for Favorite Soul/R&B Album 2013, Billboard Music Awards for Top Billboard 200 Album 2014, for Top R&B Album 2014) 2013, The 20/20 Experience 2 of 2 2013. *Publication:* Justin Timberlake (autobiography) 2004. *Honours:* American Music Awards for Favorite Pop/Rock Band, Duo or Group 2002, for Favorite Pop/Rock Male Artist 2007, 2013, for Favorite Soul/R&B Male Artist 2013, MOBO Award for Best R&B Act 2003, MTV Award for Best Pop Video (for Cry Me A River) 2003, BRIT Award for Best Int. Male Solo Artist 2004, 2007, Grammy Awards for Best Male Pop Vocal Performance (for Cry Me A River) 2004, (for What Goes Around...Comes Around) 2008, for Best Dance Recording (for Sexy Back) 2007, (for LoveStoned/I Think She Knows) 2008, for Best Rap/Sung Collaboration (with T.I.) 2007, (for Holy Grail, with Jay-Z) 2014, for Best R&B Song (for Pusher Love Girl) 2014, MTV Europe Music Award for Best Male Artist, for Best Pop Act 2006, Meteor Ireland Music Award for Best Int. Male Artist 2007, MTV Video Music Award for Best Male Artist 2007, for Best Video (for Mirrors) 2013, MTV Video Music Michael Jackson Video Vanguard Award 2013, Billboard Music Awards for Top Artist 2014, Top Male Artist 2014, for Top Billboard 200 Artist 2014, for Top Radio Songs Artist 2014, for Top R&B Artist 2014. *Current Management:* Wright Entertainment Group, PO Box 590009, Orlando, FL 32859-0009, USA. *Website:* www.justintimberlake.com; www.nsync.com.

TIMMINS, Margo; Canadian singer and songwriter; b. 1961, Montréal, QC. *Career:* fmr social worker; mem., The Cowboy Junkies 1985–; formed independent label, Lament 1986–88, 1998–. *Recordings include:* albums: Whites Off Earth Now! 1986, The Trinity Session 1988, The Caution Horses 1989, Black Eyed Man 1992, Pale Sun, Crescent Moon 1993, 200 More Miles 1996, Studio: Selected Studio Recordings 1996, Lay It Down 1996, Miles From Our Home 1998, Waltz Across America 2000, Open 2001, Radio Sessions 2002, Open Road 2002, In The Time Before Llamas 2003, One Soul Now 2004, Early 21st Century Blues 2005, At the End of Paths Taken 2007, Renmin Park 2010. *Address:* c/o Cooking Vinyl, PO Box 1845, London, W3 0ZA, England (office). *E-mail:* junkieinfo@aol.com (office). *Website:* www.cowboyjunkies.com (home).

TIMMINS, Michael; Canadian songwriter and musician (guitar); b. 21 April 1959. *Career:* mem. Hunger Project 1979; mem. Germinal 1984; Founder-mem. Cowboy Junkies 1985–; formed independent label Lament 1986–88, 1998–; has composed and written numerous songs for films. *Recordings include:* albums: Whites Off Earth Now! 1986, The Trinity Session 1988, The Caution Horses 1989, Black Eyed Man 1992, Pale Sun, Crescent Moon 1993, 200 More Miles 1996, Studio: Selected Studio Recordings 1996, Lay It Down 1996, Miles From Our Home 1998, Waltz Across America 2000, Open 2001, Radio Sessions 2002, Open Road 2002, In The Time Before Llamas 2003, One Soul Now 2004, Early 21st Century Blues 2005, At the End of Paths Taken 2007, Renmin Park 2010, Demons 2011, Sing in My Meadow 2011, The Wilderness 2012, The Kennedy Suite 2013. *Address:* c/o Cooking Vinyl, PO Box 1845, London, W3 0ZA, England (office). *E-mail:* junkieinfo@aol.com (office). *Website:* www.cowboyjunkies.com.

TIMMINS, Peter; Canadian musician (drums); b. 29 Oct. 1965. *Career:* mem. Cowboy Junkies 1985–; formed ind. label Lament 1986–88, 1998–. *Recordings include:* albums: Whites Off Earth Now! 1986, The Trinity Session 1988, The Caution Horses 1989, Black Eyed Man 1992, Pale Sun, Crescent Moon 1993, 200 More Miles 1996, Studio: Selected Studio Recordings 1996, Lay It Down 1996, Miles From Our Home 1998, Waltz Across America 2000, Open 2001, Radio Sessions 2002, Open Road 2002, In The Time Before Llamas 2003, One Soul Now 2004, Early 21st Century Blues 2005, At the End of Paths Taken 2007, Renmin Park 2010, Demons 2011, Sing in My Meadow 2011, The Wilderness 2012, The Kennedy Suite 2013. *Address:* c/o Cooking Vinyl, PO Box 1845, London, W3 0ZA, England (office). *E-mail:* junkieinfo@aol.com (office). *Website:* www.cowboyjunkies.com; www.latentrecordings.com/ cowboyjunkies.

TINETA; Canadian singer, songwriter and musician (guitar, piano, drums); b. (Tineta Michelle Couturier), 24 Aug. 1972, Red Deer, Alberta. *Career:* solo artist 1989–; support act for Steve Wariner, Pam Tillis; major concerts: Grand Ole Opry, Big Valley Jamboree, Craven, Saskatchewan, Big Valley Jamboree, Camrose, Alberta; mem. CCMA, SOCAN, CMN, CARAS, ARIA. *Compositions include:* Slippin Away, Love On The Line, Let's Make Up, It's Rainin', Too Bad So Sad, Walkin' That Line, That's What Love's About. *Recordings include:* albums: Love On The Line, Drawn To The Fire.

TINIE TEMPAH; British rapper and songwriter; b. (Patrick Chukwuemeka Okogwu), 7 Nov. 1988, Plumstead, London. *Education:* St Paul's Catholic School, Abbey Wood, St Francis Xavier Sixth Form Coll., Clapham. *Career:* collaborated with Ultra and Agent X 2007; Co-founder Disturbing London ind. record label; signed to Parlophone Records 2009; toured with Chipmunk 2010; performed with Snoop Dogg 2010 at Glastonbury Festival; supported Rihanna on UK tour 2010; first solo tour of UK in 2010; numerous collaborations including with Tinchy Stryder, Kelly Rowland, Ellie Goulding. *Recordings include:* albums: Disc-Overy 2010, Demonstration 2013. *Honours:* MOBO Awards for Best Newcomer and Best Video 2010, for Best UK Hip Hop/Grime Act 2011, 2013, MP3 Music UGG Award 2010, Urban Music Awards for Best Newcomer, Best Hip Hop Act and Best Collaboration 2010, BT Digital Music Award for Best Newcomer 2010, UK Festival Award for Breakthrough Artist 2010, BRIT Awards for Best Breakthrough Act and Best Single 2011, Ivor Novello Award for Best Contemporary Song 2011, BET Award for Best International Act UK 2011. *Address:* Disturbing London Records, Unit 4, Waterhouse, 8 Orsman Road, London, N1 5QJ (office); c/o Parlophone Records, Warner Music Group, 28 Kensington Church Street, London, W8 4EP, England (office). *Website:* www.disturbinglondon.com (office); www .parlophone.co.uk (office); www.tinietempah.com.

TINSLEY, Boyd Calvin; American musician (violin); b. 16 May 1964. *Education:* Walker Middle School, Charlottesville and Univ. of Virginia. *Career:* part-time model, including work for JanSport, Tommy Hilfiger, Gucci; as teenager helped found the Charlottesville-Albermarle Youth Orchestra; formed duo Down Boy Down 1987, expanded group and changed name to The Boyd Tinsley Band; mem., Dave Matthews Band 1992–; numerous tours and live appearances world-wide; first album released on group's own Bama Rags label. *Recordings:* albums: Remember Two Things 1993, Under The Table And Dreaming 1994, Crash 1996, Live At Red Rocks 8.15.95 1997, Before These Crowded Streets 1998, Listener Supported (live) 1999, Everyday 2001, Live In Chicago 12.19.98 2001, Busted Stuff 2002, Live At Folsom Field, Boulder, Colorado 2002, Central Park Concert 2003, Live Trax, Vol. 1–12 2004–08, The Gorge 2004, Stand Up 2005, Big Whiskey and the GrooGrux King 2009, Away from the World 2012. *Honours:* Grammy Awards for Best Rock Performance by a Duo or Group with Vocal 1997, VH-1 Awards for Favorite Group, Must Have Album, Song of the Year 2001. *E-mail:* fanmail@davematthewsband .com (office). *Website:* www.davematthewsband.com; www.boydtinsley.com.

TIPLER, Paul; British record producer and engineer. *Career:* worked with artists as producer, co-producer: Stereolab, TransGlobal Underground, Pop Will Eat Itself, Loop Guru, Mambo Taxi, Voodoo Queens; as engineer: Kingmaker, Miranda Sex Garden, Julian Cope, Elastica, Stereolab, Trans-Global Underground, Vibrators, Dr Feelgood, Jah Wobble, New Fast Automatic Daffodils.

TISHMA; Bangladeshi singer, songwriter and musician (guitar, keyboards); b. (Tasbiha Binte Shahid Tishma), 20 Jan. 1990, Dhaka. *Recordings include:* albums: Tara 2002, Chand 2003, Shurjo 2004, Baula Prem 2005, Sham Rakhi Na Kul Rakhi 2006, Mair Putul 2006, Cholonar Daba 2007, Xperiment 2011. *E-mail:* Princesstishma@yahoo.com. *Website:* www.tishmaonline.com.

TISO, Wagner; Brazilian musician (piano, keyboards), composer, arranger, conductor and music director; b. 12 Dec. 1945, Tres Pontas, Minas Gerais; m. Giselle de Andrade Goldoni; two d. *Career:* numerous concerts and festival appearances include Montreux Jazz Festival with Flora Purim, Airto Moreira and Ron Carter 1974, 1982, Festival de Música Latina, Cuba 1983, Paris 1986, Festival de Música Brasileira, Rome 1984, and jazz festivals in São Paulo, Berlin, Montmartre and Rio de Janiero; mem. AMAR, OMB. *Stage appearances:* soloist, Rhapsody in Blue 1997, Encontro de Violoncellos 1997. *Film soundtracks:* O Guarani (Norma Bengell) 1995, A Ostra e o Vento (Walter Lima Jr) 1997. *Television soundtracks:* Meu Marido (Walter Lima Jr, TV Globo), O Sorriso do Lagarto (Roberto Talma, TV Globo). *Compositions include:* Coraçao de Estudante (for film Jango), Chorata suite for piano and orchestra, Lenda Ao Boto, Choro de Mae, Cafezais Sem Fim, Suite Tom Jobim 1995, Cenas Brasileiras 1995. *Recordings include:* Wagner Tiso 1978, Wagner Tiso Ao Vivo na Europa 1982, Giselle 1986, A Floresta Amazônica (Villa Lobos) 1987, Cine Brasil (original soundtracks) 1989, Baobab 1990, O Livro de Jó 1993, Wagner Tiso Ao Vivo (with Rio Cello Ensemble) 1995, Brazilian Scenes 1997, Crooner 1999, Millennium 1999, Tocar a Poética do Som 2003, Samba and Jazz 2005, Ensaio 2008. *Honours:* Award for Best Arranger (for Sentinela, Milton Nascimento) 1981, Award for Best Instrumental Recording (for Todas as Teclas, with Cesar Camargo Mariano) 1983, Awards for Best Soundtrack (for Jango) 1984, (for Chico Rei) 1987. *Address:* Rua Cesário Alvim 55/107 Bla, Humaitá, 22261-030 Rio de Janeiro, Brazil. *Telephone:* (21) 25398493. *Fax:* (21) 22868836. *Website:* www.wagnertiso.com.br.

TISSENDIER, Claude; French musician (saxophone, clarinet); b. 1 Oct. 1952, Toulouse. *Education:* six years at conservatoire. *Career:* played at all major jazz festivals in France; mem. Claude Bolling Band for 38 years; leader, own band Saxomania for 12 years. *Recordings:* Benny Carter 1988, Spike Robinson 1991, Phil Woods 1991, Guy Lafitte 1993, Marlene Verplanck 1994, Clark Terry 1995, Teddy Edwards 2002; 20 albums with Claude Bolling 1978–2001, Paris Swings 2001. *Honours:* Sidney Bechet Prize 1987, Best Jazz Recording Prize 1986, 1988, Bill Coleman Prize 1989, Django d'Or 1996. *Address:* 9 rue des Grimettes, 92190 Meudon, France (office). *Telephone:* 1-45-07-81-64 (office). *E-mail:* claudetissendier@yahoo.fr (home).

TITELMAN, Russ; American record company executive and record producer; b. 16 Aug. 1944, Los Angeles, California; m. Carol Wikarska 1978. *Career:* Vice-President, A & R Department, and record producer, Warner Brothers Records, New York 1971–. *Recordings include:* as producer: with Randy Newman: Sail Away 1972, Good Old Boys 1974, Little Criminals 1977; with Ry Cooder: Paradise and Lunch 1973; with James Taylor: Gorilla 1975, In The Pocket 1976; with Rickie Lee Jones: Rickie Lee Jones 1979, Pirates 1981; with Paul Simon: Hearts and Bones 1983, with George Benson: 20/20 1985; with Steve Winwood: Back In The High Life 1986, Higher Love 1986; with Miriam Makeba: Sangoma 1988; with Eric Clapton: Journeyman 1989; Monkees, Anthology 1998, Love Shouldn't Hurt 1998, Very Best of Meatloaf 1998, Clapton Chronicles 1999; also featured on recordings by: Rufus and Chaka Khan, Ladysmith Black Mambazo, Little Feat, George Harrison, B-52s, Brian Wilson. *Honours:* numerous Grammy Awards (with Rickie Lee Jones, Rufus and Chaka Khan, Steve Winwood, Eric Clapton).

TITIYO; Swedish singer; b. (Titiyo Jah), *Recordings include:* albums: Titiyo 1991, This Is Titiyo 1993, Extended 1998, Come Along 2002, Best of Titiyo 2004, Hidden 2008, Tough Love 2010. *Honours:* Grammy Award for Newcomer of the Year 1989, for Best Female Pop/Rock Artist 1990, for Best Female Pop/Rock Artist 1997, for Song of the Year (Come Along) 2001. *E-mail:* per@autonomanagement.se. *Website:* www.autonomanagement.se; www .titiyo.com.

TIWARI, Ankit; Indian playback singer, composer and musical director; b. 6 March 1986, Kanpur, Uttar Pradesh; s. of R.K. Tiwari and Suman Tiwari. *Career:* composer of background music and jingles for television 2008–10; made singing debut in theme song to film Saheb Biwi Aur Gangster 2011. *Films include:* as music director or composer: Do Dooni Chaar 2011, Sai Ki Tasveer 2011, Saheb Biwi Aur Gangster 2012, Aashiqui 2 (Filmfare Award for Best Music Director 2014, Global Indian Music Acad. Award for Best Music Debut 2014, Int. Indian Film Acad. Award for Best Music Director 2014, Mirchi Music Awards for Upcoming Male Vocalist of the Year, Upcoming Music Composer of the Year, Best Song, Album of the Year 2014, Zee Cine Award for Best Music Director 2014) 2013, Samrat & Co. 2014, Ek Villain (Apsara Film and Television Producers Guild Award for Best Music Director 2014, for Best Male Playback Singer 2014, BIG Star Entertainment Award for Most Entertaining Male Singer 2014, Filmfare Award for Best Male Playback Singer 2014, Global Indian Music Acad. Award for Best Film Song 2015, Stardust Award for Best Male Playback Singer 2015, all for song Galliyan, also Mirchi Music Award for Album of the Year 2015, Screen Award for Best Music Director 2015) 2014, Singham Returns 2014, PK 2014, Alone 2015, Khamoshiyan 2015, Roy 2015, Mr X 2015, Airlift 2015, Rocky Handsome 2015, Yaara Silly Silly 2015; as singer: Issaq 2013, Dee Saturday Night 2014, Kaanchi... 2014, Purani Jeans 2014, The Xposé 2014, Action Jackson 2014, Badmashiyaan 2015, Ishqedarriyaan 2015, Tanu Weds Manu Returns 2015, All is Well 2015, Bhaag Johnny 2015. *Current Management:* c/o Brotherhood Entertainment Pvt Limited, Morya Landmark 1, Andheri, Mumbai, 400 053, India. *Telephone:* 9833482091 (mobile); 9967981178 (mobile). *E-mail:* beplofficial@gmail.com. *Website:* www.ankittiwari.com (home).

TOBIN, Karen; American singer, songwriter, musician (guitar) and producer; b. Drexel Hill, Pa; m. Tim Boyle (divorced); two d. *Education:* Bryn Mawr Conservatory of Music. *Career:* mem. American Fed. of TV and Radio Artists, Screen Actors Guild, CMA. *Recordings include:* album: Carolina Smokey Man 1991, Karen Tobin & Crazy Hearts, That's What You Get 2003. *Address:* 12345 Ventura Blvd, Suite A, Studio City, CA 91604, USA (home). *E-mail:* karentobin@worldnet.att.net (home); karentobinmusic@gmail.com. *Website:* www.karentobinmusic.com.

TOCANNE, Bruno; French jazz musician (drums) and bandleader; b. 19 March 1955, Paris; two s. *Career:* played in trio with Sophia Domancich and Paul Rogers, tour of Europa and Canada with Michel Saulnier and Jean Vanasse; f. Bruno Tocanne Réunion with Laurent Dehors, Malo Vallois, Daniel Casimir, Patrick Fradet 1990; f. Polysons collective with Jean-Rémy Guédon, Serge Adam 1993; played with Résistances trio with Lionel Martin, Benoît Keller 2001–; f. imuZZic network 2003; f. new dreams nOw! trio 2007; performed at festivals throughout Europe; also played with Laurent Cugny, Serge Lazarevitch, Jean Philippe Viret, Michel Bénita, Serge Adam, Manuel Villaroel, Philippe Sellam, Michel Saulnier, Pierre Tiboum Guignon, Antoine Hervé, Renaud Garcia-Fons, Denis Badault, Emmanuel Bex, Philippe Laccarrière, Franck Tortiller, Laurent Dehors, Catherine Delaunay, Francesco Bearzatti, Régis Huby, Xavier Garcia, Hasse Poulsen, John Greaves, Louis Sclavis, Alain Blesing, Rémi Gaudillat, Dave Burell, Itaru Oki, Yuri Kusnetsov, Vladimir Volkoff, Quinsin Nachoff, Tom Walsh, Jean Méreu, Guy Villerd, Jean Bolcato, Nacim Brahimi, Takayuki Kato, Nobuyoshi Ino, John Greaves, Quinsin Nachoff. *Recordings:* played on albums including: Hors Série 1989, Funerals 1991, Odessa 1993, Tocade(s) 2000, Résistances 2002, Global Songs 2004, Etats d'urgence 2006, new dreams nOw! 2007, Passeur de Temps 2007, 5 New Dreams 2008. *Address:* Le Bourg, 69640 Montmelas Saint Sorlin, France (home). *Telephone:* 4-74-67-31-20 (home); 9-54-70-28-39 (office). *E-mail:* btocanne@free.fr (home); laffiche@imuzzic.net (office). *Website:* www .brunotocanne.com; www.imuzzic.net.

TOD, A.; American singer and musician (bass); b. (Tod Ashley), New York, NY. *Career:* singer, Cop Shoot Cop 1988–96; founder mem., Firewater 1995–; several international tours and festival appearances. *Recordings include:* albums: with Cop Shoot Cop: Consumer Revolt 1990, White Noise 1991, Ask

Questions Later 1993, Release 1994; with Firewater: Get Off the Cross, We Need the Wood for the Fire 1996, The Ponzi Scheme 1998, Psychopharmacology 2001, The Man on the Burning Tightrope 2003, Songs We Should Have Written 2004, The Golden Hour 2008. *Website:* www.copshootcop.com.

TODOROV, Dimo; Bulgarian musician (guitar). *Career:* mem. Konkurent 1986–; numerous concerts, TV and radio appearances, Bulgaria. *Recordings include:* Konkurent 1989, Something Wet 1995, Escape from Paradise 2002, Give me Time 2007. *Honours:* Top Rock Band, Youth Festival Vidin 1989, Rock Ring, Sofia 1990, Top Rock Composition: The Cavalry 1991, Top Rock Singer, Bulgaria 1994, Group of the Year, The Darik Radio Countdown 1994. *E-mail:* emil.anchev@abv.bg (office). *Website:* www.konkurentrockband.com.

TOIVANEN, Pekka, M.Mus; Finnish musician (tenor saxophone); *Lecturer, Music Theory, Savonia University of Applied Sciences;* b. 1961. *Education:* Sibelius Acad. *Career:* played piano from age 10, clarinet from age 12; concerts with Kulttis Big Band, Brushane Big Band; joined Jazz Dept, Sibelius Acad., Helsinki 1983; formed own quartet 1987; performed with numerous groups including Espoo Big Band 1988–92, Uuden Musiikin Orkesteri 1990–92, Oiling Boiling Rhythm And Blues Band; currently Lecturer, Music Theory, Savonia Univ. of Applied Sciences; co- leader, experimental group Analemma Orchestra, Pekka Toivanen-Wade Mikkola Quintet; saxophonist, R & B band Zekosto. *Compositions include:* She Didn't Like the Wallpaper 1994; works for big bands include Breakfast, commissioned by UMO 1990, Kantelettaren parhaat 2000, Arctic Brambles 2006. *Honours:* winner, Finnish Jazz Fed. band competition 1987. *E-mail:* contact@pekkatoivanen.com (home). *Website:* www.pekkatoivanen.com.

TOLHURST, Laurence (Lol); British musician (drums, keyboards); b. 3 Feb. 1959, Horley, Sussex; m. Cindy Levinson; one c. *Career:* Founder-mem., drummer, Easy Cure (with Robert Smith and Michael Dempsey) while at school 1976, band changed name to The Cure, moved from drums to keyboards 1982–88; numerous world tours with The Cure; mem., Presence 1992–93; Founder-mem. Levinhurst (with wife, Cindy) 1999–. *Recordings:* albums: with The Cure: Three Imaginary Boys 1979, Seventeen Seconds 1980, Faith 1981, Pornography 1982, The Top 1984, Concert 1984, The Head On The Door 1985, Staring At The Sea 1986, Kiss Me, Kiss Me, Kiss Me 1987; with Presence: Inside 1993; with Levinhurst: Perfect Life 2004. *Honours:* BRIT Award for Best British Band 1992. *Current Management:* c/o Lynn Hasty, Green Galactic, 1680 N Vine Street, Suite 211, Los Angeles, CA 90028, USA. *Telephone:* (323) 466-5141. *E-mail:* lynn@greengalactic.com. *Website:* www .greengalactic.com; www.levinhurst.com.

TOLJA, Davor; Croatian singer, musician (keyboards), songwriter and arranger; b. 31 May 1957, Rijeka. *Education:* Rijeka Univ. *Career:* fmr keyboard player, Vrijeme Zemlja; fmr leader, author, player, singer, Denis and Denis; solo singer, composer, arranger, musician, producer; owner, recording studio; mem. Croatian Music Union. *Compositions include:* Probudi Me (sung by ENI) 1997. *Recordings include:* albums: with Vrijeme I Zemlja: Vrijeme I Zemlja 1979; with Denis and Denis: Cuvaj Se (Rock music magazine Best Pop Album of the Year) 1984, Ja Sam Lazljiva 1985, Budi Tu 1988, The Best Of Denis & Denis 2006, 2 na 1 2010; solo: Stari Macak 1990.

TOLLIVER, Charles; American musician (trumpet) and composer; b. 6 March 1942, Jacksonville, Fla. *Education:* Howard Univ. *Career:* began professional career with saxophone player Jackie Mclean, mid-1960's; formed quartet Music Inc. 1969; has performed in concerts and festivals worldwide; numerous recordings and performances with leading jazz musicians including Roy Haynes, Horace Silver, McCoy Tyner, Sonny Rollins, Booker Ervin, Gerald Wilson Orchestra, Oliver Nelson, Roy Ayers, Art Blakey and the Jazz Messengers, Max Roach; Co-founder, with Stanley Cowell, Strata East Records 1971; currently performs with Charles Tolliver Big Band, appearances include London Jazz Festival 2007. *Recordings include:* solo albums: The Ringer 1969, Music Inc. and Big Band 1971, Impact 1975, Paper Man 1975, Live in Berlin Vols 1 and 2, Live at Loosdrecht Festival, Live in Tokyo, Compassion, Live at Historic Slugs Vols 1 and 2, With Love 2007, Emperor March 2009; with Jackie Mclean: It's Time 1964, Action 1964, Jacknife 1965; with Booker Ervin,: Structurally Sound 1966, Booker and Brass 1967; Gerald Wilson Orchestra, Live and Swinging, Roy Ayers, Virgo Vibes, Stoned Soul Picnic, Red, Black & Green, Gary Bartz, Another Earth, Horace Silver, Serenade to a Soul Sister, Max Roach, Members Don't Git Weary, McCoy Tyner, Song For My Lady, Doug Carn, Sprit of the New Land, Oliver Nelson, Swiss Suite; with Andrew Hill: One for One, Dance With Death, Time Lines. *Honours:* Downbeat Critics Choice 1968. *E-mail:* muffco@serecs.com. *Website:* www.serecs.com; www.charlestolliver.com.

TOLLY, Maria, BA; British composer, writer and singer; b. (Maryrose Warren), 10 Feb. 1933, Islington, London, England; d. of John Crisp Warren and Mary Margaret Warren (née Crick); m. Valeriano Rocca 1958 (divorced 1980); three s. one d. *Education:* Dartington Coll., Univ. of Birmingham, Morley Coll., Music Tech. Dept, City Lit, London. *Career:* flamenco guitarist with various groups 1970s; toured Mauritius with Rae Woodland, John Lawrenson, Paul Ferris 1977; lead singer, Ballet Rambert's Cruel Garden (Christopher Bruce, Lindsay Kemp) 1979, 1980; composer/singer/guitarist/ songwriter, Broadside Theatre Co., Banner Theatre 1983–89; singer, songwriter, guitarist, tours Belgium, Netherlands, USSR, Germany, Cuba, Yugoslavia, Italy, Czechoslovakia 1985–90; performer, composer, Compact Theatre 1990–92; performer, composer, electro-acoustic concerts 1992–95; festivals in London and Sheffield 1993–97; composed electro-acoustic music for new ballet, Women Unbound, performed by Conundrum Dance Co., premiered at The Place, followed by tour of the UK 1997; songwriter, Musical Dir for Banner Theatre's production Redemption Song, premiered in Birmingham followed by tour of the UK 1997; Musical Dir, Telling Tales production Rise and Run, followed by tour of the UK 1998; performed own songs at Central Hall Westminster and Hackney Empire, with dance interpretations by Lisa Grivello and Suzette Rocca; Oral History Recordings commissioned by Hounslow Council for Museum on London Waterways; Musical Dir, Bonner Theatre 2002–; received a grant from Unltd to compose and record the music for a school dance-drama project 2003; commissioned by Enfield Council to compose and record music based on Macbeth for schools to be used throughout London schools 2004; composed and recorded music for Crash Landing; composed music for Sea-Story (funded by Enfield Community Chest); composed music for nine six-week projects used in schools in North London 2000–09; composed Book-Rap, performed by children in Enfield for the opening of a new library; involved with a team making a documentary about the Women's Irish Centre in the 1980s; writing short stories and memoirs; mem. Equity, Writers' Guild of GB. *Plays:* Billy (actor, Play for Today, BBC 2) 1979, Cargo (writer, The London New Play Festival). *Compositions:* for dance: Women Unbound, for Conundrum Dance Co. (premiered at The Place, London); also music for dance drama classes to be used in schools – nine projects under the umbrella of Dancing Stories. *Recordings:* albums: Gonna Get Up, Voices, Up To Here, touring dance-drama: About Time 1991, touring musical play: Mrs Columbus Speaks Out 1992, play: Cargo 1999, albums of music composed for school projects: My Day, Delightful Differences, Aquababy, Sea Story, Crash Landing, I'm Alive, Rainbow Rucksack, Georgie's Journey, Segments, Jo's Yard, Georgie's Journey, Our Park. *Publications:* article in Women Live, issue in syllabus of Women's Studies 1989; chapter on songwriting, Taking Reality By Surprise, Women's Press Ltd 1990, Dancing Stories 2010. *Honours:* winner GLC Songwriting Competition, Victor Jara Song Competition 1983, winner of competition for opening of Innova Science Park 1998, Millennium Award to compose music for 3 to 5 year-olds in schools 2001, Senior Award of the Year, NIACE. *E-mail:* tollyhouse@blueyonder.co.uk (home). *Website:* www .dancingstories.co.uk; www.mariatolly.co.uk.

TOLONEN, Jukka Jorma; Finnish musician (guitar, piano) and composer; b. 16 April 1952, Helsinki; m. Liisa-Elina 1992; three s. one d. *Education:* Sibelius Acad. *Career:* mem. Tasavallan Presidentti 1967–74; formed Jukka Tolonen Band 1976; also worked with Bill's Boogie Band (with Bill Öhström), Piirpauke, Christian Sievert and Gilberto Moreira; several concert tours, festival appearances, TV broadcasts; mem. Musicians Union (Sweden). *Recordings include:* albums: Tolonen 1974, Hysterica 1974, Crossection 1976, Impressions 1977, High Flyin 1979, Mountain Stream 1980, In a This Year Time 1981, Big Time 1997, JTB 2005, Last Mohican 1995, A Passenger to Paramaribo 2007, The Hook 2007, Tolonen! 2007, Summer Games 2007, Juudan Leijona 2011, Blaboly 2012. *Honours:* Finnish Jazz Fed. Yrjö Award 1972. *E-mail:* deniz.bedretdin@akbazar.fi (office). *Website:* www.jukkatolonen .com; www.curmusic.com.

TOLOUCHE, Radik; Russian (Tuvan) singer. *Career:* fmr mem. various rock and folk collectives; mem. folk singing quartet Huun-Huur-Tu 2005–. *Recordings include:* 60 Horses In My Herd 1993, The Orphan's Lament 1994, Where Young Grass Grows 1999, Live 1 2001, Live 2 2001, Altai Sayan Tandy-Uula 2004, Live at Fantasy Studios 2008, Mother-Earth! Father-Sky! 2008. *Address:* c/o JARO Record Company, Bismarckstr. 43, 28203 Bremen, Germany; Metisse Music 1 villa Juge, 75015 Paris, France. *E-mail:* mail@jaro .de. *Website:* www.jaro.de; www.metisse-music.com.

TOLSTOY, Viktoria; Swedish jazz singer; b. 29 July 1974, d. of Erik Kjellberg; great-great-granddaughter of Leo Tolstoy. *Career:* discovered while performing at jazz club in Stockholm, offered a recording contract; performed with Swedish jazz musicians including Svante Thuresson, Putte Wickman, Arne Domnerus, Ulf Wakenius, Jojje Wadenius, Esbjörn Svensson, Nils Landgren, and int. musicians McCoy Tyner, Ray Brown, Toots Thielemans; concerts throughout Scandinavia and in UK, Germany, Switzerland, Italy, Spain, South Africa, Japan, Malaysia, Mexico. *Recordings include:* albums: Smile, Love and Spices 1994, För Älskad 1996, White Russian 1997, Blame It On My Youth 2001, Shining on You Richard Spencer 2004, My Swedish Heart 2005, Pictures Of Me 2006, My Russian Soul 2008, Letters to Herbie 2011, A Moment of Now 2013. *Current Management:* c/o Eva Maria Thiessen, Worldwide Management, Oberstraße 14b, 20144 Hamburg, Germany. *Telephone:* (40) 414788. *Fax:* (89) 122497-79. *E-mail:* eva.thiessen@karsten -jahnke.de. *Website:* www.karsten-jahnke.de; www.viktoriatolstoy.com; www .actmusic.com.

TOMATITO; Spanish musician (guitar) and composer; b. (José Fernández Torres), 1958, Almería, Andalucía. *Career:* flamenco guitarist; began musical career in Málaga playing in tablaos (flamenco nightclubs); accompanied Camarón de la Isla for many years; collaborations with Paco de Lucia, José Mercé, Pansequito, Enrique Morente, Carmen Linares. *Film appearances:* Sevillanas 1992, Flamenco 1995, Vengo (César Award for Best Music Written for a Film 2001) 2000, Camarón: When Flamenco Became Legend 2005. *Recordings include:* albums: Rosas del Amor 1987, Barrio Negro 1991, Guitarra Gitana 1997, Spain (with Michel Camilo) (Latin Grammy Award) 2000, Paseo de los Castaños 2001, Aguadulce (Latin Grammy for Best Flamenco Album) 2004, Spain Again (with Michel Camilo) 2006, Sonanta

Suite (Latin Grammy Award for Best Flamenco Album) 2010, Soy Flamenco 2013. *Website:* www.macande.com; www.tomatito.com.

TOMCRAFT (see Brückner, Thomas)

TOMICH, Michael Robert; British musician (bass guitar) and DJ; b. 24 Feb. 1948, Chiswick, London, England; m. 1st Anita Kaarinä Viero 1971 (divorced 1986); m. 2nd Janet Anne Corbett 2013. *Education:* Nescot Coll., Ewell, Surrey, Stafford Coll., Kensington, studied acoustic guitar in Harrow School of Music, RSA Stage 2. *Career:* played with more than 150 different acts 1966–83; numerous tours of UK, Europe and USA, TV appearances and radio broadcasts; acts include Clyde McPhatter, The Isley Brothers, Bonzo Dog Doo Dah Band, The Skatalites, Joan Armatrading, Peter Banks, Bill Bruford, Heron, Karl Wallinger, Atomic Rooster, Pickettywitch, The Gods, If, The Fantastics; mem. Wycombe Hosp. Radio Asscn, Wexham Park Radio Asscn. *Recordings:* early records with: Pickettywitch; album: Diamond of Dreams, Heron; many session recordings with various acts. *Honours:* Wycombe Radio Personality 1994, Wexham Park Radio Martin Fellow Trophy 2005. *Address:* 10 Sandford Gardens, High Wycombe, Bucks., HP11 1QT, England (home). *Telephone:* (1494) 536497 (home).

TOMIIE, Satoshi, (Loop 7, Black Shells); Japanese producer, remixer and DJ; b. 1966, Tokyo. *Career:* formed first band in Tokyo, early 1980s; met Frankie Knuckles at a fashion party and joined the Def Mix crew; collaborations with Frankie Knuckles, Robert Owens, Diane Charlemagne; remixed: Madonna, Simply Red, Janet Jackson, Michael Jackson, Gabrielle. *Recordings include:* albums: Full Lick 2001, Club, Home, Studio 2006; singles: Tears (with Frankie Knuckles) 1989, And I Loved You (with Arnold Jarvis) 1990, The Anthem (as Black Shells) 1994, Darkness 1998, Inspired 2000, Love In Traffic, Up In Flames 2001, Ice (7): Scandal in New York 2003, Straight Up 2012. *Current Management:* c/o Judy Weinstein, 928 Broadway, Suite 904, New York, NY 10010, USA. *Telephone:* (212) 505-7728. *Fax:* (212) 505-8041. *E-mail:* jw@defmix.com; info@defmix.com. *Website:* www.defmix.com; www.satoshitomiie.com.

TOMLINSON, Louis William; British singer and actor; b. (Louis Troy Austin), 24 Dec. 1991, Doncaster, S Yorks. *Education:* Hayfield School, Hall Cross School. *Career:* mem. One Direction 2010–; finished third in The X Factor (UK), ITV 1 2010; signed to Syco Records 2010; participated in X Factor Live Tour 2011; released debut single 2011; debut album first by a British group to debut at number one on USA Billboard 200 album chart 2011; numerous TV appearances and tours; group hiatus 2016–. *Television:* as actor: If I Had You 2006. *Recordings include:* with One Direction: albums: Up All Night 2011, Take Me Home (American Music Award for Favorite Album 2013) 2012, Midnight Memories (American Music Award for Favorite Album 2014) 2013, Four 2014, Made in the A.M. 2015. *DVDs:* Up All Night: the Live Tour 2012. *Publications:* One Direction: Forever Young 2011, One Direction: The Official Annual 2012 2011, Dare to Dream: Life as One Direction 2011, Where We Are: Our Band, Our Story 2013, Who We Are: Our Official Autobiography 2014. *Honours:* numerous including: with One Direction: Bambi Pop Int. Award 2012, BBC Radio 1 Teen Awards for Best British Music Act 2012, for Best British Single 2012, 2013, 2014, 2015, for Best British Group 2013, 2015, BRIT Awards for Best British Single (What Makes You Beautiful) 2012, for BRITs Global Success 2013, for Best British Video (for You & I) 2015, JIM Awards (Flemish TV) for Best International Newcomer 2012, for Best Group 2013, for Best Pop 2013, MTV Europe Music Awards for Best New Act 2012, for Best UK & Ireland Act 2012, 2013, 2014, for Biggest Fans 2012, 2014, for Best Pop Act 2013, 2014, for Best Live Act 2014, for Best Worldwide Act (Europe North) 2014, MTV Video Music Awards Brazil Award for International Artist 2012, MTV Video Music Awards for Best New Artist 2012, for Best Pop Video and Most Share-Worthy Video (both What Makes You Beautiful) 2012, for Song of the Summer (for Best Song Ever) 2013, 4Music Video Honours Awards for Best Breakthrough and Best Group 2012, ARIA Music Awards for Best Int. Artist 2012, 2013, 2014, Billboard Music Awards for Top Duo/Group 2013, 2015, for Top New Artist 2013, for Top Pop Artist 2013, for Top Touring Artist 2015, American Music Awards for Favorite Band, Duo or Group 2013, 2014, 2015, for Artist of the Year 2014, 2015. *Current Management:* c/o Modest! Management, The Matrix Complex, 91 Peterborough Road, London, SW6 3BU, England. *E-mail:* info@modestmanagement.com. *Website:* www.modestmanagement.com; www.onedirectionmusic.com.

TOMMEY, Glenn, Cert. Ed.; British recording engineer and musician (guitar, keyboards, trombone); b. 27 Aug. 1951, Ross-On-Wye, Herefords., England; s. of John Tommey and Pamella Tommey; m. Carolyn Jane Kellett 1981; three s. *Education:* Newton Park Coll., Bath, Univ. of Bristol. *Career:* resident engineer, Crescent Studios, Bath 1974–87; freelance engineer 1987–; projects for CBS/Sony, Tokyo, Toshiba/EMI, Tokyo, Peter Gabriel IV 1982, XTC; Big Express 1984, Fossil Fuel 1996, Stranglers, Rupert Holmes, Korgis, Icehouse; plays keyboards and co-writer with Stackridge; Lecturer in Music (dedicated micro-technology), Bath Coll. of Higher Educ. *Recordings include:* album: with Stackridge: A Victory For Commonsense 2009; with Islo Mob: Wir Sind Das Abendland 2009. *Honours:* Best Recorded Album of the Year, Precious, Hajime Mizoguchi 1990. *Address:* 99 Fairfield Park Road, Fairfield Park, Bath, Avon, BA1 6JR, England (home). *Telephone:* (310) 492-5632 (Beverly Hills, Calif.) (office). *E-mail:* glenn@sundriedsongs.com (office). *Website:* www.sundriedsongs.com; www.stackridge.net.

TOMSON, Christopher (Chris) William; American musician (drums, percussion) and songwriter; b. 6 March 1984, New York, NY. *Education:* The Peddie School, Columbia Univ. *Career:* raised in Imlaystown, New Jersey; fmr mem. L'Homme Run; Founder-mem. Vampire Weekend 2006–; signed to XL Recordings 2007; numerous festival appearances and tours. *Recordings:* albums: with Vampire Weekend: Vampire Weekend 2008, Contra 2010, Modern Vampires of the City (Grammy Award for Best Alternative Music Album 2014) 2013. *Honours:* with Vampire Weekend: NME Award for Best New American Alternative/Indie Band 2008, Q Magazine Awards for Best Video (for Giving Up the Gun) 2011, for Best Act in the World Today 2013. *Current Management:* c/o Ian Montone, Monotone, Inc., 820 Seward Street, Hollywood, CA 90038, USA. *Telephone:* (323) 308-1818. *Address:* c/o Kris Chen, XL Recordings, 304 Hudson Street, 7th Floor, New York, NY 10013, USA (office). *Telephone:* (212) 995-5882 (office). *E-mail:* krischen@xlrecordings.com (office); vampireweekend@gmail.com (home). *Website:* www.xlrecordings.com (office); www.vampireweekend.com.

TONE THEORY (see Carter, Derrick)

TONG, Des; British music producer, musician, composer and arranger; *Director of Music and Light Entertainment, City TV Broadcasting;* b. 30 April 1951, Woking, Surrey, England; one s. one d. *Career:* played bass guitar with Sad Café; producer, Time Warp for Damian; has worked with artists including Real Thing, Lisa Stansfield, Joe Cocker, Alvin Stardust, Cissy Stone, Engelbert Humperdinck; fmr Head of Music for US Gold computer games co.; fmr music producer at Granada TV, BBC Radio 1 and Radio 2, ILR Radio; currently Dir of Music and Light Entertainment, City TV Broadcasting, Birmingham. *Recordings include:* with Sad Café: Sad Café, Ole, The Politics of Existing, Whatever It Takes, Anthology 2001; hit singles include: Every Day Hurts 1979, My Oh My 1980; producer: Ultimate Party Animal Album. *Address:* Charter House, Birmingham, B4 7EU, England (office). *E-mail:* des.tong@citytvbroadcasting.co.uk (office). *Website:* www.citytvbroadcasting.co.uk.

TONG, Matt; British musician (drums); b. 29 April 1979. *Career:* mem., Union, later renamed Bloc Party 2003–. *Recordings include:* albums: with Bloc Party: Silent Alarm 2005, Silent Alarm Remixed 2005, A Weekend in the City 2007, Intimacy 2008, Four 2012. *Current Management:* Press Here Publicity, 138 W 25th Street, Seventh Floor, New York, NY 10001, USA. *Telephone:* (212) 246-2640. *Fax:* (212) 582-6513. *E-mail:* info@pressherepublicity.com. *Website:* www.pressherepublicity.com. *Address:* c/o V2 Music, 131 Holland Park Avenue, London, W11 4UT, England. *E-mail:* matt@blocparty.com. *Website:* www.blocparty.com.

TONG, Pete, MBE; British DJ, music producer and A & R executive; b. 31 July 1960, Dartford, Kent, England. *Education:* King's School, Rochester. *Career:* became DJ aged 15; freelance DJ on leaving school; worked at Blues and Soul and Black Music 1979–83; radio broadcaster, Radio Invicta, Capital Radio and Radio London; Radio 1; originally on Peter Powell show, layer DJ with own dance music show; host of programmes including Essential Mix and Essential Selection; Head of A & R, London/FFRR Records; involved with organizing the Int. Music Summit in Ibiza 2008 (now held annually). *Recordings include:* albums: Ministry of Sound—The Annual, Vol. I 1995, Vol. II 1996, Vol. III 1997, Ministry of Sound—Dance Nation, Vol. I 1995, Vol. II 1996, Vol. III 1997, Vol. IV 1997, Vol. V 1999, Essential Mix 1996, 1996, 1998, 2000, 2001, Essential Selection, Winter 1997, Spring 1998, Spring 1999, Ibiza 1999, Spring 2000, Ibiza 2000, Pete Tong's Essential Collection 1997, Platinum On Black: The Final Chapter, 1998, Ministry of Sound—Clubber's Guide to Ibiza 1998, Essential Millennium 1999, Human Traffic (film soundtrack) 1999, The Beach (film soundtrack) 2000, Twisted Beats 2001, Essential Selection Presents The Clubber's Bible Winter 2002 2001, Fashion TV Presents Pete Tong 2003, Essential Selection Pete Tong 2003, Pure Pacha Ibiza: Mixed by Pete Tong and Andy B 2004, It's Showtime! (Pete Tong Presents Pure Pacha Vol. II Summer Season 2005, 2005, Essential Classics 2005, Pure Pacha Vol. 1 (mixed by Pete Tong & Sarah Main) 2006, Essential Dance Mix 2006, Pure Pacha 3 (mixed by Pete Tong and Sarah Main) 2007, Wonderland 2008, Pete Tong Presents Wonderland 2009, 2009, Pete Tong Presents Wonderland 2010, 2010, Pete Tong and Riva Starr: Future Underground 2011, All Gone Pete Tong & Felix da House Cat Ibiza '11 2011, All Gone Pete Tong & Groove Armada Miami '12 2012, All Gone Pete Tong & Skream Miami '13 2013, The Pete Tong Collection 2013. *Current Management:* c/o Anglo Management, Fulham Palace, Bishops Avenue, London, SW6 6EA, England. *Telephone:* (20) 7384-7373. *Fax:* (20) 7384-7375. *E-mail:* paul@anglomanagement.co.uk. *Website:* www.anglomanagement.co.uk; www.petetong.com.

TONG, Simon; British musician (guitar, keyboards). *Career:* mem. The Verve 1995–99; numerous live performances, festival appearances; Founder-mem. The Shining 2002–03; Founder-mem. The Good The Bad and The Queen 2006–. *Recordings include:* albums: with The Verve: Urban Hymns (BRIT Award for Best British Album 1998, Q Award for Classic Album 2007) 1997; with The Shining: True Skies 2002; with The Good The Bad and The Queen: The Good The Bad and The Queen 2007. *Honours:* BRIT Award for Best British Group (with The Verve) 1998. *Current Management:* International Talent Booking, First Floor, Ariel House, 74a Charlotte Street, London, W1T 4QJ, England. *Telephone:* (20) 7637-6979. *Fax:* (20) 7637-6978. *E-mail:* mail@itb.co.uk. *Website:* www.thegoodthebadandthequeen.com.

DJ TONKA; German producer and remixer. *Recordings include:* Peak Time (In One Go) 1999, Essential Streetparades 2000, Proved 2000, Don't Be Afraid (To Let Yourself Go) 2000, DJ Tonka 2001, Never 2001, Keep Klimbing 2002, Get Back 2003, 84 2004. *Current Management:* c/o Harald Wilm, Marienweg

12, 97688 Bad Kissingen, Germany. *Telephone:* (971) 62068. *Fax:* (971) 7850650. *E-mail:* harald@mfm-booking.de. *Website:* www.mfm-booking.de; www.djtonka.de (home).

TONTOH, Frank; musician (drums), writer and composer; b. 22 May 1964, Kumasi, Ghana. *Education:* Trinity Coll. of Music. *Career:* mem. Osibisa for four years; mem. Aztec Camera for four years; collaborations with Tanita Tikaram, Tasmin Archer, Level 42, Omar, Mica Paris, Zucchero, Roachford, Courtney Pine, Jason Rebello, Edwyn Collins, Misty Oldland, Irene Grandi; Lecturer (drums), Acad. of Contemporary Music, Guildford. *Recordings include:* Aztec Camera: Stray; Misty Oldland: Supernatural; Kimiko Yamashita: Love and Hate; Tony Remy: two albums; Theme to Wired (TV programme); Kiko Veneno: two albums; Bachology: one album; Gang of Four: 100 Flowers Bloom 1998; Jarabe de Palo: Depende 1998; others: Lewis II 2000, Irek 2001, Crazy Vibes and Things 2002, Play to Win 2004, Together as One 2005, Future Past 2006, Back to Black 2006, The Secret Life of Us 2012. *Address:* Academy Of Contemporary Music, Rodboro Buildings, Bridge Street, Guildford, Surrey, GU1 4SB, England. *Telephone:* (1483) 500800. *Website:* www.acm.ac.uk.

T.O.P.; South Korean singer, rapper, songwriter and actor; b. (Choi Seunghyun), 4 Nov. 1987, Seoul. *Career:* mem. Big Bang 2006–; collaborations include G-Dragon, Lexy, Gummy, Uhm Jung Hwa, NBK Gray, Zia, Se7en. *Recordings:* albums: with Big Bang: Bigbang Vol 1 2007, Remember 2008, Number 1 2008, Big Bang 2009, Big Bang 2 2011, Alive 2012; with G-Dragon: GD&TOP 2010. *Television:* I Am Sam 2007, Music Core 2007-08, Iris 2009, Absolutely Him 2012; numerous TV commercials. *Films:* My 19 2009, 71: Into the Fire (Daejong Film Award for Hallyu Popularity 2010, Style Icon Award for Best Actor 2010, Blue Dragon Film Awards for Best New Actor and for Popularity 2010, Max Movie Award for Best New Actor 2010, PaekSang Awards for Best New Actor and Popularity Award (Actor in a Motion Picture 2010)) 2010. *Honours:* Mnet KM Music Festival Awards for Best Male Group 2007, 2008, 2012, for Song of the Year 2007, for Digital Music 2008, for Artist of the Year 2008, 2012, for Guardian Angel Worldwide Performer 2012, Golden Disk Bonsang Award 2007, Mnet Music Portal Award 2008, Seoul Music Awards for Digital Music 2008, for Bonsang 2008, 2009, for Best Album 2009, for Popular Mobile 2009, Nickelodeon Korea Kids' Choice Best Male Artists Award 2008, 2009, Hiwon Award 2009, Korea PD Best Singer Award 2009, Best Hits Song Festival Gold Artist Award 2009, Japan Cable Broadcasting Best Newcomer Award 2009, Ministry of Culture, Sports and Tourism Artist of the Year 2009, Japan Record Awards for New Artist and Best New Artist 2009, Gold Award 2010, Japanese Grand Prix du Disque for Best Newcomer 2010, Japan Gold Disc Awards for Best Five New Artists and Best New Artist 2010, MTV Video Music Awards Japan for Best New Artist Video and Best Pop Video 2010. *Address:* c/o YG Entertainment, 397–5 YG Building, Hapjeong-Dong, Mapo-Gu, Seoul 109-819, South Korea (office). *Telephone:* (2) 3143-1105 (office). *Fax:* (2) 544-1546 (office). *E-mail:* web@ ygmail.com (office). *Website:* eng.ygfamily.com/main/main.html (office); www .ybigbang.com (home); www.ybigbang.jp (home).

TORK, Peter; American musician (bass, guitar, keyboards), singer and actor; b. (Peter Halsten Thorkelson), 13 Feb. 1944, Washington, DC. *Career:* folk musician with Au Go Go Singers, Los Angeles; mem., The Monkees 1966–68, 1986–89; 1986–89; founder of own groups, Release 1969, The New Monks 1981, Peter Tork and Shoe Suede Blues; high school teacher, Santa Monica early 1970s. *Television:* Monkees (comedy series) 1966–68, 33 1/3 Revolutions Per Monkee (NBC). *Film appearances:* Head 1968, The Brady Bunch Movie 1995. *Recordings include:* albums: with The Monkees: The Monkees 1966; More of The Monkees 1967; Headquarters 1967; Pisces, Aquarius, Capricorn and Jones Ltd 1967; The Birds, The Bees and The Monkees, 1968; Then and Now, 1986; Pool It, 1987; Anthology, 1998; solo: Stranger Things Have Happened, 1994, Two Man Band 1996, Once Again 2001. *Honours:* NARM Awards for Best Selling Group, Best Album 1967, Emmy Award for Outstanding Comedy Series 1967, three BMI Awards 1968. *Address:* c/o Nationwide Entertainment Services, 2756 N Green Valley Parkway, Suite 449, Las Vegas, NV 89014-2100, USA (office). *E-mail:* publicity@petertork .com. *Website:* www.petertork.com; www.shoesuedeblues.com.

TORO ORTIZ, Raymond (Ray); American musician (guitar) and singer; b. 15 July 1977, New Jersey; m. Christa Toro Ortiz 2008, one s. *Career:* mem. rock band, My Chemical Romance 2001–. *Recordings include:* albums: I Brought You My Bullets, You Brought Me Your Love 2002, Three Cheers for Sweet Revenge 2004, The Black Parade 2006, Danger Days: The True Lives of the Fabulous Killjoys 2010. *Honours:* Kerrang! Award for Best Int. Band 2006, 2007, NME Award for Best Int. Band 2007. *E-mail:* infomcr@ mychemicalromance.com. *Website:* www.mychemicalromance.com; www.ray -toro.com.

TORRENCE, Dean; American singer; b. 10 March 1940, Los Angeles, CA. *Education:* studied graphics. *Career:* mem. of duo, Jan and Dean (with Jan Berry) 1957–66, 1973–; solo artist 1966–; numerous live performances, founder, Kittyhawk Graphics 1967; mem., Legendary Masked Surfers 1972. *Recordings include:* albums: with Jan and Dean: Jan and Dean Take Linda Surfin', 1963; Surf City and Other Swingin' Cities, 1963; Drag City, 1964; Dead Man's Curve/The New Girl In School, 1964; The Little Old Lady From Pasadena, 1964; Ride The Wild Surf, 1964; Command Performance/Live In Person, 1965; Jan and Dean Meet Batman, 1966; One Summer Night – Live,

1982, Port to Paradise 1986, Carnival of Sound 2010; solo: Save for a Rainy Day, 1967. *E-mail:* bill@paradiseartists.com. *Website:* www.jananddean.com.

TORRES, Tico; American musician (drums); b. 7 Oct. 1953. *Career:* Founder-mem. rock group Bon Jovi 1983–88, 1992–; numerous tours, television, radio and live appearances worldwide. *Recordings include:* albums: Bon Jovi 1984, 7800° Fahrenheit 1985, Slippery When Wet 1986, Bon Jovi Live 1987, New Jersey 1988, Keep The Faith 1991, Cross Road 1994, These Days 1995, Crush 2000, One Wild Night 1985–2001 2001, Bounce 2002, Distance 2003, This Left Feels Right 2003, Have A Nice Day 2005, Lost Highway 2007, The Circle 2009, What About Now 2013, Burning Bridges 2015. *Film:* Skum Rocks! 2013. *Honours:* American Music Awards for Favorite Pop/Rock Band 1988, for Favorite Pop/Rock Single 1991, Nordoff-Robbins Music Therapy Silver Clef 1990, BRIT Award for Best Int. Group (with band) 1995, VH-1 Award for Favorite Video (for It's My Life) 2000, Billboard Music Award for Top Touring Artist 2014. *Current Management:* c/o Bon Jovi Management, 809 Elder Circle, Austin, TX 78733, USA. *Telephone:* (512) 329-0668. *Fax:* (512) 328-1629. *Website:* www.bonjovi.com.

TORRES, Tommy; Puerto Rican singer, songwriter and record producer; b. (Tommy Torres Carrasquillo), 25 Nov. 1971, Santurce, San Juan. *Education:* Berklee Coll. of Music, USA. *Career:* fmr studio asst, Sony Music Studios, New York; songwriter and producer for Latin and pop artists 1999–; solo recording artist 2001–; numerous hit songs as writer or co-writer including No Puedo Olvidar (for MDO) 1999, Llegar a Ti (for Jaci Velasquez) 1999, Cuando Seas Mia (for Son By Four) 2001, Tal Vez (for Ricky Martin) 2003, Tu Recuerdo (for Ricky Martin) 2006, Quien (for Ricardo Arjona) 2007, Desde Cuando (for Alejandro Sanz) 2009, Corre (for Jesse & Joy) 2012. *Recordings include:* albums: as solo artist: Tommy Torres 2001, Estar de Moda No Está de Moda 2004, Tarde o Temprano 2008, 12 Historias 2012; as producer: Acustico, Ednita Nazario 2002, Almas del Silencio, Ricky Martin (Billboard Latin Music Award for Best Pop Album (Male) 2004) 2003, Por Ti, Ednita Nazario (Billboard Latin Music Award for Best Pop Album (Female) 2004) 2003, Adentro, Ricardo Arjona (Grammy Award for Best Latin Pop Album 2005, Latin Grammy Award for Best Pop Album 2005) 2004, MTV Unplugged, Ricky Martin (Latin Grammy Award for Best Pop Album 2007) 2007, Paraiso Express, Alejandro Sanz (Grammy Award for Latin Pop Album of the Year 2009, Latin Grammy Award for Pop Album of the Year 2009) 2009. *Honours:* ASCAP Song of the Year Award (for Llegar a Ti) 1999, ASCAP Pop Song of the Year Award (for Tu Recuerdo) 2007, Billboard Magazine Hot Latin Tracks Producer of the Year 2007, ASCAP Latin Music Composer of the Year Award 2010, Latin Grammy Award for Song of the Year (for Corre) 2012. *Address:* c/o Warner Music Latina, Warner Music Group, 75 Rockefeller Plaza, New York, NY 10019, USA (office). *Website:* www.tommytorres.com.

TORRINI, Emilíana; Icelandic singer and songwriter; b. 16 May 1977, Kópavogur. *Career:* fmr mem. Spoon, GusGus; solo artist 1995–; songs recorded by artists including Kylie Minogue, Thievery Corporation. *Recordings include:* albums: Crouçie d'où là 1995, Merman 1996, Love in the Time of Science 1999, Fisherman's Woman (Icelandic Music Award for Pop Album of the Year) 2005, Me and Armini 2008, Rarities 2009. *Honours:* Icelandic Music Award for Singer of the Year, for Video of the Year (for Sunny Road) 2005. *Address:* c/o Rough Trade Records, 66 Golborne Road, London, W10 5PS, England (office). *Website:* www.roughtrade.com (office); www.emilianatorrini .com.

TORROJA, Ana; Spanish singer; b. 28 Dec. 1959, Madrid. *Career:* mem. Mecano 1980–93; solo career 1992–. *Recordings include:* albums: with Mecano: Mecano 1982, ¿Dónde Está El País De Las Hadas? 1983, Ya Viene El Sol 1984, En Concierto 1985, Lo Ultimo De Mecano 1986, Entre El Cielo Y El Suelo 1986, Descanso Dominical 1988, Aidalai 1991, Ana José Nacho 1998; solo: Puntos Cardinales 1997, Pasajes De Un Sueño 2000, Girados En Concierto (with Miguel Bosé) 2000, Ana Torroja 2001, Frágil 2003, Esencial 2004, Me Cuesta Tanto Olvidarte 2006, Sonrisa 2010. *Honours:* Billboard Latin Music Award for Best Hot Latin Track by a Vocal Duet, for Best Latin Pop Airplay Track by a Duo or Group (both for Duele el amor, with Aleks Syntek) 2005. *Website:* www.anatorroja.info.

TORVINEN, Juha Ensio; Finnish musician (guitar); b. 24 March 1959. *Career:* Founder-mem. Eppu Normaali 1976–. *Recordings include:* albums: Aknepop 1978, Maximum Jee&Jee 1979, Akun tehdas 1980, Cocktail Bar – Musiikkia Rantalasta 1981, Tie vie 1982, Aku ja köyhät pojat 1983, Rupisia riimejä karmeita tarinoita 1984, Kahdeksas ihme 1985, Valkoinen kupla 1986, Imperiumin vastaisku 1988, Historian suurmiehiä 1990, Studio etana 1993, Sadan vuoden päästäkin 2004, Syvään päähän 2007, Tuuliajolla 2007, Mutala 2011. *Address:* Poko Records, Universal Records Ltd, Merimiehen-katu 36 D, PO Box 140, 00151 Helsinki, Finland. *Telephone:* (6) 154677. *E-mail:* poko@poko.fi. *Website:* www.eppunormaali.fi.

TOSCHES, Nick; American writer; b. 1949, Newark, New Jersey. *Career:* began writing in small music magazines; worked with Lester Bangs at Creem; has written liner notes for compilation albums by numerous artists, including Jerry Lee Lewis and Carl Perkins; collaborated with Hubert Selby, Jr; Contributing Ed., Vanity Fair. *Recordings include:* albums: Blue Eyes and Exit Wounds (with Hubert Selby Jr) 1998, Nick & Homer (with Homer Henderson) 1998. *Publications include:* Country 1977, Hellfire (biography) 1982, Unsung Heroes of Rock 'N' Roll 1984, Power on Earth 1986, Cut Numbers (novel) 1988, Dino: Living High in the Dirty Business of Dreams (Italian-American Literary Achievement Award for Distinction in Literature

1993) 1992, Trinities (novel) (New York Times Book Review Notable Book of the Year) 1994, Chaldea (poems) 1999, The Devil and Sonny Liston 2000, The Nick Tosches Reader (anthology) 2000, Where Dead Voices Gather 2001, The Last Opium Den 2002, In The Hand of Dante 2002, King of the Jews: The Arnold Rothstein Story 2006, Never Trust a Loving God 2009, Save the Last Dance for Satan 2011, Me and the Devil 2012; contributed poems to publications, including Contents, Esquire, GQ, Long Shot, Open City, Smokes Like a Fish. *Website:* www.nicktosches.com.

TOUHAMI, Alassane, (Abin-Abin); Malian singer and musician (percussion, guitar); b. 1959, Kidal. *Career:* mem. Touareg group Tinariwen. *Recordings include:* albums: The Radio Tisdas Sessions 2000, Amassakoul 2004, Aman Iman: Water is Life 2007, Imidiwan (Uncut Music Award) 2009, Tassili 2011. *Honours:* BBC Radio 3 Award for World Music (Africa) 2005. *Address:* c/o Independiente Ltd, The Drill Hall, 3 Heathfield Terrace, London, W4 4JE, England (office). *E-mail:* tinariwen@apartment22.com (office); info@ independiente.co.uk (office); wavelabinc@gmail.com. *Website:* www.tinariwen .com.

TOUNKARA, Djelimady; Malian musician (guitar) and songwriter; b. 1947, Kita. *Career:* born into a griot family; mem. Orchestre Misira, Orchestre Nat. A, Pioneer Jazz (first modern dance bands in Mali); mem. Super Rail Band early 1970s; later played with acoustic trio Bajourou; Dir and conductor with Super Rail Band; currently leader, Djelimady Tounkara Septet; mem. AfroCubism project 2010–. *Recordings include:* albums: Djali Madi Tounkara and Rail Band 1983, Mansa (with Rail Band) 1995, In Griot Time (compilation) 2000, Sigui 2001, Big String Theory (with Bajourou) 2002, Solon Kono 2005, Allo Bamako 2007, AfroCubism (with AfroCubism) 2010. *Honours:* BBC Radio 3 Awards for World Music Award, Best African Artist 2002. *Address:* World Circuit Records, First Floor, Shoreditch Stables, 138 Kingsland Road, London, E2 8DY, England. *E-mail:* post@worldcircuit.co.uk. *Website:* www .worldcircuit.co.uk.

TOURÉ, Daby; Mauritanian singer, musician and songwriter; b. 1971, Boutilimit, Nouakchott. *Career:* fmr mem. Touré Touré; solo artist 2004–. *Recordings include:* albums: with Touré Touré: Ladde 1999; solo: Diam 2004, Stereo Spirit 2007, Call My Name 2009. *Website:* www.dabytoure.com.

TOURETTE, Jean-Michel; German musician (guitar, keyboards); b. 1975, Hannover. *Career:* mem. Wir sind Helden 2001–. *Recordings include:* albums: Die Reklamation 2003, Von hier an blind 2005, SoundSo 2007, Bring mich nach Hause 2010. *Honours:* ECHO Award for Best Nat. Band 2006. *Address:* c/o Labels Germany, Leuschnerdamm 13, 10999 Berlin, Germany. *Website:* www.wirsindhelden.com.

TOURNAS, Konstantinos (Kostas); Greek composer, lyricist, singer, musician (guitar) and producer; b. 23 Sept. 1949, Tripolis; m. Maria Tournas 1977. *Education:* studied harmony and composition. *Career:* numerous tours around Greece, USA, Germany, Poland and Cyprus; club appearances; mem. AEPI Greece, ETE Greece, FIA. *Compositions:* more than 660 titles released 1971–. *Television:* Jury mem. 'Just the 2 of Us'. *Recordings:* Aperanta Horafia, Kiries Kai Kirioi, Poll/Anthrope, Klise, Klevei o kairos. *Publication:* Kostas Tournas' Songs. *Honours:* awarded various prizes at Greek and int. song festivals, mainly as composer and lyricist. *Address:* 133 Kafkassou Street, Kipseli, Athens 11364, Greece (home). *Telephone:* (210) 8628677 (office). *Fax:* (210) 8628908 (office). *E-mail:* tournaskostas@gmail.com (office); tour@hol.gr (office). *Website:* www.tournas.gr.

TOURNIER, Michael James; British programmer and producer; b. 24 May 1963, High Wycombe, Buckinghamshire, England. *Career:* mem. Fluke 1988–99; contributed remixes for Talk Talk, Björk, Simple Minds, Smashing Pumpkins, The Rolling Stones, Yello, New Order and others. *Recordings include:* albums: The Techno Rose Of Blighty 1990, Out 1991, Six Wheels On My Wagon 1993, Oto 1995, Risotto 1997, Progressive History X (compilation) 2001; singles: Thumper 1989, Joni 1989, Philly 1990, Slid 1993, Electric Guitar 1993, Groovy Feeling 1993, Bubble 1994, The Peel Sessions 1994, Bullet 1995, Tosh 1995, Atom Bomb 1996, Absurd 1997, Squirt 1997. *Address:* One Little Indian Records, 34 Trinity Crescent, London, SW17 7AE, England. *Telephone:* (20) 8772-7600. *E-mail:* info@indian.co.uk. *Website:* www.indian.co .uk.

TOUSSAINT, Jean-Baptiste Nazaire; Aruban jazz musician (tenor and soprano saxophones); b. 27 July 1960. *Education:* Miami State Univ. with Charles Cox, Berklee Coll. of Music, USA. *Career:* mem. Art Blakey's Jazz Messengers, 1982–86; concerts world-wide; Teacher, Guildhall School of Music, 1987–; formed own bands Jean Toussaint Quartet, 1987; Nazaire, 1992; tours of Europe and Middle East with Max Roach, 1989; mem. Julian Joseph's band, 1992–94; also worked with Jason Rebello, Bheki Mseleku, Lenny White, UK, Europe and USA, 1995; mem. MCPS, PRS: Broadcast Music Inc. *Recordings include:* albums: with Art Blakey's Jazz Messengers: The New York Scene 1984, Live At Kimballs 1985, Blue Night 1985; solo: Impressions of Coltrane 1987, Silvershine (with Andy Hamilton) 1990, What Goes Around 1991, The Language Of Truth (with Julian Joseph) 1991, Who's Blues 1992, Reality 1993, Jamaica By Night (as producer) 1994, Life I Want 1995, Metropolis 1998, Back To Back 1998. Live At Ronnie Scott's 2000, Coast To Coast 2000, The Street Above The Underground 2001, Blue Black 2002. *Current Management:* c/o Fish Krish, 6 Carlton House, 319 West End Lane, London, NW6 1RN, England.

TOWNEND, Richard (Rick) James Patrick; British musician (banjo, guitar, fiddle); b. 4 July 1948, London, England; s. of Brian ('Fuzz') Townend and Bett Townend. *Career:* formed first school bluegrass group in UK; played at Royal Albert Hall, Hammersmith Odeon, Cambridge Folk Festival; appeared on BBC radio and TV folk and country music programmes, Kaleidoscope (BBC Radio 4); partner in Wadhurst Bluegrass Day Venture; mem. Musicians' Union, British Bluegrass Music Asscn, currently London and SE England Rep. *Recordings include:* Make The Old Times New (with Rosie Davis) 1995, The Echo Mountain Band 1975, Fraces on the Frets 1997, The Lily and the Rose 2002, Just The Tune 2003, All Traditional 2006, A Tribute to Bill Clifton (with the Kent Carters). *Publications include:* numerous articles in magazines. *Honours:* elected to British Bluegrass Hall of Honour 2000, winner, European World of Bluegrass Asscn Bluegrass Pioneer Award 2004. *Address:* St Julians, Sevenoaks, Kent, TN15 0RX, England (home). *Telephone:* (1732) 458261 (home). *E-mail:* rick@ricktownend .co.uk. *Website:* www.ricktownend.co.uk.

TOWNSHEND, Peter (Pete) Dennis Blandford; British composer, musician (guitar), publisher and author; b. 19 May 1945, Isleworth, London, England; s. of Clifford Townshend and Betty Townshend; m. Karen Astley 1968; one s. two d. *Education:* Acton Co. Grammar School and Ealing Art Coll. *Career:* mem. rock group, The Detours, renamed The Who 1964– (various reunion tours and recordings); solo artist 1979–; appearances include: Nat. Jazz and Blues Festival 1965, 1966, 1969, Monterey Pop Festival 1967, Woodstock 1969, Rock at the Oval 1971, Farewell tour 1982–83, Live Aid, Wembley 1985, Reunion tour 1989, Quadrophenia 1996/1997, Concert for NYC 2001, Live8 2005; owner Eel Pie Recording Productions Ltd and Eel Pie Publishing Ltd 1972–; est. Eel Pie (bookshops and publishing co.) 1976–83; est. Meher Baba Oceanic (UK archival library) 1976–; Ed., Faber & Faber (publrs) 1983–. *Compositions include:* Tommy (rock opera) (Tony Award for score 1993, Grammy Award for original cast recording 1993, Dora Mavor Moore Award 1994, Olivier Award 1997) 1969, Quadrophenia (rock opera) 1973, The Boy Who Heard Music (rock opera) 2007. *Recordings include:* albums: with The Who: My Generation 1965, A Quick One 1966, Happy Jack 1967, The Who Sell Out 1967, Magic Bus 1968, Tommy 1969, Live At Leeds 1970, Who's Next 1971, Meaty Beefy Big And Bouncy 1971, Quadrophenia 1973, The Who By Numbers 1975, The Story Of The Who 1976, Who Are You 1978, The Kids Are Alright (live) 1979, Face Dances 1981, Hooligans 1982, It's Hard 1982, Rarities Vols. 1 and 2 1983, Who's Last (live) 1984, Two's Missing 1987, Join Together (live) 1990, Live At The Isle of Wight Festival 1970 1996, The BBC Sessions 2000, Moonlighting 2005, Endless Wire 2006; solo: Who Came First 1972, Rough Mix 1977, Empty Glass 1980, All The Best Cowboys Have Chinese Eyes 1982, Scoop 1983, White City: A Novel 1985, Another Scoop 1987, The Iron Man: A Musical 1989, Psychoderelict 1993, Pete Townshend Live 1999, Lifehouse Chronicles 2000, The Oceanic Concerts 2001, Live: La Jolla 2001, Live: Sadler's Wells 2001. *Films:* music for: Tommy 1975, Quadrophenia 1979, The Kids Are Alright 1979. *Television:* music for CSI: Miami and CSI: Crime Scene Investigation. *Publications:* The Story of Tommy (with Richard Barnes), Horse's Neck 1985, Tommy: The Musical 1995, London 1996. *Honours:* Gold Ticket Madison Square Garden 1979, Ivor Novello Award for Contribution to British Music 1982, British Phonographic Industry Award 1983, BRIT Lifetime Achievement Award 1983, BRIT Award for Contribution to British Music 1988, International Rock Living Legend Award 1991, Q Lifetime Achievement Award 1997, Ivor Novello Lifetime Achievement Award 2001, BMI Pres.'s Award 2002, BMI TV Music Awards 2004, 2005, 2006, 2007, Silver Clef Award 2005, The Who were inducted into the UK Music Hall of Fame in 2005, Q Legend Award 2006, South Bank Show Outstanding Achievement Award 2007, Kennedy Center Honor 2008, Les Paul Award 2013. *Current Management:* c/o Trinifold Management, 12 Oval Road, Camden, London, NW1 7DH, England. *Telephone:* (20) 7419-4300. *Fax:* (20) 7419-4325. *E-mail:* info@trinifold.co.uk. *Website:* www.trinifold.co.uk. *Address:* Eel Pie Publishing Ltd, 4 Friars Lane, Richmond, Surrey, TW9 1NL, England (office). *Telephone:* (20) 8940-8171 (office). *Fax:* (20) 8940-8172 (office). *Website:* www.eelpie.com (office); www.thewho.com.

TOWNSHEND, Simon John; British songwriter, musician (guitar, piano) and singer; b. 10 Oct. 1960, Ealing, London, England; m. Janie Harris 1978; two s. one d. *Career:* Founder-mem. On The Air 1980; solo artist; Founder-mem. Animal Soup; singer, Rise, Rise on Smash the Mirror; mem. Musicians' Union, ASCAP, PRS, PAMRA. *Recordings include:* albums: Sweet Sound 1984, Moving Target 1986, Among Us 1997, Looking Out Looking In 2012, Simon Townshend's Moving Target. *Address:* 20 Woodgrange Avenue, Ealing Common, London, W5 3NY, England. *Website:* www.simontownshend.com.

TRAASDAHL, Jan Ole, MA; Danish academic, musician (piano) and composer; b. 21 Aug. 1958, Odense; m. Hanne Mulvad 1981. *Education:* Univ. of Århus, Berklee Coll. of Music, USA. *Career:* performed and recorded with many international jazz soloists, including Thad Jones, Richard Boone and Bent Jaedig; conducted big bands and musicals and composed music for big bands, vocal choirs and theatre; Vice-Pres., Musicians' Union, Copenhagen 1996; mem. Bd, Copenhagen Jazz Festival. *Recordings include:* Panta Rei 1984, Stig Moller 1994, Musam Big Band 1995. *Publications include:* Rhythmic Music Education 1996, Music Education in a Multicultural Society 1999. *Address:* c/o Copenhagen Jazz Festival, Sankt Peders Straede 28C, 2nd Floor, 1453 Copenhagen, Denmark (office). *Telephone:* 33-93-20-13 (office). *E-mail:* info@jazz.dk (office). *Website:* jazz.dk (office).

TRACEY, Clark; British jazz musician (drums), composer, arranger and teacher; *Manager, Tento Ten Records;* b. 5 Feb. 1961, London; s. of Stan Tracey CBE and Jackie Tracey; m. Sylvia Rae Tracey; one s. one d. *Education:* Battersea Grammar School. *Career:* freelance musician 1978–; toured with Stan Tracey to USA, India, Australia, Middle East, Europe from 1978; many television and radio appearances; jazz concerts; f. own groups, Clark Tracey Trio, Clark Tracey Quintet, Clark Tracey Sextet; Man. Tento Ten Records, Resteamed Records, Herts Jazz Club; mem. PRS, MCPS, PPL, Musicians' Union. *Compositions include:* Stiperstones Suite, for own quintet 1988, Full Speed Sideways, for own sextet, Playing In The Yard, with Charlie Rouse and Stan Tracey, Suite for Quintet at Finnish Festival 1997, Continental Drift with Stan Tracey 2000–07. *Recordings include:* albums: with Clark Tracey Quintet: Suddenly Last Tuesday, Stiperstones 1987, We've Been Expecting You, Full Speed Sideways, Bootleg Eric (with Dave Newton), The Calling 2003, The Mighty SAS 2006, Given Time 2008; with Clark Tracey Sextet: Current Climate 2009; solo: Stability 2000, British Standard Time 2005, Given Time 2008, Meantime 2014. *Publication:* Exploring Jazz Drums 2012. *Honours:* four-times winner, British Jazz Award for Best Drummer, Birmingham Jazz Club Award for Best Performance 2006, Ronnie Scott Award for Best Drummer 2007. *Telephone:* (7721) 324491 (home). *E-mail:* enquiries@tentotenrecords.com (office); mail@clarktracey.com. *Website:* www .tentotenrecords.com (office); www.clarktracey.com.

TRAERUP, Birthe, MA; Danish musicologist and academic; b. (Birthe Traerup Larsen), 9 Oct. 1930, Kolding; m. Erik Elias 1966; one s. *Education:* Univ. of Copenhagen, studied in Yugoslavia, Bulgaria, Albania, Greece, Poland, Czechoslovakia, Hungary. *Career:* Research Assoc., Danish Folklore Archives, Dept of Ethnomusicology, Copenhagen 1961–64, 1967–68; consultant, South Slavic Linguistics and Literature, Royal Library of Copenhagen 1967–86; Adjunct Prof., Inst. of Musicology, Univ. of Copenhagen 1968–72, Assoc. Prof. of Ethnomusicology 1972–97; radio programmes and lectures on music of Balkans, Denmark and other European countries; research projects on songs, instrumental music in the Muslim community, Gora, Kosovo, folk music of Albanian population, studies on Karol Szymanowski and Denmark. *Films include:* Auf der Spur der albanischen Volksmusik 1995, På sporet af den albanske folkemusik 1996, Musikkens sjael (The Soul of Music) 1998. *Television:* Otto Frello, Blomstertiden kommer (The Flowering Season is Coming). *Radio includes:* 122 programmes about music on Danish radio, numerous others in Norway and Sweden. *Publications include:* East Macedonian Folk Songs 1970, Makedonske Folkesange 1983, Elias Petersen, en dansk maler 1992; contrib. numerous articles to music journals. *Honours:* Hon. mem. Udruzenje Folklorista Srbije 1972; Jugoslavia Esperanto-Ligo Order of Merit 1964, Ministry for Culture and Art Order of Merit, Poland 1983; Radio Denmark Interval Signal Prize 1972. *Address:* Birkevang 158, 3250 Gilleleje, Denmark (home). *Telephone:* 48-30-16-81 (home). *E-mail:* birthe@bitrae.dk.

TRAINOR, Meghan Elizabeth; American singer, songwriter and record producer; b. 22 Dec. 1993, Nantucket, Mass; d. of Gary Trainor and Kelli Trainor. *Education:* Nauset Regional High School. *Career:* recorded three independently released albums 2009–11; songwriter in Nashville 2013–14, for artists including Hunter Hayes and Rascal Flatts; signed with Epic record label 2014; scored world-wide hit with All About That Bass 2014; featured vocalist on Charlie Puth's Marvin Gaye single 2015; collaborations with John Legend. *Recordings include:* albums: Meghan Trainor 2009, I'll Sing for You 2011, Only 17 2011, Title 2015. *Honours:* ASCAP Music Award 2015, Billboard Music Awards for Top Hot 100 Song and Top Digital Song (for All About That Bass) 2015, Music Business Asscn Award for Breakthrough Artist of the Year 2015, Grammy Award for Best New Artist 2016. *Current Management:* c/o Atom Factory, 10351 West Washington Boulevard, Culver City, CA 90232, USA. *Telephone:* (310) 828-7200. *Website:* atomfactory.com; meghan-trainor .com.

TRAJKOSKI, Goran; Macedonian singer and musician (bagpipes, flute). *Career:* mem. band Anastasia 1991–; numerous concerts and tours worldwide. *Recordings include:* albums: Mansarda (with Lola V. Stain) 1992, Pred Do'dot (Before The Rain) (soundtrack) 1994, Melurgia 1997, Nocurnal 1998. *Films:* contributed music to film Before the Rain and other film and TV projects. *Current Management:* c/o Ivo Jankoski, Third Ear Music, 1000 Skopje, Leninova 29/3/6, Macedonia. *Telephone:* (2) 3236990. *Fax:* (2) 3136906. *E-mail:* info@thirdear.com.mk. *Website:* www.thirdear.com.mk. *E-mail:* neubauten@plugin.com.mk (office). *Website:* www.unet.com.mk/anastasia/ Main.htm.

TRAMP, Mike; Danish singer; b. 14 Jan. 1961, Copenhagen. *Career:* singer, Danish rock group Mabel; singer and songwriter, White Lion 1985–92, 2005–; singer and songwriter, Freak of Nature 1992–94; also solo artist; numerous tours of UK, Europe, USA. *Recordings include:* albums: with White Lion: Fight To Survive 1985, Pride 1987, Big Game 1989, Mane Attraction 1991, Capricorn 1998, Remembering White Lion 1999, Return of the Pride 2008; with Freak of Nature: Freak of Nature 1993, Gathering of Freaks 1994, Outcasts 1998; solo: Capricorn 1998, Recovering the Wasted Years 2002, More to Life than This 2003, Songs I Left Behind 2004, Mike Tramp & The Rock and Roll Circuz 2009, Stand Your Ground 2011, Cobblestone Street 2013. *Website:* miketramp.dk.

TRANCHART, Romain; French musician (piano, guitar) and producer; b. 9 June 1976, Paris. *Education:* American School of Modern Music, Paris.

Career: fmrly lived in Mexico, Algeria and Brazil; fmr mem. rock band, Seven Tracks; released hit single with Davis Mouyal, as Funk Legacy 1999; Foundermem. Modjo 1998–; Co-founder record label, Modjo Music; also solo artist and producer. *Recording:* album: with Modjo: Modjo 2001. *E-mail:* matt@modjo .com; rtprods@wanadoo.fr. *E-mail:* mail@modjo.com. *Website:* www.modjo .com; www.romaintranchartproductions.com.

TRANS-X; Canadian composer, lyricist and singer; b. (Pascal Leguirand), Paris, France. *Career:* mem. SGAE (Spain). *Recordings include:* albums: Minos, De Harmonia, Gregorian Waves, Ishtar, Voice of The Cybicle, Living On Video/Vivre Sur Video 1986, On My Own 1998, Trans-X-cess 1995, 010101 2001, The Drag-Matic Album 2003, Hi-NRG Album 2012. *Honours:* Best Dance Artist, Adisq-Québec. *E-mail:* erick@liveonviedo.com.mx.

TRAORÉ, Boubacar; Malian singer, musician (guitar) and songwriter; b. 1942, Kayes. *Career:* began composing at an early age; acted in theatre 1957–58; started Les Pionniers Jazz early 1960s; also appeared on radio show, Les Auditeurs du Dimanche; earned a living as a tailor, shopkeeper and agricultural agent, training orchestras at night; after 20 years absence, invited to perform on Mali TV 1987; relocated to France 1989; recorded two albums and toured Europe and USA; collaborations include Ali Farka Toure, Toumani Diabate, Keletigui Diabate, Habib Koite; returned to settle in Bamako 1991. *Recordings include:* albums: Mariama 1990, Kar Kar 1992, Les Enfants De Pierrette 1995, Sa Golo 1996, Maciré 1999, Je Chanterai Pour Toi 2002, Kongo Magni 2005, Mali Denhou 2011.

TRAORÉ, Koniba; Malian musician; b. 1958, Koutiala; m. Kone Kadia; one s. three d. *Education:* private music lessons. *Career:* orchestral music, 1978–; biennial competitions and national level, song and dance, 1982, 1984, 1986; numerous TV appearances and on nat. radio; participant, various festivals, including Moscow and Paris. *Compositions include:* Ni bè joro 1996, Balani 1998. *Honours:* Biennial Artistic Prize, Bamako, 1984, Talabé Prize, Bamako, 1997.

TRAORÉ, Rokia; Malian singer, songwriter and musician (guitar); *President, Foundation Passerelle;* b. Bamako. *Education:* degree in sociology. *Career:* solo artist; collaboration with The Kronos Quartet, Peter Sellars, Toni Morrison; worldwide festivals and tours; five studio albums. *Recordings:* albums: Mouneissa 1998, Wanita (BBC Radio 3 Award for Album of the Year 2001) 2000, Bowmboï (BBC Radio 3 Award for Album of the Year 2004) 2003, Tchamantché 2008. *Honours:* Radio France Internationale African Discovery of the Year 1997, Kora Award for Most Promising Female 2001, BBC World Music Awards 2005, Songlines Music Award 2009, Victoires de la Musique. *Current Management:* c/o Long Wave, 27 rue Saint Geoffroy, 80000 Amiens, France. *E-mail:* thomas.weill@gmail.com. *Website:* www.longwave.fr. *Address:* c/o Tama Records, 13 rue Marc Sangnier, 80000 Amiens, France. *Website:* www.rokiatraore.com.

TRAVERS, Brian; British musician (saxophone, horn); b. 7 Feb. 1959, Birmingham, England. *Education:* Moseley School of Art. *Career:* fmr electrician; mem. reggae group UB40 1978–; numerous concerts, tours. *Recordings include:* Signing Off 1980, Present Arms 1981, The Singles Album 1982, UB44 1982, Labour of Love 1983, Live 1983, More UB40 Music 1983, Geffery Morgan 1984, Baggariddim 1985, Little Baggaridim 1985, UB40 File 1985, Rat In The Kitchen 1986, CCCP: Live In Moscow 1987, UB40 1988, Labour of Love II 1990, Promises and Lies 1993, Anansi 1995, Guns In The Ghetto 1997, Labour of Love III 1998, Presents The Dancehall Album 1998, Homegrown 2003, Who You Fighting For? 2005, TwentyFour-Seven 2008, Labour of Love IV 2010, Getting Over the Storm 2013. *Current Management:* Part Rock Management Ltd, 1 Conduit Street, London, W1S 2XA, England. *Telephone:* (1628) 626663. *E-mail:* stewartyoung@mindspring .com. *Address:* UB40, PO Box 15345, Birmingham, B9 9GJ, England. *E-mail:* info@ub40.co.uk. *Website:* www.ub40.co.uk.

TRAVERS, Pat; Canadian musician (guitar), songwriter and singer; b. 1954, Toronto. *Career:* performed with Ronnie Hawkins; Founder, Pat Travers Band 1976–; numerous concerts, festival appearances; worked with Nicko McBain, Scott Gorham, Pat Thrall, Tommy Aldridge, Michael Shrieve. *Recordings include:* albums: Pat Travers, 1976, Makin' Magic 1976, Putting It Straight 1977, Heat In The Street 1978, Go For What You Know – Live 1979, Crash and Burn 1980, Radio Active 1981, Black Pearl 1982, Hot Shot 1984, School of Hard Knocks 1990, Blues Tracks 1992, Just A Touch 1993, Blues Magnet 1994, Halfway to Somewhere 1995, Lookin' Up 1996, King Biscuit Live 1997, Summerdaze '97 1997, Whiskey Blues 1997, Blues Tracks 1998, Born Under a Bad Sign 1998, Boom Boom 2000, Don't Feed the Alligators 2000, P.T. Power Trio 2003, PT=MC2 2005, P.T. Power Trio, Vol. 2 2006, Stick with What You Know: Live in Europe 2007, Travelin' Blues 2009, Boom Boom at the House of Blues 2012, Blues On Fire 2012, Can Do 2013. *E-mail:* webmaster@pattravers .com; rodneyo@pattravers.com. *Website:* www.pattravers.com.

TRAVIS, Geoff; British music industry executive; b. 2 Feb. 1952, Stoke Newington, London. *Education:* Churchill Coll., Cambridge. *Career:* Founder, Rough Trade record label 1978–. *Address:* Rough Trade, 66 Golborne Road, London, W10 5PS, England (office). *Telephone:* (20) 8960-9888 (office). *Fax:* (20) 8968-6715 (office). *Website:* www.roughtraderecords.com (office).

TRAVIS, Randy; American country singer, songwriter and musician (guitar); b. (Randy Bruce Traywick), 4 May 1959, Marshville, North Carolina; m. Lib Hatcher (Mary Elizabeth Robertson) 1991. *Career:* played local clubs with brothers; resident at Charlotte nightclub (owned by Lib Hatcher) 1977; early recordings as Randy Traywick; resident singer, as Randy Ray, Nashville Palace 1992; solo artist as Randy Travis 1985–. *Recordings include:* albums: Storms Of Life (Acad. of Country Music Album of the Year 1986, Music City News Album of the Year 1986) 1986, Always And Forever (Grammy Award 1987, CMA Album of the Year 1987, Music City News Album of the Year 1988) 1987, Old 8x10 (Grammy Award 1988) 1988, An Old Time Christmas 1989, No Holdin' Back 1989, Heroes And Friends 1990, High Lonesome 1991, Wind In The Wire 1993, This Is Me 1994, Full Circle 1996, You And You Alone 1998, A Man Ain't Made Of Stone 1999, Inspirational Journey 2000, Randy Travis Live 2001, Anthology 2002, Rise And Shine (Grammy Award 2004) 2002, Worship & Faith (Grammy Award 2005) 2003, Passing Through 2004, Glory Train (Grammy Award for Best Southern, Country, Or Bluegrass Gospel Album 2007) 2005, Songs of the Season 2007, Around the Bend 2008, Blessed Assurance 2011, Influence, Vol. 1: The Man I Am 2013. *Honours:* Acad. of Country Music Top Male Vocalist 1985, 1986, 1987, 1988, Grammy Award for Best Country Newcomer 1986, CMA Horizon Award 1986, Acad. of Country Music Song of the Year (for On the Other Hand) 1986, (for Forever and Ever Amen) 1987, (for Three Wooden Crosses) 2004, CMA Single of the Year (for Forever and Ever Amen) 1987, Music City News Male Artist of the Year, Star of Tomorrow and Single of the Year (for On the Other Hand) 1987, CMA Male Vocalist of the Year 1987, 1988, Music City News Entertainer of the Year, Male Artist of the Year, Single of the Year (for Forever and Ever Amen) and Entertainer of the Year 1989, Grammy Award for Best Album Collaboration (for Same Old Train 1998, CMA Song of the Year (for Three Wooden Crosses) 2003, Grammy Award for Best Country Collaboration with Vocals (for I Told You So with Carrie Underwood) 2010, also awards from Performance magazine, AMOA Jukebox, Country Music Round Up, NECMA, TNN Viewers Choice Awards, Rolling Stone magazine, Playboy magazine, Billboard Music Awards, BBC Radio Two, Dove Awards, Christian Country Music Awards. *Current Management:* Elizabeth Travis Management, 1610 16th Avenue South, Nashville, TN 37212, USA. *Telephone:* (615) 383-7258. *Fax:* (615) 269-7828. *E-mail:* webmaster@randytravis.com. *Website:* www.randytravis.com.

TRAVIS, Theodore (Theo) John, BMus (Hons); British musician (tenor, soprano saxophones, flute, alto flute) and composer; b. 7 July 1964, Birmingham; m. Madelyn J. Cohen 1992; one s. *Education:* Univ. of Manchester. *Career:* Leader Theo Travis Quartet; played at Ronnie Scotts, all over UK and at int. jazz festivals; also mem. of groups Gong, Soft Machine Legacy, Travis & Fripp with guitarist Robert Fripp and Cipher, experimental ambient duo with bassist/producer Dave Sturt; also performed with Bill Nelson, John Etheridge, Jim Mullen, Harold Budd, Hatfield and the North, Mick Karn, David Sylvian, Anja Garbarek, John Foxx and the Tangent; Arts Council Tour for improvising trio with John Marshall (drums) and Mark Wood (guitar) 1998; played and recorded with many groups of Steven Wilson including solo albums/live band, Porcupine Tree, No-Man and Bass Communion. *Compositions:* Broad Street Changes Suite for jazz septet, commissioned by West Midlands Arts; many commissions with Dave Sturt to write and perform new music for classic silent films; composed for more than 35 albums. *Radio includes:* Jazz Parade (BBC Radio 2, playing original compositions) 1993. *Recordings:* ten solo albums, 26 collaborative albums and guested on over 110 albums in total. *E-mail:* info@theotravis.com (office). *Website:* www.theotravis.com.

TRENT, Tammy; American singer and musician (drums, percussion); b. 11 April 1968, Grand Rapids, Michigan; m. Trent Lenderink, 18 Aug. 1990. *Education:* 1 year college. *Career:* Signed to Rex Music, Brentwood, Tennessee; mem, BMI. *Recordings:* first radio single: Your Love Is 4 Always (No. 1, Christian Hits Radio charts); albums: Tammy Trent 1996, You Have My Heart 1997, Set You Free 2000, I See Beautiful 2006, Stronger 2008. *Address:* Tammy Trent Ministries, PO Box 1701, Brentwood, TN 37024, USA. *E-mail:* . *Website:* www.tammytrent.com.

TRETOW, Michael Bo; Swedish recording engineer and producer; b. 20 Aug. 1944; m. Lilian B; one s. one d. *Career:* recording engineer with around 40 Gold Records for early work; independent engineer and producer 1980–; composer of music for film, videos and commercials; mem. SSES. *Recordings as engineer include:* engineer on all ABBA albums: Ring Ring 1973, Waterloo 1974, Abba 1975, Greatest Hits 1976, Arrival 1976, The Album 1978, Voulez Vous 1979, Greatest Hits Vol. 2 1979, Super Trouper 1980, The Visitors 1981, The First Ten Years 1982, Abba Gold 1992, More Abba Gold 1993, Singles Collection 2001. *Recordings include:* Hubba Hubba Zoot Zoot 1981, Den Makalösa Manicken 1986. *Composition:* Swedish TV Station Call. *Honours:* Gold Camera Award 1988, Int. TV, Cinema and Radio Award 1988, Monaco Radio Contest 1989.

TREVI, Gloria; Mexican singer; b. (Gloria de los Angeles Treviño Ruiz), 15 Feb. 1968, Monterrey; m. Sergio Andrade (divorced); one s. *Career:* mem. all-female group Boquitas Pintadas 1985–89; solo artist 1989–, known as the 'Mexican Madonna'. *E-mail:* info@gloriatreviweboficial.com. *Website:* www.gloriatreviweboficial.com.

DR TREVIS (see Redman)

TREVISAN, Luciano, (Fricchetti); Italian music manager, promoter and music publisher; b. 25 Sept. 1959, Venice. *Education:* Univ. of Bologna. *Career:* involved in Cultural Asscn, ARCI Man.; record distributors –1986; Lion, events productions 1986–, Partner, Materiali Sonori record co.; promoter, live events; artist man. 1989–; Partner, Ossigeno, Music Publishing Co. 1993–; Partner, Evolution Music 1995–2000, Alma Music 2000–; Publr

mem. Società Italiana degli Autori ed Editori, o2digitale 2010–. *Publication:* Compra O Muori. *Address:* Via F.lli Cavanis 44/18, 30174 Chirignago, Venice, Italy (office). *Telephone:* (041) 5441558 (office). *E-mail:* lucianotrevisan@o2pub.com (office). *Website:* www.o2pub.com (office).

TREWAVAS, Peter; British musician (bass); b. 15 Jan. 1959, Middlesbrough, Cleveland, England. *Career:* fmr mem. The Metros; mem. progressive rock group, Marillion 1982–; numerous tours; mem. Transatlantic 2000–; mem. Kino 2005–. *Recordings include:* albums: with Marillion: Script For A Jester's Tear 1983, Fugazi 1984, Real To Reel 1984, Misplaced Childhood 1985, Brief Encounter 1986, Clutching At Straws 1987, B-Sides Themselves 1988, The Thieving Magpie 1988, Holidays In Eden 1991, Brave 1994, Afraid of Sunlight 1995, Made Again 1996, This Strange Engine 1997, Radiation 1998, Marillion.com 1999, Anorak In The UK Live 2002, Somewhere Else 2007; with Transatlantic: SMPTe 2000, Bridge Across Forever 2001; with Kino: Picture 2005. *E-mail:* info@knowmoremanagement.com. *Address:* PO Box 252, Aylesbury, Buckinghamshire, HP18 0YS, England. *Telephone:* (1296) 770839. *E-mail:* band@marillion.com; racket@marillion.com. *Website:* www.marillion.com.

TRIBAL UNDERGROUND (see Pilgrem, Rennie)

TRIBBLE; British musician (bass, keyboards, guitar) and singer; b. (Brian Evans), 20 March 1953, Coventry, England; m. (divorced); five s. one d. *Career:* partner, Horizon Recording Studios; extensive session work, touring with rock bands in Europe and USA; mem. rock, reggae and jazz outfits in West Indies; recording for numerous labels; advertising and video soundtrack work; mem. Chainsaw, Rumrunners, The Trial; Owner/man. STI/Pro-Audio; graphic design work, arrangements, session work; playing, programming and production of samples for dance producers; promoter for new artists; audio producer. *Compositions include:* The Last Great Bank Raid, The Hellpits of Nightfang, City Life, Accident Victim, Rock 'n' Roll Gambler, Werewolf; and many more as co-composer with other musicians. *Recordings include:* Police and Politicians, Devil's Daughter, Bolt From The Black, Pissed Again, Twisted and Dysfunktional; and many more with other artists/compilations.

TRICKY; British rap artist and songwriter; b. (Adrian Thaws), Bristol. *Career:* rap artist with Wild Bunch; solo artist with singer Martina; regular collaborations as singer/writer with Massive Attack; leader of recording project Nearly God (duets with Björk, Alison Moyet, Terry Hall, Neneh Cherry) 1996; numerous concerts and festival appearances. *Recordings include:* albums: with Massive Attack: Blue Lines (Face Magazine Best Album of the Year 1991) 1991, Protection 1995; solo: Maxinquaye 1995, Nearly God 1996, Pre-Millennium Tension 1996, Angels with Dirty Faces 1998, Juxtapose 1999, BlowBack 2001, Vulnerable 2003, Knowle West Boy 2008, Mixed Race 2010, False Idols 2013, Adrian Thaws 2014. *Honours:* Q Award for Best Producer 1995. *Address:* !K7 Records, Unit 10, The Laundry, 2-18 Warburton Road, London, E8 3FN, England. *E-mail:* charlotte@k7.com. *Website:* www.k7.com; www.trickysite.com.

TRITT, Travis; American country singer and songwriter; b. 9 Feb. 1963, Maretta, GA; m. Theresa 1997. *Career:* solo artist 1990–; recorded, toured with Marty Stuart. *Recordings include:* albums: Country Club 1990, It's All About To Change 1991, T-R-O-U-B-L-E 1992, A Travis Tritt Christmas: Loving Time of theYear 1992, Rhythm, Country and Blues 1993, Ten Feet Tall and Bulletproof 1994, The Restless Kind 1996, No More Looking Over My Shoulder 1998, Down The Road I Go 2000, The Lovin' Side 2002, Strong Enough 2002, My Honky Tonk History 2004, The Storm 2007. *Publication:* Ten Feet Tall and Bulletproof (autobiog.) 1992. *Honours:* CMA Horizon Award 1991, Grammy Award 1992. *Address:* 1012 16th Avenue S, Nashville, TN 37212, USA. *Website:* www.travistritt.com.

TROCMÉ, Elisa Andréa; French/Irish musician (counter-bass, clarinets, other wind instruments) and stage manager; b. 21 Aug. 1955, Pennsylvania, USA; widowed; three s. one d. *Education:* EHESS, Paris; private music lessons, workshops with B. Vitet, Tamia, Steve Lacy, Michel Fano, George Benjamin, Robert Aitken, Georges Aperghis, Toru Takemitsu, Barre Phillips. *Career:* Irving Plaza/BCBG, New York 1980; Le Grand Rex; New Morning; Centre Georges Pompidou; Musée d'Art Moderne; Grand Palais dance, music, plastic arts creations; Improvised music and dance encounters, Toulouse 1992–; Art Wars, La Mama, Theater, New York 1980; Cinema de Minuit, directed by Patricia Bardon, ProdA2, Paris 1984; The Weapons of The Spirits, directed by Pierre Sauvage (prize-winning documentary, Cannes 1987; 666, Julie West video-dance production, S Rougier, Paris 1985; European project in Serbia and Hungary with dance Cie Kobez 2010; experimental music org. 2011–12; mem. Euro Seminoar of Ethnomusicology. *Dance:* music for Julie West, Mireille Feyzeau, Roland Paulin, cie Kobez, cie Alise, New York Dance Workshop and others. *Film music:* music for The Weapons of the Spirit by Pierre Sauvage, music for short films for NYU and IDHEC. *Publications:* Clarinette magazine; translations for Télérama, L'Événement du Jeudi, L'Humanité, Melody Maker. *Honours:* Prix du Mécénat with composer Pierre Mariétan. *Address:* 13 rue Oeillets, Balma 31130, France (home). *Telephone:* 6-61-91-57-23 (mobile) (home). *E-mail:* elitrocme@hotmail.com (office).

TROHMAN, Joe; American musician (guitar); b. 1 Sept. 1984. *Career:* Founder-mem. and lead guitarist of band Fall Out Boy 2001–; headline act Nintendo Fusion Tour 2005, Black Clouds and Underdogs Tour 2005, Honda Civic Tour 2007, Young Wild Things Tour 2007; collaborations with Gym Class Heroes, Motion City Soundtrack. *Recordings include:* albums: Fall Out

Boy's Evening Out with Your Girlfriend (mini-LP) 2002, Take This to Your Grave 2003, From Under the Cork Tree 2005, Infinity on High 2007, Folie à Deux 2008, Save Rock and Roll 2013, American Beauty/American Psycho 2015. *Honours:* People's Choice Awards for Favorite Int. Group 2006, for Favorite Alternative Band 2014, Kerrang! Awards for Best Video (for Sugar, We're Going Down) 2006, (for This Ain't a Scene, It's an Arms Race) 2007, for Best Single (for The Phoenix) 2013, for Best Int. Band 2014, Teen Choice Awards for Best Rock Track and Best Single (for Dance, Dance) 2006, for Best Single (for Thnks Fr Th Mmrs) 2007, MTV Video Music Awards for Viewers Choice 2007, for Best Rock Video (for Uma Thurman) 2015, World Music Award for Best Alternative Act 2014, American Music Award for Favorite Alternative Rock Artist 2015. *Address:* Fall Out Boy Inc., PO Box 219, 1187 Wilmette Avenue, Wilmette, IL 60091; Island Records, 825 Eighth Avenue, New York, NY 10019, USA. *Website:* www.islandrecords.com; www.falloutboyrock.com.

TROUT, Walter; American musician (guitar, harmonica) and song writer; b. 6 March 1951, Atlantic City, New Jersey; s. of Edward Trout and Lynnette Cooper; m. Marie Braendgaard; three s. *Education:* studied classical trumpet, jazz then guitar. *Career:* played with John Lee Hooker, Big Mama Thornton, Joe Tex, Pee Wee Crayton 1979–80; lead guitarist, harmonica, Canned Heat 1984–89; lead guitar, John Mayall's Bluesbreakers 1984–89; formed the Walter Trout Band 1989, renamed Walter Trout and The Radicals 1998, later renamed Walter Trout 2008; mem. American Soc. of Composers, Authors and Publrs (ASCAP). *Recordings include:* albums: The Boogie Assault (with Canned Heat) 1981, Heat Brothers '84 1984, John Mayall's Bluesbreakers: Behind the Iron Curtain 1985, The Power of the Blues 1987, Chicago Line 1988, Walter Trout Band: Life in the Jungle 1989, Prisoner of a Dream 1990, The Love That We Once Knew 1990, No More Fish-Jokes Live 1992, Radio Records 1992, Transistion 1992, Motivation of Love 1992, Tremble 1994, Still Got the Blues 1994, Tellin' Stories 1994, Breaking the Rules 1995, Where Blues Meets Rock 1995, Jeffology (tribute to Jeff Beck) 1995, Tribute to Stevie (tribute to Stevie Ray Vaughan) 1996, Walter Trout 1998, Livin' Everyday 1999, Live Trout 2000, Go the Distance 2001, Blue Christmas 2001, Relentless 2003, Trout 2005, Full Circle 2006, The Outsider 2008, Unspoiled By Progress 2009, Common Ground 2010, Blues for the Modern Daze 2012, Luther's Blues - A Tribute to Luther Allison 2013, The Blues Came Callin' 2014, Battle Scars 2015. *Honours:* Loa Angeles Music Award for Guitarist of the Year, Best Ind. Rock Album, Best Blues Song in Arrow Classic Rock listeners' poll 2007, 2008, 2009, 2010, 2011, iTunes Best Blues Song 2012, British Blues Awards, Best Blues Artist Overseas 2013, 2014, 2015, Sena European Guitar Award 2015. *Current Management:* c/o Fish-Net Productions Inc., 5840 West Craig Road, Suite 120–228, Las Vegas, NV 89130, USA. *Telephone:* (714) 235-7749. *Fax:* (714) 960-6482. *E-mail:* management@waltertrout.com (office). *Address:* PO Box 246, Huntington Beach, CA 92648, USA (home). *Website:* www .waltertrout.com.

TROW, Zane Roderick; British composer and artistic director; b. 25 Jan. 1956, London, England. *Career:* moved to Australia 1989; CEO and Centre Dir, Footscray Community Arts Centre 1989–91; CEO and Artistic Dir, Next Wave Festival, Melbourne 1991–97; CEO and Artistic Dir, The Performance Space, Sydney 1997–99; Artistic Dir, Brisbane Powerhouse 1999–; currently Chair., Multimedia Art Asia Pacific; mem. Actors Equity; PRS. *Compositions include:* The Wolves, Hot Time, Dream Mamma. *Recordings include:* Big River, For Those Who Hear Actual Voices 2004. *Honours:* numerous Australian Council for the Arts grants. *Address:* Multimedia Art Asia Pacific, GPO Box 2505, Brisbane, Queensland 4001, Australia (office). *Telephone:* (7) 3161-7960 (office). *E-mail:* info@maap.org.au (office). *Website:* maap.org.au (office).

TROWER, Robin; British musician (guitar); b. 9 March 1945, Southend, Essex, England. *Career:* founder mem., The Paramounts 1962–66, Procol Harum 1967–71; solo artist 1971–; founder mem., Jude; founder, Robin Trower Band, BLT 1981; numerous festival appearances and tours. *Recordings include:* albums: with Procol Harum: Procol Harum 1967, Shine On Brightly 1968, A Salty Dog 1969, Home 1970; solo: Twice Removed From Yesterday 1973, Bridge of Sighs 1974, For Earth Below 1975, Robin Trower Live 1976, Long Misty Days 1976, In City Dreams 1977, Caravan To Midnight 1978, Victims of the Fury 1980, Back It Up 1983, Beyond The Mist 1985, Passion 1987, Portfolio 1987, Take What You Need 1988, No Stopping Anytime 1989, In the Line of Fire 1990, 20th Century Blues 1994, New Haven 1977, King Biscuit Flower Hour 1996, Someday Blues 1997, Go My Way 2000, Speed of Sound 2002, Living Out of Time 2004, Another Days Blues 2005, Seven Moons (with Jack Bruce) 2008. *Current Management:* Stardust Management, 4600 Franklin Avenue, Los Angeles, CA 90027, USA. *E-mail:* derek@trowerpower.com. *Website:* www.trowerpower.com.

TRUBETSKY, Tonu (Prince); Estonian singer, composer, poet, writer and actor; b. 24 April 1963, Revala, Tallinn; m. Anu Trubetsky 1988; one s. two d. *Career:* lead singer, Vennaskond 1984–, Felis Ultramarinus 1986, Prince Trubetsky and JMKE 1986, The Un Concern 1988; solo artist 1993–; business venture, Vennaskond Ltd. *Films include:* Soda 1987, Hysteria 1993, Elagu Proudhon! (video with Vennaskond) 1994, Riga My Love (video with Vennaskond) 1995, Punklaulupidu 2008. *Recordings include:* with Vennaskond: Ltn Schmidt'i Pojad (The Sons of Lieutenant Schmidt) 1991, Girl In Black 1991, Rockpiraadid (The Rock Pirates) 1992, Usk. Lootus. Armastus (Faith. Hope. Love) 1993, Voluri Tagasitulek (Return of The Wizard) 1995, Vaenlane Ei Maga (The Enemy Is Not Sleeping) 1995, Inglid Ja Kanglased (Angels and Heroes) 1995, Mina ja George 1996, Reis Kuule 1997,

Werszawianka 1999, Ma armastan Amserikat 2001, Subway 2003, Rigas Kaos 2005, Anarhia agentuur 2011. *Publications include:* Pogo 1989, Inglid Ja Kanglased (Angels and Heroes) 1992, Anarhia (Anarchy) 1994, Daam Sinises (Lady In Blue) 1994. *Honours:* Levijaagup 1990. *Address:* Vennaskond, PO Box 2225, Tallinn 0035, Estonia.

TRUE, Roger; American country singer and musician (guitar); b. 2 June, Greensboro, NC. *Career:* mem. The True Brothers; numerous live appearances, festivals; mem. BMI, ASCAP. *Film appearance:* The Dam. *Recordings include:* Crazy Arms; There Stands the Glass; Your Cheatin' Heart; Walk Through This World With Me; Tonight the Bottle Let Me Down; El Paso; Before the Next Teardrop Falls; Good Hearted Woman; Take This Job and Shove It; Don't Rock the Jukebox; We'll Burn that Bridge; Friends in Low Places, Sing the Hits of Webb Pierce 2000, The Third Man 2001, Wanted: the True Brothers – Country Outlaw Tribute 2006, Hymns and Other Songs We Wrote Ourselves 2006. *Honours:* NCCMA Award. *Website:* www.myspace .com/thetruebrothers.

TRUESDALE, Tommy; British singer, entertainer, actor and radio presenter; b. 17 Nov. 1947, Annbank, Ayr, Scotland; m. Marjory Truesdale 1972. *Career:* numerous television appearances, radio broadcasts, festivals; presenter and producer, Radio West; columnist, Country Music News and Roots Magazine, Ayrshire World Newspaper; mem. British Country Music Asscn. *Recordings include:* albums: C'mon Everybody 1979, Sings Country 1985, The Best of T. T. Album 1990, A Tree in the Meadow 1993, Tommy Truesdale Favourites 2000. *Honours:* Scottish Country Music Fellowship Award for Top Male Vocalist 1989, 1990. *Telephone:* (1292) 268822. *E-mail:* ttsun@lineone .net. *Website:* website.lineone.net/~ttsun.

TRUESDELL, Ryan, MA; American jazz composer, arranger and record producer. *Education:* Univ. of Minnesota, New England Conservatory of Music. *Career:* studied composition with Bob Brookmeyer and Lee Hyla; copyist for Maria Schneider, Bob Brookmeyer, Luciana Souza, Miles Evans, Gil Evans Estate, Jim Hall, Geoffrey Keezer; Founder, Ryan Truesdell's Gil Evans Project. *Recordings:* albums: as producer and arranger: Sky Blue, Maria Schneider (Village Voice Critics Poll Jazz Album of the Year 2007, Choc Award 2007, Grammy Award for Best Instrumental Composition 2008) 2007, Centennial: Newly Discovered Works of Gil Evans, Ryan Truesdell's Gil Evans Project (Jazz Journalists Asscn Award for Record of the Year 2013) 2012. *Honours:* Jazz Journalists Asscn Award for Large Ensemble of the Year (for Ryan Truesdell's Gil Evans Project) 2013; as arranger: Grammy Award for Best Instrumental Arrangement (for How About You by Gil Evans) 2013. *Current Management:* c/o Myles Weinstein, Unlimited Myles, 6 Imaginary Place, Aberdeen, NJ 07747, USA. *Telephone:* (732) 566-2881. *Fax:* (732) 566-8157. *E-mail:* myles@unlimitedmyles.com. *Website:* www.unlimitedmyles .com. *E-mail:* ryan@gilevansproject.com (home). *Website:* www.ryantruesdell .com (home); www.gilevansproject.com (home).

TRUJILLO, Robert; American musician (bass guitar); b. 23 Oct. 1964, Santa Monica, Calif. *Career:* mem. Suicidal Tendencies 1990–94; mem. Infectious Grooves 1992–; played with Ozzy Osbourne's band; mem. Metallica 2003–. *Film:* Some Kind Of Monster (Independent Spirit Award for Best Documentary 2005) 2004. *Recordings include:* albums: with Suicidal Tendencies: Lights, Camera, Revolution 1990, Possessed To Skate 1990, The Art of Rebellion 1992, Still Cyco After All These Years 1993, Suicidal For Life 1994, Six the Hard Way 1998, Friends & Family 1998, FreeDumb 1999, FNG 2000, Free Your Soul And Save My Mind 2000; with Infectious Grooves: The Plague That Makes Your Booty Move 1991, Sarsippius' Ark 1993, Groove Family Cyco 1994, Mas Borracho 2000; with Metallica: St Anger 2003, Death Magnetic 2008, Orgullo, Pasión, y Gloria: Tres Noches en la Ciudad de México 2009, The Big Four: Live from Sofia, Bulgaria 2010, Lulu 2011, Beyond Magnetic 2012. *Honours:* Grammy Award for Best Metal Performance (for My Apocalypse) 2009. *Current Management:* Q-Prime Inc., 729 Seventh Avenue, 16th Floor, New York, NY 10019, USA. *Telephone:* (212) 302-9790. *Fax:* (212) 302-9589. *Website:* www.qprime.com; www.metallica.com.

TSAI, Jolin; Chinese singer, dancer and actor; b. 15 Sept. 1980. *Education:* Fu Jen Catholic Univ. *Recordings include:* Living With the World 1999, Pirates; albums: Jolin 1019 1999, Don't Stop 2000, Show Your Love, Lucky Number, Magic, Castle, J-Game 2005, Dancing Diva 2006, Agent J 2007, Love Exercise 2008, Butterfly 2009, Myself 2010. *Soundtrack:* Warriors of Heaven and Earth 2003. *Honours:* Golden Melody Award 2007. *Address:* c/o Warner Music Taiwan Ltd, No.117, Sec.4, Minsheng East Road., Songshan District, Taipei 105, Taiwan. *Website:* www.warnermusic.com.tw/artist/jolin.

TSE, Nicholas; Hong Kong singer and actor; b. (Nicholas Tse Ting Fung), 29 Aug. 1980, s. of Patrick Tse Yin and Deborah Lai. *Education:* professional vocal training in Japan. *Career:* moved with family to Vancouver, Canada aged 7; teen pop star and high profile actor; records in Mandarin and Cantonese languages. *Films as actor:* Young and Dangerous – The Prequel 1998, Gen-X Cops 1999, Time and Tide 2000, Master Q 2001, New Police Story 2004, Invisible Target 2007, Bodyguards and Assassins 2009, Hot Summer Days 2010, Shaolin 2011, The Bullet Vanishes 2012, The Midas Touch 2013, From Vegas to Macau 2013. *Film as co-director:* Heroes in Love 2001. *Recordings include:* albums: My Attitude 1997, Fun 1997, Horizons 1998, Music Video Karaoke 1998, Believe 1999, Grateful For Your Love 1999, Most Wanted 1999, Zero Distance 2000, Understand 2000, 20 Twenty 2000, Viva 2000, Senses 2001, Jade Butterfly 2001, ME 2002, Reborn 2003, One Inch Closer 2005, Last of Nicholas Tse 2009. *Honours:* Hong Kong Film Award for

Best New Actor 1999, World Music Award 2002, World Music Award for World's Best Chinese Artist 2003, Hong Kong Film Award for Best Actor 2011. *Address:* Fitto Entertainment Co. Ltd, 28/F Emperor Group Centre, 288 Hennessy Road, Wanchai, Hong Kong Special Administrative Region, People's Republic of China.

TSHAMALA, Mufubela; Democratic Republic of the Congo researcher, musician (flute, guitar), singer and composer; b. 11 March 1957, Ilebok Kasai Occidental; m. Petronie Mbombo Malumba 1988, four s. three d. *Career:* composed music for film, La Pipe 1983; composed jingles for African Radio, 1983; numerous TV and radio broadcasts, and work as producer; puppeteer and drag artist; played in nightclubs and hotels, Kinshasa; flautist; teacher of music; researcher into traditional and modern mixing techniques; guitarist, flautist and singer in groups, Msumuenu, Ya' Kongo; mem. Asscn des Musiques de Recherche du Congo. *Compositions include:* music for Le Refuge, Le Crapeaud chez ses Beaux Parents, Revue Noire à Kinshasa No. 21 1996. *Recording:* Naza Balado Te 1982. *Publication:* La Vie de Robert le Diable (lyric drama, Colmar, France) 1984. *Honours:* First Prize for orchestration, Festival of Central African Music 1982, Festpam 1996, Brazzaville Festijazz, Kinshasa 1999.

TSISKARIDZE, Kakha; Georgian musician (drums, piano, percussion) and singer; b. 4 June 1976, Batumi. *Education:* Batumi Musical Coll. *Career:* several concerts with S. Pavliashvili on stage in Georgia, Russia and Miami, Fla, USA; mem. Dianaland Club, Batumi. *Recording:* album: Is Erti (The One) 1999. *Honours:* Jazz Music Festival Award for Best Drummer, Batumi 1992, Margarette Festival Drummer of the Year 1996, Best Drummer of the Year, Georgia 1996.

TSUI, Trix Ko-chuan; Taiwanese musician (guitar), concert promoter and DJ; b. 20 Oct. 1953, Taipei; m. Farie Hsiu-Ching Le 1979; one d. *Education:* World Coll. of Journalism and Communication. *Career:* concert promoter and stage man. for Chick Corea's Acoustic and Electric Band, Lee Ritenour, Brecker Brothers, Peabo Bryson and Patti Austin; stage man. for INXS, B. B. King, Hard Rock Cafe, Taipei 1992–94; leader and guitarist, Rock City Band 1971–80, (as house band of Hard Rock Cafe, Taipei) 1994–95; mem. Diplomats 1980–93; radio DJ, BBC, TBC; technical dir Gibson and Digitech; musical consultant, Taipei Communicating Arts (from the system of MIT); producer for Miss Jade Lee, Blindman pop group, Welfare Foundation; columnist, Non-Classical Music Magazine, Audio and CD Shopper, Liberty Time newspaper; mem. Musical Mountain Communication. *Address:* 3F No. 16, Alley 88, Sec 2, Pao-Fu Road, Yung-Ho, Taipei, Taiwan.

TSUJI, Hitonari, (Jinsei Tsuji); Japanese novelist, scriptwriter and musician; b. 4 Oct. 1959, Tokyo; m. Nakayama Miho. *Career:* fmr singer rock band, Echoes; solo artist 1993–. *Recordings include:* albums: with Echoes: Welcome to the Lost Child Club 1985, Heart Edge 1986, Goodbye Gentle Land 1987, Hurts 1988, Foolish Game 1988, The History of Echoes 1985–89 1989, Dear Friend 1989, Eggs 1990, Gold Water 1990, Silver Bullet 1991, No Kiddin' 1994; solo: The Best of Jinsei Songs 1993, New Wall 1996, Best Wishes 1997, Echoes 2000. *Film scripts:* Tenshi no wakemae 1994, Sennen tabito 1999, Hotoke 2001, Filament 2001, Calmi Cuori Appassionati 2001, Mokka no koibito 2002. *Publications include:* novels: Pianishimo (Pianissimo) (Subaru Literature Prize) 1989, Kuraudi (Cloudy) 1989, Tabibito no ki (The Tree of the Traveller) 1992, Haha naru nagi to chichi naru shike (Motherly Calm, Fatherly Storm) 1993, Passajio 1994, Kaikyô no hikari (Lights in the Channel) (Akutagawa Prize) 1996, Antinoise 1996, Hakubutsu (The White Buddha) (Prix Fémina Étranger 1999) 1997, Ai no Kumeni (Objective) 1997, Reisei to jônetsu no aida (with Ekuni Kaori) 1999, Sitto No Kaori 2000, Mokka no Koibito 2002, Ai to Eien no Aoisora 2002, Ima Kono Kono Syunkan Aishiterutoiukoto 2003, Daihitsy Ya 2004, Acacia Ashita no Yakusoku 2005, Ai no atoni Kurumono 2006, Ugan 2008, Madam to Okusama 2009, Mokka no Koibito 2009, Dahlia 2009, Acacia no Hana no sakidasukoro Acacia 2009, Kuroe to Enzō 2010. *Current Management:* c/o Japan Foreign-Rights Centre, Sun Mall No. 3, Room 201, 1-19-10 Shinjuku, Shinjuku-ku, Tokyo 160-0022, Japan. *Telephone:* (3) 5738-5397. *Fax:* (3) 5738-5398. *Website:* www.j-tsuji-h.com.

TSUNEOKA, Akira; Japanese musician (drums). *Career:* Founder-mem. Hi-Standard 1991–. *Recordings include:* albums: Growing Up 1992, Angry Fist 1995, Making the Road 1999, Kids Are Alright 2002; solo: Turbulence 2007, Halcali 2007, Misono 2009; singles: California Dreamin', Survival Of The Fattest, Punk Uprising, Love Is A Battlefield 2001, Last Of Sunny Day 2002. *Address:* c/o Fat Wreck Chords, 2196 Palou Avenue, San Francisco, CA 94119-3690, USA. *E-mail:* mailbag@fatwreck.com. *Website:* www.fatwreck.com.

TUCKER, Maureen; American musician (drums); b. 1945, New Jersey. *Career:* Musician, Velvet Underground, 1965–71; Solo artiste, 1982–; Residency, Café Bizarre; House band, Andy Warhol's Factory arts collective, New York; Member, Warhol's multimedia show, The Exploding Plastic Inevitable, 1966; Concerts include: Montréal World Fair, Canada, 1967; Reunions with Velvet Underground, France, 1990; Wembley, London, 1993. *Recordings:* albums: with The Velvet Underground: The Velvet Underground and Nico 1967, White Light, White Heat 1968, The Velvet Underground 1969, Loaded 1970, VU, 1985, Peel Slowly And See 1993, The Quine Tapes 2001; various compilations and collections; solo: Playing Possum 1982, Moejadkatebarry 1987, Life In Exile After Abdication 1989, I Spent A Week There The Other Night 1991; Dogs Under Stress 1994. *Honours:* Inducted into Rock 'n' Roll Hall of Fame (with Velvet Underground), 1996. *Address:* PO Box 2371, Douglas,

GA 31534, USA. *E-mail:* moesite@charter.net. *Website:* www.spearedpeanut .com/tajmoehal.

TUCKER, Paul; British musician (keyboards) and songwriter; b. 12 Aug. 1968, Cambridge, England. *Education:* Univ. of Newcastle. *Career:* Founder-mem. (with Tunde Baiyewu), The Lighthouse Family 1993–2001, band reformed 2010; Founder-mem. The Orange Lights 2007. *Recordings include:* album: Ocean Drive 1995, Postcards from Heaven 1997, Whatever Gets You Through The Day 2001. *Current Management:* c/o Creative Artists Agency, 5th Floor, 3 Shortlands, Hammersmith, London, W6 8DA, England. *Telephone:* (20) 8846-3000. *Fax:* (20) 8846-3090. *Website:* www.caatouring.com.

TUCKER, Tanya; American country singer; b. 10 Oct. 1958, Seminole, Tex.; d. of Jesse Tucker and Juanita Tucker; two d. *Career:* sang at country fairs as a teenager; recording artist 1972–; regular concerts include Grand Ole Opry; film appearance Jeremiah Johnson. *Compositions include:* Save Me, Leave Them Boys Alone (co-writer with Hank Williams Jr). *Recordings include:* albums: Delta Dawn 1972, What's Your Mama's Name? 1973, Would You Lay With Me 1974, Lovin' and Learnin' 1975, Tanya Tucker 1975, Here's Some Love 1976, You Are So Beautiful 1977, Ridin' Rainbows 1977, TNT 1978, Tear Me Apart 1979, Dreamlovers 1980, Should I Do It? 1981, Changes 1982, Live 1982, Love Me Like You Used To 1987, Strong Enough To Bend 1988, Tennessee Woman 1990, Greatest Hits – Encore 1990, What Do I Do With Me 1991, Lizzie and The Rainman 1992, Hits 1992, Can't Run From Yourself 1992, Fire To Fire 1995, Complicated 1997, 20 Greatest Hits 2000, Country Classics 2001, Tanya 2002, Tanya – Live at Billy Bob's Texas 2005, My Turn 2009. *Television:* Tuckerville 2005–06. *Honours:* Acad. of Country Music Top New Female Vocalist Award 1972, 1993, Country Music Association (CMA) Award for Female Vocalist of Year 1991, named amongst Country Music Television (CMT) 40 Greatest Women of Country Music 2002. *Address:* Tanya Tucker Inc., 109 Westpark Drive, Suite 400, Brentwood, TN 37027-5032, USA (office). *Telephone:* (615) 377-1308 (office). *Fax:* (615) 370-4560 (office). *E-mail:* ttuckerfc@aol.com (office). *Website:* www.tanyatucker.com.

TULLY, Nigel, MA; British bandleader, singer and musician (guitar, saxophone); b. 22 July 1943, Barnsley, Yorkshire, England; m. Prue Lyell 1978; one s. one d. *Education:* Univ. of Oxford, studied with Pat Crumly. *Career:* bandleader, The Dark Blues 1962–; numerous live concerts; Fellow, British Computer Society; Master, Worshipful Company of Musicians. *Recordings include:* Overdue 1983, Live At Ashdown 1985, 25 And Going For Gold 1988, Midsummer Dance 1992, Up All Night 1998, Six By Six 2003. *Current Management:* Dark Blues Management Ltd, Puddephat's, Markyate, Hertfordshire, AL3 8AZ, England. *E-mail:* nigeltully@darkblues.co.uk. *Website:* www.darkblues.co.uk.

TUNSTALL, Kate Victoria (K. T.); British singer, songwriter and musician; b. 1975, St Andrews, Fife, Scotland; m. Luke Bullen 2008. *Education:* Kent School, Conn., USA, Royal Holloway Coll., Egham, Surrey. *Career:* fmr mem. of bands, including The Happy Campers. *Recordings include:* albums: Eye to the Telescope 2004, Acoustic Extravaganza 2006, Drastic Fantastic 2007, Tiger Suit 2010, Invisible Empire/Crescent Moon 2013. *Honours:* Q Award for Best Track (for Black Horse and the Cherry Tree) 2005, BRIT Award for Best British Female Artist 2006, Ivor Novello Award for Best Song (for Suddenly I See) 2006. *Website:* www.kttunstall.com.

TUREK, Jan; Czech composer; b. 19 Oct. 1957, Most; m. Hana Pegrímková 1982; one s. one d. *Education:* Univ. of Economics; pvt. study of classical guitar. *Career:* more than 100 works (songs and lyrics) for theatres in Czech Repub., Poland and Norway, commercials, radio designs. *Current Management:* c/o F Agency, Zizkova 1616, 434 01 Most; c/o DILIA, Krátkého 1, 190 03 Prague 9; c/o Aura-Pont, Radlická 99, 150 00 Prague 5, Czech Republic. *Address:* Hasicska 147, 434 01 Most-Vtelno, Czech Republic (home). *E-mail:* turekvtelno@volny.cz (home).

TURNER, Alexander David (Alex); British singer, songwriter and musician (guitar); b. 6 Jan. 1986, Sheffield; s. of David Turner and Penny Turner. *Education:* Stockbridge High School, Sheffield. *Career:* founder mem. and lead singer, Arctic Monkeys 2002–; founder mem., side project, The Last Shadow Puppets 2007–; solo artist 2011–; numerous collaborations including Dizzee Rascal, Reverend and the Makers, Miles Kane, Queens of the Stone Age. *Recordings include:* albums: with Arctic Monkeys: Five Minutes with the Arctic Monkeys (EP) 2005, Whatever People Say I Am, That's What I'm Not (Mercury Music Prize 2006, Q Award for Best Album 2006, Meteor Ireland Music Award for Best Int. Album 2007, BRIT Award for Best British Album 2007, NME Award for Best Album 2007, Ivor Novello Award for Best Album 2007) 2006, Favourite Worst Nightmare (BRIT Award for Best British Album 2008) 2007, Humbug 2009, Suck It and See (MOJO Award for Best Album 2011) 2011, AM 2013; with The Last Shadow Puppets: The Age of the Understatement 2008; solo: Submarine (film soundtrack) 2011. *Honours:* with Arctic Monkeys: BRIT Awards for Best British Breakthrough Artist 2006, for Best British Group 2007, 2008, NME Awards for Best British Band 2006, 2008, for Best Track (for I Bet You Look Good on the Dancefloor) 2006, (for Flourescent Adolescent) 2008, for Best Music DVD (for Scummy Man) 2007, (for Arctic Monkeys at the Apollo) 2009, for Best Live Band 2010, 2012, Q Magazine Awards for People's Choice 2006, for Best Act in the World Today 2007, for Best Live Act 2009, for Best Track (for Do I Wanna Know?) 2013. *Current Management:* Press Here Publicity, 138 West 25th Street, Seventh Floor, New York, NY 10001, USA. *Telephone:* (212) 246-2640. *Fax:* (212) 582-

6513. *E-mail:* info@pressherepublicity.com. *Website:* www.pressherepublicity
.com. *E-mail:* arctic.monkeys@gmail.com. *Website:* www.arcticmonkeys.com.

TURNER, Andrew (Andy) Peter; British programmer and producer. *Career:* mem., Black Dog Productions 1988–95, Plaid 1995–. *Films:* as composer: Tekkonkinkreet 2006, Heaven's Door 2008. *Recordings include:* albums: with Black Dog Productions: Bytes 1993, Temple Of Transparent Balls 1994, Spanners 1995, Parallel (compilation) 1995; with Plaid: Not For Threes 1997, Rest Proof Clockwork 1999, Trainer 2000, Double Figure 2001, Parts In The Post 2003, Spokes 2003, Greedy Baby (with Bob Jaroc) 2006. *Address:* c/o Warp Records, Spectrum House, 32–34 Gordon House Road, London, NW5 1LP, England (office). *E-mail:* editor@warp.net (office). *Website:* www.plaid.co.uk.

TURNER, Carl; British DJ, writer, producer and musician (keyboards); b. 2 June 1969, Wolverhampton, England. *Education:* Stafford Coll., Wolverhampton Coll. *Career:* Founder-mem., Bizarre Inc.; writer, producer, Perfecto Records. *Recordings include:* Bizarre Theme 1990, Such A Feeling 1991, Playing With Knives 1992, I'm Gonna Get You 1992, Took My Love 1993, Energique 1993, Love in Motion 1993, Mosaic 1996, Do I, Gifted 1997. *Honours:* Music Week Award, Top Dance Single 1991. *Website:* www .carlturner.net.

TURNER, Geraldine Gail, OAM, DipEd; Australian actress and singer; b. 23 June 1950, Brisbane; m. Brian Castles-Onion 1993. *Education:* Queensland Conservatoire. *Career:* internationally renowned in concert and cabaret, particularly as Sondheim interpreter; performed in Australia, UK, Canada, USA and Africa; mem. and Fed. Pres. Australian Actors' Equity. *Plays:* Don's Party, Present Laughter, Summer of The Seventeenth Doll, Inheritance, These People, The Forest, Steel Magnolias, Melba, M.P.. *Musicals:* Oliver! (Green Room Award 1984), Chicago, Anything Goes (Green Room Award 1989, Mo Award 1989), Company, Sweeney Todd (Mo Award 1988), A Little Night Music, Into The Woods, Ned Kelly, Guys and Dolls, Call Me Madam, Kismet, Grease, Cabaret, The Witches of Eastwick, Summer Rain, Present Laughter, Jacques Brel is Alive and Well and Living in Paris, Wicked, Ruthless. *Operas and operettas:* La Belle Hélène, HMS Pinafore, The Mikado. *Film appearances:* Careful He Might Hear You, Summerfield, The Wog Boy, Break of Day. *Television appearances:* The Box, The Sentimental Bloke, The Restless Years, Michael Parkinson, A Country Practice, G.P., Beauty and the Beast, All Saints, Home and Away, An Audience with Stephen Sondheim, Sydney Dance Company Farewell, House Husbands. *Recordings include:* The Stephen Sondheim Song Book –Vols One and Two, Torch Songs – and Some Not So Tortous, Once In A Blue Moon, Gala Night, One Life To Live, When We Met, Great Moments in Australian Music Theatre, Tilbury Gala, Number One Musicals, All the Colours of the Rainbow; cast albums include: Anything Goes, Chicago. *Honours:* Medal of the Order of Australia; numerous Theatre Awards. *Current Management:* c/o James Laurie Management, 12 Raglan Street, South Melbourne, VIC 3205, Australia. *Telephone:* (3) 9682-9100. *Fax:* (3) 9682-9044. *E-mail:* sydney@jameslaurie.com. *Website:* www.jameslaurie .com.

TURNER, Howard, BA, PGCE; British producer, engineer, musician (guitar, vocals), songwriter and studio designer; *Managing Director, Studio Wizard*; b. 24 Feb. 1959, Thornage, Holt, Norfolk. *Education:* Univ. of East Anglia, Norwich. *Career:* spent childhood in war-torn Indo-China; began Raven Recording as a studio 1984; developed reputation as freelance indie/rock producer and engineer; worked with Peter DeFreitas (Echo and the Bunnymen), Steve Johnson (Teardrops) and others; Raven developed as a residential facility 1987, sold studios 1991; cr. Raven Recording Services and The Studio Wizard Organisation; primarily guitar-orientated material; developed reputation working with successful major rock and indy bands; own band, The Nivens; Founder and Man. Dir StudioWizard early 1990s; involved in building, commissioning and operating audio facilities since 1980s; also involved in music technology education and assists educational insts in specification and devt of facilities and curricula; fully qualified teacher, delivering training at all levels, from primary school to professorial seminars. *Recordings:* four albums as musician under name The Nivens; as producer/ engineer, albums by Jacob's Mouse, Red Harvest, Jazz Butcher, Perfect Disaster, The Pollen, Bad Manners, Close Lobsters, Girlschool, Eden, Green On Red, Crome Yellow; other recordings for Captain Sensible and The Damned. *Publications:* numerous magazine articles. *Address:* Studio Wizard, Melton Park, Melton Constable, Norfolk, NR24 2NJ, England (office). *Telephone:* (1263) 862999 (office); 7092-123666 (office). *Fax:* 7092-123666 (office). *E-mail:* info@studiowizard.com (office). *Website:* www.studiowizard .com (office); www.studiowizard.wordpress.com.

TURNER, Joe Lynn; American singer. *Career:* lead singer rock groups, Fandango 1977–80, Last Kiss 1979, One Night Stand 1979, Cadillac 1980, Rainbow 1980–85, Yngwie Malmsteen 1987–89, Deep Purple 1990–91; also solo artist. *Recordings include:* albums: four with Fandango 1977–80; with Rainbow: Difficult To Cure 1981, Straight Between The Eyes 1982, Bent Out Of Shape 1983, Finyl Vinyl 1986; solo: Fandango 1982, Rescue You 1985, Nothing Changes 1995, Under Cover 1997, Hurry Up And Wait 1998, Waiting for a Girl Like You 1999, Under Cover 2 1999, Holy Man 2000, Slam 2001, JLT 2003, Usual Suspects 2005, Sunstorm 2006, Second Hand Life 2007, Sunstorm: House of Dreams 2009; with Yngwie Malmsteen: Odyssey 1988, Live In Leningrad 1989, Heaven Tonight 1999; with Deep Purple: Slaves and Masters 1990; with Brazen Abbot: Guilty as Sin 2003, My Resurrection 2005;

with The Jan Holberg Project: Sense of Time 2011, At Your Service 2013. *Current Management:* c/o Mark Wexler, Jolt Productions Inc., PO Box 4174, River Edge, NJ 07661-4174, USA. *E-mail:* lisawalker@tothemax1.com. *Website:* www.joelynnturner.com.

TURNER, Juliet; British singer, songwriter and musician (guitar); b. 16 July 1973, Tummery, Co. Tyrone, NI. *Education:* Trinity Coll., Dublin. *Career:* began performing at univ.; support slots for acts, including Tracy Chapman, Natalie Merchant, U2, Brian Kennedy, Gabrielle, Sting and Bryan Adams; collaboration with John Spillane on single, Will We Be Brilliant Or What?; Owner, record label, Hear This!. *Recordings include:* albums: Let's Hear It For Pizza 1996, Burn The Black Suit 2000, Season Of The Hurricane 2003, People Have Names 2008. *Honours:* Irish Post Best Newcomer in Music award 2002, Tatler Magazine Women of the Year award for contribution to music 2002, Meteor Award for Best Irish Female Artist 2005. *Current Management:* c/o Derek Nally, Nally Management, 39 Silverstream Avenue, Stameen, Drogheda, County Louth, Ireland. *E-mail:* dereknally@oceanfree.net. *Website:* www.julietturner.com.

TURNER, Lee; American musician (piano), composer, arranger and music publisher; b. Jacksonville, Florida, USA; m. Dianne Gross, 3 s. *Education:* University of Florida; Southern Baptist Theological Seminary. *Career:* professional pianist since high school; Studio work, Nashville and Jacksonville; regular television and radio appearances, dances, shows and concerts; accompanist and soloist; Appeared with The Dream Weavers, Ed Sullivan Show; minister of music, 29 years; Director, choirs and groups, religious and secular; owner, publishing company, TurnerSong, 1981–; mem, ASCAP; AFofM. *Compositions include:* Into The Night, The Dream Weavers. *Recordings include:* It's Almost Tomorrow, The Dream Weavers; Rhapsody in Stained Glass, solo piano; There's a Meetin' Here Tonight, musical; Make Every Day a Good Day!; I Love a Piano; I Still Love a Piano. *Honours:* Annual ASCAP Award, 1974–. *E-mail:* turnersong@earthlink.net. *Website:* www .turnersong.com.

TURNER, Nik; British musician (saxophone, flute), singer, composer, arranger and teacher; b. 26 Aug. 1940, Oxford, England. *Career:* Founder-mem. Hawkwind 1969–76; numerous television and radio broadcasts, tours; Founder-mem. Inner City Unit/Sphynx 1976, Nik Turner's Fantastic All Stars 1988, Nik Turner's Space Ritual 1994, Hawklords 2007, Nik Turner's Galaktikos 2007, Nik Turner Band 2008, Nik Turner's Sphynx 2010; mem. Musicians' Union. *Recordings include:* with Hawkwind: twenty three albums, including Conscience of Hawkwind 2000; with Inner City Unit: six albums; with Sphynx: one album 1978; with Nik Turner's Space Ritual: five albums; with Nik Turner's Fantastic All Stars: Kubano Kickasso, Otherworld, Past or Future Space Ritual, Sonic Attack, Transglobal Friends and Relations, Travellers of Space; Space Gypsy 2013. *Address:* Cadillac Ranch, Pencraig Uchaf, Cwm Bach, Whitland, Dyfed, SA34 0DT, Wales (home). *Telephone:* (1994) 484466 (home). *E-mail:* thunderrider@googlemail.com; loki@nikturner .com. *Website:* www.nikturner.com.

TURNER, Peter (Pete) James; British musician (bass guitar) and songwriter; b. 28 Aug. 1974, Manchester. *Career:* formed band Mr Soft with Guy Garvey, Richard Jupp and Mark Potter 1990, renamed Soft and eventually renamed Elbow 1997–; numerous concerts and tours throughout UK, Europe and USA; played concerts in Cuba 2004, becoming first British band to perform outside Havana; headlined UKULA Bright Lights Festival, Toronto, Canada 2006. *Recordings:* albums: Asleep in the Back 2001, Cast of Thousands 2003, Leaders of the Free World 2005, The Seldom Seen Kid (Mercury Music Prize) 2008, Build a Rocket Boys! 2011, The Take Off and Landing of Everything 2014. *Honours:* BRIT Award for Best British Group 2009, Ivor Novello Awards for Best Song Musically and Lyrically (for One Day Like This) 2009, for Best Contemporary Song (for Grounds for Divorce) 2009, South Bank Show Pop Prize Award 2009, Mojo Sond of the Year 2009. *Current Management:* TRC Management, 10c Whitworth Court, Manor Park, Manor Farm Road, Runcorn, Cheshire, WA7 1TE, England. *Telephone:* (1928) 571111. *E-mail:* mail@trcmanagement.com. *Website:* www.trcmanagement .com; www.elbow.co.uk.

TURNER, Ruby; Jamaican/British singer and actress; *Managing Director, RTR Productions*; b. 22 June 1958, Clarendon, Jamaica. *Career:* backing singer with Culture Club 1980s; solo artist; appeared in numerous stage musicals and TV programmes; collaborated with Bryan Ferry, Jools Holland, UB40, Mick Jagger; Man. Dir, RTR Productions record label. *Television includes:* Eastenders, Holby City, Little Britain Christmas Special 2006. *Films include:* Love Actually 2005, Little Britain Abroad 2006. *Recordings include:* albums: Motown Songbook 1988, Paradise 1989, The Other Side 1991, Live In Concert: Glastonbury Festival 1986 1994, Restless Moods 1994, Guilty 1996, Call Me By My Name 1998, Ruby Turner 1998, Women Hold Up Half The Sky 1998, Call Me By My Name 1999, So Amazing 2005, Live at Ronnie Scott's 2007, The Informer 2008, I'm Travelling On 2009. *Honours:* LAMDA Gold Award for Acting. *Address:* 26 Denholme Grove, Kings Heath, Birmingham, B14 3BP (home); Miracle Artists, 1 York Street, London, W1U 6PA, England (office). *Telephone:* (20) 7935-9222 (office). *Fax:* (20) 7935-6222 (office). *E-mail:* rtr.productions@ntlworld.com (office); email@rubyturner .com. *Website:* www.rubyturner.com.

TURNER, Tina; American singer and songwriter; b. (Annie Mae Bullock), 26 Nov. 1939, Brownsville, Tenn.; m. 1st Ike Turner 1956 (divorced 1978); four s.; m. 2nd Erwin Bach 2013. *Career:* singer with Ike Turner Kings of Rhythm, Ike and Tina Turner Revue 1958–78; numerous concert tours worldwide; solo artist 1978–. *Films include:* Gimme Shelter 1970, Soul to Soul 1971, Tommy 1975, Mad Max: Beyond Thunderdome 1985, What's Love Got to Do with It (vocals) 1993, Last Action Hero 1993. *Recordings include:* albums: with Ike Turner: River Deep, Mountain High 1966, Outa Season 1969, The Hunter 1969, Proud Mary 1970, Come Together 1970, Workin' Together 1971, 'Nuff Said 1971, Blues Roots 1972, Feel Good 1972, Nutbush City Limits 1974, The Gospel According to Ike and Tina 1974; solo: Let Me Touch Your Mind 1972, Tina Turns the Country On 1974, Acid Queen 1975, Rough 1978, Private Dancer 1984, Break Every Rule 1986, Foreign Affair 1989, Wildest Dreams 1996, Dues Paid 1999, Twenty Four Seven 1999. *Publication:* I, Tina (autobiography) 1985. *Honours:* Chevalier, Ordre des Arts et des Lettres; Grammy Awards include for Record of the Year, Song of the Year, Best Female Vocal Performance, Best Female Rock Vocal, MTV Music Video Award 1985, American Music Awards for Favorite Soul/R&B Female Artist, for Best Video Artist 1985, for Best Female Pop/Rock Artist 1986, World Music Award for Outstanding Contribution to the Music Industry 1993, Kennedy Center Honor 2005. *Current Management:* c/o RD Worldwide Management, 1158 26th Street, Suite 564, Santa Monica, CA 90403, USA. *Website:* www .tinaturnerofficial.com.

TURRE, Stephen (Steve) Johnson; American jazz musician (trombone, conch shells) and educator; *Member Faculty, Jazz Trombone and Jazz Studies, The Juilliard School;* b. 12 Sept. 1948, Omaha, Neb.; s. of James Boles Turre and Carmen Marie Johnson; m. 1st Susan J. Beard 1970 (divorced); m. 2nd Akua Dixon 1978 (divorced); two c. *Education:* California State Univ., Sacramento, Univ. of North Texas Coll. of Music, Univ. of Massachusetts, Amherst. *Career:* fmr mem. Escovedo Brothers salsa band; toured with Ray Charles 1972; joined Art Blakey's Jazz Messengers 1973; Founder-mem. Sanctified Shells; teacher of jazz trombone, Manhattan School of Music 1988–; mem. Faculty in Jazz Trombone and Jazz Studies, Juilliard School 2001–03, 2008–; numerous collaborations as sideman. *Television:* house band mem., Saturday Night Live 1984–. *Recordings:* Viewpoint 1987, Viewpoints and Vibrations 1987, Fire and Ice 1988, Dedication 1989, Right There 1991, Sanctified Shells 1993, Rhythm Within (with Herbie Hancock and Pharoah Sanders) 1995, Steve Turre 1997, In the Spur of the Moment 1999, Lotus Flower 1999, TNT (Trombone-N-Tenor) 2000, One4J: Paying Homage to J.J. Johnson 2003, The Spirits Up Above 2004, Keep Searchin' 2006, Rainbow People 2008, Spiritman: The Smoke Sessions 2009, Delicious and Delightful 2010, Woody's Delight 2012, The Bones of Art 2013. *Honours:* Down Beat Reader's Poll Award for Best Trombonist 1998, 1999, 2001, 2002, 2006, Jazz Journalists' Asscn Award for Trombonist of the Year 2015. *Current Management:* c/o Vernon H. Hammond III, CFP, The Management Ark, 116 Village Boulevard, Suite 200, Princeton, NJ 08540, USA. *Telephone:* (609) 734-7403. *E-mail:* managearkeast@comcast.net. *Website:* managementark.com. *Address:* The Juilliard School, 60 Lincoln Center Plaza, New York, NY 10023, USA (office). *Telephone:* (212) 799-5000 (office). *E-mail:* sturre@ juilliard.edu (office); shellman48@aol.com (home). *Website:* www.juilliard.edu (office); steveturre.com (home).

TURULL, Xavi; Spanish musician (percussion); b. Barcelona; m. (divorced); one d. *Career:* brought up in UK and Spain; travelled in India, China and Thailand, played and studied at Karnataka Coll. of Percussion, Bangalore, played drums with Dalau; formed Amalgama and Fula flamenco fusion groups in Barcelona; collaborated with musicians including Ketama, Paixarinho, Gerardo Nuñez, Riqueni, de Melchor, Cañizares, Manolo Sanlucar, Joaquin Cortes, Rosario, Antonio, and Lolita Flores; studied congas with Changuito and batas with Octavio Rodriguez in Cuba; joined Ojos de Brujo 1996, a group which fuses gypsy and flamenco music with Latin American, punk, hip hop, reggae and electronic influences, set up own label La Fábrica de Colores 2001; several tours in Europe, Latin America and USA; collaborations with Nitin Sawhney, Asian Dub Foundation; toured with rock/rumba group Estopa. *Recordings include:* albums: Vengue 1999, Barí 2002, Barí: Remezclas de la Casa 2003, Techarí 2006, Aocaná 2009; other: Girando Bari (DVD) 2005, A Lo Lejos Del Río 2008. *Film compositions include:* Pau i el seu germà 2001, 7 Days in Havana 2012. *Honours:* World Music Award for Europe, BBC Radio 3 2004. *E-mail:* xavi@ojosdebrujo.com (office). *Website:* www.ojosdebrujo.com.

TUTUNJIAN BERGER, Nancy; American/Armenian speaker, singer, songwriter, writer and actress; *Contemporary Worship Leader, First Armenian Church;* b. 7 Dec. 1959, Needham, Mass; m. Richard. *Education:* studied solfège under Rouben Gregorian. *Career:* regional theatre; series of concerts sponsored by WNGN-FM, New York; numerous US festival and concert appearances; guest on several radio programmes and Jericho cable show; Power Hour cable show; own record co., Paraclete Records; mem. Broadcast Music, Inc. (BMI) as songwriter and publr; Contemporary Worship Leader, First Armenian Church; spiritual speaker, musician, worship leader at numerous retreats, confs and special events; performs with area orchestras as soloist for pops and holiday concerts; Great American Songbook jazz-cabaret performances; classical recitals and parlour concerts; guest soloist with area chorus groups. *Plays:* three one-act Biblical theatre pieces (book, lyrics and music). *Compositions include:* numerous contemporary Christian songs (lyrics and music). *Recordings include:* Songs For The Bridegroom 1992, Christmas Glow 1994, If You Have Faith 1999, All of My Days 2006. *Honours:* Trailblazers Award, Int. Airplay Asscn, Hon. Mention Certificate, Billboard Songwriting Contest. *Telephone:* (617) 926-4026 (office). *E-mail:* paraclete .music1@verizon.net (office). *Website:* www.ntbmusic.net.

TWAIN, Shania; Canadian country singer and songwriter; b. (Eileen Regina Edwards), 28 Aug. 1965, Windsor, Ont.; d. of Gerry Twain and Sharon Twain; m. 1st Robert John Lange 1993 (divorced); one s.; m. 2nd Frederic Thiebaud 2011. *Career:* fmr cabaret singer. *Recordings:* albums: Shania Twain 1993, The Woman in Me (Grammy Award for Best Country Album 1996) 1995, Come On Over 1997, On The Way 1999, Beginnings 1989–1990 1999, Wild and Wicked 2000, Complete Limelight Sessions 2001, Up! (Billboard Award for Top Country Album 2003) 2002, Greatest Hits 2004; singles: What Made You Say That 1993, Dance With The One That Brought You 1993, You Lay A Whole Lotta Love On Me 1993, Whose Bed Have Your Boots Been Under 1995, Any Man of Mine 1995, Woman In Me 1995, You Win My Love 1996, God Bless The Child 1996, I'm Outta Here 1996, Love Gets Me Every Time 1997, Don't Be Stupid 1997, You're Still The One 1998, From This Moment On 1998, When 1998, That Don't Impress Me Much 1998, Man I Feel Like A Woman 1999, You've Got A Way 1999, Don't Be Stupid (You Know I Love You) 2000, I'm Gonna Getcha Good 2002, Ka-Ching 2003, Up 2003, Forever & Always 2003, Thank You Baby For Making Someday Come So Soon 2003, When You Kiss Me 2003, Party For Two 2005. *Publications:* From This Moment On 2011. *Honours:* Country Music Television Europe Rising Video Star of the Year 1993, Female Artist of the Year 1996, Canadian Country Music Award for Female Vocalist 1995, American Music Awards for Favorite New Country Artist 1995, Favorite Female Pop/Rock Artist 2000, Favorite Female Country Artist 2000, Grammy Awards for Best Female Country Vocal Performance, Best Country Song 2000, Juno Award for Songwriter of the Year 2000, Best Country Female Artist 2000, Billboard Award for Top Country Artist 2003, inducted into Canadian Music Hall of Fame 2011. *Current Management:* c/o Sandbox Entertainment, 54 Music Square East, Nashville, TN 37203, USA. *E-mail:* info@sandboxmgmt.com. *Website:* www.sandboxmgmt.com; www .shaniatwain.com.

TWEED, Karen, BA; British musician (accordion) and composer; b. 27 May 1963, London. *Education:* Leeds Polytechnic, studied under Lawry Eady and John Whelan. *Career:* with Kathryn Tickell Band –1993; with all-female folk band, The Poozies and Anglo-Swedish ensemble, Swap; with May Morning 2001; mem. MU, PAMRA, PRS. *Composition:* Walking Up in Wonderful Wark. *Recordings include:* Chantoozies 1993, Dansoozies 1995, Infinite Blue 1998, Fyace 1997, Swap 1997, Infinite Blue 2000, Raise Your Head: A Retrospective 2001, Faerd 2003, Each Step on the Way 2005, Du Da 2005, Essentially Invisible to the Eye 2012. *E-mail:* karen@karentweed.dk. *Website:* www .karentweed.dk.

TWEEDY, Jeff; American singer, songwriter and musician (guitar); b. (Jeffrey Scot Tweedy), 1967, Belleville, Ill. *Career:* mem., Uncle Tupelo 1989–94; mem., Wilco 1994–; co-composer of music for film, Chelsea Walls 2001; mem. Loose Fur 2002–; mem. of collective, The Minus 5. *Recordings include:* albums: with Uncle Tupelo: No Depression 1990, Still Feel Gone 1991, March 16-20-1992 1992, Anodyne 1993, Songs From Uncle Tupelo 89/93: An Anthology 1994; with Wilco: A.M. 1995, Being There 1996, Summerteeth 1998, Yankee Hotel Foxtrot 2002, A Ghost is Born 2004, Sky Blue Sky 2007, Wilco (The Album) 2009, The Whole Love 2011, Star Wars 2015; with Loose Fur: Loose Fur 2002, Sleeps With Fishes 2003, Born Again in the USA 2006; with The Minus 5: The Gun Album 2006. *Film:* I Am Trying To Break Your Heart 2002. *Current Management:* c/o Tony Margherita Management, 116 Pleasant Street, Suite 245, Easthampton, MA 01027, USA. *E-mail:* info@ tmmchi.com. *Website:* tmmchi.com; www.wilcoworld.net.

2 CHAINZ, (Tity Boi); American rapper and songwriter; b. (Tauheed Epps), 12 Sept. 1977, College Park, Ga. *Education:* North Clayton High School, Ala State Univ. *Career:* as Tity Boi: Founder mem. with Earl Conyers (aka Dolla Boy) of hip hop duo Playaz Circle 1992–; solo career 2007–, name change to 2 Chainz 2011; numerous collaborations as solo artist including singles with Drake (No Lie), Kanye West (Mercy) 2012, Nicki Minaj (Beez in the Trap). *Recordings include:* with Playaz Circle: United We Stand, United We Fall 2002, Supply & Demand 2007, Flight 360: The Takeoff 2009; solo: mixtapes: Me Against the World 2007, Trap-A-Velli 2009, All Ice on Me 2009, Me Against the World 2: Codeine Withdrawal 2010, Trap-A-Velli 2: (The Residue) 2010, Codeine Cowboy (A 2 Chainz Collective) 2011, T.R.U. REALigion 2011; album: Based on a T.R.U. Story 2012. *Honours:* BET Hip Hop Awards for People's Champ (for No Lie) 2012, for Rookie of the Year 2012, for Sweet 16 Best Featured Verse (for Mercy) 2012, for Reese's Perfect Combo (for Mercy) 2012, Soul Train Award for Best Hip Hop Song of the Year (for Mercy) 2012. *Address:* c/o Def Jam Records, Island Def Jam Group, Universal Music Group, Worldwide Plaza, 825 Eighth Avenue, 28th Floor, New York, NY 10019, USA (office). *Website:* www.defjam.com (office); www.2chainz.com.

2D; singer and musician (keyboards). *Career:* animated mem. of virtual band, Gorillaz 1998– (see creator and Musical Dir, Damon Albarn and creator and Visual Dir, Jamie Hewlett). *Website:* www.gorillaz.com.

2NA, Chali; American rap artist; b. (Charles Stewart). *Career:* mem., Jurassic 5 1993–2006; numerous live performances; also mem., Ozomatli. *Recordings include:* albums: with Jurassic 5: Jurassic 5 (EP) 1997, Quality Control 2000, Power in Numbers 2002, Feedback 2006; with Ozomatli: Ozomatli 1998; with Supernatural: S.P.I.T. 2005; with Dino 5: Baby Loves Hip Hop 2008; solo: Fish Outta Water 2009. *E-mail:* info@chali2na.com (home). *Website:* www.chali2na .com (home).

'TWO-TONE' TOMMY; American musician (bass guitar); b. Louisville, Ky. *Career:* Founder-mem. My Morning Jacket 1999–. *Film:* Elizabethtown 2005.

Recordings include: albums: The Tennessee Fire 1999, At Dawn 2001, It Still Moves 2003, Early Recordings Chapter 1: The Sandworm Cometh 2004, Early Recordings Chapter 2: Learning 2004, Z 2005, Okronokos 2006, Evil Urges 2008, Circuital 2011. *Current Management:* c/o Flatiron Management, 37 West 20th Street, Suite 1008, New York, NY 10011, USA. *Telephone:* (212) 616-4787. *Fax:* (646) 341-8111. *E-mail:* jamie@flatironmgmt.com. *E-mail:* twotonetommy@mymorningjacket.com. *Website:* www.mymorningjacket.com.

TYAS, Michael; British musician (bass, guitar, mandolin, dulcimer, violin) and singer; b. 21 June 1957, Durham; m. Margaret Tyas 1992; one d. *Career:* worked in amateur folk groups in North East England; professional musician 1991–; joined the Whisky Priests 1989–95; formed The Wickermen 1998; solo career 2000–; toured 14 European countries; appeared on Anglia and Tyne Tees TV, BBC Radio 1 and 2, and on nat. radio in Belgium, Holland, Spain, Italy and Germany. *Compositions include:* Geronimo's Blues, The Scissorman, Leap of Faith, England My England. *Recordings include:* five albums with The Whisky Priests, including one live album.

TYLER, Bonnie; Welsh singer; b. (Gaynor Sullivan), 8 June 1951, Skewen; m. Robert Sullivan 1973. *Career:* lead vocalist, local bands; solo artist 1976–. *Recordings:* Lost In France 1976, It's A Heartache 1978, Natural Force 1978, Faster Than The Speed of Night 1983, Total Eclipse of The Heart 1983, Holding Out For A Hero 1985, Secret Dreams 1986, Hide Your Heart 1987, Bitterblue 1991, The Best Of 1993, Free Spirit 1996, All In One Voice 1998, Greatest Hits 2001, Heart Strings 2003, Simply Believe 2004, Wings 2005, Rocks and Honey 2013; also recorded with Shakin Stevens, Steve Hackett, Rick Derringer, Mike Oldfield, Rick Wakeman, Nelson Miranda & Rochester. *Honours:* winner Yamaha World Song Contest 1978, Echo Best Female Vocalist 1994, Variety Club of Great Britain 1984. *Current Management:* LPO, 8 Glenthorne Mews, 115a Glenthorne Road, Hammersmith, London, W6 0LJ, England. *Telephone:* (20) 8741-4453. *Fax:* (20) 8741-4289. *E-mail:* info@l-po.com. *Website:* www.l-po.com; bonnietyler.com.

TYLER, Steven; American singer and musician (harmonica); b. (Stephen Tallarico), 26 March 1948, New York; s. of Victor A. Tallarico and Susan Tallarico. *Career:* singer rock band, Aerosmith 1970–; numerous concerts, festival appearances. *Television:* co-judge, American Idol 2010–. *Film appearance:* as the Future Villain Band in Sgt Pepper's Lonely Hearts Club Band 1978. *Recordings include:* albums: Aerosmith 1973, Toys In The Attic 1975, Get Your Wings 1975, Rocks 1976, Draw The Line 1978, Night In The Ruts 1980, Greatest Hits 1981, Rock In A Hard Place 1982, Classic Live! 1986, Done With Mirrors 1986, Permanent Vacation 1987, Pump 1989, Pandora's Box 1992, Get A Grip 1993, Little South Of Sanity 1998, Young Lust – The Aerosmith Anthology 2001, O'Yeah! Ultimate Aerosmith Hits 2002, Honkin' On Bobo 2004, Music from Another Dimension! 2012. *Honours:* three Boston SKC Music Awards 1990, American Music Award 1991, Grammy Award for Best Rock Performance 1991, Rolling Stone and Billboard magazine awards. *Current Management:* c/o Richard De La Font Agency, 4845 South Sheridan Road, Tulsa, OK 74145, USA. *Telephone:* (918) 665-6200. *Website:* www.delafont.com. *Address:* c/o Aero Force One, 40 Washington Street, Suite 3000, Westborough, MA 01581, USA. *Telephone:* (508) 791-3807. *Website:* www.aerosmith.com.

TYNES, Gunnar Örn; Icelandic musician (electronics). *Career:* mem. experimental group, Múm 1997–. *Recordings include:* albums: Yesterday Was Dramatic – Today Was OK 2000, Please Smile My Noise Bleed 2001, Finally We Are No One 2002, Summer Make Good 2004, Go Go Smear the Poison Ivy 2007, Sing Along to Songs You Don't Know 2009, Smilewound 2013. *Address:* Fat Cat Records, PO Box 3400, Brighton, BN1 4WD, England. *Website:* mum.is; www.randomsummer.com.

TYRESE; American singer, rapper and actor; b. (Tyrese Darnell Gibson), 30 Dec. 1978, Watts, Calif.; s. of Lurk Gibson and Priscilla Murray Gibson (née Durham). *Career:* actor in TV and films 1996–; recording career 1998–; appeared in music videos for Usher, Monica, Chris Brown, Lady Gaga; formed supergroup TGT with Tank and Ginuwine 2007–, debut album 2013. *Films:* as actor: Love Song 2000, Baby Boy 2001, 2 Fast 2 Furious 2003, Flight of the Phoenix 2004, Four Brothers 2005, Annapolis 2006, Waist Deep 2006, Transformers 2007, The Take 2007, Transformers: Revenge of the Fallen 2009, Death Race, Legion 2010, Transformers: Dark of the Moon 2011, Fast Five 2011. *Television:* as actor: guest appearances in several series including: Hangin' with Mr Cooper 1996, Martin 1997, The Parent 'Hood 1998, Blue's Clues 1999, Moesha 2000. *Recordings include:* albums: Tyrese 1998, 2000 Watts 2001, I Wanna Go There 2002, Alter Ego 2006, Open Invitation 2011; with TGT: Three Kings 2013. *Honours:* American Music Award for Favorite New R&B/Soul Artist 2000, Soul Train Award for Song of the Year (for Stay) 2012. *Current Management:* c/o Rodney Harris, Slamm Management, 931 Monroe Drive, Suite A-102, Atlanta, GA 30308, USA. *E-mail:* Rodney@slammmanagement.com. *Website:* www.slammmanagement.com. *Address:* c/o Atlantic Records, Warner Music Group, 75 Rockefeller Plaza, New York, NY 10019, USA (office). *E-mail:* contact@atlanticrecords.com (office). *Website:* atlanticrecords.com (office); www.wmg.com (office).

TYRRELL, John William; Australian musician (drums) and manager; b. 14 March 1961, Melbourne. *Career:* manager and drummer, Abba Tribute Band, Björn Again (with Rod Leissle) 1988–; toured 50 countries world-wide, performed over 3,000 shows; mem. UK Music Union. *Recordings:* A Little Respect/Stop, Santa Claus Is Coming to Town, So You Win Again, Flashdance – What a Feeling; albums: Live At The Royal Albert Hall. *Address:* The Music Group Pty, 146A Cotham Road, Kew, Vic. 3101, Australia (office). *Telephone:* (3) 9817-5566 (office). *Fax:* (3) 9817-5533 (office). *E-mail:* john@themusicgroup.com.au (office). *Website:* www.themusicgroup.com.au (office); www.bjornagain.com.au.

TYSON, Liam, (Skin); British musician (guitar); b. 7 Sept. 1969, Liverpool, England. *Career:* mem. Cast –2002; Founder-mem. The Strange Sensation 2002–. *Recordings include:* albums with Cast: All Change 1995, Mother Nature Calls 1997, Magic Hour 1999, Beetroot 2001; with Strange Sensation: Mighty ReArranger 2005.

TZUKE, Judie; British singer and songwriter; b. 1955, London, England. *Education:* *Career:* solo artist; songwriting partnership with Mike Paxman 1975. *Recordings include:* albums: Welcome to the Cruise 1979, Sports Car 1980, I Am the Phoenix 1981, Road Noise 1982, Shoot the Moon 1983, Ritmo 1983, Judie Tzuke 1985, The Cat is Out 1985, Turning Stones 1989, Left Hand Talking 1991, Wonderland 1996, Under the Angels 1997, Welcome to the Cruise and Sports Car 2001, Songs 2 2010, One Tree Less 2012. *E-mail:* paul@tzuke.com. *Website:* www.tzuke.com.

U

U-GOD, (Baby U, 4-Bar Killer, Golden Arms, Lucky Hands); American MC and rap artist; b. (Lamont Hawkins). *Career:* mem., Wu-Tang Clan 1993–; solo artist 1999–. *Recordings include:* albums: with Wu-Tang Clan: Enter The Wu-Tang (36 Chambers) 1993, Wu-Tang Forever 1997, The W 2000, Iron Flag 2001, Disciples Of The 36 Chambers: Chapter 1 (live) 2004, The 8 Diagrams 2007, Return of the Swarm, Vol. 5 2008, Soundtracks from the Shaolin Temple 2008, Chamber Music 2009, Legendary Weapons 2011; solo: Golden Arms Redemption 1999, Mr. Xcitement 2005, Dopium 2009, The Keynote Speaker 2013. *Address:* c/o Sony Music Entertainment, 550 Madison Avenue, New York, NY 10022-3211, USA. *Website:* www.wutangcorp.com.

UBAGO, Álex; Spanish singer, songwriter and musician (guitar); b. (Alejandro Martínez de Ubago Rodríguez), 29 Jan. 1981, Vitoria-Gasteiz. *Career:* began writing songs at age 15; signed as solo artist to DRO Atlantic 2000; mem. Alex, Jorge y Lena 2010–, recorded album with singer, songwriter and producer Aureo Baqueiro; performed at Lo Nuestro Awards 2011. *Recordings:* albums: solo: ¿Qué Pides Tu? 2003, Fantasia o Realidad 2004, Aviones de Cristal 2006, Calle Ilusión 2009; with Alex, Jorge y Lena: Alex, Jorge y Lena (Latin Grammy Award for Best Pop Album by a Duo or Group with Vocals 2011) 2010. *Address:* c/o Warner Music Latina, Warner Music Group, 75 Rockefeller Plaza, New York, NY 10019, USA (office). *Website:* www .alexjorgeylena.com; www.alexubagooficial.net; www.alexubago.com.

UKIĆ, Zoran, (Zoki); Croatian musician (drums), composer and manager; b. 31 May 1962, Split; m. Vesna 1984; one s. one d. *Education:* high school in Croatia. *Career:* with Daleka Obala: Faraway Coast tours 1990, 1993–95; toured Croatia, Germany, Switzerland 1996–98; concerts in New York and Chicago, USA 1998, 2000; numerous TV appearances; tour of Croatia with The Obala 2007; mem. Croatian Musicians' Union. *Recordings:* with Daleka Obala: Faraway Coast 1990, Ludi Mornari Dolaze U Grad (Crazy Sailors Come On The Town), Mrlje (Dirty) 1993, Morski Pas (Shark) 1994, Di SI Ti (Where Are You) 1997, 1999–2000, live album Uspomena (memory) 1999, And Vith The Obala Instinite Priće (True Story) 2001, U Ime Zakona (In The Name Of Law) 2002, Marjanska pisma (Marjan song) 2007. *Publications:* Blue and Green, Croatian Rock Encyclopedia. *Honours:* The Best Debutant, Split Festival 1990, Silver Record for all recorded albums, Croatian Discography Awards 2001, Best Song, Sibenik Festival 2007. *Address:* Teutina 15, 21 000 Split (office); Put Svete, Mande 8, 21 000 Split, Croatia (home). *Telephone:* 98-264452 (mobile) (office); (21) 385904 (home). *Fax:* (21) 345358 (office). *E-mail:* zoran.ukic@st.t-com.hr (office).

ULRICH, Lars; Danish/American musician (drums); b. 26 Dec. 1955, Gentofle, Denmark; three c. *Career:* fmr tennis player; compiled New Wave of British Heavy Metal album (with Geoff Barton) 1979; fmr mem. Diamond Head; Founder-mem. heavy rock group, Metallica 1981–; world- wide tours and concerts; Owner, record label Music Company. *Films include:* Some Kind Of Monster (Independent Spirit Award for Best Documentary 2005) 2004, Heavy Metal in Baghdad 2007. *Recordings include:* albums: Kill 'Em All 1983, Ride The Lightning 1984, Master Of Puppets 1986, …And Justice For All 1988, The Good, The Bad And The Live 1990, Metallica 1991, Load 1996, Reload 1997, Early Days 1997, S&M (live) 1999, St Anger 2003, Death Magnetic 2008; singles: Whiplash 1985, Garage Days Revisited 1987, Creeping Death 1990, Harvester Of Sorrow 1988, One (Grammy Award for Best Heavy Metal Performance) 1989, Stone Cold Crazy (Grammy Award for Best Heavy Metal Performance) 1991, Jump In The Fire 1991, The Unforgiven (Grammy Award for Best Heavy Metal Performance 1992) 1991, Enter Sandman 1991, Nothing Else Matters 1992, Wherever I May Roam 1992, Sad But True 1992, Until It Sleeps 1996, Hero Of The Day 1996, Mama Said 1996, King Nothing 1997, The Memory Remains 1997, Fuel 1998, Turn The Page 1998, Whisky In The Jar (Grammy Award for Best Hard Rock Performance 2000) 1999, Die Die My Darling 1999, No Leaf Clover 2000, I Disappear 2000, Call Of The Ktulu (Grammy Award for Best Rock Instrumental Performance) 2001, St Anger 2003, Frantic 2003, Unnamed Feeling 2003. *Honours:* American Music Award for Favorite Heavy Metal Artist (with Metallica) 1993, Grammy Award for Best Metal Performance (for My Apocalypse) 2009. *Current Management:* c/o Q-Prime Inc., 729 Seventh Avenue, 16th Floor, New York, NY 10019, USA. *Telephone:* (212) 302-9790. *Fax:* (212) 302-9589. *Website:* www.metallica.com.

ULRICH, Shari; American composer, musician (violin, mandolin, piano, guitar, dulcimer, flute), singer and broadcaster; b. 17 Oct. 1951, Marin Co., Calif.; one s. one d. *Education:* coll. and studied violin. *Career:* mem. Pied Pumpkin String Ensemble 1972–76, Hometown Band 1976–78, UHF (Ulrich, Bill Henderson, Roy Forbes) 1989–; solo artist 1978–; composer of theme music for several Canadian TV series, documentaries, pieces for Sesame Street; host, Future Scan 1984, 1985, Inside Trax (also writer) 1989–94; Assoc. Prof. of Lyrics, Univ. of British Columbia 2006–11; mem. Songwriters' Assen of Canada, American Fed. of Musicians, Alliance of Canadian Cinema, Television and Radio Artists, Soc. of Composers, Authors and Music Publrs of Canada (SOCAN). *Recordings include:* five albums with Pied Pumpkin 1974, 1975, Plucking DeVine 1998, Pied Alive 2000, Pumkids 2007; with Hometown Band: Flying 1976, Hometown Band 1977; with Raffi: Bananaphone 1994; with UHF: UHF 1990, UHF II 1994; solo albums: Long Nights 1978, One Step Ahead 1980, Talk Around Town 1982, Every Road 1989, The View From Here

1998, Find Our Way 2010; with Barney Bentall & Tom Taylor: Live at Cates Hill 2009. *Plays:* Tapestry (cast), Arts Club Theatre, Vancouver 1996, Baby Boomer Blues (cast/writer), Vancouver 2005. *Honours:* Juno Awards 1977, 1981, Inducted into BC Entertainment Hall of Fame 2008. *Address:* PO Box 152, Bowen Island, BC V0N 1G0, Canada (home). *E-mail:* shari@shariulrich .com (office). *Website:* www.shariulrich.com.

ULRIK, Hans Jensen; Danish musician (saxophone, flute); b. 28 Sept. 1965, Copenhagen. *Education:* Berklee Coll. of Music, USA. *Career:* Founder Hans Ulrik Quartet; mem. Marilyn Mazur Future Song; tours of Europe, mostly Scandinavia and numerous TV and radio broadcasts; numerous collaborations including with Gary Peacock, Adam Nussbaum, Niels Lan Doky, Audun Kleive, Marilyn Mazur; leader in various bands including Pinocchio 1987, Hans Ulrik Fusion 1988–89, Hans Ulrik Group 1991–95, Wombat 1995–98. *Recordings include:* Day After Day (with Gary Peacock, Adam Nussbaum, John Abercrombie), Strange World (with Marilyn Mazur), Jazz and Mambo 2000, Shortcuts: Jazzpar Combo 2000, Light Extracts (with Eivind Aarset) 2001, Danish Standards (with Niclas Knudsen and Nikolai Munch Hansen) 2003, Tin Pan Aliens (with Steve Swallow) 2004, Believe in Spring (with Steve Swallow and Jonas Johansen) 2008, Slow Procession 2009, The Adventures Of A Polar Expedition (with Jon Balke and Benjamin Koppel) 2010. *Honours:* Leverkusen Int. Jazz Competition Award for Best Soloist 1988, 1990, numerous Danish Jazz Awards. *E-mail:* hulrik@me.com. *Website:* www .hansulrik.com.

ULSTRUP, Thomas Viderø; Danish musician (moog synthesizers, keyboards, modified piano), composer, agent and teacher; b. 31 Aug. 1968, Frederiksberg; s. of Anders Ulstrup. *Education:* Teacher's Acad. of Art, Music and Multimedia; High Schools of Jazz and Rock; private tuition. *Career:* mem. various experimental groups in Copenhagen 1984–; Co-founder legendary Danish group Gone Fishin', 1989–96; solo, duo keyboard performances; recording artist; founder, Native Music Denmark 1997, alternativemusic.dk 2000; toured with Dick Solberg & The Sun Mountain Experience, Caribbean; recordings/live performances with Moussa Diallo, Tobias Trier, Kenneth Thordal Alouise etc.; live appearance with George Duke 2004; radio host, Copenhagen radio-jazz show; writer for Danish magazine Jazz Special; founder & leader alternative Music School, Limusik.dk; mem. Gramex, Danish Jazz and Folk Authors (DJBFA), Composers in Denmark (KODA). *Compositions:* 10 x Cai 1988, Jack Daniels 1994, Meditations 1998. *Recordings:* with Gone Fishin': Gone Fishin', 1994; more than 50 CDs with children and youngsters singing. *Publications:* Native Music Compilation Vols I and II; Alternative Music Denmark. *Honours:* Gold Talent Prize, Berlingske Tidende 1988. *Address:* H/F Grænsen 8, Finsensvej 263, 2720 Vaniose, Denmark (home). *E-mail:* thomas@thomasulstrup.com (office). *Website:* www .thomasulstrup.com (office).

ULTRA (see Kool Keith)

ULVÆUS, Björn Kristian; Swedish songwriter, musician (guitar), singer and producer; b. 25 April 1945, Gothenburg; m. Agnetha Fältskog 1971 (divorced 1979). *Career:* songwriter with Benny Andersson 1966–; duo with Andersson as The Hootennanny Singers; partner in production with Andersson at Polar Music 1971; mem. pop group ABBA 1973–82; winner Eurovision Song Contest 1974; world-wide tours; concerts include Royal Performance, Stockholm 1976, Royal Albert Hall, London 1977, UNICEF concert, New York 1979, Wembley Arena 1979; reunion with ABBA, Swedish TV This Is Your Life 1986; continued writing and producing with Andersson 1982–; produced musical Mamma Mia! with Andersson, West End, London 1999. *Film:* ABBA: The Movie 1977. *Compositions include:* ABBA songs (with Benny Andersson); musicals: Chess (with lyrics by Tim Rice) 1983, The Immigrants 1994, Mamma Mia! (with Andersson) 1999. *Recordings include:* albums: with Andersson: Happiness 1971; with ABBA: Waterloo 1974, ABBA 1976, Greatest Hits 1976, Arrival 1977, The Album 1978, Voulez-Vous 1979, Greatest Hits Vol. 2 1979, Super Trouper 1980, The Visitors 1981, The Singles: The First Ten Years 1982, Thank You For The Music 1983, Absolute ABBA 1988, ABBA Gold 1992, More ABBA Gold 1993, Forever Gold 1998, The Definitive Collection 2001; singles include: with ABBA: Ring Ring 1973, Waterloo 1974, Mamma Mia 1975, Dancing Queen 1976, Fernando 1976, Money Money Money 1976, Knowing Me Knowing You 1977, The Name Of The Game 1977, Take A Chance On Me 1978, Summer Night City 1978, Chiquitita 1979, Does Your Mother Know? 1979, Angel Eyes/Voulez-Vous 1979, Gimme Gimme Gimme (A Man After Midnight) 1979, I Have A Dream 1979, The Winner Takes It All 1980, Super Trouper 1980, On And On And On 1981, Lay All Your Love On Me 1981, One Of Us 1981, When All Is Said And Done 1982, Head Over Heels 1982, The Day Before You Came 1982, Under Attack 1982, Thank You For The Music 1983. *Publication:* Mamma Mia! How Can I Resist You? (with Benny Andersson and Judy Craymer) 2006. *Honours:* World Music Award for Best Selling Swedish Artist 1993, Ivor Novello Special International Award (with Benny Andersson) 2002. *Address:* Södra Brobänken 41A, 111 49 Stockholm, Sweden. *Website:* www.abbasite.com.

ULVANG, Stelth; American musician (piano, guitar, mandolin, accordion); b. 1986. *Career:* mem. Dovekins; mem. The Lumineers 2012–; numerous tours. *Recordings:* albums: with Dovekins: Assemble the Aviary 2010, (A)live 2011;

with the Lumineers: The Lumineers 2012. *Current Management:* c/o Christen Greene and David Meinert, Onto Entertainment, 2611 5th Avenue, Seattle, WA 98121-1517, USA. *Address:* c/o Dualtone Records, Dualtone Music Group, 203 North 11th Street, Suite B, Nashville, TN 37206, USA (office). *Telephone:* (615) 320-0620 (office). *Fax:* (615) 320-0692 (office). *E-mail:* info@dualtone.com (office); info@thelumineers.com. *Website:* www.dualtone.com (office); www .thelumineers.com.

UNCLE KRACKER; American DJ, singer and songwriter; b. (Matthew Lynford Shafer), 6 June 1974, Mount Clemens, Mich.; m. Melanie; two d. *Career:* owns Mount Clemens tyre store run by father and Sunny's Tavern bar in suburban Detroit; recruited to Kid Rock's Twisted Brown Trucker touring group as DJ following release of Rock's album Grits Sandwiches For Breakfast 1991; became Rock's co-producer/co-songwriter; achieved success with solo side project recorded whilst on tour; many solo tv and live appearances backed by Twisted Brown Trucker group 2001. *Recordings include:* albums: Double Wide 2000, No Stranger To Shame 2002, Seventy Two and Sunny 2004, Happy Hour 2008, Happy Hour: The South River Road Sessions 2010, Midnight Special 2012. *E-mail:* contactus@unclekracker.com. *Website:* www .unclekracker.com.

THE UNDERDOG (see Jackson, Trevor)

UNDERWOOD, Carrie; American country singer; b. 10 March 1983, Oklahoma; d. of Stephen Underwood and Carole Underwood; m. Mike Fisher 2010; one s. *Education:* Northeastern State Univ., Okla. *Career:* winner, TV's American Idol 2005; released debut album 2005; mem. Grand Ole Opry 2008–; collaborations with Brad Paisley, Randy Travis. *Television includes:* American Idol (series winner) 2005, Grand Ole Opry 2007, New in Town 2009, Glee 2009–10, The Sound of Music 2013. *Recordings include:* albums: Some Hearts (Billboard Awards for Album of the Year and Country Album of the Year 2006, ACM Award for Album of the Year 2007, American Music Award for Favorite Country Album 2007) 2005, Carnival Ride 2007, Play On (American Music Award for Favorite Country Album 2010) 2009, Blown Away (American Music Award for Favorite Country Album 2012) 2012, Storyteller 2015. *Films include:* as actor: How I Met Your Mother 2010, Sesame Street 2010, The Buried Life 2010, Soul Surfer 2011, Blue Bloods 2011. *Honours:* Acad. of Country Music Awards for Top New Female Vocalist 2006, 2007, for Single of the Year (for Jesus, Take the Wheel) 2006, for Entertainer of the Year 2009, 2010, for Top Female Vocalist 2009, Triple Crown Award 2010, Country Music Asscn (CMA) Awards for Female Vocalist of the Year 2006, 2007, 2008, CMA Horizon Award 2006, for Single of the Year (for Before He Cheats) 2007, American Music Awards for Favorite New Breakthrough Artist 2006, for Favorite Female Country Artist 2007, 2014, 2015, Billboard Award for New Country Artist of the Year, Female Country Artist of the Year, and Female Billboard 200 Album Artist of the Year 2006, Grammy Awards for Best New Artist 2007, for Best Female Country Vocal Performance (for Jesus, Take the Wheel) 2007, (for Before He Cheats) 2008, (for Last Name) 2009, for Best Country Song (for Before He Cheats) 2008, for Best Country Collaboration with Vocals (for I Told You So with Randy Travis) 2010, for Best Country Solo Performance (for Blown Away) 2013, (for Something in the Water) 2015, Artist of the Year, American Country Awards 2010, 2011, CMT Artist of the Year Awards 2010, 2012. *Current Management:* c/o 19 Entertainment Inc., CORE Media Group Inc., 8560 West Sunset Boulevard, 8th Floor, West Hollywood, CA 90069, USA. *Telephone:* (310) 777-1940. *Website:* coremediagroup.com; www.carrieunderwoodofficial.com.

UNDERWOOD, Scott; American musician (drums) and songwriter; b. 2 Jan. 1974. *Career:* Founder-mem. Train 1994–; supported bands including Barenaked Ladies, Counting Crows, Cracker, Hootie & the Blowfish; also played drums for Greg Laswell, Food Pill, Club 33. *Recordings:* albums: with Train: Train 1998, Drops of Jupiter 2001, My Private Nation 2003, For Me, It's You 2006, Save Me, San Francisco 2009, California 37 2012. *Honours:* Grammy Awards for Best Rock Song and Best Instrumental Arrangement 2002, for Best Pop Performance by a Duo or Group with Vocal 2011, Billboard Music Awards for Top Rock Artist and Top Rock Song 2011, ASCAP Pop Music Award for Song of the Year 2011. *Current Management:* c/o Crush Management, 60-62 East 11th Street, 7th Floor, New York, NY 10003, USA. *Telephone:* (646) 688-1729. *E-mail:* info@crushmm.com. *Website:* www .crushmm.com; www.trainline.com.

UNGER-HAMILTON, Ferdy; British music industry executive; *President, Polydor Records. Career:* Man. Dir Go! Beat record label 1996–2002; A&R Exec. Island Records 2002–06; Man. Dir Virgin Records 2006–08, Pres. of A&R Labels April–May 2008; Pres. Polydor Records 2008–. *Address:* Polydor Records, 364–366 Kensington High Street, London, W14 8NS, England (office). *Telephone:* (20) 7471-5400 (office). *Fax:* (20) 7471-5401 (office). *Website:* www.polydor.co.uk (office).

THE UNKNOWN (see Carter, Derrick)

UNRUH, N. U.; American musician (percussion); b. (Andrew Chudy). *Career:* mem., Einstürzende Neubauten 1980–; solo artist 2000–; mem. Bombus. *Recordings include:* albums: with Einstürzende Neubauten: Kollaps 1981, Zeichnungen des Patienten O. T. 1983, Halber Mensch 1985, Fünf Auf der Nach Oben Offenen Richterskala 1987, Haus der Lüge 1989, Tabula Rasa 1993, Ende Neu 1996, Silence is Sexy 2000, Perpetuum Mobile 2004, Grundstück 2005, Alles wieder offen 2007; solo: Euphoria in the Age of Digital Information Transfer 2000. *Website:* www.neubauten.org.

UNTOUCHABLES (see Gonzalez, Kenny)

UOTILA, Jukkis; Finnish musician (drums, piano), composer and educator; *Professor, Sibelius Academy;* b. 23 Aug. 1960, Helsinki. *Career:* jazz performances and recordings 1976–; moved to New York 1980; worked with artists including Randy Brecker and Eliane Elias, Ted Curson, Mike Stern, Dave Samuels, Jack McDuff; returned to Finland 1984; Head of Jazz Dept, Sibelius Acad., Helsinki 1986–93, Prof. 1994–; bandleader Jukkis Uotila Band; performed world-wide at all major festivals and clubs; band sidemen featuring among others Randy Brecker, Bob Mintzer, Mike Stern, Bob Berg, Lars Jansson, Lars Danielsson, Wayne Krantz, Jeff Andrews, Anders Jormin, Tim Hagans, Dick Oatts; worked and recorded with artists including Toots Thielemans, Randy Brecker, Billy Cobham, Joey Calderazzo, Gil Evans, McCoy Tyner, Joe Henderson, Chet Baker, Tim Hagans, Bob Rockwell, Joe Lovano, McCoy Tyner, Bob Mintzer, Dave Liebman, Jerry Bergonzi, Freddie Hubbard, Kenny Wheeler, Bob Brookmeyer, The Stockholm Jazz Orchestra, Ulf Wakenius, Tim Ries, Lennart Åberg, Thomas Clausen, Doug Raney, Gustavo Bergalli, Cæcilie Norby, Eddie Lockjaw Davis, Zoot Sims, Maria Schneider, Jim McNeely; tours of Scandinavia and Europe, Japan, USA, S America, SA, SE Asia, Australia. *Recordings include:* recordings as a leader: Introspection 1984, Avenida 1987, Jukkis Uotila Band Live 1990, Fast Company 1998, Hunters & Gatherers 2000, Meninas 2005, The Music of Jukkis Uotila (with Stockholm Jazz Orchestra) 2012, The Herbie Hancock Legacy 2015; plays on over 890 jazz recordings; with Toots Thielemans: Live Takes 1998, Hard to Say Goodbye 2000; with Bob Rockwell: No Rush 1985, On the Natch 1985; with Chet Baker: When Sunny Gets Blue 1986; with Joe Bonner: Lost Melody 1987; with Doug Raney: Quintet 1988; with Stockholm Jazz Orchestra: Live at Fasching 1994, Soundbites 1996, Tango 1999, Lakes 2000, Sailing 2004, Homage 2003, Waves from the Vanguard 2006, Plays SJO 2007, Ikaros 2009, In the Blink of an Eye 2013; with Ulf Wakenius: Dig In 1999; with Vladimir Shafranov: Live at Groovy 1981, Movin Vova 2000, Portrait in Music 2002, Live in Helsinki 2002, Russian Lullaby 2003, Kids are Pretty People 2005, I'll Close My Eyes 2009; with Tim Hagans: Future North 1998, The Moon is Waiting 2011. *Honours:* 1st Class Kt Medal, Order of the Finnish Lion 2005; Georgie Award, Finnish Jazz Fed. 1991, State Prize for Music 2011. *Address:* Puolaharju 32 A, 00930 Helsinki, Finland (home). *E-mail:* avenida@kolumbus.fi. *Website:* www.jukkis.com.

UPPAL, Shiraz, MBA; Pakistani singer, songwriter and producer. *Career:* f. S.U. Studios, Lahore 2003. *Recordings include:* albums: Tera Te Mera 2003, Jhuki Jhuki 2005, Ankahi 2009. *Soundtrack:* Aashayein. *Honours:* Indian Mirchi Music Award for Best Upcoming Music Director 2010. *Website:* www .shirazuppal.com.

UPTON, Eddie, BA; British folk singer and musician (concertina, harmonica, percussion); *Director, Folk South West;* b. 4 Oct. 1944, Brighton, Sussex. *Education:* Univ. of Sussex. *Career:* full-time folk performer 1980–, specializing in traditional English songs, music and dance; fmr mem. Albion Dance Band and Etchingham Steam Band; Co-founder and Artistic Dir Folk South West, folk development soc. for SW of England 1992–; mem. Folklore Soc., English Folk Dance and Song Soc., Equity, Musicians' Union, Performing Right Soc. *Recordings include:* albums: The Prospect Before Us, Albion Dance Band; A Tale of Ale, Various Artists; Music for Christopher Columbus and his Crew, St Georges Canlona; Prospect Before Us, Albion Band; Guv'nor, Vol. 2 1996; The BBC Sessions 1998; solo: First Orders, Where the Parrett Winds Peaceful 1997, Songs of Somerset Folk 1998, Westcountry Christmas 1998, Fanfare for the South West 2003, Bud, Blossom and Bloom 2009, Past Delights 2013. *Publication:* Caedmon Capers – A Collection of New Folk Dances and Folk Dance Tunes, Singing Times: teaching English folk songs in schools, Still Growing: songs from the Cecil Sharp Collection (co-ed) 2003. *Honours:* awarded Gold Badge of the English Folk Dance and Song Society for outstanding services to the folk arts 2012. *Address:* Folk South West, 2 Church Farm Cottages, Chetnole Road, Leigh, Sherborne, Dorset, DT9 6HJ, England (office). *Telephone:* (1935) 873889 (office). *E-mail:* eddie@folksw.org.uk (office). *Website:* www.folksw.org.uk (office).

URBAN, Keith Lionel; Australian country singer and musician (guitar); b. 26 Oct. 1967, Caboolture, Qld; m. Nicole Kidman 2006; one d. *Education:* learned guitar from age of six. *Career:* moved to Nashville 1997; founder mem., The Ranch 1997–; session player for artists, including Garth Brooks, The Dixie Chicks; tours with Faith Hill, Tim McGraw, Dwight Yoakam. *Recordings include:* albums: solo: 1991 1991, Golden Road 2002, Be Here 2004, Days Go By (Acad. of Country Music Award for Best Album) 2005, The Velvet Room 2006, Welcome to the Sweat Hotel 2006, Love, Pain and the Whole Crazy Thing 2006, Defying Gravity 2009, Get Closer 2010, Fuse 2013; with The Ranch: Keith Urban in the Ranch 1997. *Honours:* ACM Awards for Best Male Vocalist 2005, 2006, for Video of the Year (for Highway Don't Care) 2014, for Vocal Event of the Year (for We Were Us, with Miranda Lambert) 2014, CMA Awards for Entertainer of the Year 2005, for Male Vocalist of the Year 2005, 2006, for Musical Event of the Year (for Highway Don't Care, with Tim McGraw and Taylor Swift) 2013, (for We Were Us, with Miranda Lambert) 2014, (for Raise 'Em Up, with Eric Church) 2015, Grammy Award for Best Male Country Vocal Performance (for You'll Think of Me) 2006, (for Stupid Boy) 2008, (for Sweet Thing) 2010, (for 'Til Summer Comes Around) 2011, American Music Award for Favorite Male Country Artist 2009, American Country Award for Single of the Year: Vocal Collaboration (for Highway Don't Care) 2013. *Address:* c/o Capitol Records Nashville, 3322 West End Avenue, Suite 11, Nashville, TN 37203, USA (office). *Website:* www.keithurban.net.

URBAN, Stan; British musician (piano) and singer; b. (Stanislaw Frank Urban), 10 Jan. 1944, Dundee, Scotland; s. of Stanislaw Urban and Martha Golden; m. 1st Erika Kuhnert 1963 (divorced 1984); two s.; m. 2nd Annette Wetterberg 1986 (died 1987); one adopted s.; m. 3rd Evelyn Jetzschmann 1996. *Education:* Brechin Lawside Acad., Dundee. *Career:* rock 'n' roll pianist; formed own band of German musicians, following tour of Germany with Long John Baldry 1962; lived and played in Ibiza late 1960s–1984; tours of Scandinavia, Middle East, South Africa, USA, Germany, UK, Spain; now lives in Denmark, solo tours, also touring band (with Michael Wedgwood, Henrik Skriver, Frank Thøgersen); coaches two finger rock 'n' roll piano technique, lectures in the history of rock 'n' roll. *Recordings include:* albums: Rock 'N' Roll Cocktail 1982, M'Roccan Rollers 1986, Live 1988, Through My Door 1992, Can't Hold On Can't Let Go 1995, The Devil Made the Boogie 1997, Dundee Jivin' 2003, Urban Friends 2010. *Fax:* 40-93-84-74. *Address:* Skaering Sandager 18, 8250 Egå, Denmark (home). *Telephone:* 86-22-84-74 (home). *E-mail:* stanurban@webnetmail.dk (home). *Website:* www.stanurban.dk.

URBANOWICZ, Chris; British musician (guitar); b. 22 June 1981, Nottingham. *Education:* Staffordshire Univ. *Career:* Founder mem., Snowfield 2003, renamed Editors 2004–12. *Recordings include:* albums: The Back Room 2005, An End Has a Start 2007, In This Light And On This Evening 2009.

URE, James (Midge), OBE; British singer, songwriter, musician (guitar), producer and director; b. 10 Oct. 1953, Glasgow, Scotland; m. 1st Annabel Giles 1985; one d.; m. 2nd Sheridan Forbes; three d. *Career:* mem., Salvation 1972, renamed Slik 1974–77; mem., Rich Kids 1977–78; founder mem., Visage 1978–82; mem., Thin Lizzy (during tour) 1979–80; mem., Ultravox 1980–87, 2008–; solo artist 1982–; producer 1980–, for artists including Antrix, Ronny, Cold Fish, Phil Lynott, Pete Godwyn, Modern Man, Fatal Charm, Steve Harley, Strasse, The Messengers, Rodeo, Michel Van Dyke, Countermine; dir of music videos, for artists including Fun Boy Three, Bananarama, Phil Lynott, Monsoon, Martha Ladly, Truth, Andrew Strong; formed Band Aid with Bob Geldof 1984, writing and recording the charity single Do They Know it's Christmas? (also trustee of Live Aid), also organized Live 8 concerts 2005; Musical Dir, Prince's Trust 1987–88. *Soundtrack compositions:* Max Headroom (TV) 1985, Turnaround (film) 1987, Boca (film) 1994, Went to Coney Island on a Mission from God... Be Back by Five 1998, October 22 1998. *Film appearances:* The Hunting of the Snark 1987, The Bogie Man (TV) 1992. *Recordings include:* albums: with Slik: Slik 1976; with Rich Kids: Ghosts of Princes in Towers 1978; with Visage: Visage 1980, The Anvil 1982; with Ultravox: Vienna 1980, Three Into One 1980, New Europeans 1981, Rage In Eden 1981, Quartet 1982, The Collection 1984, Lament 1984, U-Vox 1986, Brilliant 2012; solo: The Gift 1985, Answers to Nothing 1988, Pure 1991, Breathe 1996, Move Me 2001, Little Orphans: The Black and White Sessions 2001, 10 2008, Fragile 2014. *Honours:* Dr hc (Univ. of Abertay, Dundee) 2005; Ivor Novello and Grammy Awards. *E-mail:* midge@midgeure.com (office). *Website:* www.midgeure.com.

URTREGER, René; French musician (piano), bandleader and composer; b. 6 July 1934, Paris; m. 1st; one d.; m. 2nd Jacqueline Fornari; one s. *Career:* concerts and festivals throughout the world 1953–; started working at age 19 with Don Byas-Buck Clayton Band 1953; worked with Dexter Gordon, Zoot Sims, Stéphane Grappelli, Allen Eager, Stan Getz, Dizzy Gillespie, J. J. Johnson, Double Six; trio with Pierre Michelot and Kenny Clarke; house pianist for (Nicole) Barclay Records, France 1954–65; European tours as pianist within Miles Davis Quartet 1956, Miles Davis Quintet 1957; break from jazz music 1967–77, touring with Sacha Distel and Claude Francois; returned to jazz ensembles 1977; pianist with Sonny Stitt's French tour 1982. *Recordings include:* albums with: Lionel Hampton, Chet Baker, Bobby Jaspar, Hubert Fol, Maurice Meunier, Lester Young, Kenny Clarke, Michael Hausser, Stéphane Grappelli, Gary Burton, Stan Getz, Miles Davis, Pat Metheny and Stuff Smith; film music: Ascenseur Pour L'Echafaud, within Miles Davis Quintet, Le Poulet (Oscar short film 1965); other albums include: Recidive 1978, Humair/Urtreger/Michelot (H.U.M.) Trio 1979, Collection Privée 1981, En Direct Du Festival D'Antibes 1981, Jazzman (Prix Boris Vian, L'Academie Du Jazz 1985) 1985, Masters 1987, Avec Chet Baker 1989, Serena 1990, Chet Baker in Paris 1998, Film: René Urtreger/Homme De Jazz 1991, Saint Germains Des Presents, Telefilm by J. Ch. Averty 1993, HUM (Victoire de le Musique) 2000, Tentatives 2006. *Honours:* Officier des Arts et des Lettres 2006; winner National Jazz Tournament 1953, Prix Django Reinhardt, L'Academie Du Jazz 1961, Prix Boris Vian, L'Academie Du Jazz, Grand Prix, SACEM 1997, Grand Prix du Disque 2000, Hon. Victoire de la Musique 2005.

USHER; American R&B singer, rap artist and songwriter; b. (Usher Raymond), 14 Oct. 1978, Chattanooga, Tenn.; two s. *Education:* North Springs High School, Sandy Springs, Georgia. *Films include:* The Faculty 1998, She's All That 1999, Light It Up 1999, Texas Rangers 2001, Unchain My Heart: The Ray Charles Story 2004. *Television:* Moesha (series) 1996, The Bold and the Beautiful (series) 1987, Geppetto 2000. *Stage appearance:* Billy Flynn in Chicago (Broadway) 2006. *Recordings include:* albums: Usher 1994, My Way 1997, Live 1999, All About U 2000, 8701 2001, Confessions (American Music Award for Best Album, MTV Europe Best Album Award 2004, Grammy Award for Best Contemporary Album 2005) 2004, Here I Stand 2008, Raymond v. Raymond (Grammy Award for Best Contemporary R&B Album 2011) 2010, Looking 4 Myself 2012. *Honours:* Soul Train Award for Best R&B Single by a Male (for You Make Me Wanna) 1997, World Music Awards for Best Male Artist, Best Pop Male Artist, Best R&B Artist 2004, MTV Europe Best Male Award 2004, American Music Awards for Best R&B/Soul Artist, Best Pop/Rock Singer 2004, Source Hip Hop Award for Male of the Year 2004, NRJ Music Award for Best Int. Male, France 2005, Smash Hits Awards for Best Solo Artist, for Best R & B Act 2005, Grammy Awards for Best R&B Vocal Performance (for U Remind Me) 2002, for Best R&B Vocal Performance (U Don't Have To Call) 2003, for Best Rap/Sung Collaboration (for Yeah!) 2005, Best R&B Performance By a Duo or Group with Vocals (for My Boo) 2005, for Best R&B Vocal Performance (for There Goes My Baby) 2011, for Best R&B Performance (for Climax) 2013. *Current Management:* c/o J-Pat Management, 3996 Pleasantdale Road, Suite 104A, Dorville, GA 30340, USA. *Telephone:* (770) 416-8619. *Fax:* (770) 409-2386. *Website:* www.jpatmgntrehearsalhall .com.

USSING, Joachim; Danish musician (bass player) and composer; b. (Henrik Joachim Ussing), 9 Oct. 1952, Copenhagen; s. of Kjeld Ussing and Elsebet Ussing; m. Henriette Rolffes Becker 1989; one s. one d. *Career:* toured Scandinavia, recordings and TV appearances with Terje, Jesper & Joachim, Moirana, Phantom Band, Lone Kellermann and Rockband, Jomfru Ane Band, Doraz, Small Talk, Big Talk, Peter Thotup, Anne Grete, Peter Abrahamsen, Peter Viskinde, Bruce Daigrepoint, Paa Slaget 12, Ann-Mette Elten, Ussing/Negrain; mem. Danish Artist Union, DJBFA, KODA, GRAMEX, NCB. *Compositions include:* Een Stor Familie, score for TV series 1982–83, Sort Arbejde 2013. *Recordings:* Terje, Jesper and Joachim 1970; Phantom Band: OP and the Phantom Band; Lone Kellermann and Rockband: Før Natten bli'r til dag, Tilfældigt Forbi; Jomfru Ane Band: Blodsugerne, Bag din Ryg; Sanne og Birgit Brüel: Den hemmelige Rude; Anne Grete and Peter Thorup: Hvis ikke Nu, Regnbuen; Doraz: Tourist, Mere Frugt; Ewald and Littauer: For your Love; Peter Abrahamsen and the Bellpepper Boys: Frihed ret og Tro, Borrowed and Blue, Chicken Feet, No shirts, no shoes, no Service, Tit er jeg Glad; Janne Lærkedal: Natten har tusind Øjne; På Slaget 12: Let's Dance; Joachim Ussing & Thomas Negrain: Nattens Latter; Ann-Mette Elten: Hot-Hot, Solo, Close To You. *Honours:* numerous platinum and gold records. *Address:* Springdamvej 3, 2820 Gentofte, Denmark (home). *E-mail:* ju@ussing .net (home). *Website:* www.ussing.net (home).

UTADA, Hikaru (Hikki), (Cubic U); Japanese/American singer and songwriter; b. 19 Jan. 1983, New York; d. of Utada Teruzane and Utada Junko (Keiko Fuji); m. Kazuaki Kiriya 2002 (divorced 2007). *Education:* American School, Tokyo, Columbia Univ., New York. *Career:* recorded demos in downtime at father's studio, releasing them in USA under pseudonym Cubic U; first Japan releases as Utada Hikaru 1999, while continuing education in Tokyo; simultaneously maintained US and Japanese careers under respective names. *Radio:* hosted own radio shows in Japan, incl. Très Bien Bohemian. *Recordings include:* albums: Precious (as Cubic U) 1998, First Love 1999, U3*Star (live) 2000, Distance 2001, Deep River 2002, Singles Collection Vol. I 2004, Exodus (in English) 2005, Ultra Blue 2006, Heart Station 2008, This is the One 2009. *Honours:* World Music Award for Bestselling Asian Artist 2000. *Address:* c/o EMI Music Japan, 3-taku, Room 2–2–17, Akasaka Minato-Ku, Tokyo 107-8510, Japan (office). *Website:* www.emimusic.jp/hikki/index_e.htm.

UTHUP, Usha; Indian popular music and playback singer; b. (Usha Iyer), 8 Nov. 1947, Mumbai; m. Jani Chacko Uthup; one s., one d. *Career:* made debut as singer aged nine; contribs to numerous films as playback singer; numerous recorded albums. *Films include:* as playback singer: Purab Aur Pachhim 1970, Hare Rama Hare Krishna 1971, Shalimar 1978, Shaan 1980, Hum Paanch 1980, Wardaat 1981, Disco Dancer 1982, Bhavani Junction 1985, Dushman Devta 1991, Keechurallu 1991, Anjali 1991, Ek Tha Raja 1996, Daud 1998, Godmother 1999, Kabhi Khushi Kabhie Gham 2001, Bhoot 2003, Jogger's Park (Kalakar Award for Best Playback Singer 2004) 2003, Jajantaram Mamantaram 2003, June R 2005, Dhol 2007, Bow Barracks Forever 2007, Hattrick 2007, 7 Khoon Maaf (Filmfare Award for Best Playback Singer) 2011, Bombay March 12 2011, Don 2 2011, Kaafiron Ki Namaaz 2012, DoloGovinda 2012, Shirin Farhad Ki Toh Nikal Padi 2012; as actress: Pothan Vava 2006, Manmadan Ambu 2010, 7 Khoon Maaf 2011, Parie 2012. *Television:* as co-judge: Indian Idol 2007, 2008, Idea Star Singer 2010. *Recordings include:* albums: Door Deep Basini (Kalakar Award for Best Audio Album (Bangla) 1999) 1999, Chai Silpir Samman (Kalakar Award for Best Audio Album (Bangla) 2002) 2002. *Honours:* Padma Shri Award from Govt of India 2010. *Address:* c/o Studio Vibrations, 4G, Radhanath Chowdhury Road, Kolkata, 700 015, India (office). *E-mail:* usuthup@gmail.com; usuthup@vsnl.com (office). *Website:* www.ushauthup.com.

UTLEY, Adrian; British musician (guitar); b. 1958. *Career:* fmr mem. Big John Patton, Jazz Messengers; mem. Portishead 1991–; played guitar on Tom Jones' Reload 1999, Goldfrapp's Felt Mountain 2000; composed music for numerous films and tv series. *Film:* To Kill A Dead Man (short feature, also projected on MI5 building, London) 1995. *Recordings include:* albums: Dummy (Mercury Music Prize for Best Album) 1994, Herd Of Instinct 1995, Portishead 1997, PNYC (live) 1998, Glory Times 1998, Roseland, New York (DVD) 2002, Third 2008. *Current Management:* c/o Fruit, Ground Floor, 37 Lonsdale Road, London, NW6 6RA, England. *Telephone:* (20) 7326-0848. *Fax:* (20) 7326-8078. *E-mail:* fruitmanagement@btconnect.com. *Website:* www .portishead.co.uk.

UTTERBACK, Joe, DMA; American jazz musician (piano), composer and academic; *Associate Professor of Music, Sacred Heart University;* b. 8 Oct. 1944, Hutchinson, Kan. *Education:* Univ. of Kansas. *Career:* jazz pianist in

New York and Connecticut; solo jazz piano concerts, USA; currently Assoc. Prof. of Music, Sacred Heart Univ.; Dir of Music/Organist for First Congregational Church, Stratford, Conn.; selected for numerous seminars for regional and nat. orgs for piano and organ on improvisation, including AGO, MTA, Shubert Club, RCCO; mem. American Soc. of Composers, Authors and Publrs (ASCAP), American Guild of Organists, Coll. Music Soc. *Compositions:* jazz-influenced compositions for organ, piano, chorus, vocal solo, instrumental ensmbles. *Recordings include:* albums: Blues and Ballads at the Movies, Christmas on the Mountain, Night and Day, Gershwin: Porgy and Bess Jazz Suite, Joe Utterback, Night Train, Dr Joe's Jazz Gospel, Stardust, Jazz Dreamz. *Publications:* more than 350 published works, including Tuxedo Blues, Three Spirituals For Organ in Jazz Styles, Three Spirituals For Piano, Dr Joe's Long Ragtime Special, Missa Jazzis, Newtown Requiem, Joshua Fit the Battle of Jericho (for organ). *Honours:* Annual ASCAP Award 1991–. *Current Management:* c/o Bill Todt, 80 Rumson Place, Little Silver, NJ 07739, USA. *Telephone:* (732) 747-5227. *E-mail:* wmtodt@aol.com. *Telephone:* (203) 384-9992 (office). *E-mail:* jutterback56@aol.com (office). *Website:* www .jutterback.com; www.jazzmuze.com.

V

VAERNES, Knut, MA, MMus; Norwegian musician (guitar), composer, bandleader and record company executive; b. 1 April 1954, Trondheim; one s. *Education:* Univ. of Bergen, Univ. of Oslo. *Career:* 15 years as professional musician; concerts at nat. jazz festivals, tours of Europe; British tour with Cutting Edge, including Ronnie Scott's 1983; played with Jan Garbarek, Jon Christensen, Oslo 1982; Head of Jazz record label, Curling Legs; mem. Musicians' Union. *Recordings include:* albums: with Cutting Edge: Cutting Edge 1982, Our Man In Paradise 1984, Duesenberg 1986; solo: Admission For Guitars and Basses 1992, Roneo 1993, Jacques Tati 1995, 8:97 1998, Super Duper 1999, 4 g 2000, Tributes 2013. *Address:* Curling Legs A/S, PO Box 5298, Majorstua, 0303 Oslo, Norway (office). *Telephone:* 22-60-61-90 (office). *E-mail:* info@curlinglegs.no (office). *Website:* www.curlinglegs.no; www.knutvarnes.no.

VAI, Steve; American musician (guitar); b. 6 June 1960, Long Island, New York. *Education:* Tutored by Joe Satriani; Jazz and Classical music, Berklee College of Music, Boston. *Career:* Lead guitarist, Frank Zappa, 1979–84; Built own recording studio, 1984; Lead guitarist with Alcatrazz, 1985; David Lee Roth, 1986–89; Whitesnake, 1989–90; Also solo artiste; World-wide concerts and television/radio appearances with the above include: World Series of Rock, USA; Monsters of Rock, UK; Super Rock, Germany; Film appearance: Crossroads. *Recordings:* Albums include: with Frank Zappa: Tinseltown Rebellion, 1981; You Are What You Is, 1981; Shut Up and Play Yer Guitar, 1981; Ship Arriving Too Late, 1982; The Man From Utopia, 1983; Thing Fish, 1984; Jazz From Hell, 1986; Guitar, 1988; You Can't Do That On Stage Anymore, 1988; with Alcatrazz: Disturbing The Peace, 1985; with David Lee Roth: Eat 'Em and Smile, 1986; Skyscraper, 1988; with Whitesnake: Slip of The Tongue, 1989; solo albums: Flex-able 1984, Passion and Warfare 1990, Sex and Religion 1993, Alien Love Secrets 1995, Fire Garden 1996, Flex-Able Leftovers 1998, The Ultra Zone 1999, The 7th Song 2000, Alive In An Ultra World, 2001, Real Illusions: Reflections 2005; guest appearances include: Inferno, Motorhead 2004, Loudspeaker, Marty Friedman 2006, Bat out of Hell III: The Monster is Loose, Meat Loaf 2006, Big Neighborhood, Mike Stern 2009, Hang Cool Teddy Bear, Meat Loaf 2010. *Website:* www.vai.com.

VAIL, Frederick Scott; American recording studio executive; *President and CEO, Treasure Isle Recorders*; b. 24 March 1944, San Francisco, CA; m. 1st Brenda Joyce Howard 1972 (divorced 1977); m. 2nd Deborah J. Kirley 1996; one d. *Education:* California State University, Industrial College of the Armed Forces, Voluntary State Community College, Nashville. *Career:* radio announcer, Sacramento, 1958–62; Frederick Vail Productions, 1962–66; producer, sales manager, Teen-age Fair Inc. 1966–69; Artist Man., Beach Boys, 1969–71; Promotion Man., Capitol Records, 1972–73; Pres., Frederick Vail and Associates, 1974–80; Pres., Gen. Man., Treasure Isle Recording Studios, 1980–; Consultant, Promotion and Marketing: Waylon Jennings, 1974–75; GRT Records, 1976–78; RSO Records, 1978–79; lecturer at numerous colls and univs; event producer for: Beach Boys; Glen Campbell; Righteous Brothers; Four Seasons; Dave Clark Five; The Crickets; mem. Bd of Govs NARAS 1981–83, Bd of Trustees Asscn for Ind. Music 2001–04, CMA. *Publications:* Beach Boys – The California Myth (contrib.) 1978, Beach Boys – Heroes and Villains (contrib.) 1987; contrib. to Mix Magazine. *Address:* c/o Treasure Isle Recording Studios, Nashville, TN, USA (office). *Telephone:* (615) 297-0700 (office). *Fax:* (615) 297-6959 (office). *E-mail:* fredvail@treasureislenashville.com (office). *Website:* www.treasureislenashville.com (office); www.myspace.com/tresureislenashville.

VALDÉS, Chucho; Cuban jazz musician (piano, keyboards) and bandleader; b. (Jesús Valdés), 9 Oct. 1941, Quivican, Cuba; s. of Bebo Valdés and Pilar Rodríguez. *Education:* studied with Oscar Muñoz Boufartique, Zenaida Romeu, Rosario Franco, Leo Brower. *Career:* began playing piano aged 3; leader of own group by age 15; mem. Orquesta Sabor de Cuba 1957–61; played in salon of Hotel Havana Riviera 1961–63; played piano with Musical Theatre of Havana Orchestra; mem. Orquesta Cubana de Música Moderna 1967–; Founder Cuban jazz group, Irakere 1973–; f. Cresol ensemble with Roy Hargrove 1996; f. new quartet 1998; collaborations include Cesoria Evora, Herbie Hancock, Wynton Marsalis, Carlos Santana, Dizzy Gillespie, Max Roach, George Benson and numerous others. *Recordings include:* albums: with Irakere: Felicidad 1991, Live At Ronnie Scott's 1993, Exuberancia 1994, Indestructible 1998, Babalu Aye 1999, Yemayà 2002, Toda Cuba 2002 Irakere–30 años 2006; with Arturo Sandoval and Chucho Valdes Quartet: Straight Ahead 1994; with Cresol: Havana (Grammy Award); solo: Chucho Valdés y su Combo 1963, Jazz Batá 1972, Solo Piano 1993, Grandes Momentos De La Música Cubana 1994, Pianissimo 1997, Solo 1997, Bele Bele en la Habana 1998, Briyumba Palo Congo 1999, Live At The Village Vanguard 2000, Invitación 2000, Bele Bele En La Habana 2001, Fantasia Cubana 2002, Canciones Inéditas (Latin Grammy Award for Best Pop Instrumental Album) 2002, New Conceptions (Grammy Award) 2003, Cancionero Cubano 2005, Canto a Dios 2008, Juntos para Siempre (with Bebo Valdés) (Latin Grammy Award for Best Jazz Album 2009, Grammy Award for Best Latin Jazz Album 2010) 2009, El Último Trago (with Concha Buika) 2009, Chucho's Steps 2010, Cuban Dreams 2010, Border-Free 2013. *Honours:* Félix Varela Cross; Dr hc (Victoria Univ., Canada) 1997; Grammy Award (with Irakere) 1980, Nat. Music Prize of Cuba. *Current Management:* c/o Tobias Tumarkin, CAMI Music LLC, 1790 Broadway, 16th Floor, New York, NY 10019, USA. *E-mail:* management@comanchemusic.net. *Website:* www.camimusic.com; www.valdeschucho.com.

VALDY; Canadian singer, songwriter, musician (guitar) and producer; b. (Paul Valdemar Horsdal), 1 Sept. 1945, Ottawa; m. Kathleen Mary Fraser 1986; two s. *Education:* Usgar Collegiate, St Pat's Coll., Victoria School of Music. *Career:* numerous live appearances; mem. AFofM, NSAI, SAC, FEPRA, CARAS, CIRPA. *Recordings include:* albums: Country Man 1971, Landscapes 1973, Family Gathering 1974, Valdy and The Home Town Band 1976, Hot Rocks 1978, 1001 1979, Valdy's Kid Record 1981, Notes From Places 1986, Heart At Work 1993, Smorgasbard 1996, Contenders 1999, Contender Two 2007, Read Between the Lines 2012. *Honours:* two Juno Awards, BMI Song of the Year (for Landscapes) 1974. *E-mail:* kathyhahn@sympatico.ca. *Address:* Box 23, Fulford Harbour, Salt Spring Island, BC V8K 2P2, Canada (office). *E-mail:* valdy@saltspring.com (office). *Website:* www.valdy.com.

VALENSI, Nick; American musician (guitar); b. 16 Jan. 1981, New York, NY. *Education:* Dwight School, Manhattan. *Career:* mem., The Strokes 1998–. *Recordings include:* albums: with The Strokes: Is This It (NME Award for Album of the Year) 2001, Room on Fire 2003, First Impressions of Earth 2006, Angles 2011; collaborations with: Devendra Banhart, Regina Spektor, Sia. *Honours:* NME Awards for Band of the Year, Best New Act 2001, for Best Int. Band 2006, BRIT Award for Best Int. Newcomer 2002. *Current Management:* Wiz Kid Management, 123 E Seventh Street, New York, NY 10009, USA. *Website:* www.thestrokes.com.

VALENTIN, David Peter; American musician (flute); b. 29 April 1952, New York. *Education:* High School Music and Art, Bronx Community Coll.; studied with Hubert Laws. *Compositions include:* film soundtracks. *Recordings include:* Legends 1979, The Hawk 1980, I Got It Right This Time 1981, In Love's Time 1982, Mind Time 1987, Flute Juice 1990, Jungle Garden 1990, Kalahari 1990, Light Struck 1990, Two Amigos 1990, Musical Portraits 1991, Red Sun 1982, Tropic Heat 1993, Primitive Passions 1996, Sunshower 1999, World on a String 2005, Come Fly With Me 2006, Pure Imagination 2011. *Honours:* voted Best Flute (six years consecutively) Jazz Iz Magazine, Entertainer of Year NHAMAS 1993, Vista 2000 Excellence In The Arts 1995. *E-mail:* francois@saubadumanagement.com. *Website:* www.saubadumanagement.com.

VALENTINE, James; American musician (guitar); b. 5 Oct. 1978, Lincoln, NE. *Career:* mem., Maroon 5 2001–. *Recordings include:* albums: with Maroon 5: Songs About Jane 2002, It Won't Be Soon Before Long (Billboard Music Award for Top Digital Album 2007) 2007, Hands All Over 2010, Overexposed 2012, V 2014. *Honours:* with Maroon 5: Grammy Awards for Best New Artist 2004, for Best Pop Performance by a Duo or Group with Vocals (for Makes me Wonder) 2008, American Music Awards for Favorite Pop/Rock Band/Duo/Group 2011, 2012, for Favorite Adult Contemporary Artist 2013, Billboard Music Award for Top Hot 100 Artist 2013, People's Choice Award for Favorite Band 2013. *Current Management:* c/o Career Artist Management, 1100 Glendon Avenue, Suite 1100, New York, NY 90024, USA. *Telephone:* (310) 776-7640. *Fax:* (310) 776-7659. *Website:* camanagement.com; www.maroon5.com.

VALENTINE, Kathy; American musician (bass guitar); b. 7 Jan. 1959, Austin, Tex.; m. Steven Weisburd (divorced); one d. *Career:* mem., Textone; joined the Go-Go's 1980–85; The Go-Go's re-formed briefly for PETA benefit concert 1990; mem., re-formed Go-Go's 1994, shows in Las Vegas; formed the Bluebonnets 1992–94, re-named the Delphines 1994–; The Go-Go's re-formed 2000–13, for an album and tours, including US tour with B-52s. *Recordings include:* albums: Beauty And The Beat 1981, Vacation 1982, Talk Show 1984, Return To The Valley Of The Go-Go's 1994, God Bless The Go-Go's 2001, Lightyears 2005. *E-mail:* info@kathyvalentine.com. *Website:* www.kathyvalentine.com.

VALERIYA; Russian singer; b. (Alla Yuryevna Perfilova), 17 April 1968, Atkarsk; d. of Yuri Ivanovich and Galina Nikolaevna; m. 1st Leonid Yaroshevsky; m. 2nd Alexandr Shulgin, three c.; m. 3rd Iosif Prigozhin. *Education:* Gnesin Acad. of Music. *Career:* solo artist 1989–. *Recordings include:* albums: The Taiga Symphony 1989, Pobud' so mnoi 1989, Anna 1995, Familia Chast' 1 1997, Glaza Tsveta Neba 2001, Strana Lyubvi 2003, Nezhnost' Moya 2006, Nepodkontrolno/Out of Control (versions in English and Russian) 2008. *Publication:* Life, Tears and Love (autobiography) 2006. *Honours:* Order for the Revival of Russia 2003, Honoured Artist of Russia 2005; MuzTV Award for Best Female Artist 2004, MTV Russia Award for Best Female Artist 2004, for Best Duet 2004, Mariinskiy Order for Professional Achievement 2005, Golden Gramophone Prizes 2003, 2004, 2005, 2006, 2007. *Address:* c/o Tatiana Kononova, NOX Music, 3d street of Yamskogo poliya, bld. 26, office 40, Moscow, Russia (office). *Telephone:* (495) 739-1212 (office). *E-mail:* valeriya.prg@gmail.com; kononova-t@nm.ru (office). *Website:* www.valeriya.net.

VALLANCE, Jim, OC; Canadian songwriter and music producer; b. 31 May 1952; m. Rachel Paiement; one s. *Education:* private music study in piano, cello. *Career:* mem. Bd of Dirs Canadian Soc. of Composers, Authors and

Publishers 1996–98, 2000–15, PROCAN, 1987–90; mem. Bd of Dirs, Song-writers Asscn of Canada 1990–; mem. SOCAN (Canada), ASCAP (USA). *Compositions include:* for Aerosmith: Other Side, Ragdoll, Eat The Rich; for Bryan Adams: Heaven, Run To You, Summer of '69, Cuts Like A Knife; for Heart: What About Love; for Joe Cocker: When The Night Comes; for Tina Turner: It's Only Love, Back Where You Started; for Glass Tiger: Don't Forget Me When I'm Gone; for Bonnie Raitt, No Way To Treat A Lady; for Roger Daltrey: Rebel; for Ozzy Osbourne: Just Want You; also wrote songs with Lita Ford, Joan Jett, Motley Crue, Diane Warren, Alice Cooper. *Honours:* four Juno Awards for Composer of the Year, ASCAP Award, BMI Award, SOCAN Award. *E-mail:* jimvallance@mac.com. *Website:* www.jimvallance.com.

VALLGREN, Carl-Johan; Swedish writer and musician; b. 26 July 1964, Linköping. *Recordings include:* albums: Klädpoker med Djävulen 1996, Easy listening för masochister 1998, Kärlek och andra katastrofer 2001, 2000 mil 400 nätter 2003, I provinsen 2004, Livet 2007. *Publications include:* novels: Nomaderna 1987, Längta bort 1988, Fågelkvinnan 1991, Berättelser om sömn och vaka 1994, Dokument rörande Spelaren Rubashov 1996, För herr Bachmanns broschyr 1998, Berlin på 8 kapitel 1999, Den vidunderliga kärlekens historia (Augustpriset 2002) 2002, Kunzelmann & Kunzelmann 2009, Sea Man 2012. *Honours:* Årets bok-Månadens boks litterära pris 2002, Tylösandspriset 2004. *Address:* c/o Bonnier Books, PO Box 3159, 103 63 Stockholm, Sweden (office). *E-mail:* bonnierforlagen@bok.bonnier.se (office). *Website:* www.vallgren.nu.

VALLI, Frankie; American singer; b. (Francis Castelluccio), 3 May 1937, Newark, NJ. *Career:* mem., Four Seasons 1954–77, 1980s; solo artist 1958–. *Recordings include:* albums: with The Four Seasons: Sherry and 11 Others 1962, Ain't That A Shame and 11 Others 1963, The 4 Seasons Greetings 1963, Born To Wander 1964, Dawn and 11 Other Great Songs 1964, Rag Doll 1964, Entertain You 1965, The Four Seasons Sing Big Hits By Bacharach, David and Dylan 1966, Working My Way Back To You 1966, Lookin' Back 1967, Christmas Album 1967, Genuine Imitation Life Gazette 1969, Edizione D'Oro 1969, Chameleon 1972, Streetfighter 1975, Inside You 1976, Who Loves You 1976, Helicon 1977, Reunited Live 1981; solo: Timeless 1968, Inside You 1975, Close Up 1975, Story 1976, Frankie Valli Is The Word 1978, The Best of Frankie Valli 1980, Heaven Above Me 1981, Off Seasons 2001, Romancing the '60's 2007. *Current Management:* Steve Levine, International Creative Management, 8942 Wilshire Blvd, Beverly Hills, CA 90211, USA. *Telephone:* (310) 550-4436. *E-mail:* slevine@icmtalent.com. *Website:* www.icmtalent.com; www.frankievallifourseasons.com.

VALLÍN, Sergio; Mexican musician (guitar), songwriter and record produ-cer; b. 26 May 1973, Mexico City. *Career:* moved with family to Aguascalientes 1983; taught guitar lessons as teenager; fmr mem. of teenage band Wando – 1993; mem. rock group Maná 1994–; group f. Salva Negra Foundation (financing and supporting projects to protect environment) 1995–; over 25 million records sold worldwide; numerous int. tours; solo artist 2009–; record producer for artists including Chio, Serralde. *Recordings include:* albums: with Maná: Falta Amor 1990, ¿Dónde Jugarán Los Niños? 1992, Cuando los Ángeles Lloran 1995, Sueños Liquidos (Grammy Award for Best Latin Rock/Alternative Performance 1999, Premio Lo Nuestro for Pop Album of the Year 1999) 1997, Maná MTV Unplugged (Ritmo Latino Music Award for Album of the Year 2000) 1999, Revolución de Amor (Billboard Latin Music Awards for Latin Rock Album of the Year 2003, for Latin Pop Album of the Year – Duo or Group 2003, Grammy Award for Best Latin Rock/Alternative Album 2003, Latin Grammy Award for Best Rock Album by a Duo or Group 2003, Premio Lo Nuestro for Rock Album of the Year 2003, Ritmo Latino Music Award for Album of the Year 2003) 2002, Amar es Combatir (Billboard Latin Music Award for Latin Rock/Alternative Album of the Year 2007, Grammy Award for Best Latin Rock/Alternative Album 2007, Premio Lo Nuestro for Rock Album of the Year 2007) 2007, Arde el Cielo (Billboard Latin Music Awards for Latin Pop Album of the Year – Duo or Group 2009, for Latin Rock/Alternative Album of the Year 2009) 2008, Drama y Luz (Latin Grammy Award for Best Rock Album 2011, Premio People en Español Award for Best Album 2011, Grammy Award for Best Latin Pop, Rock or Urban Album 2012, Premio Lo Nuestro Award for Rock/Alternative Award of the Year 2012) 2011, Cama Incendiada (Latin Grammy Award for Pop/Rock Album of the Year 2015) 2015; solo: Bendito Entre las Mujeres 2009; other contribs include: Supernatural, Santana 1999. *Honours:* FAO Goodwill Amb. 2003; with Wando: first place, Valores Juveniles Bacardi Contest 1993; with Maná: Premios Lo Nuestro for Best Pop Group 1997, 1999, 2000, for Pop Song of the Year (for Mariposa Traicionera) 2004, for Rock Song of the Year (for Labios Compartidos) 2007, (for Bendita Tu Luz) 2008, for Rock Artist of the Year 2007, 2008, for Lifetime Achievement 2011, for Rock/Alternative Artist of the Year 2012, Ritmo Latino Music Award for Best Solo or Rock Group Artist 1999, Premios Oye! Special Social Prize to Music 2002, Award for Best Solo or Group Artist 2003, Mexican Public Commercial Award 2004, MasterTone Award (for Labios Compartidos) 2007, Latin Grammy Awards for Record of the Year 2000, for Best Rock Performance by a Duo or Group (both with Santana, for Corazón Espinado) 2000, for Best Pop Performance by a Duo or Group with Vocal (for Se Me Olvidó Otra Vez) 2000, Latin Grammy Special Award for Musical Accom-plishments 2006, Billboard Latin Awards for Pop Airplay Song of the Year – Duo or Group (for Labios Compartidos) 2007, for Latin Tour of the Year 2008, for Hot Latin Song of the Year – Duo or Group (for Si No Te Hubieras Ido) 2009, for Latin Pop Airplay Song of the Year – Duo or Group (for Si No Te Hubieras Ido) 2009, for Latin Duet or Group Songs 2012, for Latin Duet or

Group Album 2012, for Latin Pop Duet or Group of the Year Songs 2012, for Latin Pop Duet or Group of the Year Album 2012, Premio Juventud Supernova Award 2006, Premios Juventud for Favorite Rock Artist 2007, 2008, 2009, 2011, 2012, World Music Awards for World's Best Selling Latin Group 2007, for Best Selling Latin American Artist 2007, Los Premios 40 Principales for Best Concert/Tour 2007, 2011, Pan American Health Org. Champions of Health (for Salva Negra Foundation), World Health Day 2008, Premios Telehit for Best Int. Mexican Band 2011, Premio People en Español Award for Best Rock Artist or Group 2011, Premio Cadena Dial 2011, Premio Casandra Internacional 2012. *Address:* c/o Warner Music Mexico, SA de C.V. Leibnitz 32 Col., Nueva Anzures, México, DF 11590, Mexico (office). *Website:* www.vallin.com.mx; www.mana.com.mx.

VALTÝSDÓTTIR, Kristín Anna; Icelandic musician (electronics). *Career:* mem. experimental group, Múm 1997–2006. *Recordings include:* albums: Yesterday Was Dramatic – Today Was OK 2000, Please Smile My Noise Bleed 2001, Finally We Are No One 2002, Summer Make Good 2004. *Address:* c/o Fat Cat Records, PO Box 3400, Brighton, BN1 4WD, England.

VAN BAVEL, Boudewijn; Dutch producer and composer; *Managing Director, Sky Trance International;* b. 9 Jan. 1952, Breda; one s. *Education:* Music High School, Rotterdam. *Career:* producer, composer, Black Lee, Breda 1973–79; Man. Dir Bo Easy Studios, Breda 1980–89, Artists and Business, Rotterdam 1990, Sky Trance International (studios and theatre), Hilversum and Antwerp, Belgium 1990–. *Recordings:* California Fried Scene, Black Lee 1979, I Got To Spend More Time, Bo Easy 1983. *Address:* PO Box 64, 1200 AB Hilversum, The Netherlands.

VAN BEST, Peter; Dutch music publisher, songwriter and singer; b. 15 Oct. 1951, Kaatsheuvel. *Education:* music school. *Career:* entered Castlebar Int. Song Contest (RTE) 1986, Cavan Int. Song Contest 1988, Artemare Italy 1992, Europa Song France (Radio France) 1992, Europa Song Brussels 1993, Top Artist Show, Italy 1993, Midem Showcase 1994; invited guest, 70th anniver-sary in Paris of Peter Ustinov 1991; mem. BUMA/Stemra (Dutch collecting soc. for composers and music publrs), SENA (Foundation for the Exploitation of Neighbouring Rights). *Compositions include:* Souvenir 2002, London 2009, A Strange Night 2011, Bon Voyage 2012; own compositions published world-wide. *Publication:* Globetrotter 2011. *Honours:* Fidof (Festival Fed.) Award 1988, 1990. *Address:* Best Music, Wilhelminaplein 20, 5171 Kaatsheuvel KX, The Netherlands (office). *Telephone:* (416) 273270 (office). *E-mail:* bestmusic@ziggo.nl (office).

VAN DEN BRINK, Bert; Dutch composer and arranger; b. 24 July 1958, Geldrop; m. Medy Doves; one s. *Education:* Utrecht Conservatory with Herman Uhlhorn. *Career:* teacher of jazz music, Utrecht Conservatory; played with Dee Dee Bridgewater, Toots Thielemans, Denise Jannah, Philip Catherine, Chet Baker, Nat Adderly, Rick Margitza, Charlie Mariano. *Composition:* Wondering Why. *Recordings include:* Live at Montréal Dee Dee Bridgewater, 1990; Deepest to Dearest (solo album); Hazy Hugs, Amstel Octet with Guest Chet Baker, Bert van den Brink Invites Clare Fischer 2001, Bert's Bytes 2007, Friendship: Live At The Muziekgebouw Aan Het IJ 2009, Reflections 2010, Standards & Other Pieces 2010; Denise Jannah albums. *Honours:* First Prize, International Concours for Visually Handicapped Musicians, Hungary. *Address:* Brink Productions BV, Akkerse Straat 6A, 4061 BH Ophemert, The Netherlands (office). *Telephone:* (34) 4651740. *E-mail:* info@bertvandenbrink.com. *Website:* www.bertvandenbrink.com.

VAN DORT, Elizabeth (Liz), BA; Australian singer and composer; b. Melbourne, Vic.; partner Roger (now separated); one s. *Education:* Univ. of Melbourne. *Career:* singer, composer, various film and TV projects; singer, composer, Faraway during early 1990s; singer, Sting and The Radioactors; backing singer and session singer for various artists; formed Faraway (with Harry Williamson); completed music for several TV soundtracks; mem. Mechanical-Copyright Protection Soc. *Television includes:* vocalist and com-poser, Geschichte Mitteldeutschlands (Ottonia, Germany); other TV docu-mentaries. *Recordings include:* with Faraway: Far From The Madding Crowd 1998, 2001; with Sting & the Radioactors: Nuclear Waste 1995; with Lys: Lightwaves 2004; Effleurement (collection of female voices) 2006. *Current Management:* PO Box 1507, St Kilda South, Vic. 3182, Australia. *Website:* www.lizvandort.com.

VAN DYKE, Leroy Frank; American country musician and auctioneer; b. 4 Oct. 1929, Pettis County, MO; m. Gladys Marie Daniels 1980; three s. one d. *Education:* Univ. of Missouri, Reppert's School of Autioneering. *Career:* numerous tours, USA and abroad; played Las Vegas and various venues, especially agricultural events (fairs, rodeos, livestock events); mem. CMA, CAP, ACM, NATD, IEBA, IAFE. *Film appearance:* What Am I Bid?. *Radio:* co-host Country Crossroads. *Television:* host Leroy Van Dyke Show, Red Foley's Ozark Jubilee, Grand Ole Opry. *Recordings:* albums: Walk On By 1962, Movin' Van Dyke 1962, The Great Hits 1963, Songs for Mom and Dad 1964, At the Trade Winds 1964, Out of Love 1965, The Leroy Van Dyke Show 1965, Country Hits 1966, Movin' 1966, Auctioneer 1966, Have a Party 1967, What Am I Bid 1967, Lonesome Is 1968, Just a Closer Walk with Thee 1969, I've Never Been Loved Before 1969, Just for You 1975, Rock Relics 1978, Cross Section 1982. *Publication:* Auctioneering, Motivation, Success. *Honours:* Billboard Award for Biggest Ever Country Hit (for Walk On By) 1994. *Current Management:* Leroy Van Dyke Enterprises, 29000 Hwy V, Smithton, MO 65350, USA. *Telephone:* (660) 343-5373 (home); (660) 343-5392 (office).

Fax: (660) 343-5292 (office). *E-mail:* gvandyke@iland.net (office). *Website:* www.leroyvandyke.com.

VAN HALEN, Alex; musician (drums); b. 8 May 1955, Nijmegen, The Netherlands. *Career:* founder mem. rock group, Van Halen 1974–; numerous tours worldwide, festival appearances. *Recordings include:* albums: Van Halen 1978, Van Halen II 1979, Women and Children First 1980, Fair Warning 1981, Diver Down 1982, 1984 1984, 5150 1986, OU812 1988, For Unlawful Carnal Knowledge 1991, Right Here Right Now 1993, Balance 1995, Twister 1996, Van Halen 3 1998, A Different Kind of Truth 2012. *Honours:* Grammy Award for Best Hard Rock Performance 1992, American Music Award for Favorite Hard Rock Album 1992, MTV Video Awards 1984, 1992. *Website:* www.van-halen.com.

VAN HALEN, Eddie; rock musician (guitar); b. 26 Jan. 1957, Nijmegen, The Netherlands; m. Valerie Bertinelli 1981; one s. *Education:* Pasadena City Coll. *Career:* founder mem. rock group, Van Halen 1974–; numerous tours worldwide and festival appearances. *Recordings include:* albums: Van Halen 1978, Van Halen II 1979, Women and Children First 1980, Fair Warning 1981, Diver Down 1982, 1984 1984, 5150 1986, OU812 1988, For Unlawful Carnal Knowledge 1991, Right Here Right Now 1993, Balance 1995, Twister 1996, Van Halen 3 1998, A Different Kind of Truth 2012. *Honours:* Grammy Award for Best Hard Rock Performance 1992, American Music Award for Favorite Hard Rock Album 1992, MTV Music Video Awards 1984, 1992. *Website:* www .van-halen.com.

VAN HELDEN, Armand; American DJ, remixer and producer; b. 1972, Boston, Mass. *Career:* mem. X-Mix Productions, Boston; began remixing many Euro-pop acts; parallel solo performing career; remixer and producer for Jimmy Somerville, C. J. Bolland, Tori Amos, DJ Icey, Jocelyn Brown, Sneaker Pimps, Apollo Four Forty, Tuff and Jam; mem. duo Duck Sauce with A-Trak. *Recordings include:* albums: Old School Junkies 1996, Da Club Phenomena 1997, Enter the Meatmarket 1997, Armand Van Helden Phenomenon 1999, 2 Future 4 U 1999, Killing Puritans 2000, Gandhi Khan 2001, Repro 2001, New York: A Mix Odyssey 2004, Ghettoblaster 2007, New York: A Mix Odyssey Part 2 2008, The Best of Armand Van Helden 2012. *Website:* www .armandvanhelden.com.

VAN HOVE, Frederik (Fred); Belgian musician (piano, church organ, accordion); b. 19 Feb. 1937, Antwerp; m. 2nd Mie Van Cakenberghe 1986; three s. *Education:* Music Acad., Antwerp. *Career:* free improvised music: concerts, radio, TV; Festivals: Europe, Japan, USA, Canada, People's Republic of China, South Africa, Morocco, Lebanon, Slovenia, Taiwan; Chair. Wim vzw Asscn for Improvised Music, Antwerp. *Compositions:* for mixed instrument groups and improvising soloists; for Big Band and own groups: MLB III, Piano Kwartet, Nonet, B3B; for theatre. *Recordings:* more than 75 including Lust, Pyp, Suite for B-City, Flux 1998, Passing Waves 1998, Spraak & Roll 2004, Journey 2008, Asynchronous 2010. *Honours:* Cultural Ambassador of Flanders, 1996, 1997; SABAM Jazz Award 2010. *Address:* St Vincentiusstr. 61, 2018 Antwerp, Belgium (home). *Telephone:* (3) 2306075 (home). *Fax:* (3) 2306075 (home). *E-mail:* vanhave.fred@skynet.be (home). *Website:* www .fredvanhove.be.

VAN SLEEN, Harm; Dutch musician (bass, pedal steel) and composer; b. 31 Dec. 1965, Utrecht; m. Kerstin Lucia Venhuizen 1995; one d. *Education:* Hilversums Conservatory. *Career:* played with various pop groups 1980–89; recorded single with Burt and the Brand New Lifestyle 1989; played with Jaap Dekker's Jazz and Boogie Set 1989–93; playing with Capelino and with Mr Boogie Woogie and the Fire Sweep Blues Band, also with Dichy Greenwood, Anke Angel, Lisa Otey, The Sleen Gang, Wouters Kiers Trio. *Compositions:* Take Me To Swine Lane, Goodbye, Gossip, Bad Day, If You Went Away, Trouble, Lovin On My Mind, Holy Boogie, Young Boys and Girls (On the Old Side of Town), Dichy Greenwood, A Long Way, Mr. Boogie Woogie, Three Band Fist, Dichy Greenwood, Feeling Blue 2003. *Recordings:* Relite! Revelation 1993, Capelino, Way To Go 1997, Mr Boogie Woogie and The Fire Sweep Blues Band, Live At the Pub 1997, Bassman's Holiday. *Publications:* Mag Die Radio War Harder?!! 1993. *Address:* Resedahof 29, 3434 XC, Nieuwegein, Netherlands (home). *E-mail:* harmvansleen@hetnet.nl (office). *Website:* www .harmvansleen.nl (office).

VANDENBROUCQUE, Gérard; French musician (violin); b. 15 May 1961. *Education:* Conservatoire Hauts de Seine. *Career:* performances with Stéphane Grappelli, David Savourel, Fabrice Evain, Didier Lockwood, Tchavolo Schmidt; appearances at: Montréal Festival, SOPS, New York, Radio France Inter; mem. Asscn Jazz et Violon. *Recordings:* Tango, Violin Onztet. *Address:* 14B rue Pierre Loti, 44300 Nantes, France (home). *Telephone:* 9-50-63-34-09 (home).

VANDENDRIESSCHE, Johan, BMus, MMus, BMusicology; Belgian musician (saxophone, flute, bass clarinet, drums, bass guitar, keyboard) and teacher of music; *Teacher, HAMW & AHA Podium;* b. 30 May 1958, Leuven; m. Hilde Pollet 1991; one s. one d. *Education:* Conservatorium of Leuven, Lemmensinstituut, Leuven, Katholieke Universiteit Leuven. *Career:* appearances with Belgium Radio and TV Orchestras, BRT Big Band, BRT Jazzorkest/Philharmonic Orchestra, Eurojazz Orchestra; with own band Milkshake Banana, played in jazz festivals in Atlanta, USA, Montreux, Switzerland, Århus, Denmark; concerts with Zoot Money, Georgie Fame, Randy Crawford and John Miles as a soloist in Belgium and Holland, WDR Big Band, Cologne, Germany, with Clare Fisher, with Calvin Owens, with singer Tony Christie

band (UK, Germany), British bandleader/remixer Matthew Herbert, own bands The Demagogue Reacts, The Belgian Swingjazz Orchestra, Gezelle Gezongen, Tom Robinson; teacher of jazz and pop history, harmony, organology, saxophone and woodwinds at HAMW and AHA Podium. *Compositions:* Move, Nathalie, Cool Bird, ISIRO, Teo. *Recordings:* With Milkshake Banana, ACT Bigband, Caude Maurane, Soulsister, Claude Nougaro, Indochine, Johan Verminnen, Marc Moulin (Blue Note). *Publications:* Articles on jazz in KNACK magazine 1981–82, Soundslike magazine. *Honours:* First Prize, Int. Jazz Contest, Hoeilaart 1979. *Current Management:* c/o BVBA VDDR, Hellichtstraat 1, 3110 Rotselaar, Belgium. *Telephone:* 479-204996 (mobile). *Address:* Groenstraat 33, 3110 Rotselaar, Belgium (office). *Telephone:* (16) 44-70-01 (home). *E-mail:* johanvddr@gmail.com (home); info@ johanvandendriessche.be; info@belgianswingjazzorchestra.com (home). *Website:* www.thebelgianswingjazzorchestra.be (office); www .johanvandendriessche.be.

VANGELIS; Greek composer, musician (keyboards) and conductor; b. (Evangelos Papathanassiou), 29 March 1943, Volos. *Education:* Acad. of Fine Arts, Athens and private tuition with Aristotelis Coudourof. *Career:* began performing own compositions aged six; moved to Paris in late 1960s; composed and recorded symphonic poem Faire que ton rêve soit plus long que la nuit; returned to Greece, after period in London 1989; formed band Formynx in Greece 1960s; mem. Aphrodite's Child (with Demis Roussos) 1966–71; composer 1972–, in Paris, France, then established Nemo recording studio, London 1974; partnership with Jon Anderson as Jon & Vangelis 1980–84. *Composition for film:* O Adelfos mou o trohonomos 1963, To prosopo tis medusas 1966, 5000 psemata 1966, Sex Power 1970, scores for French wildlife films 1972, Salut, Jerusalem 1972, L'Apocalypse des animaux 1972, Amore 1973, Le Cantique des créatures: Georges Mathieu ou La fureur d'être 1974, Le Cantique des créatures: Georges Braque ou Le temps différent 1975, Ignacio 1975, Ace Up My Sleeve 1976, La Fête sauvage 1976, Prkosna delta 1980, Die Todesgöttin des Liebescamps 1981, Chariots of Fire (Acad. Award for Best Original Score 1982) 1981, Missing 1982, Le Cantique des créature: Pablo Picasso pintor 1982, Blade Runner 1982, Nankyoku monogatari 1983, Wonders of Life 1983, The Bounty 1984, Sauvage et beau 1984, Nosferatu a Venezia 1988, Le Dîner des bustes 1988, Russicum - I giorni del diavolo 1989, Francesco 1989, Terminator II 1990, La Peste 1992, Bitter Moon 1992, 1492: Conquest of Paradise 1992, De Nuremberg à Nuremberg 1994, Rangeela 1995, Kavafis 1996, I Hope 2001, Alexander 2004, El Greco 2007, Trashed 2012. *Composition for television:* L'Opera sauvage (series) 1977, Cosmos (series, BBC 1) 1980. *Recordings include:* albums: with Aphrodite's Child: Aphrodite's Child 1968, Rain & Tears 1968, End Of The World 1969, It's Five O'Clock 1970, 666 1972; solo: Terra, Dragon 1971, L'Apocalypse des animaux 1972, Earth 1973, Heaven and Hell 1975, Albedo 0.39 1976, The Vangelis Radio Special 1976, Spiral 1977, Beauborg 1978, Hypothesis 1978, China 1979, Odes 1979, See You Later 1980, To The Unknown Man 1981, Soil Festivities 1984, Invisible Connections 1985, Magic Moments 1985, Mask 1985, Direct 1988, The City 1990, Themes 1989, Voices 1995, El Greco 1995, Oceanic 1996, Reprise 1990–1999 2000, Mythodea: Music for the NASA Mission – 2001 Mars Odyssey 2001; as Jon & Vangelis: Short Stories 1980, The Friends of Mr Cairo 1981, Private Collection 1983, Page of Life 1991.

VANIAN, Dave; British singer; b. (David Letts), 12 Oct. 1956; m. Patricia Morrison 2000. *Career:* fmr grave digger; Founder-mem. punk rock band, The Damned 1976–77, 1979–89, 1991–; mem., Doctors of Madness 1978; worldwide concerts; mem. side projects, Naz and the Nomads 1984–88, The Phantom Chords 1990–95. *Recordings include:* albums: with The Damned: Damned, Damned, Damned 1977, Music For Pleasure 1977, Machine Gun Etiquette 1979, The Black Album 1980, Live At Shepperton 1980 1982, Strawberries 1982, Live At Newcastle 1983, Damned But Not Forgotten 1985, Phantasmagoria 1985, Anything 1986, Not The Captain's Birthday Party? 1986, The Captain's Birthday Party 1986, Light At The End Of The Tunnel 1987, Mindless, Directionless, Energy: Live At The Lyceum 1987, Final Damnation 1989, Live 1991, Ballroom Blitz 1992, Music For Pleasure 1995, Eternally Damned 1995, Fiendish Shadows 1996, Not Of This Earth 1996, Testify 1997, Eternal Damnation Live 1999, Molten Lager 2000, Grave Disorder 2001, So, Who's Paranoid? 2008, Machine Gun Etiquette: Anniversary Live Set 2011, 35th Anniversary Tour: Live in Concert 2012; with Naz and the Nomads: Give Daddy The Knife, Cindy 1988; with The Phantom Chords: Dave Vanian and The Phantom Chords 1995. *E-mail:* booking@ officialdamned.com (office). *Website:* www.officialdamned.com.

VANNELLI, Joseph (Joe) Anthony; Canadian producer, arranger and musician (keyboards); b. 28 Dec. 1950, Montréal. *Education:* three years univ., private music lessons. *Career:* worked with Gino Vannelli, Gary Morris, David Meece, Kudasai, Marilyn Scott, Jimmy Haslip, Don Sebesky and The Royal Philharmonic Orchestra, Gregory Hines; co-producer, commercials, including Pontiac, Honda; Owner, recording studio; concerts include Gino Vannelli's World Tour 1990–92; television includes Arsenio Hall Show (Europe), Juno Award Show (Canada), Dick Clark Night Time, documentary on rain forests of Costa Rica. *Recordings include:* Crazy Life 1973, Powerful People 1974, Storm At Sunup 1975, The Gist of The Gemini 1976, Brother To Brother 1978, Nightwalker 1981, Black Cars 1985, Big Dreamers Never Sleep 1987, Inconsolable Man 1991, Gino Vannelli Live In Montréal 1992, Yonder Tree 1995, Awakening, with Joseph Curiale 2000. *Publications include:* contributions to REP Magazine, Midi Magazine, Keyboard Magazine (Japan). *Address:* 28205 Agoura Road, Agoura Hills, CA 91301, USA.

VANNUCCI, Ronnie; American musician (drums); b. Las Vegas, NV. *Education:* Univ. of Las Vegas. *Career:* founder mem., The Killers 2002–. *Recordings include:* albums: Hot Fuss 2004, Sam's Town (BRIT Award for Best Int. Album 2007) 2006, Sawdust 2007, Day and Age 2008, Battle Born 2012. *Honours:* NME Award for Best Int. Band 2005, for Best Video 2007, MTV Video Award for Best New Artist 2005, MTV Europe Music Award for Best Rock Act 2006, BRIT Award for Best Int. Group 2007, ASCAP Vanguard Award 2010. *E-mail:* lauren.schneider@umusic.com. *Website:* www.thekillersmusic.com.

VANROBAEYS, Filip; Belgian folk musician (fiddle, harp, guitar, whistles, badhan). *Career:* mem., The Swigshift 1985–; numerous festival performances; several regional radio and TV appearances; mem. Volksmuziekfederatie. *Recordings include:* albums: Tales From the Great Whiskey Book 1996, Witness of a Celtic Past 1998, The Swigshift and Friends 2001, Walking Home 2008. *Address:* c/o Peter Derudder, Tenbrielensesteenweg 25, 8940 Wervik, Belgium (office). *E-mail:* info@swigshift.com (office). *Website:* www.swigshift.com.

VARILO, Antto; Finnish musician (guitar) and composer. *Education:* Univ. of Helsinki. *Career:* professional guitarist 1985–, performing with bands, including Hasse Walli, Badu N'Djay; mem., Värttinä 1993–. *Music for theatre:* co-wrote score to stage musical, The Lord of the Rings (with A. R. Rahman) (Princess of Wales Theatre, Toronto) 2006. *Recordings include:* albums: Aitara 1994, Kokko 1996, Vihma 1998, Ilmatar 2000, 6.12 2001, iki 2003, Miero 2006, 25 2007, Utu 2012. *Honours:* Arts Council of Finland State Prize for Merit in Music 1993, Finnish Nat. Group of IFPI Emma Award 1993. *Current Management:* c/o Phillip Page, Hoedown Arts Oy, Neitsytpolku 9 F 81, 00140 Helsinki, Finland. *Telephone:* (50) 5692982. *Fax:* (9) 628950. *E-mail:* pap@hoedown.com. *Website:* www.varttina.com.

VARIS, Francis; French musician (accordion); b. 4 Feb. 1957, Clamart; m. Françoise Niay. *Education:* Univ. of Paris VIII. *Career:* tours and European jazz festivals with Tal Farlow, Nazaré Pereira, Lee Konitz, The Paris-Musette, Titi Robin; performs with own group Bolovaris. *Recordings include:* Cordes Et Lames 1983, Medium Rare (with Lee Konitz) 1986, Accordion Madness (with Kenny Kotwitz) 1989, Paris-Musette 1 and 2 1991, 1993; Bolovaris 1994, Ombre (with Romane) 1998, Identities (with Idir) 1999, Ivory Port (with Jacques Bolognesi) 1999, Ciranda (with Marcio Faraco) 2000, Olympia 2000 2000, O March (with Maria Teresa) 2003, La Vida! (with Rumberos Catalans) 2004, Anita! (with Titi Robin) 2006, Chayara (with Nathalie El Baze) 2007, Kali Sultana 2008, Jaadu 2009, Ropes and Blades 2012, Bach Cello Suites 2, 3 and 4 2012, Bach Cello Suites 1, 5 and 6 2012. *Honours:* Grand Prix du Disque de l'Academie Charles Cros. *Address:* c/o Music Mixed Production, 31 rue Raspail, 94200 Ivry-sur-Seine, France. *Website:* www.francis-varis.com.

VÄRJÖ, Daniel; Swedish musician (guitar). *Career:* mem., The Concretes 1999–; band founded label, Licking Fingers. *Recordings include:* albums: Boyoubetterunow 2000, The Concretes 2003, Layourbattleaxedown 2005, In Colour 2006, Hey Trouble 2007, WYWH 2010. *Current Management:* EC1 Music Agency, 1 Cowcross Street, London, EC1M 6DR, England. *Telephone:* (20) 7490-8990. *Fax:* (20) 7490-8987. *E-mail:* jack@ec1music.com. *E-mail:* theconcretes@theconcretes.com; theconcretessweden@gmail.com. *Website:* www.theconcretes.com.

VARLEY, Gerard (Gez); British programmer and producer. *Career:* mem., LFO 1989–96; Founder, G Records, Swim Records, GMR. *Recordings include:* albums: with LFO: Frequencies 1991, Advance 1996; as G-Man: Kushti 1996, Beautful 1999, Avanti 2002; solo: Gez Varley Presents Tony Montana 1998, Bayou Paradis 2001, Personal Settings 2 2002. *Website:* www.g-man-techno.com.

VARSÁNYI, Juraj; Slovak musician (drums, percussion, cimbalom) and business executive; b. 14 May 1961, Bratislava; s. of Ladislav Varsányi and Barbora Varsányi; m. Mariya Gladska. *Education:* People's Conservatory of Bratislava, Julius Kovacs's School, Budapest, studied with Imre Koszegi, Budapest. *Career:* int. tours; numerous TV and radio shows with: Vus-Orchestra, Gravis, Knock-Out, Jully's Orchestra, Just Jazz, Bratislava Jazz Days 1991; Burg Mautendorf Jazzwettbewerb-Aut; King's Fest, Morocco 1986; Hajnal Quintet 1987; Varsanyi Habsburg-Wedding 1993; mem. Slovak Jazz Soc. 1989/90–. *Recordings include:* Vus LP 1983, Varsanyi, Hungarian Folk Anthologies 1984–90, Gombitova and Gravis LP 1986, Knock Out, LP 1987, Gravis, LP 1989, Varsanyi, LP 1991, La Rubia, CD 1995, Slovak Jazz Anthology, CD 1992. *Honours:* Gorizia, Int. Festival Contest 1986 Second Prize, Slovak Jazz Festival 1995. *Address:* Varsányi Juraj, Hlavna 20, 90044 Tomasov, Slovakia (home). *Telephone:* (2) 4595-8401 (office). *Fax:* (2) 4595-8555 (home). *E-mail:* georg@vav.sk (home).

VARTAN, Sylvie; French singer and entertainer; b. 15 Aug. 1944, Iskretz, Bulgaria; d. of Georges Vartan and Ilona Vartan (née Rudolf-Mayer); m. 1st Johnny Hallyday 1965 (divorced 1980); one s.; m. 2nd Tony Scotti 1984; one d. *Education:* Lycée Hélène-Boucher, Paris. *Career:* singing debut in duet with Frankie Jordan (Panne d'essence); nat. tours 1961–, int. tours 1965–, including Paris Olympia 1961, 1962, 1963, 1964 (with The Beatles), 1967, 1968, 1970, 1972, 1996, 1999, 2009, 2010, Palais des Congrès, Paris 1975–76, 1977–78, 1983, 2004, 2008, Palais des Sports, Paris 1981, 1991, Las Vegas, USA 1982, Los Angeles, USA 1983, Atlantic City, USA 1984, Sofia, Bulgaria 1990, 2009, Casino de Paris 1995, Théâtre du Châtelet 2010, 2011, New York, USA 2011, Théâtre Marigny 2011, Salle Pleyel 2011, Folies Bergère 2014.

Songs include: Tous mes copains, En écoutant la pluie, I'm Watching, Si je chante, La plus belle pour aller danser, Quand tu es là, Par amour par pitié, 2'35 de bonheur, Le Kid, Comme un garçon, La Maritza, La chasse à l'homme, Loup, Dilindam, L'heure la plus douce de ma vie, Pour lui je reviens, Mon père, J'ai un problème (with Johnny Hallyday), Toi le garçon, Bye bye Leroy Brown, La drôle de fin, Qu'est-ce qui fait pleurer les blondes?, Le temps du swing, Petit rainbow, I Don't Want the Night to End, Nicolas, Merveilleusement désenchantée, L'amour c'est comme une cigarette, Aimer, Des heures de désir, Double exposure, Virage, Femme sous influence, C'est fatal, Qui tu es, Je n'aime encore que toi, Sensible, Ce n'est pas rien, J'attendrai, Toutes peines confondues, Personne, I Like It, I Love It. *Films:* Un clair de lune à Maubeuge 1962, D'où viens-tu Johnny? 1963, Cherchez l'idole 1964, Patate 1964, Les Poneyttes 1967, Malpertuis 1971, Mon amie Sylvie 1972, L'ange noir 1994. *Television includes:* Show Averty 1965, Jolie poupée 1968, Doppia coppia (Italy) 1969, Sacha Sylvie Show 1969, Sylvissima 1970, Top à Sylvie Vartan 1972, Top à Sylvie Vartan 1972, Top à Sylvie et Johnny 1973, Je chante pour Swanee 1974, Sylvie 1975, Punto e basta (Italy) 1975, Dancing Star 1977, La Maritza 1990, Sylvie sa vie 1994, Irrésistiblement… Sylvie 1998, Qu'est-ce qui fait rêver Sylvie? 2000, Mausolée pour une garce (film) 2001, Au rythme du coeur 2005, Entre l'ombre et la lumière 2005, Tout le monde l'appelle Sylvie 2010. *Recordings:* albums: Sylvie 1962, Twiste et Chante 1963, A Nashville 1964, A Gift Wrapped from Paris 1965, Il y a Deux Filles En Moi 1966, 2mn 35 de Bonheur 1967, Comme un Garçon 1967, La Maritza 1968, Aime-moi 1970, Sympathie 1971, J'ai un problème 1973, Shang Shang a Lang 1974, Qu'Est-Ce Qui Fait Pleurer Les Blondes? 1976, Ta Sorcière Bien Aimée 1976, Georges 1977, Fantaisie 1978, I Don't Want the Night to End 1979, Deraisonnable 1979, Bienvenue Solitude 1980, Ça Va Mal 1981, De Choses et D'Autres 1982, Danse ta Vie 1983, Des Heures de Desir 1984, Virages 1986, Confidanses 1989, Vents D'Ouest 1992, Sessions Acoustiques 1994, Toutes les Femmes ont un Secret 1996, Sensible 1998, Sylvie 2004, Nouvelle Vague 2007, Toutes Peines Confondues 2009, Soleil Bleu 20100, Sylvie in Nashville 2013. *Publications include:* Si je chante 1981, Beauty Book 1985, Entre l'ombre et la lumière 2004, Dans la lumière 2007, Mot à mot 2012. *Honours:* Chevalier, Ordre du Cavalier de Madara (Bulgaria) 1996, de la Stara Plamina (Bulgaria) 2004; Officier, Ordre nat. du Mérite 2006, Légion d'honneur 2010; Commdr des Arts et des Lettres 2011; Triomphe des Variétés Award 1970. *Address:* c/o Charley Marouani, 176 avenue Charles de Gaulle, 92200 Neuilly sur Seine, France. *Website:* www.sylvie-vartan.com.

VASCONCELLOS, Joe; Chilean musician (percussion), singer and composer; b. 9 March 1959, Santiago; m. Irene Gonzalez Peña 1985. *Education:* colls in Brazil, Ecuador, Japan, Italy, Conservatorio Musicale Nicolo Paganini, Genoa, Italy. *Career:* played with Maria Creuza, tours throughout Brazil, Argentina, Uruguay, Spain, USA; mem., Congreso; as singer with own band, tours and TV appearances; mem. Sociedad Chilena del Derecho de Autor. *Recordings include:* with Congreso: Viaje por la Cresta del Mundo, Ha Llegado Carta, Joe Vasconcellos: Esto es Solo una Canción, Verde Cerca, Toque 1995, Vivo 2004, Esto Es Sólo Una Canción 2005, Verde Cerca 2005, En Paz 2005. *Honours:* Award for Best Group, Chile (with Congreso). *Telephone:* (562) 3432503. *Fax:* (562) 3432504. *E-mail:* cmonrroy@laraizproducciones.cl. *Address:* c/o Hernando de Aguirre 944, Providencia, Santiago, Chile (home). *Website:* www.joevasconcellos.com; www.joevasconcellos.cl.

VASCONCELOS, Mônica; Brazilian musician, singer and lyricist; b. 13 Nov. 1966, São Paulo. *Education:* São Paulo Univ., Brazil. *Career:* started singing at 17, at bars, parties, backing vocals for record producers; joined vocal and drama group, Beijo 1987; toured Brazil, sang on television and radio; recorded with musicians in London, including Roland Perrin, Ashley Slater, John O'Neall, Tim Garland, Christine Tobin, Jacqui Dankworth; with own band, toured England; mem. Musicians' Union. *Compositions:* Sabonete Do Mato, Mudanca Oragao, Ivan Da Caverna, Vestidinho, Guizim, Xotemo, Bossa Zangada, Outono, Maracatu Do Pomso, Samba Da Ponte, Atabaque. *Recordings:* Beijo, Nóis 1994, Nóis Dois 1999, Oferenda 2001. *Address:* c/o Graham Stansfield, 48 Bridle Way, Colehill, Wimborne, Dorset BH21 2UE, England. *E-mail:* mv@monicavasconcelos.com. *Website:* www.monicavasconcelos.com.

VAUGHN, Danny; American singer and lyricist; b. 18 July 1961, Cleveland, Ohio. *Career:* singer rock group, Waysted 1987; singer and lyricist rock group, Tyketto 1988–98; numerous concerts, tours and festivals; Founder-mem., Vaughn. *Recordings include:* albums: with Waysted: Save Your Prayers 1987; with Tyketto: Don't Come Easy 1990, Strength In Numbers 1994, Shine 1995, Take Out & Served Up Live 1996, Inishmore 1998, The Last Sunset: Farewell 2007, Dig In Deep 2012; with Vaughn: Soldiers & Sailors on Riverside 2000, Fearless 2001, Standing Alone 2001, Forever Live 2002, Traveller 2007, The Road Less Travelled 2009, Reprise 2010. *E-mail:* band@vaughn.de. *Website:* www.vaughn.de.

VAZQUEZ, Roland, MMus; American musician (drums), composer and clinician; b. 4 July 1951, Pasadena, Calif.; m. Susan Botti 1988; one d. *Education:* Manhattan School of Music. *Career:* leader, composer, producer and sideman, numerous recordings on USA and Int. jazz radio 1979–; appearances as composer/leader at major jazz festivals and venues throughout the USA and in Canada, Scandinavia and Central America; mem. jazz faculty, Manhattan School of Music 1988–98, Univ. of Michigan 2000–05; Visiting Artist, American Acad. in Rome 2005–06, Eastman School of Music 2008, Berklee School of Music 2008; mem. American Soc. of Composers, Authors and Publishers, Nat. Acad. of Recording Artists and Sciences; numerous tours and performances with Roland Vazquez Quintet, Roland Vazquez Big Band and

Octet, Clare Fischer's Salsa PicanteRiccardo Fassi Quartet. *Compositions include:* over 60 compositions recorded and published for jazz quintet, octet, dectet, big band and chamber groups. *Recordings as composer/leader:* Urban Ensemble: The Music of Roland Vazquez 1979, Feel Your Dream 1982, The Tides of Time 1988, No Separate Love 1991, Best of the LA Jazz Ensemble 1994, Further Dance 1997, Quintet Live 2007, The Visitor 2010, Triospeak 2015. *Honours:* grants include from NEA 1977, ASCAP, IAJE 1997, Michigan Council for the Arts 2003, Aaron Copland Fund for Music, Inc 2010. *Address:* PO Box 33, Red Hook, NY 12571, USA. *E-mail:* romu@rolandvazquez.com (office). *Website:* www.rolandvazquez.com.

VEDDER, Eddie; American singer and songwriter; b. (Edward Louis Seversen), 23 Dec. 1966, Evanston, Ill. *Career:* lead singer rock group Pearl Jam 1991–; numerous concert tours, festival appearances, numerous collaborations with various musicians including Nusrat Fateh Ali Khan, Cat Power, The Who, Neil Young. *Recordings include:* albums: with Pearl Jam: Ten 1991, Vs. 1993, Vitalogy 1994, Merkin Ball 1995, No Code 1996, Yield 1998, Live on Two Legs 1998, Binaural 2000, Riot Act 2002, Pearl Jam 2006, Backspacer 2009, Lightning Bolt 2013; solo: Into the Wild 2007, Ukulele Songs 2011. *Film appearances:* Singles 1992, Hype! (documentary) 1996, Runnin' Down a Dream (documentary) 2007, Off the Boulevard 2011. *Honours:* American Music Award for Favorite New Artist, Pop/Rock and Hard Rock categories 1993, Rolling Stone Readers' Awards for Best Male Singer, Best New American Band, Best Video 1993, SIMA Waterman's Honorees Environmentalist of the Year 2007. *Website:* www.pearljam.com.

VEE, Bobby; American singer; b. (Robert T. Velline), 30 April 1943, Fargo, North Dakota; m. Karen Velline; two s. *Career:* Founder-mem. US group The Shadows 1958; solo singer 1960–; world-wide appearances include Hollywood Bowl, with Jerry Lee Lewis, Brenda Lee, The Shirelles 1961, British tour with The Crickets 1962, Dick Clark's Caravan of Stars US tour 1963, British tour with Dusty Springfield, The Searchers 1964, British tour, with Dusty Springfield, The Searchers, The Zombies 1965, UK tour with Rick Nelson, Del Shannon, Bo Diddley 1985, British tour, with Brian Hyland 1988, annual appearances, Buddy Holly Memorial Concerts, Giants of Rock 'n' Roll, Wembley Arena, with Little Richard, Duane Eddy 1992, UK tours with The Crickets 1989, with The Searchers 1995, with Brian Hyland, The Chiffons and Johnny Tillotson 2002; performed in All American Solid Gold Rock 'n' Roll Show tour 1998; Sir Andrew Lloyd Webber's 50th Birthday Party 1998; Rubber Ball for 25,000th time suspended by a bungy cord from London Bridge 2003. *Recordings include:* albums: Bobby Vee 1961, Bobby Vee Sings Hits of The Rockin' 50s 1961, Take Good Care of My Baby 1962, Bobby Vee Meets the Crickets 1962, A Bobby Vee Recording Session 1962, Golden Greats 1962, Merry Christmas From... 1962, The Night Has A Thousand Eyes 1963, Bobby Vee Meets The Ventures 1963, Bobby Vee Sings The New Sound From England 1964, Come Back When You Grow Up 1967, Just Today 1968, Nothing Like A Sunny Day 1972, The Bobby Vee Singles Album 1980, Favorites 1997, Down the Line 1999, The EP Collection 1999; hit singles include: Devil Or Angel 1960, Rubber Ball 1961, More Than I Can Say 1961, Take Good Care of My Baby 1961, How Many Tears 1961, Run To Him 1961, Sharing You 1962, A Forever Kind of Love 1962, The Night Has A Thousand Eyes, from film Just For Fun 1963, Charms 1963, Come Back When You're Grown Up 1967, Just Today 1968, Gates, Grills and Railings 1969, Legendary Masters Series 1973, The Very Best Of Bobby Vee 1975, Tribute to Buddy Holly 1978, Singles Album 1980. *Films include:* Play It Cool 1962, Just For Fun 1963, C'mon, Let's Live a Little 1967. *Honours:* The Beat Goes On magazine readers polls: Best American Act 1991, Best Live Performer 1992, Favourite Male Singer 1993, Theodore Roosevelt Rough Rider Award, North Dakota state 1999. *Address:* Rockhouse Management, PO Box 757, St. Joseph, MN 56374, USA. *Website:* www.bobbyvee.com.

VEGA, Louie, (Little Louie Vega, Groovebox); American producer, remixer and DJ; b. 12 June 1965, New York. *Career:* began as a DJ in New York, 1980s; starting doing mixes for artists, including The Cover Girls; worked with Todd Terry before teaming up with Kenny 'Dope' Gonzalez as Masters At Work; duo also recorded as Nu Yorican Soul; co-founder, MAW Records; collaborations: India, Marc Anthony, Jocelyn Brown, James Ingram, Stephanie Mills; remixed: Debbie Gibson, St Etienne, Shanice, Tito Puente, Barbara Tucker, Jamiroquai, Atmosfear, Incognito, Luther Vandross, Ce Ce Peniston, Martha Wash, Ballistic Brothers. *Recordings include:* albums: Elements of Life 2004; with Masters at Work: Nu Yorican Soul 1997, Our Time Is Coming, 2002. *Address:* Strictly Rhythm, PO Box 703, Merrick, NY 11566-0703, USA. *Website:* www.myspace.com/mawrobbi.

VEGA, Sergio; American musician (bass guitar) and songwriter. *Career:* Founder mem. Quicksand 1990–95, 1997–99, 2012–; touring bass guitarist with Deftones 1999, full-time mem. 2009–. *Recordings include:* with Quicksand: Slip 1993, Manic Compression 1995; with Deftones: Diamond Eyes 2010, Koi No Yokan 2012. *Current Management:* c/o Velvet Hammer Management, 9911 West Pico Boulevard, Suite 350, Los Angeles, CA 90035-2703, USA. *Website:* www.velvethammer.net; www.deftones.com.

VEGA, Suzanne; American singer and songwriter; b. Santa Monica, Calif.; m. 1st Mitchell Froom 1995 (divorced 1998); one d.; m. 2nd Paul Mills 2006. *Education:* High School for the Performing Arts, NY, Barnard Coll. *Recordings include:* albums: Suzanne Vega 1985, Solitude Standing 1987, Days of Open Hand 1990, 99F° 1992, Nine Objects of Desire 1996, Songs in Red and Gray 2001, Beauty & Crime 2007, Close-Up Vol. 1: Love Songs 2010, Close-Up

Vol. 2: People and Places 2010, Close-Up Vol. 3: States of Being 2011, Close-Up Vol. 4: Songs of Family 2012. *Current Management:* Opus 3 Artists, 470 Park Avenue South, 9th Floor North, New York, NY 10015, USA. *Telephone:* (212) 584-7500. *E-mail:* info@opus3artists.com. *Website:* www.opus3artists.com; www.suzannevega.com.

VEGUILLA MALAVÉ, Llandel (Yandel); Puerto Rican rapper and singer; b. 14 Jan. 1977, Cayey; m.; two s. *Career:* mem. reggaeton duo Wisin & Yandel 1995–; numerous collaborations with hip-hop artists including 50 Cent and Akon; co-f. WY Records. *Recordings include:* albums: as Wisin & Yandel: Los Reyes del Nuevo Milenio 2000, De Nuevos a Viejos 2001, De Otra Manera 2002, Mi Vida...My Life 2003, Pa'l Mundo 2005, Wisin vs. Yandel: Los Extraterrestres (Grammy Award for Best Latin Urban Album 2008) 2007, La Revolución 2009; solo: Who Me? 2004, From Leader to Legend 2013. *Honours:* Latin Rhythm Award for Album Of The Year, Duo Or Group, Latin Billboard Music Awards 2009, MTV Latinoamérica Awards for Artist of the Year 2009, for Video of the Year (for Abusadora) 2009. *E-mail:* contact@wisinyandelpr.com (office). *Website:* www.wisinyandelpr.com.

VEIRS, Laura Pauline; American folk singer, songwriter and musician (guitar); b. 24 Oct. 1973, Colorado. *Education:* Carleton Coll. *Recordings include:* albums: Laura Veirs 1999, The Triumphs And Travails Of Orphan Mae 2001, Troubled By Fire 2003, Carbon Glacier 2004, Year Of Meteors 2005, Saltbreakers 2007, July Flame 2010, Tumble Bee 2011, Warp and Weft 2013. *Address:* PO Box 12713, Portland, OR 97212, USA (office). *Website:* www.lauraveirs.com.

VEJSLEV, Jakob; Danish musician (guitar) and composer; b. 25 July 1957, Copenhagen; m. Astrid Dyssegaard 24 July 1987; one s. *Career:* played harmonica from age 13; guitar 1975–; full-time guitarist with several groups and musicians (free jazz, fusion, latin, rock) 1977–; composed jazz, classical music, worked with own trio and duo 1985–; moved to Norway to work as composer, musician and music teacher 1992–; numerous collaborative projects with various artists including David Scott Hamnes; mem. Danish Jazz, Beat and Folk Composers Asscn, KODA (Danish Composers Copyright Asscn), Norwegian Jazz Asscn;. *Compositions include:* Flute quartet in 8 movements 1992, Trio (trombone, violin and marimba) 1993, Piece for 10 instruments 1994. *Recordings include:* solo: Håndslag Til Frank 1987, Til Dine Ojnes Åndmusik 1990, Throughout 2001, Choir and Chamber Music 2004. *Publications include:* Jakob Vejslev: Music for Trumpet 2009, Jakob Vejslev: Music for Organ 2009. *E-mail:* info@jakobvejslev.com. *Website:* www.jakobvejslev.com.

VEJSLEV, Tony; Danish composer, singer and musician (guitar); b. 25 Oct. 1926, Copenhagen; m. Benthe Kolding 1954; one s. *Career:* concerts in Denmark; radio broadcasts 1938–, tv appearances 1949–; mem. Danish Jazz, Beat and Folk Authors. *Recordings include:* Tony Vejslev Synger 1983, Haandslag Til Frank 1988, Til Dine Oejnes Aaandemusik 1990, 50 Danske Viser Og Sange 1993, Old Poems –New Songs 2001. *Publications include:* 19 Jaegerviser 1953 1967, 26 Viser 1987, Fem Farum Digte 1988, 18 Danske Sange 1990, 50 Danske Viserog 2002. *Honours:* Danish Jazz, Beat and Folk Authors Prize of Honour 1998. *Current Management:* Olafssongs, Paarupvej 44, Græsted, Denmark. *E-mail:* ol@olafssongs.dk. *Website:* www.olafssongs.dk.

VELASQUEZ, Regine; Philippine singer, actress and director; b. 22 April 1970, Manila. *Career:* solo artist 1986–; actress, appearing in films and TV series; est. Songbird Records 2000. *Films include:* The Untouchable Family 1987, Pik pak boom 1989, Elvis and James 2 1990, Wanted Perfect Mother 1996, Do Re Mi 1997, Honey nasa langit na ba ako 1998, Dahil may isang ikaw 1999, Kailangan ko'y ikaw 2000, Pangako... ikaw lang 2001, Ikaw lamang hanggang ngayon 2002, Huling yakap sa tag-araw 2003, Pangarap ko ang ibigin ka 2003, Captain Barbell 2003, Masikip sa dibdib 2004, I Love You, Goodbye 2005, Till I Met You 2006. *Television includes:* Bubble Gang (episode: 11th Anniversary) 2006. *Recordings include:* albums: Regine 1987, Nineteen '90 1990, Reason Enough 1993, Listen Without Prejudice 1994, Retro 1996, R2K 1999, Reigne 2001, Duets 2005, Till I Met You 2006. *Honours:* Female Artist of the Year, MTV Philippines 2001, MTV Asia 2002. *Address:* c/o Viva Records, East Tower, Philippines Stock Exchange Centre, Exchange Road, Ortigas Centre, Pasig City 1605, The Philippines. *Website:* www.reginevelasquez.net.

VELGHE, Rudy; Belgian musician (violin, guitar, nyckelharpa), composer and arranger; b. 4 Jan. 1960, Oudenaarde. *Education:* State Univ. of Ghent. *Career:* professional musician 1987–; Founder-mem. Celtic band, Orion; composed and arranged music for different short films and TV programmes; performed in many shows on radio and TV/BRT, RTB, BBC, Irish Radio; studio musician for many artists. *Compositions include:* Wailing Reel; Restless Home; Shores of Marsannay; Reel of Notes. *Recordings include:* Histoires de Rue 1990, Blue Room, Restless Home, Dao Dezi 1995, Orion 1990, 1996, About to Go, Strawberry Town. *Website:* www.orionceltic.com.

VELOSO, Caetano Emanuel Viana Teles; Brazilian singer, musician (guitar) and songwriter; b. 7 Aug. 1942, Santo Amaro da Purificação, Bahia; s. of José Teles Veloso and Claudionor Viana Teles Veloso; brother of Maria Bethânia; m. 1st Andréa Gadalha (divorced 1983); one s.; m. 2nd Paula Lavigne 1986 (divorced 2005); two s. *Career:* won a lyric competition in mid 1960s with Um Dia; part of MPB (Musica Popular Brasileira) wave of young artists, along with artists such as Gal Costa and Gilberto Gil; experimental nature of Veloso's music was not favoured by the military dictatorship, resulting in arrest 1968; two months in prison before going into exile in London; returned to Brazil 1972; his knowledge of old Brazilian songs led to him reviving the careers of older musicians, including Luiz Gonzaga; hosted a TV show with Chico Buarque 1980s; leader, Banda Nova 1984–. *Recordings include:* albums: Alegria, Alegria 1967, Domingo 1967, Caetano Veloso 1967, Atrás do Trio Eléctrico 1969, Caetano E. Chico – Ao Vivo Na Bahia 1972, Araçá Azul 1973, Jóia 1975, Doces Barbaros 1976, Bicho 1977, Maria Bethania and Caetano Veloso Ao Vivo 1978, Cinema Transcendental 1979, Outras Palavaras 1981, Cores Nomes 1982, Uns 1983, Velo 1984, Caetano 1987, Estrangeiro 1989, Muito 1990, Circulado 1992, Tropicália 2 1994, Fina Estampa en Vivo 1995, Divina Estampa 1996, Tieta Do Agresta 1997, Livros (Latin Grammy Award for Best MPB Album 2000, Grammy Award for Best World Music Album 2000) 1998, Noites Do Norte 2001, A Foreign Sound 2004, Onqôto 2005, Cê (Latin Grammy Award for Best Singer-Songwriter Album 2007) 2006, Multishow ao Vivo Cê 2007, Zii e Zie (Latin Grammy Award for Best Singer-Songwriter Album) 2009, Abraçaço (Latin Grammy Award for Best Singer-Songwriter Album 2013) 2012. *Honours:* Latin Grammy Award for Best Brazilian Song (for Não me Arrependo) 2007, Latin Recording Acad. Person of the Year 2012. *Website:* www.caetanoveloso.com.br.

VENEGAS (PERCEVAULT), Julieta; Mexican singer, songwriter and musician (guitar, accordion, keyboards); b. 24 Nov. 1970, Long Beach, Calif., USA. *Career:* solo artist 1986–. *Recordings include:* albums: Aquí 1998, Bueninvento 2000, Sí (Latin Grammy Award for Best Rock Solo Vocal Album 2004) 2003, Limón y sal (Latin Grammy Award for Best Alternative Music Album 2006, Grammy Award for Best Latin Pop Album 2007) 2006, MTV Unplugged (Latin Grammy Award for Best Alternative Music Album 2008) 2007. *Honours:* MTV Latin America Video Music Award for Best Solo Artist 2004, 2006, for Best Artist (Mexico) 2004, for Artist of the Year 2004, for Best Pop Artist 2007. *Website:* www.julietavenegas.net (office).

VENIER, Glauco; Italian musician (piano) and composer; b. 8 Sept. 1962, Sedegliano, Udine. *Education:* Berklee Coll. of Music, USA, Conservatory of Music, Udine, Italy, studied privately with Franco D'Andrea, Enrico Rava, Hal Crook, Ray Santisi, George Garzone. *Career:* private piano instructor, Udine 1985–90; music educator at several grammar schools 1985–90; educator, Conservatory of Music, Gorizia, Italy 1993–98; performed with: Kenny Wheeler, Lee Konitz, Jack Walrath, Enrico Rava, Paolo Fresu, Valery Ponomarev, Flavio Boltro, Hal Crook, George Garzone, Massimo Urbani, Stefano Di Battista, Gianni Basso, Chriss Speed, Matt Garrison, Abe Laboriel Jr., Roberto Dani. *Recordings include:* Massimo De Mattia, Poesie Pour Pasolini 1993, The Silent Drama 1995, Enrica Bacchia, Ancora 1995, Monografie By New Age (compilation) 1996, Diego Sandrin, Millionaire 1996, Tamara Obrovac, Triade 1996, Enzo Pietropaoli, Stolen Songs 1998, Fondazione Luigi Bon, Il Vieli, Il Dragon e Il Cavalir, Music for Fairytale By Glauco Venier 1998, Klaus Gesing and Glauco Venier Play Bach 2000, Ides of March (with Lee Konitz) 2001, Gorizia (with Kenny Wheeler) 2001. *Compositions include:* Finland 1991, Faces 1995, Seasons 1999, The Ballad of Hope 2000, Chamber Music 2004, Hommage to Duke 2007, Distances 2008, Stories Yet to Tell 2010, Waits 2013. *Honours:* Finalist, Thelonious Monk Piano Jazz Competition, Washington, DC 1989, Best Group (Glauco Venier Trio), Jazz Festival in Vienne France 1997. *E-mail:* orpheus@serenacom.net. *Website:* www.orpheusmanagement.it.

VENTO, Joseph; American composer, conductor and band leader; b. 16 Dec. 1926, Los Angeles, CA. *Education:* University of South Califonia, Fresno State College, Juilliard School, New England Conservatory of Music. *Career:* accordion solo, Radio KFI, Los Angeles, The William Tell Overture, 10 years old, 1937; films, Counterpoint, Man's Favorite Sport, This Earth is Mine, The Competition, Guide for a Married Man, Made in Paris, Girl Happy, Those Lips Those Eyes; mem. ASCAP; ASMAC; AFofM, New York and Los Angeles; NARAS; American Academy of Sciences; Disabled American Veterans, SR, CDR; Music Teachers' National Asscn, USA. *Compositions:* The Three Suns; I Can't Forget; Our Love is Gone; City of The Angles; Sacro Sanctum; Warsaw Connection; Sarah Suite; Ole Joe, 1997; Joes Bach, 1997. *Recordings:* Artist of The Three Suns, Twilight Time; Joe Vento Golden Hits, Vol. I and II; Surfside Records; Bells of Christmas; The Best of Joe Vento; The Best of The Three Suns; Film Soundtrack, True Friends. *Publications:* I Can't Forget, 1939; City of The Angels, 1968; Sacro Sanctum, 1979; Love Is Gone, 1995; Edulerp III, 1995; contrib. to Midi'ing in Music Composition, Moorpark College, 1991; Nurturing Music in the Nineties. *Honours:* Best Accordionist Grand Prize, 1939. *E-mail:* joevento@gmail.com. *Website:* www.joevento.com.

VERA, Billy; American singer, actor, songwriter, producer and music historian; b. (William Patrick McCord), 28 May 1944, Riverside, Calif.; s. of Bill McCord and Ann Ryan; m. 1st Barbara Young 1966; m. 2nd Rosalee Mayeux 1988; one s. one d. *Education:* Fordham Univ. *Career:* numerous concert performances; mem. American Soc. of Composers, Authors and Publrs (ASCAP), American Fed. of TV and Radio Artists, Screen Actors Guild, American Fed. of Musicians. *Plays include:* Line, Geography of a Horse-dreamer (lead role, West Coast premiere). *Films include:* Buckaroo Banzai, Blind Date, The Doors, Tonight's The Night, Baja Oklahoma. *Radio includes:* own shows on WBAI, NY and KCRW, Los Angeles. *Television includes:* Wise Guy, Alice, Scarecrow and Mrs King, Knots Landing, Beverly Hills 90210, Baywatch, Tonight Show with Johnny Carson, American Bandstand. *Compositions include:* recorded by Ricky Nelson: Mean Old World, Barbara Lewis: Make Me Belong To You, Dolly Parton: I Really Got The Feeling, Bonnie Raitt:

Papa Come Quick, Robert Plant: Don't Look Back, Lou Rawls: Room With A View, If I Were A Magician, Etta James: You've Got Me, At This Moment: Michael Bublé. *Recordings include:* Storybook Children 1967, With Pen In Hand 1968, I Can Take Care of Myself 1981, At This Moment 1987, Out of the Darkness 1994, Oh What A Night 1996, Hopeless Romantic: The Best of Billy Vera & the Beaters 2008, The Billy Vera Story 2011, Singular Genius: The Complete ABC Singles (Grammy Award for Best Album Notes 2013) 2011, Billy Vera: Big Band Jazz 2012. *Publications include:* liner notes to more than 200 historical albums; contrib. articles to magazines. *Honours:* ASCAP Award 1979, 1987, Gold Prize, Tokyo Music Festival 1981, George Peabody Award for Excellence in Broadcasting 1994, Grammy Award for Best Album Notes 2013. *Current Management:* c/o Danny Robinson, Agency for the Performing Arts, 405 South Beverly Drive, Beverly Hills, CA 90212, USA. *Telephone:* (310) 888-4232. *Website:* www.billyvera.com.

VERA, Salim; Peruvian singer, musician (guitar) and songwriter; b. 9 April 1970. *Career:* Founder-mem. Libido 1996–; numerous live performances and festival appearances; worked on projects including Royalvalet 2010. *Recordings include:* albums: Libido 1998, Hembra 2000, Pop*Porn 2003, Libido Acústica 2004, Lo Último Que Hablé Ayer 2005, A New Day 2009, Rarities 2010. *Honours:* Latin American MTV Video Music Award for Best Artist 2002, 2003, Terra Rock for Outstanding Talent 2008. *E-mail:* management@libidonet.com. *E-mail:* salim@libidonet.com (office). *Website:* www.libidonet.com.

VERA, Stephane; French musician (drums); b. 11 May 1965, Paris. *Education:* Boulogne Conservatory. *Career:* numerous collaborations including with Gilbert Becaud, Dany Brillant, Jeane Manson, Vivian Reed, David Koven, I Muvrini, Karim Kacel, Eric Lelann, Ultra Marine, Angelique Kidjo, Jacky Quartz, Idrissa Diop, Yvan Dautin, Georges Macintosh; Chief of Music Operations, waveDNA 2000–; mem. SACEM, SPEDIDAM, SDRM. *Recordings include:* Dany Brillant, Jacky Quartz, Imurvine, Karim Kacel, Richard Bona, Scenes from My Life 1999; Film: Le Nouveau Monde 1994. *Publications include:* Drummer's Magazine, Paris, VAC Magazine. *Website:* www.svera.ca.

VEREEN, Ben; American singer, actor and entertainer; b. 10 Oct. 1946, Miami, FL. *Career:* one-man show, with concert tours throughout USA, Europe, Asia, Caribbean Islands; formed organization, Celebrities for a Drug-Free America 1991; developed performing arts centre in Chicago. *Stage performances include:* on Broadway: played the Chimney Man in Jelly's Last Jam (musical) 1993, Sweet Charity, Hair, Jesus Christ Superstar, Pippin, Grind, I'm Not Rappaport, A Christmas Carol 1995. *Films include:* Sweet Charity 1969, Funny Lady 1975, Why Do Fools Fall in Love? 1998, I'll Take You There 1999, The Painting 2001, Idlewild 2006, And Then Came Love 2007, Tapioca 2007, An Accidental Friendship 2008. *Television includes:* The Fresh Prince of Bel Air, The Nanny, Webster, New York Undercover, Star Trek – The Next Generation, Intruders, They Are Among Us, Silk Stockings, own series Tenspeed and Brownshoe 1980, J.J. Starbuck, Booker, Ben Vereen: His Roots, The Jesse Owens Story, Ellis Island, All That Jazz, Funny Lady. *Honours:* Israel Humanitarian Award 1978, NAACP Image Award 1978, 1979, Eleanor Roosevelt Humanitarian Award 1983, Victory Award 1990, Tony Award for Best Actor (for Pippin), American Guild of Variety Artists Entertainer of the Year, Rising Star, Song and Dance Star; Dr hc (Emerson Coll., Boston), (St Francis Coll., Brooklyn), (Columbia Coll., Chicago).

VERHAEREN, Gert J. M., (Skummy U.N.M.); Belgian singer, songwriter and musician (guitar, bass guitar); b. 30 July 1973, Neerpelt. *Career:* mem. Ivy 1996–, mem. Supergum 1997–; mem. SABAM. *Recordings include:* with Ivy: Bo(o)s(e), Goozehand, Liquid Courage, Watermelon; with Supergum: Airplane 1997, Eating Bullets, Last Song, Local Hero 1998, Indecision, Airplane (engineless), Bitch! 1999, Doctor Y, Surfin' Suspect, Unstoppable Noise-machine 2006. *Honours:* Weerter Amateur Festival Award 2004.

VERITY, John; British singer, musician (guitar) and producer; b. 2 May 1944, Bradford, Yorkshire; m. Karen Verity 1994; two s. one d. (from previous relationships). *Career:* guitarist with various groups during 1960s; leader, John Verity Band 1969–73; lead singer, Argent 1973–76; mem. Phoenix, Charlie, John Coughlan's Diesel Band; owns recording studio; producer, guitarist and singer, Saxon; worked with John Parr, Motörhead, Ringo Starr, Russ Ballard, Tank, The Zombies, Colin Blunstone, Matthew Fisher; mem. MRCS, PRS. *Recordings include:* albums: with Verity/John Verity Band: John Verity Band 1972, Interrupted Journey 1983, Truth of The Matter 1985, Rock Solid 1989, Hold Your Head Up 1994, From the Heart 2001, Unplugged and Unhinged 2005, Say Why? 2007; with Argent: Circus 1975, Counterpoints 1975, Hold Your Head Up 1978; with Phoenix: Phoenix 1976, In Full View 1979; with Charlie: Good Morning America 1981. *Address:* c/o Linn Records, Glasgow Road, Waterfoot, Eaglesham, Glasgow, G76 0EQ, Scotland. *Website:* www.johnverity.com.

VERLAINE, Tom; American singer and musician (guitar); b. (Thomas Miller), 13 Dec. 1949, Morristown, NJ. *Career:* mem., The Neon Boys; Goo Goo; founder mem., Television 1973–78, 1991–; solo artist 1979–; various festival appearances and tours. *Recordings include:* albums: with Television: Marquee Moon 1978, Adventure 1979, The Blow Up 1990, Television 1993; solo: Tom Verlaine 1979, Dreamtime 1981, Words From The Front 1982, Cover 1984, Flash Light 1987, Warm and Cool 1992, The Miller's Tale 1996, Around 2006, Songs And Other Things 2006; with Jimmy Rip: Music for Experimental Film 2006. *Honours:* Rolling Stone Magzine Critics Award for Comeback of the Year (with Television) 1993. *Address:* c/o Thrill Jockey Records, PO Box

08038, Chicago, IL 60608, USA. *E-mail:* info@thrilljockey.com. *Website:* www .thrilljockey.com.

VERLY, François, BEPC; French jazz musician (piano, tabla, drums, percussion); b. 5 April 1958, Paris; one d. *Career:* numerous concerts on tv and radio; world tours; jazz festivals in Canada, Mexico, Colombia, Ecuador, India, Hong Kong, Europe, Africa; played with Michel Portal, David Friedman and Martial Solal. *Recordings include:* Andy Emler, National French Jazz Orchestra 1986, 1987, News from the Front (with Mark Ducret) 1999, Brume (with Frédérique Carminati) 1993, Mingus Cuernavaca (with Padovani/ Cormann) 1996, 86 (with François Jeanneau) 1997, Other Worlds (with David Friedman) 1998, Mauve (with Emmanuel Bex) 2000, Light of the Shadow (with Eric Plande) 2002, Crouch, Touch, Engage (with Andy Emler) 2009, Sketches of Ethiopia (with Mulatu Astatke) 2013. *Honours:* First Prize (percussion), Creteil 1978, First Prize (piano soloist), Défense 1986.

VERNEY, Frannie; British singer, arranger, composer and musician (piano, percussion); b. 14 May 1963, Buckinghamshire. *Education:* Purcell School for Young Musicians, Guildhall School of Music and Drama. *Career:* radio appearances include BBC Radio 5, BBC Radio Scotland, Newstalk AM; tours throughout Europe; repeat performances at jazz venues throughout Great Britain including Jazz Cafe, Royal Festival Hall Foyer, Bull's Head Barnes, Chicken Shed Theatre, Jazz Club Ascot, Edinburgh Festival Fringe, West Wales Jazz Festival, Vortex Jazz Club, Covent Garden Festival, Cork International Jazz Festival, Greenwich and Docklands Jazz Festival; performs with her band The Big Idea; bandleader and promoter of party band Happy Feet; f. The Frannie Verney Group, The Hit Squad; also performs as soloist, with duos, performs, writes and arranges for smaller bands and a cappella groups; mem. PRS, MCPS, BAC&S, Musicians' Union. *Recordings include:* The Big Idea? 1998, If I Could 2003. *E-mail:* mail@dig-it-promotions .co.uk. *Website:* www.frannieverney.co.uk.

VERNHETTES, Daniel (Dan); French musician (trumpet, cornet) and singer; b. 20 May 1942, Paris; m. Lill Vernhettes 1965. *Career:* Founder, Jazz O'Maniacs 1966; Founder and leader, Six Cats 1990–93; mem. Eddie Louis' Multicolor Fanfare 1991–93; Leader and second trumpet, Swing Feeling 1992–; Founder, trumpet player, singer, bandleader, Vintage Jazzmen (sextet) 1992; formed Brother D Blue Band (septet) 1999. *Recordings include:* Swing Feeling with Screamin' Jay Hawkins and Spanky Wilson 1995, Vintage Jazzmen live at the Hot Club du Gatinais 1996, Swing Feeling Live in Langen 1998, Vintage Jazzmen with Reverend Garrett and Brian Lewis, Vols I and II 1998, Jazz Around the World 2000, Vintage Jazzmen of France in New Orleans 2000, New Orleans Gospel Live, Vintage Jazzmen with Tori Robinson 2002, Vintage Jazzmen with Jacques Gauthé in New Orleans 2002, Swing Feeling with Tori Robinson 2004, Messin Around 2005, Sing On 2006. *Honours:* Prix Sidney Bechet De L'Académie de Jazz 1997. *Address:* 45 rue Roger Buessard, 94200 Ivry-Sur-Seine, France (home). *Telephone:* 1-46-70-24-01 (home). *E-mail:* d-vernhettes@club-internet.fr (home).

VERNON, Justin DeYarmond Edison; American singer and songwriter; b. 30 April 1981, Eau Claire, Wis. *Education:* Univ. of Wisconsin-Eau Claire. *Career:* f. bands Mount Vernon, DeYarmond Edison (both now disbanded); f. band Bon Iver 2007; mem. band Volcano Choir. *Recordings include:* albums: For Emma, Forever Ago 2008, Blood Bank (EP) 2009, Bon Iver (Q Award for Best Album 2011, Grammy Award for Alternative Music Album 2012) 2011. *Honours:* Grammy Award for Best New Artist 2012. *Address:* c/o Jagjaguwar, 1499 West Second Street, Bloomington, IN 47403, USA. *E-mail:* info@ jagjaguwar.com. *Website:* www.boniver.org.

VERNON, Mike; British record producer and songwriter; b. 20 Nov. 1944, Harrow, Middlesex; two d. *Education:* Croydon Coll. of Art. *Career:* production assistant, later staff producer Decca Record Co. 1962–66; Founder and producer Blue Horizon Label 1966; Ed. R&B Monthly (early Blues Fanzine); formed Indigo Records 1992, became Code Blue (through East/West) 1994; headed Blueside Label 1998; Assoc. Mem. Re-Pro, PRS. *Recordings include:* as producer: singles include: with Fleetwood Mac: Albatross, Need Your Love So Bad, Man of The World; with David Bowie: The Laughing Gnome; with Focus: Hocus Pocus, Sylvia; with Bloodstone: Natural High; with Roachford: Family Man; with Oli Brown: Heads I Win, Tails You Lose 2010; with Jerry Cole: Psychedelic Guitars 2012; with Dr. Feelgood: Taking No Prisoners 2013. *Honours:* WC Handy Award 1987–88.

VERSACE, Gary; American jazz pianist, organist and accordionist; b. 25 April 1968, Greenwich, Conn. *Education:* Eastman School of Music. *Career:* fmr Assoc. Prof., Jazz Studies Dept, Univ. of Oregon-Portland (for eight years); relocated to New York City 2002; formed Refuge Trio with John Hollenbeck and Theo Bleckmann. *Recordings include:* albums: Winter Sonata 2004, Time and Again 2005, Many Places 2006, Reminiscence 2007, Outside In 2008; with the Nuttree Quartet: Standards 2008; with Refuge Trio: Refuge Trio 2008; with the Claudia Quintet: Royal Toast 2010; with Cameron Brown, Dick Oatts and Lorenzo Lombardo: Black Nile 2011; numerous recording credits as sideman including albums for 17 Reasons Why, Rez Abbasi, Ari Ambrose, David Ashkenazy, Sheryl Bailey, Dan Balmer, David Brandom, Regina Carter, Eli Degibri, Christian Eckert Quartet, John Ellis, Wayne Escoffery, David Friesen, Dave Glenn, Tom Guarna, Joel Harrison, Owen Howard, Ingrid Jensen, Lee Konitz, Jonathan Kreisberg, Steve LaSpina, Andy LaVerne, Joe Magnarelli, Thomas Marriott, Kate McGarry, Chris McNulty, Chuck Owen, Dave Pietro, Tim Ries, Dave Scott, Maria Schneider, Kendra Shank, Brad Shepik, Loren Stillman, Valgardena, Matt Wilson.

Honours: Jazz Journalists' Asscn Jazz Award for Keyboard Player of the Year 2012. *Website:* www.garyversace.com.

VIBERT, Luke Francis; British producer, programmer and remixer; b. Cornwall. *Career:* fmr mem. Hate Brothers; performs as Wagon Christ, Vibert/ Simmonds, Plug, Kerrier District, Spac Hand Luke and other pseudonyms; remixer or producer of several artists including Aphex Twin, Coldcut, DJ Food, Funky Porcini, Ken Ishii. *Recordings include:* albums: as Vibert/ Simmonds: Weirs 1993, Rodulate 2008; as Wagon Christ: Phat Lab Nightmare 1994, Throbbing Pouch 1995, Tally Ho! 1998, Sorry I Make You Lush 2004, Toomorrow 2011; solo: Big Soup 1996, Stop The Panic 2000, Nuggets 2001, Further Nuggets 2002, YosepH 2003, Lovers Acid 2005, Amen Andrews Vs Spac Hand Luke 2006, Kerrier District 2 2006, Moog Acid (with Jean Jacques Perrey) 2007, Chicago, Detroit, Redruth 2007, We Hear You 2009. *Website:* www.wagonchrist.com.

VIBSKOV, Per Nielsen; Danish composer and musician (bass); b. 23 May 1962, Viborg. *Career:* bass player, Peyote 1978–85, Rosegarden 1986, Janes Rejoice 1986–87, TAO 1988–, Bayou Brothers 1990–94; bass player and producer Home Sweet Home 1994–; bass fiddle player Luksus 1996–; mem. Danish Jazz, Beat and Folk Authors. *Recordings include:* with Peyote: 84; with Janes Rejoice: Wievs To Keep 1987; with TAO: Senor Maski 1995; with Home Sweet Home: Divine 1996.

VICH, Michal; Czech singer, musician (guitar) and educator; b. 5 Nov. 1952, Prague; m. Vera Vichova 1977; one d. *Education:* School of Economics, Prague, Prague Musical School, J Jezek Conservatoire, guitar and voice studies. *Career:* with recital group Vpred; mem. The Prague Five; film music for the films of T Vorel including Olda's Party 1988, Kour, musical 1990, La Serra, opera, Prague 1994, Songs for the Children; mem. The Protective Syndicate of Authors (Czech Republic). *Compositions include:* Kour film soundtrack 1990, La Serra opera score 1994. *Recordings include:* albums: Monday Tells To Tuesday 1995, Oh, The Sails, Where Are They? (with members of the Czech Philharmonic Orchestra) 1997. *Play includes:* songwriter for numerous theatre productions. *Publications include:* books for children: Monday Tells to Tuesday 1995, Oh, The Sails, Where Are They? 1996. *Address:* Ke Kouli 84, 252 62, Unětice, Czech Republic. *Telephone:* 220970005. *Fax:* 602194546. *E-mail:* info@michalvich.cz. *Website:* www.michalvich.cz.

VICKREY, Dan; American musician (guitar); b. 26 Aug. 1966, Walnut Creek, CA. *Career:* founder mem., Counting Crows 1993–; numerous tours and live appearances. *Recordings include:* albums: August & Everything After 1993, Recovering the Satellites 1996, Across a Wire: Live in New York 1998, This Desert Life 1999, Hard Candy 2002, Saturday Nights and Sunday Mornings 2008, Underwater Sunshine 2012, Somewhere Under Wonderland 2014. *Current Management:* International Talent Booking, First Floor, Ariel House, 74a Charlotte Street, London, W1T 4QJ, England. *Telephone:* (20) 7637-6979. *Fax:* (20) 7637-6978. *E-mail:* mail@itb.co.uk. *Website:* www.countingcrows .com.

VIDAL, Jacques Henri; French musician (double bass), composer and teacher; b. 13 Oct. 1949, Athis-Mons; m. 1993; one s. *Education:* Nat. Versailles Acad. of Music. *Career:* with Christian Vander's group Magma 1970; Leader Trijoums 1976; toured France with American drummer Philly Joe Jones 1977; played with guitarist Frederic Sylvestre 1978, Jacques Vidal Quintet 1995; Prof of Double Bass, Conservatoire du 11e arrondissement de Paris; mem. SACEM, SACD, ADAMI. *Recordings include:* Return with Christian Escoudé and A Romano 1979, Be Bop, Pepper Adams and B Altschul 1979, Live A L'Olympia, J P Debarbat 1979, A Live In Paris, Glenn Ferris 1980, Rencontre J P Debarbat 1981, Music Band, Teddy Lasry 1983, Under The Magnolias, Richard Raux 1989; with Frederic Sylvestre: Premier Grand Cru with J L Chautemps 1980, 2 Plus with Eric Lelann 1982, Hommages with Eric Lelann, A Jean-Marie 1983, Trio Live, S Huchard 1986, Capricorne 1989, Bass For Ever 1995, News of Bop, Jacques Vidal Quintet 1995, Mingus Spirit 2007, Fables of Mingus 2011, Cuernavaca 2014. *E-mail:* do.matray@yahoo.fr. *Website:* www.jacquesvidal.com.

VIDOVIC, Ana; Croatian musician (guitar); b. 8 Nov. 1980, Karlovac. *Education:* Music Acad., Zagreb. *Career:* performed solo and with orchestras in music centres in Warsaw, Vienna, Salzburg, Budapest, Tel-Aviv, Paris, London, Oslo, Århus, Bergen, Rome, Bari, Vaduz, Copenhagen. *Recordings include:* Ana Vidovic 1994, Ana Vidovic Gitara 1996, Ana Vidovic Guitar Recital 1998, Ana Vidovic: The Croatian Prodigy 1999, Ana Vidovic Live! 2001, Federico Moreno Torroba Guitar Music Volume 1 2007, Guitar Artistry in Concert 2009. *Honours:* First Prize, Albert Augustine Int. Competition, Bath, First Prize, Fernando Sor competition, Rome, First Prize, Francisco Tárrega competition, Spain. *Current Management:* c/o Diane Saldick 225 East 36th Street, New York, NY 10016, USA. *E-mail:* manager@anavidovic.com. *E-mail:* diane.saldick@verizon.net. *Website:* www.anavidovic.com.

VIG, Butch; American record producer and musician (drums); b. 8 Dec. 1957, Viroqua, WI. *Career:* record prod. for various artists, including Nirvana, Smashing Pumpkins, U2, Nine Inch Nails, House of Pain, Depeche Mode, Ash, Chainsaw Kittens; fmr mem., Spooner; founder mem., Garbage 1994–; numerous tours, festivals, TV and radio appearances. *Recordings include:* albums: Garbage 1995, Version 2.0 1998, Beautifulgarbage 2001, Androgyny 2003, Bleed Like Me 2005, Absolute Garbage 2007, Not Your Kind of People 2012. *Film music:* The World is Not Enough (theme to James Bond: The World is Not Enough) 1999. *Current Management:* Free Trade Agency, 20–22

Curtain Road, London, EC2A 3NF, England. *Telephone:* (20) 7655-6900. *Fax:* (20) 7655-6909. *E-mail:* info@freetradeagency.co.uk. *Website:* www .freetradeagency.co.uk; www.garbage.com.

VIKEDAL, Ryan; Canadian musician (drums); b. 9 May 1975. *Career:* mem. rock band Nickelback 1998–2005; extensive tours. *Recordings include:* albums: Curb 1996, The State 1999, Silver Side Up (Juno Award for Best Rock Album 2002) 2001, The Long Road 2003, All The Right Reasons (Juno Award for Best Rock Album 2006, American Music Award for Favorite Pop/Rock Album 2006, Billboard Award for Rock Album of the Year 2006) 2005; with Travis Tritt: The Storm 2007, The Calm After 2013, Latest & Greatest Driving Rock Anthems 2014. *Honours:* Juno Award for Best New Group 2001, Best Group, Best Single (for How You Remind Me) 2002, MuchMusic Video Award for Best Video (for Too Bad), Best Rock Video (for How You Remind Me) 2002, Juno Award for Best Group 2006, 2009, Billboard Award for Artist Duo/Group of the Year, for Hot 100 Artist Duo/Group of the Year 2006.

VILLAMIZAR, Jorge; Colombian musician, singer and composer; b. 14 Oct. 1970, Monteria. *Education:* Univ. of Miami. *Career:* lived in Ecuador from age 10 to 18, then returned to Colombia; studied political science in London, England; fmr mem. King Salsa; resident in Miami, USA 1992–; Founder-mem. Bacilos 1995–2007, signed with Warner Music 2000; mem. Alex, Jorge y Lena 2010–, recorded album with singer, songwriter and producer Aureo Baqueiro; performed at Lo Nuestro Awards 2011. *Recordings:* with Bacilos: Madera 1999, Bacilos 2000, Caraluna (Grammy Award for Best Latin Pop Album 2003) 2002, Sin Vergüenza 2004, Grandes Éxitos 2006; with Alex, Jorge y Lena: Alex, Jorge y Lena (Latin Grammy Award for Best Pop Album by a Duo or Group with Vocals 2011) 2010. *Address:* c/o Warner Music Latina, Warner Music Group, 75 Rockefeller Plaza, New York, NY 10019, USA (office). *Website:* www.alexjorgeylena.com.

VILLEGER, André Franucin Raymond; French musician (saxophone); b. 12 Aug. 1945, Rosny-sous-Bois; one s. one d. *Career:* mem. Los Angeles Jazz Soc., Nat. Orchestra of France 2000. *Recordings include:* Albums: Something To Live For 1986, A Villeger Connections 1991; Also appears: with Claude Bolling: Jazz Gala, Live at the Meridien, Bolling Plays Ellington, Tone Parallel to Harlem, Paris Swings 2001. *Honours:* Prix Sidney Bechet, Academie Du Jazz 1973. *Address:* 28 rue Gallows, 95100 Argenteuil, France. *E-mail:* contact@andrevilleger.com. *Website:* www.andrevilleger.com.

VINCENT, Amanda, BMus; Australian musician (keyboards); b. 20 Jan. 1958, Perth. *Education:* Univ. of Western Australia. *Career:* tours with: Eurogliders in UK, USA, Philippines, Australia 1980–87, with Tim Finn in Australia, New Zealand 1986, with The Thompson Twins in UK, Ireland, USA, Canada 1987, with Boy George in UK, Europe, Australia 1987–93, with Jenny Morris in UK, Europe, Australia supporting Prince 1990, with Gang of Four in UK, USA, Canada 1991, with Billy Bragg in Australia, New Zealand, Japan 1992, with Black in UK, Turkey 1993, with Yazz in UK 1994; mem. PRS, MCPS, Musicians' Union. *Recordings include:* Escapade (with Tim Finn) 1983, Les Patterson Saves The World (soundtrack) 1987; with Eurogliders: Pink Suit Blue Day 1981, This Island 1983, Absolutely 1985, Groove 1988, Eurogliders 2005, Blue Kiss 2007; with Jenny Morris: Animal Magic 1986, Body and Soul 1987, Shiver 1989; with Boy George: Clause 28 (single) 1988, Boyfriend 1989, High Hat 1988, Tense Nervous Headache 1988, Don't Try This At Home 1991, Bloke On Bloke 1997, Spiritual High, Moodswings featuring Chrissie Hynde (single) 1991. *E-mail:* mail@eurogliders. *Website:* www.eurogliders.com.

VINCENT, Eric; French singer and musician (guitar, violin); b. 27 June 1946, Force; m. 1987. *Career:* performances worldwide; mem. SCPP, SACEM, ADAMI, SPEDIDAM. *Recordings include:* Faut-il encore 2000 ans, Un pays quelquepart, Survol, Il n'y a de nouveau que c'qui est oublié, Je Suis Fatigué, Il n'y a plus de crocodiles à Cocody, Operation Boule de Neige. *Publications include:* Cest Comme Ça 1987, Iles 1987, Sans Borne 1990, Reflets Francais 1992. *Current Management:* Marie-Claude Barbin, Madura, 11 boulevard de la Bastille, 75012 Paris, France. *Telephone:* 1-43-07-44-34. *E-mail:* madura@wanadoo.fr. *E-mail:* DHarris887@aol.com. *Website:* www.eric-vincent.com.

VINCENT, Julian (Jules) Francis Vincent, MA, DSc, PhD, MIMechE, CEng; British engineer and academic; b. (Julian Francis Vincent Hills), 19 Jan. 1943, London; m. Elizabeth May 1968; one d. *Education:* Univ. of Cambridge, Univ. of Sheffield. *Career:* concerts at Purcell Room as solo recitalist; appearances at 100 Club; TV appearances for BBC, ITV and Radio RTE with tenor banjo; organizer, Reading Banjo Festival 1983–99, Bath Banjo Festival 2000–; later Prof. of Mechanical Eng, Univ. of Bath. *Recordings include:* Stomp Off, Tenor Banjo with Paramount Theatre Orchestra. *Publications include:* Banjoists' Broadsheet journal 1973–. *Address:* Laburnum Cottage, Odd Down, Bath, BA2 2QB, England (home). *Telephone:* (1225) 835076 (home). *E-mail:* julianbanjos@mac.com. *Website:* bathbanjofestival.com.

VINDING, Mads; Danish musician (bass); b. 7 Dec. 1948, Copenhagen. *Career:* professional musician aged 16; house bass player, Montmartre Jazz Club, Copenhagen; worked with many jazz masters including Herbie Hancock, Wayne Shorter, Stan Getz, Gary Burton, Hank Jones, Dexter Gordon, Bob Brookmeyer, Ben Webster, Benny Goodman, Dizzy Gillespie, Quincy Jones, Johnny Griffin, Eddie 'Lockjaw' Davis, Gerry Mulligan, Tony Williams, Ed Thigpen, Sir Roland Hanna, Dollar Brand, Clark Terry, Monty Alexander and Toots Thielemans. *Films include:* Round Midnight 1988, Between a Smile and a Tear 2004. *Recordings include:* solo albums: Danish

Design 1974, The Kingdom (Where Nobody Dies) 1997; with Ed Thigpen: Action-Re-Action 1974, Mr Taste 1991; with Tony Williams and Wlodek Gulgowsky, Pop-Workshop 1974; with Kai Winding: Trombone Summit 1980; with Doug Raney: Guitar Guitar Guitar 1985; with Dexter Gordon and Herbie Hancock: Cinema Jazz 1986, The Other Side of Midnight 1986; with Hanne Boel and Jorgen Emborg: Shadow of Love 1987; with Roland Hanna and Jesper Thilo: This Time It's Real 1987; with Thomas Clausen Trio: She Touched Me 1988, Psalm 1995; with Sven Asmussen: Fiddler Supreme 1989; with Thomas Clausen Trio and Gary Burton: Cafe Noir 1991, Flowers and Trees 1992; with Danish Radio Big Band: Endangered Species 1993; with Trine Lise Væring: When I Close My Eyes 1996; with Jesper Thilo: Jesper Thilo Meets Thomas Clausen 1997; with Bob Brookmeyer: Old Friends 1998; with Great Jazz Trio: Great Standards Vols 1–5 1998, Daddio Don 2000; other albums with Duke Jordan, Johnny Griffin, Ernie Wilkins, Kenny Drew, Hank Jones. *Address:* Boegevej 8, 3500 Vaerloese, Denmark (home). *E-mail:* madsvinding@gmail.com. *Website:* www.vinding.dk.

VINTON, Stanley Robert (Bobby); American singer and musician (trumpet); b. 16 April 1935, Canonsburg, Pa. *Career:* mem. The Tempos; solo artist 1962–; numerous TV appearances including host of weekly variety show 1975–78; opened The Bobby Vinton Blue Velvet Theater, Branson, Mo. 1993. *Films include:* Surf Party, Big Jake, The Train Robbers. *Recordings include:* albums: Roses Are Red 1962, Bobby Vinton Sings The Big Ones 1963, Blue Velvet 1963, Bobby Vinton's Greatest Hits 1964, Tell Me Why 1964, Bobby Vinton Sings For Lonely Nights 1965, Satin Pillows And Careless 1966, Please Love Me Forever 1968, Take Good Care of My Baby 1968, I Love How You Love Me 1969, Vinton 1969, Bobby Vinton's Greatest Hits of Love 1970, My Elusive Dreams 1970, Every Day of My Life 1972, Sealed With A Kiss 1972, Bobby Vinton's All-Time Greatest Hits 1972, Melodies of Love 1974, Bobby Vinton Sings The Golden Decade of Love 1975, Heart of Hearts 1975, The Bobby Vinton Show 1976, The Name of Love 1977, Timeless 1990, A Very Merry Christmas 1994, Kissin' Christmas 1995, Branson City Limits 1998, Blue On Blue 2000, The Legend 2002, Love Songs 2003, The Great Bobby Vinton 2005, Because of You: The Love Songs Collection 2006. *Honours:* Hon. DMus (Duquesne Univ.) 1978; Hon. Citizen of Chicago, City's Certificate of Merit 1975. *E-mail:* admin@bobbyvinton.com; rob@ivalve.net. *Website:* www .bobbyvinton.com; www.robbievintonentertainment.com.

VIRTANEN, Heikki; Finnish musician (bass); b. 4 Sept. 1953. *Education:* Studied Contrabass and Musicology. *Career:* mem. jazz-rock group Tasavallen Presidenttiin early 70's; Concerts with Juhani Aaltonen, Jarmo Savolainen, Severi Pyysalo, Jukkis Uotila in 1980s–; Bass player Conjunto Baron (with Seppo Paakkunainen); Bassist for Olli Ahvenlahti; backing singer Vesa-Matti Loiri on Olli Ahvenlahti's compositional projects; Featured on recordings by: Charlie Mariano, Jukka Tolonen; mem. Aboriginal Pig Band. *Honours:* Yrjö Award, Finnish Jazz Fed. Georgie Award 1987.

VIRTANEN, Johanna; Finnish singer, teacher and musician (harmonium, kantele); b. 16 June 1976, Rovaniemi; m. Jussi Kannaste; one s. *Education:* Central Ostrobothnian Conservatory, Kokkola and Sibelius Acad. *Career:* mem. Värttinä 2001–, DuoKuunkuiskaajat/Moonwhispers 2008–; Artistic Dir Ingrid Music Limited; numerous concerts and stage appearances. *Music for theatre:* co-wrote score to stage musical, The Lord of the Rings (with A. R. Rahman) (Princess of Wales Theatre, Toronto) 2006, (Theatre Royal, London) 2007. *Recordings include:* albums: 6.12 2001, Iki 2003, Snow Angel 2005, Miero 2006, Utu 2012. *Honours:* Suomi Palkinto (with Värttinä) 2005, World Music Womex Award 2012. *Current Management:* c/o Phillip Page, Hoedown Arts Oy, Neitsytpolku 9 F 81, 00140 Helsinki, Finland. *Telephone:* (50) 5692982. *Fax:* (9) 628950. *E-mail:* pap@hoedown.com. *E-mail:* johanna .virtanen@varttina.fi (office); johanna@kuunkuiskaajat.com (office); jvirtane@ siba.fi (office). *Website:* www.varttina.com; www.duokuunkuiskaajat.com.

VIRTUE, Michael (Mickey); British musician (keyboards); b. 19 Jan. 1957, Birmingham, England. *Education:* Golden Hillock comprehensive school. *Career:* mem. reggae group UB40 1978–2008; numerous concerts, tours. *Recordings include:* albums: Signing Off 1980, Present Arms 1981, The Singles Album 1982, UB44 1982, Labour of Love 1983, Live 1983, More UB40 Music 1983, Geffery Morgan 1984, Baggariddim 1985, Little Baggaridim 1985, UB40 File 1985, Rat In The Kitchen 1986, CCCP: Live In Moscow 1987, UB40 1988, Labour of Love II 1990, Promises and Lies 1993, Anansi 1995, Guns In The Ghetto 1997, Labour of Love III 1998, Presents The Dancehall Album 1998, Homegrown 2003, Who You Fighting For? 2005, TwentyFour-Seven 2008. *Current Management:* Part Rock Management Ltd, Kendal House, 1 Conduit Street, London, W1S 2XA, England. *Telephone:* (20) 8207-1418. *E-mail:* stewartyoung@mindspring.com. *Address:* DEP International Ltd, PO Box 117, Birmingham, B5 5RG, England (office). *E-mail:* info@ub40 .co.uk (office). *Website:* www.ub40.co.uk.

VISCONTI, Tony; American record producer and musician (guitar, bass guitar, double bass, tuba, piano, keyboards); b. 1944, Brooklyn, NY; m. 2nd May Pang (divorced 2000). *Education:* studied guitar with Leon Block. *Career:* mem. jazz duo, Tony and Sigrid; joined Richmond Organization, Essex Music, working in England, signed Tyrannosaurus Rex (later T-Rex); independent prod.; mem., The TV Show; worked with Adam Ant, Argent, Badfinger, Richard Barone, David Bowie, Boomtown Rats, Carmen, Dandy Warhols, Alejandro Escovedo, Gasworks, Gentle Giant, John Hiatt, Mary Hopkin, Marsha Hunt, Kaiser Chiefs, Luscious Jackson, Legend, Manic Street Preachers, Ralph McTell, Mercury Rev, Moody Blues, Morrissey, The Move,

Hazel O'Connor, Omaha Sheriff, Osibisa, Elaine Paige, Tom Paxton, Iggy Pop, Prefab Sprout, Procol Harum, Sarstedt Brothers, Sparks, The Stranglers, Strawbs, Surprise Sisters, Thin Lizzy, T-Rex, Wings, Kristeen Young. *Recordings:* numerous albums as producer including: The Man Who Sold the World, David Bowie 1970, Electric Warrior, T. Rex 1971, Band on the Run, Paul McCartney and Wings 1973, Diamond Dogs, David Bowie 1974, Scary Monsters, David Bowie 1980, Stage, Elaine Paige 1983, Heathen, David Bowie 2002, Reality, David Bowie 2003, Ringleader of the Tormentors, Morrissey 2006, Djin Djin, Angelique Kidjo 2007, Real Animal, Alejandro Escovedo 2008, Music for Strippers, Hookers and the Odd On-Looker, Kristeen Young 2009, Street Songs of Love, Alejandro Escovedo 2010, You Love You, Semi-Precious Weapons 2010, The Future is Medieval, Kaiser Chiefs 2011, The Next Day, David Bowie 2013, Blackstar, David Bowie 2016. *Publication:* The Autobiography: From Bowie to Bolan and Back Again 2007. *Address:* c/o The Looking Glass Studios, 632 Broadway, 9th Floor, New York, NY 10012, USA. *Website:* www.tonyvisconti.com.

VISKINDE, Peter; Danish musician (guitar), composer and songwriter; b. 14 Nov. 1953, Copenhagen; m. Susan Kjeldsen 1992; two s. two d. *Career:* formed band Buffalo 1972, pop group WormWood (with Michael Falch) 1979, Big Fat Snake (with Anders Blichfeldt) 1990; mem. of groups including Hualsospille-mandene, Malurt Doraz; also recorded as solo artist; mem. DJBFA. *Recordings include:* albums: two with Buffalo, two with Hualsospillemandene, seven with Malurt; five solo albums; seven with Big Fat Snake 1991–2004. *E-mail:* info@peterviskinde.dk. *Website:* www.peterviskinde.dk.

VITEK, Pavel; Czech singer, actor, composer and lyricist; b. 30 Sept. 1962, Olomouc. *Education:* Acad. of Musical Art, Prague. *Career:* theatre and musical actor and singer 1990s-; numerous TV and radio broadcasts; own talk show on radio; mem. Czech Asscn of Authors, Intergram. *Stage appearances:* Pop Festival 1984, Gypsies Go to Heaven 1986, Some Like it Hot 1987, Dracula 1995. *Films include:* Creation of the World 1988. *Recordings include:* albums: Má svůj den 1986, Vůně tvý kůže 1992, Zahrada přání 1994, Šťastná hvězda 1995, Muzikál 1997, Procitni 2000, Největší hity 2001, Stíny duší 2006, Hity mého Srdce 2010. *Honours:* Second Prize, OIRT Festival, Budapest 1988, Midnight Sun Song Festival Prize, Finland 1992. *Address:* Pavel Vitek, Nota Bene Musical, Londy'nska' 53, 12000 Prague 2, Czech Republic (office). *E-mail:* janis@sidovsky.cz (office); lukas@celebritymanagement.cz. *Website:* www.pavelvitek.cz.

VIVES, Carlos; Colombian singer and actor; b. (Carlos Alberto Vives Restrepo), 7 Aug. 1961, Santa Marta, Departamento del Magdalena. *Education:* Jorge Tadeo Lozano Univ. *Career:* formed band La Provincia 1991–; est. Gaira Música Local label. *Film appearances include:* La Estrategia del Caracol 1994, La Tele 1995, La Voz Colombia 2012. *Television includes:* appeared in seven series on Colombian TV. *Recordings include:* albums: Por Fuera y Por Dentro 1986, Escalona: Un Canto a La Vida 1991, Clásicos De La Provincia 1993, La Tierra Del Olvido 1995, Tengo Fe 1997, El Amor De Mi Tierra 1999, Déjame Entrar (Latin Grammy Award for Best Contemporary Tropical Album 2002) 2001, Colección De Oro 2002, El Rock de Mi Pueblo (Latin Grammy Award for Best Contemporary Tropical Album 2005) 2004, Clásicos de la Provincia II 2009, Corazón Profundo (Latin Grammy Awards for Best Tropical Fusion Album 2013, for Best Contemporary Tropical Album 2014) 2013, Más + Corazón Profundo (Grammy Award for Best Tropical Latin Album 2015) 2014. *Honours:* Latin Grammy Award for Best Tropical Song (for Déjame Entrar) 2002, Latin Grammy Award for Song of the Year and Best Tropical Song of the Year (for Volví a Nacer) 2013. *Address:* Gaira Producciones, Calle 103 A, No. 18-02, Bogotá, Colombia. *E-mail:* gaira@colmsat.net.co; walter@walterkolm.com. *Website:* www.carlosvives.com.

VOISINE, Roch, OC; Canadian singer and actor; b. (Joseph Armand Roch Voisine), 26 March 1963, Edmundston, NB; m. Myriam Saint-Jean; two s. *Education:* Univ. of Ottawa. *Career:* regular tours in Canada, USA, Europe 1989–; performs in French and English; relocated to Los Angeles, USA 1995; Special Rep., UNICEF Canada 1999. *Television appearances include:* actor: Lance et Compte 1989, Armen and Bullik 1992, Le Grand Blond avec un Show sournois; other: Top Jeunesse (host). *Recordings include:* albums: Hélène 1989, Double 1990, Roch Voisine 1990, I'll Always Be There 1993, Coup de Tête 1994, Kissing Rain 1996, Chaque Feu 1999, L'Album de Noël (French) and Christmas is calling (English) 2000, Éponyme 2001, Kyrie 2002, Je Te Serai Fidèle 2003, Sauf Si L'Amour 2005, Best of Roch Voisine 2007, Americana 2008, Americana II 2009, California: Americana, Vol. 3 2010, Duophonique 2012. *Honours:* Chevalier, Ordre des Arts et des Lettres (youngest ever recipient) 1992; Male Vocalist of the Year, Juno Award 1994, Male Francophone Artist of the Year, NRJ Music Awards 2005. *Address:* c/o Sony/BMG Entertainment France, rue de Châteaudun, 75342 Paris Cedex 09, France. *Telephone:* 1-57-64-60-60. *Fax:* 1-44-40-66-66. *Website:* www.sonymusic.fr; www.rochvoisine.com.

VOLCKE, Ivan; Belgian folk musician (guitar); b. (Ivan Albert René Volcke), 9 Nov. 1954, Wervik; s. of Rogier Volcke; m. Christien Hollebeke; two s. *Education:* School of Sports, VILO, Meulebeke. *Career:* mem. The Swigshift 1985–; numerous festival appearances; several regional radio and TV broadcasts; mem. Volksmuziekfederatie. *Recordings include:* albums: Tales From the Great Whiskey Book 1996, Witness of a Celtic Past 1998, The Swigshift and Friends 2001, Walking Home 2008, The Swigshift Legacy 2011. *Address:* Speiestraat 22, 8940 Wervik, Belgium (office). *Telephone:* 475-

851346 (mobile) (office). *E-mail:* isermael@skynet.be (office). *Website:* www.swigshift.com.

VOLCY, Jean-Marc, BMus; musician (guitar, banjo, percussion) and singer; b. 29 Jan. 1966, Anse Royal, Seychelles; m. Eudoxie Volcy. *Career:* TV appearances, festivals. *Compositions include:* Three (dir, musical) 1995, 1996, 1997. *Recordings include:* albums: Sanmoi Swar Lo Zil St Pierre, Oseselwa and Sega of Seychelles, Various—Nouvelles Seychelles—New Beats From Paradise 2000, Various—Segavibes Vol. 1 Hits Of Seychelles 2004. *Honours:* winner, Grand Prix D'Afrique Decouvert Des RFI 1993, winner, Festival Creole Song Contest 1993, 1996. *Website:* www.jeanmarcvolcy.com.

VOLKOVA, Julia Olegovna; Russian singer; b. 20 Feb. 1985, Moscow. *Career:* mem., Neposedy –2000; mem., t.A.T.u. late 1990s–. *Recordings include:* albums: 200 km/h In The Wrong Lane 2002, Dvesti Po Vstrechiy 2002, Dangerous and Moving 2005, Happy Smiles 2008, Waste Management 2009. *Film appearances include:* You and I 2011, Zombie Fever 2013. *E-mail:* info@tatu.ru; ig@juliavolkova.com. *Website:* www.tatu.ru; www.juliavolkova.com.

VOLLENWEIDER, Andreas; Swiss musician (harp, multi-instrumentalist); b. 4 Oct. 1953, Zurich. *Career:* composer of numerous musical productions for theatre, film and ballet; Alvin Ailey Co. on world tour with ballet based on own music. *Compositions include:* Pace Verde, anthem of European Peace Movement 1983, Pearls and Tears, anthem in black townships of South Africa 1990, The Essential 2000. *Recordings include:* Eine Art Suite in XIII Teilen 1979, Behind the Gardens 1981, Caverna Magica 1982, White Winds 1984, Down to the Moon 1986, Dancing with the Lion 1988, Traumgarten 1990, Book of Roses 1991, Eolian Minstrel 1993, Kryptos 1994, Cosmology 1999, The Essential 2001, VOX 2004, The Storyteller 2005, Midnight Clear 2006, The Magical Journeys of Andreas Vollenweider 2006, Eolian Minstrel 2007, Andreas Vollenweider and Friends 2007, AIR 2009. *Honours:* Edison Award 1983, Grammy Award 1987, World Music Award 1992. *Current Management:* Andreas Vollenweider, c/o Impact Music Inc, Zollikerstr 144, 8008 Zurich, Switzerland. *Telephone:* (1) 3886060. *Fax:* (1) 3886061. *E-mail:* vollenweider@impactmusic.ch; info@impactmusic.ch. *Website:* www.vollenweider.com.

VOLLMER, Brian Joseph; Canadian singer, songwriter and singing teacher; b. 30 June 1955, Kitchener, Ont.; m. Lynda Cowgill 1991; one d. *Education:* studied Bel Canto singing technique with Edward Johnson. *Career:* singer in heavy rock group, Helix; several tours and TV appearances; solo artist 1999–; teacher of Bel Canto singing technique; wrote a vocal instruction column for Canadian Musician. *Recordings include:* albums: with Helix: White Lace and Black Leather 1978, Breaking Loose 1979, No Rest For The Wicked 1982, Walking The Razor's Edge 1984, Long Way To Heaven 1985, Wild In The Streets 1988, Back For Another Taste 1990, It's A Business Doing Pleasure 1992, Half Alive 1998, Best of Helix: Deep Cuts 1999; solo: When Pigs Fly 1999, B-Sides 1999, Rockin' In My Outer Space 2000, 30 years of Helix 2004, Never Trust Anyone Over 30 2004, Get Up! 2006, The Power of Rock 'n' Roll 2007, Vagabond Bones 2010, Smash Hits Unplugged 2011, Skin in the Game 2011. *Honours:* Heavy Metal Video of Year (for Running Wild in the 21st Century); four gold, two platinum albums. *Address:* 52 Terrence Street, London, ON N5Z 1C4, Canada (home). *Telephone:* (519) 452-0565 (office). *E-mail:* bvollm0656@rogers.com (home). *Website:* www.planethelix.com; www.brianvollmer.com.

VON ARBIN, Carl; Swedish musician (guitar) and graphic designer. *Career:* Founder-mem., Luca Brasi, renamed Shout Out Louds 2001–. *Recordings include:* albums: 100° (EP) 2003, Oh, Sweetheart (EP) 2004, Howl Howl Gaff Gaff 2005, Very Loud (EP) 2005, Our Ill Wills 2007, Work 2010, Optica 2013. *Current Management:* c/o Filip Wilén, Bud Fox Management, Saturnusgatan 13, 224 57 Lund, Sweden. *Telephone:* (46) 13-81-20. *E-mail:* filip@budfox.se. *Website:* www.budfox.se; www.shoutoutlouds.com.

VON HELVETE, Hank; Norwegian singer; b. (Hans Erik Dyvik Husby), 16 June 1972. *Career:* mem. punk band, Turbonegro 1988–98, 2002–. *Recordings include:* albums: Turboloid 1990, Hot Cars and Spent Contraceptives 1992, Helta Skelta 1993, Never is Forever 1994, Ass Cobra 1996, Apocalypse Dudes 1998, Scandinavian Leather 2003, Party Animals 2005, Retox 2007, Sexual Harassment 2012. *Honours:* MTV Europe Music Award for Best Norwegian Act 2005. *Address:* c/o Burning Heart Records, PO Box 441, 70148 Örebro, Sweden. *Website:* www.turbonegro.com.

VOROS, George Ladislaus; South African musician (drums) and drum teacher; b. 5 March 1958, Swaziland. *Career:* mem., South African bands: Neil Solomon; E'Void, Wozani; numerous South African TV appearances and sessions; Wworked with Jimmy James and The Vagabonds, UK; mem., Stu Page Band, UK; private drum studio, The Drum Workshop for five years; mem., Musicians' Union (registered teacher). *Recordings include:* The Love We Can Share, World Vision (charity single); album: Come and Dance, Wozani. *Publication:* Book on drums, practice and performance endorsed by Virgil Donati, Steve White and others. *Honours:* Best British Country Band (Stu Page Band) 1994. *Telephone:* (11) 7910497. *E-mail:* rhythmhead@mweb.co.za. *Website:* www.georgvoros.com.

VOWLES, Andrew (see Mushroom)

VRIENDS, Peter; Dutch musician (midi instruments); b. 31 Oct. 1963, Rotterdam. *Career:* co-owner of record cos, Essential Dance Music, Basic Beat

Recordings; Owner and engineer of recording studio; producer of own compositions, productions for third parties, mixing dance mix albums; mem. SENA, IFPI, Stermra, Buma. *Recordings include:* Emotional Travellogue, Quadripart Project 1995. *Honours:* Best House Record of the Year, Benelux (for Pot of Gold) 1991. *Address:* Peter Vriends Mastering, Noordeinde 166, 3341 LW Hendrik Ido Ambacht, The Netherlands (office). *Telephone:* (78) 6848788 (office). *Fax:* (78) 6817041 (office). *Website:* www .petervriendsmastering.nl.

VUDI; American musician (guitar); b. (Mark Pankler). *Career:* Founder-mem., American Music Club 1983–96, 2003–. *Recordings include:* albums: The Restless Stranger 1986, Engine 1987, California 1988, United Kingdom 1990, Everclear 1991, Mercury 1993, San Francisco 1994, Love Songs for Patriots 2004, A Toast to You 2005, The Golden Age 2008. *Current Management:* Undertow Music Management, 4217 West Grace Street, Chicago, IL 60641, USA. *Telephone:* (773) 205-9823. *E-mail:* chris_metzler@ undertowmusic.com. *Website:* www.undertowmusic.com; www .americanmusicclub.com.

VUJICA, Matija; Croatian singer and fashion designer; b. 19 July 1963, Metkovic. *Education:* Faculty of Economics, Zagreb; private piano lessons. *Career:* singer with group Gracia 1990–; concerts, tours and rock festivals in Croatia, Austria, Germany, Slovenia and Sweden; numerous TV and radio appearances; mem., Croatian Musicians' Union. *Recordings include:* albums: with Gracia: Gracia 1990, Jer Tu Ima Neki Crni Vrag 1994, Dancetheria 1994, 4 1995, Arena 1996, Etno Baš Hoću 1997, Cvijet s Juga 1999, Dancemix 2001; solo: Carica 2003, Etnofest Neum 2004. *Honours:* Ethno Dance Award 1994. *Address:* Zagreb, Butik se nalazi u Gajevoj 4, Croatia (office). *Telephone:* (9) 2251904 (office). *E-mail:* matija.vuica@zg.t-com.hr (office). *Website:* www .matijavuica.com.

VYAS, (Pandit) Satish; Indian musician (santoor); b. 16 Nov. 1952. *Career:* performed at Mostra Mozart festival, Venice, Italy 1997 and Barbican, UK; Artistic Dir, Navras Records. *Recordings include:* albums: Strings of Your Soul, Cascade, Dreamwaves. *Honours:* Padmashri Award 2003. *E-mail:* vyassatish@hotmail.com.

VYVÉRE, Pascale, BFA; Belgian singer, composer, songwriter, musician (piano, accordion) and actress; b. 31 May 1966, Brussels. *Career:* numerous festival appearances, concerts; roles in Chants de Femmes (film) 1994, La Voix Humaine 1996, La Dame de Chez Maxim 1996, Les Poules 1997–99, Les Miroirs d'Ostende 1998, 2000, Les Feux de Babel 1998–99; mem. SABAM (Brussels). *Recordings include:* solo album: Je Vous Attends 1997. *Honours:* Prix Sentier des Halles, Prix Adiam-92, Tremplin Chorus Hauts-de-Seine 1993, Prix Auditeurs France-Inter/RTBF/RSR 1994. *E-mail:* pascalevyvere@ hotmail.com. *Website:* www.pascalevyvere.net.

WAAKTAAR, Pål; Norwegian musician (guitar), singer and composer; b. (Pål Garnst), 6 Sept. 1961, Manglerud, Oslo; m. Lauren; one c. *Career:* mem. a-ha 1982–94, 1999–2010, 2015–; mem. Savoy; Owner record label Eleventeen Records; worked on project Weathervane (with Jimmy Gnecco) 2011. *Recordings include:* albums: Hunting High And Low 1985, Scoundrel Days 1986, Stay On These Roads 1988, East Of The Sun West Of The Moon 1990, Memorial Beach 1992, Lifelines 2002, How Can I Sleep With Your Voice In My Head (live) 2003, Singles 1984–2004 2005, Analogue 2005, Foot of the Mountain 2009, 25 2010, Ending on a High Note 2011; with Savoy: Mary is Coming 1996, Lackluster Me 1997, Mountains of Time 1999, Reasons to Stay Indoors 2001, Savoy 2004, Savoy Songbook Vol. 1 2007. *Honours:* Order of St Olav 2012; eight MTV Music Video Awards (for Take On Me and The Sun Always Shines On TV) 1986, BMI Award for One Million Broadcast Performances (for Take On Me) 1991, World Music Award for Best Selling Norwegian Artist of the Year 1993, Spellemannsprisen for Pop Group 1999, 2001. *Website:* www.a-ha.com.

WADGE, Amy Victoria, BA; British singer, songwriter and musician (guitar); b. 22 Dec. 1975, Backwell, Avon, England; d. of Michael Wadge and Jenny Wadge; m. Alun ap Brinley. *Education:* Welsh Coll. of Music and Drama. *Career:* mem. Two of a Mind 1990; mem. Hummingbird 2006–07; solo artist 2001–; has worked with Ed Sheeran, Mahalia, Shannon Saunders, Lewis Watson, Josh Kumra, Ryan Ashley, Jody Brock, Katy & The Elders, Eliza Doolittle, Gabrielle Aplin, Aquilo, Zak Able, Dua Lipa. *Radio:* presenter, I'll Show You Mine, with Frank Hennesey, BBC Radio Wales. *Recordings include:* albums: solo: The Famous Hour 2003, Woj 2004, No Sudden Moves 2006; with Hummingbird: Tougher than Love 2007. *Honours:* Welsh Music Award for Best Female Solo Artist 2002, 2003, Grammy Award for Song of the Year (for Thinking Out Loud, with Ed Sheeran) 2016. *Current Management:* c/o Spilt Milk Management, Sarm Music Village, 105 Ladbroke Grove, London, W11 1PG, England. *Telephone:* (207) 229-1229. *Website:* spiltmilkmusic.co.uk. *E-mail:* amy@amywadge.com. *Website:* www.amywadge .com.

WADSWORTH, Tony, CBE; British music industry executive; b. 1957. *Education:* Newcastle Univ. *Career:* mem. Archie Brown & The Young Bucks 1975–87; fmrly worked for Logo Records, RCA Records; joined EMI Records 1982, Strategic Marketing Div. –1987; Marketing Dir, Parlophone Records 1987–93, Man. Dir 1993–98; Pres., EMI Records Group UK and Ireland 1998–2002, Chair. and CEO EMI Recorded Music UK and Ireland 2002–08; Chair., Brit Awards Cttee 2000–03; apptd Visiting Fellow in Popular Music, Univ. of Gloucester 2005; Visiting Prof., Music and Business Schools, Newcastle Univ.; Chair. British Phonographic Industry (BPI) 2007–14; mem. Bd Brits Trust; Trustee, Music Sound Foundation, EMI Archive Trust. *Recording:* album: Bring Me the Head of Jerry Garcia (with Archie Brown & The Young Bucks) 1987. *Honours:* Strat Award, Music Week Awards 2008. *Address:* BPI, Riverside Building, County Hall, Westminster Bridge Road, London, SE1 7JA, England (office). *Telephone:* (20) 7803-1300 (office). *Fax:* (20) 7803-1310 (office). *E-mail:* general@bpi.co.uk (office). *Website:* www.bpi.co .uk (office).

WAGER, Henrik Rickard, BA; British/Swedish singer and songwriter; b. 14 March 1969, Manchester. *Education:* Univ. of Birmingham , Birmingham Conservatoire. *Career:* mem. The Flying Pickets; singer/songwiter with The Heavytones; singer/songwriter with Tape Five CDs, Swing FoodMood, Taxi to Bombay, Tonight Josephine, Swing Patrol, Circus Maximus; producer for Basta. *Musical theatre roles include:* Jesus in Jesus Christ Superstar, Frederick Trumper in Chess, Ché in Evita, Berger in Hair, Frank'n'Furter in The Rocky Horror Show, Dr Jekyll in Jekyll and Hyde, Frank Sinatra in Swing the Ratpack, Rock Tenor in Bernsteins Mass. *Recordings include:* Politics of Need, Vox, Next Generation; solo: Confessions. *Radio:* Taking It Up the Octave (Radio Four). *E-mail:* mail@henrikwager.com. *Website:* www .henrikwager.com.

WAGHORN, Gary; British musician (guitar, banjo); b. 9 May 1949, Chatham, Kent, England; m. Linda Evans 1970; one d. *Career:* Lead guitarist for Bonnie Tyler; Lead guitarist, vocalist, Slack Alice; Lead guitarist, backing vocals, Mountain Child; mem. PRS, Musicians' Union. *Recordings include:* Album: Diamond Cut, Bonnie Tyler; 6 singles with Bonnie Tyler; Single: Night Pilots, Mountain Child; Trevithick's Train.

WAGNER, Heribert, (Art Wakuna); Austrian musician (violin) and composer; *Owner, Art In Music*; b. 24 Dec. 1952, Vienna; m. Fredo Wagner; one s. *Education:* Conservatory of Vienna and Enschede, Netherlands, Univ. of Applied Arts, Vienna. *Career:* composed Gaia, a Story for Jazzgroup and Symphony Orchestra 1987–91, performed with Taijiro Iimori, New Association and Het Gelders Orkest 1992; Dutch TV, NL3, Jazz uit het BIM-Huis; festival performances include at Berliner Jazztage Philharmonie, North Sea Festival, The Hague, Montreux Jazz Festival, Jazzfest, Vienna, Nürnberg Ost-West, Nancy Jazz Pulsations, Stuttgarter Jazzfest; mem. BUMA/ STEMRA, BIM, Omroep NTR; Owner, Art In Music. *Exhibitions:* several group art expositions with Kunstpost The Hague. *Compositions:* Gaia, a Story for Jazzgroup and Symphony Orchestra; LP 'To Be Continued', CD 'Four Wheel Drive', Homage 5, Ballad for a Lonesome Guy Somewhere on This

Earth, Horizontal Curve. *Television:* Live at the BIM Huis (Nederlandse Programma Stichting), Live from Berliner Jazztage (WDR) 1987. *Recordings:* LP, To Be Continued, with New Association; CD, Four Wheel Drive, with New Association; Disco Compacto, with Trio Famoso. *Honours:* Jaromir Prize (Netherlands) 1988. *Current Management:* Art In Music, Altingstraat 38, 2593 SX The Hague, The Netherlands. *Telephone:* 68-5265500 (mobile) (office). *E-mail:* heribert_wagner@hotmail.com (office); art_wakuna@hotmail .com.

WAGNER, Kurt; American singer, musician (guitar) and songwriter; b. 1958, Bethseda, MD. *Education:* Art School, Memphis, TN. *Career:* founder mem. and lead singer of collective, Posterchild 1986, renamed Lambchop 1992–, mixing country, soul, folk and jazz music. *Recordings include:* albums: with Lambchop: I Hope You're Sitting Down/Jack's Tulips 1994, How I Quit Smoking 1996, Thriller 1997, What Another Man Spills 1998, Nixon 2000, Tools in the Dryer: A Rarities Compilation 2001, Is A Woman 2002, The Decline of Country & Western Civilization 2006, Damaged 2006, OH (Ohio) 2008, Mr M 2012; with Josh Rouse: Chester 1999. *Current Management:* High Road Touring, 751 Bridgeway, 3rd Floor, Sausalito, CA 94965, USA. *Telephone:* (415) 332-9292. *Fax:* (415) 332-4692. *E-mail:* info@ highroadtouring.com. *Website:* www.highroadtouring.com. *Address:* Lambchop Office, 2304 White Avenue, Nashville, TN 37204, USA (office). *E-mail:* lambchop@lambchop.net (office). *Website:* www.lambchop.net.

WAGNER, Sune Rose; Danish singer and musician (guitar); b. 7 Oct. 1973. *Career:* Founder-mem. The Raveonettes 2002–. *Recordings include:* albums: Whip It On (EP) 2002, Chain Gang Of Love 2002, Pretty In Black 2005, Lust Lust Lust 2007, In and Out of Control 2009; solo: Sune Rose Wagner 2008. *E-mail:* scott@theorchard.com (office).

WAGNER, Windy; American singer; b. 6 Dec. 1971, Los Angeles, CA. *Career:* vocals for Walt Disney records, Baywatch, Fame LA, various TV commercials; backing vocalist on recordings by k. d. lang, Michael Bublé, Neil Young, Walter Becker, Bette Midler, Barbra Streisand, Meredith Brooks, Natalie Grant, Julio Iglesias, Britney Spears, Miley Cyrus, Diana Ross, Jennifer Lopez; mem. SAG; AFTRA; LA Singers United. *Recordings include:* solo album: Simplest Things 2002; other credits include: Glee: The Music (Vols 1–7) 2009–11. *Honours:* Los Angeles Music Award for Best Female Vocalist. *Address:* PO Box 17551, Beverly Hills, CA 90209, USA. *Website:* www .windywagner.com.

WAHAMAKI, Benjamin (Ben) Michael; American folk rock musician (bass guitar). *Career:* mem. The Lumineers 2012–; numerous tours. *Recordings:* albums: with The Lumineers: The Lumineers 2012. *Current Management:* c/o Christen Greene and David Meinert, Onto Entertainment, 2611 5th Avenue, Seattle, WA 98121-1517, USA. *Address:* c/o Dualtone Records, Dualtone Music Group, 203 North 11th Street, Suite B, Nashville, TN 37206, USA (office). *Telephone:* (615) 320-0620 (office). *Fax:* (615) 320-0692 (office). *E-mail:* info@ dualtone.com (office); info@thelumineers.com. *Website:* www.dualtone.com (office); www.thelumineers.com.

WAHLBERG, Ulf; Swedish producer, songwriter and musician (keyboards); *Managing Director, XTC Productions/Studios AB and SPM Publishing;* b. 11 April 1951, Stockholm; m. Catherina; two s. two d. *Education:* studied piano for five years, musical high school. *Career:* Ola Hakansson, The Group Secret Service 1979; producer 1979–; mem. STIM, SAMI, SKAP. *Compositions:* Som Stormen River Oppet Hav, Heden, Ögon Man Aldrig Glömmer, Fire Into Ice, Om Kärlek (film score) 1986. *Recordings:* Secret Service, Freestyle, Susan Alfvengren, Magnum Bonum, Martin, Lake Of Tears, YSA Ferrer, Last Autumn's Dream, Reeperbahn, Docent Död, Bogart Co, Monica Törnell. *Publications:* Popcorn, Jukebox. *Honours:* Golden Leaf for Secret Service from Radio Luxembourg 1980, Swedish Grammy Award (as producer) 1986, 26 gold and platinum albums as producer. *Current Management:* c/o XTC Productions AB, PO Box 2065, 12502 Alvsjo, Sweden. *Telephone:* (8) 7492506. *Fax:* (8) 7492506. *E-mail:* info@xtc-productions.com. *Website:* www.xtc-productions .com.

WAILER, Bunny; Jamaican singer and songwriter; b. (Neville O'Riley Livingston), 10 April 1947, Kingston. *Career:* harmony singer, songwriter, and occasional lead singer, reggae group Bob Marley and the Wailers 1960s and 1970s; solo recording artist; owner, Solomonic record label 1974–. *Recordings inlcude:* Albums include: with the Wailers: Catch A Fire, Burnin'; Solo albums: Blackheart Man, Protest, Struggle, In A Fathers House, Bunny Wailer Sings The Wailers, Tribute To The Hon. Robert Nesta Marley, Rock 'n' Groove, Hook Line and Sinker, Roots Radics Rockers Reggae, Marketplace, Bunny Wailer Live, Roots Man Skanking, Rule Dancehall, Liberation, Gumption, Hall of Fame: A Tribute to Bob Marley's 50th 1995, Complete Bob Marley and the Wailers 1998; with Bob Marley: Rock to the Rock 1999, Dubdisco 1999, Communication 2000, World Peace 2003, Rub A Dub 2007, Cross Culture 2009, Reincarnated Souls 2013.

WAINWRIGHT, Loudon, III; American singer, songwriter, musician (guitar) and actor; b. 5 Sept. 1946, Chapel Hill, NC; s. of Loudon Wainwright Jr and Martha Taylor; m. 1st Kate McGarrigle (divorced 1977, died 2010); m. 2nd RitaMarie Kelly; one s. three d. *Education:* Carnegie Mellon Univ.,

Pittsburgh. *Career:* singer, folk clubs, New York and Boston 1968; recording artist 1969–; numerous festival and other live appearances, TV and radio broadcasts; compositions for ABC Nightline; radio NPR, USA continues to commission topical songs on events and individuals in the news. *Television appearances:* several episodes M.A.S.H., episode Soldier Soldier, own show Loudon and Co. (BBC Scotland), played Hal Karp in Undeclared (TV series, Fox/Dreamworks), episode of Ally McBeal. *Stage appearances:* The Birthday Party, Pump Boys and Dinettes, Caryl Churchill's Owners (at the Young Vic). *Film appearances:* The Slugger's Wife 1985, Jacknife 1989, 28 Days 2000, Big Fish 2003, The Aviator 2004, The 40-Year Old Virgin 2005, Elizabethtown 2005, For Your Consideration 2006, Knocked Up 2007, G-Force 2009. *Compositions include:* Dead Skunk, Your Mother and I, I Wish I Was a Lesbian, YK2, Glad To See You've Got Religion, The Man Who Couldn't Cry, Swimming Song, Motel Blues, Be Careful, There's A Baby In The House, The Picture 1992, Dreaming 1995. *Recordings include:* albums: Loudon Wainwright III 1970, Album II 1971, Album III 1972, Attempted Moustache 1973, Unrequited 1975, T-Shirt 1976, Final Exam 1978, A Live One 1979, Fame and Wealth 1983, I'm Alright 1985, More Love Songs 1986, Therapy 1989, History 1992, Career Moves 1993, One Man Guy: Best Of Loudon Wainwright III 1994, Grown Man 1996, Little Ship 1998, BBC Sessions 1998, Social Studies 1999, Last Man On Earth 2001, So Damn Happy 2003, Here Come The Choppers 2005, Strange Weirdos 2007, Recovery 2008, High Wide and Handsome (Grammy Award for Best Traditional Folk Album 2010) 2009, 10 Songs for the New Depression 2010, Older Than My Older Man Now 2012. *Current Management:* c/o Bernett Management, 4440 Morse Avenue, Studio City, CA 91604, USA. *Telephone:* (818) 907-8300. *Fax:* (818) 501-7544. *E-mail:* info@bernett.us. *Website:* www.lwiii.com.

WAINWRIGHT, Martha; Canadian/American singer, songwriter and musician (guitar); b. 8 May 1976, Montréal; d. of Loudon Wainwright III and the late Kate McGarrigle; sister of Rufus Wainwright; m. Brad Albetta 2007. *Recordings include:* albums: Martha Wainwright 2005, I Know You're Married But I've Got Feelings Too 2008, Sans Fusils, Ni Souliers, à Paris 2009, Come Home to Mama 2012, Trauma: Chansons de la serie tele Saison 4 2013. *Current Management:* c/o Gold Village Entertainment, 260 West 35th Street, 13th Floor, New York, NY 10001, USA. *Website:* www .marthawainwright.com.

WAINWRIGHT, Rufus; American singer, musician (piano) and songwriter; b. 22 July 1973, Rhinebeck, NY; s. of Loudon Wainwright III and the late Kate McGarrigle. *Career:* sang backing vocals on tour with mother and aunt (folk duo Kate and Anna McGarrigle) 1980s; left univ. to perform own songs in and around Montréal; Co-founder Kate McGarrigle Foundation. *Contributions to film soundtracks:* The Myth of Fingerprints 1997, Big Daddy 1999, Shrek 2001, Moulin Rouge! 2001, Zoolander 2001, I Am Sam 2001. *Opera:* Prima Donna (premiere with Opera North, Manchester) 2009. *Recordings include:* albums: Rufus Wainwright 1998, Poses 2001, Want One 2003, Want Two 2004, Release the Stars 2007, Rufus Does Judy at Carnegie Hall 2007, Milwaukee at Last! 2009, All Days are Nights: Songs for Lulu 2010, House of Rufus 2011, Out of the Game 2012, Live from the Artists Den 2014. *Current Management:* c/o Mark Adelman, Career Artist Management, 9350 North Civic Center Drive, Los Angeles, CA 90210, USA. *E-mail:* mark.adelman@ camanagement.com. *Website:* www.rufuswainwright.com.

WAITE, John; British singer, songwriter and musician (bass, harmonica); b. 4 July 1955, England. *Career:* mem. The Babys 1976–81; solo artist 1981–; singer, Bad English 1989–91. *Recordings include:* albums: with The Babys: The Babys 1976, Broken Heart 1977, Head First 1978, Union Jacks 1980, On The Edge 1980, Anthology 1981; solo: Ignition 1982, No Brakes 1984, Mask of Smiles 1985, Rovers Return 1987, The Essential 1991, Temple Bar 1995, When You Were Mine 1997, The King Biscuit Flower Hour 1999, These Times are Hard for Lovers 1999, Driver's Eyes 1999, Figure In A Landscape 2001, The Hard Way 2004, Downtown: Journey of a Heart 2006, Rough & Tumble 2011; with Bad English: Bad English 1989, Backlash 1991. *Current Management:* c/o Artists International Management, Inc, 2901 Clint Moore Road, #420, Boca Raton, FL 33496, USA. *Website:* www.johnwaite.com; www .johnwaiteworldwide.com.

WAITS, Tom; American singer, songwriter, musician (piano, guitar, percussion) and actor; b. 7 Dec. 1949, Pomona, Calif.; m. Kathleen Brennan 1980; two s. one d. *Career:* recording artist 1971–. *Theatre:* Frank's Wild Years (co-writer, play and music) 1986, The Black Rider 1989, Alice 1992, Woyzeck 2002. *Films:* Paradise Alley 1978, Wolfen 1981, One From the Heart 1982, The Outsiders 1983, Rumblefish 1983, The Cotton Club 1984, Down By Law 1986, Ironweed 1987, Candy Mountain 1988, Cold Feet 1989, Mystery Train 1989, Bearskin: An Urban Fairytale 1989, The Two Jakes 1990, Queen's Logic 1991, The Fisher King 1991, At Play in the Fields of the Lord 1991, Bram Stoker's Dracula 1992, Short Cuts 1993, Mystery Men 1999, Coffee and Cigarettes 2003, Domino 2005, Wristcutters: A Love Story 2006, Seven Psychopaths 2012. *Compositions include:* Ol' 55, The Eagles 1974, Angel Wings, Rickie Lee Jones 1983, Downtown Train, Rod Stewart 1990, The Long Way Home, Norah Jones 2004, Temptation, Diana Krall 2004, Jersey Girl, Bruce Springsteen, Domino 2005. *Recordings include:* albums: Closing Time 1973, The Heart of Saturday Night 1974, Nighthawks at the Diner 1975, Small Change 1976, Foreign Affairs 1977, Blue Valentine 1978, Heartattack and Vine 1980, Bounced Checks 1981, One from the Heart 1982, Swordfishtrombones 1983, Anthology 1983, Asylum Years 1984, Rain Dogs 1985, Frank's Wild Years 1987, Big Time 1988, The Early Years 1991, The Early Years Vol. 2 1992,

Night on Earth (with Kathleen Brennan) 1992, Bone Machine (Grammy Award for Best Alternative Music 1993) 1992, The Black Rider 1993, Beautiful Maladies 1998, Mule Variations 2000, Used Songs 1973–80 2001, Alice 2002, Blood Money 2002, Real Gone 2004, Orphans: Brawlers, Bawlers & Bastards 2006, Bad As Me 2011. *Honours:* Grammy Award for Best Alternative Album 1992, for Best Contemporary Folk Album 2000, inducted into Rock N Roll Hall of Fame 2011. *Current Management:* c/o Anti-Inc, 2798 Sunset Blvd, Los Angeles, CA 90026, USA. *E-mail:* info@anti.com. *Website:* www.anti.com; www.tomwaits.com.

WAKEFIELD MILLSAPS, Wilma; American singer, songwriter and musician (guitar); b. 13 Feb. 1949, Monroe Co., TN; m. Bill Millsaps 1967, one s. one d. *Education:* studied with Tommy Scott. *Career:* travelled extensively across USA with husband, Bill Millsaps and their Snowbird Mountain Band; appeared on satellite TV on Snowbird Mountain Bluegrass; mem. BMI, IBMA. *Recordings include:* albums: Legendary Friends of The Snowbird Mountain Band, The Singing Waterfall, 35 Years of Bluegrass Gospel. *Address:* Millsaps Music, PO Box 985, Robbinsville, NC 28771, USA. *E-mail:* millsapsmusic@yahoo.com. *Website:* billandwilmamillsaps.tripod.com.

WAKEMAN, Adam; British musician (keyboards, guitar, vocals) and songwriter; b. 11 March 1974, Windsor, Berks., England; s. of Rick Wakeman; m. Terri Wakeman; three c. *Education:* Grade 8, Associated Bd of the Royal Schools of Music. *Career:* toured the world with Wakeman band alongside father, Rick 1992–2003; Musical Dir Atomic Kitten 2002–03; toured with Artful Dodger 2001, Victoria Beckham 2001–02, Travis 2003–07, Annie Lennox 2003, Ozzy Osbourne 2003–, Black Sabbath 2004–05, 2012–13, Will Young 2008–11; currently mem. Headspace; mem. Performing Right Soc. *Films:* wrote credit music for The Woman and the Machine (Winner of Best Short Film) 2011, Nothing Man (musical score for full-length feature) 2013. *Radio:* co-hosted monthly progressive rock radio show on Total Rock Radio 2011–12. *Television:* Live 8 performance with Travis; Jools Holland, Jay Leno, Jimmy Kimmel, Letterman, Ellen, CD:UK, Top of the Pops, The Chart Show (T4). *Recordings:* albums: Wakeman with Wakeman, No Expense Spared, Romance Of A Victorian Age, The Official Bootleg, Tapestries 1995, Vignettes 1996, Return To The Centre Of The Earth 1999, Tales Of Future And Past 2001; solo: Soliloquy, 100 Years Overtime, Real World Trilogy 1997, The Classical Connection 2000, Neurasthenia; contribs to Yes Tribute album, Tales of Yesterday, co-wrote five songs for Ozzy Osbourne's platinum-selling album Scream 2010, co-wrote Headspace's debut album I Am Anonymous 2012, Snakecharmer's self-titled debut album 2013. *Honours:* Best New Talent, Keyboard Player magazine 1994. *Address:* Boundary Barn, Chetwode Road, Barton Hartshorn, Bucks., MK18 4DL, England (office). *Telephone:* 7773-771405 (mobile) (office). *E-mail:* adamwakeman@gmail.com (office). *Website:* www.headspaceonline.com (office); www.adamwakeman.co.uk.

WAKEMAN, Dusty; American musician (bass guitar), record producer and engineer; b. 31 Aug. 1953, Houston, Tex.; m. Szu Wang 1986. *Education:* Univ. of Texas, studied music with Jamie Faunt. *Career:* mixer, engineer, bassist, numerous recordings 1986–; Founder and Pres., Mad Dog Studios for 28 years; joined Mojave Audio 2005, currently Pres. *Recordings include:* mixer, engineer, producer, bassist on albums by Dwight Yoakam, Rosie Flores, Lucinda Williams, Buck Owens, Michelle Shocked, Los Lobos, Jackson Browne, Wynton Marsalis, Tom Russell, Ralph Stanley, American Pie, Giant Sand, Steve Forbert, Heather Myles. *Honours:* two Grammy Awards (for Cryin', Roy Orbison/kd lang 1987), (Ain't That Lonely Yet, Dwight Yoakam 1993). *Address:* Mojave Audio, 2711 Empire Avenue, Burbank, CA 9150, USA (office). *Website:* www.mojaveaudio.com (office).

WAKEMAN, Rick; British musician (keyboards); b. 18 May 1949, London, England. *Career:* mem. progressive rock group, Yes 1971–74, 1976–80, formed group, Anderson Bruford Wakeman Howe 1989, then re-adopted the name Yes 1991–; numerous int. concert performances; solo artist 1974–. *Recordings:* albums: with Yes: The Yes Album 1971, Fragile 1971, Close To The Edge 1972, Yessongs 1973, Tales From The Topographic Oceans 1973, Relayer 1974, Yesterdays 1975, Going For The One 1977, Tormato 1978, Drama 1980, Yesshows 1980, Union 1991, Yesstory 1991, Symphonic Music Of Yes 1993, History Of The Future 1993, Talk 1994, An Evening Of Yes Music Plus 1994, Keys To Ascension 1996, Open Your Eyes 1997, Something's Coming 1998, The Ladder 1999, House Of Yes: Live From House Of Blues 2000, Magnification 2001, Keystudio 2001, Yestoday 2002, Yes Remixes 2003, Yes And Friends 2003, Re(Union) 2004; as Anderson Bruford Wakeman Howe: Anderson Bruford Wakeman Howe 1989; solo: Piano Vibrations 1971, The Six Wives of Henry VIII 1973, Journey To The Centre Of The Earth 1974, Lisztomania 1975, Myths And Legends Of King Arthur And The Knights Of The Round Table 1975, No Earthly Connections 1976, White Rock 1976, Criminal Record 1977, Rhapsodies 1979, 1984 1981, Rock & Roll Prophet 1982, The Burning 1982, Golé! (soundtrack) 1983, Crimes Of Passion 1984, Beyond The Planets 1984, Country Airs 1986, Cost Of Living 1987, Family Album 1987, The Gospels 1987, A Suite Of Gods 1988, Zodiaque 1988, In The Beginning 1990, Silent Nights 1991, Time Machine 1991, Black Knights At The Court Of Ferdinand IV 1991, 2000 AD Into The Future 1991, Phantom Power 1991, Aspirant Sunset 1991, The Classical Connection 1991, With Wakeman 1992, African Bach 1993, Heritage Suite 1993, Prayers 1993, Word And The Gospels 1994, The Official Bootleg 1994, Sea Airs 1994, Lure Of The Wild 1994, No Expense Spared 1994, Romance Of The Victorian Age 1994, Night Airs 1995, Cirque Surreal 1995, Piano Album 1995, Softsword (King John And The Magna Carta) 1995, The New Gospels 1995, The Seven

Wonders Of The World 1995, Visions 1995, Fields Of Green 1996, Winterland 1975 1996, Tapestries 1996, Aspirant Sunrise 1996, Aspirant Sunshadows 1996, Voyager 1996, Can You Hear Me? 1996, Orisons 1996, The Word And Music 1996, Vignettes 1996, Simply Acoustic: The Music 1997, Tribute To The Beatles 1998, Themes 1998, The Art In Music Trilogy 1999, White Rock II 1999, Preludes To A Century 2000, Stella Bianca 2000, Chronicles Of Man 2000, Christmas Variations 2000, Morning Has Broken 2000, The Definitive Music Of Rick Wakeman 2002, A Tribute To The Lord Of The Rings 2002, Hummingbird 2003, My Inspiration 2003, The Real Lisztomania 2003, Missing Half 2003, Into Orbit 2003, Medium Rare 2003, Almost Classical 2004, Mixture 2004, Revisited 2004. *Current Management: c/o* Trudy Green, HK Management, 9200 Sunset Boulevard, Suite 530, Los Angeles, CA 90069, USA. *E-mail:* yes@yesworld.com (office). *Website:* www.yesworld.com; www .rwcc.com.

WALDEN, Chris; German composer and arranger (trumpet); b. 10 Oct. 1966, Hamburg; m. Beate Walden 1996; one s. one d. *Education:* Music Univ., Cologne. *Career:* mem. GEMA, American Soc. of Composers, Authors and Publrs, SCL. *Compositions:* A Deadly Vision, suite for symphony orchestra; Opus 3, for orchestra. *Recordings include:* Smokie 1994, Harlem Gospel Singers 1998; solo: Chris Walden-Ticino 1995, Chris Walden Big Band-Home Of My Heart 2005, Chris Walden Big Band-No Bounds 2006, Chris Walden Big Band & St. John's Choir-Kurt Marti Suite 2007, Chris Walden-Symphony No.1, The Four Elements 2008, Chris Walden Big Band-Full-On 2014. *Honours:* Ernst Fischer Prizes 1993, 1997. *Current Management: c/o* Patty Macmillan, Allegro Talent Group, 30700 Russell Ranch Road, Suite #250, Westlake Village, CA 91362, USA. *E-mail:* pattymac@allegrotalentgroup.com. *E-mail:* info@chriswalden.com. *Website:* www.chriswalden.com.

WALDEN, John 'White Boy'; British musician (harmonica) and blues singer; b. 23 Oct. 1948, London; m. Natalie Marjory Gellineau 1982; one s. one d. *Career:* took up harmonica as a child; started to play blues aged 13 with Bespoke Tailor Unit; several European tours with John Walden Workshop, late 1960s, Madison Blues Band 1990s; re-formed John Walden's Blues Band 1997; mem. Musicians' Union. *Recordings:* many sessions, soundtracks, commercials; John Walden's Blues Band 1997; collaborators include Brian Green. *Honours:* Medal Winner, European Harp (Harmonica) Festival, Trossingham, Germany 1996.

WALDEN, Myron; American jazz musician (alto saxophone), songwriter and arranger; b. 18 Oct. 1972, Miami, Fla. *Education:* La Guardia High School of Music and Art, Harlem School of the Arts, Manhattan School of Music. *Career:* fmr mem. LaGuardia Senior Jazz Band, LaGuardia Jazz Sextet, All City Jazz Band, All State Jazz Ensemble; has performed and recorded with Nat Adderley, Jon Hendricks, James Spaulding, Jimmy Owens, Jimmy Cobb, Wynton Marsalis, Freddie Hubbard, Joe Chambers, Joe Williams, Roy Hargrove, Jon Ore, Cecil Payne, Harry Connick Jr, Walter Booker, Ron Carter, Benny Golson, Winard Harper, Eddie Henderson, Kevin Hays, Mulgrew Miller. *Recordings include:* albums: Hypnosis 1996, Like a Flower Seeking the Sun 1999, Higher Ground 2002, This Way 2005, Momentum 2009, In This World: What We Share 2010, In This World: To Feel 2010, Countryfied 2010, Apex Live: Volume I 2010, Apex Live: Volume II 2010. *Honours:* Young and Upcoming Artist, Yamaha Corporation 1990, Saxophonist of the Year, Harlem School of The Arts, winner, Charlie Parker Competition 1993. *Current Management: c/o* Shore Fire Media, 32 Court Street, Suite 1600, Brooklyn, NY 11201, USA. *Telephone:* (718) 522-7171. *E-mail:* nlosseaton@shorefire.com. *Website:* www.shorefire.com. *E-mail:* myronwalden@earthlink.net (office). *Website:* www.myronwalden.com.

WALDEN, Narada Michael; American singer, musician (drums, keyboards), record producer and songwriter; b. 23 April 1952, Kalamazoo, Michigan; m. Anukampa Coles. *Education:* Western Michigan Univ. *Career:* drummer, with John McLaughlin 1974–76; Pres., Perfection Light Productions 1976–; Owner Tarpan Studios; currently mem. Temple of Soul; Bd of Dir, Bay Area Music Awards, San Francisco 1992. *Recordings include:* solo albums: Garden of Love Light 1977, I Cry, I Smile 1978, Awakening 1979, The Dance of Life 1979, Victory 1980, Confidence 1982, Looking At You, Looking At Me 1983, The Nature of Things 1985, Divine Emotion 1985, Thunder 2012; with John McLaughlin: Apocalypse 1974, Visions of The Emerald Beyond 1975, Inner Worlds 1976; with Temple of Soul: Brothers in Arms 2008; other recordings as musician: Teaser, Tom Bolin 1975, Wired, Jeff Beck 1976, My Spanish Heart, Chick Corea 1976, Jaco Pastorius, Jaco Pastorius 1976, Black Market, Weather Report 1976, Loading Zone, Roy Buchanan 1977, Velvet Darkness, Allan Holdsworth 1977, Exposure, Robert Fripp 1979, Oneness, Santana 1979, Clarke Duke Project 2, Stanley Clarke 1983, Patti Austin, Patti Austin 1984, Teaser, Angela Bofill 1984, Who's Zoomin' Who, Aretha Franklin 1985, Through The Storm, Aretha Franklin 1989; as musician and producer: Hero, Clarence Clemons 1985, While The City Sleeps, George Benson 1986; as producer: with Sister Sledge: Love Somebody Today 1980, All American Girls 1981, Rose is Still a Rose, Aretha Franklin 1998, Ladies and Gentlemen, George Michael 1998, Definitive Collection, Angela Bofill 1999, Best of Bond...James Bond 1999, Love Songs, Jefferson Airplane 2000; with Whitney Houston: Whitney Houston 1985, I'm Your Baby Tonight 1990; other artists include: Phyllis Hyman, Gladys Knight, Mica Paris, Regina Belle, Al Jarreau. *Honours:* NARAS Award for Songwriter of the Year 1986, Grammy 1986, ASCAP Awards for Producer of the Year, Songwriter of the Year, Publisher of the Year 1987, Billboard Magazine Producer of the Year 1986, 1987. *Address:* Tarpan Studios, 1925 East Francisco Boulevard, Suite 1, San Rafael, CA 94901, USA (office). *Telephone:* (415) 485-1999 (office). *Fax:* (415) 459-3234 (office). *E-mail:* info@narandamichaelwalden.com. *Website:* www .naradamichaelwalden.com; www.tarpanstudios.com (office).

WALDEN, Natan, MFA; musician (bass, keyboards) and composer; b. 3 Nov. 1947, Bystrzyca, Klodska, Poland; m. Ewa Kryger-Walden 1974, one s. one d. *Education:* Lund Univ., Sweden, Malmö Acad. of Music, Sweden. *Career:* in Poland mem., Nastolatki (Teenagers); bass player with singer, Niemen; in USA live work, studio work commercials with Billy Cobham and Valerie Simpson; in Sweden, studio work, theatre-musical, Röda Orm; Animalen; Blood Brothers; TV and live works with Toots Thielemans; Nestor Marconi; Lill Babs, Eurovision Song Contest; Musical Dir many TV shows on Swedish TV; many theme songs for TV serials, Sköna Söndag; Vem Tar Vem; Helt Apropa; in Denmark, mem. The Most; bass player, in live concert versions of a musical Chees; with three orchestras, Danish Radio Orchestra, Odense Symphonic Orchestra, Sonderjisk Symphonic Orchestra; mem. Swedish Soc. of Popular Music Composers. *Honours:* Golden Rose Montreux for music production of The Prize, Emmy Award 1987. *Address:* 14 Henrietta Street, London, WC2E 8QH, England.

WALI, Ahmad; Afghan singer and songwriter; b. Kabul; s. of Mohammad Akram Nawabi; m. 1st; one s.; m. 2nd. *Education:* studied tabla with Ustad Mohammad Hashim. *Career:* solo artist 1970–; exiled in Germany 1980, later USA. *Recordings include:* albums: numerous recordings for radio 1967–80 and cassette recordings in 1980s–90s in Germany and the USA; Atish 1996, Ba yaad daari 1996, Safar 1997, Henna 1998, Sahib nazaraan 1999, Tamana 1999, Shaam-e ghazal 2000, Par-e taawoos 2001, Awaragee (Vol. I and II) 2001, Khaak-e Kabul 2002, Chashm-e shokh 2005, Aarezo 2005. *E-mail:* ahmad.wali@sbcglobal.net. *Website:* www.ahmadwalimusic.info.

WALKER, Clay; American country singer, songwriter and musician (guitar); b. (Ernest Clayton Jr), 9 Aug. 1969, Beaumont, Texas. *Education:* taught guitar by his father. *Career:* played bars in Beaumont, Texas area from age 16, before giving concerts more extensively in Louisiana, Oklahoma and New Mexico; resident singer at Neon Armadillo bar, Beaumont, securing record contract with Giant Records. *Recordings include:* albums: Clay Walker 1993, If I Could Make A Living 1994, Hypnotize The Moon 1995, Self Portrait 1996, Rumor Has It 1997, Live Laugh Love 1999, Say No More 2001, Christmas 2002, A Few Questions 2003, Fall 2007, She Won't Be Lonely Long 2010; singles: What's It to You 1993, Live Until I Die 1993, Dreaming with My Eyes Open 1994, If I Could Make a Living 1994, This Woman and This Man 1995. *Publication:* Jesus Was a Country Boy 2013. *Honours:* Radio & Records Award for Best New Male Artist 1993, Country Song Roundup Award for Best New Male Vocalist 1995. *Current Management: c/o* Upward Management, 2409 21st Avenue South, Suite 205, Nashville, TN 37212, USA. *Telephone:* (615) 297-6919. *E-mail:* liesl@upward-management.com. *Website:* www.upward -management.com. *E-mail:* info@claywalker.com (office). *Website:* www .claywalker.com.

WALKER, Eddie; British singer, musician (guitar) and songwriter; b. 31 Oct. 1948, Middlesbrough, Cleveland, England; m. Judith Ann 1969; one s. *Education:* diploma in public health, Charles Trevelyan Tech. Coll., Newcastle. *Career:* concert, folk festival and club appearances throughout UK, Germany, Belgium, Netherlands, Italy, Austria, Denmark, Slovenia, Croatia, Switzerland, Ireland, Luxembourg, Hong Kong, Bangkok, NZ; radio and TV appearances; currently working solo and with Fraser Speirs (Glasgow) harmonica, ex-Paolo Nutini Band; mem. Performing Right Soc., Mechanical-Copyright Protection Soc., Musicians' Union, PPL. *Recordings:* albums: solo: Everyday Man 1977, Castle Cafe 1981, Red Shoes On My Feet 1983, Picking My Way 1985; with guitarist John James: Carolina Shout! 1990, Sidesteppin 1993, Live At The Albert Hole! (solo video album) 1996, Mind To Ramble 2000, Breakfast in Delhi? 2003, The Blues Ain't Nothin' 2003, You Better Sell It! (DVD) 2004, Red Shoes and Blues 2012. *Honours:* Northumbria Trophy for Songwriting 1975, solo winner Slough Arts Festival 1977, winner Songwriter Competition (for Stolen My Heart Away) 1982. *Address:* 33 The Grove, Brookfield, Middlesbrough, Cleveland, TS5 8DT, England (office). *E-mail:* eddie.walker13@ntlworld.com (office). *Website:* www.eddiewalker.net; www .myspace.com/eddiewalker.

WALKER, Johnny; American singer and musician (guitar). *Career:* mem., Henry & June 1994–96, Soledad Brothers 1998–2006, Cut in the Hill Gang 2007–. *Recordings include:* albums: with Soledad Brothers 2000, Steal Your Soul (And Dare Your Spirit To Move) 2002, Live 2003, Voice Of Treason 2003, The Hardest Walk 2006; with Cut in the Hill Gang: Cut Down 2009, Mean Black Cat 2011. *Address:* 1203 Ferdinand, Detroit, MI 48209, USA. *Website:* www.myspace.com/cutinthehillgang.

WALKER, Mark Robert Thomas; British musician (drums), lyricist, songwriter and journalist; b. 7 March 1962, London; m. Claire Cooper 1988; one s. two d. *Education:* BEd Hons. *Career:* tours with the Tin Gods, UK, Europe; appeared at Lausanne Festival, Switzerland 1991; television: Hangar 17, BBC 1; radio: live sessions for Capital Radio and GLR with Peachey Keen and World of Leather; TV appearances: house band drummer for the Jack Dee Show, National Lottery Show, Blue Peter, This Morning, Night Fever, London Tonight, The Big Stage and the Esther Show with Rolf Harris; solo performer of drum shows and clinics; British tours and live concert appearances with Rolf Harris including Glastonbury Festival (three times) 1997–2003, Ireland 1999, Capetown, South Africa 2000; solo performer of The Have-A-Go Drum Show, appearances include GMTV, This Morning, Rhythmsticks 1998, 1999,

2000, Festival Hall, National Music Show, Wembley, BBC Music Live, Mad About Music, Docklands Arena, Duo Drum 'n' Didg, appearances include Rhythmsticks 1999 and Horniman Museum, Drumming in London West End production, Walt Disney's The Lion King; mem. Musicians' Union, PAMRA, PAS. *Recordings:* St Mark's Place, World of Leather (debut album), The Coronation Street Album, Invisible History Of The Black Celt, Martin Okasili, Private Party, Akin; numerous recording sessions with producers Robin Miller, Faney, Colin Fairley, Jeff Foster; composed theme tune for Airdrum (cartoon series); with Rolf Harris: albums: Bootleg 1 and 70/30; single: Christmas in the Sun, Fine Day. *Publications:* The Court of King Rolf – a tribute book to Rolf Harris 2000; regular features writer for Rhythm magazine, including series The Secret Diary of a Session Drummer Aged 33 3/4, The Rudiments of Time, Rhythm Beginners, Xtreme Drums 2004. *Current Management:* Active Entertainment Management. *Address:* Myrtus, Eridge Road, Crowborough, East Sussex, TN6 2SP, England. *E-mail:* mark@mark-walker.co.uk. *Website:* www.mark-walker.co.uk.

WALKER, Scott; American singer, songwriter and musician (bass); b. (Noel Scott Engel), 9 Jan. 1944, Hamilton, OH; m. Mette Teglbjaerg (divorced); one d. *Education:* studied fine art and the double bass. *Career:* mem., The Routers 1963, Dalton Brothers 1964, Walker Brothers 1965–67, 1975–78; regular television appearances, concert tours; solo artist 1967–. *Recordings include:* albums: with the Walker Brothers: Take It Easy With The Walker Brothers 1966, Portrait 1966, Images 1967, No Regrets 1976, Lines 1977, Nite Flights 1978, After The Lights Go Out 1990; solo: Scott 1967, Scott 2 1968, Scott 3 1969, Scott 4 1970, Til The Band Comes In 1971, The Moviegoer 1972, Any Day Now 1973, Stretch 1974, We Had It All 1974, Scott Walker Plays Jacques Brel 1981, Climate of Hunter 1984, Boy Child 1990, Tilt 1995, Pola X 1999, Classics and Collectibles 2005, The Drift 2006, And who shall go to the ball? And what shall go to the ball? 2007, Bish Bosch 2012, Soused 2014. *Address:* c/o 4AD, 17–19 Alma Road, London, SW18 1AA, England. *E-mail:* 4ad@4ad.com. *Website:* www.4ad.com/scottwalker.

WALKER SMITH, Nicola, BA, MA; British singer; b. 18 Feb. 1964, Batley, West Yorkshire; m. Geoff Smith 1989; two s. (twins). *Education:* Keele Univ., Birmingham Univ. *Career:* world-wide concert appearances; television and radio includes: In Tune (BBC Radio 3), Midnight Oil, Music In Our Time, The Late Show (BBC 2); other radio broadcasts world-wide; performances include: Spindle And Shuttle, by Phillip Flood, 1992. *Recordings:* albums: The Garden 1991, Gas Food Lodging 1993, Fifteen Wild Decembers 1995, Black Flowers, with the Geoff Smith Band 1997, L'imboscata, with Franco Battiato 1997. *Publications:* American Originals (with Geoff Smith) 1994. *Honours:* Winston Churchill Fellowship 1992. *Current Management:* Kitchenware Management, 7 The Stables, Saint Thomas Street, Newcastle Upon Tyne, NE1 4LE, England. *Telephone:* (191) 230-1970. *Fax:* (191) 232-0262. *E-mail:* info@kitchenwarerecords.com. *Website:* www.kitchenwarerecords.com.

WALL, Jack; American composer and producer; *Senior Director, Game Audio Network Guild. Career:* fmr recording/mix engineer in New York, working with artists including David Byrne, John Cale, Patti Smith and Dr John; composer, especially scores for computer games as Wall of Sound 1995–; co-founder and Sr Dir Game Audio Network Guild (GANG) 2002–, co-creator of Video Games Live exhibition. *Computer game scores:* Evil Dead: Hail to the King 2000, Myst III: Exile 2001, Unreal II: The Awakening 2003, Splinter Cell: Pandora Tomorrow 2004, Myst IV: Revelation 2004, Wrath Unleashed 2004, Jade Empire 2005, Neopets 2005, Mass Effect 2007. *Address:* Game Audio Network Guild, PO Box 1001, San Juan Capistrano, CA 92393, USA (office). *E-mail:* info@audiogang.org (office). *Website:* www.audiogang.org; www.jackwall.net.

WALLACE, Angus (Gus), MA; British recording studio owner, sound designer, lecturer and farmer; b. 7 April 1968, Guilsborough, Northants, England. *Education:* School of Recording, Brixton, London. *Career:* owner, Far Heath recording studio 1986–; worked with Love and Rockets, David J, Unisex, Wishbone Ash, Spiritualized, The Fall, Natacha Atlas (Transglobal Underground), The Prodigy, Devon Sproule, Toyah Willcox, Seafood. *Honours:* Ampex Golden Reel Award 1994. *Current Management:* Heathen Management, Coton, Northants., NN6 8RF, England. *Address:* Far Heath, Guilsborough, Northants., NN6 8RH, England (office). *Website:* www.farheath.com (office).

WALLACE, Robert Andrew; Scottish musician (pipes); b. 21 Nov. 1951, Glasgow; one s. one d. *Career:* Member, folk band Whistlebinkies, 1974–; Appeared on television and radio with RSNO, Scottish Ensemble, John Cage, Yehudi Menuhin; mem, Musicians' Union; CPA; Piobaireachd Society. *Recordings:* 5 albums with Whistlebinkies; Solo albums: Chance Was A Fine Thing, 1982; Piper of Distinction, 1990; Also features on: On The West Side, Donnie Munro, 2000. *Publications:* Glasgow Collection of Bagpipe Music. *Honours:* Gold Medal, Oban, 1985; Bratach Gorm (Blue Banner), London, 1989. *Address:* The College of Piping, 16-24 Otago Street, Glasgow, G12 8JH, Scotland. *E-mail:* mail@whistlebinkies.net. *Website:* www.whistlebinkies.net.

WALLEMME, Christophe; French musician (acoustic bass); b. 1964. *Education:* studied with M. Kazoran, Hein van de Guyn, Césarius Alvim. *Career:* mem., PRYSM, Manuel Rocheman Trio, David Patrois Trio, David Patrois Quintet, Sarah Lazarus Quartet, Lois Winsberg Quintet, Jean-Pierre Como Quintet, Jean-Loup Longnon Sextet and Big Band; played numerous clubs in Paris, festival appearances; played with Tom Harrell, Ted Curson, Jean-Loup Longnon, Rick Margitza, Sylvain Beuf, Eric Barret, Richard

Galliano, Philip Catherine, Christian Escoudé, N'Guyen Lee, Stephanie Crawford, Walter Davis Jr, Barry Altschul, René Urtreger, Michel Graillier, Alain Jean-Marie, Georges Arvanitas, Jacky Terrasson, Jean-Pierre Como, Denuis Badault, Bob Mover, George Brown, Aldo Romano; teacher, EDIM 1986–. *Recordings include:* Bop For Sale, Ludovic de Preissac Quintet 1989, Correspondence, Daniel Beaussier Quartet 1990, Ciao Mon Coeur, Elizabeth Caumont 1993, Sanscrit, Daniel Beaussier Quartet 1993, Impro Primo, Sylvain Beuf Quartet 1993, Cyclades, Jean-Loup Lognon Big Band 1994, PRYSM, PRYSM 1995, Tropic City, Manuel Rocheman Trio 1995, Express Paris-Rome, Jean-Pierre Como Quintet 1996, Louis Winsberg Quintet. *Honours:* La Défense Nat. Jazz Contest Soloist Award 1988, first prize Jazz et Polar Contest 1991, first prize La Défense Nat. Jazz Contest 1994. *Address:* 25 rue Eugène Prévot, 77400 Lagny sur Marne, France (home). *Telephone:* 1-60-07-01-44 (home). *Website:* /www.christophe-wallemme.com.

WALLEN, Errollyn, BMus, MMus, Mphil, MBE; British composer and musician (keyboard); *Visiting Composer-in-Residence, Birmingham Conservatoire;* b. 10 April 1968, Belize City, Belize. *Education:* Dance Theatre of Harlem, New York, USA, Goldsmiths' Coll., London, King's Coll., London, King's Coll., Cambridge. *Career:* joined alternative cabaret band, Pulse as composer, singer and keyboardist 1983–85; freelance keyboard player 1985; opened Wallen Parr recording studio and music-production co., London 1986; composer for corporate video, film and TV 1986–; featured composer for Huddersfield Contemporary Music Festival; mem. and composer, Nanquidno 1987; composer-in-residence, Newcastle Electric Music 3 Festival 1988; founder mem. Women in Music 1987, Ensemble X 1990; part-time lecturer, Nottingham Trent Univ. 1991; guest performer and lecturer, Ga State Univ., Atlanta 1991, Lincoln Centre, New York 2003; external examiner, Brighton Univ.; leader of composition workshops in various schools, and in asscn with London Sinfonietta and Hayward Gallery 1998; founder mem. Women in Music 1987–; mem. Performing Rights Soc., British Asscn of Songwriters, Composers and Authors; Research Assoc., Middlesex Univ.; commission to compose Community Opera for Oldham 2002; Composer in Residence, Trinity Coll. of Music, Birmingham Conservatoire; mem. Bd of Trustees, Children's Music Workshop 2005–. *Compositions:* It's a Quarter to Nine 1968, Song Cycle 1976, Deaths and Entrances 1979, Concert 1980, Three Piano Pieces 1980, Three Elizabethan Songs 1980, Violin 1981, We Four Kings 1981, Quartet for wind instruments and cello 1982, Trio for two flutes and vibraphone 1982, Lines 1982, Music for small orchestra 1983, Still Lives 1983, Variations for string quartet 1983, Pulse Songs 1983–85, Psalm 150 1986, Second String Quartet 1988, Big Business 1988, Take 1988, Mythologies 1988, Memorias de un corazón en un pueblo pequeño 1989, It All Depends on You 1989, Jelly Dub Mix 1990, The Girl in My Alphabet 1990, Favourite Things 1990, In Our Lifetime 1990, The Singing Ringing Tree 1991, Dark Heart 1991, Until You Do 1991, Having Gathered his Cohorts 1991, I Hate Waiting 1991, Mondrian 1992, Heart 1992, E.D.R. 1993, Four Figures with Harlequin (opera) 1993, 1-2-3-4 (ballet) 1993, Waiting (ballet) 1993, Concerto for percussion and orchestra 1993–94, My Lazy Goodheart 1994, Are You Worried about the Rising Cost of Funerals?: Five Simple Songs 1994, Gastarbeiter 1994, Teeth 1994, Dogness 1994, Phonecalls from Besieged Cities 1994, Chorale 1995, Jig 1995, Look! No Hands! (opera) 1995, The Constant Nymph (for radio) 1996, Prelude 1996, Hunger 1996, Music for Alien Tribes 1996, Earth Stood Hard as Iron 1996, The Devil and the Doctor 1997, One Week Short of a Valentine 1997, Shit in her Eyes 1997, Chrome 1997, Never Ending 1997, Horseplay (ballet) 1997, Oil 1997–98, Peace on Earth (voice and piano) 2007. *Television:* Documentary on composer Samuel Coleridge-Taylor (BBC) 2001. *Recordings:* The Girl In My Alphabet 1990, Meet Me At Harold Moore's 1998, Errollyn 2004, Spirit Symphony – Speed-Dating for Two Orchestras (BBC Radio 3 Listeners Award British Composer Awards British Acad. of Composers and Songwriters 2005). *Publications:* Art Not Chance (contrib.), Private Views (contrib. *Honours:* Arts Council Bursary 1987, Holst Award 1991, Cosmopolitan Achievement Award 1993, Peter Whittingham Award 1995. *Address:* c/o Volker Schirp, Peters Edition, 10–12 Baches Street, London, N1 6DN, England (office). *E-mail:* errollyn@errollynwallen.com (office). *Website:* www.errollynwallen.com.

WALLER, Paul; British record producer, remixer, programmer and songwriter; b. 1961, London; two s. one d. *Career:* mem. Musicians' Union. *Recordings include:* producer of records by Björk, Soul II Soul, Naughty By Nature, Lisa Stansfield, Babyface, Eric Clapton, Elton John, Heather Small, The Spice Girls, Art Of Noise, Louise, Shola Ama.

WALLET OUMAR, Mina; Malian singer and musician (percussion); b. 1982, Kidal. *Career:* mem. Touareg group, Tinariwen. *Recordings include:* albums: The Radio Tisdas Sessions 2000, Amassakoul 2004, Aman Iman: Water is Life 2007, Imidiwan (Uncut Music Award) 2009, Tassili 2011, Emmaar 2014. *Honours:* BBC Radio 3 Award for World Music (Africa) 2005. *E-mail:* wavelabinc@gmail.com. *Website:* www.tinariwen.com.

WALLGREN, Henrik; Swedish singer and songwriter; b. 10 Sept. 1965, Gothenburg; m. Katarina Wallgren 1988; two d. *Career:* formed ORO 1990; numerous live appearances; solo artist 1996–; mem. Swedish Composers of Popular Music. *Compositions:* new score to Mother Courage 1994, Nosferatu 1995. *Recordings include:* Milk and Concrete 1990, Iron-Storm 1992, Ragamedon... 2048 1993, Quake! 1995, Walk On By 1996. *Honours:* Grammy Award, Sweden 1993, City of Gothenburg Prize 1997.

WALSH, Greg; record producer; b. England. *Career:* producer for Heaven 17, Tina Turner, Xymox; Chicago, Elkie Brooks, Lucio Battisti, British Lions, Trainspotting, Ron. *Address:* Shmusicmusic/Veracruz Music, PO Box 4232, Dunstable, Bedfordshire LU5 4XR, England. *Telephone:* (1582) 609720. *Website:* www.shmusismusic.com.

WALSH, James; British singer, (musician (guitar) and songwriter; b. 9 June 1980, Chorley, Lancashire, England; one d. *Career:* mem. Starsailor 2000–. *Recordings include:* albums: Love Is Here 2001, Silence Is Easy 2003, On the Outside 2005, All the Plans 2009; solo: Lullaby 2012, Turning Point 2014. *Website:* www.jameswalshmusic.com; www.starsailor.mu.

WALSH, Joe; American singer, musician (guitar, keyboards) and record producer; b. 20 Nov. 1947, Wichita, Kan. *Education:* Kent State Univ. *Career:* fmr mem. James Gang; solo artist, with own group, Barnstorm 1971–; mem. The Eagles 1975–; numerous tours world-wide. *Recordings include:* with The James Gang: Yer Album 1969, James Gang Rides Again 1970, Thirds 1971, Live In Concert 1971; with The Eagles: One Of These Nights 1975, Hotel California (Grammy Award for Record of the Year 1978, American Music Award for Favorite Pop/Rock Album 1977) 1976, The Long Run 1979, Long Road out of Eden 2007; solo/with Barnstorm: Barnstorm 1972, The Smoker You Drink... 1973, So What 1974, You Can't Argue With A Sick Mind 1976, But Seriously Folks 1978, There Goes The Neighbourhood 1981, You Bought It, You Name It 1983, The Confessor 1985, Got Any Gum? 1987, Ordinary Average Guy 1991, Songs For A Dying Planet 1992, Night Riding 1992, Future To This Life 1995, Robocop (TV series soundtrack) 1995, Analog Man 2012, All Night Long: Live in Dallas 2013. *Honours:* Grammy Awards for Best Vocal Arrangement (for New Kid In Town) 1978, Best Rock Vocal Performance (for Heartache Tonight) 1980, for Best Country Performance by a Duo or Group with Vocals (for How Long) 2008, for Best Pop Instrumental Performance (for I Dreamed There Was No War) 2009, American Music Award for Favorite Pop/Rock Album 1981, Favorite Pop/Rock Band 1981, Nordoff-Robbins Music Therapy Lifetime Achievement Award (with The Eagles) 2006. *Website:* www.joewalsh.com.

WALSH, Kimberley Jane; British singer, actress, dancer and presenter; b. 20 Nov. 1981, Bradford, Yorks., England; d. of John Walsh and Diane Walsh. *Education:* Univ. of Leeds. *Career:* mem. Girls Aloud, pop group created from winning contestants on reality TV show Popstars: The Rivals 2002–13. *Musical:* Shrek The Musical 2011–12. *Films:* St Trinian's 2007, Horrid Henry 2011, All Stars 2013. *Television:* This Is Personal: The Hunt for the Yorkshire Ripper 2000, Focus (BBC TV educational programme) 2001, Dream Back 2001, Girls Aloud: Off the Record 2006, Suck My Pop 2010, MTV Bafta's Red Carpet 2010, EE Bafta's Red Carpet 2011. *Recordings:* albums with Girls Aloud: Sound of the Underground 2003, What Will the Neighbours Say? 2004, Chemistry 2005, Tangled Up 2007, Out of Control 2008, Girls Aloud Greatest Hits 2012; solo album: Kimberley Walsh Centre Stage 2013. *Publication:* A Whole lot of History (autobiog.). *Honours:* Best Single, Disney Channel Awards 2003, Popjustice Music Prize 2003, 2005, 2006, BRIT Award for Best British Single (for The Promise) 2009. *Current Management:* c/o Shaw Thing Management, Unit 12A Utopia Village, 7 Chalcot Road, London, NW1 8LH, England. *Telephone:* (20) 7722-6161. *Fax:* (20) 7722-9661. *E-mail:* hills@ shawthingmanagement.com. *Website:* www.shawthingmanagement.com; www.girlsaloud.co.uk.

WALSH, Louis; Irish artist manager; b. 5 Aug. 1952, Kiltimagh, Co. Mayo. *Career:* worked with Eurovision Song Contest winner Johnny Logan, early 1980s; has managed numerous Irish and British pop acts including Bellefire, Boyzone, Ronan Keating, G4, Six, Girls Aloud, Samantha Mumba, Westlife, Shayne Ward, Eton Road, Code 5, Cilla Black; made first TV appearance as talent show judge in Irish version of Popstars 2001, judge in Popstars: The Rivals (ITV), UK 2002, The X Factor (ITV), UK 2004–, You're A Star (RTE), Ireland. *Address:* Louis Walsh Management, 24 Courtney House, Appian Way, Dublin 6, Ireland (office). *Telephone:* (1) 6680309 (office). *Fax:* (1) 6680721 (office). *E-mail:* info@louiswalsh.net (office).

WALSH, Peter; record producer; b. England. *Career:* producer for Simple Minds, China Crisis, Boomtown Rats, Alphaville, The Church, Scott Walker, Peter Gabriel, Miguel Bose, The Charlatans, Pulp. *Address:* c/o 4AD, 17–19 Alma Road, London, SW18 1AA, England.

WALSH, Steve; American singer, musician (keyboards) and songwriter; b. 1951, St Joseph, MO. *Career:* mem. of rock group, Kansas 1972–80, 1986–; Streets 1982–85; also solo artist. *Recordings include:* albums: with Kansas: Kansas 1974, Songs For America 1975, Masque 1975, Leftoverture 1976, Point of Know Return 1977, Two for the Show 1978, Monolith 1979, Audio-Visions 1980, Power 1986, In The Spirit of Things 1988, At the Tower Theatre in Philadelphia 1998, Somewhere to Elsewhere 2000, There's Know Place Like Home 2009; solo: Schemer Dreamer 1980, Glossolalia 2000, Shadowman 2005; with Streets: 1st 1983, Crimes in Mind 1985. *Honours:* UNICEF Deputy Goodwill Ambassador 1978. *Current Management:* Chipster Entertainment Inc., 168 West Ridge Pike, Suite 226, Limerick, PA 19468, USA. *E-mail:* info@ chipsterpr.com. *Website:* www.kansasband.com.

WALTER, Rémy; French singer, actor and record producer; b. 1 Sept. 1964, Paris; one d. *Education:* SACEM. *Career:* music producer 1986–; first int. success: Etienne by Guesh Patti; producer, 20 singles and 7 albums; formed own record label; actor; mem., GRAF; SACEM. *Recordings include:* Albums include: Ziskakan: Kasasnicola; Rosina de Peira: Anveit; Pascal Mathieu: En

Attendant Des Jours Pires; A3: Les Fous Du Large; Clément Masdonoar: Anastasia; First solo album: Face To the Ground, 1995. *Honours:* Clément Masdonoar: Anastasia, Best World Music Record of Year, Le Monde 1990. *Current Management:* c/o Agence A., 34, rue Vivienne, 75002, Paris, France. *Telephone:* 1-44-88-20-88. *Fax:* 1-44-88-20-89. *E-mail:* derrieuxm@aol.com. *Website:* www.agencea.fr.

WALTERS, Hannelore Liesemarie (Fil), BA; British singer, songwriter and lyricist; b. 31 Jan. 1970, Dartford, Kent. *Career:* mem., various bands from age 16; singer, songwriter, lyricist, Back To The Planet; appearances on radio and television; concerts in England and Europe for six years; festivals include Glastonbury, Phoenix, Reading. *Recordings:* albums: Mind and Soul Collaborators 1993, Messages After The Bleep 1994; singles include: Teenage Turtles 1993, A Small Nuclear Device 1994. *Address:* 8 Roberts Road, Belvedere, Kent DA17 6NP, England. *Website:* filplanet.co.uk.

WANDALL, Marietta; Danish jazz musician (piano), composer and music teacher; b. 21 Nov. 1956, Copenhagen; m. Kristian Sparre Andersen 1988; two d. *Education:* Univ. of Copenhagen. *Career:* played piano, synthesizer in jazz ensembles, including Krystal Quintet (with Marylin Mazur); Concerts in Denmark, Norway, Finland; solo pianist at several Copenhagen Jazz Festivals; duo concerts with Chris Poole (flute); jazz duo with Hanne Romer (saxophone) 1980–; numerous appearances on Danish radio and television; piano teacher in digital piano-lab. *Recordings:* with Hanne Romer: Akijava 1990, Ametyst 1994, Between Pain and Joy 2000, Walking With The Slow Turtle 2005; for Big Band: Sondagsfrihed 1995, Silly's Head 1999; for classical quartet: Gulvspurvens sange 2004. *Address:* C F Richsvej, 101 C, 2000 Frederiksberg, Denmark (office). *Telephone:* 33-88-33-80 (office). *E-mail:* marietta.wandall@oncable.dk. *Website:* www.amanda-music.dk (office).

WANG, Cyndi; Taiwanese singer and actress; b. (Wáng Jūnrú), 5 Sept. 1982, Hsinchu, Taiwan. *Recordings include:* Begin 2003, Cyndi Loves You 2004, Honey 2005, Shining Cyndi 2005 2005, Cyndi With U 2006, Magic Cyndi 2007, Fly! Cyndi 2007, Red Cyndi 2008, Beautiful Days 2009, H2H 2009, Sticky 2011, Love or Not 2012. *Plays include:* as actor: Che Zheng Zai Zhui 1999, Westside Story 2003, La Robe de Mariage des Cieux 2004, Smiling Pasta 2006. *Film:* as actor: Candy Rain 2008; soundtracks include: Momo Love 2008, Love Keeps Going 2011. *Honours:* HITO Radio Music Award 2005, 2007. *Address:* c/o Gold Typhoon, 8F, No. 35, Guangfu South Road, Songshan District, Taipei 10563, Taiwan. *Website:* www.gold-typhoon.com.tw/artist/info/1120.

WANG, Leehom; Chinese/American singer, songwriter, musician, record producer and actor and film director; b. 17 May 1976, Rochester, NY. *Education:* Eastman School of Music, Williams Coll., Berklee Coll. of Music. *Career:* participant in BMG talent competition 1995, offered a contract with the label; signed to Decca Records 1996, Sony Music Entertainment 1997; first major world tour 2006; guest conductor with Hong Kong Philharmonic Orchestra 2008; collaborations with many artists including Ashin of Mayday, Jin, Li Yan, Rain, Lim Jeong-hee, Liu Fang. *Recordings include:* albums: Love Rival, Beethoven 1995, If You Heard My Song 1996, Missing You 1996, White Paper 1997, Revolution (Golden Melody Award Taiwan and Golden Melody Award Singapore for Best Producer 1998) 1998, Impossible to Miss You (Golden Melody Awards Malaysia for Best Composer and Best Male Vocalist 2000) 1999, Forever's First Day 2000, The One and Only (Golden Melody Awards Malaysia for Best Composer-Artist 2001, for Best Producer 2001, for Best Composer-Artist 2002, for Best Lyricist 2002) 2001, Unbelievable (Golden Melody Music Award for Best Album Producer 2004, Golden Melody Award Singapore for Most Popular Asian Male Singer 2004, Global Chinese Music Award for Best Album 2004) 2003, Shangri-La 2004, Heroes of Earth (Golden Melody Award for Best Male Mandarin Artist 2006) 2005, Change Me 2007, Heart Beat 2008, The 18 Martial Arts (Global Chinese Music Award for Best Album 2011) 2010, Mnet Asian Music Award for Best Asian Artist 2012. *Films:* as actor: China Strike Force 2000, The Avenging Fist 2001, Moon Child 2003, Starlit High Noon 2005, Lust, Caution 2007, Little Big Soldier 2009, The Founding of a Party 2011, Wu Wen Xi Dong 2012; as actor and director: Love in Disguise 2010. *Honours:* People's Daily Newspaper Taiwan Best New Artist 1996, Push Magazine Taiwan Best New Artist 1996, Golden Melody Awards for Best Producer 1998, for Best Mandarin Male Singer 1998, Channel V Awards for Best Singer-Songwriter 2001, for Media's Choice Artist 2003, for Best Male Singer 2004, MTV Asia Awards for Best Male Vocalist 2000, for Best Song 2001, 1st Asia Chinese Music Awards for Best Male Performer and Best Composer 2000, Global Chinese Music Awards for Best Composer 2001, for Most Popular Composer 2003, 2004, for Most Popular Male Artist 2005, for Best Music Composition 2005, for Best Producer 2006, CCTV-MTV Asia Awards for Best Song 2001, for Best Male Vocalist 2002, TVB Jade Solid Gold Music Award for Best Mandarin Song 2002, for Favorite Mandarin Song 2006, HITO Radio Music Awards for Most Popular Male Artist 2003, for Best Song of the Year 2003, for Best Male Singer 2006, 2007, 2008, for Most Popular Voted Composing Artist 2006, for Best Music Arrangement 2006, for Best Singer-Songwriter (joint award) 2008, Cosmopolitan China Award for Top Fashion Trendsetter 2003, MusicRadio Awards for Best Composer Song 2006, Best Producer and Best Taiwan Male Singer 2006, Chinese Music Awards for Best Composing Singer 2007, for Most Popular Male Artist 2007, for Most Popular Song of the Year 2007, Global Chinese Music Awards for Best Newcomer Director Award, 2011, and for Best Male Singer (Hong Kong and Taiwan Region) 2011. *Address:* c/o Sony Music Entertainment, 6F, No. 35, Lane 11, Kwang-Fu North Road, Songshan District, Taipei, 10560, Taiwan (office).

Telephone: (02) 27668900 (office). *Fax:* (02) 27657680 (office). *Website:* www
.sonybmg.com.tw/pop/leehom (office); www.wangleehom.com.

WANGFORD, Hank, MA, MB, BChir, FFSRH; British country singer, musician
(guitar) and doctor; *Associate Specialist, National Health Service;* b. (Samuel
Hutt), 15 Nov. 1940, Wangford, Suffolk, England; m. Nicola Wangford.
Education: Univ. of Cambridge. *Career:* solo artist 1976–, with band, The Lost
Cowboys; Founder Sincere Products (including Sincere Sounds record label);
works in sexual healthcare, lecturing and training doctors and nurses world-
wide, Assoc. Specialist, Nat. Health Service (NHS); Fellow, Faculty of Sexual
and Reproductive Healthcare. *Radio series:* Nine Pound Hammer, Ghengiz
Khan was a Cowboy Too, Way Out West, He'll Have To Go, Looking for the
Lonesome Yodel. *Television series:* Big Big Country, The A to Z of C&W.
Recordings include: albums: Hank Wangford 1980, Hank Wangford Band Live
1982, Rodeo Radio 1984, Stormy Horizons 1990, Hard Shoulder (To Cry On)
1993, Wake Up Dead 1997, Best Foot Forward 2003, Whistling in the Dark
2008, Save Me The Waltz 2014. *Publications:* Hank Wangford Volume III: The
Middle Years (as Sam Hutt) 1989, Lost Cowboys 1997. *Current Management:*
c/o Mark Ringwood, The Barn, Fordwater Lane, Chichester, West Sussex
PO19 4PT, England. *Telephone:* (1243) 789786. *Fax:* (1243) 789787. *E-mail:*
markringwood@btinternet.com. *Address:* 30 Colville Terrace, London, W11 2
BU, England. *E-mail:* hankwangford@gmail.com. *Website:* www
.hankwangford.com.

WANSTALL, Tim; British musician (keyboards) and singer. *Career:* mem.
Athlete 1999–; tours throughout Europe. *Recordings include:* albums:
Vehicles & Animals 2003, Tourist 2005, Beyond the Neighbourhood 2007,
Black Swan 2009. *Honours:* Ivor Novello Award for Best Contemporary Song
(for Wires) 2006. *Website:* www.athlete.mu.

WARBECK, Stephen; British composer; b. (Stephen Robert Wood), 1948,
Southampton, England. *Education:* Univ. of Bristol. *Career:* Head of Music
and Assoc. Artist, RSC. *Music for television:* Prime Suspect 1990–96, The
Student Prince 1997, Bramwell 1996–98. *Music for theatre:* An Inspector Calls
(Nat. Theatre), Proof (Donmar Warehouse), To The Green Fields Beyond
(Donmar Warehouse), The Triumph of Love (Almeida Theatre). *Music for film:*
Femme Fatale 1993, Skallagrigg 1994, O Mary This London 1994, The
Changeling 1994, The Mother 1994, Bambino Mio 1994, Sister My Sister 1994,
Nervous Energy 1995, Brothers In Trouble 1995, Devil's Advocate 1995, Truth
or Dare 1996, Element of Doubt 1996, Different for Girls 1996, Bright Hair
1997, Shakespeare in Love (Acad. Award for score) 1998, Toy Boys 1999,
Mystery Men 1999, My Son The Fanatic 1999, Heart 1999, Fanny and Elvis
1999, A Christmas Carol 1999, Quills 2000, Billy Elliot 2000, Very Annie Mary
2001, Gabriel and Me 2001, Charlotte Gray 2001, Captain Corelli's Mandolin
2001, Secret Passage 2002, Birthday Girl 2002, Desco 2003, Mystics 2003,
Dreamkeeper 2003, Blackball 2003, The Alzheimer Case 2003, Two Brothers
2004, Proof 2004, Pour le plaisir 2004, The Oyster Farmer 2004, Mickybo and
Me 2004, Love's Brother 2004, Goal II: Living the Dream 2006, Flawless 2007.
Address: c/o Sony Classical, 10 Great Marlborough Street, London, W1V 2LP,
England (office). *Website:* www.sonymusic.co.uk (office).

WARD, Bill; British musician (drums); b. 5 May 1948, Birmingham, England.
Career: drummer with UK heavy rock group Black Sabbath (formerly Earth)
1967–80, 1983; concerts include Hollywood Music Festival 1970, Madison
Square Garden, New York 1975. *Recordings include:* albums: Black Sabbath
1970, Paranoid 1970, Master of Reality 1971, Black Sabbath Vol. 4 1972,
Sabbath Bloody Sabbath 1974, Sabotage 1975, We Sold Our Souls For Rock 'n'
Roll 1976, Technical Ecstacy 1976, Never Say Die 1978, Heaven and Hell
1980, Live At Last 1980, Born Again 1983, Black Sabbath, Reunion 1998, Past
Lives 2002, The Dio Years 2007; solo album: Two Hands Clapping 1999;
singles: Evil Woman 1970, Paranoid 1970, Iron Man, 1972, Never Say Die
1978, Hard Road 1978, Neon Knights 1980. *E-mail:* bward@billward.com.
Website: billward.com.

WARD, John Robert; British singer, songwriter and musician (guitar,
bodhran, bass guitar, harmonica); b. 28 June 1964, Halesworth, Suffolk,
England; s. of James Stuart Ward and Dawn Jerman; m. Lynne 1996; one s.
one d. *Education:* Kirkley High School. *Career:* bass player, singer in rock and
pop bands 1980s; full-time acoustic singer/songwriter 1988–; TV appearances,
festivals; elected to the folk section, Cttee of Musicians' Union 1999–2006; Co-
founder Broad Roots 2011; mem. Performing Right Soc., PPL, Musicians'
Union. *Recordings include:* albums: The Shrinking World 1988, Water on the
Stone 1992, Waking Dreams 1998, Common Ground 2005, Praying for the
Alien 2008, East of the Sunrise 2011. *Publication:* The Iron Bridge (epic poem)
2004. *E-mail:* info@johnward.org.uk (office). *Website:* www.johnward.org.uk.

WARDELL, Anita; British/Australian jazz singer; b. Guildford, UK. *Educa-
tion:* Adelaide Univ., Australia, Guildhall School of Music and Drama, UK.
Career: emigrated to Australia as a child; mem. Adelaide Connection jazz
choir 1979–89; returned to UK 1989; performed many concerts throughout
UK, Europe, Australia including appearances at Ronnie Scott's, Royal
Festival Hall, Nat. Theatre, London, yearly concerts at Paradise Festival,
Cyprus; performs in UK with own trio: pianist Robin Aspland, bassist Jeremy
Brown and drummer Gene Calderazzo; teacher of vocal improvisation,
conducts masterclasses and teaches at various insts including Guildhall
School of Music, Leeds Coll., Colchester Inst., Brunel Univ., Trinity Coll. of
Music, Adelaide Univ., Australia. *Television:* Jazz Heroes (BBC TV). *Record-
ings:* albums with Adelaide Connection: Makin' Whoopee, Nice and Easy; solo:
Why Do You Cry? 1995, Straight Ahead 1999, Until the Stars Fade 2002, If

You Never Come To Me 2004, Noted 2006. *Honours:* Best of Jazz, BBC Jazz
Awards 2007. *Current Management:* Air, 27 The Quadrangle, 49 Atalanta
Street, London SW6 6TU, England. *Telephone:* (20) 7386-1600. *E-mail:* info@
airtmtm.com. *Website:* www.airmtm.com. *E-mail:* info@anitawardell.com
(office). *Website:* www.anitawardell.com.

WARE, Martyn; British musician and record producer; b. 19 May 1956,
Sheffield, Yorkshire, England; m. Landsley Ware; two c. *Career:* founder
mem., Human League 1977–80; founder mem. production team, British
Electronic Foundation (BEF) 1980, renamed Heaven 17 1981–88; worldwide
tours; formed The Clarke & Ware Experiment with Vince Clarke 2000;
Creative Dir Sonic-ID; Visiting Prof., Queen Mary Coll., Univ. of London;
Visiting Lecturer, Royal Coll. of Art and Harvard Graduate School of Design;
ind. record producer, working with artists, including Marc Almond, Terence
Trent D'Arby, Erasure, Lena Fiagbe, Pauline Henry, Sanna Kurki-Suonio,
Alison Moyet, Conner Reeves, Joe Roberts, Scritti Politti, Shabba, Tina
Turner, Urban Cookie Collective, Mario Vasquez, Paul Weller; Fellow, Royal
Soc. for the Arts; mem. Writers Guild of America. *Recordings include:* albums:
with Human League: Reproduction 1979, Travelogue 1980; with BEF: Music
for Stowaways 1981, Music of Quality And Distinction Vol. 1 1982, Vol. 2 1991;
with Heaven 17: Penthouse and Pavement 1981, Heaven 17 1982, The Luxury
Gap 1983, How Men Are 1984, Endless 1986, Pleasure One 1986, Teddy Bear,
Duke & Psycho 1988, Higher and Higher 1993, Bigger than America 1996,
Retox/Detox 1999, Live at Last 1999, Temptation: Live in Concert 2001,
Before After 2005, Naked as Advertised 2008; as The Clarke & Ware
Experiment: Pretentious 2000, Spectrum Pursuit Vehicle 2001. *Current
Management:* c/o Red Bull Music Academy, Boisseréestr. 9-11, 50674 Cologne,
Germany. *Telephone:* (22) 13550530. *Fax:* (22) 135505350. *E-mail:* info@
redbullmusicacademy.com. *Website:* www.redbullmusicacademy.com; www
.heaven17.com; www.illustriouscompany.co.uk.

WARINER, Steve; American musician (bass), songwriter and singer; b. 25
Dec. 1954, Noblesville, IN. *Career:* bass player with Dottie West, Bob Luman,
Chet Atkins; solo artist 1978–. *Recordings include:* albums: Steve Wariner
1982, Midnight Fire 1983, One Good Night Deserves Another 1985, Life's
Highway 1985, Down in Tennessee 1986, It's A Crazy World 1987, I Should Be
With You 1988, I Got Dreams 1989, I Am Ready 1991, Drive 1993, No More Mr
Nice Guy 1996, Christmas Memories 1998, Burnin' the Roadhouse Down
1998, Two Teardrops 1999, Faith in You 2000, Steal Another Day 2003, Guitar
Christmas 2003, This Real Life 2005, Steve Wariner c.g.p. – My Tribute to
Chet Atkins 2009. *Honours:* CMA Vocal Event Award (for Restless) 1991,
Grammy Award for Best Country Instrumental Performance (for Producer's
Medley) 2010. *Address:* c/o Selectone Records, 320 Main Street, Suite 210,
Franklin, TN 37064, USA (office). *E-mail:* fanclub@stevewariner.com (office).
Website: www.stevewariner.com.

WARNES, Jennifer; American singer; b. 3 March 1947, Seattle, WA. *Career:*
singer 1967–. *Stage appearance:* Hair (Los Angeles) 1968. *Recordings include:*
albums: I Can Remember Everything 1968, See Me, Feel Me, Touch Me, Heal
Me 1969, Jennifer 1972, Jennifer Warnes 1976, Shot Through The Heart
1979, Famous Blue Raincoat 1987, Just Jennifer 1992, The Hunter 1992, The
Well 2001. *Honours:* Academy Award for Best Original Song (for It Goes Like
It Goes) 1980, (for Up Where We Belong) 1983, (for (I've Had) the Time of My
Life) 1988, Grammy Award for Best Pop Performances (for Up Where We
Belong) 1983, (for (I've Had) the Time of My Life)) 1987. *E-mail:*
correspondence@jenniferwarnes.com. *Website:* www.jenniferwarnes.com.

WARREN, Diane; American songwriter; b. 1956, Calif. *Education:* California
State University. *Career:* lyric writer, UK entry to Eurovision Song Contest
2009; f. Diane Warren Foundation; worked on numerous projects including
Music in the Schools 2000. *Compositions include:* If I Could Turn Back Time,
Cher; Solitaire, Laura Branigan; If You Asked Me To, Céline Dion; I Get
Weak, Belinda Carlisle; Rhythm of The Night, Debarge; Look Away, Chicago;
Who Will You Run To, Heart; When I'm Back On My Feet Again, Michael
Bolton; Not A Dry Eye In The House, Meat Loaf; Also composed for Gloria
Estefan, Al Green, Olivia Newton-John, Roy Orbison, Joe Cocker, Christina
Aguilera; *NSYNC. *Honours:* ASCAP Songwriter of the Year 1990, 1991,
1993, Billboard Singles Publishers of the Year 1990, 1993, ASCAP Voice of
Music Award 1995. *Website:* realsongs.com.

WARREN, (Robert) Huw, BMus; British musician (piano, accordion,
keyboards) and composer; b. 18 May 1962, Swansea, West Glamorgan.
Education: classical piano and cello. *Career:* crosses many genre boundaries
including jazz, folk, contemporary classical, world music; early musical
experiences included playing organ in working men's clubs, South Wales;
moved to London to study for a music degree 1980; involved with the British
experimental music scene and London jazz musicians; collaborated with
musicians from Brazil, Democratic Republic of the Congo, Iran, Indian sub-
continent; began long-running collaboration with June Tabor, late 1980s; co-
founder Perfect Houseplants (with Mark Lockheart and Dudley Phillips);
collaborations with Billy Bragg, Christine Tobin, The Orlando Consort, Mose
Se Fan Fan (African guitarist). *Compositions:* commissions include Riot for
Piano Circus, Steamboat Bill Jr (new score for the Buster Keaton film), music
for a production of Jean Cocteau's Monologues, Lyric Theatre, London.
Recordings: albums: A Barrel Organ Far From Home 1997, Infinite Riches In
A Little Room 2000, Everything we Love 2006, Hermeto+ 2009; with Perfect
Houseplants: Perfect Houseplants 1993, Clec 1995, Snap Clatter 1997,
Extempore (with Orlando Consort) 1998, New Folk Songs 2000; with June

Tabor: Some Other Time 1989, Aqaba Topic 1990, Angel Tiger 1992, Against The Streams 1994, Aleyn 1997, A Quiet Eye 2000, Rosa Mundi 2001; with Maddy Prior and June Tabor: No More To The Dance 1988; features on: Through Rose Coloured Glasses, Mark Lockheart 1998, Mirmama, Eddi Reader 1992, Busy Listening, Steve Arguelles 1994, Entertainment USA, Billy Jenkins 1994, Tales From The Sun, Tim Garland 1995, Mayfest 95, Billy Jenkins and the Fun Horns of Berlin 1995, Aililiu, Christine Tobin 1995, Yell of The Gazelle, Christine Tobin 1996, East Meets West 95, Billy Jenkins and the Fun Horns of Berlin 1996, Circuits, Steve Arguelles 1998, House of Women, Christine Tobin 1998. *E-mail:* huw@huwwarren.com (office). *Website:* website.lineone.net/~huw.warren.

WARWICK, Dionne; American singer; b. (Marie Dionne), 12 Dec. 1941, East Orange, NJ; m. Bill Elliott (divorced 1975); two s.; pnr Bruce Garrick. *Education:* Hartt Coll. of Music. *Career:* as teenager formed Gospelaires; later sang background for recording studio 1966; début, Philharmonic Hall, Lincoln Center, New York 1966; appearances at London Palladium, Olympia, Paris, Lincoln Center; named UN FAO Amb. 2002; Co-founder Carr/Todd/Warwick Production, Inc., Dionne Warwick Design Group Inc. *Films:* The Slaves 1969, No Night, So Long, Hot! Live and Otherwise. *Television includes:* co-host, Solid Gold; host, A Gift of Music 1981; Dionne Warwick Special; appeared in Sisters in the Name of Love 1986. *Albums include:* Valley of the Dolls and Others 1968, Promises, Promises 1975, Dionne 1979, Then Came You, Friends 1986, Reservations for Two 1987, Greatest Hits 1990, Dionne Warwick Sings Cole Porter 1990, Hidden Gems: The Best of Dionne Warwick (Vol. 2) 1992, Friends Can Be Lovers (with Whitney Houston) 1993, Dionne Warwick and Placido Domingo 1994, Aquarela do Brasil 1994, From the Vaults 1995, Dionne Sings Dionne 1998, I Say a Little Prayer For You 2000. *Publications:* My Point of View 2003, My Life, As I See It 2010. *Honours:* Dr hc (Lincoln Coll., Ill.) 2010; five Grammy Awards, Luminary Award, American Soc. of Young Musicians 1997, Chairman's Award for Sustained Creative Achievement, Nat. Asscn of Record Merchandisers 1998, History Maker, History Makers Org. of Chicago 2001, Heroes Award, New York Chapter of Recording Acad. 2002, Lifetime Achievement Award, R&B Foundation 2003, named one of Top Faces of Black History 2003. *Website:* www.dionnewarwick.net.

WARWICK, Ricky; singer and rock musician (guitar); b. Belfast, Northern Ireland; m. 1st Vanessa Young (divorced); m. 2nd Christina Warwick. *Career:* founder mem. heavy rock group, The Almighty 1988–; invited to join new lineup of Thin Lizzy 2009; co-founded Thin Lizzy spin-off band Black Star Riders 2012; numerous live performances. *Recordings include:* albums: with The Almighty: Blood Fire and Love, 1989; Blood Fire and Live, 1990; Soul Destruction, 1991; Powertrippin', 1993; Crank, 1995; Just Add Life, 1996; Almighty Almighty, 2000; Psycho Narco, 2001; solo albums: Tattoos & Alibis 2003, Love Many Trust Few 2005, Belfast Confetti 2009, Hearts on Trees 2014, When Patsy Cline Was Crazy (And Guy Mitchell Sang the Blues) 2014; with Black Star Riders: All Hell Breaks Loose 2013, The Killer Instinct 2015. *Current Management:* Triple T Management Co, 21 Napier Place, London W14 8LG, England.

WASHBURN, Dan; Canadian singer, songwriter and musician (bass); b. 28 May 1956, Coburg, Ont.; m. Jane 1984, three s. one d. *Career:* lead singer, South Mountain 1992; appeared with Marty Stuart, Waylon Jennings, Toby Keith, Merle Haggard, Prairie Oyster; mem. American Fed. of Musicians, Canadian Country Music Asscn. *Recordings include:* album with South Mountain: Where There's a Will 1995; solo: They Don't Make 'em Like That Anymore 2012. *Address:* 5503 Highway, 62 South Prince Edward Square, R. R. # 7, Belleville, ON K8N 47Z, Canada. *E-mail:* danialwashburn@sympatico .ca. *Website:* www.danwashburn.net.

WASHINGTON, Sabrina; British singer, rap artist and songwriter; b. London. *Career:* Founder mem. and lead singer, Mis-Teeq 2001–05; live appearances include 'Party at the Palace' for Golden Jubilee celebrations 2002; solo artist 2005–. *Recordings:* albums: Lickin' On Both Sides 2001, Eyecandy 2003; singles: Why? 2001, All I Want 2001, One Night Stand 2001, B With Me 2002, Roll On 2002, Scandalous 2003, Can't Get It Back 2003, Style 2003, Shoo Shoo Baby 2005. *Honours:* UK Garage Award for Best Artist 2001, MOBO Award for Best Garage Act 2002. *Website:* www.sabrinawashington .com.

WASSOUF, George; Syrian/Lebanese singer; b. 23 Dec. 1961, Kafroun, Homs; m. Shalimar; three c. *Career:* solo artist 1975–. *Recordings include:* albums: El-hawa sultan 1984, Rouh el-rouh 1992, She' ghareeb 1993, Kalam en-nass 1994, Irda bil naseeh 1995, Leil el-ashiqeen 1996, Lissa ed-dounya bi khair 1998, Tabeeb garrah 1999, Dol mush habayib 2000, Zaman el-ajayib 2001, Inta gherhom 2002, Salaf wi dein 2003, Etakhart kteer 2004, Hiyya el-ayyam 2006, Kalamak ya habibi 2008, Allah Kareem 2009.

WATERHOUSE, David Boyer, MA, LRAM, FRSC, FRAS; British/Canadian musician (piano, Highland bagpipes) and academic; *Professor Emeritus, University of Toronto;* b. 13 July 1936, Harrogate, N Yorks., England; s. of Geoffrey Waterhouse and May Waterhouse; m. Naoko Matsubara; one s. *Education:* King's Coll., Cambridge, studied piano with M. Denny, Highland bagpipes with the late P/M John Wilson and others. *Career:* Research Asst, Cambridge Inst. of Criminology 1959–60; Asst Keeper, Dept of Oriental Antiquities, British Museum 1961–64; Research Fellow, Center for Asian Arts, Univ. of Washington 1964–66; Asst Prof., Dept of East Asian Studies, Univ. of Toronto 1966–70, Assoc. Prof. 1970–75, Prof. 1975–2002, Prof. Emer. 2002–; consultant to numerous museums, publrs on Asian art and other

subjects; with Pipes and Drums, 48th Highlanders of Canada 1966–72, City of Toronto Pipe Band 1972–74; mem. Int. Council for Traditional Music, Pipers' Soc. of Ontario, Pipes and Drums Asscn of 48th Highlanders of Canada, Soc. for Asian Music (USA), Soc. for Ethnomusicology (USA), Toyo Ongaku Gakkai (Japan), Piobaireachd Soc. (Scotland), Billy Mayerl Soc. *Publications include:* Harunobu and his Age: The Development of Colour Printing in Japan 1964, Tawaraya Sotatsu and the Deer Scroll 1966, Images of Eighteenth-Century Japan 1975, Japanese Woodblock Prints from the J. Bruce Varcoe Collection 1976, Early Japanese Prints in the Philadelphia Museum of Art 1983, Ukiyo-e shuka: Suzuki Harunobu (2 vols) 1982, Dance of India (ed.) 1998, Warriors and Entertainers 2008; contribs to books include The New Grove Dictionary of Music and Musicians 1980, 2001, Kodansha Encyclopedia of Japan 1983, Encyclopaedia of Music in Canada 1992, The Dictionary of Art 1996, The Harunobu Decade (two vols) 2013, numerous articles on music theory, Japanese music, Buddhist music, Highland bagpipes, judo. *Address:* Department of East Asian Studies, University of Toronto, Robarts Library, 14087, 130 St. George Street, Toronto, ON M5S 3H1 (office); 324 Coral Terrace, Oakville, ON L6J 4C4, Canada (home). *Telephone:* (905) 844-4879 (home). *Fax:* (905) 844-4893 (home). *E-mail:* david.waterhouse@utoronto.ca. *Website:* www.eas.utoronto.ca (office).

WATERMAN, Peter (Pete) Alan, OBE; record producer and songwriter; *Chairman, Pete Waterman Limited (PWL);* b. 15 Jan. 1947. *Career:* soul DJ; promoter, record producer and remixer for artists including Adrian Baker, Susan Cadogan; mem. group, Agents Aren't Aeroplanes 1984; mem. songwriting and production team Stock/Aitken/Waterman (SAW), with Matt Aitken and Mike Stock 1984–93; founder, Chair. Pete Waterman Limited (PWL) record label 1988–, later including PWL Management International; founder, PWL America, PWL Continental, PWL Black 1991–. *Television:* The Hit Man and Her (ITV) 1988–92, judge, Pop Idol (ITV 1) 2001, 2003, Popstars–The Rivals (ITV 1) 2002. *Radio:* presenter, Sunday night show, Smooth Radio 2009–. *Recordings as producer:* albums: Hit Factory 1987, Hit Factory Vol. 2 1988, Hit Factory Vol. 3 1989, The Best of Stock, Aitken and Waterman 1990; singles: You Spin Me Round by Dead Or Alive 1984, Say I'm Your Number One by Princess 1985, Showing Out by Mel and Kim 1986, Venus by Bananarama 1986, So Macho by Sinitta 1986, Respectable by Mel and Kim 1987, Never Gonna Give You Up by Rick Astley 1987, Together Forever by Rick Astley 1988; with Kylie Minogue: I Should Be So Lucky 1988, Got To Be Certain 1988, The Locomotion 1988, Especially For You (duet with Jason Donovan) 1988, Hand On Your Heart 1989, Better The Devil You Know 1990, Rhythm of Love 1993, 50+1 1998; with Steps: Steptacular 2000; also recordings for Jason Donovan, Divine, Hazell Dean, Sonia, Brother Beyond, Big Fun, Donna Summer. *Publication:* I Wish I Was Me (autobiog.). *Honours:* Hon. DMus Univ. Coll. Chester 2004. *Address:* PWL, 222–224 Borough High Street, London, SE1 1JX, England. *Telephone:* (20) 7403-0007. *Fax:* (20) 7403-8202. *Website:* www.pwl-empire.com.

WATERS, Peter Russell; Australian jazz musician (piano); b. 4 Aug. 1953, Broken Hill; m. Sybille Waters 1997; one d. *Education:* piano studies in Adelaide with Rolland May and Clemens Leske, and in London with Peter Walfisch. *Career:* concert Pianist, Salzburg Festival with Gundula Janowitz; solo and duo recitals with Janowitz in Paris, Vienna, Berlin, London, Lyon, Rome, Stockholm, Cologne, Frankfurt, Munich, Zürich and numerous festivals; Bach Festival Schaffhausen; numerous tours, live concerts and recordings in Europe and South America 1992–; Musical Dir, Solo Pianist, Mozart and Modern exchange project in St Petersburg and Switzerland 1996; solo tour with Orchestre de Lille 1997; formed Treya Quartet with Sardinian Trumpeter Paolo Fresu, Peter Waters Tri O 2003–; mem. Tonkünstlerverein, Switzerland, World Wildlife Fund. *Recordings include:* Gates Beyond, music of John Adams, Ravel and Satie, Treya Quartet plays Gabriel Fauré. *Honours:* ABC FM Best Classical Recording in Australia, for Gates Beyond 1997.

WATERS, Roger; British singer, musician (bass guitar) and composer; b. 6 Sept. 1944, Great Bookham, Surrey. *Education:* Regent Street Polytechnic, London. *Career:* founder mem., Pink Floyd 1965–83; numerous live performances and festival appearances; solo artist 1983–. *Compositions include:* Ça Ira (opera) 2005. *Recordings include:* albums: with Pink Floyd: The Piper At The Gates Of Dawn 1967, A Saucerful Of Secrets 1968, More (film soundtrack) 1969, Ummagumma 1969, Atom Heart Mother 1970, Meddle 1971, Obscured By Clouds 1972, The Dark Side Of The Moon 1973, Wish You Were Here 1975, Animals 1976, The Wall 1979, The Final Cut 1983; solo: Music From 'The Body' (film soundtrack) 1970, The Pros And Cons of Hitch Hiking 1984, When The Wind Blows 1986, Radio K.A.O.S. 1987, The Wall: Live In Berlin 1990, Amused To Death 1992, In The Flesh Live 2000, Ça Ira: An Opera In Three Acts 2005. *Honours:* Nordoff-Robbins Silver Clef Award (with Pink Floyd) 1980, Ivor Novello Award for Outstanding Contribution to British Music (with Pink Floyd) 1992, Polar Music Prize 2008. *Current Management:* c/o William Morris Endeavor, Centre Point, 103 New Oxford Street, London, WC1A 1DD, England. *Telephone:* (20) 7534-6800. *Fax:* (20) 7534-6900. *Website:* www.wma .com; www.roger-waters.com.

WATERSON, Norma Christine, MBE; English singer; b. 15 Aug. 1939, Kingston-upon-Hull, Humberside; m. Martin Carthy; one s. one d. (Eliza Carthy). *Career:* mem. folk group The Watersons 1960s; toured with her d., her sister Lal Waterson and Lal's d. Maria as the Waterdaughters 1980s; formed family band, Waterson:Carthy 1990s; solo artist 1996–. *Recordings:* albums with The Watersons: New Voices, Frost and Fire 1965, Watersons, A Yorkshire Garland 1966, For Pence and Spice Ale 1975, Sound Sound Your

Instruments 1977, Greenfields 1981; with Lal Waterson: A True Hearted Girl 1977; with Waterson:Carthy: Waterson:Carthy 1994, Common Tongue 1997, Broken Ground 1999, A Dark Light 2002, Fishes and Fine Yellow Sand 2004, Holy Heathens and The Old Green Man 2006; solo: Norma Waterson 1996, The Very Thought Of You 1999, Bright Shiny Morning 2000, Gift (with Eliza Carthy) 2010. *Honours:* Gold Badge and Hon. Life mem. English Folk Dance and Song Soc.; Hon. DMus (Hull) 2004. *Current Management:* c/o Alan Bearman Music, The Music Base, Kings Place, 90 York Way, London, N1 9AG, England. *Telephone:* (20) 7014-2821. *E-mail:* bearman@btinternet.com. *Website:* www.alanbearmanmusic.co.uk; www.watersoncarthy.com.

WATES, Matthew (Matt) James, BMus; British musician (saxophone, flute, clarinet) and composer; b. 1964, London, England. *Education:* Berklee Coll. of Music, Boston, Mass, USA. *Career:* jazz musician, arranger and composer; recorded with Roadside Picnic, PAZ, Sax Appeal, NYJO, The Michael Garrick Big Band; leader, the Matt Wates Sextet; appeared with many top jazz musicians, including Bucky Pizzarelli, Humphrey Lyttelton, Georges Arvanitas, Helen Shapiro, John Colianni, Don Weller, Bobby Wellins, Dusko Goykevich, Duncan Lamont, Ian Shaw, Norma Winston, Peter King. *Recordings:* albums: with Matt Wates Sextet: Relaxin' At The Cat 1993, Two 1996, Smallbill's Garage 1999, Ghost Dance 2005, Plum Lane 2006, A Picture of You 2007, People Will Talk 2010; with PAZ: Dancing In The Park 1995, Samba, Samba 2000, Laying Eggs 2001; with Itchy Fingers: Full English Breakfast 1993; with Roadside Picnic: La Famille 1995. *Honours:* BT British Jazz Rising Star Award 1997, BT British Jazz Award for Best Small Group (for the Matt Wates Sextet) 2001. *Address:* c/o audio-b Ltd, PO Box 16797, London, W3 6ZS, England (office). *E-mail:* mattwates@hotmail.com (office).

WATKINS, Ian; Welsh singer; b. 30 July 1979, Pontypridd. *Career:* lead singer, Lostprophets 1997–2013; sentenced to 35 years for child sex offences 2013. *Recordings include:* albums: thefakesoundofprogress 2000, Start Something 2004, Liberation Transmission 2006, The Betrayed 2010. *Honours:* Kerrang! Award for Best British Band 2007.

WATKINS, Tionne Tenese, (T-Boz); singer; b. 26 April 1970, Des Moines, Iowa, USA. *Career:* began as singer in church choir; mem., lead singer TLC 1991–; owner, Shee Inc, Grunge Girl Music; co-owner, line of clothes, Grungy Glamorous. *Film appearance:* Belly 1998. *Recordings:* Albums: Ooooooohhh… On The TLC Tip 1992, Crazysexycool 1994, Fanmail 1999, 3D 2002, Now and Forever 2003, Crazy Sexy Hits 2007; solo single: Touch Myself (for film Fled). *Publications:* Thoughts (poems) 1999. *Honours:* Grammy Awards, Best R&B Performance by Duo/Group, Best R&B Album, for Crazysexycool, two Lady of Soul Awards, two Billboard Music Awards, three Soul Train Awards; Blockbuster Entertainment Award; four MTV Music Video Awards for Waterfalls. *Address:* LaFace Records, 1 Capital City Plaza, 3350 Peachtree Road, Suite 1500, Atlanta, GA 30326, USA.

WATSON, Robert (Bobby) Michael, Jr, BM; American musician (alto saxophone), composer, bandleader and teacher; *William D. and Mary Grant/ Missouri Distinguished Professor of Jazz Studies, University of Missouri, Kansas City;* b. 23 Aug. 1953, Lawrence; s. of Robert Watson and Lahoma Watson; m. Pamela Watson 1976; one s. one d. *Education:* Univ. of Miami. *Career:* Musical Dir with Art Blakey and The Jazz Messengers 1977–81; mem. Leads Horizon 1980–; alto with Zahir Batin 1980–; alto with Art Blakey and The Jazz Messengers 1981–; alto with Mickey Bass Quartet 1981–; mem. 28th Street Saxophone Quartet 1983–; lead alto with Panama Francis and The Savoy Sultans 1983–; lead alto with The Duke's Men 1987–; performs with Charlie Mingus Epitaph Project 1989–; alto with Smithsonian Jazz Masterworks Orchestra 1982; lead alto with Carnegie Hall Jazz Orchestra 1992; premiered Tailor Made big band 1993; own publishing co. Lafiya Music 1979–, record label, New Note Records 1983–; William D. and Mary Grant/Missouri Distinguished Prof. of Jazz Studies, Univ. of Missouri, Kansas City 2000–. *Film:* A Bronx Tale. *Recordings include:* as leader: E.T.A. 1977, All Because of You 1979, Beatitudes 1983, Gumbo 1983, Jewel 1983, Advance 1984, Appointment in Milano 1985, Round Trip 1985, Love Remains 1986, The Year of the Rabbit 1987, No Question About It 1988, The Inventor 1989, Post Motown Bop 1991, This Little Light of Mine 1991, Present Tense 1992, Tailor Made 1992, Midwest Shuffle 1993, Urban Renewal 1995, Project 1998, Quiet As It's Kept 1998, Live At Someday In Tokyo 2000, Live and Learn 2002, Horizon Reassembled 2004, Soulful Serendipity 2006, From the Heart 2008, The Gates BBQ Suite 2010; recordings with artists including Bill Cosby, Art Blakey and The Jazz Messengers, 29th Street Quartet, Duke Ellington, Charlie Mingus, Cornelius Kreusch. *Honours:* Nat. Endowment Composers' Grant 1980, Downbeat Critics' Poll Wins: Best Alto Saxophonist 1989–92, Jazz Musician of the Year 1990, inducted into Kansas Music Hall of Fame 2011. *Current Management:* J. Chriss & Co., 300 Mercer Street, New York, NY; Jon Poses, 21 North Tenth Street, Columbia, MO 65201, USA. *Telephone:* (212) 353-0855 (New York); (573) 449-3009 (Columbia). *Fax:* (212) 353-0094 (New York); (573) 875-0356 (Columbia). *E-mail:* executivedirector@ wealwaysswing.org. *Address:* Department of Jazz Studies, University of Missouri, Performing Arts Center, 4949 Cherry Street, Kansas City, MO 64110-2229, USA (office). *Telephone:* (816) 235-2905 (office). *E-mail:* watsonr@ umkc.edu (office). *Website:* conservatory.umkc.edu/faculty-profile.cfm?id=40 (office); www.bobbywatson.com.

WATSON, (Gary) Gene; American country singer, songwriter and musician (guitar); b. 11 Oct. 1943, Palestine, TX. *Career:* formed first band, Gene Watson and the Other Four, with brothers and cousins, Houston, Texas, aged

14; nearly 50 Billboard country chart singles on labels including Capitol, MCA, Epic, Warner Bros; continues to record on independent labels and tour with own band, the Farewell Party Band; mem. Texas Country Music Hall of Fame. *Recordings include:* albums: Gene Watson 1969, Love In The Hot Afternoon 1975, Because You Believed in Me 1976, Paper Rosie 1977, Beautiful Country 1977, Reflections 1978, Should I Come Home 1979, No One Will Ever Know 1980, Between This Time and Next Time 1981, Old Love Never Dies 1981, This Dream's On Me 1982, Sometimes I Get Lucky 1983, Heartaches, Love and Stuff 1984, Texas Saturday Night 1985, Memories to Burn 1985, Starting New Memories 1986, Honky Tonk Crazy 1987, Back in the Fire 1988, Little by Little 1990, At Last 1991, In Other Words 1992, Uncharted Mind 1993, The Good Ole Days 1996, Jesus is All I Need 1997, A Way to Survive 1997, From the Heart 2001, Gospel at its Best 2006, In a Perfect World 2007, Matters of the Heart 2008, A Taste of the Truth 2009. *Honours:* Citadel Media Country Legend of the Year Award 2010. *Current Management:* Lytle Management Group, PO Box 128228, Nashville, TN 37212, USA. *Telephone:* (615) 770-2688. *E-mail:* artist@lytlemgmt.com. *Website:* www.genewatsonmusic.com.

WATSON, James (Jamie), (Badger); Canadian recording engineer, producer and musician (guitar, drums, keyboards); *Studio Engineer/Manager, Chamber Recording Studio;* b. 3 June 1954, Hamilton, Ont.; s. of Dr James Wreford Watson and Jessie Watson; m. Beverley Watson 1990. *Education:* Edinburgh Acad., George Watsons Coll., Edinburgh Art Coll., Murray House Coll. *Career:* mem. Solos, Persian Rugs; currently owns and runs Chamber Recording Studio, Edinburgh; producer for The Vaselines, Foil, Eugenius, Long Fin Killie, Snow Patrol, Idlewild, Ganger; mem. Performing Right Soc., Mechanical-Copyright Protection Soc., PPL. *Recordings include:* singles: Talking Pictures (Solos), singles and album by Persian Rugs on various independent labels. *Address:* 120A West Granton Road, Edinburgh, EH5 1PF, Scotland (office). *Telephone:* 7748-306375 (mobile) (office). *E-mail:* jamiechamber@gmail.com.

WATSON, Jay Wesley; Australian musician (drums, guitar, keyboards), singer and songwriter. *Career:* drummer, Tame Impala 2007–, signed to Modular Recordings label 2008, numerous live appearances; guitarist and keyboard player, Pond 2008–. *Recordings:* albums: with Pond: Psychedelic Mango 2009, Corridors of Blissterday 2009, Frond 2010, Beard, Wives, Denim 2012, Hobo Rocket 2013; with Tame Impala: Innerspeaker (Triple J's J Award for Album of the Year 2010) 2010, Lonerism (Triple J's J Award for Album of the Year 2012, ARIA Awards for Album of the Year 2013, for Best Rock Album 2013) 2012. *Honours:* with Tame Impala: EG Music Award for Best Song (for Elephant) 2012, ARIA Award for Best Group 2013. *Current Management:* c/o Spinning Top Music, PO Box 769, Fremantle, WA 6959, Australia. *E-mail:* tameimpala@spinningtopmusic.com. *Website:* www.spinningtopmusic.com; www.tameimpala.com (home).

WATSON, Jeff; American musician (guitar), singer, writer, record producer and sound engineer; b. 4 Nov. 1959, Sacramento, Calif. *Career:* guitarist, US rock group, Night Ranger 1982–91; guitarist, Mothers Army; also solo artist; mem. BMI, American Fed. of TV and Radio Artists, Japanese Soc. for Rights of Authors Composers and Publrs. *Recordings include:* albums: with Night Ranger: Dawn Patrol 1982, Midnight Madness 1983, Seven Wishes 1985, Big Life 1987, Man In Motion 1988, Live In Japan 1990, Seven 1998, Live In Japan: Greatest Hits, Live 1999; solo: Lone Ranger 1992, Around The Sun 1993; with Steve Morse: Southern Steel; with Chris Isaac: San Francisco Days, Forever Blue; with Mothers Army: Mothers Army I and II.

WATSON, Russell; British singer (tenor); b. 1974, Salford. *Career:* professional singer 1996–; numerous TV and radio broadcasts; concert performances include Wembley Arena, Royal Albert Hall, Carnegie Hall, Sydney Opera House, opening ceremony of the Commonwealth Games, Manchester 2002. *For film and television* sang Pelagia's Song (from film, Captain Corelli's Mandolin) 2001; sang theme tune to Star Trek Enterprise (TV series) 2002. *Recordings include:* albums: The Voice 2000, Encore 2001, Reprise 2002, Amore Musica 2004, The Ultimate Collection 2006, That's Life 2007, Outside In 2007, People Get Ready 2008, La Voce 2010, The Platinum Collection 2010. *Current Management:* Merlin Elite Ltd, Hammersmith Studios, 55 Yeldham Road, London, W6 8JF, England. *Telephone:* (20) 8834-8900. *Fax:* (20) 8834-8901. *E-mail:* info@merlinelite.co.uk. *Website:* www.merlin-elite.com; www .russell-watson.com.

WATT, Ben; British musician (guitars, keyboards), singer and songwriter; b. 6 Dec. 1962; m. Tracey Thorn 2009; three c. *Education:* Hull Univ. *Career:* solo artist 1981–82; founder mem. of duo, Everything But The Girl 1983–; f. Buzzin' Fly record label 2003, Strange Feeling Records 2007; numerous live appearances, tours. *Recordings include:* albums: solo: North Marine Drive 1983; with Everything But The Girl: Eden 1984, Love Not Money 1985, Baby, The Stars Shine Bright 1986, Idlewild 1988, The Language of Life 1990, Worldwide 1991, Amplified Heart 1994, Walking Wounded 1996, Temperamental 1999, Back To Mine (mix album) 2001; with Deep Dish: Future of the Future 1998, Junk Science 1999, Lazy Dog 2000; with Splendour: Splendour 1999; with Next Best Thing: Next Best Thing 2000. *Address:* Strange Feeling Records, 31 Camden Lock Place, London, NW1 8AL, England (office). *E-mail:* marianne@buzzinfly.com (office). *Website:* www.strangefeelingrecords.com (office).

WATT, Michael (Mike) David; American musician (bass), singer and songwriter; b. 20 Dec. 1957, Portsmouth, Va; s. of James Richard Watt and

Jean V. Watt; m. Kira Roessler. *Career:* co-f. bands Minutemen (disbanded 1985), dos, Firehose; mem. Banyan Project; bassist for reunited Stooges 2003–; host, The Watt from Pedro Show (radio show). *Recordings include:* albums (both solo and group): Justamente Tres 1996, Live In Detroit 2004, The Secondman's Middle Stand 2004, Telluric Chaos 2005, The Weirdness 2007, Dos y Dos 2011, Hyphenated-Man 2011. *Film:* Brand Upon the Brain! (narrator) 2007. *Publication:* Spiels Of A Minuteman 2003. *Honours:* Lifetime Achievement Award, Bass Player Magazine 2008. *Website:* www.hootpage .com.

WATTS, Andy; British musician (shawn, Flemish bagpipes, clarinet, recorders, curtal) and singer; b. Macclesfield, England. *Education:* Univ. of Cambridge, Guildhall School of Music and Drama, Royal Conservatory, The Hague, Netherlands. *Career:* recorder teacher; freelance musician with early music groups; Musical Dir, Medieval Players; baroque and classical bassoon with the Orchestra of the Age of Enlightenment, English Baroque Soloists, Academy of Ancient Music; teacher, baroque bassoon, Royal Academy of Music; founder mem., The Carnival Band, 1984–; appearances include: Glasgow Cathedral; Birmingham Symphony Hall; Barbican Centre; arts theatres and centres; plays material from: Sweden; Croatia; USA; Bolivia; Spain; UK; France. *Recordings include:* Christmas Carols (with Maddy Prior); also recorded with: Frances Eustace; Colin Lawson; Lisa Beznosiuk and Nigel North.

WATTS, Charles (Charlie) Robert; British musician (drums); b. 2 June 1941, London, England; m. Shirley Anne Shepherd 1964; one d. *Career:* fmr mem. Blues Incorporated; mem. The Rolling Stones 1963–, numerous tours world-wide; toured with Charlie Watts Orchestra 1985–86. *Recordings include:* albums: with The Rolling Stones: The Rolling Stones 1964, The Rolling Stones No. 2 1965, Out Of Our Heads 1965, Aftermath 1966, Between The Buttons 1967, Their Satanic Majesties Request 1967, Beggar's Banquet 1968, Let It Bleed 1969, Get Yer Ya-Ya's Out 1969, Sticky Fingers 1971, Exile On Main Street 1972, Goat's Head Soup 1973, It's Only Rock And Roll 1974, Black And Blue 1976, Some Girls 1978, Emotional Rescue 1980, Tattoo You 1981, Still Life 1982, Undercover 1983, Dirty Work 1986, Steel Wheels 1989, Flashpoint 1991, Voodoo Lounge 1994, Stripped 1995, Bridges to Babylon 1997, Forty Licks 2002, Live Licks 2004, A Bigger Bang 2005; solo: Live at Fulham Town Hall 1986, From One Charlie 1992, Tribute To Charlie Parker With Strings 1991, Warm & Tender 1993, Long Ago and Far Away 1996, Charlie Watts/Jim Keltner Project 2000, Watts At Scott's 2004, The Magic of Boogie Woogie 2010, The ABC&D of Boogie Woogie Live In Paris 2012. *Films include:* Sympathy For The Devil 1969, Gimme Shelter 1970, Ladies and Gentlemen, The Rolling Stones 1977, Let's Spend the Night Together 1983, Flashpoint 1991, Shine a Light 2007. *Publications include:* Ode to a High Flying Bird 1965, According to the Rolling Stones (autobiog., jtly) 2003. *Honours:* Nordoff-Robbins Silver Clef 1982, Grammy Lifetime Achievement Award 1986, Ivor Novello Award for Outstanding Contribution to British Music 1991. *Current Management:* c/o Rosebud Agency, PO Box 170429, San Francisco, CA 94117, USA. *Telephone:* (415) 386-3456. *E-mail:* info@ rosebudus.com. *Website:* www.rosebudus.com; www.rollingstones.com.

WATTS, Dave, (Impi-D, D. WattsRiot); British musician, producer and artist representative. *Career:* mem. radical rap group, Fun-Da-Mental; mem. Ear Conditioning. *Recordings include:* albums: Seize the Time 1994, With Intent to Pervert the Cause of Injustice 1995, Erotic Terrorism 1998, Why America Will Go to Hell 1999, There Shall Be Love! 2001, Voice of Mass Destruction 2003, All is War (The Benefits of G-Had) 2006. *Website:* www.davewattsmusic .com.

WATTS, Trevor Charles; British musician (alto, soprano saxophones, piano, percussion) and composer; b. 26 Feb. 1939, York, Yorks., England; s. of Paul Watts and Phyllis Hilton; two s. one d. *Education:* Ostler County Secondary Modern , Halifax, RAF School of Music, Uxbridge. *Career:* Founder-mem. Spontaneous Music Ensemble, Amalgam, Moiré Music, Celebration Band 2000; toured with Drum Orchestra in NZ, Burma, India, Caribbean, USA, Canada, Venezuela, Mexico, Botswana, South Africa, Lesotho, Colombia, Ecuador, Bolivia, Malaysia, People's Repub. of China; first group to play Burma for ten years; Arte TV show 1994; collaborated with traditional musicians, Khartoum Int. Festival, Sudan 1996; collaborations with Afro-Venezuelan Barlovento musicians 1992, 1995; toured in Cameroon, West Africa; festivals with Moiré Music include San Francisco Jazz Fest 2001, Chicago World Music Fest 2001, Monterey Jazz Fest 2002; attended Roaring Hooves Festival, Gobi Desert, Mongolia 2003, 2005; London Jazz Festival 2006; toured Brazil, Mexico, Dominican Repub. 2005; three tours of Mexico 2006; mem. Mexican band, Urukungolo; toured USA, Canada, Brazil 2007; duos with Steeleye Span violinist Peter Knight and with pianist Veryan Weston; collaboration with Adama Drame and Moroccan musicians in Burkina Faso 2010; US tour 2011; Guelph Festival Canada 2011; London Jazz Fest 2011; tours in Australia, NZ and USA with Veryan Weston 2012; Incubate Festival, Netherlands, London Jazz Festival and BBC broadcast 2012, Ad Libitum Festival, Warsaw 2013, London Jazz Fest, John Stevens Memorial Concert 2014; mem. Performing Right Soc., Mechanical-Copyright Protection Soc., Musicians' Union, PPL. *Compositions include:* Bracknell Festival Comm.: Mr Sunshine 1984, comm. for compositions to the '11 Songs' project in Burkina Faso 2010–11, Arts Council choral comm., The Light Vessel, first performed at Harwich Sing 2013. *Play:* music for The Connection (Hampstead Theatre) 1973. *Films include:* Moiré Music Drum Orchestra: Live in Karlsruhe Jazz Festival, Arte TV (Mongolia) 2003, DVD for New Music

Assen of Mongolia 2005; interviewed for film Play Your Own Thing on innovations in European Jazz 2005; music used animated films by artist Roland Jarvis 2009–10; music for film on Roland Jarvis and his work, Simply Not Cricket, filmed at festival in Berlin of that name (dir Antoine Prum), Hear Now interview film (dir Mark French), Kongsberg Jazz Festival, Norway 2013. *Radio includes:* Mixing It (BBC Radio 3) with Gibran Cervantes 2005, Jazz Britannica (BBC Radio 4), Jazz on 3 (with Peter Knight, violin) (BBC Radio 3) 2008, DRS 2 Swiss Radio/Berlin Brandenburg radio and BBC Radio 3 (with Veryan Weston), Czech Radio 3 (four dedicated programmes), Jazz Library 2011 (hour long programme on Trevor Watts' recorded music history), Jazz Record Requests (BBC Radio 3) 2015. *Television includes:* interviewed on the history of British jazz since the war (BBC 4), Jazz Brittania, and samples of music. *Recordings include:* with M. M. Drum Ork: A Wider Embrace; with Moiré Music: With One Voice, Intakt 1995, Live at the Athens Concert Hall 2000; with The Celebration Band: Trevor Watts & The Celebration Band 2001, World Sonic solo saxophone recording 2005, Ancestry 2006, Live in Sao Paulo Brasil 2006, Drum Orchestra: Drum Energy 2007, The Deep Blue (solo project for Jazzwerkstatt, Berlin) (voted one of best CDs of the year by Jazzwise magazine), Hear Now (DVD) 2013, Dialogues in Two Places (double CD with pianist Veryan Weston) 2013, Veracity (voted Best of Year by Wire Magazine) 2014. *Publications include:* Music Outside, Ian Carr 1973, Leonard Feathers Encyclopaedia of Jazz, Innovations in British Jazz, Vol. 1 1999; contrib. to Penguin Guide to Jazz (seventh edn), also special feature on best UK recordings (eighth edn) 2010, included in Penguin Guide Best Jazz CDs of all time for 'Prayer for Peace' 2010, Plink, Plonk & Scratch 2015. *E-mail:* altowatts@btinternet.com. *Address:* 20 Collier Road, Hastings, East Sussex, TN34 3JR, England. *Telephone:* (1424) 443424. *Fax:* (1424) 443424. *E-mail:* trevor510@gmail.com. *Website:* trevorwatts.co.uk.

WAVERLY, Josie; American entertainer; m.; two s. *Career:* appearances with band Genuine Country; past appearances with country artists including John Michael Montgomery, Lorrie Morgan, Tracy Lawrence, Charlie Daniels, Randy Travis, Neal McCoy, John Anderson, Sawyer Brown, Doug Stone; mem. CMA, The American Soc. of Composers, Authors and Publrs, BMI, NAFE. *Recordings include:* CD and cassette: Who Cries This Time. *Website:* www.josiewaverly.com.

WAY, Bryan Douglas; Canadian singer and songwriter; b. 20 Jan. 1953, Cornerbrook, NF; one s. one d. *Career:* numerous live appearances; mem. Canadian Country Music Assen, Nashville Songwriters' Assen Int. *Compositions:* Goodbye To The Rain, recorded by Roger Whittaker; Your Memory Lays Down With Me, recorded by James Owen Bush; End of Money, written and recorded by Bryan Way. *Address:* 20 Gamble Avenue, Suite 105, Toronto, ON M4K 2G9, Canada.

WAY, Gerard; American singer and songwriter; b. 9 April 1977, Newark, New Jersey. *Education:* School of Visual Arts, New York. *Career:* mem. and lead singer, My Chemical Romance 2001–13; currently solo artist; collaborated with numerous musicians including Kyosuke Himuro. *Recordings include:* albums: I Brought You My Bullets, You Brought Me Your Love 2002, Three Cheers for Sweet Revenge 2004, The Black Parade 2006, Danger Days: The True Lives of the Fabulous Killjoys 2010, Conventional Weapons 2013; solo: Hesitant Alien 2014. *Publications include:* On Raven's Wings (comic book series) 1993, The Umbrella Academy (comic book mini-series) 2007. *Honours:* Kerrang! Award for Best Int. Band 2006, 2007, NME Award for Best Int. Band 2007. *Website:* www.gerardway.com.

WAY, Mikey; American musician (bass guitar); b. 10 Sept. 1980, Newark, NJ. *Career:* mem. rock band, My Chemical Romance 2001–. *Recordings include:* albums: I Brought You My Bullets, You Brought Me Your Love 2002, Three Cheers for Sweet Revenge 2004, The Black Parade 2006, Danger Days: The True Lives of the Fabulous Killjoys 2010. *Honours:* Kerrang! Award for Best Int. Band 2006, 2007, NME Award for Best Int. Band 2007. *Address:* c/o Warner Bros. Records Inc., PO Box 6868, Burbank, CA 91510, USA (office). *E-mail:* infomcr@mychemicalromance.com. *Website:* www .mychemicalromance.com.

WAY, Pete; British musician (bass). *Career:* Founder-mem. UFO 1969–83; Founder-mem. Waysted 1983–88; rejoined UFO 1991–. *Recordings include:* albums: with UFO: UFO 1971, UFO 2 –Flying 1971, Live In Japan 1972, Phenomenon 1974, Face It 1975, No Heavy Pettin' 1976, Lights Out 1977, Obsession 1978, Strangers In The Night 1979, No Place To Run 1980, The Wild, The Willing and The Innocent 1981, Mechanix 1982, High Stakes and Dangerous Men 1992, Covenant 2000, Sharks 2002, You Are Here 2004, The Monkey Puzzle 2006; with Waysted: Vices 1983, The Good The Bad The Waysted 1985, Save Your Prayers 1986; solo recording: Amphetamine 2001. *Website:* www.ufo-music.info.

WAYBILL, Fee; American singer; b. (John Waldo), 17 Sept. 1950, Omaha, Neb. *Education:* drama student. *Career:* lead singer, The Tubes 1972–; regular int. tours and concerts, festival appearances. *Film:* band appeared in film Xanadu 1980. *Recordings include:* albums: Read My Lips 1984, Don't Be Scared by These Hands 1996; With The Tubes: The Tubes 1975, Young and Rich 1976, The Tubes Now 1977, What Do You Want From Live 1978, Remote Control 1979, Completion Backwards Principle 1981, TRASH (Tubes Rarities and Smash Hits) 1982, Inside Outside 1983, Love Bomb 1986, Genius of America 1996, Hoods from Outer Space 2002, White Punks on Dope 2003, Wild in London 2005, Alive in America 2006, Goin' Down the Tubes 2008, Mondo Birthmark 2009; singles: White Punks On Dope 1975, Don't Touch Me

There 1976, Prime Time 1979, I Don't Want To Anymore 1981, She's A Beauty 1983, Tip of My Tongue 1983, The Monkey Time 1983, Piece By Piece 1985; other recordings: Richard Marx, Richard Marx 1988, contrib. to film soundtrack Nobody's Perfect 1990, Days In Avalon, Richard Marx 2000. *Website:* www.thetubes.com.

WAYNE, Jeff; American composer and arranger; b. New York, NY. *Education:* Journalism Graduate; Juilliard School of Music, New York; Trinity College of Music, London. *Career:* member, The Sandpipers, 1960s; arranger, The Righteous Brothers; composer for TV commercials, 1970s; producer, musical director, David Essex, 1970s. *Compositions include:* A Tale of Two Cities, 1969. *Recordings:* albums: War of The Worlds 1978, War of The Worlds: Highlights 1981, Spartacus 1992, Ulladubulla: War Of The Worlds Remix Album 2000; as contributor: Beyond The Planets, Rick Wakeman and Kevin Peek, 1984. *Address:* Jeff Wayne Music Group, London House, 271–273 King Street, London W6 9LZ, England. *E-mail:* info@jeffwaynemusic.com. *Website:* www.jeffwaynemusic.com.

WAYNE, John Phil; British musician (guitar, keyboards, bass, drums), singer and actor; b. 14 July 1946, London; s. of George Henry Wayne and Julie Guilbeau; one s. one d. *Education:* . *Career:* sideman with Wild Bill Davis, David Bowie, Tom Jones, John Littleton, Stéphane Grappelli, Count Basie; solo artist and trio 1975; conducted The Paris Opera Musicians; solo concerts: most int. festivals and concerts (jazz); tours: Africa, Europe; played with: Shirley Bassey, David Bowie, Tom Jones, Memphis Slim, Babik Reinhardt, Christian Escoude, Willy Mabon, Sugar Blue, Vic Pitts, Jerome Van Jones, Bruce Grant, Sangoma Everett, Jack Greg, Yos Zoomer, Milford Chambers, Adrian White, among others; Business: Music Producer Tunecore/Universal; mem. PRS, MCPS, Musicians' Union, SACEM, SDRM, Steam Train Co. *Recordings include:* Let's Rock 1968, Nunchaku 1974, Nostalgia 1980, Broadway By Night 1981, 1981 Guitar Solo 1981, John Phil Wayne Live In Europe 1986, Fairy Queen 1987, Heavy Metal of The '90s 1991, Express X 1992, Trio Compilation 1995, Solo Compilations 1995, Heavy Steel of the 2000's 2000, Standard Times for Standards 2 2001, JazzPot 2002, Instant Music 2005, Fusion Jazz 2007. *Honours:* Godfather of the Int. Monte Carlo Racing Car, Twice Best Jazz Guitarist, First Prize Jazz USA 1980–82. *E-mail:* lordwayne3@hotmail.co.uk. *Website:* www.johnphilwayne.com.

WAZIMBO; Mozambican singer and songwriter; b. (Benfica Humberto Carlos), 1948, Chibuto. *Career:* mem. The Silverstars 1964; The Geiziers; Grupo Radio Mocambique, 1975; Orchestra Marrabenta Star de Mocambique, lead vocalist, 1979; Song, Nwahulwana, used in Microsoft commercial and film The Pledge, 2001. *Recordings:* with Orchestre Marrabenta Star de Mocambique: Independence, 1985; Marrabenta Piquenique, 1996; solo: Makweru, 1997; Nwahulwana, 2001. *E-mail:* records@piranha.de. *Website:* www.piranha.de.

WEATHERALL, Andrew (Andy); British producer, remixer and DJ; b. 6 April 1963, Windsor. *Career:* began DJ career at Danny Rampling's Shoom club night; remixed Primal Scream's Loaded and went on to produce their Mercury Music Prize-winning Screamadelica album; Co-founder Boy's Own fanzine; Founder, Sabres of Paradise, Emissions Audio Output, Rotter's Golf Club Recordings; collaborations with Terry Farley, Keith Tenniswood, Jagz Kooner; mem., Bocca Juniors, Sabres of Paradise, Two Lone Swordsmen; remixed Texas, Primal Scream, Future Sound of London, My Bloody Valentine, The Orb. *Recordings include:* albums: Sabresonic (with Sabres of Paradise) 1993, Haunted Dancehall (with Sabres of Paradise) 1994, Stay Down (with Two Lone Swordsmen) 1998, Tiny Reminders (with Two Lone Swordsmen) 2001, Wrong Meeting (with Two Lone Swordsmen) 2007, Sci-Fi Lo-Fi, Vol. 1 2007, A Pox on the Pioneers 2009, Masterpiece 2012, Ruled by Passion, Destroyed by Lust 2013.

WEAVER, Derek (Blue); British producer and musician (keyboards); b. 11 March 1947, Cardiff, Wales; m. Ann; one d. *Education:* Royal College of Music, Cardiff. *Career:* keyboard player, Amen Corner 1965–70; mem. The Strawbs 1971–73; session work included T Rex, Lou Reed, Family, Alice Cooper, Graeme Edge (Moody Blues); mem. Mott The Hoople, US tour supported by Queen, first rock band to play Broadway 1973–74; also played keyboards for Streetwalkers; mem. Ian Hunter/Mick Ronson Band, European tour 1974–75; moved to USA 1975; mem. Bee Gees 1975–82; returned to London 1982; played keyboards, produced, programmed computers for artists including: Pet Shop Boys, Art of Noise, Stevie Wonder, Miguel Bose, Duran Duran, Propaganda, The Damned, Billy Ocean, Swing Out Sister, Five Star; own digital studio; tutor, popular music, Westminster Univ., London; Dir, Music Producers Guild; mem, PRS, BMI, BAC&S, Musicians' Union, Re-Pro. *Compositions include:* co-wrote songs for Bee Gees; film soundtracks for Palace Pictures. *Recordings include:* with Amen Corner: Gin House Blues 1967, World Of Broken Hearts 1967, Bend Me Shape Me 1968, High In The Sky 1968, If Paradise Is Half As Nice 1969, Hello Suzie 1969, Strawbs 1970–73, Get It On, T Rex; Mott The Hoople Live; Berlin, Lou Reed; Bee Gees, 1974–82; Keyboards on albums by: Chicago; Stephen Stills; Neil Young; McGuinn Clark Hillman; The Osmonds; John Cougar Mellencamp; KC and the Sunshine Band 1999. *E-mail:* blue@blueweaver.com (office). *Website:* www.blueweaver.com.

WEBB, Sarah Anne; British singer; b. 1971. *Career:* lead singer of jazz funk quartet, D-Influence 1990–; tours, television appearances; also producer of R&B music; group owns Freakstreet label; session work with Seal, Digable Planets, Keziah Jones. *Recordings:* albums: Good 4 We 1992, Prayer 4 Unity 1995, London 1997, D-Influence Presents D-Vas 2002. *Address:* c/o Dome Records Ltd, PO Box 3274, East Preston, Sussex BN16 9BD, England (office). *Website:* www.domerecords.co.uk (office).

WEBBE, Simon Solomon; British singer; b. 30 March 1979, Manchester, England. *Career:* mem. band, Blue 2001–05; solo artist 2005–. *Recordings include:* albums: with Blue: All Rise 2001, One Love 2002, Guilty 2004; solo: Sanctuary 2005, Grace 2006. *Honours:* Smash Hits Awards for Best Newcomer 2001, Best Live Act, Best UK Band 2002, Interactive Music Award for Artist of the Year 2002, BRIT Award for Best British Newcomer 2002, NRJ Music Award for Best Int. Group (France) 2005. *Website:* www.simonwebbe.net.

WEBBER, Mark; British musician (guitar); b. 14 Sept. 1970, Chesterfield, Derbyshire, England. *Career:* mem. Pulp 1995–2002; numerous tours, TV appearances and festival dates; contrib. to film soundtrack, Mission Impossible 1996. *Recordings include:* albums: Different Class (No. 1, UK) 1995, This Is Hardcore (No. 1, UK) 1998, We Love Life 2001, Hits 2002; singles: Common People (No. 2, UK) 1995, Sorted For E's and Whizz/Misshapes (No. 2, UK) 1995, Disco 2000 1995, Something Changed 1996, Help The Aged 1997, This Is Hardcore 1998, A Little Soul 1998, Party Hard 1998, The Trees/Sunrise 2001, Bad Cover Version 2002.

WEBBER, Stephen, BM, MM; American composer, producer, academic and musician (guitar); *Professor of Music Production and Engineering, Berklee College of Music;* b. 14 April 1958; m. Susan Matthews 1981; two d. *Education:* Univ. of North Texas, Western Kentucky Univ. studied guitar with Sharon Isbin, Aspen, and John Johns, Vanderbilt. *Career:* owner, Mid South Recording Studios 1987–94; Prof. of Music Production and Engineering, Berklee Coll. of Music 1994–; Music Dir, Americana 2009–; Music Dir, National Tour, off Broadway, Cotton Patch Gospel, Bandleader, Stephen Webber Swing Band, Guitar, Cumberland Consort; mem, NARAS, AES, AFM, GFA. *Recordings include:* as guitarist: Timeless 1988, Hymns 1990, Cumberland Consort 1992, Angel Christmas 1994; as producer: He Calms the Storm in Me, Brenda Stuart 1992, No Solid Ground, Donna Carey 1993, Kevin Gallagher 1994, Manhattan Guitar Duo 1997. *Publications:* Turntable Technique: The Art of the DJ. *Honours:* Outstanding New Leader Award, Berklee Coll. of Music 1995, Emmy Award for Outstanding Achievement, Individual Excellence/Composer, Southern region 1997. *Address:* Department of Music Production and Engineering, Berklee College of Music, 1140 Boylston Street, Boston, MA 02215, USA (office). *Website:* stephenwebbermusic.com.

WEBER, Eberhard; German musician (bass guitar, double bass); b. 22 Jan. 1940, Stuttgart; m. Maja Weber 1968. *Education:* studied violoncello. *Career:* mem., Dave Pike Set 1972–73, Volker Kriegel Spectrum 1973–75, Eberhard Weber Colours 1975–81, United Jazz and Rock Ensemble 1975–87; collaborations include Jan Garbarek 1982–, Kate Bush, Monty Alexander, Pat Metheny, Stephane Grappelli; world-wide solo performances; composer of music for TV and film 1975–; mem. Union of German Jazz Musicians (UDJ). *Recordings:* The Colours of Chloe (German Phono Acad. Award for Record of the Year 1975) 1973, Yellow Fields 1975, The Following Morning 1976, Silent Feet 1977, Fluid Rustle 1978, Little Movements 1980, Later That Evening 1982, Chorus 1984, Works 1985, Orchestra 1988, Pendulum 1993, Endless Days 2001, Stages of a Long Journey 2005, Colours 2009. *Honours:* German Phono Acad. Award for Artist of the Year 1975. *Current Management:* Bremme and Hohensee, Hauptstrasse 25, 69117 Heidelberg, Germany. *Telephone:* (221) 25672. *Fax:* (221) 29460. *E-mail:* concert@bremme-hohensee.de. *Website:* www.bremme-hohensee.de.

WECKL, Dave; American musician (drums); b. 8 Jan. 1960, St Louis, Mo.; m. Joyce 1989; one d. *Education:* Marching Bands Coll. *Career:* performances with Simon and Garfunkel, Paul Simon, Chick Corea, Brecker Bros, Michel Camit, Mike Stern, Dave Weckl Band. *Recordings include:* albums: solo: The Next Step 1990, Ultimate Play-Along for Drums, Vol. 2 1996, Rhythm of the Soul 1998, Synergy 1999, Transition 2000, The Zone 2001, Perpetual Motion 2002, Multiplicity 2005; with Jay Oliver: Convergence 2014; also with Chick Corea Elektric Band, Robert Plant (Honeydrippers), Diana Ross (Swept Away), Dave Grushin, Chick Corea Akoustic Band. *Publications include:* Instructional – On Warner Bros 1988, Back to Basics, Next Step 1989, Working It Out, I and II 1994, The Ultimate Play Along, I and II 1994, 1995. *Honours:* Grammy Award (with Chick Corea Akoustic Band 1988), Best Electric Jazz Drummer, Modern Drummer 1987–92. *Current Management:* c/o Janet Williamson Music Agency, 600 Gainsborough Avenue, Los Angeles, CA 90027, USA. *Telephone:* (323) 661-0800. *Website:* www.janetwilliamsonmusicagency.com. *E-mail:* questions@daveweckl.com. *Website:* www.daveweckl.com.

WEEKES, Alan Noel; British musician (guitar), tutor, producer and composer; *Director, Bimsha Music Productions;* b. 25 Dec. 1958, London, England; four s. *Education:* Guildhall School of Music and Drama. *Career:* involved with British reggae scene 1980s; performed at festivals and concert venues worldwide including BBC Proms at Hyde Park, London; performed on Joss Stone multi-platinum album helping to create Lover's Rock; recording session credits include Art Blakey, Aswad, Carroll Thompson, Caron Wheeler, Lynden David Hall, Wynton Marsalis, Ernest Ranglin, Jamelia, Joss Stone, Jean Adebambo, Jackie Mitto, Jazz Warriors, Jazz Jamaica, Maxi Priest, Miss Lou, Sugar Minott, Sandra Cross, Trevor Walters, Victor Romero Evans, Skatroniks and Janet Kay; numerous radio and TV broadcasts; host (with Alan Weekes Quartet), Uncle Sam's Jazz & Blues Nite, now at the

Haggerston, London 1993–; Dir, Bimsha Music Productions. *Compositions:* composer, performer, Breath (series of music commissioned by Arts Council), Shaw Theatre 1992, Just a Dream (album) 1996, Dreams Come True 1998. *Plays:* Regina, Tooth of the Crime, 65 with a Bullet, Harder They Come 2006–07. *Recordings include:* with Sugar Minott, Carroll Thompson, Trevor Walters, Jean Adebambo, Jacky Mitto, Janet Kay, Art Blakey, Dick Heckstall-Smith, Courtney Pine, Jazz Jamaica, Byron Wallen's Sound Advice, Jazz Warriors, Jazz Jamaica All Stars, Soothsayers, Hugh Masekela, Alan Weekes' Jazz Quartet, Joss Stone (Mind, Body, Soul album), two albums with Sandra Cross. *Honours:* BBC Radio 3 Best Jazz Band Award (with Jazz Jamaica All Stars) 2002. *Address:* 30 Eastbourne Road, London, N15 6NT, England (home). *Telephone:* (7917) 703914 (mobile) (home). *E-mail:* alanbimsha@ hotmail.com (home). *Website:* www.myspace.com/alanweekesquartet.

WEERAMAN, Santhush; Sri Lankan singer and rapper; b. 5 Sept. 1977. *Education:* Royal Coll., Mary Anne David's School for Singing, Colombo. *Career:* mem. Bathiya & Santhush pop/rap duo (with Bathiya Jayakody) 1998–, released several albums; achieved 25 number one singles in Sri Lanka, many live concerts; collaborated with Indian singers including Hariharan and Asha Bhosle, co-f. BNS Production Group; composed and performed official Sri Lankan cricket anthem. *Recordings:* albums: with Bathiya & Santhush: Vasanthaye – A New Beginning 1998, Life 2000, Tharunyaye 2002, Neththara 2005, Resvihidena 2007, Ayubowan 2007, Shaheena 2008, Lanka Matha 2009, Sara Sihina 2010. *Honours:* with Bathiya & Santhush: Azia Dauysy Music Festival in Kazakhstan Silver Award Winners 2001, Shanghai Music Festival Bronze Award Winners 2001, TYOP (Ten Young Outstanding Persons) Award for contribution to Culture and Arts 2002, Golden Clef Award for Best Fusion Band 2002, Male Icon Award, Colombo Hilton 2006. *Address:* c/o Saregama Digital, Saregama Records, 33 Jessore Road, Kolkata, 700028, India (office); c/o BNS Music, Colombo, Sri Lanka (office). *E-mail:* info@bnsmusic.com (office). *Website:* www.saregama.com/portal/pages/music.jsp (office); www .bnsmusic.com (office).

WEHBE, Haifa; Lebanese singer; b. 10 March 1976, Mahrouna. *Career:* solo artist 2002–. *Recordings include:* albums: Howa el-zaman 2002, Baddi eish 2005, Al-wadi (TV show soundtrack) 2005, Sea of Stars (soundtrack) 2008, Habibi ana 2008. *Honours:* Al-Jamhouria Best Arab Young Female Singer 2002, Golden Lion (Egypt) 2002, Oscar for Best Video Clip (for Baddi Eich) 2005, Murex d'Or for Artist of the Year 2005, 2006, Sawt al-Musika Award for Song of the Year (for el-Wawa) 2006. *Address:* c/o Rotana, Burj al-Ghazal, 11th Floor, al-Tabaris, Achrafieh, Beirut, Lebanon (office). *E-mail:* info@rotana.net (office). *Website:* www.rotana.net (office); www.haifawehbe.com.

WEI, Wei; Chinese singer; b. 28 Sept. 1963, Hohhot, Inner Mongolia; m. Michael J. Smith (divorced 2004); three s. *Career:* singer at 11th Asian Games, Beijing 1990, performed a duet with Julio Iglesias at East Asian Games, Shanghai 1993; represented Asia at the ceremony of the Olympic Games, Atlanta, USA 1996; performed at closing ceremony, Beijing 2008 Summer Olympics. *Film appearance:* The Singer's Story. *Recordings include:* albums: The Album 1986, Bright Eyes 1987, Endless Love 1989, I Love My Motherland 1990, Famous Songs 1992, The Twilight 1994, Wei Wei 1998, Wei Wei's Devotion 1999, Dedication of Love 2001, Myths of China 2005, Yang-Chin 2006, 20x20 2008. *Honours:* winner Nat. Young Singers' contest on Chinese TV 1986, Sopot Int. Music Festival 1987. *Current Management:* Wei Wei International Management, Jing Da International 4E, Chao Yang Park West Road 11, 100026 Beijing, People's Republic of China. *E-mail:* info@weiweiint .com (office).

WEIDNER, Tim; British mix engineer, engineer and programmer. *Career:* Worked with Seal on the Spacejam Soundtrack; Worked with Trevor Horn for The Art of Noise and Seal. *Recordings:* Tina Turner, Wildest Dreams; Seal, Seal I, Seal II, Human Being, Kiss From a Rose (Engineer), Prayer For the Dying (Engineer, Programmer); Future Love Paradise (Engineer); Janet Jackson and Luther Vandross, Best Things in Life Are Free (Engineer, Remixer); Mike Oldfield, Tubular Bells II (Engineer, Mixed, Programmer), 1992; Shara Nelson, I Fell (Engineer, Mixed); Brand New Heavies, Back To Love (Engineer, Mixed); Sweetback; Art of Noise: Seduction of Claude Debussy, 1999; Frames, Dance the Devil, 1999; Genesis: Turn it on Again: The Hits, 1999; Other. *Recordings include:* XTC; Steve Howe. *Address:* Sarm Studios, 8–10 Basing Street, London, W11 1ET, England. *E-mail:* jill@spz .com.

WEINRICH, Detlef, (Tolouse Low Trax); German DJ and musician (electronics); b. 4 May 1966, Waldshut. *Education:* Düsseldorf Art Academie. *Career:* mem. electro-pop group, Kreidler 1994–; mem. techno project Binford Tolouse Low Trax. *Recordings include:* albums: Weekend 1996, Appearance and the Park 1998, Circles 2000, Kreidler 2000, Chicks on Speed/Kreidler Sessions 2001, Eve Future 2002, Eve Future Recall 2006, Tolouse Low Trax: Boarding to Rio 2005, Tolouse Low Trax: Mask Talk 2010, Kreidler: Tank 2011. *Address:* c/o Wonder Records, Herbert-Weichmann-Strasse 47, 22085 Hamburg, Germany (office). *E-mail:* wonder@wonder-records.com. *Website:* www.ikreidler.de.

WELCH, Brian 'Head'; American musician (guitar). *Career:* founder mem., L.A.P.D. (Love and Peace, Dude) 1989, renamed KoRn 1992–2005; solo artist 2007–; numerous tours and live appearances. *Recordings include:* albums: with L.A.P.D.: Love And Peace, Dude (EP) 1989, Who's Laughing Now 1991, L.A.P.D. 1997; with KoRn: Korn 1994, Life Is Peachy 1996, Follow The Leader 1998, Issues 1999, Untouchables 2002, Take A Look In The Mirror 2003, See

You On The Other Side 2005; solo: Save Me From Myself 2008. *E-mail:* info@ drivenmusicgroup.net. *Address:* 4025 East Chandler Road, Suite 70-B3, Phoenix, AZ 85048, USA (office). *Website:* www.brianheadwelch.net.

WELCH, Bruce, OBE; British singer, songwriter, musician (guitar) and producer; b. (Bruce Cripps), 2 Nov. 1941, Bognor Regis, W Sussex, England. *Education:* Rutherford Grammar School, Newcastle. *Career:* mem., The Railroaders 1957–58, The Five Chesternuts 1958, The Drifters 1958–59, The Shadows 1959–68, Marvin Welch and Farrar 1970–72, The Shadows 1973–1990; formed Bruce Welch's Shadows (occasional live group) late 1990s–; producer for Sir Cliff Richard 1974–79, for Olivia Newton-John. *Films:* The Young Ones 1961, Summer Holiday 1963, Wonderful Life 1964, Finders Keepers 1966. *Television:* Oh Boy! (ATV) 1958–59. *Recordings include:* albums: with The Shadows: The Shadows 1961, Out Of The Shadows 1962, Dance With The Shadows 1964, The Sound Of The Shadows 1965, Shadow Music 1966, Jigsaw 1967, From Hank Bruce Brian And John 1967, Rockin' With Curly Leads 1973, Specs Appeal 1975, Live At Olympia 1975, Rarities 1976, Tasty 1977, Shadows At The Movies 1978, Rock On With The Shadows 1980, Change Of Address 1980, The Shadows Salute The Ladies 1981, Life In The Jungle 1982, The Shadows Silver Album 1983, XXV 1983, The Shadows Vocals 1984, Guardian Angel 1984, Shadow Music 1985, Moonlight Shadows 1986, Showcase The Shadows 1986, Simply Shadows 1987, Steppin' To The Shadows 1989, The Shadows At Their Very Best 1989, Life Story 2004; with Cliff Richard and The Shadows: Cliff 1959, 21 Today 1961, The Young Ones 1962, Summer Holiday 1963, Wonderful Life 1964, Aladdin 1964, Finders Keepers 1966, Established 1958 1968, Thank You Very Much 1979; singles: with The Five Chesternuts: Jean Dorothy 1958; with The Drifters: Feelin' Fine 1959, Jet Black 1959; with The Shadows: Saturday Dance 1959, Apache 1960, Man Of Mystery/The Stranger 1960, FBI 1961, Frightened City 1961, Kon-Tiki 1961, The Savage 1961, Wonderful Land 1962, Guitar Tango 1962, Dance On 1962, Foot Tapper 1963, Atlantis 1963, Shindig 1963, Geronimo 1963, Theme For Young Lovers 1964, The Rise And Fall Of Flingel Bunt 1964, Rhythm And Greens 1964, Genie With The Light Brown Lamp 1964, Mary Anne 1965, Stingray 1965, Don't Make My Baby Blue 1965, War Lord 1965, I Met A Girl 1966, A Place In The Sun 1966, The Dreams I Dream 1966, Maroc 7 1967, Somewhere 1967, Running Out Of World 1968, Dear Old Mrs Bell 1968, Slaughter On 10th Avenue 1969, Turn Around And Touch Me 1973, Let Me Be The One 1975, Run Billy Run 1975, It'll Be Me Babe 1976, Another Night 1977, Love Deluxe 1978, Don't Cry For Me Argentina 1978, Cavatina 1979, Rodrigo's Guitar Concerto 1979, Riders In The Sky 1980, Equinoxe (Part V) 1980, Mozart 40 1980, The Third Man 1981, Telstar 1981, Imagine-Woman 1981, Treat Me Nice 1982, Theme From Missing 1982, Diamonds 1983, Going Home 1983, On A Night Like This 1984, Moonlight Shadow 1986, Dancing In The Dark 1986, Pulaski 1987, Theme From The Snowman 1987, Mountains Of The Moon 1989; with Cliff Richard and The Shadows: Move It 1958, High Class Baby 1958, Livin' Lovin' Doll 1959, Mean Streak 1959, Living Doll 1959, Travellin' Light 1959, Expresso Bongo (EP) 1960, Voice In The Wilderness 1960, Fall In Love With You 1960, Please Don't Tease 1960, Nine Times Out Of Ten 1960, I Love You 1960, Theme For A Dream 1961, Gee Whiz It's You 1961, A Girl Like You 1961, The Young Ones 1962, I'm Looking Out The Window/Do You Wanna Dance 1962, It'll Be Me 1962, The Next Time/Bachelor Boy 1962, Summer Holiday 1963, Lucky Lips 1963, Don't Talk To Him 1963, I'm The Lonely One 1964, On The Beach 1964, I Could Easily Fall 1964, The Time In Between 1965, Blue Turns To Grey 1966, Time Drags By 1966, In The Country 1966, Don't Forget To Catch Me 1968; with Marvin Welch and Farrar: Mr Sun 1971, Lady Of The Morning 1971, Marmaduke 1972; solo: Please Mr Please 1974. *Publications:* Rock 'n' Roll: I Gave You the Best Years of My Life (autobiog.) 1989.

WELCH, Ed; British composer, arranger and musician (piano); b. 22 Oct. 1947, Oxford, England; m. Jane Welch 1968; two s. one d. *Education:* , Trinity College of Music. *Career:* staff arranger, plugger, orchestrator, United Artists Music 1967–76; freelance composer 1977–; guest conductor with all major British orchestras; mem. BAC&S, PRS, Musicians' Union. *Compositions include:* films: The Thirty Nine Steps 1974, The Snow Goose 1976; TV: Shillingbury Tales 1980, Blockbusters 1983, Catchphrase 1985, TV AM News 1986, Knightmare 1986, $64,000? 1989, One Foot In The Grave, all series, BBC 1989–2000, Jim Henson's Animal Show (all music) 1994, The National Lottery 1994, Wolves Witches Giants 1995.

WELCH, Florence Leontine Mary; British singer and songwriter; b. 28 Aug. 1986, London; d. of Nick Welch and Prof. Evelyn Welch. *Education:* Camberwell Coll. of Arts. *Career:* lead singer, Florence and the Machine 2006–. *Recordings include:* albums: Lungs (BRIT Award for Best British Album 2010) 2009, Ceremonials 2011, How Big, How Blue, How Beautiful 2015. *Honours:* Critics' Choice Award, BRIT Awards 2009, Meteor Ireland Music Award for Best Int. Band 2010, Q Awards for Best Female and Best Song (for You've Got the Love) 2010, for Best Video (for Ship to Wreck) 2015. *Website:* florenceandthemachine.net.

WELCH, Gillian Howard; American singer, musician (guitar, banjo) and songwriter; b. 2 Dec. 1967, California; m. David Rawlings. *Education:* Berklee Coll. of Music, Boston. *Career:* listened to bluegrass and early country music as a child and, whilst studying at Berklee, began performing in this style along with her own material as part of a duo with fellow student David Rawlings 1996–; featured solo on film soundtracks; guested on albums by: Mark Knopfler, Ryan Adams, Nanci Griffith, Emmylou Harris, Kimmie Rhodes, Guy Clark, The Chieftains, Robyn Hitchcock, Rodney Crowell, Sara Watkins,

Jenny Lewis, Norah Jones, Dave Rawlings Machine, The Decemberists, Steve Earle; songs recorded by artists including: Ryan Adams, Cindy Church, Christine Collister, Emmylou Harris, Alison Krauss and Union Station. *Recordings include:* albums: Revival 1996, Hell Among The Yearlings 1998, Time (The Revelator) 2001, Soul Journey 2003, The Harrow & the Harvest 2011; as contributor: O Brother, Where Art Thou? (Grammy Award for Album of the Year 2002) 2000. *Address:* c/o Acony Records, PO Box 60007, Nashville, TN 37206, USA (office). *Telephone:* (615) 228-7708 (office). *Fax:* (615) 228-7709 (office). *E-mail:* information@aconyrecords.com (office). *Website:* www.aconyrecords.com (office); www.gillianwelch.com.

WELCH, Justin Stephen; British musician (drums); b. 4 Dec. 1972, Nuneaton. *Career:* drummer with Psychedelic Rockers Spitfire; mem., Elastica 1992–95, Lush 2015–; toured extensively world-wide. *Recordings:* albums: Elastica 1995; singles: Stutter 1993, Connection 1994, Line Up 1994, Waking Up 1995. *Honours:* NME Readers Award for Best New Band 1994. *Current Management:* Jonathan Morley, Northern Lights Management. *E-mail:* jonathan@northernlightsmgt.co.uk. *Website:* www.northernlightsmgt.co.uk; lushofficial.com.

WELCH, Sean; British musician (bass); b. 12 April 1965, Enfield, England. *Career:* mem. The Beautiful South 1989–2007. *Recordings include:* albums: Welcome To The Beautiful South 1989, Choke 1990, 0898 1992, Miaow 1994, Blue Is The Colour 1996, Quench 1998, Painting It Red 2000, Gaze 2002, Golddiggas, Headnodders and Pholk Songs 2004, Superbi 2006.

WELDEN, Judy; American singer, songwriter, promoter, musician (piano) and inventor; b. (Judith Ann Ernst), 1 April 1938, Buffalo Valley, Pa; d. of Malcolm Ernst and Lillian Ernst; m. William Blecha 1983; one s. two d. *Education:* voice and piano lessons, Storesonline Univ. *Career:* mem. of numerous bands; Owner of two record labels and two publishing cos; numerous top ten recordings on ind. charts; performed at festivals in many countries; Founder, Treasure Coast Songwriters Asscn 1993, Fairness in Royalty Payments 1995; mem. Atlanta CMA Hall of Fame, Broadcast Music, Inc. (BMI), Reverbnation.com, numberonemusic.com. *Recordings include:* Come on Home, Fishin' For a New Love, You are there for Me, Daddy's Army Whistle, Every Day's a Holiday, Confusion, What's The Solution, Grandma's Quilts, I'm Pain Shy, I'm Hittin' the Road, Chasing A Dream, Forever Grateful, Guide My Heart, I'm a Survivor, Macho Man with a Marshmallow Heart, Kisses, This Christmas (Spread His Love Around the World), Shades of Blue, Let's Make America Great Again, and many more. *Publication:* 68 Unforgettable Days in Europe 1998. *Honours:* First Place Vocal Award 1990, Hollywood Song Jubilee 1992, Woman of the Year in Arts 1995, New Gospel Division Most Promising Female Vocalist 1999, Modern Country Album of the Year (for Judy Welden Country Hits) 1999, Female Int. Recording Artist of the Year 1999, American Horizon Award 1999, Horizon Co-Writer Award (Best of Texas, for Grandma's Quilts and Confusion (What's the Solution, with Terrance Alan and Mia Heylen) 1999, CO Hall of Fame Award 2006, GCR Artist of the Year (Great Country Radio) 2012, No. 1 Singer-songwriter on Reverbnation.com June 2013, Ind. Superstar Hall of Fame Songwriter 2013. *Telephone:* (770) 503-0096 (office). *Fax:* (770) 503-0096 (office). *E-mail:* judywelden@bellsouth.net (office). *Address:* 4008 Soapstone Lane, Gainesville, GA 30506, USA (home). *E-mail:* judy@judywelden.com. *Website:* www.judywelden.com; www.bandana-hat.com.

WELDING, Paul Daniel; British record producer and remixer; b. 14 May 1971, St Helens. *Career:* dance music record producer; various radio appearances on local stations; remixes for major record companies and also DJ at The Opera House, Toronto, Canada; mem, Musicians' Union. *Recordings:* albums: Void 1 and 2, Rebound; as Foundation: Prisoner Of Love. *E-mail:* paul@djwelly.net (office). *Website:* www.djwelly.net.

WELDON, Joel; American singer and songwriter; b. 1958; m. 1986 (divorced 1995); one s. one d. *Career:* touring artist in contemporary Christian music. *Recordings include:* albums: Mistaken Identity 1985, Terror and Love 1987, Pure Adventure 1988, Wisdom Street 1989, Cross The World 1990, Catch Fire America 1991, Rock It 1993, Rise Up America 1994. *Address:* 909 East Glencrest Drive, Spokane, WA 99208, USA. *E-mail:* debbiejill@comcast.net; joelweldon@gmail.com. *Website:* www.joelweldon.com; www.joelweldonmusic.com.

WELLER, Paul; British musician (guitar, piano), singer and songwriter; b. 25 May 1958, Woking, Surrey. *Career:* founder mem. and lead singer, The Jam 1972–82, The Style Council 1983–89, The Paul Weller Movement and solo artist 1990–; own record label Freedom High. *Recordings include:* with The Jam: In the City 1977, This is the Modern World 1977, All Mod Cons 1978, Setting Sons 1979, Sound Affects 1980, The Gift 1982; with The Style Council: Introducing The Style Council 1983, Café Bleu 1984, Our Favourite Shop 1985, Home and Abroad 1986, The Cost of Loving 1987, Confessions of a Pop Group 1988, Singular Adventures of the Style Council 1989, Here's Some That Got Away 1993, Modernism: A New Decade 1998; solo: Paul Weller 1992, Wild Wood 1993, Live Wood 1994, Stanley Road 1995, Heavy Soul 1997, Modern Classics 1998, Heliocentric 2000, Days of Speed 2001, Illumination 2002, Fly on the Wall: B-Sides and Rarities 2003, Studio 150 2004, As Is Now 2005, Catch-Flame! 2006, Hit Parade 2006, 22 Dreams 2008, Wake Up the Nation 2010, Sonik Kicks 2012. *Film:* JerUSAlem 1987. *Honours:* Ivor Novello Award, BRIT Awards for Best Male Artist 1995, 1996, 2009, Mojo Award for Best Songwriter 2005, Q Award for Outstanding Contribution to Music 2005, BRIT Award for Outstanding Contribution 2006, Silver Clef

Award 2007, Ivor Novello Award for Lifetime Achievement 2010. *Current Management:* c/o Z Management, The Palm House, PO Box 19734, London, SW15 2WU, England. *Telephone:* (20) 8874-3337. *Fax:* (20) 8874-3599. *E-mail:* dionne@zman.co.uk; alex@zman.co.uk. *Website:* www.zman.co.uk; www.paulweller.com.

WELLMAN, Samuel Edison, BA, MM, DM; American academic, composer and musician (piano); *Professor of Music, Liberty University*; b. 15 May 1951, Anderson, Ind.; m. Deborah Eileen Moyer 1971; four s. (two deceased three d. *Education:* Lenoir Rhyne Coll., Florida State Univ. *Career:* Coll. Prof., Warner Southern Coll., Lake Wales, Fla 1974–92, Liberty Univ., Lynchburg, Va 1992–; concert pianist and accompanist; church pianist and organist 1962–; mem. American Composers' Alliance, Music Teachers' Nat. Asscn, American Music Center. *Plays:* three plays. *Compositions:* more than 1,240 works. *Publications:* Four American Pieces 1991, Anna Magdalena Revisited 1993, Hometown, USA 1997, Hymn Favourites 1997, Beyond Boundaries 2002, Five Fingers in Motion 2004, Five Fingers at Play 2005; 60 essays and short stories. *Honours:* Commissioned Composer, Florida State Music Teachers' Asscn 1989. *Address:* School of Music, Liberty University, 1971 University Boulevard, Lynchburg, VA 24502 (office); 125 Temple Circle, Lynchburg, VA 24502, USA (home). *Telephone:* (434) 582-2097 (office). *E-mail:* swellman@liberty.edu (office).

WELLS, Robert Henry Arthur; Swedish composer and musician (piano and vocal); b. 7 April 1962, Stockholm; Engaged to Maria Sköld. *Education:* Adolf Fredriks Music School, 1969–78; Academy of Music, 1978–82; Private piano lessons, 1969–78. *Career:* Professionally working in Scandinavia and Russia, 1987–; Toured with different bands and singers, 1977–87; Featuring in major TV-shows; Played for Swedish Royalties several times; Concerts and TV performances in USA and Canada, 1998–99. *Recordings:* Upp Pa Berget, 1987; The Way I Feel, 1988; Rhapsody in Rock I, 1989; Rhapsody in Rock II, 1990; Norman Vs Wells, 1991; Rhapsody in Rock III, 1993; Nordic Rhapsody, 1996; Boogie Woogie Norman and Wells, 1996; Rhapsody In Rock Complete, 1998. *Honours:* Gold Record, 1998. *E-mail:* info@wellsmusic.se. *Website:* www.wellsmusic.se.

WELSFORD, Andy Wells; British musician (drums); b. 14 March 1959, Bristol; one d. *Education:* technical coll. *Career:* drummer with Meat Loaf 1985–86; March Violets 1987; Romeo's Daughter 1989; Then Jerico 1994, The Slaves 1996–; world tours, television and radio broadcasts; sessions for Roxette, Whitney Houston, John Parr, Dee Lewis, Daniel Weaver, Andy Leek. *Recordings:* two albums with Romeo's Daughter, one track on Meat Loaf album, one album with Then Jerico. *Address:* c/o Sandridgebury Stables, Sandridgebury Lane, Sandridge, St Albans, AL3 6JB, England (office).

WELSH, Dave; American musician (guitar). *Career:* mem., The Fray 2002–. *Recordings include:* album: How to Save a Life (Billboard Award for Digital Album of the Year 2006) 2005, The Fray 2009. *Honours:* Billboard Award for Digital Album Artist of the Year, for Digital Songs Artist of the Year 2006. *Address:* c/o Sony BMG, 550 Madison Avenue, New York, NY 10022, USA. *E-mail:* fraymanagement@gmail.com. *Website:* www.thefray.net.

WELTY, Ron; American musician (drums); b. 1 Feb. 1971, Long Beach, CA; m. Erica; one s. *Education:* California trade school. *Career:* played alto saxophone and drums in high school bands; fmr mem., FQX; mem., The Offspring 1986–2003; numerous live shows, festival appearances and tours; mem., Spinning Fish 1990–, Steady Ground 2003–. *Recordings include:* albums: The Offspring 1989, Ignition 1992, Smash! 1994, Ixnay On The Hombre 1997, Americana 1998, Conspiracy Of One 2000. *Honours:* Kerrang! Award for Classic Songwriter (with The Offspring) 2002. *Address:* 1100 Irvine Boulevard, Suite 73, Tustin, CA 92780, USA (office). *E-mail:* contact@steadyground.com (office). *Website:* www.steadyground.com.

WELZ, Joey; American singer, musician (piano), record producer and record company executive; *President and CEO, Canadian American Records*; b. (Joseph Welzant), 17 March 1940, Baltimore, Md; one s. one d. *Education:* Harford Coll. *Career:* pianist, Bill Haley and the Comets 1960s–80s; played with Beatles, Link Wray, Roy Buchanan; re-formed Original Comets 1981; numerous worldwide tours and TV appearances; A&R Exec., Canadian American Records 1966–70, Palmer Records, Detroit 1971–73, Music City Records, Nashville 1974–81, Caprice Records, Pennsylvania 1982–84; Pres. and CEO Caprice Int. Records 1984–, Canadian American Records 1989–; Pres. and Owner, Rock Mill Studios, Pa 1990–; mem. The American Soc. of Composers, Authors and Publrs (ASCAP); Sergeant in the Army Nat. Guard. *Compositions include:* Hey Little Moonbeam, Baby Let Your Head Hang Down, Candle In The Wind, Forever, Everyday For The Rest of My Life, Universal Love, One Stormy Love, In The Middle of The Night Time, Hey Baby, Life on Mars 1997, Your Love Means Everything with Amy Beth, A Ring Between Us with Amy Beth, Rang-a-Tang Boogie. *Recordings include:* albums: The Turn of the Century 2000, Radio Rock 2000, Song and Dance Man 2001, Rock and Roll Remembers 2001, W A K E 2006, Breakaway 2007, Hops & Hopscotch 2007, The Power And The Glory 2008, Rewind The Pop/the 90s 2008, From The Rockin' Of My Cradle To The Rollin' Of My Hearse 2008, My Rock-A-Billy Life – Rewind My Rock And Roll 2011, Touched By An Angel 2011, Rock-A-Billy Son 2011, Rock Around The Clock Forever 2011, I Remember The Song 2011, Hip Hoppin' The Rock 2011, Forever More 2011, Bring Back The Music 2011, It's All About Love And Money 2011, 21st Century Rocker 2011, Still Like To Boogie With A Texas Swing 2011, Top Ten Radio Hits Of The 50s 2011, Top Ten Radio Hits Of The 60s 2011, The Best Of

Joey Welz Country 2011, City Of Stone 2011, Born Again Country 2011, Tsunami 2011, Casino Life 2014, Lifespan 2014. *Achievement:* Duncan World Yo Yo Champion. *Honours:* Country Rock Pioneer Award, EIA Award for Most Promising Country Male Vocalist, CMA Award for Video of Year 1993, Independent Country Male Vocalist of Year, Legendary Performer of Year, Songwriter of Year, Gold Charter Member, The Rock and Roll Hall of Fame, inducted into Rockabilly Hall of Fame and The Memphis Music Heritage Hall of Fame, selected by Rolling Stone magazine as one of the top 100 Immortals of Rock and Roll. *Address:* Canadian American & Caprice International Records, PO Box 808, Lititz, PA 17543, USA (office). *Telephone:* (717) 627-4800 (office). *Fax:* (717) 627-4800 (office). *E-mail:* canadianamerican@dejazzd.com (office). *Website:* www.capricerecording.com (office); www.joeywelz.com.

WEMBA, Papa; Belgian singer and songwriter; b. (Jules Shungu Wembadio Pene Kikumba), 14 June 1949, Kasai, Democratic Republic of Congo. *Career:* began singing in church choir 1966; Co-founder, Zaiko Langa Langa 1969–74; Founder-mem., Isife Lokole 1974; formed Viva La Musica (with Ringo Starr) 1977; worked with Koffi Olomide; collaboration with Rochereau Tabu Ley's orchestra, Afrisa International 1979. *Recordings include:* albums: Zaiko Langa Langa Hits Inoubliables Vol. VIII 1970–73, Yoka Lokole Dans Matembele Bangi 1975–76, Papa Wemba and Koffi Olomide 1978–79, Événement 1981–82, Papa Wemba – Destiny Ya Moto 1985, Papa Wemba 1988, Le Voyageur 1991, The Kershaw Sessions 1994, Emotion 1995, Molokai 1998, 1977–1997 2004, New Morning 2006, Notre Père Rumba 2010, Trait d'union 2011, Maître d'école 2014. *Honours:* Elima (newspaper) Award for Best Vocalist, Kinshasa, Best Song of the Year (for Mere Superiere) 1977, Grammy Award for Best African Performer 2001. *E-mail:* shunguwemba@hotmail.com. *Website:* www.papawemba.fr.

WENDLING-PARDON, Charlotte; German trumpet player; b. 20 June 1953; m. Manfred Pardon 1982; one d. *Education:* music studies in Saarbrücken. *Career:* plays trumpet duets with her brother Jürgen Wendling; has performed at nat. and int. concerts and on radio and TV; Man. Dir 3w.Records; Fed. winner young musicians' competitions 1965, 1967, 1969, 1971; apptd Consul, Hohoe, Ghana 2001. *Honours:* Carl-Orff Prize. *Address:* 3w.Records, Steinkopfweg 10, 66386 St Ingbert, Germany (office). *Telephone:* (6894) 8233 (office). *Fax:* (6894) 870740 (office). *E-mail:* drei-w.records@t-online.de (office). *Website:* www.3w-records.de (office).

WENER, Louise; British singer, songwriter and writer; b. 1966, Ilford, Essex, England; partner Andy MacLure; one d. *Education:* Manchester Univ. *Career:* lead singer, Sleeper 1993–98; numerous tours, festival appearances; mem. PRS, MU, PAMRA. *Recordings include:* albums: Smart 1995, It Girl 1996, Pleased To Meet You 1997. *Publications include:* novels: Goodnight Steve McQueen 2002, The Big Blind (aka The Perfect Play) 2003, The Half Life of Stars 2006, Worldwide Adventures in Love 2008; memoir: Different for Girls: My True-Life Adventures in Pop 2010. *Website:* www.louise-wener.co.uk.

WENHAM, Alison, OBE; British music industry executive; *Chair and CEO, Association of Independent Music;* m.; two c. *Career:* fmrly Head of Conifer Records for 20 years; Man. Dir Classics and Jazz Divs, BMG Entertainment 1995–98; Chair. and CEO, Asscn of Independent Music (AIM) 1999–; Chair., Worldwide Independent Network 2009–; Panel mem., Second Annual Popkomm Innovations in Music and Entertainment Awards (IMEA), Berlin 2005; fmr council mem., British Phonographic Industry (BPI); fmr bd dir, PPL; currently Vice-Pres. IMPALA (European Independent Music Publishers and Labels Asscn); mem. British Library Nat. Sound Archive Advisory Cttee; mem. Culture and Creativity Cttee, Dept of Culture, Media and Sport. *Address:* Association of Independent Music, Lamb House, Church Street, London, W4 2PD, England (office). *Telephone:* (20) 8994-5599 (office). *Fax:* (20) 8994-5222 (office). *E-mail:* info@musicindie.com (office). *Website:* www.musicindie.org (office).

WENNER, Jann S.; American publisher; *Editor and Publisher, Rolling Stone;* b. 7 Jan. 1946, New York; m. Jane Schindelheim (divorced); six c. *Education:* Univ. of California, Berkeley. *Career:* Founder, Ed. and Publisher, Rolling Stone magazine 1967–; TV appearances include Crime Story 1987–88; Chair. Wenner Media Inc., Rock & Roll Hall of Fame Foundation, Inc.; Owner, Us and Men's Journal magazines. *Film appearances:* Up Your Legs Forever 1970, Perfect 1985, Jerry Maguire 1996, Almost Famous 2000. *Publications include:* Lennon Remembers (ed.) 1972, 20 Years of Rolling Stone: What a Long Strange Trip It's Been 1987, Rolling Stone Environmental Reader 1992, Gonzo: The Life of Hunter S. Thompson (edited with Corey Seymour) 2007, Fear and Loathing at Rolling Stone: The Essential Writing of Hunter S. Thompson (ed.) 2011. *Honours:* inducted into American Soc. of Magazine Eds Hall of Fame 1997, Publishing Exec. of the Year, Adweek 1994, Lifetime Achievement Award (non-performer category), Rock & Roll Hall of Fame 2004, Norman Mailer Prize for Lifetime Achievement in Magazine Publishing 2010. *Address:* Rolling Stone, Wenner Media Inc., 1290 Avenue of the Americas, New York, NY 10104-0298, USA (office). *Telephone:* (212) 484-1616 (office). *E-mail:* editors@rollingstone.com (office). *Website:* www.rollingstone.com (office); www.jannswenner.com.

WENNIKE, Ole B; Danish musician and composer; b. 15 May 1958, Copenhagen; 1 s. *Career:* Founder, Copenhagen Based The Sandmen, 1985–92, support gigs in Copenhagen for Nico, Jeffrey Lee Pierce, Long Ryders, 1985–86; USA Tour, 1989, London's Borderline, 1989; Founder, Copenhagen Based Nerve, 1995, support gigs in Copenhagen for David Bowie.

Compositions: Western Blood, House in the Country, Heart of Steel, 1989; 5 mins Past Loneliness, Can't Cry No More, 1993; Slave Song, 1994. *Recordings:* The Sandmen Albums: Western Blood, 1988; Sleepy Head, 1993; In the House of Secrets, 1994; Nerve Album: Speedfreak Jive, 1996. *Honours:* Danish Grammy, 1993; Gold Record, Denmark. *Address:* Rosenörns Alle 6, 4Tv, 1634 Copenhagen V, Denmark.

WENTZ, Pete; American musician (bass guitar); b. (Peter Lewis Kingston Wentz III), 5 June 1979, Wilmette, Ill.; m. Ashlee Simpson 2008; one s. *Education:* DePaul Univ. *Career:* fmr mem. various bands including First Born, Arma Angelus, Yellow Road Priest, Racetraitor; Founder-mem., bass guitarist, backing vocalist and lyricist for band Fall Out Boy 2001–09, 2013–; formed Black Cards (with Bebe Rexha, Nate Patterson and Spencer Peterson) 2010; headline act Nintendo Fusion Tour 2005, Black Clouds and Underdogs Tour 2005, Honda Civic Tour 2007, Young Wild Things Tour 2007; collaborations with Gym Class Heroes, Motion City Soundtrack; Owner Clandestine Industries, a co. distributing clothing and other merchandise; Head, Decaydance Records and Bartskull Films. *Recordings include:* albums: Fall Out Boy's Evening Out with Your Girlfriend (mini-LP) 2002, Take This to Your Grave 2003, From Under the Cork Tree 2005, Infinity on High 2007, Folie à Deux 2008, Save Rock and Roll 2013, American Beauty/American Psycho 2015. *Publications include:* The Boy With the Thorn In His Side, Fall Out Toy Works 2009. *Honours:* People's Choice Awards for Favorite Int. Group 2006, for Favorite Alternative Band 2014, Kerrang! Awards for Best Video (for Sugar, We're Going Down) 2006, (for This Ain't a Scene, It's an Arms Race) 2007, for Best Single (for The Phoenix) 2013, for Best Int. Band 2014, Teen Choice Awards for Best Rock Track and Best Single (for Dance, Dance) 2006, for Best Single (for Thnks Fr Th Mmrs) 2007, MTV Video Music Awards for Viewers Choice 2007, for Best Group 2007, for Best Rock Video (for Uma Thurman) 2015, World Music Award for Best Alternative Act 2014, American Music Award for Favorite Alternative Rock Artist 2015. *Website:* www.petewentz.com; www.falloutboy.com.

WENTZEL, Magni; Norwegian musician (classical guitar) and jazz singer; b. 28 June 1945, Oslo; m. 1976 (divorced 1986); one s. *Career:* numerous national and international performances; regular appearances on Norwegian television and radio; mem. Norsk Musikerforbund (Norwegian Musicians' Union). *Recordings include:* as guitarist with Radio Symphony Orchestra: with Einar Iversen's Trio: That Old Feeling/My One and Only Love, 1959; Magni Wentzel Plays, 1969; Guitar and Flute, with Torkil Bye, 1975; Sofies Plass, 1983; All Or Nothing At All, 1986; with Art Farmer: My Wonderful One, 1988; with Roger Kellaway and Red Mitchell: New York Nights, 1991; with Roger Kellaway and Niels H. O. Pedersen: Come Away With Me, 1993; with Roger Kellaway and Mads Vinding: Turn Out the Stars, 1996; Gershwin: Porgy & Bess, 2000; Divergence, 2002. *Honours:* Gamleng Prize, Norwegian Jazz Federation Buddy Award. *Address:* Neuberggaten 6 A, 0367 Oslo, Norway. *E-mail:* magniwentzel@hotmail.com.

WERMAN, Thomas Ehrlich, BA, MBA; American record producer and musician (guitar, percussion); b. 2 March 1945, Newton, Massachusetts; m. 1968; one s. two d. *Education:* Columbia College, Columbia Business School. *Career:* A & R Epic Records 1970–82; Senior Vice-President, A & R Elektra Records 1982; Independent producer 1983–; signed REO Speedwagon, Ted Nugent, Cheap Trick, Molly Hatchet, Boston, The Producers, Mother's Finest; mem, NARAS. *Recordings:* produced Ted Nugent, Cheap Trick, Molly Hatchet, Twisted Sister, Jeff Beck, Poison, Mötley Crüe, Kix, LA Guns, Jason and the Scorchers, Lita Ford, Gary Myrick, The Supersuckers, Blue Oyster Cult, The Cult, Dokken, Krokus. *Address:* Stonover Farm, 169 Under Mountain Road, Lenox, MA 01240, USA (home). *Telephone:* (413) 637-9100 (home). *E-mail:* stonoverfarm@aol.com (home).

WERNICK, Peter, (Dr Banjo), BA, PhD; American musician (banjo), writer and teacher; b. 25 Feb. 1946, New York; m. Joan Nondi Leonard 1974; one s. *Education:* Columbia Univ. *Career:* founder mem. Country Cooking, Ithaca, New York 1970–76, Rambling Drifters, Denver, Colorado 1976–78, Hot Rize, Boulder, Colorado 1978–90, Pete Wernick's Live Five 1992–, renamed Flexigrass; US and international tours with Hot Rize; appeared on Austin City Limits, Grand Ole Opry, Nashville Now, Prairie Home Companion; Pres., IBMA (International Bluegrass Association); mem, President IBMA, ASCAP, NARAS. *Recordings include:* albums: solo: On A Roll 1993, Dr Banjo Steps Out; with Hot Rize: Untold Stories, Take It Home, Traditional Ties, In Concert; with Five Live: I Tell You What!. *Publications:* Bluegrass Banjo 1974, Bluegrass Song Book 1976, How to Make a Band Work 1991, Acutab Transcriptions, Vol. I 1996, I Tell You What 1996; with Tony Trischka: Early Years 1998; with Marshall Wilborn: Brass and Piano 1999, Choice Picks 2000. *Honours:* IBMA Entertainer of the Year with Hot Rize 1989. *Address:* 7930-P Oxford Road, Niwot, CO 80503, USA (office). *E-mail:* pete@drbanjo.com (office). *Website:* www.drbanjo.com.

WERRASON; Democratic Republic of the Congo musician; b. (Ngiama Makanda), 25 Dec. 1965. *Career:* mem., Wenge Music Orchestra 1981. *Recordings include:* albums: Intervention Rapide 1998, Kubuisa Mpimpa, Témoignage 2005. *Honours:* Kora Award for Best Male African Artist 2001. *Website:* www.werrason.org.

WERTICO, Paul David; American musician (drums, percussion), educator, clinician, recording artist and producer and composer; *Associate Professor of Jazz, Chicago College of Performing Arts, Roosevelt University;* b. 5 Jan. 1953, Chicago, Ill.; m. Barbara Ungerleider 1986; one d. *Education:* Western Illinois

Univ. *Career:* mem. Pat Metheny Group 1983–2001; tours world-wide as clinician 1986–; N American tours with Simon & Bard Group 1980–82; tours world-wide with Paul Wertico Trio 1994–; mem. Pat's Metheny's Secret Story Band 1992–93; tours world-wide with Kurt Elling 1995–97; tours of Europe with Niels Lan Doky Band 1999–2000; mem. SBB 2000–07; Larry Coryell Trio 2000–; performed with numerous jazz artists, including Lee Konitz, Herbie Mann, Terry Gibbs, Buddy DeFranco, Lew Tabakin, Randy Brecker, Jaco Pastorius, Chico Freeman, Charlie Haden, George Coleman, Ramsey Lewis, Dave Liebman, Eddie Harris, Sam Rivers, Bob Mintzer, Jay McShann; Assoc. Prof. of Jazz, Chicago Coll. of Performing Arts, Roosevelt Univ.; mem. Chicago Fed. of Musicians, Nat. Acad. of Recording Arts & Sciences, Inc. (also mem. Bd of Govs), Jazz Inst. of Chicago, The Jazz Educ. Network, Nat. Asscn for Music Educ., Broadcast Music, Inc. (BMI). *Recordings include:* albums: solo/as bandleader: The Yin And The Yout 1993 Live in Warsaw! 1998, Don't Be Scared Anymore 2000, StereoNucleosis 2004, Another Side 2006, Impressions Of A City 2009; as co-leader: Earwax Control, Spontaneous Composition, 2 LIVE, BANG!, The Sign of 4, Union, State of The Union, Jazz Impressions 1, Ampersand, Feast For The Senses, Sound Portraits, Out in Space, Organic Architecture, Realization, Free the Opera!, Topics of Conversation; with Pat Metheny/Pat Metheny Group: First Circle 1984, Still Life (Talking) 1987, Letter From Home 1989, Secret Story 1992, The Road To You 1993, We Live Here 1995, Quartet 1996, Imaginary Day 1997; as sideman: recordings with Larry Coryell, Kurt Elling, Terry Callier, Bobby Lewis, Niels Lan Doky, SBB, Vangelis Katsoulis, John Moulder, Simon & Bard Group, Ken Nordine, Paul Winter and many others; performance videos/DVDs: Pat Metheny Group, Pat Metheny's Secret Story Band, SBB, Muriel Anderson, Modern Drummer Festival, PASIC, Paul Wertico's Mid-East/Mid-West Alliance, David Cain & Paul Wertico, Wertico Cain & Gray; instructional drum videos/DVDs: Fine Tuning Your Performance, Paul Wertico's Drum Philosophy (also titled Sound Work of Drumming in Japan). *Publications include:* contrib. to Drums and Drumming, DRUM!, Drum Tracks, Modern Drummer, Downbeat, musician.-com, Thinking in Jazz, Percussion Profiles, The Cymbal Book, Real World Digital Audio, Sticks 'n' Skins, The New Face of Jazz. *Honours:* seven Grammy Awards (with Pat Metheny Group, three for Best Jazz Fusion Performance 1984, 1987, 1989, three for Best Contemporary Jazz Performance 1993, 1995, 1998, one for Best Rock Instrumental 1998), NARAS Outrageous Recording Award 1990, NAIRD Best Rock Record Award (with Ellen McIlwaine) 1981, DRUM! magazine DRUMMIE! Award 1997, Chicago Tribune Chicagoan of the Year Award 2004, Life Time Achievement Award 2010, Career Achievement Award 2010, Independent Music Award (Best Live Performance Album) 2014. *Address:* 8728 North Drake Avenue, Skokie, IL 60076, USA (home). *E-mail:* paul@paulwertico.com. *Website:* www.paulwertico.com.

WESLEY, Fred A., Jr; American musician (trombone) and arranger; b. 4 July 1943, Mobile, AL; m. *Education:* Ala State Univ., Mobile, Army School of Music, VA. *Career:* served in US Army 1964–67; performed with Ike and Tina Turner 1962–63, James Brown 1968–70, 1971–75, Sam and The Goodtimers 1970–71, George Clinton 1975–78, Bootsy's Rubber Band 1976–78, Count Basie 1978–79; freelance producer and arranger 1979–; founder mem., Fred Wesley and The Horny Horns; mem., The Maceo Parker Band 1990–96; appeared on albums by artists, including Albert King, Bernie Worrell, Bobby Byrd, Bobby Womack, Bootsy's Rubber Band, Cameo, Candy Dulfer, Charles Wright and The Watts, Color Me Badd, Curtis Mayfield, De La Soul, Deee-Lite, Dr John, Earth Wind and Fire, The Four Tops, George Benson, George Clinton, Gov't Mule, James Brown, Johnnie Taylor, The Maceo Parker Band, Marcus Miller, Natalie Cole, 103rd Street Rhythm Band, Parliament, P-Funk All-Stars, Randy Brecker, Randy Crawford, Red Hot Chili Peppers, The S.O.S. Band, Terry Reid, 10,000 Maniacs, Vanessa Williams. *Recordings include:* as Fred Wesley and The Horny Horns: A Blow For Me, A Toot For You 1977, Say Blow By Blow Backwards 1979; solo: To Someone 1988, New Friends 1991, Comme Ci Comme Ca 1992, Swing And Be Funky 1992, Amalgamation 1994, The Final Blow 1994, Full Circle: From Be-Bop To Hip-Hop 1999, Wuda Cuda Shuda 2003. *Publications:* Hit Me, Fred: Recollections of a Side Man 2002. *E-mail:* joyawesley@aol.com (office). *Website:* www.funkyfredwesley.com.

WESSELTOFT, Jens-Christian (Bugge); Norwegian jazz musician (keyboards, piano), composer and producer; b. 1 Feb. 1964, Skien. *Career:* fmr mem., The Arild Andersen Band 1990, The Terje Rypdal Quintet 1991, Jon Eberson's Jazzpunkensemble 1992; f., New Conception of Jazz 1995; f., Jazzland Records 1995; collaborations with artists, including Sidsel Endresen, Michy Mano, Jan Garbarek, Billy Cobham, Joyce and Banda Maluca. *Recordings include:* albums: solo: New Conception Of Jazz 1995, Sharing 1998, Moving 2001, It's Snowing On My Piano 2001, Filming 2004, IM 2008. *Honours:* Grammy Award 1996. *Address:* c/o Jazzland Recordings, Mølleparken 2c, 0459 Oslo, Norway (office). *E-mail:* artist@buggesroom.com (office). *Website:* www.buggewesseltoft.com.

WEST, Kanye; American hip-hop and rap artist and producer; b. 8 June 1977, Atlanta, Ga; s. of Ray West and the late Donda West; m. Kim Kardashian 2014; one d. *Career:* producer working with artists, including Alicia Keys, Jay-Z, Talib Kweli, Twista, Donell Jones, Beanie Siegel, Dead Prez, Ludacris, Scarface, Paul McCartney; solo artist 2004–; Founder Kanye West Foundation 2003. *Recordings include:* albums: The College Dropout (Source Hip-Hop Music Award for Album of the Year 2004, Grammy Award for Best Rap Album 2005) 2004, Late Registration (Grammy Award for Best Rap Album 2006) 2005, Late Orchestration 2006, Graduation (Grammy Award for Best Rap Album 2008) 2007, 808s and Heartbreak 2008, My Beautiful Dark Twisted

Fantasy (BET Hip-Hop Award for CD of the Year 2011, Grammy Award for Best Rap Album 2012) 2010, Yeezus 2013; with Jay-Z: Watch the Throne 2011. *Publication:* Thank You and You're Welcome (with J. Sakiya Sandifer) 2007. *Honours:* Dr hc (School of Art Inst. of Chicago) 2015; Source Hip-Hop Music Awards for Breakthrough Artist 2004, for Video of the Year (for Through The Wire) 2004, Grammy Award for Best Rap Song (for Jesus Walks) 2005, MTV Award for Best Male Video (for Jesus Walks) 2005, Vibe Award for Best Rapper 2005, Billboard Artist Achievement Award 2005, BRIT Award for Best Int. Male Solo Artist 2006, 2008, 2009, Grammy Awards for Best Rap Solo Performance (for Gold Digger), for Best Rap Song (for Diamonds from Sierra Leone, with D. Harris) 2006, for Best Rap Solo Performance (for Stronger) 2008, for Best Rap Song (for Good Life) 2008, for Best Rap/Sung Collaboration (for Run This Town with Jay-Z and Rihanna) 2010, for Best Rap Song (for Run This Town) 2010, for Rap Performance (Otis with Jay-Z), for Rap Song (for All of the Lights), for Rap/Sung Collaboration 2012, for Best Rap Performance, Best Rap Song (for N****s in Paris), for Best Rap/Sung Collaboration (for No Church In The Wild) 2013, NME Award for Best Solo Artist 2006, BET Awards for Best Male Hip-Hop Artist 2005, 2008, 2010, for Best Duet/Collaboration (for Gold Digger, with Jamie Foxx) 2006, BET Hip-Hop Award for Producer of the Year 2009, MTV Europe Music Award for Best Hip-Hop Act 2006, MOBO Awards for Best Hip-Hop Act and Best Video (for Stronger) 2007, MTV Man of the Year 2010, MTV Video Michael Jackson Vanguard Award 2015. *Address:* c/o Roc-A-Fella Records, Island Def Jam Group, Worldwide Plaza, 825 Eighth Avenue, 28th Floor, New York, NY 10019, USA. *Website:* www.kanyewest.com.

WEST, Leslie; American musician (guitar); b. (Leslie Weinstein), 22 Oct. 1945, Queens, NY. *Career:* guitarist, Vagrants; founder mem. rock group, Mountain 1969–85, 2008–; concerts include Woodstock Festival 1970, European tour, support to Deep Purple 1985; also recorded as West, Bruce, Laing (with Jack Bruce, Corky Laing) 1974; song Nantucket Sleighride used as theme for TV series Weekend World (LWT) 1970s–80s. *Recordings:* albums: Mountain 1969, Mountain Climbing 1979, Nantucket Sleighride 1971, Flowers of Evil 1971, The Road Goes On Forever – Mountain Live 1972, Best Of... 1973, Twin Peaks 1974, Avalanche 1974, Go For Your Life 1975, Dodgin' the Dirt 1994, Over The Top 1995, As Phat as It Gets 1999, Sessions 1999, Guitar on: New Day Yesterday, Joe Bonamassa 2000. *Current Management:* c/o John M. Aubel, Forecast Productions Inc., PO Box 217, East Islip, NY 11730-9998, USA. *Telephone:* (631) 277-2352. *E-mail:* info@mountaintheband.com. *Website:* www.mountaintheband.com.

WEST, Steve; American musician (drums); b. 8 Dec. 1967, Richmond, Va. *Career:* mem., Pavement 1993–2000, reunited for live performances 2010; tours world-wide; solo project Marble Valley 2000–. *Television appearance:* Space Ghost Coast to Coast (cartoon) 1997. *Recordings include:* albums: Crooked Rain, Crooked Rain 1994, Wowee Zowee 1995, Brighten the Corners 1997, Terror Twilight 1999, Crooked Rain, Crooked Rain (expanded edn) 2004, Slash & Laugh 2008.

WESTBROOK, (James Lee) Jimi; American country music singer, songwriter and musician (guitar); b. 20 Oct. 1971, Ark.; m. Karen Fairchild 2006, one s. *Education:* Dora High School. *Career:* raised in Sumiton, Ala; worked as salesman in Birmingham, Ala 1990s; Founder-mem. Little Big Town (with Karen Fairchild and Kimberly Schlapman) 1998, appeared at Grand Old Opry 1999; toured with Keith Urban 2006, Sugarland and Jake Owen 2007, Martina McBride 2007–08, George Strait 2008, Carrie Underwood 2009, Sugarland 2010, Rascal Flatts 2012; numerous collaborations including Ashley Monroe, John Mellencamp, Collin Raye. *Recordings:* albums: with Little Big Town: Little Big Town 2002, The Road to Here 2005, A Place to Land 2007, The Reason Why 2010, Tornado 2012, Pain Killer 2014. *Honours:* Acad. of Country Music Awards for Top New Vocal Duo/Group 2007, for Top Vocal Group 2013, for Music Video of the Year (for Tornado) 2013, for Vocal Group of the Year 2014, 2015, Country Music Asscn Awards for Vocal Group of the Year 2012, 2013, 2014, 2015, for Single of the Year (for Pontoon) 2012, for Single and Song of the Year (both for Girl Crush) 2015, for American Country Award for Music Video of the Year: Group or Collaboration (for Pontoon) 2012, Daytime Emmy Award for Outstanding Original Song (for Good Afternoon) 2013, Grammy Awards for Best Country Duo/Group Performance (for Pontoon) 2013, (for Girl Crush) 2016, for Best Country Song (for Girl Crush) 2016. *Current Management:* c/o Sandbox Entertainment, 54 Music Square East, Nashville, TN 37203, USA. *E-mail:* info@sandboxmgmt.com. *Website:* sandboxmgmt.com; littlebigtown.com.

WESTBROOK, Katherine (Kate) Jane; British singer, songwriter, librettist and painter; b. Guildford, Surrey, England; m. 1st; one s. two d.; m. 2nd Mike Westbrook 1976. *Education:* Bath Acad. of Art, Univ. of Reading, Inst. of Educ., Univ. of London. *Career:* joined Mike Westbrook Brass Band 1974, formed Kate Westbrook and the Skirmishers 1994; tours of Europe, Far East, Australia, Canada; co-author with Mike Westbrook of theatre, dance pieces including The Ass 1985, Pier Rides 1986, London Bridge Is Broken Down 1987, Platterback 1998, Jago (opera) 2000; played role of Anna in Seven Deadly Sins, by Brecht/Weill, with London Symphony Orchestra, Barbican, London 1989–90; sang Big Band Rossini, Royal Albert Hall, Proms 1992, Good Friday 1663, TV opera 1995; soloist, KlangWeltReligion with Heribert Leuchter's Lux Orchestra, Germany 2001, Michael Finessy's Transgressive Gospel; The Serpent Hit première 2013; mem. Musicians' Union, Performing Right Soc., Soc. des auteurs, compositeurs et éditeurs de musique (SACEM), Chelsea Arts Club, Vout-O-Reenees, ensemble Lavolta 2015. *Exhibitions:* has exhibited paintings in UK and USA, Europe and Australia 1963–. *Recordings include:* appears on albums: Goose Sauce 1978, Mama Chicago 1979, Bright as Fire 1980, The Cortege 1982, The Ass 1985, On Duke's Birthday 1985, Pierides 1986, London Bridge is Broken Down 1988, Westbrook Rossini 1988, Off Abbey Road 1989, Goodbye Peter Lorre 1991, Good Friday 1993, Stage Set 1995, Bar Utopia 1996, Love or Infatuation 1997, Platterback 1998, The Orchestra of Smith's Academy 1998, Glad Day 1999, L'Ascenseur 2002, Chanson Irrresponsable 2002, Kate Westbrook and the Skirmishers 2004, Art Wolf 2005, The Nijinska Chamber 2006, Reset 2006, Waxeywork Show 2007, Allsorts 2009, Fine 'n' Yellow 2010 Three into Wonderfull 2012, The Serpent Hit 2013, Glad Day Live 2014, A Bigger Show with the Uncommon Orchestra 2015. *Honours:* Diaspason d'Or, for Goodbye Peter Lorre, for Love For Sale with The Westbrook Trio 1992. *Address:* PO Box 92, Dawlish, EX7 9WN, England. *E-mail:* admin@westbrookjazz.co.uk. *Website:* www.westbrookjazz .co.uk.

WESTBROOK, Michael (Mike) John David, OBE, NDD, ATD; British composer, musician (piano) and bandleader; b. 21 March 1936, High Wycombe, Bucks., England; m. Katherine Jane 1976; one s. one d. (from previous m.). *Education:* Plymouth Coll. of Art, Hornsey Coll. of Art. *Career:* formed first band, Plymouth Art School 1958; led groups, including Mike Westbrook Brass Band 1973–, Mike Westbrook Orchestra 1974–, The Westbrook Trio 1982– Kate Westbrook/Mike Westbrook Duo 1995–, West-brook & Company 1998–, New Westbrook Orchestra 2001–, The Village Band 2005; tours of Britain, Europe, Australia, Singapore, Hong Kong, Canada, USA; mem. Musicians' Union, Duke Ellington Soc., Chelsea Arts Club. *Compositions:* music for theatre, opera, dance, radio, TV, films. *Recordings include:* Marching Song 1967, Metropolis 1969, Tyger (A celebration of William Blake) 1971, Citadel/Room 315 1974, The Westbrook Blake 1980, Caught on a Train (BBC TV) 1980, On Duke's Birthday 1984, Love For Sale 1986, Big Band Rossini 1987, Off Abbey Road 1988, Bean Rows and Blues Shots 1991, Coming Through Slaughter (opera) 1994, Bar Utopia 1995, Blues For Terenzi 1995, Cable Street Blues 1997, The Orchestra of Smith's Academy 1998, Classical Blues 2001, Moulin Rouge (film) 1990; with Kate Westbrook: The Cortege 1979, London Bridge Is Broken Down 1987, Measure For Measure 1992, Chanson Irresponsable 2001, Turner in Uri 2003, Art Wolf 2003, Waxeywork Show 2006, English Soup 2008, Allsorts 2009, Fine 'n' Yellow 2010, The Serpent Hit 2011, Three into Wonderful 2013, Glad Day Live 2014; A Bigger Show 2015, music theatre with Kate Westbrook includes: Mama Chicago 1978, Westbrook Rossini 1984, Pier Rides 1987, Quichotte (opera) 1989, Good Friday 1663 (TV opera) 1995, Stage Set 1996, Love or Infatuation 1997, Platterback 1998, Jago (opera) 2000, L'ascenseur/The Lift 2002, The Nijinska Chamber 2005, Cape Gloss, Mathilda's Story (opera) 2007. *Honours:* Hon. DMus (Plymouth) 2004. *E-mail:* admin@westbrookjazz.co.uk (office). *Website:* www.westbrookjazz.co.uk (office).

WESTENRA, Hayley Dee; New Zealand singer; b. 10 April 1987, Christchurch; d. of Gerald and Jill Westenra; m. Arnaud Sabard 2013. *Career:* performer in classical, pop and traditional Maori choral styles; fmr Amb. to Save The Children, Hong Kong; Amb. for UNICEF. *Recordings include:* albums: Hayley Westenra 2001, Pure 2003, My Gift To You 2004, Odyssey 2005, Treasures 2007, River of Dreams 2008, Winter Magic 2009, Paradiso 2011, Hushabye 2013, Hayley Westenra- The Best 2014. *Publication:* In Her Own Voice (auto-biog.) 2007. *Current Management:* c/o Giselle Allier, Bedlam Management Ltd, PO Box 34449, London, W6 0XU, England. *E-mail:* hayleyw@bedlammanagement.com. *Website:* www.hayleywestenra.com.

WESTERGAAD MADSEN, Benedicte (Dicte); Danish singer, songwriter and musician; b. 9 Sept. 1966. *Career:* formed band, Her Personal Pain 1989; numerous Danish club tours, including Roskilde Festival 1991, 1994, 1997, 2000, Popkomm, Germany 1997, Sopot Festival, Poland 1997; wrote and performed music for play, Searching Hamlet 2002; founder of record label, Velvet Recording 2003–; formed band Dicte and the Sugarbones 2006. *Film appearance:* Smukke Dreng (Beautiful Boy) 1992. *Play:* lead actress in play by Hotel Pro Forma 1998. *Recordings:* albums: with Her Personal Pain: Songs From Cinema Cafe 1992; solo: Between Any Four Walls 1994, Voodoo Vibe 1996, House of the Double Axe 1998, This Is Cool 2000, Gone to Texas 2003; with Dicte and the Sugarbones: Dicte and the Sugarbones 2006; contrib. to Secrets II Live 1990, Rock Love and Understanding (Amnesty International) 1991, Gaa Ikke Over Sporet (Don't Pass the Trail, Danish Nat. Railways) 1997. *Honours:* Grammy Award for Best New Name 1992. *Current Management:* c/o Peter Sorensen, Beatbox Booking and Concerts, Jorcks Passage Opgang C, 1. sal, 1162 Copenhagen, Denmark. *Website:* www.beatboxbooking .dk. *Telephone:* 35-20-01-90 (office). *E-mail:* voiceact@post.tele.dk (office). *Website:* www.dicte.dk.

WESTERGAARD, Torben; Danish musician (bass guitar) and composer; b. 9 Oct. 1960, Århus. *Education:* Musicians' Inst., Los Angeles, USA, New School, New York, USA. *Career:* plays in own groups and freelance work in many music styles including jazz, Brazilian, pop, funk, Latin; studio musician; teacher, Rhythmic Music Conservatory, Copenhagen; mem DJBFA. *Recordings:* albums: What I Miss 1990, Brazilian Heart 1996, Oktober 2006, Penelope 2007, Tangofied 2010; featured on: Dig This Samba, Hendrik Meurkens & Manfredo Fest, Flor de Verão, Silvana Malta and the Danish Radio Big Band. *Honours:* Outstanding Bass Player of the Year, Musicians' Inst. 1985. *E-mail:* bentor@mac.com (office). *Website:* www .torbenwestergaard.dk.

WESTFALL-KING, Carmen Sigrid; Canadian singer, songwriter and musician (guitar); b. 24 Aug. 1962, Burlington, ON; m. Kenny King 1989, one d. *Career:* numerous television appearances, concerts; mem. SOCAN, CCMA. *Recordings include:* Your Old Girlfriend; You're An Angel; I Wanna Hear It From You; Talk Around Town. *Honours:* Big Country Award for Outstanding New Artist 1989. *Address:* 1050 Barnardo Avenue, Peterbor-ough, ON K9H 5X2, Canada.

WESTFIELD, Steve; American singer, songwriter and musician (guitar); b. 2 May 1965, Massachusetts. *Education:* Univ. of Massachusetts. *Career:* mem., Pajama Slave Dancers 1981–, Steve Westfield Slow Band 1993–; tours and live appearances. *Recordings include:* with Pajama Slave Dancers: All You Can Eat, 1982; Problems of Sects, 1983; Blood, Sweat and Beers, 1984; Pajama Beach Party, 1984; Heavy Petting Zoo, 1985; Full Metal Underpants, 1989; It Came From The Barn, 1996; It's Heartbreak the Sells, 1999; with Steve Westfield Slow Band: Mangled, 1994; Reject Me... First, 1996; Underwhelmed, 1998; solo: Alone with the Lonesome Brothers 2010. *Address:* c/o Glitterhouse Records, Grüner Weg 25, 37688 Beverungen, Germany. *E-mail:* info@glitterhouse.com. *Website:* www.glitterhouse.com; www .myspace.com/swestfield.

WESTHEAD, Barry; British musician (keyboards); b. 13 May 1977, Wigan, Lancashire, England. *Career:* mem., Starsailor 2000–. *Recordings include:* albums: Love Is Here 2001, Silence Is Easy 2003, On the Outside 2005, All the Plans 2009. *Current Management:* Heavenly Management, 47 Frith Street, London, W1D 4SE, England. *Telephone:* (20) 7494-2998. *Fax:* (20) 7437-3317. *E-mail:* info@heavenlymanagement.com. *Website:* www.starsailor.mu.

WESTLAKE, David; musician (drums). *Career:* mem., Sneaker Pimps 1995–; band founded Splinter Recordings 1999. *Recordings include:* albums: Becoming X 1996, Splinter 1999, Bloodsport 2002. *Current Management:* Tommy Boy Entertainment, 32 W 18th Street, New York, NY 10011-4612, USA. *E-mail:* parmesanchic@aol.com. *Website:* www.sneakerpimps.com.

WESTON, Randy; American jazz pianist, composer and bandleader; b. (Randolph E. Weston), 6 April 1926, Brooklyn, New York; m. Fatoumata Weston. *Education:* Bedford-Stuyvesant Boys High School. *Career:* early work with bandleaders including Frank Culley, Eddie 'Cleanhead' Vinson, Bullmoose Jackson during 1940s and early 1950s; collaborations with Kenny Dorham 1953, Cecil Payne 1954; formed own trio and quartet 1954; debut recording as bandleader 1954; tour of Africa with US cultural delegation 1967; f. African Rhythms Club, Tangier 1967–72; numerous collaborations with artists, arrangers and musicians including Melba Liston, Roy Brooks, Charles Mingus, Billy Harper. *Films:* Tanger Randy on the Road, Life in St Lucia (documentary). *Recordings include:* albums: as bandleader: Cole Porter in a Modern Mood 1954, The Randy Weston Trio 1955, Get Happy with the Randy Weston Trio 1955, With These Hands... 1956, Jazz à la Bohemia 1956, The Modern Art of Jazz 1956, Piano à la Mode 1957, New Faces at Newport 1958, Little Niles 1959, Destry Rides Again 1959, Uhuru Afrika 1960, Highlife 1963, Randy 1964, Berkshire Blues 1965, African Cookbook 1969, Little Niles 1969, Blue Moses 1972, Tanjah 1973, Carnival 1974, Informal Solo Piano 1974, Blues to Africa 1974, African Nite 1975, African Rhythms 1975, Randy Weston Meets Himself 1976, Perspective 1976, Rhythms-Sounds Piano 1978, The Healers (with David Murray) 1980, Blue 1984, Portraits of Thelonious Monk: Well You Needn't 1989, Portraits of Duke Ellington: Caravan 1989, Self Portraits: The Last Day 1989, The Spirits of Our Ancestors 1991, Marrakech in the Cool of the Evening 1992, The Splendid Master Gnawa Musicians of Morocco 1992, Volcano Blues 1993, Saga 1995, Earth Birth (with Montreal String Orchestra) 1997, Khepera 1998, Spirit!: The Power of Music 1999, Ancient Future 2002, Nuit Africa 2004, Zep Tepi 2006, The Storyteller 2009, The Roots of the Blues (with Billy Harper) (Jazz Journalists' Asscn Award for Duo of the Year 2014) 2013. *Publication:* African Rhythms: The Autobiog-raphy of Randy Weston 2010. *Honours:* Ordre des Arts et des Lettres 1997; Dr hc (Brooklyn Coll., CUNY) 2006, (Colby Coll.) 2012, (New England Conser-vatory of Music) 2013; Down Beat Int. Critics' Poll Awards for New Star Pianist 1955, for Composer of the Year 1994, 1996, 1999, Swing Journal Award, Japan 1999, Arts Critics and Reviewers Asscn of Ghana Black Star Award 2000, NEA Jazz Master 2001, Guggenheim Fellowship Award 2011, Doris Duke Award 2014, Jazz Journalists' Asscn Award for Trio or Duo of the Year (with Billy Harper) 2014, Lifetime Achievement in Jazz Award 2015. *E-mail:* fatou@randyweston.info. *Website:* RandyWeston.info.

WESTWOOD, Elizabeth Rose; American singer and musician; b. Washing-ton DC. *Education:* art school, Washington, DC. *Career:* mem. and lead singer, Westworld 1986–91; numerous radio and television appearances, concerts; mem. and lead singer, Moondogg 1994–; mem. PRS, Musicians' Union. *Recordings:* albums: with Westworld: Rockulator 1987, Beatbox Rock 'N' Roll 1988, Movers And Shakers 1991; with Moondogg: Fat Lot Of Good 1996, God's Wallop, All the Love in the World 2004. *Address:* PO Box 517, Richmond, Surrey, TW9, England (office). *E-mail:* mabel@moondogg.com (office). *Website:* www.moondogg.com.

WESTWOOD, Tim; British hip-hop DJ and television and radio presenter; CEO, Justice Promotions Limited. *Career:* highly influential figure in hip hop in Europe and a pioneer of the UK scene; broadcasts live from London on Capital Xtra, 9pm–11pm on Saturday nights; YouTube channel, Tim West-wood TV, has over 207 million video views; more than 426,000 Twitter followers; works closely with all major urban artists from Jay Z to Lil Wayne, Nicki Minaj to Drake; regularly tours UK each year performing to hundreds of thousands of club goers; presented Pimp My Ride UK, the most successful MTV UK production of all time and the second-highest rated show in the history of MTV Europe, still shown in every country world-wide. *Television:* ITV Night Network, Bad Meaning Good (2 documentary), Westwood Presents (UK Play) 2000, Westwood TV (Channel U) 2004–05, Pimp My Ride UK (MTV) UK season 1 2005, Pimp My Ride UK (MTV) UK season 2 2006, Westwood's Trick It Out (MTV) 2006, Pimp My Ride UK season 3 (MTV) (commissioned for 2007), Pimp My Riot Van charity episode (MTV) 2008, Flava channel season 1 2010, Flava channel season 2 2010, Flava channel season 3 2011. *Recordings:* Westwood – The Album Volume One (Silver), Westwood – Volume 2 (Gold), Westwood – Volume 3 (Gold), Westwood – Platinum Edition (Platinum), Westwood – The Jump Off (Gold), Westwood – The Takeover (Gold), Westwood – The Big Dawg (Gold), Westwood – The Invasion (Gold), Westwood – Heat (Gold), Westwood – Volume 10 (Gold), Westwood – Ride With The Big Dawg (Gold), Westwood – The Greatest (Gold), Westwood – The Big Dawg Is Back, Westwood Raw DVD; has sold over two million albums to date, with the biggest selling urban compilation in history with The Big Dawg Is Back 2010. *Honours:* Sony Radio Awards: Best Music Broadcaster 1996, 2000, Best Specialist Music Programme 1990, 1991, 1999, Silver Best Entertainment 2011, Best Community Radio Programming 2013; Best DJ, MOBO Awards 2000, 2003, 2005, 2007, 2008, John Peel Award for Outstanding Contribution to Music, Radio Academy 2010, Europe DJ of the Year, US Global Spin Awards 2012. *Address:* Justice Promotions Ltd, PO Box 6933, London, W1A 6UT, England (office). *Telephone:* (20) 7637-9219 (office). *E-mail:* helen@timwestwood.com (office). *Website:* www.timwestwood.com.

WETTON, John; British singer, songwriter and musician (bass, keyboards); b. 12 June 1949, Derby, England; m. Jill Briggs 1987. *Education:* Bournemouth College. *Career:* mem., Family 1971–72, King Crimson 1973–75, Roxy Music 1975, Uriah Heep 1976, UK 1978–79, Asia 1982–91; solo artist 1980, 1991–; mem. PRS, National Academy of Songwriters, ASCAP. *Recordings include:* with Family: Fearless 1971, Bandstand 1972; with King Crimson: Larks Tongues In Aspic 1973, Starless and Bible Black 1974, Red 1974, USA 1975, Night Watch 1998, Collectors' King Crimson, Vol. 1; with Roxy Music: Viva! 1976; with UK: UK 1978, Danger Money 1979, Live Roxy Music Album 1999; with Asia: Asia 1982, Alpha 1983, Astra 1985, Then and Now 1990; solo: Battle Lines 1994, Chasing The Deer 1998, Live in Tokyo 1998, Monkey Business 1999, Arkangel 1999, Live at the Sun Plaza Tokyo 2001. *Honours:* three ASCAP Awards. *Current Management:* QEDG Management, PO Box 6249, Leighton Buzzard, Bedfordshire, LU7 0WS, England. *E-mail:* qedg@btinternet.com. *Website:* www.johnwetton.co.uk.

WETTRE, Petter; Norwegian musician (saxophone); b. 11 Aug. 1967, Sandefjord; one s. *Education:* Berklee Coll. of Music, Boston, USA. *Career:* has recorded 40 albums as a sideman, 11 under own name; est. own record co., Household Records 2003–; has played with Dave Liebman, Adam Nussbaum, Rick Margitza, Gene Perwi, Jon Christensen, Arind Andersen, Hamid Drake; numerous tours of Norway and abroad with own bands, The Trio, Petter Wettre Trio, Petter Wettre Quintet, Wettre/Johansen duo. *Recordings include:* as leader: Petter Wettre Quartet – Pig Virus (Norwegian Grammy Award) 1996, The Trio – Meet the Locals 1999, The Trio – In Color 2000, Wettre/Johansen – The Only Way to Travel 2000, Petter Wettre Trio: The Mystery Unfolds 2001, Petter Wettre Trio – Live at Copenhagen Jazzhouse (HR) 2003, Petter Wettre Quintet – Household Name (HR) 2003, Petter Wettre/Dave Liebman – Tour de Force 2004, Petter Wettre – Hallmark Moments 2004, Petter Wettre – Paramount 2005, Petter Wettre – State of the Art 2005, Petter Wettre – Appetite for Structure 2007, Petter Wettre – Fountain of Youth (Norwegian Grammy Award) 2007, Petter Wettre & The Norwegian Radio Orchestra, Fountain of Youth – Live! 2008, The Only Way To Travel 2 2010; as sideman: Stavanger Gospel Choir – A Touch From Up Above 1994, Blunch/Mathisen – Mysteriet med den falske bonden 1995, Jan Werner – All By Myself 1995, Madeleine & Mr. Double – Second to Nobody 1995, Stephen Ackles – One For The Moon 1995, Jan Rodhe – A New Side Of 1995, Angel & Heart – One by One 1995, Sandefjord Storband – 3 1996, Polygram Oslo Groove Company – Live 1996, Frode Alnæs – Frode 1996, Øystein Sevåg – Bridge 1997, Brødrene Dal – På vikingtokt 1997, Arcade Jens Wendelboe – Strolling with the Groove 1997, Bluesband – Så dritkult 1997, Vettene på Sporet – NVCD Bryggerigangen 1997, Act Staffan W. Olsson – Smile 1998, Grappa Thorbjørn Sunde – Meridians 1998, Odd Børresen/Anita Skorgan – Våre beste barnesanger 4 1998, Kirkelig Kulturverksted 1999, Knut Reiersrud – Soul of a Man 1999, ISRC Element – Shaman 1999, Gisle Torvik – Naken uten gitar 1999, Sølvi Hansen – met Sir Jones 2000, Staffan W. Olsson – Oak Road Boogaloo 2000, Sandefjord Storband – Swinging Christmas 2001, UHU – Musikken fra Barne tv (NRK) 2001, Wenche Myhre – Viva la Diva 2002, UHU 2 – Musikken fra Barne tv (NRK) 2002, UHU 3 – Musikken fra Barne tv (NRK) 2003, LAVA – Polarity 2003, Claudio Daulsbergh – Ventos do Norte 2003, Marianne Krogness – Jeg skal bare 2004, Frode Berg – Dig It 2004, Sphinx – Sweet Maladies 2004, Turbulens – Footprint 2005, Helge Sunde – Denada 2006, New Light – Live in Oslo 2007, Elisabeth Andreassen – Spellemann 2009, Øyvind Nypan – Elements 2010, Øystein Sevåg – The RED album 2010. *Publications:* Lighthouse Omni Book, complete solo transcription of Dave Liebman and Steve Grossman's solos from E. Jones's album, Live at the Lighthouse Vols I & II. *Honours:* Berklee Coll. of Music Outstanding Achievement Award. *Address:* Hekkveien 9F, 0571 Oslo, Norway (office). *Telephone:* 90-00-53-93-1 (office). *E-mail:* mail@petterwettre .com (office). *Website:* www.petterwettre.com.

WEYLER, Javier; Argentine musician (drums). *Career:* mem. Stereophonics 2004–. *Recordings include:* albums: Language.Sex.Violence.Other? 2005, Live From Dakota 2006, Pull the Pin 2007, Keep Calm and Carry On 2009. *Honours:* Digital Music Award for Best Rock Artist 2005. *Current Management:* c/o Natalie Seymour, Nettwerk Management, 59–65 Worship Street, London, EC2A 2DU, England. *Telephone:* (20) 7456-9500. *Fax:* (20) 7456-9501. *E-mail:* natalie@nettwerk.com. *Website:* www.stereophonics.com.

WHARTON, Darren Dean; British musician (keyboards, guitar), singer and songwriter. *Career:* keyboard player for Phil Lynott 1980; mem., Thin Lizzy 1981–83; numerous concerts, tours, festival appearances; founder mem., Dare 1987–91. *Recordings include:* albums: with Thin Lizzy: Chinatown, 1980; Adventures of Thin Lizzy, 1981; Renegade, 1981; Thunder and Lightning, 1983; The Boys Are Back In Town, 1983; Thin Lizzy Live, 1992; One Night Only, 2000; with Dare: Out of the Silence, 1988; Blood from Stone, 1991; with Phil Lynott: Solo in Soho, 1980. *E-mail:* legend@darrenwharton.demon.co.uk. *Website:* www.dare-music.com.

WHEATLEY, Martin Russell, BA, MA; British musician; b. 29 Aug. 1958, London, England; m. Angela; three s. *Education:* Colchester Coll., Univ. Coll. London. *Career:* broadcasts on radio and TV, BBC and commercial; concert appearances at the Purcell Room and Queen Elizabeth Hall; extensive touring of Canada, USA, including Hawaii; specialist in acoustic fretted instruments playing in authentic early styles, jazz, blues, ragtime, Hawaiian. *Recordings:* New Orleans Hop Scop Blues, with Bent Persson and Alain Marquet; Charleston Mad, with Neville Dickie; Syncopated Jamboree, I Like To Do Things For You, The Henderson Project, Harlem's Arabian Nights, all with Keith Nichols; with Roger Eno, Long Walk, 2000; with Hula Bluebirds: Stowaways In Paradise. *E-mail:* ot39@aol.com.

WHEELER, Alison; British singer; b. 4 March 1972. *Education:* Trinity Coll. *Career:* mem. and lead singer, The Beautiful South 2003–07; currently mem. The South. *Recordings include:* albums: Gaze 2002, Golddiggas, Headnodders & Pholk Songs 2004, Superbi 2006; with The South: Sweet Refrains. *Website:* www.thesouth.co.uk.

WHEELER, Timothy; British musician (guitar), singer and songwriter; b. 4 Jan. 1977, Downpatrick, Co. Down. *Career:* founding mem. Ash 1992–; numerous headline UK and worldwide tours, UK festivals and television appearances. *Recordings include:* albums: Trailer 1994, 1977 1996, Live At The Wireless 1997, Nu-Clear Sounds 1998, Free All Angels 2001, Cosmic Debris 2002, Intergalactic Sonic 7"s: The Best Of Ash 2002, Meltdown 2004, Twilight of the Innocents 2007. *Honours:* NME BRAT Award for Best Single (for Burn Baby Burn) 2002, Q Award for Best Single (for Burn Baby Burn) 2002, Ivor Novello Award for Best Contemporary Song (for Shining Light) 2002, Kerrang! Classic Songwriter Award 2004. *Current Management:* Out There Management Ltd, 120–124 Curtain Road, London, EC2A 3SQ, England. *Telephone:* (20) 7739-6903. *Fax:* (20) 7613-2715. *E-mail:* outthere@outthere.co.uk. *Website:* www.ash-official.com.

WHELAN, Bill; Irish composer; b. (William Michael Joseph Weldon), 22 May 1950, Limerick. *Education:* Univ. Coll. Dublin. *Career:* toured and recorded with Planxty for 2 years; Composer-in-Residence, Yeats Festival, Abbey Theatre, Dublin; collaborations with U2, Van Morrison, Andy Irvine, The Dubliners, Kate Bush. *Films:* score composer: Lamb 1986, Some Mother's Son 1996, Dancing at Lughnasa 1998, Poitin 2007. *Compositions include:* The Seville Suite 1992, The Spirit of Mayo 1993, The Life of Reilly 1995, Riverdance The Show 1995; music for 15 plays for the W.B. Yeats Int. Festival, Abbey Theatre, Dublin. *Honours:* Riverdance single stayed at number 1 for 18 weeks in Ireland, went platinum in the USA and Ireland, Grammy Award for Best Musical Show Album (for Riverdance) 1997, Billboard Awards for Top World Music Artist 1996, 1997. *Current Management:* McGuinness/Whelan Music Publishing Ltd, 30/32 Sir John Rogerson's Quay, Dublin 2, Ireland. *Website:* www.billwhelan.com.

WHELAN, Gary (Gaz); British musician (drums); b. 12 Feb. 1966. *Career:* founder mem., Happy Mondays 1985–92, 1999–2000, 2004–; numerous tours and festival appearances. *Recordings include:* albums: Squirrel and G-Man Twenty-Four Hour Party People Plastic Face Carnt Smile (White Out) 1986, Bummed (Q Magazine Classic Album Award 2013) 1988, Pills 'n' Thrills and Bellyaches 1990, ...Yes Please! 1992, Uncle Dysfunctional 2007. *Honours:* DMC World DJ Award for Best Indie Act 1991. *Current Management:* c/o Warren Askew Management, Woodhead House, 44/46 Market Street, Hyde, Cheshire, SK14 1AH, England. *Telephone:* (7818) 888368 (mobile). *E-mail:* weaentertainment@gmail.com. *Website:* www.happymondaysonline.com.

WHELAN, Gavan; British musician (drums). *Career:* founder mem., James 1983–90; numerous tours, festival dates and television appearances; producer 1990–. *Recordings include:* albums: Stutter 1986, Strip Mine 1988, One Man Clapping 1989, Gold Mother 1990.

WHILE, Chris Mills; British singer, musician (guitar, banjo, bodhram, percussion) and songwriter; b. 22 Dec. 1955, Barrow-in-Furness; m. Joe While 1974 (divorced 1993); one s. one d. *Education:* Bolton Art Coll. *Career:* lead singer, The Albion Band 1993–97; duo with Julie Matthews; tours of UK, USA, Australia, Europe; numerous television and radio broadcasts, festival appearances; mem. Mechanical-Copyright Protection Soc., Performing Right Soc., Musicians' Union. *Compositions:* 100 Miles 1992, Young Man Cut Down In His Prime, co-written with Julie Matthews 1996, The Light In My Mother's Eye 1999, co-wrote music for BBC documentary, Tales from the Towpath.

Recordings include: albums: solo: Look At Me Now 1993, In the Big Room 1997, Rosetta Red 2007; with Julie Matthews: Piecework 1997, Higher Potential 1999, Stages (live) 2000, Quest 2001, Perfect Mistake 2003, Here and Now 2005, Live at the Firehouse, Germany 2007, Together Alone 2008. *Website:* www.chriswhile.co.uk; www.whileandmatthews.co.uk.

WHITAKER, Michael Whiteley; musician (keyboards, harmonica, percussion) and singer; b. 26 May 1948, Ploughley, Oxfordshire, England; m. Helen 1969; two s. *Education:* Newcastle Coll. of Arts and Technology School of Music. *Career:* mem., Halfbreed; various tours, television and radio broadcasts; mem. PRS, Equity, Musicians' Union. *Recordings include:* four albums. *Publication:* contrib. to Out Now (Rock fanzine). *Address:* 58 Hedley Street, Gosforth, Newcastle upon Tyne, NE3 1DL, England.

WHITE, Adam Peter; British public relations executive; *Vice-President of Communications, Universal Music Group International;* b. 22 Sept. 1948, Bristol. *Career:* reporter, news ed., Music Week 1974–77; Int. Ed., Billboard 1978–80, Man. Ed. 1981–83, Ed.-in-Chief 1983–85, Int. Ed.-in-Chief 1989–2001; New York Bureau Chief, Radio and Records 1985–88; London correspondent, Rolling Stone 1988–89; Vice-Pres. of Communications, Universal Music Group International, London 2002–. *Publications include:* The Billboard Book of Gold and Platinum Hits 1990, The Billboard Book of No. 1 Rhythm and Blues Hits (co-author) 1993. *Address:* Universal Music Group International Ltd, 364-366 Kensington High Street, London, W14 8NS, England (office). *Telephone:* (20) 7471-5665 (office). *E-mail:* adam.white@umusic.com (office). *Website:* www.universalmusic.com (office).

WHITE, Alan; British musician (drums); b. 14 June 1949, Pelton, Co. Durham, England; s. of Raymond White and May White; m. Gigi; two c. *Career:* mem., Airforce 1968, Plastic Ono Band 1969; mem. progressive rock group, Yes 1972–81, 1983–89, 1991– solo artist 1975–. *Recordings:* albums: with Yes: Tales From Topographic Oceans 1973, Relayer 1974, Yesterdays 1975, Going For The One 1977, Tormato 1978, Drama 1980, Yesshows 1980, 90125 1983, 9012 Live: The Solos 1985, Big Generator 1987, Union 1991, Yesstory 1991, Symphonic Music Of Yes 1993, History Of The Future 1993, Talk 1994, An Evening Of Yes Music Plus 1994, Keys To Ascension 1996, Open Your Eyes 1997, Something's Coming 1998, The Ladder 1999, House Of Yes: Live From House Of Blues 2000, Magnification 2001, Keystudio 2001, Yestoday 2002, Yes Remixes 2003, Yes And Friends 2003, Re(Union) 2004, Far From Here 2011, Heaven & Earth 2014; solo: Ramshackled 1975. *Current Management:* c/o Trudy Green, HK Management, 9200 Sunset Boulevard, Suite 530, Los Angeles, CA 90069, USA. *E-mail:* alanwhite@alanwhite.net (office). *Website:* www.yesworld.com; www.alanwhite.net.

WHITE, Alex; British musician (drums); b. Brighton. *Career:* mem., Brakes 2002–; numerous live performances. *Recordings include:* albums: Give Blood 2005, The Beatific Visions 2006, Touchdown 2009. *E-mail:* brakes@brakesbrakesbrakes.com (office). *Website:* www.brakesbrakesbrakes.com.

WHITE, Andrew; British musician (guitar); b. 28 Aug. 1974, Leeds, England. *Career:* founder mem., Runston Parva 1997, renamed Parva, renamed Kaiser Chiefs 2003–. *Recordings include:* albums: Employment (Meteor Ireland Music Award for Best Int. Album 2006, NME Award for Best Album 2006, Ivor Novello Award for Best Album 2006) 2005, Yours Truly, Angry Mob 2007, Off With Their Heads 2008, The Future Is Medieval 2011, Start the Revolution Without Me 2012, Education, Education, Education & War 2014. *Honours:* Meteor Ireland Music Award for Best Int. Group 2006, BRIT Awards for Best British Rock Act, Best British Live Act, Best British Group 2006, Nordoff-Robbins Silver Clef Award for Best Group 2006, Q Award for Best Video (for 'Ruby') 2007. *Current Management:* c/o James Sandom, Red Light Management, Unit 4.16, The Paintworks, Bath Road, Bristol BS4 3EH, England. *E-mail:* james.sandom@redlightmanagement.com. *Website:* redlightmanagement.com; www.kaiserchiefs.com.

WHITE, Andrew Nathaniel, III, BMus; American musician (saxophone, oboe, English horn, bass), composer, arranger, conductor and musicologist; b. 6 Sept. 1942, Washington, DC; m. Jocelyne H. J. Uhl. *Education:* Howard Univ., Washington, DC. *Career:* jazz saxophonist, JFK Quintet 1960–64, New Jazz Trio 1965–66; oboist and English horn player, Center of Creative and Performing Arts 1965–67; Principal Oboe and English Horn, American Ballet Theater 1968–70; electric bassist, Stevie Wonder and Motown Records 1968–70, Fifth Dimension 1970–76, Weather Report (recordings) 1970–73, The Jupiter Hair Company 1971–; solo debut at Carnegie Hall 1974; jazz saxophonist with Elvin Jones 1980–81, Beaver Harris 1983–; staff writer, Saxophone Journal; mem. Int. Double Reed Soc., Soc. for American Music, Pi Kappa Lambda. *Compositions include:* Concerto 1963, Concertina 1963, Shepherd Song 1963, Andrew with Strings 1987, A Jazz Concerto (five versions) 1988, 20 Jazz Caprices for string quartet 2007. *Recordings:* 48 self-produced recordings, collaborations include JFK Quintet, McCoy Tyner. *Publications include:* Saxophone Transcriptions – The Works of John Coltrane (15 vols), The Eric Dolphy Series Limited, The Charlie Parker Collection (four vols), The Andrew White Transcription Series (10 vols), Andy's Song Book, Chamber Music Series, Saxophone Recital Series, Saxophone Etudes, Saxophone Trios, Quartets, Quintets, Two Symphonies for Eight Saxophones, Four Jazz Duets, 12 Jazz Miniatures; books on improvisation, practice, transcription, jazz education, self-production, Coltrane's music, five comedy books; Everybody Loves The Sugar – The Book (autobiog.) 2001; contrib. of numerous articles to trade journals. *Honours:* numerous study grants; Dean Dixon Memorial Award for oboe playing 1984, Washington Area Music Asscn Award

1985, Soc. of Arts, Sciences and Letters Gold Medal, Paris, France 2006. *Address:* Andrew's Musical Enterprises Inc., 4830 South Dakota Avenue, NE, Washington, DC 20017, USA (office). *Telephone:* (202) 526-3666 (office). *Fax:* (202) 526-4013 (office).

WHITE, Eg; British songwriter, producer and musician; b. (Francis Anthony White), 22 Nov. 1966. *Career:* started career in band, Yip Yip Coyote, and duos Brother Beyond and Eg & Alice; has written or co-written songs for Will Young, James Morrison, James Blunt, Take That, Duffy, Adele, Joss Stone, Pink, Kylie Minogue, Beverley Knight and Natalie Imbruglia; f. Spilt Milk Records, Spilt Milk Management 2009. *Songs include:* Leave Right Now (Ivor Novello Award for Best Song 2004) 2003; as co-writer: Say It 2002, Going My Way 2004, Out of My Mind 2004, You Had Me 2004, Free, Keep On, Save Yourself, Think About It, Who Am I?, You Give Me Something, Wonderful World, Just A Little Bit, Cosmic, Chasing Pavements, Warwick Avenue, Changes 2008, Let It Go 2008, Water and a Flame 2009. *Recordings include:* as Eg and Alice: 24 Years of Hunger 1991; solo: Turn Me on, I'm a Rocket Man 1996, Adventure Man 2009. *Honours:* Ivor Novello Award for Songwriter of the Year 2009. *Address:* Spilt Milk Management Ltd, 215 Goldhawk Road, London, W12 8EP, England (office). *Website:* spiltmilkmusic.co.uk (office).

WHITE, Freddie; Irish singer, songwriter and musician (guitar); b. 22 Sept. 1951, Cobh, County Cork; m. Ann O'Sullivan 1979; one s. one d. *Career:* solo artist; numerous concerts, TV appearances; mem. PRS. *Recordings include:* albums: Freddie White 1979, Do You Do 1981, Long Distance Runner 1985, Close To You 1991, Straight Up 1993, My Country 1999, Lost And Found 2002, Four Days In May 2004, Stormy Lullaby 2008, Here With You 2012, Better Days 2014. *Honours:* Hot Press Award for Best Folk Specialist 1981. *Current Management:* c/o Madeleine Seiler, The Headline Agency, 39 Churchfields, Milltown, Dublin 14, Ireland. *E-mail:* info@musicheadline.com. *Website:* www.theheadlineagency.com. *E-mail:* freddie@freddiewhite.com. *Website:* www.freddiewhite.com.

WHITE, Jack; American singer and musician (guitar, drums); b. (John Anthony Gillis), 9 July 1975, Detroit, Mich.; m. 1st Meg White 1996 (divorced 2000); m. 2nd Karen Elson 2005 (divorced 2013); one s. one d. *Career:* fmrly played in a number of Detroit-based bands; Founder-mem. The White Stripes 1997–2011; Founder-mem. The Raconteurs 2006–, The Dead Weather 2009–; f. Third Man Records 2001. *Film appearances:* Cold Mountain 2003, Coffee and Cigarettes 2003. *Recordings include:* albums: with The White Stripes: White Stripes 1999, De Stijl 2000, White Blood Cells 2001, Elephant (Grammy Award for Best Alternative Album) 2003, Get Behind Me Satan (Grammy Award for Best Alternative Music Album 2006) 2005, Icky Thump (Grammy Award for Best Alternative Music Album 2008) 2007, Under Great White Northern Lights 2010; with The Raconteurs: Broken Boy Soldiers 2006, Consolers of the Lonely 2008; with The Dead Weather: Horehound 2009, Sea of Cowards 2010; solo: Blunderbuss 2012, Lazaretto (Grammy Award for Best Rock Performance 2015) 2014. *Honours:* MTV Europe Music Award for Best Rock Act 2003, BRIT Award for Best Int. Group 2004, Grammy Awards for Best Rock Song (for Seven Nation Army) 2004, for Best Rock Performance by a Duo or Group with Vocals (for Icky Thump) 2008, Music City Amb. Award, City of Nashville 2011. *Current Management:* Third Man Records, 623 7th Avenue South, Nashville, TN 37203; Monotone Management, 820 Seward Street, Hollywood, CA 90038, USA (office). *Telephone:* (615) 891-4393 (Nashville); (323) 308-1818 (office). *Fax:* (323) 308-1819 (office). *Website:* jackwhiteiii.com; www.thirdmanrecords.com; www.whitestripes.com; www.theraconteurs.com; www.thedeadweather.com.

WHITE, Jason; American musician (guitar, bass guitar), songwriter and singer; b. 11 Nov. 1973, North Little Rock, Ark.; m. Janna Rollins. *Career:* mem. many rock bands; guitarist, Numbskulz 1988; vocalist, Step by Step 1989–90; bass guitarist, Chino Horde 1990–93; guitarist, Fishwagon 1991; touring guitarist, Monsula 1992–93; bass guitarist, Sixteen Bullets 1994; guitarist and singer, Pinhead Gunpowder 1995–; bass guitarist, The Big Cats 1996–2000; guitarist 2000–; Founder mem. The Influents 1999–2003; touring guitarist with Green Day 1999–, full-time mem. 2012–; Founder mem. The Network (as Balducci) 2003–05; mem. Foxboro Hot Tubs 2007–; currently oversees operation of Adeline record label. *Recordings include:* albums: with Pinhead Gunpowder: Carry the Banner 1995, Goodbye Ellston Avenue 1997; with The Influents: Check Please 2000, Some of the Young 2003; with the Big Cats: Worrisome Blues 2002, On Tomorrow 2007, The Ancient Art of Leaving: High & Low 2011, The Ancient Art of Leaving: Two Parts 2012; with The Network: Money Money 2020 2003; with Foxboro Hot Tubs: Stop Drop and Roll!!! 2008; with Green Day: ¡Tré! 2012. *Honours:* with Green Day: MTV Europe Music Award for Best Rock Act 2013. *Address:* c/o Adeline Records LLC, 543 Encinitas Blvd, Suite 101, Encinitas, CA 92024, USA (office). *E-mail:* info@adelinerecords.net (office). *Website:* www.adelinerecords.net (office); www.greenday.com.

WHITE, Jim Ronald; Australian drummer and songwriter; b. 1962, Melbourne, Vic. *Career:* mem. Happy Orphans 1980–81, The People with Chairs Up Their Noses 1981–83; mem. Feral Dinosaurs 1982–86; Founder-mem. Venom P. Stinger 1985–96; mem. Hessian Sax 1988–89; Founder-mem. Dirty Three 1992–; Founder-mem. The Tren Brothers 1998–; Founder-mem. Xylouris White (with Giorgos Xylouris) 2013–; drummer for numerous acts including Bonnie Prince Billy, Nick Cave, Marianne Faithfull, PJ Harvey, Nina Nastasia, Beth Orton, Cat Power, Smog, White Magic. *Recordings include:* albums: with Venom P. Stinger: Meet My Friend Venom 1986, What's

Yours Is Mine 1990, Tear Bucket 1996; with Dirty Three: Dirty Three 1994, Sad & Dangerous 1994, Horse Stories 1996, Ocean Songs 1998, Whatever You Love, You Are (ARIA Award for Best Alternative Release 2000) 2000, She Has No Strings Apollo 2003, Cinder 2005, Toward the Low Sun 2012; with Nina Nastasia: You Follow Me 2007; with Xylouris White: Goats 2014. *E-mail:* whitexylouris@gmail.com. *Website:* xylouriswhite.com; dirtythree.com.

WHITE, John Paul; American folk and country music singer, songwriter and musician (guitar); b. 1973, Loretto, Tenn.; m.; four c. *Education:* Loretto High School, Univ. of North Alabama. *Career:* fmr Founder-mem., group Nuthin' Fancy; solo artist 2008; Founder-mem., The Civil Wars duo (with Joy Williams) 2008–; recording debut 2009; many TV and live appearances; supported Emmylou Harris and Adele on tour; collaborations with other artists including Taylor Swift, The Chieftains, T-Bone Burnett. *Films:* The Hunger Games (soundtrack; contributed song Safe & Sound) 2012. *Recordings:* albums: solo: The Long Goodbye 2008; with the Civil Wars: Barton Hollow (Grammy Award for Best Folk Album 2012) 2011, The Civil Wars 2013. *Honours:* with the Civil Wars: ASCAP Country Music Vanguard Award 2011, Grammy Awards for Best Country Duo/Group Performance 2012, 2014, Americana Music Asscn Honors & Awards Award for Duo/Group of the Year 2012. *Current Management:* c/o Asha Goodman and Holly Smith, Sacks & Co., 1300 Clinton Street, Suite 205, Nashville, TN 37203, USA. *Telephone:* (615) 320-7753. *E-mail:* asha.goodman@sacksco.com; holly.smith@sacksco.com. *Website:* www.sacksco.com. *Address:* c/o Sensibility Music LLC, Columbia Records, Sony Music Entertainment, 550 Madison Avenue, New York, NY 10022, USA (office). *Telephone:* (212) 833-8000 (office). *Website:* sensibilitymusic.com (office); www.sonymusic.com (office); thecivilwars.com.

WHITE, Katie; British singer, musician (guitar) and songwriter; b. 1983, Manchester. *Career:* fmr mem. TKO; fmr mem. Eskiimo; mem. The Ting Tings 2006–. *Recordings:* album: We Started Nothing (Ivor Novello Award for Best Album 2009) 2008. *Honours:* MTV Video Music Award for Best Video (for Shut Up and Let Me Go) 2008. *Address:* c/o Columbia Records, 9 Derry Street, London, W8 5HY, England (office). *Website:* www.thetingtings.com.

WHITE, Megan (Meg) Martha; American musician (drums); b. 10 Dec. 1974, Grosse Pointe, Mich.; m. 1st Jack White 1996 (divorced 2000); m. 2nd Jackson Smith 2009. *Career:* Founder-mem., The White Stripes 1997–2011. *Film appearance:* Coffee and Cigarettes 2003. *Recordings include:* albums: White Stripes 1999, De Stijl 2000, White Blood Cells 2001, Elephant (Grammy Award for Best Alternative Album) 2003, Get Behind Me Satan (Grammy Award for Best Alternative Music Album 2006) 2005, Icky Thump (Grammy Award for Best Alternative Music Album 2008) 2007, Under Great White Northern Lights 2010. *Honours:* MTV Europe Music Award for Best Rock Act 2003, BRIT Award for Best Int. Group 2004, Grammy Awards for Best Rock Song (for Seven Nation Army) 2004, for Best Rock Performance by a Duo or Group with Vocals (for Icky Thump) 2008. *Current Management:* Monotone Management, 820 Seward Street, Hollywood, CA 90038, USA. *Telephone:* (323) 308-1818 (office). *Fax:* (323) 308-1819 (office). *Website:* www.whitestripes .com.

WHITE, Peter; British musician and composer; b. 20 Sept. 1954, Luton, Beds., England. *Career:* 20 years, Al Stewart; tours, recordings, with Basia; solo tours, recordings 1990–; mem. The American Soc. of Composers, Authors and Publrs (ASCAP), American Fed. of Musicians. *Recordings:* solo albums: Reveillez-Vous 1990, Excusez-Moi 1991, Promenade 1993, Reflections 1994, Caravan of Dreams 1996, Songs of the Season 1997, Perfect Moment 1998, Glow 2001, Confidential 2004, Playin' Favorites 2006, A Peter White Christmas 2007, Good Day 2009; albums with Al Stewart: Year of The Cat 1976, Time Passages 1978, 24 Carrots 1980; with Basia: Time and Tide 1987, London Warsaw New York 1990, The Sweetest Illusion 1994, Live on Broadway 1995, It's That Girl Again 2009; with Skipper Wise: Standing Outside In The Rain 1990; with Roberto Perrera: In the Mood 1999. *Recordings include:* Philip Bailey, Rick Braun, Richard Elliot, Snowy White, Dave Koz. *Honours:* BMI Adult Contemporary Song of the Year, Time Passages 1978. *Address:* PO Box 15906, North Hollywood, CA 91615, USA (home). *E-mail:* email@peterwhite.com (office). *Website:* www.peterwhite.com.

WHITE, Terence Charles (Snowy); British musician (guitar) and singer; b. 3 March 1948, Devon. *Career:* guitarist with Peter Green; guitarist with Pink Floyd (touring band); Thin Lizzy, 1979–81; tours, Europe, UK, Japan, USA, Australia, 1979–81; solo artist 1982–. *Recordings:* Albums: with Thin Lizzy: Chinatown, 1980; Renegade, 1981; Adventures of Thin Lizzy, 1981; Solo: White Flames, 1984; Snowy White, 1985; That Certain Thing, 1987; Change My Life, 1991; Little Wing, 1998; Melting, 1999; Singles: with Thin Lizzy: Chinatown; Killers Live (EP); Solo: Bird of Paradise, 1983; Recordings with Peter Green include: Songbook, 2000; Clown, 2000; Time Traders, 2001; with Roger Waters: In The Flesh Live, 2000.

WHITE, Tom; British musician (guitar); b. Brighton. *Career:* mem., Brakes 2002–; numerous live performances. *Recordings include:* albums: Give Blood 2005, The Beatific Visions 2006, Touchdown 2009. *E-mail:* brakes@ brakesbrakesbrakes.com (office). *Website:* www.brakesbrakesbrakes.com.

WHITE, Tony Joe; American singer, musician (guitar) and songwriter; b. Oak Grove, LA. *Career:* solo artist; produced for Tina Turner, Joe Cocker, Etta James, Waylon Jennings, John Anderson, Isaac Hayes, Roy Orbison, Kris Kristofferson, Charlie Rich, Chet Atkins, Hank Williams Jr, Jessi Colter, Christine McVie, Ray Charles, Aretha Franklin and Wild Cherry. *Recordings*

include: albums: Black and White 1969, Continued 1970, Live in Europe 1971, Tony Joe, Tony Joe White 1971, The Train I'm On 1972, Snakey, Dangerous Eyes 1983, One Hot July 1999, The Beginning 2001, The Heroines 2004, Uncovered 2006, Deep Cuts 2008, The Shine 2010. *E-mail:* manager@ tonyjoewhite.com. *Website:* www.tonyjoewhite.com.

WHITE, Verdine; American singer, musician (bass) and producer; b. 25 July 1951, Chicago, Ill.; brother of Maurice White. *Career:* Founder-mem. Earth, Wind and Fire 1969–84, 1987–; live performances and tours include numerous special effects; collaborated with numerous artists including Jennifer Lopez, Deniece Williams, The Emotions, Ramsey Lewis. *Recordings include:* albums: Earth, Wind And Fire 1971, The Need Of Love 1972, Last Days And Time 1972, Head To The Sky 1973, Open Our Eyes 1974, That's The Way Of The World (soundtrack) (Grammy Award) 1975, Gratitude 1975, Spirit 1976, All 'N' All 1977, I Am 1979, Faces 1980, Raise! 1981, Secret Messages 1982, Powerlight 1983, Electric Universe 1983, Touch The World 1987, Heritage 1990, Millennium 1993, In The Name Of Love 1997, Take Two 2001, The Promise 2003, Avatar 2003, Illumination 2005, Now, Then & Forever 2013. *Honours:* American Music Award for Favorite Soul/Rhythm and Blues Band 1977, 1979, Grammy Award for Best R&B Vocal Performance (for All 'N' All) 1979, (for After The Love Has Gone) 1980, Best R&B Instrumental (for Boogie Wonderland) 1980, MTV Music Video Award 1985, Ivor Novello Award (for Easy Lover) 1986, Grammy Award for Best Gospel Performance 1987. *E-mail:* band@earthwindandfire.com. *Website:* www.earthwindandfire.com; www .verdinewhite.com.

WHITE, Will; British musician (drums) and DJ. *Career:* mem. Propellerheads 1996–2003. *Recordings include:* albums: with Properllerheads: Bang On! 1997, Decksandrumsandrockandroll 1998; with Eat Static: Crash and Burn 2001; with Jungle Brothers: VIP 2000.

WHITEHEAD, Tim, BA; British jazz musician (saxophone), composer and educator; b. 12 Dec. 1950, Liverpool, England; m. Linda Jones 1978; two s. two d. *Career:* mem., Loose Tubes (modern jazz orchestra) 1984–89; founder, Tim Whitehead Quartet 2000–, Tim Whitehead Band; formed sextet, TW6 2002–; regular recordings on TV and radio, festival appearances and tours; regular appearances at Ronnie Scott's Club, London; also performed, toured, broadcast with Ian Carr's Nucleus, Graham Collier, Jim Mullen's Meantime, Breakfast Band, Woodworks, Martin Drew Quartet; Chair. and co-founder, Jazz Umbrella (London jazz musicians' co-operative); Chair., Way Out West Jazz Collective 2004–; mem., Homemade Orchestra 2001–; Artist-in-Residence, Tate Britain 2009. *Compositions:* Silence Between Waves (Arts Council commission) 1992, Nine Sketches for solo saxophone (Jazz Umbrella/ Arts Council commission for London Jazz Festival on the South Bank) 1996, Heart and Soul (Jazz North East commission 1998), Sound Tracks 1998, Let Her Rave (Teignmouth Jazz Festival commission) 2003, Colour Beginnings (music about J.M.W. Turner's later work) 2009. *Recordings include:* English People (with Tim Whitehead Band) 1983, Decision (with Tim Whitehead Band) 1988, Authentic (with Tim Whitehead Quartet) 1992, Silence Between Waves (with Tim Whitehead Quartet) 1994, Personal Standards (with Tim Whitehead Quartet) (BBC Music Magazine Critics' Choice of the Year) 1999, Loose Tubes (with Loose Tubes), Delightful Precipice (with Loose Tubes), Open Letter (with Loose Tubes), Tides (with Colin Riley and the Homemade Orchestra) (Peter Whittingham Award 2000) 2001, Inside Covers (with Colin Riley and the Homemade Orchestra) 2003, Close To You (with Gwilym Simcock and Kathleen Willison) 2004, Lucky Boys (with Giovanni Mirabassi Quartet) 2006, Too Young to Go Steady (with Tim Whitehead Quartet) 2007, Nonsense (Michael Rosen's Nonsense poetry set to music by Tim Whitehead, Colin Riley and Liam Noble) 2009. *Honours:* Young Jazz Musician 1977, Andrew Milne Award for Jazz (for Soundtracks) 1998, Peter Whittingham Award for Jazz and Popular Music 2000. *Address:* 5 Willowbank, Ham, Richmond, Surrey (home); Basho Music, 18 Linhope Street, London, NW1 6HT, England (office). *Telephone:* (20) 8948-0687 (office). *E-mail:* timwhitehead@yahoo.com (home); info@bashomusic.co.uk (office). *Website:* www.timwhitehead.co.uk.

WHITFIELD, George William; musician (accordion) and singer; b. 29 Feb. 1964, Worcester, England. *Education:* Warwick Univ. *Career:* accordion player, vocalist with Pressgang 1988; solo appearances; work with outcast band, WOB, Steve Hunt; numerous concerts, tours and festival appearances; mem. Musicians' Union, PRS. *Recordings include:* albums: with Pressgang: Burning Boats 1994; with Outcast Band: Devil's Road 1993; with Steve Hunt: Head the Heart and the Hand 1993; with Roy Bailey: Coda 2000. *Address:* c/o Vox Pop, 1 Donnington Gardens, Reading, Berks, England.

WHITFIELD, Mark Adrian; American musician (guitar); b. 6 Oct. 1966, New York, NY; two s. *Education:* BMus, Berklee College of Music, Boston. *Career:* Appearances include: The Tonight Show; Good Morning America; The Today Show; CNN Showbiz Today; CBS Sunday Morning. *Recordings:* Albums: The Marksman; Patrice; Mark Whitfield; True Blue; Seventh Avenue Stroll; Forever Love; Take the Ride, 1999; Raw, 2000; Soul Conversation, 2000. *Publications:* Mark Whitfield Guitar Transcriptions. *Honours:* Hon. Mayor of Baton Rouge, Louisiana, USA. *Address:* 38 Laurel Ledge Court, Stamford, CT 06903, USA. *E-mail:* qpikwit@hotmail.com. *Website:* www .markwhitfield.com.

WHITMORE, Andrew David; British producer and musician (keyboards, guitar); b. 31 March 1962, Coventry, England; m. 1988; one s. one d. *Education:* Desborough Comprehensive School. *Career:* fmr mem., Terence

Trent D'Arby band, keyboard player; currently programmer, producer, working with artists including Peter Andre, East 17, Barrington Levy, Atomic Kitten, Cathy Dennis, Des'ree, Erasure, Kool & The Gang, Lisa Scott-Lee; mem. PRS, MCPS. *Compositions:* Flava (writer, with Peter Andre) 1996, Lemar: Time to Grow (writer and prod.) 2004. *Address:* 39 Greystoke Parr Terrace, Ealing, London, W5 1JL, England. *Telephone:* (20) 8998-5529 (office). *Fax:* (20) 8566-7885 (office). *E-mail:* andy@greystokeproductions.co.uk. *Website:* www.greystokeproductions.co.uk.

WHITTAKER, Roger; British singer, musician (guitar) and songwriter; b. 22 March 1936, Nairobi, Kenya. *Career:* fmr teacher and part-time folk singer; recording artist 1961–; numerous television appearances; launched UNESCO songwriting competition, 1975. *Recordings include:* albums, including compilations and special German-language recordings 1965–; Legendary 2001. *Publications include:* So Far So Good (with Natalie Whittaker). *Honours:* B'nai B'rith Humanitarian Award 1975. *Current Management:* Howard Elson Promotions, 16 Penn Avenue, Chesham, Bucks., HP5 2HS, England. *E-mail:* HElson1029@aol.com. *Website:* www.howardelson.co.uk; www .rogerwhittaker.com.

WHITWAM, Jan Barry; British musician (percussion, guitar); b. 21 July 1946, Prestbury, Cheshire, England; m. Anne Patricia 1987; one s. one d. *Education:* studied drums. *Career:* Founder-mem. Herman's Hermits 48 years, with tours world-wide, numerous concerts and TV appearances; mem. Musicians' Union, Equity. *Film appearances:* Hold On 1966, Mrs Brown You've Got a Lovely Daughter 1967. *Recordings include:* hits include: I'm Into Something Good 1964 Mrs. Brown You've Got A Lovely Daughter 1965, I'm Henry The Eighth I Am 1965, Silhouettes 1965, Wonderful World 1965, No Milk Today 1966, Something's Happening 1968. *Honours:* NME Award. *Address:* 26 South Park Road, Gatley, Cheadle, Cheshire, SK8 4AN, England.

WHYLIE, Marjorie Arnoldene Gregory, BA; Jamaican music educator, composer, cultural consultant and actress; *Staff Tutor, Philip Sherlock Centre for the Creative Arts, University of the West Indies;* b. 31 Oct. 1944, St Andrew; d. of Halcot L. and Florrie Whylie. *Education:* St Andrew High School for Girls, Univ. of the W. Indies and Jamaica School of Music. *Career:* teacher of Spanish Music, Kingston Coll. 1966–74; Cultural Officer Penal Insts and Bellvue Mental Hosp. 1974; Head Folk Music Research Dept, Jamaica School of Music 1975–85, Dir of Studies 1982–85, Prin. (acting) 1983, Consultant, External Examiner 1989; apptd Resource Tutor Music Unit, Univ. of the W. Indies 1981–83, 1991, currently staff tutor in music, Philip Sherlock Centre for the Creative Arts; Lecturer Orientation Programs for US Peace Corps Volunteers 1988; Music Dir Nat. Dance Theatre Co. of Jamaica 1967–; Consultant to CBC 1979; Artist-in-Residence Oberlin Univ., OH, USA, Cave Arts Centre, Birmingham, UK; Visiting Lecturer Ministry of Educ., Virgin Islands, Univ. of the W. Indies, Cave Hill, Barbados; devised and presented several radio programmes 1976–79; compositions include 24 ballet scores, 15 choral works and 29 instrumental pieces 1968–; has appeared at numerous Jazz festivals throughout the Caribbean 1989–. *Recordings include:* Mystic Revelation of Rastafari 1973, Traditional Music of the Caribbean 1979, Heritage 1980, Rhythm Kit (cassette and notes) 1983. *Honours:* Award for Music, Univ. of the W. Indies 1965, Bronze Musgrave Medal 1974, Silver Medal Best Supporting Actress 1976, Centenary Medal, Inst. of Jamaica 1982, Prime Minister's Medal of Appreciation 1983, Prime Minister's Aaward for Excellence in Theatre and Music 2004, Grace, Kennedy Foundation Lecturer 2005. *Address:* Philip Sherlock Centre for the Creative Arts, University of the West Indies, Mona Campus, Kingston 7 (home); 10 Milverton Crescent, Kingston 6, Jamaica. *Telephone:* 927-8183.

WICKENS, Paul 'Wix'; British record producer and musician (keyboards); b. 27 March 1956, Chelmsford, Essex; m. Margo Buchanan 1992. *Career:* recorded with The Pretenders, Dave Stewart, Mike and The Mechanics, Céline Dion, Nik Kershaw, Boy George, Status Quo, Alison Moyet, John Hiatt, The The, Prefab Sprout, The Kane Gang, Emmylou Harris, Linda Ronstadt, Jackson Browne, Bonnie Raitt; performed live with Joni Mitchell, Jon Bon Jovi, Ry Cooder, The Kane Gang, The Chieftains, Bob Dylan, Jim Diamond; worked with Paul McCartney on albums and world tours 1989–; mem. Buckingham Palace House Band, Party at the Palace (Queen's Jubilee concert) 2002; production credits include The Kane Gang, Jim Diamond, The Big Dish, Freddie McGregor, Mel Garside, Carmel, Alisha's Attic, Shakin Stevens, Texas, Kevin Coyne, Edie Brickell, Leann Rimes, Tasmin Archer; mem. Musicians' Union, PRS, MCPS, MPG.

WICKHAM, Steve; Irish musician (violin, keyboards); b. 28 Oct. 1960, Dublin; m. 1st Barbara Kernal; m. 2nd Heidi Ansell 1996. *Education:* Coll. of Music. *Career:* mem., The Waterboys 1985–90, 2000–; worked with U2, Texas Kellys, Elvis Costello, Sinead O'Connor, Sharon Shannon, Deirdre Cunningham, Maria McKee, In Tua Nua; mem. IMRO. *Theatre score:* Caoineadh Art O'Laoghaire (Abbey Theatre) 1998. *Recordings include:* albums: This Is The Sea 1985, Fisherman's Blues 1988, Room To Roam 1990, Rock in the Weary Land 2000, Universal Hall 2003, Book of Lightning 2007. *Publication:* Sofa So Good 1986. *Honours:* Hot Press Musician of the Year 1986. *Website:* www .mikescottwaterboys.com.

WIDMARK, Anders; Swedish musician (piano) and composer; b. 25 Nov. 1963, Uppsala. *Education:* Royal Acad. of Music. *Career:* collaborated with Stockholm Jazz Orchestra, Swedish Radio Jazz Orchestra, Eddie Harris, Bob Brookmeyer, Clark Terry, Rebecka Törnqvist, Bengt-Arne Wallin; solo performances with Sundsvall Symphony Orchestra and Uppsala Chamber

Soloists; mem. STIM, SKAP. *Recordings include:* solo albums: Sylvesters sista resa 1991, Anders Widmark and the Soul Quartet 1993, Holly Hannah 1994, Freewheelin' 1995, Anders Widmark 1996, Anders Widmark Trio –Psalmer 1997, Carmen 2000, Hymn 2004, Waiting for a Train 2006, Supervisor 2010, Dag Hammarskjold-Road 2012, Horses on the Run 2014; contrib.: Dreams, Bob Brookmeyer and Stockholm Jazz Orchestra 1989, A Night Like This, Rebecka Törnqvist 1993, Obsession! Live at Fasching, Egil Bop Johansen 1994, Quel Bordel, Christian Falk 1999, Pool of Happiness 2008. *E-mail:* anderswidmarkmusik@gmail.com. *Website:* www.anderswidmark.se.

WIEDLIN, Jane; American singer, musician (guitar), songwriter, fashion designer and actress; b. 20 May 1958, Oconomowoc, Wis. *Career:* Founder-mem. all-female group, The Go-Go's (formerly The Misfits) 1978–85, re-formed briefly for PETA benefit concert 1990, for shows in Las Vegas 1994, re-formed for an album and tours 2000–; numerous int. tours; collaboration with Sparks 1984; solo artist 1985–93. *Film appearance:* Bill and Ted's Excellent Adventure 1989. *Recordings include:* albums: with The Go-Go's: Beauty and The Beat 1981, Vacation 1982, Talk Show 1984, Greatest 1991, Return To The Valley of The Go-Go's 1994, God Bless The Go-Go's 2001; solo: Jane Wiedlin 1985, Fur 1988, Tangled 1990, Very Best of Jane Wiedlin 1993, Kissproof World 2000. *Compositions include:* Our Lips Are Sealed (co-writer with Terry Hall). *Publication:* Lady Robotika (comic book with Bill Morrison). *Current Management:* c/o Deb Klein & Larry Mestel, Primary Wave Talent Management, 116 East 16th Street, 9th Floor, New York, NY 10003, USA. *Telephone:* (212) 661-6990; (424) 239-1207. *Fax:* (212) 661-8890. *Website:* www .primarywavemusic.com. *Address:* 2261 Market Street, Suite 332, San Francisco, CA 94114, USA. *E-mail:* gogos@beyondmusic.com. *Website:* www .janewiedlin.com; www.gogos.com.

WIENEUSKI, Matthew; British composer, film-maker and musician (saxophone, flute); b. 20 Sept. 1965, London, England. *Education:* Bristol Univ. *Career:* European tour 1993, Japan 1994; mem. PRS. *Screenplays:* Hardcore Nation, The Kabbalist of Lincoln. *Compositions:* D*votions, The Garden of Earthly Delights. *Recordings:* albums: Babel, Criminal Justice. *Address:* c/o Dorado Records, 76 Brewer Street, London W1R 3PH, England.

WIGGS, Josephine Miranda Cordelia Susan, BA, MA; British musician (bass guitar) and composer; b. 26 Feb. 1963, Letchworth, Hertfordshire; d. of Richard John Wiggs and Florence Margaret Wiggs. *Education:* Univ. of London and Sussex. *Career:* bass, cello and backing vocals with Perfect Disaster 1987–90; bass, vocals, guitar, cello, drums with The Breeders 1990–94, bassist 2012–; bassist with Ultra Vivid Scene, US tour 1990, Honey Tongue 1992, Ladies Who Lunch; co-producer and touring drummer Kostars 1995–97, The Josephine Wiggs Experience 1996, Dusty Trails 1999–2001. *Composer:* Happy Accidents 2000, Built On Narrow Land 2012, Appropriate Behaviour 2014. *Recordings:* with Perfect Disaster: Asylum Road 1988, Up 1989, Heaven Scent 1990; with Breeders: Pod 1990, Safari 1992, Last Splash 1993, Nude Nudes, Honey Tongue 1992; with Ladies Who Lunch: Kims we Love, Everybody's Happy Nowadays Kostars: Klassics with a K 1995, The Josephine Wiggs Experience, BonBon Lifestyle 1996, Dusty Trails: Dusty Trails 2001; guest appearances on recordings by Sonic Boom (Spacemen3), Luscious Jackson, Amy Ray. *Honours:* BRIT Award for Best Single (for Cannonball) 1993. *E-mail:* jo@josephinewiggs.com (office). *Website:* www .josephinewiggs.com.

WIGGS, Pete; British musician (keyboards, programming) and producer; b. (Peter Stewart Wiggs), 15 May 1966, Reigate, Surrey, England. *Career:* Founder-mem. Saint Etienne 1988–; launched own label, Emidisc; artist in residence (with Andrew Hinton and Bob Stanley), The Southbank Centre, London 2006; soundtrack composer. *Films:* What Have You Done Today Mervyn Day 2006, This Is Tomorrow 2008, How We Used To Live 2013, The Mistletoe Bough (1904) re-scored 2013. *Recordings include:* albums: Foxbase Alpha 1991, So Tough 1993, Tiger Bay 1994, Continental 1997, Good Humor 1998, The Misadventures Of Saint Etienne (soundtrack) 1999, Sound Of Water 2000, Finisterre 2002, Tales From Turnpike House 2005, Words and Music by Saint Etienne 2012. *Current Management:* c/o Martin Kelly, Heavenly Management, 47 Frith Street, London, W1D 4SE, England. *Telephone:* (20) 7494-2998. *Fax:* (20) 7437-3317. *E-mail:* martin@ heavenlymanagement.com. *Website:* www.heavenly100.com; www.saint .etienne.net.

WILBER, Bob, BA; American bandleader, composer, arranger, writer and musician (clarinet, saxophones); b. (Robert Sage), 15 March 1928, New York, NY; m. Joanne Horton; two s. one d. *Education:* State Univ. of New York, Juilliard School, Eastman School of Music, Manhattan School of Music; studied with Sidney Bechet, Lennic Tristano, Leon Russianoff. *Career:* subbed for Sidney Bechet, Nice Festival 1948; also leading bands at Savoy, Storyville clubs, Boston; played with Bobby Hackett, Benny Goodman, Jack Teagarden, Eddie Condon; founding mem. World's Greatest Jazz Band 1969; began Soprano Summit with Kenny Davern 1973–78, re-formed as Summit Reunion 1990; performed, recorded with jazz artists including Duke Ellington, Billy Strayhorn, Louis Armstrong, Sidney Bechet; performed, presented Carnegie Hall Tribute to Benny Goodman; premiered orchestral version of Duke Ellington's Queens Suite; toured with Bechet Legacy Band; helped organize New York jazz Repertory Company; Director, Smithsonian Jazz Repertory Ensemble; leads big band in Benny Goodman re-creations; Musical Dir The Cotton Club; soloist, Pittsburgh, Baltimore, Colorado Symphony Orchestras; mem. ASCAP, Rotary, Senior Statesman of Jazz. *Compositions:* The Piscean

Suite, Portraits In Jazz. *Recordings:* over 1,500 titles including saxophones on: Horns A-Plenty; more recent releases include Fletcher Henderson's Unrecorded Arrangements 2000, Vital Wilber 2000, Moments Like This 2000, Nostalgia. *Publications:* Music Was Not Enough (autobiog.) 1987. *Honours:* Hon. DMus (Hamilton Coll.) 1998; Grammy Award for Music for Film (for The Cotton Club) 1985. *Address:* Endymion House, Church Street, Chipping Campden, Gloucestershire GL55 6JG, England (home). *Telephone:* (1386) 841217 (home).

WILDE, Danny; American singer, songwriter and musician. *Career:* mem., The Quick, Great Buildings, The Rembrandts 1991–; also solo artist. *Recordings include:* albums: with The Quick: Mondo Deco 1976; with Great Buildings: Apart from the Crowd 1981; solo: The Boyfriend 1986, Any Man's Hunger 1988, Danny Wilde 1989, Spin This! 1998, Beesides 1999, N-Progress/Scragglers 2000; with The Rembrandts: Rembrandts 1991, Untitled 1992, LP 1995, Lost Together 2001. *Address:* 9744 Wilshire Blvd, Suite 305, Beverly Hills, CA 90212, USA. *E-mail:* infomusic@aol.com. *Website:* www.therembrandts.com; www.DannyWildeMusic.net.

WILDE, Kim; British singer; b. (Kim Smith), 18 Nov. 1960, Chiswick, London, England; d. of Marty Wilde and Joyce Baker; m. Hal Fowler 1996; one s. one d. *Education:* Presdales School, Ware, St Albans Coll. of Art & Design, Capel Manor Horticultural Coll. *Career:* backing singer to father Marty; solo artist 1980–; numerous concerts, live performances; has also pursued career as landscape gardener 1998–. *Stage appearance:* played female lead in West End production of Pete Townshend's Tommy 1996. *Recordings include:* albums: Kim Wilde 1981, Select 1982, Catch As Can Can 1983, Teases and Dares 1984, Another Step 1986, Close 1988, Love Moves 1990, Love Is 1992, The Singles Collection 1981–93 1993, Now and Forever 1995, Never Say Never 2006, Come Out & Play 2010, Snapshots 2011, Wilde Winter Songbook 2013. *Publications:* Gardening with Children 2005, Harry's Garden 2006, How to Make a Scarecrow 2006, The First-time Gardener 2006. *Honours:* BRIT Award for Best British Female Artist 1983, Gold Medal, Chelsea Flower Festival 2005. *Website:* www.kimwilde.com.

WILDE, Marty; British singer and songwriter; b. (Reginald Leonard Smith), 15 April 1939, Greenwich, London, England; m. Joyce Baker; two s. two d. *Career:* performed as Reg Patterson, and with The Hound Dogs; changed name, with backing group The Wildcats, 1957; numerous TV appearances; formed the Wilde Three, vocal trio, with Justin Haywood 1965; Owner Wilde Productions Ltd. *Films:* The Helions 1961, What A Crazy World 1964. *Theatre:* Bye Bye Birdie (London) 1961. *Television:* Boy Meets Girls 1959, Six Five Special-Oh Boy Show. *Compositions include:* co-writer (with Ronnie Scott), Ice In The Sun, Status Quo; Jesamine, The Casuals; co-writer (with Ricky Wilde), Kim Wilde 1981–, Kids in America. *Recordings:* albums: Diversions 1969, Good Rocking, Now and Then 1973, Solid Gold 1994, It's Been Nice 1996, Born To Rock 'n' Roll 1999, The Best Of Marty Wilde, Hit singles include: Endless Sleep 1958, Donna 1959, A Teenager In Love 1959, Sea of Love 1959, Bad Boy 1960, Little Girl 1961, Rubber Ball 1961, Jezebel 1963. *Address:* Thatched Rest, Queen Hoo Lane, Tewin, AL6 0LT, England (home). *Telephone:* (14) 3879-8625 (office); (14) 3879-8395 (office). *E-mail:* wildeproductionstv@gmail.com (office). *Website:* www.martywilde.com (office).

WILDER, Alan; British musician; b. 1 June 1959, London, England. *Career:* mem., Depeche Mode 1982–95; numerous world tours, TV and radio appearances worldwide; currently producer. *Recordings include:* albums: Speak and Spell 1981, A Broken Frame 1982, Construction Time Again 1983, Some Great Reward 1984, The Singles 81–85 1985, Black Celebration 1986, Music For The Masses 1987, 101 1989, Violator 1990, Songs Of Faith & Devotion 1993.

WILDHORN, Frank N.; American composer and producer; b. 29 Nov. 1958, New York; one s. *Education:* college. *Career:* long-term relationship with Warner Brothers Pictures to develop and compose both musical feature-length animated films and live-action projects; Creative Dir, Atlantic Theatre; composed over 200 songs; Music Dir, Opening Ceremony, Goodwill Games 1998; mem, ASCAP, NAS, DGA, WGA. *Musical theatre:* compositions: Jekyll and Hyde, The Scarlet Pimpernel, Victor/Victoria, Svengali, The Civil War, Rudolf, Carmen, The Count of Monte Cristo, Wonderland: Alice's New Musical Adventure, Havana, Bonnie and Clyde, Never Say Goodbye, Cyrano de Bergerac, Tears from Heaven, Camille Claudel, Waiting for the Moon; compositions included in Victor/Victoria, Dracula: The Musical. *Honours:* ASCAP writing awards. *Current Management:* c/o Michael Staringer, Diabelli Management, Pfeilgasse 35/4, 1080 Vienna, Austria. *Telephone:* (1) 603-14-48. *Fax:* (1) 603-14-48. *E-mail:* michael@diabelli.com. *Website:* www.diabelli.com; www.frankwildhorn.com.

WILEY; British MC, songwriter and record producer; b. (Richard Kylea Cowie), 19 Jan. 1979, London, England. *Career:* mem., Roll Deep Crew, with 'grime' music genre, formerly performing as Wiley Kat; also solo artist. *Recordings include:* album: Treddin' on Thin Ice 2004, In At the Deep End (Urban Music Award for Best Album) 2005, Playtime is Over 2007, See Clear Now 2008, Race Against Time 2009, 100% Publishing 2011, Evolve or Be Extinct 2012, The Ascent 2013. *Honours:* MOBO Award for Best Male Act 2013. *E-mail:* bookings@eski-beat.com (office). *Website:* www.rolldeepcrew.co.uk.

WILFRIED; Austrian singer and actor; b. (Wilfried Scheutz), 24 June 1950, Bad Goisern; m. Marina 1982; one s. *Education:* Trades Acad. *Career:* mem. 4xang; tours in Austria, Germany, France. *Recordings include:* solo:

BuchstabenBlues, Wunschkonzert, Ganz normal, Poptakes, Sehr sehr arg, Berg und Tal, Der weiche Kern, Gemms, Wilfried, Feuer auf dem Dach, Leivht; with 4xang: Blues and Boogie, Mad and Madley, Affi and Alm, Welt and Weit, Die Vier Goschen Oper, Alp Fiction, 4xang4, Alles1, 4mas, Schöne Bescherung.

WILK, Bradley; American musician (drums); b. 5 Sept. 1968, Portland, OR. *Career:* mem., Rage Against the Machine 1991–2000, re-formed 2007–; involvement in various causes, incl. Fairness and Accuracy in Reporting, Rock for Choice and Refuse and Resist; numerous tours and live appearances; founder mem. Audioslave 2002–; collaborations with: Cypress Hill, Puscifier, Street Sweeper Social Club; drummer with Black Sabbath 2013. *Recordings include:* albums: with Rage Against the Machine: Rage Against the Machine 1992, Evil Empire 1996, The Battle Of Los Angeles 1998, Renegades 2000, Live And Rare 2002; with Audioslave: Audioslave 2002, Out Of Exile 2005, Revelations 2006; with Black Sabbath: 13 2013. *Honours:* with Black Sabbath: Grammy Award for Best Metal Performance (for God is Dead?) 2014. *Website:* www.ratm.com; www.audioslave.com.

WILKIE, Chris; British songwriter and musician (guitar); b. 25 Jan. 1973, Gateshead. *Career:* mem., Dubstar. *Recordings include:* albums: Disgraceful 1995, Goodbye 1997, Make It Better 2000, Stars-The Best of Dubstar 2004. *Website:* www.dubstar.com.

WILKINS, Keith Allen; American studio musician (drums), songwriter, lyricist, syndicated music columnist and public speaker and concert promoter; *Syndicated Music Columnist, St Pete Examiner;* b. 12 Sept. 1974, Detroit, Mich.; s. of Fritz G. Wilkins and Tina C. Wilkins; one d. *Education:* diploma in music business management. *Career:* co-formed rock band Gateway 1989; studio session drummer, contract songwriter (lyricist), early to mid-1990s; f. KAM Music Publishing 1992; co-f. KAM-BABS Promotions 2011; consultant for Bay Area Band Source; Pres. Tampa Bay Music Scene Historical Soc.; Vice-Pres. Florida Musicians Hall of Fame, Tampa Bay Music Hall of Fame; currently Syndicated Music Columnist for the St Pete Examiner and The Bay Buzz; fmr cover story writer for Mayhem Magazine; has collaborated with or written for record cos, musicians and songwriters world-wide, including Dave Sharky, Jon Clarke, Stephanie Allen, Don Hecht, Ralph Lake, Andrei Cheine, Jennifer Lindbo and Cathy Clark; charter mem., Rock 'N' Roll Hall of Fame & Museum; mem. American Press Asscn; fmr mem. BMI, Nat. Acad. of Recording Arts and Sciences Inc., American Fed. of Musicians, Songwriters' Guild of America, Florida Music Asscn, Nashville Songwriters Asscn Int., South West Virginia Songwriters Asscn, Memphis Songwriters Asscn, Nat. Acad. of Songwriters, Songwriters of Wisconsin, Central Florida Musicians Asscn. *Radio includes:* has appeared on several radio stations and shows, including The Live Concert Series, Black Pearl Rock Radio, Social Network Radio, WFLA, WPRN 102.1FM Tampa. *Television includes:* appeared in three commercials for Ocean Jewel Casino 1995. *Compositions include:* singles: Always 1993, Hard Promises 1993, News For You Baby 1993, Everytime I Cry 1995, Together 1995, Good Lovin' Gone Bad 1995, You're A Part of Me 1996, Could It Be You 1996, Down By The Ocean Shore 1996, They'll Come A Runnin' 1996, Magic Moment 1996. *Recordings include:* albums: Music of America 1993, Hollywood Gold 1993, America Sings 1994. *Publications include:* contribs to JAM Magazine, Mayhem Magazine, San Antonio Examiner, The Bay Buzz, ROC Magazine, EContent Magazine. *Honours:* Composer and Lyricist Certificate, Songwriters Guild of America 1994, Most Read Examiner Columnist for 2010, 2011, Media Source Award, Tampa Bay Music Network 2011. *Address:* KAM Music Publishing, 620 Clearwater-Largo Road, Suite 216, Largo, FL 33770, USA (office).

WILKINS, Mark Thomas, BA; American music organization executive; b. 14 Dec. 1956, Seattle, WA. *Education:* CSULA, Sherwood Oaks Experimental College, LACC, CSULA. *Career:* mem., Quincy Jones Workshops; Head of Promotion, Mystic Records 1983–90; Founder, Affiliated Independent Record Labels (AIR Co), and International Record Promotion (IRP) 1990–93; Co-founder, CEO, Independent Network (Indy Net) 1993–; CEO, IMRA, AIM, ILTPA; Founder, CEO, The Independent Network; Vice-President, Independent Music Asscn (IMA); co-founder, Independent Music Retailer's Asscn (IMRA), Independent Live Talent Presenter's Asscn (ILTPA), Asscn of Independent Media (AIM). *Recordings:* with Mandrill: Love Attack; with Bandit: 1 World 1 People. *Publications:* Soundtrack Mag; Author: Music Biz 411 (USA), 411 International (Europe, Asia), The Right Way To Run A Record Label 1996, Forms and Contracts For Success 1996, International Success In The Music Business 1996.

WILKINSON, Alan James, BA (Hons); British musician (saxophone), singer and teacher; b. 22 Aug. 1954, Ilford, Essex, England; s. of Leonard Tenant Wilkinson and Margaret Elsie Wilkinson; partner Gina Southgate; two s. *Education:* Leeds Polytechnic. *Career:* joined Crow, with Matthew Coe (aka Xero Slingsby), drummer Paul Hession 1978; Art Bart and Fargo with Hession (toured in Europe) 1979; trio with Akemi Kuniyoshi and Hession 1982; tour, Europe with drummer Steve Hubback; duo with Hession, played 10th Free Music Festival, Antwerp and Netherlands 1983; Art Initiative, Eindhoven; started Termite Club, Leeds, Derek Bailey's Company 1987; tour of Italy, 1988, 1993; Sound Symposium, St Johns, Newfoundland, with Hession, Wilkinson, Fell 1994; Radio 3, Jazz Today 1987; Mixing It 1993; CBC: Two New Hours 1994; tour with Peter Brotzmann 1997; Musique Action w Stefan Jaworzyn 1998; WOMAD festival 1988, 1989, 2007; Freedom of the City 2002, 2004, 2005, 2006, 2008; Avaanto, Helsinki with Eddie Prevost 2007; tour with

Eddie Prevost, Schlippenbach, Williams 2008; Ulrichsberg with Steve Noble, John Edwards 2008; gigs with Spiritualized 2009–10; Norwegian tour with Johannesen, Hoyer, Knedal Andersen; gigs with Talibam!. *Recordings:* albums: with Hession, Wilkinson, Fell: Bogey's 1991, foom! foom! 1992, The Horrors of Darmstadt 1994, The Saxophone Phenomenon 1992, Registered Firm 1998, St John's 1999, Two Falls and a Submission 2011; with John Law Quartet: Exploded on Impact 1992; others: Seedy Boy 1994, Music for 10(0) with Simon Fell 1995, In a Sentimental Mood with Stefan Jaworzyn 1996, Composition No 30 with Simon Fell 1998, Composition 12.5 with Simon Fell 2000, London with Derek Bailey 2001, The Ins and Outs with Free Base 2005, So Are We, So Are We with Eddie Prevost 2006, Obliquity with Noble, Edwards 2007, One Night In Burmantofts with Brotzmann, Fell, Kellers 2007, Live at Cafe Oto 2009, Noble, Edwards, Dem Ol Apple Pie Melodies with Talibam! 2010, Practice (solo) 2011. *Honours:* several ACGB and ACE touring and study awards 1985–95, LAB travel grant 1994. *Address:* 36 Arbor Court, Queen Elizabeth's Walk, London, N16 0QU, England (home). *Telephone:* 7814-734704 (mobile) (office). *E-mail:* a.shakeywilko@btinternet.com (home). *Website:* www.flimflam.org.uk (office).

WILKINSON, Gary; British record producer. *Recordings:* records produced and remixed for Fire Island, Farley and Heller, The Farm, Sunscreen, Janet Jackson, Roach Motel, Jimmy Somerville, Happy Mondays, M People, Pet Shop Boys, Run DMC, U2; recordings: as remixer/producer: Inspiral Carpets, Life 1990, The Farm, Spartacus 1991, New Order, Regret 1993, One Dove, Morning Dove White 1993, Kylie Minogue, Confide in Me 1994, Janet Jackson, Runaway 1995, Michael Jackson, Blood on the Dance Floor 1997, Sneaker Pimps, Spin Spin Sugar 1997, Glasgow Gangster, Deeva Feeva 1999, Badly Drawn Boy 2000.

WILKINSON, Peter; British musician (bass); b. 9 May 1969, Liverpool, England. *Career:* mem., Shack 1988–93, 2005–; founder mem., Cast 1993–2002; numerous tours, festival, TV and radio appearances; founder mem., Aviator 2002–. *Recordings include:* albums: with Cast: All Change 1995, Mother Nature Calls 1997, Magic Hour 1999, Beetroot 2001; with Aviator: Huxley Pig—Pt 1 2002. *Website:* www.shacktheband.com.

WILL.I.AM; American rap artist and producer. *Career:* fmr mem., Atban Klann; founder mem., Black Eyed Peas 1995–; simultaneous solo artist 2001–. *Films include:* Madagascar: Escape 2 Africa (voice) 2008, X-Men Origins: Wolverine 2009, Date Night 2010, Bouncing Cats 2010, Rio 2011, Rio 2 2014. *Television includes:* The Voice UK (BBC One) (judge and mentor) 2012–, The Voice Australia (judge and mentor) 2014. *Recordings include:* albums: with Black Eyed Peas: Behind The Front 1998, Bridging The Gap 2000, Elephunk (NRJ Music Award for Best Int. Album, France 2005) 2003, Monkey Business (Juno Award for Int. Album of the Year 2006, American Music Award for Favorite Rap/Hip-Hop Album 2006) 2005, The E.N.D. (Grammy Award for Best Pop Vocal Album 2010) 2009, The Beginning 2010; solo: Lost Change 2001, Must B 21 2003, Songs About Girls 2007, #willpower 2013. *Honours:* MTV Europe Award for Best Pop Act 2004, 2005, Australian MTV Awards for Best R&B Video, for Sexiest Video (both for Hey Mama) 2005, American Music Awards for Favorite Pop/Rock Band, Duo or Group 2005, 2009, for Favorite Rap/Hip-Hop Band, Duo or Group 2005, 2006, 2009, Grammy Award for Best Rap Performance by a Duo or Group (for Don't Phunk with my Heart) 2006, MOBO Award for Best Group 2006, American Music Award for Favorite Soul/R&B Band, Duo or Group 2006, Grammy Awards for Best Pop Performance by a Duo or Group with Vocal (for My Humps) 2007, (for I Gotta Feeling) 2010, BMI Award 2010, Daytime Emmy Award for Best Original Song (What I Am) 2011. *Website:* www.blackeyedpeas.com; will.i.am.

WILLARD, Atom; American musician (drums); b. (Adam Willard), 15 Aug. 1973, San Diego, Calif.; m. *Career:* fmr mem. Moth and the Alkaline Trio; mem. Rocket from the Crypt ten years; mem. The Offspring 2003–07; Founder-mem. Angels & Airwaves 2005–11. *Recordings include:* album: with The Offspring: Splinter 2003; with Angels & Airwaves: We Don't Need to Whisper 2006, I-Empire 2007, Love 2010, Love: Part Two 2011; others: Southern Medicine 2013. *Current Management:* ITB, First Floor, Ariel House, 74A Charlotte Street, London, W1T 4QJ, England. *E-mail:* info@itb.co.uk. *Website:* www.itb.co.uk.

WILLETTS, Carey; British musician (bass guitar) and singer. *Career:* Founder-mem. Athlete 1997–; tours throughout Europe. *Recordings include:* albums: Vehicles & Animals 2003, Tourist 2005, Beyond the Neighbourhood 2007, Black Swan 2009. *Honours:* Ivor Novello Award for Best Contemporary Song (for Wires) 2006. *Website:* www.athlete.mu.

WILLIAM-OLSSON, Staffan; Norwegian jazz musician (guitar), composer and arranger; b. 13 Dec. 1959, Gothenburg, Sweden; 1 d. *Career:* Member, Norwegian hard-rock group Sons of Angels, 1989–91; Tours, USA, UK, Germany; Band disbanded, 1991; Now working with Norwegian soul/jazz group The Real Thing. *Recordings:* Albums: with Sons of Angels: Sons of Angels, 1990; with The Real Thing: The Real Thing, 1992; The Real Thing In New York, 1993; A Perfect Match, 1994; Shades of Blue, 1996; Contribution to: Jukka Linkola, Pegasos, 1996; Matz Nilsson, Moonroom. *E-mail:* w-olsson@online.no.

WILLIAMS, Andy; British musician (drums). *Career:* mem. Sub Sub late 1980s, changed name to Doves 1998–; co-f. (with Jez Williams) band Black Rivers 2014. *Recordings include:* albums: with Doves: Lost Souls 2000, The

Last Broadcast 2002, Some Cities 2005, Kingdom of Rust 2009. *Website:* www.dovesmusicblog.com.

WILLIAMS, Cliff; British musician (bass guitar); b. 14 Dec. 1949, Romford, England. *Career:* mem., Home late 1960s–74; founder mem., Bandit 1974–77; mem. Australian heavy rock group, AC/DC 1977–; numerous tours worldwide, festival appearances. *Recordings include:* albums: with Home: Pause For A Hoarse Horse 1971, Home 1972, The Alchemist 1973; with Bandit: Bandit 1977; with AC/DC: Powerage 1978, Highway to Hell 1979, Back in Black 1980, For Those About to Rock 1981, Flick of the Switch 1983, Fly on the Wall 1985, Who Made Who (soundtrack) 1986, Blow Up Your Video 1988, The Razor's Edge 1990, Ballbreaker 1995, Volts 1997, Private Parts 1997, Bonfire 1997, Stiff Upper Lip 2000, Satellite Blues 2001, Black Ice 2008, Rock or Bust 2014. *Honours:* Grammy Award for Best Hard Rock Performance (for War Machine) 2010. *Current Management:* AC/DC Management, Sony Music Entertainment, 550 Madison Avenue, New York, NY 10022-3211, USA. *Website:* www.acdc.com.

WILLIAMS, Dar, BA; American singer, musician (guitar) and songwriter; b. (Dorothy Snowden), 19 April 1967, Mount Kisco, NY. *Education:* Wesleyan Univ., CT. *Career:* has had material recorded by Joan Baez; active in environmental issues and set up Snowden Environmental Trust. *Recordings include:* albums: I Have No History 1990, All My Heroes Are Dead 1991, The Honesty Room 1993, Mortal City 1996, End of Summer 1997, Cry Cry Cry (with Lucy Kaplansky and Richard Shindell) 1998, The Green World 2000, Out There Live 2001, The Beauty of the Rain 2003, My Better Self 2005, Promised Land 2008; features on Gone From Danger (with Joan Baez) 1997, Badlands – Bruce Springsteen Tribute 2000. *Current Management:* c/o Russell Carter Artist Management, 567 Ralph McGill Boulevard, Atlanta, GA 30312, USA. *Telephone:* (404) 377-9900. *Fax:* (404) 377-5131. *E-mail:* russell.rcam@gmail.com. *Website:* www.darwilliams.com.

WILLIAMS, Deniece; American soul and gospel singer; b. (Deniece Chandler), 1951; m. 2nd Brad Westering; two s. by previous marriage. *Education:* Purdue Univ. *Career:* solo gospel/soul singer; fmr mem. Wonderlove (Stevie Wonder's backing group). *Recordings include:* albums: This is Niecy 1976, I'm So Proud 1983, Let's Hear it for the Boy 1984, Hot on the Trail 1986, Water Under the Bridge 1987, So Glad I Know 1988, As Good as it Gets 1989, Special Love 1989, Lullabies to Dreamland 1991, Love Solves It All 1996, This Is My Song 1998, Love Songs 2000, Love, Niecy Style 2007. *Honours:* Grammy Award for Best Female Soul Gospel Vocal 1986, Best Group Gospel Performance 1986, Best Female Gospel Performance 1987. *Current Management:* c/o BookingEntertainment.com, 275 Madison Avenue, 6th Floor, New York, NY 10016, USA. *E-mail:* agents@bookingentertainment.com. *Website:* www.deniecewilliams.net.

WILLIAMS, Don; American songwriter, singer and musician (guitar); b. 27 May 1939, Floydada, TX. *Career:* mem., Strangers Two, Pozo-Seco Singers; solo artist 1971–. *Film appearances:* W. W. and the Dixie Dancekings, Smokey and the Bandit 2. *Recordings include:* albums: with Poco-Seco Singers: Time 1966, I Can Make It With You 1967, Shades of Time 1968; solo: Don Williams Vols 1–3 1973, 1974, You're My Best Friend 1975, Harmony 1976, Visions 1977, Country Boy 1977, Expressions 1978, Portrait 1979, I Believe In You 1980, Especially For You 1981, Listen To The Radio 1982, Yellow Moon 1983, Cafe Carolina 1984, New Moves 1986, Traces 1987, One Good Well 1989, As Long As I Have You 1989, True Love 1990, Currents 1992, I've Got a Winner in You 1993, Lord I Hope This Day Is Good, 1993, Borrowed Tales 1995, Flatlands 1996, I Turn the Page 1998, Follow Me Back Home 2000, My Heart to You 2004. *E-mail:* management@don-williams.com. *Website:* www.don-williams.com.

WILLIAMS, Doug; American singer and musician (bass guitar); b. 22 Oct. 1950, Chicago, Ill.; m. Milly Williams; three d. *Career:* f. Von Ryan's Express with brother, Emery Williams; mem. Powerhouse 1975–76, My Old School 1985, Missing in Action, Marcia Hines Band, Renee Geyer Band, Hip Hop 1988, Duffhead 1990, The Black Mass 1992, The Rockmelons 1992, D. Williams and The Black Mass 1993, Doug Williams and The Mix 2000; mem. APRA (Australia). *Current Management:* c/o PO Box 650, Surry Hills, NSW 2010, Australia. *E-mail:* management@dougwilliams.com.au. *E-mail:* doug@dougwilliams.com.au. *Website:* www.dougwilliams.com.au.

WILLIAMS, Enid; British musician (bass guitar) and singer. *Career:* founder mem. of heavy metal band, Painted Lady, band renamed Girlschool 1978–81, 1992–; formed band Framed; worked with Dave Parsons, Biddu; mem., Moho Pack; teacher of performance and vocal skills; formed band, Strangegirls. *Recordings include:* albums: Demolition 1980, Hit 'N' Run 1981, Live 1995, Race With The Devil (Live) 1998, Live On The King Biscuit Flower Hour 1998, Can't Keep A Good Girl Down 1999, 21st Anniversary: Not That Innocent 2002, Second Wave 2003, Believe 2004, Emergency/London 2005, Legacy 2008. *Address:* PO Box 33446, London, SW18 3XN, England (office). *E-mail:* girlschool@hotmail.com (office). *Website:* www.girlschool.co.uk.

WILLIAMS, Geoffrey; British songwriter, singer and musician (guitar); b. 25 April 1964, London. *Career:* mem. Musicians' Union. *Compositions:* songs for Beverly Hills 90210 album, Eternal, Color Me Badd. *Recordings include:* albums: The Drop 1997, Lost in Dinosaur World 1997, Prisoner of Love 1997, Move into Soul 2007; singles: It's Not a Love Thing 1992, Drive 1996, I Guess I Will Always Love You 1996, Sex Life 1997, Deliver Me Up 1997; also worked with Jimmy Somerville, Alison Limerick, Shaun Escoffery.

WILLIAMS, (Randall) Hank, Jr; American country singer and musician; b. 26 May 1949, Shreveport, LA; s. of Hank Williams; m. Mary Jane Williams; two s. three d. *Career:* performer since age of eight; debut appearance Grand Ole Opry 1960; solo artist 1963–; recorded with his father, and with Connie Francis, Ray Charles, Willie Nelson, John Lee Hooker, Johnny Cash, Reba McEntire, Huey Lewis, Tom Petty, Waylon Jennings, George Jones, George Thorogood and Travis Tritt; recorded as Luke The Drifter 1960s–70s; career halted by mountaineering accident 1975–77; mem. BMI, ASCAP, NEA, CMA, NARAS, ACM, AMA, AFTRA, SAG. *Recordings include:* albums: Your Cheatin' Heart (film soundtrack) 1964, Living Proof 1974, Hank Williams Jr and Friends 1976, One Night Stands 1977, The New South 1977, Family Tradition 1979, Rowdy 1981, Hank Live 1987, Born To Boogie 1987, Pure Hank 1991, Maverick 1992, Out of Left Field 1993, Hog Wild 1995, Wham Bam Sam 1996, Three Generations of Hank 1996, Stormy 1999, Stormy 1999, I'm One of You 2003, 127 Rose Avenue 2009. *Publication:* Living Proof (with Michael Bane). *Honours:* five Entertainer Awards for country music, Emmy Award (for Monday Night Football theme, ABC) 1990, Grammy Award (for There's A Tear In My Bear) 1990, gold medal Int. Film and TV Festival, New York, Pulitzer Prize Special Citation 2010. *Current Management:* c/o Ken Levitan and Ross Schilling, Vector Management, PO Box 120479, Nashville, TN 37212, USA. *Website:* www.hankjr.com.

WILLIAMS, Hayley Nichole; American singer, songwriter and musician (keyboards, guitar); b. 27 Dec. 1988, Meridian, Miss. *Career:* moved to Franklin, Tenn. at age of 13; fmr mem. The Factory; signed to Atlantic Records as a solo artist 2003; Founder-mem. Paramore 2004–, signed to Fueled by Ramen Records 2004; also featured on records by October Fall, The Chariot, B.o.B. *Recordings:* albums: with Paramore: All We Know is Falling 2005, Riot! 2007, Brand New Eyes (Kerrang! Best Album Award 2010) 2009, Paramore 2013. *Film:* Jennifer's Body (soundtrack) 2009. *Honours:* solo: Los Premios MTV Latinoamerica Fashionista Award 2009; with Paramore: Kerrang! Best New Band Award 2006, MTV Europe Music Award for Best Alternative Act 2010, NME Best Int. Band Award 2010, People's Choice Favorite Rock Band Award 2010, 2011, MTV Clubland Award (with Zedd for Stay the Night) 2014, Grammy Award for Best Rock Song (for Ain't It Fun) 2015. *Current Management:* c/o The Agency Group, 142 West 57th Street, Sixth Floor, New York, 10019, USA. *Telephone:* (212) 581-3100. *Fax:* (212) 581-0015. *E-mail:* KenFermaglich@theagencygroup.com. *Website:* www.theagencygroup.com; www.paramore.net.

WILLIAMS, J. Owen; singer, songwriter and musician (acoustic guitar); b. 1 Feb. 1959, Ireland. *Education:* studied Irish traditional music. *Career:* solo artist, with numerous festival appearances, radio broadcasts; mem. Musicians' Union, PRS. *Recordings:* albums: Ribbonmen 1991, Sean One Shoe 1994. *Address:* 18c Alwyne Place, Islington, London N1 2NL, England.

WILLIAMS, James Kimo; American composer and academic; b. 8 Jan. 1950, Amityville, New York; m. Carol Williams. *Education:* Berklee Coll. of Music, Army School of Music, , Pacific Lutheran Univ., Webster Univ., De Paul Univ. *Career:* served in US Army as combat engineer 1970–71, formed and played guitar with Soul Coordinators, Viet Nam 1970–71, rejoined in Hawaii 1977, stationed with US Army Admin Corps, Tacoma, Wash. 1979 and Fort Sheridan Ill. 1980–87, Marketing Officer, Chicago Recruiting District 1983–86; Bandmaster Commander, US Army Reserve Warrant Officer and Commander of the 85th Div. Reserve Band, Fort Sheridan, Ill. 1989–94; Music Dir and performer, Boston Repertoire Co. 1972–76; formed Paumalu Symphony 1975, later renamed Kimotion; f. Little Beck Music and One Omik Music 1992–; teacher, Berklee Coll. of Music 1976–77, Northeastern Ill. Univ., Chicago 1984, New Trier High School, Winnetka, Ill. 1987; Dir of Commercial Music and Jazz Ensembles, Sherwood Conservatory of Music, Chicago 1987–89; Artist-in-Residence, Columbia Coll., Chicago 1996–97, Assoc. Prof., Arts Entertainment and Media Management Department 1996–2010, Assoc. Prof., Music Dept 2010–; co-f. Lt Dan Band with actor Gary Sinise 2003, performing for USO worldwide; mem. Nat. Asscn of Recording Arts and Sciences (Vice-Pres. Chicago chapter 1990, Gov. 1991), BMI (publisher mem. 1990–). *Compositions include:* Dragon Lady 1969, Once More for Love 1972, Mystic Reflections of Days Gone By 1973, A New Understanding 1973, Wait for the Band 1973, We've Got the Music 1973, Stolen Butterflies 1973, Paumalu Place 1973, I Do Love You 1974, The Real Thing 1974, Ask Me Not 1974, Larorituptoo 1974, To Kiss a Rose 1974, Leilehua Waltz 1974, Walking with Your Sot 1974, The Life and Death of Life 1974, Into the Liquid 1974, Su de Lu 1975, I Know 1975, Opizmes 1975, Fique 1975, Wahiawa 1975, Take Me to Your Disco 1975, Cambimorof 1976, Carols Babyfingernail 1976, Loracsti 1976, Old Doats 1976, Chunkypeanutbutterfluff 1976, Bleath 1976, Quiet Shadows 1978, Federated 1978, Biofort Ballad 1978, Obowlap 1979, Rare Twelve 1979, Midnite Sandwich 1980, Art Perkins 1981, Perk's Eyes 1983, Kimo's Funk 1983, Inside the Rainbow 1983, Plush Mush 1983, Brothian 1984, Seven to Ten 1984, From You 1984, Dorothy's Song 1985, Mad Soap 1985, Baby Blues 1985, Ramona 1986, Still Loving You 1986, Space Limosine 1986, Rebecca 1987, Dragon Queen 1989, Kimotion 1989, Too Raw 1989, Symphony for the Sons of Nam 1990, Quartet for the Sons of Nam 1990, New Born 1992, Fanfare for Life 1993, A Child in Crisis 1994, Quartet for a New Beginning 1994, Two Gether 1995, All From You 1995, Silent Watch 1996, Testimony of Lucy Smith 1996, All Things 1996, Affection (ballet) 1997, A Streetcar Named Desire 1997, Lullaby for Maeve 1997, Buffalo Soldier 1997, Get Up 1997, Hold On 1997, Only Angels 1997, Winners and Losers 1997. *Honours:* US Army medal for work as music performer for troops stationed in remote fighting locations, Viet Nam 1971, League of Black Women, Chicago Chapter Black Rose Award for services to the community 1991, Lancaster Symphony Composers' Award 1998, Chicagoan of The Year, Chicago Magazine 2007. *E-mail:* kimo@omik.com (office); admin@littlebeckllc.com. *Website:* www.kimowilliams.com; www.omik.com (office).

WILLIAMS, Jez; British musician (guitar) and songwriter. *Career:* mem., Sub Sub late 1980s, changed name to Doves 1998–; tours in UK and USA. *Recordings:* albums: with Doves: Lost Souls 2000, The Last Broadcast 2002, Some Cities 2005, Kingdom of Rust 2009. *Address:* c/o Heavenly Recordings, 47 Frith Street, London W1D 4SE, England (office). *E-mail:* info@heavenlyrecordings.com (office). *Website:* www.doves.net.

WILLIAMS, John Charles; British composer, arranger and musician; b. 8 Feb. 1941, Hammersmith, London, England; m. Frances Margaret; three s. one d. *Education:* Acton Tech. Coll. 1957–59. *Career:* Leader Resident Big Band, Marquee Club, London 1961–63; formed Octet 1969, Big Band 1973; ensembles include saxophone quartet Changing Face 1976–78, Trio Spectrum 1985, Baritone Band 1985; played and recorded with Keith Tippett, Alan Cohen, Don Rendell; instituted annual Summer Music Festival, Shropshire; mem. Musicians' Union. *Compositions:* four pieces for Jazz Soloists and Orchestra, Out of Focus, When Summers End Is Nighing, Tenorama 2001. *Recordings:* Year of The Buffalo, Five Housman Settings and other jazz works; War Horse/The Adventures of Tintin (Classic BRIT Awards Composer Award 2012); other collaborations include Centipede, New Perspectives, with John Williams' Baritone Band: Spotlite. *Honours:* Classic BRIT Award for Lifetime Achievement 2012. *Address:* Leasowes Bank Farm, Ratlinghope, Shrewsbury, SY5 0SW, England.

WILLIAMS, John Towner; American composer, conductor and pianist; b. 8 Feb. 1932, Flushing, NY. *Education:* Juilliard School, New York, Univ. of California, Los Angeles, studied composition with Mario Castelnuovo-Tedesco. *Career:* pianist, Columbia Pictures; jazz pianist working with Henry Mancini on television scores; Conductor, Boston Pops Orchestra 1980–98. *Film scores:* The Secret Ways 1961, Diamond Head 1962, None But the Brave 1965, How to Steal a Million 1966, Valley of the Dolls 1967, The Cowboys 1972, The Poseidon Adventure 1972, Tom Sawyer 1973, Earthquake 1974, The Towering Inferno 1974, Jaws (Acad. Award) 1975, The Eiger Sanction 1975, Family Plot 1976, Midway 1976, The Missouri Breaks 1976, Raggedy Ann and Andy 1977, Black Sunday 1977, Star Wars (Acad. Award) 1977, Close Encounters of the Third Kind 1977, The Fury 1978, Jaws II 1978, Superman 1978, Dracula 1979, 1941 1979, The Empire Strikes Back 1980, Raiders of the Lost Ark 1981, E.T.: The Extra Terrestrial (Acad. Award) 1982, Return of the Jedi 1983, Indiana Jones and the Temple of Doom 1984, The River 1985, Space Camp 1986, The Witches of Eastwick 1987, Empire of the Sun (BAFTA Award for Best Score) 1988, Always 1989, Born on the Fourth of July 1989, Indiana Jones and the Last Crusade 1989, Stanley and Iris 1990, Presumed Innocent 1990, Home Alone 1990, Hook 1991, JFK 1993, Far and Away 1993, Home Alone 2: Lost in New York 1993, Jurassic Park 1993, Schindler's List (Acad. Award) 1993, Sabrina 1995, The Reivers 1995, Nixon 1995, Sleepers 1996, Rosewood 1996, Land of the Giants 1997, Seven Years in Tibet 1997, The Lost World: Jurassic Park 1997, Amistad 1997, Lost in Space 1997, Time Tunnel 1997, Saving Private Ryan 1998, Star Wars: Episode I – The Phantom Menace 1999, Angela's Ashes 1999, Harry Potter and the Sorcerer's Stone 2001, Star Wars: Episode II – Attack of the Clones 2001, Minority Report 2002, Harry Potter and the Chamber of Secrets 2002, Catch Me if You Can 2002, Harry Potter and the Prisoner of Azkaban 2004, The Terminal 2004, Star Wars: Episode III – Revenge of the Sith 2005, War of the Worlds 2005, Harry Potter and the Goblet of Fire 2005, Memoirs of a Geisha (Golden Globe for Best Original Score in a Motion Picture 2006, BAFTA Anthony Asquith Award for Achievement in Film Music 2006, Grammy Award for Best Score Soundtrack Album for Motion Picture 2007) 2005, Munich 2005, Superman Returns 2006, Harry Potter and the Order of the Phoenix 2007, Indiana Jones and the Kingdom of the Crystal Skull 2008, Harry Potter and the Half-Blood Prince 2009, Lincoln (Critics Choice Award 2013) 2012, The Book Thief 2013. *Recordings include:* John Williams Plays The Movies 1996, Music From The Star Wars Saga 1999, Jane Eyre 1999, Themes From Academy Award Winners, Over The Rainbow: Songs From The Movies 1992, John Williams Conducting The Boston Pops 1996, The Hollywood Sound 1997, From Sousa To Spielberg, Best Of John Williams 1998, Treesong 2001, Call Of The Champions (official theme of 2002 Winter Olympics, Salt Lake City) 2001, John Williams Trumpet Concerto 2002, American Journey 2002; recordings of film scores. *Honours:* numerous hon. degrees; five Academy Awards, seven BAFTA Awards, three Emmy Awards, four Golden Globes, 21 Grammy Awards, recipient of Kennedy Center Honors 2004, Classical BRIT Award for Soundtrack Composer of the Year 2005, Grammy Awards for Best Instrumental Composition (for A Prayer for Peace, from Munich) 2007, (for The Adventures of Mutt, from Indiana Jones and the Kingdom of the Crystal Skull) 2009, Nat. Medal of Arts 2009, Ken Burns Lifetime Achievement Award 2013. *Current Management:* c/o Michael Gorfaine, Gorfaine/Schwartz Agency, 4111 West Alameda Avenue, Suite 509, Burbank, CA 91505, USA. *Website:* www.johnwilliams.org.

WILLIAMS, Joy Elizabeth; American folk and country music singer, songwriter and musician (piano, concertina); b. 1982, Mich.; m. Nate Yetton; one s. *Education:* Valley Christian High School, San Jose, Calif. *Career:* raised in Calif.; signed as solo artist to Reunion Records 1999–2005; Co-founder, Sensibility Music 2008–; Founder-mem., The Civil Wars duo (with John Paul

White) 2008–; recording debut 2009; numerous TV and live appearances; supported Emmylou Harris and Adele on tour; collaborations with other artists including Taylor Swift, The Chieftains, T-Bone Burnett. *Films:* The Hunger Games (soundtrack; contributed song Safe & Sound) 2012. *Recordings:* albums: solo: Joy Williams 2001, By Surprise 2002, Genesis 2005; with the Civil Wars: Barton Hollow (Grammy Award for Best Folk Album 2012) 2011, The Civil Wars 2013. *Honours:* solo: ASCAP Music Award for Most Performed Song (for Hide) 2005; with the Civil Wars: ASCAP Country Music Vanguard Award 2011, Grammy Awards for Best Country Duo/Group Performance 2012, 2014, Americana Music Asscn Honors & Awards Award for Duo/Group of the Year 2012. *Current Management:* c/o Asha Goodman and Holly Smith, Sacks & Co., 1300 Clinton Street, Suite 205, Nashville, TN 37203, USA. *Telephone:* (615) 320-7753. *E-mail:* asha.goodman@sacksco.com; holly.smith@sacksco.com. *Website:* www.sacksco.com. *Address:* c/o Sensibility music LLC, Columbia Records, Sony Music Entertainment, 550 Madison Avenue, New York, NY 10022, USA (office). *Telephone:* (212) 833-8000 (office). *Website:* sensibilitymusic.com (office); www.sonymusic.com (office); thecivilwars.com.

WILLIAMS, Kathryn, BFA; British singer; b. 1974, Liverpool. *Education:* Univ. of Newcastle Upon Tyne. *Recordings include:* albums: Dog Leap Stairs 1999, Little Black Numbers 2000, Old Low Light 2002, Relations 2004, Over Fly Over 2005, Beachy Head 2005, Leave to Remain 2006, Two (with Neill MacColl) 2008. *Current Management:* c/o Nigel Morton, Moneypenny, Westwood House, Main Street, North Dalton, East Yorkshire YO25 9XA, England. *Telephone:* (1377) 217815. *E-mail:* nigel.morton@moneypennymusic.co.uk. *Website:* www.moneypennymusic.co.uk. *E-mail:* kath@kathrynwilliams.net (office). *Website:* www.kathrynwilliams.net.

WILLIAMS, Linda, BA; American musician (guitar, banjo, mouth harp), singer and songwriter; b. 7 July 1947, Anniston, AL; m. Robin Williams 1973. *Education:* Michigan State Univ. *Career:* duo with husband, Robin Williams 1973–; worked with Garrison Keillor's A Prairie Home Companion 1975–; touring mem., Their Fine Group 1989–; founder mem., The Hopeful Gospel Quartet; numerous appearances, Grand Ole Opry, Nashville, TN; numerous television appearances, festivals, tours; mem. Country Music Asscn, Int. Bluegrass Music Asscn, The Folk Alliance. *Recordings include:* albums: Robin & Linda Williams 1975, Shenandoah Moon 1977, Welcome Table 1978, Dixie Highway Sign 1979, Harmony 1981, Close as We Can Get 1984, Nine Till Midnight 1985, All Broken Hearts Are The Same 1989, The Rhythm Of Love 1990, Turn Toward Tomorrow 1994, Good News 1995, Sugar For Sugar 1996, Devil Of A Dream 1998, In The Company Of Strangers 2000, Visions of Love 2002, Deeper Waters 2004, The First Christmas Gift 2005, Radio Songs 2007, Buena Vista 2008, Stonewall Country 2011, These Old Dark Hills 2012, Back 40 2013. *Honours:* Peabody Award for Broadcasting (for work on Prairie Home Companion) 1980. *Current Management:* Music Tree Artist Management, 1414 Pennsylvania Avenue, Pittsburgh, PA 15233-1419, USA. *Telephone:* (412) 323-2707. *Fax:* (412) 323-1817. *Website:* www.music-tree.com. *E-mail:* robin@robinandlinda.com (office). *Website:* www.robinandlinda.com.

WILLIAMS, Lucinda; American singer and songwriter; b. 26 Jan. 1953, Lake Charles, LA. *Career:* played folk clubs in Texas; solo artist 1979–; appeared on various tribute albums; song, Still I Long For Your Kiss, for the film The Horse Whisperer 1998. *Recordings include:* albums: Ramblin' On My Mind 1979, Happy Woman Blues 1980, Lucinda Williams 1988, Sweet Old World 1992, Car Wheels On A Gravel Road 1998, Essence 2001, World Without Tears 2003, Live at the Fillmore 2005, West 2007, Little Honey 2008, Blessed 2011, Down Where the Spirit Meets the Bone 2014. *Honours:* Grammy Award for Best Songwriter 1994, for Best Female Rock Vocal Performance (for Get Right With God) 2002. *Address:* c/o Lost Highway Records, Universal Music Group, Universal Studios, 100 Universal City Plaza, Universal City, CA 91608, USA. *Website:* www.lucindawilliams.com.

WILLIAMS, Mason, BMus; American composer, writer, musician (guitar) and singer; b. 24 Aug. 1938, Abilene, Tex.; m. 1st; one d.; m. 2nd; m. 3rd 1993; m. 4th 2005. *Education:* Oklahoma City Univ., North Texas State Coll. *Career:* college student/folk singer 1959–61; served in USN 1962–63; folk singer, songwriter, sideman 1964–65; TV writer, Smothers Brothers, Andy Williams, Glen Campbell and Petula Clark 1966–69; musical performances at clubs, concerts, festivals, symphony orchestra, TV 1972–; mem. AFofM, AFTRA, WGAW, NARAS, NAS, SGA. *Art exhibitions:* Word & Image (BUS) MOMA 1968, Pasadena Museum of Art (BUS), California Artist Books, The Armory Pasadena (BUS) 1991, Radical Past, Norton Simon Museum Pasadena 1999, Art in LA, The Getty 2006, Graphics Retrospective Merc Gallery Temecula 2007, Artist's Gifts (Michael Asher), MOCA 2007, Roots & Ties, Untitled Art Space, Oklahoma City 2007. *Dance:* 'Triskelion' – Oklahoma City Univ. American Spirit Dancers (Jo Rowan), 'Triskelion' – Dance Theatre of Oregon, Eugene, Ore.. *Film:* Premium – MW Crackers Story/Ed Ruscha film. *Television:* scriptwriter: The Roger Miller Show, various Smothers Brothers shows, Saturday Night Live, Rolling Stone Magazine 10th Anniversary Special; miscellaneous TV pilots. *Recordings include:* three folk albums 1960–63, six folk anthologies and Them Poems 1963–65, five albums 1968–71; Fresh Fish 1978, Of Time and Rivers Flowing 1984, Classical Gas (with Mannheim Steamroller) 1987, A Gift of Song 1992, Of Time and Rivers Flowing 1996, EP 2003 2003, Electrical Gas (with Joe McCulloch) 2005. *Publications:* Bicyclists Dismount 1964, Next to the Windows 1965, Tosadnessday 1966, The Night I Lost my Baby 1967, Royal Road Test 1967, Boneless Roast 1967, Bus 1967, Pat Paulsen for President, The Mason Williams

Phonograph Song Album 1968, Songs from the Smothers Brothers Show 1968, The Mason Williams Reading Matter 1969, Road Sign Business 1969, Crackers (with Ed Ruscha) 1969, The MW FCC Report 1969, Flavors 1971, Cancer Society Script 1970, The MW Guitar Pieces Book 1971, Them Poems 1991, Classical Gas: The Music of Mason Williams 1995, Them Poems 2000, Classical Gas: The Music of Mason Williams 2003, The Book of Answers 2005. *Honours:* Hon. DMus (Oklahoma City Univ.) 1995; two Grammy Awards 1968, Emmy Award 1969, one Writers' Guild Award 1975, Writers' Guild Award 1981, Oregon Trout 'Wild Trout' Award 1985, Oregon Gov.'s Art Award 1990, Classical Gas/American Gramophone Gold Record 1991, BMI Special Citation of Achievement (for Classical Gas) 1999, Univ. of Oregon Distinguished Service Award 1999, State of Oregon Musician's Laureate 2000, Chet Atkins Appreciation Soc. Award 2003. *Address:* PO Box 5105, Eugene, OR 97405, USA (office). *Telephone:* (541) 345-1418 (office). *Fax:* (541) 343-6205 (office). *E-mail:* info@masonwilliams-online.com (office). *Website:* www.classicalgas .com (office).

WILLIAMS, Melanie Joy; singer and songwriter; b. 28 Oct. 1964, London, England. *Career:* solo artist; numerous television appearances; mem. Musicians' Union, Equity. *Recordings:* albums: Temper Temper, Human Cradle 1995. *Address:* 222 Lambolle Place, London NW3 4PG, England.

WILLIAMS, Mervyn; Jamaican audio engineer; b. 8 May 1957, St James; Fiancée, Kaye Troy E Janagalee, 1 s., 2 d. *Education:* Aquarius recording studio, studios overseas. *Career:* Several tours with Burning Spear; mem, MFM. *Recordings:* with Jimmy Cliff; Burning Spear; Beres Hammond; Judy Mowatt; Mikey Dread; Roots Radics; Dwight Pinkney; Delroy Wilson; Vocalist on Tiger, Ras Portraits, 1997. *Honours:* Jamaica Federation of Music (JFM).

WILLIAMS, Michelle; American singer; b. 23 July 1980, Rockford, IL. *Career:* mem., Destiny's Child 2000–05; numerous live performances; solo artist 2001–. *Recordings include:* albums: with Destiny's Child: Survivor (American Music Award for Favorite Pop/Rock Album 2002) 2001, Eight Days Of Christmas 2001, Destiny Fulfilled (Lady of Soul Award for Best Group Album 2005, American Music Award for Favorite Soul/R & B Album 2005) 2004; solo: Heart To Yours 2002, Do You Know? 2004, Unexpected 2008, Hello Heartbreak 2009. *Stage appearances include:* Aida, The Color Purple, Chicago (London) 2009. *Honours:* (with Destiny's Child) Billboard Award for Artist of the Year, Group of the Year, Hot 100 Singles Artist of the Year, Hot 100 Group of the Year 2000, Grammy Award for Best R&B Song, Best R&B Performance by a Duo or Group with Vocal (for Say My Name) 2001, NAACP Image Award for Outstanding Duo or Group (for Say My Name) 2001, MTV Video Award for Best R&B Video (for Say My Name) 2001, American Music Award for Favorite Soul/R&B Group 2001, Soul Train Sammy Davis Jr Award for Entertainer of the Year 2001, American Music Award for Favorite Pop/Rock Band, Duo or Group 2002, BRIT Award for Best Int. Group 2002, MOBO Award for Best Gospel Act 2002, World Music Award for World's Best Pop Group 2005, Lady of Soul Award for Best Group Single (for Soldier) 2005, American Music Award for Favorite Soul/R&B Band, Duo or Group 2005, Billboard Music Award for R&B/Hip-Hop Group of the Year 2005. *Current Management:* Music World Entertainment, 9898 Bissonnet, Suite 625, Houston, TX 77036, USA. *Website:* www.destinyschild.com.

WILLIAMS, Oritsé Jolomi; British singer and songwriter; b. 27 Nov. 1986. *Education:* British Int. School, Lagos, Nigeria. *Career:* mem. UFO 2006–08, changed group name to JLS (Jack the Lad Swing) 2008–13; competed in The X Factor (UK version) 2008, placed second; signed to Epic Records 2009; toured with Lemar 2009; debut single Beat Again released 2009; debut album released 2009; first headline tour 2010; recorded single Love You More for Children in Need charity 2010; collaborations include Tinie Tempah, Dev; recorded Sport Relief charity single Proud 2012; performed at Diamond Jubilee concert, outside Buckingham Palace 2012; songwriter for Jedward; Patron for National Multiple Sclerosis Society charity. *Television:* with JLS: The X Factor (as competitors) 2008, JLS Revealed (special) 2009. *Film:* JLS: Eyes Wide Open 3D (concert film and documentary) 2011. *Recordings include:* albums: with JLS: JLS (MOBO Award for Best Album 2010) 2009, Outta This World 2010, Jukebox 2011, Evolution 2012. *Publications:* Our Story So Far 2009, Just Between Us: Our Private Diary 2010. *Honours:* with UFO: Urban Music Award for Best Unsigned Act 2007; with JLS: MOBO Awards for Best UK Newcomer 2009, for Best Song (for Beat Again) 2009, for Best UK Act 2010, BBC Switch Live Award for Outstanding Artist 2009, BRIT Awards for British Breakthrough 2010, for Best British Single (for Beat Again) 2010, BT Digital Music Awards for Best Group 2010, 2011, for Best Video (for Everybody in Love) 2010, (for Eyes Wide Shut) 2011, (for Do You Feel What I Feel?) 2012, Urban Music Awards for Best Group 2010, for Best R&B Act 2010, solo: Multiple Sclerosis Society of Great Britain Inspiration Award 2010. *Current Management:* c/o Modest! Management, The Matrix Complex, 91 Peterborough Road, London, SW6 3BU, England. *E-mail:* info@ modestmanagement.com. *Website:* www.modestmanagement.com; www .jlsofficial.com.

WILLIAMS, Otis Clayborn; American singer, songwriter and producer; b. 30 Oct. 1941, Texarkana, Tex.; m. 1982; one d. *Education:* high school. *Career:* mem., The Temptations 1960–; television specials; Motown revue tours; countless tours; mem. ASCAP. *Recordings include:* albums: Meet The Temptations 1964, The Temptations Sing Smokey 1965, The Temptin' Temptations 1965, Gettin' Ready 1966, Temptations Live! 1967, In A Mellow Mood 1967, With A Lot O' Soul 1967, TV Show 1967, Wish It Would Rain 1968,

Diana Ross & The Supremes Join The Temptations 1968, Live At The Copa 1968, Cloud Nine 1969, The Temptations Show 1969, Puzzle People 1969, On Broadway 1969, Psychedelic Shack 1970, Live At London's Talk Of The Town 1970, The Christmas Card 1970, Together 1970, Sky's The Limit 1971, Solid Rock 1972, All Directions 1972, Masterpiece 1973, Zoom 1973, Song For You 1975, House Party 1975, Wings Of Love 1976, The Temptations Do The Temptations 1976, Bare Back 1978, Hear To Tempt You 1978, Power 1980, Give Love At Christmas 1980, The Temptations 1981, Reunion 1982, Back To Basics 1983, Surface Thrills 1983, Truly For You 1984, Touch Me 1985, To Be Continued... 1986, Together Again 1987, Special 1989, Milestone 1991, For Lovers Only 1995, My Girl 1997, Phoenix Rising 1998, Ear-Resistable 2000, Awesome 2001, Legacy 2004, In Japan (live) 2004, Back to Front 2007, Still Here 2010. *Publications:* Temptations (autobiog.) 1988. *Current Management:* c/o Star Direction Inc., 9200 Sunset Boulevard, Ph 20, Los Angeles, CA 90069, USA. *E-mail:* stardirection@sbcglobal.net. *Website:* www.temptationssing.com; www.otiswilliams.net/main.aspx.

WILLIAMS, (David) Paul Gifford, MA; composer and music producer; b. (Terry Day), 3 Sept. 1940, Kingston, Surrey, England; m. Rosalind Anne Burns 1965; one s. two d. *Education:* Cambridge University, Royal College of Music, Jesus College, Cambridge. *Career:* BBC Senior Producer, 1980; Sony Award winner, McCartney, BBC series, 1988; Composer for film, television; Worked with Phil Manzanera on Nowomowa album, 1988; TV music, House of Gristle, BBC TV, 1994; BBC TV Out of This World, 1994; Mysteries, BBC TV, 1997–98; Growing Places, BBC TV, 1999; mem. BACS; PRS; Musicians' Union. *Compositions:* over 1,200 published for television, films. *Recordings:* 22 albums. *Honours:* 3 Sony radio awards, 1988, 1990, 1992; Stemra Award, Netherlands, 1994. *E-mail:* paul@paulwilliamsmusic.com.

WILLIAMS, Paul Hamilton; American composer and actor; *President and Chairman, American Society of Composers, Authors and Publishers (ASCAP)*; b. 19 Sept. 1940, Bennington, Nebraska; m. Mariana Williams; one s. one d. *Career:* actor 1965–; began composing career 1970; songwriter, A&M Records; songs have been recorded by artists including Elvis Presley, Frank Sinatra, Willie Nelson, Ella Fitzgerald, David Bowie, Ray Charles, R.E.M., Tony Bennett, Sarah Vaughan, Johnny Mathis, Luther Vandross; Vice-Chair., American Soc. of Composers, Authors and Publishers (ASCAP) 2007–09, Pres. and Chair. 2009–. *Compositions:* hits include We've Only Just Begun, Rainy Days and Mondays, Evergreen, Just an Old Fashioned Love Song, Rainbow Connection, I Won't Last a Day Without You. *Films:* as composer: Phantom of the Paradise 1974, Bugsy Malone 1976, A Star is Born (Golden Globe Award for Best Score) 1976, One on One 1977, The End 1978, The Muppet Movie (Grammy Award 1980) 1979, Ishtar 1987, The Muppet Christmas Carol 1992, Lucky Ducks 2009; has made over 70 appearances in film and TV as actor. *Recordings:* albums: Just An Old-Fashioned Love Song 1972, Life Goes On 1972, Here Come Inspiration 1973, A Little Bit of Love 1974, Ordinary Fool 1975, Classics 1977, And Crazy for Loving You 1981, Back to Love Again 1997, Love Wants to Dance 2003. *Honours:* Acad. Award for Best Original Song (for Evergreen) 1976, Grammy Award for Best Song (for Evergreen), Golden Globe Award for Best Song (for Evergreen). *Address:* PO Box 100, Sunset Beach, CA 80742, USA (office). *E-mail:* pwconnection2@aol.com (office). *Website:* paulwilliamsconnection.org.

WILLIAMS, Pharrell; American producer, remixer, songwriter and musician; b. 5 April 1973, Virginia; s. of Pharaoh Williams and Carolyn Williams; m. Helen Lasichanh 2013; one s. *Education:* Princess Anne High School. *Career:* formed The Neptunes production duo with Chad Hugo 2000–; co-formed recording act, N.E.R.D. (Nobody Ever Really Dies) 2001–, with Chad Hugo and Shay Hayley; Co-founder Star Trak Entertainment label; worked with numerous artists, including Air, Mary J. Blige, Foxy Brown, Daft Punk, Jay-Z, Kelis, Ludacris, Mystikal, Nelly, No Doubt, *NSYNC, Ol' Dirty Bastard, Pitbull, P. Diddy, Ray J, Busta Rhymes, Snoop Dogg, Britney Spears, Robin Thicke, T.I., Justin Timberlake, Usher. *Television includes:* The Voice (as series judge) 2014–. *Recordings include:* albums: with N.E.R.D.: In Search Of... 2001, Fly Or Die 2004, Seeing Sounds 2008, Nothing 2010; with The Neptunes: The Neptunes Present... Clones 2003; solo: In My Mind 2005, G I R L (Grammy Award for Best Urban Contemporary Album 2015, Billboard Music Award for Top R&B Album 2015) 2014. *Honours:* Source Award for Producer of the Year (The Neptunes) 2001, MOBO Award for Best Producer (The Neptunes) 2002, Grammy Awards for Producer of the Year 2004, 2014, for Best Rap Song (for Money Maker, with Ludacris) 2007, for Record of the Year, for Best Pop Duo/Group Performance (both for Get Lucky, with Daft Punk) 2014, for Best Pop Solo Performance, for Best Music Video (both for Happy) 2015, Billboard Music Awards for Top Hot 100 Song, for Top Digital Song, for Top Radio Song, for Top R&B Song (all for Blurred Lines, with Robin Thicke and T.I.) 2014, for Top R&B Song (for Happy) 2015, for Top R&B Artist 2015, iHeartRadio Innovator Award 2014, MTV Video Music Award for Best Male Video (as producer) (for Sing) 2014, BET Award for Best Male R&B/Pop Artist 2014, BRIT Award for Int. Male Solo Artist 2015, Grammy Award for Best Rap Song (for Alright) 2016. *Website:* www.n-e-r-d.com; iamother.com.

WILLIAMS, Robert (Robbie) Peter; British singer; b. 13 Feb. 1974, Stoke-on-Trent, Staffs., England; s. of Pete Williams and Theresa Janette Williams; m. Ayda Field 2010; one d. *Career:* played the Artful Dodger in Oliver 1982; mem. group Take That 1991–95, 2010–; solo artist 1995–; tours: The Show Off Must Go On 1997, The Ego Has Landed 1998, One More for the Rogue Tour/For a Few Dollars More... Tour 1998–99, Robbie Williams North American Tours 1999, The Sermon on the Mount Tour 2000–01, Weddings, Barmitzvahs & Stadiums Tour/Sing When You're Pacific Rimming Tour 2001, Weekends of Mass Distraction Tour/Cock of Justice/Aussie Typo Tour 2003, Close Encounters Tour 2006, Take the Crown Stadium Tour 2013; recording collaborators as soloist include: Kylie Minogue, Nicole Kidman, Maxi Jazz, Pet Shop Boys, Dean Martin, Gary Barlow, Thalia; mem. Equity, Musicians' Union, Mechanical-Copyright Protection Soc., Performing Right Soc., ADAMI, GVC, AURA. *Films:* Nobody Someday 2002, De-Lovely 2004, The Magic Roundabout (voice) 2005. *Recordings include:* albums: with Take That: Take That And Party 1992, Everything Changes 1993, Nobody Else 1995, Greatest Hits 1996, Progress 2010; solo: Life Thru' a Lens 1997, I've Been Expecting You 1998, The Ego Has Landed 1999, Sing When You're Winning 2000, Swing When You're Winning 2001, Escapology 2002, Live At Knebworth 2004, Intensive Care 2005, Rudebox 2006, Reality Killed the Video Star 2009, Take the Crown 2012, Swings Both Ways 2013. *Publications:* F for English 2000, Robbie Williams: Performance (with Mark McCrun) 2001, Robbie Williams: Somebody Someday 2001, Feel (with Chris Heath) 2004, You Know Me (with Chris Heath) 2010. *Honours:* numerous including: nine Smash Hits Awards 1992–98, 16 BRIT Awards (13 solo), Levi's Nordoff-Robbins Music Therapy Original Talent Award 1998, MTV Award for Best Male 1998, Echo Award for Best Int. Male Rock and Pop Artist, Germany 2005, 2006, MTV Europe Music Award for Best Male 2005, MTV Latin America Music Award for Best Int. Pop Artist 2006, Q Idol Awards (with Take That) 2006, (solo) 2013, BRIT Award for Outstanding Contrib. to Music 2010, Echo Award for Best Int. Male 2010, NRJ Music Award for Best Int. Male Artist 2010, Virgin Media Award for Best Male Artist 2010, BRIT Award (with Take That) for Best British Group 2011. *Current Management:* IE Music Ltd, 111 Frithville Gardens, London, W12 7JG, England. *Telephone:* (20) 8600-3400. *Fax:* (20) 8600-3401. *E-mail:* info@iemusic.co.uk. *Website:* www.iemusic.co.uk; www.takethat.com; www.robbiewilliams.com.

WILLIAMS, Robin, BA; American musician (guitar, banjo, mouth harp), singer and songwriter; b. 16 March 1947, Charlotte, NC; m. Linda 1973. *Education:* Presbyterian coll. *Career:* solo artist 1969–73; duo with wife, Linda Williams 1973–; worked with Garrison Keillor's A Prairie Home Companion 1975–; touring mem., Their Fine Group 1989–; founder mem., The Hopeful Gospel Quartet; numerous appearances, Grand Ole Opry, Nashville, TN; numerous television appearances, festivals, tours; mem. Country Music Asscn, Int. Bluegrass Music Asscn, The Folk Alliance. *Recordings include:* albums: Robin & Linda Williams 1975, Shenandoah Moon 1977, Welcome Table 1978, Dixie Highway Sign 1979, Harmony 1981, Close as We Can Get 1984, Nine Till Midnight 1985, All Broken Hearts Are The Same 1989, The Rhythm Of Love 1990, Turn Toward Tomorrow 1994, Good News 1995, Sugar For Sugar 1996, Devil Of A Dream 1998, In The Company Of Strangers 2000, Visions of Love 2002, Deeper Waters 2004, The First Christmas Gift 2005, Radio Songs 2007, Buena Vista 2008, Stonewall Country 2011. *Honours:* Peabody Award for Broadcasting (for work on Prairie Home Companion) 1980. *Current Management:* Music Tree Artist Management, 1414 Pennsylvania Avenue, Pittsburgh, PA 15233-1419, USA. *Telephone:* (412) 323-2707. *Fax:* (412) 323-1817. *Website:* www.music-tree.com. *E-mail:* robin@robinandlinda.com (office). *Website:* www.robinandlinda.com.

WILLIAMS, Simon; British record company executive. *Career:* fmr NME journalist; founder, record label Fierce Panda 1994–, released early singles from bands, including Coldplay, Ash, Supergrass, The Polyphonic Spree, Keane, The Bluetones, Gorky's Zygotic Mynci, Placebo, Embrace, Kenickie, Three Colours Red, Tiger, Idlewild, Ultrasound and others. *Address:* Fierce Panda Records, 1s Leroy House, 436 Essex Road, London, N1 3QP (office); c/o Fierce Panda Records, PO Box 21441, London, N7 6WZ, England. *E-mail:* jess@fiercepanda.co.uk (office). *Website:* www.fiercepanda.co.uk (office).

WILLIAMS, Tim; American songwriter and musician (Multi Instrumentalist); b. 11 Aug. 1948, California; m. Johanne Deleevw, 2 s. *Career:* Coffee Houses; Concerts; Signed with Epic Records, 1968. *Compositions:* My Heart Can't Take Another Rodeo; Trying to Rope the Wind; Au Contraire Mon Frere. *Recordings:* Blues Full Circle, 1969; Writing This Song, 1977; Enough to be Remembered, 1982; Riverboat Rendezvous, 1995; Creole Nightingale, 1996; Indigo Incidents, 1997. *Honours:* Magazine Awards; Betty Mitchell Theatre Award. *Address:* Cayuse Music, 833 17th Ave SE, Calgary, AB T2G 1J2, Canada. *E-mail:* dtwcayuse@shaw.ca. *Website:* www.telusplanet.net/public/belzners/main.htm; www.cayusemusic.com.

WILLIAMS, Victoria Ann; American singer, songwriter and musician (guitar, banjo, dulcimer, piano, mandolin, harmonica); b. 23 Dec. 1958, Shreveport, LA; m. Mark Olson 1993. *Education:* college. *Career:* solo artist 1987–; numerous live and TV appearances; backing vocals for recordings by The Jayhawks, Giant Sand, Jimmie Dale Gilmore, Tammy Rogers, Ron Surrey, Jim White; mem. Musicians' Union, AFTRA, SAG. *Recordings include:* albums: Happy Come Home 1987, Swing The Statue 1990, Loose 1994, This Moment Live In Toronto (with the Loose Band) 1995, Gas, Food and Lodging (film soundtrack) 1995, Lilith Compilation 1997, Musings of a Creek Dipper 1998, The Original Harmony Ridge Creek Dippers 1998, Pacific Coast Rambler 1998, Zola and the Tulip Tree 1999, Water to Drink 2000, My Own Jo Ellen 2001, Mark Olson and the Creekkdippers 2002, Sing Some ol' Songs 2003, Political Manifest 2004, Mystical Theatre 2004. *Current Management:* c/o Celia Blackwool, Litterbox Music Services, PO Box 342, Joshua Tree, CA 92252, USA. *E-mail:* celia@litterboxmusic.com. *Website:* www.litterboxmusic.com; www.victoriawilliams.net.

WILLIAMSON, Astrid, BA; British singer, songwriter and musician (piano, guitar); b. 28 Nov. 1968, Shetland Islands, Scotland. *Education:* Royal Scottish Acad. of Music and Dance. *Career:* fmr mem. Goya Dress mid-1990s; solo artist 1998–; launched record label Incarnation 2003–; 2012, mem. touring band of Dead Can Dance as keyboardist and vocalist 2012–; numerous collaborations including with Oskar, The Bilderberg Groop;. *Recordings include:* albums: with Goya Dress: Rooms 1996; solo: Boy For You 1998, Astrid 2003, Day Of The Lone Wolf 2006, Here Come the Vikings 2009, Pulse 2011. *Website:* astridwilliamson.co.uk.

WILLIAMSON, Cris, BA; American singer, songwriter and musician (keyboards, guitar); b. 15 Feb. 1947, Deadwood, SD. *Education:* University of Denver. *Career:* numerous live performances, tours; composer of several documentary scores, film scores; mem. AFofM, AFTRA. *Recordings include:* albums: Artistry of Cris Williamson, 1963; The World Around Cris Williamson, 1965; Cris Williamson, Ampex, 1971; The Changer and The Changed, 1974; Live Dream, 1977; Strange Paradise, 1978; Lumiere, 1981; Blue Rider, 1982; Meg and Cris at Carnegie Hall, 1983; Portrait, 1983; Prairie Fire, 1984; Snow Angel, 1985; Wolf Moon, 1988; Country Blessed, 1989; Circle of Friends, 1991; Postcards From Paradise (with Tret Fure), 1993; Between the Covers (with Tret Fure) 1997, Radio Quiet 1999, Ashes 2001, Cris & Holly 2003, Real Deal 2005, Fringe 2007, Winter Hearts 2008. *Honours:* Parents' Choice Award (for Lumiere) 1982, Cable Car Award for Outstanding Recording Artist 1983, 1990, City and County of San Francisco State of California Honour Award for Outstanding Performer and Musician 1988. *Address:* PO Box 970, Marcola, OR 97454-0970, USA. *E-mail:* cris@criswilliamson.com. *Website:* www .criswilliamson.com.

WILLIAMSON, Daniel, (LTJ Bukem); British producer, remixer, DJ and multi-instrumentalist; *Founder, Good Looking Records;* b. 1967, Croydon, Surrey, England. *Career:* drum 'n' bass music pioneer and producer; started career as DJ late 1980s, now world-wide; got break playing at the Biology raves; Founder Good Looking Records; promoter of Logical Progression and Speed club nights, London; club residency at The End, London; collaborations with artists, including MC Conrad, Peshay; remixed Jodeci, The Shamen, Grace, Michelle Gayle; mem. Performing Right Soc. *Recordings:* albums: Journey Inwards 2000, LTJ Bukem: Producer 2001; singles: Logical Progression 1991, Bang The Drums 1992, Demon's Theme 1993, Atlantis 1993, Music 1994, Horizons 1995, 19.5 1995, Moodswings – Earth 1 1996, Cosmic Interlude – Earth 2 1997, Constellation – Earth 3 1998, Rhodes To Freedom 1999, Sunrain 2000, Switch 2006, Coolin' Out – Logical Progression 1; EPs: Suspended Space 2000, Mystical Realms 2001. *Address:* c/o Good Looking Records, 84 Queen's Road, Watford, Herts., WD17 2LA, England (office). *Telephone:* (1923) 690700 (office). *Fax:* (1923) 249495 (office). *E-mail:* info@ goodlooking.org (office). *Website:* www.goodlooking.org.

WILLIAMSON, (John Robert) Graeme, MA; Canadian musician (guitar), singer and songwriter; b. Montréal, QC; m. Iris Jamieson 1995. *Education:* Glasgow University. *Career:* frequent live television CBC (national) television and local television 1984–85; Radio: Live concert broadcasts and tours, Canada; Retired from live performance, 1985; mem. SOCAN (Canada). *Compositions:* Might As Well Be On Mars, Every Man and Every Woman Is A Star, Let Your Light Shine, Rubber Girl. *Recordings:* three tracks, album 1970; albums with Pukka Orchestra: Pukka Orchestra 1984, Palace of Memory 1986, Dear Harry 1993. *Honours:* Casby Award, Canada 1984. *Address:* 38 Victoria Crescent Road, Glasgow G12 9DE, Scotland.

WILLIAMSON, Harry; British/Australian composer, musician, producer, director and inventor; *Manager, Spring Studio, Spring Innovations, Melbourne;* b. 12 May 1950, Ilfracombe, Devon, England; s. of Henry Williamson and Christine Williamson; m. (divorced); one d. *Education:* Exeter Cathedral (Head Chorister), Millfield School, Imperial Coll., London. *Career:* Stage Man., Rainbow Theatre, London; crew for Rolling Stones, Europe; collaborated with Anthony Phillips (ex-Genesis) on two albums, Tarka and Gypsy Suite; writer with Gong/Mother Gong on 16 albums and five tours of USA, Europe 1979–91; performed at Glastonbury 1979, 1981, 1989, 1994; producer of more than 300 albums and 20 one-hour DVDs; world premiere of Tarka Symphony, Melbourne 2010; mem. Faraway, Men In Suits, Soleluna, Endymion; Owner and Man. Spring Studio, Spring Innovations, Melbourne; mem. PRS, MCPS, Musicians' Union, RMYC, ORCV; inventor of Angel Guitar and other electromechanical devices 1975–2013; acoustic consultancy 1983–2013; vinyl record mastering 1987–2008; innovated dynamic carillon actuator system for Federation Bells, Melbourne 2012; cr. adaptive eco-lighting systems 2013. *Films:* GongUncom 2006, Acid Mothers Gong 2007, University of Errors 2007, Our Home Our Land 2007, Limpopo 2008, Waterscape 2009, six concert DVDs. *Recordings include:* albums: with Sphynx: Xitintoday; with Anthony Phillips: Tarka 1988, The Gypsy Suite, Battle of the Birds; with Gong/Mother Gong: Fairytales 1979, Robot Woman 1, 2 & 3 1981–86, Wild Child 1989, Gongmaison 1989, Buddha's Birthday 1990, Owl in Tree 1991, Fish in Tree 2004, Live at Glastonbury '79 & '81 2005; with Daevid Allen: Australia Aquaria 1989, Far From The Madding Crowd 1998, 22 Meanings 1999; solo: Life in the World Unseen 2000; with Soleluna: Soleluna 2005; with jeltje: Dreaming in English 2005; with Khalil Gudaz: Migration 2013. *Honours:* Best Ind. Producer, USA 1986, Best Folk Production CD, Nat. Archives (Australia) 2010. *Address:* PO Box 3070, Prahran East, Melbourne, Vic. 3181, Australia (home). *Telephone:* (3) 9529-7779 (office). *E-mail:* harrymwilliamson@gmail.com (office). *Website:* www.springstudio.com.au (office); www.tarkamusic.net.

WILLIAMSON, John Robert, AM; Australian singer and songwriter; b. 1 Nov. 1945, Victoria; m., two c. *Career:* singer-songwriter for over 30 years; best known for True Blue (Australian Made Campaign and anthem for Australian Cricket Team) and Waltzing Matilda and a Number on My Back (Rugby), Rip Rip Woodchip, Home Among the Gumtrees; mem. Country Music Asscn of Australia, Wildlife Warrios, Save the Bilby Fund, Bush Heritage Foundation, Koala Preservation Society, Landcare Australia. *Compositions include:* Old Man Emu, True Blue, Home Among The Gum Trees, Rip Rip Woodchip, This Is Australia Calling, Raining On The Rock, Galleries of Pink Gallahs. *Recordings:* 38 albums. *Publications:* books and songbooks. *Honours:* 24 Golden Guitars, for Album of the Year, Biggest Selling Album of the Year, Male Vocalist of the Year, Song of the Year, Heritage Award, Video Clip of the Year; Inducted to Roll of Renown 1997, numerous MO Awards, for Best Male Country Performer, Best Country Performer, Most Successful Attraction of the Year, two ARIA Awards, Best Australian Country Record, Advance Australia Award, for contribution to the arts and environment, Advance Australia Foundation Ambassadorship. *Address:* PO Box 399, Epping, NSW 1710, Australia (office). *Telephone:* (2) 9555-1066 (office). *Fax:* (2) 9555-1031 (office). *E-mail:* promotions@johnwilliamson.com.au (office). *Website:* www .johnwilliamson.com.au.

WILLIAMSON, Steve; British saxophonist; b. 28 June 1964, London, England. *Career:* began career with reggae group Misty in Roots; mem. Louis Moholo's Viva La Black 1988, Chris McGregor's Brotherhood of Breath 1990, Julian Joseph Quartet; Founding mem. The Jazz Warriors; collaborations with Maceo Parker, Bheki Mseleku, Art Blakey, Archie Shepp, John Mayer, Donald Byrd and Julian Joseph; appeared at Nelson Mandela 70th birthday concert duetting with Courtney Pine. *Recordings:* Waltz For Grace 1991, Rhyme Time 1991, Journey to Truth 1992.

WILLIS, Doug (see Lee, Dave)

WILLIS, Gary Glen; American musician (electric bass) and composer; b. 28 March 1957, Longview, Texas; m. Pamela Nichols, 11 April 1991. *Education:* Kiljore Jr College; East Texas State University; North Texas State University. *Career:* Co-founder, co-leader of Tribal Tech, with Scott Henderson, 1983–; Annual tours: USA; Europe; South America; Performed, recorded with: Allan Holdsworth; Wayne Shorter; Hubert Laws; Wayne Johnson; Tim Weston & Shelby Flint. *Recordings:* albums: with Tribal Tech: Spears 1985, Dr Hee 1987, Nomad 1989, Tribal Tech 1991, Illicit 1992, Face First 1993, Primal Tracks 1994, Reality Check 1995, Thick 1999, Rocket Science 2000; solo: No Sweat 1997, Bent 1998, Slaughterhouse 3 2006, Actual Fiction 2007. *Publications:* Instructional Video: Progressive Basics, 1991; Book: Lessons With The Greats For Bass, 1995. *Website:* www.garywillis.com.

WILLOUGHBY, Brian; British musician (guitar); b. 20 Sept. 1949, Glenarm, Co. Antrim, Northern Ireland. *Education:* postgraduate level French. *Career:* toured and recorded with The Strawbs, Mary Hopkin, Cathryn Craig, Nanci Griffith, Joe Brown, Roger Whittaker, New World, Brian Connolly, Jim Diamond, The Monks, Monty Python and numerous other artists; mem. Musicians' Union, Inst. of Linguists. *Recordings include:* albums: with The Strawbs: Dave Cousins and Brian Willoughby: Old School Songs 1979, Don't Say Goodbye 1987, Ringing Down the Years 1991, Greatest Hits Live 1993, Dave Cousins and Brian Willoughby: The Bridge 1994, The Complete Strawbs (Chiswick '98) 2000, Acoustic Strawbs: Baroque & Roll 2001, Strawbs: Blue Angel 2003, Acoustic Strawbs: Full Bloom 2004: with Cathryn Craig: Pigg River Symphony, I Will (jt album), Calling All Angels 2009, Real World 2013, Painting by Numbers 2014; solo: Black and White 1998, Fingers Crossed 2005, In America 2016. *Publications include:* contrib. of guitar reviews to Musicians Only, article to Fender Frontline, features in Guitar Buyer, Guitar, Guitar Player. *Honours:* Canadian Gold Album (for Suspended Animation by The Monks). *E-mail:* brianwilloughby1@aol.com. *Website:* www .craigandwilloughby.com.

WILLS, Mark; American country singer; b. (Daryl Mark Williams), 8 Aug. 1973, Cleveland, Tenn.; m. Kelly Wills; two d. *Career:* multi-platinum selling country music artist with eight Top 10 hits, including Nineteen Something, Wish You Were Here, and Don't Laugh At Me (all nominated by Country Music Asscn for Single, Song, and Video of the Year); host of TV series 3 Gun Nation on Versus Network; has made several Christmas trips to Iraq to perform for US armed forces; lives in Atlanta, Ga. *Recordings include:* albums: Mark Wills 1996, Wish You Were Here 1998, Permanently 2000, Loving Every Minute 2001, And the Crowd Goes Wild 2003, Familiar Stranger 2008, 2nd Time Around 2009, Looking For America 2010; singles include: 19 Something 2002 (spent six weeks at No. 1, was Billboard's top country hit of the year and second most-played song of the decade 2009). *Honours:* Top New Male Vocalist Award, Acad. of Country Music 1998. *Current Management:* c/o Scott Welch Management, 24 Music Square West, Nashville, TN 37203, USA. *E-mail:* mw@markwills.com (office). *Website:* www.markwills.com.

WILLSON-PIPER, Marty; British musician (guitar), singer and songwriter; b. 7 May 1958, Liverpool. *Career:* mem. The Church 1980–2013; collaborated with All About Eve and Andy Mason, among others; solo artist 1987–. *Recordings include:* albums: with The Church: Of Skins and Hearts 1980, The Blurred Crusade 1982, Séance 1983, Heyday 1986, Starfish 1988, Gold Afternoon Fix 1990, Priest=Aura 1992, Sometime Anywhere 1994, Magician Among the Spirits 1996, Hologram of Baal 1998, After Everything Now This 2002, Parallel Universe 2002, Forget Yourself 2003, El Momento Descuidado 2004, Uninvited, Like the Clouds 2006, El Momento Siguiente 2007; as

Noctorum: Sparks Lane 2004, Offer the Light 2006, Honey Mink Forever 2011; solo: In Reflection 1987, Art Attack 1988, Rhyme 1989, Spirit Level 1992, Hanging Out in Heaven 2000, Nightjar 2008.

WILSON, Allan; British conductor; b. 5 Sept. 1949, London, England; m. 1986; two d. *Education:* State Univ. of New York, USA, Royal Acad. of Music. *Career:* taught conducting and orchestral training, State Univ. of New York; lecture recitals in the UK, USA, Canada; appearances as trumpet player. *Films:* music conducted for numerous film soundtracks, including Shipping News 2001, Slither 2006, Fury 2014. *Recordings as conductor include:* classical works by Mozart, Holst, Wagner, with orchestras and ensembles including National Studio Orchestra, London Wind Ensemble, Munich Symphony Orchestra, Hungarian State Orchestra, The Mercury Players, Festival Brass of London, Symphonie-Orchester Graunke.

WILSON, Ann D.; American rock singer and musician (flute, guitar, bass guitar, autoharp, keyboards); b. 1950, d. of John Wilson and Lou Wilson; sister of Nancy Wilson. *Education:* Cornish Allied Inst. of Fine Arts, Seattle. *Career:* lead singer, Heart 1975–; mem. side project, The Lovemongers 1992–. *Recordings include:* albums: with Heart: Dreamboat Annie 1975, Little Queen 1977, Magazine 1978, Dog & Butterfly 1978, Bebe Le Strange 1980, Private Audition 1982, Passionworks 1983, Heart 1985, Bad Animals 1987, Brigade 1990, Rock The House 1991, Desire Walks On 1993, The Road Home 1995, Here Is Christmas 1998, Alive In Seattle 2003, Jupiter's Darling 2004, Red Velvet Car 2010; with The Lovemongers: The Battle of Evermore 1993, Whirlygig 1997, A Lovemonger's Christmas 1998. *Current Management:* Borman Entertainment Inc., 1250 Sixth Street, Suite 401, Santa Monica, CA 90401, USA. *Website:* www.heart-music.com.

WILSON, Brian; American musician (bass, keyboards), singer, songwriter and producer; b. 20 June 1942, Inglewood, Calif.; m. 2nd Melinda Ledbetter 1995; two d. *Career:* Founder-mem., The Beach Boys 1961–; retired from live performance to concentrate on composing and recording 1964; numerous live appearances, tours; band est. Brother Records label 1967–; simultaneous solo artist 1988–. *Recordings include:* albums: with The Beach Boys: Surfin' Safari 1962, Surfer Girl 1963, Little Deuce Coupe 1963, Shut Down Vol. 2; All Summer Long 1964, Christmas Album 1964, The Beach Boys Today! 1965, Summer Days (and Summer Nights) 1965, Beach Boys Party 1966, Pet Sounds 1966, Smiley Smile 1967, Wild Honey 1968, Friends 1968, 20/20 1969, Sunflower 1970, Surf's Up 1971, Carl and the Passions – So Tough 1972, Holland 1973, The Beach Boys in Concert 1973, Endless Summer 1974, 15 Big Ones 1976, The Beach Boys Love You 1977, M.I.U. 1978, LA (Light Album) 1979, Keepin' The Summer Alive 1980, The Beach Boys 1985, Still Cruisin' 1989, Two Rooms 1991, Summer in Paradise 1992, The Sounds of Summer – The Very Best of The Beach Boys 2003, Smile Sessions (Grammy Award for Best Historical Album 2013) 2011, That's Why God Made the Radio 2012; solo: Brian Wilson 1988, I Just Wasn't Made For These Times 1995, Imagination 1998, Pet Projects: The Brian Wilson Productions 2003, Smile 2004, What I Really Want For Christmas 2005, That Lucky Old Sun 2008, Brian Wilson Reimagines Gershwin 2010, No Pier Pressure 2015. *Compositions for stage:* Shine 2002, That Lucky Old Sun (a Narrative) 2007. *Honours:* American Music Awards Special Award of Merit 1988, Grammy Lifetime Achievement Award 2001, US Recording Acad. Musicares Award 2004, Kennedy Center Honor 2007. *Current Management:* c/o Elliott Lott, Boulder Creek Entertainment, PO Box 91002, San Diego, CA 91269, USA. *Telephone:* (858) 793-4141. *Website:* www.thebeachboys.com; www.brianwilson.com.

WILSON, Brian Scott, BMus, MA, DMus; American composer, conductor, jazz musician (piano) and academic; *Chair and Professor of Music, Sonoma State University;* b. 12 Nov. 1962, Mass; m. Ruth; one s. *Education:* New England Conservatory, Univ. of Chicago, Univ. of Arizonia. *Career:* Prof. of Music and Composer-in-Residence, Hartwick Coll., NY 1992–2001; Chair and Prof. of Music, Sonoma State Univ. 2001–; mem. Faculties, Hartwick Coll. Summer Music Festival and Inst., Oneonta; mem. American Composers Forum, American Music Center, American Soc. of Composers, Authors and Publrs (ASCAP), College Band Dirs' Nat. Asscn, Conductors' Guild, World Asscn of Symphonic Bands and Ensembles. *Recordings:* orchestral: My Mother's Irises, Wandering The River, The First Sea Shell, The Flat Top Roof, Symphony No. 1, Desert Scenes, Symphony No. 2, Modes of Transportation; band: Fastfare, Melting Pot; choral: Jabberwocky, Three Songs of Nature, Joy, Wings; chamber music including: The Avanti Feels Glued to the Road, Sentiments, Tuba Cat Fanfare, The Season, Avinu Malkaynu; musicals including: The Birds, Speak of The 20s, The Knights; operas including: Agamemnon; incidental music to Medea, The Bachal. *Honours:* Winner, Int. Trombone Asscn Composition Competition 1998, Fellow, Composers Conf. Center for New Music, Duquesne Univ., James Madison Flute Choir Composition Competition Prize, ASCAP Distribution Award. *Address:* 6557 Jubilee Court, Rohnert Park, CA 94928, USA (home). *Telephone:* (707) 664-2468 (home). *E-mail:* brian.wilson@sonoma.edu (office). *Website:* www.brianswilson.com.

WILSON, Cassandra; American jazz singer; b. Jackson, MS; d. of Herman B. Fowlkes. *Career:* started playing guitar aged six, songwriting at 12; solo performer as folk and blues singer, turned to jazz; regular collaborations with saxophonist Steve Coleman; f. Ojah Media Group, Mississippi 2000. *Recordings include:* albums: Point of View 1986, Days Aweigh 1987, Blue Skies 1988, Jumpworld 1990, She Who Weeps 1991, After the Beginning Again 1991, Dance to the Drums Again 1992, Blue Light 'Til Dawn 1993, New Moon Daughter 1996, Songbook 1996, Blue Moon Rendezvous 1998, Traveling Miles 1999, Belly Of The Sun 2002, Glamoured 2003, Thunderbird 2006, Loverly (Grammy Award for Best Jazz Vocal Album 2009) 2008. *E-mail:* adam@bluenote.net. *Website:* www.cassandrawilson.com.

WILSON, Cindy; American singer; b. 28 Feb. 1957, Athens, GA. *Career:* founder mem., The B-52s 1976–, numerous live performances, particularly as successful touring band 1989–. *Recordings include:* albums: The B-52s 1979, Wild Planet 1980, Whammy! 1983, Bouncing Off The Satellites 1986, Cosmic Thing 1989, Good Stuff 1992, Associate, Associate 1996, Nude on the Moon: the B-52's Anthology 2002, Funplex 2008; singles: Rock Lobster 1980, Party Mix! 1981, Mesopotamia 1982, Channel Z 1989, Deadbeat Club 1989, Love Shack 1989, Roam 1990, Megamix 1991, Good Stuff 1992, Is That You Mo-Dean? 1992, Revolution Earth 1992, Tell It Like It T-I-Is 1992, Hot Pants Explosion 1993, Meet The Flintstones 1994, Time Capsule 1998. *Current Management:* Vector Management, PO Box 120479, Nashville, TN 37203, USA. *E-mail:* info@vectormgmt.com. *Website:* www.theb52s.com.

WILSON, Damian Augustine Howitt; British singer and songwriter; b. Guildford, Surrey, England. *Career:* mem. Landmarq, Maiden uniteD, Threshold, LaSalle, Headspace. *Play:* Les Miserables. *Recordings include:* albums: with Landmarq: Solitary Witness 1992, Infinity Parade 1993, The Vision Pit 1995; with Threshold: Wounded Land 1993; with LaSalle: LaSalle 1994. *Honours:* Classic Rock Soc. Award for Best Vocalist 1993. *Current Management:* c/o Matt Glover, Defiant Artists, Blueprint Management, PO Box 593, Woking, Surrey GU23 7YF, England. *Telephone:* (1296) 624874. *E-mail:* matt@blueprint-management.com. *Website:* www.blueprint-management.com. *E-mail:* contact@damian-wilson.net (office). *Website:* www.headspaceonline.com; www.damian-wilson.net.

WILSON, Dennis Edward, MusB, MM, PhD; American musician (trombone), producer, arranger and conductor; *Associate Professor of Jazz and Contemporary Improvisation, University of Michigan;* b. 22 July 1952, Greensboro, NC; m. Rebecca Elvert 1986; one s. *Education:* Berklee Coll. of Music, Boston, Hamilton Univ. *Career:* trombonist and Musical Dir Lionel Hampton Orchestra 1974–76; teacher and Choral Dir, New York schools 1976–77; trombonist arranger, Count Basie Orchestra 1977–87; Music Production Man., Count Basie Enterprises 1987–; trombonist and arranger, Frank West Orchestra 1990–; also arranger and conductor, Manhattan Transfer, Blee Blop Blues 1985; trombonist, Dizzy Gillespie Orchestra 1988; creator and Exec. Producer, Count Basie Orchestra Big Band Festival; also collaborated with Mel Torme, Ella Fitzgerald, Buddy Guy, Sarah Vaughan, Milt Jackson; mem. Nat. Asscn of Jazz Educators; Dir Detroit Jazz Festival Orchestra; Assoc. Prof. of Jazz and Contemporary Improvisation, Univ. of Michigan 2000–. *Recordings:* performed on over six Grammy winning albums. *Address:* Jazz Studies Department, School of Music, University of Michigan, 1100 Baits Drive, Ann Arbor, MI 48109-2085, USA (office). *Telephone:* (734) 615-4104 (office). *Fax:* (734) 763-5097 (office). *E-mail:* dwjazz@umich.edu (office). *Website:* www.denniswilson.org.

WILSON, Gretchen Frances; American singer, songwriter, musician (guitar) and producer; b. 26 June 1973, Pocahontas, IL; one d. *Career:* moved to Nashville 1996; solo artist. *Recordings include:* albums: Here for the Party 2004, All Jacked Up 2005, One of the Boys 2007, I Got Your Country Right Here 2010. *Honours:* American Music Award for Best Newcomer 2004, Acad. of Country Music Awards for Best Female Vocalist, for Best New Artist 2005, CMA Award for Female Vocalist of the Year 2005, American Music Award for Favorite Female Country Artist 2005. *Address:* c/o Epic Records, Sony BMG Music Entertainment, 550 Madison Avenue, New York, NY 10022, USA (office). *Website:* www.gretchenwilson.com.

WILSON, Mari; British singer; b. 29 Sept. 1957, London, England. *Career:* solo artist 1981–, with TV and concert tours; with 12-piece band, The Wilsations; regular Ronnie Scott Club appearances; mem. Musicians' Union, Equity, PRS, MCPS. *Stage performances:* Sweet Charity, Chainsaw Manicure. *Recordings include:* albums: Show People 1983, The Rhythm Romance 1992, Beat The Beat 1992, Dolled up 2005, Emotional Glamour 2008, Emotional Glamour 2012. *Current Management:* c/o Sue Harris, Republic Media, 7 Broadbent Close, Highgate Village, London, N6 5JW, England. *E-mail:* contact@mariwilson.co.uk. *Website:* www.mariwilson.co.uk.

WILSON, Mark; Australian rock musician (bass guitar); b. Aug. 1980, Geelong, Vic. *Career:* fmr mem. band The Casinos; joined rock band Jet 2002–; toured as support act with the Rolling Stones, Australia 2003; toured USA with other Australian bands The Vines and The Living End 2004; tours of USA, UK, Europe, Japan, Australia 2006–07; currently resides in Los Angeles, USA. *Recordings:* albums: Get Born 2003, Shine On 2006, Shaka Rock 2009. *Address:* c/o Atlantic Records, 1290 Avenue of the Americas, New York, NY 10104, USA (office). *Website:* www.atlanticrecords.com (office); www.jettheband.com; www.jetmusic.co.uk.

WILSON, Mary; American singer and entertainer; b. 3 June 1944, Greenville, Mississippi; m. Pedro A. Ferrer 1973, two s. (one deceased) one d. *Career:* mem., Supremes 1959–77; world tours, TV appearances. *Recordings include:* albums: with Supremes: Meet the Supremes 1962, Where Did Our Love Go 1964, A Bit of Liverpool 1964, The Supremes Sing Country, Western and Pop 1965, We Remember Sam Cooke 1965, The Supremes at the Copa 1965, Merry Christmas 1965, I Hear a Symphony 1966, The Supremes A' Go-Go 1966, The Supremes Sing Holland-Dozier-Holland 1967, The Supremes Sing Rodgers & Hart 1967, Reflections 1968, Live at London's Talk of the Town 1968, Love

Child 1968, Let the Sunshine In 1969, Cream of the Crop 1969, Farewell 1970, Right On 1970, New Ways But Love Stays 1970, Touch 1971, Floy Joy 1972, The Supremes 1975, High Energy 1976, Mary, Scherrie & Susaye 1976; solo: Red Hot 1979, Walk the Line 1992, U 1995, I Am Changing 2010. *Publications include:* Dreamgirl: My Life as a Supreme 1986, Supreme Faith: Someday We'll Be Together 1990. *Current Management:* c/o Andrew Leff, Morey Management Group, 1100 Glendon Avenue, 11th Floor, Los Angeles, CA 90024, USA. *E-mail:* mary@marywilson.com. *Website:* www.marywilson.com.

WILSON, Matt; American musician (drums) and composer; b. 27 Sept. 1964, Knoxville, Ill.; m. Felicia Wilson; three c. *Education:* Wichita State Univ. *Career:* f. Matt Wilson Quartet (MWQ) 1996–, Matt Wilson's Arts & Crafts 2001–; performed as sideman with artists including Dewey Redman Quartet, Lee Konitz, Andrew Hill, Bill Mays Trio, Herbie Nichols Project; also Matt Wilson jazz workshops. *Recordings include:* as MWQ: Going Once, Going Twice 1998, Humidity 2003, That's Gonna Leave a Mark 2009; as MW's Arts & Crafts: Matt Wilson's Arts & Crafts 2001, Wake Up! 2004, The Scenic Route 2006; other: As Wave Follows Wave 1996. *Current Management:* c/o Amy Cervini, Orange Grove Artists. *Telephone:* (917) 971-7156. *E-mail:* amy@orangegroveartists.com. *Website:* www.orangegroveartists.com. *E-mail:* matwiljazz@aol.com (office). *Website:* mattwilsonjazz.com.

WILSON, Nancy; American rock singer and musician (guitar, mandolin, keyboards, harmonica); b. 16 March 1954, San Francisco, CA; d. of John and Lou Wilson; sister of Ann Wilson; m. Cameron Crowe. *Career:* fmr mem., Bordersong; solo folk singer; mem. rock group, Heart 1974–; numerous int. tours, festival appearances; mem. side project, The Lovemongers 1992–. *Film appearances:* Fast Times at Ridgemount High, The Wild Life. *Recordings include:* albums: with Heart: Dreamboat Annie 1975, Little Queen 1977, Magazine 1978, Dog & Butterfly 1978, Bebe Le Strange 1980, Private Audition 1982, Passionworks 1983, Heart 1985, Bad Animals 1987, Brigade 1990, Rock The House 1991, Desire Walks On 1993, The Road Home 1995, Here Is Christmas 1998, Alive In Seattle 2003, Jupiter's Darling 2004, Red Velvet Car 2010; with The Lovemongers: The Battle of Evermore 1993, Whirlygig 1997, A Lovemonger's Christmas 1998; solo: Live At McCabe's Guitar Shop 1999, Meant To Be (with Ramsey Lewis) 2002, Turned to Blue (Grammy Award for Best Jazz Vocal Album 2007) 2006. *Current Management:* Borman Entertainment Inc., 1250 Sixth Street, Suite 401, Santa Monica, CA 90401, USA. *Website:* www.heart-music.com.

WILSON, Olly W., Jr, BMus, MMus, PhD; American composer, professor and scholar; *Professor of Music Emeritus, University of California at Berkeley*; b. 7 Sept. 1937, St Louis, MO. *Education:* Washington Univ., St Louis, Univ. of Ill. at Urbana-Champaign, Univ. of Iowa, Univ. of Ill. Studio for Experimental Music, studied African music in Ghana. *Career:* played jazz piano with local groups in St Louis; played double bass in several orchestras including St Louis Philharmonic, St Louis Summer Chamber Players, Cedar Rapids Symphony; studied electronic music at Studio for Experimental Music, Univ. of Illinois 1967; faculty positions at Florida A & M Univ. 1960–62, 1964–65, Oberlin Conservatory of Music 1965–70; with faculty, Univ. of California, Berkeley 1970–, Asst Chancellor for Int. Affairs 1986–90, Chair. Dept Music 1993–97, Jerry and Evelyn Hemmings Chambers Distinguished Chair. in Music 1995–98, currently Prof. Emer. of Music; compositions include chamber works, orchestral works and works for electronic media; works have been performed by numerous orchestras including Boston, Chicago, New York Philharmonic, Cleveland, Moscow Philharmonic, St Louis, San Francisco, Baltimore, Houston, Atlanta, Louisville, Oakland, Detroit, Minneapolis, Dallas, All Netherlands Symphony orchestras; Resident Fellow, Rockefeller Foundation Center, Bellagio, Italy 1991; Lila Wallace Meet the Composer commission for Youth Symphony Consortium 1991; Visiting Artist, American Acad. in Rome 1978, Fromm Composer in Residence 2008; elected to American Acad. of Arts and Letters 1995. *Compositions:* Trio for flute, cello and piano 1957–58, Prelude and Line Study 1959, String Quartet 1960, Structure for orchestra 1960, Two Dutch Songs 1960, Wry Fragments 1961, Gloria 1961, Violin Sonata 1961, Soliloquy 1962, Dance Suite 1962, And Death Shall Have No Dominion 1963, Sextet 1963, Dance Music No. 1 1963, Three Movements for orchestra 1964, Chanson Innocent 1964, Dance Music No. 2 1965, Piece for Four 1966, Biography 1966, Cetus 1967 (Dartmouth Arts Council Prize for electronic compositions 1968), In Memoriam Martin Luther King Jr 1968, Piano Piece 1969, Voices 1970, The Eighteen Hands of Jerome Harris (ballet) 1971, Black Mass (incidental music) 1971, Black Martyrs 1972, Akwan 1972, Spirit Song 1973, Echoes 1974, Sometimes 1976, Trio for piano, violin and cello 1977, Reflections 1979, Expansions 1979, Trilogy for orchestra 1979–80, Lumina 1981, Sinfonia 1983–84, No More 1985, Houston Fanfare 1986, Expansions II 1987, Moe Fragmenti 1987, A City Called Heaven 1988, Viola Concerto 1990, Of Visions and Truth 1990–91, I Shall Not Be Moved 1991–92, Expansions III 1993, Soweto's Children 1994–95, Shango Memory 1995, Fanfare for the Millennium for brass quintet and electronic sound 1996, Hold On 1997–98. *Recordings include:* Sinfonia (Boston Symphony), Akwan (Baltimore Symphony), Cetus (electronic sound), Sometimes (William Brown, tenor and electronic sound), Trio (Francesco Trio), A City Called Heaven (Boston Musica Viva, Thamyris Ensemble). *Publications:* several scholarly articles on African and African American music; contrib. numerous articles to Black Perspective in Music, Black Music Research Journal, American Organist, New Perspectives on Jazz and others. *Honours:* Guggenheim Fellowship 1971–72, 1977–78, American Acad. of Arts and Letters and Nat. Inst. of Arts and Letters Achievement in Music Composition Award 1974, Washington Univ. Distinguished Alumni Award 1991, Missouri Historical Soc. Award 1991, Lincoln Center Chamber Music Soc. Elise Stoeger Prize 1992. *Address:* Department of Music, University of California at Berkeley, 104 Morrison Hall, Room 1200, Berkeley, CA 94720-1200, USA (office). *E-mail:* ollywil@berkeley.edu (office).

WILSON, Paul; Scottish musician (bass guitar) and backing singer. *Career:* mem., Snow Patrol 2005–. *Recordings include:* album: Eyes Open (Meteor Ireland Music Award for Best Irish Album 2007) 2006, A Hundred Million Suns 2008. *Honours:* Meteor Ireland Music Awards for Best Irish Band 2007, for Most Downloaded Song and Best Live Performance 2007. *E-mail:* qprimeuk@qprime.com. *Website:* www.qprime.com. *E-mail:* info@snowpatrol.com. *Website:* www.snowpatrol.com.

WILSON, Peter, (Emerson Peters), LTCL, LGSMD, AMusTCL, MISM; British musician (piano), composer, arranger and teacher; b. 28 July 1956, Newport, Isle of Wight. *Education:* Royal Artillery Band, City of Leeds Coll. of Music, Trinity Coll. of Music, London. *Career:* keyboards for Helen Shapiro and Neil Reid, including TV and radio; freelance pianist, ballet, dance, cocktail, bands 1984–; first keyboards for Robin Cousins tour of UK, Electric Ice 1984; first keyboards for rock opera Jeanne, and musical Judy 1985; keyboards for Bruce Forsyth, Val Doonican, Michael Barrymore, other cabaret acts 1985–; teacher, Blackheath Conservatoire of Music 1981–83; mem. Tower Hamlets Strings Project 1981–92; tutor, Greenwich Music Service 1981–2010, Arts Educational Coll. 1983–85, St Thomas the Apostle Coll. 1997–, THAMES (Tower Hamlets Arts and Music Educ. Service) 2005–; Dir Greenwich Strings Project 1993–2003; mem. The Inc. Soc. of Musicians, Radio Soc. of Great Britain, Clifton Amateur Radio Soc., British Inter-Planetary Soc., The Light Music Soc., The Billy Mayerl Soc. *Compositions:* overture and suite for string orchestra, one symphony for string orchestra, two horns and oboe, The Pirate Suite for strings and piano, The Wild West Suite for strings and piano, Concert March The Militaire Orchestra for light orchestra, Caribbean Carnival Medley for light orchestra, Concert Waltz at the Mansion House for light orchestra, Concert March Team Spirit for light orchestra, Concert March Guard of Honour for light orchestra, Concert March The Field Marshal's Baton for light orchestra, three piano suites, one piano sonata and many small pieces. *Publications:* Ragtime Preludes, Go Canon Go, Palm Court Trios, Fanfares, The 2001 Piano Collection, Stringpops Series: James Bond, Harry Potter, Film, Christmas (Music Industries Asscn Music Award for Best Educational Publication 2009). *Honours:* two awards of The Van Someren-Godfrey Gold Medal, Royal Artillery Band, Hannah Brooke Prize for Piano at TCM, scholarship at TCM 1981–82. *Address:* 74 Coleraine Road, Blackheath, London, SE3 7PE, England (office). *Telephone:* (20) 8858-0720 (office).

WILSON, Reuben; American musician (organ); b. 9 April 1935, Mounds, Okla. *Recordings include:* Walk on By 1966, On Broadway 1968, Love Bug 1969, Blue Mode 1969, Groovy Situation 1970, Set Us Free 1971, Got to Get Your Own 1971, The Sweet Life 1972, Bad Stuff 1973, The Cisco Kid 1974, And the Cost of Living 1975, Straight No Chaser 1993, New York Funkies 1995, Organ Blues 2002, Fun House 2005, Movin' on 2006, The Godfathers of Groove Allegro 2007, Azure Te 2009.

WILSON, Ricky, BA, MA; British singer; b. 17 Jan. 1978, Leeds. *Career:* Founder-mem. Runston Parva 1997, renamed Parva, renamed Kaiser Chiefs 2003–. *Television:* The Voice UK (BBC One) (judge and mentor) 2014–. *Recordings include:* albums: Employment (Meteor Ireland Music Award for Best Int. Album 2006, NME Award for Best Album 2006, Ivor Novello Award for Best Album 2006) 2005, Yours Truly, Angry Mob 2007, Off With Their Heads 2008, The Future Is Medieval 2011, Souvenir: The Singles 2004–2012 2012, Education, Education, Education & War 2014. *Honours:* Meteor Ireland Music Award for Best Int. Group 2006, BRIT Awards for Best British Rock Act, Best British Live Act, Best British Group 2006, Nordoff-Robbins Silver Clef Award for Best Group 2006, Q Award for Best Video (for 'Ruby') 2007. *Current Management:* c/o James Sandom, Red Light Management, 10-16 Scrutton Street, Ground Floor, Shoreditch, London, EC2A 4RU, England. *E-mail:* james.sandom@redlightmanagement.com. *E-mail:* mail@kaiserchiefs.co.uk. *Website:* www.kaiserchiefs.co.uk.

WILSON, Roger; British folk musician and songwriter; b. 22 July 1961, Leicester, England; divorced; one d. *Education:* BA, Graphic Design. *Career:* Solo, 1986–; Urban Folk, 1990–; Touring with the House Band, 1995–98; Wood, Wilson, Carthy, 1997–. *Compositions:* Ultrasound, The Zakynthos Jig; Payday; Indian Tea; Sick of the Working Life; Many Re-workings of Folk Songs Including Hey Joe; Delia; Fair and Tender Lovers; Ramble Away, Two Sisters. *Recordings:* The Palm of your Hand; Stark Naked; Wood, Wilson, Carthy; Urban Folk Volumes I and II; Rockall; October Song. *Current Management:* TightSqueezeMusic, 30 Manor Road, Moulton, Northampton NN3 7QU, England. *E-mail:* tightsqueezemusic@hotmail.co.uk. *Website:* www.tightsqueezemusic.co.uk.

WIMBISH, Doug; American musician (guitar, bass guitar); b. 22 Sept. 1956, Bloomfield, Conn. *Education:* Hartfield Conservatory. *Career:* began career as bass player for groups Wood, Brass and Steel and Musique; mem. in-house band of SugarHill Records (Sugarhill Gang), New York 1979–84; mem. Tackhead 1984–; mem. Living Colour 1992–95, 2000–; mem. Jungle Funk 1996–99; solo artist and session musician for numerous artists and bands. *Recordings include:* albums: with Sugarhill Gang: Be a Winner 1983, The Word is Out 1983; with Tackhead: Friendly as a Hand Grenade 1989, Strange Things 1990, Videohead 1991, Power Inc. (two Vols) 1993; with Living Colour:

Stain 1993, Pride 1995, Collideøscope 2003, The Chair in the Doorway 2009; with Jungle Funk: Jungle Funk 1999; solo: Don't Forget That Beat 1985, Trippy Notes for Bass 1999, CinemaSonics 2008. *Honours:* Elvis Award for Best New Band, Int. Rock Awards 1989, MTV Award for Best New Artist, for Best Group Video, for Best Stage Performance 1989, Grammy Awards for Best Hard Rock Performance (for Cult of Personality) 1990, (for Time's Up) 1991, Rolling Stone Critics' Poll Winner of Best Band 1991. *E-mail:* doug@ dougwimbish.com; livingcolourinfo@yahoo.com. *Website:* www .livingcolourmusic.com; www.dougwimbish.com.

WINANS, Bebe; American singer; b. 17 Sept. 1962, Detroit; brother of Cece Winans; m. Debra Winans (divorced); one s. one d. *Career:* sang in PTL Singers, duo with sister, Cece Winans 1982–87; sang as duo, Bebe and Cece Winans 1987–; solo artist 1997–; founded TMG record label. *Plays:* Civil War, Don't Get God Started, What's on the Hearts of Men, King Solomon Lives: A Nubian Love Story. *Films:* as actor: The Manchurian Candidate 2004. *Recordings:* albums: as PTL: Lord Lift Us Up 1984; as Bebe & Cece Winans: Bebe & Cece Winans 1987, Heaven (Soul Train Award for Best Gospel Album 1990) 1988, Different Lifestyles (Soul Train Award for Best Gospel Album, Grammy Award for Best Contemporary Soul Gospel Album) 1991, First Christmas 1993, Relationships 1994, Still 2009; solo: Bebe Winans 1997, Love and Freedom 2000, Live and Up Close 2002, My Christmas Prayer 2003, Dream 2004, Cherch 2007. *Honours:* Grammy Awards for Best Male Soul Gospel Performance (for Abundant Life) 1988, for Best Male Soul Gospel Vocal Performance (for Meantime) 1989. *Current Management:* Strategic Artist Management, 1100 Glendon Avenue, Suite 1000, Los Angeles, CA 90024, USA. *Telephone:* (310) 208-7882. *Website:* www.bebewinans.net.

WINANS, Cece; American singer; b. (Priscilla Winans), 8 Oct. 1959, Detroit; sister of Bebe Winans; m. Alvin Love; two c. *Career:* sang in PTL Singers, duo with brother, Bebe Winans 1982–87; sang as duo, Bebe and Cece Winans 1987–; solo artist 1994–; f. Pure Springs Gospel record label 1999. *Recordings:* albums: as PTL: Lord Lift Us Up 1984; as Bebe & Cece Winans: Bebe & Cece Winans 1987, Heaven (Soul Train Award for Best Gospel Album 1990) 1988, Different Lifestyles (Soul Train Award for Best Gospel Album, Grammy Award for Best Contemporary Soul Gospel Album) 1991, First Christmas 1993, Relationships 1994, Still 2009; solo: Alone in His Presence (Grammy Award for Best Contemporary Soul Gospel Album) 1995, Everlasting Love 1998, His Gift 1998, Alabaster Box 1999, Cece Winans (Grammy Award for Best Pop/Contemporary Gospel Album) 2001, Throne Room 2003, Purified (Grammy Award for Best Contemporary Soul Gospel Album) 2005, Cece Winans presents Kingdom Kidz 2007, Cece Winans presents Pure Worship 2007, Thy Kingdom Come (Grammy Award for Best Pop/Contemporary Gospel Album) 2008. *Honours:* Grammy Awards for Best Female Soul Gospel Performance (for For Always) 1987, for Best Female Soul Gospel Performance (for Don't Cry) 1989, for Best Gospel Performance (for Pray) 2005. *Address:* Pure Springs Gospel, 115 Penn Warren Drive, Suite 300–377, Brentwood, TN 37027, USA (office). *Telephone:* (615) 371-1575 (office). *Fax:* (615) 371-1571 (office). *E-mail:* booking@purespringsgospel.com (office). *Website:* www.purespringsgospel.com; www.cecewinans.com.

WINDRICH, Erik Rudolph; Dutch singer, songwriter and musician (multi-instrumentalist); b. 5 Feb. 1960; two d. two step-s. one step-d. *Education:* Univ. in South Africa. *Career:* Evoid 1982–86; campus tour, 1984; Operation Hunger, Ellis Park Stadium, South Africa 1985; European tours; mem. South African Music Rights Org., Performing Right Soc., PPL, Musicians' Union, COBRA. *Compositions include:* with Evoid: Shadows; Taximan; I Am A Fadget; with The Vision Thing: Fist In The Air; Wyah; Brother Sistem. *Recordings include:* with Evoid: Evoid; Here Comes The Rot; A Space In Which To Create; with The Vision Thing: The Vision Thing. *Honours:* Sarie Award, South Africa 1984. *Address:* Multi Kulti Music, PO Box 347, Harrow, London, HA2 8ZN, England. *E-mail:* erik@multikultimusic.com. *Website:* www.erikwindrich.com.

WINK, Josh, (Josh Winkelman, Winks, Winx, Size 9, Dinky Dog, WiNK); American producer, remixer and DJ; b. Philadelphia, Pa. *Education:* Temple Univ., Philadelphia, Pa. *Career:* producer of electronic music 1989–; early recordings on US labels Strictly Rhythm, Sorted, Nervous; co-founder Ovum Records (with King Britt), Philadelphia 1994; maj. int. success with singles Don't Laugh, I'm Ready, Higher State of Consciousness; worldwide DJ appearances. *Recordings:* singles: Tribal Confusion (as E-Culture) 1991, I'm Ready (as Size 9), Hypnotizin', Higher State of Consciousness, Don't Laugh (as Winx) 1995, Thoughts of a Tranced Love 1996, Are You There? 1996, How's Your Evening So Far? (with Lil' Louis) 2000, Evil Acid 2001, Swirl 2007, Thick as Thieves 2007; albums: Left Above the Clouds 1996, Herehear 1998, 20 to 20 2003; remixes for artists including: Sting, Depeche Mode, Slam, Mood II Swing, Moby, Dave Clarke, Paul Oakenfold, Ladytron. *Current Management:* Elite Music Management, PO Box 3261, Brighton, East Sussex, BN2 4WA, England. *Telephone:* (1273) 621999 (office). *Fax:* (1273) 623999 (office). *E-mail:* info@elitemm.co.uk. *Website:* www.elitemm.co.uk. *Address:* Ovum Recordings, 1528 Walnut Street, #202, Philadelphia, PA 19102, USA. *Website:* www.ovum-rec.com.

WINSTEAD, Joshua (Josh); American musician (bass guitar). *Education:* Univ. of North Texas. *Career:* mem. Metric 1998–; founding mem. Bang Lime. *Films* soundtrack contributions: Scott Pilgrim vs the World 2010, The Twilight Saga: Eclipse 2010. *Recordings:* albums: with Metric: Old World Underground Where Are You Now 2003, Live it Out 2005, Grow Up and Blow

Away 2007, Fantasies (Juno Award Alternative Album of the Year 2010) 2009; with Bang Lime: Best Friends in Love 2007. *Honours:* Juno Award for Group of the Year 2010. *Address:* c/o Last Gang Records, 171 East Liberty Street, Suite 330, Toronto, ON M6K 3P6, Canada (office). *Telephone:* (416) 534-3000 (office). *Fax:* (416) 534-3005 (office). *E-mail:* management@ilovemetric.com (office); contact@banglime.com (office). *Website:* www.ilovemetric.com; www .banglime.com.

WINTER, Edgar; American musician (multi-instrumentalist) and composer; b. 28 Dec. 1946, Beaumont, Texas; m. Monica Winter, 23 March 1979. *Career:* Member, various groups: Black Plague; Johnny Winter's group (brother); Founder, White Trash, 1971; Founder, the Edgar Winter Group, 1972; Session musician with: Meat Loaf, Dan Hartman, Bette Midler, Tina Turner, 1981–. *Recordings:* Albums: with Johnny Winter: Second Winter 1970, Johnny Winter And… 1970; with White Trash: Edgar Winter's White Trash 1971, Roadwork 1972; with the Edgar Winter Group: They Only Come Out At Night 1973, Shock Treatment 1974, The Edgar Winter Group With Rick Derringer 1975, Recycled 1977, The Edgar Winter Album 1979, Standing On Rock 1981; solo: Entrance 1975, Jasmine Nightdreams 1975, Not a Kid Anymore 1994, The Real Deal 1996, Live in Japan 1998, Winter Blues 1999, Hits You Remember 2000, Edgar Winter 2002, Jazzin' the Blues 2004, Rebel Road 2008; singles include: with White Trash: Keep Playin' That Rock and Roll; I Can't Turn You Loose; with the Edgar Winter Group: Frankenstein; Free Ride; Hangin' Around; River's Risin'; Easy Street. *Current Management:* Hook Entertainment, Rock Lodge, 26033 Mulholland Highway, Malibu, CA 91302, USA. *E-mail:* hookent@earthlink.net. *Website:* www.edgarwinter.com.

WINTER, Paul Theodore, BA; American musician (saxophone), composer and bandleader; b. 31 Aug. 1939, Altoona, Pennsylvania; m. Chez Liley 1991. *Education:* Northwestern Univ., studied with John Monti, Joe Allard. *Career:* concert, recording artist 1961–; Paul Winter Sextet won Intercollegiate Jazz Festival 1961; founded Paul Winter Consort 1967–; founded Living Music Records 1980. *Recordings include:* albums: The Paul Winter Sextet 1961, Jazz Meets the Bossa Nova 1962, Jazz Premiere: Washington 1963, NewJazz on Campus 1963, Jazz Meets the Folk Song 1963, The Song of Ipanema 1963, Rio 1963, The Winter Consort 1968, Something in the Wind 1969, Road 1970, Icarus 1972, Common Ground 1977, Callings 1980, Earth Mass 1981, Sunsinger 1983, Concert for the Earth 1984, Canyon 1985, Wintersong 1986, Whales Alive 1987, Earthbeat 1988, Wolf Eyes 1989, Earth: Voices of a Planet 1990, Solstice Live 1992, Spanish Angel 1993, Prayer For The Wild Things 1994, Canyon Lullaby 1997, Brazilian Days 1998, Celtic Solstice 1999, Journey with the Sun 2000, Silver Solstice (Grammy Award for Best New Age Album 2006) 2005, Crestone (Grammy Award for Best New Age Album 2008) 2007, Flyways 2009. *Honours:* Hon. DHL (Juniata Coll.); Grammy Awards 1993, 1994, 1999, 2000, UN Global 500 Award, UN Environmental Programme Award of Excellence, US Humane Soc. Joseph Wood Krutch Medal, Governor of the State of Pennsylvania Distinguished Arts Award. *Address:* c/o Living Music, PO Box 72, Litchfield, CT 06759, USA (office). *Website:* www .livingmusic.com (office).

WINTER-HART, Paul; British musician (drums); b. 19 Sept. 1971, London, England. *Career:* mem. The Objects of Desire, renamed The Kays, then Kula Shaker 1995–; numerous TV appearances and live festival gigs. *Recordings:* Albums: K 1996, Peasants, Pigs and Astronauts 1999, Strangefolk 2007. *Website:* www.kulashakermusic.com.

WINWOOD, Mervyn (Muff); British musician (bass) and music company executive; b. 15 June 1943, Birmingham, England. *Career:* folk/blues soloist; mem., Muff-Woody Jazz Band (with brother Steve); Rhythm and Blues Quartet; mem., Spencer Davis Group 1963–67; concerts include National Jazz and Blues Festival, Grand Gala du Disques, Amsterdam, British tours with The Rolling Stones, The Who, The Hollies; Man. Exec., West End Promotions; Exec., CBS Records; Man. Dir, Sony Soho Square (S^2) Records, London 1978–2003. *Recordings:* albums: Their First LP 1966, The Second Album 1966, Autumn '66 1966; singles include: Strong Love 1965, Keep On Running 1966, Somebody Help Me 1966, Gimme Some Lovin' 1966, I'm A Man 1967; producer, Sutherland Brothers Band, Sutherland Brothers Band 1972, Sparks, Kimono My House 1974, Sparks, Propaganda 1974, Kevin Ayers, Yes We Have No Mananas 1976, Dire Straits, Dire Straits 1978, Steve Winwood: 20th Century Masters 1999. *Honours:* Carl Alan Award, Most Outstanding Group 1966.

WINWOOD, Stephen (Steve) Lawrence; British musician and composer; b. 12 May 1948, Birmingham; s. of Lawrence Samuel Winwood and Lillian Mary Winwood (née Saunders); m. Eugenia Crafton 1987; one s. three d. *Career:* singer and musician, Spencer Davis Group 1964–67, Traffic 1967–74, Blind Faith 1969; British tours with The Rolling Stones 1965, The Who 1966, The Hollies 1967; solo artist 1974–; Dir F.S. Ltd/Wincraft Music Ltd. *Recordings:* albums include: three with Spencer Davis Group 1966; with Traffic: Mr Fantasy 1968, Traffic 1968, John Barleycorn Must Die 1970, The Low Spark of High Heeled Boys 1972, When the Eagle Flies 1974; with Blind Faith: Blind Faith 1969; solo: Steve Winwood 1977, Arc of a Diver 1980, Talking Back to the Night 1982, Back in the Highlife 1986, Roll With It 1988 (Grammy Award 1989), Chronicles, Refugees of the Heart 1991, Far from Home 1994, The Finer Things 1995, Junction 7 1997, About Time 2003, Nine Lives 2008; singles: with Spencer Davis Group: Keep On Running 1966, Somebody Help Me 1966, Gimme Some Lovin' 1966, I'm a Man 1967; with Traffic: Paper Sun 1967, Hole in My Shoe 1967, solo singles: While You See A

Chance 1980, Freedom Overspill 1986, Higher Love (two Grammy Awards: Record of the Year and Best Pop Vocal Performance 1987) 1986, The Finer Things 1987, Valerie 1987, Roll With It 1988, Don't You Know What the Night Can Do 1988, Holding On 1989, One and Only Man 1990, I Will Be Here 1991, Reach for the Light 1995, Spy in the House of Love 1997; other session work includes: Lou Reed, Berlin 1973, John Martyn, Inside Out 1973, Viv Stanshall, Men Opening Umbrellas Ahead 1974, Marianne Faithfull, Broken English 1979, Talk Talk, The Colour of Spring 1986, Paul Weller, Stanley Road 1995, Eric Clapton, Back Home 2005, Eric Clapton, Clapton 2010, Slash, Hey Joe 2010, Miranda Lambert, Four the Record 2011, Eric Clapton, Old Sock 2013, Gov't Mule, Shout! 2013. *Honours:* 14 Gold Record Awards, four Platinum Record Awards. *Address:* Wincraft Music, Ltd, PO Box 41, Cheltenham, Glos., GL54 4WA, England (office). *E-mail:* management@wincraftmusic.com (office). *Website:* www.stevewinwood.com.

WIRE, Nicky; Welsh musician (bass) and songwriter; b. (Nick Jones), 20 Jan. 1969, Tredegar, Gwent; m.; one s. one d. *Education:* Oakdale Comprehensive School, Univ. of Swansea. *Career:* founder mem., Betty Blue 1986, renamed Manic Street Preachers 1988–; numerous tours, festival appearances, TV and radio appearances; first Western group to play concert in Cuba since 1979, Feb. 2001; solo work 2006–. *Recordings include:* albums: with Manic Street Preachers: Generation Terrorists 1992, Gold Against The Soul 1993, The Holy Bible 1994, Everything Must Go (BRIT Award for Best British Album 1997) 1996, This Is My Truth, Tell Me Yours (BRIT Award for Best British Album 1999) 1998, Know Your Enemy 2001, Forever Delayed 2002, Lipstick Traces: A Secret History Of Manic Street Preachers 2003, Lifeblood 2004, Send Away the Tigers 2007, Journal for Plague Lovers 2009, Postcards from a Young Man 2010, Rewind the Film 2013, Futurology 2014; solo: I Killed the Zeitgeist 2006. *Honours:* numerous including: with Manic Street Preachers: BRIT Awards for Best British Group 1997, 1999, Q Awards for Best Live Act 2001, for Best Track (for Your Love Alone is Not Enough) 2007, for Best Video (for Show Me the Wonder) 2013, MOJO Maverick Award 2009. *Current Management:* Gillian Porter, Hall or Nothing Independent Publicity, 2 Archer Street, Soho, London, W1D 7AW, England. *E-mail:* gillian@hallornothing.com. *Website:* www.hallornothing.com; www.manicstreetpreachers.com; www.nickyssecretsociety.com.

WISE, Denny; British bandleader, singer, musician and composer; *Founder and CEO, Forces Children's Trust;* b. 12 Sept. 1947, Bedford, Beds., England; m. Teresa Wise 1955; one s. one d. *Education:* Leicester Coll. of Art and Technology, private piano and vocal lessons. *Career:* radio appearances include BBC, Capital Radio, local stations, TV appearances in Germany; mem. Musicians' Union, Variety and Allied Entertainments Council; Founder and CEO Forces Children's Trust. *Recordings include:* Wise One, Time, A Toast To Gilbert O'Sullivan (Denny Wise Sings). *Publications include:* Wise One, Love In The Night, Where Did We Go Wrong. *Honours:* Sun Military Award. *Website:* www.dennywise.co.uk.

WISEFIELD, Laurence (Laurie) Mark; British musician (electric, acoustic guitars, slide, banjo), singer and songwriter; b. London; m. Patricia France Rousseau 1986. *Career:* formed group Home 1971–73; joined Al Stewart Band 1973; mem., group Wishbone Ash 1974–86; joined Tina Turner Band 1987; solo performance, Night of the Guitars; tours with Joe Cocker, Tom Jones, Roger Chapman, Eros Ramazzotti, Tina Turner, band mem., We Will Rock You musical, London 2002–, The War of the Worlds 2005; mem, Musicians' Union, PRS, MCPS, PAMRA. *Recordings:* albums: with Home Pause for a Hoarse Horse 1971, Home 1972, The Alchemist 1973; with Wishbone Ash: There's the Rub 1974, Locked In 1976, New England 1976, Front Pages News 1977, Classic Ash 1977, No Smoke Without Fire 1978, Just Testing 1980, Hot Ash 1980, Number the Brave 1981, Twin Barrels Burning 1982, Raw to the Bone 1985; solo: Night of Guitars. *E-mail:* info@lauriewisefield.com (office). *Website:* www.lauriewisefield.com.

WISEMAN, Debra (Debbie), MBE, FGSM, FTCL; British composer and conductor; b. 10 May 1963, London; d. of Paul Wiseman and Barbara Wiseman; m. Tony Wharmby 1987. *Education:* Trinity Coll. of Music, Kingsway Princeton/Morley Coll., Guildhall School of Music and Drama. *Career:* composer and conductor of music for film and TV productions 1989–; Visiting Prof. of Film Composition, Royal Coll. of Music 1995–; mem. Performing Right Soc., BAFTA, Musicians' Union, British Acad. of Composers and Songwriters. *Compositions include:* Inside Looking Out 1989, Squares and Roundabouts 1989, Echoes of Istria 1989, The Guilty, Lighthouse, Female Perversions, The Dying of the Light, Shrinks (Silents to Satellite Award for Best Original TV Theme Music 1991), The Good Guys (Television and Radio Industries Club Award for TV Theme Music of the Year 1993), Tom and Viv 1994, The Project, Judge John Deed, P.O.W., Wilde Stories, The Upper Hand, The Churchills, Serious and Organised, The Second Russian Revolution, Little Napoleons, Children's Hospital, Death of Yugoslavia, Haunted 1995, Wilde 1997, The Fairy Tale of the Nightingale and the Rose 1999, The Fairy Tale of the Selfish Giant 1999, It Might be You, A Week in Politics, People's Century, What Did You Do In The War, Auntie?, The Cuban Missile Crisis, Vet's School, The Missing Postman, Tom's Midnight Garden, Absolute Truth, Warriors (Royal TV Soc. Award) 2000, My Uncle Silas 2001, Othello 2001, Oscar Wilde Fairy Stories 2002, Freeze Frame 2004, He Knew He Was Right 2004, The Andrew Marr Show, The Truth About Love 2004, Arsène Lupin 2004, Johnny and the Bomb 2005, Middletown 2005, Feather Boy: The Musical 2005, Middletown (film music) 2006, Jekyll 2007, Walter's War 2008, Stephen Fry in America 2008, The Passion 2008, Lesbian Vampire Killers

2009, The Hide 2009, Land Girls 2009, 2010, 2011, Joanna Lumley's Nile 2010, Martin Clunes: Horsepower 2010, The Promise 2011, Joanna Lumley's Greek Odyssey 2011, Fry's Planet Word 2011, Lost Christmas 2011, The Whale 2013, Father Brown 2013–16, WPC 56 2013–14, A Poet in New York 2014, Wolf Hall 2015, The Coroner 2015, Dickensian 2015–16. *Honours:* Hon. Fellow, Trinity Coll. of Music, London 2006, Guildhall School of Music and Drama 2007; Hon. DMus (Univ. of Sussex) 2015. *Current Management:* c/o Roz Colls, Music Matters International, Crest House, 102–104 Church Road, Teddington, Middx, TW11 8PY, England; c/o Rich Jacobellis, First Artists Management, 4764 Park Granada, Suite 210, Calabasas, CA 91302, USA. *Telephone:* (20) 8979-4580 (Teddington). *E-mail:* dwiseman10@aol.com (office). *Website:* www.debbiewiseman.co.uk.

WISHMOUNTAIN (see Herbert, Matthew)

WISIN; Puerto Rican rapper and singer; b. (Juan Luis Morera Moon), 19 Dec. 1978, Cayey; m. 2008; one s. one d. *Career:* mem. reggaeton duo, Wisin & Yandel 1995–; debut release 2000; launched clothing line Los Lideres 2011; numerous collaborations with hip-hop artists including Aventura, Bone Thugs-n-Harmony, Hector El Bambino, 50 Cent, Enrique Iglesias, T-Pain, Jennifer Lopez, Daddy Yankee, Chris Brown, Don Omar, Ricky Martin, Akon; co-f. WY Records. *Recordings include:* with Wisin & Yandel: Los Reyes del Nuevo Milenio 2000, De Nuevos a Viejos 2001, De Otra Manera 2002, Mi Vida... My Life 2003, Pa'l Mundo 2005, Los Extraterrestres (Grammy Award for Best Latin Urban Album 2008, Premio Juventud for CD to Die For 2008, Billboard Music Award for Latin Rhythm Album of the Year – Duo or Group 2009) 2007, La Revolución 2009, Los Vaqueros: El Regreso 2011, Líderes 2012; solo: El Sobreviviente 2004, El Regreso del Sobreviviente 2014. *Films:* Mi vida... My Life 2003, Revolución 2011. *Television:* La Voz... México 2013. *Honours:* Premios Juventud for Favorite Video 2008, for Favorite Ringtone 2008, for Favorite Urban Artist 2008, Premios MTV Latinoamérica for Artist of the Year 2009, for Video of the Year (for Abusadora) 2009. *Address:* c/o Universal Music Latin Entertainment, Universal Music Group, 2220 Colorado Avenue, Santa Monica, CA 90404, USA (office). *Telephone:* (310) 865-5000 (office). *E-mail:* contact@wisinyandelpr.com. *Website:* www.universalmusica.com (office); www.wisinyandel.com.

WISNIAK, Alain; French composer, arranger and record producer; *Composer, Tralala Music;* b. 23 Sept. 1947, Boulogne, Seine; m. Mariline Raichenbach 1975; one s. one d. *Education:* Marguerite Long piano school, studied harmony with André Hodeir in Paris. *Career:* musician for sessions and tours with major French pop artists; co-producer, writer for Bob Sinclar III; mem. Sociétaire Définitif, SACEM. *Film scores include:* Je vous trouve tres beau (dir Isabelle Mergault), La Femme Publique (dir Andjew Zulawski), On peut toujourd rever (dir Pierre richard), L'Année des Méduses. *Recordings include:* show theme for television series Maguy; producer, composer, Cerrone's Supernature album, Victoire de la Musique 1992, Made in Jamaica (Bob Sinclar) 2010, co-composer, Love Generation by Bob Sinclar 2013. *Honours:* Médaille de la SACEM. *Address:* 16 rue Paira, 92190 Meudon, France (office). *Telephone:* 1-41-14-04-30 (office). *E-mail:* alain@tralalamusic.com (office). *Website:* tralalamusic.com (office).

WITHERS, Bill; American singer, songwriter and producer; b. 4 July 1938, Slabfork, WV; m. Marcia Johnson; two c. *Career:* US Navy –1965; solo artist 1970–; numerous live and TV appearances. *Recordings include:* albums: Just As I Am 1971, Still Bill 1972, Live at Carnegie Hall 1973, +Justments 1974, Making Music, Making Friends 1975, Naked & Warm 1976, Menagerie 1977, 'Bout Love 1978, Watching You, Watching Me 1985, numerous compilations. *Honours:* Grammy Award for Best R&B Song of the Year (for Ain't No Sunshine) 1971, (for Just the Two of Us) 1981, (for (Lean on Me) 1987, NAACP Image Award for Male Singer of the Year, and Single Record of the Year 1972, ASCAP Pop Award (for Just the Two of Us) 1999, Songwriters Hall of Fame 2005, ASCAP Rhythm and Soul Heritage Award 2006, Grammy Hall of Fame (for Lean on Me) 2007, R&B Foundation Pioneer Award 2008; Dr hc (Middlebury Coll., VT) 1999, (Mountain State Univ., Beckley, WV) 2002. *Address:* Mattie Music Group, PO Box 16698, Beverly Hills, CA 90209-1698, USA (office). *Telephone:* (323) 866-1820 (office). *E-mail:* mattiemusic@sbcglobal.net (office). *Website:* www.billwithersmusic.com.

WITHERS, Pick; British musician (drums); b. (Pique Withers), 4 April 1948, Leicester. *Career:* mem. Dire Straits 1977–82; numerous tours and TV appearances. *Recordings include:* albums: Dire Straits 1978, Communiqué 1979, Making Movies 1980, Love Over Gold 1982; with others: Slow Train Coming (with Bob Dylan), Giant From The Blue (with Gary Fletcher Band); singles: Sultans of Swing 1978, Lady Writer 1979, Romeo and Juliet 1980, Making Movies 1980, Tunnel of Love 1981, Private Investigations 1982. *E-mail:* justmusic@mac.com. *Website:* www.pickwithers.com.

WITT, Marcos; Mexican singer and musician (piano, percussion); b. (Jonathan Mark Witt Holder), 19 May 1962, San Antonio, Tex., USA; s. of Jerry Witt and Nola Witt; m. Miriam Lee 1986, three s. one d. *Education:* Univ. of Juarez, Durango, Oral Roberts Univ., Tulsa, Okla, USA. *Career:* f. CanZion Producciones 1986–, renamed CanZion Group 2002; f. CanZion Inst. 1994–; solo artist 1986–; pastor of the Spanish congregation Lakewood Church, Houston, Tex., USA. *Recordings include:* Canción a Dios 1986, Te anhelo 1992, Te exaltamos 1992, ¡Alabadle! 1994, Recordando... una misma senda 1995, Venció 1996, Es Navidad 1996, Preparad el camino 1998, Lo mejor de instrumentales 1998, Enciende una luz 1999, Homenaje a Jesús 2000, Vencéu 2000, El Volverá 2000, Vivencias 2001, Sana nuestra tierra (Latin

Grammy Award for Best Christian Album 2003) 2001, El Encuentro 2002, Dios de pactos 2003, Amazing God 2003, Recordando otra vez (Latin Grammy Award for Best Christian Album) 2004, Tiempo de Navidad 2004, Antología 2004, Dios es bueno (Latin Grammy Award for Best Christian Album 2006) 2005, Christmas Time 2005, Alegría (Latin Billboard Award for Best Christian/Gospel Album of the Year 2007) 2006, Sinfonía del alma (Latin Grammy Award for Best Christian Album) 2007, Sobrenatural 2008. *Publications include:* ¡Adoremos! 1988, Proyecto AA 1991, Poderoso 1993, Tú y yo 1994, Qué hacemos con estos músicos. *Honours:* Ritmo Latino Award by the People 2001. *Address:* CanZion Group LP, 914 W Greens Road, Houston, TX 77067, USA (office). *Telephone:* (800) 725-5125 (office). *E-mail:* contacto@canzion.com (office). *Website:* www.canzion.com/marcoswitt (office).

WITTER, Rick; British singer; b. 23 Nov. 1972, Stockport, Cheshire, England. *Career:* mem., Shed Seven 1996–2003; numerous live appearances, festivals and tours; founder mem., Rick Witter & The Dukes 2004–; mem. PRS, Musicians' Union. *Recordings include:* albums: Change Giver 1996, A Maximum High 1996, Let It Ride 1998, Truth Be Told 2001.

WITTMAN, William; record producer; b. 16 Sept. 1952, Richmond-on-Thames, Surrey, England; m. Barbara Solomon 1975; one s. *Career:* mixer, record producer, New York 1978–87, RCA Records 1987–90, CBS Records 1990–; mem. NARAS. *Recordings include:* as producer include: with Cyndi Lauper: She's So Unusual 1982, Hat Full of Stars 1992, 12 Deadly Cyns 1995; with Graham Parker: Steady Nerves 1985, Passion Is No Ordinary Word 1993; with Fixx: Calm Animals 1988, Ink 1991; with Lloyd Cole: Negatives 2000. *Honours:* Grammy Award (Kinky Boots) 2012. *E-mail:* william@weedywet.com. *Website:* weedywet.com.

WOBBLE, Jah; British musician (bass guitar); b. (John Wardle), London. *Career:* mem. Public Image Ltd (PiL) 1978–80; Founder, Human Condition; Jah Wobble's Invaders of the Heart; collaborated with Holger Czukay, Gary Clail, Bill Laswell, Dub Syndicate, The Orb, Primal Scream, The Wolfgang Press; Owner, record label 30 Hertz Records. *Compositions include:* The River, Ku-cheng concerto performed by the Royal Liverpool Philharmonic Orchestra. *Recordings include:* albums: with PiL: Public Image Ltd 1978, Metal Box 1979, Second Edition 1980; solo: Rising Above Bedlam 1991, Take Me to God 1994, Heaven and Earth 1995, Spinner (with Brian Eno) 1995, The Inspiration of William Blake 1996, Requiem 1997, Umbra Sumus 1998, Celtic Poets 1998, Deep Space 1999, Full Moon Over The Shopping Mall 2000, Passage To Hades 2001, English Roots Music 2003, Mu 2005, Alpha One Three 2006, Chinese Dub 2009, Japanese Dub 2010, 7 2011, Psychic Life 2011, Yin & Yang 2012. *Publication:* Memoirs of a Geezer: Music, Life, Mayhem 2009. *Address:* 30 Hertz Records Ltd, PO Box 34, Bramhall, Stockport, SK7 3FZ, England (office). *Telephone:* (161) 439-0464 (office). *E-mail:* data@30hertzrecords.com (office). *Website:* www.30hertzrecords.com (office).

WOHLERT, Johan; Danish musician (bass guitar); m. Pernille Rosendahl. *Career:* Founder-mem. Mew 1996–2006, 2014–; the band formed record label, Evil Office 2000–06; co-f. band, The Storm 2008. *Recordings include:* albums: with Mew: A Triumph For Man 1997, Half The World Is Watching Me 2000, Frengers (Danish Music Critics Award for Album of the Year) 2003, Mew And The Glass Handed Kites 2005; with Storm: Where the Storm Meets the Ground 2008. *Honours:* Danish Music Critics Award for Band of the Year 2003, MTV Europe Music Award for Best Danish Act 2005.

WOLANIN, Vincent M., BS; American record producer, business executive, entrepreneur and investor; *Chairman and CEO, Wolanin Companies Limited;* b. 13 Dec. 1947, Philadelphia, Pa; s. of Vincent John Wolanin and Julia Solecki; m. Illona Koch Dove 1981; two d. *Education:* Philadelphia Univ., Union Coll. *Career:* fmr professional athlete; Chair. and CEO TopNotch® Entertainment Corpn (Management-Entertainment Asset Co.); Founder TopNotch Music, Records; CEO TopNotch Man. Co.; Chair. Wolanin Cos Ltd 1973–; holds musical trademarks for Studiolive Sound™, Thoughts™, Top-Notch®; Founder, The Rockin' Christmas Fund charitable music holiday event; co-producer and songwriter with recording artist Whitney Wolanin; cr. media campaigns in Spin Magazine, Aviation International News, R&R, FMQB, and media branding and internet campaigns for artists, an airline co. and others; Founder, Chair. and CEO PrivateSky® Aviation Services, Inc. 1988–; mem. Nat. Asscn of Recording Merchandises, Nat. Acad. Recording Arts/Science, ASCAP; Grammy voting mem. *Recordings as producer:* albums as producer, co-producer or songwriter: Breaking Through 1995, Angry Room, Lyndal's Burning 1995, Lingerie-Natalia 1995; Whitney Wolanin albums: Funkology XIII 2005, Christmasology™ 2006, Girl 2009; Whitney Wolanin Billboard Top 20 songs 2004–14: Whitney Wolanin (#1) 2011, It Takes Two, Whitney Wolanin (featuring Jimi Jamison), So Close (#7), Christmas (The Warmest Time of the Year), Honesty (#20) 2012, Good, Frosty the Snowman (#13) 2012, Wrong Guy (I Did It This Time) (#15) 2013, Run, Run Rudolph (#2 Billboard) 2013, and other records for various artists. *Honours:* voted into Father Judge High School Hall of Fame, Philadelphia, Pa 2005, Lifetime Innovation Award, Philadelphia Univ. 2010, inducted into Athletic Hall of Fame, Philadelphia Univ. 2012. *Current Management:* c/o Box 1515, Sanibel Island, FL 33957-1515, USA. *Address:* TopNotch Entertainment Corpn, TopNotch Music and Records, Sanibel Island, FL 33957-1515, USA (office). *Telephone:* (518) 456-9200 (ext. 10) (office). *Website:* www.wolanin.com (office); www.whitneywolanin.com (office); www.privatesky.net (office).

WOLDE-MARIAM, Yosef; Norwegian singer; b. 3 June 1978, Oslo. *Career:* mem. Madcon 1992–; co-presenter, The Voice of Madcon (The Voice TV

channel) 2005. *Recordings include:* albums: It's All a Madcon (Spellemann-prisen for Best Hip Hop Album) 2004, So Dark the Con of Man 2009, An InCONvenient Truth 2008, Contraband 2010, Contakt 2012, Icon 2013. *Honours:* Spellemannprisen for Best Song (for Beggin') 2008. *Current Management:* c/o Peter Peters, Friendly Entertainment AS, POB 2654 Solli, 0203 Oslo, Norway. *E-mail:* peter.peters@friendly.no. *Website:* www.friendly.no; www.madconlive.com.

WOLF, Karl; Canadian (b. Lebanese) singer and songwriter; b. (Carl Abouh Samah), 18 April 1979, Beirut. *Career:* singer, songwriter and producer 2001–; has collaborated with several artists including Snoop Dogg, Diana Haddad, Choclair, Gabrielle Destroismaisons; f. own record label LW Records; performed at launch of MTV Arabia 2007, MTV Europe Music Video Awards, Liverpool 2008. *Recordings:* albums include Face Behind the Face 2006, Bite the Bullet 2007, Nightlife 2009; singles include Africa 2008, Yalla Habibi 2009, Hurting 2010. *Honours:* MTV Europe Music Awards Best Arabia Act 2008, Canadian Radio Music Awards Best New Solo Artist of the Year 2010, SOBA Anglophone Single of the Year 2010. *Address:* c/o Universal Republic Records, 1755 Broadway, New York, NY 10019, USA (office). *E-mail:* info@karlwolf.com (office). *Website:* www.karlwolf.com (office).

WOLFSON, Mark; American record producer, sound engineer, songwriter and music supervisor; *Director of Production and Development, Playtone/Epic Records;* b. 1 Sept. 1951, Chicago, IL. *Career:* producer for UB40, Talking Heads, Natalie Cole, Jane Child, Stone Temple Pilots, Kimberly Bass, School of Fish; sound engineer for Sir Mix-A-Lot, Talking Heads, Smokey Robinson, Ice-T, Natalie Cole, Thelma Houston, Phil Everly, Melle Mel, Kim Carnes, Celia Cruz, Jane Child, Michael Des Barres; producer of film soundtracks, including Philadelphia, Silence of The Lambs, That Thing You Do, 12 Bucks, Police Academy, Police Academy III, Down and Out in Beverly Hills, K2; producer of television commercials, including Burger King, Coors, Toyota, 7 Up, Pizza Hut, Circle K; Dir of Production and Devt, Playtone/Epic Records 1999–; mem. NARAS. *Address:* Reel Entertainment LLC, 11684 Ventura Blvd, Suite 134 Studio City, CA 91604, USA. *E-mail:* reelent@yahoo.com (office); mwolfson@playtone.com (office). *Website:* www.reelent.com (office).

WØLLO, Erik; Norwegian composer, musician and producer; b. 6 Jan. 1961, Hemsedal; one s. *Career:* professional artist since 1980; musical experience covers wide range of styles, from rock and jazz, to experimental electronic and classical music; best known for electronic ambient music; composer and performer of music for film, theatre, ballet and exhbns; also composes for strings, woodwind and larger orchestras; as guitarist, has led groups, playing at clubs, concert halls and festivals in Europe, USA and Canada; produces own solo albums at his Wintergarden Studio and released on CD world-wide since 1985; creates music that is both lyrical and rhythmical, emphasizing melodic and structural formations; integrates elements of pop, rock and classical, as well as ethnic and electronic ambient music styles; as guitarist, albums mix sounds of technology with acoustics gathered from the environment; mem. NOPA, Norwegian Soc. of Composers. *Compositions:* Formations (string quartet) 1982, En Brottsjø (saxophone quartet) 1986, Solar for tape and woodwinds 1986, Windows (sinfonietta) 1988, Pre Sense for two pianos, clarinet, trumpet and tape 1990, Vidder for organ and horn 1992, Accordance (string quartet) 1992, Lost in Legoland for flute, guitar and voice 1994, Magnushymnen for voice, flute, guitar and brass 1997, Ceramics for flute, percussion and tape 1998, Imaginations (string quartet) 1998, Millennium 2000 (sinfonietta for soprano, choir and organ) 1999, Transitions (sinfonietta for ensemble and soprano) 2000, Unity (string quartet) 2002, Snowflakes for choir and small orchestra 2011, Elementa Ultra (guitar and electronics) 2013, Fragmenter fra en Aftenstemning (soprano) 2015. *Dance:* music for ballet: Pyramider (Trine Thorbjørnsen) 1986, Jeg Drømte (Kjersti Engebrigtsen) 1992, Ursula X (Teet Kask) 1999, Gips (Spig Wibrodux) (Wøllo/Bry/Kask) 1999, Shadowgraph (Teet Kask) 2001, Cascade (Jane Hveding) 2002, Distant Buddha (Teet Kask) 2004, Fragile (Kjersti Engebrigtsen) 2004, Breathing Space (Kjersti Engebrigtsen) 2007. *Video/film/exhibitions/installations:* Transit (music video to the album) 1996, Antebellum America (video/installation) 1997, Rift (Continental Drift) (video from Iceland) 1998, Lay Out (video/installation) 1998, Street Lights (video/installation) 1999, Fun House (video/installation) 1999, Crash Course (video/installation) 2000, Ice Works – Music to Icesculpture 2000, Kulturstreif Hallingdal – Internet project (www.kulturstreif.no) 2000, En Transformert Reise (video/installation) 2000, Chat Chat Chat (animations/Internet interactive) 2001, Sprawlville (video/installation) 2002, Under Overflaten (video) 2003, Consuming Pleasures (video/installation) 2003, Falling Down (video/installation) 2003, Balling Games (video/installation) 2005, Playing Games Paying Games (video/installation) 2005, Beacons (light/sound installation at Asker Train station) 2005, Elevator (photo and sound installation 2005, Year (dramatic feature film by Mike Carroll) 2005, Eventyrsøppel (installation with music) 2006, Lille Øistein (computer game) 2007, Emotions (video/installation) 2011. *Theatre:* Motspillerne (Kittelsen/Thorbjørnsen) 1988–91, Aldri Verden (Vik/Schjøll) 1992, Fossegrimen (Bry/Springgard/Wøllo) 1992, 1995, 1996, Abiriels Løve (Kittelsen/Thorbjørnsen) 1996, Livskraften (Thor Rummelhoff) 2005, Heimen vår (Bry/Springgard/Wøllo) 2007. *Radio:* music for radio documentaries. *Television:* multimedia/exhbns/films/TV documentaries for NRK/TV2 and other TV cos in Norway, Europe, USA and Japan. *Recordings:* solo albums: Where It All Begins 1983, (CD) 1999, Dreams of Pyramids 1984, Traces 1985, (CD) 1988, Silver Beach 1986, 1988, (CD) 2005, Images of Light 1990, Solstice 1992, Transit 1996, Guitar Nova 1998, Wind Journey 2001, Emotional

Landscapes 2003, The Polar Drones 2003, Blue Sky, Red Guitars 2004, Elevations 2007, Gateway 2010, Silent Currents 2011, Airborne 2012, Crystal Bells 2012, The Nocturnes 2012, Silent Currents 3 2013, Celestia 2013, Timelines 2014, Tundra 2014, Blue Radiance 2015, Echotides 2015; with other artists/Projects: Celeste – Design by Music (LP) 1984, Wiese/Wøllo/Waring – Oboe/Guitar/Vibraphone 1984, (CD) 2008, New Music Composers Group – In Real Time 1992, Bry/Springgard/Wøllo – Fossegrimen (book/CD) 1995, Pacemaker – Pacemaker (EP) 1996, EXILE – Dimension D 1997, Erik Wøllo/Hyperlinkto – Musikk til en Meny 2001, Steve Roach/Erik Wøllo – Stream of Thought 2009, Frank Van Bogaert with Erik Wøllo – Air Machine 2009, Deborah Martin/Erik Wøllo – Between Worlds 2009, Erik Wøllo/ Bernhard Wöstheinrich – Arcadia Borealis 2009, Kouame Sereba with Erik Wøllo – Bako 2010, Steve Roach/Erik Wøllo – The Road Eternal 2011, Erik Wøllo/Bernhard Wöstheinrich – Weltenuhr (DiN46 CD) 2014; selected compositions licensed for collection albums: Northern Nights 1999, Music from the Edge 2000, The Echoes Living Room Concerts, Vol. 7 2001, Lights Out – VIII 2002, The Echoes Living Room Concerts, Vol. 9 2003, Event/ Horizon 2004, Tribute to Michael Garrison 2004, Lights Out – IX 2005, Lights Out – X 2006, Star's End 30th Anniversary Anthology 2007, The Projekt Sampler 2009, Afar 2010, E-Day 2011: Grosskopf/Wøllo/Remy/Splinter 2011, The Rope 25 2011, The Echoes Living Room Concerts, Vol. 17 2011, Paws (animal shelter benefit CD compilation) 2011; other: Off The Wall (world music concert project for schools, produced by Rikskonsertene) 2005; as producer/arranger: Karsten Brustad: Intarsia 1991, New Music Composers Group: In Real Time 1992, Kouame Gerard Sereba: Kilimandjaro 1993, Sverre Knut Johansen: Distant Shore 1993, Eyeman Reel: Bird Colony (also single) 1995, Current: Enter The Dream 1997, Ola og Knut Fausko: Huldrehatten, Folkemusikk frå Hemsedal 1997, Kouame Sereba with Erik Wøllo: Bako 2010, Kouame Sereba: Shama Shama 2010. *E-mail:* monumental@wollo.com (home). *Website:* www.wollo.com.

WOLSTENHOLME, Chris Tony; British musician (bass guitar); b. 2 Dec. 1978; m. Kelly Wolstenholme 2003; six c. *Career:* formed group Fixed Penalty aged 13, group became Gothic Plague, then Rocket Baby Dolls before finally settling on name Muse 1997–; numerous festival appearances, broadcasts. *Recordings include:* albums: Showbiz 1999, Origin Of Symmetry 2001, Hullabaloo 2002, Absolution 2003, Time Is Running Out 2004, Black Holes and Revelations 2006, HAARP 2008, The Resistance (Grammy Award for Best Rock Album 2011) 2009, The 2nd Law 2012, Drones (Grammy Award for Best Rock Album 2016) 2015. *Honours:* Dr hc (Univ. of Plymouth) 2008; NME Awards for Best New Band 2000, for Best Live Band 2005, 2008, 2009, for Best British Band 2007, 2010, 2011, Kerrang! Awards for Best British Band 2001, for Best British Live Act 2002, for Best Live Act 2006, Q Awards for Innovation in Sound 2003, for Best Live Act 2004, 2006, 2007, for Best Act in the World Today 2009, 2012, MTV Europe Music Awards for Best Alternative Act 2004, 2006, for Best UK and Irish Act 2004, 2007, for Headliner 2007, BRIT Awards for Best Live Act 2005, 2007, American Music Award for Favorite Alternative Artist 2010, Ivor Novello Award for Int. Achievement 2011. *Website:* www .muse.mu.

WOMACK, Lee Ann; American country singer; b. 19 Aug. 1966, Jacksonville, Texas; m. 1st Jason Sellers 1990 (divorced); m. 2nd Frank Liddell; two c. *Education:* South Plains Jr Coll., Bellmont Univ. *Career:* mem. coll. band, Country Caravan; intern, A&R dept, MCA Records; started to write songs, perform at artist showcases and sing on demo sessions; wrote material with Bill Anderson, Mark Wright, Ed Hill and Jason Sellers; solo artist. *Recordings include:* albums: Lee Ann Womack (British Country Music Award for Best Int. Country Album of the Year) 1997, Some Things I Know 1998, I Hope You Dance 2000, Something Worth Leaving Behind 2002, The Season For Romance 2002, There's More Where That Came From (CMA Award for Album of the Year) 2005, Call Me Crazy 2008. *Honours:* ACM Top New Female Vocalist 1997, AMA Award for Favorite New Country Artist 1998, ACM Awards for Single of the Year, Song of the Year, Vocal Event of the Year (all for I Hope You Dance) 2000, CMA Awards for Song of the Year, Single of the Year (both for I Hope You Dance) 2000, Grammy Award for Best Country Song (for I Hope You Dance) 2001, CMA Award for Female Vocalist of the Year 2001, Billboard Award for Adult Contemporary Song of the Year (for I Hope You Dance) 2001, Grammy Award for Country Vocal Event of the Year (for Mendocino County Line with Willie Nelson) 2002, CMA Award for Vocal Event of the Year (for Mendocino County Line with Willie Nelson) 2002, ACM Award for Vocal Event of the Year (for Mendocino County Line with Willie Nelson) 2002, CMA Award for Single of the Year (for I May Hate Myself in the Morning) 2005, CMA Award for Musical Event of the Year (for Good News Bad News, with George Strait) 2005. *Current Management:* c/o WME Entertainment, 9601 Wilshire Blvd, Beverly Hills, CA 90201, USA. *Website:* www .leeannwomack.com.

WONDER, Stevie; American singer, musician and composer; b. (Steveland Judkins Morris), 13 May 1950, Saginaw, Mich.; step-s. of Paul Hardaway; m. 1st Syreeta Wright 1971 (divorced 1972, died 2004); m. 2nd Yolanda Simmons; m. 3rd Kai Millard Morris; seven c. *Education:* Michigan School for the Blind. *Career:* first appeared as solo singer at Whitestone Baptist Church, Detroit 1959; recording artist with Motown, Detroit, initially as Stephen Judkins, 1963–70; f. and Pres. Black Bull Music Inc. 1970–, Wondirection Records 1982–; Owner, KJLH, LA. *Film appearances:* Bikini Beach 1964, Muscle Beach Party 1964. *Recordings include:* albums: Little Stevie Wonder: The Twelve-Year-Old Genius 1963, Tribute To Uncle Ray, Jazz Soul, With A Song

In My Heart, At The Beach, Uptight 1966, Down To Earth 1966, I Was Made To Love Her 1967, Someday At Christmas 1967, For Once In My Life 1969, My Cherie Amour 1969, Signed Sealed and Delivered 1969, Music Of My Mind 1972, Talking Book 1972, Innervisions (Grammy Award 1974) 1973, Fulfillingness' First Finale (Grammy Award 1975) 1974, Songs in the Key of Life (Grammy Award 1977) 1976, Journey Through the Secret Life of Plants 1979, Hotter than July 1980, Original Musiquarium 1982, Woman in Red (soundtrack) 1984, Love Songs 1984, In Square Circle 1985, Characters 1987, Jungle Fever (film soundtrack) 1991, Conversation Peace 1995, Motown Legends 1995, Natural Wonder 1996, Song Review 1996, At The Close Of A Century 1999, A Time To Love 2005. *Honours:* Edison Award 1973, Nat. Asscn of Record Merchandisers Best Selling Male Soul Artist of Year 1974, and Presidential Award 1975, Golden Globe (for I Just Called To Say I Love You) 1985, numerous American Music Awards, including Special Award of Merit 1982, Acad. Award for Best Song 1984, Soul Train Heritage Award 1987, numerous Grammy Awards, including Grammy Award (for Superstition) 1974, Grammy Award (for You are the Sunshine of My Life) 1974, Grammy Award (for Living For The City) 1975, Grammy Award (for Boogie on Reggae Woman) 1975, Grammy Award (for I Wish) 1977, Grammy Lifetime Achievement Award 1990, Nelson Mandela Courage Award 1991, IAAAM Diamond Award for Excellence 1991, National Acad. of Songwriters Lifetime Achievement Award 1992, NAACP Image Award 1992, Polar Music Prize, Swedish Acad. of Music, Grammy Award for Best Male Pop Vocal Performance (for From the Bottom of my Heart) 2006, Grammy Award for Best R&B Performance by a Duo or Group with Vocals (for So Amazing, with Beyoncé) 2006, Grammy Award for Best Pop Collaboration with Vocals (with Tony Bennett) 2007, Gershwin Prize for Popular Song, US Library of Congress 2009, Presidential Medal of Freedom 2014. *Current Management:* Steveland Morris Productions LLC, 4616 West Magnolia Boulevard, Burbank, CA 91505, USA. *Website:* www.steviewonder.net.

WONDER, Wayne; Jamaican reggae singer and rap artist; b. (Von Wayne Charles), 26 July 1972, Buff Bay, Portland. *Career:* solo artist, with numerous collaborations; founder mem. band, Alias, under pseudonym Surprise; formed record label, Singso 2000–. *Recordings:* albums: Wayne Wonder 1987, Part 2 1991, Da Vibe 2000, Schizophrenic 2001, No Holding Back 2003, Singles and Unreleased 2006, Foreva 2007. *E-mail:* reggaeruss@aol.com (office). *Website:* www.waynewonder.com.

WONDER MIKE; American rap artist; b. (Michael Wright). *Career:* mem. The Sugarhill Gang 1979–85. *Recordings include:* albums: Rapper's Delight: Hip Hop Remix 1980, The Sugarhill Gang 1980, 8th Wonder 1982, Jump On It! 1999; single: Rapper's Delight 1979.

WONG, Faye, (Shirley Wong); Chinese singer and actress; b. (Xia Lin), 8 Aug. 1969, Beijing; m. 1st Dou Wei 1996 (divorced 1999); one d.; m. 2nd Li Ya Peng 2005. *Education:* studied in Hong Kong. *Career:* song, 'Eyes on Me' used as the theme to computer game, Final Fantasy VIII. *Films:* Beyond ri zi zhi mo qi shao nian qiong 1991, Chong qing sen lin (Swedish Film Festival Award for Best Actress) 1994, Luen chin chung sing 2000, Tian xia wu shuang (Hong Kong Best Actress Award 2003) 2002, Dai sing siu si 2004, Jiu mei hu 2004, 2046 2004. *Television:* Dexter's Laboratory (series, voice) 1996, Toshinden xinde chansheng (series) 2000, Usokoi (series) 2001. *Recordings include:* albums: Shirley Wong 1989, Everything 1990, You Are The Only One 1990, Coming Home 1992, No Regrets 1993, 100,000 Whys 1993, Mystery 1994, Random Thinking 1994, Sky 1994, Ingratiate Oneself 1994, Di-Dar 1995, Restless 1996, Wong Faye 1997, Sing and Play 1998, Only Love Strangers 1999, Fable 2000, Faye Wong 2001, To Love 2003. *Website:* www.sonymusic .com.cn.

WOOD; British musician (drums); b. (Matthew Wood), Cumbria. *Career:* founder mem., British Sea Power 2000–; the band runs Club Sea Power, a monthly variety show in Brighton, England; numerous live performances and festival appearances. *Recordings include:* albums: The Decline of British Sea Power 2003, Open Season 2005, Do You Like Rock Music? 2008, Man of Aran (film soundtrack) 2009. *Honours:* Time Out Award for Live Band of the Year 2004. *Address:* British Sea Power, PO Box 5123, Hove, East Sussex BN52 9ET, England. *Website:* www.britishseapower.co.uk.

WOOD, Christopher (Chris) Barry; American musician (bass); b. Pasadena; s. of Bill and Renatte Wood. *Education:* New England Conservatory of Music, Boston. *Career:* co-founder Madeski Martin and Wood jazz band 1991, festivals and concerts USA, Europe and Japan; co-founder, Indirecto Records; collab. with Marc Ribot, John Zorn, the Jass Passengers and Elliot Sharp; also performs with brother Oliver in The Wood Brothers. *Recordings include:* as Medeski Martin and Wood: Notes From The Underground 1991, It's a Jungle In Here 1993, Friday Afternoon in the Universe 1994, Shack-Man 1996, Farmer's Reserve 1997, Bubblehouse 1998, Combustication 1998, Last Chance to Dance Trance (Perhaps) 1999, Tonic 2000, The Dropper 2000, Electric Tonic 2001, Uninvisible 2002, End of the World Party (Just in Case) 2004, Out Louder 2006, Mago 2007, Let's Go Everywhere (for children) 2008, Zaebos 2008, Radiolarians II 2009; as The Wood Brothers: Ways Not To Lose 2006. *Address:* Blue Note Group, 150 5th Avenue, New York, NY 10011, USA (office). *Telephone:* (212) 786-8600 (office). *Fax:* (212) 786-8613 (office). *E-mail:* info@mmw.net (office). *Website:* www.bluenote.com (office); www.mmw.net.

WOOD, Christopher (Chris); British musician (drums, samples); b. 6 July 1985. *Career:* Founder-mem., Bastille 2010–; released debut single 2011; signed to Virgin Records 2011. *Recordings:* album: with Bastille: Bad Blood

2013. *Honours:* BRIT Award for British Breakthrough Act 2014. *Address:* c/o Virgin EMI Records, Universal Music Group, 364–366 Kensington High Street, London, W14 8NS, England (office). *Telephone:* (20) 7471-5000 (office). *E-mail:* contact@virginemirecords.com (office). *Website:* www .virginemirecords.com (office); bastillebastille.com.

WOOD, Danny; American musician (bass guitar) and producer. *Career:* fmr mem. band The Rise; mem. And You Will Know Us By The Trail Of Dead 2004–. *Recordings include:* albums: And You Will Know Us By The Trail Of Dead 1998, Madonna 1999, Source Tags and Codes 2002, The Secret of Elena's Tomb 2003, Worlds Apart 2005, So Divided 2006, The Century of Self 2009, Tao of the Dead 2011, Lost Songs 2012. *E-mail:* band@trailofdead.com. *Website:* trailofdead.com.

WOOD, Jeffrey, BA; American record producer and composer; b. 5 Sept. 1950, Chicago, Ill.; m. Carine F. Verheyen 1992. *Education:* Univ. of Illinois, studied with Helen Beidel. *Career:* produced numerous recording artists including Luka Bloom, The Housemartins, The Origin, Pauline Black, Penelope Houston. *Recordings include:* Twist of Destiny, The Surrendering Room, three feature film soundtracks. *Address:* Fantasy Studios, Saul Zaentz Media Center, 2600 10th Street, Berkeley, CA 94710, USA (office). *Telephone:* (510) 486-2038 (office). *E-mail:* jeffreywoodmusic@gmail.com (office). *Website:* jeffreywoodmusic.com (office).

WOOD, Patte, BA; American musician (piano) and arts administrator; b. 29 Jan. 1949, Seattle, WA. *Education:* San Jose State University. *Career:* instructor, Piano Performance and Accompanist, San Francisco Bay Area, 1965–76; Administrative Director, Stanford University Center for Computer Research in Music and Acoustics, 1984–95; Visiting Scholar, Stanford University, 1995–99; Director, Blue Ridge Association for Community, Culture, Art and Technology, Eagle Rock, Virginia, 1999–; staff writer, Rockbridge Weekly; Solo Performances at festivals and concerts; Coproducer, numerous music projects; Consultant for numerous musical conferences; mem, International Computer Music Asscn; Bay Area New Music Coalition, 1986–90; ICMA Commission Awards Selection Panel, 1992; Officer, Board of Directors, ICMA, 1992–2000; Advisory Board, Electronic Music Foundation, 1995. *Publications:* Early History of the Center for Computer Research in Music and Acoustics, 1988; Conversations with John Robinson Pierce, 1991; Interview with French composer Jean-Claude Risset, 1992–98. *Honours:* National Piano Auditions, Outstanding and Superior Grades, 1956–66, International Standing, Superior Grade, 1967; Community Action Grant, AAUW, 1999. *Address:* 572 Poorhouse Road, Lexington, VA 24450, USA. *E-mail:* patte@rockbridge.net; patte@chartwellcorp.com. *Website:* www .rockbridgeweekly.com.

WOOD, Paul; British singer; b. (Paul Richard Woodcock), 16 Nov. 1964, Romford, Essex, England. *Career:* mem. The Ray Ward Trio; worked with artists including Don Lusher, George Chisholm, Kenny Ball, Terry Lightfoot; numerous live performances, radio and TV broadcasts; mem. Glenn Miller Memorial Orchestra 1987–, Lex Van Wel and His Swing Orchestra; concert tours in France, Switzerland, Spain, Italy, Germany, Belgium, Austria; works regularly with various bands on the continent; mem. Musicians' Union, The Coda Club. *Recordings include:* albums with Glenn Miller Memorial Orchestra: Recorded Live The Sporting Club Monte Carlo; two albums with Lex Van Wel and his Swing Orchestra. *Honours:* Freedom of the City of London.

WOOD, Ronald (Ronnie) David; British musician (guitar, bass guitar); b. 1 June 1947, Hillingdon, London, England; m. 1st; one s.; m. 2nd Jo Howard 1985 (divorced 2009); one s. one d. *Career:* guitarist with Jeff Beck Group 1968–69, The Faces 1969–75, The Rolling Stones 1976–; tours worldwide; has also played with Bo Diddley, Rod Stewart, Jerry Lee Lewis. *Recordings include:* albums: with Jeff Beck Group: Truth 1968, Beck-Ola 1969; with The Faces: First Step 1970, Long Player 1971, A Nod's As Good As A Wink... To A Blind Horse 1971, Ooh La La 1973, Coast To Coast Overtures and Beginners 1974; with The Rolling Stones: Black And Blue 1976, Some Girls 1978, Emotional Rescue 1980, Tattoo You 1981, Still Life 1982, Undercover 1983, Dirty Work 1986, Steel Wheels 1989, Flashpoint 1991, Voodoo Lounge 1994, Stripped 1995, Bridges to Babylon 1997, Forty Licks 2002, Live Licks 2004, A Bigger Bang 2005; solo: I've Got My Own Album To Do 1974, Now Look 1976, Mahoney's Last Stand 1976, Gimme Some Neck 1979, 1234 1981, Live At The Ritz 1988, Slide On This 1992, Slide On Live: Plugged In And Standing 1994, Live & Eclectic 2000, Not For Beginners 2002, Live At Electric Ladyland 2002, Always Wanted More 2003, Buried Alive 2006, The First Barbarians 2007, I Feel Like Playing 2010. *Film:* Shine a Light 2007. *Publications include:* According to the Rolling Stones (autobiography, jtly) 2003, Ronnie Wood: The Autobiography 2007. *Honours:* Nordoff-Robbins Silver Clef 1982, Grammy Lifetime Achievement Award 1986, Ivor Novello Award for Outstanding Contribution to British Music 1991. *Website:* www.rollingstones.com; www .ronniewood.com.

WOOD, Roy; British singer, musician (guitar) and songwriter; b. 8 Nov. 1947, Birmingham, England. *Education:* Moseley School Of Art. *Career:* mem. Mike Sheridan and The Nightriders (later named Idle Race), The Move 1966–72; Founder-mem. Electric Light Orchestra (ELO) 1971–72, Wizzard 1972–75; formed The Wizzo Band, The Helicopters; writer, producer for various artists, including Darts 1977. *Recordings include:* albums: with The Move: Move 1968, Shazam 1970, Looking On 1970, Message From The Country 1971; with ELO: Electric Light Orchestra 1972; with Wizzard: Wizzard Brew 1973, Introducing Eddy and The Falcons 1974; with The Wizzo Band: On The Road

Again 1977, Super Active Wizzo 1977; solo: Boulders 1973, Mustard 1976, Main Street 2000, Starting Up 1987. *E-mail:* www.roywood.co.uk.

WOODRUFF, Bob; American singer, songwriter and musician (guitar, drums); b. 14 March 1961, Suffern, NY. *Career:* solo artist; numerous television appearances; mem. CMA, NARAS, AFTRA, AFofM. *Recordings include:* albums: Dreams and Saturday Nights 1994, Desire Road 1997. *Honours:* Charleston Int. Film Festival Silver Award for Best Country Music Video (for Alright) 1994.

WOODWARD, Keren; British singer; b. 2 April 1961, Bristol, Somerset, England. *Career:* worked at BBC; mem. Bananarama 1981–; numerous concerts, TV and radio performances. *Recordings include:* albums: Deep Sea Skiving 1983, Bananarama 1984, True Confessions 1986, Wow! 1987, Pop Life 1991, Please Yourself 1993, Ultraviolet 1996, Exotica 2001, I Found Love 2002, Drama 2005, Viva 2009. *Current Management:* c/o ArminRahn Agency & Management, Dreimühlenstr 7, D-80469 Munich, Germany. *E-mail:* info@ arminrahn.com. *Website:* www.arminrahn.com. *E-mail:* agent@bananarama .co.uk. *Website:* www.bananarama.co.uk.

WOOLLER, Lukas; British musician (keyboards); b. West Yorks., England. *Career:* founder mem., Maxïmo Park 2001–. *Recordings include:* albums: A Certain Trigger 2005, Our Earthly Pleasures 2007, Quicken the Heart 2009, The National Health 2012, Too Much Information 2014. *Current Management:* Prolifica Management, Unit 1, 32 Caxton Road, London W12 8AJ, England. *Telephone:* (20) 8740-9920. *Fax:* (20) 8740-2976. *E-mail:* info@ prolifica.co.uk. *Website:* www.prolificamanagement.co.uk; www.maximopark .com.

WOOMBLE, Roddy; British singer and musician (guitar); b. 13 Aug. 1976. *Career:* Founder-mem. Idlewild 1995–; mem. project, The Reindeer Section 2002–; solo artist 2006–. *Recordings include:* albums: with Idlewild: Captain 1998, Hope Is Important 1998, 100 Broken Windows 2001, The Remote Part 2002, Warnings/Promises 2005, Make Another World 2007, Scottish Fiction: Best of Idlewild 2007, Post Electric Blues 2009; with The Reindeer Section: Son Of Evil Reindeer 2002; solo: My Secret is Silence 2006, Before the Ruin 2008, The Impossible Song & Other Songs 2011, Listen to Keep 2013. *Current Management:* c/o Steve Nice, Nice Management, 2109 Cooley Place, Pasadena, CA 91104-4111, England. *Telephone:* (626) 345-9794. *E-mail:* steve@ nicemgmt.com. *Website:* www.idlewild.co.uk; www.roddywoomble.com.

WORLLEDGE, Terry, (Whirligig); British musician (guitar, harmonica), singer, songwriter, producer and sound engineer; *Musician/Producer/Director*, *Whirligig Music*; b. 31 Jan. 1945, Essex; m. Jean Worlledge 1964; two d. *Education:* Peavey Foundation, USA, Middlesex Univ. *Career:* Producer/Dir Whirligig Music 1990–; mem. Country Shack, Jackson Queen; numerous recordings, live appearances, TV and radio broadcasts world-wide; feature writer for various int. magazines; mem. Musicians' Union, PRS. *Recordings include:* albums: with Country Shack: Your Country Needs You, Portrait, Which Way Is Gone?, BBC's 20 C&W Greats; with Jackson Queen: Jackson Queen (EP), On The Rewind, Jackson Queen (Old, New, Borrowed, Blue). *Honours:* British Country Music Asscn Award for Most Promising Act 1980, Radio 2 Country Club Award for Best Band (over three years), and others. *Address:* Pipers, Maypole Road, Tiptree, Essex, CO5 0EP, England (home). *Telephone:* (1621) 819343 (home). *E-mail:* terryworlledge@gmail.com.

WORRELL, Bernie; American musician (keyboards); b. 19 April 1944, Long Beach, NJ. *Education:* New England Conservatory of Music. *Career:* performed in first classical music concert aged four years, wrote first concerto aged eight, performed with Washington Symphony Orchestra aged ten; toured as musician and arranger with Maxine Brown; joined George Clinton's Parliament and Funkadelic as musical dir and keyboard player, numerous recordings and tours –1981; co-writer of numerous Parliament and Funkadelic songs; a pioneer in the use of synthesizers in funk and soul music; numerous albums and tours with Talking Heads 1981–92; collaborations with Keith Richards, Albert King, Ginger Baker, Jack Bruce, Sly and Robbie; mem. or fmr mem. David Letterman's CBS Orchestra, Gov't Mule, Black Jack Johnson Band, Colonel Claypool's Bucket of Bernie Brains; leader Bernie Worrell and the WOO Warriors 1997–; currently mem. Baby Elephant with Prince Paul and Newkirk. *Recordings:* with Funkadelic: Funkadelic 1970, Free Your Mind . . . And Your Ass Will Follow 1970, Maggot Brain 1971, America Eats Its Young 1972, Cosmic Slop 1973, Standing on the Verge of Getting It On 1974, Let's Take It to the Stage 1975, Tales of Kidd Funkadelic 1976, Hardcore Jollies 1976, One Nation Under a Groove 1978, Uncle Jam Wants You 1979, The Electric Spanking of War Babies 1981; with Parliament: Osmium 1970, Up for the Down Stroke 1974, Chocolate City 1975, Mothership Connection 1975, The Clones of Dr. Funkenstein 1976, Funkentelechy Vs. the Placebo Syndrome 1977, Live: P-Funk Earth Tour 1977, Motor Booty Affair 1978, Gloryhallastoopid 1979, Trombipulation 1980; solo: All the Woo in the World 1977, B.W. Jam (Rock the House) 1990, Funk of Ages 1990, Blacktronic Science 1993, Free Agent: A Space Odyssey 1997, Bernie Worrell and the WOO Warriors Live 1998, True DAT 2002, Improvisczario 2007; with Baby Elephant: Turn My Teeth Up 2007. *Honours:* Rock 'n' Roll Hall of Fame 1997. *Current Management:* Scott Simoneaux, Infectious Publicity, 1214 Long Beach Avenue, Los Angeles, CA 90021, USA. *Telephone:* (213) 995-5449. *Fax:* (213) 995-5450. *E-mail:* info@infectiouspublicity.com (office). *Website:* www .infectiouspublicity.com. *E-mail:* info@godforsakenmusic.com (office). *Website:* www.godforsakenmusic.com (office); www.bernieworrell.com.

WORTLEY, Barry George; British musician (drums, guitar) and singer; b. 19 May 1951, Norwich, Norfolk; m. Susan Read 1986; five s. *Career:* mem., The Aytons 1966–68, Norma and The Shade of Pale 1968–71, Edentree (touring comedy/showband) 1972–75, Fresh 1975– (name changed to Monte Carlo for last 12 of Song For Europe and Dooleys Tour Support Band, name returned to Fresh); currently a trio working functions and summer seasons; mem., Musicians' Union. *Recordings:* Valentino, Win A Few, Lose A Few, Home Again. *Honours:* winner, New Faces (ITV) 1978, Music Award, Ljubljana Song Festival, Yugoslavia 1979.

WORTLEY, J.; British singer, songwriter and musician (guitar); b. 5 June 1971, Grimsby. *Career:* mem. Illustrious Gy 1989; Founder-mem. Giant Killers; mem. Musicians' Union. *Recordings include:* album: No No No.

WRAIGHT, Jeffrey Charles; British musician (keyboards, bass guitar), singer, arranger, composer and music director; b. 17 Aug. 1954, West Sussex. *Education:* studied with Cyril Winn. *Career:* accompanied many modern jazz artists 1973–79; experimental free jazz workshop, Reading 1977–79; founder mem., early punk group, Billy and the Conquerors; joined big band on QEII 1979, became band leader of own band on the same ship; worked with The Bachelors, Bob Monkhouse, Tommy Dorsey Orchestra, Peter Gordeno, Joe Loss, Faith Brown, Elaine Delmar, Lorna Dallas; started business venture in 1983 becoming Heartrate Entertainments 1989–; keyboard player, vocalist, arrangements for A Tribute To The Blues Brothers, London West End 1992; Musical Director, and rewriter of show 1994–. *Recordings include:* Soulstice, Tony Visconti; several live sessions by Pendulum; recordings for BBC TV and Radio including several Blues Brothers appearances. *Honours:* John Dankworth Award for Best Instrumentalist Under 25 (piano) 1977.

WRAY, John; British musician (keyboards) and producer; *Director, AIR Entertainments Agency;* b. 16 Jan. 1943, Ramshaw, County Durham; m. Karen Anne Western 1986; one s. one d. *Education:* private tuition. *Career:* band leader; Dir, AIR Entertainments Agency; prod. of concert tours, including Moscow Ballet La Classique; owner, Bullseye Recording Studios. *Address:* AIR Entertainments, 17 Clyde Terrace, Spennymoor, Co Durham DL16 7SE, England (office). *Telephone:* (1388) 814632 (office). *Fax:* (1388) 812445 (office). *E-mail:* john@airagency.com (office).

WRAY, Walter, BA; British singer, songwriter and musician (guitar); b. 7 Feb. 1959, Portsmouth, Hampshire, England; m. Joanne Redfearn 1989; one d. *Education:* Sheffield Univ. *Career:* fmr mem. Junk; mem. of rock band, King Swamp 1988; solo artist; mem. Musicians' Union, PRS. *Recordings include:* albums: with Junk: Cuckooland 1986, Drop City Souvenirs 1987; with King Swamp: King Swamp 1988, Wiseblood 1990; solo: Foxgloves and Steel Strings 1992, Heaven is on Our Side 1993.

WRETZKY-BROWN, D'Arcy; American musician (bass guitar); b. 1 May 1968, South Haven, MI. *Career:* mem., Smashing Pumpkins 1989–99; numerous headlining tours, television and radio sessions; other credits include: Catherine, Filter, James Iha. *Recordings include:* albums: with Smashing Pumpkins: Gish 1991, The Peel Sessions 1992, Siamese Dream 1993, Pisces Iscariot 1994, Mellon Collie and the Infinite Sadness 1995, The Aeroplane Flies High 1996, Adore 1998, Earphoria 2002.

WRIGHT, Chely; American country singer and musician (guitar); b. 25 Oct. 1970, Kansas City, MO. *Career:* formed band, County Line; moved to Branson, Missouri, securing a job singing on the Ozark Jubilee before finishing high school; moved to Nashville and secured a job impersonating country artists, aged 18; solo artist; recording and writing with Brad Paisley, including the hit duet Hard To Be A Husband – Hard To Be A Wife. *Recordings include:* albums: Woman in the Moon 1994, Right In The Middle Of It 1996, Let Me In 1997, Single White Female 1999, Never Love You Enough 2001, The Metropolitan Hotel 2005, Lifted Off the Ground 2010. *Honours:* ACM Award for Top New Female Vocalist 1995. *Address:* c/o Country Music Asscn, 1 Music Circle S, Nashville, TN 37203, USA. *Website:* www.chely.com.

WRIGHT, Christopher Norman, CBE; British music and media executive; *Executive Chairman, Chrysalis Group plc;* b. 1944, Louth, Lincs.; m. 1st (divorced); m. 2nd. *Education:* Louth Grammar School, Univ. of Manchester. *Career:* mem. of band Gas Board mid-1960s; co-f. Ellis-Wright Agency (with Terry Ellis) 1967, signing Jethro Tull, Ten Years After; co-f. Chrysalis Records and Publishing 1969, signing The Specials, Blondie, Leo Sayer, Sinead O'Connor, Ultravox, Huey Lewis & The News, Frankie Miller, Pat Benatar, Billy Idol, Spandau Ballet; sold record div. to EMI 1991; f. subsidiary label, Echo Records 1993; f. Chrysalis Radio Group 1994 (launched Heart FM West Midlands 1994, Heart FM London 1995, acquired Galaxy Radio 1995, LBC Radio 2003); f. Chrysalis Television mid-1990s, sold to All3Media 2003; Chair. Chrysalis Group PLC –2007, Exec. Chair. 2007–, acquired by BMG Rights Management 2010; Owner Queen's Park Rangers Football Club 1996–2001; Chair. London Wasps Holdings Ltd 1996–; Owner Stratford Place stud farm, Glos.; fmr Chair., British Phonographic Inst. early 1980s. *Honours:* British Phonographic Inst. Special Award 1983. *Address:* BMG Chrysalis US, 1745 Broadway, 19th Floor, New York, NY 10019, USA (office). *Telephone:* (212) 561-3000 (office). *Fax:* (212) 683-2040 (office). *Website:* www.chrysalis.com (office); www.bmgchrysalis.com (office).

WRIGHT, David, BSc, MSc; British musician, songwriter, producer and environmental scientist; *Permitting Officer, The Environment Agency;* b. 2 Feb. 1958, Colombo, Sri Lanka; m. Nicola Wright 1987; three s. *Education:* studied environmental sciences. *Career:* solo performer and with band The

Blue Mangoes 2006–; numerous live performances; currently Permitting Officer, The Environment Agency; mem. PRS/MCPS, PPL, PAMRA, Musicians' Union; own label Blue Balloon Records. *Compositions:* Kathy's Eyes 1996, Sign Your Life Away 1996, Lost in the Wilderness 2000, Distant Trains 2000, Shotgun 2000, Who's Kissing My Baby at Christmas? 2008, Slick 2008. *Recordings:* albums: Kathy's Eyes 1996, Lost in the Wilderness 2001, The Handkerchief Lady 2008. *Honours:* Top 10% Achievement Award, Unisong Song Contest 1998, featured in Mojo magazines Local Heroes section 1998, rootsmusic.co.uk Songwriter of the Month in Nov. 2004. *E-mail:* dwpublishing@tiscali.co.uk (home).

WRIGHT, Eugene Joseph; American musician (bass) and composer; b. 29 May 1923, Chicago, Illinois; m. 1st Jacqueline Winters, 29 May 1945, divorced 1954, 1 s., 1 d., m. 2nd Phyllis Lycett, 10 Aug. 1962. *Education:* Tilden Tech, Chicago, 1938. *Career:* nicknamed The Senator; Bandleader, Dukes of Swing Orchestra, 1943–46; Bassist with: Count Basie Orchestra; Gene Ammons/Sonny Stitt Quintet; Buddy DeFranco; Red Norvo; Arnett Cobb; Cal Tjader; Dave Brubeck; Monty Alexander, 1947–72; Billie Holiday, US and European tours, 1954; Duo, Money Tree, 1975–86; Bandleader, Eugene J Wright Ensemble, 1986–; Private music teacher, 1969–; Performed with B. B. King Blues Band, Linda Hopkins International Jazz Festival, Switzerland, 1988; Performed with Dave Brubeck Quartet, US State Dinner (for Presidents Reagan and Gorbachev), Moscow, 1988; mem, NARAS; AFofM. *Recordings include:* Monty Alexander; Count Basie; Dave Brubeck Quartet, Gerald Wiggins, Harry Belafonte. *Publications:* Bass Solos; Modern Music For Bass; Jazz Giants. *Honours:* Playboy Jazz Poll Award, 1964–66; Outstanding Voluntary Service Award, Los Angeles Human Relations Commission, 1988.

WRIGHT, Finbar; Irish singer (tenor); b. 26 Sept. 1959, Kinsale, Co. Cork; m. Angela Wright 1990; one s. one d. *Education:* studied with Ileana Cotrubas and Veronica Dunne. *Career:* Australian Tour, performed with Melbourne Symphony Orchestra 1994; performed with Montserrat Caballe, Dublin 1993; USA tour 1995; mem. The Irish Tenors vocal trio, appearances worldwide; mem. IMRO. *Compositions:* Blackwind 1998. *Recordings include:* albums: Because, Whatever You Believe, Live Tribute To John McCormack, Lift The Wings, I Give My Heart, Another Season 1999, The Essential Finbar Wright 2006; with The Irish Tenors: Live In Belfast 2000, Ellis Island 2001, We Three Kings 2003, Heritage 2004, Sacred 2005. *Honours:* IRMA Best MOR Artist 1992, IRMA Best Male Artist 1993. *E-mail:* kd@wmeentertainment.com. *E-mail:* finbarwright@hotmail.com. *Website:* www.finbarwright.com; www.theirishtenorsmusic.com.

WRIGHT, Mary Jean, (Gee Karlshonn); Panamanian musician, composer and conductor; b. 12 Oct. 1945. *Education:* Instituto Nacional de Música de Panamá, Univ. of Chile, Palacio de Bellas Artes, Dominican Repub., Acad. de Santa Cecilia, Rome, Univ. de Rosario, Argentina, Fla State Univ., USA). *Career:* teacher of Musical Educ., Panamá 1962–66; founder, Dir children's choir of Panama 1962–66; Prof. of Harmony, History and Musical Form, Conservatorio Nacional de Música de El Salvador 1975; writer of musical arrangements; Man. Artistic Dept and Production Chief of DECESA (subsidiary of RCA in Cen. America and Panama), El Salvador 1975–76; Dir of El Salvador Orchestra at Int. song festival, Caracas (Venezuela) 1979; Pres., Dir-Gen. Tukan Productions (jingles), Tukan Record and Tapes and Tukan-Alba Productions, Panamá 1981–; Nat. Supervisor of Music, Instituto Nacional de Cultura, Panamá, then Dir Instituto Nacional de Música 1991; has written jingles for Cen. and S American countries; composer of many works for orchestra and choirs. *Publications:* The Jingle as Substantial Element in Modern Advertising 1988, Compendio de Armonía Funcional 1989, Canciones para Lectura a Primera Vista 1991; Music: Elegía a Victoriano Lorenzo 1968, Rondo Espacial 1982, Fantasía Burlesque 1984. *Honours:* prize-winner at Festival of Children's Song, San Salvador 1979, Panama Rep. (composer, music arranger and conductor) to OTI Int. Song Festival, Brazil 1973, Acapulco, Mexico 1974, El Salvador Rep. to OTI Int. Song Festival, Madrid (fourth prize) 1977, First Prize First Belmont Song Fes. *Address:* Tukan-Alba Productions, Panamá, Panama.

WRIGHT, Maxwell; Spanish musician (percussion); b. Paris, France. *Education:* Dartington Coll. of Arts, UK. *Career:* brought up in Formentera and London; joined Ojos de Brujo 2000, a group which fuses gypsy and flamenco music with Latin American, punk, hip hop, reggae and electronic influences; Ojos de Brujo set up own label La Fábrica de Colores 2001 and since then operate as a completely ind. org.; plays the cajón drum and performs vocal 'beatboxing'; several tours in Europe, Latin America and USA; collaborations with Nitin Sawhney, Asian Dub Foundation; also performs with Acción-Reacción-Percusión trio. *Recordings include:* with Ojos de Brujo: Barí 2002, Barí: Remezclas de la Casa 2003, Techarí 2006, Aocaná 2009; other: Girando Bari (DVD) 2005. *Honours:* World Music Award for Europe, BBC Radio 3 2004. *E-mail:* max@ojosdebrujo.com. *Website:* www.ojosdebrujo.com.

WRIGHT, Michelle; Canadian singer, songwriter and musician (guitar); b. 1 July 1961, Chatham, Ont. *Career:* mem. Nat. Acad. of Recording Arts and Sciences, Acad. of Country Music, Country Music Asscn, Canadian Country Music Asscn, Canadian Acad. of Recording Arts and Sciences. *Recordings include:* Do Right By Me 1988, Michelle Wright 1990, Now and Then 1992, The Reasons Why 1994, For Me It's You 1996, Greatest Hits 2000, Shut Up and Kiss Me 2002, A Wright Christmas 2006, Everything and More 2008, Strong 2013. *Honours:* Canadian Country Music Asscn Awards for Top

Female Vocalist 1989, Top Female Vocalist 1991, Artist of the Year 1991, Top Country Single (for Take It Like a Man) 1992, Top Female Vocalist 1993, Artist of the Year 1993, Top Country Album (for Now and Then) 1993, Top Country Single (for He Would Be Sixteen) 1993, Top Female Vocalist 1994, Top Female Vocalist 1995, Hon. Spokesperson for Special Olympics 1996. *Current Management:* c/o Jump Events Inc., 15 Hazelton Avenue, Toronto, ON M5R 2E1, Canada. *E-mail:* ben@jumpevents.ca. *Website:* www.michelle -wright.com.

WRIGHT, Alexander James (Nod); British musician (drums, percussion, guitar, keyboards); b. 14 June 1966, Hertfordshire. *Education:* North Hertfordshire College. *Career:* mem., Fields of The Nephilim, renamed Rubicon; numerous European tours, two American tours, Reading Festival 1987, 1988, Loralei Festival (Germany); mem, PRS, Musicians' Union, BPI. *Recordings:* Fields of The Nephilim Discography 1984–91, Rubicon 1992–95; co-wrote, produced, albums: Dawnrazor, The Nephilim, Elizium, Revelations, What Starts Ends, Room 101, One More Nightmare. *Honours:* Best Album and Band, Melody Maker Readers Poll.

WRIGHT, Tony; British singer; b. Bradford, Yorkshire, England. *Career:* Founder-mem. rock group, The Spoilt Bratz 1986, renamed Terrorvision 1991–2001; numerous tours, TV appearances; Founder-mem. Laika Dog 2002; Owner and woodcut and letterpress artist, Oldfield Press, Haworth, West Yorkshire. *Recordings include:* albums: with Terrorvision: Formaldehyde 1993, How To Make Friends And Influence People 1994, Regular Urban Survivors 1996, Shaving Peaches 1998, Good To Go 2001, Whales And Dolphins: The Very Best Of Terrorvision 2001, The First And The Last 2001, B-Sides And Rarities 2005; with Laika Dog: Forever and A Day 2005.

WU, Bai; Taiwanese rock singer, songwriter, musician and actor; b. (Wu Chun-lin), 14 Jan. 1968, Suantou, Lioujiao, Chaiyi Prov., Taiwan; m. Chen Wen-pey 2003. *Career:* formed the band Wu Bai & China Blue, with Dean 'Dino' Zavolta (drums), Yu Ta-hao (keyboards), Chu Chien-hui (bass guitar) and himself on lead guitar and lead vocals 1992; commercial advertisements for Vitalon-P Plus-C, Taiwan Beer, Hey Song Sarsi, Golden Life Gold Jewellery Co. *Films include:* Zheng hun qi shi (The Personals) 1998, Meili xin shijie (A Beautiful New World) 1999, Seunlau ngaklau (Time and Tide) 2000, San ging chaat goo si (New Police Story) 2004, Arthur and the Minimoys (voice) 2007. *Television includes:* Say Yes Enterprise (series) 2004, In a Good Way 2014. *Albums include:* Loving Others is a Happy Thing 1992, Wanderer's Love Song 1994, The End of Love 1996, Lonely Tree, Lonely Bird 1998, (EP) 1998, White Dove 1999, Wu Bai & China Blue Movie Song Book/Time and Tide Soundtrack 2000, Dream River 2001, Tear Bridge (CD and VCD) 2003, Two Faced Man 2005, GO PA 2005, Innocent Years (CD and DVD) 2006, 1015 CD and DVD) 2007, Spacebomb 2008, Rock and Poetry (CD and DVD) 2009, One Way Ticket 2011. *Publications:* Moonlight Symphony 2001, Wandering Soul 2002, Scenery (book of his photography) 2007, Story 2009. *E-mail:* clubwubai@ gmail.com. *Website:* wubai.com.

WU, Bai; Taiwanese actor, musician, singer and songwriter; b. 1968, Chaiyi Province. *Career:* singer, songwriter with Wu Bai and China Blue 1993–. *Films:* A Beautiful New World 1998, The Personals, Time and Tide 2000. *Recordings include:* Fall in Love with Someone Else is Happy Thing 1992, End of Love 1996, Branches Solitary Bird 1998, White Dove 1999, Dreams of Rivers 2001, Tear Bridge 2004, Two-Face 2005, The Age of Innocence 2006, Drunkenly 1015 hits 2007, Space Bomb 2008, Poetic Rock 2009, One-way Ticket 2011, Endless Sorrow Shiny 2013. *Website:* www.wubai.com.

WU, Man; Chinese musician (pipa) and composer; b. 1963, Hangzhou, Zhejiang; m.; one s. *Education:* studied with Lin Shicheng, Kuang Yuzhong, Chen Zemin, and Liu Dehai, Cen. Conservatory of Music, Beijing. *Career:* an exponent of the Pudong School of pipa playing (Chinese lute); moved to USA 1990; fmr Bunting Fellow, Radcliffe Inst. of Advanced Study, Harvard Univ.; performs regularly with Yo-Yo Ma's Silk Road Project and the Kronos Quartet; collaborations with musicians and conductors including David Zinman, Yuri Bashmet, Cho-liang Lin, Dennis Russell Davies, Christoph Eschenbach, Gunther Herbig, Esa-Pekka Salonen, Michael Stern, David Robertson; first Chinese musician to perform at the White House; has performed numerous world premieres including Chen Yi's Ning! with Yo-Yo Ma, Bright Sheng's Nanking! Nanking! with NDR Radio Symphony Orchestra, Bright Sheng's Songs for Cello and Pipa with Yo Yo Ma, Ye Xiaogang's Pipa Concerto with RSO Radio Symphony Orchestra, Tan Dun's Ghost Opera with Kronos Quartet, Terry Riley's Cusp Of Magic with Kronos Quartet 2005, Chen Yi and Wu Man's Ancient Dances multimedia work 2005, Philip Glass' Sound of a Voice 2005; collaborated with Philip Glass and five other world musicians to create Orion, Cultural Olympiad, Athens 2004; has performed with leading orchestras including Austrian ORF Radio Symphony Orchestra, Boston Symphony Orchestra, Los Angeles Philharmonic New Music Group, Moscow Soloists, Nashville Symphony, German NDR and RSO Radio Symphony Orchestras, New York Philharmonic, Seattle Symphony Orchestra, Stuttgart Chamber Orchestra; concerts at venues including Carnegie Hall, New York, Amsterdam's Concertgebouw, Moscow Great Hall, Kennedy Center, Washington, DC, Lincoln Center, New York, Opera Bastille, Paris, Royal Albert Hall and Royal Festival Hall, London, Theatre de la ville, Paris; festival appearances include Bang on a Can Festival, Festival d'Automne, Paris, BBC Proms, Hong Kong Arts Festival, La Jolla Summerfest, Le Festival de Radio France, Lincoln Center Festival, NextWave!/BAM, Ravinia Festival, Silk Road Festival, Tanglewood, Wien Modern, Yatsugatake Kogen Festival,

Japan. *Honours:* first prize, First Nat. Music Performance Competition, China 1989, City of Toronto Glenn Gould Protégé Prize 1999. *Current Management:* Opus 3 Artists, 470 Park Avenue South, 9th Floor North, New York, NY 10016, USA. *Telephone:* (212) 584-7500. *Fax:* (646) 300-8200. *E-mail:* info@ opus3artists.com. *Website:* www.opus3artists.com; www.wumanpipa.org.

WU, Vanness; Taiwanese actor and singer; b. USA. *Career:* actor, Taiwanese television series, Meteor Garden, based on Japanese cartoon strip, Boys Are Prettier Than Flowers; mem. boy band, F4 (Flowers 4). *Television includes:* Meteor Garden 2002, Meteor Garden II 2003, Peach Girl 2002, Wish to See You Again 2008. *Recordings:* albums: Meteor Rain 2002, Fantasy 4ever 2003, Waiting For You 2007. *Address:* c/o Sony Music Entertainment (Taiwan) Ltd, c/o Sony/ATV Music Publishing Asia, Suite 2801-13, 28th Floor, Citic Tower, No. 1 Tim Mei Ave, Admiralty, Hong Kong (office).

WYATT, Robert; British composer and singer; b. 28 Jan. 1945, Bristol, England; m. Alfreda Benge 1974; one s. *Career:* numerous radio broadcasts; mem. PRS, MCPS, Musicians' Union, PAMRA. *Compositions:* Heaps of Sheeps, with Alfreda Benge 1997, September 9th, Alien, Out of Season, A Sunday in Madrid. *Recordings:* albums: The End of an Ear 1971, Rock Bottom 1974, Ruth Is Stranger Than Richard 1975, Robert Wyatt 1981, The Animals Film 1982, Old Rottenhat 1985, Dondestan (with poems by Alfreda Benge) 1991, Floatsam Jetsam 1994, Short Break 1996, Shleep 1997, Cuckooland 2003, Comicopera 2007, For the Ghosts Within (with Ros Stephen and Gilad Atzmon) 2010. *Publications:* MW (with J. M. Marchetti). *Honours:* Grand Prix du Disque, Academie Charles Cros. *Address:* c/o Domino Recording Company, PO Box 47029, London, SW18 1WD, England (office). *Website:* www .dominorecordco.com (office).

WYKES, Debsey; British singer, songwriter and musician (bass guitar); b. 21 Dec. 1960, London. *Career:* mem. all-girl band, Dolly Mixture 1978–84; numerous tours; backing vocalist, Saint Etienne. *Recordings include:* album: Demonstration Tapes 1983; with Captain Sensible: six singles include: Happy Talk 1982; with Coming Up Roses: I Said Ballroom (mini album); various backing vocals for Saint Etienne.

WYLIE, Pete; British singer, songwriter and musician (guitar); b. 22 March 1958, Liverpool. *Career:* Founder mem. Crucial Three 1977–78; Founder mem. Wah! Heat, later renamed Wah! 1979–84; mem. Sinful 1986; mem. Pete Wylie and Wah! The Mongrel 1991; solo artist; mem. Mighty Wah! 1998–. *Recordings include:* albums: with Wah!: Nah Poo: The Art Of Bluff 1981, The Maverick Years 1980–81 1982, A Word To The Wise Guy 1984, The Way We Wah! 1984; with Sinful: Sinful 1987; with Wah! The Mongrel: Infamy! or How I Didn't Get Where I Am Today 1991; with Mighty Wah!: Songs of Strength & Heartbreak 2000, The Handy Wah! Hole 2000. *Website:* www .petewylie.co.uk.

WYMAN, Bill; British musician (bass guitar); b. (William George Perks), 24 Oct. 1936, Lewisham, London; m. 1st Diane Cory 1959 (divorced 1968); one s.; m. 2nd Mandy Smith 1989 (divorced 1991); m. 3rd Suzanne Accosta 1993; three d. *Career:* Founder-mem. The Rolling Stones 1962–91; numerous tours and concerts world-wide; solo artist and mem. Willie and the Poor Boys 1985, Bill Wyman's Rhythm Kings 1998–2004; Owner WGW Holdings, WGW Enterprises, Wytel Music, Ripple Records, Ripple Music, Ripple Publications, Ripple Productions, KJM Nominees, Sticky Fingers Restaurant; Lord of the Manor of Gedding and Thormwoods 1968–. *Films include:* Sympathy for the Devil 1970, Gimme Shelter 1970, Ladies and Gentlemen the Rolling Stones 1974, Let's Spend the Night Together 1982, Digital Dreams 1983. *Recordings include:* albums: with The Rolling Stones: The Rolling Stones 1964, The Rolling Stones No. 2 1965, Out Of Our Heads 1965, Aftermath 1966, Between The Buttons 1967, Their Satanic Majesties Request 1967, Beggar's Banquet 1968, Let It Bleed 1969, Get Yer Ya-Ya's Out 1969, Sticky Fingers 1971, Exile On Main Street 1972, Goat's Head Soup 1973, It's Only Rock And Roll 1974, Black And Blue 1976, Some Girls 1978, Emotional Rescue 1980, Tattoo You 1981, Still Life 1982, Undercover 1983, Dirty Work 1986, Steel Wheels 1989, Flashpoint 1991; solo: Monkey Grip 1974, Stone Alone 1976, Green Ice (film soundtrack) 1981, Bill Wyman 1981, Digital Dreams (film soundtrack) 1983, Stuff 1991, Struttin' Our Stuff 1998, Anyway the Wind Blows 1999, Groovin' 2000, Double Bill 2001, Blues Odyssey 2001, Rude Dudes 2003, Just For The Thrill 2004; singles: with The Rolling Stones: Come On 1963, I Wanna Be Your Man 1963, Not Fade Away 1964, It's All Over Now 1964, Little Red Rooster 1964, The Last Time 1965, (I Can't Get No) Satisfaction 1965, Get Off Of My Cloud 1965, 19th Nervous Breakdown 1966, Paint It Black 1966, Have You Seen Your Mother Baby, Standing In The Shadow 1966, Let's Spend The Night Together/Ruby Tuesday 1967, We Love You 1967, Jumping Jack Flash 1968, Honky Tonk Women 1969, Brown Sugar 1971, Tumbling Dice 1972, Angie 1973, It's Only Rock 'N' Roll 1974, Fool To Cry 1976, Miss You 1978, Emotional Rescue 1980, Start Me Up 1981, Waiting On A Friend 1981, Undercover Of The Night 1983, Harlem Shuffle 1986, Mixed Emotions 1989, Rock And A Hard Place 1989, Highwire 1991; solo: (Si Si) Je Suis Un Rock Star 1981, Come Back Suzanne 1981, A New Fashion 1981, Groovin' 2000. *Publications include:* Stone Alone – The Story of a Rock and Roll Band (with Ray Coleman) 1990, Wyman Shoots Chagall 2000, Bill Wyman's Blues Odyssey (with Richard Havers) 2001, Rolling With The Stones (with Richard Havers) 2002, Bill Wyman's Treasure Islands 2005, The Stones: A History in Cartoons 2006. *Honours:* Nordoff-Robbins Silver Clef 1982, Grammy Lifetime Achievement Award 1986, Ivor Novello Award for Outstanding Contribution to British Music 1991, Blues Foundation Memphis Literary Award 2002. *Website:* www.billwyman.com.

WYNENS, René; Belgian musician (drums); b. 21 Aug. 1954, Bouwel; m. Helsen Anita 1974; one s. *Education:* Acad. of Music Herentals, studied with Jan Cuyvers. *Career:* music clip for Nova Star; founder, drummer rock and roll/beatgroup, Big Problem; mem. Belgian Drumclub, Dutch Slagwerkkrant, Modern Drummer. *Film appearances:* Brylcreem Boulevard, Karakter, Elixir d'Anvers, Gastons War, Left Luggage, Sono Pazzo di Iris Blond, De Bal, Lijmen Het Been, Iederee Beroemd. *Television appearances:* Wittekerke, Familie, Levensgevaar, Vennebos, Dokters, Gaston Berghmansshow '98 I and II, De Kampioenen, Engeltjs. *Recordings:* albums: Big Problem 1, Big Problem Rockers Look Out, Big Problem Look Out Again.

WYNNE, Michael Alexander, BA; composer, songwriter, record producer, arranger and musician (electric, acoustic guitars, mandolin, banjo); b. West Kirby, Merseyside, England. *Education:* Univ. of Newcastle. *Career:* part-time recording, live work, with Irish group Flynn and Wynne; tours include Holland, Germany, Singapore; worked in Karachi, 1989; producer, live all-star show, and pop album, singer Mohammed Ali Shiakhi; also film score

composition; producer, dance album, New York, 1993; television apperance with band Posh Monkeys, UK; mem, Musicians' Union; PRS; BAC&S. *Compositions:* musical, Baby and 3 Devils. *Recordings:* Shiakhi Speaks, The Wise Guys.

WYNONNA (see Judd, Wynonna)

WYSOCKI, Ben; American musician (drums, percussion). *Career:* mem., The Fray 2002–. *Recordings include:* album: How to Save a Life (Billboard Award for Digital Album of the Year 2006) 2005, The Fray 2009. *Honours:* Billboard Award for Digital Album Artist of the Year, for Digital Songs Artist of the Year 2006. *Address:* c/o Sony BMG, 550 Madison Avenue, New York, NY 10022, USA. *E-mail:* fraymanagement@gmail.com. *Website:* www.thefray.net.

WYSOCKI, Jon; American musician (drums); b. 17 Jan. 1971, Northampton, Mass. *Career:* mem. Staind 1995–2011. *Recordings include:* albums: Tormented 1996, Dysfunction 1999, Break The Cycle 2001, 14 Shades of Grey 2003, Chapter V 2005, The Illusion of Progress 2008. *Honours:* VH-1 'Your Song Kicked Ass But Was Played Too Damn Much' Award 2001.

X, Alan, BA, DipArch; British producer, writer, musician (keyboards) and DJ; b. 8 March 1958, London, England. *Education:* Sheffield Univ. *Career:* founder mem., Chakk; signed to MCA Records/Publishing 1985; signed solo publishing deal with Warner Chappell; f. XTrax record label, London 1991. *Compositions:* film soundtracks. *Recordings:* Set Me Free, Clubland; So In Love/Real Deal, Judy Cheeks; Lost 1996, Decibel 1996, Down 2 Da Disco 1999, Come 'N' Geddit 1999, The Carry On Gang 1999, Mardi Gras 2000, @It, 2000, Black Heat 2000, Magic & Miracles 2002, 2005. *Address:* PO Box 966, London, SE11 5SA, England.

X, Richard; British producer and songwriter; b. (Richard John Phillips), 1973. *Career:* fmrly released singles as Girls On Top 2001–02; writer and producer of many hit songs for numerous artists, including Annie, Ciara, Sugababes, Rachel Stevens, Kelis, Liberty X, Javine, Alesha Dixon, Saint Etienne, Pet Shop Boys, Soft Cell, Roisin Murphy, M.I.A.; remixed tracks by Depeche Mode, New Order, Nine Inch Nails, TLC, Yazoo. *Recordings include:* albums: Richard X Presents His X Factor Volume 1 2003, Back to Mine 2004. *Address:* Black Melody, PO Box 28057, London, SE27 0YB, England (office). *E-mail:* info@blackmelody.com (office). *Website:* www.blackmelody.com.

XIMENES, Charlson Pedro Vasconcelos; Brazilian songwriter, musician (guitar, bass guitar, drums, saxophone) and singer; b. 8 May 1965, São Caitano, Pernambuco. *Education:* Morley Coll., London. *Career:* mem. Esquadrilha da Fumaça, Déjà Vu, Nando Lynch; numerous radio broadcasts, TV appearances; mem. Musicians' Union. *Recordings include:* albums: with Esquadrilha da Fumaça: Tora Tora Tora 1984; with Deja Vu: Black Angel 1987, Love Me Tonite 1988, Collision Course 1998; with Nando Lynch: Never Around 2000. *Honours:* Amateur Theatre Background Music Award 1980 Second Prize, Northeastern Popular Music Festival, Belo Jardim Pe. *Current Management:* Charleston Firle, Lewes, BN8 6LL, England. *E-mail:* info@charleston.org.uk. *Website:* www.charlson.org.uk.

XIUMIN; South Korean singer; b. (Kim Min-seok), 26 March 1990, Guri, Gyeonggi Prov. *Career:* placed second, S.M. Everysing Contest 2008; trainee, SM Entertainment 2008–12; mem. K-pop boy band Exo 2012–; mem. subgroup Exo-M 2012–; debut single 2012; numerous TV and live appearances.

Television: EXO's Showtime 2013–. *Recordings:* albums: Mama 2012, XOXO (Mnet Asian Music Award for Album of the Year 2013) 2013. *Honours:* numerous awards including: for Exo: Mnet Asian Music Award for Best New Asian Artist/Group 2012, MTV Europe Music Award for Best Japan/Korea Act 2013, MelOn Music Award for Song of the Year (for Growl) 2013; for Exo-M: Top Chinese Music Award for Most Popular Group 2013. *Address:* c/o SM Entertainment, 521 Apgujeong 2-dong, Gangnam-gu, Seoul, South Korea (office). *Telephone:* (2) 6240-9800 (office). *Website:* www.smtown.com (office); exo.smtown.com (home).

XYLOURIS, Giorgos, (Psarogiorgis); Greek singer and musician (lute); b. 1965, Anogeia, Crete; s. of Psarantonis (Antonis Xylouris); three c. *Career:* Founder-mem. Xylouris Ensemble 1995–; Founder-mem. Xylouris White (with Jim White) 2013–; other collaborations including with Psarogiannis (uncle), All Together Now. *Recordings:* albums: with Xylouris Ensemble: Xylouris Ensemble 1995, Daphne 1996, Antipodes 1998, Drakos 2002, Antipodes 2003, Live in Melbourne 2010, In a Strange Land 2011; with Xylouris White: Goats 2014. *E-mail:* whitexylouris@gmail.com. *Website:* www.xylourisensemble.com; www.xylouriswhite.com.

XZIBIT; American rap artist and actor; b. (Alvin Nathaniel Joiner), 18 Sept. 1974, Detroit, Mich. *Career:* fmr mem. Likwit Crew; Founder-mem. Strong Arm Steady 1995–2006; solo artist 1996–; collaborations with numerous artists, including Snoop Dogg, Dre. *Films include:* The Breaks 1999, Tha Eastsidaz 2000, The Wash 2001, 8 Mile 2002, Full Clip 2004, Hoodwinked! (voice) 2005, xXx: State of the Union 2005, Derailed 2005, Gridiron Gang 2006, The X-Files: I Want to Believe 2008, Malice n Wonderland 2010, Something from Nothing: The Art of Rap 2012. *Television include:* CSI: Miami (episode, Rap Sheet) 2004, Pimp My Ride (host) 2004–06. *Recordings include:* albums: The Foundation 1996, At the Speed of Life 1996, 40 Dayz & 40 Nightz 1998, Restless 2000, Man vs Machine 2002, Weapons of Mass Destruction 2004, Full Circle 2006, Napalm 2012. *Current Management:* 360 Management, 9111 Wilshire Blvd, Beverly Hills, CA 90211, USA. *Telephone:* (310) 272-7000. *Fax:* (310) 272-0070. *Website:* www.management360.com; www.xzibit.com.

Y

YA KID K; Congolese/Belgian rap artist; b. (Manuela Barbara Moasco Kamosi), 26 Jan. 1973, Zaire. *Career:* moved to Belgium aged 11; mem. Antwerp-based rap group, Fresh Beat; mem., Technotronic; rap partnership with MC Eric. *Recordings include:* albums: with Technotronic: Pump Up the Jam 1990, Trip on this: Remixes 1990, Body to Body 1991, Back to Back 1999; solo: One World Nation 1992; singles: Pump Up the Jam 1989, Get Up 1990, This Beat is Technotronik 1990, Rockin' Over the Beat 1990; with Hi Tek: Spin that Wheel 1990; solo: Awesome 1991, Let this Housebeat Drop 1992, That Man 1993; with Robi-Rob's Clubworld: Shake that Body 1996. *Current Management:* c/o Nene Musik Productions, 1406 SW Santiago Avenue, Port St Lucie, FL 34953, USA. *Telephone:* (772) 807-8305. *Fax:* (772) 807-8306. *E-mail:* nenemusic@hotmail.com. *Website:* www.yakidk.com.

YAFFA, Sami; Finnish musician (guitar); b. (Sami Takamäki), 4 Sept. 1963; m. Karmen Guy. *Career:* mem. Hanoi Rocks during 1980s; mem. various other rock bands during 1990s; mem. Mad Juana 1995–; mem. New York Dolls 2004–06. *Recordings include:* albums: with Hanoi Rocks: Bangkok Shocks, Saigon Shakes, Hanoi Rocks 1981, Oriental Beat 1982, Self Destruction Blues 1982, Back to Mystery City 1983, Two Steps from the Move 1984; with New York Dolls: One Day It Will Please Us to Remember Even This 2006, Cause I Sez So 2009. *Address:* c/o Roadrunner Records, 902 Broadway, Eighth Floor, New York, NY 10010, USA (office). *Telephone:* (212) 274-7500. *E-mail:* roadrunner@roadrunnerrecords.com. *Website:* www.roadrunnerrecords.com; www.nydolls.org; www.samiyaffa.com.

YAGNIK, Alka; Indian singer; b. 20 March 1966. *Career:* film playback singer; All-India Radio artist in Kolkata; sang regularly for top dirs throughout 1980s; sang in Gujarati, Avadhi, Oriya, Assamese, Manipuri, Nepali, Rajasthani, Bengali, Bhojpuri, Punjabi, Marathi, Telugu, Tamil, English and Malayalam. *Films as singer:* Payal Ki Jhankar 1979, Hamari Bahu Alka (duet with Amit Kumar), Laawaris 1981. *Recordings include:* soundtracks: Mera Jawaab, 1985; Biwi Ho To Aisi, Qayamat Se Qayamat Tak, Tezaab, 1988; 100 Days, Saajan, Afsana Pyar Ka, Akayla, 1991; Deewana, Khiladi, Raju Ban Gaya Gentleman, 1992; Darr, Hum Hain Rahi Pyaar Ke, Anari, 1993; Akele Hum Akele Tum, Barsaat, Coolie No 1, Karan Arjun, 1995; Gupt, Ishq, Judaai, Pardes, Yes Boss, 1997; China-Gate, Ghulam, 1998; Baadshah, Dil Kya Kare, Dillagi, Hum Aapke Dil Mein Rehte..., Hum Dil De Chuke Sanam, Hum Saath-Saath Hain, Jaanam Sanjha Karo, Taal, 1999; Champion, Deewane, Dulhan Hum Le Jayenge, Har Dil Jo Pyar Karega, Josh, Kahin Pyaar Na Ho Jaaye, Kaho Naa... Pyaar Hai, Refugee, 2000; Albela, Bas Itna Sa Khwaab Hai, Choori Choori Chupke Chupke, Daman, Dil Chahta Hai, Ek Rishtaa – The Bond of Love, Kasoor, Lagaan, One 2 Ka 4, Pyaar Ishq Aur Mohabbat, Pyaar Tune Kya Kiya, Rahul, Yaadein, 2001; Dil Hai Tumhaara, Raaz, Kya Yehi Pyaar Hai, The Legend of Bhagat Singh 2002, Dil Ka Rishta, Tere Naam, Kal Ho Naa Ho, Mumbai Se Aaya Mera Dost, Koi... Mil Gaya 2003, Bride and Prejudice, Lakshya, Hum Tum, Swades 2004, Bewafaa, Lucky: No Time for Love, Maine Pyaar Kyun Kiya? 2005, Kabhi Alvida Naa Kehna, Umrao Jaan 2006, Saawariya, Big Brother, Marigold 2007, Slumdog Millionaire, Love Story 2050, Yuvvraaj 2008, Short Kut: The Con is On, Sanam Teri Kasam, Ada... A Way of Life 2009, Milenge Milenge, Judaaiyaan: The Separation 2010, My Husband's Wife, Kya Yahi Sach Hai 2011, Rajnigandha, Rang 2012, Bombay Talkies, Kaash Tum Hote 2013. *Honours:* Sugam Sangeet Award, four Filmfare Awards, two Nat. Awards.

YALE, Brian, BMus; American musician (bass guitar); b. 14 Nov. 1968. *Education:* Univ. of Miami. *Career:* mem. Tabitha's Secret 1993–96; bass player for Matchbox Twenty 1996–, numerous tours worldwide. *Recordings include:* albums: Yourself or Someone Like You 1996, Mad Season 2000, More than You Think You Are 2002, Exile on Mainstream 2007, North 2012. *Honours:* People's Choice Awards for Favorite Musical Group (Matchbox Twenty) 2004. *Website:* www.matchboxtwenty.com.

YAMAKOSHI, Brian Seiji; American musician (koto—Japanese harp) and composer; b. 29 Dec. 1957, Chicago, Ill. *Education:* Middlesex Polytechnic, Arizona State Univ. *Career:* TV appearances: numerous in Japan; Concon C'est Nous (France), NHK TV and radio, Japan, BBC Radio; mem. ASCAP, JASRAC, SACEM. *Films:* soundtrack: C'est quoi la vie? 1999. *Recordings include:* Snowflake (with Peter Gabriel), Akiko Yano (with Akira Inoue), World Diary (with Tony Levin), Manu Katché, Shanker 1996.

YAMASHITA, Tatsuro; Japanese singer, songwriter, musician (guitar, keyboards, percussion) and producer; b. 4 Feb. 1953, Tokyo. *Recordings include:* albums: Circus Town 1976, Spacy 1977, Go Ahead! 1978, Moonglow 1979, Ride on Time 1980, On the Street Corner 1 1980, For You 1982, Melodies 1983, Big Wave 1984, Pocket Music 1986, On the Street Corner 2 1986, Boku no Naka no Shonen 1988, Artisan 1991, Cozy 1998, On the Street Corner 3 1999, Sonorite 2005, Niagara Triangle Vol. 1 (with Ei-ichi Ōtaki and Ginji Ito) 2006, Ray of Hope 2011. *Current Management:* c/o Warner Music Japan Inc., 3-1-2 Ktta-Aoyama, Minato-ku, Tokyo 107-8639, Japan. *Telephone:* (3) 5412-3111. *Website:* www.smile-co.co.jp/tats.

YAN; British singer, musician (guitar) and songwriter; b. (Jan Scott Wilkinson), Cumbria. *Career:* Founder-mem. British Sea Power 2000–; the band runs Club Sea Power, a monthly variety show in Brighton, England; numerous live performances and festival appearances. *Recordings include:* albums: The Decline of British Sea Power 2003, Open Season 2005, Do You Like Rock Music? 2008, Man of Aran (film soundtrack) 2009, Valhalla Dancehall 2010, Machineries of Joy 2013. *Honours:* Time Out Award for Live Band of the Year 2004. *Address:* British Sea Power, 95 Beaconsfield Road, Hastings, TN34 3TW, England. *E-mail:* bspmanagement@googlemail.com. *Website:* www.britishseapower.co.uk.

YAN, Jerry; Taiwanese actor and singer; b. 1 Jan. 1977. *Career:* mem. boy band, F4 (Flowers 4) 2001–03, 2007–. *Television includes:* Meteor Garden 2002, Meteor Garden II 2003, The Hospital 2006, Hot Shot 2008, Down With Love 2009, My Splendid Life 2011, In Love We Trust 2012, Unforgettable Love 2013. *Recordings include:* albums: Meteor Rain 2002, Fantasy 4ever 2003, Waiting For You 2007; solo: Jerry for You 2004, Freedom 2009, My Secret Lover 2010. *Address:* c/o Sony/ATV Music Publishing Asia, Suite 2801-13, 28th Floor, Citic Tower No. 1 Tim Mei Avenue, Admiralty, Hong Kong Special Administrative Region, People's Republic of China (office). *E-mail:* jerryyan .info@gmail.com (office). *Website:* www.jerryyan.info.

YANDEL; Puerto Rican singer; b. (Landel Veguilla Malavé Salazar), 14 Jan. 1977, Cayey; m. Yomaira Ortiz 2008; one s., one d. *Career:* mem. of reggaeton duo Wisin & Yandel 1998–, debut release 2000; launched clothing line Los Lideres 2011; numerous collaborations including Aventura, Bone Thugs-n-Harmony, Hector 'El Bambino', 50 Cent, Enrique Iglesias, T-Pain, Jennifer Lopez, Daddy Yankee, Chris Brown, Don Omar, Ricky Martin. *Films:* Mi Vida 2003, Revolución 2011. *Recordings include:* albums: with Wisin & Yandel: Los Reyes del Nuevo Milenio 2000, De Nuevos a Viejos 2001, De Otra Manera 2002, Mi Vida... My Life 2003, Pa'l Mundo 2005, Los Extraterrestres (Premio Juventud for CD to Die For 2008, Billboard Music Award for Latin Rhythm Album of the Year – Duo or Group 2009) 2007, La Revolucion 2009, Los Vaqueros: El Regreso 2011, Lideres 2012. *Honours:* Premios Juventud for Favorite Video 2008, for Favorite Ringtone 2008, for Favorite Urban Artist 2008, Premios MTV Latinoamérica for Artist of the Year 2009, for Video of the Year 2009. *Address:* c/o Universal Music Latin Entertainment, Universal Music Group, 2220 Colorado Avenue, Santa Monica, CA 90404, USA (office). *Telephone:* (310) 865-5000 (office). *Website:* www.universalmusica.com (office); www.wisinyandelpr.com.

YANKOVIC, Alfred ('Weird Al'), BA; American musician (accordion), songwriter and actor; b. 23 Oct. 1959, Lynwood, Calif. *Education:* California Polytechnic San Luiz Obispo. *Career:* concert appearances, television and radio broadcasts; film, UHF 1989; f. Ear Booker Enterprises (production co.); mem. NARAS, BMI, AFofM. *Recordings include:* albums: Ricky 1983, Weird Al Yankovic In 3-D 1984, Dare To Be Stupid 1985, Polka Party 1986, Fat (parody of Michael Jackson: Bad) 1988, Peter And The Wolf 1988, UHF (soundtrack) 1989, Off The Deep End 1992, The Food Album 1993, Apalooza 1993, Bad Hair Day 1996, Running with Scissors 1999, Poodle Hat 2003, Straight Outta Lynwood 2006, Alpocalypse 2011, Mandatory Fun (Grammy Award for Best Comedy Album 2015) 2014; singles include: Eat It 1984, Like A Surgeon, 1985, Smells Like Nirvana 1992; compilation albums: Greatest Hits, 1989; Greatest Hits Vol. 2, 1994. *Publications:* The Authorized Al, autobiography by Al Yankovic and Tino Insana, 1985. *Honours:* Grammy Award for Best Comedy Recording (Eat It) 1988, for Best Video (for Fat) 1988. *Current Management:* Jan Levey, Imaginary Entertainment, 923 Westmount Drive, Los Angeles, CA 90069, USA. *Website:* www.weirdal.com.

YANNI; Greek composer and musician (keyboards); b. (Yanni Chryssomallis), 14 Nov. 1955, Kalamata. *Education:* Univ. of Minnesota, USA. *Career:* live performances and Tvv broadcasts world-wide; collaborations with World Wildlife Fund; spokesperson for NASA; soundtracks for TV and major sporting events such as Olympic Games, Super Bowl, Tour De France, PGA Gold Championships; concerts include: The Acropolis, Greece 1993, Royal Albert Hall, London 1995, Taj Mahal, India 1997, Forbidden City, People's Republic of China 1997, Yanni Voices El Morrow, Puerto Rico 2012. *Recordings include:* albums: Optimystique 1984, Keys to Imagination 1986, Out of Silence 1987, Chameleon Days 1988, Niki Nana 1989, Reflections of Passion 1990, In Celebration of Life 1991, Dare to Dream 1992, In my Time 1993, Yanni Live at the Acropolis 1993, In the Mirror 1997, Tribute 1997, If I Could Tell You 2000, Ethnicity 2003, Voices 2008, Voices 2009, Inspiring Journey 2010, Yanni Mexicanisimo 2010, Truth of Touch 2011, Yanni: Live at El Morro Puerto Rico 2011, My Passion for México 2012. *Honours:* two Grammy Awards. *Current Management:* c/o Disney Music Group, 500 South Burbank Vista Street, Burbank, CA 91521-0007, USA. *E-mail:* bmurray@ yanniwake.com. *Website:* www.yanni.com.

YANO, Akiko; Japanese singer and musician (piano, keyboards); b. 1955, Tokyo; m. Ryuichi Sakamoto (divorced 2006). *Education:* classical training. *Career:* child piano prodigy; familiar with jazz, pop and R&B at early age; working musician in Tokyo club scene during high school and began singing at this time; played on many albums as session musician in Japan; appeared in concert with Tin Pan Alley; recorded track album by Little Feat, Los Angeles; first solo album Japanese Girl 1976; participated in Yellow Magic Orchestra world tour 1979–80; double solo album co-produced by herself and her husband titled Gohan Ga Dekitayo (Dinner's Ready!) 1980; founded Akiko Yano Trio 2009. *Albums include:* Nagatsuki Kan Nazuki 1976, I Rohani

Konpeitou 1977, To Ki Me Ki 1978, Gohan Ga Dekitayo 1980, Tadaima 1981, Ai Ga Nakuchane 1982, O.S.O.S. 1984, Brooch 1986, Granola 1987, Welcome Back Akiko Yano 1989, Love Life 1991, Super Folk Song 1992, Love Is Here 1993, Elephant Hotel 1994, Piano Nightly 1996, Oui Oui 1997, Ego Girl 1999, Home Journey Girl 2000, Reverb 2002, Honto No Kimochi 2004, Hajimete No Yano Akiko 2006, Akiko 2008, Ongakudo 2010, Yano Akiko, Imawano Kiyoshirō o Utau 2013, Tobashite Ikuyo 2014. *Website:* www.akikoyano.com.

YARED, Gabriel; French film score composer; b. 7 Oct. 1949, Beirut, Lebanon; two c. *Education:* Saint Joseph Univ., Ecole Normale de Musique. *Compositions include:* Miss O'Gynie and the Flower Man 1974, Every Man for Himself 1979, Malevil 1981, Invitation au Voyage 1982, Sarah 1983, The Moon in the Gutter 1983, Hanna K. 1983, Adieu Bonaparte 1984, Dangerous Moves 1984, Fire on Sight 1984, Nemo 1984, Flagrant Desire 1985, Scout Toujours... 1985, Betty Blue 1986, Désordre 1986, Beyond Therapy 1987, Agent Trouble 1987, The Veiled Man 1987, Les Saisons du Plaisir 1988, Clean and Sober 1988, Camille Claudel 1988, Tennessee Nights 1989, Romero 1989, Vincent & Theo 1990, Tatie Danielle 1990, Sheherazade 1990, The King's Whore 1990, The Lover 1991, Map of the Human Heart 1992, L'Instinct de l'Ange 1992, The Ark and the Deluge 1992, IP5: The Island of Pachyderms 1992, The Girl in the Air 1992, The Groundhogs 1993, Low Profile 1994, Poorly Extinguished Fires 1994, Wings of Courage 1995, Hercule et Sherlock 1996, The English Patient (Acad. Award for Best Original Dramatic Score 1996, Golden Globe for Best Original Score 1996) 1996, La Dame du Cirque 1996, Tonka 1997, Premier de Cordée 1998, City of Angels 1998, The Talented Mr Ripley 1999, Message in a Bottle 1999, The Next Best Thing 2000, Autumn in New York 2000, Lisa 2001, L'Idole 2002, Possession 2002, The One and Only 2002, Bon voyage 2003, Les Marins perdus 2003, Sylvia 2003, Cold Mountain 2003, Shall We Dance 2004, L'Avion 2005, Das Leben der Anderen 2006, Azur et Asmar 2006, Breaking and Entering 2006, 1408 2007, Coco Chanel & Igor Stravinsky 2009, Amelia 2009, The Hedgehog 2009, In the Land of Blood and Honey 2011, A Royal Affair (with Cyrille Aufort) 2012, A Promise 2013, Haute Cuisine, 2013, In Secret 2013, Belle du seigneur 2013, Kahlil Gibran's The Prophet 2014, Tom at the Farm 2014. *Honours:* Commandeur, Ordre des Arts et des Lettres 1997; Grand prix de la musique 1984, Victoire de la musique 1986, 1989, 1992, 1998, César de la musique 1993, Indie award 1997, Grammy Award 1998, Critic's Choice Award 2000, British Acad. of Arts and Television Award 1997, 2004, Best Original Soundtrack of the Year (Cold Mountain) 2004, ASCAP Award. *Current Management:* c/o Laura Engel, kraft-Engel Management, 15233 Ventura Blvd, Suite 200, Sherman Oaks, CA 91403, USA. *Telephone:* (818) 380-1918. *Fax:* (818) 380-2609. *E-mail:* laura@kraft -engel.com. *Website:* www.gabrielyared.com. *Address:* 9 rue Jean-François Gerbillon, 75006 Paris, France (office). *Telephone:* 1-42-22-87-47 (office); 1-45-44-50-73 (office). *E-mail:* yad@yadmusic.fr. *Website:* www.gabrielyared.com.

YARLING, Nicole, BA, MA; American musician (violin) and singer; *Professor of Music, Florida Memorial College;* b. 31 July 1957, Brooklyn, New York. *Education:* Baruch Coll., Columbia Univ., studied violin, composition and arranging privately. *Career:* freelance, formed Ensemble Strings 1981–84; formed R&B rock band, Little Nicky and the Slicks 1985; featured soloist with Jimmy Buffett 1990–94; Prof. of Music, Florida Memorial Univ. 2003–, also at Univ. of Miami 2008–; mem. AFTRA. *Recordings include:* Strings Attached 1984, Little Nicky and the Slicks 1988, Fruitcakes 1994, Afro Blue Band 1997, N. Yarling 1999. *Publication:* Here's to Life. *Address:* Florida Memorial University, 15800 Northwest 42nd Avenue, Miami Gardens, FL 33054, USA (office). *Telephone:* (305) 626-3600. *E-mail:* info@nicoleyarling.net. *Website:* www.nicoleyarling.com.

YARROW, Peter; American singer, songwriter and film and television producer; b. 31 May 1938, New York. *Career:* mem. Peter, Paul & Mary 1960–70, 1978–; also solo artist 1970–; Co-founder, Kerrville Folk Festival, Tex.; mem. Bd of Dirs Newport Folk Festival, Center for Global Educ., N American Congress on Latin America, Friends of Vista. *Recordings include:* albums: with Peter, Paul & Mary: Peter, Paul & Mary 1962, (Moving) 1963, In the Wind 1963, In Concert 1964, A Song Will Rise 1965, See What Tomorrow Brings 1965, (untitled) 1966, 1700 1967, In Japan 1967, Late Again 1968, Peter, Paul & Mommy 1969, Ten Years Together 1970, Reunion 1978, Such is Love 1983, No Easy Walk to Freedom 1986, A Holiday Celebration 1988, Flowers and Stones 1990, Peter Paul & Mommy Too 1993, PP M& (LifeLines) 1995, Lifelines Live 1996, Around the Campfire 1998, Songs of Conscience and Concern 1999, In These Times 2004, Carry it On 2004, The Solo Recordings 1971–1972 2008, The Prague Sessions 2010, Live In Japan 1967 2010; solo: Peter 1972, That's Enough for Me 1973, Hard Times 1975, Love Songs 1975. *Publications include:* Favorite Folk Songs, Sleepytime Songs, Let's Sing Together!. *Honours:* Allard K. Lowenstein Award (for Human Rights, Peace and Freedom) 1982, Vista Citizen Action Leadership Award, World Folk Music Asscn Kate Wolf Memorial Award, Grammy Awards 1962, 1963, 1969, Songwriters Hall of Fame Lifetime Achievement Award 2006. *Current Management:* c/o Martha Hertzberg, Walk Street Management, 22 Wavecrest Avenue, Venice, CA 90291, USA. *Telephone:* (310) 399-5001. *Fax:* (310) 399-6350. *E-mail:* information@peterpaulandmary.com (office). *Website:* www .peterpaulandmary.com.

YASINITSKY, Gregory Walter, AA, BM, DMA; American composer, musician (saxophone) and academic; *Regents Professor of Music, Washington State University;* b. 3 Oct. 1953, San Francisco, Calif.; s. of Walter Yasinitsky and Gloria Yasinitsky; m. Ann Marie Kelley 1977; one d. *Education:* San Francisco State Univ., Eastman School of Music, composition studies with Joseph Schwantner, Wayne Peterson, Lou Harrison, Samuel Adler, Robert Morris, saxophone studies with Ramon Ricker, Joe Henderson, Donald Carroll, James Matheson and Jerry Vejmola. *Career:* Lecturer in Music, San Francisco State Univ. 1977–81; Lecturer in Music, San Jose State Univ. 1978–82, Lecturer, Jazz Studies 1977–80; Prof. of Music and Co-ordinator of Jazz Studies, Washington State Univ. 1982–2011, Dir School of Music 2011–, currently Regents Prof. of Music; Prin. Saxophonist, Spokane Symphony 1991; orchestral saxophonist with San Francisco Symphony, Oakland Symphony, Cabrillo Festival Orchestra; performances as jazz saxophonist with Sarah Vaughan, Lionel Hampton, Stan Getz, Clark Terry, Louis Bellson, Randy Brecker, Tom Harrell, Gary Burton, Mark Isham, Art Lande and Ray Charles; mem. American Soc. of Composers, Authors and Publrs (ASCAP), Jazz Educ. Network, Nat. Asscn for Music Educ., Soc. of Composers Inc. *Compositions include:* more than 185 works. *Publications include:* articles for Jazz Educators Journal, Band World, New Ways, Aftertouch, Saxophone Symposium, The Instrumentalist, Saxophone Journal. *Honours:* Mullen Award Excellence in Teaching, Washington State Univ. 1989, Jazz Fellowship, Nat. Endowment for the Arts 1986, ASCAP Special Awards for Composition 1986, Jazz Educator Award, Nat. Band Asscn 1989, Washington State Composer-in-Residence Award, The Commission Project 2000–03, Washington State Composer of the Year, Washington State Music Teachers Asscn 2002–03, Washington State University Eminent Faculty Award, Marian E. Smith Faculty Achievement Award, College of Liberal Arts Distinguished Achievement Award, Edward R. Meyer Distinguished Professorship Award 2005–08, Distinguished Faculty Address Award, Washington State Univ. 2008, Regents Professor Award, Washington State Univ. 2008, Marian E. Smith Distinguished Achievement Award in Teaching 2008, Washington Artist Trust Fellowship 2009–10, Eminent Faculty Award, Washington State Univ. 2011, inducted into Washington Music Educators Hall of Fame 2014. *Telephone:* (509) 335-2509 (office). *Fax:* (509) 335-4245 (office). *E-mail:* yasinits@wsu.edu (office). *Website:* libarts.wsu.edu/music (office).

YASU; Japanese musician (guitar); b. Tokyo. *Career:* Founder-mem. punk band, Nicotine 1994–; band formed its own record label, Sky Records 1997. *Recordings include:* albums: Royal Mellow Day 1996, ¡Hola Amigo! 1997, Will Kill You... (EP) 1998, Pleeeeeeeez! Who are You? 2000, Fitness Dayz 2001, Samurai Shot 2002, School of Liberty 2003, Hey Dude! We Love the Beatles 2005, Desperado 2006, Carnival 2006, Sound from the Schizoid Core 2006, Probably the Best 2007, Achromatic Ambitious 2007. *E-mail:* nicotine@ skyrecords.co.jp (office).

YATES, Mark; British musician (guitar); b. 4 April 1968. *Career:* Founder-mem. rock group, The Spoilt Bratz 1986, renamed Terrorvision 1991–2001; numerous tours, TV appearances. *Recordings include:* albums: Formaldehyde 1993, How To Make Friends And Influence People 1994, Regular Urban Survivors 1996, Shaving Peaches 1998, Good To Go 2001, Whales And Dolphins: The Very Best Of Terrorvision 2001, The First And The Last 2001, B-Sides And Rarities 2005, Super Delux 2011. *Current Management:* c/o Townsend Records, 30 Queen Street, Great Harwood, BB6 7QQ, England. *Website:* www.terrorvision.com.

YEARWOOD, Trisha; American country singer; b. 19 Sept. 1964, Monticello, Ga; m. 3rd Garth Brooks 2005. *Education:* Belmont Univ. *Career:* session singer, Nashville 1985–; solo artist 1991–. *Recordings include:* albums: Trisha Yearwood 1991, Hearts In Armor 1992, The Song Remembers When 1993, The Sweetest Gift 1994, Thinkin' About You 1995, Everybody Knows 1996, Songbook 1997, Where Your Road Leads 1997, Real Live Woman 2000, Inside Out 2001, Jasper County 2005, Heaven, Heartache and the Power of Love 2008. *Publications:* Georgia Cooking in an Oklahoma Kitchen 2008, Home Cooking with Trisha Yearwood 2010. *Honours:* American Music Award for Best New Country Artist 1991, Country Music Asscn Award for Female Vocalist of the Year 1997, 1998, British Country Music Award for Female Vocalist of the Year 1997, Grammy Award for Best Country Vocal Collaboration, for Best Female Country Performance 1998, Acad. of Country Music Award for Top Female Vocalist 1998. *Current Management:* c/o O'Neil Hagaman, PLLC, 3310 West End Avenue Suite 400, Nashville, TN 37203, USA. *Website:* www.trishayearwood.com.

YEEUN; South Korean singer and songwriter; b. (Park Ye-eun), 26 May 1989, Goyang Co. *Career:* collaborations with 8eight, San-E, H-Eugene; mem. Wonder Girls 2006–; first int. tour (including Thailand and USA) 2009; first S Korean group to enter the Billboard Hot 100 chart (with Nobody) 2009; world tour with Jonas Brothers 2009; supported Justin Bieber at Valentine's Day Concert 2010; toured USA and Canada with Wonder World Tour 2010; collaborated with Akon on single Like Money 2012; numerous festival appearances and tours. *Films:* The Last Godfather 2010, The Wonder Girls 2012. *Television includes:* MTV Wonder Girls 2006–10, Welcome to Wonderland 2009, Made in Wonder Girls 2010; numerous guest appearances. *Recordings include:* albums: The Wonder Years (Golden Disk Main Award Winners (Bonsang) 2007) 2007, The Wonder Years: Trilogy (Seoul Music Awards for Record of the Year in Digital Release 2009, Bonsang Award 2009, Daesang Award 2009) 2009, Wonder World 2011. *Honours:* Golden Disk Awards for Popularity 2007, Seoul Music Award for Best New Artist 2008, Korean Music Awards for Best Dance and Electronic Song (for Tell Me) 2008, for Group Musician of the Year Netizen Vote (for Wonder Girls) 2009, Golden Disk Awards Main Award Winners 2008, MNet KM Music Festival Awards for Best New Female Group 2007, for Song of the Year 2008, for Best Music Video (for Nobody) 2008, for Best Female Group 2008. *Current Management:* c/o

Creative Artists Agency, 162 Fifth Avenue, 6th Floor, New York, NY 10010, USA. *Address:* c/o JYP Entertainment, JYP Center, 123-50 Cheongdam-dong, Gangnam-gu, Seoul, South Korea (office). *Telephone:* (2) 3438-2300 (office). *Website:* www.jype.com (office); www.wondergirlsworld.com.

YELLE; French singer and songwriter; b. (Julie Budet), 17 Jan. 1983, Saint-Brieuc; d. of François Budet. *Career:* Founder-mem., Yelle (with Grand-Marnier and Tepr) 2005–; released debut single Je veux le voir 2005; debut album 2007; supported Mika on tour of France 2007; featured as MTV Artist of the Week, USA 2008; f. own record label, Recreation Center 2010; supported Katy Perry on UK tour 2011. *Recordings:* albums: Pop Up 2007, Safari Disco Club 2011, Complètement fou 2014. *E-mail:* yelle.mgmt@gmail.com. *Website:* www.yelle.fr.

YELLOW SOX (see Diesel)

YEN, Wen-hsiung, BA, MA, PhD; American (b. Taiwanese) musician (piano, erhu, guzheng), composer and conductor; *Music Director and Conductor, Chinese Music Orchestra of Southern California;* b. 26 June 1934, Tainan, Taiwan; m. Yuan Yuan 1961; three s. *Education:* Nat. Taiwan Normal Univ., Chinese Culture Univ., Univ. of California, Los Angeles, World Univ., studied piano with Qing-Yan Zhou, Fu-Mei Lee, composition with Paul Chihara Hsu, Chang-Houei and Mike Mitacek, ethnomusicology with Mantle Hood, Nazir Jarazbhoy, Timothy Rice and Ali Jihad Racy. *Career:* instructor, Taiwan Provincial Taichung Teacher Coll. 1961–62; Prof., Chinese Culture Univ. 1964–69; Founder, Music Dir and Conductor Chinese Music Orchestra of Southern California 1974–, The Yue You Chorus; Founder, Chinese Culture School, Los Angeles 1976–; Lecturer, West Los Angeles Coll. 1978–82; Faculty, Dept of Music, Univ. of Maryland 1982–83; Instructor, Los Angeles City Coll., California State Univ., Los Angeles 1984–, California State Univ., Northridge and Santa Monica City Coll. 1986–; Founder and Pres. Chinese Musicians' Asscn of Southern California 1990–; conducted orchestra for Dragon Boat Festival at Chinese Cultural Center, Chinatown, Los Angeles 1993 and for opening ceremony of annual Chinese Writers' Asscn of Southern California Conf. 1993; Prof. of Music, American Purlinton Univ. 2009–; Pres. Chinese Writers Asscn of Southern California 2008–; mem. Soc. for Ethnomusicology, Int. Council for Traditional Music, Soc. for Asian Music; Fellow, UCLA. *Compositions:* Drinking Alone in the Moonlight (words by L. Bai), Song of 911, Pure Even Tune (words by L. Bai), Roc Flies Ten Thousand Miles, Mother Earth – Four Seasons, The Phoenix Hair Pin (words by Lu You), Piano Suite for A Happy Reunion, Elements. *Recording:* East-West Music Concert (DVD) 2004. *Publications:* Taiwan Folk Songs Vol. I 1967, Vol. II 1969, A Dictionary of Chinese Music (co-author) 1967, A Collection of Wen-hsiung Yen's Songs Vol. I 1968, Vol. II 1987, Vol. III 2002, Chinese Musical Culture and Folk Songs 1989, A Study of Si Xiang Qi (article) 1989, Silk and Bamboo Expresses Emotion of Meaning 2000, Wen-hsiung's Composition Vol. 3 2000, Ethnomusicology Series. *Honours:* Confucius Commemorative Day Ceremony Outstanding Teacher Award, Los Angeles 1984, UCLA Assocs of Ethnic Artists Award, Fed. of Overseas Chinese Assocs Award 2000, 2002, Outstanding Teacher Award, Jt Teacher Coll. and Normal Univ. of Taiwan Alumni Assocn 2005, 16th World Chinese Cultural and Artistic Heritage Award 2010, Outstanding Chinese Purlinton Cerebrity Award 2013. *Address:* Chinese Culture School of Los Angeles, 615 Las Tunas Drive, Suite B, Arcadia, CA 91007 (office); 9458 Pentland Street, Temple City, CA 91780, USA (home). *Telephone:* (626) 447-3823 (office); (626) 318-7210 (home). *Fax:* (626) 447-3823 (office); (626) 447-3823 (home). *E-mail:* wenhyen2000@yahoo.com (office). *Website:* www.chinesecultureschool.net (office).

YERNJAKYAN, Lilit, PhD, DA; Armenian musicologist, ethnomusicologist, pianist and academic; *Professor, Komitas State Conservatory and Institute of Art of National Academy of Sciences;* b. 8 Feb. 1950, Yerevan; d. of Vardges Yernjakyan and Sona Odabashyan; m. Vladimir Gasparian; two s. *Education:* music school after Tchaikovsky, Yerevan, Komitas State Conservatory. *Career:* Bd mem. Union of Composers and Musicologists of Armenia. *Publications include:* four books and more than 80 articles, including From the History of Armenian-Persian Musical Ties 1991, Armenia : Hymn to the Sun, 'Sahari' (Armenian Musical Culture and EthnoMusicological Study) 1998, Armenia: Current Issues of Ashoogh Study in Armenia 2005, Ashogh Love Romance in the Context of Neareastern Musical Interrelations 2009. *Honours:* Honoured Artist of Armenia 2012; Certificate for Distinguished Work (Vastakagir), Presidium of Nat. Acad. of Armenia 2011. *Address:* Nalbandian Street 47, Apartment 19A, 0025 Yerevan, Armenia (home). *E-mail:* lilituk@yahoo.com.

YETNIKOFF, Walter R.; American record company executive; b. 11 Aug. 1933, Brooklyn, NY; m. June Yetnikoff, 24 Nov. 1957, two s. *Education:* BA, Brooklyn College, New York Bar, 1953; LLB, Columbia University, 1956. *Career:* Lawyer, New York, 1958–61; Attorney, CBS Records, 1961–65; General attorney, CBS Group, 1965–69; Vice-Pres., International Division, CBS, 1969–71; Pres., CBS International, 1971–75; Pres., CBS Group, 1975–; founder Velvet Records 1995, Commotion Records; mem, International Federation of Producers of Phonographs and Videograms. *Publications:* Howling at the Moon (autobiography; with David Ritz) 2004.

YILMAZ, Efe; Turkish musician (turntables); b. 3 Oct. 1979, Ankara. *Career:* mem., alternative rock band maNga 2002–13; concerts, festivals include Sziget Festival, Mannheim Turkish Rock Festival, also London. *Recordings include:* albums: maNga 2004, Şehr-i Hüzün 2009, e-akustik 2012. *Honours:* MTV Europe Music Award for Best European Act 2009. *Current Management:*

c/o Hadi Elazzi, GRGDN, Mübayacı sok. 5, Rumelihisarı, 34470 İstanbul, Turkey. *E-mail:* iletisim@grgdn.com. *Website:* www.grgdn.com. *Address:* c/o Sony Music Entertainment, Sony Music Türkiye, Ticaret A.Ş. Oteller Sokak 1/ 5, Tepebaşı, 34430 İstanbul, Turkey (office). *Website:* manga.web.tr.

YO! YO! HONEY SINGH, Honey Singh; Indian rapper, singer, arranger, record producer and actor; b. (Hirdesh Singh), 15 March 1983, Hoshiarpur. *Education:* Guru Nanak Public School, Punjabi Bagh, New Delhi, Trinity School, UK. *Career:* session and recording artist; Bhangra producer; collaborator, musical dir, arranger and producer for numerous acts including Alfaaz, Bai Amarjit, Raja Baath, Badshah, Nishawn Bhullar, Bopaz, Raj Brar, Varinder Brar, Dilijit Dosanjh, Preet Harpal, Garry Hothi, Karran Jesbir, Sunny Leone, Ashok Masti, Inderjit Nikku, Balli Riar, Rimz J, Bill Singh, Dolly Singh, Jassi Sidhu, Resham Singh Anmol. *Films:* as actor: Mirza 2012, Tu Mera 22 Main Tera 22 2013; contrib. to numerous Bollywood movie soundtracks including Punjaban 2010, Jihne Mera Dil Luteya 2011, Shakal Pe Mat Ja 2011, Cocktail 2012, Son of Sardaar 2012, Luv Shuv Tey Chicken Khurana 2012, Race 2 2012, Bajatey Raho 2013, Chennai Express 2013, Boss 2013, Yaariyan 2013, Dedh Ishqiya 2014, London 2014. *Recordings:* albums: I.V. (International Villager) (PTC Punjabi Best Music Dir Award 2012, UK Asian Music Award for Best Int. Album 2012), Brown Rang (MTV VMAI Award for Best Indi Artist (Male) 2013. *Honours:* ETC Award for Best Sound 2006, PTC Best Folk Pop Award 2009, PTC Punjabi Best Music Dir 2010, 2011, BritAsia Best Int. Act 2012, MTV Europe Music Award for Best Indian Act 2013. *Website:* www.acmeentertainment.in. *Address:* c/o Mafia Mundeer Records, India (office). *Telephone:* (91) 9814044124 (office); (91) 9872666363 (office). *Website:* www.yoyohoneysingh.com (home).

YOAKAM, Dwight; American country singer, musician (guitar), songwriter and actor; b. 23 Oct. 1956, Pikeville, Ky. *Education:* Ohio Univ. *Career:* solo artist 1978–; numerous tours. *Films:* Red Rock West 1992, The Little Death 1995, Sling Blade 1996, Painted Hero 1996, The Newton Boys 1998, The Minus Man 1999, South of Heaven, West of Hell (also dir) 2000, Panic Room 2002, Hollywood Homicide 2003, 3-Way 2004, The Three Burials of Melquiades Estrada 2005, Wedding Crashers 2005, Bandidas 2006, Crank 2006, Four Christmases 2008, Crank: High Voltage 2009, The Last Rites of Ransom Pride 2010, Bloodworth 2010. *Television films:* Roswell 1994, Don't Look Back 1996, When Trumpets Fade 1998. *Recordings include:* albums: Guitars, Cadillacs, Etc., Etc. 1986, Hillbilly Deluxe 1987, Buenas Noches From A Lonely Room 1988, Just Looking For A Hit 1989, If There Was A Way 1990, La Croix D'Amour 1992, This Time 1993, Dwight Live 1995, Gone 1996, Under The Covers 1997, Come On Christmas 1997, A Long Way Home 1998, dwightyoakamacoustic.net 2000, Tomorrow's Sounds Today 2000, South Of Heaven, West Of Hell 2001, Population Me 2003, In Others' Words 2003, Blame The Vain 2005, Dwight Sings Buck 2007, 3 Pears 2012, Second Hand Heart 2015. *Honours:* Acad. of Country Music Award for Best New Male Artist 1986, Music City News Country Award for Best Vocal Collaboration (for Streets of Bakersfield, with Buck Owens) 1988, Grammy Awards for Best Country Male Vocal Performance 1994, for Best Country Collaboration with Vocals 1999, Cliffie Stone Pioneer Award 2011, Americana Music Award for Artist of the Year 2013. *Current Management:* c/o Gary Ebbins/Fitzgerald Hartley Company, c/o Etc. Etc. Communications, 7920 Sunset Blvd, Suite 460, Los Angeles, CA 90046, USA. *Website:* www.dwightyoakam.com.

YOAV; Israeli/South African musician (guitar); b. (Yoav Sadan), 15 Oct. 1979, Israel. *Career:* grew up in South Africa; solo artist 2006–. *Recordings include:* album: Charmed & Strange 2008, A Foolproof Escape Plan 2010, Blood Vine 2012. *Address:* PHI Group Inc., 356 rue Le Moyne, Suite 100, Montréal, PQ H2Y 1Y3, Canada (office). *E-mail:* info@phi-montreal.com (office). *Website:* phi -montreal.com (office). *E-mail:* yoavcontact@gmail.com. *Website:* www .yoavmusic.com.

YODA, Mustafa, (Frestylity); Argentine hip-hop artist. *Career:* mem. La Organización 1998–2001; solo artist 2001–. *Recordings include:* album: Cuentos de Chicos Para Grandes 2004, Prisma Elemental 2006, Imaquinar 2008, La Poderosa 2012. *Honours:* Freestyle Nat. Champion 2002, 2003. *E-mail:* management@mustafayoda.com.

YOGESWARAN, Manickam; Sri Lankan singer and musician (South Indian flute, drums); b. 3 March 1959. *Education:* studied accountancy, CIMA. *Career:* concert singer, musician, Indo-pop music; lead singer, Dissidenten 1993–; Visiting Lecturer for Music Workshop Skills, Goldsmiths Coll., London, England; regular appearances in the December Music Festival, Chennai 1994–; mem. Musicians' Union. *Recordings include:* seven albums 1990–94. *Honours:* London Sri Murugan Temple Kalai Mamani Award, Oslo Music Asscn Suranaya Devan Award. *E-mail:* yoga@yogeswaran.com. *Website:* www.yogeswaran.com.

YOKOHAMA, Ken; Japanese singer and musician (guitar). *Career:* founder mem., Hi-Standard 1991–. *Recordings include:* albums: Growing Up 1992, Angry Fist 1995, Making the Road 1999, Kids Are Alright 2002; singles: California Dreamin', Survival Of The Fattest, Punk Uprising, Love Is A Battlefield 2001, Last Of Sunny Day 2002. *Address:* c/o Fat Wreck Chords, PO Box 193690, San Francisco, CA 94119-3690, USA (office). *E-mail:* mailbag@ fatwreck.com (office). *Website:* www.fatwreck.com (office).

YÖLNEN, Lauri Johannes; Finnish singer and songwriter; b. 23 April 1979, Helsinki. *Career:* mem. The Rasmus 1994–; solo artist; collaborations with numerous artists including Ville Valo. *Recordings include:* albums: Peep 1996,

Playboys (Emma Award) 1997, Hell Of A Tester 1998, Into 2001, Dead Letters 2003, Hide From The Sun 2005, Black Roses 2008, Best of 2001-2009 2009, The Rasmus 2012; solo: New World 2011. *Honours:* Emma Award for Best New Artist 1996, MTV Europe Music Award Best Finnish Act 2005.

YORK, Taylor Benjamin; American guitarist and songwriter; b. 17 Dec. 1989, Nashville, Tenn.; s. of Peter York. *Career:* touring mem. Paramore 2007–09, full-time mem. 2009–. *Recordings:* album: with Paramore: Brand New Eyes (Kerrang! Best Album Award 2010) 2009, Paramore 2013. *Honours:* with Paramore: Kerrang! Best New Band Award 2006, MTV Europe Music Award for Best Alternative Act 2010, NME Best Int. Band Award 2010, People's Choice Favorite Rock Band Award 2010, 2011, Grammy Award for Best Rock Song (for Ain't It Fun) 2015. *Current Management:* c/o Fly South Music Group, 189 South Orange Avenue #1100, Orlando, FL 32801, USA. *Telephone:* (407) 841-6169. *Fax:* (407) 650-2664. *E-mail:* info@flysouthmusic .com. *Website:* www.flysouthmusic.com. *Address:* c/o Fueled by Ramen Records, PO Box 1803, Tampa, FL 33601, USA (office). *Website:* www .fueledbyramen.com (office); www.paramore.net.

YORKE, Thomas (Thom) Edward; British singer, songwriter and musician (guitar, keyboards); b. 7 Oct. 1968, Wellingborough, Northamptonshire, England; one s. *Education:* Univ. of Exeter. *Career:* mem. and lead singer, On A Friday 1985, renamed Radiohead 1991–; also designer of record sleeves; numerous tours, festivals and television appearances; guest vocalist with Drugstore on White Magic for Lovers and El President 1998; guest vocalist with Velvet Goldmine 1998, MTV's 120 Minutes Live 1998; other collaborations include UNKLE, P. J. Harvey; founding mem. Atoms for Peace 2009–. *Recordings include:* albums: with Radiohead: Pablo Honey 1993, The Bends 1995, OK Computer (Grammy Award for Best Alternative Music Performance) 1997, Kid A (Grammy Award for Best Alternative Music Album) 2000, Amnesiac 2001, I Might Be Wrong (live recordings) 2001, Hail To The Thief 2003, In Rainbows (Ivor Novello Album Award 2008, Grammy Award for Best Alternative Music Album 2009) 2007, The King of Limbs 2011; solo: The Eraser 2006, Tomorrow's Modern Boxes 2014; with Atoms for Peace: Amok 2013. *Honours:* Q Award for Best Act in the World Today 2001, 2002, 2003. *Current Management:* Courtyard Management, 21 The Nursery, Sutton Courtenay, Abingdon, Oxfordshire OX14 4UA, England. *Website:* www.radiohead.com.

YORN, Peter J.; American singer and songwriter; b. 27 July 1974, New Jersey. *Education:* Montville High School and Syracuse Univ. *Recordings include:* albums: musicforthemorningafter 2001, Day I Forgot 2003, Nightcrawler 2006, Back and Fourth 2009, Break Up (with Scarlett Johansson) 2009, Pete Yorn 2010. *Current Management:* c/o Fresh and Clean Media, 12701 Venice Blvd, Los Angeles, CA 90066, USA. *E-mail:* sandee@ freshcleanmedia.com. *Website:* www.peteyorn.com.

YOSHIDA, Takuro; Japanese folk singer; b. 5 April 1946, Okuchi, Kagoshima. *Education:* Sophia Univ., Tokyo. *Career:* solo artist 1970–. *Recordings include:* albums: Seishun no Uta 1968, Ningen nante 1971, Oinaru Hito 1977, Roringu 30 1978, Shangri-la 1980, Mujinto de 1981, Jonetsu 1983, Forever Young 1984, Ore ga Aishita Baka 1985, Samarukando Buru 1986, Much Better 1988, Himawari 1989, 176.5 1990, Yoshida-cho no Uta 1992, Long Time No See 1995, Kando Ryoko Namitakashi 1996, Minna Daisuki 1997, Hawaiian Rhapsody 1998, The Best Penny Lane 1999, Yoshida no Uta 2001.

YOSHIHIDE, Ōtomo; Japanese musician (guitar and turntable) and composer; b. 1 Aug. 1959, Yokohama. *Education:* Meiji Univ. *Career:* joined Player Piano 1990; mem. Ground Zero 1990–98; f. electronic groups Filament and I. S. O; f. Ōtomo Yoshihide's New Jazz Ensemble; led Double Unit Orchestra 1992–94; mem. quartet FEN (Far East Network); fmr mem. Mosquito Paper, Sampling Virus Project. *Recordings include:* numerous albums, including Yoshihide Otomo 1987, Null and Void 1993, Cathode 1999, Anode 2001, Otomo Yoshihide's New Jazz Orchestra 2005, Modulation With 2 Electric Guitars and 2 Amplifiers 2008, Donaueschinger Musiktage 2005: Allurements of the Ellipsoid 2011; numerous recordings with various groups. *E-mail:* postmaster@doubtmusic.com.

YOUNG, Adrian; American musician (drums); b. 26 Aug. 1969, Long Beach, CA; one s. *Career:* mem., No Doubt 1989–. *Recordings:* albums: No Doubt, 1992; Beacon Street Collection, 1994; Tragic Kingdom, 1995; Return Of Saturn, 2000; Rock Steady, 2001; Everything In Time 2004, Push and Shove 2012; singles: Just A Girl, 1995; Don't Speak (No. 1, UK), 1997; New, 1999; Ex-Girlfriend, 2000; Simple Kind Of Life, 2000; Bathwater, 2000; Hey Baby, 2001; Hella Good, 2002; Tour (EP), 2002; Underneath It All, 2002. *Address:* c/o Interscope Records, 2220 Colorado Avenue, Santa Monica, CA 90404, USA. *Website:* www.nodoubt.com.

YOUNG, Angus; British musician (guitar); b. 31 March 1959, Glasgow, Scotland. *Career:* Founder mem. Australian heavy rock group, AC/DC 1973–; numerous tours worldwide, festival appearances. *Recordings include:* albums: High Voltage 1975, TNT 1975, High Voltage 1975, Dirty Deeds Done Dirt Cheap 1976, Let There Be Rock 1977, Powerage 1978, Highway to Hell 1979, Back in Black 1980, For Those About to Rock 1981, Flick of the Switch 1983, Fly on the Wall 1985, Who Made Who (soundtrack) 1986, Blow Up Your Video 1988, The Razor's Edge 1990, Ballbreaker 1995, Volts 1997, Private Parts 1997, Bonfire 1997, Stiff Upper Lip 2000, Satellite Blues 2001, Black Ice 2008, Rock or Bust 2014. *Honours:* Kerrang! Legend Award 2006, Grammy Award for Best Hard Rock Performance (for War Machine) 2010. *Website:* www.acdc.com.

YOUNG, Christopher; Composer and Musician (drums); b. 28 April 1957, Red Bank, NJ, USA. *Education:* UCLA. *Career:* mem. BMI. *Compositions:* for television: The Twilight Zone 1985, Vietnam War Story 1987, American Harvest 1987, Vietnam War Story: The Last Days 1989, Hider in the House 1989, Last Flight Out 1990, Max and Helen 1990, Norma Jean and Marilyn 1996; for film: The Power 1980, Highpoint 1980, The Dorm That Dripped Blood 1981, Wheels of Fire 1984, The Oasis 1984, Def-Con 4 1984, Wizards of the Lost Kingdom 1985, A Nightmare on Elm Street Part 2: Freddy's Revenge 1985, Barbarian Queen 1985, Godzilla 1985, Avenging Angel 1985, Trick or Treat 1986, Torment 1986, Getting Even 1986, Invaders from Mars 1986, Hellraiser 1987, Flowers in the Attic 1987, Hellbound: Hellraiser II 1988, Haunted Summer 1988, Bat-21 1988, The Fly II 1989, Bright Angel 1991, Jennifer Eight 1992, The Vagrant 1992, Rapid Fire 1992, Dark Half 1993, Judicial Consent 1994, Dream Lover 1994, Murder in the First 1995, Tales from the Hood 1995, Species 1995, Virtuosity 1995, Copycat 1995, Unforgettable 1996, Set It Off 1996, Head Above Water 1996, Murder at 1600 1997, Man Who Knew Too Little 1997, Rounders 1998, Hard Rain 1998, Hush 1998, Urban Legend 1998, Entrapment 1999, In Too Deep 1999, Hurricane 1999, Bless the Child 2000, Big Kahuna 2000, Wonder Boys 2000, Scenes of the Crime 2001, The Devil and Daniel Webster 2001, Madison 2001, The Warden 2001, The Gift 2001, Sweet November 2001, The Glass House 2001, Bandits 2001, The Shipping News 2001, Dragonfly 2002, The Tower 2002, The Country Bears 2002, Something's Gotta Give 2003, The Core 2003, Shade 2003, Runaway Jury 2003, Something the Lord Made 2004, The Grudge 2004, An Unfinished Life 2005, Miss Congeniality 2: Armed & Fabulous 2005, Beauty Shop 2005, The Exorcism of Emily Rose 2005, Ask the Dust 2006, The Grudge 2 2006, Dark Ride 2006, Ghost Rider 2007, Lucky You 2007, Spider-Man 3 2007, The Messengers 2007, Untraceable 2008, Sinister 2012. *Honours:* Composer of the Year, Scorelogue.com 1999; BMI Scoring Award, for Entrapment, Swordfish, The Grudge; Best Score, Saturn Award, for Hellbound: Hellraiser II; LA Film Critics Award, for Swordfish. *Current Management:* First Artists Management, 16000 Ventura Blvd, Suite 605, Encino, CA 91436, USA. *E-mail:* cyoung4700@aol.com. *Website:* www.christopher-young .com.

YOUNG, James Jeffrey; American country music guitarist; m. Abby Young 2012. *Education:* Univ. of North Texas. *Career:* formed Eli & Young duo with Mike Eli, during late 1990s; Founder-mem. Eli Young Band 2000–. *Recordings:* albums: with Eli Young Band: Eli Young Band 2002, Level 2005, Jet Black & Jealous 2008, Life at Best 2011, 10,000 Towns 2014. *Honours:* Acad. of Country Music Award for Song of the Year 2012, MusicRow Breakthrough Artist Award 2012. *Current Management:* c/o George Couri, Triple 8 Management, 5524 West Highway 290, Austin, TX 78735, USA. *Telephone:* (512) 444-7600. *Fax:* (512) 444-7601. *Website:* www.eliyoungband.com.

YOUNG, Jesse Colin, (Perry Miller); American singer and musician (guitar, bass); b. 11 Nov. 1944, New York. *Career:* began as solo folk singer, New York early 1960s; founder mem., The Youngbloods 1965–72; numerous festival and concert appearances; resumed solo career 1972–2004. *Film:* No Nukes 1979. *Compositions include:* Get Together (recorded by Dave Clark Five) 1970. *Recordings include:* albums: with The Youngbloods: The Youngbloods 1967, Earth Music 1967, Elephant Mountain 1969, Rock Festival 1970, Ride The Wind 1971, Good 'n' Dusty 1971, High On A Ridgetop 1972; solo: Soul of a City Boy 1963, Young Blood 1964, Together 1972, Song For Juli, 1973, Light Shine 1974, Songbird 1975, On The Road 1975, Love On The Wing 1976, American Dreams 1978, Perfect Stranger 1979, Highway is for Heroes 1987, Makin' It Real 1993, Swept Away 1994, Sweetwater 1995, Greatest Hits 1998, Walk the Talk 2001, Songs for Christmas 2002, Living in Paradise 2004, Keep On Burning 2004, Celtic Mambo 2006. *Current Management:* Skyline Music, PO Box 31, Lancaster, NH 03584, USA. *Address:* BeanBag1 Entertainment, 37101 Highway 1, Monterey, CA 93940, USA (office). *Telephone:* (831) 625-1851 (office). *Fax:* (831) 625-1809 (office). *E-mail:* db@beanbag1.com (office). *Website:* www.beanbag1.com; www.jessecolinyoung.com (home).

YOUNG, Malcolm; British musician (guitar); b. 6 Jan. 1953, Glasgow, Scotland; m. Linda Young; two c. *Career:* Founder-mem. Australian heavy rock group, AC/DC 1973–2014; numerous tours worldwide, festival appearances. *Recordings include:* albums: High Voltage 1975, TNT 1975, High Voltage 1975, Dirty Deeds Done Dirt Cheap 1976, Let There Be Rock 1977, Powerage 1978, Highway to Hell 1979, Back in Black 1980, For Those About to Rock 1981, Flick of the Switch 1983, Fly on the Wall 1985, Who Made Who (soundtrack) 1986, Blow Up Your Video 1988, The Razor's Edge 1990, Ballbreaker 1995, Volts 1997, Private Parts 1997, Bonfire 1997, Stiff Upper Lip 2000, Satellite Blues 2001, Black Ice 2008. *Honours:* Grammy Award for Best Hard Rock Performance (for War Machine) 2010. *Website:* www.acdc .com.

YOUNG, Neil, (Bernard Shakey); Canadian singer, songwriter and musician (guitar); b. 12 Nov. 1945, Toronto, Ont.; m. Pegi Young; one s. one d. *Career:* fmr lead singer, The Squires; with Buffalo Springfield 1966–69; with Crosby, Stills, Nash and Young 1969–74; solo artist with own backing group, Crazy Horse 1969–. *Films:* Journey Through the Past (dir) 1974, Rust Never Sleeps (dir) 1979, Human Highway (writer and dir) 1982, Made in Heaven (actor) 1987, '68 (actor) 1988, Freedom (actor) 1989, Love at Large (actor) 1990, Weld (actor) 1990, Year of the Horse (exec. producer) 1997, Greendale (writer, dir, actor, producer) 2003, Neil Young: Heart of Gold 2006, CSNY/Déjà Vu (writer, dir, score) 2008. *Recordings include:* albums: with Buffalo Springfield: Buffalo Springfield 1967, Last Time Around 1968; with Crosby, Stills, Nash and

Young: Déjà Vu 1970, Four Way Street 1971; solo: Neil Young 1969, Everybody Knows This Is Nowhere 1969, After The Goldrush 1970, Crazy Horse 1971, Harvest 1972, Journey Through The Past 1972, Time Fades Away 1973, On The Beach 1974, Tonight's The Night 1975, Zuma 1975, Long May You Run 1976, American Stars 'N' Bars 1977, Comes A Time 1978, Rust Never Sleeps 1979, Live Rust 1980, Where The Buffalo Roam (OST) 1980, Hawks & Doves 1980, Re-ac-tor 1981, Trans 1983, Everybody's Rockin' 1983, Old Ways 1985, Landing On Water 1986, Life 1987, This Note's For You 1988, Freedom 1989, Ragged Glory 1990, Arc 1991, Weld 1991, Harvest Moon 1992, Unplugged 1993, Sleeps With Angels 1994, Mirror Ball 1995, Dead Man (OST) 1996, Broken Arrow 1996, Year Of The Horse 1997, Silver & Gold 2000, Are You Passionate? 2002, Greendale (OST) 2003, Prairie Wind (Juno Award for Best Adult Alternative Album 2006) 2005, Living With War 2006, Chrome Dreams II 2007, Fork in the Road 2009, Le Noise 2010, Psychedelic Pill 2012, A Letter Home 2014, Storytone 2014, The Monsanto Years 2015. *Publication:* Waging Heavy Peace (memoir) 2012. *Honours:* Grammy Award for Best New Artist 1970, Melody Maker Poll Winner for Best Int. Group 1971, MTV Video Award 1989, Rolling Stone Critics' Award for Best Album 1989, Bay Area Music Award for Outstanding Album 1993, Q Award for Best Live Act 1993, Juno Award for Best Producer 2006, Americana Award for Artist of the Year 2006, Grammy Award for Best Rock Song (for Angry World) 2011, inducted into Rock and Roll Hall of fame 1995 (as solo artist) and 1997 (as mem. of Buffalo Springfield). *Current Management:* c/o Elliot Roberts, Lookout Management, 1460 Fourth Street, Suite 210, Santa Monica, CA 90404, USA. *Website:* www.neilyoung.com.

YOUNG, Paul; British singer and musician (guitar); b. 17 Jan. 1956, Luton, Bedfordshire; m. Doris Elizabeth Young; one s. two d. *Career:* mem. the Streetband –1979, the Q-Tips 1979–82; solo artist 1982–, with backing band the Royal Family; numerous tours and live performances world-wide; Founder-mem. country/rock band, Los Pacaminos mid-1990s. *Recordings include:* albums: No Parlez 1983, The Secret of Association 1985, Between Two Fires 1986, Other Voices 1990, Crossing 1993, Reflections 1995, Paul Young 1997, From Time to Time 1998, Love Songs 2000, Love Will Tear Us Apart 2003, Love Swings 2006. *Current Management:* c/o What Management, 3 Belfry Villas, Belfry Avenue, Harefield, UB9 6HY, England. *Telephone:* (1895) 824674. *E-mail:* whatmanagement1@blueyonder.co.uk. *Website:* www.paul-young.com.

YOUNG, Amita Marie (Tata); Thai singer and actress; b. 14 Dec. 1980, Bangkok. *Recordings include:* albums: Amita Tata Young 1995, Amazing Tata 1997, Tata Young 2001, Real TT 2003, I Believe 2004, Dangerous Tata 2005, Temperature Rising 2006. *Honours:* MTV Asia Award for Favourite Artist (Thailand) 2006. *Current Management:* c/o Tim Young, Tata Entertainment Co., Kamoi Sukosol Bldg, Floor 12A, Suite E, 317 Silom Road, Bangkok 10500, Thailand. *Website:* www.tatayoung.com.

YOUNG, William (Will) Robert, BA; British singer; b. 20 Jan. 1979, Reading, Berks, England. *Education:* Univ. of Exeter. *Career:* winner, Pop Idol television programme 2002; numerous live appearances and tours; mem. jury, BBC Nat. Short Story Award 2009. *Film appearance:* Mrs Henderson Presents 2005. *Theatre:* The Vortex (Royal Exchange Theatre, Manchester) 2007, Cabaret (Savoy Theatre, London) 2013. *Recordings include:* albums: From Now On (Nat. Music Award for Favourite Album 2003) 2002, Friday's Child 2003, Keep On 2005, Let it Go 2008, Echoes 2011, 85% Proof 2015. *Publications:* Anything is Possible (autobiog., with Marie Claire Giddings) 2002, By Public Demand (with Richard Galpin) 2002, On Camera: Off Duty (with Richard Galpin) 2003, Funny Peculiar (autobiography) 2012. *Honours:* Top of the Pops Award for Top Newcomer, for Top Single 2002, Nat. Music Award for Favourite UK Male Singer, Favourite Newcomer 2002, BRIT Award for Best British Breakthrough Artist 2003, BRIT Award for Best British Single (for Your Game) 2005, Commercial Music Awards for UK's Favourite Artist 2006, 2007. *Current Management:* XIX Entertainment, Unit 33, Ransomes Dock, 35–37 Parkgate Road, London, SW11 4NP, England. *Telephone:* (20) 7801-1919. *Fax:* (20) 7801-1920. *E-mail:* info@xixentertainment.com. *Website:* www.xixentertainment.com; willyoung.co.uk.

YOUNGBLOOD, Mary; American musician (Native American flute) and singer; b. Sacramento, CA. *Career:* learned numerous musical instruments in childhood, including classical flute; worked as session musician and singer; received first wooden 'native flute' as gift; solo artist 1998–. *Recordings include:* albums: The Offering 1998, Heart of the World 1999, Beneath the Raven Moon (Grammy Award for Best Native American Music Album) 2002, Feed the Fire 2004, Dance with the Wind (Grammy Award for Best Native American Music Album 2007) 2006, Sacred Place 2008. *Honours:* Flutist of the Year 1999, 2000, Native American Music Award for Best Female Artist 2000. *Address:* c/o Silver Wave Records, POB 7943, Boulder, CO 80306, USA (office). *E-mail:* mary@maryyoungblood.com. *Website:* www.maryyoungblood.com.

YUAN, Enfeng; Chinese folk singer; b. 22 Jan. 1940, Shaanxi Prov.; d. of Yuan Zaiming and Li Dexian; m. Sun Shao, composer; one s. two d. *Education:* Dong Yangshi Elementary School, Xian. *Career:* joined Cultural Troupe of Provincial Broadcasting Station 1951; participated in over 3,000 performances, including numerous solo concerts and 1,000 radio and TV programmes; appearances abroad include Romania, Bulgaria, fmr Czechoslovakia, fmr USSR, Japan, Thailand, Philippines and USA; Hon. Dir and Chair. Folk Music Section, Shaanxi Broadcasting Station 1986–; Vice-Chair. Shaanxi TV Station; mem. Chinese Musicians' Asscn; mem. of Bd, Shaanxi Br., Chinese

Cultural Exchange Centre; mem. of many other official orgs. *TV film:* Silver Bell. *Compositions (with Sun Shao) include:* Millet is Delicious and Caves are Warm, Nowhere is Better than Our North Shaanxi; many recordings and song books; 300 songs on record, cassette and compact disc. *Honours:* State Actress Award 1987, May Day Labour Medal Award 1993. *Address:* Folk Music Section, Provincial Broadcasting and Television Station, Xian, Shaanxi, People's Republic of China (office).

YUBIN; South Korean singer, rapper and actress; b. (Kim YuBin), 4 Oct. 1988, Gwangiu. *Education:* Leland High School, Calif., USA, Myongji Univ. *Career:* mem. Wonder Girls 2006–; first int. tour (including Thailand and USA) 2009; first S Korean group to enter the Billboard Hot 100 chart (with Nobody) 2009; world tour with Jonas Brothers 2009; supported Justin Bieber at Valentine's Day Concert 2010; toured USA and Canada with Wonder World Tour 2010; collaborated with Akon on single Like Money 2012; numerous festival appearances and tours. *Films:* The Last Godfather 2010, The Wonder Girls 2012. *Television includes:* MTV Wonder Girls 2006–10, Welcome to Wonderland 2009, Made in Wonder Girls 2010; numerous guest appearances. *Recordings include:* albums: The Wonder Years (Golden Disk Main Award Winners (Bonsang) 2007) 2007, The Wonder Years: Trilogy (Seoul Music Awards for Record of the Year in Digital Release 2009, Bonsang Award 2009, Daesang Award 2009) 2009, Wonder World 2011. *Honours:* Golden Disk Awards for Popularity 2007, Seoul Music Award for Best New Artist 2008, Korean Music Awards for Best Dance and Electronic Song (for Tell Me) 2008, for Group Musician of the Year Netizen Vote (for Wonder Girls) 2009, Golden Disk Awards Main Award Winners 2008, MNet KM Music Festival Awards for Best New Female Group 2007, for Song of the Year 2008, for Best Music Video (for Nobody) 2008, for Best Female Group 2008. *Current Management:* c/o Creative Artists Agency, 162 Fifth Avenue, 6th Floor, New York, NY 10010, USA. *Telephone:* (212) 277-9000. *Fax:* (212) 277-9099. *Website:* www.caa.com. *Address:* c/o JYP Entertainment, JYP Center, 123-50 Cheongdam-dong, Gangnam-gu, Seoul, South Korea (office). *Telephone:* (2) 3438-2300 (office). *Website:* www.jype.com (office); www.wondergirlsworld.com.

YUNG, Joey; Hong Kong singer and actress; b. 16 June 1980; pnr Wilfred Lau. *Career:* Cantopop singer 1999–; numerous albums and concerts; film and TV actress 1999–. *Films:* as actress: The Accident 1999, Winner Takes All 2000, Feel 100% II 2001, Expect a Miracle 2001, My Schoolmate, the Barbarian 2001, Demi-Haunted 2002, The Attractive One 2004, Crazy N' the City 2005, The Jade and the Pearl 2010, Toy Story 3 (voice for Cantonese dubbed version) 2010, Diva 2012. *Television:* as actress: The Green Hope 2000, Not Just a Pretty Face 2003, Sunshine Heartbeat 2004, Kung Fu Soccer 2004, On the First Beat 2007, Stage of Youth 2009. *Recordings include:* albums: Who Will Love Me 2000, All Summer Holiday 2001, Solemn on Stage 2001, Something About You 2002, My Pride 2003, Show Up! 2003, Nin9 2 5ive 2004, Give Love a Break 2004, Bi-Heart 2005, Ten Most Wanted 2006, Close Up 2006, Glow 2007, In Motion 2008, A Time for Us 2009, Joey and Joey 2011; in Mandarin (English titles): Honestly 2001, A Person's Love Song 2002, Lonely Portrait 2003, Jump Up – 9492 2006, Little Little 2007, Very Busy 2009, Moment 2012. *Honours:* Metro Female Singer Awards 2001–09, JSG Most Popular Female Singer 2003–07, 2010, 2011, RTHK Best Female Singer Awards 2004–11, IFPI Best Selling Female Singer Awards 2004–06, 2008, 2011, Mnet TVB Choice Award 2012. *Current Management:* c/o Emperor Entertainment Group (EEG), 28/F, Emperor Group Centre, 288 Hennessy Road, Wanchai, Hong Kong Special Administrative Region, People's Republic of China. *E-mail:* enquiry@emperor.com.hk. *Website:* www.emperorgroup.com; www.joeyyung.hk.

YUNUPINGU, Geoffrey Gurrumul; Australian singer and musician; b. 1970, Elcho Island. *Career:* mem. Gumatj clan; sings in Yolngu language; mem. Yothu Yindi 1986–92; currently mem. Saltwater Band; also solo artist. *Recordings include:* albums: with Saltwater Band: Gapu Damurrun 1999, Djarridjarri 2004, Malk 2009; solo: Gurrumul (ARIA Awards for Best Independent Album and Best World Music Album) 2008, Rrakala 2011. *Honours:* NT Indigenous Music Award for Song of the Year 2008. *Current Management:* c/o Skinnyfish Music, PO Box 36873, Winnelie, NT 0821, Australia. *Telephone:* (8) 8941-8066. *Fax:* (8) 8941-9066. *E-mail:* penny@skinnyfishmusic.com.au. *Website:* www.skinnyfishmusic.com.au; www.gurrumul.com.

YUSA, BA; Cuban singer, songwriter and musician (guitar, piano, bass); b. (Yusmil Bridon Lopez), 1973, Havana. *Education:* Institute of Music. *Career:* formed own band 1999, has toured extensively in Europe, Japan, N America. *Recordings include:* albums: Yusa 2002, Breathe 2004, Haiku 2008, Live at Ronnie Scott's (DVD). *Honours:* two Cuba Disco awards. *Address:* 132 BIS N° 453 e/ 470 y 473 1896 Buenos Aires, Argentina (office). *E-mail:* yusamusic@gmail.com. *Website:* www.yusamusic.com.

YUSUF, Sami; British singer; b. July 1980, Tehran, Iran; m. Maryam Yusuf 2005. *Career:* involved in setting up Awakening record label; has performed in UK, USA, Canada, Egypt, Kuwait, UAE, Saudi Arabia, Syria, Yemen, Jordan, Qatar, Morocco, Azerbaijan, Sudan, Bosnia and Herzegovina, Germany, France, Sweden, Holland, Turkey, Austria, Belgium; performed at various charity concerts and visited Darfur for Islamic Relief 2007. *Recordings include:* albums: Al Mu'alim 2003, My Ummah 2005, Wherever You Are 2010, Salaam 2012, The Centre 2014. *E-mail:* info@samiyusufofficial.com. *Website:* www.samiyusuf.com.

Z

Z FACTOR (see Lee, Dave)

ZAAKIR; American rap artist. *Career:* mem., Jurassic 5 1993–2006; numerous live performances. *Recordings include:* albums: with Jurassic 5: Jurassic 5 (EP) 1997, Quality Control 2000, Power in Numbers 2002, Feedback 2006.

ZABALA, Fernando; Spanish promoter and musician (saxophone); b. 19 April 1962, Madrid. *Career:* promoter in Spain for: U2; Bruce Springsteen; Whitney Houston; REM; Michael Jackson; Pink Floyd; Tina Turner; Bryan Adams; Bon Jovi; Mike Oldfield; Paul McCartney; Dire Straits; Joe Cocker; Simply Red; Keith Richards; Red Hot Chili Peppers; Cirque Du Soleil; David Copperfield; current man. of Radio Tarifa, Macaco; mem. APCI (International Concert Promoters Asscn). *Publications:* contrib. to Guiá de la Música, El País, Año de Rock. *Address:* Sold Out, Alcalá 114–6B, 28009 Madrid, Spain. *Telephone:* (1) 4358428. *Fax:* (1) 4318185. *E-mail:* soldout@soldout.es. *Website:* www.soldout.es.

ZAFAR, Ali; Pakistani singer and actor; b. 18 May 1980, Lahore; s. of Mohammad Zafarullah and Kanwal Ameen; m. Ayesha Fazli; one s. *Education:* Govt Coll. Univ., Nat. Coll. of Arts. *Recordings include:* albums: Huqa Pani (Indus Music Award for Best Album 2004, Lux Style Award for Best Music Album 2004) 2003, Masty 2006, Jhoom 2011. *Films include:* Shararat (as singer); as actor: Tere Bin Laden 2010, Love Mein Gum 2011, Luv Ka The End 2011, Mere Brother Ki Dulhan 2011, London Paris New York 2012. *Television includes:* Lunda-Bazar, Kanch Ke Par, Kollege Jeans. *Honours:* Indus Music Awards, Best Debut Artist 2004, Best Pop Artist 2005, Asian Bollywood Music Awards, Best Pop Music Album in Pakistan 2005, Lux Style Awards, Youth Icon Award 2007, MTV Style Awards, Most Stylish Artist 2008, Best Male Singer 2009. *E-mail:* ammara@alizafar.net. *Website:* www.alizafar.net.

ZAKARIN, Michael; American musician (guitar); b. New York. *Career:* mem. The Bravery 2003–. *Recordings include:* albums: Unconditional (EP) 2004, The Bravery 2005, The Sun and the Moon 2007, The Sun and the Moon Complete 2008, Stir the Blood 2009. *E-mail:* petegalli@cybercom.net.

ZELATI, Marco; Italian musician (bass guitar, keyboards); b. 19 Aug. 1975, Milan. *Career:* mem. metal band Lacuna Coil 1994–. *Recordings include:* albums: In a Reverie 1999, Unleashed Memories 2001, Comalies 2002, Karmacode 2006, Shallow Life 2009, Dark Adrenaline 2012. *Website:* www.lacunacoil.it.

ZAMFIR, Gheorghe; Romanian musician (pan-pipes); b. 6 April 1941, Găeşti, nr Bucharest; m. Marie-Noele Zamfir. *Education:* self-taught and Bucharest Acad. of Music (studied under Fănică Luca). *Career:* graduated in conducting at Ciprian Porumbescu Conservatory, Bucharest 1968; toured numerous countries in Europe as student and won first prize in many int. competitions; conductor of 'Ciocirlia' Folk Ensemble in Bucharest 1969; Prof. of Pan-Pipes 1970; formed own orchestra 1970; numerous trips to Europe, Australia, S America, Canada and USA. *Recordings include:* Hora Romanilor & Tiganiada, Magic of the Panpipe, Legenda Romaneasca (muzica populara), Casa de discuri Media services, Romania, Gheorghe Zamfir en France (CD of popular music), Les Années 70, Mes Plus Belles Doina, Pan d'Amour – Kiss From a Rose, Recording with Gheorghe Zamfir – Archive, Music by Candlelight 1983, Romance 1984, Harmony 1987, The Lonely Shepherd 1988, A Return To Romance 1988, Doina din Arges 1990, Christmas at Notre Dame Basilica 1992, Panflute & Organ 1995, Harmony – Zauber der Panflöte (Beliebte Melodien) 1997, Magic of the Panpipes 2001, Like a Breeze 2008, Spirit of the Andes 2008. *Current Management:* c/o Michow Concerts and Management GmbH, Postfach 202364, 20216 Hamburg, Germany. *Telephone:* (40) 4800808. *Fax:* (40) 484443. *E-mail:* info@gheorghe-zamfir.com. *Website:* www.gheorghe-zamfir.com.

ZAMORA, Tye; American musician (bass guitar); b. 30 May 1977, Artesia, Calif. *Career:* played with local bands NOW, UVOD, The Color Red, Carpet, Stank Toof, Tyemus; mem., Alien Ant Farm 1996–2006, 2008–; self-financed independent LP 1999, signed to Papa Roach's New Noize label, second album released in conjunction with DreamWorks Records label 2001. *Recordings include:* albums: Greatest Hits (LA Music Award, Best Independent Album) 1999, ANThology 2001, Truant 2003, Up In the Attic 2006, Always and Forever 2013. *Website:* www.alienantfarm.com.

ZANDER, Robin; American singer and musician (guitar); b. 23 Jan. 1953. *Career:* learned to play guitar at age 12; joined The Destinations; later Butterscotch Sundays; Founder-mem. Cheap Trick 1974–; numerous concerts and festival appearances; tours; formed The Robin Zander Band (with Steve Luongo) 2013. *Recordings include:* albums: with Cheap Trick: Cheap Trick 1977, In Color 1977, Heaven Tonight 1978, Cheap Trick At Budokan 1979, Dream Police 1979, Found All The Parts 1980, All Shook Up 1980, One On One 1982, Next Positions Please 1983, Standing On The Edge 1985, The Doctor 1986, Lap of Luxury 1988, Busted 1990, The Greatest Hits 1991, Gift 1996, Silver 2001, Special One 2004, Rockford 2006, The Latest 2009; solo: Robin Zander 1993, Countryside Blvd 2010. *Film:* Daddy Day Care 2003. *Current Management:* c/o Bitsa Talent Inc., South Cleveland Avenue, Suite 56, Fort Myers, FL 13300, USA. *E-mail:* bitsamail@aol.com. *Website:* www

.robinzanderband.com. *Address:* c/o Trick International, 8225 Fifth Avenue, Suite 803, Brooklyn, NY 11209, USA (office). *Website:* www.cheaptrick.com.

ZANKLAN; Benin musician (percussion); b. 22 Aug. 1966, Atchoukpa. *Education:* Benin National Gendarmerie. *Career:* Nat. TV Programme ORIRE 1998; TV LC2 First Anniversary 1998; Radio Atlantique FM 1998; Radio Golfe FM 1998; mem. BUBEDRA; UMC. *Compositions include:* Sotie, Ohovive, Repos, Mi N'Danase, Gbehobada, Sorcier, ata N'De Kuku. *Recordings include:* album: Ohovive. *Honours:* Most Experienced Singer in Lomé Prize 1996. *Address:* PO Box 1135, Porto-Novo, Benin.

ZANNOU, Guy Dossa; Benin musician (guitar) and singer; b. 15 June 1962, Porto-Novo; m. Blandine Ayi, two s. one d. *Career:* appearances on Beninoise radio and TV including Coup de Pouce, Stars' Music; participated in shows with famous African stars including François Louga, Aïcha Koné, Aurlus Mabélé, Afia Mala, Gadji Céli; musical arrangements for Beninoise artists; band leader for Suka-Siko; mem. Local Union of Pop, Musicians' Local Asscn of Artists for Environment, National Federation of Artists' Asscn (sec.-gen.). *Compositions:* Corruption; Ce sera la Fête; Time is Money. *Recordings include:* Corruption. *Address:* 01 PO Box 447, Porto-Novo, Benin.

ZAPPELLINI, Marino, MMus; French musician (saxophone, flute), composer and actor; b. 17 May 1955, Bourges. *Education:* Univ. of Paris, Berklee School of Music, USA. *Career:* Leader Madzano Quartet; with MJC Marcel Cachin de Romainville 1988–; administrator and Artistic Dir L' Asscn loi 1991, Big Band Paris; worked with numerous artists including Mama Bea Tiekelski, Toure Kunda, Antoine Tome, Urban Sax, Pierre Henri, Bernard Lubat Gérard Marais, Mico Nissim, Corazón Rebelde, Pajaro Canzani, Salif Keita, Ousmane Kouyate, Kaba Mane, Manfila Kante, Carlos Nascimiento, Gery Burtin; organizer of tours for artists from Africa, UK, Spain, Portugal, Italy; agent for shows in France and internationally; mem. admin cultural division SPEDIDAM; mem. Jazz Comm., SNAM, Jazz Players' Union. *Films:* as actor: 10 Seconds; as dir and composer: Le Onzième Comandment. *Play:* as actor: Du Vent dans les Branches de Sassafras. *Recordings include:* Au Printemps de Bourges, Mama Bea, Mandinka Dong, Toure Kunda, L'Amour Titant, Antoine Tome; with Urban Sax: Urban Sax II, Urban Sax III, Les Noces Alchymiques, Pierre Henry, Kunga Kungaké, Kaba Mane; Madzano Live Concert, Corazon Rebelde, Pajaro Canzani, Kabe Mane.

ZARAÏ, Rika; Israeli singer and writer; b. 19 Feb. 1938, Jerusalem; d. of Eliezer Gozman and Fruma Gozman (née Yosefovitch); m. Johanan Zaraï (divorced); one c. *Education:* Lemel Girls' School, Jerusalem, Hatirhon School and Conservatory of Music, Jerusalem. *Career:* Musical Dir Israeli Army variety group 1960; singer and songwriter 1963–; has toured Europe, North America and Asia; Co-founder Pronatura 1986. *Songs include:* Alors je chante, L'olivier, Hava Naguila, Et pourtant le temps, Sans chemise, sans pantalon, Quand je faisais mon service militaire, Balapapa, Une étoile d'or, Israël et Ismaël, Tu t'appelais Belz, Les drapeaux de la Méditerranée, Mon tour de France, Prague, Un beau jour je partirai, Viens danser avec moi, Ami, Hochana; Albums: D'amour et de paix 1999, Hava 2000. *Publications include:* Ma médecine naturelle 1985, Mes secrets naturels 1988, Mes recettes saines et gourmandes 1990, Ces émotions qui guérissent, Le code secret de votre personnalité 1996, L'espérance a toujours raison 2006. *Honours:* Médaille d'Argent Ville de Paris, Médaille de Vermeil, Acad. Française. *Address:* Villa Montmorency, 2 bis ave des Tilleuls, 75016 Paris, France. *Website:* www.rikazarai.fr.

ZÉ, Tom; Brazilian composer, singer, arranger and actor; b. (Antonio José Santana Martins), 11 Oct. 1936, Irará, Bahia; s. of Everton C. Martins and Maria Helena Martins; m. Neusa S. Martins 1970; one s. *Education:* Univ. of Bahia Music School, studied with Ernst Widmer, Prof. H. J. Koellreuter, Piero Bastianelli and Yulo Brandao. *Career:* tropicalist movement 1967; MoMA, New York, Latin American Artists of 20th Century concert 1993; opened London Int. Festival of Theatre, Queen Elizabeth Hall, London 1993; Walker Art Center, USA 1993; Lincoln Center, New York and Avery Fisher Hall 1996; jazz festivals in USA, Canada and Europe; Only Connect, Barbican Centre Festival, London 2001; Banlieues Bleues Festival, acting with multi-ethnic community, Paris 2002; MC, Brazilian MusicNight, Midem, Cannes 2003; concerts in Germany, Spain, Argentina, Portugal 2004, Banlieues Bleues Festival, Paris, Montreux Festival, Switzerland, Portugal 2005; mem. Broadcast Music, Inc. (BMI) (USA), RZO (USA), Abramus (Brazil), Fermata (Brazil), Arlequim (Brazil), Irará Edições Musicais (Brazil). *Theatrical roles:* Arena Canta Bahia 1965, Rocky Horror Show 1975. *Film appearances:* Sábado 1994, Mater Dei 2001, Fabricando Tom Zé (documentary) 2007. *Recordings:* Sao Benedito 1965, Tropicália 1968, Todosos Olhos 1973, Estudando o Samba 1976, The Best of Tom Zé 1990, The Hips of Tradition 1993, Fabrication Defect 1999, Enciclopedia Musical Brasiliera 2000, Parabelo (soundtrack for Grupo Corpo, with José Miguel Wisnik) 2001, Jogos de armar 2001, Santagustin (soundtrack for Grupo Corpo, with Gilberto Assis) 2002, Imprensa Cantada, Estudando o Pagode 2005, Danç-Êh-Sá 2006, Estudando a Bossa: Nordeste Plaza 2008, O Pirulito da Ciência 2010, Studies of Tom Zé – Explaining Things So I Can Confuse You 2010, Tropicália Lixo Lógico 2012. *Publications:* Tropicalista lenta luta 2003, Ilha deserta – Discos 2003, As Cidades do Brasil – Salvador 2005. *Honours:* Festival Composer to Composer, Telluride Inst.

(USA), Down Beat magazine awards third place (Readers Poll), fourth place (Critics Poll), for album The Best of Tom Zé 1991, Billboard Top Alternative Album 1991, Music Festival TV Record first place, Golden Viola and Silver Sabiá (song São São Paulo, Meu Amor) 1968, fourth place (song 2001), Award for best lyrics, APCA Best Composer 1998, Citizen-Artist Prize 2000, Multicultural Estadão (São Paulo) Prize 2001, Prime Artist, Bravo! Magazine 2006, Best CD of Ind. Pop Music, Danç-Êh-Sá 2007, Best Brazilian Popular Music, Shell Prize 2007. *Address:* Rua Dr Homem de Mello 714, 05007-002 São Paulo, Brazil (home). *Telephone:* (11) 3762-9801 (office). *E-mail:* tomze@uol .com.br (office); tomze@tomze.com.br (home). *Website:* www.tomze.com.br.

ZECIC, Drazen; Croatian musician, singer and songwriter; b. 24 July 1967, Split; m. Bozena Poljak 1992; one s. two d. *Career:* began as songwriter for numerous musicians including Mate Bulić, Zlatko Pejaković, Mišo Kovač; concerts in Slovenia, Croatia; mem. Croatian Musicians' Union, HGU. *Recordings include:* albums: Zagrli Me Nocas Jace 1990, Govore Mi Mnogi Ljudi 1993, Boem U Dusi 1995, Nitko nema dva Zivota 1998, Zura 2006, Oprosti Svijete 2008, U čast svim dobrim ljudima 2009. *Honours:* Spilt Fest Croatia, Composer I Award 1992, Melodije Jadrana-Cro/Grand Prix, Singer, Composer 1993, Cardinal Stepinac Fest Croatia, Composer I Award 1993, Croatian Music Award 1998, HRF Award 2007. *Address:* Dobrilina 6, 21000 Split, Croatia (home). *Website:* www.crorec.hr.

ZEDD; German electronic music DJ, musician and record producer; b. (Anton Zaslavski), 2 Sept. 1989, Moscow, Russia. *Career:* recorded collaborations include Foxes, Matthew Koma, Hayley Williams; record producer, tracks by Lady Gaga, Justin Bieber featuring Nicki Minaj, Eva Simons, Namie Amuro; remixer of numerous tracks for artists including Armand Van Helden, Fatboy Slim, FLX, David May, Black Eyed Peas, Swedish House Mafia, Skrillex & The Doors, Empire of the Sun. *Recording:* solo album: Clarity (Grammy Award for Best Dance Recording 2014) 2012. *Honours:* MTV Clubland Award (featuring Hayley Williams for Stay the Night) 2014. *Current Management:* c/o Tim Smith, Blood Company, 727 Barton Run Boulevard, Marlton, NJ 08053, USA. *Telephone:* (856) 334-5820. *Fax:* (208) 330-8065. *E-mail:* tsmith@ bloodcompany.net; Dave.Rene@umusic.com. *Website:* www.bloodcompany .net/artists; www.zedd.net.

ZELENKA, Karel; Czech musician (alto and tenor trombone) and composer; b. 27 May 1946, Prague. *Education:* Prague Conservatory and Acad. of Arts, Prague. *Career:* mem. The Prague Big Band; played Prague Jazz Club Reduta, Berlin Jazz Club, Germany, Lucerna Hall in Prague, Warsaw Jazz Club, Poland. *Recordings include:* Poste Restante, Prague Big Band, Lucerna Hall Roth, Anniversary Concert, The Romantic Trombone. *Address:* Hlohovičky 9, 338 08 Zbiroh, Czech Republic (home). *Telephone:* (60) 7568448 (home). *E-mail:* karel.zelenka99@gmail.com.

ZEMFIRA; Russian singer; b. (Zemfira Talgatovna Ramazanova), 26 Aug. 1976. *Education:* Ufa Coll. of Fine Arts, Moscow State Univ. *Career:* worked as sound engineer, Europe Plus radio station, Ufa; formed rock band Zemfira 1998; numerous Russian and Soviet tours and festival appearances; took a break from music industry 2003, returned 2005. *Recordings include:* albums: Zemfira 1999, Forgive Me My Love 2000, 14 Weeks of Silence 2002, Vendetta 2005, Zemfira Live 2006, Thank You 2007, Z-Sides 2009, Zemfira.Live2 2010, To Live in Your Head 2013. *E-mail:* office@zemfira.ru; zemfira@zemfira.ru. *Website:* www.zemfira.ru.

ZENÓN, Miguel, BMus, MMus; Puerto Rican musician (saxophone) and composer; b. 30 Dec. 1976, Santurce, San Juan; m. Elga Castro. *Education:* Escuela Libre de Musica, Berklee Coll. of Music, Manhattan School of Music, USA. *Career:* founding mem., SF Jazz Collective 2004; mem. jazz faculty, New England Conservatory 2009–; has also taught at Banff Centre, Univ. of Manitoba, LeMoyne Coll., Univ. of Massachusetts at Amherst, Brubeck Inst., Berklee Coll. of Music, Conservatoire de Paris, Rotterdam Conservatory, Manhattan School of Music, Amsterdam Conservatory, Diaz Inst.; Kennedy Center Jazz Amb. 2003. *Recordings:* albums: as leader: Looking Forward 2002, Ceremonial 2004, Jibaro 2005, Awake 2008, Esta Plena 2009, Alma Adentro: the Puerto Rican Songbook 2011, Rayuela (with Laurent Coq) 2012, Identities are Changeable 2014; also appeared on recordings by Edu Tancredi, Gabriel Rodriguez, Gilson Schachnik, David Sanchez, Stephan Crump, Greg Tardy, William Cepeda, Guillermo Klein, Ray Barretto, Hans Glawischnig, Kendrick Oliver, Paoli Mejias, Luis Perdomo, Charlie Haden, Chiara Civello, Brian Lynch, Mingus Big Band, Edsel Gomez, Miles Okazaki, Kenny Werner, Julien Labro. *Honours:* Guggenheim Fellowship 2008, MacArthur Fellowship 2008, Jazz Journalists' Asscn Award for Alto Saxophonist of the Year 2015. *Current Management:* Mariah Wilkins Management, 315 East 86th Street, Suite 2#EE, New York, NY 10028, USA. *Telephone:* (212) 426-3282. *E-mail:* mariahwilkins@earthlink.net. *Website:* www.mariahwilkins.com. *E-mail:* miguelmusic@miguelzenon.com (office). *Website:* www.miguelzenon.com (home).

ZEPHANIAH, Benjamin Obadiah Iqbal; British poet, writer, dramatist, musician and singer and academic; *Professor of Poetry and Creative Writing, Brunel University;* b. 15 April 1958, Birmingham. *Education:* Deykin Avenue Primary School, Birmingham Ward End Hall Comprehensive School, Birmingham Broadway Comprehensive School, Birmingham Boreatton Park Approved School, Baschurch. *Career:* Writer-in-Residence, Africa Arts Collective, Liverpool 1989, Hay-on-Wye Literature Festival 1991, Memphis State Univ., USA 1991–95, Keats House, Hampstead 2011; currently Prof. of Poetry and Creative Writing, Brunel Univ.; numerous radio performances,

acting roles, appearances; mem. Musicians' Union, Equity, Performing Rights Soc., Authors' Licensing and Collecting Soc. *Recordings include:* albums: Rasta 1983, Us and Dem 1990, Back To Our Roots 1995, Belly Of The Beast 1996, Heading For The Door 2000, Naked 2006; singles: Dub Ranting (EP) 1982, Big Boys Don't Make Girls Cry 1984, Free South Africa 1986, Crisis 1992, Naked 2004. *Compositions include:* contrib. to Dancing Tribes (single, with Back To Base) 1999, Illegal (with Swayzak) 2000, What is In Between (with Mieko Shimizo) 2006, The Imagined Village 2007, The Police in Dub 2008, Skanny Skannky (Toddla T) 2009. *Plays include:* Playing the Right Tune 1985, Job Rocking 1987, Delirium 1987, Streetwise 1990, The Trial of Mickey Tekka 1991. *Radio plays include:* Hurricane Dub 1988, Our Teacher's Gone Crazy 1990, Listen To Your Parents 2000, Face 2002. *Television plays include:* Dread Poets Society 1991, Peaky Blinders 2013, 2014. *Publications include:* fiction: Face 1999, Refugee Boy 2001, Teacher's Dead 2007; poetry: Pen Rhythm 1980, The Dread Affair 1985, Inna Liverpool 1988, Rasta Time in Palestine 1990, City Psalms 1992, Talking Turkeys 1994, Funky Chickens 1996, Propa Propaganda 1996, School's Out 1997, We Are Britain 2002, Too Black, Too Strong 2002, The Little Book of Vegan Poems 2002, Gangsta Rap 2004, My Story 2011, When I Grow Up 2011, Kung Fu Trip 2011, Liam 2012, Terror Kid 2014; contrib. to periodicals, radio, TV. *Honours:* Dr hc (Univ. of North London) 1998, (Univ. of West of England) 1999, (Staffordshire Univ.) 2001, (Oxford Brookes Univ.) 2002, (South Bank Univ., London) 2002, (Univ. of East London) 2003, (Univ. Coll. Northampton) 2003, (Open Univ.) 2004, (Univ. of Central England) 2005; Hon. DLitt (Westminster Univ.) 2006, (Univ. of Birmingham) 2008, (Univ. of Hull) 2010, (Univ. of Glamorgan) 2011, (De Montfort Univ.) 2015; BBC Young Playwrights Festival Award 1988. *Current Management:* c/o United Agents, 12–26 Lexington Street, London, W1F 0LE, England. *Telephone:* (20) 3214-0800. *Fax:* (20) 3214-0801. *E-mail:* info@ unitedagents.co.uk. *Website:* unitedagents.co.uk; www.benjaminzephaniah .com.

ZETLITZ, Bertine; Norwegian singer and songwriter; b. (Bertine Axeliane Robberstad Zetlitz), 9 April 1975, Oslo; one d. *Career:* solo artist 1998–. *Recordings include:* albums: Morbid Latenight Show 1998, Beautiful So Far 2000, Sweet Injections 2003, Rollerskating 2004, My Italian Greyhound 2006, Electric Feet 2012. *Honours:* Spellemannprisen for Best Debut Album, Best Pop Album 1998, Pop Soloist of the Year 2000, Hitaward for Female Artist of the Year 1998, 2000. *Current Management:* c/o Heartbeat Management, Upper Slottsgate 15B, 0157 Oslo, Norway. *Telephone:* 90-74-20-44. *E-mail:* pernille@heartbeatmanagement.com. *Website:* www.heartbeatmanagement .com; www.bertine.com.

ZGUROVA, Kalinka Kaneva; Bulgarian folk singer; b. 25 Sept. 1945, Debelt, Bourgas District; m. Stefan Kanev 1976, one s. *Career:* debut at Nat. Singing Competition, Gramatikovo 1960; concert tours in Europe, Asia, America and Africa. *Recordings include:* over 350 songs recorded. *Honours:* Grammy Award (with Mystery of Bulgarian Voices Folk Ensemble), numerous Bulgarian and int. awards and distinctions.

ZHANG, Jane; Chinese singer and songwriter; b. (Zhang Liangying), 11 Oct. 1984, Chengdu, Sichuan. *Education:* Sichuan Univ. *Career:* placed third in Super Girl contest 2005; released debut single and album 2006; made USA live debut 2007; involved in recording We Are Ready song for Beijing Olympic Games 2007. *Stage:* The Song of the Movie 2005. *Recordings:* albums: The One 2006, Update 2007, Jane@Music 2009, Believe in Jane 2010, Reform 2011, The Seventh Sense 2014. *Honours:* numerous awards, including Music Chart Awards Best Singer Award 2007, New York China Film Festival Award for Most Popular Chinese Singer 2010, Asia Song Festival Award for Best Asian Artist 2010, Mnet Asian Music Award for Best Asian Artist 2011, Top Chinese Music Awards for Best Female Artist and Most Poular Female Artist 2013, MTV Europe Music Awards for Best Asian Act and Best Worldwide Act 2015. *Address:* c/o Sony Music Entertainment, 550 Madison Avenue, New York, NY 10022, USA (office). *Website:* www.sonymusic.com (office); en.janezhang.com.

ZHOU, Bibi; Chinese singer and songwriter; b. (Zhou Bichang), 26 July 1985, Changsha, Hunan; d. of Zhou Zhongzhan and Lu Yuanyuan. *Education:* Futian High School, Xinghai Conservatory of Music. *Career:* relocated to Shenzhen, Guangdong Prov. 1991; several collaborations including Epik High; China Women Devt Foundation Young Amb. for Land of Love, Water Cellars for Mothers project 2005, Amb. of HIV/AIDS Prevention 2005. *Films:* McDull, the Alumni 2006, The 601st Phone Call 2006, Who Touched My Violin String? 2006. *Television:* Super Girl Competition (first runner-up) 2005. *Recordings include:* albums: Who Touched My Violin String? 2006, NOW 2007, WOW 2007, Time 2009, <<i, yu, guang, jing>>(i, fish, light, mirror) (Jeanswest Entertainment Award for Most Influential Music Album 2011) 2010, Black Apple (Mandarin Golden Melody Award for Most Popular Album 2012) 2011, Unlock (Global Chinese Music Award for Best Album 2013, Channel V China Music Award for Best Album 2014) 2013. *Honours:* Global Chinese Music Awards for Most Popular New Female Artist 2006, for Allround Artist 2006, Channel V China Music Awards for Best Newcomer 2007, for Mainland's Most Popular Female Singer 2013, 2014, Beijing BQ Red List Awards for Most Popular Singer of the Year 2010, for Best Singer of the Year 2011, Baidu Entertainment Boiling Point Award for Mainland's Most Popular Female Singer 2011, China Charity Rank and Charity Ceremony Award for Charity Star 2011, Mandarin Golden Melody Award for Mainland's Most Popular Female Singer 2012, for Nationwide's Most Popular Singer 2012, MTV Europe Music Award for Best Act from Southeast Asia/China & Hong Kong/Taiwan 2014. *Website:* www.yhfamily.cn.

ZHOU, Vic; Taiwanese actor and singer; b. 9 June 1981. *Education:* Hsing Wu Coll., China Univ. of Tech. *Career:* mem. boy band F4 (Flowers 4) 2001–03, 2007–. *Television includes:* Meteor Garden 2002, Meteor Garden II 2003, Love Storm 2003, Mars 2004, Silence 2006, Sweet Relationship 2007, Black and White 2009, The Last Night of Madam Chin 2009, Home 2011. *Recordings include:* albums: with F4: Meteor Rain 2002, Fantasy 4ever 2003, Waiting For You 2007; solo: Make a Wish 2002, Remember I Love You 2004, I'm Not F4 2007, Vic Chou: The Best Collection 2009. *Films include:* Linger 2008, Tea Fight 2008, Love You 10000 Years 2010, Sleepless Fashion 2011, Perfect Two 2012, Saving General Yang 2013, Day of Redemption 2013, A Moment of Love 2013. *Honours:* Golden Bell for Best Actor (for drama Home) 2013. *Website:* www.vicpower.net.

ZHU, Ken; Taiwanese actor, singer and composer; b. 15 Jan. 1979, Taiwan. *Career:* mem. boy band F4 (Flowers 4) 2001–03, 2007–. *Television includes:* Meteor Garden 2002, Meteor Garden II 2003, Sunflower 2002, Love Storm 2003, City of Sky 2004, Wish to See You Again 2008, Momo Love 2009, No Promise Love 2011, Hero 2012. *Films include:* Sky of Love 2003, The Tokyo Trial 2006, Batanes 2007, L-O-V-E 2009. *Recordings include:* albums: with F4: Meteor Rain 2002, Fantasy 4ever 2003, Waiting For You 2007; solo: On Ken's Time 2005, Getting Real 2009. *Play:* Love on A Two Street/He and His Two Wives. *Publications include:* Mei Wei Guan Xi; F4 Music Party 2001, Comic Man -The First Anniversary of F4 2002, Meteor In Barcelona 2002, F4@Tokyo 2005.

ZIEGLER, Pablo; Argentine musician (piano), composer and arranger; b. 2 Sept. 1944, Buenos Aires; m. Sandra Sicbert 1977; one s. one d. *Education:* Music Conservatory of Buenos Aires. *Career:* formed Pablo Ziegler Terceto aged 18; pianist with Astor Piazzolla, New Tango Quintet 1978–89; formed various groups including New Tango Duo with Quique Sinesi; has performed with Orquestra Filarmónica de Buenos Aires, Orquestra Sinfónica de Buenos Aires, Orquestra Sinfónica de Tucumán, Orpheus Chamber Orchestra, Sydney Symphony Orchestra, Royal Philharmonic, Stavanger Symphony Orchestra, North Country Chamber Players, Orquestra Municipal de Rosario, Seoul Philharmonic Orchestra, Filarmónica de Méjico, Wellington Chamber Orchestra; mem. American Soc. of Composers, Authors and Publishers. *Compositions include:* Milonga in the Wind, La Conexion Portena Album. *Recordings include:* with Piazzolla Quintet: Live in Montreaux, Live in Vienna, Be As Zero Hour, Symphonic Tango, Los Tangueros 1996, La Camorra; with New Tango Quartet: La Conexion Porteña 1991; with Quintet for New Tango: Tango Romance 1998, Asfalto: Street Tango 1998, Quintet for New Tango 2000; with New Tango Duo: Bajo Cero (Latin Grammy Award for Best Tango Album) 2003, Buenos Aires Report 2007, Amsterdam Meets New Tango 2013; also appears on recordings by Gary Burton, Ettore Stratta. *Honours:* Hon. Citizen of New Orleans; Arlequin Nat. Prize 1992. *E-mail:* music@pabloziegler.com (office). *Website:* www.pabloziegler.com; www .bernsarts.com.

ZIGNAGO ALCÓVER, Gianmarco Javier; Peruvian singer and song-writer; b. 17 Aug. 1970, Lima. *Career:* moved to Miami, USA 2000. *Recordings include:* albums: Historias (Parte I) 1989, Personal 1992, Entre la Arena y la Luna 1994, Señora Cuénteme 1997, Al Quinto Día 1997, A Tiempo 2002, Resucitar (Latin Grammy Award for Best Singer–Songwriter Album 2005) 2004, Ocho 2006, Desde Adentro 2008, Días Nuevos (Latin Grammy Award for Best Singer–Songwriter Album 2011) 2011, 20 Años (Latin Grammy Award for Best Singer–Songwriter Album 2012) 2012, Versiones 2013. *E-mail:* info@ gianmarco.com.pe (office). *Website:* www.gianmarco.com.pe.

ZIMMER, Hans Florian; German film score composer; b. 12 Sept. 1957, Frankfurt am Main; m. Vicki Carolyn (separated); one d. *Education:* in England. *Career:* mem. The Buggles (produced hit song Video Killed the Radio Star); pioneered use of digital synthesizers with computer tech. and traditional orchestras; mem. BMI. *Film scores include:* Moonlighting 1982, Histoire d'O: Chapitre 2 1984, Success is the Best Revenge 1984, Insignifi-cance 1985, Separate Vacations 1986, The Wind 1987, Terminal Exposure 1987, Rain Man 1988, Twister 1988, Taffin 1988, Spies Inc 1988, The Fruit Machine 1988, Burning Secret 1988, A World Apart (with Stanley Myers) 1988, Wiezien Rio 1989, Paperhouse 1989, Dark Obsession 1989, Black Rain 1989, Driving Miss Daisy 1989, Green Card 1990, Pacific Heights 1990, Nightmare at Noon 1990, Fools of Fortune 1990, Chicago Joe and the Showgirl 1990, Bird on a Wire 1990, Days of Thunder 1990, K2 (European version) 1991, Backdraft 1991, Regarding Henry 1991, Thelma & Louise 1991, Where Sleeping Dogs Lie 1992, The Power of One 1992, A League of Their Own 1992, Radio Flyer 1992, Toys 1992, Cool Runnings 1993, Calendar Girl 1993, Point of No Return 1993, True Romance 1993, Younger and Younger 1993, The House of the Spirits 1993, The Lion King (Acad. Award, Golden Globe) 1994, Africa: The Serengeti 1994, I'll Do Anything 1994, Renaissance Man 1994, Drop Zone 1994, Two Deaths 1995, Crimson Tide (Grammy Award) 1995, Nine Months 1995, Something to Talk About 1995, Beyond Rangoon 1995, Muppet Treasure Island 1996, Broken Arrow 1996, The Preacher's Wife 1996, The Whole Wide World, 1996, The Fan 1996, The Peacemaker 1997, As Good As It Gets 1997, The Last Days 1998, The Thin Red Line 1998, The Prince of Egypt 1998, Chill Factor 1999, Gladiator (Golden Globe) 2000, The Road to El Dorado 2000, Mission: Impossible II 2000, An Everlasting Piece 2000, Hannibal 2001, Pearl Harbor 2001, Riding in Cars with Boys 2001, Invincible 2001, Black Hawk Down 2001, Spirit 2002, The Ring 2002, Tears of the Sun 2003, Matchstick Men 2003, The Last Samurai 2003, Something's Gotta Give 2003, King Arthur 2004, Thunderbirds 2004, Shark Tale 2004, Lauras Stern 2004, Spanglish 2004, The Ring Two 2005, Madagascar 2005, Batman Begins 2005, The Weather Man 2005, The Little Polar Bear: The Mysterious Island (with Nick Glennie-Smith) 2005, Pirates of the Caribbean: Dead Man's Chest 2006, The Holiday 2006, Pirates of the Caribbean: At World's End 2007, The Simpsons Movie 2007, Casi divas 2008, Kung Fu Panda 2008, The Dark Knight (Grammy Award for Best Score Soundtrack Album for Motion Picture 2009, Classical BRIT Award for Soundtrack of the Year 2009) 2008, The Burning Plain 2008, Frost/Nixon 2008, Madagascar: Escape 2 Africa 2008, The Dark Knight Rises 2012, Man of Steel 2013, 12 Years a Slave 2013, The Amazing Spider-Man 2 2014, Interstellar 2014. *Television scores:* Wild Horses 1985, First Born 1989, Millennium 1992, Space Rangers 1993, The Critic (theme) 1994, High Incident (theme) 1996, Die Motorrad-Cops: Hart am Limit 1999, El Candidato 1999, Carnivàle (series) 2003, Threat Matrix (series title theme) 2003, The Contender (series) 2005, The Pacific (mini-series) 2010, Through the Wormhole 2011–14. *Recordings:* Wings of Film 2001, numerous soundtrack recordings. *Honours:* Lifetime Achievement Award in Film Composition, Nat. Board of Review' Frederick Loewe Award, Palm Springs Int. Film Festival 2003, ASCAP Henry Mancini Award for Lifetime Achieve-ment. *Current Management:* William Morris Endeavor Entertainment, LLC, 9601 Wilshire Blvd, Beverly Hills, CA 90210, USA. *Website:* www.hans -zimmer.com.

ZIMMERMANN, André François; French musician (piano) and composer; b. 19 Jan. 1965, Fort de France, Martinique. *Education:* music school, conservatory. *Career:* appearances on TV France; concerts as soloist, duo, trio, big band, including Bucharest 1990, with the Big Band de Jazz, Metabetch-ouan, Canada, International Festival of Brasov, Transylvania 1990; festivals at Mulhouse, Nitting, Avoriaz; piano solo, St Louis, France 1991; teacher, School of Music, Sundgau-Alsace. *Compositions:* Theatre: Les Estivants, Gorki, 1986; La Mouette, Chekov, 1990; Derrière les 7 Papiers Peints, Wilfred Grote, with Haute Alsace, 1990; Un Chapeau de Paille d'Italy, Labiche, 1991; Children's pieces (2 selections for piano and orchestra); music for flute and strings; composition for regional cinema. *Recordings:* albums: Jazz Concep-tions, music for popular songs, Jazz réplique. *Address:* Domaine Saint-Ange, 07000 Coux, France.

ZINNER, Nicolas Joseph; American musician (guitar); b. 8 Dec. 1974. *Education:* New York Univ. *Career:* mem. band Yeah Yeah Yeahs 2000–; formed band Head Wound City 2005. *Recordings include:* albums: Fever To Tell 2002, Show Your Bones 2006, It's Blitz! 2009, Mosquito 2013. *Publica-tions include:* No Seats on the Party Car 2001, Slept in Beds 2003, I Hope You Are All Happy Now 2004, Please Take Me Off the Guest List 2010. *E-mail:* mail@ciullamgmt.com. *E-mail:* yeahyeahyeahsctc@hotmail.com. *Website:* www.yeahyeahyeahs.com.

ZLOKIC, Jasna; Croatian musician (guitar) and economist; b. 15 March 1955, Vela Luka; m. Boris Zlokic 1977; one s. *Career:* first public performance aged 10; amateur career sustained until first solo album 1980; mem. HGU (Hrvatska Glazbena Unija). *Recordings include:* albums: Pusti Me Da Prodem 1983, Skitnica 1984, Ja Sam Ti Jedini Drug 1985, Vjeruj Mi 1986, Kad Odu Svi 1987, Lutajuce Srce 1988, Vrijeme Je Uz Nas 1989, Tiho Sviraj Pjesmu Ljubavnu 1990, Bez Predaha 1992, Nisam Ti Se Tugo Nadala 1994, Sunce moga neba 1996, Žena od mota 1999, Putevima vjetra 2002, Ljubavni parfemi 2006. *Honours:* Zagreb Fest, Grand Prix 1984, 1988, Split Musical Festival Award 1982, 1984, 1987, 1993, 1994, MESAM Award, Female Singer of the Year 1984, 1988, Sarajevo Festival 1988, Bratislava Festival 1985, Madeira Festival 1988.

ZOGHBI, Nawal George al-; Lebanese/Canadian singer; b. 29 June 1972, Byblos, Lebanon; m. Elie Deeb 1990 (divorced 2008); twin s. one d. *Career:* appeared in Studio al-Phan music competition; solo artist 1991–; Owner, Tia Productions. *Recordings include:* albums: Wehyati andak 1992, Ayza el-rad 1994, Balaee fi zamany 1995, Habeit ya leil 1997, Mandam aleik 1998, Malom 1999, El-layali 2000, Tool omry 2001, Elli etmaneito 2002, Eineik kaddabin 2004, Yama alou 2006, Khalas sameht 2008, Ma'rafsh Leh 2011. *Honours:* Lions Club Award for Best Singer (Lebanon and Jordan) 1997, Murex d'Or for Best Female Lebanese Singer of the Year 2004, Arab Music Award for Best Female Singer 2004, for Best Song 2004, Best Arabic Singer 2005, 2006, 2007, Lebanese Female Singer of the Year 2012. *Address:* c/o Rotana, Burj al-Ghazal, 11th Floor, al-Tabaris, Achrafieh, Beirut, Lebanon (office). *E-mail:* info@nawalalzoghbi.net (office). *Website:* www.rotana.net (office); www .nawalalzoghbi.net.

ZOLA; South African singer; b. (Thuthukani Bonginkosi Dlamini), 1976, Soweto. *Education:* Jabulani Technical High, South Africa. *Career:* stage named after Zola, suburb of Soweto; early acting roles included youth series Teens On A Tightrope; Starred as Papa Action in TV series Yizo Yizo 2, 2001; followed by rise to fame as kwaito/rap/hip hop music artiste; own TV talk show Take 5/Zola On 5, also Zola 7 2003–. *Recordings:* albums: Umdlwembe (Stray Dog) 2001, Khokhovuka 2002, Bhambatha 2004. *Films:* Drum 2004, Tsotsi 2005, Catch a Fire 2006. *Honours:* Metro FM Music Awards: Album of the Year, Artist of the Year; Song of the Year, 2001. *Address:* c/o Ghetto Ruff Records, 25 7th Avenue, Parktown North, Johannesburg, South Africa (office). *Telephone:* (11) 4471943 (office). *Fax:* (11) 4471607 (office). *E-mail:* info@ ghettoruff.co.za (office). *Website:* www.zola7.co.za (home).

ZOLOTHUHIN, Adrian Dimitri, BMus; British musician (guitar), arranger and producer; b. 22 July 1970, Cleveland, Middlesbrough, England. *Educa-tion:* Univ. of Surrey. *Career:* mem. Kabak; fmr sound recordist, Sands Music;

guitarist, World of Leather; with The Better Button 1994–. *Recordings include:* with World of Leather: St Mark's Place 1994, Russian Part 1994; guitar, arranger Blow; as solo artist on album: Bacology 1995, Moonlight Express. *Address:* 110 Grove Ave, Hanwell, London, W7 3ES, England. *E-mail:* info@thebetterbutton.com. *Website:* www.thebetterbutton.com.

ZORN, John; American musician (saxophone, keyboards) and composer; b. 2 Sept. 1953, New York. *Career:* fmr mem. Naked City, Masada, Painkiller; associated with the avant garde tradition, performing with numerous artists including Wayne Horvitz, David Moss; works performed world-wide; compositions commissioned by groups including the New York Philharmonic Orchestra, Brooklyn Philharmonic, Bayerische Staasoper, WDR Orchestra Köln, American Composers Orchestra, Stephen Drury and The Kronos Quartet; f. Tzadik record co. 1995. *Compositions include:* Christabel 1972, Conquest of Mexico 1973, Mikhail Zoetrope 1974, Lacrosse 1977, Hockey 1978, Fencing 1978, The Book of Heads 1978, Pool 1979, Archery 1979, Track and Field 1980, Locus Solus 1982, Sebastopol 1983, Rugby 1983, Cobra 1984, Xu Feng 1985, Godard 1985, Spillane 1986, Hu Die 1986, Ruan Lingyu 1987, Hwang Chin-ee 1988, Cat O'Nine Tails 1988, Qúê Trân 1988, For Your Eyes Only 1989, Bézique 1989, Torture Garden 1990, Grand Guignol 1990, Dead Man 1990, Elegy 1991, Leng Teh'e 1991, Carny 1992, Memento Mori 1992, Kristallnacht 1992, Absinthe 1992, Angelus Novus 1993, Masada 1993–97, The Sand's Share 1994, Redbird 1995, Dark River 1995, Aporias 1995, Music For Children 1996, Duras 1996, Kol Nidre 1996, Orchestra Variations 1996, Etant Donnés 1997, Shibboleth 1997, Cycles du Nord 1998, Rituals 1998. *Recordings include:* solo: The Book of Heads 1995, Redbird 1995, Duras: Duchamp 1997, Angelus Novus 1998, Aporias 1998, Downtown Lullaby 1998, Circle Maker 1998, Bribe 1998, Masada Live in Jerusalem 1999, The String Quartets 1999, Lacrosse 2000, Cartoon S&M 2000, The Gift 2001, Madness Love and Mysticism 2001, Songs From The Hermetic Theatre 2001, Chimeras 2003, Magick 2004, Mysterium 2005, Rituals 2005, From Silence to Sorcery 2007, Alhambra Love Songs 2009, Interzone 2010, Nova Express 2011, Mount Analogue 2012, The Concealed 2012, Lemma 2013, Shir Hashirim 2013, Dreamachines 2013. *Publications include:* as Ed.: Arcana: Musicians on Music 2000, Arcana: Musicians on Music (Volume II) 2007, Arcana: Musicians on Music (Volume III) 2008, Arcana: Musicians on Music (Volume IV) 2009, Arcana: Musicians on Music (Volume V) 2010, Arcana: Musicians on Music (Volume VI) 2012. *Honours:* Magister Artium Gandensis, Univ. of Ghent; Jewish Cultural Award in Performing Arts, National Foundation for Jewish Culture 2001, William Schuman Award, Columbia Univ.'s School of the Arts 2007, inducted into Long Island Music Hall of Fame by Lou Reed 2011. *Address:* Tzadik, 200 East 10th Street, pmb 126, New York, NY 10003, USA (office). *E-mail:* info@tzadik.com (office). *Website:* www.tzadik.com (office).

ZULFIKARPAŠIĆ, Bojan, (Bojan Z); Serbian/French musician (piano, keyboards) and producer; b. 2 Feb. 1968, Belgrade; m. Alice Arwert 2005; two s. one d. *Education:* Kosta Manojlovic music school, Belgrade 1973–80, Stevan Mokranjac music school, Belgrade 1983–87, Blue Lake fine arts camp, Mich., USA 1986, CIM, Paris 1988–92. *Career:* played with: Henri Texier, Michel Portal, Jack DeJohnette, Julien Lourau, Kudsi Erguner, Scott Colley, Nasheet Waits, Ben Perowsky, Ari Hoenig, Josh Roseman, Vlatko Stefanovski; Leader, Bojan Z Quartet; concerts include Montreal Jazz Festival, Montreux Jazz Festival, La Roque d'Anthèron Piano Festival, London Jazz Festival, Copenhagen Jazz Festival, Marciac Jazz Festival, North Sea Jazz, Palau di Musica Catalana Barcelona, Stockholm Jazz Festival, Edinburgh Jazz Festival; La Salle Playel, Paris, Banlieues Bleues Festival; Halle That Jazz Festival, Jazz Across The Border, Berlin, Paris Jazz Festival and many others. *Recordings include:* with Bojan Z Quartet: Bojan Z Quartet 1994, Yopla! 1995; solo: Koreni 1999, Solobsession 2000, Transpacifik 2003, Xenophonia (Victoires du Jazz for Best Album of the Year 2006) 2006, Bozilo Live 2009, Humus 2010, Soul Shelter 2012; with Henri Texier: Indian's Week 1993, Mad Nomad 1995, Mosaîc Man 1998, String Spirit 2002; with Michel Portal: Dockings 1997, Baïlador 2010; with Simon Spang-Hanssen: Instant Blue 1997; with Nguyên Lê: Maghreb and Friends 1997, Purple: Celebrating Jimi Hendrix 2002; with Karim Ziad: Ifrikyia 2000; with Julien Lourau: The Rise 2001, Fire and Forget 2005; as producer: Bailador-Michel Portal 2011, Amulette-Amira Medunjanin 2011. *Honours:* Chevalier des Arts et des Lettres 2002; Best Young Jazz Musician of Yugoslavia 1989, First Prize for Soloist, La Défense Concours, Paris 1990, Grand Prix, La Défense, Paris 1992 Django Reinhardt Prize for Musician of the Year 2002, Hans Koller Prize for Best European Jazz Musician 2005, Victoires du Jazz 2006, Victoires du Jazz – Artist of the Year 2012. *Current Management:* c/o Sébastien Hamard, Next Door Agency, Antibes, France. *E-mail:* nda.agency@gmail.com. *E-mail:* info@bojanz.com (office). *Website:* www.bojanz.com.

ZURSTRASSEN, Pierre, (Pirly Zurstrassen); Belgian musician (piano, accordion), composer and teacher; *Teacher, Conservatoire Royal de Bruxelles*; b. 15 April 1958, Heusy; m. Bouhon Zurstrassen; one s. one d. *Education:* Conservatoire de Verviers, Seminaire de Jazz de Liege, Classe d'Improvisation du Conservatoire Royal de Liège. *Career:* many compositions for theatre, TV and dance; teacher of jazz harmony, jazz composition, Royal Conservatory, Brussels. *Plays:* music for Irène K, Arts & Couleurs, and others. *Recordings include:* 'H' Septet: Hautes Fagnes, 'H' Septet: Horizons Azur, Zurstrassen/Stokart Duo, Septimana, Musique à 9: Traces, Pour l'Ivoire, Musicazur, Musica Dal Vivo, Musicazur, PiWiZ trio, Tric Trac Trio, and others. *Honours:* Saxe Best Young Musician 1988, Prix Andre Grosjean 1993, Prix Madame de la Hault. *Address:* 4 Wayai, 4845 Sart, Belgium. *Telephone:* (87) 475327. *E-mail:* pirly@skynet.be. *Website:* www.pirlyzurstrassen.net.

Directory

APPENDIX A: MUSIC FESTIVALS

Australia

Adelaide Fringe Festival: PO Box 3242, Rundle Mall, Adelaide, SA 5000. *Telephone:* (8) 8100-2000. *Fax:* (8) 8100-2020. *E-mail:* buzz@adelaidefringe .com.au. *Website:* www.adelaidefringe.com.au. f. 1960; annual festival, held in March.

Big Day Out: 212 Palmer Street, East Sydney, NSW 2010. *E-mail:* info@ bigdayout.com. *Website:* www.bigdayout.com. Alternative music event, held annually in various locations.

East Coast International Blues & Roots Music Festival (Bluesfest): PO Box 1606, Byron Bay, NSW 2481. *Telephone:* (2) 6685-8310. *Fax:* (2) 6685-8370. *E-mail:* admin@bluesfest.com.au. *Website:* www.bluesfest.com.au. Annual festival of blues and roots music, held over the Easter weekend in various locations.

Falls Festival: PO Box 184, Lorne, Vic. 3232; c/o Copping PO, Copping, Tasmania 7174. *Website:* www.fallsfestival.com. f. 1993 as the Rock Above the Falls; annual festival, now held in two venues (Victoria and Tasmania) in December–January; capacity 20,000.

Perth International Arts Festival: UWA Festival Centre, M418, The University of Western Australia, 3 Crawley Avenue, Crawley, WA 6009. *Telephone:* (8) 6488-2000. *Fax:* (8) 6488-8555. *E-mail:* festival@perthfestival .com.au. *Website:* www.perthfestival.com.au. f. 1953 as the Festival of Perth; multi-arts festival held in February–March.

Port Fairy Folk Festival: Festival Office, PO Box 176, Port Fairy, Vic. 3284. *Telephone:* (3) 5568-2227. *Fax:* (3) 5568-1819. *E-mail:* pfff@ portfairyfolkfestival.com. *Website:* www.portfairyfolkfestival.com. f. 1977; world and folk music event held in Port Fairy Village in March.

Queensland Music Festival: PO Box 5188, West End, Qld 4101. *Telephone:* (7) 3010-6600. *Fax:* (7) 3010-6666. *E-mail:* info@qmf.org.au. *Website:* www .queenslandmusicfestival.com.au. Annual festival of local, national and international musical talent of all genres, held in July.

Summadayze: c/o Future Entertainment, PO Box 306, South Melbourne, Vic. 3205. *Telephone:* (3) 9686-1166. *Fax:* (3) 9686-8711. *E-mail:* enquiries@ futureentertainment.com.au. *Website:* www.summadayze.com. Annual dance festival held in Melbourne, the Gold Coast and Perth (Australia), and Auckland (New Zealand).

Sydney Festival: Sydney Festival Office, Level 2, 10 Hickson Road, The Rocks, NSW 2000. *Telephone:* (2) 8248-6500. *Fax:* (2) 8248-6599. *E-mail:* mail@sydneyfestival.org.au. *Website:* www.sydneyfestival.org.au. Annual cultural festival held in January for more than 100,000 people.

Telstra Country Music Festival Tamworth: Tourism Tamworth Ltd, PO Box 552, Tamworth, NSW 2340. *Telephone:* (2) 6767-5300. *Fax:* (2) 6767-5312. *E-mail:* tourism@tamworth.nsw.gov.au. *Website:* www.tcmf.com.au. Annual ten-day country music festival held in January.

WOMADelaide: Arts Projects Australia Pty Ltd, 12 King William Road, Unley, SA 5061. *Telephone:* (8) 8271-1488. *Fax:* (8) 8271-9905. *E-mail:* apadmin@artsprojects.com.au. *Website:* www.womadelaide.com.au. Annual three-day music festival, part of World of Music, Arts and Dance (WOMAD) network.

Austria

Art Club Imst: Sirapuit 54, 6460 Imst. *Telephone:* (5412) 62760. *Fax:* (5412) 62760. *E-mail:* artclubimst@tomorrow-sys.com. *Website:* www.riha.bz/ artclub. Open-air rock held in multiple venues.

Sunsplash: Wiesen Event, Hauptstrasse 140, 7203 Wiesen. *Telephone:* (2626) 81648-0. *Fax:* (2626) 81648-29. *E-mail:* office@wiesen.at. *Website:* www .wiesen.at. Open-air afro, reggae and Latin-American music festival held in late August.

Belgium

Belgium Rhythm 'N' Blues Festival: Breakaway vzw, Deusterstraat 11A, PO Box 2, 3990 Peer. *Telephone:* (1) 161-11-25. *Fax:* (1) 161-11-26. *E-mail:* info@brbf.be. *Website:* www.break-away.be. R&B festival held in July.

Cactusfestival: Cactus vzw Muziekcentrum, St Sebastiaansstraat 4, 8200 Bruges. *Telephone:* (5) 033-20-14. *Fax:* (5) 033-06-97. *E-mail:* info@ cactusmusic.be. *Website:* www.cactusfestival.be. f. 1981; three-day festival of a variety of music genres; capacity 20,000.

Couleur Café Festival: *E-mail:* news@couleurcafe.org. *Website:* www .couleurcafe.be. f. 1990; three-day festival with four stages of music from all over the world; capacity 70,000; organized and managed by Zig Zag, a non-profit organization.

Dour Music Festival: 10 rue du Marché, 7370 Dour. *E-mail:* info@ dourfestival.be. *Website:* www.dourfestival.be. f. 1989; three-day festival, capacity 35,000 each day.

Durbuy Rock Festival: rue Saint-Monon 33, 6940 Durbuy. *E-mail:* xavier@ durbuyrock.be. *Website:* www.durbuyrock.be.

European Forum of Worldwide Music Festivals (EFWMF): EFWMF Office, Jan Frans Willemsstraat 10A, 2530 Boechout. *Telephone:* (3) 455-69-44. *Fax:* (3) 454-11-62. *E-mail:* info@efwmf.org. *Website:* www.efwmf.org. Network of festivals, f. 1993.

Graspop Metal Meeting: Graspop Office vzw, Stenehei 30, PO Box 12, 2480 Dessel. *E-mail:* info@graspop.be. *Website:* www.graspop.be. f. 1986; metal music festival.

Jazz à Liège: Maison du Jazz, 11 rue sure les Foulons, 4000 Liège. *Telephone:* (4) 221-10-11. *Fax:* (4) 221-22-32. *E-mail:* jazz@skynet.be. *Website:* www .jazzaliege.be. Jazz festival held in May.

Klinkers: Bruges Cultural Department, Stadsbestuur, Burg 12, 8000 Bruges. *Telephone:* (5) 044-81-11. *Fax:* (5) 044-80-80. *E-mail:* info@klinkers-brugge.be. *Website:* www.klinkers-brugge.be. f. 1993; 15-day festival in July–August of multi-cultural music; capacity 50,000.

Leffingeleuren: vzw De Zwerver, Hennepstraat 8, 8400 Ostende. *Telephone:* (5) 970-08-22. *Fax:* (5) 970-08-20. *Website:* www.leffingeleuren.be. Festival featuring all styles of music, held in September.

Marktrock: Krakenstraat 6, 3000 Leuven 1. *Telephone:* (1) 689-73-89. *E-mail:* info@marktrock.be. *Website:* www.marktrock.be. Festival of rock, pop and blues music, held in August.

Nandrin Festival: GML Events, rue Renory 93, 4032 Angleur. *Telephone:* (8) 519-14-22. *E-mail:* libera@nandrinfestival.be. *Website:* www.nandrinfestival .com.

Polé Polé Festival: Lammerstraat 25, 9000 Gent. *Telephone:* (9) 356-67-00. *Fax:* (9) 356-67-10. *E-mail:* info@polepole.be. *Website:* www.polepole.be. Three-day festival of tropical music; capacity 30,000.

Pukkelpop: Diestersteenweg 152, 3970 Leopoldsburg. *E-mail:* info@ pukkelpop.be. *Website:* www.pukkelpop.be. f. 1985; three-day festival, capacity 50,000 each day.

Rock Werchter: Beverlaat 3, 3118 Werchter. *Website:* www.rockwerchter.be. f. 1975; held in June–July; capacity 70,000 each day.

Sfinks Festival: Sfinks Animatie vzw, Jan Frans Willemsstraat 10a, 2530 Boechout. *Telephone:* (3) 455-69-44. *Fax:* (3) 454-11-62. *E-mail:* info@sfinks.be. *Website:* www.sfinks.be. Annual world music festival, held in July.

Bulgaria

Varna Summer International Jazz Festival: c/o AVA Records, 9005 Varna, Chaika 50-D-47. *Telephone:* (2) 30-23-22. *Fax:* (2) 30-23-22. *E-mail:* vapirov@telecoms.bg. *Website:* www.vsjf.com. f. 1992; held in July–August.

Canada

Beaches International Jazz Festival: 1798 Queen Street East, Toronto, ON M4L 1G8. *Telephone:* (416) 698-2152. *Fax:* (416) 698-2064. *E-mail:* infobeachesjazz@rogers.com. *Website:* www.beachesjazz.com. Week-long festival held in July.

Big Valley Jamboree: c/o Panhandle Productions, 4238 37 Street, Camrose, AB T4V 4L6. *Telephone:* (780) 672-0224. *Fax:* (780) 672-9530. *E-mail:* bvj@ bigvalleyjamboree.com. *Website:* www.bigvalleyjamboree.com. Country music festival.

Edmonton Folk Festival: PO Box 4130, Edmonton, AB T6E 4T2. *Telephone:* (780) 429-1899. *Fax:* (780) 424-1132. *E-mail:* admin@efmf.ab.ca. *Website:* www .efmf.ab.ca. Three-day folk festival held annually in August, in Gallagher Park, Edmonton.

Festival International de Jazz de Montréal: 400 Maisonneuve West Blvd, Ninth Floor, Montréal, QC H3A 1L4. *Telephone:* (514) 523-3378. *Fax:* (514) 525-8033. *E-mail:* commentaires_jazz@equipespectra.ca. *Website:* www .montrealjazzfest.com. Held in June–July.

Folk on the Rocks: PO Box 326, Yellowknife, NT X1A 2N3. *Telephone:* (867) 920-7806. *Fax:* (867) 873-6535. *E-mail:* fotr@ssimicro.com. *Website:* www .folkontherocks.com. Annual four-day summer music festival, held in July.

Mariposa Folk Festival: Mariposa Folk Foundation, PO Box 383, Orillia, ON L3V 6J8. *Telephone:* (705) 326-3655. *Fax:* (705) 326-3655. *E-mail:* festival@mariposafolk.com. *Website:* www.mariposafolk.com. Traditional and contemporary folk festival, held in July.

Mill Race Festival of Traditional Folk Music: PO Box 22148, Galt Central PO, Cambridge, ON N1R 8E3. *Telephone:* (519) 621-7135. *E-mail:* mill_race@ yahoo.com. *Website:* www.millracefolksociety.com. Festival of traditional folk music and dance.

NewMusicWest: c/o 29 Productions Inc., 1062 Homer Street, Suite 301, Vancouver, BC V6B 2W9. *Telephone:* (604) 689-2910. *Fax:* (604) 689-2912.

E-mail: info@29productions.ca. *Website:* www.newmusicwest.com. Annual music festival held in April.

Ottawa International Jazz Festival: 61A York Street, Ottawa, ON K1N 5T2. *Telephone:* (613) 241-2633. *Fax:* (613) 241-5774. *E-mail:* info@ottawajazzfestival.com. *Website:* www.ottawajazzfestival.com. Jazz festival with emphasis on Canadian artists.

Vancouver Folk Music Festival: 468-411 Dunsmuir Street, Vancouver, BC V6B 1X4. *Telephone:* (604) 602-9798. *Fax:* (604) 602-9790. *E-mail:* info@thefestival.bc.ca. *Website:* www.thefestival.bc.ca. Three-day folk and world music festival held in Jericho Beach Park, in July.

Winnipeg Folk Festival: 203–211 Bannatyne Avenue, Winnipeg, MB R3B 3P2. *Telephone:* (204) 231-0096. *Fax:* (204) 231-0076. *E-mail:* info@winnipegfolkfestival.ca. *Website:* www.winnipegfolkfestival.ca. f. 1974; folk music festival, held in July.

Croatia

Zagreb Festival of Popular Music (Zagreb-fest): c/o Cantus Ltd, Baruna Trenka 5, 10000 Zagreb. *Telephone:* (1) 4922362. *Fax:* (1) 4825361. *E-mail:* cantus@hds.hr. f. early 1950s; popular music festival held in mid-December.

Denmark

Århus International Jazz Festival: Vester Allé, 8000 C Århus. *Telephone:* 87-30-883-00. *Fax:* 87-30-83-19. *E-mail:* mail@aarhusfestuge.dk. *Website:* www.aarhusfestuge.dk. Festival held in August–September.

Copenhagen Jazz Festival: Nørregade 6, 1165 K Copenhagen. *Telephone:* 33-93-20-13. *Fax:* 33-93-20-24. *E-mail:* info@jazzfestival.dk. *Website:* www.jazzfestival.dk. Festival of jazz, blues and world music, held in July.

Roskilde Festival: Havsteensvej 11, 4000 Roskilde. *Telephone:* 46-36-66-13. *Fax:* 46-32-14-99. *E-mail:* info@roskilde-festival.dk. *Website:* www.roskilde-festival.dk. f. 1971; four-day music festival held in Roskilde, near Copenhagen, in June–July; capacity 70,000.

Skagen Festival: Drosselvej 18, 9990 Skagen DK. *Telephone:* 98-44-49-69. *Fax:* 98-44-63-77. *Website:* www.skagenfestival.dk. Held in late June.

Estonia

Beach Party Festival: PBP Productions, PO Box 5822, Tallinn 13402. *E-mail:* mail@beachparty.ee. *Website:* www.beachparty.ee. f. 1994; two-day festival, capacity 15,000.

Tudengijazz: PO Box 3641, Tallinn. *E-mail:* ahven@hot.ee. *Website:* www.tudengijazz.ee. Student jazz festival held in February.

Finland

April Jazz: c/o Espoo Big Band Society, Ahertajantie 6B, 02100 Espoo. *Telephone:* (9) 4550003. *Fax:* (9) 465172. *E-mail:* info@apriljazz.fi. *Website:* www.apriljazz.fi. International indoor jazz festival, with special focus on vocal and big-band jazz; held in April.

Baltic Jazz: Masugnvägen 5, 25900 Dalsbruk. *Telephone:* (4) 0790340. *E-mail:* baltic.jazz@dragsfjard.fi. *Website:* www.balticjazz.com. f. 1987; national and international swing and traditional jazz event, held in July.

EloJazz&Blues: Veräjätie 36, 90530 Oulu. *Telephone:* (2) 2925870. *E-mail:* info@jazz20.com. *Website:* www.elojazz.com. National jazz festival covering all styles, held in June–July.

Helsingin juhlaviikot (Helsinki Festival): Lasipalatsi, Mannerheimintie 22–24, 00100 Helsinki. *Telephone:* (9) 61265100. *Fax:* (9) 61265161. *E-mail:* info@helsinkifestival.fi. *Website:* www.helsinkifestival.fi. f. 1968; festival of a range of national music, held August–September.

Imatra Big Band Festival: Heikinkatu 1, 55100 Imatra. *Telephone:* (2) 7479400. *Fax:* (2) 7479400. *E-mail:* ibbf@ibbf.fi. *Website:* www.ibbf.fi. Nine-day festival of jazz, swing, blues, soul music, held indoors and outdoors during June–July; capacity 50,000.

KaamosJazz (Jazz Under Northern Lights): Kauko Leinonen, 99695 Tankavaara. *Telephone:* (1) 6626158. *Fax:* (1) 6626261. National indoor jazz festival, held in late November.

Kainuun Jazzkevät (Kainu Jazz Spring): Kainuun Jazzkevät Oy, Teknologiapuisto PL 116, 87400 Kajaani. *Website:* www.jazzkevat.fi. f. 1980; international indoor event with all jazz styles, held in May.

Kalottjazz & Blues Festival: Tornio Cultural Office, Keskikatu 22, 95400 Tornio. *E-mail:* kulttuuritoimisto@tornio.fi. *Website:* www.kalottjazzblues.net. Four-day jazz and blues festival, held in the border towns of Tornio (Finland) and Haparanda (Sweden).

Kansantaiteenkeskus (Kaustinen Folk Music Festival): Jyväskyläntie 3, PL 11, 69601 Kaustinen. *Telephone:* (2) 072911. *Fax:* (2) 07291200. *E-mail:* folk.art@kaustinen.fi. *Website:* www.kaustinen.net. Held in July.

Keitele Jazz: PL 83, 44101 Äänekoski. *Telephone:* (40) 5106795. *Fax:* (40) 5742324. *E-mail:* keitelejazz@aanekoski.fi. *Website:* www.aanekoski.fi/keitelejazz. All jazz styles featured, held in July.

Nummirock: Nummijärventie 385, 61910 Nummijärvi. *Telephone:* (6) 2332213. *E-mail:* nrock@kauhajoki.fi. *Website:* www.nummirock.fi. Rock festival held in June.

Pori International Jazz Festival: Pohjoisranta 11D, 28100 Pori. *Telephone:* (2) 6262200. *Fax:* (2) 6262225. *E-mail:* festival@porijazz.fi. *Website:* www.porijazz.fi. Annual jazz festival of all jazz, rhythm and blues music styles, held in July.

Provinssirock: PO Box 180, 60101 Seinäjoki. *Telephone:* (6) 4212700. *Fax:* (6) 4148622. *E-mail:* info@provinssirock.fi. *Website:* www.provinssirock.fi. Three-day rock festival held in June; capacity 25,000 each day.

RMJ Festival (Midsummer): *E-mail:* media@rmj.fi. *Website:* www.rmj.fi. Three-day festival of many music genres, held in Rauma in June; 90,000 capacity.

Ruisrock: c/o Vantaan Festivaalit Oy, Merikotkanpolku 2, 01450 Vantaa. *Telephone:* (9) 8724446. *Fax:* (9) 2924770. *E-mail:* palaute@ruisrock.fi. *Website:* www.ruisrock.fi. Rock festival held by the sea in Turku, in mid-summer; capacity 65,000.

Tampereen Musiikkijuhlat (Tampere Music Festivals): Tullikamarinaukio 2, 33100 Tampere. *Telephone:* (3) 56566172. *Fax:* (3) 2230121. *E-mail:* juhamatti.kauppinen@tt.tampere.fi. *Website:* www.tampere.fi/festival/music. Series of music festivals.

Turku Jazz: Turku Jazz ry, Uudenmaankatu 1, 20500 Turku. *Telephone:* (4) 5829366. *E-mail:* info@turkujazz.fi. *Website:* www.turkujazz.fi. f. 1969; festival of mainly contemporary jazz styles, held in March.

Tuska Festival: Fredrikinkatu 61 A, 4 krs, 00100 Helsinki. *E-mail:* niklas@fme.fi. *Website:* www.tuska-festival.fi. Open-air metal music festival, held in June; capacity 10,000.

Valtakunnalliset Jazzpäivät (Finnish National Jazz Days): c/o Finnish Jazz Federation, Arabiankatu 2, 00560 Helsinki. *Telephone:* (9) 7572077. *Fax:* (9) 7572067. *Website:* www.jazzfin.com. Annual national jazz festival involving all styles, held in a different town each year, in November.

Ylläs Jazz Blues: Ylläs Soikoon ry, Tunturintie 22, 95970 Äkäslompolo. *Telephone:* (4) 5709666. *E-mail:* music@yllas.fi. *Website:* www.yllasjazzblues.net. Festival of all jazz and R&B styles, held in February.

France

Africolor: 5 rue Arthur Groussier, 75010 Paris. *Telephone:* 1-47-97-69-99. *Fax:* 1-47-97-65-44. *E-mail:* concerts@africolor.com. *Website:* www.africolor.com. Festival focusing on music from Western Africa and Indian Ocean; held in December.

Banlieues Bleues: 9 rue Gabrielle Josserand, 93500 Pantin. *Telephone:* 1-49-22-10-10. *Fax:* 1-49-22-10-11. *E-mail:* bb@banlieuesbleues.org. *Website:* www.banlieuesbleues.org. f. 1984; jazz and blues events throughout Paris in March and April.

Dock des Suds: 12 rue Urbain V, 13002 Marseille. *Telephone:* 4-91-99-00-00. *E-mail:* fiesta.des.suds@wanadoo.fr. *Website:* www.dock-des-suds.org.

Les Eurockéennes de Belfort: c/o Association Territoire de Musiques, 30a Grande rue François Mitterand, 90800 Bavilliers. *Telephone:* 3-84-22-46-58. *E-mail:* festival@eurockeennes.fr. *Website:* www.eurockeennes.com. f. 1989; three-day festival held in July; capacity 95,000.

Festival Les Vieilles Charrues: Association Les Vieilles Charrues, 17 place de la Mairie, BP 204, 29834 Carhaix cedex. *Telephone:* 2-98-99-25-45. *Fax:* 2-98-99-25-46. *E-mail:* contact@vieillescharrues.asso.fr. *Website:* www.vieillescharrues.asso.fr. f. 1992; three-day festival of a diverse range of music held in Carhaix, Brittany in July; capacity 65,000 each day.

Le Festival Synthèse de Bourges: IMEB, Place André Malraux, BP 39, 18001 Bourges cedex. *Telephone:* 2-48-20-41-87. *Fax:* 2-48-20-45-51. *E-mail:* imeb-bourges@orange.fr. *Website:* www.imeb.net. Organized by the Institut International de Musique Electroacoustique Bourges (IMEB).

Le Lieu Unique: 2 rue de la Biscuiterie, Quai Ferdinand Favre, 44013 Nantes cedex 01. *Telephone:* 2-51-82-15-00. *Fax:* 2-40-20-20-12. *E-mail:* info@lelieuunique.com. *Website:* www.lelieuunique.com. Popular music and video events and festivals.

Nice Jazz Festival: Nice Jazz Festival Organization, Viviane Sicnasi Promotion, 28 avenue Marceau, 75008 Paris. *Fax:* 1-47-23-07-58. *E-mail:* info@nicejazzfestival.fr. *Website:* www.nicejazzfestival.fr. Annual jazz festival held in July; capacity 45,000.

La Route du Rock: Rock Tympans, 4 mail François Mitterrand, 35000 Rennes. *Telephone:* 2-99-54-01-11. *Fax:* 2-99-54-22-46. *E-mail:* info@laroutedurock.com. *Website:* www.laroutedurock.com. f. 1991 as one festival; now two electronic and pop festivals held in Saint-Malo, Brittany in February (winter collection) and August (summer collection); capacity 20,000.

Germany

Africa Festival: Afro Project eV, Kaiserstrasse 16, 97070 Würzburg. *Telephone:* (931) 15060. *Fax:* (931) 15080. *E-mail:* info@africafestival.org.

Website: www.africafestival.org. f. 1989; four-day festival of African music and culture; capacity 100,000.

Alandia Jazz Festival: Norra Esplanadgatan 4B, 22100 Mariehamn. *Telephone:* (18) 16508. *Fax:* (18) 16507. *E-mail:* alandia.jazz@aland.net. *Website:* www.alandiajazz.aland.fi. Held in July.

Hurricane Festival: c/o FKP Scorpio Konzertproduktionen GmbH, Grosse Elbstrasse 277–279, 20257 Hamburg. *Telephone:* (40) 85388888. *Fax:* (40) 85388999. *E-mail:* info@fkpscorpio.com. *Website:* www.hurricane.de. f. 1997; two-day festival; capacity 50,000.

M'era Luna Festival: c/o FKP Scorpio Konzertproduktionen GmbH, Grosse Elbstrasse 277–279, 22767 Hamburg. *Telephone:* (40) 85388888. *Fax:* (40) 85388999. *E-mail:* info@fkpscorpio.com. *Website:* www.fkpscorpio.com/meraluna. f. 2000; two-day festival of darkwave, gothic and EBM music, held in August; capacity 25,000.

NatureOne: c/o I-Motion GmbH, Am Hohen Stein 8, 56218 Mülheim-Kärlich. *Telephone:* (261) 9215840. *Fax:* (261) 92158490. *E-mail:* info@i-motion.ag. *Website:* www.nature-one.de. f. 1995; three-day festival in numerous venues; capacity 40,000.

RhEINKULTUR: RhEINKULTUR GmbH, Gluckstrasse 2, 53115 Bonn. *Telephone:* (228) 2070806. *Fax:* (228) 2070808. *E-mail:* info@rheinkultur.com. *Website:* www.rheinkultur-festival.de. Germany's largest open-air festival, held in late June–early July.

Rock am Ring: c/o Marek Lieberberg Konzertagentur GmbH & Co. KG, Mörikestrasse 14, 60320 Frankfurt am Main. *Telephone:* (69) 9562020. *Fax:* (69) 568199. *E-mail:* info@mlk.com. *Website:* www.rock-am-ring.com. Held in June.

Rock im Park: c/o Marek Lieberberg Konzertagentur GmbH & Co. KG, Mörikestrasse 14, 60320 Frankfurt am Main. *Telephone:* (69) 9562020. *Fax:* (69) 568199. *E-mail:* info@mlk.com. *Website:* www.rock-im-park.com. Held in June.

Southside Festival: c/o FKP Scorpio Konzertproduktionen GmbH, Grosse Elbstrasse 277–279, 22767 Hamburg. *Telephone:* (40) 85388888. *Fax:* (40) 85388999. *E-mail:* info@fkpscorpio.com. *Website:* www.southside.de. f. 1999; three-day festival; capacity 40,000.

Summerjam: c/o Contour Music Promotion GmbH, Alexanderstrasse 78, 70182 Stuttgart. *Telephone:* (711) 238500. *Fax:* (711) 2361311. *E-mail:* info@summerjam.de. *Website:* www.summerjam.de. f. 1985; three-day festival of reggae, dancehall and world music; capacity 25,000.

TFF Rudolstadt: Stadtverwaltung Rudolstadt, Bürgermeister Jörg Reichl, Markt 7, 07407 Rudolstadt. *Telephone:* (3672) 486401. *E-mail:* kultur@rudolstadt.de. *Website:* www.tff-rudolstadt.de. Tanz & Folkfest (TFF), annual folk, roots and world music festival, held on the first weekend in July.

Greece

Athens and Epidaurus Festival: Hadjichristou 23 and Makriyianni, 117 42 Athens. *Telephone:* (210) 9282900. *Fax:* (210) 9282941. *E-mail:* info@greekfestival.gr. *Website:* www.greekfestival.gr. Festival of diverse music styles, held in July–August.

Hungary

Sziget Festival: 1033 Budapest, Óbidai-sziget, Május 9. *Telephone:* (1) 372-0650. *Fax:* (1) 372-0651. *E-mail:* info@sziget.hu. *Website:* www.szigetfestival.com. f. 1993; seven-day arts festival, held on Óbudai Island, Budapest in August; capacity 360,000.

Iceland

Iceland Airwaves: c/o Mr Destiny, PO BOX 326, 121 Reykjavík. *Telephone:* 5520380. *Fax:* 5520390. *E-mail:* info@destiny.is. *Website:* www.icelandairwaves.com. City-wide music festival held in Reykjavík, in October.

Ireland

Boyle Arts Festival: Festival Office, King House, Boyle, Co. Roscommon. *Telephone:* (7196) 63085. *E-mail:* info@boylearts.com. *Website:* www.boylearts.com. Held annually, in July–August.

Cork Jazz Festival: 80 Haddington Road, Dublin 4. *Telephone:* (1) 6375219. *E-mail:* jack@questcom.iol.ie. *Website:* www.corkjazzfestival.com. Jazz festival with Irish and international acts, held in October.

The Electric Picnic: c/o Aiken Promotions, 58–59 Thomas Street, Dublin 8. *Telephone:* (1) 4546656. *Fax:* (1) 4546787. *E-mail:* office@aikenpromotions.ie. *Website:* www.electricpicnic.ie. f. 2004; two-day festival held on the Stradbally Estate, Co. Laois, in August; capacity 25,000.

Festival of World Cultures: Dún Laoghaire Rathdown County Council, Marine Road, Dún Laoghaire, Co. Dublin. *Telephone:* (1) 2719555. *Fax:* (1) 2360217. *E-mail:* fwc@dlrcoco.ie. *Website:* www.festivalofworldcultures.com. Annual world music event, held in August.

Galway Arts Festival: Black Box Theatre, Dyke Road, Galway. *Telephone:* (91) 509700. *Fax:* (91) 562655. *E-mail:* info@galwayartsfestival.ie. *Website:* www.galwayartsfestival.ie. Arts festival held in July.

Oxegen: MCD, 7 Park Road, Dún Laoghaire. *E-mail:* contact@oxegen.ie. *Website:* www.oxegen.ie. Replaced the Witnness festival in 2004; held on the Punchestown Racecourse, Co. Kildare, in July; capacity 60,000.

Israel

Israel Festival: PO Box 4409, Jerusalem 91044. *Telephone:* 2-6237000. *Fax:* 2-5669850. *E-mail:* israel_f@zahav.net.il. *Website:* www.israel-festival.org.il. Festival of performing arts, held in Jerusalem in May–June.

Italy

Arezzo Wave: Fondazione Arezzo Wave Italia, Via Buonconte da Montefeitro 4/10, 52100 Arezzo. *Telephone:* (0575) 401722. *Fax:* (0575) 296270. *E-mail:* info@arezzowave.com. *Website:* www.arezzowave.com. European rock festival held in the first week of July.

Cremona Rock (CROCK) Festival: Centro Musica Il Cascinetto, Via Maffi 2a, 26100 Cremona. *E-mail:* info@cantieresonoro.it. *Website:* www.centromusicacremona.it. Annual rock festival held in June.

Festambiente: Segreteria Organizzativa, Località Enaoli, 58100 Rispescia (Grosseto). *Telephone:* (056) 448771. *Fax:* (056) 4487740. *E-mail:* info@festambiente.il. *Website:* www.festambiente.it. Ecological festival.

Gods of Metal: *E-mail:* info@godsofmetal.it. *Website:* www.godsofmetal.it. Two-day festival of metal music, held in Idroscalo, Milan; capacity 20,000 each day.

Independent Days Festival: *Telephone:* (434) 208631. *Fax:* (434) 20656. *E-mail:* info@indipendente.com. *Website:* www.indipendente.com. f. 1999; one-day rock music festival, held late summer in Bologna; capacity 20,000.

Neapolis Festival: *E-mail:* info@neapolis.it. *Website:* www.neapolis.it. f. 1997; two-day rock festival held in Naples; capacity 25,000.

Rockin' Umbria: Via Della Viola 1, 06100 Perugia. *E-mail:* info@rockinumbria.it. *Website:* www.rockinumbria.it. Two-day international music festival.

Roma Incontra il Mondo (Rome Meets the World): *E-mail:* roma@arciroma.it. *Website:* www.villaada.org. World music festival held in August.

Japan

Fuji Rock Festival: Naeba Ski Resort, Japan. *Website:* www.fujirockfestival.com. Held in July; capacity 60,000.

Mali

Festival au Désert: *E-mail:* fad-info@festival-au-desert.org. *Website:* www.festival-au-desert.org. f. 2001; three-day festival held in Essakane.

The Netherlands

Amsterdam Dance Event: PO Box 929, 1200 AX Hilversum. *Telephone:* (35) 6218748. *Fax:* (35) 6212750. *E-mail:* ade@bumacultuur.nl. *Website:* www.amsterdam-dance-event.nl. Weekend festival of international dance music artists and DJs, held in October; capacity 50,000.

Dance Valley Festival: *Website:* www.dancevalley.nl. f. 2004; one-day festival held in July; 60,000 capacity.

Dunya Festival: c/o DUCOS Productions, Postbus 13108, 3004 BC Rotterdam. *Fax:* (10) 4049630. *E-mail:* info@ducos.com. *Website:* www.dunya.nl. Held in June.

Dynamo Open Air Festival: Juliusstraat 45, 5621 GC Rotterdam. *E-mail:* toon@dynamo.nl. *Website:* www.dynamo.nl. Heavy rock festival.

A Campingflight to Lowlands Paradise: *Website:* www.lowlands.nl. f. 1993; three-day festival of music and the arts, held in August; capacity 60,000.

Metropolis Festival: Postbus 131, 3000 AC Rotterdam. *Telephone:* (10) 4331300. *Fax:* (10) 4134622. *E-mail:* info@metropolisfestival.nl. *Website:* www.metropolisfestival.nl. Pop festival for up-and-coming bands, held in Zuiderpark, Rotterdam, in July.

North Sea Jazz Festival: PO Box 3325, 2601 DH Delft. *Telephone:* (15) 2148900. *Fax:* (15) 2148393. *E-mail:* info@northseajazz.com. *Website:* www.northseajazz.nl. Indoor jazz festival.

Parkpop: c/o DUCOS Productions, Postbus 13108, 3004 HC Rotterdam. *Fax:* (10) 4049630. *E-mail:* info@ducos.com. *Website:* www.parkpop.nl. f. 1981; one-day free festival held in The Hague, in June; capacity 350,000.

Pinkpop: PO Box 117, 6160 AC Geleen. *Telephone:* (46) 4756717. *Fax:* (46) 4752520. *E-mail:* info@pinkpop.nl. *Website:* www.pinkpop.nl. f. 1969; three-day pop festival held in Landgraaf, in June; capacity 60,000.

Reggae Sundance Festival: *Telephone:* (40) 2908564. *Fax:* (40) 2908566. *E-mail:* info@reggaesundance.nl. *Website:* www.reggaesundance.nl. f. 1995;

open-air reggae and world music festival, held in Genneperparken, Eindhoven, in August; capacity 12,500.

Schollenpop: Stichting Schollenpop, Kranenburgweg 21, 2581 XX The Hague. *Fax:* (847) 179804. *E-mail:* info@schollenpop.nl. *Website:* www.schollenpop.nl. Annual festival held on Zuiderstrand beach, Scheveningen, in August; capacity 50,000.

Wantijpop: Stichting Popprojecten, Postbus 21450, 3001 AL Rotterdam. *Telephone:* (10) 4123455. *E-mail:* info@popprojecten.nl. *Website:* www.wantijpop.nl. f. 1995; one-day festival held in Dordrecht, in June; capacity 25,000.

New Zealand

Bay of Islands Country Rock Festival: PO Box 355, Kerikeri Bay of Islands. *Telephone:* (9) 404-1063. *Fax:* (9) 404-1065. *E-mail:* maysplace@actrix.co.nz. *Website:* www.country-rock.co.nz. Annual country music festival, held on the second weekend in May.

New Zealand International Festival of the Arts: PO Box 10-113, Wellington 6143. *Telephone:* (4) 473-0149. *Fax:* (4) 471-1164. *E-mail:* nzfestival@festival.co.nz. *Website:* www.nzfestival.telecom.co.nz. Biennial festival of the arts.

Taranaki Festival of the Arts: Festival Trust, PO Box 4251, New Plymouth, Taranaki. *Telephone:* (6) 759-8412. *Fax:* (6) 759-8458. *E-mail:* office@artsfest.co.nz. *Website:* www.artsfest.co.nz. Biennial festival, held in July–August.

Norway

Førde Internasjonale Folkemusikkfestival (Førde International Folk Music Festival): Postboks 395, 6801 Førde. *Telephone:* 57-72-19-40. *Fax:* 57-72-19-41. *E-mail:* info@fordefestival.no. *Website:* www.fordefestival.no. Held in July.

Glopperock: Musikkforeininga Gloppen Musikkforum, Postboks 222, 6821 Sandane. *Telephone:* 57-86-66-16. *Fax:* 57-82-70-03. *E-mail:* post@glopperock.no. *Website:* www.glopperock.no. f. 1980; rock festival held in June.

Molde International Jazz Festival: PO Box 415, 6401 Molde. *Telephone:* 71-20-31-50. *Fax:* 71-20-31-51. *E-mail:* post@moldejazz.no. *Website:* www.moldejazz.no. Jazz festival held in July.

Notodden Blues Festival: Postboks 211, 3672 Notodden. *Telephone:* 35-02-76-50. *E-mail:* nbf@bluesfest.no. *Website:* www.bluesfest.no. Blues festival held in August.

Quart Festivalen: Boks 260, 4663 Kristiansand. *Telephone:* 38-14-69-69. *Fax:* 38-14-69-68. *Website:* www.quart.no. Five-day festival, held in Kristiansand in July; capacity 10,000 each day.

Poland

Open'er: *E-mail:* kontakt@alterart.pl. *Website:* www.opener.pl. f. 2001; three-day festival held in Babie Doły air field in Gdynia, in July.

Przegladu Piosenki Aktorskiej (Review of Actors' Songs): 50-020 Wrocław, Teatr Muzyczny Capitol, ul. Pilsudskiego 72. *Telephone:* (71) 7890457. *Fax:* (71) 7902635. *E-mail:* ppa@teatr-capitol.pl. *Website:* www.ppa.art.pl. f. 1979; concert and recitals of Polish musical theatre of the season.

Portugal

Festival Sudoeste: Música no Coração, Rua Viriato 25, 2o Esq., 1050-234 Lisbon. *Telephone:* (21) 0105700. *Fax:* (21) 3156555. *E-mail:* musicanocoracao@musicanocoracao.pt. *Website:* www.musicanocoracao.pt/festivais/fest_sudoeste.html. Four-day festival of national and international artists, held in Zambujeira do Mar in August; capacity 35,000.

Rock in Rio: *E-mail:* contacto@rockinrio-lisboa.sapo.pt. *Website:* rockinrio-lisboa.sapo.pt. Occasional rock festival held in Rio de Janeiro, Brazil (f. 1985) and Lisbon, Portugal (f. 2004).

Romania

Golden Stag Festival: Cerbul de Aur, Bucharest 1, Calea Dorobantilor nr. 191. *Telephone:* (21) 3199033. *Fax:* (21) 3058892. *E-mail:* golden.stag@tvr.ro. *Website:* www.cerbuldeaur.ro. f. 1968; international music festival held in Braşov.

Serbia

Exit Festival: Srpsko narodno pozoriste, Novi Sad, 21000 Vojvodina. *Telephone:* 21 424 451. *Fax:* 21 424 453. *E-mail:* admin@exitfest.org. *Website:* www.exitfest.org. Annual weekend festival, held at the Petrovaradin Fortress, Novi Sad in July; capacity 55,000 each day.

Slovenia

Druga Godba: 1000 Ljubljana, Kersnikova 4. *Telephone:* (1) 4308260. *Fax:* (1) 4308265. *E-mail:* info@drugagodba.si. *Website:* www.drugagodba.si. Held in June.

Festival Ljubljana: 1000 Ljubljana, Koseskega 11. *Telephone:* (1) 2416000. *Fax:* (1) 2416037. *E-mail:* info@ljubljanafestival.si. *Website:* www.ljubljanafestival.si. Open-air arts festival, held in June–September.

No Border Jam Festival: 2000 Maribor, Klub MKC, Ljubljanska ulica 4. *Telephone:* (2) 3002990. *Fax:* (2) 3002992. *E-mail:* mkc.maribor@guest.arnes.si. *Website:* www.mkc.si. f. 1992; two-day annual punk, rock, pop, ethno, garage festival, held in August.

Spain

Barcelona International Jazz Festival: The Project, Diagonal, 482, 08006 Barcelona. *Telephone:* (93) 4817040. *Fax:* (93) 4817041. *E-mail:* theproject@the-project.es. *Website:* www.the-project.es. Jazz festival, held in October–November.

Festival Internacional de Benicàssim (FIB): *E-mail:* info@fiberfib.com. *Website:* www.fiberfib.com. f. 1994; three-day festival of indie, pop and electronic music, held in Benicàssim, Valencia, in July; capacity 30,000.

El Festival de la Guitarra de Córdoba: IMAE Gran Teatro de Córdoba, Avenida Gran Capitán 3, 14008 Córdoba. *Telephone:* (957) 480644. *Fax:* (957) 487494. *E-mail:* granteatro.prensa@ayuncordoba.es. *Website:* www.guitarracordoba.com. Annual festival, held in July.

Pirineos Sur: Diputación de Huesca, Porches de Galicia 4, 22002 Huesca. *Telephone:* (974) 294151. *Fax:* (974) 294150. *E-mail:* info@pirineos-sur.es. *Website:* www.pirineos-sur.es. Arts festival held in July–August.

Primavera Sound: *E-mail:* info@primaverasound.com. *Website:* www.primaverasound.com. Held on the site of the Olympics in Barcelona, in May.

Sónar: Advanced Music SL, PO Box 21.109, 08080 Barcelona. *E-mail:* sonar@sonar.es. *Website:* www.sonar.es. Three-day festival of music and multimedia arts; held in Barcelona in June; capacity 30,000 per day.

Sweden

Arvikafestivalen: PO Box 99, 671 23 Arvika. *Telephone:* (5) 701-36-66. *E-mail:* info@arvikafestivalen.se. *Website:* www.arvikafestivalen.se. f. 1992; rock and indie music festival, held in July.

Bluesfestivalen Mönsterås: Kuggåsvägen 2, 383 30 Mönsterås. *Telephone:* (4) 991-74-47. *E-mail:* mail@bluesfestival.nu. *Website:* www.bluesfestival.nu. f. 1994.

Hultsfred Festival: PO Box 170, 577 24 Hultsfred. *Telephone:* (4) 956-95-00. *Fax:* (4) 956-95-50. *E-mail:* info@rockparty.se. *Website:* www.rockparty.se. f. 1986.

Kalottjazz & Blues Festival: Keskikatu 22, 95400 Tornio, Finland. *Website:* www.kalottjazzblues.net. Four-day jazz and blues festival, held in the border towns of Tornio (Finland) and Haparanda (Sweden).

Re:Orient Festival: PO Box 4215, 102 65 Stockholm. *Telephone:* (8) 702-15-99. *Fax:* (8) 640-08-28. *E-mail:* fornamn@reorient.se. *Website:* www.reorient.se. f. 1993; held in August.

Stockholm Jazz Festival: Regeringsgatan 74, 2 tr, 111 39 Stockholm. *Telephone:* (8) 505-33-17-0. *Fax:* (8) 453-34-47. *E-mail:* info@stockholmjazz.com. *Website:* www.stockholmjazz.com. f. 1980; nine-day festival on the island of Skeppsholmen, in Stockholm; capacity 12,000 each day.

Switzerland

Balélec: c/o EPFL, Station 11, 1015 Lausanne. *Telephone:* 216934644. *Fax:* 216934647. *Website:* www.balelec.ch. f. 1980; one-day festival held in Lausanne, in May; capacity 15,000.

Caribana Festival: Association Caribana, rue de la combe 4, 1260 Nyon. *Telephone:* 223630280. *Fax:* 229901503. *E-mail:* presse@caribana-festival.ch. *Website:* www.caribana-festival.ch. Four-day festival of rock, folk, tropical, rap and acid jazz, held in Crans-sur-Nyon.

Jazz Festival Willisau: PO Box, 6130 Willisau. *Telephone:* 419702731. *Fax:* 419703231. *E-mail:* troxler@jazzwillisau.ch. *Website:* www.jazzwillisau.ch. Festival of jazz, held in August–September.

Lugano Estival Jazz: Lugano, 6992 Vernate. *E-mail:* info@estivaljazz.ch. *Website:* www.estivaljazz.ch. Free open-air jazz festival.

Montreux Jazz Festival: Fondation du Festival de Jazz de Montreux, Sentier de Collonge 3, CP 126, 1820 Montreux. *Telephone:* 219664444. *Fax:* 219664433. *E-mail:* info@mjf.ch. *Website:* www.montreuxjazz.com. f. 1967; annual festival, held in June–July, consisting of jazz, pop, rock, blues and soul music.

OpenAir Gampel: Postfach 82, 3945 Gampel. *Telephone:* 279325010. *Fax:* 279325014. *E-mail:* info@openairgampel.ch. *Website:* www.openairgampel.ch. f. 1986; three-day festival, held in Gampel in August; capacity 50,000.

OpenAir St Gallen: *Website:* www.openairsg.ch. f. 1977; three-day festival, held in St Gallen in June–July; capacity 30,000 each day.

Paléo Festival Nyon: Route de St-Cergue 312, CP 1320, 1260 Nyon 1. *Telephone:* 223651010. *Fax:* 223651020. *Website:* www.paleo.ch. f. 1977 as

First Folk Festival, later renamed Nyon Folk Festival; changed name in 1985; open-air festival held in July; capacity 30,000 per day.

Turkey

International İstanbul Jazz Festival: c/o İstanbul Foundation for Culture and Arts, Istiklal Caddesi 146, Beyoglu 34435, İstanbul. *Fax:* (212) 3340708. *Website:* www.iksv.org/caz. f. 1986 as part of the International İstanbul Festival, later a festival in its own right; held June–July; capacity 60,000.

Ukraine

Tavria Games International Festival: 01135 Kyiv, PO Box 14. *Telephone:* (44) 236-17-44. *Fax:* (44) 486-70-06. *Website:* www.tavriagames.com. f. 1992; annual popular music festival, held in Kakhovka in May.

United Kingdom

Americana International: Americana Promotions Ltd, Jacksonville, 1 Middle Orchard Street, Stapleford, Nottingham, NG9 8DD, England. *Telephone:* (870) 863-2100. *Fax:* (115) 949-0856. *E-mail:* silvereagleuk@aol.com. *Website:* www.americana-international.co.uk. American lifestyle event, held in July; 70,000 capacity.

Bath International Music Festival: Bath Festivals Trust, Abbey Chambers, Kingston Buildings, Bath, BA1 1NT, England. *Telephone:* (1225) 462231. *Fax:* (1225) 445551. *E-mail:* info@bathfestivals.org.uk. *Website:* www.bathmusicfest.org.uk. Arts festival f. 1993; held May–June.

BBC Electric Proms: BBC, Wood Lane, London, W12 7RJ, England. *Website:* www.bbc.co.uk/electricproms. f. 2006; five-day event, held in October.

Bestival: Bestival Ltd, Third Floor, 25 Denmark Street, London, WC2H 8NJ, England. *Telephone:* (20) 7379-3133. *E-mail:* hello@bestival.net. *Website:* www.bestival.net. Three-day music festival, held in Robin Hill, Isle of Wight, in September.

The Big Chill: Chillfest Ltd, PO Box 58279, London, N1P 1EU, England. *E-mail:* info@bigchill.net. *Website:* www.bigchill.net. f. 1994; multimedia three-day festival held in August, in association with a bar, club event and record label, covering a wide variety of music genres; 29,000 capacity.

Cambridge Folk Festival: The Guildhall, Cambridge, CB2 3QJ, England. *Telephone:* (1223) 457512. *Fax:* (1223) 457529. *E-mail:* folkfest@cambridge.gov.uk. *Website:* www.cambridgefolkfestival.co.uk. Annual folk festival with a programme including folk, blues and country; held in July–August.

The Carling Weekend: Festival Republic Ltd, 2nd Floor, Regent Arcade House, 19-25 Argyll Street, London, W1F 7TS, England. *E-mail:* info@festivalrepublic.com. *Website:* www.leedsfestival.com; www.readingfestival.com. f. 1999; rock and pop festival held in two venues: Bramham Park, Wetherby (near Leeds) and Rivermead, Reading, over three days in August; 50,000 capacity.

Creamfields: Cream Group Nation, Wolstenholme Square, 1-3 Parr Street, Liverpool L1 4JJ, England. *Telephone:* (151) 707-1309. *Fax:* (151) 707-1761. *E-mail:* info@cream.co.uk. *Website:* www.cream.co.uk. f. 1998; held on Old Liverpool Airfield, Speke Merseyside, August bank holiday weekend.

Cropredy Festival: c/o Fairport Convention, PO Box 263, Chipping Norton, Oxfordshire OX7 9DF, England. *Website:* www.fairportconvention.com. f. 1978; festival headlined by Fairport Convention; 20,000 capacity.

Download Festival: Live Nation UK Ltd, 2nd Floor, Regent Arcade House, 19-25 Argyll Street, London, W1F 7TS, England. *E-mail:* info@downloadfestival.co.uk. *Website:* www.downloadfestival.co.uk. f. 2003; rock and metal music festival held in Donington Park, Leicestershire, over a weekend in June.

Fleadh: Mean Fiddler Music Group PLC, 59-65 Worship Street, London, EC2A 2DU, England. *Telephone:* (20) 7688-9000. *Fax:* (20) 7688-8999. *Website:* www.meanfiddler.com. Irish and Scottish folk festival held in Finsbury Park, London, in June.

Glastonbury Festival: Glastonbury Festival Office, 28 Northload Street, Glastonbury, Somerset BA6 9JJ, England. *Telephone:* (1458) 834596. *Fax:* (1458) 833235. *E-mail:* office@glastonburyfestivals.co.uk. *Website:* www.glastonburyfestivals.co.uk. Festival held on Worthy Farm, Pilton, Shepton Mallet, Somerset, in June.

Isle of Wight Festival: Wight Leisure, 17 Quay Street, Newport, PO30 5BA, Isle of Wight. *Telephone:* (1983) 823828. *Fax:* (1983) 823369. *E-mail:* info@isleofwightfestival.org. *Website:* www.isleofwightfestival.org. Annual festival (ceased between 1970 and 2002), held in Newport, in June; capacity 35,000.

Monsters of Rock Festival: Live Nation UK Ltd, 2nd Floor, Regent Arcade House, 19-25 Argyll Street, London, W1F 7TS, England. *Website:* www.monstersofrock.co.uk. Annual heavy-metal festival held at Milton Keynes National Bowl in August.

Notting Hill Carnival: 5 Baseline Studios, Whitchurch Road, London, W11 4AT, England. *Telephone:* (20) 7727-0072. *Fax:* (20) 7727-0023. *E-mail:* info@nottinghillcarnival.biz. *Website:* www.lnhc.org.uk. Annual street carnival and music event, held in Notting Hill, London in August.

Sidmouth International Festival: Tourist Information Centre, Ham Lane, Sidmouth, Devon EX10 8XR, England. *Telephone:* (1395) 578627. *E-mail:* info@sidmouthfolkweek.com. *Website:* www.sidmouthfolkweek.co.uk. f. 1955; eight-day folk and roots festival, held early August; capacity 65,000.

T in the Park: Big Day Out Ltd, PO Box 28241, Glasgow, G2 5XS, Scotland. *E-mail:* media@tinthepark.com. *Website:* www.tinthepark.com. f. 1994; festival held in Balado, Scotland, in July; capacity 69,000.

V Festival: PO Box 34286, London, NW5 2XQ, England. *E-mail:* contact@vfestival.com. *Website:* www.vfestival.com. Two-day festival held at two venues: Hylands Park, Chelmsford and Weston Park, Staffordshire, in August; capacity 60,000 at each venue.

02 Music Wireless Festival: Live Nation UK Ltd, 2nd Floor, Regent Arcade House, 19-25 Argyll Street, London, W1F 7TS, England. *E-mail:* info@wirelessfestival.co.uk. *Website:* www.wirelessfestival.co.uk. f. 2005; four-day festival held in Hyde Park, London and Harewood House, Leeds, in June; 30,000 capacity.

WOMAD: Mill Side, Mill Lane, Box, Corsham, Wiltshire SN13 8PN, England. *Telephone:* (1225) 743188. *Fax:* (1225) 743481. *E-mail:* info@womad.org. *Website:* www.womad.org. Annual festival held in Charlton Park, Wiltshire, in July; 22,000 capacity.

United States of America

AmsterJam: *Website:* www.heineken.com/usa. f. 2005; one-day festival held on Randall's Island, New York, in August; rap, rock, pop, funk, and dance music; sponsored by Heineken.

Austin City Limits Festival: *E-mail:* info@austincitylimits.com. *Website:* www.aclfestival.com. Three-day festival covering diverse music genres, including R&B, rock and jazz; capacity 65,000.

Coachella Valley Music and Arts Festival: Coachella, 1100 South Flower Street, Suite 3200, Los Angeles, CA 90015. *Website:* www.coachella.com. f. 1999; diverse music festival, held in Empire Polo Field, Indio, California; capacity 68,000.

Lollapalooza: *E-mail:* info@lollapalooza.com. *Website:* www.lollapalooza.com. Three-day festival held in Grant Park, Chicago.

New Orleans Jazz & Heritage Festival: New Orleans Jazz & Heritage Festival and Foundation Inc., 336 Camp Street, Suite 250, New Orleans, LA 70130. *Telephone:* (504) 410-4100. *Website:* www.nojazzfest.com. f. 1970; annual festival, held in April–May.

Ravinia Festival: 418 Sheridan Road, Highland Park, IL 60035. *Telephone:* (847) 266-5000. *Fax:* (847) 433-7983. *E-mail:* ravinia@ravinia.org. *Website:* www.ravinia.org. Annual festival of a range of music, held in June–September.

South by Southwest (SXSW): PO Box 4999, Austin, TX 78765. *Telephone:* (512) 467-7979. *Fax:* (512) 451-0754. *E-mail:* sxsw@sxsw.com. *Website:* www.sxsw.com. Annual music and media conference and festival, held in March.

APPENDIX B: MUSIC ORGANIZATIONS

It would be impossible to list all the music organizations that exist worldwide. Therefore, we include the large international music organizations (listed once only, under the head office) and the principal national music or arts organizations of each country. Many of these organizations have websites with information on, or links to smaller or more specific groups, covering all aspects of the musical community.

Albania

Albanian National Music Committee: Pallatet 9 kate, Shkalla 2, Ap. 4, Tirana. *Telephone:* (4) 374127. *Fax:* (4) 222857. *E-mail:* vasitole@hotmail.com.

Argentina

Fondo Nacional de las Artes: Alsina 673 (1087), Buenos Aires. *Telephone:* (11) 4343-1590. *Fax:* (11) 4343-1590. *E-mail:* fnartes@fnartes.gov.ar. *Website:* www.fnartes.gov.ar.

Sindicato Argentino de Músicos (SADEM): Avenida Belgrano 3655, 2007 Buenos Aires. *Telephone:* (11) 4957-3522. *E-mail:* internacionales@sadem.com.ar. *Website:* www.sadem.org.ar.

Sociedad Argentina de Autores y Compositores de Música (SADAIC): Lavalle 1547, 1048 Buenos Aires. *Telephone:* (11) 4379-8600. *Fax:* (11) 4379-8633. *E-mail:* consultas@sadaic.org.ar. *Website:* www.sadaic.org.ar.

Australia

APRA/AMCOS: 6–12 Atchison Street, St Leonards, NSW 2065. *Telephone:* (2) 9935-7900. *Fax:* (2) 9935-7999. *E-mail:* apra@apra.com.au. *Website:* www.apra.com.au; www.amcos.com.au. The Australasian Performing Right Association (APRA) is a non-profit organization that collects royalties on behalf of its members; since 1997, it has been associated with the Australasian Mechanical Copyright Owners Society (AMCOS).

Australia Council for the Arts: PO Box 788, Strawberry Hills, NSW 2012. *Telephone:* (2) 9215-9000. *Fax:* (2) 9215-9111. *E-mail:* mail@australiacouncil.gov.au. *Website:* www.australiacouncil.gov.au. Government arts funding and advisory body.

Australian Recording Industry Association (ARIA): PO Box Q20, Queen Victoria Building, NSW 1230. *Telephone:* (2) 8569-1144. *Fax:* (2) 8569-1183. *E-mail:* aria.mail@aria.com.au. *Website:* www.aria.com.au. Organization aiming to advance the interests of the Australian record industry.

International Council for Traditional Music (ICTM): ICTM Secretariat, School of Music, Australian National University, Building 100, Canberra, ACT 0200. *Telephone:* (2) 6125-5700. *Fax:* (2) 6125-9775. *E-mail:* secretariat@ictmusic.org. *Website:* www.ictmusic.org/ICTM. Organization aiming to increase the study, preservation and dissemination of the traditional music of all countries.

International Society for Music Education (ISME): International Office, PO Box 909, Nedlands, WA 6909. *Telephone:* (8) 9386-2654. *Fax:* (8) 9386-2658. *E-mail:* isme@isme.org. *Website:* www.isme.org. Worldwide network for music educators.

Musicians' Union of Australia: c/o Federal Secretary, 150 Bell Street, Coburg, VIC 3058. *Telephone:* (3) 9355-7620. *Fax:* (3) 9355-7621. *E-mail:* federal.secretary@musicians.asn.au. *Website:* www.musicians.asn.au.

TasMusic: PO Box 435, Level 2, 54 Brisbane Street, Launceston, TAS 7250. *Telephone:* (3) 6331-4470. *E-mail:* info@tasmusic.com.au. *Website:* www.tasmusic.com.au. Independent, not-for-profit organization, supporting the Tasmanian music industry.

Austria

Gesellschaft der Autoren, Komponisten und Musikverleger (AKM): Baumannstrasse 10, 1030 Vienna. *Telephone:* (1) 050-71-70. *E-mail:* direktion@akm.co.at. *Website:* www.akm.co.at. Performing rights organization.

International Music and Media Centre (IMZ): Stiftgasse 29, 1070 Vienna. *Telephone:* (1) 889-03-15. *Fax:* (1) 889-03-15-77. *E-mail:* office@imz.at. *Website:* www.imz.at.

Musiker-Komponisten-Autoren Gilde: Gartengasse 22, 1050 Vienna. *Telephone:* (1) 54-55-99. *Fax:* (1) 545-65-10. *E-mail:* text@musikergilde.at. *Website:* www.musikergilde.at. f. 1989; musicians' union.

Musikverleger Union Österreich (MUO): Baumannstrasse 8–10, Postfach 3, 1030 Vienna. *Telephone:* (1) 337-23-0. *Fax:* (1) 337-23-40-0. Musicians' union.

Belgium

European Forum of Worldwide Music Festivals (EFWMF): Jan Frans Willemsstraat 10a, 2530 Boechout. *Telephone:* (3) 455-69-44. *Fax:* (3) 454-11-62. *E-mail:* info@efwmf.org. *Website:* www.efwmf.org. f. 1991.

European Music Office (EMO): Rue du Trône 51, 1050 Brussels. *Telephone:* (2) 213-14-00. *Fax:* (2) 213-14-01. *E-mail:* info@emo.org. *Website:* www.musicineurope.org. International non-profit organization linking the national professional organizations, associations and federations of Europe.

The Global Entertainment Retail Association-Europe (GERA-Europe): Chaussée de Wavre 214d, 1050 Brussels. *Telephone:* (2) 626-19-91. *Fax:* (2) 626-95-01. *E-mail:* info@gera-europe.org. *Website:* www.gera-europe.org. f. 2000; trade association of entertainment retailers in Europe.

Independent Music Companies Association (IMPALA): Coudenberg 70, 1000 Brussels. *Telephone:* (2) 503-31-38. *Fax:* (2) 503-23-91. *E-mail:* info@impalamusic.com. *Website:* www.impalasite.org. f. 2000 to represent European independent music companies and promote the competitiveness and development of the sector.

International Association of Music Information Centres (IAMIC): Steenstraat 25, 1000 Brussels. *Telephone:* (2) 504-90-99. *Fax:* (2) 502-81-03. *E-mail:* iamic@iamic.net. *Website:* www.iamic.net. Worldwide network of organizations that document and promote contemporary music.

International Organisation of Performing Artists (GIART): GIART Permanent Representation, La Maison des Auteurs, Rue Prince Royal 87, 1050 Brussels. *Telephone:* (2) 290-44-38. *Fax:* (2) 551-08-92. *E-mail:* giart@chello.be. *Website:* www.giart.org. f. 2003; a group of management societies of performing artists' rights, aiming to defend and promote intellectual property rights of performing artists.

Jeunesses Musicales International: Palais des Beaux Arts, 13 rue Baron Horta, 1000 Brussels. *Telephone:* (2) 513-97-74. *Fax:* (2) 514-47-55. *E-mail:* mail@jmi.net. *Website:* www.jmi.net. Youth and music network with members and contact organizations worldwide.

La Société Belge des Auteurs, Compositeurs et Editeurs (SABAM): Rue d'Arlon 75/77, Arlenstraat, 1040 Brussels. *Telephone:* (2) 286-82-11. *Fax:* (2) 230-05-89. *E-mail:* info@sabam.be. *Website:* www.sabam.be.

Benin

Organisation des Musiciens du Bénin (OMB): 04 BP 0066, Cotonou. *Telephone:* 95-96-01-59. *Fax:* 91-30-95-35. *E-mail:* omuzbenin@yahoo.fr. Musicians' union.

Bolivia

Sociedad Boliviana de Autores y Compositores de Música (SOBODAYCOM): PO Box 5107, La Paz. *Telephone:* (2) 248-9888. *Fax:* (2) 248-9882. *E-mail:* informaciones@sobodaycom.org. *Website:* www.sobodaycom.org. Society of writers and composers of music.

Brazil

Fundação Nacional de Arte (Funarte): Centro da Música, Rua da Imprensa 16, 5° andar Centro, 20030-120 Rio de Janeiro, RJ. *Telephone:* (21) 2279-8003. *Fax:* (21) 2232-3431. *E-mail:* faleconosco@funarte.gov.br. *Website:* www.funarte.gov.br.

Ordem dos Músicos do Brasil (OMB): SCS QD. 04, Edifício Israel Pinheiro 3°, Brasília DF 70300-500. *Telephone:* (61) 226-0311. *E-mail:* ombcf@ombcf.com.br. National organization, with chapters in various areas of the country, defending the rights of musicians.

Sociedade Brasileira de Música Contemporânea: SQS 105, Bloco B, Apt 506, 70344-020 Brasília, DF. *Telephone:* (11) 3672-3115. *Fax:* (11) 3673-0321.

Bulgaria

Musicautor: 1000 Sofia, ul. Budapest 17, Floor 4. *Telephone:* (2) 9801035. *Fax:* (2) 9800253. *E-mail:* musicautor_bg@musicautor.org. *Website:* www.musicautor.org. Society of authors and composers for performing and mechanical rights.

Burkina Faso

Syndicat National des Artistes Musiciens (SYNAM): 01 BP 2091, Ouagadougou 01. *Telephone:* 50-31-15-91. *Fax:* 50-30-06-82. *E-mail:* studio.des@fasonet.bf. Musicians' union.

Cameroon

Syndicat Camerounais des Artistes et Compositeurs de Musique (SCACOM): BP 3978, Yaoundé. *Telephone:* 7765-687. *Fax:* 2205-152. *E-mail:* sycamu@yahoo.fr. Musicians' union.

Canada

American Federation of Musicians: 75 The Donway West, Suite 1010, Don Mills, ON M3C 2E9. *Telephone:* (416) 391-5161. *Fax:* (416) 391-5165. *E-mail:*

afmcan@afm.org. *Website:* www.afm.org. Organization representing the interests of professional musicians in the USA and Canada.

Canada Council for the Arts—Conseil des Arts du Canada: PO Box 1047, 350 Albert Street, Ottawa, ON K1P 5V8. *Telephone:* (613) 566-4414. *Fax:* (613) 566-4390. *Website:* www.canadacouncil.ca.

Canadian Academy of Recording Arts and Sciences (CARAS): 345 Adelaide Street West, 2nd Floor, Toronto, ON M5V 1R5. *Telephone:* (416) 485-3135. *Fax:* (416) 485-4978. *E-mail:* info@carasonline.ca. *Website:* www .carasonline.ca.

Canadian Music Centre—Centre de Musique Canadienne (CMC): Chalmers House, 20 St Joseph Street, Toronto, ON M4Y 1J9. *Telephone:* (416) 961-6601. *Fax:* (416) 961-7198. *E-mail:* info@musiccentre.ca. *Website:* www .musiccentre.ca. Promotes the work of its members worldwide; extensive library and archive.

Canadian Musical Reproduction Rights Agency (CMRRA): 56 Wellesley Street W, Suite 320, Toronto, ON M5S 2S3. *Telephone:* (416) 926-1966. *Fax:* (416) 926-7521. *Website:* www.cmrra.ca. Non-profit music licensing agency.

The Canadian Recording Industry Association—L'Association de l'industrie canadienne de l'enregistrement (CRIA): 85 Mowat Avenue, Toronto, ON M6K 3E3. *Telephone:* (416) 967-7272. *Fax:* (416) 967-9415. *E-mail:* info@cria.ca. *Website:* www.cria.ca. f. 1964; non-profit trade organization representing the interests of Canadian companies that create, manufacture and market recordings.

Société du droit de reproduction des auteurs, compositeurs et éditeurs au Canada (SODRAC): 759 Victoria Square, Suite 420, Montréal, QC H2Y 2J7. *Telephone:* (514) 845-3268. *Fax:* (514) 845-3401. *E-mail:* sodrac@ sodrac.ca. *Website:* www.sodrac.com. Organization promoting copyright of its members.

The Society of Composers, Authors and Music Publishers of Canada— La Société canadienne des auteurs, compositeurs et éditeurs de musique (SOCAN): 41 Valleybrook Drive, Toronto, ON M3B 2S6. *Telephone:* (416) 445-8700. *Fax:* (416) 445-7108. *E-mail:* socan@socan.ca. *Website:* www .socan.ca. Organization administering the communication and performing rights of copyright-protected music, when used in Canada.

Chile

Asociación Nacional de Compositores (ANC): Almirante Moritt 453, Santiago. *Website:* www.anc.scd.cl.

Sociedad Chilena del Derecho de Autor (SCD): Bernarda Morin 440, Providencia, Santiago. *Telephone:* (2) 370-8731. *Fax:* (2) 370-8030. *E-mail:* comunicaciones@scd.cl. *Website:* www.musica.cl.

People's Republic of China

Chinese Musicians' Association: No.10, Nanli, Nong Zhanguan, Beijing 100026. *Telephone:* (71) 88852485. *Fax:* (71) 88852485. *Website:* www .musician.org.cn.

Colombia

La Asociación Colombiana de Músicos Profesionales: Calles 17, 10–16, Oficina 607, Santafé de Bogotá, DC.

La Asociación de Artistas de Colombia: Calle 13, 9-63, Interior 104, PO Box 24627, Bogotá, DC.

La Sociedad de Autores y Compositores de Colombia (SAYCO): Carrera 19, 40-72, PO Box 6482, Santafé de Bogotá, DC. *Website:* www .sayco.org.

The Democratic Republic of the Congo

Syndicat National des Artistes et Musiciens du Congo (SYNAMCO): BP 16668, Kinshasa 1. *Telephone:* 89 21 550. *Fax:* (12) 7278619. *E-mail:* samc_aug@yahoo.fr. Musicians' union.

The Republic of the Congo

Centrale Syndicale Congolaise des Artistes: BP 5340, Brazzaville. *Telephone:* 81-16-12. *Fax:* 81-03-30. Musicians' union.

Croatia

Hrvatska Glazbena Unija: 10000 Zagreb, Ivana Broza 8a. *Telephone:* (1) 3668227. *Fax:* (1) 3668216. *E-mail:* hgu@hgu.hr. *Website:* www.hgu.hr. Musicians' union.

Hrvatsko Društvo Skladatelja: 10000 Zagreb, Berislavićeva 9. *Telephone:* (1) 4872370. *Fax:* (1) 4872372. *E-mail:* info@hds.hr. *Website:* www.hds.hr. Composers' society.

Cuba

Centro Nacional de Derecho de Autor (CENDA): Calle 15 #604, entre B y C, Vedado, Havana. *Telephone:* (8) 32-3571. *E-mail:* cenda@cenda.cu. *Website:*

www.cenda.cu. f. 1978; oversees numerous other organizations, including La Agencia Cubana de Derecho de Autor Musical.

Centro Nacional de Música Popular: Avenida 1a, esq. 10 y 12, Playa, Havana.

Unión Nacional de Escritores y Artistas de Cuba (UNEAC): Calle 17 No. 354, esquina G y H, Vedado, CP 10400, Havana. *Telephone:* (7) 83-24551. *Fax:* (7) 33-3158. *E-mail:* uneac@cubarte.cult.cu. *Website:* www.uneac.org.cu. f. 1961.

Czech Republic

Český hudební fond: Besední 487, 110 00 Prague 1. *Telephone:* 257320008. *Fax:* 257312834. *E-mail:* info@hudebnifond.cz. *Website:* www.hudebnifond.cz. Czech music fund.

Ochranný svaz autorský pro práva k dílům hudebním (OSA): Čs. armády 20, 160 56 Prague 6. *Telephone:* 220315111. *Fax:* 233343073. *E-mail:* osa@osa.cz. *Website:* www.osa.cz. Performing and mechanical rights society for composers, authors and publishers.

Denmark

Dansk Musiker Forbund (DMF): Sankt Hans Torv 26, 2200 Copenhagen N. *Telephone:* 35-24-02-40. *Fax:* 35-24-02-50. *E-mail:* dmf@dmf.dk. *Website:* www.dmf.dk. Musicians' union.

Nordisk Copyright Bureau (NCB): Hammerichsgade 14, 1611 Copenhagen V. *Telephone:* 33-36-87-00. *Fax:* 33-36-46-90. *E-mail:* ncb@ncb.dk. *Website:* www.ncb.dk.

Ecuador

Sociedad de Autores y Compositores Ecuatorianos (SAYCE): Avenida Diez de Agosto 43147 y Río Coca, Quito. *Telephone:* (2) 224-3083. *Fax:* (2) 246-2638. *Website:* www.sayce.com.ec. f. 1973; performing rights society.

El Salvador

Centro Nacional de Artes (CENAR): Calle Valero Lecha, Colonia San Mateo, San Salvador. *Telephone:* 2298-1839. *Fax:* 2298-1843.

Estonia

Eesti Autorite Ühing (EAU): Lille 13, Tallinn 10614. *Telephone:* 668-4360. *Fax:* 668-4361. *E-mail:* eau@eau.org. *Website:* www.eauthors.ee. Represents authors' rights (principally works music and drama) and gives legal advice concerning copyright.

Fiji

Fiji Performing Right Association Ltd: GPO Box 15061, Suva. *Telephone:* 3312494. *Fax:* 3303340. *E-mail:* fpra@connect.com.fj. *Website:* www.fpra.com .fj.

Finland

Suomen Muusikkojen Liitto ry: Pieni Roobertinkatu 16, 00120 Helsinki. *Telephone:* (9) 68034070. *Fax:* (9) 68034087. *E-mail:* sml@muusikkojenliitto.fi. *Website:* www.musicfinland.com/sml/. Musicians' union.

TEOSTO: Säveltäjäin Tekijänoikeustoimisto Teosto ry, Lauttasaarentie 1, 00200 Helsinki. *Telephone:* (9) 681011. *Fax:* (9) 677134. *E-mail:* teosto@teosto .fi. *Website:* www.teosto.fi. f. 1928; organization protecting the copyright of Finnish composers and songwriters.

France

ADAMI: 14–16 rue Ballu, 75311 Paris cedex 09. *Telephone:* 1-44-63-10-00. *Fax:* 1-44-63-10-10. *Website:* www.adami.fr. Formed an alliance with SPEDIDAM in 2004, to manage common activities, called the Société des Artistes-Interprètes.

Confédération Internationale des Sociétés d'Auteurs et Compositeurs (CISAC): CISAC Secretariat, 20–26 Boulevard du Parc, 92200 Neuilly-sur-Seine. *Telephone:* 1-55-62-08-50. *Fax:* 1-55-62-08-60. *E-mail:* cisac@cisac .org. *Website:* www.cisac.org. f. 1926; a non-governmental, non-profit organization working for increased recognition and protection of creators' rights.

Fédération Internationale des Musiciens (FIM): 21 bis, rue Victor Massé, 75009 Paris. *Telephone:* 1-45-26-31-23. *Fax:* 1-45-26-31-57. *E-mail:* office@fim-musicians.com. *Website:* www.fim-musicians.com. f. 1948; international organization representing musicians of all genres of music.

International Federation for Choral Music (IFCM): International Office, Z.A. Le Mesnil, Chemin des Carreaux, 14111 Louvigny. *Telephone:* 2-31-73-38-81. *Fax:* 2-31-73-54-15. *E-mail:* info@ifcm.net. *Website:* www.ifcm.net. f. 1982 to facilitate communication between choral musicians worldwide.

International Music Council (IMC): 1 rue Miollis, 75732 Paris cedex 15. *Telephone:* 1-45-68-48-50. *Fax:* 1-43-06-87-98. *E-mail:* imc@unesco.org. *Website:* www.unesco.org/imc. f. 1949 by UNESCO; worldwide network of organizations and individuals in the field of music, promoting musical diversity and supporting cultural rights for all.

MIDEM Organization: 11 rue du Colonel Pierre Avia, BP 572, 75726 Paris cedex 15. *Telephone:* 1-41-90-44-60. *Fax:* 1-41-90-44-50. *E-mail:* info.midem@reedmidem.com. *Website:* www.midem.com.

Société des Auteurs, Compositeurs et Editeurs de Musique (SACEM): 225 avenue Charles de Gaulle, 92528 Neuilly-sur-Seine Cedex. *Telephone:* 1-47-15-47-15. *Website:* www.sacem.fr. Represents French performers.

SPEDIDAM: 16 rue Amélie, 75007 Paris cedex 07. *Telephone:* 1-44-18-58-58. *Website:* www.spedidam.fr. Monitors artist remuneration and artistic property rights; formed an alliance with ADAMI in 2004, to manage common activities, called the Société des Artistes-Interprètes.

Union Nationale des Syndicats d'Artistes Musiciens de France (SNAM): 14–16 rue des Lilas, 75019 Paris. *Telephone:* 1-42-02-30-80. *Fax:* 1-42-02-34-01. *E-mail:* snam-cgt@wanadoo.fr. *Website:* www.snam-cgt.org.

Gabon

Syndicat National des Artistes Musiciens (SYNAM): c/o Mme Véronique Eboa, BP 2206, Libreville. *Telephone:* 26-06-71. *Fax:* 73-39-09. Musicians' union.

Germany

Deutscher Musikverleger-Verband eV (DMV): Friedrich-Wilhelm-Strasse 31, 53113 Bonn. *Telephone:* (228) 539700. *Fax:* (228) 5397070. *E-mail:* info@dmv-online.com. *Website:* www.dmv-online.com. Represents the interests of music publishers throughout Germany.

Gesellschaft für Musikalische Aufführungs und Mechanische Vervielfältigungsrechte (GEMA): Postfach 30 12 40, 10722 Berlin. *Telephone:* (30) 2124500. *Fax:* (30) 21245950. *E-mail:* gema@gema.de. *Website:* www.gema.de. Performing rights organization.

Internationaler Arbeitskreis für Musik eV (IAM): Am Kloster 1a, 49565 Bramsche-Malgarten. *Telephone:* (5461) 99630. *Fax:* (5461) 996310. *E-mail:* iamev@t-online.de. *Website:* www.iam-ev.de.

Ghana

Musicians' Union of Ghana (MUSIGA): PO Box CT 2240, Cantonments, Accra. *Telephone:* (21) 775128. *Fax:* (21) 775128. *E-mail:* sidiku@dslghana.com. *Website:* www.musiga.com.gh.

Greece

Panhellenic Musicians' Union: 10 Sapfous str, 10553 Athens. *Website:* www.pmu.gr.

Société Hellenique pour la Protection de la Propriété Intellectuelle (AEPI): Fragoklisias 51, Samou Str, Amarousio, 15125 Athens. *Telephone:* (211) 11029000. *Fax:* (210) 6851576. *E-mail:* info@aepi.gr. *Website:* www.aepi.gr. Intellectual property organization.

Guatemala

Asociación Guatemalteca de Autores y Compositores (AGAYC): 14 Calle 11-42, Zona 1, 01001 Guatemala City. *Telephone:* 2384-921. *Fax:* 2513-057. *E-mail:* agayc@intelnet.net.gt.

Guinea

Association des Musiciens Interprètes de Guinée (AMIG): Centre Culturel de la Paillote, BP 53 Conakry. *Telephone:* 45-49-48. *Fax:* 45-49-48. *E-mail:* barrysko@yahoo.fr. Musicians' union.

Hong Kong

Asian Composers' League: c/o Dr Joshua Chan, Department of Music, University of Hong Kong, Pokfulam Road, Hong Kong. *Telephone:* 28597045. *Fax:* 28584933. *Website:* www.asiancomposersleague.com. f. 1973; member countries and regions: Australia, Azerbaijan, People's Republic of China, Hong Kong, Indonesia, Israel, Japan, Republic of Korea, New Zealand, The Philippines, Taiwan, Thailand and Viet Nam; holds annual conference and festival.

Composers' and Authors' Society of Hong Kong Ltd (CASH): 18/F Universal Trade Centre, 3 Arbuthnot Road, Central, Hong Kong. *Telephone:* 28463268. *Fax:* 28463261. *E-mail:* general@cash.org.hk. *Website:* www.cash.org.hk.

Music Office: Wanchai Tower 25/F, 12 Harbour Road, Wanchai. *Telephone:* 2582-5314. *Fax:* 2802-8440. *E-mail:* cmooffice@lcsd.gov.hk. *Website:* www.lcsd.gov.hk. Government organization to promote music.

Hungary

Hungarian Musicians' and Dancers' Union: 1068 Budapest, Vàrosligeti Fasor 38. *Telephone:* (1) 342-8927. *Fax:* (1) 322-5446. *E-mail:* mztszgyimesi@axelero.hu.

Magyar Zenei Tanács: 1537 Budapest, PO Box 401. *Telephone:* (1) 318-4243. *Fax:* (1) 317-4243. *E-mail:* info@hunmusic.hu. *Website:* www.hunmusic.hu. Music council, f. 1990.

Iceland

Samband tónskálda og eigenda flutningsréttar (STEF): Laufásvegi 40, 101 Reykjavík. *Telephone:* 5616173. *Fax:* 5626273. *E-mail:* info@stef.is. *Website:* www.stef.is.

India

Musicians' Federation of India: Redwood A-103, Evershine Green, New Link Road, Oshivara, Andheri (W) Mumbai 400053. *Telephone:* (22) 26399009. *E-mail:* kishorjawade@rediffmail.com.

Indonesia

Karya Cipta Indonesia: Golden Plaza Fatmawati C-12, Jl. RS. Fatmawati 15, Jakarta 12420. *Telephone:* (21) 75905884. *Fax:* (21) 7656051. *E-mail:* kci@kci.or.id. *Website:* www.kci.or.id. Copyright protection agency.

Ireland

An Chomhairle Ealaíon (The Arts Council): 70 Merrion Square, Dublin 2. *Telephone:* (1) 6180200. *Fax:* (1) 6761302. *Website:* www.artscouncil.ie. f. 1951 to promote the knowledge, appreciation and practice of the arts.

Irish Music Rights Organisation (IMRO): Regus House, 30 Upper Pembroke Street, Dublin 2. *Telephone:* (1) 6614844. *Fax:* (1) 6763125. *E-mail:* info@imro.ie. *Website:* www.imro.ie. Non-profit organization, administering performing rights and copyright of music in Ireland.

Israel

Israeli Musicians' Union: 6 Malkay Israel Square, 64951 Tel-Aviv. *Telephone:* 3-6959355. *Fax:* 3-6963528. *E-mail:* eilam@netvision.net.il. *Website:* www.eilam.org.il.

Society of Authors, Composers and Music Publishers in Israel (ACUM): Tuval 9st. (Hilazon Corner), PO Box 1704, Ramat-Gan 52117. *Telephone:* 3-6113400. *Fax:* 3-6122629. *E-mail:* info@acum.org.il. *Website:* www.acum.org.il. f. 1936.

Italy

Associazione di Informatica Musicale Italiana (AIMI): c/o Davide Rocchesso, Giudecca 494, 30133 Venice. *E-mail:* info@aimi-musica.org. *Website:* www.aimi-musica.org.

Sindacato Nazionale Musicisti (SNM): 22 via Domodossola, 00183 Rome. *E-mail:* snm@snm.it. *Website:* www.snm.it.

Società Italiana degli Autori ed Editori (SIAE): Viale della Letteratura 30, 00144 Rome. *Telephone:* (06) 59901. *Fax:* (06) 59647050. *Website:* www.siae.it. Performing rights and copyright society.

Japan

Japanese Society for Rights of Authors, Composers and Publishers (JASRAC): 3-6-12 Uehara, Shibuya-ku, Tokyo 151-8540. *Telephone:* (3) 3481-2121. *Website:* www.jasrac.or.jp.

Recording Industry Association of Japan (RIAJ): 11F Kita-Aoyama Yoshikawa Building, 2-12-16 Kita-Aoyama, Minato-ku, Tokyo 107-0061. *Telephone:* (3) 6406-0510. *Fax:* (3) 6406-0520. *E-mail:* info@riaj.or.jp. *Website:* www.riaj.or.jp.

Kenya

Kenya Union of Entertainment and Music Industry Employees (KUEMIE): Off Shimo la Tewa Road, Industrial Area, PO Box 4622, 00506 Nairobi. *Telephone:* (20) 545317. *Fax:* (20) 251938. *E-mail:* kuemie@hotmail.com.

Republic of Korea

Korea Music Copyright Association (KOMCA): KOMCA Building, Naebalsan-dong 649, Kangseo-gu, Seoul 57-824. *Telephone:* (2) 2660-0400. *Fax:* (2) 2660-0429. *E-mail:* webmaster@komca.or.kr. *Website:* komca.or.kr.

Music Association of Korea: 1-117 Tong-Sung Dong, Chongro-ku, Seoul 110-765. *Telephone:* (2) 744-8060. *Fax:* (2) 741-2378. *Website:* www.mak.or.kr.

Macao (China)

Cultural Affairs Bureau: Praça do Tap Seac, Edif. do Instituto Cultural, Macao (China). *Telephone:* 83996699. *Fax:* 28366899. *E-mail:* webmaster@icm.gov.mo. *Website:* www.icm.gov.mo. Government organization to promote the arts.

Malawi

Musicians' Association of Malawi (MAM): Private Bag 127, Blantyre. *Telephone:* 5633012. *Fax:* 5624186. *E-mail:* goodson@accessmalawi.com.

Mali

Association Nationale des Artistes du Mali (ANAM): BP E 4005, Bamako. *Telephone:* 223-52-60. *Fax:* 222-36-70. *E-mail:* nicole .sounfountera@delmli.cec.eu.int. Musicians' union.

Mexico

Sociedad de Autores y Compositores de Música (SACM): Mayorazgo 129, 03330 México, DF. *Telephone:* (56) 0477-33. *Fax:* (56) 0479-23. *E-mail:* sacm@sacm.org.mx. *Website:* www.sacm.org.mx.

Mozambique

Associaçao dos Musicos Moçambicanos: Avenida Magiguana, N° 710 R/C, Predio Macau, 6°, Maputo. *Telephone:* 1428706. *Fax:* 1301604. *E-mail:* h_langa1@hotmail.com. Musicians' union.

Namibia

Namibian Artists' Union: PO Box 22287, Windhoek. *Telephone:* (61) 240535. *Fax:* (61) 248097. *E-mail:* artistna@iway.na.

The Netherlands

BUMA/STEMRA: Siriusdreef 22–28, 2132 WT Hoofddorp. *Telephone:* (23) 7997999. *Fax:* (23) 7997777. *E-mail:* info@bumastemra.nl. *Website:* www .bumastemra.nl. Performing rights organization.

International Society for Contemporary Music (ISCM): ISCM Secretariat, c/o Muziek Centrum Nederland, ROKIN 111, 1012 KN Amsterdam. *Telephone:* (20) 3446060. *E-mail:* info@iscm.org. *Website:* www.iscm.org. f. 1922; an international network devoted to the promotion and presentation of contemporary music.

SENA: Catharina van Renneslaan 8, 1217 CX Hilversum. *Telephone:* (35) 6251700. *E-mail:* sena@sena.nl. *Website:* www.sena.nl. Promotes the rights of both performers and producers of music.

New Zealand

Creative New Zealand: National Office, Old Public Trust Building, 131–135 Lambton Quay, PO Box 3806, Wellington. *Telephone:* (4) 473-0880. *Fax:* (4) 471-2865. *E-mail:* info@creativenz.govt.nz. *Website:* www.creativenz.govt.nz. Government arts council.

Recording Industry Association of New Zealand (RAINZ): Private Bag 78 850, Grey Lynn, Auckland 1245. *Telephone:* (9) 360-5085. *Fax:* (9) 360-5086. *E-mail:* music@rianz.org.nz. *Website:* www.rianz.org.nz.

Niger

Association Nationale des Auteurs, Compositeurs et Interprètes de Musique Moderne (ANACIMM): BP 11 203, Niamey. *Telephone:* 740895. *Fax:* 743123. *E-mail:* zibo_ali@yahoo.fr.

Norway

Musikernes Fellesorganisasjon (MFO): Postboks 8806, Youngstorget, 0028 Oslo. *Telephone:* 23-06-21-50. *Fax:* 23-06-21-51. *E-mail:* mfo@musikerorg .no. *Website:* www.musikerorg.no. Musicians' union.

TONO: Galleriet, Tøyenbekken 21, Postboks 9171, Grønland, 0134 Oslo. *Telephone:* 22-05-72-00. *Fax:* 22-05-72-50. *E-mail:* tono@tono.no. *Website:* www.tono.no. Represents artists in Norway.

Paraguay

Asociación de Músicos del Paraguay: Calle 15 de agosto 1365, Asunción. *Telephone:* (21) 44-3276. *Fax:* (21) 44-3276. *E-mail:* cesar_burian@hotmail .com.

Peru

Asociación Peruana de Autores y Compositores (APDAYC): Avenida Petit Thouars 5038, Miraflores, Lima 18. *Telephone:* (1) 7158122. *Fax:* (1) 2423248. *E-mail:* dirgen@apdayc.org.pe. *Website:* www.apdayc.org.pe.

The Philippines

Filipino Society of Composers, Authors and Publishers Inc. (FILSCAP): 140 Scout Rallos St., Brgy. Sacred Heart, Quezon City, Metro Manila. *Telephone:* (2) 4156277. *Fax:* (2) 9289852. *E-mail:* info@filscap.com.ph. *Website:* www.filscap.com.ph. f. 1965; non-profit organization administering public performance and mechanical reproduction rights.

Philippine Association of the Record Industry (PARI): Suite 207 Greenhills Mansion, 37 Annapolis Street, Greenhills, San Juan, Metro Manila. *Telephone:* (2) 7250770. *Fax:* (2) 7250786. *E-mail:* writeus@pari.com .ph. *Website:* www.pari.com.ph.

Poland

Stowarzyszenie Muzykow Rozrywkowych w Polsce (STOMUR): 00-660 Warsaw, Ul. Lwowska 13. *Telephone:* (22) 6214709. *Fax:* (22) 6292854. *E-mail:* stomur@stoart.org.pl. *Website:* stomur.stoart.org.pl. Association of musicians.

Zwiazek Polskich Autorów i Kompozytorów (ZAKR): 00-093 Warsaw, Daniłowiczowska 18/5A. *Telephone:* (22) 8283735. *Fax:* (22) 8283735. *E-mail:* zakr@zakr.pl. *Website:* www.zakr.pl. f. 1946; association of authors, lyricists and composers.

Zwiazek Producentów Audio Video (ZPAV): 00-380 Warsaw, Ul. Kruczkowskiego 12 m 2. *Telephone:* (22) 6229219. *Fax:* (22) 6251661. *E-mail:* biuro@zpav.pl. *Website:* www.zpav.pl. Polish society of the recording industry.

Portugal

Associação Fonográfica Portuguesa (AFP): Rua Augusto dos Santos No. 2, 4°, 1050-028 Lisbon. *Telephone:* (21) 3529189. *Fax:* (21) 3147325. *E-mail:* contactar@afp.org.pt. *Website:* www.afp.org.pt.

Romania

Union des Musiciens Professionnels: 70149 Bucharest, Str Franklin nr 1, sect. 1. *Telephone:* (21) 6504118. *Fax:* (21) 01788. Musicians' union.

Union of Composers and Musicologists: 70149 Bucharest, Calea Victoriei 141, Sector 1. *Telephone:* (21) 2127966. *Fax:* (21) 2107211. *E-mail:* ucmr@ itcnet.ro.

Russia

Russian Authors' Society: *Telephone:* (495) 697-37-77. *Fax:* (495) 609-93-63. *E-mail:* rao@rao.ru. *Website:* www.rao.ru. Legal support for musicians.

Russian Phonographic Association: 125047 Moscow, 1 Miusskaya Str., Bld. 24/22, Office 62A. *Telephone:* (495) 626-44-47. *Fax:* (495) 626-44-47. *E-mail:* international@fonogram.ru. *Website:* www.rpa-society.com.

Senegal

Association des Métiers de la Musique du Sénégal (AMS): 758 Sicap Baobab, BP 166 12, Dakar-Fann. *Telephone:* 21-633-0672. *Fax:* 21-822-2459. *E-mail:* malickmusic@yahoo.fr. Musicians' union.

Singapore

Composers' and Authors' Society of Singapore Ltd (COMPASS): 37 Craig Road, Singapore 089675. *Telephone:* 63236630. *Fax:* 63236639. *Website:* www.compass.org.sg.

National Arts Council: 140 Hill Street, # 03-01 MICA Building, Singapore 179369. *Telephone:* 67464622. *Fax:* 68373010. *Website:* www.nac.gov.sg. Government organization for the promotion of the arts.

Recording Industry Association (Singapore) (RIAS): 4 Leng Kee Road, 03-07 SiS Building, Singapore 159088. *Telephone:* 62204166. *Fax:* 62209452. *E-mail:* oinfo@rias.org.sg. *Website:* www.rias.org.sg. f. 1976 as Singapore Phonogram & Videogram Association; fosters and maintains fair business practices within the industry.

Slovakia

Hudobné Centrum: Michalská 10, 815 36 Bratislava 1. *Telephone:* (2) 5920-4811. *Fax:* (2) 5443-0379. *E-mail:* hc@hc.sk. *Website:* www.hc.sk. Music centre.

Odborovczvaz profesionalnych orchestralnych hudobnikov Slovenska: Jakubovo nam 15, 811 09 Bratislava. *Telephone:* (2) 5296-4555. *Fax:* (2) 5296-4555. *E-mail:* karol@petocz.sk. Union of orchestral musicians.

South Africa

Musicians' Union of South Africa (MUSA): PO Box 35, Newtown, Johannesburg 2113. *Telephone:* (11) 3391676. *Fax:* (11) 3391677. *E-mail:* musa2@absamail.co.za.

Recording Industry of South Africa (RiSA): PO Box 367, Randburg 2125. *Telephone:* (11) 8861342. *Fax:* (11) 8864169. *Website:* www.risa.org.za.

South African Music Rights Organisation (SAMRO): PO Box 31609, Braamfontein, Johannesburg 2017. *Telephone:* (11) 7128000. *Fax:* (11) 4031934. *E-mail:* webmaster@samro.org.za. *Website:* www.samro.org.za.

South African Recording Rights Association Ltd (SARRAL): PO Box 31091, Braamfontein, Johannesburg 2017. *Telephone:* (11) 3391333. *Fax:* (11) 3391403. *E-mail:* info@sarral.org.za. *Website:* www.sarral.org.za.

Spain

Sindicato Profesional de Músicos Españoles (SPME): Calle de Alcalá 182, 1° Izquierda, 28028 Madrid. *Telephone:* (91) 3554870. *Fax:* (91) 3554870. *E-mail:* forma-spme@teleline.es.

Sociedad General de Autores y Editores (SGAE): Fernando VI 4, 28004 Madrid. *Telephone:* (91) 3499550. *Fax:* (91) 3499500. *Website:* www.sgae.es. Organization for performing rights.

Swaziland

Swaziland Arts and Music Association (SWAMA): PO Box 5836, Manzini. *Telephone:* 5058785. *Fax:* 5058785. *E-mail:* artsandculture@africaonline.co.sz.

Sweden

International Association of Music Libraries, Archives and Documentation Centres (IAML): c/o Statens musikbibliotek, Box 16 326, 103 26 Stockholm. *E-mail:* secretary@iaml.info. *Website:* www.iaml.info. f. 1951 to promote international co-operation and to support the interests of the profession; has individual and institutional members worldwide.

Nordic Music Committee (NOMUS): Nybrokajen 11, 111 48 Stockholm. *Telephone:* (8) 407-16-00. *Fax:* (8) 407-17-21. *E-mail:* nomus@nomus.org. *Website:* www.nomus.org. The Nordic Council expert group in matters regarding Nordic music collaboration.

Svenska Artisters och Musikers Intresseorganisation (SAMI): Döbelnsgatan 3, 111 40 Stockholm. *Telephone:* (8) 453-34-00. *Fax:* (8) 453-34-40. *Website:* www.sami.se. Swedish artists' and musicians' organization.

Svenska Tonsättares Internationella Musikbyrå (STIM): PO Box 27327, 102 54 Stockholm. *Telephone:* (8) 783-88-00. *Fax:* (8) 662-62-75. *E-mail:* info@stim.se. *Website:* www.stim.se. Performing right society.

Switzerland

Fédération Mondiale des Concours Internationaux de Musique (FMCIM): Headquarters, 104 rue de Carouge, 1205 Geneva. *Telephone:* 223213620. *Fax:* 227811418. *E-mail:* info@wfimc.org. *Website:* www.fmcim.org. f. 1957; world federation of international music competitions.

International Confederation of Music Publishers—Confédération Internationale des Editeurs de Musique (ICMP/CIEM): 6 rue de Bourg, 1002 Lausanne. *E-mail:* 101374.25@compuserve.com. *Website:* www.icmp-ciem.org. International trade association representing the interests of the music-publishing industry worldwide.

International Musicological Society (IMS): POB 1561, 4001 Basel. *E-mail:* imsba@swissonline.ch. *Website:* www.ims-online.ch. f. 1927 to advance musicological research through international co-operation.

SUISA: Bellariastrasse 82, Postfach 782, 8038 Zürich. *Telephone:* 444856666. *Fax:* 444824333. *E-mail:* suisa@suisa.ch. *Website:* www.suisa.ch; www.fondation-suisa.ch. Performing rights society; includes the Fondation SUISA pour la Musique.

World Intellectual Property Organization: Information Centre, 34 chemin des Colombettes, Geneva. *Telephone:* 223389111. *Fax:* 227335428. *E-mail:* information.center@wipo.int. *Website:* www.wipo.int. International organization promoting respect for intellectual property throughout the world.

Tanzania

Tanzania Musicians' Network: PO Box 32429, Dar es Salaam. *Telephone:* (741) 274747. *E-mail:* musicnettz@yahoo.com.

Thailand

Thai Composers' Association: 107–108 Siripong Road, Sao Chingcha, Samranrat, Bangkok 10200.

Turkey

Muzik Yapimcilari Dernegi (MUYAP): IMC 6, Blok 6437, 34470 Unkapani, İstanbul.

United Kingdom

Arts Council England: 14 Great Peter Street, London, SW1P 3NQ, England. *Telephone:* (845) 300-6200. *Fax:* (20) 7973-6590. *E-mail:* enquiries@artscouncil.org.uk. *Website:* www.artscouncil.org.uk. National development agency for the arts in England, distributing public money from the Government and the National Lottery.

British Academy of Composers and Songwriters (BAC&S): British Music House, 26 Berners Street, London, W1T 3LR, England. *Telephone:* (20) 7636-2929. *Fax:* (20) 7636-2212. *E-mail:* info@britishacademy.com. *Website:* www.britishacademy.com. Formerly the Association of Professional Composers (APC), the British Academy of Songwriters, Composers & Authors (BASCA), and the Composers' Guild of Great Britain; changed name as above

1999; activities include lobbying for music writers, providing membership services, honouring achievements through award ceremonies (Ivor Novello and British Composer Awards).

British Phonographic Industry (BPI): Riverside Building, County Hall, Westminster Bridge Road, London, SE1 7JA, England. *Telephone:* (20) 7803-1300. *Fax:* (20) 7803-1310. *E-mail:* general@bpi.co.uk. *Website:* www.bpi.co.uk.

Celfyddydau Cymru—Arts Council of Wales: 9 Museum Place, Cardiff, CF10 3NX, Wales. *Telephone:* (29) 2037-6500. *Fax:* (29) 2022-1447. *Website:* www.artswales.org. f. 1994 to fund and develop the arts in Wales.

Incorporated Society of Musicians: 10 Stratford Place, London, W1C 1AA, England. *Telephone:* (20) 7629-4413. *Fax:* (20) 7408-1538. *E-mail:* membership@ism.org. *Website:* www.ism.org. Professional body for all musicians: performers, composers, teachers, conductors, organists, etc.; represents musicians' interests, raises professional standards, and provides services (insurance, legal advice, etc.) to members.

International Artist Managers' Association (IAMA): Headquarters, 23 Garrick Street, Covent Garden, London, WC2E 9BN, England. *Telephone:* (20) 7379-7336. *Fax:* (20) 7379-7338. *E-mail:* info@iamaworld.com. *Website:* www.iamaworld.com. Worldwide association for classical music artist managers and concert agents.

International Federation of the Phonographic Industry (IFPI): Secretariat, 10 Piccadilly, London, W1J 0DD, England. *Telephone:* (20) 7878-7900. *Fax:* (20) 7878-7950. *E-mail:* info@ifpi.org. *Website:* www.ifpi.org. Promotes the interests of the recording industry worldwide.

International Music Managers' Forum (IMMF): IMMF Headquarters, British Music House, 26 Berners Street, London, W1T 3LR, England. *Telephone:* (870) 8507-800. *Fax:* (870) 8507-801. *Website:* www.musicmanagersforum.co.uk. Non-governmental organization representing the interests of music managers worldwide, through national-level Music Managers Forums.

MCPS-PRS: Copyright House, 29–33 Berners Street, London, W1T 3AB, England. *Telephone:* (20) 7580-5544. *Fax:* (20) 7306-4455. *Website:* www.prs.co.uk. Collects and distributes licence fees for the public performance and broadcast of musical works; formed as alliance between two royalty collection societies, MCPS and PRS, in 1997, to manage common activities.

Musicians' Union (MU): National Office, 60–62 Clapham Road, London, SW9 0JJ, England. *Telephone:* (20) 7582-5566. *Fax:* (20) 7582-9805. *E-mail:* info@musiciansunion.org.uk. *Website:* www.musiciansunion.org.uk. UK trade union for musicians of all genres.

PPL: 1 Upper James Street, London, W1F 9DE, England. *Telephone:* (20) 7534-1000. *Fax:* (20) 7534-1111. *E-mail:* info@ppluk.com. *Website:* www.ppluk.com. Established in 2007 following merger between Performing Artists' Media Rights Association (PAMRA) and The Association of United Recording Artists (AURA). Licenses recorded music and music videos for public performance, broadcast and new media use.

Pro-Music: c/o IFPI Secretariat, 10 Piccadilly, London, W1J 0DD, England. *Telephone:* (20) 7878-7900. *Fax:* (20) 7878-7950. *E-mail:* info@ifpi.org. *Website:* www.pro-music.org. f. 2003; international website promoting legitimate online music services and answering questions about copyright law for online music.

Scottish Arts Council: 12 Manor Place, Edinburgh, EH3 7DD, Scotland. *Telephone:* (131) 226-6051. *Fax:* (131) 225-9833. *E-mail:* help.desk@scottisharts.org.uk. *Website:* www.scottisharts.org.uk. Funds and develops the arts in Scotland.

UK Music: British Music House, 26 Berners Street, London, W1T 3LR, England. *Telephone:* (20) 7306-4446. *Fax:* (20) 7306-4449. *E-mail:* contact@ukmusic.org. *Website:* www.ukmusic.org. Formerly known as British Music Rights. Established in 1996 by the British Academy of Composers & Songwriters, the Music Publishers Association, the Mechanical-Copyright Protection Society and the Performing Right Society, to represent the interests of composers, songwriters and music publishers.

United States of America

American Academy of Arts and Letters: 633 West 155th Street, New York, NY 10032-1799. *Telephone:* (212) 368-5900. *Fax:* (212) 491-4615. *E-mail:* academy@artsandletters.org. *Website:* www.artsandletters.org.

American Federation of Musicians: 1501 Broadway, Suite 600, New York, NY 10036. *Telephone:* (212) 869-1330. *Fax:* (212) 764-6134. *Website:* www.afm.org. Organization representing the interests of professional musicians in the USA and Canada.

American Mechanical Rights Agency Inc. (AMRA): 149 S Barrington Avenue, Suite 810, Los Angeles, CA 90049. *Telephone:* (310) 440-8778. *Fax:* (310) 440-0059. *E-mail:* info@amermechrights.com. *Website:* www.amermechrights.com.

American Society of Composers, Authors and Publishers (ASCAP): ASCAP Building, 1 Lincoln Plaza, New York, NY 10023. *Telephone:* (212) 621-

6000. *Fax:* (212) 724-9064. *E-mail:* info@ascap.com. *Website:* www.ascap.com. f. 1914; performing rights organization.

Broadcast Music Inc. (BMI): 320 West 57th Street, New York, NY 10019-3790. *Telephone:* (212) 586-2000. *Website:* www.bmi.com. Performing rights organization, representing songwriters, composers and music publishers.

National Academy of Recording Arts and Sciences (NARAS): 3402 Pico Boulevard, Santa Monica, CA 90405. *Telephone:* (310) 392-3777. *Fax:* (310) 399-3090. *Website:* www.naras.org. Incorporates the Grammy Foundation and the MusiCares charity.

National Endowment for the Arts (NEA): 1100 Pennsylvania Avenue NW, Washington, DC 20506-0001. *Telephone:* (202) 682-5400. *E-mail:* webmgr@arts.endow.gov. *Website:* www.nea.gov.

National Music Council: c/o Dr David Sanders, Director, 425 Park Street, Montclair, NJ 07043. *E-mail:* sandersd@mail.montclair.edu. *Website:* www.musiccouncil.org. f. 1940 to strengthen the importance of music in US life and culture.

Recording Industry Association of America (RIAA): 1025 F Street N.W., 10th Floor, Washington, DC 20004. *Telephone:* (202) 775-0101. *Fax:* (202) 775-7253. *Website:* www.riaa.com. f. 1972 as the National Association of Independent Record Distributors & Manufacturers (NAIRD).

SESAC: 55 Music Square East, Nashville, TN 37203. *Telephone:* (615) 320-0055. *Fax:* (615) 329-9627. *Website:* www.sesac.com. f. 1930 as the Society of European Stage Authors & Composers (now simply known as SESAC); performing rights organization; also SESAC Latina (Spanish-language section).

Uruguay

Asociación Uruguaya de Músicos (AUDEM): Calle Maldonado 983, CP 11 100 Montevideo. *Telephone:* (2) 9087370. *Fax:* (2) 9080477. *E-mail:* audem@adinet.com.uy. *Website:* www.audem-uy.org.

Federación Uruguaya de Músicos (FUDEM): Gutemberg 6334, Montevideo. *Telephone:* (2) 6984376. *Fax:* (2) 3228477. *E-mail:* fudemuru@yahoo.com.

Venezuela

Sociedad de Autores y Compositores de Venezuela (SACVEN): Avenida Andrés Bello, Edificio VAM, Torre Oeste, Pisos 9 y 10, Caracas DC 1050. *Telephone:* (212) 507-7211. *Fax:* (212) 507-7287. *Website:* www.sacven.org.

APPENDIX C: MUSIC AWARDS

Academy Awards: Academy Communications Department, 8949 Wilshire Boulevard, Fifth Floor, Beverly Hills, CA 90211-1972, USA. *Telephone:* (310) 247-3000. *Fax:* (310) 271-3395. *E-mail:* publicity@oscars.org. *Website:* www.oscars.org. Academy Award for Achievement in Music Written for Motion Pictures (Original Score), Academy Award for Achievement in Music Written for Motion Pictures (Original Song).

Academy of Country Music Awards: Academy of Country Music, 4100 West Alameda Avenue, Suite 208, Burbank, CA 91505, USA. *Telephone:* (818) 842-8400. *Fax:* (818) 842-8535. *E-mail:* info@acmcountry.com. *Website:* www.acmcountry.com. f. 1965, to promote country music.

Alarmprisen: Vestbygdveien, 2743 Harestua, Norway. *Website:* www.alarmprisen.no. f. 2000; the Alarm Prize awards musicians in numerous categories, through votes from the public.

American Music Awards: c/o ABC Inc., 500 South Buena Vista Street, Burbank, CA 91521-4551, USA. *Website:* www.americanmusicawards.com. Annual awards, f. 1973, with several categories.

APRA Silver Scroll Award: Australasian Performing Right Association (APRA), PO Box 6315, Wellesley Street, Auckland, New Zealand. *Telephone:* (9) 623-2173. *Fax:* (9) 623-2174. *Website:* www.apra.co.nz/silverscroll.htm. f. 1965 to award creative excellence in songwriting.

ARIA Awards: Australian Recording Industry Association (ARIA), PO Box Q20, Queen Victoria Building, NSW 1230, Australia. *Telephone:* (2) 8569 1144. *Fax:* (2) 8569 1183. *E-mail:* aria.mail@aria.com.au. *Website:* www.ariaawards.com.au. f. 1987 to recognise excellence and innovation in all genres of Australian music.

ASCAP Awards: American Society of Composers, Authors and Publishers (ASCAP), One Lincoln Plaza, New York, NY 10023, USA. *Telephone:* (212) 621-6000. *Fax:* (212) 724-9064. *E-mail:* info@ascap.com. *Website:* www.ascap.com. Awards include: Henry Mancini Award, Creative Voice Award, Founders Award, Golden Note Award, Golden Soundtrack Award, Latin Heritage Award, Opus Award, Pied Piper Award, Rhythm & Soul Heritage Award, Silver Pen Award.

BAFTA Anthony Asquith Award for Achievement in Film Music: The British Academy of Film & Television Arts (BAFTA), 195 Piccadilly, London, W1J 9LN, UK. *Telephone:* (20) 7734-0022. *Fax:* (20) 7734-1792. *E-mail:* info@bafta.org. *Website:* www.bafta.org. One of the annual BAFTA Film Awards.

BargaJazz: Segreteria Concorso, c/o Comune di Barga, via di Mezzo 45, 55051 Barga (LU), Italy. *Telephone:* (058) 3724770. *E-mail:* bargajazz@barganews.com. *Website:* www.barganews.com/bargajazz. Annual international competition for the best arrangement and composition for a jazz orchestra.

BBC Jazz Awards: BBC TV Centre, Wood Lane, London, W12 7RJ, UK. *Website:* www.bbc.co.uk/music.

BBC Radio 3 Awards for World Music: BBC TV Centre, Wood Lane, London, W12 7RJ, UK. *Website:* www.bbc.co.uk/radio3/worldmusic. f. 2001.

Billboard Music Awards: *E-mail:* info@billboard.com. *Website:* www.billboard.com. f. 1990; annual US awards based on Billboard's year-end music charts. Also organizes conferences for various geographical areas of the music industry.

Broadcast Music Inc. (BMI) Icon Award: c/o BMI London Office, 84 Harley House, Marylebone Road, London, NW1 5HN, UK. *Website:* www.bmi.com. Recognizes songwriters and artists who have had 'a unique and indelible influence on generations of music makers'.

BRIT Awards: BPI, Riverside Building, County Hall, Westminster Bridge Road, London, SE1 7JA, UK. *Telephone:* (20) 7803-1300. *Fax:* (20) 7803-1310. *E-mail:* general@bpi.co.uk. *Website:* www.brits.co.uk. Annual awards in numerous categories.

Buma Cultuur Awards: PO Box 929, 1200 AX Hilversum, The Netherlands. *Telephone:* (35) 621 87 48. *Fax:* (35) 621 27 50. *E-mail:* info@bumacultuur.nl. *Website:* www.bumacultuur.nl. Formerly the CONAMUS Foundation Awards; annual awards: the Golden Harp (for achievement), the Silver Harp (for potential), the Export Award (for sales abroad); given at the Harpen Gala award show.

Canadian Aboriginal Music Awards: 10 Woodway Trail, Brantford, ON N3R 5Z6, Canada. *Telephone:* (519) 751-0040. *Fax:* (519) 751-2790. *E-mail:* info@canab.com. *Website:* www.canab.com.

CCMA Awards: Canadian Country Music Association (CCMA), 626 King Street West, Suite 203, Toronto, ON M5V 1M7, Canada. *Telephone:* (416) 947-1331. *Fax:* (416) 947-5924. *E-mail:* country@ccma.org. *Website:* www.ccma.org.

Choice Music Prize Irish Album of the Year: *E-mail:* info@choicemusicprize.com. *Website:* www.choicemusicprize.com. f. 2005 to select the album that best sums up the year in Irish music. Chosen by a panel of 12 media professionals from Irish print, radio and TV, the winner receives €10,000 from the Irish Music Rights Organisation and the Irish Recorded Music Association, and a specially-commissioned award from the Recorded Artists and Performers Ltd.

Concours de piano-jazz Martial Solal: ACDA, 3 rue des Couronnes, 75020 Paris, France. *Telephone:* 1 40 33 45 35. *Fax:* 1 40 33 45 38. *E-mail:* civp@civp.com. *Website:* www.civp.com/solal. Contest f. 1989 and held sporadically as part of the Concours internationaux de la Ville de Paris, organized by the Association pour la Création et la Diffusion Artistique (ACDA). Open to jazz pianists of all nationalities, with an age limit of 33 years old; first prize: €12,000.

Concours de trompette Maurice André: ACDA, 3 rue des Couronnes, 75020 Paris, France. *Telephone:* 1 40 33 45 35. *Fax:* 1 40 33 45 38. *E-mail:* civp@civp.com. *Website:* www.civp.com/andre. Contest f. 1979 and held sporadically as part of the Concours internationaux de la Ville de Paris, organized by the Association pour la Création et la Diffusion Artistique (ACDA). Open to trumpeters of all nationalities, with an age limit of 30 years old; first prize: €12,000.

Country Music Association Awards: CMA Headquarters, One Music Circle South, Nashville, TN 37203, USA. *Telephone:* (615) 244-2840. *Fax:* (615) 726-0314. *Website:* www.cmaawards.com. Annual awards for country music, f. 1967.

Digital Music Awards: *E-mail:* sam@dma06.com. *Website:* www.btyahoo.com/dma06. UK awards based around digital music technology, including best podcast, best use of mobile and broadband, best music site and best music web log (or blog).

Dove Awards: Gospel Music Association (GMA), 1205 Division Street, Nashville, TN 37203, USA. *Telephone:* (615) 242-0303. *Fax:* (615) 254-9755. *Website:* www.gmamusicawards.com. Annual awards in gospel music.

ECHO Awards: Deutsche Phono-Akademie eV, Oranienburger Strasse 67–68, 10117 Berlin, Germany. *Telephone:* (30) 59 00 38-0. *Fax:* (30) 59 00 38-38. *E-mail:* phono-akademie@phono.de. *Website:* www.echopop.de. f. 1992; annual popular music awards in numerous categories, both national and international.

Eurovision Song Contest: *E-mail:* program@eurovision.net. *Website:* www.eurovision.tv. Annual song contest between the European nations, organized by Eurovision, the operational service of the European Broadcasting Union.

Grammis: *Website:* www.grammis.se. f. 1969; annual awards in numerous categories for the Swedish popular music industry.

Grammy Awards: The Grammy Foundation, 3402 Pico Blvd, Santa Monica, CA 90405, USA. *Telephone:* (310) 392-3777. *Fax:* (310) 392-2188. *E-mail:* grammyfoundation@grammy.com. *Website:* www.grammy.com. Annual awards, f. 1958.

The Hungarian Music Awards: Magyar Hanglemezkiadók Szövetsége (MAHASZ), 1025 Budapest, Csévi utca 18, Hungary. *Telephone:* 391-42-00. *Fax:* 200-26-79. *E-mail:* info@mahasz.hu. *Website:* www.mahasz.hu. f. 1992 as the Golden Giraffe Awards; annual awards for Hungarian music of outstanding success and artistic value.

The International Songwriting Competition (ISC): 1307 Eastland Avenue, Nashville, TN 37206, USA. *Telephone:* (615) 251-4441. *Fax:* (615) 251-4442. *E-mail:* info@songwritingcompetition.com. *Website:* www.songwritingcompetition.com. f. 2002; annual songwriting contest for both aspiring and established songwriters; three prizes in each music genre category, people's choice prizes and the Grand Prize.

Jazzpar Prize: c/o Jazz Centret, Borupvej 66, 4683 Rönnede, Denmark. *Telephone:* 5671-1749. *E-mail:* jazzpar@mail.tele.dk. *Website:* www.jazzpar.dk. f. 1990; annual international award for one of five nominated performers of jazz music.

JUNO Awards: c/o Canadian Academy of Recording Arts and Sciences (CARAS), 355 King Street West, Suite 501, Toronto, ON M5V 1J6, Canada. *Telephone:* (416) 485-3135. *Fax:* (416) 485-4978. *E-mail:* info@juno-awards.ca. *Website:* www.juno-awards.ca. Annual awards for outstanding Canadian achievement in the field of recorded music.

Latin Grammy Awards: Latin Academy of Recording Arts & Sciences Inc. (LARAS), 3841 NE Second Avenue, Suite 301, Miami, FL 33137, USA. *Telephone:* (305) 576-0036. *Fax:* (305) 576-0037. *Website:* www.grammy.com/Latin/. Annual awards, f. 2002 to recognize artistic and technical achievements of Latin recording artists and creators, both national and international.

Nationwide Mercury Music Prize: *E-mail:* mh@nationwidemercuryprize.com. *Website:* www.nationwidemercurys.com. Award for one of a shortlisted 12 'albums of the year', selected to promote UK music; sponsored by Nationwide.

Meteor Ireland Music Awards: c/o Meteor Mobile Communications Ltd, 4030 Kingswood Avenue, Citywest Business Park, Naas Road, Dublin 24, Ireland. *E-mail:* info@meteor.ie. *Website:* www.meteor.ie.

MOBO Awards: The Music of Black Origin (MOBO) Organisation Ltd, 22 Stephenson Way, London, NW1 2HD, UK. *Website:* www.mobo.com.

MTV Awards: MTV Networks, 1515 Broadway, New York, NY 10036, USA. *Website:* www.mtv.com. Numerous awards are given, including the original MTV Awards and MTV Music Video Awards, and location-based awards, such as the MTV Asia Awards, MTV Japan Awards, etc.; also runs the VH1 Music Awards.

MUZ-TV Awards: *E-mail:* www@muz-tv.ru. *Website:* www.muz-tv.ru. Annual national awards in numerous categories, from the Russian music television channel, MUZ-TV.

Native American Music Awards: Native American Music Awards Inc., 511 Avenue of the Americas, Suite 371, New York, NY 10011, USA. *Telephone:* (212) 228-8300. *E-mail:* nammys@aol.com. *Website:* www.nativeamericanmusic.com.

New Zealand Music Awards: Recording Industry Association of New Zealand Inc. (RIANZ), Private Bag 78 850, Grey Lynn, Auckland, New Zealand. *Telephone:* (9) 360-5085. *Fax:* (9) 360-5086. *E-mail:* music@rianz.org.nz. *Website:* www.nzmusicawards.co.nz.

Nordoff-Robbins Silver Clef Awards: Nordoff-Robbins Music Therapy, 2 Lissenden Gardens, London, NW5 1PP, UK. *Telephone:* (20) 7267-4496. *Fax:* (20) 7267-4369. *Website:* www.silverclef.com.

Ivor Novello Awards: British Academy of Composers & Songwriters, British Music House, 25–27 Berners Street, London, W1T 3LR, UK. *Telephone:* (20) 7636-2929. *Fax:* (20) 7636-2212. *E-mail:* info@britishacademy.com. *Website:* www.britishacademy.com. Annual awards recognizing excellence in music writing.

NRJ Music Awards: NRJ, 22 rue Boileau, 75203 Paris cedex 16, France. *Website:* nrjmusicawards.nrj.fr. Annual music awards f. 2000 by NRJ radio station; held in Cannes at the opening of Marché international de l'édition musicale (MIDEM).

Laurence Olivier Awards: Society of London Theatre, 32 Rose Street, London, WC2E 9ET, UK. *Telephone:* (20) 7557-6700. *Fax:* (20) 7557-6799. *E-mail:* enquiries@solttma.co.uk. *Website:* www.solt.co.uk. Annual theatre awards, including awards for actors, directors and producers of musicals.

Polar Music Prize: Blasieholmstorg 8, 111 48 Stockholm, Sweden. *Telephone:* (8) 407 18 02. *Fax:* 611 87 18. *E-mail:* kim.pettersson@polarmusicprize.com. *Website:* www.polarmusicprize.com. A Royal Swedish Academy of Music Award; an international music prize, f. 1989 to recognize the exceptional achievements by individuals, groups or institutions in the creation and advancement of music; prize: 1 m. krona.

Polaris Music Prize: *E-mail:* steve@polarismusicprize.ca. *Website:* www.polarismusicprize.ca. f. 2006 by Steve Jordan; Canadian prize for the country's best album, based on creative quality. Prize of $20,000.

Porin Award: Institut hrvatske glazbene industrije diskografska nagrada 'PORIN', Brozova 8a, 10000 Zagreb, Croatia. *Telephone:* (1) 3668198. *Fax:* (1) 3668072. *E-mail:* porin@ihgi.hr. *Website:* www.porin.info. f. by the Croatian Phonographic Association, Croatian Musicians' Union, Croatian Radio-Television and the Croatian Composers' Society.

Premio Tenco: Club Tenco, via Matteotti 226, casella postale 1, 18038 Sanremo, Italy. *Telephone:* (184) 505011. *Fax:* (184) 577289. *E-mail:* club@clubtenco.org. *Website:* www.clubtenco.org. f. 1974 and named after singer Luigi Tenco; annual prize for career achievement of an international singer-songwriter.

Los Premios de la Música: Academia de las Artes y las Ciencias de la Música, Calle Abdón Terradas, n° 3-3bis, 28015 Madrid, Spain. *E-mail:* academia@acamu.com. *Website:* www.academiadelamusica.com. f. 1996 to recognize the work of composers, songwriters, artists and professionals in the Spanish music industry.

Premios Gardel a la Música: CAPIF, Lavalle 534 Piso 4 (C1047AAL), Buenos Aires, Argentina. *Telephone:* (11) 4326-6464. *Fax:* (11) 4326-7830. *E-mail:* comunicacion@capif.org.ar. *Website:* www.capif.org.ar. Awarded by the Cámara Argentina de Productores e Indus de Fonogramas y sus Reproduciones (CAPIF).

Pulitzer Prize in Music: The Pulitzer Prizes, Columbia University, 709 Journalism Building, 2950 Broadway, New York, NY 10027, USA. *Telephone:* (212) 854-3841. *Fax:* (212) 854-3342. *E-mail:* pulitzer@www.pulitzer.org. *Website:* www.pulitzer.org.

Ronnie Scott Awards: 47 Frith Street, London, W1D 4HT, England. *Telephone:* (20) 7439-0747. *E-mail:* ronniescotts@ronniescotts.co.uk. *Website:* www.ronniescotts.co.uk. f. 2007; held at Ronnie Scott's jazz club, London.

Soul Train Music Awards: c/o Rogers & Cowan, Pacific Design Center, 8687 Melrose Avenue, Seventh Floor, Los Angeles, CA 90069, USA. *Telephone:* (310) 854-8100. *Fax:* (310) 854-8101. *Website:* www.soultrain.com.

South African Music Awards: c/o Recording Industry of South Africa (RiSA), PO Box 367, Randburg 2125, South Africa. *Telephone:* (11) 886 1342. *Fax:* (11) 886 4169. *E-mail:* nono@samusicawards.co.za. *Website:* www.samusicawards.co.za. f. 1995; annual awards to recognize excellence in the South African recording industry.

Spellemannprisen: Sandakerveien 52, 0477 Oslo, Norway. *Telephone:* 22 22 17 88. *Fax:* 22 22 17 68. *E-mail:* spellemann@spellemann.no. *Website:* www.spellemann.no. Awarded by the Norwegian centre of the International Federation of the Phonographic Industry.

Tony Awards: American Theatre Wing, 570 Seventh Avenue, Suite 501, New York, NY 10018, USA. *Telephone:* (212) 765-0606. *Fax:* (212) 307-1910. *E-mail:* mailbox@americantheatrewing.org. *Website:* www.tonyawards.com. Annual theatre awards, including awards for actors, directors and productions of musicals.

World Music Awards: IFPI Secretariat, 54 Regent Street, London, W1B 5RE, UK. *Telephone:* (20) 7878-7900. *Fax:* (20) 7878-7950. *E-mail:* info@worldmusicawards.com. *Website:* www.worldmusicawards.com. Annual awards given for international record sales, awarded by the International Federation of the Phonographic Industry (IFPI). Award ceremony held in different locations each year.

APPENDIX D: DIGITAL MUSIC

In the early 1990s websites offering digital music to promote unsigned music artists began to appear. The first commercial download site, Emusic.com, was launched in 1998. There are now hundreds of authorized digital music services worldwide.

For details on organizations in the digital music industry, see Appendix B. For advice and information on downloading digital music, copyright law, and further lists of authorized digital music sites, see www.pro-music.org.

The following is not an exhaustive list of authorized digital music services, as the industry is constantly changing; however, every attempt has been made to give a broad range of sites.

A8: *Website:* music.a8.com. Area of operation: People's Republic of China.

Åhléns: *Website:* www.ahlens.com. Area of operation: Sweden.

AigoMusic: *Website:* www.aigomusic.com. Area of operation: worldwide.

Alapage: *Website:* www.alapage.com. Area of operation: France.

Americanas: *Website:* www.americanas.com.br. Area of operation: Brazil.

Amplifier: *Website:* www.amplifier.co.nz. Area of operation: New Zealand.

AOL Musik Downloads: *Website:* www.aol.de. Area of operation: Germany.

AonMusicdownload: *Website:* musicdownload.aon.at. Area of operation: Austria.

Archambault: *Website:* www.archambault.ca. Area of operation: Canada.

Audiojelly: *Website:* www.audiojelly.com. Area of operation: UK.

A–Z: *Website:* www.a-z.dk. Area of operation: Denmark.

Azzurra Music: *Website:* www.azzurramusic.it. Area of operation: Italy.

Beatport: *Website:* www.beatport.com. Area of operation: USA.

Belgian Music Online: *Website:* www.belgianmusiconline.be. Area of operation: Belgium.

Bengans: *Website:* www.bengans.cd. Area of operation: Sweden.

BigNoiseMusic: *Website:* www.bignoise.com. Area of operation: UK.

BigPondMusic: *Website:* www.bigpondmusic.com. Area of operation: Australia.

Biisi: *Website:* www.biisi.fi. Area of operation: Finland.

Bijenkorf: *Website:* www.bijenkorf.nl. Area of operation: The Netherlands.

Bild: *Website:* www.bild.de. Area of operation: Germany.

Bilka: *Website:* www.bilka.dk. Area of operation: Denmark.

Bleep: *Website:* www.bleep.com. Area of operation: worldwide.

BlipBeat: *Website:* blipbeat.blip.se. Area of operation: Sweden.

Box: *Website:* www.box.dk. Area of operation: Denmark.

Bugs: *Website:* www.bugs.co.kr. Area of operation: Republic of Korea.

Bulldog: *Website:* www.bulldogmusicshop.com. Area of operation: UK.

BuyMusic: *Website:* www.buymusic.com. Area of operation: USA.

Carrefour Online: *Website:* www.music.carrefour.es. Area of operation: Spain.

CD rai: *Website:* www.cd.rai.it. Area of operation: Italy.

Cdigix: *Website:* www.cdigix.com. Area of operation: USA.

CDON: *Website:* www.cdon.com. Area of operation: Europe.

Chaos Music: *Website:* www.chaos.com. Area of operation: Australia.

Chello: *Website:* www.musiczone.at. Area of operation: Austria.

Classical: *Website:* www.classical.com. Area of operation: worldwide.

Clear Channel Music New!: *Website:* www.clearchannelmusic.com/new. Area of operation: USA; new and unsigned artists.

Coke Tunes: *Website:* www.cokefridge.co.nz. Area of operation: New Zealand.

Commodore Music Store: *Website:* www.commodoreworld.com. Area of operation: The Netherlands.

CompuServe: *Website:* www.compuserve.nl. Area of operation: The Netherlands.

Connect Store: *Website:* www.connect.com. Area of operation: Europe, USA.

Cora Music: *Website:* www.coramusic.fr. Area of operation: France.

CountDownload: *Website:* www.countdownload.nl. Area of operation: The Netherlands.

Crimson Bay: *Website:* www.crimsonbay.com. Area of operation: India; Indian labels.

digiRAMA: *Website:* www.digirama.co.nz. Area of operation: New Zealand.

Disaudio: *Website:* www.disaudio.com. Area of operation: UK; Welsh music.

DJ Download: *Website:* www.djdownload.com. Area of operation: UK.

Dosirak: *Website:* www.dosirak.com. Area of operation: Republic of Korea.

Download: *Website:* www.download.nl. Area of operation: The Netherlands.

E-Compil: *Website:* www.ecompil.fr. Area of operation: France.

easyMusic: *Website:* www.easymusic.com. Area of operation: UK.

eClassical: *Website:* www.eclassical.com. Area of operation: worldwide.

Eircom: *Website:* www.eircom.net. Area of operation: Ireland.

Elatinmusic: *Website:* www.elatinmusic.com. Area of operation: USA.

eMusic: *Website:* www.emusic.com. Area of operation: Europe, USA. f. 1998 as GoodNoise; subscription-based site.

EOL Asia: *Website:* www.eolasia.com. Area of operation: Hong Kong.

Epitonic: *Website:* www.epitonic.com. Area of operation: worldwide.

Eventim: *Website:* www.eventim.de. Area of operation: Germany.

Ex Libris: *Website:* www.exlibris.ch. Area of operation: Switzerland.

Excite Music Store: *Website:* www.excite.co.jp. Area of operation: Japan.

Fame Music Megastore: *Website:* www.fame.nl. Area of operation: The Netherlands.

Finetunes Music Shop: *Website:* www.finetunes.de. Area of operation: Germany.

Fnac: *Website:* www.fnac.com. Area of operation: France.

For Your Entertainment (F.Y.E.): *Website:* www.fye.com. Area of operation: USA.

Fotex: *Website:* www.fotex.dk. Area of operation: Denmark.

Fox Music Online: *Website:* www.foxmusic.com. Area of operation: USA.

Free Record Shop: *Website:* www.freerecordshop.com. Area of operation: Europe.

Funcake: *Website:* www.funcake.com. Area of operation: Republic of Korea.

Funman: *Website:* www.funman.fi. Area of operation: Finland.

Futureshop: *Website:* www.futureshop.ca. Area of operation: Canada.

Go MP3: *Website:* www.gomp3.gr. Area of operation: Greece.

Göteborgs-Posten: *Website:* www.gp.se. Area of operation: Sweden.

Graze Music: *Website:* www.grazemusic.com. Area of operation: USA.

Gunvor: *Website:* www.gunvor.se. Area of operation: Sweden.

HearItBuyItBurnIt: *Website:* www.hearitbuyitburnit.com. Area of operation: UK.

HiMusic: *Website:* himusic.hinet.net. Area of operation: Taiwan.

HMV: *Website:* www.hmv.com. Area of operation: Australia, Europe.

Home Downloads: *Website:* www.homedownloads.se. Area of operation: Sweden.

Ilta-Sanomat Musiikki: *Website:* musiikki.iltasanomat.fi. Area of operation: Finland.

i-m Music Download: *Website:* www.i-m.ch. Area of operation: Switzerland.

iMusica: *Website:* www.imusica.com.br. Area of operation: Brazil.

Independent Dance: *Website:* www.independentdance.com. Area of operation: Europe.

India Times Digital Music Download: *Website:* www.indiatimes.com. Area of operation: India.

Indieburn: *Website:* www.indieburn.com. Area of operation: USA.

iplay: *Website:* www.iplay.pl. Area of operation: Poland.

iTunes: *Website:* www.apple.com/itunes. Area of operation: worldwide.

JB HiFi: *Website:* www.jbhifi.com.au. Area of operation: Australia.

Jubii: *Website:* www.jubii.dk. Area of operation: Denmark.

JukeOn: *Website:* www.jukeon.com. Area of operation: Republic of Korea.

KarmaDownload: *Website:* www.karmadownload.com. Area of operation: UK.

Karstadt: *Website:* www.karstadt.de. Area of operation: Germany.

KKBOX: *Website:* www.kkbox.com.tw. Area of operation: Taiwan.

Kontor: *Website:* www.kontor.cc. Area of operation: Germany.

Label Gate: *Website:* www.labelgate.com. Area of operation: Japan.

Libero iMusic: *Website:* imusic.libero.it. Area of operation: Italy.

Life Way Christian Stores: *Website:* www.lifewaystores.com. Area of operation: USA; Christian music.

Listen Japan: *Website:* www.listen.co.jp/music. Area of operation: Japan.

Loot Tunes: *Website:* www.loottunes.com. Area of operation: UK.

Los40: *Website:* www.los40.com. Area of operation: Spain.

M6 Music: *Website:* www.m6music.fr. Area of operation: France.

Magix Music Shop: *Website:* www.magixmusic.de. Area of operation: Germany.

Media Markt: *Website:* www.hotvision.de. Area of operation: Germany.

Media Milkshake: *Website:* www.mediamilkshake.se. Area of operation: Sweden.

Melo: *Website:* www.melo.pl. Area of operation: Poland.

MelOn: *Website:* www.melon.com. Area of operation: Republic of Korea.

MessaggerieMusicali: *Website:* www.messaggeriedigitali.it. Area of operation: Italy.

MetroTunes: *Website:* www.metrotunes.co.uk. Area of operation: UK.

Ministry of Sound: *Website:* www.ministryofsound.com. Area of operation: UK.

mMode Music Store: *Website:* www.attwireless.com/music. Area of operation: USA.

Mora: *Website:* www.mora.jp. Area of operation: Japan.

MP3: *Website:* www.mp3.com. Area of operation: Australia, Europe, USA.

Mperia: *Website:* www.mperia.com. Area of operation: USA.

mpGreek: *Website:* www.mpgreek.com. Area of operation: Greece.

MSN: *Website:* www.msn.com. Area of operation: worldwide.

MTV Digital Downloads: *Website:* www.mtv.com. Area of operation: Europe.

Mukebox: *Website:* www.mukebox.com. Area of operation: Republic of Korea.

Mule Music: *Website:* www.mulemusic.com.au. Area of operation: Australia.

Music: *Website:* www.music.jp. Area of operation: Japan.

Music.Dir: *Website:* m.dir.bg. Area of operation: Bulgaria; Bulgarian record companies.

Music 4 Us: *Website:* www.mu4us.com. Area of operation: Spain.

Music Minutes: *Website:* www.musicminutes.com. Area of operation: The Netherlands.

Music Store: *Website:* www.musicstore.jp. Area of operation: Japan.

Music Store: *Website:* musicstore.cdondemand.nl. Area of operation: The Netherlands.

Musica: *Website:* www.musica.co.za. Area of operation: African countries.

Musica360: *Website:* www.musica360.com. Area of operation: USA.

MusicBrigade: *Website:* www.musicbrigade.com. Area of operation: worldwide.

MusicGiants: *Website:* www.musicgiants.com. Area of operation: USA.

MusicMatch: *Website:* www.musicmatch.com. Area of operation: USA.

MusicNet: *Website:* www.musicnet.com. Area of operation: USA.

MusicNOW: *Website:* www.fullaudio.com. Area of operation: USA.

MusicON: *Website:* www.musicon.co.kr. Area of operation: Republic of Korea.

MusicOnline: *Website:* www.musiconline.no. Area of operation: Norway; Norwegian independent labels.

MusicRebellion: *Website:* www.musicrebellion.com. Area of operation: USA.

MusicShop: *Website:* www.musicshop.se. Area of operation: Sweden.

Musiikki Lataamo: *Website:* musiikkilataamo.hs.fi. Area of operation: Finland.

Musik: *Website:* www.musik.dk. Area of operation: Denmark; Danish independent labels.

Musik ElGiganten: *Website:* musik.elgiganten.dk. Area of operation: Denmark.

Muz: *Website:* www.muz.co.kr. Area of operation: Republic of Korea.

MY3UKA: *Website:* music.gbg.bg. Area of operation: Bulgaria; Bulgarian record companies.

Mycokemusic: *Website:* www.mycokemusic.com. Area of operation: Europe.

Mylisten: *Website:* www.mylisten.com. Area of operation: Republic of Korea.

Napster: *Website:* www.napster.com. Area of operation: Canada, Europe, USA; offers subscription service.

Naxos Music Library: *Website:* www.naxosmusiclibrary.com. Area of operation: worldwide.

Nervous Records: *Website:* www.nervous.co.uk. Area of operation: UK.

NetAnttila: *Website:* download.netanttila.com. Area of operation: Finland.

9Sky: *Website:* www.9sky.com. Area of operation: People's Republic of China.

NumeriCable: *Website:* www.numericable.fr. Area of operation: France.

OCN Music Store: *Website:* music-store.ocn.ne.jp. Area of operation: Japan.

OiMusic: *Website:* www.oi.co.kr. Area of operation: Republic of Korea.

Ongen: *Website:* www.ongen.net. Area of operation: Japan.

Onmusicplay: *Website:* www.onmusicplay.com. Area of operation: Spain.

Oricon Style: *Website:* www.oricon.co.jp. Area of operation: Japan.

Oxfam Music Store: *Website:* www.oxfam.org.uk. Area of operation: UK; a contribution from each purchase goes to the charity.

Ozmusicweed: *Website:* www.ozmusicweed.com. Area of operation: Australia; independent and unsigned artists.

Packard Bell: *Website:* www.packardbell.com. Area of operation: Europe.

Pass Along: *Website:* www.passalong.com. Area of operation: USA.

Payload: *Website:* www.payload.dk. Area of operation: Denmark.

Peoplesound: *Website:* www.peoplesound.com. Area of operation: UK.

Pepsi Max Music: *Website:* www.maxmusic.fi. Area of operation: Finland.

phnet musiikki: *Website:* www.phnetmusiikki.fi. Area of operation: Finland.

Planet Internet Music Stream: *Website:* www.planetinternet.nl. Area of operation: The Netherlands.

Playlouder: *Website:* www.playlouder.com. Area of operation: Europe.

Pop City: *Website:* pop.city.fi. Area of operation: Finland.

Pop Life: *Website:* www.poplife.se. Area of operation: Sweden.

Puretracks: *Website:* www.puretracks.com. Area of operation: Canada, USA.

QBand: *Website:* www.qband.com.tw. Area of operation: Taiwan.

QQ: *Website:* www.qq.com. Area of operation: People's Republic of China.

Radio 538: *Website:* www.radio538.nl. Area of operation: The Netherlands.

RCN Music: *Website:* www.rcninteraction.com/music. Area of operation: USA.

RealPlayer Music Store: *Website:* www.real.com/musicstore. Area of operation: USA.

reco-choku: *Website:* recochoku.jp. Area of operation: Japan.

Rhapsody: *Website:* www.listen.com. Area of operation: USA.

RossoAlice: *Website:* www.rossoalice.it. Area of operation: Italy.

Rough Trade: *Website:* www.roughtrade.com. Area of operation: UK.

RTL Musik: *Website:* www.rtlmusik.de. Area of operation: Germany.

SA MP3: *Website:* www.samp3.com. Area of operation: African countries.

Sanity: *Website:* www.sanity.com.au. Area of operation: Australia.

SAPO: *Website:* www.sapo.pt. Area of operation: Portugal.

7digital: *Website:* www.7digital.com. Area of operation: Europe.

Skivhugget: *Website:* digital.skivhugget.se. Area of operation: Sweden.

Soho: *Website:* www.soho.pl. Area of operation: Poland.

SongTouch: *Website:* www.songtouch.com. Area of operation: USA; Christian music.

Soundbuzz: *Website:* www.soundbuzz.com. Area of operation: worldwide.

StarHub: *Website:* play.starhub.com. Area of operation: Singapore.

StarZone: *Website:* www.starzone.cz. Area of operation: Czech Republic.

StreamWaves: *Website:* www.streamwaves.com. Area of operation: USA.

Streets Online: *Website:* www.streetsonline.co.uk/digital. Area of operation: UK.

Tarabu: *Website:* www.tarabu.com. Area of operation: Mexico.

TDC Online: *Website:* musik.tdconline.dk. Area of operation: Denmark.

Tellas Music: *Website:* music.tellas.gr. Area of operation: Greece.

10 Música: *Website:* www.10musica.com. Area of operation: Argentina.

Terra Música Premium: *Website:* musicapremium.terra.es. Area of operation: Spain.

Tesco: *Website:* www.tesco.com. Area of operation: UK.

Tiscali: *Website:* www.tiscali.com. Area of operation: Europe.

Tonlist: *Website:* www.tonlist.com. Area of operation: worldwide; Icelandic labels.

ToosT Tunes: *Website:* www.toostmusic.nl. Area of operation: The Netherlands.

Top100: *Website:* www.top100.cn. Area of operation: People's Republic of China.

Trax2Burn: *Website:* www.trax2burn.com. Area of operation: UK; independent dance labels.

TubeMusic: *Website:* www.tubemusic.com. Area of operation: Republic of Korea.

TuneTribe: *Website:* www.tunetribe.com. Area of operation: UK.

United Music: *Website:* www.unitedmusic.it. Area of operation: Italy.

Urge: *Website:* www.urge.com. Area of operation: USA.

vanLeest: *Website:* www.vanleest.nl. Area of operation: The Netherlands.

Virgin Digital: *Website:* www.virgindigital.com. Area of operation: Europe, USA.

Vitaminic Music Club: *Website:* www.vitaminic.com. Area of operation: Europe.

Vodafone Musicstation: *Website:* www.vodafonemusic.co.uk. Area of operation: UK.

Voy Music: *Website:* www.voymusic.com. Area of operation: Latin America, USA.

Wal-Mart: *Website:* www.walmart.com. Area of operation: USA.

War Child Music: *Website:* www.warchildmusic.com. Area of operation: UK; a contribution from each purchase goes to the charity.

WAVAA: *Website:* www.wavaa.com. Area of operation: Republic of Korea.

Woolworths: *Website:* www.woolworths.co.uk. Area of operation: UK.

Yahoo!: *Website:* www.yahoo.com. Area of operation: worldwide.

Zabavaj: *Website:* www.zabavaj.se. Area of operation: Slovenia.

ZapMusica: *Website:* www.zapmusica.com. Area of operation: Argentina.

GROUP INDEX

This index lists bands, popular-music orchestras, music collectives and, where a cross-reference to members is considered useful, production teams. The list under each group name includes those (current and former) members who have an entry in the book. For example, if you look at the band Röyksopp, you will see that the members are Svein Berge and Torbjörn Brundtland, each of whom has a biographical entry in the book.

A Camp: Nina Persson.
A Great Big World: Ian Axel, Chad King.
A Guy Called Gerald: Gerald Simpson.
A Touch of Jazz Inc.: DJ Jazzy Jeff.
A Tribe Called Quest: Q-Tip.
AAA (Advanced Acoustic Armorments): Jimmy Cauty.
AAAHS: Jana Heller.
ABBA: Benny Andersson, Agnetha Fältskog, Frida Lyngstad, Björn Ulvaeus.
Abba Vision: Marie-Claire Follett.
ABC: Gardner Cole, Martin Fry.
Aberjaber: Delyth Jenkins.
Absalon Orchestra: Paul Strandberg.
Acacia: Imogen Heap.
Academica: Mircea Romcescu.
Accordion Tribe: Maria Kalaniemi.
AC/DC: Brian Johnson, Phil Rudd, Cliff Williams, Angus Young, Malcolm Young.
Ace in the Hole: George Strait.
Ace of Base: Jenny Berggren, Jonas Berggren, Linn Berggren, Ulf Ekberg.
Acoustic Grinder: Jan Frederickx.
Acoustic Mania: Antonio Forcione.
Acoustic Sense: John Sund.
Acoustic Triangle: Tim Garland.
Acoustic Version: Hilda Kazassian, Vassil Petrov.
Act Big Band: Ben Sluijs.
Activity Center: Burkhard Beins.
Adam and The Ants: Adam Ant, Oscar Blandamer, Chris Constantinou, Christopher Hughes, Jon Moss.
Adamski: Seal.
Adrian Bentzon's Jazzband: Theis Jensen.
Advent: Anthony Davis.
The Advent: Colin McBean.
The Adventure Babies: Eddie Morton.
The Aeona Flute Quartet: Paul Cheneour.
Aerobic Christians: Stephen Harcourt.
Aerodrom: Paolo Sfeci.
Aerosmith: Joe Perry, Steven Tyler.
Afraid of Mice: Ronald Stone.
Africa All-Stars: Dizzy Mandjeku, Sam Manguana, Mansiamina M'Foko.
Africa Fiesta Sukisa: Mansiamina M'Foko, Dr Nico.
Africa Libre: Manecas Costa.
African Beats: King Sunny Ade.
The African Brothers: Lincoln Minott.
African Jazz: Manu Dibango.
African Project: Philippe Sellam.
Afro Celt Sound System: Iarla Ó Lionáird.
Afro-Cuban All Stars: Juan de Marcos González.
AfroCubism: Kasse Mady Diabaté, Fode Lassana Diabaté, Toumani Diabaté, Bassekou Kouyate, José Angel Martinez Nieves, Jorge Maturell Romero, Eliades Ochoa, Eglis Ochoa Hidalgo, Osnel Odit Bavastro, Baba Sissoko, Djelimady Tounkara.
Afrobeat Blaster: Chief Udoh Essiet.
Afro-Latin Jazz Orchestra: Arturo O'Farrill.
After Dark: Steve Gresswell.
After Hours: Steve Kershaw.
After Tea: Raymond Fenwick.
After the Fire: Nicholas Battle.
Afterhours: Giles Lewin.
Agathocles: Jan Frederickx.
Aghia Triada: Guillaume Orti.
a-ha: Magne Furuholmen, Morten Harket, Pål Waaktaar.
Air: Jean-Benoît Dunckel, Nicolas Godin.
Air Condition: Zbigniew Namysłowski.
Air Supply: Graham Russell.
Airforce: Ginger Baker, Alan White.
Airrace: Jason Bonham.
Akasa: John Millar.
Akimbo: Simon Bartholomew, Nick Seymour.
Akombaliha: Rajery.
The Akoustic Band: Chick Corea, Tim Garland, Scott Henderson.
Akvarium: Boris Grebenshchikov.
Al DiMeola Project: Al DiMeola.
Al Green and The Soul Mates: Al Green.
Al Stewart Band: Al Stewart, Laurie Wisefield.
Alabama: Jeff Cook, Teddy Gentry, Mark Herndon, Randy Owen.
Alabama Shakes: Zach Cockrell, Heath Fogg, Brittany Howard, Steve Johnson.

Alabama 3: Jake Black, Johnny Delafons, Simon Edwards, Orlando Harrison, John Jennings, Piers Marsh, Mark Sams, Rob Spragg.
Alafia: Angélique Kidjo.
Alain Brunet Quartet: Alain Brunet.
Alan Barnes All Stars: Alan Barnes.
The Alan Bown: Alan Bown.
The Alan Elsdon All-Star Jazz Band: John Armatage, Alan Elsdon, Adrian MacIntosh.
The Alan Parsons Project: Alan Parsons, Christopher Thompson.
Alan Price (various bands): Alan Price, William Stanger.
Alan Silva Celestial Communication Orchestra: Thierry Bruneau.
The Alarm: Mike Peters.
Albany: Billy Anderson.
Albert Mangelsdorff Band: Jean-Louis Chautemps.
Albion Band: Steve Ashley, Keith Hinchliffe, Ashley Hutchings, John Kirkpatrick, Julie Matthews, Ken Nicol, Simon Nicol, John Tams, Graeme Taylor, Linda Thompson, Richard Thompson, Eddie Upton, Christine While.
Alcatrazz: Yngwie Malmsteen, Steve Vai.
Aldargaz Ensemble: Timo Alakotila, Maria Kalaniemi.
Aldo Romano's Prosodie: Stefano di Battista, Aldo Romano.
Alejandro Escovedo Orchestra: Alejandro Escovedo.
Alex Cline Ensemble: Aina Kemanis.
Alex Cuba Band: Alex Cuba.
Alex, Jorge y Lena: Lena Burke, Alex Ubago, Jorge Villamizar .
Alex Riel Trio: Alex Riel.
Alexis Korner's Blues Incorporated: John Marshall, William Stanger.
Alfonso Ramos Orchestra: Ruben Ramos.
Alias: Wayne Wonder.
Alias Ron Kavana: Ron Kavanagh.
Alice in Chains: Jerry Cantrell, William DuVall, Mike Inez, Sean Kinney.
Alien Ant Farm: Terry Corso, Mike Cosgrove, Dryden Mitchell, Tye Zamora.
Alien Project: Steve Perry.
Alim Qasimov Ensemble: Alim Qasimov.
All About Eve: Andy Cousin, Julianne Regan.
All in Together Now: GZA, RZA.
All Saints: Nicole Appleton, Natalie Appleton-Howlett, Melanie Blatt, Shaznay Lewis.
Allan Bo Band: Palle Bolvig.
Allan Fawn and The State of the Art: Herman de Rycke.
The Alliance: Tony Martin.
Alligator Jug Thumpers: Andy Leggett.
Allman Brothers: Gregg Allman, Warren Haynes.
The Almighty: Ricky Warrick.
Almost Big Band: Nikolaj Bentzon, Palle Bolvig, Jens Winther.
Alone Again Or: Colin Angus.
Alpha Band: T Bone Burnett.
Alpha Wave: Broz Rowland.
ALT: Tim Finn, Liam Ó Maonlaí, Andy White.
Altan: Donal Lunny, Mairéad ní Mhaonaigh.
Altered Images: Johnny McElhone.
Alternative TV: Karl Blake.
Altissimo: Guillaume Orti.
Alvin Roy Saratoga Jazz Band: Colin Kellard.
Amadeus: Paddy Burton.
Amadou & Mariam: Amadou Bagayoko, Mariam Doumbia.
Amaryllis: Tracey Middleton.
Amazulu: Margo Sagov.
The Amboy Dukes: Ted Nugent.
Amen Corner: Andy Fairweather-Low, Derek Weaver.
The American Analog Set: Lee Gillespie, Tom Hoff, Andrew Kenny, Craig McCaffery, Sean Ripple, Lisa Roschmann, Mark Smith.
The American Blues: Frank Beard, Dusty Hill.
American Music Club: Mark Eitzel, Bruce Kaphan, Tim Mooney, Dan Pearson, Vudi.
The Amorphous Androgynous: Garry Cobain, Brian Dougans.
The Amps: Kim Deal.
Amsterdam: Ian Prowse.
Amsterdam: Shahin Shahida.
Anachronic Jazz Band: Marc Richard.
Anaphase: Julien Jacob.
Anastasia: Zlatko Oridjanski, Zoran Spasovski, Goran Trajkoski.
Ancient Beatbox: Nigel Eaton.
...And You Will Know Us By The Trail Of Dead: Kevin Allen, Conrad Keely, David Longoria, Jason Reece, Doni Schroader, Danny Wood.
Anderson Bruford Wakeman Howe: Jon Anderson, Bill Bruford, Steve Howe, Rick Wakeman.

Andrej Seban Band: Peter Lipa.
The Andrews Sisters: Patti Andrews.
Andy Lloyd and The Wedge: Andrew Lloyd.
Andy Prior Big Band: Bob Howard.
Andy Stewart Show: Gordon Pattullo.
Andy Summers Duo: John Etheridge, Andy Summers.
Angels & Airwaves: Tom DeLonge, Atom Willard.
Angels 1–5: Jimmy Cauty.
Anger/Marshall Band: Darol Anger.
Angus and Julia Stone: Angus Stone, Julia Stone.
Anima: Kenneth Knudsen.
Animal House: Laurence Colbert.
Animal Logic: Stanley Clarke, Stewart Copeland.
Animal Soup: Zak Starkey, Simon Townshend.
The Animals: Alan Price.
The Animatori: Kresimir Blazević.
Anjel: LeToya Luckett, LaTavia Roberson.
Ann-Marie Henning Sextet: Ann-Marie Henning.
Ann Wilson and The Daybreaks: Ann Wilson.
Anna Kaisa Liedes Group: Maria Kalaniemi.
Anne Linnet Band: Anne Linnet.
Anni and The Countrysun: Anni Filt.
Annie Haslam Band: Annie Haslam.
Annie Hawkins' New Orleans Legacy: Louis Lince.
Anssi Tikanmäki Film Orchestra: Ippe Kätkä.
The Anteaters: Jennifer Maidman.
Anthony Braxton Big Band/Duo/Quartet: Anthony Braxton, George Lewis.
Anthrax: John Bush.
Anthropology: Melvyn Dadswell.
Anti-Cappella: Fixx-It.
The Anti-Pop Consortium: Beans, Priest, M. Sayyid.
Antoine Hervé Big Band: Jean-Christophe Béney, François Chassagnite.
Antony and the Johnsons: Antony Hegarty.
Antti Sarpila Swing Band: Keith Hall, Antti Sarpila.
Anuna: Hozier, Eimear Quinn.
The Anxious Brothers: Paul Hobbs.
Any Trouble: Clive Gregson.
Aphrodite's Child: Vangelis.
Apitos: David Hassell.
Apna Sangeet: Kulwant Bhamrah.
Apollo: Alain Gibert.
The Apollos: Kandia Kouyate.
Appleton: Nicole Appleton, Natalie Appleton-Howlett.
Aqua: René Dif, Claus Norreen, Lene Nystrom, Soeren Rasted.
The Aquabats: Travis Barker.
Aquarium Rescue Unit: Jimmy Herring.
Aquila: David Richey.
Ar Jazz: Bernard Lepallec.
Arabesque: Raf Mizraki.
Arbejdersanggruppen: Ole Knudsen.
Arbuusi: Raoul Björkenheim.
Arcade Fire: William Butler, Win Butler, Régine Chassagne, Jeremy Gara, Tim Kingsbury, Sarah Neufeld, Richard Parry.
Arcadia: Bill Badley, Simon Le Bon, Nick Rhodes, Roger Taylor.
Arcady: Seán Keane, Niamh Parsons.
Arcane V: Youval Micenmacher.
Archimedes Badkar: Jörgen Adolfsson, Tommy Adolfsson.
Arctic Monkeys: Jamie Cook, Matthew Helders, Nick O'Malley, Alex Turner.
The Ardells: Steve Miller, Boz Scaggs.
Argent: Rod Argent, John Verity.
The Arian Band: Ninef Amirkhas, Borzouyeh Badihi, Sharareh Farnejad, Sahar Kashmari, Sanaz Kashmari, Siamak Khahani, Ali Pahlavan, Payam Salehi, Alireza Tabatabaee.
Ariel: Anders Müller, Tom Rowlands.
The Arild Andersen Band: Arild Andersen, Jens-Christian Wesseltoft.
The Arkells: Anthony Carone, Mike DeAngelis, Nick Dika, Dan Griffin, Max Kerman, Tim Oxford.
The Arlenes: Patrick McGarvey.
Armored Saint: John Bush.
Army of Lovers: Alexander Bard.
Arrested Development: Speech.
The Arrows: Jake Hooker.
Ars Antiqua Musicalis: Fain Sanchez Dueñas, Vincent Molino, Jordi Savall.
Art Bart and Fargo: Paul Hession, Alan Wilkinson.
Art Blakey and The Jazz Messengers: Terence Blanchard, Lou Donaldson, Billy Harper, Geoff Keezer, Chuck Mangione, Wynton Marsalis, Jymie Merritt, Wayne Shorter, Jean Toussaint, Steve Turre, Bobby Watson.
Art Ensemble of Chicago: George Lewis.
Art Farmer Quartet: Pasquale Michaelis, Steve Swallow.
Art of Noise: David Bronze, Lol Crème, Anne Dudley, Trevor Horn.
Art Pepper Quartet: Milcho Leviev.
Art Reynolds Singers: Thelma Houston.
Artery: Simon Hinkler.
Artful Dodger: Pete Devereux, Mark Hill.

Artwoods: Jon Lord.
A/S Rockkompagniet: Peter Walicki.
ASAP (Adrian Smith And Project): Adrian Smith.
Ascension: Henrik Wager.
ASCO: Afel Bocoum.
Ash: Mark Hamilton, Charlotte Hatherley, Rick McMurray, Tim Wheeler.
Ashtray Heart: Brian Molko, Stefan Olsdal.
Asia: Geoffrey Downes, Steve Howe, Carl Palmer, John Wetton.
Asian Dub Foundation: Aniruddha Das, Pandit G, Steve Chandra Savale, Sun-J.
Asiatic Disciples: Professor Griff.
ASK: Martin Archer.
Asleep at the Wheel: Ray Benson.
Aspect: David Gleeson.
The Associates: Nigel Glockler.
Aston Reymers Rivaler: Carl Aborg, Wilfredo Stephenson.
Astral Project: Steve Masakowski.
Aswad: Brinsley Forde, Michael Martin.
At the Drive In: Cedric Bixler-Zavala, Omar Rodríguez-López.
At the Racket: John Carty.
Atakor: Souad Massi.
A*Teens: Dhani Lennevald, Sara Lumholdt, Amit Paul, Marie Serneholt.
Athlete: Joel Pott, Stephen Roberts, Tim Wanstall, Carey Willetts.
Atlas: Dony.
ATM Trio: John Marshall.
Atomic Kitten: Jenny Frost, Natasha Hamilton, Kerry Katona, Liz McClarnon, Heidi Range.
Atomic Playboys: Steve Stevens.
Atoms for Peace: Nigel Godrich, Flea, Thom Yorke.
The Attractions: Elvis Costello.
Au Bonheur des Dames: Jean Davis.
Au Go Go Singers: Stephen Stills, Peter Tork.
Au Pairs: Paul Foad.
Aubrey Dunham and The Party Machine: Aubrey Dunham.
Audio de Luxe: Colin Hudson.
Audioslave: Tim Commerford, Chris Cornell, Tom Morello, Bradley Wilk.
Aunt Fuzz: Kajsa Grytt, Nike Markelius.
The Aural Tradition: Gerry Armstrong.
The Australians: Paul Hemmings.
Autechre: Sean Booth, Robert Brown.
The Auteurs: Luke Haines.
Automatic Dlamini: John Parish.
The Autumn Defense: John Stirratt.
The Avalanches: Robbie Chater, James De La Cruz, Tony Diblasi, Darren Seltmann.
Avanti: Hannu Rantanen.
Aventura: Lenny Santos, Max Santos, Romeo Santos, Henry Santos Jeter.
Aventure Dupont: Gilbert Paeffgen.
Average Joe and the Men in the Street: Alan Clayson.
Average White Band: Alan Gorrie, James Stuart.
Avia: Nickolai Gusev.
Aviator: Peter Wilkinson.
Axel and Coe: Tony Coe.
Axiom: Glenn Shorrock.
The Aytons: Barry Wortley.
Azra: Max Juricic, Boris Leiner.
Aztec Camera: Thomas Barlow, Roddy Frame, Frank Tontoh.
Azteca: Neal Schon.
The Azur Quintet: Henri Texier.

B. B. King Blues Band: George Coleman, B. B. King.
The B-52s: Kate Pierson, Fred Schneider, Keith Strickland, Cindy Wilson.
Babalet: Karel Babuljak.
Babes in Toyland: Kat Bjelland, Courtney Love.
Baby Bird: Steven Jones.
Babylon Zoo: Jas Mann.
The Babys: John Waite.
Babyshambles: Pete Doherty.
The Bachelors: Kevin Neill.
Bachman-Turner Overdrive: Randy Bachman.
Bachué: Corrina Hewat.
Backlund Big Band: Teppo Hauta-aho.
Backstreet Boys: Nick Carter, Howard Dorough, Brian Littrell, Alexander McLean, Kevin Richardson.
Bad Brains: Mackie.
Bad Company: Brian Howe, Simon Kirke, Mick Ralphs, Paul Rodgers.
Bad English: Jonathan Cain, Neal Schon, John Waite.
Bad Lieutenant: Phil Cunningham, Bernard Sumner.
Bad Sneakers: Shane Faber.
The Bags: Patricia Morrison.
Baho: Char.
Bajourou: Djelimady Tounkara.
Baker-Gurvitz Army: Ginger Baker.
Balaam and the Angel: Ian McKean.
BALL: Kramer.
Ballistic Brothers: Ashley Beedle, Diesel, Rocky.

Balls of Fire: Peter Criss.
Baltic Trio: Tõnu Naissoo.
Bamada: Habib Koité.
Bambis: Ingela Forsman.
Bamboo: Mikael Rickfors.
Banana: César Pueyrredon.
Bananarama: Sara Dallin, Siobhan Fahey, Keren Woodward.
Banco de Gaia: Toby Marks.
The Band: Robbie Robertson, Pat Travers.
Band of Angels: P. P. Arnold.
Band of Hope: John Kirkpatrick.
Band of Joy: Robert Plant.
Band of Susans: Page Hamilton.
The Band Perry: Kimberly Perry, Neil Perry, Reid Perry.
Banda Nova: Carlinhos Brown, Caetano Veloso.
Bang Bang Lulu: Gavin Knight.
Bang Lime: Joules Scott-Key, Josh Winstead.
The Bangles: Susannah Hoffs, Deborah Peterson, Victoria Peterson, Michael Steele.
Bantu Success: Remmy Ongala.
Banyan: Stephen Perkins.
B.A.P.: Wolfgang Niedecken.
Barbara Thompson's Paraphernalia: Malcolm MacFarlane.
Barbarossa: Leonardo Pedersen.
Barca do Sol: Fernando Carneiro.
Barclay James Harvest: John Lees.
The Barcodes: Alan Glen.
Baritone Band: John Williams.
Bark Psychosis: Graham Sutton.
Barker's Knee: Richard Churchley.
The Barney McAll Sextet: Barney McAll.
The Barneys: John Bickersteth.
Barnstorm: Joe Walsh.
Barry & Holly Tashian: Barry Tashian, Holly Tashian.
Barry & The Remains: Barry Tashian.
Barry Melton Band: 'Country' Joe McDonald.
Barut Trio: Sylvie Nawasadio.
Basement Jaxx: Felix Buxton, Simon Ratcliffe.
The Basics: Raul Malo.
Basin Street Six: Peter Fountain.
Bassa Bassa: Mark Priestley.
Bastille: Will Farquarson, Kyle Simmons, Dan Smith, Chris Wood.
Bathiya and Santhush: Bathiya Jayakody, Santhush Weeraman.
The Battlefield Band: John McCusker.
Bay City Rollers: Leslie McKeown, Ian Mitchell.
Bayou Brothers: Per Vibskov.
Bazaar: Anders Koppel.
BBC (various music orchestras): Bill Charleson, Jay Craig, Mike Mower.
BBMak: Mark Barry, Christian Burns, Stephen McNally.
The Beach Boys: Al Jardine, Mike Love, Brian Wilson.
Beady Eye: Gem Archer, Andrew Bell, Liam Gallagher, Chris Sharrock.
Bearcats: Chris Hall.
The Bears: Adrian Belew.
Beastie Boys: Adrock, Mike D.
Beat the Heat: Karl Ratzer.
The Beatles: Paul McCartney, Ringo Starr.
Beatnik Beatch: Roger Manning.
Beats International: Norman Cook.
Beausoleil: Michael Doucet.
The Beautiful Losers: Chris Rea.
The Beautiful South: Jacqueline Abbott, Gary Birtles, Kevin Brown, Briana Corrigan, Paul Heaton, Dave Hemingway, David Rotheray, Dave Stead, Sean Welch, Alison Wheeler.
Beaver Service: Finn Roar.
The Bee Gees: Barry Gibb.
Bees Make Honey: Ron Kavanagh.
Beggar's Mantle: Bruce Davies.
Beggar's Opera: Gordon Sellar.
Begley & Cooney: Séamus Begley, Steve Cooney.
Beijo: Monica Vasconcelos.
Bekummernis of Luc Le Masne: Guillermo Felloué.
Belfast Gypsies: Jackie McAuley.
Bellamy Brothers: David Bellamy, Howard Bellamy.
Belle & Sebastian: Isobel Campbell, Richard Colburn, Mick Cooke, Chris Geddes, Stevie Jackson, Bobby Kildea, Sarah Martin, Stuart Murdoch.
The Bellestars: Clare Hirst.
Belleville Rendezvous: Gavin Marwick.
Belleville Three: Juan Atkins, Derrick May, Kevin Saunderson.
Bellowhead: Jon Boden.
Belly: Tanya Donelly.
Belmondo Big Band: Lionel Belmondo, Stéphane Belmondo, Jean-Christophe Béney, Thomas Bramerie, Didier Havet, Clovis Nicolas.
The Beloved: Guy Gausden.
Bembeya Jazz: Sékou Diabaté.
Ben Folds Five: Ben Folds, Darren Jessee, Robert Sledge.
Benefit Group: Stanislav Kubes.

Benet: Eric Benet.
Benny Goodman's Orchestra: Eddie Bert.
Benoît Blue Boy and The Tortilleurs: Benoît Blue Boy.
Bertrand Denzler Cluster: Bertrand Denzler.
Bess Snyder and Co.: John Densmore.
Beth Custer Ensemble: Beth Custer.
The Betterdays: Michael Hayne.
Bex: Emmanuel Bex, Aldo Romano.
Bex Machine: Emmanuel Bex.
The Bex'tet: Emmanuel Bex.
The Bible: Boo Hewerdine.
Biff Bang Pow!: Alan McGee.
Big Arm: Paul Ryder.
Big Bad Family: Janne Murto.
Big Band Lumière: Denis Barbier, Stéphane Belmondo, Thierry Bruneau, François Chassagnite, Laurent Cugny, Andy Sheppard.
Big Bang: Daesung, G-Dragon, Seungri, Taeyang.
Big Black: Steve Albini.
Big Co-Motion Band: Andy Sheppard, Charles Underwood.
Big Dish: Craig Armstrong, Allan Dumbreck.
Big Dumb Face: Wes Borland.
Big Fat Snake: Anders Blichfeldt.
Big Festival Orchestra: Mario Igrec.
Big in Japan: Ian Broudie, Bill Drummond, Holly Johnson.
Big Problem: René Wynens.
The Big Push: Bryan Smith.
Big Sky Band: Charlie McKerron.
Big Town Playboys: Al Nicholls.
Bijele Strijele: Sinisa Doronjga.
Bijelo Dugme: Goran Bregovic.
Bill Bruford's Earthworks: Bill Bruford, Mick Hutton.
Bill Haley and The Comets: Dick Richards, Joey Welz.
Bill Harrell and The Virginians: Larry Stephenson.
Bill Sluijs Kwartet: Ben Sluijs.
Bill Wyman's Rhythm Kings: Martin Taylor, Bill Wyman.
Billy and The Conquerors: Alan Clayson, Jeffrey Wraight.
Billy Cobham Band: Billy Cobham, Milcho Leviev.
Billy Harper (various bands): Billy Harper.
Billy Hill: Dennis Robbins, Pam Tillis.
Billy Pilgrim: Kristian Bush.
Billy Taylor's New York Jazz Sextet: Billy Cobham.
Billy Tipton Memorial Saxophone Quartet: Amy Denio.
Binford: Andreas Reihse, Detlef Weinrich.
Bird X: Stéphane Ianora.
The Biréli Lagrène Ensemble: Biréli Lagrène.
The Birthday Party: Nick Cave, Mick Harvey.
Bitches Brew: Ann-Marie Henning.
Bitter Funeral Beer Band: Jörgen Adolfsson, Tommy Adolfsson.
Björn Again: Teresa Davis, John Tyrrell.
Blab Happy: Jon Dennis.
The Black: David Longoria.
Black: James Hughes.
The Black Arm Band: Mark Atkins.
Black Box: Simon Britton.
Black Box Recorder: Luke Haines.
Black Coffee: Gwyneth Herbert.
The Black Crowes: Luther Dickinson, Steve Gorman, Eddie Harsch, Chris Robinson, Rich Robinson.
Black Dog Productions: Edward Handley, Andy Turner.
Black Eyed Peas: Apl de Ap, Fergie, Taboo, Will.I.Am.
Black Flag: Henry Rollins.
Black Grape: Mark Berry, Shaun Ryder.
Black Jack Johnson: Mos Def.
The Black Keys: Dan Auerbach, Patrick Carney.
Black Light Burns: Wes Borland.
Black Liner Star: Choque Hosein.
The Black Mass: Doug Williams.
Black Randy: Belinda Carlisle.
Black Rebel Motorcycle Club: Peter Hayes, Nick Jago, Robert Turner.
The Black Rockers: Graham Parker.
Black Sabbath: Terry Butler, Ian Gillan, Tony Iommi, Tony Martin, Neil Murray, Ozzy Osbourne, Bill Ward.
Black Science Orchestra: Ashley Beedle.
Black Sheep: Lou Gramm.
Black Spirits: Thomas Mapfumo, Oliver Mtukudzi.
Black Tie: Randy Meisner.
Black Uhuru: Junior Reid.
Black Widow: Carleen Anderson.
Blackbyrd: Norbert Meijs.
Blackfoot: Ken Hensley.
The Blackhearts: Joan Jett.
Blackie: Phil Murray.
Blackmore's Nights: Ritchie Blackmore.
Blacks Unlimited: Chartwell Dutiro, Thomas Mapfumo.
Blacksand: Nick Franglen.
The Blackshaw Brothers: Vanessa Rubin.

Blackstreet: Teddy Riley.
Blake Babies: Juliana Hatfield.
Blancmange: Stephen Luscombe.
Blasé: Charles Angelopulo.
Blast: Peter Rasted.
Blee Blop Blues: Dennis Wilson.
The Blessing: Simon Hanson.
Blind Faith: Ginger Baker, Eric Clapton, Steve Winwood.
Blink: Thomas Negrijn.
Blink-182: Travis Barker, Tom de Longe, Mark Hoppus.
Blip: Tim Gane.
Bliss: Paul Ralphes.
Blizzard of Ozz: Ozzy Osbourne.
Bloc-notes Quintet: Didier Havet.
Bloc Party: Russell Lissack, Gordon Moakes, Kele Okereke, Matt Tong.
The Blockheads: Gilad Atzmon.
Blodwyn Pig: Mick Abrahams.
The Blokes: Billy Bragg.
Blondie: Debbie Harry.
Blood Sweat and Tears: David Clayton-Thomas, Al Kooper.
Bloodred Bacteria: Jan Frederickx.
The Bloomsbury Set: Andrew Lloyd.
The Blow Monkeys: Dr Robert.
Blowin' Smoke: Larry Knight.
Blowzabella: Nigel Eaton.
BLT: Robin Trower.
B.L.U.: Kelis.
Blue: Antony Costa, Duncan James, Lee Ryan, Simon Webbe.
Blue Aeroplanes: Ian Kearey.
Blue Angel: Cyndi Lauper.
Blue Angels: David Clarke.
Blue Birds: Ivan Myslikovjan.
Blue Bot: Michael Schack.
Blue Cluster: Ann-Marie Henning.
Blue Effect: Olda Kellner.
Blue Ensemble: Alexandre Ouzounoff.
The Blue Flames: Georgie Fame.
Blue Harlem: Al Nicholls.
Blue Mink: Madeleine Bell, Roger Coulam, Herbie Flowers, Mike Moran, Ann Odell, Alan Parker.
The Blue Moon Orchestra: Nanci Griffith.
Blue Night Express: Martie Maguire, Emily Robison.
Blue Note 7: Nicholas Payton.
Blue Notes: Paul Foad, Andy Hamilton.
Blue Öyster Cult: Eric Bloom, Donald Roeser.
Blue Pearl Band: Vincent Mills, Broz Rowland.
The Blue Planet Orchestra: Roland Perrin.
Blue Sun: Stefan Borum, Bo Jacobsen.
The Blue Tones: Brian Hunt.
Blue Train: Simon Husbands, Jartsa Karvonen, Jarmo Savolainen.
Blue Zone: Lisa Stansfield.
Bluegrass Alliance: Vince Gill.
Bluegrass Boys: Bobby Atkins, Tom Ewing.
Bluegrass Cardinals: William Bryson, Larry Stephenson.
Blues Brothers: Steve Cropper.
Blues Corporation: Paul Hobbs, Nicky Moore.
Blues Five: Peter Lipa.
Blues Inc.: George Stuart.
Blues Nite: Kenn Lending.
The Blues Project: Al Kooper.
Blues Pumpm: Zappa Cermak, Wolfgang Frosch, Friedrich Glatzl, Bernd Rommel.
The Blues Syndicate: John Mayall.
Bluesdog: Aubrey Dunham.
Bluesology: Elton John.
Bluesounds: Dave Lindholm.
The Bluetones: Eds Chesters, Adam Devlin, Mark Morriss, Scott Morriss.
Blur: Damon Albarn, Graham Coxon, Alex James, Dave Rowntree.
Blush Response: Brandon Flowers.
Bo Jacobsen World Jazz Orchestra: Bo Jacobsen.
Bo Stief 5: Bo Stief.
Boa: Paolo Sfeci.
Boards of Canada: Marcus Eoin, Michael Sandison.
Boat Rockers: Karl Hyde.
Bob and Marcia: Marcia Griffiths.
Bob Davenport and The Rakes: Bob Davenport.
bob hund: Mats Andersson, John Essing, Mats Hellquist, Jonas Jonasson, Conny Nimmersjö, Rolf Oberg.
Bob Kerr Whoopee Band: John Percival.
Bob Marley and The Wailers: Bunny Wailer.
The Bob Seger System: Bob Seger.
Bobby Few Trio: Bobby Few.
Bobri: Karel Tampier.
Bocca Juniors: Pete Heller, Andy Weatherall.
Bodast: Steve Howe.
Bodies Without Organs: Alexander Bard.

Body Count: Ice-T.
Body 'n' Soul: Ib Nielsen.
Boehm Quintette: Donald Stewart.
Bohuslän Big Band: Jukka Linkola.
Bolovaris: Francis Varis.
Bombay Hotel: Kenneth Knudsen.
Bombay1: Kurt Dahlke, Stoya.
Bomonstre: Alain Gibert.
Bon Iver: Justin Vernon.
Bon Jovi: Jon Bon Jovi, David Bryan, Richie Sambora, Alec John Such, Tico Torres.
The Bone Orchestra: Charlie Collins.
Bongo Maffin: Thandiswa Mazwai, Adrian Mupemhi, Oscar, Tshepo Seate.
Bongwater: Kramer.
Bonham: Jason Bonham.
Boo Radleys: Martin Carr, Steve Hewitt, Simon Rowbottom.
Book of Days: David Tompkins.
Booker T and The MGs (Memphis Group): Steve Cropper, Booker T. Jones.
Boomtown Rats: Bob Geldof.
Boone Creek: Ricky Skaggs.
Boothill: Karel Babuljak.
Boots Electric: Jesse Hughes.
Boots for Dancing: Jo Callis.
Bootsy's Rubber Band: Bootsy Collins.
Bootzilla Orchestra: Bootsy Collins.
Bop Brothers: Jon Taylor.
Boquitas Pintadas: Gloria Trevi.
Border Spirit: Pauline Cato.
The Boris Gardiner Happening: Boris Gardiner.
Boss Hog: Jon Spencer.
Boston: Tom Scholz.
Boston Pops Orchestra: Harry Rabinowitz, John Williams.
Both Hands Free: Bob Helson.
The Bothy Band: Donal Lunny, Matt Molloy.
Bow Wow Wow: Annabella Lu Win.
Bowers/Ducharme Trio: Annette Ducharme.
The Box: Charlie Collins.
Boy Better Know: Skepta.
Box Car Racer: Tom DeLonge.
Box Codax: Nick McCarthy.
The Boy Hairdressers: Raymond McGinley.
The Boyd Tinsley Band: Boyd Tinsley.
Boys Next Door: Nick Cave, Mick Harvey.
Boys of the Lough: Aly Bain.
Boy's Own: Terry Farley, Pete Heller.
Boys Wonder: Tony Barber.
Boyz from Brazil: Philippe Cohen Solal, Christoph H. Müller.
Boyz II Men: Michael McCary, Nathan Morris, Wanya Morris, Shawn Stockman.
Boyzone: Keith Duffy, Mikey Graham, Ronan Keating, Shane Lynch.
Brad: Stone Gossard.
Brad Mehldau Trio: Brad Mehldau.
The Bradford Singers: Madeleine Bell.
Brain Damage and Death: Floch Delvaux.
The Brain Surgeons: Ken Lyons.
Brainbox: Jan Akkerman.
Brakes: Marc Beatty, Eamon Hamilton, Alex White, Tom White.
The Brand New Heavies: Carleen Anderson, Simon Bartholomew, Siedah Garrett, Jan Kincaid, Andrew Levy.
Brand X: Phil Collins, Philip Spinelli.
Branford Marsalis: Branford Marsalis, Wynton Marsalis.
Brass Monkey: Martin Carthy, John Kirkpatrick.
Brave Belt: Randy Bachman.
Brave New World: Henrik Wager.
The Bravery: Anthony Burulcich, John Conway, Sam Endicott, Mike Hindirt, Michael Zakarin.
Braxtonia Project: Anthony Braxton, Seppo Paakkunainen.
Brazilliance: Ken Mathieson.
The Brazz Brothers: Stein Tafjord.
Bread: Anders Melander.
Break Big Band: Kari Komppa.
Breakaway: Tony Ansems.
The Brecker Brothers: Randy Brecker.
Breed: Steve Hewitt.
The Breeders: Kim Deal, Tanya Donelly, Josephine Wiggs.
Brewer's Droop: Mark Knopfler.
Brian Bennett Band: Brian Bennett.
Brian Leakes' Sweet and Sour: Adrian MacIntosh.
Brian MacLean Band: Maria McKee.
Brian Poole and The Tremeloes: David Munden, Brian Poole.
Bridewell Taxis: Sean McElhone.
Brigada S: Sergey Galanin.
Brigadiry Ser'ga: Sergey Galanin.
Bright Eyes: Jason Boesel, Conor Oberst.
Brilliant: Jimmy Cauty.

British Racing Green: Karl Blake.
British Sea Power: Hamilton, Noble, Wood, Yan.
Broadcast: James Cargill, Tim Felton, Roj Stevens.
Broken Social Scene: Brendan Canning, Kevin Drew.
Bronski Beat: Jimmy Somerville.
Brooks & Dunn: Kix Brooks, Ronnie Dunn.
Brother Beyond: Eg White.
Brother D Blue Band: Dan Vernhettes.
Brotherhood of Breath: Julian Argüelles, Chris McGregor.
Brotherhood of Man: Tim Ridley.
Brothers in Blues: Ludo Beckers.
Brown Sugar: Paul Rodgers.
The Browns: Jim Brown.
Bru Boru: Bobby Gardiner.
Bruce Adams/Alan Barnes Quintet: Alan Barnes, Jim Simpson.
Bruce Adams/P. Michaux Quintet: Pasquale Michaux.
Bruce Turner Jump Band: John Armatage, John Chilton.
Brunning Sunflower Blues Band: Bob Brunning.
Bruno Tocanne Réunion: Bruno Tocanne.
Brushane Big Band: Pekka Toivanen.
Brutus: Zbynek Maulis.
The Bryn Haworth Band: Bryn Haworth.
Bryron Lee and The Dragonaires: Marcia Griffiths.
The Bucket Band: Ronald Howe.
Buckingham Nicks: Lindsey Buckingham, Stevie Nicks.
The Bucks: Ron Kavanagh.
The Buckskin Boys: Leonard Cohen.
Buckwheat and The Hitchikers: Stanley 'Buckwheat' Dural.
Buckwheat Zydeco: Stanley 'Buckwheat' Dural.
Buddy Curtess and The Grasshoppers: Michael Henry.
Buddy DeFranco Group/Orchestra: Buddy DeFranco.
Buddy Holly and The Three Tunes: Sonny Curtis.
Buddy Rich Band: Jay Craig.
Budweiserova and Friends: Irena Budweiserova.
Buena Vista Social Club: Ry Cooder, Juan de Marcos González, Eliades Ochoa, Omara Portuondo.
The Buff Medways: Billy Childish.
Buffalo: Peter Viskinde.
Buffalo Springfield: Jim Messina, Stephen Stills, Neil Young.
Buggles: Geoffrey Downes, Trevor Horn, Hans Zimmer.
Buick MacKane: Alejandro Escovedo.
Bullit: Bob Helson.
Bumblebees: Laoise Kelly.
Bumcello: Vincent Ségal.
Burach: Sandy Brechin, Gavin Marwick.
Burning Spear: Winston Rodney, Jamaka Tee-Birdd.
Burton MU Big Band: John M. Taylor.
Bush: Robin Goodridge, Nigel Pulsford, Gavin Rossdale.
Bushwackers: Steve Cooney.
Butch Thompson Trio: Butch Thompson.
Butterfield 8: Thomas Barlow, Terry Edwards.
Butthole Surfers: Kramer.
The Butts Band: John Densmore, Robby Krieger.
Buzzcocks: Tony Barber.
Bwana Zoulou Gang: Raymond Lema.
B*Witched: Lyndsay Armaou, Edele Lynch, Keavy-Jane Lynch, Sinéad O'Carroll.
The Byrds: David Crosby, Chris Hillman, Roger McGuinn.
The Byron Band: Roger Flavell.

C Department: Karl Ratzer.
C. V. Jorgensen Band: C. V. Jorgensen.
C. Y. Laurie's Band: Alan Elsdon.
Cab Calloway Band: Robin Eubanks.
Cabestan: Bernard Simard.
Cacophony: Jason Becker.
Cadentia Nova Danica: Hugh Steinmetz.
Cadillac: Joe Turner.
Café con Leche: Francis Cromphout.
Cafe Racers: Mark Knopfler.
Café Society: Charles Angelopulo, Tom Robinson.
Café Tacvba: Elfego Buendía, Emmanuel del Real, Enrique Rangel, Joselo Rangel.
Caifanes: Saúl Hernandez.
Cajones: Lars Frederiksen.
Calennig: Patricia Carron-Smith, Mick Tems.
Caliban: David Dimond.
California Arts Trombone Quartet: Joey Sellers.
Calixto Chinchile: Damian Kulash Jr..
Calle 13: Eduardo Cabra Martínez, René Pérez Joglar.
Calypsocapellet: Niels Mosumgaard.
Camila: Mario Domm, Pablo Hurtado, Samuel Parra.
Campo Alegre: Celina González.
Canned Heat: Walter Trout.
The Cantels: James MacLeod.
Canterach: Steven Lawrence.

Cantrip: Gavin Marwick.
Canyon: Michael Britt, Keech Rainwater.
Capelino: Harm van Sleen.
Capercaillie: Manus Lunny, Michael McGoldrick, Charlie McKerron, Karen Matheson, Donald Shaw.
Capital Cities: Ryan Merchant, Sebu Simonian.
Capital Queue: Vince Ford.
Capital Swing: Rex Bennett, John Rees-Jones, Jerry Senfluk.
Cappella: Kelly Overett.
Captain & Tennille: Daryl Dragon, Toni Tennille.
Captain Howdy: Kramer.
Captain Rat and The Blind Rivets: Mark Rubel.
Carcrash International: Matthew Best.
The Cardigans: Lasse Johansson, Bengt Lagerberg, Nina Persson, Magnus Sveningsson, Peter Svensson.
The Cardinals: Ryan Adams.
Care: Ian Broudie.
Carl Story's Rambling Moutaineers: Ray Harper.
Carl Wayne and The Vikings: Beverley Bevan.
Carla Bley (various bands): Julian Argüelles, Carla Bley, George Lewis, Karen Mantler, Arturo O'Farrill Jr, Andy Sheppard, Steve Swallow, Stein Tafjord, Charles Underwood.
Carlos Malcolm Afro Jamaican Rhythm Band: Boris Gardiner, Carlos Malcolm.
Carlos Manuel y su Clan: Carlos Manuel.
Carma (Central Africa Rock Machine): Raymond Lema.
The Carnival Band: Bill Badley, Jub, Giles Lewin, Raf Mizraki, Maddy Prior, Andy Watts.
Carpe Diem: Eddie Lock.
Carpenters: John Bettis, Richard Carpenter.
The Cars: Ric Ocasek.
Carte de Séjour: Rachid Taha.
Carter the Unstoppable Sex Machine (USM): Fruitbat, Jim Bob.
Carterbar: Jimmy Powells.
Cast: Keith O'Neill, John Power, Liam Tyson, Peter Wilkinson.
Catapult: Tony Elliott.
Catatonia: Dafydd Ieuan, Paul Jones, Cerys Matthews, Owen Powell, Guto Pryce, Aled Richards, Mark Roberts.
The Catholics: Frank Black.
Causa Bibendi: Václav Harmacek.
Cayenne: Roberto Pla.
Cecil Taylor (various bands): Johannes Bauer, Teppo Hauta-aho, Heinrich Lindenmaier, Tomasz Stańko, Cecil Taylor.
Celebration of Joe: Richard Howell-Jones.
Cellofans: Marie-Ange Martin.
Celtus: John McManus.
Center of the World: Bobby Few.
Ceolteoiri Chaulann Folk Orchestra: Paddy Moloney, Sean O'Raida.
Ceramic Dog: Marc Ribot.
The Chadbournes: Kramer.
Chain Reaction: Bruce Ruffin.
Chainsaw: Tribble.
Chaka Demus and Pliers: Chaka Demus, Pliers.
Chakk: Diarmuid Boyle.
Chameleon: Yanni.
Changing Face: John Williams.
Channel Light Vessel: Kate St John.
Chantan: Corrina Hewat.
Chantelle: Olga Tañón.
The Chaps: Mark Haley.
Chapter 8: Anita Baker.
The Charlatans: Martin Blunt, Tim Burgess, Mark Collins, Tony Rogers.
The Charleston Chasers: Nicholas Payton.
Charley Marlowe: Piers Faccini.
Charlie: John Verity.
Charlie Daniels' Volunteer Jam: Charlie Daniels, Noah Gordon.
Charlie Mingus Epitaph Project: Bobby Watson.
Charlie Parker's All-Stars: Toots Thielemans.
Charlie Watts Orchestra: Charlie Watts.
Charlotte and The Volunteers: Charlotte McClain.
Chas & Dave: Chas Hodges, Dave Peacock.
Chasing Dreams: Bo Stief.
Cheap Trick: Rick Nielsen, Robin Zander.
Check Point Charlie: Eric Taminiaux.
The Chemical Brothers: Tom Rowlands, Ed Simons.
Cheneour: Paul Cheneour.
The Cherolees: Val Clover.
The Cherry Bombs: Rodney Crowell, Vince Gill.
Chesed: Katerina Hajdovska-Tlusta.
Chet Baker Quartet/Trio: Riccardo del Fra.
Chic: Nile Rodgers.
Chicago: Peter Cetera.
Chico O'Farrill's Afro-Cuban Jazz Orchestra: Arturo O'Farrill Jr.
Chief Inspector: Médéric Collignon.
The Chieftains: Kevin Conneff, Seán Keane, Matt Molloy, Paddy Moloney.
The Chills: Martin Phillipps.

China Blue: Wu Bai.
China Crisis: Ronald Stone.
Chochek Brothers: Claus Mathiesen.
Choob: Alexander Mitchell.
Chris Anderson Band: Chris Anderson.
Chris Barber Jazz and Blues Band: Chris Barber.
Chris Cross: Marcos Jimenez-Olariaga.
Chris Farlowe and The Thunderbirds: David Bronze, Dave Greenslade, Ron Kavanagh, Albert Lee.
The Christians: Garry Christian, Roger Christian, Russell Christian, Henry Priestman.
Christie: Roger Flavell.
Christophe Marguet Quartet: Christophe Marguet, Guillaume Orti.
Chuck Berry Trio: Chuck Berry.
Chuck Mangione Quartet: Chuck Mangione.
The Chuckerbutty Ocarina Quartet: Giles Lewin.
The Church: Steve Kilbey, Peter Koppes, Tim Powles, Marty Wilson-Piper.
Chute Libre: Olivier Hutman.
CIA: Ice Cube.
Ciccone Youth: Kim Gordon, Thurston Moore, Lee Ranaldo.
Ciocirlia Folk Ensemble: Gheorghe Zamfir.
Circle: Anthony Braxton, Chick Corea, Dave Holland.
Circulasione Totale Orchestra: Frode Gjerstad.
City Zones: Tim Sanders.
The Civil Wars: John Paul White, Joy Williams.
Clannad: Maire Brennan, Enya.
Clark Sisters: Elbernita Clark, Jacky Clark Chisholm, Dorinda Clark Cole, Karen Clark Sheard.
Clark Terry Big Band/Quartet: Ladislav Fidri, Pasquale Michaelis.
The Clarke & Ware Experiment: Vince Clarke, Martyn Ware.
Class: Momchil.
Classical Turkish Music Chorus: Süleyman Erguner.
The Classics: Lou Christie.
Classix Nouveaux: Sal Solo.
Claude Bolling Big Band: Claude Bolling, Jean-Louis Chautemps, Michel Delakian.
Claude Bottom and The Lion Tamers: Steve Kershaw.
Clayson and The Argonauts: Alan Clayson.
Clean Bandit: Milan Neil Amin-Smith, Grace Chatto, Jack Patterson, Luke Patterson.
Cleopatra Wong: Lindy Morrison.
The Cleveland Jazz All-Stars: Vanessa Rubin.
Cliff Bennett and The Rebel Rousers: Chas Hodges.
Clinch: Peter Jorgens.
Clinch Mountain Boys: Ralph Stanley.
Clinic Q: Lise Cabble.
Clinton: Ben Ayres, Tjinder Singh.
Clock DVA: Charlie Collins.
Closet Queens: Svein Hoier.
Cloud 9: Mark Brydon.
Clouseau: Michael Schack.
Clover: Huey Lewis.
Clowns of Death: Noodles.
CN Blue: Jung Yong Hwa, Kang Min Hyuk, Lee Jong Hyun, Lee Jung Shin.
The Coal Porters: Sid Griffin, Patrick McGarvey.
The Coasters: Billy Kramer.
Cochise: Paul Hobbs.
Cockney Rebel: Steve Harley.
Cockpit Music: Thorsten Høeg, Peter Jorgens, Søren Tarding.
CocoRosie: Bianca Casady, Siera Casady.
Cocteau Twins: Elizabeth Fraser, Robin Guthrie, Simon Raymonde.
Coincidence: Jean-Pierre Llabador.
Coke Tale: Fabien-David Haimovici.
Cold, Bold and Together: Kenny G.
Cold Chisel: Jimmy Barnes.
Cold Memory: Andy Ross.
Cold Turkey: Danny Budts.
Coldplay: Guy Berryman, Jonny Buckland, Will Champion, Chris Martin.
Coldstream Guards: Tony Hatch.
Coled Jazz Renegades: Alan Barnes.
Colin Kellard Band: Colin Kellard.
Collapsed Lung: Stephen Harcourt.
Collectif Incidences: Gérard Siracusa.
Collier/Dean: Tom Collier.
Colosseum: Dave Greenslade.
Colosseum II: Don Airey, Neil Murray.
The Colour Mary: John Forrester.
Colourfield: Terry Hall.
Colours: Loïc Dequidt.
Colours of Blue: Viggo Steincke.
Coma: Viggo Steincke.
Combo 5: Ivica Bobinec.
Comes With the Fall: William DuVall.
The Commodores: Lionel Richie.
The Communards: Sarah Morris, Jimmy Somerville.
Communio Musica: Hugh Steinmetz, Robin Taylor.

Co-Motion: Andy Sheppard.
Companhia Clic: Daniela Mercury.
The Company of Wolves: Steve Conte.
Company Week: Charlie Collins.
Concerto for Constantine: Gavin Fox.
Concrete Blonde: Johnette Napolitano.
The Concretes: Victoria Bergsman, Maria Eriksson, Martin Hansson, Ulrik Karlsson, Lisa Milberg, Per Nyström, Ludvig Rylander, Daniel Värjö.
The Congregation: Alan Parker.
Congreso: Joe Vasconcellos.
Conjunto Baron: Reino Laine, Seppo Paakkunainen, Mircea Stan, Heikki Virtanen.
Conjunto Latino: Rubén Blades.
The Contenders: Timothy Schmit.
The Contes: Steve Conte.
Continental: Mansiamina M'Foko.
Continental Heat: Tchando.
Contraband: Mae McKenna.
The Cook Family Singers: David Cook.
Cool Hand: Patrick McGarvey.
Coolfin: Donal Lunny, John McSherry, Sharon Shannon.
The Cooper Temple Clause: Tom Bellamy, Dan Fisher, Benedict Gautrey, Didz Hammond, Jon Harper, Kieran Mahon.
Cop Shoot Cop: A. Tod.
The Coral: Paul Duffy, Nick Power, Bill Ryder-Jones, Ian Skelly, James Skelly, Lee Southall.
Coral Reef Band: Jimmy Buffett, Elliot Scheiner.
Cordero et los Gran Daneses: Peter Rasted.
Cornershop: Ben Ayres, Tjinder Singh.
The Cornish Connection: Paul Cheneour.
Cornwell, Cook and West: Hugh Cornwell.
Coronarias Dans: Kenneth Knudsen.
The Corporation: Brian Poole.
Corpus Christi: Katy Moffatt.
The Corrs: Andrea Corr, Caroline Corr, Jim Corr, Sharon Corr.
Corvettes: Lenni.
Cosmetic: Jamaaladeen Tacuma.
The Cosmic Dots: Thomas Mapfumo.
Coteau: Michael Doucet.
Count Basie (various bands): Carmen Bradford, Buddy DeFranco, Roberta Fabiano, Irene Reid, Marlena Shaw, Mary Stallings, Dennis Wilson, Eugene J. Wright.
Counting Crows: David Bryson, Adam Duritz, Charlie Gillingham, Matt Malley, Ben Mize, Dan Vickrey.
Country Cooking: Peter Wernick.
Country Fever: Albert Lee.
Country Gazette: William Bryson.
Country Gentlemen: Ricky Skaggs.
Country Joe and The Fish: 'Country' Joe McDonald.
Country Shack: Terry Worlledge.
Countryfuga: Karel Tampier.
The Countrymen: Bobby Atkins.
Coup d'Etat: Neil Hannan.
Coverdale/Page: David Coverdale, Jimmy Page.
Cowboy Junkies: Alan Anton, Margo Timmins, Michael Timmins, Peter Timmins.
Coy Bowles and the Fellowship: Coy Bowles.
Cracker: David Lovering.
Craig Taborn Trio: Craig Taborn.
The Cranberries: Michael Hogan, Noel Hogan, Fergal Lawler, Dolores O'Riordan Burton.
Crawler: John Bundrick.
Crazy Horse: Neil Young.
Crazy Wolf: Kerr Donnelly.
Cream: Ginger Baker, Eric Clapton.
The Creations: Al Green.
The Creative Jazz Orchestra: June Tabor.
The Creatures: Siouxsie Sioux.
Credo Band: Djonimbo Ashilaako Bilanso.
Creedence Clearwater Revival: John Fogerty.
The Creepers: Marc Riley.
Creme Fraiche Big Band: John Sund.
Crepe Soul: John Mellencamp.
Crescent: Bo Jacobsen.
The Crewnecks: Lou Christie.
The Crickets: Sonny Curtis, Don Groom, Albert Lee.
Crime and the City Solution: Mick Harvey.
Crisp: Sia.
Crissy Lee and her All-Female Orchestra: Crissy Lee.
The Croco Jazz Big Band: Christian Goupy.
The Crocodiles: Moses Ngwenya.
Cromagnons: Mackie.
Cromlech: Delyth Jenkins.
Crosby Stills and Nash: David Crosby, Graham Nash, Stephen Stills.
Crosby Stills Nash and Young: David Crosby, Graham Nash, Stephen Stills, Neil Young.

Crosbys: William Stanger.
The Cross: Roger Taylor.
Crossing Point: Luther Rix.
Crossover: Dryden Mitchell.
Crow: Paul Hession, Alan Wilkinson.
Crowded House: Neil Finn, Tim Finn, Nick Seymour.
Crowe and McLaughlin: David McLaughlin.
The Crowns: Ben King.
Crucial Three: Julian Cope, Ian McCulloch, Pete Wylie.
Cruiser: John Bickersteth.
The Crushed Tomatoes: Tony Rombola.
Crystal: Geoffrey Gurd.
Crystal Quintet: Marilyn Mazur, Marietta Wandall.
CSS: Lovefoxxx.
Cuarteto las d'Aida: Omara Portuondo.
Cuarteto Patria: José Angel Martinez Nieves, Jorge Maturell Romero, Eliades Ochoa, Eglis Ochoa Hidalgo, Osnel Odit Bavastro.
Cuban Orchestra of Modern Music: Paquito d'Rivera, Artuo Sandoval, Chucho Valdes.
¡Cubanismo!: Jesús Alemaňy.
Cubismo: Hrvoje Rupčič.
CUE: Anders Melander.
Cuisine Cajun: Francis Cromphout.
Cult: Jackie McAuley.
The Cult: Ian Astbury, Billy Duffy.
Culture Club: Boy George, Mikey Craig, Roy Hay, Jon Moss, Ruby Turner.
The Cure: Robert Smith, Lol Tolhurst.
Curlew: Amy Denio, Bill Laswell.
Curly: Oscar Blandamer.
Curve: Dean Garcia, Alexander Mitchell.
Curved Air: Sonja Kristina, Ian Mosley.
Cut 'n' Move: Jens Larsen.
Cut 2 Taste: Michael Henry.
Cybotron: Juan Atkins.
Cypress Hill: B-Real, DJ Muggs, Sen Dog.
Cythara: Jenny Crook.

D: Dulce Maria.
Da Lench Mob: Ice Cube.
Daande Lenol: Baaba Maal.
Daara J: N'Dango D, Faada Freddy, Aladji Man.
Dada and Vinegar Joe: Peter Gage.
Daft Punk: Thomas Bangalter, Guy-Manuel de Homem-Christo.
The Dakotas: Billy Kramer.
Dalek I Love You: Andy McCluskey.
Dalek 1: David Hughes.
Dali's Car: Mick Karn.
Dalton Brothers: Scott Walker.
Dama Dama: Daniel Forró.
Damn Yankees: Jack Blades, Ted Nugent, Tommy Shaw.
The Damned: Captain Sensible, Patricia Morrison, Jon Moss, Rat Scabies, Dave Vanian.
Dance Macabre: Jason Isaacs.
Dancing Moon: Bo Jacobsen.
The Dandy Warhols: Brent DeBoer, Peter Holmstrom, Zia McCabe, Courtney Taylor.
Dane T. S. Hawk and his Great Mongo Dilmuns: Thorsten Høeg.
Dane T. S. Hawk & The Locomotion Starsemble: Thorsten Høeg.
Dangerous Girls: Robert Peters.
Daniel-John Martin Group: Daniel-John Martin.
Daniel Rovai and Friends: John Bickersteth.
Daniel Smith Blues Band/Duo: Jon Taylor.
Daniela Mühleis and Band: Daniela Mühleis.
Danish Grand Prix: Jesper Thorup.
Danish Radio (various bands): Nikolaj Bentzon, Palle Bolvig, Allan Botschinsky, Lee Gibson, Torben Kjaer, Jukka Linkola, Palle Mikkelborg, Hugh Steinmetz, John Sund, Jesper Thorup, Natan Walden, Jens Winther.
Danny King and The Mayfair Set: Beverley Bevan.
Danny White and The Shadds: Paul Hobbs.
Danny Wilson: Ged Grimes.
Danzig: Glenn Danzig.
Dardanelle: Philip Lee.
Dare: Darren Wharton.
The Dark Blues: Nigel Tully.
Darker Than Blue: Juliet Kelly.
The Darkness: Richie Edwards, Ed Graham, Daniel Hawkins, Justin Hawkins, Frankie Poullain.
Darktown: Roy Brazier.
The Darling Buds: James Hughes.
Darts: Rob Davis.
Daryl Hall Band: Alan Gorrie, Daryl Hall.
Das Pferd: Jan Kazda.
DAST Quartet: Tommy Adolfsson.
The Datsuns: Phil Buscke, Dolf de Borst, Christian Livingstone, Matt Osment.
Dave Bramage Band: Dave Grohl.

Dave Corsby Quartet: Dave Corsby.
Dave Gordon Trio: David Goodier.
Dave Holland (various bands): Dave Holland.
Dave Lambert Singers: Jon Hendricks.
Dave Lindholm and Ganpaza Gypsies: Ippe Kätkä, Dave Lindholm.
Dave Matthews Cover Band: Jimmy de Martini.
Dave Matthews Band: Carter Beauford, Stefan Lessard, Dave Matthews, Boyd Tinsley.
Dave O'Higgins and The Oblivion Brothers: Dave O'Higgins.
Dave Patrois Quintet/Trio: Benjamin Henocq, Christophe Walleme.
Dave Pike Set: Eberhard Weber.
Dave Thompson Quartet: Kevin Sanders.
The Davey Arthur Band: Davey Arthur.
Davichi: Minkyung Kang, Haeri Lee.
David Allan Coe Band: William 'Flash' Gordon.
David Davis and The Warrior River Boys: Tom Ewing.
David Feehan Band: David Feehan.
David Grisman Quintet: Darol Anger.
David L. Cook and The Trinidetts: David L. Cook.
David Moss/P. O. Jorgens Duo: Peter Jorgens.
David S. Ware Quartet: Matthew Shipp.
David Sanchez Quintet/Sextet: David Sanchez.
Davy Moving Hearts: Davy Spillane.
Dawn: Tony Orlando.
De Dannan: Mary Black, Frankie Gavin, Dolores Keane.
De Tampier: Karel Tampier.
Deacon Blue: Ricky Ross.
The Dead: Jimmy Herring.
Dead After Dark: Steff Hutchinson.
Dead by Sunrise: Chester Bennington.
Dead City Radio: Michael Kulas.
The Dead Horses: (George) Ryan Bingham.
Dead or Alive: Wayne Hussey.
The Dead Weather: Jack Lawrence, Jack White.
The Deadbeats: Damian Stanley.
The Dear Janes: Barbara Marsh.
The Deason Sisters: Kitty Wells.
Death Bang Party: Wilson Reid.
The Debonairs: Brian Bannister.
Decameron: Johnny Coppin.
Deco: Loïc Dequidt.
Deconstruction: Dave Navarro.
Dédé Ceccarelli Quartet: Thomas Bramerie, Andre Ceccarelli.
The Dedications: Francesco Ronchetti.
Deep Cut: Graham Parker.
Deep Dish: Dubfire, Sharam.
Deep Forest: Eric Mouquet, Michel Sanchez.
Deep Purple: Don Airey, Ritchie Blackmore, David Coverdale, Ian Gillan, Roger Glover, Jon Lord, Steve Morse, Ian Paice, Joe Satriani, Joe Turner.
Def Leppard: Rick Allen, Vivian Campbell, Phil Collen, Joe Elliott, Rick Savage.
Def Mix: David Morales, Satoshi Tomiie.
Defaid: Huw Owen.
The Defectors: Martin Budde.
Deftones: Stephen Carpenter, Abe Cunningham, Frank Delgado, Chino Moreno, Sergio Vega.
Defunk: Vernon Reid.
Defunkt: Kim Clarke.
Deirdre Cartwright Group: Deirdre Cartwright.
Déjà Vu: Charleson Ximenes.
Del Amitri: Andy Alston, David Cummings, Justin Currie, Chris Dollimore, Ian Harvie.
Delaney and Bonnie: Eric Clapton.
Delightful Precipice: Julian Argüelles, Django Bates, Mark Lockheart.
The Delinquents: Terry Francis.
Delirium: Simon Butcher.
The Delmonas: Billy Childish.
The Delphines: Kathy Valentine.
Delta Rae: Grant Emerson, Brittany Hölljes, Eric Hölljes, Ian Hölljes, Elizabeth Hopkins, Mike McKee.
Delta Rhythm Kings: Roy Rogers.
The DeLuxe Blues Band: Bob Brunning.
D-ELZ: Simon Butcher.
Denécheau Jâse Musette: Didier Roussin.
Denim: Lawrence Hayward.
Denis and Denis: Davor Tolja.
Denise Jannah Quintet: Denise Jannah.
Denise Lawrence (various bands): Denise Lawrence.
Denny Laine and The Diplomats: Beverley Bevan, Gordon Sellar.
Deo Dezi: Eric Mouquet.
Deolbeg: Katie Harrigan.
Depeche Mode: Vince Clarke, Andrew Fletcher, David Gahan, Martin Gore, Alan Wilder.
Depp Jones: Bela B.
Derby Big Band: John M. Taylor.
Derek and The Dominoes: Eric Clapton.

Derek Baileys Company: Johannes Bauer.
Derringer: Rick Derringer, Neil Geraldo.
Dervish: Cathy Jordan.
Desert Rose Band: William Bryson, Chris Hillman.
The Desert Sessions: Josh Homme.
Design for Living: Geoffrey Gurd.
Desmond Child and Rouge: Desmond Child.
Desperado: Dee Snider.
Destiny: M. K. Shine.
Destiny's Child: Beyoncé, LeToya Luckett, LaTavia Roberson, Kelly Rowland, Michelle Williams.
Destroyers: George Thorogood.
Detail: Frode Gjerstad.
Detente: Ross Robinson.
dEUS: Tom Barman, Alan Gevaert, Klaas Janzoons, Stéphane Misseghers, Danny Mommens, Mauro Pawlowski.
Device: Holly Knight.
The Devils: Stephen Duffy.
Dewolfe: Andrew Quin.
Dextexter: Even Dextexter.
Dexy's Midnight Runners: Kevin Rowland, Paul Speare.
The DFA (Death From Above): Tim Goldsworthy, James Murphy.
Di Derre: Jo Nesbo.
Dialog: Eero Koivistoinen.
Dialogue: Valery Meladze.
Diamond Head: Sean Harris.
Diana Express: Georgi Stanchev.
Dice: Orjan Strandberg.
Dickey Betts Band: Warren Haynes.
Didier Geers Jazz and Blues Band: Didier Geers.
Die Ärzte: Bela B, Rodrigo González, Farin Urlaub.
Die Hummel: Silke Reichmann.
Die Pilzfreunde: Heinrich Lindenmaier.
Diefenbach: Nicolaj Christophersen, Stefan Gejsing, Lasse Lyngbo, Allan Mattsson, Kenneth Sarup.
Digital Improvisation Ensemble: Marianne Joan.
Dillard and Clark: Doug Dillard.
Dillard-Hartford-Dillard: Doug Dillard, Rodney Dillard.
The Dillards: William Bryson, Doug Dillard, Rodney Dillard.
Din-Din: Thalía.
D-Influence: Ned B, Kwame Kwaten, Steve Marston, Sarah Webb.
The Dinky Toys: Kid Coco.
Dinosaur Jr: Lou Barlow.
Dio: Vivian Campbell.
Diplomats: Trix Ko-chuan Tsui.
Dire Straits: John Illsley, David Knopfler, Mark Knopfler, Hal Lindes, Pick Withers.
Dirty Dot: Noodles.
Dirty Pretty Things: Carl Barât, Didz Hammond.
The Dirty Scums: Dirty Pik.
Dirty Three: Jim White.
Disciples: Simon Campbell.
Disclosure: Guy Lawrence, Howard Lawrence.
Disco Evangelists: Ashley Beedle, David Holmes.
Disco 2000: Jimmy Cauty, Bill Drummond.
Dissidenten: Manickam Yogeswaran.
Distraction: George Stuart.
District Six: Steve Lodder, Ruthie Smith.
Diver: Bengt Lagerberg.
The Divine Comedy: Neil Hannon, Joby Talbot.
The Dixie Chicks: Martie Maguire, Natalie Maines, Emily Robison.
The Dixie Dregs: Steve Morse.
Dixie Fried: Tommi Lievemaa.
Dizrhythmia: Gavin Harrison.
Dizzy Gillespie (various bands): Paquito d'Rivera, Jymie Merritt, David Sanchez, Dennis Wilson.
DJ Jazzy Jeff and the Fresh Prince: DJ Jazzy Jeff, Will Smith.
Djata Band: Lobi Traore.
Djioliba: Oumou Sangare.
The DNA Band: Didier Geers.
DOA: Joseph Keithley.
Doc Pomus: Roberta Fabiano.
Doc Severinsen (various bands): Luther Rix, Doc Severinsen.
Doc West: Cyndi Lauper.
Doctor Phill: Peter Walicki.
Doctors of Madness: Dave Vanian.
Dodgy: Andy Miller.
Dog Days: Simon Le Bon.
Dog God: Peter Jorgens.
Doina Klezmer: Markku Lepistö.
Dokken: Don Dokken.
The Doky Brothers: Chris Minh Doky, Niels Lan Doky.
Dolenz, Jones, Boyce and Hart: Mickey Dolenz.
The Dolls: Beverley de Schoolmeester.
Dolly Mixture: Debsey Wykes.
The Dolphin Brothers: Richard Barbieri, Steve Jansen.

The Dolphins: Vincent Martucci.
Don Cherry's Band: Trilok Gurtu, Bo Stief.
Don Ellis Connection Orchestra: Milcho Leviev, Kenneth Orton.
Donny and Marie: Donny Osmond, Marie Osmond.
Dony and Momchil: Dony, Momchil.
Doobie Brothers: Michael McDonald.
The Doors: Ian Astbury, John Densmore, Robby Krieger.
Dorge, Becker, Carlsen: Irene Becker, Pierre Dorge.
Double Trouble: Lou Ann Barton.
Doudou Swing: Doudou Cuillerier.
Doves: Jimi Goodwin, Andy Williams, Jez Williams.
Down: Phil Anselmo.
Downfall: Tim Armstrong.
Dr Buzzard's Original Savannah Band: Kid Creole.
Dr Feelgood: David Bronze, Wilko Johnson.
Dr Fray: Mark Priestley.
Dr John and The Blues Preachers: Paul Hobbs.
DraculaZombieUSA: Andy Ross.
Drag: Darren Middleton.
Dragonphlie: Dryden Mitchell.
DramaGods: Nuno Bettencourt.
D:Ream: Peter Cunnah.
Dream: Steve Gresswell.
The Dream: Terje Rypdal.
Dream Academy: Kate St John.
Dream City: Bo Jacobsen.
Dream Machine: Paul Hobbs, Bo Stief.
Dream of Eden: Bret Pemelton.
Dream Police: James Stuart.
The Dream Syndicate: John Cale.
Dreams: John Abercrombie, Billy Cobham, Randy Brecker.
Drill: David Craig.
The Drinkard Singers: Dionne Warwick.
Drompojkarna: Carl Aborg.
The Drones: Fiona Kitschin, Gareth Liddiard, Mike Noga, Rui Pereira.
Dru Hill: Sisqó.
Drugi način: Branko Pozgajec.
Drumming Birds: Bob Moses.
Drumpact: Christian 'Ton-Ton' Salut.
D'semble: David Tompkins.
Duane Eddy Band: David Bronze, Duane Eddy.
Dubstar: Sarah Blackwood, Chris Wilkie.
The Dufay Collective: Giles Lewin, Raf Mizraki.
Duffhead: Doug Williams.
Duffy: Stephen Duffy.
Duke Ellington (various bands): Robin Eubanks, Kenny Garrett, Abdullah Ibrahim, Nicholas Payton, Bobby Watson.
The Dukes: Steve Earle.
The Dukes of Stratosphear: Andy Partridge.
Dukes of Swing Orchestra: Eugene J. Wright.
Dúlamán: Seoirse O Dochartaigh.
Dulce Ana: Mario Domm .
Duo Concertinissimo: Ivan Myslikovjan.
Duojazz: David Dimond.
Duran Duran: Stephen Duffy, Simon Le Bon, Nick Rhodes, Andy Taylor, John Taylor, Roger Taylor.
Dust: Neil Tennant.
The Dynamics: Randy Meisner, Pops Mohamed.
Dynamos Band: Manson Grant.

E. Bex Quartet: Emmanuel Bex.
The Eagles: Don Henley, Randy Meisner, Timothy Schmit, Joe Walsh.
Eagles of Death Metal: Josh Homme, Jesse Hughes.
Earl Taylor and The Stoney Mountain Boys: Tom Ewing.
Earplay: John Lunn.
Earth, Wind and Fire: Philip Bailey, Ralph Johnson, Verdine White .
East: Michael Fix.
East Orange: Mark Barrett.
East 17: Terry Coldwell, Brian Harvey, John Hendy, Tony Mortimer.
East Village: Spencer Smith.
Easter: John Phillips.
Easy Money: Toby Keith.
Ebb: Paul Luther.
Eberhard Weber Colours: John Marshall, Eberhard Weber.
EBU Big Band: Tõnu Naissoo.
Ecaroh: Laurent Gianez.
Echo & The Bunnymen: Ian McCulloch, Will Sergeant.
Echo Base: Oscar Harrison.
Echobrain: Jason Newsted.
Echoes of Friends: Doudou Cuillerier.
Eddie Condon's NY: Edward Polcer.
Eddie Louis' Multicolor Fanfare: Dan Vernhettes.
Edentree: Barry Wortley.
The Edgar Winter Group: Edgar Winter.
ED/GE: Ed Jones.
Editors: Edward Lay, Russell Leetch, Tom Smith, Chris Urbanowicz.

Edouard Ferlet Trio: Gary Brunton.
Edward Vesala's Sound and Fury: Raoul Björkenheim, Pertti Päivinen, Teemu Salminen, Mircea Stan, Edward Vesala.
Eek-A-Mouse: Jon Gorr, Rohan Heath.
Eero Koivistoinen Octet: Pentti Lahti, Reino Laine.
Eg and Alice: Eg White.
Eggstone: Patrik Bartosch, Maurits Carlsson, Per Sunding.
Egil Kapstad Trio: Karin Krog.
The Egtved Chronicle: Kim Soerensen.
The Egypt 80: Femi Kuti, Seun Kuti.
Einstürzende Neubauten: Jochen Arbeit, Blixa Bargeld, Alexander Hacke, Rudolph Moser, N. U. Unruh.
Ekhymosis: Juanes.
El Canto del Loco: Daniel Martín García, David Otero Martín, Chema Ruiz Casares, Alejandro Velázquez Insua.
El Cuarteto del Rey: Pablo Milanés.
El Setze Jutges: Lluís Llach.
El Tanbura: Zakaria Ibrahim.
Elastica: Justine Frischmann, Annie Holland, Donna Matthews, Justin Welch.
Elbow: Guy Garvey, Richard Jupp, Craig Potter, Mark Potter, Pete Turner.
The Elected: Jason Boesel, Blake Sennett.
Electra Strings: Caroline Lavelle.
Electrafixion: Ian McCulloch, Will Sergeant.
Electribe 101: Billie Ray Martin.
Electric Be Bop Band: Paul Motian.
Electric Company: Andrew Kenny, Lisa Roschmann, Mark Smith.
The Electric Crayons: Tim Burgess, Steve Hewitt.
Electric Light Orchestra (ELO): Don Airey, Beverley Bevan, Bill Hunt, Jeff Lynne, Roy Wood.
Electric Soul: Phil Asher.
Electric Volunteered Slaves: Olivier Temime.
Electrix: Brian Poole.
Electronic: Johnny Marr, Bernard Sumner, Neil Tennant.
Elegato: Nester Haddaway.
The Elektric Band: Chick Corea.
Elektrobus: Mikoláš Chadima.
Eleventh House: Larry Coryell.
Eli Young Band: Mike Eli, Jon Jones, Chris Thompson, James Young.
Elise Einarsdotter Ensemble: Elise Einarsdotter.
Emanon: Manfred Mann.
Embers: John Butcher.
Embrace: Mick Dale, Steven Firth, Mike Heaton, Danny McNamara, Richard McNamara.
Emerson Lake and Palmer (ELP): Keith Emerson, Greg Lake, Carl Palmer.
Emerson Lake and Powell: Keith Emerson, Greg Lake.
EMF: Ian Dench.
Emigrate: Richard Z. Kruspe.
Eminence Group: Stanislav Kubes.
Emmett Spiceland: Donal Lunny.
Emmylou Harris' Hot Band: Rodney Crowell, Emmylou Harris, Ricky Skaggs.
Empire: Bob Andrews.
Empire Bakuba: Papy-Tex Matolu-Dode.
Empire of the Sun: Nick Littlemore, Luke Steele.
The Emsland Hillbillies: Hermann Lammers Meyer.
Encore Plus Grande: Guigou Chenevier.
Endless Summer: Mike Love.
Energit: Lubos Andrst.
Energy: Ginger Baker.
Energy Crisis: 'Country' Joe McDonald.
The Enforcers: Darrel Higham.
English Country Blues Band: Ian Anderson.
Erguner Ensemble Instrumental-Choeur Musique Turque: Süleyman Erguner.
Enigma: Michael Cretu.
Enormous: Steve O'Toole.
Enrico Quartet: James Chadwick.
Ensemble Aldargaz: Maria Kalaniemi.
Ensemble InterContemporain: Jean-Louis Chautemps.
Ensemble Kaboul: Hossein Arman, Khaled Arman, Osman Arman.
Ensemble Musique Vivante: Gérard Siracusa.
Ensemble Niafunké: Afel Bocoum.
Ensemble Strings: Nicole Yarling.
Entrance: Palle Mikkelborg, Bo Stief.
The Entropics: Amy Denio.
Entropology: John Brennan, Simon Picard, Eddie Prévost.
Enya: Enya, Nicky Ryan, Roma Ryan.
Epik High: Tablo, Mithra Jin, DJ Tukutz.
Episode Six: Ian Gillan, Roger Glover.
Eppu Normaali: Sami-Kalle Ruusukallio, Aku Syrjä, Martti Syrjä, Mikko Syrjä, Juha Torvinen.
The Equals: Eddy Grant, Mzwakhe Mbuli.
Equation: Cara Dillon.
Equip Out: Patrice Meyer.

Era: Eric Levi.
Erasure: Andy Bell, Vince Clarke.
Erguner Dervishes Tourneurs: Süleyman Erguner.
Erguner Musique Ottoman: Süleyman Erguner.
Eric B. & Rakim: Eric B., Rakim.
Eric Burdon (various bands): Eric Burdon.
Eric Clapton Band: David Bronze, Eric Clapton.
Eric Delaney Band: Elkie Brooks, Jim Lawless.
Eric Dolphy Memorial Band: Heinrich Lindenmaier.
Eric Lelann Quartet: Olivier Hutman.
Eric Lohrer Trio: Eric Lohrer.
Eric Martin Band: Eric Martin.
Eric Schultz (various bands): Eric Schultz.
Errorhead: Marcus Deml.
Erykah Free: Erykah Badu.
Escape: Peter Frampton.
Escovedo Brothers: Steve Turre.
Esperanto: Glenn Shorrock.
Espoo Big Band: Keith Hall, Janne Murto, Mika Mylläri, Eerik Siikasaari, Kari Tenkanen.
Esquadrilha da Fumaça: Charleson Ximenes.
Essentials: Jamaka Tee-Birdd.
Ester: Katerina Hajdovska-Tlusta, Alexandr Hajdovsky-Potapovic.
E-Street Band: Nils Lofgren, Bruce Springsteen.
Estúdio da Glória: Tim Rescala.
ETC... Band: Stanislav Kubes.
Etchingham Steam Band: Ashley Hutchings, Eddie Upton.
Eternal: Easther Bennett, Vernie Bennett, Kelle Bryan, Louise.
Eugene J. Wright Ensemble: Eugene J. Wright.
Europe: Joey Tempest.
The Europeans: Steve Hogarth.
Eurythmics: Annie Lennox, Dave Stewart.
Eva Pilarová Ensemble: Vít Fiala, Eva Pilarová.
Evanescence: Terry Balsamo, Will Boyd, Rocky Gray, John LeCompt, Amy Lee.
The Evans Family Band: Sara Evans.
The Everglades: Michael Brook.
The Everly Brothers: Sonny Curtis, Don Everly.
Evermore: Dann Hume, Jon Hume, Peter Hume.
Everything But The Girl: Tracey Thorn, Ben Watt.
Evidence: Roland Perrin.
Evil Twin: Karl Blake, David Mellor.
E'Void: George Voros.
The Executive: George Michael, Andrew Ridgeley.
Exile: Hiro.
Exo: Baekhyun, Chanyeol, Chen, D.O., Lu Han, Kai, Kris, Lay, Lu Han, Sehun, Suho, Tao.
Exo-K: Baekhyun, Chanyeol, D.O., Kai, Sehun, Suho.
Exo-M: Chen, Lu Han, Kris, Lay, Lu Han, Tao.
Exodus: Björk.
Expresso Bongo Orchestra: Paul Speare.
Extempore: Mikoláš Chadima, Alexandr Hajdovsky-Potapovic.
Extra Ball: Jarek Smietana.
Extreem: Jan Frederickx.
Extreme: Nuno Bettencourt, Gary Cherone.
Eye of the Hurricane: David Doruzka.
Eyuphuro: Zena Bacar.

F4 (Flowers 4): Vanness Wu, Jerry Yen, Vic Zhou, Ken Zhu.
The Fabulous Dorseys: William Cronk.
Fabulous Night Train: Steve Miller.
Fabulous Thunderbirds: Lou Ann Barton.
FACE: Steve Cooney.
Face to Face: Flemming Agerskov, Julian Argüelles, Martin France, Jesper Nordenstroem.
The Faces: Rod Stewart, Ronnie Wood.
Fairground Attraction: Eddi Reader.
Fairport Convention: Ashley Hutchings, Dave Mattacks, Iain Matthews, Simon Nicol, David Pegg, Richard Thompson.
Faith No More: Roddy Bottum, Courtney Love, Mike Patton.
Faithless: Rollo Armstrong, Jamie Catto, Maxi Jazz, Sister Bliss.
The Falcons: Eddie Floyd.
The Fall: Marc Riley, Mark E. Smith.
Fall Out Boy: Andy Hurley, Patrick Stump, Joe Trohman, Pete Wentz.
The Fallen Angels: Knox.
False Idols: Steve Kershaw.
The Family: Kirk Franklin, John Wetton.
Family Affair Band: Sean Gourley.
Family Funkton: Carleen Anderson.
Famous Last Words: Martin Carthy, Keith Hancock.
The Fanatics: Simon Fowler, Oscar Harrison, Damon Minchella.
Fancy: Raymond Fenwick.
Fandango: Joe Turner.
Fanfasio: Paul Ada.
Fania All-Stars: Rubén Blades.
Fantastic All-Stars: Nik Turner.

Fantômas: Mike Patton.
The Far East Family Band: Kitaro.
Far from the Madding Crowd: Harry Williamson.
Faraway: Liz van Dort.
The Farm: Leon Caffrey.
Fa-Sol Band: Djonimbo Ashilaako Bilanso.
Fast Buck: Scott Gorham.
Fastway: Eddie Clarke.
Fat Freddy's Drop: Chris Faiumu, Iain Gordon, Tehimana Kerr, Tony Laing, Joe Lindsay, Warren Maxwell, Dallas Tamaira.
Fat Sam's Band: Thomas Chalmers, Ken Mathieson.
The Fatima Mansions: Aindrías O'Gruama.
FBI: Rick Astley.
Feast or Famine: Shahin Shahida.
Feeder: Taka Hirose, Grant Nicholas, Mark Richardson.
Feeling B: Paul H. Landers, Christian 'Flake' Lorenz.
The Feetwarmers: John Chilton.
Felis Ultramarinus: Prince Trubetsky.
Felt: Lawrence Hayward.
Fenn O'Berg: Christian Fennesz, Jim O'Rourke.
Feral Dinosaurs: Jim White.
Ferdo Livadic Tambura Orchestra: Sinisa Leopold.
Fernando Jazz Gang: Doudou Cuillerier.
Ferris: Dave Lindholm.
Fever Pitch: Martin Speake.
The Fiddlers 4: Darol Anger.
Field Music: David Brewis.
Fiestacita: Janne Murto.
The Fifth Dimension: Copeland Davis, Marilyn McCoo.
58: Nikki Sixx.
50 Foot Wave: Kristin Hersh.
Fifth Harmony: Ally Brooke, Camila Cabello, Dinah Jane Hansen, Lauren Jauregui, Normani Kordei.
Fiction Family: Jon Foreman.
Fight: Rob Halford.
Figure of Fun: Thomas Fersen.
Final Fantasy: Owen Pallett.
Fine Young Cannibals: Roland Gift.
The Finn Brothers: Neil Finn, Tim Finn.
Finnforest: Jarmo Savolainen.
Fire Island: Pete Heller.
Firedaze: Steff Hutchinson.
The Fireman: Paul McCartney.
Firetown: Duke Erikson.
The Firm: Paul Rodgers, Anthony Thorpe.
First Aid Kit: Johanna Söderberg, Klara Söderberg.
First Edition: Mike Post, Kenny Rogers.
First Light: Roy Shipston.
First National Band: Mike Nesmith.
Fishbone: Angelo Moore.
The Five Chestnuts: Bruce Welch.
The 5 O'Clock Shadows: Brendan Croker.
5 Seconds of Summer: Michael Clifford, Luke Hemmings, Calum Hood, Ashton Irwin.
The 5.6.7.8s: Sachiko Fujii, Ronnie Fujiyama.
5XKAJ: Bertel Abildgaard.
Fixx: Cy Curnin.
The Flaming Lips: Wayne Coyne, Steven Drozd, Michael Ivins, Kliph Scurlock.
The Flaming Methodists: Marc Catley.
Flaming Youth: Phil Collins.
Flanagan-Ingham Quartet: Kevin Flanagan.
Flash: Christopher Cross.
The Flat Back Four: Steve Kershaw.
Flat Hedgehog: Richard Howell-Jones.
The Flatlanders: Joe Ely.
Flavour Country: Michael Kerr, Ben Thatcher.
The Flecktones: Bela Fleck.
Fleetwood Mac: Lindsey Buckingham, Mick Fleetwood, Christine McVie, John McVie, Dave Mason, Stevie Nicks.
Flesh: Ken Lyons.
Fleur de Lys: Bryn Haworth.
Flint: Keith Flint.
Flint Hill Playboys: Bobby Atkins.
Flip City: Elvis Costello.
The Flirtations: Nigel Moyse.
Flivva: Michael Brook.
Floetry: Marsha Ambrosius, Natalie Stewart.
Flook!: Michael McGoldrick.
Florence and the Machine: Florence Welch.
Florida Georgia Line: Tyler Hubbard, Bryan Kelley.
Flotsam and Jetsam: Jason Newsted.
Flowered Up: Tim Dorney.
Flowerpot Men: Jon Lord.
Flowers and Frolics: Roger Digby.
The Fluence Band: Lynne Percival.

The Fluffers: Glenn Tilbrook.
Fluke: Michael Bryant, Jon Fugler, Michael Tournier.
Flumgummery: Katie Harrigan.
Flyer: Cyndi Lauper.
Flying Burrito Brothers: Chris Hillman, Thad Maxwell.
The Flying Fratellinis: Geoffrey Gurd.
The Flying Lizards: Brian Nevill.
Flying Perfect: Broz Rowland.
The Flying Pickets: Michael Henry, Hereward Kaye, Henrik Wager.
Flying Saucers: Peter Pritchard.
Flynn and Wynne: Michael Wynne.
Flyte Tyme: Jimmy Jam, Terry Lewis, Alexander O'Neal.
Foals: Jack Bevan, Edwin Congreave, Walter Gervers, Andrew Mears, Yannis Philippakis.
F.O.C.: Ian Haug.
Focus: Jan Akkerman.
FOK: Katerina Hajdovska-Tlusta, Alexandr Hajdovsky-Potapovic.
Folk Implosion: Lou Barlow.
Folkus: Nigel Moyse.
FoMoFlo: Amy Denio.
Fonográf: Levente Szörényi.
Foo Fighters: Dave Grohl, Taylor Hawkins, Nate Mendel, Chris Shiflett, Pat Smear.
The Footprints Quintet: Christian Goupy.
Forcefield: Jan Akkerman, Raymond Fenwick.
Foreigner: Lou Gramm, Mick Jones.
Forerunner Jazz Orchestra: Jymie Merritt.
Forever More: Alan Gorrie.
F-Orkestra: Heinrich Lindenmaier.
Formynx: Vangelis.
42nd Street Swing: Gren Horabin.
The Four Accordionists of the Apocalypse: Amy Denio.
The Four Bs: Ben King.
4 Etoiles: Muta Mayi, Nyboma-Syran Mbenza, Mansiamina M'Foko.
Four Fifths: John Hiatt.
4hero: Mark Clair, Dego MacFarlane.
4 Men and a Dog: Gerry O'Connor.
4 Non-Blondes: Linda Perry.
4.40: Juan Guerra.
The Four Ramblers: Val Doonican.
Four Seasons: Frankie Valli.
The Four Seeds: Don Henley.
The Four Strings: Ahmad Jamal.
4xang: Wilfried.
Fourth World: José Neto.
Foxboro Hot Tubs: Billie Joe Armstrong, Tre Cool, Mike Dirnt.
Foxhunters: Bjarne Schmidt.
Fragile Friends: Michael King.
Framed: Enid Williams.
The Frames: Glen Hansard.
Framus Five: Josef Kucera.
François Laudet Big Band: François Laudet.
François Merville Quintet: Guillaume Orti.
Frank Brooker New Orleans Swingtet: Paul Russell.
Frank West Orchestra: Dennis Wilson.
Frankie Goes to Hollywood: Holly Johnson.
The Franks: Peter Rasted.
Frantic Elevators: Mick Hucknall.
Franz Ferdinand: Bob Hardy, Alex Kapranos, Nick McCarthy, Paul Thomson.
The Fray: Joe King, Isaac Slade, Dave Welsh, Ben Wysocki.
Freak of Nature: Mike Tramp.
Freakpower: Norman Cook.
Freckle Face: Arno Hintjens.
Fred Wesley and The Horny Horns: Fred Wesley.
Fred Wesley and The JBs: Bootsy Collins, Barney McAll, Fred Wesley.
Freda: Uno Svenningsson.
The Freddie Starr Band: Gordon Sellar.
Freddy Delagaye Clan: Freddy Delagaye.
Freddy King Quintet: David Swanson.
Free: John Bundrick, Simon Kirke, Paul Rodgers.
The Free Association: David Holmes.
Free Flight Quartet: Milcho Leviev.
Free Form Funky Freqs: Jamaaladeen Tacuma.
Free Kitten: Kim Gordon.
Free Spirits: Larry Coryell.
Freebop: Nigel Moyse.
The Freehold: Phil Collins.
Freelectronic: Tomasz Stańko.
Freeze Frame: Ronald Stone.
Frehley's Comet: Ace Frehley.
Freja: Hanne Thordsen.
French Impression: Duncan Kenyon, Bryan Smith.
The Frenchies: Chrissie Hynde.
Frente: Angela Hart.
Frères Bernard Orchestra: Jean-Claude Montredon.

Fresh: Barry Wortley.
Fresno: Gustavo Mantovani, Lucas Silveira.
Freur: Karl Hyde, Rick Smith.
Fridge: Kieran Hebden.
Friends and Love: Philip Bailey.
Friendship: Lee Ritenour.
F.R.I.S.K.: Liam Howe.
Frisque Concordance: John Butcher.
Fritz: Lindsey Buckingham, Stevie Nicks.
Frode Gjerstad Duo/Trio/Quartet: Frode Gjerstad.
Frode Thingnaes Quintet: Karin Krog.
Frogwings: Jimmy Herring.
From the Underworld: Mark Priestley.
The Front: Heikki Sandren.
Frontline: Caecilie Norby.
The Frosties: Sid Griffin.
Frou Frou: Imogen Heap.
Fruitcake: Steve Cooney.
Fruko y sus Tesos: Joe Arroyo.
Fuat Saka Band: Claus Mathiesen.
The Fugees: Lauryn Hill, Wyclef Jean, Pras Michel.
The Fugs: Kramer, Edward Sanders.
Fujara: Ole Knudsen.
Fullface Storband: Carsten Ortmann.
Fun.: Jack Antonoff, Andrew Dost, Nate Ruess.
Fun Boy Three: Lynval Golding, Terry Hall, Neville Staple.
Fun-Da-Mental: Phil Pickering, Aki Qureshi.
Fun Lovin' Criminals: Fast, Mackie Jayson, Huey Morgan, Steve O'Brien.
Fun-Da-Mental: Aki Nawaz, Dave Watts.
Funeral for a Friend: Chris Coombs-Roberts, Gareth Davies, Matt Davies, Ryan Richards, Darran Smith.
Funk Brothers: Oscar Blandamer.
The Furey Brothers: Davey Arthur, George Furey.
The Fureys and Davey Arthur: Davey Arthur, Eddie Furey, Finbar Furey.
Fusion: Nik Kershaw.
Futon: Simon Gilbert.
Future: Roy Shipston.
Future Song: Klavs Hovman, Marilyn Mazur, Hans Ulrik.
Future Sound of London: Garry Cobain, Brian Dougans.

G. S. Duo, Quartet, Trio: André Jaume, Gérard Siracusa.
G Unit: 50 Cent.
The Gaither Vocal Band: Michael English.
The Gajna: Jan Frederickx.
Galaxy: Ippe Kätkä.
Gallagher & Lyle: Benny Gallagher, Graham Lyle.
Galliano: Rob Gallagher, Ski, Cripsin Robinson.
Galliards Folk Group: Leon Rosselson.
Gamble's Romeos: Thom Bell.
Game Over: Dirty Pik.
Gamma Ray: Kai Hansen, Josh Homme.
Gang of Four: Andy Gill.
The Gang of Three: Dave O'Higgins.
Gang Starr: Guru, DJ Premier.
Garbage: Duke Erikson, Shirley Manson, Steve Marker, Butch Vig.
Gary Bartz Quartet/Quintet: Barney McAll.
Gary Burton Quartet/Quintet: Gary Burton, Pat Metheny, Steve Swallow.
Gary Crosby's Nu Troop: Denys Baptiste.
Gary Moore Band: Don Airey, Neil Murray.
Gary Myrick and The Figures: David Dennard.
Gateway: John Abercrombie, Jack de Johnette, Dave Holland.
Gatlin Brothers: Larry Gatlin.
Gecko Moon: Ringo Madlingozi.
Geiziers: Wazimbo.
Gene Ammons/Sonny Stitt Quintet: Eugene J. Wright.
Gene Chandler and The Dukays: Gene Chandler.
Gene Krupa Orchestra: Buddy DeFranco.
Gene Loves Jezebel: Michael Aston, Chris Bell.
Gene Watson and the Other Four: Gene Watson.
General Havoc: Ben Ayres, Tjinder Singh.
Generation Gap: Ken Tardley.
Generation X: Bob Andrews, Billy Idol.
Genesis: Tony Banks, Bill Bruford, Phil Collins, Peter Gabriel, Steve Hackett, Mike Rutherford.
The Gentle Waves: Isobel Campbell.
Genuine Country: Josie Waverly.
Geoff: Brett Anderson.
Geoff Keezer Quartet/Trio: Geoff Keezer.
Geoff Overon Band: Geoff Overon.
George Robert/Tom Harrell Quintet: George Robert.
Geordie: Brian Johnson.
George Benson Group: George Benson, Earl Klugh.
George Maycock Trio: Ali Haurand.
George Robert Quartet: George Robert.
George Shearing Duo/Quintet/Trio: Warren Chiasson, George Shearing, Toots Thielemans.

George Webb's Dixielanders: Owen Bryce.
Georgie Fame Band: Georgie Fame.
Geraldo Orchestra: Bob Adams.
Gerard Badini Big Band: François Chassagnite.
Gérard Kazembe Orchestra: Raymond Lema.
Gerry and The Pacemakers: Keith Hall, Gerry Marsden.
Gerry Mulligan's International Big Band: Ladislav Fidri.
Ghetto Blaster: Chief Udoh Essiet.
Ghost Cauldron: DJ Kaos.
Ghost in the Machine: Peter Jorgens.
Giant Blonder: Wolfgang Frosch, Friedrich Glatzl.
Giant Killers: Michael Brown, J. Wortley.
Gil Evans Orchestra: Tom Malone, Marilyn Mazur.
Gilgamesh: Philip Lee, Neil Murray.
Gillan: Raymond Fenwick, Janick Gers, Ian Gillan, Mike Moran.
Gillan and Glover: Ian Gillan, Roger Glover.
Ginger Baker's Nutters: Ginger Baker, Keith Hale.
Gipsy Kings: Diego Baliardo, Paco Baliardo, Tonino Baliardo, Andre Reyes, Canut Reyes, Nicolas Reyes, Pablo Reyes, Patchai Reyes.
Gipsy Love: Karl Ratzer.
Gipsy Project: Biréli Lagrène.
Giraffe: Bengt Lagerberg.
Girl: Phil Collen.
Girls Aloud: Cheryl Cole, Nadine Coyle, Sarah Harding, Nicola Roberts, Kimberley Walsh.
Girls' Generation: Taeyeon.
Girlschool: Jackie Chambers, Denise Dufort, Tracey Lamb, Kim McAuliffe, Enid Williams.
Glad: Timothy Schmit.
Gladiators: Jon Gorr, Lenni.
Gladys Knight and The Pips: Gladys Knight.
Glay: Hisashi, Jiro, Takuro, Teru.
Glen Campbell and The Western Wranglers: Glen Campbell.
Glenn Branca's Guitar Orchestra: Page Hamilton, Wharton Tiers.
Glenn Miller Memorial Orchestra: Paul Wood.
Glenn Miller Orchestra: Buddy DeFranco.
The Gloaming: Dennis Cahill, Doveman, Martin Hayes, Iarla Ó Lionaird, Caoimhín Ó Raghallaigh.
Global Guaranty Orchestra: Peter Jorgens.
Globe Unity Orchestra: Johannes Bauer, Anthony Braxton.
Glorious: Anju Sharda.
Glove: Robert Smith.
GMT: Kate Cameron.
Gnags: Per Frost, Jens Nielsen, Peter Nielsen, Jacob Riis-Olsen.
Gnarls Barkley: Cee-Lo Green, Danger Mouse.
The Go-Betweens: Robert Forster, Lindy Morrison.
The Go-Gos: Charlotte Caffey, Belinda Carlisle, Gina Schock, Kathy Valentine, Jane Wiedlin.
Go Plus: Johannes Przygodda.
Go West: Peter Cox, Richard Drummie.
Goah: Gérard Siracusa.
Goat: Phil Pickering.
Godless Wicked Creeps: Martin Budde.
Godley and Crème: Lol Crème, Kevin Godley.
The Gods: Ken Hensley, Greg Lake.
Godsmack: Sully Erna, Robbie Merrill, Tony Rombola, Tommy Stewart.
Gogmagog: Janick Gers.
Gogol Bordello: Eugene Hütz, Sergey Ryabtsev.
Goldberg-Miller Blues Band: Steve Miller.
Golden Diamond: Peter Walicki.
Golden Earring: Rinus Gerritsen, Barry Hay, George Kooymans.
Golden Gate Jazzmen: Derek Sarjeant.
Golden Mercury: King Sunny Ade.
Golden Palominos: Jamaaladeen Tacuma.
Golden Rodeo: Chris Geddes.
Golden State Boys: Chris Hillman.
Goldfrapp: Alison Goldfrapp, Will Gregory.
Golem: Vivian Peres.
Golubiye Gitari: Alexander Malinin.
Gomez: Ian Ball, Paul Blackburn, Dajon Everett, Tom Gray, Ben Ottewell, Olly Peacock.
Gominak: Hamouka Dagara.
Gone Fishin': Thomas Ulstrup.
Gong: Bill Bruford, Kramer, Harry Williamson.
Good Day: Mario Igrec.
Good News: Rohn Lawrence.
The Good Sons: Michael King.
The Good The Bad and The Queen: Damon Albarn, Tony Allen, Paul Simonon, Simon Tong.
Goodacre Country: Tony Goodacre.
Goodbye Mr McKenzie: Shirley Manson.
Gordon Giltrap Band: Gordon Giltrap, Ian Mosley.
Gorge: Mark Haley.
Gorillaz: Damon Albarn, Jamie Hewlett, Russel Hobbs, Murdoc Nicalls, Noodle, 2D.
Goroh-e-Baran: Farhad Darya.

Gorse-Franolic Duo: Drazen Franolic, Vesna Gorse.
The Gospelaires: Dionne Warwick.
Gossip: Hannah Blilie, Beth Ditto, Brace Paine.
Gotan Project: Philippe Cohen Solal, Edouardo Makaroff, Christoph Müller.
Government Mule: Warren Haynes.
Goya Dress: Astrid Williamson.
Goyasnada: Floch Delvaux.
The Graces: Meredith Brooks, Charlotte Caffey.
Gracia: Matija Vujica.
Graduate: Curt Smith.
Graham Collier Septet/Sextet: Philip Lee, John Marshall.
Graham Parker and The Rumour: Graham Parker.
Graham Stewart 7: Alan Elsdon.
Grand Mike Jazz: Remmy Ongala.
Grand Slam: Brian Downey.
Grandmaster Flash and The Furious Five: Grandmaster Flash, Melle Mel.
Grandmaster Flash and The 3 MCs: Grandmaster Flash.
The Grateful Dead: Philip Lesh.
Grauzone: Stephan Eicher.
Gravediggaz: RZA.
Great Buildings: Phil Solem.
Great Society: Grace Slick.
Great White: Jack Russell.
Greedy Beat Syndicate: Matthew Best.
Green Day: Billie Joe Armstrong, Tre Cool, Mike Dirnt, Jason White.
Green Pajamas: Jeff Kelly.
Green River: Jeff Ament, Stone Gossard.
The Greenhornes: Patrick Keeler, Jack Lawrence.
Greenslade: Dave Greenslade.
Greg Kihn Band: Joe Satriani.
Gren Horabin Combo: Gren Horabin.
Greta and The Stray Shots: Robert Childs.
Grethe Ingmann and Sunset: Peter Walicki.
The Grid: David Ball, Richard Norris.
Grin: Nils Lofgren.
Grinderman: Nick Cave.
Gronvirke: Peter Jorgens.
Groove Armada: Andy Cato, Tom Findlay.
Groove Nation: Eddie Saunders.
Groovebusters: Ken Mathieson.
Grooveyard: Jon Taylor.
The Group: Olli Ahvenlahti.
Group 87: Mark Isham.
Grubstreet: Robb Johnson.
Grupo Baruc: Sergio George.
Grupo Mazz: Jimmy Gonzalez.
Grupo Patria: Eglis Ochoa Hidago, Osnel Odit Bavastro.
Grupo Radio Mocambique: Wazimbo.
Grussner Band: Gary Heckard.
Grymlings: Mikael Rickfors.
Gryphon: Graeme Taylor.
Guarare: Rubén Blades.
Guardian Angel: Steve Gresswell.
Guess Who: Randy Bachman.
The Guest Stars: Ruthie Smith.
Guitar Hell: Gary Brunton.
The Guitar Orchestra: Christopher Baylis.
Gulf String: Pierre Blanchard.
Gulliver: Sergey Galanin, Daryl Hall, John Oates.
Gun: Mark Rankin.
Gun Club: Patricia Morrison.
Guns N' Roses: Axl Rose, Slash, Izzy Stradlin.
Gustav Brom Big Band: Gustav Brom, Jaromír Hnilička.
Guttermaendene: Carsten Ortmann.
Guy: Teddy Riley.
Guy Barker International Septet: Guy Barker.
Gwazigan: Bernard Simard.
Gwerinos: Huw Owen.
Gwerz: Soïg Siberil.
Gyllene Tider: Per Gessle.
Gym Class Heroes: Disashi Lumumba-Kasongo, Travie McCoy, Matt McGinley, Eric Roberts.
Gyroscope: Robert Mackay.

H2O: Alan McGee.
Hackensack: Nicky Moore.
Haim: Alana Haim, Danielle Haim, Este Haim.
Haircut 100: Nick Heyward.
Haley Brothers: Mark Haley.
Half Japanese: Kramer.
Halfbreed: Michael Whitaker.
Halfnelson: Tommy Adolfsson, Ron Mael, Russell Mael.
Hall and Oates: Daryl Hall, John Oates.
Hall Brothers Jazz Band: Butch Thompson.
Halla Da: Soren Fledelius.

Hallelujah Chicken Run Band: Thomas Mapfumo.
Hallmark Swingtet: Jerry Senfluk.
The Hallucinations: Jerome Geils.
Hamilton Pool: Iain Matthews.
Hammond Swing Machine: Pasquale Michaelis.
Hana Hegerová Ensemble: Vit Fiala.
Hand/Dupré Guitar Duo: Richard Hand.
Hanne Romer Quartet: Hanne Romer.
Hanoi Rocks: Sami Yaffa.
Hans Knudsen Jumpband: Hans Knudsen.
Hans Ulrik Quartet: Hans Ulrik.
Hanson: Neil Murray.
The Happy End: Sarah Morris.
Happy Fellows: Alla Pugacheva.
Happy Mondays: Mark Berry, Paul Ryder, Shaun Ryder, Gary Whelan.
Happy Orphans: Jim White.
Hard Fi: Richard Archer, Steven Kemp, Ross Philips, Kai Stephens.
Hard Time: Pishta Penava.
Hardline: Jonathan Cain, Neal Schon.
Haricots Rouges: Marc Richard.
Harkalidid: Annika Hoydal.
Harlan County: Peter Skellern.
Harley's John: Ales Zimolka.
The Harmonics: Iain McKinna.
Harrison and Stewart: Dave Stewart.
Harrison-Blanchard: Terence Blanchard.
Harry-Ca-Nab: Richard Churchley.
HASK: Gilles Coronado, Guillaume Orti.
Hat Trick: Michael Fix.
Hate: Flea.
Hater: Matt Cameron.
Havana Cuban Boys of Armando Orefiche: Guillermo Felloué.
Havana Fireflies: John Freeman.
Hawklords: Nik Turner.
Hawkwind: Dave Brock, Keith Hale, John Millar, Nik Turner.
Haysi Fantayzee: Kate Garner, Jeremy Healy.
HBO: Ice Cube.
The Headless Horsemen: John Parish.
Heads Hands and Feet: Chas Hodges, Albert Lee.
Headspace: Adam Wakeman, Damian Wilson.
Heart: Ann Wilson, Nancy Wilson.
Heart to Heart Trio: Kenneth Knudsen, Palle Mikkelborg.
Heartache: Janie Fricke.
Heaven Can Wait: Peter Parker.
Heaven Factory: Ian Kearey.
Heaven on Earth: James Carter, Christian McBride, John Medeski.
Heavy Stereo: Gem Archer.
Héctor and Tito: Tito El Bambino.
HED: Barcode, Kerry Mason.
Hed Boys: Dave Lee.
Hedge Hog: Terje Berg, Sverre Fossen, Arve Gulbrandssen, Svein Hoier, Morten Kristiansen.
Hedgehoppers Anonymous: Alan Avon.
Hege Tokle: Soren Fledelius.
Heikki Sarmanto Ensemble: Heikki Sarmanto, Mircea Stan.
Helicopters: Phil Bennett, Roy Wood.
Helix: Brian Vollmer.
The Hellions: Dave Mason.
Hello: Duncan Kenyon.
Hello Sailor: Neil Hannan.
Helloween: Kai Hansen.
Hellsaw: Jan Frederickx.
Helmet: Page Hamilton.
Helsinki Melodeon Ladies: Maria Kalaniemi.
Hemisphere: Valanga Khoza.
Hendricks and Ross: Jon Hendricks, Annie Ross.
The Hendricks Family: Jon Hendricks.
Henrik Johansen's Jazzband: Theis Jensen.
Henry & June: Ben Swank, Johnny Walker.
Henry Rollins Band: Henry Rollins.
The Hepburns: Aled Richards.
Her Personal Pain: Benedicte Westergaad Madsen.
Herb Miller Orchestra: Clive Copland, Bob Howard.
Herbie Hancock Trio: Herbie Hancock, Dave Holland.
Herbie Mann and The Deep Pocket Band: Cornell Dupree.
Herbie Nichols Project: Ben Allison.
Hercules and the Love Affair: Antony Hegarty.
The Herd: Andrew Bown, Peter Frampton.
Here and Now: Robert Peters.
Here Lies a Crime: Christina Staël von Holstein.
Heritage New Orleans Brass Band: Dave Brennan.
Herman's Hermits: Peter Noone, Jan Whitwam.
Hermeto Pascoal Group: Hermeto Pascoal.
Hessian Sax: Jim White.
Hexagone: Pierre Dutot.
Hexethyl Big Band: Hanne Romer.

HeXtet: John Brennan.
The Hi-Fi's: Marilyn McCoo.
Hi-Life Parade Band: John M. Taylor.
Hi-Standard: Akihiro Nanba, Akira Tsuneoka, Ken Yokohama.
Hickory: Phil Collins.
The Hideaways: Judd Lander.
The High Fidelity: Sean Dickson.
The Highwaymen: Kris Kristofferson, Willie Nelson.
The Higsons: David Cummings, Terry Edwards.
The Hilltops: John Stirratt.
Himmelexpressen: Kenn Lending.
Hindu Love Gods: Bill Berry, Peter Buck, Mike Mills.
Hip Hop: Doug Williams.
The Hip Jazz Trio: Christian 'Ton-Ton' Salut.
Hipsway: Craig Armstrong, Johnny McElhone.
Hiss and Hum: Jason Creasey, Hamish Hutchison.
Hit 'n' Run: Alison Clarkson, Grieg Clifford.
Hit the Hay: Peter Walicki.
The Hives: Pelle Almqvist, Nicholaus Arson, Vigilante Carlstroem, Chris Dangerous, Dr Matt Destruction.
Hljomar: Gunnar Thordarson.
Hokey Pokey: Richard Thompson.
Hole: Courtney Love.
The Hollies: Graham Nash, Mikael Rickfors.
Hollyweird: Christopher Nettleton.
Holy Barbarians: Ian Astbury.
Holy Ghost Boys: Hammer.
Hombres G: Rafael Gutiérrez Muñoz, Daniel Mezquite Hardy, Javier de Molina Burgos, David Summers Rodríguez.
Home: Laurie Wisefield.
Home Fire: Ron Kavanagh.
Home Service: John Tams, Graeme Taylor.
Home Sweet Home: Per Vibskov.
Homemade Orchestra: Tim Whitehead.
Homespun: David Rotheray.
Honey Tongue: Josephine Wiggs.
The Honeydrippers: Jeff Beck, Robert Plant, Jimmy Page, Nile Rodgers.
Honeymoon Stitch: Chad Smith.
The Honkin' Hep Cats: Steve Kershaw.
Hoof: Andrew Barlow.
The Hootennanny Singers: Benny Andersson, Björn Ulvaeus.
Hootie and the Blowfish: Darius Rucker.
The Hopeful Gospel Quartet: Linda Williams, Robin Williams.
Horizon: Edward Simon, Bobby Watson.
Hornweb: Martin Archer.
Horse: Allan Dumbreck.
Hos Anna: Hanne Romer.
Hot Club de Norvege: Jon Larsen.
Hot Club Zagreb: Mario Igrec.
Hot Kings: Marie-Ange Martin.
The Hot Rats: Gaz Coombes, Danny Goffey.
Hot Rize: Peter Wernick.
Hot Salsa: Wilfredo Stephenson.
Hot Savoury Souffles: Brian Madigan.
Hot Tuna: Jack Casady, Jorma Kaukonen.
Hot Vultures: Ian Anderson.
Hothouse: Heather Small.
Hothouse Flowers: Liam O Maonlai.
The Hound Dogs: Marty Wilde.
House of Pain: DJ Lethal.
House of Schock: Gina Schock.
The Housemartins: Norman Cook, Stan Cullimore, Paul Heaton, Dave Hemingway.
How To Grow A Band: Chris Thile.
How We Live: Steve Hogarth.
HRT Tambura Orchestra: Ladislav Fidri, Sinisa Leopold.
HSAS: Neal Schon.
Hualsospillemandene: Peter Viskinde.
Hubble Bubble: Plastic Bertrand.
Hudson River Sloop Singers: Don McLean.
Hue and Cry: Gregory Kane, Patrick Kane.
Huey Lewis & The News: Huey Lewis.
Hugh Hopper Band: Patrice Meyer.
Hugh Scott Band II: Carl Aborg.
Hugh Steinmetz Octet: Hugh Steinmetz.
Human Chain: Django Bates.
Human Condition: Jah Wobble.
Human League: Jo Callis, Philip Oakey, Martyn Ware.
Humble Pie: Peter Frampton.
The Humdingers: Bradley Leftwich.
Humphrey Lyttelton Band: Alan Barnes, Tony Coe, Mick Hutton, Adrian MacIntosh.
Hunk Ai: Carsten Ortmann.
Hunkpapa: Leon Caffrey.
The Hunters: Jan Akkerman.
Hurricane #1: Andrew Bell.

Hurts: Adam Anderson, Theo Hutchcraft.
Hustler: Ken Lyons.
Huun-Huur-Tu: Sayan Bapa, Kaigal-ool Khovalyg, Alexei Saryglar, Radik Tolouche.
Hybryds: Sandy Nys.
Hypnotix: Karel Babuljak.

I Am Arrows: Andy Burrows.
I Am X: Chris Corner.
I-Level: Duncan Bridgeman.
I-Threes: Marcia Griffiths, Rita Marley.
I-Tones: Jon Gorr.
Ian and The Muscletones: John Bickersteth.
Ian Campbell Folk Group: David Pegg.
Ian Dunlop's Babylon Babies: John Bickersteth.
Ian Mitchell Band: Ian Mitchell.
Ib Glindemann Orchestra: Palle Bolvig.
ICE: Zak Starkey.
Ich + Ich: Annette Humpe, Adel Tawil.
Ichthyornis: Youval Micenmacher.
Icicle Works: Ian McNabb.
Id: Andy McCluskey.
Identity Kit: Ron Kavanagh.
Idle Race: Jeff Lynne.
Idle Vice: Dave Rowntree.
Idlewild: Gavin Fox, Rod Jones, Colin Newton, Allan Stewart, Roddy Woomble.
Idoli: Vladimir Divljan.
If 6 Was 9: Grieg Clifford.
Ifang Bondi: Badou Jobe.
Ignis: Katerina Hajdovska-Tlusta.
Ikettes: P. P. Arnold.
Ikwezi: Ringo Madlingozi.
Il Divo: Urs Bühler, Sébastien Izambard, Carlos Marín, David Miller.
Il Nuovo Canzionere Italiano: Giovanna Marini.
Ildfuglen: Claus Mathiesen.
Illés: Levente Szörényi.
Illinois Jacquet's Big Band: Eddie Bert.
Illustrious Gy: J. Wortley.
Ilya Kuryaki and the Valderramas: Emmanuel Horvilleur, Dante Spinetta.
The Image: Dave Edmunds.
Imagination: Lee John.
Imagine Dragons: Ben McKee, Daniel Platzman, Dan Reynolds, Wayne Sermon.
Immaculate Fools: Andrew Ross.
Immigration Union: Courtney Barnett.
Imperial Drag: Roger Manning.
Imperial Teen: Roddy Bottum.
Impromptu: Paul Cheneour.
The In Crowd: Steve Howe, Jamaka Tee-Birdd.
IN2á3: Pentti Lahti, Ilkka Niemeläinen.
The Inadequates: Gillian Gilbert.
Inclassificable: Steve Lodder, Andy Sheppard.
Incognito: Jean-Paul Maunick, Paul 'Tubbs' Williams.
Incomparable Benzini Brothers: Fiachna O'Brainain, Liam O Maonlai.
Incredible Blues Puppies: Alan Glen.
Incubus: Brandon Boyd, Mike Einziger, Ben Kenney, Chris Kilmore, José Pasillas.
Indus Creed: Taufiq Qureshi.
Infectious Grooves: Mike Muir, Stephen Perkins, Robert Trujillo.
The Infidels: Robert Lee.
Infinitum: Michael Mondesir, Nicola Yeoh.
Inner Circle Band: Bruce Ruffin.
Inner City: Kevin Saunderson.
Inner City Unit: Nik Turner.
The Innocent Criminals: Ben Harper.
Inrou: Mikoláš Chadima.
Instant Life: Rolf Oberg.
Instinct: Pentti Lahti, Ilkka Niemeläinen.
Institute: Gavin Rossdale.
The Intellectuals: Nils Maaetoft.
Interpol: Paul Banks, Carlos Dengler, Sam Fogarino, Daniel Kessler.
Intombi Zesi Manje Manje: Moses Ngwenya.
Invaders of the Heart: Justin Adams, Jah Wobble.
Invocator: Jacob Hansen.
INXS: Garry Beers, Andrew Farriss, Jon Farriss, Tim Farriss, J. D. Fortune, Kirk Pengilly.
Ioan Gyuri Pascu and The Blues Workers Band: Ioan Gyuri Pascu.
Iona: Teri Bryant, Barbara Ryan.
Ippe Kätkä Band: Ippe Kätkä, Kari Komppa.
Irakere: Carlos Manuel, Chucho Valdés.
Irakli Louis Ambassadors: Irakli de Davrichewy.
Iris: Andrew Jans-Brown.
Iron Horse: Randy Bachman, Steven Lawrence, Gavin Marwick.

Iron Maiden: Bruce Dickinson, Janick Gers, Steve Harris, Nicko McBrain, Dave Murray, Adrian Smith.
Isife Lokole: Papa Wemba.
ISKRA: Jörgen Adolfsson, Tommy Adolfsson, Viorgos Fakanas.
The Isley Brothers: Ernie Isley, Marvin Isley, Ronald Isley, Rudolph Isley.
Isley Jasper Isley: Ernie Isley, Marvin Isley.
Ismo Alanko: Ippe Kätkä.
Istanbul Mevlevi Ensemble: Süleyman Erguner.
Itchy Fingers: Mike Mower, Martin Speake.
It's Alive: Max Martin.
Ivan Hicks and Maritime Express: Ivan Hicks.
Ivy: Gert Verhaeren.
Izzy Stradlin and The Ju Ju Hounds: Izzy Stradlin.

J. B. Hutto and The Hawks: Mark Rubel.
The J. Geils Blues Band: Jerome Geils.
J. M. Albertucci-Gianez: Laurent Gianez.
Jack Bruce (various bands): Larry Coryell, John Marshall.
Jack Duff Quintet: David Swanson.
Jack Parnell Orchestra: Bob Adams, Martin Kershaw.
Jackie Lynton Band: Gordon Sellar.
Jackie on Assid: Chris Constantinou.
The Jackson 5: Jackie Jackson, Jermaine Jackson, Marlon Jackson, Tito Jackson.
Jackson Queen: Terry Worlledge.
The Jacksons: Jackie Jackson, Janet Jackson, Jermaine Jackson, LaToya Jackson, Marlon Jackson, Randy Jackson, Tito Jackson.
Jacob's Optical Stairway: Mark Clair, Denis MacFarlane.
Jacques Doudelle Orchestra: Jacques Doudelle.
Jacques Vidal Quintet: Jacques Vidal.
Jacqui Hicks Band: Jacqui Hicks.
Jaguares: Saúl Hernandez.
Jaguars: Gilles Gabriel.
The Jam: Rick Buckler, Bruce Foxton, Paul Weller.
James: David Baynton-Power, Tim Booth, Saul Davies, Jim Glennie, Larry Gott, Mark Hunter, Michael Kulas, Adrian Oxaal, Gavan Whelan.
James Chadwick Quartet: James Chadwick.
James Dapogny's Chicago Jazz Band: James Dapogny.
James Gang: Joe Walsh.
James Last Orchestra: Martin Kershaw.
Jamiroquai: Jay Kay, Derrick McKenzie.
JAMS: Bill Drummond.
Jan and Dean: Dean Torrence.
Jan Garbarek Group: Jan Garbarek, Marilyn Mazur, Terje Rypdal.
Jan Levander's Oktett: Jan Levander.
Jane's Addiction: Perry Farrell, Dave Navarro, Stephen Perkins.
Janes Rejoice: Per Vibskov.
Jani Malmi Quartet/Trio: Jani Malmi, Jorma Ojanperä, Markku Ounaskari, Kari Tenkanen.
Jansen, Barbieri, Karn: Richard Barbieri, Steve Jansen, Mick Karn.
Janusz Muniak Quartet: Juraj Kalasz.
Japan: Richard Barbieri, Rob Dean, Steve Jansen, Mick Karn, David Sylvian.
Japancakes: John Neff.
Jarek Smietana Quintet: Jarek Smietana.
Jarmo Savolainen Nonet: Teemu Salminen, Jarmo Savolainen.
Jaromir Honzak Trio: David Doruzka.
Jason's Fleece: K. Franzén.
The Javelins: Ian Gillan.
Jazz Baltica Ensemble: Stein Tafjord.
Jazz Big Band HGZ: Mario Igrec.
Jazz Brothers: Chuck Mangione.
Jazz Celebrities: Ken Mathieson.
Jazz Composers Collective: Ben Allison.
Jazz Crusaders: Hubert Laws.
Jazz Écosse All-Stars: Ken Mathieson.
The Jazz Epistles: Abdullah Ibrahim, Hugh Masekela.
Jazz is Dead: Jimmy Herring.
Jazz Jamaica: Alan Weekes.
Jazz Oil Quintet: Jean-Sebastien Daurat.
Jazz O'Maniacs: Dan Vernhettes.
Jazz Rockers: Zbigniew Namysłowski.
Jazz Umbrella: Tim Whitehead.
Jazz Warriors: Cheryl Alleyne, Denys Baptiste, Gail Thompson, Alan Weekes, Nicola Yeoh.
Jazzee-Czech: Vìt Fiala.
The Jazztones: Nitin Sawhney.
Jean-Christophe Béney Quartet: Jean-Christophe Béney, Pierre de Bethmann, Benjamin Hénocq.
Jean-Christophe Cholet Quartet: Jean-Christophe Cholet, Benjamin Henocq.
Jean-Loup Longnon Big Band/Sextet: François Chassagnite, Jean-Loup Longnon, Christophe Walleme.
Jean-Pierre Como Quintet: Christophe Walleme.
Jean Quillivic Quartet: Jean Quillivic.
Jean Toussaint Quartet: Jean Toussaint.
Jeans: Dulce Maria.

The Jeevas: Crispian Mills.
The Jeff Beck Group: Jeff Beck, Rod Stewart, Ronnie Wood.
Jeff Lorber Fusion: Kenny G.
Jefferson Airplane: Jack Casady, Paul Kantner, Jorma Kaukonen, Grace Slick.
Jefferson Starship: Paul Kantner, Grace Slick.
Jellyfish: Roger Manning.
jeltje: Harry Williamson.
Jennifer Nettles Band: Jennifer Nettles.
The Jennifers: Danny Goffey.
Jenny and Johnny: Jenny Lewis.
Jericho: David Bellamy, Howard Bellamy, Pierre Dutot.
Jerry Allen Trio: Alan Grahame.
The Jesus & Mary Chain: Bobby Gillespie, Jim Reid, William Reid.
Jesus Jones: Jerry Deborg.
Jet: Christopher Cester, Nic Cester, Cameron Muncey, Mark Wilson.
The Jet Blacks: Barrie Martin.
Jethro Tull: Mick Abrahams, Don Airey, Ian Anderson, David Goodier, Jonathan Noyce, David Pegg.
The Jets: Wayne Fontana.
JetSet: Orjan Strandberg.
The Jewels: Lady Bo.
JFK Quintet: Andrew White III.
JIFT Schelinger Group: Stanislav Kubes.
Jim and Jesse and The Virginia Boys: Tom Ewing.
Jim Kweskin Jug Band: Maria Muldaur.
Jim Mullen Quartet/Quintet: David Dimond, Mick Hutton.
Jimmy Brown Sound: Ken Hensley.
Jimmy Giuffre Trio: Jim Hall.
Jimmy James and The Vagabonds: Oscar Blandamer.
Jimmy Owens Plus: Jimmy Owens.
Jimmy Sturr and His Orchestra: Jimmy Sturr.
Jim's Super Stereoworld: Jim Bob.
The Jitters: Blair Packham.
The Jive Aces: Ian Clarkson.
Jivi Honk and Band: Jivi Honk.
JLS: J.B. Gill, Marvin Humes, Aston Merrygold, Oritsé Williams.
JoBoxers: Chris Bostock.
Joby Talbot Quartet: Joby Talbot.
The Jodimans: Marshall Lytle.
Joe Henderson Quartet: Kim Clarke.
Joe Jackson Band: Joe Jackson.
Joe Perry Project: Joe Perry.
Joel Plaskett and the Emergency: Joel Plaskett.
John Barry Seven: Alan Bown, Leslie Reed.
John Burch Octet: Dave Corsby.
John Coughlan's Diesel Band: John Verity.
John Dankworth Big Band: Martin Kershaw.
John Dankworth Seven: Tony Kinsey.
The John Hoare 4: Steve Kershaw.
John Latham's Jazztimers: John Latham.
John Lurie's Lounge Lizards: Marc Ribot.
John Martyn Band: Charles Underwood.
John Mayall's Bluesbreakers: Eric Clapton, Mick Fleetwood, John McVie, John Mayall, William Stanger, Mick Taylor, Walter Trout.
John Mayers Inov-Jazz Fusions: John Millar.
John Miles Band: Barry Black.
John Miller Orchestra: Bob Howard.
The John Morgan Band: John Morgan.
John Petters Swing Band: John Petters.
John Shepherd Combo: Gren Horabin.
John Stevens' Away and Dance Orchestra: Nigel Moyse.
John Stevens' Spontaneous Music Ensemble: Maggie Nicols.
John Sund Group: John Sund.
John Tchicai and his Festival Band: Thorsten Høeg, Peter Jorgens.
John Tchicai Workshop Orchestra: Heinrich Lindenmaier, Paco Sanchez.
John Verity Band: John Verity.
Johnnie Wright and The Harmony Girls: Kitty Wells.
Johnny and Sipho: Johnny Clegg.
Johnny and The Cellar Rockers: Jan Akkerman.
Johnny Davis Band: Buddy DeFranco.
Johnny Griffin Quartet: Pasquale Michaelis.
Johnny Marr & The Healers: Alonza Bevan, Johnny Marr, Zak Starkey.
Johnny Mars Band: Chris Cozens, Raymond Fenwick.
Johnny Thompson Singers: John Thompson.
The Johnson Mountain Boys: David McLaughlin.
Jokleba: Jon Balke.
Jompson Brothers: Chris Stapleton.
Jon Eberson's Jazzpunkensemble: Jens-Christian Wesseltoft.
Jon Spencer Blues Explosion: Judah Bauer, Russell Simins, Jon Spencer.
Jon Strong Band: Mark Priestley.
Jonas Brothers: Joe Jonas, Kevin Jonas, Nick Jonas.
Jonathan Lewis Quartet: Gary Brunton.
Jonsí & Alex: Jonsí Birgisson.
Jools Holland Big Band: Thomas Barlow, Jools Holland.
Jordy Boys: Rick Springfield.

Journey: Jonathan Cain, Steve Perry, Neal Schon.
Joy Division: Peter Hook, Stephen Morris, Bernard Sumner.
Joy Quintet: Chris Francis.
JPP: Timo Alakotila.
Jubilee Jazz Band: Dave Brennan.
Jubilee New Orleans Brass Band: Dave Brennan.
Judas Jump: Andrew Bown.
Judas Priest: Rob Halford.
The Judds: Naomi Judd, Wynonna Judd.
Jude: Robin Trower.
Juhani Vilkki Sextet: Eero Ojanen.
Juice Leskinen: Ippe Kätkä.
Juice on the Loose: Ron Kavanagh.
Jukka Linkola (various bands): Pentti Lahti, Jukka Linkola, Teemu Salminen, Eerik Siikasaari.
Jukka Perko Quartet: Jukka Perko, Eerik Siikasaari.
Jukka Syrenius Band: Jartsa Karvonen.
Jukka Tolonen Band: Pertti Päivinen, Jukka Tolonen.
Jukkis Uotila Band: Jukkis Uotila, Teemu Salminen, Eerik Siikasaari.
Julian Argüelles Quartet: Julian Argüelles.
Julian Joseph Band: Julian Joseph, Jean Toussaint.
Juliana Hatfield Three: Juliana Hatfield.
Juliette & The Licks: Juliette Lewis.
Juliette et les Independants: Mirwais.
Juluka: Johnny Clegg.
Junebug: Ambrosia Parsley.
Jungle Funk: Doug Wimbish.
Jungle Jim: Ronald Risdon.
Junior M.A.F.I.A.: Lil'Kim.
Junip : José González.
Juniper: Damien Rice.
Junk: Walter Wray.
Junoon: Salman Ahmad, Ali Azmat, Brian O'Connell.
Junta: Paul Barrett.
Jurassic 5: Akil, Cut Chemist, DJ Nu-Mark, Marc 7even, Chali 2NA, Zaakir.
Just Good Friends: Joolz.
Justice: Gaspard Augé, Xavier de Rosnay.
Justified Ancients of Mu Mu: Jimmy Cauty, Bill Drummond.
Justine: Val Clover.

K-Creative: Ski.
The K-Foundation: Jimmy Cauty, Bill Drummond.
K-Klass: Steve Hewitt.
K. S. & The Mystery Jet Set: Khalid Siddiqui.
Kabak: Adrian Zolothuhin.
Kaiser Chiefs: Nick Baines, Nick Hodgson, Simon Rix, Andrew White, Ricky Wilson.
Kajagoogoo: Nick Beggs.
Kalinka Zigeunertrio: Herman de Rycke.
Kallai: Herman de Rycke.
Kalmisto-Klang: Teppo Hauta-aho.
Kamel Kombo: Jan Levander.
Kandahar: Herman de Rycke.
Kande: Rafli.
Kane Gang: David Brewis.
Kansas: Steve Morse, Steve Walsh.
Kantner Balin Casady (KBC) Band: Jack Casady, Paul Kantner.
KapelaSNOO: Karel Babuljak.
Karel Babuljak and his Band of Dreams: Karel Babuljak.
Karelia: Seppo Paakkunainen.
The Karelia: Alex Kapranos.
Kari Larne Group: Ippe Kätkä.
Kari Tenkanen Quintet: Janne Murto, Kari Tenkanen.
Karl Brothers: Jörgen Adolfsson, Tommy Adolfsson.
Karl Denver Trio: Kevin Neill.
Kartet: Benjamin Henocq, Guillaume Orti.
Kasabian: Chris Edwards, Christopher Karloff, Tom Meighan, Sergio Pizzorno.
Katastroof: Jozef Hermans.
Katharine Chase Band: Katharine Chase.
Kathryn Tickell Band: Kathryn Tickell, Karen Tweed.
Katia Labèque Band: Marque Gilmore, Katia Labèque, Dave Maric.
Katmandu: Ray Dorset.
Katrina and The Waves: Katrina Leskanich.
Katzenjammer: Josh Homme.
KAZDA: Jan Kazda.
KB Hallen: Martin Heurlin.
KC and The Sunshine Band: Harry Casey.
Keane: Tom Chaplin, Richard Hughes, Tim Rice-Oxley.
Kefir: Claus Mathiesen.
Keith Jarrett (various bands): Jack de Johnette, Jan Garbarek, Keith Jarrett.
Keith Tippett's Canoe: Bob Helson.
Keith Tippett's Centipede: Maggie Nicols.
Kekele Project: Papa Noel.
Kelvin Christiane Band: Kelvin Christiane.

Kemia: Soïg Siberil.
Ken Colyer Allstars: Louis Lince.
Ken Mathieson's Classic Jazz Orchestra: Ken Mathieson.
Ken Meyers Band: Ken Meyers.
Ken Sims Dixie Kings: John Petters.
Ken Stevens Orchestra: Thomas Chalmers.
Kenn Lending Blues Band: Kenn Lending.
Kenny Baker Dozen: Brian Dee.
Kenny Ball's Jazzmen: Martin Litton.
Kenny Gamble and The Romeos: Kenny Gamble, Daryl Hall.
Kenny Graham Afro Cubist Band: Duncan Lamont.
Kenny Wheeler Big Band: Julian Argüelles.
Kent Carter String Trio: Kent Carter.
Kentucky Thunder: Ricky Skaggs.
Kentucky Travellers: Tom T. Hall.
Kerr Donnelly Band: Kerr Donnelly.
Kevin Richard: Kevin Hotte.
Khaval: Terry Riley.
Kick Horns: Simon C. Clarke.
Kicks Like a Mule: Richard Russell.
Kid Creole and The Coconuts: Kid Creole, Paul Gerimon.
Kidjo Brothers Band: Angélique Kidjo.
Kiki Dee Band: Kiki Dee.
Kilhets: Mikoláš Chadima.
Kilimandjaro: Tchando.
The Kill: Will Sexton.
Killer Loop: Mr C, Layo Paskin.
The Killers: Brandon Flowers, David Keuning, Mark Stoermer, Ronnie Vannucci.
Killing for Company: Aled Richards.
Killing Joke: Jaz Coleman.
Killing the Rose: John Forrester.
The Killjoys: Kevin Rowland.
Kindness: Katharine Chase.
The Kindness of Strangers: Craig Armstrong.
Kindred Spirit: Giles Cooper, Deborah Peterson, Elaine Samuels.
King Crimson: Adrian Belew, Bill Bruford, Robert Fripp, Greg Lake, Peter Sinfield, John Wetton.
King Curtis Band: Cornell Dupree.
King Kong: Farin Urlaub.
King Pleasure and The Biscuit Boys: Al Nicholls.
King Swamp: Walter Wray.
Kings of Convenience: Erik Glambek Bøe, Erlend Øye.
Kings of Leon: Caleb Followill, Jared Followill, Matthew Followill, Nathan Followill.
Kings of Tomorrow: Sandy Rivera.
The Kinks: Ray Davies, Ian Gibbons, Mark Haley.
Kinky: Gilberto Cerezo, Carlos Chairez, Omar Gongora, Ulises Lozano, César Pliego.
The Kinshasha Band: Roger Flavell.
Kirka and Islanders: Ippe Kätkä.
Kiss: Peter Criss, Ace Frehley, Bruce Kulick, Gene Simmons, Paul Stanley.
Kiss 'N' Tell: David Campbell.
Kit and The Saracens: Ken Hensley.
Kjell Karlsen Quartet: Karin Krog.
Klepper: Herman de Rycke.
The KLF: Jimmy Cauty, Bill Drummond.
Klinik: Sandy Nys.
The Knife: Karin Dreijer Anderssen, Olof Dreijer.
Knights of the Occasional Table: Aquamanda.
Kodeks: Goran Bregovic.
Kominikayson: Jean-Claude Montredon, Richard Raux.
Konkurent: Emil Anchev, Dragomir Manov, Julian Naumov, Petar Petrov, Dimo Todorov.
Konono No. 1: Mawangu Mingiedi.
KoRn: Reginald Arvizu, Jonathan Davis, James Shaffer, David Silveria, Brian Welch.
Kornog: Soïg Siberil.
K-0z Office: Floch Delvaux.
Kraftwerk: Wolfgang Flür, Ralf Hütter, Florian Schneider.
Krakatau: Tommy Adolfsson, Raoul Björkenheim, Ippe Kätkä.
Kreidler: Thomas Klein, Andreas Reihse, Detlef Weinrich.
The Krew: Nik Kershaw.
Kries: Mojmir Novakovič.
Krosswindz: Chandrani Banerjee, Ratanjit Banerjee, Vikramjit Banerjee.
Kryzsztof Komeda Group: Tomasz Stańko.
Kudsi Erguner Ensemble: Kudsi Erguner.
Kula Shaker: Alonza Bevan, Jay Darlington, Crispian Mills, Paul Winter-Hart.
The Kult: Paul Brady.
Kulttis Big Band: Pekka Toivanen.
Kultur Shock: Amy Denio.
Kung Lir: Jan Levander.
Kurt Edelhagen Orchestra: Jean-Louis Chautemps.
Kurt Rosenwinkel's Heart-Core Band: Barney McAll.

Kxutrio: Heinrich Lindenmaier.
Kyuss: Josh Homme.

La Bottine Souriante: Bernard Simard.
La Campagnie du Jazz: Vivian Peres.
La Capela Reial de Catalunya: Jordi Savall.
La Charanga Habanera: David Calzado.
La Chitarra Rotta: Franco Fabbri.
La Clave: James Le Messurier.
La Fábrica de Tonadas: Santiago Auserón.
La Famille: Alan Weekes.
La Grande Bande de Cornemuse: Robert Amyot.
La Peña de los Ugarte: Eva Ayllón.
La Perfecta: Edward Palmieri.
La Protesta: Joe Arroyo.
La Provincia: Carlos Vives.
La Rouchta: Soïg Siberil.
La Roux: Elly Jackson, Ben Langmaid.
La Verdad: Joe Arroyo.
Labelle: Patti Labelle.
Lack of Knowledge: Tony Barber.
Lacuna Coil: Marco Biazzi, Andrea Ferro, Cristiano Migliore, Cristiano Mozzati, Christina Scrabbia, Marco Zelati.
Lacy and The Lovers: Kevin Rowland.
Lady Antebellum: Dave Haywood, Charles Kelley, Hillary Scott.
Lady Bo and the BC Horns: Lady Bo, Wally Malone.
Ladysmith Black Mambazo: Joseph Shabalala.
Laelia Anceps: Morten Harket.
Laferrière: Rolf Buhrer.
Laika Dog: Tony Wright.
Laine: Tõnu Naissoo.
Lamb: Andrew Barlow, Louise Rhodes.
Lambchop: Kurt Wagner.
Lambert Hendricks and Ross: Jon Hendricks, Annie Ross.
Lammas: Tim Garland.
Lard: Al Jourgensen.
The Larks: Thomas Barlow.
The Larry Stephenson Band: Larry Stephenson.
The La's: Paul Hemmings, John Power.
Last Exit: Bill Laswell.
The Last Hard Men: Jimmy Chamberlin.
The Last Heard: Bob Seger.
Last Kiss: Joe Turner.
Latin Fever: Sue Hadjopoulos.
Lau: Kris Drever, Martin Green, Aidan O'Rourke.
The Laughing Apple: Alan McGee.
Laurel Canyon: Janis Siegel.
Laurent Coq Quartet: Jean-Christophe Béney.
Laurie & John: John Stirratt.
Laurie Anderson Band: Laurie Anderson, Wharton Tiers.
Laurie Chescoe's Good Time Jazz: Laurie Chescoe.
Lavantairyhmä: Jorma Tapio.
The Law: Paul Rodgers.
Lawrence Walk Orchestra: Peter Fountain.
Layo and Bushwacka!: Bushwacka!, Layo Paskin.
The Lazy Ramblers: Ralph Stanley.
Le Degara-Band: Moussa Poussi.
Le Grand Julot: Eddy van Mouffaert Govert.
Le Quintette de Cornemuse: Robert Amyot.
Le Sacre du Tympan: Guillaume Orti.
Le Trio Joubran: Adnan Joubran, Samir Joubran, Wissam Joubran.
Leaders of the New School: Busta Rhymes.
The League of Gentlemen: Robert Fripp.
Leather Charm: James Hetfield.
Leaves: Andri Ásgímsson, Noi Steinn Einarsson, Arnar Gudjonsson, Hallur Hallsson, Arnar Olafsson.
Led Zeppelin: John Paul Jones, Jimmy Page, Robert Plant.
Lee Curtis and The All Stars: Wayne Bickerton.
Lee Evans Trio: Lee Evans.
Left Hand Right Hand: Charlie Collins.
Leftfield: Neil Barnes, Paul Daley.
Leftwich and Higginbotham: Bradley Leftwich.
Legen: Mojmir Novakovič.
Legend: Kerr Donnelly.
The Legendary Brats: Roy Shipston.
Legendary Masked Surfers: Dean Torrence.
Leif Johansson Orchestra: Anders Müller.
Leke Leke: Olu Shola Adedayo.
Lemon Interrupt: Darren Emerson, Karl Hyde, Rick Smith.
Lemon Jelly: Fred Deakin, Nick Franglen.
Lemon Kittens: Karl Blake.
The Lemon Trees: Guy Chambers.
The Lemonheads: Evan Dando.
Leonardo Pedersen's Jazzkapel: Ib Nielsen, Leonardo Pedersen.
Les Ambassadeurs Internationaux: Mory Kanté, Salif Keita.
Les Bantous de la Capitale: Papa Noel.

Les Batteries: Guigou Chenevier.
Les Chats Suavages: Andre Ceccarelli.
Les Étoiles du Raï: Cheb Faudel.
Les Figures: Guigou Chenevier.
Les Howard's Northern Dance Orchestra (NDO): Bob Howard.
Les Milieus Branches: Mory Kanté.
Les Parisiennes: Claude Bolling.
Les Pieds Mobiles: Christian Goupy.
Les Pionniers Jazz: Djelimady Tounkara, Boubacar Traoré.
Les Primitifs du Futur: Jean Davis, Didier Roussin.
Les Standardistes: Benjamin Henocq.
Les Triaboliques: Justin Adams.
Les Trianas d'Algers: Souad Massi.
Les Valiants: Pops Mohamed.
Lester Bowie's Brass Fantasy: Kim Clarke.
Lester Bowie's New York Organ Ensemble: James Carter.
Lester Lanin Orchestra: Roberta Fabiano.
Level 42: Mark King, Mike Lindup.
Levellers: Mark Chadwick, Jeremy Cunningham, Simon Friend, Charlie Heather, Matt Savage, Jon Sevink.
Levinhurst: Lol Tolhurst.
Levity Lancers: Keith Nichols.
Lex Van Wel and his Swing Orchestra: Paul Wood.
LFO (Low Frequency Oscillation): Gez Varley.
Liar: Steve Mann.
The Libertines: Carl Barât, Pete Doherty, John Hassall, Gary Powell.
Liberty-N-Justice: Robert Sliger.
Libido : Manolo Hidalgo, Antonio Jauregui, Iván Mindreau, Salim Vera.
Lifetime: John McLaughlin.
The Lift: Rohn Lawrence.
Light of the World: Mike Collins, Jean-Paul Maunick.
The Lightfingered Gentry: Richard Hand.
Lighthouse: Howard Shore.
The Lighthouse Family: Tunde Baiyewu, Paul Tucker.
The Lightning Seeds: Ian Broudie, Paul Hemmings.
Lights in a Fat City: Phil Pickering.
Likwit Crew: Xzibit.
Lil Jon and The Eastside Boyz: Lil Jon.
The Lilac Time: Stephen Duffy.
Lilith: Pia Rasmussen.
Limburgs Dansorkest: Leo Rutten.
Limp Bizkit: Wes Borland, Frederick Durst, DJ Lethal, John Otto, Sam Rivers.
L'Impossible Tri: Youval Micenmacher.
Lindisfarne: Raymond Laidlaw.
Line of Flight: Liam Howe.
Linie 3: Soren Reiff.
Linkin Park: Chester Bennington, Rob Bourdon, Brad Delson, Dave Farrell, Joe Hahn, Phoenix, Mike Shinoda.
Lionel Hampton Jazz Orchestra: Quincy Jones, George Robert, Dennis Wilson.
Lionrock: Mark Stagg.
Lipservice: Merlin Rhys-Jones.
Lisa Loeb and Nine Stories: Lisa Loeb.
Listen: Robert Plant.
Little Axe: Alan Glen.
Little Big Band: Stephane Dambry.
Little Big Company: Ales Zimolka.
Little Big Town: Karen Fairchild, Kimberly Schlapman, Philip Sweet, Jimi Westbrook.
Little Brother: Simon Campbell.
Little Douglas Band: Rhonda Finlayson.
Little Joy: Fabrizio Moretti.
Little Nicky and The Slicks: Nicole Yarling.
Little River Band: John Farnham, Glenn Shorrock.
Little Village: Ry Cooder, John Hiatt.
The Little Willies: Norah Jones.
Living Colour: William Calhoun, Corey Glover, Vernon Reid, Muzz Skillings, Doug Wimbish.
Living Dead: Andrew Farrow.
Living Time Orchestra: Steve Lodder, Andy Sheppard.
Lizl: Bernd Rommel.
Lloyd Cole & The Commotions: Lloyd Cole, David Cummings.
Loaded Bluegrass: Kevin Kienlein.
Lock & Burns: Eddie Lock.
Lock Up: Tom Morello.
Locomotive: Jim Simpson.
Loggins and Messina: Kenny Loggins, Jim Messina.
Loïc Dequidt Trio: Loïc Dequidt.
Lois Winsberg Quintet: Christophe Walleme.
Lo'jo: Guillaume Bourreau, Nicholas Meslien, Nadia Nid el-Mourid, Yasmina Nid el-Mourid, Denis Péan, Matthieu Rousseau.
London: Nikki Sixx.
The London Big Band: Laurie Johnson.
London City Stompers: Max Collie.
London Cowboys: Robert Lee.

London Electric Guitar Orchestra: John Bisset.
Lone Justice: Maria McKee.
Lonesome and Blue: Dennis Cyporyn.
Lonestar: Michael Britt, Cody Collins, Richie McDonald, Keech Rainwater, John Rich, Dean Sams.
Long Distanz: Chris Cozens.
The Long Ryders: Sid Griffin.
Longdancer: Dave Stewart.
The Longpigs: Diarmuid Boyle, Richard Hawley, Crispin Hunt, Simon Stafford.
Lonnie Donegan Band: Roger Flavell.
Look Twice: Lenni.
The Loose Connections: Niamh Parsons.
Loose Fur: Glenn Kotche, Jim O'Rourke, Jeff Tweedy.
Loose Tubes: Cheryl Alleyne, Julian Argüelles, Django Bates, Mark Lockheart, Julian Nicholas, Tim Whitehead.
L'Orange: Daniel Biro.
The Lorne Gibson Trio: Dale Harris.
Los Amigos de las Americas: Michael Kissel.
Los Bucaneros: Pablo Milanés.
Los Bukis: Marco Solis.
Los Caporales: Flaco Jiménez.
Los Carminantes: Flaco Jiménez.
Los Gemelos: Ana Tijoux.
Los Gran Daneses: Jorge Cordero.
Los Guachos: Gullermo Klein.
Los Hijos del Sol: Eva Ayllón.
Los Incontrolados: Guillaume Orti.
Los Kipus: Eva Ayllón.
Los Lobos: Steve Berlin, David Hidalgo, Conrad Lozano, Louie Pérez, César Rosas.
Los Mundialistas o Callejón: Eva Ayllón.
Los Pacaminos: Paul Young.
Los Salseros: Guillermo Felloué.
Los Salvajes del Ritmo: Rubén Blades.
Los Super Seven: Ruben Ramos.
Los Temerarios: Adolfo Angel Alba, Gustavo Angel Alba.
Los Tetas: Ana Tijoux.
Los Tigres del Norte: Eduardo Hernandez, Hernan Hernandez, Jorge Hernandez, Luis Hernandez, Oscar Lara.
Los Vobos: Ales Zimolka.
The Lost Cowboys: B. J. Cole, Hank Wangford.
The Lost Jockey: Orlando Gough, Giles Lewin.
Lost Kids: Stefan Borum.
Lost Tribe: Adam Rogers.
Lostprophets: Lee Gaze, Mike Lewis, Jamie Oliver, Stuart Richardson, Ian Watkins.
Lou Ann Barton Band: Lou Ann Barton.
Loudest Whisper: Ron Kavanagh.
Love Affair: Morgan Fisher.
Love Bites: Phil Bennett.
Love Construction: Sos Fenger.
Love Sculpture: Dave Edmunds.
Love-Sister-Hope: Boris Leiner.
Love Unlimited Orchestra: Kenny G.
LoveCut dB: Sarah Cracknell.
The Lovemongers: Ann Wilson, Nancy Wilson.
Loverboy: Mike Reno.
The Lovin' Spoonful: John Sebastian.
LTD (Love Togetherness and Devotion): Jeffrey Osborne.
Lubos Andrst Blues Band: Lubos Andrst.
Luc Rène and The Jumps: Bobby Marty.
Lucky Luciano: Mike Peters, Robert Peters.
Lucy Pearl: Raphael Saadiq.
Lugee and The Lions: Lou Christie.
Luksus: Per Vibskov.
Lulu and The Luvvers: Lulu.
Lumineers: Jeremiah Fraites, Neyla Pekarek, Wesley Schultz, Steth Ulvang, Ben Wahamaki.
Luna Nova: Timo Alakotila.
Lunasa: Michael McGoldrick, John McSherry.
Lush: Emma Anderson, Justin Welch.
Lusus Naturae: Bruce Coates.
Lynn Morris Band: Lynn Morris.
Lynyrd Skynyrd: Gary Rossington.
Lyra and The Fianna: David Richey.
Lysis Steve Berry Trio: Mark Lockheart.

M People: Paul Heard, Mike Pickering, Shovell, Heather Small.
M. T. Purse: Nils Maaetoft.
Maarifa Street: Jon Hassell.
Mabel: Mike Tramp.
Mabulu: Dilon Djindi.
McAlmont: David McAlmont.
McAlmont and Butler: Bernard Butler, David McAlmont.
MacAlpine: Tony MacAlpine.

McCoy: Nikki Brooks.
The McCoys: Rick Derringer.
McCulloch's Mysterioso Show: Ian McCulloch.
The Maceo Parker Band: Fred Wesley Jr.
McFly: Tom Fletcher, Danny Jones, Harry Judd, Dougie Poynter.
McGuinn Clark and Hillman: Chris Hillman, Roger McGuinn.
McGuinness Flint: Benny Gallagher, Graham Lyle.
Machine Head: Dirty Pik.
Machine of Time: Andrei Makarevich.
Macho Frog: Alex Brown.
Mack and The Boys: Brian Bannister, Richard Bywater.
McKitty: Nicko McBrain.
The MacLeods: James MacLeod.
Mad: Damian Stanley.
Mad Dogs and Englishmen: Gary Miller.
Mad Juana: Sami Yaffa.
Mad Nomads: Henri Texier.
Madball: Mackie Jayson.
Madcon: Tshawe Baqwa, Yosef Wolde-Mariam.
Maddie and Tae: Taylor Dye, Madison Marlow.
The Madisons: Roger Glover.
Madness: Chrissy Boy, Graham 'Suggs' McPherson.
Madzano Quartet: Marino Zappellini.
Magazin: Tonci Huljic.
The Magic Band: Ry Cooder, Cliff Martinez.
Magic Lantern: John Kirkpatrick.
The Magic Numbers: Angela Gannon, Sean Gannon, Michele Stodart, Romeo Stodart.
Magic Roundabout: Roger Flavell.
Magma: Didier Lockwood, Jacques Vidal.
Magmouat Hakmoun: Hassan Hakmoun.
Magnetic North Orchestra: Jon Balke, Dave Clarke.
Magnum: Bob Catley, Tony Clarkin.
Mahavishnu Orchestra: Bill Cobham, Jan Hammer, John McLaughlin, Jean Luc Ponty.
Mahogany: Paul Hobbs.
Mahogany Rush: Frank Marino.
Maische: Christian Fennesz.
Makesome Breaksome: Bushwacka!.
Makiza: Ana Tijoux.
Makossa: Benny Tetteh-Lartey.
Mal Waldren Trio: Jesper Thorup.
Malachy Sweeney Band: Bobby Gardiner.
Malaika: Tshedi Mholo, Bongani Nchanga, Jabulani Ndaba.
Malibu Stacey: Leigh Marklew.
Malin Head: Lorraine Jordan.
Malta: Göran Fristorp.
Malurt Doraz: Peter Viskinde.
Ma'ma Bubo: Karel Babuljak.
The Mamas and the Papas: Michelle Phillips.
Mama's Boys: John McManus.
The Mambas: Marc Almond.
Mammoth: Nicky Moore.
Man Jumping: Orlando Gough, John Lunn.
Man Size Safe: Ben Allison.
Maná: Juan Calleros, Alex González, Fher Olvera, Sergio Vallín.
Manassas: Chris Hillman, Stephen Stills.
Mandanga: Natacha Atlas.
Mando Diao: Björn Dixgård, Carl-Johan Fogelklou, Samuel Giers, Gustaf Norén.
The Mandrells: Barbara Mandrell.
Manfred Mann: Paul Jones, Martin Kershaw, Manfred Mann.
Manfred Mann Earth Band: Manfred Mann, Christopher Thompson.
maNga: Ferman Akgül, Cem Bahtiyar, Özgür Öney, Yagnur Sarigul, Efe Yilmaz.
Manhattan Transfer: Luther Rix, Janis Siegel, Dennis Wilson.
Manic Street Preachers: James Dean Bradfield, Sean Moore, Nicky Wire.
Manigance: Bernard Simard.
Manitoba: Caribou.
Manitou: Harry Skinner.
Manix: Mark Clair.
Mannheim Steamroller: Chip Davis.
Mano Negra: Manu Chao.
Mansun: Dominic Chad, Paul Draper, Stove King, Andie Rathbourne.
Manuel Rocheman Trio: Manuel Rocheman, Christophe Walleme.
The Mar-Keys: Steve Cropper.
Marc Ducret Trio: Joël Allouche.
March of Crimes: Ben Shepherd.
March Violets: Andy Welsford.
Marcia Hines Band: Doug Williams.
Maria Excommunikata: Carola Grey.
The Maria McKee Band: Maria McKee.
Maria Schneider Jazz Orchestra: Maria Schneider.
Marillion: Fish, Steve Hogarth, Mark Kelly, Ian Mosley, Steve Rothery, Peter Trewavas.
Marilyn Manson: Marilyn Manson.

Marina and the Diamonds: Marina Diamandis.
Marine Girls: Tracey Thorn.
Mario Igrec Quintet: Mario Igrec.
Marion: Phil Cunningham.
Marius Cultier and The Surfs: Jean-Claude Montredon.
Markku Johansson Quintet: Markku Johansson, Jorma Ojanperä.
Markovic-Gut Sextet: Milivoje Markovic.
The Marksmen: Boz Scaggs.
Marksmen Combo: Steve Miller.
Marmite Infernale: Alain Gibert.
Maroon 5: Jesse Carmichael, Ryan Dusick, Matt Flynn, Adam Levine, Mickey Madden, James Valentine.
Maroontown: Gavin Knight.
Marquis de Sade: Anne Linnet.
MARS: Tony MacAlpine.
The Mars Volta: Juan Alderete, Cedric Bixler-Zavala, Isaiah Owens, Marcel Rodríguez López, Omar Rodríguez-López.
Marshwinds: Ivan Hicks.
Martha Reeves and The Vandellas: Martha Reeves.
Martial Solal Big Band: Jean-Louis Chautemps.
The Martinis: David Lovering, Joey Santiago.
Marty Gillan and The Sweetwater Band: Lisa Brokop.
Marvelous Band: Alain Gibert.
The Marvelous Marbles: Sheena Ringo.
Marvin Welch and Farrar: Bruce Welch.
Mary Halvorson Quintet: Mary Halvorson.
Mary Mary: Erica Campbell, Tina Campbell.
Mary My Hope: Steve Gorman.
The Mary Stokes Band: Mary Stokes.
März Combo: Johannes Bauer.
Masada: John Zorn.
Mashupheadz: Bushwacka!.
Masqualero: Arild Andersen, Jon Balke, Tore Brunborg.
Massive Attack: Daddy G, Nellee Hooper, Mushroom, Shara Nelson, 3-D.
Massukos: Feliciano dos Santos.
The Masters: John Oates.
Masters at Work: Kenny Gonzalez, Todd Terry, Louie Vega.
The Masters of Percussion: Vijay Chauhan, V. Selva Ganesh.
The Matadors: Smokey Robinson.
Matchbox: Graham Fenton.
Matchbox Twenty: Kyle Cook, Paul Doucette, Rob Thomas, Brian Yale.
Material: Bill Laswell.
Matheran: Mark Lockheart.
Matrix: Tony Coe.
The Matt Wates Sextet: Matt Wates.
Matt Wilson Quartet: Matt Wilson.
Matt Wilson's Arts and Crafts: Matt Wilson.
Matthew Herbert Big Band: Matthew Herbert.
Matthews Southern Comfort: Iain Matthews.
Maurice Magnoni Quartet: Joël Allouche.
The Mavericks: Noddy Holder.
The Mavericks: Raul Malo.
Max and The Broadway Metal Choir: Jan Cyrka.
Max Collie Jazz Kings/Max Collie Rhythm Aces: Max Collie.
Max Roach-Clifford Brown Quintet: Jymie Merritt.
Maxïmo Park: Tom English, Duncan Lloyd, Paul Smith, Archis Tiku, Lukas Wooller.
Maximum Balloon: David Sitek.
May Morning: Karen Tweed.
Mayfield: Curt Smith.
Mayflowers Band: Helene Hanzick.
Maynard Ferguson Octet: Paul Mitchell-Davidson.
Mayohuacan: Carlos Manuel.
Mazelé: Alexandr Hajdovsky-Potapovic.
M-Base: Steve Coleman.
MCH Band: Mikoláš Chadima, Blanka Strayblova.
MDC: Matt Freeman.
Meat Loaf: Meat Loaf, Kasim Sulton.
Mecano: José Cano, Nacho Cano, Ana Torroja.
Medeski Martin and Wood: Billy Martin, John Medeski, Chris Wood.
Medford Slim Band: Ludo Beckers.
Medicine Wheel: Ben Allison.
Meditations Singers: Della Reese.
Mediterrán and Balassa: Levente Szörényi.
Mega City Four: Gerry Bryant, Chris Jones.
Megadeth: Dave Mustaine, Chris Poland.
The Mel Lewis Orchestra: Kenny Garrett.
Melbourne Max Collie Jazz Bandits: Max Collie.
Melbourne New Orleans Jazz Band: Max Collie.
Melody Ranch Girls: Jean Shepherd.
Melt : Kate Ryan.
Melting Pot: Sonia Jacobsen.
The Menaces: Nigel Lindridge.
Mentaur: Tim Ridley.
Menudo: Ricky Martin.
The Mercan Dede Ensemble: Mercan Dede.

The Mercey Brothers: Eric Mahar, Larry Mercey.
Mercia Jazz Band: Paul Russell.
Mercoledi & Co.: Guillaume Orti.
Mercury Rev: Jonathon Donahue, Dave Fridmann, Grasshopper, Jeff Mercel, Carlos Molina.
Mercy: Morten Harket.
Meredith Monk & Vocal Ensemble: Meredith Monk.
Meridian Folk Trio: Frank Hamilton.
The Merry Makers: Hugh Masekela.
Merv Griffin with Side Street Strutters: Joey Sellers.
Messiah: Mark Davies.
Metak: Matko Jelavic.
Metallica: Kirk Hammett, James Hetfield, Dave Mustaine, Jason Newsted, Robert Trujillo, Lars Ulrich.
Métarythmes de l'Air: Christian Leroy.
The Meters: Art Neville, Cyril Neville.
The Method: Simon Campbell.
Methods of Mayhem: Tommy Lee.
Metric: Emily Haines, Joules Scott-Key, Jimmy Shaw, Josh Winstead.
Metro Squad: Belinda Carlisle.
Metropolis: Paul Barrett.
The Metros: Peter Trewavas.
Mew: Jonas Bjerre, Silas Graae, Bo Madsen, Johan Wohlert.
The Mexican Revolution: Ruben Ramos.
Meyerheim and Co.: Soren Reiff.
Mezzoforte: Dave O'Higgins.
MFSB (Mother Father Sister Brother) Band: Thom Bell.
Miami Sound Machine: Gloria Estefan.
Mica, Goran and Zoran: Goran Bregovic.
Michael Schenker Group (MSG): Steve Mann, Michael Schenker.
Michel Cusson and The Wild Unit: Michel Cusson.
Michel Portal's New Unit: Joël Allouche.
Michele Hendricks Quintet: Thomas Bramerie, Michele Hendricks.
Mick Fleetwood Band: Mick Fleetwood.
Mickey Bass Quartet: Bobby Watson.
Mickey Jazz: Remmy Ongala.
Mickey Jupp Band: David Bronze.
Mickey Mouse Revival: Andrew Lloyd.
Micky Askman Ragtime Jazzband: John M. Taylor.
Midge Marsden's Country Flyers: Neil Hannan.
Midi: Robo Grigorov.
Midland Allstars: John M. Taylor.
Midnight Court: Dennis Cahill, Martin Hayes.
Midnight Oil: Peter Garrett.
Midnight Sun: Allan Mortensen, Bo Stief.
Midnite Follies Orchestra: Laurie Chescoe, Keith Nichols.
Mighty Diamonds: Jon Gorr.
The Mighty Vikings: Bobby Ellis.
Mighty Wah!: Pete Wylie.
Mika Mylläri Quintet: Mika Mylläri.
Mike and The Mechanics: Paul Carrack, Mike Rutherford.
Mike Berry and The Outlaws: Don Groom, Chas Hodges.
Mike Gibbs Orchestra: Julian Argüelles, John Marshall.
Mike Mower Quartet: Mike Mower.
Mike Sheridan and The Nightriders: Roy Wood.
Mike Taylor Jazzmen: Mike Taylor.
Mike Westbrook Brass Band/Orchestra: Kate Westbrook, Mike Westbrook.
Miles & Milner: Richard Thomas.
Miles Davis Group: Dave Holland, Marilyn Mazur, John Scofield, Wayne Shorter.
The Milkshakes: Billy Childish.
Milli-Medjilis: Polad Byul-Byul Oglu.
Milltown Brothers: Matthew Nelson.
Mind Your Own Business: Richard Churchley.
The Mindbenders: Wayne Fontana.
Ministry: Paul Barker, Al Jourgensen.
Ministry of Humour: Robb Johnson.
Mint Juleps: Debbie Charles.
Mínus: Bjarni, Bjossi, Frosti, Johnny, Krummi Munis.
The Minus 5: Peter Buck, Jeff Tweedy.
Mirage: Michael Stock.
Mircea Stan Quartet: Pentti Lahti.
Mirror: Thomas Clausen.
Mis-Teeq: Alesha Harvey, Su-Elise Nash, Sabrina Washington.
Misbeat: Giles Cooper.
Misha Mengelberg Trio/Quartet: Misha Mengelberg.
Miss B Haven: Lise Cabble.
Missing in Action: Doug Williams.
The Mission: Andy Cousin, Simon Hinkler, Wayne Hussey.
The Mission City Playboys: Moe Bandy.
Mission Impossible Big Band: Dave Corsby.
Mistikana: Valery Meladze.
MJT + 3: Muhal Abrams.
MMMPP: Paul Okoye, Peter Okoye.
MMPP: Paul Okoye, Peter Okoye.

Mo James Soul Band: Mo James.
Mobb Deep: Havoc, Prodigy.
Mobben: Peter Ericson.
Modern Dixielanders: Zbigniew Namysłowski.
Modern Kids: Broz Rowland.
Modjo: Yann Destagnol, Romain Tranchart.
Modulations: Jean Davis.
Module: Alain Brunet.
Moe and Joe: Moe Bandy, Joe Stampley.
Moho Pack: Enid Williams.
Moloko: Mark Brydon, Roisin Murphy.
Molto Mobile: Gérard Siracusa.
Momentum: John Brennan.
MoMo (Music of Moroccan Origin): Tahir el-Edrissi, Lahcen Lahbib, Farid Nainia.
Momoiro Clover Z: Momoka Ariyasu, Kanako Momota, Ayaka Sasaki, Shiori Tamai, Reni Takagi.
Monaco: Peter Hook.
Monad: Paul Mitchell-Davidson.
Monade: Laetitia Sadier.
The Monarchs: Van Morrison.
Money Tree: Eugene J. Wright.
Monique Weiss Quartet: Paul Speidel.
The Monkees: Mickey Dolenz Jr, Mike Nesmith, Peter Tork.
Monopacific: Zak Starkey.
Monrad and Rislund: Jan Monrad.
Monsoon: Sheila Chandra, John Millar.
Monsters of Folk: Jim James, Conor Oberst.
Mont Jóia: Jan-Mari Carlotti.
Montreux Band: Darol Anger.
Montrose: Sammy Hagar.
Moody Blues: Justin Hayward, John Lodge.
The Moody Brothers: Greg Auch.
The Moog Cookbook: Roger Manning.
Moonalice: Jack Casady.
Moonbaker Abbey: Ron Mael, Russell Mael.
Mooncoin: Lorraine Jordan.
Moondogg: Bob Andrews, Elizabeth Westwood.
The Moondogs: P. J. Proby.
The Moonglows: Ben King.
Moonjam: Morten Kaersaa, Rasmus Kaersaa.
Morand Cajun Band: Roger Morand.
Moravigne: Olivier Hutman.
Morcheeba: Skye Edwards, Paul Godfrey, Ross Godfrey.
Morgan: Morgan Fisher.
Morris Ellis Orchestra: George Lewis.
Morten Kargaard Group: Makiko Hirabayashi.
Mosaic Orchestra: Sonia Jacobsen.
Mostly Other People Do the Killing: Jonathan (Jon) Irabagon.
Mother Blues Band: Patrick Hazell.
Mother Earth: Tracy Nelson.
Mother Gong: Harry Williamson.
Mother Love Bone: Jeff Ament, Stone Gossard.
Mothers' Army: Jeff Watson.
Mötley Crüe: Tommy Lee, Mick Mars, Vince Neil, Nikki Sixx.
Motörhead: Eddie Clarke, Brian Robertson.
Mott the Hoople: Morgan Fisher, Ian Hunter, Mick Ralphs, Derek Weaver.
Mountain: Leslie West.
Mountain Child: Gary Waghorn.
Mountain City Four: Anna McGarrigle.
Mountain People: Julian Nicholas.
Mourning Widows: Nuno Bettencourt.
The Move: Beverley Bevan, Jeff Lynne, Roy Wood.
The Movies: Jamie Lane.
Moving Hearts: Donal Lunny, Christy Moore.
The Moving Sidewalks: Billy Gibbons.
Moxy: Mike Reno.
Mozamba: Bob Moses.
Mr Big: Paul Gilbert, Eric Martin, Billy Sheehan.
Mr Boogie Woogie and The Fire Sweep Blues Band: Harm van Sleen.
Msumuenu: Mufubela Tshamala.
Mt Desolation: Tim Rice-Oxley.
Mud: Rob Davis.
Mudcrutch: Tom Petty.
Muddy Waters Blues Band: Bob Margolin.
Muldoon Brothers: Paul Muldoon.
Muleskinner: Ken Tardley.
Mulford/MacFarlane Group: Malcolm MacFarlane.
Muluankh: Simon Spang-Hanssen.
Múm: Örvar Smárason, Gunnar Örn Tynes, Kristín Anna Valtýsdóttir.
Mumbo's Brain: Chris Poland.
Mumford and Sons: Ted Dwane, Marcus Johnston, Ben Lovett, Winston Marshall .
Mungo Jerry: Ray Dorset.
Muse: Matthew Bellamy, Dominic Howard, Chris Wolstenholme.
Musique Vivante: Jean-Louis Chautemps.

Muszikás: Márta Sebestyén.
My Bloody Valentine: Liam O Maonlai.
My Chemical Romance: Bob Bryar, Frank Iero, Raymond Toro Ortiz, Gerard Way, Mikey Way.
My Darling Clementine: Lou Dalgleish.
My Morning Jacket: Carl Broemel, Patrick Hallahan, Jim James, Bo Koster, 'Two-Tone' Tommy.
My Old School: Doug Williams.
Mynta: Fazal Qureshi.
The Myrol Brothers: Keith Myrol, Myles Myrol, Rick Myrol.
Myslovitz: Jacek Kuderski, Wojciech Kuderski, Przemysław Myszor, Wojciech Powaga, Artur Rojek.
Myster Black: Gilles Gabriel.
Mystere Five: John Johnson.
Mystic Deckchairs: Steve Hewitt.
Mystic Music Ensemble: Süleyman Erguner.
MyTown: Danny O'Donoghue, Mark Sheehan.

Nação Zumbi: Jorge du Peixe, Lucio Maia, Toca Ogan, Gilmar Oito, Pupilo Paupequeno.
Nada: Bo Jacobsen.
Nagisa Ni te: Shinji Shibayama, Masako Takeda.
Naima: Chris Francis.
Naïve: Claus Berthelsen.
The Nakayashi Group: Inoue Yosui.
Naked City: Bill Frisell, John Zorn.
Naked Skinnies: Mark Eitzel.
Naked Voices: Dee Jarlett.
Nando Lynch: Charleson Ximenes.
The Nash Ramblers: Jon Stewart.
Nashville Strings: Mark O'Connor.
Natalie Cole's Malibu Music Men: Daryl Dragon.
The National: Matt Berninger, Aaron Dessner, Bryce Dessner, Bryan Devendorf, Scott Devendorf.
National Ensemble of Mali: Oumou Sangare.
National Health: Neil Murray.
Nationalteatern: Anders Melander.
Native Tongues: Mos Def.
Natural Born Deejays: Dimitri Lambrecht.
Natural Born Lovers: Billy Childish.
Natural Gas Jazz Band: Robert Murphy.
Naturalna Mistika: Boris Leiner.
Naz and The Nomads: Rat Scabies, Dave Vanian.
Nazaire: Jean Toussaint.
Nazareth: Dan McCafferty.
The Nazz: Todd Rundgren.
Nebesna Kopalyna: Yuri Polchenko.
Ned's Atomic Dustbin: John Penney.
Negative Trend: Tim Mooney.
Negramaro: Ermanno Carlà, Andrea de Rocco, Andrea Mariano, Giuliano Sangiorgi, Emanuele Spedicato, Danilo Tasco.
Neil Christian and The Crusaders: Jimmy Page.
Neil Solomon Band: George Voros.
Neil Sparkes & The Last Tribe: Neil Sparkes.
Nelly Pouget Quartet: Nelly Pouget.
Nelstar: Nelly Furtado.
Nemesis Avenue: A. R. Rahman.
Neposedy: Lena Katina, Julia Volkova.
The Neptunes: Chad Hugo, Pharrell Williams.
N.E.R.D. (Nobody Ever Really Dies): Shay Hayly, Chad Hugo, Pharrell Williams.
Nerve: JXL.
Netoband: José Neto.
The Network: Billie Joe Armstrong, Tre Cool, Mike Dirnt.
Neurotic Outsiders: Steve Jones, John Taylor.
Nev and Norris: Brendan Croker.
The Neville Brothers: Aaron Neville, Art Neville, Charles Neville, Cyril Neville.
The Neville Sound: Art Neville, Cyril Neville.
New Age Orchestra: Paul Cacia.
New Breed: Timothy Schmit.
The New Bushbury Mountain Daredevils: Brian Bannister, Eric Barlow, Richard Bywater, Eddie Morton.
New Celeste: Graeme Duffin.
New Christy Minstrels: Kim Carnes, Kenny Rogers.
New Commitments: Trace Adkins.
New Conception of Jazz: Jens-Christian Wesseltoft.
New Delta Ahkri Band: Anthony Davis.
New Dixie Syncopators: John Petters.
New Edition: Bobby Brown.
New Electron Moscovites: Alla Pugacheva.
New Grass Revival: Bela Fleck.
New Jazz Trio: Andrew White III.
New Jungle Orchestra: Irene Becker, Pierre Dorge.
The New London Consort: Bill Badley, Giles Lewin.
New Model Army: Ricky Warwick.

The New Monks: Peter Tork.
New Order: Tom Chapman, Phil Cunningham, Gillian Gilbert, Peter Hook, Stephen Morris, Bernard Sumner.
New Orleans Stompers: Zbigniew Namysłowski.
New Power Generation: Prince.
The New Quartet: Christina Staël von Holstein.
The New Radicals: Gregg Alexander.
New Sector Movements (NSM): Ig Culture.
The New Seekers: Paul Layton, Keith Potger.
New Song: Wambali Mkandawire.
New Westbrook Orchestra: Mike Westbrook.
New World Rising: Nile Rodgers.
New York Art Quartet: Roswell Rudd.
New York Dolls: Steve Conte, Brian Delaney, David Johansen, Brian Koonin, Sylvain Sylvain, Sami Yaffa.
New Yorkers: Chris Poland.
NeWorks: Yuzuru Sadashige.
News from the Shed: John Butcher.
Newspeak: Alan McGee.
The Next: Zak Starkey.
The Next Step: Christopher Marshall.
Niadem's Ghost: David Tompkins.
Niafunke District Troupe: Ali Farka Touré.
The Nice: P. P. Arnold.
Nick Cave & The Bad Seeds: Blixa Bargeld, Nick Cave, Mick Harvey.
Nickel Creek: Chris Thile, Sara Watkins.
Nickel Eye: Nikolai Fraiture.
Nickelback: Chad Kroeger, Mike Kroeger, Ryan Peake, Ryan Vikedal.
Nicolas Folmer Quintet: Jean-Christophe Béney.
Nicotine: Full, Howie, Naoki, Yasu.
Niekku: Maria Kalaniemi.
Niels Husum Septet: Ib Nielsen.
Niels Lan Doky Trio: Niels Lan Doky, Alex Riel.
Nigel Moyse Quartet: Nigel Moyse.
Night: Christopher Thompson.
Night Ranger: Jack Blades, Jeff Watson.
Night Timers: William Stanger.
Nightmares on Wax: George Evelyn.
Nightwork: Michael Stock.
Nike: Nike Markelius.
Nikolaj Bentzon (various bands): Nikolaj Bentzon.
Nine Below Zero: Mark Feltham, Alan Glen.
Nine Inch Nails: Trent Reznor.
99ers: Dave Edmunds.
Nirvana: Dave Grohl, Kris Novoselic.
Nisajo: John Brennan.
Nitebreed: Buggy Lees.
N-Joi: Saffron.
No Devotion: Lee Gaze, Mike Lewis, Jamie Oliver, Stuart Richardson.
No Doubt: Tom Dumont, Tony Kanal, Gwen Stefani, Adrian Young.
No Fit State: Stephen Roberts.
No Romance in China: Vince Clarke.
No Smoking Orchestra: Emir Kusturica.
Nocturnal Emissions: Nigel Ayers.
Noel Redding Band: Eric Bell.
Noise Boys: Stephan Eicher.
Nom: Dimitri Tikhonov.
Nomos: John Spillane.
Nordic All-Women Big Band: Hanne Romer.
Norma and the Shade of Pale: Barry Wortley.
Norman Beaker Band: Norman Beaker, Lenni.
Norrin Radd: Patrick McGarvey.
North of Cornwallis: Spencer Smith.
Northstar: Sam Roberts.
Northwest Jazz Quintet: Tom Collier.
Not Drowning, Waving: John Phillips.
Notorious: Sean Harris.
Notting Hillbillies: Brendan Croker, Mark Knopfler, Steve Phillips.
Notturno: Zeljen Klasterka.
Noty Spices: Yemi Alade.
Nozzle: John Forrester.
NQB: Ann-Marie Henning.
***NSYNC:** Lance Bass, JC Chasez, Joey Fatone, Chris Kirkpatrick, Justin Timberlake.
NTU Troop: Barney McAll.
Nu-Era: Denis MacFarlane.
Nu Yorican Soul: Kenny Gonzalez, Louie Vega.
The Nubiles: Christopher Nettleton.
Nucleus: Karl Jenkins, John Marshall.
Nudes/Pale Nudes: Amy Denio.
The Nuns: Alejandro Escovedo.
Nursery Crimes: Rusty Hopkinson.
The Nutty Boys: Chrissy Boy.
N.W.A.: Dr Dre, Ice Cube.
Ny Bris: Dag Arnesen.

Oak Ridge Boys: Duane Allen, Joseph Bonsall.
Oasis: Gem Archer, Andrew Bell, Liam Gallagher, Noel Gallagher, Chris Sharrock.
Oasis: Julian Lloyd Webber, Peter Skellern.
Objects of Desire: Alonza Bevan, Crispian Mills.
Obote: Jivi Honk.
Obsession: James Hetfield.
O'Cajunal Playboys: Richard Churchley.
Ocean Colour Scene: Steve Cradock, Simon Fowler, Oscar Harrison, Damon Minchella.
Octavo: Guigou Chenevier.
Octurn: Guillaume Orti.
The Offbeats: Justin Hayward.
Office: Lacy Dalton.
The Offspring: Dexter Holland, Greg Kriesel, Noodles, Pete Parada, Ron Welty, Atom Willard.
Ohilyönti: Tommi Lievemaa.
OHM: Chris Poland.
Oige: Cara Dillon.
Oiling Boiling: Matti Oiling.
Oingo Bongo: Danny Elfman.
OJJ!600: Carl Aborg.
Ojos de Brujo: Marina Abad, DJ Panko, Ramón Giménez, Paco Lomeña, Javi Martin, Sergio Ramos, Carlos Sarduy, Xavi Turull, Maxwell Wright.
OK Go: Daniel Konopka, Damian Kulash Jr., Tim Nordwind, Andy Ross.
Oklahoma Wind: Mel McDaniel.
Old Teenagers: Mikoláš Chadima.
Old Town School of Folk Music: Gerry Armstrong.
Oleg Lundstrem Jazz Orchestra: Alla Pugacheva.
Olsen: Jørgen Olsen, Noller Olsen.
Olympia Brass Band: Paul Spedding.
Olympic: Petr Janda.
Omar Rodríguez-López Group: Omar Rodríguez-López.
On Fillmore: Glenn Kotche.
On the Air: Mark Brzezicki, Simon Townshend.
On the Steps of Armstrong's Hot Five: Irakli de Davrichewy.
O.N.E.: Corneille.
OneRepublic: Drew Brown, Zach Filkins, Eddie Fisher, Brent Kutzle, Ryan Tedder.
One Direction: Niall Horan, Zayn Malik, Liam Payne, Harry Styles, Louis Tomlinson.
One Giant Leap: Duncan Bridgeman, Jamie Catto.
One Nation: Kipper.
One Night Stand: Barrie Martin, Joe Turner.
1000 Homo DJs: Al Jourgensen, Trent Reznor.
One Truth Band: John McLaughlin.
One Two: Caecilie Norby.
The Onset: Paul Hemmings.
Onxtet de Violon Jazz: Daniel-John Martin.
Oortcloud: Funkey.
Open Air: Eric Lohrer.
Operation Ivy: Tim Armstrong, Matt Freeman.
Opisthodromiki Kompania: Eleftheria Arvanitaki.
Opus Incertum on C: Guillaume Orti.
Orage: Olu Shola Adedayo.
Orange: Jean-Benoît Dunckel, Nicolas Godin.
Orange Juice: Edwyn Collins, Paul Heard.
The Orb: Jimmy Cauty.
Orbital: Paul Hartnoll, Phil Hartnoll.
Orchestra Baobab: Barthélemy Attisso, Issa Cissoko, Rudy Gomis, Balla Sidibe.
Orchestra Makassy: Remmy Ongala.
Orchestra Marrabenta Star de Mocambique: Wazimbo.
Orchestra Super Matimila: Remmy Ongala.
Orchestra Tivoli: Michala Petri.
Orchestra Volta Jazz: Cheikh Lô.
Orchestral Manoeuvres in the Dark (OMD): Andy McCluskey.
Orchestre African Jazz: Papa Noel.
Orchestre Afrisa International: Mansiamina M'Foko.
Orchestre Bamboula: Mansiamina M'Foko.
Orchestre Bella Mambo: Kanda Bongo Man.
Orchestre de Contrebasses: Renaud Garcia-Fons.
Orchestre Diamono: Youssou N'Dour.
Orchestre Misira: Djelimady Tounkara.
Orchestre National A: Djelimady Tounkara.
Orchestre National de Jazz (France): Denis Barbier, Eric Barret, Lionel Benhamou, Laurent Blumenthal, Jean-François Canape, François Chassagnite, Laurent Cugny, Geoffrey de Masure, Benoit de Mesmay, Michel Delakian, Xavier Desandre-Navarre, Didier Havet, Serge Lazarevitch, Nguyên Le, Philippe Sellam, Simon Spang-Hanssen.
Orchid Waltz: Brian Doran.
Oregon: Trilok Gurtu.
Orera: Nani Bregvadze, Vakhtang Kikabidze.
Orfeus: Dave Lindholm.
Oriental Mood: Claus Mathiesen.
The Original Danish Polcalypso Orchestra: Leonardo Pedersen.

Original Mirrors: Ian Broudie.
Oriole Brass Band: Paul Russell.
Orion: Dee Jarlett, Soïg Siberil, Rudy Velghe.
Ornicar Big Band: Philippe Laudet.
ORO: Henrik Wallgren.
Orphéon Celesta: Emmanuel Hussenot.
Orphesians: Oscar Blandamer.
Orquesta Aragón: Omara Portuondo.
Orquesta Cubana de Música Moderna: Chucho Valdés.
Orquesta La Inspiración: Roberto Pla.
Orquesta Lucho Bermudez: Roberto Pla.
Orquesta Ritmo Oriental: David Calzado.
Os Ipanemas: Wilson das Neves.
Os Mutantes: Sergio Días, Arnaldo Dias Baptista, Zélia Duncan, Ronaldo Leme.
Osibisa: Teddy Osei, Frank Tontoh.
Osiris: Bo Jacobsen.
Oskorri: Kepa Junkera.
Oslo Groove Company: Jukka Linkola.
Oslo 13: Jon Balke.
The Osmonds: Donny Osmond, Marie Osmond.
Osmosis: Guillaume Orti.
Osprey: Buggy Lees.
Ostjydsk Musikforsyning: Marius Knudsen.
Otawa: Sari Kaasinen.
OTC4: Bob Helson.
The Other Two: Gillian Gilbert, Stephen Morris.
The Others: Brian May.
Otis Grand and The Big Blues Band: Barrie Martin.
The Otto Donner Treatment: Otto Donner, Seppo Kantonen, Eero Ojanen.
Ottopasuuna: Janne Lappalainen.
Oui Oui: Nomiya Maki.
Out Loud: Bob Helson, Nile Rodgers.
Out of Order: Dryden Mitchell.
Outkast: Andre 3000, Big Boi.
Outlandish: Isam Bachiri, Lenny Martinez, Waqas Qadri.
Overview: Damian Stanley.
Owlkatraz: Billie Jo Spears.
Oxyde de Cuivre: Jean Quillivic.
Oxymore Quintet: Guillaume Orti.
Oysterband: Ian Kearey, June Tabor.
Oysters Rockefeller: Harold Nino.
Ozomatli: Cut Chemist, Chali 2NA.

P. J. Harvey Trio: P. J. Harvey.
Paco de Lucía Sextet: Paco de Lucía.
Paddy Corn Band: Bernd Rommel.
The Pagans: Eric Burdon.
Page One: Thomas Blachman.
Page/Plant: Jimmy Page, Robert Plant.
Pago Libre: John Brennan, Arkady Shilkloper.
Paice Ashton Lord (PAL): Jon Lord, Ian Paice.
Painkiller: Bill Laswell, John Zorn.
Paintings: Guillaume Orti.
Pajama Slave Dancers: Steve Westfield.
Palais Congrés: Hamouka Dagara.
Palatino: Aldo Romano.
Paley's Watch: Marc Catley.
Palle Mikkelborg Trio: Palle Mikkelborg.
Palm Skin Productions: Ski.
Pam Tillis Band: Pam Tillis.
Pan L Beaters Steel Band: Dave Edwards.
Panama Francis and The Savoy Sultans: Bobby Watson.
Panama Red: Ron Kavanagh.
Pandémonium: Joël Allouche, François Chassagnite, Katia Labèque.
Pankrti: Peter Lovsin.
Pantera: Phil Anselmo.
Papa Bue's Viking Jazz Band: Didier Geers, Jørgen Svare.
Pape & Cheikh: Cheikhou Coulibaly, Papa Fall.
Paper Fish: Christina Staël von Holstein.
Paquito D'Rivera Ensemble: Paquito D'Rivera.
Paradise: Simo Salminen.
Parakou: Angélique Kidjo.
The Paramounts: Robin Trower.
Paramore: Jeremy Davis, Hayley Williams, Taylor York.
The Paramours: Bill Medley.
Paranoid Earthling: Asela Bandara, Mirshad Buckman, Dhanushka Samarasinghe, Shanka Samarasinghe.
Pardesi: Silinder Pardesi.
Pardy Quintet: Richard Pardy.
Paris: Bret Michaels.
Paris-Barcelona Swing Connection: Ramon Fossati.
The Paris Gun: Steven Gregory Drozd.
Paris-Musette: Didier Roussin.
Paris Washboard: Louis Mazetier.
Parksorch: David Campbell.

Parliament/Funkadelic: George Clinton, Bootsy Collins.
Parni Valjek: Hasanfendic Husein, Drazen Scholz, Paolo Sfeci.
The Pasadena Roof Orchestra: Alan Barnes, Nicholas Payton.
Pascal's Bongo Massive: Phil Asher.
Pat and the Blue Wizards: Gilles Gabriel.
Pat Hammond's Reflections: Paul Hobbs.
Pat Metheny Group: Jack de Johnette, Pat Metheny, Paul Wertico.
Pat Travers Band: Pat Travers.
Patchwork: Zeljen Klasterka.
Pat's Secret Story Band: Paul Wertico.
Patti Smith Group: Patti Smith.
Patty Duke Syndrome: Ryan Adams.
Paul and his Gang: Paul Strandberg.
Paul and Linda: Linda Eder.
Paul Ayick Quintet: Paul Ayick.
Paul Bley Quintet: Bill Frisell, Paul Motian.
Paul Butterfield Group: David Sanborn.
Paul Carrack Band: David Bronze, Paul Carrack.
Paul Ehlers Quartet: Bo Jacobsen.
Paul Mauriat Orchestra: Raymond Gimenes.
Paul Motian Trio: Bill Frisell, Joe Lovano, Paul Motian.
Paul Russell and The Rebels: Gary Glitter.
Paul Severson and Friends Jazz Quintet: Paul Severson.
Paul Speidel Band: Paul Speidel.
The Paul Weller Movement: Paul Weller.
Paul Winter Consort: Chris Brown, Paul Winter.
Pavement: Mark Ibold, Scott Kannberg, Stephen Malkmus, Bob Nastanovich, Steve West.
Paws for Thought: Paul Mitchell-Davidson.
PBS Radikal: Didier Awadi.
Peace: Marian Bradfield, Paul Rodgers.
Peace Pipe: Ben Allison.
Peaky Blinders: Richard Churchley.
Pearl Jam: Jeff Ament, Matt Cameron, Stone Gossard, Jack Irons, Mike McCready, Eddie Vedder.
The Pearlfishers: David Scott.
The Peddlars: Roy Phillips.
Pedrito Martinez Group: Pedrito Martinez.
Pekka Pohjola Group: Ippe Kätkä.
Pekka Pöyry Quartet: Teppo Hauta-aho.
Pekka Toivanen Quartet: Heikki Sandren, Pekka Toivanen.
Pele: Wayne Morgan, Ian Prowse.
Pen Lee and Co.: Dave Lindholm.
Pendulum: Peredur ap Gwynned, Paul Harding, Gareth McGrillen, Ben Mount, Kevin Sawka, Rob Swire.
Pennou Skoulm: Soïg Siberil.
Pentagon: Mario Igrec, Wambali Mkandawire.
Pentangle: Bert Jansch, Claire-Louise Powell, Danny Thompson.
Penthouse: Herman de Rycke.
The People With Chairs Up Their Noses: Jim White.
Pepa Päivinen Trio: Guillaume Orti, Pepa Päivinen, Hannu Rantanen.
Peper: Leo Rutten.
Per Goldschmidt Orchestra: Anders Müller.
Perfect Disaster: Josephine Wiggs.
Perfect Houseplants: Mark Lockheart, Dudley Phillips, Huw Warren.
Perkana Percussion: Stephen Perkins.
Perko-Pyysalo Poppoo: Jukka Perko, Eerik Siikasaari.
Perlonex: Burkhard Beins.
Peruna Jazzmen: Paul Strandberg.
Pet Hate: Stephen Roberts.
Pet Shop Boys: Chris Lowe, Neil Tennant.
Pete Allen Jazz Band: Pete Allen, John Armatage.
Pete Best Four: Wayne Bickerton.
Pete Fountain Sextet: Peter Fountain.
Pete Wernick's Live Five: Peter Wernick.
Pete 'Wyoming' Bender Band: Josef Kucera.
Peter and Gordon: Peter Asher.
The Peter Band Band: Herman de Rycke.
Peter Brötzmann Alarm Orchester: Johannes Bauer.
Peter Duchin Orchestra: Roberta Fabiano.
Peter Herboltzheimer's Rhythm and Brass Combination: Bo Stief.
Peter Lipa Combo: Peter Lipa.
Peter, Paul & Mary: Noel Paul Stookey, Peter Yarrow.
Peter Thorup and Jesper Band: Jesper Thorup.
The Peth: Dafydd Ieuan.
Peto: Ringo Madlingozi.
Petter Wettre Quintet: Petter Wettre.
Petter Wettre Trio: Petter Wettre.
Peyote: Per Vibskov.
Phantastique Orchestre Modulaire: Benjamin Henocq.
The Phantom Chords: Dave Vanian.
The Phantoms: Jana Heller, Billy Kramer.
The Pharaohs: Richard Mackie.
Phil Lesh and Friends: Jimmy Herring, Philip Lesh.
Phil Seamen Quartet: Danny Thompson.
Phil Tate Orchestra: Peter Jeffries.

Phil Woods (various bands): Henri Texier.
Philip Catherine Trio: Ben Sluijs.
Philippe Duchemin Trio: Philippe Duchemin, Patricia Lebeugle.
Philippe Sellam Quintet: Benjamin Henocq, Philippe Sellam.
Phoenix: Laurent Brancowitz, Deck D'Arcy, Thomas Mars, Christian Mazzalai.
Phoenix: John Verity.
Phosphor: Burkhard Beins.
PI Seadust: Francisco Alburo.
Piano Kvartet: Christian Leroy.
Piccadilly Dance Orchestra: Michael Law.
Pickettywitch: Keith Hall.
Picnic: Carsten Ortmann.
The Pictures: David Lane.
Pieces of Eight: Martin Litton.
Pied de Poule: Gérard Siracusa.
Pied Pear: Rick Scott.
The Pied Pipers: Thomas Mapfumo.
Pied Pumpkin String Ensemble: Rick Scott, Shari Ulrich.
Pierre Sellin Big Band: Jean Quillivic.
Pigalle: François Hadji-Lazaro.
Pigbag: Christopher Lee, Brian Nevill.
Pigface: Steve Albini, Paul Barker, Al Jourgensen.
Pigsty Hill Light Orchestra: Andy Leggett.
Piirpauke: Sakari Kukko.
Pili Pili: Angélique Kidjo.
The Pilots: Broz Rowland.
Pinhead Gunpowder: Billie Joe Armstrong, Tre Cool, Mike Dirnt.
Pink 'n' Black: Paul Hobbs.
Pink Cloud: Char.
Pink Floyd: Andrew Bown, David Gilmour, Nick Mason, Roger Waters.
Pipelines: John Brennan.
Pipschips&videoclips: Mario Boršcak, Tin Osteš, Nikola Radman, Dubravko Ripper.
The Pixies: Frank Black, Kim Deal, David Lovering, Joey Santiago.
Pizzicato Five: Nomiya Maki, Konishi Yasuharu.
Placebo: Steve Hewitt, Brian Molko, Stefan Olsdal.
Plaid: Edward Handley, Andy Turner.
Plain Jane: Buggy Lees.
Plainsong: Iain Matthews.
Plakband: Norbert Meijs.
Planet Earth Rock 'n' Roll Orchestra: Paul Kantner.
Planet Jazz: Vivian Peres.
Planete Lolingo Band: Djonimbo Ashilaako Bilanso.
Plank Road: Bradley Leftwich.
Planxty: Paul Brady, Donal Lunny, Matt Molloy, Christy Moore, Liam O'Flynn, Bill Whelan.
Plasma: Bob Helson.
Plastic Ono Band: Alan White.
PLB System: Dimitri Lambrecht.
(+44): Travis Barker, Mark Hoppus.
Pnau: Nick Littlemore.
PO!: Ruth Miller.
Poco: Randy Meisner, Jim Messina, Timothy Schmit.
Pogues: Jem Finer, Shane MacGowan.
Poi Dog Pondering: Abra Moore.
Poiema: Steve Gresswell.
The Pointer Sisters: Anita Pointer, Ruth Pointer.
Poison: Bret Michaels.
The Police: Stewart Copeland, Sting, Andy Summers.
The Politicians: Timothy Armstrong.
Polwechsel: Burkhard Beins.
Polygone: Pierre Dutot.
The Polyphonic Spree: Tim DeLaughter, St Vincent.
Polytown: Mick Karn.
The Poor: Randy Meisner.
The Poor Mouth: Jackie McAuley.
Poors of Reign: Christopher Cunningham.
The Poozies: Kate Rusby, Karen Tweed.
Pop Rivets: Billy Childish.
Popeluc: Pete Castle.
The Popes: Shane MacGowan.
Popman and the Disciple: Andrew Lloyd.
Popman and the Raging Bull: Andrew Lloyd.
Porcupine Tree: Richard Barbieri.
Pori Big Band: Jorma Ojanperä, Jari Perkiömäki.
Pori Jazz: Seppo Paakkunainen.
Pork Pie: Aldo Romano, Bo Stief.
Porno for Pyros: Perry Farrell, Stephen Perkins.
Portejoie-Lagarde: Philippe Portejoie.
Portishead: Geoff Barrow, Beth Gibbons, Dave McDonald, Adrian Utley.
Positive Force: Femi Kuti.
Poutnici: Miroslav Hulan.
Powderfinger: Jon Coghill, John Collins, Bernard Fanning, Ian Haug, Darren Middleton.
The Power Station: Andy Taylor, John Taylor.

Power Tools: Bill Frisell.
Powerhouse: Yngwie Malmsteen, Doug Williams.
Poyut Gitari: Alexander Malinin.
Pozo-Seco Singers: Don Williams.
The Prague Big Band: Karel Zelenka.
The Prague Five: Michal Vich.
Precious: Jenny Frost.
Prefab Sprout: Paddy McAloon, Wendy Smith.
Presence: Lol Tolhurst.
Pressgang: John Forrester, George Whitfield.
Pressure Point: Matthew Best.
Preston School of Industry: Scott Kannberg.
Pretenders: Martin Chambers, Chrissie Hynde.
Pretty Blue Gun: Dale Harris.
Pride: Paul Cooke, Sade.
Primal Scream: Martin Duffy, Bobby Gillespie, Andrew Innes, Gary Mounfield.
Prime Time: Jamaaladeen Tacuma.
Primi Band: Lise Dynnesen, Marilyn Mazur.
The Primitives: Jay Farrar.
Prince and The Revolution: Prince.
Prince Trubetsky and JMKE: Prince Trubetsky.
Prins Lätt: Carl Aborg.
Pro-Gress: Mark Stagg.
Problem Kids: Rocky.
Probot: Dave Grohl.
The Proclaimers: Charlie Reid, Craig Reid.
Procol Harum: David Bronze, Robin Trower.
Prodigal Sons: Michael Fix, Ian McCulloch.
The Prodigy: Keith Flint, Liam Howlett, Maxim.
The Producers: Harry Skinner.
The Professionals: Paul Cook.
Progmatics: Janne Lappalainen.
The Promise: Jason Isaacs.
Propellerheads: Alex Gifford, Will White.
Prvni Republika: Karel Babuljak.
PRYSM: Pierre de Bethmann, Benjamin Henocq, Christophe Walleme.
P$C (Pimp Squad Click): T.I..
P-Square: Paul Okoye, Peter Okoye.
Psychedelix: Char.
Psychic TV: Matthew Best.
Psycho Motel: Adrian Smith.
Psychograss: Darol Anger.
Public Announcement: R Kelly.
Public Enemy: Chuck D, Flavor Flav, Professor Griff, Terminator X.
Public Image Limited (PiL): Jah Wobble.
The Puentes Brothers: Alex Cuba.
Pula't Asul Band: Francisco Alburo.
Pulp: Nick Banks, Jarvis Cocker, Candida Doyle, Richard Hawley, Simon Hinkler, Steve Mackey, Russell Senior, Mark Webber.
Pulse Unit: Klavs Hovman, Marilyn Mazur.
Punch Brothers: Chris Thile.
Pure Prairie League: Vince Gill.
Purple Fleas: Mikoláš Chadima.
Push: Eddie Saunders, Cripsin Taylor.
Pussy Galore: Jon Spencer.
Pyewackett: Ian Blake.
The Pyramid: Iain Matthews.

Q Lazzarus: Mark Barrett.
The Q-Tips: Oscar Blandamer, Paul Young.
Quadrisect: George Lewis.
Quando Quango: Mike Pickering.
The Quarrymen: Paul McCartney.
The Quartet: Ali Haurand.
Quartet Gianez: Laurent Gianez.
Quarteto Novo: Hermeto Pascoal.
Quartier Latin: Koffi Olomide.
Quartz: Dina Carroll.
Queen: John Deacon, Morgan Fisher, Brian May, Paul Rodgers, Roger Taylor.
Queens of the Stone Age: Josh Homme, Mark Lanegan.
Queensrÿche: Geoff Tate.
Quickdraw: Pamela Cole.
Quintet Moderne: Teppo Hauta-aho.
Quinteto Oriente: Eliades Ochoa.
Quintette a Cordes de Pierre Blanchard: Pierre Blanchard.
Quintetto alla Busara: Amy Denio.
The Quireboys: Ginger.
Quiz: John Howard.
Quoi de Neuf Docteur Big Band: Benjamin Henocq.
Quotations: Barrie Martin.

R. Cajun and The Zydeco Brothers: David Blant, Chris Hall, Freddy Hopwood.
Racer X: Juan Alderete, Paul Gilbert.

The Raconteurs: Brendan Benson, Patrick Keeler, Jack Lawrence, Jack White.
Radcliffe Rollers Steel Band: Jo Servi.
Radio Authority: Feargal Sharkey.
Radio Bemba Sound System: Manu Chao.
Radio Futura: Sanitago Auserón.
Radio Prague Big Band: Petr Dvorsky, Václav Harmacek, Jukka Linkola.
Radio Science Orchestra: Chris Elliott, Simon Hanson, Matthew Seligman.
Radio Tarifa: Benjamin Escoriza, Vincent Molino, Fain Sanchez Dueñas.
Radio Telefís Éireann (RTÉ) Orchestra: Fionnuala Sherry.
Radiohead: Colin Greenwood, Jonny Greenwood, Ed O'Brien, Phillip Selway, Thom Yorke.
RadioKijada: Christoph H. Müller.
Radiotones: Dave Arcari.
Ragairne: Mairead Ni Mhaonaigh.
Rage Against the Machine: Tim Commerford, Zack de la Rocha, Tom Morello, Bradley Wilk.
Ragged Laughter: David Campbell.
Ragged Robin: Steve Ashley.
Raglin Street Rattle: David Campbell.
Ragnarö: Hans Bryngelsson.
The Raiders: Dave Edmunds.
The Railroaders: Bruce Welch.
Rain Tree Crow: Richard Barbieri, Steve Jansen, Mick Karn, David Sylvian.
Rainbow: Don Airey, Ritchie Blackmore, Roger Glover, Joe Turner.
Rainbow Chasers: Ashley Hutchings.
Rajaton: Hannu Rantanen.
Rakes of Kildare: Donal Lunny, Christy Moore.
Ralph Sharon Sextet: Alan Grahame.
Ram Jam Band: Roger Flavell, Peter Gage, Dave Greenslade.
Rambling Drifters: Peter Wernick.
Rammstein: Richard Z. Kruspe, Paul Landers, Till Lindemann, Christian Lorenz, Oliver Riedel, Christoph Schneider.
Ramona 55: Angie Brown.
Ramunder: Maria Kalaniemi.
The Ranch: Keith Urban.
Rancid: Tim Armstrong, Lars Frederiksen, Matt Freeman, Brett Reed.
Randy Brecker Band: Randy Brecker.
Randy Weston (various bands): Randy Weston.
Randy Weston and Billy Harper: Billy Harper, Randy Weston.
Rank and File: Alejandro Escovedo.
Raoul Björkenheim Triad: Hannu Rantanen.
Rapeman: Steve Albini.
Rapid Transit: Courtney Barnett.
Rapination: Charlie Mallozzi, Marco Sabiu.
Rapino Brothers: Charlie Mallozzi, Marco Sabiu.
The Rapture: Gabe Andruzzi, Luke Jenner, Vito Roccoforte, Mattie Safer.
Rascal Flatts: Jay DeMarcus, Gary LeVox, Joe Don Rooney.
The Rascals of Rhythm: Steve Kershaw.
The Rasmus: Aki Hakala, Eero Heinonen, Pauli Rantasalmi, Lauri Johannes Yölnen.
Raspberries: Eric Carmen.
Rat: Rat Scabies.
Ratz: Hugh Moffatt.
Ravens: Robert Fripp.
The Raveonettes: Sharin Foo, Sune Rose Wagner.
Ravishing Beauties: Kate St John.
Raw Stylus: Ski.
Ray Harper and Friends: Ray Harper.
The Ray McVay Band: Tony Clout.
Ray Shields Orchestra: Clive Copland.
The Ray Ward Trio: Paul Wood.
Raydio: Ray Parker.
Razorlight: Björn Ågren, Johnny Borrell, Andy Burrows, Carl Dalemo.
RBD: Christopher Casillas von Uckermann, Christian Chavez Garza, Dulce Espinoza Saviñon, Alfonso Herrera Rodríguez, Dulce Maria, Maite Perroni Beorlegui, Anahí Puente Portillo.
Re-Pro: Robin Millar.
The Real Thing: Phil Collins, Staffan William-Olsson.
The Rebels: Duane Eddy.
The Reclines: kd lang.
The Red and the Black: Mike Scott.
Red Ball Jets: David Roth.
Red Cluster: Ann-Marie Henning.
Red Gum: Steve Cooney.
Red Hot Chili Peppers: Flea, John Frusciante, Jack Irons, Anthony Kiedis, Cliff Martinez, Dave Navarro, Chad Smith.
Red House Snakes: Buggy Lees.
Red Rooster: Walter Stes.
Red Whale: Eric Lohrer.
Redkaya Ptitsa: Sergey Galanin.
The Redlands Palomino Company: Patrick McGarvey.
Reel Union: Seán Keane.
The Reese Project: Kevin Saunderson.
Reflexionen: Joël Allouche.
The Reggae Revolution: Pato Banton.

Reik: Gilberto Marín Espinoza, Jesús Navarro Rosas, Julio Ramirez Eguía.
The Reindeer Section: Norman Blake, Richard Colburn, Mick Cooke, Gary Lightbody, John Quinn, Roddy Woomble.
Relaxace: Karel Babuljak.
Release: Peter Tork.
Relentless7: Ben Harper.
R.E.M.: Bill Berry, Peter Buck, Mike Mills, Michael Stipe.
The Rembrandts: Phil Solem, Danny Wilde.
The Remnant Kings: Jon Boden.
Rempsetti: Matti Oiling.
Renee Geyer Band: Doug Williams.
REO Speedwagon: Kevin Cronin.
Reprazent: DJ Krust, Roni Size.
The Republic: Sarah Morris.
Republic of Strings: Darol Anger.
Republica: Tim Dorney, Johnny Male, Saffron.
Rero: Nani Bregvadze.
Reset: Julien Blais.
Respect Group: Stanislav Kubes.
Restless Soul: Phil Asher.
Return to Forever: Chick Corea, Stanley Clarke, Al DiMeola, Earl Klugh.
Revenge: Peter Hook.
Rever d'Aventures: Paul Ada.
Reverse: Guillaume Orti.
Revival Jazz Band: Peter Lipa.
Revolting Cocks: Al Jourgensen.
The Rezillos: Jo Callis.
The Rhinocats: Josh Smith.
Rhizome: Jean-Louis Chautemps.
Rhonda: Rhonda Finlayson.
The Rhythm and Blues Orchestra: Jools Holland, Gilson Lavis.
Rhythm and Reeds: Harry Pitch.
Rhythm Dandies: King Sunny Ade.
Rhythm Doctors: David Lucas.
The Rhythm Experience: Zakir Hussain, Bhavani Shankar.
Rhythm Rising: Stephen Laffy.
Rhythm Section: Rennie Pilgrem.
Ricet Barrier: Valentin Clastrier.
Rich Kids: Midge Ure.
Richard III: Brian Doran.
Richard Reiter Swing Band: Luther Rix.
Richard Sudhalter's New Paul Whiteman Orchestra: Keith Nichols.
The Richard Thompson Band: Clive Gregson, John Kirkpatrick, Richard Thompson.
Richter and Chadima: Mikoláš Chadima.
Rick Norcross and The Nashfull Ramblers Western Swing Band: Rick Norcross.
Rick Scott Band: Rick Scott.
Rick Witter & The Dukes: Rick Witter.
Ride: Andrew Bell, Laurence Colbert, Stephen Queralt.
Riel/Mikkelborg Quintet: Palle Mikkelborg, Alex Riel.
The Righteous Brothers: Bill Medley.
The Rigmor Gustafsson Quintet: Rigmor Gustafsson.
Rilo Kiley: Jason Boesel, Pierre de Reeder, Jenny Lewis, Blake Sennett.
Rinconcito Monsefuano: Eva Ayllón.
Ringo Starr and his All-Starr Band: Simon Kirke, Todd Rundgren, Ringo Starr.
Rinôçérôse: Patrice Carrié, Jean-Philippe Freu.
Rio: Emilio.
Rio Diamond: T. Graham Brown.
The Rishi Rich Project: Jay Sean, Rishi Rich.
Rising: Yngwie Malmsteen.
Rising Force: Yngwie Malmsteen.
The Rising Sons: Ry Cooder.
Ritmo Loco: Mario Igrec, Zeljen Klasterka.
Riverdogs: Vivian Campbell.
Roach Motel: Pete Heller.
Roachford: Andrew Roachford.
Road Vultures: Eric Martin.
Roadrunners: Paul Rodgers.
Roadside Picnic: Dave O'Higgins.
Robby Krieger and Friends: Robby Krieger.
Robert Cray Band: Robert Cray.
Robert Santiago's Latino-Américain: Didier Roussin.
Roberto Pla Latin Ensemble: Roberto Pla.
Robin Trower Band: David Bronze, Robin Trower.
Rocco and the Saints: Bobby Rydell.
Rock-a-Mambo: Mansiamina M'Foko, Papa Noel.
Rock and Hyde: Bob Rock.
The Rock and Joces Extempore Band: Blanka Strayblova.
Rock Candy: Vince Neil.
Rock City Band: Trix Ko-chuan Tsui.
Rock Goddess: Tracey Lamb.
Rock Island Line: Peter Garrett.
Rock N Roll Gypsies: Tracey Lamb.

The Rockets: Dennis Robbins, Sal Solo.
The Rockmelons: Doug Williams.
Rockpile: Dave Edmunds.
Rococo: Roy Shipston.
Rod Mason's Hot Five: Andy Leggett.
Rodger Fox Big Band: David Feehan.
Rodrigo y Gabriela: Gabriela Quintero, Rodrigo Sánchez.
Roger Nobes Quartet: Roger Nobes.
Roll Deep: Skepta.
The Rolling Stones: Mick Jagger, Keith Richards, Mick Taylor, Charlie Watts, Ronnie Wood, Bill Wyman.
Rolling Thunder: Jorma Tapio.
Romen: Valentina Ponomareva.
Romeo's Daughter: Andy Welsford.
The Rondelles: Delbert McLinton.
The Ronettes: Ronnie Spector.
Roogalator: Jon Taylor.
Roommushklahn: Raoul Björkenheim.
Roosters: Eric Clapton.
The Roots: Nicola Yeoh.
Roots Radics: Jamaka Tee-Birdd.
Rory Storme and The Hurricanes: Ringo Starr.
Rosegarden: Per Vibskov.
Rosenhontz: Luther Rix.
Rosenstolz: Peter Plate.
Rosetta Stone: Ian Mitchell.
Rossington-Collins Band: Gary Rossington.
The Rough Squirrels: Steve Forbert.
The Routers: Scott Walker.
The Rover Girls: Emma Anderson.
Roxette: Marie Fredricksson, Per Gessle.
Roxx Gang: Kevin Steele.
Roxy Music: Brian Eno, Bryan Ferry, John Wetton.
Roy Haynes Quartet: Eric Barret.
Roy Pellett Jazzband: Andy Lawrence.
Roy Woodward Big Band: Richard Howell-Jones.
Royal Blood: Michael Kerr, Ben Thatcher.
Royals: Ippe Kätkä.
Röyksopp: Svein Berge, Torbjörn Brundtland.
RSD (Rida, Sita, Dewi): Dewi Lestari.
RSJ and The Decoding Society: Ronald S. Jackson, Vernon Reid.
Rub Ultra: Sarah Matthews.
The Rubettes: Mark Haley, Anthony Thorpe.
Rubicon: Marc de Maeyer, Nod Wright.
The Rubisa Patrol: Mark Isham.
Rudimental: Piers Agget, Amir Amor, Kesi Dryden, DJ Locksmith.
Rufus and Chaka Khan: Chaka Khan, Karl Ratzer.
Rufus Foreman Band: Buddy Guy.
Rumi Ensemble: Hafez Nazeri.
Rumrunners: Tribble.
Run-D.M.C.: Darryl McDaniels, Joseph Simmons.
The Runaways: Lita Ford, Joan Jett, Michael Steele.
Runrig: Iain Bayne, Calum MacDonald, Rory MacDonald, Donnie Munro.
Rural Still Life: David Paich.
Rush: Geddy Lee, Alex Lifeson, Neil Peart.
The Russ Morgan Orchestra: John Morgan.
The Rustics: Jesper Thorup.
Ruth's Refrigerator: Ruth Miller.
The Rye: Zebadi Fisk.

S-Express: Mark Moore, Sonique.
Sabres of Paradise: Andy Weatherall.
Sacred Harp Singers: Gerry Armstrong.
Sad Cafe: Lenni, Des Tong.
The Sadista Sisters: Geoffrey Gurd.
Safika: Valanga Khoza.
Sailor: Henry Marsh.
Saint Etienne: Sarah Cracknell, Paul Kelly, Spencer Smith, Bob Stanley, Pete Wiggs.
Saints and Sinners: Red Richards.
Sajkedelik Sraml Band: Karel Babuljak.
Salsanama: Lise Dynnesen.
Salt: Ginger Baker.
Salt-N-Pepa: Pepa, Salt, Spinderella.
Salta: Daniela Mercury.
Saltwater Band: Geoffrey Yunupingu.
Salty Dog: Brian Bannister.
Sam and Dave: Sam Moore.
Sam Mitchel Blue Vikings: Jesper Thorup.
Sam Rivers Big Band: George Lewis.
Sam Roberts Band: Sam Roberts.
Samara: Stephen Rubie.
The Same: Martin Phillipps.
Samson: Nicky Moore.
The Sandkings: Jas Mann.
The Sandmen: Ole Wennike.

Sandoval Group: Arturo Sandoval.
The Sandpipers: Jeff Wayne.
Sandpit: Stephanie Ashworth.
Sands Family: Colum Sands, Tommy Sands.
Sandunga: Sergio Mulet.
Sandy Brechin Band: Sandy Brechin.
Santana Blues Band: Carlos Santana.
Santo El Diablo: Patrick McGarvey.
Sara Evans Band: Sara Evans.
Sarah Lazarus Quartet: Christophe Walleme.
Savage Garden: Darren Hayes, Daniel Jones.
The Savage Rose: Klavs Hovman, Anders Koppel, Annisette Koppel, Alex Riel.
Savannah Rose Band: Anni Filt.
Savoy: Pål Waaktaar.
Savoy Gang: Jerry Senfluk.
Savoy Jazzmen: Louis Lince.
Savuka: Johnny Clegg.
The Saw Doctors: Johnny Donnelly, Anthony Thistlethwaite.
The Saxist: Aubrey Dunham.
Saxon: Nigel Glockler.
Saxperiment: Janne Murto, Pertti Päivinen.
Scaniazz: Paul Strandberg.
The Scapegoats: Terry Edwards.
Scare Dem Crew: Elephant Man.
Scarlet: Paul Luther.
Scars on Broadway: John Dolmayan, Daron Malakian.
Schola Antiqua: Marianne Joan.
The Scholars: Kenny Rogers.
Scissor Sisters: Babydaddy, Paddy Boom, Del Marquis, Ana Matronic, Jake Shears.
Scool Band: Peter Walicki.
Scorch Trio: Raoul Björkenheim.
Scorpio: Steve Gresswell.
The Scorpions: Klaus Meine, Michael Schenker, Rudolph Schenker.
Scottsville Squirrel Barkers: Chris Hillman.
Scream: Dave Grohl.
The Screaming Jets: David Gleeson.
Screaming Lord Sutch: Jeff Beck.
Screaming Trees: Josh Homme, Mark Lanegan.
Screeching Weasel: Billie Joe Armstrong, Tre Cool, Mike Dirnt.
The Screen Gemz: Karl Hyde, Rick Smith.
The Script: Danny O'Donoghue, Glen Power, Mark Sheehan.
Scritti Politti: Green Gartside.
The Seahorses: John Squire.
The Sealed Knot: Burkhard Beins, Rhodri Davies.
Sean Jones Sextet: Sean Jones.
Seannachie: Simon Thoumire.
The Searchers: John McNally, Mike Pender.
Seb Jarrousse Sextet: Loïc Dequidt.
Sebadoh: Lou Barlow.
Sebastian's Men: Tony Elliott.
Sebö Halmos Group: Márta Sebestyén.
Second City Jazzmen: John M. Taylor.
2nd Line: Allan Mortensen.
Second National Band: Mike Nesmith.
Secret Dakota Ring: Andy Ross.
Secret Garden: Rolf Lovland, Fionnuala Sherry.
Secret Machines: Ben Curtis, Brandon Curtis, Josh Garza.
Secret Oyster: Kenneth Knudsen.
The Secret Show: Matt Davies.
Secret Society: Speech.
Secrets: Carter Beauford.
The Sect Maniacs: Andy Fairweather-Low.
Sector 27: Tom Robinson.
The Seekers: Judith Durham, Athol Guy, Keith Potger, Bruce Woodley.
Seelyhoo: Sandy Brechin.
Seis del Solar: Rubén Blades.
The Seldom Scene: Phil Rosenthal.
The Selecter: Neol Davies, Richard Mackie.
Selecter Instrumental: Neol Davies.
The Selfish Gene: Rui Pereira.
The Selofane: Judd Lander.
Senser: James Barrett.
Sensurround: Paul Hemmings.
Sentridoh: Lou Barlow.
The Seppo Kantonen Trio: Seppo Kantonen, Jorma Ojanperä.
Septeto Típico: Eliades Ochoa.
Septeto Turquino: Jorge Maturell Romero, Osnel Odit Bavastro, .
Sepultura: Max Cavalera.
The Sequence: Angie Stone.
Serebro: Anastasia Karpova, Olga Seryabkina, Elena Tennikova.
Seu Jorge and Almaz: Seu Jorge, Lucio Maia, Pupilo Paupequeno.
Seven Tracks: Romain Tranchart.
7 Wheels: Guillaume Orti.
Severi Pyysalo's No Hope Band: Heikki Sandren.

The Sex Pistols: Paul Cook, Steve Jones, John Lydon.
Sexteto: Peter Rasted.
The Sexton Sextet: Will Sexton.
SF Jazz Collective: Miguel Zenón.
Shabbey Road: Zoe McCulloch.
The Shades: Richard Howell-Jones, Bruce Ruffin.
Shades of Blue: Stefan Borum.
Shadow King: Vivian Campbell, Lou Gramm.
The Shadows: Brian Bennett, Hank Marvin, Cliff Richard, Bruce Welch.
Shahin and Sepehr: Sepehr Haddad, Shahin Shahida.
Shake: Jo Callis.
Shakespears Sister: Marcella Detroit, Siobhan Fahey.
Shakin' Street: Eric Levi.
Shakti: Zakir Hussain, John McLaughlin, V. Selva Ganesh.
Sham69: David Parsons.
The Shamen: Colin Angus, Mr C, Gavin Knight.
The Shamrocks: Bobby Marty.
Sharkey and Co.: Emmanuel Hussenot.
Shaskeen: Seán Keane.
Shaw Blades: Jack Blades, Tommy Shaw.
Shawn Loescher Trio: Juraj Kalasz.
She-Rockers: Alison Clarkson.
Shed Seven: Paul Banks, Tom Gladwin, Alan Leach, Rick Witter.
SheDaisy: Kassidy Osborn, Kelsi Osborn, Kristyn Osborn.
Shegui: Seán Keane.
Shellac: Steve Albini.
Shiloh: Don Henley.
The Shining: Simon Jones, Simon Tong.
The Ship: Birgit Lokke Larsen.
Ship of Fools: Stephen Tilston.
Shirtsville: Carsten Ortmann.
Shit and Chanel: Anne Linnet.
Shiva: Teresa Davis.
Shivanova: Orphy Robinson.
Shivaree: Ambrosia Parsley.
Shock-Headed Peters: Karl Blake.
Shockabilly: Kramer.
Shotgun Express: Rod Stewart.
The Shots: Ken Lyons.
The Shout: Orlando Gough.
Shout Out Louds: Eric Edman, Ted Malmros, Adam Olenius, Bebban Stenborg, Carl von Arbin.
Showdown: Richie McDonald.
Shriekback: Brian Nevill.
Siam: Christopher Baylis.
Siddharta: Primož B., Jani H., Boštjan M., Tomi M., Tomaž O. R., Cene R..
Sierra Maestra: Jesús Alemañy, Juan de Marcos González.
Sigur Rós: Jónsi Birgisson, Orri Páll Dýrason, Goggi Holm, Kjarri Sveinsson.
Silly Sisters: Maddy Prior, June Tabor.
Silly Wizard: Gordon Jones.
The Silver Bullet Band: Bob Seger.
Silverlead: John Forrester.
The Silverstars: Wazimbo.
Silverwing: Stephen Roberts.
Simcess: Thomas Negrijn.
Simmerfield Blues: Andy Carr.
Simon & Garfunkel: Art Garfunkel, Paul Simon.
Simon Campbell Band: Simon Campbell.
Simon Thoumire Three: Simon Thoumire.
Simple Minds: Charlie Burchill, Jim Kerr.
Simply Red: Mick Hucknall.
Sine Dramatic: Youssou N'Dour.
Sinful: Pete Wylie.
Sing-Sing: Emma Anderson.
Singing McEntires: Reba McEntire.
Singing Zoo: Jens Norremolle.
The Sinister Cleaners: Len Liggins.
Siouxsie & The Banshees: Siouxsie Sioux, Robert Smith.
Sirmakka: Sari Kaasinen.
Sista: Missy Elliott.
The Sisterhood: Andrew Eldritch, Patricia Morrison.
The Sisters of Mercy: Andrew Eldritch, Wayne Hussey, Patricia Morrison.
Sisters Unlimited: Sandra Kerr.
6 Cadde: Emre Aydin.
Six Cats: Dan Vernhettes.
Six Winds: Marilyn Mazur, Alex Riel.
606 Club Big Band: Stephen Rubie.
16 Tambourines: Tony Elliott, Michael Moran.
Sked: Soïg Siberil.
Skid Row: Sebastian Bach.
Skunk Anansie: Ace, Cass Lewis, Mark Richardson, Skin.
Sky: Herbie Flowers, Tristan Fry, John Williams.
Skymasters: Lee Gibson.
Slack Alice: Gary Waghorn.
Slade (II): Don Powell, Dave Hill, Noddy Holder.
Slam: Stuart McMillan, Orde Meikle.

Slank: Bim Bim, Kaka.
Slash's Snakepit: Slash.
Slaughterhouse 5: Steve O'Toole.
The Slaves: Andy Welsford.
Slawterhaus: Johannes Bauer.
Slax: Vivian Peres.
Sleeper: John R. Green, Louise Wener.
Sleepers: Tim Mooney.
The Sleeping Giants: Tom Cunningham.
Sleepless Knights: Paul Barrett.
The Sleepy Jackson: Luke Steele.
SLEMP: Leo Rutten.
Slide Hampton and The Jazzmasters: David Sanchez.
Slik: Midge Ure.
Slinky: Jon Dennis.
Slip: Lars Frederiksen.
Slow Food Music: Annika Fehling.
SLS Group: Stanislav Kubes.
Sly and Robbie: Sly Dunbar, Robbie Shakespeare.
Sly and The Family Stone: Sly Stone.
Small Talk: Hans van Pol.
SMAP (Sports Music Assemble People): Kimura Takuya.
Smashing Pumpkins: Jimmy Chamberlin, Billy Corgan, James Iha, D'Arcy Wretzky-Brown.
Smile: Brian May, Roger Taylor.
Smisk: Nike Markelius.
The Smiths: Johnny Marr, Steven Morrissey.
Smithsonian Jazz Masterworks Orchestra: Bobby Watson.
Smokey Robinson and The Miracles: Smokey Robinson.
Smokie: Christopher Norman, Alan Silson.
Smooth Criminals: Paul Okoye, Peter Okoye.
S.M.V.: Stanley Clarke, Marcus Miller.
Snake: Michael Anthony.
Sneaker Pimps: Chris Corner, Liam Howe, David Westlake.
Sneakers: Morten Kaersaa.
Sneeze: Rusty Hopkinson.
Sniff 'n' The Tears: Jamie Lane.
Snow Patrol: Nathan Connolly, Gary Lightbody, John Quinn, Tom Simpson, Paul Wilson.
Snowbird Mountain Band: Wilma Wakefield Millsaps.
Snug: Ed Harcourt.
Societies of Air Mines: Hamouka Dagara.
Society's Children: Pops Mohamed.
The Soft Boys: Andy Metcalfe, Matthew Seligman.
Soft Cell: Marc Almond, David Ball.
Soft Machine: John Etheridge, Karl Jenkins, John Marshall.
Soft on the Inside Big Band: Andy Sheppard.
SOH Trio: Ali Haurand.
The Soil: Daron Malakian, Serj Tankian.
Soil & "Pimp" Sessions: Akita Goldman, Josei, Midorin, Motoharu, Shacho, Tabu zombie.
The Sojourners: David Craig.
Sokoli: Peter Lovsin.
Solar Plexus: Monica Dominique.
Solas: Karan Casey.
Soldier Blue: Morten Harket.
Soledad Brothers: Ben Swank, Johnny Walker.
Soleluna: Harry Williamson.
Solid Senders: Wilko Johnson.
The Solutions: Bernd Rommel.
Somair: Hamouka Dagara.
Some Girls: Juliana Hatfield.
Somesax: Thorsten Høeg.
Something for Kate: Stephanie Ashworth, Paul Dempsey, Clint Hyndman.
The Sommers Rosenthal Family Band: Phil Rosenthal.
The Somnambulists: Tony Elliott.
Son Caribeño: Joe Arroyo.
Son Volt: Jay Farrar.
Sonic Renegades: Amy Denio.
Sonic Youth: Kim Gordon, Mark Ibold, Thurston Moore, Jim O'Rourke, Lee Ranaldo, Steve Shelley.
Sonichar: Hamouka Dagara.
Sonido de Londres: Roberto Pla.
Sons of Angels: Staffan William-Olsson.
Sons of Champlin: Mark Isham.
Sons of Kemet: Shabaka Hutchings, Oren Marshall, Seb Rochford, Tom Skinner.
Sons of Kyuss: Josh Homme.
Sons of the Desert: Ron Mael.
Sophisticated Movement: Norbert Meijs.
Soprano Summit: Bob Wilber.
Sort Sol: Thorsten Høeg, Knud Odde.
Sosterrock: Pia Rasmussen.
Soul Brothers: Moses Ngwenya.
Soul Clan: Ben King.
Soul Machine: Cyril Neville.

Soul Miner's Daughter: Jennifer Nettles.
Soul Satisfiers: Gloria Gaynor.
Soul Syndicate: Jamaka Tee-Birdd.
Soul II Soul: Jazzie B, Nellee Hooper.
Soul Vision: Sandy Rivera.
Soulfly: Max Cavalera.
Soulset: Seppo Paakkunainen.
Soulshape: Bo Jacobsen.
Soulsister: Jan Leyers, Hervé Martens, Paul Michiels.
Sound in Mind: Ken Tardley.
Sound Pool: Patrick Hazell.
Soundgarden: Matt Cameron, Chris Cornell, Ben Shepherd, Kim Thayil.
The Soup Dragons: Sean Dickson.
Sour Grapes: Richard Thompson.
South Mountain: Dan Washburn, Laurie La Porte-Piticco, Steve Piticco.
Southern Feeling: W. C. Clark.
Southern Hillman Furay Band: Chris Hillman.
Southlanders: Jo Servi.
The Soweto Kinch Quartet/Trio: Soweto Kinch.
Space: Leon Caffrey, Jimmy Cauty, Franny Griffiths, Jamie Murphy, Dave Palmer, Tommy Scott.
Space Age Playboys: Kory Clarke.
Space and Rhythm Jazz: Jan Kaspersen.
Space Ritual: Nik Turner.
Spacemen 3: Jason Pierce.
Spandau Ballet: Tony Hadley, Gary Kemp, Martin Kemp.
Spanking Violets: Katharine Chase.
Sparks: Ron Mael, Russell Mael.
Sparky Lightbourne: Alexander Mitchell.
SPC ECO: Dean Garcia.
Spear of Destiny: Chris Bell.
Special Venture: John Sund.
The Specials: Rodney Byers, Jerry Dammers, Lynval Golding, Terry Hall, Neville Staple.
The Spectors Three: Phil Spector.
The Spectres: Bret Michaels.
Spectrum: John Abercrombie, Billy Cobham, Bela Fleck, Eberhard Weber.
The Spencer Davis Group: Spencer Davis, Raymond Fenwick, Muff Winwood, Steve Winwood.
Sphere: Andy Sheppard.
Sphynx: John Millar, Nik Turner, Harry Williamson.
The Spice Girls: Victoria Beckham, Melanie Brown, Emma Bunton, Melanie Chisholm, Geri Halliwell.
Spider: Holly Knight.
The Spider's Webb: Francisco Alburo.
Spiers and Boden: Jon Boden.
Spill: Beth Orton.
Spillane Band: Davy Spillane.
The Spin Doctors: Chris Barron.
Spinal Tap: Loudon Wainwright III.
Spirit Level: Charles Underwood.
Spirit of Django: Alan Barnes, Martin Taylor.
Spirit Talk Mbira: Chartwell Dutiro.
Spirits: Mozez.
Spirits of Rhythm: Paul Russell.
The Spiritual Cowboys: Dave Stewart.
Spiritual Kvintet: Irena Budweiserova.
Spiritualized: Jason Pierce.
Spirou: Paul Ada.
Spitfire: Justin Welch.
Splat!: David Parsons.
Splinter: Giles Cooper.
Split Enz: Neil Finn, Tim Finn.
Spoiler: Stephen Harcourt.
Spooner: Doug Erikson.
The Sports: Andrew Pendlebury.
The Springfields: Thomas Mapfumo.
Spyro Gyra: Scott Ambush, Jay Beckenstein, Bonny Bonaparte, Julio Fernandez, Tom Schuman.
The Squares: Joe Satriani.
Squealer: Rudy Roberts.
Squeeze: Paul Carrack, Chris Difford, Jools Holland, Gilson Lavis, Andy Metcalfe, Glenn Tilbrook.
The Squeegees: Pierre de Reeder.
St Louis Union: Lenni.
St Lunatics: Nelly.
Stafford James Project: Stafford James.
Staind: Johnny April, Aaron Lewis, Mike Mushok, Jon Wysocki.
Stan Getz Quartet: Dave Holland.
Stan Rubin's Tigertown Five: Edward Polcer.
Stańko-Vesala Quartet: Tomasz Stańko, Edward Vesala.
The Stanley Brothers: Ralph Stanley.
Stanley's Joyful Noise: Daniel Konopka, Damian Kulash Jr., Tim Nordwind.
Starboys: Ippe Kätkä.
Starsailor: Benjamin Byrne, James Stelfox, James Walsh, Barry Westhead.

The Statesiders: Mel Tillis.
Status Quo: Andrew Bown, Rick Parfitt, Francis Rossi.
The Staubgolds: Markus Detmer.
Steady Ground: Ron Welty.
Steampacket: Rod Stewart.
SteelDrivers: Chris Stapleton.
Steel Pulse: Selwyn 'Bumbo' Brown, David Hinds, Steve Nisbett.
Steel Spirit Steel Band: Dave Edwards.
Steeler: Yngwie Malmsteen.
Steeleye Span: Martin Carthy, Ashley Hutchings, John Kirkpatrick, Maddy Prior.
Steely Dan: Walter Becker, Donald Fagen, Michael McDonald.
Stefano di Batista Quintet: Clovis Nicolas.
Stekpanna: Steve Kershaw.
Stellastarr: Shawn Christensen, Michael Jurin, Arthur Kremer, Amanda Tannen.
Stephane Furic Project: Stephane Furic.
Stephen Barry Band: Michael Browne.
Stephen Malkmus and The Jicks: Stephen Malkmus.
Stereo MCs: Rob Birch, Catherine Coffey, Nick Hallam, Owen If.
Stereo Total: Françoise Cactus, Brezel Göring.
Stereolab: Tim Gane, Laetitia Sadier.
Stereophonics: Kelly Jones, Richard Jones, Javier Weyler.
Steve Ashley Band: Steve Ashley.
Steve Coleman and Five Elements: Steve Coleman.
Steve Coleman and Metrics: Steve Coleman.
Steve Coleman and The Council of Balance: Steve Coleman.
Steve Coleman and The Mystic Rhythm Society: Steve Coleman.
The Steve Gibbons Band: Steve Gibbons.
Steve Gresswell Band: Steve Gresswell.
Steve Hillage Band: John Millar.
Steve Klink Quartet: Mario Igrec.
Steve Lacy Quintet/Sextet: Kent Carter, Bobby Few.
Steve Miller Band: Steve Miller, Boz Scaggs.
The Steve Morse Band: Steve Morse.
Steve Phillips and The Rough Diamonds: Steve Phillips.
Steve Westfield Slow Band: Steve Westfield.
Steve Williamson Quintet: Cheryl Alleyne.
The Stewart Four: Sly Stone.
The Stiff Upper Lips: Lynval Golding.
The Stills: Julien Blais, Olivier Corbeil, Tim Fletcher, Dave Hamelin, Liam O'Neil.
Stockton's Wing: Steve Cooney, Michael Hanrahan.
Stolle and Svare Jazz Quintet: Jørgen Svare.
Stone Canyon Band: Randy Meisner.
Stone Dome: Fish.
Stone Gods: Richie Edwards, Dan Hawkins, Robin Goodridge, Ed Graham.
The Stone Poneys: Linda Ronstadt.
Stone Roses: Ian Brown, Mani, John Squire.
Stone Soup: Carrie Newcomer.
Stone the Crows: Mike Moran.
The Stoners: Sly Stone.
The Stooges: Iggy Pop.
Storm Warning: Keith Hall.
Storms/Nocturnes: Tim Garland, Geoffrey Keezer.
The Stormtroopers: Gary Hall, Michael King.
The Storytellers: Tom T. Hall.
The Straightjackets: Delbert McClinton.
Strangegirls: Denise Dufort, Kim McAuliffe, Enid Williams.
Strangelove: Alex Lee.
The Strangers: Merle Haggard.
Strangers Two: Don Williams.
Stranglers: Jean-Jacques Burnel, Hugh Cornwell.
Strannye Igry: Nickolai Gusev.
The Strawbs: Derek Weaver.
The Streaplers: Gert Lengstrand.
Street Beat: Caecilie Norby.
Street Sweeper Social Club: Tom Morello.
The Streetband: Roger Kelly, Paul Young.
Streetfighters: John Sykes.
Streetwalkers: Nicko McBrain.
Strider: Mark Reader.
Strings: Peter Lipa.
Stripmind: Sully Erna.
The Strokes: Julian Casablancas, Nikolai Fraiture, Albert Hammond Jr, Fabrizio Moretti, Nick Valensi.
Stu Page Band: George Voros.
The Style Council: Paul Weller.
Styx: Tommy Shaw.
Sub Zero: Tony Mortimer, Eddie Morton.
Success Mwachame: Remmy Ongala.
Suede: Brett Anderson, Bernard Butler, Neil Codling, Justine Frischmann, Simon Gilbert, Alex Lee, Richard Oakes, Mat Osman.
Sugababes: Amelle Berrabah, Keisha Buchanan, Mutya Buena, Siobhan Donaghy, Jade Ewen, Heidi Range.
Sugar Mice: Claire-Louise Powell.

Sugar Ray: Stan Frazier, DJ Homicide, Murphy Karges, Mark McGrath, Rodney Sheppard.
The Sugarcubes: Björk.
The Sugarhill Gang: Master Gee, Wonder Mike, Doug Wimbish.
Sugarland: Kristian Bush, Jennifer Nettles.
Suicidal Tendencies: Mike Muir, Robert Trujillo.
Suka-Siko: Guy Zannou.
The Sultans: Ludo Beckers.
Summerfield Blues: Dave Arcari.
Summit Reunion: Bob Wilber.
Sun Quartet: Stefan Borum.
Sunburst Band: Dave Lee.
The Sundays: Patrick Hannan.
Suns of Arqa as Ireti: Clare Durrant.
The Sunsets: Shakin' Stevens.
Sunspeak: John Forrester.
Super_Collider: Jamie Liddell.
Super Eagles: Badou Jobe.
Super Etoile: Youssou N'Dour.
Super Furry Animals: Huw Bunford, Cian Ciárán, Dafydd Ieuan, Guto Pryce, Gruff Rhys.
Super Monkeys: Namie Amuro.
Super Rail Band: Mory Kanté, Salif Keita, Djelimady Tounkara.
Superbus: Jennifer Ayache, Francois Even, Patrice Focone, Michel Giovannetti, Guillaume Rousé.
Supercharge: Lenni.
Supergrass: Gareth Coombes, Rob Coombes, Danny Goffey, Mick Quinn.
Supergum: Gert Verhaeren.
Superjazz: David Dimond.
Supersilent: Helge Sten.
The Supremes: Diana Ross, Mary Wilson.
Survivors: Kenn Lending.
Surya: Fazal Qureshi, Taufiq Qureshi.
Suspicion: Stromae.
Svare/Thoroddsen: Jørgen Svare.
Svehlik: Alexandr Hajdovsky-Potapovic.
SVT: Anders Melander.
Swansea Jack: Mick Tems.
Swap: Karen Tweed.
Swedish House Mafia: Steve Angello, Axwell, Sebastian Ingrosso.
Sweet: Steve Mann.
Sweet Aliana: Taylor Dye, Madison Marlow.
Sweet Inspirations: Cissy Houston.
Sweet Magnolia: Al Kooper.
Sweet 75: Kris Novoselic.
Sweet Soul Sisters: Dee Jarlett.
Sweet Substitute: Andy Leggett.
Sweetblood: Choque Hosein, Wajid Rehman.
Sweethearts: Niels Mosumgaard.
Sweethearts in a Drugstore: Peter Jorgens.
Sweethearts of the Rodeo: Kristine Arnold, Janis Gill.
The Swigshift: Peter Derudder, Filip Vanrobaeys, Ivan Volcke.
Swing: Vivian Peres.
Swing Feeling: Dan Vernhettes.
The Swinging Laurels: Gary Birtles.
Swinging Singing Eight: Gordon Lightfoot.
Switchfoot: Chad Butler, Jerome Fontamillas, Jon Foreman, Tim Foreman, Drew Shirley.
Sy-Daff: Martin Heurlin.
Sylk: King Britt.
Symmetric Orchestra: Fode Lassana Diabaté, Toumani Diabaté.
The Syndicats: Raymond Fenwick, Steve Howe.
Syriana: Bernard O'Neill.
System of a Down: John Dolmayan, Daron Malakian, Shavo Odadjian, Serj Tankian.
System 7: Paul Oakenfold.

T. Graham Brown's Rock of Spam: T. Graham Brown.
Tabernacle: Charlie Mallozzi, Marco Sabiu.
Tabu Ley Rochereau's Africa Fiesta: Sam Mangwana.
Tackhead: Doug Wimbish.
Tad Newton's Jazzfriends: Colin Kellard, Tad Newton.
The Taffbeats: Andy Fairweather-Low.
Take That: Gary Barlow, Howard Donald, Jason Orange, Mark Owen, Robbie Williams.
Talas: Billy Sheehan.
Talis Mantra: Colin Hudson.
Talisker: Ken Hyder.
Talking Heads: David Byrne.
Tam Linn: Davey Arthur, Eddie Furey, Finbar Furey.
Tam Tam Top: Thomas Negrijn.
Tama: Sam Mills.
Tamalin: John McSherry.
Tamara Obrovac Quartet: Tamara Obrovac.
The Tambourines: Tony Elliott.
Tampere Jazz Orchestra: Ippe Kätkä, Kari Komppa.

Tangerine Dream: Richard Vanceunebrouck-Werth.
Tangerine Peel: Mike Chapman.
Tango Mano: Edouardo Makaroff.
Tangopojat: Ippe Kätkä.
Tant Strul: Kajsa Grytt, Nike Markelius.
Tantrum: Buggy Lees.
TAO: Drazen Franolic, Vesna Gorse, Per Vibskov.
Tapehead: Thorsten Høeg.
Tapestry: David Feehan.
Tapiola Big Band: Jartsa Karvonen, Simo Salminen.
Tappi Tikarras: Björk.
The Tarantinos: Wilson Reid.
Tarantula: Thad Maxwell.
Tarika: Hanitra Rasoanaivo.
Tasavallan Presidentti: Juhani Aaltonen, Jukka Tolonen, Heikki Virtanen.
Tasty Licks: Bela Fleck.
Tatool Altounian National Song and Dance Ensemble: Djivan Gasparyan.
t.A.T.u.: Lena Katina, Julia Volkova.
Taurus: Sven Gaul.
The Taverners: Nigel Lindridge.
Taxi Girl: Mirwais.
Taylor's Free Universe: Robin Taylor.
T-Bone Boogie Band: Paul Hobbs.
The T-Bones: Keith Emerson.
TC Matic: Arno Hintjens.
Tchikai/Dorge Quartet: Pierre Dorge, Peter Jorgens.
Tea for Three: Bobby Marty.
Team Sleep: Chino Moreno.
The Teardrop Explodes: Julian Cope.
Tears: Anne Linnet.
The Tears: Brett Anderson, Bernard Butler.
Tears for Fears: Chris Hughes, Roland Orzabal, Curt Smith, Ian Stanley.
The Techniques: Rick Levy, Bruce Ruffin.
Ted Heath (various bands): Brian Dee, Laurie Johnson.
Ted Nugent Band: Brian Howe, Ted Nugent.
The Teddy Bears: Phil Spector.
Teddy Fullick Quintet: Paul Russell.
The Tee Set: Raymond Fenwick.
Teemu Salminem Quartet: Teemu Salminen.
Teen Commandments: Paul Anka, Johnny Nash.
Teenage Fanclub: Norman Blake, Raymond McGinley.
Teenager: Nick Littlemore.
Teenager: Norbert Meijs.
Television: Tom Verlaine.
Temper, Temper: Vince Ford.
The Temper Trap: Jonathon Aherne, Toby Dundas, Joseph Greer, Dougy Mandagi, Lorenzo Sillitto.
Temple of Soul: Narada Michael Walden.
Temple of Sound: Count Dubulah, Neil Sparkes.
Temple of the Dog: Jeff Ament, Matt Cameron, Chris Cornell, Stone Gossard, Mike McCready.
The Temptations: Otis Williams.
10cc: Lol Crème, Kevin Godley, Graham Gouldman.
10,000 Maniacs: Natalie Merchant.
The Tennessee Fat Cats: Joe Stampley.
Tennessee Flash Cats: Kerr Donnelly.
Tennessee Mountain Boys: Kitty Wells.
The Teplo: Zbynek Maulis.
The Terence Blanchard Quartet: Terence Blanchard, Edward Simon.
The Terje Rypdal Quintet: Terje Rypdal, Jens-Christian Wesseltoft.
Terraplane: Nick Linden.
Terrorvision: Leigh Marklew, David Shuttleworth, Tony Wright, Mark Yates.
Terry, Blair and Anouchka: Terry Hall.
Terry Lightfoot Band: John Armatage, Alan Elsdon.
Testament: Alex Skolnick.
Texas: Craig Armstrong, Michael Bannister, Eddie Campbell, Richard Hynd, Johnny McElhone, Ally McErlaine, Sharleen Spiteri.
TGT: Ginuwine, Tank, Tyrese.
That's How It Is: Ski.
The The: Matt Johnson.
Theatre of Hate: Billy Duffy.
theaudience: Sophie Ellis-Bextor.
Thebe: Adrian Mupemhi.
Thee Headcoats: Billy Childish, Holly Golightly.
Thee Mighty Caesars: Billy Childish.
Their Fine Group: Linda Williams, Robin Williams.
Theis/Nyegaard Jazzband: Theis Jensen.
Them: Jackie McAuley, Van Morrison.
Them Crooked Vultures: Dave Grohl, Josh Homme, John Paul Jones.
Then Jerico: Mark Shaw, Andy Welsford.
Then There Were Six: Steve Kershaw.
Theo Travis Band: Theo Travis.
Therapy?: Andy Cairns, Neil Cooper, Michael McKeegan.
Thieves Like Us: John Parish.

Thin Lizzy: Eric Bell, Brian Downey, Scott Gorham, Brian Robertson, John Sykes, Darren Wharton.
Third Eye: Ali Haurand.
The Thirsty Scums: Dirty Pik.
13 1/2: Ilham al-Madfai.
The 13th Guest: Keven Fitzsimmons.
30 Seconds to Mars: Jared Leto, Shannon Leto, Tomo Milicevic.
This Is How We Fly: Caoimhín Ó Raghallaigh.
Thomas Talks: Ruthie Smith.
The Thomas Wright Affair: David Wright.
Thompson Square: Keifer Thompson, Shawna Thompson.
The Thompson Twins: Chris Bell, Matthew Seligman.
Thôt Agrandi: Guillaume Orti.
Thôt Twin: Guillaume Orti.
Thrash Peninsula: Lloyd Hanson.
Three City Four: Martin Carthy.
Three Lanes Over: Marianne Joan.
The Three Ronstadts: Linda Ronstadt.
The Three Strings: Ahmad Jamal.
Thrill of a Lifetime: Craig Stevens.
The Throbs: Ginger.
Throwing Muses: Tanya Donelly, Kristin Hersh.
Tiefschwarz: Alexander Schwarz, Sebastian Schwarz.
Tiger: Nicky Moore.
Tiger Moth: Ian Anderson.
Tigger and Paul: Paul Hobbs.
Tihai Trio: Nitin Sawhney, Talvin Singh.
Tijuana Brass: Herb Alpert.
Til Tuesday: Aimee Mann.
Tim Whitehead Band/ Quartet: Tim Whitehead.
Timbersound: Mags Furuholmen.
Timbiriche: Paulina Rubio, Thalía.
The Time: Jimmy Jam, Terry Lewis.
Time: Peco Petej.
Timeless: John Abercrombie.
The Timelords: Jimmy Cauty, Bill Drummond.
The Times: Georgi Stanchev.
Tinariwen: Alhousseini Abdoulahi, Ibrahim Ag Alhabib, Said Ag Ayad, Elaga Ag Hamid, Eyadou Ag Leche, Alassane Touhami, Mina Wallet Oumar.
The Ting Tings: Jules de Martino, Katie White.
Tintin og Hårtgírrerne: Carsten Ortmann.
Típica 73: José Alberto.
Tired Pony: Peter Buck, Richard Colburn, Gary Lightbody.
Tito Rodriguez's Mambo Orchestra: Edward Palmieri.
Tjens Couter: Arno Hintjens.
TKO: Katie White.
TLC: Rozanda Thomas, Tionne Watkins.
TMA: Ales Zimolka.
Together: Rohan Heath.
Toiling Midgets: Tim Mooney.
Tok Trio: Kent Carter.
Tokio Hotel: Bill Kaulitz, Tom Kaulitz, Georg Listing, Gustav Schäfer.
Tom, Brad and Alice: Bradley Leftwich.
Tom Petty and The Heartbreakers: Tom Petty.
Tom Robinson Band (TRB): Charlie Morgan, Tom Robinson.
Tom T. Hall's Band: Tom T. Hall, Johnny Rodriguez.
Tomahawk: Mike Patton.
Tomasz Stańko Quintet: Tomasz Stańko.
Tommy Barlow Quartet: Tommy Barlow.
Tommy Chase Quartet: Alan Barnes.
Tommy Dorsey Orchestra: Buddy DeFranco.
Tommy Hunt Band: Roger Flavell.
Tommy Sampson Orchestra: Thomas Chalmers, Jay Craig.
Tomorrow: Steve Howe.
Tomorrow's Warriors: Soweto Kinch.
Ton-Ton Quartet: Christian 'Ton-Ton' Salut.
Tone Dogs: Amy Denio.
Toni and The Movers: Michael Steele.
Tõnu Naissoo Quartet/Trio: Tõnu Naissoo.
Tony and Sigrid: Tony Visconti.
Tony Oxley's Contemporary Music Ensemble: Johannes Bauer.
Tony! Toni! Toné!: Raphael Saadiq.
Toot Sweet: Jim Dvorak, Ruthie Smith.
Toots and The Maytals: Toots Hibbert.
Top Notch: Jamaka Tee-Birdd.
Torch Song: William Orbit.
Toshiko Akiyoshi Jazz Orchestra: Toshiko Akiyoshi, George Robert.
Toss the Feathers: Michael McGoldrick.
Total Issue: Aldo Romano.
Toto: Bobby Kimball, Steve Lukather, David Paich, Steve Porcaro.
Touch: Terence Trent D'Arby.
Touchers: Gérard Siracusa.
Touchstone: Mark Orchin.
Tout Grand Nania Band: Djonimbo Ashilaako Bilanso.
Town Choice: Jimmy Powells.

The Town Criers: Bob Seger.
TPOK (Tout Pouissant Ochestre Kinshasa) Jazz: Papa Noel, Sam Mangwana.
TR3: Dave Matthews.
Traction Ailleurs: Vivian Peres.
Trader Horn: Jackie McAuley.
Traffic: Dave Mason, Steve Winwood.
The Tragically Hip: Rob Baker, Gordon Downie, Johnny Fay, Paul Langlois, Gord Sinclair.
Train: Patrick Monahan, Jimmy Stafford, Scott Underwood.
Trains and Boats and Trains: Soma Allpass.
The Trammps: Paul Damen.
Tramp: Bob Brunning.
Trans-Europe Diatonic: Kepa Junkera, John Kirkpatrick.
Trans-Global Underground: Natacha Atlas, Count Dubulah, Neil Sparkes.
The Transatlantics: Tony Clout.
Transient v Resident: Martin Archer.
Transparent Music Ensemble: B. J. Cole.
Transsylvania Phoenix: Nicu Covaci.
Trash: John Mellencamp.
Traste Linden's Kvintette: Traste Linden.
The Traveling Wilburys: Bob Dylan, George Harrison, Jeff Lynne, Tom Petty.
Travis: Andy Dunlop, Francis Healy, Douglas Payne, Neil Primrose.
Trax: Peter Bellotte.
The Tremblers: Peter Noone.
The Tren Brothers: Jim White.
T-Rex: Herbie Flowers.
Treya Quartet: Paolo Fresu, Gilbert Paeffgen, Peter Waters.
The Trial: Tribble.
Triangulus: Hans Bryngelsson.
Tribal Drift: Duncan Bridgeman, Phil Pickering.
Tribal Tech: Scott Henderson, Gary Willis.
Tribu: Geoffrey de Masure.
The Trick: Eddie Morton.
The Tridents: Jeff Beck.
Triggerfish: Jason Isaacs.
Trigon: John Sund.
Trijoums: Jacques Vidal.
Trinity: Bonny Bonaparte.
Trinity: Vivian Campbell.
Trinovox: Francesco Ronchetti, Julian Spizz.
The Trio: Petter Wettre.
Trio Bal(l)ade: Gérard Siracusa.
Trio BraamDeJoodeVatcher: Michiel Braam.
Trio Eckert-Gaivoronski-Naissoo: Vojtech Eckert, Tõnu Naissoo.
Trio Grande: Silke Reichmann.
The Trio of Doom: Keven Fitzsimmons.
Trio Ozi: Alexandre Ouzounoff.
Trio Paillard-Bismut-Roucan: Michel Bismut, Jean-Yves Roucan.
Trio Sowari: Burkhard Beins.
Trio Spectrum: John Williams.
Trio Töykeät: Eerik Siikasaari.
Triode: Jean-Yves Roucan.
Triple Gee: Guillaume Orti.
Triple Threat Review: Lou Ann Barton.
Tripping Daisy: Tim DeLaughter.
Triumph: Rik Emmett.
The Triumphs: Jorma Kaukonen, B. J. Thomas.
Troka: Timo Alakotila.
Trompolis: Pierre Dutot.
Tropicana Orchestra: Jean-Claude Montredon.
Troya Cubano: Eliades Ochoa.
Trubrot: Gunnar Thordarson.
True Believers: Alejandro Escovedo.
Trulio Disgracias: Flea.
Trust: Nicko McBrain.
Tsilavena: Rajery.
Tsunami One: Adam Freeland.
Tubby Hayes Quartet/Quintet: Danny Thompson.
Tuberkuloited: Alar, Juks, Olav Kund, Meelis Laidvee, Summer.
The Tubes: Fee Waybill.
Tubeway Army: Gary Numan.
Tula Jazz: Valentina Ponomareva.
Tulla Céili Band: Martin Hayes.
Tuohi Quartet: Teppo Hauta-aho, Seppo Paakkunainen.
Turbonegro: Euroboy, Happy-Tom, Pål Pot Pamparius, Rune Rebellion, Chris Summers, Hank von Helvete.
Turin Brakes: Olly Knights, Gale Paridjanian.
The Turks: Gary Bonds.
Turn-On: Tim Gane.
Turnpike: Alan Clayson.
Turntable Terranova: DJ Kaos.
Turtle Island String Quartet: Darol Anger.
Tuxedo Big Band: Philippe Laudet, Paul Spedding.
TV on the Radio: Tunde Adebimpe, Kyp Malone, David Sitek.

The TV Show: Tony Visconti.
TV-2: Sven Gaul.
TW6: Tim Whitehead.
Twas Brillig: Paul Hobbs.
12 Bar: Dave Lindholm.
Twentieth Century Saints: Geoffrey Gurd.
28th Street Saxophone Quartet: Bobby Watson.
Twenty Flight Rockers: Ian McKean.
Twenty 4 Seven: Fixx-It.
Twenty-Miles: Judah Bauer.
21 Guns: Scott Gorham.
23 Skidoo: Sam Mills.
The Twilights: Glenn Shorrock.
Twin Q: Michal Filek.
The Twin Set: Davey Lane, Tim Rogers.
Twins: Helene Hanzick, Poul Hanzick.
Twisted Brown Trucker: Uncle Kracker.
Twisted Sister: Dee Snider.
The Twisters: Ilham al-Madfai.
Two: Ivan Myslikovjan.
2AM: Changmin, Jinwoon, Jo Kwon, Seulong.
2Kool: Rishi Rich.
Two Lone Swordsmen: Andy Weatherall.
2NE1: Bom, CL, Dara, Minzy.
Two of a Mind: Amy Wadge.
213: Snoop Dogg.
Two Shiny Heads: Phil Asher.
2 Smokin' Barrels: Terry Francis.
Two Tones: Gordon Lightfoot.
2 Unlimited: Anita Doth, Ray Slijngaard.
Tygers of Pan Tang: John Sykes.
Tyketto: Danny Vaughn.
Tystion: Robert Mackay.

U2: Bono, Adam Clayton, The Edge, Larry Mullen Jr.
UB40: Astro, Jimmy Brown, Ali Campbell, Robin Campbell, Earl Falconer, Norman Hassan, Brian Travers, Mickey Virtue.
U Boat: Phil Murray.
UFO: Phil Mogg, Michael Schenker, Pete Way.
UHF: Shari Ulrich.
UHO-Trio: Matti Oiling.
UK: John Wetton.
UK Subs: Lars Frederiksen.
The Ukrainians: Len Liggins.
Ulcerrhoea: Jan Frederickx.
Ulrich Gumpert Trio: Johannes Bauer.
Ultralyd: Frode Gjerstad.
Ultramagnetic MCs: Kool Keith.
Ultramarine: Mario-Laurent Canonge, Simon Kay, Nguyên Le.
Ultrasound: Kevin Figes.
Ultravox: Midge Ure.
UMO (New Music Orchestra): Lee Gibson, Keith Hall, Kari Heinila, Markku Johansson, Seppo Kantonen, Jartsa Karvonen, Eero Koivistoinen, Kari Komppa, Pentti Lahti, Jukka Linkola, Janne Murto, Mika Mylläri, Pertti Päivinen, Jukka Perko, Hannu Rantanen, Teemu Salminen, Heikki Sarmanto, Pekka Sarmanto, Mircea Stan.
Umps and Dumps: John Kirkpatrick.
The Un Concern: Prince Trubetsky.
Un Drame Musical Instantané: Gérard Siracusa.
The Unclaimed: Sid Griffin.
Uncle Tupelo: Jay Farrar, John Stirratt, Jeff Tweedy.
The Uncool: Ron Sexsmith.
Underground Resistance: Mike Banks, Jeff Mills.
Underground Sound of Lisbon: Rui Da Silva.
The Undertones: Feargal Sharkey.
Underworld: Darren Emerson, Karl Hyde, Rick Smith.
Unhelig: Bernd Heinrich Graf.
Union: Randy Bachman.
Union Jack: Claudio Giussani.
Union of South Africa: Hugh Masekela.
Union Station: Alison Krauss.
The Uniques: Joe Stampley.
Unit 4: Greg Lake, John Wetton.
United Jazz and Rock Ensemble: Tony Coe, Eberhard Weber.
United Nations Band: Arturo Sandoval.
United Nations of Sound: Richard Ashcroft.
Unity Committee: Cut Chemist.
U.N.K.L.E.: James Lavelle, DJ Shadow.
Unkommuniti: Tim Gane.
Unsacred Hearts: Andy Ross.
Unto Tango Orchestra: Hannu Rantanen.
Upper Space Group: Gary Brunton.
The Upsetters: Little Richard.
Urban Cookie Collective: Rohan Heath.
Urban Dogs: Matthew Best, Knox.
Urban Mood: Gilles Coronado, Guillaume Orti.

Urban Renewal Project: Ron Mael, Russell Mael.
Urban Sax: Viviane Ginapé, Andy Sheppard.
Urban Shakedown: Claudio Giussani.
Urban Thermo Dynamics: Mos Def.
Urban Turban: Hans Bryngelsson.
Uriah Heep: Mick Box, Ken Hensley, John Wetton.
Urmas Lattikas Quintet: Urmas Lattikas.
Usch: Nike Markelius.
Utopia: Todd Rundgren, Kasim Sulton.
UU: Thomas Fersen.
UZEB: Michel Cusson.

V8: Palle Mikkelborg.
V Twin: Chris Geddes.
Vacuum: Alexander Bard.
Vagrants: Leslie West.
Valdez: Roberto Pla.
Vale of Atholl Pipe Band: Katie Harrigan.
Valeriu Sterian and Compania de Sunet: Valeriu Sterian.
Vali and Carmen: Valeriu Sterian.
Van Dango: Leonardo Pedersen.
Van Der Graaf Generator: Peter Hammill, David Jackson.
Van Gogh: Marc de Maeyer.
Van Halen: Michael Anthony, Gary Cherone, Sammy Hagar, David Roth, Alex van Halen, Eddie van Halen.
The Vandals: Travis Barker.
The Vanguards: Terje Rypdal.
Vantaa Pops Orchestra: Markku Johansson.
Vargavinter: Jörgen Adolfsson.
Värttinä: Susan Aho, Mari Kaasinen, Sari Kaasinen, Janne Lappalainen, Markku Lepistö, Lassi Logrén, Jaakko Lukkarinen, Hannu Rantanen, Antto Varilo, Johanna Virtanen.
Vaughn: Danny Vaughn.
Vaughn Monroe Orchestra: John Pizzarelli.
Vegas: Terry Hall, Dave Stewart.
Veltto and Heru: Ippe Kätkä.
Velvet Palm: Rhonda Finlayson.
Velvet Revolver (VR): Slash.
The Velvet Rodeo Band: Kevin Kienlein.
The Velvet Underground: John Cale, Maureen Tucker.
Venini: Russell Senior.
Vennaskond: Prince Trubetsky.
Vernon P Stinger: Jim White.
Vers La Flammes: Christina Staël von Holstein.
Vertical Hold: Angie Stone.
The Verve: Richard Ashcroft, Simon Jones, Nick McCabe, Peter Salisbury, Simon Tong.
Vesa Matti Loiri Group: Maria Kalaniemi.
Veselye Rebyata Ensemble: Alla Pugacheva.
The Vibrators: Knox.
Vic Godard's Subway Sect: Chris Bostock.
Vice Bishop's Blues Band: Freddy Hopwood.
Vicious Circle: Rusty Hopkinson.
Vicious Rumours: Vinnie Moore.
Victor: Alex Lifeson.
The Vikings: Alan Gorrie.
Villi Kazassyan's Big Band: Vassil Petrov.
Vinegar Joe: Elkie Brooks.
The Vines: Ryan Griffiths, Patrick Matthews, Craig Nicholls, Hamish Rosser.
Vintage Jazzmen: Dan Vernhettes.
Violet Indiana: Robin Guthrie.
Virgin: Doda.
The Virgin Prunes: Gavin Friday.
Virginia Wolf: Jason Bonham.
Virgo: Marshall Jefferson.
Visage: Midge Ure.
Vital Signs: Salman Ahmad.
Vitezi Om'a: Peter Lovsin.
Viva La Musica: Koffi Olomide, Papa Wemba.
Viviane Ginapé/Eric Schultz Duo: Viviane Ginapé, Eric Schultz.
Viviane Ginapé Quartet: Viviane Ginapé.
Vjestice: Boris Leiner.
Vladimir Tarasov's Baltic Art Orchestra: Tõnu Naissoo.
Voice of Progress: Junior Reid.
Voice of the Beehive: Martin Brett.
Void: Andy Bell.
Volapék: Guigou Chenevier.
Voodoo Guru: Zebadi Fisk.
Voodoo Sioux: Nicholas Flaherty.
Vopruz: Karel Babuljak.
Vow Wow: Neil Murray.
Vox Office: Marc Brochet.
Voz de Cabo Verde: Joaquim Almeida.
Vrijeme Zemlja: Davor Tolja.

Vujicsics: Márta Sebestyén.
Vulcano: Hans van Pol.

W. C. Clark Bires Band: Will Sexton.
Wagon Wheels: Thomas Mapfumo, Oliver Mtukudzi.
Wah!: Pete Wylie.
Wah! The Mongrel: Pete Wylie.
Wakeman Band: Adam Wakeman, Rick Wakeman.
Walden's Blues Band: John Walden.
Walker & The All Stars: Junior Walker.
Walker Brothers: Barrie Martin, Scott Walker.
The Walkie Talkies: Wayne Hussey.
Wall of Voodoo: Stanard Ridgway.
The Wallflowers: Jakob Dylan.
Wally Fawkes Band: John Armatage.
Waltari: Kärtsy.
Walter Trout and The Radicals: Walter Trout.
Wamdue Kids: Chris Brann.
The Wanderers: David Parsons.
Warm Guns: Lars Muhl.
Warrior Soul: Kory Clarke.
The Warriors: Walter Afanasieff, Jon Anderson.
W. Arts and All: Paul Hobbs.
Wasama Quartet: Pentti Lahti, Ilkka Niemeläinen.
The Waterboys: Guy Chambers, Nick Linden, Ian McNabb, Richard Naiff, Mike Scott, Sharon Shannon, Steve Wickham.
Waterdaughters: Norma Waterson.
Waterson:Carthy: Eliza Carthy, Martin Carthy, Norma Waterson.
The Watersons: Martin Carthy, Norma Waterson.
WATT: Carla Bley.
Wave Play: Ann-Marie Henning.
Wavestar: John Dyson.
The Way Forward: King Sunny Ade.
Wayne County and The Electric Chairs: John Johnson.
Wayne Shorter Quartet: Wayne Shorter.
Waysted: Pete Way.
Wayward Sheikhs: Justin Adams.
Wayzgoose: David Richey.
Weather Report: Wayne Shorter.
The Weavers: Frank Hamilton.
Web: Charles Angelopulo.
Webcore: Phil Pickering.
The Wedding and Funeral Band: Goran Bregovic.
The Wedding Present: Len Liggins.
Weekend at Waikiki: JXL.
Ween: Kramer.
Weezer: Rivers Cuomo.
The Weirdos: Murphy Karges.
Wellingbrook Singers: Mike Post.
Wellwater Conspiracy: Matt Cameron.
Wendy and Lisa: Lisa Coleman, Wendy Melvoin.
West Bruce and Laing: Leslie West.
West India Company: Stephen Luscombe.
Westbrook and Company: Kate Westbrook, Mike Westbrook.
The Westbrook Trio: Mike Westbrook.
Western Electric: Patrick McGarvey.
Westlife: Nicky Byrne, Kian Egan, Mark Feehily, Shane Filan, Brian McFadden.
Westside Connection: Ice Cube.
Westworld: Bob Andrews, Elizabeth Westwood.
Wet Wet Wet: Graeme Clark, Tom Cunningham, Graeme Duffin, Neil Mitchell, Marti Pellow.
Wetton/Downes: Geoffrey Downes.
Wettre/Johansen Trio: Petter Wettre.
Wham!: George Michael, Andrew Ridgeley.
Whatever: Danny Thompson.
Wheeler and Coe: Tony Coe.
The Wheels of Fortune: Val Clover.
When in Rome: Clive Farrington.
Whirling Pope Joan: Nigel Eaton.
Whiskeytown: Ryan Adams.
The Whisky Priests: Gary Miller, Glenn Miller, Michael Tyas.
Whistlebinkies: Stuart Eydmann, Robert Wallace.
White Bread: Bernd Rommel.
The White Cats: Rat Scabies.
The White Ducks: John Hiatt.
White Lion: Mike Tramp.
White Rabbit: Mo James.
White Spirit: Janick Gers.
The White Stripes: Jack White, Meg White.
White Trash: Edgar Winter.
Whitefire: Simon Campbell.
Whites: Ricky Skaggs.
Whitesnake: Don Airey, Vivian Campbell, David Coverdale, Jon Lord, Neil Murray, John Sykes, Steve Vai.
The Who: John Bundrick, Roger Daltrey, Pete Townshend.

Wicked Lester: Gene Simmons.
The Wickermen: Michael Tyas.
Widowmaker: Dee Snider.
The Wigs: Boz Scaggs.
WigWam: Alison Clarkson, Alex James.
Wilco: Leroy Bach, Glenn Kotche, John Stirratt, Jeff Tweedy.
Wild!: Nikki Brooks.
The Wild Bunch: Daddy G, Nellee Hooper, Mushroom, Tricky.
Wild Choir: Gail Davies.
Wild East: Claus Mathiesen.
Wild Horses: Brian Robertson.
The Wild Mans Band: Peter Jorgens.
Wild Ones: Stephen Roberts.
The Wild Tchoupitoulas: Charles Neville, Cyril Neville.
The Wildcats: Marty Wilde.
The Wilde Three: Raymond Fenwick, Justin Hayward, Marty Wilde.
The Wildhearts: Ginger.
Wilko Johnson Band: Wilko Johnson.
Willie and The Poor Boys: Bill Wyman.
The Willing Sinners: Marc Almond.
Wilsations: Mari Wilson.
Wind o Four: Svend Hedegaard.
Wings: Paul McCartney.
Winter Consort: Luther Rix.
Wir sind Helden: Judith Holofernes, Pola Roy, Mark Tavassol, Jean-Michel Tourette.
Wise Wound: Brian Madigan.
Wisin y Yandel: Juan Luis Morera, Llandel Veguilla Malavé.
Witness: Phil Bennett.
The Wizards: Stanislav Kubes.
Wizzard: Roy Wood, Bill Hunt.
The Wizzo Band: Roy Wood.
WOB: John Forrester.
The Wolfmen: Chris Constantinou.
Wolfstone: Ivan Drever.
Wonder Girls: Hyelim, Sohee, Sunye, Yeeun.
Wonderlove: Deniece Williams.
Wood, Wilson, Carthy: Roger Wilson.
The Wooden Birds: Andrew Kenny.
Woodoo: Ippe Kätkä.
Woody Herman Big Band: Tom Malone.
Woody Shaw Quintet: Dag Arnesen.
Woody's Truck Stop: Todd Rundgren.
Work 4: Herman de Rycke.
World Class Wreckin' Crew: Dr Dre.
World on a String: John Sund.
World Party: Guy Chambers, Karl Wallinger.
World's Greatest Jazz Band: Bob Wilber.
Wozani: George Voros.
Writz: Nicholas Battle.
Wu-Tang Clan: Cappadonna, Ghostface, GZA, Inspectah Deck, Masta Killa, Method Man, Raekwon, RZA, U-God.
Wynton Marsalis Septet: Wynton Marsalis.

Xavier Richardeau Quartet: Xavier Richardeau.
XLarge: Julien Blais.
X-Press 2: Ashley Beedle, Diesel, Rocky.
XTC: Andy Partridge.
The xx: Romy Madley-Croft, Oliver Sim, Jamie Smith.
Xylouris Ensemble: Giorgios Xylouris.
Xylouris White: Jim White, Giorgios Xylouris.

Y Celtiaid Anyhsbus: Huw Owen.
Y Cyrff: Paul Jones, Mark Roberts.
Ya Toupas: Ray Lema, Mansiamina M'Foko, Manuaku.
Yahoos: Ippe Kätkä.
Yamo: Wolfgang Flür.
The Yardbirds: Jeff Beck, Eric Clapton, Alan Glen, Jimmy Page.
Yat-Kha: Albert Kuvezin.
Yazoo: Vince Clarke, Alison Moyet.
Yeah Jazz: David Blant.
Yeah Yeah Yeahs: Brian Chase, Karen O, Nicolas Zinner.
Yelle: Grandmarnier, Yelle.
Yellow City Big Band: Ben Sluijs.
Yellow Defect: Mikoláš Chadima.
Yellow Magic Orchestra: Ryûichi Sakamoto.
Yellow Moon: Karl-Erik Pedersen.
Yellowbelly: Gary Birtles.
Yeni Türkü: Fatih Ahiskali, Furkan Bilgi, Erkin Hadimoglu, Derya Köroglu, Raci Pişmişoglu, Erdinç Şenol.
Yerba Buena Blues Band: Tom Ball.
Yes: Jon Anderson, Bill Bruford, Geoffrey Downes, Trevor Horn, Steve Howe, Trevor Rabin, Rick Wakeman, Alan White.
The Yes Boys: Raymond Lema.
Yip Yip Coyote: Eg White.
Yngwie Malmsteen: Joe Turner.

Yo La Tengo: Georgia Hubley, Ira Kaplan, James NcNew.
Yo Yo Honey: Anita Jarrett.
Yothu Yindi: Geoffrey Yunupingu.
You Am I: Rusty Hopkinson, Andy Kent, Davey Lane, Tim Rogers.
The Young and the Useless: Adrock.
Young Disciples: Carleen Anderson.
Young Fathers: Kayus Bankole, Graham Hastings, Alloysious Massaquoi.
The Young Generation: Janis Siegel.
Young Snakes: Aimee Mann.
The Youngbloods: Jesse Young.
Yummy Fur: Paul Thomson.
Yusef Lateef Quartet: Kim Clarke.

Zac Brown Band: Coy Bowles, Zac Brown, Clay Cook, Jimmy de Martini, Chris Fryar, John Driskell Hopkins.
Zagreb Jazz Portrait: Mario Igrec.
Zagreb Jazz Quartet/Quintet/Sextet: Silvestar Glojnaric.
Zagreb Radio Big Band: Silvestar Glojnaric.
Zahar: Hassan Hakmoun.
Zaiko Langa Langa: Papa Wemba.
Zap Mama: Sylvie Nawasadio.
Zap-Pow: Jamaka Tee-Birdd.
Zawinul Syndicate: Scott Henderson.
Zbigniew Namysłowski Quartet/Quintet: Zbigniew Namysłowski.
Zebra: Tchando.
Zechs Marquise: Marcel Rodríguez López.

Zemfira: Zemfira.
Zero: Lindy Morrison.
Zero Degree Atoll: Ahmed Nashid.
Zero Pop: Mark Howell.
Zero 7: Sophie Barker, Henry Binns, Tina Dico, Sam Hardaker, Mozez, Sia.
Ziggy Marley and The Melody Makers: Ziggy Marley.
Zirenes: Marilyn Mazur.
Zlatni Dukati: Stanko Saric.
Zodiac Mindwarp and The Love Reaction: Jan Cyrka.
Zöhar: Erran Baron Cohen, Andrew Kremer.
The Zombies: Rod Argent, Colin Blunstone.
The Zone: John Mellencamp, Mika Mylläri.
Zoo: Mick Fleetwood, Ales Zimolka.
Zoo: Hiro.
Zoot: Rick Springfield.
The Zoots: Ludo Beckers.
Zridlo: Karel Tampier.
Zu: Amy Denio.
The Zutons: Boyan Chowdhury, Abi Harding, Paul Molloy, David McCabe, Sean Payne, Russell Pritchard.
Zuvuya: Phil Pickering.
Zwan: Billy Corgan.
Zydeco Hot Rods: Freddy Hopwood.
Zydecomotion: Chris Hall.
Zygmunt Wichary Group: Zbigniew Namysłowski.
ZZ Top: Frank Beard, Billy Gibbons, Dusty Hill.